CUMULATIVE AUTHOR INDEX
FOR
POOLE'S INDEX
TO
PERIODICAL LITERATURE
1802–1906

Cumulative Author Index Series

Number one: Cumulative Author Index for
Poole's Index to Periodical Literature.

Number two: Cumulative Author Indexes for the
Monthly Catalog of United States
Government Publications.

Number three: Cumulative Author Index for
Public Affairs Information Service. Bulletin.

Number four: Cumulative Author Index for the
A.L.A. Index to General Literature.

CUMULATIVE AUTHOR INDEX
FOR
POOLE'S INDEX
TO
PERIODICAL LITERATURE
1802–1906

Compiled and Edited by

C. Edward Wall
Head Librarian, The University of Michigan
Dearborn Campus Library

With the Technical Assistance of

Edward Przebienda
Lead Programmer, The Center for Urban Studies
The University of Michigan

And the Editorial Assistance of

Wayne Somers
Bibliographer, Schaffer Library
Union College

The Pierian Press
Ann Arbor, Michigan
1971

Library of Congress Catalog Card Number: 77-143237
International Standard Book Number: 87650-006-8

DEDICATION

To my wife, Mary Ellen, and my children, Annette, Jannette and Heather, with love and appreciation for their understanding support during the years required to complete this project.

PREFACE.

PURPOSE.

"The work is an index to subjects and not to writers, except when writers are treated as subjects." The words of William Frederick Poole in his "Preface" to the 1882 Edition of his Index to Periodical Literature take on a special significance here, insofar as they serve as the jumping off point for the present volume. The need for an author approach to Poole's Index has been the "mote" troubling the eye of every indexer, scholar, researcher, librarian and general reader ever to come in contact with the tool and, at long last, that approach has been supplied.

When, in their "Preface" to the Fourth Supplement (1903), William I. Fletcher and Mary Poole further elaborated upon the reasons dictating the exclusion of an author approach from the Index, they neatly summarized the basic problem which this author now knows to be so very true:

> "It has always seemed so very desirable that the Index should contain entries under the names of the writers of the articles....But such entries added to those now included would nearly double the amount of matter and the consequent size and cost of the volumes, which consideration is simply prohibitive from a commercial point of view, as the sales but little more than cover the cost of printing as it is."

Matter, size and costs notwithstanding, the sheer magnitude and classic nature of Poole's Index has exerted its irresistable attraction, culminating in the present Cumulative Author Index. The volume has been done with a view to providing not only a reliable companion to the Index itself, but also in the hope that, by demonstrating the unlimited possibilities for improvements by librarians within their own field, it will stimulate and foster a renewal of the professional commitment and dedication to learning which so fully characterized the career of William Frederick Poole.

SCOPE AND INCLUSIVENESS.

The Cumulative Author Index displays in one alphabetical sequence all personal names which appear within parentheses in the 1882 Edition and the five Supplements of Poole's Index to Periodical Literature. It contains in excess of 300,000 references to the names of authors hitherto totally inaccessible, adding a much needed and long awaited dimension to this most famous of cooperatively compiled indexes.

FORMAT AND SYSTEM OF DEVELOPMENT.

Entries have been arranged in triple column pages for maximum economy. Each letter of the alphabet (except X and Y) begins a new page, with headers for the first and last citation appearing on each page. Citations for every reference have been displayed in a ten character field which indicates their location by volume (positions 1 & 2), page (positions 3 through 7), and column (positions 8 & 9). Additionally, single and multiple references within columns have been so identified with the letters 's' or 'm' (position 10). A typical citation, v3p0012c2m, is therefore read as "volume 3, page 12, column 2, multiple references." Volume numbers, 1 through 6, correspond respectively to the initial 1882 Edition, and the five Supplements of 1888, 1893, 1897, 1903 and 1908.

FORM OF ENTRY.

Due to extensive variations in the form of entry of the names indexed in Poole's over more than five decades, certain non-standard guidelines for the choice of form of entry have been adopted for this Author Index. They are essentially uncomplicated and few in number, and have been selected because they provide the most expeditious and reasonable solution to form of entry problems which could otherwise be resolved only through a prolonged, intensive and costly program of verification.

The basic underlying principles of this scheme of arrangement are an attempt to circumvent the inconsist practices and entry variations found in all elements of proper names within Poole's Index, especially prefixed and compound surnames, but including simple surnames, forenames and initials. Indexing by the least variable of these elements--the last unique word in the surname--allows more consistent access to surnames represented and abbreviated in several different ways, and has therefore been the rule applied to most prepositionally prefixed and unhyphenated compound surnames of Germanic (English, Dutch, German), and Romance (French, Italian, Spanish, Portuguese) origin. This procedure brings together such entries as "Campen, E." and "Campen, E.van" or "Gerstner, F.A.de" and "Gerstner, F.A.von". Some exceptions and qualifications to this rule have also been established: the more consistently recorded Celtic and other compound surnames with attributive prefixes (M', Mac, Mc, O', St., Ste., Saint, Sainte) have been entered in proper alphabetical sequence, while those that were inconsistently recorded (A', L') appear under the last unique word; hyphenated compound names of primarily Germanic origin appear under the first element of the compound; Germanic names marked with umlauts have for the most part not been transliterated, so that citations to a name recorded in Poole's in both an umlauted and a transliterated form have not been merged but appear as separate entries. A check of both diacritically rendered names, whatever their origin, and all possible transliterated versions of that name is therefore essential to assure complete recovery of works by a single author. Finally, English forename compounds are entered under the forename while similar entries for non-English names are entered under the object of the preposition. For the most part, entries are indexed exactly as they appear in Poole's. Errors in Poole's are therefore reflected in the Author Index. All similar spellings of a name (e.g., Greene for Green, Smyth for Smith, Gardner for Gardiner), should be checked for possible mispelled names. Less obvious possibilities are numerous (e.g., Cheny, E.D. for Cheney, E.D. or Mallone, M. for Malloni, M.) and should be checked to the limits of one's imagination.

ARRANGEMENT OF ENTRIES.

Names in the Author Index have been arranged alphabetically, word by word, according to the forms of entry described above. For the same name, single surnames, hyphenated and attributive compounds and forename compounds are entered in that order. Similarly, for the same name, lowercase entries precede uppercase entries (e.g., Macleod, H.D. precedes MacLeod, H.D.).

Three classes of authorship are noted: single authorship, joint authorship, and multiple authorship (involving more than two persons), and have been recorded sequentially. The names of two joint authors are cited under each name, while the participation of three or more multiple authors is simply indicated in the entry for each author by the abbreviation "et al."

Titles of all kinds--nobility, office and address, as well as ecclesiastical, governmental, military, academic and professional titles--have been retained in the entry as they are recorded in Poole's. This includes abbreviated titles, which are not filed as if spelled out. In the great majority of instances this scheme produces the same order of entries as would otherwise have occurred if all abbreviations had been spelled out, with variations so slight as to be trivial. Titles appearing as parts of entries without forenames or initials have been filed alphabetically as if they were forenames. Prepositional prefixes or subordinated elements of surnames appear after the title when citations do not contain forenames or initials.

By the arrangement discussed above, references to the same name can be seen to have been broken down into two distinct categories: classes of authorship--single, joint, multiple--attributed to the name, and; title variations associated with the name, one or more of which may be a reference to the same person cited in the classed arrangement immediately preceding.

PROBLEMS OF VERIFICATION.

The far-reaching problems attached to verification of authorship and consistent forms of entry which have dictated the practices outlined herein will hopefully encourage scholars to act upon the availability of this index in a positive way. Only the long drawn out nature of such an undertaking, together with the reluctance to render an entry within the text difficult to locate by citing it in a far different manner in the Author Index, has kept this writer from pursuing the matter further. We look now to a day when a definive supplement to the Author Index will appear, establishing standard forms of entry and referring users from the variant forms which so obviously fill the pages of this volume. Suggestions and contributions to this end will be appreciated, and should be sent to the attention of the Editor, Pierian Press, Ann Arbor, Michigan.

ACKNOWLEDGEMENTS.

I wish to express special appreciation to Edward Przebienda who wrote the computer programs and supervised much of the data gathering and sorting of entries for this index, to Wayne Somers who, for five months, patiently and carefully proofread and corrected the initial printout of sorted entries, and to Thomas Schultheiss for extensive assistance with the final proofreadings and preparation of photo-ready copy. I also wish to thank Cheryl Boyer, Josephine Przebienda, June Rowe, and Doris Boyer for keypunching the materials for this volume, and William Romej for assistance with data processing routines.

C. Edward Wall
March 3, 1971

A. v5p0283c1s
A., S. v6p0654c1s
Aaron, E.M. v3p0086c1s
v4p0043c1s
v4p0145c1m
v5p0581c2s
Ababrelton, R. v6p0442c2s
Abad, L.V.de and Thurber, F.B.
v6p0161c1s
Abain, G.d' v1p0190c1s
v1p0402c1s
v1p1013c1s
v1p1193c2s
Abbadie, A.d' v1p0003c2s
v1p1301c1m
v2p0259c1s
v2p0462c1s
Abbadie, A.d' et al. v2p0426c1s
Abbay, R. v1p0214c1m
v1p0271c1s
v1p0666c2s
v3p0007c1s
Abbe, C. v1p0074c1s
v1p0282c1s v1p0381c2s v1p0903c2s
v1p1267c2s v1p1269c1s v1p1293c1s
v1p1395c1s v2p0035c1s v3p0005c1s
v3p0088c2m v3p0192c1s v3p0275c2s
v3p0331c2s v3p0439c1s v3p0457c2s
v4p0190c1s v4p0252c2s v4p0367c1s
v5p0035c2s v5p0184c2s v5p0225c1s
v5p0254c1s v5p0449c2s v6p0250c1s
v6p0316c1s v6p0361c1s v6p0413c1s
v6p0415c2s v6p0667c2s
Abbey, E.A. v6p0034c1s
v6p0294c2s
Abbey, E.A. and Hodge, H.. v6p0587c2s
Abbey, E.A. and Lang, A. . v3p0388c1m
v4p0517c1s v4p0518c1s v4p0519c1m
Abbey, E.A. and Rhys, E. . v6p0587c2m
Abbey, E.A. and Swinburne, A.C.
v6p0588c1s
Abbey, E.A. and Symons, A.
v6p0588c1s
Abbey, E.A. and Watts-Dunton, T.
v6p0587c2s
Abbey, H. v1p0497c2s
Abbey, H. et al. v5p0086c1s
Abbey, R. v1p0306c1m
v1p1058c2s v1p1120c1s
Abbot, A.W. v1p0447c2s
v1p0575c2s v1p0697c2s v1p0809c1s
v1p1324c1s v3p0035c1s v3p0386c1s
v6p0109c1s
Abbot, C.C. v3p0307c1s
Abbot, C.G. and Fowle, F.E., jr.
v4p0459c2s
Abbot, C.W. v5p0290c1s
Abbot, E. v1p0127c1s
v1p0129c1s v1p0129c2s v1p0235c2s
v1p0347c1s v1p0588c2s v1p0685c2s
v1p0879c2s v1p0966c1s v1p1054c2s
v1p1312c2s v3p0043c1m
Abbot, E. and Hedge, F.H.. v1p1302c2s
Abbot, E.H. v1p0854c2s
v1p1183c1s v1p1187c1s v3p0190c2s
v4p0046c1s v4p0075c1s v6p0084c2s
Abbot, E.V. v6p0366c2s
Abbot, F.E. v1p0125c1s
v1p0134c2s v1p0241c2s v1p0288c1s
v1p0347c1s v1p1001c2m v1p1037c2s
v1p1065c1s v1p1074c1s v1p1095c1s
v1p1214c2s v1p1228c1s v1p1300c2s
v1p1304c1s v2p0274c1s v2p0339c2s
v3p0190c2s v3p0428c1s v4p0069c2s
v4p0187c2s v4p0478c2s
Abbot, F.E. and Neale, E.V.
v1p1228c1s
Abbot, H.E. v3p0147c1s
Abbot, H.L. v1p0376c1s
v1p0618c2s v1p0854c1s v1p0854c2s
v1p1110c1m v1p1241c1s v2p0211c2s
v2p0466c1s v5p0124c2s v5p0200c1s
v5p0429c1m v5p0480c2s v5p0558c2s
v6p0197c1s v6p0476c2s v6p0477c1m
v6p0477c2s
Abbot, H.L. and Humphreys, A.A.
v1p0854c2s
Abbot, H.L. and Morison, G.S.
v6p0477c1s
Abbot, J.B. and Hill, T.P.
v1p0816c2s v1p0911c2s
Abbot, J.H. v1p0401c2s
Abbot, J.M. v6p0107c1s
Abbot, L. v3p0047c2s
Abbot, S.W. v6p0408c2s
Abbot, W. v1p0511c1s
v1p1017c2s
Abbot, W.A. v5p0603c2s
Abbot, W.J. v4p0027c2s
v4p0077c1s v4p0100c1m v4p0304c2s
v5p0158c1s v6p0515c1s
Abbot, W.J. and Small, A.W.
v5p0002c1s
Abbot, W.T. v6p0113c1s
Abbott, A. v1p0190c2s
v1p0293c2s v1p0430c2s v1p0753c1s
v1p0886c2s v1p0917c2s v1p1074c1s
v1p1432c2s v3p0009c2s v3p0437c1s
v4p0198c1s v4p0277c2s v4p0325c1s
v5p0191c1s v5p0192c1s v5p0192c2s
v6p0207c1s v6p0532c2s
Abbott, A.A. v5p0128c2s
Abbott, A.D. v5p0102c2s
Abbott, A.E. v4p0202c2s
v4p0229c2s v4p0251c1s v4p0321c1s
v4p0361c1s v4p0503c2s v5p0146c1s
Abbott, A.F. v2p0356c1s
Abbott, A.R. v1p0118c1s
v1p0301c1s v1p0426c1s v1p0503c2s
v1p0560c1s v1p0687c2s v1p1161c1s
v1p1344c2s v1p1346c2s
Abbott, A.V. v2p0436c1m
v4p0403c2s v5p0185c2s
Abbott, Austin v4p0277c2s
v4p0323c2s v4p0553c1s
Abbott, B. v1p0374c1s
v1p0462c2s
Abbott, B.N. v1p0753c2s
Abbott, B.V. v2p0102c2s
v2p0150c2s
Abbott, C.A. v3p0265c2s
Abbott, C.C. v1p0135c2s
v1p0136c1s v1p0136c2s v1p0137c1s
v1p0394c2s v1p0456c2m v1p0457c1s
v1p0460c2s v1p0626c1s v1p0636c1m
v1p0638c1s v1p0638c2m v1p0803c2s
v1p0907c1s v1p1255c2m v1p1256c1m
v2p0003c2s v2p0010c2s v2p0015c1s
v2p0018c2s v2p0036c1s v2p0046c2s
v2p0047c2s v2p0093c2s v2p0102c1s
v2p0115c1s v2p0149c1s v2p0157c1m
v2p0168c2s v2p0202c2s v2p0223c2s
v2p0274c2s v2p0307c1s v2p0360c1s
v2p0406c2s v2p0426c1s v2p0442c1s
v2p0469c1s v2p0475c2s v2p0480c2s
v3p0016c2m v3p0045c2s v3p0055c1s
v3p0153c1s v3p0165c1s v3p0194c2s
v3p0214c1s v3p0254c2s v3p0359c1s
v3p0272c1s v3p0272c2s v3p0277c2s
v3p0289c2s v3p0309c1s v3p0315c2s
v3p0316c1s v3p0397c1m v3p0458c2s
v3p0466c1s v3p0471c2s v4p0049c1s
v4p0127c2s v4p0129c2s v4p0151c2s
v4p0161c2s v4p0162c2s v4p0319c1s
v4p0332c1s v4p0352c1s v4p0411c1s
v4p0432c2s v4p0528c2s v4p0575c1s
v4p0624c1s v5p0041c1s v5p0064c1m
v5p0358c1s v5p0400c2s v5p0525c1s
v5p0605c2s v5p0617c1s v6p0013c2s
v6p0021c1s v6p0125c1s v6p0189c1s
v6p0242c2s v6p0407c2s v6p0444c1s
v6p0459c1s v6p0691c1s v6p0709c1s
Abbott, C.Y. v6p0410c1s
v6p0496c2s v6p0579c2s
Abbott, D.P. v6p0409c1m
v6p0647c1s
Abbott, E. v1p0038c2s
v1p0539c2s v1p0748c1s v1p1397c2s
v2p0190c1s v6p0652c2s v6p0682c2s
v6p0704c1s
Abbott, E. and Breckinridge, S.P.
v6p0704c1s
Abbott, E.A. v1p0085c1s
v1p0417c1s v1p0805c2s v2p0044c2s
v3p0081c2s v3p0302c1s v3p0357c2s
v4p0057c1s v4p0149c1s v4p0588c1s
v5p0344c1s v6p0209c2s v6p0248c1s
v6p0420c1s
Abbott, E.H. v5p0403c2s
v5p0484c2m v5p0641c1s v6p0180c1s
v6p0308c1s v6p0428c2s v6p0447c1s
v6p0451c2s v6p0538c2s v6p0563c2s
v6p0582c1s v6p0605c2s v6p0712c1m
Abbott, E.L. v6p0065c2s
Abbott, Edith v6p0132c1s
v6p0355c2s v6p0403c2s v6p0682c2s
v6p0705c2s
Abbott, Eleanor H. v6p0554c2s
Abbott, Ernest H. v6p0215c2s
Abbott, F. v1p0056c2s
v1p0903c2s v3p0085c1s v3p0195c2s
v5p0442c1s
Abbott, F.E. v1p0437c2s
v1p1117c2s
Abbott, F.E. et al. v3p0260c1s
Abbott, F.F. v5p0441c2s
v5p0442c2s
Abbott, F.L. v1p0887c1s
v3p0454c1m
Abbott, F.M. v4p0123c2s
v4p0128c1s v4p0233c2s v4p0262c2s
v4p0266c2s v4p0494c2s v4p0600c2s
v4p0627c1m v5p0536c1s v5p0638c1s
v6p0137c2s
Abbott, G.F. v6p0392c1s
Abbott, G.N. v1p0424c2s
v1p0440c1s v1p0651c1s v1p0684c2s
v1p0687c2s v1p0702c2s v1p0793c2s
Abbott, G.S. v1p0189c1s
Abbott, Geo.M. v3p0396c2s
Abbott, H.C.DeS. v3p0333c2s
v3p0334c1m
Abbott, H.V. v5p0311c1s
v6p0152c1s
Abbott, J. v1p0008c2s
v1p0084c2s v1p0325c2s v1p0329c2s
v1p0375c1s v1p0390c1s v1p0399c1s
v1p0450c2s v1p0483c2s v1p0580c1s
v1p0665c1s v1p0746c2s v1p0748c2m
v1p0867c2s v1p0961c1s v1p0967c2s
v1p1003c2s v1p1068c2s v1p1113c2s
v1p1158c2s v1p1233c2s v1p1240c2s
v1p1250c1s v1p1268c2s v1p1288c1s
v5p0338c1s
Abbott, J.C. v4p0359c2s
Abbott, J.E. v5p0284c1s
Abbott, J.F. v6p0335c1s
Abbott, J.G. v4p0174c1s
Abbott, J.H. v1p0426c1s
v1p0426c2s v1p1082c1s
Abbott, J.H.M. v6p0206c1s
Abbott, J.J. v1p0239c2s
v1p0840c1s
Abbott, J.S.C. v1p0080c1s
v1p0115c2s v1p0141c2s v1p0201c1s
v1p0220c2s v1p0280c1s v1p0379c1s
v1p0475c2s v1p0476c1m v1p0480c1s
v1p0485c1s v1p0668c1s v1p0696c1m
v1p0771c1s v1p0771c2s v1p0772c1s
v1p0813c2s v1p0832c2s v1p0871c1s
v1p0893c1s v1p1033c1s v1p1035c1s
v1p1088c1s v1p1134c1s v1p1142c2s
v1p1331c1s v1p1343c1m v1p1344c1s
v1p1344c2m v1p1345c1m v1p1345c2m
v1p1346c1s v1p1346c2s v1p1347c1s
v1p1347c2s v1p1369c2s v1p1387c1s
Abbott, K. v6p0696c2s
Abbott, K.M. v6p0143c1s
Abbott, L. v1p0128c2s
v1p0140c2s v1p0377c2s v1p0526c1s
v1p0531c2s v1p0679c1s v1p0682c2s
v1p0806c2s v1p0852c1s v1p0891c1s
v1p0899c1s v1p0936c2s v1p1012c2s
v1p1076c2s v1p1124c2s v1p1223c2s
v1p1230c1s v1p1402c1s v1p1438c2s
v2p0042c2s v2p0081c1m v2p0149c1s
v2p0333c1s v2p0352c1s v2p0407c2s
v3p0081c2s v3p0095c2s v3p0103c1s
v3p0204c1s v3p0215c1s v3p0216c1s
v3p0230c1s v3p0266c2s v3p0324c1s
v3p0349c1s v3p0356c2s v3p0357c2s
v3p0398c1s v3p0398c2s v3p0427c2s
v3p0452c2s v3p0454c2s v4p0022c1s
v4p0097c1s v4p0109c1s v4p0301c2s
v4p0456c1s v4p0462c1s v4p0466c2s
v4p0480c1s v4p0596c1s v5p0002c1s
v5p0016c1s v5p0018c1s v5p0019c2s
v5p0057c1s v5p0057c2m v5p0058c1m
v5p0078c2s v5p0079c2s v5p0140c2s
v5p0169c2s v5p0174c1s v5p0182c1s
v5p0201c2s v5p0209c2s v5p0236c2s
v5p0237c1s v5p0260c2m v5p0261c1s
v5p0270c1s v5p0288c2s v5p0305c2s
v5p0306c1m v5p0306c2s v5p0307c1m
v5p0327c1s v5p0332c1s v5p0332c2s
v5p0378c1s v5p0385c1s v5p0414c2s
v5p0418c1s v5p0436c2s v5p0444c2s
v5p0463c1s v5p0465c2s v5p0468c2m
v5p0484c2s v5p0489c1s v5p0521c1s
v5p0530c2s v5p0534c2s v5p0547c2s
v5p0562c1s v5p0577c1m v5p0578c1s
v5p0590c2s v5p0604c2s v6p0018c1s
v6p0019c2s v6p0055c1s v6p0056c1m
v6p0085c2s v6p0093c1m v6p0123c1s
v6p0125c2s v6p0140c2s v6p0166c2s
v6p0194c1s v6p0213c1s v6p0278c1s
v6p0280c1s v6p0293c1s v6p0309c1s
v6p0309c2s v6p0310c2s v6p0340c2s
v6p0342c2s v6p0377c2s v6p0419c1s
v6p0419c2m v6p0446c2s v6p0485c1s
v6p0507c1s v6p0509c2s v6p0510c1s
v6p0513c2s v6p0523c2s v6p0551c1s
v6p0568c1s v6p0605c1s v6p0625c1s
v6p0681c2s v6p0692c2m v6p0703c2s
v6p0705c2s v6p0711c2s
Abbott, L. and Hadley, A.T.
v5p0177c1s
Abbott, L. and Potter, H.C.
v5p0506c1s
Abbott, L. et al. v2p0106c2s
v4p0567c1s
Abbott, L.D. v5p0033c2s
v5p0070c1s v5p0387c2m v5p0500c2m
v5p0536c2s
Abbott, L.F. v5p0640c2s
Abbott, Lyman v4p0001c2s
v4p0403c2s v4p0581c1s v5p0198c1s
v6p0109c2s
Abbott, M. v4p0565c2m
Abbott, M.E. v5p0263c1s
Abbott, Mabel A.R. v6p0020c1s
Abbott, N.R. v5p0220c2s
Abbott, O. v4p0244c2s
Abbott, O.C. v6p0067c1s
Abbott, R.G. v4p0601c2s
v5p0613c2s
Abbott, S.A. v1p0019c2s
Abbott, S.A.B. v3p0051c1s
Abbott, S.W. v3p0101c1s
v3p0379c1s v4p0599c1s v5p0155c1s
v6p0134c1s v6p0146c2s
Abbott, S.W. et al. v4p0108c1s
Abbott, T. v1p0016c2s
v1p0528c2s v1p0901c1s v1p1101c1s
v1p1101c2s v2p0181c1s
Abbott, T.C. v5p0334c1s
Abbott, T.K. v3p0336c1s
v6p0424c1s
Abbott, W. v1p0068c2s
v1p0849c1m

Abbott, W.C. v4p0420c1s
v4p0628c1s v5p0257c2s v5p0620c2s
v6p0481c1s
Abbott, W.J.L. v4p0202c1s
v4p0250c1s v4p0352c1s v4p0410c1s
v4p0516c1s v5p0454c1s
Abbott, W.S. v3p0459c1s
v5p0399c1s
Abd-ur-Rashid, M. v3p0349c2s
Abderhalden, Emil v6p0011c1s
Abdy, A.J. v6p0319c1s
Abdy, J.T. v1p1023c2s
Abdy, Mrs. v1p0574c1s
v1p0879c1s v1p0924c2s v1p0983c1s
v1p1335c1s
v1p1418c2s
Abdy-Williams, E.M. v4p0630c1s
v4p0633c1s
Abe, F.K. v5p0302c2s
Abe, K. v5p0303c1s
Abeel, D. v1p0853c2s
Abel, C. v1p0396c1s
v2p0016c2s v2p0104c2s v2p0249c1s
Abel, C.D. v6p0483c2s
Abel, Dr. v6p0228c2s
Abel, F. v2p0090c2s
v2p0150c2s v3p0147c1s v3p0165c1s
v3p0209c2s
Abel, F.A. v1p0146c1s
v1p0437c1m v1p0563c1s v1p0664c1s
v2p0067c2s v2p0126c1s v2p0138c1s
v2p0419c2s
Abel, H.F. v6p0626c2s
Abel, M.H. v5p0212c2s
v5p0520c2s
Abel, Prof. v1p0225c1m
v1p0346c2s v1p0562c2s
Abell, E.L., Mrs. v1p0895c1s
Abell, F. v2p0016c2s
v2p0232c2s v2p0233c2m v2p0234c1s
v2p0241c1s v2p0366c2s v2p0373c2s
v2p0381c2s v2p0412c1s v2p0436c2s
v2p0445c2s v2p0460c2s v2p0470c2s
v3p0227c2m v4p0339c2s v6p0385c2s
Abell, H.F. v1p0678c2s
v2p0427c2s v3p0193c2s v3p0227c2s
v3p0235c2s v3p0362c1s v3p0463c1s
v4p0036c2s v4p0081c2s v4p0476c1s
v4p0489c2s v4p0617c2s v5p0018c2s
v5p0143c1s v5p0263c1s v5p0498c1s
v5p0538c2s v6p0232c1s v6p0337c1s
v6p0603c2s
Abell, W.M. v6p0553c1s
Abell, W.P. v4p0477c2s
Abelson, P. v6p0308c1s
Abely, Mrs. v1p0308c2s
Aber, M.A. v3p0289c2s
v4p0169c1s
Aber, W.M. v4p0170c2s
v4p0418c1s v5p0326c2s
Abercorn, Duke of et al.
v5p0296c2m
Abercrombie, D.W. v4p0320c2s
v5p0517c2s
Abercrombie, D.W. et al. . v4p0506c2s
v4p0512c1s
Abercrombie, E.B. v4p0263c2s
v4p0264c2m v4p0585c1s v5p0214c1s
v5p0270c2s
Abercrombie, W.H. v6p0149c1s
Abercromby, J. v4p0012c2s
v4p0093c1s v4p0199c2m v4p0357c1s
v4p0382c2s v4p0501c2s v5p0223c1s
v5p0357c1m
Abercromby, J. and Taylor, I.
v3p0153c1s
Abercromby, R. v2p0048c2s
v2p0201c2s v2p0304c2m v2p0323c2s
v2p0413c2s v2p0469c1m v2p0475c1s
v3p0088c2m v3p0133c1m v3p0238c1s
v3p0251c1s v3p0286c1s v3p0306c1s
v3p0445c2s v3p0458c2m v3p0465c2s
Aberdeen, Countess of v4p0120c1s
v4p0629c1s v5p0637c1s v6p0407c2s
v6p0704c2s
Aberdeen, Earl of v1p1402c1s
v2p0352c2s v5p0610c2s
Aberdeen, Earl of and
Gordon, J.C.H. v2p0187c2s
Aberdeen, Earl of and
Hamilton-Gordon, J.C. . v2p0318c2s
Aberdeen, I. v5p0637c2m
Aberdeen, Lady v4p0101c2s
Aberdeen, Lord et al. v3p0199c1s
Aberly, J. v4p0374c1s
v6p0390c1s v6p0421c2s
Abernethy, J.W. v4p0028c1s
v4p0118c1s v4p0628c2s v5p0087c1s
v5p0341c2s v6p0459c1s
Abetti, G. and Crommelin, A.C.D.
v6p0037c1s
Abhedananda, Swami and
Farnsworth, E.C. v5p0608c2s
Able, F. v3p0223c1s
Ablett, J. v5p0125c1s
Ablett, T.R. v3p0122c2s
v5p0168c1s
Ablett, W.H. v3p0292c2s
Abney, Capt. v1p1003c1s
v3p0403c2s
Abney, W. v6p0575c2s
Abney, W.D.W. v3p0092c2s
v3p0250c2s
Abney, W.deW. v1p1004c1s
v1p1233c2s v2p0340c1s v2p0413c2s
v2p0425c1m v3p0250c2s v3p0330c2m
v3p0331c1s v3p0416c1s v4p0080c1s
v4p0124c2m v4p0125c1s v4p0193c1s
v4p0331c2s v4p0440c2m v4p0441c1s
v4p0443c1s v4p0541c1s v5p0449c1s
v6p0576c2s
About, E. v1p0019c1s
v1p0197c1s v1p0427c2s v1p0430c2s
v1p0577c2s v1p0677c1s v1p0708c1s
v1p0847c2m v1p0863c1s v1p0982c1s
v1p1193c1s v1p1333c2s v1p1360c2s
v2p0125c2s
Abrahall, J.H. v2p0238c2s
Abraham, A.P. v6p0433c2s
Abraham, G.D. v6p0013c2m
v6p0433c1m v6p0433c2s
Abraham, H. v3p0434c1s
Abraham, P.S. v3p0247c1s
Abraham, W.H. v4p0268c2s
Abrahams, A. v6p0384c1s
Abrahams, B.L. v4p0302c1s
Abrahams, I. v4p0021c1s
v4p0210c2s v4p0233c2s v4p0357c1s
v4p0623c1s v4p0636c2s v5p0023c1s
v5p0254c1s v5p0307c2m v5p0411c1s
v5p0436c2s v6p0029c2s v6p0249c2s
Abrahams, L. v5p0369c2s
v6p0058c1s
Abram, D.W. v4p0157c1s
Abram, E.W. v4p0062c2s
v4p0207c1s v4p0318c1s v4p0383c1s
Abram, W.A. v1p0720c2s
v1p1431c2s v2p0238c1s v2p0261c2s
v4p0318c1s
Abrams, L. v6p0330c2s
Abramsen, A.v. v2p0122c2s
Abreu, G.de Vasconcellos . v4p0005c2s
Abt, R. v2p0383c1s
Academicus and Stobart, W.L.
v5p0497c1s
Accola, O.E. v3p0229c1s
Achard, M.A. v1p1040c2s
Ache, Caran d' v6p0306c2s
Achelis, T. v4p0188c2m
v4p0194c1s v5p0020c2s v6p0212c1s
Acheson, A. v6p0109c1s
v6p0586c1s
Acheson, C.B. v5p0646c2s
Acheson, E.G. v4p0089c1s
v5p0242c2s
Acheson, H. v2p0425c2s
Acheson, H.C. v5p0280c2s
v5p0576c1s
Achkinasi, M. v2p0381c2s
Achorn, E.O. v4p0272c1s
v4p0333c2s
Achurch, J. v4p0344c1s
Achurch, J. and Charrington, C.
v4p0128c2s
Ackerman, A.A. v3p0019c1s
Ackerman, A.W. v5p0058c1s
v5p0309c2s
Ackerman, C.F. v6p0118c2s
Ackerman, G.E. v5p0387c1s
Ackerman, J.D. v5p0534c1s
Ackerman, J.Y. v1p1434c2s
Ackerman, W.K. v2p0363c2s
Ackermann, A.S.E. v6p0132c2s
Ackers, B.St.J. v1p0336c2s
v2p0113c2s v3p0112c2s
Ackland, J. v3p0152c2s
v4p0169c1s v5p0136c1s v5p0245c2s
v5p0516c2s v5p0568c1s
Ackroyd, L.G. v4p0277c1m
v4p0343c1s v5p0085c2s v5p0282c2s
v5p0628c2s
Ackroyd, W. v2p0124c1s
v2p0150c2s v2p0284c2m v6p0527c1s
Ackworth, W.M. v5p0080c1s
v6p0528c2s
Acland, A.H.D. v2p0101c2m
v2p0247c2s
Acland, C.T.D. v1p0308c2s
v3p0353c1s v4p0169c2s
Acland, E.A., Mrs. v3p0011c2s
v3p0066c1s
Acland, F. v6p0473c1s
v6p0542c2s
Acland, F.A. v6p0108c1s
v6p0208c1s v6p0385c1s
Acland, H.W. v1p0619c1s
Acland, J. v1p0986c1s
Aconaqua v6p0354c2s
Aconcagua v6p0676c1s
Acreff, E.M. v5p0201c2s
Acros, Duke of v5p0018c1s
Acton, E. v1p0703c2s
Acton, F. v1p0943c1s
Acton, F.S., Mrs. v1p1123c1s
Acton, Lord v2p0174c2s
v2p0203c2s v2p0328c1s v3p0119c2s
v3p0138c1s v3p0172c2s v3p0201c2s
v3p0216c2s v3p0262c1s v3p0419c2s
v3p0441c2s v4p0578c1s
Acton, W. v1p0624c1s
Acworth, H.A. v5p0331c1s
Acworth, W.M. v3p0075c1s
v3p0183c2s v3p0256c1s v3p0257c2m
v3p0266c1s v3p0278c1s v3p0352c1m
v3p0352c2s v3p0353c1s v3p0376c2s
v3p0381c2s v3p0402c1s v4p0471c1s
v4p0472c1m v4p0472c2m v4p0530c2s
v4p0582c1s v5p0391c2s v5p0476c1s
v5p0476c2s v5p0477c2m v6p0098c1s
v6p0530c1s
Adair, A. v2p0254c2s
v2p0306c1s v3p0259c2s v3p0411c1s
v3p0439c1s v4p0021c1s
Adair, Alan v3p0275c1s
Adalet v3p0189c2s
v3p0438c2s v3p0469c2s v4p0356c2s
Adam, A. v1p0475c2s
Adam, C. v1p0793c1s
v1p1040c2s
Adam, E., Mme v2p0170c2s
Adam, G.M. v1p0301c1s
v5p0324c1s v6p0598c1s
Adam, G.N. v4p0198c1s
Adam, George v6p0526c2s
Adam, J. v3p0011c1s
v3p0039c2s v3p0164c1s v3p0380c1s
v4p0172c2s v4p0626c1s
Adam, J., Mme. v2p0170c2s
v3p0160c1m v3p0161c1s v3p0320c2s
v4p0163c1s v4p0211c2s v4p0215c1s
Adam, J., Mme. and Curzon, G.N.
v4p0522c2s
Adam, M. v4p0603c2s
Adam, Madame v2p0165c2s
v4p0313c1s
Adam, Paul v6p0087c1s
v6p0674c2s
Adam, S.H. and White, S.E.
v6p0440c2s
Adam, T. v6p0376c2s
Adam, W. v1p0629c1s
v1p0791c1s v1p0802c2s
Adam, W.L. v5p0340c2s
Adami, J.G. v4p0177c2s
Adami, J.G. and Roy, C.S.. v3p0453c1s
Adams, A. v5p0422c1s
v6p0003c2s
Adams, A.D. v4p0175c1s
v5p0068c2s v5p0135c2s v5p0183c1m
v5p0183c2m v5p0184c1m v5p0184c2s
v5p0185c1s v5p0226c2m v5p0260c2s
v5p0283c2s v5p0429c2s v5p0462c2m
v5p0551c1s v5p0554c2s v6p0014c1s
v6p0197c1s v6p0198c1s v6p0198c2m
v6p0199c1m v6p0248c1s v6p0295c1s
v6p0321c1s v6p0425c2s v6p0435c1s
v6p0435c2s v6p0456c2m v6p0531c2s
v6p0659c1s v6p0659c2s v6p0688c1m
Adams, A.F. v5p0334c1s
Adams, A.H. v6p0207c2s
v6p0266c2s v6p0354c2s v6p0379c2s
v6p0400c1s
Adams, A.H.D. v3p0450c1s
Adams, A.J.S. v2p0136c2s
Adams, A.L. v1p0104c2s
v1p0135c2s v1p0136c1s v1p0147c2s
v1p0209c1s v1p0396c2s v1p0456c1s
v1p0899c1s
Adams, A.W. v2p0438c2s
Adams, B. v1p0283c1s
v1p0325c2s v1p0610c2s v1p1285c2m
v2p0096c2s v2p0452c1s v3p0170c1s
v4p0231c1s v5p0111c2s v5p0130c1s
v5p0289c2s v5p0400c1s v5p0480c2s
v5p0543c1s v5p0626c1s v6p0188c2s
v6p0284c1s v6p0530c2s v6p0621c1s
v6p0667c1s v6p0669c2s
Adams, B.B. v6p0528c1s
Adams, Brooks v2p0453c2s
v5p0030c2s v5p0621c2s v6p0684c2s
Adams, C. v1p0087c1s
v1p0114c2s v1p0207c1s v1p0308c2s
v1p0668c2s v1p0756c1s v1p0805c1s
v1p0831c1s v1p0879c1s v1p0957c1s
v1p1138c1s v1p1142c2s v1p1206c2s
v1p1363c2s v1p1365c2s v1p1398c2s
v2p0024c1s v2p0045c2s v2p0293c2s
v2p0301c2s v2p0384c1s v2p0448c2s
v3p0017c1s v3p0253c2s v3p0262c1s
v3p0284c2s v3p0329c1s v3p0472c2s
v4p0029c1s v4p0091c2s v4p0369c2s
v5p0548c1s v5p0596c1s v5p0629c1s
Adams, C., Mrs. v4p0221c1s
Adams, C.A. v1p0052c2s
Adams, C.B. v1p0509c1s
v1p0809c1s
Adams, C.C. v2p0082c2s
v2p0384c2s v3p0065c2s v3p0383c1s
v3p0425c2s v4p0005c2m v4p0006c2s
v4p0019c2s v4p0192c2s v4p0275c1s
v4p0355c1s v4p0392c1s v4p0432c2m
v4p0582c1s v5p0011c1s v5p0027c1s
v5p0048c2s v5p0130c1s v5p0130c2s
v5p0197c1s v5p0200c1s v5p0231c2s
v5p0238c1s v5p0255c2s v5p0318c1s
v5p0360c2s v5p0456c2s v5p0599c2s
v5p0600c1s v6p0023c1s v6p0250c1s
v6p0360c2s v6p0395c1s v6p0460c2s
v6p0562c2s v6p0613c2s
v6p0668c1s

Adams, C.D. v6p0109c1s
v6p0137c1s
Adams, C.E. v6p0653c2s
Adams, C.F. v1p0018c2s
v1p0031c1s v1p0033c2s v1p0092c1m
v1p0154c1s v1p0179c1s v1p0227c1s
v1p0272c1s v1p0313c2s v1p0319c1s
v1p0326c1s v1p0326c2s v1p0567c2s
v1p0569c1s v1p0649c2s v1p0698c2s
v1p0786c1s v1p0808c2s v1p0860c2s
v1p0913c1s v1p1012c1s v1p1066c2s
v1p1099c1s v1p1134c1s v1p1208c2s
v1p1244c2s v1p1245c1s v1p1262c1s
v1p1350c2s v1p1353c2s v1p1362c1s
v1p1383c1m v3p0009c1s v3p0413c1s
v4p0079c1s v4p0119c1m v4p0183c2s
v4p0184c1s v4p0341c1s v4p0387c1s
v4p0457c2s v4p0469c2s v4p0596c2s
v4p0603c2s v5p0191c2s v5p0267c1s
v6p0136c2s v6p0137c2s v6p0282c1s
v6p0292c2s v6p0355c1s v6p0366c1s
v6p0448c1s v6p0507c1s v6p0601c2s
v6p0622c1s
Adams, C.F. and Cranch, C.P.
v3p0351c1s
Adams, C.F. and Goodwin, W.W.
v4p0170c1s
Adams, C.F. et al. v5p0496c2s
Adams, C.F., jr. v1p0089c1s
v1p0151c2m v1p0168c1s v1p0206c1s
v1p0325c2s v1p0413c1s v1p0424c1m
v1p0437c1s v1p0451c1s v1p0540c1m
v1p0714c1s v1p0714c2s v1p0743c1m
v1p0752c1s v1p0814c1s v1p0941c1s
v1p0988c1s v1p1048c1s v1p1075c2m
v1p1076c1m v1p1077c2m v1p1079c1m
v1p1079c2s v1p1080c1m v1p1145c2s
v1p1181c1s v1p1251c1s v1p1261c2s
v1p1352c2s v1p1383c2s v1p1400c2m
v2p0096c2s v2p0171c1s v2p0364c1s
v2p0396c1s
Adams, C.Frederic v1p1040c1s
v2p0248c1s v2p0370c1s
Adams, C.H. v4p0135c2s
Adams, C.K. v1p0111c2s
v1p0231c2s v1p0261c2s v1p0275c1s
v1p0386c1s v1p0477c2s v1p0483c1s
v1p0515c1s v1p0895c1s v1p0896c1s
v1p1137c2s v1p1158c1s v1p1330c2m
v1p1357c2s v2p0092c2s v2p0103c1s
v2p0164c2s v2p0210c2s v2p0439c1m
v2p0452c1s v2p0454c2s v2p0469c2s
v3p0091c2m v3p0144c1s v3p0171c2s
v3p0197c1s v3p0325c1s v3p0366c1s
v3p0370c1s v3p0443c2s v3p0444c1s
v4p0126c1s v4p0507c1s v5p0128c1s
v5p0178c2m v5p0572c2s v5p0601c1s
Adams, C.K. and Coy, E.W.. v4p0122c2s
Adams, C.K. et al. v3p0091c2m
Adams, C.W. v1p0837c2s
Adams, Charlotte v2p0381c2s
v3p0253c1s v6p0261c1s
Adams, Crosby, Mrs. v5p0100c2s
v5p0394c2s
Adams, D. v1p1402c2s
v5p0069c2s
Adams, Daisy W. and
Adams, W.I.Lincoln v6p0625c1s
Adams, E. v6p0243c1s
Adams, E.B. v6p0294c2s
Adams, E.D. v5p0218c1s
v5p0228c2s v5p0361c1s v6p0094c2s
v6p0206c1s v6p0213c1s v6p0242c1s
v6p0258c1s v6p0391c2s v6p0442c1s
v6p0545c2s v6p0678c1s
Adams, E.D., Mrs. v5p0557c1s
Adams, E.E. v1p1064c1s
Adams, E.F. v1p0540c1s
v3p0375c1s v3p0400c1s v4p0132c1s
v4p0195c1s v4p0217c1s v5p0410c1s
v5p0548c2s v5p0593c1s
Adams, E.G., jr. v5p0136c2s
Adams, E.L. v4p0330c1s
v5p0107c1s v5p0337c1s v6p0373c1s
v6p0501c2s v6p0517c2m
Adams, E.P. v4p0331c2s
v5p0185c2s v6p0286c2s
Adams, E.P. and Trowbridge, J.
v5p0356c1s
Adams, E.T. v4p0145c2s
v4p0180c1s v5p0551c1s
Adams, E.W. v4p0075c2s
v4p0344c2s v5p0513c2s
Adams, Edw.W. v4p0080c2m
Adams, F. v3p0027c2s
v3p0028c1m v3p0237c1s v3p0238c2s
v4p0038c2s v4p0117c2s v4p0232c2s
v4p0247c2s v4p0311c2m v4p0398c1s
v4p0408c2s v4p0520c1s v4p0534c1s
v4p0569c2s
Adams, F. and Brown, C.M.L.
v6p0490c1s
Adams, F.A. v1p0058c1s
v1p0118c1s v1p0290c1s v1p0426c2s
v1p0555c1m v1p1062c1s
Adams, F.D. v4p0011c2s
v4p0165c2s v4p0322c1s v4p0447c2s
v4p0560c2s v5p0154c2m v6p0096c2s
v6p0449c1s v6p0546c2s
Adams, F.D. and Coker, E.G.v6p0546c1s
Adams, F.D. et al. v5p0091c2s
Adams, F.S. v2p0446c2s
Adams, F.U. v6p0344c2s
Adams, F.U. et al. v6p0234c2s
Adams, F.V. v6p0160c2s
Adams, Franklin and Brown, G.M.L.
v6p0080c1s v6p0117c2s
Adams, G. v4p0106c2s
v5p0149c1s v5p0284c2s v6p0413c1s
Adams, G.B. v3p0151c2m
v3p0472c2s v4p0259c1s v4p0437c1s
v4p0532c1s v4p0591c2s v4p0597c2s
v5p0020c1m v5p0189c2s v5p0205c2s
v6p0177c1s v6p0237c2s v6p0287c1s
v6p0292c1s v6p0383c2s
Adams, G.E. v5p0318c2s
Adams, G.F. v4p0168c1s
v4p0293c1s
Adams, G.H. v2p0150c2s
Adams, G.I. v4p0156c1s
v4p0196c2s v5p0204c2s v5p0481c1s
v6p0349c1s
Adams, G.M. v1p0903c1s
v4p0121c2s v4p0347c1s v5p0631c2s
v6p0090c2s
Adams, H. v1p0090c2s
v1p0184c1s v1p0194c1s v1p0210c2s
v1p0212c1s v1p0408c1s v1p0410c2s
v1p0487c2s v1p0509c2s v1p0540c2s
v1p0544c2s v1p0545c1s v1p0573c1s
v1p0675c1s v1p0759c2s v1p0910c1s
v1p0962c1s v1p1019c1s v1p1145c2s
v1p1211c1m v1p1295c2s v1p1309c2s
v1p1321c1s v1p1350c1s v1p1373c2s
v1p1421c2s v1p1427c2s v4p0139c1s
Adams, H. and Lodge, H.C.. v1p1348c2s
Adams, H.B. v1p0031c1s
v1p0259c1s v1p0265c2s v1p0291c2s
v1p0508c1s v1p1321c2s v1p1351c1s
v1p1438c1s v2p0032c2m v2p0067c1m
v2p0070c2s v2p0100c1m v2p0142c1s
v2p0142c2s v2p0167c1s v2p0176c1s
v2p0204c1m v2p0248c1s v2p0256c1s
v2p0279c1s v2p0310c2s v2p0315c2s
v2p0345c2s v2p0350c2s v2p0383c1s
v2p0384c1s v2p0387c1s v2p0431c2s
v2p0442c1s v2p0455c2s v2p0456c1s
v2p0461c1s v2p0466c2s v2p0471c1s
v2p0474c2s v3p0001c2s v3p0073c2s
v3p0128c2s v3p0197c1s v3p0249c2s
v3p0307c1s v3p0316c1s v3p0384c2s
v3p0403c1s v3p0445c1m v3p0445c2m
v4p0016c1s v4p0071c1s v4p0214c2m
v4p0580c2s v5p0544c2s v5p0581c2s
Adams, H.B. and Trent, W.P.
v3p0183c2s
Adams, H.B. and Wood, H. . v4p0125c2s
Adams, H.B. et al. v3p0091c2s
v3p0197c1s
Adams, H.C. v1p0339c1m
v1p0342c2s v1p0657c2s v1p1215c2s
v2p0013c1s v2p0130c1m v2p0132c1s
v2p0156c1m v2p0418c1s v2p0431c2s
v2p0452c2s v2p0465c2s v3p0032c2s
v3p0033c1s v3p0072c1s v3p0104c1s
v3p0113c1s v3p0120c2s v3p0197c2s
v3p0214c2s v3p0285c2s v3p0408c1s
v3p0416c2s v4p0015c2s v4p0170c2s
v4p0194c2s v4p0288c1s v4p0369c1s
v4p0471c1m v4p0472c2m v4p0532c2s
v4p0615c1s v5p0294c1s v5p0478c1s
v5p0568c1s v6p0009c1s v6p0435c2s
v6p0523c1s v6p0658c2s
Adams, H.C. et al. v6p0318c1s
Adams, H.G. v1p0136c2s
v1p0463c1m v1p0645c1s v1p0922c1s
v1p0940c1s v1p0949c1s v1p1409c2s
Adams, H.J. v6p0612c1s
Adams, H.S. v4p0049c1s
v4p0555c1s
Adams, H.W. v1p0160c2m
Adams, I.H. v3p0331c1s
Adams, J. v1p0218c2s
v1p0683c1s v1p1356c2s v1p1384c1s
v4p0445c1s v6p0349c1s v6p0675c2s
Adams, J. and Dicey, E. .. v4p0172c2s
Adams, J.A. v5p0446c1s
Adams, J.B. v1p0227c2s
v1p0297c2s
Adams, J.C. v1p0247c2s
v1p0648c2s v1p0993c2s v1p1161c1s
v1p1356c1s v2p0085c2s v2p0440c1s
v3p0010c1s v3p0024c1s v3p0106c1s
v3p0253c1s v3p0292c1s v3p0355c2s
v3p0434c2s v4p0101c2s v4p0115c2s
v4p0183c2s v4p0300c1s v4p0333c1s
v4p0367c1s v5p0233c1s v6p0077c2s
v6p0576c2s
Adams, J.C. et al. v4p0144c1s
Adams, J.D. v5p0317c1s
Adams, J.F.A. v4p0441c2s
Adams, J.G. v1p0172c1s
v1p0313c2s v1p0535c1s v1p0536c2s
v1p0688c1m v1p0689c2s v1p0978c1s
v1p0994c1s v1p1064c2s v1p1150c1s
v1p1197c1s v1p1292c2s v1p1326c1s
v1p1355c2s v1p1368c2s v2p0183c2s
v2p0236c1s v2p0237c1s v2p0415c1s
v4p0390c1s
Adams, J.G.B. v3p0400c1s
Adams, J.H. v1p0691c1s
v4p0047c1m v4p0185c1m v4p0363c1s
v4p0380c1s v4p0392c2s v4p0393c1s
v4p0498c2s v4p0500c1s v4p0511c2s
v4p0537c1s v5p0341c1s
Adams, J.Q. v1p0474c1s
v1p0476c2s v1p0479c1m v1p0516c2s
v1p0548c1m v1p0552c1s v1p0680c2s
v1p0798c1s v1p0907c2s v1p1023c2s
v1p1037c1s v1p1216c2s v1p1229c1m
v1p1276c2s v1p1332c1s v1p1349c2s
v5p0153c1s v5p0407c1s v6p0033c2s
Adams, J.R. v4p0052c2s
Adams, J.W. v1p1081c1s
Adams, John v5p0257c1s
Adams, L. v1p0288c1s
v1p0434c2s v1p0435c1s v1p0623c1m
v1p0740c1s v1p0839c1s v1p0904c1s
v1p1001c1s v1p1002c1s v1p1053c2s
v1p1062c1s v1p1235c1m
Adams, L., Mrs. v1p0703c1s
v1p0934c1s v2p0173c1s
Adams, L.H. and Merrill, S.
v1p1359c1s
Adams, L.T. v1p0333c2s
Adams, Laura M. v5p0448c2m
Adams, Leith v3p0167c2s
Adams, Louise H. v6p0295c1s
v6p0515c2s
Adams, M. v5p0373c2s
v5p0411c1s v5p0582c1s v5p0637c2s
Adams, M.B. v1p0293c2s
Adams, M.D. v3p0111c2s
Adams, M.E. v4p0149c2s
v6p0349c1m
Adams, M.G. v1p0567c1s
Adams, M.L. v3p0186c1s
v3p0409c2s v4p0194c2s v4p0452c2s
v4p0563c1s
Adams, M.N. v1p0697c1s
Adams, Mary v6p0144c1s
Adams, Myron E. v6p0116c1s
Adams, N. v1p0254c1s
v1p0330c1s v1p0847c2m v1p0848c1s
v1p1065c1s v1p1286c2s v1p1399c2s
v6p0434c1s
Adams, O.F. v1p0199c2s
v1p0599c1s v1p1131c2s v1p1408c2s
v2p0062c2s v2p0357c1s v3p0027c1s
v3p0463c1s v4p0023c1s v4p0037c2s
v4p0191c2s v4p0341c1s v4p0346c1s
v4p0515c2s v6p0041c1s v6p0052c1s
v6p0079c2s v6p0111c2s v6p0236c1s
v6p0532c1s v6p0623c2s
Adams, O.S. v1p0142c2s
v1p0667c2s v3p0291c1s v3p0303c1s
Adams, R. v4p0131c1s
v6p0155c1s v6p0600c2s
Adams, R., jr. v4p0206c1m
Adams, R.C. v4p0314c1s
Adams, R.D. v1p0079c1s
Adams, R.J. v2p0034c2s
Adams, Robert W. v6p0074c1s
Adams, S. v1p0041c1s
v1p0262c2s v1p0287c1s v1p0333c2s
v1p0711c1s v1p0747c1s v1p0793c2s
v1p0816c2s v1p0899c1s v1p1037c2s
v1p1062c2s v1p1096c1s v1p1161c2s
Adams, S.A. v3p0274c2s
Adams, S.F. v1p0170c1s
v3p0034c2s
Adams, S.H. v5p0158c2s
v5p0340c1s v6p0161c2s v6p0185c1s
v6p0230c1s v6p0351c2s v6p0380c2s
v6p0397c2s v6p0407c1s v6p0512c2s
v6p0533c1s v6p0614c2s v6p0623c2m
v6p0627c2s v6p0660c1s v6p0663c2s
v6p0711c1s
Adams, Samuel H. v6p0045c2s
Adams, T. v1p1309c2s
v1p1761c2s v5p0515c1s v6p0247c1s
Adams, T.P. v1p0201c1s
v1p0571c1s
Adams, T.S. v5p0284c1s
v5p0364c2s v5p0460c1s v5p0460c2m
v6p0312c2s v6p0510c1s v6p0622c1s
v6p0652c2s v6p0701c1s
Adams, W. v1p0033c1s
v1p0068c1s v1p0234c2s v1p0240c2s
v1p0242c1m v1p0242c2s v1p0243c1s
v1p0244c1s v1p0254c2s v1p0273c2s
v1p0314c1s v1p0357c2s v1p0422c2s
v1p0690c1s v1p0726c1s v1p0846c2s
v1p0870c1s v1p1055c1s v1p1064c1s
v1p1065c1s v1p1140c2s v1p1175c2s
v2p0129c1s v2p0153c1s v5p0481c2s
Adams, W.A. v1p1079c2s
v6p0031c1s v6p0031c2s
Adams, W.B. v1p0065c2s
v1p0083c1m v1p0116c1s v1p0195c2s
v1p0301c1s v1p0376c2s v1p0465c1s
v1p0520c1s v1p0551c1m v1p0562c1m
v1p0651c2s v1p0763c2s v1p0783c2s
v1p0824c2s v1p0877c1s v1p0978c1s
v1p1011c2s v1p1055c1s v1p1075c2s
v1p1076c1s v1p1078c1m v1p1079c1s
v1p1080c1s v1p1080c2s v1p1091c1s
v1p1173c1s v1p1181c1s v1p1191c2m
v1p1192c1m v1p1320c2m v1p1391c2s
v1p1392c2s v3p0029c2s v3p0212c2s

v3p0353c2s v3p0369c1s v3p0412c1m
v6p0221c1s
Adams, W.D. v1p0060c2s
v1p0318c1s v1p0521c2s v1p0882c2s
v2p0144c2s v2p0249c1s v2p0261c2s
v2p0328c1m v2p0416c2s v2p0435c2s
v3p0122c1s v3p0231c1s v3p0257c1s
v3p0275c1s v3p0316c1s v3p0357c1s
v3p0387c1s v3p0462c1s v3p0464c1s
v4p0003c1m v4p0079c2s v4p0141c1s
v4p0146c2s v4p0147c1s v4p0272c2s
v4p0309c1s v4p0328c1s v4p0335c1s
v4p0415c1s v4p0572c2s v5p0576c1s
Adams, W.Davenport v1p1386c2s
Adams, W.G. v1p0387c2s
v1p0399c2m v1p0815c2s v1p1005c2s
v2p0271c2s v3p0107c1s v3p0132c2s
Adams, W.G.S. v6p0106c2s
Adams, W.H. v6p0703c1s
Adams, W.H.D. v1p0975c1s
v1p1022c1s v3p0028c2s v3p0089c1s
v3p0089c2s v3p0102c1s v3p0112c2s
v3p0160c2s v3p0183c2m v3p0253c1s
v3p0331c2s v3p0333c1s v3p0349c2s
v3p0461c2s v4p0445c1s
Adams, W.I.L. v3p0330c2m
v3p0331c1m v4p0440c1s v4p0440c2s
v5p0447c2s
Adams, W.I.Lincoln and
Adams, Daisy W. v6p0625c1s
Adams, W.J. v1p1159c2s
Adams, W.M. v2p0104c1s
v2p0177c1s v3p0141c1s v3p0465c1s
v4p0034c1s v4p0172c1s v5p0430c1s
Adams, W.S. v5p0554c1s
Adams, W.T. v4p0506c2s
Adams, W.W. v1p0685c2s
v2p0275c2s
Adams, Z.B. v2p0273c1s
Adams, Z.F. v5p0333c2s
Adamson, J. v1p0040c1s
v1p0272c1s v1p0724c1s
Adamson, R. v1p0427c1s
v1p0702c1s v1p0760c1s v1p0760c2m
v1p0812c1s v1p0839c2s v1p1002c1s
v1p1160c1s v1p1162c2s v1p1228c1s
v2p0200c1s v2p0240c2m v2p0262c2s
v2p0266c2s v2p0339c1s v2p0358c2s
v3p0329c2s
Adamson, W. v2p0274c1s
v6p0480c2m
Adamson, W.A. v1p1146c1s
Adamson, W.S. v1p0243c2s
Adcock, A.St.J. v5p0342c2s
v5p0365c2s v5p0539c1s
Addams, J. v4p0158c2s
v4p0268c2m v4p0532c2s v5p0102c1m
v5p0105c2s v5p0127c1s v5p0327c2s
v5p0535c2s
Addams, J. et al. v4p0030c2s
Addams, Jane v5p0072c1s
v5p0391c2s v5p0584c2s v6p0114c2s
v6p0115c1m v6p0194c1s v6p0309c1s
v6p0318c1s v6p0435c1s v6p0638c1s
v6p0651c2s v6p0660c2s v6p0707c2s
Addenbrooke, G.L. v4p0012c2m
v5p0184c2s v6p0198c1s
Adderley, A., Sir v5p0626c1s
Adderley, J. v4p0530c1s
v5p0117c2s
Adderley, J.G. v4p0553c1s
Adderly, J. v4p0109c2s
v6p0141c1s
Addicks, L. v6p0149c1s
Addis, A. v1p0727c1s
v1p1221c1s
Addis, C.S. v3p0079c1s
v5p0319c2s
Addis, J. v1p1185c2s
Addis, M.E.L. v6p0299c2s
Addis, M.E.Leicester v5p0257c2s
v5p0579c1s
Addis, W. v4p0170c1s
Addis, W.E. v1p1098c2s
v2p0432c1s
Addis, Y.H. v2p0462c1s
v3p0341c1s v6p0679c1s
Addison, D.D. v2p0343c1s
v5p0469c1s
Addison, H.R. v1p0143c2s
v1p0185c2s v1p0294c1s v1p0445c2s
v1p0790c2s v1p1145c2s v1p1213c1s
v1p1273c2s v2p0033c2s
Addison, J. v1p1005c2s
v2p0047c2s
Addison, J.E. v1p1218c2s
Addison, P.L. v4p0227c1s
v4p0516c1s
Addison, T. v6p0190c2s
Addleshaw, P. v4p0064c2m
v4p0080c2s v4p0248c2s v4p0325c1s
v4p0405c2s
Addleshaw, Stanley v5p0435c2s
Addy, E.O. v4p0558c2s
Addy, S.O. v3p0140c2s
v3p0152c1s v3p0295c2s v3p0474c2s
v5p0227c1s
Addy, S.O. et al. v6p0230c2s
Ade, G. v6p0217c1s
v6p0463c2s
Ade, George v6p0384c1s
Adee, A.A. v1p0746c2s
v1p0786c1s v1p1277c1s v2p0070c1s
Adee, D.A. v3p0116c2s
Adee, D.G. v1p0902c1s
v1p1230c1s v4p0042c2s v4p0189c1s
v4p0351c1s v4p0595c1s
Adee, S. and Pettingal, J.
v1p0026c1s
Adelung, E.von v4p0373c1s
Adeney, W.F. v2p0007c2s
v2p0042c2s v2p0134c1s v2p0151c2s
v2p0214c2s v2p0216c2s v2p0236c1s
v2p0327c1s v2p0348c1s v2p0360c1s
v2p0450c2s v3p0042c2s v4p0057c2s
v4p0193c2s v4p0255c2s v5p0058c2s
v5p0305c2s v5p0310c2s v5p0388c1s
v6p0063c1s v6p0342c1s v6p0642c2s
Adeney, W.P. v5p0305c2s
Adenry, W.F. v2p0254c2s
Adger, J.B. v2p0439c2s
Adickes, E. v4p0308c1s
v4p0439c2s v5p0230c2s v5p0446c2s
v5p0447c1s
Adie, A.J. v1p1255c2s
Adie, R. v1p0304c2s
Adiline, Jules v6p0104c2s
Adkins, E. v2p0099c2s
Adkins, F.J. v6p0193c2s
Adkins, F.S. v5p0177c1s
Adkins, H. v4p0479c2s
Adkins, M.T. v3p0011c1s
v3p0047c1s v3p0124c1s v3p0292c1s
v3p0408c1s v3p0444c1s v3p0456c2s
Adlard, G. v1p0909c2s
Adler, C. v2p0043c1s
v2p0130c2s v2p0414c1s v3p0209c1s
v3p0230c1s v3p0231c1s v4p0299c2s
v5p0072c1s v5p0514c1m v6p0339c2s
v6p0576c2m
Adler, C. and Medlicott, M.
v5p0393c1s
Adler, D. v3p0427c1s
v4p0078c2m v4p0099c2s v4p0572c1s
v5p0026c1s v5p0082c2s
Adler, E.N. v4p0286c2s
v5p0056c2s v5p0308c1s v5p0314c1s
v5p0397c1s v5p0585c2s v6p0043c1m
v6p0398c1s
Adler, E.N. and Broyde, I.
v5p0071c1s
Adler, E.N. and Kayserling, M.
v5p0041c1s
Adler, E.N. and Schechter, S.
v5p0174c1s
Adler, F. v1p0173c1s
v1p0691c1s v1p0691c2s v1p0697c1s
v1p0707c2s v2p0106c2s v2p0146c2s
v2p0275c2s v2p0297c1s v3p0128c2s
v3p0143c1s v4p0143c1s v4p0157c2s
v4p0187c2m v4p0188c1s v4p0354c1s
v4p0439c1s v4p0528c2s v4p0636c1s
v5p0529c1s v5p0601c1s v6p0114c2s
v6p0349c2s v6p0494c2s v6p0637c1s
Adler, F. et al. v2p0132c1s
v4p0109c2s
Adler, G. v3p0399c1s
Adler, G.J. v1p0559c1s
v1p0614c1s v1p0789c1s
Adler, G.T. v1p0008c2s
Adler, H. v1p0689c2m
v2p0236c2s v2p0239c1s v3p0230c2s
v3p0287c2s v4p0303c1s
Adler, H. et al. v3p0458c2s
Adler, H.M. v5p0408c2s
v6p0378c2s v6p0384c1s v6p0506c2s
Adler, M. v4p0302c1s
v4p0306c2s v5p0307c2s
Adler, M.N. v4p0302c1s
v6p0058c1s
Adler, N. v6p0115c2s
Admire, W.W. v3p0015c1s
v3p0234c2s
Adney, T. v5p0092c2s
v5p0164c2s v5p0385c2s v6p0099c1s
v6p0315c2s v6p0420c2s v6p0428c1s
v6p0461c1s
Adolphus, J.L. v1p0007c1s
Adolphus, T.A. v1p0967c2s
Adsit, C.D., Mrs. v3p0063c1s
Ady, F., Mrs. v3p0146c2m
Ady, H., Mrs. v3p0139c1s
Ady, J.E. v2p0157c2m
v2p0199c1s
Ady, J.M. v3p0173c1s
v3p0279c2s v3p0366c2s
Ady, J.M., Mrs. v4p0304c2s
Ady, Julia, Mrs. v3p0279c2s
Ady, Julia C. v6p0211c1s
Ady, Julia Cartwright v5p0374c2s
Ady, Julia M., Mrs. v3p0366c2s
Adye, F. v4p0104c1s
v4p0419c2m
Adye, J. v1p0067c2s
v3p0023c2s v3p0183c1m v4p0225c2s
v4p0235c2s v5p0216c2s v5p0217c1s
v5p0258c1m
Adye, J., Lt.Gen.Sir v1p0633c1s
Adye, J., Sir v1p0542c2s
v3p0179c2s v3p0180c1s v4p0236c1m
Adye, John v5p0518c2s
Adye, John, Sir v3p0180c1s
Affleck, T. v1p0226c1s
Afghanistan, Ameer of v2p0003c2s
Aflalo, A.G. v5p0387c2s
Aflalo, F.G. v4p0505c1s
v5p0003c2s v5p0020c2m v5p0021c1m
v5p0039c1s v5p0040c1s v5p0051c1s
v5p0199c1s v5p0208c2m v5p0209c1s
v5p0209c2s v5p0255c1s v5p0346c2s
v5p0383c2s v5p0397c2s v5p0434c2s
v5p0435c1s v5p0442c1s v5p0451c1s
v5p0494c2s v5p0505c2s v5p0507c2s
v5p0510c2s v5p0516c2s v5p0547c1m
v5p0579c1s v5p0646c1s v6p0053c2s
v6p0211c1s v6p0226c2s v6p0227c1m
v6p0304c1s v6p0394c1s v6p0397c1s
v6p0570c2s v6p0611c2m v6p0615c1s
v6p0713c2s
Aflalo, J. v6p0012c1s
Agar, J.G. v5p0119c1s
Agar, W.T. v3p0188c1s
Agard, A.F. v5p0197c2s
Agarwala, M.L. v4p0357c1s
Agassiz, A. v1p0200c2s
v1p0215c1s v1p0311c1s v1p0313c1s
v1p0347c1s v1p0462c1s v1p0466c2s
v1p0565c1s v1p0587c2s v1p0960c1m
v1p1040c1s v1p1440c2s v2p0013c1s
v2p0073c2s v2p0090c2s v2p0107c1s
v2p0455c1s v3p0325c2s v3p0328c1s
v4p0038c1s v4p0052c1s v4p0095c1s
v4p0420c2s v5p0011c1m v5p0206c2s
v5p0339c1s v6p0011c1m v6p0396c1s
v6p0474c1s
Agassiz, A.R. v4p0353c1s
Agassiz, E.C. v1p0497c1s
v1p0524c1s v1p0786c2s
Agassiz, E.C., Mrs. v1p0562c1s
Agassiz, L. v1p0026c2s
v1p0030c2s v1p0040c2s v1p0041c2m
v1p0042c1m v1p0042c2s v1p0200c1s
v1p0295c2s v1p0366c1s v1p0435c1s
v1p0456c1m v1p0508c1s v1p0509c2s
v1p0523c2m v1p0524c1m v1p0613c2s
v1p0614c1s v1p0621c2s v1p0876c2s
v1p0899c1m v1p1073c1s v1p1187c2s
v1p1271c1s v1p1293c1s v1p1296c2s
Agassiz, L. et al.
v5p0153c2m
Agassiz, L., Mrs. v1p0158c1m
Ager, H.C. v4p0423c2s
v4p0533c2s
Ager, H.G. v4p0157c2s
v4p0169c1s v4p0614c2s
Agg-Gardner, J.T. v2p0434c1m
Agha, S. v1p0289c2m
Aglipay, G. v6p0494c1s
Agnew, B.L. v4p0457c1s
Agnew, D. v3p0008c2s
v5p0274c2s
Agnew, D.C.A. v2p0352c2s
Agnew, D.H. v1p1263c2s
Agnew, Daniel v5p0258c2s
Agnew, J.H. v1p1046c1s
v1p1288c1s
Agnew, Mary C. v4p0085c1s
v4p0087c2s v4p0539c1s
Agnus, O. v5p0273c2s
Agrell, A. v4p0321c1s
Agresti, O.R. v6p0152c1s
v6p0478c1s
Agudio, T. v1p1076c2s
Aguilar, A. v1p0382c1s
Aguilar, F. v6p0012c1s
Aguilar, G. v2p0457c1s
Aguillon, Col.d' v1p1115c1s
Aguirre, C.M. v6p0160c2s
Aguirre, G.C.de v3p0200c1s
Aguirre, G.G.de v5p0412c1s
Ah-Nen-La-De-Ni v6p0315c2s
Ahern, M.E. v5p0333c1s
v6p0535c1s
Ahern, W. v1p1291c1s
Aherne, C. v5p0513c2s
v5p0514c1s v6p0040c1s
Ahmad, R. v4p0027c1s
v4p0166c2s v4p0376c1s v5p0005c1s
v5p0286c1s v5p0287c1s v5p0381c2s
v5p0420c2s
Ahmad, Rafiuddin v3p0196c2s
v3p0469c2s v4p0376c1s v4p0628c1s
v5p0286c2s
v5p0299c1m
Ahnfelt, A.
v2p0428c1m
v3p0417c2m
Aicard, Jean v6p0633c2s
Aide, H. v1p0554c2s
v1p0805c1s v1p1361c1s v2p0002c2s
v2p0123c1s v2p0359c1s v3p0010c1s
v3p0011c2s v3p0012c1s v3p0092c2s
v3p0139c1s v3p0143c2s v3p0286c1s
v3p0292c1s v3p0362c1s v3p0392c1s
v3p0405c1s v4p0002c2s v4p0076c2s
v4p0267c1s v5p0138c2s v5p0235c2s
v5p0331c2s
Aiglun, Vicomte d' v4p0322c1s
Aiken, C.A. v1p0132c2s
v1p0254c2s v1p0420c2s v1p0724c2s

v1p0857c2s v2p0043c1s v2p0081c1m v2p0082c1s v2p0290c2s
Aiken, C.E. v1p0279c1s
Aiken, C.F. v5p0041c2s v6p0045c1s v6p0301c2s v6p0342c1s v6p0487c1s v6p0537c1s v6p0540c2s
Aiken, E.E. v3p0078c2s
Aiken, Ednah v6p0159c2s
Aiken, J. v1p1152c2s
Aiken, R. v2p0051c1s
Aiken, S. v1p0977c2s
Aiken, W.B. v3p0065c2s
Aiken, W.E. v6p0208c2s
Aiken, W.M. v4p0024c2s v5p0025c2s v5p0026c2s v5p0642c1s
Aikin, A. v1p0147c2s v1p0604c1s v1p0664c2s v1p1317c1s
Aikin, J. v1p1271c1s
Aikin, W.A. v6p0680c2s
Aikin, W.E. v6p0190c2s
Aikin, W.E.A. v1p0501c2s
Aikins, A. v1p1039c1s
Aikins, H.A. v4p0149c2s v4p0446c2s v6p0522c1s
Aikins, H.A. and Hodge, C.F. v4p0463c1s
Aikman, C.M. v3p0006c1s v4p0008c2s v4p0026c1s v4p0104c2s v4p0225c1s v4p0337c1s v4p0369c1s v4p0370c2s v4p0405c1s v4p0429c2s v5p0009c2s v5p0164c1s v5p0374c1s
Aikman, G. v6p0069c2s v6p0245c1s v6p0276c2s v6p0552c1s v6p0620c1m
Aikman, R. v1p0189c2s v1p1140c1s
Aikman, W. v1p0404c1s v1p0681c1s v1p1040c2s
Ailes, M.E. v5p0027c1s v5p0600c1s
Aimar, M. v2p0283c1s
Aime, V. v1p1265c1m
Aimee, L.d' v5p0179c2s
Aimes, H.H.S. v6p0160c2s
Aimes, Hubert H.S. v6p0007c2s
Ainey, W.H. v4p0393c2s
Ainger, A. v2p0075c2s v2p0246c2m v2p0247c1s v2p0398c1s v3p0091c1s v3p0140c2s v3p0240c2s v3p0411c2s v4p0448c2s v4p0569c1s v6p0147c1s v6p0359c2s
Ainger, A. and Besant, W.. v4p0085c1s
Ainley, D. v1p1181c2s
Ainsa, S. v2p0286c2s
Ainsbury, W.F. v3p0396c2s
Ainscough, J.A. v4p0216c1s
Ainslee, A. v1p0813c2s
Ainslee, G. v1p0156c2s v1p0803c2s v1p1128c1s v1p1273c1s v1p1321c1s v1p1421c1s
Ainslee, Guy v1p0930c2s
Ainsleigh, N. v4p0217c1s v5p0262c2s
Ainslie, G. v2p0219c2s
Ainslie, W.L. and Voxall, J.H. v5p0077c2s
Ainsworth, D.E. v5p0178c2m
Ainsworth, J. v4p0347c1s
Ainsworth, W.F. v1p0002c2s v1p0012c1s v1p0013c1s v1p0069c2s v1p0084c2m v1p0214c1s v1p0377c2s v1p0429c1s v1p0434c1m v1p0439c1s v1p0467c1s v1p0559c2s v1p0621c1s v1p0623c1s v1p0644c2s v1p0691c1s v1p0746c1s v1p0901c1s v1p0977c1s v1p0992c1s v1p1088c2s v1p1099c2s v1p1278c2s v1p1310c2s v1p1332c1m v1p1337c2s v1p1338c1s v2p0067c2s v2p0432c2s v3p0023c2s v3p0046c2s v3p0110c2s v3p0257c2s v3p0290c2s v4p0023c1s v4p0189c1s v5p0167c1s
Ainsworth, W.H. v1p0077c1s v1p0151c1s v1p0209c2s v1p0280c2s v1p0293c2m v1p0460c2s v1p0563c2s v1p0590c2s v1p0607c2m v1p0674c2s v1p0693c2s v1p0768c2s v1p0889c1s v1p0940c1s v1p0953c1s v1p1235c2s v1p1317c2s v2p0067c2s
Aird, T. v1p0065c1s v1p0239c1s v1p0256c1s v1p0343c1s v1p0903c2s v1p0941c1s v1p1266c2s
Airlie, Earl of v1p0015c2s v1p0111c1s v1p0907c2s v1p1342c1s v3p0180c1s v4p0235c2s v4p0444c4s
Airy, G.B. v1p0146c1s v1p0184c2s v1p0375c1s v1p0375c2s v1p0573c2s v1p0787c2s v1p0986c2s v2p0163c1m v3p0064c1s v3p0363c2s
Airy, G.B. and Lewin, T. . v1p0184c2s
Airy, G.B. et al. v1p0286c2s
Airy, H. v1p0732c2s v1p0986c2s v2p0047c1s
Airy, H. et al. v2p0046c2s
Airy, O. v2p0250c2s v3p0307c1s v5p0618c2s
Airy, W. v1p0051c1s v1p0326c2s v1p1076c1s
Aisle, H. v2p0123c1s
Aitchison, G. v2p0019c1s v2p0019c2m v2p0020c1s v2p0093c2s v2p0114c1s v2p0156c1s v2p0180c1s v2p0229c1s v2p0276c1s v2p0299c1m v2p0417c1m v3p0113c1s v3p0113c2s v3p0210c2s
Aitchison, George v4p0024c1s v6p0139c1s
Aitchison, Prof. v3p0035c2s
Aitken, E. v4p0627c2s
Aitken, E.H. v6p0315c1s
Aitken, F.W. v6p0188c2s
Aitken, G.A. v2p0204c2s v2p0420c1m v3p0002c2s v3p0113c2m v3p0114c1s v3p0168c1s v3p0344c1s v3p0409c1s v3p0427c1s v4p0022c2s v4p0151c1m v4p0221c1m v5p0440c2s v5p0564c1m
Aitken, H. v5p0506c1s
Aitken, J. v1p0373c1m v1p0464c1s v1p0524c1s v1p0621c2s v1p0875c1s v2p0126c1s v3p0088c2s v3p0125c1s v4p0164c2m v5p0184c2s
Aitken, J. and Tarr, R.S.. v4p0317c1s
Aitken, J.B. v2p0081c2s
Aitken, Jessie T. v5p0154c2s
Aitken, K.L. v6p0286c1s
Aitken, R. v5p0276c2s v5p0319c1s v6p0581c1s
Aitken, R.G. v5p0549c1s v5p0549c2s v6p0107c1s v6p0613c2s v6p0614c1m v6p0647c1s
Aitken, Robert v6p0166c2s
Aitken, W.C. v3p0275c2s
Aiton, G.B. v5p0192c1s v5p0518c1s
Ajano, R.B.d' v4p0193c2s
Aked, C.F. v4p0346c1m v4p0397c1s
Akehurst, F.E. v3p0144c2s
Akeman, T.B. v4p0194c1s
Aken, A.G.Van v2p0479c1s
Akerlind, G.A. v6p0328c2s
Akerman, J.H. v1p0933c2s
Akerman, J.Y. v1p0039c2m v1p0040c1m v1p0040c2s v1p0046c1s v1p0100c1s v1p0100c2s v1p0103c2s v1p0104c1s v1p0139c2s v1p0156c1s v1p0163c2s v1p0198c2s v1p0272c1s v1p0336c2s v1p0349c2s v1p0356c1s v1p0695c1s v1p0790c2s v1p0791c1s v1p0949c1s v1p1039c2s v1p1108c1s v1p1122c2s v1p1129c2s v1p1394c2s
Akerman, J.Y. and Stone, S. v1p0211c1s
Akerman, J.Y. and Wright, T. v1p1403c1s
Akerman, R. v1p0493c2m v1p0663c2m v1p1250c2m
Akers, C. v5p0187c1m v5p0350c1s
Akers, E.A.C. v1p1372c2s
Akers, P. v1p0957c1s
Akin, C.K. v1p0747c1s v1p1006c2s
Akin, K. v2p0413c2s
Akin, L. v6p0296c2s
Akm, C.von v1p0677c2m
Akrabova, E.S. v6p0011c2s
Akroyd, E. v1p0439c1s
Akroyd, H. v5p0435c2s
Alabaster, E. v5p0113c1s
Alabaster, H. v1p0173c2s
Alain, A. v4p0148c2s
Alarcon, P.A.de v5p0011c1s v5p0137c2s v5p0248c2s v5p0480c2s v5p0596c1s
Alarcon, P.Antonia de v5p0627c2s
Albaro, P.d' v5p0144c1s
Albee, E. v4p0143c1s v4p0188c1s v4p0188c2s v4p0270c2s v4p0517c1s v4p0599c1s v5p0196c1m v5p0227c2s v5p0275c2s v5p0606c1s v6p0517c1s
Albee, H.R. v5p0289c2s v6p0155c2s v6p0554c1m v6p0554c2s
Albee, Helen R. v6p0690c2s
Albee, J. v1p0131c1s v1p0582c1s v1p1017c1s v2p0198c1s v4p0016c2s v4p0385c2s v4p0540c2s v5p0013c1s v5p0036c2s v5p0329c1s v5p0575c2s v5p0633c1s v6p0202c2s
Albee, S. v1p0014c1s v1p0976c1s
Albemarle, Earl of v4p0175c2s
Alberger, L.R. v5p0132c1s
Albers, A.C. v6p0314c1s v6p0631c1s
Albert, A.D. v6p0018c2s
Albert, A.D., jr. v5p0304c1s v6p0057c2s v6p0099c1s
Albert, A.E.P. v4p0112c1s
Albert, C.S. v1p0248c2s v1p0275c1s v1p0639c1s v1p1304c2s v2p0121c1s v2p0269c1s v3p0238c2s v3p0347c1s v3p0404c1s v3p0454c2s v4p0037c1s v4p0286c1s v4p0345c1s v4p0633c1s v5p0177c1s v6p0165c2s
Albert, F.X.E. v6p0458c1s
Albert, J.J. v1p0649c2s v1p0956c2s
Albert, L.E. v1p0076c1s v1p0847c2s
Albert, Prince v1p1245c2m
Albert, Prince of Monaco . v4p0182c2s v5p0037c1s v5p0417c2s
Albert of Godesberg v5p0393c2s
Alberti, C. v3p0164c2s v6p0479c1s
Albertson, C. v6p0177c1s v6p0335c1s
Albertson, J.W. v5p0348c2s
Albery, F.F.D. v4p0163c2s v6p0415c1s
Albi, G.C.d' v5p0140c1s
Albinson, J. v5p0321c1s
Albion, J. v2p0180c2s
Albrecht, A. v6p0557c1s
Albrecht, G.E. v6p0336c2s
Albree, C.B. v5p0298c1s
Albro, J.A. v1p0118c1s v1p0882c2s
Albro, W.C. v4p0318c2s
Albuquerque, J.P.D' v5p0009c2s v6p0692c2s
Alburger, L.R. v4p0200c1s
Alcho, A.D. v5p0625c2s
Alcho, A.D' v5p0555c2s
Alciphron v6p0048c1s v6p0369c1s v6p0550c2s
Alcock, C.W. v3p0157c2s
Alcock, N. v3p0250c2s
Alcock, N. et al. v2p0309c1s
Alcock, R. v2p0078c2s v2p0328c2s
Alcock, R., Sir v1p0011c1s v1p0063c1s v1p0067c2s v1p0068c1s v1p0231c2s v1p0232c2s v1p0233c2s v1p0677c2s v1p0678c2s v1p0679c1s v1p0861c2s v1p0944c2s v1p0985c2s v2p0078c2s v3p0313c1s
Alcom, F.G. v4p0307c2s
Alcott, A.B. v1p0335c2s v1p0504c1s v1p0587c2m v1p0949c2s v1p0998c2s v1p0999c1s v1p1016c2s v1p1301c1s v1p1419c2s
Alcott, A.N. v4p0597c1s
Alcott, L.M. v1p0168c1s v1p0338c2s v1p0773c1m v1p1155c2s v1p1430c2s
Alcott, W.A. v1p1427c2s
Alcott, W.P. v1p0557c1s
Alcott, W.S. v6p0076c2s
Alcott, Winfield S. v6p0309c1s
Aldama, M.Carrillo v6p0160c2s
Alden, A.D. v2p0130c1s
Alden, B. v6p0665c1m
Alden, C.L., Mrs. v4p0010c1s v5p0011c2s v5p0534c2s
Alden, E. v1p0808c2s v1p0809c2s v1p0816c2s v1p1178c2s
Alden, E.K. v1p0362c2s v1p0977c2s v4p0398c2s v4p0481c2s
Alden, G.H. v5p0550c1s v6p0239c2s
Alden, G.I. v4p0517c1s
Alden, H.M. v1p0003c1s v1p0111c2s v1p0197c1s v1p0268c2s v1p0345c1m v1p0377c2s v1p0987c2s v1p1051c2s v1p1109c1s v1p1252c2s v5p0256c1s v6p0394c2s
Alden, J. v1p0180c2s v1p0417c2s v1p0528c1s v1p0820c2s v1p0868c2s v1p1093c2s v1p1253c2s v4p0139c1s v4p0185c2s
Alden, J.E. v5p0625c2s
Alden, L. v1p0755c1s v1p1418c1s
Alden, L.P. v4p0103c2s v5p0263c1s
Alden, M.L.T., Mrs. v4p0531c2s
Alden, P. v5p0302c2s v5p0433c1s v6p0383c2s v6p0384c1s
Alden, P. and Dawes, H.L.. v5p0445c1s
Alden, Percy v4p0598c1s v5p0437c2s v6p0019c1s
Alden, Prof. v1p1273c1s
Alden, R.M. v4p0335c1s v5p0374c2s v6p0503c2s
Alden, T. v1p0356c2s
Alden, W.H. v4p0615c1s v5p0561c2s v6p0115c2s
Alden, W.L. v1p0196c2m v1p0204c2s v1p0451c1s v1p0471c2s v1p0534c1s v1p0575c2s v1p0692c1s v1p0735c1s v1p0814c2s v1p1053c2s v1p1258c1s v1p1383c1s v2p0066c2s v2p0171c1s v2p0382c2s v2p0404c2s v2p0409c2s v4p0035c2s v4p0128c1s v4p0154c1s v4p0204c2s v4p0206c2s v4p0211c1s v4p0225c2s v4p0263c1s v4p0267c1s v4p0342c1s v4p0380c1s v4p0417c2s v4p0418c1s v4p0460c2m v4p0490c2s v4p0529c2s v4p0578c2s v4p0588c2s v4p0600c2s v4p0608c2s v4p0623c1s v5p0248c2s v5p0295c1s v5p0310c2s v5p0348c1s v5p0348c2s v5p0381c1s v5p0389c2s v5p0395c1s v5p0396c2s v5p0492c1s v5p0507c2s v5p0564c2s v5p0610c1s v5p0645c1s

v6p0014c2s v6p0105c1s v6p0157c1s
v6p0482c2s v6p0623c1s v6p0690c1s
Alden, W.L. and Dillon, W.
v4p0378c1s
Alden, W.S. v4p0140c2s
Aldenham, Lord v4p0230c1s
v5p0061c2s
Alder, Dankmar v4p0025c1s
Alder, E. v1p0522c2s
Alder, R. v1p0931c1s
Alderman, E.A. v4p0538c1s
v5p0540c2m v6p0192c2s v6p0333c2s
v6p0604c2s v6p0605c2s
Alderman, L.A. v3p0268c1s
Alderson, Bernard v6p0102c1s
Alderson, V.C. v6p0635c2s
Aldis, H.G. v5p0514c2s
v6p0229c2s
Aldis, J. v1p0451c1s
v1p0891c1s v1p1042c2s
Aldis, J.A. v2p0203c2s
Aldis, M.S. v4p0628c1s
Aldis, Mary v6p0298c2s
Aldis, Mary S. v3p0445c2s
v3p0468c2s
Aldis, O.F. v1p1345c2s
Aldis, S. v3p0084c2s
Aldis, W.S. v1p0721c1s
v1p0952c2s v2p0074c1m v2p0291c1s
v3p0404c1s
Aldrich, C. v1p1410c2s
v3p0046c2s v3p0119c2s v3p0168c1s
v3p0191c2s v3p0231c2s v3p0243c1s
v3p0382c1s v4p0333c1s v4p0620c1s
Aldrich, C.J. v6p0259c1s
Aldrich, Charles and Hubbard, N.M.
v2p0363c2s
Aldrich, E. v5p0018c1s
v5p0062c1s
Aldrich, G.I. and Balliet, T.M.
v6p0581c2s
Aldrich, H.I. v3p0300c2s
Aldrich, H.L. v3p0461c1m
v4p0618c2s
Aldrich, J. v1p0283c2s
v1p0295c2s
Aldrich, J.K. v1p0685c1s
Aldrich, J.M. v4p0156c2s
v4p0202c1s
Aldrich, J.M. and Turley, L.A.
v5p0210c1s
Aldrich, M. v4p0356c1s
v4p0501c1s v4p0537c1s
Aldrich, M.A. v5p0015c2s
Aldrich, N.W. v4p0563c2s
Aldrich, P.D. v4p0527c2s
v5p0195c1m v5p0530c2s
Aldrich, P.E. v2p0356c1s
Aldrich, R. v3p0345c2s
v3p0452c2s v5p0421c2s v5p0513c1s
v6p0076c2s v6p0289c2s v6p0679c2s
v6p0683c1s
Aldrich, T.B. v1p0012c1s
v1p0430c2s v1p0490c2s v1p0491c1s
v1p0500c2s v1p0706c2s v1p0735c1s
v1p0785c2s v1p0801c1s v1p0823c1s
v1p0834c1s v1p0837c1s v1p0851c2s
v1p0866c2s v1p0941c2s v1p0962c2s
v1p0988c2s v1p1013c1s v1p1020c2s
v1p1036c2s v1p1060c1s v1p1071c1s
v1p1072c2s v1p1110c2s v1p1240c1s
v1p1254c1s v1p1403c2s v2p0276c1s
v2p0449c2m v3p0082c1s v3p0127c1s
v3p0243c1s v3p0294c1s v3p0306c1s
v3p0310c1s v3p0324c1s v3p0461c1s
v4p0099c2s v4p0206c2s v4p0231c2s
v4p0254c2s v4p0306c1s v4p0408c1s
v4p0428c2s v4p0453c2s v4p0620c1s
v5p0096c1s v5p0213c2s v5p0263c2s
v5p0266c1s v5p0329c1s v5p0517c1s
v5p0524c2s v5p0559c1s v5p0605c2s
v6p0012c2s v6p0054c2s v6p0311c1s
v6p0409c2s v6p0552c2s v6p0649c1s
v6p0696c2s v6p0711c2s
Aldrich, T.B. and Oliphant, M.O.W.
v3p0383c2s
Aldrich, T.H. v2p0435c2s
Aldrich, T.H. and Smith, E.A.
v6p0264c1m
Aldrich, W. v4p0008c1s
v4p0195c1s v4p0575c2s v4p0619c1s
v4p0628c2s
Aldrich, W.S. v4p0177c1s
v4p0180c2s v4p0536c1s v4p0541c1s
v4p0547c2s v4p0610c2s v5p0183c1s
v5p0188c1s
Aldrich, W.S. and Sims, G.C.
v5p0401c2s v5p0615c1s
Aldrich, W.S. et al. v4p0180c1s
v4p0395c2s
Aldrich, Wilbur v4p0135c1s
Aldridge, A.F. v5p0591c1s
v5p0643c1s
Aldridge, J. v2p0239c2s
Aldridge, L. v2p0476c2s
Alencar, J.Martiniano de . v4p0243c2s
Alexander and Morfit v1p0036c2s
Alexander, A. v1p0002c1s
v1p0071c2s v1p0075c1s v1p0106c2s
v1p0107c2s v1p0117c1s v1p0131c1s
v1p0140c2s v1p0176c1s v1p0206c2m
v1p0208c2s v1p0215c1s v1p0278c1m
v1p0344c2s v1p0361c1s v1p0493c2s
v1p0514c1s v1p0563c1s v1p0575c1s
v1p0585c2s v1p0608c2s v1p0636c1m
v1p0637c2s v1p0646c2s v1p0651c1m
v1p0680c1s v1p0688c2s v1p0707c1s
v1p0741c1s v1p0777c1s v1p0783c2s
v1p0812c2s v1p0847c2s v1p0853c1s
v1p0868c1s v1p0868c2s v1p0907c1s
v1p0944c2s v1p0977c2s v1p0985c2s
v1p0993c2s v1p1001c1s v1p1009c1s
v1p1046c1s v1p1047c1s v1p1091c2s
v1p1157c2s v1p1160c1s v1p1165c2m
v1p1167c1s v1p1199c2s v1p1200c2s
v1p1205c1s v1p1211c1s v1p1252c2s
v1p1278c1s v1p1301c2m v1p1306c1s
v1p1328c2s v1p1355c2s v1p1393c2s
v1p1404c2s v2p0040c1s v2p0311c2s
v4p0439c1s v6p0320c1s v6p0421c2s
v6p0479c1s v6p0601c1s
Alexander, A. and Alexander, J.A.
v1p0215c1s v1p0406c2s
Alexander, A. and Alexander, J.W.
v1p1046c1s
Alexander, A. and Hodge, C.
v1p0003c1s
Alexander, A. and Miller, S.
v1p1046c1s
Alexander, A.C. v6p0283c2s
Alexander, Anna v6p0562c2s
Alexander, Archibald v6p0212c1s
Alexander, B. v5p0063c2s
Alexander, B.S. v1p0986c2s
Alexander, Boyd v6p0623c2s
Alexander, C.A. v1p0009c1s
v1p0496c2s v1p0565c1s v1p0836c2s
Alexander, C.F. v1p0432c1s
v1p0541c2s v1p0735c1s
Alexander, C.G. v5p0283c1s
Alexander, C.K. v3p0426c2s
Alexander, C.L. v1p1057c1s
v1p1293c2s
Alexander, E.A. v4p0206c1s
v4p0254c2s v4p0350c2s v4p0607c1s
v5p0362c2s v5p0379c1s v5p0467c1s
Alexander, E.P. v1p0048c2s
v1p0288c1s v1p0518c2m v1p0734c1s
v1p1343c2s v1p1345c1s v1p1347c1s
v2p0166c2s v2p0266c1s v2p0482c2s
v3p0172c1s v3p0353c1s v3p0386c2s
v4p0538c1s v6p0366c1s
Alexander, E.P. et al. ... v5p0541c2s
Alexander, E.T. v2p0453c1s
Alexander, G. v2p0056c2s
v3p0219c2s v4p0029c2s v4p0140c2s
v5p0288c1s
Alexander, G. et al. v4p0557c2s
Alexander, G.G. v1p0232c2m
v5p0566c2s
Alexander, H. v6p0394c2s
v6p0467c2s
Alexander, H.B. v6p0055c2s
v6p0680c2s
Alexander, H.C. v1p0020c2s
v1p0567c1s v1p1183c1s v2p0366c1s
Alexander, Hartley B. v6p0306c2s
Alexander, J. v4p0213c1s
v4p0296c2s v4p0419c1s v4p0441c1s
v5p0639c1s
Alexander, J.A. v1p0047c2s
v1p0048c1m v1p0050c1m v1p0076c1s
v1p0118c1s v1p0118c2s v1p0121c1s
v1p0122c1s v1p0123c1s v1p0123c2s
v1p0124c2s v1p0125c2m v1p0127c2s
v1p0128c1s v1p0131c1s v1p0132c1s
v1p0254c1m v1p0328c2s v1p0368c1s
v1p0392c2s v1p0398c1s v1p0421c1m
v1p0421c2m v1p0423c2s v1p0483c2s
v1p0537c1s v1p0550c2s v1p0554c2s
v1p0565c2s v1p0581c2m v1p0659c1s
v1p0690c1s v1p0712c2s v1p0818c1s
v1p0836c2s v1p0840c2s v1p0961c1s
v1p0976c2s v1p0979c1s v1p0992c1s
v1p1042c2s v1p1043c1s v1p1045c2s
v1p1046c1s v1p1047c2s v1p1056c1s
v1p1058c1s v1p1067c1s v1p1128c1s
v1p1140c2m v1p1178c1s v1p1301c2m
v1p1303c1s v1p1332c1s v1p1357c2s
v1p1404c1s
Alexander, J.A. and Alexander, A.
v1p0215c1s v1p0406c2s
Alexander, J.A. and Hodge, C.
v1p1140c1s v1p1165c1s
Alexander, J.A. and Miller, S.
v1p0238c2s
Alexander, J.G. v4p0342c2s
v4p0415c1s v4p0415c2s
Alexander, J.H. v1p0004c1s
v1p0829c1s v1p1034c1s v1p1362c2s
v1p1390c1s v1p1396c2s
Alexander, J.H. and Morfit, C.
v1p0267c2s v1p1265c1s
Alexander, J.L. v2p0475c1s
Alexander, J.M. v2p0280c2s
Alexander, J.W. v1p0040c1s
v1p0059c2s v1p0060c2s v1p0068c1s
v1p0096c1s v1p0120c1s v1p0158c1s
v1p0189c1s v1p0206c2s v1p0215c1s
v1p0242c2s v1p0254c2s v1p0275c1s
v1p0315c1s v1p0320c1s v1p0348c1s
v1p0358c1s v1p0381c1s v1p0391c1s
v1p0405c2s v1p0495c1s v1p0500c1s
v1p0515c2s v1p0556c1s v1p0582c2s
v1p0584c2s v1p0597c2s v1p0603c1s
v1p0620c2s v1p0677c2s v1p0697c1s
v1p0702c1s v1p0754c1s v1p0757c2s
v1p0777c1s v1p0777c2s v1p0781c2s
v1p0805c2s v1p0808c1s v1p0825c1s
v1p0826c2s v1p0840c1s v1p0847c2s
v1p0850c1s v1p0852c1s v1p0884c1s
v1p0903c1s v1p0905c2s v1p0923c1s
v1p0953c1s v1p0966c1s v1p0977c1s
v1p0989c1s v1p0999c2s v1p1040c1s
v1p1043c1m v1p1043c2s v1p1045c1s
v1p1047c1s v1p1047c2m v1p1062c1s
v1p1071c2s v1p1089c2m v1p1093c1s
v1p1093c2s v1p1095c2s v1p1158c1s
v1p1178c2m v1p1180c1s v1p1191c1s
v1p1221c2s v1p1240c1s v1p1270c1s
v1p1288c1s v1p1288c2s v1p1304c1s
v1p1334c1s v1p1357c2s v1p1373c2s
v1p1374c1s v1p1409c1s v1p1442c2s
v2p0054c1s v4p0611c1s v5p0293c1s
v5p0466c1s v6p0633c1s
Alexander, J.W. and Alexander, A.
v1p1046c1s
Alexander, J.W. and Dod, A.B.
v1p1321c1s
Alexander, J.W. and Hall, J.
v1p0935c2s
Alexander, J.W. et al. ... v2p0440c1s
Alexander, L.H. v6p0700c1s
Alexander, Mrs. v1p0490c2s
v1p1081c2s v2p0168c1s v2p0168c2s
v2p0383c1s v3p0250c2s v3p0461c2s
v3p0467c2s
Alexander, N. v5p0195c1s
Alexander, N.D. v3p0241c2s
Alexander, P.W. v2p0098c1s
Alexander, S. v1p0288c2s
v1p0811c1s v1p0900c2s v2p0191c2s
v2p0200c1s v2p0214c2s v2p0255c1s
v2p0274c2s v2p0379c2s v3p0185c1s
v4p0096c1s v4p0188c2s v4p0382c1s
v4p0419c2s v4p0599c2s v6p0177c1s
Alexander, S.A. v4p0032c2s
v4p0057c2s v4p0436c2s
Alexander, S.D. v1p0176c1s
v1p1051c1s
Alexander, T. and Blakiston, T.
v2p0289c2s
Alexander, T.P. v3p0323c1s
Alexander, T.S. v6p0138c1m
Alexander, W. v1p0076c2s
v1p0675c1s v1p0686c1s v1p0688c1s
v1p0754c2s v1p0790c1s v1p1098c2s
v1p1391c1s v3p0080c2s v3p0384c2s
v4p0574c1s v5p0489c1s v5p0577c1s
v6p0088c2s
Alexander, W.A. v6p0650c1s
Alexander, W.C. v1p1360c1s
Alexander, W.D. v1p0566c1s
Alexander, W.E. v4p0371c1s
Alexander, W.F. v5p0166c2s
v6p0104c2s v6p0441c1s v6p0541c2s
v6p0604c2s
Alexander, W.H. v6p0509c2s
v6p0692c2s
Alexander, W.J. v2p0191c1s
Alexander, W.J. and Whitman, E.A.
v3p0402c1s
Alexander, W.L. v1p0118c1s
v1p0122c1s v1p0128c2s v1p0581c2s
v1p0585c2s v1p0858c1m v1p1120c2s
v2p0042c1s v2p0044c2s v2p0144c1s
Alexander, W.S. v3p0247c2s
Alexander, W.W. v2p0441c2s
v2p0459c1s
Alexandre, A. v4p0058c2s
v4p0089c2s v4p0454c2s v5p0094c1s
v5p0330c1s v6p0059c1s
Alexandrenko, B. v3p0362c1s
Alexei v6p0457c2s
Alexis, W. v1p0570c1s
Aley, R.J. v6p0137c1s
Aleyne, J. v1p0062c1s
v1p0819c2s v1p1141c2s
Alfonso, N.d' v2p0477c2s
Alford, C.J. v6p0260c2s
Alford, D.P. v2p0431c1s
Alford, E.M. v1p0349c1s
v3p0187c1s v4p0413c1s v5p0406c2s
Alford, H. v1p0118c2s
v1p0119c2s v1p0128c1s v1p0239c2s
v1p0241c2s v1p0243c2s v1p0249c1s
v1p0249c2m v1p0251c1s v1p0251c2s
v1p0252c1s v1p0292c2s v1p0303c2m
v1p0312c2s v1p0410c1s v1p0417c1s
v1p0433c1s v1p0442c2s v1p0473c2s
v1p0672c1s v1p0746c1s v1p0874c1s
v1p0980c2s v1p1060c1s v1p1065c1s
v1p1092c1s v1p1095c2s v1p1120c1s
v1p1126c1s v1p1167c1s v1p1295c1s
v1p1328c1s
Alford, H.C. v4p0028c2s
Alford, M. v1p0064c2s
v5p0261c1s
Alford, M. and Watts, G.F.
v1p0904c2s

Alfriend, E.M. v3p0361c1m
v6p0332c2s
Alfriend, F.H. v2p0098c1s
v2p0453c2s
Alger, A.H. v5p0140c1s
Alger, A.L. v4p0138c2s
v4p0576c1s
Alger, A.M. v4p0134c2s
v5p0131c2s
Alger, A.R. v1p1043c1s
v1p1355c2s
Alger, F. v1p0506c2s
v1p1440c1s
Alger, F. and Jackson, C.T.
v1p0931c1s
Alger, F.M. v6p0218c2s
Alger, F.S. v5p0601c2s
Alger, G.H. v6p0428c2s
Alger, G.W. v4p0520c1s
v4p0569c2s v5p0201c1m v6p0157c2s
v6p0158c1s v6p0216c2s v6p0239c1s
v6p0249c2s v6p0346c2s v6p0356c1s
v6p0380c1s v6p0614c2s
Alger, H. v1p0370c2s
v1p1056c2s
Alger, H., jr. v1p1170c2s
v4p0010c2s
v4p0550c2s
Alger, J.G. v3p0035c2s
v3p0123c2s v3p0130c2s v3p0226c1s
v4p0001c2s v4p0211c2s v4p0364c1s
v4p0478c1s v4p0564c1s v5p0148c2s
v5p0170c1s v5p0218c1m v5p0252c1s
v5p0354c2s v5p0398c1s v5p0430c2s
v5p0491c1s v5p0494c1s v5p0521c2s
v6p0082c2s v6p0161c1s v6p0480c1s
Alger, M. v6p0378c2s
Alger, P.R. v5p0468c1s
v6p0223c2s
Alger, R.A. v5p0189c1s
v5p0599c1s
Alger, T.L. v5p0545c1s
Alger, W.R. v1p0047c1s
v1p0074c2s v1p0130c2s v1p0207c1s
v1p0331c2s v1p0337c2s v1p0347c2s
v1p0356c1s v1p0365c1s v1p0405c2s
v1p0420c2s v1p0428c2s v1p0491c2m
v1p0495c2m v1p0496c2m v1p0528c1s
v1p0560c2m v1p0592c1s v1p0717c1s
v1p0745c1s v1p0746c1s v1p0793c2s
v1p0805c2s v1p0851c1s v1p0900c2s
v1p0975c2s v1p0976c2s v1p0986c1s
v1p0995c1s v1p1022c1s v1p1043c1s
v1p1065c1s v1p1086c2s v1p1094c2s
v1p1107c1s v1p1184c2s v1p1221c2s
v1p1235c1s v1p1265c1s v1p1275c1s
v1p1288c2s v1p1302c2s v1p1307c1s
v1p1321c2s v1p1323c1s v1p1370c2s
v1p1385c1s v1p1424c1s v1p1430c1s
v1p1440c1s v2p0357c2s
v4p0127c1s
Alglave, E. v1p1015c2s
Algue, J. v5p0360c1s
Ali, A.Y. v6p0313c1s
Ali, Mehdi v3p0210c2s
Ali, S.A. v1p0634c2s
Alington, C.W. v6p0665c1s
Alison, A. v1p0168c1s
v1p0300c2s v1p0383c2s v1p0412c1s
v1p0476c2s v1p0479c1s v1p0489c1s
v1p0510c2s v1p0672c1s v1p0719c1s
v1p0849c1s v1p0907c2s v1p0919c1s
v1p0974c1s v1p1065c1s v1p1228c2s
v1p1230c1s v1p1241c1s v4p0356c1s
v4p0395c2s v4p0593c2s
Alison, A., Gen. v4p0189c2s
Alison, A., Sir v3p0161c1s
Alison, Archibald v4p0235c2s
Alison, F. v1p1047c1s
Alison, R.E. v2p0434c2s
Alison, S.A. v2p0396c2s
Alison, S.S. v1p0238c1s
Alison, W. v4p0245c1s
Alison, W.P. v1p1031c1s
Allaben, A.E. v4p0002c1s
v4p0075c1s v4p0322c1s v4p0579c1s
Allaben, F. v4p0033c2s
v4p0045c1s v4p0045c2s
v4p0197c1s v4p0233c1s v4p0259c2s
v4p0312c1s v4p0459c1s v4p0543c1s
v4p0624c1s
Allain, A. v6p0027c2s
Allain, E. v4p0068c1s
v4p0488c1s
Allaire, E.M. v4p0406c2s
v5p0100c1s v5p0524c1s v5p0527c2s
Allan, A.G. v4p0613c2s
v5p0188c2s
Allan, A.S. v2p0276c2s
Allan, J.C. v3p0431c2s
Allan, J.M. v1p0795c1s
Allan, J.McG. v2p0396c2m
Allan, J.T. v1p1324c1s
Allan, N. v1p0323c2s
Allan, P.L. v6p0139c1s
Allan, S. v6p0497c1s
Allan, T. v3p0134c2s
Allan, T.J. v6p0207c2s
Allan, U. v5p0428c1s
Allan, W. v1p0051c1s
v1p0210c1s v1p0216c2s v1p0518c2m
v2p0027c1s v2p0098c1s v2p0252c2s
v2p0275c1s v2p0279c1m v2p0349c1m
v2p0400c1s v2p0453c1m v5p0246c2s
Allan, W. and Walker, F.A.
v3p0246c1m
Allan, W. et al. v1p0518c2s
Allardyce, A. v1p0592c1s
v1p0878c1s v1p1065c2s v1p1069c2s
v4p0165c2s
Allardyce, I. v5p0606c1s
Allardyce, J. v1p0186c1s
Allaria, A. v4p0065c2s
v4p0143c1s
Allaway, H. v5p0617c1s
Allbutt, E. v4p0574c1s
Allbutt, G.L. v5p0236c2s
Allbutt, T. v4p0483c2s
Allbutt, T.C. v1p0157c1s
v3p0077c2s v4p0397c2s v5p0577c1s
Allbutt, T.H. v5p0104c2s
Allchin, A. v4p0075c2s
Allchin, J.H. v6p0707c1s
Allcott, S.M. v1p0143c1s
Allderice, E.W. v2p0067c1m
Alldridge, E.L. v5p0583c2s
Alldridge, L. v1p0708c1s
v2p0264c1s v4p0201c2s v4p0518c1s
Alldridge, Lizzie v3p0389c1s
Alldridge, T.J. v4p0523c1s
Alleman, H.C. v5p0426c1s
v5p0572c1s
Allen, A. v4p0320c2s
v4p0439c2m
v5p0225c1s
v5p0258c2s
v5p0400c1s
v6p0064c2s
v6p0651c2s
Allen, A.B. v1p0108c1s
Allen, A.C. v6p0125c2s
Allen, A.E. v5p0223c1s
v6p0300c2s
Allen, A.H. v5p0556c1s
v6p0093c2s
Allen, A.J. v2p0014c1s
v6p0177c1s
Allen, A.M. v6p0353c1s
v6p0677c2s
Allen, A.S. v6p0090c1s
Allen, A.V.G. v2p0437c2s
v3p0200c2s v3p0427c2s v4p0074c2s
v4p0545c1s v4p0580c2s v6p0288c1s
v6p0579c1s
Allen, Anne S. v6p0478c2s
Allen, Anne Story v6p0178c2s
Allen, Annie T. v6p0137c2s
Allen, C. v1p1399c2s
v3p0243c2s
Allen, C.A. v3p0081c1s
v3p0081c2m v3p0229c2s v3p0354c2s
v5p0114c1s
Allen, C.C. v3p0132c2s
v3p0372c2s v4p0007c1s v4p0284c2s
v4p0314c2s v6p0093c1s v6p0689c1s
Allen, C.D. v4p0067c1s
v5p0071c1s
Allen, C.E. v5p0462c2s
v5p0633c2s v6p0647c1s
Allen, C.F. v6p0204c1s
Allen, C.H. v2p0135c2s
v4p0090c1s v6p0509c2s v6p0510c1s
Allen, C.J. v1p0376c1s
v1p0564c2s v6p0300c1s
Allen, C.J.M. v5p0426c1s
Allen, C.L. v4p0049c2m
v4p0332c1s
Allen, C.L. and Hellier, C.E.
v4p0131c2s
Allen, C.N. v3p0046c1s
v3p0272c2s
Allen, C.R. and Nichols, W.R.
v2p0396c1s
Allen, C.S. v4p0046c1s
v5p0405c1s
Allen, C.V. v6p0197c2m
v6p0351c1s v6p0351c2s v6p0414c2s
v6p0419c1s
Allen, D.O. v1p0632c2s
Allen, D.P. v2p0002c1s
v2p0008c2s v2p0243c2s v2p0265c1s
v2p0471c1s
Allen, E. v1p0086c1s
v1p0166c2s v1p0421c2s v1p0422c1s
v1p0757c2s v1p0807c2m v1p0808c1s
v1p1314c2s v2p0469c2m
Allen, E.A. v1p0586c1s
v1p1059c1s v1p1246c2s v2p0300c1s
v3p0178c2s v3p0228c1s v3p0390c2s
v3p0413c2s v3p0452c1s v5p0440c1s
Allen, E.A.H. v2p0322c2s
v3p0267c1s v3p0380c1s
Allen, E.B. v6p0470c1s
Allen, E.E. v3p0047c2s
v6p0070c2m
Allen, E.G. v1p0149c1s
Allen, E.H. and Ware, W.R.
v2p0240c2m
Allen, E.J. v5p0237c1s
v5p0558c1m
Allen, E.P. v2p0287c1s
v3p0072c1s v3p0411c2s v4p0012c2s
v4p0273c2s
Allen, E.P. and Denby, C. v5p0477c2s
Allen, E.P. and Fearon, J.S.
v5p0111c2s
Allen, E.T. v5p0298c1s
Allen, E.T. and Day, A.L.. v6p0221c2s
Allen, E.W. v5p0009c2s
v5p0042c2s v6p0008c1m
Allen, Ezra v5p0397c1s
Allen, F. v1p0552c1s
v6p0216c2s
Allen, F.A. v1p0966c1s
Allen, F.C. v5p0013c1m
Allen, F.D. v2p0222c1s
v4p0093c1s v4p0461c2s
Allen, F.H. and Bacon, H.. v1p0063c1s
Allen, F.J. v6p0471c2s
v6p0502c1s
Allen, F.O. v4p0433c2s
v5p0608c1s
Allen, F.W. v6p0013c1s
Allen, G. v1p0106c2s
v1p0170c2s v1p0278c2m v1p0300c2s
v1p0329c1s v1p0337c2s v1p0352c2s
v1p0358c1s v1p0380c2s v1p0407c2s
v1p0410c1s v1p0410c2s v1p0434c1s
v1p0447c1s v1p0462c2s v1p0465c1s
v1p0505c1s v1p0506c2s v1p0507c1s
v1p0512c1s v1p0542c1s v1p0551c2s
v1p0552c1s v1p0564c1s v1p0565c2s
v1p0594c1s v1p0612c2s v1p0613c1s
v1p0668c1s v1p0695c1s v1p0704c1s
v1p0721c2s v1p0838c2s v1p0897c1s
v1p0935c1s v1p0943c1s v1p0949c2s
v1p0957c2s v1p1007c2s v1p1094c2s
v1p1127c2s v1p1171c1s v1p1196c1s
v1p1210c1s v1p1263c1s v1p1278c1s
v1p1368c2s v1p1434c1s v2p0004c2s
v2p0010c1s v2p0015c1m v2p0016c1m
v2p0034c2s v2p0037c1s v2p0038c1s
v2p0046c1s v2p0046c2s v2p0053c1s
v2p0054c2s v2p0062c2m v2p0090c1s
v2p0091c1s v2p0094c1s v2p0103c1s
v2p0108c1s v2p0109c2s v2p0112c1s
v2p0116c2s v2p0122c1s v2p0142c2s
v2p0149c2s v2p0157c1m v2p0159c2m
v2p0160c1m v2p0160c2s v2p0161c2s
v2p0169c1s v2p0172c2m v2p0173c2s
v2p0182c1s v2p0182c2s v2p0184c2s
v2p0185c1m v2p0197c1s v2p0201c2s
v2p0202c2s v2p0206c2m v2p0211c1s
v2p0211c2s v2p0212c2s v2p0214c2s
v2p0215c2s v2p0222c2s v2p0232c1s
v2p0233c1s v2p0249c1s v2p0252c1s
v2p0267c1s v2p0269c2s v2p0274c1m
v2p0274c2s v2p0277c1s v2p0291c1s
v2p0295c1s v2p0301c1s v2p0344c1m
v2p0351c1s v2p0354c1s v2p0355c2s
v2p0372c2s v2p0391c1s v2p0394c1s
v2p0406c1s v2p0426c1s v2p0427c2m
v2p0430c2s v2p0431c1s v2p0432c1s
v2p0436c2s v2p0439c1s v2p0448c1s
v2p0469c2s v2p0470c1s v2p0471c2s
v3p0001c1s v3p0021c1s v3p0029c2s
v3p0064c2s v3p0067c1s v3p0085c1s
v3p0087c2s v3p0110c2s v3p0452c1s
v4p0021c2s v4p0024c1s v4p0029c1s
v4p0029c2s v4p0034c2s v4p0047c1s
v4p0051c2s v4p0062c1s v4p0064c1s
v4p0081c1s v4p0082c1s v4p0092c2s
v4p0093c2s v4p0120c1s v4p0143c1s
v4p0149c1s v4p0152c2s v4p0185c1m
v4p0190c1s v4p0193c2s v4p0202c1s
v4p0213c1s v4p0225c2s v4p0226c2s
v4p0228c2s v4p0235c1s v4p0253c1s
v4p0255c2s v4p0273c2s v4p0275c2s
v4p0281c1s v4p0305c1s v4p0337c1s
v4p0338c1s v4p0348c1s v4p0373c2s
v4p0381c2s v4p0392c1s v4p0418c1s
v4p0418c2s v4p0436c2s v4p0454c2s
v4p0469c2s v4p0473c2s v4p0482c1s
v4p0494c1s v4p0502c1s v4p0510c1s
v4p0514c2s v4p0541c1s v4p0541c2s
v4p0569c2s v4p0583c1s v4p0588c2s
v4p0612c2s v4p0623c1s v4p0625c1s
v4p0633c1s
Allen, G. and Smith, H.A.. v4p0094c1s
Allen, G. et al. v4p0070c1s
Allen, G.H. v1p0023c1s
Allen, G.M. v5p0156c2s
v6p0694c1m
Allen, G.W. v2p0003c1s
v2p0031c1s v2p0107c1s v2p0121c2s
v2p0125c1s v2p0144c2s v2p0197c1s
v2p0210c1s v2p0233c1s v2p0421c1s
v6p0441c1s
Allen, Grant v1p0009c1s
v1p0135c1s v1p0300c2s v1p0338c1s
v1p0493c1s v1p0551c1s v1p0635c2s
v1p0884c1s v2p0057c1s v2p0197c2s
v2p0307c1s v2p0312c2s v2p0413c1s
v2p0422c2s v2p0462c1s v2p0482c1s
v3p0003c2s v3p0004c2m v3p0010c2s
v3p0014c2s v3p0046c1s v3p0095c1m
v3p0098c2s v3p0116c2s v3p0124c1s
v3p0140c2s v3p0143c2s v3p0152c1s
v3p0157c1s v3p0168c2s v3p0178c1s
v3p0190c2s v3p0194c2s v3p0218c2s

v3p0247c1s v3p0254c2s v3p0257c2s
v3p0273c2s v3p0291c1s v3p0291c2s
v3p0297c2s v3p0303c2s v3p0341c1s
v3p0345c1s v3p0358c1s v3p0359c1s
v3p0374c2s v3p0380c1s v3p0384c1s
v3p0398c1s v3p0410c2s v3p0416c2s
v3p0419c1s v3p0426c2s v3p0428c2s
v3p0429c2s v3p0436c2s v3p0457c2s
v3p0462c2s v3p0467c1s v3p0467c2m
v3p0474c2s v4p0172c2s v4p0507c1s
v4p0587c2s v5p0021c2s v5p0023c2s
v5p0028c1s v5p0081c2s v5p0085c1s
v5p0115c2s v5p0123c2s v5p0126c2s
v5p0153c2s v5p0173c1m v5p0196c2s
v5p0198c2m v5p0216c1s v5p0240c2s
v5p0261c1s v5p0264c1s v5p0265c1s
v5p0310c2s v5p0337c1s v5p0343c1s
v5p0351c1s v5p0358c1s v5p0379c1s
v5p0388c2s v5p0400c2s v5p0475c1s
v5p0496c2s v5p0517c2m v5p0538c1s
v5p0545c2m v5p0546c1s v5p0572c1s
v5p0621c2s v5p0636c1s v5p0643c2s
v6p0610c1s
Allen, Grant and Sully, J.
v1p0009c1s
Allen, Grant et al. v3p0250c2s
Allen, H. v1p0883c1s
v2p0138c1s v3p0246c2s v3p0335c2s
v4p0017c1s v4p0075c2s v4p0448c1s
v4p0470c2s v4p0497c1s v4p0507c1s
v4p0610c1s v5p0162c2s
Allen, H.F. v5p0599c1s
Allen, H.H. v6p0510c1s
Allen, H.J. v2p0179c1s
v3p0058c2m v3p0105c2s v5p0102c2s
Allen, H.P. v6p0519c1s
Allen, H.S. v5p0088c2s
v5p0520c2s v6p0009c2s v6p0643c1s
Allen, H.T. v2p0006c2s
v5p0004c1s v5p0098c2s v5p0375c1s
v6p0105c2s
Allen, H.W. v4p0155c1s
v4p0368c1s v4p0368c2s
Allen, Horace v6p0616c1s
Allen, I. v4p0168c2s
v4p0611c2s v5p0096c1s v5p0194c1m
v5p0200c2s v5p0234c1s v5p0241c1s
v5p0263c2s v5p0366c2s v5p0467c1s
v5p0500c1s v5p0585c1s v6p0625c2s
v6p0690c2s
Allen, I.D. v6p0301c1s
v6p0446c2m
Allen, Inglis v5p0018c2s
Allen, J. v1p0219c2m
v1p0255c1s v1p0386c1s v1p0412c1s
v1p0591c1s v1p0704c2s v1p0928c1s
v1p0973c1s v1p0993c1s v1p1228c2s
v1p1270c1s v2p0132c2s
Allen, J.A. v1p0135c2m
v1p0136c1s v1p0136c2s v1p0138c2s
v1p0174c1s v1p0329c1s v1p0333c2s
v1p0340c2s v1p0374c1s v1p0435c1s
v1p0681c2s v1p0791c2s v1p0867c1s
v1p0869c2s v1p0899c1s v1p0945c2s
v1p0949c1m v1p1005c1s v1p1041c1m
v1p1232c2s v1p1292c2s v1p1419c1s
v2p0046c2m v3p0383c1s v4p0061c1s
v5p0139c1m v5p0389c2s v5p0547c2s
v6p0068c1s v6p0288c1s v6p0330c2s
v6p0608c2m
Allen, J.A. and Coues, E.. v5p0413c1s
Allen, J.A. and Holder, J.B.
v2p0471c2s
Allen, J.A., Dr. v6p0101c1s
Allen, J.B. and Carr, H. . v6p0643c2s
Allen, J.C. v2p0140c2s
v6p0091c1s v6p0340c2s v6p0342c1s
v6p0587c2s v6p0588c2s v6p0626c1s
Allen, J.E. v4p0464c1s
v4p0542c1s v6p0312c1s v6p0378c2s
Allen, J.G. v4p0459c1s
Allen, J.H. v1p0027c1s
v1p0044c1s v1p0109c2s v1p0121c2s
v1p0124c2s v1p0189c2s v1p0218c1s
v1p0242c2s v1p0244c1s v1p0252c2s
v1p0289c1s v1p0291c2s v1p0313c1m
v1p0316c1s v1p0390c1s v1p0429c2s
v1p0447c1s v1p0527c1s v1p0587c2m
v1p0601c1s v1p0646c1s v1p0686c1s
v1p0687c1s v1p0690c1m v1p0700c2s
v1p0727c1s v1p0730c1s v1p0740c2s
v1p0741c1m v1p0750c1s v1p0768c1s
v1p0792c2s v1p0821c1s v1p0847c1s
v1p0847c2s v1p0857c1s v1p0933c1s
v1p0957c1s v1p0972c2s v1p0989c2s
v1p1001c1m v1p1037c2s v1p1090c1s
v1p1094c2s v1p1096c1s v1p1120c2s
v1p1161c1s v1p1200c2s v1p1206c1s
v1p1208c1s v1p1214c2s v1p1300c2s
v1p1302c2s v1p1304c1s v1p1341c1s
v1p1344c1s v1p1345c1s v1p1345c2m
v1p1346c1m v1p1347c2m v1p1352c2s
v1p1353c2m v1p1378c1s v1p1441c2s
v2p0008c2s v2p0079c2s v2p0102c2s
v2p0121c1s v2p0212c1s v2p0255c1s
v2p0289c1s v2p0295c2s v2p0328c2s
v2p0339c2s v2p0349c2s v2p0388c1s
v2p0438c1m v2p0451c2m v3p0080c2s
v3p0193c1s v3p0281c1s v3p0297c2s
v3p0314c2s v3p0358c1s v3p0395c2s
v3p0421c1s v3p0441c1m v4p0479c1s
v4p0516c1s
Allen, J.H. and Hale, E.E.
v1p1352c2s
Allen, J.J. v1p1343c1s
v6p0247c2s
Allen, J.L. v2p0109c2s
v2p0112c2s v2p0200c1s v2p0233c1s
v2p0241c1s v2p0242c1s v2p0262c1s
v2p0335c2s v2p0371c2s v2p0443c1s
v3p0028c2s v3p0102c2s v3p0105c2s
v3p0107c2s v3p0148c1s v3p0156c2s
v3p0235c2s v3p0236c1s v3p0236c2s
v3p0322c1s v3p0340c2s v3p0394c2s
v3p0395c1s v3p0435c1s v3p0439c1s
v3p0440c2s v3p0462c2s v4p0060c2s
v4p0081c1s v4p0185c1s v4p0303c2s
v4p0310c1m v5p0205c2s v5p0214c2s
v6p0310c2s v6p0663c1s v6p0673c2s
Allen, J.L. and Potts, W.J.
v2p0033c1s
Allen, J.L. et al. v6p0461c2s
Allen, J.M. v1p1420c1s
v4p0065c1s
Allen, J.R. v1p1382c1s
v3p0157c1s v3p0306c2s v4p0029c1s
v4p0074c2s v4p0088c2s v4p0199c2s
v4p0300c1s v4p0366c2s v4p0396c1s
v4p0406c1s v5p0053c1s v5p0078c1s
v5p0371c2s v5p0461c2s v5p0464c1s
v5p0495c1s v5p0516c1s v5p0574c2s
v5p0639c1s v6p0231c1s v6p0470c2s
Allen, J.Romilly v5p0018c2s
v5p0145c2s
Allen, J.T. v1p0903c2s
Allen, J.W. v4p0635c1s
v5p0204c1s
Allen, John v1p0040c1s
Allen, K. v5p0350c2s
v6p0688c2s
Allen, L. v1p1247c1s
v3p0192c2s v3p0448c1m v4p0180c2s
v4p0252c2m v4p0272c2s v4p0277c2s
v4p0288c2s v4p0602c2m v5p0188c2s
v5p0201c1s v5p0353c1s v5p0469c2s
v6p0417c2s v6p0674c1s
Allen, L.E. v5p0103c2s
Allen, L.F. v2p0071c1s
Allen, Leicester v6p0142c2s
Allen, M.A. v3p0366c1s
v4p0124c1s
Allen, M.C. v4p0563c1s
Allen, M.E. v4p0151c1s
v5p0157c1s v5p0450c2s
Allen, M.H. v6p0462c2s
Allen, M.J. et al. v3p0083c2s
Allen, M.L. v3p0029c1s
Allen, M.M., Mrs. v6p0011c2s
Allen, M.V. v4p0129c1s
Allen, N. v1p0356c2s
v1p0378c1s v1p0631c2s v1p0944c2s
v1p1034c1s v1p1034c2s v2p0001c2s
v2p0211c1s v2p0310c2m v2p0349c2s
Allen, N.R. v4p0256c1s
v5p0200c2s v5p0205c2s
Allen, O.D. and Comstock, W.J.
v1p0101c2s
Allen, O.P. v4p0011c1s
Allen, P.L. v6p0004c1s
v6p0048c2m v6p0056c2s v6p0106c2s
v6p0121c2s v6p0142c1s v6p0145c2s
v6p0170c1s v6p0173c2s v6p0189c1s
v6p0197c1s v6p0216c2s v6p0221c1s
v6p0230c2s v6p0231c1m v6p0263c1s
v6p0307c1s v6p0308c2s v6p0367c1s
v6p0404c2s v6p0428c2s v6p0429c1s
v6p0443c1s v6p0446c2s v6p0482c1m
v6p0483c2s v6p0494c2s v6p0515c1m
v6p0516c1m v6p0524c2s v6p0528c1s
v6p0535c1s v6p0541c1s v6p0583c2s
v6p0615c1s v6p0615c2s v6p0633c2s
v6p0635c1s v6p0680c2s v6p0681c2s
v6p0694c1s v6p0701c1m
Allen, P.S. v4p0505c1s
v6p0008c1s v6p0047c2s v6p0135c1s
v6p0377c2s
Allen, Percy R. v6p0156c1s
Allen, R. v1p1382c1s
v4p0273c1s v4p0598c2s v5p0438c2m
Allen, R.H. v1p1418c1s
v6p0102c2s v6p0232c1s
Allen, R.L. v1p0772c1s
v6p0159c2s
Allen, R.M. v4p0092c2s
v5p0213c2s
Allen, R.McD. v6p0231c1s
Allen, R.McDonald v4p0039c1s
Allen, R.W. v1p0117c1s
v1p0397c1s v1p1094c1s v1p1412c1s
v2p0279c2s
Allen, S. v6p0094c2s
v6p0275c1s
Allen, S.H. v3p0360c2m
v6p0530c2s
Allen, S.M. v1p0023c2s
v2p0469c2s v3p0331c2s v3p0459c1s
Allen, S.N. v3p0459c1s
Allen, S.R. v4p0267c1s
v5p0305c2s
Allen, T. v1p0854c1s
v5p0160c1s v6p0224c2s
Allen, T.E. v3p0210c2s
v3p0284c1s v4p0130c1s v4p0163c1s
v4p0286c1s v4p0464c1m v4p0479c1s
v4p0479c2s v4p0482c2s v4p0567c2m
v5p0546c2s
Allen, T.E. and Dolbear, A.E.
v4p0540c2s
Allen, T.F. v2p0074c2s
Allen, T.G. v4p0052c2s
v4p0132c1s v4p0155c2s v4p0206c1m
v5p0033c2s v5p0150c2s
Allen, T.G., jr. v4p0035c1s
v4p0058c1s v4p0145c1s v4p0384c1s
v4p0564c1s
Allen, T.G., jr. and
Sachtleben, W.L. v4p0032c2s
v4p0058c2s
Allen, T.H. v4p0502c2s
Allen, T.J. v3p0473c1s
v5p0126c2m v5p0130c1s v5p0325c1s
Allen, T.W. v4p0262c1s
v4p0561c2s
Allen, Viola v5p0003c1s
Allen, W. v1p0156c1s
v1p0291c1s v1p0795c2s v1p0855c2s
v1p1056c2s v1p1261c1s v1p1358c2s
v1p1404c2s v2p0024c1m v2p0074c1s
v2p0087c1s v2p0335c2s v2p0423c1s
v2p0453c1m v2p0453c2s v3p0074c2s
v3p0194c1s v3p0404c1s v5p0084c2s
v5p0406c1s v5p0521c2s v6p0127c2s
Allen, W.A. v5p0061c2s
v6p0706c2s
Allen, W.A.T. v6p0163c1s
Allen, W.B. v2p0440c1s
v4p0458c1s v5p0416c1s
Allen, W.C. v5p0059c1s
Allen, W.C. and Badham, F.C.
v4p0561c2s
Allen, W.D. v4p0209c2s
Allen, W.F. v1p0069c1s
v1p0153c2s v1p0173c1s v1p0176c2s
v1p0184c2s v1p0208c2s v1p0258c1s
v1p0271c1s v1p0275c1s v1p0300c2s
v1p0410c2s v1p0411c1s v1p0480c2s
v1p0487c1m v1p0492c1s v1p0515c1s
v1p0516c1s v1p0516c2s v1p0525c1s
v1p0551c2s v1p0556c2s v1p0561c1s
v1p0671c2s v1p0693c2s v1p0720c2s
v1p0721c2s v1p0772c2s v1p0842c1s
v1p0879c2s v1p0890c2s v1p0891c1m
v1p0891c2m v1p0905c1s v1p0905c2s
v1p0992c2m v1p1008c1m v1p1030c1s
v1p1032c1s v1p1047c2s v1p1056c1s
v1p1081c2s v1p1092c2s v1p1121c2s
v1p1123c2s v1p1124c1m v1p1124c2m
v1p1125c2s v1p1126c1s v1p1132c2s
v1p1159c1s v1p1166c2s v1p1223c2s
v1p1224c1s v1p1225c2m v1p1254c2s
v1p1264c2s v1p1280c1s v1p1295c2s
v1p1318c1m v1p1327c2s v1p1347c2s
v1p1348c2m v1p1350c1s v1p1353c1s
v1p1353c2s v1p1371c2s v2p0022c2s
v2p0097c1m v2p0108c1m v2p0140c1s
v2p0142c1m v2p0142c2s v2p0166c1s
v2p0167c2s v2p0177c2s v2p0207c1s
v2p0228c1m v2p0231c2s v2p0244c2s
v2p0271c2s v2p0279c1s v2p0295c2s
v2p0297c1s v2p0330c1s v2p0377c1s
v2p0381c1s v2p0381c2s v2p0406c2s
v2p0407c2s v2p0441c2s v2p0450c1s
v2p0452c2s v2p0461c2s v3p0008c2s
v3p0021c2s v3p0023c2s v3p0087c2s
v3p0144c1s v3p0151c2s v3p0197c1s
v3p0216c2s v3p0221c2s v3p0246c2s
v3p0273c1s v3p0285c1s v3p0319c1s
v3p0356c2s v3p0366c1s v3p0447c1s
v3p0464c2s
Allen, W.F. and Hosmer, J.K.
v1p0924c2s v3p0047c1s
Allen, W.F. and Norton, G.
v2p0016c2s
Allen, W.H. v1p0313c1s
v1p0400c2s v1p0483c2s v1p0576c1s
v1p0906c2s v1p0913c1s v1p1001c2s
v1p1102c1s v1p1162c2s v1p1436c2s
v3p0131c2s v3p0438c1s v5p0134c1s
v5p0260c1s v5p0279c2s v5p0508c1s
v5p0572c1s v5p0603c2s v6p0109c1s
v6p0117c1s v6p0143c2s v6p0189c2s
v6p0195c1s v6p0206c1s v6p0242c2s
v6p0261c2s v6p0298c1s v6p0451c1s
v6p0522c2s v6p0569c2s v6p0573c2s
v6p0574c1m v6p0580c1s v6p0615c1m
v6p0638c1s v6p0651c2s
Allen, W.J. v1p1089c2s
Allen, W.S. v2p0266c1s
v4p0331c2s v5p0338c2s v5p0556c2s
v6p0621c1s
Allen, W.V. v4p0166c1s
v4p0617c1s v6p0347c1s v6p0488c2s
Allen, W.V. et al. v6p0667c1s
Allen, W.W. v1p1053c1s
Allen, Z. v1p0919c2s
v2p0306c1s
Allerton, C. v1p0057c1s
Allerton, W.S. v5p0408c1s
Alles, F.L. v6p0329c1s
v6p0329c2s v6p0687c2s

Alleyne, F.M. v5p0301c2s
v5p0428c2s
Allibone, A. v2p0234c2s
Allibone, S.A. v1p0132c2s
v1p0345c1m v1p0384c2s v1p0694c1s
v1p0694c2s v1p0729c2s v1p0855c1s
v1p0990c2s v1p1103c1s v1p1132c2s
v2p0368c1s
Allier, R. v3p0360c1s
v3p0365c1s v6p0302c1s
Allies, F.W. v1p0804c2s
Allies, J. v1p1178c2s
Allies, M. v1p0372c2s
v1p0475c2m v1p0741c2s v1p1117c1s
Allies, M.A. v2p0250c1s
Allies, M.H. v1p0565c1s
v2p0016c1s v2p0272c2s v2p0381c2s
v3p0267c2s
Allies, T.W. v1p0238c2s
v1p0387c1s v1p1067c2s v3p0240c2s
Allin, A. v4p0434c2s
v4p0475c2s v5p0198c1s v6p0363c1s
v6p0601c2s
Allin, A. and Hall, G.S. . v5p0327c1s
v5p0579c2s
Alling, A.N. v3p0432c2s
Alling, J.T. v3p0172c2s
v3p0288c2s
Alling, M.R. v1p1163c2s
v2p0432c1s
Allingham, W. v1p0140c2s
v1p0266c2s v1p0656c1s v1p0658c2s
v1p0731c1s v1p0774c1s v1p0824c2s
v1p0892c1s v1p0913c2s v1p1021c1s
v1p1335c2s v1p1366c2s v1p1429c1s
v2p0151c2s v2p0421c2s v4p0063c1s
v4p0560c1s v5p0096c1s v5p0362c1s
v5p0371c1s v5p0516c2s v5p0626c2s
v6p0449c1s v6p0463c2s v6p0580c1s
v6p0589c1s v6p0591c2s
Allinson, A.C.E. v6p0257c1s
Allinson, E.P. and Penrose, B.
v2p0338c2s v3p0086c1s v3p0186c1s
v3p0329c1s v3p0359c1s
Allinson, F.G. v2p0021c1s
v2p0224c2s v3p0322c1s
Allinson, F.G. and Joynes, E.S.
v6p0296c1s
Allinson, L.C. v1p0181c1s
Allinson, T.R. v2p0054c2s
v2p0124c1s v2p0161c1s v2p0257c2s
v3p0066c2s
Alliott, J.B. v5p0246c1s
Alliott, R. v1p1094c2s
Allis, S. v5p0344c1s
Allis, W.P. v5p0292c1s
Allison, A. v3p0017c2s
v4p0023c1s v4p0207c1s
Allison, C. v6p0130c1s
Allison, C.H. v6p0524c1s
v6p0528c1s v6p0656c2s
Allison, H.E. v5p0291c2s
Allison, J.W. v3p0323c1s
Allison, L.C. v1p0497c2s
v5p0068c1s
Allison, S.S., Mrs. v4p0526c2s
Allison, T.R. v2p0118c2s
v2p0160c2s
Allison, W.B. v2p0110c1s
v3p0096c2s v6p0387c2s
Allison, W.B. and Jones, J.K.
v5p0464c2s
Allison, W.T. v5p0246c1s
v5p0526c2s v6p0022c1s v6p0062c1s
v6p0467c2s
Allison, Y.E. v2p0296c2s
v2p0382c1s v3p0258c1s v4p0198c1s
v4p0429c2s v4p0549c1s
Alliston, N. v5p0130c2s
v5p0461c1s v6p0520c2s
Allman, G.J. v1p0134c2s
v1p0366c1s v1p0619c1s v1p0642c1s
v1p1059c1s v2p0062c1s
Allman, G.J. and Romanes, G.J.
v1p0681c2s
Allman, J. v6p0556c1s
Allman, Prof. v1p0366c1s
Allnutt, W.H. v4p0459c1s
v5p0227c1s v5p0466c1s v6p0466c2s
Allon, H. v1p0250c1s
v1p0754c2s v1p0962c1s v1p1061c2s
v1p1175c1s v2p0081c1s v2p0301c2s
v3p0205c1s v3p0342c1s v4p0301c2s
v4p0456c1s
Alloway, R.M. v3p0325c1s
Allport, F. v5p0200c2s
v5p0613c1s
Allsop, R.O. v3p0306c2s
v3p0308c1s v4p0522c1s
Allsop, R.Owen v3p0438c2s
Allsopp, H. v6p0428c2s
Allston, C. v6p0598c1s
Allston, F. v3p0264c2s
v4p0551c2s
Allston, Gov. v1p1205c1s
Allston, J.B. v1p0461c2s
v1p0716c1s v1p0995c1s
Allston, R.F.W. v1p1106c1s
Allum, T.C. v6p0409c2s
Allyn, R. v1p0172c1s
v1p0667c2s v1p1407c2s
Alma-Tadema, L. v2p0194c2s
v4p0029c2s
Almack, E. v5p0102c2s
Almack, R. v1p1243c1s
v2p0335c1s v5p0439c2s
Almack, R. and Bruce, J. . v1p0977c2s
Almar, J. and Jayare v6p0558c2s
Almirall, R.F. v6p0374c2s
v6p0660c2s
Almond, H.H. v1p0072c2s
v1p0384c2s v1p1005c2s v4p0206c2s
v5p0198c2s v5p0449c1s v5p0471c2s
v5p0505c2s
Almond, T.L. v6p0172c1s
Almy, A.H. v3p0037c2m
Almy, C., jr. v1p0457c2s
Almy, C., jr. and Godkin, E.L.
v1p0195c1s v1p0457c2s
Almy, F. v4p0078c1s
v4p0097c1s v4p0315c2s v5p0102c1s
v5p0118c1s v5p0221c2s v5p0425c2s
v6p0086c2s v6p0348c2s
Almy, J.E. v5p0162c2s
Almy, J.J. v3p0063c1s
Almy, P.H.W. v4p0058c2s
v4p0088c1s v4p0178c1s v4p0311c2s
v4p0454c2s v4p0615c2s v4p0622c1s
v5p0125c2s
Alonzo-Alonzo, A. v6p0510c1s
Aloysia, Sister v3p0098c1s
Alpe, E.M. v5p0152c2s
Alpers, O.T.J. v6p0454c2s
Alsop, F.J.O. v6p0058c1s
Alsted, D.B. v4p0265c1s
Alstine, H.J.Van v3p0066c2s
Alstine, N.Van v1p0253c1s
v1p0441c1s v1p0685c2s
Alt, F.M. v5p0152c1s
Altamira, R. v5p0544c2m
v6p0608c1m
Altemson, B.J.R. v6p0443c1s
Alten, Lieut.-Gen.von v6p0036c2s
Alter, D. v1p0399c2s
v1p0747c1s
Altgeld, J.P. v3p0208c2s
v4p0597c1s
Altham, E.A. v3p0071c1s
Althaus, J. v1p0157c1s
v4p0284c1s
Altman, F.D. v3p0091c1s
v5p0378c1s
Altman, S.P. v6p0506c2m
Altmann, C.K. v1p0388c1s
Altmann, S.P. v6p0425c1s
Alton, E.A.D' v5p0295c2s
v6p0326c1m
Alton, Margaret v6p0142c2s
Altschule, H. v3p0089c2s
Altsheler, J. v5p0419c2s
v6p0691c1s
Altsheler, J.A. v4p0072c2s
v4p0519c2s v4p0543c2s v5p0008c2s
v5p0036c2s v5p0065c2s v5p0318c2s
v5p0326c1s v5p0396c1s v5p0396c2s
v5p0481c1s v6p0291c2s v6p0540c2s
Alvarez, S. v4p0142c2s
Alvey, R.H. v4p0184c1s
Alviella, G.d' v2p0369c1s
v2p0456c1s v3p0026c1m
v3p0418c1s
Alviella, G.d', Count v5p0035c1s
Alvin, F. v4p0621c2s
Alvord, B. v1p0154c1s
v1p1024c2s v2p0097c1s
Alvord, F. v3p0041c1s
Alvord, H.C. v4p0226c1s
Alvord, H.E. v3p0399c2s
Alvord, T.G. v5p0443c1s
v5p0621c1s
Alvord, T.G., jr. v5p0147c2s
v5p0148c1s
Alward, Silas v6p0211c1s
Alwis, J. v1p0173c2s
v1p0962c1s
Amadi, G. v4p0452c2s
Amagat, E.H. v3p0167c2s
v3p0252c2s
Aman-Jean, E. v5p0030c2s
v5p0405c2s v5p0498c2s
Amandoline, A. v3p0060c2s
v6p0458c2s
Amarga, N. v5p0119c1s
v6p0160c2s
Amari, M. v1p1195c1s
Amaron, C.E. v3p0065c1s
v3p0364c1s v3p0365c1s v3p0440c1s
Amberg, W.A. v4p0393c2s
Amberley, K. v1p0814c2s
Amberley, Lady v1p0471c2s
Amberley, Lord v1p0173c2s
v1p0249c2s v1p0741c1s v1p0872c1s
v1p1093c1s v1p1238c1s v1p1384c1s
Amberley, Viscountess v1p1421c2s
Ambers, C.H. v1p1259c1s
Ambler, C.H. v6p0447c2s
v6p0693c1s
Ambler, R.P. v1p0242c1s
v1p0850c2s v1p1084c1s v2p0117c1s
Ambros, A.W. v6p0552c2s
Ambrose, J.C. v1p0277c1s
v1p1075c2s v1p1113c2s v2p0184c2s
v3p0208c1s v3p0451c2s
Ambrose, L. v4p0123c2s
v4p0329c2s v4p0330c2s v4p0407c1s
v5p0336c2s
Ambrose, Lodilla v6p0104c1s
v6p0522c1s
Ambrose, R.J. v5p0296c1s
Ambrose, W.J.L. v6p0211c1s
Ambruster, W. v1p0089c1s
Ambulo, J. v3p0070c2s
Amedroz, H.F. v1p0448c2s
Ameer, Ali v2p0039c2s
v2p0218c1s v3p0284c2s v4p0293c1s
v4p0293c2s v4p0525c1s v5p0635c1s
v6p0123c1s v6p0312c2s v6p0313c2s
v6p0314c2s
v6p0607c2s
Ameghino, F. v4p0430c1s
v5p0532c2s
Ameisen, A. v5p0168c2s
v5p0231c2s
Amelineau, E. v4p0154c1s
Amen, H.P. v5p0518c1s
Amenomori, N. v6p0285c1s
Amenomori, Nobushige v6p0336c2s
Ament, W.S. v3p0090c2s
American, S. v6p0673c2s
American, Sadie v5p0454c2s
v5p0606c2s
American Fenian v1p0448c2s
Americus v6p0661c2s
Amery, L.S. v5p0040c1s
Ames, A. v1p1193c1s
v5p0017c2s v5p0209c1s v5p0460c2s
Ames, A.F. v4p0287c2s
Ames, A.H. v1p1140c2s
v4p0518c1s v6p0040c1s
Ames, A.P. v6p0653c2s
Ames, C.G. v1p0219c1s
v1p1352c2s v2p0478c1s v4p0068c2s
v4p0076c1s v4p0217c2s v4p0254c1s
Ames, C.H. v6p0230c2s
Ames, C.R. v6p0010c1s
v6p0257c2s
Ames, E.F. v5p0373c1s
Ames, E.S. v6p0642c2s
Ames, F., jr. v5p0064c1s
Ames, F.B. v3p0074c1s
Ames, F.S.D. v2p0103c2s
Ames, H.B. v4p0043c1s
v4p0174c1s v6p0197c1s
Ames, H.V. v5p0439c2s
Ames, J.A. v3p0104c1s
Ames, J.B. v4p0585c2s
v6p0043c2s v6p0233c2s v6p0361c1s
v6p0420c2s v6p0432c1s v6p0608c2s
Ames, J.B. et al. v6p0641c1s
Ames, J.S. v4p0540c2s
v5p0184c2s v5p0361c1s v5p0472c2s
v5p0571c1s
Ames, J.W. v1p0175c1s
v1p0373c1s v1p0457c2s v1p0485c2s
v1p1148c2s v1p1344c2s v1p1345c1s
Ames, L.T. v4p0568c2s
Ames, M. v2p0121c1s
v2p0122c1s
Ames, M.C. v1p0593c1s
v1p1420c1s
Ames, Minnie B. v6p0177c1s
Ames, O. et al. v3p0031c1s
Ames, P.W. v1p1149c1s
Amherst, A., Lady v5p0211c1s
Amherst, M.T. v3p0179c1s
Amherst, W. v4p0114c2m
Amherst, W.J. v1p1119c2s
v2p0268c1s v2p0376c1s v3p0453c2s
v4p0320c1s
Ami, H.M. v5p0499c1s
v6p0553c2s
Ami, Henry H., Dr. v5p0090c2s
Amicis, De v1p0797c2s
Amicis, E.de v3p0375c2s
v3p0475c1s v5p0509c1s v5p0609c2s
Amicis, Edmondo de v6p0409c2s
Amidon, C.F. v6p0025c1s
v6p0210c2s
Ammen, D. v1p0650c2s
v2p0184c2s v2p0314c1m v3p0218c2s
v3p0305c1s v4p0423c2s v4p0595c1s
Ammidon, P.R. v3p0191c2s
Ammidown, E.H. v3p0471c2s
Ammon, O. v5p0467c1s
Amor, E. v2p0193c1s
v2p0324c2s
Amor, J.V.W. v2p0286c2s
Amores, E.M. v4p0538c2s
Amory, H. v1p0986c2s
Amory, I. v1p1325c2s
Amory, J. v1p0476c2s
Amory, R. v6p0506c1s
Amory, T.C. v1p0035c1s
v1p0190c2s v1p0415c1s v1p0424c1s
v1p0733c1s v1p1139c2s v1p1266c1m
v1p1307c2s v3p0324c1s
Amos, E.C. v5p0353c2s
v5p0582c2s
Amos, J. v4p0390c1s
Amos, M.S. v6p0448c1s

Amos, S. v1p0059c2s v1p0156c2s v1p0257c2s v1p0315c1s v1p0342c2s v1p0409c2s v1p0437c2s v1p0730c1s v1p1384c2s v2p0017c2s v2p0102c1m v2p0133c1s v2p0133c2m v2p0134c1m v2p0134c2m v2p0227c1s v2p0348c1m
Amos, S. and Barnard, C.I. v1p0396c1s
Amos, S. and Bryce, J. ... v2p0187c2s
Amos, S. and Keay, J.S. .. v2p0135c1s
Amos, S. et al. v1p0380c1s
Amos, S., Mrs. v5p0638c2s
Amos, S., Mrs. et al. v4p0628c2s
Amos, S.A. v5p0637c2s
Amos, S.M. v4p0148c2s
Amos, S.M.S. v4p0630c1s
Amos, S.M.S. et al. v4p0353c2s
Amouretti, F. v4p0269c2s v4p0313c1s
Amouroux, M.W.L' v1p0837c2s
Ampere, J.J. v1p0028c2s v1p0204c2s v1p0917c2s v1p0997c2s v1p1389c1s
Amphlett, J. v1p0138c1s v1p0309c1s v1p0504c1s v1p1272c2s
Amphlett, W. v1p1400c1s
Amphori, A. v1p1288c2s
Amram, B.B. v6p0462c1s
Amram, D.W. v3p0119c1s v4p0302c1m v4p0323c1s v5p0001c1s v5p0003c2s v5p0060c2s v5p0066c2s v5p0291c1s v5p0304c2m v5p0308c2s v5p0323c2s v5p0329c2s v5p0503c1s v5p0645c2s v6p0065c1s v6p0319c2s v6p0516c2s
Amringe, J.H.Van v1p0647c1s v3p0093c1s
Amringe, W.F.Van v1p1292c1s
Amsbary, W.B. v6p0127c2s v6p0231c2s
Amsden, D.E. v5p0302c2s
Amstel, A.van v5p0108c1s v5p0418c2s
Amundsen, E. v5p0517c2s
Amundsen, R. v6p0395c1s
Amyot, T. v1p0103c2s v1p0147c1s v1p0393c1s v1p0410c2s v1p0445c2s v1p0550c1s v1p0709c2s v1p0881c1s v1p0926c2s v1p1034c2s v1p1106c1m v1p1337c2s
Anagnos, J.R. v1p0577c2s v2p0275c2s
Anagnos, M. v3p0235c1s v5p0066c2s
Ancrum, B. v4p0516c2s
Ancrum, Beswicke v4p0516c2s
Ander, P. v3p0208c2s
Anderdon, J. v1p0166c1s
Anderdon, W.H. v1p0156c1s v1p0353c1s v1p0361c1s v1p0806c1s v1p1095c1s v1p1098c1s v1p1371c1s v2p0056c2m v2p0166c1s v2p0179c2s v2p0459c2s
Anders, J.M. v1p1014c2s v1p1016c1s v2p0162c1s v2p0325c2s
Andersen, C. v1p1196c2s
Andersen, H.C. v1p0175c1s v1p0332c1s v1p0351c1s v1p0459c2s v1p0500c1s v1p0529c2s v1p0539c2s v1p0700c2s v1p0750c2s v1p0776c1s v1p0940c1s v1p0985c1s v1p1008c2s v1p1061c2s v1p1088c1s v1p1172c2s v1p1231c1s v1p1274c1m v1p1274c2s v1p1307c2s v1p1337c2s v1p1403c2m
Anderson, A. v1p0228c1s v1p1226c1s v2p0258c1s v2p0459c2s v3p0323c1s v5p0086c2s v6p0480c1s v6p0539c1s v6p0546c2s
Anderson, A.C. v1p0637c1s
Anderson, A.D. v5p0017c1s v5p0349c1s
Anderson, A.H. v6p0154c2s
Anderson, A.J. v4p0620c2s
Anderson, A.M. v4p0179c2s v5p0201c1s
Anderson, A.P. v5p0284c2s
Anderson, A.W. v5p0478c2s v6p0518c1s v6p0664c2s
Anderson, Ada W. v6p0515c2s
Anderson, Alice L. v5p0281c2s
Anderson, Arnold M. v6p0022c2s
Anderson, C.A. v6p0064c2s
Anderson, C.N. v6p0483c2s
Anderson, D. v2p0397c1s v4p0028c2s v4p0126c2s
Anderson, D.J. v2p0196c2s
Anderson, David v5p0510c1s
Anderson, E. v1p1043c1s v2p0320c2s v5p0071c1s v6p0666c1s
Anderson, E.C. v1p0442c1s v1p0689c1s
Anderson, E.G. v1p1182c1s v1p1423c1s v4p0627c1s
Anderson, E.H. v5p0340c1s v6p0371c2s
Anderson, E.P. v2p0141c2s v3p0011c2s v3p0061c1s v3p0109c2s v3p0214c2s v3p0311c2s v3p0411c2s v3p0460c1s v4p0263c1s
Anderson, E.R. v6p0419c2s
Anderson, F.A. v4p0613c1s
Anderson, F.F. v5p0014c2s v5p0623c2s
Anderson, F.M. v5p0315c1s v5p0416c1s v5p0613c1s v6p0516c1s
Anderson, G. v1p0048c1s v1p0193c1s v1p0336c1s v1p0848c1s v1p0855c1s v3p0166c1s v4p0273c1s
Anderson, G. and Wakeman, T.B. v2p0351c2s
Anderson, G., Mrs. v4p0008c2s
Anderson, G.B. v6p0218c2s v6p0329c1s v6p0588c2s
Anderson, G.E. v6p0118c2s
Anderson, G.L. v5p0377c2s
Anderson, G.W. v1p0268c1s v1p1068c1s v1p1154c1s v5p0417c2s v6p0100c1s
Anderson, H.J. v1p0672c2s v1p1163c2s
Anderson, H.M. v6p0685c2s
Anderson, H.T. v1p0095c2s v1p0738c2s
Anderson, I. v1p0221c1s v1p0376c2s v1p0957c1s v1p1365c1s
Anderson, J. v1p0109c2s v1p0113c1s v1p0236c1s v1p0336c1s v1p0469c1s v1p0636c1s v1p0637c1m v1p0637c2s v1p0846c1s v1p0858c1s v1p0898c2s v1p1076c2s v1p1165c1m v1p1291c1s v1p1311c2s v1p1439c2s v3p0185c1s v3p0272c2s v3p0328c2s v4p0383c2s v5p0179c2s v5p0208c2s v5p0330c2s v6p0655c2s
Anderson, J., Sir v1p1290c2s
Anderson, J.A. v4p0131c2s v6p0605c2s
Anderson, J.D. v2p0003c2s v5p0285c1s v6p0614c1s
Anderson, J.E. v5p0273c2s
Anderson, J.G. v1p0760c1s v1p0761c1s
Anderson, J.G.C. v5p0267c1s v5p0458c2s
Anderson, J.L. v3p0201c1s
Anderson, J.M. v1p0206c1s v1p0742c1s v1p0743c2s v2p0205c1s v3p0057c1s v3p0129c2s v4p0095c2s v4p0498c1s v6p0333c1s
Anderson, J.P. v2p0057c1s
Anderson, J.R. v1p0472c1s v1p0742c2s v1p0874c1s v1p1069c2s
Anderson, J.S. v3p0062c2s
Anderson, Jos. v5p0311c2s
Anderson, K. and Tanner, A. v4p0515c1s
Anderson, K.C. v5p0489c2s
Anderson, L. v6p0451c1s
Anderson, L.A. v6p0321c2m v6p0323c1s
Anderson, L.F. v6p0573c1s
Anderson, L.M. v1p0142c2s v1p0460c2s v1p0931c2s v1p1082c1s
Anderson, M. v3p0406c1s v4p0094c2s v4p0146c2s v5p0556c1s
Anderson, M., Capt. v4p0604c2s
Anderson, M.B. v1p0244c1s v1p0418c1s v1p1163c1s v2p0002c2m v2p0031c1m v2p0058c2s v2p0143c2s v2p0144c2m v2p0155c1s v2p0176c1s v2p0181c2m v2p0210c2s v2p0230c2s v2p0267c2s v2p0298c1m v2p0304c1s v2p0333c1s v2p0428c2m v3p0020c2m v3p0029c1s v3p0057c1s v3p0057c2s v3p0075c1s v3p0115c2s v3p0139c2s v3p0140c1m v3p0154c2s v3p0231c2s v3p0260c1m v3p0351c1s v3p0358c2s v3p0463c1s v4p0183c2s v4p0184c1s v4p0305c1s v4p0319c1s v4p0520c1s v5p0037c1s v5p0086c1s v5p0522c2m v5p0523c1s v5p0523c2s v6p0090c2s v6p0586c2s
Anderson, M.E. v6p0164c2s
Anderson, M.S. v4p0410c2s v5p0205c2s v5p0432c2s v5p0500c2s
Anderson, N.J. v1p1378c2s
Anderson, Neal L. v6p0115c1s
Anderson, P. v1p0461c1s v1p0695c2s v3p0102c1s v4p0136c1s v4p0544c1s
Anderson, R. v1p0556c2s v1p0580c2s v1p0658c2s v1p0701c2s v1p0702c2s v1p0749c1s v1p0853c1s v1p0853c2s v1p0878c2s v1p1309c2s v2p0226c1s v2p0226c2s v3p0287c2s v4p0056c1s v4p0139c2s v4p0141c2s v5p0143c1m v6p0055c2s v6p0158c1m v6p0296c1s v6p0517c2s
Anderson, R., Sir v6p0065c1s
Anderson, R.B. v1p0096c1s v1p0926c1s v1p0926c2s v1p1098c1s v1p1155c1s v1p1307c1s v1p1417c1s v2p0111c1s v2p0175c2s v2p0213c2s v2p0233c1s v2p0244c1s v2p0314c1s v2p0387c1s v2p0436c1s v2p0443c1s v3p0038c1s v3p0093c2s v3p0307c1s v3p0450c1s v4p0013c1m v4p0407c2s v4p0495c2s
Anderson, R.C. v1p0277c2s
Anderson, R.G. v5p0328c1s
Anderson, R.H. v1p0518c2s v2p0365c2s
Anderson, Robert v5p0236c2s
Anderson, S.L. v2p0377c1s
Anderson, S.M. v1p0849c2s
Anderson, S.T. v2p0045c1s v2p0290c2m v2p0367c2s v2p0385c2s
Anderson, T. v1p0945c1s v4p0273c1s v6p0622c1s v6p0681c1m
Anderson, T.D. v5p0058c2s v5p0645c2s
Anderson, T.D., jr. v2p0043c2s
Anderson, T.F. v4p0408c1m v6p0465c2s v6p0625c1s
Anderson, T.M. v1p0032c1s v1p0380c1s v5p0029c2m v5p0120c2s v5p0232c2s v5p0375c2s v5p0445c1s v5p0550c1s v6p0674c1s
Anderson, T.O. v6p0411c1s
Anderson, W. v2p0005c1s v2p0069c2s v2p0103c1s v2p0114c2s v2p0178c2s v2p0315c1s v2p0382c2s v2p0467c2s v2p0474c2s v3p0192c2s v3p0242c1s v3p0284c2s v3p0291c2s v3p0457c1m v4p0024c2s v4p0180c2s v4p0507c1s v4p0631c1s v5p0018c2s v5p0317c1s
Anderson, W. and Good, A.. v3p0100c2s
Anderson, W.B. v5p0132c1s
Anderson, W.C. v4p0323c1s
Anderson, W.F. v5p0145c1s v5p0437c1s v5p0576c2s
Anderson, W.G. v3p0470c1s v4p0441c1s v5p0449c1s v6p0038c2s v6p0498c1s v6p0710c2m
Anderson, W.G. et al. v3p0025c2s
Anderson, W.H. v4p0076c2s
Anderson, W.J. v1p0195c1s v1p1387c1s v6p0634c1s
Anderson, W.P. v4p0331c2s
Anderson, W.W. v3p0432c2s
Andersson, A. v6p0373c1s v6p0628c2s
Andersson, J.G. v6p0023c1s v6p0023c2s v6p0218c2s v6p0646c2s
Anderton, B. v5p0337c1s
Anderton, I.M. v4p0358c2s v4p0413c1s v4p0587c2m v4p0616c1s v5p0027c1s v5p0182c1s v5p0216c1s v5p0386c2s
Anderton, Isabella M. v5p0210c2s
Anderton, Q.M. v5p0208c1s
Andras, G. v5p0532c1s
Andre, Ch. v2p0467c2s
Andre, E. v6p0403c2s v6p0470c2s
Andre, E.C. v6p0492c2s
Andre, E.M. v5p0560c1s
Andre, G.G. v1p0269c1s v1p1366c2s v2p0157c2s v2p0214c1s
Andre, J. v1p0310c1s
Andre, J.L. v2p0061c1s v2p0089c2s v2p0091c2s v2p0098c2s v2p0156c1s v2p0160c2s v2p0204c1s v2p0207c2s v2p0258c1s v2p0296c1s v2p0318c2s v2p0359c2s v2p0393c2s v3p0407c1s v4p0166c1s v4p0206c1s v4p0458c1s v5p0097c2s v5p0563c1s
Andre, J.Lewis v3p0275c1s
Andre, P. v4p0388c1s
Andre, P.F. v1p0207c1s v1p0322c1s v1p0530c2s v1p1016c2s v1p1114c1s v1p1243c1s v1p1342c1s v1p1421c2s
Andreades v6p0272c1s
Andreades, A. v6p0272c1s v6p0392c1s
Andreae, P. v4p0062c2s v4p0257c1s v4p0342c1s v4p0391c2s v4p0469c1s v4p0590c2s
Andree, R. v4p0020c1s
Andrew, A. v1p0395c2s
Andrew, A.P. v5p0383c1s v6p0413c2m v6p0694c2s
Andrew, A.P. and Kinley, D. v6p0156c2s
Andrew, A.W. v6p0105c2s
Andrew, E.F. v4p0529c1s
Andrew, F. v5p0219c1s v5p0367c2s
Andrew, F.J. v3p0156c1s
Andrew, J. v4p0433c1s
Andrew, J.A. v1p0910c2s
Andrew, M.F. v6p0317c2s
Andrew, S.A. v2p0222c2s
Andrew, S.R. v1p0239c1m v1p0426c1s v1p0538c2s v1p0539c1s v1p0566c1s v1p0847c1s v1p0870c2s v1p1096c2s v1p1105c2s v1p1286c1s
Andrew, V.R. v4p0085c1s v4p0393c2s
Andrew, W.P. v1p0429c1s v1p0634c2s v3p0144c1s v3p0211c2s v3p0352c1s
Andrewes, F.W. v4p0516c1s
Andrewes, F.W. and Miers, H.A. v4p0429c2s

Andrews, A. v1p0159c2s v1p0271c2s v1p0305c2s v1p0306c2m v1p0315c2s v1p0370c2s v1p0397c2s v1p0413c1s v1p0413c2s v1p0417c2s v1p0439c1s v1p0498c2s v1p0797c1s v1p0887c2s v1p0914c2s v1p0915c1s v1p1242c2s v6p0358c1s v6p0605c2s v6p0696c1s
Andrews, A.C. v2p0311c1s
Andrews, A.D. v5p0182c1s v5p0599c1s v6p0506c2s
Andrews, A.P. v6p0159c2s
Andrews, A.W. v5p0228c2s
Andrews, Alice N. v6p0203c2s
Andrews, B.R. v6p0040c2s v6p0277c1s
Andrews, C. v4p0101c2s v6p0540c2s
Andrews, C.C. v1p0322c1s v1p0537c1s v1p0636c1s v1p0751c2s v1p0832c2s v1p1353c2s v4p0542c2s
Andrews, C.C., Gen. v6p0233c1s
Andrews, C.D. v2p0342c2s
Andrews, C.G. v2p0308c2s
Andrews, C.L. v5p0075c2s
Andrews, C.M. v3p0097c1m v3p0190c1s v3p0412c2s v3p0461c1s v3p0465c2s v4p0127c2s v4p0129c2s v4p0212c2s v4p0226c1s v4p0286c2s v4p0288c1s v4p0609c1s v5p0165c1s v5p0193c1s v5p0217c2s v5p0248c1s v5p0398c1s v5p0398c2s v6p0016c1s v6p0213c1s v6p0353c2s
Andrews, C.S. v5p0291c1s v5p0368c1s v6p0158c1s
Andrews, C.W. v1p0422c1s v4p0330c1s v4p0422c1s v4p0508c1s v5p0116c1s v5p0334c2s v5p0440c2s v6p0400c1s
Andrews, C.W. and Kroeger, A.B. v5p0334c2s
Andrews, Clement W. v6p0074c2s
Andrews, Dr. v1p0400c1s v1p0812c1m v1p0955c2s
Andrews, E. v1p0155c1s v1p0523c2s v1p0793c1s v1p0794c1s v1p0810c1s v2p0143c1s v2p0219c1s v2p0244c2s v5p0355c1s v6p0218c1s
Andrews, E.A. v2p0015c2s v3p0014c2s v3p0094c1s v3p0103c2s v4p0019c1s v4p0072c1s v4p0138c2s v4p0178c2s v5p0078c2s v5p0222c1s v6p0080c2s v6p0156c2s v6p0195c1s v6p0226c1s
Andrews, E.B. v1p0267c2s v1p0268c1s v1p0268c2s v1p0269c2m v1p0853c2s v1p0938c2m v1p0995c2m v2p0135c2s v2p0191c1s v2p0240c2s v2p0337c1s v2p0347c2s v3p0091c2m v3p0099c2s v3p0114c2s v3p0120c1s v3p0152c2s v3p0285c2s v3p0323c2s v3p0378c1s v3p0393c2s v3p0397c2s v3p0437c1s v4p0059c1s v4p0088c1s v4p0126c1s v4p0167c2s v4p0170c2s v4p0223c2s v4p0283c1s v4p0377c2m v4p0378c1s v4p0452c2s v4p0483c1s v4p0486c2s v4p0507c1s v4p0520c2s v4p0524c1s v4p0532c1s v4p0563c2s v4p0584c1s v5p0105c1s v5p0126c2s v5p0467c2s v5p0471c2s v6p0105c1s v6p0170c1s v6p0272c2s v6p0281c1s v6p0600c2s v6p0670c2s v6p0671c2s
Andrews, E.B. and Howe, W.W. v5p0592c2s
Andrews, E.B. et al. v1p0828c2s
Andrews, E.Benj. v6p0188c2s
Andrews, E.F. v2p0053c1s v3p0077c1s v3p0253c2s v4p0110c1s v4p0183c2s v4p0234c1s v4p0245c2s v4p0276c2s v4p0366c2s v4p0551c2s v4p0607c2s v4p0632c1s v5p0329c1s v5p0457c1s v5p0555c2s
Andrews, E.G. v6p0061c1s
Andrews, E.L. v3p0353c2s v6p0026c2s v6p0528c2s
Andrews, E.P. v5p0334c1s v5p0334c2s v5p0434c1s
Andrews, E.R. v1p1311c2s
Andrews, Edith H. v6p0100c1s
Andrews, Edward L. v2p0363c1s
Andrews, F. v1p0931c2s
Andrews, F.B. v6p0052c1s
Andrews, F.F. v6p0479c1s
Andrews, G. v2p0013c2s v6p0418c1s v6p0612c2s
Andrews, G.K. v3p0254c2s
Andrews, G.L. v1p1401c2s v5p0626c1s v5p0626c2s
Andrews, Grace A. v5p0168c1s
Andrews, H., jr. v2p0446c2s
Andrews, I. v6p0217c1s
Andrews, I.M. v6p0184c2s v6p0681c2s
Andrews, I.W. v2p0131c1s v2p0294c2s v2p0316c2s v2p0322c2s v3p0200c2s v3p0236c1s v3p0268c1s v3p0310c2s v3p0424c2s
Andrews, J.B. v4p0365c2s v5p0397c2s v5p0634c1s
Andrews, J.W. v2p0096c2s
v4p0473c1s
Andrews, L.R. v6p0592c1s
Andrews, M.E. v6p0711c1s
Andrews, M.R.S. v6p0158c2s v6p0173c1s v6p0236c1s v6p0261c2s v6p0311c2s v6p0351c1s
Andrews, Mary R.S. v6p0066c1s v6p0069c2s v6p0095c1s v6p0159c2s v6p0244c1s v6p0264c1s v6p0359c1s v6p0378c1s v6p0380c2s v6p0387c1s v6p0395c2s v6p0412c1s v6p0501c2s v6p0503c2s v6p0507c1s v6p0645c1s v6p0663c1s v6p0680c2s v6p0693c1s v6p0694c1s v6p0702c1s
Andrews, P. v4p0416c2s
Andrews, P., Lt. v5p0401c2s
Andrews, R.D. v4p0025c1s v5p0015c1s v6p0027c2s v6p0154c1s
Andrews, S. v1p0233c2s v1p0235c1s v1p0487c1s v1p0905c1s v1p1388c2s
Andrews, S.A.P. v4p0186c1s
Andrews, S.J. v1p0687c1s v3p0418c2s v6p0126c2s
Andrews, S.P. v1p0283c1s v1p0702c2s v1p0715c1s v1p0724c2m v1p1002c2s v1p1343c2s v1p1344c2s
Andrews, S.R. v1p0348c1s v1p1287c1s
Andrews, Sara v6p0515c2s v6p0647c2s
Andrews, T. v1p0164c2s v1p1161c2s v1p1233c2s
Andrews, T.J. v5p0365c2s
Andrews, W. v1p0245c1s v1p0810c1s v1p0936c2s v2p0013c2s v3p0245c1s v4p0518c1s v5p0191c1s v5p0264c1s v5p0595c2s v6p0055c1s v6p0232c2s v6p0244c1s
Andrews, W.C. v5p0410c1s
Andrews, W.E. v3p0156c1s v5p0203c1s v6p0485c2s
Andrews, W.G. v1p0870c1s
Andrews, W.L. v4p0011c2s v4p0015c2s v4p0453c2s v4p0497c2s v5p0048c2s v5p0070c1s v5p0070c2s v5p0074c2s v5p0193c1s v5p0205c2s v5p0242c2s v5p0257c2s v5p0310c2s v5p0406c2s v5p0407c1s v5p0487c1s v5p0509c2s v6p0074c1s v6p0547c1s v6p0616c2s
Andrews, W.P. v2p0459c2s v3p0175c2s v3p0176c1s v3p0356c2s v4p0477c1s v6p0643c2s v6p0678c1s
Andrews, W.S. v3p0146c2s v6p0073c2s v6p0211c2s v6p0230c1s v6p0394c2s
Andrews, W.S. and Baker, A.L. v6p0394c2s v6p0612c1s
Andrews, W.S. and Carus, P. v6p0395c1s
Andrews, W.V. v1p1198c1s
Andrews, W.W. v1p0207c2s v1p0594c1s v1p0666c2s v1p0692c2s v1p0710c2s v1p0729c1s v1p0791c2m v1p0898c1s v1p1095c2s v1p1271c2s
Andria, A.T.M.d' v4p0636c2s
Andrieu, J. v1p0285c2s v1p0718c1s v1p1104c1s
Andrieux, L. v4p0423c2s
Andrus, G.M. v6p0497c2s v6p0522c1s
Andrus, S.C. v6p0009c1s v6p0414c2s
Andrus, S.G. v6p0414c1s v6p0414c2m v6p0440c1s v6p0639c2s
Andrus, W.I. v5p0539c1s
Andrusoff, N. v4p0063c1s
Anesaki, M. v6p0086c1s v6p0123c1s
Anet, C. v6p0244c1s
Anet, C. and Schopfer, J.. v6p0546c2s
Anet, L. v2p0038c2s
Ange, E. v2p0032c2s v2p0324c2s
Angell, E.A. v5p0568c2s
Angell, F. v5p0121c1s
Angell, F. and Harwood, Henry v5p0369c2s
Angell, G.T. v1p0042c2s v2p0003c1s
Angell, H.C. v1p0616c2s v1p1196c2s
Angell, I.B. v1p1393c2s
Angell, J. v6p0373c1s
Angell, J.B. v1p0275c1s v1p0417c2s v1p0489c1s v1p0503c2s v1p0513c2s v1p0531c1s v1p0650c2s v1p0755c1s v1p0790c1s v1p1073c2s v1p1130c2s v1p1143c1s v2p0078c2m v2p0233c1s v3p0037c2s v3p0281c1s v3p0445c1s v5p0109c2s v5p0595c1s v6p0135c2s v6p0190c2s v6p0426c1s
Angell, J.B. et al. v2p0126c2s v3p0090c1s v3p0091c2m v4p0131c1s v4p0542c2s
Angell, J.D. v1p0406c1s
Angell, J.K. v1p0284c1s
Angell, J.R. v5p0280c1s v5p0470c2s v5p0471c1s v5p0578c2s v6p0134c2s v6p0172c1s v6p0521c1s v6p0521c2s v6p0522c1s v6p0604c2s v6p0623c1s
Angell, J.R. and Fite, W.. v5p0540c1s
Angell, J.R. and McLennan, S.F. v4p0549c2s
Angell, J.R. and Moore, A.W. v4p0036c2s v4p0245c1s
Angell, J.R. and Pierce, A.H. v4p0036c2s
Angell, J.R. and Simons, Sadie E. v5p0193c1s
Angell, J.R. and Thompson, H.B. v5p0133c2s
Angell, James R. v6p0004c2s v6p0122c2s
Angell, L. v1p0373c2s
Angell, T.B. v2p0131c1s
Angelo, Michael v4p0128c1s
Angier, Belle S. v5p0583c1s
Angier, C.B. v4p0074c1s v4p0084c2s v4p0225c2s v5p0152c1s v5p0170c2s v5p0265c1s
Angier, F.H. v1p0863c2s
Angier, N. v5p0509c1s
Anglicanus, M. v6p0365c2s
Anglin, S. v5p0215c2s
Anglin, T.W. v4p0506c1s
Anglo-American v6p0561c1s
Anglo-Indian v6p0162c2m v6p0313c1s v6p0352c2s
Angot, A. v4p0568c2s
Angstman, C.S. v5p0165c1s
Angstrom, A.J. v1p0077c2s
Angstrom, C. v2p0457c2s
Angus, C. v5p0316c1s v5p0372c1s
Angus, G.A. v6p0098c2s
Angus, H.C. v5p0041c2s
Angus, J. v1p0550c1s
Angus, J.K. v4p0079c2s v4p0413c1s
Angus, M.E. v4p0536c1s
Angus, O. v5p0468c1s v5p0634c2s v5p0645c2s
Anichkoff, E. v4p0031c1s
Anketell, J. v1p0145c1m v1p0422c2s v1p0620c1m v1p0870c1m
Annan, A.M.F. v1p1305c2s
Annan, A.M.F., Mrs. v1p0084c1s v1p0877c2s v1p1439c1s
Annan, A.R. v1p0581c1s
Annand, J. v4p0428c1s v5p0457c2s
Annand, James v4p0240c1m v4p0328c2m
Annandale, N. v5p0176c1s
Annesley, C. v6p0303c1s v6p0440c1s
Annunzio, G.d' v5p0278c1s v5p0300c2s v6p0181c2m v6p0331c2s
Anrooy, A.Van v6p0710c1s v6p0714c2s
Anscombe, A. v4p0125c2m v4p0429c1s v5p0051c2s v5p0264c1s
Anscombe, A. et al. v4p0226c1s
Ansell, E. v6p0007c1s v6p0012c2s v6p0240c2s v6p0300c1s v6p0387c1s v6p0506c2s v6p0539c1s v6p0634c1s
Ansell, F.G. v6p0663c2s v6p0687c2s v6p0688c1s
Ansell, F.G. and Walker, J.B. v6p0685c1s
Anselm, S. v1p0686c1s
Anslow, R. v4p0560c1s
Anson, J.C.I. v6p0362c1s
Anson, W.R. v3p0199c2s v4p0052c2s v4p0131c2s v4p0238c2s v5p0034c2s
Ansot, H. v4p0058c2s v4p0196c2s
Anspach, F.R. v1p1238c1s
Anstadt, P. v2p0266c1s v2p0475c2s v3p0465c2s v5p0387c1s v6p0390c1s
Ansted, A. v4p0025c1s v4p0045c2s v4p0148c2s v4p0500c1s v4p0616c2s
Ansted, Alex v5p0210c1s
Ansted, D. v1p0011c1s
Ansted, D.F. v1p0211c2s
Ansted, D.T. v1p0003c1s v1p0052c2s v1p0053c1s v1p0073c1s v1p0174c2s v1p0209c1s v1p0211c2s v1p0223c2s v1p0263c1s v1p0268c1s v1p0316c1s v1p0428c1s v1p0506c2m v1p0617c2m v1p0652c1s v1p0661c1s v1p0718c2s v1p0747c1s v1p0826c1m v1p0828c2s v1p0879c1s v1p0922c2s v1p1005c2s v1p1110c2s v1p1147c1s v1p1148c2s v1p1151c1s v1p1151c2s v1p1218c2s v1p1255c2s v1p1316c1m v1p1322c1s v1p1337c1m v1p1369c1m v1p1377c1m v1p1390c2m v1p1391c2s v2p0102c1s v3p0059c2s v3p0386c2s
Ansted, Prof. v1p0266c1s v1p0876c2s v1p0959c1s
Ansted, T.D. v1p0762c2s
Anster, J. v1p0245c2s

v1p0934c1s v1p1156c2s v1p1257c2s
Anstey, F. v2p0048c2s
v2p0152c2s v2p0177c2s v2p0401c2s
v2p0451c1s v3p0030c1s v3p0177c1s
v3p0187c1s v3p0256c2s v3p0279c2s
v3p0291c1s v3p0416c2s v4p0104c2s
v4p0259c1s v5p0525c2s
Anstie, F.E. v1p0817c1s
v1p0957c2s v1p1254c1m v1p1431c1s
Anstruther, E. v4p0166c2s
v5p0071c2s v5p0283c2s v5p0638c2s
v6p0073c1s v6p0628c1s
Anstruther, Eva v4p0146c2s
Anstruther, Mrs. v3p0318c2s
v6p0247c1s
Anstruther-Thomson, C. and Paget, V.
v5p0051c1s
Anthon, C.E. v2p0423c1s
Anthony, A.W. v4p0057c1s
v6p0126c1s v6p0538c2s
Anthony, C. v4p0187c2s
Anthony, C., jr. v1p1065c1s
Anthony, C.V. v4p0195c2s
v5p0486c2s v6p0285c2s
Anthony, E. v3p0103c1s
v3p0450c2s v4p0430c2s v6p0102c1s
v6p0167c2s
Anthony, F. v6p0057c2s
v6p0316c1s
Anthony, H.B. v2p0372c1s
v2p0424c1s
Anthony, H.M. and Munro, J.A.R.
v5p0396c2s
Anthony, J.B. v5p0069c2s
v5p0284c1m
Anthony, J.P. v1p0413c1s
v1p0463c2s v1p0531c2s v1p1148c2s
Anthony, J.T. v1p0343c1s
Anthony, J.V.S. v1p0212c2s
v1p0376c2s
Anthony, M.H. v6p0596c1s
Anthony, S.B. v5p0022c2s
v5p0635c2s
Anthony, Susan B. v6p0705c2s
Anthony, W.A. v1p0401c2s
v1p0580c2s v1p0748c1s v3p0133c2s
v4p0174c2s v4p0175c1m v4p0277c1s
v5p0423c1s v5p0571c2s
Antimaco, G. v2p0459c2s
Antisdel, C.B. v6p0144c1s
Anton, P. v1p0574c2s
Antona, A.H. v6p0249c1s
Antona, A.J.H. v4p0010c2s
v4p0088c1s v4p0168c1s v4p0250c1s
v4p0444c1s v6p0414c1s
Antoniadi, E. v5p0123c2s
v5p0571c2s
Antoniadi, E.M. v5p0363c1s
v5p0509c1s v5p0549c2s v6p0146c1s
v6p0402c2s v6p0403c1s v6p0564c2s
Antoniadi, E.M. and Burkett, F.C.
v6p0146c1s
Antoniadi, E.M. and Mathieu, G.
v5p0123c2s
Antrim, E. and Goebel, H.. v5p0597c1s
Antrim, E.I. v5p0230c2m
v5p0231c2s v5p0336c2s
Antrim, Minna T. v6p0358c1s
v6p0625c1s v6p0657c1s
Antrobus, B.W. v4p0348c1s
Antrobus, C.L. v5p0225c2s
v5p0315c2s v5p0351c2s v5p0426c1s
v5p0455c1s v5p0596c2s v6p0184c2s
v6p0200c2s v6p0246c2s v6p0586c1s
v6p0691c1s
Antwerp, W.H.Van v3p0454c2s
Apache, A. v4p0045c1s
Apache, Antonio v4p0636c1s
Apel, F.L. v1p1296c2s
Apel, Lilian v5p0513c1s
Apgar, A.C. v4p0583c2s
Apgar, E.A. v6p0502c2s
Apgar, Genevieve v6p0142c2s
Aplin, O.V. v6p0067c1s
Aplin, W. v1p0069c1s
Apoikos v6p0654c2s
Apparent, A.de L' v3p0123c2s
Appel, J.W. v4p0214c1s
v5p0483c1s v6p0421c2s
Appel, T. v1p0074c1s
v1p0114c1s v1p0243c1s v1p0248c1s
v1p0305c1s v1p0515c1s v1p0527c2s
v1p0581c1m v1p0685c1s v1p0689c2s
v1p0727c1s v1p0792c1s v1p0793c2s
v1p0811c1s v1p0812c1s v1p0818c1s
v1p0823c2s v1p0900c2s v1p1058c1s
v1p1215c1s v1p1215c2s v1p1243c2s
v1p1432c2s v2p0285c1s v2p0339c2s
v2p0437c2s v2p0452c1s v3p0084c2m
v3p0269c2s v4p0183c2s v5p0510c2s
Appel, Theo. v2p0367c2s
Appelbee, A.S. v5p0041c2s
v5p0271c1s v5p0274c1s v5p0383c2s
v5p0389c1s
Apperley, C.J. v1p0472c2s
v1p0479c1s v1p0605c1s v1p0818c2s
v1p1062c2s v1p1110c2s v1p1239c2s
v1p1330c1s
Apperson, G.L. v3p0092c1s
v3p0139c2s v3p0471c2s v4p0066c1s
v4p0189c1s v4p0405c2s v4p0423c1s
v4p0448c1s v5p0061c1s v5p0136c2s
v5p0252c2s v5p0347c1s v5p0352c1s
v5p0524c1s v5p0582c1s v6p0296c2s
v6p0426c2s v6p0478c1s v6p0526c1s
Apple, A.T.G. v6p0122c2s
v6p0262c2s
Apple, H.H. v6p0483c1s
Apple, J.H. v1p1042c2s
v2p0483c2s
Apple, J.W. v1p0258c2s
v1p1352c1s
Apple, T. v1p0003c2s
v1p0285c2s v1p0392c1s v1p1023c1s
v1p1102c2s v1p1120c2s v1p1354c2s
v3p0300c1s
Apple, T.G. v1p0047c2s
v1p0075c1s v1p0095c2s v1p0096c1s
v1p0096c2s v1p0120c2s v1p0189c2m
v1p0241c1m v1p0241c2s v1p0254c2s
v1p0255c2m v1p0275c1s v1p0296c2s
v1p0312c2s v1p0313c2s v1p0319c2s
v1p0357c2s v1p0393c1s v1p0427c1s
v1p0440c1s v1p0441c1s v1p0487c1s
v1p0514c2m v1p0528c1m v1p0570c2s
v1p0686c1m v1p0688c2s v1p0692c2s
v1p0746c1s v1p0756c2s v1p0777c2m
v1p0848c1s v1p0889c2s v1p0898c2s
v1p0992c2s v1p0999c2s v1p1001c1s
v1p1058c1s v1p1085c2s v1p1090c2m
v1p1094c2s v1p1097c1s v1p1109c2s
v1p1122c2s v1p1158c1s v1p1161c1s
v1p1200c1s v1p1237c2s v1p1301c2m
v1p1304c1s v2p0011c1s v2p0081c1s
v2p0082c1m v2p0085c2s v2p0147c1m
v2p0180c2s v2p0240c2s v2p0367c1s
v2p0388c2s v2p0414c1s v3p0042c2s
v3p0125c1s v3p0143c1s v3p0171c1s
v3p0397c2s v4p0054c1s v4p0190c2s
v4p0300c2s v4p0301c1s v4p0477c1s
Apple, T.G. et al. v3p0300c1s
Appleby, B. v1p0897c1s
Appleby, H.C. v1p0067c1s
v1p0445c2s v1p1272c1s v2p0017c2s
Applegarth, A.C. v2p0412c1s
v4p0139c2s v4p0307c1s v4p0324c1s
v4p0468c2m
Applegate, J. v1p0406c1s
Appleton, A. v6p0044c2s
v6p0279c2s
Appleton, A.I. v3p0070c1s
v5p0509c2s
Appleton, C.E. v1p0300c2s
v1p0332c2s v1p0385c2s v1p0826c2s
v1p0869c1s v1p1100c2s v1p1164c1s
Appleton, E.E. v1p1260c1s
Appleton, E.H. v1p0566c1s
v1p1365c2s v1p1403c2s
Appleton, E.J. v4p0352c2s
Appleton, J.M.W. v1p1380c1s
Appleton, J.N. v1p0956c2s
Appleton, N. v1p0714c1s
v1p0731c1s v1p1100c1s v3p0190c2s
Appleton, T.G. v1p0453c2s
v1p0482c2s v1p0623c1s v1p0928c1s
v1p1237c2s v1p1262c1s v1p1335c2s
Appleton, T.H. v2p0058c1s
Appleton, W.H. v5p0269c1s
Appleton, W.S. v1p0086c1s
v1p0542c1s v1p0681c2s v1p1154c1s
v1p1231c2s v1p1397c1s v2p0191c2s
v3p0029c2s v3p0194c2s v3p0325c1s
v4p0456c1s v4p0583c2s v5p0262c2s
v5p0405c1s v5p0438c1s
Appleyard, R. v5p0124c2s
v5p0246c1s v5p0247c1m v6p0268c2s
Appleyard, Rollo v5p0585c2s
Appleyard, W.A. v3p0020c2s
Applin, A. v5p0165c1s
Applin, A. and Warwick, H.S.
v5p0608c2s
Appold, G.N. v2p0121c1s
Apponyi, A. v6p0042c2m
v6p0303c2m v6p0324c1s
Apponyi, Albert v6p0303c2s
Apponyi, F.H. v2p0232c2s
Appy, E.P. v3p0280c2s
Appy, H. v5p0339c2s
Apsey, W.S. v3p0417c2s
Apthorp, W.F. v1p0084c2s
v1p0114c2s v1p0834c1s v1p0885c2s
v1p0938c1s v1p1330c1s v3p0030c1s
v3p0274c1s v3p0452c2m v4p0161c2s
v4p0165c1s v4p0213c1s v4p0320c1s
v4p0416c1s v4p0426c2s
Arago, F. v1p0065c1s
v1p0265c1s v1p0281c2s v1p0452c2s
v1p0580c1s v1p0590c1s v1p0715c2s
v1p0748c2s v1p0783c2s v1p0903c2s
v1p1268c2s v1p1309c1s v1p1377c2s
v1p1393c1s
Arago, M. v1p0145c2s
v1p1248c2s
Arai, S. v4p0453c1s
Aranjo, F. v5p0212c1s
v5p0300c1s
Arber, E. v1p0132c2s
Arbes, J. v4p0403c1s
v4p0590c1s
Arbib, E. v5p0232c1s
Arbouville, Mad.d' v1p0489c2s
v1p1100c2s v1p1371c2s
Arbuckle, J. v1p0086c2s
v1p0551c2s v1p0719c2s v1p0724c2s
v1p0876c2s v3p0304c1s
Arbuthnot, A. v1p0633c2s
Arbuthnot, A.J. v1p0630c2s
v2p0322c1s
Arbuthnot, C.E. v4p0605c1s
Arbuthnot, E. v5p0042c1s
Arbuthnot, F.F. v4p0477c2s
Arbuthnot, G. v3p0389c1s
v5p0164c2s
Arbuthnot, R.H. v1p0084c1s
Arcet, M.d' v1p0147c2s
Arch, J. v4p0314c1s
Arch, J. and Potter, G. .. v1p0715c1s
Archard, E. v1p0949c2s
v1p1420c2s
Archbald, J. v1p0188c1s
v1p1085c2s
Archbold, E. v1p0198c2s
Archbold, J.D. v5p0592c2s
Archbold, W.A. v5p0548c2s
Archbold, W.A.J. v5p0433c1s
v5p0470c1s v5p0615c2s v6p0481c1s
Archbold, W.J. v5p0073c2s
Archbutt, L. v4p0411c2s
Archdekan-Cody, B. v3p0237c2s
v3p0320c2s v3p0321c1s v4p0425c2s
Archer, A. v1p0294c1s
Archer, A.T. v1p1297c2s
Archer, C.M. v1p1003c2s
Archer, E. v6p0631c2s
Archer, E.M. v1p0244c2s
v2p0006c1s v3p0401c1s
Archer, G.W. v1p0056c1s
v1p0940c1s v1p1347c1s v4p0494c2s
v4p0547c1s
Archer, H.G. v5p0028c2s
v5p0201c2s v5p0208c1s v5p0291c1s
v5p0294c2s v5p0344c1s v6p0199c2s
v6p0262c2s v6p0278c1s v6p0384c1s
v6p0529c2s v6p0530c1s v6p0595c1s
v6p0660c2s v6p0696c2s
Archer, H.S. v6p0013c2s
v6p0080c1s v6p0127c2s v6p0198c2s
v6p0611c2s
Archer, J.A. and Norgate, K.
v4p0250c1s
Archer, J.H.L. v1p0237c1m
v1p1035c1s
Archer, J.W. v1p0210c2s
v1p0695c1s v1p0765c2s v1p0928c2s
v1p1008c1s v1p1333c2s
Archer, Prof. v1p0939c2s
v1p1039c2s v3p0146c2s
Archer, S. v2p0315c1s
Archer, T. v1p0075c1s
v1p0506c2s v1p0836c2s v1p1233c1s
Archer, T.A. v3p0228c2s
v3p0354c2s v4p0119c1s v4p0214c1s
v4p0250c1s v4p0516c2s v4p0586c2s
v6p0008c1s v6p0256c1s v6p0259c2s
Archer, T.C. v1p0436c1s
v1p0650c1s v1p0691c2s
Archer, W. v1p0364c1s
v1p0521c2s v1p0621c1s v1p1186c1s
v2p0002c1m v2p0013c2s v2p0088c1m
v2p0108c1s v2p0123c1m v2p0213c2m
v2p0257c1s v2p0299c1s v2p0316c2s
v2p0336c1s v2p0342c2s v2p0345c1s
v2p0378c1s v2p0398c1s v2p0398c2m
v2p0416c1s v2p0416c2s v2p0420c2s
v3p0002c1s v3p0013c1s v3p0110c1s
v3p0122c1m v3p0206c2s v3p0207c1s
v3p0235c2m v3p0263c2s v3p0362c2s
v3p0388c1s v3p0389c1m v3p0406c1s
v3p0409c2s v3p0427c1s v3p0433c2s
v4p0002c2s v4p0094c1s v4p0132c2s
v4p0160c2m v4p0164c2s v4p0272c1s
v4p0317c2s v4p0328c1s v4p0335c1s
v4p0358c2s v4p0389c2s v4p0544c1m
v4p0560c1s v4p0572c1s v4p0616c1s
v5p0016c2s v5p0017c2s v5p0038c2s
v5p0099c1s v5p0141c1m v5p0167c1m
v5p0167c2m v5p0233c2m v5p0255c2s
v5p0256c1s v5p0262c1s v5p0273c2s
v5p0278c2s v5p0281c2s v5p0327c1s
v5p0355c2s v5p0365c2m v5p0385c2s
v5p0441c2s v5p0446c2m v5p0451c2s
v5p0523c2s v5p0543c2s v5p0547c2m
v5p0573c1s v5p0575c2s v5p0588c2s
v5p0626c2s v6p0158c2s v6p0220c1s
v6p0281c1s v6p0305c2m v6p0306c1s
v6p0352c2m v6p0359c2s v6p0495c1s
v6p0588c1s v6p0589c2s v6p0609c2s
v6p0642c1s v6p0698c2s
Archer, W. and Lowe, R.W.. v3p0388c1s
v4p0518c1s
Archer, W. et al. v5p0456c1s
Archer, W.W. v3p0245c1s
v3p0401c1s
Archer, William v4p0215c1s
v4p0272c1s v4p0517c1s v4p0549c2s
Archer, Wm. v4p0549c2s
Archibald, A.W. v4p0456c2s
Archibald, C. v5p0091c1s
Archibald, C.D. v1p0946c2s
Archibald, D. v4p0204c2s

v4p0279c1s v4p0615c2m v5p0258c2s
Archibald, E.D. v1p1270c2s
v2p0014c1s v2p0028c2s v2p0110c2s
v2p0469c1s v2p0475c1s v3p0088c2s
v3p0237c1s v3p0410c2s v3p0462c1s
v4p0380c1s
Archibald, E.D. and Siemens, C.W.
v2p0425c1s
Archibald, G., Mrs. v3p0116c2s
v3p0462c1s
Archibald, J. v1p1153c2s
Archibald, J.F.J. v4p0569c1s
v5p0088c2s v5p0258c1s v5p0329c2s
v5p0354c1s v5p0508c1s v5p0543c2s
v5p0619c1s v6p0166c1m
Archibald, S.G. v6p0087c1s
Archibald, T.H. v1p1005c1s
Arckland, J. v6p0230c1s
Arctowski, H. v5p0022c1m
v5p0022c2s v5p0038c2m v6p0506c1s
Arcy, C.F.D' v6p0484c2s
Arcy, E.D' v3p0147c1s
v5p0144c1s v5p0425c1s
v6p0311c2s
Arcy, H.W.D' v1p0257c2s
Arcy, N.D' v1p0363c2s
Ardan, I. v6p0561c1s
Arde, J. and Potter, G. .. v1p0483c1s
Arden, C. v2p0069c1s
v2p0141c1s v2p0213c1s v2p0289c2s
Arden, E. v4p0394c1s
v5p0409c2m
Arden, H.I. v3p0315c2s
v3p0431c1s v5p0099c2s v6p0110c1s
v6p0222c1s v6p0353c1s
Arden, H.J. v5p0374c1s
Arden, H.L. v5p0553c2s
Arden, K. v5p0622c2s
Ardon, E. v4p0314c2s
Ardrey, W.B. v4p0092c1s
Arendt, O. v4p0231c1s
v4p0525c2s v5p0061c2s
Arendzen, J. and Pass, H.L.
v5p0332c1s
Arene, E. v5p0266c2s
Arens, E. v3p0438c2s
Arens, E.J. v3p0192c1s
Arensberg, W.C. v6p0544c1s
Arey, A.L. v3p0331c2s
Argall, P. v4p0230c1s
v4p0530c1s
Argand, M. v1p0625c1s
Argent, E.d' v4p0316c2s
Argles, M. v2p0296c2s
v2p0469c2s v3p0209c2s v3p0240c1s
v3p0440c2s
Argles, M., Mrs. v3p0306c2s
v3p0473c1s
Argo, F.H. v6p0125c2s
Argout, M.d' v1p0091c1s
Argyll v2p0307c2s
v3p0159c1s v4p0041c1s v4p0261c2s
v4p0271c1s v4p0272c2m v4p0533c1s
v4p0569c2s
Argyll and Stoney, G.J. .. v2p0439c2s
Argyll et al. v2p0413c1s
v3p0145c1s v3p0194c2s
Argyll, Duke of v1p0010c1s
v1p0028c2s v1p0052c1s v1p0250c1s
v1p0426c2s v1p0430c1s v1p0589c2s
v1p0646c2m v1p0657c2s v1p0711c2m
v1p0901c1m v1p0901c2s v1p0926c2s
v1p1028c2s v1p1041c2s v1p1042c2s
v1p1094c2s v1p1166c1s v2p0005c2s
v2p0115c1s v2p0161c1s v2p0174c2m
v2p0184c2s v2p0191c2s v2p0202c2s
v2p0247c2s v2p0248c1s v2p0352c1s
v2p0390c2s v2p0391c1m v3p0007c1s
v3p0081c1s v3p0100c2m v3p0111c1s
v3p0114c2s v3p0145c1s v3p0145c2s
v3p0165c2s v3p0193c1s v3p0205c2s
v3p0224c1s v3p0241c2s v3p0248c1s
v3p0281c2s v3p0355c2s v3p0379c2m
v3p0432c1s v4p0052c2s v4p0317c1s
v5p0198c2s v5p0247c2s v6p0159c2s
v6p0266c2s v6p0278c1s v6p0290c2s
v6p0578c1s
Aria, E. v6p0503c2s
v6p0641c1s
Ariosto v1p1323c1s
Arkel, G.Van v6p0142c1s
Arkwright, R. v3p0258c1s
v3p0336c1s
Arkwright, W. v3p0261c2s
v4p0089c2s v4p0345c2s
Arling, N. v3p0470c1s
v4p0534c2s v5p0635c2s
Arlington, H. v3p0029c2s
Armagnac, T. v3p0129c1s
Armas, M.T. v5p0529c2s
Armbruster, C. v2p0464c1s
Armengaud, M. v1p0495c1s
Armengaud, M., jr. v1p0502c1s
Armer, Laura A. v6p0660c2s
Armes, E. v6p0478c2s
Armes, Ethel v6p0038c2s
v6p0080c1s v6p0281c1s v6p0345c2s
Armes, W.D. v3p0191c1s
v3p0265c2s v5p0580c1s v6p0338c1s
v6p0390c2s
Armfield, H.T. v1p0109c1s
v1p0690c1s v1p1278c1s
Armistead, C.J. v4p0191c2s
Armit, A.M.D' v4p0579c2s
v5p0089c2s
Armit, R.H. v1p0911c1s
Armitage, B.F. v5p0479c2m
Armitage, E. v3p0209c2s
v6p0314c1s v6p0423c1s v6p0576c2s
v6p0577c1s
Armitage, E.S. v2p0214c2s
v5p0173c1s v6p0459c1s
Armitage, E.S. and Pryce, T.D.
v6p0103c2s
Armitage, E.S., Mrs. v2p0049c1s
v2p0118c2s v2p0348c1s
Armitage, F. v3p0039c1s
Armitage, H. v5p0250c2s
v5p0349c1s
Armitage, J. v1p0919c1s
v1p1298c2s
Armitage, Mrs. v3p0058c1s
Armitage, T. v3p0033c2m
Armitage, T.R. v3p0047c1s
v3p0047c2m
Armitt, A. v1p1424c2s
v2p0028c2s v2p0057c2s v2p0273c2s
v2p0462c2s v3p0130c2s v3p0424c1s
v4p0074c2s v4p0149c2s v4p0520c1s
Armond v6p0622c1s
Armond, D.A.De and Cochran, C.F.
v5p0587c1s
Armor, S. v6p0469c1s
Armour, M. v4p0029c1s
v4p0048c1s v5p0014c1s v6p0323c2s
v6p0352c1s v6p0678c1s
Armour, S.B. v4p0318c1s
Arms, H.P. v1p0290c1s
v4p0354c2s
Arms, J.M. v3p0380c1s
Arms, J.M. and Hyatt, A. . v4p0366c2s
Arms, M.S. v3p0392c1s
Arms, M.W. v6p0101c1s
Armsby, H.P. v1p0881c2s
v1p1040c2s v1p1218c1s v2p0005c2m
v2p0006c1s v2p0060c2s v2p0062c2s
v2p0072c2s v2p0118c2m v2p0315c1m
v2p0409c1s v3p0399c2s v6p0008c2s
v6p0462c2s v6p0540c2s
Armsby, W.H. v5p0552c1s
Armsden, J. v4p0318c2s
Armstead, H.W. v5p0018c2s
Armstead, M. v5p0203c2s
Armstrong, A. v4p0216c1s
v4p0585c1s
Armstrong, A.C. v4p0274c2s
v5p0169c1s v5p0266c2s v5p0513c1s
v6p0318c2s v6p0495c2s v6p0600c1s
v6p0609c2s
Armstrong, A.C., jr. v2p0147c1s
v2p0414c1s v4p0194c1s v4p0439c1s
v4p0575c1s v5p0447c1s v5p0531c2s
Armstrong, A.L. v6p0470c2s
Armstrong, A.W. v5p0301c1s
Armstrong, E. v1p0504c1s
v1p0824c1s v3p0007c2s v3p0048c2s
v3p0070c1s v3p0204c1m v3p0282c1s
v3p0374c2s v3p0376c2s v3p0446c1s
v4p0211c1s v4p0327c1s v5p0011c1s
v5p0528c2s v5p0543c1s v6p0110c1s
v6p0639c2s
Armstrong, E.J. v4p0547c1s
Armstrong, F. v1p1337c1s
v3p0251c2s
Armstrong, F.A.W.T. v3p0438c2s
Armstrong, F.C. v3p0144c2s
v6p0060c1s v6p0081c2s v6p0535c2s
v6p0663c1s
Armstrong, F.L. v5p0105c1s
Armstrong, G.B. v4p0305c2s
v4p0389c2s
Armstrong, G.E. v6p0623c1s
v6p0650c1s
Armstrong, G.E., Lieut. .. v5p0558c2s
Armstrong, G.F. v1p0840c2s
v1p1375c2s
Armstrong, G.W. v4p0086c1s
Armstrong, H. v3p0371c2s
Armstrong, H.E. v1p0237c1s
v2p0076c1s v2p0389c2s v2p0390c1s
v3p0380c1s v3p0380c2s v3p0446c2m
v4p0171c1m v4p0174c1s v4p0481c2s
v4p0506c1s v4p0507c1s v4p0507c2s
v4p0508c1m v4p0512c1s v5p0264c1s
v5p0514c1s v6p0094c2s v6p0193c2s
v6p0204c1s v6p0431c1s v6p0473c1m
Armstrong, I.J. v4p0254c2s
v4p0258c2m v4p0572c2s v5p0337c2s
v5p0381c2s
Armstrong, J. v1p0864c2s
v1p1393c2s v3p0236c2s v4p0148c2s
Armstrong, J., jr. v1p0353c2s
Armstrong, J.E. v6p0134c1s
Armstrong, J.E. et al. ... v6p0039c1s
Armstrong, J.G. v3p0173c1s
Armstrong, J.P. v6p0001c1s
Armstrong, J.W. v1p0440c1s
v1p0812c1s v1p1203c1s
Armstrong, K. v1p0476c1s
v1p0523c1s v1p0719c1s
Armstrong, L. v3p0132c1s
v4p0120c2s v4p0281c2s
Armstrong, L.H. v3p0079c2s
v3p0104c2s v3p0375c2s v3p0393c1s
v4p0386c2s v4p0399c1s v4p0407c2s
Armstrong, Le R. v3p0385c2s
v4p0305c2s
Armstrong, Lord v3p0182c1s
v3p0422c2m
Armstrong, M.F. v1p0569c1s
v1p0871c1s v3p0468c2s
Armstrong, M.W. v4p0210c2s
Armstrong, Mrs. v4p0265c1s
Armstrong, R. v1p0231c1s
v1p1250c1s v5p0048c1s v5p0048c2s
v5p0084c2s v5p0116c1s v5p0138c2s
v5p0140c2s v5p0213c1s v5p0309c2s
v5p0552c2s v5p0638c2s v6p0478c2s
Armstrong, R.A. v1p0173c1s
v1p0980c1s v2p0092c2s v2p0132c1s
v2p0255c1s v3p0206c2s v3p0220c2s
v4p0081c1s v4p0573c1s v5p0123c2s
v5p0234c2s v5p0359c1s
Armstrong, R.B. v6p0647c1s
Armstrong, Regina v5p0082c1s
v5p0280c1m
Armstrong, S.T. v4p0020c2s
v4p0108c1s v4p0599c1s
Armstrong, T. v3p0214c2s
v6p0049c2s
Armstrong, T.H. v6p0250c2s
Armstrong, T.P. v6p0351c1s
v6p0508c1s v6p0559c1s v6p0559c2s
v6p0564c2s
Armstrong, W. v2p0023c2s
v2p0073c1s v2p0122c1s v2p0146c2s
v2p0170c1s v2p0212c1s v2p0231c1s
v2p0262c1s v2p0262c2s v2p0289c1s
v2p0298c1s v2p0326c2s v2p0329c2s
v2p0349c2s v2p0379c1s v2p0449c1s
v2p0477c2s v3p0018c2s v3p0021c2m
v3p0035c2s v3p0101c2s v3p0157c2s
v3p0193c2s v3p0200c2s v3p0291c2s
v3p0317c2m v3p0320c1s v3p0332c1s
v3p0358c2s v3p0362c1s v3p0371c1s
v3p0382c2s v3p0402c1s v3p0409c2s
v3p0429c1s v3p0448c2s v3p0456c1s
v3p0457c1s v4p0030c1s v4p0118c1m
v4p0159c2s v4p0161c2s v4p0163c1s
v4p0163c2s v4p0166c1s v4p0168c1s
v4p0218c2s v4p0227c2s v4p0260c1s
v4p0339c2s v4p0364c1s v4p0369c1s
v4p0387c2s v4p0394c1s v4p0398c1s
v4p0416c1s v4p0421c2s v4p0426c1s
v4p0480c1m v4p0493c2s v4p0549c1m
v4p0564c1s v4p0605c1s v5p0171c2s
v5p0353c2s v5p0413c1s v5p0436c1s
v5p0564c1s v5p0612c2s v6p0046c1s
v6p0103c2s
Armstrong, W. and Spielmann, M.H.
v4p0029c1s
Armstrong, W., Sir v1p0161c1s
v1p0268c1s
Armstrong, W.C. v6p0688c1s
Armstrong, W.E., Sir v1p0162c1s
Armstrong, W.G. v2p0086c2s
v2p0114c2s v3p0320c1s
Armstrong, W.G., Sir v1p0562c2s
v1p0947c1s
Armstrong, W.J. v1p0553c1s
v1p1229c2s v2p0006c1s v2p0070c1s
v3p0036c1s v4p0265c2s v4p0284c2s
v4p0608c1s v5p0347c2s
Armstrong, W.J. et al. ... v5p0229c2s
Armstrong, W.L. v5p0248c2s
Armstrong, W.N. v4p0308c1s
Armstrong, W.R. v5p0575c1s
Armstrong, Walter v3p0152c2s
v3p0227c2s v3p0368c2s v4p0416c1s
v5p0461c1s v5p0484c2s
Armstrong, Walter, Sir ... v5p0612c2s
Armstrong, Wm. v5p0084c1s
v5p0287c2s v5p0539c1s
Armstrong, Wm.H. v3p0415c2s
Armstrong, Z. v6p0143c2s
v6p0480c2s
Armytage, C.F. v2p0114c1s
Armytage, F.F. v5p0240c1m
v5p0343c1s
Armytage, G, Mrs. v2p0124c1s
Armytage, G.F. v2p0169c2s
Armytage, Mrs. v3p0061c2s
v3p0188c2s v3p0266c2s v3p0338c2s
Armytage, R. v2p0237c1s
Arnaud, E. v1p0131c1s
Arnault, C. v1p1316c2s
Arndt, F.B. v5p0393c2s
Arndt, P. v6p0254c1s
Arndt, W.T. v6p0435c2s
Arnett, D. v6p0604c2s
Arnett, F.S. v6p0153c2s
v6p0179c1s v6p0297c1s v6p0452c2s
v6p0515c2s v6p0559c1s v6p0612c2s
v6p0641c2s v6p0664c2s v6p0710c2s
Arnett, Frank S. v6p0135c2s
Arnett, L.D. v6p0153c2s
v6p0194c1s v6p0295c1s v6p0463c2s
Arngrimsson, F.B. v3p0396c1s
Arnim, Countess Von v5p0452c1s
Arnim, M.A.B. v6p0239c2s

Arnold, A. v1p0068c1s
v1p0250c1s v1p0372c1s v1p0486c2m
v1p0552c1s v1p0589c1s v1p0649c1s
v1p0661c1s v1p0720c2s v1p0721c1s
v1p0721c2m v1p0722c1m v1p0751c2s
v1p0762c1s v1p0791c1s v1p0804c1s
v1p0929c1s v1p0992c1s v1p1075c2s
v1p1086c2s v1p1116c2s v1p1135c2s
v1p1163c1s v1p1330c2s v1p1331c1s
v1p1425c1s v1p1426c1s v2p0142c2s
v2p0143c1s v2p0188c1s v2p0188c2s
v2p0190c1s v2p0198c2s v2p0226c1s
v2p0331c1s v3p0158c2s v3p0256c1s
v3p0258c2s v3p0289c2s v3p0307c1s
v3p0361c1s v3p0398c2s v4p0446c1s
v5p0619c2s
Arnold, A. and Brett, R.B.
v2p0189c2s
Arnold, A. and Courtney, L.
v2p0330c2s
Arnold, A. and Lyttleton, C.G.
v1p0546c2s
Arnold, A.N. v1p0096c1m
v1p0096c2s v1p0126c1s v1p0130c1s
v1p0313c1s v1p0553c1s v1p0554c1m
v1p0852c2s v1p1139c1s v1p1142c1s
v2p0190c1s
Arnold, A.U. v1p0652c1s
Arnold, A.W. v4p0344c1s
v5p0036c1s v5p0213c2s v6p0138c2s
v6p0300c2s v6p0584c1s
Arnold, Arthur v2p0330c2s
v3p0241c1s
Arnold, B. v4p0075c1s
Arnold, B.J. v4p0175c1s
v6p0189c2s
Arnold, B.W. v5p0445c1s
Arnold, B.W., jr. v5p0477c1s
v5p0581c2s
Arnold, C.H. and Patterson, A.H.
v4p0175c1s
Arnold, E. v1p0066c1s
v1p0336c2s v1p0365c2s v1p0446c2s
v1p0710c2s v1p0789c1s v1p1240c1s
v1p1258c1s v1p1301c1s v1p1308c2s
v1p1326c2s v1p1367c2s v2p0036c1s
v2p0045c2s v2p0113c2s v2p0141c1s
v2p0169c2s v2p0272c1s v2p0310c1s
v2p0373c1s v3p0226c2s v3p0227c2s
v3p0306c1s v3p0425c1s v4p0034c1s
v4p0245c2s v4p0281c1s v4p0298c1s
v4p0376c1s v4p0390c2s v4p0588c2s
v4p0603c2s v5p0285c1s
Arnold, E., Sir v4p0297c2s
v4p0298c1s v4p0331c1s v4p0343c1s
Arnold, E., Sir et al. ... v4p0214c2s
Arnold, E.A. v2p0160c1s
v2p0317c1s v3p0366c1s
Arnold, E.L. v2p0202c2s
v4p0161c2s v4p0497c1s v5p0269c2s
v5p0520c1s v6p0332c1s v6p0500c2s
v6p0548c2s
Arnold, E.M. v3p0316c2s
Arnold, Edwin v4p0018c2s
Arnold, Edwin, Sir v4p0173c1s
v5p0560c1s v6p0164c2s v6p0353c2s
Arnold, Ethel M. v2p0301c1s
v3p0127c2s
Arnold, F. v1p0011c2s
v1p0097c2s v1p0524c2s v1p0562c1s
v1p0605c2s v1p0817c1s v1p0986c1s
v1p1007c2s v1p1017c1s v1p1235c2s
v1p1280c2s v1p1434c2s v2p0065c1s
v2p0083c2s v2p0288c2s v2p0349c2s
v2p0414c2s v3p0060c1s v3p0282c2s
v3p0316c1s v3p0430c1s v3p0433c2s
v4p0545c1s v6p0323c1s
Arnold, F.A. v2p0357c2s
v3p0307c2s
Arnold, F.R. v6p0153c1s
v6p0241c2s
Arnold, F.S. v5p0456c1s
Arnold, Felix v6p0145c2s
v6p0286c1s
Arnold, G. v1p1408c1s
Arnold, G.F. v1p0516c2s
v1p0742c2s
Arnold, H. v2p0385c2s
Arnold, H.L. v4p0347c1s
v4p0371c1s v4p0460c2s v4p0548c1s
v5p0353c1s v6p0066c1s v6p0153c1s
v6p0217c2s v6p0508c1s
Arnold, H.P. v6p0076c2s
Arnold, I.H. v1p0750c1s
Arnold, I.N. v1p0060c1s
v1p0274c2s v2p0022c1s v2p0259c1m
Arnold, J. v1p0239c2s
Arnold, J.M. v2p0440c2s
Arnold, J.N. v2p0012c1s
v2p0406c1s v2p0432c2s v3p0200c2s
v3p0290c1s v3p0296c1s v3p0360c2s
v3p0361c1s v3p0396c2s v3p0402c2s
v3p0410c2s
Arnold, J.O. v3p0020c2s
v5p0551c2s v6p0328c2s v6p0412c1s
Arnold, J.R. v1p0287c2s
Arnold, Lady v3p0139c1s
v4p0183c1s
Arnold, M. v1p0003c2m
v1p0036c2s v1p0046c2s v1p0159c2s
v1p0165c2s v1p0177c1s v1p0180c2s
v1p0181c2s v1p0210c2s v1p0248c2s
v1p0249c1s v1p0256c2s v1p0266c2s
v1p0273c2s v1p0285c1s v1p0300c2s
v1p0323c1s v1p0331c1s v1p0363c2s
v1p0369c2s v1p0387c1s v1p0387c2s
v1p0413c2s v1p0415c1s v1p0417c2s
v1p0423c1s v1p0441c2s v1p0489c2s
v1p0503c2s v1p0539c2s v1p0560c2m
v1p0583c1s v1p0653c1s v1p0657c2s
v1p0694c1s v1p0696c1s v1p0741c1m
v1p0753c2s v1p0754c2s v1p0819c2s
v1p0977c1s v1p0980c1s v1p0992c1s
v1p1058c2s v1p1061c2s v1p1067c1s
v1p1097c1s v1p1143c1s v1p1215c1s
v1p1236c2m v1p1243c1s v1p1243c2s
v1p1429c2s v1p1431c2s v1p1440c1s
v2p0010c1m v2p0043c2s v2p0082c2s
v2p0139c2s v2p0147c2s v2p0230c1s
v2p0255c1s v2p0260c2s v2p0268c1s
v2p0272c2s v2p0304c1s v2p0349c1s
v2p0388c1s v2p0389c1s v2p0417c1s
v2p0455c1s v2p0471c1s v2p0479c2s
v3p0010c1s v3p0012c2s v3p0083c1s
v3p0097c2s v3p0164c2s v3p0179c1s
v3p0182c2m v3p0220c2s v3p0279c2s
v3p0420c2s v3p0431c2s v3p0441c2s
v5p0196c2s v5p0564c2s v6p0294c2s
Arnold, M.A. v6p0631c2s
Arnold, M.L.H. v5p0512c1s
Arnold, Matthew v3p0389c2s
Arnold, N.J. v3p0068c1s
v3p0324c2s v3p0414c1s
Arnold, R. and Spencer, A.C.
v6p0567c2s
Arnold, R. and Wiley, D.C.
v6p0250c2s
Arnold, R.A. v1p0015c1s
v1p0017c1s v1p0270c1s v1p0346c1s
v1p0471c1s v1p0721c1s v1p1052c2s
v1p1054c2s v1p1122c2s v1p1141c2s
v1p1150c2s v1p1261c1s v1p1263c2s
v1p1337c1s v1p1391c2s
Arnold, S.B. v4p0093c1s
v4p0498c1s
Arnold, S.G. v1p0230c2s
v1p0319c1s v1p0319c2s v1p0412c1s
v1p0462c1s v1p0486c1s v1p0487c1s
v1p0540c2s v1p0638c1s v1p0713c2s
v1p0802c1s v1p0893c2s v1p0956c1s
v1p1252c1s v1p1256c2s v1p1265c1s
v1p1321c2s v1p1395c2s v1p1412c1s
v2p0405c1s
Arnold, S.J. v1p0210c1s
Arnold, S.L. v6p0572c2s
Arnold, Sarah L. v5p0511c1s
Arnold, T. v1p0215c1s
v1p0310c2s v1p0857c1s v1p0932c2s
v1p0954c2s v1p1110c1s v1p1124c1s
v1p1235c2s v3p0084c1s v3p0123c2s
v3p0127c2s v3p0259c1s v4p0303c2s
v4p0420c1s v5p0123c2s v5p0170c1s
v6p0455c1s
Arnold, T. and Littledale, Dr.
v1p1118c1s
Arnold, T.H. v5p0239c1s
Arnold, T.J. v1p1149c1s
Arnold, W. v6p0507c2s
Arnold, W.H. v2p0150c1s
Arnold, W.J. v4p0241c1s
Arnold, W.R. v6p0259c2s
Arnold, W.S. v4p0634c1s
Arnold, W.T. v2p0377c1s
v3p0029c1s v3p0266c1s v6p0032c1s
v6p0545c1s
Arnold-Forster, H.O. v1p0652c2s
v2p0032c1s v2p0185c2s v2p0186c1s
v2p0187c1m v2p0227c1s v3p0179c2s
v3p0182c1s v3p0220c1s v3p0221c2m
v3p0321c2s v4p0236c2s v4p0237c2m
v4p0238c1m v4p0290c1s v4p0290c2s
v4p0579c2s v4p0582c1s v4p0601c2s
v4p0610c1s v5p0049c2s v5p0243c1s
v5p0244c2m v5p0248c1s
Arnold-Forster, H.O. and
Lubbock, J., Sir v2p0370c1s
Arnold-Forster, H.O. et al.
v4p0239c2s
Arnot, M. v4p0501c1s
Arnot, R.H. v5p0491c2s
Arnot, W. v1p0375c1m
v1p1110c1s v3p0319c2s
Arnoth, S. v4p0531c2s
Arnott, Dr. v1p0619c1s
Arnott, W. v2p0445c2s
Aronson, M. v5p0219c2s
v5p0344c2s v5p0457c1s v5p0512c2s
v5p0513c1s v5p0565c1s
Aronson, R. v4p0552c2s
Arpe, R.N. v6p0031c1s
Arpee, L. v6p0484c2s
Arper, E.A.N. v6p0475c2s
Arran, Earl of v5p0375c2s
Arreat, L. v4p0221c2s
v4p0439c1s v5p0447c1s v5p0484c1s
v6p0238c1s v6p0361c1s v6p0469c2s
Arrhenius, S. v6p0199c2s
v6p0603c1s
Arrington, A. v1p0341c2s
Arrol, W. v3p0158c2s
Arrow, F., Sir v1p1264c2s
Arrowsmith, M. v6p0010c2s
Arrowsmith, R. v6p0276c1s
Arsdale, J.W.Van
v6p0558c1s
Arthur, G. v5p0117c1s
v5p0117c2s v6p0069c1s v6p0125c2s
v6p0242c2s v6p0603c1s v6p0702c2s
Arthur, G., Sir v5p0007c2s
v6p0024c1s v6p0082c1s v6p0162c2s
v6p0234c1s v6p0352c2s v6p0513c1s
Arthur, H. v4p0468c1s
v5p0113c2s
Arthur, J. v3p0359c1s
v3p0470c1s
Arthur, J.C. v2p0334c1s
v4p0018c1s v4p0154c1s v4p0220c2m
v4p0445c2m v4p0513c1s v4p0601c1s
Arthur, J.P. v6p0449c1s
Arthur, Josephine v6p0619c2s
Arthur, Marion v5p0232c2s
Arthur, R. v5p0155c2s
v5p0310c2s v6p0140c1s v6p0301c2s
v6p0464c1s
Arthur, T.S. v1p0141c2s
v1p0219c1s v1p0229c2s v1p0442c1s
v1p0443c2s v1p0505c2s v1p0588c1s
v1p0592c2s v1p0640c1s v1p0699c2s
v1p0738c2s v1p0804c1s v1p0846c1s
v1p0877c1s v1p0930c2s v1p0982c2s
v1p1142c1s v1p1210c1s v1p1218c1s
v1p1260c2s v1p1275c1s v1p1295c2s
v1p1408c2s v1p1429c1m v1p1433c2s
Arthur, W. v1p0205c2s
v1p0282c2s v1p0477c1s v1p0545c1s
v1p0588c1s v1p0629c1s v1p0671c2s
v1p0857c2s v1p0889c2s v3p0119c2s
v3p0229c1s v3p0276c2s v3p0364c1s
Arthy, E. v1p0796c1s
Artiaga, S. v6p0668c1s
Artmeter v6p0084c1s
Artois, E.d' v5p0061c2s
Artz, V.T. v5p0427c1s
Arunachalam, P. v6p0390c1s
Arundale, Lord v2p0444c2s
Arundell of Wardour, Lord. v1p1373c1s
v3p0023c1s v2p0473c1s
Asakawa, K. v6p0354c1m
v6p0398c2s v6p0560c2s v6p0561c1s
Asaph, A.G. v4p0112c2s
v4p0608c2s v5p0588c1s
Asbury, A. v1p0173c2s
v1p0886c2s v1p1379c2s
Asch, G.Van v2p0113c2s
Ascham, R. v1p1159c2s
Ascher, B.H. v2p0478c1s
Ascher, I.G. v1p0060c2s
v1p0851c1s
Ascherson, P. and Engler, A.
v4p0069c2s
Ash, W. v4p0236c1s
Ashbaugh, T.D. v5p0396c1s
Ashbee, C.R. v4p0174c2s
v4p0301c2m v4p0456c2s v5p0026c1s
v5p0149c1s v5p0298c2s v5p0565c1s
v6p0182c2s v6p0276c1s v6p0513c2s
Ashbee, E.W. v2p0052c1s
v2p0402c1s
Ashbee, H.S. v1p0985c2s
v2p0012c2s v2p0045c2s v2p0240c2s
v2p0298c1s v4p0151c2s v4p0385c1s
v4p0607c1s
Ashbourne, Lord v4p0289c2m
v4p0530c2s
Ashbrook, W.S. v3p0159c2s
Ashburner, C.A. v1p0701c2s
v1p0939c2s v2p0090c1s v2p0158c2s
v2p0171c2s v3p0311c1s
Ashburner, C.E. v5p0580c1s
Ashburner, J. v1p0824c2s
v1p1209c2s
Ashburner, L. v2p0218c2s
v3p0212c1s v3p0268c2s v5p0143c2s
v5p0286c2s
Ashburner, S. v1p1078c1s
Ashburton, Lord v1p0963c1s
Ashbury, A. v1p0136c1s
v1p0563c2s
Ashby, E. v1p0560c2s
Ashby, G. v1p0272c1s
Ashby, G.J.M. v6p0499c2s
Ashby, H.W. v5p0235c2s
Ashby, Irene M. v5p0107c1s
Ashby, J. and King, B. ... v4p0604c2s
Ashby, S.R. v6p0473c1s
v6p0542c2m
Ashby, T. v6p0215c1s
Ashby-Macfadyen, Irene ... v6p0006c2m
v6p0311c1s
Ashby-Sterry, J. v1p0036c1s
v3p0117c1s
Ashcourt, W. v3p0146c2s
Ashe, E. v6p0462c2s
Ashe, E.D. v1p0195c1s
Ashe, I. v1p0579c1s
v1p0613c2s v1p1204c1s
Ashe, R.P. v4p0589c2s
Ashe, T. v1p0384c1s
v2p0008c2s v2p0202c1s
Ashe, W.A. v3p0142c2s

v3p0203c2s v4p0037c2s
Asher, D. v2p0024c2s
v2p0224c2s
Asher, Edward v4p0058c1s
Asher, G.M. v1p0610c2s
v1p0790c2s
Asher, L. v4p0344c2s
Asheton, F. v1p0066c1s
v1p0451c1s v1p0489c2s v1p0856c2s
v1p1312c2s
Ashford, J. v6p0392c2m
v6p0649c2s
Ashhurst, J. v5p0334c2s
Ashhurst, J., jr. et al. . v1p0500c1s
Ashhurst, R.L. v3p0388c1s
Ashitzu, Zitsuzen v4p0077c2s
Ashleigh, C. v5p0617c2s
Ashley, C. v2p0004c2s
Ashley, C.D. v5p0329c2s
v6p0519c1s
Ashley, C.S. v2p0468c2s
v3p0108c1s v3p0137c1s v3p0218c2s
v3p0346c2s v4p0191c1s v4p0230c2s
Ashley, C.W. v6p0694c1s
Ashley, D.D. v6p0386c2s
Ashley, E. v5p0226c1s
v5p0234c2s v5p0467c1s
Ashley, G.H. v6p0568c1s
Ashley, Grace v6p0074c1m
Ashley, H.D. v4p0090c2s
Ashley, H.P. v5p0210c1s
v5p0278c2m
Ashley, J. v1p1208c2s
Ashley, J.M. v3p0251c2s
v3p0386c2s v4p0083c1s v4p0481c1s
v4p0558c2s
Ashley, K.L. v4p0370c1s
Ashley, Lord v1p0269c1s
v1p0439c1s v1p0641c1s v1p0714c1s
v1p0961c1s
Ashley, M.L. v6p0176c1s
Ashley, O.D. v4p0472c1s
v5p0567c1s
Ashley, P. v5p0392c1s
v6p0382c1s v6p0436c2s v6p0458c1s
v6p0614c2s
Ashley, P.W.L. v5p0345c1s
Ashley, Percy v6p0385c2s
Ashley, R.H. v6p0176c1s
v6p0624c2m
Ashley, W.B. v6p0021c2s
v6p0025c2s v6p0276c2s v6p0497c2s
v6p0512c1s v6p0544c1s v6p0673c2s
v6p0695c1s
Ashley, W.J. v3p0050c1s
v3p0256c1s v3p0360c2s v3p0363c2s
v3p0418c1s v3p0425c1s v3p0471c2s
v4p0026c2s v4p0046c2s v4p0165c1s
v4p0167c1s v4p0281c1s v4p0283c2s
v4p0305c2s v4p0346c2s v4p0352c2s
v4p0491c1s v4p0498c1s v4p0513c1s
v4p0515c2s v4p0580c2m v4p0604c2s
v5p0052c2s v5p0130c2s v5p0136c2s
v5p0175c2s v5p0190c1s v5p0193c1s
v5p0217c1s v5p0220c1s v5p0221c2s
v5p0288c2s v5p0311c1m v5p0410c2s
v5p0438c1s v5p0457c1s v5p0548c2s
v5p0584c1s v5p0592c2s v5p0625c1s
v6p0141c1s v6p0632c2s v6p0633c1s
v6p0639c2s v6p0652c1s v6p0670c2s
Ashley, W.J. and Lawton, W.C.
v5p0548c2s
Ashman, W.N. v4p0283c1s
Ashmead, A.S. v4p0051c2m
v4p0327c1s v4p0370c2s v4p0483c2s
Ashmead-Bartlett, E. v4p0239c2s
Ashmore, A. v5p0270c2s
v5p0396c2s
Ashmore, S.G. v4p0118c1s
Ashmore, W. v1p0235c2s
v1p0820c2s
Ashmun, G. v6p0377c2s
Ashmun, M. v6p0287c2s
v6p0302c2s
Ashpitel, A. v1p0323c2s
Ashpitel, A. and Parker, J.H.
v1p0237c2s
Ashton, A. v2p0373c1s
v5p0258c1s
Ashton, E. v3p0243c2s
Ashton, Howard v6p0674c2s
Ashton, J. v2p0103c1s
v2p0191c2s v3p0189c1s v4p0182c2m
v4p0604c1s v6p0069c2s
Ashton, R. v1p1112c1s
v2p0426c1s v5p0363c1s
Ashton, R.S. v2p0113c1s
v2p0329c1s
Ashton, S. v1p0684c2s
Ashton, W. v2p0074c2s
Ashurst, R.L. v6p0046c2s
Ashwell, F.E. v3p0468c2s
Ashworth, D. v4p0065c1s
v4p0252c2s
Ashworth, H. v3p0102c1s
v3p0180c2s
Ashworth, J.H. v6p0082c2s
Ashworth, R.A. v5p0415c1s
Askew, Sarah B. v6p0372c2s
Askowith, H. v6p0450c1s
Asling, S.E. v4p0578c1s
Aspden, H. v4p0570c2s
Aspden, N.H. v2p0400c1s
v2p0470c1s
Asperge, P. v1p0490c2s
Aspinwall, J.L. v6p0693c2s
Aspinwall, W.B. v6p0361c2s
v6p0635c1s
Aspray, E. v5p0111c1s
v5p0528c1s
Asquith, H.H. v5p0062c1s
v6p0066c2s
Asquith, H.H. and Goodby, E.
v3p0031c1s
Asquith, M. v6p0154c2s
Assikinack, F. v1p0937c2m
Astbury, T.H. v6p0677c1s
Astle, T. v1p0334c1s
v1p0383c1s v1p0384c1m v1p0551c1s
v1p0985c2s v1p1173c2s v1p1194c2s
v1p1256c1s
Astley, A.F. v2p0208c1s
Astley, H.D.J. v5p0076c2s
Astley, H.J.D. v6p0643c1s
Astley, L.P.C. v5p0164c2s
Aston, A. v1p1361c2s
Aston, W.G. v4p0298c1s
v5p0303c1s
Astor, W.W. v2p0052c2s
v2p0376c2s v3p0472c2s v5p0013c1s
v5p0035c1s v5p0123c1m v5p0203c2s
v5p0215c1s v5p0354c1s v5p0442c2s
Astor, W.W. et al. v3p0360c2s
Astrup, E. v4p0187c1s
v4p0242c2s v4p0364c1s v4p0432c2s
Atchison, D.R. v1p0702c1s
Atchison, H.D. v4p0328c2s
v6p0708c2s
Atherley-Jones, L.A. v3p0248c1s
v4p0471c1m v6p0356c1s
Atherstone, E. v1p0805c1s
v1p0923c1s v1p0958c1s
Atherton, C. v3p0113c1s
v3p0409c1s v3p0432c2s
Atherton, E.L. v5p0309c1s
Atherton, G. v4p0052c2s
v4p0159c1s v4p0197c2s v4p0344c2s
v4p0629c2s v5p0163c2s v6p0016c2s
v6p0164c1s v6p0278c2s
Atherton, G.F. v2p0321c2s
v3p0038c2s v3p0117c2s v3p0291c2s
v3p0448c1s
Atherton, Gertrude v5p0415c2s
v5p0526c2s v6p0017c1s v6p0018c1s
v6p0029c2s v6p0234c1s
Atherton, Gertrude F. v3p0063c1s
Atherton, N.B. v5p0398c2s
Atkey, B. v5p0307c1s
Atkins, B.R. v4p0372c2s
Atkins, C.G. v1p0457c1s
Atkins, D. v6p0255c2s
Atkins, David v6p0210c1s
Atkins, E. v3p0017c2s
v5p0358c2s
Atkins, E.F. v5p0146c2s
v5p0559c2s
Atkins, H.A. v2p0333c2s
Atkins, J.B. v5p0619c1s
v6p0266c1s
Atkins, T. v5p0243c1s
Atkinson, A. v5p0067c2s
Atkinson, A.D. v1p0559c2s
v1p1196c1s v2p0035c1s v2p0308c2s
v2p0350c2s
Atkinson, A.D.B. v4p0632c1s
Atkinson, A.G. v1p0459c2s
Atkinson, A.G.B. v4p0112c1s
v4p0143c2s v4p0498c2s v5p0117c2s
Atkinson, A.L.C. v6p0283c1s
Atkinson, A.R. v6p0454c2s
v6p0586c2s
Atkinson, A.S. v6p0490c2s
v6p0676c2m
Atkinson, A.S. and Lang, A.
v3p0107c2s
Atkinson, B. v4p0090c1s
v4p0137c1s v4p0373c2s v4p0381c2m
v4p0390c2s v4p0635c2s v5p0061c1s
v5p0100c1s v5p0116c1s v5p0141c2s
v5p0282c1s v5p0308c2s v5p0309c1s
v5p0379c2s v5p0413c1s v5p0503c2s
v5p0504c1s v5p0616c1s v6p0012c2s
Atkinson, Blanche v4p0179c1s
v4p0186c1s v5p0140c2s v5p0195c1s
Atkinson, C.J. v6p0487c2s
Atkinson, E. v1p0031c1s
v1p0093c2s v1p0275c2s v1p0306c1s
v1p0306c2s v1p0325c1s v1p0382c2s
v1p0385c2s v1p0640c1s v1p0649c2s
v1p0706c1s v1p0714c2s v1p0797c2s
v1p0815c2s v1p0861c1s v1p1053c1s
v1p1077c2s v1p1206c2s v1p1224c1s
v1p1282c2s v1p1341c2s v1p1358c1s
v1p1394c1s v2p0027c1s v2p0097c1s
v2p0104c2m v2p0161c1m v2p0245c1s
v2p0371c1s v2p0387c1s v2p0464c1s
v3p0011c2s v3p0072c1s v3p0099c1m
v3p0102c1m v3p0118c2s v3p0152c2s
v3p0153c2m v3p0241c1s v3p0250c2s
v3p0296c2s v3p0321c1s v3p0337c1s
v3p0339c2s v3p0341c1m v3p0343c2s
v3p0345c2m v3p0356c2s v3p0380c1s
v3p0393c1s v3p0396c1m v3p0397c2s
v3p0399c2s v3p0401c2s v3p0408c2m
v3p0413c2s v3p0416c2s v3p0420c1s
v3p0421c1m v3p0442c1s v3p0444c1s
v3p0452c1m v3p0472c2s v4p0045c1s
v4p0068c2s v4p0078c1s v4p0080c2s
v4p0132c2s v4p0194c2s v4p0200c1s
v4p0202c2s v4p0230c1m v4p0247c2s
v4p0275c1s v4p0283c2s v4p0303c1m
v4p0319c1s v4p0378c1s v4p0378c2s
v4p0458c1s v4p0523c2s v4p0525c2s
v4p0526c2s v4p0565c1s v4p0580c2s
v4p0600c1s v4p0602c1s v4p0610c1s
v5p0124c1s v5p0130c1m v5p0139c1s
v5p0324c1s v5p0370c1s v5p0419c2s
v5p0524c2s v5p0567c1s v5p0568c2s
v5p0615c1s v5p0627c2m v6p0141c2s
v6p0182c1s v6p0225c2m v6p0250c2s
v6p0446c2s v6p0518c1s v6p0632c2s
Atkinson, E. and Cabot, E.T.
v4p0328c2s
Atkinson, E. and George, H.
v3p0241c2s v3p0421c1s
Atkinson, E. and Hyde, W.D.
v4p0398c2s
Atkinson, E.A. v4p0396c1s
Atkinson, E.C. v4p0493c1s
v5p0498c1s
Atkinson, E.G. v5p0252c2s
v5p0376c2s v5p0463c1s
Atkinson, E.G. and Lang, A.
v5p0364c2s
Atkinson, E.G. and Lee, S.L.
v2p0024c2s
Atkinson, E.G. et al. v4p0291c1s
Atkinson, E.S. v4p0046c1s
v4p0409c1s v4p0412c2s v4p0627c1s
v5p0046c2s v5p0390c2s v5p0425c1s
v5p0451c2s v5p0486c2s v5p0630c2s
Atkinson, E.V. v4p0554c2s
Atkinson, Edward v3p0059c2s
v5p0207c2m v5p0338c1s v5p0480c1s
v6p0132c2s v6p0486c1s
Atkinson, Edward and Norton, C.L.
v6p0087c1s
Atkinson, F.J. v5p0062c1s
v5p0529c2s v6p0313c1s v6p0313c2s
Atkinson, F.M. v6p0494c1s
Atkinson, F.W. v4p0466c1s
v5p0106c1s v5p0264c2s v5p0518c1s
v6p0493c2m
Atkinson, G. v3p0180c2s
Atkinson, G.F. v2p0414c2s
v4p0192c1s v4p0445c1s v4p0445c2s
v4p0457c1s v4p0542c2s v4p0605c1s
v5p0387c2m v5p0453c2s
Atkinson, G.M. v2p0151c1s
Atkinson, H. v5p0120c2s
Atkinson, H.G. v1p0398c1s
v1p0623c1s v1p1004c2s
Atkinson, J. v1p0009c1s
v1p0805c2s v1p0830c1s v1p0867c2s
v1p1089c2s v1p1442c1s v2p0286c1s
v3p0343c1s
Atkinson, J.B. v1p0052c2s
v1p0059c1s v1p0061c2s v1p0062c2m
v1p0063c1m v1p0105c2m v1p0310c2s
v1p0366c2s v1p0425c2s v1p0461c1s
v1p0521c1s v1p0607c2s v1p0736c2m
v1p0801c2s v1p0813c2s v1p0874c1s
v1p0879c2s v1p0958c2m v1p1036c1s
v1p1045c2s v1p1097c2s v1p1160c2s
v1p1307c2s v1p1393c1s v1p1402c1s
v1p1408c2s v2p0023c1m v2p0024c1s
v2p0077c2s v2p0093c1s v2p0114c2s
v2p0268c1s v2p0272c2s v2p0283c2s
v2p0294c2s v2p0326c2s v2p0372c2s
v3p0164c2s v4p0387c2s
Atkinson, J.B., Mrs. v1p1160c2s
Atkinson, J.C. v1p0265c1s
v2p0305c1s v3p0152c1s v3p0295c2s
v3p0333c2s v4p0225c2s v4p0540c1s
Atkinson, J.E. v4p0086c1s
Atkinson, J.H. v6p0514c2s
Atkinson, J.J. v1p0017c1s
v1p0269c1s v1p0844c1s v6p0450c1s
Atkinson, J.L. v4p0077c2s
v4p0296c2s v4p0298c1s v4p0592c1s
v6p0336c2s
Atkinson, J.W. and Murray, D.C.
v6p0271c2s
Atkinson, L. v4p0310c2s
Atkinson, L.B. v4p0120c2s
Atkinson, M. v6p0578c1s
v6p0651c2s v6p0659c1s
Atkinson, M.A. v1p0705c1s
Atkinson, R. v1p0331c1s
v1p0908c2s
Atkinson, R.W. v1p0160c1s
Atkinson, S.B. v6p0375c2s
Atkinson, T. v1p0586c1s
v1p1001c2s v1p1094c2s
Atkinson, W. v3p0202c2s
v3p0263c1s v3p0293c2s v3p0411c2s
v4p0362c1s v4p0484c2s v4p0519c2s
v5p0061c2s v6p0470c2s
Atkinson, W.A. v5p0190c2s
v6p0346c2s v6p0634c1s v6p0700c2s

Atkinson, W.G. v1p1324c1s
Atkinson, W.N. v4p0120c2s
Atkinson, W.P. v1p0190c1s
v1p0261c2s v1p0262c1s v1p0390c1s
v1p0392c1s v1p0451c1s v1p0619c1s
v1p0865c2s v1p0993c2s v1p1356c2s
v1p1391c1s v1p1393c2s
Atkinson, W.Y. v4p0036c1s
Atkinson, William v5p0552c1s
Atlay, J.B. v4p0530c2s
v5p0047c2s v5p0590c2s v6p0217c1s
v6p0442c1s v6p0633c2s
Atlee, B.C. v4p0635c1s
Atlee, L.W. v2p0089c2s
v2p0459c1s v2p0464c2s
Atlee, S.Y. v1p0957c2m
v1p1040c2s
Atlee, W. v2p0468c1s
v4p0151c2s
Attee, E.A. v1p1125c2s
Attenborough, F. v5p0455c2s
Attenborough, J. v6p0304c1s
Attenborough, J.M. v5p0157c1s
v5p0433c2s v6p0100c2s v6p0126c1s
v6p0131c1s v6p0183c1s v6p0189c2s
v6p0569c2s v6p0604c1s v6p0611c2s
Atter, R. v6p0506c1s
Atterberg, G. v2p0448c2s
Atterbury, A.P. v5p0065c2s
v5p0151c1s v6p0341c2s
Atterbury, Eleanor v6p0282c2s
Atterbury, G. v6p0638c2s
Atterbury, W.W. v3p0415c2s
Atteridge, A.H. v1p0563c1s
v1p0641c2s v1p1033c2s v1p1140c2s
v1p1290c1s v1p1316c2s v2p0009c1s
v2p0025c1s v2p0056c2s v2p0071c2s
v2p0091c1s v2p0186c2s v2p0218c1s
v2p0271c2s v2p0292c1m v2p0376c1s
v3p0029c1s v3p0040c1s v3p0161c1s
v3p0212c1s v3p0225c1s v3p0282c2s
v3p0283c1s v3p0360c1s v4p0236c2s
v5p0558c2s v6p0560c2s
Atteridge, C.H. v3p0028c2s
Atteridge, H. v2p0112c2s
v2p0122c2s v2p0152c2s v5p0540c1s
Atteridge, M.E. v1p0814c1s
Atteridge, R. v2p0265c2s
Attfield, J. v1p0966c2s
Attwell, H. v2p0337c2s
v5p0100c2s
Attwell, Henry v5p0055c1s
Attwell, J.S. v4p0025c2s
Attwill, R.I. v4p0183c2s
v4p0402c2s
Attwood, J.S. v3p0052c2s
Atwater, C. v1p0636c2s
v1p0938c2s v1p1041c1s
Atwater, C.G. v6p0244c1s
Atwater, H.D. v5p0166c2s
Atwater, I. v3p0155c1s
v3p0281c2s
Atwater, L.A. v1p0253c2s
v1p1004c2s v2p0236c1s
Atwater, L.H. v1p0093c1s
v1p0096c2s v1p0119c2s v1p0166c1s
v1p0171c1s v1p0180c1s v1p0241c2s
v1p0274c1s v1p0275c2s v1p0276c2s
v1p0287c2s v1p0290c1m v1p0290c2s
v1p0292c1s v1p0292c2s v1p0313c2s
v1p0326c1s v1p0390c1s v1p0392c1s
v1p0393c2s v1p0394c1s v1p0426c2s
v1p0441c1s v1p0447c1s v1p0500c1s
v1p0528c2m v1p0623c1s v1p0627c2s
v1p0644c1s v1p0684c1s v1p0685c2s
v1p0711c1s v1p0760c2s v1p0823c1s
v1p0839c2s v1p0843c1s v1p0849c2s
v1p0853c2s v1p0860c2s v1p0868c2s
v1p0869c2s v1p0953c1s v1p0954c1s
v1p0999c2s v1p1001c1s v1p1027c1m
v1p1044c1m v1p1046c1m v1p1046c2m
v1p1047c1s v1p1078c2s v1p1083c2m
v1p1086c1s v1p1094c1m v1p1102c1s
v1p1103c1m v1p1109c2s v1p1140c2s
v1p1149c1s v1p1203c2s v1p1217c1s
v1p1232c2s v1p1235c1m v1p1240c1s
v1p1274c2s v1p1287c1m v1p1302c2s
v1p1321c1s v1p1328c2s v1p1342c2s
v1p1366c2s v1p1410c2m v1p1418c2s
v1p1428c2s v2p0064c1s v2p0064c2s
v2p0092c2s v2p0096c1s v2p0110c1s
v2p0130c2s v2p0184c1s v2p0220c2s
v2p0245c1s v2p0245c2s v2p0328c2m
v2p0336c1s v2p0352c1s v2p0352c2m
v2p0363c2s v2p0371c2m v2p0405c2s
v2p0408c1s v2p0431c2s v2p0437c2s
v2p0439c2s v2p0443c2s
Atwater, L.W. v1p0096c1s
Atwater, R.M. v4p0228c1s
Atwater, R.S. v1p0928c2s
Atwater, W.O. v1p0638c1s
v1p1254c2s v3p0157c1m v3p0316c2s
v4p0007c2s v4p0206c1m v5p0011c2m
v5p0212c2s v5p0486c1s v6p0637c2m
Atwell, C.L. v4p0121c1s
Atwell, H. v3p0034c2s
Atwood, A.W. v6p0018c2s
Atwood, E.C. v5p0266c1s
Atwood, I.M. v1p0248c2s
v1p0313c2s v1p0527c2s v1p0646c1s
v1p0843c2s v1p1103c1s v1p1159c1s
v1p1355c2s v2p0145c2s v2p0455c2s
Atwood, J.M. v1p0688c2s
v1p0814c2s v3p0244c1s
Atwood, M. v1p1035c1s
Atwood, W.B. v6p0306c2s
Auber, E. v4p0444c1s
Auberlen, C.A. v1p0121c2s
v1p0580c2s v1p0818c2s
Aubert, F. v1p1088c1s
Aubertin, C.J. v6p0641c1s
Auberville, D. v1p0949c1s
Aubigne, C.L.Merle d' v6p0238c1s
Aubigne, J.H.M.d' v1p0778c2m
Aubigne, J.H.Merle d' v1p0255c2m
v1p0328c1m
Aubigne, Mlle.d' v5p0356c2m
Aubrey, D. v3p0093c1s
Aubrey, Dr. v3p0012c1s
v3p0213c1s v3p0238c2s v3p0458c2s
v3p0468c2s
Aubrey, F. v5p0545c2s
Aubrey, W.H.S. v1p1291c1s
v2p0099c2s v3p0010c2s v3p0178c1s
v3p0239c1s v3p0397c2s v4p0015c1m
v5p0073c2s v5p0453c2s v6p0382c1s
v6p0423c2s v6p0507c1s
Aubrey-Vitet, M.E. v1p1181c1s
Aubry, G. v4p0200c1s
Aucaigne, F. v5p0129c2s
Auchincloss, H.B. v1p0187c2s
v1p0322c1s v1p0322c2s v1p0519c1s
v1p0649c2s v1p1187c2s v1p1265c2s
Auchmuty, R.T. v2p0444c1s
v3p0016c2s
Auden, H.W. v5p0249c2s
Auden, T. v6p0592c2s
Audenried, J.C. v1p0377c2s
v1p0431c2s v1p1190c2s
Audley, C.F. v3p0472c1s
Audley, H. v1p1359c2s
Audsley, G.C. v4p0017c2s
Audubon, J.J. v1p0023c2s
v1p0307c2s v1p0340c2s v1p0854c2s
v1p1084c1m
Audubon, Miss v1p0076c1s
Auerbach, B. v1p0005c2s
v1p0102c2s v1p0228c2s v1p0308c1s
v1p0726c2s v1p0755c2s v1p0892c1s
v1p1112c2s v1p1438c2s
Auerbach, F. v2p0004c2s
Auerbach, J.S. v5p0593c1s
v6p0170c1s v6p0659c2s
Aughey, S. v1p0406c1s
v1p0777c2m v1p1084c1s
Augonarde, P. v5p0005c2s
Augsburg, D.R. v4p0161c1s
Augu, H. v1p0451c2s
Augustine, M., Sister v6p0103c2s
Auld, F. v6p0684c1s
Auld, J.B. v1p0283c1s
Auld, R.C. v3p0046c2s
v3p0070c2m v3p0200c2m v3p0337c2s
v3p0368c2s v4p0308c1s v4p0487c1s
Auld, W. v6p0269c1s
Aulick, H.P. v5p0544c2s
Auria, L.d' v3p0135c2s
v1p0538c2m v1p0618c2m v1p1310c1m
v2p0419c1m v3p0117c2m v3p0189c2m
v3p0286c2m v3p0430c1m v3p0458c1m
v5p0549c1m v6p0211c2m
Auria, L.d' and Briggs, R.
v1p0640c2m
Auringer, O.C. v3p0130c2s
Austen, Col. v1p1081c1s
Austen, D.E. v3p0037c1s
Austen, E.J. and Sheldon, L.V.
v4p0342c1s
Austen, G. v2p0203c1s
Austen, H.H.G. v1p0500c2s
v1p0706c2m
Austen, J. v2p0344c2s
Austen, L.F. v6p0329c2s
Austen, Nellie M. v5p0563c2s
Austen, P.T. v3p0146c1s
v3p0152c2m v4p0099c1s v4p0192c1s
v4p0364c2s v5p0177c1s v5p0621c2s
Austen, W. v5p0071c2s
v5p0334c1s v6p0087c1s v6p0371c2s
v6p0373c2s
Austen, W.C.R. v3p0275c2m
v6p0013c1s
Austen, W.C.Roberts v6p0257c2s
Austen, W.Roberts v5p0298c1s
Austin v4p0171c2s
Austin, A. v1p0071c1s
v1p0082c2s v1p0350c2s v1p0432c1s
v1p0444c2s v1p0550c1s v1p0627c2s
v1p0716c2s v1p0901c1s v1p0993c1s
v1p1022c1s v1p1276c1s v1p1288c2m
v1p1313c1s v2p0020c2s v2p0021c1m
v2p0069c1s v2p0096c2s v2p0104c1s
v2p0126c2s v2p0159c1s v2p0179c2s
v2p0186c1s v2p0189c1m v2p0208c2s
v2p0231c2s v2p0260c2m v2p0331c2s
v2p0346c1s v2p0346c2s v2p0348c1s
v2p0399c2s v2p0416c1s v2p0437c2s
v3p0020c2m v3p0052c2m v3p0077c1s
v3p0261c2s v3p0337c2s v3p0389c2s
v3p0424c2s v3p0425c1s v4p0028c1s
v4p0039c2s v4p0110c1s v4p0194c1s
v4p0219c2s v4p0267c1s v4p0290c2s
v4p0291c1m v4p0357c2s v4p0437c1s
v4p0490c2s v4p0543c1s v4p0570c1s
v5p0136c2s v5p0152c2s v5p0240c1s
v5p0419c2s v5p0472c1s v6p0496c1s
v6p0505c1s v6p0505c2s v6p0689c1s
Austin, A. and Cranbrook, Viscount
v3p0307c1s
Austin, A. and Maccoll, M.
v1p0104c1s
Austin, A.C. v1p0135c1s
Austin, Alfred v3p0253c1s
v4p0250c1s v5p0458c1s v6p0247c1s
Austin, B.F. v5p0470c1s
Austin, B.M. v6p0569c2s
Austin, Beau v3p0409c2s
Austin, C. v1p1050c2s
Austin, C.H. v5p0258c1s
Austin, E. v4p0377c1s
Austin, F. v3p0293c1m
v3p0313c1s
Austin, F.J. v2p0275c1s
v3p0339c2s v4p0096c1s v5p0339c1s
Austin, F.T. v2p0262c1s
Austin, F.W. v5p0170c1s
Austin, Frank v4p0607c1s
Austin, G. v2p0252c2s
Austin, G.A. v1p0068c1s
Austin, G.B. v3p0041c1s
Austin, G.C. v4p0165c1s
v4p0323c2s
Austin, G.L. v1p0066c1s
v1p0135c2s v1p0197c1s v1p0425c2s
v1p0834c1s v1p1082c2s v1p1372c1s
v1p1415c1s v3p0185c2s v3p0246c1m
v3p0251c2s v3p0390c1s v3p0430c1s
v3p0442c2s v3p0443c1s
Austin, H. v1p1312c1s
v4p0486c1s v5p0053c1s v5p0061c2s
v5p0316c1s v5p0317c1s v5p0350c2s
v5p0455c1s v5p0580c2m
Austin, H.H. v5p0534c2s
v6p0466c2s
Austin, H.H., Maj. v5p0499c2s
Austin, H.H.G. v2p0203c1s
Austin, H.W. v2p0342c1s
v2p0345c2s v3p0246c1s v3p0335c1s
Austin, J. v1p0212c2s
Austin, J.B. v1p0027c2s
Austin, J.G. v1p0007c2s
v1p0084c2s v1p0098c2s v1p0186c1s
v1p0257c1s v1p0296c1s v1p0323c1s
v1p0563c1s v1p0571c2s v1p0573c2s
v1p0925c2s v1p0952c2s v1p0965c2s
v1p1308c2s v1p1323c1s v1p1378c2s
v2p0377c1s v3p0343c2s
Austin, J.G., Mrs. v1p0726c2s
Austin, J.J. v1p0794c1s
v1p1059c1s v1p1121c1s
Austin, J.O. v2p0008c2s
v3p0035c1s v3p0061c2s v3p0341c2s
v3p0459c1s
Austin, J.T. v1p0572c2s
v1p0730c2s v1p0780c2s v1p0935c1s
v1p1063c1s v1p1065c2s v1p1214c2s
v1p1216c2s v1p1283c1s v1p1342c1s
v1p1401c2s
Austin, Jane G. v1p0013c2s
Austin, L.F. v1p0667c1s
v2p0085c2s v2p0303c2s v3p0156c2s
v4p0033c2s v4p0381c2s v5p0582c1s
v5p0611c1s
Austin, L.F. and Ropes, A.R.
v4p0619c2s
Austin, L.R. v6p0450c2s
Austin, M. v4p0384c2s
v5p0017c2s v5p0135c2s v5p0359c2s
v5p0447c2s v5p0461c2s v5p0525c1s
v5p0640c1s v6p0178c1s v6p0496c1s
Austin, M. and Gooch, F.A.
v5p0017c2s v5p0359c2m v5p0426c2s
Austin, M.A. v6p0567c1s
Austin, Mary v6p0053c1s
v6p0171c2s v6p0261c1s v6p0330c1s
v6p0344c1s v6p0360c1s v6p0362c1s
v6p0380c2s v6p0387c1s v6p0395c2s
v6p0568c1s v6p0658c2s v6p0696c2s
Austin, Mary T. v6p0093c2s
Austin, Mrs. v1p0673c2s
Austin, O.P. v5p0006c1s
v5p0111c2s v5p0128c1s v5p0128c2m
v5p0130c1s v5p0155c2s v5p0200c1s
v5p0302c1m v5p0506c2s v5p0599c2s
v5p0602c1s v5p0603c1s v5p0603c2s
v6p0098c2s v6p0140c2m v6p0141c1s
v6p0309c1s v6p0400c1s v6p0401c2s
v6p0414c1s v6p0474c1s v6p0561c1s
v6p0657c2s v6p0666c2s v6p0667c1s
v6p0668c1s v6p0669c2m
Austin, R.W. v6p0524c1s
Austin, S. v1p0516c1m
v1p0517c2s v1p0723c1s v1p1185c1s
Austin, S. Mrs............ v1p0820c1s
Austin, S.F. and Rather, E.Z.
v6p0640c1s
Austin, S.P. v4p0137c2s
Austin, W. v4p0067c1s
v4p0134c2s v4p0423c1s
Austin, W.H. v4p0329c1s

Austria, Crown Prince of . v1p1239c1s
Austrian, D. v6p0018c2s
Autcliffe, H. v6p0575c2s
Authwise, E. v1p1338c2s
Auvergne, E.B.D' v6p0554c1m
Auvergne, M.d' v1p0105c1m
v1p0166c1m
Avebury, Lord v5p0277c1m
v5p0391c2s v5p0392c1s v5p0399c1s
v6p0021c2s v6p0074c1s v6p0213c1s
v6p0267c1s v6p0626c2s
Avebury, Lord et al. v6p0271c1s
Aveling, E. v2p0213c2s
v2p0397c2s v3p0307c2s v4p0314c2s
v4p0333c1s v6p0020c2s
Aveling, E. and Aveling, E.M.
v2p0477c1s v3p0012c2s v3p0389c2s
Aveling, E.B. v2p0081c2s
Aveling, E.M. and Aveling, E.
v2p0477c1s v3p0012c2s v3p0389c2s
Aveling, Edw. v4p0412c1s
v4p0589c1s
Aveling, F. v5p0483c2s
v6p0203c1s v6p0218c1s v6p0307c1s
v6p0319c1s v6p0449c1s v6p0495c2s
v6p0496c1s v6p0574c2s v6p0610c1s
Aveling, F.W. v2p0368c1s
v2p0456c1s v6p0523c2s v6p0549c1s
Aveling, S.T. v4p0482c1s
Aveling, T.W. v1p0253c1s
v1p0253c2m v1p0254c2s v1p0336c1s
Avenarius, F. v5p0230c1s
Avenel, G.d' v3p0131c2m
v5p0529c1m
Avenel, W. v5p0310c2s
Avequin, M. v1p1265c2s
Avery, A.C. v4p0257c2s
Avery, B.P. v1p0041c2s
v1p0062c1s v1p0081c2s v1p0187c2s
v1p0261c1s v1p0519c1s v1p0534c1s
v1p0639c1s v1p0900c2s v1p0956c2s
v1p1140c2s v1p1188c1s v1p1196c1s
v1p1326c1s
Avery, E.A. v2p0301c2s
Avery, E.M., Mrs. v4p0433c1s
Avery, Eliz.H. v6p0380c1s
Avery, H.O. v2p0024c1s
v2p0467c1s v3p0320c2s
Avery, I.W. v3p0376c1s
Avery, J. v1p0464c2s
v1p0631c1s v1p1148c1s v1p1220c1s
v1p1364c1s v2p0017c1s v2p0024c2s
v2p0216c2s v2p0217c2s v2p0218c1s
v2p0348c1s v2p0348c2s v2p0440c2s
v2p0481c1s
Avery, J.H. v1p0846c1s
Avery, J.W. v1p1346c2s
Avery, S.P. v5p0466c2s
Avery, T. v1p0258c1s
Avery, T.M. v4p0134c2s
Aves, E. v5p0321c1s
v5p0557c1s
Avirett, P.W. v4p0078c2s
Avis, E.S. v5p0290c1s
Avonmore, T. v1p1037c1s
Awdry, H. v5p0473c2s
Axford, G. v1p0001c2s
v1p0333c2s
Axon, E. v5p0359c2s
Axon, W. v1p0185c1s
v1p0236c1s v1p0242c1s v1p0328c2s
v1p0464c1s
Axon, W.E.A. v1p0132c2m
v1p0150c2s v1p0165c1s v1p0206c1s
v1p0226c2s v1p0232c2s v1p0354c2s
v1p0436c1s v1p0732c2s v1p0742c2m
v1p0743c1s v1p0743c2s v1p0744c1s
v1p1062c2s v1p1313c2s v1p1314c1s
v2p0006c1s v2p0014c1s v2p0015c2s
v2p0018c1s v2p0019c2s v2p0022c2s
v2p0023c1s v2p0031c2s v2p0040c2s
v2p0045c2s v2p0046c2s v2p0051c1s
v2p0058c1s v2p0062c1s v2p0076c1s
v2p0100c2s v2p0101c2m v2p0104c2s
v2p0108c2s v2p0113c2s v2p0133c1s
v2p0144c1s v2p0158c2s v2p0160c2s
v2p0161c1s v2p0184c1s v2p0193c1s
v2p0195c1s v2p0195c2s v2p0222c1s
v2p0236c2s v2p0252c1s v2p0255c2s
v2p0256c2m v2p0257c1s v2p0265c1s
v2p0269c1s v2p0275c1m v2p0279c2s
v2p0289c2s v2p0321c2s v2p0332c2s
v2p0336c1s v2p0339c1s v2p0383c1s
v2p0397c1s v2p0405c2s v2p0434c1s
v2p0442c1s v2p0445c1s v2p0447c2s
v2p0466c1s v2p0467c1s v3p0030c2s
v3p0118c2s v3p0162c1s v3p0177c2s
v3p0181c2s v3p0185c1s v3p0189c2s
v3p0210c2s v3p0267c1s v3p0344c1s
v3p0375c2s v3p0391c1s v3p0458c1s
v4p0014c2s v4p0356c2s v5p0137c2s
v5p0166c1s v5p0203c2s v5p0299c1s
v5p0313c1s v5p0333c2s v5p0569c1s
v5p0633c1s v6p0026c1s v6p0108c2s
v6p0122c1s v6p0133c2s v6p0195c1s
v6p0372c1s v6p0478c1s v6p0662c2s
v6p0707c1s
Axson, S. v4p0116c2s
v4p0334c2s v4p0408c2s v4p0490c1s
v4p0520c1s v5p0580c2s v6p0208c2s
Axtell, J.L. v3p0214c1s
v3p0392c2s
Axtell, S.J. v5p0041c2s
Axtell, S.P. v4p0613c1s
Axtens, F. v4p0247c2s
Ayamat-Batuk v1p0886c2s
Aycard, M. v1p1111c1s
Aycard, Marie v1p0223c2s
Aycock, C.B. v6p0190c1s
v6p0605c1s
Ayer, C. v1p0130c2s
Ayer, C.C. v6p0423c1s
Ayer, C.W. v6p0372c2s
Ayer, F.D. v2p0097c2m
Ayer, I. v5p0580c2s
Ayer, J.C., jr. v6p0367c1s
Ayer, L.M. v2p0215c2s
Ayer, M. v5p0582c1s
Ayer, M.F. v6p0076c2s
Ayer, W.E. v6p0030c2s
Ayers, S.G. v6p0302c1s
Ayles, H.H.B. v6p0562c1s
Aylett, E. v2p0033c2s
Ayling, E.M. v2p0153c2s
v4p0110c2s
Aylmer, I.E. v1p0918c2s
Aylmore, C. v6p0338c1s
v6p0570c1s
Ayloffe, J. v1p0213c1s
v1p0393c1s v1p0411c1s v1p0585c1s
Aylsworth, G.M. v4p0271c2s
Aylward, A. v2p0004c1s
v2p0466c1s v3p0035c2s
Aylward, E.M. v4p0425c1s
Aymar, M.F. v1p1154c2s
Aymonier, E. v4p0565c2s
Aynsley, C.M. v1p1247c2s
Ayrault, H. v1p0371c2s
v1p1420c1s v2p0422c1s
Ayre, G.L. v5p0238c1s
Ayres, A. v5p0191c2s
Ayres, B. v1p1291c2m
Ayres, E.F. v3p0107c1s
v3p0436c2s
Ayres, H.B. v4p0207c2s
v4p0209c1s v4p0543c1s
Ayres, I. v5p0527c1s
Ayres, J.C. v4p0461c1s
v5p0276c2s v5p0516c2s
Ayres, P.W. v4p0096c1s
v4p0097c1s v5p0214c1s v5p0443c1s
v5p0443c2m v5p0560c2s v6p0232c2s
v6p0381c1s v6p0512c1s
Ayres, S.A. v6p0370c2s
Ayres, S.G. v4p0317c1s
v5p0155c2s v6p0373c1s v6p0642c1s
Ayres, W. v6p0302c2s
Ayres, W.A. v1p0651c2s
Ayres, W.O. v2p0052c2s
v2p0273c2s v2p0460c2s v3p0229c1s
Ayres, W.P. v5p0163c1s
Ayrton, E. v5p0268c1s
v5p0342c2s v6p0127c2s v6p0179c1s
v6p0423c2s v6p0663c2s
Ayrton, E. and Zangwill, I., Mrs.
v6p0631c1s
Ayrton, Hertha v5p0182c2s
v6p0197c1s
Ayrton, J.C. v1p0385c1s
v1p1425c1s v3p0455c1s
Ayrton, O.M. v6p0674c2s
Ayrton, Prof. and Perry, Prof.
v1p0788c2s
Ayrton, W.E. v1p0400c2m
v1p0850c2s v2p0137c1m v2p0141c1m
v2p0172c1s v2p0463c2s v3p0133c1s
v4p0176c1s v5p0099c2s v5p0183c1s
v5p0310c1s v6p0198c1s v6p0296c2s
v6p0512c2m
Ayrton, W.E. and Perry, J.
v2p0281c2s v3p0383c2s
Ayrton-Zangwill, E. v6p0169c2s
Ayscough, J. v4p0139c1s
v5p0013c2s v5p0082c2s v5p0093c2s
v5p0094c1s v5p0405c1s v5p0425c1s
v5p0425c2s v5p0472c2s v5p0487c1s
v5p0494c1s v6p0434c1s
Ayscough, S. v1p0544c2s
Aytoun, W.E. v1p0088c1s
v1p0177c2s v1p0291c1s v1p0383c2s
v1p0455c2s v1p0526c2s v1p0600c2s
v1p0603c2s v1p0731c2s v1p0865c1s
v1p0926c1s v1p1075c1s v1p1083c1s
v1p1114c2s v1p1188c1s
Azarias, Brother v1p0040c1m
v1p0184c2m v1p0305c1s v1p0415c1m
v1p1001c1m v2p0111c2s v2p0260c1s
v2p0390c2m v2p0440c1s v3p0012c2s
v3p0049c1s v3p0057c1s v3p0082c2s
v3p0306c2s v3p0364c2s v3p0378c1s
v3p0378c2s v4p0326c2s v4p0387c1s
v4p0597c2s v4p0598c1s
Azcarate, G.de v6p0607c2m

B., A. v3p0194c1s
B., C.V. v6p0623c1s
B., E. v4p0456c2s
B., E.J. and Bolton, W.W.. v4p0157c2s
B., E.S. v5p0008c2s
B., G.A. v6p0227c1s
B., H. v5p0510c1s
B., I.H. v5p0042c1s
B., J. v5p0486c1s
B., J.C. v2p0193c1s
B., L. v6p0060c1s
B., L.A. v6p0673c2s
B., M. v1p0304c1s
B., N.T. v6p0055c2s
B., R.E. v1p0250c2s
B., W.F.H. v5p0292c1s
Baart, P.A. v3p0314c2s
v3p0365c1s
Babad, N.M. v4p0501c2s
v5p0108c2s
Babb, C.C. v4p0021c2s
v4p0454c2s
Babb, J.E. v3p0076c2s
v3p0208c1s
Babbitt, B.B. v2p0171c2s
Babbitt, D.R. v6p0391c1s
Babbitt, E.H. v4p0154c2s
v4p0376c1s v5p0126c1s v5p0127c1s
v6p0135c2s v6p0605c2s
Babbitt, F.C. v5p0137c2s
Babbitt, F.E. v2p0274c1s
v2p0361c1s
Babbitt, G.F. v5p0224c2s
Babbitt, I. v5p0080c1s
v5p0122c1s v5p0170c2s v5p0544c1s
v6p0282c1s v6p0302c2s v6p0379c2s
Babbitt, J.A. v5p0103c1s
Babbitt, Juliette M. v5p0166c2s
v5p0354c1s v5p0509c1s v5p0635c2s
Babbitt, Z.B. v6p0636c2s
Babcock, B.W. v6p0182c2s
v6p0630c2s
Babcock, C. v1p1363c2s
Babcock, C.C. v6p0414c1s
Babcock, E.S. v6p0311c2s
v6p0580c2s v6p0651c1m v6p0672c2s
Babcock, G.H. v1p0639c1s
v1p1003c1s v4p0547c1s
Babcock, H.S. v3p0341c1s
v5p0462c1m v6p0512c1m
Babcock, J.B. v5p0206c2m
Babcock, J.H. v5p0148c1s
v5p0402c2s v5p0613c1s
Babcock, J.W. v5p0603c2m
v6p0030c1s v6p0451c2s
Babcock, J.W. and Faulkner, C.J.
v4p0595c2s
Babcock, J.W. et al. v6p0633c1s
Babcock, K.C. v4p0504c2m
v6p0293c1s
Babcock, R. v1p0011c2s
v1p0097c1m v1p0117c2s v1p0582c1s
v1p0847c1s v1p0927c1s v1p0987c1s
v1p1096c1s v1p1403c1s v2p0309c2s
Babcock, R., jr. v1p0393c1s
Babcock, W.H. v1p0259c1s
v1p0340c1s v1p0651c2s v1p0978c2s
v2p0077c2s v2p0170c2s v2p0241c2s
v2p0409c2s v3p0170c1s v3p0219c1s
v3p0270c1s v4p0612c1s v5p0032c1s
v5p0073c2s v6p0663c1s
Babelon, E. v2p0223c1s
v2p0336c2s
Baber, G. v3p0231c2s
v4p0206c2s
Baber, J.A. v5p0249c2s
Babine, A.V. v4p0329c2s
Babington, W.M. v2p0438c1s
Babson and Sinclair v3p0159c1s
Babson, H. v4p0072c2s
v4p0079c1s v4p0486c2s v5p0387c2s
Babson, J.E. v1p0719c1s
v1p0720c1m v1p0942c1s
Babut, C.E. v2p0165c2s
Baccelli, Alfredo v6p0678c1s
Bacchus, F. v5p0429c2s
v5p0495c1s v6p0484c1s
Bach, R. v5p0338c2s
Bache, A.D. v1p0077c1s
v1p0145c2s v1p0195c2s v1p0270c1s
v1p0278c2s v1p0377c1s v1p0387c2s
v1p0484c2s v1p0562c1m v1p0706c2s
v1p0728c1s v1p0787c2m v1p0788c1m
v1p0827c2m v1p0865c2m v1p0898c2s
v1p0915c2s v1p1061c1s v1p1074c1s
v1p1080c2s v1p1150c1s v1p1292c1s
v1p1293c1s v1p1310c1m v1p1316c1s
v1p1414c1s v1p1414c2s
Bache, A.D. and Hilgard, J.E.
v1p0788c2s
Bache, D. v5p0416c2s
Bache, H. v1p0748c1s
Bache, R. v5p0160c1s
v5p0621c1s v6p0044c2s v6p0124c1s
v6p0226c1s v6p0297c1s v6p0432c1s
v6p0432c2s v6p0551c1s v6p0667c2s
Bache, R.M. v1p1172c2s
v2p0116c2s v2p0274c2s v2p0299c2s
v2p0360c1s v3p0123c2s v4p0163c1s
v4p0244c2s v4p0371c2s v4p0474c1s
v5p0044c1s v5p0219c1m v6p0239c2s
v6p0647c1s
Bache, Rene v5p0241c1s
v5p0601c1s v6p0665c2s
Bache, W. and Dean, J.W. . v1p0484c1s
Bacheler, A.W. v5p0596c2s
Bacheler, A.W. et al. v5p0265c1s
Bacheler, O.R. v1p0216c1s
v2p0086c1s
Bacheller, I. v5p0169c1s
v6p0664c1s
Bacheller, I. et al. v6p0055c1s
Bacheller, Irving v5p0042c1s
v5p0350c1s v5p0434c2s v5p0521c2s
v5p0555c1s v5p0599c1s v5p0599c2s
Bacheller, M. v4p0003c1s
v4p0052c1s v4p0068c1s v4p0069c2s
v4p0299c1s v4p0420c2s
Bachellor, A.S. v3p0106c2s
Bachelor, A. v1p0773c2s
Bachelor, J.B. v5p0598c2s
Bachelor, M. v6p0500c1s
Bachelor, N. v6p0156c1s
Bachelor Maid, The v6p0222c2s
Bacher, O.H. v6p0676c2s
v6p0696c1s
Bacher, W. v4p0269c2s
v4p0435c1s v4p0468c2s v5p0174c1m
v5p0260c2s v5p0356c2s v5p0531c1s
v5p0567c1s v5p0572c1s v6p0030c2s
v6p0343c1s v6p0593c1s
Bacher, W. and Porges, N.. v5p0228c1s
Bacher, W., Prof. et al. . v6p0343c1s
Bachman, J.
v1p0136c1s
v1p0837c2s
Backhouse, J.W. et al. ... v2p0404c2s
Backhouse, T.W. v2p0028c2s
v2p0090c1s v2p0462c2s
Backhouse, T.W. and Stromeyer, C.E.
v3p0093c1s
Backhouse, T.W. et al. ... v2p0090c1s
v2p0426c1s
Backhouse, W. v3p0407c2s
Backman, F.P. v5p0292c2s
v6p0490c2s v6p0635c1s
Backup, E.E. v3p0077c1s
Backus, C.K. v2p0287c2s
v2p0316c2s v2p0422c1s
Backus, E. v1p0461c2s
v1p0864c1s v1p1140c1s
Backus, E.M. v4p0138c1s
v4p0225c2s v4p0558c1s v5p0475c1s
Backus, Emma M. v5p0212c2s
v5p0402c2m
Backus, H.H. v5p0388c2s
Backus, J.T. v2p0039c2s
Backus, J.W. v2p0010c1s
v2p0290c2s v2p0369c2s
Backus, M. v6p0497c1s
Backus, W.H. v6p0531c2m
Bacon et al. v1p1360c1s
Bacon, A.M. v6p0221c1s
v6p0312c2s
Bacon, A.O. v6p0550c1s
v6p0656c1s
Bacon, A.S. v5p0599c1s
Bacon, A.T. v1p0279c2m
v1p1082c1s v1p1195c1s
Bacon, Alice M. v5p0255c1s
Bacon, B.W. v3p0041c1s
v3p0041c2m v3p0043c2s v3p0091c2s
v3p0228c1s v3p0427c2s v4p0148c2s
v4p0298c2s v4p0301c1s v5p0001c2s
v5p0055c2s v5p0059c2m v5p0196c2s
v5p0201c2s v5p0305c2s v5p0307c1s
v5p0430c1s v5p0434c2s v5p0567c2s
v6p0063c1m v6p0063c2m v6p0064c1m
v6p0065c1s v6p0123c1s v6p0123c2s
v6p0157c1s v6p0176c1s v6p0286c1s
v6p0340c1s v6p0342c2s v6p0345c2s
v6p0412c1s v6p0478c2s v6p0653c2s
Bacon, B.W. et al. v6p0340c2s
Bacon, C. v6p0372c2s
Bacon, C.F. v5p0127c1s
v5p0155c2s v5p0603c2s
Bacon, Capt. v1p0322c2s
Bacon, D.F. v1p0263c1s
v1p0307c1s v1p0398c2s
Bacon, D.M. v6p0187c2s
Bacon, Delia v1p1183c1s
v1p1183c2s
Bacon, E.M. v1p0501c1s
v3p0431c2s v3p0436c2s v3p0475c1s
v4p0151c2s v5p0071c1s v5p0079c1s
v5p0084c1s v5p0167c1s v5p0210c1s
v5p0329c2s v5p0342c1s v5p0631c2s
v6p0301c2s v6p0330c1s v6p0694c2s
v6p0697c2s
Bacon, E.P. v6p0324c2s
Bacon, Edgar M. v6p0053c1s
Bacon, F. v1p0577c2s
v1p0619c2s v6p0603c1s
Bacon, F. and Cowdrey, S.G.
v1p1360c1s
Bacon, F.H. v2p0025c1s
v4p0323c1s
Bacon, G. v1p0486c2s
v1p1361c2s v5p0075c1s v5p0081c1s
v5p0145c2s v5p0169c2s v5p0240c1s
v6p0187c2s v6p0350c2s
Bacon, G.A. v3p0087c1s
v3p0128c1s v3p0368c2s
Bacon, G.B. v1p0090c2s
v1p0123c2s v1p0235c1m v1p0679c1s
v1p0808c1s v1p1069c1s v1p1193c2s
v1p1194c1s v1p1204c1s v1p1238c2s
v1p1270c2s v1p1295c1s v1p1399c1s
v2p0312c1s
Bacon, G.W. v1p0678c1s
v1p0679c1s v1p1270c1s
Bacon, Gertrude v5p0377c2s
v5p0451c1s v5p0644c1s v6p0385c1s
Bacon, H. v1p0239c1s
v1p0242c1s v1p0320c1s v1p0337c2s
v1p0470c2s v1p0624c2s v1p1302c2s
v2p0051c1s v2p0168c1s v4p0393c2s
v4p0546c1s
Bacon, H. and Allen, F.H.. v1p0063c1s
Bacon, H. and Gibbs, H.H.. v4p0524c1s
Bacon, I.M. v6p0636c1s
Bacon, J. v2p0337c1s
v6p0005c1s
Bacon, J.C. v1p0957c1s
Bacon, J.D. v6p0226c1s
Bacon, J.E. v4p0250c2s
Bacon, J.F. v6p0596c1s
Bacon, J.M. v5p0037c1s
v5p0044c1m v5p0066c1s v5p0123c1s
v5p0212c1s v5p0338c2s v5p0345c2s
v5p0384c2s v5p0517c2s v5p0540c1m
v5p0554c2s v5p0579c1s v5p0624c1m
v6p0009c2m v6p0026c1s v6p0048c2s
v6p0132c1s v6p0289c2s v6p0383c1m
v6p0415c2s v6p0582c1s v6p0604c2s
v6p0619c1s v6p0636c2s v6p0645c1s
v6p0688c1s
Bacon, J.S. v2p0328c1s
v6p0121c2s
Bacon, Josephine D. v6p0259c2s
v6p0369c1s v6p0381c1s v6p0571c2s
Bacon, Josephine Daskam, Mrs.
v6p0017c1s
Bacon, L. v1p0048c1s
v1p0085c1s v1p0112c1s v1p0129c1s
v1p0157c1s v1p0169c1s v1p0180c1s
v1p0198c2s v1p0200c1s v1p0219c1s
v1p0220c2s v1p0228c2s v1p0236c1s
v1p0243c1s v1p0244c1s v1p0252c2s
v1p0254c2s v1p0262c1s v1p0278c1s
v1p0279c2s v1p0290c1s v1p0294c2s
v1p0296c2s v1p0306c1s v1p0375c2s
v1p0381c1s v1p0393c1s v1p0411c2s
v1p0421c1m v1p0422c1m v1p0422c2s
v1p0432c1s v1p0471c1s v1p0571c2s
v1p0575c1s v1p0591c1m v1p0595c2s
v1p0603c1s v1p0646c1s v1p0668c1s
v1p0702c1s v1p0725c1s v1p0775c2s
v1p0781c2s v1p0806c1s v1p0832c1s
v1p0852c1s v1p0852c2s v1p0903c2s
v1p0905c1s v1p0905c2s v1p0909c2s
v1p0910c2s v1p0932c2s v1p0942c2s
v1p0963c1s v1p0976c2s v1p0982c2s
v1p0988c1s v1p0990c1s v1p0990c2s
v1p1009c1s v1p1025c2s v1p1028c2s
v1p1038c1s v1p1038c2s v1p1042c1s
v1p1046c1m v1p1046c2s v1p1047c2s
v1p1062c2s v1p1065c1s v1p1066c2m
v1p1067c1s v1p1075c2s v1p1088c2s
v1p1094c1s v1p1115c2s v1p1116c1s
v1p1118c2s v1p1139c2s v1p1158c1s
v1p1169c2s v1p1206c1m v1p1206c2s
v1p1207c1s v1p1208c1s v1p1209c1s
v1p1217c1s v1p1240c1s v1p1258c2m
v1p1262c1s v1p1264c2s v1p1265c1s
v1p1267c1s v1p1286c2s v1p1318c2s
v1p1331c2s v1p1336c2s v1p1343c2s
v1p1346c2s v1p1352c1s v1p1355c1s
v1p1378c1s v1p1395c2s v1p1396c1s
v1p1399c1s v1p1399c2s v1p1409c2s
v1p1412c1s v1p1432c1s v1p1436c1m
v2p0099c2s v4p0152c2s v5p0195c1s
v5p0609c1s v6p0709c1s
Bacon, L. and Hall, E.E. . v1p0910c1s
Bacon, L. and Hastings, T.
v1p0882c2s v1p0883c2s
Bacon, L.W. v1p0148c1s
v1p0177c1s v1p0230c2s v1p0286c1s
v1p0290c2s v1p0291c1m v1p0422c2s
v1p0440c2s v1p0466c1s v1p0483c1s
v1p0504c2s v1p0599c2s v1p0620c2s
v1p0683c2s v1p0775c2s v1p0855c2s
v1p0923c2s v1p1038c2s v1p1042c1s
v1p1058c2s v1p1109c1s v1p1117c2s
v1p1118c2s v1p1121c1s v1p1157c1s
v2p0010c2s v2p0013c2s v2p0031c1s
v2p0058c1s v2p0120c1s v2p0171c2s
v2p0257c1s v2p0302c2s v2p0348c2s
v2p0356c1m v3p0054c2s v3p0118c1s
v3p0148c2s v3p0249c2s v3p0264c1s
v3p0326c1s v3p0337c1s v3p0340c1s
v3p0346c1s v3p0431c1s v4p0104c2s
v4p0111c2m v4p0213c1s v4p0220c1s
v4p0221c2s v4p0310c1s v4p0407c2s
v4p0463c1s v4p0488c1s v4p0503c2s
v4p0588c2s v5p0443c2s
Bacon, L.W. et al. v4p0503c2s
Bacon, Lee v4p0202c2s
Bacon, Leonard W. v5p0445c2s
Bacon, M.A. v4p0223c2s

v5p0013c1s v5p0265c2s v5p0325c2s
v5p0538c2s v6p0045c1s v6p0108c2s
v6p0114c2s v6p0251c2s v6p0292c1s
v6p0318c1s v6p0380c2s v6p0605c1s
v6p0625c1s v6p0690c2s v6p0697c2s
Bacon, N.G. v6p0694c2s
Bacon, N.S. v6p0159c2s
Bacon, N.T. v5p0158c1s
v5p0600c2s v5p0602c1s v6p0334c1s
v6p0558c1s v6p0560c2s v6p0702c1s
Bacon, R.C. v1p0480c1s
Bacon, R.H. v1p0521c2s
v1p0934c2s v1p1016c2s v1p1325c2s
Bacon, S.L. v4p0002c2s
Bacon, T. v1p0412c2s
v1p0493c1s v1p0576c1s v1p0976c2s
v1p1078c1s v1p1084c1s v1p1285c2s
v1p1374c2s v2p0147c1s v2p0192c2m
v2p0355c2s v3p0161c2s v4p0205c2s
Bacon, T.D. v6p0025c1s
v6p0065c1s v6p0538c2s
Bacon, T.R. v1p1361c2s
v3p0020c2s v3p0154c2s v3p0270c2s
v3p0425c1s v4p0169c1s v4p0259c1s
v4p0393c1s v4p0553c1s v6p0370c1s
v6p0539c1s v6p0576c1s v6p0710c2s
Bacon, T.S. v5p0459c2s
Bacon, W.J. v3p0098c1s
Bacon, W.T. v1p0577c2s
v1p0824c1s v1p0893c2s
Bacot, J.T.W. v1p0603c2s
Bacourt, M.de v2p0452c2s
Baddeley, R.W. v1p0082c2s
Baddeley, St.C. v6p0549c1s
v6p0549c2s
Baddeley, St.Clair v6p0387c1s
Bade, W.F. v6p0688c1s
Badeau, A. v1p0477c2s
v1p0540c2s v1p1335c2s v1p1341c2s
v1p1342c2s v2p0179c2s v2p0184c2m
v2p0400c1s v3p0166c2s v4p0048c1s
v4p0200c2s v4p0234c2s v4p0288c2s
v4p0552c2s v4p0608c2s
Badeau, Adam v4p0068c1s
Baden, A.J. v6p0305c2s
Baden, J. v6p0631c2s
Baden-Powell v3p0037c2s
Baden-Powell, A. v6p0230c1s
Baden-Powell, B. v5p0019c1s
v6p0005c1s v6p0009c2s v6p0570c1s
Baden-Powell, B.F.S. v3p0031c1s
v5p0317c2m
Baden-Powell, B.H. v3p0450c1s
v4p0051c1m v4p0584c1s v4p0604c2s
v4p0636c2s v5p0252c1s v5p0286c1s
v5p0287c1s v5p0472c2s
Baden-Powell, G. v1p0543c2s
v1p0544c2m v2p0089c2s v2p0176c2s
v2p0186c1s v2p0186c2s v2p0187c1s
v2p0223c1s v2p0330c1s v2p0424c1s
v3p0065c1s v3p0066c1s v3p0180c2m
v3p0181c1m v3p0182c2s v3p0199c2s
v3p0298c1s v5p0220c1s v5p0245c1s
v5p0626c1s
Baden-Powell, G., Sir v3p0321c2s
v3p0350c2s v4p0239c1s v4p0276c1s
v5p0142c2s v5p0174c1s v5p0559c2s
Baden-Powell, G., Sir and
Ebrington, Lord v3p0005c1s
Baden-Powell, H.H. v4p0279c2s
Badenoch, G.R. v5p0038c2s
v5p0145c2s
Badenoch, L.N. v4p0200c2s
v4p0250c2s v4p0280c2s v4p0286c1m
v4p0384c2s v4p0609c1s v5p0089c2s
v6p0393c1s
Badenoch, M.T.D. v5p0388c2s
Bader, A.J. v6p0254c2s
Badger, E.W. v4p0217c1s
Badger, Eliza, H. v6p0156c1s
Badger, G.H. v2p0210c1s
Badger, G.P. v1p0857c1s
v1p0885c2s v1p1332c1s v2p0018c1s
v2p0230c2s v2p0244c1s
Badger, H. v4p0608c2s
Badger, H.C. v1p0046c1s
v1p0796c2s v2p0103c1s v3p0081c1s
v3p0136c1s v3p0190c2s v3p0404c1s
v4p0355c1s
Badger, J.E. v5p0050c2s
Badger, J.E., jr. v5p0389c2s
Badger, S.C. v1p0824c2s
Badger, W.I. v2p0027c1s
Badger, W.W. v1p0874c2s
Badham, C. v1p1387c1s
v2p0483c1s
Badham, D.C. v1p0202c2s
v1p0447c2s v1p0456c2m v1p0457c1m
v1p0503c2s v1p0563c1s v1p0880c1s
v1p0945c1s v1p0990c2s v1p1009c2s
v1p1108c2s v1p1164c2s v1p1187c2s
v1p1329c2s
Badham, F.P. v4p0056c2s
v4p0057c1s v4p0300c1s v4p0437c1m
v4p0605c2s v5p0043c1s v5p0309c1s
v5p0397c2s v6p0344c2s
Badham, F.P. and Allen, W.C.
v4p0561c2s
Badham, F.P. and Laughton, J.K.
v5p0404c1s
Badington, A. v4p0529c2s
Badley, B.H. v1p0632c2s
v1p0853c2s v1p1361c2s v2p0336c2s
v2p0471c1s
Badoureau, M. v2p0086c1s
Baer, A.W. v2p0342c2s
Baer, B.F. v1p0038c1s
v1p0394c1s v1p0790c2s v1p0987c2s
Baer, G.F. v1p0513c1s
v1p0988c1s v4p0477c1s v6p0621c2s
Baer, H.M. v5p0026c2s
Baer, J.A. v6p0152c1s
v6p0337c1s v6p0654c1s
Baer, J.W. v4p0117c2s
Baer, Von v1p1309c2s
Baerenbach, F.v. v2p0414c1s
Baermann, P.H. v1p1081c1s
Bagby, A.M. v2p0260c1s
v3p0252c2s
Bagby, G.W. v1p0374c2s
v1p0681c1s v1p1344c2s v1p1388c2s
Bagehot, W. v1p0026c1s
v1p0134c1s v1p0297c1s v1p0544c2s
v1p0549c2s v1p0734c2s v1p0766c2s
v1p0793c1s v1p1006c2s v1p1026c1s
v1p1112c1s v1p1177c2s v1p1210c2s
v1p1314c2s v1p1425c2s v4p0599c2s
v5p0234c2s
Bagen, B.D. v5p0325c1s
Bagenal, P.H. v1p0659c1s
v2p0223c2s v2p0224c2s v2p0228c1s
v2p0451c1s v3p0219c2s v3p0221c2s
v3p0364c2s v5p0542c2s
Bagg, E.N. v4p0617c2s
v5p0362c2s
Bagg, L.H. v1p1401c2s
v2p0470c2s
Bagger, L. v1p0336c1s
v1p0406c1s v1p0619c1s v1p0916c1s
v1p1038c1s v1p1218c1s
Bagley, Florence N. v6p0221c1s
Bagley, W.C. v5p0370c1s
v5p0520c1s
Bagnall, W.R. v1p0649c2s
v1p1066c1s
Bagot, A.G. v3p0473c2s
v4p0238c1s v5p0276c2m v5p0643c1s
Bagot, C., Mrs. v5p0086c1s
v5p0440c2s
Bagot, D. v1p0130c1s
v1p1325c2s v4p0174c1s
Bagot, Dosia v5p0332c1s
Bagot, R. v5p0355c2s
v5p0494c1m v5p0608c1s v6p0223c1s
v6p0501c1m
Bagwell, R. v1p0656c1m
v1p0659c2s v1p0662c2m v1p0973c1s
v1p1069c2s v6p0327c2s
Bahadurji, K.N. v4p0280c1s
Bahlsen, L. v6p0699c1s
Bahn, J.A. v3p0364c1s
Baier, Julius v5p0632c2s
Baigent, F.J. v5p0235c2s
Baigneres, A. v2p0275c1s
Baildon, H.B. v1p0024c2s
v2p0120c2s
Baildon, H.C. v4p0549c2s
Baildon, H.P. v5p0553c1s
Baildon, W.P. v6p0679c2s
Bailey, A. v2p0251c1s
v2p0334c1s v4p0138c1s v5p0589c2s
Bailey, A.H. v1p0873c1s
v3p0016c1s
Bailey, A.S. v4p0516c1s
v5p0564c1s
Bailey, A.W. v3p0035c2s
v3p0201c2s v3p0218c2s v3p0219c1s
v3p0421c2s v4p0016c1s v4p0192c2s
v4p0363c2s v6p0081c2s v6p0381c2s
v6p0467c1s v6p0500c1s v6p0533c1s
Bailey, Alfred v5p0456c1s
Bailey, Anne Stuart v5p0128c2s
Bailey, C. v4p0580c2s
v5p0385c2s
Bailey, C.A. v2p0482c2s
Bailey, D.P. v1p0272c2s
v1p0313c2s v1p0860c1s v1p1153c2m
v2p0034c1s v2p0088c2s v3p0087c2s
Bailey, D.P., jr. v1p0092c2s
v1p0094c1s v1p0193c2s v1p0647c1s
v1p0735c1s v1p1153c2s v1p1232c2s
v1p1349c1s
Bailey, E. v3p0154c2s
Bailey, E.A. v4p0564c1s
Bailey, E.H. v4p0215c2s
Bailey, E.H.S. v3p0009c2s
v3p0188c2s v3p0276c1s
Bailey, E.H.S. and Michols, E.L.
v2p0405c2s v3p0420c2s
Bailey, E.J. v6p0207c2s
Bailey, E.L. v5p0585c2s
Bailey, F. v1p0382c1s
v3p0132c2s
Bailey, F.C. v6p0207c1s
Bailey, G. v1p0117c1s
v1p0495c2s v1p0820c1s v1p0889c2s
v1p1093c1s v3p0439c2s v3p0453c2s
v5p0023c1s v6p0080c1m v6p0278c1s
v6p0628c1s
Bailey, G.E. v6p0092c1s
v6p0093c2s
Bailey, G.H. v2p0390c1s
v4p0084c1s
Bailey, Gervase, Mrs. v6p0369c1s
Bailey, Grace H. v6p0342c2s
v6p0352c1s v6p0380c2s v6p0416c1s
Bailey, Grace Helen v6p0165c2s
Bailey, H.C. v5p0165c1s
v5p0396c1s v6p0055c2s v6p0179c1s
v6p0261c1s v6p0516c2s v6p0596c1s
v6p0611c2s
Bailey, H.D. v6p0611c2s
Bailey, H.L. v5p0491c1s
Bailey, H.T. v5p0066c1s
v5p0080c2s v5p0126c1s v6p0034c2s
v6p0036c1s v6p0224c2s
Bailey, J.B. v1p0628c2s
v2p0070c2s v2p0088c1s v2p0282c1s
v5p0498c2s
Bailey, J.C. v3p0103c1m
v3p0105c2s v3p0179c2s v4p0073c1s
v4p0186c1s v4p0241c1s v4p0317c1s
v5p0104c1s v5p0233c1s v5p0263c1s
v5p0553c1s v6p0022c2s v6p0026c2s
v6p0032c1s
Bailey, J.E. v2p0036c2m
v2p0051c1s v2p0062c2s v2p0063c1s
v2p0295c2s v2p0331c2s v2p0473c1s
v6p0185c1s
Bailey, J.F. v3p0081c1s
Bailey, J.G. v6p0286c2s
Bailey, J.J. v1p0742c1s
Bailey, J.T. v5p0533c1s
v6p0178c1s v6p0638c2s
Bailey, J.W. v1p0041c1s
v1p0073c1s v1p0349c2s v1p0470c1m
v1p0835c2s v1p0836c1m v1p0935c2s
v5p0403c1s v5p0540c2s v6p0024c2s
v6p0344c2s
Bailey, L.H. v4p0007c2s
v4p0014c1s v4p0021c2s v4p0040c1s
v4p0082c1s v4p0101c1s v4p0134c2s
v4p0191c1s v4p0195c2s v4p0216c2m
v4p0217c1m v4p0219c2s v4p0233c2s
v4p0242c2s v4p0264c2m v4p0265c1s
v4p0292c2s v4p0312c1s v4p0364c1s
v4p0397c2s v4p0409c1s v4p0445c2s
v4p0446c1s v4p0483c2s v4p0491c2s
v4p0513c1s v4p0552c2s v4p0600c2s
v4p0623c2s v5p0009c1s v5p0075c2s
v5p0198c2s v5p0203c1m v5p0226c1s
v5p0271c2s v5p0400c2s v5p0556c1s
v5p0623c1s v6p0008c1s v6p0009c1s
v6p0022c2s v6p0059c1s v6p0111c2s
v6p0123c2s v6p0159c2s v6p0163c1s
v6p0163c2s v6p0193c1s v6p0219c2m
v6p0220c1m v6p0246c2s v6p0410c1s
v6p0417c1s v6p0485c2m v6p0502c2m
v6p0552c1s v6p0552c2s v6p0590c1s
Bailey, L.H. et al. v6p0221c2s
v6p0318c1s
Bailey, L.W. v1p0349c2s
v1p0490c2s v2p0246c2s
Bailey, L.Y. v2p0027c2s
Bailey, M. v5p0009c2s
v6p0695c1s
Bailey, Muriel v6p0678c1s
Bailey, P. v5p0579c1s
Bailey, P.J. v1p0356c2s
v1p0621c1s v1p0746c2s
Bailey, R. v1p0266c1s
Bailey, R.W. v1p0179c2s
v1p0323c1s v1p0600c1s v1p0723c2s
v1p1431c2s
Bailey, S. v1p0096c2s
v1p0133c2s
Bailey, S.C.H. v3p0003c2s
v3p0276c1s
Bailey, S.I. v5p0194c2s
v6p0029c1s v6p0490c2s v6p0511c2s
v6p0614c2s v6p0626c1s
Bailey, S.L. v1p0287c2s
v1p0313c2s
Bailey, T. v6p0248c2s
Bailey, T.P., jr. v4p0439c1s
v6p0212c1s v6p0672c1s
Bailey, Temple v6p0466c2s
Bailey, V. v5p0357c2s
v6p0597c2s
Bailey, V.H. v6p0076c1s
v6p0094c2s v6p0301c2s v6p0452c1s
v6p0472c2s v6p0492c1s v6p0687c2s
Bailey, W. v1p0847c1s
v5p0067c2s
Bailey, W.B. v5p0199c2s
v5p0289c1s v6p0137c1s v6p0624c2s
Bailey, W.F. v4p0006c1m
v5p0011c1s v5p0458c2s v6p0007c1s
v6p0447c1s
Bailey, W.H. v4p0406c2s
v5p0570c1s
Bailey, W.H., Sir v6p0325c1s
v6p0359c2s
Bailey, W.M. v5p0371c1s
Bailey, W.S. v4p0274c1s
Bailey, W.W. v1p0083c2s
v1p0541c1s v1p0614c1s v1p1023c2s
v1p1141c2s v1p1176c1s v1p1327c2s
v1p1396c2s v1p1428c1s v2p0299c2s
v3p0193c2s v3p0440c1s v5p0622c1s

v6p0173c1s v6p0375c2s v6p0502c2s
v6p0503c1s v6p0582c1s
Bailey, W.W. et al. v3p0051c2s
Bailey, Whitman v6p0639c1s
Bailey-Kempling, W. v6p0134c2s
v6p0439c1s
Bailhache, C.M. v4p0318c2s
Bailie, W. v6p0708c1s
Baillie, A.F. v4p0424c2s
Baillie, Col. v3p0259c1s
v3p0277c1s v3p0283c1s v3p0302c2s
v3p0310c2s
Baillie, H. v6p0375c1s
Baillie, J.B. v5p0266c2s
v5p0577c1s v6p0143c2s
Baillie, M.H. v5p0272c1s
Baillie-Grohman, F. and
Baillie-Grohman, W. ... v6p0245c1s
v6p0304c1s
Baillie-Grohman, W. and
Baillie-Grohman, F. ... v6p0245c1s
v6p0304c1s
Baillie-Grohman, W.A. v2p0374c2s
v4p0020c2s v4p0095c2m v4p0486c2s
v4p0514c2s v4p0551c2s v5p0008c1s
v5p0033c2s v5p0093c1s v5p0100c2s
v5p0101c1s v5p0212c1s v5p0216c1s
v5p0240c2s v5p0248c1s v5p0276c2s
v5p0318c1s v5p0360c2s v5p0362c2s
v5p0488c2m v5p0547c1m v5p0547c2s
v5p0555c2s v5p0597c1s
Baillie-Grohman, W.A. et al.
v4p0030c2s
Baillie-Hamilton, Mary A.. v5p0364c2s
Baillie-Scott, M.H. v5p0223c2s
v6p0201c2s
Baillot, E.P. v6p0192c1s
Bailward, W.A. v6p0110c1s
Baily, F. v1p0459c1s
Bain, A. v1p0259c1m
v1p0262c2s v1p0271c2s v1p0304c1s
v1p0342c1s v1p0385c1s v1p0417c1s
v1p0427c1m v1p0436c2s v1p0447c2s
v1p0467c1s v1p0625c1s v1p0648c2m
v1p0723c2s v1p0819c1s v1p0826c2s
v1p0839c1m v1p0843c1m v1p0843c2s
v1p0868c1s v1p0889c2s v1p0993c2s
v1p1004c2m v1p1005c1m v1p1016c2s
v1p1055c2s v1p1062c1s v1p1177c2s
v1p1178c1s v1p1217c2s v1p1222c1s
v1p1235c1s v1p1277c2s v1p1305c2s
v1p1410c1s v1p1410c2m v2p0147c1s
v2p0273c1s v2p0289c2s v2p0438c2s
v2p0456c1s v2p0466c1s v3p0024c1s
v3p0136c2s v3p0150c2s v3p0264c2s
v3p0331c2s v3p0413c2s v3p0451c2s
v4p0130c1s v4p0421c1s v4p0447c1s
v4p0465c1s v4p0486c1s
Bain, A. and Barnett, P.A.
v3p0140c2s
Bain, B. v5p0196c1m
Bain, C. v1p0693c1s
Bain, C.W. v5p0042c1s
v5p0121c2m
Bain, G.G. v3p0343c1s
v3p0442c2s v4p0129c2s v4p0148c2s
v4p0155c1s v4p0201c2s v4p0402c2s
v4p0482c2s v4p0556c1s v5p0133c1s
v5p0252c2s v5p0589c2s v6p0311c2s
Bain, G.McK. v3p0471c2s
Bain, H.F. v5p0339c1s
v5p0437c1s v6p0251c1s v6p0667c2s
v6p0671c2s
Bain, J. v5p0333c2s
v6p0097c1s
Bain, J. et al. v5p0334c1s
Bain, J., jr. v3p0066c1s
v3p0249c1s v4p0329c2s v5p0333c1s
v5p0474c1s
Bain, J.W. v5p0570c1s
Bain, Mrs. v4p0188c1s
Bain, Prof. v1p1000c1s
Bain, R. v4p0242c1s
Bain, R.N. v3p0187c1s
v3p0336c1m v4p0045c2s v4p0050c1s
v4p0221c1s v4p0261c1s v4p0548c2s
v5p0055c1s v5p0207c1s v5p0240c2s
v5p0309c2s
Bain, R.V. v4p0443c2s
Bainbridge, E. v4p0173c2s
v4p0553c1s v5p0108c2s
Bainbridge, J. v5p0271c1s
Bainbridge, W.F. v1p0121c1s
Baines, A.C. v3p0045c2m
v4p0060c1s
Baines, E. v1p1428c2s
Baines, J.A. v4p0091c2s
v4p0170c1s v4p0278c2m v4p0280c1s
v4p0280c2s v4p0428c1s v5p0099c2m
v5p0248c1s v5p0284c2s v5p0285c2s
v5p0570c1s v6p0266c1s v6p0270c2s
v6p0313c1s v6p0314c2s v6p0324c1m
Baines, T. v2p0004c2s
v2p0008c2s v2p0024c2s v2p0034c2s
v2p0067c1s v2p0139c1s v2p0203c2s
v2p0460c2s v6p0671c1s v6p0678c2s
Bair, J.H. v6p0209c2s
v6p0318c2s
Baird, A. v4p0425c1s
v5p0433c2s
Baird, A., Sir v6p0508c2s
Baird, C.M. v1p0946c2s
Baird, C.W. v1p0329c1s
v1p0765c1s v1p1046c1s v2p0120c1s
v2p0352c2s
Baird, Dr. v1p1353c2s
Baird, E.M. v6p0104c1s
Baird, F. v5p0365c2s
v5p0436c2s
Baird, G. v5p0227c2s
Baird, G.D. v6p0433c1s
Baird, G.J. v1p0529c1s
Baird, G.W. v1p0502c1s
v1p0919c2s v2p0136c2s v2p0157c1s
v3p0213c2s v3p0278c2s v4p0028c1m
Baird, H.C. v1p0223c2s
v1p0486c2s v1p0860c1s v1p1026c2s
v1p1044c2s v1p1057c1s v1p1163c2s
v3p0032c1s v3p0152c2s
Baird, H.M. v1p0025c2s
v1p0056c2s v1p0115c1s v1p0151c1s
v1p0328c2s v1p0388c1s v1p0402c2s
v1p0524c2s v1p0552c1m v1p0552c2s
v1p0553c1s v1p0554c1s v1p0601c1s
v1p0770c1s v1p0889c1s v1p0892c2s
v1p0907c2s v1p0921c1s v1p0950c2s
v1p0965c1s v1p0996c1s v1p1124c1s
v1p1142c2s v1p1157c2m v1p1301c2s
v2p0442c1s v3p0073c1s v3p0164c1s
v3p0216c2s v3p0418c2s v4p0265c2s
v4p0327c2s v4p0477c2s
Baird, J.H. v1p0096c2s
Baird, J.W. v6p0171c1s
Baird, R. v1p0243c1s
v1p0316c1s v1p0331c1s v1p0479c2s
v1p0490c1s v1p0518c1s v1p0741c2s
v1p0855c1s v1p0920c2s v1p0930c1s
v1p1043c2s v1p1270c2s v1p1356c1s
v1p1357c1s
Baird, S.F. v1p0136c2s
Baird, S.F. and Baird, W.M.
v1p0136c2s
Baird, S.J. v1p0097c1s
v1p0230c1s v1p0278c1s v1p1042c1s
v1p1047c2s
Baird, W. v1p0043c1s
v1p0519c1s v1p0681c1s v1p0780c1s
v1p0896c1s v1p1019c2s v1p1060c1s
v1p1223c2m v1p1305c2s v1p1346c1s
v1p1391c1s v4p0606c1s v5p0281c1s
v5p0613c1s v6p0130c2s
Baird, W.M. and Baird, S.F.
v1p0136c2s
Baird-Huey, H.J. v4p0298c1s
Bairnsfather, P.R. v6p0646c1s
v6p0653c1s
Bairnsfather, P.R., Lt.-Col.
v6p0329c2s
Bakeman, F.W. v2p0438c1s
Baker, A. v2p0273c1s
Baker, A.A. v1p0688c1s
Baker, A.F. v3p0032c2s
Baker, A.G. v6p0433c1s
Baker, A.J. v4p0194c1s
Baker, A.L. v6p0012c1s
v6p0030c1s v6p0199c2s v6p0251c1m
v6p0435c1s
Baker, A.L. and Andrews, W.S.
v6p0394c2s v6p0612c1s
Baker, A.R. v1p0406c2s
v1p0648c2s v2p0320c2s v2p0338c1s
v3p0167c2s
Baker, Abby G. v6p0551c1s
v6p0696c2s
Baker, B. v1p0104c2s
v1p0377c1s v1p0922c1s v2p0055c2s
v2p0212c2s v3p0158c2m v4p0404c2s
Baker, B. and Fowler, J. . v2p0135c1s
v3p0158c2s
Baker, B., Sir v3p0391c1s
Baker, B.R. v1p0970c2s
Baker, B.S. v6p0333c2s
Baker, C. v6p0338c1s
Baker, C.A. v5p0074c1s
Baker, C.Collins v6p0200c1s
Baker, C.D. v3p0056c1s
Baker, C.F. v6p0228c2s
v6p0502c1s
Baker, C.S. v1p1075c2s
v5p0134c1s
Baker, D.W. v4p0235c1s
Baker, E. v3p0180c1s
v6p0159c1s v6p0516c1s
Baker, E., Mrs. v1p0245c2s
Baker, E.A. v5p0335c2s
v6p0058c1s v6p0108c1s v6p0290c2s
v6p0372c1s
Baker, E.B. v1p0383c2s
v5p0482c2s
Baker, E.B. and Baker, M.N.
v6p0569c2s
Baker, E.C. v6p0568c2s
Baker, E.H. v3p0121c1s
v3p0351c1s
Baker, E.J. v3p0030c2s
Baker, E.M. v6p0347c1s
Baker, E.N. v4p0415c1s
Baker, E.P. v2p0198c1s
Baker, Ernest A. v6p0168c2s
v6p0345c1s
Baker, F. v2p0024c1s
v6p0279c1s v6p0376c2s
Baker, F.A. v6p0485c1s
Baker, F.C. v4p0377c1s
v5p0382c1s v5p0393c2s v6p0390c2s
v6p0440c1s v6p0524c1s v6p0674c2s
Baker, F.G. v5p0247c1s
Baker, F.H. v2p0019c2s
v3p0094c1s
Baker, F.L. v3p0037c1s
Baker, F.T. v6p0514c2s
Baker, G.A., jr. v1p0878c2s
Baker, G.B. v3p0257c1s
v3p0353c2s v6p0018c1s
Baker, G.E. v1p0006c1s
v1p0556c1s v1p1181c2s v1p1396c2s
v2p0396c1s v2p0466c2s
Baker, G.F. v4p0230c1s
Baker, G.H. v5p0335c2s
Baker, G.P. v3p0077c2s
v3p0427c1s v4p0304c2s v5p0155c2m
v6p0081c2s v6p0137c1s v6p0180c2m
v6p0542c2s v6p0664c2s
Baker, G.P., jr. v2p0035c1s
v2p0153c1s v3p0056c1s v3p0141c2s
v3p0274c2s
Baker, G.S. v1p0177c1s
v2p0083c2s
Baker, G.S., Sir v5p0246c1s
v5p0316c2s
Baker, H. v3p0009c2s
v3p0050c1s v4p0521c1s
Baker, H.A. v4p0376c2s
Baker, H.B. v1p0081c1s
v1p0089c2s v1p0098c1s v1p0140c1s
v1p0141c2s v1p0227c1s v1p0256c1s
v1p0485c2s v1p0510c1s v1p0584c1s
v1p0602c2s v1p0863c1s v1p0943c2s
v1p0944c1m v1p0970c2s v1p1183c2s
v1p1190c1s v1p1261c2s v1p1284c2s
v1p1300c2m v1p1410c1s v2p0031c2m
v2p0037c2s v2p0080c2s v2p0093c1s
v2p0094c2s v2p0198c2s v2p0239c2s
v2p0261c1s v2p0269c2s v2p0283c1m
v2p0287c2s v2p0288c1s v2p0297c2m
v2p0321c1s v2p0345c2s v2p0416c2m
v2p0436c2m v2p0437c1s v2p0445c1s
v3p0090c1s v3p0264c2s v3p0344c1s
v3p0371c2s v4p0162c2s v4p0340c1s
v6p0379c2s v6p0663c1s
Baker, H.Barton v5p0251c2s
Baker, H.C. v5p0279c1s
Baker, H.F. v1p0094c1s
v1p0094c2s v4p0178c1s
Baker, H.G.A. v6p0528c2s
Baker, H.L. v2p0067c2s
v2p0232c1s
Baker, H.N. v2p0029c1s
Baker, H.S. v3p0378c1s
v4p0156c2s
Baker, H.T. v6p0289c2s
v6p0352c2s v6p0353c2s
Baker, H.W. v1p0133c2s
v1p0886c1s v1p1031c2s
Baker, H.W., Mrs. v1p1068c1s
Baker, I. v5p0274c2s
Baker, I.A. v5p0508c1s
Baker, I.O. v1p0491c1s
v2p0213c2s v3p0288c2m
Baker, Ida A. v5p0325c2s
Baker, Ira O. v3p0159c1m
v3p0399c2s
Baker, Isadore v5p0305c1s
Baker, J. v2p0040c2s
v2p0102c1s v3p0054c1s v3p0100c2s
v3p0188c2s v3p0243c1s v3p0324c2s
v3p0325c2s v3p0341c2s v3p0372c1s
v3p0373c1s v3p0379c1s v4p0446c2s
v4p0449c1s v4p0565c2s v5p0404c1s
v6p0069c2s v6p0258c2s
Baker, J.C. v6p0009c2s
Baker, J.E. v3p0271c1s
v6p0591c1s
Baker, J.F. v3p0053c1s
Baker, J.G. v2p0154c2s
v5p0089c2s
Baker, J.G. and Muller, M.
v2p0409c1s
Baker, J.H. v4p0123c1s
v4p0171c2s v4p0257c1s v6p0190c2s
Baker, J.O. v2p0416c1s
Baker, Jas. v3p0050c2s
Baker, K.W. v6p0644c1s
Baker, L. v6p0475c2s
v6p0501c2s
Baker, L.R. v4p0226c2s
Baker, L.W. v2p0208c1s
Baker, M. v2p0271c2s
v3p0442c1s v4p0009c2s v4p0157c1s
v4p0381c1s v4p0593c2s v5p0073c2s
v5p0228c2m v5p0609c1m v5p0621c1s
v6p0512c2s
Baker, M. and Hubbard, G.G.
v5p0228c2s
Baker, M. and Ogden, H.G.. v3p0417c1s
Baker, M.A. v3p0307c1s
Baker, M.A. et al. v2p0312c1s
Baker, M.N. v5p0105c1s
v5p0119c2s v5p0407c1s v5p0622c2m
Baker, M.N. and Baker, E.B.

v6p0569c2s
Baker, M.S. v5p0105c2s
Baker, Marcus v6p0570c2s
Baker, Minnie S. v5p0466c1s
Baker, Mrs. v2p0336c2s
Baker, O. v5p0061c1s
Baker, O.S., Mrs. v1p0717c1s
Baker, R. v1p0438c2s
v1p0692c2s v4p0563c2s v6p0263c2s
v6p0308c1s v6p0370c1s
Baker, R.B. v1p0069c2s
v1p0364c1s v1p0369c1s
Baker, R.H. and Todd, D. . v6p0188c1m
Baker, R.M. v6p0329c2s
Baker, R.S. v5p0004c1m
v5p0010c1m v5p0036c1s v5p0041c1s
v5p0052c1s v5p0071c2s v5p0074c1s
v5p0082c2s v5p0094c1s v5p0230c2m
v5p0232c1s v5p0232c2s v5p0235c2s
v5p0253c2s v5p0263c2s v5p0275c2s
v5p0330c2s v5p0338c2s v5p0386c2s
v5p0417c2s v5p0496c1s v5p0507c1s
v5p0551c2s v5p0555c1s v5p0561c1s
v5p0597c2s v5p0603c2s v5p0604c2s
v5p0619c1s v5p0627c2s v5p0631c2s
v5p0639c1s v5p0643c2s v6p0001c1s
v6p0090c1s v6p0139c1s v6p0185c1s
v6p0203c1s v6p0231c2s v6p0232c2s
v6p0277c1m v6p0281c1s v6p0289c1s
v6p0315c2s v6p0355c2s v6p0356c1m
v6p0356c2s v6p0359c1s v6p0400c2s
v6p0418c2s v6p0425c2s v6p0429c1s
v6p0434c2s v6p0448c2s v6p0454c1s
v6p0460c1s v6p0528c1m v6p0528c2s
v6p0529c1s v6p0530c2m v6p0540c1s
v6p0551c2s v6p0566c1s v6p0567c2s
v6p0602c2s v6p0607c1s v6p0631c1s
v6p0661c1s v6p0711c2m
Baker, R.S. and Lake, S. . v5p0027c2s
Baker, Ray S. v4p0100c1s
v5p0027c2s v6p0391c1s
Baker, S. v2p0177c2s
v2p0288c1s v5p0291c2s v5p0511c2s
v5p0519c1s
Baker, S., Sir v1p0935c1s
v1p1070c1s v3p0401c1s
Baker, S.W. v1p0757c2s
v1p1207c1s v1p1386c1s v2p0135c1s
v3p0004c2s v3p0430c1s
Baker, S.W., Sir v2p0134c1s
v3p0212c2s
v3p0268c1s
Baker, S.W., Sir and Vambery, A.
v2p0129c1s
v2p0380c2s
Baker, Samuel, Sir v2p0410c1s
Baker, T. v1p0736c2s
v2p0052c2s v2p0464c1s v3p0353c1s
v3p0386c1s v3p0451c2s v6p0492c1s
Baker, T.B.L. v1p0315c2s
v1p1090c2s
Baker, T.J.L. v1p0527c1s
Baker, T.S. v5p0258c1s
Baker, T.W. v4p0477c2s
Baker, V. v5p0365c2s
v5p0542c1s v5p0624c2s v6p0686c1s
Baker, W. v1p1250c2s
Baker, W.H. v1p0161c2s
Baker, W.J. v4p0357c2s
Baker, W.M. v1p0324c2s
v1p0593c1s v1p0824c1s v1p0874c2s
v1p0878c1s v1p0900c2s v1p0904c2s
v1p0908c2s v1p1084c2s v1p1087c2s
v1p1203c1s v1p1227c2s v1p1273c1s
v1p1296c2s v1p1375c1s v2p0150c1s
v2p0267c1s v2p0436c1s
Baker, W.S. v1p0425c2s
v3p0245c2s v3p0455c2m v3p0456c1s
v4p0015c2s v4p0244c2s v4p0611c2m
v5p0620c2s
Baker-Penoyre, J. v6p0491c2s
Baker-Penoyre, J. and
Hopkinson, J.H. v6p0409c2s
Bakewell, A. v3p0245c2s
Bakewell, C.M. v5p0154c1s
v5p0383c2s v5p0455c1s v5p0485c1m
v6p0032c2s v6p0202c2s v6p0412c2s
v6p0418c2s v6p0554c1s v6p0644c2s
Bakewell, Charles M. v5p0411c1s
Bakewell, J.H. v4p0430c1s
v6p0313c1s
Bakewell, R. v1p0919c2s
v1p1147c1s
Bakewell, R.H. v3p0180c2s
v4p0401c2s v6p0266c2s v6p0553c2s
Bakewell, T. v1p0326c2s
Bakewell, T.W. v1p0145c2s
v1p0146c2s v1p0213c1s v1p0403c2s
v1p0442c1s v1p1248c2s
Balair, O. v3p0009c1s
Balalchano, Z.de v6p0200c2s
Balbirnie, J. v3p0202c2s
Balcarres, Lord v5p0541c2s
Balch, A. v2p0290c1s
v2p0332c2s v3p0064c2m v3p0303c1s
v4p0085c1s
Balch, C.L. v1p0190c1m
Balch, E. v3p0023c1s
v3p0039c1s v3p0080c1s v3p0142c1s
v3p0196c2s v3p0315c1s v3p0320c2s
Balch, E.G. v4p0452c1s
v6p0596c2s
Balch, E.S. v4p0385c1s
v4p0498c1s v5p0022c1s v5p0278c2m
v5p0566c1s v5p0631c1s v6p0005c2s
v6p0023c2m v6p0182c1s v6p0253c2s
v6p0609c2s v6p0639c1s
Balch, E.W. v1p0322c1s
Balch, Edwin S. v6p0023c1s
v6p0698c2s
Balch, Edwin Swift v6p0023c1s
Balch, Eliz. v6p0338c2s
Balch, Emily G. v3p0421c1s
Balch, F.N. v5p0163c1s
Balch, F.V. v1p1342c2s
Balch, J. v1p0648c1m
Balch, S.W. v4p0110c2s
v4p0483c1s
Balch, T. v1p0272c2s
v1p1192c2m v2p0064c2s
Balch, T.W. v6p0010c1m
v6p0591c2s v6p0629c1s
Balch, W.F. v1p0087c2s
Balch, W.R. v2p0338c2s
v2p0347c1s v2p0385c1s
Balch, W.S. v1p0361c2s
v1p1106c1s v1p1355c2s v2p0106c2s
Balcomb, J.T. v2p0229c1s
Balcombe, E. v1p0895c1s
Bald and Mactear v1p1147c1s
Baldacci, L. v2p0230c2s
Baldgh, F. v2p0371c1s
Baldock, J.S. v3p0180c1s
Baldry, A.L. v4p0001c1s
v4p0003c2s v4p0030c2s v4p0233c2s
v4p0304c2s v4p0486c1s v4p0519c2s
v4p0550c1s v5p0029c1s v5p0030c2s
v5p0031c1m v5p0033c2s v5p0036c2s
v5p0039c1s v5p0049c1s v5p0094c2s
v5p0104c2s v5p0121c1s v5p0134c1s
v5p0156c1s v5p0168c1s v5p0170c1m
v5p0240c2s v5p0256c1s v5p0263c1s
v5p0294c1s v5p0309c1m v5p0330c1s
v5p0332c2s v5p0345c1s v5p0345c2s
v5p0346c1m v5p0352c1s v5p0352c2s
v5p0359c2s v5p0370c1m v5p0385c1s
v5p0385c2s v5p0399c2s v5p0413c2s
v5p0433c2s v5p0435c1s v5p0448c2s
v5p0458c1s v5p0465c2s v5p0487c1m
v5p0488c2s v5p0499c1s v5p0509c1m
v5p0516c1m v5p0524c2s v5p0538c2s
v5p0545c2s v5p0557c2s v5p0563c2m
v5p0598c2s v5p0615c1s v5p0622c2s
v5p0623c1s v5p0625c2s v5p0639c1s
v6p0084c2s v6p0126c2s v6p0182c2s
v6p0233c1s v6p0279c2s v6p0294c2s
v6p0303c2s v6p0422c2s v6p0427c2s
v6p0499c1s v6p0526c1s v6p0541c2m
v6p0553c1s v6p0553c2s v6p0643c2s
v6p0662c2s v6p0686c1s v6p0691c1s
v6p0696c1s v6p0712c2s
Baldry, Alfred lys v5p0013c1s
Baldwin, A., Mrs. v4p0576c2s
v5p0135c2s v5p0211c1s v5p0503c1s
Baldwin, A.C. v1p0099c1s
v1p0492c2s
Baldwin, A.H. v1p0049c1s
v1p0101c2s v1p0181c2s v1p0202c2s
v1p0245c2s v1p0247c1s v1p0270c2s
v1p0327c1s v1p0328c1s v1p0346c2s
v1p0394c1s v1p0456c1s v1p0457c1s
v1p0458c1s v1p0471c2s v1p0542c1s
v1p0564c2s v1p0565c2s v1p0573c1s
v1p0587c1s v1p0708c2s v1p0758c2s
v1p0770c2s v1p0773c2s v1p0784c1s
v1p0799c1s v1p0880c1s v1p0933c1s
v1p0962c2s v1p0989c1s v1p1009c2m
v1p1035c1s v1p1110c2s v1p1210c1s
v1p1240c1s v1p1309c1s v1p1323c1m
v1p1327c1s v1p1336c1s v1p1375c2s
v6p0646c1s
Baldwin, A.S. v2p0445c2s
v5p0507c1s v5p0622c2s
Baldwin, A.W. v1p0066c1s
Baldwin, B.A. v1p0087c2s
Baldwin, C. v1p0236c1s
v1p1148c2s
Baldwin, C.C. v2p0087c2s
v2p0320c1m v2p0460c2s v2p0473c1s
v3p0463c1m v4p0248c1s
Baldwin, C.G. v6p0087c1s
Baldwin, C.S. v4p0483c1s
v6p0136c2s v6p0207c1s v6p0256c2s
Baldwin, Clara F. v6p0370c2s
Baldwin, D.P. v5p0031c1s
Baldwin, DeF. and Gooch, F.A.
v5p0002c2s
Baldwin, E. v4p0098c1s
Baldwin, E.B. v5p0027c1s
v5p0443c1s
Baldwin, E.F. v4p0224c1s
v4p0431c2s v5p0054c2s v5p0095c2s
v5p0172c1s v5p0263c1m v5p0348c2s
v5p0430c2s v5p0450c2s v5p0461c1s
v5p0490c1s v5p0566c2s v5p0602c2s
v5p0605c2s v5p0623c1s v6p0086c1s
v6p0104c2s v6p0475c2s v6p0678c1s
v6p0687c1m v6p0703c2s
Baldwin, E.F. et al. v5p0558c1s
Baldwin, E.H. v5p0132c1s
v5p0262c1s v5p0340c2s v6p0245c2s
v6p0451c1s
Baldwin, E.I. v6p0373c1s
Baldwin, E.T. v5p0069c2s
v5p0154c2s
Baldwin, Emma V. v6p0084c1s
v6p0372c2s v6p0469c2s
Baldwin, Evelyn B. v5p0625c1s
Baldwin, F. v3p0169c2s
Baldwin, F.C. v6p0419c1s
Baldwin, F.S. v5p0126c2s
v5p0297c1s v5p0351c2s v5p0537c2s
v6p0256c1s v6p0319c2s v6p0573c1s
Baldwin, F.S. et al. v5p0446c1s
Baldwin, G.A. v6p0484c2s
Baldwin, H. v1p0181c1s
v1p0214c2s v1p0314c1s v1p0503c1s
v1p0731c1s v1p0749c2s v1p0875c2s
v1p1262c2s v4p0537c1s v6p0183c2s
Baldwin, H.D. v5p0406c2s
Baldwin, H.deF. v5p0407c1s
Baldwin, H.P. v4p0251c1s
Baldwin, J. v1p0067c1s
v3p0022c2s v3p0295c1s v3p0441c2s
Baldwin, J.A. v6p0605c1s
Baldwin, J.B. v1p1345c2s
v1p1399c1s v1p1418c2s
Baldwin, J.D. v1p0050c1s
v1p0543c2s v1p0653c2s
Baldwin, J.F. v6p0153c1s
v6p0352c1m v6p0518c1s
Baldwin, J.G. v1p0187c2s
v1p0463c2s v1p0567c2s
Baldwin, J.H. v6p0022c1s
v6p0289c1s v6p0569c1s v6p0628c1s
Baldwin, J.L. v6p0341c2s
Baldwin, J.M. v3p0053c1s
v3p0207c2s v3p0215c2s v3p0271c1s
v3p0348c2m v3p0414c2s v4p0015c2s
v4p0046c2s v4p0103c1m v4p0103c2s
v4p0130c1m v4p0135c2s v4p0140c1s
v4p0170c2s v4p0179c1s v4p0190c2s
v4p0191c2s v4p0196c2s v4p0221c2s
v4p0255c1s v4p0272c1s v4p0274c2s
v4p0284c1m v4p0286c1s v4p0381c2s
v4p0436c2s v4p0439c1s v4p0454c1s
v4p0464c2m v4p0465c1s v4p0465c2s
v4p0474c1m v4p0484c1s v4p0507c2s
v4p0528c1s v4p0541c1s v4p0555c2s
v4p0574c1s v5p0043c2s v5p0076c2m
v5p0196c1s v5p0198c1s v5p0293c2s
v5p0325c1s v5p0514c1s v5p0519c1m
v5p0534c2s v5p0535c2s v5p0546c1s
v6p0221c1s v6p0249c2s v6p0307c2s
v6p0383c1s v6p0414c1m v6p0418c2s
v6p0513c1s v6p0522c1s
Baldwin, J.M. and Bosanquet, B.
v6p0307c2s
Baldwin, J.M. and Ladd, G.T.
v4p0130c1s v4p0190c2s
Baldwin, J.M. and Shaw, W.J.
v4p0364c2s
Baldwin, J.S. v1p0455c2s
Baldwin, J.W. v3p0404c2s
Baldwin, James v4p0505c2s
Baldwin, L. v1p1373c1s
v1p1429c1s v3p0459c2s v4p0590c1s
Baldwin, M. v3p0122c2s
v5p0147c1s v5p0463c1s v6p0333c1s
v6p0696c1s
Baldwin, M.M. v3p0113c1s
v3p0455c2s v3p0464c2s
Baldwin, M.R. v1p1028c2s
Baldwin, N. v4p0195c1s
Baldwin, Nelson v4p0314c2s
Baldwin, O.H. v6p0419c1s
Baldwin, R.S. v3p0063c2s
v4p0635c1s
Baldwin, R.S., jr. v3p0305c1s
Baldwin, S.E. v1p0572c2s
v1p0730c2s v1p1245c1s v1p1358c1s
v2p0481c2s v3p0011c2s v3p0105c2s
v3p0178c1s v4p0019c1s v4p0322c2s
v4p0592c1s v4p0592c2s v4p0597c1s
v5p0001c2s v5p0003c2s v5p0126c1s
v5p0126c2s v5p0142c1s v5p0155c1s
v5p0293c2s v5p0386c1s v5p0525c2s
v5p0562c2s v5p0600c2s v5p0602c1s
v5p0628c2s v6p0012c2s v6p0147c2s
v6p0151c1s v6p0324c1s v6p0364c2s
v6p0634c1s
Baldwin, S.L. v2p0079c1s
v2p0322c2s
Baldwin, S.L., Mrs. v5p0111c1s
Baldwin, S.P. v6p0450c1s
Baldwin, T. v1p0014c2s
v1p0016c1s v1p0290c2s v1p1176c1s
v1p1181c1s
Baldwin, T.T. v6p0281c2s
Baldwin, W. v1p0162c1s
v1p1261c1s
Baldwin, W.A. v6p0247c1s
v6p0573c2s
Baldwin, W.B. v4p0116c1s
Baldwin, W.C. v2p0283c1s
v2p0396c2s
Baldwin, W.E. v3p0243c1s
v3p0259c2s v4p0120c1s v4p0411c1s
v4p0561c2s
Baldwin, W.H. v5p0403c1s

v6p0114c2s v6p0171c2s v6p0219c1s
Baldwin, W.H., jr. v5p0535c2s
Baldwin, W.W. v2p0083c1s
v5p0477c1s
Baldwin-Childe, Mrs. v3p0238c1s
Baldy, F.C. v5p0132c2m
Bale, E. v4p0322c2s
v4p0422c1s v4p0631c1s v5p0137c1m
Balestier, C.W. v2p0065c1s
Balestier, J. v1p0167c2s
v1p0283c1s v1p0790c2s
Balestier, W. v2p0155c1s
v3p0094c2s v4p0051c1s v4p0088c2s
v4p0476c2s
Balestier, W. and Kipling, R.
v3p0297c2s v4p0395c1s
Balet, J.C. and Defrance, L.
v6p0338c2s
Balfour, A. v1p0744c1s
v6p0007c2s v6p0151c2s v6p0210c1s
v6p0623c2s v6p0689c1s v6p0701c2s
Balfour, A.J. v1p0426c2s
v1p0435c1s v1p0630c1s v1p1321c1m
v2p0040c1s v2p0091c1s v2p0147c1s
v2p0244c1s v2p0347c2s v2p0348c1s
v4p0239c1s v4p0261c2s v4p0273c2s
v4p0335c1s v4p0394c2s v5p0117c1s
v5p0412c1s v6p0082c1s v6p0407c1s
Balfour, Alice v4p0006c1s
Balfour, Andrew v5p0096c1s
Balfour, C.L. v1p0448c1s
Balfour, D.M. v1p0015c1s
v1p0173c1s v1p0629c1s v1p0652c2s
v1p0759c1s v1p0963c1s v1p1077c1s
v1p1078c1s v1p1146c2s v3p0051c1m
v3p0176c2s v3p0393c2s
Balfour, David v4p0549c1s
Balfour, E. v1p0359c2s
v1p0578c2m v1p0608c1s v1p0632c2s
v1p1218c2s v3p0108c2s v3p0187c2s
v3p0260c2s v4p0159c2s v4p0218c1m
v4p0561c1s v5p0151c1s v5p0244c1s
v5p0244c2s v5p0251c1s v6p0589c2s
v6p0653c1s
Balfour, Edith v6p0327c2s
Balfour, F., Lady v4p0340c1s
v6p0705c1s
Balfour, F.H. v3p0177c1s
v4p0105c2s v4p0374c1s v5p0277c2s
Balfour, Frances, Lady ... v4p0240c1s
v6p0577c2s
Balfour, G. v1p0473c2s
v1p0474c2s v1p0545c1s
Balfour, H. v4p0150c2s
v5p0202c1s v5p0531c1s v5p0532c2s
v6p0235c2s
Balfour, H.H. v5p0322c2s
Balfour, M.C. v4p0333c1s
Balfour, Miss v3p0097c1s
Balfour, R. v6p0403c2s
Balfour, R.G. v2p0027c2s
v3p0359c2s
Balfour, T.G. v1p0578c2s
v1p0604c2s v1p0873c1s
Balfour-Murphy, K. v5p0021c1s
v6p0102c1s
Balfour of Burleigh v3p0381c1s
Balfour of Burleigh, Lord. v2p0391c1s
Balgarnie, F. v4p0275c1s
Balgarnie, R. v2p0084c2s
v2p0385c1s v2p0409c1s v3p0042c1s
Balkwill, F.W. v6p0225c1s
Ball, A.E. v5p0352c2s
Ball, A.H. v5p0083c2s
Ball, A.M. v4p0420c1s
Ball, B.W. v1p0008c2s
v1p0465c2s v1p0810c2s v1p0841c2s
v1p0891c2s v1p0980c1s v1p1425c2s
v4p0517c2s v4p0568c2s
Ball, C.B. v6p0638c1s
v6p0648c2s
Ball, C.J. v2p0024c2s
v2p0030c2s v2p0042c2m v2p0133c1s
v2p0204c1s v3p0228c1s v3p0228c2s
Ball, C.M. v4p0292c1s
Ball, E.S. v1p1101c2s
Ball, G.J. v6p0219c1s
Ball, H. v5p0050c2s
Ball, H.W. v5p0437c1s
Ball, J. v1p0937c1s
v1p1273c1s v5p0315c2s
Ball, J., jr. v2p0223c2s
Ball, J.Rodney v6p0221c2s
Ball, J.W. v1p0205c2s
v1p0603c1s v1p0700c2s v4p0488c2s
v5p0380c1s
Ball, L.C. v1p0087c2s
Ball, M.A. v2p0313c1s
Ball, M.V. v4p0041c1s
Ball, Mrs. v1p0958c2s
Ball, R. v4p0089c1s
v4p0132c2s v4p0272c2s v4p0445c1s
v4p0492c1s v4p0556c2m v5p0363c1s
v4p0307c1s v4p0381c1s v4p0445c1s
v4p0597c1s v5p0152c1s
Ball, R., Sir v3p0330c2s
v4p0034c1m v4p0036c1s v4p0071c2s
v4p0218c2s v4p0256c1m v4p0310c1s
v4p0331c1s v4p0357c2s v4p0370c2s
v4p0406c2s v4p0597c1s v5p0035c1s
v5p0174c2s v5p0372c1s v6p0038c1s
v6p0614c1s
Ball, R.S. v1p0828c2s
v1p1243c2s v2p0026c1s v2p0095c2s
v2p0112c2s v2p0127c1s v2p0139c1s
v2p0180c2s v2p0185c1s v2p0213c2s
v2p0296c2m v2p0308c2s v2p0425c1s
v2p0440c2s v3p0024c2s v3p0238c1s
v3p0382c1s v3p0391c1s v4p0306c2s
Ball, R.S., jr. v5p0013c2s
v5p0226c2s
Ball, R.S., Sir v4p0167c1s
v4p0265c1s v4p0633c1s
Ball, Robert v4p0246c1s
v4p0403c1s v6p0354c2s v6p0446c1s
Ball, Robert, Sir v4p0034c1s
Ball, Robert S.
v3p0415c1s
Ball, S. v4p0314c1s
v4p0450c1s v4p0533c1s v4p0534c1m
v5p0193c1s v5p0283c2s v5p0535c1s
v5p0536c1m v6p0041c2s v6p0100c1s
v6p0682c1s
Ball, S. and Hirst, F.W. . v5p0536c2s
Ball, S.H. v6p0139c1s
Ball, T.S. v4p0174c1s
Ball, V. v1p0349c1s
v3p0088c2s v3p0212c1s v3p0237c2s
v3p0280c2s v4p0154c2s v4p0163c1s
v4p0333c2s v4p0576c2s v5p0303c2s
Ball, V. and Maskelyne, N.S.
v3p0237c2s
Ball, W. v5p0181c2s
Ball, W.D. v3p0068c1s
Ball, W.E. v3p0324c1s
v3p0365c2s v5p0309c1s v5p0446c2s
v6p0258c2s
Ball, W.E. and Hughes, H.P.
v4p0589c2s
Ball, W.H. v4p0221c1s
Ball, W.P. v4p0286c1s
v4p0513c2s
Ball, W.S. v6p0438c1s
Ball, W.T.W. v4p0293c1s
v4p0519c1s
Ball, W.V. v6p0204c2s
Ballagh, J.C. v1p0679c1s
v4p0529c2s v4p0606c1s v5p0403c2s
v5p0532c2s v5p0602c1s v5p0613c1s
v6p0597c1s
Ballaigne, C. v4p0388c2s
Ballantine, E. v1p0684c1s
Ballantine, H. v3p0299c2s
Ballantine, J.W. v2p0039c2s
v2p0042c1s v3p0043c1s
Ballantine, S. v3p0244c2s
Ballantine, Serj. v2p0250c2s
Ballantine, W.G. v2p0191c1s
v3p0041c2s v3p0042c2s v3p0043c1s
v3p0371c1s v5p0402c2s v6p0341c1s
Ballantyne, A. v3p0109c2s
v3p0140c1s v4p0011c1s v5p0201c2s
v5p0452c2s
Ballantyne, A.G. v1p0102c2s
Ballantyne, E. v3p0122c1s
v3p0293c2s v4p0038c2s v4p0544c1s
Ballantyne, R.M. v1p0930c1s
Ballantyne, T. v1p0438c2s
Ballantyne, W.G. v6p0137c2s
Ballard, A. v2p0348c2s
v5p0189c2s v5p0504c2s v5p0639c2s
v6p0178c2s v6p0396c2s
Ballard, Anna v4p0571c2s
Ballard, C.R. v4p0063c1s
v4p0159c1s
Ballard, F. v1p1152c1s
Ballard, F.A. v1p1033c2s
Ballard, F.W. v1p1193c2s
v1p1438c2s
Ballard, H.H. v3p0005c2m
v3p0029c1s v3p0185c2s v3p0380c1s
Ballard, H.O. and Crosby, W.O.
v4p0520c2s
Ballard, I.H. v3p0038c2s
v3p0250c1s v3p0267c2s v5p0349c2s
Ballard, J. v6p0465c2s
Ballard, J.P. v2p0222c2s
Ballard, M.A. v5p0203c2s
v6p0432c2s
Ballard, M.L. and Townsend, B.L.
v3p0424c2s
Ballard, R.L. v6p0031c1s
Ballard, S. v5p0302c1s
v5p0302c2s v5p0303c2s v6p0036c1s
Balle, C. v4p0269c1s
Ballen, F.T. v5p0547c2s
Ballentine, E. v1p0681c1s
Ballentine, F.S. v5p0068c1s
Balliet, H.S. and Rosenberg, C.C.
v6p0198c1s
Balliet, L. v5p0326c1s
Balliet, T.M. v4p0432c2s
v5p0512c2s
Balliet, T.M. and Aldrich, G.I.
v6p0581c2s
Ballin, A.S. v2p0249c1s
v2p0249c2s v3p0242c2s
Ballin, Ada S. v2p0439c2s
Ballinger, J. v5p0094c1s
v5p0333c2s v6p0374c1s v6p0375c1s
v6p0586c1s v6p0656c2s
Ballinger, L. v5p0028c1s
Balliol, M.A. v6p0495c1s
v6p0653c1s
Ballore, Montessus de v6p0185c2s
Ballou, A. and Tolstoi, Count
v3p0306c2s
Ballou, E. v1p1355c1s
Ballou, G.H. v1p0061c2s
v1p0959c1s
Ballou, H. v1p0019c1s
v1p0127c2s v1p0496c2s v1p0528c2s
v1p0689c1s v1p1060c1s v1p1293c2s
Ballou, H., jr. v1p0356c1s
v1p1406c2s
Ballou, H., 2d v1p0016c2s
v1p0048c1s v1p0089c2s v1p0127c1s
v1p0127c2s v1p0128c2s v1p0130c1m
v1p0130c2s v1p0131c2s v1p0198c2s
v1p0201c2s v1p0248c2s v1p0293c1s
v1p0424c1s v1p0441c1s v1p0471c1s
v1p0471c2s v1p0496c1m v1p0529c1s
v1p0577c1s v1p0687c1s v1p0700c1s
v1p0700c2s v1p0813c2s v1p0832c2s
v1p0840c1s v1p0898c1s v1p0904c1s
v1p0921c1s v1p0923c2s v1p0998c2s
v1p1083c2s v1p1089c1s v1p1147c2s
v1p1200c1s v1p1208c1s v1p1355c2m
v1p1407c2s
Ballou, H., 2d et al. v1p1355c2s
Ballou, H.S. v5p0161c1s
v6p0387c2s v6p0631c2s
Ballou, L.W. v2p0169c2s
v2p0370c2s v2p0403c2s
Ballou, M. v1p0346c2s
v1p0426c1s v1p1064c2s v1p1101c1s
v1p1175c1s
Ballou, W.H. v1p0394c1s
v2p0002c2s v2p0047c1s v2p0159c1m
v3p0010c2s v3p0014c2s v3p0228c1s
v3p0277c2s v3p0316c1s v3p0414c1s
v3p0416c1s v5p0228c2s v5p0509c2m
v5p0630c2s v6p0593c1s
Ballou, W.H. and Proctor, R.A.
v2p0193c1s
Balmain, Count v6p0442c1s
Balmer, R. v2p0472c1s
Balmes, J. v2p0353c1s
v2p0372c1s
Balmforth, R. v4p0240c1s
v4p0243c2s v4p0564c2s v5p0093c1s
v5p0588c2s v6p0118c2s v6p0165c2s
v6p0310c1s
Balogh, F. v2p0212c1s
v6p0303c2s
Balsillie, D. v4p0240c1s
Baltimore, J.M. v2p0109c1s
v3p0059c1s v3p0314c1s v5p0171c1s
v5p0338c2s v5p0491c1s v6p0099c2s
v6p0315c1s v6p0524c1s v6p0562c1s
Baltzell, W.J. v5p0530c2s
v5p0539c1m
Baltzley, J.B. v1p0769c1s
Baltzly, J.M. v1p0649c2s
Baly, G.H. v2p0213c2s
Baly, M.F. v4p0391c2s
Balz, H. v5p0607c1s
Balzac, E.de v5p0575c2s
Balzac, H. v1p0422c2s
v2p0099c2s v2p0284c2s
Balzac, H.de v1p1277c2s
v1p1365c1s v2p0026c2s v3p0146c2s
v3p0195c1s v4p0186c1s v5p0217c2s
v6p0482c2s
Balzac, M.de v1p0790c1s
Balzani, U., Count v1p0743c1s
Bamber, E.F. v4p0175c2s
Bamber, G. v4p0497c1s
Bamberger, L. v3p0171c1s
v3p0171c2s v3p0303c1s
Bambord, M.E. v2p0243c1s
Bamburgh, W.C. v6p0085c1s
Bamfield, J.H. v2p0159c2s
Bamford, M.E. v2p0216c1s
v4p0081c1s
Bamford, Mary E. v2p0077c1s
Bamfylde, H. v3p0002c1s
Bancroft, C.F. v5p0182c2s
Bancroft, C.F.P. v4p0438c2s
v4p0512c1s v4p0512c2s
Bancroft, C.P. v3p0216c2s
Bancroft, E.A. v6p0486c1s
Bancroft, E.P. v4p0118c2s
Bancroft, Edgar A. v6p0529c1s
v6p0531c2s
Bancroft, F.T. v3p0251c2s
v3p0386c2s v3p0442c2s v4p0368c1s
v4p0379c2s v4p0516c2s v5p0003c2s
v5p0103c1s v5p0384c1s v5p0521c2m
v5p0548c2s v5p0552c2s v5p0560c2s
v5p0574c1s v6p0366c1s v6p0521c1s
v6p0606c2s
Bancroft, F.J. v3p0192c2s
Bancroft, F.J. and Bancroft, R.M.
v2p0078c2m v3p0059c1s v3p0078c1s
Bancroft, G. v1p0029c2s
v1p0033c1s v1p0091c1s v1p0217c1s
v1p0262c1s v1p0373c2s v1p0482c2s
v1p0485c1s v1p0530c1s v1p0530c2s
v1p0539c1s v1p0554c2s v1p0555c1m
v1p0555c2s v1p0572c2s v1p0584c2s

v1p0587c1s v1p0726c2s v1p0732c2s
v1p0815c2s v1p0876c1s v1p1047c2s
v1p1124c2s v1p1156c2s v1p1208c2s
v1p1219c2s v1p1378c2s v1p1387c2s
v2p0011c1s v2p0088c1s v2p0140c1s
v2p0148c2s v2p0394c2s v3p0002c2s
Bancroft, H. v6p0660c2s
Bancroft, H.H. v1p0259c2s
v3p0063c1m v3p0091c1s v3p0196c2s
v3p0277c1s v3p0446c1s v4p0083c2s
v6p0120c1s
Bancroft, J.M. v2p0478c1s
v3p0389c1s
Bancroft, Jane v3p0372c1s
Bancroft, R.H. v1p0259c1s
v1p0978c1s
Bancroft, R.M. and Bancroft, F.J.
v2p0078c2m v3p0059c1s v3p0078c1s
Bancroft, S. v6p0181c2s
v6p0513c2s
Bancroft, W.A. v4p0115c2s
v6p0621c1s
Bancroft, W.D. v3p0018c2s
v6p0112c1s v6p0199c2s
Bancroft, Wilder D. v6p0112c1s
Band, H.Meade v6p0284c1s
Bandelier, A.F. v1p0832c1s
v1p0960c2s v1p0993c1s v1p1216c1s
v2p0017c1m v2p0018c2s v2p0063c1s
v2p0287c1s v2p0307c2s v2p0312c1m
v2p0457c1s v3p0069c2s v3p0223c2s
v3p0241c2s v3p0243c1s v3p0277c1s
v3p0317c1s v3p0339c1s v3p0351c1s
v6p0014c2s v6p0159c2s v6p0186c1s
v6p0312c1s v6p0594c2s v6p0598c1s
v6p0605c2s v6p0648c1m v6p0656c2s
Bandini, A. v6p0414c1s
Bandini, Don Arturo v6p0246c1s
Bandini, H.E. v3p0063c2s
v4p0083c2s v4p0084c1s v4p0325c2s
v4p0420c2s v4p0539c2s v4p0621c2s
Banditz, Sophus v5p0052c2s
Bandmann, D.E. v1p1242c1s
v1p1261c2s
Banfield, F. v2p0390c2s
v3p0149c1s v3p0380c2s v4p0124c2s
v4p0244c1s v4p0288c1s v4p0346c1s
v4p0434c1s v4p0469c1s
Banfield, T.C. v1p1061c1s
Banga, H. v5p0147c1s
Bangs, C.E. v5p0463c1s
Bangs, Dr. v1p1093c2s
v1p1287c1s
Bangs, E.L. v1p0584c2s
v1p0886c1s
Bangs, E.M. v6p0386c1s
v6p0710c2s
Bangs, H.M. v3p0120c1s
Bangs, J.K. v4p0089c2s
v4p0362c1s v4p0397c2s v4p0417c1s
v4p0475c1s v5p0015c2s v5p0359c2s
v5p0390c2s v5p0566c1s
Bangs, J.K. et al. v6p0222c2s
v6p0461c2s
Bangs, L.B. v6p0676c1s
Bangs, N. v1p0252c1s
v1p0257c1s v1p0311c1s v1p0698c1s
Bangs, O. v4p0353c1s
v5p0321c2s v5p0357c2m
Bangs, O. and Zappy, W.R.. v6p0068c1s
Bangs, W.M. v1p1358c2s
v1p1410c2s v6p0279c1s
Bangs, W.McK. v3p0147c1s
v3p0280c2s v4p0269c2s
Banim, M. v1p0266c2s
v2p0124c2s v3p0166c2s
Banister, H. v1p0843c2s
Banister, J.A. v5p0139c1s
Banister, J.M. v5p0488c2s
Banker, C.A. v3p0280c2s
Bankes, G.N. v5p0131c2s
Bankes, W.J. v1p0960c2s
Banking, B.M. v4p0369c2s
Banks, Adeline M. v5p0546c1s
Banks, C.E. v1p0499c2s
v2p0051c1s v2p0069c2s v2p0272c2m
v2p0284c2s v2p0421c2s v3p0033c2s
v4p0262c1s v4p0304c1s v4p0358c1s
v4p0602c2s v5p0171c1s v5p0363c2m
v5p0594c1s v5p0612c2s
Banks, Carrie W. v5p0258c2s
Banks, D.C. v5p0210c1s
v6p0346c2s
Banks, E. v6p0069c1s
v6p0703c2s
Banks, E.J. v6p0162c2s
v6p0165c2s v6p0210c1s v6p0362c1s
v6p0470c1s v6p0583c1s v6p0583c2s
v6p0675c1s
Banks, E.L. v4p0123c1s
v4p0180c2s v4p0627c1s v5p0002c2s
v5p0065c1s v5p0182c1s v5p0275c1s
v5p0311c1s v5p0402c2s v5p0637c1s
v6p0215c1s
Banks, E.L. et al. v4p0267c1s
Banks, E.M. v6p0251c2s
Banks, Edgar J. v6p0069c1s
Banks, Eliz. v6p0584c2s
Banks, F.D. v4p0137c1s
Banks, G. v2p0033c2s
Banks, G.L. v1p0815c1s
Banks, J. v1p0428c2s
Banks, J., Sir v1p0608c1s
v1p0708c1s v1p0773c1s v1p1122c2s
v1p1273c2s
Banks, J.S. v4p0573c1s
v5p0374c2s v5p0447c1s v5p0465c2s
v5p0469c1s v5p0483c2s
Banks, L. v1p0943c2s
Banks, L.A. v3p0173c2s
v6p0692c1s
Banks, N. v6p0325c1s
Banks, N.H. v4p0011c1s
v4p0217c2s v4p0372c2s v4p0624c2s
Banks, W.B. v4p0438c1s
Bannard, H.C. v3p0311c2s
Bannatyne, D. v1p1431c2s
Bannerman, D. v6p0555c2s
Bannerman, D.D. v2p0064c2s
v2p0352c2s
Bannerman, Frances v5p0067c2s
Banning, H.E. v3p0464c2s
v4p0404c2s
Banning, H.G., Mrs. v4p0605c1s
Banning, Kendall v6p0089c1s
v6p0110c2s
Bannister, A. v3p0063c2s
Bannister, H. v1p0343c2s
v1p0816c1s v1p1056c1s v1p1161c2s
Bannister, H.M. v1p0055c1s
v1p0358c2s v1p0507c1s v6p0022c2s
Bannister, R. v3p0061c2s
v3p0075c2s v3p0090c1m v3p0279c1s
v3p0414c1s v3p0421c2s v3p0465c2s
Bannister, S. v1p0918c2s
Bansemer, C.S. v5p0075c2s
Banta, D.D. v2p0341c2s
v3p0436c2s
Banvard, J. v1p0007c2s
v1p1013c2s
Bapst, G. v4p0355c2s
v4p0392c2s v4p0584c1s v6p0406c2s
Baquero, E.G. v5p0224c1s
Baquero, E.Gomez de v5p0400c1s
Bar, A.De v1p0459c1s
Bar, G.B. v3p0150c2s
Barail, Count Du v5p0587c2m
Barakatullah, M. v6p0200c1s
v6p0392c1s v6p0560c1s
Barakatullah, Mohammed ... v4p0293c2s
v4p0537c1s v6p0330c1s
v6p0645c2s
Baranowsky, M.T. v6p0343c2s
Barba, J. v1p1251c1s
Barba, W.P. v6p0616c1s
Barbas, Brother v2p0439c1s
v3p0120c1s v3p0242c1s v3p0344c1s
v3p0378c2s
Barbe, L. v2p0154c1s
v2p0257c2s v2p0278c2s v2p0361c1s
v2p0382c2s v2p0462c2s v2p0465c1s
v2p0466c1s v3p0270c1s v3p0271c1s
v4p0096c1s
Barbe, Louis v4p0246c2s
Barbeck, W. v1p0213c1s
v1p0494c2s
Barbee, W.J. v1p0289c1s
v1p0440c1s v1p0441c1s v1p0684c1s
v1p1147c2s v2p0183c2s v3p0287c1s
Barbek, C.A. v5p0559c2s
Barber, A.D. v1p0842c2s
v4p0359c2s v5p0456c1s
Barber, A.E. v1p1307c2s
Barber, A.W. v4p0579c2s
v6p0122c2s v6p0363c2s
Barber, C.A. v4p0555c1s
v4p0576c2s v5p0559c2s
Barber, E.A. v1p0279c1s
v1p0494c1s v1p0498c2s v1p0638c2s
v1p0867c2m v1p1063c2m v1p1255c2s
v1p1269c2s v1p1360c1s v2p0012c1s
v2p0020c1s v2p0071c1s v2p0219c2s
v2p0220c1s v2p0300c1s v2p0342c2s
v2p0351c1s v2p0442c1s v3p0341c1s
v4p0106c1m v4p0345c2s v4p0455c1m
Barber, F.C. v1p0872c1s
Barber, F.M. v3p0147c1m
v3p0187c1s v3p0390c2s v6p0623c1s
Barber, H. v3p0295c2s
v4p0361c2s
Barber, H.H. v1p0001c1s
v1p0034c2s v1p0119c2s v1p0141c1s
v1p0148c1s v1p0156c2s v1p0297c2s
v1p0330c1s v1p0402c2s v1p0450c1s
v1p0501c1s v1p0589c2s v1p0599c2s
v1p0610c1s v1p0615c2s v1p0635c1s
v1p0715c1s v1p0810c2s v1p0865c1m
v1p0983c2s v1p0985c1s v1p1012c2s
v1p1059c1s v1p1116c1s v1p1221c2s
v1p1261c1s v1p1341c1s v1p1341c2s
v1p1369c2s v4p0314c2s v4p0329c1s
v4p0330c1s
Barber, J.H. v5p0214c1s
Barber, La V.A. v6p0424c1s
Barber, R. v1p0737c1s
Barber, S. v2p0027c2s
v2p0386c1s v3p0206c2s v3p0257c2s
v4p0371c2s v4p0520c2s v4p0557c2s
v5p0099c1s v5p0427c1s
Barber, T. v2p0210c1s
v2p0470c2s
Barber, W. v1p1321c2s
v5p0529c1s
Barber, W.J. v2p0390c1s
Barber, W.N. v1p0120c2s
v1p0613c1s
Barbier, M. v1p0894c2s
Barbier, M.E. v1p1304c2s
Barbier, Pierre v5p0272c1s
Barbieri, Isabella De v4p0384c1m
Barbour, A.M. v6p0147c1s
v6p0617c2s
Barbour, B.J. v1p1373c1s
Barbour, C. v3p0449c2s
Barbour, D. v4p0144c1s
v4p0279c1s
Barbour, E.H. v3p0433c1s
v4p0146c1s v5p0043c1s v6p0234c2s
v6p0542c1s
Barbour, E.H. and Fisher, C.A.
v6p0091c2s
Barbour, E.H. and Torrey, J., jr.
v3p0312c2s
Barbour, E.H. and Ward, H.B.
v6p0432c2s
Barbour, F.A. v3p0013c2s
v4p0183c2s v5p0160c2s v5p0191c1s
Barbour, F.C.W. v3p0008c2s
v3p0068c2s v3p0309c1s v4p0059c1s
v4p0311c1s v4p0539c1s v6p0012c1s
v6p0331c2s
Barbour, Fannie C.W. v4p0355c1s
v6p0456c2s
Barbour, I.H. v4p0210c1s
Barbour, J.F. and Pratt, E.A.
v5p0215c1s
Barbour, J.H. v5p0060c1m
Barbour, M. v5p0239c2s
Barbour, R.H. v6p0004c2s
v6p0038c1s v6p0124c2s v6p0183c1s
v6p0286c2s v6p0310c2s v6p0353c1s
v6p0469c2s v6p0487c1s v6p0649c2s
v6p0678c2s
Barbour, R.W. v2p0004c2s
v2p0268c2s
Barbour, Ralph H. v6p0079c1s
v6p0294c1s
Barbour, T. v6p0599c1s
Barbour, T.S. v2p0322c2s
Barbour, W.M. v1p0201c1s
v1p0657c1s v1p1262c1s v2p0299c1s
v2p0351c2s v2p0481c2s
Barca, C.de la v1p0787c1s
Barcena, M.de la v2p0273c2s
Barcenas, J.J.D. v5p0608c2s
Barck, C. v6p0609c1s
Barclay, A. v6p0543c2s
Barclay, Armiger v6p0003c1s
Barclay, B.S. v1p0112c1s
Barclay, E. v3p0067c2s
v4p0550c2s v4p0577c2s
Barclay, J.W. v1p0279c1s
v2p0298c2s v6p0396c2s v6p0526c1s
Barclay, R. v3p0158c1s
v4p0230c1s
Barclay, S. v5p0152c1s
Barclay, T. v4p0157c2s
v4p0232c2s v4p0394c1s v5p0096c1s
v5p0131c1s v5p0212c2s v5p0216c2m
v5p0217c1s v5p0243c1s v5p0468c2s
v6p0007c1s v6p0026c2m v6p0236c1s
v6p0253c1s v6p0277c2s
Barclay, W.C. v6p0513c2s
Barclay, W.S. v6p0029c2s
v6p0072c2s v6p0307c1s v6p0394c2s
v6p0646c2m
Barcroft, J. v6p0082c2s
Barcroft, Joseph v6p0082c2s
Barczinsky, A. v3p0023c1s
v3p0173c1s v3p0208c1s v3p0451c1s
v4p0231c2s v4p0484c1s
Bard, E.F. and Maltbie, M.R.
v5p0105c1s
Bard, T.R. v6p0480c2s
Bard, W.H. v6p0010c2s
Barde, F.S. v6p0465c1s
Bardeen, C.W. v3p0377c2s
v3p0475c2s v4p0126c2s v5p0179c2s
v5p0512c1s
Barden, G. v4p0335c2s
Bardoux, J. v6p0238c1s
Bardsley, C.W. v2p0172c2s
Bardsley, H.J. v5p0130c2s
v6p0192c1s
Bardsley, J. v1p0415c1s
Bardsley, J.W. v3p0077c2s
v3p0389c2s
Bardwell, W.A. v3p0249c2s
v3p0293c1s v3p0382c1s v4p0330c1s
Bare, H.B. v5p0014c1s
v5p0061c2s v6p0152c2s v6p0644c2s
Barff, F.S. v1p0225c1s
v1p0663c2s v1p1023c1s v2p0161c1s
v3p0068c1s v3p0089c1s v3p0092c2s
v3p0174c2s
Barff, Prof. v1p0664c1s
Barfield, S. v3p0355c1s
Bargen, O.Van v6p0132c1s
Barger, B.L. v6p0276c2s
Barger, S. v1p0266c2s

Barham, C. v4p0119c1s
Barham, C.M. v3p0004c2s
Barham, C.N. v3p0027c1s
v3p0230c2s v3p0266c1s v3p0268c2s
v3p0349c1s v3p0430c2s v4p0271c2s
v4p0320c1s v4p0339c1s
Barham, F. v1p0581c2s
v1p1408c1s
Barham, G.B. v6p0679c1s
Barham, R.H. v1p0308c2s
v1p0534c1s v1p0682c1s v1p0886c2s
v1p1185c2s
Barham, R.H.D. v1p0627c1s
v1p0861c2s
Barhydt, D.P. v6p0640c1s
Barl, E.V. v3p0126c2s
Barine, A. v3p0081c2s
v3p0327c1s v4p0313c1s
Baring, E. v2p0217c2s
Baring, F. v4p0158c2s
v5p0165c1s v5p0264c2s v5p0405c2s
v5p0426c2s v5p0631c2s v6p0282c2s
v6p0460c1s
Baring, M. v6p0526c1s
v6p0561c1s
Baring-Gould, S. v1p0103c2s
v1p0105c2s v1p0208c2s v1p0237c2s
v1p0257c1s v1p0561c1s v2p0146c1s
v2p0170c2s v2p0172c1s v2p0204c2s
v2p0261c1s v3p0016c1s v3p0016c2s
v3p0048c1s v3p0090c1s v3p0124c1s
v3p0142c1s v3p0144c2s v3p0226c1s
v3p0313c1s v3p0329c2s v3p0366c2s
v3p0461c2s v3p0465c1s v4p0049c1s
v4p0050c1s v4p0113c2s v4p0114c1s
v4p0148c1s v4p0205c2s v4p0218c1s
v4p0242c2s v4p0312c1s v4p0313c1s
v4p0327c2s v4p0389c2s v4p0412c2s
v4p0456c2s v4p0467c1s v4p0480c1s
v4p0500c2s v4p0550c1s v4p0580c1s
v5p0022c2s v5p0127c2s v5p0131c2s
v5p0154c2s v5p0195c1s v5p0305c2s
v5p0311c2s v5p0339c1m v5p0418c1s
v5p0441c1s v5p0495c1s v5p0496c2s
v5p0528c1s v5p0566c1s v5p0612c1s
v5p0640c1s v6p0108c2s v6p0506c1s
v6p0598c2s v6p0616c2s
Barker, A. v2p0350c2s
v3p0416c2s v5p0082c2s
Barker, A.D. v2p0130c2s
Barker, A.R.R. v2p0395c1s
v2p0448c2s
Barker, A.W. v6p0148c1s
v6p0632c2s
Barker, C. v1p0220c1s
v1p0341c1s v1p0368c2s v1p0994c2s
v6p0611c1s
Barker, C.A. v3p0310c1s
v3p0357c1s
Barker, C.M. v1p0764c2s
v6p0548c1s
Barker, Canon et al. v4p0372c2s
Barker, D.W. v6p0132c1s
Barker, E. v3p0026c2s
v3p0320c1s v3p0360c2s v3p0372c1s
Barker, E.C. v6p0597c1s
v6p0632c1s v6p0640c1m
Barker, E.D. v3p0352c2s
Barker, E.F. v5p0291c1s
v5p0481c2s
Barker, E.H. v1p1129c2s
v3p0007c2s v3p0168c1s v4p0009c2s
v4p0087c2s v4p0162c1s v4p0162c2s
v4p0380c1s v4p0435c1s v4p0469c2s
v4p0492c2s v4p0513c2s v4p0564c1s
v4p0582c2s v4p0598c2s v4p0603c2s
v5p0153c2s
Barker, E.H.L. v2p0441c1s
Barker, E.M. v6p0590c1s
Barker, E.P. v6p0641c1s
Barker, E.R. v2p0005c1s
v2p0064c2s v2p0167c2s v2p0268c2s
v2p0324c2s
Barker, F.C. v5p0618c1s
Barker, G.F. v1p0077c1s
v1p0077c2s v1p0225c2s v1p0382c1s
v1p0498c2m v1p0745c2s v1p0955c1s
v1p0996c2s v1p1233c2s v2p0067c2s
v2p0354c2s v3p0156c2s v5p0010c1s
v5p0340c1s v5p0571c1s v6p0644c2s
Barker, G.F. and Rowland, H.A.
v1p0399c2s
Barker, G.F.R. v3p0461c1s
Barker, G.R. v1p0166c1s
Barker, H. v5p0484c1s
v6p0143c2s v6p0212c1s
Barker, H.J. v3p0204c2s
v3p0379c1s v3p0466c2s
Barker, I.B. v1p0149c1s
Barker, J. v5p0372c2s
Barker, J.E. v6p0205c1s
v6p0253c1s v6p0255c1s v6p0267c2s
v6p0294c1s v6p0336c2s v6p0556c1s
Barker, J.Ellis v6p0192c1s
Barker, J.H. v2p0257c2s
v2p0280c1s v5p0223c1s
Barker, J.S. v1p0673c2s
v1p0814c2s
Barker, L.D.S. v1p0887c2s
Barker, L.F. v6p0409c1s
v6p0576c1s
Barker, L.F. and Flexner, S.
v5p0444c2s
Barker, L.M. v1p0159c2s
Barker, Lady v1p0012c2s
v1p0013c1s v1p0436c2s v1p0701c1s
v1p0897c1m v1p1417c2s v2p0374c2s
Barker, M. v1p0160c1s
v1p0246c1s v4p0069c2s v4p0093c2s
v4p0111c1s v4p0119c2s v4p0136c2s
v4p0145c1s v4p0219c2s v4p0220c1s
v4p0249c2s v4p0416c1s v4p0624c1s
Barker, M.A. v1p1435c1s
Barker, M.A., Lady v1p0813c1s
Barker, M.E. v3p0139c2s
Barker, M.R. v1p0251c2s
v1p0970c2s
Barker, Mrs. v1p0166c1s
Barker, R. v1p0287c1s
v1p0970c2s v1p1178c2s
Barker, R., Mrs. v1p0253c1s
v1p0386c1s v1p0482c1s v1p0537c2s
v1p0597c1s v1p0845c1s v1p0863c1s
v1p0991c1s v1p1029c2s v1p1071c2s
v1p1126c2s
Barker, R.J., Mrs. v4p0148c2s
Barker, R.K. v5p0498c1s
Barker, R.M. v5p0097c2s
v6p0246c1s
Barker, S. v2p0138c1s
Barker, S.W. v1p0036c1s
Barker, Sale, Mrs. v1p0013c2s
Barker, T. v1p1379c2s
Barker, T.B. v1p0842c2s
Barker, V. v3p0139c1s
Barker, W. v1p0487c2s
v5p0289c2s v6p0016c1s v6p0162c1s
v6p0528c1s v6p0557c1s
Barker, W.C. v5p0105c1s
Barker, W.R. v1p0455c2s
Barkley, Flora E.S. v6p0325c2s
Barkley, T.J. v1p0248c2s
Barkly, H. et al. v2p0004c1s
Barksdale, F.N. v5p0096c1s
v6p0112c2s
Barkworth, T. v3p0029c1s
Barler, O.L. v6p0611c1s
Barley, W.F. v5p0007c2s
Barlow, A.E. v4p0322c1s
Barlow, A.E. et al. v5p0091c2s
Barlow, C.A.M. v6p0188c2s
Barlow, D. v1p0648c2s
Barlow, D.H. v1p0882c1s
Barlow, G. v4p0215c1s
v4p0293c1s v4p0544c1s v4p0562c1s
v6p0388c1s v6p0629c1s v6p0702c2s
Barlow, H. v1p1071c1m
Barlow, H.C. v1p1323c2s
v1p1324c1s
Barlow, J. v1p0573c2s
v5p0038c2s v5p0232c2s v5p0481c1s
v5p0629c1s v6p0169c1s v6p0218c2s
Barlow, J.R. v4p0284c1s
Barlow, Jane v4p0386c2s
v4p0603c1s v5p0066c1s v6p0167c1s
v6p0328c1s v6p0425c1s
Barlow, M. v5p0138c1s
v5p0175c1s v5p0245c1m v5p0247c2s
v5p0293c1s v5p0580c2s v5p0641c1s
v6p0188c2s v6p0367c1s
Barlow, P. v1p0664c2s
v1p1261c1s
Barlow, P.W. v1p0161c1s
v1p0195c2s v1p0522c2s v1p0919c2s
Barlow, W. v2p0108c2s
Barlow, W.H. v1p0104c2s
v1p0408c1s v1p0761c1s v1p0919c2s
Barmby, C. v1p1420c2s
Barmby, Cuthbert v5p0304c1s
Barmby, G. v1p0019c1s
v1p0140c2s v1p0267c1s v1p0286c1s
v1p0335c2m v1p0405c1s v1p0442c2s
v1p0969c2s v1p1002c2s v1p1021c2s
Barmby, J. v3p0209c1s
Barn, F. v2p0016c1s
Barnabas, J.H. v3p0195c1s
v4p0149c1s
Barnabel, F. v2p0001c2s
Barnaby, C.W. v6p0557c1s
Barnaby, H.C.G. v6p0529c2s
Barnaby, N. v5p0136c1s
Barnaby, N., Sir v5p0619c1s
v6p0337c1s
Barnaby, S.W. v2p0212c2s
v5p0253c1s v5p0643c2s
Barnam, G. v6p0257c1s
Barnard v2p0095c2s
Barnard, C. v1p0015c1s
v1p0047c1s v1p0048c2s v1p0174c2s
v1p0226c2s v1p0299c1m v1p0424c1s
v1p0463c1s v1p0493c1s v1p0599c2s
v1p0605c2s v1p0703c1s v1p0759c2s
v1p0996c2s v1p1198c2s v1p1290c1s
v1p1313c2s v2p0102c1s v2p0224c1s
v2p0344c2s v2p0432c2s v3p0089c1s
v3p0092c2s v3p0106c2s v3p0133c1s
v3p0134c1s v3p0216c1s v3p0253c1s
v3p0304c1s v3p0316c2s v3p0330c2s
v3p0340c2s v3p0352c2s v3p0356c1s
v3p0408c2s v3p0415c1s v3p0417c2s
v3p0462c1s v4p0064c1s v4p0168c2s
v4p0287c2s v4p0335c1s v4p0431c2s
v4p0467c1s v4p0487c1s v4p0507c1s
v4p0606c2s v5p0462c2s v5p0570c2s
v5p0571c2s v5p0574c1s v5p0616c1s
v6p0698c1s
Barnard, C. and Mayer, A.M.
v1p0747c2m
Barnard, C.F. v1p0218c2s
v1p0297c1s v1p0763c2s
Barnard, C.G. v4p0028c2s
Barnard, C.I. v1p0021c2s
v1p0116c2s v1p0395c1s v1p0395c2s
v1p0396c1m v1p0396c2s v1p0473c2s
v1p0478c1s v1p0668c1s v1p1060c2s
v2p0135c2s v5p0095c2s
Barnard, C.I. and Amos, S.
v1p0396c1s
Barnard, Charles v4p0316c1s
v4p0630c2s
Barnard, Charles and Flood, T.L.
v4p0179c2s
Barnard, D.D. v1p0046c2s
v1p0282c2s v1p0832c1m v1p0834c1s
v1p1028c2s v1p1169c2s v1p1287c1s
v1p1342c1s v1p1348c1s v1p1362c1s
v1p1405c1s
Barnard, E.E. v2p0014c1m
v2p0095c1m v2p0095c2m v2p0239c2s
v2p0285c1m v2p0308c2m v2p0319c1s
v2p0404c2s v2p0459c1s v3p0330c2s
v4p0033c2s v4p0037c2s v4p0126c2m
v4p0167c1s v4p0306c2m v4p0307c1s
v4p0357c2s v4p0358c1s v4p0371c1s
v4p0396c1m v4p0447c1s v4p0567c2s
v4p0637c1s v5p0174c2s v5p0227c2s
v5p0402c1s v5p0448c1s v5p0448c2s
v5p0453c2s v6p0596c2s
Barnard, E.E. and Wilson, H.C.
v2p0239c2s
Barnard, E.W. v4p0042c2s
v5p0282c1s v5p0418c1s
Barnard, Edith v6p0108c2s
v6p0211c1s v6p0248c2s v6p0534c2s
v6p0658c1s
Barnard, F. v5p0386c1s
Barnard, F.A.P. v1p0017c1s
v1p0077c1s v1p0189c1m v1p0275c1m
v1p0275c2s v1p0329c1s v1p0337c1m
v1p0398c2s v1p0579c2s v1p0831c1s
v1p0854c1s v1p0986c1s v1p1160c2s
v1p1198c2s v1p1440c2s v2p0131c1s
v2p0286c1s v3p0239c2s v3p0337c2s
v3p0442c1s
Barnard, F.A.P. et al. ... v2p0049c1s
v2p0131c2s v2p0353c1s
Barnard, H. v1p0223c2s
v1p0292c1m v1p0385c1s v1p0388c2s
v1p0389c1s v1p0389c2m v1p0486c1s
v1p0497c2s v1p0571c2s v1p0572c1s
v1p0731c1s v1p0910c2s v1p0925c2s
v1p0990c2s v1p1397c2s v1p1401c2s
v1p1417c1s
Barnard, J.E. v6p0046c2s
Barnard, J.E. and Carver, T.A.B.
v5p0449c1s
Barnard, J.E. and Macfadyen, A.
v5p0042c2s
Barnard, J.G. v1p0340c2s
v1p0469c1s v1p0564c2s v1p0570c2s
v1p0854c1m v1p0927c2s v1p0986c2s
v1p1075c2s v1p1310c1s v2p0194c1s
Barnard, J.L. v6p0071c1s
Barnard, L. v6p0358c1s
Barnard, P.L. v5p0461c2s
v5p0466c2s
Barnard, P.M. v5p0059c2s
Barnard, W.L. v6p0249c1s
v6p0363c2s v6p0395c2s
Barnard, W.S. v1p0835c1s
v1p0945c1s v1p1059c1s
Barnard, W.T. v2p0363c2s
v3p0031c2s v3p0215c1s v3p0353c2s
Barneby, J. v3p0112c2s
Barnes, A. v1p0037c1s
v1p0085c2s v1p0123c2s v1p0157c1s
v1p0180c2s v1p0241c2s v1p0242c2s
v1p0283c2s v1p0378c1s v1p0398c2s
v1p0421c2m v1p0433c2s v1p0847c1s
v1p0848c1s v1p0979c1s v1p0982c2s
v1p0997c1s v1p1001c1s v1p1044c1s
v1p1047c1s v1p1055c1s v1p1094c1s
v1p1200c1s v1p1302c1s v1p1304c2s
v3p0089c2s v3p0319c2s
Barnes, A.A.S. v6p0121c1s
v6p0439c2s v6p0596c2s
Barnes, A.M. v5p0068c2s
v5p0095c1m v5p0328c1s v5p0578c2s
v5p0591c2s
Barnes, A.S. v6p0003c1s
v6p0063c2m v6p0110c1s v6p0386c2s
v6p0478c2s v6p0548c2s v6p0700c1s
Barnes, B. v6p0217c1s
Barnes, C.E. v4p0064c1s
Barnes, C.M. v2p0466c1s
Barnes, C.M.S. v1p0293c2s
v1p1280c2s
Barnes, C.R. v4p0069c2s
v4p0070c1s v4p0503c1s v5p0073c1s
v5p0453c2s v5p0514c1s v6p0122c2s

v6p0540c2s
Barnes, C.W. v5p0239c1s
v5p0573c1s v6p0085c1s v6p0273c1s
v6p0538c1s
Barnes, D.L. v4p0337c2m
Barnes, E. v2p0372c1s
v3p0019c2s v4p0103c2s v4p0104c1s
v4p0171c1s v4p0467c2s v4p0516c2s
Barnes, E. and Barnes, M.. v5p0267c1s
Barnes, E. et al. v4p0104c1s
Barnes, E.W. v1p1023c2s
Barnes, Earl v5p0138c1s
v5p0472c2s
Barnes, F.E. v6p0323c2s
Barnes, G.A. v6p0695c1s
Barnes, G.F. v1p1181c1s
Barnes, G.H. v1p0472c2s
Barnes, G.N. v5p0584c2s
v6p0682c2s
Barnes, G.S. v6p0169c1s
Barnes, G.W. v1p1148c1s
Barnes, H. v1p1086c1s
v2p0472c1s
Barnes, H.E. v1p0646c2s
v1p0977c2s
Barnes, H.F. v4p0246c2s
Barnes, H.J. v2p0396c1s
v6p0540c2s
Barnes, H.W. v4p0304c1s
Barnes, J. v4p0216c1s
v4p0456c1s v4p0562c1s v4p0571c2s
v5p0006c1s v5p0068c1s v5p0160c2s
v5p0316c1m v5p0317c2s v5p0355c2s
v5p0408c1s v5p0465c1m v5p0490c2s
v5p0539c1s v5p0587c1s v5p0587c2s
v5p0588c1s v5p0588c2s v5p0589c1s
v5p0602c2s v5p0616c2s v5p0621c2s
v6p0054c1s v6p0345c2s v6p0467c2s
v6p0642c1s v6p0669c1s v6p0676c1m
v6p0676c2s v6p0693c1s
Barnes, J.A. v5p0056c1s
Barnes, J.E. v1p1096c2s
Barnes, J.N. v1p0932c2s
v1p1298c1s
Barnes, James v5p0327c1s
v6p0622c1s
Barnes, L.C. v4p0533c1s
v6p0008c1s
Barnes, L.C. et al. v4p0056c2s
Barnes, M. and Barnes, E.. v5p0267c1s
Barnes, M.C. v5p0269c1s
v6p0693c2s
Barnes, M.S. v3p0197c1s
v4p0258c2s v4p0259c1s v5p0088c2s
Barnes, P. v2p0155c2s
Barnes, S.G. v6p0323c2s
v6p0388c1s v6p0478c1s
Barnes, T.M., jr. v5p0631c1s
Barnes, T.W. v3p0232c2s
Barnes, W. v1p0098c2s
v1p0105c2s v1p0648c1s v1p0699c2s
v1p0938c1s v1p1013c2s v1p1022c1s
v1p1381c2s v2p0122c1s v3p0443c2s
Barnes, W.C. v3p0016c1s
v4p0544c2s
Barnes, W.E. v5p0057c1s
v5p0057c2m v5p0058c1s v5p0626c2s
v6p0062c1s v6p0062c2s
Barnes, W.H. v1p0229c1s
v1p0310c2s v1p0575c2s v1p0616c1s
v1p0719c2s v1p1275c1s
Barnes, W.R. v2p0140c1s
v2p0414c2s
Barnes, Will C. v5p0555c1s
Barnett, A.T. v5p0224c2s
Barnett, B.A. v4p0559c2s
v5p0101c1s
Barnett, C.T. v6p0432c2s
Barnett, Canon v5p0468c1s
v5p0635c1s
Barnett, E.A. v5p0121c1s
v6p0607c2s
Barnett, G.E. v5p0414c1s
v6p0050c2s v6p0378c1s v6p0404c2m
v6p0708c1s
Barnett, H.A. v2p0186c1s
Barnett, H.O. v1p1431c1s
v2p0023c2s v4p0104c1s v5p0512c1s
v6p0348c2s
Barnett, H.V. v4p0130c2s
v4p0143c1s v4p0161c1s v4p0218c2s
v4p0274c1s v4p0274c2s v4p0406c1s
v4p0418c1s v4p0444c1s v4p0493c1s
v4p0493c2s v4p0503c2s v4p0623c2s
v4p0631c1m v4p0634c1s
Barnett, H.W. v1p1366c2s
Barnett, Henrietta O. v6p0247c1s
v6p0279c1s
Barnett, I.W. v5p0351c2s
Barnett, J. v6p0641c1s
Barnett, J.F. v6p0174c2s
Barnett, M. v4p0550c2s
Barnett, M.J. v2p0017c2s
Barnett, P.A. v2p0134c1s
v2p0236c2s v2p0346c2s v3p0131c1s
v3p0264c1s v3p0429c2s
Barnett, P.A. and Bain, A.
v3p0140c2s
Barnett, R.C. v4p0410c2s
Barnett, R.W. v2p0033c1s
v2p0088c2s
Barnett, S. v1p0831c1s
Barnett, S., jr. v1p0859c1s
Barnett, S.A. v2p0083c2s
v2p0263c1s v2p0407c1s v2p0408c1s
v2p0455c2s v3p0434c2s v3p0441c1s
v3p0462c2s v4p0040c2s v4p0097c1s
v4p0112c2s v4p0166c1s v4p0306c1s
v4p0351c2s v4p0452c1m v4p0506c1s
v4p0557c2s v4p0590c2s v4p0598c1m
v5p0097c1s v5p0102c1s v5p0107c2s
v5p0269c1s v5p0273c1s v5p0345c1s
v5p0380c1s v5p0394c1s v5p0459c1s
v5p0521c1s v5p0605c2s v6p0109c1s
v6p0116c1s v6p0190c1s v6p0191c2s
v6p0573c2s v6p0665c1s
Barnett, S.A. and Brabazon, Lord
v2p0086c1s
Barnett, S.A. and
Westminster, Duke of .. v5p0311c2s
Barnett, S.A. et al. v4p0557c2s
Barnett, S.A., Mrs. v2p0367c2s
v3p0256c1s v6p0651c1s
Barnett, V.H. v6p0332c1s
Barnett-Smith, G. v5p0094c2s
Barney, C.N. v6p0178c1s
Barney, E.C. v4p0015c2s
v4p0627c2s
Barney, E.G. v2p0093c1s
Barney, J.D. v6p0070c1s
Barney, J.K. v3p0467c2s
Barney, J.K., Mrs. v3p0336c2s
Barnhurst, H.R. v5p0068c2s
Barnicoat, C.A. v6p0191c1s
v6p0468c2s v6p0532c2s v6p0589c2s
Barnicoat, Constance A. .. v6p0683c2s
Barnitz, P. v5p0031c1s
Barns, C. v3p0167c2s
v6p0230c2s
Barns, C.E. v4p0581c2s
v5p0272c2s
Barns, T. v6p0642c1s
Barnsley, S.H. v4p0186c2s
Barnstein, H. v5p0567c1s
Barnum, C.K. v4p0580c1s
Barnum, F. v4p0513c2s
Barnum, G. v6p0377c1s
Barnum, P.T. v3p0034c2s
v3p0091c2s v3p0138c2s v3p0139c1s
v3p0252c1s v3p0444c2s
Barnum, S.W. v1p0581c1s
Barnwell, J.G. v1p0206c1s
v1p1087c2s v1p1316c2s
Barnwell, R.G. v2p0114c1s
v2p0117c2s v2p0443c2s
Baron, A.H.N. v6p0675c2s
Baron, G.Le v4p0260c2s
Baron, Grace Le v6p0441c2s
Baron, J. v2p0182c1s
v5p0238c1s
Baron, R. v2p0030c1s
v2p0271c1s v2p0463c1s
Baroncelli, F.de v3p0367c2s
Barr, A. v2p0172c2s
v2p0200c1s v2p0246c2s v2p0404c2s
Barr, A.E. v1p0088c1s
v1p0330c1s v1p0582c1s v1p0884c1s
v2p0171c1s v2p0309c1s v2p0351c2s
v2p0397c1s v2p0398c1s v2p0409c2s
v3p0098c2s v3p0164c2s v3p0253c2s
v3p0257c2s v3p0367c1s v3p0473c1s
v4p0039c1s v4p0148c1s v4p0408c1s
v4p0408c2s v4p0459c2s v4p0534c2s
v4p0627c2s v5p0499c2s v5p0540c1s
Barr, A.E. et al. v3p0119c1s
v3p0269c1s
Barr, A.E., Mrs. v4p0202c2s
v4p0384c2s
Barr, A.F. v1p1297c1s
Barr, A.L. v2p0132c2s
Barr, Amelia E. v5p0213c1s
Barr, C.J. v6p0371c1s
v6p0372c2s
Barr, D. v6p0313c2s
Barr, E.A. v4p0449c2s
Barr, F. v4p0550c2s
Barr, J. v2p0196c1s
Barr, J.H. v4p0547c1s
v4p0547c2s v4p0586c2s
Barr, J.M. v3p0345c1s
v5p0448c1s v5p0450c2s
Barr, M. v2p0442c1s
Barr, M.W. v5p0107c1s
v5p0279c1m v5p0280c2s v6p0410c2s
Barr, Mrs. v2p0250c1s
Barr, R. v4p0012c1s
v4p0070c2s v4p0072c2s v4p0110c2s
v4p0149c2s v4p0159c1s v4p0160c1s
v4p0161c1s v4p0162c1s v4p0165c1s
v4p0196c1s v4p0198c2s v4p0253c2s
v4p0265c2s v4p0271c1s v4p0276c2s
v4p0307c2s v4p0310c2s v4p0366c2s
v4p0376c1s v4p0380c1s v4p0418c2s
v4p0447c1s v4p0475c2s v4p0482c2s
v4p0519c1s v4p0528c1s v4p0570c2s
v4p0588c1s v4p0589c1m v4p0590c2s
v4p0602c1s v4p0619c1m v4p0626c2m
v5p0003c1s v5p0025c1s v5p0030c1s
v5p0091c2s v5p0095c2s v5p0122c1s
v5p0139c2s v5p0228c1s v5p0233c1s
v5p0251c1s v5p0295c1s v5p0316c1s
v5p0316c2m v5p0322c1s v5p0347c1s
v5p0358c2s v5p0420c2s v5p0434c2s
v5p0578c2s v5p0605c2s v5p0634c1s
v6p0019c2s v6p0030c2m v6p0057c2s
v6p0096c2s v6p0098c1s v6p0179c1s
v6p0267c2s v6p0283c1s v6p0364c2s
v6p0393c1s v6p0619c2s v6p0667c2s
v6p0688c2s
Barr, R. and Crane, S. ... v6p0471c1s
Barr, R. and Whibley, C. . v6p0084c2s
Barr, R. et al. v5p0527c1s
Barr, R.D. v2p0297c2s
Barr, Robert v6p0179c2s
Barr, W. v5p0283c1s
v5p0609c2s v5p0635c2s
Barr, W.M. v4p0467c1s
v6p0304c2m v6p0392c2s v6p0688c1m
Barr, Walter v5p0325c2s
v6p0413c2s
Barracleugh, S.H. v5p0551c1s
Barraclough, F. v3p0288c1s
Barraclough, G. v1p0934c2s
v1p1005c1s
Barraclough, T. v5p0478c2s
Barrand, C.W. v6p0051c2s
v6p0276c1s
Barrass, E. v1p0204c1s
v2p0382c1s v3p0060c1s
Barratt, A. v1p1028c1s
Barratt, A. and Sidgwick, H.
v1p0394c1s
Barratt, M. v5p0053c2s
Barratt, R. v6p0676c2s
Barraud, A.R. v1p0377c1s
Barre, L. v2p0441c2s
Barreaux, J.V.des v1p1220c2s
Barrell, C.H. v6p0099c1s
Barrell, F.E. v5p0519c2s
Barrell, J. v6p0146c2s
Barrell, J.S. and Capen, S.B.
v3p0287c1s
Barrere, C. v1p0140c2s
v1p0345c2s v1p0424c2s v1p0477c1s
v1p0611c2s v1p0716c1s v1p0737c1s
v1p0808c1s v1p1010c2s v1p1117c1s
v1p1332c2s
Barres, Maurice v4p0423c2s
Barrett, A. v1p0426c2m
v4p0178c2s
Barrett, A.R. v4p0151c1s
v4p0213c2s
Barrett, B.F. v1p0684c2s
v1p0686c2s v1p1019c1s v1p1274c2s
v1p1275c1s
Barrett, D.C. v6p0366c2s
Barrett, D.M. v5p0105c2s
v5p0515c2s
Barrett, E.B. v1p0321c2s
Barrett, E.R. v1p0233c1s
v2p0079c1m
Barrett, E.W. v4p0077c1s
v4p0251c2s v4p0293c1s v4p0341c1s
Barrett, Ellen v6p0238c2s
Barrett, F. v1p0786c2s
v1p0856c2s v1p1335c2s
Barrett, F.T. v5p0336c1s
Barrett, G. v5p0564c2s
Barrett, G.C. v1p0317c1s
v3p0233c2s
Barrett, G.S. v2p0243c2s
v3p0342c1s
Barrett, J. v4p0033c1s
v4p0106c2s v5p0108c1s v5p0108c2s
v5p0109c2s v5p0110c1s v5p0112c1s
v5p0113c2s v5p0160c1s v5p0379c2s
v5p0427c1m v5p0444c1m v5p0445c2m
v5p0446c1m v5p0491c2s v5p0527c2s
v5p0602c1s v5p0628c1s v6p0029c2s
v6p0336c1s v6p0362c2s v6p0477c1s
v6p0544c2s v6p0592c2m v6p0666c1s
Barrett, J. et al. v5p0445c1s
Barrett, J.H. v1p0169c2s
v1p0179c1s v1p0201c2s v1p0202c1s
v1p0720c1s v3p0034c2s v4p0332c2s
Barrett, J.O. v1p1087c1s
Barrett, J.P. v2p0137c1s
Barrett, John v5p0088c2s
v6p0476c2s
Barrett, L. v1p0144c1s
v1p0468c2s v1p0908c1s v3p0122c1s
v3p0387c1s
Barrett, M. v1p0147c2s
v1p0337c1s v5p0482c1s v5p0505c1s
v5p0514c2s v5p0520c1s v5p0558c2s
v5p0625c2s v6p0045c1s v6p0127c2s
v6p0577c2s
Barrett, R.M. v5p0270c1s
v5p0313c1s
Barrett, Rosa M. v5p0297c1s
v6p0179c1s
Barrett, S. v1p0123c2s
v1p0266c2s v1p1275c1s v1p1341c2s
v1p1398c1s
Barrett, S.A. v6p0508c1s
Barrett, S.E. v6p0053c1s
Barrett, T. v6p0176c2s
Barrett, T.S. v3p0405c2s
Barrett, W. v3p0188c2s
v3p0404c2s

Barrett, W.F. v1p0307c2s
Barrett, W.F. v1p0073c2s
v1p0278c1s v1p0343c1s v1p0443c2s
v1p0502c1s v1p0524c1s v1p0580c2s
v1p0619c1s v1p0835c1s v1p0907c1s
v1p1177c2s v1p1232c1s v1p1291c1s
v1p1291c2s v2p0028c2s v2p0258c1s
v2p0272c1m v3p0348c1s v3p0418c2s
v6p0521c1s
Barrett, W.F. et al. v2p0440c1s
Barrett, W.G. v1p1379c2s
Barrett-Leonard, J. v4p0324c1s
Barrickman, J.M. v6p0599c1s
Barrie, J.M. v2p0192c1s
v3p0056c2s v3p0178c1s v3p0189c2s
v3p0237c1s v3p0254c1s v3p0274c2s
v3p0358c2s v3p0430c2s v4p0515c1s
v5p0086c2s v5p0552c2s v5p0582c1s
v5p0624c2s v6p0381c1s
Barrie, M.M. v6p0193c2s
v6p0240c1s
Barriger, J.W. v5p0558c2s
Barring, F.M.De v2p0165c1s
Barringer, C.L. v4p0482c1s
v4p0537c2s
Barringer, P.B. v5p0403c1s
Barringer, R. v1p1343c2s
Barringer, V.C. v1p1230c1s
Barrington, D. v1p0051c2s
v1p0200c1s v1p0205c1s v1p0226c2s
v1p0266c1s v1p0303c1m v1p0500c1s
v1p0642c2s v1p0700c2s v1p0885c1s
v1p1012c1s v1p1050c2s v1p1168c1s
v1p1372c1s v1p1376c1s v1p1380c2s
v1p1381c1s v1p1441c2s
Barrington, D. and Morrell, T.
v1p0026c1s
Barrington, E.I. v1p0064c1s
v2p0289c1s v2p0378c2s v2p0468c1s
v3p0451c1s
Barrington, M. v6p0074c1s
v6p0130c2s v6p0172c1s v6p0684c2s
Barrington, R., Mrs. v4p0476c1s
v5p0330c1s
Barrington, R.H., Mrs. ... v1p0713c2s
Barrington, Viscountess .. v6p0584c2s
Barrois, C. v1p0469c2s
v5p0614c1s
Barroll, H.H. v3p0345c1s
v4p0522c1s v5p0509c1s
Barron, A.J. v6p0651c1s
Barron, E. v6p0625c1s
Barron, E.A. v4p0068c1s
v4p0160c2s
Barron, G.B. v3p0433c2s
Barron, H., Sir v1p0453c1s
Barron, J. v1p0368c2s
Barron, J., Sir v1p1403c1s
Barron, J.A. v4p0322c1s
Barron, L. v6p0364c2s
v6p0552c1s
Barron, O. v5p0389c2s
Barrow, A.J. v4p0499c1s
Barrow, D.C., jr. v1p0512c2s
v1p0905c1s v2p0103c1s
Barrow, E. v6p0266c1s
Barrow, E.G. v4p0297c2s
v5p0303c1s v6p0186c2s
Barrow, F. v1p0081c2s
v1p0198c1s v1p0979c2s v1p1037c2s
v1p1069c2s v1p1197c1s
Barrow, F., Mrs. v1p1069c1s
Barrow, F.H. v6p0116c1s
v6p0508c2s
Barrow, G. v1p0566c1s
v4p0573c2s
Barrow, J. v1p0257c1s
Barrow, J., Sir v1p0007c2s
v1p0010c1s v1p0010c2s v1p0011c1m
v1p0011c2m v1p0012c1s v1p0012c2m
v1p0050c1s v1p0055c1m v1p0078c1s
v1p0078c2s v1p0104c1s v1p0107c2s
v1p0109c1s v1p0146c2s v1p0150c2s
v1p0231c1s v1p0368c2m v1p0395c1s
v1p0457c2m v1p0535c1s v1p0591c2m
v1p0611c1s v1p0614c1s v1p0633c2s
v1p0647c1s v1p0675c2s v1p0678c1s
v1p0678c2s v1p0713c1s v1p0800c2s
v1p0834c1s v1p0854c2s v1p0885c2s
v1p0913c2m v1p0921c2m v1p0927c2s
v1p0929c1m v1p0933c1s v1p0956c1s
v1p0975c1m v1p0991c1s v1p1024c1s
v1p1024c2m v1p1128c1s v1p1177c1s
v1p1324c1s v1p1378c2s v1p1441c2s
Barrow, Meta E. v2p0296c2s
Barrow, P.W. v5p0646c2s
Barrowman, J. v5p0124c1s
Barrows, A. v4p0402c2s
v6p0178c2s v6p0290c1s
Barrows, A.C. v6p0295c2s
Barrows, A.C. and Sheldon, C.
v5p0455c2s
Barrows, C.E. v1p0261c2s
v1p1412c1s v2p0473c1s
Barrows, C.H. v1p1394c2s
Barrows, C.M. v3p0026c2s
v3p0121c1s v3p0325c1s
Barrows, D.P. v5p0129c1s
v6p0132c2m v6p0139c1s v6p0315c2s
v6p0493c2s
Barrows, E.P. v1p0132c1s
v1p0242c2s v1p0312c2s v1p0496c2s
v1p0646c1m v1p0676c1s v1p0685c1s
v1p0853c2s v1p1056c1s v1p1102c1s
v1p1206c2s v1p1208c1s v1p1208c2s
v1p1417c1s
Barrows, E.P., jr. v1p0334c2s
v1p0825c1s v1p0980c1s v1p1102c2s
Barrows, F., Mrs. v1p0991c1s
Barrows, H.D. v1p0325c1s
v6p0329c1s v6p0686c1s
Barrows, I.C. v4p0196c2s
v4p0346c2s v4p0354c1s v5p0090c1s
v5p0133c1s v5p0309c2s v5p0369c2s
v5p0384c2s v5p0467c1s v6p0248c1s
v6p0354c2s v6p0517c1s
Barrows, I.C. and Barrows, S.J.
v3p0386c2s
Barrows, I.C., Mrs. v4p0149c1s
v4p0477c1s
Barrows, J.C. v5p0525c1s
v6p0510c2s
Barrows, J.H. v4p0077c2s
v4p0102c1m v4p0479c1s v4p0479c2m
v5p0111c2s v5p0115c1s v5p0177c1s
v5p0360c2s v5p0417c1s v5p0483c1s
v6p0016c2s
Barrows, J.H. and Harper, W.R.
v4p0100c1s
Barrows, J.L. v2p0081c1s
Barrows, J.S. v3p0026c2s
v4p0217c1s v4p0276c2s v6p0360c1s
Barrows, L.D. v1p0840c1s
v1p1174c2s
Barrows, M. v4p0536c2s
Barrows, M.E. v6p0056c1s
v6p0483c2s
Barrows, Mary M. v6p0697c2s
Barrows, N. v2p0261c2s
Barrows, S.J. v1p0057c1s
v1p0069c2s v1p0236c1s v1p0343c2s
v1p0347c1s v1p0565c1s v1p0879c2s
v1p0941c2s v1p1197c2s v2p0009c1s
v2p0237c2s v3p0213c2s v3p0299c1s
v3p0321c1s v4p0094c1s v4p0131c2s
v4p0169c1s v4p0287c2s v4p0434c1m
v4p0459c2s v5p0036c2s v5p0143c2s
v5p0166c1s v5p0197c1s v5p0294c1s
v5p0440c1s v5p0467c1s v5p0619c2s
v6p0157c2s v6p0158c1s v6p0348c2s
v6p0367c1s v6p0517c1m v6p0517c2m
v6p0583c2s v6p0666c2s
Barrows, S.J. and Barrows, I.C.
v3p0386c2s
Barrows, S.T. v5p0058c2s
Barrows, W. v1p0096c2s
v1p0180c1s v1p0291c1s v1p0590c1s
v1p0623c1s v1p0625c2s v1p0631c2s
v1p0770c2s v1p0802c1s v1p0809c1s
v1p0855c1s v1p0863c2s v1p0977c2s
v1p1091c1s v1p1120c1s v1p1302c2s
v1p1346c2s v2p0011c1s v2p0077c1s
v2p0082c1s v2p0087c1s v2p0096c1s
v2p0219c1s v2p0286c2s v2p0297c1s
v2p0342c2s v2p0364c1s v2p0373c1s
v2p0452c1s v2p0470c2m v3p0010c2s
v3p0076c1s v3p0197c2s v3p0213c1m
v3p0333c1s v3p0427c2s v3p0460c1s
Barrows, Wm. v3p0441c2s
Barrs, J.E. v6p0130c1s
Barrus, C. v6p0706c2s
Barrus, G.H. v4p0120c2s
v5p0551c1s v6p0244c1s v6p0615c2m
Barry, A. v1p0435c2s
v1p1001c2s v2p0333c1s v4p0181c1s
v5p0117c1s v5p0490c1s v6p0065c1s
v6p0394c2s
Barry, A., Bishop v3p0180c2s
Barry, A.C. v1p0242c1s
v1p0338c1s v1p0495c2s v1p0673c2s
v1p0719c1s v1p0846c1s v1p0949c2s
v1p1237c2s v2p0324c1s v2p0415c1s
v3p0258c1s
Barry, C. v4p0265c2s
v6p0299c1s
Barry, D. v6p0145c2s
v6p0259c2s
Barry, D.S. v5p0409c1s
v6p0151c2s v6p0583c1s
Barry, E.E. v4p0497c1s
Barry, E.M. v1p0052c2s
v1p0054c2m
Barry, F. v5p0384c1s
Barry, G.A. v6p0660c2s
Barry, H. v5p0399c1s
v6p0105c2s v6p0417c1s
Barry, H.H. v6p0677c1s
Barry, Harriet H. v6p0706c1s
Barry, J.A. v4p0390c2s
v4p0556c1s v4p0625c1s v5p0036c1s
v5p0064c2s v5p0065c1s v5p0075c1s
v5p0274c1s v5p0282c1s v5p0322c1s
v5p0326c1s v5p0347c2s v5p0379c2s
v5p0424c1s v5p0481c1s v6p0596c1s
Barry, J.D. v3p0449c1s
v4p0070c2s v4p0198c2s v4p0250c1s
v4p0377c2s v4p0555c1s v5p0081c1s
v5p0141c1s v5p0352c2s v5p0492c2s
v5p0554c1s v6p0011c2s v6p0641c1s
Barry, J.G. v3p0052c1s
Barry, J.J. v1p0020c2m
Barry, J.S. v1p0189c2s
v1p0220c2s v1p0746c1s v1p1187c2s
v1p1324c1s v1p1355c2s
Barry, J.W. v4p0180c1s
v5p0346c2m
Barry, K.M. v3p0475c1s
Barry, L.J. v6p0147c1s
Barry, M. v1p0140c2s
v2p0208c2s
Barry, M.N. v5p0216c1s
Barry, M.N. and Hicks, M.R.
v6p0304c1s v6p0705c1s
Barry, P. v1p0459c1s
v3p0076c2s v3p0094c2s v5p0007c1s
v6p0006c1s v6p0048c2s v6p0083c1s
v6p0267c1s v6p0299c1s v6p0604c1s
v6p0630c1s v6p0655c1s
Barry, R. v6p0509c1m
v6p0593c2s
Barry, R., Sir v1p0149c1s
v1p0743c1s
Barry, W. v1p0088c1s
v1p0464c1s v1p1017c1s v1p1027c2s
v1p1352c1s v2p0028c1s v2p0068c2s
v2p0081c1s v2p0083c2s v2p0105c2s
v2p0123c2s v2p0167c2s v2p0315c1s
v2p0370c1s v2p0375c1s v2p0376c1s
v2p0389c1s v2p0437c1s v3p0006c1s
v3p0120c1s v3p0177c2s v3p0285c2s
v3p0302c1s v3p0306c1s v3p0346c2s
v3p0357c2s v3p0358c1s v3p0360c1s
v3p0361c2s v3p0364c1s v3p0380c2s
v3p0397c2s v3p0404c1s v3p0418c1s
v3p0437c1s v4p0042c1s v4p0152c1s
v4p0253c1s v4p0270c2s v4p0313c2s
v4p0456c1s v4p0488c1s v4p0489c1s
v4p0560c1s v4p0614c2s v4p0637c1s
v5p0017c2s v5p0083c2s v5p0151c2s
v5p0197c2s v5p0341c2s v5p0409c1s
v5p0427c2s v5p0485c1s v5p0490c1s
v5p0492c2s v5p0493c2s v5p0494c1s
v6p0008c1s v6p0159c1s v6p0164c1s
v6p0192c1s v6p0241c1s v6p0307c1s
v6p0363c1s v6p0368c1s v6p0369c2s
v6p0455c2s
Barry, W.F. v1p0065c2s
Barry, Wm. v5p0282c1s
Barrymore, H.J. v5p0378c1s
Barss, J.E. v5p0326c2s
Barstow, N. v4p0047c1s
Barstow, N.S. v5p0185c1s
Barstow, W.S. v4p0174c2s
v6p0199c2s
Barstow, Z.S. v1p0128c2s
v1p0129c1s v1p0343c2s v1p0685c1s
v1p0692c2s v1p1042c2s
Bart, P. v2p0030c2s
Barter, F. v5p0526c1s
Barter, Frank v6p0025c2s
Barth, C.H. v5p0360c1s
Barth, T. v4p0088c2s
v4p0259c2s v4p0575c2s v5p0231c2s
v5p0232c1s v5p0243c1s
Barth, Theodor v4p0062c2s
Barthelemy, A. v4p0029c2s
v5p0430c2s
Barthelemy, H. v2p0164c1s
Bartholdi, M. v2p0094c1s
v2p0392c2s
Bartholdt, R. v6p0323c2s
v6p0481c1s v6p0485c1s
Bartholeyns, A.O'D. v3p0086c2s
v3p0201c2s v3p0246c1s v3p0338c2s
v6p0181c1s
Bartholomew, E. v1p1070c1s
Bartholomew, E.F. v4p0039c1s
v5p0394c2s
Bartholomew, E.G. v1p0400c1s
Bartholomew, F. v1p0206c2s
Bartholomew, H. v6p0086c2s
Bartholomew, J. v5p0121c1s
Bartholomew, J.I. v5p0074c1s
Bartine, H.F. v4p0593c1s
Bartlet, B. v1p0272c1s
Bartlet, V. v5p0059c2m
v5p0323c2s v6p0052c1s v6p0341c2s
Bartlet, Vernon v6p0125c2s
Bartlet, W.S. v1p0176c2s
Bartlett, A. v1p1396c2s
Bartlett, A.A. v1p0481c2s
v1p1126c1s
Bartlett, A.D. v1p0137c1s
Bartlett, A.K. v6p0285c2s
v6p0427c1s v6p0468c2s v6p0646c2s
v6p0647c1s v6p0713c1s
Bartlett, A.L. v3p0191c1s
v3p0301c1s
Bartlett, B.L. v3p0255c1s
Bartlett, Boyd and Smith, F.M.
v6p0095c1s
Bartlett, C.A.H. v3p0097c1s
v3p0361c1s
Bartlett, C.H. v5p0288c1s
Bartlett, C.J. v4p0459c2s
Bartlett, Dr. v3p0037c2s
Bartlett, E. v1p0648c2s
v6p0338c1s
Bartlett, E.E. v4p0461c2s
Bartlett, E.J. v6p0039c1s

Bartlett, E.S. v4p0585c2s v5p0017c2s v5p0084c2s v6p0699c1s
Bartlett, Ellen Strong ... v6p0053c1s
Bartlett, F.G. v2p0134c2s v2p0463c2s v3p0147c1s v3p0463c1s
Bartlett, F.O. v6p0036c1s v6p0167c2s
Bartlett, G. v4p0216c1s v4p0276c1s
Bartlett, G.B. v2p0366c2s v3p0095c1s
Bartlett, H.L. v2p0297c2s
Bartlett, H.M. v4p0460c1s
Bartlett, J. v6p0497c1s v6p0497c2m
Bartlett, J.A. v3p0152c2s
Bartlett, J.B. v5p0175c1s v5p0324c1s
Bartlett, J.F. v4p0435c1s v4p0595c1s
Bartlett, J.G. v6p0057c1s v6p0291c1s
Bartlett, J.R. v1p0193c1s v1p0280c2s v1p1105c1s v2p0068c1s v2p0114c2m v5p0124c2s v5p0544c1s
Bartlett, J.V. v4p0502c1s v4p0605c1s v6p0064c1m v6p0123c2s v6p0626c2s
Bartlett, J.W. v5p0021c1s
Bartlett, L. v6p0631c2s
Bartlett, L.C. v6p0518c1s
Bartlett, Lancler v6p0059c2s
Bartlett, M.K. v5p0420c2s
Bartlett, M.V. v5p0428c2s
Bartlett, Messrs. v1p1255c2s
Bartlett, N. v1p0557c2s v6p0064c1s
Bartlett, R.E. v2p0083c2s v3p0083c2s v4p0112c1s v4p0194c1s
Bartlett, R.M. v1p0649c2s
Bartlett, S.C. v1p0043c2s v1p0118c1s v1p0122c1s v1p0122c2s v1p0126c2s v1p0241c2s v1p0398c2s v1p0618c1s v1p0646c2s v1p0668c2s v1p0825c1s v1p0852c1s v1p0978c1s v1p1161c1s v1p1237c1s v1p1238c1s v2p0112c1s v2p0131c1s v2p0152c1s v2p0274c1s v2p0352c1s v2p0415c1s v3p0091c2m v3p0110c2s v3p0461c2s v4p0055c2s v4p0067c2s v5p0057c1s v5p0265c1s v5p0269c1s
Bartlett, S.C. et al. v3p0091c2s
Bartlett, S.S. v1p1322c1s
Bartlett, T.H. v1p0865c1s v2p0296c1s v2p0418c2s v3p0026c2s v3p0034c1s v3p0163c1s v3p0166c2s v3p0188c1s v3p0244c1s v3p0279c2s v3p0286c2s v3p0363c1s
Bartlett, V. v4p0109c1s v4p0185c2s v6p0436c2s
Bartlett, V. and Carlyle, A.J. v5p0024c1s
Bartlett, W. v5p0199c2s
Bartlett, W.A. v1p0227c2s
Bartlett, W.C. v1p0187c2s v1p0188c2s v1p0499c2s v1p0607c2s v1p0759c2s v1p0770c1s v1p0820c1s v1p1143c2s v1p1339c1s v1p1428c1s v3p0014c2s v3p0148c1s v3p0162c2s v3p0226c1s v3p0278c1s v5p0214c1s v5p0425c2s v6p0644c1s v6p0699c2s
Bartlett, W.H. v1p0329c2s v1p0598c2s v1p1070c2s v1p1160c1s v4p0129c2s v5p0504c1s
Bartlett, W.H., Mrs. v6p0714c2s
Bartlett, W.H.C. v1p0282c1s v1p0747c2s
Bartlett, W.K. v2p0053c2s
Bartlett, W.P.G. v1p1070c2s
Bartlett, W.R. v6p0284c2s
Bartlett, W.S. v1p1376c2s
Bartley, A.G. v3p0007c2s v4p0574c2s
Bartley, C.T. v2p0100c1s
Bartley, G.C.T. v3p0074c1s v3p0165c1s v3p0311c1s v3p0324c2s v3p0376c1s v5p0007c2s v6p0504c1s
Bartning, L. v6p0168c1s v6p0444c2s
Bartol, C.A. v1p0074c1s v1p0100c1s v1p0111c1s v1p0152c1s v1p0218c1s v1p0241c1s v1p0243c2s v1p0252c1s v1p0312c2s v1p0405c2m v1p0475c2s v1p0528c1s v1p0530c2s v1p0599c1s v1p0684c1s v1p0687c1s v1p0750c1s v1p0846c1s v1p0847c1s v1p0847c2s v1p0849c2s v1p0876c1s v1p0889c2s v1p0920c2s v1p0982c2s v1p1021c1s v1p1031c1s v1p1083c2s v1p1095c1s v1p1171c2s v1p1185c1s v1p1203c2s v1p1271c2s v1p1301c2m v1p1303c1s v1p1381c2s v1p1387c1s v1p1393c2s v1p1397c1s v2p0039c1s v2p0041c2s v2p0074c1s v2p0140c2s v2p0171c2s v2p0244c1s v2p0268c2s v2p0298c1s v2p0328c1s v2p0341c2s v2p0359c2s v2p0424c1s v2p0451c2s v3p0037c1s v3p0054c1s v3p0148c1s v3p0193c1s v3p0280c1s v3p0287c2s v3p0345c2s v3p0358c1s v3p0432c1s v3p0434c2s v4p0069c1s v4p0074c2s v4p0096c1s v4p0178c2m v4p0478c2s v4p0565c2s
Bartol, C.A. and Champlin, E.R. v3p0136c1s
Bartol, H.W. v1p1265c1s v3p0355c2s v4p0175c2s
Bartol, Mary v2p0331c2s
Bartoli, A. v3p0224c1s
Barton, A. v5p0643c2s v6p0346c2s
Barton, B. v1p0143c1s v1p0674c2s v1p1021c1s
Barton, B.S. v1p0637c2s
Barton, B.W. v4p0196c1s
Barton, C. v2p0465c2s v4p0511c1s v5p0148c1m
Barton, Clara v3p0231c2s v5p0481c1m
Barton, E. v5p0039c1s v6p0041c2s
Barton, E.M. v2p0125c2s v2p0255c2s
Barton, E.S. v4p0511c2s
Barton, F. v5p0354c1s
Barton, F.S. v5p0211c1s
Barton, G.A. v3p0023c2s v4p0229c2s v5p0010c1s v5p0057c2s v5p0058c1s v5p0060c1s v5p0436c2s v5p0519c2s v6p0062c1s v6p0340c1s v6p0369c1s v6p0485c1s
Barton, G.A. and Spoer, H.H. v6p0633c2s
Barton, G.B. v5p0039c1m v5p0143c1s v5p0481c2s
Barton, G.F. v6p0412c1s
Barton, G.H. v2p0250c2s v5p0250c2s v5p0258c1s v6p0458c1s
Barton, G.H. and Crosby, W.O. v1p0200c1s
Barton, H.J. v6p0136c1s
Barton, I.M. v1p0808c1s
Barton, J. v1p0580c1s v1p1056c1s v1p1122c2s
Barton, J.L. v6p0194c1s v6p0212c1s v6p0421c2s v6p0546c1s v6p0642c2s
Barton, J.S. v5p0327c2s
Barton, M. v1p0502c2m
Barton, N.T. v5p0388c2s
Barton, P.P. v6p0456c2s
Barton, R. v5p0301c1s
Barton, R.F. v2p0117c2s
Barton, R.T. v4p0323c1s
Barton, S.M. v5p0229c2s v5p0628c1s v6p0406c2s
Barton, W.E. v4p0054c2s v4p0300c1s v4p0399c1s v4p0574c1s v5p0048c2s v5p0054c1s v5p0277c2m v5p0403c1s v5p0412c1s v5p0453c2s v5p0582c2s v6p0061c2s v6p0122c2s v6p0180c1s v6p0350c2s v6p0436c2s v6p0513c2s
Barton, W.H. v1p0506c2s
Bartram, Clara v6p0287c2s
Bartram, G. v6p0208c2s v6p0465c2s v6p0586c2s
Bartram, R. v2p0131c2s v2p0208c2s v2p0442c1s
Barum, Gertrude v6p0218c2s
Barus, A.H. v4p0103c1s
Barus, C. v3p0098c1s v3p0133c1s v3p0133c2s v3p0156c1s v3p0174c2m v3p0223c1s v3p0252c2m v3p0264c1s v3p0284c2m v3p0334c1s v3p0363c1s v3p0409c1s v3p0451c1s v3p0452c1s v3p0456c2s v4p0089c1s v4p0110c2s v4p0128c1s v4p0232c1s v4p0252c2s v4p0486c1s v4p0524c1s v4p0568c2s v4p0573c2s v4p0579c1s v4p0606c1s v5p0010c1s v5p0065c2s v5p0127c2s v5p0235c2s v5p0289c2s v5p0293c2s v5p0338c1s v5p0370c2s v5p0447c2m v5p0451c1s v5p0473c2s v5p0531c1s v5p0571c1s v5p0583c1m v5p0608c1s v5p0610c1s v5p0621c2s v6p0040c1s v6p0058c2s v6p0143c2s v6p0150c2m v6p0217c1s v6p0248c2s v6p0325c2m v6p0377c1s v6p0462c1m v6p0498c2s v6p0526c2s v6p0527c1s v6p0625c2s v6p0674c2s v6p0709c2m
Barus, C. and Iddings, J.P. v4p0174c2s
Barus, C. and Kingsley, J.S. v6p0474c1s
Barus, C. and Strouhal, V. v2p0101c2s v2p0419c2m v3p0409c1s
Barus, C., Mrs. v3p0194c2s v3p0314c1s v3p0444c1s v3p0456c1s v3p0456c2s v3p0468c1s
Barus, Carl v5p0388c2s v6p0682c1s
Barus, T. v6p0377c2s
Barwick, G.F. v5p0070c1s v6p0083c1s v6p0684c2s
Barydardt, P.S. v4p0288c1s
Barzellotti, G. v4p0295c1s
Barzellotti, J. v1p1000c2s
Bas, C.J.Le v1p0633c1s
Bas, C.T.Le v1p0342c1s
Bas, H.V.Le et al. v4p0557c2s
Baschet, A. v1p0331c1s
Bascom, E.C. v2p0078c1s
Bascom, J. v1p0208c2s v1p0259c2s v1p0275c2s v1p0293c1m v1p0305c1s v1p0417c2s v1p0435c2s v1p0458c1s v1p0603c1s v1p0646c1s v1p0646c2s v1p0648c2s v1p0651c1s v1p0651c2s v1p0724c1s v1p0760c2s v1p0820c2s v1p0826c1s v1p0843c2s v1p0850c2s v1p1000c1s v1p1026c2s v1p1048c2s v1p1064c2s v1p1215c1m v1p1233c1s v1p1235c1s v1p1357c2s v1p1360c2s v1p1421c1s v2p0042c1s v2p0097c2s v2p0129c1s v2p0147c1m v2p0149c2s v2p0152c1s v2p0266c2s v2p0289c2s v2p0339c2m v2p0353c2s v2p0368c2s v2p0389c2s v2p0408c2s v2p0437c1s v2p0474c1m v3p0039c1s v3p0049c2s v3p0145c1s v3p0233c2s v3p0238c2s v3p0378c1s v3p0398c1s v3p0427c1s v4p0188c1m v4p0301c1s v4p0558c1s v4p0599c2s v5p0131c1s v5p0236c1s v5p0483c2s v6p0105c1s v6p0136c2s v6p0188c2s v6p0356c1s v6p0356c2s v6p0417c2s v6p0448c2s v6p0468c1s v6p0521c1s v6p0528c2s v6p0533c1s v6p0627c1s v6p0665c1s v6p0667c1m v6p0708c2s
Bascom, John v5p0158c1s
Basden, H. v1p0759c2s
Basevi, C.E. v4p0026c1s v4p0606c1s
Bash, A. v1p0068c1s
Bashfield, E.H. and Bashfield, E.W. v3p0069c2s v4p0172c2s
Bashfield, E.W. v6p0194c1s
Bashfield, E.W. and Bashfield, E.H. v3p0069c2s v4p0172c2s
Bashford, H. v5p0013c1s v5p0414c1s v6p0473c2s
Bashford, H.F. v3p0319c1s
Bashford, H.H. v6p0333c2s
Bashford, J.L. v6p0205c1s v6p0252c1s v6p0252c2s v6p0253c1m v6p0253c2s v6p0254c1s v6p0255c1s v6p0265c1s v6p0635c2s
Bashford, J.W. v2p0250c1s v3p0073c2s v3p0218c2s v4p0074c2s v6p0118c2s v6p0519c1s v6p0692c1s
Bashforth, F. v2p0356c1m v3p0346c1s
Bashore, H.B. v4p0222c2s v4p0227c1s v4p0235c1s v4p0248c2s v4p0559c1s v5p0358c1m
Baskerville, B.C. v6p0506c1s
Baskerville, C. v5p0015c1s v5p0104c1s v5p0514c2s v6p0011c1s v6p0111c2m v6p0112c1s v6p0133c1s v6p0200c1s v6p0354c2s v6p0575c2s v6p0644c2s v6p0648c1s v6p0664c1s
Baskerville, C. and Kunz, G.F. v6p0355c1s v6p0473c2s v6p0527c2s
Baskerville, C. and Lockhart, L.B. v6p0527c2s v6p0713c1s
Baskerville, W.M. v2p0197c1s v3p0028c2s v3p0141c1s v3p0197c1s v3p0335c2s v4p0248c2s v4p0320c2s v5p0086c2s v5p0392c2s
Baskett, J.N. v5p0064c1s
Bass, C.C. v4p0369c2s
Bass, J.L. v1p0460c1s
Basset, A.B. v4p0177c1s v4p0477c1s
Bassett, A.B. v4p0165c1s
Bassett, A.L. v1p0464c2s v1p0927c2s v1p1336c1s v1p1339c2s v1p1387c1s
Bassett, D.A. v2p0107c2s
Bassett, E. v3p0303c2s
Bassett, E.P. v5p0558c1s
Bassett, F. v1p1395c2s
Bassett, F.S. v3p0149c2s v3p0297c2m v3p0298c1s v3p0339c2s v3p0382c2s v3p0403c2s v4p0211c2s v4p0218c2s v4p0511c1s v4p0607c1s
Bassett, G.H. v4p0289c1s v4p0290c2s v5p0297c1s
Bassett, H.H. v5p0541c1m
Bassett, J. v2p0449c1s
Bassett, J.H. v1p0310c1s
Bassett, J.S. v4p0050c2s v4p0377c1s v4p0406c2m v4p0529c1s v4p0555c1s v5p0017c1s v5p0023c1s v5p0095c1s v5p0532c1s v6p0147c2s v6p0158c2s v6p0183c1s v6p0243c2s v6p0447c1s v6p0459c2s v6p0480c2s v6p0544c1s v6p0605c1s v6p0605c2m v6p0606c2s v6p0680c1s v6p0686c2s
Bassett, M.E.S. v5p0597c2s
Bassett, R.E. v6p0010c1s v6p0608c1s
Bassett, R.E. and Lena, Hazde v6p0462c1s
Bassett, W. v6p0710c1s
Bassett, W.F. v4p0190c1s v4p0552c2s
Bassett-Smith, P.W. v4p0038c1s

Bassford, F. v4p0634c2m
Bassford, H. v6p0644c2s
Bassin, E. v2p0236c2s
Bastable, C. v6p0326c2s
Bastable, C.F. v3p0285c2s
v3p0434c1s v4p0243c2s v4p0290c2s
v4p0450c1s v5p0207c1s v5p0245c2m
v5p0295c2s v5p0296c1s v6p0256c1s
v6p0267c1s v6p0326c2s v6p0634c1s
v6p0713c2s
Bastian, A. v2p0059c2s
Bastian, H.C. v1p0086c1s
v1p0142c2s v1p0157c1m v1p0354c1s
v1p0434c1s v1p0434c2m v1p0512c2m
v1p0579c2s v1p0651c2s v1p0746c1m
v1p0906c2s v1p0907c1s v1p0947c2s
v1p1059c1s v1p1177c2s v1p1209c1s
v1p1239c1s v1p1305c2s v1p1359c1s
v6p0228c1s v6p0244c1s v6p0376c1s
v6p0381c2s v6p0520c2s
Bastide, C. v5p0027c2s
v5p0080c1s v5p0485c1s v6p0553c1s
v6p0612c1s v6p0683c2s
Bastide, Ch. v5p0086c2s
v5p0187c1s v5p0221c1m
Bastide, L. v3p0227c2s
Bastin, E.B. v3p0076c2s
v3p0169c2s
Bastin, S.L. v6p0131c2s
Bastin, S.L. and Henslow, G.
v6p0229c2s
Bastin, S.Leonard v6p0502c1m
Bataille, A. v2p0139c2s
Batalha-Reis, J. v5p0228c2s
v5p0541c1m
Batchelder, A.I. v3p0084c1s
Batchelder, C.E. v2p0234c2s
v4p0041c1s v4p0047c1s
Batchelder, F.R. v4p0144c2s
v4p0276c2s v5p0578c1s v5p0621c1s
v6p0604c1s
Batchelder, G.F. v3p0281c1s
Batchelder, J. v1p1158c1s
Batchelder, L.H. v5p0094c1s
v5p0103c2s v5p0104c1m v5p0423c2s
v5p0449c1s
Batchelder, S. v1p0306c1s
v3p0447c2s
Batchelder, S.F. v5p0384c2s
v5p0507c1s v6p0281c2s v6p0361c1s
Batchelder, W.J. v6p0218c1s
v6p0459c1s v6p0464c1s v6p0700c2s
Batcheller, B.C. v3p0125c2s
v5p0455c1s
Batcheller, G.S. v6p0423c2s
v6p0705c1s
Batchellor, A.S. v3p0121c2s
Batchelor, G. v1p0426c2m
v1p0587c1s v1p0951c1s v1p1055c1s
v1p1093c2s v1p1145c2s v1p1217c1s
v2p0147c1m v2p0167c1s v2p0272c2s
v2p0367c1s v2p0368c2m v2p0384c1s
v2p0407c1m v2p0459c2s v3p0281c2s
v3p0361c2m v3p0373c1s v3p0441c1s
v4p0188c2s v4p0255c2m v4p0359c2s
v4p0436c2s
Batchelor, J. v4p0008c2s
Batchelor, W. v1p0928c1s
Batdorf, Sam F. v6p0365c2s
Bate, C.S. v1p1121c1s
Bate, F. v5p0123c2s
v5p0405c2s
Bate, J. v1p0599c1s
Bate, J.D. v5p0065c2s
v5p0381c2s
Bate, P. v5p0235c2s
v5p0552c2s v6p0156c2s v6p0287c1s
v6p0569c2s
Bate, S. v1p0460c2s
Batell, A.F. v4p0497c2s
Bateman, A.E. v2p0431c1s
v2p0475c2s v3p0181c2s v3p0209c2s
v4p0580c2s
Bateman, A.H. v1p0405c2s
Bateman, A.Z. v6p0487c2s
Bateman, C.C. v6p0109c1s
v6p0218c2s v6p0418c2s v6p0429c2m
v6p0430c2s v6p0544c2s
Bateman, G.J. v2p0018c2s
Bateman, M. v6p0022c2s
v6p0169c1s
Bateman, May v5p0283c2s
v6p0362c2s
Bateman, S. v4p0229c1s
v4p0393c2s v6p0577c2s
Bateman, T. v1p0743c1s
Bateman, T. and Jewitt, L.
v1p1039c2s
Bateman, W.B. v1p0432c1s
Bates v3p0155c1s
v3p0203c1s
Bates, A. v2p0017c2s
v2p0058c2s v2p0115c1s v2p0386c2s
v3p0035c1s v3p0262c1s v3p0274c2s
v3p0295c2s v3p0345c1s v3p0355c1s
v3p0376c2s v3p0389c1s v3p0394c2s
v3p0420c2s v3p0466c2s v4p0288c1s
v4p0537c1s v5p0037c1s v5p0072c2s
v5p0539c1s v5p0556c1s v6p0049c2s
v6p0157c2s v6p0420c2s
Bates, A.B. v4p0392c2s
Bates, A.E. v5p0599c1s
v5p0599c2s
Bates, A.J. v2p0254c1s
Bates, A.L. v4p0459c2s
Bates, Arlo v3p0292c2s
v5p0144c2s v6p0312c1s
Bates, B. v1p1037c2s
v6p0297c2s
Bates, C. v3p0322c2s
Bates, C.F. v1p0141c2s
v4p0621c1m v5p0562c2s
Bates, D. v2p0277c1s
v3p0102c1s v3p0289c2s v3p0454c1s
v5p0122c1s v6p0121c2s
Bates, D.H. v5p0119c1s
Bates, D.M. v1p0853c1s
v2p0079c1m v2p0164c2s v2p0309c2s
v6p0688c2s
Bates, E. v1p0015c1s
v3p0086c2s
Bates, E.B. v4p0058c2s
v5p0601c1s
Bates, E.C. v3p0102c1s
Bates, E.S. v3p0108c1s
v3p0321c1s v3p0325c2s v3p0329c1s
v4p0106c1s v4p0469c1s v4p0501c2s
v4p0557c2s v6p0280c2s v6p0586c2s
Bates, F. v4p0198c1s
Bates, F.D.W. v6p0217c1s
Bates, F.O. v5p0087c1s
Bates, Francis W. v6p0006c2s
Bates, G.F. v6p0446c1s
Bates, G.H. v2p0357c1s
v3p0374c1s
Bates, G.L. v3p0043c2s
Bates, H. v3p0291c1m
v3p0367c2s v4p0352c2s v6p0405c2s
Bates, H.F. v4p0545c2s
Bates, H.H. v2p0280c2s
v2p0338c1s
Bates, H.P. v5p0039c2s
v6p0348c2s
Bates, H.R. v6p0419c2s
Bates, H.W. v1p0960c1s
Bates, J. v1p0393c1s
v1p0648c2s v1p0837c1s v1p0867c2s
Bates, J.C. v1p0918c1s
Bates, J.W. v3p0217c1s
Bates, K.L. v3p0031c1s
v3p0306c2s v3p0468c1s v4p0184c1s
v4p0492c1s v4p0616c2s v5p0634c1s
v6p0075c2s
Bates, K.L. et al. v2p0265c2s
v4p0335c2s
Bates, Katherine L. v5p0452c1s
v6p0205c2s v6p0359c1s v6p0569c1s
Bates, L.B. v4p0480c2s
Bates, L.J. v1p0756c1s
Bates, L.P. v4p0627c1s
Bates, L.W. v6p0477c2s
Bates, Lindon, jr. v6p0477c2s
Bates, M. v1p0186c2s
Bates, N.D. v3p0433c1s
Bates, President v3p0191c1s
v3p0473c1s v4p0497c2s
Bates, R.C. v5p0186c2s
Bates, S. v4p0553c2s
Bates, S.P. v1p0740c2s
Bates, W. v5p0124c2s
v5p0318c2s v5p0623c1s v5p0631c1s
Bates, W.C. v1p0314c2s
v1p1346c1s v3p0473c1s v4p0139c1s
v4p0296c1s v5p0073c1s v5p0642c1s
v6p0650c1s
Bates, W.G. v1p0386c1s
v3p0019c2s v3p0312c2s v3p0457c2s
Bates, W.H. v5p0335c2s
v6p0145c2s v6p0484c1s
Bates, W.N. v5p0002c2s
v6p0019c1s v6p0132c1s v6p0298c1s
v6p0466c2s v6p0608c1s
Bates, W.N. and Tarbell, F.B.
v4p0568c2s
Bates, W.O. v1p0008c2s
v2p0182c2s v2p0281c1s
Bates, W.W. v1p0006c2s
v4p0378c2s v4p0521c1m v4p0521c2s
v4p0525c1s v4p0525c2s v5p0526c1m
v6p0401c1s v6p0591c2m
Bateson, A. v3p0447c2s
Bateson, H.D. v4p0131c2s
v4p0179c2s
Bateson, M. v3p0138c2s
v4p0112c1s v4p0172c1s v4p0377c1s
v4p0632c1s v5p0075c2s v5p0330c1s
v5p0515c2s v5p0635c2s v6p0076c1s
v6p0194c2s v6p0304c1s v6p0384c2s
v6p0490c2s v6p0578c2s v6p0612c2s
Bateson, Mary v3p0285c1m
v6p0178c2s v6p0424c2s
Bateson, T. v5p0069c1s
v5p0157c1s
Bateson, W. v5p0607c2s
v6p0082c1s v6p0288c1s
Bateson, W. et al. v4p0114c2s
Bath, J. v5p0506c2s
Bather, A.G. v4p0035c1s
v4p0040c2s
Bather, F.A. v4p0060c1s
v4p0094c2s v4p0101c2s v4p0297c2s
v4p0343c2s v4p0356c1s v5p0393c1s
v5p0429c1s v6p0249c2s v6p0437c2s
v6p0464c1s
Bather, F.A. and Buckman, S.S.
v4p0016c1s
Bathon, W. v5p0141c1s
v5p0381c2s v6p0181c1s
Bathon, Wingrove v5p0142c1s
v5p0326c1s v6p0551c2s
Bathurst, F. v5p0208c1s
Bathurst, G. v5p0004c1s
Bathurst, K. v6p0116c1s
v6p0117c2s v6p0257c1s v6p0462c2s
Batson, H.M. v4p0626c1s
v5p0225c2s v5p0433c2s
Batson, H.M. and Wyndham, P.
v5p0321c2s
Batson, R. v1p0977c1s
v1p1320c2s
Batson, S., Mrs. v3p0150c1s
v4p0314c1s v4p0324c1s v4p0454c2s
Batson, S., Mrs. et al. .. v4p0318c1s
Batt, N.G. v1p0052c2s
v1p0242c1s v1p0893c1s v1p0920c1s
v1p0957c1s v4p0571c2s
Batt, W.J. v3p0344c2s
Batte, J.D. v5p0254c1s
Battell, P. v1p0808c1s
Batten, G.H.M. et al. v4p0415c1s
Batten, J.H. v5p0220c1s
v5p0349c1s
Batten, L.W. v3p0042c1s
v4p0055c1s v4p0057c2s v4p0439c1s
v5p0057c1s v5p0308c1s v6p0095c2s
Batten, S.Z. v5p0118c1s
v6p0214c2s
Batten, T.Z. v6p0125c1s
Battenberg, M.H. v6p0344c2s
Battersby, C. v2p0327c2s
v4p0070c2s v4p0332c1s v4p0613c2s
v5p0554c2s
Battersby, F.J. v5p0133c1s
Battersby, H.F.P. v6p0296c1s
v6p0571c1s v6p0587c2s
Battersby, I.P. v3p0144c2s
Battersby, J.C. v1p0911c1s
Battersby, Maj. v4p0045c2s
Battersby, P.T. v5p0621c2s
Battersby, T.P. v1p0589c2s
v4p0149c2s v5p0076c1s v5p0626c1s
Battersea, Lady v5p0014c2s
v5p0019c1s v5p0268c1s
Battersea, Lord v4p0190c1s
Battershall, J.P. v1p1024c2s
Battershall, W. v5p0513c1s
Battershall, W.W. v1p0241c2s
v5p0463c1s
Battey, A.H. v4p0610c2s
Battey, E.V. v1p0230c2s
v1p0715c2s
Battine, C. v6p0352c2s
Battine, C.W. v4p0236c1s
Battis, E.C. v6p0565c1s
Battle, K.P. v3p0415c1s
Battles, A. v1p1208c1s
Battles, F. v3p0047c1s
v3p0093c1s
Battles, W.W. v6p0620c1s
Batton, L.W. v5p0525c2s
Batts, R.L. v6p0640c1s
Batty, B, Mrs. v3p0474c2s
Batty, J.H. v6p0634c2s
Battye, A. v3p0274c1s
v3p0316c1s v3p0391c2s v3p0445c2s
Battye, A.T. v6p0712c2s
Battye, A.Trevor v5p0027c1s
Baty, T. v5p0293c2s
v6p0104c2s v6p0132c2s v6p0147c1m
v6p0154c2s v6p0177c2s v6p0208c1s
v6p0364c1s v6p0556c1s v6p0574c2s
v6p0601c1s
Baty, W. v2p0162c1s
Baudens, M.L. v1p0316c2s
Baudin, P. v6p0237c2s
Bauditz, S. v5p0211c2s
Baudot, A.de v4p0024c1s
Baudot, V. v3p0003c1s
v3p0318c1s
Baudrillart, H. v2p0165c1s
v3p0261c2s
Baudrimont, M.A. v1p0825c2m
Bauer, G. v3p0068c1s
Bauer, L.A. v4p0349c2m
v6p0185c2s v6p0395c1m v6p0474c1s
v6p0486c2s v6p0568c1s
Bauer, L.A. and Trowbridge, J.
v5p0356c1s
Bauer, L.A., Dr. v5p0602c1s
Bauer, L.A.O. v6p0187c2s
Bauer, S. v3p0336c2s
v3p0351c1s v4p0469c2m v6p0356c2s
Baugh, J. v6p0375c2s
v6p0418c2s v6p0495c2s v6p0604c2s
Baugh, Lillian M. v5p0318c2s
Baughan, E.A. v6p0620c2s
v6p0683c1s
Baugher, H.L. v1p0038c2s
v1p0130c1s v1p0229c1s v1p0385c1s
v1p0404c1s v1p0440c1s v1p0564c1s

v1p0599c2s v1p0625c1s v1p0686c2s
v1p0688c1s v1p0777c2s v1p0778c1m
v1p0847c2s v1p1262c2s v1p1284c2s
v1p1301c2s v1p1360c2s
Baugher, L.H. v2p0167c1s
Baum, A. v2p0110c1s
v2p0371c2s
Baum, Frank v5p0486c2s
Baum, H.M. v2p0372c1s
v3p0084c1s v3p0321c1s v3p0347c1s
v3p0408c1s
Baum, L.F. v5p0200c1s
Baum, R. v4p0576c2s
Baum, W.M. v1p0384c2s
v1p1140c2m v4p0456c2s
Bauman, J.A. v1p0124c1s
Baumann, A.A. v3p0147c2s
v3p0256c2s v3p0321c2s v3p0417c1m
v3p0433c1s v4p0152c1s v4p0227c2s
v4p0238c2s v4p0338c2s v4p0582c1s
v5p0583c1s v6p0127c1s v6p0640c2s
v6p0650c2s
Baumann, F. v1p0471c1s
v3p0018c2s
v4p0362c2s
Baumann, H. v4p0184c2s
Baumann, J. v2p0105c2s
v3p0071c1s
Baumes, J.R. v2p0210c1s
Baumfeld, M. v6p0042c2s
Baumfeld, Maurice, Dr. ... v6p0661c2s
Baumfield, M. v5p0040c1s
Baumgarten, C. v6p0109c2s
v6p0512c1s
Baumgartner, A. v5p0178c2s
Baumgartner, A.L. v4p0616c2s
Baumhauer, E.H.von v1p1296c1s
Baun, J.A.De v1p1047c1s
v2p0114c1s v4p0573c1s
Baunard, Abbe L. v1p0980c2s
Baur, F.C. v1p0074c2s
Baur, G. v1p0386c1s
v1p1157c1s v3p0118c1s v3p0166c1s
v3p0315c1s v3p0318c1s v3p0425c2s
v4p0191c1s v5p0063c2s v5p0224c1m
Baur, P. v6p0648c1s
Baur, P.V.C. v6p0196c2s
Bauschinger, J. v2p0135c2s
v2p0354c2s
Bausemer, W.S. v6p0647c1s
Bauslin, D.H. v3p0281c1s
v4p0007c1s v4p0039c1s v4p0328c2s
v4p0374c2s v5p0060c2s v5p0463c2s
v5p0489c2s v5p0576c2s v6p0193c1s
Bausman, F. v5p0204c1s
v5p0258c2s v6p0004c1s v6p0347c1s
v6p0583c2s v6p0667c1s
Bausman, W. v1p1238c2s
Bautain, L. v1p0869c2s
v1p0964c1s
Baverstock, E.H. v1p0640c2s
Bavinck, H. v4p0084c2s
v5p0141c2s
Bawden, H.H. v5p0075c1s
v6p0001c2s v6p0478c2s v6p0497c2s
v6p0521c1m v6p0521c2s
Bawden, H.H. and Small, A.W.
v6p0602c1s
Bawden, J. v1p1216c1s
v1p1272c2s
Bawer, Julius A. v6p0534c1s
Bawolle, W.C. v5p0375c2s
Bawtree, E.W. v1p0637c2s
Bax, A.N. v5p0117c1s
Bax, E.B. v1p0799c1s
v2p0038c2s v2p0408c1m v3p0175c1s
v3p0209c1s v3p0372c1s v3p0399c1s
v4p0259c1s v4p0328c2s v4p0621c2m
v5p0536c1s
Bax, E.B. and Besant, A. . v3p0399c1s
v3p0467c2s
Bax, E.B. and Marson, C.L.
v3p0398c1s
Bax, E.Belfort v4p0136c2s
v4p0420c2s
Baxendell, J. v2p0008c1s
v2p0360c1s
Baxter, A.H. v5p0161c2s
Baxter, C.J. v6p0192c2s
Baxter, D. v5p0456c2s
v5p0482c1s v6p0054c2s v6p0206c1s
Baxter, Edwin C. v6p0131c1s
Baxter, G.H. v6p0156c1s
Baxter, G.M. v6p0675c1s
Baxter, J.P. v2p0310c2s
v3p0001c1s v3p0231c1s v4p0453c2s
v4p0485c2s v5p0392c1s
Baxter, L.E. v4p0030c1s
v4p0031c1s v4p0032c1s v4p0043c1s
v4p0043c2s v4p0068c1s v4p0088c1s
v4p0135c1s v4p0148c2s v4p0154c2s
v4p0164c1s v4p0202c2s v4p0255c1s
v4p0368c2s v4p0397c2s v4p0473c2s
v4p0577c2s v5p0072c1s
Baxter, R. v1p0649c2s
v2p0047c1s
Baxter, R.D. v1p0897c2s
v1p1076c1s
Baxter, R.W. v5p0570c1s
Baxter, S. v1p0468c1s
v1p1242c1s v2p0108c2s v2p0286c2s
v2p0287c1m v2p0298c1s v2p0373c1s
v2p0483c2m v3p0019c2s v3p0038c2s
v3p0039c2s v3p0143c2s v3p0214c1s
v3p0219c1s v3p0297c2s v3p0340c1s
v3p0341c1s v3p0384c2s v3p0431c1s
v3p0444c1s v4p0048c1s v4p0058c2s
v4p0068c2m v4p0116c2s v4p0267c2s
v4p0281c2s v4p0368c2s v4p0427c1s
v4p0471c2s v4p0534c1s v4p0605c1s
v4p0608c2s v4p0620c2s v5p0030c1s
v5p0053c1s v5p0072c1s v5p0072c2s
v5p0134c2s v5p0148c2s v5p0183c2s
v5p0201c2s v5p0258c1s v5p0304c1s
v5p0334c2s v5p0428c1s v5p0455c1s
v5p0471c2m v5p0544c2s v5p0554c2s
v5p0558c2s v5p0591c2m v5p0607c1s
v6p0033c1s v6p0055c2s v6p0080c1s
v6p0129c1m v6p0247c2s v6p0395c2s
v6p0432c2s v6p0453c1s v6p0477c2m
v6p0570c2s v6p0581c1s v6p0606c1s
v6p0612c1s v6p0637c1s v6p0669c2s
v6p0679c1s v6p0693c1s
Baxter, S.S. v1p0749c2s
v1p1003c2s
Baxter, Sylvester v4p0069c1s
v4p0319c2s v4p0427c1s v4p0555c1s
v5p0072c2s v5p0324c2s v5p0433c1s
v5p0590c1s v6p0033c1s v6p0435c1s
Baxter, W. v4p0090c2s
v4p0176c1s
Baxter, W., jr. v4p0174c2s
v4p0176c2s v4p0177c2s v5p0041c1m
v5p0183c2s v5p0184c1s v5p0294c2s
v5p0622c1s
Baxter, W.E. v1p0244c1s
v2p0208c2s
Baxter, W.L. v4p0303c1s
v5p0056c2s
Baxter, Wm.J. v4p0142c1s
Bay, E.B. v2p0408c1s
Bay, J.C. v4p0060c1s
v4p0449c1s v4p0530c1s v5p0158c2s
v5p0237c1s v6p0444c2s
Bayard, E. v2p0206c2s
Bayard, M.T. v4p0074c1s
v4p0127c2s v4p0150c2s v4p0168c1s
v4p0229c2s v4p0417c2s
Bayard, P.F. v6p0430c1s
Bayard, S.J. v1p0409c2s
Bayard, T.F. v3p0408c1s
v4p0214c1s v5p0610c2s
Bayard, T.F. and Hoar, G.F.
v4p0595c2s
Bayard, T.F. et al. v4p0526c1s
Bayes, W. v6p0094c2s
v6p0450c2s
Bayfield, Jas. v5p0462c2s
Baylee, J.T. v4p0230c1s
v4p0278c1s v4p0412c1s v5p0244c1s
v5p0416c2s v5p0436c2s v5p0440c1s
v5p0450c2s v5p0459c1s v5p0598c1s
v5p0615c2s v6p0708c1s
Bayles, G. v1p0314c1s
Bayles, G.J. v5p0118c1s
Bayles, J.C. v1p0054c2s
v1p0332c2s v2p0229c1s v3p0040c1s
v3p0351c2s v3p0409c1s v4p0100c2s
v4p0224c2s v5p0583c2s v6p0497c2s
v6p0663c2s
Bayley, A.R. v6p0110c2s
Bayley, E. v1p0103c1s
Bayley, E.H. v4p0331c1s
v5p0337c2s
Bayley, G. v2p0429c2s
Bayley, G.W.R. v1p0739c2s
Bayley, J. v1p1142c2s
Bayley, J.A.A.S. v2p0055c1s
Bayley, R.A. v2p0452c2s
Bayley, R.C. v6p0497c1s
Bayley, W.S. v3p0332c1s
v3p0363c1s v3p0399c2s v4p0037c1s
v4p0217c2s
Baylies, F. v1p0270c1s
Baylis, F.G. v1p0373c2s
Baylis, S.M. v3p0133c1s
v3p0436c2s
Baylis, W.J. v5p0550c1s
v5p0618c1s v6p0468c2s
Baylis, W.T. v5p0159c1s
Bayliss v4p0301c1s
Bayliss, D. v1p0919c1s
Bayliss, J.H. v3p0190c1s
Bayliss, W. v3p0022c1s
v3p0388c1s v4p0029c1m v4p0029c2m
v4p0115c2s v4p0137c2s v4p0319c1s
v4p0493c1s v4p0493c2s v4p0577c2s
v4p0602c2s v5p0276c1s v5p0306c1m
v5p0310c1s v5p0330c1s v5p0376c1s
v5p0623c1s v6p0033c2s v6p0151c2s
v6p0415c1s v6p0417c2s v6p0531c2s
v6p0648c1s v6p0679c2s
Bayliss, W., Sir v6p0342c1s
Bayliss, Wyke, Sir v5p0524c1s
Baylor, F.C. v2p0028c1s
v2p0119c2s v2p0216c1s v2p0321c2s
v2p0336c1s v2p0401c1s v2p0429c2s
v3p0103c2s v3p0123c1s v3p0195c2s
v3p0216c1s v3p0355c2s v3p0430c2s
v4p0050c2s v4p0192c2s v4p0362c2s
v4p0585c1s v4p0621c2s v5p0085c2s
v5p0132c2s v5p0147c1s v5p0215c2s
v5p0258c1s v5p0273c1s v5p0366c2s
Baylor, M. v6p0687c2s
Bayly, A.E. v3p0189c2s
v4p0578c1s v5p0623c2s
Bayly, E.B. v2p0396c1s
Bayly, J.C. v4p0457c1s
Bayly, T.H. v1p0922c1s
v1p0924c1s
Bayma, A. v1p0173c2s
v1p0434c1s v1p0812c1s v1p0999c2s
v1p1232c2s
Bayma, F. v1p0109c1s
v1p0372c2s v1p0528c2s v1p0826c2s
v1p0875c2s v1p1040c2s v1p1051c1s
v1p1162c1s v1p1228c1s
Bayma, J. v1p0072c1s
v1p0333c2s v1p0434c2m v1p0495c2s
v1p0584c1s v1p0737c2s v1p0901c1s
v1p0964c1s v1p1000c1s v1p1162c2s
v1p1306c1s v2p0439c1s
Bayma, P. v1p0247c1s
v1p1063c2s
Bayne, C.J. v4p0599c1s
v5p0592c1s
Bayne, I. v1p0361c2s
Bayne, J. v1p0758c2s
Bayne, J.T. v4p0245c1s
Bayne, P. v1p0056c2s
v1p0060c1s v1p0219c2s v1p0249c2s
v1p0261c1s v1p0310c1s v1p0319c1s
v1p0328c1s v1p0441c1s v1p0500c1s
v1p0584c2s v1p0676c1s v1p0685c2s
v1p0688c2s v1p0841c2s v1p0865c1s
v1p0872c2s v1p0906c2s v1p0974c2s
v1p0999c2s v1p1048c2s v1p1064c2s
v1p1094c1s v1p1260c1s v1p1275c2s
v1p1362c2s v1p1407c1s v2p0335c2s
v4p0275c2s v4p0611c1s
Bayne, R. v3p0191c1s
v3p0288c2s
Bayne, S.G. v5p0141c2s
Bayne, T. v1p0060c2s
v1p0170c1s v1p0170c2s v1p0179c1s
v1p0642c1s v1p0709c1s v1p0780c1s
v1p0872c2s v1p0873c1s v1p1022c2s
v1p1128c2s v1p1189c2s v1p1235c2s
v1p1257c1s v1p1276c1s v1p1286c2s
v1p1333c2m v2p0378c2s v2p0428c2s
v4p0080c1s v6p0009c2s v6p0392c2s
v6p0435c1s v6p0441c1s
Bayne, W. v6p0698c2s
Baynes, A.H. v1p0514c2s
v2p0176c1s v5p0398c2s
Baynes, C.D. v5p0487c2s
Baynes, E.H. v4p0494c2s
v5p0400c1s v5p0448c2s v6p0021c2s
v6p0415c1s v6p0554c2s v6p0653c1s
Baynes, H. v5p0111c2s
v6p0431c2s
Baynes, H.M. v2p0249c2s
v2p0259c2s v2p0410c2s
Baynes, John v4p0617c2s
Baynes, N.H. v6p0287c2s
Baynes, R.E. v2p0135c2s
v3p0125c2s
Baynes, T.S. v1p0568c1s
v1p1070c1s v1p1183c2s v3p0068c2s
Baynham, G.W. and Coleman, J.
v4p0267c2s
Baynham, W. v2p0002c1s
v2p0416c2s
Bayrhoffer, K.T. v1p0812c1s
v1p0843c1s v1p1336c2s
Bazalgette, C.N. v1p1181c1s
v2p0468c1s
Bazalgette, J.W. v2p0086c2s
Bazan, E.P. v3p0403c1s
v5p0543c1s v5p0544c1s
Bazan, E.Pardo v3p0469c2s
Bazin, Col. v5p0290c2s
v6p0319c1s
Bazin, H. v2p0373c2s
Bazin, R. v5p0331c2s
v6p0463c1s
Bazin, Rene v5p0089c2s
v5p0243c1s v5p0389c2s v5p0441c1s
v5p0486c2s v5p0596c1s v5p0634c1s
Bazley, T. v1p0306c1s
v1p0307c2s
Bazley, T., Sir v1p0796c1s
Bazouk, Bashi v6p0164c1s
Bazzini, A. v5p0131c2s
Beach, A. v6p0663c2s
Beach, C.F. v6p0194c1s
Beach, C.F., jr. v3p0437c1s
v4p0580c2s v6p0020c2s v6p0241c2s
Beach, D.N. v1p1073c2s
v3p0011c1s v3p0190c2s v3p0445c1s
v4p0143c1s v4p0182c1s v4p0232c2s
v4p0317c1s v4p0373c1s v5p0577c1s
v5p0643c2s v6p0123c1s
Beach, F.C. v3p0330c2s
Beach, F.E. v6p0498c2s
Beach, H.C. v4p0555c2s
Beach, H.H.A., Mrs. v5p0552c1s
Beach, H.P. v4p0064c2s
v4p0266c2s v4p0585c1m v6p0119c1s
Beach, J.K. v4p0277c2s

Beach, J.W. ... v6p0389c2s
Beach, L.H. ... v5p0595c1s
Beach, L.K. ... v1p0837c1s
Beach, M.Y. ... v4p0305c1s
v4p0402c2s v6p0367c2s
Beach, R.E. ... v6p0138c1s
v6p0434c2s v6p0459c2s v6p0479c1s
v6p0579c1s v6p0592c2s v6p0596c1s
v6p0639c2s v6p0641c1s
Beach, Rex E. ... v6p0010c2s
v6p0364c1s v6p0536c1s v6p0611c1s
v6p0709c1s
Beach, S.A. ... v4p0111c1s
Beach, S.C. ... v1p0949c2s
v2p0098c2s v2p0367c2s v2p0395c2s
v3p0399c2s
Beach, T.J. ... v1p0337c1s
Beach, T.W. ... v6p0362c2s
Beach, W.G. ... v2p0139c2s
v5p0039c1s
Beachcroft, R.M. and Harris, H.P.
v4p0338c2s
Beackley, W. ... v2p0144c2s
Beadle, C. ... v4p0094c1s
v5p0429c2s v5p0613c1s v6p0478c2s
v6p0688c1s
Beadle, H.M. ... v5p0102c1s
v5p0497c1s
Beadle, J.H. ... v1p0872c1s
v1p1199c1s v1p1214c2s v1p1360c1m
Beadon, R. ... v4p0236c2s
v4p0276c1s
Beadon, R.J. ... v3p0027c1s
Beal, B.L. ... v5p0072c2s
Beal, E.M. ... v2p0104c1s
v2p0217c2s
Beal, H.M. ... v4p0318c1s
Beal, J. ... v1p1179c2s
Beal, N.L. ... v4p0285c1s
Beal, S. ... v1p0173c1s
v1p0173c2s v1p0233c2s v1p0680c1s
v1p1094c2s v1p1228c2s v2p0022c1s
v2p0059c2s v2p0207c2s v3p0451c2s
Beal, W.B. ... v5p0399c1s
Beal, W.F. ... v4p0208c1s
Beal, W.J. ... v1p0009c1s
v1p0288c1s v1p0645c1s v1p0732c2s
v1p0835c1s v1p1014c2m v1p1015c1m
v1p1306c1s v2p0005c2s v4p0070c1s
v4p0208c1s v4p0485c2s v4p0552c2s
v5p0222c2s v5p0518c2s v6p0444c2m
v6p0503c1s v6p0618c2s
Beale, A. ... v1p0305c2s
v1p0308c1s v1p0605c2s v1p0703c2s
v1p0763c2s v1p0785c1s v1p0856c2s
v1p0891c1s v1p0951c2s v1p0955c2s
v1p1271c1s v1p1381c1s v1p1381c2s
v2p0160c1s v2p0208c1s v2p0214c2s
v2p0277c1s v2p0318c1s v2p0416c1s
v2p0420c1s v2p0471c1s v3p0077c1s
v3p0173c1s v3p0201c2m v3p0256c1s
v3p0282c1s v3p0362c2s
Beale, D. ... v3p0377c2s
v4p0570c1s v5p0638c1s
Beale, Dorothea ... v3p0173c2s
v6p0532c1s
Beale, E.J. ... v3p0431c1s
Beale, E.P. ... v6p0439c1s
Beale, G.W. ... v2p0177c2s
Beale, J., jr. ... v3p0036c2s
Beale, J.H. ... v4p0249c2s
v5p0456c2s v6p0402c2s
Beale, J.H., jr. ... v6p0145c2s
v6p0151c1s v6p0158c1s v6p0176c2s
v6p0348c1s v6p0437c1s v6p0518c1s
v6p0618c1s
Beale, J.S. ... v2p0363c2s
Beale, Joseph H., jr. ... v6p0176c2s
v6p0319c2s
Beale, L.S. ... v1p0207c2s
v1p0336c1s v1p0745c2s v1p0746c1s
v1p0788c2s v1p0810c2s v1p0850c2s
v1p1005c2s v1p1097c2s v4p0331c1s
Beale, Miss ... v2p0131c1s
Beale, O.C. ... v6p0308c2s
Beale, O.J. ... v6p0249c1s
Beale, R. ... v1p0034c1s
Beale, R.L.T. ... v1p1107c1s
Beale, S. ... v2p0023c1s
v2p0023c2s v2p0036c2s v2p0121c2s
v2p0269c2s v2p0329c1s v2p0329c2s
v2p0349c2s v2p0365c1s v2p0368c1s
v2p0382c2s v2p0384c1s v2p0475c1s
v3p0022c1s v3p0051c2s v3p0076c2s
v3p0227c2s v3p0314c2s v3p0317c2s
v3p0320c1m v3p0320c2m v3p0329c1s
v3p0404c2s v3p0446c2s v3p0449c2s
v4p0062c1s v4p0214c2s v4p0281c1s
v4p0363c1s v4p0364c1s v4p0371c1s
v4p0408c1s v4p0421c2s v4p0453c2s
v4p0477c2s v4p0493c2s v4p0520c2s
v4p0577c2s v4p0603c2s v4p0637c2s
v5p0049c1s v5p0049c2s v5p0054c1s
v5p0069c2s v5p0074c2m v5p0076c2s
v5p0143c1s v5p0166c1s v5p0216c1s
v5p0220c2s v5p0310c1s v5p0330c2s
v5p0357c2s v5p0376c1s v5p0417c1s
v5p0430c2s v5p0473c1s v5p0484c1s
v5p0492c2s v5p0494c2s v5p0495c2s
v5p0500c1s v5p0544c1s v5p0550c2s
v5p0615c1s v5p0619c2s v5p0632c2s
v5p0640c1s v5p0641c2s v6p0001c2s
v6p0005c2s v6p0012c1s v6p0045c1s
v6p0055c2s v6p0103c1m v6p0146c1s
v6p0174c1m v6p0234c1s v6p0238c1s
v6p0307c1s v6p0359c2s v6p0391c1s
v6p0523c2s v6p0563c1s v6p0695c2s
Beale, Sophia ... v3p0138c2s
v4p0043c1s v4p0257c2s v4p0413c1s
v4p0425c2s v5p0080c1s v5p0103c1s
v6p0055c1s v6p0491c1s v6p0657c1s
Beale, Sophia et al. ... v4p0557c2s
Beale, Sophia S. ... v4p0018c1s
Beale, T. ... v5p0133c1s
v5p0376c2s v5p0441c1s v5p0445c2s
v5p0501c2s v5p0591c2s
v6p0120c1s
Beam, S.J. ... v6p0600c1s
Beam, S.Z. ... v2p0183c2s
v2p0236c1s v2p0245c1s v3p0026c1s
v3p0084c2s v3p0145c1s v3p0214c2s
v3p0287c1s v3p0359c2s v3p0360c1s
v4p0103c2s v4p0190c2s v4p0477c1m
v5p0116c2s v5p0261c1s v5p0530c1s
v5p0535c1s v6p0576c1s
Beaman, A. ... v2p0135c1s
Beaman, C.C. ... v1p0928c2s
Beaman, C.C., jr. ... v1p0017c2s
v1p0050c2s v1p0294c2s
Beaman, E.Hulme ... v5p0139c2s
Beaman, E.O. ... v1p0279c2s
Beaman, G.W. ... v3p0378c2s
Beaman, S. ... v1p0283c2s
v1p0626c2s
Beames, D. ... v5p0222c2s
v5p0282c2s v5p0531c1s
Beames, J. ... v4p0077c2s
v4p0278c2s v5p0081c2s v5p0646c2s
Beames, John ... v4p0051c1s
Bean, A.W. ... v3p0406c2s
Bean, J.S. ... v2p0378c1s
Bean, J.S., jr. ... v1p0963c2s
v2p0411c1s
Bean, L.S. ... v3p0119c1s
v4p0111c2s
Bean, M.A. ... v1p0450c2s
v2p0077c2s
Bean, M.D. ... v1p1310c1s
Bean, R.B. ... v6p0446c2s
v6p0448c2s
Bean, S. ... v5p0305c1s
Bean, S.A. ... v1p0554c1s
v1p0891c1s
Bean, S.C. ... v3p0322c2s
Bean, T.H. ... v3p0373c1s
v5p0208c2s v5p0629c1s
Bean, T.H. and Goode, G.B.
v1p0456c2s v1p0457c1s
Bean, W.H. ... v6p0686c2s
Beane, S.C. ... v1p0866c2s
v1p1237c1s v6p0648c2s
Bear, B.De ... v5p0130c2s
Bear, E. ... v1p0015c1s
Bear, W. ... v1p0015c1s
Bear, W.E. ... v1p0015c2s
v1p0444c1s v1p0444c2m v1p0550c1s
v1p0741c1s v1p1261c1s v2p0005c2m
v2p0071c1s v2p0187c1s v2p0227c2s
v2p0247c2m v3p0221c1s v3p0241c1s
v4p0007c2s v4p0008c1m v4p0025c2s
v4p0092c2s v4p0206c1s v4p0219c1s
v4p0290c2s v4p0356c1s v4p0415c2s
v5p0009c1s v5p0009c2m v5p0285c1s
v5p0324c1s v5p0362c1s v6p0243c2s
Bear, W.E. et al. ... v4p0314c1s
v4p0318c1s
Bear, W.S. ... v2p0434c2s
Beard, A.E.S. ... v6p0573c2s
Beard, A.F. ... v2p0165c2s
v2p0210c2s v6p0609c1s
Beard, Annie E.S. ... v6p0095c2s
v6p0228c2s v6p0625c1s v6p0712c1s
Beard, C. ... v1p0098c1s
v1p0113c1s v1p0115c2s v1p0133c2s
v1p0205c2s v1p0243c2s v1p0247c2s
v1p0285c2s v1p0289c2s v1p0355c1s
v1p0368c1s v1p0409c2s v1p0488c2s
v1p0525c1s v1p0583c1s v1p0626c1s
v1p0720c1s v1p0863c2s v1p0941c1s
v1p0997c2s v1p1010c1s v1p1119c1s
v1p1260c1s v1p1286c1s v1p1305c2s
v1p1313c1s v1p1363c2s v1p1369c1s
v1p1432c2s v2p0368c2s
Beard, C.A. ... v6p0238c1s
Beard, D. ... v6p0025c2s
v6p0049c1s v6p0081c1s v6p0095c1m
v6p0095c2m v6p0170c2s v6p0179c1s
v6p0353c1s v6p0382c2m v6p0524c2s
v6p0596c1s v6p0597c1m v6p0599c1s
v6p0629c1s v6p0650c1s
Beard, D.C. ... v2p0309c2s
v3p0394c2s v6p0474c1m
Beard, Dr. ... v1p0112c1m
Beard, Emma E. ... v6p0420c1m
Beard, F. ... v2p0068c1s
v3p0068c1s v4p0030c2s v4p0159c2s
v4p0402c2s v4p0412c2s v5p0561c2s
v5p0562c1s v6p0626c2s
Beard, F.E. ... v4p0418c1s
Beard, G. ... v5p0298c2s
Beard, G.H. ... v4p0436c2s
v6p0312c1s
Beard, G.M. ... v1p0032c2m
v1p0134c2s v1p0156c2s v1p0264c2s
v1p0273c1s v1p0418c1s v1p0436c2s
v1p0644c1s v1p0644c2s v1p0698c2s
v1p0767c2s v1p0843c2s v1p0907c1s
v1p0955c2s v1p0989c2s v1p1203c2s
v1p1238c2s v1p1296c2s v1p1321c1s
v2p0161c2s v2p0239c2s v2p0265c2s
v2p0290c1s v2p0309c2s
Beard, G.M. et al. ... v2p0221c2s
Beard, J. ... v3p0154c1s
v3p0290c2s v3p0295c1s v3p0448c2s
v4p0514c2s
Beard, J.C. ... v1p0340c1s
v1p0800c2s v1p0842c2s v1p0936c2s
v1p0983c2s v2p0046c2s v4p0511c1s
v4p0565c2s
Beard, J.R. ... v1p0118c2s
v1p1304c2s
Beard, R. ... v2p0028c1s
v2p0109c2s v2p0371c1s v2p0438c1s
Beard, R.O. ... v2p0282c2s
v2p0317c2s v6p0498c2s
Beard, W.H. et al. ... v2p0184c2s
Beard, W.L. ... v5p0079c1s
v5p0271c1s
Beard, W.LeC. ... v4p0062c2s
v4p0358c2s v4p0540c1s v5p0342c2s
v5p0498c1s v5p0581c1s v6p0303c1s
Beard, W.S. ... v4p0261c2s
Beardmore, W.G. ... v4p0369c2s
Beardshear, W.M. ... v4p0171c1s
v5p0202c2s
Beardslee, C.S. ... v6p0061c1s
v6p0341c1s v6p0351c2s v6p0352c1s
v6p0377c2s
Beardslee, J.W. ... v5p0057c2s
Beardslee, L.A. ... v5p0565c2s
Beardslee, W.A. ... v3p0021c1s
v4p0122c2m
Beardsley, A. ... v3p0153c2s
Beardsley, C. ... v4p0256c1s
v5p0592c1s
Beardsley, C., jr. ... v4p0173c2s
Beardsley, E.E. ... v1p0005c2s
v1p0114c1s v1p0610c2s v1p0896c2s
v2p0242c2s v2p0324c1s
Beardsley, G. ... v5p0098c1s
v5p0192c1m v5p0578c2s
Beardsley, I.L. ... v2p0256c2s
Beardsley, J.J. ... v1p0297c1s
Beardsley, M.W. ... v6p0691c1s
Beare, H. ... v4p0291c2s
Beare, J.I. ... v4p0514c1s
Bearer, A. ... v2p0200c2s
Bearn, G.E. ... v5p0592c2s
v6p0145c1s
Bearn, S.Z. ... v6p0240c2s
Bearne, D. ... v3p0314c1s
v3p0431c2s v4p0107c2s
Beasley, C.O. ... v3p0442c1s
Beasley, F. ... v1p0309c2s
Beasley, H.R. ... v6p0581c1s
Beasley, W.L. ... v4p0305c1s
v4p0358c2s v6p0297c1s v6p0433c1s
v6p0636c2s v6p0650c1s
Beasley, Walter L. ... v6p0025c2s
Beatley, T.S. ... v6p0392c2s
Beaton, A.H. ... v5p0267c2s
v6p0293c2s
Beaton, D. ... v6p0419c1s
v6p0538c1m
Beaton, P. ... v1p0315c2s
v1p0372c1s v1p0542c2s v1p1218c2s
Beaton, P.C. ... v1p0783c1s
Beaton, W.W. ... v6p0257c2s
v6p0433c1s
Beatrice, Princess ... v2p0006c1s
Beatson, W.B. ... v6p0314c1s
v6p0503c1s
Beattie, A.S., Mrs. ... v1p1404c2s
Beattie, F. ... v4p0414c1s
Beattie, F.R. ... v5p0464c1s
Beattie, F.R. and Witt, J.De
v5p0464c1s
Beattie, F.R. and Minton, H.C.
v6p0514c2s
Beattie, H.P. ... v6p0493c2s
Beattie, J.A. ... v2p0082c1s
v2p0092c2s v2p0132c1s
Beattie, R.H. ... v4p0021c1s
v6p0464c1s
Beattie, W.R. ... v5p0292c1s
Beatty, A. ... v1p0189c1s
v1p0486c1s v1p0580c1m v1p0983c1s
v1p1207c2s v1p1258c2m v1p1353c1s
v1p1410c2s
Beatty, J. ... v3p0404c1s
Beatty, W. ... v4p0414c1s
Beatty, W.A. ... v2p0298c2s
v3p0420c1s v4p0501c2s
Beatty, W.T. ... v2p0371c1s
Beatty-Kingston, W. ... v3p0273c2s
v4p0388c1s v4p0447c1s v4p0492c2s
v5p0144c2s
v5p0615c2s
Beattys, H.H. ... v6p0513c2s
Beaty, J. ... v1p1323c2s

v2p0205c2s v3p0096c1s v3p0177c2s
Beaty, J., jr. v1p0598c2s
Beaty, S.A. v6p0316c1s
Beaty-Pownall, D.F. v4p0348c2s
Beau, E.Le v1p0858c2s
Beaucaire, R.de v2p0176c1s
Beauchamp, Earl v2p0277c2s
Beauchamp, H. v4p0280c1s
Beauchamp, S. v1p0309c2s
v1p0848c2s
Beauchamp, W.M. v2p0219c2s
v2p0220c1s v2p0229c2m v2p0322c1s
v2p0465c1s v3p0071c1s v3p0075c1s
v3p0094c2s v3p0099c2s v3p0126c2s
v3p0213c2s v3p0312c2s v4p0205c1m
v4p0205c2s v4p0256c2s v4p0281c2s
v4p0282c1s v4p0282c2s v4p0292c2m
v4p0363c1s v4p0376c2s v4p0384c1s
v4p0414c2m v4p0455c2s v5p0195c1s
v5p0239c2s v5p0287c2s v5p0298c2m
v5p0455c1s v5p0617c2s v6p0315c1s
v6p0329c1s v6p0467c2s
Beauclerk, R. v1p0014c2s
v1p1123c2s v3p0447c2s v4p0300c1s
Beauclerk, T. v4p0279c1s
Beaufain, A. v1p0468c1s
v1p0579c1s
Beaufort, Duke of v3p0205c1s
Beaufort, E.V. v5p0373c1s
v5p0413c1s v5p0496c2s
Beaufort, F. v2p0124c1s
Beaufort, M.de v1p0515c2s
v1p0597c1s
Beaufort, W.H.De v1p1322c1s
Beaufoy, P. v5p0586c1s
Beaugeard, T. v4p0133c1s
Beaugrand, H. v3p0065c2s
v4p0313c2s v4p0469c2s v5p0625c2s
Beaulieu, A.L. v1p1136c2s
v4p0480c1s v4p0496c2s v4p0532c1s
Beaulieu, B. v5p0607c1s
Beaulieu, G.von v4p0156c1s
Beaulieu, M.P.L. v5p0015c2s
Beaulieu, P.L. v1p0970c1s
v2p0096c1s v2p0475c2s v4p0345c2s
Beaulieu, P.Leroy v4p0615c1s
Beaulieu, T.H. v3p0283c1s
Beaumes, H. v6p0182c1s
Beaumont v5p0574c2s
Beaumont, A. v5p0442c1s
Beaumont, C.M. v5p0121c1s
Beaumont, Caroline M. v4p0463c2s
Beaumont, F. et al. v2p0143c2s
Beaumont, G.F. v3p0090c1s
Beaumont, H. v2p0276c1s
Beaumont, J. v1p0711c1s
v1p1102c2s
Beaumont, J.T.B. v1p0268c2s
v1p1364c2s
Beaumont, J.W. v3p0005c2s
Beaumont, M. v4p0407c2s
v4p0418c2s v5p0012c2s v5p0349c2s
v5p0616c2s
Beaumont, M.Elie de v1p0166c2s
Beaumont, Major v1p0367c1s
v1p1113c1s
Beaumont, Mary v5p0260c1s
Beaumont, R. v6p0690c2s
Beaumont, W.M. v4p0193c1s
Beaumont, W.W. v1p1080c2s
v1p1250c2s v1p1251c1s v4p0090c2s
v4p0475c2s v5p0041c1m v5p0095c2s
v6p0044c2s
Beaupre, A.M. v5p0023c1s
v6p0138c1s
Beauregard, G.T. v1p0221c1s
v1p0288c2s v1p0368c1s v1p0795c2s
v1p0873c1s v1p1107c1s v1p1346c1m
v2p0060c2s v2p0075c1s v2p0400c2s
v3p0328c1s v3p0442c2s
Beauvoir, A. v6p0022c2s
Beavan, A.H. v4p0041c2s
v5p0193c1s v5p0362c2s v5p0499c1s
v5p0507c2s
v5p0611c2s
Beaver, A. v2p0023c1s
v2p0024c1m v2p0326c2s v3p0022c1m
v3p0280c2s v3p0412c1s v4p0030c2s
v4p0031c1s v4p0070c2s v4p0218c1s
v4p0340c2s v4p0347c2s v4p0434c2s
v4p0442c2s v4p0517c2s v4p0561c1s
v6p0183c2s v6p0460c2s v6p0590c2s
Beaver, Alfred v2p0326c1m
v2p0371c2s
Beaver, B. v1p1011c2s
v1p1113c2s
Beaver, J.A. v3p0231c2s
v4p0485c2s
Beazeley, M. v3p0196c2s
v3p0449c2s
Beazell, Mabel v6p0142c2s
Beazley, C.R. v5p0354c2s
v5p0361c1m v5p0391c1s v5p0413c1s
v5p0499c2s v5p0645c2s v6p0098c2s
v6p0164c1s v6p0200c2s v6p0250c2s
v6p0258c2s v6p0400c1s v6p0510c2s
Beazley, S. v6p0021c1s
Bebb, C.H. v4p0200c1s
Bebb, M.S. v4p0623c1s
Bebok, H.M. v5p0288c1s
Becczner v6p0196c2s
Becelaere, F.L.van v6p0643c2s
Becerra, R. v3p0092c1s
Bechamp, A. v1p0086c1s
Beche, H.de la, Sir v1p0508c1s
Becher, E. v6p0392c2s
Becher, F.A. v3p0337c1s
v3p0442c2s
Bechler, W.H. v6p0669c1s
Bechtel, F.A. v5p0612c2s
Beck, C. v1p0513c2s
v1p0727c2s v1p1180c2s v1p1334c2s
Beck, C.F. v5p0080c2s
Beck, E. v4p0452c2s
v6p0365c1s
Beck, F.C. v1p1038c2s
Beck, H. v6p0040c2s
Beck, J.M. v4p0156c2s
v4p0610c1s v5p0233c2s v6p0019c2s
v6p0659c1s
Beck, J.N. v6p0322c1s
Beck, J.R. v1p1012c1s
Beck, J.T. v1p0119c1s
Beck, L. v4p0629c1s
Beck, L.C. v1p1316c1s
v1p1415c2s
Beck, M. v4p0260c1s
Beck, M.E. v1p0733c1s
Beck, S.W. v2p0180c2s
v4p0228c2m v4p0468c1s v4p0517c2s
v4p0590c2s
Beck, T. v4p0116c2s
v4p0280c1s
Beck, T.R. v1p0127c1s
v1p0131c1s v1p1017c1s v2p0282c2s
v2p0333c1s v4p0297c1s
Beckaby, J. v1p0076c1s
Becke, H. v1p1122c2s
Becke, L. v4p0064c2s
v4p0153c2s v4p0345c1s v4p0405c1s
v5p0203c2s v5p0337c2s v5p0406c1s
v5p0429c1s v5p0456c2s v5p0467c2s
v5p0513c1s v6p0228c1s v6p0619c2s
Becke, L. and Jeffery, W.. v4p0210c1s
v5p0039c2s v5p0250c2s v5p0566c2s
Becke, L. et al. v4p0354c2s
Becke, Louis v5p0210c1s
v5p0524c1s v5p0555c1s v6p0440c1s
Becker, A. v1p1118c1s
Becker, B.H. v2p0054c2s
v2p0079c2s v2p0142c1s v2p0170c2s
v2p0245c2s v2p0382c2s v2p0393c2s
Becker, Bernard H. v4p0546c2s
Becker, C. v3p0293c1m
v5p0408c1m v5p0598c1s v5p0603c1s
v6p0016c2s v6p0018c1m v6p0089c1s
v6p0146c2s v6p0452c1s v6p0542c1s
v6p0667c1s
Becker, G.F. v1p0224c1s
v2p0064c1s v2p0089c2s v2p0107c1s
v2p0119c2s v2p0127c1s v2p0173c2s
v2p0174c1s v2p0199c1s v2p0463c1m
v3p0085c1s v3p0126c1s v3p0363c1s
v3p0392c2s v4p0006c1s v4p0006c2s
v4p0165c2s v4p0227c1s v4p0231c1s
v4p0454c2s v4p0552c1s v4p0576c2s
v5p0007c2s v5p0038c2s v5p0146c2s
v5p0161c2s v5p0313c2s v5p0443c2s
v5p0453c1s v5p0491c2m v5p0586c2s
v6p0251c1s
Becker, G.P. v1p0287c1s
Becker, H. v3p0202c2s
Becker, I. v4p0540c2s
Becker, L.E. v1p1426c1m
Becker, M.J. v3p0137c1s
Becker, O.M. v6p0025c2s
v6p0708c2s
Becker, O.M. and Brown, Walter
v6p0616c1s
Becker, T.A. v1p0066c2s
v1p0127c1s v1p0262c1s v1p0356c2s
v1p1050c1s v1p1119c2m v1p1120c1s
v1p1175c1s v2p0097c1s v3p0416c2s
v4p0171c1s
Becker, W.F. v5p0520c1s
Becket, J.a v3p0400c2s
Becket, J.J.a v2p0023c2s
v2p0110c2s v3p0120c2s v3p0151c1s
v3p0170c1s v3p0367c1s v4p0011c2m
v4p0040c1s v4p0259c2s v4p0343c2s
v4p0492c2s v5p0043c1s v5p0309c2s
v5p0434c2s v6p0110c2s
Beckett, A.a v1p0082c2s
v2p0068c1s v2p0434c2s v3p0037c1s
v4p0446c2s v4p0447c1m
Beckett, A.a and Burnand, F.C.
v2p0359c2s v3p0349c2s
Beckett, A.W.a v4p0146c2s
v4p0196c1s v4p0229c2s v4p0475c1s
v5p0576c1s
Beckett, Arthur v5p0534c1s
Beckett, E. v2p0022c2s
v2p0096c1s v2p0359c2s v2p0389c1s
v2p0468c2s v5p0234c2s
Beckett, E.W. v3p0027c2s
v3p0085c1s v3p0183c1s v4p0237c1s
Beckett, E.W. et al. v3p0004c1s
Beckett, Edmund v6p0553c2s
Beckett, Ernest v5p0492c1s
Beckett, R.A. v3p0462c2s
Beckett, W.H. v3p0102c2s
v3p0323c1s
Beckford, A. v5p0022c2s
Becknell, W.L. v2p0345c1s
Beckner, W.M. v2p0388c1s
Beckton, J.G. v1p0495c1s
Beckurts, C.L. v5p0159c1s
v5p0290c1s
Beckwith, A. v1p0211c1s
v1p0268c1s
Beckwith, C. v3p0051c2s
Beckwith, C.A. v4p0301c1s
Beckwith, D.H. v2p0206c2s
v2p0320c1s v3p0200c1s
Beckwith, G.C. v1p1035c2s
Beckwith, H.T. v1p0142c2s
Beckwith, H.W. v4p0274c1s
Beckwith, I.T. v4p0031c2s
Beckwith, J. v3p0290c1s
Beckwith, N.W. v1p0174c1s
v1p0194c2s v1p0284c1s v1p0467c2s
v1p0635c2s v1p0708c2s
Beckwith, S.H. v6p0668c1s
Beckwith, T.D. and Kellerman, K.F.
v6p0046c2s
Beckwith, W.P. v2p0202c2s
v3p0146c1s
Becole, Louis v5p0030c1s
Becoulet, C. v1p1370c2s
Becquard, M.F. v1p0288c1s
Becquerel, E. v1p0399c1s
Becquerel, H. v5p0475c2s
Becquerel, M. v1p0400c2s
Becquerel, M.E. v1p0825c2s
Bedard, T.P. v4p0399c1s
Beddard, F.E. v2p0128c2s
v3p0014c2s v3p0070c2s v3p0092c2s
v3p0126c2s v4p0166c1m v4p0226c2s
v4p0371c2s v4p0413c1s v5p0050c2s
v5p0071c2s v5p0098c2s v5p0418c2s
v5p0482c2s
Beddoe et al. v1p0196c1s
Beddoe, D. v5p0023c2s
v5p0139c2s v5p0269c2s v5p0555c2s
Beddoe, J. v1p0174c2s
v1p0565c2s v2p0093c2s v2p0212c1s
v2p0418c2s v4p0020c1m v4p0513c2s
v4p0617c2s v5p0297c2s v5p0358c2s
v5p0519c1s
Beddoe, J. and Moore, A.W.
v5p0359c1s
Beddoes, H.R. v6p0007c2s
Bede, C. v1p0056c2s
v1p0158c1s v1p0188c2s v1p0327c1s
v1p0439c2s v1p0590c2s v1p0922c1s
v2p0001c1s v2p0035c1s v2p0077c1s
v2p0108c2s v2p0153c1s v2p0154c1s
v2p0158c2s v2p0163c2s v2p0177c2s
v2p0273c2s v2p0297c1s v2p0316c2s
v2p0325c2s v2p0334c2s v2p0382c2s
v2p0404c1s v2p0459c1s v2p0461c1s
Bedel, F. and Ryan, H.J. . v4p0384c2s
Bedel, J. v2p0311c1s
Bedell, C.H. v4p0165c1s
Bedell, G.T. v2p0044c1s
v2p0368c2s
Bedford, Bishop of v3p0256c1s
Bedford, G.A. v1p1091c1s
Bedford, G.S. v1p1007c1s
Bedford, H. v1p0053c1s
v1p0114c2s v1p0216c1s v1p0366c2s
v1p0407c2s v1p0513c1s v1p0518c1s
v1p0570c1s v1p0573c2s v1p0579c2s
v1p0590c2s v1p0597c1s v1p0676c2s
v1p0682c1s v1p0775c2s v1p0912c1s
v1p0930c1s v1p0934c1s v1p1041c1s
v1p1074c1s v1p1084c1s v1p1105c2s
v1p1126c2s v1p1132c2s v1p1147c2s
v1p1218c1s v1p1252c1s v1p1268c2s
v1p1269c1s v1p1291c2s v1p1337c2s
v1p1381c1s v1p1440c1s v2p0481c1s
v3p0260c1s
Bedford, H.L. v2p0121c2s
Bedford, J.R. v1p1376c1s
Bedford, R. v6p0254c1s
Bedford, R.C. v4p0397c1s
v4p0587c2s v5p0595c2s
Bedford, W. v6p0409c2s
Bedford, W.K.R. v3p0135c1s
v4p0071c1s v4p0072c1s v4p0139c1s
v5p0361c1s
Bedford, Wimer v6p0668c1s
Bedier, J. v6p0657c1s
Bedloe, E. v3p0078c2s
Bedo, G. v1p0409c1s
Bee, H.F. v1p1017c2s
Beebe, C.W. v6p0021c2s
v6p0067c2m v6p0226c1s v6p0539c2s
v6p0713c2s
Beebe, H.L. v4p0392c1s
Beebe, J.A. v3p0309c2s
v3p0371c2s
Beebe, Katherine v5p0106c1s
Beebe, M.L. v3p0475c1s
Beebe, R. v1p1077c2s
Beeby, C.F. v6p0340c2s
Beecher, C. v1p1337c1s
v2p0266c1s v3p0012c2s
Beecher, C.E. v1p0373c2s
v1p0578c2s v1p1197c1s v3p0022c2s

v3p0044c2s v3p0052c2s v3p0237c2s
v3p0247c1s v3p0404c2s v3p0413c1s
v3p0432c2s v4p0071c1s v4p0417c2s
v4p0468c1s v4p0573c2s v4p0584c1m
v4p0584c2s v5p0089c1s v5p0197c2s
v5p0363c1s v5p0546c1s v5p0558c2s
v5p0565c1s v5p0590c2s v5p0597c1s
v6p0550c1s v6p0657c1s v6p0709c2s
Beecher, C.E. and Call, R.E.
v2p0309c2s v2p0360c2s
Beecher, C.E. and Dodge, W.W.
v4p0524c1s
Beecher, E. v1p0035c2s
v1p0095c2s v1p0121c1s v1p0131c2s
v1p0263c2s v1p0290c1s v1p0290c2s
v1p0603c1s v1p0612c2s v1p0689c1s
v1p0754c1s v1p0793c2s v1p0843c1s
v1p0920c2s v1p1151c2s v1p1386c1s
Beecher, F. v6p0188c2s
Beecher, F.A. v3p0165c2s
v6p0594c2s
Beecher, H.W. v1p0689c1s
v2p0438c1s v3p0250c2s
Beecher, H.W. and Dyke, J.Van.
v2p0088c2s
Beecher, H.W. et al. v2p0106c2s
Beecher, L. v1p0296c1s
v1p0496c1s v1p1088c2s v1p1100c1s
v1p1103c1s
Beecher, T.K. v5p0440c1s
Beecher, W.J. v1p0121c2m
v1p0246c2s v2p0034c2s v2p0150c2s
v2p0151c2s v2p0244c2s v2p0434c1s
v2p0443c2m v3p0041c2s v3p0042c1s
v3p0145c1s v3p0246c2s v3p0408c1s
v4p0054c1s v4p0058c1s v4p0431c1s
v5p0056c2s v5p0057c1s v5p0058c1s
v6p0343c2s v6p0650c1s
Beeching, H.C. v2p0058c2s
v2p0185c1s v2p0249c1s v2p0263c1s
v2p0277c1s v2p0389c2s v2p0402c2s
v3p0054c2s v3p0410c1s v3p0425c1s
v4p0108c2s v5p0122c2s v5p0192c1s
v5p0192c2s v5p0364c1s v5p0455c2s
v5p0456c1s v5p0483c1s v5p0489c2s
v5p0617c2s v6p0009c1s v6p0040c2s
v6p0208c1s v6p0587c1s v6p0587c2s
v6p0588c1s v6p0689c1s
Beede, C.W. v6p0438c2s
Beede, F.H. v6p0451c1s
Beede, V.V.M. v5p0050c2s
v5p0070c1s v5p0274c2s v5p0302c2s
v5p0326c1s v5p0380c1s v6p0130c2s
v6p0273c1s v6p0286c2s v6p0331c1s
v6p0466c2s v6p0656c1s
Beede, V.Van M. v6p0120c2m
v6p0228c2s
Beedham, L.E. v6p0094c1s
Beedy, H.B.C. v4p0007c1s
v4p0433c2s
Beedy, M.E. v1p0352c1s
v1p1176c2s v1p1423c2s
Beedy, Mary E. v3p0170c1s
Beehler, W.H. v3p0310c2s
v5p0543c2s v6p0337c1s
Beek, H.L. v4p0356c2s
Beeke, L. v6p0389c1s
v6p0635c2s
Beeker, A. v1p1055c1s
Beeker, G.F. v2p0215c2s
Beekman, J.S. v2p0117c1s
Beelars, M.F. v6p0090c1s
Beeman, J.S. v2p0137c2s
Beemer, N.H. v1p0816c1s
Beer, G.L. v5p0209c2s
v5p0226c1s v5p0245c1s v6p0127c1s
v6p0243c2s v6p0266c2s v6p0273c2s
v6p0354c2s v6p0670c1s v6p0685c2s
v6p0693c2s
Beer, J.T. v2p0382c1s
Beer, M. v5p0303c1s
Beer, R. v4p0405c1s
v4p0409c1s v4p0491c1s v5p0496c1s
Beer, T.H.de v3p0388c1s
v4p0164c2m v4p0260c1s
Beer, W. v4p0329c2s
v5p0334c2s v5p0406c1s
Beer, W. and Maedler, J.H.
v1p0866c1s
Beerbohm, C. v3p0307c1s
v4p0502c2s
Beerbohm, J. v1p0945c2s
Beerbohm, M. v4p0160c1s
v4p0217c1s v5p0003c1m v5p0005c1m
v5p0025c1s v5p0040c2s v5p0044c2s
v5p0051c1s v5p0053c1s v5p0073c2s
v5p0084c1s v5p0087c1s v5p0100c2m
v5p0115c2s v5p0140c2s v5p0141c1s
v5p0154c1s v5p0167c1m v5p0167c2m
v5p0171c2s v5p0174c2s v5p0191c2s
v5p0195c1m v5p0202c2s v5p0205c1s
v5p0208c1s v5p0209c2s v5p0224c1s
v5p0233c2s v5p0251c2m v5p0256c2s
v5p0257c2s v5p0259c1s v5p0262c1s
v5p0278c1s v5p0278c2m v5p0299c1s
v5p0303c2s v5p0304c2s v5p0310c1m
v5p0311c2s v5p0319c1s v5p0324c2s
v5p0341c1s v5p0355c2s v5p0360c1s
v5p0363c2s v5p0364c1s v5p0369c1s
v5p0377c1s v5p0392c2s v5p0393c1s
v5p0394c2s v5p0417c2s v5p0425c1s
v5p0439c1s v5p0446c2m v5p0451c2m
v5p0454c2s v5p0465c1s v5p0468c1s
v5p0478c2m v5p0480c1s v5p0480c2s
v5p0496c2s v5p0497c2m v5p0508c2s
v5p0509c1s v5p0515c1s v5p0522c2m
v5p0523c1m v5p0523c2m v5p0524c1s
v5p0524c2m v5p0525c2s v5p0527c1s
v5p0538c1s v5p0552c2m v5p0564c1s
v5p0575c2s v5p0585c1s v5p0610c1s
v5p0617c1s v5p0623c2s v5p0628c2s
v5p0631c1s v5p0644c1s v5p0645c1s
v6p0003c1m v6p0003c2s v6p0011c2s
v6p0029c1s v6p0029c2s v6p0048c2s
v6p0052c2m v6p0059c1s v6p0060c1s
v6p0077c2s v6p0086c1s v6p0100c2s
v6p0103c1s v6p0112c2s v6p0121c2s
v6p0138c1s v6p0156c1m v6p0158c2m
v6p0163c2s v6p0165c2m v6p0169c1s
v6p0180c1s v6p0180c2m v6p0181c1m
v6p0181c2s v6p0195c1m v6p0201c2s
v6p0208c2s v6p0210c2s v6p0212c2m
v6p0217c2m v6p0221c2s v6p0245c1s
v6p0246c2s v6p0256c1s v6p0256c2m
v6p0262c1s v6p0275c2s v6p0276c1s
v6p0276c2s v6p0279c2m v6p0280c1s
v6p0283c1s v6p0283c2s v6p0284c1s
v6p0286c1s v6p0288c2s v6p0289c2s
v6p0298c1s v6p0302c1s v6p0305c2s
v6p0306c1m v6p0306c2s v6p0329c2m
v6p0345c2m v6p0350c2s v6p0352c2s
v6p0365c2s v6p0367c2s v6p0379c2s
v6p0388c2s v6p0393c1s v6p0393c2s
v6p0397c1s v6p0403c1s v6p0419c2s
v6p0439c1s v6p0449c2s v6p0450c2s
v6p0473c1s v6p0478c1s v6p0480c2s
v6p0483c1s v6p0495c1m v6p0499c2s
v6p0500c1m v6p0504c1s v6p0536c1s
v6p0545c2s v6p0561c2m v6p0570c2s
v6p0578c1s v6p0586c2s v6p0587c2s
v6p0588c1m v6p0589c1s v6p0589c2m
v6p0620c2s v6p0627c2m v6p0630c1m
v6p0630c2s v6p0641c2m v6p0643c2s
v6p0649c1s v6p0649c2s v6p0654c1s
v6p0662c1s v6p0663c2s v6p0685c2s
v6p0691c2m v6p0698c2m v6p0699c2s
v6p0711c1s
Beerbohm, Max v5p0261c2s
v5p0490c2s v5p0575c2s v6p0102c2s
v6p0103c1s v6p0439c1s v6p0495c1s
v6p0582c1s v6p0689c1s
Beers, F.A., Mrs. v2p0422c1s
Beers, G.W. v1p0658c2s
Beers, H. v6p0218c2s
Beers, H.A. v1p0541c2s
v1p1436c1s v2p0077c2s v2p0092c1s
v2p0094c2s v2p0267c1s v2p0293c1s
v2p0303c2s v2p0307c2s v2p0415c1s
v3p0074c2s v3p0099c1s v3p0253c2s
v3p0278c1s v3p0449c1s v4p0183c2s
v4p0623c1s v5p0467c2s v5p0601c2s
v6p0201c1s v6p0207c2s v6p0588c1s
v6p0653c2s
Beers, R.W. v5p0387c1s
Beers, W.A. v2p0268c1s
Beers, W.G. v1p0073c2s
v1p0194c1s v1p0195c1s v1p0223c2s
v2p0065c2s v2p0244c2s v3p0123c2s
Beery, E.D. v5p0523c2s
Beesley, E.S. v1p1037c2s
v1p1309c2s v1p1319c2s v1p1431c1s
Beesly, A.H. v1p0340c2s
v1p0499c1s v1p0499c2s v2p0403c2s
Beesly, E.S. v1p0207c2s
v1p0256c1s v1p0478c2s v1p0482c1s
v1p0498c2s v1p0546c1s v1p0650c1s
v1p0904c1s v1p1320c1m v4p0266c1s
Beeson, Emma B. v6p0088c1s
Beeson, S.V. v1p1085c1s
v2p0326c1s
Beeston, C. v2p0483c2s
Beet, J.A. v3p0081c1s
v5p0059c2s v5p0280c2s v6p0063c1s
v6p0294c1s
Beet, Thomas v6p0172c1s
Beeton, H.C. v3p0055c1s
Beeton, H.R. v4p0144c1s
Beeton, M.M. v5p0559c2s
v5p0626c1s
Beeton, Mary and Pearson, K.
v5p0347c1s
Beets, N. v1p1362c1s
Beetz, W. v1p1390c1s
Beever, J. v6p0622c1s
Beevor, C.E. and Horsley, V.
v3p0285c2s
Beevor, H.R. v6p0498c2s
Begbie, A.H. v5p0155c1s
v5p0342c2s v5p0355c1s v5p0421c1s
v5p0556c2s
Begbie, A.J. v1p0047c2s
Begbie, E.H. v5p0605c2s
Begbie, H. v5p0203c2s
v6p0153c1s v6p0263c1s v6p0319c2s
v6p0534c1s
Begetsky, A.N. v5p0356c2s
Begg, A. v3p0066c1s
Begg, H. v4p0461c2s
Begg, J.H. v5p0002c1s
Begg, R.B. v3p0437c1s
Begg, W.P. v1p0784c1s
Beggs, F.S. v4p0382c2s
Beggs, T. v3p0017c1s
v3p0099c1s v3p0125c1s v3p0457c2s
Begle, G.G. v5p0263c1s
Begley, W. v6p0461c1s
Begoras, W. v6p0593c1m
Behan, W.P. v6p0063c2s
Behenna, Kathleen A. v5p0377c2s
Behn, H.E. v6p0164c1s
Behr, F.B. v5p0183c2s
v6p0425c2m v6p0530c2s
Behr, H.H. v1p0998c1s
Behrend, B.A. v6p0013c2s
Behrend, H. v3p0118c2s
v3p0272c2m v3p0437c2s
Behrends, A.J.F. v2p0081c1s
v2p0235c2s v3p0314c2s v3p0373c2s
v4p0129c1s v4p0379c1s
Behrends, A.J.F. et al. .. v3p0073c2s
Behrens, T.T. v6p0561c2s
Behrens, W.J. v2p0160c1s
v2p0222c2s
Behringer, G.F. v1p0777c1s
v1p1045c1s v4p0270c1s v4p0345c1s
v5p0369c1s
Beighton, E.E. v2p0208c1s
Beighton, J.T. v3p0361c1s
Beighton, T.D. v1p0117c1s
v6p0314c1s v6p0315c1s
Beigitz, J.H. v6p0642c2s
Beitler, A.M. v6p0348c2s
Beke, C.T. v1p0012c1s
v1p0724c2s v1p0805c2s v1p0922c2m
Belaney, R. v2p0199c2s
Belasco, D. v6p0180c2s
v6p0181c2s v6p0642c1s
Belasco, David v6p0003c1s
Belasco, G. v6p0523c1s
Belcher, D. v1p1066c2s
Belcher, E. v6p0505c2s
Belcher, J. v1p0148c2s
v1p0288c1s v1p0847c2s v1p1060c1s
v1p1094c1s v6p0709c1s
Belcher, J.H. v1p0867c2s
Belcher, J.J. v1p0008c1s
v1p0424c2s v1p1209c2s
Belcher, S.W., Mrs. v5p0156c2s
Belcher, T.W. v2p0382c2s
Belcher, W.E. v6p0508c1s
Belcikowski, A. v2p0347c1m
v3p0336c2m v4p0449c2m v5p0457c1m
v6p0506c2m
Beldam, J. v1p1131c1s
v1p1363c1s
Belden, A.L. v3p0165c2s
Belden, D. v3p0375c1s
Belden, H.M. v5p0352c1s
v5p0517c1s v6p0422c2s
Belden, J.VanZ. v5p0384c1s
v5p0414c2s v5p0582c2s
Belden, W.P. v5p0452c1s
Belderson, S.W. v5p0201c1s
v5p0550c1s v6p0263c1s
Belding, A.M. v4p0253c1s
v4p0574c2s v5p0405c1s v5p0504c2s
v6p0216c1s
Belfield, H.H. v3p0267c1s
Belfield, Jane v6p0285c1s
v6p0299c2s
Belford, S.W. v5p0112c2s
v5p0444c1s v5p0444c2s
Belford, W.H. v6p0694c2s
Belgrave, D. v2p0122c1s
v2p0239c2s
Belgrave, D.J. v2p0243c2s
v4p0223c1s
Belin, H.E. v5p0205c2s
v5p0403c2s v6p0102c2m v6p0597c1m
v6p0667c2s
Belisle, D.W. v1p1090c2s
Belknap, G.E. v1p0936c2s
v3p0327c1s v4p0399c1s v5p0017c2s
v5p0219c1s
Belknap, H.W. v6p0155c2s
v6p0342c2s
Belknap, M.G. v1p0968c2s
Belknap, W.R. v2p0204c2s
Bell, A. v1p0056c2s
v2p0462c2s v3p0282c2s v5p0638c1s
Bell, A., Mrs. v5p0001c1s
v5p0038c1s v5p0051c1s v5p0575c2s
Bell, A.F. v5p0095c2s
v6p0155c1s v6p0404c2s
Bell, A.G. v1p0835c1s
v1p1004c1m v1p1176c2s v1p1222c1s
v1p1222c2m v1p1234c2s v1p1291c1s
v2p0113c2s v2p0395c1s v3p0112c2s
v3p0331c1s v3p0423c1s v4p0149c2s
v4p0177c1s v5p0161c2s v5p0268c1s
v5p0399c1s v5p0524c2s v6p0047c1s
v6p0590c1s v6p0691c1s
Bell, A.G., Mrs. v4p0541c1s
Bell, A.H. v1p1291c1s
v5p0478c1s v5p0561c2s v6p0277c2s
v6p0319c1s v6p0530c2s v6p0599c1s
v6p0627c1s v6p0636c1s
Bell, A.J. v5p0367c2s
v5p0519c2s v6p0679c2s
Bell, A.M. v1p0421c1s

v2p0009c1m v2p0249c1s v2p0326c2s
v2p0414c1s v3p0112c2s v3p0330c1s
v3p0404c1s v3p0451c1s v3p0451c2s
v4p0104c2s v4p0146c2s v4p0202c1s
v4p0469c2s v5p0210c2s v5p0223c1s
v6p0465c1s
Bell, A.N. v1p0011c1s
v1p1013c2s v1p1070c1s v6p0613c1s
Bell, A.N. and Troebridge, W.P.
v2p0199c2s
Bell, Acton v1p1308c2s
Bell, Arthur, Mrs. v5p0012c2s
v6p0102c2s
Bell, Arthur H. v6p0645c1s
Bell, B. and Gale, R. v1p0604c1s
Bell, C. v1p0110c1s
v3p0123c1s v3p0204c2s v4p0140c2s
v4p0534c2s v5p0367c1s
Bell, C.A. v2p0236c1s
v5p0490c1s v5p0508c1s
Bell, C.E. v2p0155c2s
Bell, C.F. v6p0472c2s
Bell, C.F.M. v2p0134c1s
Bell, C.H. v1p0028c2s
v1p0110c1s v1p0464c2s v1p1053c1s
v2p0150c1s v2p0233c1s v3p0301c2s
Bell, C.J. v1p0399c1s
Bell, C.L. v6p0630c2s
Bell, C.N. v4p0385c1s
Bell, C.R. v1p1239c1s
Bell, C.S.M. v2p0133c2s
Bell, Canon et al. v4p0113c2s
Bell, Charlotte v6p0426c1s
Bell, Clark v4p0534c2s
Bell, E. v1p0009c2s
v1p0379c2s v1p1332c2s v2p0047c2s
v4p0606c2s
Bell, E.C. v4p0297c2s
Bell, E.D. v5p0281c2s
v5p0626c1s
Bell, E.H. v3p0191c1s
v3p0436c2s v4p0047c2s v4p0303c2s
v5p0170c2s v5p0269c2s v5p0356c2s
Bell, E.I. v2p0019c1s
v2p0093c2s v2p0123c2s v2p0326c2s
v2p0416c1s v3p0425c2s v4p0023c2m
v4p0024c1s v4p0072c2s v4p0182c2s
v4p0194c2s v4p0510c1s v4p0538c2s
v4p0546c2s
Bell, E.Ingress v2p0346c1s
Bell, E.J. v4p0493c1s
Bell, E.K. v3p0261c1s
Bell, E.Q. v2p0104c2s
Bell, E.Y. v1p1348c2s
Bell, F. v4p0578c1s
v5p0256c2s v5p0360c1s v5p0374c1s
v5p0579c1s v6p0584c2s
Bell, F.H. v5p0100c2s
Bell, F.J. v1p0817c2s
v2p0205c2s
Bell, F.L. v6p0600c2s
Bell, Florence v5p0388c2s
v6p0532c2s v6p0712c1s
Bell, G. v1p1091c2s
v6p0668c1s
Bell, G.J. and Jenkin, F.. v2p0402c1s
Bell, G.L. v5p0154c1s
v5p0389c2s v6p0012c2s v6p0186c1s
Bell, G.M. v1p0334c2s
v1p0761c2s v1p1044c2s v1p1370c1s
Bell, G.M. et al. v6p0406c2s
Bell, G.W. v5p0039c1s
Bell, Gertrude L. v5p0258c1s
Bell, H. v1p1063c2s
v3p0211c2s v3p0212c2s v4p0132c1m
v4p0202c1s v4p0258c2s v4p0562c1s
v4p0608c1s v5p0008c1s v5p0285c1s
v5p0420c2s v5p0548c1s v6p0219c1s
v6p0267c2m v6p0314c2m v6p0373c2s
Bell, H.H. v5p0635c2s
v6p0353c1s
Bell, H.J. v1p0456c1s
v4p0197c2s
Bell, H.P. v1p1080c2s
Bell, H.T.M. v3p0049c1s
v3p0254c1s
Bell, H.W. v5p0215c1s
v5p0553c1s
Bell, Hamilton v6p0453c2s
Bell, Horace v5p0286c2s
v6p0528c2s
Bell, Hugh, Mrs. v4p0341c1s
Bell, I. v1p0288c1s
Bell, I.L. v1p0268c1s
v1p0493c2s v1p0663c2m v1p0665c1s
v1p0665c2m v1p0666c1s v1p0749c2s
Bell, J. v1p0351c2s
v1p0866c1s v1p1415c1s v3p0037c2s
v3p0179c1s v3p0408c2s v3p0465c2s
v4p0442c2s v4p0602c2s v5p0631c1s
v5p0642c1s
Bell, J.C. v4p0087c2s
v4p0106c1s v4p0537c2s v4p0585c2s
Bell, J.C. et al. v4p0129c1s
Bell, J.D. v1p0082c1s
v5p0643c1s
Bell, J.J. v3p0173c1s
v3p0350c2s v4p0086c2s v4p0469c1s
v4p0498c2s v4p0499c2s v5p0091c2s
v5p0202c1s v5p0342c2s v5p0360c1s
v5p0481c1s v6p0012c2s v6p0065c2s
v6p0147c1s v6p0231c1s v6p0368c2s
v6p0403c1s v6p0427c1s v6p0434c1s
v6p0482c1s v6p0532c1s v6p0551c2s
v6p0591c2s v6p0691c1m
Bell, J.M. v1p0780c2s
v5p0090c2s v6p0121c1s v6p0455c1s
v6p0648c2s
Bell, J.S. v1p0188c1s
v1p0759c2m v1p1248c1s v2p0084c2s
v3p0313c2s
Bell, J.T. v5p0199c1s
Bell, J.W. v1p0514c2s
v1p1215c2s v2p0048c1s v2p0456c1s
v3p0065c2s v3p0288c1s v3p0398c1s
Bell, James M. v6p0455c1s
Bell, L. v2p0063c2s
v2p0364c1s v2p0393c2s v2p0413c2s
v2p0450c2s v3p0076c1s v3p0133c2s
v3p0168c1s v3p0223c1s v3p0251c1m
v3p0458c1m v4p0079c1s v4p0175c2s
v4p0176c2s v4p0384c2s v5p0183c1m
v5p0183c2m v5p0184c1s v5p0184c2s
v5p0185c1s v5p0185c2s v5p0237c2s
v5p0252c2s v5p0377c2s v5p0531c1s
v6p0197c1s v6p0198c2s v6p0204c1s
v6p0400c1s v6p0512c2s
Bell, L. and Rowland, H.A.
v3p0263c2s
Bell, L., Sir v3p0223c2s
Bell, Lilian v6p0100c2s
v6p0663c2s
Bell, Louis v6p0197c2s
v6p0198c2s
Bell, M. v1p1183c1s
v2p0016c1s v2p0036c1s v2p0037c1s
v2p0037c2s v2p0046c2s v2p0047c1s
v2p0105c2s v2p0168c2s v2p0294c1s
v2p0295c1s v2p0324c1s v2p0365c1s
v2p0393c2s v3p0048c1s v3p0188c1s
v3p0200c2s v3p0252c1s v3p0270c1s
v3p0275c1s v3p0467c1s v4p0032c2s
v4p0033c1s v4p0383c1s v4p0455c1s
v5p0173c2s v5p0310c1s v6p0304c2s
Bell, M.S. v3p0327c2m
v5p0480c2s
Bell, Mark v4p0105c1s
Bell, Mary v4p0267c1s
v5p0113c1s v5p0530c1s v5p0581c1s
Bell, Mrs. v1p1100c1s
Bell, N. v6p0152c1s
Bell, Nancy v6p0693c2s
Bell, P.G. v2p0130c2s
Bell, R. v1p0036c1s
v1p0111c1s v1p0170c2s v1p0244c2s
v1p0320c1s v1p0426c1s v1p0459c2s
v1p0492c2s v1p0716c1s v1p1059c1s
v1p1127c2s v1p1143c2s v1p1154c1s
v1p1186c2s v1p1217c2s v1p1242c1s
v1p1260c1s v1p1262c2s v1p1299c2s
v1p1322c1s v2p0185c1s v4p0268c1s
v5p0043c1s v5p0103c2s v5p0275c1s
v5p0305c1s v5p0376c1s v5p0532c2s
v6p0356c1s
Bell, R. and Dilke, C. ... v6p0652c1s
Bell, R.F. v3p0413c1s
v6p0195c2s
Bell, R.G. and Kellogg, W.L.
v6p0594c2s
Bell, R.M. v5p0534c2s
Bell, S. v5p0569c1s
v6p0115c1s v6p0231c2s v6p0388c1s
v6p0506c2s v6p0516c1s v6p0687c1s
Bell, S.D. v1p0911c2s
Bell, S.L. v4p0074c2s
Bell, W. v1p0051c1s
v1p0200c1s v1p0370c2s v1p1261c1s
Bell, W.A. v1p0956c2s
Bell, W.H. v1p1254c1s
v3p0089c2s v5p0163c2s v6p0640c1s
Bell, W.T. v5p0424c2s
v6p0167c1s
Bellacombe, A.de v1p0030c2s
Bellaigne, C. v6p0274c2s
Bellairs, C. v5p0246c2s
v5p0247c1s v5p0401c1s v6p0268c1m
v6p0445c1s
Bellairs, C.W. v5p0124c1s
v6p0132c2s
Bellairs, K.G. v6p0230c2s
Bellairs, N. v6p0670c1s
Bellairs, S. v2p0253c1s
v3p0414c1s
Bellamy, C. v1p0560c1s
Bellamy, C.S. v1p0724c1s
v1p0924c2s
Bellamy, E. v1p0273c2s
v1p0346c1s v1p0770c1s v1p0940c1s
v1p1039c1s v1p1266c2s v1p1271c1s
v1p1391c1s v2p0049c2s v3p0025c1s
v3p0038c2s v3p0259c2s v3p0296c2s
v3p0297c1s v3p0340c1s v3p0431c1s
v3p0466c2s v4p0394c1m v5p0045c2s
Bellamy, E.W. v1p0755c2s
v2p0026c2s v3p0127c1s v3p0152c2s
v3p0189c1s v3p0266c2s v4p0207c1s
v4p0377c1s v4p0458c1s
Bellamy, F. v3p0114c2s
v5p0273c2s v6p0623c2s
Bellamy, F.A. v2p0426c1s
Bellamy, M. v5p0237c2s
Bellangee, J. v4p0516c2s
Bellanti, L.F. v6p0361c2s
Bellargue, C. v4p0256c1s
Bellaris, C. v5p0109c2s
Bellars, H.J. v1p0137c1s
Bellars, M.E. v6p0376c1s
Bellars, W. v1p0330c2s
v1p0796c1s v1p0977c2s v1p1057c1s
v1p1430c2s
Bellas, H.H. v4p0151c2s
Bellas, M.R.J. v4p0267c2s
Bellasis, E. v3p0302c1s
Bellei, G. v6p0410c2s
Belleli, L. v6p0289c2s
Bellesheim, A. v3p0365c1s
Bellesort, A. v5p0092c2m
v5p0269c2m v5p0352c1m v5p0444c2s
v5p0530c1m
Bellesort, Andre v5p0303c1m
v5p0446c1s
Bellew, F. v2p0140c2s
Bellew, F.H.T. v4p0349c1s
Bellew, H.W. v1p0009c2s
v3p0223c2s v4p0004c2s
Bellew, J.C.M. v1p0083c1s
v1p0733c1s
Bellew, J.M. v1p0420c2s
Bellew, K. v6p0221c2s
Belling, K.J. v4p0388c2s
v4p0389c1s v4p0446c1s v4p0506c2s
Bellingham, H. v1p0459c2s
v1p0479c2s v1p0653c2s v1p0654c2s
v1p0657c1s v1p0659c1s v1p0659c2m
v1p0940c1s v1p0979c1s v1p1057c2s
v1p1061c1s v1p1090c2s v1p1109c2s
v1p1117c1s v1p1276c2s v2p0107c1s
v2p0225c1s v2p0384c2s v3p0079c2s
Bellingham, J. v1p1116c2s
Bellman, J.J. v6p0154c1s
Belloc, B.R. v3p0165c2s
v4p0091c1s v4p0177c2s v4p0458c2s
Belloc, H. v4p0211c1s
v5p0153c1s v6p0183c1s v6p0271c1s
v6p0284c1s v6p0319c2s v6p0396c1s
v6p0398c1s v6p0400c2s v6p0401c2s
v6p0420c2s v6p0470c2s v6p0520c1m
v6p0533c2s v6p0550c1s v6p0562c2s
v6p0580c1s v6p0679c2s
Belloc, Hilaire v5p0266c1s
v6p0038c1s v6p0171c1s v6p0550c2s
v6p0631c1s
Belloc, L.S. v3p0372c1m
v3p0448c2s
Belloc, M.A. v3p0023c1s
v3p0177c1s v3p0430c1s v4p0089c1s
v4p0132c1s v4p0148c1s v4p0235c1s
v4p0385c2s v4p0426c2s v4p0486c1s
v4p0509c1s v4p0522c1s v4p0600c1s
v5p0052c1s v5p0094c1s v5p0474c2s
Belloc, M.A.De v3p0114c1s
Belloc, Marie A. v4p0080c1s
v4p0248c2s
Belloc-Lowndes, M. v5p0169c1s
Belloc-Lowndes, Mrs. v5p0137c2s
v5p0180c1s v6p0368c1s
Bellot, H.H.L. v4p0052c2s
v4p0085c1s v4p0085c2s v4p0086c1s
v4p0120c2s v4p0183c1s v4p0239c2s
v4p0240c1s v4p0289c2m v4p0306c1m
v4p0318c2m v4p0322c2s v4p0328c2s
v4p0337c1m v4p0353c2s v4p0372c2s
v4p0471c2s v4p0472c2s v5p0007c2s
v6p0108c1s v6p0258c1s v6p0555c2s
Bellows, B. v1p0275c1s
Bellows, H.I. v1p0867c2s
Bellows, H.W. v1p0028c2s
v1p0029c1s v1p0100c2s v1p0179c2s
v1p0247c2s v1p0259c1s v1p0276c1s
v1p0394c2s v1p0431c2s v1p0441c1s
v1p0487c1s v1p0573c1s v1p0605c2s
v1p0646c1s v1p0745c1s v1p0750c1s
v1p0792c2s v1p0850c1s v1p0916c1s
v1p0931c2s v1p0972c1s v1p1040c2s
v1p1064c1s v1p1092c2s v1p1094c1s
v1p1101c1s v1p1234c1s v1p1238c2s
v1p1301c2s v1p1304c1s v1p1308c1s
v1p1325c2s v1p1331c2s v1p1342c2s
v1p1348c2s v1p1407c1s v1p1417c1m
v2p0235c2s v2p0395c1s
Bellows, H.W. and Bruch, Prof.
v1p0740c2s
Bellows, I.F. v2p0010c2s
v2p0241c2s v4p0076c2s v6p0098c2s
v6p0237c1s
Bellows, Isabel F. v5p0148c2s
v5p0269c1s
Bellows, J.A. v2p0012c2s
v2p0039c1s v2p0106c2s v3p0031c2s
v3p0141c1s
Bellows, J.F. v2p0397c2s
Bellows, J.N. v1p0256c2s
v1p0821c1m v1p1288c1s v1p1319c1s
v1p1320c1s
Bellows, R.P. v5p0161c2s
Bellson, Miss v1p1254c1s
Bellville, A. v1p0010c2s
Belmas, M. v4p0380c1s
Belmont, C. v5p0502c2m
Belmont, F. v2p0125c2s

Belmont, P. v1p1285c2s
v3p0097c2s v5p0158c1s v5p0158c2s
v5p0444c1s v5p0536c1s v5p0567c1s
v5p0568c1s v5p0619c1s
Belmont, Perry v6p0196c2s
Belmore, Earl of v2p0227c1s
Belopolsky, A. v4p0255c1s
Belrose, L., jr. v4p0128c1m
v4p0223c1s v4p0336c1s
Belshaw, R.R. v1p1388c1s
Belt, T. v1p0523c2s
v1p0792c1s v2p0158c2s v2p0179c1m
v2p0262c2s v2p0314c1s v2p0421c1s
Beltrami, G. v5p0132c1s
Beltz, G.F. v1p0314c2s
v1p0562c2s v1p1195c2s
Beman, I. v2p0242c1s
v2p0242c2s
Beman, S. v1p0486c1s
Beman, W.W. v3p0261c2s
v5p0366c1s
Bement, A. v5p0550c2s
Bement, W. v1p0625c2s
Bemis, Alfred W. v6p0072c2s
Bemis, E.G. v6p0154c2s
Bemis, E.W. v2p0184c1s
v2p0262c1s v2p0287c2s v2p0407c2s
v3p0016c2s v3p0099c1s v3p0168c1s
v3p0170c1m v3p0209c1s v3p0238c2s
v3p0280c1s v3p0352c1s v3p0375c1s
v3p0398c1s v3p0405c2s v3p0421c1m
v3p0434c1m v3p0443c2s v4p0115c2m
v4p0195c1s v4p0220c2m v4p0275c2s
v4p0314c2s v4p0315c1s v4p0378c1s
v4p0524c2s v4p0525c2s v4p0533c2s
v4p0553c1s v4p0553c2s v5p0002c1s
v5p0136c2s v5p0227c1s v5p0391c2s
v5p0556c2m v5p0568c2s v5p0569c2s
v5p0584c2s v5p0593c1s v6p0131c1s
v6p0131c2s v6p0345c1s
Bemis, E.W. et al. v4p0337c1s
Bemis, Edward W. v6p0436c1s
Bemis, F.W. and Ingram, E.E.
v6p0436c1s
Bemis, G. v3p0038c1s
Bemrose, W. v1p1433c2s
Benard, C. v1p0063c2s
v1p0582c2s
Benard, Chas. v6p0029c1s
Bence-Jones, H. v5p0340c2s
Bencini, I.M. v5p0080c1s
Benda, W.T. v6p0245c2s
v6p0303c2s
Bendall, C. v3p0040c2s
v4p0492c2s v5p0390c2s v5p0624c1s
Bendall, C. and Wenzel, H.
v3p0428c2s
Bendall, E.A. v1p0081c2s
v1p0564c2s v1p0753c1s v3p0232c1s
Bendall, W. v5p0440c2s
Bendavid, I.B. v3p0230c2s
Bender, A.P. v4p0302c1s
Bender, C. v1p0016c2s
v1p0162c1s v1p0523c1s
Bender, C.H. v1p0162c1s
Bender, Dr. v1p0850c2s
Bender, H.R. v4p0374c2s
Bender, P. v2p0065c2m
v2p0086c2s v3p0065c1m v3p0065c2m
v3p0163c2m v3p0167c1s v3p0301c2s
v3p0350c2s v4p0087c1s
Bender, W. v4p0382c1s
Bendix, Max v5p0612c2s
Bendt, F. v5p0185c1s
Benecke, E.C. v1p0341c1s
v5p0344c2s
Benecke, E.F.M. v4p0092c2s
Beneden, P.J.Van v1p0042c2s
Beneden, P.J.von v1p0967c1s
Benedetti, F. v5p0478c1s
v5p0556c2s
Benedict, A. v1p0007c1s
Benedict, A.K. v5p0316c1s
Benedict, A.L. v3p0214c1s
v4p0131c1s v4p0363c1m v4p0363c2s
v5p0126c1s v5p0227c2s v5p0287c2s
v5p0288c1s v5p0368c1m v5p0389c1s
v6p0169c1s v6p0389c1s v6p0397c1s
Benedict, A.M. v1p0443c1s
Benedict, C. v6p0291c2s
v6p0323c1s v6p0388c1s
Benedict, E. v6p0133c1s
Benedict, E.C. v1p0334c2s
v1p0885c2s v1p1046c2s
Benedict, E.F. v3p0443c1s
Benedict, E.R. v4p0409c1s
Benedict, F.G. v6p0112c1s
Benedict, F.L. v1p0851c1s
v1p0851c2s v1p0931c1s v1p1049c2s
v1p1213c2s v1p1316c1s v5p0339c2s
Benedict, G.G. v4p0079c2s
Benedict, G.W. v1p1367c2s
v6p0207c2s
Benedict, H.A. v1p1358c2s
v5p0507c1s
Benedict, Hester A. v5p0313c2s
Benedict, J., Sir v1p0750c2s
v2p0303c1s
Benedict, J.E. v1p0006c2s
Benedict, L.E.W. v5p0097c1s
v5p0334c2s
Benedict, M. v5p0394c2s
Benedict, M.E. v6p0498c2s
Benedict, Marie v5p0114c1s
Benedict, Mary K. v6p0521c2s
Benedict, Mrs. v6p0031c2s
Benedict, N.R. v6p0525c1s
Benedict, R.D. v6p0013c1s
Benedict, S. v2p0153c1s
v2p0444c2s
Benedict, W.K. v4p0596c2s
Benedict, W.R. v2p0099c2s
v2p0131c1s v2p0149c1s v2p0309c2s
v3p0143c1s v6p0273c2s v6p0536c2s
Benedite, L. v5p0351c2s
v6p0367c1s
Benest, H. v5p0558c2s
Benet, S.E. v4p0460c2s
Bengless, J.D. v1p0857c2s
Bengough, C.B. v6p0031c1s
Bengough, H.M. v5p0029c1s
v5p0618c1s
Bengough, J.W. v4p0318c1s
Bengough, S.E. v4p0320c2s
v4p0518c2s v4p0519c1s
Benham, C. v5p0137c2s
v5p0611c2s
Benham, C.E. v6p0280c2m
v6p0317c2s v6p0627c1s
Benham, Canon v3p0103c1s
v4p0623c2s
Benham, G.A. v4p0558c2s
Benham, W. v1p0684c1s
v1p0972c1s v2p0002c2s v2p0084c1s
v2p0142c2s v2p0379c2s v3p0263c2s
v3p0311c2s v3p0356c2s v3p0428c1s
v3p0465c1s v5p0491c2s
Benham, W.B. v4p0508c1s
Beni, D.S. v5p0186c1s
Benisch, A. v2p0239c1s
Benites, J. v1p0748c1s
Benjafield, H. v4p0216c2s
Benjamin, A.N. v5p0206c2s
v5p0501c2s v5p0505c2s v6p0593c1s
v6p0680c2s
Benjamin, Anna N. v5p0114c2s
v5p0291c1s v5p0508c1s v5p0560c1s
Benjamin, C.F. v3p0407c1s
v5p0032c1s v5p0089c2s v5p0548c2s
Benjamin, C.H. v5p0211c2s
v5p0353c1s v5p0462c2s v5p0533c2s
v6p0393c1m v6p0464c1s v6p0502c1s
v6p0598c2m v6p0615c2s v6p0682c2s
Benjamin, E.B., Mrs. v2p0026c1s
Benjamin, E.H. v4p0501c2s
Benjamin, F. v5p0259c1s
Benjamin, G.H. v3p0132c2s
Benjamin, J.P. v1p0015c1s
v1p0142c2s v1p1265c2s
Benjamin, J.P. and Davis, J.
v1p1346c1s
Benjamin, M. v3p0010c2s
v3p0263c2s v3p0296c2s v4p0099c1s
v4p0100c2s v4p0114c2s v4p0124c2s
v4p0159c1s v4p0430c2m v5p0015c1s
v5p0289c2s v6p0073c1s v6p0111c2s
v6p0689c1s
Benjamin, P. v1p0642c2s
v1p0711c2s v1p0739c1s v1p0787c1s
v1p0885c2s v1p0928c1s v1p1425c2s
v2p0241c2s v3p0067c2s v3p0133c2s
v3p0134c1s v3p0298c1s v3p0323c1s
v3p0382c2s v4p0430c1s v4p0610c2s
v5p0050c1s v5p0401c1m v5p0401c2m
v5p0508c2s v5p0510c2m v5p0544c1s
v5p0558c2s v5p0595c1s v5p0602c2m
v5p0603c1m v5p0604c2s v5p0626c2s
v6p0032c1s v6p0142c1s v6p0232c1s
v6p0292c1s v6p0345c2m v6p0422c2s
v6p0567c1s v6p0650c1s v6p0668c2m
v6p0669c1m
Benjamin, P., jr. v1p0876c1s
Benjamin, Park v5p0553c2s
v6p0022c1s v6p0054c1s v6p0181c2s
v6p0337c2s v6p0650c1s v6p0668c2s
Benjamin, S.G.W. v1p0062c1m
v1p0062c2m v1p0083c2s v1p0086c2s
v1p0166c1s v1p0171c2s v1p0197c2s
v1p0217c1s v1p0482c2s v1p0511c1s
v1p0527c1s v1p0553c1s v1p0609c2s
v1p0616c2s v1p0633c2s v1p0642c2s
v1p0785c2s v1p0786c2s v1p0910c2s
v1p0936c2s v1p0952c1s v1p1036c2s
v1p1037c1s v1p1050c2s v1p1171c1s
v1p1172c2s v1p1227c2s v1p1294c1s
v1p1331c2s v2p0008c1s v2p0036c2s
v2p0067c1s v2p0068c1s v2p0071c2s
v2p0102c2s v2p0109c1s v2p0260c1s
v2p0271c2s v2p0332c1s v2p0336c2m
v2p0342c1s v2p0383c2s v2p0419c1m
v2p0432c2s v2p0471c2s v2p0481c1s
v3p0010c2s v3p0020c1s v3p0128c1m
v3p0153c2s v3p0158c2s v3p0162c1s
v3p0223c2s v3p0232c2s v3p0263c1s
v3p0267c2s v3p0284c2s v3p0303c1s
v3p0303c2s v3p0306c2s v3p0327c1m
v3p0327c2m v3p0459c1s v3p0473c2m
v4p0075c2s v4p0304c1s v4p0371c1s
v4p0374c2s v4p0382c2s v4p0494c2s
v4p0600c1s v4p0625c1s
Benjamin, S.W. v2p0336c2s
Benjamin, W.R. v3p0055c1s
Benn, A.W. v1p0173c1s
v1p0427c1s v2p0115c2m v2p0191c1s
v2p0194c1s v3p0019c2s v3p0042c1s
v3p0043c2s v3p0145c2s v3p0231c1s
v3p0242c2s v3p0337c2s v3p0358c1s
v3p0384c1s v4p0042c1s v4p0054c2m
v4p0055c2m v4p0057c2s v4p0077c2s
v4p0242c1s v4p0264c2s v4p0351c1s
v4p0419c1s v4p0439c1m v4p0478c2s
v4p0480c2m v4p0532c1s v4p0533c1s
v4p0545c1s v4p0548c2s v4p0558c1s
v4p0572c2s v4p0589c1s v5p0009c1s
v5p0198c1s v6p0286c2s v6p0482c1s
v6p0503c2s
Benn, J.W. v2p0020c1s
v2p0478c2s v3p0067c2s
Benn, R.D. v4p0016c2s
v4p0218c1s v5p0416c2s v5p0442c2s
v6p0616c2s
Benner, J. v1p1249c2s
v2p0227c1s
Benners, C.E. v1p0771c1s
Benners, E., Mrs. v1p1174c2s
Benners, E.S., Mrs. v1p1298c2s
Bennet, J.K. v1p0668c2s
Bennet, M. v1p0633c1s
Bennet, M.S. v6p0261c2s
Bennett, A. v4p0264c2s
v4p0473c2s
Bennett, A.B. v6p0346c1s
Bennett, A.H. v1p0619c2s
v1p1422c2s
Bennett, A.W. v1p0021c2s
v1p0025c1s v1p0153c1m v1p0279c1s
v1p0449c2m v1p0462c2s v1p0601c2s
v1p0644c2s v1p0645c1s v1p0645c2s
v1p0842c2s v1p0900c1s v1p1007c1s
v1p1014c2m v1p1015c1s v1p1015c2m
v1p1016c1s v1p1232c2s v1p1233c1s
v1p1324c1s v1p1364c2s v1p1372c1s
v1p1378c2s v2p0159c2s v2p0429c1s
v2p0445c2s v3p0179c2s v4p0568c2s
v5p0608c2s
Bennett, A.W. and Berkeley, M.J.
v1p1404c1s
Bennett, C. v3p0404c2s
v3p0473c1s v4p0330c2s v4p0546c2s
Bennett, C.A. v3p0410c1s
v6p0181c2s
Bennett, C.E. v4p0321c2m
v5p0326c2s v6p0163c1s v6p0243c2s
Bennett, C.N. v4p0121c2s
v6p0691c2s
Bennett, C.P. v2p0115c1s
Bennett, C.W. v1p0061c2s
v1p0206c1s v1p1058c1s v1p1120c1s
v1p1284c2s
Bennett, Col. v5p0074c2s
Bennett, Dr. v1p0865c1s
Bennett, E.A. v5p0171c1s
v6p0222c2s v6p0691c2s
Bennett, E.F.T. v5p0208c2s
Bennett, E.H. v3p0119c1s
v3p0269c1s v4p0007c2s
Bennett, E.N. v5p0142c2m
v5p0420c2s v5p0537c2s
Bennett, Ella C. v6p0472c1s
Bennett, F.A. v6p0117c2s
Bennett, F.E. v1p0851c2s
Bennett, F.E. et al. v3p0057c1s
Bennett, F.M. v4p0009c2s
v4p0594c2s v4p0595c1s v5p0383c2s
v5p0401c1s v5p0551c2s
Bennett, F.P. v4p0180c1s
Bennett, F.S.M. v4p0334c1s
Bennett, F.W. v6p0275c2s
Bennett, G. v2p0029c1s
Bennett, G.H. v5p0280c2s
v5p0292c2s v5p0327c2s v6p0218c2s
Bennett, G.W. v1p0462c2s
Bennett, H. v2p0164c1s
v3p0298c2s
Bennett, H.C. v6p0247c2s
v6p0573c2s
Bennett, H.G. v1p0966c1s
Bennett, H.H. v5p0035c2s
v5p0101c2s v5p0120c2s v5p0139c1s
v5p0200c2s v5p0236c1s v5p0375c2s
v5p0474c2s
Bennett, H.M. v3p0083c1s
v3p0362c1s
Bennett, H.T. v1p0586c2s
Bennett, Helen C. v6p0573c2m
Bennett, J. v1p0017c1m
v1p0124c2s v1p0142c2s v1p0143c1s
v1p0161c2s v1p0500c2s v1p0569c2s
v1p0646c1s v1p0943c2s v1p1414c2s
v4p0389c2s v4p0390c1s v4p0527c1s
v5p0422c1s v6p0541c2s
Bennett, J.B. v1p1300c2s
Bennett, J.D. v6p0298c2s
Bennett, J.E. v4p0324c1s
v4p0617c1m v5p0088c1m v5p0088c2s
v5p0129c1s v5p0183c1s v5p0237c2s
v5p0298c2m v5p0299c2s v5p0303c2s
v5p0362c1s v5p0377c2s v5p0378c1s
v5p0423c1s v5p0525c1s v5p0577c1s
v5p0622c1s v6p0689c2s

Bennett, J.H. v1p0642c1s
Bennett, J.I. v6p0026c2s
Bennett, J.R. v1p0019c2s
v2p0197c1s v3p0251c2s
Bennett, J.R., Sir v2p0234c2s
Bennett, J.W. v1p0768c2s
v4p0136c1s v4p0423c2s v5p0537c1s
v6p0170c1s v6p0601c1s
Bennett, L.E. v6p0494c2s
Bennett, L.T. v1p0567c1s
Bennett, L.V. v4p0434c2s
Bennett, M. v1p0214c2s
Bennett, Mrs. v1p1335c1s
Bennett, R.A. v4p0318c2s
Bennett, R.T. v3p0110c1s
Bennett, S.R. v2p0414c1s
Bennett, T. v1p1146c2s
Bennett, T.J. v1p0109c1s
v6p0489c2s
Bennett, W. v1p0590c1s
Bennett, W.C. v1p0056c2s
v1p0815c1s v1p0919c2s v2p0401c1s
Bennett, W.H. v4p0302c1s
v5p0056c2s v5p0057c1s v6p0063c1s
v6p0063c2s v6p0065c1m v6p0341c2s
Bennett, W.W. v2p0286c1s
Bennetts, G.A. v5p0337c1s
Benni, A.W. v1p1137c1s
Benning, H.L. v3p0389c2s
Benning, H.L. et al. v1p0518c2s
Bennink, C. v6p0421c1s
Bennion, F. v6p0440c2s
Bennoch, F. v3p0172c2s
v3p0426c2s
Benoist, C. v4p0539c2s
v5p0148c1s v5p0542c1s
Benoiston, M. v1p0873c2s
Benonville, P. v3p0018c1s
v3p0165c2s
Benouville, L. v4p0210c1s
v4p0471c2s
Bensall, Cecil v5p0081c2s
Bensel, J.B. v2p0243c1s
Bensel, P.W. v6p0701c1s
Bensemer, W.S. v4p0413c2s
Bensley, B.A. v5p0040c1s
v5p0358c1s v5p0363c2s
Bensley, M.S. v6p0704c2s
Bensley, Martha S. v6p0034c1s
v6p0035c2s v6p0116c1s v6p0499c1s
Bensly, R.L. v2p0238c2s
Benson, A. v2p0054c1s
v3p0179c2s v3p0194c2s v3p0244c1s
v3p0287c2s
Benson, A.C. v2p0143c2s
v3p0143c2s v3p0323c2s v3p0385c2s
v4p0052c2s v4p0070c1s v4p0184c2s
v4p0189c1s v4p0309c1s v4p0319c1s
v4p0336c2s v4p0448c2s v4p0492c1s
v4p0615c2s v5p0036c1s v5p0038c1s
v5p0055c1s v5p0324c1s v5p0343c1s
v6p0002c1s v6p0034c1s v6p0130c1s
v6p0193c1s v6p0212c2s v6p0222c1s
v6p0243c1s v6p0353c2s v6p0445c1s
v6p0538c1s v6p0541c2s v6p0584c1s
v6p0682c1s
Benson, A.C. and Fletcher, F.
v6p0382c2s
Benson, A.C. and Lubbock, P.
v6p0622c2s
Benson, A.L. v6p0659c2s
Benson, Allan L. v6p0263c1s
v6p0415c2s v6p0425c2s v6p0522c2s
Benson, C. v1p0275c1s
v1p0714c2s v1p0823c1s v1p1032c1s
v1p1061c2s v1p1411c2s
Benson, C.E. v6p0340c1s
v6p0584c1s
Benson, D. v1p0199c1s
Benson, E. v1p0326c2s
v1p0343c1s v1p0366c2s v1p0369c2s
v1p0455c1s v1p0480c1s v1p0492c1s
v1p0503c2s v1p0529c2m v1p0567c2s
v1p0575c2s v1p0617c1s v1p0753c1s
v1p0753c2s v1p0754c1s v1p0915c2s
v1p0918c1s v1p0958c2s v1p0967c2s
v1p1008c1s v1p1019c2s v1p1218c2s
v1p1263c2s v1p1311c1s v1p1314c1s
v1p1420c2s v1p1421c1s v4p0033c1s
Benson, E. and King, R. .. v1p0917c2s
Benson, E.F. v4p0004c2s
v4p0136c2s v4p0284c2s v4p0332c2s
v4p0342c2s v4p0386c2s v4p0419c1s
v4p0481c1s v4p0482c1s v4p0551c1s
v4p0564c1s v4p0624c2s v5p0165c2s
v5p0171c1s v5p0204c2s v5p0453c1s
v6p0013c1s v6p0090c1s v6p0333c2s
v6p0600c2s
Benson, E.I. v4p0198c1s
Benson, E.N. v3p0441c1s
Benson, E.W. v5p0151c2s
Benson, Eugene v4p0453c2s
v4p0490c2s
Benson, F.H. v4p0058c1s
Benson, F.R. v5p0575c2s
Benson, G. v6p0622c2s
Benson, G.E. v5p0252c2s
Benson, G.R. v6p0267c1s
Benson, G.V. v3p0397c2s
Benson, H.M. v1p0340c1s
v1p0538c2s
Benson, J. v1p0687c2s
v1p0811c1s
Benson, J.Knowles v6p0007c2s
Benson, J.S. v1p0222c1s
Benson, L.F. v5p0464c1s
Benson, M. v5p0317c2s
Benson, M.E. v6p0672c2s
Benson, M.E., Miss v3p0385c2s
Benson, R. v1p0266c1s
Benson, R.A. v1p0153c2s
Benson, R.H. v6p0292c1s
v6p0424c2s
Benson, W.A.S. v3p0243c2s
v3p0275c2s v6p0679c1s
Bensted, Clara v5p0385c1s
v6p0550c1s
Bensusan, S.L. v4p0002c2s
v4p0018c2s v4p0078c2s v5p0083c1s
v5p0087c1m v5p0099c2s v5p0274c1s
v5p0344c2s v5p0387c1s v5p0430c2s
v6p0048c2s v6p0263c1s v6p0311c2s
v6p0402c1s v6p0429c2m v6p0430c1m
v6p0597c1s
Bent, A.H. v4p0051c1s
v4p0126c2s v5p0013c1s v5p0205c1s
v5p0257c2s v6p0080c2s
Bent, A.S. v6p0656c2s
Bent, G.L. v4p0422c1s
Bent, I.T. v3p0079c2s
Bent, J.L. v4p0209c2s
Bent, J.S. v3p0072c2s
Bent, J.T. v1p0328c2s
v1p0393c1s v1p1136c1s v1p1149c1s
v1p1365c2s v2p0012c2s v2p0016c2s
v2p0024c1s v2p0035c1s v2p0061c1s
v2p0073c1s v2p0080c1s v2p0110c2s
v2p0128c2s v2p0142c1s v2p0159c1s
v2p0190c1m v2p0190c2m v2p0226c1s
v2p0226c2s v2p0232c1s v2p0241c1m
v2p0263c2s v2p0275c1s v2p0304c1s
v2p0305c1s v2p0318c2s v2p0326c1s
v2p0358c1s v2p0372c1m v2p0377c1s
v2p0385c1m v2p0429c2s v2p0437c2s
v2p0442c2s v2p0464c2s v3p0005c2s
v3p0023c2s v3p0024c2s v3p0030c2s
v3p0043c2s v3p0081c2s v3p0085c1m
v3p0103c1s v3p0108c1s v3p0116c1s
v3p0124c1s v3p0183c2m v3p0184c1s
v3p0184c2s v3p0188c2s v3p0200c1s
v3p0212c1s v3p0247c2s v3p0264c1s
v3p0272c2s v3p0285c1s v3p0294c2s
v3p0300c2s v3p0305c1s v3p0311c1s
v3p0312c1s v3p0315c2s v3p0317c1s
v3p0323c2s v3p0327c2m v3p0370c2s
v3p0373c2s v3p0374c1m v3p0375c2s
v3p0416c1s v3p0420c2s v3p0426c2s
v3p0428c2s v3p0459c1s v4p0002c1s
v4p0022c1m v4p0027c2s v4p0048c2s
v4p0114c1m v4p0154c2s v4p0188c2s
v4p0245c1m v4p0359c1m v4p0388c1s
v4p0413c2s v4p0436c1s v4p0537c2s
v4p0616c1s v4p0637c1s v5p0537c2s
Bent, J.Theodore v4p0391c1s
Bent, M. v6p0511c2s
Bent, S. v2p0285c2s
Bent, S.A. v4p0153c1s
Bent, T. v2p0108c1s
v3p0062c1s v3p0234c2s v3p0423c2s
Bent, T., Mrs. v5p0643c2s
Bent, T.A. v1p0523c1s
Bent, Theo. v3p0097c2s
Benthall, W. v5p0481c2s
v6p0535c1s
Bentham, G. v1p0134c1s
v1p0153c1s v1p0898c2s v1p1164c1s
v1p1364c1s
Bentham, J. v1p0404c2s
v1p0928c2s
Bentham-Edwards, M. v1p0534c1s
Bentinck, F.O. v5p0175c1s
Bentley, A. v3p0286c1s
v3p0326c1s v4p0412c1s
Bentley, A.F. v4p0195c1s
v4p0288c2s
Bentley, H. v1p0036c1s
v1p0846c1s
Bentley, I.M. v5p0241c2s
v5p0369c2s v5p0565c1s v6p0130c2s
v6p0139c1s v6p0145c2s v6p0244c2s
v6p0285c1s v6p0410c2s
Bentley, I.M. and Sabine, G.H.
v6p0649c2s
Bentley, I.M. and Tichener, E.B.
v6p0055c1s
Bentley, M. v6p0470c1s
Bentley, R. v1p0850c2s
Bentley, R.C. v5p0326c2s
Bentley, W. v1p1387c2s
Bentley, W.A. v5p0534c2s
Bentley, W.A. and Perkins, G.H.
v5p0534c2s
Bentley, W.H. v5p0132c2s
Benton, A.A. v1p0075c2m
v1p1296c2s v2p0230c2s v3p0097c2s
v5p0135c2s v5p0204c1s
Benton, A.B. v6p0028c1s
v6p0483c2s
Benton, C.C. v3p0201c2s
Benton, C.E. v4p0024c2s
v4p0195c1s v4p0261c2s v4p0533c1s
v4p0564c2m v6p0054c1s
Benton, D. v2p0065c1s
v3p0085c1s v3p0284c1s
Benton, E.E. v4p0447c2s
v4p0633c2m v5p0040c2s
Benton, E.J. v5p0313c2s
v6p0682c1s
Benton, H.S. v6p0155c2s
Benton, J. v1p0060c1s
v1p0179c2s v1p1307c1s v2p0022c1s
v2p0121c2s v2p0241c1m v2p0302c2s
v2p0378c2s v2p0381c2s v2p0400c1s
v2p0439c2s v2p0469c2m v3p0035c1s
v3p0049c2s v3p0054c2s v3p0056c1s
v3p0058c1s v3p0109c1s v3p0125c2s
v3p0137c1s v3p0149c2s v3p0184c2s
v3p0204c2s v3p0259c2s v3p0260c1s
v3p0284c2s v3p0315c1s v3p0357c1s
v3p0360c2s v3p0440c2s v4p0429c2s
v4p0450c2s v4p0457c2s v4p0492c2s
v5p0040c2s v5p0113c2s v5p0187c1s
v5p0329c1s v5p0455c2m v5p0463c2s
v6p0052c1s
Benton, J.A. v2p0064c1s
Benton, J.H. v6p0058c2s
Benton, J.H., jr. v4p0597c1s
Benton, J.R. v4p0163c1s
v4p0243c2s v4p0447c2s v4p0543c2s
v5p0251c2s v5p0591c2s v6p0104c2s
v6p0229c2s
Benton, Joel v4p0219c2s
v4p0314c2s v4p0315c1s v4p0436c1s
v4p0555c1s v6p0303c1s
Benton, M. v1p0646c2s
v4p0410c2s
Benton, M.B. v1p0042c2s
v1p1183c2s v2p0055c1s v3p0462c1s
v4p0122c1s
Benton, M.H. v4p0177c2s
Benton, R.H. v6p0126c1s
Benton, T.H. v1p0091c2s
v1p0092c1s
Benton, W.A. v1p0294c2s
v1p0328c1s
Benton, W.G. v3p0058c2s
v3p0096c1s v3p0419c2s
Bentwich, H. v5p0645c2m
Bentwich, N. v6p0384c1s
v6p0461c1s
Bentwick, K.K. v4p0049c2s
Bentzon, F. v6p0489c1s
Bentzon, T. v4p0103c2s
v4p0131c2s v4p0163c1s v4p0194c2s
v4p0214c2s v5p0080c1s v5p0115c2s
v5p0161c2s v5p0166c2s v5p0491c2s
v6p0402c1s v6p0649c1s
Bentzon, T. et al. v4p0100c2s
Bentzon, Th. v4p0371c2s
v5p0036c1s v5p0069c2s v5p0134c1s
v5p0220c2s v5p0221c1s v5p0385c1s
v5p0431c2s v6p0018c2s v6p0242c1s
Benyon, R. v4p0009c1s
v4p0417c2s
Benzel, G. v6p0411c1s
Beranger, P.J.de v1p0328c2s
Berard-Varagnac, M. v2p0269c1s
Berberich, A. v2p0095c1s
Berckmans, P.J. v6p0552c1s
Berdan, J.M. v6p0017c1s
Berdoe, E. v3p0057c2m
v3p0098c1s v3p0217c2s v4p0076c2s
v4p0343c1s v4p0363c1s
Berdrow, W. v5p0592c2s
v6p0252c1s
Bere, De La v5p0395c2s
Bere, H.P.de la v5p0353c1s
Bereman, T.A. v3p0127c1s
Berens, A. v2p0340c1s
Berens, L.H. v4p0233c1s
v6p0360c2s v6p0525c2s v6p0628c1s
v6p0700c2s
Berenson, B. v2p0181c2s
v2p0239c2s v2p0438c2s v3p0020c2s
v3p0230c2s v3p0284c1s v3p0372c1s
v3p0432c1s v4p0114c1s v4p0135c1s
v4p0147c1s v4p0440c2s v4p0600c2s
v5p0234c1s v5p0374c2s
Beresford, A. v3p0362c1s
v3p0372c2s v3p0419c1s v4p0122c2s
v4p0209c2s v4p0424c1s v4p0580c1s
v5p0017c2s v5p0038c1s v5p0083c2s
v5p0144c2s v5p0279c1s v5p0283c1s
v5p0355c1s v5p0363c2s
Beresford, C. v3p0296c2s
v5p0019c2s v5p0020c1s v5p0108c2s
v5p0130c1s v5p0246c2m v5p0287c1s
v5p0367c2s v5p0501c2s
Beresford, C. and Mahan, A.T.
v4p0017c2s
Beresford, C., Lord v3p0181c2m
Beresford, C.E.de la P. .. v5p0320c1s
v5p0430c2s v5p0501c2s v5p0528c1s
v5p0594c2s v6p0398c1s v6p0434c2s
v6p0489c2s v6p0556c1s v6p0557c2s
Beresford, C.E.de la Poer. v5p0206c2s
v5p0207c1s v6p0509c1s
Beresford, C.E.de la Poer, Col.
v6p0101c1s v6p0105c1s
Beresford, Charles, Lord . v5p0404c1s

Beresford, E. v5p0640c1s
Beresford, F. v2p0123c2s
Beresford, J.J. v4p0051c2s
v4p0174c1s
Beresford, W. v1p0345c1s
v6p0411c1s
Beresford-Hope, A.J. v2p0084c1s
v2p0277c2s
Berg, A.Van B. v4p0375c2s
v4p0440c1s
Berg, C. v4p0285c2s
Berg, L.D. v3p0059c1s
v4p0292c1s
Berg, L.de v2p0178c2s
Berg, L.deC. v2p0060c1s
v4p0440c1s
Bergami, F. v4p0440c1s
Berge, A.de la v3p0393c1s
Bergen, B.L. and Newell, W.W.
v4p0205c2s
Bergen, F.D. v2p0014c2s
v2p0077c2s v2p0344c1s v3p0014c1m
v3p0333c2s v4p0205c2s v4p0403c2s
v4p0423c2s v4p0429c2s v4p0558c1s
v4p0563c1s v5p0105c2s v5p0211c2s
Bergen, F.D. and Newell, W.W.
v4p0103c2s v4p0149c2s v4p0615c2s
Bergen, F.D., Mrs. v4p0079c2s
v4p0291c2s v4p0358c2s v4p0445c2m
v4p0500c1s v4p0623c2s
Bergen, F.D., Mrs. and Newell, W.W.
v4p0558c1s
Bergen, F.Y. v3p0331c2s
Bergen, Fanny D. v5p0072c1s
v5p0454c1s
Bergen, J. v1p0647c1s
v1p1339c2s
Bergen, J.T. v5p0241c2s
Bergen, J.Y. v6p0136c2s
v6p0169c2s
Bergen, R.Van v5p0109c2s
v5p0111c2s v5p0303c1s v6p0333c2s
Bergen, T.D. v6p0331c1s
v6p0441c2s v6p0491c1s
Bergengren, R. v4p0097c2s
v5p0101c1s v5p0119c1s v5p0146c1s
v5p0290c2s v6p0108c2s v6p0139c2s
v6p0248c1s v6p0305c2s v6p0591c1s
v6p0614c1s v6p0618c1s v6p0642c1s
v6p0698c2s
Bergengren, Ralph v6p0428c2s
v6p0637c1s
Berger, E.W. v6p0011c1s
Berger, F.K. v1p0773c2s
v1p1437c1s
Berger, G. v3p0472c2s
Berger, H.H. v3p0227c1s
Berger, S. v3p0452c1s
Bergerat, E. v4p0002c1s
Bergerat, E. and Leloir, M.
v5p0369c1s
Bergerat, Emile v5p0554c2s
Bergeron, J. v2p0296c2s
v4p0009c2s
Bergerot, E. v5p0031c1s
Bergh, G.A. v1p1268c1s
Bergh, H. v1p0321c1s
v2p0457c1s
Berghaus, A. v1p0734c1s
v2p0089c1s
Bergsman, M. v2p0089c2s
v2p0458c1s
Bergstresser, P. v1p0112c1s
v1p0528c1s v1p0847c2s v1p1139c1s
v2p0027c2s v2p0152c1s v2p0351c2s
v3p0095c2s v3p0121c1s v4p0037c1s
Bergstrom, J.A. v4p0364c2s
v4p0365c1s v5p0116c1s v6p0210c1s
Bergtheil, J. v3p0296c2s
Bergthora v5p0209c2s
Beringer, A. v2p0351c1s
Beringer, O.L. v6p0005c2s
Beringer, P.N. v5p0047c2s
v5p0310c2s v5p0347c2s v6p0092c1s
v6p0224c1s v6p0494c1s v6p0636c1s
Beringer, P.N. et al. v6p0463c1s
Berkeley, C. v5p0272c2s
Berkeley, G.F. v1p1193c1s
Berkeley, G.F.H. v5p0068c1s
v5p0243c2s v5p0533c2s v5p0618c1s
v6p0002c1m v6p0327c1s
Berkeley, H. v2p0187c1s
Berkeley, L.E. v2p0224c2s
Berkeley, M. v5p0500c2s
Berkeley, M.J. v1p0153c1s
v1p0494c2m v1p0706c2s v1p0875c1s
v1p1307c1s v1p1328c1s
Berkeley, M.J. and Bennett, A.W.
v1p1404c1s
Berkeley, R.C. v1p1327c1s
Berkey, H.E. v6p0125c1s
Berkley, H. v1p0147c2s
Berkowitz, H. v6p0111c1s
v6p0343c2s v6p0428c2s
Berkshire, Earl of and
Suffolk, Earl of v5p0216c1s
Berle, A.A. v4p0007c2s
v4p0053c1s v4p0140c2s v4p0334c2s
v4p0479c2s v6p0122c1s v6p0144c2s
v6p0333c2s v6p0450c1m v6p0536c2s
v6p0544c2s v6p0642c2s
Berle, A.A. and Spencer, E.C.
v3p0208c2s
Berlin, A.F. v2p0421c1s
v5p0441c2s
Berlin, M. v5p0057c2s
v5p0332c1s
Berliner, E. v3p0178c2s
v4p0234c1s
Berly, J.A. v2p0089c2s
v3p0088c2s
Berlyn, A. v2p0096c1s
v3p0356c1s v4p0037c1s v4p0112c2s
v4p0529c1s
Berman, P. v6p0162c1s
Bermingham, J.A. v2p0291c1s
Bernac, J. v4p0051c2s
v4p0070c1s v4p0082c2s v4p0307c2s
v4p0345c2s v4p0426c1s v4p0468c1s
v4p0485c2s
Bernac, Jean v5p0498c1s
Bernacchi, L. v5p0022c1m
Bernacchi, L.C. v6p0023c1s
Bernadou, J.B. v3p0100c2s
v4p0133c2s v5p0633c1s
Bernard, C. v1p0157c1s
v1p1171c1s v2p0061c2s
Bernard, E.G. v5p0183c1s
v5p0526c2s
Bernard, F. v3p0461c2s
Bernard, F.A.P. v1p0563c1s
Bernard, G. v4p0564c2m
Bernard, G.S. v3p0265c1s
v3p0328c2s
Bernard, H. v3p0397c1s
v6p0398c2s
Bernard, H.M. v4p0022c1s
v4p0584c1s v5p0610c1s v5p0632c2s
Bernard, H.N. v3p0145c2s
v3p0231c1s v3p0323c2s v3p0328c1s
Bernard, J. v2p0416c1s
Bernard, J.H. v5p0059c1s
v5p0122c2s v5p0263c1s v5p0378c2s
v6p0043c1s v6p0051c2s v6p0058c1s
v6p0259c1s v6p0347c1s v6p0519c2s
v6p0582c1s v6p0629c1s v6p0653c2s
Bernard, J.H. et al. v4p0437c1s
Bernard, L.S. v5p0412c2s
Bernard, M. v1p1111c1s
v5p0204c2s v5p0255c1s
Bernard, Prof. v4p0300c2s
Bernard, St. v1p0619c2s
Bernard, T.D. v4p0190c2s
Bernardy, Amy A. v6p0400c2s
Bernays, A.E. v5p0474c2s
Bernays, C.L. v1p0108c2s
v1p1083c1s
Bernays, J. and Paget, J., Sir
v1p0019c2s
Bernays, S.F.L. v5p0122c2s
Berne-Bellecour, G. v4p0364c1s
Bernhard, C. v1p0076c2s
v1p0309c2s v1p0330c1s
Bernhardt, Sarah v4p0350c2s
v6p0014c2s v6p0641c2s
Bernhardt, W. v3p0007c2s
v3p0075c2s v3p0118c2s v3p0342c1s
v5p0400c1s
Bernheim, A. v4p0400c1s
Bernheim, A.C. v3p0031c1s
v3p0304c1s v3p0304c2s v3p0322c2s
v4p0399c2s v4p0442c2s
Bernheim, A.C. et al. v4p0030c2s
Bernheim, H. v4p0312c2s
Bernheimer, C.S. v5p0307c2s
v5p0601c1s v6p0343c1s v6p0600c2s
Bernstein, A. v3p0230c1s
Bernstein, C. v5p0279c1s
Bernstein, E. v4p0533c2s
v6p0254c1s v6p0255c1s v6p0599c2s
Bernstein, Eduard v4p0533c1s
Bernstein, H. v6p0519c2s
Bernstorff, Count v3p0171c1s
Berolinensis.O. v6p0253c2s
Berquier, J.L. v2p0167c2s
Berra, M.O.y v2p0211c1s
Berrian, W. v1p0770c1s
Berridge, H.D. v3p0369c1s
Berry, A.B. v2p0316c2s
Berry, A.D. v5p0305c2s
Berry, A.G. v5p0611c2s
Berry, B. v6p0352c2s
Berry, C.A. v3p0096c2s
v3p0300c2s v5p0051c2s
Berry, C.W. v5p0194c1s
Berry, E.C. v6p0275c1s
Berry, E.O. v6p0528c2s
Berry, E.R. v6p0703c2s
Berry, E.W. v6p0077c1s
v6p0142c2s v6p0214c2s v6p0264c2s
v6p0463c1s v6p0475c2s v6p0502c2s
v6p0584c1s v6p0656c1s
Berry, G.E. v6p0689c2s
Berry, G.R. v5p0236c2s
v6p0061c1s
Berry, G.S. v5p0152c1s
Berry, J. v4p0315c1s
Berry, J.F. v4p0186c1s
Berry, J.R. v1p1378c2s
v3p0084c1s
Berry, L.F. v5p0307c1s
v5p0468c2s
Berry, L.G. v5p0028c2s
Berry, Louis F. v5p0257c1s
Berry, M. v6p0508c2s
v6p0573c1s
Berry, Martha v6p0046c2s
Berry, O.S. v6p0068c2s
Berry, Olive S. v6p0497c1s
Berry, P. v1p0255c2s
v1p0422c2m v1p0847c2s v1p1304c1s
Berry, V. v4p0385c2s
Berry, V.H. v4p0296c2s
Berryman, J.B. v5p0643c1s
Berryman, J.R. v3p0292c1s
v3p0310c1s v4p0624c2s
Berryman, V. v4p0312c1s
Bersier, E. v2p0236c1s
Bersier, M. v2p0017c1s
v2p0029c2s v2p0235c1m v2p0236c1s
v2p0267c1s v2p0418c1s
Bert, P. v1p0017c1s
v1p0073c2s v1p0907c1s v2p0165c2s
Bertaux, Emile v5p0451c2s
Berth, J.L.C. and Moore, F.
v6p0392c2s
Bertheau, F. v1p0122c2s
Berthelot and Vieille v2p0150c2s
Berthelot, M. v1p0224c1s
v1p0224c2s v1p0281c1s v2p0150c2s
Berthelot, M.E. v5p0104c1s
Berthelot, P.E. v3p0072c2s
v4p0025c2s v4p0098c2s v5p0513c1s
Berthelot, P.E.M. v4p0008c2s
v4p0009c2s
Berthelot, P.M. v5p0386c1s
v5p0513c1s
Berthelt, M. v6p0260c1s
v6p0503c1s
Bertholf, E.P. v5p0627c1s
Berthon, E.L. v3p0048c1s
Berthoud, E.L. v1p0621c2s
v2p0009c2s v2p0024c1s v2p0038c2s
v2p0063c2s v2p0064c2s v2p0090c1s
v2p0094c1s v2p0214c1s v4p0160c2s
Bertie, E. v1p0756c1s
Bertillon, A. v3p0039c2s
v3p0207c2s
Bertillon, J. v1p0035c2s
v2p0120c1s v4p0410c2m v5p0217c2s
Bertin, G. v2p0018c1s
v2p0030c2s v2p0394c2s v3p0024c2m
v3p0029c2s v6p0046c1s
Bertin, L.E. v1p1393c1s
Bertini, L.E. v6p0676c2s
Bertolett, F.F. v5p0207c2s
Berton, H.A. v1p0652c2s
v1p0866c1s v1p1071c2s
Bertouch, Baroness de v4p0485c1s
Bertram, A. v4p0315c2s
v4p0469c1s
Bertram, J. v4p0364c1s
Bertram, J.G. v1p0049c1s
v1p0142c2s v1p0287c2s v1p0457c2m
v1p0588c2s v1p0955c2m v1p1146c1s
v1p1406c2s v2p0157c2m v2p0158c1s
v2p0202c1m v2p0384c1s v2p0392c1s
v3p0130c2s v3p0154c1s v3p0316c2s
v3p0341c1s v3p0381c1s
Bertrand, A. v5p0563c1s
Bertrand, A. and Jamin, J.
v1p0502c1s
Bertrand, H. v5p0353c1s
Berwick, E. v3p0017c1s
v3p0149c2s v5p0122c1s v5p0427c1s
v5p0627c1s v6p0324c2s
Berwick, J. v5p0446c2s
Berwick, Thomas v4p0095c1s
Berzelius, Prof. v1p0828c1s
Besant, A. v2p0151c1s
v2p0408c1s v4p0186c2s
Besant, A. and Bax, E.B. . v3p0399c1s
v3p0467c2s
Besant, A. and Lunn, H.S.. v4p0258c1s
Besant, A., Mrs. v3p0053c1s
Besant, Annie v4p0271c2s
v4p0505c2s v4p0517c1s v4p0573c2s
Besant, J.F. v5p0365c1s
Besant, W. v1p0017c2s
v1p0115c1s v1p0153c2s v1p0345c2s
v1p0451c1s v1p0492c1s v1p0668c1s
v1p0819c2s v1p0858c2m v1p0864c2s
v1p0881c1s v1p0961c2s v1p1011c2s
v1p1072c1s v1p1257c2s v1p1322c2s
v1p1371c1s v1p1371c2s v2p0008c1s
v2p0013c1s v2p0023c2s v2p0078c1s
v2p0131c2s v2p0148c2s v2p0155c1s
v2p0180c2s v2p0211c2s v2p0239c1s
v2p0254c2s v2p0263c1s v2p0327c2s
v2p0365c2s v3p0028c2s v3p0038c1s
v3p0120c1s v3p0137c1s v3p0231c2s
v3p0243c1s v3p0255c2s v3p0256c2s
v3p0257c1m v3p0308c2s v3p0326c2m
v4p0013c2s v4p0015c1s v4p0017c2s
v4p0039c1m v4p0052c1s v4p0100c2s
v4p0101c1s v4p0122c2s v4p0249c1s
v4p0277c1s v4p0334c2m v4p0335c1s
v4p0339c1s v4p0339c2m v4p0360c1s
v4p0408c2s v4p0460c2s v4p0466c2s
v4p0470c2s v4p0475c2s v4p0533c1s

v4p0542c2s v5p0012c1s v5p0037c1s
v5p0040c2s v5p0098c2s v5p0189c1s
v5p0192c2s v5p0202c2m v5p0205c2s
v5p0345c1m v5p0345c2s v5p0346c1s
v5p0346c2s v5p0415c2s v5p0435c2s
v5p0506c2s v5p0575c1s
Besant, W. and Ainger, A.. v4p0085c1s
Besant, W. and Burges, A.M.
v4p0466c2s
Besant, W. and Nutt, A. .. v5p0070c1s
Besant, W. and Rice, J. .. v1p0181c2s
v1p0199c1s v1p0674c1s v1p0861c2s
v1p0888c1s v1p0952c1s v1p1085c2s
v1p1174c1s v1p1264c1s v1p1306c1s
v1p1418c1s v2p0008c1s v2p0067c2s
v4p0511c2s
Besant, W. et al. v3p0151c2s
v3p0152c1s
Besant, W., Sir v5p0317c2s
v5p0595c2s
Besant, Walter v4p0295c2s
Besant, Walter and Pollock, W.H.
v4p0097c2s
Besnard, A. v5p0498c2s
Bessels, E. v1p0055c2s
v1p0806c1s v2p0020c2s
Bessemer, H. v1p0074c1s
v1p0663c2s v1p1080c2s v1p1250c2m
v1p1292c1s
Besser, M. v1p0639c2s
v1p1302c2s v1p1303c2s
Besser, W.F. v3p0471c2s
Bessey, C. v6p0232c2s
v6p0431c2s
Bessey, C.E. v4p0143c1s
v4p0190c2s v4p0209c1s v4p0297c1s
v4p0443c2s v4p0507c1s v4p0574c1s
v4p0583c2s v4p0598c2s v5p0019c1s
v5p0073c1s v5p0128c2s v5p0137c2s
v5p0198c1s v5p0402c1m v5p0454c1s
v5p0469c1s v5p0608c2s v6p0012c1s
v6p0077c1m v6p0077c2m v6p0165c2s
v6p0222c1s v6p0229c2s v6p0233c2m
v6p0244c1s v6p0245c2s v6p0312c2s
v6p0376c2s v6p0420c1s v6p0422c2s
v6p0424c1s v6p0444c2s v6p0479c1s
v6p0491c2s v6p0502c2m v6p0625c1s
v6p0656c2s v6p0680c1s v6p0688c1s
v6p0691c1s v6p0706c1s
Bessey, E.A. v5p0015c1s
v6p0264c2s
Bessey, E.E. v1p0153c1s
Best, C.L. v5p0033c1s
Best, E.F. v5p0324c1s
Best, G.A. v5p0531c1s
Best, G.H. v4p0412c2s
Best, L.S. and Bramwell, M.
v3p0206c1s
Best, M.A. v6p0632c2s
Bests, N. v1p0388c1s
Beswick, S. v4p0173c1s
v4p0559c2s
Beta, O. v6p0410c2s
Betham-Edwards, M. v1p0082c2s
v1p0422c2s v1p0924c2s v1p0949c2s
v2p0175c2s v3p0163c2s v3p0241c1s
v4p0065c1s v4p0172c1s v4p0194c2s
v4p0605c1s v5p0217c1s v6p0075c2s
v6p0145c2s v6p0147c1s v6p0480c1s
Betham-Edwards, M.B. v6p0237c1m
v6p0238c2s v6p0241c2s v6p0299c2s
v6p0300c1s
Betham-Edwards, Miss v4p0018c1s
v4p0332c2s v4p0498c2s v6p0390c2s
Bethards, J.H. v5p0306c1s
Bethencourt, G.de v6p0343c2s
Bethune, A.N. v1p0255c1s
Bethune, Archdeacon v1p1326c1s
Bethune, C.C. and Boulton, H.E.
v3p0338c2s
Bethune, G.A. v1p0438c1s
Bethune, G.W. v1p0026c2s
v1p0736c2s v1p1217c2s
Bethune, J.S. v1p0738c1s
Bethune, R. v4p0489c2s
Beton, F. v6p0066c1s
Bettany, F.G. v6p0657c2s
Bettany, G.T. v1p0042c2s
v1p0044c1s v1p0044c2s v1p0190c1s
v1p0586c1s v1p0899c2s v1p0947c2s
v1p1145c2s v3p0144c2s v3p0187c1s
v3p0441c1s
Bettany, J.G. v2p0401c1s
v3p0012c2s v3p0240c1s v3p0254c1s
v3p0258c1s v3p0294c1s v3p0294c2s
v3p0413c2s v3p0417c2s
Bettany, W.A.C. v4p0161c1s
Bettany, W.A.L. v4p0003c1s
v4p0010c1s v4p0160c2s v4p0179c1s
v4p0304c2s v4p0497c1s v4p0570c2s
v4p0572c1s v4p0572c2s v4p0582c2m
v4p0609c2s
Bettelheim, P. v5p0216c2s
v5p0308c1s
Betteridge, W. v4p0568c2s
Betteridge, W.B. v5p0468c2s
Betteridge, W.R. v4p0056c1s
v5p0058c2s v5p0468c2s v6p0062c2s
v6p0063c1s v6p0631c2s
Bettinger, L.F. v6p0488c1s
Betton, C.S. v6p0005c2s
Betts, B.N. v1p0280c1s
Betts, B.R. v2p0096c2s
Betts, C.W. v1p1113c2s
Betts, F. v1p1308c1s
Betts, F.H. v3p0141c1s
v3p0474c1s
Betts, F.J. v1p0179c2s
v1p1296c1s
Betts, G.F. v1p0111c2s
Betts, L.W. v5p0082c1s
v5p0234c1s v5p0236c1s v5p0350c1s
v5p0352c1s v5p0360c2s v5p0362c2s
v5p0384c2s v5p0452c2s v5p0474c1s
v5p0488c2s v5p0555c1s v5p0557c1s
v5p0572c2m v5p0583c2s v5p0621c1s
v6p0110c1s v6p0114c1m v6p0116c2s
v6p0161c1s v6p0504c1s v6p0585c1s
v6p0599c2s
Betts, P. v3p0293c1m
Betts, R. v2p0139c2s
Betts, R.G. v6p0043c2s
Betts, W.C. v5p0443c1s
v6p0321c2m
Betts, X. v1p0681c2s
Beugless, J.D. v1p0271c1s
v1p1108c2s v1p1148c2s v1p1356c2s
v2p0106c2s
Beule, F. v1p0586c2s
Beust, F. v2p0168c2s
v2p0243c1s v2p0337c1s
Bevan, A.A. v4p0504c2s
v5p0510c1s
Bevan, B. v1p0211c1s
Bevan, C.P. v2p0072c2s
Bevan, D. v4p0157c1s
Bevan, D. and Coplin, W.M.L.
v4p0521c2s
Bevan, D.W. v6p0581c1s
Bevan, E.N. v6p0186c2s
Bevan, E.R. v5p0023c1s
v5p0157c1s v6p0024c1s v6p0036c1s
v6p0582c2s
Bevan, G.P. v1p0008c1s
v1p0268c1s v1p0360c2s v1p0413c1s
v1p0524c2s v1p0546c2m v1p0654c2s
v1p0657c1s v1p0947c2s v1p1261c2s
v1p1294c1s v1p1381c1m v1p1434c1s
v2p0240c2s v2p0396c1s v3p0221c1s
Bevan, L.D. v2p0133c1s
v2p0236c1s
Bevan, P. v1p0268c1s
v1p0269c1s v1p1339c2s
Bevan, T.P. v1p0155c2s
Bevan, W.L. v5p0474c2s
Bevan, Wm.L. v4p0437c2s
Bevens, T. v5p0272c2s
Beveridge, A.J. v5p0147c1s
Beveridge, H. v1p0630c1s
v5p0005c1s v5p0042c1s v5p0148c2s
v5p0182c1s v5p0225c2s v5p0319c2s
v6p0045c2s v6p0072c1s v6p0312c2s
Beveridge, J. v3p0156c2s
v3p0307c2s v5p0325c2s v6p0077c2s
v6p0460c2m v6p0461c1s
Beveridge, P.J. v2p0416c1s
Beveridge, W. v5p0514c2s
Beveridge, W.H. v6p0356c1s
v6p0652c1s
Beveridge, W.H. and Maynard, H.W.
v6p0665c1s
Beverley, E. v1p0807c1s
Beverley, H. v1p0112c1s
Bevier, I. v5p0212c2s
Bevier, L. v4p0265c1s
Bevington, J.A. v4p0363c1s
Bevington, L.J. v1p1083c2s
Bevington, L.S. v1p0071c2s
v1p0346c2s v1p0373c2s v1p0465c2s
v1p0791c1s v1p1101c1s v1p1288c2s
v2p0215c1s
Bevis, E. v4p0519c2s
Bevis, J.L. v5p0152c2s
Bewer, J.A. v5p0058c2s
v5p0565c1s v6p0062c2s v6p0341c1s
Bewer, Julius A. v6p0047c2s
Bewes, W.A. v4p0218c1s
Bewsker, J.E. v2p0048c1s
Bey, Brugsch v2p0133c2s
Bey, Ismail Kemal v5p0586c2s
Beyer, G.E. v5p0534c1s
Beyerle, H.J. v1p1056c1s
Beyfuss, A.E. v6p0043c1s
Beyle, H. v1p0773c1s
Beymer, W.G. v6p0584c1s
Beynon, E. v4p0586c1s
Beynon, Marie E. v5p0366c2s
Beynon, R. v3p0092c2s
v3p0094c2s v3p0156c2s v3p0310c2s
v3p0328c2s v3p0473c2s v4p0036c1s
v4p0043c1m v4p0179c1s v4p0539c2s
Beyschlag, W. v1p0129c1s
v1p0850c2s
Bezold, C. v3p0265c1s
v5p0412c2s
Bhimgee, A.M. v6p0314c1s
Bhownaggree, M.M. v3p0468c2s
Bhownaggree, M.M., Sir ... v5p0286c2s
Biagi, G. v4p0520c1s
v5p0299c2m v6p0331c1m v6p0372c2s
v6p0374c1s v6p0712c2s
Biagi, Guido v4p0202c2s
Bianciardi, E.D.R. v1p1111c1s
v1p1196c1s v1p1261c2s v2p0170c1s
v2p0171c2s v2p0267c2s v2p0321c1s
v2p0342c2s v2p0402c1s v2p0457c2s
v2p0459c2s
Bianco, O.F. v5p0372c2s
Biart, L. v1p1199c2s
v1p1404c1s v4p0192c2s
Bibb, A.B. v3p0018c1m
v3p0464c2s v4p0114c1m v4p0228c1s
v4p0362c1s v4p0387c1s v4p0498c2s
v4p0499c1s v4p0500c1s v4p0512c1s
v4p0616c2s v5p0137c1s v5p0214c2s
v5p0609c1s v5p0622c1s
Bibb, B. v5p0194c2s
v5p0518c2s v5p0531c1s
Bibb, G.C. v1p0060c2s
v1p0925c2s v1p0931c2s v1p1185c2s
v1p1298c1s v1p1430c2s
Bibb, G.C., Miss v1p0140c1s
Bibber, T.E.Van v1p0053c1s
Bibbins, J.R. v6p0248c1s
v6p0248c2s v6p0661c1s
Bibby, E. v1p0972c2s
Bibby, G.H. and Woodrow, E.A.E.
v4p0285c1s
Bice, H.H. v4p0465c2s
Bick, B. v2p0213c2s
Bickaby, J. v1p0039c1s
Bickerdike, C.F. v6p0596c1s
v6p0634c2s
Bickerdyke, J. v4p0200c2s
v4p0201c1s v4p0407c2s v4p0511c1s
v4p0585c1s v5p0591c2s
Bickersteth, R. v1p0120c1s
v1p0282c2s v1p0652c2s v1p1090c1s
v1p1120c1s
Bickerton, A.W. v6p0614c1s
Bickerton, C. v6p0103c2s
v6p0317c2s
Bickerton, J.H. v3p0092c2s
Bickerton, W.H. v5p0439c1s
Bickford, F.T. v3p0071c1s
v4p0102c1s
Bickford, L.H. v6p0525c2s
Bickley, A.C. v2p0113c1s
v2p0164c1s v2p0304c2s v2p0308c1s
v2p0360c2s v2p0476c2s v3p0383c1s
v3p0467c1s v4p0073c2s v4p0499c2s
v4p0527c2s v4p0530c2s v4p0618c1s
v4p0622c2s
Bickley, F.B. v4p0509c1s
Bickmore, A.S. v1p0016c2s
v1p0232c2m v1p0508c2s v1p0678c1s
Bicknel, A.
v2p0165c2s
Bicknell, A.H. v1p0304c1s
Bicknell, A.L. v3p0144c1s
v3p0320c2s v3p0470c2s v4p0212c1s
v4p0586c1s v5p0221c2s v5p0348c2s
v5p0361c2m
Bicknell, A.S. v2p0058c2s
v3p0201c1s v5p0617c1s
Bicknell, E. v5p0320c2s
v5p0425c2s
Bicknell, E.P. v4p0196c2s
v6p0109c2s v6p0307c1s v6p0492c2s
v6p0568c1s
Bicknell, F.M. v4p0019c2s
v4p0153c2s v4p0311c2s v5p0482c2s
v5p0605c2s
Bicknell, G. v6p0497c2s
Bicknell, G.T. v4p0633c2s
Bicknell, H.S. v3p0235c2s
Bicknell, J.M. v6p0446c2s
Bicknell, P. v5p0383c2s
Bicknell, P.F. v4p0183c2m
v5p0116c2s v5p0161c2s v5p0209c2s
v5p0279c2s v5p0304c2s v5p0479c2s
v5p0488c1s v5p0499c2s v5p0522c1s
v5p0605c1s v5p0629c1s v6p0014c2s
v6p0020c1s v6p0043c2s v6p0054c2s
v6p0057c2s v6p0077c1s v6p0084c1s
v6p0101c2m v6p0110c1s v6p0147c2s
v6p0155c1s v6p0159c1s v6p0166c1s
v6p0179c1s v6p0183c2s v6p0243c2s
v6p0251c2s v6p0263c1s v6p0273c1s
v6p0281c2s v6p0283c2s v6p0293c1s
v6p0303c1s v6p0339c2s v6p0353c1s
v6p0359c2s v6p0367c2s v6p0369c1m
v6p0375c2s v6p0407c1s v6p0417c2m
v6p0474c2s v6p0482c1s v6p0488c2s
v6p0525c2s v6p0532c1s v6p0545c2s
v6p0555c2s v6p0598c1s v6p0622c2s
v6p0631c1s v6p0634c2s v6p0656c2s
v6p0692c1s v6p0702c2s
Bicknell, P.R. v6p0505c1s
Bicknell, Percy F. v6p0173c2s
Bicknell, R.E. v6p0158c2s
v6p0281c2s v6p0429c2s
Bicknell, T.W. v2p0105c1s
v2p0132c1s v2p0368c1s v2p0443c2s
v3p0033c2s v3p0149c1s
Bicknell, W.M. v1p0641c2s
v1p0867c2s v1p0889c2s v3p0218c1s
v3p0472c2s
Bickshu, Subhadra v4p0078c1s
Bidder, Dr. v1p0565c2s

Bidder, G.P. v4p0120c2s
Biddle, A. v1p0740c2s
Biddle, A.J.D. v6p0156c1s
Biddle, A.S. v1p0294c2s
Biddle, C. v1p0132c2s
Biddle, C.J. v1p0038c1s
Biddle, C.W. v2p0181c1s v3p0229c2s
Biddle, G.B. v6p0101c2s
Biddle, G.W. v3p0354c2s
Biddle, H.D. v4p0483c1s
Biddle, H.J. v3p0314c1s
Biddle, H.L. v4p0117c2s v4p0306c1s v4p0623c1s v5p0085c1m
Biddle, J.A. v5p0577c1s
Biddle, N. v1p0522c2s
Biddle, T. and Jordan, J.. v1p0240c2s
Biddle, W.A. v1p1391c2s
Biddle, W.F. v2p0302c2s v4p0346c2s v4p0415c1s
Biddle, W.L.C. v1p0270c2s
Biddle-Cope, Marquis v2p0385c1s v2p0450c1s v3p0319c1s
Biddlecombe, J. v6p0042c1s
Biddulph, C.E. v3p0115c2s v3p0211c1s v3p0353c2s v4p0004c2s v4p0153c2s v4p0435c2s v4p0436c1m v4p0567c2s
Biddulph, D.W., Mrs. v6p0652c2s
Biddulph, J.M. v5p0550c2s
Biddulph, M.A.S. v4p0102c2s
Biddulph, R. v2p0072c1s
Biden, S.P. v5p0219c2s
Bidie, G. v1p0450c2s
Bidlake, W.H. v3p0123c2s v6p0126c2s
Bidwell, A.K. v4p0363c1s
Bidwell, Belle J. v3p0315c1s
Bidwell, J. v3p0063c1m v3p0163c1s v4p0048c1s v4p0083c1s v6p0093c1s
Bidwell, S. v1p1004c1s v1p1291c2s v2p0138c2s v2p0272c1s v2p0413c2s v2p0463c1s v3p0250c2s v3p0251c1s v3p0264c1s v4p0547c1s v5p0008c2s v5p0128c2s v5p0129c1s v5p0470c1s v6p0497c2s
Bidwell, W. v5p0640c1s
Bidwell, W.H. v1p0022c1s v1p0364c2s
Bieberstein, R.von v3p0097c2s v3p0341c1s v4p0130c2s
Bieberstein, Rogalla von . v5p0287c1s
Biedenbach, C.L. v4p0257c1s
Biedermann, C., Baron v5p0547c1s
Biedermann, Dr. v2p0121c1s
Bienkowski, P. v4p0186c2s
Bienstock, J.W. v5p0502c1s
Bienstock, Vladimir v6p0246c2s
Bierbower, A. v1p0138c2s v1p0286c1s v1p0431c2s v1p0441c1m v1p0594c1s v1p0738c2s v1p0869c1s v1p1045c2s v1p1073c1s v1p1117c1s v1p1162c2s v1p1175c1s v1p1216c1s v1p1292c2s v1p1342c2s v2p0038c1s v2p0152c1s v2p0225c1s v2p0286c1s v2p0366c2s v2p0388c1s v2p0439c1m v3p0231c1s v3p0245c1s v4p0015c1s v4p0301c1s v4p0314c2s v4p0460c2s v5p0042c1s v5p0305c2s v5p0462c2s v5p0479c2s v5p0536c1s v6p0015c1s v6p0217c2s v6p0296c2s
Bierbower, Austin v1p0053c2s v5p0148c2s v6p0125c1s
Bierce, A. v6p0144c1s v6p0176c1s v6p0322c1s v6p0348c1s v6p0603c1s v6p0603c2s v6p0694c1s
Bierce, A.G. v1p0574c1s v1p1160c2s
Bierhoff, F. v4p0404c2s v4p0408c2s
Bierstadt, A. v4p0126c1s
Bierstadt, C.A. v2p0381c1s
Bierstadt, O.A. v2p0164c2s v2p0473c2s v3p0394c2s
Bierwirth, H.C. v2p0441c2s v3p0171c2s v4p0480c1s
Bierwith, C. v4p0516c1s
Bierwith, H.C. v4p0065c1s
Biesen, C.van den v4p0054c2s v4p0515c2s
Biesenthal, J.H.R. v1p0128c2s v1p0903c1s
Biethen, J. v6p0710c1s
Biffen, R.H. v6p0694c2s
Bigelow, A. v1p0876c2s v1p0982c2s v1p1390c2s v3p0445c2s
Bigelow, A.G. v2p0106c2s
Bigelow, B. v6p0384c2s
Bigelow, C.H. v6p0567c1s
Bigelow, E. v5p0266c1s
Bigelow, E.B. v1p0713c1s
Bigelow, E.E. v2p0010c2s v3p0037c1s v3p0263c1s v4p0034c2s
Bigelow, E.V. v3p0403c2s
Bigelow, F.H. v3p0027c1m v3p0095c1s v3p0415c1m v3p0416c1s v4p0120c1s v4p0165c2s v4p0253c2s v4p0545c2s v4p0556c2m v4p0557c1s v4p0568c1s v4p0568c2s v5p0123c2m v5p0144c1s v5p0151c1s v5p0174c2m v5p0356c1s v5p0560c2s v6p0052c2s v6p0132c1s v6p0280c2s v6p0413c1s v6p0433c1s v6p0625c2s
Bigelow, G.I. v4p0498c2s
Bigelow, H.A. v6p0401c1s
Bigelow, H.B. v6p0260c2s
Bigelow, H.R. v2p0080c2s
Bigelow, J. v1p0024c2s v1p0058c1s v1p0105c1s v1p0212c1s v1p0265c2s v1p0354c2s v1p0371c2s v1p0390c1s v1p0472c1s v1p0478c2s v1p0573c1s v1p0576c2s v1p0876c1s v1p1018c1s v1p1149c1s v1p1181c2s v2p0166c1s v2p0208c2s v2p0232c1s v2p0234c1s v2p0287c1s v2p0319c2s v3p0095c2s v3p0162c1s v4p0164c2s v4p0219c1s v4p0538c2s v4p0576c2s v5p0083c1s v5p0098c1s v5p0347c2s v5p0503c1s v5p0601c1s v6p0239c1s v6p0666c1s
Bigelow, J., jr. v3p0172c1s v6p0361c2s
Bigelow, John v4p0577c1s
Bigelow, L.J. v1p0356c2s v1p0730c1s v1p1153c1s v1p1266c1s
Bigelow, M.M. v4p0065c1s v4p0213c2s v4p0323c1s v5p0171c2s v6p0364c1s v6p0405c1s v6p0451c2s v6p0650c2s
Bigelow, Melville M. v6p0364c2s
Bigelow, N.M.W. v6p0465c2s
Bigelow, P. v1p0266c1s v1p0756c1s v1p1400c1s v3p0015c2s v3p0171c1s v3p0464c2m v4p0005c2s v4p0006c2m v4p0022c1s v4p0062c1s v4p0062c2s v4p0108c1s v4p0135c2s v4p0147c2s v4p0224c1s v4p0224c2s v4p0264c1s v4p0302c2s v4p0313c1s v4p0495c2s v4p0496c1s v4p0496c2m v4p0622c2m v5p0008c1m v5p0049c1s v5p0068c1m v5p0093c1s v5p0110c1s v5p0111c1s v5p0158c1s v5p0189c1s v5p0189c2s v5p0195c1s v5p0230c2s v5p0231c1m v5p0269c2s v5p0303c1s v5p0303c2s v5p0315c2s v5p0320c1s v5p0398c2s v5p0410c2s v5p0422c2s v5p0496c1s v5p0530c1s v5p0538c1s v5p0542c1s v5p0553c2s v5p0558c1s v5p0589c1s v5p0601c1s v5p0610c2s v5p0624c2s v5p0631c2s v6p0045c2s v6p0059c1m v6p0085c2s v6p0118c2s v6p0187c1s v6p0252c1s v6p0252c2s v6p0254c1s v6p0254c2s v6p0256c1s v6p0287c1m v6p0307c1s v6p0416c2s v6p0421c1s v6p0434c1s v6p0435c1m v6p0450c2m v6p0476c1m v6p0477c1s v6p0579c2s v6p0643c2s v6p0670c2s v6p0683c1s v6p0699c1s v6p0710c1m
Bigelow, P., Mrs. v3p0124c1s v6p0619c2s
Bigelow, Poultney v4p0130c2s v4p0224c1s v5p0225c1s v5p0230c1s v5p0439c1s v5p0586c2s v5p0631c2s
Bigelow, Poultney, Mrs. .. v3p0121c2s
Bigelow, R.P. and Rathbun, E.P. v6p0381c1s
Bigelow, S.L. v6p0200c1s v6p0357c1s
Bigelow, T. v1p0775c2s
Bigelow, W. v6p0659c2s
Bigelow, W.B. v5p0116c2s
Bigelow, W.D. v5p0212c2s v6p0231c1s
Bigelow, W.P. v5p0114c1s
Bigelow, W.R. v3p0190c2s
Bigelow, W.S. v5p0169c2s
Bigg, A.H. v2p0478c1s v4p0195c2s v4p0621c2s
Bigg, A.H. and Hatchard, M.L. v3p0429c2s
Bigg, J.S. v1p0716c1s
Bigg, L. v1p0360c2s
Bigg-Wither, G., Mrs. v3p0173c1s
Biggar, C.R.W. v4p0490c2s
Biggar, E.B. v1p0349c1s v2p0324c1s v4p0393c1s v4p0398c1s v4p0550c2s v4p0637c2m v5p0006c1s v5p0320c1s v5p0586c1s
Biggar, E.R. v6p0064c2s
Biggar, H.P. v5p0331c1s
Biggart, A.S. v5p0030c1s
Biggs, H.M. v4p0020c2s v4p0131c1s v5p0319c1s v5p0357c1s v5p0594c1s
Biggs, K.A.A. v4p0568c1s v4p0611c1s v5p0253c2s
Bigham, J. v4p0016c1m v4p0123c1s v4p0513c2s v5p0126c2s v5p0463c1s
Bigham, John v4p0465c1s
Bignami, E. v5p0183c2s v5p0184c1s v5p0185c1s v5p0300c2s v6p0197c1s v6p0197c2s v6p0198c1s v6p0527c2s v6p0550c1s v6p0624c2s
Bignani, Enrico v6p0198c1s
Bignell, F.H. v2p0293c1s
Bignold, H.B. v6p0042c1s v6p0474c1s
Bignon, F. v4p0394c2s
Bigot, M.H. v6p0052c1s v6p0538c2s
Bigourdan, G. v6p0188c1s
Bikelas, D. v1p0553c2s v2p0063c1s v2p0190c1s v3p0062c1m v3p0183c2m v3p0184c1s v5p0036c2s v5p0142c2s
Bikelas, Demetrios v4p0587c1s
Bikle, P.M. v1p0443c2s v1p0580c1s v1p1268c2s v1p1422c2s v2p0269c1s v3p0230c1s v3p0281c1s
Bilbie, H.G. v5p0306c1s
Bilderbeck, J.B. v6p0110c2s
Bildt, Baron de v6p0123c2s
Bildt, C.di v5p0475c1s
Biles, J.H. v4p0548c1s v5p0526c1m
Biley, E. v1p0016c1s v1p0581c2s
Bilgram, H. v1p1249c1s v1p1416c2s v2p0319c2s v2p0425c2s v4p0088c1s v6p0089c2s
Bilinski, A.R.B.de v6p0557c1s
Bilinski, A.Rustem Bey de. v6p0661c1s
Bilkey, P.E. v5p0041c2s
Bill, C. v4p0225c2s v4p0236c1s v5p0245c2s v6p0255c2s v6p0267c1s
Bill, E. v2p0101c1s
Bill, M.B. v2p0122c1s
Billberg, H. v3p0187c1s v3p0417c2s
Billheimer, T.C. v3p0233c2s
Billia, L.M., Prof. v4p0091c1s
Billiani, C.C. v4p0031c1s v4p0415c1s
Billing, A.H. v5p0344c2s
Billing, R.C. v3p0441c1s v3p0472c2s v4p0116c1s
Billing, S. v2p0161c2s v2p0213c1s v2p0222c2s v2p0307c2s v2p0450c2s
Billingham, H. v1p0292c2s v1p0706c2s
Billings, E. v1p0193c1s v1p0195c1s v1p0301c1s v1p0317c2s v1p0469c2s v1p1367c2s
Billings, F.P. v3p0071c1s
Billings, F.S. v4p0542c1s
Billings, Frank v6p0408c2s
Billings, G. v6p0228c1s v6p0405c1s v6p0668c1s
Billings, J.S. v1p0494c2m v1p0816c1s v1p1436c2s v2p0080c2s v2p0175c2s v2p0282c1s v2p0390c2s v2p0396c1s v2p0457c1s v3p0121c2s v3p0192c1s v3p0273c1s v4p0062c1s v4p0131c1s v4p0252c1s v4p0265c1m v4p0363c2m v4p0383c2s v4p0438c1s v4p0441c2s v4p0453c1s v4p0502c2m v5p0334c1s v5p0375c1s v5p0407c2m v6p0372c2s v6p0373c1s
Billings, J.S., Dr. v4p0594c1s
Billings, John S. v3p0457c2s
Billings, L.G. v4p0254c1s
Billings, W.R. v1p1311c1s
Billington, M.F. v4p0119c2s
Billman, I.C. v1p0777c2s
Billows, F.H. v5p0536c1s
Billroth, Prof. v1p0256c1s
Bills, G.M.W. v4p0535c1s
Billson, C.J. v2p0314c2s v2p0346c1s v4p0166c1s v4p0205c2s v4p0408c1s
Billson, W.W. v1p0317c2s
Bilsinger, Dr. v4p0397c2s
Bilson, J. v4p0052c2s
Bilson, W.W. v2p0401c2s
Binckley, J.M. v1p0198c2s v1p0227c1s v1p0228c1s v1p0333c2s v1p0492c1s v1p1042c2s v1p1056c1s v1p1218c2s
Binckley, J.W. v1p1253c2s
Binckley, M.L. v1p0728c2s
Binder, R.M. v6p0033c2s
Bindley, T.H. v3p0254c1s v3p0275c1s v4p0045c2s v4p0550c1s
Bindloss, H. v4p0447c1s v4p0551c2s v4p0562c1s v5p0036c1s v5p0051c1s v5p0082c2s v5p0088c2s v5p0148c1s v5p0151c2s v5p0155c2s v5p0157c1s v5p0213c1s v5p0238c1s v5p0257c2s v5p0263c2s v5p0274c1m v5p0283c1m v5p0283c2s v5p0304c2s v5p0326c1s v5p0348c1s v5p0383c2s v5p0392c2s v5p0411c2m v5p0412c2s v5p0437c2s v5p0494c2s v5p0508c2s v5p0509c2s v5p0518c1s v5p0572c1s v5p0584c1s v5p0585c1s v5p0597c1m v5p0597c2s v5p0605c2m v5p0607c2s v5p0627c2s v5p0628c1s v6p0006c1s v6p0381c2s v6p0410c1s v6p0554c2s v6p0616c1s v6p0620c1s
Bindloss, Harold v5p0414c2s v5p0503c2s v6p0243c1s
Bindon, E. v3p0254c1s
Bindseil, H.E. v1p0097c2s
Binet, A. v2p0215c1s v3p0097c1s v3p0209c1s v3p0216c1s

v4p0021c1s v4p0037c1s v4p0122c1s
v4p0125c1s v4p0130c1m v4p0193c1s
v4p0211c2s v4p0277c1m v4p0284c2s
v4p0285c2s v4p0365c1s v4p0369c2m
v4p0464c1s v4p0515c1s v4p0575c1s
v5p0003c1s v5p0062c1s v5p0369c2s
v5p0441c2s v5p0455c1s
Binet, A. and Fere, C. ... v3p0206c1s
Binet, A. and Vaschide, N.
v5p0293c1s
Binet, M.A. v4p0417c1s
Binet-Valmer, G. and Vaschide, N.
v6p0170c1s
Bing, J. v1p0259c1s
Bing, S. v4p0260c1s
v5p0606c1s v6p0033c2m
Bingham, C. v3p0078c1s
v3p0109c1s v3p0120c1s v3p0168c2s
v3p0177c1s v3p0199c1s v3p0259c2s
v3p0306c1s v3p0373c1s v4p0267c1s
Bingham, D. v3p0035c2s
Bingham, E. v6p0535c2s
Bingham, G., Sir et al. .. v5p0504c1s
Bingham, G.C. v3p0157c1s
Bingham, H. v6p0164c2s
Bingham, H.A., Mrs. v1p0496c2s
Bingham, J.A. v5p0598c1s
Bingham, J.W. v4p0009c1s
Bingham, R. v6p0605c2s
Bingham, T.A. v4p0059c2s
v5p0098c2s v5p0230c1s v5p0470c1s
Bingham, T.F., Mrs. v4p0083c2s
Binion, S.A. v3p0130c2s
Binkley, C.A. v5p0400c2s
Binkley, S.H. v2p0010c1s
v2p0300c1s
Binney, C.C. v3p0031c1s
v4p0043c1s
Binney, E.W. v1p0470c2s
Binney, H. v1p0431c2s
v1p1178c2s v3p0216c1s v3p0248c1s
v3p0329c1s v3p0430c1s
Binney, J. v4p0056c1s
Binney, T. v1p0081c2s
v1p0181c2s v1p0384c2s v1p1220c1s
Binney, W.G. v1p0859c1s
Binnie, W. v2p0039c2s
v2p0042c1s v2p0269c1s v2p0432c1s
v2p0480c2s
Binns, C.E. v6p0511c2m
Binns, C.F. v4p0094c2s
v6p0107c1s v6p0130c2s v6p0225c1s
v6p0321c1s v6p0511c2s
Binns, R.W. v2p0351c1s
Binns, W. v1p0060c1s
v1p0364c1s v1p0435c1s v1p0830c2s
v1p0869c2s v1p1096c1s v1p1161c2s
v2p0082c1s v2p0147c1s
Binns, W. et al. v4p0557c2s
Binsse, H. v5p0360c2s
Binsse, H.B. v4p0371c1s
v5p0151c1s v5p0353c2s
Binsse, L.B. v2p0075c1s
v2p0113c1s v2p0233c1s v2p0286c2s
v2p0367c2s v2p0388c1s v3p0096c1s
v3p0143c2s v3p0314c2s v3p0320c1s
v3p0344c2s
Binyon, L. v5p0323c2s
v6p0033c2s v6p0070c1s v6p0167c1s
v6p0168c1s v6p0479c1s v6p0541c2s
v6p0588c2s v6p0664c1s v6p0689c1s
Binyon, Lawrence v4p0164c2s
Biorkman, E. v5p0378c2s
v6p0506c2s
Birch, G.H.
v2p0020c1s
v3p0275c2s
Birch, L.G. v5p0163c1s
Birch, S. v1p0013c2s
v1p0036c1s v1p0069c2s v1p0395c1s
v1p0396c1s v1p0427c1s v1p0533c2s
v1p0590c1s v1p1082c1s v1p1199c1s
v1p1307c2s v1p1363c1m v1p1435c1s
Birch, T. v1p0219c2s
v1p0676c1s
Birch, T.B. v5p0435c1s
Birch, W.de G. v1p0644c2s
v1p0732c1s v3p0014c1s v3p0464c1s
Birchall, F.T. v6p0415c1s
v6p0504c2s v6p0536c1s v6p0546c1s
v6p0696c2s
Birchard, C.C. v5p0394c1s
Birchenough, H. v5p0006c2s
v5p0157c1s v5p0181c1s v5p0231c2s
v5p0244c1s v5p0248c1m v5p0584c1s
v6p0006c2s v6p0107c2s v6p0271c2s
v6p0416c2s
Birchenough, H., Mrs. v5p0376c2s
Birchenough, M.C. v3p0113c1s
v4p0080c1s v4p0213c2s v4p0311c1s
v5p0290c2s
Birchenough, Mabel C. v6p0318c2s
Birchmere, J.W. v2p0045c1s
Birckel, J.J. v1p1127c1s
Bird, A.A. v4p0115c1s
v4p0116c1s v4p0438c1m v4p0438c2m
v5p0622c2s
Bird, A.B. v4p0433c2s
Bird, C. v3p0030c1s
v3p0110c1s v3p0336c2s v3p0463c2s
Bird, F.M. v1p0105c2s
v1p0521c2s v1p0620c1m v1p0620c2s
v1p0778c2s v1p0933c2s v1p1398c2s
v3p0296c2s v3p0432c1s v4p0126c1s
v4p0197c2s v4p0198c1s v4p0234c1s
v4p0271c2s v4p0287c1s v4p0331c1s
v4p0349c1m v4p0420c2s v4p0470c1s
v4p0554c2s v5p0135c1s v5p0206c1s
v5p0352c1s v5p0355c2s v5p0382c1s
v5p0435c2s v5p0486c1s v5p0555c2s
Bird, F.M. and Bird, R.M.. v3p0038c1s
Bird, F.W. v2p0223c2s
Bird, G.F. v5p0344c1m
Bird, H.S. v3p0464c2s
v5p0550c1s v6p0510c1s
Bird, I. v1p0535c2s
Bird, I.A. v1p0620c1s
v1p1398c2s
Bird, I.L. v2p0029c1s
v2p0273c1s v2p0374c2s v2p0460c2s
Bird, J. v1p0284c2s
v1p0578c2s v1p0629c1s v2p0096c2s
Bird, J.T. v6p0140c2s
Bird, M. v1p0576c2s
Bird, P.R. v6p0166c2s
Bird, R.M. v1p0007c2s
v1p0338c2s v6p0228c1s v6p0376c2s
Bird, R.M. and Bird, F.M.. v3p0038c1s
Bird, S.R. v2p0055c1s
v2p0056c1s v2p0108c2s
Bird, T. v4p0542c2s
v5p0200c2s v5p0518c2s v5p0561c1s
Bird, W.D. v5p0411c2s
Birdilove, Robin v5p0063c2s
Birdsall, O. v6p0671c2s
Birdsall, W.R. v4p0119c2s
Birdseye, C.E. v6p0135c2s
Birdseye, G. v1p0261c1s
v1p0331c1s v1p0405c1s v1p0471c1s
v1p0704c2s v1p0840c1s v1p1127c1s
v1p1220c2s v1p1416c1m v1p1430c2s
Birdwood, F. v6p0120c1s
v6p0271c2s
Birdwood, G. v3p0088c2s
v3p0146c1s v3p0197c2s v3p0211c1s
v3p0264c1s v3p0341c1s v3p0343c2s
v5p0089c2s v5p0204c2s v5p0286c2s
v5p0355c1s v5p0388c1m v5p0422c1s
v5p0532c1s v6p0032c2s v6p0094c2s
v6p0524c2s
Birdwood, G. and Skeat, W.W.
v5p0488c1s
Birdwood, G., Sir v2p0083c1s
v4p0366c2s v5p0462c1s
Birdwood, George v4p0327c1s
v6p0098c2s
Birdwood, H. v6p0517c2s
Birdwood, H.M. v5p0284c2m
v5p0285c2s v5p0453c1s
Birge, E.A. v5p0335c1m
v6p0074c2s v6p0374c2s v6p0664c2s
v6p0671c2s v6p0672c1s
Birge, F.E. v4p0151c2s
Birge, W.S. v6p0226c2s
v6p0694c1s
Birger-Morner, Count v5p0031c1s
Birgham, F. v2p0285c2s
Birkbeck, A.M. v1p0142c2s
v1p0318c2s v1p1180c1s
Birkbeck, Dr. v1p1010c2s
Birkbeck, J. v1p1265c1s
Birkbeck, Miss. v1p1279c2s
Birkedal, H. v2p0078c1m
v2p0337c1s v2p0411c2s
Birkenbine, H.P.M. v1p1081c1s
Birkenbine, J. v5p0378c1s
Birkhaeuser, J.A. v3p0464c1s
Birkhimer, W.E. v5p0032c1s
v5p0032c2m v5p0033c1s v5p0271c1s
v5p0290c1s v5p0591c1s v5p0626c1s
v6p0442c1s
Birkinbine, H.P.M. v1p1065c1s
v1p1065c2s v1p1160c1s v1p1391c2s
Birkinbine, J. v1p0141c1s
v3p0223c1m v3p0353c2s v3p0457c2s
v4p0064c1s v4p0151c2s v4p0180c2s
v4p0292c1m v4p0368c1s v4p0438c1s
v5p0219c2m v5p0227c2s v5p0323c1s
v5p0377c2s v5p0621c2s v6p0070c2s
v6p0499c2s
Birkinbine, John v6p0132c2s
Birkmyre, R. v6p0218c1s
Birmingham, J. v1p0281c1s
v1p0699c1m v1p0865c2s v1p1269c1s
Birnage, A. v6p0131c1s
v6p0390c1s
Birnbaum, D. v6p0654c1s
Birney, E.C. v4p0141c2s
Birney, Elizabeth C. v5p0486c1s
Birney, W. v6p0130c1s
v6p0362c2s
Birnie, J.B.L. v4p0484c2s
Birnie, R. v5p0252c2s
Birnie, T.C. v4p0414c2s
Birrell, A. v2p0061c1s
v2p0139c2s v2p0204c1s v2p0237c2s
v2p0247c1s v3p0020c2s v3p0028c2s
v3p0076c2s v3p0240c2s v3p0260c2s
v3p0302c1s v3p0339c1s v3p0459c2s
v4p0039c1s v4p0112c2s v4p0141c1s
v4p0216c2s v4p0265c2s v4p0337c1s
v4p0477c1s v4p0564c1s v4p0579c1s
v5p0069c2s v5p0140c2s v5p0189c2s
v5p0207c1s v5p0272c1s v5p0309c2m
v5p0330c2s v5p0343c2s v5p0438c2s
v5p0487c1s v5p0553c1s v5p0625c2s
v6p0003c1s v6p0072c1s v6p0101c2s
v6p0192c1s v6p0194c1s v6p0194c2s
v6p0258c1s v6p0264c1s v6p0264c2s
v6p0332c1s v6p0359c2s v6p0459c1s
v6p0468c2s v6p0484c1s v6p0577c2s
Birrell, Aug. v5p0041c1s
Birrell, O.M. v2p0240c1s
Birt, H.N. v5p0117c2s
v5p0122c2s v5p0194c2s v6p0385c1s
Birt, W.R. v1p0074c1s
v1p0748c2s v1p0866c1m v1p1080c2s
v2p0296c1s
Birtwell, C.W. v4p0329c1m
Birtwell, M.L. v4p0096c2s
Bisbee, M.D. v2p0297c1s
v5p0061c1s v6p0366c2s
Bisbee, R.E. v4p0486c1s
v5p0464c2s v6p0234c2s v6p0443c1s
v6p0495c1s
Bisby, F.L. v5p0337c2s
Bischof, G. v1p0375c1s
v1p0376c2s v1p0377c1s v1p0793c1s
v1p1377c1m v1p1390c2s
Bischoff, T. v1p0792c1s
Biscoe, E.D. v5p0070c2s
Biscoe, M.B. v6p0125c1s
v6p0126c2s
Biscoe, Maurice B. v6p0028c1s
Biscoe, T.D. v1p0732c2s
Biscoe, W.S. v1p0628c2s
v1p1062c2s v2p0255c2s v4p0423c1s
Biscoe, W.S. and Dewey, M.
v5p0334c2s
Bishard, A. v5p0113c2s
Bishop, A.G. v5p0635c2s
Bishop, C. v3p0087c2s
Bishop, C.E. v3p0109c1s
v3p0176c1s v3p0188c2s v3p0202c2s
v4p0537c1s v5p0573c2s
Bishop, C.F. et al. v3p0085c2s
Bishop, C.S. v6p0068c2s
Bishop, E. v2p0194c2s
v2p0278c2s v2p0383c2s v4p0058c2s
v4p0359c2s v5p0097c1s v5p0136c2s
v5p0348c1s
Bishop, E.C. v1p0177c1s
Bishop, E.F. v2p0312c2s
Bishop, E.K. v5p0344c1s
v5p0516c2s
Bishop, E.L. v6p0446c1s
Bishop, G.B. v1p0252c1s
v1p1399c2s v2p0049c1s
Bishop, H. v5p0399c1s
v5p0484c2s
Bishop, H.B. v5p0597c2s
Bishop, I.B. v2p0403c2s
Bishop, I.Bird v3p0221c1s
Bishop, I.I. v4p0576c1s
Bishop, I.L. v3p0020c1s
v3p0438c1s v5p0109c2s
Bishop, I.P. v2p0429c2s
Bishop, Isabella v5p0565c1s
Bishop, Isabella B. v5p0387c1s
Bishop, J.B. v2p0089c1s
v2p0136c1s v2p0312c2s v2p0353c1s
v2p0354c2s v2p0356c1m v2p0423c1s
v2p0431c1s v2p0444c2s v3p0024c1s
v3p0031c1s v3p0031c2s v3p0033c1s
v3p0095c2s v3p0132c1s v3p0209c1s
v3p0214c1s v3p0233c2s v3p0254c2s
v3p0259c1s v3p0285c2s v3p0304c2s
v3p0311c1m v3p0326c1s v3p0337c2s
v3p0346c1s v3p0419c2m v3p0423c1s
v3p0454c1m v4p0043c1m v4p0058c2s
v4p0089c2s v4p0115c1s v4p0116c2s
v4p0119c1m v4p0135c2s v4p0236c2s
v4p0278c1s v4p0314c1s v4p0396c1s
v4p0449c2s v4p0457c2s v4p0595c2s
v4p0607c2s v5p0051c2s v5p0072c1m
v5p0098c1s v5p0120c2s v5p0144c2m
v5p0182c1s v5p0214c1s v5p0332c1s
v5p0407c1s v5p0456c2s v5p0464c2s
v5p0496c1s v5p0506c2s v5p0566c2s
v6p0259c2s v6p0284c1s v6p0390c2s
v6p0476c1s v6p0515c1s
Bishop, J.B. et al. v4p0174c1s
Bishop, J.F., Mrs. v5p0643c2s
Bishop, J.Le M. v1p0646c2s
Bishop, J.M. v3p0264c1s
Bishop, J.P. v2p0253c1s
v4p0269c1s v4p0328c1s v4p0509c2s
Bishop, J.R. v4p0122c2s
v4p0257c1s v5p0126c1s v5p0404c2s
v6p0240c2s v6p0324c1s v6p0362c2s
v6p0367c1s v6p0447c1s v6p0494c2s
v6p0616c1s
Bishop, J.T. v6p0071c2s
v6p0095c1s v6p0109c2s v6p0174c2s
v6p0284c2s v6p0533c2s v6p0554c2s
v6p0664c1s
Bishop, K.M. v2p0214c2s
Bishop, Kate M. v2p0482c1s
Bishop, L. v1p1159c2s
Bishop, M.C. v1p0312c1s

v1p1116c2s
Bishop, P.P. v3p0094c2s
Bishop, R.F. v4p0088c2s
v4p0360c1s v5p0115c1s v5p0595c2s
Bishop, R.P. v4p0012c1s
Bishop, S. v2p0426c2s
v4p0251c1s
Bishop, S.E. v2p0244c1s
v3p0191c1s v3p0271c2s v3p0416c1s
v4p0250c2s v4p0310c2s v5p0258c2s
v6p0169c2s v6p0283c1s v6p0351c1s
v6p0485c2s
Bishop, S.H. v5p0054c1s
v5p0102c1s v5p0426c1s v6p0109c2s
v6p0242c2s v6p0537c2s
Bishop, S.J.B. v5p0119c1s
Bishop, W.D. v1p0650c2s
Bishop, W.F. v6p0342c1s
Bishop, W.H. v1p0065c2s
v1p0066c1s v1p0079c1s v1p0102c2s
v1p0216c1s v1p0322c1s v1p0344c2s
v1p0346c2s v1p0384c1s v1p0439c1s
v1p0450c1s v1p0758c1s v1p0783c2s
v1p0789c2s v1p0851c2s v1p0911c1s
v1p0942c2s v1p1177c1s v1p1258c1s
v1p1381c1s v2p0007c1s v2p0021c1s
v2p0055c1s v2p0058c2s v2p0064c2s
v2p0080c2s v2p0118c1s v2p0119c2s
v2p0182c1s v2p0207c2s v2p0209c1s
v2p0210c1s v2p0286c2s v2p0287c1m
v2p0383c1s v2p0385c1s v2p0461c2s
v3p0029c1s v3p0101c2s v3p0228c2s
v3p0254c1s v3p0263c2s v3p0308c2s
v3p0320c1s v3p0373c1s v3p0474c1s
v4p0001c1s v4p0129c2s v4p0189c2s
v4p0194c2m v4p0311c2s v4p0455c1s
v4p0539c2s v4p0585c1s v4p0633c2s
v5p0023c1s v5p0061c1s v5p0139c2s
v5p0180c2s v5p0189c2s v5p0232c2s
v5p0326c1s v5p0507c2s v5p0606c2s
v6p0087c2s v6p0196c2s v6p0520c2s
Bishop, W.I. v2p0415c1s
Bishop, W.M. v6p0065c2s
Bishop, W.S. v6p0210c1s
Bishop, W.W. v5p0071c1s
v5p0335c2s v5p0518c1s v5p0577c2s
v5p0608c1s v6p0039c2s v6p0104c1m
v6p0130c2s v6p0157c1s v6p0370c2s
v6p0372c1s v6p0431c1s
Bisland, E. v3p0037c1s
v3p0058c1s v3p0095c2s v3p0109c2s
v3p0156c1s v3p0202c2s v3p0255c2s
v3p0275c1s v3p0309c1s v3p0312c2s
v3p0326c2s v3p0413c2s v3p0420c2s
v3p0435c2s v4p0124c1s v4p0148c1s
v4p0161c2s v4p0244c1s v4p0339c1s
v4p0626c1s v4p0627c2s v5p0016c2s
v5p0259c2s v5p0358c1s v5p0595c2s
v6p0601c1s
Bisland, E. et al. v4p0270c1s
Bisland, M. v3p0052c1s
v3p0068c2s v3p0123c1s v3p0151c1s
v3p0296c2s v3p0330c2s v3p0468c1s
v6p0526c1s
Bismark, K. v1p0233c1s
Bispham, C.T. v2p0251c1s
Bispham, D. v6p0437c2s
Bispham, D. and Lucas, C.. v6p0383c2s
Bispham, G.T. v1p1351c1s
v5p0252c2s
Bispham, W. v4p0068c1s
Bisschop, W.R. v6p0007c1s
Bissell, C. v1p0583c1s
v3p0166c2s v4p0140c1s v4p0273c2s
v4p0431c2s
Bissell, E.C. v1p0047c1s
v1p0122c1s v1p0394c1s v1p0424c2m
v2p0042c2s v2p0043c1s v2p0043c2s
v3p0041c2s v3p0347c2s v4p0054c2s
v4p0055c1s v6p0061c2s
Bissell, E.C. and Gregory, D.S.
v2p0045c1s v2p0082c1s
Bissell, F.S. v6p0371c2s
Bissell, G.E. v6p0032c2s
Bissell, G.P. v1p0093c2s
v1p0094c1s
Bissell, G.W. v4p0288c2s
v5p0418c2s v6p0002c2s
Bissell, J.W. v2p0299c2s
Bissell, M.L. v1p1299c2s
v1p1387c1s
Bissell, M.T. v3p0136c2s
v3p0469c1s v4p0035c2s
Bissell, W.A. v6p0567c2s
Bisset, A. v1p0220c1s
v1p0485c1s
Bissinger, E. v3p0197c2s
Bisson, I.H. v6p0285c2s
Bithell, R. v1p0026c1s
v1p0224c2s v1p0272c1s v1p0401c2s
v1p0498c1m v1p0579c2s v1p0746c2s
v1p0955c2s v1p1263c2s v1p1291c1s
Bitler, F.L. v4p0061c2s
Bitter, K. v5p0391c2s
Bitter, K.T. v6p0564c1s
Bitting, W.C. v4p0385c1s
Bittinger v5p0214c2s
Bittinger, J.B. v1p0118c2s
v1p0138c1s v1p0315c1s v1p0315c2s
v1p0980c2m v1p1208c1s v1p1395c1s
v2p0043c2s v2p0107c2s v2p0146c1s
v2p0352c2s
Bittinger, J.O. v3p0459c1s
Bittinger, J.Q. v1p0052c2s
v1p0850c1s v1p1043c1s v1p1347c1s
v3p0371c1m
Bixby, A.C. v6p0405c1s
v6p0617c1s
Bixby, J.F. v5p0437c1s
Bixby, J.T. v1p0084c1s
v1p0134c2s v1p0210c1s v1p0235c1s
v1p0236c2s v1p0238c2s v1p0346c1s
v1p0686c2s v1p0687c1s v1p0711c1s
v1p0729c1s v1p0802c1s v1p0859c2s
v1p0875c2s v1p0890c1s v1p0905c2s
v1p0937c1s v1p0964c1s v1p0993c2s
v1p1060c1s v1p1062c2s v1p1072c1s
v1p1094c1s v1p1094c2s v1p1095c1s
v1p1101c1s v1p1161c1m v1p1222c1s
v1p1236c2s v2p0006c1s v2p0059c2s
v2p0147c1m v2p0177c1s v2p0212c1s
v2p0215c2s v2p0354c1s v2p0368c1s
v2p0369c1m v2p0369c2s v2p0449c2s
v2p0480c2s v3p0057c2s v3p0058c2s
v3p0121c1s v3p0145c1s v3p0205c1s
v3p0234c1s v3p0273c1s v3p0302c1s
v3p0357c2s v3p0358c1m v3p0401c1s
v3p0424c2s v3p0444c2s v3p0454c2s
v4p0188c2s v4p0191c2s v4p0296c1s
v4p0320c2s v4p0376c1s v4p0382c1s
v4p0487c1s v4p0537c2s v4p0600c2s
v4p0637c2s v5p0042c1s v5p0114c2s
v5p0279c2s v5p0397c1s v5p0412c2s
v5p0483c1s v5p0514c2s v5p0604c2s
v6p0649c1s
Bixby, J.T. and Mountford, W.
v1p0857c1s v1p0858c1s
Bixio, M. v1p0604c2s
Bizet, G. v4p0357c1s
v5p0099c2s
Bjerknes, M. v2p0271c2s
Bjerregaard, C.H.A. v4p0496c2s
Bjerring, N. v5p0321c1m
Bjorck, A. v4p0300c2s
v5p0055c2s
Bjorkman, E. v6p0078c1s
v6p0122c1s v6p0257c1s
Bjorkman, Frances M. v6p0117c2s
v6p0462c2s
Bjornson, B. v1p0929c2s
v2p0278c2s v2p0311c2s v3p0307c2s
v4p0228c2s v4p0384c2s v4p0407c2s
v5p0321c2s v5p0579c1s
Bjornson, B. and Frederiksen, N.C.
v2p0387c1s
Bjornson, B. et al. v6p0237c1s
Blaauw, W.H. v1p0732c1s
v1p0811c2s
Blach, E. v3p0196c1s
Blach, E.S. v5p0278c2s
Blachford, Lord v1p0012c2s
v1p0545c1s v1p0618c1s v1p0839c1s
v1p0877c2s v1p1441c2s
Black, A. v1p0719c2s
v3p0272c1s v4p0063c2s v4p0274c2s
v4p0485c1s v4p0600c1s v5p0057c2s
v5p0058c1s v5p0161c2s v5p0263c2s
v5p0310c2s v6p0062c1s v6p0083c1s
v6p0154c2s v6p0461c2s v6p0497c1s
v6p0698c1s
Black, A. and Bradby, L.B.
v5p0201c1s
Black, A. and Huntington, D.W.
v3p0330c2s
Black, A.A. v4p0250c2s
v4p0289c2s v4p0424c2s
Black, Alex. v4p0062c2s
v4p0440c1s
Black, Archibald v6p0463c1s
Black, C. v1p0016c2s
v1p0579c1s v1p0824c1s v2p0067c2s
v2p0069c1s v2p0296c2s v3p0071c1s
v3p0080c1s v3p0147c2s v3p0152c1s
v3p0256c1s v3p0256c2s v3p0282c1s
v3p0345c1s v3p0412c2s v3p0452c1s
v3p0470c2m v4p0159c1s v4p0360c2s
v4p0459c1s v4p0581c1s v4p0606c2s
v4p0608c2s v6p0002c2s v6p0114c1s
v6p0357c2s v6p0616c2s v6p0651c2s
Black, C. and Simon, T. .. v3p0468c1s
Black, C. et al. v4p0452c1s
Black, C.E.D. v3p0003c2s
v3p0047c1s v3p0112c2s v4p0240c2s
v4p0279c2s v4p0280c2s v4p0281c1m
v4p0576c1s v5p0034c1s v5p0112c1s
v5p0286c2s v6p0057c2s v6p0646c1s
Black, C.F. v4p0262c2s
Black, C.R. v3p0008c2s
Black, Clementina v3p0413c1s
v3p0472c2s v4p0080c1s v4p0581c1s
v6p0631c1s
Black, E. v2p0420c2s
Black, E.C. v5p0527c1s
Black, F. v5p0082c2s
Black, G. v3p0268c2s
Black, G.D. v4p0620c1s
Black, H. v6p0010c1s
v6p0158c2s v6p0707c2s
Black, H. and Clark, E.G.. v3p0387c1s
Black, H.C. v2p0154c2s
v2p0223c1s v2p0347c1s v3p0026c2s
v3p0248c1s v3p0336c2s v4p0006c2s
v4p0127c2s v4p0190c2s v4p0541c2s
Black, H.E. v6p0607c2s
Black, Hugh v6p0490c1s
Black, J.C.C. v2p0203c1s
Black, J.G. v6p0194c2s
Black, J.M. v1p0855c2s
Black, J.R. v1p0047c2s
v1p0354c1s v1p1150c2s
Black, J.S. v1p0424c1s
v1p0540c2s v1p0772c2s v1p1181c2s
v1p1243c2s v1p1413c1m v3p0146c2s
v4p0515c1s v4p0522c2s
Black, J.S. and Ingersoll, R.G.
v1p0240c2s
Black, J.S. and Stoughton, E.W.
v1p1048c1s
Black, J.W. v4p0086c2s
v4p0358c2s v4p0504c1s v5p0364c2s
Black, P.Y. v5p0036c1s
Black, R.L. v6p0233c1s
Black, R.M. v3p0113c1s
Black, R.W. v3p0209c1s
v3p0357c2s v3p0449c1s
Black, S. v1p1146c1s
v6p0041c2s
Black, W. v1p0404c2s
v1p0556c2s v1p0584c2s v1p0740c1s
v1p0782c2s v1p0784c2s v1p0785c2s
v1p0795c1s v1p0803c1s v1p0817c2s
v1p0859c2s v1p0955c2s v1p1051c1s
v1p1080c2s v1p1082c1s v1p1131c1s
v1p1150c2s v1p1259c1m v1p1308c2s
v1p1406c2s v2p0137c1s v2p0142c1s
v2p0203c1s v2p0239c1s v2p0332c2s
v2p0399c1s v2p0427c1s v2p0472c2s
v3p0113c2s v3p0188c1s v3p0209c2s
v3p0397c1s v4p0073c2s v4p0247c1s
v4p0274c2s v4p0349c2s v6p0701c2s
Black, W.F. v4p0156c2s
Black, W.G. v1p1045c2s
v1p1187c1s v2p0247c1s v2p0282c1s
v2p0288c1s v2p0304c2s v2p0399c1s
v3p0194c1s v4p0215c2s v4p0508c2s
Black, W.H. v1p0163c2s
v1p0754c1s v1p0765c1s v2p0005c1s
v2p0351c2s v2p0367c2s v2p0371c1s
v2p0438c1s
Black, W.H. and Franks, A.W.
v1p0596c2s
Black, W.H. and Lewin, T.. v1p1037c1s
Black, W.J. v1p0535c1s
v2p0325c2s
Black, W.M. v5p0208c1s
v6p0031c2s
Black, W.N. v4p0023c2s
v4p0024c1m v4p0078c1s v4p0137c2s
v4p0175c1s v4p0387c1s v4p0400c1s
v4p0400c2s v4p0533c1s v4p0553c2s
v4p0595c1s v4p0615c1s
Black, W.P.M. v5p0430c1s
Black, W.T. v2p0006c2s
v2p0125c2s
Black, Winifred v6p0260c1s
Black, Wm. v5p0095c1s
Blackader, A. v1p0786c2s
v1p0957c1s
Blackall, C.H. v2p0013c1s
v2p0020c1m v2p0050c2s v2p0057c1m
v2p0060c1s v2p0060c2s v2p0135c2s
v2p0159c1s v2p0199c2m v2p0208c1m
v2p0256c1s v2p0263c2s v2p0301c2s
v2p0329c1s v2p0337c1s v2p0366c1s
v2p0384c1s v2p0388c2s v2p0442c2s
v2p0443c2s v2p0458c2s v2p0459c1s
v2p0460c2s v2p0480c1m v3p0059c1s
v3p0076c2s v3p0121c1m v3p0196c2s
v3p0349c1s v4p0023c2s v4p0024c1s
v4p0025c1s v4p0451c2s v4p0543c2s
v4p0548c1s v5p0026c1s v5p0072c1s
v5p0082c2s v5p0105c1s v5p0144c2s
v5p0552c1s v6p0641c2s
Blackall, W.W. v6p0542c2s
Blackbird, E.G. v5p0180c2s
Blackburn, D. v6p0543c1s
v6p0654c2s
Blackburn, Douglas v6p0007c1s
Blackburn, E.J.M. v2p0113c2s
Blackburn, E.V. v2p0287c1s
Blackburn, H. v1p0237c1s
v1p0572c2s v1p0639c1s v1p0926c1m
v1p0935c1s v1p1318c2s v2p0023c1s
v2p0215c1s v2p0306c2s v2p0477c1s
v3p0022c1s v3p0208c2m v4p0274c1m
v4p0425c2s v4p0451c2s
Blackburn, J. v1p0290c1s
v1p0386c2s
Blackburn, J.C.S. v3p0359c1s
Blackburn, J.S. v1p1176c2s
Blackburn, K. v5p0596c1s
Blackburn, Mrs. v1p0622c2s
Blackburn, S. v4p0627c1s
Blackburn, T. v6p0666c1s
Blackburn, V. v3p0457c2s
v4p0164c2s v4p0449c1s v4p0522c1s
v4p0608c2s v5p0385c2s v6p0286c2s
v6p0438c2s v6p0482c1s
Blackburn, V. and Carr, J.C.
v5p0560c1s

Blackburn, V., Mrs. v2p0113c2s
Blackburn, W. v1p0926c1s
Blackburn, W.J. v1p1191c2s
Blackburn, W.M. v1p0167c1s
v1p0189c2m v1p0240c2s v1p0323c1s
v1p0430c1s v1p1089c2s v1p1098c1s
v1p1212c1s v2p0241c2s
Blackburne, E.O. v1p0695c2s
v1p0951c1s v2p0108c2s
Blackburne, T. v1p1430c1s
Blackford, A.L. v2p0148c1s
Blackford, C.M. v5p0086c2s
v5p0205c1s v5p0403c1s v5p0505c1s
v5p0516c2m v5p0537c2s
Blackford, T.A. v5p0269c2s
Blackhall, C.H. v6p0027c2s
Blackie, J.A. v2p0058c2s
v2p0309c1s
Blackie, J.S. v1p0071c2s
v1p0262c2s v1p0313c1s v1p0338c1s
v1p0405c2s v1p0441c1s v1p0500c2s
v1p0517c2s v1p0526c2s v1p0554c1s
v1p0555c2s v1p0601c1s v1p0714c1s
v1p0721c1s v1p0724c2s v1p0725c1s
v1p0826c2s v1p0885c1s v1p0922c2s
v1p0948c2s v1p1016c2s v1p1060c2s
v1p1157c2s v1p1164c2s v1p1378c2s
v2p0037c2s v2p0044c1s v2p0181c2s
v2p0190c2s v2p0202c2s v2p0284c1s
v2p0369c1s v2p0392c1s v2p0456c1s
v3p0044c1s v3p0081c1s v3p0184c1s
v3p0188c2s v3p0233c1s v3p0242c2s
v3p0258c1s v3p0261c2s v3p0381c2s
v3p0387c2s v4p0241c1s v4p0312c2s
v4p0320c1s v4p0320c2s v4p0392c1s
v4p0445c1s v4p0509c1s v5p0249c1s
Blackie, J.S. and Geddes, W.D.
v1p0601c1s
Blackie, L.S. v1p0429c2s
Blackie, W.G. v2p0053c1s
Blackiston, A.H. v6p0107c1s
v6p0414c2s
Blackiston, G.H. v6p0102c2s
Blackiston, G.P. v6p0580c2s
v6p0624c1s
Blackley, Canon v3p0141c1s
Blackley, H. v5p0228c1s
Blackley, W.C. v2p0247c2s
Blackley, W.L. v1p0059c2s
v1p0088c2s v1p0299c2s v1p0382c2s
v1p0416c1s v1p0574c1s v1p0648c1m
v1p0981c2m v1p1016c2s v1p1038c2s
v1p1153c2s v2p0039c2s v2p0084c1s
v2p0223c1s v2p0244c2s v2p0440c1m
v3p0141c1s v3p0218c1s v4p0412c1s
Blackley, W.L. and Glennie, J.S.S.
v1p0898c1s
Blacklock, A.D. v4p0508c2s
Blackman, F.F. v4p0550c1s
Blackman, V.H. and Murray, G.
v5p0125c1s
Blackman, W.F. v4p0535c1s
v6p0446c2s
Blackman, W.F. and Wallace, A.R.
v5p0591c2s
Blackmar, F.W. v3p0063c2s
v3p0230c2s v3p0403c1s v4p0152c2s
v4p0282c1s v4p0434c1s v4p0461c1s
v4p0555c1s v5p0054c1s v5p0313c2s
v5p0507c1s v5p0533c2s v5p0544c2s
v6p0533c2s v6p0534c1s v6p0600c1s
Blackmore, E.G. v1p0707c1s
v1p1227c2s
Blackmore, J.J. v5p0260c2m
v5p0551c1s
Blackmore, R.D. v1p0022c2s
v1p0246c1s v1p0311c2s v1p0423c2s
v1p0789c1s v1p0807c1s v2p0415c2s
v3p0405c2s v4p0063c1s v4p0147c2s
v4p0435c2s v5p0153c1s
Blacknall, O.W. v2p0309c1s
v4p0136c2s v4p0552c2m
Blackshaw, R. v2p0022c1s
v2p0429c2s v6p0112c2s v6p0166c1s
v6p0286c2s v6p0330c1s v6p0384c1s
v6p0453c1s v6p0604c1s
Blackshaw, Rand v6p0444c2s
Blackstock, G.T. v4p0602c1s
Blackstock, W.S. v4p0022c1s
v4p0225c2s
Blackstone, S. v1p0538c1s
Blackstone, W., Sir v1p0381c1s
v1p1173c2m
Blackstone, W.E. v3p0230c2s
Blackstone, W.S. v4p0140c2s
Blackwall, J. v1p0135c2m
v1p0647c1s v1p1236c1s
Blackwelder, E. v6p0233c1s
Blackwell, A. v1p0457c1s
v1p0470c2s v1p0665c2s
Blackwell, A.B. v1p0625c2s
v1p0820c2s v1p1099c2s
Blackwell, Alice Stone ... v6p0705c2s
Blackwell, Anna v5p0071c1s
Blackwell, C. v5p0396c2s
Blackwell, E. v1p0816c2s
v1p1421c1s v2p0478c1s
Blackwell, E.R. v1p0919c2s
Blackwell, F.O. v4p0176c2s
v4p0372c2s v6p0197c2s
Blackwell, H.B. v1p0949c2s
v1p1094c1s v1p1341c1s v3p0470c1s
Blackwell, J.E. v3p0059c2s
Blackwell, J.K. v3p0223c1s
Blackwell, R. v4p0509c1s
Blackwell, R.W. v5p0183c2s
Blackwell, S.C. v1p1204c2s
Blackwell, S.H. v1p0495c1s
Blackwell, T. v3p0368c1s
Blackwell, T.E. v1p1390c1s
Blackwell, T.S. v3p0048c2s
v3p0064c2s v3p0119c2s v3p0148c2s
v3p0186c1s v3p0222c1s v3p0278c2s
v3p0351c1s v3p0383c1s v3p0436c2s
v4p0088c2s v4p0201c2s v4p0265c2s
v4p0418c2s v4p0420c2s v4p0548c1s
Blackwood, A. v3p0294c2s
v5p0096c1s v5p0153c1s v5p0258c1s
v5p0395c2s v5p0546c2s v6p0164c2s
Blackwood, F.T. v5p0285c1s
Blackwood, Isabella C. ... v6p0611c1s
Blackwood, S.A. v3p0086c1s
Blackwood, W. v1p0052c2m
v1p0053c1s v1p0053c2s v1p0054c1m
v1p0396c2s
Blackwood, W.C. v2p0245c1s
v2p0452c2s
Blackwood, W.G. v1p0336c2s
Bladen, E.S., Mrs. v6p0174c1s
Blades, R.H. v6p0105c2s
Blades, W. v1p1016c1s
v1p1051c2s v1p1312c1s v1p1383c2s
v2p0040c1s v2p0051c2s v2p0354c2s
v3p0453c2s v3p0457c1s v4p0589c1s
v5p0333c1s v5p0335c1s v5p0429c2s
Blagden, C.M. v5p0114c1s
Blagden, G.W. v1p0183c1s
v1p1416c2s
Blagden, I. v1p0856c2s
v1p1420c1s
Blagden, L. v1p1334c2s
Blagg, D. v5p0290c2s
Blagg, T.M. v5p0067c1s
v5p0431c1s
Blagrove, B.H. v2p0459c1s
Blaikie, J.A. v2p0006c2s
v2p0040c1s v2p0040c2s v2p0058c1s
v2p0112c1s v2p0169c1s v2p0194c2s
v2p0383c1s v2p0441c2s v2p0448c1s
v2p0476c1s v2p0481c1s v4p0010c2s
v4p0030c1s v4p0031c2s v4p0126c1s
v4p0147c2s v4p0161c1s v4p0226c1s
v4p0348c1s v4p0405c2s v4p0411c1s
v4p0414c1s v4p0421c2m v4p0453c2s
v4p0475c2s v4p0600c1s v4p0613c1s
Blaikie, W. v1p0072c2s
v1p0881c2s v1p1129c2m v2p0078c1s
v3p0331c1s
Blaikie, W.G. v1p0432c2s
v1p0745c1s v1p0757c2s v1p0952c2s
v1p1095c1s v1p1286c2m v1p1389c1s
v2p0004c1s v2p0050c2s v2p0066c1s
v2p0082c1s v2p0083c2s v2p0098c2s
v2p0100c2s v2p0126c2s v2p0148c1s
v2p0150c1s v2p0155c2s v2p0171c1s
v2p0175c1s v2p0191c2s v2p0199c1s
v2p0235c1m v2p0235c2m v2p0245c2s
v2p0258c1s v2p0261c2m v2p0296c1s
v2p0312c2s v2p0338c2s v2p0352c2m
v2p0353c1m v2p0355c2s v2p0389c2s
v2p0391c2s v2p0407c1s v2p0408c1s
v2p0434c1s v2p0438c1s v2p0454c1s
v3p0034c1s v3p0061c2s v3p0093c1s
v3p0128c1s v3p0215c2s v3p0235c1s
v3p0342c1s v3p0381c1s v3p0381c2s
v3p0432c2s v3p0446c2s v3p0447c1s
v4p0054c1s v4p0063c1s v4p0068c2s
v4p0113c1s v4p0206c1s v4p0467c2s
v4p0509c1s v4p0532c2s v4p0533c2s
v4p0626c1s v5p0005c2s v5p0469c1s
v5p0490c1s v6p0013c1s
Blaikie-Murdoch, W.G. v6p0110c1s
Blaikley, J.D. v6p0439c2s
Blaine, J.G. v1p0178c1s
v3p0088c1s v3p0355c2s v4p0595c2s
Blaine, J.G. and Gladstone, W.E.
v3p0162c2s
Blaine, J.G. et al. v4p0526c1s
Blaine, R. v1p0301c1s
Blaine, R.G. v5p0141c2s
v5p0367c2s
Blaine, W. v3p0444c1s
Blainey, A.B. v5p0183c1s
Blair, A.A. v1p0026c1s
v1p0246c1s v1p0663c2s
Blair, A.H. v5p0462c1s
Blair, A.L. v5p0304c1s
Blair, C.M., Mrs. v1p1405c1s
Blair, E.H. v4p0435c1s
v6p0654c1s
Blair, F.N. v4p0398c1s
Blair, F.P. v5p0054c2s
v6p0145c2s
Blair, G. v5p0466c2s
Blair, H.C. v5p0064c2s
v5p0488c2s
Blair, H.M. v1p0230c1m
Blair, H.W. v2p0007c1s
v2p0434c1m v3p0423c2s
Blair, H.W., Mrs. v3p0456c1s
Blair, J.H. v5p0614c2s
Blair, J.P. v5p0219c2s
Blair, L.H. v4p0346c1s
v4p0538c1s
Blair, M. v1p1100c1s
v6p0577c2s
Blair, M.E. v1p0031c2s
v1p0334c1s v1p0737c2s v1p1308c2s
Blair, R. v3p0374c2s
Blair, R. and Cox, C. v4p0247c1s
Blair, T.S. v1p0663c2s
v4p0450c2s
Blair, W. v1p0259c2s
v1p0417c1s v1p0944c2s v2p0253c1s
Blair, W.T. v1p1426c1s
Blair-Watson, A. v4p0310c2s
Blaisdell, J.A. v6p0060c1s
v6p0061c1s
Blaisdell, J.J. v1p0847c1s
Blaisdell, T.C. v5p0341c1s
Blake, A.B. v1p0786c2s
v1p0971c1s v1p1000c1s v2p0069c1s
v2p0160c2s v2p0164c2s v2p0165c1s
v2p0248c2s v2p0394c1s
Blake, A.B., Mrs. v1p0883c1s
Blake, A.J. v2p0367c1s
Blake, B. v6p0335c1s
Blake, C. v1p0722c2s
Blake, C.C. v1p0045c2s
v1p0613c1m v1p0643c2s v1p0961c1s
v1p0962c2s
Blake, C.C. and Charnock, R.S.
v1p1382c2s
Blake, C.E. v4p0369c2s
v4p0543c1s v5p0203c1s v6p0207c2s
v6p0574c2s
Blake, C.J. v5p0449c2s
v6p0617c2s
Blake, E. v3p0030c2s
v3p0301c1s v4p0231c2s v4p0290c2s
v5p0301c2s v5p0362c2s
Blake, E., Lady v5p0626c1s
Blake, E.A. v1p0176c2s
v1p0888c2s v1p0983c2s
Blake, E.F. v1p0144c1s
v1p0276c1s
Blake, E.J. v5p0066c1s
Blake, E.M. v5p0463c1s
Blake, E.T. v1p0221c2s
Blake, E.V. v1p0315c2s
v1p0514c1s v1p1184c2s v3p0273c1s
Blake, E.V., Mrs. v1p0197c1s
Blake, E.W. v1p0271c2s
v1p0463c1m v1p0467c1s v4p0590c2s
Blake, E.W., jr. v1p0065c1s
v1p0399c2s
Blake, Edith, Mrs. v3p0030c2s
Blake, F. v5p0401c2s
Blake, F.E. v3p0047c1s
v4p0015c2m v4p0016c1s v4p0071c1s
v4p0091c1s v4p0159c2m v4p0323c2s
v4p0401c2s v4p0434c2s v5p0048c1s
v5p0125c1s v5p0166c1s v5p0274c1s
v5p0365c2s v5p0479c2s v5p0616c1s
Blake, F.L. v4p0357c2s
Blake, G. v4p0316c1s
v4p0407c1s v4p0617c2s
Blake, H.A. v2p0031c2s
v3p0155c1s v4p0125c2s v4p0296c1m
v5p0112c1s
Blake, H.A. et al. v1p0657c1s
Blake, H.A., Sir v3p0226c1s
Blake, H.B. v1p0972c1s
v1p1103c2s
Blake, H.T. v1p0831c2s
v1p0956c2s v1p1044c1s v1p1087c1s
v1p1348c1s v3p0031c1s v3p0239c1s
v4p0043c1s
Blake, H.W. v3p0359c1s
Blake, Harriet M. v5p0558c1s
Blake, I.W. v5p0013c1s
Blake, J. v1p0187c1s
v2p0341c1s v2p0426c2s v5p0618c2s
Blake, J.B. v4p0214c1s
Blake, J.C. v6p0080c2s
v6p0260c1s v6p0260c2s v6p0594c2s
Blake, J.C. and Gooch, F.A.
v6p0083c2s
Blake, J.F. v1p1036c1s
v1p1255c2s v4p0320c1s
Blake, J.G. v6p0643c2s
Blake, J.H. v1p0456c2s
Blake, J.L. v1p0966c1s
Blake, J.M. v1p0352c1s
Blake, J.P. v1p0883c2s
Blake, J.R. v1p0042c2s
v1p0560c1s
Blake, J.V. v1p0245c1s
v1p0253c1s v1p0464c1s v1p0464c2m
v1p0623c2s v1p0745c2s v1p0763c1s
v1p0883c1s v1p1043c1s v1p1264c1s
v3p0097c2s v3p0194c2s v3p0351c2s
v3p0441c1s v3p0474c2s
Blake, J.W. v4p0375c2s
Blake, J.Y.F. v5p0487c2m
Blake, Katherine G. v6p0543c1s
Blake, L.A. v4p0180c1s
Blake, L.D. v1p1387c1s
v3p0225c2s
Blake, L.D. and Denslow, V.B.

v2p0478c1s
Blake, L.D. et al. v2p0477c1s
Blake, L.I. v3p0353c2s
Blake, L.I. and Franklin, W.S.
v4p0125c1s
Blake, Lady v3p0039c1s
v3p0213c1s v3p0301c1s v3p0383c1s
Blake, M. v1p0435c2s
v1p0608c1s
Blake, M.E. v3p0234c1s
v3p0276c2s v3p0277c1m v3p0364c1s
v4p0388c1s v4p0540c1s v5p0065c2s
v5p0411c1s v5p0417c1s v6p0704c1s
Blake, M.M. v4p0627c1s
Blake, M.W. v3p0070c2s
Blake, Matilda M. v4p0452c1s
v4p0627c1s v4p0628c2s
Blake, R.P. v5p0583c1s
Blake, S.L. v1p0117c1s
v1p0336c1s v1p0357c2s v1p1043c2m
v2p0465c1s v3p0453c2s v5p0378c2s
Blake, T.A. v1p0029c1s
Blake, W. v4p0013c2s
Blake, W.H. v4p0269c2s
Blake, W.P. v1p0018c1s
v1p0187c2s v1p0432c2s v1p0509c1s
v1p0524c1s v1p0533c2s v1p0845c1s
v1p0947c1s v1p1349c2s v2p0161c1s
v2p0214c1s v2p0285c2s v2p0314c2m
v3p0046c2s v3p0093c2s v5p0595c1s
v6p0325c2s v6p0427c1s
Blake, W.W. v2p0287c1s
v3p0029c2s
Blake, Wm. v6p0482c2s
Blakelock, R.B.S. v5p0177c2s
v5p0384c1s
Blakely, Bertha E. v6p0433c1s
Blakely, E.T. v1p0544c1s
v3p0392c2s v4p0228c1s
Blakely, Laurie J. v6p0466c2s
Blakely, T.E. v6p0391c2s
Blakeman, W.C. v5p0205c2s
v6p0505c2s
Blakemore, W. v5p0124c1s
v5p0127c2s
Blakeney, E.H. v5p0578c2s
Blakeney, W. v5p0112c2s
v5p0459c2s
Blaker, H. v5p0016c2s
v6p0598c2s v6p0616c2s
Blakeslee, A.F. v6p0714c2m
Blakeslee, E. v3p0041c1s
v3p0416c1s v4p0557c2s v6p0626c2s
Blakeslee, F.G. v6p0012c1s
v6p0083c2s v6p0230c2s
Blakeslee, G.H. v6p0506c1s
Blakeslee, S.V. v1p1094c1s
v1p1162c1s
Blakeslee, T.H. v2p0170c2s
Blakeslee, T.M. v6p0518c2s
Blakesley, G.H. v4p0354c1s
v4p0360c1s
Blakesley, J.W. v1p0872c2s
v1p1264c1s v2p0439c1s
Blakesley, T.H. v4p0567c2s
Blakie, J.S. v1p0433c2s
Blakie, W.G. v4p0374c2s
Blakiston, H.E.D. v4p0611c1s
Blakiston, T. v1p1113c2s
Blakiston, T. and Alexander, T.
v2p0289c2s
Blames, D. and Jepson, E.. v5p0534c1s
Blanc, H.W. v5p0352c1s
v5p0509c1s
Blanc, L. v1p0431c1s
v1p0448c2s v1p0546c1m v1p0714c2m
v1p0895c2m v1p0896c1s v1p1122c2s
Blanc, M. v2p0296c1s
Blanc, M.Le v1p0162c1m
v1p0211c1s v1p0772c2s v6p0589c2s
Blanc, M.T. v5p0225c1s
v5p0487c1s
Blanc, Mme. v4p0312c2s
v5p0325c1s v5p0380c2s v6p0406c2s
Blanch, J.M. v6p0426c2s
Blanchamp, H. v4p0268c2s
Blanchan, N. v5p0309c2s
Blanchard, A. v4p0281c1s
Blanchard, C.A. v3p0383c2s
v4p0512c2s
Blanchard, C.A. et al. ... v5p0334c1s
Blanchard, C.J. v6p0139c2s
v6p0329c2s v6p0533c2m
Blanchard, D.C. v2p0242c2s
Blanchard, D.H. v5p0038c1s
Blanchard, E. v1p0042c1s
v1p0745c1s v1p1376c2s v3p0404c2m
v4p0410c2s
Blanchard, E.F. v6p0115c2s
Blanchard, E.L. v1p0165c1s
v1p0270c1s v1p0443c2s v1p0861c2s
Blanchard, E.R. v6p0243c1s
v6p0358c2s v6p0695c1s
Blanchard, F. v4p0293c1s
Blanchard, F.J. v6p0148c1s
Blanchard, F.M. v6p0522c2s
Blanchard, F.Q. v6p0419c2s
Blanchard, G. v3p0439c2s
v4p0543c2s
Blanchard, G.R. v1p1080c1s
v3p0338c2s v3p0353c1s v5p0478c1s
Blanchard, Grace v6p0641c1s
Blanchard, H. v1p1065c1s
v1p1355c2s v2p0455c2s
Blanchard, H.S. v4p0178c1s
Blanchard, J. v1p0398c1s
v1p1214c1s
Blanchard, J.G. v2p0122c1s
Blanchard, J.P. v1p0487c1s
v1p0702c1s v1p0732c2s v1p0903c2s
v1p0983c1s
Blanchard, J.T. v4p0173c2s
Blanchard, L. v1p0289c1s
v1p0295c2s v1p0446c1s v1p0459c1s
v1p0465c2s v1p0560c2s v1p0568c2s
v1p0628c1s v1p0704c2s v1p0779c1s
v1p0992c1s v1p1048c1s v1p1054c1s
v1p1059c2s v1p1062c2s v1p1175c1s
v1p1217c1s v1p1219c1s v1p1234c2s
v1p1338c2s
Blanchard, M.L. v4p0064c2s
Blanchard, N. v3p0041c1s
Blanchard, N.C. v4p0485c1s
Blanchard, R.H. v6p0091c2s
Blanchard, S.H. v1p0309c1s
Blanchard, S.L. v1p0505c2s
v1p0542c2s v1p0601c2s v1p0631c2s
v1p0754c2s v1p0839c1s v1p0878c1s
v1p0938c1s v1p1215c2s v1p1280c1s
Blanchard, S.S., Mrs. v4p0338c2s
Blanchard, V. v6p0561c2s
Blanche, A. v2p0240c2s
Blanching, E.M. v6p0049c2s
Blanchon, M. v6p0035c2s
Blanco, Y.de v6p0012c1s
Bland, F. v2p0049c2s
v2p0151c1s v2p0482c2s v3p0312c2s
v3p0462c1s
Bland, H. v3p0399c1s
Bland, H.M. v6p0093c2s
v6p0383c1m v6p0613c1s v6p0694c2s
Bland, H.Meade v6p0618c1s
Bland, J.P. v1p0435c1s
Bland, P.E. v1p0793c2s
Bland, R.P. v2p0403c1s
v3p0393c2s v4p0144c1s v4p0524c2m
v4p0525c1s v5p0529c2s
Bland, R.P. and Miller, W.
v4p0596c1s
Bland, R.P. and Poor, H.V.
v1p0273c1s
Bland, R.P. and Rhoades, J.H.
v4p0524c1s
Bland, R.P. et al. v4p0230c2s
v4p0525c1s v4p0526c1s
Bland, T. v1p0859c1s
Bland, T., jr. v1p0033c1s
Bland, T.A. v1p1074c1s
v3p0213c2s v5p0368c1s
Bland, W. v1p1192c1s
Bland-Strange, T. v6p0138c2s
Blandford, G.F. v1p0406c2s
Blandford, Marquis of v1p0410c1s
v1p0450c1s v1p0587c1s v1p0721c1m
v2p0189c2s v2p0348c1s
Blandford, Marquis of and
McCarthy, J. v2p0206c1s
Blandford, W.F.H. v4p0586c1s
v5p0573c2s
Blanding, E.M. v5p0045c1s
Blanding, W.F. v6p0051c1s
Blandy, J.F. and Williams, C.P.
v1p0300c1s v1p1271c1s
Blaney, J.H. v5p0053c2s
Blanford, H.F. v1p0099c2s
v1p1003c2s v1p1268c1s v1p1269c1s
v2p0364c1s v2p0404c2s v3p0034c2s
v3p0108c2m v3p0353c2m v3p0416c1s
v4p0551c1s
Blanford, H.F. and Curtis, G.E.
v3p0353c2s
Blanford, W.T. v1p0632c2s
v2p0173c2s v2p0326c2s v3p0280c2s
v4p0089c1s v5p0021c1s
Blank, M. v1p0347c1s
v1p1192c1s v1p1366c2s
Blanke, E.N. v4p0399c2s
Blankenburg, R. v6p0234c2s
v6p0487c2s v6p0524c2s
Blanstein, D. v6p0468c2s
Blaquiere, D.de v2p0124c1m
v2p0156c2s v2p0429c2s
Blaram, W.D.Van v5p0644c1s
Blarcom, C.R.Van v4p0494c2s
Blascom, W.D.Van, jr. v4p0231c1s
Blasdale, W.C. v6p0288c1s
Blashfield, E.H. v5p0156c1s
v5p0391c1s v5p0391c2s v6p0278c2m
v6p0294c1s v6p0465c2s v6p0500c1s
v6p0549c1s v6p0549c2s
Blashfield, E.H. and
Blashfield, E.W. v3p0155c2s
v3p0265c2s v3p0305c2s v3p0320c2s
v3p0406c1s v4p0202c2s v4p0474c1s
v4p0523c1s
Blashfield, E.W. v5p0377c2s
v5p0513c1s v5p0528c1s
Blashfield, E.W. and
Blashfield, E.H. v3p0155c2s
v3p0265c2s v3p0305c2s v3p0320c2s
v3p0406c1s v4p0202c2s v4p0474c1s
v4p0523c1s
Blashill, T. v2p0401c1s
v2p0441c1s v3p0202c1s
Blasius, W. v1p0829c1s
Blatch, H.S. v4p0604c2s
v4p0629c2s
Blatch, Harriot S. v3p0129c2s
Blatchford, A.N. v2p0131c1s
Blatchford, E.H. v5p0360c1s
v5p0446c1s v5p0591c1s
Blatchley, W.S. v5p0020c2s
v5p0453c2s
Blatherwick, C. v1p1146c2s
v2p0125c1s v2p0360c2s v3p0198c2s
v3p0210c1s v3p0440c2s v4p0508c2s
Blathwayt, R. v3p0062c1s
v3p0260c1s v3p0369c1s v4p0051c2s
v4p0080c1s v4p0243c1s v4p0274c1s
v4p0304c2s v4p0337c2s v4p0402c1s
v4p0426c2s v4p0495c1s v4p0579c1s
v4p0621c2s v5p0303c2s v5p0461c1s
Blatt, W.M. v6p0363c2s
Blattner, D. v5p0242c2s
Blau, L. v4p0360c1s
v5p0056c1s v5p0365c2s v6p0405c1s
v6p0631c2s
Blauvelt, A. v1p0688c1s
v1p0689c1s v1p0850c1m v1p1058c1s
v1p1203c2s v2p0236c1s v6p0225c1s
Blauvelt, M.T. v4p0004c2s
v5p0048c2s v5p0636c2s v6p0473c1s
Blauvelt, Mary T. v5p0403c2s
Blauvelt, W.H. v4p0220c2s
Blaxter, H.V. v6p0358c1s
Bleasdale, J.I. v6p0112c2s
v6p0466c1s
Bleby, H. v1p0404c2s
Blechynden, K. v5p0087c2s
Bleckley, L.E. v4p0346c1s
v4p0397c1s
Bled, V.Du v6p0406c2m
Bledsoe, A.T. v1p0085c1s
v1p0198c2s v1p0239c1s v1p0291c2s
v1p0296c1s v1p0335c1s v1p0342c2s
v1p0391c1m v1p0440c1s v1p0510c1s
v1p0528c1s v1p0567c2s v1p0584c1s
v1p0648c1s v1p0689c1s v1p0734c1s
v1p0741c2m v1p0742c1s v1p0855c1s
v1p0926c2m v1p1019c1s v1p1129c2s
v1p1206c2s v1p1223c1m v1p1314c1s
v1p1342c1s v1p1343c1s v1p1343c2s
v1p1344c1s v1p1345c2s v1p1348c2s
v1p1354c1s v1p1410c2m
Bleecker, Lieut. v1p0575c1s
v1p0601c2s
Bleek et al. v1p0196c1s
Bleek, W.H.I. v1p0079c1s
Blei, F. v5p0052c1s
Bleloch, W. v6p0654c2s
Bleneowe, G. v3p0435c1s
Blend, H.Meade v6p0256c1s
Blennerhassett, C. v1p1241c1s
Blennerhassett, Lady v3p0173c2s
v5p0390c2s
Blennerhassett, R. v1p0721c1s
v2p0260c1s v5p0040c1s v5p0189c1s
v5p0231c2s v5p0243c1m v5p0500c2s
v5p0611c2s v6p0042c2m v6p0205c1s
v6p0205c2s v6p0236c1m v6p0239c1s
v6p0253c1m v6p0254c1m v6p0254c2s
v6p0303c2s v6p0327c2s v6p0331c1s
v6p0332c1s v6p0385c2s v6p0572c1s
v6p0643c1s v6p0688c2s
Blennerhassett, R., Sir .. v1p1332c2s
v2p0227c2s v3p0046c1s v3p0337c2s
v3p0348c1s v5p0409c1s v6p0455c2s
Blennerhassett-Adams, T. . v5p0066c2s
Blerzy, H. v1p0025c2s
v4p0008c1s
Blessington, Lady v1p0182c1s
v1p1294c1s
Blesson, L. v1p0624c1s
Blethen, J. v6p0058c1s
v6p0132c1s v6p0301c1s v6p0329c2s
v6p0398c1s v6p0460c2s v6p0534c1s
v6p0708c2s
Blethen, Joseph v6p0142c2s
Blew, W. v3p0201c1s
Blew, W.C.A. v4p0418c2s
Blewett, J. v4p0195c1s
v4p0198c2s v4p0390c2s v5p0012c2s
v5p0135c2s v5p0250c2s v5p0266c1s
v5p0415c1s v6p0177c1s v6p0216c1s
v6p0226c1s v6p0280c1s v6p0533c2s
Blewitt, J. v4p0134c2s
v4p0347c1s v4p0449c1s v5p0251c2s
v6p0117c1s v6p0187c1s v6p0467c1s
Blewitt, O., Mrs. v2p0460c2s
Bleyer, H.W. v3p0280c1s
Blichfeldt, E.H. v6p0389c1s
Blicq, J.De v6p0714c1s
Bligh, E.V. v2p0271c2s
Blight, J.T. v1p1397c2s
Blight, R. v5p0225c2s
v5p0277c2s v5p0380c2s v6p0071c1s
v6p0140c1s v6p0247c1s v6p0321c1s
v6p0463c1s
Blind, K. v1p0058c2s
v1p0080c2s v1p0109c2s v1p0145c1s

v1p0314c2s v1p0337c2s v1p0342c2s
v1p0379c1s v1p0382c2s v1p0431c2s
v1p0459c2s v1p0474c2s v1p0479c1s
v1p0487c2s v1p0513c2s v1p0514c1s
v1p0515c1s v1p0515c2s v1p0517c2s
v1p0552c1s v1p0614c1s v1p0615c1s
v1p0706c2s v1p0733c2s v1p0777c2s
v1p0814c2m v1p0891c1m v1p0896c2s
v1p0937c2s v1p0954c1s v1p1024c1s
v1p1073c1s v1p1090c1s v1p1118c1s
v1p1129c1s v1p1133c2m v1p1134c2s
v1p1136c1s v1p1138c1s v1p1152c1s
v1p1179c1s v1p1179c2s v1p1230c1s
v1p1296c2m v1p1324c2s v1p1327c1s
v1p1330c1s v1p1383c2s v1p1391c2s
v1p1399c2s v1p1418c2s v2p0171c2s
v2p0176c2s v2p0205c2s v2p0212c1s
v2p0268c1s v2p0269c1s v2p0304c1s
v2p0314c1s v2p0362c1s v2p0371c2s
v2p0400c2s v2p0404c2s v2p0435c2s
v2p0447c2m v2p0464c1m v3p0003c1s
v3p0047c1s v3p0058c1s v3p0167c1s
v3p0171c1s v3p0174c1m v3p0183c1s
v3p0230c1s v3p0261c1s v3p0272c2m
v3p0350c1s v3p0371c2s v3p0377c1s
v3p0382c2s v3p0389c1s v3p0436c2s
v3p0438c1s v3p0464c1s v4p0010c1s
v4p0017c1m v4p0125c2s v4p0146c1s
v4p0163c2s v4p0166c1s v4p0174c1s
v4p0186c2s v4p0213c2s v4p0280c2s
v4p0312c1s v4p0313c1s v4p0348c1s
v4p0393c1s v4p0482c2s v4p0495c2m
v4p0496c1s v4p0496c2s v4p0497c2s
v4p0520c2s v4p0577c2s v4p0582c1s
v4p0586c2s v4p0587c1s v4p0625c1s
v5p0044c1s v5p0048c2s v5p0052c2s
v5p0064c2s v5p0124c1s v5p0144c1s
v5p0180c1s v5p0197c1s v5p0218c2s
v5p0230c2s v5p0231c1s v5p0232c1s
v5p0283c2s v5p0287c2s v5p0363c1s
v5p0390c2s v5p0418c1s v5p0501c2s
v5p0505c1s v5p0581c2s v5p0586c2s
v5p0587c1s v5p0587c2m v5p0594c2s
v5p0631c2s v6p0013c2s v6p0164c2s
v6p0238c1s v6p0253c1s v6p0253c2s
v6p0254c2s v6p0255c1s v6p0258c1s
v6p0295c2s v6p0331c2s v6p0349c2s
v6p0392c1m v6p0414c1s v6p0478c1s
v6p0480c1s v6p0556c1s v6p0556c2m
v6p0557c1s v6p0559c2s v6p0626c1s
v6p0629c1s v6p0661c1s v6p0679c2s
v6p0699c1s v6p0702c1s
Blind, K. and Evans, A.J.. v2p0440c1s
Blind, Karl v3p0054c2s
v3p0162c2s v3p0170c2s v3p0242c1s
v3p0336c1s v4p0212c2s v4p0505c1s
v4p0536c2s v4p0560c2s v5p0623c2s
v6p0571c2s v6p0628c1s
Blind, M. v1p0067c1s
v1p1230c1s v2p0446c2s v4p0040c1s
v5p0381c1s
Blinn, L.M. v1p1083c1s
Bliss, A. v1p0900c1s
Bliss, A.J. v6p0502c1s
Bliss, Arthur J. v6p0304c2s
Bliss, C. v1p0752c1s
Bliss, C.B. v5p0470c2s
Bliss, C.R. v1p0333c1s
v4p0399c2s
Bliss, D.W. v2p0171c1s
Bliss, E.E. v1p0293c1s
Bliss, E.M. v1p0378c2s
v4p0166c2s v5p0174c1s v5p0437c2s
v5p0484c2s v6p0105c1s v6p0421c2s
Bliss, E.W. v2p0244c2s
Bliss, F. v6p0537c2s
Bliss, F.J. v3p0419c1s
v5p0388c1s v6p0288c2s v6p0475c2s
Bliss, G., jr. v1p0476c1s
Bliss, G.A. v5p0389c1s
Bliss, G.R. v1p0096c1s
Bliss, H.E. v6p0074c1m
v6p0370c2m
Bliss, H.L. v4p0094c1m
v4p0261c2s v5p0321c2s v5p0550c2m
v5p0598c1s v5p0636c1s v6p0114c2s
Bliss, J.C. v4p0559c1s
Bliss, J.G. v6p0375c2s
Bliss, J.M. v5p0347c2s
Bliss, L. v1p0635c2s
Bliss, M. v1p0799c2s
Bliss, P. v3p0150c2s
Bliss, P.C. v1p0967c1s
Bliss, R. v3p0248c2m
Bliss, R., jr. v1p0013c2s
v2p0256c1s
Bliss, R.P. v6p0487c2s
Bliss, S. v1p0221c2s
Bliss, T.H. v5p0455c1s
Bliss, W. v2p0099c2s
v2p0481c2m v3p0014c2s v4p0356c1s
v5p0088c1s
Bliss, W.D.P. v3p0398c2s
v4p0581c1s v5p0482c1s v5p0535c2s
v5p0598c1s v6p0038c2s v6p0059c2s
v6p0065c2s v6p0125c2s v6p0127c1s
v6p0269c1s v6p0452c1s v6p0462c2s
v6p0600c1s v6p0601c1m
Bliss, W.D.P. and Sheldon, C.M.
v6p0125c1s
Bliss, W.H. v2p0055c1s
Bliss, W.P. v3p0005c2s
Bliss, W.R. v3p0209c2s
v3p0433c2s v3p0454c2s
Bliss, Z.R. v6p0666c1s
Blissett, N.K. v5p0104c2s
v5p0228c1s v5p0329c2s v5p0584c1s
v5p0590c2s v5p0634c1s v6p0218c2s
v6p0397c2s v6p0586c1s
Blissett, Nellie K. v4p0376c2s
Blix, M. et al. v3p0045c2s
Bloch, Albert v6p0510c2s
Bloch, J.de v5p0066c2s
v5p0243c2s v5p0588c1s v5p0589c1s
v5p0618c2s v6p0006c1s
Block, C.C. v1p1195c1s
Block, L.J. v1p0883c2s
v2p0344c2s v3p0179c1s v3p0309c2s
v4p0039c2s v4p0155c2s v4p0198c2s
v4p0319c2s v4p0439c1s v4p0466c1s
v4p0506c1s v4p0520c2s v4p0570c1m
v4p0575c1s v5p0044c2s v5p0160c1s
v5p0387c2s v5p0585c2s
Block, L.J. and Whitney, M.A.
v6p0622c2s
Block, M. v1p1027c1s
v4p0167c1s
Blocksom, A.P. v5p0619c1s
v6p0685c1s
Blodget, H. v2p0474c2s
Blodget, L. v1p0018c1s
v1p0174c2s v1p0996c2s v1p1080c2s
v1p1192c1s v1p1215c2s v1p1343c1s
v1p1349c1s v2p0402c2s
Blodgett, A.D. and Blodgett, G.W.
v2p0137c1s
Blodgett, A.N. v2p0124c2s
v2p0220c2s
Blodgett, B.C. v2p0030c2s
v2p0195c2s
Blodgett, G.W. v1p0401c1s
Blodgett, G.W. and Blodgett, A.D.
v2p0137c1s
Blodgett, J.H. v3p0129c2s
v4p0213c2s v4p0274c1s v4p0506c2s
v4p0512c1s v5p0129c2s v5p0256c2s
v5p0550c2s v5p0574c2s
Blodgett, K.N. v1p0101c2s
Blodgette, G.B. v1p0314c2s
Bloede, G. v1p0443c2s
v1p0564c2s v1p0782c2s v1p0790c1s
v1p1295c1s
Blois, E.A.De v6p0660c2s
Blom, G.P. v1p1092c1s
Blomefield, A.H. v5p0320c1s
Blomfield, A. v4p0054c2s
Blomfield, C.J. v1p0113c1s
v1p0555c1m
Blomfield, D. v4p0476c1s
Blomfield, D.F. v3p0239c2s
v5p0344c1s
Blomfield, R. v4p0024c1m
v4p0218c1s v4p0286c2s v4p0509c1s
v4p0510c2s v6p0028c1s v6p0539c1s
Blomfield, R.T. v2p0229c2s
v3p0017c2s v3p0018c2s v3p0121c1s
v3p0167c1m v3p0187c2s v3p0188c1s
v3p0200c2s v3p0232c1s v3p0400c1s
Blond, A.Le, Mrs. v6p0433c1s
Blond, Aubrey Le, Mrs. ... v6p0648c2s
Blond, E.Le v6p0549c2s
v6p0647c2s
Blondeau, C. v1p1177c2s
Blondel, L. v1p0675c2s
Blondin, J.F. v3p0367c1s
Blood, B. v1p1022c1s
Blood, B.P. v1p1328c2s
v2p0339c1s
Blood, J.J. v2p0157c1s
Blood, M.E. v5p0636c2s
Blood, Mrs. v3p0305c2s
Bloodgood, C.D. v1p1202c2s
Bloodgood, D.W. v1p0829c1s
Bloodgood, E.A. v2p0478c2s
v3p0260c2s
Bloodgood, G. v6p0647c2s
Bloodgood, J.H. v1p0189c1s
Bloodgood, S.D.W. v1p0567c1s
v1p0610c2s
Bloom, A.E. v4p0302c2s
Bloom, J.E. v5p0538c1s
Bloomfield, G., Lady v2p0276c2s
Bloomfield, Georgiana v3p0223c1s
Bloomfield, J.C. v3p0221c1s
Bloomfield, J.E. v1p0267c2s
v1p0269c2s v1p0306c1s v1p0649c2s
v1p0650c1s v1p0854c2s v1p1076c2m
v1p1079c2s v1p1144c1s v1p1246c2m
v1p1319c2s
Bloomfield, M. v2p0190c2m
v2p0339c2s v2p0386c1s v2p0458c1s
v3p0001c2s v3p0025c1s v3p0355c2s
v3p0414c1s v3p0447c2s v4p0077c2s
v4p0078c1s v4p0280c2s v4p0470c1s
v4p0601c1s v5p0489c1s v5p0608c1s
v6p0102c1s v6p0107c1s v6p0161c2s
v6p0398c2s v6p0675c2s
Bloomfield-Moore, C.J. ... v3p0235c1m
Bloor, A.J. v1p0054c1s
v1p1294c1s v2p0060c1s v2p0114c2s
v2p0389c1s v3p0464c1s v6p0452c1s
v6p0511c2s v6p0695c2m
Blose, G. v1p0551c1s
Bloss, E.B. v5p0213c1s
v6p0649c2s
Bloss, J.O. v3p0047c2s
Bloss, J.O. et al. v4p0081c1s
Blossom, E.L. v3p0439c2s
Blossom, H.M., jr. v5p0078c2s
v6p0140c2s
Blossom, M.C. v5p0168c2s
v5p0265c1s v5p0295c2s v5p0448c1s
Blossom, Mary C. v6p0009c1s
Blot, P. v1p0297c2m
v1p0352c2m v1p0605c1s
Blouet, P. v3p0012c1s
v3p0014c1s v3p0161c1s v3p0164c2s
v3p0232c2s v5p0455c1s
Blouet, P. and Lang, A. .. v3p0010c2s
Blouet, P. et al. v4p0557c2s
Bloundelle-Barton, J. v3p0062c1s
Blount, A. v5p0001c2s
v5p0263c2s
Blount, B. v6p0199c2s
Blount, C. v3p0259c2s
Blount, G. v6p0651c1s
Blount, Godfrey v6p0153c2s
Blount, J. v6p0408c1s
Blow, B. v6p0365c1s
v6p0467c2s v6p0564c1s
Blow, S.E. v2p0111c2m
v5p0316c1s
Blow, W.N. v5p0489c2s
v5p0531c2s
Blowitz, de v4p0212c1s
Blowitz, De v3p0160c1s
v3p0171c2s
Blowitz, H.de v6p0069c1s
Blowitz, H.G.de v5p0169c1s
v5p0217c2s
Blowitz, M.de v4p0010c2s
v4p0189c2m v4p0305c1s
Blowitz, S.de v4p0068c2s
Bloxam, G.W. v2p0332c2s
Bludau, A. v5p0490c1s
Blue, A. v6p0095c2s
v6p0097c1s
Blue, B.B. v1p1345c1s
Blue, F.K. v6p0647c1s
Blue, L.A. v5p0550c1s
Bluefield, C. v4p0390c1s
Bluemner, O. v5p0336c2s
Bluff, Oliver v4p0583c1s
Blum, E. v4p0038c2s
v4p0223c2s
Blum, Emil v3p0370c1s
Blum, R. v2p0110c1s
v2p0458c2s v4p0296c2s
Blume, G.O. v6p0053c2s
v6p0280c2s
Blumenfeld, R.D. v6p0208c1s
Blumenstein, W.H. v6p0334c1s
Blumenthal, C.E. v1p0919c2s
Blumentritt, F. v3p0351c1s
v5p0445c2s
Blundell, A.S.M. v5p0218c2s
Blundell, C.W. v2p0115c1s
Blundell, Francis, Mrs. .. v5p0219c1s
v6p0698c2s
Blundell, H.W. v5p0002c1s
Blundell, H.Weld v6p0002c1s
v6p0022c2s
Blundell, J.W.F. v1p0078c2s
v1p0079c1s v1p0079c2m v1p0196c2s
Blundell, M.E.F. v6p0153c2s
Blundell, M.E.Francis, Mrs.
v6p0222c2s
Blundell, M.E.S. v6p0052c1s
v6p0230c1s
Blundell, Mary E.F. v6p0116c2s
Blunden, G.H. v4p0237c1s
v4p0277c2s v4p0278c1s v5p0283c2m
v5p0567c2s v5p0568c2s
Blunt, A.C. v5p0430c2s
Blunt, C.D.McK. v6p0685c1s
Blunt, H.W. v5p0468c2s
v5p0501c2s v5p0615c1s v6p0142c1s
v6p0713c1s
Blunt, J. v1p0269c2s
v1p0307c1s
Blunt, J.C. v1p0339c1s
Blunt, J.J. v1p0180c2m
v1p0255c1s v1p0261c2s v1p0312c1s
v1p0386c2s v1p0566c2s v1p0571c1s
v1p0630c1s v1p0841c2s v1p0961c2s
v1p0975c1s v1p1089c2s v1p1121c2s
v1p1226c2s v1p1318c1s v1p1371c2s
Blunt, M. v2p0016c2s
v3p0150c1s v3p0269c2s
Blunt, Maria v3p0322c1s
Blunt, R. v3p0426c2s
v5p0094c2s
Blunt, R. and Prideaux, W.F.
v5p0103c2s
Blunt, W.G. v6p0161c1s
Blunt, W.S. v1p0050c1s
v1p0604c2s v1p0634c1s v1p0857c2s
v1p1075c2s v1p1331c1s v2p0134c1s
v2p0207c2s v2p0216c2s v2p0218c1m
v2p0218c2s v2p0230c2s v2p0293c2s

v2p0294c1s v4p0022c1m v4p0141c1s
v4p0172c2s v4p0263c2s v4p0346c2s
v4p0448c1s v4p0537c2s v5p0271c1s
v6p0127c1s v6p0153c2s v6p0166c1s
v6p0277c1s v6p0297c1s v6p0627c2s
Blunt, W.S. and Cane, E.F.Du
v4p0587c1s
Blunt, W.S. and Griffin, L., Sir
v2p0217c2s
Blunt, Wilfrid S. v6p0196c1s
Bluntschli, J.C. v1p0744c2s
Blyden, E.W. v1p0010c1s
v1p0011c2m v1p0012c1s v1p0741c1m
v1p0857c2m v1p0858c1s v1p0904c2s
v1p0905c2m v4p0005c2s
Blyth, A.W. v2p0118c2m
v2p0154c1s v2p0160c2s
Blyth, B.S. v1p0039c1s
v1p0299c2s v1p0513c2s
Blyth, E. v1p0375c1s
v6p0661c2s
Blyth, E.K. v4p0318c2s
Blyth, J. v1p0835c1s
v2p0136c2s
Blyth, J. et al. v5p0085c1s
Blyth, J.A.St.J. v1p0138c2s
Blyth, K. v4p0224c2s
v5p0232c1s
Blyth, P. v2p0478c1s
Blyth, P.A. v3p0198c1s
Blyth, T.A. v1p0348c2s
Blythe, S.G. v5p0081c2s
v5p0182c1s v5p0385c1s
Blytt, A. v2p0089c1s
Boaden, J. v1p0627c2s
Boag, G.W. v5p0484c1s
v6p0571c2s
Boalt, F.L. v6p0599c1s
Boalt, J.H. v2p0403c1s
Boardman, D.S. v1p0179c2s
v1p1386c2s
Boardman, F. v3p0198c2s
Boardman, G.D. v1p0688c2s
v1p0794c2s v1p1200c1s v1p1326c1s
v2p0031c2s v2p0354c2s v3p0041c1s
v3p0258c1s v3p0345c2s v4p0113c2s
v4p0479c1s v6p0072c1s
Boardman, G.N. v1p0242c1s
v1p0289c2s v1p0447c2s v1p0847c1s
v1p1026c1s v1p1304c1s v1p1316c1s
v1p1422c2s v2p0222c2s v5p0432c2s
Boardman, H.A. v1p0386c1s
Boardman, M.T. v6p0495c1s
Boardman, S.L. v1p0567c1s
v2p0162c2m
Boardman, S.W. v2p0465c2s
Boardman, V.L. v5p0211c2s
v5p0481c2s
Boardman, W.H. v5p0489c1s
v6p0351c2s
Boas, F. v2p0020c2m
v2p0045c2s v2p0109c2s v2p0146c1s
v3p0015c1s v3p0055c1m v3p0142c2m
v3p0169c1s v3p0213c2m v3p0305c1s
v3p0348c2s v3p0377c2s v3p0441c2s
v3p0447c1s v4p0013c2s v4p0020c1m
v4p0101c1s v4p0103c2s v4p0107c1m
v4p0187c1s v4p0282c1m v4p0282c2s
v4p0389c1s v4p0406c2s v4p0431c2s
v4p0505c2s v4p0586c1s v5p0022c2s
v5p0023c1s v5p0099c2s v5p0107c1s
v5p0195c1m v5p0254c1s v5p0320c2s
v5p0358c2s v5p0527c2s v5p0593c2s
v6p0023c2m v6p0121c1s v6p0210c2s
v6p0212c1m v6p0284c2s v6p0316c2s
v6p0441c1s v6p0459c2s v6p0470c1s
v6p0596c2s v6p0679c2s
Boas, F. and Chamberlain, A.F.
v3p0142c2s
Boas, F. and Dall, W.H. .. v3p0143c2s
Boas, F. and Powell, J.W.. v3p0143c2s
Boas, F. and Rink, H. v4p0187c1s
Boas, F.S. v4p0580c2s
v4p0598c1s v5p0320c2m v5p0362c2s
v6p0109c1s v6p0543c1s
Boas, Franz v4p0009c1s
v4p0073c2s v4p0179c1s v4p0225c2s
v4p0313c2s v5p0580c1s v6p0316c2s
Boas, H.B. v6p0242c2s
Boase, C.W. v2p0072c2m
v2p0191c1s v2p0432c1s v3p0087c2s
v3p0101c1s v3p0138c2s
Boase, G.C. v2p0055c1s
v2p0103c1s
Boate, E.W. v2p0013c2s
Boboulieff, D. v1p0400c2s
Bocher, F. v1p0488c2s
v1p0489c1s v1p0518c1s v2p0381c2s
v2p0397c2s v3p0372c1s v3p0475c1s
Bock, J.P. v5p0386c2s
Bockett, F.W. v6p0658c2s
Bockus, C.E. v1p0326c1s
Bocock, J. v5p0308c2s
Bocock, J.A. v1p0741c2s
Bocock, J.P. v4p0115c2s
v4p0291c1s v4p0399c1s v5p0162c1s
v5p0297c2s v5p0567c2s v5p0571c1s
v6p0500c2m
Bocock, K. v4p0333c2s
v4p0396c2s v4p0569c1s v4p0581c1s
v6p0600c1s
Bocock, Kemper v4p0315c1s
Bod, A. v4p0213c2s
Boddington, H. v5p0033c1s
Boddington, Helen v5p0250c2s
Boddy, C.A.S. and Kingstone, A.C.
v4p0206c2s
Bode, B.H. v6p0216c1s
Bode, C.A.De v1p1333c2s
Bode, E.A.de v1p1329c1s
Bode, G.H. v1p0384c2s
v1p0518c1s v1p1356c2s v1p1357c1s
Bode, W. v3p0039c2s
v4p0412c1s
Boden, G.H. v5p0532c2s
Bodfish, J.P. v1p0389c2s
v1p1118c2s v1p1119c2s v4p0119c2s
Bodge, G.M. v2p0338c2s
v3p0013c1m v3p0329c2s v4p0498c1s
Bodichon, De v1p0894c1s
Bodie, J. v1p1290c2s
Bodin, T. v2p0427c1s
v2p0475c2s
Bodine, W.B. v1p0706c1s
Bodine, W.L. v6p0658c1s
Boding, H.Annette v6p0653c1s
Bodington, A. v3p0145c1s
v4p0007c2s v4p0087c1s v4p0095c1s
v4p0130c1s v4p0225c2s v4p0285c2s
v4p0479c1s v4p0493c2s v4p0514c1s
v4p0556c1s v4p0559c1s
Bodington, Alice v3p0269c1s
v3p0280c1s v3p0299c1s
Bodington, C. v5p0337c1s
Bodington, N. v3p0448c1s
Bodington, O.E. v5p0221c1s
Bodio, L. v4p0293c2s
Bodkin, F.E. v1p1391c1s
v3p0457c1s
Bodkin, M.McD. v6p0327c1s
v6p0327c2s v6p0328c1s
Bodley, C. v3p0255c1s
Bodley, C., Mrs. v4p0098c1s
Bodley, D.F. v6p0025c2s
Bodley, G.E. v5p0026c2s
Bodley, G.F. v6p0036c1s
Bodley, J.E.C. v3p0004c1s
v3p0053c2s v3p0234c1s v3p0365c1s
v4p0562c1s v4p0636c2s v5p0361c2s
v6p0237c1s v6p0241c2s v6p0406c2s
Bodley, T. v1p1048c2s
v2p0350c2s
Bodley, W.H. v2p0258c1s
Bodley, W.S. v6p0388c1s
Bodmer, J.J. v1p0160c2s
v1p1204c2s
Bods, F. v2p0192c2s
Bodwell, J.C. v1p1043c1s
Body, C.W.E. v5p0117c1s
Boeckh, R. v6p0308c1s
Boedeker, Augusta v5p0573c1s
Boehl, E. v4p0345c1s
Boehm, L. v3p0196c2s
v4p0598c2s
Boehm, Lise v4p0386c1s
Boehm-Bawerk, E. v4p0088c2m
v4p0287c2s
v6p0100c1s
v6p0123c2s
Boehm-Bawerk, E. and Bonar, J.
v3p0067c2s
Boehm-Bawerk, E.v v3p0336c2s
v3p0337c1s
v4p0599c2s
Boehm-Bawerk, E.v and
Edgeworth, F.G. v4p0599c2s
Boehm-Bawerk, E.von v3p0127c2s
v5p0509c2s
Boehmer, G.H. v2p0137c2s
Boekelman, B. v4p0078c1s
Boemond, B.R.S. v2p0309c2s
Boeringer, P.N. v4p0203c1s
v4p0274c2s v4p0454c1s v4p0474c1s
v4p0502c1s v4p0625c1s v5p0160c1s
Boeringer, P.N. and Greene, C.S.
v4p0083c1s
Boerner, C.G. v2p0285c1s
Boevey, S.M.C. v5p0382c1s
v5p0395c2s v5p0459c2s v5p0555c2s
Boevey, S.M.Crawley v6p0328c2s
Bogardus, A. v3p0330c2s
v6p0163c1s
Bogart, E.L. v4p0199c2s
v5p0105c1s v5p0273c1s v5p0557c1m
v5p0584c2s v5p0644c2s v6p0198c1s
v6p0621c2s
Bogart, J. v3p0353c1s
v4p0403c2s
Bogart, L.E. v5p0187c2s
Bogart, W.H. v1p1014c2s
Bogart, W.S. v2p0320c1s
v3p0062c2s v3p0267c2s
Bogdanovitch, L.A.de v5p0502c2s
Bogen, B.D. v5p0009c1s
v5p0325c1s v6p0646c1s
Boger, C.G. v4p0183c1s
Boger, C.G., Mrs. v4p0010c2s
v4p0031c2s v4p0277c1s v4p0397c2s
Boger, E. v1p0303c1s
Boger, H. v6p0022c1s
Bogert, B. v4p0259c2s
Bogert, M.T. v6p0101c1s
Bogert, N.J.M. v5p0378c1s
Bogg, J.S. v5p0223c2s
v6p0040c1s
Boggs, E.B. v1p0011c2s
v1p0138c1m v1p0422c1m v1p0422c2s
v1p0732c1s v1p0852c2s v1p0917c2s
v1p1090c2s v1p1109c1s v1p1269c2s
Boggs, L.P. v6p0221c2s
Boggs, Lucinda P. v6p0532c2s
Boggs, R. v1p1105c2s
Boggs, W. v5p0342c1s
v6p0244c2s
Boggs, W.B. v1p0422c1s
Boggs, W.D. v3p0383c2s
Boggs, W.E. v1p1223c1s
v5p0541c2s
Bogh, E. v1p0139c2s
v5p0451c2s
Bogle, D.B. v5p0472c1s
Bogle, W.R. v3p0352c1s
Boglietti, G. v2p0231c1m
v3p0225c1s v4p0017c1s
Bogoras, W. v5p0116c2s
v6p0036c2s
Bogouschefsky, N.C.de v1p0693c1s
v1p1171c2s
Bogue, E.E. v3p0029c1s
Bogue, K. v6p0680c1s
Bogue, S.R. v3p0274c2s
v3p0448c2s v4p0332c2s v4p0457c2s
Bogue, V.G. v1p1288c2s
Boguslawski, G.von v2p0393c1s
Boguslawski, Von v3p0419c1s
v4p0561c2s v5p0231c1s
Boh, F. v4p0181c1s
Bohan, E. v1p0402c2s
Bohannon, E.W. v4p0104c1s
v5p0106c1s
Bohasseck, C. v6p0279c2s
v6p0427c2s
Bohl, E. v3p0028c1s
v3p0427c2s v5p0275c2s
Bohl, H. v6p0011c2s
Bohlen, F.H. v6p0544c2s
Bohlman, H.T. and Finley, W.L.
v6p0067c1s
Bohme v2p0421c1s
Bohn, E. v6p0086c2s
Bohun, C. v2p0155c1s
Boies, H. v5p0529c2s
Boies, H.M. v1p0839c1s
v5p0543c2s
Boies, J. v1p0965c2s
Boies, J.S. v1p0152c1s
Boies, W.E. v1p0155c2m
Boies, W.J. v5p0208c1s
v5p0441c1s v5p0566c2s v6p0050c1s
v6p0050c2s v6p0174c1m
Boileau, F.F.R. and Wallace, L.A.
v5p0416c2s
Boileau, J.P. v1p0820c1s
Boileau, J.P.H. v2p0054c2s
Boileau, L.C. v4p0380c2s
Boileau, M. v5p0497c2s
Boillat, E. v2p0016c2s
Bois, A.A.Du v1p0526c1m
v1p0882c2s
Bois, A.J.Du v1p0051c1m
v1p0522c2m v1p0541c1s v1p1127c1m
v1p1382c1m v2p0427c2s v3p0209c1s
v3p0281c2s v3p0379c2m v4p0478c1s
v4p0507c1s
Bois, B.H.Du v4p0013c1m
Bois, C. v1p0485c2s
Bois, C.G.Du v5p0054c1m
v5p0161c2m v6p0316c1m v6p0390c1m
v6p0604c2m
Bois, Constance G.Du v6p0421c1m
v6p0421c2m
Bois, E.E.Du v1p0244c1m
v1p0738c1m
Bois, E.E.Du, Mrs. v1p0715c2m
Bois, E.N.G.Le v4p0447c2s
Bois, E.V.Du v5p0463c1m
Bois, G.P.Du v4p0512c2m
Bois, H.A.Du v1p0120c1m
v1p0305c1s v1p0435c1m v1p0793c1m
v1p0794c1m v4p0313c2s
Bois, H.Du v4p0313c2s
Bois, H.M.Du v2p0471c2s
Bois, H.P.Du v6p0074c1m
Bois, J.T.Du v2p0193c1s
Bois, K.Du v3p0232c2m
Bois, P.Du v6p0538c1m
Bois, W.E.B.Du v5p0220c1s
v5p0402c2m v5p0403c1s v5p0403c2m
v5p0620c1s v6p0039c2m v6p0248c1s
v6p0446c2m v6p0447c2m v6p0448c1m
v6p0448c2m v6p0597c1m
Bois, W.E.B.Du and Graves, J.T.
v6p0039c2m
Bois, W.E.B.Du and Stone, A.H.
Bois-Reymond, E.Du v1p0333c1m
v1p0497c1m v1p0901c1m v2p0150c1m
v2p0211c2m v2p0390c1m v2p0480c2s
v3p0073c1s v3p0332c1s v3p0380c1m
v4p0199c2m v4p0394c2m v4p0507c1m
v6p0547c1m

v6p0447c2m
Boise, J.R. v1p0008c2s
v1p0072c2s v1p0262c2s v1p0389c2s
v1p0601c1s v1p0643c1s v1p1221c1m
v1p1406c1s v4p0554c2s
Boissier, G. v1p1125c1s
v6p0630c2s
Boissier, Gaston v5p0575c2s
Boistiniere, L.C. v1p0051c2s
v1p0526c1s
Bok, E. v6p0126c2s
v6p0456c2s
Bok, E.W. v3p0029c1s
v3p0149c1s v4p0080c2s v4p0179c2s
v4p0335c1s v4p0636c1m v6p0154c1s
Boker, G.H. v1p0088c1s
v1p0308c1s v1p1107c1s
Boker, G.H. et al. v1p0534c1s
Bokum, H. v1p0513c1s
v1p0514c1s
Bolam, G. v6p0706c2s
Boland, M.A. v4p0132c1s
Bolas, T. v1p0635c2s
v2p0063c2s v2p0136c2s v2p0340c2s
v2p0479c1s v3p0029c1s v3p0062c2s
v3p0132c2s v3p0187c1s v3p0330c2s
v3p0331c1s v3p0368c2s v3p0409c2s
v5p0448c2m
Bolavier, E.E. v2p0127c2s
Bolce, H. v6p0014c2s
v6p0118c2m v6p0146c1s v6p0174c2s
v6p0260c2s v6p0333c2s v6p0335c2s
v6p0336c1s v6p0336c2m v6p0337c2s
v6p0426c1s v6p0474c1s v6p0477c1s
v6p0533c2s v6p0667c2m
Bolce, H. and Vanderlip, F.A.
v5p0314c1s
Bolce, Harold v6p0334c1s
v6p0651c2s
Boldrewood, R. v4p0038c2s
v4p0484c1s v5p0039c1s
Bolen, G.L. v5p0258c1s
v5p0460c1s v5p0567c1s
Bolet-Paraza, N. v4p0601c2s
Bolfield, B. v1p1123c1s
Bolitho, C. v5p0314c1s
Bolivar, J. v3p0276c2s
Boll, J. v1p1297c1s
Bollaert, M. v1p0993c1s
Bollaert, W. v1p0288c1s
v1p0832c1s v1p0992c2m v1p0993c1s
v1p1440c2s v3p0373c2s
Bolland, G.H. v4p0333c2s
Bolland, S. v4p0292c1s
Bolland, W.C. v6p0378c1s
Bollard, R.S. v6p0669c1s
Boller, A.P. v1p0054c1s
v1p0161c2m v1p0539c1s v2p0390c2s
Boller, H.A. v1p1196c1s
Bolles, A.S. v1p0180c1s
v1p0295c2m v1p0326c2s v1p0640c1s
v1p0699c2s v1p0714c2s v1p0735c1s
v1p0861c1s v1p0862c2s v1p1026c1m
v1p1283c2s v1p1285c2s v1p1323c1s
v1p1351c1s v1p1361c2m v1p1385c1s
v2p0033c1s v2p0033c2m v2p0034c1s
v2p0091c2s v2p0092c2s v2p0110c1s
v2p0408c2s v2p0452c1s v2p0452c2m
v3p0087c2s v6p0356c2s v6p0443c1s
v6p0460c2s
Bolles, D.H. v4p0450c2s
Bolles, E.C. v1p0507c1s
v1p0626c1s v1p0792c2s v1p1093c1s
Bolles, E.C., Mrs. v4p0431c2s
Bolles, F. v3p0219c1s
v4p0060c2m v4p0061c2s v4p0064c1s
v4p0105c1s v4p0107c2s v4p0228c2s
v4p0249c1s v4p0269c1s v4p0284c2s
v4p0408c1s v4p0419c1s v4p0624c1s
Bolles, J.A. v1p0120c1s
v1p0144c1s v1p0148c2s v1p0255c2s
v1p0485c2s v1p0641c1s v1p0649c1s
v1p0697c1s v1p0703c2s v1p1035c2s
v1p1083c1s v1p1177c1s v1p1347c2s
v1p1418c2s v3p0253c1s v3p0303c1s
Bolles, J.H. v1p1207c2s
Bolley, H.L. v4p0008c1s
v4p0370c2s v6p0694c2s
Bolling, G.M. v5p0426c2s
v6p0289c1s v6p0361c1s
Bolmberg, A.M.Von v5p0402c2s
Bolt, B. v6p0226c1s
v6p0653c2s
Bolt, Ben v6p0310c2s
v6p0396c1s
Bolte, A. v1p1408c2s
Bolton, A.D. v4p0051c1s
v4p0349c1s
Bolton, A.T. v4p0582c2s
Bolton, C.E. v5p0123c1s
v5p0559c1s
Bolton, C.K. v2p0006c2s
v4p0220c1s v4p0249c1s v4p0329c1s
v4p0329c2s v4p0330c2s v4p0580c1s
v5p0230c1s v5p0334c1s
Bolton, C.R. v5p0168c2s
Bolton, E.S. v5p0533c2s
v6p0058c2s v6p0592c1s v6p0603c1s
Bolton, F., Sir v3p0456c2s
Bolton, F.E. v4p0410c1s
v4p0475c2s v5p0277c2s v5p0279c2s
v5p0413c2s v6p0194c2s v6p0290c2s
Bolton, G. v5p0023c2s
v5p0567c2s v5p0580c1s
Bolton, G. and Lawrence, A.
v5p0340c1s
Bolton, H. v6p0702c1s
Bolton, H.C. v1p0452c2m
v1p0746c2s v1p1421c1s v2p0051c1s
v2p0076c1s v2p0076c2s v2p0247c1s
v2p0282c1s v2p0477c1s v3p0131c1s
v3p0290c1s v3p0339c2s v3p0374c2m
v4p0022c1s v4p0027c2s v4p0052c1s
v4p0067c1s v4p0092c2s v4p0136c2s
v4p0209c2s v4p0217c2s v4p0219c1s
v4p0232c1s v4p0235c1s v4p0251c1s
v4p0284c1s v4p0329c1s v4p0435c1s
v4p0490c2s v4p0513c1s v4p0530c2s
v5p0011c1s v5p0035c1s v5p0040c1s
v5p0067c1s v5p0083c1s v5p0103c2s
v5p0139c2s v5p0449c2s v5p0463c2s
v5p0577c2s v6p0011c1s v6p0052c2s
v6p0059c2s v6p0089c1s v6p0344c1s
v6p0378c2s v6p0527c1s
Bolton, H.C. and Julien, A.A.
v2p0036c2s v2p0403c2s
Bolton, H.Carrington v5p0278c1s
Bolton, H.E. v5p0015c2s
v5p0267c1s v6p0607c1s v6p0640c1s
Bolton, H.I. v5p0637c1s
Bolton, J. v4p0602c1s
Bolton, M. v4p0041c1s
Bolton, M.P. v4p0103c2m
v4p0262c1s
Bolton, R.K. v5p0159c1s
Bolton, R.P. v4p0121c1s
v5p0185c1s v5p0327c2s v6p0024c2s
v6p0027c1s v6p0200c1m v6p0204c1m
v6p0268c2s v6p0352c2s v6p0615c2s
Bolton, S.H., Mrs. v2p0140c2s
Bolton, S.K. v2p0477c2m
v3p0464c1s v4p0067c2s
Bolton, S.T. v1p0205c1s
Bolton, Sarah K. v2p0432c2s
Bolton, T. v3p0467c1s
Bolton, T.C. v4p0364c2s
Bolton, T.L. v4p0483c2s
v6p0432c2s
Bolton, T.L. and Haskell, E.M.
v5p0034c2s v5p0319c1s
Bolton, T.L. and Miller, E.T.
v6p0210c1s
Bolton, W.W. and E.J.B. .. v4p0157c2s
Bolton, W.W. and Laing, J.W.
v4p0600c1s v5p0607c2s
Boltwood, B.B. v6p0298c2s
v6p0526c2m v6p0527c1m
Boltwood, B.B. and Rutherford, E.
v6p0527c1s
Boltwood, B.B. and Wells, H.L.
v4p0082c2s
Boltwood, E. v5p0127c1s
v6p0069c1s v6p0069c2s v6p0130c1s
v6p0142c1s v6p0161c2s v6p0162c2s
v6p0165c2s v6p0166c1s v6p0167c2s
v6p0170c2s v6p0178c2s v6p0231c1s
v6p0256c2s v6p0273c2s v6p0323c1s
v6p0342c2s v6p0353c2s v6p0365c1s
v6p0402c2s v6p0405c2s v6p0417c2s
v6p0434c1s v6p0466c1s v6p0472c1m
v6p0531c1s v6p0608c2s v6p0620c2s
v6p0664c2s v6p0673c1s v6p0679c2s
v6p0697c2s v6p0702c1s
Boltwood, H.L. et al. v3p0025c2s
v5p0265c1s
Boltzmann, L. v4p0221c1s
v5p0037c2s v5p0449c2s
Bomberger, J.H.A. v1p0097c1s
v1p0218c2s v1p0537c2s v1p0686c1s
v1p0700c1s v1p0756c2m v1p0769c1s
v1p0908c1s v1p1000c2s v1p1053c1s
v1p1093c2s v1p1442c2m
Bompas, H.M. v2p0384c1s
v4p0050c1s v4p0112c2s v4p0169c2s
v4p0261c2s v4p0632c2s v6p0191c1s
Bompiani, S. v1p1126c1s
v2p0021c2s v2p0147c2s v3p0004c2s
v5p0414c1s
Bon, G.Le v3p0351c2s
v4p0032c1s v4p0117c2s v4p0191c1s
v5p0514c1s v6p0406c2s v6p0407c1s
v6p0526c2s
Bonaparte, C.J. v3p0086c2s
v3p0442c2s v4p0097c1m v4p0359c1s
v4p0430c2s v4p0597c2s v5p0602c2s
v6p0515c1s
Bonaparte, L.L. v2p0016c2s
Bonaparte, R. v2p0249c2s
Bonar, A. v2p0462c1s
Bonar, H. v2p0268c1s
Bonar, J. v1p0387c2s
v3p0067c1m v3p0239c1s v3p0446c2s
v4p0119c1s v4p0180c1s v4p0483c2s
v5p0136c2s v5p0175c1s v5p0283c2s
v5p0346c1s v5p0357c2s v5p0467c2s
v5p0491c2s v6p0323c1s
Bonar, J. and Boehm-Bawerk, E.
v3p0067c2s
Bonar, J. and Collet, C.E.
v3p0452c1s
Bonaventura, St. v1p0619c2m
v3p0401c1s
Bonavia, E. v4p0576c1s
Bonavia, E. et al. v2p0160c1s
Bonavia, G. v3p0165c1s
v3p0211c2s
Boncoeur, J. v1p0007c1s
v1p0697c1s
Bond, A.C. v2p0432c2s
Bond, A.T. v5p0069c1s
Bond, C.E. v5p0121c2s
Bond, E. v1p0039c1s
v4p0005c2s v4p0049c2s v4p0237c2s
Bond, E.A. v1p0223c1s
v1p0393c1s v1p0545c2s v1p0624c2s
v1p0667c2s v1p0669c1s v1p1294c1s
Bond, E.S. v5p0135c2s
v5p0283c1s v5p0534c1s v5p0583c2s
v5p0589c1s v5p0629c1s
Bond, Ed.S. v5p0151c2s
v5p0597c1s
Bond, F. v6p0709c2s
Bond, F.B. v6p0579c1s
Bond, F.S. v2p0362c2s
Bond, F.T. v1p0144c2s
v1p0844c2s v6p0053c2s v6p0597c2s
Bond, G.M. v2p0172c1m
v2p0281c2m
Bond, G.P. v1p0281c1m
v1p1003c2s v1p1152c2s
Bond, H. v4p0454c1s
v6p0372c2s
Bond, H.F. v1p0322c1s
v1p0638c1s v1p1306c2s v2p0219c2s
v2p0456c2s v4p0599c1s v5p0072c2s
Bond, J. v1p0339c1s
v1p1416c2s v4p0588c1s
Bond, J.J. v2p0083c1s
Bond, J.V. v6p0619c2s
Bond, L.A. v4p0122c1s
v4p0156c1s v4p0210c1s v4p0347c2s
v4p0481c2s v4p0503c1s v4p0530c1s
v4p0555c2s v4p0574c2s
Bond, O.Z. v6p0369c2s
Bond, R. v1p1080c1s
v1p1423c1s v6p0455c2s
Bond, R.W. v4p0090c2s
v4p0517c2s v4p0519c1s v5p0500c1s
v5p0502c1s v6p0390c2s v6p0555c1s
Bond, T. v1p0578c1s
Bond, T.E. v1p0830c2s
v1p0831c1s v1p1237c2s
Bond, T.E., jr. v1p0120c1s
v1p0319c2s
Bond, W. v5p0119c2s
v5p0141c2s
Bondfield, M.G. v5p0527c1s
Bondy, M.W. v1p0653c2s
Bone, H.A. v5p0222c1s
v6p0032c1s v6p0632c2s
Bone, J.H.A. v1p0561c1s
v1p1137c2s v1p1319c2s
Bone, J.R. v5p0559c2s
Bone, W.P. v2p0358c1s
Boner, C. v1p0723c1s
v1p0815c1s v1p1008c2s
Boner, E.G. v4p0436c2s
v4p0497c1s
Boner, J.H. v5p0551c2s
Bonet-Maury, G. v3p0441c1s
v4p0488c2s v5p0432c1s
Bonfield, J. and M'Claughry, R.W.
v4p0102c1s
Bonfort, H. v4p0204c2s
v4p0256c2s
Bonghi, R. v2p0230c2m
v2p0231c1s v2p0253c2s v3p0224c1m
v3p0367c1m v4p0293c2m v4p0294c1s
v4p0294c2s
Bonghi, R. and Zannoni, G.
v4p029 c s v4p0293c2s
Bonheur, Rosa v6p0073c1s
v6p0203c2s
Bonhote, J.T. v6p0139c2s
Boni, G. v2p0019c2s
v2p0114c1s v2p0279c2s v2p0396c1s
v2p0458c2m v5p0411c2s v5p0495c1s
v5p0495c2s v6p0549c2s
Bonifas, F. v1p1302c2s
Bonin, H.R. v2p0022c2s
Bonis, H. v5p0281c1s
Bonjour, C. v1p0363c1s
Bonnafous, J. v5p0092c1s
Bonnar, W. v4p0279c1s
Bonne, B.P. v1p0810c2s
Bonnean, J.X. v6p0696c2s
Bonnefoux, L. v1p0326c1s
v1p1349c2s
Bonnefoux, N. v1p0095c1s
Bonnefoux, S. v1p0453c1s
Bonnell, C.R. v2p0085c1s
v3p0084c2s v3p0341c2s
Bonnell, J.F. v6p0555c1s
Bonner, G. v3p0049c1s
v3p0209c2s v4p0084c1s v4p0493c2s
v5p0266c1s v6p0461c2s
Bonner, G.M. v2p0216c1s
Bonner, Geraldine v5p0555c2s
Bonner, H. v5p0207c2s
Bonner, H.B. v4p0071c1s

v4p0181c2s
Bonner, I. ... v1p0732c2s
Bonner, J. ... v1p0041c2s
v1p0105c1s v1p0154c1s v1p0171c1s
v1p0172c1s v1p0348c2s v1p0532c2s
v1p0751c2s v1p0814c2s v1p0832c1m
v1p0929c1s v1p0949c1s v1p0956c1s
v1p1123c2s v1p1228c2s v3p0078c1s
v3p0093c1s v3p0223c2s v3p0413c2s
v4p0159c2s v4p0519c2s v6p0010c1s
v6p0120c1s v6p0356c2s
Bonner, J.S. ... v5p0365c2s
Bonner, S. ... v1p0590c1s
v1p0626c2s v1p0852c1s v1p1103c2s
v1p1202c2s v1p1342c2s v1p1361c1s
v1p1376c2s
Bonner, T.R. ... v1p0797c2s
v1p1017c2s
v1p1088c1s
Bonner, W.G. ... v4p0476c1s
v5p0481c2s
Bonner, W.T. ... v5p0068c2s
Bonnet, J. ... v1p0863c2s
Bonnett, V. ... v2p0294c2s
Bonnetty, A. ... v1p0775c2s
Bonneville, A.De ... v1p1240c2s
Bonney ... v3p0244c2s
Bonney, C.C. ... v1p0228c1s
v1p0700c1s v1p1078c1s v2p0348c1s
v3p0094c1s v3p0146c2s v3p0292c1s
v3p0297c1s v4p0101c1s v4p0479c1m
v5p0014c2s v5p0016c2s v5p0120c2s
v5p0201c2s v5p0241c1s v5p0293c2s
v5p0327c2s v5p0421c2s v6p0347c1s
Bonney, J.G. ... v3p0476c1s
v6p0173c1s v6p0213c1s
Bonney, T.C. ... v6p0223c2s
Bonney, T.G. ... v1p0025c2m
v1p0166c1s v1p0190c1s v1p0812c1m
v1p0899c2s v1p1196c1s v1p1286c1s
v1p1404c2s v2p0009c1s v2p0173c2s
v2p0462c2s v2p0463c1s v3p0125c2s
v3p0159c1s v3p0173c2m v3p0240c1s
v3p0268c1s v3p0287c1s v4p0088c1s
v4p0227c1m v4p0247c1s v4p0369c2s
v4p0609c2s v5p0066c1s v5p0161c1s
v5p0265c2s v5p0389c2s v6p0149c2s
v6p0165c2s v6p0169c2s
Bonney, T.G. et al. ... v3p0100c2s
v3p0328c2s
Bonney, W.L. ... v5p0636c1s
Bonnier, C. ... v5p0193c1s
Bonnier, P. ... v3p0192c2s
Bonnycastle, R.H. ... v1p0077c1s
Bonomi, J.I. ... v6p0535c2s
Bonquillon, T. ... v6p0642c2s
Bonsal, L. ... v3p0395c2s
Bonsal, S. ... v4p0043c1s
v4p0197c2m v4p0343c1s v5p0078c2s
v5p0079c1s v5p0101c1s v5p0108c2s
v5p0111c2s v5p0147c2s v5p0182c1s
v5p0453c1s v5p0507c2s v5p0508c2s
v5p0527c2s v5p0528c1s v5p0542c2m
v5p0543c1s v5p0623c2s v6p0103c2s
v6p0392c1s v6p0421c1s v6p0430c2s
v6p0492c2s v6p0493c2s v6p0494c1s
v6p0499c2s v6p0606c1s
Bonsal, Stephen ... v5p0521c1s
v5p0581c2s
Bonsall, J. ... v1p0006c2s
v1p0341c2s v1p0511c1s v1p0736c1s
v1p0917c2s v1p0987c2s v1p1392c2s
Bonsall, S. ... v1p0186c2s
v1p1311c2s
Bonser, A.E. ... v3p0072c2s
v5p0270c1s
Bonser, F.C. ... v6p0410c2s
Bonser, F.G. ... v6p0125c1s
Bonsfield, R.W.G. ... v2p0019c2s
Bonsfield, W. ... v2p0406c1s
Bontemps, C. ... v1p1019c1s
Bontems, G. ... v1p0525c2s
Bonter, H.M. ... v5p0328c2s
Bonus, A.R. ... v6p0313c1s
v6p0313c2s
Bonwick, J. ... v2p0029c1s
v2p0101c1s v4p0237c1s
Bonwill, W.G.A. ... v3p0146c1s
Bonyer, R. ... v6p0219c1s
Boodin, J.E. ... v6p0418c2s
Boodle, R.W. ... v1p0065c1s
v1p0410c1s v1p0512c1s v1p0791c1m
v1p0993c2s v1p1021c1s v1p1295c1s
v2p0394c1s
Book, W.F. ... v6p0290c1s
v6p0290c2s
Books, C.T. ... v1p0620c2s
Bookwalter, J.W. ... v3p0149c2s
Boole, M. ... v2p0052c1s
Boole, Mary E. ... v6p0211c2s
Boone, Grace R. ... v6p0441c1s
Boone, H.B. ... v6p0141c2s
v6p0287c2s v6p0708c1s
Boone, M.S. ... v6p0351c2s
Boone, R.G. ... v4p0174c1s
v4p0281c2s v5p0366c2s v5p0558c1s
v5p0569c2s v6p0193c1m v6p0193c2s
v6p0399c2s v6p0515c2s v6p0517c1s
v6p0582c2s
Boone, W.J. ... v1p0233c1s
Booraem, H.T. ... v4p0024c2m
Boose, J.R. ... v2p0256c2s
v5p0128c1s v5p0333c2m v5p0498c2s
v6p0371c1s
Boosey, W. ... v4p0388c1s
Boot, W.H. ... v4p0266c2s
Booth, A. ... v1p1265c1s
Booth, A.J. ... v1p0471c2s
Booth, B. ... v4p0430c1s
v6p0566c1s
Booth, B., Mrs. ... v4p0628c2s
Booth, C. ... v2p0319c1s
v3p0256c1s v3p0257c1s v3p0324c1s
v3p0326c1s v4p0315c1s v4p0339c1s
v4p0340c2s v4p0412c1s v4p0431c2s
v4p0452c2s v5p0419c1s v6p0271c1s
Booth, C., jr. ... v6p0267c2s
v6p0591c2s
Booth, C.A. ... v4p0370c2s
v4p0434c1s
Booth, E.C. and Tufts, L.T.
v5p0594c1s
Booth, E.E. ... v6p0403c2s
Booth, E.G. ... v4p0578c1s
Booth, E.M.J.von, Mrs. ... v4p0303c1s
Booth, F. ... v1p0670c2s
Booth, G. ... v1p0492c2s
Booth, G.S. ... v2p0262c1s
Booth, G.Sclater ... v3p0255c1s
Booth, H.C. ... v4p0201c1s
Booth, H.M. ... v4p0113c2s
Booth, H.W.G. ... v3p0389c1s
Booth, J. ... v1p0933c2s
Booth, J.C. ... v1p0225c1s
v1p0527c1s v1p0639c1s v1p0732c1s
v1p1147c1s
Booth, J.C. and Garrett, T.H.
v1p0624c2s v1p0939c1s
Booth, James ... v1p0628c1s
Booth, Maud B. ... v4p0500c2s
Booth, N. ... v1p0759c1s
Booth, O. ... v3p0095c2s
Booth, O, Mrs. ... v3p0240c1s
Booth, R.R. ... v1p0853c1s
Booth, S.M. ... v1p1264c2s
v1p1291c1s
Booth, W. ... v3p0050c1s
v3p0141c2s v3p0374c1s v4p0501c1s
v4p0532c2s v6p0016c1s
Booth, W. et al. ... v2p0384c2s
Booth, W.H. ... v2p0018c2s
v2p0071c1s v3p0255c1s v4p0161c2s
v4p0547c1s v5p0066c2s v5p0167c2s
v5p0183c1s v5p0226c2s v6p0143c2m
v6p0204c2s v6p0216c1s v6p0248c1s
v6p0248c2m v6p0249c1s v6p0260c2s
v6p0512c2s v6p0527c2s v6p0615c2s
v6p0649c2s
Booth, Wm. ... v5p0471c1s
Booth-Daphne, O., Mrs. ... v3p0185c1s
v4p0365c2s
Booth-Tucker ... v6p0566c2s
Booth-Tucker, F.DeL. ... v5p0506c2m
Booth-Tucker, F.Deh ... v5p0436c2s
Booth-Tucker, H.Deh ... v4p0501c1s
Boothby, G. ... v4p0195c2s
v4p0582c2s v5p0106c1s v5p0481c1s
Boothby, Guy ... v4p0059c1s
v4p0147c2s v4p0551c1s v5p0083c1s
v5p0376c2s v5p0552c2s v6p0440c1s
Boott, F. ... v1p0265c1s
v2p0309c2s
Boraston, J.M. ... v4p0037c2s
v6p0067c2s v6p0496c2s
Borcena, M. ... v1p0834c1s
Borchers, W. ... v5p0185c2s
Borchgrevink, C.E. ... v4p0019c2m
v5p0022c1m v5p0022c2s v5p0541c2s
v6p0023c1m
Borcke, H.von ... v1p1345c1s
Bordage, E. ... v4p0200c2s
Borden, F. ... v6p0097c1s
Borden, J. ... v1p0423c1s
Borden, P.D., jr. and Nichols, W.R.
v2p0229c2s
Borden, W.H.C. ... v4p0411c2s
Bordier, A. ... v1p0425c1s
Bordwell, P. ... v6p0094c1s
Borgan, Mary H.B. ... v6p0307c2s
Borgeaud, C. ... v4p0130c2s
v6p0094c1s v6p0535c1s
Borger, P. ... v5p0547c2s
Borgerhoff, J.L. ... v6p0256c2s
Borges, E. ... v4p0010c1s
Borglum, G. ... v5p0102c2s
v5p0492c1s
Borgquist, A. ... v6p0160c1s
Borgstedt, M. ... v3p0018c2s
Boring, Blanche M. ... v5p0279c1s
Boring, W.A. ... v5p0567c2s
Borland, C. ... v3p0361c1s
Borland, J.E. ... v6p0439c2s
Borland, S. ... v1p0225c1s
Borland, W. and Orr, J. .. v6p0514c2s
Borlase, N.C. ... v5p0048c2s
Borlase, W.C. ... v1p1327c2s
v1p1329c1s v2p0084c1s v2p0330c1s
v4p0134c2s v4p0470c2s
Born, H. ... v5p0629c2s
Born, P. ... v1p0848c1s
Borne, O.S. ... v5p0304c1s
v5p0384c1s v5p0578c1s
Bornemann, K.R. ... v1p1390c1m
Borneo, F. ... v3p0150c1s
Bornhak, C. ... v4p0228c2s
v4p0337c1s
Borodine, N. ... v4p0135c2s
Boron, G. ... v6p0009c1s
v6p0525c1s
Bororykine, P. ... v4p0495c2s
Boros, G. ... v3p0126c2s
Borowski, F. ... v6p0438c2s
Borradaile, A.A. ... v4p0379c1s
Borradaile, H.E. ... v4p0120c1s
v4p0206c1s
Borrajo, E.M. ... v2p0349c2s
Borret, B. ... v5p0192c1s
v5p0193c1s v5p0279c1s v5p0329c1s
v5p0438c2s v5p0441c1s v5p0530c1s
Borrett, B. ... v5p0402c2s
Borries, A.von ... v4p0337c2s
v6p0382c2s
Borries, H.von ... v1p0759c2s
Borring, A.C.de ... v3p0374c1s
Borring, F.M.De ... v3p0115c1s
Borroughs, J. ... v3p0148c1s
Borrow, G. ... v1p0795c1s
v1p1138c2s v5p0299c2s
Borrowe, H.A. ... v3p0234c1s
Borsa, M. ... v6p0258c2s
Borsari, L. ... v5p0495c1s
Borsch, J.L. ... v6p0609c1s
Borthvick, J. ... v5p0038c2s
Borthwick, A., Sir ... v2p0354c1s
Borthwick, A.B. ... v3p0469c1s
Borton, Fred ... v5p0203c2s
Bosanquet, B. ... v2p0097c1s
v2p0148c2s v2p0151c1s v3p0143c1s
v3p0207c2s v3p0464c1s v4p0096c2s
v4p0179c1s v4p0446c2s v4p0475c1s
v4p0476c2s v4p0478c2s v4p0622c1m
v5p0036c2s v5p0192c2s v5p0241c1s
v5p0261c1s v5p0322c1s v5p0534c2s
v5p0536c1s v5p0537c2s v5p0550c1s
v6p0147c1s v6p0164c2s v6p0167c1s
v6p0286c1s v6p0539c1s v6p0593c2s
v6p0709c2s
Bosanquet, B. and Baldwin, J.M.
v6p0307c2s
Bosanquet, B. and Marshall, A.
v4p0452c1s
Bosanquet, B. et al. ... v5p0580c1s
Bosanquet, B., Mrs. ... v5p0123c2s
v5p0425c1s
Bosanquet, F.A. ... v5p0328c1s
Bosanquet, H. ... v4p0150c1s
v5p0273c1s v5p0289c1s v5p0327c1s
v5p0535c2s v6p0109c2s v6p0682c2s
v6p0703c2s
Bosanquet, Helen ... v5p0102c1s
v5p0341c2s v5p0585c2s v6p0704c2s
Bosanquet, I.W. ... v1p0123c1s
v1p0332c2s
Bosanquet, J.W. ... v1p0395c2s
v1p0825c1s
Bosanquet, Mrs. ... v6p0497c2s
Bosanquet, R. ... v6p0427c2s
Bosanquet, R.C. ... v4p0326c1s
v5p0248c2s v5p0458c2s v6p0675c1s
Bosanquet, R.C. and Tod, M.N.
v6p0272c1s
Bosboom-Toussaint, Mme. .. v2p0272c2s
Boscanten, W.S.C. ... v2p0030c2s
Boscawen, A.G. ... v4p0113c1s
v4p0296c2s v5p0122c2s v6p0279c1s
Boscawen, A.G. and Webster, R.E.
v4p0112c2s
Boscawen, G. ... v4p0624c1s
Boscawen, W.S. ... v3p0416c1s
Boscawen, W.St.C. ... v1p0084c2s
v2p0024c1s v2p0094c2s v4p0095c1m
v4p0172c1s v4p0219c2s v5p0563c1s
Boscawen, W.St.C. and Ward, W.H.
v5p0517c1s
Bose, H.M.Du ... v4p0251c2s
Bose, J.C. ... v5p0449c2s
Bose, R.C. ... v1p0592c1s
Bose, W.P.Du and Henneman, J.B.
v6p0218c1s
Bosher, K.L. ... v6p0333c2s
v6p0674c1s
Boss, H.R. ... v1p0148c2s
Boss, L. ... v1p0281c2s
v2p0095c2m v3p0309c2s v6p0037c2s
Bossard, J. ... v1p0416c2s
Bosscha, H.C. ... v1p0564c1s
Bossut, C. ... v1p0976c2s
Bost, E. ... v4p0463c1s
Bostedo, L.G. ... v4p0615c1s
v5p0509c2s
Bostwick, A. ... v4p0210c1s
Bostwick, A.E. ... v2p0137c2s
v2p0284c2s v2p0462c1s v3p0001c2s
v4p0329c2s v4p0474c2s v5p0070c1s
v5p0333c2s v5p0334c1s v5p0335c2s
v5p0337c1s v5p0479c2s v6p0074c2s
v6p0223c1s v6p0372c1m v6p0372c2m
v6p0373c1m v6p0374c1s v6p0375c1m
v6p0453c2m v6p0532c2s v6p0546c1s
v6p0577c1s

Bostwick, A.E. et al. v5p0334c1s v6p0017c1s
Bostwick, Arthur E. et al. v6p0374c1s
Bostwick, Kate M. v4p0630c2s
Boswell, C.S. v3p0085c2s v3p0148c1s v3p0185c2s v3p0295c1s v4p0559c2s
Boswell, E. v6p0547c1s
Boswell, J.I. v1p1406c2s
Boswell, J.W. v1p0454c2s
Boswell, R.B. v5p0019c1s v5p0158c2s v5p0311c2s
Boswell, R.Bruce v4p0154c1s v5p0160c1s
Boswell, W.L. v3p0153c2s
Bosworth, E.I. v3p0342c1s v5p0306c1m v5p0307c1s v5p0436c1s v6p0484c2s
Bosworth, F. v1p0581c2m
Bosworth, L.A.M. v4p0551c2s v6p0429c1s
Botassi, D.N. and Cleveland, L. v5p0597c2s
Botassi, D.N. and Dilke, C.W. v5p0249c1s
Botcherby, B. v1p0050c2s v2p0301c2s
Boteler, A.R. and Sanborn, F.B. v2p0058c1s
Boteler, F.M. v6p0295c1s
Botfield, B. v1p0078c1s
Both, V. v1p0769c1s
Botha, L. v6p0072c1s
Botham, W. v4p0318c1s
Bothamley, C.H. v5p0447c2s
Bothams, W. v4p0438c1s
Bothmer, A. v4p0338c1s v4p0633c2s v5p0532c1s
Bothmer, Countess von v1p0525c1s
Bothmer, M.von v1p0513c1s v1p1058c2s v1p1392c2s
Botkin, A.C. v1p0568c2s
Botkine, P. v4p0496c2s
Botsford, A.H. v5p0507c2s
Botsford, Anna v6p0090c1s
Botsford, C.H. v2p0026c2s v2p0171c2s v2p0183c2s
Botsford, G.W. v6p0548c2s v6p0582c2s
Botsford, M.W. v2p0287c1s v2p0337c1s
Botta, V. v1p0389c1s v1p0814c2s
Bottalla, F. v1p0602c1s
Bottome, M. et al. v4p0630c1s
Bottomley, J.T. v1p0077c1s v1p0525c2s v1p0621c2s v1p1416c2s v2p0199c2s v2p0238c2s
Bottomley, W. v3p0094c2s v3p0264c1s
Bottwood, L.M. v1p0637c1s
Boucher, H. v5p0386c2s
Boucher, W.M. v4p0284c2s
Boucherett, J. v1p0482c2s v1p1424c1s
Boucherie, M.A. v1p1311c2s
Bouchette, E. v5p0090c1s
Bouchot, H. v4p0097c2s v4p0537c1s v5p0038c1s v5p0132c1s
Bouchot, Henri, ... v4p0195c2s
Boucicault, D. v1p0363c1s v1p0364c2s v3p0002c2s v3p0051c2m v3p0100c1s v3p0122c1s v3p0303c2s v3p0312c2s v3p0343c2s v3p0387c2s v3p0388c1s v3p0427c1s
Boucicault, D. and Reade, C. v1p0471c1s
Boue, A. v1p1332c2m v1p1333c1s
Boughey, A.H.F. v5p0604c2s v5p0636c2s v6p0272c2s
Boughton, D., Mrs. v4p0166c2s
Boughton, D.H. v6p0364c1s v6p0493c2s
Boughton, E.M. v4p0052c1s
Boughton, G.B. v2p0243c2s
Boughton, G.H. v2p0205c1s v2p0283c2s v2p0474c2s v2p0481c1s v3p0159c2s
Boughton, W. v3p0445c1s v4p0337c1s v4p0397c1s v4p0411c2s v4p0620c1s
Boughton, W. et al. v4p0597c2s
Boughton, W.E.R. v1p0395c1s
Bougle, C. v5p0537c2s
Bougler, D.C. v2p0079c1s v6p0691c1s
Bougler, G.S. v2p0139c2m v2p0145c2m
Bouland, L. v3p0365c1s
Boulden, H.B. v5p0023c1s
Boulden, H.B., Mrs. v4p0629c1s
Boulden, Jane L. v5p0637c2s v5p0642c1s
Bouldin, P. v4p0473c2s
Boulenger, G.A. v3p0360c2s v4p0216c1s v4p0531c1s v5p0049c2s v5p0263c2s v5p0485c2s
Boulger, C.S. v2p0445c2s
Boulger, D. v2p0003c2s v2p0025c1m v2p0183c1s v2p0216c2s v3p0003c2s v3p0152c2s v3p0211c1s v3p0212c1s v3p0227c1s v3p0327c1m
Boulger, D.C. v1p0231c2s v1p0232c2s v1p1133c2s v2p0003c2s v2p0078c2s v2p0251c2s v2p0284c1m v2p0362c2s v3p0060c2s v3p0078c2s v3p0079c1s v3p0079c2s v4p0020c2s v4p0105c1s v4p0133c2s v4p0283c1s v4p0328c1s v5p0005c1s v5p0108c2s v5p0109c2s v5p0110c2m v5p0111c1m v5p0111c2s v5p0112c2s v5p0132c2m v5p0173c2s v5p0190c2s v5p0203c2s v5p0246c2s v5p0253c2s v5p0338c2s v5p0501c1s v5p0622c2s v5p0641c2s v6p0005c2m v6p0036c2m v6p0057c1m v6p0118c1s v6p0119c1s v6p0127c1s v6p0144c1s v6p0146c2s v6p0205c1s v6p0213c1s v6p0237c1s v6p0253c2s v6p0294c2s v6p0369c2s v6p0440c2s v6p0449c2s v6p0527c2s v6p0589c1s v6p0711c1s
Boulger, Demetrius C. v6p0042c2s
Boulger, G.S. v2p0038c1s v2p0046c1s v2p0059c2s v2p0077c1s v2p0135c2s v2p0162c2m v2p0198c1s v2p0205c2s v2p0207c2m v2p0249c2s v3p0363c1s
Boulion, S.B. and Means, D.M. v4p0080c2s
Boult, Ella M. v6p0307c2s
Boult, H. v4p0530c2s
Boult, J. v2p0440c2s
Boult, S.H. v4p0075c1s v4p0152c2s v4p0597c2s
Boulter, S. v4p0089c2s
Boulter, W.C. v4p0317c1s
Boulting, W. v2p0112c2s v3p0175c1s
Boulton, A.C.F. v6p0299c1s
Boulton, A.C.Forster v5p0244c2s
Boulton, A.J. v6p0665c2s
Boulton, C.A. v5p0220c1s
Boulton, C.B. v4p0294c1s
Boulton, C.R. v4p0058c1s v4p0392c1s v4p0490c1s v5p0495c1s
Boulton, E.B. v3p0092c2s
Boulton, H. v4p0126c1s v4p0339c1s
Boulton, H.E. v3p0338c2s v4p0344c2s v4p0469c1s
Boulton, H.E. and Bethune, C.C. v3p0338c2s
Boulton, L.M. v5p0373c2s
Boulton, O. v5p0030c1s
Boulton, S.B. v2p0441c1s v3p0017c1s v3p0181c1s v3p0239c1s v3p0262c1s v4p0382c1s
Boulton, W.B. v5p0141c2s v6p0277c1s v6p0301c2s
Boulton, W.R. v6p0645c2s
Boulvin, J. v6p0204c2s
Bouquillon, T. v2p0403c1s v4p0021c1s v4p0170c1s v6p0065c2s v6p0428c2s v6p0548c1s
Bouran, T. v5p0386c2s
Bourassa, H. v6p0241c2s
Bourbaugh, C.C. v1p0237c1s
Bourchier v3p0434c2s
Bourchier, H. v5p0018c1s
Bourchier, H.J. v5p0478c2s
Bourchier, J.D. v3p0028c1m v3p0031c1m v3p0036c2s v3p0059c2m v3p0104c2s v3p0183c2s v3p0189c2s v3p0360c2s v3p0367c2s v3p0385c2s v3p0404c1s v4p0010c1s v4p0078c2s v4p0451c2s v4p0584c1s v5p0384c2s
Bourchier, M. v3p0247c2s
Bourchier, W. v4p0149c1s v4p0580c1s
Bourdeau, L. v4p0008c1s v4p0578c2s
Bourdillon, F.W. v5p0413c1s v5p0502c1s v6p0433c2s v6p0517c1s
Bourdillon, James, Sir ... v6p0058c1s
Bourdon, G. v6p0641c2s
Bourgault-Ducoudray, L.A.. v4p0048c1s v4p0608c2s
Bourget, M.J. v1p0580c1s
Bourget, P. v2p0370c1s v3p0151c2s v3p0259c2s v4p0101c1s v4p0197c2s v4p0198c1s v4p0215c1s v4p0475c1s v5p0008c2s v5p0023c1s v5p0195c1s v5p0210c1s v5p0221c1s v5p0275c1s v5p0415c2s v5p0437c1s v6p0461c2s v6p0562c2s
Bourget, P. et al. v3p0152c1s
Bourget, Paul v3p0336c1s v5p0432c2s v5p0531c2s
Bourinot, J.G. v1p0193c2m v1p0194c1s v1p0194c2s v1p0195c1m v1p0195c2s v1p0804c2s v1p0931c1s v1p0940c1s v1p0951c1s v1p0974c2s v2p0066c1s v3p0065c1m v3p0065c2s v3p0150c2s v3p0255c1s v4p0085c1s v4p0085c2m v4p0086c1s v4p0174c1s v4p0342c2s v4p0498c2s v5p0086c2s v5p0090c1m v5p0090c2m v5p0091c1m v5p0125c1s v5p0405c1s v5p0415c1m v5p0499c1s v5p0504c2s v5p0598c2s
Bourke, A. v3p0245c2s
Bourke, C.F. v5p0344c2s v5p0625c2s v6p0500c1s
Bourke, J.G. v3p0106c2s v4p0020c2m v4p0022c1s v4p0204c2s v4p0368c1s v4p0373c1s v4p0376c2s v4p0484c2m v4p0531c1s v4p0558c1s v5p0353c2s v6p0544c2s
Bourke, John G. v3p0214c1s
Bourn, A.O. v4p0101c2s
Bourn, H.H. v3p0229c2s
Bourne, A. v1p0463c1s v1p1041c1s
Bourne, A.G. v3p0246c1m
Bourne, A.N. v6p0175c2s v6p0421c1s v6p0597c1s
Bourne, E.E. v1p0909c2s v1p0989c1s v1p1033c2m
Bourne, E.G. v2p0112c2s v2p0204c1s v2p0481c2m v3p0156c2s v3p0169c1s v3p0186c2s v3p0305c1m v3p0393c2s v3p0406c2s v4p0010c1s v4p0158c1s v4p0216c2s v4p0246c2s v4p0254c2s v4p0259c1s v4p0473c2s v4p0515c1s v4p0530c1s v5p0017c1s v5p0128c1s v5p0204c1s v5p0204c2s v5p0479c1s v5p0598c2s v5p0629c2s v6p0092c1s v6p0103c1s v6p0140c1s v6p0286c2s
Bourne, E.G. and Ford, P.L. v5p0204c1s
Bourne, Francis v6p0191c2s
Bourne, G. v6p0192c2s v6p0486c1s v6p0542c2s v6p0555c1s v6p0585c1s v6p0679c1s
Bourne, G.C. v3p0026c1s v4p0094c1s v4p0185c2s
Bourne, H.C. v3p0050c1s v4p0156c1s v4p0265c1s v4p0315c1s v4p0434c1s
Bourne, H.E. v3p0369c2s v4p0119c1s v4p0166c1m v4p0268c2s v4p0610c1s v5p0014c2s v5p0153c1s v5p0197c1s v5p0217c1s v5p0218c2s v5p0397c2s v5p0404c1s v5p0442c1s v6p0094c2s v6p0237c2s v6p0433c2s v6p0442c1s v6p0479c2s v6p0480c1s
Bourne, H.H. v3p0281c1s
Bourne, H.R.F. v1p0098c2s v1p0758c2s v1p0791c1s v1p0823c2s v1p0987c2s v1p1128c2s v2p0068c2s v3p0004c2s v3p0005c1s v3p0015c2s v5p0006c2s v5p0528c2s v6p0144c1s
Bourne, H.R.Fox v2p0175c1s v2p0407c2s v3p0091c1s v3p0314c2s v5p0005c2s v5p0008c1s v5p0128c1s v5p0132c2m v5p0597c1s
Bourne, J. v1p0714c2s v1p0783c2s v1p1248c2s
Bourne, J. et al. v1p1247c1s
Bourne, J.H.F. v2p0171c1s
Bourne, M. v3p0128c2s
Bourne, May E. v6p0025c2s v6p0691c1s
Bourne, R. v5p0361c2s
Bourne, S. v1p0544c1s v1p0544c2s v1p1198c2s v2p0007c1s v2p0161c1s v2p0431c1s v3p0065c2s v3p0209c2s v4p0237c1s
Bourne, T. v2p0053c2s
Bourne, T.J. v5p0476c2s
Bourne, W.O. v1p0360c2s v1p1029c1s
Bourniot, J.G. v4p0038c1s
Bourns, F.S. and Worcester, D.C. v5p0445c2s
Bouroff, B.A. v6p0557c1s
Bourrier, A. v5p0217c1s v5p0469c1s
Bouscaren, G. v1p0280c2s
Bousfield, E.G.P. and Green, F.W.E. v6p0305c2s
Bousfield, W.R. v4p0590c2s
Boussard v2p0019c2s
Boussin, J. v1p0423c1s
Boussingault, J.B. v1p0230c2s v1p0467c2s v1p1081c1s
Boussingault, M. v1p0533c1s v1p1251c1s
Boutall, W. v5p0570c1s
Boutan, L. v5p0449c1s
Bouteiller, J.de v1p0971c1s
Boutell, C. v1p0397c1s v1p0459c1s v1p0864c2s v1p1174c1s
Boutell, H.L. v4p0597c1s
Boutell, H.S. v5p0399c1s v5p0500c1s v5p0574c1s v6p0667c1s
Boutell, L.H. v2p0195c1s v3p0315c1s
Boutelle, C.O. v2p0090c2s v2p0128c2s v2p0173c1s v2p0455c1m v5p0262c1s
Boutelle, J.A. v1p0237c2s
Boutflower, C.H. v6p0693c1s
Boutillier, A.Le v6p0646c2s
Bouton, E. v2p0144c1s v3p0287c1s
Bouton, Eugene v6p0207c1s
Bouton, N. v1p0398c2s

v1p0846c2s v1p0911c2s v1p1039c1s
Bouton, W. v1p0523c1s
v1p1322c2s v2p0155c2s
Boutwell, G.A. v4p0149c2s
v4p0317c1s
Boutwell, G.S. v1p0016c1s
v1p0284c1m v1p0453c1s v1p0540c2s
v1p0544c2s v1p0947c2s v1p1100c1s
v1p1245c1s v1p1264c1s v1p1319c1m
v1p1344c1s v2p0237c2s v3p0099c2s
v3p0272c1s v3p0300c2s v3p0393c1s
v4p0277c2s v4p0313c1s v4p0437c1s
v4p0593c1s v5p0065c2s v5p0066c1s
v5p0074c1s v5p0283c2s v5p0292c2s
v5p0309c1s v5p0532c1s v5p0604c2s
v6p0147c1m
Boutwell, G.S. and Seymour, H.
v2p0454c2s
Boutwell, G.S. et al. v2p0034c1s
v2p0454c1s
Boutwood, A. v5p0037c2s
v5p0279c1s v5p0396c2s
Bouve, E.T. v3p0195c2s
Bouve, P.C. v5p0406c1s
v6p0554c1s v6p0711c2s
Bouve, Pauline C. v6p0155c2s
v6p0161c2s v6p0168c1s v6p0243c1s
v6p0259c1s v6p0544c1s
Bouve, T.S. v1p1225c1s
Bouve, T.T. v1p0911c1s
v5p0169c1s v5p0646c1s
Bouverie, J.F. v1p0203c1s
v1p0535c1s v1p0878c2s
Bouvet, Marguerite v5p0154c2s
Bouvier, A. v2p0172c2s
Bouvier, G.A. v6p0101c1s
v6p0563c1s
Bovard, F.D. v4p0138c1s
v4p0565c1s
Bovel, J. v1p0194c2s
Bovell, J. v1p0642c1s
Boveri, T. v5p0099c1s
Bovet, De v3p0221c2s
Bovet, M.A.de v4p0357c1s
Bovet, M.A.de and Widor, C.M.
v4p0233c1s
Bovet, M'lle.de v3p0178c1s
Bovey, S.M.C. v5p0074c1s
Bovoruikin, P. v1p0922c1s
Bow, J.B.De v1p0854c1s
Bow, J.D.B.De v1p0031c2s
v1p0186c2s v1p0212c1s v1p0272c2s
v1p0282c2m v1p0283c1s v1p0283c2m
v1p0284c1s v1p0295c1s v1p0307c1s
v1p0322c2s v1p0375c1s v1p0461c2s
v1p0539c1s v1p0638c1s v1p0648c1s
v1p0649c2s v1p0650c2s v1p0718c1s
v1p0729c1s v1p0748c1s v1p0772c1s
v1p0772c2s v1p0792c1s v1p0809c1s
v1p0819c2s v1p0854c2s v1p0913c1m
v1p1005c2s v1p1025c2s v1p1034c1s
v1p1078c1s v1p1079c2s v1p1208c2s
v1p1225c1s v1p1226c1s v1p1231c1s
v1p1245c2m v1p1265c1s v1p1290c1s
v1p1314c1s v1p1353c1s v1p1386c1s
v1p1401c1s v2p0096c1s v2p0098c1s
v2p0286c2s v2p0363c2s v2p0411c1m
v2p0452c1s v2p0453c1m
Bowden, A.C. v5p0285c1s
Bowden, A.J. v2p0052c1s
Bowden, E.M. v3p0287c2s
v3p0355c2s v3p0394c1s v4p0031c1s
v4p0048c2s v4p0078c1s v4p0188c2s
v4p0258c1s v5p0301c2s
Bowden, H.P. v4p0554c2s
Bowden, S., Father v3p0355c2s
v3p0357c2s
Bowdish, B.S. v6p0068c1m
Bowditch, A. v6p0067c2s
Bowditch, A.M. v4p0140c2s
Bowditch, C.P. v5p0088c1s
v5p0347c2s v5p0367c1s
Bowditch, E.W. and Philbrick, E.S.
v2p0122c2s
Bowditch, H. v6p0059c1s
Bowditch, H.I. v1p0295c1s
v3p0098c1s v3p0435c1s
Bowditch, H.P. v1p0736c2s
v2p0207c2s v2p0309c2s v3p0190c2s
v4p0363c2s v4p0440c1s v4p0508c1s
v5p0368c1s
Bowditch, H.P. and Cummings, E.
v4p0101c1s
Bowditch, N. v1p0069c2s
v1p0070c2s v1p0281c1s v1p0513c1s
Bowdle, S.E. v6p0519c2s
Bowdler, J. v1p1253c2s
Bowdoin, H. v4p0194c2s
Bowdoin, J. v1p0747c1s
Bowdoin, W.G. v5p0070c2m
v5p0071c1s v5p0377c2s v5p0645c1s
v6p0074c1m
Bowen, A.C. v5p0075c1s
Bowen, A.M. v5p0237c1s
v5p0635c2s
Bowen, B.B. v1p0141c2s
v1p0142c1m v1p0337c1s v1p1060c1s
v1p1149c2s v1p1427c2s
Bowen, C.W. v3p0455c2s
Bowen, D. v1p0047c2s
v1p0450c1s v1p0688c2s
Bowen, D.V. v6p0376c1s
Bowen, E. v1p0230c1s
v1p0268c2s v1p1096c1s
Bowen, E.A. v2p0026c1s
v2p0076c2s v4p0033c1s v4p0070c2s
v4p0306c2s
Bowen, E.M. v6p0202c1s
Bowen, E.W. v4p0273c2s
v5p0043c2s v5p0097c2s v5p0121c2s
v5p0232c1s v5p0446c2s v5p0455c2s
v5p0525c1s v5p0612c2s v5p0617c2s
v6p0018c2s v6p0081c2s v6p0180c2s
v6p0200c2s v6p0211c1s v6p0239c1s
v6p0242c2s v6p0330c1s v6p0461c2s
v6p0491c1s v6p0519c1s v6p0596c2s
v6p0609c2s v6p0618c1s
Bowen, F. v1p0008c2s
v1p0012c2s v1p0032c2s v1p0033c1s
v1p0042c2s v1p0085c1s v1p0086c1s
v1p0092c2s v1p0114c1s v1p0116c1s
v1p0151c2m v1p0152c1m v1p0154c2s
v1p0169c2s v1p0173c1s v1p0188c1s
v1p0208c2m v1p0241c2s v1p0242c1s
v1p0244c1s v1p0249c1s v1p0259c2s
v1p0262c1s v1p0276c1s v1p0280c1s
v1p0287c2s v1p0292c1s v1p0298c2m
v1p0309c2s v1p0313c1m v1p0323c2s
v1p0329c2s v1p0339c1s v1p0342c2s
v1p0345c2s v1p0362c1s v1p0368c2s
v1p0370c1s v1p0371c2s v1p0373c2s
v1p0414c2s v1p0430c2m v1p0434c2s
v1p0475c1s v1p0475c2s v1p0477c1s
v1p0482c1s v1p0484c1s v1p0488c2s
v1p0509c2s v1p0522c1s v1p0528c1s
v1p0532c2s v1p0537c2s v1p0554c1s
v1p0572c2m v1p0594c2s v1p0595c1s
v1p0598c1s v1p0604c1s v1p0614c1s
v1p0616c1s v1p0623c1s v1p0637c2s
v1p0643c2s v1p0646c2s v1p0647c1s
v1p0650c1s v1p0671c1s v1p0681c1s
v1p0698c1s v1p0702c2s v1p0712c1s
v1p0750c2s v1p0754c2s v1p0758c2s
v1p0761c1s v1p0771c2s v1p0772c2s
v1p0774c2m v1p0779c1s v1p0791c2s
v1p0796c2s v1p0809c1s v1p0810c2s
v1p0815c2s v1p0819c1s v1p0826c2s
v1p0839c2s v1p0843c2s v1p0861c1s
v1p0868c2s v1p0876c1s v1p0879c2s
v1p0900c2s v1p0923c2s v1p0927c1s
v1p0931c2s v1p0947c2s v1p0950c2s
v1p0976c2s v1p0993c1s v1p1000c1s
v1p1002c1s v1p1013c1s v1p1020c1s
v1p1021c2s v1p1026c1s v1p1026c2m
v1p1027c1m v1p1030c1s v1p1034c1s
v1p1041c1s v1p1052c2s v1p1055c2s
v1p1057c1s v1p1082c2s v1p1103c2s
v1p1104c1s v1p1105c1s v1p1122c2m
v1p1170c1s v1p1184c1s v1p1202c1s
v1p1205c2s v1p1211c1s v1p1213c1s
v1p1214c1s v1p1226c2s v1p1245c2s
v1p1253c2s v1p1283c1s v1p1303c2m
v1p1321c1m v1p1344c1s v1p1348c1s
v1p1350c1s v1p1350c2s v1p1356c2s
v1p1359c1s v1p1386c1s v1p1393c2m
v1p1396c1s v1p1405c2s v1p1416c2s
v2p0041c2s v4p0504c2s
Bowen, F. and Felton, C.C.
v1p0413c2s
Bowen, F. and Whittlesey, C.
v1p0725c1s
Bowen, G.F. v3p0101c2s
v4p0135c2s
Bowen, H.C. v3p0355c2s
v3p0422c1s v4p0296c2s
Bowen, H.H. v5p0097c2s
v5p0415c2s v5p0474c1s v5p0587c1s
v6p0669c2s
Bowen, Herbert W. v6p0676c1s
Bowen, Herbert W. and Foster, J.W.
v6p0550c1s
Bowen, J.E. v2p0133c2s
v2p0134c2s v3p0135c1s v3p0191c2s
v3p0360c1s
Bowen, J.W.E. v3p0360c1s
Bowen, M.K. v5p0478c1s
Bowen, Marian v4p0516c1s
Bowen, Marion P. v6p0100c2s
v6p0103c2s
Bowen, R.A. v4p0110c1s
v5p0580c2s v6p0103c1s
Bowen, R.S. v6p0498c2s
Bowen, W.A. v6p0175c2s
v6p0469c1s
Bowen, W.H.C. v4p0129c2s
v4p0370c2m v4p0399c1s
Bowen-Colthurst, M. v6p0366c2s
v6p0380c2s
Bowen-Graves, F. v1p0607c1s
Bowen-Jones, J. v2p0005c2s
Bowen-Rowlands, E. v4p0190c2s
Bowen-Rowlands, E.B. v6p0347c1s
Bower, A.F. v5p0475c2s
Bower, A.S. v2p0053c2s
Bower, B.M. v6p0255c2s
Bower, F.O. v2p0252c1s
v2p0269c2s v4p0197c1s v4p0384c2s
v6p0502c2s
Bower, G.S. v1p0201c2s
v1p0364c1s v1p0556c1s v1p0584c1s
v1p1017c1s v1p1189c2s v2p0116c2s
Bower, H. v2p0076c1s
v4p0576c1s v4p0587c1s
Bower, J.A. v1p0400c2s
v1p1004c1s v3p0230c1s
Bower, L.F. v3p0162c1s
v4p0009c1s
Bower, M. v5p0204c1s
v6p0703c1s
Bower, Marian v6p0288c1s
Bower, P.B. v2p0393c2s
Bower, R.L. v6p0170c2s
Bowerman, G.F. v6p0074c1m
v6p0075c1s v6p0372c2m v6p0374c1s
v6p0687c1s
Bowers, A.F. v6p0297c1s
Bowers, C.G. v5p0149c1s
v5p0578c1s
Bowers, D.P., Mrs. v6p0075c2s
Bowers, E.A. v3p0158c1s
Bowers, L.W. v6p0365c1s
Bowers, S. v2p0071c2s
Bowers, W.W. v6p0134c2s
Bowes, A. v1p1255c1s
Bowes, R. v2p0065c1s
v2p0354c2s v5p0054c1s
Bowes, Robert v3p0397c1s
Bowie, A.G. v1p0084c2s
v1p0259c1s v1p1017c2s v1p1290c1m
v1p1380c1s v2p0328c1s v2p0359c2s
v3p0196c1s v3p0340c1s v3p0340c2s
v4p0257c2s v4p0544c2s
Bowie, A.J.J., jr. v2p0119c2s
Bowie, J. v6p0648c2s
Bowie, R.C. v6p0140c1s
Bowie, S.J. v6p0605c2s
Bowie, W.W.W. v1p1313c2s
Bowker et al. v1p0196c1s
Bowker, J. v3p0277c2s
v3p0417c1s
Bowker, Jas. v4p0291c1s
Bowker, R.R. v1p0359c2s
v1p0511c1s v1p0511c2s v1p0743c2s
v1p1027c2s v1p1085c1s v1p1238c1s
v1p1353c1s v2p0092c1s v2p0255c2m
v2p0402c2s v2p0424c1s v2p0455c1s
v2p0455c2s v2p0480c1s v3p0028c2s
v3p0049c2s v3p0088c2s v3p0249c1s
v3p0255c2s v3p0319c2s v3p0471c2s
v4p0129c2s v4p0176c1s v4p0283c2m
v4p0291c2s v4p0330c2s v4p0400c2s
v4p0403c1s v4p0453c2s v4p0548c1s
v4p0561c2s v5p0218c2s v5p0334c1s
v6p0065c2s v6p0511c1s
Bowker, S.D. v2p0282c1s
Bowlby, A.A. v5p0007c2s
Bowlby, H. v6p0592c1s
Bowle, Eliz.H. v6p0401c2s
v6p0613c2s
Bowle, J. v1p0155c1s
v1p0200c1s v1p0488c2s v1p0885c1s
v1p0950c1s v1p0972c1s v1p1123c2m
Bowles, B.F. v1p0282c2s
v2p0096c1s
Bowles, C. v1p0190c2s
v1p0256c1s v1p0451c2s v1p0557c2s
v1p0735c2s v1p0881c1s v1p1082c2s
v1p1383c1s
Bowles, E. v1p0177c2s
v1p0217c2s v1p0368c1s v1p0800c2s
v1p0820c2s v1p0850c2s v1p0855c2s
v1p1230c1s v3p0165c2s
Bowles, E.E. v5p0524c2s
Bowles, G. v1p0887c1s
v1p1277c1s v1p1314c2s v5p0189c2s
v5p0345c2s
Bowles, G.S. v5p0190c2s
Bowles, J. v3p0366c1s
Bowles, J.M. v6p0074c2s
v6p0229c2s v6p0283c2s v6p0453c1s
Bowles, J.P. v6p0115c2s
Bowles, M.E. v4p0249c2s
Bowles, P. v1p0088c2s
Bowles, R.H. v6p0215c2s
v6p0495c1s
Bowles, R.L. et al. v3p0397c1s
Bowles, R.N. v6p0207c1s
Bowles, S. v1p0258c1s
v1p0538c1s v1p0570c2s v1p0880c2s
v1p0956c1s v1p1245c1s v6p0515c2s
Bowles, S.P. v6p0503c1s
Bowles, T.G. v1p0067c1s
v1p0723c2s v1p0897c1s v2p0186c2s
v2p0187c1s v2p0312c2s v3p0384c2s
v4p0145c2s v5p0008c1s v5p0191c1s
v5p0218c1s v5p0248c1s v5p0285c1s
v5p0584c1s v5p0594c2s v5p0618c2s
Bowley, A.L. v4p0315c2s
v4p0608c1m v5p0009c2s v5p0099c2s
v5p0284c1s v5p0615c1m v5p0615c2m
v6p0082c2s v6p0268c1s v6p0271c2s
v6p0682c2m v6p0707c1s
Bowley, A.L. and Edgeworth, F.Y.
v6p0615c1s
Bowley, A.L. and Hopkinson, A.
v5p0615c2s
Bowley, A.L. and Wood, G.H.
v6p0682c2s
Bowley, F.S. v1p1008c1s
v1p1343c1s

Bowling, E.W. v3p0088c1s
Bowlker, C.A.C. v3p0133c2s
Bowman, A. v1p0187c1s
v1p0792c2s
Bowman, E.M. v5p0125c2s
Bowman, F.H. v4p0177c1s
Bowman, H.B. v1p1189c2s
Bowman, H.M. v6p0004c1s
Bowman, I. v6p0422c1s
v6p0514c1s
Bowman, J.C. v2p0008c2s
v2p0039c2s v3p0041c1s v3p0104c1s
v5p0023c2s v5p0305c2s v5p0482c1s
v5p0488c1s v5p0576c2s v6p0342c1s
Bowman, J.E. v1p1247c2s
v1p1389c2s
Bowman, J.F. v1p0002c1s
v1p0064c1s v1p0197c1s v1p0526c2s
v1p0942c1s v1p1180c1s
Bowman, L. v6p0458c2s
Bowman, Larrey v6p0218c2s
Bowman, M.M. v6p0045c2s
v6p0260c1s v6p0330c1s v6p0386c2s
v6p0387c1s v6p0551c2s v6p0570c1s
Bowman, R. v5p0312c1s
v6p0474c2s v6p0558c2s
Bowman, S.L. v1p1423c2s
v3p0041c1s v3p0217c1s v4p0017c1s
v4p0300c2s v4p0305c1s v4p0431c1s
v6p0412c1s
Bowman, S.M. v1p0624c2s
v1p1190c2m v1p1347c1s
Bowman, W. v1p0046c1s
v1p0776c1s
Bowne, B.P. v1p0434c2s
v1p0527c2s v1p0651c1s v1p0711c1s
v1p0761c1s v1p0901c1s v1p1062c1s
v1p1235c1m v1p1260c1s v1p1300c2s
v1p1301c1s v1p1338c1s v1p1358c1s
v1p1360c2s v1p1433c2s v2p0050c1s
v2p0280c1m v2p0283c2s v2p0369c1s
v3p0025c1s v3p0207c2s v3p0255c2s
v4p0190c2s v4p0191c2s v4p0214c1s
v4p0558c1s v5p0196c1s v6p0420c2s
v6p0521c2s v6p0610c1m
Bowne, C.W. v4p0284c2s
Bowne, E.G. v6p0014c2s
Bowne, E.S. v3p0173c1s
Bowne, M. v2p0153c2s
Bownell, A. v1p0773c1s
Bowra, H. v2p0108c2s
Bowring, Dr. v1p1436c1s
Bowring, E.A. v1p0444c1s
v1p1227c1s v1p1416c1s
Bowring, J. v1p0109c1s
v1p0113c1m v1p0220c2s v1p0233c2s
v1p0257c1s v1p0332c1s v1p0339c2m
v1p0373c1s v1p0377c2s v1p0382c2s
v1p0402c1s v1p0472c1s v1p0486c2s
v1p0553c2s v1p0795c1s v1p0942c1s
v1p1052c1s v1p1070c1s v1p1082c1s
v1p1228c2s v1p1278c2s v1p1301c1s
v1p1334c1s v2p0343c1s v2p0346c1s
Bowring, J., Sir v1p0234c1s
v1p0235c2s v1p0289c1s v1p0680c1s
v1p0806c1s v1p0962c2s v1p1194c1s
v1p1229c2s v3p0078c1s
Bowring, L.B. v4p0279c1s
Bowring, W.B. v3p0199c1s
v3p0301c1s
Bowyer, G. v1p0204c2s
Bowyer, G., Sir v1p0247c2s
Box, G.H. v6p0386c2s
Box, M.H. v4p0436c1s
v4p0462c1s v4p0475c1s
Boxall, C., Sir v6p0327c2s
Boxall, C.G. v4p0031c2s
v4p0470c2s
Boxall, G.E. v4p0022c1s
v4p0038c2s v5p0039c2s v6p0447c2s
v6p0576c2s
Boyan, W.H. v4p0499c1s
Boyce, A.S. v2p0482c2s
Boyce, C. v1p1112c1s
Boyce, Florence A. v5p0293c2s
Boyce, H. v6p0337c1s
Boyce, J.P. v1p0689c1s
Boyce, M. v5p0409c1s
Boyce, N. v4p0231c1s
v4p0249c2s v4p0624c1s v5p0160c2s
v5p0415c1s v6p0520c2s
Boyce, Neith v6p0223c1s
v6p0389c1s
Boyce, R. et al. v6p0659c2s
Boyce, W.W. v1p1285c1s
v2p0237c2s v2p0366c2s v2p0410c2s
v2p0455c1s
Boyd, A. v1p1328c2s
Boyd, A.K.H. v1p0007c1s
v1p0022c2s v1p0043c2s v1p0064c2s
v1p0074c1s v1p0104c2s v1p0137c2s
v1p0191c2s v1p0207c1m v1p0223c2s
v1p0229c1s v1p0256c1s v1p0286c2s
v1p0308c1s v1p0310c1s v1p0316c1s
v1p0335c2s v1p0344c2s v1p0353c2m
v1p0366c1s v1p0371c1s v1p0375c2s
v1p0425c2s v1p0459c2s v1p0491c1s
v1p0496c2s v1p0531c2s v1p0535c1s
v1p0560c1m v1p0584c1s v1p0590c1s
v1p0596c2s v1p0617c2s v1p0625c2s
v1p0688c1s v1p0708c2s v1p0736c2s
v1p0740c1s v1p0767c2s v1p0784c1s
v1p0813c1s v1p0826c2s v1p0851c1s
v1p0855c1s v1p0939c2m v1p0947c2s
v1p0976c1s v1p0979c1s v1p0988c2m
v1p1021c1s v1p1041c1s v1p1047c1s
v1p1064c2s v1p1070c1s v1p1100c2m
v1p1111c1s v1p1165c1s v1p1171c2s
v1p1211c2s v1p1218c2s v1p1221c2s
v1p1243c1s v1p1263c2s v1p1266c2s
v1p1270c1s v1p1305c2s v1p1310c2s
v1p1315c1s v1p1335c1s v1p1337c1s
v1p1339c1s v1p1358c1s v1p1371c1s
v1p1430c2s v1p1432c1s v1p1432c2s
v2p0001c1s v2p0037c2s v2p0152c1s
v2p0156c1s v2p0182c1s v2p0206c1s
v2p0209c2s v2p0269c2s v2p0293c1s
v2p0421c2s v2p0431c2s v2p0436c2s
v2p0447c1s v2p0472c1s v3p0017c2s
v3p0040c1s v3p0116c1s v3p0117c2s
v3p0204c1s v3p0206c1s v3p0315c2s
v3p0363c1s v3p0381c1s v3p0419c1m
v3p0438c1s v3p0460c2s v4p0111c1s
v4p0260c2s v4p0364c2s v4p0432c2s
v4p0435c2s v4p0545c1s v4p0558c2s
v5p0131c2s v5p0347c2s v5p0355c2s
v5p0418c1s v5p0440c1s
Boyd, A.S. v3p0462c2s
Boyd, A.S., Mrs. v5p0127c2s
v5p0408c2s v5p0541c2s v5p0598c1s
Boyd, C. v4p0115c2s
Boyd, C.E. v4p0115c1s
v5p0076c2s v5p0120c1s v5p0279c2s
v5p0601c1s v5p0627c1s
Boyd, C.W. v5p0008c2s
v5p0586c2s
Boyd, D. v1p1160c2s
Boyd, D.K. v5p0025c2s
v6p0154c2s
Boyd, Dr. v1p1047c2s
Boyd, E. v3p0090c2s
Boyd, E.E. v4p0600c2s
Boyd, F. v3p0278c1s
Boyd, G., Mrs. v5p0530c2s
Boyd, H.S. v1p0684c1s
Boyd, Harriet A. v5p0142c2m
Boyd, J. v3p0023c1s
Boyd, J.A. v1p0073c1s
Boyd, J.F. v2p0093c2s
v2p0140c2s
Boyd, J.H. v4p0545c1s
Boyd, J.O. v5p0057c2s
Boyd, J.S. v6p0178c2s
Boyd, M. v3p0417c1s
v5p0096c1s
Boyd, M.S. v5p0617c2s
v6p0004c1s v6p0281c2s v6p0344c1s
Boyd, Mabel v4p0343c2s
Boyd, Mary S. v5p0052c1s
v5p0254c1s v6p0103c2s v6p0131c2s
v6p0324c2s v6p0429c1s v6p0619c1s
Boyd, P. v1p0887c1s
v1p0988c2s v1p0998c1s
Boyd, R. v1p1042c1s
Boyd, R.J. v6p0624c2s
Boyd, T. v3p0002c1s
Boyd, T.M. v2p0232c2s
Boyd, W. v1p0618c2s
v2p0157c2s
Boyd, W.G. et al. v4p0081c1s
Boyd, W.K. v6p0012c1s
v6p0424c2s v6p0489c2s v6p0605c1s
Boyden, A.C. v4p0507c1s
Boyden, A.G. v3p0054c2s
v4p0026c2s v5p0413c2s
Boyden, A.G. et al. v5p0413c2s
Boyden, E. v2p0405c1s
Boyden, J. v1p0495c2s
Boyden, U.A. v1p0437c1s
v1p0923c2s
Boyden, W.C. v5p0028c1s
Boye and Rogers v1p0750c1s
Boye, M.H. v1p0666c1s
Boyer, A. v3p0156c2s
Boyer, E.M.Nicholl, Mrs. . v6p0004c1s
Boyer, H. v6p0167c1s
Boyer, Harriet v6p0098c2s
Boyer, J. v4p0500c1s
v5p0008c2s v5p0338c2s v5p0430c2s
v5p0431c1s v5p0432c1s v6p0143c1s
v6p0230c1s v6p0489c1s v6p0708c1s
Boyer, Jacques v5p0005c1s
Boyer, M.G. v4p0021c1s
v4p0300c2s v4p0497c2s
Boyer, M.T. v5p0499c1s
Boyer-Brown, E. v4p0571c2s
Boyerson, N. v5p0478c2s
Boyes, H.C. v1p0053c1s
v2p0263c2s
Boyes, J.F. v2p0101c1s
v3p0007c1s v3p0020c1s v3p0061c1s
v3p0093c2s v3p0126c2s v3p0162c1s
v3p0315c2s v3p0343c2s v3p0377c1s
v4p0324c1s v4p0433c1s
Boyesen, A. v6p0517c2s
Boyesen, H.H. v1p0043c2s
v1p0066c2s v1p0114c2s v1p0137c2s
v1p0139c1s v1p0160c2s v1p0189c1s
v1p0433c2s v1p0441c2s v1p0490c2s
v1p0535c1s v1p0562c2s v1p0570c2s
v1p0590c2s v1p0609c1s v1p0612c1s
v1p0624c1s v1p0677c1s v1p0710c2s
v1p0795c1s v1p0926c2m v1p0929c2s
v1p0930c1s v1p1071c1s v1p1084c1s
v1p1123c2s v1p1126c2s v1p1164c1s
v1p1257c2s v1p1274c1s v1p1286c1s
v1p1307c1s v1p1317c2m v1p1328c1s
v1p1339c1s v2p0013c1s v2p0013c2s
v2p0048c1m v2p0077c1s v2p0148c2s
v2p0176c1s v2p0203c1s v2p0242c2s
v2p0276c2s v2p0317c1m v2p0355c2s
v2p0407c1s v2p0426c1s v2p0448c2m
v3p0066c2s v3p0074c1s v3p0093c1s
v3p0100c1s v3p0101c1s v3p0106c2s
v3p0115c1s v3p0135c1s v3p0136c1s
v3p0151c2s v3p0162c2s v3p0171c1s
v3p0176c2s v3p0206c2m v3p0209c1m
v3p0239c2s v3p0250c2s v3p0306c1s
v3p0306c2s v3p0307c2s v3p0308c2m
v3p0317c1s v3p0326c2s v3p0334c2s
v3p0376c2s v3p0378c2s v3p0410c2s
v3p0439c1s v3p0468c1s v4p0062c2s
v4p0070c2s v4p0098c2s v4p0100c1s
v4p0101c2s v4p0141c1s v4p0160c2s
v4p0179c1s v4p0201c2s v4p0217c2s
v4p0256c1s v4p0267c2m v4p0272c1m
v4p0272c2m v4p0276c1s v4p0303c2s
v4p0320c2s v4p0356c2s v4p0384c2s
v4p0391c1s v4p0405c2s v4p0407c2m
v4p0408c2s v4p0421c2s v4p0427c2s
v4p0475c1s v4p0498c1m v4p0504c2m
v4p0533c1s v4p0586c2s v4p0604c2s
v4p0625c1s v4p0626c1s v4p0626c2s
v4p0636c2m v5p0414c2m v6p0022c1s
v6p0039c1s v6p0121c2s v6p0459c2s
Boyesen, H.H. et al. v3p0091c2s
Boyesen, H.H., Jr. v6p0152c1s
Boyesen, H.H., 2d v5p0516c2s
v6p0018c2s v6p0180c2s v6p0571c2s
Boyesen, I.K. v6p0460c2s
Boyington, W.W. v3p0018c2s
Boykin, J.C. v5p0511c2s
v5p0636c1s
Boyle, B. v4p0072c1s
v4p0347c2s v4p0536c2s
Boyle, C. v1p0082c1s
v1p0087c2s v5p0587c2s v5p0640c1s
Boyle, C.B. v1p0866c1s
Boyle, D. v4p0171c1s
v4p0605c1s
Boyle, E. v2p0316c1s
Boyle, E.R. v1p0560c1s
Boyle, E.V. v5p0276c2s
Boyle, F. v1p0067c1s
v1p0150c2s v1p0357c1s v1p0366c1s
v1p1322c1s v2p0001c1s v2p0049c2s
v2p0069c2s v2p0108c2s v2p0117c2s
v2p0144c2s v2p0210c2s v2p0319c2s
v2p0332c2s v2p0359c2s v2p0362c1s
v2p0395c1s v2p0413c1s v2p0427c2s
v3p0086c2s v3p0205c2s v3p0313c2m
v3p0383c2s v4p0048c2s v4p0124c2s
v4p0159c2s v4p0416c2s v4p0528c1s
v5p0237c1s v5p0509c2s v5p0555c1s
v5p0635c1s v6p0002c2s v6p0247c1s
v6p0469c2s v6p0526c1s v6p0536c1s
v6p0571c1s
Boyle, Frederick v4p0584c2s
Boyle, G.D. v4p0500c1s
v5p0182c1s
Boyle, H.E. v6p0216c2s
Boyle, H.R. v6p0585c2s
Boyle, J. v5p0464c2s
v5p0502c2s v6p0206c1s v6p0436c2s
Boyle, J.E. v6p0153c2s
v6p0448c2s v6p0665c2s
Boyle, J.F. v1p0629c1s
Boyle, J.R. v4p0485c1s
Boyle, James v6p0601c1s
Boyle, R. v4p0193c1s
Boyle, R., Mrs. v4p0077c1s
Boyle, R.C., Mrs. v5p0169c2s
v5p0255c1s
Boyle, S.P. v4p0255c1s
Boyle, V.F. v3p0203c1s
v3p0416c1s v4p0247c2s v4p0412c1s
v5p0034c2s v5p0065c2s v5p0106c1s
v5p0153c1s v5p0160c1s v5p0316c2s
v5p0419c1s v5p0424c2s v5p0440c1s
v5p0566c1s v5p0591c1s v6p0287c2s
Boyle, W. v6p0170c2s
Boylston, J. v4p0305c2s
Boyne, S.R. v2p0047c2s
Boynton, A.J. v6p0634c1s
Boynton, C.B. v1p0440c2s
Boynton, E.C. v1p0554c2s
v1p0563c1s
Boynton, E.M. v6p0547c1s
Boynton, E.N. v1p0453c1s
Boynton, F.D. v5p0264c2s
v5p0408c1m v5p0466c1s v6p0290c1s
Boynton, G.M. v1p0290c1s
Boynton, H. v1p1250c1s
v5p0462c2s v5p0639c2s
Boynton, H.C. v6p0616c2s
Boynton, H.V. v1p0163c2s
v1p1389c1s v1p1405c2s v3p0343c2s
v3p0444c2s v4p0102c2s v4p0426c2s
Boynton, H.W. v4p0232c2s
v6p0033c2s v6p0075c1s v6p0076c1s

v6p0155c2s v6p0173c1s v6p0287c1s
v6p0303c1s v6p0346c2s v6p0359c2s
v6p0360c2s v6p0426c2s v6p0485c2s
v6p0489c2s v6p0505c2s v6p0523c1s
v6p0532c2m v6p0629c1s v6p0635c2s
v6p0684c2s v6p0711c1s
Boynton, L. v5p0631c2s
v6p0003c2s
Boynton, M., Lady v4p0247c1s
Boynton, P.H. v6p0154c1s
Boynton, S.S. v3p0003c1s
v3p0048c1s v3p0088c2s v3p0111c2s
v3p0210c1s v3p0354c2s v3p0374c1s
v3p0419c2s v4p0083c2s v4p0089c1s
v4p0372c1s v4p0562c1s v4p0585c2m
v6p0594c1s
Boynton, W.E. v5p0396c2s
Boys, C.V. v2p0045c2m
v2p0127c1s v2p0138c1s v2p0286c1s
v2p0405c2s v3p0044c1s v3p0062c2s
v3p0071c1s v3p0192c2s v3p0350c2s
v3p0404c2s v3p0436c1s v4p0235c1s
v4p0440c2s v5p0061c1s v5p0131c2s
v5p0163c2s v5p0321c2s v6p0643c1m
Boys, H. v1p0197c2s
v1p1301c1s
Boys, J.De v4p0017c2s
Boys, Jaques de v5p0532c1s
Boys, W. v1p0710c1s
Boys-Smith, E.P. v5p0037c2s
Braam, J.W. v6p0555c1s
Brabant, E. v6p0007c1s
v6p0654c2s
Brabant, E.H. v6p0654c2s
Brabant, E.Y. v6p0565c1s
Brabazon, Lord v1p0258c1s
v2p0010c1s v2p0127c1s v2p0140c2s
v2p0340c2s v2p0468c2s v2p0477c1s
v3p0092c2s v3p0202c1s v3p0331c1s
v3p0433c2s v4p0013c2s v4p0566c2s
Brabazon, Lord and Barnett, S.A.
v2p0086c1s
Brabourne, Lord v2p0143c2s
v2p0187c2s v2p0208c2s v2p0225c2s
v3p0049c1s v3p0137c2s v3p0174c1s
v3p0219c2s v3p0221c1s v3p0222c1m
v3p0241c1s v3p0321c2s v3p0322c1s
v3p0431c1s v4p0174c1m v4p0183c1s
v4p0236c2s v4p0239c1s v4p0258c2s
Brabrook, E. v6p0296c1s
Brabrook, E.W. v1p0299c1s
v1p0299c2s v1p0491c2s v1p1153c2s
v2p0057c1s v2p0168c2s v3p0061c1s
v4p0215c2s v6p0230c2s v6p0242c2m
v6p0408c2s
Bracchi, A. v5p0128c2s
Brace, C.L. v1p0024c2s
v1p0030c2s v1p0219c1s v1p0229c2s
v1p0230c1s v1p0330c2s v1p0333c2s
v1p0485c2s v1p0615c2m v1p0675c2s
v1p0695c1s v1p0760c1s v1p0840c1s
v1p0915c2s v1p0916c1s v1p0917c1m
v1p0981c2m v1p1179c2s v1p1337c2m
v2p0077c1s v2p0081c2s v2p0134c2s
v5p0107c2s v5p0144c1s v6p0658c1s
Brace, D.B. v6p0376c2s
Brace, E.C. v1p0927c2s
v1p1374c1s
Brace, Emma v5p0074c2s
Brace, H. v1p0207c2s
v2p0349c1s v2p0351c1s
Brace, S.C. v1p0058c2s
Brace, W. v2p0255c2s
Brackenbury, C.B. v1p0665c2s
v1p0947c1s v3p0180c2s v3p0201c1s
v5p0556c2s
Brackenbury, H. v2p0223c1s
v2p0410c2s v4p0286c2s v5p0127c2s
v5p0301c1s v5p0505c1s
Brackenbury, H., Sir v5p0586c2s
Brackenbury, L. v4p0236c1s
Brackett, A. v1p0527c2s
Brackett, A.C. v1p0134c2s
v1p0271c1s v1p0303c1s v1p0392c1s
v1p0582c2s v1p0636c2s v1p0735c2s
v1p0842c1s v1p0950c1s v1p1187c1s
v1p1363c1s v3p0161c2s v3p0163c2s
v3p0201c1s v3p0359c2s v3p0411c2s
v4p0580c2s v4p0583c1s v4p0628c1s
v5p0586c1s
Brackett, A.G. v1p0058c1s
v1p0188c1s v1p0209c1s v1p0908c1s
v1p1435c1s v3p0026c1s v3p0052c2s
v3p0071c1s v3p0101c2s v3p0231c2s
v3p0267c2s v3p0272c1s v3p0277c1s
v3p0302c1s v3p0310c2s v3p0392c1s
v4p0083c2s v4p0520c2s v5p0098c2s
Brackett, C.F. v1p0498c2s
v3p0134c1s
Brackett, C.F. and Young, C.A.
v1p0384c1s
Brackett, F.P. v5p0372c2s
Brackett, J.R. v3p0299c1s
v4p0097c1s v5p0101c2s v5p0102c1s
v5p0179c2s v5p0187c2s v5p0613c1s
v5p0633c2s v6p0049c1s v6p0125c2s
v6p0627c1s
Brackett, J.S. v3p0459c1s
Brackett, R.N. and Branner, J.C.
v3p0326c2s
Brackett, R.N. and Williams, J.F.
v3p0303c2s
Brackett, W. v1p0755c1s
v1p0793c2s v1p1160c2s v2p0429c1s
Brackett, W.S. v1p1083c1s
Brackstad, H.L. v2p0048c1s
v4p0407c2s
Bracq, J.C. v3p0164c1s
v4p0376c2s v5p0011c2s v5p0216c2s
v5p0217c1s v5p0217c2s v5p0340c1s
v5p0503c1s v6p0393c2s v6p0455c2s
v6p0562c2s
Bradbrook, W. v4p0285c1s
v5p0028c2s v5p0432c2s v6p0689c1s
Bradbury, A.W. v1p0715c2s
Bradbury, E. v2p0075c2s
v2p0295c1s v4p0098c1s v4p0247c2s
v4p0299c2s v4p0352c2s v4p0369c2s
v4p0432c1m v4p0453c1m v4p0471c2s
v4p0495c1s v4p0498c2s v4p0633c2s
Bradbury, G.H. v4p0268c1s
Bradbury, H. v1p0901c2s
v1p1051c2s
Bradbury, H.B. v5p0618c1s
Bradbury, J.M. v1p0113c1s
Bradbury, R.H. v5p0103c2s
v5p0340c1s v5p0475c2s v5p0538c1s
v6p0222c1s v6p0489c1s v6p0526c2s
v6p0527c1s
Bradbury, R.H. and Partridge, E.A.
v6p0526c2s
Bradby, G.F. v6p0282c2s
Bradby, H.C. v5p0438c1s
Bradby, L.B. and Black, A.
v5p0201c1s
Braddeley, R.W. v1p0943c1s
Braddon, E. v4p0038c1s
v4p0270c1m v4p0495c2s v4p0521c1s
v4p0526c2s v4p0543c1s v4p0564c1m
Braddon, E. and Murray, D.C.
v3p0027c2s
Braddon, E.N. v4p0576c2s
Braddon, E.N.C. v4p0038c1s
Braddon, E.N.C., Sir v3p0420c2s
Braddon, E.N.Coventry v4p0037c2s
Braddon, J.B. v4p0502c1s
Braddon, M.E. v1p0018c2s
v1p0068c2s v1p0077c2s v1p0137c2s
v1p0154c1s v1p0221c2s v1p0277c2s
v1p0336c2s v1p0357c1s v1p0357c2s
v1p0432c2s v1p0449c1s v1p0606c1s
v1p0655c1s v1p0693c2s v1p0696c1s
v1p0716c2s v1p0731c1s v1p0770c2s
v1p0774c1s v1p0780c1s v1p0841c1s
v1p0888c2s v1p0889c2s v1p0942c1s
v1p0943c1s v1p0956c2s v1p1182c2s
v1p1200c2s v1p1202c1s v1p1237c1s
v1p1238c2s v1p1259c2s v1p1313c1s
v1p1376c2s v2p0294c1s v2p0409c1s
v3p0150c1s v3p0284c2s v4p0555c1s
v6p0376c2s
Braddon, Miss v4p0160c2s
Braden, C. v1p1095c1s
v2p0041c2s v2p0042c1s v2p0082c2s
v2p0195c1s v2p0221c1s v2p0284c2s
v3p0338c1s
Braden, G. v2p0244c2s
v4p0141c1s
Bradfield, C.M., Mrs. v6p0014c1s
Bradfield, T. v4p0015c1s
v4p0028c2s v4p0075c2s v4p0077c1s
v4p0093c2s v4p0197c2s v4p0198c1s
v4p0251c2s v4p0327c2s v4p0346c2s
v4p0448c2s v5p0087c1s v5p0192c2s
Bradford, A. v1p0015c2s
v1p0151c2s v1p0282c2s v1p0569c1s
v1p0572c2s v1p0731c2s v1p0758c1s
v1p1133c1s v1p1264c2s v1p1411c1s
Bradford, A.H. v2p0235c1s
v2p0415c1s v3p0128c2s v3p0194c2s
v3p0356c2s v4p0128c2s v4p0382c1s
v4p0426c2s v4p0438c1s v4p0531c1s
v5p0011c1s v5p0024c2s v5p0077c1s
v5p0083c1s v5p0133c1s v5p0145c1s
v5p0151c2s v5p0236c2s v5p0380c1s
v5p0414c1s v5p0473c1s v5p0562c1s
v6p0122c2s v6p0285c2s v6p0523c2s
v6p0537c2s v6p0623c2s v6p0670c1s
Bradford, A.H. and Briggs, C.A.
v4p0478c2s
Bradford, A.H. et al. v4p0185c2s
Bradford, A.S. v5p0072c1s
v5p0415c1s
Bradford, C. v6p0227c2s
Bradford, C.B. v3p0154c2s
v3p0373c1s v3p0437c1s
Bradford, E.A. v4p0013c2s
Bradford, G. v1p0048c2s
v1p0130c1s v1p0151c2m v1p0184c1s
v1p0272c2s v1p0294c2s v1p0341c2s
v1p0453c1s v1p0453c2s v1p0515c2s
v1p0545c2s v1p1025c2s v1p1077c2s
v1p1232c2s v1p1233c1s v2p0087c1s
v2p0151c2s v2p0165c2s v2p0295c1s
v2p0309c1s v2p0452c2s v2p0454c2s
v3p0096c2s v3p0292c1s v3p0343c1s
v3p0442c2s v4p0129c1s v4p0159c1s
v4p0202c1s v4p0211c1s v4p0273c2s
v4p0277c2s v4p0359c2s v4p0387c2s
v4p0546c1s v5p0637c1s
Bradford, G. and Bridgman, R.L.
v4p0127c1s
Bradford, G., jr. v3p0135c2s
v3p0207c2s v3p0323c1s v3p0377c1s
v3p0448c2s v4p0013c2s v4p0178c1s
v4p0326c2s v4p0436c2s v5p0520c2s
v6p0072c2s v6p0089c1s v6p0158c2s
v6p0657c2s v6p0684c2s
Bradford, G.B. v1p1267c1s
Bradford, G.P. v4p0074c2s
Bradford, I. v5p0078c1s
Bradford, J. v4p0389c2s
Bradford, J.E. v2p0172c1s
Bradford, J.S. v1p1223c1s
Bradford, L.C. v1p1297c1s
v5p0630c1s
Bradford, R. v6p0571c1s
Bradford, R.A. v5p0363c2s
Bradford, R.B. v5p0124c2s
v6p0636c2s
Bradford, S.S. v1p1262c2s
Bradford, T. v1p0731c1s
v1p0816c1s v1p1004c2s v1p1104c1s
Bradford, W. v1p0132c2m
v1p0220c1s
Bradford, W.J.A. v1p0079c1s
v1p0212c1m v1p0679c1s v1p0872c1s
v1p0901c2s
Bradford-Whiting, M. v4p0010c2s
v4p0619c1s v5p0168c1s v5p0523c2s
Bradford-Whiting, Mary ... v5p0634c1s
Bradish, A. v1p1328c1s
Bradlaugh, C. v3p0131c2m
v3p0183c1s v3p0212c1s v3p0239c1m
v3p0337c2s v3p0398c2s v3p0440c1s
v4p0533c2s
Bradlaugh, Chas. v4p0265c2m
Bradlaugh, W.R. v3p0053c1s
Bradlee, C.D. v1p0448c2s
v4p0519c2s
Bradlee, J.E. v2p0358c1s
Bradley, A.A. v6p0309c1m
Bradley, A.C. v1p0170c2s
v1p0890c2s v2p0307c1s v2p0394c1s
v6p0218c2s v6p0586c2s v6p0587c1s
v6p0588c1s v6p0653c1s
Bradley, A.G. v1p0141c2s
v1p0905c1s v2p0027c1s v2p0059c1s
v2p0089c1s v2p0187c1s v2p0195c1s
v2p0247c2s v2p0277c1s v2p0324c2s
v2p0360c2s v2p0447c2s v3p0011c1s
v3p0126c2s v3p0166c2s v3p0214c1s
v3p0315c2s v3p0321c1s v3p0339c1s
v3p0381c2s v3p0450c2s v3p0465c1s
v4p0041c1s v4p0133c2s v4p0201c1s
v4p0254c2s v4p0291c1s v4p0427c1s
v4p0506c1s v4p0587c2s v4p0605c2s
v4p0618c1s v5p0018c2s v5p0275c1s
v5p0322c2s v5p0453c2s v5p0592c1s
v5p0598c2s v5p0616c2m v6p0020c2s
v6p0097c2s v6p0236c1s v6p0239c2s
v6p0263c1s v6p0437c1s v6p0459c2s
v6p0545c1m v6p0592c2s v6p0683c2s
Bradley, C.B. v2p0445c2s
v3p0385c1s v6p0209c2s v6p0211c1s
v6p0380c1s v6p0458c1s
Bradley, C.F. v2p0290c2s
v3p0043c1s v3p0184c2s
Bradley, C.F. and Votaw, C.W.
v5p0058c2s
Bradley, C.S. v4p0455c2s
Bradley, C.W. v2p0340c2s
Bradley, E. v1p0024c2s
v1p0197c2s v1p0464c1s v1p0588c1s
v1p0754c2s v1p0770c1s v1p0773c2s
v1p1239c2s v1p1254c1s v1p1307c2s
v2p0036c2s v2p0430c2s v5p0636c1s
Bradley, E.T. v3p0461c1s
Bradley, Emily T. v3p0410c2s
Bradley, F.E. v4p0237c2s
Bradley, F.H. v1p0048c1s
v1p0457c1s v1p0506c2s v1p0509c1s
v1p1198c1s v1p1296c1s v1p1349c2s
v2p0027c2s v2p0097c1s v2p0273c1s
v2p0415c1s v2p0429c2s v3p0024c1s
v3p0334c2s v3p0355c2s v3p0429c1s
v4p0130c1s v4p0131c2s v4p0161c2s
v4p0464c1m v4p0465c1s v4p0467c2s
v4p0475c1s v4p0481c2s v4p0497c2s
v4p0537c2s v5p0131c2s v5p0369c2s
v5p0443c1s v6p0040c2s v6p0229c1s
v6p0410c2s v6p0659c2s v6p0698c2s
Bradley, G.G. v1p1063c1s
v2p0088c1s v2p0131c2s v3p0130c1s
Bradley, H. v1p0335c2s
v1p0409c2s v1p0892c1m v2p0009c1s
v2p0014c2s v2p0045c1s v2p0070c1s
v2p0086c1s v2p0143c2s v2p0144c2m
v2p0192c1s v2p0304c2s v2p0305c1s
v2p0305c2s v2p0374c1s v2p0380c1m
v3p0026c2s v3p0071c2s v3p0135c2s
v3p0140c1s v3p0168c1s v3p0175c1s
v3p0178c1s v3p0224c1s v3p0250c1s
v3p0416c2s v3p0425c1s v3p0451c2s
v4p0144c2s v4p0188c2s v4p0197c2s
v4p0302c1s v4p0339c1s v5p0011c2s
v5p0248c1s v5p0254c2s v5p0274c2s
v5p0359c1s v6p0121c2s v6p0470c2m
v6p0499c2s
Bradley, H. and Mayhew, A.L.

v3p0388c2s
Bradley, H. and Neilson, G.
v6p0709c2s
Bradley, H. et al. v4p0332c2s
Bradley, H.C. v6p0149c1s
v6p0633c2s v6p0713c1m
Bradley, H.G. v5p0188c2s
Bradley, H.L. v2p0472c2s
v3p0193c2s v3p0445c2s v4p0073c1s
v4p0110c1s v4p0153c2s v4p0159c2s
v4p0554c2s v4p0579c2s v5p0268c1s
v5p0268c2s v5p0425c1s v6p0250c1s
Bradley, J.C. v3p0328c1s
Bradley, J.E. v2p0132c1s
v3p0328c1s v3p0421c2s v3p0422c1s
v4p0123c2s v4p0170c2s v4p0512c1s
v5p0400c2s v5p0454c2s v5p0631c1s
v6p0503c2s
Bradley, J.P. v1p0178c2s
v3p0269c2s
Bradley, J.P. et al. v3p0119c1s
Bradley, J.W. v2p0275c2s
v2p0290c1s v2p0342c2s v4p0163c1s
v4p0244c1s v4p0602c2s
Bradley, L. v1p0628c1s
Bradley, M. v1p0983c2s
Bradley, M.C. v4p0072c2s
Bradley, M.E. v1p0076c1s
v1p0837c2s v1p1081c1s v2p0128c2s
Bradley, R.M. v6p0229c1s
v6p0566c1s v6p0593c2s v6p0693c2s
Bradley, Rose M. v6p0479c2s
Bradley, S.M. v1p0078c1s
Bradley, T.B. v1p0038c1s
v1p1030c1s v1p1088c2s v1p1375c2s
Bradley, T.W. v4p0354c2s
v4p0473c1s
Bradley, W.A. v6p0181c2s
v6p0213c2s v6p0700c1s
Bradley, W.E. v2p0007c1s
v4p0619c2s
Bradley, W.H. v4p0402c2s
v5p0436c2s
Bradley, W.P. v5p0558c2s
Bradley-Birt, F.B. v5p0559c2s
v6p0005c2s
Bradner, L., jr. v4p0056c2s
Bradsby, H.C. v3p0322c2s
Bradshaw, A. v2p0315c1s
Bradshaw, G. v5p0285c1s
Bradshaw, H. v2p0194c2s
Bradshaw, H. and Duff, E.G.
v2p0017c1s v2p0382c2s
Bradshaw, J. v4p0371c2s
Bradshaw, J.W. v4p0582c1s
v6p0262c2s
Bradshaw, K. v4p0499c2s
Bradshaw, M. v4p0568c2s
Bradshaw, W.R. v5p0230c1s
Bradwin, G. v3p0002c1s
Bradwood, W. v1p0147c1s
v1p0767c2s
Brady, A.C. v6p0414c1s
Brady, A.N. v5p0185c1s
Brady, C.J. v6p0224c1s
Brady, C.T. v5p0047c2s
v5p0064c2s v5p0078c2m v5p0093c2s
v5p0156c1s v5p0197c2s v5p0214c2s
v5p0222c2s v5p0259c2s v5p0282c1s
v5p0293c1s v5p0310c1s v5p0326c1s
v5p0349c1s v5p0386c2s v5p0474c1m
v5p0482c2s v5p0539c2m v5p0593c2s
v5p0608c1s v5p0625c2s v5p0628c1s
v5p0628c2m v6p0002c2s v6p0016c2s
v6p0025c1s v6p0037c2s v6p0045c2s
v6p0129c2s v6p0159c1m v6p0183c2s
v6p0211c1s v6p0240c1s v6p0263c2s
v6p0275c1s v6p0277c1s v6p0300c2s
v6p0310c2s v6p0345c2s v6p0358c1s
v6p0362c1s v6p0374c1s v6p0394c2s
v6p0465c1s v6p0476c1m v6p0482c2s
v6p0489c1s v6p0490c1s v6p0593c2s
v6p0608c1s v6p0630c1s v6p0648c1s
v6p0694c1s
Brady, C.T. et al. v6p0170c2s
Brady, E.B. v3p0070c1s
v3p0082c2s v3p0220c1s v3p0310c1s
v3p0339c1s v3p0365c1s v4p0020c1s
Brady, G. v1p0980c1s
Brady, G.S. v1p0292c2s
v1p0321c2s v1p0420c1s v1p0800c2s
v1p0836c1s v1p0950c2s v1p1173c1s
v1p1244c1s v4p0536c1s
Brady, H.B. v1p0256c2s
v1p0466c2s v1p0960c1s v1p0996c1s
Brady, J. v4p0347c1s
Brady, J.B. v3p0046c1s
v6p0259c1s
Brady, J.E. v5p0585c2m
Brady, J.E., jr. v5p0158c2s
Brady, J.F. v6p0122c1s
Brady, J.G. v4p0009c1s
v5p0011c1s v6p0701c2s
Brady, M. v2p0353c2s
v2p0423c1s
Brady, M.W. v1p1116c1s
Brady, Muriel A. v6p0472c1s
Brady, S.M. v1p0287c2s
v2p0113c2s
Brady, W.M. v1p0653c2s
v1p0654c1m v1p0658c2s v1p0661c1s
v1p1013c1s v2p0224c2s
Brae, A.E. v2p0377c1s
v2p0441c1s
Braekstad, H.L. v5p0414c2s
v6p0240c1s
Braekstad, H.L. and Staaff, K.
v6p0460c2s
Bragdon, C. v5p0081c2s
v6p0027c2s v6p0300c1s v6p0333c1m
v6p0394c1s v6p0544c1s v6p0546c1s
Bragdon, C.E. v6p0354c2s
Bragdon, C.F. v4p0024c1s
v4p0294c2s v4p0500c1s v6p0055c2s
v6p0338c1s
Bragdon, G.C. v3p0114c2s
Bragg, B. v2p0157c2s
Bragge, W. v1p0783c2s
Braham, A.D. v5p0215c1s
Braham-Barton, A. v4p0112c2m
Brahm, Otto v4p0505c1s
Braid, H.M. v5p0087c2s
Brailsford, H.N. v6p0087c2s
v6p0157c1s v6p0186c2s v6p0272c1s
v6p0274c2m v6p0369c1s v6p0392c1m
v6p0561c2s v6p0661c2s
Brailsford, W. v2p0009c1s
v2p0017c2s v2p0021c2s v2p0039c2s
v2p0089c1s v2p0089c2s v2p0163c2s
v2p0172c1s v2p0309c2s v2p0383c1s
v2p0445c2s v2p0481c1s v3p0030c1s
v3p0040c1s v3p0137c1s v3p0300c2s
v3p0307c1s v4p0020c1s
Brain, E. v4p0160c2s
v4p0501c1s v4p0517c2s v4p0544c1s
Brainard, C.G. v6p0296c1s
Brainard, C.R. v4p0459c1s
Brainard, D.L. v4p0406c1s
Brainard, E.P. v3p0460c2s
Brainard, F.R. v3p0020c1s
v3p0125c2s v3p0335c1s v3p0354c1s
Brainard, J.M. v5p0409c2s
Brainard, J.S. v6p0388c2s
Brainard, M.L. v1p0709c2s
v1p1309c1s
Brainard, Maggie D. v6p0298c1s
Brainard, O. v5p0082c2s
Brainard, T. v1p0215c1s
v1p1395c2s
Braine, C.D.H. v5p0185c2s
v5p0527c2s
Braine, S.E. v4p0285c1s
v4p0327c2s v4p0386c2s v5p0038c2s
v5p0331c2s
Braine, Sheila E. v4p0141c2s
v5p0318c1s
Brainerd, C. v1p1215c2s
Brainerd, C., jr. v5p0122c2s
v5p0468c2s
Brainerd, D.S. v1p0975c2s
Brainerd, E. v2p0167c2s
v2p0196c2s v2p0206c2s v2p0428c2s
Brainerd, E. and Harrison, J.A.
v2p0033c1s
Brainerd, E.P. v2p0405c2s
Brainerd, Eleanor H. v6p0100c1s
v6p0182c1s
Brainerd, Eleanor Hoyt ... v6p0020c1s
Brainerd, Ezra v5p0397c1s
Brainerd, I.H. v4p0143c1s
v4p0265c2s
Brainerd, M.B. v2p0118c2s
Brainerd, T.H. v4p0485c2s
Brainerd, W. v1p0759c2s
Braislin, W.C. v4p0407c2s
Braithwaite, E.E. v6p0062c2m
Braithwaite, R. v1p0875c1s
Braithwaite, W. v6p0472c2s
Braithwaite, W.J. v5p0457c2s
Brakspear, H. v5p0322c1s
Brale, S. v2p0195c2s
Braley, A.W. v4p0075c2s
Braley, E.W. v2p0285c1s
Braley, G. v4p0068c2s
Bram, H.A. v6p0122c1s
Bram, S.Z. v2p0041c2s
Bramah, E. v6p0712c2s
Braman, H.D. v5p0640c1s
Braman, M.P. v1p0310c2s
Bramble, C.A. v5p0022c2s
v5p0050c2s v5p0094c2s v5p0156c2s
v5p0225c1s v5p0327c1s v5p0385c2s
v5p0395c2s v5p0524c2s v5p0617c2s
Bramble, C.H. v5p0635c1s
Brame, C.E. v1p1440c2s
Brame, C.M. v1p0361c2s
Brame, J.S.S. v5p0200c1s
v6p0244c1s
Bramerton, A.E.H. v6p0012c1s
Bramhall, E.C. v5p0146c1s
Bramhall, F.J. v5p0477c1s
Bramhall, J.T. v5p0604c1s
Bramley, E.H. v2p0265c1s
v2p0465c1s
Bramston, M. v3p0309c1s
v5p0218c1s v5p0609c1s
Bramwell, F. v2p0281c2s
v3p0055c1s v4p0091c1s
Bramwell, F., Sir v3p0137c1s
Bramwell, F.J. v1p0502c1s
v1p0783c1s v1p0815c2s v1p1041c1s
v1p1078c2s v1p1248c2s v1p1249c1s
v1p1250c1s v2p0141c1s v2p0141c2s
v3p0353c1s
Bramwell, F.J. and Easton, E.
v1p0766c2s
Bramwell, F.J., Sir v2p0281c2m
Bramwell, Lord v2p0107c1s
v2p0124c1s v2p0221c2s v2p0277c2s
v3p0170c1s v3p0220c1s v3p0268c2s
v3p0346c1s v3p0431c1s v4p0141c2s
Bramwell, M. and Best, L.S.
v3p0206c1s
Branch, A.H. v5p0260c1s
v5p0521c2s v5p0539c1s v5p0578c2s
v5p0645c1s v6p0128c2s
Branch, Anna H. v5p0490c1s
v6p0584c2s v6p0664c2s
Branch, C. v1p1254c2s
Branch, C.J. v1p1272c1s
v1p1401c2s
Branch, L.C. v4p0457c2s
Branchi, E. v2p0111c2s
Brand, A.E. v4p0390c1s
v4p0398c2s v4p0453c2s v5p0390c1s
v5p0390c2s
Brand, A.H. v3p0462c2s
Brand, C. v3p0164c2s
Brand, H.R. v1p0720c2s
v1p0762c2s
Brand, J. v1p0393c1s
v1p0547c2s v1p0676c2s v1p0907c2s
v1p1114c2s v1p1129c1s v1p1318c1m
v2p0292c1s v4p0057c1s v6p0125c2s
Brand, J.E. v6p0624c2s
Brand, R.H. v6p0007c2s
v6p0266c2s v6p0656c2s
Brand, W.F. v2p0175c2s
v2p0282c2s v5p0100c2s
Brand, W.H. v1p0734c1s
v1p1049c2s v1p1346c2s
Brandeis, L.D. v3p0190c2s
v6p0322c1s v6p0364c1s v6p0652c1s
v6p0652c2s
Brandenburg, B. v6p0015c2s
v6p0069c1s v6p0090c2s v6p0094c1s
v6p0120c1s v6p0223c2s v6p0256c1s
v6p0268c2s v6p0308c1m v6p0309c1s
v6p0562c1s v6p0606c1s v6p0632c2s
v6p0655c2s
Brander, G. and Pegge, S.. v1p0135c1s
Brander-Dunbar, Lieut. and
Parkinson, F.B. v5p0538c2s
Brandes, F.H. v2p0126c1s
v2p0196c1s v2p0204c2s v2p0387c1s
v2p0425c2s
Brandes, G. v5p0158c2s
v6p0130c2s v6p0262c1s v6p0305c2s
v6p0532c1s v6p0539c1s
v6p0677c1s
Brandi, S.M. v2p0333c1s
v2p0376c2s v3p0228c2s v4p0326c2s
Brandicourt, V. v4p0286c1s
v4p0360c2s
Brandin, L. v6p0479c1s
Brandin, L. and Seccombe, T.
v6p0288c1s
Brandini, Arturo v6p0124c1s
Brandis, A.von v6p0670c2s
Brandis, D. v3p0158c1s
v3p0367c1s v4p0208c2s v4p0209c1s
v4p0566c2s v5p0214c2s v5p0285c2s
v6p0319c1s
Brandl, A. v3p0091c1s
Brandl, S.M. v4p0452c2s
Brandon, C. v1p0753c2s
v1p0783c1s
Brandon, R. v3p0352c1s
Brandreth, H. v1p0787c1s
v1p1122c2s
Brandt, A. v6p0690c1s
Brandt, B. v4p0605c1s
Brandt, C. v6p0676c1s
Brandt, E. v1p1011c2s
Brandt, G.R. v6p0559c1s
Brandt, H.C.G. v3p0139c2s
Brandt, L. v5p0365c1s
v5p0532c1s v6p0146c2s v6p0170c2s
v6p0331c1s v6p0446c2s v6p0453c1s
v6p0472c2s v6p0564c1s v6p0568c2s
v6p0580c1s v6p0660c1s
Brandt, Lilian v6p0448c1s
Brandt, M.von v5p0020c1s
v5p0108c2m v5p0111c2s v5p0230c2s
v5p0231c1s v5p0446c1s v5p0542c1s
v5p0586c2s v6p0119c2s
Brandt, V.De v6p0619c1s
Brandt, Van v5p0502c2s
Brandt, W.V. v5p0231c1s
Branford, G. v1p0184c1s
Branford, V. v6p0188c1s
Branford, V.V. v5p0399c2s
v5p0515c1s v6p0602c1m
Branford, Victor V. v6p0128c1s
Brangwyn, F. v5p0235c2s
v5p0543c1s
Brann, H.A. v1p1083c2s
v2p0034c2s v2p0052c2s v2p0106c2s
v2p0140c1s v2p0158c1s v2p0167c1s
v2p0195c2s v2p0244c2s v2p0277c1s

v2p0294c1s v2p0306c1s v2p0313c1s
v2p0331c1s v2p0358c2s v2p0388c1s
v3p0170c1s v3p0246c2s v3p0247c1s
v3p0364c2s v4p0488c1s v5p0290c2s
v5p0492c2s v6p0473c2s
Brannan, J.W. v5p0257c1s
Branner, J.C. v2p0213c2s
v2p0222c1s v2p0249c2s v2p0440c2s
v3p0003c1s v3p0009c2s v3p0151c1m
v3p0169c2s v4p0026c2s v4p0070c1s
v4p0136c1s v4p0394c2s v4p0463c2s
v5p0024c1s v5p0042c2s v5p0491c2s
v6p0222c1s v6p0234c2s v6p0433c1s
v6p0568c1s
Branner, J.C. and Brackett, R.N.
v3p0326c2s
Branner, J.C. and Means, J.H.
v4p0385c2s v4p0472c1s
Branner, J.C. and Walcott, C.D.
v6p0667c2s
Brannigan, F. v5p0445c1s
Branscombe, A. v4p0612c1s
Bransen, E.C. v6p0605c1s
Branson, D. v4p0477c2m
Branson, D.C. v6p0332c1s
v6p0501c2s
Branson, F. v1p1214c1s
Branson, W.J. v5p0098c1s
v5p0413c1s
Branson, W.P. v3p0090c1s
Branston, M. v4p0536c2s
Brant, H.C.G. v2p0192c1s
Brant, J.R. v1p0664c2s
Brant, T.L. v6p0515c1s
Brantegham, A.van v6p0587c2s
v6p0627c2s
Branthwayt, E. v1p0776c1s
v1p0795c1s v1p1147c1s v1p1304c2s
v1p1315c1s
Brantley, E. v2p0026c2s
Brantley, J.T. v1p0392c1s
Brantley, W.T. v1p0020c2s
Brantly, W.T. v5p0261c2s
Braren, J.S. v6p0123c1s
Braschi, V.M. and Ordonez, E.
v6p0414c1s
Brashear, J.A. v2p0343c2s
v2p0374c2s v3p0272c2s v4p0117c2s
v4p0410c1s v4p0568c1m v5p0012c2s
v5p0095c1s v5p0235c2s v5p0367c2s
v5p0563c2m v6p0361c1s
v6p0671c1s
Brashear, J.A. and Perrine, C.D.
v5p0314c2s
Brasher, R.I. v3p0397c1s
Brashfield, T.N. v2p0051c2s
Brassey v4p0278c2s
Brassey, A. v1p0583c2s
v1p0961c1s v2p0179c2s v4p0634c1s
Brassey, Lady v2p0134c2s
Brassey, Lord v2p0455c1s
v3p0050c2s v3p0141c1s v3p0181c1s
v3p0391c1s v4p0237c1s v4p0280c2s
v4p0617c2s v5p0136c1s v5p0246c2s
Brassey, Lord and Colomb, P.H.
v3p0182c1s
Brassey, Mrs. v1p1269c2s
Brassey, T. v1p0165c2s
v1p0299c1s v1p0415c1s v1p0547c1s
v1p0714c1m v1p0901c2s v1p1129c2s
v1p1174c1s v1p1192c1s v1p1269c2s
v1p1319c1s v2p0187c1s v2p0223c1s
v2p0382c2s v2p0425c2s v3p0297c2s
v5p0039c1s v5p0611c2s v6p0268c1s
Brassey, T., Sir v2p0481c2s
v5p0244c2s
Brassey, T.A. v3p0027c2s
v3p0223c2s v4p0237c2s v4p0238c1s
v5p0245c2s v5p0246c1s v6p0267c2s
Brassler, C.A. v6p0291c1s
v6p0594c2s
Brastow, L.O. v2p0016c2s
v2p0081c1s v2p0132c2s v2p0357c2s
v2p0384c2s v3p0136c1s v3p0281c1s
v6p0040c2s v6p0642c2s
Brathwaite, J.W. v5p0469c1s
Bratton, J. v2p0395c2s
Brauer, A. v4p0516c2s
Braun, A. v1p1364c1s
v6p0253c2s
Braun, Dr. v1p0247c2s
Braun, E. v1p0064c2s
v1p1195c2s
Braun, H.A. v1p0580c2s
v1p1033c1s
Braun, K. v2p0193c2s
Braun, O. v3p0170c2s
Braun, X. v1p1369c2s
Braun-Gizychiu, Lucy v6p0252c1s
Braune, E. v2p0176c1s
Brauner, B. and Young, S.. v3p0009c2s
Brauns, Prof. v2p0006c1s
Brausewetter, E. v5p0510c1s
Brawley, W.H. v6p0668c1s
Braxton, A.C. v6p0151c2s
v6p0348c1s v6p0680c1s
Bray, A. v2p0291c2s
Bray, C. v1p0157c1s
v1p1006c2s
Bray, Caroline and Hennell, Sara
v6p0200c2s
Bray, E. v3p0081c2s
Bray, F.C. v5p0240c2s
v6p0529c2s
Bray, F.G. v6p0528c2s
Bray, Isaiah v4p0369c1s
Bray, J.W. v4p0632c1s
v5p0522c1s
Bray, R.A. v5p0116c2s
Bray, S. v5p0509c1s
Bray, Vicar of v6p0095c1s
Bray, W. v1p0015c2s
v1p0245c2s v1p0585c2s v1p0708c1s
v1p0770c2s v1p1008c2s v1p1067c2s
v1p1102c1s v1p1122c2s v1p1219c1s
v1p1318c1s v1p1385c2s
Bray, W. and Willis v1p1122c2s
Bray, W.F. v6p0058c1s
Braybook, E.M. v6p0307c2s
Brayley, A.W. v4p0069c1m
v4p0521c2s v6p0470c1s
Brayley, E.W. v1p1091c1s
v2p0425c1s
Brayley, G. v4p0389c1s
Brayton, A.P. v6p0688c1s
Brayton, G.A. v1p0425c2s
Brayton, J.G. v6p0093c1s
Brayton, L.F. v6p0143c1s
Braz, A.Le v5p0077c2s
v6p0167c1m
Braz, Anatole Le v5p0012c2s
v5p0077c2s
Brazer, J. v1p0037c1s
v1p0090c1s v1p0112c1s v1p0176c1s
v1p0215c1s v1p0242c2s v1p0336c1s
v1p0356c1m v1p0392c1s v1p0499c1s
v1p0555c1s v1p0610c1s v1p0684c1s
v1p0798c1s v1p1030c2s v1p1094c1s
v1p1132c1s v1p1176c2s v1p1250c1s
Brazier, A. v6p0369c1s
Brazier, A.O. v5p0239c2s
Brazier, J. v1p0176c2s
Brazier, S. v6p0492c2s
v6p0651c2s
Breakell, M.L. v6p0704c1s
Breaker, J.M.C. v1p0096c2s
v1p0397c2s v1p0496c1s
Breal, A. v5p0191c1s
v5p0220c2s
Breal, M. v5p0325c1s
v5p0468c1s
Brearey, F.W. v1p0008c2s
v1p0463c2m v2p0158c2m
Breasted, J.H. v4p0172c2m
v4p0458c2s v4p0465c2s v5p0173c2s
v5p0181c1m v5p0571c2s v6p0196c1s
v6p0410c1s v6p0495c2s
Breazeale, J.F. v6p0694c2s
Brebner, A. v5p0267c1s
Breck, E. v6p0561c2s
Breck, H.G. v6p0497c1s
Breck, H.S. v6p0093c1s
v6p0095c1s v6p0416c1s
v6p0695c1s
Breck, Katharine H. v6p0628c1s
Breck, M. v4p0254c2s
Breck, M.H. v1p0138c2s
Breck, R.L. v1p0240c1s
Brecke, Edward v5p0631c2s
Breckenridge, C.P. v3p0202c1s
Breckenridge, Dr. v1p1342c2s
Breckenridge, J.E. and Kreider, D.A.
v4p0454c2s v4p0535c2s
Breckenridge, R.M. v4p0044c1s
v4p0086c1s v4p0424c2s v5p0046c1s
v5p0149c2s v5p0162c2s
Breckenridge, S.F. v4p0057c2s
v5p0363c1s
Breckenridge, W.L. v1p0275c2s
Breckinridge, J. v1p0852c1s
v1p1103c2s
Breckinridge, J.C. v1p0228c1s
v1p0881c1s v1p1388c1s
Breckinridge, J.S. v3p0201c2s
Breckinridge, R.J. v1p0332c1s
v1p0706c1s v1p1155c2s
Breckinridge, S.P. v6p0355c2s
v6p0704c2s
Breckinridge, S.P. and Abbott, E.
v6p0704c1s
Breckinridge, W.C.P. v3p0299c1s
v3p0420c1m
Breckinridge, W.C.P. and
Republican, A. v3p0443c2s
Bredin, J. v5p0513c2s
Bredius, A. v2p0126c1s
Breed, D. v1p1003c1s
Breed, D.R. v4p0051c1s
v4p0108c2s
v4p0461c2s
Breed, M.B. and Keiser, E.H.
v4p0349c2s
v4p0011c2s
Breed, W.P. v2p0352c2s
v2p0353c1s
Breed, W.R. v6p0122c1s
Breen, A.E. v4p0469c2s
Breen, H. v2p0035c2s
Breen, J. v1p0281c2s
v1p0804c1m v1p0865c2s v1p1267c2s
v1p1291c2s
Breen, J.D. v4p0358c2s
Breen, J.W. and Walker, A.
v1p1342c1s
Breese, J.L. v4p0440c2s
Breets, Dr. v1p0980c1s
Breeze, S.N. v3p0468c2s
Bregy, K. v6p0607c1s
v6p0644c1s
Bregy, Katherine v6p0156c1s
v6p0277c1s v6p0345c1s
Brehm, A.E. v2p0018c1s
v2p0046c2s v2p0157c1s v2p0295c1s
v2p0401c2s
Breidenbaugh, E.S. v1p0745c2s
v1p0844c1s v1p1161c1s v1p1239c1s
Breitenbach, L.M. v6p0508c1s
Breitenbach, W. v2p0357c1s
Bremen, W.N. v6p0497c2s
Bremen, W.V. v5p0330c2s
v5p0398c1s
Bremen, W.von v5p0616c2s
Bremer, F. v1p0072c2s
v1p0245c1s v1p0413c1s v1p1274c2s
v1p1375c2s v1p1414c2s
Bremner, C.S. v4p0194c2s
v4p0245c1s v4p0628c1s v5p0344c2s
Bremner, Christina v3p0469c1s
Bremont, A.de v3p0002c2s
v3p0037c1s
Bremont, F. v2p0406c1s
Bren, R. v6p0484c2s
Brenan, B. v6p0186c2s
Brenan, G. v5p0032c1s
v5p0242c2s v5p0315c2s v5p0491c2s
v5p0619c2s v6p0377c2s
Brenan, Gerald v5p0152c2s
Brenan, J.C. v1p0178c1s
v1p0605c1s v1p0689c2s v1p0705c2s
v1p0757c1s v1p0886c1s v1p0981c1s
v1p0993c2s v1p1174c2s v1p1258c1s
Brench, D.C. v4p0150c2s
Brenchley, J. v5p0369c1s
Brenda v3p0390c1s
Brendel, F. v1p0153c1s
v1p0461c2s
Brendle, D.F. v1p0564c2s
v3p0013c2s
Brendlinger, P.F. v3p0106c2s
Brenet v5p0351c1s
Brenet, M. v5p0094c2s
Brengle, F. v2p0291c2s
Brengle, H.G. v3p0005c2s
Brennan, E. v6p0218c1s
Brennan, Eliz. v6p0351c2s
Brennan, G.H. v4p0359c2s
Brennan, M.S. v2p0443c1s
v3p0133c1s
Brenner, J.C. v6p0283c1s
Brenon, E.St.J. v2p0072c2s
Brenon, F.St.J. v4p0361c1s
Brenon, St.J., Mrs. v2p0266c2s
Brent, C. v2p0016c1s
Brent, C.H. v6p0016c1s
v6p0334c1s v6p0418c2s v6p0492c2s
v6p0494c2m v6p0712c1s
Brent, G.L. v1p0967c1s
Brent, H.J. v1p0504c1s
v1p0618c1s v1p0773c2s
Brent, J. v1p0040c1s
v1p0184c2s v6p0053c2s v6p0081c2s
v6p0419c2s v6p0687c1s
Brent, J.C. v1p0011c2s
v1p0203c1s v1p0889c2s
Brent, J.L. v1p1343c1s
Brent, W.C. v1p0903c1s
v1p1399c2s
Brentano, E. v4p0450c1s
Brentano, L. v5p0469c2s
v6p0205c2s
Brentnall, C.F. and Day, L.F.
v6p0307c2s
Brenton, D.G. v4p0550c2s
Brents, T.W. v3p0357c1s
Brentworth, S. v4p0154c2s
Brereton, A. v2p0001c1s
v2p0035c2m v2p0123c1s v2p0161c1s
v2p0200c2s v2p0230c1s v2p0302c1s
v2p0328c1s v2p0361c1s v2p0372c2s
v2p0400c1s v3p0117c1s v3p0388c2s
v3p0427c1s v4p0003c1s v4p0293c1s
v4p0512c1s v4p0543c2s v4p0570c2s
v5p0547c2s v5p0574c1s
Brereton, Austin v6p0329c2s
Brereton, C. v5p0178c2m
v5p0517c2s v6p0191c1s v6p0192c1m
v6p0194c1s v6p0273c1s v6p0384c1s
v6p0423c2s v6p0581c1s
Brereton, C.S.H. v5p0177c2s
Brereton, H.C. v6p0130c2s
v6p0238c1s
Brereton, J.J. v3p0327c1s
Brereton, J.L. v1p0209c1s
v2p0388c1s
Brereton, K. v6p0072c1s
v6p0654c2s
Brereton, O.S. v1p0272c1s
v1p0585c1s v1p1129c1s v1p1380c2s
Brereton, R.P. v6p0571c2s
Breschkovsky, C. v6p0246c2s

Breschkovsky, Catherine .. v6p0557c1s
Breslin, J.W. v4p0152c1s
v5p0203c2s v5p0216c1s v5p0296c2s
Breslin, J.William v5p0309c1s
Bresslau, M.H. v2p0075c2s
Brester, A. v4p0545c2s
Brester, A., jr. v4p0545c2m
v4p0556c2m v4p0557c1s
Bretherton, B.J. v5p0186c2s
Bretherton, R.H. v5p0157c1s
v5p0160c2s v6p0609c1s
Breton, Adela C. v6p0023c2s
Breton, J.Le v5p0316c2s
Breton, John C. v5p0127c2s
Breton, John Le v5p0361c2m
v5p0499c2s v5p0555c1s
Breton, P. v1p0349c1s
Brett, A.J. v2p0152c2s
Brett, E.H. v4p0435c1s
Brett, F. v2p0477c2s
Brett, G.P. v6p0512c1s
v6p0523c1s v6p0595c1s
Brett, G.P. et al. v6p0532c2s
Brett, Geo.P. v6p0149c1s
v6p0595c1s
Brett, J. v1p0382c1s
v1p0899c2s v4p0165c1s v4p0319c1s
v4p0473c2s v4p0571c1s v5p0480c1s
Brett, J.E. v5p0567c1s
Brett, M.P. v5p0571c1s
Brett, P.B. v3p0306c1s
Brett, R.B. v3p0239c2s
v3p0337c2s v4p0105c1s v4p0364c1s
v4p0372c2s v4p0423c1s v4p0444c2s
v4p0603c2m
Brett, R.B. and Arnold, A.
v2p0189c2s
Brett, R.B. and Cowper, Earl
v3p0182c2s
Brett, W.H. v2p0482c2s
v3p0088c1m v3p0249c1m v3p0400c1s
v4p0329c1s v4p0330c1m v5p0333c1s
v5p0337c1s v6p0131c2s v6p0374c1s
v6p0374c2s v6p0522c2s
Brettingham, M. v2p0326c1s
Bretton, A. v2p0470c2s
Breuer, J.B. v4p0522c2s
Brevoort, I. v5p0496c2s
Brevoort, J.C. v1p0028c1s
v1p0184c1s v1p0272c2s v1p0280c2s
v1p0833c1s v1p1230c2s v2p0459c2m
Brew, M.W. v3p0339c1s
v3p0445c2s
Brewer, C.D. v1p0367c2s
Brewer, D.C. v5p0094c1s
Brewer, D.J. v3p0346c2s
v5p0125c1s v6p0025c1s v6p0151c1s
v6p0365c1m v6p0537c1s v6p0669c2s
v6p0687c2s
Brewer, D.T. v6p0348c1s
Brewer, E. v2p0029c2s
v2p0050c2s v2p0260c1s v2p0314c2s
v3p0092c1s v3p0380c2s v5p0120c2s
v5p0440c2s
Brewer, F. v1p0928c1s
Brewer, F.N. v6p0114c2s
Brewer, F.P. v1p0272c2s
v1p1273c2s v2p0356c1s
Brewer, G.W. v1p1169c1s
Brewer, H.W. v1p0052c2s
v1p0515c2s v1p0683c2s v3p0256c1s
v4p0107c2s v4p0339c2s v4p0407c2s
v4p0490c2s v4p0613c2s v5p0013c2s
v5p0255c1s v5p0346c1s v6p0385c1s
Brewer, J.A. v5p0059c2s
Brewer, Mrs. v3p0323c1s
v4p0302c1s v4p0339c1s v4p0542c1s
Brewer, R. v3p0375c1s
Brewer, R.H. v6p0132c2s
v6p0545c2s
Brewer, T.A. v1p0882c1s
Brewer, T.M. v1p0076c1s
v1p0135c1s v1p0135c2m v1p0136c1s
v1p0136c2s v1p0137c2s v1p0430c2s
v1p0949c1s v1p1212c1s
Brewer, W.H. v1p0187c2m
v1p0279c1s v1p0508c2s v1p0565c1s
v1p0876c2s v1p1016c1s v1p1217c2s
v1p1320c2s v1p1354c1s v2p0088c1s
v2p0207c2s v3p0300c2s v3p0301c1s
v4p0166c2s v4p0550c1s v5p0027c1s
v5p0346c2s v6p0512c1s
Brewer, W.M. v5p0385c1s
v6p0010c2s v6p0082c2s v6p0598c1s
Brewer, W.W. v5p0271c1s
Brewerton, G.D. v1p0203c1s
v1p0912c2s v1p1400c2s
Brewster, A. v1p0066c1s
v1p0469c2s v1p0627c1s v1p0739c1s
v1p1124c2s v1p1378c2s
Brewster, A.H. v2p0164c1s
v2p0329c2s v3p0392c1s
Brewster, A.R. v4p0590c2s
Brewster, B., Sir v1p0976c2s
Brewster, B.B. v6p0076c1s
Brewster, C.B. v3p0328c1m
v4p0188c1s v4p0558c1s
Brewster, C.E. v4p0630c2s
Brewster, D. v1p0004c2s
v1p0041c2s v1p0218c2s v1p0279c1s
v1p0333c1s v1p0437c2s v1p0746c2s
v1p0747c1s v1p0850c2s v1p1091c1s
v1p1390c2s
Brewster, D., Sir v1p0010c2s
v1p0029c1s v1p0044c2s v1p0050c2s
v1p0055c1s v1p0055c2s v1p0056c1s
v1p0067c2s v1p0070c1s v1p0070c2m
v1p0071c1m v1p0150c2s v1p0162c1s
v1p0164c2m v1p0202c2s v1p0206c1s
v1p0278c1s v1p0278c2s v1p0281c2s
v1p0305c1s v1p0313c1m v1p0327c2s
v1p0329c2s v1p0348c2s v1p0400c2s
v1p0408c1s v1p0412c1s v1p0437c2m
v1p0468c2s v1p0497c2s v1p0508c1m
v1p0509c1s v1p0524c1s v1p0525c2s
v1p0531c2s v1p0558c1s v1p0613c2s
v1p0639c2s v1p0698c2m v1p0746c2s
v1p0747c2s v1p0748c1s v1p0748c2m
v1p0749c1s v1p0762c2s v1p0787c1s
v1p0794c1s v1p0820c2s v1p0829c2s
v1p0835c1s v1p0835c2s v1p0836c1s
v1p0900c1s v1p0900c2s v1p0906c2m
v1p0923c1s v1p0923c2s v1p0936c1s
v1p0945c1s v1p0968c2s v1p0976c2s
v1p0978c2s v1p0982c2s v1p0983c1s
v1p1003c2s v1p1004c1s v1p1005c2m
v1p1035c2s v1p1070c2s v1p1073c2s
v1p1077c1s v1p1079c1s v1p1130c2s
v1p1135c1s v1p1161c2s v1p1162c2s
v1p1163c1m v1p1165c1s v1p1172c1s
v1p1196c1s v1p1212c1s v1p1238c2s
v1p1252c2s v1p1289c2s v1p1291c2s
v1p1292c1s v1p1303c2s v1p1309c2s
v1p1356c1s v1p1375c1m v1p1390c1s
v1p1393c1m v1p1394c2s v1p1404c2s
v1p1416c1s v1p1432c2s v1p1438c2s
Brewster, E.H.G. v5p0482c2s
Brewster, E.T. v5p0405c2s
v5p0624c1s v6p0165c2s v6p0214c2s
v6p0585c2s
Brewster, F. v2p0362c2s
Brewster, H. v6p0638c2s
Brewster, H.L. v6p0163c1s
Brewster, H.P. v4p0266c2s
Brewster, L.D. v6p0141c1s
Brewster, Margaret v6p0597c1s
Brewster, W.L. v6p0371c1s
Brewster, W.N. v5p0109c2s
v5p0112c1s v5p0302c1s v6p0421c2s
v6p0509c1s
Brewster, W.T. v4p0349c1s
Brewtnall, E.F. v4p0136c2s
v4p0624c1s
Briant, R. v5p0448c2s
v5p0534c1s
Brice, A.M. v4p0025c1s
v4p0295c2s v5p0094c1s v5p0173c1s
v5p0187c1s v5p0382c1s v5p0415c1s
v5p0419c1s v5p0502c2s v5p0503c2s
v5p0504c1s v6p0008c2s v6p0128c1s
v6p0148c2s v6p0692c1s
Brice, J. v1p0698c1s
Brice, J.J. v3p0297c2s
Brice, L.S. v3p0278c2s
Bricka, M. v2p0467c1s
Brickdall, C.F. v5p0324c1s
Brickman, W.E. v5p0106c2s
v5p0563c2s
Bricknell, A.J.G. v5p0426c1s
Brickwell, A.J. v4p0240c2s
v4p0337c2s
Bridel, G. v2p0448c2s
Bridell-Fox, E.F. v3p0057c1s
Bridenbaugh, S.R. v1p1090c1m
v1p1118c1s v5p0118c1s
Bridge, A. v6p0709c1s
Bridge, C. v1p0468c2s
v1p1263c2s v1p1316c2s v2p0090c1s
v2p0411c2s v5p0246c2s v6p0449c1s
Bridge, C., Capt. v4p0237c2s
Bridge, C., Sir v5p0186c1s
v5p0246c2s v6p0336c1s v6p0445c2s
Bridge, C.A. v1p0301c2s
Bridge, C.A.G. v1p0234c2s
v1p0305c1s v1p0678c2m v1p0710c1s
v1p1032c2s v5p0128c1s v5p0401c1s
v6p0130c1s v6p0268c1s v6p0269c1s
v6p0428c2s v6p0448c2s v6p0667c2s
Bridge, C.H.M. v1p0446c1s
v1p0461c1s v1p1195c1s
Bridge, H. v4p0251c2s
Bridge, J.F. v4p0618c1s
Bridge, J.H. v5p0277c2s
v5p0359c2s v5p0425c1s v5p0542c1s
v6p0293c2s v6p0659c1s
Bridge, J.R. v2p0220c2s
v3p0398c2s v4p0063c2s v4p0478c1s
Bridge, Norman v6p0230c2s
Bridge, W.C. v6p0407c1s
Bridge, W.Cyprian v5p0608c2s
Bridgeman, C.G.O. v4p0201c2s
Bridgeman, R.L. v6p0485c1s
Bridgeman, W.S. v4p0012c1s
v6p0293c2s
Bridger, E.A. v5p0493c1s
Bridges, A.F. v1p0171c2s
v1p0696c1s v1p0840c2s v1p0990c2s
Bridges, E.T. v1p0021c2s
v1p0918c2s
Bridges, F. v3p0090c1s
Bridges, Flora v6p0653c1s
Bridges, J.A. v5p0283c1s
v5p0426c1s
Bridges, J.H. v1p0287c1s
v1p0434c1s v1p0573c1s v1p0578c1m
v1p0690c2s v1p0745c1s v1p1037c2s
v1p1217c2s v1p1376c1m v3p0150c1s
v6p0663c1s
Bridges, Philippa v5p0538c1s
Bridges, R. v4p0138c2s
v4p0371c2s v4p0591c1s v5p0277c2s
v5p0317c1s v6p0088c2s v6p0216c2s
v6p0262c1s v6p0272c2s v6p0418c1s
v6p0438c1s v6p0550c2s v6p0700c1m
Bridges, R. and Hodge, H.. v6p0350c2s
Bridges, Robert v6p0071c2s
v6p0164c2s
Bridges, T. v4p0634c2s
Bridges, T.C. v6p0225c2s
Bridges, W. v1p0612c2s
v1p1079c1s
Bridgett, T.E. v1p0353c2s
v1p0611c1s v1p1013c1s v2p0201c1s
v2p0278c2s v2p0320c2s v2p0436c2s
v3p0163c2s v3p0367c1s v3p0464c1s
v4p0112c2s v4p0134c2s v4p0480c1s
v5p0141c2s v5p0492c2s v5p0633c2s
Bridgman, A.L. v1p1009c1s
Bridgman, F.A. v3p0008c2s
Bridgman, H.A. v3p0087c1s
v3p0274c1s v4p0114c1s v4p0162c2s
v5p0135c1s v5p0595c2s v6p0623c2s
Bridgman, H.L. v6p0623c2s
v6p0700c2s
Bridgman, H.L. and Peary, R.E.
v5p0438c1s
Bridgman, L.B. v4p0096c1s
v4p0478c1s v4p0590c2s v4p0614c2s
v5p0521c1s
Bridgman, L.P. v4p0178c2s
Bridgman, R.L. v4p0064c2s
v4p0115c2s v4p0135c1s v4p0174c1m
v4p0325c2m v4p0430c1s v4p0608c1s
v4p0615c2s v5p0068c1s v5p0330c1s
v5p0343c1s v5p0365c1s v5p0598c2s
v6p0148c1s v6p0179c2s v6p0323c2s
v6p0367c1s v6p0405c1s v6p0443c2s
v6p0485c2m v6p0522c2s v6p0708c2m
Bridgman, R.L. and Bradford, G.
v4p0127c1s
Bridgman, S.E. v5p0414c1s
Bridgman, W.S. v4p0033c2s
v4p0401c1m v4p0431c2s v4p0591c2s
v4p0600c1s v6p0039c1s v6p0536c1s
v6p0551c1s v6p0563c2s v6p0674c1s
Bridle, A. v5p0151c2s
v5p0402c2s v5p0539c1s v6p0708c1s
Bridle, A. and Macdonald, J.K.
v5p0083c1s
Bridport, V. and Hood, A.N.
v5p0076c2s
Brie, F.W.D. v6p0663c1s
Brier, J.W. v6p0167c1s
Briere, P. v6p0591c1s
Brierley, F. v3p0351c1s
Brierley, G.H. et al. v3p0074c2s
v3p0432c2s
Brierley, H. v4p0245c1s
v5p0563c1s v5p0629c1s v6p0378c1s
Brierley, J. v2p0149c1s
Brierly, J. v3p0069c2s
v3p0260c2s
Briesen, E.von v6p0281c2s
Briesen, F.v. v2p0182c1s
Briggs and Davis v1p1065c2s
Briggs, A. v1p0464c1s
Briggs, A.C. v5p0585c2s
Briggs, A.F.A. v2p0357c1s
Briggs, A.H. v5p0272c2s
v5p0344c1s
Briggs, C.A. v1p0132c1s
v1p0646c1s v1p1045c2s v1p1047c1s
v1p1060c1s v1p1302c2s v1p1402c2s
v2p0042c2m v2p0043c1s v2p0152c1s
v2p0196c1s v2p0313c2s v2p0360c1m
v2p0437c2m v3p0016c1s v3p0043c2s
v3p0080c2m v3p0082c2s v3p0104c1s
v3p0215c2s v3p0229c1s v3p0342c2s
v3p0350c1s v3p0356c1s v3p0392c2s
v3p0427c2s v3p0449c1s v4p0073c1s
v4p0111c2s v4p0113c2s v4p0457c1s
v4p0500c2s v4p0557c2s v4p0572c2s
v4p0618c1s v5p0057c1s v5p0115c1s
v5p0116c2s v5p0117c1s v5p0117c2s
v5p0404c1s v5p0499c2s v5p0519c1s
v5p0537c1s v5p0577c1s v6p0063c2s
v6p0104c2m v6p0158c2s v6p0177c2s
v6p0383c1s v6p0469c2s v6p0547c2s
v6p0642c2s
Briggs, C.A. and Bradford, A.H.
v4p0478c2s
Briggs, C.A. and Green, W.H.
v2p0042c1s
Briggs, C.A. et al. v3p0084c2s
v3p0141c2s v4p0109c2s
Briggs, C.E. v4p0210c1s
Briggs, C.F. v1p0036c1s
v1p0300c2s v1p0401c2s v1p0753c2s
v1p0892c2s v1p0928c1s v1p1048c1s
v1p1068c1s v1p1307c2s v1p1339c1s

v1p1342c1s v1p1436c1s
Briggs, E. v5p0598c2s
Briggs, E.B. v5p0444c1s
v5p0444c2s v5p0541c2s v6p0493c2s
Briggs, E.G. v5p0059c2s
Briggs, E.L. v3p0404c2s
v4p0116c1s
Briggs, F.H. v5p0103c1s
Briggs, F.H. et al. v5p0263c1s
Briggs, F.Z. v5p0105c2s
Briggs, G.P. v1p0677c2s
Briggs, G.W. v1p0260c1s
v1p0460c1s v1p0566c2s
Briggs, G.W. and Hale, E.E.
v1p1009c1s v1p1380c2s
Briggs, J. v1p0628c2s
Briggs, J.A. v3p0191c2s
v3p0245c1s
Briggs, J.E. et al. v3p0245c1s
Briggs, J.J. v1p0708c1s
v2p0446c1s
Briggs, J.J. and Jewitt, L.
v1p0409c1s v1p0708c1s
Briggs, L.B.R. v3p0139c2s
v3p0140c1s v3p0413c1s v5p0126c1s
v5p0126c2s v5p0127c1s v5p0179c1s
v6p0281c2s v6p0405c2s
Briggs, L.G. and McCall, A.G.
v6p0602c2s
Briggs, L.J. v6p0172c2s
Briggs, L.J. et al. v4p0487c1s
Briggs, L.L. v1p1270c1s
Briggs, M.C. v1p1045c1s
v2p0286c1s
Briggs, M.N. v5p0317c2s
Briggs, N.B. v5p0056c1s
Briggs, R. v1p0017c1s
v1p0111c1s v1p0111c2s v1p0145c2m
v1p0231c1s v1p0246c1s v1p0339c2s
v1p0359c2s v1p0399c1s v1p0408c1s
v1p0501c2s v1p0502c1s v1p0503c1s
v1p0783c2s v1p0831c2s v1p0858c1s
v1p0978c2s v1p0996c2s v1p0997c1s
v1p1065c2s v1p1170c2s v1p1248c1s
v1p1251c1s v1p1265c1s v1p1312c1s
v1p1366c1s v1p1366c2s v1p1390c1s
v2p0294c1s v2p0418c2s v2p0419c1s
v2p0466c1s v6p0592c2s
Briggs, R. and Auria, L.D'
v1p0640c2s
Briggs, R.A. v5p0083c1s
Briggs, S. v2p0034c2s
v2p0436c2s
Briggs, W.M. v3p0402c2s
Brigham, A. v1p0295c1s
v1p0643c2s
Brigham, A.D. v4p0441c1s
Brigham, A.F. v6p0250c1s
Brigham, A.P. v4p0070c2s
v4p0222c2s v5p0127c1s v5p0229c1s
v5p0381c2s v5p0449c1m v6p0037c1s
v6p0135c2s v6p0422c1s v6p0454c2s
v6p0460c2s v6p0545c1s
Brigham, Albert P. v6p0025c1s
Brigham, C. v3p0412c2s
Brigham, C.B. v1p0049c1s
Brigham, C.H. v1p0001c1s
v1p0010c2s v1p0011c1s v1p0011c2s
v1p0013c1s v1p0071c2s v1p0101c1s
v1p0118c1m v1p0122c1s v1p0123c2s
v1p0124c1s v1p0177c2s v1p0202c1s
v1p0222c1s v1p0256c2s v1p0329c2m
v1p0332c1s v1p0346c2s v1p0347c2s
v1p0356c1s v1p0368c2m v1p0384c2s
v1p0424c2s v1p0468c2s v1p0481c2s
v1p0495c2s v1p0497c2s v1p0513c2s
v1p0551c2s v1p0587c2s v1p0619c2s
v1p0672c2s v1p0678c2s v1p0682c1m
v1p0682c2s v1p0689c2s v1p0690c1s
v1p0690c2m v1p0691c1m v1p0697c2s
v1p0702c2s v1p0705c1s v1p0733c1s
v1p0740c2s v1p0774c2s v1p0791c2s
v1p0802c1s v1p0835c1m v1p0856c1s
v1p0871c2s v1p0872c1s v1p0903c1s
v1p0934c1s v1p0960c2m v1p0961c1m
v1p0998c1s v1p1053c1s v1p1054c1s
v1p1120c2s v1p1125c1s v1p1125c2s
v1p1141c2s v1p1148c1m v1p1187c2s
v1p1221c2s v1p1276c1s v1p1278c2m
v1p1279c2s v1p1324c1s v1p1341c1m
v1p1341c2s v1p1417c1s
Brigham, C.S. v5p0441c1s
Brigham, H.O. v6p0017c2s
v6p0084c2s v6p0370c2s
Brigham, Herbert O. v6p0017c1s
Brigham, J. v1p0230c2s
v1p1224c2s v5p0242c1s v5p0266c1s
v5p0304c1s v5p0311c1s v5p0335c2s
v5p0344c1s v5p0500c2s v5p0626c2s
v5p0629c2m v5p0645c1s v6p0374c2m
v6p0589c2s
Brigham, Johnson v5p0261c2s
v6p0161c2s v6p0429c1s
Brigham, M.T. v1p0580c1s
Brigham, W. v1p0910c1s
Brigham, W.E. v3p0218c2s
Brigham, W.T. v1p0365c1s
v1p0376c2s v1p0377c1s v1p0493c1s
v1p0956c1s v2p0242c2s v3p0090c1s
v3p0146c2s v3p0186c1s v3p0236c1m
v5p0044c2s
Brigham, W.Y. v1p0214c1s
Bright, A. v4p0010c1s
v4p0164c1s
Bright, A.W. v5p0036c1s
Bright, C. v5p0529c1s
v5p0558c2s v5p0570c2s v6p0270c2s
v6p0442c2s v6p0611c2s v6p0636c1m
v6p0636c2m
Bright, Charles v5p0571c1s
Bright, D. v4p0446c1s
Bright, D. and Carus, P. . v5p0461c2s
Bright, H. v1p0791c1s
Bright, J. v1p1057c2s
Bright, J. et al. v4p0557c2s
Bright, J.F. v3p0412c1s
Bright, J.S. v1p1181c1s
Bright, J.T. v1p1263c2s
Bright, J.W. v2p0050c2s
Bright, L. v6p0380c1s
Bright, N.K. v6p0085c1s
v6p0307c2s v6p0514c2s
Bright, W. v3p0418c2s
Brightly, S. v1p1419c2s
Brightman, F.E. v4p0397c2s
Brightmen, F. v4p0052c2s
Brill, J.A. v5p0556c2s
Brimblecom, C.E. v3p0270c2s
v3p0418c1s v4p0045c2s
Brimblecom, C.F. v4p0413c2s
Brimley, C.S. v6p0539c2s
Brimley, G. v1p0038c2s
Brimmer, M. v2p0023c2s
Brimmer, M. and Hooper, E.W.
v4p0204c2s
Brin, C.E. v1p1055c2s
Brinchmann, C. v4p0407c2m
Brinckle, A.P. v3p0216c2s
Brinckle, J.G. v1p0882c1s
Brinckman, J. v1p1107c1s
Brinckmann, C. v5p0414c2m
Brincourt v3p0018c2s
v3p0406c2s
Brincourt, M. v3p0320c1s
v3p0320c2m v3p0321c1s
Brindisi, R. v6p0330c2s
Brindle, D.F. v1p0685c1s
Brindle, E. v6p0398c2s
Brindley, R. v3p0056c1s
v3p0110c2s v3p0116c1s v3p0170c2s
v3p0305c1s v3p0387c1s v3p0454c1s
Brindley, R.B. v6p0422c2s
Brindley, T.H. v4p0121c2s
Brindley, W.E. v6p0233c1s
v6p0509c2s
Brindley, William v5p0361c1s
Brine, L. v1p0320c2s
Brine, P.J. v1p0811c1s
v1p0901c1s
Brink, C.M. v3p0243c2s
Brinkerhoff, H.R. v3p0361c1s
v4p0355c1s v4p0370c2s v4p0477c2s
v4p0520c2s v4p0584c2s v4p0592c1s
v5p0599c1s
Brinkerhoff, M.B. v6p0134c2s
Brinkerhoff, R. v3p0105c1s
v5p0466c2s
Brinkley, C.H. v2p0300c1s
Brinkley, Capt. v6p0555c2s
Brinkley, F. v6p0337c1m
v6p0560c1s
Brinkley, V. v3p0227c2s
Brinkman, C. v6p0110c1s
Brinley, F. v1p0311c2s
v1p0339c1m v1p0378c1s v1p0484c2s
Brinley, T. v1p0075c2s
Brinnistool, E.A. v5p0273c2s
Brinsov, V. v5p0502c2s
v6p0559c2m
Brintnell, O.S. v2p0091c2s
Brinton, C. v5p0068c1s
v5p0082c1m v5p0166c1s v5p0216c1s
v5p0220c2s v5p0237c2s v5p0240c2s
v5p0264c1s v5p0330c2s v5p0403c2s
v5p0502c2s v5p0582c1s v5p0594c2s
v5p0610c2s v6p0088c2s v6p0111c2s
v6p0262c1s v6p0282c2s v6p0305c2s
v6p0354c2s v6p0367c2s v6p0393c2s
v6p0407c2s v6p0410c1s v6p0434c2s
v6p0441c1s v6p0488c1s v6p0517c1s
v6p0539c2s v6p0557c1s v6p0558c1s
v6p0570c2s v6p0579c1s v6p0582c1s
v6p0589c1m v6p0674c1s v6p0687c1s
v6p0695c2s v6p0696c1s v6p0714c1s
Brinton, Christian v5p0051c1s
v5p0240c2s v5p0484c2s v6p0028c1s
v6p0072c2s v6p0103c2s v6p0136c1s
v6p0293c1s v6p0453c1s
Brinton, D.G. v1p0027c1s
v1p0157c2s v1p021 c s v1p0212c2s
v1p0636c2s v1p0637c1s v1p0638c2s
v1p0810c2s v1p0897c1s v1p1002c1s
v1p1017c2s v1p1326c2s v1p1439c2s
v2p0008c1s v2p0219c1s v2p0281c1s
v2p0300c1s v2p0305c1s v2p0430c1s
v3p0010c2s v3p0012c1s v3p0057c1s
v3p0057c2m v3p0142c2s v3p0143c2s
v3p0175c1s v3p0213c1s v3p0213c2s
v3p0295c2s v4p0012c1s v4p0016c2s
v4p0020c1m v4p0066c1s v4p0075c2s
v4p0076c1m v4p0114c2s v4p0173c1s
v4p0282c1m v4p0282c2s v4p0326c1s
v4p0351c2s v4p0433c2s v4p0448c2s
v5p0083c2s v5p0087c2s v5p0254c1s
v5p0359c1s v5p0395c1s v5p0443c2s
v5p0562c2s
Brinton, G. v6p0300c2s
v6p0377c2s
Brinton, S. v2p0153c1s
v3p0051c2s v3p0072c2s
Brinton, T.L. v2p0221c2s
Brinton, T.S. v2p0341c1s
Brisbane, A. v1p0069c1s
v1p0471c2s v4p0144c1s v6p0285c1m
Brisbane, Arthur v5p0283c2s
v5p0409c2s
Brisbane, W.H. v1p0769c1s
Brisbin, J.S. v1p0636c1s
v1p0637c2s v1p1351c1s v1p1435c2s
Briscoe, G. v5p0584c1s
Briscoe, J.P. v1p1039c2s
v2p0256c1s v2p0317c1s v4p0153c1s
v4p0401c2s v4p0408c1s v5p0054c1s
Briscoe, M.S. v3p0298c2s
v4p0019c1s v4p0021c2s v4p0288c2s
v4p0303c1s v4p0581c2s v5p0131c2s
v5p0141c2s v5p0266c1m v5p0274c1s
v5p0442c1s v5p0466c1s v5p0531c1s
v5p0572c1s v6p0292c1m v6p0311c1s
Briscoe, Margaret S. v5p0424c2s
v6p0406c2s v6p0534c2s
Briscoe, P. v6p0640c1s
Brisson, A. v5p0204c2s
Brisson, Ad. v5p0168c2s
Bristed, C.A. v1p0008c2s
v1p0026c1s v1p0029c2s v1p0034c1s
v1p0086c1s v1p0145c1s v1p0190c1s
v1p0205c1s v1p0225c2s v1p0267c1s
v1p0298c2s v1p0300c2s v1p0318c1s
v1p0351c2s v1p0366c2s v1p0370c1s
v1p0390c1s v1p0398c2s v1p0417c1s
v1p0423c2s v1p0437c2s v1p0551c2s
v1p0564c2s v1p0600c2s v1p0601c1s
v1p0611c2s v1p0626c1s v1p0704c1s
v1p0745c1s v1p0752c2s v1p0798c2s
v1p0831c2s v1p0838c1s v1p0869c1s
v1p0931c2s v1p0968c1s v1p0969c2s
v1p1005c2s v1p1017c1s v1p1018c2m
v1p1034c1s v1p1048c2s v1p1087c1s
v1p1100c1s v1p1212c2s v1p1217c1s
v1p1295c2s v1p1298c2s v1p1326c2s
v1p1352c1s v1p1352c2s v1p1357c2s
v1p1372c2s v1p1417c1s v1p1420c2s
v1p1425c2s
Bristol, A.C. v1p1419c2s
Bristol, C.L. v5p0054c1s
v5p0406c2s
Bristol, C.L. and Mark, E.L.
v6p0059c1s
Bristol, F.M. v3p0042c2s
v4p0029c1s v4p0121c2s v4p0478c1s
v5p0513c1s v6p0393c2s v6p0696c1s
Bristow, A.T. v6p0409c1s
v6p0673c2s
Bristow, H.G. v1p1436c2s
Bristowe, H. v6p0235c2s
Bristowe, L.S. v4p0096c2s
Bristowe, L.W. and Marriott, H.P.F.
v5p0554c2s
Britan, H.H. v6p0437c2s
Britt, Gisela D. v6p0068c2s
Brittain, M.L. v6p0575c1s
Brittan, C.H. v1p0648c1s
v1p0883c2s v1p1123c1s v4p0536c2s
v4p0541c1s
Britten, B. v1p1204c2s
Britten, F.J. v5p0621c2s
Britten, J. v1p0044c1s
v1p1127c2s v2p0083c2s v2p0153c2s
v2p0159c1s v2p0246c1s v2p0255c2s
v2p0375c2s v2p0376c1s v3p0021c1s
v3p0046c1s v3p0070c2s v3p0185c1s
v3p0203c2s v3p0240c1s v3p0298c2s
v3p0355c1s v3p0364c2m v4p0205c1s
v5p0074c1s v5p0095c1s v5p0097c2m
v5p0135c1s v5p0189c2s v5p0275c2s
v5p0315c1s v5p0469c1s v5p0493c1s
v5p0510c1s v6p0077c2s v6p0078c2s
v6p0305c1s v6p0520c2s v6p0547c2m
v6p0548c1s
Brittle, J.R. v2p0136c2m
Britton, E. v5p0508c1s
Britton, E.E. v5p0399c1s
v5p0591c1s v6p0223c2s v6p0417c1s
Britton, G.H. v6p0658c1s
Britton, J. v4p0069c2s
v5p0635c2s
Britton, J.B. v1p0268c1s
Britton, J.J. v4p0076c1s
v5p0053c1s v5p0426c1s v5p0631c1s
Britton, J.R. v6p0569c2s
Britton, N.L. v4p0069c2m
v4p0166c2s v6p0077c1s v6p0540c1s
Britton, N.S. v6p0127c2s
v6p0296c1s
Britton, T.A. v1p1311c1s
Britton, W.E. v4p0579c1s
v5p0271c2s v6p0046c2s
Broad, C.D. v6p0466c2s
v6p0575c1s

Broad, C.E. v1p0934c2s
Broad, F.B. v5p0379c2s
Broadbent, B. v6p0498c1s
Broadbent, W., Sir v6p0393c2s
Broadfoot, Maj. v4p0001c1s
Broadfoot, W. v4p0003c2m
v4p0296c1s v4p0348c1s v5p0061c2s
v5p0313c1s v5p0329c2s v5p0437c2s
v5p0472c1s v6p0036c2s
Broadhead, A. v2p0054c2s
Broadhead, Davis v2p0297c2s
Broadhead, E. v2p0311c2s
Broadhead, G.C. v1p0098c2s
v2p0048c1s v2p0094c1s v2p0173c2m
v2p0174c1s v2p0240c2s v2p0276c1s
v2p0279c2s v2p0285c1s v2p0445c2s
v2p0470c2s v4p0084c2s v4p0375c1s
v4p0420c1s v4p0617c1m
Broadhead, G.C. and De Wyl, N.
v1p0855c1s
Broadhead, G.E. v1p0702c1s
Broadhouse, J. v2p0137c2s
v2p0209c2s
Broadhouse, J. and Marx, K.
v2p0067c1s
Broadhurst, H. v2p0166c1s
v2p0247c2s v2p0252c1s
Broadhurst, H. et al. v2p0188c2s
Broadley, A.G. v3p0299c1s
Broadley, A.M. v2p0004c1s
v2p0135c1s
Broadus, E.K. v5p0017c1s
v6p0208c1s v6p0514c1s
Broadus, J.A. v1p0097c1s
v1p0554c2s v1p1043c2s v1p1044c1s
v2p0017c1s
Broadus, T.A. v5p0440c1s
v6p0488c1s
Broadwell, A.H. v5p0020c2s
v5p0083c1s v5p0270c2s v5p0458c1s
v5p0533c2s v5p0617c1s
Broadwood, B.M. v3p0062c2s
Broadwood, J. v4p0292c2s
Broca, P. v1p0045c1s
v1p0045c2s v1p0209c1s v1p0971c2s
v2p0016c2s v2p0071c2m
Brocas, F.Y. v1p0494c2s
v1p0875c1m
Broch, O.I. v2p0005c2s
Brochner, G. v5p0393c1s
v6p0035c2s
Brochner, Jessie v6p0305c2s
Brock, A.C. v6p0361c1s
v6p0430c2s
Brock, A.D. v3p0408c2s
v3p0423c1s
Brock, A.Ten v1p0928c2s
v1p0935c1s
Brock, D.H. v6p0460c1s
v6p0469c2s
Brock, E.P.L. v2p0085c1s
v2p0387c1s
Brock, E.P.L. et al. v3p0076c1s
Brock, F. v5p0078c1s
v5p0553c1s
Brock, H.M. v6p0498c1s
Brock, I.A. v1p0853c2s
Brock, R.A. v1p0191c1s
v1p0906c2s v1p1438c1s v3p0098c2s
v3p0165c1s v3p0450c2s
Brock, S.G. v4p0591c2s
Brock, W. v1p0330c2s
v1p0613c1s v1p0823c1s v1p0979c2s
v1p1438c2s
Brockelbank, T.A. v3p0216c1s
v3p0353c1m v6p0528c1s v6p0530c2s
Brockett, L.P. v1p0010c2s
v1p0049c2s v1p0101c1s v1p0142c1m
v1p0156c2s v1p0173c2s v1p0337c1m
v1p0574c2s v1p0613c2s v1p0623c2m
v1p0643c1s v1p0643c2s v1p0707c2s
v1p0738c1s v1p0975c2s v1p0997c2s
v1p1190c1s v1p1408c1s v2p0331c2s
v2p0435c1s
Brockett, W. v2p0331c2s
Brocklehurst, F. v5p0014c1s
v5p0391c2s v5p0571c1s v6p0398c1s
Brocklesby, J. v1p0348c1s
v1p1081c1s v1p1269c1s
Brocklesby, W.C. v1p0572c1s
v1p1326c1s
Brockman, F.S. v6p0428c1s
Brockmeyer, H.C. v1p0531c1s
v3p0175c2s
Brocks, R.L. v5p0465c2s
Brockton, S.R. v1p0770c2s
v1p0776c2s v1p0951c1s
Brockway, A.L. v5p0175c1s
Brockway, C.J. v2p0012c1s
Brockway, Z.R. v1p1053c1s
v2p0107c1s v2p0107c2s v2p0355c1s
v3p0344c2m v4p0178c1s v5p0143c2s
v6p0517c2s
Broderick, A. v4p0375c1s
Broderick, B.F. v4p0027c1s
Broderick, E. v5p0085c2s
v5p0331c2s
Broderick, J.T. v5p0185c1s
Broderip, F.F. v1p0906c1s
Broderip, W.J. v1p0018c2s
v1p0107c2s v1p0135c1s v1p0136c1s
v1p0302c1s v1p0320c2s v1p0340c2s
v1p0358c1s v1p0562c1s v1p0680c1s
v1p0708c2s v1p0788c2s v1p0795c2s
v1p0882c1s v1p0900c1s v1p0934c2s
v1p0949c2s v1p0985c2s v1p1084c1s
v1p1114c2s v1p1127c1s v1p1187c2s
v1p1213c1s v1p1428c1s
Brodgate, W.K. v2p0095c2s
Brodhead, D. v2p0012c1s
v2p0253c1s v2p0308c1s v2p0325c2s
v2p0466c2s
Brodhead, E. v2p0313c2s
v2p0335c2s
Brodhead, E.W. v5p0195c2s
v5p0201c2s
Brodhead, J. v6p0011c2s
Brodhead, J.R. v1p0038c2s
v1p0303c1s v1p0636c2s v1p0909c2s
v1p0912c1s v1p0912c2s v1p0916c1s
Brodhurst, J.P. v4p0421c2s
v4p0571c1s v4p0617c1s
Brodhurst, J.P. and Talmeyr, M.
v4p0206c1s
Brodhurst, J.Penderel v3p0473c2s
Brodhurst, S. v4p0133c1m
v5p0133c2s v5p0181c2s v5p0218c1s
v5p0339c1s v5p0370c2s
Brodie, A.D. v4p0087c1s
v4p0336c1s
Brodie, A.D. and Cook, W.V.
v6p0220c2s
Brodie, A.O. v6p0329c2s
v6p0692c2s
Brodie, B.C. v1p0639c2s
v1p1164c1s v1p1314c1s
Brodie, B.C., Sir v1p0041c1s
v1p0157c2s v1p0601c2s v1p0816c2m
Brodie, D.E. v6p0542c2s
Brodie, F.J. v2p0364c1s
v3p0216c1s v3p0257c1s
Brodie, H.S. v3p0291c2s
v4p0283c1s v4p0354c2s
Brodie, J.F. v3p0437c2s
Brodie, J.S. v1p0664c1s
Brodie, M. v5p0440c2s
Brodie, M.G. v1p0519c1s
Brodie, P.B. v1p0314c2s
v1p0508c2s v1p0557c1s
Brodie, R.H. v6p0159c1s
Brodie, T.G. v4p0397c2s
v4p0462c2s v5p0099c1s
Brodie, W. v1p0030c1s
v1p1345c2s
Brodie-Innes, J.W. v4p0271c2s
Brodlique, E.H. v4p0276c2s
Brodlique-Summers, E. v6p0404c2s
Brodribb, W.J. v1p1018c1s
v1p1018c2m
Brodrick, A. v4p0148c1s
Brodrick, G. v1p1356c2s
Brodrick, G.A. v1p0652c2s
Brodrick, G.C. v1p0657c1s
v1p0741c1m v2p0005c2s v2p0105c1s
v2p0115c1s v2p0115c2m v2p0227c1s
v2p0284c1m v2p0325c1s v2p0407c2s
v3p0144c2s v3p0221c1s v3p0316c2s
v4p0271c1s v4p0289c2s v4p0533c2s
v5p0014c1s v5p0191c1s v5p0426c2s
v5p0646c2s
Brodrick, G.C. and Lankester, E.R.
v5p0426c2s
Brodrick, H. v5p0426c2s
Brodrick, M. v5p0096c2s
Brodrick, Mr. et al. v6p0312c2s
Brodrick, St.J. v2p0348c2s
v4p0544c2s v6p0265c2s
Brodrick, W.St.J. v1p0974c2s
Brodrick, W.St.John v2p0209c1s
v2p0322c2s v2p0330c2s
Broeck, A.Ten v1p0103c1s
v1p0108c1s
Broeke, J.T. v6p0293c2s
Broeke, J.Ten v4p0026c2s
v4p0058c1s v6p0259c1s
Brogan, J.C. v6p0673c1s
Brogan, T.C. v6p0172c1s
Brogden, H.H. v1p1227c1s
Broglie, A.de v1p0151c1s
v1p0736c2s
Broglie, Prince de v3p0456c1s
Brokaw, E.B. et al. v4p0318c2s
v4p0564c2s
Brokaw, R.W. v5p0363c1s
Brokaw, W.E. v4p0283c1s
v4p0516c1s v4p0564c2s v4p0582c1s
Bromby, C.H. v1p0252c1s
v3p0338c2s v6p0496c1s
Bromby, C.H. and Darlington, T.
v4p0112c2s
Bromel, A. v1p0115c1s
Bromer, E.S. v6p0342c1s
v6p0535c1s
Bromfield, A.W. v1p0288c1s
Bromfield, E.T. v4p0557c2s
v5p0562c1s
Bromhead, H.B. v4p0264c1s
Bromhead, H.M. v5p0350c2s
Bromhead, H.W. v4p0168c2s
v4p0245c2s v4p0530c2s v5p0066c1s
v5p0240c1s v5p0280c1s v5p0332c1s
v5p0407c1s v5p0438c1s v6p0179c2s
v6p0235c1s v6p0383c1s v6p0531c1s
Bromilow, A.H. v1p0056c1s
v1p0167c2s v1p0212c1s v1p0364c2s
v1p0946c2s v1p1097c1s v1p1129c2m
v1p1281c1s v1p1393c2s
Bromley, I.H. v1p1324c1s
v3p0101c1s v4p0332c2s
Bromley, J. v3p0472c1s
Bromley, J.H. v1p1438c1s
Bromley, R. v5p0410c1s
Bromley-Davenport, W. v2p0338c1s
Brommage, W.H. and Inkersley, A.
v4p0226c1s
Brondgeest, J.T. v1p0465c2s
Brongniart, A. v1p0037c1s
Bronner, M. v6p0042c1s
v6p0289c2s v6p0483c2s
Bronson, B.F. v1p0046c1s
v1p0651c1s v1p0809c1s v1p1412c1s
Bronson, D. v5p0233c1s
Bronson, F.M. v4p0262c1s
v5p0269c1s v5p0350c2s
Bronson, H. v1p0162c2s
v1p0569c1s v1p0578c1s v1p0613c1s
v1p0816c1s v1p1073c2s v1p1209c2s
v1p1292c2s
Bronson, H. and Roseboro, V.
v5p0282c2s
Bronson, H.L. v6p0286c2s
v6p0526c2s v6p0527c1s
Bronson, K.C. v5p0034c2s
v5p0079c2s
Bronson, K.DeK. v6p0085c1s
Bronson, T.B. v3p0171c1s
v3p0171c2s v4p0123c1s v4p0370c2s
Bronson, W.C. v3p0140c1s
v5p0016c1s
Bronson, W.W. v1p1406c1s
Bronson-Howard, G. v6p0070c1s
v6p0226c1s v6p0397c2s
Bronte, C. v1p0406c2s
v1p1054c2s v1p1389c2s v1p1404c2s
v4p0364c2s v5p0004c2s
Bronte, E.J. v1p0952c1s
Broode, H. v1p0286c1s
Brook, A.T. v5p0419c1s
Brook, A.Ten v1p0069c1s
v1p0682c2s v1p0833c1s v1p0880c1s
v1p0912c2s v1p0919c2s v1p1118c1s
v1p1414c1s v3p0305c1s
Brook, H.E. v6p0093c2s
v6p0387c1s v6p0712c2s
Brook, J.G. v4p0224c1s
Brook, M. and Steward, J.E.
v2p0172c1s
Brook, S. v2p0163c2s
Brook, W. v4p0195c2s
Brooke, A. v5p0128c1s
Brooke, A.Ten v1p0810c1s
Brooke, C. v1p0426c1s
v1p0466c2m
Brooke, C.W.A. v4p0339c2s
Brooke, E. v6p0691c1s
Brooke, Emma v4p0516c2s
v6p0397c2s
Brooke, G. v2p0233c1s
Brooke, G.C. v6p0094c1s
Brooke, G.H. v5p0213c1s
v6p0526c1s
Brooke, G.M. v6p0133c2s
Brooke, H. v4p0304c2s
Brooke, H.S. v3p0003c1s
Brooke, H.W. v2p0266c2s
Brooke, J. v4p0614c2s
v5p0555c1s
Brooke, J.C. v1p0206c2s
v1p0708c1s v1p1154c2m v1p1173c2m
Brooke, J.C. and Milles, J.
v1p1173c2s v1p1433c1s
Brooke, J.M. v3p0275c1s
Brooke, J.T. v1p0731c2s
Brooke, J.W. v6p0554c1s
Brooke, M. v3p0125c1s
v4p0343c1s v5p0084c2s v5p0581c1s
Brooke, O.G. v6p0221c1s
Brooke, R.S. v1p0953c1s
Brooke, S. v3p0258c2s
v3p0389c2s
Brooke, S.A. v1p0063c2s
v1p0223c1s v1p0565c1s v1p0639c1s
v1p0695c2m v1p1042c2s v1p1132c2s
v1p1189c2s v2p0449c1s v3p0057c1s
v3p0388c1s v4p0076c1s v4p0553c1s
v4p0569c1s v6p0032c1s
Brooke, St. G.T. v4p0129c1s
Brooke, Stopford A. v6p0085c1s
Brooke, V. v1p0340c2s
Brooke, Vivian v4p0373c2s
Brooke-Alder, Isabel v5p0373c2s
Brooke-Hunt, V. v6p0207c1s
Brookfield, A.M. v2p0100c1s
v6p0278c1s
Brookfield, Col. et al. .. v5p0244c2s
Brookfield, F. v4p0046c2s
Brookfield, F.M. v6p0391c2s
Brooking, J.H.C. v6p0197c1s
Brookman, F.W. v4p0477c2s
Brooks, A. v3p0236c2s

v4p0074c2s
Brooks, A. et al. v3p0282c2s
Brooks, A.H. v6p0010c1m v6p0010c2m v6p0250c2m
Brooks, A.H. and Raeburn, D.L. v6p0393c2s
Brooks, A.M. v5p0031c1s
Brooks, B. v6p0099c2s v6p0432c2s v6p0607c1s v6p0616c1s v6p0631c2s
Brooks, B.A. v1p0019c2s v4p0109c1s
Brooks, B.S. v1p0346c2s v1p1148c2m v1p1245c1s
Brooks, Benj. v6p0203c2s
Brooks, C. v1p0167c2s v1p0481c2s v1p0641c1s v1p0867c2s v1p0898c2s v1p1058c2s v1p1150c2s v1p1159c2s
Brooks, C.E. v1p0245c2s v1p0708c1s
Brooks, C.G. v1p0784c1s v1p1336c1s
Brooks, C.S. v1p0958c1s v6p0346c2s v6p0490c2s
Brooks, C.T. v1p0077c2s v1p0121c2s v1p0131c2s v1p0170c1s v1p0423c2s v1p0610c2s v1p0611c1s v1p0687c2s v1p0688c1s v1p0774c2s v1p0786c1s v1p0830c1s v1p0874c2s v1p1021c1s v1p1105c1s v1p1107c1s v1p1124c2s v1p1442c2s
Brooks, C.T. and Brooks, M.E.M. v1p0855c2s
Brooks, C.W. v1p0168c1s v1p0236c1s
Brooks, D. v1p0748c2s
Brooks, D.C. v1p0227c1s v1p0228c1s v1p0451c1s v1p0574c2s
Brooks, E. v1p0028c2s v1p0261c1s v1p0291c2s v1p0294c2s v1p0410c1s v1p0556c2s v1p0594c1s v1p0714c1s v1p0729c2s v1p1277c2s v1p1314c1s v1p1435c1s v2p0139c2s v4p0040c1s v5p0512c1s
Brooks, E.C. v5p0290c1s v6p0290c1s v6p0574c1s
Brooks, E.G. v1p0087c2s v1p0089c2m v1p0128c2s v1p0493c2s v1p0684c1s v1p0684c2s v1p0727c1s v1p0867c2s v1p0874c2s v1p0881c2s v1p0956c1s v1p1089c2s v1p1101c1s v1p1106c2s v1p1261c1s v1p1333c2s v1p1342c2s v1p1355c2m v1p1407c2s
Brooks, E.S. v3p0246c2s v4p0345c1s
Brooks, E.W. v4p0293c1s v4p0299c2s v4p0303c2s v4p0637c1s v5p0086c1m v5p0288c2s
Brooks, F. v1p0058c1s v1p0831c1s
Brooks, F.E. v6p0264c2s
Brooks, F.H. v6p0674c2s
Brooks, Florence v6p0003c1s v6p0470c2s v6p0559c2s
Brooks, Florence E. v6p0649c2s
Brooks, G. v3p0137c2s v3p0248c1s v3p0444c1s
Brooks, G.B. v4p0086c1s
Brooks, G.W. v4p0575c2s
Brooks, H. v5p0411c1s v6p0217c1s
Brooks, H.E. v6p0387c1s
Brooks, H.S. v1p0834c1s v2p0023c2s v2p0071c1s v2p0106c1s v2p0121c2s v3p0025c1s v3p0264c1s v3p0275c2s v3p0277c1s v3p0322c1s v3p0327c2s v3p0344c1s v3p0430c1s v3p0450c2s v4p0526c1s v5p0154c2s v5p0193c2s v5p0271c2s v5p0373c1s v6p0414c2s
Brooks, I.T. v1p0383c2s v3p0353c1s
Brooks, Ida L. v6p0407c1s
Brooks, J. v4p0446c2s v6p0101c1s
Brooks, J.A. v1p1050c1s
Brooks, J.C. v4p0559c2s
Brooks, J.E. v3p0239c1s
Brooks, J.G. v3p0398c1s v4p0096c2m v4p0097c1s v4p0132c2s v4p0248c1s v4p0286c2s v4p0287c1s v4p0333c2m v4p0372c1s v4p0412c1s v4p0430c2s v4p0532c2s v4p0533c2m v4p0534c1s v4p0535c1s v4p0591c1m v5p0124c2s v5p0159c1s v5p0209c2s v5p0289c1s v5p0321c1s v5p0593c1s v6p0109c1s v6p0141c2s v6p0209c1s v6p0308c2s v6p0318c2s v6p0425c1s v6p0434c2s v6p0468c1s v6p0601c2s v6p0621c2s v6p0652c1m v6p0691c2s
Brooks, J.G., Mrs. v1p0625c1s
Brooks, J.Graham v6p0115c1s
Brooks, J.W. v4p0032c2s v4p0278c2s
Brooks, K. v1p0096c2s v1p1393c2s v2p0382c1s
Brooks, L. v1p1041c1s v6p0279c1s
Brooks, M. v2p0411c1s v4p0567c2s
Brooks, M.E. v1p0222c1s v4p0629c2s
Brooks, M.E.M. and Brooks, C.T. v1p0855c2s
Brooks, M.H. v1p1270c2s v3p0355c1s
Brooks, M.S. v4p0076c1s
Brooks, M.W. v2p0402c2s v3p0217c1s
Brooks, Mrs. v1p0677c1s
Brooks, N. v1p0048c1s v1p0232c1s v1p0321c1s v1p0349c1s v1p0443c1s v1p0505c2s v1p0572c1s v1p0574c1s v1p0678c1s v1p0678c2s v1p0679c1s v1p0750c1m v1p0851c2s v1p1101c1s v1p1146c1s v1p1149c1s v1p1380c1s v2p0070c1s v2p0103c1s v2p0201c1s v2p0272c2s v2p0338c1s v2p0383c1s v2p0387c1s v3p0303c1s v4p0098c1s v4p0234c2s v4p0332c2m v4p0333c1s v4p0428c2s v4p0529c2s v4p0612c1s v4p0619c2s v5p0017c1s v5p0122c2s v5p0128c1m v5p0256c2s v5p0390c2s v5p0419c2s v6p0502c1s v6p0692c2s
Brooks, Noah v4p0475c2s v5p0425c2s v6p0281c1m v6p0296c1s v6p0387c2s
Brooks, P. v1p1064c1s v1p1203c2s v1p1243c1s v2p0235c1s v2p0359c1s v2p0387c2s v3p0080c2s v4p0068c2s v4p0069c1s v4p0110c2s v4p0371c2s
Brooks, Phillips v2p0372c1s v5p0422c2s v5p0539c1s
Brooks, R.C. v5p0054c1s v5p0073c1s v5p0119c2m v5p0120c2s v5p0391c1s v5p0392c1s v5p0457c1s v5p0469c2s v6p0059c1s v6p0248c2s v6p0310c2s v6p0368c2s v6p0585c2s
Brooks, R.O. v6p0231c2s
Brooks, Robert C. v6p0059c1s v6p0089c1s
Brooks, S. v1p0068c2s v1p0976c1s v1p1086c2s v1p1153c1s v1p1199c1s v1p1378c1s v1p1407c2s v5p0006c1s v5p0006c2s v5p0040c1s v5p0080c2s v5p0109c1s v5p0133c1s v5p0150c1s v5p0182c1s v5p0182c2s v5p0194c1s v5p0196c2s v5p0218c1s v5p0219c1m v5p0245c2s v5p0281c1s v5p0384c1s v5p0433c1s v5p0501c1s v5p0566c1s v5p0586c2m v5p0587c1m v5p0600c2s v5p0631c2s v6p0014c2s v6p0176c2s v6p0186c2s v6p0205c1s v6p0206c2s v6p0213c2s v6p0238c2s v6p0266c2s v6p0267c1s v6p0269c2s v6p0302c2s v6p0327c1s v6p0334c1s v6p0383c2s v6p0384c1s v6p0396c1s v6p0402c1s v6p0426c1s v6p0452c2s v6p0453c1s v6p0515c1s v6p0550c1m v6p0550c2s v6p0561c1s v6p0565c2s v6p0607c2s v6p0665c2s v6p0676c1s v6p0691c2s v6p0699c1s
Brooks, S. et al. v3p0156c2s
Brooks, S.D. v5p0182c2s v5p0265c1s v6p0290c1s v6p0505c1s v6p0572c2s v6p0573c1s v6p0574c1s
Brooks, S.W. v3p0178c1s v3p0261c2s v3p0404c1s v3p0416c2s v3p0473c1s
Brooks, Sidney v5p0300c2s
Brooks, Stratton D. and Morss, C.H. v6p0290c1s
Brooks, Sydney v6p0172c2s v6p0186c2s v6p0245c1s
Brooks, T. v6p0068c2s
Brooks, T.B. v1p0787c2s v1p0802c1s v1p0844c2s v1p1112c2s v1p1113c1s
Brooks, T.B. and Pumpelly, R. v1p0300c1s v1p1271c1s
Brooks, W. v3p0203c2s v4p0341c2s v6p0120c1s
Brooks, W.A. v4p0064c2s v4p0087c2s v4p0249c2s v4p0423c1s v4p0635c1s v5p0092c2s
Brooks, W.C. v4p0600c2s
Brooks, W.G. v3p0034c2s v3p0064c1s v3p0102c1s
Brooks, W.H. v1p0390c2s v1p0955c2s v1p1288c2s
Brooks, W.H.J. v1p0945c2s
Brooks, W.K. v1p0135c2s v1p0463c2s v1p0646c2s v1p0963c1s v1p1014c2s v1p1146c2s v1p1421c2s v2p0031c2s v2p0102c2s v2p0108c2s v2p0113c2s v2p0149c2s v2p0274c1s v2p0340c2s v2p0384c2s v2p0396c2s v2p0483c2s v3p0154c1s v3p0228c1s v3p0260c2s v3p0439c2s v4p0219c1s v4p0225c1s v4p0270c2s v4p0284c2s v4p0317c2s v4p0331c1s v4p0345c2s v4p0448c2s v4p0507c2s v4p0617c2s v4p0626c1s v5p0374c2s v5p0400c1s v5p0412c2s v5p0513c2s v5p0605c1s v6p0202c1s
Brooks, W.K. and Ward, L.F. v5p0447c1s
Brooks, W.R. v2p0094c2s v2p0095c1m v2p0285c1s v5p0448c1s v5p0609c1s
Brooks, W.R. and Egbert, H.V. v2p0095c1s
Brooks, W.R. and Frisby, E. v2p0095c1s
Brooksbank, B. v2p0230c1s v2p0346c1s
Brooksbank, F.C. v4p0502c1s
Broome, E.C. v6p0295c2s
Broome, F.N. v1p0019c1s v1p0071c1s v1p0418c1s v1p0918c2s v1p1270c2s
Broome, J. v5p0210c2s v5p0338c2s v5p0477c1s v5p0478c1s v5p0531c2s
Broome, Lady v5p0062c2s v5p0063c2s v5p0135c2s v5p0294c2s v5p0367c1s v5p0398c2s v5p0520c2s v6p0455c1m v6p0546c2s
Broome, M.A. v5p0039c2s
Broome, M.A., Lady v5p0590c2s
Broomell, G.D. v6p0669c2s
Brophy, W. v3p0133c1s v4p0176c2s
Brosch, L. v6p0648c1s
Brosius, H.M. v5p0238c2s v5p0250c2s
Brosius, M. v4p0195c1s v4p0266c1s v5p0149c1s
Brosnahan, T. v6p0190c2s
Bross, W. v1p1321c2s
Broster, D.K. v6p0029c2s v6p0085c2s v6p0425c2s
Brot, L.Teisserenc de and Rotch, A.L. v6p0040c1s v6p0412c2s
Brothers, A. v1p0382c1m v2p0340c1s
Brotherton, A.W. v1p1142c1s v3p0253c1s v4p0399c2s
Brotherton, Alice W. v6p0278c2s
Brotherton, C. v1p0073c1s
Brotherton, G.H. v5p0233c2s
Brotherton, M. v1p0500c2s v1p0702c2s v1p0722c2s v3p0075c2s
Brotherton, Mary v4p0579c1s
Brotherton, Mrs. v1p1320c2s v1p1402c2s
Brotherton, R.H. v6p0264c1s
Brotherton, T.W. v1p0187c1s v1p0188c1s v1p0533c2s v1p1254c1s
Brough, B.H. v3p0204c2s v4p0006c1s v4p0372c1s v5p0124c1s v5p0298c2s v5p0304c2s v5p0371c2s v5p0377c2s v5p0378c1s v5p0563c2s v6p0328c2s v6p0419c1s v6p0619c1s
Brough, C.H. v5p0380c2s
Brough, E. v3p0047c2s
Brough, J. v3p0233c2s v4p0465c2s
Brough, L. v4p0247c1s
Brough, R.B. v2p0435c2s
Brough, S. v5p0200c1s
Brough, W. v5p0285c1s
Brougham, A. v1p0202c2s v1p0251c2s
Brougham, H. v1p0003c2s v1p0004c1s v1p0027c2s v1p0032c2s v1p0040c2s v1p0057c1s v1p0087c2s v1p0113c1s v1p0139c1s v1p0140c2s v1p0155c2s v1p0181c2s v1p0182c2m v1p0217c1s v1p0219c1s v1p0271c1s v1p0272c1s v1p0375c2s v1p0387c1s v1p0390c2s v1p0435c2s v1p0473c1s v1p0476c2s v1p0480c2s v1p0482c1s v1p0510c2m v1p0511c1s v1p0532c1s v1p0544c2s v1p0546c1s v1p0546c2s v1p0548c1m v1p0548c2s v1p0561c2s v1p0589c1s v1p0604c1s v1p0625c1m v1p0635c1m v1p0681c1s v1p0729c2s v1p0730c2s v1p0742c1s v1p0746c2s v1p0758c2s v1p0802c1s v1p0842c1s v1p0849c1s v1p0907c2s v1p0915c1s v1p0915c2s v1p0945c1m v1p0973c1s v1p0973c2m v1p0974c1s v1p1012c1m v1p1030c2s v1p1075c1s v1p1111c2s v1p1116c2s v1p1174c1s v1p1217c1s v1p1228c2s v1p1265c2s v1p1281c2s v1p1285c1s v1p1306c2s v1p1317c1s v1p1381c2s v1p1383c1s v1p1394c1m v1p1401c1s v1p1409c1s
Brougham, H. and Jeffrey, F v1p0395c1s
Brougham, H. and Parry, C.H. v1p0959c1s
Brougham, L.H. v1p0915c1s
Brougham, Lord v1p0227c1s v1p0387c1s v1p0524c1s v1p0533c1s v1p0552c2s v1p0580c1s v1p0616c2s v1p1216c2s v1p1356c1m v1p1384c2s
Brougham, R. v5p0076c2s
Brougham, W.F. v5p0404c1s
Broughman, H. v1p1062c2s
Broughton, F.C. v2p0028c1s
Broughton, F.W. v3p0314c1s v4p0136c2s v4p0494c2s
Broughton, G.H. v6p0696c1s
Broughton, J. v1p0040c2s

v1p0465c1s
Broughton, L. v1p0084c1s
v1p0559c2s v1p0608c2s
Broughton, Mrs. v1p0842c2s
Broughton, R. v1p0282c1s
v1p0535c2s v1p0795c1s v1p0930c2s
v1p1032c1s v1p1087c2s v1p1328c2s
v1p1339c1s v1p1403c2s v2p0038c2s
v3p0007c1s v4p0049c2s v5p0155c1s
v5p0212c1s v5p0225c1s v5p0509c2s
Broughton, Rhoda v3p0199c1s
v4p0386c1s v4p0481c1s v4p0510c2s
v6p0363c2s
Broughton, U.H. v4p0516c2s
Broughton, W.H. v4p0121c2s
Broun, J.A. v1p0099c2m
v1p0634c1s v1p1268c1s v1p1269c1m
v1p1395c1s
Broun, W.H. v6p0386c2s
Broun, W.Le R. v1p0399c1s
Brower, E. v3p0436c1s
v4p0173c2s v4p0196c2s v4p0347c1s
v4p0358c1s v4p0389c1s v5p0419c2s
Brower, Edith v3p0049c1s
Brown and Cabot v6p0305c1s
Brown, A. v2p0115c1s
v2p0150c2s v2p0462c1s v2p0476c2s
v3p0030c1s v3p0048c1s v3p0442c2s
v4p0088c2s v4p0154c2s v4p0179c2s
v4p0195c1s v4p0221c2s v4p0252c1s
v4p0296c1s v4p0304c1s v4p0312c2s
v4p0384c1s v4p0406c1s v4p0529c2s
v4p0537c2s v4p0605c2s v4p0606c1m
v5p0056c1s v5p0141c2s v5p0150c1s
v5p0188c1s v5p0206c2s v5p0265c2s
v5p0298c2m v5p0325c2s v5p0358c1s
v5p0361c1s v5p0378c1s v5p0516c2s
v5p0517c2s v5p0577c2s v6p0005c1s
v6p0159c2s v6p0166c1s v6p0173c1s
v6p0414c2s v6p0632c2s v6p0701c1s
Brown, A. and Dickson, M.W.
v1p0328c1s
Brown, A.A. and Pomeroy, E.
v5p0162c1s
Brown, A.A., Mrs. v1p0819c2s
Brown, A.B.A. v6p0512c1s
v6p0709c1s
Brown, A.C. v1p0139c1s
v1p0374c1s v3p0289c2s v6p0199c2s
v6p0325c2s v6p0607c1s
Brown, A.D. v1p0043c1s
v1p0090c2s v1p0901c2s v1p1192c1s
v1p1352c1s v2p0150c2s v2p0443c2s
v3p0133c1s v3p0430c2s
Brown, A.E. v1p0047c1s
v1p0231c1s v1p1179c1s v1p1202c1s
v2p0274c1s v4p0049c1s v4p0063c2s
v4p0069c1s v4p0624c2s v5p0023c2s
v5p0072c2s v5p0267c2s v5p0384c1s
v5p0551c2s v6p0024c2s v6p0030c2s
v6p0076c1s v6p0123c2s v6p0410c2s
Brown, A.E. and Caton, J.D.
v1p0340c2s
Brown, A.F. v1p1362c1s
v2p0458c2s v4p0080c2s v5p0116c1s
v5p0377c1s v5p0505c1s v5p0590c1s
v6p0024c1s v6p0326c1s v6p0410c1s
v6p0448c2s
Brown, A.G. v6p0044c2s
v6p0657c2s
Brown, A.G. and Remnitz, V.Y.
v5p0463c1s
Brown, A.H. v5p0626c1s
Brown, A.J. v3p0241c1s
v4p0158c1s v5p0220c1s v6p0036c2s
v6p0119c2s v6p0354c2m v6p0708c2s
Brown, A.J.J. v1p0460c2s
Brown, A.M. v5p0086c1s
Brown, A.N. v2p0255c2s
Brown, A.R. v3p0259c1s
v4p0009c1s v4p0196c2s v4p0342c2s
v4p0570c1s v5p0272c2s v5p0332c1s
Brown, A.W. v1p0169c2s
v1p0990c2s v1p1396c1s v3p0047c2s
Brown, Abbie F. v5p0531c1s
Brown, Addison v4p0508c1s
Brown, Alice v5p0166c1s
v5p0574c2s v6p0046c1s v6p0073c2s
v6p0105c2s v6p0230c1s v6p0264c2s
v6p0274c2s v6p0275c2s v6p0279c2s
v6p0287c2s v6p0288c2s v6p0291c2s
v6p0324c2s v6p0347c1s v6p0386c1s
v6p0397c2s v6p0398c1s v6p0420c1s
v6p0442c2s v6p0465c2s v6p0500c1s
v6p0504c1s v6p0552c2s v6p0594c2s
v6p0596c1s v6p0614c2s v6p0650c1s
v6p0656c1s v6p0662c2s v6p0702c1s
v6p0703c1s
Brown, Anna Robeson v6p0681c2s
Brown, B. v4p0477c2s
v6p0483c1s
Brown, B.C. v4p0031c1s
v5p0557c1s v6p0434c2s v6p0474c1s
Brown, B.F. v5p0229c1s
Brown, C. v1p0237c2s
v2p0275c1s v3p0424c2s v4p0403c2s
Brown, C.B. v1p0561c1s
v4p0072c2s v4p0552c1s v6p0386c2s
v6p0568c2s
Brown, C.C. v2p0438c2s
Brown, C.E. v6p0612c1s
Brown, C.F. v5p0019c1s
Brown, C.G. v6p0533c1s
Brown, C.H. v6p0065c2s
Brown, C.L. v2p0109c2s
Brown, C.M.L. v6p0676c1s
Brown, C.M.L. and Adams, F.
v6p0490c1s
Brown, C.O. v5p0082c2s
Brown, C.R. v1p0384c1s
v2p0043c1s v3p0042c1s v4p0054c2s
v4p0055c1s v5p0058c2s v6p0176c1s
v6p0185c1s
Brown, C.S. v2p0266c1s
v3p0142c1s v4p0371c1s v5p0049c1s
v5p0103c1s v5p0487c1s v5p0507c2s
v6p0476c1s v6p0485c2s
Brown, C.S.V. v5p0183c2s
v5p0184c2s v5p0215c2s v5p0431c1s
v6p0197c2m
Brown, C.T. v3p0076c2s
Brown, Caroline v4p0590c1s
v5p0161c1s v5p0319c2s
Brown, Carroll N. v6p0655c2s
Brown, Clara S. v5p0251c2s
v5p0373c1s v5p0472c1s v6p0476c1s
v6p0649c2s
Brown, Colvin B. v6p0618c1s
Brown, Cram, Prof. v5p0506c1s
Brown, D. v1p0529c1s
v1p0688c1s v1p0688c2s v2p0044c1m
v2p0082c1s v2p0167c1s v2p0181c1s
v2p0212c2s v2p0473c1s v3p0015c2s
v3p0026c1s v4p0056c1s v4p0056c2s
v5p0067c2s
Brown, D.H. v5p0554c1s
Brown, D.J. v1p0283c2s
Brown, D.K. v1p0019c2s
v1p1270c1s
Brown, D.W. v5p0087c2s
Brown, Demetra Vaka v6p0661c2s
Brown, Dr. v1p1128c2s
Brown, E. v1p0605c1s
v1p0888c2s v1p1248c2s v1p1313c2s
v1p1422c2s v2p0071c2s v2p0331c1s
v3p0223c1s
v5p0558c2s
Brown, E.B. v4p0539c1s
v4p0608c2s v5p0013c1s v5p0576c2s
v6p0202c1s v6p0461c2s
Brown, E.C. v5p0170c2s
v5p0339c1s v5p0640c1s
Brown, E.E. v1p0230c1s
v4p0171c1s v5p0127c1s v5p0180c1s
v5p0230c1s v5p0274c2s v5p0399c2s
v5p0517c2s v5p0518c1s v5p0569c2m
v6p0190c1s v6p0289c2s v6p0518c2s
v6p0671c2s
Brown, E.F. v1p0052c2s
Brown, E.H. v5p0427c2s
Brown, E.L. v2p0426c2s
v4p0034c2s
Brown, E.O. v3p0263c1m
v4p0179c1s
Brown, E.P. v5p0229c1s
Brown, E.S. v3p0470c2s
Brown, E.V. v4p0466c2s
Brown, E.W. v1p0741c2s
v2p0211c1s v2p0255c1s v5p0277c2s
v6p0007c2s v6p0082c1s v6p0626c1s
v6p0690c2s
Brown, Elmer E. v6p0193c2s
Brown, F. v1p0016c1s
v1p0035c2s v1p0557c1s v1p0884c1s
v1p0891c2s v1p1312c1s v1p1338c1s
v2p0043c2s v2p0199c2s v2p0204c1s
v2p0249c2s v2p0382c1s v3p0029c2m
v3p0041c1s v3p0084c1s v3p0193c1m
v3p0445c2s v4p0033c2s v4p0182c2s
v5p0056c1s v5p0057c2s v5p0412c2m
v5p0424c1s v6p0062c1s v6p0069c1s
Brown, F.C. v5p0092c1s
v5p0331c2s v6p0074c1s v6p0094c2s
v6p0298c2s v6p0369c1s v6p0459c1s
v6p0552c2s
Brown, F.C. and Stewart, G.
v5p0090c1s
Brown, F.F. v1p0216c2s
v2p0077c1s
Brown, F.H. v5p0285c1s
v5p0572c2s v6p0278c2s v6p0282c1s
v6p0330c1s
Brown, F.J. v1p0925c2s
v4p0286c2s
Brown, F.M. v4p0029c1s
v4p0319c1s v4p0393c2s
Brown, F.Madox v4p0029c2s
Brown, F.R. v2p0296c1s
Brown, F.T. v2p0082c1s
v6p0202c2s
Brown, F.W. v5p0159c2s
v6p0249c1s v6p0565c2s
Brown, F.W., Mrs. v5p0274c2s
Brown, Francis v4p0054c2s
Brown, G. v1p0539c2s
v2p0019c2s v2p0467c2s v3p0059c1s
v3p0059c2s v4p0024c1s v4p0047c2s
v4p0233c2s v4p0447c2s v5p0241c1s
v5p0506c1s v6p0024c1s v6p0131c2s
v6p0368c2s v6p0561c1s
Brown, G.B. v1p0062c2s
v1p1171c1s v1p1414c1s v2p0023c1s
v2p0190c2s v2p0336c1s v2p0392c2s
v4p0168c2s v6p0294c1s
Brown, G.Baldwin v2p0176c1s
v2p0301c2s v6p0262c2s
Brown, G.F. v2p0088c1s
Brown, G.G. v4p0333c2s
Brown, G.L. v2p0426c2m
Brown, G.M.L. v6p0029c1s
v6p0161c2s v6p0189c2s v6p0470c2s
v6p0608c1s v6p0676c1m v6p0705c1s
Brown, G.M.L. and Adams, Franklin
v6p0080c1s v6p0117c2s
Brown, G.P. v1p1263c1s
v3p0266c2s
Brown, G.R. v6p0117c2s
v6p0380c2s
Brown, G.S. v6p0436c1s
Brown, G.T. v4p0192c1s
v4p0338c2s v5p0565c1s
Brown, G.W. v1p0259c1s
v2p0217c1s
Brown, Glenn v4p0520c2s
v4p0575c1s v4p0612c1s v5p0093c2s
v6p0033c1s v6p0687c1s
Brown, H. v1p0092c1s
v1p0525c2s v2p0169c1s v4p0244c1s
v4p0324c1s
Brown, H., Mrs. v3p0414c2s
Brown, H.A. v1p0961c1s
v6p0712c2s
Brown, H.B. v2p0446c1s
v3p0064c2s v3p0110c1s v3p0233c1s
v3p0319c1s v4p0462c1s v4p0588c1s
v5p0464c2s v6p0348c1s
Brown, H.D. v3p0445c1s
Brown, H.E. v1p0059c1s
v5p0029c2s
Brown, H.F. v2p0230c2s
v2p0446c2s v2p0458c2s v2p0461c1s
v3p0173c2s v3p0210c2s v3p0247c1s
v3p0448c1m v4p0092c2s v4p0226c1s
v4p0272c1s v4p0312c2s v4p0435c2s
v4p0561c1s v4p0606c1s v5p0293c2s
v5p0429c2s v6p0282c2s
Brown, H.H. v3p0111c1s
v3p0265c1s v5p0353c2s v5p0467c2s
v6p0155c1s v6p0181c2s v6p0210c1s
v6p0353c2s v6p0395c2s v6p0476c1s
v6p0535c1s v6p0589c1s v6p0656c2s
Brown, H.N. v1p1178c2s
v1p1236c2s v1p1271c2s v2p0119c2s
v2p0255c1s v2p0347c2s v2p0368c1s
Brown, H.P. v3p0146c2s
Brown, H.S. v1p0102c2s
v1p0127c2s v1p0340c2s v1p0796c2s
v1p1434c2s v6p0324c2s v6p0496c1s
Brown, H.T. v1p1304c2s
v5p0097c1s v5p0161c2s v6p0100c2s
Brown, H.V. v3p0024c1s
v3p0463c1s v4p0028c1s v4p0296c2s
Brown, H.W. v1p0536c2s
v1p1301c2s v4p0090c1s v4p0104c2s
v4p0553c2s
Brown, Harry H. v6p0531c1s
Brown, Henry H. v6p0424c2s
Brown, Hume v6p0578c2m
Brown, I. v5p0138c1s
Brown, I.C. v6p0109c1s
Brown, J. v1p0068c1s
v1p0229c1s v1p0405c1s v1p0459c2s
v1p0578c1s v1p0591c2s v1p0758c2s
v1p0816c2s v1p0818c2s v1p0958c1s
v1p1069c2s v1p1072c1s v1p1089c1s
v1p1431c2s v2p0194c2s v2p0252c1s
v3p0062c2s v3p0124c2m v3p0135c2s
v3p0136c1s v3p0194c2s v3p0267c1s
v3p0374c1s v3p0464c2s v5p0133c1s
Brown, J. and Putnam, J.P.
v3p0435c1s
Brown, J., Dr. v1p0215c2s
v1p1363c2s
Brown, J.A. v1p0044c2s
v1p0045c1s v1p0048c1s v1p0076c1m
v1p0076c2s v1p0096c1s v1p0120c2s
v1p0130c1s v1p0130c2m v1p0296c2s
v1p0314c1m v1p0344c2s v1p0398c1s
v1p0432c1s v1p0447c2s v1p0468c2s
v1p0497c1s v1p0640c2m v1p0687c2s
v1p0688c2m v1p0700c2s v1p0743c2s
v1p0769c2s v1p0777c2m v1p0778c1m
v1p0778c2s v1p0788c1m v1p0788c2m
v1p0813c1s v1p0823c2m v1p0829c2s
v1p0839c2s v1p0847c1s v1p1009c1s
v1p1089c2s v1p1118c2s v1p1161c1s
v1p1175c2s v1p1303c2s v1p1336c2s
v4p0422c1s v4p0505c1s v5p0259c1s
v5p0510c2m
Brown, J.B. v1p0036c2s
v1p0055c1m v1p0133c2s v1p0139c2s
v1p0239c1s v1p0249c1s v1p0321c2s
v1p0355c2s v1p0362c2s v1p0494c1s
v1p0504c2s v1p0524c2s v1p0707c2s
v1p0859c2s v1p1064c2s v1p1101c1s
v1p1199c2s v1p1230c2s v2p0215c2s
v2p0366c2s v2p0462c1s
Brown, J.C. v1p0344c1s
v1p0468c1s v2p0029c1s v2p0038c2s
v2p0162c2s v2p0412c2s v4p0585c2s

v6p0096c1s
Brown, J.C.J. v1p0072c2s
v1p0271c2s v1p1439c1s v2p0310c1s
Brown, J.Carter v2p0256c2s
v2p0357c2s
Brown, J.D. v4p0119c1s
v4p0329c1s v5p0097c1s v5p0123c1s
v5p0205c2s v5p0284c1s v5p0333c1m
v5p0335c2s v5p0337c1s v6p0065c2s
v6p0373c1s
Brown, J.E. v2p0162c1s
v6p0325c1s v6p0524c2s v6p0614c1s
v6p0643c1s
Brown, J.F. v6p0575c1s
Brown, J.H. v1p0332c1s
v1p0834c1s v1p1227c2s v4p0144c2s
v4p0478c2s v4p0526c1s
Brown, J.J. v4p0160c1s
Brown, J.M. v1p0140c1s
v1p0905c1s v1p1220c1s v2p0200c2s
v3p0050c1s v3p0235c2s v3p0336c1s
v3p0338c1s v3p0405c2s
Brown, J.M. and Davie, G.M.
v2p0118c2s
Brown, J.M.A. v5p0457c2s
Brown, J.N. v1p0097c2s
v1p0711c1s v6p0657c1s
Brown, J.P. v1p0116c1s
v1p0294c1s v1p0294c2s v1p0345c2s
v1p0377c2s v1p0948c1s v1p1331c2m
v6p0104c1s
Brown, J.R. v1p0420c1s
v4p0066c2s v4p0225c2s v5p0060c2s
Brown, J.S. v3p0039c2s
v5p0309c2s v6p0290c1s v6p0524c2s
v6p0581c2s
Brown, J.S. and Soldan, F.L.
v6p0136c1s
Brown, J.T. v1p0897c2s
v1p1051c2s v1p1362c2s v2p0035c1s
v2p0434c1s v4p0618c2s
Brown, J.T., jr. and Halliday, Carl
v6p0284c1s
Brown, J.T.T. v6p0051c2s
v6p0390c2s
Brown, J.T.T. and Neilson, G.
v5p0047c2s
Brown, J.W. v1p0095c2s
v1p0319c1s v2p0400c1s
Brown, James v6p0305c1s
Brown, John, Dr. v1p0054c2s
v1p1277c2s
Brown, Julius A. v6p0542c2s
Brown, K. v4p0093c1s
v5p0421c1s v6p0507c1s v6p0695c1s
Brown, K.H. v5p0480c2s
v5p0596c1s v6p0166c1s v6p0285c1s
v6p0301c1s v6p0482c2s v6p0645c1s
v6p0649c2s
Brown, Katharine H. v5p0397c2s
v6p0081c1s v6p0217c1s
v6p0539c2s
Brown, L.B. v4p0439c2s
Brown, L.C. v5p0379c2s
Brown, M. v6p0132c2s
Brown, M.A. v1p1350c2s
v1p1419c2s
Brown, M.B. v5p0225c2s
v5p0620c1s
Brown, M.E. v1p1041c1s
v3p0066c2s
Brown, M.F. v4p0334c1s
v4p0461c2s
Brown, M.R. v1p0904c2s
v1p0905c2s
Brown, Mabel H. v6p0092c2s
v6p0136c2s v6p0350c1s
Brown, Maria A. v4p0125c2s
Brown, Marie A. v2p0428c1s
v4p0559c2s
Brown, Mary W. v5p0409c1s
Brown, May B. v5p0121c1s
v5p0558c1s
Brown, Miss v1p1387c2s
Brown, N.C. v1p0135c1s
v2p0118c2s v2p0364c1s v4p0061c2s
Brown, Nannie v4p0437c1s
Brown, O. v1p1423c2s
Brown, P. v1p0728c1s
Brown, P.A. v1p0507c2s
Brown, P.H. v4p0077c1s
v4p0285c1s
Brown, R. v1p0353c2s
v1p1015c1s v1p1107c2s v1p1113c1s
v2p0078c1s v2p0088c2s v2p0148c1s
v2p0298c2s v2p0310c2s v2p0316c1s
v2p0323c2s v2p0329c2s v2p0374c2s
v2p0445c1s v2p0452c2s v3p0066c1s
v3p0079c2s v3p0350c2s v4p0025c2s
v4p0048c2s v4p0484c2s v5p0026c1s
v5p0131c1s v5p0134c1s v5p0251c2s
v5p0639c2s v5p0645c2s v6p0127c2s
v6p0147c1s v6p0565c1m
Brown, R. and Fleming, G.. v1p0055c2s
Brown, R., Dr. v3p0288c2s
Brown, R., jr. v1p1269c2s
v2p0105c2s v2p0483c1s v3p0018c1s
v3p0143c2m v3p0153c1s v3p0474c2s
v4p0052c1s v4p0130c2s v4p0577c2s
Brown, R., jr. and Lang, A.
v2p0196c2s
Brown, R., jr. et al. v2p0249c1s
Brown, R.C. v4p0358c2s
Brown, R.C.E. v5p0421c2s
Brown, R.M. v6p0077c1s
v6p0422c1m
Brown, R.M.G. v3p0218c1s
Brown, R.S. v4p0304c1s
Brown, R.W. v2p0141c1s
v2p0432c2s
Brown, Robert M. v6p0127c2s
v6p0422c1s
Brown, S. v1p0335c1s
v1p0431c1s v1p0596c1s v1p0647c1s
v1p0673c1s v1p0758c1s v1p0907c2s
v1p1002c1s v1p1077c1s v1p1168c1s
v1p1245c2m v3p0276c2s v4p0139c2s
Brown, S.C., Mrs. v1p0806c1s
Brown, S.G. v1p0034c2m
v1p0061c1s v1p0215c1m v1p0330c1s
v1p0331c1s v1p0345c1s v1p0393c2s
v1p0482c2s v1p0945c2s v1p1133c1s
v1p1168c1s v1p1332c1s v1p1398c2s
Brown, S.J. v2p0026c1s
v5p0561c1s
Brown, S.S. v3p0136c2s
Brown, Sam., Dr. v1p0041c1s
v1p0519c2s v1p1005c2s
Brown, T. v5p0548c1s
Brown, T., jr. v1p0867c1s
Brown, T.C. v6p0251c1s
v6p0499c2s
Brown, T.D. v1p0966c1s
v6p0200c1s
Brown, T.E. v4p0080c2s
v4p0304c2s v4p0352c2s v4p0489c2s
v4p0523c1s v4p0620c1s v5p0545c2s
Brown, T.E., jr. v4p0177c2s
Brown, T.F. v3p0089c2s
v5p0124c1s
Brown, T.J. v1p1438c1s
v3p0342c2s
Brown, T.K. v1p0657c2s
Brown, T.L. v4p0481c1s
Brown, T.O. v3p0179c2s
Brown, T.S. v1p1149c2s
v1p1311c2s
Brown, T.W. v4p0209c2s
v5p0034c2s v5p0327c2s v5p0475c1s
Brown, V. v5p0255c2s
v5p0553c1s
Brown, W. v1p0289c2s
v1p0435c2s v1p0514c2s v1p0517c2s
v1p0625c2s v1p0861c1s v1p1215c2s
v1p1216c1s v1p1351c2s v1p1359c2m
v2p0063c1s
Brown, W. and Weeden, W.B.
v1p1040c1s
Brown, W.A. v3p0215c1s
v3p0408c1s v5p0115c1s v5p0256c1s
v5p0480c1s v6p0439c2s v6p0514c2s
Brown, W.B. v1p0291c1s
v1p0594c1s v1p0685c1s v1p0912c1s
v1p1179c1s v5p0124c2s
Brown, W.C. v5p0418c1s
v6p0543c2s
Brown, W.E. v6p0647c1s
Brown, W.F. v6p0053c1s
v6p0169c2s v6p0481c2s
Brown, W.Forster v6p0348c2s
Brown, W.G. v3p0132c2s
v4p0249c1s v5p0256c2s v5p0257c1s
v5p0320c1s v5p0328c1s v5p0434c1s
v5p0541c2s v5p0643c2s v6p0142c2s
v6p0144c2s v6p0179c2s v6p0261c1s
v6p0292c1s v6p0293c2s v6p0344c2s
v6p0377c2s v6p0422c1s v6p0448c2s
v6p0489c2s v6p0515c1s v6p0551c1s
v6p0605c1s v6p0669c2s v6p0686c2s
Brown, W.Garrott v6p0201c2m
v6p0550c1s
Brown, W.H. v1p0995c2s
v1p1007c2s v4p0428c2s v4p0455c2s
v6p0083c1s v6p0316c1s v6p0319c2s
v6p0522c2s
Brown, W.J. v5p0039c1s
v5p0091c2s v5p0256c1s v5p0316c2s
v6p0151c1s v6p0170c1s v6p0364c2m
v6p0607c1s
Brown, W.J., Prof. v6p0147c2s
Brown, W.L. v1p0008c1s
v1p1107c1s v1p1243c2s v2p0131c2s
v2p0411c1s v5p0023c2s v5p0038c2s
v5p0361c2s
Brown, W.N. v3p0054c1s
v3p0059c1s v3p0288c2s
Brown, W.P. v3p0044c2s
v3p0050c1s v3p0143c1s v3p0195c1s
v3p0253c1s v3p0290c2s v3p0335c1s
v3p0411c1s v4p0293c1s
Brown, W.R. v1p1110c1s
v6p0435c2s
Brown, W.S. v3p0466c1s
Brown, W.T. v5p0264c1s
Brown, W.V. v2p0270c2s
Brown, W.W. v4p0061c2s
Brown, W.W., Mrs. v4p0102c2s
v4p0607c2s
Brown, Walter and Becker, O.M.
v6p0616c1s
Brown-Jast v5p0333c1s
Brown-Sequard, C.E. v2p0113c2s
v3p0053c1s v3p0072c1s
Brownbill, J. v2p0053c2s
v2p0088c1s v2p0146c2s v4p0019c2s
Browne, A. v6p0142c2s
Browne, A.F. v3p0001c2m
v3p0016c2s v3p0055c1s v3p0308c1m
Browne, A.G. v3p0010c1s
Browne, A.G., jr. v1p0038c1s
v1p0872c1s v1p1360c1s v1p1385c2s
Browne, A.J.J. v3p0071c1s
Browne, A.J.Jukes v5p0011c1s
Browne, A.P. v3p0100c1s
Browne, A.S. v4p0377c2s
Browne, A.W. v2p0028c2s
Browne, B.C. v3p0138c2s
v3p0389c1s v5p0598c2s
Browne, B.C., Sir v5p0188c1s
v5p0188c2m v5p0451c1s
Browne, B.E. v2p0467c2s
Browne, B.P. v1p0305c1s
v1p0427c1s v3p0147c1s v6p0408c2s
Browne, C.A., jr. v6p0394c2s
v6p0651c1s
Browne, C.D. v1p0088c2s
Browne, C.E. v1p0056c2s
v1p0809c2s v1p1186c2s v6p0103c2s
Browne, C.E. and Hall, G.S.
v6p0117c2s
Browne, C.F. v1p0102c2s
v1p0622c1s v5p0083c2s v5p0105c2s
v5p0121c2s v5p0256c2s v5p0580c2s
v5p0614c2s v5p0625c2s
Browne, C.H. v6p0134c1s
Browne, C.O. v1p0946c2s
v1p1428c2s v3p0020c1s
Browne, C.R. v6p0030c1s
Browne, C.T. v1p0258c2s
Browne, C.W. v4p0476c2s
Browne, D. v6p0249c1s
Browne, D.H. v3p0260c2s
Browne, D.H. and Gayley, C.M.
v3p0312c1s
Browne, D.J. v1p1396c2s
Browne, D.K. v1p0178c2s
Browne, E. v1p0178c1s
v4p0589c1s
Browne, E.A. v6p0052c2s
v6p0081c2s v6p0165c2s
Browne, E.C. v5p0233c1s
Browne, E.G. v4p0145c2s
v4p0435c2s v6p0255c2s
Browne, E.L. v4p0393c1s
Browne, E.M.Thomas v4p0395c1s
Browne, Evelyn H. v5p0644c2s
Browne, F. v1p0139c2s
v2p0242c2s v2p0261c1s v2p0395c2s
v2p0457c1s
Browne, F.C. v1p0709c2s
v1p0718c2s
Browne, F.F. v1p0060c1s
v1p0183c1s v1p0357c1s v1p0471c1s
v1p0610c2s v1p0628c2s v1p0706c1s
v1p0744c1s v1p0767c2s v1p1021c1s
v1p1021c2s v1p1032c2s v1p1113c2s
v1p1187c2s v1p1276c1s v1p1381c2s
v1p1407c1s v1p1407c2s v1p1409c2s
v1p1430c1s v2p0051c2s v2p0068c1s
v2p0125c1s v2p0176c1s v2p0246c2s
v2p0249c2s v2p0271c1m v2p0336c1s
v2p0398c1s v2p0439c2s v2p0453c1s
v4p0012c1s v4p0596c1s v5p0472c1s
Browne, G. v3p0395c1s
Browne, G.DeH. v4p0067c2s
v4p0414c1s
Browne, G.E. v3p0267c1s
v5p0019c1s v5p0092c2s
Browne, G.F. v2p0018c2s
v2p0141c1s v2p0327c1s v3p0371c1m
v3p0444c2s v4p0442c2s v4p0451c2s
v4p0510c2m v4p0627c2s v5p0049c1s
v6p0398c1s
Browne, G.H. v1p0183c2s
v4p0183c2s v5p0531c1s
Browne, G.L. v2p0056c1s
v2p0422c1s v6p0264c2s v6p0405c2s
v6p0673c1m
Browne, G.M. v2p0058c2s
v2p0086c2s
Browne, G.Waldo v6p0097c1s
Browne, H. v3p0026c1s
v3p0145c2s v3p0271c1s v3p0357c1s
v3p0377c2m
Browne, H.A. v1p0270c1s
v6p0712c2s
Browne, H.C. v3p0351c1s
Browne, H.J. v2p0086c2s
v3p0025c2s
Browne, H.L. v2p0191c2s
Browne, H.M. and Hodgkin, L.V.
v3p0051c2s v3p0130c2s
Browne, H.R. v6p0566c2s
Browne, Hugh M. v6p0446c2s
Browne, I. v3p0007c1s
v3p0152c1s v3p0244c2s v3p0270c1s
v3p0304c2s v3p0463c2s v4p0136c1s
v4p0190c2s v4p0303c2s v4p0336c2s
v4p0356c2s v4p0401c1s v4p0410c2s
v4p0484c2s v4p0501c2s v4p0609c2s

v5p0013c1s v5p0067c2s v5p0309c2s
v5p0328c1s v5p0433c2s
Browne, J. v1p0079c1s
v1p1094c1s
Browne, J.A. v1p0038c2s
Browne, J.B. v4p0310c2s
Browne, J.C. v1p0338c1s
v1p0643c1s v1p0720c1s v3p0216c2s
Browne, J.C., Sir v4p0060c1s
v4p0187c2s v4p0516c2s
Browne, J.D. v1p0272c2s
Browne, J.G. v6p0030c2s
v6p0633c2s
Browne, J.H. v1p0032c1s
v1p0116c2s v1p0151c1s v1p0170c1s
v1p0171c2s v1p0177c1s v1p0201c1s
v1p0293c2s v1p0338c1m v1p0397c2s
v1p0473c2s v1p0489c1s v1p0498c2s
v1p0504c2s v1p0517c2s v1p0553c2s
v1p0556c1s v1p0574c1s v1p0583c1s
v1p0597c1s v1p0625c1s v1p0658c2s
v1p0728c2s v1p0774c2s v1p0819c2s
v1p0892c1s v1p0913c1s v1p0936c1s
v1p0969c2s v1p1045c2s v1p1059c2s
v1p1084c1s v1p1106c2s v1p1112c2s
v1p1128c2s v1p1138c1s v1p1147c2s
v1p1186c1s v1p1194c2s v1p1209c2s
v1p1229c1s v1p1236c2s v1p1242c1s
v1p1421c1m v1p1424c2s v1p1425c2s
v2p0030c1s v2p0312c2s v2p0313c1s
v2p0398c2s v3p0031c2s v3p0112c2s
v3p0118c2s v3p0128c1s v3p0263c2s
v3p0268c1s v3p0358c1s v3p0468c1s
v4p0043c1s v4p0072c1s v4p0336c2s
v4p0378c2s v5p0369c1s
Browne, J.H.B. v6p0600c1s
Browne, J.M. v1p0703c2s
v2p0006c2s v3p0333c2s
Browne, J.R. v1p0058c1s
v1p0187c1m v1p0187c2s v1p0188c1s
v1p0234c1s v1p0257c1s v1p0321c2s
v1p0515c1s v1p0622c1s v1p0697c1s
v1p0874c2s v1p0908c1m v1p0908c2s
v1p0929c2s v1p0956c2s v1p1024c1s
v1p1151c1s v1p1297c1s v1p1297c2s
v1p1389c1s v1p1403c1s
Browne, J.Ross v1p1439c1s
Browne, James, Dr. v1p1165c1s
Browne, L. v3p0400c2s
v3p0403c2s v4p0020c2s
Browne, L.C. v1p0979c2s
v1p1179c1s v1p1200c1s v1p1356c1s
Browne, M. v1p0041c1s
v1p0063c1s v1p0106c2s v1p0148c2s
v1p0170c2s v1p0308c1s v1p0341c1s
v1p0350c2s v1p0371c2s v1p0446c2s
v1p0511c2s v1p0746c1s v1p0773c2s
v1p0884c2s v1p0892c2s v1p0907c1s
v1p1021c1s v1p1025c1s v1p1178c1s
v1p1287c2s v1p1300c1s v1p1317c1s
v1p1426c1s v5p0080c1s
Browne, M.A. v1p0303c1s
v1p1371c2s
Browne, M.J.B. v1p0027c1s
Browne, M.T.B. v1p0259c2s
Browne, Miss v1p1203c2s
Browne, N.F. v4p0330c2s
v5p0334c2s
Browne, O. v2p0229c1s
Browne, P. v1p0067c1s
v4p0261c2s v4p0277c2s
Browne, P.A. v1p0447c2s
v1p0744c2s v1p0815c2s v1p0978c2s
v1p1374c1s
Browne, P.E. v6p0142c1s
v6p0295c2s
Browne, Porter E. v6p0174c2s
Browne, Porter Emerson ... v6p0036c1s
Browne, R. v1p0055c1s
Browne, R.C. v2p0032c1s
v2p0139c2s v2p0246c2s v2p0335c1s
v3p0235c2s v3p0240c2s v3p0314c2s
v4p0011c1s v4p0097c2s v4p0155c2s
v4p0201c2s v4p0322c1s v4p0599c1s
Browne, R.E. v2p0119c2s
v2p0153c2s
Browne, R.G.M. v3p0409c2s
v4p0034c1s v4p0222c2s v4p0558c1s
Browne, R.K. v1p0399c1s
Browne, R.W. v2p0127c1s
Browne, S.C. v1p0985c2s
Browne, T.B. v1p0600c1s
v1p1327c2s
Browne, T.S. v5p0511c1s
Browne, W. v1p0574c1s
v4p0209c2s v4p0545c2s
Browne, W.H. v1p0009c1s
v1p0014c2s v1p0015c1s v1p0015c2s
v1p0061c2s v1p0081c2s v1p0138c1s
v1p0170c2s v1p0203c2s v1p0226c2s
v1p0283c1s v1p0311c2s v1p0326c1s
v1p0350c2s v1p0413c1s v1p0417c2s
v1p0419c1m v1p0474c1s v1p0474c2s
v1p0476c2s v1p0488c2s v1p0496c1s
v1p0511c2s v1p0512c1s v1p0527c1s
v1p0538c1s v1p0557c2s v1p0560c2s
v1p0570c2s v1p0574c1s v1p0611c1s
v1p0611c2s v1p0618c1s v1p0638c1s
v1p0725c1s v1p0735c2s v1p0741c2s
v1p0750c1s v1p0771c1s v1p0786c2s
v1p0799c1s v1p0799c2s v1p0807c2m
v1p0832c1s v1p0833c2s v1p0836c1s
v1p0848c2s v1p0873c1m v1p0884c1s
v1p0893c2s v1p0979c1s v1p0982c2s
v1p1005c2s v1p1015c2s v1p1019c2m
v1p1020c1s v1p1028c1s v1p1049c1s
v1p1068c2s v1p1094c1s v1p1132c2s
v1p1135c1s v1p1143c1s v1p1164c1s
v1p1176c1s v1p1184c1s v1p1184c2s
v1p1224c1s v1p1224c2m v1p1236c1s
v1p1237c2s v1p1260c1s v1p1261c1s
v1p1273c1s v1p1279c2s v1p1295c1m
v1p1295c2s v1p1317c2s v1p1319c2s
v1p1347c1m v1p1380c1s v1p1412c2s
v1p1418c1s v2p0216c2m v2p0279c1s
v4p0231c2s v5p0016c1s v5p0044c2m
v5p0420c2s v5p0511c1s v5p0620c2s
v6p0090c2s
Browne, W.H. and Ewbank, H.
v1p1223c1s
Browne, W.K. v2p0183c1s
Browne, W.M. v4p0411c1s
v5p0252c1s v5p0266c1s v5p0487c1s
v5p0498c2s v5p0499c1s
Browne, W.R. v1p0387c1s
v1p0924c2s v1p1030c2s v1p1079c2s
v1p1214c2s v2p0065c2s v2p0179c2s
v2p0360c2s v2p0363c2s v2p0389c1s
v2p0467c2s v3p0366c2s v6p0148c1s
v6p0228c1s
Browne, W.R. et al. v2p0080c2s
Browne, W.T. v4p0098c1s
Brownell, A. v4p0069c1s
v4p0146c2s v4p0376c1s v4p0383c1s
v4p0528c2s v6p0089c2s v6p0398c2s
v6p0429c2s v6p0655c1s
Brownell, Atherton v6p0160c1s
v6p0160c2s
Brownell, C.F. v6p0022c1s
Brownell, C.L. v5p0303c2s
Brownell, D.W. v1p0837c1s
Brownell, Edith v6p0291c2s
Brownell, F.C. v4p0611c1s
Brownell, H.H. v1p0562c1s
v1p0750c1s
Brownell, H.M.K. v2p0121c2s
Brownell, J.L. v4p0062c1s
Brownell, L. v5p0173c1s
Brownell, L.W. v6p0094c2s
v6p0230c1s v6p0320c2s v6p0367c2s
v6p0437c2s v6p0497c1m
Brownell, T.F. v1p0427c1s
v1p0930c2s v1p0992c2s v1p1305c2s
v1p1307c2s
Brownell, W.A. v3p0062c1s
Brownell, W.C. v1p0029c1s
v1p0030c1m v1p0031c2s v1p0060c1m
v1p0064c2m v1p0103c2s v1p0184c1s
v1p0191c1s v1p0202c1s v1p0340c1s
v1p0350c2s v1p0357c4s v1p0368c2s
v1p0417c1s v1p0417c2s v1p0419c1s
v1p0451c1s v1p0492c1s v1p0511c2s
v1p0610c2s v1p0722c2s v1p0796c2s
v1p0841c1s v1p0918c1s v1p0958c1s
v1p1032c2s v1p1176c2s v1p1226c2s
v1p1298c1s v1p1354c2s v1p1405c2s
v1p1409c2s v1p1430c1s v2p0013c1m
v2p0198c1s v2p0233c1s v2p0265c1s
v2p0392c2s v3p0109c1s v3p0164c1m
v3p0303c2s v3p0320c1s v3p0363c1s
v3p0382c1s v3p0382c2s v4p0029c2s
v4p0047c1s v4p0402c1s v4p0421c2m
v4p0426c1m v4p0601c1s v5p0029c2s
v5p0031c2s v5p0085c1s v5p0094c2s
v5p0186c1s v5p0446c2s v5p0492c1s
v5p0500c1s v5p0574c2s v6p0032c1s
v6p0103c2s v6p0148c1s v6p0200c2s
v6p0209c1s v6p0287c1s v6p0333c1s
Browning, A. v3p0296c2s
Browning, C.H. v5p0558c1s
v6p0031c1s v6p0095c1s v6p0276c2s
Browning, E.B. v1p0467c2s
v1p0756c1s v1p0885c1s v1p1220c2s
v2p0230c2s v6p0619c1s
Browning, E.B. and Horne, R.H.
v1p1061c2s
Browning, E.G. v5p0336c2s
Browning, G. v2p0231c1s
Browning, H.E. v6p0098c1s
Browning, H.Ellen v6p0544c1s
Browning, J. v1p0699c1s
v1p0804c1s v1p1152c2s v2p0045c2s
v2p0151c1s v2p0402c1s v2p0446c1m
v2p0446c2m v2p0450c1s v2p0469c1s
Browning, J.B. v2p0018c2s
v2p0213c2s v2p0340c2s
Browning, O. v1p0051c2s
v1p0461c1s v2p0045c2s v2p0065c1s
v2p0141c2s v2p0164c1s v2p0266c2s
v2p0445c2s v2p0446c2s v3p0020c2s
v3p0064c1s v3p0069c1s v3p0128c1s
v3p0134c2s v3p0135c1m v3p0176c1s
v3p0197c2s v3p0245c2s v4p0118c1s
v4p0147c2s v4p0202c2s v4p0295c1s
v6p0206c2s v6p0646c2s
Browning, Oscar v3p0068c2s
v3p0295c2s v5p0636c2s v6p0219c1s
v6p0500c1s v6p0655c1s
Browning, P.E. v3p0360c2s
v4p0016c2s v4p0045c2s v4p0046c1s
v4p0083c1s v4p0133c1s v4p0554c1s
v4p0600c1s v5p0087c1s v5p0100c1s
v5p0575c1s
Browning, P.E. and Flora, C.P.
v6p0107c1s
Browning, P.E. and Gooch, F.A.
v3p0021c1s v3p0219c1s v4p0288c2s
Browning, P.E. and Goodman, R.J.
v4p0600c1s
Browning, P.E. and Hartwell, J.B.
v5p0411c1s
Browning, P.E. and Howe, E.
v5p0560c1s
Browning, P.E. and Hutchins, G.P.
v5p0575c1s
Browning, P.E. and Jones, L.C.
v4p0082c1s
Browning, R. v1p0533c2s
v1p0589c1s v1p1339c1s
Browning, T.B. v1p0286c1s
v4p0049c2s v4p0402c1s v6p0099c2s
v6p0267c2s
Browning, W. v1p0380c2s
Brownlee, E.V. v6p0603c2s
Brownlee, J.H. v3p0140c1s
Brownlee, W.M. and Grace, W.G.
v3p0104c2s
Brownlie, A. v6p0646c1s
v6p0646c2s
Brownlow, Canon v3p0385c1m
v3p0395c2m
Brownlow, E.B. v3p0400c2s
v3p0473c1s v4p0536c2s v4p0537c1s
v4p0634c1s
Brownlow, Earl v5p0244c2s
Brownlow, Monsignor v4p0192c1s
Brownlow, W.P. v6p0545c1s
Brownlow, W.R. v1p0957c1s
v3p0269c2s v4p0459c2s v5p0010c2s
Brownrigg, H. v1p0966c1s
Brownsmith, S. v2p0361c2s
Brownson, C.L. v4p0026c1s
v4p0035c1s v4p0600c2s
Brownson, C.L. et al. v4p0186c2s
Brownson, O.A. v1p0069c1m
v1p0107c2m v1p0114c1s v1p0171c1s
v1p0201c2s v1p0203c2s v1p0218c2s
v1p0239c2s v1p0241c2s v1p0247c1s
v1p0247c2s v1p0252c1s v1p0260c1s
v1p0261c2s v1p0293c2s v1p0309c2m
v1p0342c2s v1p0364c2s v1p0385c1s
v1p0386c1s v1p0391c1m v1p0398c2s
v1p0440c2s v1p0472c1s v1p0486c1s
v1p0527c2s v1p0538c1s v1p0571c2s
v1p0587c1s v1p0595c1s v1p0623c1s
v1p0625c1s v1p0648c2s v1p0650c1s
v1p0673c2s v1p0715c1s v1p0730c1s
v1p0741c2s v1p0797c1s v1p0810c2s
v1p0819c1s v1p0861c2s v1p0869c1s
v1p0869c2s v1p0898c2s v1p0900c2m
v1p0912c2s v1p0964c2s v1p1001c1s
v1p1001c2m v1p1002c1s v1p1037c2s
v1p1055c1s v1p1058c2s v1p1062c1s
v1p1083c2s v1p1085c1s v1p1086c1s
v1p1089c2s v1p1095c2s v1p1096c2s
v1p1103c2s v1p1115c2m v1p1117c2m
v1p1118c1m v1p1119c2s v1p1120c1m
v1p1120c2s v1p1121c1s v1p1124c1s
v1p1142c1s v1p1216c2s v1p1217c1s
v1p1235c1s v1p1238c1m v1p1238c2s
v1p1271c1s v1p1304c1s v1p1363c2s
v1p1412c1s v1p1420c2s
Brownson, S.G. v1p0587c1s
Brownson, W.H. v3p0356c1s
Browski, L.E. v3p0116c1s
v3p0474c2s
Broxap, E. v6p0302c1s
Broyde, I. and Adler, E.N.
v5p0071c1s
Brubacher, A.R. v6p0581c2s
Brubaker, J. v1p0252c2s
v1p0852c2s v4p0300c1s v5p0467c1s
Bruce, A. v6p0408c2s
Bruce, A.A. v6p0203c1s
v6p0580c2s
Bruce, A.B. v1p0980c1s
v2p0044c2s v2p0183c2s v4p0057c1m
v4p0057c2s v4p0109c1s v4p0109c2s
v4p0188c1s v4p0300c2m v4p0301c2s
v4p0302c2s v4p0384c1s v4p0500c2s
v4p0530c1s v5p0009c1s v5p0174c1s
v5p0305c2m v5p0306c1s v5p0371c1s
v5p0577c1s
Bruce, A.B. et al. v2p0438c1s
v4p0108c2s
Bruce, A.F. v3p0137c1s
Bruce, A.T. v2p0140c2s
v2p0340c2s
Bruce, B.E. v3p0327c2s
Bruce, B.S. v5p0430c1s
Bruce, C. v1p0891c2s
v2p0009c1m v3p0055c1s v6p0281c1s
Bruce, C., Sir v3p0211c1s
Bruce, C.A. v1p1287c2s
Bruce, C.D. v5p0110c2s
v6p0036c2s
Bruce, D. v1p0135c2s
v1p0361c2s v3p0300c1s v6p0007c2s
v6p0082c2s v6p0617c2s
Bruce, E.B. v1p0807c2s

Bruce, E.C. v1p0054c1s
v1p0185c2s v1p0199c1s v1p0212c1s
v1p0701c1s v1p0703c1s v1p0723c1s
v1p0901c1s v1p1107c2s v1p1284c1s
v1p1299c1s v1p1346c2s v1p1364c1s
v1p1373c1s v1p1377c1m v2p0010c1s
v2p0011c2s v2p0047c1s v2p0136c2s
v2p0152c2s v2p0160c1s v2p0295c1s
v2p0312c1s v2p0363c2s v2p0400c1s
v2p0482c2s
Bruce, E.H.Stuart v6p0048c2s
Bruce, E.L. v5p0351c1s
Bruce, E.S. v3p0031c1m
v3p0380c1s v4p0204c2s
Bruce, E.V. v2p0338c2s
Bruce, F. v5p0285c2s
Bruce, G.E. v6p0646c1s
Bruce, G.L. v4p0340c1s
v5p0165c1s v6p0383c2s v6p0385c2s
Bruce, H.A. v5p0557c2s
v6p0009c1s v6p0058c1s v6p0066c2s
v6p0127c1s v6p0165c2s v6p0287c1s
v6p0404c1s v6p0408c2s v6p0490c1s
v6p0501c1s v6p0521c2s v6p0593c2s
v6p0645c2s v6p0660c2s
Bruce, H.Addington v6p0611c1s
Bruce, H.G. v2p0071c2s
v2p0098c1s v2p0431c2s v2p0467c1s
v3p0071c1s v3p0172c2s v3p0264c1s
v3p0306c2s
Bruce, H.J. v1p0136c2s
Bruce, H.W. v1p1107c1s
Bruce, J. v1p0172c2s
v1p0192c1s v1p0219c2s v1p0256c1s
v1p0348c2s v1p0425c1s v1p0457c1s
v1p0459c2s v1p0536c1s v1p0538c2m
v1p0563c1s v1p0733c1s v1p0764c2s
v1p0808c2s v1p0870c2m v1p0877c1s
v1p0913c2s v1p0987c1s v1p1138c2s
v1p1244c1m
Bruce, J. and Almack, R. . v1p0977c2s
Bruce, J.C. v1p0538c1s
v2p0141c2s v2p0376c2s v5p0119c1s
v5p0541c2s
Bruce, J.D. v6p0049c1s
v6p0461c1s v6p0588c1s v6p0640c2s
Bruce, J.M. v1p0612c1s
v1p0849c2s v5p0500c2s
Bruce, L.Knight v3p0236c1s
Bruce, N.B. v4p0148c2s
Bruce, P. v4p0032c2s
Bruce, P.A. v2p0442c1s
v5p0088c1s v5p0196c2s v5p0402c2m
v5p0598c2s
Bruce, R. v3p0219c2s
v5p0041c1m v5p0150c2s v5p0151c1s
v5p0159c2s v5p0225c1s v5p0528c1s
v6p0150c2s
Bruce, R.E. v6p0626c1s
Bruce, S.M. v6p0348c1s
Bruce, T.B. v4p0294c2s
Bruce, Viola v5p0420c2s
Bruce, W. v1p0135c2s
v4p0371c1s
Bruce, W.J. v1p0483c2s
v1p0947c2s
Bruce, W.S. v4p0019c2m
v4p0331c2s v4p0511c2s v5p0022c1s
v5p0053c1s v5p0413c1s
Bruce, Wallace v4p0413c1s
Bruce-Angier, C. v5p0094c1s
Bruch, G.J. v1p0828c1s
Bruch, J.F. v1p1222c1s
Bruch, Prof. and Bellows, H.W.
v1p0740c2s
Bruckmann, A.E. v3p0022c2s
Bruckner, G. v1p0024c2s
v1p0689c1s v1p1321c2s
Brudno, E.S. v5p0308c1s
v6p0017c2s v6p0343c2s v6p0344c1s
Bruel, K. v4p0637c2s
Bruen, A.J. v4p0096c2s
Bruen, M. v1p0504c2s
v1p1216c1s
Bruere, R.W. v6p0456c1s
Brues, C.T. v6p0024c2s
Bruggen, Baron von der ... v2p0176c2s
Brugmann, K. v3p0172c1s
Bruhl, G. v2p0077c1s
Bruhl, J.W. v6p0609c1s
Bruhl, M. v4p0424c2s
Bruhmet, M.A. v1p0677c2s
v1p0679c1s v1p0701c2s
Brumback, F.F. v4p0153c2s
Brumbaugh, M.G. v4p0597c2m
v4p0598c1s v6p0428c1s v6p0509c2s
Brumby, Prof. v1p0017c2s
Brumell, H.P. v4p0094c1s
Brummitt, D.B. v6p0588c2s
Brumner, J. v6p0055c2s
Brun, Le v1p1288c2s
Brun, S.J. v4p0157c2s
v5p0218c1s
Bruncken, E. v5p0253c1s
v6p0615c1s
Brune, A. v5p0114c1s
Bruneau, J. v6p0062c2s
Brunel, A. v1p0493c2s
Brunel, M.I. v1p1299c1s
Bruner, F.M. v2p0083c2s
v2p0085c1s
Bruner, J.D. v6p0302c1s
Bruner, J.W. v6p0163c1s
Bruner, Jane W. v5p0011c1s
Bruner, W.H. v1p0707c1s
Brunet-Debaines, A. v6p0481c1s
v6p0660c2s
Brunetiere, F. v4p0193c1s
v4p0215c1s v4p0324c2s v5p0014c2m
v5p0017c1s v5p0030c1s v5p0089c1s
v5p0104c1s v5p0189c1s v5p0221c1m
v5p0221c2s v5p0558c1s v6p0049c1s
Brunetiere, F. et al. v5p0221c1s
Brunhes, H.J. v6p0114c2s
Brunin, L. v1p1391c1s
Brunlees, J. v1p1079c1s
v2p0363c2s
Brunner, A. v1p0759c1s
Brunner, H. v4p0323c1s
Brunner, H.C. and Matthews, B.
v2p0395c2s
Brunner, J. v6p0275c1s
Brunner, Josef v6p0612c1s
Brunner, M. v1p0073c2s
Brunot, F.R. v1p0939c1s
Brunowe, M.J. v4p0400c2s
Bruns, H.D. v6p0048c2s
Bruns, P. v5p0106c2s
v5p0580c2s
Bruns, R.M. v5p0233c2s
Brunson, A. v1p0273c1s
v1p0831c1s v1p1399c1s
Brunt, C.Van v1p0400c1s
Brunt, H.Van v1p0054c2s
v1p0062c1s v1p0063c1s v1p0063c2s
v1p0339c2m v1p1236c2s v2p0020c1m
v2p0025c2s v2p0253c1s v2p0372c1s
v3p0018c2s v4p0023c2s v4p0100c2m
v4p0269c2s v5p0082c2s v5p0496c1s
Brunt, H.Van and Walker, C.H.
v2p0208c2s
Brunt, H.Van and Winsor, J.
v1p0743c2s
Brunt, H.Van et al. v2p0184c2s
Brunton, C. v6p0689c1s
Brunton, L. v6p0365c2s
Brunton, L.M. v4p0048c2s
Brunton, Lander v6p0284c2s
Brunton, T.C. v1p0639c1s
Brunton, T.L. v1p0019c2s
v1p0354c1s v2p0076c1s v4p0064c1s
v4p0135c1s v4p0249c2s v5p0449c2s
Brunton, W. v4p0607c2s
Brush, A.A. v3p0105c1s
Brush, C.F. v1p0399c1s
v5p0226c2s v5p0260c1s v6p0026c2s
Brush, C.F. and Morley, E.W.
v6p0249c1s
Brush, E. v5p0131c1s
Brush, E.F. v2p0413c2s
v5p0143c2s
Brush, E.H. v5p0062c2s
v5p0082c1s v6p0012c1s v6p0436c2s
v6p0564c1s
Brush, F. v5p0260c1s
Brush, G.de F. v2p0219c1s
Brush, G.J. v1p0823c2s
v1p0845c1m v2p0290c1s
Brush, G.J. and Dana, E.S.
v1p0439c2s v1p0844c2s v3p0053c1s
v3p0280c2s
Brush, G.J. and Smith, J.L.
v1p0844c1s
Brush, M.E. v3p0358c2s
v3p0392c1s
Brushfield, T.N. v2p0364c2s
Brushingham, J.P. v5p0199c1s
v6p0213c2s
Brusie, C.F. v4p0335c1s
Brussler, C.A. v6p0059c1s
Bry, H. v1p0772c2m
Bry, R.M. v1p0772c2s
Bryan, A.J. v6p0567c2s
Bryan, A.S. v5p0640c2s
Bryan, Alfred C. v5p0046c2s
Bryan, C. v1p0339c1s
v5p0118c2s v5p0229c2s v5p0348c1s
v5p0428c1s v5p0628c1s
Bryan, C.P. v3p0076c2s
Bryan, E.B. v5p0398c2s
Bryan, E.L. v1p1023c1s
Bryan, F.C. v6p0360c2s
Bryan, G. v4p0585c2s
Bryan, G.H. v4p0036c1s
v4p0221c1s v5p0004c2s v5p0053c1s
v5p0054c2s v5p0194c2s v5p0210c2s
v5p0263c1s v5p0316c1s v5p0513c2s
v5p0577c2s v5p0614c1s v6p0005c1s
v6p0091c2s v6p0134c2s v6p0196c1s
v6p0211c2s v6p0220c2s v6p0245c2s
v6p0255c2s v6p0294c2s v6p0471c1s
v6p0486c2s v6p0671c1s v6p0678c1s
v6p0689c1s
Bryan, J.P.K. v2p0339c1s
Bryan, J.T. v5p0174c1s
Bryan, J.W. v6p0319c2m
Bryan, L.R. et al. v5p0327c1s
Bryan, R.S. v2p0340c2s
Bryan, T.W.G. v5p0274c2s
Bryan, W.H. v1p0332c2s
v4p0160c1s v4p0552c2s v5p0025c1s
v5p0082c2s v5p0533c2s v5p0551c2s
v6p0564c1s
Bryan, W.J. v4p0144c1m
v4p0525c1s v5p0304c1s v5p0464c2s
v5p0603c1s v5p0603c2s v6p0170c1s
v6p0220c1s v6p0317c2s v6p0485c1s
v6p0601c1s
Bryan, W.J. et al. v4p0563c2s
v5p0382c2s
Bryan, W.L. v4p0384c2s
v6p0643c1s v6p0670c2s
Bryan, W.L. and Harter, N.
v5p0570c2m
Bryan, W.S.P. v5p0004c1s
v5p0464c1s
Bryant, A.P. and Day, W.C.
v4p0062c2s
Bryant, C. v1p0597c2s
v3p0383c1s
Bryant, C.S. v1p0392c1s
v2p0028c2s
Bryant, E. v1p0187c2s
Bryant, E.E. v5p0633c2s
Bryant, E.J. v3p0467c2s
Bryant, F.E. v6p0645c1s
Bryant, H.F. v5p0559c1s
Bryant, H.G. v4p0025c1s
v4p0316c1s
Bryant, J. and Marsden, W.
v1p0522c2s
Bryant, J.D. v2p0367c1s
Bryant, J.H. v1p0014c1s
v4p0573c2s
Bryant, L.M. v6p0707c2s
Bryant, L.T. v5p0349c2s
v5p0395c2s v5p0589c1s v6p0658c2s
Bryant, Lilian T. v6p0128c2s
v6p0215c1s
Bryant, P. v4p0072c2s
Bryant, R.C. and Chetwood, J.
v6p0309c1s
Bryant, S. v3p0242c2s
v4p0020c1s v4p0171c2s v4p0514c1s
v4p0561c1s v4p0566c1s v5p0099c1s
v5p0370c1s v5p0519c1s
Bryant, S., Mrs. v2p0078c1s
Bryant, S.C. v5p0424c2s
v6p0303c2s v6p0662c2s
Bryant, T.H. v5p0512c2s
v6p0290c2s v6p0701c2s
Bryant, W.C. v1p0032c2s
v1p0035c1s v1p0103c1s v1p0310c1s
v1p0330c1s v1p0338c1m v1p0460c1s
v1p0460c2s v1p0558c2s v1p0567c1s
v1p0591c1s v1p0603c2s v1p0621c1s
v1p0676c1s v1p0678c1s v1p0876c1s
v1p0918c1s v1p0941c1s v1p1016c1s
v1p1102c1s v1p1131c2s v1p1172c1s
v1p1175c2s v1p1191c1s v1p1292c1s
v1p1336c1s v1p1393c1s
Bryant, W.H. v4p0515c1s
Bryant, W.M. v1p0323c1s
v1p0385c2s v1p0392c2s v1p0702c1s
v1p0891c1s v1p1006c2m v1p1083c1s
v1p1144c1s v1p1356c1s v2p0059c2s
v2p0072c1s v2p0323c2s v2p0342c2s
v3p0093c2s v3p0098c1s v3p0127c2m
v3p0209c1s v3p0218c2s v3p0314c2s
v4p0147c1s
Bryant, W.McK. v5p0249c2s
Bryce, C. v4p0353c2s
Bryce, G. v3p0266c1s
v4p0170c1s
Bryce, J. v1p0030c2s
v1p0104c1s v1p0127c1s v1p0201c2s
v1p0294c1s v1p0511c2s v1p0525c1s
v1p0539c1s v1p0550c1s v1p0611c1s
v1p0622c2m v1p0734c2m v1p0796c2s
v1p0954c1s v1p0973c1s v1p1030c2s
v1p1134c1s v1p1331c1m v1p1440c2s
v2p0004c1s v2p0012c1s v2p0036c2s
v2p0054c1m v2p0056c1s v2p0060c2s
v2p0063c2s v2p0064c2s v2p0084c2s
v2p0111c1s v2p0112c1s v2p0124c2s
v2p0133c2m v2p0134c1m v2p0135c1s
v2p0142c2m v2p0143c1m v2p0153c2s
v2p0166c2s v2p0170c2s v2p0173c1s
v2p0179c2s v2p0186c1s v2p0186c2m
v2p0187c1m v2p0187c2m v2p0188c1m
v2p0188c2m v2p0189c1m v2p0191c2m
v2p0200c1s v2p0205c1s v2p0208c2m
v2p0209c1s v2p0217c1s v2p0218c1s
v2p0218c2s v2p0224c2m v2p0225c1s
v2p0225c2s v2p0226c1m v2p0226c2m
v2p0227c1m v2p0227c2s v2p0228c1s
v2p0234c2s v2p0240c1s v2p0251c2s
v2p0277c2s v2p0294c2s v2p0312c2s
v2p0327c2s v2p0330c2m v2p0331c1m
v2p0353c2s v2p0373c1s v2p0379c1s
v2p0380c2m v2p0384c2s v2p0386c2s
v2p0388c2s v2p0408c1s v2p0423c2m
v2p0424c2s v2p0430c1s v2p0447c1s
v2p0451c2s v2p0454c2s v2p0455c2s
v2p0456c1m v2p0458c2s v2p0473c2s
v2p0477c2s v2p0478c1s v3p0088c2s
v3p0118c1s v3p0124c2s v3p0188c2s
v3p0199c2s v3p0201c2s v3p0202c1s
v3p0222c1s v3p0234c1s v3p0295c2s
v3p0299c1s v3p0302c2s v3p0307c1s

v3p0337c1s v3p0431c2s v4p0006c1m
v4p0027c1s v4p0116c2m v4p0214c1m
v4p0238c2s v4p0353c2s v4p0370c1s
v4p0397c1s v4p0415c2s v4p0450c1s
v4p0520c2s v4p0530c2s v4p0582c1s
v4p0596c2s v4p0601c2s v5p0006c1m
v5p0012c1s v5p0095c2s v5p0128c2s
v5p0234c2m v5p0248c1s v5p0315c1s
v5p0391c2s v5p0406c2s v5p0462c1s
v5p0515c1s v5p0528c2s v5p0588c1s
v5p0600c2s v6p0003c1m v6p0036c1s
v6p0084c1s v6p0094c2m v6p0151c2s
v6p0160c1s v6p0160c2s v6p0161c1s
v6p0170c2s v6p0186c2m v6p0191c2s
v6p0237c1s v6p0250c2s v6p0258c1s
v6p0283c1s v6p0291c1s v6p0326c2s
v6p0360c2s v6p0366c2s v6p0369c2s
v6p0434c2s v6p0445c2s v6p0475c2s
v6p0542c1s v6p0549c2s v6p0562c1s
v6p0578c1s v6p0593c1m v6p0605c2s
v6p0610c1s v6p0630c2s v6p0667c2s
v6p0678c2s
Bryce, J. and Amos, S. ... v2p0187c2s
Bryce, J. and Dicey, A.V.. v5p0606c1s
Bryce, J. and Laugel, A. . v2p0423c2s
Bryce, J. and Nettleship, R.L.
v2p0191c2s
Bryce, J. and Webb, A. ... v5p0611c1s
Bryce, James v5p0021c2s
v5p0194c1s v6p0006c1s v6p0014c2s
v6p0301c1s
Bryce, L. v3p0099c1s
v3p0122c2s v5p0089c2s v5p0477c2s
v5p0593c2s
Bryce, L. et al. v3p0360c2s
Bryce, L.S. v1p1239c2s
v3p0013c1s v3p0096c2m v3p0399c1s
v3p0441c2s
Bryce, M. v2p0477c2s
Bryce, M.R.L. v4p0304c2s
Bryce, N.J. v1p1243c1s
Bryce, P. v2p0289c2s
Bryce, P.H. v4p0107c2s
v4p0368c1s v4p0577c1s v6p0308c2s
Bryce, T.H. v6p0578c2s
Bryceson, H. v3p0314c1s
Bryden, H.A. v3p0173c1s
v3p0193c2s v3p0234c1s v3p0258c2s
v4p0065c1m v4p0080c2s v4p0173c2s
v4p0219c1s v4p0243c2s v4p0325c1s
v4p0350c1s v4p0403c1s v4p0415c2s
v4p0447c2s v4p0460c2s v4p0483c1s
v4p0512c2s v4p0582c1s v4p0583c2s
v5p0006c1s v5p0007c1m v5p0007c2s
v5p0022c2m v5p0051c2s v5p0062c2s
v5p0084c2s v5p0182c1s v5p0202c2s
v5p0225c1s v5p0256c1m v5p0276c2m
v5p0324c2s v5p0486c2s v5p0487c2s
v5p0547c2s v5p0576c1s v6p0020c1s
v6p0047c1s v6p0200c1s v6p0256c2s
v6p0280c2m v6p0329c1s v6p0440c2s
v6p0491c1s v6p0598c1s v6p0618c2s
Bryden, H.A. et al. v5p0510c2s
Brydges, E., Sir v1p0165c2m
v1p0505c1s v1p0648c2s v1p0948c2s
v1p0985c1s v1p1433c2s v4p0235c1s
Brydges, H. v3p0323c2s
v3p0334c2s
Brydon, J. v4p0332c1s
Bryent, W. v1p1416c1s
Bryer, J. v5p0130c2s
Bryne, A. v4p0567c2s
Bryne, J.C. v1p0406c1s
Bryson, L.F. v4p0185c2s
v4p0226c2s v5p0496c2s
Bryson, M. v6p0350c2s
Bryson, Mrs. v5p0579c2s
Bryson, W. v1p1010c2m
Bubna, A.de v1p0110c1s
v6p0484c1s
Buch, L.von v1p0196c1s
v1p0785c2s v1p1377c1s
Buchan, A. v1p0073c2s
v1p0265c2s v1p0543c2s v1p0632c2s
v1p0829c1s v1p0873c2s v1p1081c1s
v1p1165c2s v1p1395c1s v2p0039c2s
v2p0285c2m v2p0364c1s v5p0369c1s
v6p0556c1s
Buchan, J. v4p0017c2s
v4p0127c1s v4p0201c1s v4p0428c2s
v4p0451c1s v4p0485c1s v5p0036c1s
v5p0202c2s v5p0215c2s v5p0309c1s
v5p0360c2s v5p0392c2s v5p0412c2s
v5p0465c1s v5p0494c2s v5p0539c1s
v5p0621c2s v6p0007c2m v6p0472c1s
Buchan, J. et al. v5p0553c1s
Buchan, J.M. v1p0153c1s
v1p0265c1s v1p0287c1s v1p0346c2s
v1p0595c1s
Buchan, John v5p0081c1s
v5p0254c1s v5p0282c2s
Buchan, W. v5p0129c2s
v5p0154c1s
Buchan, Wm. v5p0205c1s
Buchanan, A.E. v4p0487c2s
Buchanan, A.H. v2p0258c1s
Buchanan, Agnes F. v6p0568c2s
Buchanan, C.M. v5p0049c1s
v5p0288c2s
Buchanan, E.M. v1p0978c1s
Buchanan, F. v1p0663c2s
v1p0856c2s
Buchanan, G. v1p0162c1s
v3p0414c1s v3p0447c2s
Buchanan, H.B.M. v4p0568c2s
v6p0219c2s
Buchanan, J. v2p0138c2s
v4p0409c2s v5p0164c1s
Buchanan, J.G. v1p1171c2s
Buchanan, J.R. v1p1062c2s
v1p1215c1s v2p0208c1s v3p0010c1s
v3p0015c1s v3p0144c1s v3p0168c2s
v3p0241c1s v3p0398c1s v3p0467c1s
v4p0109c2s v4p0169c2s v4p0170c2m
v4p0176c2s v4p0300c1s v4p0465c2m
v4p0573c2s v5p0481c2s v6p0112c2s
v6p0356c1s
Buchanan, J.R. and Wright, C.D.
v5p0585c1s
Buchanan, J.T. v3p0015c1s
v6p0232c2s
Buchanan, J.Y. v1p0340c1s
v1p0340c2s v1p0718c1s v2p0027c1s
v2p0319c1s v2p0393c2s v2p0434c1s
v2p0467c1s v3p0207c1s v3p0382c2s
v3p0390c2s v4p0410c2s v4p0618c2s
v5p0022c1s v5p0089c1s v5p0234c1s
v5p0537c2s v5p0561c1s
Buchanan, Jos.R. v3p0098c1s
Buchanan, L. v6p0430c2s
Buchanan, Lloyd v6p0031c1s
v6p0086c1s v6p0635c2s
Buchanan, M.F. v1p1087c2s
Buchanan, R. v1p0087c2s
v1p0106c2s v1p0139c1s v1p0202c1s
v1p0257c1s v1p0330c1s v1p0331c1s
v1p0357c1s v1p0405c1s v1p0424c1s
v1p0440c1s v1p0472c2s v1p0520c2s
v1p0527c1s v1p0529c2s v1p0570c1s
v1p0580c2s v1p0612c1s v1p0625c2s
v1p0668c1s v1p0698c1s v1p0700c2s
v1p0725c2s v1p0726c2s v1p0767c1m
v1p0773c2s v1p0837c1s v1p0871c2s
v1p0877c1s v1p0906c1s v1p0937c1s
v1p0942c1s v1p0985c1s v1p1028c1s
v1p1122c2s v1p1165c2s v1p1175c1s
v1p1182c2s v1p1219c2s v1p1237c1s
v1p1240c1s v1p1259c1s v1p1307c2s
v1p1310c2s v1p1362c2s v1p1396c1s
v1p1410c2s v2p0059c2s v2p0120c2s
v2p0167c1s v2p0310c1s v2p0320c2s
v2p0365c2m v2p0385c2s v3p0058c2s
v3p0105c2s v3p0122c1s v3p0453c2s
v4p0023c1s v4p0077c2s v4p0157c1s
v4p0296c1s v4p0316c2s v4p0381c2s
v5p0054c2s v5p0144c1s v5p0192c2s
v5p0270c1s v5p0317c2s v6p0103c2m
v6p0235c1m v6p0403c1s v6p0502c1m
Buchanan, R. and Caine, H.
v3p0434c2s
Buchanan, R. et al. v5p0464c1s
Buchanan, R.W. v1p0084c1m
v1p0160c2s v1p0521c1s v1p0603c1s
v1p0626c2s v1p0704c1s v1p0774c1s
v1p0789c1s v1p0824c1s v1p0870c1s
v1p1020c2s v1p1201c2s v1p1227c2s
v1p1242c2s v1p1358c2s v1p1408c2s
v1p1418c1s
Buchanan, Roberdean v6p0091c2s
Buchanan, Robert v4p0121c1s
v4p0320c1s v4p0636c1s v6p0235c1s
Buchanan, S.H. v2p0082c1s
v2p0274c2s v2p0427c1s
Buchanan, W. v1p0065c2s
v1p0181c2s v1p0324c2s v1p0336c1s
v1p1335c1s
Buchanan, W.F. v3p0302c2s
Buchanan, W.I. v5p0200c1s
v6p0018c1s
Buchard, R.B. v4p0634c2s
Bucher, H.W. v1p0404c2s
v1p0613c1s
Bucher, K. v6p0300c1s
Bucherer, A.B. v6p0199c2s
Bucherer, A.H. v4p0176c2s
Buchler, A. v4p0323c1s
v5p0304c2s v5p0305c1s v5p0310c2s
v5p0410c1s v5p0565c1s v6p0052c1s
Buchner, E.F. v4p0216c1s
v5p0319c1s v5p0447c1s v5p0614c1s
v6p0190c1s v6p0290c1s v6p0521c2s
v6p0522c1s v6p0680c2s
Buchner, L. v4p0071c2s
v4p0352c1s v4p0627c1s v5p0514c2s
Buchner, M. v2p0154c2s
v2p0309c1s
Bucholz, C.W. v2p0141c1s
Buchrucher, Dean v1p0005c1s
Buck, C.D. v2p0235c1s
v3p0002c1s v3p0022c2s v3p0025c1s
v3p0183c2m v3p0208c1m v4p0001c2s
v5p0080c1s v5p0319c2s
Buck, C.D. and Tarbell, F.B.
v3p0015c1s
Buck, C.H. v6p0313c1s
v6p0329c1s v6p0523c2s
Buck, C.K. v6p0105c1s
Buck, C.W. v1p1215c1m
v1p1222c1s v1p1341c1s v4p0615c1s
Buck, D.D. v1p0688c2s
v1p0840c1s v1p1174c2s v1p1303c2s
Buck, D.D.D. v1p0441c1s
Buck, Dudley v5p0394c1s
Buck, E.C. v2p0218c2s
v3p0210c2s
Buck, E.D. v3p0002c1s
Buck, F.T. v4p0614c2s
Buck, G. v4p0170c2s
v4p0466c1s v5p0160c2s v5p0191c1s
v5p0241c2m v5p0471c1s
Buck, G.M. v4p0515c1s
Buck, Gertrude v5p0434c1s
Buck, H.W. v5p0410c1s
v6p0456c2m
Buck, J.H.W. v2p0178c2s
Buck, L.L. v6p0235c1s
Buck, M.K. v4p0200c1s
Buck, W. v5p0120c1s
v5p0149c1s v5p0239c2s v6p0499c1s
v6p0575c1s v6p0600c2s
Buck, W.B. v5p0147c1s
v6p0454c2s
Buck, W.E. v3p0474c1s
Buck, W.J. v1p0267c2s
v1p1387c2s v2p0249c1s v2p0249c2s
v3p0356c1s v5p0558c1s
Buckalew, C.R. v1p1048c2s
Bucke, R.M. v2p0182c1s
v2p0403c1s v5p0522c2m v5p0629c2m
Bucke, W.F. v6p0159c2s
Bucke, W.W. v6p0163c1s
Buckell, G.T. v6p0168c1s
Buckell, G.T.T. v6p0321c1s
Buckham, H.M. v2p0152c2s
Buckham, J. v1p1034c1s
v1p1164c1s v3p0140c1s v3p0255c1s
v3p0327c2s v3p0336c1s v3p0342c1s
v3p0376c1s v4p0141c1s v4p0337c2s
v4p0436c1s v4p0631c2s v5p0253c1s
v6p0388c2s
Buckham, J.R. v6p0642c2s
Buckham, J.W. v3p0229c1s
v4p0394c2s v4p0413c1s v4p0531c2s
v5p0012c2s v5p0101c1s v5p0200c1s
v5p0341c1s v5p0400c2s v5p0510c1s
v6p0403c1s
v6p0697c2s
Buckham, M.H. v1p0416c2m
v2p0251c2s v2p0437c2s
Buckham, R.B. v5p0080c2s
v5p0251c2s v6p0364c1s
Buckhout, W.A. v4p0203c2s
Buckingham, C. v5p0503c1s
v5p0608c1s
Buckingham, C.E. v1p0816c1s
v5p0170c1s
Buckingham, C.L. v3p0422c2s
Buckingham, E. v1p0625c2m
v1p1043c1s v1p1064c2s v1p1096c2s
v1p1178c2s v1p1179c1s v2p0448c1s
v3p0301c1s v3p0349c2s v3p0471c2s
Buckingham, E.M. v5p0613c2s
Buckingham, Elinor, M. ... v6p0235c2s
Buckingham, H.A. v1p0098c1s
v1p1319c1s
Buckingham, J.A. v1p0869c1s
v1p1042c2s
Buckingham, J.S. v1p0378c1s
v1p0395c2s v1p0948c1s v1p0961c2s
v1p1060c2s
Buckingham, J.T. v1p1070c1s
v1p1393c1s
Buckingham, L.F.A. v1p1323c1s
Buckingham, L.H. v3p0058c2s
Buckingham, S.G. v1p1176c2s
v2p0211c2s
Buckinghamshire, Countess of
v5p0321c2s
Buckland, A.A. v1p0103c1s
Buckland, A.R. v2p0193c2s
v2p0263c2s v2p0298c1s v3p0067c2s
v3p0084c2s v3p0107c2s v3p0256c2s
v3p0322c1s v3p0326c2s v3p0334c2s
v4p0006c2s v4p0040c2s v4p0103c1s
v4p0226c2s v4p0232c2s v4p0256c1s
v4p0258c1s v4p0263c2s v4p0340c1s
v4p0374c2s v4p0374c2s v4p0413c2s
v4p0484c1s v4p0528c2s v4p0552c2s
v4p0574c2s v4p0586c1s v4p0628c2s
v4p0630c2s v6p0388c2s
Buckland, A.R. et al. v4p0111c2s
v4p0457c2s
Buckland, A.W. v1p0016c1s
v1p0136c1s v1p0356c1s v1p0890c2s
v1p1104c2s v1p1198c1s v1p1254c1s
v2p0054c2s v2p0096c1s v2p0112c1s
v2p0128c2s v2p0138c2s v2p0399c2s
v2p0481c1s v3p0030c1s v3p0214c1s
v3p0420c2s v4p0210c1s v4p0391c2s
v5p0155c1s v5p0371c1s v5p0534c1s
Buckland, A.W. et al. v3p0118c2s
Buckland, A.W., Miss v2p0309c2s
Buckland, C. v1p1230c1m
Buckland, C.E. v6p0091c2s
Buckland, C.T. v2p0039c2s
v2p0171c1s v2p0322c2s v3p0014c2s
v3p0045c1s v3p0062c2s v3p0143c2m
v3p0153c2s v3p0211c1s v3p0211c2m
v3p0213c1s v3p0217c1s v3p0218c1s
v3p0397c1s v4p0011c1s v4p0060c2s

v4p0083c1s v4p0107c1s v4p0326c2s v4p0516c1s
Buckland, E.G. v3p0093c2s v3p0437c1s
Buckland, E.S.L. v4p0339c1s
Buckland, F. v1p0276c2s v1p0311c2s v1p0491c2s v1p0592c2s v1p0862c1s v1p1272c2s v1p1414c1s v3p0154c1s
Buckland, F.T. v2p0125c1s v2p0160c1s v2p0169c1s v2p0178c1m v2p0183c1s v2p0203c2s v2p0301c2m v2p0307c1s v2p0365c1s v2p0384c1m v2p0393c1s v2p0449c1s v3p0002c1s
Buckland, J. v4p0194c1s v4p0229c2s v4p0263c2s v4p0309c1s v4p0336c2s v4p0586c1s v5p0011c1s v5p0074c1s v5p0608c2s v6p0164c2s v6p0610c2s
Buckland, S. v1p0329c1s
Buckland, W. v1p0065c1s v1p1313c2s
Buckland, W.W. v4p0307c1s v5p0494c1s
Bucklar, W.H. v5p0494c2s
Buckle, G. v1p0900c1s
Buckle, H.T. v1p0403c1s v1p0741c2s v1p1424c1s
Buckle, T.H. v1p1386c1s
Buckler, A. v4p0077c2s v4p0358c2s v4p0558c2s v5p0404c2s v6p0059c2s v6p0396c1s
Buckler, Alison v4p0097c2s v5p0093c2s v5p0219c2s
Buckler, G.G. v5p0079c2s v5p0635c1s
Buckler, W.H. v5p0437c2s v6p0529c1s
Buckley, A.B. v1p0746c1s v2p0015c2s v3p0380c1s
Buckley, E. v4p0007c1s v4p0109c1s v4p0297c1s v4p0298c1s v4p0479c1s v4p0521c1s v5p0109c2s v5p0386c1s v5p0483c1s v6p0113c1s v6p0335c2m v6p0537c2s v6p0591c1s
Buckley, E.B. v6p0201c1s
Buckley, E.P. v3p0248c2s
Buckley, E.R. v4p0546c2s v5p0575c2s v6p0434c2s
Buckley, Edmund v6p0337c2s
Buckley, G.W. v3p0355c2s v5p0307c1s
Buckley, J.M. v1p0620c1s v1p0831c1s v2p0152c1s v3p0016c2s v3p0024c2s v3p0037c1s v3p0067c2s v3p0090c2s v3p0118c2s v3p0122c2s v3p0148c2s v3p0190c1s v3p0204c1s v3p0280c1s v3p0281c1s v3p0343c1s v3p0355c1s v3p0398c1s v3p0400c2s v3p0435c2s v3p0451c1s v4p0150c1m v4p0367c2s v4p0441c1s v4p0456c2s v4p0599c1s v4p0624c2s v4p0630c1s v5p0034c2s v5p0114c2m v5p0508c1s v5p0620c2s v6p0157c2s v6p0180c1s v6p0219c1s v6p0413c1m v6p0692c1s
Buckley, J.M. and MacArthur, R.S. v4p0615c1s
Buckley, J.M. et al. v2p0123c1s v2p0460c1s
Buckley, L.W. v5p0318c1s
Buckley, R. v5p0283c1s
Buckley, R.B. v6p0006c1s v6p0315c1s
Buckley, R.P. v6p0526c1s
Buckley, S.B. v1p0265c2s v1p0796c2s v1p1324c1s v2p0436c1s
Buckley, T.W. v5p0472c1s
Buckley, W. v5p0282c2s v5p0612c1s v6p0407c1s v6p0642c1s
Buckman, G.R. v1p1063c2s v2p0094c1s v2p0364c2s
Buckman, J. v1p0302c1s v1p0541c1s v1p0934c1s v1p0990c2s v2p0222c1s
Buckman, P. v5p0180c2s
Buckman, S.S. v4p0040c2s v4p0191c1s v5p0325c1s v6p0079c1m
Buckman, S.S. and Bather, F.A. v4p0016c1s
Buckman, S.S. and Schuchert, C. v6p0663c2s
Buckman, W. v6p0552c2s
Buckmaster, C.A. v2p0389c2m
Buckmaster, G.A. v4p0020c2s v4p0255c1s v4p0351c1s v5p0453c1s
Buckmaster, J.C. v3p0356c2s
Buckminster, L.N.H. v1p0573c2s
Bucknam, C.A. v2p0466c1s
Bucknell, J.C. v1p0843c2s
Buckner, H.F. v6p0316c1s
Buckner, Inez v6p0569c2s
Buckner, S.B. v1p1033c2s
Bucknill, Dr. v2p0428c1s
Bucknill, J.C. v1p0649c1s v2p0221c2s
Bucknill, J.T. v2p0258c2s
Buckstaff, F.G. v4p0160c1s v4p0628c2s
Buckton, G.B. v1p1012c1s v2p0017c1s v2p0220c2s
Budd, E.G. v5p0472c1s
Budd, G.D. v1p0513c1s
Budd, Geo.D. v1p0005c2s
Budd, H. v4p0429c1s v4p0592c1s
Budd, H., jr. v1p0809c2m
Budd, K.C. v5p0092c1s v6p0087c2s v6p0154c1s v6p0230c1s v6p0298c2s v6p0353c1s v6p0478c1s
Budd, Katharine C. v5p0119c2s v6p0338c1s v6p0570c2s
Budd, P. v1p0502c2s
Budd, S.C. v4p0458c2s v4p0626c2s
Budde, K. v4p0055c2m v4p0056c1s v4p0405c2s v5p0033c2s v5p0174c1s v6p0061c1s v6p0061c2s
Buddensieg, R. v3p0364c2s v4p0621c2s
Buddington, Z.B. v1p0230c1s v1p0942c1s v1p1053c1s
Buddington, Z.B., Mrs. ... v1p0351c1s v1p1168c1s v1p1404c2s
Budenberg, F. v4p0547c2s
Budge, E.A.W. v3p0097c2s v5p0136c2s v5p0181c2s v6p0449c2s
Budinbaugh, S.R. v1p0890c2s
Budington, W.I. v1p0617c1s v1p1111c2s v1p1149c2s v1p1250c1s v1p1254c2s
Budwell, J.T. et al. v6p0429c1s
Buehl, B. v6p0464c2s
Buehler, D.A. v2p0367c1s
Buehler, G. v5p0081c1s
Buehler, H.G. v4p0127c2s v5p0280c1s
Buehrle, R.K. v2p0132c1s v3p0421c2s v4p0506c1m
Bueknill, J.T. v3p0433c1s
Buel, A.W. v5p0076c1s v5p0460c2s v6p0152c1m
Buel, C.C. v1p0001c1s v1p0114c1s v1p0321c1s v1p0332c2s v1p0915c2s v1p0918c1s v1p1039c1s v2p0262c2s v2p0421c1s v4p0102c1s v4p0342c1s v4p0400c1s v5p0464c2s
Buel, E.C.B. v6p0201c1s
Buel, M. v3p0282c1s
Buel, R.H. v1p0408c2s v1p0759c2s v1p1249c1s v1p1293c1s v2p0419c1s v2p0467c1s v3p0100c2s
Buel, S. v1p0700c1s v1p0769c2s v1p0912c1s v1p1140c2s v1p1277c2s v1p1308c1s v2p0371c1s v2p0388c1s
Buell, A.C. v5p0408c1s
Buell, C.E. v3p0207c2s v3p0376c1m
Buell, C.J. v4p0275c1s v4p0292c1s v4p0318c2s v4p0472c2s v4p0525c2s
Buell, C.S. v4p0188c1s v4p0464c2s v5p0523c1s
Buell, D.C. v1p1190c2s v1p1347c1s v2p0400c2s
Buell, Don C. et al. v5p0541c2s
Buell, J. v6p0407c2s
Buell, J.F. v6p0112c2s
Buell, J.I. v5p0306c1s
Buell, L.B. v6p0116c1s
Buell, M.D. v2p0005c1s
Buell, W. v2p0030c1s v2p0065c2s v2p0074c1s v2p0117c1m v2p0122c1s v2p0125c1s v2p0178c1s v2p0204c2s v2p0210c1s v2p0271c1s v2p0287c2m v2p0302c1s v2p0330c1s v2p0464c2s v2p0466c2s v2p0476c2s v2p0481c1s
Buell, W.P. v2p0031c2s
Buell, W.S. v5p0078c1s v5p0498c1s
Bueno, A.D. v5p0044c2s
Buerstatte, R.T. v4p0231c1s
Buff, H. v1p0459c1s
Buffen, F.F. v2p0276c2s
Buffenoir, H. v5p0390c1s
Buffet, C.H. v3p0036c2s v3p0060c1s
Buffet, E.P. v1p0107c2s v1p0222c1s v1p0261c1s v1p0338c1s v1p0889c1s v1p1433c1s v3p0125c2s v3p0144c2s v3p0331c2s v6p0062c1s v6p0157c2s
Buffum, D. v3p0178c1s v4p0296c1s v4p0398c2s v6p0657c2s
Buffum, E.G. v1p0211c2s v1p0416c2s v1p0498c2s v1p0599c1s v1p0738c2s v1p0855c2s v1p0983c2s
Bugbee, A.M. v4p0009c2s v4p0574c1s
Bugbee, J.M. v1p0151c2s v1p0454c2s v3p0051c1s v3p0086c1s
Bugbee, L.G. v5p0532c1s v6p0381c1s v6p0563c1s
Bugbee, M.G. v3p0396c1s
Bugbee, Saidee G. v5p0151c2s
Bugeia, Julia H.S. v6p0554c1s
Bugg, G. v1p0509c2m
Bugg, L.H. v4p0481c1s v5p0351c2s v5p0493c2s v5p0494c1s
v6p0155c1s
Bugg, Lelia H. v6p0482c2s
Buhl, F. v5p0057c2s v5p0308c1s
Buhler, G. v3p0024c1s v3p0226c1s v3p0375c1s v4p0033c1s v4p0361c1s
Buisson, A. v1p0100c1s v1p0519c2s v1p0886c1s v1p1339c1s
Bukhsh, Khuda v4p0280c2s v6p0371c1s
Bukhsh, S.K. v5p0286c1s v5p0420c2s v5p0605c1s
Bukhsh, S.Khuda v5p0024c2s v5p0146c1s v5p0519c1s
Buksh, K. v6p0484c1s
Bulbring, K.D. v3p0113c2s v4p0151c1s
Bulfin, W. v6p0059c2s v6p0219c1s v6p0234c1s v6p0249c1s v6p0525c1s v6p0606c1s
Bulfinch, S.G. v1p0047c2s v1p0124c2s v1p0127c2s v1p0242c2s v1p0308c2s v1p0582c1s v1p0688c2s v1p0708c2s v1p0768c2s v1p0769c2s v1p0840c1s v1p0847c1m v1p0871c2s v1p0967c1s v1p1042c2s v1p1093c2s v1p1137c1s v1p1150c1s v1p1157c1s v1p1172c1s v1p1180c1s v1p1203c2s v1p1260c1s
Bulfinch, T. v1p0124c1s v1p0680c2s v1p0690c2s v1p0756c2s
Bulgardo, I. v1p0906c2s
Bulgarin, T. v1p0220c2s v1p0994c1s
Bulger, G.E. v1p0198c1s v1p0591c2s v1p1315c2s
Bulkeley, M.G. et al. v3p0031c1s
Bulkeley, R.W. v5p0247c1s v5p0503c2s v6p0710c1m
Bulkeley, W.L. v6p0448c1s
Bulkley, B. v5p0133c1s
Bulkley, J.E. v4p0081c1s v5p0428c2s v5p0535c1s v5p0637c1s
Bulkley, J.M. v2p0010c1s v6p0381c2s
Bulkley, L. v2p0175c1s
Bulkley, W.L. v6p0572c2s
Bull, J. v2p0105c2s
Bull, J.C. v4p0062c2s v4p0277c1s v4p0374c1s v4p0420c2s v5p0002c2s v5p0205c1s v5p0600c1s v6p0471c2s v6p0641c1s
Bull, John, jr. v1p0651c2s
Bull, L. v2p0260c1s
Bull, L.C. v4p0441c1s v4p0589c1s v5p0361c2s v5p0635c1s
Bull, M. v1p0493c2s v1p0580c1m v1p0580c2s
Bull, S.C. v3p0142c1s v3p0307c1s
Bull, Storm v5p0188c2s
Bullard, A. v1p0406c2s v1p0527c2s v6p0564c2s
Bullard, E.F. v5p0087c1s v5p0583c2s
Bullard, H.A. v1p0772c2s v1p0805c1s v1p0832c2s v1p1297c1s
Bullard, J.E. v3p0027c2s v4p0038c1s v4p0038c2s v4p0314c1s
Bullard, L.C. v1p1179c2s v1p1257c2s
Bullard, R.L. v5p0402c2s v6p0128c1s v6p0430c2m v6p0494c1s v6p0541c2s v6p0602c2m
Bullard, W. v1p0741c1s
Bullen, A.H. v3p0064c2s v6p0250c1s
Bullen, C.W. v2p0101c2s v2p0363c1s
Bullen, F.J. v6p0366c1s
Bullen, F.T. v4p0269c2s v5p0001c2s v5p0022c1s v5p0022c2s v5p0053c2s v5p0067c1s v5p0159c1s v5p0160c1s v5p0223c2s v5p0246c2s v5p0258c1s v5p0273c2s v5p0279c1s v5p0320c1s v5p0340c1s v5p0348c1m v5p0360c1s v5p0417c2m v5p0424c1s v5p0459c2s v5p0516c2m v5p0517c1s v5p0524c1s v5p0526c2s v5p0527c1s v5p0562c2s v5p0579c1s v5p0581c2s v5p0595c1s v5p0623c2s v5p0624c1s v5p0627c1m v5p0644c2s v6p0051c2s v6p0235c1s v6p0352c1s v6p0463c2s v6p0476c1s v6p0491c1s v6p0566c2s v6p0646c1s v6p0700c2s
Bullen, Frank T. v5p0050c1s v6p0589c1s
Bullen, M.W. v2p0050c2s v3p0048c2s
Bullen, R.A. v5p0454c1s
Buller, A.P. v5p0159c1s
Buller, C. v1p0067c1s v1p0154c1s v1p1071c1s
Buller, F.T. v6p0700c2s
Buller, H.M. v5p0462c2s
Buller, W. v2p0069c2s
Buller, W.A. v1p0288c1s
Bulley, A.A. v3p0470c1s v4p0407c2s v4p0628c1s

Bulley, A.Amy v3p0120c2s
Bulley, H.A. v2p0296c2s
Bullinger, A. v3p0098c1s
Bullitt, J.F. v4p0423c2s
Bullitt, T.W. v2p0452c1s
Bullman, C. v4p0333c2s
Bulloch, J.M. v4p0093c2s
v4p0143c2s v4p0500c1s v5p0171c1s
v5p0206c2s v5p0240c1m v5p0310c1s
v5p0440c2s v5p0501c2s v5p0575c1s
v6p0052c2s v6p0173c2s
Bullock, Amy H.W. v6p0707c1s
Bullock, C.J. v3p0215c1s
v3p0336c2m v5p0166c2s v5p0568c1s
v5p0568c2m v5p0584c1s v5p0592c1s
v5p0593c1s v5p0615c1s v6p0051c1s
v6p0132c1s v6p0184c1s v6p0253c1s
v6p0261c2s v6p0318c1s v6p0321c2s
v6p0334c1s v6p0435c1s v6p0435c2s
v6p0469c1s v6p0518c1m v6p0591c1s
v6p0652c2s v6p0667c1s v6p0684c2s
v6p0699c2s
Bullock, E. v6p0130c2s
Bullock, E.D. v5p0097c1s
Bullock, H.A. v6p0322c2s
v6p0659c2s
Bullock, J.G. v4p0293c1s
Bullock, J.M. v5p0233c1s
v5p0233c2s v5p0339c2s v6p0181c1s
v6p0223c2s v6p0307c2m v6p0343c2s
v6p0346c2s v6p0372c1s v6p0379c2m
v6p0380c1m v6p0438c1s v6p0458c2s
v6p0461c1s v6p0578c2s v6p0612c2s
Bullock, J.R. v3p0460c2s
Bullock, L. v3p0159c2s
Bullock, M.A. v6p0013c2s
Bullock, R.B. v6p0534c1s
Bullock, R.H. v2p0413c1s
Bullock, S. v5p0048c2s
v6p0386c1s
Bullock, S.F. v4p0258c2s
v4p0485c1s v4p0542c2s v5p0266c1s
v5p0453c2s v5p0480c1s v5p0594c2s
v5p0624c2s v6p0345c1s v6p0415c2s
Bullock, Shan F. v6p0328c1s
Bullock, Starr v6p0133c2s
Bullock, T.L. v4p0105c1s
v5p0108c2s
Bullock, W.D. v5p0076c1s
Bullock, W.E. v3p0442c1s
Bullock, W.F. v6p0094c1s
v6p0661c2s
Bullock, W.R., Mrs. v5p0212c1s
Bullock, Waller Irene v6p0375c1s
Bullon, F.T. v4p0618c2s
Bullwinkle, C.W. v5p0442c2s
v6p0278c2s
Bulman, C.W. v5p0417c2s
Bulman, G.W. v2p0093c2s
v3p0089c1s v3p0111c1s v3p0439c2s
v4p0041c1s v4p0061c1m v4p0222c2s
v4p0237c1s v4p0429c2s v5p0051c2s
v5p0519c1s v5p0614c1s v6p0582c2s
Bulmer, E.F. v6p0206c2s
Bulmer, Maud A. v5p0474c1s
Bulow, Von v6p0610c1s
Bulwer, Dr. v4p0152c2s
Bulwer, E.G. v5p0243c1s
Bulwer, E.L. v1p0319c2s
v1p0888c1s v1p1156c2s
Bulwer, E.L., Mrs. v1p0064c2s
Bulwer, E.L., Sir v1p0141c1s
v1p0209c2m v1p0856c2s
Bulwer, H.L. v1p1231c2s
v1p1281c2s
Bulwer, H.L., Sir v1p1025c1s
Bulwer-Lytton, E., Sir ... v1p0293c1s
Bum, J.W. v3p0229c1s
Bump, C.W. v4p0013c1s
v4p0126c1s
Bump, O.F. v2p0075c2s
Bumpus, H.C. v4p0060c2s
v4p0566c2s v5p0208c1s v5p0343c2s
v5p0570c2s v6p0193c1s v6p0437c1s
Bumpus, M.L. v6p0672c2s
Bumstead, A. v5p0059c2s
v6p0051c1s v6p0285c2s v6p0342c1s
v6p0484c2s
Bumstead, H. v1p1292c1s
v2p0308c2s v3p0345c2s
Bumstead, H.A. v6p0198c2s
v6p0255c2m v6p0526c2s v6p0546c2s
Bumstead, H.A. and Wheeler, L.P.
v6p0526c2m
Bumstead, S.J. v3p0255c2s
Bunbury, C. v1p0519c1s
v1p0918c2s v2p0139c1s v2p0316c2s
Bunbury, C.J.F. v1p1225c1s
Bunbury, E.H. v1p0314c2s
v1p0553c1s
Bunce, J.T. v1p0062c2s
v1p0310c2s v1p0928c1s v4p0111c2s
v4p0457c2s
Bunce, Louise M. and Owen, E.S.D.
v6p0171c2s
Bunce, O.B. v1p0005c1s
v1p1054c1s v1p1153c1s v3p0050c1s
v3p0241c2s v3p0355c1s v3p0469c2s
Bundle, D.F. v1p0441c2s
Bundy, J.M. v1p0354c2s
v1p0907c2s v1p1345c1s v3p0022c2s
Bundy, W.C. v6p0230c2s
Bungay, G.W. v1p0317c2s
Bunge, G. v3p0123c1s
Bunker, Alfr. v5p0569c2s
Bunker, W.M. v6p0423c2s
v6p0594c1s
Bunn, A.C. v2p0292c1s
Bunnell, S.H. v5p0183c1s
v6p0535c2s
Bunner, H.C. v1p0917c1s
v1p1187c2s v2p0027c1s v2p0267c1s
v2p0366c2s v3p0291c2s v3p0297c1s
v3p0383c2s v3p0385c1s v3p0405c2s
v3p0411c1s v3p0475c1s v4p0032c2s
v4p0070c2s v4p0098c2s v4p0100c2s
v4p0138c2s v4p0214c2s v4p0216c2s
v4p0277c1s v4p0299c2s v4p0327c2s
v4p0342c1s v4p0361c2s v4p0408c2s
v4p0417c1s v4p0418c2s v4p0454c2s
v4p0551c2s v4p0576c2s
Bunner, H.C. and Matthews, J.B.
v1p0357c2s
Bunner, M.T. v6p0679c2s
Bunny, R.W. v4p0143c1s
Bunsen and Playfair v1p0495c1s
v1p0502c1s v1p0502c2s
Bunsen, E. v3p0319c1s
v3p0324c1s v3p0328c1s v3p0375c2s
Bunsen, E. et al. v3p0284c1s
Bunsen, G.von v1p0395c1s
v1p0515c1s v2p0166c2s v2p0176c2s
v3p0171c2s
Bunsen, M. v4p0079c1s
Bunsen, Prof. v1p0459c1s
v1p1016c2s
Bunsen, R.W.E. v1p0189c1s
Bunsen, T.von v3p0307c2s
v3p0324c2s
Bunsen, Th.von v3p0174c1s
v3p0199c1s
Bunsen, Victoria Buxton de
v6p0646c2s
Bunte, H. and Schilling, Dr.
v2p0172c1s
Bunting, C.Van A. v6p0272c1s
v6p0464c1s v6p0643c2s
Bunting, H.M. v6p0372c2s
Bunting, H.P.W. v4p0340c2s
Bunting, J. v1p0113c1s
v1p0515c1s v2p0287c2s v4p0114c2s
v4p0365c1s
Bunting, M. v5p0153c1s
Bunting, P.W. v5p0389c1s
Bunts, H.C. v3p0286c1s
Bunyard, G. v5p0222c2s
Bunyea, E.P. v5p0061c1s
v5p0622c1s
Buoy, C.W. v3p0296c2s
Burbank, C.B. v1p1021c1s
Burbank, E.A. v5p0287c2s
v5p0288c1s
Burbank, E.M. v4p0632c2s
v5p0054c1s
Burbank, J.E. v5p0492c1s
v6p0378c2s
Burbank, J.E. and Trowbridge, J.
v5p0447c2s v5p0492c1s
Burbank, L.F. v5p0567c2s
Burbank, L.S. v1p0420c2s
Burbeck, H. v1p0176c1s
Burbidge, E. v4p0138c1s
Burbidge, F.W. v2p0322c2s
v3p0156c1m v4p0203c2s v4p0285c2s
v4p0355c1s
Burbridge, A.F. v5p0572c1s
Burbridge, A.T. v5p0059c1s
v5p0201c2s v6p0639c2s
Burbridge, M. v6p0291c2s
Burbury, Mrs. v1p0257c2s
Burbury, S.H. v3p0214c2s
Burce, A.B. v4p0158c1s
Burce, C., Sir v6p0281c1s
Burce, H.A. v6p0301c2s
Burce, J.M. v3p0384c2s
Burch, A.De v5p0148c2s
v5p0186c1s v5p0255c2s
Burch, C.N. v6p0216c2s
Burch, G.J. v2p0158c1s
v3p0277c2s
Burch, H.R. v6p0138c2s
Burchall, P.H. v6p0262c1s
Burchard, E.M. v4p0132c2s
v4p0178c2s v4p0315c2s v4p0455c2s
v4p0481c2s
Burchard, George v6p0534c2s
Burchard, P.R. v1p0389c2s
Burchard, R.B. v4p0087c2s
v4p0401c2s v4p0506c2s v4p0634c2m
v5p0092c2m v5p0643c1s
Burchard, R.E. v4p0243c1s
Burchard, W.C. v3p0200c1s
Burchell, H.F. v6p0044c1s
Burchell, H.P. v6p0043c2s
v6p0044c1s v6p0045c1s v6p0432c1s
Burchett, G. v3p0029c2s
Burchett, R. v1p0365c1s
Burchill, W.E. v3p0336c2s
Burckhabter, C. v3p0415c1s
Burckhardt, J.L. v1p0106c2s
Burckhart, R. v5p0499c2s
Burd, A.A. v5p0060c1s
Burde, J. v5p0587c1s
Burder, S.F. v2p0426c1s
Burder, W.C. v1p0824c1s
v1p1291c2s
Burdett, C.D. v1p1284c1s
Burdett, E.W. v6p0436c1s
Burdett, G. v1p0304c2s
v1p1151c2s
Burdett, G.A. v4p0511c2s
Burdett, H.C. v1p0606c1m
v1p0934c2s v2p0013c1s v2p0208c1s
v4p0238c1s
Burdett, Henry C. v4p0237c1s
Burdett, S.S. et al. v4p0434c1s
Burdett, W.H. v1p0314c1s
Burdett-Coutts, Baroness . v4p0338c1s
Burdette, R.J. v2p0028c1s
v3p0012c1s v3p0164c2s v3p0204c2s
v6p0218c1s
Burdette, R.J. et al. v3p0236c2s
Burdick, A.J. v6p0091c1s
Burdick, C.L. v4p0009c1s
v6p0009c2s
Burdick, E.E. v4p0299c2s
Burdick, F.H. v2p0117c1s
Burdick, F.M. v6p0365c1s
Burditt, F. v1p0451c1s
v1p0602c1s
Burdon-Sanderson, J. v5p0170c1s
v5p0368c2s v5p0388c2s
Buren, A.W.Van v6p0320c2s
v6p0615c1s
Buren, J.D.Van v1p0956c2s
v1p1361c2s
Buren, J.H.Van v6p0510c1m
Buretk, H.A. v1p0003c2s
Burette, H.A. v1p1301c1s
Burg, Dr. v1p0825c2s
Burger, G.A. v1p0088c1s
Burger, V., Dr. v1p0769c1s
Burger, W.H. v6p0414c1s
Burges, A. v1p1259c2s
Burges, A.M. and Besant, W.
v4p0466c2s
Burges, W. v1p0214c2s
v1p0959c2s v2p0018c2s
Burgess, A.F. and Ingram, B.
v6p0526c2s
Burgess, C.F. v6p0373c1m
Burgess, C.W. v6p0298c2s
Burgess, E. v1p0175c2s
v1p0181c1s v1p0592c2s v1p1320c1s
v3p0265c2s v6p0614c1s
Burgess, E.S. v3p0008c1s
Burgess, G. v1p0090c2s
v1p0163c2s v1p0222c1s v1p0250c2s
v1p0421c2s v1p0526c2s v1p0758c1s
v1p1063c1s v1p1093c1s v1p1112c2s
v4p0128c2s v4p0207c1s v5p0222c1s
v5p0235c2s v5p0310c2s v5p0325c2s
v5p0345c2s v5p0355c1s v5p0479c2s
v5p0494c2s v5p0553c2s v5p0574c1s
v5p0579c1s v5p0598c1s v6p0087c2s
v6p0135c1s v6p0350c1s v6p0434c2s
v6p0568c2s v6p0571c2s v6p0598c2s
Burgess, G. and Irwin, W.. v6p0536c1s
Burgess, G.K. v6p0264c2s
Burgess, Gelett v5p0161c1s
v6p0255c2s
Burgess, H. v1p0132c1s
Burgess, H.T. v5p0039c2s
v6p0026c1s v6p0705c1s
Burgess, I.B. v3p0197c2s
v3p0242c2s v3p0243c2s v4p0475c2s
v5p0011c2s v5p0087c1s v5p0121c2s
v5p0518c1s
Burgess, J. v4p0033c1s
Burgess, J.A. and Sawyer, E.M.
v6p0246c1s v6p0496c2s
Burgess, J.J.H. v4p0520c2s
Burgess, J.T. v2p0353c2s
Burgess, J.W. v2p0011c1s
v2p0094c1s v2p0316c2s v2p0451c2s
v2p0452c1s v2p0454c2s v3p0132c1s
v3p0150c2s v3p0171c2m v3p0218c2s
v3p0348c1s v3p0358c2s v4p0211c1s
v4p0224c2s v4p0380c1s v4p0427c2s
v4p0592c2s v4p0594c2s v5p0138c1s
v5p0457c2s v5p0602c1s v5p0603c1s
v6p0146c1s v6p0667c2s
Burgess, J.W. and Freund, E.
v5p0603c1s
Burgess, Kate v6p0627c2s
Burgess, O.A. v1p0247c1s
v1p0314c1s v1p0440c1s v1p0688c1m
Burgess, R. v1p0294c1s
v1p0481c2m v1p0670c1s
Burgess, T.C. v4p0408c2s
Burgess, T.C. et al. v3p0091c2s
Burgess, W.C. v6p0221c2s
Burgess, W.S. and Weysse, A.W.
v6p0540c2s
Burgh, A.De v5p0120c2s
v5p0499c1s v5p0597c1s
Burgh, N.P. v1p1248c2s
v3p0268c1s v3p0382c1s v3p0414c1s
Burgh, W.De v1p0980c2s
Burghardt, C.A. v1p0845c1s

Burghclere, Lady v6p0620c1s
Burghclere, Lord v5p0613c1s
v6p0029c2s v6p0679c2s
Burghclere, Winifred v6p0009c1s
Burgin, C. v1p0614c1s
Burgin, C.A. v1p0645c1s
v1p0760c1s
Burgin, G.B. v4p0018c1s
v4p0039c1m v4p0141c2s v4p0161c1s
v4p0164c1s v4p0198c2s v4p0206c1s
v4p0209c2s v4p0265c1s v4p0298c2s
v4p0312c1s v4p0321c1s v4p0345c2s
v4p0352c1s v4p0409c2m v4p0433c2s
v4p0482c1s v4p0504c1s v4p0550c1s
v4p0587c1s v5p0261c2s v5p0507c2s
v5p0623c2s v6p0043c1s v6p0124c2s
v6p0165c2s v6p0712c2s
Burgin, G.B. and Sharp, Luke
v4p0249c1s
Burgin, G.H. v4p0136c2s
Burgin, G.R. v4p0463c2s
Burgis, E.C. v6p0097c1s
Burgon, J.W. v2p0044c2s
v2p0198c1s v2p0275c2s v3p0356c2s
v3p0428c1s
Burgoyne, A.H. v6p0200c1s
v6p0592c2s
Burgoyne, J.M. v6p0212c2s
Burgwin, H. v1p0422c1s
v2p0119c1s v2p0357c1s
Burgwyn, C.P.E. v1p1091c1s
Burk, A.B. v2p0060c1s
v2p0205c2s v2p0338c2s
Burk, C.F. v5p0126c1s
v5p0468c1s
Burk, F. v5p0107c1s
v5p0404c2s v5p0413c2s v5p0569c2s
v6p0181c2s v6p0193c1s v6p0635c1s
Burk, F.L. v5p0570c1s
Burk, F.L. and McLellan, J.A.
v4p0026c2s
Burk, H.A.
v1p0174c2s
Burke, A.R. v4p0162c1s
Burke, Agnes J. v4p0048c2s
Burke, B.E. v4p0566c1s
Burke, C. v3p0040c1s
v4p0035c1s v4p0039c1s v4p0146c2s
v4p0178c1s v4p0185c2s v4p0276c2s
v4p0319c1s v4p0336c1s v4p0372c1s
v4p0373c2s v4p0375c1s v4p0391c1s
v4p0413c1s v4p0429c1s v4p0445c1s
v4p0457c1s v4p0536c2s v5p0012c2s
v5p0036c1s v5p0140c1s v5p0187c2s
v5p0200c1s v5p0219c2s v5p0222c1s
v5p0261c2s v5p0348c2s v5p0434c1s
v5p0521c2s v5p0539c1s v5p0579c1s
v5p0598c1s v5p0605c2s v5p0623c2s
Burke, Christian v5p0236c1s
Burke, E. v1p0978c2m
Burke, E.H. v6p0627c1s
Burke, E.M. v6p0568c1s
Burke, F. v6p0093c1s
Burke, G. v1p0452c2s
Burke, J. v5p0338c1s
Burke, J.B. v1p0178c1s
v6p0214c2s v6p0376c1s v6p0526c2m
v6p0610c1s
Burke, J.J. v6p0280c2s
v6p0368c1s
Burke, L. v1p1440c2s
Burke, M. v2p0002c2s
Burke, M.D. v4p0023c1s
Burke, Margaret S. v6p0490c2s
Burke, O.J. v1p0023c1s
v1p0291c2s v1p0368c2s v1p0653c2s
v1p0658c1s
Burke, S.H. v1p0806c2s
v1p1116c2s v2p0069c2m v2p0139c1s
v2p0142c2s v2p0154c1s v2p0157c2s
v2p0201c1s v2p0224c2s v2p0228c1s
v2p0278c2s v2p0298c1s v2p0302c1s
v2p0342c2s v2p0367c1m v2p0373c2s
v2p0476c2m
Burke, T. v5p0108c1s
v5p0459c1s v5p0535c2s v5p0568c1s
v6p0498c1s v6p0573c2s
Burke, U.R. v1p0629c1s
v1p0630c2s v1p0666c2s v3p0109c1s
Burke, W.F. v6p0093c1s
Burke, W.H. v4p0274c1s
v4p0395c2s
Burke, W.H. et al. v4p0115c1s
Burkett, C.W. v6p0009c1s
Burkett, C.W. and Poe, Clarence R.
v6p0152c2s
Burkett, F.C. and Antoniadi, E.M.
v6p0146c1s
Burkhardt, H. v5p0251c1s
Burkholder, A.I. v5p0344c1s
Burkholder, M. v6p0073c1s
Burkitt, F.C. v4p0530c2s
v5p0058c2s v5p0118c2s v5p0503c2s
v6p0442c2s v6p0638c1s
Burkitt, R. v6p0350c1m
Burland, J.B.H. v4p0527c2s
Burleigh, B. v3p0440c2s
v5p0249c1s
Burleigh, C. v1p0230c1s
Burleigh, F.A. v4p0455c1s
v4p0629c1s
Burleigh, G.S. v1p0892c1s
v1p1042c1s
Burleigh, R.C. v1p0747c1s
Burleson, W.D. v6p0274c2s
Burley, L.Le Gay v6p0108c1s
Burling, J.W. v5p0313c2s
Burlingame, E.L. v1p0235c2s
v1p0786c2s v1p0931c2s v6p0085c1s
Burlingame, L.D. v6p0392c2s
v6p0393c1s
Burlingame, W.A. v1p0800c1s
v1p0895c1s
Burlumi, T.A. v5p0469c1s
Burman, J.M. v6p0520c2s
Burmmitt, D.B. v6p0588c2s
Burn, A.E. v5p0059c2s
v5p0304c2s
Burn, A.S. v5p0145c1s
Burn, R. v1p0307c2s
Burnaby, E. v2p0473c2s
Burnaby, F. v2p0032c2s
Burnam, J.M. v5p0469c2s
Burnand, F.C. v1p0878c1s
v1p0888c2s v2p0094c2s v2p0123c1s
v2p0416c1m v3p0387c2s v4p0079c2s
v4p0339c2s v4p0544c1s v4p0572c1s
v5p0472c2s
v6p0640c2s
Burnand, F.C. and Beckett, A.a
v2p0359c2m
v3p0349c2s
Burnand, H. v1p1149c2s
Burnand, R.M. v4p0331c2s
Burnap, C.E. v4p0383c2s
Burnap, G.W. v1p0089c2s
v1p0099c1s v1p0131c2s v1p0180c1s
v1p0189c1s v1p0242c2s v1p0421c2s
v1p0515c1s v1p0570c2s v1p0589c2s
v1p0646c1s v1p0821c1s v1p1046c1s
v1p1069c2m v1p1097c2s v1p1116c1s
v1p1262c1s v1p1304c1s v1p1304c2s
v1p1319c1s v1p1321c1s v1p1326c1s
v1p1394c1s
Burnblum, E. v4p0419c2s
Burne, C. v4p0183c1s
v4p0205c1s
Burne, C.S. v3p0332c2s
v5p0212c1s
v5p0547c2s
Burne, E.Lancaster v6p0700c1s
Burne, O., Sir v2p0422c2s
Burne, O.T. v3p0211c2s
v5p0244c2s
v5p0284c1s
Burne-Jones, P. v6p0310c2s
Burnell, A. v2p0065c1s
v2p0073c2s v5p0483c1s v5p0513c1s
Burnell, G.R. v1p0150c2s
v1p0461c1s v1p0481c2s v1p1176c1s
v1p1397c2s v3p0022c2s v3p0059c2m
v3p0153c1s v3p0168c1s v3p0320c2s
v3p0457c2s
Burnet, G. v1p1170c1s
Burnet, G.W. v4p0428c1s
Burnet, J. v5p0327c2s
v6p0503c2s
Burnet, J.R. v1p0337c1s
v6p0203c1s
Burnet, W. v1p0605c2s
v1p0969c1s v1p0970c2s v1p1052c1m
v2p0043c2s v2p0283c1s v2p0333c1s
v4p0403c1s v5p0221c2s v5p0302c2s
v5p0465c2s v6p0019c1s
v6p0200c1s
Burnet, Wm., Rev. v4p0431c2s
Burnett, C.A. v3p0444c2s
Burnett, F.H. v1p0424c2s
v1p0439c1s v1p0454c2s v1p0575c1s
v1p0760c1s v1p0772c2s v1p0824c1s
v1p0862c2s v1p0942c2s v1p1180c1s
v1p1210c1s v1p1257c2s v1p1272c2s
v1p1299c1s v1p1420c1s v2p0291c2s
v2p0440c1s v4p0335c2s v4p0414c1s
v4p0551c1s v5p0357c1s
Burnett, F.H. and Gillette, W.H.
v2p0146c2s
Burnett, F.J. v6p0004c2s
Burnett, F.M. v6p0271c2s
v6p0633c1s
Burnett, Frances H. v4p0120c1s
v6p0166c1s v6p0277c2s v6p0311c1s
v6p0592c2s
Burnett, G. v1p1166c2s
v3p0381c1s
Burnett, G.W. v4p0157c1s
Burnett, J. v3p0052c2s
v4p0553c2s
Burnett, J.L.R. v4p0368c1s
v4p0557c2s
Burnett, J.LaR. v4p0123c2m
v4p0533c1s
Burnett, J.M. v4p0131c1s
Burnett, M.G. v4p0227c2s
Burnett, R.N. v6p0075c2s
v6p0226c1s v6p0262c2s v6p0281c1s
v6p0562c1s v6p0572c1s
v6p0699c2s
Burnett, R.W. v6p0674c2s
Burnett, S.C. v5p0223c2s
Burnett, S.M. v1p0438c1m
v2p0093c2s v2p0151c1s v4p0419c1s
v4p0569c1s v5p0367c2s
Burnett, Sara C. v5p0263c2s
v5p0405c2s
Burnett, T.L. v2p0384c2s
Burnett, T.R. v3p0080c2s
v3p0083c1s
Burnett, V. v6p0078c1s
Burnett, Vivian
v6p0235c2s
Burnett, W.I. v1p0036c2s
v1p0047c1s v1p0210c1m v1p0462c1s
v1p1007c2s v1p1238c2s v1p1368c1s
Burnett, W.J. v1p0295c1s
Burney, A. v3p0202c1s
v3p0325c2s
Burney, A.G. v6p0265c1s
Burney, A.M. v2p0358c2s
Burney, Arthur v3p0357c1s
Burney, Fanny v6p0026c2s
Burney, H. v1p0178c1s
Burney, S.G. v2p0013c2s
v2p0037c1s v2p0081c1s v2p0109c2s
v2p0169c2s
Burnham, A.F. v2p0151c2s
Burnham, A.W. v1p0597c2s
v1p1064c2s
Burnham, B.F. v4p0335c2s
v5p0060c2s v5p0483c2s
Burnham, C.C. v4p0313c1s
Burnham, C.G. v5p0105c2s
v5p0133c2s v5p0394c1s
Burnham, C.H. v5p0161c2s
Burnham, C.L. v5p0040c2s
Burnham, Clara L. v5p0193c2s
Burnham, D.H. v6p0687c2s
Burnham, E.B., Mrs. v5p0564c1s
Burnham, E.G. v5p0107c2s
Burnham, G. v1p0408c1s
v1p1182c2s
Burnham, G.H. v1p0894c1s
Burnham, G.M. v5p0135c1s
v5p0457c1s v5p0551c2s
Burnham, H. v4p0581c2s
Burnham, S. v1p0006c1s
v1p0023c2s v1p0038c1s v3p0416c1s
v6p0200c2s v6p0292c2s
Burnham, S. et al. v4p0054c1s
Burnham, S.W. v1p0261c1s
v1p1243c2m v2p0026c1s v2p0287c2s
v2p0417c1m v2p0417c2m v2p0433c2s
v4p0046c1m v4p0091c2s v4p0460c2s
v4p0545c1m v4p0545c2s v5p0528c2s
v5p0548c2s v5p0549c1m v5p0567c2s
v6p0613c2s v6p0614c1m
Burnham, S.W. and Wilson, H.C.
v2p0417c1s
Burnham, W.H. v3p0003c1s
v3p0077c2s v3p0218c1s v3p0274c1m
v3p0377c2s v3p0378c1s v4p0103c1s
v4p0274c2s v4p0364c2s v4p0505c2s
v5p0004c1s v5p0406c1s v5p0470c2s
v5p0511c2s v5p0512c2s v5p0569c2s
v6p0019c1s v6p0190c1s v6p0295c2s
v6p0573c1s v6p0574c1s v6p0635c2s
v6p0636c1s
Burnham, W.P. v5p0599c2s
Burnite, Caroline v6p0116c1s
v6p0116c2s
Burnley, J. v5p0376c2s
v5p0421c2s v5p0592c1s v6p0447c2s
Burnley, James v5p0289c2s
Burnly, J. v5p0421c2s
Burnouf, E. v1p0167c1s
v1p0826c1s v2p0057c2s v2p0284c2s
Burnouf, M.E. v3p0430c2s
Burns, C.H. v3p0003c1s
Burns, C.L. v4p0130c2s
Burns, D. v1p1292c1s
Burns, E.F. v3p0102c2s
v3p0400c2s
Burns, E.S. v1p0246c2s
Burns, G.J. v5p0549c1s
v5p0604c2s
Burns, J. v1p0764c2s
v3p0165c1s v4p0277c2s v4p0286c2s
v4p0314c2s v4p0339c1s v4p0509c1s
v5p0203c2s v5p0324c1s v6p0007c2s
v6p0014c2s v6p0119c2s v6p0262c1s
v6p0355c2s v6p0508c1s v6p0704c2s
Burns, J. and Manning, Cardinal
v3p0412c2s
Burns, J. and Prothero, R.E.
v4p0338c2s
Burns, J. et al. v4p0027c2s
Burns, J.A. v5p0182c2s
v5p0493c2s v6p0481c2s v6p0635c1s
Burns, John v3p0107c2s
v6p0436c1s
Burns, L.M. v6p0174c1s
v6p0324c2s
Burns, R. v2p0442c1s
Burns, W. v6p0592c1s
Burns, W.J. v1p0980c1s
Burns, W.S. v6p0312c2s
Burns-Gibson, J. v1p0624c2s
v1p1000c2s
v1p1150c2s
Burnside, H.M. v4p0091c2s

v4p0370c1s v4p0382c2s v4p0484c2s
v4p0591c1s v4p0635c1s
Burnside, M. v3p0184c1s
v4p0029c2s v4p0241c1s v5p0448c1s
v5p0461c1s
Burnside, S.M. v1p1158c1s
Burnside, W. v5p0417c2s
Burnstein, J. v1p0437c2s
Burpee, C.W. v5p0292c2s
Burpee, J.L. v6p0183c2s
Burpee, L.J. v5p0044c2s
v5p0089c2s v5p0091c1s v5p0557c1s
v6p0036c2s v6p0065c2s v6p0096c1s
v6p0096c2m v6p0097c1s v6p0097c2m
v6p0098c1s v6p0156c2s v6p0169c2s
v6p0329c1s v6p0330c1s v6p0372c2s
v6p0387c2s v6p0692c2s
Burr, A.W. v3p0199c2s
Burr, C.H., jr. v3p0387c2s
Burr, E.F. v1p0244c1s
v1p0684c1s v1p0906c2s v2p0026c1s
v2p0480c2s v3p0040c2m
Burr, F. v1p0268c2s
Burr, F.A. v3p0007c2s
v3p0107c1s v3p0218c2s v4p0039c1s
v5p0309c1s
Burr, G.L. v3p0101c1s
v3p0418c1s v3p0467c2s v4p0452c2s
v4p0619c2s v5p0252c1s v5p0421c1s
v5p0596c2s v5p0609c1s v6p0213c2s
Burr, H.H. v5p0638c2s
Burr, H.M. v6p0712c1s
Burr, H.W. v6p0278c2s
Burr, J.G. v2p0061c1s
Burr, R.D. v1p1252c1s
v2p0324c1s
Burr, R.H. v6p0320c1s
Burr, T.W. v1p0837c1s
v1p1003c2s v1p1044c2s v1p1244c1s
Burr, W.A. v6p0477c2s
Burr, W.H. v1p0126c1s
v1p0810c2s v1p1392c1s v2p0094c2m
v2p0116c2s v5p0082c2s v5p0215c2s
v6p0324c1s v6p0476c2m v6p0477c1s
v6p0635c2s
Burrage, H.S. v1p0036c1s
v1p0129c2s v1p0451c1s v1p0564c2s
v1p0682c2s v1p0834c1s v1p0879c2s
v1p1347c1s v2p0439c1m v2p0483c2s
v3p0043c1s v5p0339c1s v5p0632c1s
v6p0277c1s v6p0643c2s
Burrage, H.S. and Smyth, E.
v2p0034c2s
Burrage, H.W. v1p0689c1s
v1p1345c1s
Burrage, T.J. v6p0408c2s
Burrall, W.H. v1p0271c2s
Burrard, S.G. v6p0214c1s
v6p0433c2s
Burrell, A. v3p0099c1s
v3p0421c2s
Burrell, C.B. v5p0002c2s
Burrell, D.J. v4p0557c2s
Burrell, D.S. v4p0477c1s
Burrell, E.M. v5p0215c2s
Burrell, L. v4p0006c2s
Burrell, L.M. v5p0534c2s
v6p0240c2m v6p0270c1s v6p0271c1s
v6p0310c1s
Burrell, L.W. v6p0048c1s
Burrell, P.S. v6p0192c2s
v6p0193c2s v6p0419c2s
Burrell, W.S. v3p0457c1s
Burres, W.T. v6p0361c2s
Burridge, A.F. v2p0223c1s
Burrill, K. v6p0148c1s
v6p0573c1s v6p0631c2s
Burrill, Katharine v6p0112c2s
v6p0124c2s v6p0257c1s v6p0449c1s
v6p0584c2s
Burrill, T.J. v1p0086c1s
v4p0449c1s v6p0415c2s
Burris, S.C. v3p0396c1s
Burritt, C.H. v6p0494c1s
Burritt, E. v1p0193c2s
v1p0368c1s v1p0545c1s v1p0622c2s
v1p0623c1s v1p1038c1s v1p1148c1s
v1p1204c2s v1p1385c1s
Burritt, I.N. v1p1384c1s
Burrough, W.F. v4p0379c2s
Burroughs, F.T. v3p0106c1s
v3p0241c2s
Burroughs, G.S. v4p0053c2s
v5p0057c1s
Burroughs, J. v1p0006c2s
v1p0049c1s v1p0076c1s v1p0107c1s
v1p0107c2s v1p0135c1s v1p0135c2m
v1p0136c1s v1p0136c2m v1p0137c1m
v1p0143c2s v1p0193c1m v1p0310c1s
v1p0323c2s v1p0405c1s v1p0413c1s
v1p0444c1s v1p0472c2m v1p0505c1s
v1p0607c2s v1p0611c1s v1p0611c2s
v1p0761c2s v1p0789c2s v1p0799c1s
v1p0899c1s v1p0900c2s v1p0901c1s
v1p0916c2s v1p0917c2s v1p0988c2s
v1p1019c2s v1p1020c1s v1p1081c1s
v1p1240c2s v1p1260c2s v1p1310c1s
v1p1327c2m v1p1382c1s v1p1388c2s
v1p1395c1s v2p0026c2s v2p0033c1s
v2p0046c2m v2p0047c1m v2p0047c2s
v2p0057c1s v2p0068c2m v2p0140c1m
v2p0141c2s v2p0143c1s v2p0160c1s
v2p0238c1s v2p0294c1s v2p0307c2s
v2p0314c2s v2p0351c1s v2p0389c2m
v2p0391c1s v2p0391c2s v2p0393c2s
v2p0422c2s v2p0439c2m v2p0472c2s
v2p0478c2s v2p0479c2s v3p0012c2s
v3p0020c2s v3p0070c2s v3p0189c2s
v3p0205c2s v3p0235c2s v3p0253c1m
v3p0265c1s v3p0297c2m v3p0322c2s
v3p0379c2s v3p0380c1s v3p0429c1s
v3p0463c2s v4p0029c1s v4p0060c2s
v4p0152c1s v4p0178c2s v4p0198c2s
v4p0335c1s v4p0448c1s v4p0456c2s
v4p0475c1m v4p0478c2s v4p0528c2s
v4p0569c2s v4p0573c1s v4p0586c1s
v4p0620c1m v4p0620c2m v4p0621c2s
v5p0011c1s v5p0054c1s v5p0064c1s
v5p0067c1s v5p0144c1s v5p0144c2s
v5p0238c2s v5p0260c1s v5p0340c2s
v5p0341c2s v5p0342c1s v5p0386c1s
v5p0400c2s v5p0417c1s v5p0558c1s
v5p0585c1s v5p0629c2s v5p0631c1s
v6p0021c1s v6p0021c2m v6p0022c1s
v6p0026c2s v6p0055c2m v6p0071c2s
v6p0139c2s v6p0300c1s v6p0376c1s
v6p0379c2s v6p0386c1s v6p0443c2m
v6p0444c1m v6p0444c2s v6p0525c2s
v6p0550c2s
Burroughs, J. and Deacon, C.F.
v6p0021c2s
Burroughs, J.G. v2p0403c2s
Burroughs, John v4p0447c2s
v5p0070c1s v5p0486c1s v6p0444c1s
Burroughs, Julian v6p0089c1s
v6p0106c1s
Burroughs, W. v2p0048c2s
Burrow, C.K. v5p0023c1s
v5p0101c1s v5p0133c2s v5p0210c2s
v5p0255c1s v5p0255c2s v5p0282c2s
v5p0319c1s v5p0398c2s v5p0411c1s
v5p0416c2s v5p0435c2s v5p0474c2s
v5p0582c2s v5p0641c2s v6p0303c2s
Burrow, F.H. v6p0508c2s
Burrow, G.H. v4p0589c2s
Burrow, J.C. v6p0496c2s
Burrowes, E. v5p0390c1s
Burrowes, G. v1p0986c2s
v1p1229c2s
Burrowes, T.H. v1p0926c1s
v1p0988c1s
Burrows, A. v3p0119c1s
v3p0176c2s v6p0260c2s
Burrows, A.J. v2p0035c1s
v2p0162c1s v2p0373c2s
Burrows, C. v5p0458c1s
Burrows, C.K. v5p0123c1s
Burrows, C.W. v6p0511c1s
Burrows, G. v5p0132c2s
Burrows, H.W. v4p0002c2s
Burrows, H.W. and Holland, R.
v4p0207c1s
Burrows, J.C. v5p0018c1s
v5p0600c2s v6p0598c2s
Burrows, J.C. et al. v4p0595c2s
Burrows, J.L. v2p0255c1s
Burrows, M. v6p0248c2s
Burrows, M. and Wilson, S., Sir
v2p0215c2s
Burrows, Prof. v1p0954c1s
Burrows, R.M. v4p0468c1s
v4p0541c2s
Burrows, S.M. v3p0015c2s
v3p0072c2s v3p0134c2s
Burrows, W.A. v5p0517c2s
Burstall, F.W. v5p0188c2s
Burstall, R.A. v5p0570c1s
Burstall, S.A. v2p0423c1s
Burt, A.W. v5p0052c1s
Burt, B.C. v1p1185c1s
v2p0240c2s v3p0171c1s v4p0394c2s
v4p0439c1s v4p0439c2s
Burt, D. v1p0240c2s
v1p0253c1s v1p0291c1s v1p0946c2s
v1p1206c2s
Burt, E.A. v4p0324c2s
Burt, F.A. v4p0040c2s
Burt, G.A. v5p0429c1s
Burt, M.E. v3p0146c1s
v3p0355c1m v4p0474c2s
Burt, N.C. v1p0348c2s
Burt, P.H. v4p0477c2s
Burt, R.C. v4p0557c1s
Burt, S.S. v3p0273c1s
Burt, S.W. v4p0117c1s
v4p0251c2s
Burt, T. v2p0465c2s
v2p0480c1s v3p0238c2s v4p0266c1s
v6p0269c1s v6p0465c1s v6p0488c1s
Burt, T. et al. v4p0314c1s
Burt, W. v5p0331c1s
Burton, A.E. v6p0187c2s
v6p0625c1s
Burton, B.S. v1p0828c2s
v1p0845c1s
Burton, C. v4p0481c1s
Burton, C.E. v4p0115c2s
Burton, C.M. v6p0278c2s
Burton, C.P. v4p0445c1s
Burton, C.U.C. v1p0018c1s
v1p0292c1m v1p0329c2s v1p0537c1s
v1p0670c2s v1p1124c2s v1p1125c1m
v1p1126c2s v1p1155c1s v1p1274c1s
Burton, E.D. v4p0057c1m
v4p0057c2m v4p0301c1s v4p0431c1s
v4p0561c1s v4p0573c2s v5p0059c1m
v5p0306c1s v5p0306c2s v5p0389c1s
v5p0562c1s v6p0061c1s v6p0371c1s
v6p0373c1s v6p0626c2s v6p0642c2s
Burton, E.D. and Mathews, S.
v5p0306c1s
Burton, E.De W. v5p0294c1s
v5p0457c1s v6p0063c1s
Burton, E.L. v1p1069c1s
Burton, E.S. v6p0334c2s
Burton, E.W. v4p0196c2s
Burton, F.G. v5p0584c2s
Burton, F.R. v3p0115c2s
v3p0304c1s v4p0305c1s v4p0389c2s
v4p0634c2s v5p0341c1s v5p0394c2s
v6p0292c1s
Burton, F.W. v1p0068c1s
v1p0204c2s v1p0797c2s v2p0348c2s
v4p0605c2s
Burton, G. et al. v3p0156c2s
Burton, G.J. v4p0191c2s
Burton, G.L. v5p0140c2s
Burton, H.E. v5p0121c2s
v6p0130c1s
Burton, H.F. v2p0135c1s
v2p0271c1s v4p0490c2s
Burton, H.J. v1p0159c2s
v1p1283c1s
Burton, H.N. v1p0599c1s
Burton, I. v3p0309c1s
v4p0080c2s
Burton, J. v1p0122c1s
v1p1115c1s v3p0365c1s
Burton, J.A. v6p0457c1s
Burton, J.H. v1p0113c1s
v1p0149c1s v1p0149c2s v1p0953c1s
v5p0211c1s v5p0212c2s v5p0526c1s
v5p0559c1s
Burton, J.R. v6p0229c1s
v6p0329c1s
Burton, J.W. v1p1216c1s
Burton, Mrs. v4p0210c1s
Burton, N.S. v1p0386c1s
v2p0250c2s v3p0378c2s v4p0229c1s
v4p0300c1s v4p0479c2s v6p0233c2s
v6p0342c2s
Burton, P. v4p0037c1s
v4p0159c1s
Burton, R. v1p1126c1s
v3p0436c1s v4p0015c1s v4p0051c2s
v4p0075c2s v4p0183c2s v4p0184c2m
v4p0335c1s v4p0349c1s v4p0408c1s
v4p0408c2s v4p0417c2s v4p0489c2s
v4p0551c2s v5p0065c2s v5p0080c1s
v5p0108c1s v5p0137c2s v5p0144c2s
v5p0191c2s v5p0192c1s v5p0192c2s
v5p0195c1s v5p0205c2m v5p0233c2s
v5p0299c1s v5p0301c2s v5p0325c2s
v5p0341c2s v5p0474c2s v5p0497c1s
v5p0517c1s v5p0539c1s v5p0539c2s
v5p0619c2s v5p0637c1s v6p0210c1s
v6p0361c2s v6p0598c2s
Burton, R.E. v3p0242c2s
v3p0336c1s v4p0591c1s
Burton, R.F. v1p0045c1s
v1p0045c2s v1p0158c2s v1p0329c1s
v1p0396c2s v1p0443c1s v1p0613c1s
v1p0668c2s v1p0752c1s v1p0842c2s
v1p0960c2s v1p0962c2s v1p0996c1s
v1p1146c2s v1p1154c2s v1p1370c2s
v1p1371c1s v1p1382c1s v1p1439c1s
v2p0004c2s v2p0018c1s v2p0039c2s
v2p0045c2s v2p0098c2s v2p0133c2s
v2p0134c1s v2p0183c1s v2p0225c2s
v2p0259c2s v2p0327c1s v2p0327c2s
v2p0403c2s v2p0421c1s v3p0176c2s
v3p0178c1s v3p0278c1s v3p0412c1s
Burton, R.G. v4p0135c2s
v4p0495c2s v4p0496c2s v5p0397c2s
v5p0580c1s v5p0618c1s v6p0339c1s
v6p0392c2s v6p0416c2s v6p0646c2s
v6p0685c1s
Burton, Richard v5p0337c2s
Burton, W. v1p0385c1s
v1p1438c2s v4p0455c1s v5p0328c2s
v5p0462c1m v6p0258c2s v6p0511c2s
Burton, W.E. v5p0148c2s
Burton, W.K. v3p0375c1s
Burton, W.L. v1p0401c1s
Burton, W.S. v5p0078c2s
Burton-Brown, A. v4p0167c1s
Burton-Brown, Mrs. v6p0549c2s
Burtsell, R.L. v1p0911c2s
Burtt, E.P. v4p0057c2s
v4p0515c2s
Burty, P. v2p0051c1s
v3p0059c1s
Burtz, Lollie B. v6p0364c1s
Burwell, H. v4p0065c2s
Burwell, J.R. v1p0015c1s
Burwell, W. v1p0926c2s
Burwell, W.B. v2p0306c1s
Burwell, W.M. v1p1314c1s
v2p0096c1s v2p0101c2s v2p0142c2s
v2p0150c1s v2p0223c1s v2p0237c2s

v2p0252c2s v2p0306c1s v2p0411c1s
Burwell, W.R. v1p1289c2s
Bury, B.de v1p0023c1s
v1p0478c2s
Bury, Countess de v1p0002c2s
Bury, E. v2p0089c2s
v2p0264c1s
Bury, F.B.de v5p0465c1s
v5p0645c2s
Bury, J.B. v2p0147c2s
v3p0003c2s v3p0143c2s v3p0184c2m
v3p0330c1s v3p0365c2s v3p0427c2s
v3p0428c1s v4p0035c1s v4p0122c1s
v4p0237c1s v4p0242c1s v4p0254c1s
v4p0256c2s v4p0262c1s v4p0269c2s
v4p0295c1s v4p0370c1s v4p0489c1s
v4p0523c1s v4p0627c1s v4p0628c2s
v5p0121c2s v5p0295c1s v5p0498c1s
v5p0595c1s v6p0484c1m
Bury, Jane v5p0377c2s
Bury, S.B.de v4p0139c2s
Bury, V. v2p0110c2s
Bury, Viscount v1p0193c1s
v1p0194c1s v1p0838c1s v1p0885c2s
v2p0136c2m
Bury, Viscount and Lorne, Marquis of
v2p0186c2s
Bury, W. v2p0005c2s
v2p0143c1s v2p0348c2s
Bury, Y.Blaze de v1p0473c2s
v1p0896c1s v2p0276c2s v3p0055c2s
v3p0075c1s v3p0160c1m v3p0161c2m
v3p0163c2m v3p0164c1m v3p0171c2s
v3p0244c1s v3p0271c2s v3p0313c1m
v3p0333c1s v3p0338c1s v3p0409c2s
v3p0419c1s v3p0419c2m v3p0427c1s
v3p0449c1s v4p0076c2s v4p0096c1s
v4p0210c2s v4p0232c1m v4p0305c1m
v4p0322c1s v4p0326c1s v4p0637c1s
v5p0048c2s v5p0054c2s v5p0073c2s
v5p0221c2s v5p0415c2s v5p0560c1s
v5p0637c1s
Bury, Y.de v3p0264c2s
Bury, Yetta B.de v4p0048c2s
Bury-Palliser, Mrs. v1p0715c2s
Busberg, H. v4p0263c2s
Busbey, H. v1p0605c1s
v1p1327c1s
Busch, M. v1p0138c2s
v2p0474c2s
Buschen, A.de v1p1137c1s
Busck, A. v6p0412c1s
v6p0297c2s v6p0480c2s
Bush, A.D. v6p0176c2s
Bush, A.R. v5p0369c1s
Bush, B.F. v4p0208c1s
Bush, E.T. v6p0487c2s
Bush, Egbert T. v6p0554c2s
Bush, G. v1p0083c2s
v1p0130c1s v1p0242c1s v1p0529c2s
v1p1155c1s v1p1174c2s
Bush, G.G. v2p0096c2s
v2p0176c1s v2p0456c1s
v3p0155c2s
Bush, J.C. v5p0032c2s
v5p0098c1s v5p0377c2s v5p0556c1s
Bush, J.S. v1p0859c2s
Bush, K.J. and Verrill, A.E.
v5p0329c1s
Bush, L.P. v6p0234c2s
Bush, Mary G. v5p0126c2s
Bush, R.J. v1p0701c2s
Bush, S.S. v5p0318c2s
Bush, S.W. v1p0301c1s
v1p0582c1s v1p0740c2s v1p0848c1s
v1p0870c1s v1p1314c2s
Bush, T.F. v1p0869c2s
Bush-Brown, H.K. v5p0407c2s
Bushby, D.C. v4p0177c2s
Bushby, H.N.G. v5p0303c1s
v5p0319c2s v6p0334c1s
Bushby, J.W. v1p0622c2s
Bushby, Mrs. v1p0111c1s
v1p0139c1s v1p0331c1s v1p0344c1s
v1p0443c2s v1p0511c1s v1p0526c2s
v1p0616c2s v1p0935c1s v1p1192c2s
v1p1213c2s v1p1231c2s v1p1274c1s
v1p1335c1s v1p1344c1s v1p1408c1s
v1p1427c1s v1p1427c2s
Bushby, W.R. v6p0341c2s
Bushe, C.K. v2p0202c2s
Bushe-Fox, L.L. v3p0432c1s
Bushee, F.A. v5p0072c2s
v5p0299c2s v6p0068c2s v6p0076c1s
v6p0142c1s v6p0308c1s
Bushill, T.W. v4p0179c2s
Bushnell, A. v1p0011c2s
Bushnell, C.I. v1p1314c2s
v3p0237c1s
Bushnell, C.J. v5p0105c1s
v5p0553c2s v6p0113c2s
Bushnell, D.E. v2p0352c2s
Bushnell, D.I., jr. v6p0039c2s
v6p0397c1s v6p0432c2s v6p0459c2s
v6p0465c1s v6p0473c2s v6p0597c2s
Bushnell, D.J. v6p0433c1s
Bushnell, E. v3p0460c2s
Bushnell, H. v1p0187c1s
v1p0230c1s v1p0239c1s v1p0278c1s
v1p0282c2s v1p0390c2s v1p0421c1s
v1p0424c2s v1p0432c1s v1p0445c1s
v1p0486c2s v1p0536c2s v1p0596c2s
v1p0684c1s v1p0708c2s v1p0775c1s
v1p0868c2m v1p0910c2s v1p1017c2s
v1p1044c1s v1p1054c2s v1p1065c1s
v1p1093c1s v1p1094c1s v1p1103c1s
v1p1161c1s v1p1284c2s v1p1326c1s
v1p1435c2s v2p0337c1s v5p0008c2s
Bushnell, J.E. v2p0081c1s
v2p0130c2s v2p0131c2s v2p0269c1s
v2p0411c1s v3p0084c1s v3p0314c2s
v3p0421c2s v4p0114c1s
Bushnell, L. v1p0002c2s
v1p0082c2s v1p0799c2s
Bushnell, M. v5p0611c2s
Bushnell, S. v1p0791c1s
Bushnell, S.Morgan v6p0200c1s
Busiel, J.T. v4p0631c2s
Busk, G. v1p0113c2s
v1p0166c2s v1p0992c2s v1p1204c1m
Busk, K. v2p0202c2s
Busk, R.H. v3p0110c1s
v4p0205c2s v4p0294c2s
Buss, A.A. v6p0626c1s
Buss, J.F. v5p0253c2s
Buss, S. v6p0342c2s
Buss, W.H. v5p0207c2s
Busse, Dr. v1p0935c2s
Bussell, F.W. v6p0153c2s
Busser, S.E. v6p0529c1s
Bussey, G.B. v1p1429c2s
Bussey, G.M. v1p0357c2s
v1p0752c2s
Bussy, S. v6p0636c1s
Busteed, H.E. v1p1198c2s
Buster, J.P. v5p0574c1s
Buston, A.A.S. v2p0077c2s
Buswell, H.F. v1p0644c1m
Butcher, C.H. v2p0084c1s
v3p0365c2s
Butcher, E.L. v5p0211c1s
Butcher, F. v6p0315c1s
Butcher, J. v3p0099c1s
Butcher, J.G. v4p0140c1s
v5p0156c1s
Butcher, J.J. v2p0186c2s
Butcher, L.M. v5p0539c2s
Butcher, S.H. v2p0409c2s
v3p0204c2s v5p0249c2s v6p0079c1s
Bute, Earl of v2p0272c2s
Bute, Marquis of v2p0027c1s
v2p0213c1s v2p0332c2s v3p0381c2s
v4p0072c2s v4p0492c2s
Butler, A.G. v5p0378c2s
Butler, A.J. v4p0248c1s
v4p0284c2s v5p0083c1s v5p0092c1s
v5p0388c1s v5p0431c2s v5p0462c1s
Butler, A.M. v2p0040c2s
v6p0306c1s
Butler, A.W. v2p0202c2s
v2p0303c2s v2p0382c2s v2p0385c2s
v4p0141c2s v5p0204c2s v6p0109c1s
v6p0312c2s v6p0316c1s v6p0517c1s
Butler, A.W. and Quick, E.R.
v2p0024c2s
Butler, A.W. et al. v2p0046c2s
Butler, Amos W. v6p0508c2s
Butler, Arthur J. v6p0099c1s
Butler, B.F. v2p0010c1s
v2p0460c1s v3p0061c2s v3p0065c1s
v3p0474c1s v6p0510c1s
Butler, B.F. and Lorne, Marquis of
v4p0049c2s
Butler, B.F. et al. v1p1048c2s
Butler, C. v1p0181c1s
v1p0890c1s v2p0158c2s v5p0060c2s
v6p0256c1s
Butler, C.A. v2p0021c2s
v2p0425c2s v3p0127c1s
Butler, C.H. v5p0094c1s
v6p0084c2s
Butler, C.M. v1p0263c1s
v1p0673c1s v1p0737c2s v1p1043c2s
v1p1395c2s v2p0023c2s v2p0367c1m
Butler, C.P. v5p0509c1s
v5p0545c1s v5p0571c2s
Butler, Capt. v1p0198c1s
v1p0701c1s
Butler, D. v1p0569c1s
Butler, D.B. v6p0106c2s
Butler, D.C. v4p0331c2s
v4p0424c1s v6p0537c1s
Butler, E. v1p0637c2s
Butler, E.A. v2p0038c1s
v2p0145c1s v2p0214c1s v2p0222c1m
v2p0246c1s v2p0469c2s v2p0476c1s
v3p0037c1s v3p0090c1s v3p0104c2s
v3p0126c2s v3p0155c1s v3p0156c2s
v3p0174c2s v3p0259c1m v3p0278c1s
v3p0289c2m v3p0325c1s v3p0376c2m
v3p0393c2s v3p0430c1s v3p0456c2m
v4p0020c2s v4p0049c1s v4p0049c2m
v4p0092c1s v4p0121c1s v4p0146c1s
v4p0218c2s v4p0228c2s v4p0256c2s
v4p0285c2s v4p0286c1s v6p0134c1s
v6p0320c2s v6p0367c1s v6p0617c2s
v6p0700c2s
Butler, E.C. v1p0528c1s
v2p0202c1s v4p0196c1s v5p0024c1s
v5p0204c1s
Butler, E.E. v1p0085c2s
Butler, E.H. and Southern, H.
v1p0950c1s v1p0950c2s
Butler, E.P. v5p0043c2s
v5p0202c1s v5p0255c2s v5p0312c1s
v5p0425c1s v5p0482c1s v6p0067c1s
v6p0166c1s v6p0265c1s v6p0358c1s
v6p0407c1s v6p0416c1s v6p0421c1s
v6p0499c2s v6p0582c1s v6p0710c2s
v6p0712c1s
Butler, E.R. v3p0309c2s
v3p0437c2s
Butler, E.S., jr. v5p0119c1s
Butler, F.A. v1p0114c1s
Butler, F.K. v1p0512c2s
v1p0611c2s
Butler, F.M. v5p0539c1s
v5p0569c1s v5p0596c1s v5p0619c2s
Butler, G. v1p0004c2s
v1p0506c1s v1p0637c2s v1p0655c2s
v1p0697c1s v1p0709c1s v1p0942c1s
v1p1103c1s v1p1123c1s v3p0240c2s
Butler, G.A. v1p0325c1s
v1p1198c2s v1p1232c2m v3p0210c2s
v3p0393c1s
Butler, G.B. v1p1181c2s
Butler, Geo. v5p0460c2s
Butler, H.C. v4p0023c2s
v4p0025c1s v4p0160c1s v4p0490c1s
v5p0492c2s v6p0630c2m
Butler, H.M. v3p0080c2s
v3p0086c1s v3p0160c2s v3p0190c1s
v3p0201c2s v3p0270c1s v3p0324c1s
v4p0410c1s
Butler, H.R. et al. v5p0033c1s
Butler, J. v1p0074c1s
v1p1100c2s v3p0050c1s
Butler, J., Mrs. et al. .. v4p0628c2s
Butler, J.A. v2p0427c1s
v2p0470c2s v5p0377c1s v5p0556c2s
Butler, J.C. v1p1297c2s
Butler, J.D. v1p0032c1s
v1p0132c2s v1p0181c1s v1p0247c1s
v1p0352c1s v1p0742c1s v1p1187c1s
v1p1245c1s v2p0094c2s v2p0096c2s
v2p0102c1s v2p0132c1s v2p0195c2s
v2p0205c1s v2p0287c2s v2p0296c1s
v2p0311c1s v2p0312c1s v2p0397c1s
v2p0422c1s v2p0428c2s v2p0458c2s
v2p0460c2s v2p0464c2s v3p0022c2s
v3p0093c2s v3p0188c1s v3p0227c1s
v4p0014c1s v4p0086c2s v4p0105c1s
v4p0j21c1s v4p0131c2s v4p0147c2s
v4p0226c1s v4p0226c2s v4p0278c2m
v4p0328c1s v4p0342c2s v4p0443c1s
v4p0455c1s v4p0622c2s v5p0237c1s
v5p0285c1s v5p0633c2s v6p0080c2s
v6p0152c1s v6p0244c2s v6p0369c2m
v6p0422c1s v6p0429c2s v6p0483c2s
Butler, J.E. v1p0481c2s
v1p1057c1s
Butler, J.F. v1p1426c2s
v6p0131c2s
Butler, J.G. v1p0212c1s
v5p0604c2s
Butler, J.H. v1p0230c2s
Butler, J.O. v1p0618c2s
Butler, J.R. v3p0150c1s
Butler, J.W. v2p0370c2s
Butler, L. v1p0939c1s
v5p0210c2s v6p0265c2s
Butler, L.A. v4p0286c1s
Butler, L.G. v3p0428c2s
Butler, M. v1p0026c2s
v1p0306c2s v1p0706c1s v1p0772c2s
v1p0939c1s v1p1030c1s v1p1399c2s
v1p1400c1m v4p0525c1s v5p0006c2s
v5p0440c1s v6p0708c1s
Butler, M.B. v2p0409c1s
Butler, M.C. v3p0401c2s
Butler, M.L. v5p0366c1s
Butler, M.M. v6p0112c1s
Butler, M.N. v6p0563c2s
Butler, M.R., Mrs. v1p0475c2s
Butler, Maynard v6p0059c1s
Butler, N. v4p0122c2s
v4p0335c1s v4p0335c2s v6p0290c1s
Butler, N.C. v2p0270c2s
v4p0143c1s v6p0544c1s v6p0607c1s
Butler, N.M. v2p0101c1m
v2p0132c2s v2p0193c1s v2p0240c2s
v2p0358c1s v2p0438c1s v3p0129c2s
v3p0266c2s v3p0303c2s v3p0377c2s
v3p0378c2s v3p0422c1s v3p0442c2s
v4p0152c1s v4p0169c1m v4p0170c1s
v4p0170c2s v4p0171c2s v4p0177c2s
v4p0312c2s v4p0400c2m v4p0512c2m
v4p0532c1s v4p0597c2s v5p0082c1s
v5p0120c2s v5p0126c1s v5p0177c1s
v5p0178c2m v5p0179c1s v5p0179c2s
v5p0180c1m v5p0233c2s v5p0267c1s
v5p0316c1s v5p0399c1s v5p0406c2m
v5p0407c1s v5p0475c1s v5p0484c2s
v5p0518c1s v5p0621c1s v6p0135c1s
v6p0136c1m v6p0140c1s v6p0189c2s
v6p0193c2s v6p0224c2s v6p0482c1s
v6p0518c2s v6p0572c2s v6p0635c1s
Butler, N.M. and Field, C.
v2p0244c2s
Butler, N.M. and Rhees, R.

v6p0136c1s
Butler, N.M. et al. v6p0540c1s
Butler, Nicholas M. v6p0194c1s
v6p0635c1s v6p0671c1s
Butler, P. v6p0223c1s
Butler, Pierce v6p0403c2s
Butler, R. v1p1438c1s
v4p0096c1s
Butler, R.G. v3p0019c1s
v3p0150c1s v5p0432c2s v5p0544c2s
Butler, Reuben v4p0112c2s
Butler, S. v1p0610c2s
v4p0098c2s v4p0148c1s v4p0262c1s
v4p0497c1s v4p0505c1s v6p0063c1s
v6p0063c2s v6p0273c1s v6p0340c2s
Butler, S.A. v2p0038c1s
Butler, Samuel v4p0037c1s
v4p0380c2s
Butler, T.J. v3p0346c2s
Butler, V. v4p0325c2s
Butler, W. and Foster, J.M.
v4p0415c1s
Butler, W.A. v1p0357c1s
v1p0504c1s v1p0931c1s v1p1220c2s
v1p1338c1s
Butler, W.A. and Logan, W.S.
v4p0022c2s
Butler, W.F. v1p0009c2s
v1p0012c2s v1p0144c2s v1p0164c2s
v1p0328c2s v1p0358c1s v1p0661c2s
v1p1330c1s v1p1366c1s v1p1438c1s
v1p1441c2s v2p0185c2s v4p0246c2s
Butler, W.H. v5p0537c1s
Butler, W.R. v4p0257c1s
v6p0247c1s
Butlin, F.M. v5p0637c2s
Butlin, W.B. v6p0103c2s
Butt, A. v5p0025c1s
Butt, A.W. v5p0029c2s
v6p0077c2s
Butt, B.M. v1p0309c2s
v2p0004c2s v2p0279c2s v3p0112c1s
v3p0121c1s v3p0291c1s v4p0196c2s
Butt, Drinkwater v5p0026c2s
Butt, G. v3p0400c2s
Butt, I. v1p0275c2s
v1p0276c2s v1p1441c1s
Butt, K. v2p0125c2s
Butt, L. v4p0006c2s
v4p0308c2s v4p0373c2s
Butterfield, C.W. v2p0014c1s
v2p0064c2s v2p0077c1s v2p0105c2s
v2p0136c1s v2p0151c2s v2p0168c2s
v2p0169c1s v2p0232c2s v2p0250c1s
v2p0269c2s v2p0287c2s v2p0289c2m
v2p0300c1s v2p0316c2s v2p0320c1s
v2p0380c1s v2p0382c1s v2p0455c2s
v2p0476c1m v3p0055c2s v3p0063c1s
v3p0069c2s v3p0076c2s v3p0090c1s
v3p0118c1s v3p0119c2s v3p0124c1s
v3p0179c2s v3p0185c2s v3p0263c1s
v3p0279c2m v3p0280c1s v3p0310c2s
v3p0312c1m v3p0324c2s v3p0371c1s
v3p0453c1s v3p0466c1s v3p0470c2s
v4p0083c1s
Butterfield, H.S. and Witt, F., Dr.
v3p0084c1s
Butterfield, K.L. v5p0009c1s
v5p0202c2s v5p0242c1m v5p0264c1s
v5p0500c1s v6p0008c2m v6p0219c2m
v6p0555c1m
Butterfield, R.W. v2p0074c1s
v2p0154c1s
Butterfield, W.H. v1p0434c1s
v1p0652c1s
Butterwood, H. v3p0335c2s
Butterworth, A.I. v5p0432c1s
Butterworth, C.H. v1p0651c2s
v1p1085c1s
Butterworth, F.S. v6p0231c2s
Butterworth, H. v1p0046c1s
v1p0139c1s v1p0354c1s v1p0510c2s
v1p0643c2s v1p1181c2s v1p1367c1s
v1p1386c2s v3p0155c2s v3p0194c2s
v3p0216c1s v3p0411c1s v4p0246c1s
v4p0311c1s v4p0412c2s v5p0018c2s
v5p0040c2s v5p0100c2s v5p0202c2s
v5p0412c2s v5p0556c1s
Butterworth, S. v6p0359c2s
Buttgenbach, F. v1p0664c1s
Buttles, U.X. v4p0107c2s
Buttman, P. v1p0554c2s
Buttner, C.G. v2p0004c1s
v2p0111c1m
Buttolph, E.K. v3p0295c1s
v5p0532c2s
Button, C.P. v5p0339c1s
Button, Maude B. v6p0457c2s
Buttrick, H.E. v6p0213c2s
Butts, E.De v3p0267c2s
Butts, E.L. v5p0449c2s
Butts, E.L.De v3p0196c2s
Butts, F.B. v2p0295c1s
Butts, I. v1p0258c1s
v1p0326c1s v1p0713c2s
Butts, M.F. v3p0009c1s
v3p0462c2s
Butts, W.H. v4p0123c1s
v4p0504c2s v4p0512c2s v4p0552c1s
v5p0249c2s v5p0265c1s
Butts, W.R. v6p0490c1s
Buttz, H.A. v1p0127c1s
v2p0017c1s v2p0190c2s v3p0043c1s
v4p0057c2s v4p0095c1s v4p0279c2s
Butz, G.C. v4p0432c2s
v4p0513c1s
Buxton, B.H. v1p0492c1s
v1p0906c1s v1p1155c2s
Buxton, C. v1p0669c2s
v1p1241c2s
Buxton, C.R. v6p0122c1s
v6p0207c1s
Buxton, C.R. and Buxton, N.
v6p0392c1s
Buxton, D. v1p0337c1s
Buxton, D.W. and King, E.A.
v5p0113c2s
Buxton, E.N. v3p0023c2s
v3p0128c2s v3p0135c1s v3p0206c2s
v3p0371c2s v3p0375c2s v3p0389c2s
v4p0172c2s v4p0357c1s v4p0527c1s
v5p0095c2s v6p0246c1s
Buxton, E.N. and Johnston, A.
v3p0252c2s
Buxton, E.O. v4p0169c2s
v4p0462c1s
Buxton, F. v3p0005c1s
v4p0006c2s
Buxton, F.W. v2p0363c1s
Buxton, G.F. v1p1400c1s
Buxton, J. v1p0422c1s
Buxton, Mrs. v1p1328c1s
Buxton, N. v5p0321c1s
v5p0471c1s v6p0048c1s
Buxton, N. and Buxton, C.R.
v6p0392c1s
Buxton, S. v4p0353c2s
v5p0209c1s v5p0234c2s v5p0527c1s
v6p0227c2s v6p0654c2s
Buxton, S. and Hodgkin, H.
v4p0586c1s
Buxton, S.C. v1p0160c1s
v1p0304c2s v1p0398c2s v1p0486c1s
v1p0765c2s v2p0131c2s v2p0136c1s
v2p0225c1s v2p0388c1s
Buxton, S.C. and Farrar, J.A.
v1p0657c1s
Buxton, V.A. v6p0661c2m
Buxton, Victoria A. v6p0354c1s
Buxton, W. v1p0361c2s
v1p0878c2s
Buysman, M. v2p0426c1s
Buzelle, G.B. v4p0097c1s
v4p0632c2s
Byall, J.B. v6p0141c1s
Byerly, W.E. v5p0256c2s
v6p0282c1s v6p0499c2s
Byers, J.D. v4p0073c1s
Byers, S.H.M. v1p1105c1s
v1p1143c2s v1p1276c2s v2p0009c1s
v2p0041c1s v2p0094c1s v2p0111c1s
v2p0321c1s v2p0436c1s v3p0093c2s
v3p0231c2s v3p0240c2s v3p0372c1s
v3p0390c2s v3p0417c2s v3p0443c1s
v4p0520c2s v4p0560c2s v5p0043c2s
v6p0054c1s v6p0281c2s v6p0597c1s
v6p0673c1s
Byers, W.M. v4p0058c2s
Byers, W.N. v3p0093c1s
Byington, E.H. v1p0732c2s
v1p1054c2s v1p1157c2s v1p1270c1s
v2p0360c1s v3p0054c1s v3p0083c2s
v5p0180c1s v5p0259c2s v6p0467c2m
Byles, A.Holden v5p0292c2s
v6p0196c2s
Byles, J. v3p0056c1s
v3p0069c2s
Byles, J.B. v1p0133c1s
Byles, S.A. v3p0246c1m
v4p0195c2s v4p0568c2s v4p0587c1s
Byng, G. v6p0226c1s
v6p0240c2m v6p0632c2s
Bynner, C.N. v3p0089c1s
Bynner, F.L. v2p0301c1s
v2p0335c1s v3p0037c2s v3p0060c1s
v4p0155c1s
Bynner, E.L. and Hale, L.P.
v3p0440c2s
Bynner, W. v6p0349c1s
Bynum, W.D. v5p0602c2s
Byram, E.R. v6p0503c2s
Byrce, G. v6p0098c1s
Byrd, M.E. v2p0319c1s
v3p0024c2s v4p0381c1s v4p0556c2s
v5p0549c1s v6p0037c2s
Byrd, Mary E. v6p0037c2s
v6p0038c1m
Byrde, M. v5p0036c1s
v5p0107c2s v5p0163c2s v5p0210c1s
v5p0396c1s v5p0559c1s v6p0507c2s
Byrde, M.B. v5p0590c1s
Byrne, E. v5p0295c2s
Byrne, E.F. v4p0460c2s
Byrne, H. v1p0666c2s
Byrne, J. v1p1095c2s
v3p0179c2s v6p0534c1s
Byrne, J.H. v6p0360c1s
Byrne, J.O. v6p0599c1s
Byrne, J.P. v1p0482c2s
Byrne, O. v1p0405c1s
v1p1076c1s
Byrne, S. v1p0661c2s
v3p0160c1s v5p0384c2s
Byrne, U. v3p0209c2s
Byrne, W. v1p0770c1s
v1p0886c1s
Byrne, W.P., Mrs. v1p0471c2s
v1p0718c1s v1p0863c1s v1p1440c1s
Byrnes, C. v6p0289c2s
Byrnes, M.J. v2p0297c1s
v2p0439c1s
Byrnes, T. v4p0137c2s
v4p0139c2s
Byrns, A.G. v5p0461c2s
v6p0054c2s v6p0279c1s
Byron, G.B. v6p0148c2s
v6p0407c2s
Byron, H.J. v1p0951c1s
v1p0957c1s v2p0344c2s v2p0345c1s
v2p0416c2s
Byron, Lord v6p0269c1s
Byron, M. v5p0460c1s
v6p0380c1s
Byron, May v5p0539c1s
v6p0218c1s v6p0238c2s v6p0257c1s
v6p0285c2s
Byron, Mrs. v6p0232c2s
Byron, T.F. v3p0055c1s
Byrrne, E.F. v3p0165c1s
v4p0174c1s v4p0386c1s v4p0616c2s
Byse, C. v6p0628c2s
Bywater, S. v1p0342c1s
Byzantinos, G.P. v5p0516c2s

C., A.B. v5p0434c1s
C., A.B. and Expertus v5p0332c2s
C., A.E. v6p0111c2s
C., J.M. v6p0050c2s
C., M.A. v3p0302c2s
C., M.B. v5p0496c2s
C., R. v6p0035c2s
C., T.K. v6p0150c1s
C., W.R. v6p0325c2s
C., Wm., Mrs. v5p0552c2s
Caballero, F. v1p0334c1s
v1p0462c1s v1p0668c2s v1p1335c2s
v2p0003c1s v2p0099c2s v2p0121c2s
v2p0158c1s v2p0421c1s v2p0449c2s
v2p0451c1s
Cabaniss, C.H. v5p0599c1s
Cabeen, C.W. v3p0196c1s
Cabeen, F.V. v6p0632c1m
Cabell, De R.C. v4p0058c2s
v4p0146c1s
Cabell, E.D. v6p0207c2s
Cabell, F.B. v4p0391c2s
Cabell, G.C. v3p0417c2s
Cabell, I.C. v6p0703c1s
Cabell, J.B. v6p0003c2s
v6p0103c2s v6p0146c1s v6p0236c1s
v6p0300c1s v6p0311c2m v6p0572c1s
v6p0584c2s v6p0619c1s v6p0629c1s
v6p0639c1s
Cabell, J.L. v1p0434c2s
v1p0820c2s
Cabell, M.W. v1p1323c2s
Cabell, N.F. v1p1373c1s
Cabell, P.B. v4p0055c1s
v4p0261c1s v5p0122c2s v5p0463c2s
v6p0535c1s
Cabell, W.D., Mrs. v5p0079c1s
v5p0569c1s
Cabera, R. v4p0142c2s
Cable, G.W. v1p0111c1s
v1p0185c1s v1p0539c2s v1p0680c1s
v1p0785c1m v1p1196c1s v1p1312c2s
v2p0101c1s v2p0107c1m v2p0111c1s
v2p0120c2s v2p0267c1m v2p0308c2s
v2p0312c1m v2p0411c1s v3p0026c2m
v3p0068c1s v3p0178c2s v3p0191c1s
v3p0197c2s v3p0199c1s v3p0230c1s
v3p0259c1s v3p0299c1m v3p0299c2s
v3p0411c2s v3p0443c1s v4p0170c1s
v4p0243c1s v4p0261c2s v4p0295c2s
v4p0303c2s v4p0324c2s v4p0397c1s
v4p0551c2m v4p0565c2s v4p0617c2s
v5p0427c1s v5p0440c2s v5p0605c2s
v6p0090c2s v6p0246c2s v6p0247c2s
v6p0295c1s
Cable, G.W. and Johnston, J.W.
v2p0411c1s
Cable, George W. v5p0193c2s
Cable, M.L. v2p0114c1s
Cabot and Brown v6p0305c1s
Cabot, C.E. v4p0009c1m
v5p0095c2s v5p0119c1s
Cabot, E.T. and Atkinson, E.
v4p0328c2s
Cabot, F.E. v2p0136c2s
v2p0137c2s v4p0175c2s v6p0225c2s
Cabot, F.J. v6p0348c1s
Cabot, H.C. v1p1181c1s
Cabot, J.E. v1p0053c1m
v1p0061c2s v1p0110c1s v1p0136c2s
v1p0208c2s v1p0262c1m v1p0285c1s
v1p0305c1s v1p0385c1s v1p0390c1s
v1p0427c1s v1p0467c1s v1p0793c2s
v1p0826c2s v1p0843c1s v1p1001c1s
v1p1028c1s v1p1059c1s v1p1094c1s
v1p1228c1s v1p1308c1s v3p0136c1s
Cabot, R.C. v5p0162c2s
v5p0499c1s v6p0409c1m
Cabot, S. v6p0518c2m
Cabot, S., jr. v1p0224c1s
Cabot, W.M. v6p0338c2s
Cabrera, R. v4p0142c2s
v4p0250c1s v5p0147c2s v5p0148c1s
Caclamanos, D. v6p0276c2s
Cadawalder, B. v1p0206c1s
Cadazza, E. v4p0299c2s
Cadby, J. v6p0670c1s
Caddell, C. v1p0906c1s
v1p1145c2s
Caddell, C.M. v1p0098c1s
v1p0332c2s
Cade, J. v1p0206c1m
v1p1115c1s v1p1122c2s v1p1372c1s
Cade, J.A. v6p0154c1s
Cade, R. v5p0095c1s
Cadell, Col. v1p0838c2s
Cadell, G. v3p0063c2s
v3p0158c1s v3p0241c1s v3p0421c2s
v6p0233c1s
Cadell, H.M. v3p0290c2s
Cadell, J.F. v5p0017c2s
v6p0314c2s v6p0560c2s v6p0685c2s
Cadman, S.P. v4p0043c2s
v4p0184c2s v4p0190c1s v4p0324c1s
v4p0372c2s v4p0456c2s v4p0506c1s
v4p0603c2s v5p0350c2s v5p0426c1s
v5p0572c2s
Cadogan, A., Lady v1p0482c1s
Cadogan, A.L. v1p0488c2s
Cadogan, F. v6p0472c2s
Cadogan, Earl v2p0415c2s
Cadoux, H.W. v6p0212c2s
Cadow, H. v6p0045c2s
Cadwallader, S. v1p0154c2s
v6p0247c2s v6p0528c1s
Cadwallader, Starr v6p0131c2s
Cady, C.B. v4p0325c1s
v4p0388c2s
Cady, C.M. v4p0054c2s
v4p0106c1s v5p0055c2s
Cady, D.R. v1p0389c2s
v1p1421c1s
Cady, E.C. v6p0691c1s
Cady, G.L. v5p0537c2s
Cady, J.C. v3p0313c1s
v5p0012c2s v5p0116c2s
Cady, J.Cleveland v6p0398c1s
Cady, K. v4p0201c2s
Cady, L.F. v1p0262c1s
Cady, P. v6p0166c2m
Cady, T. v5p0407c2s
Cady, W.G. v4p0573c2s
v5p0097c2s v6p0498c2s v6p0595c2s
v6p0670c2s
Cady-Scott, W. v4p0422c2s
Caffin, B.C. v3p0282c2s
Caffin, C.H. v5p0082c1m
v5p0289c1s v5p0391c1s v6p0011c2s
v6p0018c1s v6p0033c2s v6p0052c1s
v6p0185c2s v6p0223c2s v6p0241c1s
v6p0245c1s v6p0281c1m v6p0293c2s
v6p0295c2s v6p0354c2s v6p0401c1s
v6p0437c1s v6p0475c1m v6p0497c1s
v6p0510c2m v6p0531c1s v6p0563c1s
v6p0563c2s v6p0570c2s v6p0579c1s
v6p0595c1s v6p0599c1s v6p0695c2s
v6p0700c2s
Caffin, C.H. and Fowler, F.
v6p0689c1s
Caffin, C.H. and Mills, Evan
v6p0570c2s
Caffin, C.N. v6p0076c2s
Caffrie, B.C. v3p0199c1m
Cage, H.B., Mrs. v6p0394c1s
Cagney, C. v3p0400c1s
Cahalane, D.C. v6p0256c2s
Cahall, W.C. v2p0372c2s
v3p0320c2s v3p0368c2s v3p0422c2s
v4p0295c1s v4p0508c1s v4p0617c1s
Cahan, A. v5p0023c2s
v5p0119c1s v5p0232c2s v5p0307c1s
v5p0411c2s v5p0475c1s v5p0502c2s
v5p0597c1s v5p0645c1s v6p0346c1s
v6p0557c2s v6p0558c2s v6p0559c2s
v6p0649c1s
Cahan, Abraham v5p0154c1s
v5p0171c1s v6p0559c1s
Cahill, E.F. v5p0634c1s
Cahill, W.C. v3p0085c2s
Cahoon, B.B. v4p0487c2s
Cahoon, H.H. v5p0107c1s
v5p0637c1s
Cahoon, J.B. v5p0338c2s
Cahour, A. v1p0890c1s
Caillard, E.M. v4p0065c2s
v4p0109c1s v4p0157c1s v4p0232c1s
v4p0352c1s v4p0360c2s v4p0361c1m
v4p0384c2s v4p0436c1s v4p0482c2s
v4p0507c2s v4p0542c1s v4p0582c1s
v4p0614c2s v5p0220c1s v5p0332c2m
v5p0400c2s v6p0156c2s v6p0309c1s
v6p0309c2s v6p0427c1s
Caillard, Emma M. v5p0213c2s
v5p0236c2s v6p0156c2s v6p0302c2s
v6p0387c2s v6p0490c1s v6p0538c2s
v6p0637c1s v6p0642c2s
Caillard, Emma Marie v5p0201c2s
Caillard, V. v2p0060c2s
v2p0449c1s v3p0144c1s v3p0438c2m
v6p0083c1s v6p0240c1s v6p0266c2s
v6p0267c1m v6p0633c1s
Caillard, V.H.P. v2p0006c2s
Caille, A. v5p0368c2s
Cailletet, L. v1p0281c1s
v2p0325c2s v3p0016c2s
Cailletet, M.L. v1p0017c1s
v1p0619c1s v1p0924c1s
Caillouet, S.P. v6p0489c1s
Cain, G. v3p0155c1s
v3p0234c1s
Cain, Georges v6p0033c1s
Cain, J.A. v1p1108c1s
v1p1266c1s v2p0071c2s v2p0211c2s
v3p0214c2s v3p0346c2s
Cain, J.C. v6p0133c1s
Cain, W. v1p0003c1s
v1p0051c1m v1p0161c2s v1p0408c1s
v1p1382c1s v2p0007c2s v2p0118c2s
v2p0127c2s v2p0174c1s
Cain, Wm. v2p0447c2m
v3p0093c2s
Caine, H. v3p0058c2s
v3p0151c2s v3p0366c1s v4p0335c2s
v4p0598c2s v5p0114c1s v6p0518c1s
Caine, H. and Buchanan, R.
v3p0434c2s
Caine, Hall v4p0518c2s
v6p0375c1s v6p0462c1s v6p0537c1s
Caine, Hall et al. v4p0133c1s
Caine, J.H. v3p0091c1s
Caine, L.H. v4p0492c1s
Caine, R. v3p0259c2s
Caine, T.H. v2p0022c1s
v2p0059c1s v2p0063c1s v2p0092c1m
v2p0120c1s v2p0144c2s v2p0378c2s
v2p0397c1m v2p0399c2s v2p0400c1s
v2p0420c1s v2p0429c1m v2p0435c1s
v2p0439c2s v2p0450c1s v2p0474c2s
v3p0406c2s v4p0353c1s
Caine, T.H. and Dowden, E.
v2p0399c2s
Caine, T.H.H. v1p0061c2s
v1p1022c2s v1p1028c1m v1p1128c2s
v1p1186c2s v1p1271c1s v1p1271c2s
Caine, W. v6p0227c2s
v6p0330c1s
Caine, W.S. v4p0568c1s
Caine, W.S. and Manning, H.E.C.
v3p0252c2s
Caird, C. v2p0368c2s
Caird, C.M. v1p0931c2s
Caird, E. v1p0287c2s
v1p0702c1s v1p0702c2m v1p1129c2s
v1p1160c1s v1p1321c1s v1p1429c2s
v2p0147c1s v2p0181c1s v2p0339c2s
v3p0110c2s v3p0175c2s v3p0358c1s
v4p0167c2s v4p0519c1s v5p0311c1s
v5p0523c2s v6p0215c1s v6p0484c1s
Caird, E. and Sidgwick, H.
v1p0623c1s
Caird, Edward v6p0349c2s
Caird, J. v1p0248c2s
v1p0296c2s v1p0542c2s v1p0633c2s
v1p0802c1s v1p0980c2s v1p1064c2s
v1p1093c2s v1p1161c1s
Caird, M. v3p0149c1s
v3p0268c1s v3p0268c2m v4p0630c1s
v6p0183c2s v6p0585c2s
Caird, Mona v4p0127c2s
v4p0268c2s v6p0511c1s v6p0543c2s
Caird, R. v1p0259c2s
v1p1115c2s v1p1363c1s v1p1365c2s
v5p0327c1s
Cairnes, Capt. v5p0089c2s
v5p0166c1s
Cairnes, J.E. v1p0101c2s
v1p0287c1s v1p0299c1s v1p0532c2s
v1p0534c1s v1p0543c1s v1p0545c1s
v1p0650c2s v1p0655c1m v1p0661c1s
v1p0720c2s v1p0906c1s v1p1025c2m
v1p1026c2m v1p1214c2s v1p1344c2s
v1p1357c2s v1p1426c1s
Cairnes, W.E. v5p0169c2s
v5p0243c1s v5p0243c2m v5p0244c1s
v6p0236c1s v6p0241c1s v6p0265c2s
v6p0417c1s
Cairns, D.S. v5p0114c2s
v5p0469c2s v6p0123c1s v6p0342c1s
Cairns, F.I. and Chester, A.H.
v3p0106c1s
Cairns, J. v1p0215c1s
v1p1084c1s v1p1120c1s v1p1413c1s
v2p0169c2s v2p0391c1s v2p0429c1s
v2p0438c1m v3p0081c1s v3p0198c2s
v3p0381c2s v3p0427c2s
Cairns, J. et al. v2p0438c1s
Cairns, W. v4p0505c1s
Caithness, Earl of v1p0759c2s
Cajal, Ramon y, Prof. v4p0397c2s
Cajori, F. v3p0271c2s
v4p0487c1s v5p0227c1s v5p0449c2s
Calais, S. v6p0709c1s
Calame, C.T. v6p0560c1s
Calamy, Dr. v1p1056c2s
Calamy, E. v1p0190c2s
v1p0355c2s
Calcraft, J.W. v1p0043c1s
v1p0086c2s v1p0110c1s v1p0133c2s
v1p0147c1s v1p0220c2s v1p0302c1s
v1p0318c2s v1p0364c2s v1p0369c1s
v1p0402c2s v1p0420c2m v1p0422c2s
v1p0480c2s v1p0488c2s v1p0501c1s
v1p0563c2s v1p0587c1s v1p0588c1s
v1p0612c1s v1p0683c1s v1p0753c1s
v1p0795c2s v1p0801c2s v1p0893c2s
v1p1013c2s v1p1040c2s v1p1059c2s
v1p1133c1s v1p1164c2s v1p1187c1s
v1p1190c2s v1p1242c1s v1p1300c1s
v1p1377c2s v1p1421c1s v1p1435c2s
Caldecott, R. v2p0164c1s
Calder, F.L. v2p0101c1s
v5p0570c1s
Calder, J.E. v1p1284c1s
Calder, W.J. and McDonald, T.McG.
v6p0565c1s
Calderon and Oxenford, J.. v1p0019c1s
Calderon, A.A. v6p0490c1s
Calderon, G. v5p0163c2s
v5p0337c2s v5p0502c2s v6p0549c1s
Calderon, G.L. v5p0327c1s
v5p0488c1s v5p0566c2s v5p0582c1s
Calderon, M.A. v6p0490c1s
Calderon, P. v1p1175c1s
Calderon, P.H. v2p0022c2s
v2p0023c2s
Calderon, Y. v5p0002c1s
Calderwood, H. v1p0427c1s
v1p0434c1s v1p0435c1s v1p0437c2s
v1p0564c1s v1p0612c2s v1p0651c1s
v1p0794c1s v1p0868c1s v1p0869c1m

v1p1001c1s v1p1288c2s v1p1410c2s
v2p0147c1s v2p0235c2s v2p0297c1s
v2p0352c2m v2p0413c1s v2p0414c1s
v3p0207c2s v3p0297c1s v3p0330c1s
v4p0188c1s v4p0288c1s v4p0439c2s
v4p0514c2s
Calderwood, W.G. v3p0071c1s
Calderwood, W.L. v4p0018c1s
v4p0041c2s v4p0394c1s
Caldicott, A. v2p0151c1s
Caldwell v6p0214c1s
Caldwell, A. v3p0289c2s
Caldwell, Bettie D. v6p0274c1s
Caldwell, C. v1p0927c1s
Caldwell, E.B. v5p0413c1s
v5p0472c1s
Caldwell, G.C. v2p0340c1s
v4p0197c2s v4p0413c1s
Caldwell, H.C. v3p0233c2s
v3p0245c1s v5p0312c2s v6p0148c1s
Caldwell, J.C. v4p0096c2s
v4p0431c1s
Caldwell, J.H. v1p0905c1s
Caldwell, J.P. v1p0187c1s
v1p0692c1s v1p1204c2s
Caldwell, J.W. v2p0291c1s
v3p0152c1s v3p0429c1s v4p0198c1s
v4p0538c1s v5p0052c2s
Caldwell, Mary R. v6p0074c1s
Caldwell, O.W. v6p0077c2s
v6p0444c2s
Caldwell, Prof. v1p0351c1s
v1p0404c1s v1p1293c2s
Caldwell, R.C. v1p0343c2s
v1p1081c1s
Caldwell, S.L. v1p0027c1s
v1p0111c2s v1p0205c2s v1p0360c1s
v1p0483c1s v1p0594c2s v1p0820c1s
v1p1093c1s v1p1411c2s v2p0147c1s
Caldwell, S.R. v1p1200c1s
Caldwell, W. v3p0234c2s
v4p0186c1s v4p0439c1s v5p0273c1s
v5p0370c1s v5p0446c2s v5p0447c1s
v5p0463c1s v5p0471c1s v5p0512c2s
v5p0535c1s v5p0537c2s v6p0062c2s
v6p0533c1s
Caldwell, W.C. v4p0471c2s
Calef, A.B. v5p0215c2m
Calef, B.S. v1p1346c1s
Calef, J.F. v6p0401c2s
Caley, J. v1p0105c1s
v1p0162c2s v1p0254c1s v1p0483c1s
v1p0585c1m v1p0690c2s v1p0691c2s
v1p1385c2s v1p1413c2s
Calhoun, A.R. v6p0624c2s
Calhoun, J.A. v1p1205c1s
Calhoun, J.B. v6p0244c1s
Calhoun, J.C. v1p1206c2s
v1p1208c1s
Calhoun, L.C. v1p0150c1s
Calhoun, P. v1p0811c1s
Calhoun, W.L. v5p0450c1s
Califf, J.M. v5p0032c2s
Calisch, E.N. v6p0713c1s
Calkins, A. v1p0944c2s
Calkins, A.B. v4p0365c2s
v4p0547c2s
Calkins, C. v6p0151c1s
Calkins, C.G. v5p0444c1s
v5p0444c2s v5p0445c2s v6p0494c1s
Calkins, F.W. v5p0263c2s
v5p0348c1s v5p0388c2s v5p0390c1s
v5p0634c2s v5p0644c2s v6p0066c1s
v6p0153c1m
Calkins, G.N. v3p0375c1s
v4p0606c2s v5p0357c1s v5p0469c1s
v5p0469c2s v5p0547c1s v6p0175c2s
v6p0520c2s v6p0572c1m v6p0713c2s
Calkins, Gary N. v6p0082c2s
Calkins, M.W. v4p0033c2m
v4p0161c2s v4p0241c2s v4p0360c2s
v4p0365c1s v4p0464c2m v4p0507c1s
v4p0561c1s v5p0131c2s v5p0168c1s
v5p0313c2s v5p0330c1s v5p0470c1s
v5p0470c2s v5p0542c1s v5p0580c1m
v6p0286c1s v6p0522c1s v6p0610c1s
Calkins, Mary W. v4p0104c1s
Calkins, N.A. v1p0935c2m
v2p0388c2s v2p0432c1s
Calkins, R. v4p0249c2s
Calkins, W. v1p0125c2s
v1p0415c2s v1p0688c1s v2p0266c1s
v2p0284c2s v3p0104c1s v4p0128c2s
v6p0332c1s
Calkins, W.W. v4p0330c2s
Calkins, Wolcott v6p0549c2s
Call, A.D. v6p0193c2s
v6p0201c2s
Call, A.P. v4p0482c1s
Call, Annie P. v6p0117c1s
v6p0219c1s v6p0399c1s v6p0425c2s
v6p0647c1s
Call, E.E. v4p0031c2s
v4p0394c2s v4p0535c2s
Call, R.E. v1p0760c1s
v2p0262c2s v3p0064c2s v3p0385c2s
v3p0392c2s v4p0606c2s v5p0358c1m
v6p0574c2s
Call, R.E. and Beecher, C.E.
v2p0309c2s v2p0360c2s
Call, R.E. and McGee, W.J.
v2p0262c2s
Call, W.M.W. v1p0047c2s
v1p0644c2s v1p0797c1s v1p0906c2s
v1p1194c2s v3p0036c1s
Callaghan, E. v5p0524c2s
Callaghan, J.F. v2p0086c1s
Callahan, D.T. v4p0150c1s
Callahan, J.M. v5p0189c2s
v5p0323c1s v5p0602c1s v6p0499c1s
Callahan, R.C. v6p0120c1s
Callahan, S.S.F. v6p0305c2s
Callan, M.J. v1p1162c2s
Callan, N.J. v1p1390c1s
Callan, P.A. v2p0151c1s
Callander, H.B. v3p0019c1s
Callander, T. v6p0174c2s
Callandreau, M.O. v6p0502c1s
Callandreau, O. v6p0287c1s
Callaway, C. v1p1433c2s
v2p0440c2s v6p0519c1s
Callaway, H. v1p0356c1s
v1p0897c1s
Callaway, M. v2p0068c1s
Callaway, M., jr. v3p0013c2s
Callcott, F.G. v5p0622c1s
Callendar, H.L. v5p0572c1s
Callendar, H.S. v5p0027c2s
Callender, C.R. v6p0086c2s
v6p0157c1s
Callender, E.B. v1p0606c1s
v2p0102c1s
Callender, G.S. v6p0151c2s
v6p0614c2s
Callender, M.L. v1p1316c2s
Callender, S.N. v1p0005c1s
v1p0048c1s v1p0241c1s v1p0242c1s
v1p0243c2s v1p0312c2s v1p0435c1s
v1p0769c1s v1p0845c2s v1p1042c1s
v1p1058c2s v1p1074c1s v2p0277c1s
v2p0293c2s v3p0084c2s v3p0175c1s
v4p0036c2s v4p0277c1s v4p0477c1s
Callery, M.M. and Yvan ... v5p0566c2s
Callingham, J. v1p0723c1s
Calloway, G.N. v6p0662c1s
Calloway, T.J. v5p0595c2s
v5p0620c1s v6p0446c2s
Callwell, C.E. v4p0237c1s
v5p0249c1s
Calman, E.S. v1p0691c1s
Calman, W.T. v5p0498c1s
Calmet, A. v1p0691c2s
v1p1101c2s
Calmette, A. v4p0531c1s
v5p0453c1s
Calmettes, P. v6p0342c2s
v6p0361c2s v6p0479c2s v6p0505c2s
v6p0643c1s
Calmour, A.C. v3p0319c2s
Calonne, A.de v4p0078c1s
v4p0425c1s v4p0426c1s v4p0605c1s
v5p0101c1s v5p0103c1s v5p0216c2s
v5p0217c2s v6p0083c1s
Calonne, Alphonse de v4p0265c1s
v5p0221c1s
Calonne, Alphonse de, Count
v4p0425c2s
Calonne, Vicomte de v1p0363c2s
Calpe v5p0501c1s
Calthorp, E.G. v5p0048c2s
Calthrop, A. v2p0276c2s
v2p0447c2s
Calthrop, Annette v2p0458c2s
Calthrop, C.M. v3p0279c2s
Calthrop, G. v2p0139c1s
v3p0346c2s
Calthrop, S.R. v1p0121c2s
v1p0190c1s v1p0313c1s v1p0386c2s
v1p0434c1s v1p0685c1s v1p1005c1s
v1p1092c2s v1p1161c1s v1p1345c1s
v1p1356c1s v1p1357c1s v2p0041c2s
v2p0180c2s v2p0230c2s v2p0234c2s
v2p0356c2m v4p0229c1s
Calve, Emma v6p0657c2s
Calvera, R. v5p0147c2s
Calverley, C.S. v1p0323c1s
v1p0942c1s v1p1383c2s
Calverley, M. v1p0537c2s
v1p1082c1s
Calverley, W.S. v2p0113c2s
Calvert et al. v1p0825c2s
Calvert, A.F. v4p0038c2s
Calvert, D. v4p0391c2s
Calvert, F.C. v1p0023c2s
v1p0186c2s v1p0224c1s v1p0224c2s
v1p0268c1s v1p0279c2s v1p0307c1s
v1p0665c1s v1p0825c2s v1p1214c1s
v3p0068c1s v3p0075c2m
Calvert, F.G. v1p0665c1s
Calvert, G. v6p0230c2s
Calvert, G.H. v1p0276c1s
v1p0331c1s v1p0416c1s v1p0557c1s
v1p1143c1s
Calvert, J.B. v6p0546c1s
Calvert, S. v4p0084c1s
Calvert, W. v3p0035c2s
v3p0362c2s v3p0473c2s
Calvin, Emily R. v6p0701c2s
Calvin, J. v1p0096c2s
Calvin, S. v1p0268c1s
v1p1428c1s
Cambon, J. v6p0174c2s
Cambray, P.G. and Jarvis, A.W.
v6p0383c2s v6p0385c1s
Cambridge, A. v1p0442c1s
v5p0538c2s
Cambridge, I. v1p0181c2s
Cambridge, O.P. v1p1236c1s
Camden, C. v1p0108c2s
v1p0142c1s v1p0373c1s v1p1273c1s
Camden, J.N. and Welch, J.C.
v2p0320c2s v2p0417c1s
Camden, R.de, Sir v1p0556c1s
v1p0633c1s v1p0674c2s v1p0811c1s
v1p0872c2s v1p0987c1s v1p1388c2s
v1p1395c2s v1p1418c2s
Camden, Rom de, Sir v1p0892c1s
Camerano, L. v2p0020c1s
Cameron, A. v1p0343c1s
v2p0014c1s v2p0324c1s v6p0012c1s
v6p0598c1s
Cameron, A.B. v2p0311c2s
v2p0444c1s
Cameron, A.D. v5p0179c1s
v5p0469c2s v5p0595c2s v5p0611c1s
v6p0143c2s v6p0303c1s v6p0520c2s
v6p0573c1s v6p0615c2s
Cameron, A.L.P. v2p0029c1s
Cameron, A.M. v4p0264c2s
v5p0576c1s
Cameron, A.S. v4p0049c2s
v4p0438c1s
Cameron, Agnes D. and Harper, Vincent
v6p0082c1s
Cameron, Alice v4p0473c1s
Cameron, B. v5p0141c1s
v5p0176c2s v5p0275c1s v5p0288c2s
v5p0585c2s v6p0487c1s
Cameron, C. v1p0886c2s
v1p1360c1s v2p0080c2s v2p0114c1s
v2p0433c1s v3p0104c1s
Cameron, C.A. v6p0557c2s
Cameron, C.D. v1p0626c2s
Cameron, Capt. v3p0176c2s
Cameron, D. v2p0114c2s
Cameron, D.Y. v5p0369c1s
Cameron, E. v5p0428c1s
Cameron, E.S. v6p0058c1s
Cameron, F.K. v5p0037c2s
v6p0002c2s v6p0602c2m
Cameron, G.G. v5p0278c1m
v5p0322c2s v5p0462c2s
Cameron, George G. v5p0002c1s
Cameron, H.B. v5p0590c1s
Cameron, H.C. v1p0256c1s
v1p0417c1s v1p1368c2s v5p0340c2s
Cameron, H.H.Hay v5p0447c2s
Cameron, H.L. v3p0032c1s
Cameron, H.L., Mrs. v1p0698c1s
v3p0111c2s v4p0040c2s v4p0335c2s
Cameron, I.D. v5p0421c2s
Cameron, J. v1p0796c2s
v2p0066c1s v4p0121c1s v5p0515c2s
Cameron, J.A. v2p0391c2s
Cameron, J.H. v4p0426c1s
Cameron, J.S. v1p1044c1s
Cameron, J.W. v6p0126c1s
v6p0577c2s
Cameron, L. and Lubbock, J.
v2p0410c1s
Cameron, L., Mrs. v3p0102c2s
Cameron, Laura B. v4p0356c2s
Cameron, M. v6p0103c2s
v6p0124c1s v6p0141c2s v6p0170c2s
v6p0515c2s v6p0656c2s v6p0683c1s
v6p0695c1s
Cameron, M. and Smith, A.P.
v5p0024c1s
Cameron, M.L. v4p0276c1s
Cameron, Mary S. v3p0441c1s
Cameron, P. v4p0053c2s
v4p0111c2s v4p0570c1s
Cameron, R. v4p0049c2s
v4p0070c1s v4p0203c2s v4p0217c2s
v4p0416c1s v4p0416c2s v4p0446c1s
v6p0062c1s v6p0494c1s
Cameron, R.W. v3p0027c2s
Cameron, Rosalie v5p0131c2s
v6p0274c2s v6p0347c2s
Cameron, S.E. v6p0505c2s
Cameron, T.W. v1p0201c2s
v3p0467c1s
Cameron, V.L. v1p0011c2m
v1p0012c1s v1p0634c1s v1p0639c2s
v2p0004c1s v2p0050c1s v2p0203c2s
v2p0258c1s v2p0410c2s v3p0004c2m
v3p0005c2s v3p0061c1s v3p0395c2m
Cameron, V.L. et al. v3p0004c1s
Cameron, V.Lovett v3p0147c1s
Cameron, W.B. v4p0387c1s
v4p0414c2s v5p0274c1s v5p0275c1s
v5p0597c2s
Cameron, Wm. v5p0079c2s
Camm, B. v5p0165c2s
v5p0186c2s v5p0252c2s v5p0555c2s
v5p0583c1s
Camm, D.B. v4p0483c2s
v5p0023c2s v5p0305c1s v5p0364c1m
Cammon, H.M. v1p1426c2s
Camp, C.B.De v6p0069c1s

v6p0234c2s
Camp, E.M. v2p0308c0s
v3p0302c2s v3p0303c1s v3p0303c2s
v5p0148c2s v5p0380c1s v5p0558c1s
Camp, G.S. v1p0252c2s
Camp, M.Du v1p0644c1m
v3p0230c2s v3p0311c1m v3p0344c2s
Camp, Maxime Du
v4p0579c2s
Camp, P.F. v5p0202c1s
v5p0518c1s
Camp, W. v3p0025c2m
v3p0035c1s v4p0035c2m v4p0206c2m
v4p0306c2s v4p0635c1s v5p0036c2s
v5p0213c1m v5p0585c2s v6p0039c1s
v6p0232c1m v6p0261c1s v6p0552c2s
Camp, W. et al. v5p0213c1s
Camp, W.A. v4p0118c2s
Camp, W.C. v2p0027c1s
v3p0157c2m
Campagnac, E.T. and Russell, C.E.B.
v5p0224c2s v5p0359c2s v5p0394c1s
v5p0585c1s
Campbell, A. v1p0011c2s
v1p0776c2s v3p0421c2s v5p0065c2s
Campbell, A., Lady v2p0158c2s
v6p0180c2s
Campbell, A.A. v6p0199c1s
Campbell, A.C. v1p0135c2s
v5p0045c2s v5p0091c1s
Campbell, A.D. v4p0066c1s
Campbell, A.F. v5p0456c2s
Campbell, A.G. v2p0456c2s
Campbell, A.J. v6p0105c2s
Campbell, A.R. v6p0363c2s
Campbell, A.W. v5p0490c1s
Campbell, B. v1p0799c2s
v1p1257c1s
Campbell, B.N. v1p1117c1s
Campbell, B.U. v1p0189c1s
v1p0203c1s v1p0807c2m
Campbell, C. v1p0082c2s
v1p1112c1s v1p1374c1s v2p0004c1s
v4p0149c1s v4p0209c2s v5p0091c2s
v6p0368c2s v6p0480c1s v6p0676c2s
Campbell, C., Lady v4p0530c2s
v6p0152c1s
v6p0205c2s
Campbell, C.A. v1p0033c2s
v1p0998c1s v1p1112c1s v1p1211c1s
v2p0013c2s v2p0334c2s
Campbell, C.C. v1p0038c1s
Campbell, C.F.F. v6p0070c2s
v6p0071c1s
Campbell, C.J. v1p0939c2s
Campbell, C.M. v2p0282c1s
Campbell, C.P. v6p0210c1s
Campbell, C.T. v1p0154c1s
v1p0767c2s v2p0114c1s v2p0401c2s
Campbell, C.W. v4p0134c1s
v6p0425c2s
Campbell, Colin, Lady v4p0183c1s
Campbell, D. v1p0086c2s
v1p0385c1m v1p1050c2s v1p1174c2s
v1p1223c1s v2p0091c1s v3p0307c2s
v3p0310c2s
Campbell, D. and Walker, N.L.
v5p0464c1s
Campbell, D.H. v2p0208c1s
v4p0069c2s v5p0301c2s v5p0387c2s
v5p0426c2s v5p0547c1s v6p0013c2s
v6p0020c2s v6p0077c1s v6p0210c1s
v6p0468c2s v6p0503c1s
Campbell, D.R. v3p0168c2s
v3p0200c1s
Campbell, E. v1p0609c1s
v6p0561c1s
Campbell, E.C. v5p0228c1s
Campbell, E.P. v1p0384c1s
Campbell, F. v3p0211c1s
v4p0058c1s v5p0061c1m v5p0129c2s
v5p0363c1s v5p0421c1s v5p0440c2s
v5p0474c2s v6p0223c2s
Campbell, F.B.F. v5p0550c1s
Campbell, F.J. v5p0643c1s
Campbell, Frances v5p0463c2s
v5p0582c2s v6p0594c2s
Campbell, G. v1p1330c2s
v2p0016c1s v2p0339c1s v3p0212c2s
v4p0255c2s v4p0325c2s v4p0371c1s
v4p0614c1s v5p0048c2s v5p0087c2s
v6p0610c1s v6p0677c1s
Campbell, G., Sir v1p0394c2s
v1p0395c1s v1p0396c1s v1p0599c2s
v1p0631c1s v1p0657c2s v1p0721c2s
v1p1223c1s v1p1332c2s v2p0135c1s
v3p0241c1m
Campbell, G., Sir and Rickey, A.G.
v1p0657c2s
Campbell, G.D. v1p0652c1s
v1p1096c1s v3p0040c1s v4p0238c2s
v6p0187c1s
Campbell, G.E. v3p0194c2s
v3p0198c2s v3p0332c1s v4p0485c1s
v4p0602c2m
Campbell, G.F. and Wells, H.L.
v4p0082c2s
Campbell, G.J., jr. v5p0401c2s
Campbell, G.W. v4p0508c2s
Campbell, Gertrude E. v3p0117c2s
v4p0150c2s v4p0161c2s
Campbell, H. v1p0519c1s
v1p0707c2s v1p1210c1s v2p0054c2s
v2p0161c2s v2p0476c1s v3p0077c1s
v3p0077c2s v3p0202c1s v3p0204c1s
v3p0268c1s v3p0469c1s v3p0470c2s
v3p0475c1s v4p0180c1s v4p0303c2s
v4p0367c2s v4p0568c2s v4p0626c1s
v4p0630c1s v4p0632c2s v5p0165c2s
v5p0176c2s v5p0199c1s v5p0521c1s
v5p0555c2s
Campbell, H. and Maynard, M.
v3p0120c2s
Campbell, H., Mrs. v3p0196c1s
Campbell, H.C. v4p0243c1s
v4p0470c2s v5p0369c2s
Campbell, H.D. v2p0350c2s
v6p0377c2s
Campbell, H.D. and Campbell, J.L.
v2p0174c1s
Campbell, H.D. and Howe, J.L.
v4p0102c2s v6p0412c2s
Campbell, Helen v3p0111c2s
v3p0210c1s v3p0341c1s v4p0266c2s
Campbell, Helen et al. ... v3p0077c1s
Campbell, Hugh v5p0098c2s
Campbell, I.R. v2p0360c1s
Campbell, J. v1p0210c2s
v1p0259c2s v1p0396c1s v1p0604c1s
v1p0639c2s v1p0652c1s v1p0936c1s
v1p0996c1s v1p1095c2s v2p0112c2s
v2p0207c2s v3p0242c1s v3p0429c2s
v4p0080c1s v4p0281c1s
Campbell, J.A. v1p0487c2s
v1p1165c2s v1p1343c2s v1p1344c2s
v1p1346c1m v3p0402c2s v5p0096c2s
v5p0416c1s v5p0495c2s v6p0549c1s
Campbell, J.A., Lieut. ... v3p0423c1s
Campbell, J.A.P. v3p0095c2s
Campbell, J.D. v2p0346c1s
v3p0091c1m v3p0240c2m v4p0122c1s
v4p0122c2s
Campbell, J.D. et al. v3p0028c1s
Campbell, J.F. v1p0660c2s
v1p1269c2s
Campbell, J.G. v3p0065c1s
Campbell, J.H.C. v1p1250c1s
Campbell, J.J. v6p0264c2s
v6p0618c2s
Campbell, J.L. v1p1373c2m
v1p1374c1s
Campbell, J.L. and Campbell, H.D.
v2p0174c1s
Campbell, J.M. v2p0124c2s
v3p0342c2s v4p0111c2s v5p0305c1s
v6p0371c1s v6p0371c2s
Campbell, J.Maud et al. .. v6p0374c1s
Campbell, J.P. v4p0355c2s
Campbell, J.R. v2p0459c2s
v4p0456c1s
Campbell, J.S. v4p0352c1s
v5p0106c2s v5p0597c1s v5p0621c1s
Campbell, J.T. v2p0110c2s
v2p0162c1s v2p0220c1s v2p0274c2s
v2p0441c1s v2p0445c2s
Campbell, J.V. v1p0264c1s
v1p0405c2s v1p0422c2s v1p0699c2s
v2p0031c2m v2p0067c1s v2p0117c1m
v2p0239c1s v2p0287c2s v3p0197c2s
Campbell, L. v1p0118c2s
v2p0003c1s v2p0003c2s v3p0003c2s
v3p0295c1s v3p0388c1s v4p0075c1s
v5p0123c1s v5p0332c1s v5p0454c1s
v5p0522c2s v6p0005c2s v6p0095c1s
v6p0428c1s v6p0586c1s v6p0587c1s
Campbell, L.C. v4p0437c2s
Campbell, L.H. v3p0323c1s
Campbell, Lady v1p1327c1s
Campbell, Lord v1p0548c1s
Campbell, M. v5p0096c2m
Campbell, M.G. v1p0757c1s
v6p0155c2s
Campbell, M.L. v4p0039c2s
Campbell, M.R. v4p0605c2s
v5p0173c1s v6p0078c1s
Campbell, M.R. and Hays, C.W.
v4p0021c2s
Campbell, M.T. v6p0106c1s
v6p0597c2s
Campbell, Mrs. v6p0325c1s
v6p0357c2s
Campbell, N.R. v6p0375c2s
v6p0406c2s v6p0583c2s
Campbell, Norman R. v6p0471c1s
Campbell, P.H. and Garland, H.
v5p0491c1s
Campbell, R. v2p0217c2s
v2p0352c2s v4p0318c2s v5p0015c2s
Campbell, R.F. v2p0039c2s
Campbell, R.F.G. v5p0312c1s
Campbell, R.J. v6p0065c1s
v6p0626c2s
Campbell, R.V. v4p0240c2s
v5p0515c1s
Campbell, S. v3p0031c1s
v3p0130c2s v3p0195c2s
Campbell, S.M. v1p0741c2s
v1p1092c2s v1p1342c2s
Campbell, T. v1p0006c2s
v1p0021c2s v1p0072c2s v1p0157c2s
v1p0766c2s v1p1021c2s v1p1102c1s
Campbell, V., Lady v6p0480c1s
Campbell, Vera v6p0368c2s
v6p0531c2s
Campbell, W. v2p0147c1s
v2p0333c1s v6p0013c1m v6p0603c1s
Campbell, W.A. v4p0440c2s
v4p0484c1s v4p0524c1s v4p0592c1s
Campbell, W.C. v4p0429c1s
v5p0096c2s
Campbell, W.H. v5p0287c1s
Campbell, W.H.W. v3p0340c2s
v4p0326c2s
Campbell, W.W. v1p0103c1s
v1p0582c1s v1p0647c1s v1p1398c1s
v2p0066c1s v3p0318c2s v4p0037c2m
v4p0164c2s v4p0221c2s v4p0343c2m
v4p0358c1s v4p0396c1s v4p0411c1s
v4p0528c1s v4p0540c2s v4p0545c2s
v5p0054c1s v5p0174c2s v5p0235c2s
v5p0314c2s v5p0560c2m v5p0632c2s
v6p0038c1s v6p0103c2s v6p0166c1s
v6p0187c2s v6p0375c2m v6p0604c2s
v6p0613c2s
Campbell, W.W. and Perrine, C.D.
v6p0571c1s
Campbell-Bannermann, H., Sir
v6p0268c1s
Campbell-Hyslop, C.W. v5p0614c2s
Campbell-Praed, Mrs. v3p0010c1s
v5p0314c1s
Campbell-Tipton, L. v5p0330c2s
v5p0404c2s
Campeano, Dr. v6p0105c2s
v6p0140c2s v6p0416c2s
Campen, E. v2p0205c1s
Campen, E.van v2p0205c1m
v3p0125c1m
Campen, S.R.Van v1p0055c2s
v1p0585c2s v3p0198c2m v4p0260c1s
Camperdown, Earl of v2p0159c1s
v5p0587c2s v5p0589c1s
Campin, F. v1p1240c2s
Campion, G. v3p0186c1s
v3p0471c1s
Campo, Inez de v4p0631c2s
Campo-Grande, Viscount de. v2p0477c1s
Camut, E. v3p0248c2s
Canaan, E. v5p0009c1s
v5p0119c2s v5p0391c2s
Canby, H.S. v5p0219c2s
v5p0356c2s v5p0527c1s v6p0592c1s
Canby, N. v4p0100c1m
v4p0100c2s v4p0275c1s
Canby, Ruth B. v6p0541c1s
Canby, W.M. v1p1270c2s
Candage, R.G.F. v4p0069c2s
Candee, H.C. v5p0418c2m
v5p0638c2s
Candeze, E. v1p0324c2s
Candler, A. v5p0150c2s
v6p0065c2s
Candler, E. v5p0089c1s
v6p0276c2s
Candler, H. v2p0199c2s
v2p0200c2s v6p0164c2s v6p0586c2s
Candler, J. v1p0864c2s
Candler, Warren A. v6p0160c2s
Candlin, G.T. v4p0479c2s
v5p0109c1s v5p0113c1s
Candlish, J.S. v2p0217c1s
v3p0428c1s v4p0158c2s v4p0300c2s
v5p0037c2s
Candlish, R. v1p0526c2s
Candlish, R.H. v1p0954c1s
Candlish, R.S. v1p0117c2s
v1p0239c2s v1p0292c2s v1p0324c1s
v1p0568c2s v1p0685c2s v1p0802c2s
v1p0813c1s v1p0869c1s v1p0954c1s
v1p1094c2s v1p1181c2s v1p1318c2s
Candolle, A.De v1p0327c2m
v1p0354c1s
v1p1162c1s
v2p0344c1s
Candolle, A.L.P.P.de v1p0152c2m
Candolle, A.P. v1p0346c1s
Candolle, A.P.De v1p0610c2m
Candolle, C.de v1p0732c2s
v5p0518c2s
Candolle, De v1p1324c1s
Candy, E.T. v6p0315c1s
Candy, F.H. v3p0056c1s
v3p0158c1s v4p0107c2s v4p0398c2s
v5p0191c1s v5p0285c2s
Candy, H. v4p0249c2s
Cane, B. v3p0282c1s
v4p0555c1s
Cane, E.Du v5p0120c2s
Cane, E.Du, Sir v2p0143c1m
v5p0141c2m
Cane, E.F.Du v3p0105c1m
v3p0344c2s v4p0139c2s v4p0459c2m
v5p0039c2s v5p0243c2m v5p0439c1s
v5p0622c2s
Cane, E.F.Du and Blunt, W.S.
v4p0587c1s
Cane, E.F.Du, Sir v1p1065c2m
v2p0334c2s v3p0158c2m v3p0298c1m
v5p0093c2m
Cane, F.V.Du v3p0351c1s

Canebrake, T. v2p0435c1s
Canfield, A.G. v6p0242c1s
v6p0586c2s
Canfield, A.J. v1p0690c1m
Canfield, A.S. v6p0275c1s
Canfield, C.L. v4p0585c2s
Canfield, C.S. v1p0953c1s
Canfield, C.T. v1p0529c2s
v1p1097c2s
Canfield, D. v6p0056c1s
v6p0427c2s
Canfield, Dorothy v6p0259c1s
v6p0272c1s v6p0296c2s v6p0306c2s
v6p0340c1s v6p0362c1s v6p0388c2s
v6p0492c1m v6p0540c1s v6p0582c2s
v6p0619c2s v6p0658c2s
Canfield, G.F. v1p0637c1s
v1p0637c2s
Canfield, H. v4p0040c1s
Canfield, H.S. v5p0155c2s
v5p0392c2s v5p0463c1s v5p0534c1s
v5p0639c2s v6p0168c1s v6p0183c1s
v6p0426c1s v6p0524c2s
Canfield, J.H. v4p0396c1s
v4p0617c1s v5p0127c1s v5p0180c1s
v5p0223c1s v5p0336c1s v5p0350c1s
v6p0136c2s v6p0137c1s v6p0178c2s
v6p0253c1s v6p0281c1s v6p0371c2s
v6p0373c1m v6p0373c2m v6p0496c1s
v6p0536c2s v6p0680c2s
Canfield, J.H. and Fernald, O.M.
v4p0122c2s
Canfield, J.H. et al. v6p0532c2s
Canfield, James H. v6p0014c2s
v6p0193c1s v6p0375c1s
Canfield, James H. et al.. v6p0374c1s
Canfield, S.B. v1p1047c1s
Cann, T.H. v6p0422c1s
Cannan, E. v4p0059c1s
v4p0115c2s v4p0156c1s v4p0167c1s
v4p0240c1m v4p0351c1s v4p0431c2s
v4p0453c1s v4p0483c2s v4p0565c1s
v4p0607c2s v5p0093c2s v5p0149c2s
v5p0158c2s v5p0207c1s v5p0244c2s
v5p0247c1s v5p0247c2s v5p0273c1s
v5p0533c1s v5p0550c2m v5p0568c1s
v5p0584c1s v6p0189c1s v6p0205c2s
v6p0312c1s v6p0509c1s
Cannan, Edwin v6p0436c2s
Canney, L. v6p0030c2s
Canniff, W. v1p0194c2s
Canniff, W.H. v4p0470c2s
v5p0477c1s
Canning, A.R. v6p0678c2s
Canning, E.J. v4p0235c1s
Canning, E.W.B. v1p0637c1s
v3p0214c1s v3p0310c2s v3p0461c1s
Canning, F. v3p0382c1s
Canning, G. v1p0080c2s
v1p0387c1s v1p0390c2s v4p0435c2s
Canning, J. v4p0276c1s
v4p0519c2s
Canning, T. v3p0238c2s
Cannon, E. v6p0268c1s
Cannon, G.M. v4p0411c1s
Cannon, G.Q. v1p1360c1s
Cannon, H.W. et al. v4p0593c1s
Cannon, J.G. v4p0593c1s
Cannon, J.S. v6p0554c1m
Cannon, S. v6p0188c2s
Cannon, W.A. v6p0077c2s
v6p0091c1m v6p0171c2s
Canova, L.L. v5p0595c1s
Canovas v5p0128c1s
Cantier, R. v6p0604c1s
Cantini, I. v1p0712c2s
Cantley, A.C. v5p0368c2s
v5p0427c1s
Cantley, C.H. v6p0592c1s
Cantley, L.R. v6p0352c2s
Canton, A.E. v4p0244c2s
Canton, W. v1p0725c2s
v2p0277c2s v4p0067c1s v4p0110c1s
v4p0185c1s v4p0267c1s v4p0320c1s
v4p0381c1s v4p0398c1s v4p0436c2s
v4p0500c1s v5p0054c2s v5p0079c2s
v5p0141c2s v5p0192c1s v5p0211c2s
v5p0250c2s v5p0275c1s v5p0297c2s
v5p0305c2s v5p0306c2s v5p0352c2s
v5p0397c1s v5p0398c1s v5p0420c1s
v5p0441c2s v5p0530c1s v5p0548c2s
v5p0563c1s v5p0564c2s v5p0573c1m
v5p0642c2s v6p0078c1s
Canton, Wm. v3p0008c2s
v5p0079c1s
Cantor, M. v5p0473c2s
Cantor, W. v5p0436c2s
Cantry, N. v4p0290c1s
Cantu, C. v1p0061c2s
v1p1271c1s
Cantwell, E. v3p0439c1s
v4p0013c1s
Cantwell, G.C. v6p0047c2s
Cantwell, G.D. v5p0180c2s
Cantwell, G.G. v6p0010c2s
Cantwell, J.C. v4p0009c2s
v4p0273c1s v4p0313c1s v4p0478c1s
v6p0010c1s v6p0536c1s v6p0580c2s
Cantwell, J.V. v5p0295c1s
Cantwell, W.P. v6p0548c1s
Caparn, A.H. v6p0687c1s
Caparn, H.A. v4p0219c2s
v5p0453c2s v6p0033c2s v6p0479c1s
v6p0620c2s v6p0623c2s
Caparn, H.H. v4p0319c1s
v4p0319c2s
Capehart, E.E. v5p0508c2s
Capel, Mgr. v1p0249c2s
v1p1118c2s v1p1318c2s
Capel, Yolet v6p0205c2s
v6p0266c1s
Capelle, Owen v6p0093c1s
v6p0332c2s v6p0386c2s
Capen, E.H. v1p0794c2s
v3p0282c2s v3p0378c2s v3p0397c2s
v3p0437c2s v3p0444c2s
Capen, E.W. v6p0284c1s
Capen, H.A. v4p0319c2s
Capen, L. v1p0271c1s
Capen, O.B. v6p0045c2s
v6p0130c2s v6p0154c1s v6p0202c1s
v6p0246c2m v6p0283c2s v6p0294c2s
v6p0366c1s v6p0386c1s v6p0389c1s
v6p0403c1s v6p0644c1s v6p0688c2s
v6p0690c2s v6p0710c1s
Capen, O.P. v6p0433c1s
Capen, Oliver B. v6p0085c2s
v6p0273c2s
v6p0394c1s
Capen, S.B. v3p0266c2s
v4p0387c2s
Capen, S.B. and Barrell, J.S.
v3p0287c1s
Capers, E. v2p0196c2s
Capers, F.W. v1p0385c2s
Capes, B. v5p0004c2s
v5p0101c2s v5p0348c2s v5p0455c1s
v5p0481c1s v5p0500c1s v5p0564c2s
v5p0592c1s v5p0597c1s v5p0617c2s
v5p0630c2m v5p0631c2s v6p0518c1s
Capes, B.E.J. v4p0381c1s
v5p0385c1s
Capes, F.M. v2p0304c2s
v3p0388c2s
Capes, J.M. v1p0052c1s
v1p0104c1s v1p0112c2s v1p0197c2s
v1p0252c1s v1p0284c2s v1p0388c1s
v1p0432c2s v1p0496c2s v1p0517c2s
v1p0683c2s v1p0730c1s v1p0766c1s
v1p0813c1s v1p0839c2s v1p0882c1s
v1p0883c1m v1p0912c1s v1p0935c1s
v1p1117c1s v1p1160c1s v1p1214c2s
v1p1431c2s v2p0421c2s
Capes, W.W. v1p0072c2s
v1p0275c1s v1p1125c2s
Capitain, F.de v6p0164c2m
Capitan, L. v4p0369c1s
Cappelain, J.Le v2p0262c2s
Cappelli, R. v6p0323c2s
Capper, E. v4p0084c2s
v6p0570c2s
Capper, J. v1p0214c1s
v1p0306c1s v4p0028c2s
Capper, John v3p0072c2s
Capper, R. v3p0096c1s
v3p0305c2s
Capper, S.H. v5p0082c2s
Capper, S.J. v2p0402c1s
v3p0463c1s v4p0012c1s v4p0494c1s
Cappie, J. v2p0027c2s
v2p0463c1s
Cappon, J. v6p0545c2m
Capps, E. v4p0108c1s
v4p0161c1s v4p0186c2s v4p0241c2s
v5p0161c2s v5p0249c1s v5p0250c1s
v5p0291c2s
Capps, Edward v5p0249c1s
Capron, A.J. v6p0433c1s
Capron, J.R. v2p0151c1s
Capstick, J.W. v4p0221c1s
Capuana, L. v5p0139c1s
Caracristi, C.F.Z. v4p0124c1s
Caralampi, B. v4p0499c2s
Carbaugh, H.C. v5p0032c1m
v5p0100c1s v5p0364c1s v5p0391c2s
Carbonnelle, T. v1p0185c2s
Carbutt, J. v1p0583c2s
v1p1003c2s v3p0174c2s v3p0330c2s
v6p0497c1s
Card, F.W. v4p0021c2s
v4p0061c2s v4p0264c2s v4p0445c1s
v4p0449c1s v4p0451c1s v5p0388c2s
v5p0582c1s
Carden, A.J. v1p0440c1s
Carden, E.W. v6p0354c2s
Carden, R.W. v6p0023c2s
v6p0416c1s
Cardew, P. v5p0183c2s
v6p0198c1s
Cardi, C.N.De v5p0411c2s
Cardozo, E.C. v4p0127c1s
v4p0247c2s v4p0343c2s v4p0418c2s
v5p0280c1s
Cardozo, F.L., jr. v5p0606c2s
Cardozo, J.N. v1p0093c2s
v1p0306c2m v1p0325c1s
Carducci and Oliphant, M.. v2p0210c2s
Carducci, G. v6p0331c1s
Cardwell, R. v1p0449c1s
v1p0485c1s v1p0557c2s v1p0561c1s
v1p0946c2s v1p1074c1s v1p1382c2s
Cardwill, M.E. v3p0038c2s
v3p0460c2s v4p0075c1s v4p0258c2s
Cardwill, Mary E. v3p0173c1s
v5p0255c1s v5p0523c1s
Carel, F. v6p0186c1s
Carey, A. v1p0083c2s
v1p0940c2s
Carey, A.A. v6p0115c2s
v6p0449c2s v6p0574c2s v6p0628c2s
Carey, Alice v1p0043c2s
Carey, C. v6p0004c1s
v6p0248c2s
Carey, C.W. v5p0268c1s
v5p0595c1s
Carey, D.P. v6p0167c1s
Carey, E. v1p1341c2s
v2p0302c2s
Carey, E.E. v4p0307c2s
Carey, E.L. v5p0639c1s
Carey, E.S. v1p1361c1s
Carey, E.W. v1p0025c2s
Carey, F.K. v1p1424c2s
v2p0050c1s v2p0478c1s
Carey, F.W. v5p0524c1s
v6p0119c2s
Carey, G. v1p0896c2s
v6p0050c1s
Carey, G.F. v1p0964c2s
Carey, G.L. v4p0576c1s
Carey, G.W. v5p0320c2s
Carey, H.C. v1p0092c1s
v1p0325c1s v1p0486c2s v1p0860c1s
v1p1025c2s v1p1027c1s v1p1100c1s
v1p1160c2s v1p1394c1s v2p0384c1s
Carey, H.D. v6p0005c2s
Carey, J. v1p0153c1m
Carey, M. v1p0200c2s
v1p0262c1s v1p0556c2s v1p0898c1s
v5p0284c2s v5p0369c2s
Carey, M.A. v1p0560c2m
Carey, N.E. v6p0201c2s
Carey, P. v1p0088c1s
Carey, R.N. v1p1428c1s
v4p0081c1s v4p0386c2s
Carey, S. v1p1341c1s
Carey, T. v5p0623c1s
Carey, T.G. v1p0346c2s
Carey, W. v6p0232c1s
Carey, W.A. v2p0454c1s
Carey, W.M. v3p0190c1s
Carey-Hobson Mrs. v2p0062c1s
Carfrae, G.M. v4p0363c2s
Cargill, A. v4p0609c2s
v5p0523c1s v6p0267c1s v6p0587c2s
v6p0610c2s
Cargill, Alex. v3p0376c1s
v3p0387c1s
Cargill, J.F. v6p0465c1s
Cargill, T. v1p0523c1s
v5p0477c1s
Carhart, C.L. v5p0058c1s
v6p0062c2s
Carhart, H.S. v1p0070c2s
v1p0400c2s v2p0138c1m v2p0138c2s
v2p0272c1s v2p0427c1s v3p0087c1s
v3p0133c1s v3p0134c1s v4p0165c1s
v4p0175c2s v4p0176c2m v4p0507c1m
v5p0102c2s
Carichoff, E.R. v3p0414c2s
Carington, R.S. v2p0351c1s
Carion, J. v2p0308c2s
Cariswell, M. v3p0063c1s
v3p0213c2s v3p0283c1s
Carl, K.A. v6p0118c2s
Carl, Prince v2p0217c2s
v2p0441c1s
Carle, G. v4p0387c1s
Carles, W.R. v5p0643c2s
Carleton, Attie v2p0476c1s
Carleton, E. v6p0077c2s
Carleton, F.T. v6p0539c1s
v6p0605c1s
Carleton, H. v1p0118c1s
v1p0528c2s v1p0840c1s v1p1043c2s
v1p1101c2s v1p1174c2s
Carleton, H.G. v5p0208c2s
v5p0210c2s v5p0384c2s
Carleton, J.H. v1p0912c2s
Carleton, Judge v1p0410c1s
v1p0984c1s
Carleton, M.A. v4p0598c2s
Carleton, S. v5p0323c2s
v6p0242c2s v6p0604c2s v6p0694c1s
Carleton, S.C. v6p0563c2s
Carleton, W. v1p0099c1s
v1p0139c2s v1p0439c1s v1p0444c1s
v1p0659c1s v1p0677c1s v1p0950c2s
v1p1182c2s v1p1308c2s v1p1360c2s
v2p0158c2s v2p0201c2s v4p0434c2s
v6p0451c2s
Carlile, B. v2p0015c1s
v3p0014c1s
Carlile, J.B. v3p0381c2s
v3p0432c2s v5p0346c2s
Carlile, J.C. v4p0353c2m
Carlile, W. v6p0126c2s
v6p0158c1s v6p0385c1s v6p0665c1s
Carlile, W.A. v4p0065c2s

Carlile, W.W. v4p0130c1s v4p0284c1s v4p0382c1s v4p0394c1s v4p0475c1s v5p0237c2s v5p0240c2s v5p0245c1s v5p0284c2s v5p0382c2m v5p0383c1m v5p0408c2s v5p0501c1s v6p0189c1s v6p0212c1s v6p0215c2s v6p0425c1m v6p0528c1s
Carlile, Wilson v6p0665c1s
Carlin, E.C. et al. v5p0158c2s
Carlin, E.V. v6p0394c1s v6p0474c2s
Carlin, Eva V. v5p0355c1s v5p0506c1s v5p0606c2s v5p0628c1s
Carlin, F.M. v6p0257c2s
Carlin, W.E. v5p0209c1s v5p0314c1s v5p0447c2s v6p0653c1s
Carling, G. v6p0364c2s
Carling, George v6p0244c1s
Carlisle, A., Sir v1p0272c1s
Carlisle, Bishop of v3p0146c1s
Carlisle, C.B. v1p0038c1s
Carlisle, C.W. v6p0617c1s
Carlisle, D. v1p1115c1s v2p0246c2s
Carlisle, Earl of v6p0378c2s
Carlisle, H. v1p1175c2s v2p0469c1m v2p0469c2s
Carlisle, J.C. v3p0270c2s
Carlisle, J.G. v3p0096c2s v3p0114c2s v3p0149c2s v3p0359c1m v3p0416c2s v3p0420c1s v4p0526c1s v5p0182c2s v5p0464c2s v5p0601c1s v5p0602c1s
Carlisle, J.G. and Reed, T.B. v3p0202c2s
Carlisle, J.H. v2p0355c1s
Carlisle, N. v1p0086c2s v1p0108c2s v1p0567c2s v1p0579c1s
Carlisle, T. v1p0353c2s v1p0617c1s v1p0627c1s v1p0844c1s v1p1049c1s v1p1435c1s
Carlisle, W.W. v4p0093c1m
Carll, M.M. v1p0389c2s v1p0641c1s v1p0810c2s
Carlock, J.L. v6p0492c2s
Carlson, A.J. v6p0285c1s v6p0424c1s
Carlson, E. v2p0064c2s
Carlson, P. v4p0333c2s
Carlton, E. v4p0153c1s
Carlton, E.T. v6p0317c2s
Carlton, F.T. v6p0008c2s v6p0025c2m v6p0033c1s v6p0154c1s v6p0198c1s v6p0295c1s v6p0302c2s v6p0346c1s v6p0526c1s v6p0555c1s v6p0572c2s
Carlton, H.P. v1p1148c2s
Carlton, W.N.C. v6p0136c2s
Carlton, W.W. v6p0513c2s
Carlyle, A.B. v1p1387c2s
Carlyle, A.J. v3p0270c1s v4p0369c2s v4p0574c1s v5p0022c2s v5p0273c1s
Carlyle, A.J. and Barlett, V. v5p0024c1s
Carlyle, E. v4p0409c1s
Carlyle, E.I. v6p0141c2s
Carlyle, Florence v5p0031c2s v5p0141c2s
Carlyle, J.C. v3p0463c1s
Carlyle, J.E. v2p0148c1s
Carlyle, K. v1p1339c2s
Carlyle, M. v6p0068c2s v6p0125c2s
Carlyle, R.W. v4p0574c1s v5p0285c1s
Carlyle, T. v1p0087c1s v1p0134c1s v1p0178c2s v1p0181c2s v1p0185c1s v1p0218c2s v1p0302c2s v1p0319c2s v1p0349c1s v1p0351c2s v1p0370c2s v1p0403c2s v1p0419c2s v1p0476c1s v1p0483c1s v1p0485c1s v1p0513c2m v1p0514c1m v1p0530c1m v1p0531c1m v1p0531c2s v1p0570c2s v1p0589c2s v1p0593c2s v1p0667c1s v1p0694c1s v1p0712c1s v1p0777c2s v1p0849c1s v1p0893c2s v1p0905c2s v1p0919c2s v1p0929c2s v1p1051c2s v1p1107c1m v1p1152c1s v1p1154c2s v1p1156c1s v1p1168c1s v1p1168c2s v1p1193c1s v1p1196c2s v1p1280c2s v1p1320c2s v1p1342c2s v1p1347c1s v1p1370c2s v1p1378c1s v1p1398c2s v2p0051c1s v2p0069c1s v2p0227c2s v3p0320c1s v4p0425c2s v4p0633c1s
Carlyon-Britton, P.W.P. .. v6p0462c1s
Carlyon-Jenkins, C. v4p0460c2s
Carmack, G.A. v6p0710c1s
Carman, A. v4p0396c1s
Carman, A.B. v6p0018c2s v6p0549c1s
Carman, A.R. v3p0065c1s v4p0096c2s v4p0267c2s v4p0575c2s v5p0281c2s v5p0433c1s v6p0090c1s v6p0232c2s v6p0238c1s v6p0265c1s v6p0266c2s v6p0284c1s v6p0312c1s v6p0436c2s v6p0462c1s v6p0488c1s v6p0518c1s v6p0545c1s v6p0589c2s v6p0647c2s v6p0677c2s
Carman, A.S. v4p0391c1s v5p0249c2s v6p0495c2s
Carman, Ada v5p0107c2s v5p0427c2s v5p0556c2s
Carman, B. v3p0243c1s v3p0429c2s v4p0034c2s v4p0476c1s v4p0517c1s v4p0636c2s v5p0001c2s v5p0159c1s v5p0282c1s v5p0489c1s v5p0633c1s v6p0033c1s
Carman, Bliss v4p0536c2s v6p0035c1s v6p0043c1s v6p0048c1s v6p0055c2m v6p0075c1m v6p0105c1s v6p0124c1s v6p0158c2s v6p0202c1s v6p0249c2s v6p0255c2s v6p0264c1s v6p0307c2s v6p0311c1s v6p0346c2s v6p0400c2s v6p0410c2s v6p0505c2m v6p0516c2s v6p0533c1s v6p0580c2s v6p0582c2s v6p0611c2s v6p0621c1m v6p0707c1s
Carman, E. v6p0269c2s
Carman, E.K. v6p0573c1s
Carman, F. v2p0118c1s
Carman, G.N. v6p0581c2s
Carman, I.N. v2p0371c1s v4p0113c2s
Carmany, J.H. v1p1153c2s
Carmarthen, K. v3p0124c1s
Carmarthen, Lady v3p0288c1s
Carmichael, C.H.E. v4p0005c2s
Carmichael, Dr. v1p1392c1s
Carmichael, E. v6p0038c1s v6p0249c2s v6p0420c2s v6p0450c1s
Carmichael, H. v1p1220c2s v2p0022c2s
Carmichael, H.E. v4p0211c1s
Carmichael, Henry v3p0457c1s
Carmichael, J. v4p0479c1s
Carmichael, J.H. v6p0256c2s
Carmichael, M. v4p0118c2s v4p0262c2s v4p0361c2m v5p0279c1s v5p0329c2s v5p0595c2m v6p0238c2m v6p0547c2s v6p0662c1s
Carmichael, Montgomery ... v6p0238c2s
Carmichael, N.R. et al. .. v4p0487c1s
Carmody, Prof. v5p0125c1s
Carmon, J.N. v1p0353c2s
Carnachan, J.G. v3p0381c1s
Carnahan, J. v1p0393c1s
Carnarthen, K.L. v2p0377c1s
Carnarvon, Earl of v1p0626c1s v1p0648c1s v2p0028c2s v2p0152c1s v2p0189c1s v2p0194c2s v2p0254c2s v2p0351c2s v2p0380c1s v2p0415c2s v2p0421c2s v3p0027c2s v3p0067c1s v3p0322c2s v3p0448c1s
Carne, J. v1p0644c1s v1p0658c1s v1p1312c2s
Carne, R.L. v2p0139c1s
Carne, W.F. v1p1387c1s v1p1387c2s v3p0154c2s v4p0605c2s
Carnegie, A. v2p0115c2s v2p0141c2s v2p0245c1s v2p0245c2s v2p0320c2s v3p0181c1s v3p0248c2s v3p0285c1s v3p0329c1s v3p0341c1s v3p0416c2s v3p0420c1s v3p0437c1s v3p0458c1s v4p0238c2s v4p0336c2s v4p0563c2s v4p0593c1s v4p0594c2s v4p0595c1s v4p0596c1s v4p0601c2s v4p0615c1s v5p0007c2s v5p0080c2s v5p0247c1s v5p0281c1s v5p0359c2s v5p0441c2s v5p0445c1s v5p0457c1s v5p0574c1s v5p0593c1s v5p0598c2s v5p0603c2s v5p0611c1s v6p0020c2s v6p0089c2s v6p0266c2s v6p0271c1s v6p0355c1s v6p0365c2s v6p0485c1s v6p0669c2s v6p0690c1s
Carnegie, A. and Lubbock, J. v4p0525c2s
Carnegie, A. et al. v3p0138c1s v4p0101c1s
Carnegie, Andrew v3p0458c2s v6p0671c1s
Carnegie, C. v5p0356c1s
Carnegie, D. v5p0451c1s
Carnegie, D.W. v5p0039c2s
Carnelley, T. v1p0621c1m v1p0621c2s
Carneri, B. v4p0478c2s
Carnes, W.W. v2p0077c1s
Carney, H.C. v2p0412c1s
Carney, J.W. v2p0394c2s
Carney, S.H. v6p0072c1s
Carney, S.H., jr. v6p0146c2s v6p0409c1s
Carney, W.J. v5p0222c2s v5p0585c1s
Carney, W.J. and Thomas, C. v6p0031c1s v6p0352c2s
Carnifex, J. v3p0154c2s
Carnsew, R. v6p0282c2s
Caro, E. v1p0489c1s v2p0173c1s v2p0201c2s
Caron, D.A. v1p0271c1s
Caron, H.Le v4p0324c2s
Carothers, P.W.B., Mrs. .. v1p0606c1s
Carotti, J. v4p0513c2s
Carpe, A. v4p0442c1m
Carpenter, A. v2p0160c1s v3p0123c2s v3p0156c2s v3p0386c2m
Carpenter, A.B. v1p0202c2s
Carpenter, A.H. v6p0277c1s v6p0444c1s
Carpenter, B.W. v1p0285c1s
Carpenter, Boyd, Mrs. v3p0049c1s v4p0128c2s
Carpenter, C.U. v6p0217c2m v6p0321c1s v6p0356c1s v6p0392c2s v6p0443c1s v6p0618c1s
Carpenter, E. v2p0120c2s v2p0143c1s v2p0407c1s v3p0105c1s v3p0108c1s v3p0143c1s v3p0396c2s v3p0433c2s v3p0446c2s v6p0691c1s v6p0704c2s
Carpenter, E.B. v1p0500c1s v2p0171c1s v2p0306c1s v3p0025c1s
Carpenter, E.C. v6p0087c2s v6p0263c2s v6p0420c1s
Carpenter, E.F. v3p0232c2s
Carpenter, E.J. v3p0467c2s v4p0068c2s v4p0069c1s v4p0624c1s v5p0050c1s v5p0072c2s v5p0134c1s v5p0469c2s v6p0699c2s
Carpenter, E.N. et al. ... v3p0123c1s
Carpenter, E.W. v1p0148c1s v1p0353c1s v1p0863c2s
Carpenter, Ed. v6p0259c2s
Carpenter, Edward v5p0176c2s v5p0237c2s
Carpenter, Elizabeth v6p0176c2s v6p0402c1s
Carpenter, F. v1p0187c2s v1p0666c2s v1p1273c1s
Carpenter, F.B. v1p0750c1s v2p0259c1s v5p0085c1s
Carpenter, F.C. v2p0012c2s v2p0452c1s
Carpenter, F.C.L. v5p0293c2s
Carpenter, F.D.Y. v1p0158c2s v1p0235c1s v1p0287c1s v1p1034c2s v2p0052c2s v2p0053c2s v2p0055c1m v2p0086c2s v2p0087c1s v2p0089c2s v2p0141c1s v2p0167c1s v2p0181c1s v2p0266c2s v2p0290c2s v2p0333c2s v2p0364c2s v2p0411c2s v2p0451c2s v2p0468c2s
Carpenter, F.G. v2p0098c1s v2p0353c1m v3p0011c1s v3p0029c1s v3p0050c1s v3p0062c2s v3p0077c1s v3p0096c2s v3p0100c2s v3p0126c2s v3p0212c2s v3p0227c2s v3p0237c1s v3p0325c2s v3p0343c1m v3p0368c2s v3p0391c2s v3p0431c2s v3p0439c2s v3p0456c1m v3p0469c2s v4p0195c2s v4p0326c2s v4p0377c1s v4p0545c1s v4p0594c2s v5p0055c1s v5p0069c2s v5p0550c1s
Carpenter, F.I. v2p0172c2s v4p0019c2s v4p0178c1m v5p0191c2s v5p0192c2s v6p0201c1s v6p0461c1s
Carpenter, F.I. et al. ... v4p0335c2s
Carpenter, F.J. v3p0117c2s v4p0184c1s
Carpenter, F.O. v6p0141c1s v6p0141c2s v6p0192c2s v6p0317c2s v6p0373c2s v6p0374c1s
Carpenter, G.H. v4p0124c2s v4p0285c2m v4p0618c1s v5p0292c1s v5p0546c1s
Carpenter, G.H. and Wallace, A.R. v4p0422c1s
Carpenter, G.R. v2p0051c1s v2p0200c2s v3p0106c1s v3p0110c1m v3p0110c2s v3p0203c2s v3p0206c2s v3p0287c1s v3p0463c2s v4p0147c2s v4p0183c1s v5p0171c1s v5p0263c2s v5p0415c2s v6p0363c1s
Carpenter, G.S. v5p0210c1s v5p0469c2s
Carpenter, G.T. v2p0092c2s v2p0106c1s v2p0148c2s v2p0318c2s
Carpenter, G.W. v1p0944c2s v1p1147c1s
Carpenter, H. v1p0842c2s v1p1042c2s v1p1237c2s v3p0231c2s
Carpenter, H.B. v3p0341c1s v3p0429c2s
Carpenter, H.G. v6p0462c2s
Carpenter, H.J. v6p0219c1s
Carpenter, H.M. v4p0155c2s v5p0049c1s
Carpenter, H.R. v1p0697c1s
Carpenter, Helen M. v4p0375c2s
Carpenter, J. v1p0281c1s v1p0381c2s v1p0382c1s v1p0541c1s v1p0557c1s v1p0755c1s v1p0827c1s v1p0865c2m v1p0904c1s v1p1004c1s v1p1036c2s v1p1213c2s v1p1234c1s v1p1244c1s v1p1267c2s v1p1268c2s v1p1269c1s v1p1367c1s v1p1432c1s
Carpenter, J.C. v1p0203c1s v1p0458c1s v1p0807c2s v3p0095c1s v4p0545c2s
Carpenter, J.E. v1p0045c1s v1p0047c2s v1p0124c2s v1p0131c1s v1p0173c2s v1p0297c1s v1p0366c1s v1p0394c2s v1p0512c1s v1p0685c1s v1p1056c2s v1p1281c1s v2p0043c1s v2p0043c2s v2p0356c2s v3p0229c1s v4p0078c1s v5p0281c1s

Carpenter, J.Estlin v6p0086c1s
Carpenter, L. v1p0128c1s
Carpenter, L.H. v5p0486c1s
Carpenter, M. v1p0448c1s
v1p0661c2s v1p1052c1s v1p1420c1s
Carpenter, M.T. v4p0225c2s
Carpenter, M.W. v1p0755c2s
v1p0756c1s v1p0940c1s v2p0240c1s
Carpenter, Mary A. v5p0167c1s
Carpenter, P.C. v1p1005c2s
Carpenter, P.H. v1p0447c1s
Carpenter, P.P. v1p1292c2m
Carpenter, R.C. v4p0134c2s
v4p0175c1m v4p0284c2s v4p0547c1m
Carpenter, R.H. v2p0019c2s
v2p0071c1s v2p0371c2s
Carpenter, S.H. v1p0435c1s
v1p1203c1s
Carpenter, T.D.Y. v2p0471c2s
Carpenter, W. v1p0139c1s
v1p0470c1s
Carpenter, W.A. v2p0432c1s
Carpenter, W.B. v1p0017c1s
v1p0041c1s v1p0044c1s v1p0110c1s
v1p0157c1s v1p0214c2s v1p0332c1s
v1p0340c1s v1p0342c1s v1p0354c1s
v1p0420c2s v1p0457c2s v1p0465c1s
v1p0467c1s v1p0521c1s v1p0562c1m
v1p0579c2s v1p0587c1s v1p0612c2s
v1p0642c2s v1p0729c1s v1p0747c1s
v1p0747c2s v1p0749c2m v1p0825c1s
v1p0843c1s v1p0900c2s v1p0901c1m
v1p1074c2m v1p1171c2m v1p1172c1m
v1p0936c2m v1p0938c1s v1p1007c1s
v1p1206c2s v1p1234c1s v1p1238c1s
v1p1238c2s v1p1271c2s v1p1279c2s
v1p1390c1s v1p1410c2s v1p1440c2s
v2p0039c1s v2p0112c1s v2p0116c2s
v2p0119c1m v2p0149c1s v2p0161c1s
v2p0161c2s v2p0175c2s v2p0202c2s
v2p0235c2s v2p0405c2s v2p0425c1s
v2p0451c1s v2p0457c1s v2p0483c2s
v3p0021c1s v3p0056c2s v3p0110c1s
v3p0112c2s v3p0229c1m v3p0229c2s
v3p0250c1s v3p0445c2s v4p0075c2s
v4p0232c1s v4p0300c2s v4p0426c2s
v4p0515c2s v4p0543c2s v5p0306c1s
v5p0456c1s v5p0512c2s v6p0191c2s
v6p0258c1s
Carpenter, W.B. and Coleridge, Lord
v2p0462c2s
Carpenter, W.B. and Dawson, J.W.
v1p0420c2s
Carpenter, W.B. et al. ... v3p0342c1s
Carpenter, W.B., Mrs. v4p0414c1s
Carpenter, W.Boyd v3p0048c2s
v3p0246c1m v3p0311c1s v3p0359c2s
v3p0394c1s v3p0400c2s v3p0415c2s
v4p0048c2s v4p0303c2s v5p0234c2s
v6p0123c2s v6p0333c1s v6p0419c2s
Carpenter, W.H. v2p0153c1s
v2p0249c2s v2p0443c2s v3p0207c2m
v3p0242c2s v3p0307c2s v3p0426c2s
v3p0429c1s v3p0449c2s v3p0450c1m
v4p0010c2s v4p0062c2s v4p0164c2s
v4p0215c2s v4p0253c1s v4p0272c1s
v4p0307c2s v4p0310c2s v4p0407c2m
v4p0498c1s v5p0176c1s v5p0207c2s
v5p0297c2s v5p0645c1s v6p0251c2s
v6p0263c1s v6p0679c1s
Carpenter, W.L. v1p0366c1s
v1p0645c1s v1p0919c2s v2p0131c1s
v2p0132c1s v2p0132c2s v2p0390c1s
v2p0402c1s v2p0432c2s v3p0128c2s
v3p0380c1s v3p0392c1s
Carpenter, W.M. v1p0492c1s
v1p0854c1s
Carpenter, W.P. v2p0016c1s
Carr, A. v5p0047c1s
v5p0059c1s v5p0059c2s v5p0114c1s
v5p0151c2s v5p0306c2s v5p0308c2s
v5p0325c1s v5p0366c2s v5p0436c1s
v5p0531c1s v6p0061c1s v6p0061c2s
v6p0063c2m v6p0064c1m v6p0163c1s
v6p0282c2s v6p0341c1s v6p0342c1s
v6p0484c2s
Carr, A.C. v1p0877c1s
v2p0037c2s v4p0162c1s v6p0243c1s
v6p0439c1s
Carr, Agnes J. v4p0551c1s
Carr, Arthur v6p0125c2s
Carr, B. v4p0062c2s
Carr, C., Mrs. v1p0726c1s
v1p0776c1s v3p0465c1s v4p0037c1s
v4p0074c1s
Carr, C.T. v6p0151c2s
Carr, E.S. v1p0175c1s
v4p0241c2s v4p0480c1s v4p0505c1s
v5p0447c1s v5p0483c2s v5p0545c2s
Carr, F. v3p0024c1s
v6p0168c2s
Carr, Fannie, W. v6p0389c1s
Carr, G. v1p0814c2s
v1p1039c1s
Carr, G.B. v5p0117c2s
v5p0463c1s
Carr, G.S. v3p0146c1s
Carr, H. v1p0052c1s
v3p0336c1s
Carr, H. and Allen, J.B. . v6p0643c2s
Carr, H.J. v2p0051c2s
v2p0367c1s v3p0248c2s v3p0249c2s
v4p0329c2s v4p0337c1s v5p0332c2s
v5p0336c2s v5p0409c2s
Carr, H.W. v5p0267c2s
Carr, J. v2p0041c1s
v2p0378c1s
Carr, J.C. v1p0140c2s
v1p0304c1s v1p0841c1s v1p1142c2s
v1p1313c1s v2p0002c1s v2p0052c1s
v2p0371c2s v2p0378c2s v2p0463c2s
v3p0034c2s v3p0208c2s v6p0568c2s
Carr, J.C. and Blackburn, V.
v5p0560c1s
Carr, J.Comyns v2p0478c2s
Carr, J.F. v6p0095c1s
v6p0204c2s v6p0331c1m v6p0476c2m
v6p0477c1s
Carr, J.W.C. v1p0370c2s
v1p0797c2s v1p1381c2s
Carr, Jeanne C. v6p0053c1s
v6p0434c2s v6p0645c1s
Carr, K. v3p0002c2s
v3p0118c2s v4p0373c2s
Carr, L. v2p0010c2s
v2p0219c2s v3p0289c2s v4p0013c2s
v4p0282c1s v4p0282c2s v4p0385c1s
v4p0399c2s v4p0442c2s v4p0503c2s
v4p0540c1s v5p0039c2s v5p0358c1s
Carr, M.E. v5p0528c2s
v6p0627c2s
Carr, O.A. v2p0082c1s
v2p0084c2s
Carr, R. v1p0484c1s
Carr, R.V. v5p0309c2s
v6p0321c1s
Carr-Ellison, R.H. v5p0290c1s
v5p0644c1s v6p0031c2s v6p0105c2s
v6p0711c2s
Carrau, L. v4p0001c1s
Carrel, A. v6p0351c1s
Carrel, E. v4p0629c2s
Carrel, F. v4p0211c1s
v4p0351c1s v4p0353c2s v4p0561c1s
v6p0276c2s v6p0302c2s v6p0376c1s
v6p0426c2s v6p0428c1m v6p0430c1s
Carrel, F.P. v2p0007c2s
v2p0051c2s v2p0216c2s v2p0256c1s
v2p0271c2s v2p0278c1s
Carrere, J.F. v6p0157c2s
Carrere, J.M. v4p0023c1s
v4p0023c2s v4p0200c1s
Carret, J.R. v5p0218c2s
v5p0568c1s
Carret, M.B. v1p0229c1m
v1p0463c1s v1p0606c1s v1p0754c1s
v2p0120c1s
Carrevon, H. v4p0385c2m
Carrias, V. v1p0997c2s
v1p1229c1m
Carrick, A.VanL. v5p0527c1s
Carrick, J. v2p0066c1s
v3p0395c2s
Carrick, W. v1p0118c1s
Carrie, J. v2p0047c1s
Carrigain, P. v1p0407c2s
Carrighan, J. v1p0772c2s
Carringer, M.A. v6p0190c1s
v6p0293c1s
Carrington, C.R.Earl v5p0323c2s
Carrington, Carroll v5p0274c1s
Carrington, E. v1p0101c2s
v1p0185c2s v1p0244c2s v1p0464c2s
v1p0579c2s v1p0934c1s v1p1313c1s
v2p0401c2s v4p0279c2s v4p0467c2s
Carrington, F. v1p0914c1s
v1p1392c2s v5p0094c2s v5p0168c1s
v5p0466c2s
Carrington, G. v1p0978c1s
Carrington, H. v6p0309c2s
Carrington, H.A. v1p1007c1s
Carrington, H.B. v1p0717c2s
v1p1387c2s v2p0457c2s v3p0051c1s
v3p0060c1s v3p0304c1s v3p0443c1s
v3p0453c2s
Carrington, J.B. v4p0064c2s
v4p0145c2m v4p0310c1s v4p0578c1s
v4p0605c2s v5p0012c2s v5p0064c1s
v5p0129c1s v5p0150c2m v5p0330c1s
v5p0384c1s v5p0406c2s v5p0433c2s
v5p0482c2s v5p0613c1s v5p0633c2s
v6p0496c2s v6p0594c2s v6p0617c2m
v6p0620c2s v6p0706c2s
Carrington, Jas B. v6p0307c2s
Carrington, K. v1p1127c2s
Carrington, S. v1p0409c1s
v1p1307c1s
Carrington, S.E. v6p0592c2s
Carrington, T.C. v4p0309c1s
Carrington, W.T.H. v2p0476c1s
v5p0086c2s
Carrison, T. v6p0217c2s
Carroll, A.E. v1p0186c2s
v2p0434c2s
Carroll, A.L. v1p0352c1s
v1p0465c1s v1p1017c1s v1p1159c2s
Carroll, C. v1p0275c1s
v1p0338c2s v1p0518c1s v1p0794c2s
v1p0896c2s v1p0916c2s v1p1175c2s
v1p1336c2s v1p1357c1s
Carroll, C.C. v1p0601c2s
Carroll, C.F. v4p0103c1s
v4p0168c2s v4p0169c2s v5p0179c1s
v5p0264c2s v5p0360c2s
Carroll, C.H. v1p0087c2s
v1p0093c2m v1p0095c1s v1p0325c1m
v1p0325c2m v1p0354c1s v1p0453c1m
v1p0645c2s v1p0649c2s v1p0860c2m
v1p1232c1s v1p1282c2s v1p1361c2s
Carroll, C.M. v3p0080c1s
v3p0365c1s
Carroll, H. v1p0853c2s
Carroll, H.K. v1p0830c1s
v1p1304c1s v2p0269c1s v4p0109c2s
v4p0114c1s v4p0119c1s v4p0153c1s
v4p0374c2s v4p0397c1s v4p0489c1s
v5p0199c2s v5p0372c2s v5p0460c2m
v5p0603c1s
Carroll, J. v1p0047c2s
v5p0557c1s
Carroll, J.P. v1p0280c1s
v5p0325c1s
Carroll, J.S. v6p0164c1s
Carroll, L. v1p1376c2s
v3p0062c2s v6p0418c2s
Carrow, G.D. v3p0276c2s
Carruth, E. v5p0127c1s
Carruth, F.W. v6p0076c2s
v6p0651c1s
Carruth, Frances W. v5p0072c2s
v5p0222c1s v6p0687c1s
Carruth, H. v4p0091c2s
v4p0158c2s v5p0116c1s v5p0343c1s
v5p0347c2s v5p0550c1s v5p0558c1s
v6p0465c2s
Carruth, Hayden v5p0086c1s
v5p0450c2s v5p0556c1s
Carruth, W.H. v4p0223c2s
v4p0254c2s v4p0258c2s v4p0511c1s
v4p0545c1s v5p0219c2s v5p0313c2s
v5p0340c1s v5p0412c1s v6p0053c2s
v6p0262c2s v6p0305c2s v6p0404c1s
v6p0572c1m
Carruth, W.W. v3p0219c1s
v4p0287c2s v4p0521c2s v4p0606c2s
Carruthers, J. v2p0408c2s
Carruthers, J.B. v5p0453c2s
v6p0502c2s
Carruthers, W. v1p0152c2s
v1p0153c1s v1p0268c2s v1p0423c2s
v1p0434c1s v1p0541c1s v1p0960c1s
v1p1015c2s v2p0344c1s v6p0112c2s
Carry, J. v6p0236c1s
Carryer, A.P. v6p0520c1s
Carryl, C.E. v3p0067c2s
v4p0266c2s v4p0485c1s
Carryl, G.W. v4p0034c2s
v4p0240c2s v5p0036c2s v5p0041c1s
v5p0085c1s v5p0132c1s v5p0217c1s
v5p0271c1s v6p0055c1s v6p0079c2s
v6p0161c2s v6p0169c1s v6p0226c2s
v6p0285c1s v6p0310c2s v6p0456c2s
v6p0467c2s v6p0480c1s v6p0499c2s
v6p0500c2s v6p0541c2s v6p0594c1s
v6p0596c1s v6p0699c1s v6p0714c2s
Carson and Lloyd, C.J. ... v6p0081c1s
Carson, A.C. v4p0486c2s
Carson, C. v5p0288c1s
Carson, E.L. v3p0050c1s
v3p0473c1s
Carson, H. and Hurll, E.M.
v4p0335c2s
Carson, H. et al. v4p0335c2s
Carson, H.L. v3p0441c2s
v4p0003c1m v4p0059c2s v4p0101c2s
v4p0140c1s v4p0460c1s v6p0487c2s
Carson, J. v6p0500c1s
Carson, J.C. v5p0204c2s
Carson, J.M. v6p0711c2s
Carson, Katherine v6p0070c2s
Carson, P. v3p0194c1s
Carson, W.R. v5p0279c1s
Carstairs, J.S. v6p0685c1s
Carstairs, R. v4p0279c2s
v5p0285c1s
Carstairs, W.F.W. v6p0007c2s
v6p0457c1s
Carstanjen, F. v5p0041c2s
Carstens, C.C. v6p0080c1s
v6p0109c2s v6p0125c1s v6p0599c2s
Carstensen, G.A. v4p0463c1s
v4p0479c2s
Cartaz, A. v4p0468c2s
v5p0554c2s
Carte, S. v1p0464c2s
Carter, A. v4p0124c2s
Carter, A.B. v1p0422c1s
Carter, A.C.R. v3p0022c1m
v4p0031c1s v4p0442c2s v5p0209c1s
v5p0450c2m v5p0498c2m v5p0555c2s
v6p0363c2s v6p0553c2s
Carter, A.L. v3p0231c1s
v4p0502c1s
Carter, A.P. v3p0012c1s
Carter, A.T. v4p0133c2s
v5p0328c1s v6p0153c1s
Carter, B. v1p0019c2s
v5p0529c2s
Carter, C.F. v3p0177c2s
v6p0362c1s v6p0421c2s v6p0697c2s

Carter, E.B. v3p0253c1s
Carter, E.C. v5p0308c1s
Carter, E.E. v6p0260c2s
Carter, E.K. v4p0217c1s
v5p0092c2s
Carter, E.W. v3p0333c2s
v3p0365c2s v4p0313c1s
Carter, F. v1p0380c2s
v1p0560c2s v1p0587c1s v1p0738c2s
v1p0920c1s v1p1286c1s v2p0181c2m
v6p0447c2s
Carter, G. v1p0312c2s
Carter, G.R. v6p0283c1s
Carter, H. v3p0437c2s
Carter, H.J. v5p0335c2s
Carter, J. v1p1122c2s
v2p0366c1s v3p0185c1s v4p0080c2s
v4p0382c1s v4p0533c1s v4p0533c2s
v5p0467c2s
Carter, J. and Holland, H.S.
v6p0141c1s v6p0428c2s
Carter, J.B. v6p0424c2s
v6p0680c1s
Carter, J.C. v3p0244c2m
v4p0576c2s
Carter, J.F. v6p0505c1s
Carter, J.G. v1p0506c2s
v1p0648c2s v1p1288c1s
Carter, J.H. v3p0156c1s
Carter, K. v4p0254c2s
v4p0321c1s v4p0343c2s v4p0503c1s
v4p0635c2s
Carter, L.W. v3p0047c2s
Carter, M. v3p0466c2s
Carter, M.E. v6p0699c2s
Carter, M.H. v5p0153c2s
v5p0316c1s v5p0370c1s v6p0167c2s
v6p0479c1s
Carter, O.C.S. v4p0031c2s
v4p0120c2s v4p0220c2s v4p0411c2s
v5p0513c1s v6p0002c2s v6p0167c1s
v6p0491c1s v6p0607c1s
Carter, R. v1p0563c2s
v3p0302c2s
Carter, R.B. v1p0816c2s
v1p1233c1s v2p0462c1s v3p0092c2s
v3p0093c1s v3p0147c2s v3p0451c1s
v5p0200c2m v5p0368c1s v6p0011c1s
v6p0648c1s v6p0680c1s
Carter, R.G. v3p0059c1s
Carter, R.K. v3p0148c2s
v4p0229c1s
Carter, S.D. v1p0919c1s
Carter, S.N. v1p0957c1s
v2p0101c2s v3p0263c2s v4p0609c1s
Carter, Susan N. v5p0300c2s
Carter, T. v1p0832c2s
v1p0833c2s v1p0852c2s v2p0287c1s
Carter, T.H. v4p0481c2s
Carter, T.T. v1p0250c2s
v4p0113c1s v4p0128c2s
Carter, T.T. and Shore, T.T.
v4p0112c1s
Carter, W. v2p0480c2s
Carter, W.C. v4p0557c1s
Carter, W.G. v2p0097c2s
Carter, W.H. v3p0441c2s
v5p0215c1s v6p0031c1s v6p0205c1s
v6p0493c1s v6p0551c1s v6p0666c1m
v6p0666c2s v6p0670c1s v6p0712c1s
Cartera, R.Malet de v6p0630c1s
Carton, F. v1p0451c2s
Carton, R.P. v2p0317c2s
Cartwright, A. v4p0314c2s
Cartwright, A.D. v6p0566c2s
Cartwright, E., Mrs. v4p0374c1s
v5p0199c2s
Cartwright, H. v5p0084c1s
Cartwright, J. v1p0461c2s
v2p0025c1s v2p0053c2s v2p0065c1s
v2p0066c2m v2p0067c1s v2p0184c1s
v2p0250c2s v2p0365c1m v3p0101c2m
v3p0194c1s v3p0259c1s v3p0263c1s
v3p0318c1s v3p0371c2s v3p0376c1s
v3p0440c2s v3p0453c1s v4p0009c2s
v4p0019c1s v4p0046c2s v4p0070c1s
v4p0079c1s v4p0134c1s v4p0135c2s
v4p0146c2s v4p0172c1s v4p0204c2s
v4p0220c1s v4p0301c1s v4p0304c2m
v4p0342c2s v4p0363c1s v4p0369c1s
v4p0371c1s v4p0394c1s v4p0418c1s
v4p0421c2s v4p0431c2s v4p0468c1s
v4p0473c2s v4p0484c2s v4p0503c2s
v4p0517c1s v4p0577c2s v4p0603c2s
v4p0605c1s v4p0616c2s v6p0276c1s
v6p0532c1s v6p0689c1s
Cartwright, J.D. v1p0406c1s
v1p0419c2s v1p0459c1s v1p0886c2s
v1p0888c1s v1p1430c2s
Cartwright, Julia v2p0183c2s
v2p0376c2s v2p0458c2s v5p0310c1m
v5p0479c1s v5p0504c1s v6p0088c2s
v6p0152c1s v6p0705c1s
Cartwright, Minnie v6p0053c2s
Cartwright, R. v6p0133c1s
Cartwright, R.J. v3p0347c1s
Cartwright, S. v1p1223c2s
Cartwright, S.A. v1p0613c1s
v1p0904c2s v1p0905c1s v1p1206c1s
v1p1265c2s v2p0309c1s
Cartwright, S.E. v5p0191c2s
v5p0503c1s
Cartwright, T.S. v2p0121c1s
v2p0427c1s v3p0230c1s
Cartwright, W.C. v1p0517c1s
v1p0672c2s v2p0098c2s
Cartwright-Ady, Julia v4p0047c1s
v4p0473c2m
Carty, M. v4p0227c2s
Caruana, A.A. v3p0265c1s
Carulla, F.J.R. v4p0548c1s
Carus, A. v6p0159c2s
Carus, C.G. v1p1068c2s
Carus, J.V. et al. v5p0514c1s
Carus, P. v3p0143c1s
v3p0242c1s v3p0280c1s v3p0437c2s
v4p0001c2s v4p0002c1s v4p0007c1m
v4p0007c2m v4p0014c2s v4p0019c2s
v4p0026c2s v4p0029c1s v4p0033c2s
v4p0037c1s v4p0051c2s v4p0053c1s
v4p0071c2m v4p0077c2m v4p0092c1s
v4p0093c1s v4p0101c1s v4p0106c2m
v4p0109c1s v4p0121c2s v4p0128c1s
v4p0130c1s v4p0149c2s v4p0152c2m
v4p0154c1m v4p0155c2s v4p0161c2s
v4p0162c2s v4p0172c1s v4p0186c2s
v4p0187c2s v4p0188c1m v4p0188c2m
v4p0190c2s v4p0191c1m v4p0192c1s
v4p0193c2s v4p0196c1s v4p0196c2m
v4p0209c2m v4p0229c2m v4p0232c1s
v4p0246c1s v4p0248c1s v4p0254c1s
v4p0272c1m v4p0273c2m v4p0275c2m
v4p0284c1m v4p0297c1s v4p0300c1s
v4p0307c2s v4p0308c1s v4p0308c2m
v4p0312c2s v4p0315c1s v4p0326c2s
v4p0327c2s v4p0336c1s v4p0351c2s
v4p0360c2m v4p0364c2s v4p0366c2s
v4p0371c1s v4p0372c1m v4p0379c1m
v4p0381c2s v4p0382c1s v4p0384c2s
v4p0389c1s v4p0392c1s v4p0396c1m
v4p0405c1s v4p0414c2s v4p0417c2s
v4p0421c1m v4p0423c2s v4p0424c1s
v4p0436c1s v4p0438c1s v4p0439c2m
v4p0447c1m v4p0454c1m v4p0461c2s
v4p0463c2s v4p0464c1m v4p0464c2s
v4p0465c1s v4p0476c2s v4p0478c1s
v4p0478c2s v4p0479c1m v4p0479c2s
v4p0482c2s v4p0483c2m v4p0491c2s
v4p0507c1m v4p0507c2m v4p0508c1s
v4p0514c1s v4p0515c1s v4p0516c2s
v4p0530c1s v4p0533c1s v4p0536c1s
v4p0539c1m v4p0542c1s v4p0546c1m
v4p0555c2s v4p0574c1s v4p0575c1s
v4p0577c1s v4p0581c2s v4p0585c2m
v4p0590c1s v4p0603c1s v4p0608c2s
v4p0624c2s v4p0629c2s v5p0018c1s
v5p0023c2s v5p0041c2s v5p0055c1s
v5p0055c2s v5p0056c1s v5p0056c2s
v5p0071c2s v5p0081c2m v5p0092c1s
v5p0095c1s v5p0101c2s v5p0107c2m
v5p0108c1s v5p0108c2s v5p0111c2s
v5p0115c1m v5p0145c2m v5p0146c1s
v5p0146c2s v5p0152c1s v5p0155c1m
v5p0157c2s v5p0171c2s v5p0184c2s
v5p0195c1s v5p0196c1s v5p0199c1s
v5p0199c2s v5p0224c1s v5p0231c1s
v5p0232c1s v5p0236c1m v5p0236c2m
v5p0239c2s v5p0246c1s v5p0250c1s
v5p0260c1s v5p0280c2s v5p0291c2s
v5p0306c2s v5p0307c1m v5p0313c2s
v5p0327c1s v5p0347c2m v5p0355c2s
v5p0367c2s v5p0377c1s v5p0386c1s
v5p0394c2s v5p0396c2s v5p0430c1s
v5p0437c1s v5p0443c2s v5p0446c2s
v5p0447c2s v5p0454c2s v5p0480c1s
v5p0483c2m v5p0484c1s v5p0486c2s
v5p0506c1s v5p0508c1s v5p0510c2s
v5p0512c2s v5p0519c1s v5p0521c1s
v5p0529c1s v5p0540c1s v5p0544c1s
v5p0579c2s v5p0590c2s v5p0598c1s
v5p0608c2s v5p0613c2s v5p0643c2s
v6p0002c2s v6p0008c1s v6p0009c1s
v6p0019c1s v6p0024c2s v6p0025c1s
v6p0037c1s v6p0045c2s v6p0059c2s
v6p0060c1s v6p0073c2m v6p0086c1s
v6p0086c2s v6p0090c2s v6p0103c1s
v6p0118c2m v6p0120c2s v6p0121c1m
v6p0121c2s v6p0123c1m v6p0124c2s
v6p0145c2s v6p0159c2m v6p0169c1s
v6p0172c1s v6p0187c1s v6p0195c2s
v6p0226c1s v6p0245c1s v6p0251c1s
v6p0259c2m v6p0276c2s v6p0277c1s
v6p0278c2s v6p0280c2s v6p0287c2s
v6p0294c2m v6p0307c2s v6p0309c2m
v6p0336c2s v6p0338c1s v6p0340c2s
v6p0342c1s v6p0349c2s v6p0354c1s
v6p0355c1s v6p0361c1s v6p0365c1s
v6p0383c1s v6p0392c2s v6p0394c2s
v6p0396c2s v6p0397c1s v6p0397c2s
v6p0406c1s v6p0411c2m v6p0418c1s
v6p0422c2s v6p0423c1s v6p0438c1s
v6p0444c1s v6p0465c1s v6p0470c2m
v6p0482c2s v6p0488c2s v6p0492c1s
v6p0511c1s v6p0524c2s v6p0536c2s
v6p0540c2s v6p0552c1m v6p0557c1s
v6p0560c1s v6p0563c2s v6p0572c1s
v6p0583c1s v6p0586c2s v6p0590c1s
v6p0591c1s v6p0594c2s v6p0603c1s
v6p0604c2s v6p0609c2s v6p0610c2s
v6p0616c2s v6p0618c2s v6p0626c1m
v6p0628c1s v6p0632c1m v6p0642c2s
v6p0643c1s v6p0644c2s v6p0657c1s
v6p0659c1s v6p0688c1s v6p0694c2s
v6p0698c1s v6p0699c1s v6p0709c2s
v6p0713c1s v6p0713c2s
Carus, P. and Andrews, W.S.
v6p0395c1s
Carus, P. and Bright, D. . v5p0461c2s
Carus, P. and Gordon, M.L.
v5p0081c2s
Carus, P. and Loyson, H. . v5p0236c2s
Carus, P. and Mach, E. ... v3p0150c2s
v3p0385c1s
Carus, P. and Merton, S.D.
v6p0496c1s
Carus, P. and Minton, H.C.
v6p0103c1s
Carus, P. and Starr, F. .. v5p0373c2s
Carus, P. and Suzuki, T. . v5p0325c2s
v5p0566c2s
Carus, P. and Vocke, W. .. v5p0231c1s
Carus, P. et al. v4p0109c2s
v4p0374c2s
v5p0055c1s
Carus-Wilson, C. v3p0374c2m
Carus-Wilson, C.A. v5p0183c2s
v5p0455c1s
Carvalho, C.N. v3p0294c1s
v3p0432c1s v4p0099c1s v4p0168c2s
v4p0246c1s v5p0086c2s v5p0121c1s
Carvalho, S. v1p0805c2s
Carver, C. v1p1020c1s
Carver, G.W. v6p0604c2s
Carver, J.N. v6p0450c1s
Carver, L.D. v5p0335c2s
Carver, R. v6p0620c1s
Carver, T.A.B. and Barnard, J.E.
v5p0449c1s
Carver, T.N. v4p0152c1s
v4p0157c1s v4p0275c1s v4p0287c2s
v4p0314c2s v4p0351c1s v4p0384c1s
v4p0564c2s v4p0608c1s v5p0061c2s
v5p0202c1s v5p0383c1s v5p0418c2s
v5p0467c2s v5p0568c2s v5p0592c1s
v5p0623c2s v6p0149c2s v6p0150c1s
v6p0176c1s v6p0318c1s v6p0323c1s
v6p0436c2s v6p0520c1s v6p0633c1s
v6p0634c1s v6p0674c1s v6p0690c1s
Carvere, J.M. v6p0028c1s
Carvin, O.Z. v6p0618c1s
Carvosso, B. v1p1362c1s
Cary, A. v1p0550c2s
v1p0569c2s v1p0792c1s v1p0859c1s
v1p0887c2s v1p1018c2s v1p1066c2s
v1p1128c1s v1p1408c1s v3p0239c2s
Cary, A.A. v4p0065c1s
v5p0068c2s
Cary, Austin v5p0214c1s
Cary, C. v2p0453c1s
v5p0109c2s v5p0111c2s v5p0528c1s
v6p0163c2s
Cary, E. v1p0259c1m
v1p0392c1s v2p0049c1s v2p0089c1s
v3p0130c1s v4p0361c1s v4p0593c1s
v5p0158c1s v5p0186c1s v5p0209c2s
v5p0350c1s v5p0566c1s v6p0195c2s
Cary, E.F. v3p0344c2s
Cary, E.L. v5p0144c1s
v5p0350c1s v5p0387c2s v5p0402c2s
v5p0497c1s v6p0003c2s v6p0052c2s
v6p0085c1s v6p0107c2s v6p0161c1s
v6p0180c2s v6p0214c1s v6p0260c1s
v6p0283c2s v6p0301c2s v6p0304c2s
v6p0333c1s v6p0358c2s v6p0411c1m
v6p0411c2s v6p0514c2s v6p0551c2s
v6p0552c1s v6p0588c2s
Cary, Edward v5p0154c1s
Cary, Eliz.A. v6p0256c1s
Cary, Eliz.L. v6p0317c1s
Cary, G. v6p0086c2s
Cary, G.L. v1p0042c2s
v1p0117c1s v1p0119c1s v4p0591c2s
v5p0044c1s
Cary, H.C. v1p1354c1s
Cary, H.L. v4p0067c2s
Cary, M.A. v1p0884c1s
Cary, O. v3p0238c1s
Cary, P. v1p1308c2s
v1p1335c2s
Cary, R.N. v4p0375c1s
Cary, S. v1p1036c1s
Cary, T.G. v1p0092c1s
v1p0202c2s v1p0403c2s v1p0990c2s
v1p1054c2s v1p1148c2s v1p1371c1s
Cary, W. v4p0590c1s
Cary, W.B. v2p0371c2s
Casali, G.F.S.de v1p0505c1s
v1p0615c1s v1p0670c1s v1p0671c2s
v1p1126c1s
Casamajor, E.H. et al. ... v6p0236c2s
Casamajor, G.H. v5p0003c1s
Casamajor, P. v1p0026c1s
Casanova, J.J. v1p0567c1s
v1p1378c1s
Casanowicz, I.M. v4p0428c2s
v6p0481c2s
Casartelli, L.C. v2p0153c2s
v3p0129c2s v3p0314c1s v3p0476c1s
v4p0079c2s v4p0163c1s v4p0417c1s
v4p0488c1s v4p0597c1s v5p0344c2s

v6p0045c1m v6p0314c2s v6p0394c2s
v6p0473c1s v6p0508c2m
Casas, Q.B.de Las v5p0374c2s
Casastelli, L.C. v3p0127c2s
Case, E. v2p0222c2s
Case, E., jr. v2p0305c2s
v2p0323c2s
Case, E.C. v5p0214c2s
v5p0485c2s v6p0444c2s v6p0487c1s
Case, F. v4p0182c2s
Case, F.T. v6p0321c2s
Case, G. v6p0594c1s
Case, G.L. v3p0346c1s
Case, J.W. v4p0582c2s
Case, L.J.B. v1p0404c2s
v1p1016c2s
Case, M.E. v4p0490c1s
Case, M.P. v1p0223c1s
v1p0323c1s
Case, T. v4p0627c2s
v6p0542c2s
Case, T.S. v2p0110c2s
v2p0149c2s v2p0156c2s v2p0172c1s
v2p0240c2s v2p0252c1s v2p0293c1s
v2p0312c1m v2p0386c1s v2p0390c1s
v2p0443c2s v2p0467c1s v2p0475c2s
Casey, G.E. v1p0259c2s
Casey, J.B. v6p0053c1s
Casey, J.F. v3p0008c1s
v4p0123c1s v4p0257c1s
Casey, J.K. v1p0770c2s
Casey, M.A. v1p0957c2s
Casey, M.P. v5p0287c2s
Casey, O.J. v3p0137c2s
Casey, T.L. v2p0249c1s
v6p0215c1s v6p0440c1s
Casey, W.R. v1p1075c2s
v1p1076c2s
Cash, J. v5p0529c1s
Cash, T.M. v1p0962c2s
v1p0963c1s
Cashel-Hoey, Mrs. v2p0420c1s
Casiat, M. v1p0875c2s
Casimer, N. v2p0302c2s
Caskey, Lacey D. v6p0320c1s
Casley, H.C. v2p0424c1s
Caspari, C.E. v1p0684c2s
Casper, C.N. v2p0051c2s
Cass, L. v1p0030c2s
v1p0050c1s v1p0328c1s v1p0635c2s
v1p0636c2s v1p0637c2s v1p0638c1s
v1p0767c1s v1p0832c1s v1p1252c2s
Cassard, W.G. v5p0508c2s
Cassat, A.C. v4p0379c2s
Casseday, B. v1p0823c1s
Casseday, M.M. v2p0023c2s
v2p0121c2s v2p0445c1s v4p0068c1s
v4p0614c1s
Cassel, A.H. v2p0386c2s
Cassel, G. v5p0568c2s
Cassel, H. v3p0117c2s
Casselberry, E. v1p0389c2s
v1p0855c1s
Cassell, E.F. v5p0622c1s
Casselman, A. v6p0389c1s
Casselman, A.B. v4p0128c2s
v4p0434c1s v6p0027c1s
Casselman, A.C. v5p0461c2s
Cassels, J.L. v1p0828c2s
Cassels, R. v3p0066c1s
Cassels, W.R. v1p0974c2s
v4p0564c1s v6p0025c1s v6p0213c2s
v6p0340c2s
Casseres, B.de v6p0140c2s
v6p0202c2s v6p0262c1s v6p0280c2s
v6p0283c2s v6p0617c2s v6p0630c1s
Casserley, A.L. v5p0365c2s
Casserly, C. v1p0698c1s
Casserly, D. v1p0603c1s
v1p0806c1s v1p0873c1s v1p0892c1s
v1p1018c2s v1p1020c1s v1p1020c2s
v1p1119c2s v1p1308c2s v1p1373c1s
v1p1380c1s
Casserly, D.A. v1p0485c2s
v1p0512c1s v1p0564c1s v2p0232c2s
v2p0237c1s
Casserly, G. v6p0112c1s
v6p0354c1s
Cassidy, J. v4p0104c1s
v4p0201c1s v4p0250c1s v4p0274c1s
v4p0444c1s v5p0049c1s v5p0518c2s
v5p0596c1s v6p0196c1s v6p0240c1s
v6p0520c2s v6p0663c1s
Cassidy, James v5p0090c1s
v5p0100c1s v5p0213c2s v5p0366c1s
v5p0506c1s
Cassidy, M.A. v5p0511c1s
Cassidy, P.S. v4p0087c2s
v4p0403c2s
Cassier, L. v5p0557c1s
Cassilis, I.L. v1p0717c1s
v4p0158c1s v4p0607c2s
Cassini, Comte v6p0557c1m
Cassini, M. v6p0559c1s
Cassody, J.B. v5p0363c2s
Casson, F.H. v5p0279c2s
Casson, H.N. v5p0500c2s
v5p0581c2s v5p0593c2s v6p0024c1s
v6p0098c1s v6p0184c2s v6p0207c2s
v6p0241c1s v6p0249c2s v6p0253c1s
v6p0327c2s v6p0331c1s v6p0343c2s
v6p0535c1s v6p0564c2s v6p0572c1s
v6p0577c1s v6p0601c1s v6p0607c2s
v6p0616c1s v6p0637c2s v6p0652c1s
v6p0692c1s v6p0712c1s
Casson, T. v6p0470c1s
Cassot, A. v4p0275c2s
Castaigne, A. v4p0032c1s
v4p0485c2s v5p0389c2s v5p0431c2s
v6p0080c2s v6p0156c1s v6p0242c1s
v6p0304c1s v6p0426c2s v6p0516c2s
v6p0564c1s
Castan, M. v1p0563c1s
Castanis, C.P. v1p0553c1s
Castelar, E. v1p0431c1m
v1p0452c1s v1p0482c1s v1p0673c1s
v1p0726c1s v1p1100c1s v1p1209c1s
v2p0115c2s v3p0046c1s v3p0144c1s
v3p0319c1s v3p0376c2s v3p0402c2s
v4p0125c2s v5p0064c2m v5p0352c2s
v5p0542c2s v6p0607c2s
Casteli, W.R. v1p0301c2s
Castell-Hopkins, J. v4p0237c1s
Castellane, Marquis de ... v6p0236c2s
Castellani, A. v1p0691c2m
v1p0790c1s
Castelli, E.P. v3p0392c1s
Castelot, E. v4p0212c2s
v4p0462c2s v6p0237c2s
Castiglione, G.E.Di.P. ... v6p0331c1s
Castillo, D.B. v6p0426c1s
Castle, A. and Castle, E.. v3p0300c2s
v5p0049c2s v5p0465c2s v6p0551c2s
Castle, Agnes and Castle, Egerton
v5p0518c1s
Castle, C.W. v5p0544c2s
v5p0573c2s
Castle, E. v3p0034c2s
v3p0238c1s v3p0418c1s v4p0150c1s
v4p0163c2s v4p0186c1s v4p0244c1s
v4p0269c2s v4p0371c2s v5p0188c1s
v5p0644c2s v6p0221c2s v6p0630c1s
Castle, E. and Castle, A.. v3p0300c2s
v5p0049c2s v5p0465c2s v6p0551c2s
Castle, Egerton and Castle, Agnes
v5p0518c1s
Castle, H.A. v5p0603c2s
v6p0511c1m v6p0511c2s
Castle, H.C. v6p0633c2s
Castle, M. v1p1004c2s
v1p1260c1s
Castle, M.A. v1p0445c2s
v1p1004c2s
Castle, M.L.E. v6p0085c2s
Castle, N.H. v3p0166c1s
v5p0251c2s
Castle, O.L. v1p0890c2s
Castle, W.E. v6p0021c1m
v6p0215c1s v6p0288c2m v6p0585c2s
Castle, W.E. et al. v6p0214c2s
Castle, W.R. v4p0251c1s
Castlemon, H. v4p0550c2s
Castleton, D.R. v1p1309c2s
v1p1387c1s v1p1408c1s
Castletown, Lord v2p0225c2s
v3p0387c1s v5p0242c2s
Castletown, Lord et al. .. v4p0291c1s
Castner, H.Y. v2p0008c1s
Castner, J. v5p0462c2s
Castor, G.D. v6p0280c2s
Castor, T.H. v3p0242c2s
Castro, F.de v1p0858c2s
Caswell, A. v1p0011c2s
v1p0100c2s v1p0407c1s v1p0810c2s
v1p1440c1s
Caswell, E.W. v4p0367c2s
Caswell, G.W. v5p0125c1s
Catchings, T.C. et al. ... v4p0129c1s
Catchings, W. v6p0366c2s
Catchpool, E. v2p0149c2s
Cater, J. v6p0231c2s
v6p0376c1s v6p0410c1s v6p0472c2s
Cater, R.W. v5p0044c2s
v5p0113c2s v5p0125c1m v5p0263c2s
v5p0356c1s v5p0451c2s v5p0529c1s
v5p0581c2s v5p0607c2s v6p0107c1s
v6p0317c1s
Cates, A. v2p0019c1s
Cates, Arthur v5p0175c1s
Cates, E.E. v5p0569c1s
Cath, Grace v6p0457c2s
Catham, C.T. v4p0429c1s
Cathcart, W.L. v4p0594c2s
v5p0313c1s v5p0344c1s v5p0353c1s
v5p0369c1s v5p0478c2s
v5p0603c1s
Cather, N. v4p0413c2s
Cather, W.S. v5p0182c1s
v5p0194c2s v6p0167c1s v6p0518c2s
v6p0655c2s
Cather, Willa v6p0579c1s
Cather, Willa S. v6p0484c2s
Catherwood, M.A. v3p0436c2s
v4p0212c2s
Catherwood, M.H. v1p0312c1s
v1p0749c1s v1p0791c1s v1p1041c2s
v2p0065c2s v2p0103c1s v2p0320c2s
v2p0354c1s v2p0395c1s v2p0420c1s
v2p0420c2s v2p0457c1s v3p0047c2s
v3p0240c1s v3p0254c1s v3p0366c1s
v4p0048c2s v4p0098c1s v4p0274c1s
v4p0310c2s v4p0335c2s v4p0356c2s
v4p0412c2s v4p0418c2s v4p0451c2s
v4p0485c2s v4p0620c1s v4p0623c2s
v4p0625c2s v5p0077c1s v5p0135c1s
v5p0150c1s v5p0154c2s v5p0165c2s
v5p0308c2s v5p0316c2s v5p0361c2s
v5p0388c2s v5p0531c2s v5p0564c1s
Catholic Priest v1p0640c2s
Catholicus and Lacey, T.A.
v4p0112c2s v4p0488c1s
Catlett, C. v6p0134c2s
Catlett, C. and Clarke, F.W.
v3p0334c1s
Catlin, A.A. v5p0218c2s
Catlin, C.L. v1p0750c1s
Catlin, G.DeG. v6p0139c2s
Catlin, G.L. v1p0137c2s
v3p0078c1s
Catlin, H.D. v1p0689c1s
v1p1050c1s v1p1055c1s v3p0191c1s
v3p0404c2s
Catlin, L.E. v6p0175c2s
Catly, C.S. v2p0037c2s
Caton, J.D. v1p0041c2s
v1p0044c2s v1p0340c2m v1p0877c1s
v1p1327c2s v1p1333c1m v2p0015c2s
v2p0037c1s v2p0346c2s v3p0438c2s
v3p0461c1s v4p0100c1s v4p0468c1s
Caton, J.D. and Brown, A.E.
v1p0340c2s
Cator, G. v6p0538c1s
v6p0623c1s v6p0658c2s
Cattell, F.J. v6p0029c1s
Cattell, J.M. v2p0073c1s
v3p0207c2s v3p0246c2s v5p0257c1s
v5p0542c1s v5p0613c1s v6p0018c1m
v6p0102c1s v6p0249c2s v6p0405c1s
v6p0451c2s v6p0575c2s v6p0672c1s
Cattell, J.M. and Dolley, C.S.
v4p0397c2s v4p0474c1s
Cattell, J.M. and Wallaschek, R.
v3p0293c2s
Cattell, J.McK. v3p0274c2s
v3p0429c2s v4p0362c2s v4p0410c1s
v4p0465c1s v4p0475c2s v6p0215c1s
v6p0521c1s v6p0521c2s v6p0670c2s
Cattell, J.McK. and Farrand, L.
v4p0125c2s
Cattell, J.W. v2p0402c1s
Cattell, S.W. v4p0630c2s
Cattell, W. v1p1410c2s
Catterall, C.H. v6p0302c2s
Catterall, R.C.H. v5p0045c1s
v5p0289c2s v5p0629c2s v6p0409c1s
Cauffman, S.J. v4p0425c2s
Caufland, R.M. v1p0636c1s
Caughey, B.C. v6p0218c1s
Cauldwell, R. v1p1313c1s
Caulfield, F.W. v4p0508c1s
Caulfield, M. v6p0424c1s
Caulfield, S.F.A. v1p0337c1s
v1p0726c2s
Caulkins, F.M. v1p0912c1s
Causard, M. v5p0193c2s
Cautley, L.R. v5p0317c1s
Cavada, F.F. v1p0110c2s
Cavalieri, E. v4p0195c2s
v4p0523c1s
Cavanagh, C.F. v5p0312c1s
v5p0621c1s
Cavanagh, J.R. v5p0476c2s
Cavanaugh, Catherine F. .. v6p0095c1s
Cavazza, E. v3p0011c2s
v3p0062c2s v3p0109c2s v3p0120c2s
v3p0225c1s v3p0437c1s v4p0352c1s
v4p0356c1s v4p0486c1s v4p0504c1s
v4p0619c1s
Cave, A. v1p0769c2s
v1p0874c2s v2p0205c2s v2p0301c2s
v2p0368c2s v2p0438c1s v3p0041c1m
v3p0357c2s v4p0109c2s
Cave, D. v5p0043c2s
v5p0163c2s v5p0640c2s
Cave, Dora v5p0068c2s
Cave, E. v1p0366c1s
Cave, H.J. v5p0459c1s
Cave, R.H. v1p0234c2s
v1p1108c1s
Cave-Browne, J. v1p0520c1s
v3p0052c2s v4p0070c2s v4p0317c2s
Caven, A. v6p0446c1s
Caven, W. v2p0042c1s
v2p0215c1s v2p0215c2s v2p0438c1m
v3p0065c2s v3p0091c2s v3p0215c2s
v3p0342c2s v4p0457c1s v4p0507c2s
v5p0464c1s v6p0514c2s
Caven, W. and MacVicar, H.
v5p0464c1s
Cavendish v1p1405c2s
v2p0472c1s v5p0628c2s
Cavendish, A. v6p0075c2s
v6p0227c2s v6p0639c2s
Cavendish, F., Lady v3p0105c2s
Cavendish, F., Lady et al.
v4p0452c1s
Cavendish, L.C.F. v3p0005c1s
v5p0327c1s
Caverno, C. v1p0730c1s
v1p1095c2s v1p1164c1s v3p0006c1s

v3p0271c2s v5p0133c2s v5p0160c1s
v6p0122c2s v6p0468c2s v6p0521c1s
v6p0593c1s
Caverno, D.H. v1p0053c1s
Caverno, J.H. v4p0262c1s
Caverno, J.H. and Frost, M.A.
v5p0126c2s
Cavis-Brown, J. v5p0105c2s
Cavit, T.E. v6p0155c2s
Caw, J.L. v4p0030c1s
v4p0348c1s v4p0623c2s v5p0030c2s
v5p0031c2s v5p0220c2s v5p0388c1s
v5p0514c2s v5p0589c1s v5p0624c1s
v6p0684c2s
Cawein, M. v4p0203c1s
v4p0410c2s v5p0351c2s v5p0369c2s
v5p0419c2s v5p0478c1s v6p0541c1s
Cawley, G. v4p0298c2s
Cawood, E. v5p0067c1s
Cawood, Rose v5p0638c2s
Caws, F. v2p0159c1s
Caws, Frank v5p0132c1s
Cawthorne, C.E. v4p0630c2s
Caxton, W. v5p0061c2s
Caye, G. v5p0188c1s
Cayley, A. v2p0280c1m
v3p0418c1s
Cayley, G., Sir v1p0008c1s
Cayley, G.J. v1p0064c2s
v1p0922c1s
Cayley, H. v6p0300c1s
Cayley, R.A. v3p0367c2s
Caylor, O.P. v3p0035c1s
v3p0192c2s
Cazalet, E. v5p0319c2s
Cazalet, E.A. v5p0501c2s
Cazelle, E. v1p0134c2s
Cazenove, J.G. v1p0205c1s
v1p0417c2s
Cazin, F.M.F. v2p0319c2s
v4p0537c2s v5p0452c1s
Cazin, T.M.T. v4p0521c2s
Ceard, H. v2p0210c2s
Cease, D.L. v5p0079c1s
v6p0357c1s
Cecconi, E. v2p0449c2m
v4p0355c1s v4p0380c2s
Cecil, A. v6p0054c2s
v6p0125c1s
Cecil, Algernon v6p0429c1s
Cecil, E. v5p0005c2s
v5p0307c1m v5p0346c1s v5p0412c1s
v6p0007c2s v6p0083c1s v6p0512c2s
v6p0542c1s
Cecil, E.G. v2p0189c1s
Cecil, E.G., Lord v2p0408c2s
v3p0183c1s v3p0226c2s
Cecil, G. v5p0046c1s
Cecil, H. v5p0117c1s
v5p0481c1s v6p0258c1s v6p0271c2s
Cecil, Hu. v5p0117c2s
Cecil, Hugh v5p0484c1s
Cecil, V. v6p0344c2s
Cecil, W.G. v6p0665c1s
Cecil, Wm. v6p0653c2s
Celesti, A. v6p0120c2m
Celles, A.D.De v5p0327c1m
Cellier, A. v2p0444c2s
Centanini, G.P. v6p0404c2s
Ceraski, W. v6p0626c1s
Cerf, M. v4p0058c2s
Cermak, B. v3p0048c2m
Cernuschi, H. v1p1198c1s
Cerny, G. v1p0166c2s
v1p0560c2s v1p0739c2s
Cerone, Francesco v5p0110c2s
Cervantes, M.de v1p0397c2m
v1p0697c2m
Cervin, O.Z. v4p0024c1m
v6p0148c2s v6p0608c1s v6p0628c2s
Cervin, Olaf Z. v6p0460c2s
v6p0646c2s
Cesare, R.de v4p0295c1m
v4p0490c1m v5p0009c2m v5p0459c1m
Cesareo, G.A. v5p0440c2s
Cesaresco, E.M. v2p0072c1s
v2p0113c2s v2p0160c2m v2p0262c2m
v3p0167c1s v3p0224c1s v3p0325c1s
v4p0077c2s v4p0419c1s v4p0484c2s
v4p0489c2s v4p0490c1s v4p0576c2s
v4p0605c2m v5p0020c2s v5p0248c2s
v5p0249c2s v5p0250c1s
Cesaresco, E.Martinengo .. v5p0096c2s
v5p0608c1s
Cesaresco, Evelyn Martinengo
v4p0294c2s
Cesaresco, M., Countess .. v4p0295c1s
v4p0395c1m
Cesnola, L.P.Di v1p0935c1m
Cespedes, J.A.de v1p0286c1m
Cespedes, J.de A. v1p1292c2s
Cessua, J.B. v6p0529c1s
Cestr, F.J. v4p0465c2s
Cestre, C. v5p0604c2s
Cew, J.De v1p0948c2m
Cezanne, M. v1p0161c2s
Chace, A.E. v3p0473c1s
Chace, E. v1p0228c2s
Chace, E.B. v5p0474c1s
v5p0487c2s
Chace, G.I. v1p0208c2s
v1p0441c1s v1p0528c1s v1p0528c2s
v1p1005c2m v1p1073c1s v1p1236c2s
v1p1441c1s v2p0274c1s
Chace, G.J. v1p0568c1s
Chace, J. v3p0096c2s
Chace, L.G. v6p0116c2s
v6p0453c2s v6p0573c2s
Chace, W.S. v1p1077c2s
Chadbourn, E.R. et al. ... v2p0028c2s
Chadbourne, G.S. v3p0345c1s
v3p0415c2s
Chadbourne, P.A. v1p0136c2s
v1p0276c1s v1p0346c1s v1p0714c1s
v1p1362c2s
Chadding, H. v1p0943c1s
Chadick, S.R. v2p0043c2s
v2p0109c2s v2p0244c1s
Chadlick, J.W. v5p0277c1s
Chadsey, C.E. v6p0666c2s
Chadwick, A.M. v6p0067c2s
Chadwick, C.A. v6p0065c1s
Chadwick, C.D. v4p0132c1s
Chadwick, C.N. v5p0471c2s
Chadwick, D. v1p1379c2s
Chadwick, E. v1p0258c2s
v1p0286c2m v1p0315c2s v1p0816c2s
v1p0873c2s v1p0973c2s v1p1024c2s
v1p1030c2s v1p1031c2s v1p1038c2s
v1p1153c2s v1p1261c1s v1p1376c1s
v1p1431c2s v2p0263c2s v3p0102c1s
v3p0192c1s v3p0331c2s v3p0340c2s
v3p0375c1s
Chadwick, E., Sir v3p0071c2s
v3p0180c2s
Chadwick, F.E. v3p0254c2s
v3p0409c1s v5p0508c2s v6p0580c1s
v6p0668c2s
Chadwick, F.E., Capt. v5p0602c2s
Chadwick, G.A. v6p0064c1s
v6p0340c2m
Chadwick, G.M. v6p0439c1s
Chadwick, H. v3p0017c2s
v3p0035c1m v3p0104c2s v3p0105c1s
v5p0048c2m
Chadwick, H.C. v6p0060c1s
Chadwick, H.M. v4p0576c1s
v5p0465c2s
Chadwick, J.D. v4p0621c1s
Chadwick, J.R. v1p1421c1s
v3p0087c1s v3p0153c1s v6p0157c1s
Chadwick, J.R. et al. v2p0477c2s
Chadwick, J.V. v5p0499c1s
Chadwick, J.W. v1p0120c2s
v1p0132c1s v1p0170c2s v1p0201c1s
v1p0253c1s v1p0270c1s v1p0528c2s
v1p0582c1s v1p0582c2s v1p0595c2s
v1p0625c2s v1p0668c1s v1p0684c2s
v1p0691c1s v1p0767c1s v1p0793c2s
v1p0796c2s v1p0799c1s v1p0809c1s
v1p0825c2s v1p0834c1s v1p0841c2s
v1p0848c1s v1p0859c2s v1p0863c2s
v1p0869c1s v1p0912c1s v1p0912c2s
v1p0942c1s v1p0972c2s v1p1037c2s
v1p1056c2s v1p1074c1s v1p1086c2s
v1p1162c1s v1p1210c2s v1p1296c2s
v1p1302c1s v1p1378c1m v2p0013c2s
v2p0106c2s v2p0171c2s v2p0181c1s
v2p0274c2s v2p0331c2s v2p0357c1s
v2p0365c1s v2p0368c1s v2p0368c2s
v2p0369c1s v2p0369c2s v2p0409c2s
v2p0452c1s v2p0454c1s v2p0473c1s
v3p0011c2s v3p0018c2s v3p0037c1m
v3p0042c1s v3p0073c1m v3p0081c1s
v3p0154c2s v3p0165c1s v3p0167c2s
v3p0175c1m v3p0185c1m v3p0187c2s
v3p0193c1m v3p0203c2s v3p0216c2s
v3p0233c1s v3p0245c2s v3p0259c2s
v3p0289c2s v3p0302c1m v3p0366c2s
v3p0394c1s v3p0396c2s v3p0402c1s
v3p0411c2s v3p0419c1s v3p0441c1s
v3p0441c2s v3p0458c1s v3p0472c2s
v4p0054c2s v4p0074c2m v4p0076c1s
v4p0102c1s v4p0111c1s v4p0121c1m
v4p0128c2s v4p0144c2m v4p0168c1s
v4p0178c2s v4p0216c2s v4p0217c2s
v4p0226c1s v4p0249c2s v4p0260c2s
v4p0261c1s v4p0270c2s v4p0302c2s
v4p0308c1s v4p0321c1s v4p0333c1s
v4p0343c2s v4p0346c2s v4p0354c1s
v4p0355c1s v4p0381c2s v4p0421c1m
v4p0453c2s v4p0468c1s v4p0479c1s
v4p0488c1s v4p0538c2s v4p0556c1m
v4p0569c1s v4p0579c1s v4p0591c2s
v4p0611c1s v4p0621c1s v5p0013c1s
v5p0078c2m v5p0080c1s v5p0084c2s
v5p0165c2s v5p0169c2s v5p0264c2s
v5p0277c1s v5p0307c2s v5p0330c1s
v5p0350c1s v5p0364c1m v5p0367c1s
v5p0370c2s v5p0372c2s v5p0473c1s
v5p0484c2s v5p0606c1s v5p0633c2s
v6p0017c1s v6p0031c1s v6p0056c1s
v6p0059c2s v6p0172c1s v6p0200c2s
v6p0243c2s v6p0283c2s v6p0368c1s
v6p0386c1s v6p0403c2s v6p0490c1s
v6p0616c2s v6p0618c1s v6p0639c1s
v6p0697c2s v6p0707c2s
Chadwick, J.W. et al. v5p0445c1s
Chadwick, R.A. v6p0325c1s
Chadwick, T.W. v4p0077c1s
Chaffee, A.R. v6p0039c1s
v6p0666c1s
Chaffee, F. v4p0157c2s
v4p0531c2s
Chaffee, J.F. v1p0684c2s
v4p0478c2s v4p0482c2s v5p0400c1s
v5p0484c2s
Chaffers, W. v1p0525c2s
v1p1114c2s v2p0115c1s v3p0341c1s
Chaffin, W.L. v1p0686c2s
Chahoon, G. v1p1110c2s
v5p0063c2s
Chaille-Long, C. v3p0100c2m
v3p0115c2s v3p0195c1s v6p0118c2s
Chaille-Long, Ch. v4p0098c1s
v6p0664c1s
Chaille-Long, Charles v4p0098c1s
v5p0181c2s v6p0664c1s
Chailley-Bert, J. v6p0237c1s
Chaillu, P.B.Du v3p0004c2m
Chajes, H.P. v5p0057c2s
Chalklen, C.W. v1p0394c2s
v1p0395c2s
Challamel, J. v4p0157c2s
v4p0211c2s
Challen, J. v1p0034c2s
v1p0170c1s v1p0441c1s v1p0620c1s
v1p0840c1s
Challen, J.R. v5p0061c2s
Challers, J. v1p1139c2s
Challeu, F. v6p0469c1s
Challice, J.A. v1p1206c1s
Challice, Rachel v6p0502c1s
Challinor, M. v3p0134c2m
v4p0326c2s
Challis, H.W. v1p0723c2s
Challis, J. v1p1267c2s
Challon, P.F. v3p0047c1s
Chalmers v3p0431c2s
Chalmers, A. v1p0114c2s
v1p0321c1s
Chalmers, A.B. v5p0373c2s
v6p0601c1s
Chalmers, A.K. v6p0569c2s
Chalmers, D.P., Sir v4p0124c2s
v4p0601c2s v5p0494c1m
Chalmers, G. v1p0799c1s
v1p1176c1s v1p1317c1s
Chalmers, H.H. v1p0906c1s
Chalmers, J. v5p0522c1s
v5p0581c1s
Chalmers, J.A. v5p0100c2s
Chalmers, J.B. v1p0469c1s
Chalmers, L.H. v5p0280c2s
Chalmers, M.D. v3p0113c1s
v3p0209c2s v4p0181c1s v4p0307c1s
v4p0435c1s v6p0411c1s
Chalmers, P. v1p0808c1s
Chalmers, R. v4p0447c2s
v4p0499c1m v5p0491c2s v6p0563c1s
Chalmers, T. v1p0120c2s
v1p0302c2s v1p0798c1s v1p0981c2s
v1p1000c2s v1p1026c2s v1p1030c2s
v1p1031c2s v1p1065c1s v1p1153c1s
v1p1319c1s v1p1319c2s v4p0108c2s
v5p0068c1s v5p0097c1s v6p0125c2s
Chamberlain, A. v3p0296c2s
v4p0563c1s v5p0001c1s v5p0133c2s
v5p0214c2s v5p0216c1s v5p0365c1s
v5p0559c1s v6p0233c1s v6p0378c2s
v6p0599c1s
Chamberlain, A.B. v2p0084c2s
v6p0292c1s v6p0473c1m
Chamberlain, A.C. v3p0258c2s
Chamberlain, A.F. v3p0142c2s
v3p0298c2s v3p0299c2s v4p0003c2s
v4p0017c2s v4p0020c1s v4p0063c1s
v4p0093c2s v4p0138c2s v4p0205c1s
v4p0282c2s v4p0312c1s v4p0313c1m
v4p0369c1s v4p0375c1m v4p0392c1s
v4p0441c2s v4p0529c1s v4p0543c2s
v5p0012c1m v5p0023c1s v5p0076c2m
v5p0106c2s v5p0150c1s v5p0179c2s
v5p0180c1s v5p0212c1s v5p0254c1s
v5p0267c2s v5p0288c2s v5p0294c2s
v5p0299c2s v5p0319c2s v5p0360c1s
v5p0368c2s v5p0445c1s v5p0586c1s
v5p0634c1s v6p0012c2s v6p0018c2s
v6p0041c2s v6p0115c2m v6p0207c2s
v6p0222c2s v6p0224c2s v6p0285c1s
v6p0297c1s v6p0316c1s v6p0316c2m
v6p0329c1s v6p0330c2s v6p0353c2s
v6p0354c1s v6p0359c1s v6p0402c1s
v6p0402c2s v6p0490c1s v6p0492c2s
v6p0493c2s v6p0494c1s v6p0512c1s
v6p0520c2m v6p0544c1s v6p0633c2s
v6p0674c2s v6p0699c2s v6p0700c1s
Chamberlain, A.F. and Boas, F.
v3p0142c2s
Chamberlain, A.F. and
Chamberlain, I.C. v6p0114c2s
Chamberlain, A.I. v5p0420c1s
Chamberlain, Alex.F. v5p0204c1s
Chamberlain, B.H. v4p0298c2s
v4p0341c2s v4p0344c1s
Chamberlain, C.E. v1p0710c2s
Chamberlain, C.J. v6p0015c1s
v6p0249c2s v6p0409c2s
Chamberlain, C.W. v6p0166c2s
Chamberlain, D.H. v1p0262c2s

v1p0276c2s v1p0753c2s v1p0905c1s
v1p1087c1s v2p0068c2s v2p0136c1s
v2p0249c2s v2p0253c1s v2p0411c1s
v2p0481c2s v3p0041c2s v3p0087c2s
v3p0096c2s v3p0233c2s v3p0259c2s
v3p0289c2s v3p0299c1s v3p0401c2s
v3p0441c2s v4p0546c2s v5p0078c2s
v5p0480c2s v5p0521c2s v5p0600c1s
v5p0626c1s
Chamberlain, D.H. and Wise, J.S.
v2p0370c2s
Chamberlain, E. v1p1147c1s
v1p1432c1s
Chamberlain, E.T. v4p0015c2s
v5p0017c1s v5p0034c1s v5p0526c2s
Chamberlain, E.T. et al. . v4p0251c1s
Chamberlain, G. v6p0080c1s
Chamberlain, G.A. v6p0477c2s
v6p0551c1s v6p0606c1m
Chamberlain, G.W. v6p0407c2s
v6p0623c2s v6p0694c1s
Chamberlain, Geo.A. v6p0080c1s
Chamberlain, H. v3p0182c1s
Chamberlain, H.L. v6p0020c2s
v6p0571c2s v6p0662c2s
Chamberlain, H.R. v3p0149c2s
v3p0215c2s v4p0015c1s v4p0402c2s
v5p0168c2s
Chamberlain, I.C. v2p0179c1s
v5p0212c1s
Chamberlain, I.C. and
Chamberlain, A.F. v6p0114c2s
Chamberlain, Isabel C. ... v5p0160c1s
Chamberlain, J. v1p0266c2s
v1p0385c2s v1p0547c2s v1p0549c2s
v1p0649c1m v1p0725c1s v1p1027c2s
v1p1062c2s v1p1063c2s v1p1158c2s
v2p0126c1s v3p0096c2s v3p0321c2s
v3p0399c1s v4p0115c1s v4p0215c2s
v4p0261c2s v4p0289c2s v4p0314c1s
v4p0387c2s v4p0412c1m v5p0380c1s
v5p0604c1s v6p0235c2s v6p0514c1s
Chamberlain, J.E. v5p0532c2s
v5p0631c1s
Chamberlain, J.L. v3p0020c1s
Chamberlain, J.P. v1p0040c2s
Chamberlain, L. v6p0038c1s
v6p0702c1s
Chamberlain, L.S. v5p0288c2s
Chamberlain, L.T. v1p0840c2s
Chamberlain, Lucia v6p0145c1s
v6p0261c2s v6p0361c2s v6p0579c1s
v6p0656c2s v6p0689c2s
Chamberlain, M. v1p0275c1s
v1p0451c1s v1p0743c1s v2p0155c1s
v2p0171c2s v2p0454c1s v3p0038c1s
v4p0616c1s
Chamberlain, M.E. v5p0416c2s
Chamberlain, M.H. v5p0330c2s
Chamberlain, N. v4p0307c2s
v5p0285c2s
Chamberlain, N. and Colvin, A.
v5p0285c2s
Chamberlain, N.H. v1p0207c1s
v1p0411c2s v1p0421c2s v1p0861c2s
v1p1340c2s v3p0060c1s v3p0436c2s
Chamberlain, N.Y. v3p0374c2s
v3p0474c1s
Chamberlain, R. v1p0755c1s
v1p1418c1s
Chamberlain, S. v1p1197c2s
v2p0299c2s v3p0449c1s
Chamberlain, S.E. v3p0159c1s
Chamberlain, T.C. v4p0273c1s
v4p0351c2s v4p0633c2s v5p0172c2s
v6p0671c1s
Chamberlain, W. v1p0078c1s
v1p0550c1s
Chamberlain, W.A. v6p0707c1s
Chamberlain, W.R. v4p0111c2s
Chamberlaine-Bey, T. v6p0368c2s
Chamberlayne, C.F. v2p0239c1s
v6p0214c1s v6p0364c1s
Chamberlayne, E.S. v5p0390c1s
v5p0437c1s v6p0301c2s
Chamberlayne, I. v1p0868c1s
Chamberlayne, J. v1p1147c2s
Chamberlayne, J.H. v1p0734c1s
Chamberlin, C.D. v5p0593c2s
Chamberlin, D.H. v3p0354c1s
Chamberlin, E. v1p0227c2s
v1p0228c1s v1p0609c2s v1p0967c2s
v1p1257c2s
Chamberlin, E.T. v6p0161c2s
Chamberlin, H.B. and Halstead, Murat
v3p0460c1s
Chamberlin, H.H. v4p0380c1s
Chamberlin, J. v4p0130c1s
v4p0403c2s
Chamberlin, J.E. v2p0161c2s
v2p0162c1s v2p0453c2s v5p0543c1s
v5p0601c1s
Chamberlin, J.E. and Hurd, C.E.
v3p0167c1s
Chamberlin, J.E. et al. .. v5p0508c1s
Chamberlin, J.M. v1p0432c2s
Chamberlin, N.H. v1p0248c1s
Chamberlin, T.C. v2p0024c1s
v2p0102c1s v2p0179c1s v2p0185c1s
v2p0297c1s v3p0206c2s v4p0223c1s
v4p0227c1s v4p0272c2s v4p0507c2s
v4p0555c1s v4p0593c2s v5p0137c2s
v6p0185c2s v6p0301c1s
Chamberlin, T.C. and Leverett, F.
v4p0411c2s
Chamberlin, T.C. and Salisbury, R.D.
v3p0334c2s
Chamberlin, T.C. et al. .. v6p0204c1s
v6p0577c1s
Chamberlin, W.A. v5p0230c2s
v6p0232c2s
Chambers, A. v3p0139c1s
v3p0231c1s
Chambers, B.M. v5p0356c2s
v6p0325c2s v6p0645c1s
Chambers, C., jr v2p0055c2s
Chambers, C.E.S. v5p0100c2s
Chambers, C.E.S. et al. .. v4p0474c1s
Chambers, C.H. v2p0216c1m
v2p0272c2s v2p0342c2s v2p0451c1s
v3p0294c1s v3p0440c2s v3p0462c2s
Chambers, C.Haddon v3p0210c1s
Chambers, C.K. v6p0052c2s
Chambers, C.T.D. v6p0525c1s
Chambers, D. v1p0988c1s
v1p1405c2s
Chambers, D.A. v1p1402c1s
Chambers, D.L. v6p0587c1s
Chambers, E.K. v4p0028c1s
v4p0047c1s v4p0135c1s v4p0267c2s
v4p0304c1s v4p0345c2s v4p0358c2s
v4p0368c2s v4p0422c2s v4p0436c2s
v4p0448c1s v4p0492c1s v4p0499c2s
v4p0572c2s v4p0614c1s v5p0192c2s
v6p0003c1s v6p0052c2s v6p0144c1s
v6p0214c1s v6p0352c1s v6p0394c2s
v6p0587c2s v6p0612c2s
Chambers, E.K. and G., L.I.
v6p0159c1s
v6p0675c1s
Chambers, E.K. et al. v5p0523c2s
Chambers, E.T.D. v4p0418c2m
v4p0498c1s v4p0499c1s v5p0090c2s
v6p0096c2s v6p0097c2s v6p0566c1s
Chambers, F. v1p0099c2s
v2p0426c2s
Chambers, F.T. v6p0567c1s
Chambers, F.W. v1p0713c2s
v4p0053c2s
Chambers, G. v1p0282c1s
Chambers, G.F. v1p0073c2s
v1p0282c1m v1p0829c2s v1p0945c1s
v1p1305c1s v1p1394c2s v2p0319c1s
Chambers, G.W. v1p1243c2s
Chambers, G.W.F. v1p0281c2m
Chambers, H.E. v4p0250c2s
v4p0584c1s v4p0617c1s v5p0264c2s
Chambers, J. v3p0292c1s
v3p0343c2s v3p0410c1s v4p0168c2s
v4p0577c1s
Chambers, J.W. v3p0145c1s
Chambers, M. v1p0604c2s
Chambers, M.E. v1p0388c2s
Chambers, N.P. v5p0089c2s
Chambers, O.W. v6p0215c2s
Chambers, P.F. v4p0558c2s
Chambers, R. v1p0240c2s
v1p0299c2m v1p0430c2s v1p0444c2s
v1p0524c1s v1p0622c1s v1p0755c1s
v1p1128c2s v1p1164c2s v1p1172c2s
v1p1254c2s v1p1285c1s v4p0227c1s
Chambers, R.W. v4p0063c1s
v4p0276c2s v4p0350c2s v4p0442c1s
v5p0126c1s v5p0366c2s v5p0371c1s
v5p0421c1s v5p0434c2s v5p0644c1s
v6p0021c2s v6p0081c1s v6p0103c1s
v6p0225c2s v6p0255c2s v6p0401c2s
v6p0459c1s v6p0482c2s v6p0533c2s
v6p0594c1s v6p0608c2s v6p0610c2s
v6p0657c2s v6p0712c1s
Chambers, Robert v6p0651c1s
Chambers, S. v5p0519c2s
Chambers, S.A. v6p0241c1s
Chambers, S.F. v2p0469c1s
Chambers, T.W. v1p0121c1s
v1p0127c1s v1p0131c2s v1p0166c2s
v1p1174c2s v2p0038c2s v2p0042c2s
v2p0043c1s v2p0161c2s v2p0291c1s
v2p0415c1s v2p0434c2s v2p0457c2s
v3p0042c2s v3p0054c2s v3p0113c1s
v3p0233c1s v3p0319c2s v3p0356c2s
v3p0371c1s v3p0376c1s v4p0055c2s
v4p0150c1s v4p0157c2s v4p0228c2s
v4p0229c1s v4p0286c1s v4p0460c1s
v4p0462c1s v4p0477c1s
Chambers, T.W. and Frothingham, O.B.
v1p0344c2s
Chambers, T.W. et al. v2p0106c2s
Chambers, W. v1p0028c2s
v1p0030c1s v1p0042c2s v1p0043c1s
v1p0069c1s v1p0069c2s v1p0076c1s
v1p0086c2s v1p0087c1s v1p0091c2s
v1p0112c1s v1p0117c1s v1p0138c1s
v1p0144c1s v1p0147c2s v1p0148c1s
v1p0151c1s v1p0158c1s v1p0162c2s
v1p0190c2s v1p0207c1s v1p0219c1s
v1p0271c2s v1p0279c2s v1p0293c2s
v1p0300c1s v1p0300c2s v1p0309c2s
v1p0315c2s v1p0317c1s v1p0321c1s
v1p0329c2s v1p0330c2s v1p0335c1s
v1p0342c1s v1p0349c2s v1p0358c2m
v1p0361c2s v1p0367c2s v1p0368c1s
v1p0375c1s v1p0383c2s v1p0394c1s
v1p0405c2s v1p0424c2s v1p0438c2s
v1p0439c2s v1p0442c2s v1p0445c1s
v1p0445c2s v1p0450c1s v1p0450c2s
v1p0456c1s v1p0464c2s v1p0466c2s
v1p0497c1s v1p0518c2s v1p0525c1m
v1p0526c2s v1p0536c1s v1p0539c1s
v1p0540c1s v1p0556c1s v1p0582c1s
v1p0589c1s v1p0590c2s v1p0593c2m
v1p0605c1s v1p0606c1s v1p0607c2s
v1p0623c2s v1p0625c1s v1p0651c2s
v1p0654c2s v1p0655c2s v1p0670c1s
v1p0673c2s v1p0692c1s v1p0697c1s
v1p0702c1s v1p0705c2m v1p0711c1s
v1p0721c2s v1p0722c1s v1p0734c2s
v1p0746c1s v1p0748c2s v1p0753c2s
v1p0758c2s v1p0763c1s v1p0767c2s
v1p0770c2s v1p0779c2s v1p0784c1s
v1p0787c1s v1p0811c2s v1p0820c2s
v1p0855c1s v1p0860c1s v1p0864c2s
v1p0865c2s v1p0866c2s v1p0875c1s
v1p0877c2s v1p0891c2s v1p0893c1s
v1p0893c2s v1p0914c1s v1p0915c2s
v1p0918c2s v1p0919c1s v1p0923c2s
v1p0935c2s v1p0937c2s v1p0941c1s
v1p0957c1s v1p0981c1s v1p0983c2s
v1p0985c1s v1p0997c2m v1p1034c1s
v1p1070c2s v1p1071c1s v1p1072c1s
v1p1075c2s v1p1087c1s v1p1101c1s
v1p1105c2s v1p1107c1s v1p1111c1s
v1p1111c2s v1p1123c2s v1p1125c1s
v1p1126c2s v1p1128c1s v1p1133c1s
v1p1137c1s v1p1165c2s v1p1168c1s
v1p1172c1s v1p1180c2s v1p1191c1s
v1p1191c2s v1p1201c2s v1p1206c1s
v1p1208c1s v1p1212c1s v1p1212c2s
v1p1219c2s v1p1220c1s v1p1232c1s
v1p1253c2s v1p1267c2s v1p1270c2s
v1p1275c1s v1p1309c1s v1p1342c1s
v1p1358c2s v1p1361c1s v1p1389c1s
v1p1389c2s v1p1393c2s v1p1398c1s
v1p1402c1s v1p1414c2s v1p1421c2s
v1p1429c2s v1p1442c1s v2p0136c1s
v2p0245c1s v2p0305c2s v2p0321c2s
v2p0479c2s
Chambers, W.G. v6p0306c2s
v6p0459c1m v6p0707c1s
Chambers, W.L. v5p0506c2s
Chamblin, Jean v6p0358c1s
Chambre, A.S. v1p1355c2s
v1p1356c1s
Chambre, A.St.J. v1p0118c2s
v1p0321c1s v1p0378c2s v1p0850c1s
v1p0920c1s v1p1083c2s v1p1121c2s
v2p0041c2s v2p0119c2s
Chambre, A.St.John v1p0293c2s
v1p0688c2s v1p0831c1s
Chambrun, Marquis de v4p0212c2s
v4p0332c2s v4p0556c1s
Chamerovzow, L.A. v1p0153c2s
v1p1257c2s
Chamier, D. v3p0099c2s
Chamier, E. v3p0014c1s
Chamisso, A.von v1p1148c2s
Champagny, Bishop v1p0202c1s
Champier, V. v2p0089c2s
v2p0100c1s v2p0237c1s v4p0150c2s
Champier, Victor v2p0329c2s
Champion, H.H. v2p0407c2s
v2p0408c1s v3p0131c2s v3p0182c2s
v3p0183c1s v3p0238c2m v3p0239c1m
v3p0412c2s v3p0434c2s v4p0173c2s
v4p0462c2s v4p0553c1s
Champion, J.E. v4p0590c2s
Champion, M.K. v4p0034c2s
v6p0413c1s v6p0672c2s
Champion, May K. v6p0110c1s
Champion, S.A. v5p0289c1s
Champion, T.E. v4p0164c1s
v4p0166c2s v4p0178c2s v4p0186c1s
v4p0228c2s v4p0240c1s v4p0326c2s
v4p0365c2s v4p0407c2s v4p0558c2s
v4p0604c1s v4p0623c2s v5p0011c1s
v5p0090c1s v5p0091c2s v5p0182c1s
v5p0234c2s v5p0482c2s v5p0616c2s
v6p0129c2s
Champlin, E.R. v3p0402c2s
Champlin, E.R. and Bartol, C.A.
v3p0136c1s
Champlin, G. v3p0139c2s
Champlin, J.D. v1p0505c2s
v4p0132c2s v4p0180c2s v5p0095c1s
v6p0663c2s
Champlin, J.D., jr. v1p0022c1s
v1p0142c2s v1p0799c1s v1p0840c1s
v1p0999c1s v1p1141c2s v1p1256c1s
v1p1354c1s v1p1402c1s v3p0013c1s
v3p0023c1s v3p0141c1s v6p0351c1s
Champlin, J.T. v1p0180c2s
v1p0486c2s v1p0551c2s v1p0552c2s
v1p1057c1s v1p1062c1s
Champness, E.J. v6p0703c2s
Champness, T. v3p0395c1s
v4p0061c1s
Champness, W.H. v6p0158c1s
v6p0182c2s v6p0512c1s
Champney, A.C. v3p0116c1s
Champney, E.N. v5p0226c1s

Champney, E.W. v3p0322c2s
v3p0366c1s v4p0449c1s v4p0523c1s
v4p0628c1s v5p0355c1s v5p0427c2s
v5p0608c1s v6p0084c2s v6p0533c1s
Champney, J.W. v3p0330c2s
v3p0331c1s
Champney, L.W. v1p0032c1s
v1p0067c1s v1p0104c1s v1p0446c1s
v1p0579c1s v1p0668c1s v1p0913c2s
v1p1023c1s v1p1036c2s v1p1145c2s
v1p1222c2s v1p1371c2s v1p1378c2s
v2p0024c2s v2p0120c2s v2p0377c1s
v2p0394c1s v2p0401c2s v2p0469c2s
v2p0476c1s v3p0219c1s
Champney, Lizzie W. v3p0150c1s
Champneys, B. v1p0052c1s
v1p0253c1s v1p0310c2s v1p0762c1s
v1p0980c2s v1p1126c2s v1p1139c1s
v1p1414c1s v3p0018c2s v3p0473c2s
v4p0023c1s v4p0097c2s v4p0274c1s
v4p0417c1s v4p0499c2m v4p0529c2s
v4p0633c2m
Champneys, F.H. v1p0640c2s
Champneys, W.W. v1p0021c1s
Champury, E. v6p0219c1s
Chan-Toon, M. v6p0697c1s
Chance, B. v6p0320c1s
Chance, F. v3p0049c2s
v3p0231c1s v4p0040c2s v4p0154c1m
v4p0156c1s v4p0295c2s v4p0382c2s
v4p0558c2s
Chance, F. et al. v3p0090c1s
v4p0028c2s v4p0055c2s v4p0134c1s
Chance, G.W. v2p0338c2s
Chance, H. v3p0174c2s
Chance, H.M. v1p0840c1s
v4p0120c2m v4p0217c1s v4p0230c2s
v4p0231c1s v5p0124c1s v5p0237c2s
v5p0366c1s v6p0161c1s
Chance, J.F. v4p0050c2s
v5p0189c1s v5p0354c2s
v5p0491c1s v6p0048c2s
v6p0217c1s v6p0251c1m
v6p0460c1s v6p0628c2s
Chance, W. v4p0452c1s
v5p0459c1s v6p0384c2s
Chance, W., Mrs. v5p0223c2s
Chancellor, A. v6p0102c2s
Chancellor, C.W. v4p0286c2s
v5p0621c2s
Chancellor, E.B. v4p0141c1s
Chancellor, P.S. v5p0061c1s
Chancellor, W.E. v6p0078c2s
v6p0574c1s v6p0627c1s
Chandler, A. v4p0362c2s
Chandler, A.B. v5p0092c2s
Chandler, A.D. v1p0030c2s
v4p0074c2s
Chandler, A.E. v4p0626c2s
Chandler, B. v3p0266c1s
v3p0267c2s v3p0282c1s v4p0331c2s
Chandler, B.W. v4p0186c2s
Chandler, Bessie v4p0124c2s
Chandler, C.D. v3p0227c2s
v3p0361c1s
Chandler, C.F. v2p0340c1s
v6p0179c2s
Chandler, C.F. and Pellew, C.E.
v6p0195c2s
Chandler, C.H. v5p0561c1s
Chandler, E.L. v1p0028c1s
Chandler, F.W. v6p0608c1s
v6p0638c2s
Chandler, G. v1p0558c2s
v1p1250c2s
Chandler, Geo.L. v5p0230c2s
Chandler, H.P. v5p0528c2s
Chandler, H.W. and Rost, R.
v3p0048c1s
Chandler, J. v1p0084c1s
v6p0244c1s
Chandler, J.A.C. v4p0481c1s
v4p0605c2s v5p0613c1s
Chandler, J.B. v4p0060c1m
Chandler, J.R. v1p0484c2s
v1p1053c1s v4p0469c2s v5p0410c1s
Chandler, J.S. v3p0212c2s
Chandler, K.A. v6p0092c2s
v6p0117c1s v6p0303c1s
Chandler, Katherine A. ... v6p0013c1s
v6p0081c2s
Chandler, L. v3p0402c1s
Chandler, L.B. v3p0467c2s
v4p0464c1s
Chandler, P.W. v1p0423c1s
v1p1108c1s
Chandler, R. v1p1389c2s
Chandler, S.C. v4p0178c1s
v4p0233c1s v5p0130c1s v5p0240c2m
v5p0456c2s v5p0609c1s
Chandler, S.C. and Wendell, O.C.
v2p0095c1s
Chandler, S.C., jr. v1p0727c2s
v2p0008c2s v2p0014c1s v2p0095c1s
v2p0319c1s
Chandler, W.E. v2p0126c1s
v3p0132c1s v3p0402c1s v4p0144c1s
v4p0275c2m v5p0446c1s v5p0592c2s
v5p0602c2s v6p0529c1s
Chandler, W.E. and Quincy, J.
v4p0596c1s
Chaney, G.L. v1p0156c2s
v1p0217c1s v1p0219c1s v1p0288c1s
v1p1176c2s v1p1419c2s v2p0180c2s
v3p0026c1s v3p0128c2s
Chaney, H.A. v3p0109c2s
v3p0277c2s v4p0306c1m
Chaney, L.W., jr. v4p0227c1s
Chang, T.Y. v6p0118c2s
Chang, Yow Tong v6p0118c2s
Chanler, M. v4p0570c2s
Channell, G. v6p0366c2s
Channell, L.S. v6p0096c2s
v6p0590c2s
Channell, Mary A. v6p0275c2s
Channer, C.A. v4p0012c1s
v4p0249c1s v4p0629c2s
Channing, B.M. v5p0539c1s
Channing, E. v1p1251c2s
v2p0025c1s v2p0079c1s v2p0105c1s
v2p0161c2s v2p0184c1s v2p0342c1s
v2p0372c1s v2p0380c2s v2p0382c2s
v2p0444c1s v5p0633c1s
Channing, E.P. v1p1270c1s
Channing, E.T. v1p0227c1s
v1p0310c2m v1p0330c1s v1p0403c2s
v1p0534c2m v1p0754c2s v1p0864c1s
v1p0919c2s v1p0938c1s v1p0990c2s
v1p1169c2s
Channing, Edward v2p0306c1s
Channing, F.A. v5p0009c2s
v5p0117c1s v5p0438c2s v6p0008c2s
v6p0360c1s v6p0405c1s v6p0520c1s
Channing, F.C. v5p0285c1s
v5p0598c1s
Channing, G. and Ellis, G.
v1p0175c1s
Channing, G.E. v3p0035c2s
v3p0206c2s v3p0389c1s v3p0411c2s
v4p0136c1s v4p0189c1s v4p0266c2s
v4p0276c1s v5p0215c1s v6p0090c2s
v6p0203c2s v6p0331c1s v6p0387c1s
v6p0394c1s v6p0402c2s v6p0423c2s
v6p0466c1s v6p0471c2s v6p0489c2s
v6p0490c2s v6p0545c1s v6p0549c2m
v6p0550c1s
Channing, G.G. v1p0913c2s
Channing, Grace E. v5p0219c1s
v6p0223c2s v6p0229c1s v6p0350c1s
v6p0420c2s v6p0549c1s v6p0590c1s
v6p0644c2s
Channing, Grace Ellery ... v6p0549c2s
Channing, J.P. v4p0162c1s
v5p0377c1s v6p0149c1s
Channing, S. v3p0197c1s
v3p0207c2s v3p0385c1s v3p0473c1s
v4p0169c2s v4p0188c2s v4p0451c1s
Channing, S., Mrs. v4p0093c2s
Channing, Susan v4p0068c2s
Channing, W. v1p0031c2s
v1p0032c1s v1p0034c2s v1p0152c2s
v1p0262c1s v1p0453c2s v1p0578c2s
v1p0753c1s v1p0816c1m v1p0817c1s
v1p0845c1s v1p0867c1s v1p0899c1s
v2p0213c1m v2p0222c1m v4p0441c2s
v5p0157c1s v5p0179c2s v5p0291c2s
v6p0193c1s
Channing, W.E. v1p0069c1s
v1p0240c2s v1p0385c1s v1p0392c2s
v1p0445c2s v1p0448c2s v1p0452c2s
v1p0458c2s v1p0464c2s v1p0740c2s
v1p0754c2s v1p0841c2s v1p0893c2s
v1p1151c1s v1p1176c2m v1p1200c1s
v1p1234c2s v1p1270c1s v1p1297c2s
v1p1333c2s v1p1354c2s
Channing, W.F. v1p0599c2s
v1p1003c1s v1p1290c1s v2p0368c1s
v2p0433c2s
Channing, W.H. v1p0086c2s
v1p0393c2s v1p0464c2s v1p1103c1s
v1p1203c2s v2p0139c2s v2p0373c1s
Chant, C.A. v6p0139c1s
v6p0198c2m v6p0199c1s v6p0636c2s
Chant, L.O. v4p0215c2s
v5p0635c1s
Chant, L.O., Mrs. v4p0530c1s
Chantrell, G.F. v1p0211c1s
Chanute, O. v1p0161c2s
v1p0808c2s v1p1076c2s v2p0141c2s
v2p0281c2s v3p0003c1s v4p0004c2s
v4p0631c1s v5p0004c2s v5p0211c2m
v6p0005c1s
Chanute, O. and Morison, G.
v1p0161c1s
Chapel, F.L. v2p0082c2s
Chapelle, A. v2p0333c2s
Chapham, H.S. v6p0017c1s
Chapin, A.B. v1p0029c2s
v1p0048c1s v1p0243c2s v1p0246c2m
v1p0275c2s v1p0394c2m v1p0395c2s
v1p0513c2s v1p0589c2s v1p0775c1s
v1p0903c1s v1p0923c2s v1p1402c1s
Chapin, A.C. v5p0198c2s
v5p0269c1s
Chapin, A.L. v1p0074c2s
v1p0111c1s v1p0261c2s v1p0270c1s
v1p0839c2s v1p1065c2s v1p1111c2s
v1p1265c2s v2p0046c1s v2p0056c1m
v2p0112c2s v2p0156c1s v2p0257c2s
v2p0309c1s v2p0408c1s
Chapin, B. v2p0461c1s
Chapin, C. v1p0292c1s
v1p0504c1s
Chapin, C.H.B. v6p0004c2s
Chapin, C.V. v3p0215c2s
v3p0348c2s v6p0175c2s v6p0188c1s
v6p0409c1s
Chapin, C.W.E. v3p0213c2s
v5p0221c1s v5p0249c2s
Chapin, D.D. v2p0290c2s
Chapin, E.E. v6p0639c1s
Chapin, E.H. v1p0070c1s
v1p0241c1s v1p0649c1s v1p0745c1s
v1p1054c2s v1p1089c1s v1p1195c2s
v1p1279c2s
Chapin, Ellis W. v6p0112c2s
Chapin, F.H. v3p0044c1s
v3p0088c1s
Chapin, H.D. v3p0341c1s
v3p0397c2s v4p0103c1s v4p0171c1s
v4p0506c1s v4p0559c1s v5p0277c2s
v6p0417c1s
Chapin, H.G. v5p0099c1s
v5p0392c2s v6p0158c1s v6p0262c1s
v6p0563c1s v6p0620c1s v6p0690c2s
Chapin, H.W. v6p0509c2s
Chapin, J.B. v1p0643c1s
Chapin, J.H. v1p0612c1s
v1p0852c2s v1p0870c1m v6p0034c2s
Chapin, J.R. v1p0891c1s
v1p0912c1s v1p1374c2s v1p1402c2s
v3p0097c1s v4p0274c2s
Chapin, Lillian v6p0047c1s
Chapin, Lou V. v5p0079c1s
Chapin, N.D. v3p0148c2s
Chapin, T.F. v5p0360c2s
Chapin, T.F. et al. v5p0263c1s
Chaplain, R. v5p0609c2s
Chaplin, F.D.P. v6p0654c1m
Chaplin, H.W. v6p0133c1s
v6p0168c1s v6p0701c2s
Chaplin, J. v1p0097c2s
v1p0323c1s v1p0651c1s v1p0677c2s
v1p0909c2s v1p1010c1s v1p1066c2m
v1p1069c2s v2p0477c1s
Chaplin, S. v2p0301c1s
v5p0548c1s
Chaplin, W.S. v1p1110c1s
v1p1392c1s v5p0621c1s
Chapman, A. v6p0066c1s
v6p0081c1s v6p0083c2s v6p0139c1s
v6p0155c1m v6p0155c2s v6p0233c1s
v6p0590c1s v6p0692c2s
Chapman, A.S. v5p0205c1s
Chapman, Arthur v6p0105c1s
v6p0139c1s v6p0170c2s v6p0196c2s
v6p0315c2s
Chapman, C. v4p0052c1s
v4p0109c1s v4p0229c1s v4p0468c1s
v5p0500c2s
Chapman, C.H. v4p0470c1s
v4p0630c1s v5p0170c2s v5p0353c2s
Chapman, C.T. v6p0562c2s
v6p0710c1s
Chapman, C.W. v1p0108c1s
v1p0108c2s
Chapman, D.J. v4p0489c1s
Chapman, E. v3p0267c1s
Chapman, E.F. v3p0060c2s
v4p0006c2s v6p0266c1m v6p0617c2s
Chapman, E.J. v1p0074c1s
v1p0192c2s v1p0193c1m v1p0193c2s
v1p0267c2s v1p0321c2s v1p0507c2s
v1p0508c2m v1p0509c1s v1p0524c2s
v1p0732c1s v1p0793c1s v1p0835c1s
v1p0844c2s v1p0929c1s v1p0943c1m
v1p1189c1s v1p1233c1s v1p1271c1s
v1p1325c2m
Chapman, E.M. v2p0109c1s
v3p0420c2s v4p0156c2s v4p0423c1s
v5p0017c1s v5p0080c2s v5p0135c2s
v5p0140c2s v5p0192c2s v5p0236c2s
v5p0329c1s v5p0435c2s v5p0463c1s
Chapman, E.R. v5p0636c2s
Chapman, E.T. v1p1436c2s
Chapman, Eliz. R. v3p0119c1s
v3p0269c1s
Chapman, Elmer R.B. v6p0087c2s
Chapman, F. v5p0227c1s
v6p0424c2s v6p0655c2s
Chapman, F.M. v3p0030c2s
v4p0061c1s v4p0061c2s v5p0062c2m
v5p0063c2s v5p0064c1s v5p0089c2s
v5p0504c2s v6p0017c2s v6p0067c1s
v6p0071c2s v6p0228c2m v6p0487c1s
v6p0496c2s v6p0596c2s v6p0599c2s
Chapman, F.M. and Wheeler, W.M.
v6p0386c1s
Chapman, F.R.H. v5p0539c2s
Chapman, F.W. v1p0709c2s
v5p0019c2s v5p0062c2s v5p0191c2s
v5p0397c1s v5p0403c2s
Chapman, G. v5p0318c1s
Chapman, G.A. v6p0504c1s
Chapman, G.C. v1p1163c1s
Chapman, G.W. v1p1315c1s
Chapman, H. v1p0399c2s
v6p0419c2s
Chapman, H.G. v4p0014c1s
v4p0488c1s v4p0573c1s v5p0205c2s

v5p0269c2s
Chapman, H.S. v1p0532c2s
v1p1370c1s
Chapman, J. v1p0259c1s
v1p0538c1s v1p0544c1s v1p0544c2s
v1p0631c1s v1p0791c2s v1p1217c1s
v2p0338c2s v2p0469c2s v5p0023c2s
v5p0304c2s v5p0429c2s v5p0439c1s
v6p0038c2s v6p0107c2s v6p0134c1s
v6p0490c2s v6p0585c1s v6p0643c2s
v6p0714c1s
Chapman, J.B. v5p0393c2s
v5p0455c2s
Chapman, J.E. v6p0531c1s
Chapman, J.H. v2p0336c2s
v4p0248c1s
Chapman, J.J. v3p0110c1s
v4p0075c2s v4p0369c1s v4p0519c1s
v5p0182c1s v5p0187c1s v5p0241c1s
v5p0275c2s v5p0341c1s v5p0392c1s
Chapman, J.T. v2p0242c2s
Chapman, J.W. v3p0329c1s
v5p0568c1s v6p0038c2s
Chapman, John v6p0063c1m
Chapman, K.A. v6p0203c1s
Chapman, Katharine E. v6p0707c1s
Chapman, M.J. v1p0008c2m
v1p0429c1s v1p0581c1s
Chapman, Maj-Gen. v3p0180c2s
Chapman, Mary v4p0106c1s
Chapman, Mrs. v1p1208c1s
v5p0595c2s
Chapman, P. v6p0484c1s
Chapman, R.B. v6p0449c2s
Chapman, R.H. v4p0051c2s
v6p0546c2s
Chapman, Robert H. v6p0171c2s
Chapman, Robert R. v6p0167c1s
Chapman, S.J. v5p0289c2s
v5p0585c1m v5p0615c2s v6p0203c1s
v6p0271c2m v6p0399c2s v6p0633c1s
v6p0682c2s
Chapman, S.J. and Knoop, D.
v6p0153c1s
Chapman, T. v1p0910c1s
v1p1354c2s v4p0162c1s v4p0607c2s
v5p0521c1s v5p0638c1s v6p0395c2s
Chapman, T., Mrs. v3p0206c1s
v5p0331c2s v5p0405c1s v6p0402c2s
Chapman, T.C. v4p0213c1s
Chapman, T.J. v2p0011c1s
v2p0054c1s v2p0072c2s v2p0099c2s
v2p0168c1s v2p0335c1s v2p0343c1s
v2p0350c1s v2p0466c2m v2p0470c1s
v2p0470c2s v2p0481c1s v3p0069c2s
v3p0071c2s v3p0114c1s v3p0124c2s
v3p0213c1s v3p0288c1s v3p0325c2s
v3p0395c2s v3p0417c2s v4p0015c1s
v4p0028c2s v4p0213c1s v4p0342c2s
Chapman, Theo. v5p0132c1s
v5p0447c1s
Chapman, Theo., Mrs. v2p0478c1s
Chapman, W. v1p1381c1s
v4p0066c1s v4p0067c1s
Chapolsky, F.A. v2p0027c2s
Chappel, E.J. v4p0331c1s
Chappell, G.S. v6p0194c1s
v6p0280c1s v6p0467c1s
Chappell, W. v1p0585c1s
v1p0882c1s v1p0883c2s v1p1220c1s
v2p0191c1s
v2p0303c1s
Chappellsmith, J. v1p0099c2s
v4p0386c2s
Chappie, J. v5p0294c2s
Chappie, J.M. v5p0500c1s
Chapple, B. v6p0009c2s
v6p0166c2s v6p0663c2s v6p0687c2m
Chapple, J.M. v5p0065c1s
v5p0082c1s v5p0118c2s v5p0133c1s
v5p0157c2s v5p0203c1s v5p0234c2s
v5p0256c2s v5p0262c1s v5p0322c2s
v5p0387c1s v5p0442c2s v5p0477c1s
v5p0486c1s v5p0489c1s v5p0616c1s
v5p0621c1s v5p0640c1s v6p0004c1s
v6p0054c1s v6p0069c2s v6p0102c1s
v6p0110c2s v6p0162c1s v6p0277c1s
v6p0279c2s v6p0333c1s v6p0496c1s
v6p0529c2s v6p0562c2s v6p0567c1s
v6p0620c1s v6p0677c1s v6p0687c2m
Chapple, W.H. v6p0317c1s
Chappuis, J. v3p0192c2s
Charbonnel, V. v5p0484c1s
v5p0493c2s
Charcot, J.B. v6p0023c1s
Charcot, J.M. v3p0053c1s
v3p0206c1m v3p0264c1s v4p0194c1s
v4p0429c2s
Charcot, Jean v6p0023c1s
Chard, L.C. v6p0511c2s
v6p0677c1s
Chard, T.S. v1p0735c2s
Chardin, G. v6p0150c2s
Charles, E.M. v6p0027c2s
Charles, E.R., Mrs. v1p0870c1s
Charles, Frances v6p0640c2s
Charles, Mrs. v5p0106c2s
Charles, R., Mrs. v4p0630c1s
Charles, R.H. v6p0209c1s
v6p0245c1s v6p0412c1s v6p0639c2s
Charles, R.H. and Owen, J.
v4p0056c1s v4p0185c1s
Charles, R.H. et al. v4p0056c2m
Charlesworth, E.G. v1p0952c1s
Charlesworth, F. v6p0489c1s
Charlesworth, H. v4p0304c1s
v4p0549c1s
Charlesworth, H.W. v4p0086c2s
v4p0447c1s v4p0544c1s
Charlesworth, S. v4p0036c1s
v4p0516c2s
Charleton, A.G. v4p0404c1m
v5p0039c2s v5p0377c2m
Charleton, R.J. v2p0310c1s
v4p0143c1s
Charlewood, W. v3p0239c2s
Charley, W. v3p0155c1s
Charlton, A. v3p0293c1s
v3p0456c2s
Charlton, E.W. v5p0357c2s
v5p0489c1s
Charlton, J. v4p0557c1s
v5p0017c1s v5p0090c1m v5p0090c2m
v5p0091c1s v5p0161c2s v5p0584c1s
v6p0097c2m v6p0098c1s v6p0266c2s
v6p0533c2m
Charlton, John v6p0096c1s
Charlton, M.J. v5p0193c2s
Charlton, Mrs. v1p0184c1s
v1p0238c1s
Charmes, F. v5p0232c1s
v5p0589c1s v6p0430c1s v6p0556c2s
Charnay, D. v1p0212c2s
v2p0073c1s
Charnier, E. v3p0329c2s
Charnock, R.S. v1p0724c1s
v1p0788c2s v4p0307c2s
Charnock, R.S. and Blake, C.C.
v1p1382c2s
Charpentier, J.de v1p0524c1s
Charpy, G. and Grenet, L. v6p0328c2s
Charraud, D. v1p0247c2s
v1p0473c2s v2p0268c1s
Charrier, Capt. v4p0404c2s
Charrington, C. v5p0480c2s
v6p0641c2s
Charrington, C. and Achurch, J.
v4p0128c2s
Charroppin, C.M. v3p0327c1s
v5p0379c1s
Charruaud, D. v1p0481c2m
v2p0165c2s
Charteris, A.H. v2p0081c2s
v2p0365c1s v3p0467c1s v3p0469c1s
Chartres, A.V. v4p0435c1s
Chartres, H. v3p0073c1s
v3p0092c1s v3p0098c2s v3p0139c1s
v3p0232c2s
Chartres, J. v4p0491c1s
Chartres, R. v3p0272c1s
Chartres, V. v5p0272c1s
Chartres, Vivanti v5p0187c2s
Charvet, L. v5p0325c1s
Chase, A.H. v2p0459c2s
v5p0336c2s
Chase, A.W. v1p0533c1s
v1p0638c1s v1p0749c2s v1p0876c1s
v1p1172c2s v1p1311c2s
Chase, B. v2p0077c1s
Chase, B.S. v5p0392c1s
Chase, C. v1p0529c1s
Chase, C.A. v4p0047c1s
v4p0328c1s
Chase, C.H. v4p0140c2s
v4p0574c2s v5p0133c2s
Chase, C.S. v5p0340c1s
Chase, D. v1p0015c1s
Chase, D.A. v6p0377c1s
Chase, E.E. v1p0046c2s
v3p0317c2s
Chase, E.H. v1p1150c2s
v3p0286c2s
Chase, F. v1p1307c1s
v2p0112c1s v3p0110c2s v3p0189c1s
Chase, F.H. v3p0300c2s
v5p0151c2s v6p0386c1s v6p0693c1s
Chase, F.L. v6p0393c2s
Chase, G. v3p0348c2s
v4p0249c2s v4p0401c2s
Chase, G.B. v1p0775c1s
Chase, G.E. v1p0196c2s
Chase, G.I. v1p0154c2s
Chase, G.J. v1p0527c2s
Chase, H. v1p0588c1s
Chase, H.L. v6p0012c2s
v6p0609c1s
Chase, H.S. v5p0072c2s
Chase, I. v1p0096c1m
v1p0096c2s v1p0101c1s v1p0130c2s
v1p1064c2s
Chase, J.A. v1p0531c1s
Chase, J.B. v2p0065c2s
v2p0231c2s v2p0474c1s
Chase, J.C. v5p0419c1s
v5p0536c2s
Chase, L., jr. v1p1323c1s
Chase, L.B. v5p0365c2s
Chase, M.G. v1p0752c1s
Chase, M.W. v5p0394c2s
v5p0476c1s
Chase, Maj. v1p0341c1s
Chase, Margaret H. v6p0564c2s
Chase, Mary W. v5p0394c1s
v5p0450c1s v5p0530c1s
Chase, P. v6p0287c2s
Chase, P.E. v1p0008c1s
v1p0070c1s v1p0070c2m v1p0077c2s
v1p0099c2s v1p0213c1s v1p0257c1s
v1p0257c2s v1p0268c1s v1p0541c2m
v1p0571c1m v1p0579c2s v1p0651c2s
v1p0666c2s v1p0746c2s v1p0747c2m
v1p0751c2s v1p0787c2m v1p0788c1s
v1p0788c2m v1p0829c1s v1p0866c1s
v1p0884c1m v1p1014c1s v1p1024c2s
v1p1074c1s v1p1081c1m v1p1196c2s
v1p1268c1s v1p1269c1s v1p1339c2s
v1p1395c1s v2p0196c2s v2p0299c2s
v2p0340c2s v2p0362c1s v2p0409c1s
v2p0421c2s v2p0425c1s v2p0469c1s
Chase, R.B. v5p0623c2s
Chase, R.L. v3p0125c1s
Chase, Ray E. v6p0209c2s
v6p0463c1s
Chase, S. v1p0246c2s
v1p0693c1s v1p0878c1s v1p1005c2s
v1p1163c1s
Chase, S.C. v1p0783c2s
Chase, S.P. v1p0168c1s
Chase, T. v1p0537c2s
v1p0551c2s v1p0553c2s v1p0601c1s
v1p1430c1s
Chase, T.L. v1p0043c1s
v1p1074c2s v1p1225c2s v1p1373c2s
Chase, Theodora A. v6p0586c1s
Chase, W.G. v4p0009c2s
v4p0611c2s
Chase, W.H. v2p0411c1s
Chase, W.J. v4p0241c1s
v4p0594c2s v5p0495c2m v5p0602c1m
Chase, W.J. and Thurber, C.H.
v4p0123c1s
Chasemore, A. v2p0169c1s
v4p0544c1s
Chasles, P. v1p0032c1s
Chasse, Comte La v6p0567c2s
Chasseloup-Laubat, Marquis de
v4p0100c2s v5p0041c1s
Chat, E.G. v5p0356c2s
Chatard, F.S. v1p1119c2s
v2p0112c1s v2p0253c2s v2p0414c1s
v2p0424c1s v3p0281c2s v3p0319c1s
v3p0364c1s v4p0071c2s v4p0445c1s
Chatard, T.M. v2p0268c1s
v3p0008c2s v3p0373c2s v3p0446c1s
v4p0535c2s
Chateaubriand, F. v1p0001c2s
Chateaubriand, F.A. v1p1281c2s
v1p1305c1s
Chateaubriand, F.A.de v1p0071c2s
v1p1098c2s
Chateaubriand, Visc.de v2p0375c2s
v2p0382c2s
Chatelain, H. v4p0005c2s
v4p0006c2s v4p0018c1s v4p0197c2s
v5p0212c1s
Chatelaine, H. v3p0004c2s
v3p0005c2s
Chater, A.G. v5p0522c1s
v5p0615c2s
Chater, M. v5p0577c2s
v6p0066c2s
Chater, Melville v5p0389c1s
Chatfield-Taylor, H.C. v4p0010c2s
v4p0014c1s v4p0100c2s v4p0133c2s
v4p0234c1s v4p0348c2s v4p0516c1s
v4p0539c2s v6p0379c1s v6p0424c1m
v6p0472c1s v6p0641c2s
Chatrard, F.S. v1p0276c1s
Chatterton, E.K. v6p0351c1s
Chatterton, G.C. v6p0549c2s
Chatterton, G.G. v6p0549c2s
Chatterton, J.M. v1p1041c2s
Chatwood, S. v3p0255c1s
v3p0371c2s
Chaudet, M. v1p0825c2s
Chaumont, F.de v1p1366c2m
Chaumont, Prof.De v2p0213c1s
Chausse, A. v6p0087c1s
Chauvenet, W.M. v5p0504c1s
Chavanne, J. v1p0054c2s
Chavannes, E. v6p0120c2s
Chawner, H. v6p0560c2s
Chawner, Mary G. v6p0163c2s
v6p0202c2s v6p0444c1s
Chawner, W.H. v6p0283c1s
Cheadle, W.B. v1p0164c1s
v1p0817c1s v1p0887c2s
Cheales, H.J. v5p0222c1s
v6p0684c1s
Cheatham, B.F. v1p1240c2s
v2p0336c2s v2p0415c2s
Checkley, E. v3p0331c1s
v4p0388c1s v6p0497c2s
Cheesborough, E.B. v1p1223c2s
v3p0028c2s v3p0357c1s v3p0467c1s
Cheesebrough, A.S. v3p0474c2s
v4p0108c2s v4p0255c1s
Cheeseman, J. v2p0172c1s
Cheesewright, F.H. v3p0189c2s
v4p0368c1s

Cheesman, J. v1p0015c1s v2p0184c1s
Cheesman, L.M. v2p0229c1s v2p0419c2s
Cheetham, S. v1p0252c1s v1p0972c2s v1p1109c2s v1p1118c2s v1p1294c2s v1p1340c2s v1p1432c2s v2p0254c2s v2p0269c1s v3p0124c1s v4p0053c2s
Cheever, D.W. v1p0049c1s v1p0177c1s v1p0271c1s v1p0354c1s v1p0420c2s v1p0896c2s v1p0944c2s v1p1005c1s v1p1070c1s v1p1287c2s v1p1314c1s v1p1345c1s v4p0260c2s
Cheever, G.B. v1p0120c2m v1p0176c1s v1p0242c2s v1p0274c1s v1p0345c1s v1p0377c2s v1p0381c1s v1p0440c2s v1p0470c2s v1p0495c2s v1p0527c1s v1p0539c2s v1p0555c1s v1p0563c2s v1p0582c1s v1p0698c2s v1p0852c2s v1p0929c1s v1p1066c2s v1p1094c2s v1p1098c1s v1p1118c2s v1p1208c1s v1p1404c1s v1p1410c2s v2p0149c2s v3p0040c2s v3p0265c1s
Cheever, G.B. et al. v1p0198c2s
Cheever, H.M. v6p0342c2s
Cheever, H.R. v1p0669c1s
Cheever, H.T. v1p0440c1s
Chekhov, A. v6p0559c2s v6p0597c2s
Chellis, M.D. v2p0333c2s v2p0421c2s
Chelmsford, Lord v4p0279c1s
Cheltnam, C.S. v1p1071c1s v1p1132c1s
Chemnitz, M. v1p0440c2s
Chenay, P. v6p0302c1s
Cheney, A.D. v6p0053c1s
Cheney, A.E. v4p0077c2s
Cheney, A.N. v5p0591c2s
Cheney, C.B. v6p0460c2s v6p0507c1s
Cheney, C.E. v3p0193c2s v4p0411c1s
Cheney, Chas.P. v2p0426c1s
Cheney, E.A. v4p0296c2s
Cheney, E.D. v1p0061c2s v1p0228c2s v1p0248c1s v1p0278c1s v1p0715c1s v1p0834c2s v1p0841c1s v1p1092c2s v1p1156c1s v1p1223c2s v3p0470c1s v4p0009c2s v4p0272c1s v4p0295c1s
Cheney, E.D., Mrs. v1p0063c1s
Cheney, E.P. v5p0388c1s v6p0324c1s
Cheney, E.V. v5p0546c2s
Cheney, H.V., Mrs. v1p0853c1s
Cheney, J.V. . v1p0032c2s v1p0033c2s v1p0614c2s v2p0430c1s v3p0040c2s v3p0045c1s v3p0057c1s v3p0258c1s v3p0263c1s v3p0292c2s v3p0335c2s v3p0336c1s v3p0424c2s v3p0444c1s v4p0039c2s v4p0126c1s v4p0137c2s v4p0178c2s v4p0235c1s v4p0247c2s v4p0344c1s v4p0448c2m v4p0575c2s v4p0580c1s v4p0620c2s v4p0621c1s v4p0632c1s v5p0079c1s v5p0195c2s v5p0202c2s v5p0238c2s v5p0326c1s v5p0349c2s v5p0434c1s v5p0574c2s v6p0070c1s v6p0391c1s v6p0444c1s v6p0505c1s v6p0534c2s v6p0639c1s
Cheney, J.V., Mrs. v4p0388c2s
Cheney, J.Vance v6p0234c2s
Cheney, John Vance v6p0697c1s
Cheney, L.M. v3p0291c1s
Cheney, M.L. v3p0063c2s v4p0310c2s
Cheney, Mary L. v2p0376c2s
Cheney, May L. v4p0538c2s
Cheney, S.P. v3p0045c1m v3p0045c2m v3p0258c1s v3p0403c1s
Cheney, T.P. v2p0363c2s v3p0353c1s
Cheney, W. v2p0197c1s
Cheney, Warren v6p0383c1s
Cheng, C.Liang v6p0119c1s
Chenoweth, A.C. v3p0106c2s
Chenoweth, C Van D. v3p0440c1s
Chenoweth, C.Van D., Mrs.. v4p0267c2s v4p0341c1s v6p0645c1s
Chenoweth, L.E. v6p0695c1s
Cheny, E.D. v1p0430c2s
Cher, K. v5p0613c2s
Cherbuliez, M.V. v4p0564c1s
Cherbuliez, V. v1p0367c2s v1p1142c1s v1p1261c2s
Chernoff, D. v1p1251c1s
Chernoff, M. v1p1251c1s
Cherrill, A.K. v1p0925c1s v3p0006c1s v3p0330c1s v3p0361c2s
Cherriman, J.B. v1p0212c1s v1p0281c2s v1p0423c1s v1p0709c2s v1p0967c1s v1p1128c2s
Cherry, F. v4p0456c2s
Cherry, K. v6p0677c1s
Cherry, W.S. v5p0005c2s v5p0185c2s v6p0200c1s
Cherson, F.W. v1p0141c1s
Chersonese v6p0557c2s
Cherzekov, V.F. v4p0496c1s
Chesebro', C. v1p0098c1s v1p0137c2s v1p1087c1s
Chesebro', Caroline v1p0026c2s
Chesebrough, A.S. v1p0043c2s v1p0496c1s v1p0598c2s v1p0599c2s v2p0062c1s v3p0039c1s
Chesebrough, C. v1p0336c1s v1p0439c1s v1p0464c1s v1p0466c1s v1p0492c1s v1p0565c2s v1p0577c1s v1p0583c1s v1p0586c1s v1p0627c1s v1p0668c1s v1p0710c2s v1p0728c2s v1p0738c1s v1p0787c2s v1p0851c2s v1p0942c2m v1p0951c2s v1p1049c1s v1p1053c2s v1p1066c1s v1p1272c2s v1p1323c2s v1p1369c2s
Chesebrough, E.S. v1p0346c2s v1p1329c2s
Chesebrough, T.W. v1p0148c2s
Chesen, H. v1p0536c1s
Cheshire, E. v1p0211c2s
Chesley, E.M. v1p0843c1s
Chesnaye, G.P. v5p0005c2s
Chesneau, E. v4p0029c1s v4p0164c1s
Chesney, C.C. v1p0073c1s v1p0080c2s v1p0235c2s v1p0445c1s v1p0450c2s v1p0473c1s v1p0516c2s v1p0540c2s v1p0546c1s v1p0547c1s v1p0734c1s v1p0894c2s v1p0895c1s v1p1035c2s v1p1190c2s v1p1219c2s v1p1277c1s v1p1343c1s v1p1345c2s v1p1378c1s
Chesney, E.C. v4p0380c2s
Chesney, G. v1p0102c2s v1p0630c1s v1p0631c1m v1p0634c2s v1p0635c1s v1p0952c2s v1p1133c2s v1p1198c2s v4p0280c2s v5p0029c2s v5p0243c1s
Chesney, G., Gen.Sir v4p0042c1s
Chesney, G., Sir v3p0179c2m v3p0180c1s v4p0355c1m v4p0525c1s
Chesney, G.M. v5p0286c1s v6p0219c1s
Chesney, J. v1p1040c1m v1p1424c2s v2p0021c1s
Chesnut, V.K. v6p0111c2s v6p0502c2s
Chesnutt, C.W. v3p0097c1s v3p0111c2s v3p0177c2s v3p0339c1s v5p0073c2s v5p0083c1s v5p0271c2s v5p0361c1s v5p0402c2s v5p0563c2s v5p0620c1s v5p0630c2s v6p0054c2s
Chess, H.B. v4p0200c1s
Chessar, J.A. v1p0679c1s
Chesson, F.W. v1p0452c2s v1p0546c1s v1p0944c2s v1p1036c2s v2p0171c2s
Chesson, N. v6p0161c2s
Chester, A.H. v1p0532c1s v5p0320c1s
Chester, A.H. and Cairns, F.I. v3p0106c1s
Chester, C. v1p0579c1s
Chester, C.M. v6p0187c2m v6p0250c1s v6p0669c1s
Chester, C.T. v1p0102c2s v1p1290c1s v6p0249c1s
Chester, Colby M. v6p0476c2s
Chester, E.S. v2p0108c2s v2p0115c1s v2p0241c1s v2p0312c2s v2p0387c1s v3p0195c1s
Chester, Emma S. v2p0312c2s
Chester, F. v5p0050c1s
Chester, F.D. v2p0115c1s v6p0046c2s
Chester, G.J. v1p0394c2s
Chester, G.R. v6p0052c1s v6p0524c2s v6p0596c1s v6p0621c2s v6p0664c1s v6p0703c1s
Chester, H. v1p0465c2s v1p1422c2s
Chester, J. v4p0596c2s v5p0029c1s v5p0032c2m v5p0033c1s v5p0050c1s v5p0067c2s v5p0220c2s v5p0228c1s v5p0253c1s v5p0363c2s v5p0375c1m v5p0395c2s v5p0461c1s v5p0602c2s v5p0618c1s v5p0618c2s v6p0665c2s
Chester, J. and Ingalls, J.M. v5p0252c1s
Chester, J.L. v1p0169c2s v1p0372c1s v1p0618c1s v1p0759c1s v1p0985c2s v1p1114c1s v1p1349c2s v1p1353c1s v1p1387c1s v1p1398c2s v1p1404c2s v2p0031c2s v2p0278c2s
Chester, N. v5p0152c2s v5p0273c2s v5p0456c1s
Chester, S.B. v5p0018c1s v5p0360c2s v5p0411c2s v5p0482c2s v6p0571c2s
Chester, W. v1p0952c2s
Chesterfield v6p0002c1s
Chesterfield, R. v1p0084c2s v1p0930c2s v1p1054c2s
Chesterman, E.R. v4p0154c1s
Chesterton, C. v6p0032c1s v6p0057c2s v6p0172c1s v6p0173c2s v6p0196c2s v6p0222c2s
Chesterton, G. v5p0610c2s
Chesterton, G. and Williams, J.E.Hodder .. v5p0623c1s
Chesterton, G.K. v6p0032c1s v6p0085c1s v6p0184c1s v6p0281c1m v6p0302c1s v6p0345c1s v6p0369c1s v6p0370c1s v6p0461c2s v6p0505c1s v6p0584c1s v6p0587c2m v6p0589c2s v6p0638c2s v6p0640c2s v6p0647c2s v6p0649c1s v6p0689c1s
Chesterton, G.K. and Williams, J.E.H. v5p0450c2s
Chesterton, Gilbert K. ... v6p0302c2s
Chesworth, T. v6p0325c1s
Chetlain, A.L. v1p1088c1s
Chetwood, J. v1p0339c1s v5p0384c1s
Chetwood, J. and Bryant, R.C. v6p0309c1s
Chetwood, J., jr. v4p0275c1s v5p0280c2s
Chetwynd, G., Sir v3p0351c2s
Chetwynd, H., Mrs. v3p0014c2s v4p0365c2s v4p0485c1s
Chetwynd, H.W. v1p0577c2s
Chetwynd, H.W., Mrs. v3p0112c2s
Chevalier, A. v4p0389c2s
Chevalier, M. v1p0532c1s v1p0860c2s v1p0963c1s
Chevalier, N. v3p0411c1s
Chevalier, S. v4p0637c1s
Chevallier, A.A. v3p0248c1s
Chevenix, M. v1p0414c2s v1p0473c1m v1p0754c1s
Chever, E.E. v1p0637c1s
Cheverton, B. v1p0017c1s
Chevy, E.R. v6p0251c2s
Chew, B. v5p0363c2s
Chew, Lee v6p0120c1s
Cheyne, Barbara v6p0580c2s
Cheyne, J.K. v1p0825c1s v5p0035c1s
Cheyne, J.K. and Neubauer, A. v2p0204c1s
Cheyne, T.K. v1p0118c2s v1p0123c1s v1p0695c1s v2p0022c1s v2p0043c1s v2p0043c2m v2p0356c2s v2p0369c1s v3p0023c2s v3p0041c2s v3p0042c1s v3p0114c1s v3p0135c2s v3p0165c2s v4p0053c2s v4p0054c2m v4p0055c2m v4p0056c1s v4p0057c2s v4p0099c2s v4p0140c2s v4p0155c2s v4p0275c2s v4p0504c2s v4p0535c2s v5p0017c2s v5p0055c2s v5p0056c1s v5p0056c2s v5p0057c2m v5p0058c1m v5p0058c2s v5p0060c2m v5p0200c2s v5p0277c1s v5p0299c1s v5p0364c2s v5p0395c2s v5p0403c2s v5p0465c2s v6p0045c2s v6p0060c2s v6p0061c2m v6p0065c1m v6p0215c2s v6p0415c1s
Cheyne, T.K. et al. v4p0055c2s
Cheyney, E.P. v3p0015c2s v3p0052c2s v3p0097c2s v3p0241c2s v4p0167c2s v4p0189c2s v4p0354c1s v4p0580c2s v5p0165c1s v5p0190c1m v5p0344c2s v5p0520c1s v5p0543c1s v6p0187c1s
Cheyney, W.A. v3p0246c2m
Cheysson, E. v5p0131c1s
Chiabra, Giovanni v6p0521c2s
Chiarini, G. v4p0365c2s
Chibas, E.J. v4p0142c2s v4p0353c1s v4p0470c2s v5p0153c1s
Chichester, C.R. v2p0226c2s v2p0384c2s
Chichester, E.L. v3p0107c1s v3p0317c1s
Chichester, H. v1p0041c1s
Chichester, R.C. v2p0038c2s
Chickering, I. v1p0093c1s
Chickering, J. v1p0152c1s v1p0258c1m v1p0809c1s v1p1034c2s
Chickering, J.W. v1p1097c1s
Chickering, J.W., jr. v1p0354c2s v1p0462c2s v1p0569c1s v1p1324c1s
Chidsey, C.E. v3p0322c2s
Chilcott, R.V. v1p0084c2s
Child v6p0649c2s
Child, A.B. and Gordon, A.J. v3p0283c1s
Child, A.L. v2p0445c2m
Child, B.G. v1p0843c1s
Child, C.D. v5p0371c2s
Child, C.G. v6p0346c1s
Child, C.M. v4p0094c2s v5p0553c2s v5p0646c1s v6p0036c1s
Child, C.T. v5p0185c1s v5p0551c1s v6p0198c2s
Child, Clarence G. v6p0362c2s
Child, D.L. v1p0698c2s v1p1265c1s
Child, E.B. v6p0400c2s v6p0664c1s
Child, F.J. v1p0088c1s v1p1112c1s
Child, F.S. v5p0166c1s
Child, F.W. v3p0050c1s
Child, G. v1p1239c1s
Child, G.W. v1p0373c2s v1p1150c2s v4p0112c2s
Child, H. v5p0041c2s

v5p0079c1s v5p0326c1s v5p0639c1s
Child, J. v3p0073c2s
Child, L. v4p0414c1m
Child, L.M. v1p0173c2s
v1p0501c1s v1p0599c1s v1p0605c2s
v1p0768c2s v1p0906c1s v1p1031c2s
v1p1095c2s v1p1121c1s v1p1360c2s
v1p1412c1s
Child, L.M., Mrs. v1p0928c2s
Child, M. v1p0792c1s
v6p0586c1s
Child, M.E. v4p0550c2s
Child, M.S. v4p0163c2s
Child, Mrs. v1p0135c1s
Child, N.G.L. v6p0145c2s
Child, R.W. v6p0091c2s
v6p0158c2s v6p0223c2s v6p0397c2s
v6p0400c2s v6p0609c1s
Child, Richard W. v6p0368c2s
Child, S. v6p0360c2s
Child, T. v1p1145c1s
v2p0032c2s v2p0035c1s v2p0035c2s
v2p0040c2s v2p0053c2s v2p0105c2s
v2p0112c2s v2p0114c2s v2p0123c1s
v2p0125c1s v2p0166c1s v2p0182c2s
v2p0210c2s v2p0305c2s v2p0307c1s
v2p0312c2s v2p0329c1m v2p0329c2s
v2p0330c1s v2p0379c1m v2p0383c2s
v2p0397c1s v2p0397c2m v2p0455c1s
v2p0466c2s v3p0013c1s v3p0019c1m
v3p0021c2s v3p0023c1s v3p0031c1s
v3p0039c2s v3p0051c2s v3p0059c1s
v3p0062c1s v3p0078c1m v3p0082c1s
v3p0093c2s v3p0097c2s v3p0124c1s
v3p0148c1s v3p0164c1s v3p0201c2m
v3p0209c2s v3p0217c2s v3p0238c1s
v3p0251c2s v3p0253c1s v3p0263c2s
v3p0279c2s v3p0289c1s v3p0305c2s
v3p0319c2m v3p0320c2m v3p0327c2s
v3p0334c2s v3p0339c2s v3p0342c2s
v3p0370c2m v3p0372c2s v3p0382c2s
v3p0387c2s v3p0388c2s v3p0389c1s
v3p0397c1s v3p0446c1s v3p0449c2s
v4p0126c1s v4p0186c2s v4p0358c2s
v4p0425c1m v4p0425c2s v4p0426c1s
v4p0433c1s
Child, T.E. v1p0824c1s
v1p1049c1s v1p1317c2s v1p1371c2s
Child, Theodore v2p0312c2s
v3p0110c2s
Child, W.C. v1p0598c2s
v1p0599c1s v1p1065c1s
Childar, C. v2p0449c2s
Childe, C. v4p0061c2s
v4p0095c2s v5p0477c2s
Childe, C.F. v1p0254c2s
Childe, Cromwell v5p0631c1s
v6p0043c1s
Childers, E. v5p0243c2s
Childers, H.C.E. v3p0305c1s
v3p0467c1s v4p0458c2s
Childers, H.R.E. v5p0039c1s
v6p0147c2s v6p0445c2s
Childers, H.R.E. and Knowles, J.
v5p0243c2s
Childers, R.C. v1p0173c2s
Childers, S. v6p0108c2s
Childs, C.C. v1p0666c1s
Childs, C.G. v1p0269c2s
v1p0997c2s
Childs, C.V. v5p0552c1s
Childs, D.L. v1p0108c1s
Childs, M.F. v6p0041c1s
Childs, O.W. v1p0920c1s
Childs, T.H. v2p0442c2s
Childs, T.S. v1p0667c1s
v1p1112c1s
Childs, W.M. v5p0232c2s
Chilovi, D. v6p0372c1s
Chilton, C.B. v6p0589c2s
Chilton, E. v3p0197c2s
v3p0474c1s v4p0173c2s v4p0222c1s
v4p0259c1s v4p0316c1s v4p0316c2s
v4p0327c2s v4p0587c2s
Chilton, J.M. v1p0853c2s
Chilton, R.S. v2p0254c2s
Chilton, S. v1p0579c1s
Chipman, A.J. v5p0420c2s
Chipman, N.P. v5p0088c1s
v5p0199c2s v5p0503c2s v5p0574c1s
v5p0600c1s v6p0309c1s
Chipman, R.M. v1p0236c2s
Chipman, W.P. v3p0354c1s
v3p0394c2s
Chipman, W.W.L. v4p0086c2s
Chippendale, C.V. v4p0399c2s
v6p0466c1s
Chipperfield, S. v6p0438c1s
Chirol, M.V. v2p0336c2s
Chirol, V. v1p0174c2s
v2p0429c2s v6p0186c2s v6p0478c1s
Chirol, W.V. v1p0421c1s
v1p1305c1s
Chisholm, A. v4p0236c2s
v5p0638c1s v6p0534c1s
Chisholm, G.C. v5p0248c1s
Chisholm, G.G. v2p0447c1s
v3p0089c1s v3p0245c2s v3p0402c1s
v5p0111c2s v5p0191c1s
Chisholm, H. v4p0240c1s
v5p0245c2s v5p0559c2s v5p0568c2s
v5p0578c2s v5p0588c1s v6p0266c1s
v6p0411c2s v6p0647c2s
Chisholm, H.W. v1p0831c1s
v1p0831c2s v1p1396c2s v3p0355c2s
Chisholm, J. v6p0154c2s
v6p0320c1s
Chisholm, J.A. v3p0262c1s
v4p0246c1s
Chisholm, Mrs. v5p0624c2s
Chisholm, S. v2p0013c2s
v2p0411c2s
Chisholm, W.B. v4p0096c1s
v4p0288c1s v4p0428c2m v4p0451c1s
v4p0596c1s v4p0632c2s
Chisholm, W.B. and Denison, M.A.
v4p0154c2s
Chisholm, W.C. v6p0565c1s
Chislanzoni, A. v5p0612c2s
Chismore, G. v2p0306c1s
Chittenden, A. v5p0581c2s
Chittenden, A.H. v6p0099c2s
Chittenden, C.E. v2p0308c2s
Chittenden, F.H. v6p0320c2s
Chittenden, H.M. v3p0158c2s
v6p0029c2s v6p0422c1s
Chittenden, L.E. v1p0601c2s
v3p0251c2m v3p0435c2s v3p0442c1s
v3p0444c1s v4p0307c1s v4p0322c2s
v4p0325c1m v5p0485c1s
Chittenden, N.H. v6p0134c1s
v6p0514c1s v6p0546c1s
Chittenden, R.H. v2p0358c2s
v5p0518c2s v6p0231c1s v6p0463c1s
v6p0498c2s
Chittenden, R.U. v1p0730c1s
Chitto, L. v1p0965c2s
Chiverius, W.T. v6p0022c1s
Chivot, H. v3p0387c1s
Choate, I.B. v3p0046c2s
v3p0090c1s v3p0272c2s v3p0295c1s
v3p0301c1s v3p0389c2s v4p0125c2s
v4p0184c2s v6p0651c1s
Choate, J.B. v2p0108c2s
v2p0350c2s
Choate, J.H. v5p0113c2m
v5p0341c2s v6p0202c1s v6p0239c1s
v6p0377c2s v6p0627c1s
Choate, J.H. and Hale, E.E.
v3p0009c1s
Choate, R. v5p0415c2s
Chocarne, F. v1p0716c1s
Chollet, L.E. v1p0526c1s
v1p1040c1s v1p1420c2s
Cholmeley, F. v6p0360c1s
Cholmeley, R.F. v6p0074c2s
v6p0190c2s v6p0370c2s v6p0575c1s
Cholmondeley, E.C. v6p0501c2s
Cholmondeley, F.G. v3p0230c1s
v3p0232c1s v3p0424c1s
Cholmondeley, M. v4p0154c2s
v4p0574c1s v5p0572c2s
Cholmondeley, Mary v4p0154c2s
v5p0004c2s v5p0452c2s v6p0517c2s
Chomel, M.C. v6p0544c1s
Chomley, C.H. v6p0041c2s
v6p0240c2s
Chopin, K. v4p0035c1s
v4p0040c1s v4p0405c2s v4p0420c1s
v4p0477c2s v4p0562c2s v5p0402c2s
Choquet v3p0002c1s
Chorley, C.H. v1p0944c1s
Chorley, G.F. v1p0077c2s
v1p0569c2s v1p0856c1s v1p1133c1s
Chorley, H.F. v1p0170c2s
v1p0820c1s v1p0884c2s v1p1007c2s
v3p0292c2s
Chorley, Herbert v6p0108c2s
Chorley, J.R. v1p1231c1s
Chotzner, Dr. v4p0252c2s
v4p0628c1s
Chotzner, J. v4p0186c2s
v4p0275c1s v4p0635c1s v5p0313c1s
Chouteau, P. v6p0388c1s
Chown, J.P. v1p0200c2s
Choynski, I. v6p0093c2s
Chree, C. v4p0349c2s
v5p0356c1m v6p0395c1m
Chree, C. and Milne, J. .. v6p0582c2s
Chreiman, M.A. v3p0470c1s
Chrisman, F.L. v4p0130c1s
Chrisman, O. v4p0103c1s
v4p0103c2s v4p0104c1s v4p0226c2s
v5p0106c1s v5p0106c2s v5p0413c2s
v5p0518c1s
Chrisman, Oscar v5p0107c2s
v5p0471c1s
Christ, H. v4p0129c2s
v4p0203c2s
Christall, C.W. v2p0202c2s
Christian, E. v2p0060c1s
Christian, E.B.V. v4p0517c1s
v4p0617c1s
Christian, E.E. v3p0117c1s
Christian, E.V.B. v5p0328c2s
Christian, F.W. v5p0095c1s
v5p0374c1s
Christian, I.E. v5p0227c2s
v5p0560c2s v5p0579c2s
Christian, J. v1p0942c1s
Christian, Princess v3p0298c2s
Christiani, M. v1p1144c1s
Christie, A.J. v2p0152c1s
v2p0221c2s v2p0245c2s v2p0376c1s
Christie, C. v5p0336c1s
Christie, C.C. v6p0086c1s
v6p0618c1s
Christie, F.A. v5p0024c1s
v5p0115c1s v5p0421c1s v6p0126c1s
Christie, H.C. v2p0250c2s
v2p0297c2s
Christie, J. v2p0419c2s
v4p0548c1s v5p0408c2m v6p0411c2s
Christie, J.D. v3p0361c2s
Christie, J.R. v4p0232c1s
v4p0287c2s v5p0135c1s v5p0505c1s
Christie, K. v3p0434c2s
Christie, M.E. v1p0391c1s
v2p0018c1m v5p0630c1s
Christie, Nimmo v4p0390c1s
Christie, R. v6p0277c1s
v6p0302c2s
Christie, R.C. v2p0059c1s
v4p0010c1s v4p0600c1s v5p0333c1s
Christie, R.M. v2p0128c2s
Christie, R.W.D. v3p0119c1s
v3p0308c2s
Christie, W.D. v1p0047c2s
v1p0398c2s
Christie, W.H.M. v2p0441c2s
v3p0255c1s v4p0440c1s
Christie, W.W. v5p0108c1s
v5p0550c2s v6p0118c1s v6p0221c2s
v6p0618c2s
Christison, D. v2p0172c1s
Christison, Dr. v1p0274c2s
v1p0958c1s
Christison, G.W. v4p0565c2s
Christison, J.S. v6p0309c2s
Christison, R. v3p0028c1s
Christitch, P. v1p1180c1s
Christmas, G.V. v5p0115c2s
v5p0272c1s v5p0495c1s v6p0129c2s
v6p0201c2s v6p0407c2s v6p0496c2s
Christmas, H. v1p0050c2s
v1p0817c2s
Christmas, Miss v1p0526c2s
Christophelsmeier, C. v6p0242c1s
Christopher, C. v3p0082c1s
Christopher, H. v2p0027c2m
v2p0129c2s v2p0243c1s v2p0274c1s
v2p0384c2s v2p0415c1s v3p0097c1s
v3p0210c1s
Christophers, S.W. v2p0286c1m
Christy, C.W. v1p1085c1s
Christy, D. v2p0104c1s
v2p0139c2s v2p0245c1s
Christy, H.C. et al. v5p0508c1s
Christy, M. v4p0152c2s
v6p0080c1m v6p0201c1s v6p0398c1s
Christy, M. and Porteous, W.W.
v5p0075c2m
Christy, S.B. v1p0257c1s
Christy, W. v6p0655c1s
Chrysostom, Brother v4p0572c2s
Chrystal, G. v2p0039c2s
v2p0138c1s v2p0390c2s v5p0565c2s
Chrystal, J. v1p0938c1s
Chrystie, G.K. v5p0127c2s
Chubb, E.W. v3p0387c2s
v4p0064c1s v4p0114c2s v4p0201c1s
v4p0351c1s v4p0442c1s v5p0170c2s
v6p0260c1m v6p0586c2s v6p0587c2s
Chubb, H. v1p0091c2s
v1p0501c2s v1p0763c1s
Chubb, H.W. v4p0337c2s
Chubb, P. v3p0185c1s
v3p0398c1s v3p0398c2s v6p0194c1s
Chubb, P.A. v3p0399c1s
Chubbuck, E. v1p0789c1s
Chumley, J. v4p0386c2s
v5p0472c1s
Chunder-Dutt, S. v1p0635c1s
Church, A. v1p0299c1s
v1p0385c2s v1p0657c1s v1p1246c1s
v3p0080c2s v5p0123c1s v5p0134c2s
v5p0172c2s v5p0277c1s v6p0451c1s
Church, A.H. v1p0159c1m
v1p0503c2s v1p1052c2s v1p1236c1s
v2p0041c1s v2p0086c1s v2p0169c1s
v2p0272c2s v2p0279c2s v2p0341c2s
v2p0348c2s v2p0441c2s v3p0039c1s
v3p0092c2s v3p0121c2s v3p0164c2s
v3p0174c2s v3p0227c2m v3p0341c1s
v3p0342c1s v3p0415c1s v3p0453c2s
v4p0026c1s v4p0090c2s v4p0292c2s
v4p0298c2s v4p0366c2s v4p0455c1s
v4p0456c2s v4p0586c2s v4p0613c1s
v4p0616c1m v5p0138c2s v5p0201c1m
v5p0246c1s v6p0053c1s
Church, A.J. v2p0436c2s
v3p0002c1s v3p0066c1s v3p0105c2s
v3p0155c2s v3p0225c1s v3p0260c2s
Church, Alfred v2p0436c2m
Church, B.C. and Fitzpatrick, F.W.
v5p0211c1s
Church, B.J. v2p0079c2s
Church, C. v1p1410c2s
Church, C.M. v5p0308c2s
v5p0492c1s v5p0509c2s v5p0625c1m

Church, Canon v4p0616c2s
Church, E.H. v1p0782c2s
Church, E.L. v1p0717c2s
Church, E.M. v4p0073c1s v4p0111c1s v4p0392c1s
Church, E.R. v1p0352c2s v1p0356c2s v1p0668c1s v1p0892c2s v1p0988c1s v1p1228c2s v2p0477c2s
Church, E.S. v5p0378c2s
Church, F. v1p1243c2s
Church, F.M. v1p0155c1s v1p0888c2s v1p0924c1s v1p0943c2s
Church, F.P. v3p0462c1s
Church, F.S. v4p0018c1s
Church, G.E. v1p0026c2s v1p0147c1m v1p1067c2s v4p0095c2s v5p0027c2s v5p0069c1s v5p0097c2s v5p0099c2s v5p0138c2s v5p0541c1m v6p0002c2s v6p0072c2s v6p0096c1s v6p0152c1s v6p0324c2s v6p0476c2s v6p0483c1s
Church, H. v4p0588c2s
Church, I.P. v2p0448c2s v3p0205c2s v3p0438c1m v3p0448c1s v3p0457c2s v4p0165c1s v5p0089c1s v6p0304c2s
Church, J.A. v1p0029c1s v1p0279c1s v1p0287c1s v1p0743c2s v1p0845c2m v1p1293c1s v2p0097c2s v3p0393c2s v4p0105c1s v5p0377c2s v5p0460c2s v5p0508c2s v5p0544c1s
Church, J.H. v1p0911c1s
Church, J.M. v1p0632c1s
Church, J.R. v6p0403c2s
Church, M. v6p0628c1s v6p0660c2s v6p0691c1s
Church, P. v1p0128c2s v1p0842c1s v1p0966c2s
Church, P.E. v1p0578c1s
Church, R. v1p1018c1s v4p0021c2s
Church, R., Mrs. v1p0056c2s v1p0102c1s v1p0199c1s v1p0563c1s v1p0635c1s v1p0776c1s v1p0817c2s v1p1023c1s v1p1360c2s
Church, R.W. v1p1109c1s v3p0057c2s
Church, Ross, Mrs. v1p1254c1s
Church, S.D. v1p0131c2s
Church, S.H. v5p0145c1s v5p0154c1s
Church, W.C. v1p0059c1s v1p0289c1s v1p0424c1s v1p0879c1s v1p0956c1s v3p0030c2s v3p0142c1s v4p0186c2s v5p0147c1s v5p0152c1s v5p0424c2s v6p0099c2s
Church, W.C. et al. v4p0434c1s
Churcher, D.G. v5p0286c1s
Churchill, G.B. v6p0522c2s
Churchill, H.T. v5p0461c1s
Churchill, J.W. v2p0019c2s
Churchill, L.P. v5p0506c2m v6p0567c1s
Churchill, O. v3p0182c1s v4p0238c1s v6p0445c1s
Churchill, R. v4p0154c2s
Churchill, R., Lady v3p0370c1s
Churchill, R.S., Lord v2p0037c1s v2p0330c2s
Churchill, S. v3p0404c2s
Churchill, S.B. v1p0994c1s
Churchill, W. v3p0124c1s v3p0199c2s v3p0274c1s v3p0300c1s v3p0317c1s v3p0336c1s v4p0386c1s v5p0092c2s v5p0160c2s v5p0381c1s v5p0506c2s v5p0508c2s v6p0507c2s
Churchill, W. et al. v4p0549c1s
Churchill, W.A. v4p0555c2s
Churchill, W.S. v4p0142c2s v5p0222c2s v5p0243c2s v5p0490c2s v5p0510c1s v6p0127c1s v6p0271c2s
Churchill, W.Spencer v5p0203c2s
Churchill, W.W. v6p0143c2s
Churchill, Winston v5p0085c2s
Churchman, J.W. v6p0122c1s
Churchman, P.H. v6p0642c2s
Chute, J.M. v1p1038c1s
Chydenius, W. v6p0628c2s
Cialdi, A. v1p1172c1s
Cilley, F.H. v5p0182c1s
Cione, Andrea di v3p0313c2s
Cippico, Ant. v6p0022c2s
Cisar, F. v5p0068c2s
Cisneros, F.J. v1p0993c1s
Cisneros, H. v1p1364c2s
Cist, C. v1p0307c1s
Cist, H.M. v2p0086c1s v2p0453c1s
Cist, H.N. v6p0536c1s
Citters, W. v5p0313c1s
Claflin, C.H. v6p0232c1s
Claflin, J.F. v3p0244c1s v3p0395c2s
Claflin, M.B. v4p0620c2s
Claflin, Tennessee v4p0357c1s v4p0504c1s
Clagett, S.H. v1p1420c1s
Claggett, E.B. v1p0911c2s
Claghorn, K.H. v4p0133c1s v5p0083c2s v5p0280c2m v6p0308c2m v6p0309c1s v6p0330c2s
Claiborne, J. v1p0306c1s
Claine, M.J. v4p0556c1s
Clairborne, J.F.H. v1p0854c1s
Clamantis, Vox v5p0009c2s
Clamer, G.H. v5p0371c2s v6p0013c1s
Clampitt, J.W. v1p1272c2s v3p0449c2s
Clancy, J.J. v3p0219c2s v3p0221c1s v3p0222c1s v4p0289c1s v4p0289c2m v5p0296c2s
Claparede, E. v1p0043c1s v6p0021c2s
Clapham, C. v1p0157c1s
Clapham, G.M. v4p0159c2s v4p0631c2s
Clapham, J.A. v1p0253c1s v2p0183c2s v6p0164c1s v6p0401c2s
Clapham, J.H. v5p0482c2s v6p0519c2s v6p0543c1s v6p0708c2s
Claphat, H.S. v6p0679c2s
Clapp, A.H. v1p0617c1s
Clapp, C.M. et al. v6p0713c2s
Clapp, C.W. v1p0074c1s v1p0156c2s v1p0634c1s v1p0646c2s v1p1044c1s v1p1064c2s v1p1065c1s v1p1066c1s v1p1140c1s v1p1178c1s v1p1304c1s v1p1420c2s v2p0059c2s
Clapp, C.W. and Frost, W.G. v2p0092c1s
Clapp, D. v1p0453c2s v1p0570c1s v4p0384c1s v4p0565c2s
Clapp, E. and Trask, W.B.. v1p0260c2s
Clapp, E.B. v4p0118c1s v6p0134c1s v6p0252c2s
Clapp, E.Bull v6p0272c2s
Clapp, H.A. v1p0717c1s v2p0229c2s v2p0397c1s v2p0398c1s v3p0455c1s v4p0068c1s v5p0167c2s v5p0222c2s v5p0466c1s v5p0522c2s
Clapp, H.L. v4p0104c1s v4p0104c2s v4p0168c2s v4p0324c1s v4p0395c1s v4p0410c1s v4p0469c2s v5p0074c1s v5p0198c2s v5p0204c2s v5p0226c1s v5p0511c1s v5p0511c2m v6p0150c2s v6p0193c1s v6p0246c2s v6p0438c1s v6p0574c1s
Clapp, J.B. v3p0267c1s
Clapp, J.C. v4p0410c1s
Clapp, L.A.C. v1p1271c2s
Clapp, L.A.C., Mrs. v1p0187c2s v1p1182c1s
Clapp, P.M. v1p0521c2s
Clapp, R. v5p0148c2s v5p0643c2s
Clapp, R.G. v6p0421c2s
Clapp, R.P. v5p0329c2s
Clapperton, J.H. v3p0269c1s
Clapperton, J.H. and Shorthouse, J.H. v2p0005c1s
Clapperton, J.H., Miss ... v1p0014c2s v1p1420c2s
Clarallan D. v6p0702c1s
Clare, C. v5p0525c1s
Clare, E. v1p1123c1s
Clare, J. v1p0698c2s v1p1100c2s
Clare, R.H. v6p0011c1s
Clare, W. v1p0008c2s
Clarence, L.B. v4p0095c1s
Clarendon, Lord v1p0982c2s
Claretie, J. v2p0230c1s v2p0282c2s v4p0215c1s v4p0522c1s v5p0382c1s v5p0422c2s v5p0522c1s v6p0140c1s
Claretie, J. and Roberts, W. v5p0432c1s
Claretie, Jules v5p0153c2s
Claretie, L. v6p0115c2s
Claris, L.J. v2p0230c1s v2p0345c1s
Clark, A. v1p0884c1s v1p1243c2s v1p1267c2s v4p0037c1s v4p0419c2s v4p0567c2s v5p0333c1s v5p0574c1s v6p0211c1s v6p0584c1s
Clark, A.C. v3p0206c1s
Clark, A.F.B. v6p0622c2s v6p0700c2s
Clark, A.G. v4p0567c2s
Clark, A.H. v4p0240c2s v6p0697c1s
Clark, A.I. v5p0439c1s v5p0489c1s v6p0347c2s v6p0650c1s
Clark, A.L. v3p0307c2s
Clark, A.M. v2p0124c1s v2p0130c1s v2p0140c2s v2p0289c1s v2p0298c1s v2p0420c2s v3p0064c1s v3p0229c2s v5p0089c1s v5p0493c2s
Clark, A.M.L. v5p0011c2s
Clark, A.R. v1p0846c2s
Clark, A.W. v6p0109c2s v6p0445c2s
Clark, B. v5p0634c1s
Clark, B.F. v1p0256c2s
Clark, C. v1p0645c2s v1p1086c2s v1p1134c2s v1p1137c1m v1p1138c1m v1p1138c2s v1p1319c1s v5p0199c1s
Clark, C.C.P. v1p0714c2s
Clark, C.E. v5p0508c2s
Clark, C.H. v1p0572c1s v1p1308c1s v1p1412c1s v2p0027c1s v2p0088c2s v2p0451c2s v5p0034c1s v5p0190c2s v5p0252c2s v5p0501c1s v6p0145c1s v6p0281c2s
Clark, C.S. v2p0463c2s v5p0019c2s v5p0157c1s v5p0399c1s v5p0401c1s v5p0438c1s v5p0558c2s v5p0602c2s v5p0614c2s v6p0265c1s v6p0416c2s v6p0417c1s v6p0443c1s v6p0445c1s v6p0452c1s v6p0668c2s v6p0669c2s
Clark, C.U. v5p0313c1s
Clark, C.W. v3p0017c1s v3p0415c2s v3p0423c2s v3p0444c1s v3p0470c1s v4p0109c1s
Clark, D. v1p0581c1s v1p0745c1s v1p0816c1s v1p1007c1s v1p1374c1s
Clark, D.C. v1p0783c2s v1p1247c2s
Clark, D.K. v1p0267c2s v1p0580c1s v1p0759c1s v1p0759c2s v1p1246c2s v2p0418c2s
Clark, D.S. v3p0116c1s
Clark, D.W. v1p0069c1s v1p0471c2s v1p0507c1s v1p0582c1s v1p0685c1s v1p0686c1s v1p0739c2s v1p0758c2s v1p1004c2s v5p0013c2s v6p0090c2s v6p0184c1s
Clark, E. v1p1344c2s v2p0327c2s v3p0304c1s v3p0412c1s
Clark, E.A. v2p0215c1s v3p0244c2s
Clark, E.B. v5p0183c1s v5p0544c2s
Clark, E.B.E. v1p0982c1s v1p1110c2s
Clark, E.C. v4p0307c1s v4p0325c1s
Clark, E.D. v1p1202c2s
Clark, E.E. v5p0159c2s v5p0477c1s v6p0026c1s
Clark, E.G. v3p0030c1s v3p0170c1s v3p0421c1s v4p0517c2s
Clark, E.G. and Black, H.. v3p0387c1s
Clark, E.H.G. et al. v2p0034c1s
Clark, E.M. v3p0057c2s v5p0157c1s
Clark, E.P. v2p0003c1s v2p0049c1s v2p0079c2m v2p0086c2s v2p0089c1s v2p0092c1s v2p0119c1s v2p0121c2s v2p0131c2s v2p0136c1s v2p0243c2m v2p0258c1s v2p0279c2s v2p0309c1s v2p0310c2s v2p0331c2s v2p0348c1s v2p0349c2s v2p0353c1s v2p0356c1s v2p0422c2s v2p0454c2m v2p0463c2m v3p0040c2s v3p0047c1m v3p0047c2s v3p0072c1s v3p0088c1m v3p0093c1s v3p0123c1s v3p0178c1s v3p0190c1s v3p0264c1s v3p0267c1s v3p0291c2m v3p0296c2s v3p0299c1m v3p0322c2s v3p0326c1s v3p0337c1s v3p0345c2s v3p0348c2s v3p0356c2s v3p0408c1m v3p0416c2s v3p0430c1s v3p0451c2s v3p0470c1s v4p0102c1m v4p0275c1s v4p0308c1s v4p0374c1s v4p0399c2s v4p0457c2s v4p0494c1s v4p0525c2s v4p0538c1m v4p0538c2m v4p0558c2s v4p0603c1s v5p0080c2s v5p0099c2s v5p0105c1s v5p0108c2s v5p0123c1s v5p0127c2s v5p0149c2s v5p0157c2s v5p0206c1s v5p0233c1s v5p0281c2s v5p0295c1s v5p0337c2s v5p0353c1m v5p0386c1s v5p0402c1s v5p0403c2s v5p0406c2m v5p0418c1s v5p0434c1s v5p0443c1s v5p0459c2m v5p0474c1m v5p0507c1s v5p0519c2s v5p0566c1s v5p0603c2s v5p0605c1s v5p0610c2s v5p0643c2s v5p0644c1s v6p0144c2s v6p0307c2s v6p0356c2s v6p0366c1s v6p0415c1s v6p0419c1s v6p0583c1s
Clark, E.P. and Godkin, E.L. v3p0036c1s
Clark, E.U. v4p0016c1s
Clark, E.W. v1p0678c1s v3p0404c1s v6p0273c1s
Clark, F.B. v1p0856c2s v4p0355c1s v6p0011c2s v6p0059c1s v6p0201c2s v6p0549c2s v6p0587c1s
Clark, F.C. v1p0256c1s v1p0646c2s v1p1086c1s v1p1088c1s v3p0066c2s v3p0123c2s v3p0353c1s v4p0616c2s v6p0141c2s v6p0225c1s v6p0542c1s v6p0571c2s
Clark, F.E. v3p0080c2s v4p0015c2s v4p0108c2m v4p0109c1s v4p0287c2s v4p0451c1s v4p0636c1m v5p0069c1s v5p0109c2s v5p0114c1m v5p0286c1s v5p0380c1m v5p0418c2s v5p0422c2s v5p0453c1s v5p0587c1s v6p0122c1m v6p0208c2s v6p0301c1s v6p0534c2s v6p0628c2s v6p0655c1s
Clark, F.G. v3p0288c2s
Clark, F.H. v3p0248c2s v4p0049c1s v4p0442c1s v5p0052c1m
Clark, F.M., Mrs. v5p0394c1s

Clark, F.W. v1p0224c2s
v5p0104c1s
Clark, Francis E. v4p0287c1s
Clark, G. v5p0448c2s
v5p0470c1s v5p0592c2s
Clark, G.A. and Jordan, D.S.
v5p0517c1s v6p0072c1s
Clark, G.B. v2p0445c1s
v5p0068c1s v5p0407c2s
Clark, G.C. v1p0165c1s
Clark, G.E. v6p0456c1s
Clark, G.F. v1p0820c1s
v4p0310c1s v5p0315c2s
Clark, G.H. v1p0598c1s
v1p1065c1s v5p0027c1s v5p0617c2s
Clark, G.L. v4p0175c1s
v4p0337c2s v4p0467c1m v4p0547c1m
v4p0547c2s v6p0011c1s v6p0156c1s
Clark, G.R. v1p0760c1s
Clark, G.S. v4p0591c2s
Clark, G.T. v1p0666c1s
v2p0110c1s v5p0336c1s v5p0497c2s
v5p0546c2s v6p0372c2s
Clark, G.W. v1p0058c2s
v1p0598c2s v1p1270c2s v1p1331c2s
Clark, Geo.L. v6p0441c1s
Clark, H., jr. v5p0395c2s
Clark, H.A. v2p0470c1s
v5p0389c1s
Clark, H.E. v3p0445c1m
Clark, H.F. v4p0106c1s
Clark, H.H. v4p0508c1s
Clark, H.J. v1p0835c2s
v1p1024c2s v1p1239c1m
Clark, H.L. v4p0060c1s
v5p0301c2s v6p0599c1s v6p0608c2s
v6p0650c2s
Clark, H.L. et al. v5p0295c1s
Clark, H.S. v3p0064c2s
Clark, I. v4p0163c1s
v4p0469c2s v5p0033c2s v5p0635c1s
v6p0388c1s v6p0619c2s
Clark, I.S. v1p1139c2s
Clark, Imogen v5p0361c2s
Clark, J. v1p0035c2s
v1p0086c2s v1p0166c1s v1p0218c1s
v1p0313c1s v1p0384c1s v1p0487c2s
v1p0521c1s v1p0564c2s v1p0681c1s
v1p0980c1m v1p0980c2s v1p0991c1s
v1p1118c1s v1p1162c2s v1p1203c2s
v1p1344c2s v1p1397c1s
Clark, J. and Klemm, L.R.. v3p0196c1s
Clark, J.A. v1p0651c1s
Clark, J.B. v1p0180c1s
v1p0252c2s v1p0286c1s v1p1027c1s
v1p1216c1s v1p1361c2s v1p1394c1s
v2p0130c1s v2p0245c1s v2p0464c1s
v3p0067c1s v3p0095c1s v3p0118c2s
v3p0127c2s v3p0218c1s v3p0241c2s
v3p0345c2s v3p0358c2s v3p0396c2s
v3p0437c2s v3p0452c1s v3p0452c2s
v4p0088c2m v4p0121c2s v4p0167c2m
v4p0231c1s v4p0286c2s v4p0287c2m
v4p0315c1s v4p0461c1s v4p0524c2s
v4p0599c2s v5p0175c1s v5p0175c2s
v5p0383c2s v5p0511c1s v5p0592c1s
v5p0592c2m v5p0593c1m v5p0615c1m
v6p0026c1m v6p0188c2m v6p0222c2s
v6p0425c2s v6p0492c2s v6p0518c2s
v6p0535c1s v6p0601c1s v6p0633c1s
v6p0635c1s v6p0654c2s v6p0659c2s
v6p0662c2s v6p0682c2s
Clark, J.C.L. v6p0660c2s
Clark, J.E. v2p0159c2s
v2p0426c2s
Clark, J.F. v1p1441c2s
v4p0142c2s v4p0525c2s v4p0537c2s
Clark, J.G. v1p0275c1s
v4p0088c1s v4p0214c1s v4p0283c2s
v4p0336c2s v4p0606c1s v4p0607c1s
v5p0508c1s
Clark, J.H. v4p0059c1s
v4p0167c2s
Clark, J.J. v6p0151c2s
Clark, J.M. v1p0433c2s
v2p0288c1m v3p0278c2s
Clark, J.M. and Schuchert, C.
v5p0229c1s
Clark, J.O.A. v1p0597c1s
Clark, J.P. v6p0583c2s
Clark, J.S. v1p0031c2s
v1p0206c2s v1p0230c1s v1p0253c2s
v1p0264c1s v1p0290c1s v1p0290c2s
v1p0306c1s v1p0344c2s v1p0599c2s
v1p0636c1s v1p0809c1s v1p0811c1s
v1p0846c2s v1p0853c2s v1p0868c2s
v1p0879c1s v1p0929c2s v1p1010c1m
v1p1066c2s v1p1089c1s v1p1103c2s
v1p1207c2s v1p1400c2s v3p0139c1s
v3p0140c1s v4p0030c1s v4p0169c1s
v4p0512c1s v5p0167c2s v5p0352c1s
v5p0563c1s v6p0391c1s v6p0609c2s
Clark, J.T. v4p0402c2s
v5p0229c2s v5p0515c1s v6p0261c1s
Clark, J.W. v1p1172c2s
v2p0032c1s v2p0362c1s v3p0248c2s
Clark, J.W. and Lodge, O.J.
v2p0126c1s
Clark, J.W. et al. v2p0151c1s
Clark, Jean W. v6p0505c2s
Clark, K.U. v1p1310c1s
v2p0301c1s v3p0069c2s
Clark, Kate Upson v6p0450c1s
Clark, L. v1p0700c1s
v3p0244c2s v3p0287c1s
Clark, L.D. v6p0355c2s
v6p0356c1s v6p0652c2s
Clark, L.G. v1p0038c1s
v1p0208c1s v1p0229c2m v1p0298c2s
v1p0350c1s v1p0403c2s v1p0667c2m
v1p0689c2s v1p0759c1s v1p1149c2s
v1p1168c2s v1p1396c1s v1p1413c1s
Clark, L.N. v5p0389c2s
v6p0674c1s
Clark, M.A.O. v5p0274c1s
Clark, M.B. v5p0135c2s
Clark, M.C. v3p0253c2s
v5p0192c2s
Clark, M.H. v1p0288c2s
Clark, M.L. v4p0274c2s
Clark, N.B. v2p0337c2s
v2p0400c2s
Clark, N.G. v1p0852c2s
v3p0058c2s
Clark, N.W. v4p0497c2s
Clark, O.E. v2p0432c2s
Clark, P. v1p0376c1s
v1p1077c2s
Clark, P.G. v6p0508c1s
Clark, Paul G. v6p0073c1s
v6p0124c1s
Clark, R. v5p0511c2s
Clark, R., jr. v6p0349c2s
v6p0622c2s
Clark, R.C. v6p0563c1s
v6p0639c2s v6p0640c1s
Clark, R.G. v1p1079c2s
Clark, R.H. v5p0601c1s
v6p0159c2s
Clark, S. v3p0468c2s
v5p0181c2s
Clark, S.C. v1p0136c2s
Clark, S.D. v1p0241c1s
v1p0248c2s v1p0290c1s v1p0341c2s
v1p0769c2s v1p1043c1s v1p1043c2s
v1p1287c1s v1p1340c1s v1p1429c1s
v2p0482c1s
Clark, S.F. v6p0663c2s
Clark, S.H. v1p0438c2s
Clark, S.M. v3p0187c2s
Clark, S.N. v3p0086c2s
v3p0337c2s v3p0442c1s v5p0440c1s
Clark, T.E. v1p0437c2s
v1p0639c1s v1p0936c2s v1p1023c1s
v1p1366c1s v1p1375c2s
Clark, T.H. v6p0202c2s
v6p0466c1s
Clark, T.Lindsay v5p0206c1s
Clark, T.M. v1p0140c2s
v1p0252c2s v1p0255c2s v1p0385c2s
v1p0421c2s v1p0422c2s v1p0488c1s
v1p0587c2s v1p0693c2s v1p0912c1s
v1p1159c2s v1p1341c1s v2p0060c1s
v2p0122c2s v2p0251c1s v3p0385c2s
v4p0023c1s v4p0059c2s v4p0131c2s
v4p0528c2s v6p0027c2s v6p0262c2s
v6p0285c2s v6p0470c2s v6p0629c2s
Clark, T.M. et al. v4p0166c1s
Clark, T.U. and Longfellow, W.P.
v3p0361c1s
Clark, Theodora E. v5p0203c2s
Clark, U. v1p1237c2s
Clark, V.S. v5p0460c1s
v6p0160c2s
Clark, W. v1p0058c2s
v1p0713c2s v1p1088c2s v2p0333c1s
v4p0086c2s v4p0091c1s v4p0128c1s
v4p0148c2s v4p0193c1s v4p0252c1s
v4p0259c2s v4p0311c2s v4p0346c1s
v4p0368c1s v4p0368c2s v4p0406c2s
v4p0432c2s v4p0454c2s v4p0457c2s
v4p0472c2s v4p0515c1s v4p0567c1m
v4p0596c1s v5p0095c2s v5p0152c2m
v5p0174c1s v5p0177c1s v5p0327c2s
v5p0461c2s v5p0471c2s v5p0573c1s
v5p0592c2s v5p0600c1s v5p0604c1s
v5p0610c2s v6p0088c2s v6p0347c1s
v6p0659c1s v6p0666c2s
Clark, W. and Ely, R.T. .. v4p0567c1s
Clark, W.A. v5p0470c2s
Clark, W.B. v3p0009c1s
v4p0185c1s
Clark, W.F. v1p0606c1s
Clark, W.G. v1p0072c2s
v1p0732c2s v1p0836c2s v1p1404c2s
Clark, W.J. v1p0141c1s
v1p0598c2s v1p0793c2s v1p1060c1s
v1p1069c2s v5p0183c2s v6p0651c2s
Clark, W.J.H. v2p0062c2s
Clark, W.R. v5p0528c2s
Clark, W.S. v1p0828c2s
Clark, Walter v5p0600c1m
v6p0363c2s
Clark, X. v1p0287c2s
v1p1053c2s v4p0214c1s v4p0397c1s
v4p0421c1s v4p0513c2s
Clarke, A. v1p0003c1s
v1p0522c1s v1p0710c2s v1p0989c2m
v1p1278c1s v3p0448c2s v4p0564c1s
v5p0331c2s v6p0187c1s
Clarke, A., Sir v1p0102c1s
v6p0593c1s
Clarke, A., Sir and Colomb, P.H.
v3p0155c1s v3p0158c2s
Clarke, A.C. v1p0832c2s
Clarke, A.L. v6p0013c1s
v6p0312c2s v6p0384c2s
Clarke, A.M. v2p0016c1s
v2p0074c1s v2p0116c2s v2p0172c1s
v2p0245c2m v2p0336c1s v3p0287c2s
v4p0032c2s v4p0105c2s v4p0284c1s
v4p0419c2s v5p0527c2s
Clarke, A.P. v4p0622c1s
Clarke, A.S. v6p0103c1s
Clarke, A.St.J. v1p0721c1s
Clarke, A.V. v5p0490c2s
Clarke, B. v2p0078c1s
v2p0147c2s v2p0161c1s v2p0323c2s
v3p0415c2s v3p0423c2s
Clarke, B.A. v4p0192c1s
v4p0210c1s v4p0578c2s v5p0124c1s
v5p0282c2s
Clarke, C. v1p0080c2s
v1p0086c1s v1p0105c1s v1p0214c2s
v1p0253c1s v1p0281c1s v1p0309c2m
v1p0345c2s v1p0367c1s v1p0421c2s
v1p0587c2s v1p0609c2s v1p0782c2s
v1p0904c1s v1p0941c1s v1p1011c2s
v1p1032c1s v1p1280c2s v1p1303c1s
v1p1330c1s v1p1403c2s
Clarke, C. and Clarke, M.C.
v1p0081c1s v1p0682c1s
Clarke, C.B. v1p0706c2s
v1p1256c1s v3p0313c2s
Clarke, C.B. et al. v4p0095c1s
Clarke, C.C. . v1p0006c2s v1p0105c2s
v1p0178c1s v1p0181c1s v1p0282c1s
v1p0291c2s v1p0425c1s v1p0444c2s
v1p0451c2s v1p0466c1s v1p0602c1s
v1p0641c2s v1p0695c2s v1p0704c1m
v1p1093c2s v1p1152c2s v1p1186c1s
v1p1212c2s v1p1251c2s v1p1253c1s
v1p1275c1s v1p1362c1s v1p1434c1s
v3p0376c2s
Clarke, C.J.T. v5p0461c1s
Clarke, C.L. v4p0037c1s
v5p0012c1s v5p0295c1s
Clarke, C.P. v2p0070c1s
v3p0018c2m v3p0021c2s v3p0211c1s
v4p0074c1s
Clarke, C.S. v4p0004c1s
v4p0254c2s v5p0014c2s v5p0602c2s
Clarke, D. v1p0561c2s
v1p1106c2s
Clarke, D.K. v1p0146c2s
v1p0759c1s
Clarke, Dean v6p0611c1s
Clarke, E. v1p0009c2s
v1p0113c2s v1p1377c2s v2p0186c2s
v6p0383c1s v6p0588c1s
Clarke, E., Mrs. v1p0530c1s
Clarke, E.B. v4p0083c2s
v4p0316c1s v4p0316c2s v5p0307c1s
Clarke, E.B., Mrs. v6p0357c2s
Clarke, E.D. v1p0167c1s
v1p0210c2s v1p1122c1s v6p0653c2s
Clarke, E.E. v3p0248c2m
v4p0202c2s v4p0330c2s v4p0628c2s
v5p0138c1s
Clarke, E.H. v1p0390c1s
v1p0391c1s v1p0623c2s
Clarke, E.M. v2p0160c2s
v2p0179c1s v3p0078c1s
Clarke, E.P. v2p0279c2s
v3p0346c1s v3p0415c2s v5p0467c1s
v6p0371c2s
Clarke, E.T. v5p0030c1s
v5p0033c1s v6p0555c2s
Clarke, Edith E. v6p0669c2s
Clarke, Effie v5p0307c1s
Clarke, Effie B. v5p0255c1s
v5p0321c2m
Clarke, F. v4p0562c2s
Clarke, F.C. v1p0620c2s
v5p0616c1s
Clarke, F.E. v5p0113c1s
Clarke, F.H. v5p0450c1s
Clarke, F.L. v3p0029c2s
v3p0156c2s v3p0172c2s v3p0188c1s
v3p0191c2s v3p0397c1s v3p0411c1s
v3p0432c1s v3p0447c2s v5p0258c2s
Clarke, F.M. v3p0158c2s
v6p0712c1s
Clarke, F.N. and Reid, J.. v4p0045c2s
Clarke, F.W. v1p0061c1s
v1p0152c1s v1p0225c1s v1p0275c1s
v1p0287c1s v1p0386c1s v1p0390c1s
v1p0399c1s v1p0401c2m v1p0435c1s
v1p0456c1s v1p0519c2s v1p0580c1s
v1p0751c2s v1p0844c2s v1p1160c2s
v1p1233c2s v2p0259c1s v2p0260c1s
v2p0261c1s v2p0290c1s v2p0348c1s
v2p0389c2s v2p0478c2s v3p0147c1s
v3p0187c2s v3p0219c1s v3p0277c2m
v3p0280c2s v3p0305c1s v3p0359c1s
v4p0107c2s v4p0465c2s v4p0637c1s
v5p0082c1s v5p0104c1s v5p0358c2s
v5p0583c2s v5p0605c1s v5p0605c2s
v6p0040c1s v6p0111c2s v6p0514c2s
v6p0521c1s

Clarke, F.W. and Catlett, C.
v3p0334c1s
Clarke, F.W. and Darton, N.H.
v5p0277c2s
Clarke, F.W. and Diller, J.S.
v2p0443c1s v2p0449c1s
Clarke, F.W. and Schneider, E.A.
v3p0392c2s
v4p0368c2s
Clarke, F.W. and Steiger, G.
v5p0017c2m v5p0438c1s v6p0594c2s
Clarke, F.W. et al. v5p0496c2s
Clarke, G. v4p0622c2s
v5p0415c2s
v5p0618c2m
Clarke, G.C.
v2p0082c1s
Clarke, G.H. v2p0066c1s
v6p0107c2m
Clarke, G.Herbert v6p0361c2s
Clarke, G.J. v4p0270c2s
v4p0346c2s v5p0027c2s
Clarke, G.K. v5p0320c1m
v5p0402c1m v6p0446c1m
Clarke, G.M. v1p0919c1s
Clarke, G.S. v3p0027c2s
v3p0180c2s v4p0236c2s v4p0237c2s
v4p0238c1m v4p0363c2s v5p0019c2s
v5p0189c1s v5p0215c1s v5p0231c1s
v5p0245c1s v5p0245c2s v5p0246c2s
v5p0281c1s v5p0356c1s v5p0401c1s
v5p0404c1s v6p0267c2s
Clarke, G.S., Sir v5p0246c1s
Clarke, G.W. v1p0649c2s
v1p1108c1s
Clarke, H. v1p0208c1s
v1p0389c1s v1p0625c2s v1p0666c1s
v1p0788c2s v1p0897c2s v1p0989c2s
v1p0999c1m v1p1034c2s v1p1078c2s
v1p1179c1s v1p1330c2s v1p1394c2s
v2p0027c1s v2p0056c2m v2p0204c1s
v2p0259c1s v2p0282c2s v2p0299c2s
v2p0341c1s v2p0361c2s v2p0375c1s
v2p0402c2s v2p0440c1s v2p0448c2s
v3p0176c2s v3p0196c1s v3p0211c2s
v3p0241c2s v3p0292c1s v3p0352c2s
Clarke, H.A. v1p0883c2s
v3p0057c2m v3p0292c2s v3p0404c1s
v4p0021c1s v4p0069c1s v4p0076c1m
v4p0131c1s v4p0155c2s v4p0178c2s
v4p0373c1s v4p0388c1s v4p0389c1s
v4p0448c2s v4p0449c1s v4p0461c2s
v4p0518c2s v4p0570c1s v4p0627c1s
v5p0014c1s v5p0078c2s v5p0079c2s
v5p0080c1s v5p0171c1s v5p0195c1s
v5p0455c2s
Clarke, H.A. and Porter, C.
v5p0079c2s v5p0080c1s v5p0153c2s
v5p0203c2s v5p0278c1s v5p0468c1s
v5p0522c1m v5p0523c1m v5p0523c2s
v5p0539c2s v5p0630c2s v6p0202c2s
v6p0587c2s
Clarke, H.B. v5p0542c2s
Clarke, H.E. v3p0196c1s
Clarke, H.F. v1p1393c1s
Clarke, H.J. v3p0115c1s
v3p0375c2s
Clarke, H.L. v4p0203c2s
v4p0539c1s v4p0545c2s v4p0583c1s
Clarke, H.M. v3p0184c1s
v6p0252c2s
Clarke, H.S. v1p0898c1s
v1p1036c2s v2p0153c2s v2p0293c1s
v2p0416c1s v2p0439c1s v3p0044c1s
v3p0429c1s v4p0418c2s
Clarke, H.V. v4p0260c2s
v4p0371c1s v4p0432c1s v4p0569c1s
v4p0609c2s v4p0620c2s
Clarke, Helen A. and
Porter, Charlotte v4p0519c1s
v6p0588c2m
Clarke, Hyde v4p0049c2s
v4p0183c2s v4p0420c2s v4p0587c1s
Clarke, I. v6p0705c2s
Clarke, I.E. v1p0462c2s
v1p1113c1s
Clarke, Isabel v6p0433c2s
Clarke, J. v1p0840c2m
Clarke, J.A. v3p0408c2s
Clarke, J.C.C. v1p0024c2s
v1p0261c2s v1p0527c1s v1p1016c2s
v1p1017c1s v1p1411c2s
Clarke, J.F. v1p0038c1s
v1p0042c1s v1p0129c1s v1p0156c2s
v1p0171c1s v1p0173c2s v1p0201c1s
v1p0242c1s v1p0242c2s v1p0259c2s
v1p0289c1s v1p0312c2s v1p0344c2s
v1p0356c2s v1p0433c2s v1p0451c1s
v1p0471c2s v1p0566c2s v1p0580c2s
v1p0663c1s v1p0685c2m v1p0687c2s
v1p0689c1s v1p0692c1s v1p0704c1s
v1p0706c1s v1p0805c1s v1p0818c2s
v1p0838c1s v1p0857c2s v1p0905c1s
v1p1010c1s v1p1024c2s v1p1045c2s
v1p1110c2s v1p1116c1s v1p1129c2s
v1p1139c2m v1p1158c2s v1p1164c1s
v1p1183c2s v1p1184c1s v1p1200c2s
v1p1207c1s v1p1207c2s v1p1208c1s
v1p1260c2s v1p1303c2s v1p1304c1s
v1p1318c1s v1p1336c2s v1p1342c2s
v1p1352c2s v1p1369c2s v1p1378c1s
v1p1400c1m v2p0074c1s v2p0117c1s
v3p0162c2s v3p0243c2s v5p0274c2s
Clarke, J.F. and Johnson, S.
v1p0130c2s
Clarke, J.L. v4p0270c2s
Clarke, J.L.J. v6p0265c2m
Clarke, J.M. v1p1000c2s
v2p0117c2s v3p0041c1s v4p0120c1s
v4p0210c1s v6p0250c1s v6p0417c2s
v6p0612c1s
Clarke, J.M. et al. v2p0042c1s
Clarke, J.O.A. v2p0286c1s
Clarke, J.S. v1p0640c1s
Clarke, J.T. v1p0052c1s
v1p0052c2s v1p0054c1s v1p0069c1s
v1p0376c1s v1p0941c2s v2p0025c1m
v2p0025c2s v2p0122c1s v2p0224c2s
v2p0388c1s v3p0167c1s v3p0436c2s
Clarke, J.T. and Emerson, A.
v3p0017c2s
Clarke, J.W. v1p0068c2s
v3p0012c2s v3p0218c2s v3p0391c1s
v4p0458c1s
Clarke, K. v3p0437c1s
Clarke, L.F. v3p0074c1s
v6p0405c2s
Clarke, L.G. v1p0175c2s
v1p1287c1s
Clarke, L.L. v1p0447c2s
v1p0645c1s v1p0835c1s v1p1236c1s
Clarke, L.L., Mrs. v1p0463c2m
Clarke, L.W. v6p0555c1s
Clarke, Lois W. v5p0166c1s
Clarke, M.A. v4p0344c1s
Clarke, M.B. v1p0335c1s
Clarke, M.C. v1p0672c2s
v1p0719c2s v1p1081c2s v1p1183c2s
v1p1184c2s v1p1185c1s v1p1185c2s
v1p1186c2m
Clarke, M.C. and Clarke, C.
v1p0081c1s v1p0682c1s
Clarke, M.E. v6p0084c2s
Clarke, M.K. v6p0640c2s
Clarke, M.O. v4p0536c2s
Clarke, M.S. v4p0409c2s
v5p0595c2s
Clarke, Mabel S. v5p0257c2s
Clarke, Mary A. v6p0489c2s
Clarke, Max v6p0225c2s
Clarke, N.W. v3p0083c2s
Clarke, P. v4p0265c1s
Clarke, R. v1p1196c1s
v2p0086c1s
Clarke, R.C. v1p0683c2s
Clarke, R.E. v1p0300c1s
v2p0228c1s
Clarke, R.F. v1p0036c1s
v1p0121c2s v1p0314c2s v1p0321c1s
v1p0340c1s v1p0499c1s v1p0727c2s
v1p0946c2s v1p0989c1s v1p1023c2s
v1p1124c2s v1p1177c2s v1p1217c2s
v2p0003c2s v2p0005c1s v2p0010c1s
v2p0010c2s v2p0012c1m v2p0027c1s
v2p0162c2m v2p0167c1m v2p0225c1s
v2p0242c2s v2p0260c2s v2p0288c1s
v2p0291c1s v2p0297c1s v2p0313c1s
v2p0324c2s v2p0325c1m v2p0354c1m
v2p0360c1s v2p0375c1m v2p0375c2s
v2p0382c1s v2p0384c2s v2p0387c2s
v2p0448c1s v2p0450c2m v2p0456c1s
v2p0473c2s v3p0104c1s v3p0214c2s
v3p0330c1s v4p0054c1s v4p0194c1s
v4p0254c1m v4p0300c1s v4p0453c1s
v4p0583c2s v4p0606c2s v5p0019c2s
v5p0132c1s v5p0493c1s v5p0619c2s
Clarke, R.H. v1p0159c1s
v1p0219c1s v1p0360c2s v1p0692c2s
v1p0726c1s v1p0802c1s v1p1116c1s
v2p0033c1s v2p0064c2s v2p0066c2s
v2p0170c1s v2p0369c2s v2p0375c1s
v2p0452c2s v2p0472c2s v2p0480c2s
v3p0010c1s v3p0306c2s v3p0307c1m
v3p0364c2s v3p0395c2s v4p0125c2s
v4p0359c1s v4p0483c1s v4p0488c2m
v4p0611c2m v5p0047c1s v5p0493c2s
v6p0641c1s
Clarke, R.L. v1p0812c2s
Clarke, R.S. v1p0005c2s
Clarke, R.W. v2p0376c1s
Clarke, S. v1p0784c1s
v1p1178c2s v2p0085c2s v2p0439c1s
v3p0054c2s v3p0085c1s v3p0284c1s
v3p0295c2s v5p0309c1s v5p0626c2s
v5p0627c1s
Clarke, S.A. v1p0710c1s
v1p0735c1s v1p0947c1s v1p1122c1s
v2p0323c1s v2p0359c1s v5p0291c1s
v5p0627c2s v6p0469c2s v6p0697c1s
Clarke, S.B. v3p0421c1s
Clarke, S.C. v1p0279c2s
v1p0461c2m v1p0462c1s v1p0612c2s
v1p0624c1s v1p1146c2s v4p0154c1s
v4p0268c2m
Clarke, S.D. v1p1328c1s
v1p1328c2s
Clarke, S.E.J. v4p0281c1s
Clarke, S.F. v2p0111c2m
v3p0100c2s v3p0380c1s
Clarke, S.H. v4p0064c1s
v4p0445c1s v5p0452c2s
Clarke, S.M.S. v3p0357c1s
Clarke, S.R. v4p0089c2s
v4p0381c2s
Clarke, S.W. v3p0002c2s
Clarke, Sarah v1p0024c1s
Clarke, T. v1p0141c1m
v1p0313c1s v1p0435c1s v1p0862c2s
v1p1029c2s v1p1162c2s
Clarke, T.C. v1p0052c1s
v1p0154c2s v1p0161c2s v1p0162c1s
v1p0258c2s v1p0718c1s v1p0727c2s
v1p1076c2s v1p1079c2s v1p1080c1s
v3p0158c2s v4p0473c2s v4p0614c1s
v5p0076c1s
Clarke, T.C. and Hering, R.
v1p0161c1s
Clarke, T.E. v1p1171c2s
Clarke, T.M. v2p0148c2s
Clarke, T.S. v1p0944c2s
v1p1085c1s
Clarke, T.W. v1p0703c2s
v1p1161c2s v1p1262c2s v2p0092c2s
Clarke, W. v1p0193c1s
v1p0259c1s v1p1239c1s v2p0091c1s
v2p0186c2s v3p0056c1s v3p0114c2s
v3p0160c2s v3p0161c2s v3p0174c1s
v3p0243c1s v3p0257c2s v3p0288c2s
v3p0322c1s v3p0398c2s v3p0455c1s
v4p0090c1s v4p0122c2s v4p0181c2s
v4p0187c2s v4p0214c1s v4p0339c1s
v4p0463c1s v5p0064c2s v5p0190c2s
v5p0248c1s v5p0272c2s v5p0332c2s
v5p0476c1s
Clarke, W.A. and Olmsted, D.
v1p0827c1s v1p0827c2s
Clarke, W.B. v1p0149c2s
v1p0440c2s v1p0914c1s v1p1103c2s
v2p0043c2s v3p0080c2s v6p0199c1s
Clarke, W.F. v1p0606c1s
Clarke, W.G. v5p0020c1s
v5p0278c2s
Clarke, W.N. v1p0130c1s
v2p0045c1m v2p0236c1s v2p0414c2s
v2p0428c1s v3p0111c1s v3p0119c2s
v6p0084c1s v6p0304c2s
Clarke, W.R. v3p0012c2s
Clarke, W.S. v5p0549c1s
Clarke, W.T. v1p0495c2s
Clarke, Wm. v2p0186c2s
Clarke-Nuttal, G. v6p0046c2s
Clarkin, F. v6p0624c2s
v6p0643c2s v6p0684c1s
Clarkson, A. v1p1397c2s
Clarkson, C. v1p0767c2s
Clarkson, J.S. v3p0337c1s
v5p0242c1s
Clarkson, J.S., Mrs. v5p0295c1s
Clarkson, J.W. v5p0240c2s
Clarkson, P.S. and Macfarlane, W.W.
v3p0080c1s
Clarkson, R.B. v2p0047c2s
Clarkson, R.H. v1p0853c1s
Clarkson, S. v1p0432c2s
Clarkson, S.F. v2p0122c2s
Clarkson, T. v6p0044c2s
Clarkson, W.F. v3p0096c2s
Clary, W. v1p0983c2s
Clason, A.W. v2p0075c1s
v2p0114c1s v2p0115c2s v2p0313c2s
v2p0316c1s v2p0412c1s v2p0452c1s
v2p0461c2s v3p0031c2s v3p0114c2s
v3p0121c1s v3p0325c2s v3p0383c2s
Claspell, S.K. v6p0147c1s
Classon, W.H. v6p0625c2s
Clatworthy, L.M. v6p0104c1s
Clatworthy, Linda M. v6p0375c1s
Claubry, M.H.G.de v1p0167c1s
Claude, G. v6p0009c2s
Claudet, A. v1p1003c1s
v1p1091c1s v1p1252c2s
Claudet, F. v1p1044c2s
Claudet, M. v1p0329c1s
Claudet, M.F. v1p0300c1s
v1p0532c1s
Claudin, A. v4p0459c2s
Claudy, C.H. v6p0218c2s
Claughton, T.L. v1p1385c1s
Claus, C. v1p1083c1s
v1p1204c2s v4p0411c1s
Claus, W. v3p0039c1s
Clausen, G. v4p0029c1s
Clausius, R. v1p0580c1s
v1p1248c2s
Clavel, M. v6p0047c1s
Clavering, E. v6p0044c2s
v6p0206c2s v6p0213c1s v6p0231c2s
v6p0482c1s
Claviere, R.de Maulde la . v5p0337c2s
Claxton, I. v5p0087c2s
Claxton, J. v1p0353c1s
Claxton, L. v1p0335c2s
Claxton, Mrs. v1p0558c1s
Claxton, P.P. v6p0573c1s
Claxton, W.R. v1p0085c1s
v4p0027c1s v4p0488c1s
Clay, A. v2p0391c1s
v6p0116c1s v6p0573c2s
Clay, A.T.F. v6p0665c1s
Clay, B.L. v4p0562c1s

Clay, C.E. v3p0044c1s v3p0052c2s v3p0151c1s v3p0384c1s v3p0408c1m v3p0428c2s v3p0451c2s v3p0473c2s v3p0474c1s v5p0331c1s v6p0304c1s
Clay, C.H. v6p0105c1s
Clay, C.M. v2p0063c1s v2p0411c1s v5p0265c1s
Clay, E.R. v3p0094c2s v3p0109c2s v3p0143c1s v3p0401c1s
Clay, H. v1p0789c2s v1p1362c1s
Clay, H. et al. v4p0177c1s
Clay, H.A. v6p0683c1m
Clay, J. v1p0315c1m
Clay, T.H. v3p0225c2s
Clay, T.L. v3p0470c2s
Clay, W. v1p1251c1s
Clayden, E.J. v3p0231c2s
Clayden, F.W. v1p0493c2s
Clayden, P.W. v1p0295c2s v1p0381c1s v1p0495c1s v1p0608c1s v1p0782c1s v1p0987c2s v1p1245c2s v1p1350c2s v5p0068c1s
Clayden, P.W. et al. v4p0111c2s v4p0457c2s
Claye, S.D. and Debray, P. v3p0288c2s
Clayes, S.L. v3p0354c2s v4p0110c1s
Clayes, S.L., Mrs. v3p0357c1s
Claypole, E.J. v4p0327c2s
Claypole, E.W. v1p0747c2s v1p0899c2s v2p0060c1s v2p0077c1s v2p0163c2s v2p0173c2s v2p0335c1s v3p0016c1s v3p0145c1s v3p0319c2s v4p0531c2s v4p0577c1s v4p0633c2s
Claypole, G. v1p1390c2s
Claypole, K.B. v3p0312c2s
Claypole, K.B., Mrs. v3p0173c2s
Claypoole, W. v3p0362c2s
Clayton, A. v1p1205c1s
Clayton, B.F. v4p0016c1s v4p0195c1s
Clayton, B.T. v5p0460c2s
Clayton, C. v2p0323c2s v3p0015c1s
Clayton, E. v3p0305c2m v3p0416c1s v3p0417c1s
Clayton, E.C. v1p0943c2s v2p0267c2s
Clayton, F. v6p0069c2s v6p0448c1s v6p0605c1s
Clayton, H.D. v1p0695c2s
Clayton, H.E.G. v6p0416c2s
Clayton, H.H. v2p0014c1s v2p0438c2s v2p0468c2s v3p0015c2s v3p0076c2s v3p0108c2m v3p0410c2s v3p0458c2m v4p0145c2s v4p0312c1s v4p0615c2m v5p0038c2s v5p0478c1s v6p0005c1s v6p0041c1s v6p0627c1s v6p0681c1s
Clayton, J.M. v1p1098c1s
Clayton, J.W. v1p0922c2s
Clayton, N.W. v6p0670c2s
Clayton, W. v5p0389c2s
Clayton, W.O. v6p0574c1s
Clayton, W.W. v3p0268c1s v3p0277c2s v3p0396c1s v3p0464c2s
Clear, G.Le v4p0177c1s
Cleary, J.M. v4p0287c1s
Cleary, K.M. v5p0379c2s v5p0552c2s v6p0615c1s
Cleary, W.W. v1p0750c1s
Cleaveland, A.M. v6p0121c1s v6p0232c1s v6p0389c1s v6p0458c1s
Cleaveland, Agnes M. v6p0653c2s
Cleaveland, N. v1p0133c1s v1p0779c1s v1p1240c1s
Cleaver, C. v5p0646c2s
Cleaves, A. v6p0276c2s v6p0445c2s
Cleaves, M.A. v6p0585c2s
Cleburne, P.R. v1p0228c1s
Cleef, A.Van v1p0058c1s v1p0098c1s v1p1240c2s v3p0335c1s
Cleef, Augustus Van v5p0391c1s
Cleemann, T.M. v1p0051c1s
Cleeve, F.J.S. v5p0375c1s
Clegg, S. v1p1311c2s
Cleghorn, J. v1p0351c1s
Cleghorn, Sarah N. v6p0069c2s
Cleland, A.M'Q. v5p0223c2s
Cleland, A.McF. v4p0223c1s
Cleland, H.F. v6p0081c2s
Cleland, J. v1p1004c2s v3p0145c1s
Cleland, R. v1p0098c1s
Clelland, G.M. v1p0686c1s
Clemen, C. v6p0209c2s v6p0344c2s v6p0346c1s
Clemenceau, G. v5p0218c1s v6p0014c2s v6p0236c2s
Clemenceau, G. et al. v6p0236c2s
Clemens, C. v6p0064c2s
Clemens, C.L. v6p0232c1s
Clemens, E.V. v4p0133c1s
Clemens, H. v5p0409c2s
Clemens, S.L. v1p0115c1s v1p0188c2s v1p0196c1s v1p0197c2s v1p0202c2s v1p0438c1s v1p0473c2s v1p0551c1s v1p0733c2s v1p0774c1s v1p0819c1s v1p0854c2s v1p1012c1s v1p1081c2s v1p1082c2s v1p1086c2m v1p1388c1s v2p0003c1s v2p0109c2s v2p0237c1s v2p0355c1s v2p0379c2s v3p0097c1s v3p0139c2s v3p0226c1s v3p0273c2s v3p0274c2s v3p0423c1s v4p0070c1s v4p0132c1s v4p0187c1s v4p0293c1s v4p0303c1s v4p0306c2s v4p0371c2s v4p0466c2s v4p0520c1s v4p0578c2s v4p0582c2s v5p0003c2s v5p0005c2s v5p0035c2s v5p0040c1s v5p0110c2m v5p0114c2s v5p0167c1s v5p0222c2s v5p0287c1s v5p0358c2s v5p0396c1s v5p0565c1s v5p0596c1s v5p0600c2s v6p0122c1s v6p0149c1s v6p0163c1s v6p0189c1s v6p0244c2s v6p0386c2s v6p0686c2s
Clemens, S.L. and Matthews, B. v3p0099c2s
Clemens, W.M. v2p0350c2s v2p0436c1s v3p0263c2s v3p0391c1s v4p0537c2s v5p0092c2s v5p0256c2s v5p0553c1s v6p0179c1s v6p0223c1s v6p0239c2s
Clement, B. v4p0581c1s
Clement, C.E. v4p0421c2s
Clement, E.H. v6p0346c2s v6p0686c1s
Clement, E.W. v3p0184c1s v3p0227c1s v3p0227c2s v4p0296c2s v4p0297c1m v4p0297c2m v4p0337c1s v4p0426c2s v5p0145c2s v5p0526c1s v6p0092c1s v6p0121c1s v6p0334c2s v6p0337c1s v6p0338c1s v6p0339c1s
Clement, H.N. v6p0425c1s
Clement, J. v1p0987c2s v2p0180c2s v2p0456c2s v3p0055c2s v4p0399c1s
Clement, P. v5p0595c1s
Clement, V. v4p0231c2s
Clement, W.K. v5p0193c2s v5p0278c2s v5p0290c2s v5p0326c2s v5p0605c1s
Clements, F.E. v5p0337c1s v6p0171c2s v6p0272c2s v6p0307c2s v6p0362c2s
Clements, F.E. and Pound, R. v5p0323c1s
Clements, H. v3p0458c2m v3p0459c1s
Clements, H.H. v1p1008c2s
Clements, J.M. v5p0371c2s
Clements, L.R. v5p0318c1s
Clements, W.L. v4p0138c1s
Clemons, C.F. and Gooch, F.A. v4p0514c1s
Clemson, T.G. v1p0016c1s v1p1265c2s
Clemson, W.F. v1p0732c1s
Clendenen, A.F. v1p0908c2s
Clephan, R.C. v6p0030c2s v6p0196c1s
Clerc, A. v1p0368c1s
Clergue, H. v5p0148c2s
Clergue, H. and Roscoe, E.S. v5p0323c1s
Clericetti, C. v1p0162c1s
Clerk, A. v4p0131c2s v4p0307c2s v4p0364c2s v4p0627c1s
Clerk, D. v2p0172c1s v5p0226c2s v6p0323c2s
Clerk, F.L. v2p0252c1s
Clerk, H. v1p0618c2s v1p0825c2s
Clerk, J. v1p1264c1s
Clerk, J.F. v4p0098c1s
Clerk, Janie M. v5p0314c1s
Clerk, N.M. v1p0056c2s
Clerke, A. v1p0191c1s v1p0299c2s
Clerke, A.M. v1p0281c2s v1p0348c2s v2p0345c1s v2p0425c1s v3p0024c2s v3p0027c1s v3p0067c1m v3p0101c2s v3p0205c2s v3p0298c2s v3p0309c2s v3p0407c1m v3p0407c2m v3p0415c1s v3p0416c1s v3p0439c2s v4p0037c2m v4p0271c1s v4p0447c1s v4p0503c2s v4p0545c1s v4p0545c2m v5p0035c2s v5p0087c2s v5p0542c1s v6p0037c2s v6p0214c2s
Clerke, A.St.J. v4p0444c2s
Clerke, Agnes M. v5p0549c2s v6p0152c1s v6p0446c1s v6p0625c2s
Clerke, E. v2p0018c1s
Clerke, E.M. v1p0047c1s v1p0064c1s v1p0331c1s v1p0452c2s v1p0461c1s v1p0671c2s v1p1065c2s v1p1098c2s v1p1251c2s v1p1369c2s v2p0001c2s v2p0032c1s v2p0050c1s v2p0061c2s v2p0066c2s v2p0075c2s v2p0079c1s v2p0086c1s v2p0217c2s v2p0270c1s v2p0271c1s v2p0276c1s v2p0287c1s v2p0295c1s v2p0337c2s v2p0404c2s v2p0410c2s v3p0019c1s v3p0024c1s v3p0066c1s v3p0075c1s v3p0121c2s v3p0148c2s v3p0160c2s v3p0162c1s v3p0169c1s v3p0186c2s v3p0212c1m v3p0221c1s v3p0395c1s v3p0409c1s v3p0421c2s v3p0437c1s v4p0006c1s v4p0138c1s v4p0291c2m v4p0303c1s v4p0350c1s v4p0357c2s v4p0359c1s v4p0374c1s v4p0488c1s v4p0540c1s v5p0493c1m v5p0583c1s v5p0610c1s
Clerke, Ellen M. v5p0240c1s
Clerke, J. v1p0279c2s v1p0912c2s
Clerke, R.F. v3p0077c2s
Clermont-Ganneau v3p0228c2s v5p0154c1s
Clermont-Ganneau, C. v1p0049c2s v3p0283c2s
Clermont-Ganneau, C.C. ... v1p0960c2s
Clesinger, Mme. v6p0183c2s
Cleve, J. v3p0262c1s
Cleve, J.S.Van v4p0064c1s v4p0153c2s v4p0388c2m v4p0442c1m v4p0451c2s v4p0527c2s v4p0608c2s v5p0393c1s v5p0393c2s v5p0395c1m v6p0620c2s v6p0684c2s
Cleve, J.W.Van v6p0513c2s
Cleve, M.J. v1p0468c1s
Cleve, P.T. v4p0511c1s
Cleveland, C.D. v6p0246c1s
Cleveland, C.L.W. v5p0050c1s
Cleveland, E.J. v3p0135c1s v4p0311c1s v4p0592c1s v4p0619c2s
Cleveland, E.R. v3p0362c2s v3p0455c1s
Cleveland, F.A. v4p0405c2s v5p0095c1s v5p0128c2s v5p0382c2s v5p0588c1s v6p0040c2s v6p0050c2s v6p0051c2s v6p0151c1s v6p0435c1s v6p0436c1s v6p0667c1s v6p0668c2s
Cleveland, G. v5p0101c2s v5p0603c2s v5p0609c1s
Cleveland, G.A. v2p0289c1s
Cleveland, Grover v6p0015c2s v6p0113c2s v6p0141c2s v6p0233c2s v6p0480c2m v6p0524c2s v6p0525c2s v6p0592c1s v6p0621c1s v6p0667c2s
Cleveland, H. v1p1347c1s
Cleveland, H.G. v2p0204c1s
Cleveland, H.I. v5p0028c2s v5p0477c2s v6p0451c1s v6p0529c2s v6p0550c2s
Cleveland, H.R. v1p0053c2s v1p0256c1s v1p0260c1s v1p0366c2s v1p0402c2s v1p0419c2s v1p0430c2s v1p0445c1s v1p0610c2s v1p0648c2s v1p0884c1s v1p0890c2s v1p0985c2s v1p1150c1s v1p1235c2s
Cleveland, H.W. v1p1252c1s v2p0184c2s v2p0321c1s v2p0443c1s
Cleveland, H.W.S. v1p0468c1s v1p0723c1s v1p0835c1s v1p0972c1s v1p1210c1s v4p0427c2s
Cleveland, J.T. v1p0584c2s
Cleveland, L. v5p0014c1s v5p0181c2s v5p0578c2s
Cleveland, L. and Botassi, D.N. v5p0597c2s
Cleveland, P.R. v3p0253c2s v3p0279c2s
Cleveland, R.D. v5p0346c1s v5p0642c1s
Cleveland, R.E. v3p0117c2s v3p0156c1s
Cleveland, Ralph D. v6p0208c1s
Cleveland, Sue S. v6p0486c2s
Cleveland, T., jr. v5p0385c1s
Clevenger, S.V. v1p0157c1s v1p0907c2s v2p0341c1s v2p0358c1s v2p0456c2s v3p0072c2s v3p0094c1s v3p0242c1s v3p0265c1s v3p0331c1s v3p0429c2s v4p0017c1s v4p0071c2s v4p0108c1s v4p0108c2s v4p0379c1s v4p0425c1s v4p0463c2s
Clever, C. v1p0244c1s v1p0745c2s v3p0356c2s v4p0130c1s v4p0143c1s v4p0316c1s v4p0324c1s v4p0470c2s v4p0477c1s v5p0085c1s v5p0116c2s v5p0378c1s v6p0125c1s v6p0135c2s v6p0538c1s
Clever, C. et al. v4p0477c1s
Clever, Conrad v6p0513c2s
Clews, E.W. v5p0537c1s
Clews, H. v3p0061c1s v3p0067c2s v3p0352c2s v3p0402c2s v3p0453c2m v4p0283c2s v4p0471c1s v4p0472c2s v4p0599c1s v5p0617c1m v6p0089c2s v6p0522c2s v6p0560c1s v6p0684c1m
Clews, H. et al. v2p0245c1s
Cleyre, V.de v4p0017c1s v4p0461c1s v4p0514c2s v6p0019c2s
Cliff, D.Y. v2p0179c1s v2p0198c2s
Clifford, A. v5p0121c1s v5p0345c1s v5p0628c2s
Clifford, C. v6p0156c1s
Clifford, C.J. v5p0610c1s
Clifford, C.W. et al. v6p0039c2s
Clifford, E. v3p0109c2m v3p0191c2s v3p0431c2s v4p0315c2s v5p0389c2s v6p0162c1s
Clifford, E.C. v5p0315c2s v6p0121c1s v6p0627c2s

Clifford, F. v3p0090c1s
Clifford, F.H. v6p0099c1s
v6p0566c1s
Clifford, H. v5p0113c2s
v5p0154c1s v5p0155c2s v5p0202c1s
v5p0210c2s v5p0214c1s v5p0258c1s
v5p0282c2s v5p0316c2s v5p0357c1m
v5p0478c2m v5p0530c1m v6p0075c2s
v6p0080c2s v6p0085c2s v6p0094c1s
v6p0134c1s v6p0145c1m v6p0186c1s
v6p0232c1s v6p0259c2s v6p0272c1s
v6p0295c1s v6p0305c2s v6p0366c2s
v6p0396c1m v6p0492c2s v6p0493c1s
v6p0495c1s v6p0525c1s v6p0552c1s
v6p0563c1s v6p0565c2s v6p0596c1s
v6p0647c1s v6p0692c2s
Clifford, H. et al. v6p0423c2s
Clifford, H.E. v6p0041c1s
Clifford, Hugh v6p0011c1s
v6p0526c1s v6p0584c2s v6p0631c2s
Clifford, I. v6p0418c1s
Clifford, J. v1p0020c2s
v1p0058c1m v1p0187c2s v1p0188c2s
v1p0336c1s v1p0351c1s v1p0422c2s
v1p0483c1s v1p0505c2s v1p0697c1s
v1p0716c2s v1p0770c1s v1p0791c1s
v1p0797c2s v1p0799c2s v1p0864c1s
v1p0895c2s v1p0912c2s v1p0959c2s
v1p0984c1s v1p0993c2s v1p0994c1s
v1p0996c1s v1p1023c2s v1p1108c2s
v1p1148c2m v1p1149c1s v1p1151c1s
v1p1266c2s v1p1272c2s v1p1297c2s
v1p1308c2s v1p1320c2s v1p1398c2s
v1p1308c2s v1p1320c2s v1p1398c2s
v1p1410c1s v2p0436c2s v3p0033c2s
v4p0045c2s v4p0098c2s v4p0229c1s
v4p0505c1s v5p0201c2s v6p0426c2s
v6p0482c2s
Clifford, J.H. v1p0869c2s
v1p1051c1s v4p0188c1s v4p0467c1s
Clifford, J.T. v1p1123c1s
Clifford, Josepha v5p0003c2s
Clifford, Josephine v5p0628c1s
v6p0092c2s
Clifford, K. v6p0545c1s
Clifford, L. v5p0562c2s
Clifford, Lucy v4p0243c1s
Clifford, M. v6p0381c1s
Clifford, V. v1p0773c2s
Clifford, W. v1p0313c1s
v2p0106c2s
Clifford, W. and Voysey, C.
v3p0356c2s v3p0428c1s
Clifford, W.K. v1p0058c1s
v1p0110c1s v1p0228c2s v1p0304c2s
v1p0312c2s v1p0375c1s v1p0406c2s
v1p0407c2s v1p0427c1s v1p0792c2s
v1p0812c1s v1p0843c1s v1p0869c1s
v1p0901c1s v1p1001c2s v1p1066c1s
v1p1093c2s v1p1108c1s v1p1163c2s
v1p1164c1s v1p1305c2s v1p1356c1s
v1p1432c1s v4p0455c2s v6p0580c2s
Clifford, W.K. et al. v1p0869c1s
Clifford, W.K., Mrs. v3p0210c1s
v3p0218c1s v3p0312c2s v3p0471c1s
v4p0276c1s v4p0309c1s v5p0347c1s
Clifford-Lloyd, C.D.
v1p0178c1s
Clift, A.S. v6p0198c2s
v6p0637c2s
Clift, D.H. v6p0151c2s
Clift, Denison H. v6p0312c1s
Clifton, Bishop of v4p0154c1s
Clifton, Fanny v2p0420c2s
Climenson, E.J. v5p0304c2s
Climo, W.Hill v6p0014c2s
Clinch, B. v1p0188c1s
v1p0188c2s
Clinch, B.C. v2p0286c2s
v2p0375c2s
Clinch, B.G. v5p0493c2s
Clinch, B.J. v2p0456c2s
v3p0220c2m v3p0370c2s v3p0441c1s
v4p0289c2s v4p0348c2s v4p0489c1s
v4p0495c2s v4p0514c2s v5p0020c1s
v5p0108c2s v5p0134c1s v5p0148c1s
v5p0281c2s v5p0379c2s v5p0380c1s
v5p0444c1m v5p0445c2m v5p0595c1s
v6p0057c2s v6p0092c2s v6p0093c2s
v6p0237c1s v6p0238c1s v6p0326c2s
v6p0327c2s v6p0328c1s v6p0331c2s
v6p0421c2m v6p0494c1s v6p0672c1s
Clinch, Bryan J. v5p0325c2s
v5p0444c1s v6p0275c2s
Clinch, G. v2p0002c2s
v2p0254c2s v2p0365c1s v2p0375c1s
v3p0299c2s v4p0338c1s v4p0338c2s
v4p0362c1s v4p0410c1s v4p0623c1s
v5p0061c2s v5p0463c2s v6p0024c1s
v6p0449c1m
Clinch, J.H. v1p0046c1s
v1p0279c1s
Clinche, B.J. v2p0019c2s
v2p0024c2s v2p0072c2s v2p0224c2s
v2p0225c1m v2p0227c1m v2p0227c2s
v2p0268c1s v2p0287c1s v2p0298c2s
v2p0395c1s v2p0404c1s v4p0250c2s
v4p0290c2s
Cline, L.C. v1p1339c1s
Cline, T.H. v2p0241c2s
Cline, T.S. and Dodge, R.. v5p0200c2s
Clingman, T.S. v1p0298c1s
Clinkscales, J.G. v6p0173c1s
Clintock, J. v1p0837c2s
Clinton, C.F.F. v1p0332c1s
v1p0553c1s v1p0624c2s v1p1263c1s
v1p1333c1s v1p1337c2s
Clinton, C.Pelham v3p0185c1s
Clinton, C.S.P. v3p0235c2s
Clinton, C.T. v5p0137c1s
Clinton, De W. v1p0912c1s
Clinton, G.W. v1p0508c1s
Clithero, T. v6p0404c2s
Clive, A. v1p0152c2s
v1p0227c1s v1p0368c1s v1p0661c2s
v1p0713c1s v1p0979c1s v1p1020c2s
v1p1189c2s v1p1256c1s v1p1407c1m
Clive, C. v1p0661c2s
v1p0981c1s
Clive, E. v1p0001c2s
v1p0204c1s v1p0329c1s v1p0698c1s
v1p0838c2s v1p1438c2s
Clive, P.A. v5p0428c2s
Clive-Bayley, Miss v5p0624c1s
Clizbee, J. v1p1328c1s
Clodd, E. v1p0430c2s
v1p1255c2s v2p0010c2s v2p0022c1s
v2p0045c1s v2p0106c2s v2p0110c1s
v2p0123c2m v2p0149c1s v2p0193c1s
v2p0240c2s v2p0249c1s v2p0273c2s
v2p0304c2m v3p0023c1s v3p0104c1s
v3p0112c2s v3p0145c2s v3p0185c1s
v3p0194c2s v3p0265c2s v3p0282c1s
v3p0288c2s v3p0345c1s v3p0400c1s
v4p0190c2s v4p0191c1s v4p0201c2s
v4p0464c1s v5p0483c2s v5p0514c1s
v6p0512c1s
Cloman, S.A. v5p0616c2s
Clond, V.W. v6p0291c2s
Clonel, J.L. v1p0655c1s
Clopath, H. v5p0031c2s
Close, C.F. v6p0345c2s
v6p0650c1s
Close, C.S. v1p0607c2s
v1p0877c2s
Close, F. v1p0239c1s
v1p0508c1s
Closson, C.C. v4p0189c1s
v4p0514c1s v4p0590c2s v4p0591c1s
v5p0020c1s v5p0023c1m v5p0099c2s
v5p0197c2s v5p0263c1s v5p0475c2m
v5p0535c2s
Closson, C.C., jr. v4p0591c1s
Closson, H.W. v3p0082c1s
v5p0029c2s v5p0333c2s
Closson, M.C., Mrs. v4p0550c2s
Closson, M.H. v4p0246c1s
v4p0298c2s v4p0344c2s v4p0433c1s
v4p0537c2s v4p0582c2s
Closson, Mabel H. v4p0009c1s
v4p0307c2s
Closson, W.B. v3p0471c1s
Cloth, F.de T. v5p0582c2s
Cloud, B.M. v5p0163c2s
Cloud, D.M. v5p0132c2s
Cloud, J.G., Mrs. v1p0658c1s
Cloud, J.L. v1p0061c1s
v1p0292c2s v1p1380c1s
Cloud, V.W. v4p0276c1s
v4p0352c2s v4p0581c2s v5p0021c2s
v5p0041c2s v5p0343c1s v5p0365c1s
v5p0366c2s v6p0048c2s v6p0068c2s
v6p0366c1s v6p0420c2s v6p0434c1s
Cloud, Virginia W. v5p0259c1s
v6p0365c2s
Clough, A.H. v1p0035c1s
v1p0299c1s v1p0310c2s v1p0418c2s
v1p0531c1s v1p0589c2s v1p0741c2s
v1p0955c1s v1p0967c2s v1p1275c1s
v1p1430c2s v6p0382c1s
Clough, A.J. v1p1422c1s
v3p0468c2s
Clough, A.L. v6p0398c1s
Clough, E.H. v5p0452c1s
Clough, J.A. v3p0070c2s
Clough, R.S. v2p0009c2s
Clough, S. v1p0239c1s
Clough, W.O. v2p0108c2s
v2p0116c2s v2p0283c1s v2p0406c2s
v2p0422c1s v3p0115c2s v3p0148c2s
v3p0226c1s
Clouston, J.S. v5p0311c1s
v6p0153c2s v6p0234c1s v6p0288c1s
v6p0299c2s v6p0564c2s
Clouston, K.W. v5p0166c1s
v5p0223c2s
Clouston, R.S. v4p0185c1s
Clouston, T.S. v2p0477c2s
v4p0071c2s v4p0140c1s v4p0162c2s
v4p0273c2s v4p0482c1s
Clouston, W.A. v2p0315c2s
v3p0017c2s v3p0026c2s v3p0034c1s
v3p0049c1s v3p0289c1s v3p0360c1s
v4p0057c2s v4p0067c1s v4p0216c1s
v4p0299c2s v4p0354c2s v4p0448c2s
Clouston, W.A. and MacBain, A.
v4p0041c2s
Clover, A.K. v5p0305c2s
Clover, J. v4p0521c1s
Clover, L.P. v1p1373c2s
Clover, S.B. v1p0018c2s
Clover, S.T. v4p0146c1s
Clow, F.R. v4p0114c2s
v4p0250c2s v4p0538c2s v4p0565c1s
v5p0175c2m v6p0524c2s
Clowes, F. v4p0200c1s
v4p0220c2s v5p0521c1s v6p0585c1m
Clowes, W.I. v4p0425c2s
Clowes, W.L. v3p0186c2s
v4p0107c1s v4p0121c1s v4p0225c2s
v4p0238c1m v4p0263c2s v4p0277c1s
v4p0363c2s v4p0395c2s v4p0407c1s
v4p0409c2s v4p0433c1s v4p0484c1s
v4p0580c1s v4p0581c2m v5p0015c2s
v5p0069c2s v5p0101c1s v5p0199c1s
v5p0210c1s v5p0246c2s v5p0247c1s
v5p0401c1s v5p0404c1s v5p0496c1s
v5p0516c2s v5p0533c1s v5p0598c2s
v6p0133c2s v6p0268c1s v6p0326c2s
v6p0459c1s v6p0565c1s v6p0677c2s
Clowes, W.Laird v4p0236c2s
Clowes, Wm.L. v4p0363c2s
Cloy, D.E. v6p0605c1s
Cloyd, D.E. v6p0573c1s
Clozel, F.J. v4p0045c1s
Club, W.A., Dr. v6p0045c1s
Clubbe, E.H. v3p0023c1s
v3p0034c1s v3p0119c2s v3p0203c2s
Cluer, A.R. v4p0561c1s
Clulow, G. v3p0334c2s
v5p0193c2s
Cluseret, G. v1p0448c2s
v1p0611c2s v1p0940c1s v1p1277c1s
Cluseret, Gen. v1p0285c2m
Cluss, A. v1p0982c1s
Clute, Eliz.W. v6p0420c1s
Clute, Helen F. v5p0606c2s
Clute, O. v2p0414c2s
Clute, Oscar v3p0460c1s
Clutton-Brock, A. v6p0070c1s
v6p0305c2s v6p0629c1s
Clutz, J.A. v1p0440c2s
v1p0868c1s v2p0039c2s v2p0379c1s
v3p0283c1s v5p0127c1s v5p0378c1s
v6p0513c1s
Clyde, A. v1p0076c2s
v1p0433c1s v1p0609c2s v1p1127c2s
Clyde, Mrs. v5p0146c1s
Clymer, M. v3p0122c2s
v3p0148c2s v3p0280c1s
Clymer, W.B.S. v3p0027c1s
v3p0240c2s v3p0242c1s
Clyne, J. v1p0371c2s
Clynton, R. v3p0052c2s
v3p0311c2s
Coakley, G.W. v3p0243c1s
v3p0298c2s v3p0313c2s v3p0333c2s
v3p0376c1s v4p0126c2m v4p0367c1s
Coale, G.B. v2p0172c2s
Coale, W.E. v1p0052c2s
Coan, J. v6p0187c1s
Coan, T. v1p0575c1m
v1p0707c1m v1p0812c2m v1p1376c2s
Coan, T.M. v1p0032c2s
v1p0034c2s v1p0054c2s v1p0150c2s
v1p0265c2s v1p0278c2s v1p0318c1s
v1p0323c1s v1p0359c1s v1p0437c2s
v1p0452c1s v1p0452c2s v1p0574c2s
v1p0575c1m v1p0579c1s v1p0647c2s
v1p0741c1s v1p0746c1s v1p0803c2s
v1p0848c2s v1p0883c1s v1p0886c1s
v1p0908c1s v1p0996c2s v1p1029c1s
v1p1045c2s v1p1051c2s v1p1091c1s
v1p1132c2s v1p1254c1s v1p1255c1s
v1p1263c2s v1p1266c1s v1p1292c1s
v1p1323c2s v1p1351c1s v1p1377c1s
v1p1430c1s v2p0041c1s v2p0062c2s
v2p0068c1s v2p0105c1s v2p0245c2s
v2p0290c1s v2p0296c1s v2p0348c2s
v2p0379c2m v2p0479c2s v3p0014c1m
v3p0035c2s v3p0063c1s v3p0274c1s
v3p0280c2m v3p0328c1s v3p0417c2s
v3p0456c2s v3p0473c1s v5p0258c2s
Coan, T.M. and Wilder, B.G.
v1p0392c2s
Coape, H.C. v1p1007c2s
v2p0471c2s
Coar, H.L. v3p0169c2m
v5p0366c1s
Coar, J.F. v5p0167c1s
v5p0230c1s v5p0230c2s v5p0258c1s
v5p0559c1s v5p0631c1s v6p0252c1s
v6p0252c2s v6p0423c2s
Coard, J.M. v5p0485c2s
Coate, H.A.A. v4p0106c2s
Coate, H.E.A. v4p0432c1s
Coates, B.H. v1p1112c1s
Coates, F. v3p0308c1s
v5p0018c1s v5p0203c1s v5p0464c2s
v5p0545c2s
Coates, F.E. v3p0207c2s
v3p0274c1s v4p0028c1s v4p0200c1s
v4p0293c2s v4p0318c2s v5p0486c2s
v6p0257c2s
Coates, F.M. v6p0469c2s
Coates, J.H. v6p0011c1s
Coates, T.F.G. v6p0149c2s
Coats, M.J. v5p0053c1s
v5p0394c2s
Coats, R.H. v6p0025c1s

v6p0148c1s
Cobb, A.G. v2p0106c2s
Cobb, A.W. v4p0624c1s
Cobb, B.F. v3p0131c1m v3p0392c2s
Cobb, C. v1p0065c2s v1p0883c2s v4p0507c2s v6p0700c1s
Cobb, E.B. v1p0454c2s v1p0693c1s v1p0877c2s v1p0951c2s
Cobb, H. v1p0666c1s v1p0855c1s v1p1144c1s v1p1237c1m
Cobb, H.F. v3p0050c2s
Cobb, H.N. v2p0044c2s
Cobb, J.B. v1p0312c2s v1p0667c2s v1p1066c1s v1p1412c2s
Cobb, J.H. v6p0283c1s
Cobb, J.S. v2p0143c2s v2p0389c2s v4p0122c1s v4p0138c2s
Cobb, M.E.R. v4p0103c2s
Cobb, M.L. v3p0311c1s
Cobb, M.S. v6p0495c1s
Cobb, S. v1p0496c1s v1p0528c2s v1p0847c2s
Cobb, S.H. v1p1044c1s v1p1270c2s v1p1348c1s v3p0346c1s v5p0131c1s v5p0536c1s
Cobb, T. v5p0163c1s v5p0447c1s v6p0014c1s v6p0066c1s v6p0358c2s
Cobb, W.F. v4p0462c1s v5p0117c1s v5p0117c2s v6p0305c2s v6p0535c1s
Cobb, W.H. v1p0075c1m v1p0124c2s v1p0684c1s v1p0896c2s v1p1222c1s v2p0043c2m v2p0180c2s v2p0355c2s v2p0358c1s v3p0042c1s v4p0056c1m v4p0516c1s v5p0058c1m v5p0072c1s v5p0260c2s
Cobban, G.M. v4p0279c2s
Cobban, J.M. v1p0116c2s v1p0693c1s v1p1013c2s v1p1103c1s v1p1258c1s v2p0041c1s v2p0191c2s v3p0137c1s v3p0271c1s v4p0079c1s v4p0459c1s v4p0562c1s
Cobban, J.McL. v3p0228c2s v3p0400c1s v4p0338c1s v4p0535c2s
Cobbe, E.P. v2p0152c1s
Cobbe, F.B. v1p0802c1s v1p1144c2s v4p0226c2s
Cobbe, F.C. v3p0054c2s
Cobbe, F.P. v1p0006c2s v1p0026c1s v1p0035c2s v1p0041c2s v1p0042c1m v1p0043c1s v1p0062c1s v1p0071c2s v1p0072c1s v1p0083c1s v1p0104c2s v1p0156c2s v1p0175c2s v1p0202c2s v1p0210c1s v1p0213c1m v1p0218c2s v1p0228c2s v1p0249c1s v1p0273c2s v1p0288c2s v1p0313c2s v1p0333c2s v1p0336c2s v1p0338c1s v1p0347c1s v1p0359c2s v1p0360c2s v1p0365c2s v1p0369c1s v1p0423c1s v1p0432c1s v1p0438c2s v1p0448c2m v1p0495c2s v1p0496c2s v1p0564c2s v1p0578c1s v1p0584c2s v1p0589c1s v1p0614c2s v1p0615c2s v1p0625c2s v1p0628c2s v1p0642c2s v1p0654c2s v1p0682c2s v1p0695c2s v1p0717c1s v1p0754c2s v1p0805c2s v1p0819c1s v1p0869c1s v1p0879c2s v1p0940c2s v1p1009c1s v1p1031c1s v1p1031c2s v1p1055c1s v1p1068c2s v1p1111c2s v1p1124c2s v1p1179c2m v1p1215c2s v1p1216c2s v1p1219c2s v1p1324c2s v1p1355c1s v1p1376c1s v1p1408c2s v1p1418c2s v1p1421c2m v1p1423c2s v1p1424c1m v1p1426c1s v1p1426c2s v1p1431c1s v2p0005c1s v2p0063c1s v2p0239c1s v2p0368c2s v2p0420c1s v2p0428c1s v2p0446c1s v2p0462c1s v2p0462c2m v2p0483c2s v3p0129c2s v3p0136c2s v3p0175c1s v3p0204c1s v3p0308c1s v3p0333c1s v3p0358c1s v3p0380c2s v3p0451c1s v4p0071c1s v4p0489c2s v4p0606c2s v4p0637c2s v5p0364c1s v6p0160c1s
Cobbe, F.P. et al. v2p0384c2s
Cobbe, Frances P. v6p0705c1s
Cobbe, T.P. v1p0745c1s
Cobbet, T. v1p0910c2s
Cobbett, W. v1p0091c2s v1p1313c1s
Cobbold, C.S.W. v3p0216c2s
Cobbold, P.A. v2p0426c1s
Cobbold, R.P. v5p0043c2s v5p0112c2s
Cobbold, T.S. v1p0134c2s v1p0420c1m v1p0437c2s v1p0463c2s v1p0522c2s v1p0967c1m v1p1269c2s v1p1405c2s v3p0368c2s
Cobby, E.F. v5p0232c2s v5p0380c2s v6p0472c1s
Cobden, R. v1p1331c2s
Cobden-Sanderson v5p0070c2s
Cobden-Sanderson, T.J. ... v3p0049c2s v4p0066c2s
Cobern, C.M. v4p0621c1s v6p0060c2s v6p0218c2s v6p0431c1s
Cobham, A. v4p0130c1s
Cobham, C.D. v1p0552c1s
Cobleigh, E.N. v1p0255c1s
Cobleigh, N. v1p1432c1s
Cobleigh, N.E. v1p1087c1s
Coblentz, H.E. v6p0186c2s
Coblenz, F. v6p0065c1s
Coburn, A.G. v4p0274c2s
Coburn, A.L. v6p0043c1s v6p0510c2s
Coburn, C.M. v5p0056c2s v6p0074c1s
Coburn, F.F. v6p0480c2s
Coburn, F.W. v4p0334c2s v5p0030c2s v5p0031c1s v5p0033c1s v5p0121c2s v5p0257c1s v5p0326c2s v5p0511c2s v6p0034c1m v6p0035c2s v6p0066c2s v6p0076c2s v6p0077c1s v6p0142c2s v6p0228c1s v6p0279c1s v6p0282c1s v6p0310c2s v6p0349c2s v6p0394c1s v6p0405c2s v6p0446c1s v6p0485c1s v6p0499c1s v6p0517c2s v6p0637c1s v6p0696c1s v6p0707c1s
Coburn, J. v1p0639c1s
Coburn, W.D. v6p0555c2s
Coche, W.A. v1p0182c1s
Cochet, L'Abbe v1p0039c2m v1p0211c2s v1p0435c2s v1p0824c2s v1p1411c1s
Cochin, A. v1p1258c1s
Cochin, D. v2p0090c2s
Cochran, C.B. v5p0085c2s v6p0004c2s v6p0231c2s
Cochran, C.F. and Armond, D.A.De v5p0587c1s
Cochran, D.B. et al. v3p0025c2s
Cochran, J., Gen. v4p0480c2s
Cochran, S.D. v1p0432c2s
Cochran, S.P. v6p0350c2s
Cochran, T. v1p0997c1s v1p1285c2s v1p1286c1s
Cochran, W. v1p0314c1s v1p1314c1s
Cochran, W.B. v5p0312c1s v6p0009c1s
Cochran, W.C. v5p0141c1s v5p0321c1s
Cochrane, A. v4p0037c2s v4p0439c2s v4p0487c2s v5p0152c1s v5p0575c2s
Cochrane, A.D. v5p0239c2s
Cochrane, A.H.D. v5p0232c1s
Cochrane, C.H. v5p0004c2s
Cochrane, H.A.F. v2p0251c1s
Cochrane, J. v1p0912c1s v1p0956c1s v2p0012c1s v2p0075c1s v2p0086c1s v2p0282c1s v3p0455c2s
Cochrane, J.C. v1p1359c2s
Cochrane, Lord v2p0078c1m
Cochrane, R. v6p0548c2s
Cochrane, S.D. v1p0528c2s
Cock, A. v4p0142c1s
Cock, D. v2p0342c2s
Cock, W.J. v1p0962c1s
Cockburn, A.E. v1p0222c1s
Cockburn, F.G.Le Coste ... v3p0441c2s
Cockburn, J. v1p0317c1s v1p1166c1s
Cockburn, J.A. v5p0039c1s v6p0041c2s v6p0042c1s v6p0203c1s v6p0221c1s
Cockburn, J.D. v3p0303c2s v4p0402c2s v5p0157c1s
Cockburn, W. v1p0985c1s
Cockcroft, T. v5p0185c2s
Cocke, C.P. v5p0120c2s
Cocke, J.R. v4p0271c2s v4p0372c1s v4p0464c1s
Cocke, L. v6p0463c1s v6p0479c1s
Cocke, W.A. v1p0447c1s v1p1103c1s v1p1189c1s v1p1348c1s v2p0106c2s v2p0309c2s v2p0450c1s
Cocke, Z. v3p0103c2s v3p0281c2s v3p0284c1s v3p0467c1s v4p0252c1s v4p0375c2s v6p0303c1s v6p0369c1s
Cocker, B.F. v1p0072c1s v1p0528c2s v1p0826c2s v1p0843c2s v1p0868c1s v1p1095c2s v1p1410c2s
Cockerell, D. v5p0070c2s v6p0073c2s
Cockerell, F.D.A. v6p0056c1s v6p0056c2s
Cockerell, J.D.A. v6p0122c1s
Cockerell, J.D.A. and Garcia, F. v5p0253c1s
Cockerell, S.C. v5p0280c1s
Cockerell, S.P. v4p0325c2s
Cockerell, S.R. v1p0307c1s
Cockerell, T.D.A. v4p0121c1m v4p0203c1s v4p0486c1s v4p0504c2s v4p0529c2s v4p0617c2s v5p0085c2s v5p0125c1m v5p0128c2s v5p0153c2s v5p0210c2s v5p0360c2s v5p0395c2s v5p0454c1s v5p0510c1m v5p0547c2s v6p0013c2s v6p0047c2s v6p0056c2s v6p0066c2s v6p0165c2s v6p0177c2s v6p0203c2s v6p0214c1s v6p0214c2s v6p0230c1s v6p0248c2s v6p0297c1s v6p0309c2s v6p0320c2s v6p0323c1s v6p0368c2s v6p0379c2s v6p0384c2s v6p0410c2s v6p0432c1s v6p0435c1s v6p0451c1m v6p0495c2s v6p0531c2s v6p0537c2m v6p0538c1s v6p0546c2s v6p0552c2s v6p0571c2s v6p0576c2s v6p0684c1s v6p0713c2m
Cockerell, T.D.A. and Harris, W.T. v5p0177c2s
Cockerell, W.B. v6p0657c1s
Cockerell, W.P. v6p0012c2s v6p0288c2s v6p0466c2s v6p0482c1s v6p0611c1s v6p0695c1s
Cockerill, J.A. v4p0305c1s v4p0402c2m v4p0599c1s v4p0636c1s
Cockran, H. v3p0294c2s
Cockran, Henriette v4p0475c2s
Cockran, W.B. v4p0199c1s
Cockrell, E. v5p0133c1s v5p0272c2s v6p0559c1s
Cockshott, J.J. v4p0330c2s
Cockton, H. v1p1243c2s
Coddington, V.W. v2p0003c2s
Codington, E.W. v4p0199c2s
Codman, A.A. v4p0050c1s v4p0392c1s
Codman, H.W. v3p0215c1s
Codman, J. v1p0034c1s v1p0158c1s v1p0872c1s v1p1068c1s v1p1360c1s v2p0214c1s v2p0401c1s v3p0222c2s v3p0391c2s v5p0172c1s v5p0297c2s v5p0362c1s
Codman, J., 2d v3p0074c2s
Codman, J.T. v5p0135c2s
Codman, S.P. v4p0279c1s
Codrington, R. v4p0107c1s v5p0007c1s v5p0020c1s
Codrington, R. et al. v6p0542c2s
Codrington, R.H. v2p0282c2m v4p0205c1s v4p0364c1s
Cody, A.S. v4p0015c1s v4p0163c1s
Cody, B.A. v4p0350c2s
Cody, E.G. v2p0041c1s v2p0294c2s v2p0326c2s
Cody, H.A. v4p0281c2s v6p0098c1s
Cody, L.S. v4p0097c1s
Cody, S. v6p0504c2s
Cody, W.F. v4p0270c1s v5p0498c1s
Coe, C.C. v2p0318c2s v2p0323c1s v4p0148c1s
Coe, C.H. v4p0027c1s v4p0203c1s v4p0220c1s v4p0368c1s
Coe, D.A. and Currie, J.A. v3p0065c1s
Coe, D.B. v1p0086c1s v1p0298c1s
Coe, E.B. v1p0275c1s v2p0211c1s v3p0198c2s
Coe, E.M. v3p0011c2s v4p0198c1s v4p0330c1s v4p0408c2s v4p0474c2s
Coe, G.A. v4p0439c1s v4p0479c1s v5p0023c1s v5p0319c1s v5p0483c2m v5p0576c1s v6p0536c2s v6p0537c2s v6p0538c1s v6p0538c2s
Coe, G.S. v1p1232c2m v1p1344c1s v2p0033c1s v2p0033c2s v2p0403c1s v4p0144c1s v4p0525c2s
Coe, L.W. v2p0094c1s v2p0406c2s
Coe, Mrs. and Lucas, E.V.. v6p0359c2s
Coe, Sadie E. v5p0594c1s
Coe, W.R. v5p0404c1s v6p0155c2s v6p0325c1s v6p0479c1s
Coetzee, P. v6p0333c2s
Coffey, A.B. v5p0114c1s v5p0621c1s
Coffey, F.G. v6p0605c2s v6p0624c1s
Coffey, G. v3p0221c2s v3p0322c1s v6p0470c2s
Coffin, A.F. v5p0627c2s
Coffin, B.C. v3p0324c1s
Coffin, C. v1p0181c2s v1p0847c2s
Coffin, C.C. v1p0329c1s v1p0556c2s v1p0714c1s v1p1179c2s v1p1346c2s v1p1347c2s v2p0016c2s v2p0110c1s v2p0243c1s v3p0258c1s v3p0269c2s v3p0455c2s
Coffin, C.H. v5p0119c2s v5p0215c1s
Coffin, C.P. v5p0348c1s
Coffin, C.R. v6p0239c2s
Coffin, Col. v1p0164c2s
Coffin, F.J. v5p0130c1s
Coffin, G.M. v6p0162c1s
Coffin, H.A. v6p0136c1s
Coffin, J. v1p0006c1s v1p0222c1s v1p0737c2s v1p0925c2s
Coffin, N.W. v1p0271c2s
Coffin, P. v1p0809c1s
Coffin, R.B. v1p0397c1s
Coffin, R.F. v3p0001c1s v3p0063c2s v3p0157c2s v3p0223c1s v3p0467c2s v3p0473c2s v3p0474c1m
Coffin, R.J. v3p0409c1s
Coffin, V. v4p0469c1s v5p0074c1s v5p0090c1s v5p0474c1s

v5p0505c1s v5p0601c1s v6p0650c1s
v6p0651c1s
Coffin, W.A. v3p0035c1s
v3p0103c1s v3p0320c1s v4p0036c1s
v4p0040c1s v4p0069c1s v4p0101c1s
v4p0146c1s v4p0274c1s v4p0422c1s
v4p0453c2s v4p0503c2s v4p0629c1s
v5p0048c1s v5p0098c2s v5p0133c1s
v5p0220c2s v5p0269c1s v5p0384c1s
v5p0448c2s v5p0504c1s v6p0032c2s
Coffin, W.E. v4p0048c1s
Coffin, W.F. v1p0166c1s
v1p0194c2s
Coffinbury, W.L. v2p0219c1s
Coffman, J.M. v6p0066c1s
Coggeshall, A.R. v1p1172c2s
Coggeshall, F. v2p0281c1s
Coggeshall, S.J. v1p0244c1s
Coggeshall, S.W. v1p0830c1m
v1p0831c1s v1p0879c1s v1p1118c1s
v1p1413c1s
Coggeshall, W.T. v1p0561c1s
v1p0740c1s v1p0938c2s
Coggin, F.G. v2p0078c2s
v4p0197c2s
Coggins, A.H. v5p0281c2s
Coggins, P.H. v5p0024c2s
v5p0237c2s v5p0419c2s v5p0566c1s
v5p0634c1s v6p0056c2s v6p0147c2s
Coghill, A.L. v5p0365c1s
v5p0420c1s
Coghill, R.P., Mrs. v5p0134c2s
Coghlan, H.C. v2p0457c1s
Coghlan, J.J. v6p0506c2s
Coghlan, T.A. v2p0364c1s
Cogshall, W.A. v5p0372c1s
Cogswell, F. v1p1258c2s
Cogswell, F.H. v4p0477c2s
v4p0517c1s
Cogswell, G.A. v4p0036c2s
Cogswell, G.Z. v5p0514c1s
Cogswell, J.G. v1p0752c2s
v1p0832c2s v1p1160c1s v1p1396c1s
Cogswell, W. v1p0370c1s
v1p0444c1s v1p1010c1s v1p1018c2s
v1p1272c2s
Cohen, A. v6p0322c2s
Cohen, A.H. v2p0036c1s
Cohen, A.R. v2p0073c2s
v2p0130c2s
Cohen, D.S. v1p0235c1s
Cohen, E. v2p0140c1s
Cohen, E.G. v5p0233c1s
v5p0579c1s
Cohen, Ellen G. v5p0431c2s
Cohen, F. v1p1054c1s
Cohen, H. v4p0302c2s
v5p0475c1s v6p0483c1s v6p0652c1s
Cohen, H. and Morgan-Browne, H.
v6p0355c2s
Cohen, H.A. v3p0462c1s
Cohen, J. v2p0320c1s
v3p0230c1s
Cohen, M. v3p0248c2m
Cohen, M.M. v2p0199c2s
v3p0057c1s v4p0076c1s v4p0324c1s
Cohen, N.L. v3p0238c2s
v6p0571c1s
Cohen, S.S. v5p0620c2s
Cohen, W.S. v5p0007c1s
Cohn, A. v2p0192c1s
v3p0052c1s v4p0163c2s v4p0212c2s
v5p0080c1s v5p0153c2s v5p0168c2s
v5p0302c1s v5p0508c2s v6p0423c1s
v6p0480c1s
Cohn, Ad. v3p0026c2s
Cohn, F. v2p0072c2s
v3p0167c1s
Cohn, G. v1p1026c1s
v3p0210c2s v3p0421c1s v4p0126c1s
v4p0127c2s v4p0247c2s v4p0450c1s
v4p0472c1s v5p0318c2s v5p0478c1s
v6p0156c2s v6p0254c2s v6p0506c2s
v6p0632c2s
Cohn, H. v1p0437c2s
Cohn, H.L. v6p0362c1s
Cohn, L. v4p0438c2s
v5p0446c2s
Cohn, M.M. v1p0452c2s
v3p0024c1s
Coissy, H.de v1p0806c2s
v1p1373c1s
Coit, D. v2p0123c1s
v2p0336c1s
Coit, H.A. v2p0210c1s
v3p0052c2s v3p0377c2s
Coit, J.B. v6p0041c1s
Coit, S. v2p0297c1s
v4p0187c2s v4p0300c1s v4p0485c2s
v4p0591c1s
Coit, S.T. v1p0306c1s
Coit, Stanton v6p0259c1s
Coit, T.W. v1p0117c2s
v1p0446c1s v1p0728c1s v1p1326c1s
Coke, D.F.T. v6p0245c2s
Coke, J.T. v2p0091c2s
Coke, T. v1p0830c2s
Coke, Talbot, Mrs. v5p0636c1s
Cokely, M. v5p0353c1m
v6p0355c1s
Coker, E.G. and Adams, F.D.
v6p0546c1s
Coker, R.E. v6p0471c1s
Col, Bennet v5p0030c1s
Colajanni, N. v4p0294c1s
v5p0269c2s v5p0300c1s
Colam, J. v2p0015c1s
Colam, W.N. v2p0063c2s
Colani, T. v1p0121c2s
v1p1147c2s v2p0165c2s v2p0187c2s
Colardeau, E. v4p0173c2s
Colbach, H. v2p0166c2s
v2p0246c2s
Colbeck, A. v6p0078c1s
v6p0185c1s
Colbeck, Alfred v6p0395c2s
Colbeck, Capt. v6p0023c1s
Colbert, E. v1p0227c2m
v1p0376c2s v1p0382c1s v1p1244c2s
v1p1269c1s v1p1367c1s v6p0677c1s
Colborn, G.R. v5p0127c1s
Colborne, J. v2p0410c2s
Colbron, G.I. v5p0348c2s
v6p0252c2s v6p0305c2s v6p0402c2s
v6p0678c2s
Colbron, Grace I. v5p0106c1s
v5p0171c1s v5p0548c1s v6p0003c2s
v6p0164c1s
Colburn, E.F. v6p0566c2s
Colburn, F.W. v6p0279c2s
v6p0632c2s
Colburn, G.F. v1p1289c1s
Colburn, J. v1p0111c1s
v1p0809c1s v4p0072c1s
Colburn, J.E. v6p0208c2s
Colburn, L. v1p0664c1s
Colburn, R.J. v1p0073c1s
Colburn, R.T. v1p0722c1s
v1p0956c2s v4p0420c2s v4p0531c2s
v4p0565c1s v5p0325c1s
Colburn, S.P. v5p0337c2s
Colburn, W. v1p0057c2s
v1p0281c2s
Colburn, W.G. v1p1424c2s
Colburn, Z. v1p0145c2m
v1p0162c1s v1p0665c1s v1p0759c1m
v3p0139c1s
Colby, C. v1p0560c1s
Colby, C.B. v6p0613c2s
Colby, C.W. v3p0141c1s
v4p0012c1m v4p0070c1s v4p0080c1s
v4p0181c1s v4p0248c1s v4p0303c1s
v4p0513c2s v5p0055c1s v5p0096c2s
v5p0102c2s v5p0116c2s v5p0173c2s
v5p0217c1s v5p0217c2s v5p0218c2m
v5p0221c2s v5p0252c2s v5p0260c1s
v5p0266c2s v5p0300c1s v5p0305c1s
v5p0356c2s v5p0374c1s v5p0398c1s
v5p0404c1s v5p0404c2s v5p0434c1s
v6p0022c2s v6p0096c2s v6p0110c1s
v6p0149c2s v6p0157c1s v6p0183c2s
v6p0207c1s v6p0241c1s v6p0245c1s
v6p0273c2m v6p0287c1s v6p0292c2s
v6p0332c1s v6p0353c2s v6p0358c1s
v6p0367c2s v6p0379c2s v6p0395c2s
v6p0404c1s v6p0415c1s v6p0442c1m
v6p0442c2s v6p0473c1s v6p0507c1s
v6p0525c1s v6p0539c1s v6p0577c2s
v6p0585c1s v6p0622c2s
Colby, C.W.C. v6p0206c1s
Colby, Clara B. v5p0253c1s
Colby, F.M. v1p0309c1s
v1p0367c1s v1p0439c2s v1p0461c1s
v1p0590c2s v1p0874c1s v1p0926c1s
v1p0989c1s v1p1105c2s v1p1195c2s
v1p1299c1s v1p1327c2s v1p1373c2s
v1p1411c1s v2p0031c2s v2p0035c2s
v2p0097c2s v2p0150c1s v2p0178c2m
v2p0195c2s v2p0205c1s v2p0243c2s
v2p0254c2s v2p0261c2s v2p0341c2s
v2p0350c1m v2p0361c1s v2p0375c1s
v2p0418c1s v2p0424c1s v2p0425c2s
v2p0434c2s v2p0439c2s v2p0470c1s
v3p0024c1s v3p0037c1s v3p0060c1s
v3p0100c2s v3p0180c2s v3p0240c1s
v3p0318c1s v3p0340c1s v3p0435c2s
v3p0462c2s v5p0194c1s v5p0646c1s
v6p0181c1s v6p0202c1s v6p0333c1s
v6p0352c2s v6p0379c2s v6p0450c2s
v6p0456c1s v6p0517c1s v6p0617c2s
Colby, J.F. v1p1285c1s
v2p0107c1s v2p0119c1s v4p0323c2s
Colby, J.M. v3p0465c2s
Colby, Josephine v6p0350c2s
Colby, L.W. v4p0282c1s
Colby, T.M. v2p0203c1s
Colby, W. v6p0404c1s
Colby-lucas, F. v5p0020c1s
Colchester, Baron v3p0089c2s
Colchester, Lord v2p0273c1s
v2p0404c1s v3p0137c1s v3p0419c2s
v5p0186c2s v6p0391c2s
Colchester-Wemyss, M.W. .. v6p0508c1s
v6p0508c2s
Colcleugh, E.S. v4p0035c1s
v4p0375c1s
Colclough, J.A.G. v3p0224c2s
Colclough, J.G. v4p0290c1s
v4p0303c1s v4p0353c2s v4p0480c2s
v4p0589c2s
Colcock, A.J. v5p0201c2s
Colcock, A.T. v5p0052c1s
v5p0275c2s v5p0313c1s v6p0388c2s
Colcord, A.E. et al. v6p0620c2s
Colcord, W.A. v4p0150c1s
Colden, C. v1p0458c2s
Coldridge, W. v3p0414c1s
Coldwell, M. v1p0621c1s
Coldwell, S.L. v2p0081c2s
Cole, A. v1p0288c2s
v4p0316c1s v4p0563c1s
Cole, A.D. v4p0441c2s
v6p0289c1s
Cole, A.L. v5p0578c2s
Cole, A.M.F. v6p0388c1s
v6p0547c2s
Cole, A.N. v1p0770c1s
v1p1048c1s v1p1099c2s
Cole, A.S. v2p0308c2s
v2p0407c1s v3p0135c2s v3p0239c2m
v3p0293c2s v3p0419c2s v3p0420c1s
v4p0178c2s v4p0316c1m v4p0316c2m
v6p0357c2s v6p0626c2s
Cole, A.W. v1p0175c2s
v1p0324c2s v1p0790c1s v1p0864c2s
Cole, Alan S. v2p0436c1s
v6p0202c1s
Cole, C. v1p1330c2s
Cole, C.A. v1p0525c2s
v1p0658c2s v1p1145c2s
Cole, D. v1p0261c2s
v1p0926c1s
Cole, D.U. v1p0793c1s
Cole, E.E. v6p0629c1s
Cole, E.M. v3p0474c2s
v4p0141c2s v4p0268c1s v4p0327c1s
v4p0485c2s v4p0635c2s v5p0413c2s
v5p0594c1s v6p0660c2s
Cole, F.N. v6p0017c2s
Cole, G.A.J. v4p0289c1s
v4p0289c2s v5p0013c2s v5p0020c1s
v5p0049c1s v5p0050c1s v5p0068c2s
v5p0134c2m v5p0154c1s v5p0166c2s
v5p0172c2s v5p0195c1s v5p0201c2s
v5p0229c1s v5p0297c1s v5p0314c1s
v5p0315c2s v5p0389c2s v5p0614c1s
v6p0185c2s v6p0257c2m v6p0367c1s
v6p0521c1s
Cole, G.B. v3p0277c1s
Cole, G.F. v3p0373c2s
Cole, G.R.F. v1p0235c1s
v1p0695c2s v1p1321c1s
Cole, G.W. v2p0051c2s
v3p0049c2s v3p0070c1m v3p0248c2s
v4p0058c1s v4p0198c1s v4p0329c1s
v4p0329c2m v5p0061c1s v5p0334c2s
v6p0370c2s
Cole, G.W. et al. v4p0408c2s
Cole, H. v3p0020c1s
v4p0257c2s v4p0366c2s v5p0566c2s
Cole, H. and Redgrave v1p0064c1s
Cole, J.A. v5p0098c2s
Cole, J.F. v5p0269c2s
Cole, J.J. v1p0865c2s
Cole, J.L. v3p0249c2s
Cole, J.R. v4p0122c1s
Cole, J.W. v4p0179c1s
v5p0139c2s v5p0621c2s
Cole, L.J. v6p0524c1s
Cole, L'A. v4p0022c1s
Cole, L'Aigle v4p0398c1s
v4p0447c2s
Cole, Lucy K. v5p0614c1s
Cole, M.E. v4p0575c1s
Cole, M.M. v1p0024c2s
v1p0952c2s v1p1151c2s
Cole, N. v1p1405c1s
Cole, N.A. v5p0169c2s
v5p0271c1s v5p0475c2s
Cole, P.M. v3p0053c1s
v4p0103c1s v4p0217c2s v4p0616c1s
v4p0619c1s
Cole, P.McA. v3p0143c2s
v5p0576c2s
Cole, R. v1p0220c1s
Cole, R.L. v3p0018c2m
Cole, R.S. v4p0542c2s
Cole, S.D. v6p0207c2s
Cole, S.E. v1p1129c2s
Cole, S.V. v2p0461c1s
v3p0206c1s v4p0564c2s v6p0195c1s
v6p0312c1s
Cole, S.V. et al. v2p0139c2s
Cole, S.W. v4p0389c1s
Cole, T. v1p0034c1s
v1p1195c1s v2p0396c1s v4p0065c2s
v4p0145c1s v4p0160c1s v4p0202c1s
v4p0246c1s v4p0259c2s v4p0262c2s
v4p0349c1s v4p0361c1s v4p0368c1s
v4p0418c1s v4p0454c2s v4p0480c1s
v4p0494c1s v4p0494c2s v4p0548c1s
v4p0569c1s v4p0570c2s v4p0600c1s
v6p0099c1s v6p0562c2s
Cole, T. and Stillman, W.J.
v3p0013c2s v3p0147c2s v3p0173c1s
v3p0258c2s v3p0266c2s v3p0270c1s
v3p0270c2s v3p0274c1s v3p0313c2s
v3p0317c2s
Cole, W. v1p0201c1s
v1p0604c1s

Cole, W.E. v6p0516c2s
Cole, W.I. v4p0136c2s
v5p0072c1s v5p0072c2m v5p0106c1s
v5p0242c1s v5p0356c2s v5p0423c2s
v6p0076c1s v6p0078c1s
Cole, W.M. v3p0137c1s
v3p0217c2s v4p0620c1s v6p0207c2s
Cole, W.R. v4p0534c1s
Cole, W.W. v6p0295c2s
Coleborn, M. v5p0085c2s
Colebrooke, J. v1p0207c2s
v1p0272c1s v1p0526c2s
Colebrooke, W. v2p0332c2s
Colegrove, C.P. v4p0466c2s
Colegrove, F.W. v5p0330c2s
v5p0369c2s v5p0480c2s
Coleman, A. v6p0236c2s
v6p0493c2s
Coleman, A.E. v1p0349c1s
Coleman, A.I.du P. v5p0040c2s
v5p0072c1s v5p0151c2s v5p0190c1s
v5p0278c1s v6p0110c2s v6p0228c1s
v6p0336c1s v6p0368c1m v6p0396c1s
v6p0429c1s v6p0679c2s v6p0683c1s
Coleman, A.P. v3p0044c2s
v3p0055c1s v3p0093c1s v3p0331c2s
v3p0380c2s v4p0019c2s v4p0035c1s
v4p0204c1s v4p0227c1s v6p0080c1s
v6p0186c1s v6p0449c1s
Coleman, Ambrose v6p0493c1s
Coleman, C. v3p0061c2s
v4p0012c1s v5p0472c1s v5p0548c1s
v5p0579c1s v6p0030c2s v6p0033c1s
v6p0109c1s v6p0127c2s v6p0152c1s
v6p0278c2s v6p0318c2s v6p0431c1s
v6p0537c2s v6p0649c2s
Coleman, C.W. v1p0034c1s
v3p0020c1s v3p0028c2s v3p0226c1s
v3p0401c2s v3p0450c2m v4p0554c2s
Coleman, C.W., jr. v2p0024c2s
v2p0088c1s
Coleman, Caryl v4p0228c1s
Coleman, Dr. v1p0796c2s
Coleman, E.G. and Gwin, W.M.
v3p0187c1s
Coleman, E.J. v3p0400c2s
v4p0077c1s
Coleman, E.T. v2p0325c2s
Coleman, G.D. v4p0301c1s
Coleman, G.P. v6p0022c2s
v6p0421c1s v6p0644c1s
Coleman, H.W. v5p0298c2s
v6p0412c1s
Coleman, J. v2p0002c2s
v2p0035c2s v2p0057c2s v2p0118c2s
v2p0338c1s v2p0349c1s v2p0365c2s
v2p0416c2s v2p0467c2s v3p0014c1s
v3p0112c2s v3p0157c1s v3p0262c1s
v3p0299c2s v3p0406c2s v3p0414c2s
v4p0256c2s v4p0309c2s v4p0324c2s
v4p0376c2s v5p0575c2s v5p0642c2s
Coleman, J. and Baynham, G.W.
v4p0267c2s
Coleman, J.J. v1p0791c1s
Coleman, J.S. v4p0470c2s
Coleman, John v4p0162c2s
Coleman, K.B. v5p0268c2s
v5p0481c1s v6p0475c1s
Coleman, L. v1p0336c1s
v1p0431c2s v1p0695c2s v1p0960c2s
v1p1088c1s v1p1139c2s v1p1200c2s
v1p1202c2s v2p0180c1s v2p0238c1s
v2p0369c1s v3p0083c2s v4p0479c2s
Coleman, M.W. v4p0632c2s
Coleman, R.A. v1p1149c1s
Coleman, R.E. v1p0706c1s
Coleman, R.F. v1p0706c1s
Coleman, R.T. v1p0334c2s
Coleman, W.E. v2p0007c2s
Coleman, W.H. v4p0074c2s
Coleman, W.M. v5p0320c2s
v5p0592c2s
Coleman, W.P. v6p0491c2s
Coleman, W.T. v3p0449c2s
Colenso, F.E. v1p1322c1s
v2p0483c2s
Colenso, H.E. v5p0007c2s
Colenso, H.E. and Werner, A.
v4p0393c1s
Colenso, Harriet and
Fox-Bourne, H.R. v4p0156c1s
Colenso, J.W. and Martineau, R.
v1p0313c1s
Colenso, W. v4p0354c2s
Coler, B.S. v5p0085c1s
v5p0096c2s v5p0102c1m v5p0116c2s
v5p0120c1s v5p0130c2s v5p0163c2s
v5p0391c2s v5p0406c2s v5p0407c1m
v5p0407c2m v5p0408c1s v5p0457c2s
v5p0606c1s v6p0452c1s v6p0454c1s
v6p0507c1s
Coleridge, B.J.S. v6p0108c1s
Coleridge, C. v5p0632c2s
Coleridge, C.R. v3p0150c1s
v3p0309c1s v4p0067c2s v4p0316c2s
v4p0568c2s v5p0644c1s v6p0505c2s
Coleridge, G. v5p0491c1s
v6p0168c1s
Coleridge, H. v1p0416c1s
v1p0453c2s v1p0596c1s v1p0677c1s
v1p1056c2s v1p1288c1s
Coleridge, H.A. v1p0554c1s
Coleridge, H.J. v1p0016c2s
v1p0046c2s v1p0087c2s v1p0128c1s
v1p0128c2s v1p0202c1s v1p0232c2s
v1p0324c2s v1p0432c1s v1p0446c2s
v1p0454c2s v1p0557c2s v1p0640c2s
v1p0641c1s v1p0687c1s v1p0806c1s
v1p0807c1s v1p0850c1s v1p0850c2s
v1p0861c2s v1p0966c2s v1p0977c1s
v1p0980c2s v1p1013c1s v1p1029c1s
v1p1053c2s v1p1082c1s v1p1120c1s
v1p1134c2s v1p1143c1s v1p1263c1s
v1p1359c1s v1p1373c1s v1p1435c1m
Coleridge, H.M.E. v5p0580c1s
Coleridge, H.N. v1p0401c2s
v1p0419c1s v1p0554c2s v1p0555c2s
v1p1010c2s
Coleridge, J., Sir v1p1429c2s
Coleridge, J.D. v1p0173c1s
v1p0273c2m v3p0244c2s
Coleridge, J.H. v1p0603c1s
Coleridge, Lord v1p0155c1s
v3p0020c2s v3p0307c1s v3p0346c2s
v3p0387c1s v3p0428c2s v4p0168c2s
v6p0172c2s
Coleridge, Lord and Carpenter, W.B.
v2p0462c2s
Coleridge, M.E. v5p0222c1s
v5p0322c2s v5p0534c2s v6p0284c1s
Coleridge, N.E. v6p0549c1s
Coleridge, S. v5p0020c2s
v5p0613c2m v6p0680c2m
Coleridge, S.T. v1p0516c2s
v1p0806c1s v1p0813c2s v1p0870c1s
v1p1220c2s v1p1381c1s v4p0018c1s
v4p0539c1s
Coles, A. v1p0775c1s
v2p0149c1s v2p0150c1s
Coles, C.S. v4p0365c1s
v4p0414c1s
Coles, Ed. v1p0624c2s
Coles, F.R. v5p0150c1s
v5p0156c1s v5p0163c1s v5p0279c2s
v5p0317c2s v5p0515c2s v6p0359c2s
Coles, S.C. v5p0185c2s
Coles, S.F. v4p0245c2s
v4p0350c2s v4p0436c2s v4p0491c2s
v4p0510c1s
Coles, S.L. v4p0418c2s
Coles, W.D. v4p0597c1s
Colestock, H.T. v5p0558c2s
v6p0137c1s v6p0537c1s v6p0537c2s
Coleston, R.E. v2p0134c2s
Coley, J.E. v3p0395c2s
Coley, S. v1p0141c2s
v1p0248c2s
Colfax, S. v1p0391c1s
Colford, J.K. v6p0383c2s
Colgan, N. v1p0140c2s
v1p0147c1s v1p0175c1s v1p0461c1s
v1p0672c1s v1p0837c2s v1p0872c2s
v1p1008c1s v1p1011c2s v1p1282c1s
v1p1296c2s v1p1365c1s v1p1367c2s
v2p0360c2s v2p0460c1s
Colgate, A.W. v1p0053c2s
v1p0054c1s v1p0073c2s v1p0709c2s
v1p1078c2s v4p0428c2s
Colgate, J.C. et al. v6p0002c1s
Colger, V. v1p0636c1s
Colie, E.M. v5p0304c2s
v5p0323c2s
Colin, A. v1p1248c2s
v6p0206c2s
Colinet, P. v3p0058c2s
Coll, A. v5p0115c2s
v5p0204c1s v5p0214c1s v5p0480c1s
v6p0025c2s v6p0056c2s v6p0181c2s
v6p0232c2s v6p0470c2s v6p0619c2s
Coll, B. v4p0028c2s
v4p0418c2s v4p0463c1s
Coll, J.A. v5p0539c1s
Colladon, Prof. v1p1143c2s
Collar, M.A. v6p0370c2s
Collar, W.C. v2p0408c2s
v3p0091c1s v3p0091c2s v3p0378c2s
v4p0321c2m
Collcutt, T.E. v6p0277c2s
Collen, E. v6p0183c2s
Collen, E.H.H. v6p0313c2s
Coller, E. v1p0116c1s
v1p0800c1s v1p0930c1s v1p1145c2s
v1p1202c1s v1p1204c2s
Colles, C.J. v3p0437c1s
Colles, G.W. v4p0159c2s
v4p0545c2s v5p0586c1s v6p0096c2s
v6p0415c1m
Colles, G.Wetmore v6p0325c1s
Colles, H.C. v6p0498c2s
Colles, R. v4p0398c2s
v6p0345c2s v6p0566c2s v6p0629c1s
v6p0629c2s
Colles, W.M. v2p0327c1s
v3p0154c1s v3p0257c1s v3p0338c2s
v4p0184c1s v5p0137c1s v6p0149c1m
v6p0149c2s v6p0379c1s
Colles, W.M. and Williamson, G.C.
v6p0257c1s
Collet, C.D. v4p0050c1s
v4p0402c1s
Collet, C.F. v3p0470c2s
v4p0356c2s v5p0615c2s v5p0637c1s
v5p0638c1s
Collet, C.E. and Bonar, J.
v3p0452c1s
Collet, O.W. v2p0087c2s
v2p0267c1m v2p0302c2s v2p0383c1s
v2p0383c2m v2p0471c1s v3p0307c2s
Collet, S.D. v1p0156c2s
v1p0618c1s v1p0635c1s v1p1301c1s
v2p0054c2s
Colleton, R.A. v5p0195c1s
Collett, A. v6p0058c2s
v6p0068c2s
Collett, Clara E. v5p0636c1s
Collett, H. v4p0298c2s
Collett, O.W. v2p0238c1s
v2p0293c1s
Collett, S.D. v1p0410c1s
v1p1207c1s
Collett-Sandars, W. v1p0068c1s
Colley, C.E. v3p0287c1s
Colley, Lady v6p0137c2s
Colley, R. v1p0115c1s
v4p0006c1s
Collie, J.N. v6p0617c1s
Collie, Norman v5p0491c2s
Collier, A.L. v2p0321c2s
Collier, C. v1p0818c2s
v1p1414c1s v2p0055c1s
Collier, C.V. v6p0548c2s
Collier, H.P. v3p0013c2s
Collier, J. v1p1062c1s
v1p1217c2s v4p0453c2s v5p0051c1s
v5p0128c1s v5p0128c2s v6p0026c1s
v6p0041c1s v6p0041c2s v6p0042c1s
v6p0042c2s v6p0130c1s v6p0138c2m
v6p0222c1s v6p0236c1s v6p0254c2s
v6p0465c1s v6p0582c1s v6p0600c2s
v6p0608c2s v6p0622c1s v6p0674c2s
Collier, J.F. v2p0077c2s
Collier, J.N. v6p0546c2s
Collier, J.P. v1p0085c2s
v1p0171c2s v1p0547c2s v1p0565c2s
v1p0585c1s v1p0763c1s v1p0928c2s
v1p1081c2m v1p1184c1s v1p1220c1s
Collier, J.P. and Cooper, W.D.
v1p0929c2s
Collier, J.T. v2p0303c2s
v2p0377c1s
Collier, M. v5p0458c2s
Collier, M.A. v1p1401c1s
Collier, P. v1p1016c2s
v4p0101c1s v4p0185c1s v4p0231c2m
v4p0258c1s v4p0261c2s v4p0405c1s
v4p0460c2s v4p0474c2s v4p0506c2s
v5p0037c1s v5p0239c1m v5p0547c1s
v6p0215c2s
Collier, R.L. v1p0108c1s
v2p0229c2s v2p0277c2s
Collier, R.P. v1p0959c1s
Collier, R.R. v1p1245c1s
Collier, T.S. v2p0110c1s
v2p0272c1s
Collier, W. v1p0104c2s
v1p0707c1s v1p1029c1s v3p0014c2s
Collier, W.F. v4p0555c1s
Collier, W.P. v5p0424c2s
Collin, C. v4p0062c2s
Collin, C.A. v2p0355c1s
v3p0344c2m v4p0140c1s v4p0257c2s
Collin, G.L. v5p0042c1s
v6p0020c2s v6p0448c1s v6p0524c2s
v6p0582c1s v6p0594c1s
Collingridge, G. v4p0297c2s
Collings, J. v2p0247c2s
v2p0381c1s v4p0008c1s
Collings, T.C. v4p0113c2s
v4p0404c2s v4p0516c1s
Collings, W. v1p0058c2s
Collingwood, C. v1p0835c2s
v1p1151c2s v1p1329c2s v2p0001c2s
v2p0351c2s v2p0393c1s
Collingwood, F. v1p0161c1s
v1p0280c2s v1p1414c1s v2p0008c2s
v2p0055c2s v2p0072c2s v2p0141c1s
v2p0427c2s v4p0116c1s
Collingwood, G. v2p0215c1s
Collingwood, S. v5p0164c1s
Collingwood, S.D. v5p0164c1s
Collingwood, W. v5p0255c2s
v5p0276c1s v5p0469c2s
Collingwood, W.G. v6p0099c1s
v6p0159c2s v6p0286c1s v6p0325c2s
v6p0514c2s v6p0555c1m
Collins, A. v2p0183c1s
Collins, A.C. v3p0166c2s
Collins, A.F. v6p0197c1s
v6p0636c2m
Collins, A.M. v2p0284c2s
Collins, A.S. v1p0457c1s
v1p1327c1s
Collins, C. v1p0923c2s
v1p1121c1s v4p0528c2s v6p0017c2s
Collins, C.A. v1p0108c2s
v1p0134c1s v1p0437c2s v1p1253c1s
Collins, C.H. v6p0032c1s
Collins, C.M. v4p0433c1s
Collins, C.T. v3p0217c1s
Collins, C.T., Mrs. v6p0165c2s

v6p0426c1s
Collins, Charles v6p0027c2s
Collins, Churton and Swinburne, A.C.
v2p0361c1s
Collins, D.C. v3p0032c1s
Collins, D.E. v4p0204c1s
Collins, E. v3p0282c2s
v3p0473c1s v5p0570c2s v6p0699c2s
Collins, E.D. v5p0015c1s
Collins, F. v2p0330c1s
v2p0482c1s v6p0676c2s
Collins, F.H. v3p0250c1s
v3p0287c2s v3p0314c2s
Collins, G. v1p0690c1s
v1p0794c1s v2p0081c2s v2p0117c1s
v2p0235c2s v2p0454c2s v2p0465c2s
v3p0213c1s
Collins, G.D. v2p0086c2s
v4p0116c1s
Collins, G.F. v6p0117c2s
v6p0490c1s
Collins, G.L. v6p0288c2s
Collins, G.N. v6p0576c2s
Collins, H. v3p0137c2s
v3p0283c2s
Collins, H.H. v3p0125c1s
Collins, H.L. v5p0477c1s
Collins, J. v1p0562c1s
v3p0051c2s v3p0368c2s
Collins, J.A. v4p0126c1s
v4p0261c2s
Collins, J.A. and Wood, H.
v5p0382c2s
Collins, J.B. v1p0647c1s
Collins, J.C. v1p1031c1s
v1p1183c2s v2p0144c1s v2p0183c2s
v2p0428c2s v3p0052c2m v3p0086c2s
v3p0140c2s v3p0211c1s v3p0253c1s
v3p0355c1s v3p0445c2s v4p0076c1s
v4p0265c1s v4p0320c2s v4p0340c2s
v5p0097c2s v5p0192c2s v5p0324c2s
v5p0384c1s v5p0428c2s v5p0499c2s
v5p0522c1s v5p0523c2s v5p0578c2s
v5p0605c1s v5p0612c2s v5p0640c2s
v6p0090c2s v6p0157c2s v6p0256c2s
v6p0272c2s v6p0339c2s v6p0371c1s
v6p0405c1s v6p0411c2s v6p0418c1s
v6p0427c1s v6p0461c1s v6p0542c2s
v6p0587c1m v6p0588c1s
Collins, J.F. v4p0416c1s
Collins, J.H. v3p0079c1s
v5p0137c2s v6p0016c2s v6p0275c1s
v6p0346c1s v6p0452c1s
Collins, J.J. v1p1257c1s
v2p0091c2s
Collins, J.V. v4p0287c2s
v4p0367c2s v4p0512c2s v5p0012c1s
v5p0366c1s v6p0030c1m v6p0175c1s
v6p0406c1s
Collins, J.W. v5p0209c1s
v5p0209c2s v5p0604c1s
Collins, James v6p0073c2s
v6p0379c2s
Collins, K. v6p0067c1s
v6p0511c1s
Collins, M. v1p0036c1s
v1p0044c2s v1p0057c1s v1p0071c1s
v1p0106c2s v1p0160c2s v1p0203c1s
v1p0205c1s v1p0221c2s v1p0244c2s
v1p0274c1s v1p0277c1s v1p0342c1s
v1p0421c1s v1p0447c2s v1p0525c1s
v1p0575c1m v1p0623c2s v1p0626c2s
v1p0627c2s v1p0652c1s v1p0673c2s
v1p0698c2s v1p0716c2s v1p0722c2s
v1p0787c1s v1p0817c2s v1p0878c2s
v1p0950c2s v1p0952c1s v1p0957c2s
v1p0983c1s v1p1074c1s v1p1121c2s
v1p1131c2s v1p1132c1s v1p1145c1s
v1p1201c2s v1p1255c1s v1p1275c1s
v1p1307c1s v1p1316c1s v1p1336c1s
v1p1339c1s v1p1368c1s v1p1407c2s
v1p1420c1s v2p0026c2s v2p0310c2s
Collins, M. and Lillie, J.
v2p0293c2s
Collins, M., Mrs. v1p0785c2s
Collins, M.A. v2p0460c1s
Collins, N. v1p0352c2s
Collins, P. v6p0077c2s
v6p0229c2s v6p0230c1s v6p0320c2s
v6p0321c1s v6p0404c2s v6p0418c1s
v6p0620c2s
Collins, R. v2p0405c1s
Collins, R.H. v1p0706c1s
Collins, S.C. v1p0568c1s
v1p1070c1s
Collins, S.M.A. v1p0908c1s
Collins, V. v4p0065c2s
v6p0402c2s v6p0585c2s
Collins, V.L. v6p0516c2s
v6p0532c1s v6p0697c1s
Collins, V.S. v4p0128c2s
Collins, Vere v6p0574c1s
Collins, W. v1p0139c2s
v1p0199c1s v1p0264c2s v1p0300c2s
v1p0336c1s v1p0336c2s v1p0366c1s
v1p0370c1s v1p0442c1s v1p0445c2s
v1p0492c2s v1p0496c1s v1p0574c1s
v1p0803c2s v1p0866c2s v1p0889c2s
v1p0908c1s v1p0924c1s v1p0989c2s
v1p1192c2s v1p1202c1s v1p1296c1s
v1p1335c2s v1p1339c1s v1p1420c1s
v1p1437c1s v2p0178c2s v2p0199c1s
v2p0209c2s v2p0399c1s v2p0482c2s
v3p0311c1s
Collins, W. and Dickens, C.
v1p0924c1s
Collins, W.D. and Fiske, W.E.
v5p0185c2s
Collins, W.J. v5p0345c1s
Collins, W.S. v3p0119c1s
v3p0268c2s v3p0443c2s v4p0411c2s
Collins, W.W. v1p0862c1s
v1p0878c2m v1p1114c1s v1p1143c2s
v1p1335c1s
Collins, W.W. and Dickens, C.
v1p0732c1s
Collinson, B.W. and Munro, J.K.
v6p0358c1s
Collinson, H.L. v3p0256c2s
Collinson, J. v5p0063c1s
Collinson, P. v1p1129c1s
Collis, C.H.T. v3p0310c1s
Collison, C.S. v6p0535c2s
Collitz, H. v3p0151c2s
v3p0214c2s v3p0340c2s v3p0343c2s
Collomb, E. v1p0524c2s
Colls, J.M.N. v1p0409c1s
Collum, R.F. v5p0362c1s
Collum, R.S. v3p0228c2s
v3p0251c2s v3p0329c1s v4p0595c1s
Collyer, A. v4p0500c2s
Collyer, Adelaide v4p0137c2s
Collyer, D'Arcy, Mrs. v4p0092c2s
v6p0205c1s
Collyer, R. v1p0130c1s
v1p0147c1s v1p0227c2s v1p0229c1m
v1p0451c2s v1p0575c2s v1p0581c1s
v1p0687c1s v1p0693c2s v1p0746c1s
v1p0777c2s v1p0861c2s v1p0877c1s
v1p0962c1s v1p0996c2s v1p1085c1s
v1p1111c2s v1p1345c1s v1p1407c2s
v2p0030c2s v2p0282c2s v2p0436c2s
v3p0049c2s
Collyer, R. et al. v3p0138c1s
v3p0216c1s
Collyer, R.H. v1p0613c1s
Collyer, T.H. v6p0354c1s
Colmache, G. v1p0505c2s
v4p0142c2s
Colman, A.J. v5p0239c1s
Colman, C.W., jr. v1p1329c1s
Colman, H. v1p0225c1s
v1p0240c2s v1p0404c1s v1p0544c2s
v1p0744c2s v1p0805c1s v1p1082c1s
v1p1319c1s v3p0341c2s
Colman, J. v1p1173c2s
v2p0295c2s
Colman, J.F. v1p0527c1s
Colman, K. v3p0086c1s
Colman, L. v1p1148c1s
Colmer, J.G. v3p0065c1s
v3p0066c1s v3p0262c1s
v4p0236c2m
Colnagh, D. v6p0146c1s
Colnaghi, D. v3p0155c2s
v3p0372c2s
Colnaghi, D.E. v4p0255c2s
Colne, C. v5p0235c2s
Colne, P. v2p0327c2s
Colo, V. v6p0536c1s
Cologan, W.H. v3p0271c2s
Coloma, F. v3p0141c2s
Coloma, Father v3p0430c2s
Coloma, L. v3p0153c2s
Coloma, Luis v5p0257c2s
Colomb, Admiral v3p0117c2s
Colomb, Col. v1p0339c1s
Colomb, J. v6p0448c2s
Colomb, J.C.R. v3p0181c1s
v4p0181c1s v5p0247c1s v5p0248c1s
v6p0269c1s
Colomb, J.C.R., Sir v3p0182c1s
v5p0246c2s
Colomb, John, Sir v6p0269c1s
Colomb, P.H. v3p0066c1s
v3p0089c2s v3p0092c1s v3p0181c1s
v3p0297c2s v3p0443c2s v4p0151c1s
v4p0183c1s v4p0238c1s v4p0356c1s
v4p0363c2s v4p0511c1s v4p0521c2s
v4p0548c1s v4p0579c2s v4p0604c1s
v4p0610c2s v5p0176c2s v5p0246c2m
v5p0259c1s v5p0262c2s v5p0375c1s
v5p0401c1m v5p0401c2m v5p0404c1s
v5p0516c2s v5p0526c2s v5p0543c2m
v5p0544c1s v5p0585c1s v5p0593c2s
v5p0619c1m v6p0652c2s
Colomb, P.H. and Brassey, Lord
v3p0182c1s
Colomb, P.H. and Clarke, A., Sir
v3p0155c1s v3p0158c2s
Colomb, P.L. v3p0392c2s
Colombo, Bishop of v3p0058c2s
Coloniensis v6p0334c1s
Colonies, Les and Parel, G.
v6p0564c2s
Colonna, B.A. v2p0393c1s
v6p0589c1s
Colonna, F. v5p0069c1s
Colquhoun, A.H.V. v4p0117c1s
v4p0347c1s v5p0043c1s v5p0050c2s
v5p0065c1s v5p0090c1s v5p0091c2s
v5p0111c1s v5p0229c2s v5p0474c1s
v5p0480c2s v5p0505c2s v5p0611c1s
v6p0183c2s v6p0190c1s v6p0194c2s
v6p0200c1s v6p0346c1s v6p0533c2s
v6p0552c1s
Colquhoun, A.R. v2p0078c2s
v2p0220c1s v3p0060c2s v4p0105c2s
v4p0328c1s v4p0522c1s v4p0522c2s
v4p0596c1s v5p0005c1s v5p0034c1s
v5p0064c2s v5p0108c2s v5p0110c1s
v5p0173c2s v5p0284c1s v5p0359c2s
v5p0501c2s v5p0527c2s v5p0528c1m
v5p0600c2s v6p0006c1s v6p0036c2m
v6p0118c2s v6p0119c1s v6p0120c1s
v6p0121c1s v6p0253c1s v6p0255c2s
v6p0330c1s v6p0369c2s v6p0447c2s
v6p0476c2s v6p0478c1s v6p0507c2s
v6p0560c1s v6p0713c2s
Colquhoun, Archibald R. .. v6p0107c1s
Colquhoun, J.C. v1p0560c2s
Colquhoun, P. and Wassa, Pasco, Pasha
v4p0433c1s
Colquitt, A.H. v3p0299c2s
v3p0346c1s
Colquitt, A.H. et al. v4p0248c2s
Colson, E.M. v6p0247c2s
Colson, Ethel M. v5p0295c1s
Colson, L.B. v4p0558c2s
v6p0414c1s v6p0533c2s v6p0645c2s
Colsson, C.C. v4p0532c2m
Colston, R.E. v1p0216c2s
v2p0410c1s
Colston, R.E. and Greene, S.D.
v2p0295c1s
Colt, J.D. v3p0416c2s
Colt, L.B. v6p0363c2s
Colt, P. v6p0153c2s
v6p0297c1s v6p0298c2s v6p0562c1s
v6p0623c2s
Colt, Philip v6p0297c1s
Colton, A. v1p0047c1s
v5p0133c1s v5p0182c1s v5p0210c1s
v5p0271c2s v5p0411c2s v5p0460c1s
v5p0494c2s v5p0546c1s v5p0580c2s
v5p0581c2s v5p0611c2s v6p0018c2s
v6p0032c2s v6p0098c2s v6p0153c2s
v6p0213c2s v6p0228c2s v6p0245c1s
v6p0272c1s v6p0279c1s v6p0299c2s
v6p0311c2s v6p0333c2s v6p0340c1s
v6p0351c1s v6p0352c1s v6p0380c2s
v6p0457c2s v6p0549c1s v6p0596c2s
v6p0619c2s v6p0627c2s v6p0643c1s
v6p0650c1s v6p0655c1s
Colton, A.E. v6p0232c1s
Colton, A.L. and Schaeberle, J.M.
v5p0371c2s
Colton, A.M. v1p1043c1s
v3p0459c1s
Colton, A.S. v1p0046c2s
v1p0846c1s v2p0233c1s
Colton, A.W. v4p0074c1m
v4p0166c1s v4p0354c2s v4p0498c1s
v5p0250c1s v5p0260c1s v5p0282c2s
v5p0504c1s v5p0539c2s v5p0596c1s
v5p0596c2s v5p0622c1s
Colton, Arthur v5p0187c1s
v5p0400c2s v5p0452c2s v5p0613c1s
Colton, B.P. v6p0713c2s
Colton, C. v1p0003c2s
v1p0016c1s v1p0276c1s v1p0306c2s
v1p0432c2s v1p0481c2s v1p0798c1s
v1p1382c1s v1p1411c2s
Colton, D.M. v1p0405c1s
v1p0584c2s v1p0774c2s v1p0779c2s
v1p0876c1s
Colton, F. v1p1365c2s
Colton, G.H. v1p0263c1s
v1p0577c2m v1p0583c2s v1p0686c2s
v1p0823c2s v1p0893c2s v1p0947c2s
v1p1387c2s
Colton, H. v6p0054c1s
Colton, H.E. v1p0591c1s
Colton, H.W. v1p1339c2s
Colton, J.S. v2p0046c1s
Colton, W. v1p0505c1s
v1p0886c1s v1p0944c2s v1p1332c2s
Columbine, W.B. v5p0035c2s
v5p0256c1s v5p0535c2s
Colver, N. v1p0967c2s
Colvert, F.C. v1p0664c1s
Colvile, C. v4p0264c1s
Colvill, H.H. v6p0607c2s
v6p0617c1s v6p0633c2s
Colville, C. v1p0349c1s
Colville, H.E. v4p0308c2s
Colville, J. v4p0509c1s
v6p0296c2s
Colville, W.J. v6p0571c1s
Colville, W.L. v4p0455c2s
Colville, Z. v4p0411c2s
Colvin, A. v1p0631c1s
v4p0107c1s v4p0166c1s v4p0279c2m
v4p0281c1s v5p0009c1s v5p0285c2s
Colvin, A. and Chamberlain, N.
v5p0285c2s
Colvin, F.H. v4p0547c1s
Colvin, Prof. v1p0072c2s
Colvin, S. v1p0054c2s. v1p0059c1s
v1p0061c2s v1p0062c1s v1p0062c2s

v1p0064c1s v1p0100c2s v1p0116c1s
v1p0153c2m v1p0169c1s v1p0170c2s
v1p0212c1s v1p0218c2s v1p0229c2s
v1p0318c1s v1p0370c2m v1p0447c2s
v1p0472c2s v1p0495c1s v1p0497c1s
v1p0511c2m v1p0522c1s v1p0558c1s
v1p0559c2s v1p0566c1s v1p0596c1s
v1p0611c2s v1p0695c1s v1p0714c1s
v1p0736c1s v1p0754c1s v1p0808c1s
v1p0840c1s v1p0866c2s v1p0891c2s
v1p0958c1s v1p0958c2s v1p0982c1s
v1p0988c2s v1p1008c2s v1p1023c1s
v1p1104c2s v1p1106c2s v1p1108c1s
v1p1126c2s v1p1171c1s v1p1196c1s
v1p1219c1s v1p1294c2s v1p1307c2s
v1p1367c2s v1p1381c2s v1p1393c1s
v1p1399c2s v1p1413c2s v2p0087c1s
v2p0121c2s v2p0234c2s v2p0361c1s
v2p0365c1m v2p0457c2s v3p0009c2s
v3p0072c1s v3p0108c2s v3p0184c1s
v3p0258c1s v3p0375c2s v4p0084c2s
v4p0160c1s v4p0163c2s v4p0178c2s
v4p0234c2s v4p0267c2s v4p0473c2s
v4p0492c1s v4p0555c1s v5p0446c2s
v6p0350c1s v6p0537c1s
v6p0689c1s
Colvin, S.J. v6p0307c1s
Colvin, S.S. v5p0279c1s
v6p0216c1s v6p0513c1s v6p0522c1s
v6p0533c1s v6p0671c2s
Colvin, S.S. and Meyer, I.F.
v6p0117c1s
Colvin, Sidney v3p0235c1s
Colvin, V. v1p0583c2s
v1p1113c2s
Colwell, A.W. v4p0555c2s
Colwell, C.A. v6p0514c2s
Colwell, J.V.V. v6p0235c1s
Colwell, S. v1p0091c2s
v1p0313c2s v1p0453c1s v1p0545c1s
v1p0860c2s v1p1030c2s v1p1212c1s
v1p1274c1s
Colwell, W.H. v6p0046c2s
Colwick, A.M. v5p0462c2s
Colyar, A.S. v3p0296c1s
Colyar, A.S. and Kennedy, W.
v2p0302c1s
Colyar, P.S. v4p0588c2s
Comadi, E. v6p0363c1s
Coman, K. v6p0019c2s
v6p0206c1s v6p0447c1s
Coman, Katherine v6p0283c1s
Coman, M. v6p0095c1s
Comba, E. v2p0042c1s
v2p0457c1s v3p0453c1s
Combe, G. v1p0069c1s
v1p1004c2s
Combe, T. v1p0040c1s
v1p0101c1s v1p0272c1s v1p0272c2s
v1p0782c2s v1p0988c1s v1p1154c1s
v1p1178c1s v1p1317c2s v3p0358c2s
Combes, E. v3p0122c2s
v3p0302c2s v3p0422c2s v6p0237c1s
v6p0547c2s
Combes, Emile v6p0236c2m
Comegys, C.G. v2p0441c1s
Comes, J.T. v6p0012c2s
Comey, A.M. v3p0091c1s
v4p0123c2s v4p0464c1s
Comfort, A. v5p0639c1s
Comfort, G.F. v1p0276c1s
v1p0624c2s v1p0724c2s v1p0741c1s
v1p1372c1s v6p0033c2s v6p0224c2s
Comfort, S. v1p0059c1s
v1p0074c1s v1p0206c1s v1p0343c2s
v1p0507c1s v1p0681c2s v1p0869c1s
Comfort, S. and Young, J.H.
v1p1152c1s
Comfort, W.L. v6p0173c2s
v6p0397c2s v6p0590c2s v6p0695c1s
Comfort, W.W. v5p0522c2s
Comfort, Will L. v6p0539c1s
v6p0593c2s
Comfort, Will Levington .. v6p0234c1s
Comly, I. v1p0987c2s
Commander, Lydia K. v6p0212c1s
v6p0219c1m v6p0346c2s
Commelin, A.O. v4p0322c1s
Common, A.A. v2p0136c2s
v2p0386c2s v2p0433c2s v3p0298c2s
v3p0330c2s v3p0403c2s v3p0423c2s
v4p0373c2s v4p0545c2s v5p0035c1s
v5p0048c1s v5p0077c1s v5p0312c2s
Common, T. v6p0457c1s
Commons, J.R. v3p0281c2s
v4p0115c1s v4p0115c2s v4p0225c1s
v4p0283c1s v4p0372c2s v4p0379c2s
v4p0455c2s v4p0462c1s v4p0481c1s
v4p0564c2s v5p0162c1s v5p0230c1s
v5p0321c1m v5p0391c1s v5p0391c2m
v5p0392c1s v5p0457c1s v5p0485c2s
v5p0519c1s v5p0541c2s v5p0592c2s
v6p0016c1s v6p0017c2s v6p0026c1s
v6p0113c2s v6p0128c2s v6p0170c1s
v6p0212c1s v6p0308c2s v6p0309c1s
v6p0318c2s v6p0356c1s v6p0356c2m
v6p0358c2s v6p0386c1s v6p0408c1s
v6p0435c1m v6p0436c2s v6p0439c2s
v6p0446c2s v6p0526c1s v6p0577c1s
v6p0597c1s v6p0599c2s v6p0634c2s
v6p0652c1m v6p0652c2s v6p0665c2s
v6p0691c2s
Commons, J.R. and Gunton, Geo.
v4p0152c1s
Commun, J.D. v1p1377c1s
Comparetti, D. v3p0217c1s
Compatriot v6p0226c1s
Compayre, G. v3p0129c1s
v4p0170c1s v4p0171c2m v4p0597c1s
v5p0106c1s v5p0178c1s v5p0179c2s
v5p0221c2s v5p0431c2s v5p0626c2s
v6p0192c1s v6p0237c2s v6p0459c1s
Compton, A., Lord et al. . v5p0244c2s
Compton, A.G. v2p0460c1s
Compton, C.C. v6p0641c2s
Compton, C.G. v6p0243c2s
v6p0679c1s
Compton, E.T. v4p0135c2s
Compton, Earl v3p0199c1s
v3p0318c2s v3p0338c2s
Compton, H. v1p0736c1m
v1p1175c2s v1p1432c1s v3p0208c1s
v5p0225c2s
Compton, H.W. v4p0464c2s
Compton, J.S. v6p0227c2s
Compton, R. v4p0270c1s
v4p0398c1s v4p0459c2s v4p0536c1s
v4p0608c2s
Compton, Roy v5p0216c1s
v5p0438c2s v5p0612c1s v5p0639c2s
v5p0642c1s v5p0642c2s
Compton, T.E. v6p0416c1s
v6p0614c1s
Comrie, P. v1p0911c1s
Comstock, A. v3p0002c1s
v3p0021c2s v3p0116c1s v3p0248c1s
v3p0253c2s v3p0259c1s v3p0449c1s
v4p0029c2s v4p0274c2s v4p0335c1s
v4p0451c2s v5p0341c2s
Comstock, A. et al. v2p0460c1s
Comstock, A.B. v5p0021c2s
v5p0292c1m v5p0621c2s v6p0024c2s
v6p0056c1s v6p0056c2s v6p0067c1s
v6p0068c1s v6p0114c1s v6p0132c1s
v6p0150c1s v6p0155c1s v6p0214c1s
v6p0400c1m v6p0444c1s v6p0444c2s
v6p0462c2s v6p0582c1m v6p0599c1s
v6p0612c1s v6p0656c1s
Comstock, Anna B. v6p0656c1s
Comstock, C.B. v1p1440c1s
Comstock, F.A. v4p0051c2s
v4p0283c1s v4p0566c2s
Comstock, G.C. v2p0257c2m
v3p0243c2s v3p0457c2s v4p0034c1s
v4p0331c2s v4p0357c2s v4p0477c1s
v5p0035c2s v5p0130c1s v5p0370c2s
v6p0140c2s v6p0480c1s
Comstock, Geo.C. v6p0647c1s
Comstock, Geo.O. v6p0625c2s
Comstock, H. v1p0604c2s
v2p0234c2s
Comstock, J.H. and Kochi, C.
v6p0321c1s
Comstock, J.H. and Needham, J.G.
v5p0292c1s
Comstock, M.E. v4p0329c1s
Comstock, S. v6p0421c1s
Comstock, S.M. v5p0195c1s
Comstock, Sarah v5p0112c2s
v6p0217c2s v6p0608c1s
Comstock, T.B. v1p0509c2s
v1p1435c2s v1p1437c1s v2p0284c2s
v2p0374c2s v4p0018c2s v6p0047c1s
Comstock, W.J. v1p1282c2s
v1p1359c1s
Comstock, W.J. and Allen, O.D.
v1p0101c2s
Comte, A., jr. v1p1330c2s
Comyn, F. v4p0602c1s
Conacher, H.M. v5p0149c2s
v6p0596c2s
Conant, A.J. v2p0300c1s
Conant, C.A. v3p0264c1s
v4p0393c2s v5p0046c1s v5p0130c2s
v5p0142c1s v5p0144c1s v5p0149c2s
v5p0175c1s v5p0199c2m v5p0237c2s
v5p0281c2s v5p0295c1s v5p0382c2s
v5p0383c1s v5p0434c1s v5p0482c2s
v5p0501c1s v5p0518c2s v5p0543c2s
v5p0545c1s v5p0567c1s v5p0589c2s
v5p0599c2s v6p0050c1s v6p0118c2s
v6p0162c1s v6p0224c1s v6p0318c2s
v6p0325c2s v6p0425c1m v6p0425c2s
v6p0493c1m v6p0494c1s v6p0518c1s
v6p0582c1s v6p0618c1m v6p0658c2s
v6p0659c1s v6p0670c1s v6p0684c1s
Conant, C.B. v1p0170c1m
v1p0206c2s v1p0268c2s v1p0539c2s
Conant, C.E., Mrs. v5p0638c2s
Conant, C.S. v5p0016c1s
v5p0173c2s
Conant, E. et al. v5p0413c2s
Conant, E.L. v4p0035c2s
v4p0249c1s
Conant, G.W. v4p0441c1s
Conant, H.C., Mrs. v1p0402c2s
Conant, H.J. v4p0547c2s
Conant, H.S. v1p0011c1s
v1p0135c2s v1p0212c2s v1p0322c2s
v1p0383c2s v1p1313c1s v1p1333c2s
v1p1401c1s v2p0018c1s v5p0131c2s
v6p0060c1s
Conant, L., jr. v5p0138c1s
Conant, L.L. v4p0361c1s
Conant, L.S. v6p0403c1s
v6p0544c2s v6p0646c1s
Conant, Martha P. v6p0085c2s
Conant, R.W. v3p0206c2s
v4p0178c2s v4p0188c1s v5p0341c1s
v6p0019c2s
Conant, S. v1p0924c1s
Conant, S.S. v1p0010c2m
v1p0042c1s v1p0073c2s v1p0077c2s
v1p0138c1s v1p0174c1s v1p0274c2s
v1p0393c2s v1p0759c1s v1p0813c1s
v1p0832c2s v1p0855c2s v1p0914c1s
v1p0959c2s v1p1148c2s v1p1194c1s
v1p1195c2s v1p1290c1s v2p0110c1s
v2p0153c2s
Conant, T. v4p0261c1s
Conant, T.J. v1p0126c1m
v1p0131c1s v1p1065c2s v1p1067c1s
v2p0042c2s
Conant, W.B. v6p0275c1s
Conant, W.C. v1p0067c1s
v1p0117c2s v1p0144c2s v1p0323c2s
v1p0493c2s v1p1182c1s v1p1389c2s
v1p1426c1s v2p0128c2s v2p0313c2s
v2p0469c2s v3p0457c1s
Conard, H.L. v3p0069c1s
v3p0070c2s v3p0082c2s v3p0087c2s
v3p0098c2m v3p0116c2m v3p0123c1s
v3p0136c2s v3p0143c1s v3p0155c2s
v3p0157c1s v3p0159c1s v3p0173c1s
v3p0177c1s v3p0185c2s v3p0188c1s
v3p0193c1s v3p0195c2s v3p0196c1s
v3p0198c1s v3p0203c2s v3p0228c1s
v3p0230c2s v3p0232c1s v3p0235c2s
v3p0245c1s v3p0260c2s v3p0269c2s
v3p0270c2s v3p0283c2s v3p0285c2s
v3p0299c2m v3p0305c1s v3p0310c2s
v3p0350c1s v3p0356c1s v3p0360c2s
v3p0361c1s v3p0367c2s v3p0375c1s
v3p0376c2s v3p0379c1s v3p0382c1s
v3p0390c2s v3p0391c1s v3p0396c1s
v3p0396c2m v3p0405c2s v3p0409c1m
v3p0410c2s v3p0412c2s v3p0429c1s
v3p0446c2s v3p0452c1s v3p0458c1m
v3p0464c1s v4p0011c1s v4p0040c1s
v4p0046c1s v4p0050c1s v4p0062c1s
v4p0062c2s v4p0064c1s v4p0072c1s
v4p0075c1s v4p0075c2m v4p0078c1s
v4p0080c2s v4p0084c1s v4p0090c1s
v4p0091c1s v4p0157c2s v4p0158c2s
v4p0174c1s v4p0185c1s v4p0193c2s
v4p0206c2s v4p0214c2s v4p0235c1s
v4p0243c1s v4p0257c1s v4p0262c2s
v4p0267c1s v4p0270c1s v4p0322c2s
v4p0343c2s v4p0344c2s v4p0345c1s
v4p0346c2m v4p0362c2s v4p0382c2s
v4p0391c1s v4p0433c1s v4p0483c1s
v4p0487c2s v4p0526c2s v4p0530c1s
v4p0550c1s v4p0554c1s v4p0565c2s
v4p0587c2s v4p0608c2s v4p0619c2s
v4p0635c2s
Conard, J. v6p0556c1s
Conard, Laetitia M. v6p0316c2s
v6p0401c1s v6p0525c2s
Conaty, T.J. v2p0132c2s
v3p0218c1s v6p0137c2s v6p0547c2s
Concas, D.V.M. v6p0608c1s
Concas, V.M. v4p0125c2s
Conch, J. v1p0898c2s
Concilio, J.B.De v2p0480c2s
Concilio, J.De v1p0433c2m
v1p0441c2m v1p0793c1s v1p0794c2s
v1p1120c1s v1p1200c2s v2p0439c2s
v3p0316c1s v3p0454c2s
Conder and Lukin v1p0162c1s
Conder, A.R. v5p0558c1s
Conder, C.R. v1p0116c1s
v1p0198c1s v1p0497c1s v2p0230c2s
v2p0272c1s v2p0294c1s v2p0327c1m
v2p0410c2s v2p0429c2m v3p0023c2s
v3p0081c2s v3p0174c2s v3p0197c2m
v3p0230c1s v3p0230c2s v3p0261c2s
v3p0386c1s v3p0418c2s v3p0423c2s
v4p0013c1s v4p0055c1s v4p0087c1s
v4p0145c2s v4p0259c1s v4p0299c2s
v4p0302c1s v4p0384c1s v4p0422c2m
v4p0541c1s v4p0580c2s v5p0034c1s
v5p0181c2s v5p0249c1s v5p0267c1s
v5p0428c2s v5p0505c1s v5p0645c2s
v6p0343c2s v6p0713c1s
Conder, C.R. and Smith, W.R.
v3p0041c1s
Conder, Dr. v2p0257c2s
Conder, E. v2p0266c1s
v2p0389c2s
Conder, E.R. v2p0041c2s
v2p0042c1s v2p0042c2s v2p0359c1s
v3p0229c1s
Conder, E.R. and Reynolds, H.R.
v1p1118c1s
Conder, E.R. and Romanes, G.J.
v2p0437c2s
Conder, F.D. v1p0612c2s
Conder, F.R. v1p0037c1s
v1p0066c2s v1p0129c1m v1p0241c2s
v1p0242c2s v1p0269c1m v1p0377c2s

v1p0399c1s v1p0410c2s v1p0415c1s
v1p0464c1s v1p0496c2s v1p0550c2s
v1p0562c2s v1p0565c1s v1p0586c2s
v1p0624c2m v1p0642c2s v1p0652c1s
v1p0685c2s v1p0690c1s v1p0730c1s
v1p0758c2s v1p0764c1s v1p0766c2m
v1p0770c1s v1p0825c1m v1p0849c2s
v1p0880c2s v1p0923c1s v1p0988c2s
v1p1005c2s v1p1076c1s v1p1077c1s
v1p1078c1s v1p1078c2s v1p1079c1s
v1p1096c2s v1p1150c2s v1p1177c1s
v1p1238c1s v1p1285c2s v1p1299c1s
v1p1305c2s v1p1321c2s v1p1391c2s
v1p1431c2m v2p0066c2s v2p0165c2s
v2p0226c2s v2p0245c1s v2p0340c2s
v2p0464c1s v3p0069c1s v3p0305c2s
Conder, G.W. v1p0178c2s
v1p0412c1s
Conder, J. v1p0677c2s
v3p0018c2s v5p0303c2s
Conder, R.C. v4p0561c2s
Conder, R.F. v4p0476c2s
Conder, R.F.R. v3p0071c2s
Condereau, M. v1p0646c2s
v1p0648c2s
Condict, J.C. v2p0219c1s
Condit, Ida M. v5p0031c2s
Condit, J.B. v1p1043c2s
Condon, T. v1p0509c1s
v1p0693c1s v1p1411c1s
Condon, W.J. v2p0072c2s
Condor, F.R. v1p0257c1s
v1p1391c2s
Cone, A. v5p0217c1s
v5p0221c2s
Cone, Ada v5p0030c2s
v5p0432c1s v5p0599c2s v6p0033c1s
v6p0387c2s
Cone, Corinne I. v5p0614c1s
Cone, H.G. v2p0104c1s
v2p0196c2s v2p0266c1s v2p0424c2s
v3p0011c2s v3p0194c2s v3p0225c2s
v3p0361c1s v3p0428c2s v3p0467c1s
v5p0043c2s v5p0201c2s
Cone, J.A. v6p0664c1s
Cone, J.H. v3p0008c1s
Cone, K.M. v5p0366c2s
v6p0195c1s v6p0406c2s
Cone, K.M., Mrs. v5p0108c1s
Cone, Kate M. v5p0106c2s
Cone, M. v1p0938c2s
v2p0087c2s v2p0298c1s
Cone, O. v1p0101c1s
v1p0120c1s v1p0125c2s v1p0126c2s
v1p0127c1s v1p0127c2s v1p0129c2s
v1p0467c1s v1p0529c1s v1p0553c2s
v1p0587c2s v1p0646c2s v1p0684c2s
v1p0685c1s v1p0729c2s v1p0862c2s
v1p0948c1s v1p1056c2m v1p1157c1s
v2p0149c1s v2p0169c2s v2p0251c1s
v2p0254c2s v2p0370c2s v2p0389c1s
v3p0150c1s v3p0339c2s v4p0056c1s
v4p0057c1s v4p0109c1s v4p0186c2s
v4p0301c1s v4p0301c2s v5p0059c1s
v5p0436c2s v5p0530c1s v6p0064c1s
Cone, S.W. v1p0296c1s
v1p0360c1s v1p0365c1s v1p0708c2s
v1p0938c1s v1p1028c1s v1p1048c1s
v1p1055c1s v1p1063c1s v1p1103c2s
v1p1181c2s v1p1245c1s v1p1378c1s
Cones, E. v2p0127c1s
Cones, S.E. v1p0783c2s
Conestabile, Count v2p0065c1s
Congar, S.H. v1p0908c2s
v1p0909c1s
Congdon, C.T. v1p0200c2s
v1p0491c1s v1p0756c1s v1p0932c2s
v1p0941c1s v1p1020c2s v1p1036c1s
v1p1099c1s v1p1368c1s v2p0115c2s
v2p0215c1s v2p0260c2s v2p0269c2s
v2p0312c1s v2p0355c1s
Congdon, J.B. v1p0094c1m
Conger, C.M. v4p0612c1m
Conger, C.T. v4p0222c1s
Conger, E.H. v5p0108c2s
Conger, Margaret G. v6p0584c1s
Conger, Myrtle v6p0290c2s
Conger, S.H. v1p0617c1s
Conger-Kaneko, J. v6p0195c1s
v6p0704c1s
Congreve, E.M. v6p0273c1s
v6p0444c1s
Congreve, R. v1p0287c1s
v1p0546c1s v1p1330c2s v1p1376c1s
Conine, M.A.B. v5p0639c1s
Coningsby, R. v1p0715c2s
Conington, J. v1p0284c2s
v1p0356c2s v1p0390c1s v1p0601c1s
v1p0769c2s v1p1032c2s v1p1109c2s
v1p1306c1s v1p1309c2s
Coniston, J. v5p0580c1s
v5p0630c1s
Conklin, A. v3p0341c2s
Conklin, E.G. v4p0513c2s
v5p0126c2s v5p0161c2s v5p0299c2s
v5p0639c2s v5p0646c2s v6p0157c2s
v6p0195c2s
Conklin, E.J. v5p0062c2s
Conklin, J. v5p0028c2s
Conklin, W.J. v1p0352c1s
v6p0437c1s
Conkling, D.P.B. v4p0454c2s
Conkling, F.A. v2p0104c1s
v3p0449c1s
Conley, E.M. v6p0151c2s
v6p0413c2s v6p0414c1m v6p0414c2m
v6p0636c1s
Conliffe-Owen, F. v5p0180c1s
Conn, F.W. v3p0218c1s
Conn, H.W. v2p0108c2s
v2p0139c2s v2p0149c2s v2p0258c1s
v3p0044c2s v3p0091c2s v3p0250c2s
v3p0279c1s v3p0297c1s v3p0380c2m
v4p0041c1m v4p0122c1s v4p0191c2s
v4p0429c2s v4p0463c1s v5p0016c1s
v5p0042c2m v5p0103c2s v5p0198c2s
v5p0376c1s v6p0046c2s v6p0047c1m
v6p0175c2s v6p0288c2s v6p0317c2s
v6p0675c1m
Connell, A.K. v2p0218c1s
v4p0279c1s
Connell, F. v5p0013c2s
v5p0389c2s
Connell, F.N. v5p0172c1s
v5p0238c2s v5p0396c2s v5p0476c1s
v6p0288c2s v6p0440c1s v6p0632c1s
Connell, I. v1p1081c1s
Connell, P.C. v6p0327c2s
Connell, R.E. v5p0423c2s
Connellan, C. v1p0962c2s
Connellan, D. v1p1370c2s
Connellan, P.L. v1p1313c1s
v5p0096c1s v6p0103c2s v6p0368c1s
Connelley, W.E. v5p0642c2s
Connelly, C.L. v1p1084c2s
Connelly, J. v5p0170c1s
Connelly, J.H. v3p0311c1s
v4p0021c2s v4p0090c1s v6p0676c1s
Conner, B.H. v6p0177c2s
v6p0203c1s
Conner, J.E. v6p0666c2s
Conner, P.S.P. v3p0013c2s
v4p0129c2s v4p0368c1s v5p0270c2s
v5p0507c2s
Connery, T.B. v3p0128c1s
v3p0406c2s v5p0133c1s v5p0226c1s
v5p0310c2s v5p0409c2s v5p0612c2s
Conney, Mrs. v4p0412c2s
Connolly, C.B. v5p0076c1s
v6p0346c2s
Connolly, C.M. v5p0168c2s
Connolly, C.P. v4p0071c1s
v6p0419c2s v6p0426c2s
Connolly, D. v2p0228c2s
v2p0395c2s
Connolly, Edward v5p0615c2s
Connolly, J.B. v5p0103c1s
v5p0420c2s v6p0029c1s v6p0049c1s
v6p0070c1s v6p0179c2s v6p0181c2s
v6p0185c2s v6p0226c2s v6p0227c2s
v6p0230c1s v6p0259c1s v6p0308c1s
v6p0309c1s v6p0361c2s v6p0395c1s
v6p0452c2s v6p0460c1s v6p0466c2s
v6p0467c1s v6p0484c1s v6p0566c2s
v6p0573c1s v6p0620c2s v6p0649c2s
v6p0669c1s v6p0694c1m v6p0698c1s
v6p0710c1s
Connolly, J.M. v5p0487c1s
Connolly, J.R. v6p0554c2s
Connolly, Jas B. v6p0659c2s
Connolly, Louise v6p0374c1s
Connolly, M. v5p0080c1s
Connolly, R.M. v4p0194c2s
Connor, D. v4p0300c2s
Connor, G.C. v2p0286c2s
Connor, Harriet C. v5p0267c2s
Connor, J.B. v2p0125c2s
v2p0447c1s
Connor, J.T. v4p0083c1m
v4p0084c1s v4p0454c1s v5p0049c1s
v5p0112c2s v5p0115c2s v5p0390c1s
v6p0053c1s v6p0087c2s v6p0099c2s
v6p0120c1s v6p0483c2s v6p0590c2s
Connor, P.J. v5p0326c1s
Connor, R. v1p0486c1s
v1p0602c2s v1p0868c2s v1p0897c2s
v1p0910c2s v1p1223c1s v1p1318c1s
v1p1321c1s v5p0061c2s v5p0358c2s
Connor, R.D.W. v6p0485c1s
Connor, Ralph v5p0240c1s
Connor, S.E. v5p0225c1s
Connor, W.D. v6p0527c2s
Connor, W.E. et al. v4p0462c1s
Connor-Ohlmutz, P. v6p0516c2s
Conolly, L. v2p0103c2s
Conolly, T.L. v2p0025c2s
Conover, C.R. v3p0112c1s
v3p0168c2s v3p0202c2s v4p0486c2s
Conover, D.S.B. v5p0636c1s
Conrad, A.Z. v5p0001c2s
Conrad, D.B. v3p0266c1s
v3p0424c2s v3p0440c2s v4p0375c2s
v4p0550c2s v4p0590c2s
Conrad, F.W. v1p0076c1s
v1p0096c2s v1p0276c1s v1p0313c2s
v1p0598c2s v1p0769c1s v1p0778c1s
v1p1065c1s v1p1075c1s v1p1344c2s
v2p0177c2s v2p0261c2s v2p0290c2s
v3p0143c1s v3p0342c1s v4p0611c2s
Conrad, H.L. v4p0019c2s
v4p0028c1s
Conrad, J. v5p0260c1s
v5p0314c1s v5p0322c2s v5p0347c2s
v5p0411c2s v5p0645c1s v6p0019c2s
v6p0043c2s v6p0074c2s v6p0203c2s
v6p0236c1s v6p0287c2s v6p0319c1s
v6p0333c1s v6p0591c2s v6p0649c2s
v6p0663c2s v6p0684c2s v6p0710c1s
Conrad, J.F. v6p0124c1s
Conrad, Joseph v5p0061c2s
v6p0579c2s
Conrad, M.G. v4p0223c2s
Conrad, T.A. v1p0187c1s
v1p0470c2s v1p0508c1s v1p0509c2s
v1p1189c1s
Conrad, V.L. v1p1064c1s
v1p1256c2s v5p0351c1s
Conradi, A.F. v6p0520c1s
Conradi, E. v6p0117c2s
v6p0365c2s v6p0608c1s v6p0609c1s
Conroy, J. v2p0367c1s
Cons, E. v4p0027c2s
Conscience, H. v1p0142c1s
Considine, D. v1p0771c1s
Considine, J. v1p1275c2s
Constable, A. v6p0656c2s
Constable, A.G. v1p0147c1s
v1p0293c2s v1p0800c1s v1p0975c2s
v1p1167c1s
Constable, A.H.B. v5p0323c2s
Constable, H. v1p0128c2s
Constable, Howard v5p0207c2s
Constable, J. v1p0066c1s
Constable, M.S. v4p0193c2s
v4p0407c2s v4p0559c2s
Constant, B. v3p0288c2s
v3p0419c2s v5p0134c1s v5p0275c1s
Constant, Benjamin v5p0235c1s
v5p0376c1s
Constant, D'Estournelles de
v6p0213c2s v6p0323c2s v6p0550c2s
Constant, J.J.B. v5p0617c1s
Constant, W.S. v6p0562c2s
Constantine, Crown Prince of Greece
v6p0466c2s
Conte, C.Le v2p0058c2s
Conte, Caroline Le v4p0578c1s
Conte, J.L.Le v1p0134c2m
v1p0187c1s v1p0188c1s v1p0188c2s
v1p0204c1s v1p0281c1s v1p0301c2s
v1p0375c2m v1p0376c1s v1p0392c1s
v1p0420c1m v1p0467c1m v1p0487c2s
v1p1377c1s v4p0190c2s
Conte, J.Le v1p0133c2s
v1p0434c1m v1p0435c1s v1p0461c2s
v1p0519c1s v1p0524c1m v1p0524c2s
v1p0562c1s v1p0646c2s v1p0728c2s
v1p0747c2s v1p0757c1s v1p0794c1s
v1p0804c1s v1p0828c2s v1p0862c1s
v1p0877c1s v1p0885c2s v1p0903c2s
v1p0945c1s v1p1161c1m v1p1182c1s
v1p1196c1m v1p1217c1s v1p1375c1m
v1p1377c1m v2p0015c1s v2p0028c1s
v2p0067c1m v2p0109c2s v2p0158c1s
v2p0158c2s v2p0161c1s v2p0215c2s
v2p0246c2s v2p0286c1s v2p0317c2s
v2p0372c2s v2p0382c2s v2p0395c1s
v2p0402c1s v2p0406c2s v2p0410c2s
v2p0430c1s v2p0440c1s v2p0482c2s
v3p0005c2s v3p0035c2s v3p0044c2m
v3p0063c1s v3p0083c2s v3p0088c2s
v3p0126c1m v3p0145c1m v3p0145c2s
v3p0146c1s v3p0150c1s v3p0156c2s
v3p0192c2s v3p0209c1s v3p0271c1s
v3p0283c2s v3p0314c1s v3p0401c2s
v3p0402c1s v3p0437c2s v3p0451c1s
v4p0018c1s v4p0168c2s v4p0190c2s
v4p0191c1s v4p0191c2s v4p0204c2s
v4p0352c1s v4p0385c2s v5p0062c2s
v5p0173c1s v5p0229c1s v5p0513c2s
v6p0214c2s v6p0433c2s v6p0671c2s
Conte, J.Le and Rising, W.B.
v2p0284c2s
Conte, Joseph Le v5p0100c1s
Contessa, E.W. v1p0019c1s
Conteur, P.E.Le v5p0370c2s
Converse, C.C. v3p0429c1s
v4p0389c1s v5p0619c2s
Converse, C.C. et al. v2p0356c1s
Converse, E.M. v1p0642c1s
v1p0723c2s
Converse, F. v4p0076c1s
v4p0520c1s v5p0131c1s v5p0425c1s
v6p0428c1s v6p0645c1s
Converse, Florence v5p0337c1s
Converse, H.M. v4p0292c2s
Converse, J.H. v5p0343c2s
v5p0344c1s v6p0190c2s
Converse, J.W. v6p0047c2s
Conway, B.L. v6p0176c1s
v6p0176c2s
Conway, Bertrand L. v6p0348c2s
v6p0386c2s
Conway, C. v3p0067c2s
Conway, C.H. v6p0262c2s
v6p0497c1s
Conway, D. v1p0938c1s
Conway, F. v4p0244c2s
Conway, H. v2p0069c2s
v2p0077c1s v2p0113c2s v2p0152c2s

v2p0333c1s
Conway, H.S. and Molesworth, W.
v1p0368c1s
Conway, I.J. v4p0054c1s
Conway, J. v2p0037c2s
v2p0131c1m v2p0375c2s v4p0082c2s
v4p0147c1s v4p0452c2s v4p0466c1s
v4p0487c2s v4p0489c1m v4p0618c1s
v4p0632c2s v6p0547c2s
Conway, J.J. v3p0358c1s
v6p0440c2s
Conway, K.E. v3p0314c1s
Conway, M. v3p0051c2s
v5p0069c1s v5p0095c2s v5p0275c1s
v5p0343c1s v6p0036c1s v6p0238c2s
v6p0269c1s v6p0317c2s
Conway, M., Sir v5p0002c2s
v5p0018c2s v5p0279c2s
v5p0539c2s
Conway, M.D. v1p0027c1s
v1p0032c2s v1p0035c1s v1p0053c2s
v1p0062c2s v1p0072c1s v1p0081c1s
v1p0095c2s v1p0106c2s v1p0114c1s
v1p0140c2s v1p0170c1s v1p0201c1s
v1p0226c1s v1p0277c1m v1p0339c2s
v1p0340c1s v1p0343c2m v1p0347c1s
v1p0350c1s v1p0372c1s v1p0408c2s
v1p0413c1s v1p0414c2s v1p0446c2s
v1p0463c1s v1p0472c1s v1p0473c1s
v1p0478c1s v1p0482c2s v1p0490c2s
v1p0529c2s v1p0548c1s v1p0556c1s
v1p0575c2s v1p0624c1s v1p0676c1s
v1p0693c2s v1p0713c2s v1p0714c2s
v1p0750c1s v1p0772c2s v1p0774c2s
v1p0802c1s v1p0814c2s v1p0857c1s
v1p0880c1s v1p0890c1s v1p0890c2s
v1p0904c2s v1p0935c2s v1p0954c1s
v1p0957c2s v1p0968c2s v1p0972c2s
v1p0998c2s v1p1042c2s v1p1072c1s
v1p1092c2s v1p1094c1s v1p1094c2s
v1p1133c2s v1p1139c2s v1p1141c1s
v1p1168c2s v1p1186c2s v1p1187c1s
v1p1203c1s v1p1227c1s v1p1261c1s
v1p1287c2s v1p1300c2s v1p1301c1s
v1p1317c2m v1p1324c1s v1p1342c2s
v1p1344c1s v1p1370c2s v1p1374c2s
v1p1385c1s v1p1407c1s v1p1410c2s
v1p1412c2s v1p1422c2s v1p1429c2s
v1p1437c2s v2p0091c1s v2p0139c2s
v2p0173c2s v2p0179c2s v2p0200c1s
v2p0244c2s v2p0295c2s v2p0332c2s
v2p0397c2s v2p0427c1s v2p0468c2s
v3p0001c2s v3p0007c2s v3p0009c2s
v3p0047c1s v3p0049c2s v3p0051c2s
v3p0080c1s v3p0097c2s v3p0099c2m
v3p0100c1s v3p0116c1s v3p0145c2s
v3p0162c2s v3p0233c1s v3p0288c2s
v3p0317c1m v3p0343c1s v3p0354c1m
v3p0357c2s v3p0449c1s v3p0455c1m
v3p0455c2m v3p0456c1s v3p0464c1s
v4p0007c1s v4p0011c1s v4p0040c2s
v4p0071c1s v4p0073c1s v4p0084c1s
v4p0090c1s v4p0091c1s v4p0098c1s
v4p0145c2s v4p0150c2s v4p0178c2s
v4p0179c1s v4p0188c1s v4p0191c2s
v4p0203c1s v4p0216c2m v4p0243c2s
v4p0270c2s v4p0299c1s v4p0328c2s
v4p0335c1s v4p0358c2s v4p0384c2s
v4p0402c1s v4p0405c1s v4p0413c2s
v4p0421c1m v4p0426c2m v4p0450c1s
v4p0479c2s v4p0480c2s v4p0497c1s
v4p0514c2m v4p0532c1s v4p0538c2s
v4p0542c1s v4p0562c2s v4p0570c2s
v4p0591c2s v4p0608c2s v4p0611c2s
v4p0612c1m v4p0620c1s v4p0628c2s
v5p0017c1s v5p0058c1s v5p0108c2s
v5p0168c2s v5p0195c2s v5p0198c1s
v5p0306c2s v5p0364c1s v5p0390c2s
v5p0427c2m v5p0434c2s v5p0538c2m
v5p0577c1s v5p0633c2s v6p0081c2s
v6p0202c1s v6p0202c2s v6p0248c1s
v6p0283c2s v6p0284c1s v6p0404c1s
Conway, M.D. and Corson, H.
v3p0057c2s
Conway, M.D. and Oswald, F.L.
v4p0588c2s
Conway, M.D. et al. v3p0167c1s
v4p0557c2s
Conway, Martin, Sir v5p0018c2s
Conway, R.S. v3p0124c1s
v3p0272c2s v5p0033c2m v6p0127c1s
Conway, T., jr. v6p0621c1s
Conway, W.M. v2p0019c2s
v2p0022c2s v2p0023c2s v2p0024c2s
v2p0039c1s v2p0049c2s v2p0065c1s
v2p0125c1s v2p0261c2s v2p0271c2s
v2p0283c1s v2p0329c1s v2p0335c1s
v2p0341c1s v2p0365c1s v2p0436c1s
v2p0471c1s v2p0479c1m v3p0022c1s
v3p0070c1s v3p0258c1s v3p0260c2s
v3p0344c1s v3p0354c2s v3p0471c1s
v4p0011c2s v4p0012c1m v4p0013c1s
v4p0030c1s v4p0031c1s v4p0039c1m
v4p0133c2s v4p0245c2s v4p0257c2s
v4p0258c2s v4p0260c2s v4p0308c2s
v4p0324c2s v4p0346c2s v4p0385c1m
v4p0385c2s v4p0390c1s v4p0445c2s
v4p0459c1s v4p0459c2s v4p0631c1m
v5p0389c2s v5p0546c2m v6p0611c1m
Conway, W.M., Sir v5p0170c2s
v5p0509c1s
Conwell, R.H. v6p0125c2s
Conwentz, H. v4p0013c1s
Conybeare, C.A.V. v1p1159c2s
Conybeare, F. v5p0115c2s
Conybeare, F.C. v3p0020c1s
v3p0029c1s v3p0185c1s v3p0316c1s
v3p0334c1s v3p0365c1s v4p0021c1s
v4p0046c1m v4p0056c1s v4p0057c1s
v4p0064c2s v4p0110c1s v4p0152c2m
v4p0277c2s v4p0305c1s v4p0430c2s
v4p0437c1s v4p0438c2s v4p0446c2m
v4p0515c2s v4p0537c2s v4p0605c2s
v4p0627c2s v5p0028c2s v5p0057c2s
v5p0060c1s v5p0087c2s v5p0115c1s
v5p0158c2s v5p0168c2s v5p0169c1m
v5p0218c1m v5p0218c2s v5p0308c1s
v5p0359c2s v5p0441c2s v5p0468c2s
v5p0469c2s v5p0498c1s v5p0538c2s
v5p0564c2s v5p0574c1s v6p0057c1s
v6p0063c2s v6p0172c1s v6p0425c2s
v6p0562c1s
Conybeare, F.C. et al. ... v4p0056c2s
v4p0300c1s
Conybeare, H. v1p0054c1s
Conybeare, J.C. v1p0459c1s
Conybeare, J.J. v1p0040c1m
v1p0436c1s v1p0716c1s
Conyers, S. v1p1190c1s
Conyngham, A., Lord v1p1329c2s
Conyngham, J. v6p0629c2s
Conyngton, J. v6p0659c1s
Conyngton, T. v5p0138c1s
Coocke, J.E.V. v4p0272c1s
Coocke, J.R. v4p0271c2s
Coode, Clara E. v5p0384c1s
Cook, A. v6p0091c2s
Cook, A.B. v4p0018c1s
v4p0049c1s v5p0295c1s v6p0177c1s
v6p0273c2s
Cook, A.C. v5p0092c1m
Cook, A.J. v1p0016c1s
v1p0107c1s v2p0038c1s v3p0200c1s
v3p0205c2s v6p0387c1s
Cook, A.M. v2p0384c1s
Cook, A.R. v6p0596c2s
Cook, A.S. v2p0007c2s
v2p0014c2s v2p0156c1s v2p0246c1s
v2p0463c2s v3p0030c1s v3p0057c2s
v3p0088c1s v3p0258c1s v3p0371c1s
v3p0388c2s v3p0425c1m v4p0098c2s
v4p0184c1s v4p0341c1s v4p0570c1s
v5p0192c1s v6p0587c2s
Cook, A.S. and Stevenson, W.H.
v3p0088c1s
Cook, A.S. and Westwood, J.O.
v3p0279c2s
Cook, C. v1p0052c2s
v1p0107c2s v1p0175c2s v1p0212c2s
v1p0303c1s v1p0305c2s v1p0495c1s
v1p0716c1s v1p0842c1s v1p0866c2s
v1p0897c1s v1p0916c1m v1p0958c1s
v1p1240c1s v1p1372c1s v2p0019c2s
v2p0023c1s v3p0018c2s v3p0022c2s
v3p0056c1s v3p0184c1s v3p0223c2s
v3p0317c2s v3p0382c2s v4p0029c2s
v4p0031c1s v4p0032c1s v4p0070c1s
v4p0110c1s v4p0143c2s v4p0150c2s
v4p0151c2s v4p0254c1s v4p0259c2s
v4p0455c1s v4p0554c1s v6p0469c2s
Cook, C. et al. v2p0184c2s
Cook, C., Mrs. v1p0473c2s
Cook, C.A. v3p0125c2s
Cook, C.B. v6p0178c1s
Cook, C.E. v5p0213c1s
Cook, C.S. v2p0413c2s
v3p0447c1s
Cook, C.W. v1p1437c1s
Cook, C.W. and Kraus, E.H.
v6p0165c2s
Cook, Carroll v5p0088c1s
Cook, Clarence v5p0275c1s
v5p0385c2s
Cook, D. v1p0002c1s
v1p0004c2m v1p0005c1s v1p0006c2s
v1p0007c1s v1p0064c2s v1p0088c2s
v1p0107c2s v1p0143c2s v1p0150c1s
v1p0178c1s v1p0204c1s v1p0219c2s
v1p0220c1s v1p0297c1s v1p0330c2s
v1p0335c1s v1p0358c1s v1p0363c2s
v1p0371c1s v1p0445c1s v1p0448c2s
v1p0466c1s v1p0501c1m v1p0519c1s
v1p0527c1s v1p0559c1s v1p0571c1s
v1p0577c1s v1p0577c2s v1p0586c1m
v1p0590c2s v1p0595c2s v1p0596c1s
v1p0694c1s v1p0698c2s v1p0703c2s
v1p0707c2s v1p0709c1s v1p0811c2s
v1p0877c1s v1p0941c1s v1p0943c2s
v1p0962c1s v1p0975c2s v1p0979c2s
v1p1011c1s v1p1017c2m v1p1032c2s
v1p1050c1s v1p1054c1s v1p1073c2s
v1p1082c1s v1p1112c1s v1p1126c2s
v1p1129c1s v1p1130c1s v1p1132c1s
v1p1132c2s v1p1183c2s v1p1184c1s
v1p1184c2s v1p1185c2s v1p1186c1s
v1p1187c1m v1p1211c2s v1p1212c1s
v1p1242c1m v1p1255c1s v1p1299c2m
v1p1358c2s v1p1368c1s v1p1371c1s
v1p1409c1s v1p1418c2s v1p1436c2s
v2p0002c1m v2p0035c2s v2p0061c2s
v2p0085c2s v2p0094c1s v2p0094c2s
v2p0118c1s v2p0154c1s v2p0193c2s
v2p0196c2s v2p0203c2s v2p0238c2s
v2p0275c2s v2p0289c1s v2p0300c2s
v2p0301c1s v2p0304c1s v2p0321c1s
v2p0328c1s v2p0332c1s v2p0344c2s
v2p0345c1s v2p0374c1s v2p0398c1m
v2p0435c2s v2p0436c1s v2p0436c2s
v2p0437c1s v2p0438c2s v2p0446c2s
v2p0474c1s
Cook, Dr. v1p0361c2s
Cook, Dutton v4p0003c1s
v4p0042c2s v4p0375c2s v4p0392c2s
v4p0493c1s
Cook, E. v1p0177c1s
v1p0228c2s v1p0311c2s v1p0877c1s
v1p0942c2s v1p0951c2s v1p1182c2s
v1p1266c2s v1p1309c1s v1p1313c1s
v6p0101c2s
Cook, E.C. v3p0435c2s
v4p0047c1s v4p0223c2s v4p0334c2s
v4p0417c2s v5p0522c1s v5p0575c1s
Cook, E.H. v2p0425c1s
Cook, E.P. v4p0012c1s
Cook, E.T. v3p0296c2s
v4p0031c1s v4p0355c1s v4p0495c1s
v5p0500c2s v6p0258c1s v6p0267c2s
v6p0269c2s v6p0361c2s
Cook, E.T., Mrs. v4p0267c2s
v4p0398c1s v4p0495c1m v4p0553c2s
v4p0606c1s v5p0252c1s v5p0346c2s
Cook, E.W. v2p0310c2s
v5p0423c2s v6p0122c1s v6p0122c2s
v6p0312c1s
Cook, E.Wake v6p0463c1s
Cook, Emily C. v3p0284c1s
v3p0468c2s v4p0393c2s
Cook, F.A. v4p0019c2m
v5p0022c1m v5p0022c2s v5p0027c1s
v5p0038c2s v5p0251c2s v5p0288c2s
v5p0456c2s v5p0508c2s v5p0579c2s
v6p0210c2s v6p0393c2m
Cook, F.C. v2p0240c2s
Cook, F.E. v1p1085c2s
Cook, F.G. v2p0478c1s
v3p0117c2s v3p0244c2s v3p0245c1m
v3p0245c2s v3p0268c2s v3p0269c1m
v3p0371c1s v3p0465c1s v5p0157c2s
v5p0312c1s v6p0201c1s v6p0659c1s
Cook, G. v1p0282c2s
Cook, G.A. v4p0593c2s
Cook, G.C. v5p0629c2s
Cook, G.E. v5p0089c1s
Cook, G.H. v1p0912c1s
Cook, G.L. v4p0097c2s
Cook, H. v6p0238c2s
v6p0648c1s
Cook, H.C. v1p0040c2s
v1p0213c1s v1p0644c2s v1p0705c2s
v1p0839c1s v1p1378c2s
Cook, H.O. v5p0038c1s
Cook, H.S. v1p0849c2s
Cook, H.T. v1p0185c1s
v1p0377c2s v1p1334c2s v1p1366c1s
Cook, J. v1p1083c2s
v1p1260c1s v1p1302c1s v1p1310c1s
v2p0004c1s v2p0261c2s v3p0004c1s
v3p0011c1s v3p0031c1s v3p0038c2s
v3p0040c2m v3p0050c1s v3p0054c2s
v3p0065c2s v3p0111c1s v3p0132c1s
v3p0148c1m v3p0152c2s v3p0175c1s
v3p0202c1s v3p0214c1s v3p0214c2s
v3p0229c1s v3p0244c2s v3p0252c2s
v3p0283c1m v3p0288c1m v3p0296c2s
v3p0299c1s v3p0318c2s v3p0322c1s
v3p0345c2s v3p0359c1s v3p0359c2s
v3p0364c1s v3p0364c2m v3p0365c1m
v3p0365c2s v3p0368c2s v3p0373c2s
v3p0378c1s v3p0383c2s v3p0401c2m
v3p0402c1s v3p0416c1s v3p0423c2m
v3p0437c2s v3p0441c1s v3p0454c2s
v4p0001c1s v4p0005c2s v4p0017c1s
v4p0027c1s v4p0036c2s v4p0053c1m
v4p0053c2s v4p0054c1s v4p0058c1s
v4p0075c1s v4p0091c2s v4p0102c1m
v4p0108c2s v4p0111c2s v4p0160c1m
v4p0174c1s v4p0190c2s v4p0191c1s
v4p0193c2s v4p0232c2s v4p0250c2s
v4p0261c1m v4p0275c1s v4p0297c2s
v4p0328c2s v4p0374c2s v4p0380c2s
v4p0382c2s v4p0394c1s v4p0397c1s
v4p0424c1s v4p0427c1s v4p0455c1s
v4p0461c2s v4p0464c1s v4p0466c1s
v4p0472c2s v4p0479c1s v4p0479c2s
v4p0501c1m v4p0503c2s v4p0510c1s
v4p0543c2s v4p0557c1m v4p0557c2s
v4p0568c1s v4p0572c2s v4p0599c1s
v4p0604c1s v4p0626c1s v5p0432c2s
Cook, J. and Hovey, A. ... v5p0432c2s
Cook, J. et al. v3p0454c2s
Cook, J., Mrs. v4p0160c1s
v4p0568c1s
Cook, J.A. v5p0025c1s
v5p0498c1s
Cook, J.E. v1p1373c2s
Cook, J.J. v4p0224c2s
Cook, J.W. v4p0566c2s
v5p0287c2s
Cook, J.W. et al. v5p0413c2s
Cook, Joel v3p0420c1s

Cook, K. ... v1p0002c2s
v1p0066c2s v1p0067c1s v1p0173c2s
v1p0222c1s v1p0298c2s v1p0334c1s
v1p0363c1s v1p0394c2s v1p0425c1s
v1p0527c2s v1p0553c2s v1p0575c2s
v1p0598c1s v1p0611c1s v1p0685c1s
v1p0715c1s v1p0792c1s v1p0931c2s
v1p0966c1s v1p1144c1s v1p1151c1s
v1p1264c1s v1p1272c1s v1p1356c1s
v1p1384c2s v1p1407c1s v2p0197c2s
Cook, K.R. ... v1p0458c2s
Cook, Lady ... v4p0145c1s
v4p0284c2s v4p0357c1s v4p0369c2s
v4p0467c2s v4p0504c1s v4p0623c1s
Cook, M. ... v1p0006c2s
Cook, M.E. ... v6p0134c1s
v6p0152c1s v6p0220c1s v6p0357c2s
Cook, M.W., Mrs. ... v1p0063c2s
v1p1020c2s
Cook, N. ... v1p0094c1s
Cook, O. ... v5p0338c2s
Cook, O.F. ... v4p0124c1s
v4p0548c2s v5p0198c1s v5p0403c1s
v5p0545c1s v6p0008c2s v6p0152c2m
v6p0214c2m v6p0215c1s v6p0325c1s
v6p0350c1s v6p0361c1s v6p0410c1s
v6p0459c1s v6p0514c2s v6p0554c1s
v6p0608c2m v6p0663c2s
Cook, O.K. ... v6p0024c1s
Cook, P. ... v1p1140c2s
v3p0130c2s v6p0631c2s
Cook, R.A. ... v4p0122c1s
Cook, R.B. ... v2p0179c1m
v2p0214c1s
Cook, R.E. ... v6p0616c2s
Cook, Rev.Dr. ... v1p0647c2s
Cook, S.A. ... v4p0054c1s
v6p0061c1s v6p0125c2s v6p0320c2s
v6p0650c2s
Cook, T. ... v2p0101c1s
v5p0144c1s
Cook, T.A. ... v4p0019c1s
v4p0408c1s v5p0165c1s v5p0262c1s
v5p0270c2s v5p0384c1s v6p0134c2s
v6p0295c2s v6p0409c1s v6p0496c1s
v6p0512c1s v6p0553c1s v6p0610c2s
v6p0679c2s v6p0693c2s
Cook, Theo.A. ... v6p0482c1s
Cook, W. ... v1p0416c1s
v3p0128c2s v3p0145c1s v5p0267c1s
Cook, W.B. ... v1p0935c1s
v1p1095c2s
Cook, W.F. ... v3p0343c2s
Cook, W.L. ... v5p0457c2s
v6p0158c2s v6p0277c2s v6p0685c1s
Cook, W.M. ... v4p0387c2s
Cook, W.V. ... v6p0081c2s
v6p0100c1s v6p0301c1s v6p0482c2s
v6p0491c2s v6p0566c2s v6p0648c1s
Cook, W.V. and Brodie, A.D.
v6p0220c2s
Cook, W.Victor ... v5p0343c1s
v6p0032c2s
v6p0682c1s
Cook, W.W. ... v5p0444c2s
v6p0646c2s
Cook, Walter ... v5p0025c2s
Cook, Z. ... v1p1403c1s
Cook, Z., jr. ... v1p0082c2s
v1p0648c1m
Cooke, A.B. ... v6p0302c1s
Cooke, A.H. ... v3p0183c2s
v4p0523c1s
Cooke, A.M. ... v4p0114c2s
Cooke, A.O. ... v6p0174c2s
v6p0276c1s v6p0294c1s v6p0619c2s
v6p0664c2s
Cooke, A.R. ... v3p0216c2s
Cooke, C. ... v1p0253c1s
v1p1391c1s v3p0458c2s
Cooke, C.J. ... v3p0138c1s
v3p0370c2s
Cooke, C.J.B. ... v4p0337c2s
v5p0344c1s
Cooke, C.K. ... v2p0311c2s
v2p0325c2s v2p0385c1s v4p0164c1s
Cooke, C.W. ... v3p0423c1s
Cooke, C.W.R. ... v2p0331c1s
v3p0321c2s v4p0114c1s v5p0119c1s
Cooke, E.J. ... v5p0212c1s
Cooke, E.V. ... v5p0036c2s
v5p0104c2s v5p0367c2s v5p0478c2s
v6p0306c2s
Cooke, F.H. ... v4p0080c2s
v4p0115c1s v4p0135c1s v4p0283c2s
v4p0585c2s v4p0589c2s v4p0608c1s
v5p0592c2s v5p0593c1s
Cooke, G.A. ... v4p0439c2s
Cooke, G.H. ... v1p0749c2s
Cooke, G.M. ... v4p0207c1s
v5p0453c1s v6p0094c1s v6p0392c2s
v6p0612c1s
Cooke, G.MacG. ... v6p0066c1s
v6p0100c2s v6p0220c2s v6p0398c2s
v6p0439c2s v6p0489c1s v6p0521c1s
v6p0594c2s v6p0695c1s
Cooke, G.W. ... v2p0058c1s
v2p0117c2s v2p0202c2s v2p0346c1s
v3p0198c2s v3p0321c1s v3p0398c2s
v4p0076c1s v4p0076c2s v4p0112c1s
v4p0551c2s v5p0072c2s v5p0078c2s
v5p0081c1s v5p0132c1s v5p0150c1s
v5p0170c1s v5p0405c2s v5p0509c1s
v5p0598c1s v6p0202c1m v6p0240c1s
v6p0262c1s v6p0301c1s v6p0653c2s
Cooke, George Willis ... v5p0082c2s
Cooke, Grace M. ... v6p0048c2s
Cooke, Grace MacG. ... v6p0397c2s
v6p0643c1s
Cooke, Grace MacG. and Reed, V.
v6p0464c1s
Cooke, H. ... v1p0089c2s
v1p0193c1s v1p0917c1s v1p0919c2s
v1p0996c2s v1p1388c2s
Cooke, H.M. ... v2p0097c2s
Cooke, J. ... v1p0499c1s
v1p0526c2s v1p1399c2s v2p0025c2s
v2p0397c1s v4p0584c1s v5p0083c2s
Cooke, J.D.S. ... v6p0120c2s
Cooke, J.E. ... v1p0033c1s
v1p0222c2s v1p0270c2s v1p0297c2s
v1p0298c2s v1p0312c1s v1p0314c2s
v1p0365c1s v1p0371c1s v1p0371c2s
v1p0483c1s v1p0636c2s v1p0667c1m
v1p0676c2s v1p0677c1s v1p0680c2s
v1p0681c1s v1p0701c2s v1p0734c1s
v1p0760c1s v1p0804c2s v1p0834c1s
v1p0849c1s v1p0864c1s v1p0941c1s
v1p0943c2s v1p0953c2s v1p1030c1s
v1p1070c2s v1p1190c1s v1p1211c1s
v1p1240c1s v1p1298c1m v1p1345c1s
v1p1373c2s v1p1374c1s v1p1374c2s
v1p1400c2s v1p1406c2s v1p1411c2s
v1p1427c1s v2p0057c2s v2p0058c2s
v2p0082c2s v2p0088c1s v2p0114c1s
v2p0234c1s v2p0279c1s v2p0296c2s
v2p0339c2s v2p0400c1s v2p0442c2s
v2p0461c2s v2p0476c1s v3p0109c2s
v3p0261c2s v3p0290c2s v3p0335c1s
Cooke, J.E.V. ... v4p0052c2s
Cooke, J.H. ... v4p0066c1s
v4p0617c2s v5p0343c1s v5p0358c2s
Cooke, J.P. ... v1p0102c2s
v1p0237c1s v1p0400c1s v1p0841c1s
v1p1304c2s v1p1306c2s v1p1354c2s
v2p0087c2s v2p0125c2s v2p0191c1s
v2p0197c1s v2p0390c2s v3p0134c2s
v3p0190c2s
Cooke, J.P., jr. ... v1p0046c1s
v1p0073c2s v1p0074c1m v1p0224c1s
v1p0323c2s v1p0539c1s v1p0618c2s
v1p0711c2s v1p0858c2s v1p1074c2s
v1p1233c2s v1p1268c2s
Cooke, Jane G. ... v5p0482c2s
Cooke, Jay ... v4p0525c2s
v6p0667c1s
Cooke, M.C. ... v1p0153c1s
v1p0271c2s v1p0462c2s v1p0494c2m
v1p0770c2s v1p0836c1s v1p0882c1s
v1p0965c2s v1p1015c1s v4p0072c1s
Cooke, P. ... v1p0537c1s
Cooke, P. and Cooke, R.T.. v6p0615c2s
Cooke, P.P. ... v1p1019c2s
Cooke, P.St.G. ... v3p0063c1s
v3p0426c1s
Cooke, R.J. ... v3p0033c2s
v3p0229c1s v4p0185c2s v4p0186c2s
v6p0051c2s v6p0126c2s v6p0340c2s
v6p0341c1s
Cooke, R.T. ... v1p0004c1s
v1p0043c1s v1p0088c1s v1p0185c2s
v1p0261c2s v1p0286c2s v1p0380c2s
v1p0487c1s v1p0609c2s v1p0807c1s
v1p0827c1s v1p0851c1s v1p0851c2s
v1p0878c2s v1p0891c2s v1p0908c2s
v1p0987c2s v1p1108c2s v1p1113c2s
v1p1146c1s v1p1305c2s v1p1308c1s
v1p1315c2s v1p1416c1s v2p0207c1s
v2p0319c2s v3p0098c2s v3p0433c2s
v3p0470c1s
Cooke, R.T. and Cooke, P.. v6p0615c2s
Cooke, R.T. et al. ... v3p0119c1s
v3p0202c2s v3p0269c1s v3p0470c1s
Cooke, Rose T. ... v2p0409c2s
Cooke, T. ... v5p0047c1s
v5p0149c2s v6p0050c2s
Cooke, W. ... v1p0425c2s
v2p0036c2s
Cooke, W.A. ... v1p0796c2s
Cooke, W.E. ... v6p0411c2s
v6p0647c1s
Cooke, W.Ernest ... v6p0330c1s
v6p0690c2s
Cooke, W.F. ... v3p0386c1s
Cooke, W.H. ... v1p0167c1s
v3p0362c2s
Cooke, W.M. ... v2p0324c1s
Cooke, W.W. ... v4p0370c2s
Cooke, Z. ... v6p0148c1s
Cooke-Trench, T. ... v5p0454c1s
Cooker, J.H. ... v3p0010c1s
v3p0130c2s
Cookson, M. ... v1p0697c2s
v1p0803c2s v1p0869c2s v1p0897c1s
v1p1405c1s v2p0251c1s v4p0432c2s
Coolbrith, I.D. ... v1p0339c1s
v1p0492c1s v1p0699c2s v1p0732c2s
v1p0935c2s v1p0937c2s v1p1071c2s
v1p1418c2s
Coolbrith, I.D. and Williams, S.
v1p0082c2s
Coolbrith, Ina ... v6p0281c2s
Cooley, A.S. ... v5p0036c2s
v6p0288c2s
Cooley, C.C. ... v6p0078c2s
Cooley, C.H. ... v4p0095c2s
v4p0582c1s v5p0202c1s v5p0227c2s
v5p0534c2s v5p0633c2s
Cooley, E.B. ... v6p0567c1s
Cooley, E.G. ... v5p0182c2s
Cooley, E.W. ... v5p0388c2s
Cooley, Ellen J. ... v6p0672c2s
Cooley, F. ... v4p0602c1s
Cooley, H.R. ... v3p0469c1s
v6p0157c2s
Cooley, H.S. ... v4p0399c1s
v4p0529c2s
Cooley, J.D. ... v1p0757c2s
Cooley, J.E. ... v1p0395c2s
Cooley, L.C. ... v1p0400c1s
v1p0579c2s v1p1305c1m v1p1329c2s
Cooley, L.E. ... v2p0359c1s
Cooley, Le R.C. ... v1p0858c2s
Cooley, S. ... v4p0115c2s
v4p0132c2s v4p0375c1s v4p0418c2s
v4p0481c1s
Cooley, T.M. ... v1p0180c1s
v1p0437c2s v1p0493c2s v1p0537c2s
v1p0718c2s v1p0854c2s v1p1048c2s
v2p0018c1s v2p0103c2s v2p0244c2m
v2p0287c2m v2p0394c2s v2p0452c1s
v3p0097c2s v3p0244c2s v4p0250c2s
v4p0323c2m v4p0342c1s v4p0553c2s
Cooley, T.M. et al. ... v1p1048c2s
v2p0091c1s v2p0126c2s
Cooley, W.F. ... v2p0298c2s
v3p0143c2s v4p0515c2s
Cooley, W.H. ... v6p0176c2s
v6p0662c2s v6p0706c1s
Coolidge, A. ... v1p1327c1s
Coolidge, A.A. ... v5p0384c2s
Coolidge, A.C. ... v4p0005c2s
v4p0080c2s v4p0137c2m v4p0189c2s
v4p0449c2s v4p0516c1s v4p0522c2s
v4p0576c1s v4p0587c1s v5p0024c2s
v5p0151c2s v5p0258c2s v5p0318c2s
v5p0501c2s v6p0006c1s v6p0020c2s
v6p0339c2s v6p0486c2s v6p0593c1s
Coolidge, A.H. ... v1p0528c2s
v5p0056c1s
Coolidge, D. ... v5p0118c2s
v5p0277c2s v6p0091c1s v6p0381c2s
v6p0466c1s v6p0472c1s
Coolidge, Dane ... v6p0656c2s
Coolidge, H.F. ... v6p0632c1s
Coolidge, J.I.T. ... v1p0440c2s
v1p0687c2s v1p1042c1s v1p1438c2s
Coolidge, J.L. and Maltbie, W.H.
v5p0366c1s
Coolidge, J.R. ... v1p0237c1s
v5p0026c1s v5p0226c1s v5p0554c2s
v6p0027c2s v6p0076c2s
Coolidge, K. ... v4p0108c2s
v5p0396c2s v5p0641c2s
Coolidge, L.A. ... v5p0599c1s
v5p0621c1s v6p0151c2s v6p0279c2s
v6p0353c2s v6p0427c1s
Coolidge, R. ... v5p0411c2s
Coolidge, S. ... v1p0913c2s
v2p0140c1s
Coolidge, W.A.B. ... v3p0142c1s
v3p0172c1s v3p0356c1s v3p0377c1s
v3p0394c2s v3p0418c1s v4p0560c2s
v4p0568c1s v6p0013c2s v6p0110c1s
Coombs, F.L. ... v5p0258c2s
Coombs, J.C. ... v6p0591c1s
Coombs, W.J. ... v4p0563c2s
Coon, R.R. ... v1p0689c2s
v1p1435c2s
Cooney, J. ... v5p0097c2s
v5p0466c2s
Coonley, F. ... v5p0642c2s
Coonley, L.A. ... v4p0080c1s
v4p0491c1s v5p0043c2s
Coope, A.W. ... v6p0246c2s
v6p0587c1s
Cooper, A. and Holland, C.B.
v1p1250c2m
Cooper, A.N. ... v6p0287c1s
v6p0628c2s v6p0653c2s v6p0684c1s
Cooper, A.S. ... v4p0383c2s
v5p0099c1s
Cooper, B.H. ... v2p0318c2s
v3p0309c1s
Cooper, C. ... v3p0465c2s
v4p0162c1s v4p0166c2s v4p0454c2s
v4p0616c1s v5p0595c1s
Cooper, C.A. ... v5p0176c2s
Cooper, C.C. ... v1p0077c1s
v4p0601c2s
Cooper, C.D. ... v4p0038c2s
Cooper, C.H. ... v1p1040c2s
v3p0014c1s v3p0171c2m v3p0464c2s
v4p0062c1s v4p0213c2s v4p0224c1s
v4p0544c2s v4p0589c1s v4p0594c1s
v4p0622c2s v5p0043c2s v5p0231c2s
v5p0256c2s v5p0525c2s v5p0542c2s
v6p0235c2s v6p0332c2s v6p0353c2s
v6p0377c2m v6p0557c2s v6p0686c2s
Cooper, Chas. ... v4p0263c1s

Cooper, E. v3p0326c1s
v4p0049c1s v6p0466c1s
Cooper, E.H. v5p0107c1s
v5p0107c2m v5p0135c2s v5p0273c1s
v5p0588c2s v5p0592c1s v5p0644c1s
v6p0116c2s v6p0117c2m v6p0124c1s
v6p0141c1s
Cooper, F. v4p0066c2s
Cooper, F.B. v6p0375c1s
Cooper, F.E. v5p0597c2s
Cooper, F.J. v6p0523c2s
v6p0713c2s
Cooper, F.T. v4p0019c1s
v4p0052c2s v4p0548c2s v5p0193c1s
v5p0216c2s v5p0364c1s v5p0413c2s
v5p0415c1s v5p0491c2s v6p0147c2s
v6p0209c2s v6p0219c1s v6p0222c2s
v6p0223c1s v6p0292c1s v6p0293c2s
v6p0361c2s v6p0379c1s v6p0382c1s
v6p0388c2s v6p0394c2s v6p0409c2s
v6p0461c2m v6p0468c1s v6p0489c2s
v6p0504c1s v6p0533c1s v6p0595c2s
v6p0611c1s v6p0627c2s v6p0648c1s
v6p0663c2s
Cooper, F.T. and Maurice, A.B.
v6p0101c2s
Cooper, F.Taber v6p0159c2s
v6p0171c1s v6p0280c1s v6p0317c2s
v6p0348c2s v6p0612c2s v6p0672c2s
Cooper, H.C. v5p0373c2s
v5p0514c1s v6p0112c1s
Cooper, H.T. v1p0918c2s
Cooper, I.J. v1p0637c2s
Cooper, J. v1p0275c1s
v1p0276c2s v1p0389c1s v1p0402c1s
v1p0600c2s v1p0976c2s v2p0191c1s
v2p0448c1s v4p0003c2s v4p0058c1s
v4p0081c1m v4p0109c1s v4p0229c1s
v4p0255c2s v4p0453c2s v4p0623c1s
v5p0142c1s v5p0166c1m v5p0234c2s
v5p0236c2s v5p0289c1s v5p0377c1s
v5p0378c2s v5p0400c2s v5p0454c1s
v5p0610c1s v5p0640c1s v6p0008c1s
v6p0098c2s v6p0108c2s v6p0171c2s
v6p0300c2s v6p0309c2s v6p0536c2s
v6p0642c1s
Cooper, J.A. v4p0067c1s
v4p0085c2m v4p0086c1s v4p0183c2s
v4p0185c1s v4p0267c2s v4p0413c1s
v4p0423c2s v4p0469c1s v4p0524c2s
v4p0533c1s v4p0592c1s v4p0610c2s
v5p0053c1s v5p0069c2s v5p0081c2s
v5p0090c1s v5p0090c2m v5p0091c1s
v5p0091c2m v5p0205c1s v5p0229c2s
v5p0234c2s v5p0254c1s v5p0274c2s
v5p0275c1s v5p0415c1s v5p0421c2s
v5p0477c2s v5p0556c1s v6p0010c1s
v6p0014c2s v6p0072c1s v6p0096c1m
v6p0097c1s v6p0097c2s v6p0098c1m
v6p0191c1s v6p0209c1s v6p0264c1s
v6p0267c2s v6p0274c2s v6p0310c1s
v6p0358c1s v6p0461c1s v6p0478c2s
v6p0480c2s v6p0512c2s v6p0545c2s
v6p0560c1s v6p0563c2s
Cooper, J.E. v6p0615c2s
Cooper, J.F. v1p0199c2s
v1p0294c2s v1p0381c2s v1p0666c1s
v1p1017c1s v1p1155c2s v1p1169c1s
v3p0304c2s
Cooper, J.F. et al. v2p0011c2s
Cooper, J.G. v1p0136c1s
v1p0188c1s v1p0327c2m v1p0863c2m
v4p0420c1s
Cooper, J.H. v1p0111c1m
v1p1040c2s v1p1240c2s v1p1248c1s
v1p1249c1s v1p1404c2s v3p0232c1s
v3p0272c2s v4p0220c1s v4p0467c1s
v4p0498c1s v4p0612c2s v4p0633c1s
v5p0344c1s v5p0622c2s v6p0096c1s
Cooper, J.M. v4p0251c2s
Cooper, J.T. v1p0855c1s
v6p0627c2s
Cooper, J.W. v2p0077c2s
Cooper, Jacob v6p0065c1s
v6p0244c1s v6p0670c2s
Cooper, Jeannette v6p0294c1s
v6p0306c2s v6p0540c2s v6p0687c2s
Cooper, Judge v1p1225c1s
Cooper, K. v1p1174c1s
v2p0322c1s
Cooper, L. v5p0355c1s
v6p0330c2s v6p0359c2s v6p0386c1s
Cooper, L.M. v5p0159c2s
Cooper, L.O. v4p0417c1s
v5p0008c1s v5p0051c2s v5p0052c2m
v5p0296c1s v5p0579c2s v5p0633c2s
Cooper, Lane v5p0455c2s
v6p0053c1s v6p0142c1s v6p0707c2s
Cooper, Miss v3p0220c1s
Cooper, O.H. v1p1297c2s
Cooper, P. v1p0326c1s
Cooper, S. and Jones, J. . v1p1343c2s
Cooper, S.B. v1p0158c1s
v1p0491c2s v1p0941c1s v1p1420c2s
v1p1426c1s v1p1439c1s
Cooper, S.B., Mrs. v1p0707c2s
Cooper, S.F. v1p0222c1s
v1p0454c2s v1p0557c1s v1p0610c2s
v1p0621c2s v1p0645c2s v1p0717c2s
v1p1193c2s v1p1371c2s v1p1426c1s
v3p0099c1s v4p0060c2s
Cooper, S.W. v2p0445c2s
v2p0478c1s v3p0205c1s v3p0244c2s
v3p0252c2s v3p0408c1s v3p0435c2s
v3p0470c1s
Cooper, T. v1p0061c1s
v1p0297c1s v1p0523c1s v1p0733c2s
v1p1225c1s v1p1377c1s v2p0359c1s
Cooper, T.A. v4p0339c2s
Cooper, T.C. v1p1004c2s
Cooper, W. v1p1213c1s
v5p0442c1s v5p0551c1m
Cooper, W.B. v1p0729c1s
v2p0339c2s
Cooper, W.C. v4p0291c1s
v4p0410c1s
Cooper, W.D. v1p0411c2s
v1p1013c2s v1p1095c1s v1p1173c2s
v1p1318c1s
Cooper, W.D. and Collier, J.P.
v1p0929c2s
Cooper, W.F. v1p0108c2s
v1p1364c2s
Cooper, W.R. v6p0044c2s
v6p0184c2s
Cooper, W.W. v1p0214c2s
Cooper, William v6p0197c2s
Coopwood, B. v6p0211c1s
Coore, G.B.M. and Stevenson, F.S.
v4p0027c2s
Coote, C.H. v4p0362c1s
Coote, H. v2p0309c2s
Coote, H.C. v1p0163c2s
v1p0297c2s v1p1124c1s v1p1154c2s
v2p0050c1s v2p0075c2s v2p0293c1s
v4p0092c2s v4p0193c2s v4p0205c1s
v4p0205c2s v4p0294c2s v5p0381c1s
Coote, K.V. v4p0605c2s
Coover, M. v5p0058c2s
v6p0063c1s v6p0342c1s v6p0478c2s
Copcutt, F. v1p0141c1s
v1p0154c2s v1p0336c1s v1p0384c1s
v1p0429c2s v1p0718c2s v1p1084c1s
v1p1176c1s
Cope, E.D. v1p0003c2s
v1p0023c1s v1p0041c1s v1p0134c1m
v1p0136c2s v1p0202c2s v1p0205c2s
v1p0268c2s v1p0279c2s v1p0434c1m
v1p0434c2m v1p0447c2s v1p0457c1s
v1p0466c1s v1p0470c2s v1p0508c2s
v1p0794c2s v1p0862c2s v1p0863c2s
v1p0881c2s v1p0912c2s v1p0927c1s
v1p0947c2s v1p0960c1m v1p1013c2s
v1p1059c1s v1p1105c1s v1p1152c2s
v1p1399c2s v1p1410c2s v1p1434c1s
v1p1435c2s v1p1441c1s v2p0009c2s
v2p0018c2s v2p0036c1s v2p0046c1s
v2p0065c1s v2p0070c2m v2p0080c2s
v2p0098c1s v2p0107c1s v2p0120c2s
v2p0145c1s v2p0148c2s v2p0149c1s
v2p0149c2m v2p0211c1s v2p0253c2s
v2p0257c2s v2p0273c2s v2p0341c1m
v2p0370c2s v2p0374c2s v2p0432c2s
v2p0435c2m v2p0459c2m v2p0482c1s
v3p0022c2s v3p0069c2s v3p0072c2s
v3p0127c2s v3p0153c1s v3p0254c1s
v3p0265c1s v3p0275c1s v3p0280c1s
v3p0327c1s v3p0332c2s v3p0345c1s
v3p0363c1s v3p0386c2m v3p0394c2s
v3p0422c2s v4p0047c2s v4p0095c1s
v4p0117c2s v4p0150c1s v4p0185c1s
v4p0187c2s v4p0190c2s v4p0191c1s
v4p0191c2s v4p0233c1s v4p0272c2s
v4p0273c2s v4p0351c2m v4p0352c1s
v4p0357c1s v4p0361c1m v4p0364c2s
v4p0372c1s v4p0379c2s v4p0380c2s
v4p0394c2m v4p0396c2s v4p0408c1s
v4p0481c2s v4p0516c2m v4p0531c1m
v4p0567c1s v4p0572c2s v4p0575c1s
v4p0629c1s v5p0584c1s
Cope, E.D. and Lankester, E.R.
v3p0447c1s
Cope, E.D. and Packard, A.S., jr.
v1p0920c2s
Cope, E.D. et al. v3p0250c2s
Cope, F.R., jr. v5p0572c2s
v6p0452c2s
Cope, G. v3p0195c2s
v4p0311c2s
Cope, H.F. v6p0095c2s
v6p0146c2s v6p0201c1s v6p0329c2s
v6p0546c2m v6p0590c1s v6p0711c1s
Cope, Walter v6p0360c2m
Copeland, A. v4p0632c1s
Copeland, C.T. v4p0037c2s
v4p0197c1s v4p0549c1s v5p0094c2s
v5p0095c1s v6p0283c2s
Copeland, G.A. v5p0209c2s
Copeland, H. v4p0364c1s
Copeland, H.E. v1p0900c1s
Copeland, H.E. and Jordan, D.S.
v1p1149c2s
Copeland, J.A. v4p0461c2s
Copeland, R. v2p0455c1s
v4p0037c2s v5p0219c2s v5p0534c1s
v5p0549c2s
Copeland, R. et al. v3p0094c1s
Copeland, R.M. v1p0494c2s
v1p0500c1s v1p0888c1s v1p0969c1s
v1p1349c2s
Copeland, T. v6p0489c2s
Copeland, T.M. v6p0055c1s
Copeland, W.C. v5p0019c2s
Copeland, W.E. v1p1162c2s
v1p1238c2s v1p1355c1s v6p0148c2s
Copeland, W.P. v6p0148c2s
Copeman, E. v6p0540c2s
Copinger, H. v1p0035c2s
v1p0112c2s v1p0214c1s v1p0378c1s
v1p0443c1s v1p1256c1s
Copinger, Lieut.-Col. v1p1409c1s
Copinger, Lucy v6p0034c1s
v6p0111c2s v6p0421c1s v6p0694c2s
v6p0703c1s
Copinger, W.A. v5p0060c2s
Copland, J.A. v6p0440c2s
Copland, M. v5p0285c2s
Copland, S. v1p0015c1s
Copland-Crawford, W.E.B. . v5p0528c2s
Copleston, E. v1p0325c2s
Copleston, F., Mrs. v3p0305c2s
v4p0494c1s
Copley, F.B. v6p0319c1s
v6p0424c2s
Copley, J. v2p0374c2s
Coplin, W.M.L. and Bevan, D.
v4p0521c2s
Copner, J. v4p0113c1s
Copp, G.G. v6p0112c2s
v6p0139c2s
Coppee, F. v3p0038c2s
v3p0332c1s v4p0110c1s v4p0161c1s
v4p0268c1s v4p0435c1s v4p0485c1s
v4p0530c2s v5p0041c2s v5p0268c2s
v5p0273c2s v6p0302c1s v6p0366c2s
Coppee, Fr. v5p0639c1s
Coppee, H. v1p0022c1s
v1p0061c2s v1p0411c1m v1p0428c2s
v1p0680c1s v1p0866c2s v1p0959c1s
v1p1073c1m v1p1228c1s v1p1401c2s
v2p0178c1s v2p0203c2s v3p0279c2s
v3p0442c2s v5p0373c1s
Coppee, H.S.L. and Dutton, C.N.
v4p0328c1s v4p0375c1s
Coppee, H.St.L. v4p0375c1s
v5p0380c2s
Coppens, C. v1p1175c1s
Coppersmith, Mary E. v6p0207c2s
Coppin, L.J. v6p0006c1s
Copping, E. v3p0195c1s
v3p0260c2s v4p0299c2s
Coppinger, W. v1p0113c1s
Copplestone, B. v5p0248c2s
v5p0282c2s v5p0315c2s v5p0357c1s
v5p0367c1s v5p0506c1s v5p0606c2s
v6p0090c1s v6p0638c1s
Copplestone, R. v5p0237c2s
Coppock, F.M. and Knies, K.
v1p0861c1s
Copus, J.E. v6p0368c1s
Copway, G. v1p0636c1s
Coquelin, C. v1p0963c2s
v3p0002c1m v3p0163c2s v3p0284c2s
v3p0387c1s v4p0051c2s v6p0140c1s
v6p0424c1s
Coquerel, A. v1p0243c1s
v1p0481c2s v1p0561c2s v1p0623c1s
v1p1044c1s v1p1100c2s v1p1120c1s
Coquerel, E. v1p0481c2m
Coquillet, D.W. v6p0161c1s
Cora, Angel de v5p0243c1s
Corballis, C. v6p0427c2s
Corbaux, F. v1p1088c1s
v1p1099c1s
Corbet, R.G. v5p0100c1s
v6p0086c1s v6p0107c2s v6p0334c1m
Corbet, R.S. v6p0624c1s
Corbet, W.J. v2p0222c1s
v3p0221c1s v4p0285c2s v4p0345c1s
v4p0508c1s v4p0532c2s v5p0007c2s
v5p0190c1s v5p0196c1s v5p0291c2m
v5p0351c1s v5p0618c2s v6p0007c1s
v6p0108c1s v6p0138c1s v6p0320c1m
v6p0326c2s v6p0327c2s v6p0328c1s
Corbet-Seymour v5p0052c2s
Corbet-Seymour, M., Mrs. . v5p0518c2s
Corbett, A., jr. v4p0069c1s
Corbett, Alexander, jr. .. v6p0345c2s
Corbett, E.T. v4p0381c2s
Corbett, H.R. v5p0179c1s
v5p0264c2s
Corbett, J. v4p0124c1s
v4p0348c2s v4p0496c1s v4p0581c2s
v5p0028c2s v5p0207c2s v5p0586c2s
Corbett, J.S. v5p0218c1s
v5p0398c1s v5p0631c1s v6p0022c2s
v6p0266c1s v6p0268c2s v6p0409c1s
v6p0445c1s v6p0559c2s v6p0582c2m
Corbett, Julian v4p0303c1s
v4p0313c1s v4p0348c1s v6p0180c2s
Corbett, L.C. v4p0209c1s
v4p0424c1s v5p0590c1s v6p0247c1s
Corbett, R. v1p0339c2s
Corbett, Sarah v4p0311c1s
Corbett, W.J. v4p0181c1s
v4p0285c2s v6p0265c1s v6p0289c2s
v6p0627c2s
Corbigny, B.de v1p0146c2s
v1p1440c1s
Corbin, A. v3p0239c1s

v4p0582c1s
Corbin, E.A. and Goodrich, H.G.
v1p0146c1s
Corbin, H. v1p1374c2s
Corbin, H.C. v5p0598c2s
v6p0087c2s v6p0398c1s
Corbin, J. v4p0035c2s
v4p0036c1s v4p0118c1s v4p0206c2s
v4p0394c1s v4p0419c2s v5p0037c1s
v5p0045c1s v5p0182c2s v5p0213c1s
v5p0274c1s v5p0523c2s v5p0576c1s
v6p0083c2s v6p0121c2s v6p0145c1s
v6p0206c1s v6p0232c2s v6p0473c1s
v6p0503c2s v6p0586c1s v6p0587c1s
v6p0642c1s
Corbin, John v6p0384c2s
v6p0454c1s v6p0623c2s
Corbin, L.P. v6p0629c1s
Corbin, M.A. v6p0429c2s
Corbin, R. v6p0452c1s
Corbin, W. v5p0082c2s
Corbishley, J. v5p0063c2s
Corbit, W.F. v3p0465c1s
Corbusier, W.F. v2p0017c1s
Corby, E.F. v4p0222c1s
v4p0303c1s v4p0493c2s
Corbyn, J.H. v2p0059c2s
Corcelles, F.de v2p0348c2s
Corcoran, J.A. v1p0116c2s
v1p0121c2s v1p0127c1s v1p0468c2s
v1p0683c1s v1p0737c2s v1p0850c2s
v1p0965c1s v1p1013c1s v1p1118c2s
v1p1279c1s v1p1279c2s v2p0032c2s
v2p0042c2s v2p0085c1s v2p0106c2s
v2p0268c2s v3p0026c2s v3p0146c2s
v3p0150c1s v3p0228c2s v3p0323c2s
v3p0418c2s
Corcoran, M. v2p0270c1s
Corcoran, Mgr. v2p0140c2s
Cord, E.C. v4p0306c2s
Cordeaux, J. v1p1193c1s
v4p0253c2s
Cordeiro, F.J.B. v6p0264c2s
Cordeiro, O.J.B. v6p0039c2s
Corden, V. v5p0611c1s
Corder, F. v2p0464c1s
Corderoy, E. v1p0035c2s
v1p1054c2s v1p1089c2s v1p1252c2s
Cordery, A. v1p1189c1s
Cordery, B.M. v2p0408c2s
Cordery, R. v1p1062c2s
Cordes, A. v4p0149c1s
Cordier, Constant v6p0119c1s
Cordier, L. v1p0375c2s
Cordley, C. v4p0518c2s
v4p0542c2s v4p0543c1s v5p0164c2s
v5p0522c2s v6p0168c1s
Cordley, R. v1p0290c2s
Cordner, J. v1p0260c1s
v1p0304c1s v1p0777c1s v1p1118c1s
v2p0357c1s v3p0404c2s
Cordova, R. v4p0544c1s
v5p0142c1s v6p0083c1s v6p0680c1s
Cordova, R.J.De v1p0213c2s
v1p0360c1s v1p0725c1s
Corelli, M. v2p0178c2s
v2p0203c2s v2p0237c1s v2p0321c2s
v2p0456c2s v3p0323c2s v3p0354c1s
v4p0134c1s
Corelli, Marie v3p0240c1s
v4p0412c1s v4p0635c1s
Corey, D.G. v1p0847c2s
v1p0978c1s
Corey, D.P. v1p1380c1s
v5p0250c1s v5p0257c2s v5p0357c2s
Corey, W. v6p0707c1s
Corey, W.A. v6p0418c1s
Corfield, C.R. v1p1377c1s
Corfield, C.S. v1p0574c1s
Corfield, W.A. v1p0362c2s
v1p1181c1s v1p1181c2s v1p1391c2s
Corfield, W.H. v1p0373c2s
v1p0877c1s v1p1150c1s v1p1150c2s
v1p1161c1s v1p1337c1s v2p0126c2s
v2p0459c1s v2p0468c1s v3p0125c1s
v5p0442c2s
Coriegliani, C.A. v4p0461c1s
Corille, F.V. v4p0416c2s
v4p0498c1s
Cork, Countess of v3p0468c1s
v4p0055c2s v4p0531c2s
Cork, Countess of and
Orrery, Countess of ... v5p0140c1s
Cork, Countess of and
Orrey, Countess of v5p0196c2s
Cork, E.C. v3p0299c2s
Cork, H. v5p0273c1s
Corkett, F.T. v6p0511c1s
Corkhill, Kate v5p0205c2s
Corkran, A. v2p0209c2s
v2p0271c2s v6p0640c2s
Corkran, C.J. v2p0304c1s
Corkran, H. v2p0120c1s
v2p0304c1s v2p0341c2s v3p0310c1s
v3p0426c1s v3p0429c2s v3p0449c2s
v4p0075c2s v4p0393c1s v4p0571c1m
v5p0155c1s
Corkran, Henriette v4p0003c2s
v4p0063c1s v4p0358c1s v4p0494c2s
v4p0623c1s
Corkran, S.F. v1p0503c2s
v1p0963c2s
Corkran, W. v1p1298c2s
Corlaer, P.Van v3p0350c2s
Corlass, R.W. v2p0314c2s
Corlette, H.C. v6p0028c1s
v6p0155c2s
Cormack, J.D. v5p0176c1s
v5p0314c2s
Cormack, T.J. v5p0514c1s
Cormenin, M.de v1p0719c1s
Cormer, E.B. v6p0525c2s
Cormer, Earl v6p0702c2s
Cormican, P.J. v4p0053c2s
Cormon, F. v4p0030c1s
Cornaby, W.A. v4p0105c1s
v5p0132c2s v5p0422c2s
Cornaro, C. v2p0245c2s
Cornaz, A. v6p0031c1s
Corneau, G. v6p0036c2s
v6p0394c2s
Cornelius, E. v1p0393c1s
v1p1262c2s
Cornelius, M.H., Mrs. v1p1262c1s
Cornell, A.B. v5p0464c2s
Cornell, J.J. v4p0468c2s
Cornell, O. v3p0119c1s
Cornell, R.C. v5p0406c2s
v6p0178c1s
Cornell, W.P. v5p0207c2s
Cornely, J. v6p0237c1s
v6p0238c1s
Corner, G.R. v1p0039c2s
v1p0404c2s v1p0596c2s v1p0730c2s
v1p1115c1s v1p1227c2s v1p1243c1s
v1p1383c2s v1p1386c2s v1p1402c1s
v1p1433c1s
Corner, W. v4p0063c1s
v5p0381c1s v6p0185c1s
Corner-Ohlmutz, Caroline . v5p0100c1s
v6p0594c2s v6p0628c1s v6p0702c1s
Cornet, M.F.L. v1p0845c2s
Corney, B.G. v4p0198c2s
Corney, W. v5p0250c1s
Cornfield, W.H. et al. ... v4p0557c2s
Cornford, F.M. v6p0029c2s
v6p0708c1s
Cornford, L.C. v4p0021c1s
v5p0041c1s v5p0052c1s v5p0238c2s
v6p0254c2s v6p0269c1s v6p0337c1s
Cornford, L.Cope v6p0686c1s
Cornill, C.H. v4p0016c2s
v4p0055c1s v4p0055c2m v4p0177c2s
v4p0193c1m v4p0265c1s v4p0293c1s
v4p0299c1s v4p0302c1m v4p0302c2s
v4p0303c1s v4p0304c1s v4p0384c1s
v4p0397c1s v4p0462c1s v5p0056c1s
v5p0057c2s v5p0307c2s v5p0308c1s
v5p0577c1s v6p0330c2s
Cornill, C.H. et al. v5p0055c1s
Corning, C.R. v3p0301c2s
v3p0409c1s v5p0324c2s
Corning, J.L. v2p0268c1s
v2p0269c1s
Corning, W.H. v1p0241c1s
v1p0684c1s v1p0798c1s
Cornish, B.W. v5p0461c1s
v5p0607c1s
Cornish, C. v5p0397c2s
Cornish, C.J. v3p0438c2s
v4p0018c1s v4p0061c1s v4p0245c2s
v4p0338c2s v4p0339c2s v4p0363c1s
v4p0398c2s v4p0404c2s v4p0575c1s
v4p0621c2s v5p0018c1s v5p0020c2s
v5p0064c1s v5p0139c2s v5p0164c2s
v5p0172c2s v5p0223c2s v5p0225c1m
v5p0268c1s v5p0345c1s v5p0413c1s
v5p0496c1s v5p0547c1s v6p0237c2s
v6p0482c1s v6p0518c1s v6p0592c1s
Cornish, D.H. v4p0194c2s
v4p0614c2s
Cornish, E.L. v1p0372c2s
v1p0378c1s
Cornish, F.W. v1p0063c1s
v1p0554c1s v1p0869c1s v2p0147c2s
v3p0106c1s v3p0163c1s v4p0269c2s
v4p0562c2s v6p0205c2s v6p0431c1s
Cornish, G.W. v6p0620c1s
Cornish, J.F. v5p0459c1s
Cornish, L.C. v5p0095c2s
v6p0473c2s
Cornish, R.H. v4p0069c2s
v4p0098c2s v5p0449c1s
Cornish, V. v3p0090c2s
v3p0109c1s v3p0116c2s v3p0169c2s
v3p0276c1s v3p0368c2s v3p0389c2s
v4p0063c2s v4p0098c2s v4p0221c1s
v4p0252c2s v4p0349c2s v4p0546c1s
v4p0614c2s v5p0412c1s v5p0507c2m
v5p0516c2s v5p0623c2m v6p0585c1s
v6p0599c1m v6p0689c2s
Cornish, W. v6p0171c1s
Cornish, W., Mrs. v4p0221c1s
v5p0587c2s
Cornish, W.R. v4p0108c1s
Cornish-Bond, M. v5p0096c2s
Cornu, A. v1p0747c2s
v4p0036c1s v4p0155c2s v5p0338c1s
Cornu, M. v1p0505c2s
v1p0584c1s v1p1005c1s
Cornut, E. v2p0229c1s
Cornwall, A.L. v4p0331c1s
Cornwall, A.L. and Immler, F.O.
v4p0629c1s
Cornwall, B. v1p1054c1s
Cornwall, E.E. v4p0134c2s
v4p0550c1s v5p0451c2s v6p0692c1s
Cornwall, H.B. v1p0995c2s
v3p0279c1s v4p0099c1s v6p0274c1s
Cornwall, I.J. v6p0150c1s
Cornwall, N.E. v1p0131c1s
v1p0604c1s v1p0727c2s v1p0769c1s
Cornwall, W.A. v1p0813c2s
v1p1258c1s
Cornwallis, K. v1p0007c1s
v1p0139c2s v1p0325c1s v1p0534c1m
v1p0916c2s v1p0917c1s v1p0963c2s
v1p0993c1s v1p1110c1s v1p1254c2s
v1p1348c2s v1p1351c2s v1p1382c1s
v2p0011c2s v2p0365c2s
Cornwallis-West, G., Mrs.. v6p0399c1s
Cornwell, W.C. v4p0378c2s
v4p0593c1s v5p0382c2s
Corpe, A.W. v6p0309c2s
v6p0420c2s v6p0468c2s v6p0543c1s
v6p0551c2s v6p0587c1s v6p0587c2m
Corr, M. v1p0370c2s
Corran, G.I. v1p0726c2s
Corrance, F.S. v1p0721c2m
v1p1294c1s
Corrance, H.C. v5p0019c2s
v5p0190c2s v5p0366c1s v5p0489c2s
v5p0493c2m v5p0546c2s v6p0490c2s
v6p0548c1s
Corregan, C.H. v6p0601c2s
Corresca, R. v6p0075c2s
Correvon, H. v4p0012c1m
v4p0260c2s
Corrigan, M.A. v2p0297c2s
v2p0375c2s
Corrigan, S.J. v2p0095c1s
v2p0096c1s v2p028-c1s v2p0285c2s
v4p0033c2s v4p0126c2s v4p0220c2s
v4p0470c1m v5p0293c2s v5p0453c2s
Corroyer, E. v1p1372c2s
v4p0024c1s
Corry, W.M. v1p0730c2s
Corse, M.B. v6p0301c1s
Corser, F.G. v3p0155c2s
Corsit, W.F. v1p0988c1s
Corson, C.R. v1p0366c2s
v1p0783c1s v1p0856c2s v1p1124c2s
v1p1259c1s v2p0254c2s v3p0419c2s
Corson, C.R., Mrs. v1p0530c2s
v1p0611c2s v1p1295c2s v3p0364c2s
v3p0369c2s v4p0422c2s
Corson, H. v1p0416c1s
v2p0058c2s v4p0075c2s v4p0076c2s
v4p0098c1s v4p0184c1s v4p0334c2s
v4p0517c2s v4p0606c2s
Corson, H. and Conway, M.D.
v3p0057c2s
Corson, R., Mrs. v1p1237c2s
Cort, C. v2p0477c1s
v2p0478c1s v3p0145c2s v4p0185c2s
v4p0555c2s v5p0037c2s v5p0362c2s
v5p0440c1s
Cortambert, E. v1p0768c1s
Cortelyou, G.B. v6p0554c2s
v6p0670c1s
Cortes, D. v1p0119c2s
Cortesi, D. v4p0542c1s
Cortesi, S. v5p0018c1s
v5p0027c1s v5p0144c1m v5p0216c2s
v5p0300c1m v5p0300c2s v5p0429c2s
v5p0495c1s v5p0609c2s v5p0610c2s
v6p0368c1s v6p0411c2s v6p0429c2s
v6p0440c1s v6p0494c2s v6p0501c1m
v6p0544c2m v6p0548c1s v6p0675c1m
v6p0678c1s v6p0702c1s
Cortesi, Salvatore v6p0368c1s
Corthell, E.E. v2p0432c2m
Corthell, E.L. v1p0854c2m
v3p0391c1s v4p0567c1m v5p0168c1s
v5p0475c2s v5p0526c1s v5p0527c1s
v6p0029c1s
Corthell, J.R. v6p0409c2s
Corthell, N.E., Mrs. v6p0711c2s
Corthell, W.G. v6p0706c1s
Corti, J.S. v3p0243c2s
Cortie, A.E. v3p0238c1s
Cortie, A.L. v2p0426c2m
v3p0058c1s v3p0127c1s v3p0238c1s
v3p0298c2s v3p0327c1s v3p0403c2s
v3p0415c1m v3p0415c2s v4p0034c1s
v4p0037c2s v4p0167c1s v4p0556c2s
v4p0557c1m v5p0174c2s v5p0372c2s
v5p0538c1s v5p0549c2s v5p0561c1s
v6p0626c1s
Cortissoz, R. v4p0013c2s
v4p0028c2s v4p0029c1s v4p0100c2s
v4p0154c2s v4p0155c1s v4p0187c1s
v4p0210c2s v4p0214c2s v4p0387c2s
v4p0400c2s v4p0456c1s v4p0548c1s
v4p0586c1s v5p0067c1s v5p0331c2s
v5p0354c2s v5p0392c1s v6p0033c2s
v6p0034c1s v6p0307c2s v6p0358c2s
v6p0412c2s v6p0415c1s v6p0474c2s
v6p0538c2s v6p0563c1m v6p0589c1s
v6p0679c1s v6p0689c1s v6p0695c2s

Cortissoz, Royal v6p0536c1s
v6p0570c2s v6p0621c1s
Cortlandt, R.B. v6p0089c2s
Cortright, Judge v5p0492c2s
Corvin, O. v1p0994c1s
Corwin, C.E. v4p0036c2m
v5p0535c1s
Corwin, E. v1p0575c1s
Corwin, E.F. v6p0375c1s
Corwine, W.R. v6p0403c2s
Cory, C. v6p0624c1s
Cory, F.W. v2p0364c1s
v2p0413c2s
Cory, J.E. v1p0847c2s
Cory, W. v5p0254c2s
Coryell, J.R. v2p0046c2s
v2p0399c1s v3p0045c2s v3p0156c2s
Coryell, M. v1p1321c2s
Coryn, H. v5p0377c1s
Coryton, J. v1p0178c1s
v1p0231c1s v1p0651c2s
Coryton, T. v1p1004c1s
Cosack, Dr. v1p1043c2s
Cosby, D.S.A. v5p0117c1s
v5p0117c2s v5p0296c1s v5p0296c2m
v5p0297c1s v5p0332c1s v5p0493c2s
v6p0191c2s v6p0270c1s v6p0326c2s
v6p0327c1s v6p0370c1s v6p0481c1s
Cosgrave, J.O'H. v5p0341c2s
Cossage, W. v1p0195c2s
Cosson, Baron De v3p0405c2s
v3p0437c2s v4p0027c2m
Cosson, E. v2p0053c1s
Cosson, E.A.De v2p0237c2s
v2p0410c2s
Cosson, E.de v2p0111c1s
v2p0234c2s v2p0252c1s v2p0327c1m
Cosson, Maj.De v3p0101c1s
Costa, B.F.De v1p0028c1s
v1p0060c1s v1p0186c2s v1p0198c1s
v1p0335c1s v1p0349c1s v1p0511c1s
v1p0526c2m v1p0536c2s v1p0539c2s
v1p0603c1s v1p0611c1s v1p0707c1s
v1p0793c2s v1p0861c2s v1p0928c2s
v1p0929c2s v1p0972c1m v1p1033c2s
v1p1068c1s v1p1145c1s v1p1207c2s
v1p1310c1s v1p1312c2s v1p1368c1m
v1p1388c2s v2p0033c1s v2p0053c1s
v2p0159c2s v2p0183c1s v2p0221c2s
v2p0230c2s v2p0242c1s v2p0265c2s
v2p0272c2s v2p0299c1s v2p0316c1s
v2p0345c2s v2p0385c2s v2p0436c2s
v2p0452c1s v2p0476c2s v3p0010c1s
v3p0073c1s v3p0151c1s v3p0344c1s
v3p0453c2s v4p0350c1s v4p0384c1s
v4p0398c2s v4p0406c1s v4p0575c1s
v4p0609c1s v5p0056c1m v5p0645c2s
Costa, E. v6p0491c1s
Costa, G. v5p0330c1s
Costa, J. and Nightingale, F.
v2p0040c1s
Costar, W.J. v6p0114c1s
Costard, G. v1p0644c2s
Coste, F.H.P. v3p0349c1s
v4p0191c1s v4p0285c2s v4p0535c2s
Coste, F.H.Perry v4p0121c2s
Costello, D. v1p0007c1s
v1p0007c2s v1p0020c1s v1p0100c2s
v1p0139c2s v1p0301c2s v1p0319c2s
v1p0357c1s v1p0439c1s v1p0446c1s
v1p0469c1s v1p0519c2s v1p0563c1s
v1p0570c1s v1p0595c1s v1p0694c2s
v1p0720c2s v1p0736c1s v1p0761c1s
v1p0761c2s v1p0779c1s v1p0805c1s
v1p0841c1m v1p0862c2s v1p0878c1m
v1p0908c2s v1p0924c1s v1p1111c1s
v1p1191c1s v1p1242c2s v1p1339c1s
v1p1369c1s
Costello, F.H. v6p0445c2s
v6p0685c1s
Costello, L.S. v1p0102c1s
v1p0163c2s v1p0165c2s v1p0217c2s
v1p0226c2s v1p0257c2s v1p0273c1s
v1p0345c1s v1p0452c1s v1p0502c2s
v1p0526c2s v1p0587c1s v1p0718c1s
v1p0813c2s v1p0862c1s v1p0931c1s
v1p0940c2s v1p1068c2m v1p1193c2s
v1p1277c1s v1p1411c1s
Costello, M. v4p0607c1s
Costello, M.W. v4p0030c2s
Costello, Miss v1p0076c1s
Costelloe, B.F.C. v2p0375c2s
v2p0380c2s v4p0340c1s v4p0340c2s
v4p0359c2s v4p0619c2s
Costenes, J.C. v2p0337c1s
Costigan, G.P. v6p0347c1s
v6p0349c1s
Costigan, G.P., Jr. v6p0151c1s
v6p0184c2s
v6p0360c1s
Cosulich, A. v6p0699c1s
Cotel, G.L. v5p0503c1s
v5p0518c2s
Cotes, E. v6p0489c2s
Cotes, E., Mrs. v5p0234c2s
v6p0088c2s v6p0286c1s v6p0431c2s
v6p0469c2s
Cotes, E.C. v4p0531c1s
v6p0088c2s
Cotes, K.D. v6p0153c2m
v6p0191c2s
Cotes, S.J.D. v6p0508c1s
Cotgreave, A. v5p0341c2s
Cothonay, B. v5p0111c2s
v5p0493c1s
Cothran, L. v5p0010c2s
v5p0134c2s
Cotsworth, M.B. v3p0066c1s
Cott, J.M.Van v1p0698c1s
Cott, J.Van v1p0095c1s
Cotta, B. v1p0172c1s
Cotte, A.M. v2p0013c1s
v2p0079c1s v2p0102c1s v2p0183c1s
v3p0026c2s
Cottell, H.W. v4p0212c2s
Cottell, J.McK. v4p0505c2s
Cotter, J.L. v2p0304c2s
Cotterell, C. v4p0498c2s
v5p0036c1s v5p0486c1s
Cotterell, C.A.M. v2p0456c1s
Cotterell, Constance v5p0415c1s
v6p0458c2s
Cotterell, Constance A.M.. v4p0062c2s
Cotterell, G. v3p0008c1s
v3p0027c1s v3p0058c2s v3p0262c2s
v3p0323c2s v4p0037c2s v4p0346c1s
v4p0348c1m v4p0519c2s v4p0560c1s
v4p0614c1s v4p0616c1m v5p0140c2s
Cotterell, T.S. v6p0053c2s
v6p0618c2s
Cotterill, H. v1p0544c1s
Cotterill, H.B. v3p0309c1s
Cottman, V.L. v3p0309c2s
Cotton, A. v3p0212c2s
Cotton, A., Sir v3p0149c1s
v3p0189c2s
Cotton, A.E. v2p0316c2s
v3p0301c2s
Cotton, A.L. v5p0155c2s
v5p0314c2s v5p0520c1s v6p0125c1s
v6p0517c1s
Cotton, A.T., Sir v2p0217c2s
Cotton, Albert L. v5p0424c1s
Cotton, F.A. v6p0290c1s
Cotton, F.C. v1p0362c2s
v1p0607c2s v3p0121c2s v5p0285c2s
Cotton, F.E. v6p0152c2s
v6p0515c2s
Cotton, F.W. v4p0315c2s
v4p0463c2s
Cotton, G.P. v5p0029c1s
v5p0189c1s
Cotton, H. v6p0314c2s
Cotton, H., Sir v6p0185c2s
v6p0314c2s
Cotton, H.J.S. v1p0631c1s
v1p1177c2s v2p0064c1s v2p0142c1s
Cotton, Henry v6p0313c2s
Cotton, J.C. v1p0283c2s
Cotton, J.J. v5p0241c2s
v5p0520c1s v6p0508c1s
Cotton, J.S. v2p0141c1s
v2p0269c2s v3p0003c2s v3p0039c2s
v3p0049c1s v3p0061c1s v3p0135c2s
v3p0191c1s v3p0211c2s v3p0283c2s
v3p0335c1s v3p0377c1s v3p0454c2s
v3p0455c1s v3p0465c1s v3p0475c1s
v4p0001c1s v4p0050c2s v4p0075c2s
v4p0147c2s v4p0196c1s v4p0214c1s
v4p0218c2s v4p0243c2s v4p0259c2s
v4p0278c2s v4p0305c2s v4p0316c2s
v4p0369c2s v4p0373c1s v4p0383c1s
v4p0388c1s v4p0398c1s v4p0404c1s
v4p0405c2s v4p0419c1s v4p0420c1s
v4p0430c1s v4p0432c2s v4p0474c1s
v4p0476c1s v4p0487c2s v4p0492c2s
v4p0530c2s v4p0549c1s v4p0561c1s
v4p0574c1s v4p0602c1s v4p0607c2s
v4p0618c2m v4p0623c2s
Cotton, J.S. and Poole, R.S.
v4p0171c2s
Cotton, L.G. v4p0077c2s
Cotton, P.H.G.P. v6p0663c2s
Cotton, R.H. v3p0162c2s
Cotton, R.W. v4p0111c1s
Cotton, W. v1p0204c2s
Cotton, W.J.R. v2p0264c1s
Cotton, W.L. v5p0465c2s
Cottrell, C.H. v6p0122c2s
Cottrell, C.M. v5p0609c2s
Cottrell, H. v4p0040c1s
Cottrell, S.B. v5p0343c1s
Cou, H.F.De v4p0346c1s
v5p0137c2s
Coube, E. v3p0324c2m
Coubertin, P.de v4p0211c1s
v4p0211c2s v4p0413c2m v4p0495c2s
v4p0526c2s v5p0138c2s v5p0189c1m
v5p0197c1m v5p0216c2m v5p0217c1s
v5p0217c2s v5p0218c1m v5p0218c2m
v5p0231c2s v5p0245c2s v5p0293c2s
v5p0348c2s v5p0420c1s v5p0431c1s
v5p0604c2s v6p0052c2s v6p0169c1s
v6p0238c1s v6p0574c2s
Coubertin, P.de, Baron ... v5p0078c2s
v5p0255c2s
Couch, A.F.Q. v4p0487c2s
Couch, A.Q. v4p0266c2s
v4p0414c1s
Couch, A.T. v5p0309c1s
Couch, A.T.Q. v3p0029c2s
v4p0299c1s v4p0448c2s v4p0585c1s
v5p0055c2s v5p0314c2s
Couch, A.T.Quiller v5p0142c2s
Couch, D.N. et al. v2p0166c2s
Couch, J. v1p0039c1s
v1p0215c2s v1p0456c2m v1p0720c1s
v1p1105c2s v1p1236c1s
Couch, L.Q. v4p0321c1s
v6p0124c1s
Couch, L.Quiller v4p0373c2s
v5p0135c2s
Couch, M.Q. v5p0162c2s
v5p0348c1s
Coudert, A.K. v6p0457c1s
Coudert, F.R. v4p0022c2s
v4p0121c1s v4p0595c2s v5p0024c2m
v5p0290c1s v5p0290c2s v5p0399c2s
v6p0151c2s
Coudert, F.R. and McMaster, J.B.
v4p0015c2s
Coudert, F.R. et al. v3p0216c1s
v4p0142c2s v4p0455c2s v4p0615c1s
Coues, E. v1p0102c1s
v1p0135c1s v1p0135c2m v1p0136c1s
v1p0136c2s v1p0139c2s v1p0181c2s
v1p0435c1s v1p0466c1s v1p0536c1s
v1p0575c1s v1p0625c1s v1p0637c2s
v1p0680c1s v1p0792c1s v1p0948c2s
v1p0949c1m v1p1041c2m v1p1069c1s
v1p1075c1s v1p1173c1s v1p1232c1s
v2p0414c2s v2p0438c1s v3p0448c2s
v4p0158c2s v4p0221c1s v4p0253c2s
v4p0301c2s v4p0375c1s v4p0407c1s
v4p0540c1s v4p0635c2s v5p0065c1s
v5p0330c2s v6p0568c2s v6p0643c1s
Coues, E. and Allen, J.A.. v5p0413c1s
Coues, S.E. v1p0529c1s
v1p1005c2s v1p1047c2s v1p1219c2s
Coughlan, J.P. v5p0026c2s
v5p0220c2s v5p0240c2s
Coughlin, J.J. v5p0398c2s
Coughran, Ernestine v5p0208c1s
Coughtrie, M. v2p0003c1s
Coulson, G.J.A. v1p0205c1s
v1p0308c1s v1p0452c1s v1p0937c2s
v1p1131c2s v1p1264c2s v1p1316c1s
Coulson, J.G. v1p1017c2s
Coultas, A.J. v6p0085c1s
Coultas, H. v1p0025c1s
v1p0048c2s v1p0107c2s v1p0153c1s
v1p0470c2s v1p1014c2m v1p1015c2s
v1p1016c1s v1p1127c1s v1p1252c1s
v1p1324c1m v1p1364c1m
Coulter, A.D. v6p0344c2s
Coulter, Arthur D. v6p0118c1s
Coulter, C.C. v5p0098c2s
Coulter, E.K. v6p0452c1s
Coulter, E.R. v6p0117c2s
Coulter, J. v6p0454c1s
Coulter, J.Lee v6p0402c1s
Coulter, J.M. v3p0051c2s
v3p0145c2s v4p0060c1s v4p0123c1s
v4p0395c1s v4p0507c2s v4p0512c2s
v4p0598c1s v5p0073c1s v5p0253c1s
v5p0463c2s v5p0513c2s v6p0024c2s
v6p0077c1s v6p0165c2s v6p0190c2s
v6p0428c2s v6p0430c2s v6p0540c1s
v6p0575c2s
Coulter, S.M. v6p0656c1s
Coulton, C.G. v5p0564c2s
Coulton, G.G. v6p0043c2s
v6p0058c2s v6p0104c2s v6p0238c2s
v6p0265c2s v6p0424c2m v6p0523c2s
v6p0537c2s v6p0548c1s v6p0565c2s
Councill, W.H. v5p0403c1s
v5p0403c2s
Councilman, W.T. v5p0257c1s
Countryman, G. v5p0333c2s
v5p0334c2s v5p0335c1s
Countryman, G. et al. v5p0334c1s
Countryman, G.A. v5p0336c2s
Countryman, Gratia v6p0374c1s
Countryman, Gratia A. v6p0372c2s
v6p0655c2s
County, A.J. v6p0136c2s
Coupe, C. v3p0043c1s
v3p0209c1s v4p0007c2s v4p0283c1s
v4p0560c1s v5p0459c2s v6p0487c1s
v6p0502c1s v6p0547c1s v6p0639c1s
v6p0665c2s
Couper, J.L. v5p0327c1s
Coupin, H. v4p0398c1s
v4p0575c1s v4p0609c2s v5p0211c1s
Coupland, W.C. v1p1161c2s
v2p0372c1s v3p0168c2s v3p0274c1s
v3p0348c2s v4p0269c1s
Courant, M. v5p0113c1s
v5p0584c2s
Courbiere, F. v4p0149c1s
Courcelles, E.de v1p0422c2s
Courcy, H.de v2p0377c2s
Cournay, P.F.De v2p0329c2s
Cournot, A. v1p1106c2s
Cournot, M. v1p1232c2s
Coursen, A.C. v5p0536c2s
Coursen, C.H. v6p0083c1s
v6p0407c1s
Coursen, Charlotte H. v4p0589c1s
Courser, C.H. v6p0353c1s

Coursey, W.S. v6p0393c1s
Courson, B.de v5p0029c2s
v5p0076c2s v5p0095c1m v5p0189c2s
v5p0431c2s v6p0031c2s v6p0228c2s
v6p0289c1s v6p0536c1s
Courson, Barbara, Comtesse de
v5p0504c1s
Courson, Comtesse de v4p0082c1s
v4p0091c1s v6p0083c1s v6p0241c2s
v6p0525c1s v6p0548c1s v6p0607c2s
v6p0639c1s
Courson, Countess de v6p0479c1s
v6p0479c2m v6p0480c1m
Courson, de v6p0547c2s
Courson, Della v5p0347c1s
v5p0455c2s
Courson, Mad. de v5p0504c1s
Court, C. v5p0047c1s
Court, C.A. v5p0218c1s
v5p0588c2s v6p0517c1s
Courteline, Geo. v5p0366c1s
Courtenay, A.E. v3p0194c1s
v4p0137c1s
Courtenay, A.M. v4p0555c2s
v5p0079c1s
Courtenay, E. v1p0072c2s
v1p0221c1s v1p0308c1s
Courtenay, E.H. v1p0727c2s
Courtenay, J.B. v1p0692c1s
v1p0808c2s v3p0145c1s
Courtenay, Louisa v5p0140c1s
v5p0417c2s
Courtenay, R. v2p0047c1s
v3p0423c1s
Courtenay, T.P. v1p1185c1m
v1p1185c2s v1p1186c2m
Courteney, L. v5p0603c2s
Courthope, W.J. v2p0022c2s
v2p0058c2s v2p0068c2s v2p0096c2s
v2p0099c2s v2p0135c2s v2p0144c1s
v2p0189c1s v2p0238c1s v2p0270c1s
v2p0346c1s v2p0346c2s v2p0369c1s
v2p0444c2s v2p0449c2s v2p0470c1s
v2p0479c2s v3p0073c1s v3p0180c2s
v3p0235c1s v3p0323c1s v3p0390c1s
v4p0118c1s v4p0183c1s v4p0448c2s
v5p0455c2s v6p0029c2s v6p0267c1s
Courtier, T. v4p0436c1s
Courtland, W.T. v4p0243c2s
Courtney, E. v5p0228c1s
v6p0289c1s v6p0594c1s
Courtney, J.C. v6p0596c2s
Courtney, L. v1p0640c1s
v1p0657c1s v1p0668c1s v1p0848c2s
v1p1332c2s v2p0225c2s v3p0189c2s
v3p0241c1s v3p0278c1s v3p0324c2s
v3p0339c2s v3p0398c2s v3p0408c2s
v4p0059c1s v4p0059c2s v4p0283c1s
v4p0450c1s v5p0092c1s v5p0175c2s
v5p0296c2s v5p0409c2s v5p0437c2s
v6p0007c1s v6p0232c2s v6p0260c1s
v6p0269c2s v6p0481c1s v6p0481c2s
Courtney, L. and Arnold, A.
v2p0330c2s
Courtney, L. and Masham, Lord
v4p0214c1s
Courtney, L. et al. v2p0370c1s
v4p0265c2s
Courtney, L.H. v1p0715c1s
v1p1027c2s v1p1333c1s v1p1344c1s
v4p0236c2s v4p0586c1s
Courtney, L.H. et al. v4p0630c1s
Courtney, L.M. v5p0124c1s
Courtney, W.L. v1p0201c2s
v1p1062c1s v2p0058c2s v2p0059c2s
v2p0139c2s v2p0144c1s v2p0153c2s
v2p0198c1s v2p0230c1s v2p0236c1s
v2p0283c2s v2p0325c2s v2p0346c1s
v2p0365c2s v2p0408c2s v2p0428c2s
v2p0456c1s v3p0030c1s v3p0073c2s
v3p0115c2s v3p0159c2s v3p0316c2m
v3p0322c2s v4p0003c1s v4p0007c1s
v4p0030c2s v4p0160c2s v4p0161c1s
v4p0179c1s v4p0270c2s v4p0272c1s
v4p0356c1s v4p0423c1s v4p0429c1s
v5p0451c2m v6p0180c2s v6p0181c1s
v6p0288c2s v6p0401c2s v6p0588c2s
v6p0665c1s
Courtney, W.P. v1p0165c1s
v1p0550c1s v2p0015c2s v2p0040c2s
v2p0055c1s v2p0077c1s v2p0103c2s
v2p0108c2s v2p0142c2m v2p0151c2s
v2p0163c2s v2p0174c2s v2p0198c1s
v2p0198c2s v2p0199c1s v2p0422c1s
v2p0449c1s v3p0175c2s v3p0192c2s
v4p0022c2s v4p0112c2s v4p0137c2s
v4p0304c2s v4p0454c1s v4p0576c1s
v4p0583c2s v6p0358c1s
Courtois, A. v3p0032c1s
Courtois, M. v1p0749c2s
v1p0873c2s
Courtot, Cecile de v5p0398c1s
Courty, P. v3p0246c2s
Couse, E. v3p0045c1s
Cousin, A.R. v2p0070c2s
v2p0235c1s v2p0244c1s v2p0278c2s
v2p0281c1s v2p0295c1s
Cousin, V. v1p0702c2s
v2p0465c2s v4p0605c2s
Cousins, G. v2p0271c1s
Cousins, H.T. v4p0360c1s
v4p0529c1s
Cousins, R.G. et al. v4p0596c1s
Cousins, V. v4p0324c2s
Couste, E. v1p1248c1s
Coutant, R.B. v3p0205c1s
v3p0420c2s v3p0455c1s
Couteur, J.Le v5p0448c1s
Couthouy, M. v1p0170c1s
v2p0252c1s
Coutlee, C.R. v5p0624c2m
Coutts, W.A. v5p0276c2s
v6p0533c2m
Couty, M. v1p0208c1s
Couzins, H.D. v4p0163c1s
Coventry, I. v5p0390c1s
Coventry, R.G.T. v6p0217c2s
v6p0391c1s
Coverdale, G. v2p0012c2s
Coverdale, J. v5p0595c2s
Covert, J.C. v6p0275c1s
Covert, L. v6p0038c1s
Covert, W.L.F. v5p0336c1s
Covert, W.R. v4p0337c2s
v4p0474c1s
Coves, E. v5p0035c1s
Covey, A.S. v6p0079c2s
v6p0289c1s v6p0676c2s
Coville, F.V. v4p0150c1s
v4p0263c1s v5p0243c1s v5p0591c1s
v6p0171c2s
Coville, J. v4p0509c1s
Coville, James v4p0127c2s
Covington, W. v3p0201c2s
Cowan, A.G. v4p0352c1s
Cowan, G.D. v1p0110c2s
v1p0348c2s v1p0350c1s v1p0503c1s
Cowan, G.I. v1p0061c1s
v1p0347c1s v1p0453c1s v1p0498c2s
v1p0524c2s v1p0952c2s
Cowan, Hugh v5p0525c2s
Cowan, J.F. v5p0397c1s
v5p0411c1s v5p0590c2s
Cowan, J.L. v6p0036c2s
v6p0220c1s v6p0501c1s v6p0661c2s
v6p0670c1s v6p0682c1s
Cowan, J.S. v1p1264c1s
Cowan, P.D. v3p0001c2s
Cowan, R. v1p0525c2s
Cowan, S.K. v2p0037c2s
v2p0216c1s v2p0324c2s v2p0379c1s
Cowan, W. v4p0039c2s
v4p0185c2s v4p0241c1s v5p0351c1s
Coward, E. v3p0180c1s
Coward, E.F. v5p0209c2s
Coward, J.M. v6p0498c2s
Coward, T.A. v6p0022c1s
v6p0067c2s v6p0246c1s
Coward, W.S. v4p0168c2s
Cowden, Robert v6p0078c1s
Cowdery, M.F. v1p0867c2s
v1p1063c2s
Cowdin, J.E. v6p0507c2s
Cowdrey, S.G. and Bacon, F.
v1p1360c1s
Cowdrick, E.L. v4p0171c2s
v5p0180c1s v5p0264c2s v5p0471c2s
v5p0569c1s v5p0569c2m
v6p0573c2s
Cowdrick, J.C. v4p0074c2s
Cowdrick, S. v6p0360c1s
Cowdy, S. v2p0273c2s
Cowee, A. v6p0257c2s
Cowell, A. v5p0290c1s
Cowell, C.D. v4p0195c2s
v4p0506c1s
Cowell, G. v1p0288c2s
Cowell, H. v3p0325c1s
Cowell, H.C.B. v4p0381c2s
v4p0505c2s v4p0590c2s v4p0591c1s
Cowell, J., Sir v4p0034c1s
Cowell, J.C. v4p0272c1s
Cowell, J.C., Sir v3p0024c2s
Cowell, J.E. v6p0584c1s
Cowell, P. v1p0451c1s
v1p0744c1s v2p0261c2s v4p0329c2s
Cowell, P.H. v5p0385c1s
v6p0008c1s v6p0188c1s v6p0427c2s
Cowell, Prof. v1p0112c2s
v1p0565c1s
Cowell, R.C. v5p0226c1s
v5p0641c2s
Cowell, S. v3p0137c1s
Cowen, E. v2p0161c2s
Cowen, Elsa v2p0304c1s
Cowen, H.L. v2p0071c2s
v2p0295c2s v2p0445c1s
Cowen, J. v1p0017c2s
v1p0085c2s v1p0171c2s v1p0175c1s
Cowen, P. v3p0230c2s
Cowgill, F.B. v4p0320c1s
Cowgill, T.W. v6p0380c1s
Cowie, A. v5p0517c1s
Cowie, I. v6p0387c1s
Cowing, E.K. v4p0039c1s
v4p0446c2s
Cowing, J.P. v6p0152c1s
Cowlam, G.B. v3p0443c1s
Cowles, E. v3p0207c2s
v4p0358c2s
Cowles, E.H. v1p1033c2s
v2p0009c2s
Cowles, E.H. et al. v2p0137c2s
Cowles, H. v1p0097c1s
v1p0124c2s v1p0291c1s v1p0496c1s
v1p0685c1s v1p0688c2s v1p0795c1s
v1p1091c1s v1p1174c2s v1p1200c1s
Cowles, H.C. v5p0453c2s
Cowles, J.L. v4p0415c2s
v4p0471c2s v4p0472c2s v5p0461c2s
v6p0479c1s v6p0511c1s
Cowles, J.P. v1p0129c2s
v1p0779c2s v1p1093c2s v1p1303c1s
Cowles, K.C. v6p0188c1m
Cowles, Paul v6p0567c2s
Cowles, S.H. v1p0536c2s
Cowles, W.B. v5p0082c2s
v6p0591c2s
Cowles, W.H. v3p0350c2s
Cowles, W.L. v1p0573c2s
v6p0469c2s
Cowley, A. v1p0999c1s
v4p0501c1m v6p0249c2s v6p0285c2s
v6p0567c1s
Cowley, C. v3p0071c2s
v3p0197c1s v3p0459c1s v4p0581c1s
v6p0678c1s
Cowley, E.A. v3p0123c2s
Cowley-Brown, G.J. v3p0204c1s
v3p0259c1s v4p0113c1s v4p0578c1s
Cowly, E.F. v2p0150c2s
Cowper, B.H. v1p0006c2s
v1p0124c2s v1p0126c1s v1p0263c2s
v1p0353c1s v1p0504c1s v1p0693c1s
v1p0698c1s v1p0825c2s v1p0844c1s
v1p0961c1s v1p0993c2s v1p1056c1s
v1p1109c1s v1p1279c1m v1p1279c2s
v1p1281c2s v1p1375c1s v1p1412c1s
v1p1433c1s v2p0044c1s v2p0079c1s
v2p0236c2s
Cowper, C.W. v1p0683c1s
Cowper, Countess v2p0263c1s
v2p0348c1s v3p0470c1s
Cowper, E.A. v1p0815c2s
Cowper, Earl v2p0063c2s
v2p0186c1s v2p0188c1s v2p0189c1s
v2p0282c2s v2p0472c1s v4p0436c1s
Cowper, Earl and Brett, R.B.
v3p0182c2s
Cowper, F. v3p0144c2s
Cowper, H.S. v4p0584c2m
v5p0591c1s
Cowper, J.M. v2p0153c2s
v2p0354c1s
Cowper, K. v4p0475c1s
Cowper, Lord v4p0621c2s
Cowper, W. v1p1312c2s
Cowper-Coles, S. v5p0185c2s
v5p0580c1s v6p0163c2s
Cowperthwait, J.H. v3p0069c2s
v3p0285c1s v3p0438c1s
Cox, A. v3p0142c1s
v3p0145c1s
Cox, A.A. v5p0128c2s
Cox, A.H.M. v6p0645c1s
Cox, A.S. v3p0434c2s
v4p0068c2s v5p0631c2s
Cox, C. and Blair, R. v4p0247c1s
Cox, C.F. v2p0287c2s
Cox, C.F. et al. v2p0320c2s
Cox, C.S. v5p0607c2s
Cox, E. v5p0293c2s
v5p0420c2s v5p0596c2s
Cox, E.B. v1p0488c2s
v1p0489c2s v1p0503c2s
Cox, E.C. v3p0049c1s
Cox, E.T. v1p0046c1s
v1p0268c2s v1p0639c1s
Cox, E.W. v3p0023c2s
v3p0076c2s v3p0365c2s
Cox, F.A. v1p0534c1s
v1p0842c2s v1p1070c1s
Cox, F.H. v5p0536c2s
v5p0574c1s
Cox, F.J. v6p0008c1s
Cox, F.T. v5p0273c1s
v5p0489c2s v6p0599c2s
Cox, Florence T. v6p0344c1s
v6p0377c1s v6p0465c2s
Cox, G.A. v4p0439c1s
Cox, G.D. v2p0144c1s
Cox, G.F. v1p0527c2s
v1p1101c1s
Cox, G.H. v3p0258c2s
v6p0126c2s
Cox, G.W. v1p0239c2s
v1p0411c1s v1p0416c2s v1p0447c2s
v1p0600c1m v1p0600c2s v1p0601c1s
v1p1034c1s v1p1441c2s v2p0023c1s
v2p0084c1s v2p0201c2s v2p0249c1s
v2p0305c1s v2p0359c1s v3p0206c1s
v3p0318c1s v4p0026c2s v4p0437c1s
v4p0523c1s v4p0584c2s
Cox, G.W. and Lang, A. ... v2p0304c2s
v3p0013c2s
Cox, G.W., Sir v1p0184c1s
v1p0604c2s v2p0233c1s v2p0392c2s
Cox, H. v1p0162c1s
v1p0339c2s v1p0523c1s v1p0599c2s
v1p1212c2s v3p0125c1s v3p0131c2s

v3p0211c2m v4p0280c2s v5p0155c2s v5p0245c1s v5p0559c2m v6p0108c1s v6p0150c1s v6p0266c2s
Cox, H.C. v4p0200c1s v4p0478c1s
Cox, H.C. and Warman, E.B. v4p0274c2s
Cox, H.F. v1p0719c2s v1p0941c1s
Cox, H.G. v6p0132c1s
Cox, H.J. v6p0626c1s
Cox, Harold v4p0090c2s v5p0245c1s
Cox, I. v6p0220c1s
Cox, I.J. v6p0387c2s v6p0567c1m v6p0572c2s v6p0640c1m
Cox, J. v4p0499c1m v6p0041c1s v6p0140c2s v6p0141c1s v6p0625c2s
Cox, J. et al. v6p0140c2s
Cox, J., jr. v6p0377c1s
Cox, J.B. v3p0103c1s
Cox, J.C. v1p0715c1s v3p0017c1s v3p0246c1s v3p0249c2s v3p0471c1s v4p0023c1s v4p0358c1s v5p0048c2s v6p0071c2s v6p0101c1s v6p0134c2s v6p0179c1s v6p0228c2s v6p0262c2s v6p0427c2s v6p0459c1s v6p0461c1s v6p0485c2s v6p0491c2s v6p0617c2s
Cox, J.C. and Hirst, J. .. v3p0155c1s
Cox, J.D. v1p0259c1s v1p0286c2s v1p0335c1s v1p0607c2s v1p0636c1s v1p0636c2s v1p0637c2s v1p0645c2s v1p0694c2s v1p0919c2s v1p0973c2s v1p1079c1s v1p1190c2m v1p1252c1s v1p1287c1s v1p1343c1s v1p1345c1s v1p1347c1s v2p0059c1s v2p0060c1s v2p0184c2s v2p0306c1s v2p0396c1s v2p0439c1s v2p0453c2s v3p0092c1s v3p0179c1s v3p0231c2m v3p0236c2s v3p0246c1s v3p0251c2m v3p0262c1s v3p0266c1s v3p0283c2s v3p0285c1m v3p0386c1s v3p0390c1m v3p0390c2s v3p0412c1s v3p0415c1s v3p0441c2s v3p0442c1s v3p0443c1s v3p0446c1s v4p0028c1s v4p0081c1m v4p0082c1s v4p0244c2s v4p0247c1s v4p0251c2s v4p0259c2s v4p0347c1s v4p0393c1s v4p0451c1s v4p0520c2s v4p0574c1m v4p0576c2s v4p0584c1s v4p0592c2s v4p0593c2s v4p0594c2m v4p0595c1s v4p0596c2s v4p0613c2s v5p0020c1s v5p0103c1s v5p0105c2s v5p0215c1s v5p0220c1s v5p0301c1s v5p0329c1s v5p0332c1s v5p0380c2m v5p0444c2s v5p0459c2s v5p0516c2s v5p0521c2s v5p0525c2s v5p0543c2s v5p0592c1s
Cox, J.D. et al. v5p0541c2s
Cox, J.E. v1p0883c1s
Cox, J.F., Mrs. v6p0256c1s
Cox, J.G. v2p0478c1s
Cox, J.G.S. v5p0090c2s v5p0327c1s v5p0484c2s
Cox, J.S. v1p0285c2s
Cox, J.S., jr. v5p0147c2s
Cox, K. v2p0298c1s v2p0392c2s v2p0463c1s v2p0468c1s v3p0014c1s v3p0022c1s v3p0022c2s v3p0074c2s v3p0121c1s v3p0124c1s v3p0189c2s v3p0235c1s v3p0372c1s v3p0447c2s v4p0011c2s v4p0029c2m v4p0047c1s v4p0063c2s v4p0072c2s v4p0246c2s v4p0294c1s v4p0304c2s v4p0342c2s v4p0369c1s v4p0406c1s v4p0421c2s v4p0457c1s v4p0468c1s v4p0480c1s v4p0561c1s v5p0079c1s v5p0082c1s v5p0220c2s v5p0441c2s v5p0450c2s v5p0495c2s v5p0499c2s v5p0501c2s v6p0033c1s v6p0034c1s v6p0150c1s v6p0229c1s v6p0278c2s v6p0294c1s v6p0404c2s v6p0417c2s v6p0420c1s v6p0423c1s v6p0546c2s v6p0555c1s v6p0570c2s v6p0588c1s v6p0590c2s v6p0633c1s v6p0679c2s v6p0695c2s v6p0696c1s
Cox, K. and Low, W.H. v4p0409c1s
Cox, K. and Sturgis, R. .. v5p0447c2s
Cox, K. et al. v4p0405c2s
Cox, Kenyon v4p0602c2s v6p0415c1s v6p0442c2s v6p0677c2s
Cox, L.J. v6p0362c1s
Cox, L.M. v6p0275c2s
Cox, L.O. and Eigenmann, C.H. v5p0607c2s
Cox, Mabel v5p0033c2s
Cox, Mabel M. v6p0363c1s
Cox, N.A. v4p0032c2s v4p0559c1s
Cox, P. v5p0570c1s
Cox, R. v1p0978c2s v2p0332c2s v3p0031c1s
Cox, S. v1p0240c1s v1p0614c2s v1p0942c1s v1p1203c1s v1p1417c1s v2p0190c1s v2p0267c1s v2p0353c1s v3p0175c2s v3p0187c2s v3p0209c1s v3p0232c1s v3p0265c2s v3p0458c2s v3p0471c2s v4p0475c2s
Cox, S.H. v1p0020c2s v1p0558c2s v1p0617c2s v1p1355c1s v1p1435c1s
Cox, S.S. v1p0320c2s v1p0442c1s v1p0537c1s v1p0614c2m v1p0746c2s v2p0099c1s v2p0293c2s
Cox, T. v4p0015c2s v4p0455c2s v4p0462c1s v4p0462c2s v4p0563c1s v4p0631c2s
Cox, T. and Mead, E. v4p0015c2s
Cox, T.E. v5p0374c2s
Cox, Theo. v4p0152c1s
Cox, Theo.E. v4p0094c2s
Cox, W.G. v6p0041c2s
Cox, W.J. v2p0427c1s
Cox, W.L.P. v4p0499c1s
Cox, W.R. v3p0354c1s
Cox-Stephens, A. v4p0209c2s
Coxe, A.C. v1p0003c1s v1p0032c1s v1p0039c2s v1p0249c1s v1p0263c1s v1p0288c2s v1p0320c2s v1p0421c2s v1p0422c1s v1p0422c2m v1p0576c1s v1p0611c1s v1p0892c2s v1p0910c1s v1p1013c1s v1p1063c2s v1p1093c2s v1p1157c1s v1p1217c1s v1p1343c1s v2p0012c2s v2p0106c2s v3p0008c2s v3p0011c1s v3p0137c2s v3p0138c1s v3p0208c2s v3p0287c2s v3p0295c2s v3p0323c2s v3p0343c1s v3p0365c2s v3p0416c2s v3p0440c1s
Coxe, A.C. and Tatlock, W. v1p0255c2s
Coxe, A.C. et al. v3p0084c2s v3p0141c2s
Coxe, B. v1p0259c2s
Coxe, E.B. v1p0845c2s v4p0120c2s
Coxe, Eckley B. v1p0050c2s
Coxe, H.C. v6p0167c2s v6p0237c2s
Coxe, H.O. v1p0628c2s
Coxe, J.R. v1p0322c1s
Coxe, M. v1p1416c1m
Coxe, R.C. v4p0228c2s
Coxe, T. v1p0447c1s
Coxe, W.E.C. v1p0666c1m
Coxhead, A.C. v6p0699c2s
Coxhead, Edith v6p0439c1s
Coxon, E. v2p0028c1s
Coxon, E.S. v1p0855c2s
Coxwell, H. v1p0089c1s v2p0032c2m
Coy, E.G. v2p0339c1s v3p0023c2s v3p0163c2s
Coy, E.W. v6p0696c2s
Coy, E.W. and Adams, C.K.. v4p0122c2s
Coyle, C.W. v4p0392c1s
Coyle, H. v4p0118c1s v4p0623c1s
Coyle, J.P. v1p0427c1s v4p0113c2s v4p0315c2s
Coyne, J.S. v1p0996c2s v1p1311c1s
Cozens-Hardy, W.H. v4p0380c1s
Cozzens, F.S. v1p0101c2s v1p0308c1s v1p0931c1s v1p0955c2s v1p1415c1s v3p0401c2s
Crabbe, G. v1p0253c1s
Crabbe, I. v6p0338c2s
Crabfield, J.B. v6p0408c1s
Crabtree, J. v5p0405c1s
Crace et al. v1p0825c2s
Crace, J.D. v3p0092c2s v6p0167c2s v6p0474c2s
Crace, J.G. v3p0256c2s
Crackanthorpe, B.A. v4p0148c2s v4p0335c1s v4p0411c2s v4p0629c2s v6p0641c2s
Crackanthorpe, H. v4p0127c1s v4p0583c2s
Crackanthorpe, M. v3p0182c2m v3p0437c1s v4p0140c2s v4p0285c1s v4p0323c1s v4p0339c1s v4p0340c2s v5p0520c1s v6p0158c1s v6p0267c1s v6p0509c1s
Cracroft, B. v1p0354c2s v1p0616c2s v1p0690c2s v1p0765c2s v1p0959c2s v1p1130c1s v1p1180c2s
Craddock, C.E. v1p1243c2s v2p0345c1s v4p0091c2s v4p0306c2s v4p0438c1s v5p0312c1s v5p0610c2s
Craddock, R.J. v2p0434c1s
Cradocke, T. v1p0132c2s
Craft, A.N. v5p0344c1s
Craft, M.C. v6p0259c2s v6p0482c1s
Craft, Mabel v4p0083c2s
Craft, Mabel C. v5p0112c2s v5p0114c1s v5p0566c1s
Craft, R. v6p0310c2s
Crafts, C.E. v6p0307c1s v6p0382c1s
Crafts, G.E. v6p0438c1s
Crafts, H.A. v5p0129c1s v5p0299c1m v6p0093c1s v6p0320c2s v6p0568c1s
Crafts, J.M. v4p0002c2s
Crafts, Lettie M. v6p0532c2s
Crafts, W.A. v1p1078c1s v3p0192c2s v3p0218c2s v4p0360c1s
Crafts, W.F. v2p0255c1s v3p0081c2s v3p0326c1s v3p0371c1m v3p0373c2s v3p0415c2s v3p0472c2s v4p0096c2s v4p0101c2s v4p0102c1m v4p0102c2s v4p0193c2s v4p0325c2s v4p0477c1s v4p0497c2s v4p0535c1s v4p0557c1s v4p0557c2s
Cragg, F. v6p0312c2s
Cragin, B.S. v5p0292c1s
Cragin, F.W. v2p0174c1s
Cragin, L.T. v1p0023c1s v1p0084c2s v1p0583c2s v1p1007c2s
Craick, W.A. v6p0264c1s
Craies, W.F. v4p0010c2s
Craig, A.L. v4p0105c2s v4p0134c1s v4p0147c2s v4p0519c2s
Craig, B.F. v1p1293c1s
Craig, G.C. v5p0109c1s v5p0360c1s
Craig, H. v1p0068c2s v1p0294c1s v2p0207c2s v6p0155c1s
Craig, H. et al. v4p0144c1s
Craig, H.J. v5p0222c1s
Craig, Hugh v4p0250c2s
Craig, I. v1p0245c1s v1p1143c1s v1p1375c2s v4p0614c2s
Craig, J. v1p0193c2s v1p1358c2s v4p0206c2s v6p0025c2s v6p0099c1s v6p0243c2s v6p0352c2s v6p0656c1s
Craig, J.A. v5p0042c1s v5p0057c2s v6p0590c1s
Craig, J.W. v4p0290c2s
Craig, Martha v6p0357c2s
Craig, O. v2p0414c1s v4p0431c2s
Craig, R. v6p0519c2s
Craig, R.M. v4p0320c2s
Craig, S.S. et al. v5p0530c2s
Craig, T. v1p0463c1m v1p0463c2s v1p1272c1s
Craig, W.C. v1p0759c2s
Craig, W.G. v4p0457c1s v5p0378c1s
Craig, W.G. and Drury, J.B. v5p0464c1s
Craig, W.H. v4p0180c1s
Craig, W.N. v4p0049c2s v4p0090c1m v4p0203c2s v4p0214c2s v4p0409c1s v4p0433c1s v4p0449c1s v4p0491c2s v4p0552c2s v4p0605c1s
Craighan, L. v4p0528c1s
Craighead, J.B. v2p0309c1s
Craighead, J.G. v1p0149c1s
Craigie, D.J. v4p0016c2s
Craigie, F.J., jr. v6p0349c2s
Craigie, M., Mrs. v4p0160c2s
Craigie, P.C. v5p0550c2s
Craigie, P.G. v1p0538c1s v2p0005c2s v3p0149c1s v3p0241c1s v3p0339c1s v4p0082c2s v5p0550c1s
Craigie, P.M. v5p0485c2s v6p0056c1s v6p0180c2s v6p0184c1s v6p0223c2s v6p0263c1s v6p0365c2s v6p0516c1s v6p0549c1s v6p0583c1s v6p0601c2s v6p0630c1s
Craigie, P.M.T. v6p0201c2s
Craigie, P.M.T., Mrs. v6p0653c1s
Craigie, W.A. v4p0045c2s v4p0076c2s v4p0197c2s v4p0205c2s v4p0254c2s v4p0273c1s v4p0528c1s v4p0586c2s v5p0027c2s v5p0424c2s v5p0515c1s
Craik, D.M. v1p0014c1s v1p0017c1s v1p0065c1s v1p0142c1s v1p0158c1s v1p0205c2s v1p0229c2s v1p0246c1s v1p0264c1s v1p0266c1s v1p0282c1s v1p0291c2s v1p0303c2s v1p0357c1s v1p0361c2s v1p0365c1s v1p0382c2s v1p0474c2s v1p0479c2s v1p0520c1s v1p0560c1s v1p0569c2s v1p0593c1s v1p0595c1s v1p0605c2s v1p0627c2s v1p0689c2s v1p0708c2s v1p0726c1s v1p0728c2s v1p0757c1s v1p0762c2m v1p0774c2s v1p0788c2s v1p0855c2s v1p0888c1s v1p0924c1s v1p0968c1s v1p0969c2s v1p1013c2s v1p1031c2s v1p1052c1s v1p1100c2s v1p1257c1s v1p1322c2s v1p1358c1s v1p1366c1s v1p1418c2s v1p1420c1s v1p1426c2s v1p1439c1s v2p0103c2s v2p0123c1s v2p0172c2s v2p0225c1s v2p0228c1s v2p0243c1s v2p0257c2s v2p0265c1s v2p0295c1s v2p0329c2s v2p0404c1s v2p0421c2s v3p0107c1s v3p0202c2s v3p0222c1s v3p0268c1s v3p0268c2s v3p0274c1m v3p0405c2s v3p0445c2s
Craik, G.L. v1p0415c2s
Craik, G.M. v1p0026c1s v1p0166c2s v1p0588c1s v2p0357c2s
Craik, H. v2p0131c2s
Craik, H. and Saintsbury, G. v5p0515c2s
Craik, Henry v2p0428c2s
Craik, J. v1p0297c2s v1p0441c1s v1p0810c2s v1p0950c2s v1p1037c2s v1p1073c2s v1p1088c2s v1p1091c1s v1p1093c2s v1p1354c2s v2p0083c2s
Crain, W.A. v1p1236c2s

Cram, C.W. v4p0363c1s
v4p0378c2s v4p0529c2s
Cram, J. v1p0854c1s
Cram, J.A. v1p0451c1s
Cram, R.A. v4p0024c1s
v4p0025c1m v4p0050c2s v4p0068c2s
v4p0167c1s v5p0026c2s v5p0104c2s
v5p0302c2m v6p0027c2s v6p0148c2s
v6p0166c1s
Cram, R.A. and Warren, H.L.
v5p0026c2s
Cram, S.E. v5p0255c1s
Cram, T.J. v1p0104c1s
v1p1311c1s
Cram, W.A. v1p0140c2s
v1p0810c1s v1p1221c2s v2p0358c2s
v2p0466c2s
Cram, W.E. v4p0061c2s
v5p0020c2s v5p0063c2m v5p0170c2s
v5p0211c2s v5p0259c1m v5p0547c2s
v5p0624c1s v5p0639c2s
Cramblitt, F.A. v6p0469c2s
Cramer, F. v3p0363c1s
v4p0060c1s
Cramer, J.P. v6p0568c1s
Cramer, M.J. v1p0129c2s
v1p0419c2s v1p0978c1s v3p0043c1s
v5p0306c1s
Cramer, W.E. v1p1099c2s
Cramp, C.H. v3p0094c2s
v3p0391c1s v4p0395c2s v4p0595c1s
v5p0302c1s v5p0370c2s v5p0401c2s
v6p0591c1m v6p0616c1s
Cramp, J.M. v1p0253c2s
v1p0254c1s
Crampton, C.A. v3p0401c1s
v5p0559c2m
Crampton, C.W. v6p0522c1s
Cramsie, M.I. v5p0493c2s
Cran, W. v5p0387c2s
Cranage, D.H.S. v4p0073c1s
Cranborne, Viscount v3p0378c2s
Cranborne, Viscount et al.
v4p0265c2s
Cranbrook, Viscount v2p0225c2s
v2p0333c2s v2p0475c1s
Cranbrook, Viscount and Austin, A.
v3p0307c1s
Cranch, C.P. v1p0064c1s
v1p0335c2s v1p0356c1s v1p0365c2s
v1p0529c2s v1p0731c2s v1p0774c2s
v1p0801c1s v1p0908c1s v1p0940c1s
v1p0950c1s v1p1210c1s v1p1266c2s
v1p1275c1s v1p1277c2s v1p1281c1s
v1p1429c2s v2p0023c2s v2p0139c2s
v2p0458c2s v3p0145c1s v3p0426c1s
v3p0440c2s v4p0179c1s
Cranch, C.P. and Adams, C.F.
v3p0351c1s
Cranch, E. v4p0559c2s
Cranch, E.P. v1p0786c1s
Cranch, W. v1p1289c2s
Crandall, A. v6p0645c1s
Crandall, A.F.J. v2p0309c1s
Crandall, C.H. v3p0060c1s
v3p0201c1s v3p0311c1s v3p0375c2s
v4p0136c2s v4p0162c1s v4p0264c1s
v4p0412c2s v5p0554c2s v5p0556c1s
Crandall, C.J. v6p0315c2s
Crandall, C.L. v1p0161c1s
Crandall, F.A. v5p0604c1s
v6p0378c2s v6p0655c2s
Crandall, F.C. v6p0522c1s
Crandall, F.M. v6p0175c2s
Crandall, L.A. v4p0053c2s
Crandall, L.S. v5p0455c1s
Crandall, M.I. v3p0248c2s
v3p0249c2s
Crandall, W.I. v4p0126c1s
v4p0616c1s
Crandall, W.S. v5p0119c2s
Crandall, W.T. v3p0472c2s
Cranden, E.S. v5p0451c1s
v5p0472c2s
Crandon, F.P. v3p0085c2s
Crane, A. v2p0011c2s
v2p0064c2s v2p0257c2s v2p0302c2s
v2p0317c1s v2p0412c1s v2p0452c2s
v2p0481c2s v2p0482c2s v4p0071c1s
v4p0419c1s v4p0554c2s
Crane, A.B. v1p0005c2s
Crane, A.C. v5p0288c1s
Crane, A.M. v1p0755c2s
v1p0886c2s v1p1022c1s v1p1053c1s
v6p0638c1s
Crane, A.R. v6p0432c1s
Crane, Agnes v4p0368c1s
Crane, Alice R. v5p0096c1s
Crane, C. v5p0519c2s
Crane, C.A. v4p0129c1s
v4p0367c2s
Crane, C.B. v1p0839c2s
v2p0223c1s v2p0291c1s v2p0369c1s
v2p0415c1s v6p0321c1s v6p0462c2s
Crane, C.H. v5p0643c1s
Crane, C.J. v4p0411c1s
v5p0029c1s v5p0206c2s v5p0290c1s
v5p0488c2s v6p0182c1s v6p0226c1s
v6p0307c2s v6p0319c1s

Crane, C.K. v6p0044c1s
v6p0236c2s
Crane, E.A. v5p0200c1s
Crane, F. v4p0432c2s
v4p0458c1s v5p0187c1s v5p0498c1s
v5p0539c1s v6p0099c2s v6p0307c1s
v6p0362c2s v6p0447c1s v6p0477c2s
v6p0538c2s v6p0575c1s
Crane, F.W. v4p0087c2s
v4p0440c1s v4p0619c2s v5p0620c2m
Crane, Fergus v6p0329c2s
Crane, G. v6p0081c1s
Crane, J. v6p0638c2s
Crane, J.C. v1p0144c2s
v6p0224c1s
Crane, J.E. v5p0394c1s
v5p0530c2s
Crane, J.L. v4p0234c2s
Crane, J.S. v4p0243c2s
Crane, J.T. v1p0020c2s
v1p0030c1s v1p0070c2s v1p0165c2s
v1p0228c2s v1p0356c2s v1p0367c2s
v1p0475c2s v1p0673c2s v1p0831c1s
v1p0890c1s v1p0976c2s v1p0989c2s
v1p1084c1s v1p1243c2s v1p1292c2s
v1p1318c2s v1p1342c1s v1p1350c2s
v1p1432c1s
Crane, L. v6p0232c2s
v6p0427c2s
Crane, L.B. v5p0058c2s
v5p0059c1m
Crane, L.F. v6p0390c2s
Crane, Leo v6p0380c2s
Crane, M.F. v1p0186c1s
Crane, N. v1p0997c1s
Crane, O. v1p0681c2s
Crane, R.N. v6p0363c2s
v6p0708c1s
Crane, R.T. v4p0586c1s
Crane, S. v1p0529c1s
v1p0687c1s v1p1099c1s v1p1147c2m
v1p1200c1s v2p0146c2s v2p0181c1s
v2p0222c2s v2p0324c1s v2p0368c2s
v3p0217c1s v3p0229c2s v3p0354c2s
v3p0359c2s v4p0120c2s v4p0243c1s
v4p0264c2s v4p0281c2s v4p0336c1s
v4p0364c2s v4p0562c1s v4p0571c1s
v4p0575c2s v4p0603c2s v5p0002c1s
v5p0043c1s v5p0076c1s v5p0083c1s
v5p0084c1s v5p0159c1s v5p0210c1s
v5p0236c2s v5p0251c2s v5p0253c1s
v5p0266c1s v5p0315c2s v5p0345c2s
v5p0347c1s v5p0351c2s v5p0358c2s
v5p0359c1s v5p0384c1s v5p0406c1s
v5p0421c2s v5p0455c1s v5p0465c1s
v5p0486c2s v5p0514c2s v5p0517c2s
v5p0519c1s v5p0538c1s v5p0595c2s
v5p0613c2s v5p0628c2s
Crane, S. and Barr, R. ... v6p0471c1s
Crane, Stephen v5p0068c1s
v5p0153c1s v5p0640c1s
Crane, T.F. v1p0101c2s
v1p0150c1s v1p0405c1s v1p0461c1s
v1p0464c2m v1p0489c1s v1p0571c2s
v1p0669c2s v1p0754c1s v1p0776c1s
v1p0816c2s v1p1098c1s v1p1231c1m
v1p1281c1s v1p1327c1s v1p1328c1s
v2p0007c2s v2p0231c1s v2p0270c1s
v2p0357c2s v3p0003c2s v3p0156c2s
v4p0004c2s v4p0205c2s v4p0225c2s
v4p0452c2s
Crane, W. v1p0340c1s
v2p0201c1s v2p0404c1s v3p0023c1s
v3p0208c1s v3p0208c2s v3p0215c1s
v4p0032c1s v4p0150c2m v4p0153c2m
v4p0161c1s v4p0225c1s v4p0376c1s
v4p0534c1s v5p0159c2s v5p0232c2s
v5p0402c1s v6p0167c2s v6p0555c1s
v6p0661c1s
Crane, W. and Day, L.F. .. v6p0470c2s
Crane, W.A. v5p0476c2s
Crane, W.B. v6p0405c2s
Crane, W.C. v1p1083c2s
v1p1271c1s v1p1437c1s v2p0096c1s
v2p0299c2s
Crane, W.E. v4p0589c1s
Crane, W.F. v6p0686c2s
Crane, W.H. v4p0003c1s
v4p0446c2s
Crane, W.I. v5p0519c1s
v6p0194c1s
Crane, W.M. v1p0562c2s
Crane, W.W. v1p0034c2s
v1p0457c1s v1p0506c1s v1p0513c1s
v1p1429c1s v2p0370c1s v2p0378c1s
v2p0409c2s v3p0387c2s v3p0426c2s
v4p0173c2s v5p0556c2s v6p0610c1s
Crane, W.W., jr. v1p0286c1s
v6p0059c1s v6p0413c2s v6p0680c1s
Crane, Wa. v5p0031c2s
Crane, Walter v4p0013c2s
v5p0387c2s
Crane, Walter and Day, L.F.
v5p0436c1s
Cranefield, F. v6p0260c1s
Craner, H.D. v6p0457c1s
Cranford, K. v4p0537c2s
Cranford, W.I. v6p0210c1s
v6p0610c1s v6p0672c2s
Cranmer, G. v4p0429c1s

Cranor, H.D. v6p0102c2s
v6p0404c2s
Cranson, E.S. v4p0372c2s
Cranson, J.H. v5p0371c2s
Cranston, E.M. v5p0140c2s
Cranston, M.R. v6p0016c2s
v6p0085c2s v6p0148c2s v6p0217c2s
v6p0381c1s v6p0584c2s
Cranston, Mary R. v6p0256c2s
v6p0565c2s v6p0628c2s
Cranston, Mary Rankin v6p0600c2s
Crany, A. v4p0512c1s
Cranz, A. v2p0174c1s
Crapper, W. v3p0369c1s
Crapsey, A.S. v6p0131c1s
Crapsey, E. v1p0230c1s
v1p0257c2s v1p0268c1s v1p0317c1m
v1p0346c2s v1p0444c2s v1p0498c2s
v1p0760c1s v1p0770c2s v1p0852c1s
v1p0881c1s v1p0917c1s v1p0981c2s
v1p0982c1s v1p1253c2s v1p1294c1s
v1p1305c1m
Crary, A. v5p0192c1s
Crary, Agnes v5p0021c1s
Crary, B.F. v3p0236c2s
Crary, Bessie J. v5p0137c2s
Cras, C.G.Le v5p0585c1s
Craster, H.H.E. v6p0470c2s
Crauford, O. v3p0060c1s
Craufurd, A.H. v4p0190c1s
Craufurd, C.H. v5p0240c2s
Craufurd, H.J. v6p0378c2s
Craufurd, H.J. and Lytton, Earl of
v6p0522c2s
v6p0637c2s
Craufurd, J. v1p0317c2s
v1p1166c1s
Craufurd, O. v2p0065c1s
Cravath, J.R. v4p0101c1s
Craven, A. v1p1364c2s
Craven, E.G. v5p0183c2s
v5p0431c2s
Craven, E.R. v2p0206c2s
v2p0220c2s v2p0352c2s
v3p0342c2s
Craven, Florence v2p0318c1s
Craven, R., Mrs. v1p0460c1s
Craver, Harrison W. v6p0372c2s
Craw, W.J. v1p1002c2s
Crawfoot, J.W. v5p0461c1s
Crawford, A. v2p0225c1s
v3p0197c2s
Crawford, A.B. v2p0192c1s
Crawford, A.G. v2p0041c1s
Crawford, A.W. v6p0480c2m
v6p0481c1s v6p0492c1s
Crawford, C.Alex. v6p0510c2s
Crawford, Caroline v6p0239c1s
Crawford, D. v3p0321c2s
v3p0322c1s v4p0261c2s v4p0265c2s
v4p0266c1s v4p0328c2s
Crawford, E. v1p1305c2s
v3p0160c2s v3p0320c2s v3p0475c2s
v4p0070c1s v4p0163c2s v4p0348c1s
v4p0399c2s v4p0425c2s v4p0480c2s
v4p0628c2s v5p0174c1s v5p0610c2m
v6p0161c2s v6p0213c1s v6p0213c2s
v6p0539c1s v6p0643c1s v6p0670c1s
Crawford, E., Mrs. v5p0267c2s
Crawford, Emily v4p0048c1s
v4p0212c2s v4p0294c2s v4p0426c1s
v5p0348c2s v5p0610c2s
Crawford, F.C. v5p0354c1s
Crawford, F.M. v2p0023c1s
v2p0218c1s v2p0294c1s v2p0376c2s
v2p0377c2s v2p0386c2s v3p0270c2s
v3p0324c1s v3p0375c1s v3p0375c2s
v3p0429c2s v3p0459c2s v3p0466c2m
v4p0012c2s v4p0045c2s v4p0065c2s
v4p0091c1s v4p0130c2s v4p0159c1s
v4p0279c2s v4p0310c2s v4p0326c2s
v4p0343c1s v4p0391c2s v4p0396c1s
v4p0408c1s v4p0408c2s v4p0490c2m
v4p0491c1s v4p0537c1s v4p0575c2s
v4p0601c1s v4p0612c1s v5p0137c2s
v5p0240c1s v5p0283c1s v5p0299c2s
v5p0330c2s v5p0429c2s v5p0496c2s
v5p0610c1s v6p0218c1s v6p0368c1s
Crawford, F.M. and Holmes, O.W.
v3p0442c1s
Crawford, F.M. and Mable, H.W.
v4p0610c2s
Crawford, G.F. v1p0542c2s
Crawford, G.M. v2p0213c1s
v2p0332c1s
Crawford, G.M., Mrs. v1p0141c1s
v1p0478c2s v1p0481c1s
Crawford, G.S. v4p0120c1s
Crawford, J. v1p0071c2s
v1p0226c1s v1p0271c1s v1p0286c1s
v1p1029c1s v1p1216c1s v1p1313c2s
v1p1348c2s v2p0325c1s v4p0016c1s
v4p0403c2s v4p0510c1s v4p0610c1s
v5p0017c2s v5p0410c1s
Crawford, J.C. v6p0194c2s
Crawford, J.D. v4p0007c2s
v6p0293c1s
Crawford, J.H. v4p0060c2s
v4p0061c1s v4p0164c1s v4p0198c2s
v4p0209c2s v4p0436c2s v4p0509c1m

v5p0289c2s
Crawford, J.M. and Edwards, W.H.
v4p0101c1s
Crawford, J.S. v5p0137c2s
v5p0431c1s v5p0433c1s
v6p0219c2s
Crawford, J.U. v3p0386c1s
Crawford, L.C. v6p0264c1s
Crawford, M.C. v6p0142c1s
v6p0239c1s v6p0293c1s v6p0350c1s
v6p0408c2s v6p0426c2s v6p0648c2s
v6p0704c1s
Crawford, M.S. v3p0222c2s
v4p0625c1s
Crawford, Mary C. v6p0076c2s
v6p0122c1s v6p0538c2s v6p0572c1s
Crawford, Mrs. v1p0469c2s
Crawford, O.M. v5p0369c2s
Crawford, P. v3p0432c2s
v4p0146c2s v4p0560c1s
Crawford, R. v5p0041c1s
v6p0258c1s v6p0624c1s
Crawford, R.F. v4p0618c2s
Crawford, R.T. v6p0250c1s
Crawford, Robert v6p0436c1s
Crawford, S.W. v5p0193c2s
v5p0230c1s
Crawford, Sarah M. v5p0193c2s
Crawford, T.C. v4p0039c2s
v4p0063c1s v4p0097c2s v4p0156c2s
v4p0267c2s v4p0375c2s v4p0403c1s
v4p0424c1s v4p0515c1s v4p0612c2s
v5p0169c1s v5p0234c2s v5p0270c1s
v5p0381c1s
Crawford, T.R. v3p0178c2s
Crawford, V.M. v4p0248c1s
v4p0599c2s v4p0603c1s v5p0052c1s
v5p0052c2s v5p0153c2s v5p0179c1s
v5p0193c1s v5p0217c1s v5p0355c1s
v5p0361c2s v5p0435c2s v5p0443c2s
v5p0528c2s v5p0612c1s v5p0637c1s
v5p0638c1s v5p0640c2s v6p0096c1s
v6p0230c2s v6p0479c2s v6p0562c2s
v6p0663c2s v6p0697c1s v6p0705c2s
Crawford, Virginia M. v5p0047c1s
Crawford, W. v1p1043c2s
Crawford, W.D. v3p0311c1s
Crawford, W.H. v2p0044c1s
v5p0276c2s
Crawford, W.H., jr. v5p0560c1s
Crawfurd, D. et al. v4p0289c2s
Crawfurd, J. v1p0790c2s
v1p0793c1s v1p0793c2s
Crawfurd, O. v1p1037c1s
v2p0040c2s v2p0070c1s v2p0073c1s
v3p0004c1s v3p0031c2s v3p0156c2s
v3p0206c2s v3p0313c1s v3p0340c1m
v3p0351c1s v3p0395c2s v3p0406c1m
v4p0276c2s v5p0304c1s v5p0411c1s
v5p0505c1s v5p0581c2s v6p0181c1s
v6p0444c1s
Crawley, A.E. v4p0516c2m
v4p0561c2s v4p0629c2s
Crawley, E. v6p0041c2s
Crawley, E.S. v5p0229c1s
v5p0416c1s v6p0406c1s
Crawley, H. v6p0611c1s
Crawley, H.E. v6p0120c2s
Crawley, Howard v5p0161c2s
v5p0294c2s
Crawley, Howard, Dr. v5p0002c1s
Crawley, J.S. v1p0313c2s
v1p0453c1s v1p0860c2s
Crawley-Boevey, S.M. v5p0125c2s
Crawshay, A. v4p0475c2s
Crawshay, R. v5p0020c1s
v6p0053c2s v6p0351c1s
Cray, E.L. v6p0430c2s
Creach, M. v4p0469c2s
Creagh, C.V. v4p0079c2s
Creagh, J.T. v5p0444c1s
v6p0176c2s v6p0236c2s
Creak, E.W. v1p0286c2s
v2p0097c1s v2p0229c2s v4p0349c2s
v6p0395c1s
Crease, J.F. v6p0107c1s
v6p0256c1s
Creasy, E. v1p0293c2s
v1p1323c2s v1p1367c1s
Creasy, E., Sir v1p0465c1s
v1p0736c1s v1p0739c1s
Creasy, E.R. v1p0428c1s
Creasy, E.S. v1p0020c1s
v1p0050c2s v1p0103c1s v1p0184c2s
v1p0215c2s v1p0219c2s v1p0274c2s
v1p0343c2m v1p0538c2s v1p0712c2s
v1p0799c1s v1p0826c2s v1p0863c2s
v1p0893c1s v1p1065c1s v1p1230c2s
v1p1278c2s v1p1317c2s v1p1361c2s
v1p1367c1s
Creath, J. v2p0043c2s
v2p0385c2s
Credland, W.R. v2p0031c2s
v2p0256c1s v2p0420c1s
Cree, A.T.C. v6p0046c1s
Cree, C. v5p0577c2s
Cree, J.K. v4p0009c1s
v4p0370c1s
Creed, C.A. v5p0592c1s
Creed, J.M. v5p0244c1s
v6p0041c2m v6p0057c1s
Creed, S.M. v6p0071c2s
Creedmoor, W. v5p0102c1s
v5p0132c1s v6p0453c1s
Creelman, H. v4p0616c2s
Creelman, J. v4p0168c2s
v4p0341c1s v4p0364c1s v4p0395c2s
v4p0519c2s v5p0508c2s v6p0480c2s
Creelman, James and Marshall, Edward
v5p0049c2s
Creevey, C.A. v5p0642c1s
Crehore, A.C. and Squier, G.O.
v5p0565c1s
Crehore, C.F. v2p0086c2s
v3p0086c1m v3p0130c1s v3p0178c1s
v3p0215c2s v3p0228c1s v3p0244c2s
v3p0323c2s v3p0330c2s v3p0331c2s
v3p0378c2s v3p0452c1s v3p0452c2s
Crehore, J.D. v1p0523c1s
v1p0666c1s v1p1010c2s v1p1100c2s
v1p1259c1s v1p1282c1s v2p0209c2s
v2p0342c1s
Creighton, Beatrice v5p0223c1s
Creighton, C. v2p0119c1s
v2p0145c2s v2p0482c1s v3p0148c2s
v3p0256c2s v3p0387c2s v3p0446c1s
v3p0446c2s v4p0156c2s v4p0338c1s
v6p0501c2s
Creighton, J.E. v4p0253c1s
v4p0287c1s v4p0372c1s v4p0439c2s
v4p0465c1s v4p0561c1s v4p0590c2s
v5p0180c2s v5p0281c1s v5p0319c1s
v5p0372c2s v5p0470c2s v5p0585c2s
v6p0216c1s v6p0412c2s v6p0495c2s
v6p0523c2s v6p0610c2s
Creighton, J.G.A. v4p0385c2s
Creighton, J.G.A. and Yale, L.M.
v3p0465c1s
Creighton, J.H. v3p0262c1s
Creighton, J.R. v4p0457c2s
v4p0467c1s
Creighton, L. v3p0470c1s
v6p0273c2s
Creighton, Louise, Mrs. .. v5p0636c2s
Creighton, M. v1p0331c1s
v1p0869c2s v1p1012c2s v1p1100c2s
v1p1376c1s v1p1434c2s v2p0075c1s
v2p0109c2s v2p0112c2s v2p0125c2s
v2p0144c2s v2p0232c1s v2p0237c2s
v2p0287c2s v2p0308c1s v2p0316c2m
v2p0373c1s v2p0403c1s v2p0471c1s
v2p0482c1s v3p0139c1s v3p0141c1s
v4p0011c2s v4p0178c1s v4p0259c2s
v4p0347c1s v4p0350c2s v4p0404c1s
v4p0495c2s v5p0263c2s v5p0266c2s
v5p0319c1s v5p0345c1s v6p0292c1s
Creighton, M. and Villari, L.
v2p0203c1s
Creighton, Mrs. v5p0140c1s
Creighton, R.J. v1p1348c1s
v2p0454c2s v6p0054c2s
Creitz, C.E. v5p0520c2s
Crellin, H.N. v4p0194c1s
v4p0219c1s v4p0249c2s v4p0293c2s
v4p0556c1s v4p0606c2s v4p0633c2s
Crellin, J.S. v6p0566c2s
Cremer, A.R. v3p0026c1s
Cremer, W.R. v6p0324c2s
Cremony, J.C. v1p0008c1s
v1p0046c2s v1p0321c1s v1p0370c2s
v1p0436c2s v1p0593c1s v1p0636c1s
v1p0784c1s v1p1127c2s v1p1151c1m
v1p1206c1s
Creole, A. v2p0461c1s
Crespi, A., Dr. v4p0632c2s
Crespi, A.J.H. v1p0010c1s
v1p0050c2s v1p0297c2s v1p0436c2s
v1p0465c1s v1p0535c2s v1p0612c2s
v1p0708c2s v1p0715c2s v1p0757c2s
v1p0865c1s v1p0954c1s v1p1040c1s
v1p1168c2s v1p1193c1s v1p1292c2s
v1p1319c2s v3p0010c1s v3p0046c1s
v3p0052c1s v3p0064c2s v3p0080c1s
v3p0081c2s v3p0090c1s v3p0101c2s
v3p0108c2s v3p0112c1s v3p0117c2m
v3p0118c2s v3p0127c1s v3p0143c2s
v3p0150c1s v3p0157c1s v3p0165c1s
v3p0180c2s v3p0205c2s v3p0262c1s
v3p0323c1s v3p0371c1s v3p0372c1s
v3p0380c2s v4p0150c1s v5p0155c2s
v5p0222c2s v5p0223c1s
Crespi, C.R. v1p0667c2s
v1p0988c1s
Crespi, J.G.H. v5p0013c1s
Crespigny, C.C.de v1p0837c2s
Crespigny, C.de v6p0138c2s
Crespigny, De v1p0150c2s
Crespigny, P.C.de, Mrs. .. v2p0411c2m
v3p0474c2s v6p0440c1s
Crespin, M.A. v1p1290c2s
Cressey, G.C. v3p0281c2s
Cressman, M.S. v3p0033c2s
v3p0347c1s v4p0557c2s
Cresson, C.M. v1p0146c2s
v1p0787c2s
Cresson, H.T. v2p0158c1s
v2p0343c1s v4p0256c2s
Cresson, J.C. v1p0502c1m
v1p0902c2s v1p1196c2s
Cresswell, B.F. v2p0382c2s
Cresswell, C.N. v3p0362c1s
Cresswell, H. v3p0294c1s
Cresswell, L. v4p0143c2s
Cresswell, M. v3p0308c1s
Creswell, F.H.P. v6p0654c1m
Creswell, H. v3p0441c1s
Creswicke, L. v4p0414c2s
v4p0619c2s
Creudson, W. v6p0338c1s
Creuzbaur, R. v1p1247c2s
Crevecoeur, St.J.de v1p0892c2s
v1p0916c2s v1p0919c2s
Crew, C.L. v6p0524c2s
Crew, E. v1p1075c2s
Crew, H. v3p0264c1s
v3p0415c1s v4p0470c1s v5p0279c2s
v5p0449c2s v6p0498c2s
Crew, H. and Hale, G.E. .. v4p0557c1s
Crew, H. and Tatnell, R. . v4p0540c2s
Crew, J.C. v6p0646c2s
Crewe, Earl of v4p0290c2s
Crewe, S. v4p0281c1s
Creyke, C. v4p0007c2s
v4p0257c1s v5p0150c2s v5p0531c1s
v5p0614c1s
Creyke, W. v6p0607c1s
Crichfield, G.W. v6p0477c1s
Crichton, M. v4p0307c1s
Crichton-Browne, H. v4p0165c1s
Crichton-Browne, J. v3p0189c1s
v5p0368c2s
v6p0569c2s
Crichton-Browne, J., Sir
v6p0101c2s
Crilly, D. v6p0007c2s
Crim, M. v2p0322c1s
v3p0107c1s v3p0209c2s v3p0404c1s
v3p0437c2s v3p0439c2s v3p0455c1s
v3p0475c1s v4p0141c2s v4p0553c2s
v6p0541c2s
Cringan, A.T. v4p0466c1s
Crinkle, N. v4p0424c1s
Cripps, A.S. v6p0038c1s
Cripps, C.A. v3p0095c1s
v3p0162c2m v3p0163c1s v3p0399c1s
v4p0008c1s v4p0167c2s v5p0272c2s
v6p0271c1s
Cripps, M. v5p0176c2s
Cripps, W. v3p0177c1s
v3p0334c1s v3p0402c2s v4p0446c1s
Cripps, W.J. v3p0102c2s
Crisfield, C.L. v5p0299c1s
Crisman, O. v6p0295c1s
Crisp, C.F. v4p0129c1s
v4p0462c2s
Crisp, E. v1p0899c2s
Crisp, F. et al. v3p0277c2s
Crispi v5p0590c2s
Crispi, F. v3p0224c2m
v4p0295c1s v4p0452c2s v5p0013c1s
v5p0108c2s v5p0300c1s v5p0591c1s
Crispin, E.S. v6p0457c2s
Crispolti, F. v6p0368c1s
v6p0501c1s
Crissey, F. v4p0265c1s
v5p0105c1s v5p0256c1s v5p0265c2s
v5p0476c2s v5p0592c2s v5p0645c1s
v6p0511c1s
Crissey, F. and Harwood, W.S.
v5p0223c2s
Crissey, Forest v6p0317c1s
Crissy, F. v4p0064c2s
Crist, Lawrence v6p0038c1s
Cristy, A.B. v5p0557c1s
Cristy, M. v3p0281c2s
v4p0444c2s v5p0128c2s v5p0405c1s
Criswell, R., jr. v1p1389c1s
Criswick, H.C. v1p1213c2s
v1p1233c2s
Crittenden, R.H. v4p0093c2s
Crittenden, T.L. v5p0361c1s
Croad, H. v5p0396c1s
Croal, J.P. v4p0168c1s
Croal, T.A. v1p0210c2s
v2p0125c2s v5p0176c1s v6p0277c2s
Croasdale, W.T. v3p0352c1s
Crocheron, J.J. v1p0324c2s
Crockard, F.H. v5p0125c2s
v6p0328c2s
Crocker, B. v4p0079c2s
Crocker, C.W. v1p0716c1s
v1p0889c2s v1p0962c1m v1p1012c1s
Crocker, F.B. v4p0165c1s
v4p0175c1m v4p0175c2m v6p0350c2s
Crocker, F.C. v5p0156c2s
Crocker, G.G. v5p0072c2s
Crocker, G.U. v4p0286c2s
Crocker, G.W. v5p0178c2s
v5p0511c1s
Crocker, J.H. v3p0281c1m
v4p0028c1s
Crocker, U.H. v1p0017c2s
v1p0504c2s v4p0288c2s v4p0419c1s
Crocker, U.H. and Macoane, S.M.
v3p0315c2s
Crocker, Z. v1p0359c2s
v1p0384c2s v1p0386c1s
Crockett, A.E. v5p0514c2s
Crockett, I. v5p0464c1s
Crockett, J.A. v2p0099c2s

Crockett, M.A. v5p0368c1s
Crockett, S.R. v4p0118c2s
v4p0311c2s v4p0365c1s v4p0510c1s
v4p0531c1s v5p0067c1s v5p0186c2s
v5p0207c2s v5p0238c2s v5p0326c1s
v5p0342c1s v5p0415c2s v5p0530c1s
v5p0553c2s v5p0591c2s v5p0627c2s
v6p0004c2s
Croes, J.J.R. v5p0120c2m
Crofford, F.B. v5p0288c1s
Croffut, B.B. v5p0101c2s
v5p0268c1s
Croffut, W.A. v1p0227c1s
v1p0227c2s v1p1384c2s v1p1430c1s
v3p0275c1s
Croffut, W.A. and Post, L.F.
v2p0245c2s
Croffut, W.O. v4p0462c1s
Croft, A. v1p1275c2s
v4p0576c2s
Croft, A.W. v4p0576c1s
Croft, C. v2p0364c1s
Crobt, H. v1p0016c2s
v1p0300c1s v1p0665c1s v1p1052c1s
Croft, M.L. v6p0500c2s
v6p0590c2s
Croft, W.B. v6p0174c1s
Crofton, A.F.B. v4p0273c2s
v5p0027c2s v5p0143c1s
Crofton, F.B. v1p0438c1s
v1p0758c2s v1p1216c2s v1p1425c2s
v4p0246c1s v5p0050c1s v5p0206c2s
v5p0481c2s v6p0310c1s v6p0461c1s
Crofton, F.Blake v5p0386c2s
Crofton, H.T. v2p0194c1m
Crofton, H.W. v3p0383c2s
Crofton, W. v1p0315c2s
v1p0317c1s
Crofton, W., Sir v1p0543c1s
v1p1052c1s
Crofts, E.W. v4p0310c1s
v4p0494c1s v4p0534c2s
Crofts, H.B. v5p0368c2s
Crofts, J. v2p0093c2s
Crofts, J.A. v1p0536c1s
Croke, R. v1p0555c1s
Croke, W.J.D. v4p0294c1s
v4p0404c1s v5p0429c2s v5p0495c1s
v6p0077c2s v6p0208c1s v6p0332c1s
v6p0501c1s
Crokell, T. v6p0611c1m
Croker, B.M. v3p0218c1s
v3p0431c1s v5p0560c1s
Croker, E.F. v6p0701c1s
Croker, J.W. v1p0027c2s
v1p0038c2s v1p0051c1s v1p0059c2s
v1p0066c2s v1p0139c1s v1p0146c2s
v1p0147c2s v1p0168c2s v1p0178c1s
v1p0178c2s v1p0182c1s v1p0189c2s
v1p0193c1s v1p0209c1s v1p0261c1s
v1p0288c1s v1p0302c2s v1p0309c1s
v1p0314c2s v1p0341c1s v1p0350c2s
v1p0370c1s v1p0402c1s v1p0408c2s
v1p0409c2s v1p0412c1s v1p0413c2s
v1p0429c2s v1p0458c2s v1p0475c2m
v1p0476c1m v1p0476c2m v1p0479c1s
v1p0480c1s v1p0482c1s v1p0489c2s
v1p0505c1s v1p0510c2s v1p0511c1m
v1p0548c1m v1p0548c2m v1p0561c1s
v1p0571c2s v1p0577c2s v1p0659c2s
v1p0698c2s v1p0717c1s v1p0739c2s
v1p0771c2s v1p0772c1s v1p0780c1s
v1p0784c1s v1p0791c1s v1p0800c2s
v1p0805c2s v1p0863c1s v1p0893c1s
v1p0893c2m v1p0894c2s v1p0895c1s
v1p0895c2s v1p0947c2s v1p0973c2m
v1p0974c1s v1p0985c1s v1p0987c2m
v1p1002c2s v1p1012c1s v1p1012c2s
v1p1020c2s v1p1038c2s v1p1050c1s
v1p1055c2s v1p1074c2s v1p1104c1s
v1p1111c2s v1p1126c2s v1p1133c1s
v1p1133c2s v1p1135c2s v1p1145c1s
v1p1171c1s v1p1190c2s v1p1195c2s
v1p1211c2m v1p1235c1s v1p1243c1s
v1p1284c2s v1p1366c2s v1p1368c1s
v1p1380c2s v1p1382c2s v1p1383c1m
v1p1393c1s v1p1397c2s v1p1405c1s
v1p1409c1s v1p1433c2s v2p0168c1s
Croker, R. v5p0603c2s
Croker, T.C. v1p0662c2s
v1p1263c2s
Crole, D. v5p0569c1s
Croll, J. v1p0936c2s
v1p1213c2s v1p1267c2s v1p1268c1s
v1p1293c1s v2p0020c2s v2p0089c1s
v2p0213c2s v2p0223c2s v2p0347c1s
v2p0425c1s v3p0173c2s
Croll, P.C. v3p0415c2s
v4p0374c2s v4p0616c2s
Croly, D.G. v1p0696c2s
v1p1099c1s
Croly, G. v1p0177c2s
v1p0324c2s v1p0662c1s v1p0804c2s
Croly, H. v5p0033c1s
v5p0082c1s v6p0027c1s v6p0027c2s
v6p0028c1m v6p0033c2s v6p0128c2s
v6p0153c2s v6p0280c1s v6p0281c2s
v6p0292c1s v6p0333c1s v6p0360c2s
v6p0452c1s v6p0454c1s v6p0503c2s
v6p0543c1s v6p0568c1s
Croly, H.D. v4p0029c1s
v5p0025c2s v6p0280c2s v6p0639c2s
Croly, Herbert v6p0303c2s
v6p0452c1s
Croly, J.C. v3p0119c1s
v3p0120c2s
Croly, J.J. v1p0278c2s
v1p1425c2s
Crombie, J.E. v4p0200c2s
v4p0568c2s v4p0616c1s
Crombie, J.M. v1p0744c1s
v2p0127c1s
Crombie, J.W. v2p0207c1s
v2p0374c1s v3p0001c1s v3p0351c2s
v3p0434c2s v6p0072c1s
Cromby, C.H. v6p0011c1s
Cromer, E. v5p0630c2s
Cromer, G.C. v5p0447c1s
Cromer, J.M. v2p0269c1s
v3p0254c2s v4p0113c2s v4p0121c2s
v6p0421c2s
Cromie, C.F. v1p0694c2s
v1p0870c2s v1p1362c1s
Cromie, R. v6p0661c1s
Cromie, W.H. v2p0029c2s
v2p0032c1s v2p0078c2s v2p0116c1s
v2p0231c1s v2p0288c2s v2p0316c2s
v2p0350c1s v2p0381c1s v2p0395c2s
v2p0412c2s
Crommelin, A.C.D. v5p0167c1s
v5p0175c1s v6p0037c2s v6p0188c1s
v6p0348c1s v6p0496c1s
Crommelin, A.C.D. and Abetti, G.
v6p0037c1s
Crommelin, A.D. v6p0571c1s
v6p0630c2s
Crommelin, A.G.D. v6p0427c2s
Crommelin, E.G. v5p0268c2s
Crommelin, Emeline G. v5p0186c2s
Crommelin, H.S.M.Van v4p0164c2s
Crommelin, H.S.M.Van W. .. v5p0172c1m
v6p0184c2m
Crommelin, M. v3p0125c1s
v4p0004c1s v4p0104c2s v4p0133c2s
v4p0503c1s v4p0613c1s v5p0555c2s
Crommelin, May v3p0167c1s
v5p0323c2s v5p0440c2s
Crompton, A. v1p1247c2s
Crompton, C. and Crompton, R.E.
v5p0150c2s
Crompton, H. v1p0537c2s
v1p0700c1s v1p0787c1m v1p1261c2s
v3p0205c2s v5p0163c1s
Crompton, H.W. v4p0169c1s
Crompton, J. v1p0416c2s
v2p0414c2s
Crompton, R.E. v4p0174c2s
v5p0367c2s
Crompton, R.E. and Crompton, C.
v5p0150c2s
Crompton, R.E.B. v2p0258c2s
v3p0132c2s v4p0176c1s
Cromwell, A.D. v6p0293c1s
Cromwell, O.E. v3p0361c2s
Cronan, J.F. v6p0659c2s
Cronan, R. v5p0447c2s
Cronch, W. v6p0038c2s
Crone, J.S. v4p0050c1s
Cronin, H.S. v6p0500c2s
v6p0522c1s
Cronin, J.J. v6p0117c1s
Cronin, P.F. v4p0287c1s
Cronise, E.S. v4p0248c2s
Cronwright-Schreiner, S.C.
v5p0007c2s
Cronyn, D. v1p1426c1s
Crook, A.R. v4p0224c1s
v4p0597c1s v6p0139c2s v6p0422c1s
v6p0444c1s v6p0470c2s
Crook, G. v5p0023c2s
Crook, I. v2p0439c2s
v4p0465c2s v6p0222c2s
Crook, M. v6p0416c1s
Crook, R. v2p0027c2s
v2p0201c2s
Crook, R.E. v6p0258c1s
Crook, W.H. v6p0377c2s
Crook, W.M. v6p0269c2s
Crook, Z. v5p0278c1s
Crook, Z.E. v6p0199c2s
Crooke, E.R. v1p0678c1s
Crooke, R.E. v6p0579c1s
Crooke, W. v5p0155c1s
v5p0285c2s v5p0286c2s v5p0320c1s
v5p0532c2s v6p0402c2s
Crooker, J.H. v2p0167c1s
v3p0074c1s v3p0075c1s v3p0188c2s
v3p0331c2s v3p0358c1s v4p0071c2s
v4p0129c1s v4p0152c1s v4p0381c2s
v4p0466c1s v4p0479c2s v4p0532c2s
v4p0533c2m v5p0384c2s
Crooker, W. v3p0133c1s
Crookes, W. v1p0159c1s
v1p0348c2s v1p0399c1s v1p0400c1s
v1p0502c2s v1p0747c1s v1p0812c1m
v1p0858c2m v1p0950c2s v1p1003c1s
v1p1074c1m v1p1074c2m v1p1100c1s
v1p1234c1s v2p0008c1s v2p0076c1s
v2p0118c1s v2p0129c2s v2p0136c2s
v2p0137c1s v2p0137c2s v2p0146c1s
v2p0170c1s v2p0185c1s v2p0258c2m
v2p0272c1s v2p0294c1s v2p0322c1s
v2p0358c1s v2p0362c1s v2p0385c1s
v2p0413c2m v2p0415c1m v2p0432c2s
v2p0433c2s v2p0482c2s v3p0009c2s
v3p0076c1m v3p0126c1s v3p0134c1s
v3p0359c2s v4p0176c2m v4p0177c1s
v4p0253c2s v5p0027c2s v5p0076c2s
v5p0160c2s v5p0213c1s v5p0261c2s
v5p0320c1s v5p0513c2s v6p0305c1s
v6p0526c2s v6p0527c1s
Crookes, W., Sir v5p0449c1s
v6p0173c1s
Crookes, William, Sir v5p0611c2s
v6p0406c2s
Crooklands, J. v4p0294c1s
Crooks, Ezra B. v6p0186c1s
Crooks, G.R. v1p0127c2s
v1p0128c1s v1p0180c2s v1p1398c2s
v2p0286c1s v2p0438c1s v2p0482c2s
v3p0043c1s v5p0577c1s
Crooks, W. v3p0403c2s
v4p0253c2s v6p0356c2s
Croom, E.R. v3p0169c2s
v3p0376c1s
Cropper, A.E. v6p0320c1s
Cropper, E. v6p0570c1s
Cropper, J. and Morison, J.C.
v2p0226c1s
Cropper, P. v5p0415c1s
Cropper, R.P. v6p0686c2s
Crosbie, R. v3p0145c2s
v4p0191c1s
Crosbie, W. v1p0598c2s
v1p1237c2s v2p0335c2s
Crosby, A. v1p0262c1m
v4p0505c1s
Crosby, C.C.P. v1p1400c2s
Crosby, C.E. v2p0460c1s
Crosby, D.J. v6p0573c2s
Crosby, E. v6p0055c2s
v6p0123c2s v6p0175c1s v6p0241c1s
v6p0308c2s v6p0342c2s v6p0346c1s
v6p0393c1s v6p0416c1s v6p0425c1s
v6p0425c2s v6p0458c1s v6p0583c1m
v6p0583c2s v6p0588c2s v6p0589c2s
v6p0605c1s v6p0664c1s v6p0684c1s
Crosby, E. et al. v6p0310c2s
Crosby, E.C. v2p0223c1s
v2p0390c1s
Crosby, E.H. v2p0454c2s
v3p0069c2s v3p0081c1s v3p0104c1s
v3p0107c2s v3p0229c1s v3p0249c2s
v3p0345c1s v3p0373c2s v4p0578c2m
v5p0082c2s v5p0321c1s v5p0483c2s
v6p0238c2s v6p0319c2s v6p0649c1s
Crosby, E.H. and Hall, B.. v5p0506c1s
Crosby, E.R. v5p0156c1s
Crosby, E.U. v6p0225c2s
Crosby, Ernest v6p0195c2s
Crosby, F.W. and Crosby, W.O.
v5p0100c1s v5p0516c2s
Crosby, H. v1p0118c2s
v1p0125c2m v1p0686c1s v1p0866c2s
v1p0874c1s v1p0916c1s v1p0960c2s
v1p0979c2s v2p0111c2s v2p0180c2s
v2p0251c1s v2p0313c1s v2p0323c1s
v2p0353c1s v3p0042c1s v3p0146c2s
v3p0178c1s v3p0209c2s v3p0252c2s
v3p0304c2s v3p0360c2s v3p0368c2s
v6p0406c2s
Crosby, H. et al. v2p0106c2s
Crosby, H.B. v1p0059c2s
Crosby, H.R. v1p1149c1s
Crosby, Herbert v6p0567c2s
Crosby, I.E. v1p0293c1s
Crosby, J. v1p0736c2s
v1p1185c1s v1p1186c1s
Crosby, M. v3p0077c1s
v3p0099c2s v3p0120c2s v3p0224c1s
v3p0263c1s v3p0312c1s v3p0450c2s
Crosby, M.C. v5p0208c1s
Crosby, M.L. v6p0658c1s
Crosby, M.R. v5p0637c2s
Crosby, Margaret v3p0095c1s
Crosby, N.E. v4p0437c2s
Crosby, O.K. v4p0465c2s
Crosby, O.T. v5p0002c1s
v5p0005c2s v6p0410c2s v6p0645c2m
v6p0661c1s
Crosby, P. v4p0105c2s
Crosby, S.P. and Nevitt, C.
v5p0152c1s
Crosby, W.E. v1p0286c2s
Crosby, W.I. v1p1325c2s
Crosby, W.O. v1p0139c1s
v1p0809c1s v1p1011c1s v2p0467c1s
v5p0131c2s v5p0409c1s v5p0606c1s
Crosby, W.O. and Ballard, H.O.
v4p0520c2s
Crosby, W.O. and Barton, G.H.
v1p0200c1s
Crosby, W.O. and Crosby, F.W.
v5p0100c1s v5p0516c2s
Crosfield, J. v1p0179c2s
Croskery, T. v1p0856c1s
v2p0112c1s v2p0121c1s v2p0227c2s
v2p0345c2s v2p0353c1s v2p0376c2m
v2p0385c2s v2p0471c1s
Croskey, H.W. v1p0250c1s

Croskey, J. v5p0418c2s
Croskey, Julian v5p0225c1s
Crosland, N. v1p0070c2s v1p0716c2s v2p0440c2s
Crosland, N., Mrs. v1p0878c2s
Crosland, T.W.H. v5p0038c1s v5p0200c2s
Crosoer, G. v4p0564c2s
Crosquery, T. v2p0069c2s
Cross, A.E. v6p0208c2s
Cross, A.L. v6p0384c1s
Cross, A.W. v5p0084c2s v5p0514c2s
Cross, C.F. v5p0099c1s v5p0429c2s
Cross, C.R. v1p0836c1s
Cross, D.W. v3p0066c1s v3p0088c1s
Cross, E.B. v1p0097c2s
Cross, E.S. v1p0870c1s
Cross, H.H. v6p0023c2s
Cross, Ira v6p0136c1s v6p0516c1s
Cross, J. v1p0811c1s v1p1270c1s
Cross, J.A. v1p0628c2s v3p0043c1s v5p0059c2s v5p0306c2s v5p0426c2s
Cross, J.L. v6p0122c2s
Cross, J.N. v5p0506c1s
Cross, J.W. v1p1353c2s v3p0027c1s v3p0110c1s v3p0157c1s v3p0181c1s v3p0443c2s v4p0059c1s v5p0248c1s v6p0007c1s v6p0224c1s v6p0267c1s v6p0267c2s v6p0360c1s v6p0425c1s
Cross, K.A. v1p0729c2s
Cross, L. v1p0148c1s v1p0180c1m v1p0413c1s v1p0439c1s v1p0450c2s v1p0499c2s v1p0521c2s v1p0577c1s v1p0718c1s v1p0733c1s v1p0742c1s v1p0752c2s v1p0863c1s v1p0906c2s v1p0992c2s v1p1022c1s v1p1027c1s v1p1152c1s v1p1270c1s v1p1274c1s v1p1322c2s v3p0416c1s v3p0419c2s
Cross, L.R.H. v2p0316c1s
Cross, M. v1p0166c2s v1p0357c1s
Cross, M.B. v5p0075c2s
Cross, M.F.W. v3p0291c2s
Cross, M.K. v1p0148c1s v1p0359c1s v1p0432c2s v1p0741c1s v1p0847c2s v1p1103c2s v1p1220c1s
Cross, Miss v1p0800c2s
Cross, R.A. v2p0105c1s v2p0126c1s
Cross, R.A., Sir v2p0097c1s v2p0263c1s v2p0348c2s v2p0349c1s
Cross, R.J. v3p0065c1s v3p0302c2s v4p0123c2s
Cross, R.T. v3p0259c1s v3p0332c2s v3p0363c1s
Cross, S. v5p0087c1s v5p0151c1s v5p0217c1s
Cross, T. v1p0192c1s v1p0666c2s v1p0842c2s
Cross, W. v2p0171c2s v2p0443c1s v3p0009c2s v3p0012c2s v3p0115c1s v3p0117c1s v4p0454c2s v5p0279c2s v5p0642c2s v6p0172c2s
Cross, W. and Eakins, L.G. v2p0358c2s v4p0465c2s
Cross, W. and Hillebrand, W.F. v2p0342c1s v2p0429c2s v2p0483c1s
Cross, W. and Iddings, J.P. v2p0008c1s
Cross, W.C.H. v3p0388c2s
Cross, W.L. v3p0206c2m v6p0142c2s v6p0391c2s v6p0617c1m
Cross, W.M. v4p0199c2s
Crosse, A., Mrs. v1p1339c1s v3p0177c2s v3p0236c1s v3p0297c1s v3p0326c2s v4p0229c2s v4p0232c2s v4p0312c2s v4p0321c1s v4p0327c2s v4p0345c2s v4p0394c2s v4p0541c1s
Crosse, A.F. v2p0437c2s
Crosse, Andrew, Mrs. v3p0242c1s v3p0379c2s v3p0399c2s v4p0049c1s v4p0070c2s v4p0075c2s v4p0089c2s v4p0132c1s
Crosse, C. v6p0588c1s
Crosse, C.A.H. v1p0614c2s v1p1143c1s v2p0139c2s v3p0338c2s
Crosse, G. v5p0522c2s
Crosskey, H. v1p0390c2s
Crosskey, H.W. v1p0137c2s v1p0507c2s v1p0621c2s v1p0734c1s v1p0793c1s v1p0925c1s v1p1167c2s v1p1212c1s v1p1432c1s v2p0112c2s v2p0299c1s
Crosskey, W. v1p0137c2s
Crossley, E.M. v5p0628c1s
Crossley, F.B. v6p0248c1s
Crossley, H.W. v2p0389c2s
Crosswaithe, J. v1p0339c1s v1p0904c1s
Crosswell, C.N. v2p0396c1s
Crosswell, T.R. v5p0454c1s
Crosthwait, H.L. v6p0483c1s
Crosthwaite, C.H.T. v4p0487c2s v5p0575c1s
Crosthwaite, J.G. v5p0010c1s
Croston, J. v1p0571c1s v2p0108c2s
Croswell, J.G. v2p0282c2s
Croswell, M.S. v1p1148c1s
Croswell, S.C. v2p0447c2s
Croswell, S.G. v2p0223c1s v2p0445c2s v3p0125c2s v5p0280c2s
Croswell, T.R. v5p0175c1s v5p0558c1s
Crotch, W.D. v1p0737c1s
Crothe, J.M. v1p0498c1s
Crothers, J.D. et al. v3p0123c1s
Crothers, S. v6p0492c2s
Crothers, S.M. v4p0328c2s v5p0228c1m v5p0267c1s v5p0275c2s v5p0455c2s v6p0123c2m v6p0203c2s v6p0214c1s v6p0218c2s v6p0307c1m v6p0309c1s v6p0514c1s v6p0525c2s v6p0599c2s
Crothers, S.M. et al. v5p0511c1s
Crothers, T.D. v2p0007c1s v2p0220c2m v2p0222c1s v4p0284c1s v4p0307c1s v4p0461c2s v5p0368c1s
Crothers, W.E. v1p0202c2s v2p0088c1s v6p0285c1s
Crothus, W.E. v1p1008c1s
Crottie, J.M. v2p0180c1s
Crouch, A.P. v3p0078c1s v3p0109c1s v3p0219c1s v4p0006c2s v4p0349c1s v4p0511c1s v4p0531c1s v5p0086c2s v5p0417c2s
Crouch, I.E. v4p0322c2s
Crouch, R.A. v6p0560c1s
Crouch, S.G. v5p0197c1s
Croudace, C.H. v5p0286c2s
Crounse, L. and Waite, D.H. v4p0630c1s
Crounse, L.L. v1p1229c1s
Crouter, A.L.E. v3p0112c2s v4p0149c2s
Crova, M.A. v1p1268c2s
Crow, C.L. v4p0224c1s
Crow, F.E. v5p0441c1s
Crow, J.M. v2p0025c1s
Crow, L. v1p0140c1s v1p0577c1s v1p0602c2s v1p1338c2s
Crow, M.F. v4p0121c2s v4p0168c2s v4p0628c1s
Crow, Martha F. v6p0158c2s
Crowder, C.H. v2p0035c2s v2p0281c1s
Crowder, F.W. v4p0542c1s
Crowdy, J. v2p0004c1s v2p0004c2s v2p0020c2s v2p0023c2s v2p0024c2s v2p0090c2s v2p0091c2s v2p0134c2s v2p0217c1m v2p0358c2s v2p0403c1s
Crowe, A.B. v5p0514c1s
Crowe, C. v1p0502c2s v1p0586c2s v1p0770c2s v1p0772c1s v1p0820c1s v1p1335c2s
Crowe, C., Mrs. v1p1111c1s v1p1257c2s
Crowe, E. v4p0585c1s v5p0574c2s
Crowe, F.J.W. v5p0220c1s
Crowe, J.A. v2p0365c1s v3p0317c2s v4p0333c2s v4p0444c2s v6p0256c2s
Crowe, Mrs. v1p0796c1s v1p1210c1s v1p1311c1s
Crowe, R. v6p0110c2s
Crowell, E. v4p0272c1s v4p0518c1s
Crowell, E.P. v1p0237c2s
Crowell, F. v3p0192c1s v4p0260c1s v4p0400c2s v5p0627c2s
Crowell, J. v1p0276c1s
Crowell, J.F. v2p0077c2s v5p0009c2s v5p0016c2s v5p0298c1s v5p0477c2s v5p0501c1s v5p0559c2m v5p0626c1s v5p0641c1s v6p0015c1s v6p0015c2m v6p0401c1s v6p0458c2s v6p0591c1s v6p0670c2s
Crowell, J.M. v2p0352c1s
Crowell, N.H. v5p0085c2s v5p0342c2s v5p0612c2s v6p0398c1s v6p0626c1s
Crowell, W. v1p0681c1s
Crowell, W.H. v5p0240c1s
Crowest, F.J. v3p0062c1s v3p0255c2s v3p0293c1m v3p0293c2s v3p0313c1s v3p0465c2s v4p0245c2m v4p0386c1s v4p0388c2m v4p0467c2s v4p0602c2s v5p0053c1s v5p0076c1s v5p0082c2s v5p0095c2s v5p0114c1s v5p0123c2s v5p0223c1s v5p0482c2s v5p0611c1s
Crowfoot, J.W. v5p0150c2s
Crowhurst, W.H. v2p0084c1s
Crowley, E.S. v6p0038c1s
Crowley, J.G. v6p0591c2s
Crowley, M.C. v3p0088c1s v4p0259c2s v6p0057c1s v6p0235c1s v6p0577c2s v6p0675c1s v6p0712c1s
Crowley, Mary C. v6p0586c1s
Crowley, R.O. v5p0583c1s
Crowley, T.M. v4p0487c2s
Crowne, J.V. v6p0415c2s
Crownfield, D. v6p0377c1s
Crowninshield, A.S. v3p0007c2s v3p0035c2s v4p0240c2s v5p0294c1s v5p0410c1s
Crowninshield, B.B. v6p0710c1s
Crowninshield, B.W. v1p1190c1s v5p0601c2s
Crowninshield, E. v2p0215c2s
Crowninshield, F. v1p1008c1s v2p0024c1s v2p0302c1s v2p0326c2s v2p0365c1s v2p0368c1s v3p0021c1s v4p0150c2s v4p0387c2s v5p0156c2s v6p0141c2s v6p0224c2s
Crowninshield, F. and Sturgis, R. v5p0324c2s
Crowninshield, Fred. v2p0146c2s v5p0156c1s
Crowninshield, M.B. v5p0507c2s
Crowninshield, S., Mrs. .. v5p0011c1s v5p0213c2s v5p0363c2s v5p0396c2s v5p0431c1s v6p0451c1s
Crowquil, A. v1p1180c1s
Crowquill, Sara v5p0233c1s
Crowset, F.J. v5p0277c2s
Crowther, E. v5p0076c1s
Crowther, E.P. v5p0540c1s
Crowther, G. v3p0094c2s
Crowther, J. v1p0781c1s
Crowther, S., jr. v6p0299c2s
Crowther, W.E. v2p0023c2s
Croxton, A. v4p0117c2s v4p0491c1s
Croxton, F.C. v6p0056c1m
Croz, M.C. v1p0697c1s
Crozier, G.B. v6p0020c1s v6p0232c2s
Crozier, J.A. v3p0440c1s
Crozier, J.B. v2p0097c2s v4p0301c1s v5p0608c2s v6p0147c2s v6p0205c2s v6p0206c1s v6p0240c2m v6p0269c1s v6p0333c2s v6p0351c1s v6p0507c1s v6p0610c1s v6p0691c2s
Crozier, L.G. v5p0638c2s
Crozier, W. v5p0599c1s
Cruger, J.H. v1p1153c1s
Cruger, L.N. v1p1348c1s
Cruger, V.R., Mrs. v3p0012c2s v3p0151c2s v3p0173c1s v3p0263c1s v3p0274c1s v3p0446c2s v3p0469c1s v4p0129c2s v4p0200c2s v5p0215c1s v5p0217c2s
Cruger, Van R., Mrs. v4p0177c2s v4p0332c2s v4p0473c1s v5p0390c1s v5p0581c1s v6p0174c2s v6p0448c2s
Cruice, D.L. v6p0113c1s v6p0175c1s v6p0307c1s
Cruikshank, B. v5p0353c2s
Cruikshank, E. v4p0414c2s
Cruikshank, Ernest v3p0213c1s
Cruikshank, J. v6p0220c1s
Cruikshank, M. v6p0210c1s
Cruikshank, W. v5p0146c1s v5p0261c2s
Cruise, P. v1p0028c1s v1p0089c2s v1p0735c1s v1p1011c1s
Cruls, M. v2p0095c1s
Crum, C.W.R. v4p0508c1s
Crum, F.S. v4p0357c1s v5p0064c2s v5p0365c1s v5p0559c1s
Crum, F.S. and Wilcox, W.F. v5p0559c1s
Crumbaugh, J.S. v1p0685c1s
Crumer, M.J. v4p0270c2s
Crumley, H.L. v6p0116c2s
Crump, A. v3p0152c2s v3p0343c2s
Crump, A. and Foxwell, H.S. v4p0237c1s
Crump, C.G. v6p0256c2s
Crump, C.G. and Hughes, A. v4p0143c2s
Crump, C.G. et al. v5p0125c1s
Crump, E. v1p0599c2s v1p0717c1s v1p0882c2s v1p1179c2s v1p1202c2s v1p1422c1s
Crump, G.E. v5p0061c2s
Crump, L. v5p0348c2s
Crump, W.B. and Heath, G.. v4p0507c2s
Crump, W.W. v5p0154c2s
Crundall, W. and Mowll, W. v5p0166c2s
Crunden, F.M. v1p0742c2s v1p1187c2m v2p0256c1s v3p0049c2s v3p0248c2s v3p0249c2s v4p0329c1s v4p0329c2m v5p0335c1s v5p0504c2s v6p0238c2s v6p0371c2m v6p0372c2s v6p0374c1s v6p0563c2s
Crupper, M.W. v6p0037c1s
Cruse, C.F. v1p0123c1s v1p0252c2s v1p0624c1s v1p1279c1s
Cruse, P.H. v1p0370c1s
Crutcher, E. v6p0474c2s
Crutchley, E.T. v5p0203c2s
Crutchley, W.C. v3p0181c2s
Cruttwell, C.T. v3p0038c2s
Cruttwell, M. v5p0159c2s v5p0451c1s v5p0610c1s
Cryan, R.W.W. v4p0062c1s

v4p0636c1s v5p0010c2s v5p0348c2s
v6p0009c2s v6p0157c1s v6p0643c1s
Crynkle, N. v4p0399c2s
Cubberley, E.P. v5p0507c1s
v5p0512c1s
Cubitt, G. v1p0813c1s
Cubitt, Horace v6p0087c1s
Cubitt, J. v2p0480c2s
Cubitt, W. v1p0085c1s
Cucheval-Clavigny v1p0203c2s
Cudbury, S. v4p0611c1s
Cuddell, C. v1p0773c1s
Cudlip, A. v1p0143c2s
v1p0221c1s v1p0774c1s v1p0851c2s
v1p0896c2s v1p1017c2s
Cudlip, A.P. v1p0716c2s
Cudlip, P. v1p0115c2s
Cudlip, P., Mrs. v1p0442c1s
v1p0940c2s v1p1239c1s v1p1241c1s
v2p0234c2s v2p0301c1s v3p0209c2s
v4p0011c1s v4p0262c2s v4p0333c1s
Cudlip, Pender, Mrs. v4p0343c2s
Cudworth, W. v5p0279c2s
Cuers, R.de v5p0235c2s
Cuers, Rene v5p0026c2s
Cuers, Rene de v5p0074c1s
Cuervo, T.de v6p0362c1s
Cuffe, K. v4p0148c2s
v4p0629c2s
Cui, Cesar v5p0393c2s
Culberson, C.A. v6p0300c2s
Culbertson, C.A. v3p0416c2s
Culbertson, M.S. v1p0234c1s
Cule, W.E. v4p0130c2s
v5p0021c2s v5p0022c2s v5p0116c1s
v5p0168c1s v5p0322c2s v5p0390c2s
v5p0419c2s v5p0434c2s v5p0634c2s
v6p0177c1s v6p0184c1s v6p0386c2s
v6p0579c2s
Culin, S. v4p0106c1m
v4p0106c2m v4p0159c1s v4p0194c2s
v4p0205c1s v4p0219c2m v4p0349c1s
v4p0356c1s v4p0423c1s v4p0607c2s
v5p0444c2s v6p0014c2s v6p0246c1m
v6p0316c2s v6p0613c1s
Culin, Stewart v4p0447c1s
Cullen, A.H. v2p0110c2s
v2p0221c1s v2p0228c1s v2p0328c1s
v2p0349c1s v3p0319c1s
Cullen, C.L. v6p0011c1s
Cullen, E. v1p0332c1s
Cullen, G.M. v4p0603c1s
Culler, M.L. v4p0057c2s
Culley, J.L. v2p0018c2m
v2p0469c2s
Culley, R.S. v1p1290c2s
Cullinan, M. v1p1373c1s
Cullingworth, C.J. v5p0374c2s
Cullom, S.M. v3p0149c2s
v3p0346c2s v3p0348c2s v3p0408c1s
v3p0422c2s v4p0152c1m v6p0429c1m
v6p0655c2s
Cullum, G.W. v1p0894c2s
v1p1241c1s v2p0296c1s v2p0306c1s
Culmann, F.J. v1p1055c1s
Culmer, H.A. v5p0384c2s
Culmer, H.L.A. v4p0385c1s
Culp, D.W. v5p0403c1s
Culver, A.G. v5p0314c1s
Culver, F.F. v6p0659c1s
Culver, I.O. v1p1013c2s
Culver, J.H. v2p0385c1s
Culver, J.O. v1p0471c1s
Culver, M.M. v2p0074c1s
Culver, S.W. v1p1050c1s
v1p1271c1s v1p1304c1s v2p0044c2s
v2p0135c2s v2p0356c1s v3p0371c2s
Culvert, G.H. v1p1156c2s
Culverwell, E.P. v4p0272c2s
v6p0335c1s
Cumberland, B. v4p0353c2s
Cumberland, B. and Harkness, A.H.
v5p0605c1s
Cumberland, G. v1p0089c1s
Cumberland, S.C. v2p0440c1s
v3p0429c2s
Cumby, W.P. v5p0585c1s
Cuming, E.D. v3p0060c2s
v3p0205c1s v3p0282c1s v3p0291c1s
v3p0306c2s v3p0411c1s v5p0084c1s
v5p0165c2m v5p0312c1s
Cuming, F.D. v4p0473c1s
Cuming, J. v1p1217c2s
Cuming, W.H. v1p0233c1s
Cumings, E. v1p1422c1s
v2p0291c2s v2p0309c2s v4p0443c2s
v4p0551c1s v5p0317c2s
Cumings, E.R. v6p0221c2s
Cumings, Elizabeth v5p0065c2s
v5p0292c2s v5p0506c1s
Cumming, A.N. v2p0391c1s
v3p0199c2s v3p0346c2s v3p0381c1s
v6p0059c1s v6p0577c2s
Cumming, C.F.G. v1p0452c2s
v1p0495c1s v1p0591c1s v1p1264c2s
v2p0052c2s v2p0060c1s v2p0067c1m
v2p0080c1s v2p0178c1s v2p0198c1s
v2p0203c1s v2p0213c1s v2p0214c1s
v2p0217c2s v2p0237c2s v2p0254c1s
v2p0262c1s v2p0262c2s v2p0299c2s
v2p0314c1m v2p0314c2s v2p0316c2s
v2p0320c2s v2p0326c1s v2p0356c2s
v2p0385c2s v2p0480c2s v2p0481c1s
v2p0482c2m v3p0015c2s v3p0120c1s
v3p0293c2s v3p0317c1s v3p0440c1s
v3p0452c1s v3p0460c1s
Cumming, C.F.Gordon v2p0048c1s
v2p0064c2m v2p0082c2s v2p0106c2s
v2p0110c2s v2p0116c2s v2p0135c2s
v2p0143c2s v2p0161c2s v2p0169c2s
v2p0170c2s v2p0219c2s v2p0224c1s
v2p0291c2s v2p0313c2m v2p0315c1s
v2p0334c2m v2p0351c1s v2p0366c2s
v2p0430c1s
Cumming, D. v5p0346c2s
Cumming, Duncan v5p0603c1s
Cumming, E.D. v6p0177c2s
Cumming, G. v1p0631c2s
Cumming, G., Miss v1p0452c2s
Cumming, J. v1p0014c1s
v1p0118c2s v1p0396c1s v1p0528c2m
v1p0594c1s v1p0668c2s v1p0714c2s
v1p0777c1s v1p0884c2m v1p1093c1s
v1p1162c1s v1p1196c2s v1p1397c2s
v1p1437c1s
Cumming, L et al. v3p0115c1s
Cumming, W. v5p0360c1s
v5p0637c1s
Cumming, W.H. v1p0035c1s
Cumming, W.J. v1p0488c2s
Cummings, A.M. v3p0064c1s
v3p0335c2s v3p0385c2s
Cummings, B.F., jr. v4p0359c1s
Cummings, C.A. v1p0080c2s
v1p0576c1s v1p0606c1s v1p0611c1s
v1p0714c2s v1p0840c1s v1p1009c1s
v1p1090c2s v1p1344c1s v5p0086c2s
v6p0351c1s v6p0386c1s
Cummings, E. v3p0017c1s
v3p0099c2s v3p0320c1s v3p0397c2s
v3p0434c1s v4p0233c1s v4p0429c1s
v4p0598c1s v5p0101c2s v5p0102c1s
v5p0136c2s v5p0170c1s v5p0535c1s
v5p0584c2s v5p0639c1s v5p0641c1s
v6p0013c1s v6p0155c1s
Cummings, E. and Bowditch, H.P.
v4p0101c1s
Cummings, E.C. v1p0746c1s
v4p0022c2s
Cummings, E.G. v5p0398c2s
Cummings, E.G. and Freeman, H.E.
v5p0163c1s
Cummings, E.R. v6p0086c1s
v6p0503c2s
Cummings, E.R. and Mauck, A.V.
v6p0234c2s
Cummings, F.J. v2p0117c1s
Cummings, J. v1p0398c1s
v1p0527c2s v1p1418c2s v2p0244c2s
v3p0231c2s v4p0377c2s v4p0452c1s
v5p0136c1s v5p0283c2s v5p0330c2s
v5p0459c2s v5p0584c1s v5p0584c2s
v5p0641c1s v6p0078c2s v6p0106c2s
v6p0113c2s v6p0169c2s v6p0293c2s
v6p0318c1m v6p0621c1s v6p0621c2s
Cummings, J.W. v1p0147c2s
v1p0806c2s
Cummings, L. v3p0213c1s
Cummings, P. v1p0978c1s
v5p0080c1s
Cummings, W. v3p0071c2s
v5p0076c1s v5p0115c2s v5p0520c2s
Cummins, A.H. v2p0114c1s
v2p0323c2s
Cummins, E.H. v3p0095c2s
Cummins, E.S. v3p0063c2s
v4p0262c2s
Cummins, J.J. v1p1139c1s
Cummins, J.W. v1p0448c2s
Cummins, M.L. v5p0274c1s
Cummins, M.S. v1p0561c1s
v1p0582c1s
Cummins, Mabel P. v4p0209c2s
Cummins, W.R. v4p0546c2s
Cumnock, R.L. v3p0346c1s
Cumnock, R.M. v3p0135c2m
Cumont, F. v6p0422c2m
v6p0423c1m
Cunard, Maud v5p0404c2s
Cundall, F. v3p0379c2s
v4p0296c1s v4p0443c2s v4p0486c1s
Cundall, H.M. v4p0153c1s
v4p0163c1s v4p0168c1s v4p0227c2s
v4p0336c1s v4p0353c1s v4p0408c1s
v4p0519c2s v4p0526c2s v4p0625c2s
v6p0048c1s v6p0350c1m v6p0383c1s
v6p0429c1s v6p0478c1s v6p0678c1s
Cundall, J. v1p0149c1s
Cundell, G.S. v1p1003c2s
Cundiff, Hannah M. v5p0394c2s
Cundill, M.G. v4p0513c2s
v5p0054c2s v5p0267c2s v5p0290c2s
v5p0352c1s v5p0379c1s v5p0494c2s
v5p0606c1s
Cuneo, C. v6p0696c1s
Cunes, S.A. v5p0361c1s
Cunha, G.W.Da v4p0569c1s
Cuniff, M.G. v6p0355c2s
Cuninghame, G.C. v1p1143c2s
Cuninghame, R. v2p0450c2m
v2p0456c2s
Cunisset-Carnot, M. v4p0060c2s
Cunliffe, F.H.E. v6p0560c2s
Cunliffe, J.W. v4p0293c1s
v4p0553c2s
Cunliffe-Owen, E. v3p0092c2s
Cunliffe-Owen, F. v1p1276c2s
v5p0110c2s v5p0170c1s v5p0193c1s
v5p0244c1s v5p0423c1s v5p0499c2s
v6p0184c2s v6p0196c2s v6p0252c1s
v6p0254c2s v6p0363c2s v6p0458c2s
v6p0513c2s v6p0571c2s v6p0584c2s
v6p0628c2s v6p0648c1s v6p0711c1s
Cunniff, M.G. v5p0343c2s
v5p0353c2s v5p0557c2s v6p0030c1s
v6p0128c2s v6p0173c1s v6p0340c1s
v6p0357c1m v6p0454c1s v6p0465c1s
v6p0511c1m v6p0528c2s v6p0530c1s
v6p0531c1s v6p0639c2s v6p0699c2s
Cunniff, M.G. and Goodrich, A.
v5p0407c2s
Cunningham, A. v1p0197c1s
v1p0618c2s v1p0668c2s v1p0693c2s
v1p0801c1m v1p0940c1s v1p1171c1s
v2p0093c2m v2p0117c1s v2p0213c1m
v3p0226c1s v3p0308c2s v6p0316c1s
Cunningham, A.C.F. v2p0478c1s
Cunningham, B. v6p0263c2s
v6p0418c2s
Cunningham, B.H. v1p1260c2s
v6p0397c1s
Cunningham, Brysson v6p0177c1s
v6p0182c1s v6p0591c2m
Cunningham, C. v5p0014c1s
v6p0697c1s
Cunningham, C.E. v6p0230c1s
Cunningham, C.W. v5p0156c2s
Cunningham, D.A. v2p0299c2s
v2p0477c1s
Cunningham, D.J. v2p0268c1s
v3p0360c2s
Cunningham, Dr. v1p0473c2s
v1p1318c2s
Cunningham, Dr. and James, J.A.
v1p0027c2s
Cunningham, E. v1p0233c2s
v1p0235c1s
Cunningham, E.P. v5p0098c2s
v5p0575c1s
Cunningham, Ellen T. v4p0411c1s
Cunningham, F. v1p0514c1s
v1p0514c2s v1p1083c2s v3p0103c1s
v6p0004c1m v6p0088c1s v6p0138c1s
v6p0221c2s v6p0376c1s
Cunningham, F.D. v2p0154c2s
Cunningham, G. v5p0614c1s
Cunningham, G.C. v1p0193c1s
v2p0262c1s v5p0251c2s v6p0413c2s
Cunningham, H. and Dabney, R.
v4p0196c1s
Cunningham, H., Sir v4p0588c2s
Cunningham, H.S. v3p0211c2s
v4p0279c1s
Cunningham, H.W. v5p0148c2s
Cunningham, J. v1p0365c2m
v1p1209c1s v1p1375c2s
Cunningham, J.A. v6p0548c1s
Cunningham, J.D. v5p0022c2s
Cunningham, J.T. v3p0111c1s
v3p0240c2s v3p0447c1s v4p0201c2s
v4p0286c1s v4p0443c1s v4p0637c2s
v5p0022c1s v5p0180c2s v5p0480c1s
v5p0545c1s v6p0098c2s v6p0248c1s
Cunningham, Justice v3p0192c1s
Cunningham, L.T. v2p0353c2s
Cunningham, P. v1p0789c1s
v1p1183c2s
Cunningham, P.T. v2p0483c1s
Cunningham, R. v1p0007c2s
Cunningham, R.P. v5p0096c1s
Cunningham, W. v1p1025c2s
v1p1094c2s v1p1208c1s v1p1216c1s
v1p1302c2s v1p1341c2s v2p0193c1s
v2p0228c1s v2p0273c2s v2p0349c2s
v2p0434c1s v2p0459c1s v2p0479c1s
v3p0127c2s v3p0130c1s v3p0186c2s
v3p0296c2s v4p0088c2s v4p0167c1m
v4p0168c1s v4p0181c1s v4p0239c2s
v4p0449c2s v4p0491c1s v4p0573c2s
v4p0608c1s v5p0089c1s v5p0149c1s
v5p0175c1s v5p0187c2s v5p0245c1s
v5p0281c2s v5p0383c1s v5p0437c1s
v6p0006c2s v6p0159c1s v6p0189c1m
v6p0240c2s v6p0256c2s v6p0577c1s
v6p0684c2s
Cunningham, W.C. v1p1293c1s
Cunninghame, B.A. v6p0021c1s
Cunninghame, C.F. v5p0346c1s
v5p0347c2s
Cunninghame-Graham, R.B. . v4p0264c1s
v4p0383c2s
Cunnington, H.A. v1p0579c2s
v1p1074c2s
Cunnington, W. v1p1329c2s
v6p0318c2s
Cunston, C.G. v6p0481c2s
Cuntz, J.H. v4p0277c1s
v5p0492c2s
Cunyngham, H. v3p0016c2s
Cunynghame, H. v2p0432c2s

v4p0192c1s v6p0101c2s v6p0185c1s
Cunynghame, H.H. v3p0422c1s
v3p0422c2s v4p0090c2s v5p0187c2s
v6p0244c2s
Cuppari, G. v2p0467c2s
Cupples, G. v1p0340c2s
v1p0556c1s v1p0713c2s v1p0758c2s
v3p0294c1s
Cupples, G., Mrs. v2p0202c1s
Cuppy, E.O. v5p0154c2s
Curie, S.S. v6p0527c1s
Curl, M.A. v5p0227c2s
Curl, Mattie A. v5p0419c1s
Curley, E.A. v1p0015c1s
v2p0038c1s v2p0177c1s v2p0408c1s
v4p0115c1s
Curling, H. v1p0160c2s
v1p0257c1s v1p0304c2s v1p0305c2s
v1p0362c1s v1p0403c1s v1p0409c2s
v1p0572c1s v1p0801c2s v1p0856c1s
v1p0986c2s v1p1187c1s
Curnick, F.T. v4p0328c2s
Curra, J.W. v5p0463c2s
Curran, F. v1p0385c2s
Curran, H.E. v5p0336c2s
Curran, J. v1p0657c2s
Curran, J.E. v1p0138c2s
v1p0713c2s v1p0814c2s v1p0831c2s
v1p1379c2s v3p0135c2s v3p0228c1s
v3p0231c1s v3p0294c2s v3p0337c2s
v3p0366c1s
Curran, J.J. v6p0644c1s
Curran, M.B. v6p0490c2s
Curran, R. v1p0685c1s
Curran, W. v2p0061c1s
v2p0257c2s v2p0276c1s v2p0366c2s
Curran, W., Dr. v2p0394c2s
Currell, W.S. v6p0136c1s
Curren, T.J. v6p0636c2s
Currey, E.H. v6p0147c1s
Currey, F. v1p1014c2s
Currey, F.W. v1p0013c2s
v1p0445c2s v3p0220c1s
Currey, G.B. v2p0300c2s
Currey, J.B. v3p0116c2s
Currie, B. v4p0144c1s
Currie, D. and Sandys, E.W.
v3p0186c1s
Currie, E.H., Sir v3p0256c1s
v3p0326c2s
Currie, F.I. v4p0207c1s
Currie, J. v1p0385c2s
v2p0162c2s
Currie, J.A. v4p0347c2s
Currie, J.A. and Coe, D.A.
v3p0065c1s
Currie, Lady v6p0221c1s
Currie, M.M. v5p0163c2s
v6p0182c1s v6p0379c2s
Currie, M.M., Lady v6p0538c2s
Currie, Mary M. v6p0245c2s
Currie, S. v5p0202c2s
Currier, A.F. v6p0075c1s
v6p0372c2s
Currier, A.H. v1p0560c1s
v1p1043c2s v1p1176c2s v1p1418c1s
v5p0072c1s
Currier, A.H. and Wright, G.F.
v3p0321c1s
Currier, A.N. v1p0652c1s
v3p0301c1s v6p0165c2s
Currier, C.F.A. v4p0211c2m
Currier, C.W. v2p0234c2s
v3p0005c2s v3p0258c1s v4p0125c2s
v4p0459c2s v4p0609c2s v5p0096c1s
v5p0146c2s v5p0147c1s v5p0252c1s
v5p0614c2s v6p0018c2s v6p0101c1s
v6p0692c2s
Currier, J.M. v4p0205c1s
v4p0398c2s
Currier, Mary M. v5p0573c2s
Currier, Susan L. v5p0188c1s
Currier, Susan L.J. v5p0270c1s
Curry, C. v6p0158c1s
Curry, D. v1p0012c1s
v1p0012c2s v1p0100c1s v1p0274c1s
v1p0278c1s v1p0319c1s v1p0440c2s
v1p0463c1s v1p0528c1s v1p0563c2s
v1p0582c1s v1p0646c1s v1p0666c2s
v1p0680c1s v1p0700c1s v1p0734c1s
v1p0830c1s v1p0904c2s v1p0917c2s
v1p0931c2s v1p1158c2s v1p1350c2s
v1p1402c2s v1p1434c2s v2p0016c2s
v2p0017c1s v2p0034c2s v2p0042c2m
v2p0045c2s v2p0081c2s v2p0083c2s
v2p0093c1s v2p0098c2s v2p0107c1s
v2p0117c1s v2p0190c1s v2p0222c2s
v2p0286c1m v2p0289c1s v2p0290c2s
v2p0292c1s v2p0299c2s v2p0324c1s
v2p0355c2s v2p0371c2s v2p0394c1s
v2p0415c1s v2p0438c1s v2p0456c1s
v3p0229c2s v3p0258c1s v3p0349c1s
Curry, D.J. v1p1379c1s
Curry, G.L. v1p0947c1s
Curry, J. v6p0093c2s
Curry, J.L.M. v1p0288c1s
v1p0734c1s v1p1223c2s v1p1349c1s
v2p0130c2s v2p0131c2s v2p0221c1s
v2p0431c2s v3p0142c2s v3p0155c2s
v3p0174c1s v3p0292c1s v4p0396c2s
v5p0010c2s v5p0092c2s v5p0127c2s
v5p0234c2s v5p0403c2s v5p0437c1s
v5p0540c2s v5p0542c2s v6p0092c1s
Curry, J.T. v5p0084c2s
v6p0036c1s v6p0155c1s
Curry, Miss v1p0381c2s
Curry, O. v1p1189c1s
v1p1338c1s v1p1417c2s
Curry, W.W. v1p1096c1s
Cursetjee, M. v1p0630c2s
Curteis, G.H. v1p0071c2s
v1p0177c1s v1p0248c1s v2p0005c1s
Curtin, J. v3p0295c1s
v4p0205c1s v5p0528c2s
Curtis, A.B. v3p0122c2s
v3p0175c1s v3p0204c1s v3p0217c2s
v3p0379c1s v3p0383c2s v3p0418c2s
Curtis, A.J. v1p0065c1s
v1p1081c1s
Curtis, A.M. v6p0247c2s
Curtis, B.R. v1p1245c1s
v3p0051c1s
Curtis, C.E. v5p0045c2s
v5p0122c1s v5p0556c2m
Curtis, D.A. v2p0299c2s
v3p0111c2s v3p0304c2s
Curtis, E.C. v3p0394c1s
Curtis, E.G. v1p0707c2s
v4p0630c2s v4p0636c2s
Curtis, E.J. v1p0095c2s
v1p0703c2s v1p0756c1s v1p1182c2s
v1p1219c2s v3p0192c1s
Curtis, E.L. v2p0042c2s
v2p0234c2s v2p0284c2s v3p0042c1s
v3p0175c1s v3p0259c2s v4p0054c2s
v4p0055c2s v4p0057c2s v4p0422c2s
v4p0477c2s v5p0056c1s v5p0058c1s
v5p0308c1s v5p0308c2s v5p0577c1s
v6p0062c1s v6p0065c1s
Curtis, E.L. and Dwight, J.
v6p0166c1s
Curtis, E.S. v5p0318c2s
v6p0316c1s v6p0317c1s
Curtis, F. v6p0539c2s
Curtis, F.E. v2p0290c2s
Curtis, F.L. v1p0076c2s
Curtis, G.B. v2p0331c1m
v2p0472c1s
Curtis, G.B. and Winchelsea, Lord
v4p0008c1s
Curtis, G.C. v6p0681c1s
Curtis, G.de C. v4p0614c2s
Curtis, G.E. v3p0353c2m
v3p0458c2s v3p0465c2s v4p0473c1s
Curtis, G.E. and Blanford, H.F.
v3p0353c2s
Curtis, G.H. v4p0073c2s
Curtis, G.P. v5p0084c2s
v5p0360c2s v6p0056c2s v6p0073c1s
v6p0104c1s v6p0200c2s v6p0215c1s
v6p0245c1s v6p0340c2s v6p0488c2s
v6p0569c1s v6p0633c2s
Curtis, G.T. v1p0452c1s
v1p0782c1s v1p0832c2s v1p0876c2s
v1p0936c1s v1p0973c2s v1p1078c1s
v1p1346c1s v1p1353c1s v1p1354c1s
v1p1395c2s v2p0099c1s v2p0106c2s
v2p0208c2s v2p0270c1s v2p0353c1s
v2p0445c2s v2p0466c2s v3p0077c1s
v3p0302c2s v3p0446c1s v3p0464c2s
v4p0262c1s
Curtis, G.T. and Thurston, L.A.
v4p0250c2s
Curtis, G.W. v1p0032c1s
v1p0038c1s v1p0167c1s v1p0205c1s
v1p0259c1s v1p0266c2s v1p0321c1s
v1p0349c2s v1p0352c2s v1p0361c2s
v1p0445c1s v1p0502c2s v1p0575c2s
v1p0913c1s v1p0913c2s v1p0920c2s
v1p0958c1s v1p1036c1s v1p1039c1s
v1p1168c1s v1p1172c1s v1p1210c2s
v1p1216c2s v1p1276c2s v1p1298c1s
v1p1312c2s v1p1322c2s v1p1416c2s
v2p0082c2s v2p0087c1s v2p0140c1s
v2p0230c1m v2p0265c2s v2p0342c1s
v3p0099c2s v3p0198c2s v3p0289c2s
v5p0082c2s
Curtis, H.G. v5p0460c2s
v5p0603c1s
Curtis, H.H. v2p0146c2s
v3p0273c1s v3p0308c1s
Curtis, H.N. v3p0294c1s
Curtis, H.P. v3p0432c2s
Curtis, H.S. v5p0291c1s
v6p0503c2s v6p0504c1s v6p0673c2s
v6p0687c1s v6p0687c2s
Curtis, Helen C.B. v6p0548c2s
Curtis, Isabel G. v6p0319c2s
v6p0339c2s
Curtis, J.H. v2p0056c1s
Curtis, J.K. v4p0251c2s
v6p0244c2s v6p0554c2s
Curtis, L. v1p0074c2s
v1p0435c1s v1p0626c1s v1p0887c2s
v4p0351c2s
Curtis, L.A.B. v2p0145c2s
Curtis, L.E. v4p0233c1s
v4p0315c2s
Curtis, M. v6p0115c1s
Curtis, M.A. v1p0096c1s
v1p0421c1s
Curtis, M.F. v1p0606c2s
Curtis, M.L.W. v5p0302c1s
v5p0349c2s
Curtis, M.M. v3p0115c2s
v3p0171c1s v3p0445c1s v5p0021c1s
Curtis, Martin v5p0116c1s
Curtis, N. v6p0230c2s
v6p0296c2s
Curtis, Natalie v6p0018c2s
Curtis, O.A. v4p0265c1s
Curtis, P.C. v3p0210c1s
Curtis, R. v1p0023c1s
v1p0888c2s v1p1009c1s
Curtis, R.H. v3p0101c1s
v4p0322c2s
Curtis, R.H. and Scott, R.H.
v2p0196c2s
Curtis, R.W. v1p0478c1s
Curtis, R.W. and Gooch, F.A.
v6p0278c2s
Curtis, S.R. v1p0346c1s
Curtis, T. v1p1226c1s
Curtis, T.B. v1p0606c1s
Curtis, T.C. v3p0351c2s
Curtis, T.E. v5p0205c1s
v5p0507c2s v5p0534c2s v5p0608c2s
Curtis, T.F. v1p0096c2s
v1p1303c2s
Curtis, T.W. v5p0387c1s
Curtis, T.W. and Schroeder, A.T.
v5p0490c2s
Curtis, W.A. v3p0295c2s
v4p0321c1s v4p0350c2s v4p0396c2s
v5p0466c1s v5p0565c2s v6p0134c1s
v6p0526c1s v6p0535c2s
Curtis, W.B. v3p0166c2s
v4p0035c2s v4p0064c2s v4p0635c1s
v5p0036c2s
Curtis, W.C. v5p0485c2s
Curtis, W.E. v1p0871c2s
v1p0941c1s v3p0019c1s v3p0034c2s
v3p0069c2s v3p0078c1s v3p0088c1s
v3p0092c1s v3p0101c2s v3p0127c2s
v3p0319c2s v3p0327c2s v3p0470c2s
v4p0013c1s v4p0013c2s v4p0125c2m
v4p0126c1m v4p0262c2s v4p0494c2s
v4p0602c1s v4p0611c2s v5p0069c1s
v5p0081c2s v5p0089c1s v5p0099c2s
v5p0105c2s v5p0109c2s v5p0111c1s
v5p0146c2s v5p0354c1s v5p0429c1s
v5p0432c2s v5p0543c2s v5p0562c2s
v5p0611c2s v5p0621c1s v6p0048c1s
v6p0195c2s v6p0377c2s
Curtis, W.J. v6p0151c1s
Curtis, W.N. v4p0459c2s
Curtis, W.O. v3p0335c1s
Curtis, W.O'L. v3p0462c2s
Curtis, Wilmetta v5p0166c1s
Curtis-Plim, E. v5p0396c1s
Curtiss, A.H. v1p0586c2s
v1p1233c1s
Curtiss, F.H. v5p0220c1s
Curtiss, G.T. et al. v2p0126c2s
Curtiss, H.G. v6p0068c2s
Curtiss, L.R. v1p0858c2s
Curtiss, S.I. v2p0016c1s
v2p0042c2s v2p0043c1m v2p0148c1s
v3p0043c2s v4p0056c1s v5p0055c2s
v5p0057c1s v5p0058c1s v5p0558c1s
v5p0631c2s v6p0026c1s v6p0169c1s
v6p0176c1s v6p0226c1s v6p0259c1s
v6p0396c2s v6p0536c2s v6p0562c1m
v6p0583c1m
Curtiss, S.R. v1p0858c2s
Curtiss, W.E. v6p0444c2s
Curtius, E. v1p0941c2m
v1p1087c2s v1p1430c2s
Curtius, E.von v1p0114c2s
v1p0652c1s v1p0941c2s
Curtius, F. v3p0009c1s
Curtois, M.A. v4p0156c2s
v4p0536c2s v5p0093c1s v5p0350c1s
v5p0482c2s v5p0538c2s
Curve, A. v2p0476c1s
Curwen, H. v1p0689c2s
Curwen, J.S. v1p0831c1s
v1p0883c1s v1p0925c1s v1p1061c2m
v2p0085c2s v2p0323c1s v2p0358c1s
v3p0293c2s v3p0432c2m v3p0474c2s
v5p0393c2s
Curwen, J.S., jr. v1p0620c1m
v1p1061c2m
Curwin, G.R. v1p0326c2s
Curwood, J.O. v6p0054c1s
v6p0095c2m v6p0100c2s v6p0149c1s
v6p0241c1s v6p0359c1s v6p0659c1s
Curzon v5p0274c2s
Curzon, G. v3p0285c1s
v4p0522c2s v5p0314c2s
Curzon, G.M. v2p0325c2s
v2p0346c2s
Curzon, G.N. v2p0100c1m
v3p0023c2m v3p0048c2s v3p0059c1s
v3p0078c2s v3p0097c1s v3p0134c2s
v3p0202c1m v3p0211c2m v3p0234c1s
v3p0234c2s v3p0238c1s v3p0285c1s
v3p0473c1s v3p0474c2s v4p0166c1s
v4p0278c2s v4p0283c1m v4p0377c1s
v4p0420c1s v4p0423c1s v4p0522c1s

Curzon, G.N. and Adam, J., Mme.
v4p0522c2s
Curzon, G.N. et al. v4p0476c1s
Curzon, L.H. v1p0605c1s
Curzon, Lord v5p0611c1s
v6p0313c2s
Curzon, Lord et al. v6p0312c2s
Curzon, R. v1p0424c2s
v1p1323c2s
Curzon, S.A. v4p0311c2s
v4p0452c2s
Cusack, M.F. v1p1425c1s
v3p0098c1s v3p0252c2s v3p0364c1s
v3p0365c1s
Cushing, C. v1p0034c2s
v1p0102c1s v1p0112c1s v1p0144c2s
v1p0147c1m v1p0153c1s v1p0167c2s
v1p0174c1s v1p0212c2s v1p0244c1s
v1p0254c2s v1p0256c2s v1p0267c2s
v1p0269c2s v1p0273c1s v1p0275c2s
v1p0276c1s v1p0277c2m v1p0280c1s
v1p0280c2s v1p0286c1s v1p0291c1s
v1p0314c1s v1p0353c1s v1p0384c2s
v1p0459c1s v1p0485c2s v1p0560c1s
v1p0576c2s v1p0593c2s v1p0598c2s
v1p0648c1s v1p0730c1m v1p0730c2m
v1p0733c2s v1p0772c2s v1p0809c1s
v1p0833c1s v1p0907c2s v1p0928c2s
v1p0986c1s v1p0987c2s v1p1048c1s
v1p1108c2s v1p1113c2s v1p1213c2s
v1p1255c1s v1p1368c1s v1p1368c2s
v1p1395c2s v1p1396c1s v1p1424c2s
v1p1426c1s
Cushing, D.Q. v1p0909c2s
Cushing, E.W. v1p0421c1s
v1p0816c2s v1p1269c1s
Cushing, F.H. v2p0483c2m
v3p0349c1s v4p0637c2s v5p0562c2s
Cushing, G.H. v6p0359c1s
Cushing, H.A. v3p0012c2s
v3p0025c2s v4p0434c2s v5p0486c1s
Cushing, L.S. v1p0258c2s
Cushing, Mrs. v1p1312c1s
Cushing, P. v2p0035c1s
v2p0059c2s v2p0258c2s v3p0270c1s
v3p0294c1s
Cushing, Paul v3p0326c2s
Cushing, T. v1p1299c2s
v4p0249c2s
Cushing, T., jr. v1p0647c1s
v1p1159c2s
Cushing, T.P. v1p1314c2s
Cushing, W.L. v2p0026c2s
Cushman, A.S. v6p0222c1s
Cushman, C. v1p1031c2s
Cushman, F.W. v6p0523c1s
Cushman, G.F. v1p0422c2s
v2p0064c1s
Cushman, G.H. v3p0443c1s
Cushman, H.E. v5p0080c1s
Cushman, H.I. v1p0805c2s
v1p1336c2s v2p0369c2s v3p0112c2s
v3p0394c1s v3p0444c2s
Cushman, H.W. v1p0023c2s
v1p0028c2s
Cushman, I. v4p0144c2s
Cushman, J.A. v6p0155c2s
v6p0358c2s v6p0502c1s v6p0502c2s
v6p0503c1s v6p0542c1s
Cushman, J.A. and Henderson, W.P.
v6p0026c2s v6p0542c1s
Cushman, R.S. v5p0173c2s
v5p0250c1s
Cushman, T. v5p0486c2s
Cushnie, C. v4p0503c1s
Cusin, A. v2p0045c1s
Cussans, J.E. v2p0465c2s
v5p0390c1s
Cussen, L.F. v5p0248c1s
Cust, A. v1p0672c1s
v1p0812c1s v1p0984c1s
Cust, C.N. v4p0017c2s
Cust, E. v2p0146c2s
Cust, H. v5p0006c1s
v5p0006c2s v5p0231c2s v6p0542c1s
Cust, H. et al. v4p0239c2s
Cust, H.J.G. v6p0266c1s
Cust, Henry v4p0544c2s
Cust, L. v4p0030c2s
v4p0161c2s v4p0163c2s v4p0225c2s
v4p0253c1s v4p0587c1s v5p0157c1s
v5p0172c1s v5p0495c2s
Cust, Lionel v6p0034c1s
Cust, R. v1p0378c1s
v5p0398c2s
Cust, R.N. v3p0004c2s
v4p0005c2s v4p0281c1s v4p0360c1s
v4p0383c1s v4p0582c1s v5p0005c2s
v5p0423c2s
Custer, C.A. v1p1347c2s
Custer, E.B. v5p0599c2s
v6p0093c2s
Custer, G.A. v1p0175c1s
v1p1013c2s v1p1201c2s v1p1345c1s
Custis, G. v5p0630c1s
Cutcliffe-Hyne, C.J. v4p0200c2s
v5p0134c2s
Cuthbert, E. v1p0324c1s
v1p0886c1s v2p0124c2s
Cuthbert, Father v5p0219c1s
v5p0493c1s v6p0238c2m v6p0280c2s
v6p0400c2s v6p0547c2s
Cuthbert, J.H. v1p0097c2s
Cuthbert, S. v6p0681c2s
Cuthbertson, C. v5p0034c2s
Cuthell, E.E. v5p0518c1s
v6p0698c1s v6p0698c2s
Cuthell, E.E., Mrs. v3p0074c2s
v3p0203c1s v5p0153c1s
Cuthwill, E. v4p0552c2s
Cutler, C. v1p0156c1s
v1p0684c2s
Cutler, C.G. v5p0632c1s
Cutler, C.H. v3p0084c1s
v4p0456c2s
Cutler, E. v1p0626c2s
v1p0685c1s v1p0793c2s v1p0909c1s
v1p1111c2s
Cutler, E.J. v1p0170c2s
v1p0768c1s
Cutler, H.G. v2p0431c1s
v2p0442c2s v2p0472c1s v3p0063c2s
v3p0076c2s v4p0013c2s
Cutler, J.E. v6p0390c2s
v6p0391c1s
Cutler, J.T. v4p0051c2s
Cutler, M. v3p0084c1s
Cutler, M.C. v3p0176c1s
Cutler, M.S. v3p0249c1s
v3p0249c2s v4p0329c1s v4p0330c1s
Cutler, Martha v6p0295c2s
v6p0462c2s
Cutler, R.P. v1p0697c2s
Cutler, S.P. v1p1019c2s
Cutler, U.W. v6p0574c2s
Cutler, W.A. v5p0399c1s
Cutler, W.P. v3p0313c2s
Cutten, G.B. v6p0352c1s
Cutten, W.H. v5p0408c2s
Cutter, A.E. v1p0929c1s
Cutter, C. v1p0206c1s
Cutter, C.A. v1p0001c2m
v1p0206c1m v1p0451c1s v1p0484c2s
v1p0573c1m v1p0628c2s v1p0742c1s
v1p0742c2m v1p0743c1m v1p0743c2m
v1p0891c2s v1p0899c2s v1p0962c2s
v1p1301c2s v2p0015c2s v2p0045c2m
v2p0060c1s v2p0160c2s v2p0176c2s
v2p0190c2s v2p0216c2s v2p0255c2m
v2p0256c1m v2p0256c2m v2p0257c1m
v2p0290c2s v2p0313c1s v2p0336c1s
v2p0339c1s v2p0345c1s v2p0366c2s
v2p0399c1s v2p0452c1s v3p0011c2s
v3p0028c2s v3p0128c1s v3p0248c2m
v4p0014c2s v4p0073c2s v4p0092c1s
v4p0329c1m v4p0442c1s v5p0138c1s
v5p0333c2s v5p0334c1s v5p0335c1s
v5p0633c1s v6p0017c1s v6p0372c1s
v6p0372c2s
Cutter, C.A. and Lane, W.C.
v2p0256c1s
Cutter, E. v1p0835c1s
v3p0002c1s v3p0026c2s v3p0330c1s
v4p0037c1s
Cutter, E.R. v5p0431c2s
Cutter, H.F. v4p0307c1s
v4p0495c2s v4p0593c2s
Cutter, H.G. v3p0443c2s
Cutter, H.R. v6p0245c2s
Cutter, J.E. v6p0657c2s
Cutter, N., Mrs. v4p0528c1s
Cutter, R.H. v1p1025c1m
Cutter, W. v1p0020c1s
v1p0651c1s
Cutter, W.P. v6p0074c2s
v6p0372c2s
Cutter, W.R. v2p0242c1s
v2p0481c1s v3p0467c1s v4p0131c2s
v4p0221c2s v4p0385c2s v4p0625c2s
v5p0148c2s v5p0215c2s v5p0376c1s
v5p0432c2s v5p0578c1s
Cutter, W.R. and Loring, A.G.
v5p0451c1s v6p0084c1s v6p0683c2s
Cutting, A.W. v6p0689c2s
Cutting, H.A. v1p0174c2m
v2p0060c1s
Cutting, H.P. v1p0318c2s
v1p1157c2s
Cutting, M.D. v3p0152c1s
Cutting, M.S. v4p0136c2s
v4p0193c2s v4p0254c2s v5p0272c2s
v5p0576c1s v5p0577c2s v6p0038c1s
v6p0280c1s v6p0291c1s v6p0311c1s
v6p0381c1s v6p0434c1s v6p0470c2s
v6p0630c1s v6p0639c1s
Cutting, Mary S. v6p0288c2s
v6p0311c1s v6p0467c1s v6p0488c2s
v6p0603c2s v6p0621c1s v6p0627c1s
Cutting, Mary Stewart v6p0311c2s
Cutting, R.F. v5p0471c2s
Cutting, R.Fulton v6p0454c1s
Cutting, R.L. v6p0460c1s
Cutting, S.S. v1p0097c1s
v3p0033c2s
Cutting, S.W. v1p1112c1s
v6p0423c2s v6p0572c1m
Cutts, E.L. v1p0061c2s
v1p0264c2s v1p0405c1s v1p0710c2s
v1p0823c2s v1p0848c2s v1p0861c2s
v1p1171c1s v1p1368c2m v4p0053c1s
v4p0221c2s v4p0241c2s
Cutts, E.T. v1p0587c2s
v1p1010c1s
Cutts, H. v1p0679c2s
Cuvier v1p1306c2s
Cuvier, B. v1p1163c1s
Cuvier, Baron v1p1306c2s
Cuvier, F. v1p0041c2s
Cuvier, G. v1p0057c2s
v1p0335c1s v1p0394c2s v1p0718c2s
v1p1050c1s v1p1162c2s v1p1306c2s
Cuvier, G.L. v1p0551c2s
Cuyler, R.I. v6p0530c1s
v6p0692c2s
Cuyler, T.D. v1p0244c2s
Cuyler, T.L. v1p0030c2s
v1p0081c1s v1p0211c2s v1p0222c2s
v1p0384c1s v1p0409c2s v1p0413c1s
v1p0415c1s v1p0766c2s v1p0775c1s
v1p0971c2s v1p1166c2s v1p1167c2s
v1p1368c1s v4p0450c2s v5p0388c2s
v5p0433c2s v6p0183c2s
Cygnus v6p0044c2s
v6p0432c1s
Cyon, E.De and Hutton, R.H.
v2p0462c1s
Cyples, W. v1p0216c2s
v1p0436c2s v1p0694c2s v1p1145c1s
Cyr, C.W. v3p0369c2m
v3p0370c1s v3p0453c1s
Cyr, N. v3p0160c1s
Czermak, J. v1p0042c1s
v1p0620c2s
Czerny, F. v1p0375c2s

D., A.St.C. v5p0260c1s
D., C.B. v6p0410c1s
D., F.A. v5p0198c1m
D., J. v2p0459c1s
D., L. v3p0165c1m
D., L.L. v1p1262c2m
D., M.H. v4p0521c2s
D., W.M. v5p0357c2s
Dabney, C.W. v5p0042c2s
v5p0177c1s v5p0605c1s v6p0084c1s
v6p0192c2s
Dabney, C.W., jr. v4p0170c1s
v5p0399c2s
Dabney, G.E. v1p0262c1s
v1p0389c2s v1p1097c1s v1p1373c2s
v1p1374c2s
Dabney, J.P. v1p0133c2s
v1p0290c2s v1p0572c2m v1p0694c1s
v1p0775c1s v1p1145c2s v5p0342c2s
v5p0458c2s
Dabney, Miss v1p0083c2s
v1p0196c1s
Dabney, O.F. v4p0187c1s
Dabney, Prof. v1p0875c2s
Dabney, R. and Cunningham, H.
v4p0196c1s
Dabney, R.H. v6p0011c2s
Dabney, R.L. v1p0228c1s
v1p0391c1s v1p0392c1s v1p0528c2s
v1p0675c1s v1p0795c2s v1p0841c2s
v1p0997c2s v1p1223c1s v1p1425c2s
v2p0013c1s v2p0042c1s v2p0063c1s
v2p0140c2s v2p0176c1s v2p0220c2m
v2p0232c2s v2p0340c2s v2p0437c2s
Dabney, V. v3p0278c1s
Dabney, W.D. v4p0283c2s
Dabney, W.P. v1p0786c1s
v2p0211c1s
Dabo, L.S. v6p0032c2s
v6p0695c1s
Daboll, J. v6p0357c1s
Dacosta, J. v1p0631c1s
v1p0666c2s v4p0004c2s v4p0279c1s
v4p0281c1s
Daddow, S.H. v1p0925c1s
Dade, C. v1p0238c1s
v1p0865c2s v1p1256c2s v1p1316c2s
Dadourian, H.M. v6p0199c2m
v6p0526c2m
Daell, A.N.Van v3p0163c2s
v3p0242c2s v3p0378c2s
Daell, A.N.Van et al. v4p0320c2s
Dafforne, J. v1p0227c1s
v1p0587c2m v1p0781c1s v1p1316c1s
Dafoe, J.A. v5p0088c2s
Dafoe, J.W. v5p0205c1s
v5p0410c1s
Daft, L. v5p0578c1s
Dagg, J.L. v1p0253c1s
Daggett, C.D. v6p0482c1s
Daggett, J. v1p1190c1s
Daggett, L.M. v3p0097c1s
v3p0474c1s
Daggett, M. v3p0401c1s
Daggett, M.S. v6p0378c1s
v6p0624c1s
Daggett, O.E. v1p0111c2s
v1p0976c2s v1p1043c2s v1p1240c2s
v1p1428c2s
Daggett, R.M. v4p0198c1s
v4p0551c2s v4p0585c2s
Daglish, G.H. v1p0525c2s
Daguerre, M. v1p0329c1s
Dahlgren, C.B. v4p0399c1s
Dahlgren, M.V. v3p0305c2s
v3p0463c1s
Dahlgren, U. v6p0197c2s
v6p0227c1s
Dahlgren, Ulric v5p0208c2s
v6p0629c2s
Dahlke, J. v1p0452c2s
Dahlman, A.E. v3p0281c1s
Dahn, F. v4p0224c1s
Daiches, S. v6p0169c2s
Daimler, P. v5p0041c1s
Daingerfield, E. v4p0285c1s
Daingerfield, H. v5p0315c1s
Daingerfield, J.E.P. v2p0058c1s
Daintrey, L. v3p0448c1s
Daintrey, Miss v3p0069c1s
Dairs, A.P. v6p0329c1s
Daiseaux, E. v3p0019c1s
Daish, J.B. v3p0169c1s
v3p0356c2s v3p0380c2s v6p0324c2s
Dake, L.M. v6p0672c2s
Dakin, L.J. v2p0028c1s
Dakyns, H.G., jr. and Parsons, C.G.
v6p0661c1s
Daland, J. v4p0064c1s
v4p0271c2s
Dalbac, Major v5p0451c1s
Dalby, J.W. v1p1019c1s
Dalby, Mad. v1p0969c1s
Dalby, W.B. v1p0711c1s
Dalby, W.B., Sir v4p0363c2s
v5p0260c1s
Dalby, W.E. v6p0382c2s
Daldy, F.R. v3p0099c2s
v3p0100c1s
Dale, A.B. v4p0121c2s
Dale, A.W.W. v1p0194c1s
v2p0065c2s v2p0153c2s v3p0021c1s
v3p0173c1s v3p0203c2s v3p0262c2s
v4p0530c2s
Dale, Alan v6p0003c1m
v6p0003c2m v6p0059c1s v6p0181c1s
v6p0641c2s v6p0642c1s
Dale, B. v6p0068c1s
v6p0386c2s v6p0439c2s v6p0656c2s
Dale, Bonneycastle v6p0527c2s
Dale, D. v2p0046c2s
v2p0196c1s v2p0273c1s v2p0415c2s
v3p0019c1s v3p0061c2s v3p0217c1m
v3p0338c2s v3p0382c2s v3p0397c1s
v3p0404c2s v3p0414c1s v4p0148c2s
v4p0204c2s v4p0520c1s v5p0018c1s
v5p0099c2s v5p0230c1s v5p0257c2s
v5p0324c1s v5p0388c2s v5p0578c2s
v5p0636c1s v6p0086c1s v6p0148c1s
v6p0237c1s v6p0415c2s v6p0465c1s
v6p0645c2s
Dale, Dailey v4p0590c1s
Dale, E. v1p0281c1s
v1p0696c2s v1p1177c1s
Dale, F.D. v6p0116c1s
Dale, G. v4p0066c1s
Dale, H., Mrs. v6p0242c2s
Dale, J.A. and Dodd, L.T.. v5p0500c2s
Dale, J.B. v6p0140c2s
Dale, J.W. v3p0015c2s
Dale, M. v4p0487c2s
v4p0629c1s v5p0440c2s
Dale, R.W. v1p0028c2s
v1p0029c2s v1p0035c2s v1p0060c1s
v1p0144c2s v1p0185c2s v1p0223c2s
v1p0250c1s v1p0290c2s v1p0291c1s
v1p0335c2s v1p0344c2s v1p0387c1s
v1p0389c2s v1p0397c1s v1p0440c2s
v1p0461c2s v1p0596c2s v1p0626c1s
v1p0676c2s v1p0688c1s v1p0703c1s
v1p0716c1s v1p0778c2s v1p0865c1s
v1p0893c1s v1p0922c1s v1p0922c2s
v1p0925c1s v1p0961c2s v1p1030c1s
v1p1102c2s v1p1106c1s v1p1126c2s
v1p1200c1s v1p1300c2s v1p1330c2m
v1p1340c2s v1p1429c1s v2p0068c2s
v2p0076c1s v2p0081c2s v2p0083c1s
v2p0131c1m v2p0148c2s v2p0153c2s
v2p0162c2m v2p0170c2s v2p0188c1s
v2p0235c2m v2p0275c2s v2p0310c1s
v2p0330c2s v2p0356c1s v2p0358c2s
v2p0370c1s v2p0371c2s v2p0382c2s
v2p0391c1s v2p0403c2s v2p0412c1s
v2p0426c1s v2p0429c2s v2p0480c2s
v3p0027c2m v3p0028c1s v3p0043c1s
v3p0054c2m v3p0119c1s v3p0182c2s
v3p0199c2s v3p0281c1s v3p0295c1s
v3p0357c2s v3p0437c2s v4p0011c1s
v4p0215c2s v4p0424c2s v5p0236c2s
v5p0311c2s
Dale, S.M. v6p0692c2s
Dale, S.S. v6p0413c2m
Dale, T.C. v6p0161c2s
Dale, T.F. v5p0458c1s
v6p0236c1s v6p0399c1s v6p0507c2s
v6p0612c2s
Dale, T.N. v2p0174c1s
v2p0372c1s v4p0118c2s v6p0631c1s
Dale, T.N., jr. v1p1039c2s
Dale, T.T. v6p0178c1s
Dalehaye, H. v5p0364c1s
Daley, C.P. v1p0798c2s
Daley, J.G. v5p0384c1s
v5p0385c2s v6p0388c1s
Dalgairns, J.B. v1p0528c2s
v1p0529c1s v1p0640c2s v1p1222c1s
Dalgleish, T. v4p0231c1s
Dalgleish, T.S. v1p0391c1s
Dalgleish, W.S. v1p0087c2s
v2p0155c2s v2p0200c2s v2p0206c1s
v2p0316c2s v3p0381c2s v3p0436c2s
v4p0202c2s v4p0356c1s v4p0508c2s
Dall, A. v6p0486c1s
Dall, C.H. v1p0175c2s
v1p0212c1s v1p0217c1s v1p0233c2s
v1p0289c1s v1p0528c2s v1p0603c1s
v1p0750c2s v1p0950c1s v1p1068c1s
v1p1095c2s v1p1164c2s v1p1407c2s
v1p1425c2s v1p1426c1s v2p0077c1s
v2p0130c1s v3p0178c1s v3p0191c1s
v4p0621c1s v5p0256c1s
Dall, C.H., Mrs. v1p0016c2s
v1p0099c1s v1p0395c2s v1p1221c1s
v1p1426c1s v4p0623c1s
Dall, C.H.A. v1p0632c2s
v1p0634c2s v1p1341c1s v2p0059c2s
v2p0231c1s
Dall, C.W.H. v1p0705c1s
Dall, C.W.H., Mrs. v1p0945c2s
Dall, W.D. v6p0148c1s
Dall, W.H. v1p0018c1m
v1p0055c1s v1p0055c2s v1p0188c2s
v1p0425c1m v1p0435c1s v1p0459c2s
v1p0638c1s v1p0859c1m v1p0901c2s
v1p0920c1s v1p0925c2s v1p1194c1s
v1p1213c1s v1p1308c1s v1p1439c2m
v2p0004c1s v2p0006c2m v2p0009c2s
v2p0020c2s v2p0079c2s v2p0193c1s
v2p0234c1s v2p0294c1m v2p0303c2s
v2p0334c1s v2p0401c2s v2p0458c1s
v2p0463c1s v3p0037c2s v3p0145c1s
v3p0155c2s v3p0169c2s v3p0185c1s
v3p0196c1s v3p0263c2s v3p0276c2s
v3p0290c1m v3p0316c2s v3p0325c2s
v3p0372c1s v4p0009c1m v4p0019c2s
v4p0048c1s v4p0221c1s v4p0298c2s
v4p0350c2s v4p0376c2s v4p0439c2s
v4p0567c1s v5p0011c1m v5p0027c1s
v5p0065c2s v5p0269c2s v5p0318c1s
v5p0329c1s v5p0397c2s v5p0400c1s
v5p0423c1s v5p0645c1s v6p0010c1s
v6p0023c1s v6p0047c2s v6p0056c1s
v6p0214c2s v6p0264c1s v6p0359c1s
v6p0424c1s v6p0474c1s v6p0483c1s
v6p0632c1s v6p0712c2s
Dall, W.H. and Boas, F. .. v3p0143c2s
Dall, W.H. et al. v6p0576c2s
Dall, Wm.H. v4p0049c2s
Dallas, C. v5p0320c1s
Dallas, D. v5p0351c1s
v5p0357c1s
Dallas, E.S. v1p0873c2s
v2p0250c1s
Dallas, G.M. v1p1289c2m
v3p0372c2m
Dallas, H.A. v5p0279c1s
v5p0524c1s v5p0536c1s
Dallas, J. v2p0147c2s
v2p0274c1s
Dallas, Lieut. v5p0288c2m
Dallas, M.K. v5p0554c1s
Dallas, W.L. v1p1269c1s
v1p1394c2s
Dallas, W.S. v1p0181c1s
v1p0420c1s v1p0456c2s v1p0875c1s
v1p1039c1s
Dallaway, J. v1p0163c2s
v1p0294c1s
Dallin, C.E. v6p0579c1s
Dallin, V.C. v5p0241c2s
Dallinger, F.W. v4p0093c1s
Dallinger, L. v5p0089c1s
Dallinger, W.H. v1p0589c1s
v1p1178c1s v1p1239c1m v2p0046c1m
v2p0181c1s v3p0285c1s v3p0350c1s
v4p0369c2s v4p0415c2s
Dallinger, W.H. and Drysdale, J.
v1p0953c1s
Dallmeyer, T.R. v4p0567c2s
Dallow, W. v4p0222c1s
Dally, E. v1p0802c2s
Dalma, Alma v5p0364c2s
Dalman, G. v6p0274c2s
Dalmer, N. v3p0425c1s
Dalrymple, A. v1p0957c1s
Dalrymple, C., Sir v5p0433c1s
Dalrymple, Charles, Sir .. v5p0608c1s
Dalrymple, D. v1p0640c2s
Dalson, A.T. and Wetherill, C.M.
v1p0271c1s
Dalton, A.M. v6p0091c2s
Dalton, C. v3p0235c1s
v3p0430c1s v4p0600c1s v6p0629c1s
Dalton, C.B. v6p0130c1s
Dalton, E.B. v1p0258c1s
v1p0915c2s
Dalton, F. v6p0540c1s
Dalton, J.C. v1p0142c2s
v1p0786c2s v1p1015c2s v1p1376c2m
v4p0172c2s v4p0222c1s
Dalton, J.C., jr. v1p1059c1s
Dalton, J.N. v2p0154c1s
Dalton, L.V. v6p0565c1s
Dalton, M. v2p0381c1s
v4p0290c1s v5p0295c2s v5p0296c1s
Dalton, M.S. v5p0493c2s
Dalton, O.M. v5p0053c2s
v5p0086c1s v6p0342c2s v6p0387c1s
v6p0524c1s
Dalton, O.M. and Read, C.H.
v5p0053c2s
Dalton, T. v1p0635c2s
Dalton, W. v6p0059c2s
Daly, A. v2p0122c2s
Daly, C.P. v1p0055c1s
v1p0506c1s v1p1322c2s v1p1432c1s
v2p0319c2s v4p0037c1s
Daly, D. v3p0351c1s
v6p0631c2s
Daly, D.D. v3p0050c2s
Daly, E.D. v5p0169c2s
v5p0170c1s v5p0571c2s
Daly, F.H. v1p0649c1s
v1p1212c2s
Daly, Fred. v4p0543c2s
Daly, H.D. v3p0147c2s
v3p0219c1s v3p0294c1s v3p0332c1s
Daly, Harriet W. v4p0066c1s
Daly, J.F. v5p0044c1s
Daly, M. v1p0738c1s
Daly, R.A. v5p0417c2s
v5p0439c1s v6p0181c2s v6p0264c1s
v6p0307c1s v6p0378c1s
Daly, Reginald, A. v6p0433c2s
Daly, W.H. v5p0467c2s
Daly, W.H. et al. v5p0592c2s
Dalzell, A. v1p0565c2s
Dalzell, C. v6p0596c2s
Dalzell, J. v4p0230c2s
v4p0564c1s v5p0238c2s

Dalzell, J. et al. v4p0525c1s
v4p0563c2s
Dalziel, H. v2p0120c2s
v3p0457c2s v6p0517c1s
Dam, H.J. v3p0344c2s
Dam, H.J.W. v4p0004c2s
v4p0043c2s v4p0206c1s v4p0248c2s
v4p0440c2s v4p0487c1s v4p0531c1s
v4p0637c1s v5p0056c1m v5p0172c2s
v5p0299c1s v5p0384c1s v5p0568c1s
v5p0571c1m v5p0610c1s
Damant, M. v3p0394c2s
Damant, Mrs. v2p0054c1s
v2p0427c1s v2p0450c2s v3p0186c2s
Damant, Scott v5p0385c2s
Dambeck, C. v1p0327c2s
Dame, L.L. v1p0467c2s
v2p0445c2s v3p0278c1s v3p0435c2s
Dames, M.L. v4p0043c1s
v6p0048c2s
Dames, M.L. and Seeman, F.
v6p0045c2s
Damiani, F. v1p0046c1s
v1p0321c1s
Damon, D. v1p0850c1s
Damon, F.M. v6p0057c1s
Damon, L.T. v4p0154c1s
v4p0177c2s v5p0040c1s
Damon, W.E. v1p0301c1s
v1p0347c2s
Dampier, W. v1p0734c2s
v4p0338c2s v4p0609c2s v4p0631c1s
Dampier, W.J. v1p0203c2s
Damrel, H.L. v1p0502c2s
Damrosch, F. v6p0437c2s
Damrosch, W. v3p0313c1s
Damsel, H.L. v1p0664c2s
v1p1078c1s
Damson, Lloyd v6p0277c1s
Dan, Beatrice A. v4p0072c2s
Dan, H.J.W. v4p0154c2s
Dana, A. v5p0597c2s
Dana, A.H. v1p0072c2s
v1p1005c1s v1p1034c1s v1p1034c2s
v1p1271c1s
Dana, C. v6p0203c1s
Dana, C.A. v3p0443c1s
v3p0473c1s v4p0299c2s v4p0305c1s
v4p0583c1s v5p0601c2s
Dana, C.H. v4p0305c2s
v4p0468c1s
Dana, C.L. v2p0087c1s
v2p0099c2s v2p0251c2s v2p0257c2s
v3p0300c1s v4p0016c2s v4p0151c2s
v4p0225c2s v6p0550c2s
Dana, C.L. et al. v2p0150c2s
Dana, D. v1p0096c1s
v1p0419c1s v1p0846c1s v1p0909c2s
v1p1105c2s v1p1415c2s
Dana, E.E. v5p0531c2s
Dana, E.S. v1p0500c2s
v1p0845c1s v2p0057c2s v2p0102c1s
v2p0182c1s v2p0285c2s v2p0294c2s
v3p0034c1s v3p0039c2s v3p0328c2s
v3p0375c1s v4p0146c2s
Dana, E.S. and Brush, G.J.
v1p0439c2s v1p0844c2s v3p0053c1s
v3p0280c2s
Dana, E.S. and Grinnell, G.B.
v1p0718c2s
Dana, E.S. and Hillebrand, W.F.
v3p0440c1s
Dana, E.S. and Penfield, S.L.
v2p0285c2s v3p0336c1s
Dana, E.S. and Schrauf, A.
v1p0844c2s
Dana, F. v1p1391c1s
v3p0435c1s v4p0444c2s v5p0048c2s
Dana, G. v6p0321c2s
Dana, G.W. v1p0327c1s
Dana, H.C. v4p0587c2s
v4p0628c1s
Dana, J.C. v2p0130c2s
v4p0329c1s v5p0205c2s v5p0334c1s
v5p0335c2s v5p0336c2s v5p0337c1s
v5p0479c2s v6p0017c1s v6p0074c1s
v6p0222c2s v6p0223c1s v6p0370c2s
v6p0372c2m v6p0373c2s v6p0374c2m
v6p0375c1s v6p0455c1m v6p0532c2s
Dana, J.C. et al. v6p0017c1s
v6p0532c2m
Dana, J.D. v1p0041c2s
v1p0042c1s v1p0048c1s v1p0055c1s
v1p0114c1m v1p0115c1s v1p0139c1s
v1p0185c2s v1p0188c2s v1p0213c1m
v1p0224c1m v1p0271c2s v1p0292c2s
v1p0301c2m v1p0305c1s v1p0312c2m
v1p0321c2m v1p0326c2s v1p0338c1s
v1p0375c1s v1p0375c2s v1p0424c1s
v1p0470c1s v1p0506c2m v1p0508c1m
v1p0508c2m v1p0509c2m v1p0523c2s
v1p0524c1m v1p0524c2m v1p0556c2m
v1p0616c2s v1p0701c2s v1p0707c1s
v1p0745c2m v1p0749c2s v1p0791c2s
v1p0792c2m v1p0794c1s v1p0810c1s
v1p0812c2m v1p0844c2s v1p0845c1m
v1p0866c1m v1p0898c2s v1p0899c1s
v1p0909c2m v1p0910c1s v1p0911c2s
v1p0926c2m v1p0927c1s v1p0936c2m
v1p0947c1s v1p0956c1m v1p0975c2s
v1p0986c2s v1p1041c2m v1p1113c1m
v1p1161c2s v1p1172c2s v1p1198c1s
v1p1204c2s v1p1233c1m v1p1296c1s
v1p1351c2s v1p1367c1s v1p1367c2m
v1p1368c1s v1p1368c2s v1p1377c1m
v1p1415c2s v1p1436c1s v1p1441c2s
v2p0099c2s v2p0102c2s v2p0106c2s
v2p0163c2s v2p0179c1s v2p0193c2s
v2p0214c1s v2p0284c2s v2p0311c2s
v2p0323c2s v2p0349c2s v2p0374c2s
v2p0402c2s v2p0429c2s v2p0463c1s
v2p0475c2s v3p0017c1s v3p0064c1s
v3p0101c2s v3p0169c2s v3p0179c2s
v3p0191c2s v3p0233c2s v3p0236c1s
v3p0254c2s v3p0257c2m v3p0271c2s
v3p0301c2s v3p0310c1s v3p0363c1s
v3p0384c1s v3p0393c1s v3p0419c1m
v3p0451c2m v3p0476c2s v4p0023c1s
v4p0031c2s v4p0055c1s v4p0227c1s
v4p0307c1s v4p0375c1m v4p0398c1s
v4p0398c2s
Dana, J.F. v1p0399c2s
Dana, J.I. v1p0876c2s
Dana, J.J. v1p0507c1s
v1p0509c2s
Dana, M. v5p0083c2s
v5p0496c2s v6p0129c2s v6p0413c1s
v6p0431c2s v6p0583c1s
Dana, M.M. v3p0234c1s
Dana, M.M.G. v1p0289c2s
v1p0310c2s v1p1402c1s v1p1412c1s
v3p0125c2s v3p0356c1s
Dana, M.McG. v3p0096c1s
v3p0398c1s v4p0096c2s v4p0116c1s
v4p0116c2s v4p0307c2s v4p0338c2s
v4p0387c1s v4p0431c2s v4p0580c2s
Dana, M.T. v5p0408c1s
Dana, Marvin v6p0101c1m
Dana, N.P. v6p0021c2s
Dana, O.E. v3p0077c1s
v3p0152c1s v5p0262c2s
Dana, R. v1p0537c1s
Dana, R.H. v1p0024c1s
v1p0172c1s v1p0353c1s v1p0404c2s
v1p0534c2s v1p0577c1s v1p0667c2s
v1p0729c1s v1p0941c1s v1p0977c2s
v1p1149c2s v1p1428c1s v3p0031c1s
v3p0031c2s v3p0071c1m v3p0078c2s
v3p0340c2s v3p0452c2s v4p0042c2s
v4p0117c1s v4p0290c2s v4p0493c1s
Dana, R.H., jr. v1p0186c2s
v1p0258c2s v1p0265c1s v1p0320c2s
v1p0330c1s v1p0426c2s v1p0650c2s
v1p1048c2s v1p1352c2s
Dana, R.P. v1p0231c1s
Dana, S.L. v1p0225c1s
v1p0508c1s v1p0845c1s
Dana, W.F. v3p0037c2s
v6p0590c2s
Danbogue, Lady v3p0294c1s
Danby, F. v4p0213c2s
v4p0381c1s v5p0084c2s v5p0180c2s
v5p0304c2s v5p0362c2s v5p0491c1s
v5p0512c2s v6p0161c1s
Danby, Frank v5p0166c2s
v5p0354c2s
Dance, G. v1p1009c2s
Dancy, G.W. v4p0003c1s
v4p0461c2s v4p0518c1s
Dandeno, J.B. v5p0454c1s
v6p0497c2s v6p0551c2s v6p0602c2s
Dandridge, D. v3p0195c1s
v3p0394c1s v4p0111c1s v5p0630c2s
Dandridge, Danske v4p0204c1s
Dane, B.L.R. v3p0439c1s
Dane, D. v4p0461c2s
Dane, J.B. v5p0112c1s
v5p0304c2s
Dane, W.J. v3p0289c1s
Danenbaum, R. v6p0419c2s
Danforth, A. v6p0282c1s
Danforth, A.H. v6p0430c1s
Danforth, C.F. v3p0436c2s
v4p0047c1s v4p0585c1s
Danforth, I.N. v1p0628c1s
Danforth, J.N. v1p0454c1s
Dangerfield, C. v6p0004c2s
v6p0038c1s v6p0059c2s v6p0150c1s
v6p0220c2s v6p0232c1s v6p0246c1s
v6p0274c2s v6p0291c2s v6p0405c2s
v6p0623c2s v6p0694c2s
Dangerfield, Clinton v6p0311c2s
Dangerfield, G. v6p0589c2s
Dangerfield, J. v1p1054c2s
v1p1335c1s
Daniel, A.M. and Waldstein, C.
v6p0163c2s
Daniel, A.S. v4p0103c2s
v4p0628c2s
Daniel, A.S. and White, H.
v5p0407c1s
Daniel, E. et al. v4p0477c1s
Daniel, F. v2p0166c2s
v3p0002c2s
Daniel, F.E. v5p0084c2s
v5p0291c2s
Daniel, F.S. v2p0165c1s
v3p0456c1s v4p0134c2s v4p0277c1s
Daniel, G. v1p0412c2s
Daniel, J. v4p0449c2s
v6p0211c1s
Daniel, J.M. v2p0252c2s
Daniel, J.W. v1p0605c2s
v2p0009c2s v2p0063c2s v2p0110c1s
v2p0400c1s v3p0111c2s v4p0165c2s
Daniel, P.A. v2p0398c1s
Daniell, A. v5p0294c2s
Daniell, A.E. v4p0340c2s
Daniell, C. v2p0046c1s
v3p0176c2s v3p0211c2s v4p0230c2s
v4p0279c2s
Daniell, Col. v1p1030c2s
Daniell, F.H.B. v2p0226c2s
v2p0330c2s v4p0047c2s
Daniell, H.J. v6p0080c1s
Daniell, J.F. v4p0511c1s
Daniell, M.G. v1p0331c1s
Daniell, W.C. v1p1225c2s
Daniell, W.F. v1p0012c1m
v1p0533c1s
Daniels, A.H. v4p0036c2s
v4p0364c2s v4p0477c2s v6p0383c1s
Daniels, A.J. v3p0406c2s
v4p0003c1s v4p0161c1s v4p0544c1s
Daniels, A.S. v6p0638c2s
Daniels, Adeliza v5p0054c1s
Daniels, B.K. v5p0451c2s
v5p0467c2s v6p0243c2s v6p0399c1s
v6p0484c2s v6p0494c1s
Daniels, C.F. v1p0338c2s
v1p0912c1s v1p1403c1s
Daniels, C.L. v3p0341c2s
v4p0607c1s
Daniels, Dr. v5p0388c2s
Daniels, E.D. v4p0261c1s
v4p0300c1s v4p0466c2s v5p0056c2s
v5p0283c2s v5p0569c1s v6p0394c2s
v6p0575c1s v6p0584c1s
Daniels, F. v6p0502c2s
Daniels, F.H. v4p0065c1s
Daniels, F.H.B. v6p0332c2s
Daniels, H.C. v5p0089c2s
v5p0166c1s v5p0209c1m v5p0591c1s
Daniels, H.G. v5p0052c1s
v5p0434c1s v5p0616c1s
Daniels, J. v6p0192c2s
v6p0446c2s
Daniels, J.F. v6p0449c2s
Daniels, J.L. v5p0126c1s
Daniels, M.S. v5p0196c2m
Daniels, Mary S. v6p0038c2s
Daniels, R.L. v1p0004c1s
v2p0347c1s
Daniels, R.McD. v6p0551c2s
Daniels, W.H. v1p0546c2s
v1p1335c2s
Daniels, W.M. v4p0042c1s
v4p0243c1s v4p0273c1s v4p0459c1s
v5p0376c1s v5p0519c1s v6p0120c1s
v6p0162c2s v6p0168c2s v6p0169c2m
v6p0170c1s v6p0184c1s v6p0232c2s
v6p0351c1s v6p0357c1s v6p0399c1s
v6p0435c2s v6p0436c2s v6p0495c1s
v6p0530c1s v6p0533c2s v6p0537c1s
v6p0540c1s v6p0589c2s v6p0615c1m
v6p0633c1s v6p0634c1s v6p0648c1s
v6p0658c2s v6p0659c1s v6p0667c1s
v6p0682c1s v6p0692c1s
Danielson, F.W. v6p0582c1s
Danion, T.D. v1p0690c2s
Danks, B. v3p0269c1s
v3p0285c2s v4p0079c2s
Danks, W. v5p0489c2s
Danley, W.S. v2p0042c1s
v2p0410c2s
Dannenberg, J. v6p0049c1s
v6p0128c2s
Danner, E.W. and Gooch, F.A.
v3p0015c2s v4p0454c2s
Dannreuther, E. v1p0108c1s
v1p0885c1s v1p0943c2s
Dansiger, A. v6p0341c1s
Danson, J.T. v1p0373c2s
v1p0474c1m v1p0532c1s v1p0544c1s
v1p1049c2m v1p1134c2s v1p1208c1s
Danvers, F.C. v1p0634c2s
v1p0666c2s v1p1079c1s v2p0090c2s
v2p0143c2s v2p0150c1m v2p0169c1s
v2p0217c2s v2p0218c2s v2p0229c2s
v2p0306c2s v2p0334c1s v2p0345c2s
v2p0363c1m v2p0411c2m v2p0421c1s
v2p0424c2s v2p0482c1s v3p0126c2s
v3p0149c1s v3p0210c2s v3p0211c2s
v3p0212c1s v3p0327c2s v5p0009c2s
v5p0287c1s
Danvers, F.G. v1p1019c1s
Danvers, J. v4p0280c1s
Danvers, J., Sir v2p0218c1s
v3p0212c2m v3p0352c1m
Danvers, R.C. v1p0415c1s
Danziger, G.A. v3p0238c1s
v3p0239c2m v3p0366c1s v3p0412c2s
v3p0414c2s v6p0291c1s
Danziger, G.A. and
Nesfield, D.M., Mrs. .. v4p0302c2s
Daponte, D. v2p0312c1s
Dapprich, F. and Sterling, S.A.
v6p0552c1s
Dapray, J.A. v5p0375c2s
Dar, P.B.N. v3p0124c1s

Darbers, H. v5p0262c2s
Darbishire, R.D. v1p0409c1s v2p0438c1s
Darboun, H. v5p0002c1s
Darboux, G. v6p0251c1s
Darby, J.L. v5p0104c2s
Darby, W. v1p0485c1s v1p0956c1m v1p1060c1s v1p1061c1s
Darby, W.E. v5p0437c2s
Darche, L. v4p0409c2s
Darcy, B. v2p0145c2s
Darcy, R. v4p0587c1s
Dare, A. v6p0283c1s
Dare, D. v4p0089c1s
Dare, F. v2p0242c2s
Dare, Fanny v5p0606c1s
Dare, Marion v5p0579c1s
Dare, S. v3p0468c1s
Dare, S. et al. v3p0202c2s
Darfield, J. v4p0426c2s
Dargan, E.P. v5p0186c1s v6p0200c2s
Dargan, W.F. and Tillman, B.R. v4p0331c1s
Darley, E.E. v1p0586c2s
Darley, F.O.C. v3p0315c2s
Darling, C.J. v4p0181c1s
Darling, C.R. v2p0423c2s v6p0132c1s
Darling, C.W. v3p0041c1s v3p0197c1s v3p0312c2s v4p0054c1s
Darling, Chas., Sir v6p0499c1s
Darling, E.A. v5p0037c1s
Darling, Eugene, A. v5p0037c1s
Darling, G. v5p0565c1s v6p0660c1s
Darling, Gertrude v5p0191c2s v5p0192c1s
Darling, H. v1p1043c1s v1p1102c2s
Darling, H.K. v5p0083c2s v6p0111c2s v6p0469c1s
Darling, Isabel v6p0641c1s v6p0694c1s
Darling, J.D. v5p0049c2s v6p0602c2s
Darling, J.V. v1p1212c2s
Darling, M.G. v1p0314c1s
Darling, N. v1p0617c1s
Darling, O.I. v3p0099c2s
Darling, T.G. v4p0109c1s v4p0228c2s v5p0115c1s v5p0268c2s v5p0577c1s v5p0641c2s
Darlington, L. and Talbot, E.B. v5p0038c1s
Darlington, P.J. v5p0188c2s v5p0321c1s
Darlington, T. v6p0107c1s v6p0309c1s
Darlington, T. and Bromby, C.H. v4p0112c2s
Darlington, T. and Houston, A. v4p0112c2s
Darlington, W. v1p0808c1s
Darlington, W.M. v1p0059c1s v1p0864c2s
Darlow, T.H. and Neumann, B.P. v3p0096c2s
Darmesteter, A.M.F. v3p0161c2s
Darmesteter, J. v1p0528c2s v1p0529c2s v1p0890c2s v3p0003c2s v3p0476c1s v4p0480c2s
Darmesteter, M. v4p0599c2s
Darmesteter, M.J. v5p0217c1s v5p0220c2s v5p0415c2s
Darmesteter, Mme. v3p0361c2s
Darnley, Earl v2p0147c2s
Darnton, P.W. v3p0350c1s
Darnton-Fraser, H.J. v6p0370c1s
Darr, F.J.A. v2p0385c1s v3p0186c1s
Darr, P.B.N. v3p0212c1s
Darrach, C.C. v5p0186c1s
Darrach, C.G. v6p0259c1s v6p0464c1s
Darrach, Henry v5p0153c1s
Darrach, J.M.A. v6p0087c2s
Darragh, J.T. v1p1203c1s v5p0586c2s v6p0007c1s
Darrah, E.M. v5p0108c1s
Darrell, A.V. v1p0114c2s
Darrell, J. v1p0568c2s v1p1151c1s v2p0177c2s v2p0336c1s v2p0440c1s v3p0254c1s
Darrin, K. v6p0252c1s
Darrow, A.R. v2p0003c2s
Darrow, C.S. v4p0475c1s v6p0436c1s
Darrow, Clarence S. v6p0113c2s
Darrow, P.C. v3p0108c2s
Dart, E.C.M. v5p0001c1s v5p0193c2m v5p0434c2s
Dartmoor, C. v1p0367c2s
Dartmouth, T. v5p0319c1s
Darton, F.J.H. v6p0173c2s
Darton, J.W. v5p0079c2s
Darton, N.H. v2p0210c2s v2p0429c2s v2p0456c2s v3p0035c1s v3p0244c1s v3p0330c1s v3p0412c1s v3p0459c2s v4p0023c1s v4p0349c2s v4p0519c2s v5p0230c1s v5p0541c1s v6p0186c1s v6p0427c1s v6p0592c2s
Darton, N.H. and Clarke, F.W. v5p0277c2s
Darton, N.H. and Keith, A. v5p0204c2s
Darton, N.H. and Kemp, J.F. v4p0155c2s
Daru, Comte v1p0236c2s
Darwin, C. v1p0181c1s v1p0640c2s v1p0642c2m v1p0647c1s v1p0862c1s v1p0963c1s v1p1016c1s v1p1296c1s v2p0048c1s v2p0221c1s v2p0341c2s v2p0457c2s v5p0289c2s
Darwin, C. and Wallace, A. v5p0545c1s v5p0608c1s
Darwin, E.W. v6p0584c2s
Darwin, Ellen W. v4p0266c2s
Darwin, Ellin W., Mrs. ... v3p0385c2s
Darwin, F. v1p0025c1s v1p0107c1s v1p0265c2s v1p0645c2s v1p0744c2s v1p1014c2s v1p1015c1s v1p1015c2s v2p0343c2s v2p0344c1s v4p0625c1s v5p0318c2s v5p0454c1s v5p0503c1s v5p0621c2s v6p0082c1s v6p0264c2s v6p0675c2s
Darwin, F. et al. v2p0413c1s
Darwin, F., Mrs. v6p0008c1s
Darwin, G. v1p0803c1s
Darwin, G.H. v1p0305c2s v1p0309c2s v1p0366c2s v1p0376c1s v1p0506c2m v1p0715c1s v1p0724c1m v1p0803c1m v1p0946c1s v1p1027c1s v1p1310c1s v1p1361c2s v2p0127c2s v2p0173c2s v2p0174c1s v2p0239c2s v2p0373c1s v2p0440c2m v2p0441c1s v2p0469c2s v3p0126c1s v3p0276c1m v3p0298c2s v3p0367c2s v3p0375c2s v3p0407c1s v3p0430c1s v4p0272c2s v4p0545c2s v5p0071c2s v5p0509c1s v6p0082c1s v6p0214c1s v6p0215c1s v6p0239c1s v6p0250c1s v6p0571c1m v6p0646c1s
Darwin, G.H. and Nolan, J. v2p0440c2s
Darwin, H. v2p0434c1s
Darwin, L. v4p0005c2s v4p0235c2s v4p0404c2s v5p0008c1s v5p0238c2s v5p0465c1s v6p0162c1s v6p0425c1s
Darwin, Leonard v6p0436c2s
Darwin, S.H. v2p0104c1s
Dary, G. v5p0184c2s
Daryll, A.B. v6p0226c2s v6p0603c2s
Das, D.N. v2p0203c1s v2p0473c2s
Daschbach, E.M. v6p0069c2s v6p0208c2s
Dasent, A.I. v3p0256c2s
Dasent, G. v2p0269c2s
Dasent, G.N. v1p0410c2s v1p0929c2s
Dasent, G.W. v1p0716c2s v3p0112c2s
Dasent, G.W., Sir v2p0473c2s
Dasent, J.R. v5p0626c1s
Dashiell, B.J., Jr. v4p0176c2s
Dashiell, R.B. v4p0027c2s
Dashiell, T.G. v3p0209c1s
Daskam, J. v6p0071c2s
Daskam, J.D. v5p0016c2s v5p0260c1s v5p0270c1s v5p0281c1s v5p0342c2s v5p0419c1s v5p0558c1s v5p0617c2s v6p0029c1s
Daskam, Josephine D. v5p0355c1s v6p0189c1s v6p0311c2s v6p0380c2s v6p0492c1s v6p0541c2s v6p0604c1s v6p0674c1s
Dassonville, W.E. v6p0497c1s
Dastre, A. v5p0012c2s v5p0037c1s v5p0124c2s v5p0212c2s v5p0438c1s
Dastre, M.A. v5p0298c1m v5p0442c2s
Datchet, C. v5p0452c2s
Daube, G. v3p0408c2s
Daubney, C. v2p0463c1m
Daubney, C.A. v6p0225c1s
Daubree, A. v2p0128c1s v2p0285c2s
Daubree, G.A. v1p1367c2s v2p0128c1s v3p0280c2s v3p0363c1s v3p0405c2s v3p0457c1m
Dauchy, W.E. v2p0224c1s
Daucy, G.W. v3p0122c1s
Daudeno, J.B. v6p0643c2s
Daudeno, J.P. v6p0651c1s
Daudet, A. v1p0223c2s v1p0338c1s v1p1102c2s v2p0145c1s v2p0210c2s v2p0293c1s v2p0320c2s v2p0402c1s v2p0448c2s v3p0062c1s v3p0339c1s v3p0339c2s v3p0374c1s v3p0392c1s v4p0162c2s v4p0305c1s v4p0390c2s v4p0414c1s v4p0544c1s v5p0021c2s v6p0115c2s
Daudet, Ernest v4p0090c2s
Dauge, H. v2p0243c2s
Dauglish, J. v1p0159c1s v3p0054c1s
Daulton, A.M. v6p0090c1s v6p0124c1s v6p0339c1s v6p0458c2s v6p0610c2s
Daulton, G. v6p0554c2s
Daumart, M. v5p0575c2s
Daumas, Gen. v1p0617c1s
Dauncey, Enid C. v6p0016c2s
Dauncey, S. v2p0144c2s v2p0416c1s
Daunt, A.O. v5p0157c2s v5p0296c1s
Daunt, W.J.O. v2p0142c2s
Daunt, W.J.O'N. v2p0185c1s v2p0225c2s v2p0226c2m v2p0228c1m v4p0237c1s v4p0289c2s v4p0291c1s
Dausman, E.A. v6p0157c2s
Dave, E.M. v3p0119c2s
Daveis, J.L. v1p0239c1s
Daveiss, M.T., Mrs. v4p0003c2s
Davenant, F. v1p0736c1s v1p0791c1s
Davenay, D. v3p0239c2s v3p0463c1s
Davenny, W.I. v2p0365c1s
Davenport, B. v5p0125c2s
Davenport, B.F. v1p0334c1s
Davenport, C. v5p0056c1s v5p0070c2m v5p0071c1s v5p0089c2s v5p0187c2s v5p0411c1s v5p0482c2s v5p0613c2s v6p0094c2s v6p0287c2s v6p0342c2s v6p0415c1s
Davenport, C.B. v5p0062c1m v5p0646c2s v6p0021c1s v6p0139c1s v6p0188c1s v6p0214c2s v6p0408c1s v6p0410c1s v6p0431c2s v6p0608c2s v6p0650c2s v6p0674c2s v6p0713c2s
Davenport, C.B. et al. ... v5p0295c1s
Davenport, C.D. v5p0646c1s
Davenport, C.H. v3p0106c2s v4p0231c1s v6p0590c1s
Davenport, Cyril v4p0066c1s v4p0066c2m v4p0362c2m
Davenport, E. v1p1011c1s v3p0140c1s
Davenport, F. v1p0883c2s
Davenport, F.G. v5p0165c1s v5p0188c2s v5p0573c2s
Davenport, F.M. v5p0181c1m v6p0446c2s v6p0541c2s
Davenport, F.P. v3p0347c2s
Davenport, F.W. v3p0305c1s
Davenport, Frances G. v6p0679c1s
Davenport, G.C. v4p0018c2s
Davenport, G.E. v4p0197c1s
Davenport, G.H. v6p0138c1s v6p0584c1s
Davenport, Grace F. v5p0421c1s
Davenport, H. v1p0334c1s v6p0296c2s v6p0297c2s v6p0491c2s
Davenport, H.J. v4p0497c2s v5p0567c1s v6p0100c1s v6p0152c1s v6p0188c2s v6p0215c2s v6p0263c2s v6p0506c2m v6p0583c1s
Davenport, H.W. v6p0067c1s v6p0149c2s
Davenport, J.S. v1p0180c1s v1p0769c2s v6p0341c2s
Davenport, Louise v6p0383c1s
Davenport, R.W. v1p0664c2s v5p0551c2s
Davenport, S.T. v3p0344c1s
Davenport, W.B. v2p0164c1s
Davenport, W.Bromley v2p0384c1s
Davenport, W.E. v6p0330c2s v6p0363c1s
Davenport, W.H. v1p0643c2s v1p0915c2m
Davenport-Hill, F. v4p0431c1s
Davenport-Hill, R. v3p0422c2s
Daves, E.G. v4p0473c1m
Daves, G. v4p0406c2s
Davey, F.J. v5p0084c2s v5p0098c2s v5p0401c2s v5p0412c2s v5p0422c2s v5p0425c1s v6p0046c1s v6p0147c2s v6p0242c2s v6p0362c1s
Davey, G.J. v1p0644c1m
Davey, H. v3p0280c1s v4p0070c2s v4p0616c2s v6p0455c1s
Davey, J. v6p0656c2s
Davey, R. v1p0196c1s v1p0363c2s v1p0369c2s v1p0505c2s v1p0640c2s v1p0669c2s v1p0752c1s v1p0859c2m v1p0920c1s v1p0977c2s v1p1071c1s v2p0068c1s v2p0072c2s v2p0173c1s v2p0231c1s v2p0274c1s v2p0361c1s v2p0362c1s v2p0470c2s v3p0185c2s v3p0225c2s v3p0245c2s v3p0270c1s v3p0437c2s v3p0467c2s v4p0027c1s v4p0125c2s v4p0130c2m v4p0140c2s v4p0160c2s v4p0163c2s v4p0193c1s v4p0266c2s v4p0308c2s v4p0376c2s v4p0502c1s v4p0544c1s v4p0544c2s v4p0555c2m v4p0587c1s v4p0629c1s v5p0003c1s v5p0018c1s v5p0094c1s v5p0170c1m v5p0217c2m v5p0258c1m v5p0345c1s v5p0530c2s v6p0237c1s v6p0238c1s v6p0262c2s v6p0352c1s v6p0384c1m v6p0544c2s
Davey, R.B. v1p0776c1s
Davezac, A. v1p0207c2s

v1p0341c1s v1p0451c1s v1p0500c1s v1p0731c2s
David, A. v3p0380c2s
David, A.C. v6p0051c1s v6p0081c1s v6p0091c1s v6p0113c1s v6p0138c2s v6p0247c2s v6p0298c2s v6p0431c1s v6p0444c2s v6p0452c1s v6p0453c2s v6p0589c2s v6p0619c1s v6p0622c2s v6p0641c2s
David, Arthur C. v6p0087c2s
David, F. v4p0190c2s v4p0194c1s
David, J.S. v5p0150c2s v6p0063c2s
David, L.O. v6p0363c2s
David, T. v2p0220c2s
David, W.M. v3p0276c1s
Davidge, C.S. v4p0630c2s v4p0632c2s
Davids, E. v5p0548c1s v6p0116c2s
Davids, Edith v5p0576c1s
Davids, H. v1p0053c1s v1p0958c2s v1p1171c1s
Davids, J.L. v1p0222c1s v1p1380c2s
Davids, R.W. v3p0359c2s
Davids, T.W. v2p0470c1s
Davids, T.W.R. v1p0173c1m v1p0173c2s v1p1197c1s v2p0059c2s v2p0060c1s v2p0218c1m v2p0218c2s v4p0077c2s v5p0081c2s
Davidson, A.B. v2p0043c2s v4p0056c1s v4p0259c1s v4p0275c2s v5p0037c2s v5p0057c1s v5p0307c2s v5p0352c2s v6p0332c2s
Davidson, A.C. v1p0848c1s
Davidson, A.F. v3p0419c2s v4p0197c2s v5p0153c2s v5p0171c1s v5p0239c2s v6p0402c2s
Davidson, A.T. v1p0976c2s v1p1299c2s v2p0403c1s
Davidson, Anna v6p0391c2s
Davidson, C. v4p0184c1s
Davidson, D. v4p0162c2s
Davidson, E.A. v3p0215c1s v3p0422c2s
Davidson, F.A. v3p0118c2s
Davidson, F.A.G. v6p0218c1s v6p0562c2s
Davidson, F.E. v5p0313c1s
Davidson, F.L.M. v5p0268c1s
Davidson, G. v1p0018c1s v1p0956c1s v2p0095c2s v2p0319c1s v2p0343c2s v2p0462c2s v2p0463c1s v4p0013c2s v4p0129c2s v6p0140c2s v6p0460c2s v6p0491c2s v6p0540c1s v6p0666c2s
Davidson, G. et al. v2p0239c2s
Davidson, G.B. v1p0016c1s
Davidson, G.L.O. v5p0211c2s
Davidson, H. v1p1316c2s
Davidson, H.C. v2p0013c2s v2p0039c2s v2p0199c1s v3p0087c2s v3p0310c2s v3p0311c1s v3p0318c2s v3p0324c1s v4p0420c2s v4p0618c2s
Davidson, H.M. v1p0568c1s v1p1266c2s v6p0662c2s
Davidson, I. v5p0047c2s v5p0527c2s
Davidson, J. v1p0954c1s v1p1289c1s v3p0192c1s v3p0271c1s v3p0417c2s v4p0170c1s v4p0193c2s v4p0214c2s v4p0370c1s v4p0562c2s v4p0598c1s v5p0084c2s v5p0090c1m v5p0194c1s v5p0200c1s v5p0244c2m v5p0341c2s v5p0351c2s v5p0525c2s v5p0529c2s v5p0569c1s v6p0096c1s v6p0096c2m v6p0097c1s v6p0206c1s v6p0505c2s v6p0519c1s v6p0577c2s
Davidson, J.B. and Stevenson, W.H. v2p0014c2s
Davidson, J.H. v2p0076c1s v2p0140c2s
Davidson, J.L.S. v2p0377c1s
Davidson, J.M. v6p0131c2s v6p0283c1s
Davidson, J.W. v1p0120c1s v1p0888c1s v6p0398c1s v6p0593c1s
Davidson, L.C. v4p0154c1s
Davidson, M.G. v4p0372c1s
Davidson, Olaf v5p0212c1s
Davidson, R. v1p0683c1s v1p0823c1s v1p0841c2s v1p0869c1s v1p0923c1s v6p0013c2s
Davidson, R.C. et al. v3p0085c2s
Davidson, R.T. v1p0118c1s v3p0358c2s v5p0164c1s v6p0084c1s
Davidson, R.T. et al. v2p0384c2s
Davidson, S. v1p0118c1s v1p0128c2m v1p0690c1s v1p0825c1m v1p1035c2m v1p1338c1s
Davidson, Susan M. v5p0614c1s
Davidson, T. v1p0051c2s v1p0539c2s v1p0553c1s v1p0710c1s v1p0750c1s v1p0923c2s v1p0974c2s v1p1000c2s v1p1098c2s v1p1276c1s v1p1306c1s v1p1336c2s v2p0021c1s v2p0023c1s v2p0032c1s v2p0130c2s v2p0231c2s v2p0335c2s v2p0376c1s v2p0439c1m v3p0011c2s v3p0019c2s v3p0128c2s v3p0248c1s v3p0267c1s v3p0272c2s v3p0346c1s v3p0422c1s v4p0152c2s v4p0170c2s v4p0181c1s v4p0187c2s v4p0188c1s v4p0331c1s v4p0376c1s v4p0606c1s v5p0079c1s v5p0158c1s v5p0176c2s v5p0231c2s v5p0248c1s v5p0249c1s v5p0265c1s v5p0502c1s v5p0595c2s v5p0636c2s
Davidson, T. et al. v4p0168c2s
Davidson, T.W. v6p0191c1s
Davidson, V. v6p0071c2s v6p0612c1s
Davidson, W.L. v1p0153c1s v1p0293c1s v1p0345c2s v1p0351c1s v1p1177c2s v2p0195c2s v2p0224c1s v2p0339c2s v2p0366c1s v2p0381c1s v3p0087c1s v5p0454c1s v6p0047c2s v6p0156c2s
Davidson, W.T. v5p0114c1s v5p0305c2s
Davie, E.W. v6p0108c2s
Davie, G.M. and Brown, J.M. v2p0118c2s
Davies, A. v1p0727c2s v6p0003c2m v6p0181c2s v6p0182c1s v6p0504c1s
Davies, A.E. v5p0101c1s v6p0521c1s
Davies, A.E. and Haines, T.H. v6p0534c1s
Davies, A.L. v6p0356c1s
Davies, A.M. v2p0456c2s
Davies, C. v2p0315c2s
Davies, C.M. v1p0975c2s v1p1215c2s v1p1238c2s v1p1311c1s
Davies, D.C. v2p0141c2s
Davies, D.H. v5p0391c2s v6p0436c2s
Davies, D.J. v5p0122c2s
Davies, E. v1p0625c1s v1p1422c1s v1p1423c1s v4p0080c2m v4p0577c2s v5p0418c1s
Davies, E.A. v5p0359c1s
Davies, F.J. v4p0298c2s
Davies, G. v4p0345c2s
Davies, G.C. v1p0047c1s v2p0014c1s v2p0374c2s v3p0082c2s
Davies, G.C., Mrs. v4p0637c2s
Davies, G.S. v2p0024c1s v5p0639c1s v6p0029c1s v6p0361c2s
Davies, H. v4p0609c1s v5p0005c1s v5p0031c1s v5p0386c1s v5p0470c2s v5p0471c1s v5p0535c1s v5p0558c2s v5p0571c2s v5p0614c2s v5p0631c2s v6p0054c2s v6p0059c2s v6p0194c2s v6p0211c1s v6p0612c2s
Davies, H.B. v3p0098c2s v3p0385c2s
Davies, H.H. v5p0423c2m
Davies, H.L. v4p0565c1s
Davies, H.M. v5p0395c1s
Davies, J. v1p0009c1s v1p0057c2s v1p0134c2s v1p0265c2s v1p0414c2s v1p0421c1s v1p0490c2s v1p0559c2s v1p0740c1s v1p0781c1s v1p0874c2s v1p0983c1s v1p1043c1s v1p1301c1m v1p1372c2s v2p0410c1s
Davies, J.A. v1p0467c1s v1p0746c2s v1p0835c2s v1p1080c2s v1p1088c2s v1p1244c1s v1p1293c1s
Davies, J.D. v6p0187c1s
Davies, J.J. v3p0006c1s v3p0129c1s v3p0132c1s v3p0425c1s v4p0088c1s v4p0169c1s v4p0169c2s v4p0190c1s v4p0232c2s v4p0368c2s v4p0506c1s v4p0570c1s v5p0178c1s
Davies, J.L. v1p0047c2s v1p0060c1s v1p0117c2s v1p0241c2s v1p0249c1s v1p0251c2s v1p0286c1s v1p0290c2s v1p0337c2s v1p0423c2m v1p0440c1s v1p0546c1s v1p0650c1s v1p0684c1s v1p0687c2s v1p0813c1s v1p0830c2s v1p0857c1s v1p0869c2s v1p0981c2s v1p1031c1s v1p1041c2s v1p1050c1s v1p1103c2s v1p1302c1s v1p1360c1s v1p1360c2s v2p0083c2s v2p0280c2s v2p0370c1s v2p0476c2s v3p0006c1s v3p0250c1s v4p0117c2s v4p0156c1s v4p0455c2s v5p0194c2s v6p0125c2s v6p0490c2s
Davies, J.L.L. v1p0691c2s v2p0307c1s
Davies, J.W. v6p0088c1s v6p0457c1s
Davies, L. v6p0438c1s
Davies, L.H., Sir v5p0264c1s
Davies, L.J. v5p0109c1s v5p0112c1s
Davies, L.L. v1p1422c2s
Davies, M. v1p0023c1s v1p0150c2s v1p0264c2s v1p0324c2s v1p0429c1s v1p0774c1s v1p0864c2s v1p1185c1s v1p1238c1s v1p1327c1s v4p0274c1s v5p0135c2s v6p0455c1s
Davies, M.A. v6p0148c1m
Davies, M.R. v3p0187c2s v3p0333c1s v4p0105c1s v4p0172c1s v4p0403c2s v4p0433c1s v4p0592c1s v5p0645c1s
Davies, M.Rees v4p0511c2m
Davies, N.de G. v6p0195c2s
Davies, N.E. v2p0418c1s
Davies, Oma v6p0311c2s
Davies, Randall v3p0014c2s
Davies, S.D. v2p0087c2s v2p0317c2s v2p0386c2s v2p0411c1s v2p0430c2s v4p0518c2s v4p0569c2s
Davies, S.K. v6p0157c1s
Davies, S.W. v3p0167c2s
Davies, T. v1p0104c1s
Davies, T.F. v1p1009c1s
Davies, T.H. v4p0251c1m
Davies, T.W. v3p0193c1s v4p0155c2s v4p0376c2s v4p0417c1s v5p0484c1s v6p0285c2s
Davies, V.A. v3p0385c2s
Davies, W. v2p0024c2s v2p0377c2s v4p0074c1s v4p0077c2s v4p0562c2s v4p0576c1s v4p0598c2s
Davies, W.G. v1p0271c2s v1p0293c1s v1p0760c2s
Davies, W.M. v2p0128c1s v5p0022c2s
Davies, W.W. v2p0043c2s v3p0042c1s v3p0042c2s v4p0055c2s v4p0173c2s v4p0327c2s
Davies, Wm. v4p0251c1s
Davies-Evans, M.E. v3p0459c2s
Daviess, M.T. v1p0334c2s
Davin, N.F. v1p0113c1s v1p0193c1s v1p0500c1s v1p0661c1s v1p0734c2s v1p0839c2s v1p0914c2s v1p1234c2s v5p0009c2s
Davis and Briggs v1p1065c2s
Davis, A. v1p1250c2m
Davis, A.J. v1p1039c2s
Davis, A.M. v2p0167c2s v3p0012c1s v3p0190c2s v3p0214c1s v3p0244c1s v3p0308c2s v3p0326c1s v4p0318c2s v5p0365c1s v6p0051c1m
Davis, A.M.F. v2p0027c1s
Davis, A.McF. v2p0466c2s v4p0044c1s v4p0143c2s v4p0249c1m v4p0260c2s v4p0385c2s v5p0046c2s v5p0133c2s v5p0149c1s v5p0222c2s v6p0059c1s v6p0076c1s v6p0282c1s v6p0425c1s v6p0507c1s
Davis, A.P. v4p0308c1s v5p0410c1m v5p0410c2m v5p0429c1s v6p0324c1s
Davis, A.R. v4p0085c2s v4p0086c2s v4p0087c1m v4p0472c1s v4p0499c1s v5p0622c2s
Davis, A.S. v2p0095c2s v2p0096c1s v3p0002c1s v3p0423c1s
Davis, B. v1p1279c2s v5p0423c2s v5p0540c1m v6p0020c1s v6p0198c2s v6p0325c2s
Davis, B.G. v5p0294c1s
Davis, B.M. v5p0521c2s v5p0644c1s v6p0106c1s v6p0502c1m v6p0503c1s v6p0585c2s
Davis, B.W. v4p0443c2s
Davis, C. v1p0197c2s v1p0263c2s v1p0635c2s v1p1149c2s
Davis, C.B. v1p1328c1s v4p0215c2s v4p0418c2s v4p0553c1s v5p0233c1s v5p0236c1s v5p0239c2s v5p0381c1s v5p0439c1s v6p0036c1s v6p0127c2s v6p0143c2s v6p0297c2s v6p0452c2s v6p0453c2s v6p0463c2s v6p0543c1s v6p0649c2s v6p0674c1s
Davis, C.C. v6p0093c1s v6p0531c1s
Davis, C.D. v6p0325c1s
Davis, C.E.L.B. v1p1110c1s
Davis, C.F. v6p0611c2s
Davis, C.G. v5p0067c2s v5p0129c2s v5p0408c1s v5p0643c1s v6p0296c2s v6p0710c1s v6p0710c2m
Davis, C.H. v1p0269c2m v1p0437c1s v1p0824c1s v1p0824c2s v1p0872c2s v1p0901c2s v1p0902c2s v1p0956c1s v1p1005c2s v1p1249c2s v1p1345c2s v1p1347c2s v1p1351c2s v5p0183c2s v5p0184c1s
Davis, C.H. and Forbes, H.C. v5p0183c2s v5p0184c1s
Davis, C.H. and Griggs, J.S., jr. v4p0180c1s
Davis, C.H. and Williamson, F.S. v5p0184c1s
Davis, C.K. v4p0317c2s v4p0592c2s v5p0445c1s
Davis, C.K. and Grosscup, P.S. v4p0553c2s
Davis, C.M. v1p0117c2s
Davis, C.S. v1p0154c1m v1p0294c2s v1p1257c1s
Davis, C.T. v2p0055c2m v2p0299c1s v2p0344c2s v2p0351c1m v2p0441c1s
Davis, C.W. v3p0006c2s v3p0149c2m v3p0241c2s v3p0352c1s v3p0461c2s v5p0075c2s v5p0137c2s v5p0139c1s v5p0353c2s v5p0627c2s
Davis, D. v6p0211c1s
Davis, D.T. v4p0146c1s v5p0549c1s

Davis, Delia T. v5p0071c1s
v5p0521c2s v5p0607c2s
Davis, E. v1p0067c2s
v1p0843c1s v1p0928c2s v1p1287c2s
v3p0259c1s v3p0444c2s v4p0076c2s
v4p0092c2s v4p0215c1m v4p0326c1s
v4p0387c1s v4p0493c2s v5p0013c2s
Davis, E.B. v5p0221c2s
Davis, E.G. v6p0154c2s
v6p0666c1s
Davis, E.J. v1p0197c1s
v1p1055c1s v1p1176c1s
Davis, E.W. v1p0788c1s
v4p0583c1s v6p0079c1s
Davis, Eugene v4p0361c2s
Davis, F. v1p0372c1s
v1p1338c1s v3p0456c2s v4p0507c1s
v4p0613c1s v4p0613c2m v5p0622c1s
v6p0274c1s
Davis, F.N. v6p0201c2s
Davis, F.W. v4p0453c2s
Davis, G. v1p1018c1s
Davis, G.B. v5p0290c1s
v6p0324c1s
Davis, G.C. v2p0114c2s
v5p0298c1s
Davis, G.R. v4p0100c2s
Davis, G.T. v1p0327c1s
v6p0545c2s
Davis, G.T.B. v4p0002c2s
v4p0149c1s v4p0368c2s v4p0372c2s
v4p0374c2s v4p0622c1s v6p0413c1m
v6p0423c1s v6p0541c2s
Davis, G.W. v4p0055c2s
v4p0403c2s
Davis, G.W. et al. v5p0327c1s
Davis, H. v1p0021c2s
v1p0242c1s v1p0679c2s v1p0786c1s
v1p0991c1s v1p1157c1s v1p1404c1s
v2p0011c1s v2p0093c1s v2p0100c1s
v2p0154c1s v2p0184c1s v2p0239c1s
v2p0418c1s v2p0431c2s v3p0081c1s
v3p0388c2s v3p0445c1s v3p0468c2s
v4p0083c2s v4p0133c1s v4p0346c1s
v4p0403c2s v4p0517c1m v5p0082c1s
v5p0214c2s v5p0406c2s v5p0407c1s
v5p0409c1s v5p0548c1s v5p0566c1s
v5p0642c2s v6p0052c2s v6p0133c2m
v6p0167c2s v6p0205c1s v6p0262c2s
v6p0287c1s v6p0287c2s v6p0391c2s
v6p0426c1s v6p0481c1s v6p0515c1s
v6p0539c2s v6p0616c1s v6p0628c1s
v6p0659c2s v6p0667c1s
Davis, H. and McVeagh, W.. v6p0676c1s
Davis, H. and Smyth, C. .. v6p0222c2s
Davis, H. et al. v3p0091c2s
Davis, H.C. v5p0050c1s
v5p0567c1s
Davis, H.F. v5p0399c1s
Davis, H.H. v1p0736c1s
Davis, H.J. v6p0456c2s
Davis, H.M. v5p0393c1s
Davis, H.N. v6p0456c2s
Davis, H.R. v4p0096c1s
v4p0277c1s
Davis, H.S. v4p0083c1s
v4p0484c2s v5p0035c2s v5p0430c1s
v5p0636c1s v6p0307c1s v6p0653c2s
Davis, H.W. v1p1087c1s
Davis, H.W.C. v5p0043c1s
v5p0044c1s v6p0110c2s v6p0161c2s
v6p0562c2s v6p0616c2s
Davis, Hartley v6p0675c1s
Davis, Hayne v6p0018c2s
v6p0144c2s v6p0175c1m v6p0324c2m
v6p0485c1s v6p0485c2s v6p0564c1s
Davis, Herman S. v6p0228c2s
v6p0499c1s
Davis, Horace v5p0627c2s
Davis, I. v1p1373c1s
Davis, J. v1p0789c2s
v1p0854c1s v1p1072c1s v1p1343c2s
v1p1346c1s v1p1368c1s v2p0219c2s
v2p0400c1s v2p0418c1s v3p0408c1s
v3p0443c1s v4p0043c2s v4p0065c2s
v4p0088c2s v4p0378c1m v4p0378c2s
v4p0392c2m v5p0295c2s v5p0385c2s
v6p0345c2s
Davis, J. and Benjamin, J.P.
v1p1346c1s
Davis, J., Mrs. v5p0446c1s
Davis, J.A. v4p0457c1s
Davis, J.B. v1p0266c1s
v1p0409c1s v1p0427c2s v1p0565c2s
v1p0792c2s v1p0904c2s v1p0992c2s
v1p1073c1s v1p1132c1s v1p1155c1s
v1p1204c1s v1p1241c2s v2p0280c2s
v6p0136c2s
Davis, J.C.B. v4p0200c2s
Davis, J.D. v3p0114c1s
v3p0224c1s v4p0040c2s v5p0250c1m
v5p0308c1s v6p0061c1s
Davis, J.D. and Mallory, H.F.
v4p0302c2s
Davis, J.E. v1p0073c1s
v1p0214c2s v1p1304c2s
Davis, J.G. v1p1054c2s
v3p0111c2s
Davis, J.M. v5p0339c2s
Davis, J.P. v3p0141c1s
v4p0591c2s v5p0138c1s v5p0476c2s
Davis, J.R. v2p0259c1s
Davis, J.R.A. v4p0332c2s
Davis, J.W. v1p0212c1m
v1p0377c1s v1p0640c2s v1p1052c1s
v1p1273c1s v1p1277c2s v2p0403c2s
v3p0415c2s v4p0312c1s v4p0354c2s
v5p0211c2s
Davis, J.W., Mrs. v1p0160c1s
v1p1041c1s
Davis, Jeff. v3p0245c2m
Davis, K.B. v3p0111c2s
v4p0063c2s v5p0068c2s v5p0403c1s
v5p0615c1s
Davis, L. v3p0001c1s
Davis, L.B. v6p0092c1s
Davis, L.C. v1p0005c1s
v1p0152c1s v1p0261c2s v1p0281c1s
v1p0320c1s v1p0349c2s v1p0643c2s
v1p0680c2m v1p0855c2s v1p0953c1s
v1p1178c2s v1p1182c2s v1p1259c1s
v1p1386c2s v1p1433c2s v2p0002c1s
v2p0123c1s v3p0406c1s v6p0469c2s
Davis, M. v1p0719c2s
v5p0350c1s v5p0421c1s v5p0601c2m
Davis, M.E.M. v3p0025c1s
v3p0072c1s v3p0400c2s v4p0252c1s
v4p0373c1s v4p0386c1s v4p0531c2s
v4p0537c2s v5p0597c2s v6p0232c2s
Davis, M.R.G. v6p0589c1s
Davis, M.T. v5p0422c1s
Davis, M.W. v6p0429c1s
Davis, Mary A. v6p0138c1s
v6p0172c2s
Davis, N. v1p0638c1s
v1p1266c1s v2p0119c2s v5p0168c2s
v5p0537c1s
Davis, N.D. v1p0013c1s
v3p0017c1s v3p0124c1s v3p0191c2s
v3p0368c2s v3p0460c2s v4p0014c1s
v4p0016c1s v4p0073c2s v4p0244c1m
v4p0355c1s v4p0361c1m v4p0387c2s
v4p0601c2s v5p0074c2s v5p0077c2s
v5p0156c1s v5p0191c2s v5p0219c1s
v5p0252c1s v5p0314c2s v5p0398c1s
v5p0479c2s v5p0620c2s v5p0626c1s
v6p0172c1s
Davis, N.Darnell v4p0354c2s
Davis, N.H. v1p0356c2s
Davis, N.K. v1p1042c2s
v2p0289c2s v2p0308c2s v2p0462c2s
v3p0378c2s
Davis, Nina v5p0311c2s
Davis, O.K. v4p0019c2s
v4p0232c2s v5p0010c1s v5p0160c2s
v5p0360c1s v5p0446c1s v6p0162c2s
v6p0185c1s v6p0272c1s v6p0338c1s
v6p0362c1s v6p0398c1s v6p0477c2m
v6p0492c2s v6p0493c2s v6p0494c1s
v6p0534c2s v6p0631c1s v6p0710c2s
Davis, O.S. v6p0064c1s
v6p0208c2s v6p0399c2s v6p0490c2s
v6p0545c2s
Davis, Oscar King v6p0054c1s
Davis, P. v6p0559c2s
Davis, P.S. v1p0121c2s
v1p0229c1s v1p0240c1s v1p0686c1s
v1p0732c1s v1p0980c1s v1p1140c2s
Davis, R. v2p0460c1s
Davis, R.C. v2p0045c2s
v5p0593c1s v6p0075c1s
Davis, R.G. v6p0269c2s
v6p0597c2s v6p0600c1s
Davis, R.H. v1p0004c2s
v1p0023c1s v1p0087c2s v1p0111c2s
v1p0115c2s v1p0116c1s v1p0153c2s
v1p0277c2s v1p0329c2s v1p0334c2s
v1p0359c1s v1p0376c1s v1p0511c1s
v1p0542c2s v1p0569c2s v1p0571c1s
v1p0590c1s v1p0593c1s v1p0609c2s
v1p0693c2s v1p0730c1s v1p0737c2s
v1p0746c2s v1p0776c1s v1p0897c1s
v1p0933c1s v1p0942c2s v1p0952c1s
v1p0981c1s v1p0983c2s v1p0997c1m
v1p1020c2s v1p1070c1s v1p1196c2s
v1p1252c1s v1p1258c1s v1p1259c2s
v1p1269c2s v1p1336c1s v1p1380c1s
v1p1381c2s v1p1409c1s v1p1436c2s
v2p0271c2s v2p0309c1s v2p0402c2s
v2p0468c2s v3p0014c2s v3p0108c2s
v3p0166c2s v3p0194c1s v3p0208c2s
v3p0294c1s v3p0401c2s v3p0453c1s
v4p0014c2s v4p0016c1s v4p0019c1s
v4p0032c2s v4p0070c2s v4p0089c1s
v4p0090c2s v4p0094c2s v4p0095c2s
v4p0114c2s v4p0134c1s v4p0153c1s
v4p0168c2s v4p0174c1s v4p0181c2s
v4p0234c1s v4p0254c1s v4p0258c1s
v4p0309c2s v4p0321c1s v4p0339c1s
v4p0340c2s v4p0373c2s v4p0398c2s
v4p0420c1s v4p0425c1s v4p0425c2s
v4p0426c1m v4p0459c1s v4p0489c2s
v4p0597c2s v4p0633c2s v5p0005c2s
v5p0159c1s v5p0177c1s v5p0179c2s
v5p0249c1s v5p0251c2s v5p0276c1s
v5p0316c2s v5p0317c2s v5p0322c2s
v5p0340c1s v5p0359c1s v5p0410c2s
v5p0420c2s v5p0434c2s v5p0460c1s
v5p0465c1m v5p0507c1s v5p0508c2s
v5p0538c1s v5p0543c2s v5p0589c1s
v5p0605c2s v5p0606c2s v5p0611c1s
v5p0618c2s v5p0619c1s v5p0627c1s
v6p0051c2s v6p0087c2s v6p0100c2s
v6p0353c1s v6p0450c1s v6p0568c2s
v6p0612c1s
Davis, R.H. et al. v3p0269c1s
Davis, R.H., Mrs. v1p0819c2s
Davis, R.M. v4p0195c1s
v4p0457c2s
Davis, R.O.E. v6p0355c1s
Davis, R.P. v6p0039c1s
v6p0693c1s
Davis, R.S. v1p0221c1s
Davis, Rebecca H. v3p0430c2s
v5p0342c2s v5p0597c2s v6p0014c2s
v6p0016c1s v6p0154c1s v6p0194c1s
v6p0201c1s v6p0219c1s v6p0333c2s
v6p0466c1s v6p0665c1s
Davis, Rebecca Harding ... v5p0267c2s
Davis, Richard H. v3p0055c2s
v3p0315c1s v3p0428c1s v3p0441c1s
Davis, S. v1p0870c1s
v1p1084c2s v2p0151c2s v5p0186c2s
v5p0238c2s v5p0378c1s
Davis, S.D. v2p0156c1s
Davis, S.K. v5p0463c2s
Davis, S.M. v4p0307c1s
v4p0342c2s v4p0397c1s v4p0407c1s
v4p0457c2s v4p0475c2s v4p0527c2s
v4p0630c1s v5p0294c2s
Davis, S.R. v3p0219c1s
v3p0340c2s
Davis, Sallie J. v6p0459c2s
Davis, T.A., Mrs. v1p0393c2s
Davis, T.E. v4p0430c2s
Davis, T.H. v2p0426c2s
Davis, T.K. v2p0092c2s
v6p0060c2s
Davis, T.R. v1p0174c1s
v1p0279c2s v1p1400c2m v3p0390c2s
v4p0234c2s v4p0520c2s
Davis, V.D. v2p0297c2s
Davis, W. v1p0290c1s
v6p0208c2s v6p0304c2s v6p0572c1s
Davis, W.A. v1p0774c2s
Davis, W.D. v3p0181c1s
Davis, W.G. v5p0500c2s
v6p0128c1s
Davis, W.H. v5p0257c2s
v5p0444c2s v6p0159c2s v6p0386c1s
v6p0495c2s v6p0563c2s
Davis, W.J. v2p0476c1s
v3p0303c2s v5p0036c1s
Davis, W.L. v1p0699c2s
Davis, W.M. v1p0903c2s
v2p0047c2m v2p0051c1s v2p0074c2s
v2p0089c1s v2p0092c1s v2p0099c2s
v2p0110c2s v2p0124c1m v2p0127c2s
v2p0183c1s v2p0229c2s v2p0285c2s
v2p0316c1s v2p0319c1s v2p0393c1s
v2p0424c2s v2p0440c2s v2p0443c1s
v2p0445c1s v2p0446c1s v2p0457c2s
v2p0461c1s v2p0467c2s v2p0475c1s
v3p0108c2m v3p0151c1s v3p0169c1m
v3p0240c1s v3p0301c2s v3p0326c1s
v3p0362c1m v3p0432c2s v3p0436c1s
v3p0451c2s v4p0146c2s v4p0181c1s
v4p0197c1s v4p0222c2m v4p0322c1s
v4p0343c1s v4p0355c1m v4p0365c2s
v4p0367c1s v4p0369c1s v4p0377c1s
v4p0381c1s v4p0399c1s v4p0441c1s
v4p0441c2s v4p0485c1s v4p0507c2s
v4p0512c2s v4p0513c2m v4p0566c2s
v5p0104c1s v5p0129c1s v5p0228c2m
v5p0389c2s v5p0449c1m v5p0513c2s
v5p0569c2s v5p0601c1s v6p0004c1s
v6p0006c1s v6p0013c2s v6p0029c2m
v6p0082c1m v6p0250c2m v6p0257c2s
v6p0369c1s v6p0583c1s v6p0599c1s
v6p0624c1s v6p0661c1s v6p0693c2s
Davis, W.M. and Dawson, G.M.
v2p0475c1s
Davis, W.M. et al. v2p0089c2s
Davis, W.N. v4p0556c1s
Davis, W.P. v5p0240c1s
Davis, W.S. v5p0492c2s
Davis, W.T. v2p0184c2s
v2p0342c1s v6p0656c1s v6p0690c2s
Davis, W.W. v5p0177c1s
v6p0245c2s v6p0336c1s v6p0426c1s
v6p0500c1s
Davis, W.W.H. v1p0894c2s
v1p1388c1s
Davis, Wm.M. v4p0434c1s
Davison v3p0043c2s
Davison, A. v4p0016c2s
Davison, C. v2p0243c2s
v4p0165c2s v4p0166c1m v4p0381c1s
v4p0433c2m v4p0475c1s v5p0173c1m
v5p0302c2s v5p0540c1m v5p0554c2s
v6p0186c1s v6p0216c1s v6p0567c2s
v6p0582c2s v6p0678c1s
Davison, C.S. v4p0099c2s
v4p0267c1s v4p0303c2s v4p0385c2s
v4p0418c1s
Davison, G. v3p0330c2s
Davison, G.C. v2p0398c1m
Davison, J. v1p0097c1s
v1p0317c2s v1p0383c1s v1p1054c2s
Davison, J.M. v3p0459c2s

v4p0611c1s v5p0372c1s
Davison, L.P. v5p0050c1s
v5p0460c2s
Davison, M. v3p0312c1s
v5p0112c2s
Davison, Prof. v3p0217c1s
Davison, T. v1p0815c1s
Davison, T.R. v2p0419c1s
v3p0341c2s v6p0154c1s v6p0294c2s
v6p0300c1s v6p0435c1s v6p0603c1s
Davison, T.W. v4p0055c2s
Davison, W. v2p0046c2s
v3p0227c2s
Davison, W.J. v4p0302c1s
Davison, W.T. v4p0055c2s
v5p0060c2s v5p0372c2s v5p0493c1s
Davitt, M. v2p0228c1s
v2p0334c2s v3p0183c1s v3p0221c1s
v3p0221c2m v3p0239c1s v3p0322c1s
v4p0086c1s v4p0140c1s v4p0289c1s
v4p0328c2s v4p0458c2s v5p0419c1s
v6p0328c1s
Davitt, M. and Laing, G. . v2p0227c1s
Davol, R. v5p0021c1s
v5p0581c2s v6p0303c1s v6p0474c2s
v6p0695c2s
Davol, Ralph v6p0090c1s
Davray, H.D. v6p0208c2s
v6p0679c2s
Davy, C. v1p0161c1s
Davy, E.M. v1p1339c2m
v2p0180c2s v2p0193c1s v2p0272c2s
v2p0304c1s v3p0076c2s v3p0123c2s
Davy, E.M., Mrs. v3p0191c1s
v3p0227c2s v3p0376c2s v3p0411c1s
v4p0098c1s v4p0153c2s v4p0196c1s
v4p0253c2s v4p0591c1s
Davy, G.A. v6p0241c1s
Davy, H. v1p1377c2s
Davy, H., Mrs. v1p0036c1s
Davy, J. v1p0560c1m
Davy, J.B. v6p0509c1s
v6p0654c2s
Dawbarn, C. v6p0237c2s
v6p0702c2s
Dawber, E.G. v5p0379c1s
v5p0529c1s
Dawe, C. v5p0052c1s
v5p0113c1s v5p0157c1s v5p0187c1s
v5p0280c1s v5p0462c2s v5p0496c2s
v6p0263c2s
Dawe, Carlton v5p0273.2s
v6p0287c2s
Dawe, W.J. v5p0584c2s
Dawes, A.L. v3p0038c2s
v3p0068c2s v3p0074c1s v3p0076c1s
v3p0152c1s v3p0203c2s v3p0214c1m
v3p0235c2s v3p0294c2s v3p0308c1s
v3p0336c2s v3p0344c2s v3p0396c2s
v4p0096c2s v4p0097c1s
Dawes, C.G. v5p0149c2s
v6p0590c2s
Dawes, E.C. v1p0393c1s
v3p0381c1s
Dawes, H.L. v1p0398c1s
v3p0079c2s v3p0359c1s v3p0446c1s
v4p0072c2s v4p0129c1s v4p0129c2s
v4p0220c1s v4p0246c2s v4p0282c1s
v4p0415c2s v4p0545c1m v4p0612c2s
v5p0288c1m
Dawes, H.L. and Alden, P.. v5p0445c1s
Dawes, H.L. et al. v2p0353c1s
v4p0248c2s
Dawes, S.E. v1p0083c2s
Dawes, W.R. v1p1152c2s
v1p1269c1s
Dawkins, B. v4p0422c1s
Dawkins, C.E. v2p0481c2s
v3p0228c1s v5p0155c2s v5p0181c2s
v6p0416c2s
Dawkins, K.E. v2p0176c2s
Dawkins, R.M. v6p0102c2s
v6p0174c2s v6p0440c2s
Dawkins, W.B. v1p0042c2s
v1p0077c1s v1p0100c1s v1p0101c2s
v1p0104c2s v1p0209c1m v1p0340c2s
v1p0431c1s v1p0470c1s v1p0506c2s
v1p0706c1s v1p0720c2s v1p0751c1s
v1p0792c1m v1p0793c2s v1p0794c2s
v1p0817c2s v1p0899c1s v1p1017c1s
v1p1018c1s v1p1045c1s v1p1045c2s
v1p1092c1s v1p1180c2s v1p1369c1s
v1p1419c1s v2p0010c1s v2p0016c2s
v2p0143c2s v2p0259c2s v2p0274c1m
v2p0274c2s v3p0089c1m v3p0159c1s
v3p0240c2s v4p0068c2s v4p0146c2s
v4p0352c1s v4p0433c2s v4p0609c1s
v6p0132c2s
Dawley, T.R. v5p0241c2s
v5p0258c1s
Dawley, T.R., jr. v4p0602c1s
v5p0082c1s v5p0147c2s v5p0239c2s
v5p0241c2s v5p0258c1s v5p0408c1s
v5p0429c1s v5p0442c1s v6p0026c1s
v6p0054c2s v6p0362c2s v6p0414c2s
v6p0456c2s v6p0477c2m v6p0607c2s
Dawson, A. v5p0322c1s
Dawson, A.J. v4p0032c2s
v4p0418c2s v5p0032c2s v5p0153c2s
v5p0170c2s v5p0253c2s v5p0282c1s
v5p0349c2s v5p0364c1s v5p0387c1s
v5p0425c2s v5p0589c2s v6p0035c1s
v6p0165c2s v6p0291c2s v6p0429c2m
v6p0430c1m v6p0619c2s
Dawson, B. v3p0387c1s
Dawson, B.M. v4p0606c1s
Dawson, C. v1p0655c2s
v3p0159c1s v5p0226c2s v6p0258c2s
v6p0512c1s
Dawson, C.A. v6p0061c1s
Dawson, C.W. v6p0537c2s
Dawson, D. v2p0410c1s
v2p0420c2s
Dawson, D.L. v3p0407c2s
v4p0070c2s
Dawson, E. v1p0547c2s
v3p0221c2s v5p0522c2s v5p0588c1s
v6p0005c2s v6p0104c2s v6p0329c1s
v6p0466c2s v6p0517c2s v6p0538c2s
Dawson, E.F. v1p0336c1s
Dawson, E.R. v5p0312c1s
v5p0564c2s v5p0622c1s
Dawson, F.W. v4p0581c2s
Dawson, G. v1p0039c2s
v1p1184c2s
Dawson, G.E. v4p0151c2s
v5p0055c2s v5p0358c2s v5p0386c1s
v5p0470c1s v5p0562c1s v6p0538c1m
Dawson, G.J.C. v1p0664c1s
Dawson, G.M. v1p0466c2s
v1p0718c2s v1p0983c1s v2p0179c1m
v2p0194c2s v2p0386c2s v3p0104c2m
v3p0238c1s v3p0432c2s v3p0447c1s
v4p0085c2m v4p0086c2s v4p0486c2s
v5p0491c2m
Dawson, G.M. and Davis, W.M.
v2p0475c1s
Dawson, H.B. v1p0005c2s
v1p0033c1s v1p0113c1s v1p0362c2s
v1p0876c1s v1p0912c1s v1p1033c2s
v1p1267c1s
Dawson, H.M. v5p0267c2s
v5p0506c1s v6p0325c2s
Dawson, H.P. v2p0020c2s
Dawson, J. v2p0007c1s
v4p0039c1s v5p0184c1s
Dawson, J., jr. v1p0273c2s
v1p1429c2s
Dawson, J.H. v1p0075c1s
v2p0027c1s v2p0219c2s
Dawson, J.W. v1p0040c2s
v1p0102c2s v1p0214c2s v1p0269c2s
v1p0347c2m v1p0420c2m v1p0433c2s
v1p0434c2s v1p0466c1s v1p0467c2s
v1p0469c2s v1p0470c2m v1p0504c1s
v1p0507c1s v1p0618c1s v1p0668c1s
v1p0745c1s v1p0783c1s v1p0792c2m
v1p0793c1s v1p0899c1s v1p0960c1s
v1p1015c1m v1p1161c1s v1p1161c2s
v1p1162c2s v1p1213c1s v1p1233c1s
v1p1364c2m v1p1422c2s v2p0010c1s
v2p0011c1s v2p0024c2s v2p0043c1s
v2p0067c2s v2p0086c2s v2p0106c2s
v2p0117c1s v2p0117c2s v2p0131c1s
v2p0134c2s v2p0145c1s v2p0146c1s
v2p0149c1m v2p0173c2s v2p0174c1s
v2p0204c2s v2p0273c2m v2p0274c1s
v2p0274c2m v2p0283c1s v2p0296c1s
v2p0309c2s v2p0354c1s v2p0402c2s
v2p0413c1s v2p0421c1s v3p0041c2s
v3p0114c2s v3p0142c1s v3p0145c2s
v3p0159c1s v3p0169c2s v3p0251c1s
v4p0172c1s v4p0210c1s v4p0422c2s
v5p0057c1s v5p0198c1s v5p0306c2s
Dawson, J.W. and Carpenter, W.B.
v1p0420c2s
Dawson, J.W. et al. v2p0315c1s
v3p0091c2s
v3p0250c1s
Dawson, L.A. v4p0081c1s
Dawson, M. v4p0081c1s
Dawson, M. and Dawson, R.. v6p0089c1s
v6p0420c1s v6p0483c1s v6p0646c2s
Dawson, M.L. v5p0278c1s
v5p0403c2s
Dawson, M.M. v4p0117c2s
v4p0144c1s v4p0286c2m v4p0399c2s
v4p0464c1s v4p0465c2s v4p0542c1s
v5p0403c1s v6p0321c2m v6p0322c1s
Dawson, N. v5p0371c2s
v5p0485c2s
Dawson, O. v2p0046c1s
v2p0112c1s v2p0112c2m v2p0483c2s
Dawson, O.S. v3p0379c2s
Dawson, P. v5p0183c2s
v5p0551c1s v6p0615c2m
Dawson, R. and Dawson, M.. v6p0089c1s
v6p0420c1s v6p0483c1s v6p0646c2s
Dawson, R.L. v3p0116c2s
Dawson, S. v3p0190c1s
v3p0445c2s v4p0361c1s v4p0374c1s
Dawson, S.E. v1p0033c2s
v1p0210c1s v1p0325c2m v1p1041c2s
Dawson, T.C. v5p0075c2s
v6p0080c1s
Dawson, W. v1p0165c1s
v1p0562c1s v1p0901c2s v1p0902c1s
v1p0947c1s v1p1174c1m v2p0072c2s
v2p0107c1s v2p0129c2m v2p0239c2s
v2p0285c1s v2p0308c1s v2p0393c1s
v2p0424c2s v2p0426c2m v3p0104c2s
v3p0159c1s v3p0333c2s v4p0210c1s
Dawson, W.C. v1p0254c1s
Dawson, W.H. v2p0108c2s
v4p0062c1s v4p0560c2s v4p0583c2s
v5p0231c2m v5p0273c1s v5p0585c2s
v5p0598c1m v6p0148c2s v6p0253c1m
v6p0255c1m v6p0485c1s v6p0520c1s
v6p0629c2m v6p0632c2s v6p0633c1s
v6p0653c2s v6p0708c2s
Dawson, W.J. v4p0549c2s
v4p0551c1s v4p0614c2s
Dawson, W.O. v2p0320c2s
Day, A. v3p0215c2s
Day, A.A. v6p0199c1s
Day, A.F. v3p0394c2s
Day, A.L. v6p0524c2s
Day, A.L. and Allen, E.T.. v6p0221c2s
Day, A.L. and Holborn, L.. v5p0226c2s
v5p0237c2s v5p0371c2m
Day, A.L. and Shepherd, E.S.
v6p0418c2s
Day, A.M. v6p0494c1s
Day, B. v2p0341c2s
v4p0007c1s v4p0031c1s v4p0066c1s
v4p0319c1s v4p0528c2s
Day, Beth v4p0145c1s
Day, C. v5p0321c1s
v5p0552c1s v6p0318c2s v6p0358c1s
v6p0392c2s v6p0393c1s
Day, C.D. v5p0353c2s
Day, D.T. v4p0372c1s
v5p0223c1s v5p0377c2s v5p0378c1s
v5p0418c2s v6p0133c1s v6p0376c2m
Day, E. v5p0348c2s
v5p0433c2s v6p0060c2s v6p0061c2s
v6p0285c2s v6p0287c2s v6p0330c2s
v6p0519c2s
Day, E.C.H. v1p1289c1s
Day, E.G. v6p0085c2s
Day, E.L. v2p0245c1s
Day, F. v3p0154c1s
Day, F. et al. v2p0384c1s
Day, F.E. v6p0523c1s
Day, F.H. v3p0254c2s
v5p0448c1s
Day, F.J. v1p0004c2s
Day, F.M. v5p0026c2m
v5p0492c2s v6p0246c2s
Day, F.S. v3p0340c2s
Day, G.E. v1p0337c1s
v1p0381c1s v1p0396c1s v1p0726c2s
Day, H. v6p0386c1s
v6p0466c1s
Day, H.D. v4p0573c2s
v5p0356c1s v5p0489c1s
Day, H.F. v5p0176c1s
v6p0084c1s v6p0100c1s v6p0219c2s
Day, H.M. v1p0416c2m
Day, H.N. v1p0009c1s
v1p0106c1s v1p0130c1s v1p0205c1s
v1p0235c1s v1p0246c2s v1p0417c1s
v1p0639c2s v1p0724c1s v1p0760c2s
v1p0761c1s v1p0869c1s v1p0959c1s
v1p0998c2s v1p1002c2s v1p1043c1s
v1p1065c1s v1p1104c2s v1p1132c2s
v1p1284c2s v1p1308c1s v1p1322c1s
v2p0017c2s v2p0244c1s v2p0262c2s
v2p0414c1s v2p0446c2s v2p0447c2s
v2p0480c2s v3p0326c2s v3p0348c2s
Day, Holman v6p0038c1s
Day, J. v1p0074c1s
v1p0112c1s v1p0292c2s v1p0309c2s
v1p0590c1s v1p0991c1s v1p1086c2s
v2p0336c1s
Day, J.C. v5p0604c2s
Day, J.Q. v1p0066c2s
v1p0852c1s
Day, J.W. v4p0456c2s
v4p0533c1s
Day, L.E. v6p0074c1s
Day, L.F. v2p0023c1s
v2p0114c2s v2p0116c2s v2p0192c2s
v2p0203c1s v2p0323c2s v2p0475c2s
v3p0021c1s v3p0115c2s v3p0314c2m
v3p0465c2s v3p0471c1s v4p0028c2s
v4p0029c1m v4p0029c2s v4p0032c1m
v4p0083c1s v4p0101c2s v4p0121c2m
v4p0136c1s v4p0138c1s v4p0142c1s
v4p0150c2m v4p0160c1s v4p0218c1s
v4p0228c1m v4p0286c1s v4p0324c2s
v4p0366c2s v4p0382c2s v4p0384c1s
v4p0417c2m v4p0424c2s v4p0442c2s
v4p0523c1s v4p0538c2s v4p0544c2s
v4p0548c2s v4p0561c2s v4p0577c1s
v4p0605c1s v4p0609c1m v4p0631c1m
v5p0004c2s v5p0031c1s v5p0033c1s
v5p0070c2m v5p0085c2s v5p0141c1s
v5p0156c2m v5p0159c2m v5p0187c2s
v5p0235c1s v5p0235c2m v5p0298c1s
v5p0331c2m v5p0424c1s v5p0552c1s
v5p0579c2s v5p0639c1s v6p0032c2s
v6p0035c2s v6p0167c1s v6p0287c2s
v6p0304c1s v6p0412c1s v6p0430c2s
v6p0446c1s v6p0511c2m v6p0612c2s
Day, L.F. and Brentnall, C.F.
v6p0307c2s
Day, L.F. and Crane, W. .. v6p0470c2s
Day, L.F. and Crane, Walter
v5p0436c1s

Day, Lewis F. ... v5p0330c1s v6p0033c2s v6p0541c2s
Day, Mrs. ... v1p0385c2s v1p0904c1s
Day, O.E. ... v1p0253c1s
Day, P.B. ... v1p0846c2s
Day, R.C. ... v3p0031c2s v3p0037c1s v3p0037c2m v3p0054c1s v3p0121c2s v3p0133c2t v3p0134c1s v3p0251c1s v3p0300c1s
Day, R.E. ... v5p0483c1s
Day, S. ... v2p0064c1s v2p0219c1s v2p0219c2s
Day, S.E. ... v5p0253c2s
Day, S.J.V. ... v1p0664c2s v1p0665c1s
Day, S.P. ... v1p0140c1s v1p0177c1s v1p0211c2s v1p0359c2s v1p1390c2s
Day, T.F. ... v4p0632c1s v5p0576c2s v6p0160c1s
Day, W. ... v3p0040c1s v3p0201c1s v3p0356c2s
Day, W.C. ... v1p1239c2s v2p0240c1s v4p0078c2s v4p0226c1s v5p0034c2s
Day, W.C. and Bryant, A.P. v4p0062c2s
Day, W.F. ... v4p0062c1s v4p0140c2s v4p0212c2s v4p0227c1s v4p0371c2s v4p0483c1s v4p0500c1s v4p0625c2s v6p0152c1s v6p0264c1s v6p0386c2s
Day, W.G. ... v1p0002c1s v1p0169c1s v1p0571c2s
Day, W.H. ... v4p0502c1s
Day, W.M. ... v2p0006c1s v2p0089c1s v2p0379c1m v2p0439c2s v3p0310c2s
Day, Wm. ... v3p0438c1s
Dayot, A. ... v5p0011c2s v5p0101c1s v5p0159c2s v5p0609c2s v6p0164c1s v6p0483c1s
Dayrell, V. ... v1p0199c1s v1p0800c1s
Days, H.H. ... v6p0344c1s
Dayton, C.W. v4p0454c1s
Deaburg, M.W.Van ... v4p0143c2s
Deacon, C.F. and Burroughs, J. v6p0021c2s
Deacon, G.F. ... v1p0295c1s v1p0982c1s v1p1260c2s v1p1391c2s v2p0467c1s v3p0456c2s
Deacon, H. ... v2p0027c2s
Deaderick, D. ... v1p0920c1s
Deady, M.P. ... v1p1036c1s v2p0240c1s
Deakin, A. ... v3p0027c2s
Deakin, Beatrice ... v4p0148c1s
Deakin, Dorothea ... v6p0257c2s v6p0303c1s
Deakin, R. ... v1p0584c2s
Dealey, J.Q. ... v6p0414c1s
Dealy, P.F. ... v2p0121c2s v2p0313c2s
Dean, A. ... v1p0351c1s v1p0468c2s v1p0595c1s v5p0617c1s
Dean, A., Mrs. ... v4p0515c1s v4p0529c1s v5p0278c2s
Dean, Andrew, Mrs. ... v4p0321c1s
Dean, B. ... v4p0021c2s v4p0355c2s v4p0519c2s v5p0401c1s v6p0165c1s v6p0214c1s v6p0214c2s v6p0218c2s v6p0277c1s v6p0390c1s v6p0396c1s v6p0407c2s v6p0418c1s v6p0420c2s v6p0475c2s v6p0608c2s v6p0677c2s
Dean, B. et al. ... v6p0102c1s
Dean, B.A. ... v4p0072c2s v5p0180c1s
Dean, B.S. ... v5p0134c1s v5p0241c1s v5p0421c2s v5p0481c2s
Dean, Bashford ... v5p0320c1s v5p0323c2s v6p0589c1s
Dean, C.L. ... v1p0722c2s v1p0937c2s v1p1184c1s v1p1220c2s v2p0210c1s
Dean, C.R. ... v6p0485c2s v6p0515c1s
Dean, G.R. ... v5p0026c1s v5p0235c2s
Dean, G.W. ... v1p0768c1s v1p1270c1s v2p0042c2s v2p0243c2s v2p0277c2s v4p0377c1s
Dean, Gordon ... v5p0465c1s
Dean, H.M. ... v1p0121c1s v4p0522c1s v4p0633c2s
Dean, I.E. ... v4p0199c2s
Dean, J. ... v1p0324c2s v1p1170c2s v3p0456c2s
Dean, J.M. ... v6p0283c1s v6p0493c2s
Dean, J.W. ... v1p0156c1s v1p0162c2s v1p0330c2s v1p0334c1s v1p0335c2s v1p0337c2m v1p0455c2s v1p0466c1s v1p0493c1s v1p0540c2s v1p0708c2s v1p0825c2s v1p0910c1s v1p1190c1s v1p1242c2s v1p1318c1s v1p1409c1s v2p0077c1s v2p0113c2s v2p0120c2s v2p0374c2s v3p0020c1s v3p0236c1s v3p0254c1s v3p0286c1s v3p0325c1s v3p0439c1s v3p0463c2s v4p0079c1s v4p0095c2s v4p0122c1s v4p0210c2s v4p0225c1s v4p0252c1s v4p0295c2s v4p0317c2s v4p0551c2s v4p0622c2s v5p0048c1s v5p0069c1s v5p0203c1s v5p0339c2s
Dean, J.W. and Bache, W. . v1p0484c1s
Dean, J.W. and Deane, W.R. v1p0337c2s
Dean, M. ... v1p0155c1s v1p0228c2s v1p0308c2s v1p0359c2s v1p0444c1s v1p0444c2s v1p0639c1s v1p0803c2s v2p0299c1s v2p0306c1s v4p0326c1s v4p0371c1s
Dean, R.E. ... v5p0411c2s
Dean, S. ... v4p0106c1s
Dean, S., Mrs. ... v5p0481c2s
Dean, Sara ... v5p0509c1s
Dean, T. ... v3p0107c1s
Dean, W. ... v3p0473c2s v5p0125c1s v5p0155c1s
Deane, A.C. ... v3p0184c1s v4p0161c2s v4p0536c1s v4p0544c1s v4p0590c2m v4p0625c1s v5p0117c1s v5p0149c1s v5p0151c1s v5p0412c2s v5p0415c2s
Deane, A.M. ... v2p0360c1s
Deane, B.L. ... v6p0167c1s
Deane, C. ... v1p0306c1s v1p0536c2s v1p0662c1s v1p0809c1s v1p0910c1s v2p0063c2s v2p0276c1s v2p0345c2s v3p0471c1s
Deane, C. and Lewis, J.A.. v2p0342c1s
Deane, D. ... v5p0269c1s
Deane, G. ... v1p1246c2s v1p1250c1s v3p0169c2s
Deane, G.F. ... v1p0081c2s v1p0529c2s v1p0577c1s v1p0841c1s v1p0933c1s
Deane, I. ... v2p0158c1s v4p0614c2s
Deane, Inigo ... v4p0536c2s
Deane, J. ... v1p0466c1s
Deane, J.B. ... v1p0362c1s v1p0703c1s v1p0759c1s v1p0949c1s
Deane, J.C. ... v1p0073c1s
Deane, J.E. ... v3p0106c2s
Deane, Lady ... v2p0002c2s
Deane, M. ... v1p0371c1s v1p0602c2s v3p0046c2s v3p0264c2s v3p0312c2s
Deane, M.B. ... v3p0108c1s v3p0313c2s
Deane, M.G. ... v3p0027c1s
Deane, Mary ... v4p0431c1s
Deane, O. ... v5p0273c2s
Deane, W. ... v6p0382c2s
Deane, W.J. ... v3p0041c2m v3p0141c1s v3p0224c1s v3p0231c1s v3p0323c2s v3p0348c1s v3p0376c1s v3p0392c1s
Deane, W.R. ... v1p0457c1s v1p0737c2s v1p1392c2s v1p1393c1s
Deane, W.R. and Dean, J.W. v1p0337c2s
Deans, J. ... v3p0213c2s v3p0433c1s v4p0009c2s v4p0048c1s v4p0073c2s v4p0138c2m v4p0148c1s v4p0245c2m v4p0580c1s
Deans, James ... v4p0618c2s
Dearborn, E.B. ... v1p0337c2s v1p0910c2s
Dearborn, G.V. ... v5p0280c2s
Dearborn, G.V.N. ... v5p0470c2s v5p0480c2s v5p0533c1s
Dearborn, H. ... v1p0175c2m
Dearborn, H.A.S. ... v1p0024c1s v1p0823c1s v1p0902c2s v1p1310c1s
Dearborn, W.F. ... v6p0540c2s
Dearborn, W.L. ... v1p0160c2s
Dearing, J.L. ... v5p0056c1s v6p0334c2m
Dearle, N.B. ... v6p0508c2s v6p0665c1s
Dearsly, W.A.St.J. ... v3p0465c1s
Dearth, C.V.R. ... v5p0182c1s
Deas, A.S. ... v1p0084c2s v1p0519c1s
Deas, F. ... v2p0004c2s
Deas, F.M.P. ... v2p0462c2s v3p0156c1s v3p0455c1s
Deas, Fanny M.P. ... v2p0301c1s
Deas, G. ... v1p0832c1s
Deas, H. ... v1p0332c2s v1p1328c1s
Deas, James ... v5p0163c2s
Dease, E. ... v3p0221c1s
Deasy, H.H.P. ... v5p0034c1s v5p0048c1s v5p0579c2s
Deatrick, W.W. ... v6p0635c2s
Debar, J.H.D. ... v1p0285c2s
Debauve, A. ... v2p0270c1s
Debervill, F.B. ... v4p0123c2s
Debette, M.L.P. ... v1p0525c2s
Debray and Deville ... v1p1016c2s
Debray, P. and Claye, S.D. v3p0288c2s
Debray, X.B. ... v2p0436c1s
Debre, S. ... v4p0212c1s v4p0302c1s
Debrit, M. ... v5p0197c1s v6p0441c2s
Debs, E.V. ... v4p0017c1s v4p0284c2s v4p0315c1s v4p0315c2s v5p0535c1s v6p0599c2s
Debus, H. ... v1p0579c2s
Deby, J. ... v1p1250c2s
Decharme, C. ... v1p0099c2s
Decker, A. ... v5p0288c1s
Decker, K. ... v6p0323c1s
Decker, Sarah S.P. ... v6p0706c1s
Decker, W.F. ... v5p0434c1s
Decle, L. ... v4p0483c1s v4p0582c1s v4p0614c1s v5p0203c2s v5p0221c2s v5p0566c2s
Decle, Lionel ... v4p0550c1s
Decrow, G. ... v4p0350c1s
Dedartein, F. ... v4p0024c2s
Dedriekson, C.W.A. ... v1p1024c2s
Dee, M.J. ... v1p0235c1s
Deems, C.F. ... v1p1161c1s v2p0038c1s v2p0081c1s v2p0108c2s v2p0170c1s v2p0244c2s v2p0389c1s v3p0090c1s v3p0145c1s v3p0287c2s v3p0324c1s
Deems, Clarence ... v4p0247c2s
Deen, I.E. ... v4p0144c1s
Deeping, W. ... v6p0069c2s v6p0564c2s v6p0647c2s
Deeping, Warwick ... v6p0409c2s
Deering, A. ... v2p0089c2s
Deering, G.L. ... v4p0317c2s
Deering, M.C. ... v6p0151c1s v6p0382c1s v6p0567c2s
Deering, R.W. ... v6p0252c1s v6p0259c2s v6p0286c1s v6p0368c2s v6p0572c1s v6p0691c1s
Deering, W.H. ... v3p0147c1s
Deery, J.J. ... v5p0521c1s
Deffner, A. ... v2p0388c1s v2p0442c1s
Defoe, J.W. ... v3p0059c1s
Defouri, J.H. ... v2p0130c1s v2p0386c1s v2p0431c1s v2p0439c1s
Defrance, L. and Balet, J.C. v6p0338c2s
Degelman, C.F. ... v2p0064c2s
Degener, L. ... v2p0411c2s
Degidon, N.F. ... v6p0690c2s
Degni, J. ... v1p0382c1s
Degni, J.M. ... v1p0070c2s v1p0788c2s v1p1244c1s v2p0137c2s v2p0459c1s
Deherain, P.P. ... v4p0197c1s v4p0619c1s v5p0559c2s
Dehli, A. ... v6p0027c1s
Dehn, W. ... v5p0501c1s
Deighton, H. ... v6p0080c1s
Deir, A. ... v4p0350c1s
Deitrick, E.B. ... v4p0629c2s
Deitz, A.E. ... v5p0198c1s
Deke, F.H. ... v6p0236c1s
Del, R.E. ... v6p0478c1s
Delabarre, E.B. ... v4p0130c1s v5p0200c2s
Delafield, F. ... v3p0273c1s
Delafield, L.L. ... v1p0097c2s
Delafield, M.L. ... v1p1212c1m v3p0254c2s
Delafield, W. ... v1p0847c2s v4p0103c1s
Delafosse, J. ... v6p0237c1s
Delaire, A. ... v1p1215c1s
Delambre, J.B.J. and Houston, E.J. v4p0136c1s
Delambre, M. ... v1p0718c1s
Delamere, E.S. ... v2p0046c2s v4p0449c2s
Deland, E. ... v5p0460c2s
Deland, E.D. ... v5p0148c2s v5p0390c2s v5p0424c2s
Deland, L.F. ... v4p0206c2s
Deland, M. ... v3p0025c1s v3p0291c1s v3p0392c1s v4p0193c1s v4p0210c2s v4p0305c2s v4p0438c2s v4p0551c1s v5p0289c1s v5p0415c2s v5p0419c1s v5p0633c2s v6p0014c2s
Deland, Margaret ... v4p0265c2s v4p0414c1s v6p0025c1s v6p0038c1s v6p0045c2s v6p0126c2s v6p0203c2s v6p0215c2s v6p0216c1s v6p0264c2s v6p0308c1s v6p0461c1s v6p0681c1s v6p0696c2s
Delaney, J. ... v6p0234c2s
Delaney, J.B. ... v4p0121c2s
Delaney, J.J. ... v5p0482c1s
Delaney, T.F. ... v5p0394c2s
Delano, W.H. ... v1p0068c2s
Delanoy, F.N. ... v6p0010c1s
Delany, P. ... v6p0043c2s
Delany, P.B. ... v3p0062c1s v4p0567c1s v4p0567c2s v5p0571c1s
Delap, A. ... v1p1289c2s
Delapurne, O. ... v1p0497c2s
Delary, J.C. ... v2p0154c2s
Delattre, L. ... v5p0342c2s
Delaunay, M. ... v2p0477c1s
Delauney, G. ... v2p0396c2s

Delauney, Lieut.-Col. v5p0189c1s
Delavigne, C. v1p0931c1s
Delavigne, J.C. v1p1224c2s
v1p1265c2s v2p0185c1s v2p0431c1s
Delboeuf, J. v2p0015c2s
v4p0140c1s v4p0336c2s v4p0539c1s
v5p0343c1s v5p0641c2s
Delboeuf, M. v2p0126c1s
v2p0302c2s
Delboy, P.A. v2p0412c2s
Delbruck, H. v4p0491c2s
v5p0586c2s
Deledda, G. v6p0461c1s
Delepierre, O. v1p0001c1s
v1p0021c1s v1p0220c1s v1p0483c1s
v1p0692c1s v1p0818c2s v1p1248c2s
v1p1258c1s v1p1292c1s
Delepine, S. v3p0118c2s
Delesse, A. v1p1113c1s
Delevaque, C. v1p1368c2s
Delff, H.K.H. v2p0111c2s
v2p0151c2s v2p0244c1s
Delille, E. v2p0205c2s
v3p0034c2s v3p0036c1s v3p0068c1s
v3p0163c2s v3p0164c1s v3p0166c2s
v3p0320c2s v3p0448c2s v4p0070c1s
v4p0212c1s v4p0361c2s v4p0403c1m
v4p0603c2s
Delille, H.A. v1p0895c2m
v1p0896c1s
Delines, M. v4p0223c2s
Delisle, L. v5p0450c2s
Delitzsch, F. v1p0129c2s
v1p0581c2s v1p0682c2m v1p0684c1s
v1p0761c1s v1p0769c1s v1p0961c1s
v1p0998c2s v1p1320c1s v2p0025c2s
v2p0030c2s v2p0203c1s v2p0235c1s
v2p0292c1m v3p0040c2s v6p0045c2s
v6p0425c2s
Delk, E.H. v4p0108c2s
v4p0109c1s v4p0152c1s v4p0185c2s
v4p0345c1s v5p0114c1s v5p0305c2s
v5p0378c1s v5p0380c1s v6p0122c1s
Dell, R. v3p0203c1s
v6p0072c1s v6p0237c1s v6p0237c2m
Dell, R.E. v5p0381c1s
v5p0619c2s v6p0269c2s v6p0547c1s
Dell, S. v1p0267c1s
Dellenbaugh, F.S. v5p0400c1s
v5p0462c1s v5p0491c2s v6p0511c2s
v6p0544c2s v6p0674c1s
Delmar, A. v1p0015c2s
v1p0103c1s v1p0259c1s v1p0454c1s
v1p0649c2s v1p1137c1s v1p1155c1s
v1p1425c1s v2p0452c2s v4p0144c1s
v4p0378c1s v4p0525c2s v5p0094c1s
v6p0092c1s v6p0260c2s v6p0530c1s
v6p0627c2s
Delmar, A. et al. v2p0403c1s
Delmar, Alex. v6p0260c2s
Delmar, E. v6p0240c2s
Delmard, A. v5p0044c1s
Delme-Radcliffe, C. v6p0664c1s
Deloncle, F. v4p0172c2s
Deloney, E. v1p0905c2s
Delplace, L. v2p0328c2s
v2p0473c1s
Delta, T. v3p0293c2s
v5p0498c1s
Deltour, F. v4p0149c2s
Demain-Grange, Leighton .. v6p0261c2s
Demarest, D.D. v1p0615c2s
v1p0726c1s v3p0427c2s
Demarest, G.L. v1p0881c2m
v1p1356c1s v3p0184c1s
Demarest, J.K. v2p0290c2s
v3p0043c2s
Demarest, W.H.S. v5p0562c1s
Demarest, W.T. v6p0126c2s
Dembitz, L.M. and Eaton, A.M.
v6p0515c1s
Dembitz, L.N. v3p0307c2s
v3p0424c2s v4p0042c2s v5p0328c1s
v6p0037c2s v6p0046c1s
Dembitz, Z.M. v3p0224c1s
Dembleby, J.M. v6p0083c2s
Dembry, R.E. v1p0460c2s
v1p0886c2s
Demeny, G. v3p0331c2s
Demeritt, E.H. v1p0235c2s
Demeritt, E.W. v4p0542c1s
Demetriades, D. v4p0586c2s
Demidof, A. v1p0950c2s
Demidoff, P. and Forster, J.R.
v1p1283c2s
Deming, C. v2p0423c2s
v3p0055c1s v3p0097c1m v3p0132c2s
v3p0149c1s v3p0254c2s v3p0291c2s
v3p0296c1s v3p0359c1s v3p0415c2s
v3p0443c2s v4p0129c2s v4p0175c2s
v4p0195c1s v5p0048c2s v5p0208c2s
v6p0039c1m v6p0053c1m v6p0071c2s
v6p0226c1s v6p0227c2m v6p0232c1s
v6p0450c1s v6p0463c1s v6p0542c1s
v6p0658c1m v6p0710c2s
Deming, D.D. v1p0306c2s
Deming, E.W. v4p0368c1s
v6p0432c1s
Deming, H.E. v3p0443c2s
v5p0392c1s v6p0435c2s v6p0516c1s
Deming, H.S. v6p0080c2s
v6p0159c2s v6p0303c1s
Deming, P. v2p0002c2s
v2p0016c1s v2p0232c2s v2p0379c2s
v2p0388c1s v2p0422c1s v2p0442c2s
v3p0259c2s
Deming, T.W., Mrs. v2p0124c1s
Demming, W.F. v2p0026c1s
Demmon, I.M. and Prescott, A.B.
v6p0491c1s
Demontzey, P. v2p0162c1s
Dempsey, C. v4p0107c1s
v4p0218c1s
Dempsey, C.W. v4p0028c2s
v4p0125c1s v4p0619c2s
Dempster, B. v1p0952c1s
v2p0428c1s v3p0054c1s v3p0157c2s
v3p0266c1s v3p0291c1s v4p0336c1s
Dempster, C. v1p0043c1s
v1p0148c1s v1p0370c2s v1p0418c2s
v1p0872c1s v1p1059c2s v1p1131c1s
v1p1367c1s v2p0168c1s
Dempster, C.L.H. v5p0398c1s
v5p0557c2s v6p0091c1s v6p0584c1s
Dempster, J. v1p0404c1s
v1p0651c1s v1p0685c1s v1p0830c2s
v1p1001c1s v1p1205c1s v1p1224c2s
Dempster, R. v1p1248c1s
v1p1391c1s
Denby, C. v5p0033c2s
v5p0108c1s v5p0108c2s v5p0109c1s
v5p0110c1s v5p0113c2s v5p0158c2s
v5p0173c2s v5p0444c1s v5p0445c2m
v5p0446c1m v5p0544c1s v5p0600c1s
v5p0602c1s v6p0119c1s v6p0120c1s
v6p0398c1s
Denby, C. and Allen E.P. . v5p0477c2s
Denby, C., jr. v5p0111c2s
v5p0139c1s v5p0315c2s
Denby, H.C. v5p0109c2s
Dendy, H. v4p0283c2s
v4p0338c2s v4p0356c2s v4p0581c1s
v4p0629c2s
Dendy, H., Miss v4p0534c1s
Dendy, M. v6p0221c2s
Dene, C.H. v4p0549c2s
Dene, R.M. v4p0038c2s
v4p0210c2s v4p0308c1s v4p0528c1s
Denham, H.M. v1p0748c1s
Denham, J.F. v1p0045c2s
v1p0761c1s
Denham, T. v1p1053c2s
Denig, R.C. v4p0636c2s
Denig, R.G. v4p0198c2s
v4p0624c2s
Deniker, J. v6p0163c2s
v6p0357c1s v6p0369c2s v6p0646c1s
v6p0659c2s
Denio, E. v6p0330c2s
Denio, F.B. v2p0043c1s
v2p0044c1s v4p0055c2s v4p0058c1s
v4p0140c2s v4p0261c1s v4p0548c1s
v5p0260c2s v5p0369c2m v5p0419c2s
v5p0520c2s v6p0061c2s v6p0519c2s
Denis, H. v5p0327c1s
Denis, J. v1p0678c1s
v2p0143c2s
Denison, A. v6p0048c2s
Denison, D.T.S. v6p0167c2s
Denison, F. v2p0372c1s
Denison, G.A. v3p0380c1s
Denison, G.E. v3p0044c1s
v4p0145c1m v4p0145c2s
Denison, G.F. v4p0085c1s
Denison, G.T. v1p0209c1s
v1p0734c1s v4p0625c2s v5p0190c1s
v5p0190c2s v5p0254c1s v6p0096c1s
Denison, J.H. v2p0132c1s
v3p0280c1m v4p0016c1s v4p0027c2s
v5p0280c1s v5p0378c2s v6p0272c1s
v6p0696c2s
Denison, L. v5p0072c1s
v5p0386c2s v5p0407c1s v6p0055c1s
v6p0095c1m v6p0143c2s v6p0477c1s
v6p0551c1s v6p0562c1s v6p0672c2s
v6p0696c2s
Denison, Lindsay v6p0304c2s
Denison, M.A. v2p0239c2s
v3p0028c2s v3p0349c1s v4p0088c2s
v4p0437c1s v4p0478c1s v5p0070c2s
Denison, M.A. and Chisholm, W.B.
v4p0154c2s
Denison, T.S. v5p0409c2s
Denkin, R. v1p0494c2m
v1p0618c2s
Denloh, Edward v4p0150c2s
v4p0416c2s
Denman, Lord v1p0973c1s
Denman, Thos., Baron v5p0290c1s
Denne, S. v1p0050c1s
v1p0159c2s v1p0197c2m v1p0214c2s
v1p0216c2s v1p0309c1s v1p0359c2s
v1p0464c2s v1p0596c1s v1p0789c1s
v1p0965c2s v1p1112c2s v1p1144c2s
v1p1358c2s v1p1380c2s v1p1411c2s
Dennee, Charles v5p0395c1s
Dennehy, A. v5p0635c2s
Dennehy, A.S. v6p0238c2s
Dennehy, L. v5p0529c1s
Dennehy, W. v1p0205c1s
v1p0615c1s v1p0653c1s v1p0655c1s
v1p0656c1m v2p0124c2s
Dennehy, W.F. v2p0045c2s
v2p0084c2s v2p0087c2s v2p0124c2m
v2p0186c1s v2p0224c2s v2p0227c2m
v6p0159c1s v6p0183c1s v6p0326c1s
v6p0326c2s v6p0327c1s v6p0327c2s
v6p0694c1s
Dennehy, W.F. et al. v6p0159c1s
Dennehy, W.P. v2p0228c1s
Dennell, M.B. v5p0111c1s
Dennen, G.A. v4p0389c1s
Dennen, S.R. v1p0731c2s
v3p0155c2s v3p0199c1s v3p0463c1s
Dennett, E.R. v6p0052c1s
Dennett, J.C. v2p0136c1s
Dennett, J.R. v1p0032c1s
v1p0142c1s v1p0152c1s v1p0170c2m
v1p0182c2s v1p0191c1s v1p0200c2s
v1p0215c2s v1p0239c1s v1p0318c2s
v1p0331c2s v1p0345c2s v1p0349c2s
v1p0350c2m v1p0351c1s v1p0394c1s
v1p0442c2s v1p0450c2s v1p0505c2s
v1p0531c1s v1p0572c1s v1p0575c2s
v1p0594c1s v1p0599c2s v1p0610c2s
v1p0644c1s v1p0651c1s v1p0667c2s
v1p0694c1s v1p0733c2s v1p0736c1s
v1p0750c1s v1p0774c2m v1p0779c1s
v1p0796c2s v1p0840c2m v1p0843c2s
v1p0931c2s v1p0946c1s v1p0953c1s
v1p0981c1s v1p1041c1s v1p1041c2s
v1p1084c2s v1p1112c1s v1p1128c1s
v1p1128c2s v1p1168c1m v1p1182c1s
v1p1184c1s v1p1201c2s v1p1218c2s
v1p1219c2s v1p1223c2s v1p1226c1s
v1p1250c2s v1p1258c2s v1p1286c1s
v1p1295c1m v1p1299c2s v1p1312c1s
v1p1313c2s v1p1343c1s v1p1346c2s
v1p1355c1s v1p1362c1s v1p1393c2s
v1p1401c1s v1p1407c2s v1p1420c2s
v1p1438c1s
Dennett, M.W. v6p0365c2s
Dennett, Mary W. v6p0422c2s
Dennett, R.E. v5p0083c2s
v5p0155c2s
Denney, J. v4p0042c1s
v5p0024c1s v5p0059c2s v5p0080c1s
v6p0040c1s v6p0064c1s v6p0123c1s
v6p0341c1s v6p0353c2s
Denney, J.V. v5p0192c1s
Denning, W.F. v1p0699c1s
v1p0827c1m v1p0827c2s v1p1359c1s
v2p0095c1s v2p0239c2m v2p0254c1s
v2p0278c1m v2p028-c1m v2p0285c1m
v2p0285c2s v2p0336c2s v2p0433c2s
v3p0233c1s v3p0275c2m v3p0276c1s
v4p0306c2m v4p0366c2s v4p0367c1m
v4p0435c2s v4p0522c1s v4p0545c2s
v4p0568c1s v5p0129c2s v5p0130c1m
v5p0312c2m v5p0370c2s v5p0372c1m
v5p0372c2m v5p0441c1s v6p0140c2m
v6p0347c2m v6p0348c1m v6p0402c2s
v6p0413c1m v6p0502c1s
Denning, W.F. et al. v5p0372c1s
Denninghoff, B. v5p0451c1s
Dennis, A. v5p0555c1s
Dennis, A.H. v4p0095c2s
v4p0350c1s
Dennis, A.P. v6p0147c1s
v6p0391c1s v6p0443c1s v6p0460c1s
v6p0555c2s v6p0667c1s
Dennis, A.P.L. v6p0282c1s
v6p0370c2s v6p0543c1s
Dennis, A.W. v4p0614c2s
Dennis, Alfred P. v6p0043c2s
Dennis, Arthur P. v5p0645c1s
Dennis, G. v2p0385c1s
v3p0375c2s
Dennis, J. v1p0148c2s
v1p0310c2s v1p0323c2s v1p0347c2s
v1p0600c1m v1p0694c1s v1p0957c2s
v1p1030c2s v1p1032c2s v1p1111c2s
v1p1270c1s v1p1272c2s v1p1402c2s
v2p0146c2s v2p0186c1s v2p0246c2s
v2p0260c1s v2p0293c2s v3p0056c2s
v3p0057c1s v3p0077c1s v3p0090c2s
v3p0115c1s v3p0123c2s v3p0201c2s
v3p0253c1s v3p0335c2s v3p0336c1s
v3p0363c2s v3p0382c1m v3p0402c2s
v3p0472c1s v4p0037c2s v4p0201c2s
v4p0334c2s v4p0554c2s v5p0341c1s
Dennis, J., jr. v3p0363c1s
v6p0223c2s v6p0597c2s
Dennis, J.F. v4p0323c2m
Dennis, J.G. v6p0173c1s
Dennis, J.H. v6p0686c2s
Dennis, J.S. v4p0374c2s
v5p0111c1s v6p0421c2s
Dennis, L.C. v5p0048c1s
v5p0614c1s
Dennis, M. v5p0102c2s
Dennis, T.F. v4p0434c1s
Dennis, W. v1p1293c1s
v1p1310c2s v4p0531c1s
Dennis, W.H. v3p0245c1s
Dennison, D.T.S. et al. .. v4p0629c2s
Dennison, Dr. v1p0284c1s
Dennison, E.W. v6p0161c1s
Dennison, G.T. v4p0086c2s
Dennison, H. v1p0351c1s

Dennison, H.M. v1p0282c2s
Dennison, J.H. v2p0074c2s
Dennison, U. v5p0559c1s
Dennison, W. v5p0291c2s v6p0091c1s v6p0577c1s
Dennison, W.E. v4p0269c1s
Denniston, W.T. v4p0592c2s
Denny, A. v4p0551c2s
Denny, E.I. v4p0084c2s
Denny, J. v5p0514c2s v5p0577c1s
Denny, M.B. v6p0315c2s
Denny, W.A.C. v6p0097c1s
Dennys, N.B. v1p0985c2s v1p1009c2s v4p0105c2s
Denovan, W. v3p0417c2s v4p0559c2s
Denslow, A.E. v4p0233c1s
Denslow, V. v4p0131c2s v4p0602c1s
Denslow, V.B. v1p0222c1s v1p0235c1s v1p0274c2s v1p0538c1s v1p0721c2s v1p0843c2s v1p0906c1s v1p1048c1s v1p1232c2m v1p1282c1s v1p1346c2s v1p1349c1s v1p1378c1s v2p0050c1s v2p0098c2s v2p0347c1s v4p0080c2s v4p0455c1s v5p0014c2s
Denslow, V.B. and Blake, L.D. v2p0478c1s
Denslow, Van Buren v4p0017c2s v4p0043c2s v4p0044c2s v4p0167c2s v4p0188c2s v4p0262c2s v4p0518c1s v4p0541c2s v4p0608c1s v5p0268c2s
Densmore, E. v6p0493c2s
Densmore, F. v6p0494c1s
Densmore, Frances v6p0316c2m
Densmore, H. v5p0367c1s
Dent, C. v3p0009c1s v3p0475c2s v4p0385c2s
Dent, C.T. v4p0093c1s v4p0190c1s
Dent, E.A. v6p0037c2s v6p0038c1s
Dent, E.J. v1p0246c2s
Dent, Elsie A. v6p0289c1s
Dent, J.C. v1p0556c1s v1p0957c2s v1p1069c1s
Dent, N. v6p0092c2s v6p0573c1s
Dent, R.K. v5p0070c1s v5p0236c1s v5p0333c1s
Dent, T. v6p0364c2s
Dent, T.W. v1p1317c2s
Dent, W.Y. v3p0059c2s
Denton, C.J. v4p0379c2s
Denton, H.St.A. v4p0114c1s v4p0293c2s
Denton, J.B. v1p1390c2s v1p1391c2s v3p0102c1s v3p0121c2s v3p0239c2s v3p0353c2s v3p0386c1s v3p0457c2m
Denton, S. v6p0138c1s v6p0377c2s
Denton, W. v1p0864c1m
Denyer, C.H. v4p0565c2s v5p0273c1s v5p0340c2s v6p0117c1s
Denza, F. v1p0827c2s
Depasse, H. v2p0165c2s
Depew, C. and Hall, J. v3p0449c1s
Depew, C.M. v3p0184c2s v3p0244c2m v3p0455c2s v4p0125c2s v4p0162c1s v4p0214c1s v4p0306c2s v4p0323c1s v4p0553c1s v5p0477c2s v5p0562c2s v6p0213c1s v6p0383c2s
Depew, C.M. and Flower, R.P. v5p0289c1s
Depew, C.M. et al. v4p0123c1s v4p0384c1s
Depoele, C.J.Van v2p0137c2s
Deppen, L.G. v4p0225c1s
Depping, G. v1p0206c1s v1p0744c1s
Deprez, F. v2p0250c1s
Deranco, C. v2p0411c1s
Derby, A. v2p0061c2s v2p0071c2s v2p0176c2s v2p0185c2s
Derby, C.H. v1p1232c1s
Derby, E.H. v1p0016c1m v1p0151c1s v1p0307c2s v1p0833c2s v1p0911c2s v1p0921c2s v1p0956c1s v1p1038c2s v1p1077c1m v1p1192c1s v1p1250c1s v1p1297c2s v1p1321c2s v1p1343c2s v1p1348c1s v1p1349c1s v1p1351c2s v1p1352c1s v1p1354c1s v1p1354c2s
Derby, Earl v1p1243c1s
Derby, Earl of v1p0657c2s
Derby, G.A. v5p0283c2m v5p0436c1s
Derby, L.G. v4p0421c2s
Derby, O.A. v1p0799c1s v2p0055c1m v2p0117c2m v2p0278c2s v3p0053c2s v3p0116c2s v3p0264c1s v3p0285c1s v3p0473c2s v4p0366c2s v4p0367c1s v5p0075c2s v5p0359c2s v5p0382c2s v5p0510c2s v5p0582c2s v5p0583c2s v6p0080c1m v6p0424c2s
Derby, R.A. and Woodgate, W.B. v6p0071c2s
Dercum, F. v1p0872c2s v1p1177c2s
Derechef, R. v4p0336c2s v4p0440c2s
Dering, E. v3p0359c2s
Dering, E.H. v2p0246c1s v3p0058c2s v3p0207c2s v3p0428c1s v3p0429c1s
Dering, R.G. v3p0411c2s
Derjavin, G. v2p0381c2s
Derleth, C., jr. v6p0129c1s
Dernjac, J. v3p0358c2s
Deroulede, P. v1p1178c2s v1p1330c1s v6p0254c1s
Derr, W.L. v4p0470c2s v5p0477c2s
Derrick, F. v1p0076c2s v1p0888c1s v1p1261c2s
Derry, Bishop of v2p0310c1s
Derthick, W.M. v4p0359c2s v4p0388c2s v4p0448c1s
Derwent, J.L. v2p0225c2s
Dery, V.D. v1p0328c1s v1p1249c1s v1p1304c2s
Desart, Countess of v3p0230c2s
Desart, E. v5p0388c2s
Desart, Earl of v1p0537c2s v1p0544c2s
Desart, Ellen, Countess Dowager of v6p0245c1s
Desart, H. v5p0636c1s
Desart, Lord v1p1091c2s
Deschamps, E. v6p0589c1s
Deschamps, G. v6p0236c1s v6p0666c1s
Deschanel, A.P. v1p1289c2s
Deseret, P. v1p1004c2s
Deshler, C. v1p0251c2s
Deshler, C.D. v1p0033c2s v1p0328c2s v4p0150c2s
Deshler, D. v1p0375c2s
Deshon, F. v1p0869c2s v1p1116c1s
Deshon, G. v1p0117c1s v1p0853c1s v1p1059c1s v1p1126c1s v3p0378c2s
Desi, E.D. and Smith, F.F. v4p0586c2s
Desjardins, P. v4p0017c1s
Desjardins, S.E. v6p0415c1s
Deslandres, M.H. v4p0556c2s
Desmond, A.J. v2p0248c1s
Desmond, D. v3p0233c1s v3p0296c1s v3p0418c1s
Desmond, H.J. v3p0242c1s v5p0297c2s v6p0353c2s
Desmond, H.W. v4p0023c2m v4p0024c2s v4p0474c1s v6p0055c2s v6p0113c1s v6p0158c2s v6p0453c2s v6p0546c1s v6p0596c2s
Desmond, M.E. v5p0630c1m v6p0284c1s v6p0565c1s v6p0697c2s
Desmond, R.E. v6p0041c2s v6p0091c2s v6p0326c2s v6p0454c2s
Desnoyers, C. v1p0154c1s
Desor, E. v1p0025c1s v1p1038c2s v1p1226c1s v1p1271c1s
Desor, M. v1p0524c1s v1p1155c1s
Despard, M. v1p0883c2s v1p0917c1s
Despret, M. v1p1251c2s
Desprez, F. v1p0790c1s v1p1362c2s
Dessaix, E. v5p0233c1s
Dessaulles, M.L.A. v1p0476c2s
Dessler, W.C. v1p0619c2s
Dessoir, M. v3p0206c2s v3p0263c2s v4p0325c2s v4p0373c2s v4p0542c1s
Destailleur, A. v6p0241c2s
Destree, O.G. v4p0510c2s
Detain, C. v1p0732c1s
Detlef, C. v1p0263c2s
Detmers, H.J. v2p0204c2s v2p0428c2s
Detrick, C.R. v6p0264c1s
Deulin, C. v3p0116c1s
Deusen, E.M.Van v2p0454c1s
Deusen, E.Van v6p0151c1s
Deusen, G.W.Van v4p0216c2s v5p0032c1s v5p0032c2s v5p0033c1s v5p0200c1s v5p0253c1s v5p0373c1s v5p0619c1s
Deutsch, G. v5p0308c1s v5p0645c2s
Deutsch, J. v2p0049c1s
Devar, C.S. v1p0713c1s
Devas, C.S. v2p0245c1m v2p0248c1s v2p0464c1s v3p0138c2s v3p0200c1s v3p0324c1s v3p0364c1s v3p0387c1s v3p0397c2s v3p0398c2s v3p0412c2s v4p0450c1m v4p0532c2s v4p0533c1s v5p0134c2s v5p0158c1s v5p0175c2m v5p0383c2s v5p0386c1s v5p0500c2s v6p0368c1s v6p0536c2s v6p0601c1s
Deveaux, E. v5p0644c1s
Devens, C. v1p0518c2s
Dever, M. v6p0705c1s
Dever, Mary v6p0218c1s
Devereaux, A.W. v6p0351c2s
Devereaux, G.M. v2p0412c1s
Deverell, E. v5p0527c1s
Deverell, E.M. v5p0053c2s
Deverell, W.R. v1p1154c2s
Devereux, A.F. v3p0172c1s
Devereux, E. v3p0101c1s v3p0135c1s
Devereux, G. v6p0547c1s
Devereux, G.H. v1p0780c2s
Devereux, W. v6p0198c2m v6p0225c1s
Devey, J. v2p0085c2s
Deville and Debray v1p1016c2s
Deville, H.St.C. v1p0225c1s
Devine, E.J. v3p0315c1s v4p0086c2s v5p0500c1s
Devine, E.T. v4p0116c2s v5p0202c1s v5p0273c1s v5p0340c2s v5p0384c2s v5p0425c2m v5p0458c2s v5p0459c2s v5p0558c2s v6p0059c2s v6p0109c2m v6p0144c2s v6p0308c2s v6p0405c2s v6p0436c1s v6p0453c2s v6p0492c2s v6p0509c2s v6p0518c1s v6p0536c1s v6p0568c1s v6p0568c2m v6p0638c1s v6p0660c1s
Devine, F.P. v3p0262c2s
Devinney, J.A. v1p1385c2s
Devins, J.B. v4p0104c1s
Devlin, R.T. v2p0355c1s
Devon, Charlotte D. v4p0063c1s
Devonshire, Duke of v5p0514c1s
Devonshire, E. v3p0457c1s
Devonshire, R.S. v6p0631c1s
Devoore, A. v5p0628c2s
Devoore, Ann v6p0292c1s v6p0467c1s
Devos, C.S. v2p0142c1s
Devoy, J. et al. v3p0163c1s
Devrient, H. v5p0417c1s
Dew, G.E. v2p0297c2s
Dew, L.E. v5p0395c1s v6p0264c1s v6p0336c2s v6p0680c2s
Dew, T.R. v1p1100c1s
Dewar and Liveing v1p1233c2s v3p0316c2s
Dewar, A. v3p0145c2s
Dewar, D. v4p0491c2s
Dewar, G.A. v5p0062c2s
Dewar, G.A.B. v4p0081c2s v4p0428c1s v5p0063c1s v5p0140c2s v5p0209c1s v5p0255c1s v5p0345c2s v5p0425c2s v5p0433c1s v5p0574c1s v5p0633c1s v6p0020c2s v6p0022c1s v6p0053c1s v6p0067c2s v6p0155c2s v6p0178c1s v6p0227c1s v6p0320c1s v6p0378c1s v6p0455c1s v6p0457c2s v6p0459c1s
Dewar, H. v1p0710c2s
Dewar, J. v1p0747c2s v3p0167c2s v3p0311c1s v4p0008c2s v4p0036c1s v4p0204c1s v4p0420c1s v5p0277c2m v5p0397c1s v5p0537c2s v6p0082c1s v6p0159c2s v6p0248c2m v6p0312c2s v6p0378c2m v6p0643c1s
Dewar, J. and Liveing, G.D. v4p0540c2m v5p0037c2s
Dewar, J. and Liveing, S.D. v5p0614c1s
Dewar, J. and Living, G.D. v3p0125c1s
Dewar, J. and Pattison-Muir, M.M. v4p0221c1s
Dewar, Prof. v3p0232c2s
Dewar, T.I. v3p0272c2s
Dewar, T.J. v2p0199c1s
Dewar, W. v5p0305c2s v6p0420c1s
Dewart, E.H. v1p1111c2s v4p0502c2s v5p0577c1s v6p0519c1s
Dewe, J.A. v6p0566c1s v6p0609c1s v6p0644c2s
Dewees, C. v1p0452c1s v1p0862c2s
Dewes, A. v1p0802c2s
Dewey, A. v2p0052c1s
Dewey, C. v1p0077c1s v1p0265c1s v1p0265c2s v1p0485c2s v1p0524c1s v1p0794c1m v1p0943c2s
Dewey, C.D. v1p0077c2s
Dewey, C.F. v4p0492c2s v5p0219c1s v5p0597c1s v5p0631c2s
Dewey, C.M. v1p0057c2s v1p0794c1s
Dewey, D.R. v3p0160c2s v3p0408c2s v4p0532c2s v4p0555c2s v5p0616c2s v6p0141c1s
Dewey, E.H. v5p0203c2s
Dewey, E.W. v5p0099c1s
Dewey, F.H. v5p0088c1s v5p0173c1s
Dewey, J. v2p0240c2s v2p0244c1s v2p0280c1s v2p0339c2s

v2p0358c1m v2p0410c2s v2p0414c2s
v2p0477c2s v3p0143c1s v3p0185c1s
v3p0237c2s v3p0255c2s v3p0287c1s
v3p0329c2s v3p0335c2s v3p0348c1s
v3p0348c2s v3p0384c2s v4p0103c2s
v4p0172c1s v4p0179c2m v4p0188c2m
v4p0196c2s v4p0257c1s v4p0369c1s
v4p0382c1m v4p0396c1s v4p0476c2s
v4p0480c2s v4p0481c1s v4p0514c2s
v4p0539c1s v4p0573c2s v5p0179c1s
v5p0180c2s v5p0198c1s v5p0256c2s
v5p0288c2s v5p0370c1s v5p0416c1s
v5p0465c2s v5p0470c2s v5p0511c1s
v5p0512c2s v5p0534c2s v5p0578c2s
v6p0057c2s v6p0202c2s v6p0216c1s
v6p0251c1s v6p0428c2s v6p0486c1s
v6p0521c2s v6p0563c2s v6p0581c1s
v6p0610c1s
Dewey, J. et al. v5p0511c1s
Dewey, John v6p0002c1s
Dewey, L.H. v6p0286c2s
Dewey, L.M. v6p0145c1s
v6p0156c1s v6p0320c1s
Dewey, M. v1p0149c1s
v1p0206c1m v1p0628c2s v1p0742c1m
v1p0742c2m v1p0743c1s v1p0743c2m
v1p0744c1s v1p0796c1s v2p0052c1s
v2p0070c2s v2p0256c1m v2p0257c1s
v3p0070c1s v3p0249c2s v3p0304c2s
v3p0445c2s v5p0095c1s v5p0097c1s
v5p0336c1s v5p0337c1s v5p0466c2s
v6p0193c1s v6p0371c1s v6p0374c2s
v6p0574c1s
Dewey, M. and Biscoe, W.S.
v5p0334c2s
Dewey, M. et al. v1p0742c2s
v6p0017c1s
Dewey, M.E. v4p0281c1s
v4p0282c1s v4p0282c2m
Dewey, Melvil v6p0373c1s
v6p0375c1s
Dewey, O. v1p0014c1s
v1p0029c1s v1p0035c2s v1p0109c2s
v1p0120c2s v1p0123c2s v1p0189c2s
v1p0217c1s v1p0218c2s v1p0223c2s
v1p0239c2m v1p0240c1s v1p0240c2s
v1p0243c2s v1p0253c2s v1p0257c2s
v1p0264c1s v1p0264c2s v1p0285c1m
v1p0286c1s v1p0291c1m v1p0293c1s
v1p0298c2s v1p0338c1s v1p0339c2s
v1p0348c1s v1p0391c1s v1p0404c1s
v1p0487c1s v1p0528c2m v1p0711c1m
v1p0741c2s v1p0756c2s v1p0769c1m
v1p0769c2s v1p0846c2s v1p0868c2s
v1p0869c1s v1p0869c2s v1p0932c2s
v1p0944c2s v1p0949c2s v1p0967c1s
v1p1028c1s v1p1042c2s v1p1058c1s
v1p1065c1s v1p1069c2s v1p1074c1s
v1p1085c1m v1p1087c2s v1p1093c1m
v1p1094c1s v1p1095c1s v1p1096c2s
v1p1097c1s v1p1100c1s v1p1101c2s
v1p1102c2s v1p1120c1s v1p1139c2s
v1p1160c2s v1p1177c1s v1p1206c1s
v1p1244c2s v1p1270c1s v1p1277c2s
v1p1300c2s v1p1340c1m v1p1340c2s
v1p1341c1s v1p1386c1s
Dewey, Prof. v1p1412c1s
Dewey, R. v5p0172c2s
v5p0291c2s
Dewey, R.S. v1p0477c2m
v1p0606c1s v3p0216c2m
Dewey, S. v4p0007c1s
v4p0014c2s v4p0030c1s v4p0179c2s
v4p0211c1s v4p0211c2s v4p0213c2s
v4p0356c2s v4p0425c1s v4p0528c2m
v4p0557c2s v5p0031c1s v5p0125c1s
v5p0130c1s v5p0167c1s v5p0325c1s
v5p0326c2s v5p0432c1s v6p0019c2s
v6p0238c2s v6p0395c2s v6p0480c1s
Dewey, S. and Hellig, S. . v6p0302c2s
Dewhurst, F.E. v6p0663c1s
Dewhurst, W. v5p0161c2s
v5p0382c2s v6p0310c2s v6p0474c2s
Dewi v6p0117c1s
Dewick, E.F. v1p0865c1s
Dewick, E.S. v5p0458c2s
v5p0470c1s
Dewing, B.F. v6p0172c2s
Dewing, T.W. et al. v6p0662c2s
Dewitz, J. v5p0481c1s
v5p0506c1s
Dewsnup, E.R. v6p0141c1s
Dewson, F.A. v4p0172c1s
v5p0337c2s v5p0564c1s
Dex, L. v4p0154c2s
Dexler, H. and Freund, L.. v6p0184c1s
Dexter, E. v1p0457c1s
Dexter, E.C. v6p0231c2s
v6p0518c2s
Dexter, E.G. v5p0143c1s
v5p0170c1s v5p0511c1m v5p0560c1s
v5p0624c1m v6p0008c1s v6p0025c1s
v6p0094c1s v6p0135c2m v6p0136c1s
v6p0141c2s v6p0232c1s v6p0289c2s
v6p0364c1s v6p0432c2s v6p0623c2s
Dexter, F. v1p0324c1s
v1p0453c2s v1p0596c1s v1p0958c1s
v1p1008c1s v1p1009c1s v1p1083c1s
v1p1132c2s
Dexter, F.B. v2p0129c1s
Dexter, G.B. v3p0445c2s
Dexter, H.M. v1p0148c2s
v1p0160c1s v1p0253c1s v1p0253c2s
v1p0255c1s v1p0289c2s v1p0290c1s
v1p0290c2m v1p0336c1s v1p0382c2s
v1p0398c1s v1p0646c1s v1p0731c2s
v1p0742c1s v1p0743c1s v1p0910c2s
v1p0971c2s v1p1010c1s v1p1068c1s
v1p1112c1s v1p1181c1s v1p1302c1m
v2p0342c1s v3p0080c2s v3p0096c1s
v3p0104c1s v3p0248c1s v3p0332c2s
v3p0420c1s v5p0038c2s v5p0516c1s
Dexter, H.S. v1p0424c1s
v1p0642c2s v1p0918c1s
Dexter, M. v5p0133c1s
Dexter, N. v2p0094c1s
Dexter, R. v1p0438c2s
Dexter, S. v3p0017c1s
v3p0059c1s v3p0099c2s v4p0078c2s
Dexter, S.S. v2p0451c1s
Dexter, W. v6p0179c2s
Dexter, W.P. v1p0224c1s
v1p1127c2s
Dey, F.V. v6p0354c1s
Dey, F.V.R. v5p0452c1s
Deykin, W.R. v5p0189c2s
Deyo, M. v3p0422c2s
Dharmapala, H. v5p0081c2s
Dhruva, H.H. v4p0279c1s
Dhu, M. v6p0562c2s
Dhuv, S. v1p1127c2s
Diack, E.S. v5p0635c1s
Diack, W. v4p0509c1s
v5p0084c1s v5p0095c2s v5p0475c2s
v6p0356c2s v6p0425c1s v6p0484c2s
v6p0578c2s v6p0709c1s
Diack, Wm. v6p0345c2s
Dial, G.W. v6p0249c1s
Diamond, H.W. v1p0880c1s
Diarista, A. v5p0300c1s
v5p0331c1s v5p0429c2s v6p0501c2s
Diaz, A.M. v1p0444c1s
v1p0755c2s v1p1011c1s v1p1159c2s
v1p1219c1s v3p0335c1s v3p0395c2s
v4p0269c1s v5p0455c1s v5p0532c1s
Diaz, A.M., Mrs. v4p0447c2s
v4p0630c2m
Diaz, Abby M. v3p0377c2s
Diaz, P. v3p0475c1s
Dibble, G.B. v6p0209c2s
Dibble, M.C. v5p0100c1s
Dibblee, G.B. v4p0321c1s
v6p0517c1s
Dibdin, E.R. v2p0118c1s
v4p0028c1s v4p0074c1s v4p0168c1s
v4p0182c2s v4p0336c1s v4p0352c2s
v4p0516c1s v5p0012c2s v5p0216c1s
v5p0633c1s v6p0021c1s v6p0381c1s
v6p0622c2s v6p0651c1s
Dibdin, E.Rimbauldt v5p0084c2s
Dibdin, J.C. v2p0345c1s
Dibdin, L.F. v2p0263c1s
Dibdin, L.T. v4p0527c1s
v4p0609c1s v5p0489c2s
Dibdin, T.F. v1p0132c2s
Dibdin, W.J. v3p0250c2s
v4p0331c2s
Dibert, Olive v6p0121c1s
Dicey, A.V. v1p0016c2s
v1p0031c1s v1p0086c2s v1p0099c1s
v1p0113c1s v1p0157c2s v1p0173c1m
v1p0176c1s v1p0177c2m v1p0191c2s
v1p0204c1s v1p0219c2s v1p0220c2s
v1p0270c1s v1p0270c2s v1p0293c1s
v1p0319c2s v1p0342c2s v1p0344c1s
v1p0409c2s v1p0410c2m v1p0411c2s
v1p0412c1s v1p0412c2m v1p0413c1s
v1p0427c1s v1p0430c1m v1p0472c1s
v1p0475c1s v1p0476c1m v1p0479c2s
v1p0481c1s v1p0487c1s v1p0491c2s
v1p0492c2m v1p0510c2s v1p0511c1s
v1p0511c2m v1p0521c1s v1p0529c2s
v1p0544c2m v1p0557c2s v1p0559c2m
v1p0584c1s v1p0593c2s v1p0611c2s
v1p0632c1s v1p0647c1s v1p0652c2s
v1p0653c1s v1p0655c1s v1p0656c1s
v1p0691c2s v1p0694c2s v1p0728c1s
v1p0729c1s v1p0729c2s v1p0730c1s
v1p0734c2m v1p0741c2s v1p0771c1s
v1p0782c1s v1p0783c1s v1p0839c2s
v1p0849c1m v1p0896c1s v1p0962c1s
v1p0962c2s v1p0987c2s v1p0995c2s
v1p1006c2s v1p1027c1s v1p1032c2s
v1p1033c1s v1p1058c1s v1p1067c1m
v1p1072c1s v1p1072c2s v1p1094c1s
v1p1108c1s v1p1133c1s v1p1217c2s
v1p1235c1s v1p1243c1s v1p1252c1s
v1p1280c1s v1p1304c2s v1p1305c2s
v1p1306c1s v1p1308c1m v1p1314c1s
v1p1321c1s v1p1326c2s v1p1330c2s
v1p1378c1m v1p1405c1s v2p0001c1s
v2p0045c2s v2p0056c1m v2p0084c1s
v2p0090c2s v2p0107c2s v2p0108c1s
v2p0115c2m v2p0116c1s v2p0135c2s
v2p0141c2s v2p0142c2m v2p0143c1s
v2p0153c2s v2p0154c1s v2p0154c2s
v2p0164c2s v2p0165c1s v2p0170c2s
v2p0171c1s v2p0174c2s v2p0180c1s
v2p0186c1m v2p0186c2s v2p0187c2m
v2p0189c1m v2p0189c2s v2p0191c2s
v2p0192c1m v2p0206c1m v2p0224c2m
v2p0225c1s v2p0225c2s v2p0226c1s
v2p0231c2s v2p0269c2s v2p0270c1s
v2p0277c2s v2p0280c2s v2p0282c2s
v2p0288c2m v2p0291c1s v2p0325c2s
v2p0327c2s v2p0333c1s v2p0336c2s
v2p0371c2s v2p0384c2s v2p0400c1s
v2p0428c2s v2p0429c1s v2p0438c2s
v2p0440c2s v2p0444c1s v2p0445c1s
v3p0106c1s v3p0138c1m v3p0144c1s
v3p0160c2s v3p0161c1s v3p0220c2s
v3p0226c1s v3p0296c1s v3p0321c2s
v3p0337c2s v3p0348c2s v3p0356c1s
v3p0382c1s v3p0417c2s v3p0441c1s
v3p0462c1s v3p0464c1s v4p0168c1s
v4p0181c2m v4p0196c1s v4p0211c2m
v4p0212c1s v4p0238c2m v4p0266c1s
v4p0287c2s v4p0290c2s v4p0307c1m
v4p0392c2s v4p0444c2s v4p0578c1s
v5p0016c2s v5p0066c1s v5p0145c1m
v5p0189c1s v5p0190c1m v5p0190c2s
v5p0193c1s v5p0221c1s v5p0245c1s
v5p0257c2s v5p0285c2s v5p0327c2s
v5p0329c1s v5p0439c1s v5p0600c2s
v5p0631c2s v6p0012c2s v6p0057c2s
v6p0108c1s v6p0110c2s v6p0121c2s
v6p0126c2s v6p0140c1s v6p0146c1s
v6p0192c1s v6p0196c2s v6p0205c2s
v6p0208c2s v6p0213c2s v6p0235c2s
v6p0240c1s v6p0242c1s v6p0269c1s
v6p0269c2m v6p0270c1m v6p0270c2s
v6p0293c1s v6p0293c2m v6p0295c2s
v6p0337c1s v6p0360c1s v6p0367c1s
v6p0385c2s v6p0391c2m v6p0407c1s
v6p0424c1s v6p0447c2s v6p0473c1s
v6p0481c1s v6p0492c2s v6p0508c2m
v6p0551c2s v6p0573c2s v6p0577c2s
v6p0616c2m v6p0651c2m v6p0681c2s
v6p0682c1s
Dicey, A.V. and Bryce, J.. v5p0606c1s
Dicey, A.V. and Webb, A. . v5p0433c1s
Dicey, A.V. et al. v4p0476c1s
Dicey, C. v6p0542c1s
Dicey, E. v1p0017c2s
v1p0029c2s v1p0080c2s v1p0114c2s
v1p0209c2s v1p0301c1s v1p0334c1s
v1p0395c1s v1p0395c2m v1p0396c1s
v1p0396c2s v1p0408c2m v1p0502c2s
v1p0517c1s v1p0524c2s v1p0549c1s
v1p0575c2s v1p0605c1s v1p0615c2s
v1p0634c1s v1p0641c1s v1p0671c1s
v1p0672c1s v1p0738c1s v1p0750c1s
v1p0874c2s v1p0893c1s v1p0895c2s
v1p0917c1s v1p0933c1s v1p0962c1s
v1p0969c1s v1p0977c1s v1p1024c1s
v1p1093c2s v1p1157c1s v1p1160c2s
v1p1238c1s v1p1331c1s v1p1346c2s
v1p1352c2s v1p1354c1s v1p1384c1s
v2p0133c2s v2p0134c1m v2p0134c2s
v2p0135c1s v2p0189c1m v2p0189c2s
v2p0423c2s v3p0067c1s v3p0131c1s
v3p0137c2s v3p0182c2s v3p0183c1m
v3p0337c1s v3p0360c2s v3p0437c2s
v4p0006c2m v4p0042c1s v4p0078c2s
v4p0172c2s v4p0237c2s v4p0238c2s
v4p0239c2s v4p0289c2s v4p0290c1s
v4p0296c2s v4p0472c1s v4p0491c2s
v4p0495c1s v4p0495c2s v4p0544c2s
v4p0571c1s v4p0591c2s v4p0602c1s
v5p0006c1s v5p0006c2m v5p0007c1s
v5p0007c2m v5p0181c1m v5p0281c2s
v5p0297c2s v5p0332c1s v5p0332c2s
v5p0487c2m v5p0500c2s v5p0586c2s
v5p0587c2s v6p0072c1m v6p0081c2s
v6p0099c2s v6p0100c1s v6p0195c2s
v6p0240c1s v6p0264c2s v6p0265c1s
v6p0269c2s v6p0333c2s v6p0346c2s
v6p0429c2s v6p0555c2s v6p0624c2s
v6p0654c2s
Dicey, E. and Adams, J. .. v4p0172c2s
Dicey, E. and Rogers, J.G.
v4p0239c2s
Dicey, E. et al. v6p0310c1s
Dicey, Edward v3p0004c2s
Dick, A. v1p1002c2s
Dick, A.B. v5p0200c2s
Dick, A.C. v1p0427c2s
Dick, A.H. v1p0264c1s
Dick, C. v5p0604c1s
v6p0009c2s v6p0168c2s
Dick, C.D. v4p0552c1s
Dick, C.H. v4p0611c1s
v5p0623c2s
Dick, C.J.A. v1p0167c1s
Dick, F.W. v1p1251c1s
Dick, H.A. v1p0264c1s
Dick, J. et al. v5p0084c1s
Dick, S. v6p0201c2s
v6p0279c1s
Dick, T. v1p1152c2s
v1p1356c1s
Dickens, C. v1p0090c2s
v1p0091c2s v1p0099c1s v1p0137c2s
v1p0141c2s v1p0228c2m v1p0245c1s
v1p0245c2m v1p0337c1s v1p0357c2s
v1p0410c1s v1p0442c2s v1p0451c2s
v1p0512c1s v1p0551c1s v1p0570c2s
v1p0596c2s v1p0607c2s v1p0616c2s
v1p0755c1s v1p0770c1s v1p0779c1s
v1p0809c2s v1p0878c2m v1p0879c1s

v1p0879c2s v1p0889c2s v1p0908c2s v1p0920c2s v1p0940c1s v1p0941c2s v1p0951c2s v1p0952c1s v1p0969c2s v1p1032c1s v1p1054c1s v1p1063c1s v1p1074c2s v1p1084c1s v1p1131c2s v1p1153c1s v1p1180c2s v1p1219c1s v1p1249c1s v1p1260c2s v1p1280c2s v1p1298c1s v1p1306c2s v1p1308c1s v1p1339c1s v1p1378c2s v1p1431c1s v1p1433c2s v2p0303c1s v2p0436c1s v4p0156c1s v4p0160c2m v4p0338c2s v4p0340c1s v4p0424c1s v4p0572c2m
Dickens, C. and Collins, W. v1p0924c1s
Dickens, C. and Collins, W.W. v1p0732c1s
Dickens, C. et al. v1p0598c1s
Dickens, C., jr. v1p0022c2s v3p0117c1s v4p0155c1m
Dickens, C.W. v6p0173c2s
Dickens, F. v2p0118c1s
Dickens, J. v2p0055c1s v2p0068c2s
Dickens, M.A. v3p0267c2s v4p0459c2s v4p0599c2s v5p0555c2s
Dickens, Mary A. v3p0106c2s v5p0161c1s v5p0224c1s
Dickenson, J.C. v3p0181c2s
Dickenson, J.H. v6p0533c2s
Dickenson, W. v1p0267c1s v1p0824c1s
Dicker, T.W. v3p0384c1s
Dickerman, A. v3p0103c1s
Dickerman, J. v3p0343c1s
Dickerman, L. v2p0133c1s v2p0343c1s
Dickerman, S.O. v6p0320c1s
Dickerson, E.N. v3p0408c2s
Dickerson, E.N., jr. v3p0419c2s
Dickerson, J.S. v5p0642c1s v6p0602c1s
Dickerson, James S. v6p0035c2s
Dickert, T.W. v5p0116c2s
Dickes, W.F. v3p0071c1s v3p0232c2s v4p0124c2s v4p0260c1s
Dickey, C.A. v2p0352c2s
Dickey, S.C. v5p0633c1s
Dickie, A.C. v6p0617c1s
Dickie, G.W. v5p0188c2m v5p0462c2m v5p0619c1m v6p0054c1s v6p0591c1s v6p0686c1s v6p0708c1s
Dickin, M. v6p0090c1s
Dickins, F.V. v3p0006c2s v5p0303c1s
Dickins, F.V. and Kumagusu, Minakato v3p0121c2s
Dickins, F.Victor and Kumagusu, Minakato v6p0339c1s
Dickinson, Asa D. v6p0070c2s
Dickinson, B. v1p0847c2s
Dickinson, C.A. v3p0082c2s v5p0503c1s
Dickinson, C.E.G. v4p0067c1s
Dickinson, C.H. v4p0301c1s v5p0057c2s
Dickinson, C.W. v4p0185c1s
Dickinson, D.M. v3p0340c2s
Dickinson, Dr. v1p0933c1s
Dickinson, E. v4p0113c2s v4p0345c1s v4p0388c2s v4p0389c1s v4p0474c2s v5p0042c1s v5p0133c2s v5p0277c2s v5p0393c2m v5p0394c1s v5p0493c1s
Dickinson, E.E. v1p0871c2s v2p0162c2m v3p0069c2s v3p0310c1s v5p0225c2s
Dickinson, E.W. v1p0124c1s
Dickinson, Ellen E. v2p0429c2s
Dickinson, F.H. v1p0251c2s v1p0255c2s
Dickinson, G.L. v6p0044c2m v6p0085c2s v6p0119c1s v6p0123c1s v6p0156c2s v6p0213c2s v6p0218c1s v6p0300c2s v6p0309c2s v6p0438c2s v6p0469c1s v6p0587c2s
Dickinson, G.L. and Lilley, A.L. v6p0536c2s v6p0541c1s
Dickinson, G.Lowes v6p0370c1s v6p0570c1s v6p0589c2s v6p0683c1s
Dickinson, H.C. v6p0084c1s
Dickinson, J. v1p0235c1s v3p0474c2s v6p0309c2s
Dickinson, J.J. v6p0696c2s
Dickinson, J.M. v3p0424c2s v6p0010c1s
Dickinson, J.M. et al. ... v5p0592c1s
Dickinson, J.T. v1p0067c2s v1p0259c2s v1p0591c2s
Dickinson, J.W. v1p1288c2m v2p0388c1s v2p0388c2s v3p0215c1s v3p0378c1s v4p0406c1s v5p0471c2s
Dickinson, L. v1p1036c2s
Dickinson, Lydia F. v4p0252c2s v5p0259c2s v5p0362c2s v5p0388c2s v6p0170c2s
Dickinson, M.G. v5p0053c2s v5p0122c2s v5p0266c1s v5p0289c2s v5p0621c2s v5p0641c2s
Dickinson, M.L. v3p0148c2s v3p0214c2s v4p0626c1s v5p0631c1s v5p0637c2s
Dickinson, M.L. et al. ... v3p0148c1s
Dickinson, R.L. v3p0101c2s v4p0117c1s v6p0453c1s
Dickinson, R.S. v1p0808c1s
Dickinson, R.W. v1p0099c1s v1p0120c1m v1p0189c1s v1p0528c1m v1p0641c2s v1p0685c1s v1p0916c2s v1p1044c1s v1p1059c1s v1p1064c2s v1p1139c1s v1p1139c2s v1p1406c2s v1p1413c1s
Dickinson, S. v3p0165c2s v4p0038c2s v4p0264c1s v4p0446c2s
Dickinson, T. v6p0194c1s v6p0430c2s v6p0713c2s
Dickinson, W. v1p0351c1s v2p0118c1s v2p0481c1s v3p0069c1s
Dickinson, W.H. v5p0346c2s
Dickman, J.F. v1p0180c2s
Dickman, J.T. v5p0098c1s v6p0409c2s
Dicks, W.F. v5p0267c2s
Dickson, A. v4p0567c2s
Dickson, A. and Dickson, W.K.L. v4p0168c2s v4p0311c1m
Dickson, A.K.L. v5p0008c2s
Dickson, B. v6p0351c1s
Dickson, C. v6p0101c1s
Dickson, C.A. v4p0471c1s v5p0593c2s
Dickson, C.S. v5p0454c2s
Dickson, C.W. v6p0503c1s
Dickson, D. v2p0062c2s
Dickson, E. v5p0635c1s
Dickson, E.H. v5p0315c2s
Dickson, F. v3p0264c2s
Dickson, F., Sir v3p0072c2s
Dickson, F.S. v5p0574c2s
Dickson, F.T. v5p0078c1s v5p0110c2s v5p0112c2m v5p0458c1s v5p0564c2s
Dickson, Fred.S. v4p0592c1s
Dickson, G. v6p0471c1s
Dickson, H.N. v4p0095c1s v4p0201c1s v4p0222c1s v4p0407c1s v5p0037c1s v5p0123c1s v5p0417c2s v5p0540c1s v6p0220c1s v6p0403c2s
Dickson, H.N. et al. v4p0095c1s
Dickson, H.S. v1p0686c1s
Dickson, J. v4p0219c1s v4p0414c2s
Dickson, J.A. v1p0535c2s v2p0024c2s
Dickson, J.H. v6p0096c1s
Dickson, L.E. v6p0275c1s
Dickson, M.W. and Brown, A. v1p0328c1s
Dickson, R.F. v4p0390c2s
Dickson, S.B. v1p1206c2s
Dickson, S.H. v1p0467c1s v1p0745c1s v1p0819c1s
Dickson, T.D. v4p0354c2s
Dickson, W. v2p0417c1s
Dickson, W.A. v3p0276c2s
Dickson, W.E. v1p0883c1s v4p0092c2s v4p0178c2s v5p0298c1s
Dickson, W.K. v5p0312c2s v6p0005c1s
Dickson, W.K.L. and Dickson, A. v4p0168c2s v4p0311c1m
Dickson, W.M. v2p0087c1s v2p0259c1s v3p0441c1s v3p0458c1s
Dickson, W.P. v4p0056c1s v5p0118c1s
Didden, R. v5p0235c1s v5p0289c1s v5p0545c2s
Didier, E.L. v1p0147c1s v1p0189c1s v1p0207c2s v1p0300c2s v1p0682c1s v1p0837c2s v1p0838c1s v1p0863c1s v1p0932c2s v1p1002c2s v1p1019c2s v1p1389c1s v2p0032c2m v2p0101c1s v2p0103c1s v2p0168c1s v2p0198c2s v2p0222c1s v2p0234c1s v2p0279c1s v2p0334c1s v2p0343c2s v2p0345c2s v2p0364c2s v2p0372c2s v2p0376c2s v2p0377c1s v2p0400c1s v2p0435c1s v2p0461c2s v2p0462c1s v3p0028c2m v3p0049c1s v3p0062c1s v3p0074c2s v3p0097c2s v3p0127c2s v3p0202c1s v3p0253c1m v3p0253c2m v3p0257c2s v3p0269c2s v3p0270c1s v3p0303c2s v3p0377c2s v3p0384c2s v3p0391c1s v3p0416c2s v3p0467c1s v4p0063c2s v4p0081c2s v4p0091c1s v4p0098c1s v4p0215c1s v4p0260c2s v4p0320c2s v4p0336c1s v4p0350c1s v4p0358c2s v4p0380c1m v4p0418c1s v4p0419c2s v4p0448c1s v4p0516c1s v4p0543c2s v4p0551c2s v4p0552c2s v4p0628c1s v5p0602c2s v6p0086c1s v6p0089c1s v6p0103c2s v6p0144c1s v6p0287c1s v6p0332c2s v6p0339c2s v6p0351c1s v6p0504c2s v6p0585c2s
Didier, E.S. v1p0147c2s
Didier, Eugene L. v6p0058c2s
Didier, G.L. v1p0802c2s
Diebitsch-Peary, J. v4p0025c2s v4p0529c2s
Diedrich, Dr. v2p0337c1s
Diedrich, H.W. v6p0670c2s
Dieffenbach, A.C. v6p0125c2s
Diehl, C. v3p0289c1s v6p0090c2s v6p0160c1s
Diehl, G. v1p0139c1s v1p0211c2s v1p0253c2s v1p0769c1s v1p0777c2s v1p0778c1s v1p0948c1s v1p1157c2s v1p1256c1s
Diemer, H. v5p0188c2s v5p0353c1m v6p0152c1s v6p0204c1s v6p0392c2s v6p0499c2s v6p0682c2s
Diemer, Hugo v6p0073c2s v6p0399c2s
Dienst, A. v6p0640c1s
Diercks, G. v6p0607c2s
Diescher, S. v5p0477c2s
Dieserud, J. v5p0334c2s v6p0374c2s
Diesterweg, A. v1p0993c2s
Dietler, H. v5p0477c2m
Dietrich, E.G.W. v6p0152c2s
Dietrich, F.S. v3p0295c1s
Dietrichson, P.G. v2p0476c1s
Dietrick, E.B. v3p0299c2s v4p0114c2s v4p0162c1s v4p0275c2s v4p0328c2s v4p0455c2s v4p0599c2s
Dietrick, E.W. v4p0455c1s
Dietrick, Ellen B. v3p0470c1s
Dietz, J. v2p0165c2s v2p0170c2s
Dietzel, H. v6p0240c1s v6p0255c1s v6p0355c2s
Dieuade, T.M. v5p0508c2s
Dieulafait, M. v2p0290c1s
Dieulafoy, J. v3p0417c1s
Dieulafoy, M. v3p0006c2s
Diffenderffer, F.R. v1p0378c2s v1p1397c1s v5p0439c2s v5p0474c1s
Digby, E. v4p0253c1s v6p0385c2s
Digby, E.T. v5p0286c2s
Digby, H.S. v1p1387c1s
Digby, K.E. v4p0140c1s
Digby, O. v1p0429c1s
Digby, W. v1p0214c1s v1p0600c1s v6p0314c2s
Digby, W.P. v6p0096c2s v6p0204c2m v6p0318c1s v6p0328c2s
Digby, W.Pollard v6p0216c2s v6p0652c1s
Diggle, J.R. v3p0128c2s v3p0129c1m v3p0378c2m v4p0103c2s v4p0169c2m v4p0170c1s v4p0170c2s v4p0339c2m v4p0534c1s v5p0133c2s
Diggle, J.R. and Riley, A. v4p0169c2s
Diggle, J.W. v5p0257c2s v5p0268c1s v5p0480c2s v5p0513c2s v6p0068c2s v6p0191c2s
Diggs, A.L. v4p0195c1m v6p0078c1s v6p0134c1s v6p0247c1s v6p0300c1s v6p0703c1s
Diggs, Annie L. v6p0091c1s
Dijk, P.Van v2p0175c1s
Dijon, H. v3p0276c2s v3p0324c1s
Dike, G.P. v5p0027c2s
Dike, S.W. v2p0105c1s v2p0120c1m v2p0248c1s v2p0407c2s v2p0408c2s v3p0119c1m v3p0149c1s v3p0268c2m v3p0397c2s v3p0399c2s v4p0129c1s v4p0157c2m v4p0194c2s v4p0356c2s v4p0357c1s v4p0423c2s v4p0628c1s v5p0163c2s v5p0535c1s
Dike, S.W. et al. v3p0083c2s v3p0119c1s
Dikehut, H.F. v1p0833c1s
Dilke, A.W. v1p0208c1s v1p1194c1s
Dilke, C. and Bell, R. ... v6p0652c1s
Dilke, C., Sir v5p0245c1s
Dilke, C.W. v1p0232c1s v1p0970c1s v3p0004c2s v3p0027c2s v3p0180c1m v3p0183c1s v3p0278c2s v4p0027c2s v4p0064c2s v4p0174c1s v4p0189c2s v4p0237c2s v4p0238c2s v4p0240c1s v4p0278c2s v4p0314c1s v4p0491c1s v5p0019c2s v5p0037c1s v5p0112c1s v5p0173c2s v5p0180c1s v5p0243c1s v5p0244c2s v5p0245c1m v5p0272c1s v5p0285c2s v5p0294c1s v5p0408c2s v5p0412c1s v5p0510c2s v5p0598c2s v6p0030c2s v6p0082c2s v6p0267c2s v6p0560c1s
Dilke, C.W. and Botassi, D.N. v5p0249c1s
Dilke, C.W. et al. v5p0445c1s
Dilke, C.W., Sir v1p0385c2s v1p0538c1s v1p0678c1s v1p1158c2s v3p0159c2s v3p0179c2s v3p0211c1s v4p0237c1s v4p0589c2s v5p0245c2s v5p0246c1s v5p0251c2s v6p0268c1s
Dilke, E.F.S. v2p0166c1s v3p0239c1m v3p0283c1s v3p0434c1s v3p0434c2s v4p0083c1s v4p0110c2s v4p0387c1s v4p0481c1s v5p0038c1s v5p0485c1s v5p0623c1s v5p0638c1s
Dilke, E.F.S., Lady v2p0001c2s v3p0116c1s v4p0628c2s
Dilke, Emilia v4p0004c1s
Dilke, Emilia F.S. v2p0372c2s

v4p0247c1s v4p0424c2s v4p0555c1s
v4p0584c2s
Dilke, Lady v2p0091c2s
v3p0022c2s v3p0160c1s v3p0163c2s
v3p0422c2s v3p0468c1s v3p0470c2s
Dilke, M.M. and Fawcett, M.G.
v3p0470c1s
Dilks, T.B. v4p0256c1s
Dill, E. v1p0280c1s
Dill, J.B. v5p0592c2s
Dill, J.H. v1p0291c1s
Dill, R.G. v2p0409c1s
Dill, Robert v6p0236c2s
Dillard, A.W. v2p0069c1s
v2p0237c1s v4p0635c1s
Dillard, G.M. v4p0228c2s
v4p0380c1s
Dillard, J.H. v4p0123c2s
v5p0028c1s v5p0341c1s
Dillard, R. v4p0150c2s
v4p0168c1m v4p0565c2s
Dillaway, C.K. v1p0402c2s
Dillaye, S.T. v1p1321c2s
Dille, I. v1p0844c2s
Dille, J. v1p0855c1s
Diller, J.S. v1p1402c1s
v2p0027c2s v2p0117c2s v2p0174c1s
v2p0336c1s v2p0446c2s v2p0463c1s
v3p0104c2s v3p0244c1s v4p0368c2s
v4p0607c1s v5p0141c2m v5p0367c2s
v5p0428c1s v5p0548c1s v6p0079c1s
v6p0353c1s v6p0403c2s v6p0407c2s
v6p0681c1s
Diller, J.S. and Clarke, F.W.
v2p0443c1s v2p0449c1s
Diller, J.S. and Kunz, G.F.
v3p0116c2s
Diller, J.S. and Schuchert, C.
v4p0154c2s
Dillingham, A.C. v6p0459c1s
Dillingham, Frances B. ... v6p0081c1s
Dillingham, M.W. and Thorn, C.R.
v4p0397c1s
Dillingham, P. v1p0244c1s
v4p0083c1s v4p0318c2s v4p0396c2s
Dillmann, A. v2p0199c2s
Dillon, A. v3p0179c2s
v4p0517c1s v5p0186c2s v5p0523c2s
Dillon, D.J. v6p0097c2s
Dillon, E. v4p0530c1s
v6p0662c1s
Dillon, E.J. v3p0277c2s
v4p0027c1m v4p0077c2s v4p0189c2s
v4p0224c2s v4p0232c2s v4p0237c1s
v4p0240c2s v4p0397c2s v4p0495c2s
v4p0578c2m v4p0625c2s v5p0010c1s
v5p0094c2s v5p0110c1s v5p0142c2s
v5p0162c2s v5p0182c1s v5p0197c1s
v5p0231c2s v5p0249c1s v5p0297c1s
v5p0359c2s v5p0500c2s v5p0501c1s
v5p0502c1s v5p0542c2s v5p0634c2s
v6p0010c2s v6p0042c2s v6p0047c1s
v6p0205c1s v6p0213c1s v6p0253c1s
v6p0254c1s v6p0255c1s v6p0262c1s
v6p0266c2s v6p0267c2s v6p0294c1s
v6p0334c1s v6p0392c1m v6p0398c2s
v6p0404c1s v6p0424c2s v6p0429c2s
v6p0457c1s v6p0478c1s v6p0482c2s
v6p0510c2m v6p0547c1s v6p0555c2m
v6p0556c2m v6p0557c1m v6p0557c2s
v6p0558c1m v6p0558c2m v6p0560c1s
v6p0561c1s v6p0584c2s v6p0646c1s
v6p0702c1s
Dillon, E.L. v6p0251c2s
Dillon, E.O.S. v2p0016c2s
Dillon, E.T. v4p0055c2m
Dillon, F. v1p0395c1s
v2p0467c2s v4p0404c2s v4p0438c2s
v5p0303c2s
Dillon, F.J. v5p0410c2s
Dillon, H. v3p0062c2s
v3p0113c1s v3p0135c1s v3p0157c1s
v3p0180c1s v3p0200c2s v3p0278c2s
v3p0413c1s v3p0432c1s v3p0437c2m
v4p0027c2s
Dillon, H.A. v5p0028c2s
v5p0087c2s
Dillon, Harold v3p0458c2s
Dillon, J. v1p1110c1s
v2p0226c2s v6p0325c2s
Dillon, J.A. v1p0651c1s
Dillon, J.F. v2p0011c1s
v3p0011c2s v3p0039c1s v3p0090c1s
v3p0136c2s v3p0244c2s v4p0323c1s
v4p0462c1s v5p0363c2s v6p0074c2s
Dillon, John F. v4p0322c2s
Dillon, P. v1p0331c1s
v2p0287c1s
Dillon, P.W. v1p1106c1s
Dillon, R. v6p0676c2s
Dillon, S. v3p0352c2s
v4p0591c2s
Dillon, V.B. et al. v4p0291c1s
Dillon, W. v2p0025c1s
Dillon, W. and Alden, W.L.
v4p0378c1s
Dillon, Wm. v2p0126c2s
Dillson, W.W. v4p0322c2s
Dillwyn, E.A. v2p0096c1s
v2p0321c2s
Dillwyn, L.L. v2p0208c2s
v2p0364c1s
Dilworth, W.H. v6p0673c1s
Diman, J.K. v1p1028c1s
Diman, J.L. v1p0028c1s
v1p0260c1s v1p0275c2s v1p0390c1s
v1p0637c2s v1p0842c1s v1p0877c2s
v1p0907c1s v1p0907c2s v1p0956c2s
v1p1036c2s v1p1069c1s v1p1089c2s
v1p1121c2s v1p1353c2s v1p1357c2s
v1p1393c2s v2p0368c2s
Diman, L. v5p0421c2s
Dimitry, C. v1p0033c1s
v2p0028c1s v2p0039c1s v2p0312c1m
v2p0482c2s
Dimitry, J. v2p0064c1s
v2p0075c2s v2p0312c1s v3p0244c1s
Dimm, J.R. v1p0206c2s
v1p0275c2s v1p1063c2s
Dimmock, A. v4p0416c1m
Dimmock, G. v2p0034c2s
v2p0483c1s
Dimmock, T. v3p0259c2s
Dimnet, E. v6p0547c2s
Dimock, A. v4p0341c2s
v5p0019c1s
Dimock, A.W. v6p0083c2s
v6p0229c1s v6p0259c1s v6p0433c1s
v6p0444c2s v6p0580c1s v6p0633c2s
Dimock, Arthur v5p0453c1s
Dimock, J. v6p0633c2s
Dimock, J.A. v6p0013c1s
v6p0159c1s
Dimock, Julian A. v6p0398c2s
Dimon, J.L. v1p0231c2s
v1p0540c1s
Dimond, F. v1p1088c1s
Dimond, W.H. et al. v4p0564c1s
Dimsdale, M.S. v3p0414c1s
Dimsdale, T.I. v1p0501c2s
Dines, W.H. v6p0048c2s
v6p0353c1m
Dingby, W. v2p0012c1s
Dingle, D. v3p0048c2s
Dingler and Pfeiffer v1p1247c1s
Dingley, A.L. v5p0417c1s
Dingley, B.H. v5p0356c2s
v5p0513c1s
Dingley, Blanche v6p0438c1s
Dingley, E.N. v4p0514c2s
v4p0614c2s v5p0468c2s
Dingley, F.L. v1p0551c1s
Dingley, Florence v5p0172c1s
v5p0361c1s
Dingley, N. v5p0487c1s
Dingley, N. et al. v4p0129c1s
Dingley, N., jr. v3p0264c2s
v3p0391c1s
Dingman, D.B. v1p1350c2s
Dinkerd, H.D. v6p0700c2s
Dinsmore, A. v6p0279c2s
Dinsmore, C.A. v5p0152c2s
v5p0153c1m v6p0040c1s
Dinsmore, L.J. v3p0002c2s
v3p0459c1s
Dinsmore, S.P. v1p0395c1s
Dinwiddie, E.W. v6p0184c1s
v6p0491c2s
Dinwiddie, Emily W. v5p0013c1s
Dinwiddie, W. v5p0279c2s
v5p0548c1s
Dinwiddie, W.W. v6p0637c1s
Diosy, Arthur v4p0297c2s
Diplock, A.H. v5p0073c1s
v5p0216c2s v5p0322c1s v5p0610c1s
v5p0645c1s
Diplomaticus v5p0054c1s
v5p0109c1m v5p0111c1s v5p0124c2s
v5p0502c2s v5p0505c2m
Dippold, G.T. v1p0204c2s
Dircks, H. v1p0419c2s
Dircks, R. v6p0546c2s
v6p0553c2s
Dircks, Rudolf v6p0460c1s
Dircks, W.H. v3p0243c2s
Dirnan, L. v6p0407c1s
Diserens, I.B. v5p0131c2s
Disney, A.N. v4p0512c1s
Disosway, G.P. v1p0026c2s
v1p0031c1s v1p0037c2s v1p0047c2s
v1p0190c2s v1p0301c2s v1p0612c1m
v1p0759c2s v1p0870c1s v1p0916c2s
v1p1210c2s v1p1245c2s v1p1256c2s
v1p1374c1s v1p1399c1s
Disraeli, B. v1p0641c1s
v1p0697c2s
Disraeli, I. v1p0349c2s
v1p1195c2s
Distant, W.L. v1p0199c2s
v1p0298c1s v1p0427c2s v1p0613c2s
v1p0921c1s v1p1182c1s v2p0036c1s
Ditchfield, H.H. v6p0106c1s
Ditchfield, P.H. v3p0186c2s
v3p0191c2s v3p0321c1s v3p0361c2s
v3p0403c1s v3p0450c1s v4p0257c2s
v4p0473c2s v4p0474c2s v5p0005c1s
v5p0070c1s v5p0075c1s v5p0228c1s
v5p0432c2s v5p0467c1s v5p0636c1s
v6p0247c2s
Dithmar, E.A. v5p0167c2s
v5p0415c2s v5p0578c1s v6p0213c2s
Ditmars, R.L. v6p0506c1s
v6p0539c2s
Ditson, G. v1p0300c1s
Ditson, G.L. v1p0322c1s
Diver, M. v5p0074c2s
v5p0213c1s v5p0486c1s v5p0628c1s
v6p0458c2s
Diver, Maud v5p0382c1s
Divers, E. v1p0281c2s
v1p0785c2s v1p1315c2s v1p1391c1s
v6p0040c1s
Divine, E.T. v4p0627c2s
Dix, B.M. v5p0152c1s
v5p0311c1s v6p0165c2s
Dix, Beulah M. v6p0189c1s
v6p0325c1s v6p0541c1s v6p0579c2s
Dix, D. v6p0703c1s
Dix, E.A. v5p0141c1s
v5p0203c2s v5p0265c2s v6p0213c1s
v6p0514c2s
Dix, E.A. and MacGonigle, J.N.
v6p0214c1s v6p0229c1s
Dix, E.R.McC. v5p0466c2s
Dix, G. v5p0609c2s
v6p0228c2s
Dix, Gertrude v4p0265c1s
Dix, H.L. v1p0347c2s
Dix, J. v6p0278c1s
Dix, J.A. v1p0321c1m
v1p0325c2s v1p0351c2s
Dix, J.R. v1p1381c1s
Dix, M. v1p0882c2s
v1p1109c1s v2p0096c2s v2p0150c1s
v4p0344c1s
Dix, R.S. v3p0113c1s
v3p0211c1s v3p0376c2s
Dix, W.F. v5p0628c2s
v6p0004c1s v6p0043c2s v6p0044c1s
v6p0153c2s v6p0169c1s v6p0455c2s
v6p0594c2s v6p0611c2s v6p0629c2s
Dix, W.G. v1p0037c2s
v1p1363c1s
Dixie, F., Lady v2p0073c1s
v2p0483c2s v5p0343c1s
Dixey, F.A. v5p0277c1s
v5p0343c1s v5p0519c1s v6p0359c1s
Dixey, W. v3p0473c1s
v3p0475c1s
Dixie, Florence v4p0430c1s
v4p0542c2s
Dixon, A.C. v6p0512c2s
Dixon, A.E. v6p0198c1s
v6p0595c1s
Dixon, B.H. v1p0983c2s
v2p0170c1s
Dixon, B.V.B. v1p0392c1s
v1p1006c1s
Dixon, C. v2p0046c2s
v2p0149c2s v3p0045c1s v3p0045c2s
v3p0046c1s v3p0164c2s v4p0222c1s
v5p0021c1s v5p0456c2s
Dixon, E. v3p0462c2s
v4p0138c1s v6p0707c1s
Dixon, E.F. v4p0326c2s
Dixon, E.F.R. v4p0326c2s
Dixon, E.S. v1p0186c2s
v1p1202c1s v1p1310c1s v4p0034c1s
Dixon, E.T. v1p0346c1s
v4p0153c1s v4p0338c1s v4p0360c2s
v4p0388c2s v4p0462c1s v6p0438c2s
v6p0469c2s
Dixon, F. v3p0130c1m
v3p0198c1s v3p0211c2s v3p0375c2s
v4p0031c2s v4p0079c1s v4p0082c1s
v4p0206c1s v4p0235c2s v4p0317c2s
v4p0498c1s v5p0323c1s v5p0324c1s
v5p0331c2s v5p0404c2s v5p0495c2s
v5p0510c1s v5p0552c1s v5p0607c1s
v6p0051c2s
Dixon, F.A. v1p0352c2s
v1p0601c2s v1p0756c1s
Dixon, F.F. v4p0151c1s
Dixon, F.F.R. v4p0095c1s
v4p0177c2s v5p0100c1s
Dixon, F.H. v5p0015c2s
v5p0153c1s v5p0175c2s v5p0477c2s
v5p0478c1s v6p0216c2s v6p0324c2s
v6p0528c1s v6p0530c2s
Dixon, G. v1p0163c1s
v1p0923c2s v1p1299c2m v2p0036c1s
Dixon, G.C. v1p0015c1s
Dixon, G.G. v4p0073c2s
Dixon, G.H. v4p0618c1s
Dixon, G.T., jr. v6p0068c1s
Dixon, H. v1p0085c1s
v3p0167c2s v4p0404c1s
Dixon, H.B. v2p0340c2s
Dixon, H.H. v4p0286c1s
Dixon, H.N. v4p0485c1s
Dixon, H.O'S. v4p0598c2s
Dixon, J. v1p0264c1s
v2p0088c2s v6p0081c1s
Dixon, J.H. v1p1189c2s
Dixon, J.M. v5p0118c2s
v6p0088c2s v6p0543c1s v6p0564c1s
v6p0579c1s
Dixon, L.M. and Fairbanks, H.W.
v5p0384c2s
Dixon, M.H. v2p0291c2s

v2p0420c1s v3p0035c1s v4p0096c1s v4p0104c1s v4p0193c2s v4p0207c1m v4p0327c2s v4p0380c2s v4p0387c2s v5p0073c2s v5p0213c2s v5p0276c1s v5p0301c2s
Dixon, Marion H. v5p0509c1s v6p0046c2s
Dixon, Marion Hapworth ... v5p0314c2s
Dixon, P.F. v4p0177c2s
Dixon, R.B. v5p0049c1s v5p0094c1s v5p0141c1s v6p0015c1s v6p0395c2s v6p0588c2s v6p0589c1m
Dixon, R.B. and Kroeber, A.L. v6p0093c1s v6p0316c2s
Dixon, R.F. v4p0081c2s v4p0216c1s v5p0055c1s v6p0098c1s v6p0239c2s
Dixon, R.W. v3p0094c2s v3p0426c2s
Dixon, S. v2p0099c2s
Dixon, S.B. v5p0262c1s
Dixon, T., jr. v5p0309c2s v6p0623c2s v6p0710c1s
Dixon, W. v4p0414c2s v5p0298c1s
Dixon, W., Mrs. v4p0281c2s
Dixon, W.G. v2p0233c2s v2p0234c1s
Dixon, W.H. v1p0026c1s v1p0029c2s v1p0043c1s v1p0138c2s v1p0167c2s v1p0379c2s v1p0385c2s v1p0397c1s v1p0598c2s v1p0753c2s v1p0795c2s v1p0961c1s v1p0976c1s v1p0987c1s v1p0987c2s v1p1012c2s v1p1103c2s v1p1185c1s v1p1229c2s v1p1317c2s v1p1384c2s v1p1434c1s
Dixon, W.M. v4p0334c2s v4p0422c2s
Dixon, W.W. v5p0263c2s v6p0221c2s
Dixson, Z.A. v4p0100c2m v6p0074c1s
Dixwell, E.S. v1p0555c1s
Doa, J.W. v6p0154c1s
Doak, H.M. v4p0295c2s
Doan, F.C. v6p0212c1s
Doane, C.W. v6p0177c1s
Doane, E.T. v1p0380c2s
Doane, G.W. v1p0320c2s v1p0384c2s
Doane, T. v1p0602c2s v1p1110c2s
Doane, W.C. v1p0127c1s v1p0422c1s v1p0704c1s v1p0775c2s v1p1096c1s v1p1342c2s v2p0044c1s v2p0096c2s v3p0141c2s v4p0035c2s v4p0223c2s v4p0333c2m v4p0401c1s v4p0450c2s v4p0487c2s v4p0557c1s v4p0610c1s v4p0630c1m v5p0018c1s v5p0435c2s v6p0176c2s
Doane, W.C. and Lathrop, G.P. v4p0489c1s
Dobbie, I. v6p0006c2s v6p0120c2s v6p0310c2s v6p0542c2s v6p0593c1s
Dobbie, Prof. v5p0478c2s
Dobbin, F.H. v6p0490c2s
Dobbin, O.T. v1p0126c1s v1p0243c1s v1p0395c1s v1p0514c2m v1p0515c1s v1p1398c2s
Dobbins, F.S. v2p0233c2s
Dobbins, J.L. v6p0195c2s
Dobbs, A.E. v4p0340c2s
Dobbs, C.E.W. v2p0278c2s v2p0382c1s v2p0403c2s v3p0033c2m
Dobbs, G. v4p0256c1s
Dobell, B. v2p0399c2s v5p0101c1s v5p0262c1s v5p0310c1s v5p0324c2s v5p0575c1s v5p0608c1s v6p0010c1s v6p0135c1s v6p0346c1s v6p0359c2m v6p0391c2s
Dobell, J.C. v3p0426c1s
Doberck, W. v1p1113c2s v2p0095c1s v2p0319c1s v2p0417c1s v2p0421c2s v2p0426c2s v3p0410c2s v3p0465c1s
Dobie, J.S. v4p0094c1s
Doblado, L. v1p1229c1s
Doble, C.E. v2p0135c2s v2p0241c2s v2p0473c1s v3p0029c2m v3p0168c1s v3p0348c1s v3p0411c2s v4p0089c2s
Doble, R.McF. v6p0197c2s
Dobree, L.E. v2p0435c2s
Dobschutz, E.von v5p0059c2s v6p0343c1s
Dobson, A. v1p0071c1s v1p0778c2s v1p0808c2s v2p0041c1m v2p0074c2s v2p0105c2s v2p0155c2m v2p0185c1s v2p0253c1s v2p0260c2s v2p0265c2s v2p0436c2s v2p0472c2s v3p0177c1s v3p0198c1s v3p0306c1s v3p0339c1s v3p0344c1s v3p0409c1s v3p0447c2s v4p0042c2s v4p0074c1s v4p0083c1s v4p0084c2s v4p0092c2s v4p0107c2s v4p0198c2s v4p0220c1s v4p0222c1s v4p0243c1s v4p0247c2s v4p0256c2s v4p0259c2m v4p0261c2s v4p0316c2s v4p0326c2s v4p0339c1s v4p0351c1s v4p0399c2s v4p0405c1s v4p0451c1s v4p0473c2m v4p0484c1s v4p0492c2s v4p0510c1s v4p0530c2s v4p0560c1s v4p0578c2s v4p0586c2s v4p0588c2s v4p0625c2s v5p0019c1m v5p0040c2s v5p0111c1s v5p0140c2s v5p0191c1s v5p0267c2s v5p0418c1s v5p0437c1s v5p0478c1s v5p0504c1s v5p0553c1s v5p0569c1s v6p0107c1s v6p0213c2s v6p0248c1s v6p0261c1s v6p0368c2s
Dobson, Austin v4p0198c2s v4p0362c2s v4p0466c2s v6p0274c1s
Dobson, B.A. v4p0174c2s v4p0331c2s
Dobson, C.M. v5p0238c1s v5p0377c1s
Dobson, G.E. v1p0037c1s
Dobson, J.A. v1p0030c1s
Dobson, P. v1p0622c1s v4p0119c1s
Dobson, W. v1p0720c2s
Dobson, W.A. v4p0554c2s v4p0595c1s v4p0610c2m
Dobson, W.T. v1p0753c1s v1p1337c1s v5p0451c1s
Doby, H.A. v6p0417c1s
Dock, M.L. v4p0046c2s v4p0074c1s v4p0099c2s v4p0178c1s v4p0208c2s v4p0409c2s v5p0356c1s
Dockree, E. v6p0496c2s
Dod, A.B. v1p0198c2s v1p0313c1s v1p0398c1s v1p0454c1s v1p0510c1s v1p1004c2s v1p1103c1s v1p1227c2s
Dod, A.B. and Alexander, J.W. v1p1321c1s
Dod, C.S., jr. v1p0755c1s
Dod, W. v1p1042c1s
Dod, W.A. v1p0052c2m v1p0054c2s v1p0127c2s v1p0240c2s v1p0247c1s
Dodd, A.B. v2p0246c1s v2p0260c2s v2p0419c2s v4p0406c1s v6p0201c2s v6p0661c2s v6p0702c2s
Dodd, A.F. v6p0634c1s
Dodd, C.I. v5p0106c1s v5p0107c2m v5p0511c2s v6p0573c1s
Dodd, C.J. v5p0107c2s v5p0108c1s
Dodd, C.L. v6p0218c1s v6p0574c1s
Dodd, Catherine v5p0178c1s v6p0115c2s
Dodd, Catherine I. v5p0017c1s
Dodd, Catherine J. v5p0511c2s
Dodd, E.B. v4p0538c2s
Dodd, G. v1p0064c1s v1p1077c1s v2p0074c1s v2p0148c1s v2p0186c1s v2p0218c1s v2p0258c2s v2p0259c1s v2p0291c1s v2p0327c2s v2p0332c2s v2p0338c1s v2p0350c2s v2p0363c1m v2p0423c2s v2p0432c2s v2p0433c1m v2p0433c2s
Dodd, H. v6p0677c1s
Dodd, I.E. v4p0023c2s
Dodd, I.S. v5p0162c2s v5p0601c1s v6p0181c2s
Dodd, J.A. v4p0498c2s
Dodd, J.T. v4p0452c1s v5p0459c1m
Dodd, L.T. and Dale, J.A.. v5p0500c2s
Dodd, L.W. v6p0540c1s
Dodd, Lee W. v6p0054c2s
Dodd, S. v2p0045c1s
Dodd, S.C.T. v4p0544c2s v5p0018c2s
Dodd, S.G. v3p0141c2s
Dodd, T.R. v5p0587c1s
Dodd, W.F. v6p0194c1s v6p0245c2s v6p0292c2m v6p0293c1s v6p0359c2s v6p0393c2s v6p0459c2s v6p0583c1s
Dodd, W.H. v6p0366c1s
Dodd, W.O. v1p0288c1s
Doddridge, J. v1p1400c2s
Dodds, G. v1p0436c2s v1p0795c2s v1p0862c1s v2p0162c1s
Dodge, A. v2p0167c1s v3p0120c2s v3p0404c1s
Dodge, A.J. v6p0210c2s
Dodge, A.L. v5p0544c1s
Dodge, A.P. v2p0002c2s v3p0168c1s
Dodge, C.R. v3p0362c2s v3p0436c1s v4p0203c1s v5p0205c2s v6p0280c1s
Dodge, C.Richards v6p0690c2s
Dodge, C.T. v4p0263c2s
Dodge, C.W. v5p0646c2s
Dodge, D. v2p0098c1s v2p0308c2s v3p0107c2s v3p0307c1s v3p0442c2s v3p0446c1s v4p0128c2s v4p0497c2s
Dodge, D.K. v3p0307c2s v3p0376c2s v4p0071c1s v4p0109c2s v4p0184c1s v4p0272c2s v4p0320c1s v5p0191c2s v5p0278c1s v5p0326c2s
Dodge, Daniel K. v6p0180c2s
Dodge, E. et al. v2p0017c1s
Dodge, E.A. v6p0090c2s v6p0343c1s v6p0494c1s v6p0552c2s
Dodge, E.C. v6p0427c1s
Dodge, F.S. v4p0310c2s
Dodge, F.S. et al. v3p0236c1s
Dodge, G.H. v3p0173c1s v3p0472c1s v4p0632c2s
Dodge, G.M. v1p0956c1s v6p0264c1s
Dodge, H.F. v6p0157c1s
Dodge, H.I. v6p0282c2s
Dodge, H.W. v1p0037c1s
Dodge, J.A. v5p0498c1s
Dodge, J.C. v2p0013c2s v2p0065c1s v2p0240c1s
Dodge, J.E. v1p0469c1s
Dodge, J.M. v4p0455c2s v4p0491c1s
Dodge, J.R. v2p0108c2s v3p0254c2s v4p0015c2s v4p0195c1s v4p0336c2s
Dodge, J.S. v1p0980c2s v2p0333c1s
Dodge, J.S., jr. v1p0909c2s v1p1302c1s
Dodge, J.T. v4p0158c1s
Dodge, J.W. v1p1438c2s
Dodge, L. v4p0111c1s v4p0413c1s
Dodge, L. and Preston, H.W. v3p0010c1s v3p0023c2s v3p0027c1s v3p0048c2s v3p0228c2s v3p0233c1s v3p0261c1s v3p0324c1s v3p0366c2s v3p0371c1s v3p0385c1s v3p0418c2s v4p0118c2s v4p0124c2s v4p0437c1s v4p0449c2s v4p0484c1s v4p0490c1s v4p0561c1s
Dodge, L.A. v1p0307c2s
Dodge, L.P. v2p0171c1s v2p0427c2s
Dodge, L.W. v2p0237c2s v2p0312c1s v2p0334c2s v2p0472c2s
Dodge, Louise v4p0001c1s
Dodge, M. v4p0485c1s v5p0490c2s v6p0545c1s
Dodge, M.A. v1p0134c1s v1p0140c2s v1p0176c2s v1p0199c1s v1p0497c1s v1p0500c1s v1p0572c2s v1p0606c2s v1p0717c2s v1p0856c2s v1p0882c2s v1p0886c1s v1p0931c1s v1p1040c1s v1p1067c2s v1p1080c1s v1p1214c2s v1p1388c2s v1p1416c2s v2p0033c1s v2p0068c1s v2p0082c1s v2p0087c1s v2p0113c1s v2p0159c2s v2p0171c1s v2p0193c1s v2p0356c1s v2p0361c2s v2p0418c1s v3p0013c1m v3p0041c1s v3p0076c1s v3p0096c2s v3p0193c1s v3p0213c2m v3p0224c2s v3p0345c1s v3p0469c2s v3p0470c1s v4p0362c1s v4p0541c1s v5p0621c1s
Dodge, M.A. and Lawrence, E.A. v3p0096c2s
Dodge, M.A. et al. v4p0595c2s
Dodge, M.B. v1p1002c1s v1p1374c1s
Dodge, M.E. v1p1101c2s
Dodge, M.M. v1p0185c1s v1p0916c2s
Dodge, M.M., Mrs. v5p0596c1s
Dodge, M.S. v1p0703c2s
Dodge, N.E. v1p0471c2s v1p1329c1s
Dodge, N.L. v1p0182c2s
Dodge, N.S. v1p0035c1s v1p0049c1s v1p0050c1s v1p0050c2s v1p0075c2s v1p0083c2s v1p0097c2s v1p0176c1s v1p0176c2s v1p0199c1s v1p0221c1s v1p0257c2s v1p0277c1s v1p0328c2s v1p0351c1s v1p0351c2s v1p0380c1s v1p0416c2s v1p0510c1s v1p0606c2s v1p0623c2s v1p0698c1s v1p0737c1s v1p0761c2s v1p0762c2s v1p0765c1s v1p0771c1s v1p0780c1s v1p0795c1s v1p0831c2s v1p0906c1s v1p0975c1s v1p0999c1s v1p1029c2s v1p1114c1s v1p1128c1s v1p1154c2s v1p1309c2s v1p1380c1s v1p1402c2s v2p0310c1s
Dodge, P.D. v4p0051c2s
Dodge, R. v1p0718c1s v1p0914c2s v5p0114c2s v5p0479c2s v5p0613c2s v6p0680c1s v6p0680c2s
Dodge, R. and Cline, T.S.. v5p0200c2s
Dodge, R.E. v4p0447c1s v5p0228c2s v5p0449c1s v5p0490c1s v5p0514c1m v6p0171c2s
Dodge, R.E.N. v3p0027c1s v3p0030c1s v3p0071c2s v3p0074c2s v3p0135c1s v3p0216c1s v3p0235c1m v3p0286c1s v3p0400c2s
Dodge, R.I. v5p0538c1s
Dodge, Raymond v5p0200c2s
Dodge, Raymond E. v4p0563c2s
Dodge, S.D. v3p0474c2s
Dodge, T.A. v1p0604c2s v1p0734c2s v1p0887c2s v1p1310c2s v1p1343c1s v2p0074c1s v2p0306c1s v3p0201c1s v3p0285c1s v3p0441c2s v4p0010c1s v4p0062c1s v4p0107c1s v4p0189c2s v4p0263c2s v4p0264c1m

v5p0331c1s v5p0508c2m v5p0543c2s
v6p0702c2s
Dodge, T.A. and Patch, C.A.
v3p0443c1s
Dodge, V.R. v5p0333c1s
Dodge, Virginia v5p0335c2s
Dodge, W.A. v2p0479c2s
Dodge, W.C. v4p0288c2s
v5p0294c2s v5p0435c1m
Dodge, W.E. and Strong, J.
v3p0378c1s
Dodge, W.W. v3p0159c1s
v3p0179c1s
Dodge, W.W. and Beecher, C.E.
v4p0524c1s
Dodgson, C. v4p0189c2s
v4p0273c1s v4p0430c1s v4p0446c1s
v4p0631c1s v6p0183c2s
Dodgson, C.L. v3p0008c2s
v3p0077c2s v3p0406c1s
Dodgson, D.S. v6p0673c1s
Dodgson, E.S. v4p0047c1s
Dods, M. v1p0289c1s
v3p0394c1s v3p0475c1s v4p0300c2s
v4p0301c2s v4p0303c2s v4p0478c2s
v4p0479c2s v4p0533c1s v5p0058c2s
v5p0089c1s v5p0305c2s v5p0561c2s
v6p0052c1s v6p0214c1s
Dods, Marcus v5p0055c1s
Dodsley, C.E. v6p0687c2s
Dodson, E. v2p0429c1s
Dodson, J.M. v6p0518c2s
Dodson, R. v1p1039c1s
Dodson, R.B. v2p0080c1s
Dodwell, H.H. v6p0032c1m
v6p0158c2m v6p0376c1s
Dodwell, H.Herbert v6p0631c1s
Doe, J.B. v5p0186c2s
Doebner, R. v3p0137c2s
Doellinger, J.J.I. v1p0756c2s
Doggett, K.N. v1p0461c2s
v1p1213c2s
Doggett, L.L. v5p0644c2s
Doggett, S.B. v4p0164c1s
v4p0408c2s v5p0072c2s v5p0352c1s
v5p0465c2s
Doggett, T. v1p0121c2s
v1p0684c1s v1p0754c2s
Doggett, T.P. v1p1384c1s
Doherty, D.J. v6p0631c1s
Doherty, E.P. and Ruggles, M.B.
v3p0050c1s
Doherty, F.B. v4p0573c2s
Doherty, F.M. v1p0013c2s
v1p0246c1s v1p1257c2s
Doherty, H. v1p0471c2s
Doherty, J.J. v3p0038c1m
v3p0300c2s v4p0523c2s
Doherty, T. v5p0291c1s
Dohm, A. v1p1441c1m
Dohoney, E.L. v2p0260c1s
Dohrn, A. v4p0410c2s
v4p0637c2s
Dolan, G. v5p0503c2s
Dolan, J. v4p0341c2s
Dolan, T.M. v3p0205c2s
Dolaro, S. v3p0038c2s
Dolbear, A.E. v1p0945c1s
v1p1006c2s v1p1128c2s v2p0258c1s
v2p0433c2s v3p0129c2s v3p0331c2s
v3p0380c1s v3p0423c1s v4p0036c1s
v4p0037c2s v4p0176c1s v4p0176c2s
v4p0331c2s v4p0347c1s v4p0360c2s
v4p0441c1s v4p0441c2s v4p0464c1m
v4p0487c1s v4p0507c2s v6p0576c1s
Dolbear, A.E. and Allen, T.E.
v4p0540c2s
Dolbear, E.H. v4p0441c2s
Dolbeer, W.H. v5p0106c2s
Dolby, E. v5p0342c1s
Dolby, G. v2p0401c1s
Dolby, W. v1p0821c1s
Dole, A.M. v6p0081c1s
v6p0372c1s
Dole, C.F. v1p0741c1s
v1p1055c1s v2p0351c2s v3p0083c2s
v3p0125c1s v3p0143c1s v4p0110c2s
v4p0190c1s v4p0218c1s v4p0479c1s
v4p0633c1s v5p0084c2s v5p0118c1s
v5p0593c2s v6p0008c1s v6p0145c2s
v6p0426c1s
Dole, C.H. v5p0141c2s
Dole, Catherine S. v6p0207c2s
Dole, E.P. v2p0088c2s
v2p0478c1s
Dole, G.T. v2p0121c1s
Dole, I. v1p0416c2s
v3p0258c1s
Dole, N.H. v2p0243c2s
v3p0115c2s v3p0235c2s v3p0349c2s
v3p0370c2m v3p0438c1s v4p0156c2s
v4p0321c2s v4p0496c2m v4p0568c2s
v4p0586c2s v5p0581c2s v6p0142c1s
v6p0373c2s v6p0466c2s v6p0612c2s
v6p0699c1s
Dole, S.B. v4p0250c2s
v5p0258c2s
Dolezalek, C. v1p1143c2s
Dolge, Alfred v4p0461c1s
Dollar, G. v5p0052c1s
v5p0061c2s v5p0310c1s v5p0382c2s
v5p0410c1s v5p0418c2s v5p0481c2s
Dollar, L. v5p0188c1s
Dolley, C.S. and Cattell, J.M.
v4p0397c2s v4p0474c1s
Dollinger, I.von v1p0640c2s
Dollinger, J.J.I.v. v3p0228c2s
Dollinger, J.J.I.von v1p1357c1s
Dollinger, J.v. v1p0499c2s
Dollinger, J.von v1p0629c2s
v2p0236c2s
Dolliver, C.D. v1p1438c1s
Dolliver, C.G. v1p1002c1s
Dolliver, J.P. v5p0095c2s
v5p0604c1s v6p0334c1s v6p0669c2s
Dolliver, J.P. et al. v4p0129c1s
Dolliver, Jonathan P. v6p0529c1s
Dollman, J.C. v6p0474c2s
v6p0496c2s
Dolman, F. v2p0175c1s
v3p0036c1s v3p0054c2s v3p0325c2s
v3p0336c2s v4p0077c1s v4p0080c2s
v4p0081c1s v4p0095c1s v4p0115c1s
v4p0124c1s v4p0198c1s v4p0351c2s
v4p0365c2s v4p0416c1s v4p0422c2m
v4p0559c1s v4p0623c1s v5p0007c1s
v5p0013c1s v5p0093c1s v5p0107c2s
v5p0152c1s v5p0159c2s v5p0234c1s
v5p0247c2s v5p0328c2s v5p0369c1s
v5p0384c2s v5p0526c1s v5p0564c2s
v5p0625c1s v5p0637c1s v6p0417c2s
Dolman, Frederick v4p0061c2s
v4p0387c2s v5p0020c2s v5p0638c2s
Dolman, I. v1p0626c1s
Dolman, J. v6p0436c1s
Dolman, J., jr. v4p0539c1s
Dolmetsch, A. v5p0100c2s
Dolph, J.M. v3p0119c1s
Dolph, J.N. v3p0307c2s
Dolph, J.N. and Vest, G.G.
v4p0129c1s
Dolph, J.N. et al. v4p0248c2s
Dolph, S.N. v4p0481c2s
Dolsen, H. v1p1177c2s
Dolsen, H.L. v1p0697c1s
v3p0339c2s
Dolson, E.C. v6p0504c2s
Dolson, G.N. v5p0196c1s
v5p0386c2s v5p0411c1s v6p0396c1s
Dombavand, B. v1p0661c1s
Domer, S. v4p0482c2s
Domett, Alfred v6p0124c2s
Domett, C. v6p0687c2s
Domett, C.S. v6p0348c1s
Dominic, Rene v5p0582c1s
Domojirov, A. v2p0475c1s
Domvile, F. v2p0192c1s
Domvile, M. v3p0102c2s
v3p0163c2s
Domville, M. v2p0036c1s
Don, O'C. v4p0289c2s
v4p0291c1s v5p0297c1s
Donagh, M. v6p0142c2s
Donaghe, H.R. v5p0257c1s
Donahue, J.L. v6p0220c1s
v6p0581c2s
Donajowski, R. v5p0243c2s
Donald, A.K. v4p0553c1s
Donald, C.W. v4p0019c2s
Donald, E.W. v5p0503c1s
Donald, H. and Spence, M.. v4p0119c2s
Donald, J.T. v3p0023c1s
v4p0404c1s v5p0298c2s
Donald, R. v3p0239c1s
v3p0437c2s v4p0173c2m v4p0286c2s
v4p0431c2m v4p0462c1s v4p0595c2s
v4p0632c2s v5p0131c1s v5p0217c2s
v5p0273c1s v5p0344c2s v5p0392c1m
v5p0418c2s v5p0431c1s v5p0556c2s
v5p0561c2s v5p0571c1s v5p0592c2s
v6p0088c2s v6p0183c2s v6p0435c1s
v6p0436c1m v6p0436c2s v6p0599c2s
v6p0601c1s v6p0658c2s
Donald, Robert v4p0212c2s
v4p0266c2s v4p0462c2s v4p0557c2s
v5p0556c2s v5p0640c1s
Donaldson, A. v1p0773c2s
v1p0977c1s v1p1308c2s
Donaldson, A.L. v5p0612c2s
Donaldson, A.M. v5p0598c1s
Donaldson, F. v3p0098c1s
Donaldson, F., jr. v3p0109c2s
Donaldson, H.H. v2p0054c2s
v2p0434c1s v3p0053c1s v3p0054c2s
v3p0072c1s v3p0103c2s v3p0300c1m
v4p0135c2s v4p0397c2s v6p0019c2s
v6p0203c2s
Donaldson, H.H. and Hall, G.S.
v2p0299c2s
Donaldson, I.H. v5p0450c2s
Donaldson, J. v1p0099c1s
v1p0263c2s v1p0392c1s v1p0551c2s
v1p1017c1s v1p1190c1s v1p1423c2s
v2p0131c2s v3p0107c2s v3p0363c2s
v3p0365c2s v3p0366c1s v3p0468c1s
v3p0469c1s v3p0470c1s v4p0170c1s
v6p0577c2s
Donaldson, J.A. v4p0251c1s
Donaldson, J.B. v3p0444c1s
v4p0109c1s
Donaldson, J.H. v3p0320c1s
Donaldson, J.W. v4p0475c2s
Donaldson, Jas. v6p0192c2s
Donaldson, R. v6p0390c2s
Donaldson, T. v1p1062c2s
v2p0022c2s v2p0064c2s v2p0181c2s
v5p0629c2s
Donaldson, T.B. v6p0393c1s
Donaldson, W. v1p0408c1s
v4p0343c1s
Donati, Prof. v3p0206c1s
Donbavaud, B. v2p0015c1s
Doncaster, L. v6p0165c1s
Doncot, F. v1p0697c1s
Donders, C. v6p0037c1s
Donehoo, E.R. v3p0338c2s
Doney, M. v6p0152c1s
Doniat, J.C. v6p0323c2s
Donigan, B.E. v6p0364c2s
Doniphan, J. v4p0342c2s
v4p0375c1s
Donisthorpe, W. v4p0017c1s
v4p0356c2s
Donkersley, R. v1p0143c1s
v1p1253c2s
Donkin, B. v4p0258c1s
v5p0462c2s v5p0550c2s v6p0615c1s
Donkin, E.H. v4p0436c2s
v5p0005c1s
Donkin, H. v2p0291c1s
v2p0415c1s v2p0440c1s
Donkin, H.B. v2p0282c2s
v4p0020c2s
Donlan, W.J. v6p0571c1s
Donnally, E.A. v6p0178c1s
Donne, A. v1p0619c2s
Donne, B.J.M. v5p0268c2s
Donne, W.B. v1p0364c1s
v1p0364c2s v1p1104c2s
Donne, W.B. and Liddel, H.G.
v1p1114c2s
Donnell, A.H. v5p0186c2s
v5p0342c2s v5p0368c2s v6p0004c2s
v6p0114c2s v6p0221c2s v6p0303c1s
v6p0375c2s v6p0516c2s v6p0519c1s
v6p0533c1m v6p0534c1s v6p0541c1s
v6p0644c2s v6p0664c2s v6p0677c2s
Donnell, Alice H. v6p0035c1s
Donnell, Annie H. v6p0025c1s
v6p0078c1s v6p0175c2s v6p0216c1s
v6p0504c2s v6p0525c1s
Donnelly, F.P. v6p0292c2s
Donnelly, I. v3p0030c1s
v3p0387c2m v4p0517c2s
Donnelly, J. v1p0848c2s
Donnelly, L.M. v5p0419c2s
Donnelly, S.R. v6p0651c2s
Donnelly, T. v6p0327c1s
Donnelly, T. and Herbert, H.A.
v4p0243c2s
Donner, H.M. v6p0224c2m
v6p0225c1s v6p0628c1s
Donner, W.H. v5p0431c1s
Donnithorne, V.H. v6p0383c2s
Donohoe, D., jr. v6p0401c1s
Donohue, F.L. v5p0050c2s
Donohue, L.B. v6p0246c1s
Donoughmore, Earl of v4p0266c1s
v4p0289c2s
Donovan, A. v4p0125c2s
Donovan, J. v3p0242c2s
v4p0320c1s v5p0325c1s v5p0394c1s
v6p0203c1s
Donovan, M. v6p0048c1s
Donovan, Robert v6p0327c1s
Donovan, T.M. v5p0039c2s
v5p0474c2s v6p0360c2s
Doolan, J.C. v5p0315c1m
Dooley, C. v5p0240c1s
v5p0253c1s v5p0287c1s
Dooley, E.T. v2p0077c2s
v2p0240c1s
Doolittle, C.L. v2p0095c1m
v2p0095c2s v4p0322c1s v5p0035c1s
v5p0211c1s v6p0463c2s
v6p0577c1s
Doolittle, C.S. v5p0487c1s
v5p0640c2s
Doolittle, E. v4p0321c2s
v5p0482c1s v5p0549c1s v5p0571c2s
v6p0613c2s
Doolittle, E.S. v5p0626c2s
Doolittle, Edward S. v5p0312c2s
Doolittle, J. v1p0234c1s
v1p1249c1s
Doolittle, M. v1p0109c1s
Doolittle, M.H. v1p0612c2s
v1p0684c2s v1p0850c1s
Doolittle, T.S. v2p0222c2s
Dooly, M.A. v4p0283c2s
Doone, H. v3p0474c1s
Dooner, W.T. v5p0193c2s
v5p0290c1s v5p0538c1s
Doornik, J.E. v1p0470c2s
Dopp, K.E. v6p0297c2s
v6p0656c1s
Dopp, Katherine E. v6p0199c2s
Doran, J. v1p0621c1s
v1p0763c2s v1p0863c1s v1p1123c1s
v1p1184c2s v1p1358c1s v1p1417c2s

v1p1424c1s
Doran, J.I. v1p0174c2s
v1p0996c2s
Doran, L.W. v6p0441c1s
Dorchester, D. v1p0046c2s
v1p0393c1s v1p0501c1s v1p1355c2s
v2p0286c1s v4p0076c1s v4p0109c2s
v4p0282c1s v4p0398c2s v5p0031c1s
v5p0128c1s
Dorchester, D., jr. v4p0246c2s
v4p0448c1s v4p0570c1s
Dore, J.R. v2p0041c2s
v2p0470c1s v4p0053c1s
Doremus, F.H. v6p0106c2s
Doremus, R.O. v4p0220c2s
v4p0449c1s
Doremus, R.O. et al. v3p0350c1s
Doremus, R.Ogden v6p0075c2s
v6p0087c2s
Doren, E.C. v5p0335c1s
v5p0335c2s v5p0337c1s v6p0074c2s
v6p0371c2s
Doring, A. v4p0381c2s
Doring, F. v1p1367c1s
Doring, W. v3p0093c2s
Dorington, J. v5p0178c2s
Dorland, C.P. v4p0083c2s
Dorling, W. v1p0501c1s
v2p0148c2s
Dorman, L.M. v1p0259c1s
v1p0292c2s v1p0587c2s v1p0916c1s
v2p0313c2s v2p0434c1s
Dorman, Marcus R.P. v6p0665c2s
Dormis, J. v6p0172c2s
v6p0331c2s
Dorn, Dr. v1p0820c1s
Dorn, L.Van v3p0076c2s
Dornblaser, S.G. v6p0060c1s
Dornblaser, T.F. v4p0102c2s
v4p0345c2s v4p0584c2s v5p0435c1s
v6p0122c2s v6p0575c1s
Dornbloser, E.H. v6p0299c2s
Dorner, Dr. v1p0528c1s
Dorner, I.A. v1p0529c2s
Dorner, J.A. v1p0498c1s
v1p0640c2s v1p0687c1s v1p0688c2s
v1p0700c1s v1p0777c2s v1p1058c1s
v2p0257c2s
Dorner, J.E. v1p1060c2s
Dorner, O. v5p0490c2s
Dorney, P.S. v2p0079c2s
Dorpfeld, W. v3p0430c2s
Dorpfeld, W. et al. v3p0273c2s
Dorr, A.V.N. v4p0418c1s
Dorr, D. v1p0063c2s
v2p0113c1s
Dorr, F.O. v1p0284c1s
v1p0801c1s v1p0873c2s v1p1079c2s
v1p1191c2s v1p1319c2s
Dorr, J.C.R. v1p0887c2s
v1p0981c1s v1p1403c2s v2p0040c2s
v3p0062c2s v3p0071c1s v3p0173c1s
v3p0184c1s v3p0453c1s v3p0468c1s
v5p0282c2s v5p0425c2s v5p0491c1s
v5p0503c1s
Dorr, L.S. v1p0427c2s
v1p0797c1s v1p0959c2s v1p1299c2s
Dorr, R.C. v6p0705c2m
Dorr, Rheta C. v6p0075c2s
v6p0277c1s
Dorr, T.O. v1p0832c2s
Dorrance, J.F. v5p0282c2s
Dorsey, A.V. v3p0040c1s
v3p0414c2s v3p0425c1s v5p0242c1s
v5p0266c1s
Dorsey, A.Y. v3p0399c2s
Dorsey, Anna V. v6p0359c1s
Dorsey, C.A. v6p0029c2s
Dorsey, D. v2p0403c2s
Dorsey, D.B. v1p0773c1s
v1p0773c2s
Dorsey, E.B. v2p0362c2s
Dorsey, E.L. v2p0110c2s
v2p0243c2s v3p0030c1s v3p0323c1s
v3p0469c1s v4p0210c2s v4p0295c1s
Dorsey, G.A. v4p0102c1s
v4p0436c2s v5p0022c2m v5p0206c1m
v5p0225c1m v5p0254c1s v5p0270c1m
v5p0288c1s v5p0510c1s v5p0531c2b
v5p0581c1s v5p0594c1m v5p0630c1s
v5p0634c1s v6p0301c1s v6p0409c1s
v6p0471c1s v6p0485c1m v6p0698c1s
Dorsey, G.A. and Holmes, W.H.
v5p0532c1s v5p0583c2s
Dorsey, H.C. v3p0471c1s
Dorsey, J.O. v2p0117c2s
v2p0219c2s v2p0321c2m v2p0324c1m
v2p0403c2s v2p0404c1s v3p0116c2s
v3p0295c1s v3p0314c2s v4p0059c1s
v4p0225c2s v4p0253c1s v4p0313c2s
v4p0413c2m v4p0451c2m v4p0523c2s
v4p0527c2m v4p0571c1m v4p0624c1s
Dorsey, J.Owen v2p0300c2s
Dorsey, L.R. v3p0231c2s
Dorsey, M.W. v3p0078c1s
Dorsey, N.E. v5p0015c1s
v5p0532c1s
Dorsey, S.A. v2p0028c1s
Dorsey, S.W. v3p0302c2s
Dorsheimer, W. v1p0179c1s
v1p0680c2s v1p1344c2s
Dorst, J.H. v5p0098c1s
Dorum, J. v6p0326c1s
v6p0327c1s
Dosker, H.E. v5p0048c1s
Dossie, R. v3p0071c1s
Doster, F. v5p0446c1s
Dosterzee, J.J.Van v1p0121c2s
v1p0359c1s v1p0684c1s v2p0437c2s
Dostoyevsky, T. v3p0254c1s
Doten, C.W. v6p0528c1s
Doten, Carroll W. v6p0068c2s
Doty, A.H. v4p0137c2s
v5p0259c2s v5p0474c1s v5p0644c1s
v6p0524c2s
Doty, A.H. et al. v5p0259c2s
Doty, D.Z. v5p0533c2s
Doty, F.E. v6p0081c2s
Doty, H.A. v2p0048c2s
v2p0472c2s
Doty, M.F. v6p0535c1s
Doty, T.E. v5p0466c2s
v5p0601c1s
Doubavaud, E. v2p0112c2s
Doubleday, F.N. v4p0274c2s
Doubleday, R. v5p0051c2s
v6p0151c2s v6p0530c1s
Doubleday, W.E. v3p0308c1s
v5p0333c2s v5p0336c2m v6p0374c1s
Douce, F. v1p0226c2s
v1p0366c2s v1p0446c2s v1p0465c2s
v1p0539c1s v1p0596c2s v1p0624c2s
v1p0803c2s v1p0852c1s v1p1130c2s
v1p1176c1s v1p1317c2s v1p1365c2s
v1p1413c2s
Douce, F. and Holden, R. . v1p0464c2s
v1p1307c2s
Douce, H.F. and Hamper, W.
v1p1132c1s
Doucet, J. v1p1377c2s
Doudney, E. v2p0336c1s
Doudney, S. v2p0121c2s
v2p0201c1s v3p0175c2s v4p0443c2s
v5p0314c1s
Doudney, Sarah v3p0282c1s
Douey, A.E. v2p0276c1s
Dougall, J.D. v2p0014c2s
v2p0141c2s v4p0455c2s
Dougall, L. v4p0127c1s
v4p0193c1s v4p0226c2s v4p0348c2s
v4p0575c2s v4p0618c2s v4p0625c1s
v4p0636c1s v6p0093c1s v6p0185c2s
Dougan, P. v6p0600c2s
Dougherty, A. v1p0730c2s
v1p1017c2s
Dougherty, C.A. v2p0067c2s
v4p0294c2s
Dougherty, C.J. v5p0182c2s
Dougherty, D. v3p0034c1s
Dougherty, F.C. and Parrott, J.
v6p0667c2s
Dougherty, J.E. v5p0169c2s
Dougherty, J.G. v2p0356c1s
Dougherty, J.H. v3p0304c2s
Dougherty, J.J. v2p0007c1s
v2p0037c2s v3p0048c2s
Dougherty, J.W. v4p0449c1s
Dougherty, N.C. v3p0128c1s
v5p0012c1s v5p0326c2s
Dougherty, P. v6p0531c1s
Dougherty, W.E. v4p0281c2s
v4p0633c2s v5p0318c2s
Doughty, A.G. v4p0388c1s
v4p0437c2s v5p0101c1s v5p0606c1s
Doughty, F.A. v1p0667c2s
v2p0151c2s v3p0058c1s v3p0207c2s
v3p0247c1s v4p0069c1s v4p0198c1s
v4p0627c1s v5p0012c2s v5p0042c2s
v5p0139c1s v5p0165c1s v5p0212c1s
v5p0338c1s v5p0363c1m v5p0406c1s
v5p0540c2s v5p0546c1s v6p0597c2s
Doughty, H.M. v4p0164c1s
v4p0328c1s v5p0168c1s v5p0634c1s
Doughty, J.G. v2p0032c2s
Douglas, A. v4p0120c1s
Douglas, A.F. v2p0093c1m
v2p0291c2s
Douglas, A.H. v5p0074c1s
v5p0196c1s v5p0370c1s
Douglas, A.M. v5p0419c2s
Douglas, Alice M. v5p0361c1s
Douglas, Anna v5p0404c2s
v5p0497c2s
Douglas, B. v4p0163c1s
Douglas, B.K. v1p0235c2s
Douglas, C. v6p0270c2s
v6p0577c2s v6p0582c1s
Douglas, C.H. v4p0255c1s
v4p0257c1s
Douglas, C.H.J. v4p0127c2s
Douglas, E. v5p0371c1s
v6p0183c1s
Douglas, F.J. v5p0072c2s
v5p0089c1s v5p0119c2s v5p0392c1s
Douglas, F.S. v5p0239c1s
Douglas, G. v5p0048c1s
v5p0102c2s v5p0329c2s v5p0578c2s
v6p0291c2s
Douglas, G., Sir v5p0203c1s
v5p0331c1s v5p0522c2s
Douglas, G.C. v4p0525c1s
v4p0525c2s
Douglas, G.C.M. v3p0042c1s
v3p0224c1s v4p0055c1s v4p0055c2s
v5p0056c2s v6p0062c2s
Douglas, G.W. v2p0029c2s
v2p0099c2s v2p0266c2s v2p0414c2s
Douglas, George v5p0482c2s
Douglas, George, Sir v5p0065c2s
Douglas, H.F. v1p0191c2s
Douglas, H.K. v1p0675c1s
v2p0232c2s v5p0301c1s
Douglas, H.P. v5p0081c2s
v5p0276c2s v6p0661c1s
Douglas, I.A. and Mueller, M.
v4p0408c1s
Douglas, J. v1p0078c2s
v1p0193c2s v1p0195c1s v1p0230c2s
v1p0852c1s v1p0992c2s v1p0996c2s
v1p1039c2s v1p1103c1s v2p0029c1s
v2p0102c1m v2p0182c1s v3p0005c2s
v3p0175c1s v3p0281c2s v3p0357c1s
v3p0358c1s v4p0063c1s v4p0133c1s
v4p0332c1s v4p0366c2s v4p0372c1s
v4p0402c1s v5p0124c2s v5p0146c1s
v5p0371c2s v5p0430c2s v5p0477c1s
v5p0510c1s v5p0542c1s v5p0564c1s
v6p0006c2s v6p0030c1s v6p0041c1s
v6p0057c1s v6p0059c2s v6p0111c1s
v6p0132c2s v6p0196c1s v6p0262c2s
v6p0281c1s v6p0351c1s v6p0455c2s
v6p0462c1s v6p0538c1s v6p0588c2s
Douglas, J. and Melvill, Gen.
v1p1122c2s
Douglas, J. and Mills, L.H.
v5p0587c1s
Douglas, J.A. and Muller, F.M.
v4p0301c2s
Douglas, J.N. v2p0258c2s
Douglas, James v6p0149c1s
Douglas, L. v5p0528c2s
v6p0127c2s v6p0593c2m
Douglas, M. v1p1067c1s
v1p1128c1s v2p0065c2s v2p0155c2s
v2p0216c1s v2p0288c1s v2p0422c2s
v3p0333c2s v4p0200c2s v4p0618c2s
Douglas, N. v4p0633c2s
Douglas, P. v5p0601c2s
Douglas, R. v4p0092c1s
v4p0208c1s v4p0209c1s
Douglas, R.B. v6p0479c2s
v6p0617c2s
Douglas, R.K. v1p0233c1s
v1p0233c2s v2p0061c2s v2p0078c2s
v2p0079c1m v2p0079c2s v2p0080c1s
v2p0282c1s v2p0283c1s v2p0327c1s
v3p0078c2s v3p0079c1s v3p0226c2s
v3p0309c1s v3p0439c1s v4p0105c2m
v4p0106c1m v4p0106c2s v4p0134c1s
v4p0166c2s v4p0298c1m v5p0109c2s
v5p0110c1s v5p0110c2s v5p0111c2s
v5p0112c1s v5p0122c1s v5p0240c1s
v5p0643c2s v6p0118c1s
Douglas, R.K. and Meade, L.T.
v4p0483c2s
Douglas, R.L. v6p0395c2s
Douglas, R.W. v1p0210c1s
v1p1091c2s
Douglas, S.A. v1p1296c1s
v1p1350c1s
Douglas, S.L. v6p0692c2s
Douglas, T. v5p0272c2s
Douglas, T.H. v4p0543c2s
Douglas, W.A. v4p0075c1s
v4p0111c2s v5p0053c1s
Douglas, W.L. v6p0632c2s
v6p0651c2s
Douglas, W.S. v4p0141c2s
Douglass, A.E. v2p0066c2s
v2p0159c2m v2p0299c2s v2p0300c1m
v4p0344c1s v4p0358c1s v4p0436c2s
v4p0490c2s v5p0035c1s v5p0037c1s
v5p0227c2s v5p0312c2m v5p0350c1s
v5p0363c1s v5p0389c2s v5p0453c1s
v5p0459c2s v5p0518c2s v5p0549c2s
v5p0645c2s v6p0013c1s v6p0427c1s
Douglass, A.E. and Hale, G.E.
v5p0549c2s
Douglass, C.H.J. v1p1351c1s
v4p0565c1s
Douglass, D.B. v1p1384c2s
Douglass, E. v1p1012c2s
v5p0491c1s
Douglass, E.S. v6p0411c2s
Douglass, F. v1p0905c2m
v2p0122c1s v2p0309c1s v3p0191c2s
v4p0346c1m v6p0388c1s
Douglass, G.N. v4p0514c1s
v4p0516c2s
Douglass, H.M. v1p0035c1s
Douglass, H.P. v4p0256c1s
Douglass, J. v4p0059c1s
v6p0133c1s
Douglass, J.N. v3p0036c2s
v3p0156c2s
Douglass, M.H. v6p0535c1s
Douglass, N. v3p0334c1s
Douglass, S.J. v1p0011c2s
v1p0527c2s v1p0925c2s v1p1016c2s
Douglass, W. v5p0149c1s

Douglass, W.F. v1p0263c2s
Douglass, W.T. v2p0130c1s
Doull, I.C. v5p0340c2s
Doulton, J. v1p1296c1s
Doumer, P. v6p0205c1s
Doumic, R. v5p0044c2s
v5p0050c2s v5p0221c1s v5p0373c2s
v5p0397c2s v5p0582c1s v6p0241c2s
Doumic, Rene v5p0037c2s
v5p0381c2s v5p0637c1s
Dounet, Card. v2p0250c2s
Dounet, G. v5p0217c1s
Douse, T.LeM. v5p0380c2s
v5p0545c2s
Dousman, M.E. v4p0329c2s
Dousman, M.E. and Foster, W.E.
v5p0334c1s
Douthwaite, D.W. v4p0163c1s
v4p0235c2s v4p0568c2s
Douthwaite, W.R. v2p0185c1s
v2p0465c1s
Dove, C.C. v5p0172c1s
v5p0263c1s v5p0386c1s
Dove, H.W. v1p0074c1s
v1p1080c2s v1p1256c2s
Dove, J.R. v2p0043c2s
Dove, P.E. v1p0408c1s
v1p1107c2s
Doveridge, F. v3p0226c1s
v3p0324c1s
Doveton, F.B. v5p0085c2s
v5p0159c1s v5p0539c1s
Dovidoff, Mad. v4p0578c2s
Dow, A.W. v5p0031c2s
Dow, C.M. v6p0456c2s
Dow, E.W. v5p0231c2s
v6p0241c2s
Dow, J. v3p0349c2s
v4p0310c1m v4p0346c2s v4p0453c2s
Dow, J.E.T. v4p0291c2s
Dow, J.G. v2p0180c1s
v2p0324c2s v2p0361c2s v2p0397c2s
v2p0420c1s v2p0428c2s v3p0137c2s
v3p0168c2s v3p0335c1s v3p0335c2s
v3p0349c2s v3p0446c2s v4p0302c1s
v4p0467c2s v4p0475c1s v4p0485c1s
Dow, J.W. v5p0166c1s
v5p0586c1s v6p0152c2s v6p0298c2m
v6p0300c1s v6p0452c2s v6p0677c1s
Dow, Joy W. v6p0295c1s
v6p0298c2s
Dow, L. v1p0332c2s
Dow, N. v1p1292c2s
v3p0252c2m v3p0346c1m v3p0444c1s
Dow, N. and Lewis, D. v2p0355c2s
v2p0434c1s
Dow, Neal v2p0356c1s
Dowall, L.D. v6p0441c1s
Dowd, C.F. v5p0214c1s
Dowd, C.W. v5p0494c1s
Dowd, J. v4p0538c1s
v5p0009c1s v5p0121c1s v5p0139c1s
v5p0403c1s v5p0557c2s v5p0637c2s
v6p0114c2s
Dowd, J. and Gunton, G. .. v5p0320c2s
Dowd, Jerome v4p0022c1s
Dowd, W.B. v5p0329c2s
v6p0363c2s
Dowd, W.F. v2p0266c1s
Dowdall, H.C. v5p0106c1s
Dowdall, L.D. v6p0707c1s
Dowden, E. v1p0009c1s
v1p0064c1s v1p0170c2s v1p0201c2s
v1p0293c1s v1p0473c1s v1p0475c2s
v1p0488c1s v1p0511c2m v1p0530c2s
v1p0612c1s v1p0720c1s v1p0722c2s
v1p0725c2s v1p0801c2s v1p0842c1s
v1p0901c1s v1p1020c2s v1p1060c2s
v1p1072c1s v1p1164c1s v1p1321c1s
v1p1430c1s v1p1430c2s v2p0011c2s
v2p0052c1s v2p0124c2s v2p0142c2s
v2p0174c2s v2p0181c1s v2p0181c2m
v2p0185c1s v2p0260c2s v2p0283c1s
v2p0293c1s v2p0367c1s v2p0397c2m
v2p0398c1s v2p0398c2m v2p0399c2m
v2p0409c2s v2p0428c2s v2p0429c1s
v2p0431c2s v2p0473c1s v2p0478c1s
v2p0479c2s v2p0482c1s v3p0091c1s
v3p0120c2s v3p0140c2m v3p0147c2s
v3p0154c2s v3p0161c1s v3p0164c1s
v3p0175c2s v3p0176c1m v3p0218c2s
v3p0253c2s v3p0269c2s v3p0367c2s
v3p0372c1s v3p0377c1m v3p0382c1s
v3p0388c1s v3p0390c1m v3p0460c1s
v3p0472c1m v4p0028c1s v4p0073c1s
v4p0122c1s v4p0184c2s v4p0229c2s
v4p0289c2s v4p0365c2s v4p0459c1s
v4p0574c2s v5p0261c1s v5p0317c1s
v5p0341c2s v5p0365c1s v5p0398c1s
v5p0416c2s v5p0473c1s v6p0085c1s
v6p0208c2m v6p0305c2s v6p0328c1s
v6p0483c2s v6p0586c2s v6p0655c2s
Dowden, E. and Caine, T.H.
v2p0399c2s
Dowden, E. and Salt, H.S.. v3p0390c1s
Dowden, Edward v3p0253c1s
Dowden, J. v1p0266c2s
v1p0284c2s v1p0285c1s v2p0044c2s
v2p0071c1s v2p0096c2s v2p0254c1s
v2p0261c2s v2p0351c2s v6p0184c1s
Dowden, T.B. v4p0052c1s
v4p0145c2s
Dowden, T.F. v2p0364c1s
Dowdeswell, C. v2p0464c1m
Dowdeswell, W. v3p0462c1s
Dowe, C.E. v3p0210c1s
Dowe, J.E.T. v4p0293c1s
Dowe, W. v1p0113c2s
v1p0171c2s v1p0228c1s v1p0254c1s
v1p0327c1s v1p0411c2s v1p0439c2s
v1p0484c1s v1p0538c1s v1p0551c2s
v1p0578c2s v1p0653c2s v1p0661c2s
v1p0698c2s v1p0724c1s v1p0742c1s
v1p0876c1s v1p0937c2s v1p0998c2s
v1p1013c1s v1p1024c2s v1p1029c2s
v1p1067c1s v1p1167c1s v1p1176c2s
v1p1189c2s v1p1190c2s v1p1275c1s
Dowell, G.S. v5p0268c1s
Dowie, M.M. v3p0231c1s
v3p0371c1s v4p0258c1s
Dowie, Menie M. v6p0358c1s
Dowie, R.C. v4p0521c2s
Dowker, G. v2p0385c2s
v2p0456c2s
Dowler, B. v1p0875c1s
Dowler, W.J. v4p0411c1s
Dowling, A.E.P.R. v3p0149c2s
v4p0010c2s v4p0024c1s v4p0110c1s
v4p0172c1s v4p0202c2s v4p0219c2s
v4p0452c2s v5p0434c2s v5p0528c1m
v5p0578c2s v6p0229c1s
Dowling, A.R. v4p0173c1s
v4p0301c1s
Dowling, H.M. v5p0633c2s
v6p0655c2s
Dowling, J. v1p0700c1s
v1p1033c1s v1p1222c1s v1p1324c2s
Dowling, J.A. v6p0302c2s
Dowling, J.F. v4p0038c2s
Dowling, J.W. v2p0206c2s
Dowling, R. v1p0334c1s
v1p0345c1s v1p0397c2s v1p0531c2s
v1p0800c2s v1p0889c2s v1p1260c2s
v1p1299c2s v1p1315c1s v1p1339c2s
v1p1397c1s v2p0237c2s v2p0250c1s
v2p0275c1s v2p0322c1s v2p0416c2s
v3p0278c1s v4p0598c2s
Dowling, R.D. v1p0807c2s
Dowman, J. v5p0177c2s
v5p0562c2s v5p0572c1s v6p0167c2s
v6p0226c1s v6p0520c1s v6p0637c2s
Down, T.C. v4p0353c2s
v4p0461c2s v5p0064c2s v5p0318c1m
v5p0318c2m v6p0273c1s
Downer, J.R. v4p0193c2s
Downer, S.A. v1p0438c2s
Downer, S.A., Mrs. v1p0188c2s
v1p0455c2s v1p0866c2s v1p1071c2s
Downes, A. v1p0134c2s
v2p0175c2s
Downes, H. v1p0942c2s
Downes, J. v1p0334c2s
v1p1381c1s
Downes, W. v1p0051c2s
v1p0298c1s v1p0375c2s v1p0507c2s
v1p0721c2s v2p0127c2s v3p0414c1s
Downes, W.H. v3p0034c2s
v3p0051c1s v3p0278c2s v3p0317c2m
v3p0330c2s v3p0447c2s v4p0030c1s
v4p0068c2s v4p0069c1s v4p0097c2s
v4p0101c2s v4p0276c1s v4p0393c1s
v4p0612c1s v4p0614c1s v5p0030c1s
v5p0053c2s v5p0072c2s v5p0151c2m
v5p0255c2s v5p0490c2s v5p0639c2s
v6p0076c1s v6p0165c2s v6p0393c2s
v6p0513c1s v6p0633c2s
Downes, W.H. and Robinson, F.T.
v4p0032c1s v4p0064c2s
Downey, D.G. v4p0367c2s
Downey, E. v1p0270c1s
v1p0745c2s v1p1320c2s v2p0314c2s
v2p0338c1s v2p0341c2s
Downey, J.E. v5p0008c2s
v5p0419c2s
Downey, J.G. v1p0188c1s
v1p0945c2s
Downey, R. v2p0153c1s
v2p0174c2s v2p0202c2s
Downie, J. v3p0222c1s
v3p0381c2s v4p0394c1s v4p0509c1m
Downing, A. v4p0099c1s
Downing, A.M.W. v5p0154c2s
Downing, A.M.W. and Stoney, G.J.
v5p0372c2s
Downing, E.R. v5p0592c1s
v6p0019c1s
Downing, F. v1p0089c2s
v1p1347c1s
Downing, H.P.B. v4p0618c1s
Downing, M.K. v5p0605c2s
Downing, Miss v1p1426c2s
Downing, Prof. v1p0564c1s
Downing, S.R. v4p0485c1s
Downing, W. v2p0256c2s
Downs, A.S. v3p0001c1s
Downs, C.A. v2p0282c2s
v3p0448c2s
Downs, W. v4p0388c1s
Downs, W.H. v6p0695c2s
Downton, C.E. v6p0204c2s
Dowse, T.E. v6p0266c1s
Dowsett, E. v6p0475c2s
Dowsett, F.J. v3p0230c2s
Dowsey, S. v1p1126c2s
Dowsley, E. v4p0290c2s
v4p0301c2s v5p0082c2s v5p0202c1s
Dowson, E. v3p0411c1s
Dowson, E.C. v3p0402c2s
Dowson, J.E. v2p0171c2s
v3p0113c1s v3p0167c2s
Dowson, W.H. v5p0065c1s
Dox, H.L. v1p0038c2s
v1p0433c2s v1p0847c1s v1p0848c1s
v1p0868c1s v1p1040c2s v1p1067c1s
v2p0359c1s
Doxey, J.S. v1p0272c1s
v1p0466c1s v1p1039c2s v1p1416c2s
v2p0116c1s
Doyen, E. v6p0098c2s
Doyen, J.T. v1p0236c1s
v1p1141c1s v1p1280c2s v1p1315c2s
Doyle, A.C. v2p0051c1s
v2p0257c2s v2p0274c1s v2p0394c2s
v3p0055c1s v3p0315c1s v3p0331c2s
v3p0392c1s v3p0410c1s v3p0416c2s
v3p0462c2s v4p0025c2s v4p0091c2s
v4p0149c1s v4p0158c1s v4p0207c1s
v4p0242c2s v4p0341c2m v4p0342c1s
v4p0477c2s v4p0528c2s v4p0560c1s
v4p0568c2s v5p0143c2s v5p0146c1s
v5p0155c2s v5p0241c1s v5p0243c2m
v5p0245c1s v5p0251c1s v5p0486c2s
v5p0498c1s v5p0555c1m v5p0555c2s
v5p0585c1s v5p0588c1s v5p0596c1s
v5p0597c2s v5p0614c2s v5p0627c1s
v6p0174c2s v6p0654c2s
Doyle, A.Conan v4p0475c2s
v4p0529c1s v4p0546c1s v4p0618c2s
v5p0142c1s v5p0588c1s
Doyle, A.P. v4p0488c2s
v5p0109c2s v5p0354c1s v5p0406c2s
v5p0445c2s v5p0506c1s v5p0572c1s
v6p0368c1s v6p0454c1s v6p0493c2s
v6p0547c2m
Doyle, Agnes C. v6p0668c2s
Doyle, C.W. v5p0093c2s
v5p0279c2s
Doyle, D. v3p0168c1s
Doyle, F., Sir v3p0029c2s
v3p0258c1s
Doyle, F.H. v1p0360c2s
v1p0588c1s v1p1071c2s v3p0344c1s
Doyle, F.H., Sir v1p0604c2s
v2p0207c1s
Doyle, J.A. v2p0167c2s
v2p0189c2s v2p0212c2s v2p0295c2s
v3p0010c1s v3p0262c1s v3p0301c1s
v3p0442c2s v3p0443c1s v4p0015c2s
v4p0359c2s v4p0406c2s v4p0467c2s
v4p0584c1s v5p0015c1s
Doyle, J.C. v1p1163c1s
Doyle, J.N. v4p0531c2s
Doyle, J.T. v2p0401c2s
v3p0063c1s v3p0282c2s v3p0333c1s
v3p0387c1s v4p0105c1s v4p0116c2s
v4p0117c1s
Doyle, K.D. v6p0495c2s
Doyle, L. v1p0194c1s
Doyle, L.C. v4p0350c2s
Doyle, M. v1p0330c1s
Doyle, Martin v1p0589c2s
Doyle, R.D. v4p0322c2s
Doyle, W.E. v1p0174c1s
Doyne, W.T. v1p0104c1s
Drachmann, H. v2p0333c1s
v4p0457c1s v4p0620c2s
Drachmann, H. and Mackenzie, H.
v5p0169c1s
Draecken, K.van v1p0940c2s
Drage, G. v4p0275c1m
v4p0314c2m v5p0008c2s v5p0109c2s
v5p0459c1s v5p0587c1s v6p0310c1m
v6p0557c1m
Drage, M. v4p0380c2s
Draghicesco, D. v6p0303c2s
Dragomanov, M. v4p0206c1s
Dragoumis, E.J. v3p0168c2s
Drahms, A. v4p0477c1s
Drahofe, A.B. v6p0018c1s
Drail, R. v4p0118c2s
Drake, A. v4p0341c2s
Drake, A.W. v4p0143c2s
v4p0635c1s
Drake, B. v1p0706c1s
Drake, B.V. v6p0118c2s
Drake, C. v4p0608c1s
Drake, C.D. v1p0339c1s
v1p0494c1s
Drake, C.M. v6p0129c2s
Drake, C.M. et al. v5p0259c2s
Drake, D. v5p0257c1s
Drake, E. v4p0605c1s
Drake, F.C. v4p0064c2s
v5p0043c2s v6p0587c2s
Drake, F.S. v1p0152c2s
v1p0712c1s
Drake, H.A. v4p0315c2s
v6p0621c2s
Drake, J. v3p0420c2s
v6p0172c1s

Drake, J.H. ... v5p0494c1s v5p0516c1s v6p0130c1s
Drake, J.M. ... v1p1011c1s v2p0355c1s
Drake, J.N. ... v4p0087c2s
Drake, Jeanie ... v6p0084c1s v6p0181c2s v6p0291c2s v6p0420c2s v6p0442c2s v6p0648c2s
Drake, M. ... v6p0261c1s
Drake, O.S.T. ... v4p0012c2s
Drake, O.T.S. ... v3p0121c2s
Drake, S.A. ... v1p0152c1s v1p0808c2s v1p1072c1s v1p1145c2s v1p1394c1s v1p1406c2s
Drake, S.G. ... v1p0005c2s v1p0006c1s v1p0028c1s v1p0030c2s v1p0152c1s v1p0157c2s v1p0170c2s v1p0223c2s v1p0305c2s v1p0360c2s v1p0361c1s v1p0422c2s v1p0444c1s v1p0491c2s v1p0512c1s v1p0521c1s v1p0534c1s v1p0536c2s v1p0638c1s v1p0680c2s v1p0695c2s v1p0731c1s v1p0743c1s v1p0811c1s v1p0814c1s v1p0910c1s v1p0910c2m v1p0975c2s v1p1009c1s v1p1036c1s v1p1081c2s v1p1084c2m v1p1114c2s v1p1244c2s v1p1264c2s v1p1387c1s v1p1404c2s
Drake, V.M. ... v2p0146c1s
Drake, W. ... v1p0168c1s v1p0415c2s v1p0416c2s v1p1122c2s v1p1123c2s
Drake, W.B. ... v1p0892c2s
Drake, W.R. ... v1p0550c2s v1p0786c1s
Draper, A.G. ... v1p0337c1s v5p0128c2s
Draper, A.S. ... v3p0130c1s v4p0466c1m v4p0506c1m v5p0179c1s v5p0512c2s v5p0569c1s v5p0605c1m v6p0134c1s v6p0135c2s v6p0194c2s v6p0498c1s v6p0575c1s v6p0670c2s v6p0672c1m
Draper, A.S. et al. ... v4p0506c1s
Draper, Andrew S. ... v6p0192c2s v6p0194c1s
Draper, C. ... v1p1077c2s
Draper, D. ... v1p0265c2s
Draper, E.G. ... v1p0157c2s
Draper, G. ... v1p1276c2s
Draper, H. ... v1p0073c2s v1p0281c2s v1p0382c1m v1p0699c1s v1p0817c1s v1p0955c1m v1p1003c1s v1p1003c2m v1p1014c1s v1p1113c1m v1p1233c2m v1p1234c1m v1p1268c1m v2p0308c2m v2p0337c2s v2p0413c2s
Draper, H.N. ... v1p0040c2s v1p0429c1s v1p0732c1s
Draper, J.C. ... v1p0017c1s v1p0040c2s v1p0159c1m v1p0160c1s v1p0271c1s v1p0273c2s v1p0366c2s v1p0435c1s v1p0580c1s v1p0836c1s v1p0839c1s v1p0844c2m v1p0955c1s v1p0955c2s v1p1172c1s v1p1176c1s v1p1268c2m v1p1287c2s v1p1313c2s v1p1366c1s
Draper, J.W. ... v1p0198c1s v1p0224c1s v1p0225c1s v1p0407c2s v1p0433c2s v1p0440c2s v1p0483c2s v1p0498c1s v1p0579c2s v1p0747c1m v1p0747c2s v1p0836c1s v1p0955c1s v1p1003c2s v1p1160c2s v1p1161c1s v1p1162c1s v1p1163c2s v1p1233c2m v1p1268c2s v1p1310c1s v1p1394c2s v2p0166c1s
Draper, R.D. ... v3p0339c2s
Draper, S.A. ... v6p0070c2s
Draper, T.W. ... v4p0016c1s
Draper, W.F. ... v4p0135c1m v4p0250c2s v4p0354c2s v4p0359c2s v4p0462c2s v4p0501c1s v4p0534c1s v4p0563c2s v4p0607c2s v4p0608c1s v6p0633c1s
Draper, W.H. ... v5p0012c1m v5p0137c1s v5p0287c2s v6p0200c2s
Draper, W.R. ... v5p0288c1s v6p0009c1s v6p0155c1s v6p0465c1s v6p0482c2s v6p0694c2s
Draper, Wm.R. ... v6p0355c2s
Drapes, T. ... v4p0285c2s
Dravo, E.E. ... v6p0031c1s
Draycott, C. ... v5p0200c2s v5p0614c1s v5p0631c1s
Drayson, A.W. ... v1p0012c1s v1p0070c1s v1p0070c2s v1p0162c1s v1p0602c2s v1p1088c2s v1p1213c1s v1p1239c2s v1p1244c1s v1p1268c1s v1p1311c2m v1p1409c1s v2p0096c1s v2p0127c1m v2p0129c2s v2p0268c2s v2p0296c2s v4p0072c2s v4p0192c1s v4p0272c2s
Drayson, Lieut.-Col. ... v1p1390c2s
Drayton, A.W. ... v2p0347c1s
Drayton, E. ... v1p1423c1s
Drayton, J.B. ... v6p0154c2s v6p0348c1s v6p0385c2s
Drayton, J.R. ... v6p0238c1s
Drayton, M. ... v5p0093c2s
Drayton, R.H. ... v6p0120c1s v6p0263c2s
Drechsel, E. ... v2p0076c1s
Dredd, F. ... v5p0472c1s v6p0275c1s
Dredd, F. and Ryan, E. ... v6p0346c2s
Dredge, J. ... v4p0101c1s
Dredge, J. et al. ... v4p0100c2s
Dreer, F.J. ... v3p0109c1s
Dreher, E. ... v3p0332c1s
Dreher, J.A. ... v4p0538c1s
Dreher, W.C. ... v2p0253c2s v5p0231c2s v6p0058c2s v6p0078c1s v6p0254c2m v6p0255c1s
Dreiser, T. ... v5p0080c2s v5p0222c2s v5p0235c2s v5p0477c1s v5p0551c2s v5p0569c1s v5p0592c1s
Dreiser, Theodore ... v5p0096c1s v5p0141c1s v5p0256c1s v5p0427c1s v5p0548c1s
Dreper, W.C. ... v5p0230c1s
Dresbach, M. ... v6p0071c1s v6p0151c2s
Dreslar, F.B. ... v4p0505c2s
Dresser, A.R. ... v3p0330c2s
Dresser, C. ... v1p0064c1s v1p0064c2s v1p0152c2s v3p0021c1m v3p0022c1s v3p0314c2s
Dresser, C.L. ... v1p0401c1s
Dresser, Christopher ... v1p0063c1s
Dresser, F.A. ... v5p0177c2s
Dresser, H. ... v1p1207c1s
Dresser, H.E. ... v6p0497c1s
Dresser, H.W. ... v4p0372c1s v5p0003c1s v5p0220c1s v5p0291c1s v5p0337c2m v5p0386c1s v5p0406c1s v5p0579c2s v5p0608c2s
Dresser, H.W. and Woodbury, J.C. v5p0114c2s v5p0176c1s
Dresser, J.A. ... v6p0083c2s v6p0525c1s
Dresslar, F.B. ... v4p0165c2s v4p0196c1s v4p0385c2s v4p0434c2s v4p0465c1s v4p0580c1s v4p0606c1s v5p0113c1s v5p0252c1s v5p0258c2s v6p0124c2s v6p0681c1s
Drever, W.P. ... v6p0364c1s
Drew, A.A.W. ... v4p0025c2s v4p0283c2s v4p0307c2s v5p0270c1s
Drew, B. ... v1p0879c2s
Drew, C. ... v1p0213c1s v1p0234c2s v1p0662c2s
Drew, C.H. ... v1p0360c1s v1p0521c1s v4p0373c2s v5p0024c2s v5p0056c2s
Drew, D.A. ... v5p0363c1s
Drew, E.P. ... v4p0512c2s
Drew, F. ... v3p0009c1s v4p0036c2s
Drew, F.M. ... v3p0149c2s v4p0344c1s
Drew, G.A. ... v6p0713c2s
Drew, G.L. ... v5p0301c1s
Drew, G.S. ... v1p0180c1s v1p0691c2s v1p1215c1s
Drew, H.S. ... v2p0087c1s
Drew, J. ... v4p0003c1s
Drew, M., Mrs. ... v6p0258c1s
Drew, Prof. ... v1p1206c1s
Drew, T.B. ... v3p0053c1s v3p0332c2s
Drew, W.P. ... v6p0602c1s
Drewe, Marion ... v6p0631c2s
Drewry, C.S. ... v1p0714c2s
Drewry, E.S. ... v1p0024c1s v3p0063c2s v3p0153c2s v4p0063c1s v4p0552c1s
Drewry, I.L. ... v1p1309c1s
Drewry, L.M. ... v1p0886c1s
Drewry, W.F. ... v4p0185c2s
Dreyer, J.L.E. ... v3p0377c1s v4p0540c2s v5p0074c2m v5p0277c1s
Dreyer, M. ... v6p0467c1s
Dreyfus, A. ... v5p0160c1s
Dreys, O.L. ... v6p0513c2s
Driggs, L.L. ... v6p0416c2s v6p0669c1s
Driggs, R. ... v3p0291c2s
Drinker, H.S. ... v1p0844c1s
Drinkwater, A.E. ... v3p0047c2s
Driscoll, Charles F. ... v2p0482c1s
Driscoll, Clara ... v6p0161c1s
Driscoll, J.T. ... v6p0123c2s v6p0495c2s v6p0576c1s v6p0642c1s
Driscoll, N.W. ... v5p0279c1s
Drisley, M. ... v3p0243c1s
Driver, C.H. ... v1p0408c1s v1p0663c2s
Driver, G.R. ... v3p0041c2s
Driver, J.M. ... v4p0445c1s
Driver, S.R. ... v3p0041c1s v3p0041c2s v3p0169c2s v3p0240c1s v4p0054c1s v4p0054c2s v4p0055c1m v4p0058c1s v4p0286c1s v4p0504c2s v4p0528c2s v5p0056c2s v5p0057c1s v5p0057c2s v6p0062c2m
Droch, R. ... v3p0087c2s v3p0164c1s
Dromgoole, W.A. ... v3p0040c1s v3p0152c1s v3p0178c2s v3p0192c2s v3p0265c1s v3p0311c1s v3p0471c1s v4p0037c1s v4p0110c1s v4p0114c1s v4p0149c1s v4p0267c2s v4p0269c1s v4p0288c1s v4p0327c1s v4p0413c1s v4p0470c2s v4p0510c1s v4p0560c1s v4p0599c2s v4p0610c2s v4p0621c1s v4p0630c2s v5p0188c1s v5p0262c2s v5p0628c1s v6p0070c2s v6p0071c2s v6p0218c1s v6p0244c1s v6p0280c2s v6p0376c2s v6p0451c2s v6p0466c1s v6p0664c2s
Dron, J.A. ... v5p0108c1s
Drone, E.S. ... v1p0064c1s v1p0300c2s v1p0572c2s v1p0639c2s v1p0746c2s v3p0416c2s
Droop, H.R. ... v1p0398c1s v1p0848c2s
Dropero, G. ... v4p0565c1s
Droppers, G. ... v3p0226c2s v3p0227c1s v3p0409c2s v4p0106c2s v4p0167c2s v4p0297c1s v4p0297c2m v4p0298c1m v5p0302c2m v5p0303c1m
Drought, E.T. ... v6p0187c1s
Drown, E.S. ... v6p0412c2s
Drown, T.M. ... v1p0664c1s v1p0826c1s v1p1197c2s v1p1251c1s v2p0090c2s v2p0229c2s v2p0432c2s v6p0190c2s
Drown, T.M. and Shimer, P.W. v1p0665c1s
Drowne, H.R. ... v5p0169c2s
Drowne, H.T. and Drowne, S. v2p0196c2s v2p0219c2s
Drowne, S. and Drowne, H.T. v2p0196c2s v2p0219c2s
Droz, G. ... v1p0109c1s
Droz, N. ... v4p0476c2s
Druar, M. ... v5p0334c1s
Druery, C.T. ... v4p0197c1s v4p0264c2s
Druley, T.C. ... v1p0426c1s v1p1147c2s v1p1161c1s v1p1314c2s v1p1428c2s
Druley, T.S. ... v2p0190c2s
Drum, W.F. ... v5p0014c1s
Drum, W.M. ... v6p0122c2m v6p0295c2s v6p0462c1s v6p0607c2s
Drumm, J.H. ... v1p0422c2s v1p0727c1s v1p1089c2s
Drummond, A.T. ... v1p0192c2m
Drummond, D. ... v1p0096c1s
Drummond, E.W. ... v1p0311c1s
Drummond, H. ... v2p0016c1s v2p0172c2s v3p0052c2s v3p0130c1s v3p0280c1s v3p0395c2s v4p0071c1s v4p0165c2s v4p0190c2s v4p0381c1m v5p0060c2s v5p0358c2s v5p0380c1s v5p0540c1s v6p0603c2s
Drummond, H. and Huxley, T.H. v2p0106c2s
Drummond, H.G. ... v5p0031c2s v5p0168c1s v5p0236c2s v5p0337c2s
Drummond, Hamilton ... v5p0172c2s v5p0274c1s v5p0474c2s
Drummond, J. ... v1p0129c1s v1p0528c2s v1p0529c1s v1p0700c2m v2p0044c1s v2p0359c1s v4p0046c2s v5p0309c1s v6p0544c1s
Drummond, J.H. ... v5p0019c1s
Drummond, L. ... v2p0301c1s
Drummond, Mrs. ... v4p0500c2s
Drummond, R.B. ... v1p0126c1s v1p0127c1s v1p0189c2s v1p0423c2m v1p0688c2s v1p0689c2s v1p1089c1s v1p1102c1s v1p1138c2s v1p1402c2s v2p0043c2s v2p0044c1s v2p0045c1s v2p0082c1s v2p0432c1s v3p0043c1s v3p0184c1s v4p0431c1s v4p0509c1s
Drummond, R.C. ... v4p0281c1s v4p0546c2s v5p0209c1s
Drummond, W. ... v1p0391c1s v1p1051c1s
Drummond, W.H. ... v5p0456c2s v6p0408c1s
Drumont, E. ... v6p0344c1s
Druro, B.P. ... v1p1189c1s
Drury, A.H. ... v1p0763c1s v1p1257c2s v2p0076c1s v2p0438c2s v4p0574c1s v5p0232c2s v5p0416c2s v5p0611c1s v5p0627c2s
Drury, B.P. ... v1p0345c1s v1p1000c1s v1p1235c2s
Drury, E. ... v2p0448c2s v2p0483c1s
Drury, E.C. ... v6p0632c2s
Drury, J.B. ... v1p0333c2s v6p0535c2s
Drury, J.B. and Craig, W.G. v5p0464c1s
Drury, J.B. and Good, J.I. v5p0482c1s
Drury, M.R. ... v6p0609c1s
Drury, S.H. ... v6p0021c2s v6p0396c2s
Drury, W.P. ... v5p0310c2s v5p0314c1s v5p0565c2s v5p0578c2s v6p0641c1s v6p0672c2s
Dryden, A. ... v5p0131c2s
Dryden, Alice ... v5p0321c2m v5p0414c1s
Dryden, E. ... v6p0039c1s
Dryden, H. ... v2p0224c1s v2p0391c2s v5p0363c2s

Dryden, J. v4p0059c2s v4p0232c1s
Dryden, J.F. v6p0322c1s v6p0477c1s
Dryden, V. v5p0169c2s
Dryer, C.R. v3p0380c1s v6p0249c1s
Dryer, G.H. v3p0127c1s v4p0224c2s v5p0485c1s
Drygalski, E.von v5p0022c1m v6p0023c1s
Drysdale, A.H. v2p0076c2s v2p0143c1s v2p0201c1s v2p0243c1s v2p0247c1s v2p0264c2s v2p0352c2s v4p0099c2s
Drysdale, A.T. v2p0162c2s
Drysdale, C.I. v2p0351c1s
Drysdale, C.R. v1p0177c1s v1p1076c2s v1p1421c1s v3p0339c2s
Drysdale, J. and Dallinger, W.H. v1p0953c1s
Drysdale, W. v2p0343c1s v3p0039c2s
Drysdale, W.D. v4p0007c2s
Drysdale, W.S. v1p0310c1s v1p1262c1s v4p0080c1s
Duane, A.S. v4p0256c1s
Duane, W. v1p0892c1s v5p0103c2s v6p0199c1s
Duane, W. and Lory, C.A. . v5p0577c2s
Duane, W. and Trowbridge, J. v4p0175c2s
Dub, M. v6p0042c2s
Dubassov v3p0433c1s
Dubberley, W. v1p0110c2s v1p0147c2s
Dubbs, J.H. v1p0289c1s v1p0513c2s v1p0620c1s v1p0695c2s v1p0890c2s v1p0924c2s v1p0987c2s v1p1073c2s v1p1085c2s v1p1238c1s v1p1254c1s v1p1263c2s v1p1421c2s v2p0175c2s v2p0204c2s v2p0213c2s v2p0268c1s v2p0324c2s v2p0335c2s v2p0367c2s v3p0162c1s v3p0170c2s v3p0204c1s v4p0114c1s v4p0163c1s v4p0244c1s v4p0417c1s v4p0433c2s v4p0477c1m v4p0477c2s v5p0482c1s
Dubh, S. v6p0266c1s
Dublin, L.I. v6p0396c2s
Duboc, J. v1p0513c1s
Duboin, A. v6p0014c1s
Dubois, E. v4p0444c2s v6p0114c2s
Dubois, H.A. v1p0425c1s
Dubois, L. v1p0073c2s v1p0936c2s v2p0249c2s
Dubois, L.E. v1p0834c2s v1p0842c2s v1p0996c1s
Dubois, L.L. v6p0170c2s
Dubois, T. v6p0292c1s
Dubois, W.E. v1p0326c1s v1p1397c1s
Dubor, G.De v4p0267c2s v5p0397c2s
Dubos, L. v2p0333c1s
Dubose, W.P. and Ramage, B.J. v6p0279c1s
Dubourg, A.W. v1p0101c1s v1p0139c1s v1p0749c1s v1p0940c2s v1p1376c1s
Dubray, C.A. v6p0193c1s
Dubret, M. v2p0362c2s
Dubsky, A.O. v5p0081c1s v5p0495c2s v5p0581c1s
Dubuque, H.A. v3p0233c1s
Duby, M.C. v6p0241c1s
Duc, W.B.Le v3p0035c1s
Ducarel, Dr. v1p1414c1s
Ducatel, J.T. v1p0236c2s v1p0784c1s v1p0919c2s v1p0951c1s v1p1041c2s v1p1119c1s
Duchal, Dr. v1p0074c2s
Duchesne, L. v6p0548c1s
Duchess, The v3p0016c2s
Ducie, Earl of v1p0998c1s v2p0109c2s v2p0413c1s
Duckett, G. v1p0220c1s
Duckham, F.E. v5p0241c2s
Duckwall, E.W. v6p0046c2s
Duckworth, A. v4p0319c1s v4p0553c1m v5p0039c1s
Duckworth, D. v1p0839c1s v4p0155c2s
Duckworth, G.H. v4p0591c1s
Duckworth, W.L.H. v4p0038c2s v4p0138c1s v4p0528c2s v5p0565c1s
Duclaux, E. v5p0162c2s
Duclaux, M. v6p0099c2s v6p0242c1s v6p0650c2s
Ducpetiaux, E. v1p1144c2s
Duddleston, A.C. v4p0248c2s
Dudeney, H., Mrs. v5p0313c1s v6p0014c1s
Dudevant, A.L. v3p0024c1s v3p0357c1s
Dudevant, A.L.A. v1p0626c2s v1p0800c1s v2p0132c1s
Dudevant, A.L.A., Mad. ... v1p0946c1s
Dudevant, A.L.A.D. v1p0324c1s v1p0459c2s v1p1318c1s
Dudevant, A.M. v3p0280c1s
Dudevant, Mme. v1p0481c1s
Dudfield, R. v6p0284c2s
Dudgeon, H.D. v3p0118c2s
Dudgeon, R.E. v1p1375c1s
Dudley, A. v1p1223c1s
Dudley, A.T. v3p0025c2s
Dudley, C.B. v1p0449c1s v1p1075c1s v1p1251c2m v2p0420c1s v3p0165c1s v3p0310c2s v4p0048c1s v5p0103c2s v5p0298c1s v5p0476c1s
Dudley, C.H. v6p0018c2s
Dudley, C.R. v5p0206c1s
Dudley, D. v1p0090c2s v1p0370c1s
Dudley, E. v1p1037c2s v3p0084c2s
Dudley, Earl of v1p0383c1s v1p0974c1s v1p1316c1s v1p1380c2s
Dudley, H.S. v4p0616c2s v5p0072c2s
Dudley, J. v3p0433c1s
Dudley, J.G. v1p0306c1s v1p0306c2s v5p0389c1s
Dudley, J.L. v1p0756c2s
Dudley, L.E. v1p0638c1s v3p0245c1s
Dudley, L.J. v1p0347c2s
Dudley, Lord v1p0219c2s v1p0973c2s
Dudley, M.E. v6p0093c1s
Dudley, M.S. v5p0460c1s v6p0441c2s v6p0455c2s
Dudley, Matie F. v5p0434c2s
Dudley, P.H. v2p0169c2s v6p0530c2s
Dudley, S.W. v6p0643c1s
Dudley, T.H. v4p0594c1s
Dudley, T.P. v1p0490c2s v1p1384c2s
Dudley, T.U. v2p0309c1s v3p0200c1s
Dudley, T.W. v2p0357c1s
Dudley, W.L. v2p0228c1s v3p0451c1s v6p0039c1s
Due, C.L. v6p0305c2s
Due, P. v3p0054c1s
Duer, A. v5p0200c2m v5p0322c1s
Duer, Alice and Miller, H.W. v5p0340c1s
Duer, C. v6p0121c2s
Duer, Caroline v6p0127c2s v6p0440c1s v6p0504c2s v6p0700c2s v6p0707c1s
Duer, E. v6p0154c2s v6p0273c2s v6p0453c2s
Duer, Eliz. v6p0516c2s v6p0658c1s
Duer, J.K. v1p0234c1s
Duer, W.A. v1p0917c1s v1p1387c1s
Duerden, J.E. v4p0296c1s v5p0003c1s v6p0149c2m v6p0283c1s v6p0471c1s
Dufax, Dr. v2p0336c2s
Dufernex, B. v6p0169c1s
Duff, A. v1p0122c1s v1p0435c2s v1p0630c1s v2p0042c2s v2p0043c2s v2p0234c2s v3p0042c1s
Duff, A., jr. v1p0121c1s v1p1306c1s
Duff, A.J.G. v3p0311c2s
Duff, A.W. v5p0223c1s v5p0518c2s v5p0598c1s v6p0432c1s
Duff, Beatrix v4p0210c2s
Duff, E. v4p0305c1s
Duff, E.G. v3p0053c1s v4p0067c1s v4p0152c1s v4p0546c2s v5p0180c2s v5p0415c1s v6p0077c2s
Duff, E.G. and Bradshaw, H. v2p0017c1s v2p0382c2s
Duff, G.S. v4p0588c1s
Duff, H.A. v1p0887c2s
Duff, H.L. v6p0463c1s
Duff, H.N. v1p0627c2s
Duff, J. v5p0211c1s
Duff, L.C. v6p0366c2s
Duff, M.E.G. v1p0009c2s v1p0013c1s v1p0204c2s v1p0227c1s v1p0379c1m v1p0391c2s v1p0394c2s v1p0397c1s v1p0430c2s v1p0431c1s v1p0539c1s v1p0546c2s v1p0633c2m v1p0928c1s v1p1025c1s v1p1133c2s v1p1177c2s v1p1246c1s v1p1252c1s v1p1331c1s v3p0028c1s v3p0212c2m v3p0418c2s v4p0046c2s v4p0178c2s v4p0280c2s v4p0327c2s v5p0043c1s v6p0003c1m v6p0030c1s v6p0127c1s v6p0507c2s
Duff, M.E.G. and Lemoinne, J. v1p1330c1s
Duff, M.E.Grant v3p0211c2s v4p0365c1s v4p0545c1s v5p0286c2s
Duff, M.E.Grant, Sir v3p0182c2s v3p0211c1s v5p0142c2s
Duff, M.G. v4p0237c1s
Duff, R.S. v2p0431c1s v2p0449c1s
Duff, Robert A. v6p0520c2s
Duff, U.F. v6p0418c1s v6p0607c1s
Duff, W.L. v1p0650c1s
Duff-Gordon, Lady v1p0153c2s v1p0185c1s v1p0517c2s v1p1300c2s
Dufferin and Ava, Marquis of v5p0069c1s
Dufferin, Earl v1p0267c1s v1p0622c2s
Dufferin, Lady v1p1358c1s v2p0217c2s
Dufferin, Lord v3p0212c2s
Duffey, E.B. v1p0682c1s v1p1424c1s
Duffey, E.B., Mrs. v4p0542c1s
Duffey, J. v1p1313c1s
Duffey, J.B. v1p0280c2s v1p0304c2s
Duffey, J.H. v1p1211c1s
Duffie, C.D. and Howe, L.D. v6p0071c1s
Duffie, G.C. and Lighton, W.R. v6p0624c1s
Duffield, A.J. v1p0147c1s v1p0767c1s
Duffield, D.B. v1p0392c2s
Duffield, G. v1p0131c2s v1p0454c2s v1p0528c2s v1p0900c2s v1p1046c1s v1p1303c1s
Duffield, G.W. v2p0458c2s
Duffield, J.T. v1p0435c2s v1p0541c2s v1p0811c1s v5p0242c2s v5p0464c1s
Duffield, P. v5p0148c1s v5p0380c2s
Duffield, S.P. v3p0026c2s v3p0414c1s
Duffield, S.W. v1p0881c2s v1p1014c1s v1p1064c2s v1p1314c2s v1p1363c2s v1p1372c2s v2p0203c1s
Duffield, T.W. v2p0201c2s
Duffield, W.B. v4p0536c2s v4p0564c2s v4p0586c2s v4p0617c2s v5p0023c1s v5p0089c1s v5p0173c2s v5p0300c1s v5p0378c2s v5p0398c1s v5p0408c2s v5p0417c2s v5p0452c2s v5p0591c1s v5p0631c1s v6p0138c2s v6p0269c1s v6p0270c2s v6p0606c1s v6p0633c2s v6p0650c2s
Duffy, B. v2p0377c2s
Duffy, C.G. v1p1035c1s v1p1370c1s v2p0188c2s v2p0225c1s v2p0225c2m v2p0228c1s v3p0027c1s v3p0027c2s v3p0180c2m v3p0219c2s v3p0220c1s v5p0197c1s v5p0272c1s
Duffy, C.G., Sir v6p0101c2s
Duffy, C.G., Sir et al. .. v4p0428c1s
Duffy, R. v6p0616c2s
Duffy, S.G. v3p0463c2s
Duflou, G. v4p0371c2s
Dufour, C. v1p0524c2s v2p0179c2s
Dufour, W.C. v4p0482c2s
Dufouri, J.H. v2p0311c2s
Dufrenoy, P.A. v1p0666c2s
Dufresne, L'Abbe v5p0261c1s
Dugan, C.A. v4p0158c2s
Duganne, A.J.H. v1p0116c1s v1p0597c1s v1p1161c1s v1p1222c1s v2p0115c1s
Dugard, M. v4p0628c1s
Dugdale, H.A. v2p0104c1s
Dugdale, J.B. v5p0455c2s
Dugdale, R.L. v1p0315c2s v2p0107c2s
Dugdale, W.S. v1p0219c2s
Duges v6p0227c1s
Duggar, B.M. v6p0502c2s
Dugmore, A.R. v5p0208c2s v5p0400c2s v5p0639c2s v6p0022c1s v6p0045c1s v6p0095c2s v6p0099c1m v6p0178c1s v6p0183c1s v6p0229c1s v6p0304c2s v6p0453c2s v6p0468c2s v6p0566c1s v6p0569c2s v6p0655c1s v6p0658c1m v6p0701c1s
Dugmore, A.Radclyffe v6p0698c2s
Duguid, J. v6p0292c1s
Duhern, P. v5p0577c2s
Duhigg, T.S. v4p0503c2s
Duhm, B. v4p0055c2s
Duhn, F.von v4p0294c1s v6p0215c1s
Dui, M. v1p0744c1s
Duisberg, C. v6p0375c2s
Dujardin, E. v4p0603c1s
Duke, B.W. v1p0694c2s v2p0054c2s v2p0253c1s v2p0372c2s v2p0400c2s v4p0037c1s
Duke, J.S. v1p0271c2s v1p1038c2s v1p1319c1s v1p1440c2s
Duke, R.T.W. v5p0427c1s
Dulac, A. v6p0148c1s
Dulany, D. v1p0031c1s
Duller, C.W. v6p0091c1s
Dulles, C.W. v1p0380c1s v1p0957c2s v1p1023c1s v2p0213c1s
Dulles, J.H. v4p0242c1s v6p0523c2s
Dulon, R. v6p0252c1s
Dumaresq, C. v3p0003c1s

v3p0027c2s
Dumas, A. ... v1p0500c2s
v1p0677c2s v1p0786c1s v1p0803c1s
v1p0812c1s v1p0920c2s v1p1136c2s
v1p1144c2s v1p1309c1s v1p1325c1s
v3p0372c2s
Dumas, J.P. ... v1p0224c2s
v1p0745c1s v1p0948c1s
Dumas, M. ... v2p0067c2s
Dumas-Brown ... v5p0333c1s
Dumble, A.E. ... v3p0144c2s
Dumble, D.T. and Harris, G.D.
v4p0219c1s
Dumble, E.A. ... v3p0312c1s
Dumble, E.T. ... v6p0491c1s
v6p0639c2s
Dumble, J.H. ... v1p0621c1s
v1p0621c2m
Dumon, M.S. ... v1p0474c2s
Dumont, J.A. ... v1p0145c2s
Dumont, L. ... v1p0259c2s
v1p0435c1s v1p0572c2s v1p1339c1s
Dumoulin, J. ... v1p1213c1s
Dun, H.P. ... v4p0338c2s
Dun, J. ... v1p0094c1s
Dunant, M. ... v1p1068c2m
Dunaway, T.S. ... v2p0034c2s
Dunbar, A. ... v3p0381c1s
v6p0311c1s v6p0470c2s v6p0551c2s
Dunbar, C.F. ... v1p0055c2s
v1p0326c1s v1p0331c1s v1p0484c1s
v1p0572c2s v1p0650c1s v1p0809c1s
v1p0861c1s v1p1025c2s v1p1207c2s
v1p1352c1s v1p1379c2s v1p1422c2s
v2p0130c1s v2p0347c2s v3p0032c2s
v3p0033c1s v3p0107c2s v3p0188c2s
v3p0336c2s v3p0421c1s v4p0043c2s
v4p0044c1s v4p0045c1s v4p0277c2s
v5p0046c2s v5p0238c1s v5p0383c1s
v5p0616c2s
Dunbar, C.F. et al. ... v4p0177c2s
v4p0249c1s
Dunbar, C.M. ... v1p1037c2s
Dunbar, G. ... v1p0057c2s
Dunbar, H. ... v6p0572c2s
Dunbar, J.B. ... v1p0982c1s
v1p0982c2s v2p0219c1s v2p0333c2s
v6p0007c2s
Dunbar, M.L. ... v5p0502c2s
Dunbar, N. ... v6p0702c2s
Dunbar, O.H. ... v6p0124c2s
v6p0171c1s v6p0230c1s v6p0234c1s
v6p0333c1s v6p0376c1s v6p0603c1s
v6p0678c2s
Dunbar, Olivia H. ... v6p0255c2s
v6p0695c1s
Dunbar, P.L. ... v5p0157c2s
v5p0284c1s v5p0291c1s v5p0349c1s
v5p0378c2s v5p0388c1s v5p0390c1s
v5p0495c2s v5p0524c2s v5p0539c1s
v5p0547c1s v5p0556c2s v5p0597c2s
v5p0613c2s v5p0616c1s v5p0629c1s
v6p0127c1s v6p0224c1s v6p0679c2s
Dunbar, Paul L. ... v6p0689c2s
Dunbar, R.C. ... v6p0539c2s
Dunbar, W. ... v1p0107c1s
Dunbar, W.H. ... v3p0132c1s
v4p0300c2s v4p0546c1s v5p0291c1m
v6p0642c2m
Dunbar, W.S. ... v6p0160c1s
v6p0443c2s v6p0599c1s v6p0647c2s
Dunboyne, Lady ... v2p0321c2s
v4p0207c1s
Duncan, A. ... v3p0313c2s
Duncan, B. ... v2p0452c1m
Duncan, B.O. ... v2p0018c2s
v2p0449c1s
Duncan, C. ... v4p0093c2s
v4p0163c1s v4p0344c2s v4p0369c1s
v4p0473c2s
Duncan, C.H. ... v6p0397c1s
Duncan, C.S. ... v6p0027c1s
Duncan, D. ... v1p0202c2m
v6p0313c2s
Duncan, D.W.C. ... v3p0076c1s
Duncan, Ellen ... v6p0034c2s
Duncan, Eric ... v6p0674c1s
Duncan, F. ... v1p0358c1s
v1p1143c2s v3p0131c1s v5p0303c2s
v6p0032c1s v6p0085c1s v6p0247c2s
v6p0288c1s v6p0542c2s v6p0570c2s
v6p0629c1s v6p0656c1s
Duncan, F.M. ... v4p0049c1s
Duncan, Frances ... v6p0150c1s
v6p0247c2s v6p0617c2s
Duncan, G. ... v6p0427c1s
v6p0519c2s
Duncan, G.B. ... v5p0017c2s
v5p0599c1s
Duncan, G.M. ... v5p0330c1s
v6p0367c1s
Duncan, G.S. ... v4p0242c1s
v6p0279c1s
Duncan, H. ... v1p0225c2s
Duncan, H.E. ... v4p0612c2s
v6p0260c1s v6p0455c1s
Duncan, H.J. ... v1p0667c1s
Duncan, H.M. ... v5p0596c2s
Duncan, J. ... v1p0786c2s
v1p0907c1s v1p0921c2s v2p0207c2s
v2p0242c1s
Duncan, J.A. ... v4p0306c1s
v5p0515c2s
Duncan, J.C. ... v1p0719c2s
Duncan, J.P. ... v4p0336c2s
Duncan, L. ... v1p1362c2s
v3p0134c1s v4p0176c2m v4p0455c2s
v5p0183c2s v6p0635c2s
Duncan, L.L. ... v4p0193c2s
v4p0205c1m v4p0326c1m v5p0212c2s
v5p0474c2s
Duncan, M.M. ... v1p0168c1s
v1p0266c2s v1p0703c1s v1p0837c2s
Duncan, M.Y. ... v3p0116c1s
Duncan, N. ... v5p0103c1s
v5p0213c2s v5p0282c1s v5p0323c2s
v5p0409c1s v5p0546c2s v6p0055c1s
v6p0076c1s v6p0080c2s v6p0103c2s
v6p0134c1s v6p0181c2s v6p0214c1s
v6p0231c2s v6p0243c2s v6p0274c1s
v6p0278c1s v6p0284c2s v6p0311c1s
v6p0357c2m v6p0471c2s v6p0527c2s
v6p0532c2s v6p0549c1s v6p0569c2s
v6p0580c1s v6p0580c2s v6p0621c1s
v6p0630c2s v6p0638c1s v6p0643c1s
v6p0689c2s v6p0694c1s v6p0709c1s
v6p0710c2s
Duncan, P.M. ... v1p0301c1m
v1p0509c2s v1p0527c1s v1p0645c1s
v1p0745c1s v1p0748c1s v1p0793c1s
v1p1002c2s v1p1045c1s v2p0102c2s
v2p0214c2s v2p0221c2s
Duncan, R. ... v1p1192c1s
Duncan, R.H. ... v6p0106c1s
Duncan, R.K. ... v6p0011c1s
v6p0104c1s v6p0200c1s v6p0458c2s
v6p0489c1s v6p0526c2s v6p0637c2s
Duncan, S.A. ... v1p0978c2s
Duncan, S.J. ... v3p0099c2s
v3p0152c1s v4p0279c2s v4p0437c1s
v4p0603c1s
Duncan, Sarah J. ... v5p0024c1s
Duncan, T. ... v6p0525c1s
Duncan, W. ... v1p0927c1s
v1p1038c2s
Duncan, W.C. ... v1p0855c1s
v1p0927c1s v1p1135c1s
Duncan, W.H., jr. ... v5p0553c2s
Duncan, W.S. ... v1p0447c1s
v2p0141c1s v2p0154c1s v2p0274c1s
Duncanson, J.M. ... v2p0434c2s
Dunckley, H. ... v1p0524c2s
v1p0538c1s v1p0992c2s v1p1130c2s
v2p0134c1s v3p0077c2s v3p0114c2s
v3p0139c1s v3p0160c2s v3p0181c1s
v3p0183c1s v3p0356c2s v3p0460c1s
Duncombe, C. ... v5p0323c1s
Duncombe, C.W. ... v3p0201c2s
Duncombe-Jewell, L.C.R. .. v4p0212c2s
Dundas, D. ... v6p0005c1s
Dundas, F.G. ... v4p0305c2s
v4p0536c1s
Dundas, V.V. ... v5p0105c2s
Dundee, R.R. ... v4p0206c2s
Dundonald, Earl of ... v6p0265c2s
Dundonald, Lord ... v4p0558c2s
Dunell, G.R. ... v3p0266c1s
v5p0526c1s v6p0529c2s v6p0565c2s
Dunelm, B.F. ... v4p0108c2m
v4p0132c2s v5p0199c2s v5p0289c2s
v5p0467c2s
Dunelm, J.B. ... v3p0339c1s
Dungan, D.H. ... v2p0284c2s
Dungan, D.R. ... v2p0042c2s
v2p0044c2m v2p0150c1s v2p0434c1s
v3p0042c1s
Dungate, E.J. et al. ... v2p0268c2s
Dunham, A.C. ... v2p0243c2s
Dunham, A.H. ... v6p0458c2s
Dunham, C. ... v3p0095c2s
v5p0543c2s v6p0366c1s
Dunham, H.C. ... v6p0063c2s
Dunham, L. ... v6p0482c2s
Dunham, S.A. ... v4p0009c1s
Duniway, C.A. ... v6p0667c1s
Dunkin, C. ... v1p0164c1s
v1p0193c1s v1p0868c1s
Dunkin, E. ... v1p1080c2s
v1p1213c2s v2p0003c1s v2p0094c1s
v2p0127c2s v2p0129c2m v2p0191c2s
v2p0192c1s v2p0242c2s v2p0263c2s
v2p0285c1s v2p0288c1s v2p0296c2s
v2p0307c2s v2p0319c1s v2p0421c2s
v2p0425c1s v2p0426c2s
Dunkin, E.H.W. ... v1p0001c2s
v1p0006c2s v1p0100c1s v1p0110c2m
v1p0818c1s v1p1255c2s
Dunklee, Irah ... v6p0226c2s
Dunlap, J.R. ... v4p0378c2s
Dunlap, K. ... v6p0604c2s
Dunlap, Knight ... v6p0216c2s
v6p0500c2s
Dunlap, L. ... v2p0410c2s
Dunlap, O.E. ... v5p0183c1s
v5p0410c1m v5p0462c2s v6p0456c2s
Dunlap, Orrin E. ... v6p0456c2s
Dunlap, S.F. ... v1p0891c2s
v1p1269c2s
Dunlap, T. ... v3p0271c2s
Dunlap, W. ... v1p0297c2s
v1p0454c1s
Dunlap, Z.F. ... v6p0564c1s
Dunlevy, H. ... v3p0252c1s
Dunlop, A. ... v1p0548c2s
v1p0976c1s v4p0299c2s
Dunlop, A.P. ... v4p0126c1s
Dunlop, D. et al. ... v3p0323c2s
Dunlop, H.W.D. ... v1p0206c1s
v1p0742c1s
Dunlop, J. ... v2p0299c2s
v2p0369c1s
Dunlop, M.A.W. ... v4p0228c1m
v4p0455c1m
Dunlop, R. ... v3p0138c1s
v3p0220c1m v3p0220c2s v3p0254c2s
v3p0292c1s v3p0310c1s v3p0325c1s
v3p0333c1s v3p0342c2s v4p0181c2s
v4p0291c1s v4p0344c2s v4p0579c1s
v6p0327c2s
Dunlop, W. ... v5p0040c1s
Dunlop, W.B. ... v3p0078c1s
v3p0079c1m v3p0352c1s
Dunlop-Wallace-Goodbody, F.C.
v5p0148c2s v5p0427c1m
Dunlop-Wallace-Goodbody, F.G.
v5p0242c2s v6p0005c1s v6p0099c1s
v6p0241c1s
Dunman, Lord ... v6p0271c2s
Dunmore, Earl of ... v4p0033c1s
v4p0423c1s
Dunn, A.J. ... v2p0278c1s
v4p0463c1s v6p0026c1s
Dunn, A.W. ... v4p0218c2s
v6p0493c2s v6p0551c1s v6p0606c1s
Dunn, Arthur W. ... v6p0151c1s
Dunn, B.W. ... v5p0281c1s
Dunn, E. ... v1p0407c2s
v4p0272c2s
Dunn, E.B. ... v3p0458c2s
v4p0615c2s v5p0184c2s
Dunn, G. ... v3p0294c2s
v4p0151c1s
Dunn, G.S. ... v4p0165c1s
v6p0694c2s
Dunn, H.A.C. ... v4p0196c2s
Dunn, H.P. ... v2p0066c2s
v4p0087c1s v4p0184c2s v4p0269c1s
v4p0558c2s
Dunn, J. ... v6p0245c1s
v6p0549c1s
Dunn, J.B. and Townsend, L.T.
v3p0426c1s
Dunn, J.D. ... v5p0239c2s
Dunn, J.J. ... v4p0479c2s
v4p0488c1s v6p0328c1s v6p0713c1s
Dunn, J.P. ... v4p0524c2s
Dunn, J.P., jr. ... v3p0288c2s
v3p0450c1s
Dunn, J.S. ... v5p0586c2s
Dunn, L.R. ... v1p0240c1s
v1p0845c2s v1p1067c1s v1p1149c1s
v2p0221c2s
Dunn, M. ... v4p0443c1s
v5p0141c1s v5p0150c2s v5p0209c1m
v5p0524c1s v6p0164c1s
Dunn, M.B. ... v5p0450c2s
v5p0525c2s v5p0569c1s v6p0073c2m
v6p0085c2s v6p0127c1s v6p0142c2s
v6p0189c2s v6p0426c2s v6p0495c2s
v6p0588c2s v6p0653c2s
Dunn, Matthias ... v5p0208c2s
Dunn, N.P. ... v6p0590c2s
Dunn, R. ... v1p1062c1s
v6p0001c2s v6p0039c2s v6p0078c2s
v6p0095c2s v6p0153c2s v6p0246c1s
v6p0260c2s v6p0338c2s v6p0393c2s
v6p0459c2s v6p0541c1s v6p0709c1s
Dunn, R.P. ... v1p0418c1s
v1p0560c2s v1p0620c2s v1p1329c1s
Dunn, Robert ... v6p0552c2s
Dunn, S. ... v1p0261c2s
v1p0848c1s
Dunn, S.H. ... v4p0008c2s
v4p0280c2s v4p0414c2s v4p0418c2s
v5p0044c2s v5p0049c1s v5p0214c2s
v5p0287c1s v5p0296c2s v5p0478c2s
v5p0490c1s v6p0164c1s v6p0424c2s
Dunn, Sara H. ... v5p0083c1s
Dunn, W.A. ... v5p0008c2s
Dunn-Gardner, A. ... v4p0533c2s
Dunnachie, J. ... v1p0455c1s
Dunne, E.F. ... v6p0113c2s
v6p0436c1m
Dunne, F.P. ... v5p0082c1s
v6p0074c2s v6p0179c1s v6p0434c1m
Dunne, J.W. ... v6p0605c2s
Dunnell, E.G. ... v4p0152c2s
Dunnell, M.B. ... v4p0379c2s
v4p0519c2s v5p0112c1s v6p0119c1s
Dunning, A.E. ... v3p0096c1s
v4p0112c1s v5p0352c1s
Dunning, C. ... v1p0319c2s
v2p0015c2s v2p0026c2s v2p0062c2s
v2p0106c1s v2p0114c1s v2p0301c1s
v2p0410c2s v2p0472c2s v3p0006c2s
v3p0445c2s
Dunning, D.M. ... v4p0177c1s
v4p0220c2s v6p0264c2s
Dunning, E.O. ... v1p0577c2s
v1p0681c1s v1p0805c1s v1p0893c2m

Dunning, J.F. v6p0311c1s
v6p0629c2s v6p0662c2s
Dunning, N.A. v4p0144c1s
Dunning, W.A. v2p0452c1s
v3p0355c2s v3p0408c1s v3p0442c1s
v4p0015c1s v4p0173c2s v4p0290c1s
v4p0450c1s v4p0450c2s v4p0539c1s
v5p0028c1s v5p0353c1s v5p0417c2s
v5p0457c1s v5p0480c2s v5p0552c2s
v5p0601c2s v5p0602c1s v5p0603c1s
v6p0345c1s v6p0382c1s v6p0424c2s
v6p0507c1s
Dunning, W.A. and Smith, M.
v5p0457c1s
Dunning, W.M. v6p0524c2s
Dunnington, F.P. v3p0266c1s
v3p0431c1s
Dunphy, B. v1p0044c1s
v1p0593c1s
Dunraven, Earl of v1p0194c1s
v1p0279c1s v1p0478c1s v1p0867c2s
v1p0910c2m v1p1104c1s v1p1114c1s
v1p1188c2s v1p1383c2s v2p0094c1s
v2p0187c2s v2p0209c1m v2p0399c1s
v2p0425c2s v2p1428c1s v3p0181c1s
v3p0183c1s v3p0433c1m v4p0275c1s
v4p0284c2s v4p0500c1s v4p0634c2s
v6p0326c1s v6p0327c1m
Duns, E. v3p0191c1s
Duns, J. v1p0383c1s
v1p1152c1s
Dunsany, Adm.Lord v1p0545c1s
v2p0423c2s
Dunsany, Lord v2p0143c2s
Dunsany, Lord et al. v2p0143c2s
Dunscomb, S.W. v5p0046c2s
Dunstan, A.S. et al. v5p0537c2s
Dunstan, M.J. v5p0151c2s
Dunstan, W.R. v6p0313c1s
Dunstan, Wyndham v6p0082c2s
Dunster, H.P. v2p0142c1s
v2p0328c2s v3p0006c1s v3p0156c1s
v3p0340c1s v3p0474c1s
Dunton, E.K. v5p0219c1s
v5p0362c2s v5p0479c1s v5p0590c2s
v6p0041c1s v6p0088c2s v6p0110c2s
v6p0450c2s v6p0488c2s v6p0514c2s
v6p0644c1s v6p0696c1m
Dunton, Edith K. v6p0514c2s
v6p0552c2s
Dunton, L. v3p0271c2s
v3p0287c1s v3p0287c2s v3p0422c1s
v4p0169c1s v4p0505c2s
Dunton, T.W. v5p0581c1s
Dunvell, T.L. v1p0474c1s
Dunwoody, H.H.C. v4p0499c1s
v4p0579c2s
Dupanloup, F.A.P. v1p0802c2s
v1p1422c1s v1p1424c2s
Dupanloup, Mgr. v1p1363c1s
Dupays, H. v6p0432c2s
Dupee, J.A. v2p0465c1s
Dupee, L.C. and Wells, H.L.
v4p0082c2s
Duponceau, P.S. v1p1285c2s
Dupont, E. v6p0083c1s
Dupont, Mrs. v1p1275c1s
Duppa, R. v1p0770c2s
Duppa-Crotch, W. v3p0286c2s
Dupre, A. v1p1415c1s
v5p0521c2s
Dupre, L.I. v1p0279c1s
Dupree, J.W. and Morgan, H.A.
v6p0431c2s
Dupriez, L. v6p0388c1s
Dupuy, E. v1p0587c1s
v1p0907c1s
Dupuy, E.A. v1p0296c2s
v1p0446c1s v1p1127c2s v1p1273c1s
v1p1411c1s
Dupuy, Georges v6p0043c2s
Duquesnel, F. v5p0054c2s
Duran, A. v1p1231c1s
Duran, C. v2p0125c2s
Duran-Loriga, J.J. v5p0263c1s
Durand, A. v4p0258c1s
Durand, A.F. v1p1138c1s
Durand, A.G.A. v5p0113c2s
Durand, C.A. v4p0323c1s
Durand, E. v1p0834c2s
v5p0265c1s v5p0425c2s
Durand, E.D. v4p0594c2s
v5p0119c2s v5p0330c1m v5p0602c1s
v6p0056c1s v6p0318c1s v6p0367c1s
v6p0618c1s v6p0621c1s v6p0621c2s
v6p0652c1s
Durand, J. v1p0476c1s
v1p0479c1s v1p0482c1s v1p0502c2s
v1p1186c2s v1p1371c1s v3p0011c1s
v3p0021c1s v3p0070c1s v3p0443c1s
Durand, K. v6p0114c1s
v6p0223c2s
Durand, R.A. v6p0118c1s
v6p0355c2s v6p0423c1s
Durand, W.F. v4p0176c2s
v4p0547c2s v5p0284c1s v5p0526c1s
Durand-Claye, M.A. v3p0386c2s
Durang, C. v1p1308c2s
Durant, C.F. v1p1181c2s
v1p1197c2s
Durant, H.R. v6p0001c1s
v6p0525c2s v6p0623c2s v6p0672c2s
v6p0695c1s
Durban, W. v5p0291c1s
v5p0501c1s v5p0501c2s v5p0528c1s
v6p0099c2s
Durban, William v5p0528c1s
Durbin, E.C. v6p0292c1s
Durbin, Elizabeth W. v4p0157c2s
v4p0513c1s
Durbin, J.P. v1p0336c2s
v1p0393c1s v1p0831c1s
Durbin, W.T. v6p0391c1s
Dureau, A.J.C.A. v1p0205c1s
Durell, J.C.V. v6p0539c1s
Duren, C. v1p1423c2s
Duret, T. v4p0151c2s
v4p0459c2s
Durfee, C. v1p0458c2s
Durfee, C.A. v1p0743c2s
Durfee, E.DeF. v5p0343c1s
Durfee, M. v1p0492c1s
Durfee, T. v1p0270c2s
Durfee, W.F. v3p0223c1m
v3p0223c2s v3p0409c1s v4p0180c2s
v4p0200c1s v4p0287c1s v4p0292c1s
v4p0363c1s v4p0385c2s v4p0468c2s
v4p0548c1s v4p0559c1s v5p0371c2s
v5p0473c2s
Durfee, W.F. and North, S.N.D.
v3p0011c1s
Durgin, C. v1p0898c2s
Durgin, E.T. v4p0039c2s
v4p0445c1s v4p0567c2s
Durham, B. v4p0034c2s
Durham, Bp.of v2p0472c2s
Durham, C.M. v6p0351c2s
Durham, Earl of v3p0438c1s
Durham, F.H. v6p0651c2s
Durham, J. v1p1171c1s
v5p0077c1s v5p0128c2s v5p0607c2s
v5p0611c2s
Durham, J.H. v5p0436c2s
Durham, J.S. v5p0023c1s
v5p0321c2s v6p0173c1s v6p0662c1s
Durham, M.E. v6p0048c1s
v6p0392c2s v6p0584c2s
Durham, M.Edith v6p0349c2s
Durham, N.W. v3p0437c2s
Durham, W. v2p0076c1s
v3p0075c2s v3p0359c2s
Durham, W.H. v6p0079c2s
Durham, W.W. v5p0547c1s
Durie, J. v1p1127c1s
v2p0217c2s
Durie, M.S. v6p0490c2s
v6p0653c1s
During, S.M. v5p0357c2s
v5p0425c2s v6p0147c2s
During, Stella M. v6p0645c2s
v6p0675c1s
Durivage, F.A. v1p0342c1s
v1p0627c2s v1p0940c1s
Durland, K. v6p0133c1s
v6p0557c1s v6p0616c2s
Durland, Kellogg v6p0010c1s
v6p0354c2s
Durley, R.J. v6p0661c1s
Durlin, F. v5p0089c2s
Durlin, F., jr. v6p0658c1s
Durling, L.H. v3p0306c2s
Durnford, C.D. v2p0074c2s
v4p0013c2s v6p0226c1s
Durnford, W. v4p0189c1s
v5p0196c2s
Durno, A.G. v5p0442c2s
Durnstein, Adalbert von .. v6p0086c2s
Durrant, A.I. v6p0540c1s
Durrant, A.L. v5p0228c1s
Durrant, A.W. v5p0167c1s
Durrant, W.S. v5p0617c2s
Durrett, R.T. v2p0242c1s
v2p0242c2s v4p0342c2s
Durst, J.H. v2p0004c1s
v2p0079c2s v2p0248c1s v2p0373c1s
v6p0419c1s
Durward, A. v5p0356c1s
Durward, O.H. v2p0037c1s
Duryea, C.E. v4p0204c2s
Duryea, E. v6p0566c2s
v6p0567c2s v6p0568c1s
Duryea, J.T. v3p0107c2s
v3p0460c1s
Duryee, G.V.W. v5p0350c1s
Duryee, H.G. v6p0071c2s
Duryee, J.R. v6p0243c1s
Dusck, V. v2p0451c2s
Dusek, V. v2p0029c2s
v2p0050c2m
Dusen, J.Van v5p0218c2s
Dustan, A.G. et al. v6p0512c1s
Dutcher, A. v4p0232c2s
Dutcher, S. v1p0436c2s
v2p0411c1s v3p0464c2s
Dutcher, W. v2p0046c2s
Duthie, D.W. v2p0085c1s
v5p0485c1s v6p0110c2s v6p0488c2s
Duthie, W. v1p0532c1s
v1p0691c2m v1p1202c1s v1p1270c1s
Duthiers, H.L. v2p0102c2s
Duthiers, H.deLacaze v3p0475c2s
Duthiers, M.DeL. v4p0018c2s
Duthrie, W. v1p0338c2s
Duthus, H. v1p0596c2s
Duton, Cecile I. v3p0050c1s
Dutt, R. v6p0314c2s
Dutt, R.C. v5p0202c2s
v5p0284c1s v5p0287c1s v5p0356c1s
Dutt, W.A. v4p0245c1s
v5p0067c2s v5p0072c1m v6p0403c1s
Dutt, W.A. and Larkby, J.R.
v6p0209c2s
Dutt, Wm.A. v5p0204c2s
Dutto, L.A. v3p0016c2s
v3p0299c1s v3p0343c1s v3p0364c2s
v3p0451c1s v4p0125c2m v4p0126c1m
Dutton, A. v1p0649c1s
Dutton, A.H. v6p0044c1s
v6p0072c1s v6p0092c1s v6p0138c1m
v6p0445c1s
Dutton, Arthur H. v6p0440c2s
v6p0631c2s
Dutton, C. v5p0433c2s
Dutton, C.E. v1p0279c2s
v1p0295c1s v1p0295c2s v1p0434c2s
v1p0493c2s v1p0562c2m v1p0621c2s
v1p1259c1s v1p1399c2s v2p0035c2s
v2p0094c1s v2p0106c1s v2p0179c1s
v2p0463c1m v3p0093c1s v3p0126c1m
v3p0446c1s v5p0423c1s v5p0614c1s
v6p0188c2s v6p0681c1s
Dutton, C.E. and Hayden, E.
v3p0126c1m
Dutton, C.E. and Newcomb, W.
v3p0126c1s
Dutton, C.N. v2p0099c1s
v2p0223c1s v2p0366c1s v4p0616c2s
v5p0343c2s
Dutton, C.N. and Coppee, H.S.L.
v4p0328c1s v4p0375c1s
Dutton, G. v1p0963c1s
Dutton, H. v1p0085c1s
v1p0316c1s v1p1343c2s
Dutton, J.F. v1p0999c2s
v2p0344c2s v3p0006c1s v3p0016c2s
v3p0136c1s
Dutton, J.R. v1p0871c2s
Dutton, J.T. v1p0507c1s
Dutton, M.B. v6p0274c2s
v6p0513c2s
Dutton, Maude B. v6p0165c2s
v6p0463c1s
Dutton, Maude Barrows v6p0124c2s
Dutton, O.H. v1p0297c1s
v1p1420c1s
Dutton, R.J. v5p0084c1s
Dutton, S.T. v2p0132c2s
v2p0388c2s v4p0139c2s v4p0169c1s
v4p0171c1s v4p0566c2s v5p0179c2s
v5p0180c1s v5p0264c2s v6p0059c1s
v6p0323c2s
Dutton, S.W.S. v1p0034c2s
v1p0075c1s v1p0087c2m v1p0219c1s
v1p0328c2s v1p0337c1s v1p0373c2s
v1p0389c2s v1p0421c2s v1p0441c1s
v1p0477c1s v1p0497c2s v1p0535c2s
v1p0559c1s v1p0575c2s v1p0617c1s
v1p0673c2s v1p0689c1s v1p0841c2s
v1p0908c2s v1p0911c2s v1p0941c1s
v1p0984c1s v1p1040c1s v1p1058c1s
v1p1091c2s v1p1118c2s v1p1159c1s
v1p1206c2m v1p1207c1m v1p1207c2s
v1p1208c2s v1p1255c1s v1p1287c1s
v1p1292c2s v1p1318c2s v1p1369c1s
v1p1436c1s v2p0405c1s
Dutton, S.W.S. and Eustis, W.T.
v1p0290c1s
Dutton, W. v1p0294c2s
v1p0333c1s
Dutton, W.T. v4p0277c2s
Duval, C.P. v2p0222c2s
v2p0372c2s
Duval, E. v2p0204c1s
Duval, E.R. v1p0284c2s
Duval, F. v3p0073c1m
Duval, L.M. v5p0127c1s
Duvall, C.P. v2p0351c2s
v2p0424c1s
Duvall, E. v4p0055c1s
v4p0376c2s v5p0215c2s v5p0350c1s
v5p0418c1s v5p0421c2s v5p0456c2s
v5p0467c1s v6p0706c1s
Duvall, Ellen v5p0419c2s
Duvar, H. v1p0245c1s
v1p1187c1s v4p0418c2s v5p0381c2s
Duvel, J.W.T. v6p0582c1s
Duvivier, A.D. v5p0530c2s
Duxbury, W.C. v4p0395c1s
Duyckinck, E.A. v1p0006c1s
v1p0108c1s v1p0134c1s v1p0170c1s
v1p0540c2s v1p0567c1s v1p0575c1s
v1p0704c2s v1p0754c1s v1p0786c2s
v1p0866c2s v1p0912c2s v1p1438c1s
Duyckinck, E.C. v1p0772c2s
Duykwood, E. v1p1202c2s
Duykwood, E.T. v2p0214c2s
Duyl, A.G.C.Van v4p0006c1s
v5p0172c1s v5p0238c1s
Duysters, G.F. v4p0015c1s
Duzee, I.D.Van v1p0085c1s

v1p1021c2s v1p1385c1s v1p1428c1s
Dver, M.J. v1p0064c1s
Dvorak, A. v4p0388c2s v4p0506c2s
Dvorak, V. v1p0004c2s
Dwarris, F., Sir v1p0159c2s
Dwight, B.W. v1p0144c1s v1p0275c2s v1p0277c1s v1p0386c1s v1p0428c2m v1p0529c1s v1p0639c2s v1p0999c1s v1p1423c2s
Dwight, C.P. v4p0306c1s
Dwight, E. v1p0181c2m v1p0326c1s v1p0838c1s v1p0918c1s v1p1276c2s v2p0146c1s v3p0304c1s v3p0348c2s
Dwight, E.S. v1p1261c2s
Dwight, H.E. v1p1060c2s
Dwight, H.G. v6p0018c2s v6p0053c2s v6p0146c1s v6p0232c1s v6p0287c1s v6p0291c2s v6p0452c2s v6p0474c2s v6p0594c2s v6p0622c2s v6p0661c1s v6p0672c2s
Dwight, H.O. v1p1330c2s v1p1331c2s v1p1332c2s v3p0115c2s v3p0356c2s v5p0445c1s v5p0446c1s v6p0006c1m v6p0146c1s
Dwight, J. v3p0424c2m v6p0232c1s
Dwight, J. and Curtis, E.L. v6p0166c1s
Dwight, J.S. v1p0032c2s v1p0350c2s v1p0500c1s v1p0569c2s v1p0576c1s v1p0882c2m v1p0883c1s v1p0883c2s v1p0884c1m v1p0962c2s v1p1156c2s v1p1200c1s v1p1201c2s v1p1235c2s v1p1295c2s v1p1386c1s v2p0030c2s v2p0195c2s v2p0303c1s v3p0094c2s v3p0189c1s
Dwight, M. v1p0159c1s
Dwight, M.A. v1p0062c2s v1p0064c1s v1p0365c1s
Dwight, M.E. v2p0082c1s
Dwight, S. v1p1436c1s
Dwight, S.A., Mrs. v1p0336c1s
Dwight, T. v1p0020c2s v1p0074c2s v1p0118c2s v1p0156c2s v1p0285c1s v1p0384c2m v1p0389c1s v1p0425c1s v1p0555c1s v1p0595c2s v1p0641c2s v1p0905c1s v1p0963c1s v1p0989c2s v1p1198c1s v1p1200c1s v1p1210c2s v1p1224c2s v2p0013c1s v2p0131c1s v2p0325c2s v2p0481c2s v3p0043c1s v3p0098c1s v3p0128c2s v3p0129c1s v3p0158c1s v3p0258c1s v3p0361c2s v3p0380c1s v3p0391c2s v3p0471c2m v4p0019c1s v4p0065c1s v4p0169c2s v4p0409c2s v4p0627c2s v5p0257c1s v6p0565c1s
Dwight, T., jr. v1p0285c1s
Dwight, T.F. v1p0082c1s v1p0275c1s v1p0595c2s v1p1388c1s v2p0166c1s v2p0445c2s
Dwight, T.W. v1p0916c1s v3p0093c1s v3p0155c1s v3p0190c1s v3p0437c2s v4p0324c1s
Dwight, T.W. and Harrington, James v3p0443c2s
Dwight, T.W. et al. v1p1048c2s
Dwight, Thos. v1p1115c2s v4p0260c2s
Dwight, Timothy v5p0126c2s
Dwight, W. v1p0198c2s
Dwight, W.B. v1p0155c1s v1p0311c1s v1p0469c2s v1p1384c1s v2p0163c2s v2p0465c2m v3p0251c2s v3p0454c1s
Dwight, W.B. and Ford, S.W. v2p0429c2s
Dwight, W.T. v1p0319c1s v1p0729c1s v1p0986c1s
Dwinell, I.E. v1p0095c2s v1p0119c1s v1p0201c2s v1p0242c1s v1p0290c2s v1p1092c2s v1p1093c1s v1p1175c1s v1p1238c2s v2p0005c1s v2p0042c1s v2p0120c1m v2p0355c2m v2p0356c2s v2p0406c1s v3p0130c1s v3p0148c1s v3p0280c1s
Dwinelle, J.W. v1p0895c2s
Dwire, H.B. v6p0454c2s
Dyall, C. v5p0496c2s
Dyan, M. v4p0235c1s v4p0504c1s
Dyar, H.G. v4p0327c1s
Dyar, M.C. v6p0055c1s v6p0058c1s v6p0201c1s v6p0619c2s
Dyar, W.W. v6p0081c1s v6p0673c1s
Dybowski, J. v3p0082c2s v3p0313c2s
Dybowski, M.J. v4p0379c1s
Dyche, J.A. v5p0307c2m
Dyche, L.L. v4p0025c2s v4p0187c1s v4p0609c2s
Dyck, C.V.A.Van v1p1278c2s
Dyde, S.W. v2p0262c2s v3p0143c1s v3p0270c1s v4p0154c1s v4p0190c2s v4p0214c1s v5p0143c1s v5p0472c2s v5p0550c1s
Dye, C. v6p0212c1s
Dye, E.E., Mrs. v3p0219c1s
Dyer, A.B. v5p0032c2s
Dyer, A.H. v6p0337c2s
Dyer, A.M. v4p0467c1s
Dyer, B.L. v6p0007c1s
Dyer, C.R. et al. v3p0106c2s
Dyer, D.B., Mrs. v5p0163c2s
Dyer, E. v1p1416c2s v3p0121c1s v3p0347c2m v3p0360c2s
Dyer, E.J. v6p0263c2s
Dyer, F. v1p0238c2s v1p0243c1s v1p0991c1s
Dyer, F.J. v6p0568c2s
Dyer, F.T. v2p0159c2s v2p0382c2s v2p0400c1s
Dyer, G.L. v3p0169c1s v6p0117c2s v6p0275c2s
Dyer, H. v3p0422c1s v4p0238c2s v4p0547c2s v6p0335c1s
Dyer, H.G. v6p0431c2s
Dyer, H.P. v4p0523c2s
Dyer, J. v1p0099c1s v1p0114c1s v1p0180c1s v1p0181c2s v1p0248c1s v1p0252c2s v1p0284c1s v1p0346c2s v1p0412c1s v1p0439c2s v1p0655c2s v1p0668c1s v1p0708c2s v1p0782c2s v1p0865c1s v1p0901c1s v1p0997c1s v1p1000c2s v1p1061c2s v1p1064c2s v1p1072c2s v1p1088c2s v1p1137c2s v1p1214c2s v1p1299c2s v1p1301c2s v1p1352c2s v1p1417c1s
Dyer, J.F.J. v1p0803c2s
Dyer, John v1p0926c2s
Dyer, L. v1p0551c2s v1p1309c1s v2p0386c1s v3p0008c2s v3p0016c1s v3p0019c2s v3p0113c2s v3p0219c1s v3p0401c1s v4p0004c2s v4p0075c1s v4p0130c2s v4p0242c1m v4p0305c2s v4p0430c1s v4p0490c1s v5p0012c1m v5p0042c1s v5p0093c1s v5p0120c1s v5p0177c2s v5p0257c2s v5p0311c1s v5p0332c1s v5p0353c1s v5p0396c2s v5p0426c2s v5p0600c1s v6p0012c1s v6p0027c1s v6p0045c2s v6p0072c1s v6p0195c2s v6p0262c1s v6p0272c2s v6p0273c1s v6p0353c2s v6p0392c2s v6p0466c2m v6p0542c2s v6p0601c2s
Dyer, L.C. v6p0686c1s
Dyer, Louis v6p0185c1s v6p0281c2s
Dyer, M.C. v6p0372c2s
Dyer, Margaret C. v6p0371c2s
Dyer, O. v5p0306c2s
Dyer, S. v1p0095c2s v1p0318c2s
Dyer, T.F.T. v1p0358c1s v1p0865c2s v1p1406c2s v1p1411c1s v2p0070c1s v2p0113c2s v2p0123c2s v2p0152c1s v2p0198c2s v2p0232c2s v2p0243c2s v2p0277c2m v2p0290c1s v2p0202c2s v2p0314c2s v2p0345c1s v2p0410c2s v2p0427c1s v2p0437c1s v2p0441c1s v2p0442c2s v2p0446c1s v2p0472c1m v3p0293c2s v3p0333c2s v3p0466c2s
Dyer, W.A. v6p0087c1s v6p0120c1s v6p0139c1s v6p0244c2m v6p0258c2s v6p0299c2s v6p0595c1s v6p0626c1s
Dyer, W.B. v5p0105c2s v5p0443c1s v5p0448c2s
Dyer, W.J.J. v2p0032c2s
Dyer, W.S.T. v2p0194c2s
Dyer, W.T.T. v1p0449c2s v1p0586c2s v1p0738c1s v1p1015c1s v1p1081c1s v1p1324c1s v1p1364c1s v2p0046c1s v2p0114c1s v2p0149c2s v2p0154c2s v2p0409c1m v3p0403c2s v3p0418c2s v4p0145c2s v5p0150c2s
Dyer, W.T.T. et al. v3p0007c2s v3p0257c1s
Dyer, W.T.Thiselton v3p0019c1s v6p0112c2s
Dyes, Gustave v5p0168c1s v5p0332c1s
Dyes, Gustave and Taylor, R.S. v5p0380c2s
Dyke, Apul Van v6p0407c1s
Dyke, C.B. v6p0448c2s
Dyke, H. v1p0838c2s
Dyke, H.J.Van v1p0255c1s v1p1285c2s v2p0022c2s v2p0034c2s v2p0078c1s v2p0322c2s v2p0382c2s v3p0258c1s
Dyke, H.J.Van, jr. v1p1088c1s v2p0013c1s v2p0235c2s v2p0238c1s v2p0289c1s v2p0435c1s v2p0463c2s
Dyke, H.Van v3p0015c1s v3p0094c2s v3p0229c1s v3p0263c2s v3p0309c1s v3p0425c1m v3p0466c1s v4p0055c2s v4p0085c2s v4p0201c1s v4p0300c1s v4p0309c1s v4p0317c1s v4p0459c1s v4p0537c2s v4p0551c2s v4p0570c1s v4p0585c1s v4p0600c0s v4p0620c1s v5p0048c2s v5p0116c1s v5p0209c1s v5p0236c2s v5p0306c1s v5p0338c1s v5p0350c1s v5p0352c1s v5p0373c2s v5p0435c1s v5p0436c2s v5p0450c2s v5p0499c2s v5p0573c1s v5p0581c2s v5p0596c2s v5p0607c1s v5p0617c2s v5p0643c2s v6p0020c2s v6p0114c1s v6p0122c2s v6p0156c2s v6p0169c2s v6p0190c1s v6p0190c2s v6p0209c1s v6p0259c2s v6p0302c1s v6p0366c2s v6p0376c1s v6p0417c2s v6p0514c2s v6p0524c2s v6p0536c1s v6p0573c1s v6p0590c2s v6p0593c2s v6p0612c1s v6p0644c1s v6p0644c2s v6p0653c1s v6p0686c2s v6p0708c2s
Dyke, H.Van et al. v4p0569c1s v6p0074c2s
Dyke, J.C.Van v2p0070c2s v2p0173c1s v3p0021c1s v3p0022c1m v3p0437c2s v4p0030c2s v4p0101c2s v4p0126c1s v4p0135c1s v4p0241c1s v4p0480c1s v4p0510c2s v5p0051c2s v5p0144c2s v5p0224c1s v5p0267c2s v5p0270c2s v5p0328c1s v5p0331c1s v5p0386c2s v5p0422c2s v5p0476c1s v5p0487c1s v5p0495c2s v5p0595c2s v5p0622c2s v5p0632c1s v6p0319c2s v6p0570c2s
Dyke, J.S.Van v2p0161c2s v2p0280c1s
Dyke, J.Van and Beecher, H.W. v2p0088c2s
Dyke, P. v3p0225c2s
Dyke, P.Van v3p0229c2s v4p0080c1s v5p0094c2s v5p0534c2s v6p0029c1m v6p0039c1s v6p0431c1s v6p0506c1s
Dyke, R. v6p0031c2s
Dyke, T.S.Van v2p0287c1s v3p0053c2s v3p0350c1s v3p0374c1m v4p0143c2s v4p0468c2s v4p0531c2s v4p0568c1s v4p0631c2s v5p0063c1s v5p0166c2s v5p0473c2m v6p0143c2s v6p0168c1m v6p0201c1s v6p0249c1s v6p0387c1m v6p0470c1s v6p0499c2s v6p0525c2s v6p0527c1s v6p0543c2s v6p0567c1s v6p0590c1s v6p0592c1s v6p0658c1s
Dyke, W.H. v3p0422c1s
Dyke, W.Van v3p0237c1s
Dykema, P.W. v5p0355c1s
Dykers, R. v4p0555c1s
Dykes, D.O. v6p0278c2s v6p0348c1s
Dykes, F. v1p0709c2s
Dykes, J.O. v1p0175c2s v2p0081c1s v2p0081c2s v2p0112c2s v2p0238c1s v2p0395c1s v3p0285c2s v3p0456c2s v5p0059c2m
Dykes, T. v2p0062c1s v2p0319c1s v2p0419c1s v2p0481c2s v3p0428c2s v5p0040c2s
Dykman, J.O. v3p0013c2s v3p0303c2s v3p0372c1s
Dymond, A.H. v1p0300c2s v1p0736c1s
Dymond, J. v1p0390c1s
Dymond, P. v3p0285c1s
Dyne, F.Van v4p0394c2s
Dyneley, J. v6p0278c2s
Dyneley, M. v3p0425c1s
Dynes, J.H. v5p0099c2s
Dyrenforth, R.G. and Newcomb, S. v3p0353c2s
Dyson, E. v5p0238c2s v6p0514c2s
Dyson, F.W. v6p0602c2s v6p0614c1s
Dyson, W.F. v5p0345c1s
Dziatzko, C. v2p0057c1s
Dziatzko, K. v4p0329c2s
Dziewicki, H. v3p0228c2m v5p0456c2s
Dziewicki, M.H. v3p0115c1s v3p0146c2s v3p0156c2s v4p0094c1s

E., J.W. v1p0085c1s
Eaches, O.P. v2p0222c2s
v2p0368c2s v3p0346c2s
Eachus, G.E. v2p0396c1s
Eadie, J. v1p0246c2s
v1p1348c1s
Eadie, J.H. v2p0014c1s
Eads, G.W. v6p0449c1s
Eads, J.B. v1p0161c2s
v1p0651c1s v1p0854c1m v1p1009c1s
v1p1143c2s v2p0161c1s v2p0229c1s
v2p0400c2s
Eagar, A.R. v6p0064c1s
Eagar, Alex.R. v6p0064c1s
v6p0272c1s
Eagle, P.A., Mrs. v3p0280c2s
Eagle, P.B. v5p0104c2s
v5p0287c2s v5p0606c1s
Eagle-Clark, W. v6p0067c1s
Eaglepen, S. v1p0937c2s
Eagles, J. v1p0144c1s
v1p0259c2s v1p0322c1s v1p0569c1s
v1p0816c1s v1p0883c1s v1p1202c2s
v1p1275c2s v1p1292c1s v1p1298c1s
Eagles, T.H. v1p1363c2s
Eagles, T.J. v3p0372c2s
Eaglesfield, C.B.C. v5p0040c2s
v5p0070c1s v5p0275c2s
Eaglesfield, C.C. v5p0081c2s
v5p0231c2s v5p0232c1s v5p0393c1s
v5p0394c2s v5p0570c2s
Eaglestone, C. v3p0048c2s
v3p0078c1s v3p0266c1s v3p0366c2s
v4p0072c1s v4p0163c2s v4p0392c2s
v4p0610c2s
Eaglestone, C.R. v3p0124c1s
v3p0264c2s v3p0284c1s v3p0429c1s
Eakins, G. v6p0466c1s
Eakins, J.J. v3p0203c1s
v4p0137c1s
Eakins, L.G. v3p0275c2s
v3p0276c1s v3p0414c2s v4p0367c1s
Eakins, L.G. and Cross, W.
v2p0358c2s v4p0465c2s
Eakins, W.G. v6p0097c1s
Eakle, A.S. v4p0011c1s
v5p0062c2s v5p0194c2s v6p0475c1s
Eakle, A.S. and Muthman, W.
v4p0505c1s
Eames, E.J. v1p0749c2s
Eames, E.J., Mrs. v1p0082c2s
v1p1338c2s
Eames, E.L. v3p0087c1s
v3p0172c2s v3p0219c1s v3p0234c2s
v3p0291c2s v3p0352c2s v3p0361c1s
v3p0459c2s
Eames, J.V., Mrs. v1p0791c2s
Eames, N. v3p0037c2s
v3p0272c2s v3p0294c2s v3p0375c1s
v3p0389c2s v3p0448c1s v3p0463c1s
v4p0049c1s v4p0263c1s v4p0476c1s
v4p0633c2s v5p0156c2s v5p0506c1s
Eames, Ninetta v4p0083c2s
v4p0084c1s v4p0501c2s v5p0344c2s
v6p0383c1s
Eames, R.L. and Reed, T.A.
v2p0401c1s
Eames, W. v5p0074c2s
v5p0330c2s v5p0334c1s v5p0405c2s
Eames, W.S. v6p0016c2s
Eardley, C.E. v1p0132c2s
Eardley, F. v4p0632c2s
Eardley-Wilmot, C. v5p0467c1s
Eardley-Wilmot, E. v5p0246c2s
Eardley-Wilmot, E.A. v4p0338c2s
Eardley-Wilmot, F. v3p0278c2s
Eardley-Wilmot, S. v3p0138c2s
v3p0211c2s v4p0106c2s v4p0238c1s
v4p0294c2s v4p0521c2s v4p0587c1s
v5p0287c1s v5p0401c2s v6p0669c1s
Earhart, R.F. and Foulk, C.W.
v6p0671c1s
Earl, A. v4p0579c1s
v6p0349c2s
Earl, E. v3p0315c2s
Earl, F.K. v5p0347c1s
v5p0555c1s
Earl, G.W. v1p0078c1s
v1p0911c1s v1p0966c1s
Earl, J.C. v2p0311c2s
Earland, A. v6p0232c2s
Earle, A., Mrs. v6p0179c1s
v6p0190c2s
Earle, A.M. v3p0079c1s
v3p0098c2s v3p0172c1s v3p0273c1s
v3p0273c2s v3p0296c1s v3p0350c2s
v3p0394c2s v3p0432c2s v4p0069c2s
v4p0083c2s v4p0127c2s v4p0195c2m
v4p0203c2m v4p0209c2s v4p0357c1s
v4p0401c1s v4p0444c2s v4p0454c2s
v4p0455c1s v4p0459c2s v4p0467c2s
v4p0494c1s v4p0505c2s v4p0598c1s
v4p0621c1s v4p0624c1s v5p0015c1s
v5p0137c1s v5p0273c1s v5p0287c2s
v5p0474c1s v5p0492c1s v5p0529c1s
v6p0090c2s v6p0229c2s v6p0514c2s
Earle, Alice M. v4p0124c2s
v4p0162c1s v6p0626c1s
Earle, C. v4p0019c1s
v4p0422c1s v4p0466c2s v4p0563c1s
v5p0215c1s v5p0567c2s
Earle, C.W. v5p0520c2s
Earle, E. v4p0501c1s
Earle, E.L. v5p0407c1s
v5p0546c2s
Earle, F.R. v2p0205c2s
Earle, F.S. v6p0160c1s
v6p0161c1s v6p0244c1s
Earle, H.P. v6p0569c2s
Earle, J. v1p0723c2s
v1p0724c2s v1p0843c1s v1p1166c1s
v4p0183c2s
Earle, J. and Mayhew, A.L.
v3p0215c2s
Earle, J. et al. v3p0362c2s
Earle, J.C. v1p0192c1s
v1p0762c1s v1p0934c1s v1p1119c1s
v1p1128c2s v1p1154c2s v1p1253c1s
v1p1294c2s v1p1435c2s v2p0005c1s
v2p0080c1s v2p0144c1s v2p0232c1s
v2p0266c2s v2p0325c2s v2p0346c1s
v2p0375c1s v2p0376c2s v2p0381c2s
Earle, J.G. v1p1024c2s
Earle, L.C. v6p0436c2s
Earle, M.L. v3p0392c2s
v4p0523c2s v6p0272c2s
Earle, M.L. and McMurtry, W.J.
v3p0392c2s
Earle, M.T. v4p0089c1s
v4p0233c2s v4p0435c2s v5p0011c2s
v5p0051c1s v5p0097c2s v5p0128c1s
v5p0188c1s v5p0260c1s v5p0311c1s
v5p0359c1s v5p0390c1s v5p0408c1s
v5p0420c2s v5p0421c1s v5p0427c1s
v5p0531c1s v5p0579c1s v5p0580c2s
v6p0100c2s v6p0104c2s v6p0106c2s
v6p0344c2s v6p0462c1s v6p0534c2s
v6p0649c2s v6p0669c2s
Earle, Maria T. v6p0116c1s
v6p0177c1s
Earle, Maria Theresa v4p0032c1s
v6p0432c1s
Earle, Mary T. v4p0132c1s
v6p0161c2s v6p0174c1s
Earle, P. v3p0216c2s
Earle, P.E. v2p0421c2s
Earle, R.A. v1p0525c1s
v1p1332c1s
Earle, S.C. v5p0221c1s
Earll, M. v5p0237c1s
Earll, R.E. v2p0157c2s
Earls, J.C. v1p1116c2s
Early, E.L. v5p0277c2s
Early, J.A. v1p0175c1m
v1p0435c2s v1p0485c2s v1p0518c2m
v1p0519c1s v1p0675c1m v1p0795c2s
v1p1342c2s v1p1346c1m v1p1347c1m
v1p1347c2m v1p1388c2s
v2p0453c2s
Early, J.A. et al. v1p0518c2s
Earnest, J.A. v2p0149c1s
v2p0266c1s v3p0261c1s v4p0054c1s
v4p0497c2s
Earnshaw, E.H. v5p0622c1s
Earp, F.R. v6p0166c2s
v6p0251c2s v6p0355c1s v6p0489c2s
v6p0630c2s v6p0655c2s
Earwaker, J.P. v1p0077c1s
v1p0757c1s v1p0928c1s v1p0954c2s
v1p1061c2m v2p0247c1s v3p0076c1s
Easby-Smith, J.S. v5p0318c2s
Easley, R.M. v5p0098c1s
v6p0129c1s v6p0279c2s v6p0356c2s
Eassie, E. v1p1018c1s
Eassie, L.M. v5p0164c1s
v5p0349c2s
Eassie, W. v1p0354c2s
v1p0579c1s v1p0607c2s v3p0104c1s
v3p0168c1s
East, A. v5p0167c1m
v5p0449c1s v5p0560c2s v5p0561c1m
v6p0167c2s v6p0180c1s v6p0181c2s
East, Alfred v4p0298c1s
v6p0596c2s
East, F.J. v6p0165c2s
East, F.R. v6p0509c1s
v6p0615c1s
East, J.N. v3p0182c1s
East, J.W. v2p0069c2s
East, M.B. v6p0680c1s
Easter, M.E. v1p1221c1s
Easter, S.E. v6p0332c2s
Eastin, G.B. v2p0195c1s
Eastlake, A.P. v1p1402c1s
Eastlake, C.L. v1p0639c2s
v1p1144c2s v1p1284c2s v3p0296c2s
v4p0449c2s v6p0279c2s v6p0384c2s
v6p0443c1s v6p0475c1s v6p0519c1s
v6p0640c2s v6p0684c2s
Eastlake, C.L. and Vallance, A.
v6p0167c2s
Eastlake, E.W. v3p0227c1s
Eastlake, F.W. v2p0128c1s
Eastlake, G. v6p0487c2s
Eastlake, H.Y. v2p0207c1s
v2p0244c1s v2p0270c1s
Eastlake, Lady v3p0423c2s
v3p0459c1s
Eastlake, W.D. v4p0297c1s
v4p0297c2s
Eastman, C.A. v4p0527c2s
v5p0150c1s v6p0264c2s v6p0271c2s
v6p0315c2s v6p0316c2s v6p0530c2s
Eastman, C.R. v4p0156c1s
v5p0008c2s v5p0146c2s v5p0161c2s
v5p0208c2s v5p0354c2s v5p0454c1s
v5p0471c1s v5p0532c1s v5p0566c1s
v6p0019c2s v6p0034c2m v6p0037c1s
v6p0067c2s v6p0100c2s v6p0107c1s
v6p0148c2s v6p0169c2s v6p0170c2s
v6p0172c2s v6p0189c1s v6p0214c1s
v6p0227c1s v6p0234c2m v6p0250c1s
v6p0398c2s v6p0443c2m v6p0487c1s
v6p0489c1s v6p0576c2s v6p0577c1s
v6p0677c2s v6p0679c2s v6p0681c1s
Eastman, C.W. v5p0268c2s
Eastman, E.G. v5p0288c1m
Eastman, E.V. v4p0029c2s
v4p0169c1s v4p0448c2s
Eastman, Elaine G. v5p0388c2m
Eastman, F. v4p0183c1s
v4p0451c1s v4p0617c1s v5p0375c1s
Eastman, F.F. v5p0614c2s
Eastman, G. v5p0249c1s
Eastman, J. v1p0127c2s
Eastman, J.B. and Woods, R.A.
v6p0076c2s
Eastman, J.C. v4p0101c1s
v4p0102c1s
Eastman, J.R. v2p0445c1s
v2p0459c1s v4p0034c1s v4p0594c2s
v5p0513c1s
Eastman, L.A. v4p0329c2s
v5p0069c2s v5p0334c2s v5p0335c1m
Eastman, L.R. v1p0380c1s
Eastman, L.R., jr. v1p0925c2s
v1p1219c2s
Eastman, M.H. v1p0941c1s
Eastman, M.J. v4p0626c1s
Eastman, Max F. v6p0484c1s
Eastman, O. v1p0034c2s
v1p0351c1s
Eastman, P. v6p0234c1s
v6p0329c2s v6p0349c1s v6p0694c2s
v6p0700c1s
Eastman, S.C. v1p0911c1s
v5p0164c1s
Eastman, W.R. v4p0330c1s
v4p0401c1s v5p0334c1s v5p0334c2s
v5p0336c2s v6p0104c1s v6p0375c1s
Eastman, W.R. and Marvin, C.
v6p0371c1s
Eastman, W.R. et al. v6p0371c1s
v6p0374c1s
Eastman, W.T.
v3p0405c1s
Easton, B.S. v5p0561c1s
Easton, C. v4p0370c2s
v5p0604c2s v6p0417c1s v6p0614c1s
Easton, C.C. v6p0569c1s
Easton, E. v1p1110c1s
v1p1397c2s
Easton, E. and Bramwell, F.J.
v1p0766c2s
Easton, E.E. v5p0588c1s
Easton, E.T. v5p0200c2s
Easton, H.T. v5p0046c2s
Easton, M.W. v1p1252c1s
v3p0024c1s v3p0140c1s v3p0163c2m
v3p0178c2s v4p0178c1s
Eastwick, E.B. v1p0533c1s
v1p0631c2s v2p0251c2s
Eastwick, G. v1p0228c1s
Eastwick, J. v4p0395c2s
v4p0398c1s
Eastwick, R.W.E. v4p0151c2s
v4p0161c1s
Eastwick, R.W.Egerton v4p0556c1s
Eastwood, A. v3p0429c2s
v4p0342c2s v6p0057c1s
Eastwood, A.C. v6p0395c1s
Eastwood, F. v1p0246c1s
v1p0505c2s v1p0799c1s
Eastwood, G. v1p0348c2s
v1p1236c1s
Eastwood, J. v1p0524c2s
v1p0686c1s v1p1062c2s v3p0081c2s
v3p0145c1m
Eastwood, M. v2p0450c1s
v2p0474c1s v4p0097c2s v5p0301c1s
Easum, B.C.D' v5p0215c2s
v5p0224c2s v5p0240c1s v6p0466c2s
Eaton, A. v1p0268c1s
v1p0788c1s
Eaton, A.M. v2p0168c1s
v5p0541c1m v6p0544c2s
Eaton, A.M. and Dembitz, L.M.
v6p0515c1s
Eaton, A.W. v4p0408c1s
Eaton, A.W.H. v3p0188c2s
v4p0408c1s
Eaton, B.D. v4p0457c2s
Eaton, B.S. v6p0433c1s
Eaton, C. v5p0174c1s
Eaton, C.A. v5p0114c2s
Eaton, C.H. v3p0415c2s
v4p0467c1s v4p0597c1s v5p0355c2s
Eaton, D. v5p0519c2s
Eaton, D.B. v1p0068c2s
v1p0258c1s v1p0259c1m v1p0259c2s

v1p0643c2s v1p0880c2s v1p1027c1s
v1p1239c1s v1p1295c2m v2p0086c2s
v2p0087c1m v2p0332c2s v2p0347c1s
v2p0454c2s v3p0086c2m v3p0322c2s
v3p0343c1s v4p0117c1s v4p0449c2s
Eaton, D.C. v3p0003c2m
v3p0035c1s v3p0346c2s v3p0393c1s
v5p0031c2s
Eaton, E.A. v1p0706c1s
Eaton, E.H. v5p0039c2s
Eaton, E.L. v5p0376c1s
Eaton, Edith v6p0014c1s
Eaton, F. and Hodgson, J.E.
v3p0306c1s v3p0475c2s
Eaton, F.A. v1p0208c1s
v1p0472c2s v1p1264c1s v2p0379c1s
v6p0553c2s
Eaton, F.A. and Hodgson, E.
v3p0313c1s
Eaton, F.A. and Hodgson, J.E.
v3p0034c2s v3p0073c1s v3p0166c1s
v3p0191c2s v3p0289c1s v3p0303c2s
v3p0328c1s v3p0413c1s v4p0202c1s
v4p0493c1s v4p0493c2s v4p0531c2s
v4p0587c1s
Eaton, F.A. and Leslie, G.D.
v4p0084c1s v5p0069c1s v5p0101c1s
v5p0127c2s v5p0135c2s v5p0265c2s
v5p0482c2s v5p0498c2s v5p0533c1s
v5p0619c2s v5p0626c2s v6p0047c2s
v6p0146c1s v6p0212c2s v6p0364c2s
v6p0553c2s
Eaton, F.B. v2p0066c2s
Eaton, F.H. v4p0217c2s
Eaton, Fred. and Hodgson, J.E.
v3p0102c1s
Eaton, Fred.A. v6p0553c2s
Eaton, Fred.A. and Hodgson, J.E.
v3p0165c2s v3p0360c1s v3p0368c1s
Eaton, G.F. v5p0066c2s
v6p0522c1s v6p0657c1s
Eaton, H.F. v5p0570c1s
Eaton, H.W. v2p0136c2s
v2p0137c2s v2p0430c1s
Eaton, Harriet P. v4p0385c1s
Eaton, I. v4p0607c2s
Eaton, I.G. v3p0366c1s
Eaton, J. v2p0130c2s
v2p0131c2s v2p0132c1s v2p0208c1s
v2p0220c2s v2p0386c1s v2p0390c2m
v2p0455c1s v3p0091c2s v3p0310c2s
v4p0009c1s v4p0100c2s v4p0295c2s
Eaton, J.H. v1p1152c2s
Eaton, John v3p0313c2s
Eaton, Mrs. v1p1297c1s
Eaton, Oliver v6p0379c1s
Eaton, Percival R. v6p0359c1s
v6p0684c2s
Eaton, R. v1p0008c2s
v1p0876c1s
Eaton, S.J.M. v3p0325c2s
Eaton, S.M. v1p0995c2s
Eaton, T.J. v2p0007c1s
Eaton, V.G. v2p0031c2s
v2p0432c2s v3p0313c1s v4p0424c2s
Eaton, W. v1p0086c1s
v3p0279c2s v6p0505c2s
Eaton, W.L. v3p0178c2s
Eaton, W.P. v6p0044c1s
Eaves, L. v6p0568c2s
Ebbs-Canavan, F. v6p0073c1s
Ebeling, W. v1p0920c1s
Ebell, A.J. v1p0848c2s
Ebelmen and Salvetat v1p1035c1s
Ebener, F. v1p0467c2s
Eberhart, G.L. v4p0261c2s
v4p0262c1s v4p0379c2s
Eberle, E.W. v5p0050c1s
v5p0423c2s v5p0508c2s
Eberle, F. v5p0645c2s
v6p0713c1s
Ebermeyer, A. v3p0165c1s
Ebers, G. v1p0589c2s
v1p1071c2s v2p0063c2s v2p0430c2s
v3p0131c2s v4p0424c2s v4p0634c1s
v5p0329c1s
Eberschweiler, F. v5p0287c2s
Ebersole, M.V. v5p0208c1s
Ebersole, W.S. v5p0434c1s
Ebert, A. v1p0219c2s
v1p0753c1s
Ebert, H. v4p0556c2s
Eberty, F. v1p0535c1s
Ebner-Eschenbach, M.von .. v4p0459c1s
v5p0207c1s v6p0052c2s
Ebner-Eschenbach, Marie von
v5p0207c1s
Eborall, A.C. v5p0458c1s
v6p0197c2m
Ebrard, J.H. v1p0113c2s
Ebrard, J.H.A. v1p0343c2s
v1p0514c2s v1p0692c2s v1p0769c1s
v1p1432c2s v1p1442c2s v2p0129c1s
Ebrington, Lord v2p0189c2s
v2p0227c1s v3p0221c2s
Ebrington, Lord and
Baden-Powell, G., Sir . v3p0005c1s
Ebrington, Viscount v3p0163c1s
v3p0321c2s
Ebsen, H.L. v4p0547c2s
Eby, C.S. v3p0226c2s
v3p0227c1m
Eby, F. v5p0316c1s
v5p0360c2s
Eby, S.C. v5p0267c2s
Eccles, A.S. v3p0273c1s
v4p0252c1s v4p0363c2s v4p0529c2s
v4p0596c1s
Eccles, C.O'C. v3p0397c1s
v5p0390c2s
Eccles, C.O'Conor v3p0222c2s
Eccles, D. v2p0119c2s
v2p0307c2s
Eccles, F.Y. v6p0288c1s
Eccles, H.L. v6p0129c1s
v6p0299c2s
Eccles, Miss v1p1296c1s
Eccles, R.C. v1p0810c2s
Eccles, R.G. v1p0714c2s
v2p0341c1s
Eccles, R.K. v4p0503c2s
Echols, E.S. v4p0249c1s
Echols, Emma S. v5p0540c1s
Eckard, J.R. v1p1161c1s
Eckardt, H.M.P. v6p0050c2s
v6p0571c2s
Eckart, I.R. v1p0004c2s
Eckart, W.R. v2p0083c1s
Eckel, E.C. v5p0534c1s
v6p0248c1s v6p0328c2s v6p0418c2s
v6p0447c2s
Eckel, Edwin C. v6p0106c2s
Eckels, J.H. v4p0044c1s
v4p0199c1s v4p0378c1m v4p0593c1m
v4p0596c1s v5p0062c1s v5p0289c2s
v5p0329c2s v5p0603c2s v5p0634c2s
v6p0051c1s v6p0365c2s v6p0539c2s
v6p0667c1s v6p0692c2s
Eckenrode, H.J. v6p0680c1s
Eckenstein, L. v6p0297c1s
Ecker, A. v1p1204c1s
Eckersley, W.A. v4p0359c1s
Eckerson, M.H. v1p0752c1s
Eckford, H. v1p0158c1s
v1p0560c2s v1p0713c1s v1p0919c2s
v1p1196c1s v1p1282c1s v2p0035c2s
v2p0065c1s v2p0169c1s v2p0221c2s
v2p0241c1s v3p0048c1s v3p0151c1s
v3p0371c1s v3p0455c1s v4p0437c2s
Eckford, Henry v5p0631c2s
Eckhardt, C. v4p0345c1s
Eckhardt, C.C. v6p0708c2s
Eckhartz v2p0078c2s
Eckman, G.P. v6p0341c2s
v6p0640c2s
Eckoff, W.J. v1p0802c1s
Eckstein, Consul v3p0012c2s
v3p0375c1s
Eckstein, E. v4p0244c1s
v4p0409c1s v5p0557c1s
Eckstein, L. v5p0210c2s
Eckstein, W. v5p0338c2s
Eckstorm, F.E. v6p0389c2s
Eckstrom, F.H. v6p0644c2s
Eckstrom, R.P. v6p0599c1s
Eclaire, E. v1p1264c1s
Ecob, Eleanor v6p0570c2s
Ecob, H.C. v4p0140c2s
Ecob, H.G. v5p0203c2s
Ecob, J.H. v3p0383c2s
v4p0573c1s v5p0118c1s v6p0559c2s
Ecroyd, H. v1p0993c2s
v1p1229c1s v1p1365c1s v1p1371c1s
Ecroyd, W.F. and Whittaker, T.P.
v1p0486c1s
Eddie, L.A. v4p0026c1s
v4p0167c1s v5p0478c1s
Eddis, F.E. v4p0477c2s
Eddy, A.D. v1p0421c1s
v1p0641c2s
Eddy, A.J. v5p0359c2s
Eddy, C. v4p0417c1s
v5p0393c1s v5p0423c1s v5p0423c2m
Eddy, C.W. v3p0011c1s
Eddy, D.C. v1p0598c2s
Eddy, F.M. v5p0086c1s
Eddy, H.D. v1p0541c1s
Eddy, H.T. v1p0051c1m
v1p0365c1s v1p0541c1m v1p1259c1s
v1p1304c2s v1p1390c1s v2p0027c2s
v2p0172c1s v2p0199c1s v2p0199c2s
v2p0243c1m v2p0280c1s v2p0362c1s
v3p0028c2s v6p0637c1s
Eddy, J. v1p0352c2s
v4p0191c2s
Eddy, J.M. v3p0071c2s
v5p0203c1s
Eddy, Mary Baker G. v6p0282c2s
Eddy, R. v1p0528c2s
v1p0881c2s v1p1356c1m v2p0299c2s
v2p0302c2s v2p0426c1s v3p0230c1s
Eddy, R.H. v1p0168c2s
Eddy, S.J. v5p0491c1s
Eddy, T.A. and Schurz, C.. v4p0192c2s
Eddy, T.M. v1p0158c1s
v1p0830c1m v1p1077c1s v1p1120c2s
v1p1400c1s
Eddy, T.W. v6p0398c2s
Eddy, U.D. v3p0094c2s
v4p0593c2s v6p0205c1s
Eddy, W.A. v1p0989c1s
v2p0074c1s v2p0086c1s v2p0443c1s
v3p0131c2s v3p0410c2s v4p0002c1s
v5p0317c2s
Eddy, Z. v1p0382c2s
v1p0956c2s v1p1043c1s
Ede, W.M. v3p0326c1m
v4p0412c1s
Edelfelt, A. v3p0153c1s
Edelmann, Edith v4p0037c2s
Edelmann, J.H. v4p0024c2s
Eden, E. v1p0357c2s
Eden, F. v1p1146c1s
Eden, N. v6p0628c2s
Edenburgen, J. v3p0054c1s
Edensor, M. v3p0445c2s
Eder, J.M. v1p0327c2s
Edersheim, A. v1p0129c1m
v2p0044c1s
Edersheim, Dr. v2p0268c1s
Edersheim, E. v2p0348c2s
v3p0148c1s v3p0177c2s v3p0205c1s
v3p0291c1m v3p0294c1s
Edersheim, Ella v3p0215c2s
Ederson, M. v3p0117c2s
Edes, E. v2p0193c1s
Edes, E.B. v2p0205c2s
v3p0142c1s
Edes, H.H. v4p0470c1s
v6p0701c1s
Edes, R.T. v1p0019c2s
v5p0142c2s
Edgar, C.C. v6p0330c1s
Edgar, G.G. v6p0221c1s
Edgar, J. v4p0396c1s
v4p0413c2s
Edgar, J.D. v1p0235c1s
v1p0637c2s v1p1039c1s v5p0091c1s
v5p0408c2s
Edgar, J.W. v1p0173c2s
Edgar, L.A. v1p0035c1s
Edgar, P. v4p0256c1s
v5p0221c1s v6p0090c2s v6p0429c1s
v6p0590c1s
Edgar, R. v1p0558c1s
Edgar, R.M. v2p0438c1s
v3p0040c2s v3p0145c2s v6p0657c1s
v6p0688c2s
Edgar, R.McC. v1p0218c1s
v1p1176c2s v2p0199c2s v2p0268c1s
v2p0385c2s v3p0230c1s v4p0108c2s
v4p0109c1s v5p0371c1s
Edgar, W.C. v4p0194c2s
v4p0319c1s v4p0371c1s v4p0496c1s
v6p0289c2s
Edgar, W.M. v6p0316c1s
Edgarton, R. v4p0080c2s
v4p0581c1s
Edgcombe, F.J.S. v1p0520c1s
Edgcome, J. v4p0213c2s
Edgcumbe, Ernestine, Lady. v5p0389c1s
Edgcumbe, R. v1p0222c2s
v2p0063c1s v3p0189c1s v3p0435c2s
v4p0063c2m v5p0086c1s v5p0166c1s
v5p0455c1s v5p0590c1s
Edgcumbe, R. and Harvey, F.
v2p0063c1s
Edgcumbe, R and Poland, H.B.
v6p0157c1s
Edgcumbe, R., Sir v5p0264c2s
Edge-Partington, J. v4p0361c2s
Edgecomb, D.W. v3p0309c2s
v3p0424c1s v4p0476c2s v5p0571c2s
v6p0637c1s
Edgecombe, W. v5p0544c2s
Edgell, B. v6p0647c1s
Edgell, E.Wyatt v1p0211c2s
Edger, H. v1p1057c1s
Edger, W.W. v6p0097c2s
v6p0659c2s
Edgerly, J.A. v1p0383c1s
Edgerly, J.G. v4p0201c2s
Edgerly, N.F. v1p0383c1s
Edgerton, C.C. v1p0253c2s
Edgerton, C.E. v5p0633c2s
Edgerton, H.H. v1p0501c2s
Edgerton, J.A. v5p0229c2s
v6p0012c2s v6p0669c2s
Edgerton, James A. v6p0140c2s
Edgerton, W. v1p0020c2s
Edgeworth, F.Y. v1p0582c2s
v2p0074c1s v2p0130c1s v2p0156c1s
v2p0182c1s v2p0236c1s v2p0266c2s
v2p0281c1s v2p0407c1s v2p0418c2s
v2p0462c1s v3p0033c1s v3p0146c1m
v3p0176c1s v3p0188c2s v3p0336c2s
v3p0337c1m v3p0343c2s v4p0121c2s
v4p0131c1s v4p0230c2s v4p0377c2s
v4p0378c1s v4p0450c1s v4p0458c1s
v4p0532c1s v4p0546c2s v4p0599c2s
v4p0612c2s v5p0061c2s v5p0130c1s
v5p0175c2s v5p0199c1s v5p0294c1s
v5p0384c1s v5p0550c2s v5p0568c1s
v5p0568c2s v5p0584c1m v5p0607c1s
v5p0615c1s v6p0210c2s v6p0215c2s
v6p0360c2s v6p0506c2m v6p0533c1s
v6p0651c2s
Edgeworth, F.Y. and
Böhm-Bawerk, E.V. v4p0599c2s
Edgeworth, F.Y. and Bowley, A.L.
v6p0615c1s

Edgeworth, J. v4p0344c1s v5p0364c2s
Edgeworth, R.L. v1p1213c1s v1p1389c1s
Edgington, T.B. v3p0299c1s
Edgren, A.H. v4p0257c1s
Edgren, H. v6p0386c1s
Edgren, R. v6p0078c1m v6p0344c1s
Edholm, C.L. v6p0124c2m v6p0138c1s v6p0500c2s v6p0552c2s v6p0568c1s v6p0617c2s
Edholm, E.L. v6p0132c1s
Edholm, M.G.C. v6p0519c2s v6p0597c1s
Edinger, L. v5p0075c1s
Edis, R.W. v2p0020c1s v2p0126c1s v2p0209c1s v3p0113c1s v3p0165c2s v3p0202c2s
Edison, J.A. v2p0138c1s
Edison, T.A. v1p0399c2s v1p0580c1m v1p0825c2s v1p1002c2s v1p1329c2s v1p1378c1s v2p0006c1s v2p0137c2s v2p0433c1s v3p0132c2s v3p0330c1s v6p0432c1s v6p0619c1s
Edison-Hopkinson v2p0126c2s
Edkins, E. v2p0079c1s v2p0154c1s
Edkins, J. v2p0022c1s v2p0078c2s v2p0079c1s v2p0079c2s v2p0080c1m v2p0220c1s v2p0308c1s v2p0322c1s v2p0334c2s v2p0421c1s v3p0072c2s v3p0079c2s
Edkins, Joseph v4p0320c1s
Edleston, R.H. v3p0053c2s
Edlund, E. v1p0621c1s
Edmands, I.R. v5p0183c1s
Edmands, J. v2p0257c1s v2p0358c2s v3p0009c1s v3p0190c1s v5p0458c2s
Edmands, L.W. v4p0406c2s
Edmands, M.G. v4p0482c2s
Edmands, T.F. v4p0359c2s v4p0370c2s
Edmiston, H. v6p0130c1s v6p0331c2s v6p0404c2s v6p0409c2s
Edmiston, H.J. v5p0144c2s
Edmond, J. v1p0874c1s v1p1214c2s
Edmond, J.P. v4p0509c1s v5p0333c2s
Edmonds, A. v5p0107c1s v5p0302c1s
Edmonds, C. v6p0150c2s
Edmonds, C.D. v5p0451c1s
Edmonds, E.M. v3p0201c2s v4p0312c2s v4p0313c2s v4p0321c1s v4p0425c1s v4p0451c1s v4p0606c2s
Edmonds, E.N. v1p0555c2s
Edmonds, F.B. v2p0426c2s
Edmonds, F.S. v6p0492c1s v6p0535c1s
Edmonds, J.W. v1p0085c1s v1p0729c1s v1p1344c1s v1p1347c2s
Edmonds, May B. v6p0384c1s
Edmonds, R. v1p1002c1s v2p0110c1s v2p0285c2s v2p0421c2s
Edmonds, R.H. v1p0159c1s v1p0437c1s v4p0538c1m v4p0596c2s v6p0152c2s v6p0605c1s v6p0668c2s v6p0687c2s
Edmonds, T.R. v1p1247c1s
Edmonds, W.J. v5p0199c1s
Edmonds, W.L. v4p0207c1s v5p0416c2s v5p0478c2s
Edmondson, J. v3p0294c1s
Edmondson-Joel, J. v6p0069c1s
Edmondstone, P.M. v1p0229c1s
Edmund, A.T. v6p0677c1s
Edmunds, A.J. v4p0433c2s v5p0081c1s v5p0081c2s v5p0216c2s v5p0333c1s v5p0428c2s v5p0439c1s v5p0563c2s v6p0086c1s v6p0122c2s v6p0249c2s v6p0341c1s v6p0475c2s v6p0684c2s
Edmunds, C.K. v5p0098c2s v6p0118c1s v6p0118c2m v6p0119c2s v6p0631c1s v6p0696c2s
Edmunds, E. v1p0239c1s v4p0174c1s
Edmunds, E.S. v2p0246c1s
Edmunds, F.H. v5p0565c2s
Edmunds, F.S. v6p0491c2s
Edmunds, G.F. v1p0457c2s v1p1048c1s v1p1244c2s v1p1352c2s v2p0193c1s v2p0298c2s v3p0337c1s v3p0420c1s v3p0444c1s v4p0277c2s v4p0450c2s v4p0515c1s v4p0596c2s v5p0292c2s
Edmunds, H. v3p0179c1s
Edmunds, J. v1p0427c1s v1p0702c2s v1p0993c2s
Edmunds, L. v4p0190c2s
Edmunds, M.S. v4p0012c2s v4p0025c2s
Edmunds, W.H. v4p0066c2s v5p0070c2s
Edmundson, G. v2p0099c2s v2p0389c2s v3p0168c1s v3p0198c2s v3p0279c2s v3p0313c2s v3p0451c2s v4p0072c1s v4p0263c1s v4p0419c1s v4p0559c2s v5p0075c2s v5p0252c1m v6p0184c2s v6p0399c1s
Edmundson, G. and Gosse, E. v2p0289c2s
Ednoc, N. v5p0635c1s
Edridge-Green, F.W. v4p0577c2s v6p0139c1s
Edselas, F.M. v4p0025c2s v4p0068c2s v4p0222c1s v4p0226c2s v4p0410c2s v5p0181c2s v5p0412c1m v5p0510c1s
Edser, E. v6p0527c1s
Edser, E. and Stansfield, H. v5p0338c1s
Edson, A.W. v4p0406c1s v4p0506c1s v5p0365c1s v5p0569c2s v6p0564c1s v6p0627c1s
Edson, C. v2p0160c2s v3p0123c1s v3p0141c2s v4p0149c2s v4p0350c2s v4p0356c2s v4p0363c2s v4p0369c1s v4p0627c1s v4p0629c1m v5p0051c1s v5p0259c2s v5p0453c1s v5p0532c2s
Edson, C. et al. v4p0108c1s
Edson, H.A. v2p0118c1s v2p0442c1s
Edson, H.R. v1p0003c2s v4p0216c2s v4p0485c2s
Edson, Mira B. v5p0031c2s
Edson, O. v1p0166c2s
Edson, T. v1p0273c1s v1p1158c1s
Edward, A.B. v1p0566c1s
Edward, D. v2p0177c1s
Edward, H. v2p0188c2s v3p0285c1s
Edward, Prince of Wales .. v2p0031c1s
Edwardes, A. v1p0143c2s v1p0732c2s v1p0951c1s v1p1361c1s v2p0032c2s v2p0179c1s v3p0325c1s
Edwardes, Annie v4p0004c1s
Edwardes, C. v2p0159c2s v2p0309c1s v3p0025c2s v3p0062c2s v3p0104c2s v3p0149c2s v3p0155c2s v3p0165c1s v3p0192c2s v3p0198c2s v3p0247c1s v3p0267c1s v3p0286c1s v3p0294c2s v3p0328c1s v3p0366c2s v3p0379c1s v3p0467c2s v4p0004c1s v4p0010c2s v4p0048c2s v4p0068c1s v4p0090c1s v4p0095c2s v4p0124c1s v4p0159c1s v4p0178c2s v4p0195c2s v4p0200c2s v4p0206c2s v4p0215c2s v4p0228c1s v4p0228c2s v4p0231c1s v4p0235c2s v4p0243c2s v4p0260c2s v4p0314c2s v4p0315c2s v4p0317c1s v4p0319c1s v4p0368c1s v4p0375c1s v4p0392c2s v4p0407c2s v4p0428c2s v4p0490c2s v4p0529c2s v4p0598c2s v4p0602c1s v4p0634c1s v5p0004c1s v5p0047c2s v5p0049c2s v5p0083c1s v5p0138c2m v5p0145c2s v5p0150c2s v5p0200c2s v5p0221c1s v5p0221c2s v5p0340c2s v5p0355c1s v5p0389c2s v5p0397c2s v5p0439c1s v5p0461c1s v5p0542c2s v5p0544c2s v5p0564c2s v5p0607c2s v5p0608c1s v5p0624c2s v5p0631c2s v5p0645c1s v6p0065c2s v6p0100c1s v6p0103c2s v6p0178c2s v6p0203c2s v6p0286c1s v6p0310c2s v6p0359c1s v6p0420c2s v6p0434c1s v6p0435c2s v6p0440c1s v6p0467c1s v6p0486c2s v6p0510c2s v6p0534c1s v6p0566c1s v6p0570c1s v6p0578c1s v6p0594c1s v6p0596c1s v6p0650c1s v6p0695c1s v6p0714c2s
Edwardes, C.E. v4p0263c1s
Edwardes, Charles v4p0073c2s v4p0096c1s v4p0326c2s v5p0161c1s v5p0348c2s v5p0506c1s v5p0529c2s
Edwardes, E. v4p0620c1s
Edwardes, E.C.H. v2p0259c1s
Edwardes, H.B., Sir v1p0629c2s
Edwardes, H.S. v3p0234c2s v4p0244c2s
Edwardes, T. v6p0360c1s v6p0457c2s v6p0596c2s v6p0628c1s
Edwards, A. v1p0051c2s v1p0115c2s v1p0689c2s v1p0946c2s v1p1273c1s v1p1376c1s v1p1434c1s v3p0017c1s v3p0163c1s v6p0556c2s v6p0558c1s
Edwards, A. et al. v3p0141c2s
Edwards, A., Mrs. v1p1253c2s
Edwards, A.B. v1p0857c1s v1p1156c1s v2p0018c1s v2p0046c2s v2p0073c2s v2p0128c2s v2p0133c2m v2p0134c2m v2p0135c2m v2p0150c1s v2p0202c1s v2p0279c2s v2p0307c2s v2p0321c2s v2p0333c1s v2p0360c2m v2p0385c1s v2p0387c2s v2p0430c2s v2p0474c2s v3p0034c1s v3p0058c1s v3p0130c1s v3p0131c1s v3p0131c2s v3p0234c1m v3p0274c2s v3p0291c2s v3p0376c2s v4p0197c2s v4p0408c2s v4p0551c1s
Edwards, A.B. and Proctor, R.A. v2p0360c1s
Edwards, A.B. and Sandys, J.E. v3p0401c1s
Edwards, A.C. v6p0683c2s
Edwards, A.G. v4p0113c1s v4p0430c2s
Edwards, A.M. v1p0203c2s v1p0346c1s v1p0757c1s v1p0836c1s v3p0216c1s v4p0095c2s v4p0268c1s v5p0042c2s
Edwards, Amelia B. v2p0121c2s v2p0338c1s
Edwards, B. v3p0215c1s v5p0630c2s
Edwards, B., Miss v2p0125c1s v3p0160c2s
Edwards, B.B. v1p0120c2s v1p0125c1s v1p0125c2s v1p0129c2s v1p0132c2s v1p0165c1s v1p0190c1s v1p0232c2s v1p0247c2s v1p0262c1s v1p0262c2s v1p0278c1s v1p0336c2s v1p0348c1s v1p0385c1s v1p0393c1s v1p0569c1s v1p0572c2s v1p0581c2s v1p0582c1s v1p0682c1s v1p0809c1s v1p0825c1s v1p0846c1s v1p0846c2s v1p0852c1s v1p0912c1s v1p0923c2s v1p0960c2s v1p0990c2s v1p0998c2s v1p1117c1s v1p1124c2s v1p1208c2s v1p1216c1s v1p1301c2s v1p1416c2s v1p1430c1s
Edwards, C. v1p0308c1s v1p0356c1s v1p0568c2s v1p0823c2s v1p1184c2s v1p1186c2s v1p1415c1s v3p0035c2s v4p0042c1s v4p0350c2s v4p0534c1s v4p0553c1m v4p0581c1m v5p0197c2s v5p0299c2s v5p0323c1s v6p0652c2m
Edwards, C.B. v6p0377c2s
Edwards, C.C. v1p0858c1s
Edwards, C.E. v6p0060c2s
Edwards, C.L. v2p0047c1s v3p0106c2s v4p0041c2s v4p0205c1s v5p0020c1s v6p0053c1s v6p0357c1s
Edwards, C.P. v2p0036c1s
Edwards, C.R. v5p0215c1s v6p0321c1s v6p0493c2s v6p0669c2s
Edwards, D. v2p0073c2s v2p0387c2s v4p0035c2s
Edwards, E. v1p0743c1s v1p1153c2s v2p0276c1s v2p0340c1s v3p0193c2s
Edwards, E.F. v1p0961c2s
Edwards, E.H. v1p0890c1s
Edwards, E.H., Mrs. v1p0996c1s
Edwards, E.J. v3p0473c1s v4p0063c2s v4p0104c2s v4p0119c1s v4p0141c1s v4p0234c2s v4p0248c2s v4p0266c1s v4p0401c2s v4p0403c2s v4p0415c2s v4p0427c1m v4p0514c2s v4p0541c1s v4p0562c2m v4p0565c2s v4p0588c1s v5p0071c2s v5p0271c2s v5p0387c2s v6p0325c1s v6p0429c1s v6p0528c1s v6p0565c1s v6p0621c1s v6p0689c1s v6p0696c1s
Edwards, E.J. and Gessner, F.B. v4p0347c2s
Edwards, E.P. v1p0607c1s v1p1196c2s v1p1222c2s v2p0258c2m
Edwards, E.Price v4p0331c2s
Edwards, F.A. v1p0011c1s v1p0012c2s v1p0521c2s v1p0701c1s v1p0757c2s v1p0922c2s v1p1030c1s v3p0136c2s v5p0005c2s v5p0132c2s v5p0300c1s v5p0411c1m v5p0412c1s v5p0528c2s v5p0539c2s v5p0540c1s v6p0002c1s
Edwards, F.B. v6p0133c2s
Edwards, G. v1p0141c2s
Edwards, G.C. v5p0415c1s v5p0581c2s v6p0262c1s v6p0517c2s
Edwards, G.D. v5p0212c1s
Edwards, G.V. v6p0525c2s
Edwards, G.W. v3p0052c2s v3p0284c1s v3p0430c1s v4p0032c1s v4p0065c2s v4p0118c1s v4p0210c2s v4p0465c2s v4p0485c1s v4p0576c1s v5p0280c1s v5p0504c1s
Edwards, H. v1p0044c1s v1p0302c1s v1p0814c2s v2p0016c1s v4p0267c2s v6p0264c1s v6p0469c1s
Edwards, H.M. v1p0215c2s v1p0960c1s
Edwards, H.S. v1p0009c2s v1p0171c2s v1p0185c1s v1p0446c2m v1p0593c1s v1p0791c2s v1p0883c2s v1p1004c1s v1p1136c2m v1p1137c1s v1p1242c1s v1p1384c2s v2p0111c1s v2p0126c2s v2p0134c2s v2p0135c2s v2p0153c2s v2p0203c2s v2p0244c1s v2p0294c1s v2p0322c1s v2p0377c1s v2p0381c1s v2p0381c2s v2p0416c2s v2p0449c2s v3p0050c2s v3p0104c1s v3p0203c1s v3p0208c1s v3p0280c1s v3p0311c2s v3p0362c1s v3p0394c2s v3p0432c1s v3p0446c2s v3p0448c1s v4p0047c2s v4p0088c2s v4p0244c2s v4p0247c2s v4p0293c1s v4p0359c1s v4p0495c2s v4p0619c1s v4p0620c1s v5p0078c2s v5p0249c2s v5p0299c1s v5p0320c2s v5p0339c1s v5p0349c1s v5p0352c2s v5p0631c2s v5p0639c2s v6p0004c2s v6p0244c1s v6p0381c1s v6p0447c1s v6p0586c1s v6p0663c1s

Edwards, H.S.S. v1p0149c2s
Edwards, H.T. v6p0222c2s
v6p0675c2s
Edwards, Horace v6p0013c1s
v6p0025c2s v6p0093c1s v6p0223c2s
v6p0275c2s
Edwards, I. v1p0643c2s
Edwards, J. v1p0052c2s
v1p0275c2s v1p0922c2s v1p1234c1s
v1p1432c2s v3p0404c2s v5p0354c2s
v6p0258c1s v6p0463c1s
Edwards, J. et al. v1p0743c1s
Edwards, J.E. v2p0309c1s
v2p0333c2s v2p0337c2s v2p0453c2s
Edwards, J.H. v5p0530c1s
Edwards, J.P. v1p0270c1s
v1p0408c2s v1p0433c2s v1p0474c2s
v1p0711c1s v1p0711c2s v1p0969c1s
v1p0983c1s v1p1103c2s
Edwards, J.R. v4p0405c1s
Edwards, L.B. v4p0548c2s
v4p0633c2s v5p0036c1s v5p0107c1s
v5p0262c2s v5p0559c1s v5p0635c1s
v5p0635c2s v6p0508c1s
Edwards, Louise B. v6p0641c1s
Edwards, M. v2p0034c2s
v4p0386c1s
Edwards, M.A. v1p0850c2s
v1p0962c2s
Edwards, M.B. v1p0021c2s
v1p0116c1s v1p0141c1s v1p0176c2s
v1p0183c2s v1p0185c2s v1p0229c1s
v1p0245c1s v1p0278c1s v1p0305c2s
v1p0357c1s v1p0377c2s v1p0473c2s
v1p0478c2s v1p0489c2s v1p0523c1s
v1p0573c2s v1p0701c1s v1p0710c1s
v1p0785c2s v1p0812c2s v1p0885c2s
v1p0968c1s v1p0968c2s v1p1104c1s
v1p1160c1s v1p1163c1s v1p1409c1s
v1p1430c2s v2p0101c1s v2p0123c2s
v2p0181c2s v2p0334c1s v3p0146c2s
v3p0366c1s v3p0367c2s v4p0093c1s
v4p0171c2s v4p0320c2s
Edwards, M.E. v1p0496c1s
v1p0890c1s v2p0304c2s v2p0472c2s
v2p0475c2s v4p0386c1s
Edwards, M.G. v3p0378c1s
v3p0444c2s
Edwards, M.R. v2p0236c2s
Edwards, N.M. v6p0365c1s
Edwards, O. v5p0303c1s
Edwards, P. v4p0064c1s
v4p0307c1s v4p0323c1m
Edwards, P.L. v4p0325c1s
v4p0627c1s
Edwards, R. v1p0283c2s
v1p0741c1s v1p0926c1s v1p1311c1s
Edwards, S. v1p0067c2s
Edwards, S.O. v3p0360c2s
Edwards, T. v1p0121c2m
v1p0218c2s v1p0254c2s v1p0808c1s
v1p1010c1s v1p1060c1s v1p1064c2s
v1p1066c2s v1p1176c2s v2p0152c2s
Edwards, T.C. v2p0351c2s
Edwards, T.R. v3p0297c1s
Edwards, W. et al. v5p0321c1s
Edwards, W.A. v5p0202c2s
Edwards, W.F. v5p0467c2s
v5p0471c2m v5p0512c1s v5p0605c1s
Edwards, W.H. v1p0181c1s
v4p0317c2s
Edwards, W.H. and Crawford, J.M.
v4p0101c1s
Edwards, W.S. v1p0496c1s
v2p0286c1s v5p0097c2s v6p0216c1s
Edwards, W.W. v1p0397c2s
v1p0481c1s v1p0491c2s v1p0648c1s
v1p0982c1s v1p1030c2s v1p1031c2s
v3p0052c2s v4p0071c1s
Edwin, T. v4p0047c1s
Eeles, F.C. v6p0562c2s
Eells, A.G. v6p0671c1s
Eells, J. v2p0198c1s
v2p0298c2s v2p0352c2s
Eells, M. v2p0219c1s
v2p0219c2m v2p0220c1s v2p0359c1s
v2p0449c2s v3p0213c2m v3p0349c1s
Eells, S. v1p0443c1s
Eels, M. v6p0316c2s
Effendi, Gebel v3p0305c2s
Effendi, M. v1p1212c2s
Effendi, Sadik v4p0027c2s
Egan, J.J. v6p0147c1s
Egan, L.H. v4p0396c2s
Egan, M.F. v1p0186c1s
v1p0223c1s v1p0312c1s v1p0485c1s
v1p0564c1s v1p0804c2s v1p1128c1s
v1p1227c2s v2p0116c2s v2p0169c1s
v2p0259c1s v2p0317c2s v2p0338c2s
v2p0435c1s v2p0444c2s v4p0138c2s
v4p0488c1s v4p0489c1s v4p0569c1s
v5p0163c1s v6p0073c1s v6p0111c1s
v6p0142c1s v6p0171c1s v6p0207c2s
v6p0255c2s v6p0296c1s v6p0328c1s
v6p0348c2s v6p0379c2s v6p0380c1s
v6p0484c1s v6p0536c1s v6p0548c2s
v6p0581c1s v6p0587c1m v6p0587c2m
v6p0588c1s v6p0604c2s v6p0607c2s
v6p0674c1s v6p0686c1s
Egan, P. v1p0766c1s
Egan, P.R. v5p0479c1s
Egan, R.F. v6p0461c1s
Egan, W.C. v6p0154c1s
Egar, J.H. v1p0101c1s
v1p0207c1s v1p0599c2s v1p0964c2s
v1p0971c2s v2p0104c2s
Egar, M.F. v3p0247c1s
Egbert, H.C. v4p0592c1s
v5p0215c1s
Egbert, H.V. v2p0095c2s
Egbert, H.V. and Brooks, W.R.
v2p0095c1s
Egbert, J.C., jr. v5p0458c2m
v5p0642c1s v6p0125c2s v6p0549c2m
Egerton, H. v2p0240c1s
Egerton, H.E. v2p0090c2s
v2p0158c2s v3p0197c1s v3p0308c2s
v6p0184c2s
Egerton, H.G. v4p0009c1s
v4p0227c1s v4p0383c1s
Egerton, J.C. v2p0277c2s
v2p0427c2s
Egerton, Lord v2p0005c1s
Egerton, W. v4p0386c2s
v6p0313c1s v6p0314c1s
Egerton of Tatton v4p0132c1s
v4p0353c1s v6p0298c1s v6p0408c2s
v6p0478c1s
Egerton of Tatton, Earl .. v6p0384c2s
Egge, A.E. v2p0183c2s
Eggers, H. v2p0350c1s
Eggert, C.A. v1p0477c2s
v1p1057c1s v2p0088c1s v2p0131c1s
v2p0249c2m v2p0390c2s
Eggleson, E. v5p0308c2s
Eggleston, A.R. v5p0566c2m
Eggleston, E. v1p0245c1s
v1p0264c1s v1p0612c2s v1p0707c2s
v1p0975c2s v1p1052c1s v1p1130c1s
v1p1159c2s v1p1270c2s v2p0005c2s
v2p0010c2m v2p0011c1m v2p0028c1s
v2p0093c2s v2p0096c1s v2p0102c2s
v2p0174c2s v2p0205c1s v2p0219c1s
v2p0219c2s v2p0231c1s v2p0310c2s
v2p0366c2s v2p0404c1s v2p0451c2s
v3p0030c1s v3p0049c2s v3p0082c2s
v3p0083c1s v3p0148c2s v3p0179c2s
v3p0376c2s v3p0441c2s v4p0016c1s
v4p0205c2s v4p0352c2s v4p0398c1s
v4p0407c1s v4p0476c1s v5p0128c1s
Eggleston, E. and Putnam, G.H.
v3p0099c2s
Eggleston, F.O. v3p0431c2s
Eggleston, G.C. v1p0887c2s
v1p1314c2s v1p1346c2s v1p1374c1s
v2p0220c1s v2p0353c1s v2p0477c2s
v3p0011c1s
Eggleston, J.R. v5p0314c2s
Eggleston, J.W. v6p0257c2s
Eggleston, W.G. v3p0283c2s
Eggleston, W.G. et al. ... v3p0350c1s
Egle, W.H. v1p0294c2s
v1p0864c2s v1p1083c1s v3p0196c1s
v3p0325c2s v4p0611c2s v5p0081c1s
Egleston, M. v2p0310c2s
Egleston, N.H. v1p0114c1s
v1p0236c2s v1p0404c2s v1p0467c2s
v1p0468c1s v1p0846c2s v1p0847c1s
v1p0996c2s v1p1055c1s v1p1254c2s
v1p1412c1s v2p0162c1s v2p0162c2m
v2p0207c1s v2p0311c1s v2p0441c2s
v2p0446c1m v3p0295c2s v3p0464c2s
Egleston, T. v1p1091c1s
v1p1204c2s v2p0060c1s v2p0318c2s
Egleston, Thos. v3p0059c2s
Eglestone, C. v3p0295c2s
Eglinton, L. v6p0457c2s
Egremont, G. v6p0055c2s
Egville, H.D' v6p0168c2s
Ehrehart, C.J. v1p0406c2s
v1p0649c2s
Ehrenberg, C.G. v1p0642c1s
Ehrich, L.R. v3p0093c1s
v4p0125c1s v4p0315c2s v4p0478c2s
v4p0550c1s
Ehrstroem, E. v6p0224c2s
Eichberg, A. v1p0862c2s
v1p1054c2s v1p1257c2s
Eichelberger, L. v1p0248c1s
v1p1304c1s
Eichelberger, L.A. v1p0218c1s
Eichelberger, W.S. v6p0037c2s
Eichholz, A. v5p0231c2s
Eichler, C.K. v5p0442c1s
Eichmann, A.F. v6p0190c2s
Eichtal, E.d' v1p0229c2s
Eidlitz, L. v2p0389c1s
v4p0023c1s v4p0025c1s
Eiffel, G. v3p0131c2s
Eigenmann, C.H. v2p0483c2s
v3p0082c1s v3p0153c2s v3p0475c2s
v4p0145c2s v4p0223c2s v4p0327c2s
v4p0600c2s v5p0200c2s v5p0208c1m
v5p0208c2m v5p0288c1s v5p0591c1s
v6p0102c1s v6p0104c2s v6p0195c1s
v6p0214c2s v6p0226c2s v6p0227c1m
v6p0283c1s v6p0288c2s v6p0598c2s
Eigenmann, C.H. and Cox, L.O.
v5p0607c2s
Eigenmann, C.H. et al. ... v6p0105c2s
Eights, J. v1p0913c2s
Eiloart, A. v4p0036c2s
v4p0548c2s
Eiloart, Arnold v6p0051c2s
Eilvart, A. v4p0569c1s
Eimbeck, W. v5p0491c2s
v6p0250c1s
Eimer, G.H.T. v3p0403c2s
Eimer, T. v5p0545c1s
Eimi, C.W. v1p0646c2s
Einaudi, L. v5p0427c1s
Einhorn, A. v2p0109c1s
Einsle, S. v1p0674c2s
v1p0965c2s
Einstein, L. v5p0546c1s
v6p0415c1s
Eirich, P. v1p0848c1s
Eiselen, F.C. v6p0519c2s
Eisen, G. v6p0185c2s
v6p0275c2m
Eisen, Gustave v4p0583c1s
Eitner, W. v1p1282c2s
Ekedahl, Waldemar v6p0205c1s
Ekeley, J.B. v4p0441c2s
Ekin, C.
v1p1391c2s
Ela, D.H. v2p0244c2s
Elam, C. v1p0082c1s
v1p0433c2s v1p0434c1s v1p0434c2s
v1p0565c1s v1p0792c2s v1p1161c1s
v1p1372c2s
Elam, Dr. v1p0960c1s
Elam, W.C. v1p0163c1s
v1p0397c2s v1p0881c1s v1p1417c2s
v4p0091c2s v4p0154c2s v4p0163c2s
v4p0517c2s v4p0518c2s v4p0587c1s
v5p0056c2s
Elbano, E. v6p0368c1s
v6p0501c1s
Elbogen, I. v6p0343c1s
Elcourt, E. v1p0359c2s
Elden, W. v1p0738c2s
Elder, A. v1p0587c2s
v1p1051c1s v1p1212c2s v1p1315c2s
v1p1409c1s
Elder, C. v1p1285c1s
Elder, G.W. v4p0431c2s
Elder, H.M. v2p0199c2s
v3p0115c1s
Elder, J. v1p0145c2s
Elder, J.R. v4p0118c1s
Elder, L.R. v6p0420c2s
Elder, M.T. v3p0341c2s
Elder, R.B. v1p0951c2s
v1p1179c2s v1p1373c2m v1p1374c2s
Elder, S.J. v6p0149c1m
Elder, W. v1p0486c2s
v1p0504c1s v1p0638c2s v1p0701c2s
v1p0931c1s v1p1025c2s v1p1351c2s
Elderkin, J. v1p1330c1s
Elderkin, P.B. v5p0351c1s
Elderkin, P.D. v5p0088c2s
Eldon, E. v6p0677c2s
Eldon, R. v6p0517c2s
Eldred, B. v6p0140c1s
Eldred, C.E. v6p0552c2s
v6p0602c2s
Eldredge, J. v1p0431c2s
Eldredge, L.W. v6p0295c1s
Eldredge, Z.S. v5p0171c2s
v5p0182c1s v5p0235c2s v5p0414c2s
v5p0531c2s
Eldridge, G.H. v3p0104c2s
Eldridge, G.M. v2p0332c2s
Eldridge, G.S. v6p0309c2s
Eldridge, J. v1p0229c1s
Eldridge, M.O. v6p0545c1s
Elek, B. v4p0047c2s
Eley, H. v1p0342c1s
v1p0798c2s v1p0984c1s
Elford, Bert H. v6p0470c1s
Elft, Freiherr v. v5p0006c1s
v5p0068c1s v5p0587c1s
Elfving, F. v4p0445c2s
Elgar, F. v2p0308c1m
v2p0400c2s v3p0390c2s v4p0548c1s
v4p0604c1s v4p0614c1s v6p0534c2s
Elgee, C.H. v5p0451c1s
Elgin, E.M. v5p0047c2s
v5p0340c1s
Elgin, G.H. v3p0132c1s
Elgood, G.S. v5p0225c2s
Elgood, P.G. v5p0243c2s
Elgrave, C. v3p0142c2s
Elias, F. v6p0012c2s
Elias, N. v4p0379c1s
Elias, R. v3p0278c2s
Eliot, A. v2p0119c1s
v2p0237c2s v4p0006c2s v4p0146c1s
v4p0252c1s v6p0116c2s v6p0649c2s
Eliot, Ada v5p0634c2s
Eliot, C. v3p0095c1s
v4p0068c2s v4p0319c1s v4p0319c2s
Eliot, C. and Sargent, C.S.
v5p0590c1s
Eliot, C.E. v1p0390c2s
Eliot, C.F. v6p0707c2s
Eliot, C.N. v6p0086c1s
v6p0369c2s v6p0645c2s
Eliot, C.N.E. v6p0006c1s

v6p0663c2s
Eliot, C.W. v1p0036c1s
v1p0276c1s v1p0354c2s v1p0390c2s
v1p0457c1s v1p0816c1s v1p0831c1s
v1p0835c1s v1p0924c1s v1p0946c2m
v1p0955c2s v1p0995c2s v1p1157c2s
v1p1159c1s v1p1162c2s v1p1193c2s
v1p1212c2s v1p1313c2s v1p1325c1s
v1p1356c2s v2p0132c1s v3p0011c2s
v3p0085c2s v3p0091c2s v3p0094c2s
v3p0149c1s v3p0158c1s v3p0290c1s
v3p0378c1m v4p0015c2s v4p0016c1s
v4p0022c2s v4p0117c2s v4p0170c2s
v4p0171c1s v4p0234c1s v4p0249c2s
v4p0512c1s v4p0596c2s v5p0118c1s
v5p0127c1s v5p0130c2s v5p0171c1s
v5p0214c2s v5p0233c2s v5p0329c1s
v5p0399c2s v5p0517c2s v5p0518c1s
v5p0600c2s v5p0601c1s v5p0604c1s
v6p0016c1s v6p0025c2s v6p0055c2s
v6p0074c2s v6p0135c1s v6p0136c1s
v6p0136c2s v6p0141c2s v6p0146c2s
v6p0161c1s v6p0190c2s v6p0192c2m
v6p0202c1s v6p0203c1s v6p0231c2s
v6p0239c1s v6p0282c1s v6p0325c1s
v6p0356c2m v6p0357c1m v6p0372c1s
v6p0376c1s v6p0409c1s v6p0446c2s
v6p0572c2s v6p0574c2s v6p0576c2s
v6p0581c1s v6p0581c2s v6p0670c2s
v6p0690c1s
Eliot, C.W. and McCosh, J.
v2p0455c2s
Eliot, C.W. and Peabody, E.
v5p0511c1s
Eliot, C.W. and Storer, F.H.
v1p0061c1s
Eliot, C.W. et al. v4p0074c2s
v5p0176c2s
v6p0540c1s
Eliot, D.W. v2p0290c2s
Eliot, E. v3p0393c1s
v4p0629c2s
Eliot, E.C. v2p0150c1s
v5p0294c2s v6p0363c2s v6p0573c1s
Eliot, E.L. v1p1182c1s
Eliot, E.W. v3p0190c2s
Eliot, F. v3p0292c1s
v6p0163c2s
Eliot, Geo. v1p0014c1s
v1p0058c2s v1p0276c1s v1p0331c1s
v1p0609c1s v1p0677c1s v1p0735c2s
v1p0746c2s v1p0878c1s v1p1083c2s
v1p1126c2s v1p1141c1s v1p1155c2s
v1p1335c2s
Eliot, H.R. v2p0233c1s
v3p0118c1s v4p0625c1s v6p0069c2s
Eliot, J. and Sutton, J.R.
v6p0531c1s
Eliot, John, Sir v6p0082c1s
Eliot, L.H. v5p0401c1s
Eliot, Max v3p0432c1s
Eliot, N.M. v5p0518c1s
Eliot, P.F. v6p0038c2s
v6p0167c1s
Eliot, S. v1p0028c2s
v1p0060c2m v1p0250c1s v1p0255c2s
v1p0259c1s v1p0285c1s v1p0312c2s
v1p0357c1s v1p0392c1s v1p0714c2s
v1p0786c1s v1p1131c2s v1p1350c1s
v4p0457c1s v6p0423c1s
Eliot, S.A. v1p0032c2s
v1p0062c1s v1p0151c2m v1p0219c1s
v1p0410c2s v1p0429c1s v1p0435c1s
v1p0501c2s v1p0569c2s v1p0576c1s
v1p0883c2m v1p0884c1s v1p0947c2s
v1p0981c2s v1p0987c1s v1p1008c1s
v1p1052c2m v1p1093c2s v1p1208c2s
v1p1301c2s v1p1384c1s v4p0288c1s
v5p0389c1s
Eliot, T.L. v1p0072c1s
v2p0395c2s
Eliot, W.G. v1p0317c1s
v1p0847c2s v1p0855c1s v1p1144c1s
v1p1355c1s
Eliot, W.H. v1p0808c1s
Eliot-James, A.G.F. v2p0442c1s
Eliseef, A.V. v3p0023c2s
Elizabeth, Queen of Roumania
v2p0267c2s v6p0070c2s v6p0343c2s
v6p0439c1s v6p0552c2s
Elkin, Dr. v4p0367c1s
Elkin, W.B. v4p0269c1s
v4p0590c2s
Elkin, W.L. v4p0367c1s
Elkind, L. v6p0007c2s
v6p0031c2s v6p0252c2s v6p0253c2s
v6p0254c2s v6p0294c1s
Elkind, S. v6p0288c1s
Elkington, E.W. v6p0393c1s
v6p0661c2s
Elkington, T. v3p0192c2s
v3p0448c1s
Elkins, J.R. v4p0127c1s
Elkins, L. v6p0601c1s
Elkins, S.B. et al. v2p0245c1s
Elkins, W.B. v6p0283c1s
v6p0283c2s
Elkinton, J. v6p0179c2s
Ell, H.G. v6p0454c2s
Ella, S. v5p0458c1s
Ellacombe, H.N. v2p0397c1s
v4p0454c2s v6p0230c1s v6p0247c1s
v6p0247c2s v6p0338c1s v6p0441c1s
v6p0552c1s v6p0592c2s
Ellam, T.E. v5p0281c1s
Ellard, V.G. v3p0410c2s
v5p0638c1s
Elleau, L.A. and Ennis W.D.
v5p0017c2s
Ellendorf, J. v1p0994c1s
Eller, W.H. v3p0162c2s
v4p0036c1s
Ellerbe, A.W. v1p1204c2s
Ellerton, R. v1p0483c1s
Ellery, H. v1p1367c2s
Ellery, H.C. v3p0135c1s
Ellery, R.L.J. v1p0382c1s
v1p0986c2s v2p0095c1s
Ellery, T.G. v6p0435c2s
Ellet, C. v1p1075c1s
v1p1076c1s v1p1078c2s v1p1321c2s
Ellet, C., jr. v1p1315c1s
Ellet, E.F. v1p0403c2s
v1p0576c1m v1p0712c1s v1p0862c1s
v1p0950c1s v1p1032c1s v3p0326c1s
Ellet, E.F., Mrs. v1p0019c1s
v1p0021c1s v1p0023c1s v1p0034c1s
v1p0046c2s v1p0099c1s v1p0117c1s
v1p0141c2s v1p0142c1s v1p0155c2s
v1p0158c1s v1p0171c2s v1p0173c2s
v1p0261c1s v1p0348c1m v1p0352c1s
v1p0373c1s v1p0393c2s v1p0441c2s
v1p0448c1s v1p0489c2s v1p0502c2s
v1p0520c2s v1p0521c2s v1p0527c1s
v1p0537c1s v1p0572c1s v1p0607c1s
v1p0668c2s v1p0710c2s v1p0713c2s
v1p0719c1s v1p0723c2s v1p0750c2s
v1p0752c1s v1p0773c2s v1p0799c2s
v1p0817c2s v1p0852c1s v1p0876c1s
v1p0924c2s v1p0957c1s v1p1007c2s
v1p1020c1s v1p1110c1s v1p1132c1s
v1p1148c1m v1p1152c2s v1p1156c1s
v1p1180c2s v1p1209c2s v1p1251c2s
v1p1286c1s v1p1312c2s v1p1320c1s
v1p1325c1s v1p1360c2s v1p1381c2s
v1p1420c1s v1p1425c1m
Ellet, Mrs. v1p0084c2s
v1p0108c1s v1p0111c1s
Ellice, J.H. v5p0610c2s
Ellick, J.J. v2p0035c2s
Ellicott, C.J. v1p0039c2s
v1p0247c2s v1p0251c2s v1p0338c1s
v1p1088c1s v4p0054c1m
Ellicott, J.M. v3p0063c1s
v4p0521c1s v5p0619c1s
Ellicott, W.M. v4p0024c2s
Ellinger, B. v6p0216c2s
v6p0266c2s
Ellington, E.B. v4p0339c1s
v4p0455c2s v5p0622c1s
Ellington, H. v3p0025c2s
Ellinwood, F.F. v3p0357c2s
v4p0374c2s
Ellinwood, F.F. et al. ... v5p0081c2s
Elliot, A. v4p0091c1m
v4p0330c2s v4p0580c1s v4p0591c2s
v6p0389c1s
Elliot, A.D. v2p0206c1s
v2p0391c2s v3p0369c1s
Elliot, A.R. v6p0161c2s
Elliot, C. v2p0284c2s
Elliot, C.W. v1p0233c2s
v1p0917c1s v1p0969c2s v1p1039c2s
v1p1126c1s v1p1148c2s v1p1314c2s
Elliot, D.G. v5p0022c2s
v5p0063c1s
Elliot, F. v6p0584c2s
Elliot, F. v1p1123c1s
Elliot, G., Sir v3p0182c1s
v3p0298c1s
Elliot, G.F.S. v4p0005c2s
v4p0200c1s v4p0589c1s
Elliot, G.H. v1p1148c2s
Elliot, G.S.McD. v6p0020c2s
Elliot, H. v3p0001c1s
v5p0030c1s v5p0213c1s
Elliot, H., Sir v3p0027c2s
v3p0438c2s v4p0213c1s
Elliot, H.B. v2p0236c1s
Elliot, H.F. v1p0100c1s
v1p1153c1s
Elliot, H.R. v3p0302c2s
v6p0061c1s v6p0284c1s v6p0421c2s
v6p0611c1s
Elliot, J. v5p0333c1s
Elliot, J.C. v6p0301c1s
Elliot, Mrs. v1p0474c1s
Elliot, R.H. v1p0592c1s
v1p0592c2s v1p0629c1s v1p0632c2s
v1p0633c2s v1p0814c2s v5p0285c2s
Elliot, S.R. v4p0081c2s
Elliot, W. v5p0086c2s
v5p0617c2s
Elliot, W.G. v4p0002c2s
v4p0543c2s
Elliot, W.Y. v5p0003c1s
Elliotson, J. v1p0041c1s
v1p0293c1s v1p0788c1s v1p0824c2s
v1p0825c1m v1p0843c1s v1p1004c2m
v1p1237c1s
Elliott, A.M. v2p0066c1m
v2p0167c2s v2p0249c2s v2p0314c1s
v2p0377c1s v3p0065c2s
Elliott, A.S. v6p0350c2s
Elliott, C. v1p0048c1s
v1p0116c2s v1p0252c1s v1p0262c2s
v1p0646c2s v1p0848c1s v5p0285c1m
Elliott, C.A. v4p0279c2s
v5p0285c1s v5p0346c1s v6p0099c2s
v6p0313c1s v6p0573c2s
Elliott, C.B. v3p0037c2s
v3p0103c1s v3p0246c2s v3p0292c1s
v4p0373c1s v5p0604c1s v6p0350c2s
Elliott, C.P. v5p0504c1s
Elliott, C.W. v1p0024c1s
v1p0064c2s v1p0138c1s v1p0185c1s
v1p0439c1s v1p0444c2s v1p0531c2s
v1p0570c2s v1p0605c1s v1p0790c1s
v1p0839c1s v1p1007c2s v1p1010c1s
v1p1039c2s v1p1040c1s v1p1425c1s
v2p0478c2s
Elliott, E. v1p0178c2s
v1p0302c1s v1p0302c2m v1p0310c2s
v1p0347c2s v1p0418c2s v1p0550c2s
v1p0921c1s v1p1021c2m v1p1370c1s
v5p0278c2s v5p0451c2s v6p0002c2s
v6p0044c1s v6p0057c1s v6p0247c1s
v6p0311c2s v6p0379c1s v6p0523c2s
Elliott, E.B. v1p0045c2s
v1p0058c2s v1p0410c1s v1p0933c2s
v1p1098c2s v1p1318c2s
Elliott, E.C. v5p0638c1s
Elliott, E.T. v1p0209c1s
Elliott, F., Mrs. v1p1408c2s
Elliott, G. v5p0320c2s
v5p0436c1s v6p0078c1s
Elliott, G. et al. v3p0007c2s
Elliott, G., Sir v3p0385c2s
Elliott, G.E.Scott v6p0117c2s
Elliott, G.S. v4p0005c1s
Elliott, G.W. v2p0374c1s
Elliott, H. v4p0003c1s
v4p0031c2s v4p0544c1s v5p0144c2s
v5p0573c1s
Elliott, H.R. v2p0005c1s
Elliott, H.W. v1p0018c1s
v1p0636c1s v1p1172c2s v1p1173c2s
v1p1212c1s v1p1383c1s v2p0393c2s
v4p0511c2s
Elliott, I.M. v5p0360c1s
Elliott, J.A. v4p0117c1s
Elliott, J.C. v4p0230c1s
Elliott, J.E. v6p0304c2s
v6p0370c1s
Elliott, J.H. v1p0315c2m
v1p0981c2m v3p0347c1s
Elliott, J.S. v2p0343c2s
Elliott, J.W. v6p0229c2s
Elliott, M. v5p0035c2s
v6p0368c1s
Elliott, M.H. v5p0478c2s
v6p0001c2s v6p0332c1s v6p0353c1s
v6p0546c1s v6p0549c1m v6p0549c2s
Elliott, M.R. v6p0291c2s
Elliott, O.L. v4p0450c1m
v4p0563c1s v4p0615c1s v5p0126c1s
v6p0633c1s
Elliott, R.R. v3p0160c1s
v4p0045c2s v4p0107c1s v4p0154c1s
v4p0281c1s v4p0282c1s v4p0292c2s
v5p0047c2m v5p0159c2m v5p0276c2s
v5p0297c2s v5p0560c1s v6p0143c1s
v6p0236c2s v6p0326c2s v6p0340c2m
Elliott, R.S. v1p1399c2s
Elliott, R.W. v2p0447c2s
Elliott, S. v3p0228c2s
Elliott, S.B. v3p0146c1s
v4p0194c1s v4p0373c2s v4p0457c1s
v5p0043c2s v5p0171c2s v5p0206c1s
v5p0215c1s v5p0255c1s v5p0283c2s
v5p0412c1s v5p0468c1s v5p0547c2s
v5p0634c1s v6p0304c2s v6p0637c2s
Elliott, S.R. v4p0136c2s
v4p0155c2s v4p0221c2s v4p0364c2s
v4p0535c2s v5p0131c2s v5p0355c2s
v5p0578c1s v5p0580c1s
Elliott, Sarah B. v5p0308c2s
v5p0565c1s
Elliott, T.H. v3p0421c1s
Elliott, T.M. v1p1397c2s
Elliott, W. v1p0307c1s
v1p1121c1s v2p0042c1s v2p0115c1s
v2p0358c2m v2p0376c1s v2p0376c2s
v2p0388c2m v2p0408c2s v3p0144c2s
v3p0193c1s v3p0364c1s v3p0365c1s
v4p0478c2s v4p0488c2s v5p0047c2s
v5p0218c2s v5p0379c2s v5p0612c2s
v6p0341c2s
Elliott, W. et al. v4p0129c1s
Elliott, W.A. v4p0413c2s
v5p0592c1s v6p0273c1s
Elliott, W.J. v2p0157c1s
v2p0288c2s v2p0372c2s
Elliott, W.S. v2p0342c1s
Ellis, A. v1p1198c2s
v2p0331c1s v3p0032c2s v3p0033c1s
v3p0263c1s v3p0268c1s v3p0410c1s
v4p0356c1s
Ellis, A.B. v1p0349c1s
v1p1196c1s v2p0086c2s v2p0140c2s

v2p0302c1s v2p0358c2s v3p0268c2s
v3p0338c1s v3p0404c2s v3p0451c2s
v4p0165c2s v4p0178c1s v4p0205c2m
v4p0302c2s v4p0356c2s v4p0497c2s
v4p0529c2s v4p0616c1s
Ellis, A.C. v4p0557c2s
v5p0179c1s
Ellis, A.C. and Hall, G.S.
v4p0103c1s v4p0158c2s
Ellis, A.C. and Parsons, J.R., jr.
v6p0290c1s
Ellis, A.C. and Shipe, Maud M.
v6p0220c2s
Ellis, A.G. v2p0248c1s
Ellis, A.J. v1p0885c1m
v1p1315c2s v1p1329c2s v2p0113c2s
v2p0303c2s v2p0460c1s v3p0293c2m
v3p0404c1s v6p0603c2s
Ellis, Alston v6p0290c1s
Ellis, B. v5p0322c1s
Ellis, C. v2p0219c2s
v3p0262c2s
Ellis, C.B. v6p0141c1s
Ellis, C.E. v5p0310c1s
Ellis, C.M. v1p1013c1s
v1p1117c2s v1p1282c1s
Ellis, C.P. v6p0089c2s
Ellis, D. v1p1146c1s
v5p0140c2s v5p0282c2s
Ellis, D.G. v5p0203c2s
Ellis, E. v1p0115c2s
v1p1169c2s v3p0023c2s
Ellis, E.A. v5p0094c1s
v5p0599c1s
Ellis, E.Glode v4p0389c2s
Ellis, E.S. v5p0525c2s
v5p0557c2s
Ellis, E.V., Mrs. v1p1378c2s
Ellis, E.W. v1p1365c2s
Ellis, Emily G. v3p0074c1s
Ellis, F.S. v4p0058c1s
v4p0098c1s v5p0387c2s
Ellis, G. v1p0182c1s
v1p0182c2m v1p0283c1s v1p0726c1s
v1p1168c2s v1p1169c1s v1p1228c1s
v1p1400c1s
Ellis, G. and Channing, G.
v1p0175c1s
Ellis, G.A. v1p0192c1s
v1p0449c2s v1p0712c2s v1p1116c2s
v1p1179c2s v1p1398c2s
Ellis, G.E. v1p0006c1s
v1p0010c2s v1p0029c2s v1p0032c1s
v1p0033c1s v1p0068c2s v1p0074c1s
v1p0075c1s v1p0107c2s v1p0114c1s
v1p0120c2s v1p0121c1s v1p0125c2s
v1p0126c1s v1p0127c2s v1p0128c1s
v1p0129c2s v1p0152c1s v1p0154c2s
v1p0189c2s v1p0204c1s v1p0238c2s
v1p0239c2s v1p0241c2s v1p0243c1m
v1p0244c2s v1p0250c2s v1p0253c2s
v1p0254c1s v1p0275c1s v1p0306c1s
v1p0313c2s v1p0339c2s v1p0380c2s
v1p0412c1s v1p0425c1s v1p0440c1s
v1p0443c2s v1p0504c1s v1p0556c2m
v1p0572c2s v1p0573c1s v1p0618c1s
v1p0641c1s v1p0670c1s v1p0685c1s
v1p0688c2s v1p0689c1s v1p0694c2s
v1p0741c1s v1p0746c1s v1p0754c1s
v1p0775c1s v1p0777c1s v1p0794c1s
v1p0808c1s v1p0808c2s v1p0809c1m
v1p0842c1s v1p0890c2m v1p0897c2s
v1p0909c2m v1p0921c1s v1p0927c1s
v1p0954c1s v1p0961c1s v1p0973c1s
v1p0987c2s v1p0990c1s v1p0998c1s
v1p1008c1s v1p1012c2m v1p1030c1s
v1p1033c1s v1p1067c1s v1p1067c2s
v1p1072c1s v1p1086c1s v1p1089c1s
v1p1089c2s v1p1093c2s v1p1094c1s
v1p1102c1s v1p1115c2s v1p1117c2s
v1p1118c2s v1p1157c2s v1p1160c1s
v1p1173c2s v1p1175c2s v1p1260c1s
v1p1266c1s v1p1274c2s v1p1275c1s
v1p1287c1s v1p1303c2s v1p1340c1m
v1p1340c2s v1p1344c1s v1p1350c1s
v1p1362c2s v1p1386c2s v1p1400c2s
v1p1416c1s v1p1416c2m v1p1418c1s
v2p0204c1s v2p0212c2s v2p0248c2s
v3p0038c1s v3p0367c2s v4p0050c1s
v4p0075c1s v4p0249c2s v4p0494c2s
v4p0545c1s
Ellis, G.E.R. v4p0497c2s
Ellis, G.H. v6p0132c1s
Ellis, G.Harold v6p0192c2s
v6p0222c1s
Ellis, G.S. v5p0004c2s
v5p0071c1s v5p0198c2s v5p0450c2s
v5p0496c2s v5p0520c1s v5p0520c2s
v5p0555c2s v5p0619c1s v6p0584c1s
Ellis, G.Stanley v6p0001c2s
Ellis, Grace E. v1p0061c1s
Ellis, H. v1p0167c1s
v1p0184c2s v1p0217c2s v1p0296c2s
v1p0491c2s v1p0560c2s v1p0570c2s
v1p0608c1s v1p0676c2s v1p0754c2s
v1p0762c1s v1p0764c2s v1p0925c2s
v1p0953c2s v1p1053c2s v1p1068c1s
v1p1074c2s v1p1165c1s v1p1173c2s
v2p0067c2s v3p0073c2s v4p0125c1s
v4p0161c2s v4p0211c2s v4p0221c2s
v4p0252c1s v4p0470c1s v5p0001c2s
v5p0062c1s v5p0161c2s v5p0168c1s
v5p0201c2s v5p0216c2s v5p0224c1s
v5p0227c2m v5p0329c2s v5p0345c2s
v5p0371c1s v5p0481c1s v5p0501c2s
v5p0542c2s v5p0543c1s v5p0608c2s
v6p0004c1s v6p0021c1s v6p0028c2m
v6p0081c1s v6p0106c2s v6p0139c1s
v6p0212c2s v6p0253c2s v6p0299c2s
v6p0302c1s v6p0316c1s v6p0373c2s
v6p0389c2s v6p0410c1s v6p0411c2s
v6p0475c1s v6p0488c1s v6p0553c1s
v6p0571c2s v6p0585c1s v6p0607c2m
v6p0675c1s v6p0711c1s
Ellis, H. and Grove, A. .. v6p0703c2s
Ellis, H., Sir v1p0308c2s
v1p0403c1s v1p0412c2s v1p0425c1s
v1p0446c1s v1p0670c2s v1p0768c2s
v1p0773c1s v1p0783c2s v1p0863c1s
v1p0902c1s v1p0933c2s v1p0949c1s
v1p1138c1s v1p1230c2m v1p1273c2s
Ellis, H.H. v1p0592c2s
v2p0203c2s v2p0407c2s v2p0477c1s
Ellis, Havelock v4p0140c2s
v5p0381c2s v6p0107c1s v6p0703c2s
Ellis, Horace v5p0422c1s
v5p0560c1s
Ellis, J. v1p0235c1s
v2p0124c2s
Ellis, J.B. and Everhardt, B.M.
v5p0223c1s
Ellis, J.E. v6p0047c2s
Ellis, J.T. v6p0530c2s
Ellis, J.W. v2p0081c1s
v2p0130c2s
Ellis, J.W., Sir v2p0263c2s
Ellis, L.A. v4p0290c2s
Ellis, L.B. v5p0009c1s
v5p0036c1s v5p0093c2s v5p0106c1m
v5p0139c1s v5p0147c1s v5p0148c1s
v5p0201c1s v5p0376c1s v5p0439c1s
v5p0540c2m v5p0569c1s v5p0580c1s
v6p0070c2s v6p0114c2s v6p0229c2m
v6p0380c1s
Ellis, L.D. v5p0178c2s
Ellis, L.J. v6p0308c1s
Ellis, Leonora B. v6p0033c2s
v6p0039c2s v6p0153c1s v6p0499c1s
v6p0605c1s
Ellis, M. v1p0628c2s
v3p0433c1s
Ellis, M.A. v6p0257c1s
v6p0417c2s v6p0500c2s
Ellis, M.B. and Meyer, Annie N.
v5p0232c2s
Ellis, R. v1p0058c1s
v1p0071c2s v1p0129c2s v1p0130c1m
v1p0180c1s v1p0208c1m v1p0239c2s
v1p0241c1s v1p0242c1s v1p0244c1s
v1p0248c1m v1p0440c1s v1p0440c2s
v1p0487c1s v1p0935c1s v1p1055c1s
v1p1091c1s v1p1141c1s v1p1161c1s
v1p1173c2s v1p1297c2s v1p1386c1s
v2p0007c2s v2p0071c2s v2p0185c1s
v2p0244c1s v2p0261c2s v2p0281c1s
v2p0333c1s v2p0339c2s v2p0356c1s
v2p0410c1s v2p0427c1s v2p0461c2s
v3p0048c1s v3p0070c2s v3p0085c2m
v3p0107c1s v3p0141c1s v3p0237c2s
v3p0249c1s v3p0314c2m v4p0019c2s
v4p0040c1s v4p0092c2s v4p0256c1m
v4p0419c1s v4p0437c2s v5p0162c1s
v5p0461c1s v6p0482c1s
Ellis, R. and Hosmer, G.W.
v1p1174c1s
Ellis, R.S. v1p0153c2s
Ellis, S. v1p0071c2s
v1p0626c1s v1p1016c2s v1p1064c2s
v1p1093c1s v2p0215c2s v2p0297c2s
v2p0344c2s v2p0368c1s v6p0028c2s
Ellis, T. v3p0048c1s
v3p0195c2s v4p0134c1s
Ellis, T.B. v4p0291c1s
Ellis, T.G. v1p0292c2s
v1p0460c2m v1p0564c2s v1p1110c2s
Ellis, T.H. v3p0361c1s
Ellis, T.J. v2p0263c1s
Ellis, T.S. v2p0154c1s
Ellis, W. v1p0715c2s
v1p0785c1s v1p1311c2s v2p0122c1s
v2p0128c1s v2p0283c2s v2p0425c1s
v3p0133c1s v5p0174c2s v5p0561c1s
Ellis, W.A. v4p0312c1s
v5p0512c2s v5p0615c2s v6p0683c1s
Ellis, W.B. v4p0068c2s
v4p0214c2s
Ellis, W.C. v6p0400c2s
Ellis, W.E. v5p0565c2s
v5p0642c1s v6p0296c2s
Ellis, W.H. v1p0924c1s
v5p0090c2s
Ellison, G.F. v5p0192c2s
Ellison, J.E. v2p0459c1s
Ellison, O. v6p0433c1s
Ellison, O.C. v5p0315c1s
v6p0507c1s
Ellison, R.F. v1p0832c1s
Ellison, T. v3p0094c1s
Ellison, T.H. v6p0508c2s
Elliston, M. v5p0203c2s
v5p0213c1s v6p0693c2s
Elliston, Marion v6p0070c2s
v6p0117c2s v6p0140c1s v6p0208c1s
v6p0229c1s v6p0351c2s
Elliston, W.R. et al. v4p0428c1s
Ellmore, A. v3p0148c2s
v3p0373c2s
Ells, R.W. et al. v5p0091c2s
Ellsworth, E.W. v1p0056c2s
v1p1080c1s v1p1235c2s
Ellsworth, H.W. v1p0891c2s
v1p0928c1s v1p1155c1s
Ellsworth, O.M. v1p0593c1s
Ellsworth, P.W. v1p0686c2s
Ellsworth, W.W. v1p0922c1s
v3p0130c2s v4p0401c1s v5p0011c2s
v5p0314c2s v5p0617c1s v5p0624c2s
v6p0200c2s
Ellwanger, G.H. v5p0226c1s
v5p0499c2s
Ellwanger, H.B. v2p0378c1s
Ellwanger, W.D. v4p0549c1s
v6p0060c1s v6p0623c1s
Ellwanger, W.D. and Robinson, C.M.
v4p0202c1s
Ellwood, C.A. v5p0280c1s
v5p0535c1s v5p0535c2m v6p0029c2s
v6p0109c1s v6p0422c2s v6p0541c2s
v6p0601c2s
Ellwood, G.M. v5p0156c1s
Ellzey, M.G. v2p0279c1s
Elmard, A.d' and Morland, C.E.
v4p0273c2s
Elmendorf, D.L. v5p0431c1s
v5p0449c1s v6p0562c2s v6p0592c2s
Elmendorf, Dwight L. v6p0189c1s
Elmendorf, H.L. v5p0334c1s
v5p0336c1s v6p0086c2s v6p0373c1s
v6p0532c1s
Elmendorf, H.L., Mrs. v6p0116c2s
Elmendorf, J.J. v2p0081c2s
v2p0195c1s v3p0258c2s v5p0404c1s
Elmendorf, M.L. v3p0283c2s
v3p0347c2s v3p0367c2s v4p0375c1s
v4p0492c2s
Elmer, E. v4p0578c2s
Elmer, H.C. v3p0350c2s
v4p0461c2s
Elmer, L.Q.C. v1p0404c1s
Elmer, W., jr. v4p0175c1s
Elmer, W.H. v5p0531c2s
Elmes, K.W. v6p0072c1s
Elmore, C.J. v4p0155c1s
Elmsley, P. v1p0008c2s
v1p0072c1s v1p0429c2m
Elmslie, E. v4p0005c1s
v4p0205c2s
Elmslie, Prof. v3p0121c1s
Elmslie, W.G. v2p0042c2s
v3p0041c2s v3p0341c2s v3p0397c2s
Elmy, B. v6p0702c2s
Elmy, Ben v5p0280c2s
Elout, C.K. v5p0172c1s
Elphinstone, H.W. v4p0108c1s
v4p0131c1s v4p0187c1s v4p0318c2s
v4p0356c2s v6p0360c2s v6p0364c2s
Elphinstone, K. v5p0085c2s
Elphinstone, R.W. v1p0902c2s
Elrington, H. v1p0360c1s
v5p0072c1s v5p0580c1s v5p0644c2s
v6p0548c2s
Elrod, J. v6p0116c1s
v6p0158c2s
Elrod, M.J. v6p0426c2m
Elrod, M.N. v1p1015c2s
v1p1175c2s
Elsdale, H. v1p0089c1s
v3p0005c1s v3p0316c2s v3p0359c2s
v4p0004c2s v4p0005c2s v4p0363c2s
v4p0470c1s v4p0508c1s v4p0561c2s
v4p0610c1m v5p0075c1s v5p0618c1s
Elsden, J.V. v2p0173c2s
Elsden, J.V. and Wood, S.V.
v2p0440c2s
Elseffer, L. v4p0514c1s
Elsing, W.T. v4p0569c1s
Elsner, L. v4p0555c1s
Elsom, J.F. v2p0060c1s
Elson, H.W. v6p0379c1s
Elson, L.C. v3p0051c1s
v5p0393c2s v6p0230c2s v6p0437c2s
v6p0438c2m
Elson, S.R. v3p0108c2s
v3p0457c2s
Elston, Chas.R. v4p0258c2s
Elstrie, G. v3p0399c1s
Elten, J.F. v1p0204c1s
v1p0617c1s
Elting, I. v2p0126c1s
v2p0210c1s v2p0461c1s
Eltinge, E. v4p0399c2s
Elton, C. v1p0721c1s
v2p0110c1s v2p0142c1s v2p0185c1s
v2p0386c1s v3p0039c2s v3p0140c1s
v3p0151c2s v3p0186c2s v3p0288c2s
v3p0453c2s v4p0147c2s v4p0604c2s
v5p0639c1s
Elton, C. and Elton, M. .. v4p0067c2s
Elton, C.I. v2p0142c2s
v2p0145c1s v2p0200c2s v2p0244c2s

v2p0248c1s v2p0248c2s v2p0316c1s v2p0409c2s v2p0464c1s v4p0110c1s v5p0419c2s v6p0587c1s
Elton, C.L. ... v2p0181c2s
Elton, E. ... v5p0030c1s
Elton, F. ... v3p0400c1s
Elton, J.M. ... v2p0470c1s
Elton, M. and Elton, C. .. v4p0067c2s
Elton, O. ... v3p0462c2s v4p0383c2s v6p0333c1s v6p0441c1s v6p0587c1s
Eltzbacher, E. ... v6p0253c2s
Eltzbacher, G. ... v6p0335c2s
Eltzbacher, O. ... v5p0357c2s v6p0006c2s v6p0008c2s v6p0098c2s v6p0111c2s v6p0118c1s v6p0190c2s v6p0236c1s v6p0240c2s v6p0252c2s v6p0253c1m v6p0254c1s v6p0254c2m v6p0255c1s v6p0335c1m v6p0530c1s v6p0534c1s v6p0557c1s v6p0560c2s v6p0616c1s v6p0655c1s v6p0665c1s v6p0699c1s v6p0711c1s
Elvins, A. ... v4p0126c2s
Elwell, A.M. ... v4p0374c1s
Elwell, F.E. ... v5p0081c2s v6p0033c1s v6p0355c2s v6p0403c1s v6p0452c1s
Elwell, F.E. et al. ... v6p0641c2s
Elwell, F.Edwin, Mrs. ... v6p0167c2s v6p0334c2s
Elwell, J.J. ... v2p0221c2s
Elwell, R. ... v5p0186c2s
Elwell, R.F. ... v6p0472c2s
Elwes, H.J. ... v2p0254c1s v3p0061c2s
Elwes, K.W. ... v5p0189c2s v5p0200c2s v6p0059c1s
Elwes, Katherine W. ... v5p0361c2s
Elwes, R.G. ... v5p0131c1s
Elwin, W. ... v6p0228c1s v6p0640c2m
Elwood, C.A. ... v5p0425c2s
Elworthy, F.T. ... v6p0262c1s
Ely, A.B. ... v1p0252c1s v1p0290c1s v1p0290c2s
Ely, A.H. ... v1p1073c1s
Ely, A.W. ... v1p0102c1s v1p0164c1s v1p0212c2s v1p0305c1s v1p0306c1s v1p0322c2s v1p0337c1s v1p0378c1s v1p0613c2s v1p0772c2s v1p1040c1s
Ely, A.W., Dr. ... v1p0456c1s
Ely, Dr. ... v1p0232c2s v1p0322c2s
Ely, E.P. ... v1p0628c1s v1p1308c1s
Ely, E.S. ... v1p0029c1s
Ely, G.H. ... v5p0104c2s v5p0220c2s v5p0578c1s
Ely, Helena R. ... v6p0247c2s
Ely, I.M. ... v1p0038c2s v1p0421c2s
Ely, J. ... v3p0017c1s
Ely, J.C. ... v2p0245c2s v2p0295c2s
Ely, L.B. ... v6p0712c1s
Ely, M. ... v6p0340c1s
Ely, N.B. ... v1p0334c1s
Ely, R.E. ... v5p0320c1s
Ely, R.T. ... v1p0275c1s v1p0299c1s v2p0040c2s v2p0086c1s v2p0086c2s v2p0097c1s v2p0130c1s v2p0174c2s v2p0223c2s v2p0244c2s v2p0245c2s v2p0294c2s v2p0347c2s v2p0359c1s v2p0362c2m v2p0363c1s v2p0388c1s v2p0407c2m v2p0408c1m v2p0408c2s v2p0454c2s v2p0468c2s v3p0099c1s v3p0101c1m v3p0127c2s v3p0215c1s v3p0216c1s v3p0218c2s v3p0239c1m v3p0285c2s v3p0324c1s v3p0329c1s v3p0336c2s v3p0421c1m v3p0423c1s v4p0054c2s v4p0096c1s v4p0167c2s v4p0315c2s v4p0379c2s v4p0532c1s v4p0532c2s v4p0597c2s v4p0627c2s v5p0003c2s v5p0138c1s v5p0175c1s v5p0175c2s v5p0219c2s v5p0241c1s v5p0342c1s v5p0383c2s v5p0391c2s v5p0435c2s v5p0471c2s v5p0535c2s v5p0552c1s v5p0568c2s v5p0593c1s v6p0014c1s v6p0217c1s v6p0273c2s v6p0300c2s v6p0318c1m v6p0318c2s v6p0370c1s v6p0429c1s v6p0487c1s v6p0521c1s
Ely, R.T. and Clark, W. .. v4p0567c1s
Ely, R.T. and Urdahl, T.K. v5p0536c2m
Ely, R.T. et al. ... v6p0318c1s
Ely, S.C. ... v5p0116c2s
Ely, S.M. ... v2p0249c2s
Ely, T. ... v2p0399c1s v3p0025c1s v3p0025c2s v3p0062c1s v3p0093c2s v3p0428c1s v4p0435c1s v4p0451c2s v5p0458c2s v5p0608c1m
Ely, T.N. ... v3p0352c2s
Ely, W. ... v1p0500c1s
Elyom, Josephine ... v6p0533c1s
Elze, K. ... v2p0397c1s v3p0387c2s
Elzner, A.O. ... v6p0143c2s v6p0550c1s
Emanuel, C.H.L. ... v5p0077c2s v5p0371c2s
Emanuel, F. ... v5p0621c2s
Emanuel, F.L. ... v5p0131c2s v5p0268c1s v5p0590c1s v6p0339c1s v6p0385c2s v6p0511c1s
Emanuel, L. ... v4p0174c1s v4p0240c1s
Emanuel, W. ... v5p0087c1s v5p0172c2s v5p0301c1s
Embree, C.F. ... v5p0412c2s v6p0125c1s v6p0664c2s v6p0695c1s
Embree, C.L. ... v6p0370c1s
Embree, F.B. ... v5p0273c1s v5p0521c1s
Embree, L.C. ... v4p0249c2s
Embury, E.C. ... v1p1327c2s v1p1371c2s
Embury, E.C., Mrs. ... v1p0230c1s v1p0716c2s v1p0745c2s v1p0804c1s v1p1053c1s
Emch, A. ... v5p0005c1s v6p0518c1s
Emden, A. ... v4p0135c1s v5p0138c1s v5p0327c2s
Emden, W. ... v3p0427c1s v5p0338c1s
Emerick, C.F. ... v4p0007c2s v4p0596c1s v5p0241c1s
Emerson, A. ... v2p0337c2s v2p0450c2s v3p0008c1s v3p0019c2s v3p0056c1s v3p0093c2s v3p0244c1s v4p0077c1s v4p0428c2s v5p0269c1s
Emerson, A. and Clarke, J.T. v3p0017c2s
Emerson, B.K. ... v1p0376c2s v2p0114c2s v2p0135c2s v3p0039c2s v4p0222c2s v4p0582c2s v5p0284c2s v6p0091c2s v6p0151c2s v6p0251c1s
Emerson, B.K. and Loomis, F.B. v6p0616c2s
Emerson, C. ... v1p0938c2s v1p1200c2s
Emerson, C.M. ... v1p1075c1s
Emerson, Dr. ... v1p1350c2s
Emerson, E. ... v1p0020c2s v1p0021c1s v1p0415c2s v1p0989c1s v1p1003c1s v1p1043c2s v1p1252c2s v3p0246c2s v3p0265c2s v3p0385c1s v3p0458c1s v6p0334c2s v6p0557c2s
Emerson, E., jr. ... v5p0089c2s v5p0460c1m v6p0606c1s
Emerson, E.R. ... v5p0424c2s
Emerson, E.W. ... v4p0016c2s v4p0377c1s v5p0213c2s v5p0450c2s v5p0552c2s v6p0202c1s
Emerson, E.W and Hawthorne, J. v6p0202c2s
Emerson, F.F. ... v4p0077c1s
Emerson, F.V. ... v6p0110c2s v6p0250c1s
Emerson, F.W. ... v6p0534c2s
Emerson, G. ... v1p0865c2s v1p1394c2s
Emerson, G.B. ... v1p0004c2s v1p0013c2m v1p0153c1s v1p0196c1s v1p0273c1s v1p0285c1m v1p0603c1s v1p0808c2s v1p0811c1s v1p0867c2s v1p1271c1s v1p1289c1s v1p1422c1s v1p1429c1s v1p1431c2s
Emerson, G.H. ... v1p0035c2s v1p0089c2s v1p0189c2s v1p0218c1s v1p0239c1s v1p0241c2s v1p0242c1s v1p0247c1s v1p0250c2s v1p0293c1s v1p0379c2s v1p0391c2s v1p0404c2s v1p0420c1s v1p0433c2s v1p0495c2s v1p0529c1s v1p0551c2s v1p0552c2s v1p0568c1s v1p0588c1s v1p0593c2s v1p0613c1s v1p0952c2s v1p1001c1s v1p1028c1s v1p1041c1s v1p1084c1s v1p1089c1s v1p1091c1s v1p1091c2s v1p1096c2s v1p1124c2s v1p1147c2s v1p1178c2s v1p1221c2s v1p1224c1s v1p1301c1s v1p1304c2s v1p1326c1s v1p1343c1s v1p1350c2s v1p1355c1m v1p1355c2m v2p0027c2s v2p0068c2s v2p0164c2s v2p0227c2s v2p0368c1s v2p0436c2s v2p0437c1s v3p0125c1s v3p0137c2s v3p0287c2s v3p0347c1s v3p0427c2s v3p0430c1s v3p0443c2s
Emerson, H. ... v5p0318c2s v5p0426c2s v6p0010c2s v6p0133c1s v6p0186c1s
Emerson, H.B. ... v5p0220c2s
Emerson, Harrington ... v6p0010c2s
Emerson, J. ... v1p0393c1s v1p0985c1s v1p1108c1s v1p1392c1s v1p1435c2s v2p0067c1s
Emerson, J.D. ... v1p0132c2s
Emerson, J.S. ... v4p0027c2s v6p0349c2s
Emerson, J.S. et al. ... v3p0236c1s
Emerson, J.W. ... v5p0242c1m v5p0242c2s
Emerson, M.W. ... v4p0366c1s v4p0420c2s
Emerson, Marg. ... v6p0285c1s
Emerson, N.B. ... v4p0422c1s v6p0283c2s
Emerson, O.F. ... v3p0015c1s v3p0058c1s v3p0136c1s v3p0139c2s v3p0140c1m v3p0140c2s v3p0259c2s v3p0387c1s v4p0098c2s v4p0183c2s v4p0184c2s v4p0320c2s v4p0334c2s v4p0439c1s v4p0517c1s v5p0191c2s v6p0091c2s v6p0423c1s
Emerson, P. ... v4p0632c2s
Emerson, P.H. ... v4p0440c2s
Emerson, R. ... v1p0046c1s v1p0222c1s v1p0733c2s v1p0847c1s v1p0860c1s v1p0909c2s v1p0948c1s v1p1325c2s v6p0504c2s v6p0529c2s v6p0539c1s v6p0649c2s
Emerson, R.W. ... v1p0151c1s v1p0201c2s v1p0218c1s v1p0240c2s v1p0323c1s v1p0365c2s v1p0404c1s v1p0404c2s v1p0427c1s v1p0437c1s v1p0733c2s v1p0750c1s v1p0754c2s v1p0794c2s v1p0841c2s v1p0869c1s v1p0948c2s v1p0992c1s v1p1042c2s v1p1061c2s v1p1085c2s v1p1201c1s v1p1307c1s v1p1321c1s v2p0057c2s v2p0139c2s v2p0279c2s v2p0373c1s v2p0427c1s v4p0068c2s v4p0343c2s v6p0108c2s v6p0154c1s v6p0586c1s v6p0687c1s
Emerson, S. ... v6p0336c1s
Emerson, William ... v5p0097c1s
Emerton, E. ... v2p0072c1s v2p0085c2s v2p0268c1s v2p0269c1s v3p0172c2s v3p0216c2s v3p0239c1s v3p0301c2s v4p0128c2s v4p0163c2s v4p0249c1s v4p0283c1s v5p0169c1s v5p0197c2s v5p0228c1s v5p0257c1s v5p0266c2s v6p0094c2s v6p0210c1s
Emerton, E.E. ... v5p0482c1s
Emerton, J.H. ... v1p0044c1s v1p1236c1m v2p0319c2s
Emery, A.C. ... v6p0136c1s v6p0137c2s
Emery, C. ... v4p0020c2s v6p0100c2s v6p0234c1s v6p0599c1s
Emery, C.E. ... v1p1246c2s v1p1248c1m v1p1249c1s v2p0119c2s v3p0408c2s v4p0065c2s v4p0094c2s v4p0101c2s v4p0177c1s v4p0180c1s v4p0384c2s v4p0547c2m v4p0613c2s v5p0550c2s
Emery, Clay and Pierce, V.M. v6p0299c2s
Emery, F.A. ... v5p0154c1s v6p0511c1s
Emery, G.E. ... v2p0342c1s
Emery, G.F. ... v1p0163c2s v1p0213c1s v1p1198c1s v1p1241c2s v1p1387c1s v1p1392c1s v5p0187c1s
Emery, G.L. ... v1p0677c1s
Emery, H.C. ... v4p0218c2s v5p0230c1s v5p0241c2s v6p0126c1s
Emery, H.T. ... v4p0108c2s
Emery, I.C. ... v5p0421c2s v5p0425c1s v5p0488c2s
Emery, I.S. ... v3p0353c1s
Emery, J.B. ... v2p0071c2s v2p0276c1s
Emery, J.S. ... v5p0027c2s
Emery, L.A. ... v6p0408c2s
Emery, M. ... v5p0016c2s v5p0240c2s
Emery, M.F. ... v1p0334c1s
Emery, M.G. ... v1p1257c2s
Emery, M.L. ... v1p0551c1s
Emery, M.S. ... v2p0185c1s v2p0451c1s
Emery, S. ... v3p0252c2s
Emery, S.A. ... v1p0235c1s
Emery, S.B. ... v1p0806c1s
Emery, S.G. ... v1p0921c1s
Emery, S.H., jr. ... v1p0323c1s v1p1017c1s
Emery, S.L. ... v1p0735c2s v1p1095c1s v1p1258c1s v5p0187c1s v5p0493c2s
Emery, V.J. ... v5p0157c1s
Emery, W. ... v1p0190c1s v1p1357c2s
Emery, W.G. ... v5p0517c1m
Emery, W.M. ... v5p0176c2s v5p0587c2s
Emett, F.W. ... v5p0597c1s
Emigh, M. ... v6p0649c1s
Emin Pasha ... v3p0004c1s
Emm, W. ... v5p0498c1s v6p0661c1s
Emmanuel, M. ... v5p0230c2s v5p0393c2m
Emmel, A.N. ... v6p0075c2s
Emmens, S.H. ... v4p0335c2s v5p0010c1s
Emmens, S.M. ... v5p0010c1s
Emmet, J. ... v1p0499c2s
Emmet, R.H. ... v6p0711c1s
Emmet, T.A. ... v3p0304c1s v6p0280c2s v6p0327c2s v6p0441c1s
Emmet, W.T. ... v3p0007c1s
Emmette, T. ... v1p0736c2s v1p1070c1s
Emmons, E. ... v1p0265c2s v1p0470c1s
Emmons, F.W. ... v1p1091c1s

Emmons, M. v6p0654c1s
Emmons, S.F. v2p0071c1m v3p0093c1s v4p0230c2s v5p0010c2s v5p0229c1s v5p0250c1s v6p0251c1s v6p0264c1s v6p0351c2s
Emmons, T.W. v1p0752c1s
Emmott, A. v6p0153c1s
Emmott, Constance H. v5p0343c2s
Emmott, G.H. v4p0022c2s
Emory, A.C. v6p0622c2s
Emory, E. v6p0666c2s
Emory, F. v5p0014c2m v5p0134c2s v5p0477c2s v5p0501c2s v5p0599c2m v5p0600c1s v6p0018c1s v6p0216c1s v6p0606c1s v6p0666c2m
Emory, J. v1p0831c1s
Emory, R. v1p1234c1s
Emott, J. v1p0284c2s v2p0357c1s
Empson, W. v1p0029c1s v1p0030c1s v1p0113c1s v1p0216c2s v1p0253c1s v1p0412c2s v1p0499c1s v1p0534c2s v1p0538c2s v1p0548c2s v1p0614c1s v1p0659c1s v1p0780c2s v1p0791c2s v1p0954c2s v1p1026c1s v1p1383c1s
Emrick, C.F. v5p0009c1s
Enbule-Evans, A. v1p0236c2s
Encke, J.F. v1p0648c1s
Ende, A.von v4p0299c1s v4p0389c1s v4p0407c2s v5p0230c2s v6p0306c1s
Ende, Amelia v5p0565c1s v6p0251c2s v6p0295c1s v6p0697c1s
Ende, Amelia Von v6p0163c1s
Endean, J.R. v4p0533c2s
Enderby, W.D. v2p0381c2s
Enderlein, E.H. v5p0380c1s
Enders, H.E. v6p0140c2s
Endicott, A. v3p0159c2s
Endicott, C.M. v1p0407c2m v1p0950c1s v1p0982c2s
Endicott, F. v1p0101c2s v3p0013c2s v3p0048c1s
Endicott, M. v6p0083c2s
Endicott, W., jr. v1p1351c2s
Endicott, W.E. v1p0139c1s v4p0002c2s v4p0023c1s v4p0078c2m v4p0146c1m v4p0419c1s
Endlich, F.M. v1p0342c2s v1p0348c2s v1p0400c1s v1p1113c2s v2p0034c2s v2p0312c1s v2p0356c2s v3p0067c1s v3p0280c2s
Endlick, F.M. v1p0360c1s
Endres, E. v5p0028c1s v5p0345c2s v5p0352c1s v5p0498c1s
Endres, E.R. v4p0523c2s
Enebuske, C.J. v4p0628c1s
Engberg, C.C. v6p0615c1s
Engel, C. v2p0461c1s
Engel, H. v4p0284c1s
Engelenburg, F.V. v5p0007c2s
Engelman, G.J. v6p0526c1s
Engelmann, G. v1p0213c2s
Engelmann, H. v1p1041c1s
Engelmann, T.W. v4p0388c1s
Engels, F. v4p0496c1s
Engelsman, B. v3p0112c2s
England, Bishop v1p1117c2s
England, G. v6p0261c1s
England, G.A. v6p0219c1s v6p0225c1s v6p0365c2s v6p0387c1s v6p0604c1s
England, M.T. v6p0609c1s
Engle, G.B. v4p0072c2s
Engledue, W.C. v1p0041c1s v1p0824c2s v1p0825c1s
Englefield, H., Sir v1p0750c2s v1p1085c2s v1p1437c2s
Englefield, H.C., Sir v1p1114c2s
Englehardt, B.von v3p0127c1s
Engleheart, G.H. v4p0393c1s
Engler, A. and Ascherson, P. v4p0069c2s
Engler, E.A. v2p0028c2s v2p0067c2s v2p0441c2m
Engles, J. v1p0108c2s
Englis, J.A. v6p0702c1s
English, C.D. v2p0341c1s v3p0019c1s v3p0435c1s v3p0441c2s v4p0162c1m
English, Douglas v6p0021c2s v6p0167c2s
English, E. v2p0049c1s
English, H. v3p0432c2s
English, J.E. v5p0635c2s
English, J.M. v5p0273c2s v5p0436c1s
English, J.S. v6p0696c2s
English, R.I. v6p0636c1s
English, T.D. v1p0102c2s v1p0105c1s v1p0143c1s v1p0184c2s v1p0310c1s v1p0338c1s v1p0442c1s v1p0740c2s v1p0859c1s v1p0948c2s v1p0962c2s v1p1219c2s v1p1266c1s v2p0449c2s v3p0094c2s
English, W.F. v6p0214c2s
Engstrom, C.L. v3p0308c1s v3p0454c2s
Enloe, B.A. et al. v4p0434c1s
Enneking, J.J. et al. v5p0263c2s
Ennet, J.P. v1p0787c2s
Ennis, J. v2p0409c1s v2p0417c2s
Ennis, W.D. v5p0188c2s v5p0462c2s v5p0551c1s v6p0400c1s v6p0523c2s v6p0615c2s
Ennis, W.D. and Elleau, L.A. v5p0017c2s
Ennsto, Mrs. v1p1082c2s
Eno, H.L. v5p0435c2s
Eno, J.N. v6p0315c2s
Enock, C.R. v6p0490c1s
Enock, F. v5p0051c2s v5p0052c1s v5p0210c1s v5p0292c1m v5p0546c1s
Enock, R. v6p0301c2s v6p0400c2s
Enright, J. v3p0134c1s
Enright, J.D. v5p0163c2s v5p0362c2s
Ense, B.F., Mrs. v1p0814c1s
Ensign, J.R. and Gooch, F.A. v3p0056c1s
Ensley, E. v3p0347c1s
Ensor, E. v5p0213c1s v5p0297c2s v6p0643c2s v6p0647c2s v6p0684c1s
Ensor, G. v1p0654c1s
Ensor, R.C.K. v6p0653c2s v6p0708c1s
Ent, W.N. v6p0569c1s
Enteman, M.M. v6p0687c2s
Entwistle, J. v1p0761c1s v1p1042c2s
Entz, J.F. v1p0043c2s v1p0154c1s v1p0647c2s v1p1153c2m
Eothen v6p0157c2s
Eotvos, Baron v1p1371c2s
Eppens, E.H. v6p0103c1s v6p0444c2s
Epps, A.C.Van v1p1197c2s
Epps, W. v5p0039c1s
Eps, Van v4p0624c1s
Epstein, E.M. v1p0159c1s v2p0235c2s v3p0041c1s v3p0175c1s
Eques v6p0265c1s
Erben, H. v3p0374c1s
Erben, H.F.T. and Lozano, C.A. v3p0165c2s
Erchmann, A.E. et al. v5p0163c2s
Erck, W. v2p0129c2s
Erckmann-Chatrian v5p0546c1s
Erckmann-Chatrian, MM. ... v1p0002c2s v1p0142c2s v1p0177c2s v1p0228c2s v1p0257c2s v1p0276c2s v1p0288c2s v1p0337c2s v1p0491c1s v1p0570c1s v1p0624c2s v1p0642c2s v1p0652c1s v1p0744c2s v1p0785c1s v1p0785c2s v1p0889c1s v1p1070c2s v1p1100c1s v1p1258c1s v1p1335c1s v1p1339c1s v1p1369c1s v1p1372c2s v1p1408c1s v1p1409c2s v2p0184c2s v4p0116c1s
Erdman, C.L. v2p0076c2s
Erdman, P.K. v3p0398c1s
Erdmann, B. v6p0105c1s
Erdmann, H. v5p0104c1s
Erdmann, J.E. v1p0372c1s
Eremao, J.P.Val d' v4p0144c1s v4p0237c1s v4p0281c2m v4p0402c1s
Eremao, Jose P.Val d' v4p0364c1s
Erf, E. v5p0178c2s v5p0317c1s
Erhardt, W. v5p0395c2s v5p0415c1s v6p0439c2s
Eric, A. v4p0043c2s v4p0121c1s v4p0296c1s v4p0359c2s v5p0003c2s v5p0301c2s v5p0338c2s
Eric, Allan v4p0246c1s v4p0408c1s
Erichsen, H. v4p0039c1s v6p0347c2s v6p0359c1s v6p0512c1s
Erichsen, Hugo v5p0448c2s v6p0172c1s v6p0365c1s
Erichsen, N. v2p0158c1s
Ericksen, H. v3p0028c2s v6p0552c2s
Erickson, Halford v6p0115c1s
Erickson, Hugo v6p0560c1s
Erickson, J. v4p0034c1s v4p0119c1s
Erickson, K. v3p0327c1s v4p0158c1s
Ericsson, C. v4p0556c1s v5p0446c1s
Ericsson, J. v1p0189c1s v1p0459c1s v1p0580c1m v1p0580c2m v1p0824c1m v1p1074c1m v1p1218c1s v1p1263c2s v1p1267c2m v1p1268c1m v1p1268c2m v1p1269c1m v1p1293c1s v2p0295c1s v2p0296c2s v2p0425c2s v2p0426c1m v2p0434c1s v3p0416c1s
Ericsson, J. and Wood, De V. v2p0425c2s
Erie, G.F. v3p0156c2s
Erlebach, A. v3p0143c2s v3p0314c2s v3p0471c2s
Erman, M. v1p1293c1s
Ermatinger, C.O. v5p0374c1s
Ernest, G.A.O. v3p0101c1s
Ernst, A. v2p0128c1s v2p0157c2s v2p0258c2s v2p0331c2s v3p0245c2s v4p0360c1s
Ernst, C.W. v1p0434c2s v1p0464c1s v1p1215c2s v2p0118c1s v2p0176c2s v2p0269c1s v4p0069c2s v4p0387c2s v4p0454c1s v5p0640c1s
Ernst, C.W. and Gray, A. . v2p0112c2s
Ernst, G.A.O. v6p0076c2s
Ernst, H.C. v4p0249c2s v6p0021c1s v6p0281c2s
Errant, J.W. v4p0137c1s v5p0105c1s
Errett, I. v1p0119c2s v1p0239c2s v1p0436c1s v1p0852c1s v1p0915c1s v1p1175c2s v1p1363c2s
Errett, R. v2p0220c1s v2p0345c2s v3p0114c1s v3p0213c2s v3p0214c1s v3p0326c1s v3p0333c1s v3p0359c1m
Errington, D. v2p0144c1s
Errington, J. v3p0148c2s v3p0233c2m v3p0326c2s v3p0388c1s
Errington, Lord v3p0054c1s
Errington, T. v2p0233c1s
Errol, J. v3p0168c2s v3p0344c1s v4p0193c1s v4p0295c1s
Erroll, Earl of v6p0175c1s v6p0265c1s v6p0265c2m v6p0266c2s v6p0269c1s
Erroll, H. v4p0619c2s v5p0087c1s
Errott, I. v1p1058c2s
Erskine, J. v4p0318c2s
Erskine, J.R. v6p0548c1s
Erskine, K. v5p0520c1s
Erskine, Lucile v6p0635c2s
Erskine, P. v5p0539c1s
Erskine, S. v4p0186c2s v4p0290c1s v4p0355c1s v6p0689c2s
Erskine, S., Mrs. v6p0689c2s
Erskine, S.R. v6p0400c1s
Erskine, St.V. v1p1338c2s
Ertz, E. v6p0709c2s
Ervin, J.N. v4p0414c1s
Ervin, W. v4p0526c2s
Erving, W.G. v6p0195c2s
Erwin, J. v4p0186c2s
Erwin, J.M.F. v5p0403c2s
Erwine, A. v1p0320c1s
Esbjorn, C.M. v2p0044c2s
Esby, J.P. v1p0565c1s
Esch, J.J. v6p0443c1s v6p0529c2s v6p0530c1s v6p0530c2s
Eschbach, E.P. v3p0207c2s
Eschbach, E.R. v6p0474c2s
Eschenauer, A. v1p1156c1s
Escobar, F. v6p0477c1s v6p0551c1s
Escombe, F. v5p0518c2s
Escombe, M. v6p0012c2s
Escott, A. v2p0154c1s v4p0117c2s v4p0159c1s v4p0196c2s v4p0549c2s v5p0518c2s v5p0523c1s
Escott, T.H. v4p0114c1s v4p0419c2s v4p0427c2s v4p0430c1s
Escott, T.H.S. v1p0144c1s v1p0202c1s v1p0267c1s v1p0285c2s v1p0352c2s v1p0428c2s v1p0463c2s v1p0464c2s v1p0520c1s v1p0520c2s v1p0521c2s v1p0602c1s v1p0607c1s v1p0621c2s v1p0648c2s v1p0696c2s v1p0710c1s v1p0739c2s v1p0761c2s v1p0780c1s v1p0780c2s v1p0781c1s v1p0786c2s v1p0804c1s v1p0908c1s v1p0932c2s v1p1011c2s v1p1018c1s v1p1124c2s v1p1167c2s v1p1168c2s v1p1259c2s v1p1305c1s v1p1334c2m v1p1358c2s v1p1361c1s v1p1386c2s v2p0004c1s v2p0029c2s v2p0056c1s v2p0134c1m v2p0170c1s v2p0186c2m v2p0188c1m v2p0188c2m v2p0192c1s v2p0198c2s v2p0208c2s v2p0324c1s v2p0330c2s v2p0333c2s v2p0380c2s v2p0410c1s v2p0420c2m v2p0482c1s v4p0033c1s v4p0146c2s v4p0154c2s v4p0182c2s v4p0211c1s v4p0216c2s v4p0227c1s v4p0239c2m v4p0240c1s v4p0305c2s v4p0370c1s v4p0435c1s v4p0491c2s v4p0495c2s v4p0499c2s v4p0500c1s v4p0584c2s v4p0635c1s v5p0033c1s v5p0095c1s v5p0180c1s v5p0263c1s v5p0271c2s v5p0416c1s v5p0456c1s v5p0465c2s v5p0481c2s v5p0491c1s v5p0499c1s v6p0132c1s v6p0138c2s v6p0216c2s v6p0299c1m v6p0329c2s v6p0344c1s v6p0384c1s v6p0410c1s v6p0574c2s v6p0576c2s v6p0635c1s v6p0657c2s v6p0660c2s v6p0702c2s
Esdaile, A. v6p0373c1s
Esdaile, D. v1p0362c2s v1p0494c2s v1p0955c2s v1p1146c1s
Esdaile, E. v4p0447c2s
Esenwein, J.B. v6p0337c2s
Esher, Viscount v6p0194c2s
Esler, E.R. v4p0052c2s v4p0299c2s v4p0452c2s v6p0566c2s
Esmark, Prof. v1p0506c2s
Esparbes, Georges D' v5p0269c2s

Esparlies, George d' v5p0555c2s
Espenshade, A.H. v6p0034c1s
Espin, T.E. v2p0420c1s
Espinas, A. v2p0116c2s
Espinasse, F. v2p0302c2s
Espitallier, G. and Rochas, A.de
v3p0018c2s
Esplen, S. v5p0122c2s
Esposito, M. v6p0173c2s
Espy, J.P. v1p0077c1s
v1p0099c2s v1p0266c2s v1p0348c1m
v1p0619c2s v1p0829c1s v1p0829c2s
v1p1080c2s v1p1193c1s v1p1240c1s
v1p1256c2m v1p1316c1s
Esquiros, A. v1p0412c2s
Esser, F.T. v3p0312c2s
Essex, H. v6p0500c1s
Essex, J. v1p0160c2s
v1p0174c1s v1p0190c1s v1p0253c2s
v1p0409c1s v1p0750c2s v1p1112c2s
v1p1129c1s
Essick, A. v1p0117c1s
v1p0847c2s
Esson, W.B. v5p0183c2s
Estabrook, A.M. v5p0141c1s
v6p0143c2s v6p0440c1s
Estabrook, Alma M. v5p0361c2s
v6p0378c2s v6p0389c2s
Estabrook, H.D. v6p0358c2s
Estabrook, H.K. v5p0533c1s
Estabrook, W.C. v6p0450c1s
Estagel, J. v1p0859c1s
v1p0916c2s v1p1221c1s
Estcourt, C. v2p0014c1s
v2p0040c2s
Estcourt, E.E. v1p0003c1s
Este, D' v6p0376c2s
Estee, M.M. v3p0163c1s
v5p0304c1s v6p0092c1s v6p0224c1s
Estep, E.R. v6p0044c2s
Esterbrook, A.M. v6p0540c1s
Esterbrook, H.D. v5p0254c2s
Esterline, B. v6p0012c2s
v6p0113c2s v6p0120c1s v6p0144c2s
v6p0364c1s v6p0529c1s
Esterre, C.R.D' v6p0044c2s
Esterre-Keeling, E.D' v3p0002c1s
v3p0045c1s v3p0172c1s v3p0466c2s
v4p0218c2s v4p0254c2s v4p0366c1s
v4p0560c1s v5p0078c1s v5p0152c1s
Esterre-Keeling, Elsa D' . v5p0139c2s
Estes, D. v2p0174c2s
Estes, D.F. v2p0044c2s
v2p0337c2s v5p0055c2s
Estes, W.C. v4p0136c1s
v5p0139c1s
Estevanez, N. v5p0128c2s
Estill, H.F. v6p0304c1s
Estournelles, Baron d' ... v2p0190c2s
v2p0427c1s
Estrada, E.D. v2p0478c2s
Estrange, A.A.D.L' v2p0021c2s
v2p0185c2m
Estrange, A.G.L' v3p0465c1s
Estrange, A.L' v2p0066c2s
Estrange, C.J.L' v2p0176c1s
v2p0288c2s
Estrange, C.L. v5p0100c1s
Estrange, C.L' v5p0468c1s
v5p0473c1s
Estrange, G.L' v1p1170c2s
v4p0022c1s
Estrange, G.L', Sir v1p0987c1s
Estrella, T.D' v3p0112c2s
Estrem, A. v5p0510c1s
Estrem, A. and Miller, M.M.
v4p0627c1s
Estridge, H. v1p0415c2s
Etalii, C.A. v1p1099c2s
Ethelmer, E. v4p0625c2s
v5p0134c2s v5p0204c1s v5p0204c2s
Etheredge, J. v1p0603c1s
v1p1214c2s v2p0126c1s
Etheridge, J.St.C. v5p0017c2s
Etheridge, R. v1p0508c2s
v4p0038c2s v4p0091c2s v4p0326c2s
Etheridge, R., jr. v4p0038c1s
v4p0560c2s
Etienne, E. v6p0138c2s
v6p0430c1s
Etienne, L. v1p1020c1s
Etten, I.M. v4p0303c1s
Etten, I.M.van v4p0266c1s
Etter, J.W. v4p0573c1s
Etting, F.M. v1p0987c2s
v1p0997c1s
Etting, T.M. v4p0379c2s
Ettinger, G.T. v4p0123c2s
Ettinger, P. v6p0483c1s
Etty, J.L. v5p0523c1m
v5p0523c2s v6p0028c1s v6p0586c2s
v6p0587c2s
Eu, E. v3p0161c2s
Eubule-Evans, A. v1p0569c1s
v1p0933c1s
Eucken, R. v4p0439c1s
v5p0207c1s v5p0222c1s v5p0231c1s
v5p0232c1s v5p0261c1s v5p0447c1s
v5p0483c2s v6p0376c1s
Eucken, Rudolf v5p0230c2s
Eugert, A.C. v2p0419c1s
Eustace, H.J. v6p0079c2s
Eustace, R. and Meade, L.T.
v5p0554c2s
Eustes, J.B. et al. v2p0089c1s
Eustis, E. v6p0257c1s
Eustis, G. v1p0133c1s
v1p0284c1s
Eustis, G.H. v6p0374c1s
Eustis, H.L. v1p0432c1s
Eustis, I.B. v3p0015c2s
Eustis, J.B. v3p0402c1s
v5p0168c2s v5p0216c2s
Eustis, W.T. v1p0075c1s
v1p0234c2s v1p0709c1s v1p0769c1s
v1p0872c1s v1p1075c2s v1p1224c1s
v1p1338c2s v1p1360c1s v1p1398c2s
Eustis, W.T. and Dutton, S.W.S.
v1p0290c1s
Euverte, M. v1p1251c1s
Evald, C.A. v3p0453c1s
Evan, J. v2p0351c1s
Evans, A. v1p1077c1s
Evans, A.Dudley v6p0530c1s
Evans, A.E. v1p1424c1s
v3p0385c2s v4p0224c2s v4p0361c1s
Evans, A.G. v3p0354c1s
v5p0104c1s v5p0298c2s
Evans, A.J. v1p0036c2s
v1p0080c2s v1p0087c2s v1p0151c1s
v1p0245c1s v1p0864c1s v2p0032c1s
v2p0447c2s v3p0420c1s v3p0425c2s
v4p0043c1s v4p0074c2s v4p0139c1s
v4p0365c2s v4p0442c2s v4p0487c2s
v5p0124c1s v5p0205c2s v5p0238c1s
v5p0378c2s v5p0589c2s v6p0013c2s
v6p0353c2s v6p0357c2s
Evans, A.J. and Blind, K.. v2p0440c1s
Evans, A.J. and Myers, J.L.
v4p0139c1s
Evans, A.J. and Taylor, Isaac
v2p0058c1s
Evans, A.R. v4p0310c2s
v5p0210c2s v5p0362c1s
Evans, A.S. v1p0266c2s
v1p0274c2s v1p0560c1s v1p0568c1s
v1p0761c1s v1p0797c2s v1p1282c1s
v1p1374c2s v1p1380c1s v1p1405c2s
v1p1416c1s
Evans, A.W. v4p0190c1m
v6p0241c2s v6p0243c2s
Evans, B.D. v6p0281c1s
Evans, B.G. v2p0464c2s
Evans, B.R. v1p0706c1s
Evans, Beriah G. v6p0191c2s
Evans, C. v1p0149c1s
Evans, C.A. v1p0052c1s
v1p0231c1s v1p1079c2s v1p1255c2s
v1p1318c1s v6p0262c1s v6p0386c1s
Evans, C.J. v5p0261c2s
Evans, C.R. v6p0605c2s
Evans, C.W. v5p0525c2s
Evans, D. v5p0534c1s
v6p0256c1s
Evans, D.S. v2p0480c2s
v4p0154c1s
Evans, D.T. v1p0538c2s
Evans, Dr. v1p1265c2s
Evans, E. v1p0422c1s
Evans, E.B. v4p0193c1s
v5p0488c2s
Evans, E.E. v1p0204c2s
v1p0484c2s v1p0934c1s v2p0378c2s
v3p0267c2s v4p0607c1s
Evans, E.E., Mrs. v1p0116c1s
v6p0649c1s
Evans, E.J. v6p0346c2s
Evans, E.K. v5p0180c2s
Evans, E.P. v1p0003c1s
v1p0064c1s v1p0084c1s v1p0138c1s
v1p0140c2s v1p0210c1s v1p0266c1s
v1p0390c1s v1p0454c1s v1p0518c1s
v1p0574c1s v1p0754c1s v1p0879c2s
v1p0890c2s v1p0892c1s v1p0975c2s
v1p1029c2m v1p1030c1s v1p1060c1s
v1p1131c2s v1p1183c2s v1p1185c2s
v1p1187c1s v1p1196c2s v1p1197c1s
v1p1408c2s v1p1420c1s v1p1441c1s
v2p0024c2m v2p0041c2s v2p0042c2s
v2p0060c1s v2p0081c2s v2p0194c2m
v2p0266c2s v2p0327c1s v2p0339c1s
v2p0359c2s v2p0380c1s v2p0459c2s
v3p0014c2m v3p0049c1s v3p0119c2s
v3p0170c2s v3p0185c1s v3p0206c2m
v3p0207c1s v3p0243c1s v3p0292c1s
v3p0333c1s v3p0348c2s v3p0404c1s
v4p0018c1s v4p0018c2m v4p0152c2s
v4p0216c1m v4p0352c1s v4p0373c2s
v4p0376c2s v4p0382c1s v4p0444c2s
v4p0479c2s v4p0541c1s v4p0558c1s
v4p0584c1s v5p0020c2s v5p0039c2s
v5p0562c1s v5p0568c2s v5p0634c1s
v6p0683c1s
Evans, E.P. and Winsor, J.
v4p0125c2s
Evans, E.P., Mrs. v1p0167c1s
Evans, E.W. v1p0208c2s
v1p0827c1s v1p0939c2m v1p1373c1s
v1p1401c2s
Evans, Eliz.E. v3p0475c2s
Evans, F. v5p0632c2s
v6p0084c1s v6p0142c1s v6p0364c2s
v6p0589c1s
Evans, F.D. v5p0101c2s
Evans, F.E. v6p0401c2s
Evans, F.J. v3p0173c2s
Evans, F.W. v1p1183c1s
v4p0192c2s v5p0579c1s
Evans, G. v2p0240c1s
Evans, G.H. v6p0419c1s
Evans, G.S. v6p0386c1s
v6p0698c2s
Evans, G.W. v2p0362c1s
v3p0008c1s v3p0169c2s v3p0248c2s
v3p0403c2s v5p0229c2s v6p0012c1s
v6p0030c1s v6p0251c1s
Evans, H. v2p0435c1s
v3p0245c2s v5p0484c2s v5p0518c2s
Evans, H.A. v4p0454c2s
Evans, H.C. v5p0440c1s
v6p0509c1s
Evans, H.D. v1p0035c2s
v1p0138c1s v1p0247c2s v1p0255c1s
v1p0356c2s v1p0421c2s v1p0803c1s
v1p0869c1s v1p0890c1s v1p1059c2s
v1p1089c1s v1p1102c2s v1p1214c2s
v1p1303c1s v2p0297c1s
Evans, H.R. v5p0066c2s
v5p0329c2s v5p0490c2s v6p0043c2s
v6p0070c2s v6p0091c2s v6p0145c1s
v6p0196c1s v6p0255c2s v6p0330c1s
v6p0369c1s v6p0394c2m v6p0442c1s
v6p0500c1s v6p0545c2s v6p0581c1s
v6p0645c2s v6p0656c2s
Evans, J. v1p0040c1s
v1p0051c2s v1p0145c1s v1p0375c1s
v1p0460c1s v1p0460c2m v1p0506c2s
v1p0710c2s v1p0720c2s v1p0870c2s
v1p1045c1s v1p1122c2s v1p1255c2m
v1p1396c2s v1p1439c2s v2p0006c1s
v2p0091c2s v2p0106c1s v2p0108c2s
v2p0130c2s v2p0141c2s v2p0341c1s
v4p0484c2s v4p0574c1s v5p0048c2s
v5p0078c2s v5p0176c2s v5p0264c1s
v5p0428c1s v5p0514c2s v5p0529c1s
Evans, J., Sir v4p0020c1s
v5p0025c1m v5p0358c1s
Evans, J.A. v3p0123c2m
v3p0381c2s v4p0162c2s v4p0304c2s
Evans, J.C. et al. v5p0360c1s
Evans, J.F. v1p0788c2s
Evans, J.H. v3p0243c2s
Evans, J.S. v4p0429c1s
v4p0449c2s
Evans, J.W. v5p0286c1s
v6p0072c2s v6p0419c1s
Evans, L. v5p0561c1s
Evans, L.B. v4p0171c2s
v6p0387c2s
Evans, L.I. v3p0081c2s
Evans, L.J. v2p0044c1m
Evans, L.P. v4p0538c1s
Evans, L.T. v3p0218c1s
Evans, M. v6p0362c2s
Evans, M.D. v5p0302c1s
Evans, M.G. v5p0074c2s
v5p0538c2s
Evans, M.J. v2p0250c1s
v2p0322c1s v2p0464c2s v6p0017c1s
Evans, M.N. v4p0419c2s
Evans, M.S. v1p0897c1s
Evans, Mary S. v3p0120c2s
Evans, N. v3p0256c1s
Evans, N.N. v6p0032c2s
v6p0125c1s
Evans, P.S. v2p0255c1s
v2p0442c2s
Evans, P.S., jr. and Gooch, F.A.
v4p0514c1s
Evans, R. v3p0118c2s
v4p0004c1m v5p0004c2s v5p0439c2s
Evans, R.D. v5p0508c2s
v6p0287c1s
Evans, R.D. et al. v4p0180c1s
Evans, R.G. v3p0334c1s
Evans, R.H. v6p0395c1s
Evans, R.K. v2p0219c2s
v3p0278c2s v3p0283c1s v5p0290c1s
v6p0416c2s
Evans, Robert K., Mrs. ... v6p0220c2s
Evans, S. v1p0065c1s
v1p0167c2s v1p0260c1s v1p0261c1s
v1p0706c1s v1p0775c1s v1p0920c2s
v1p1141c2s v1p1235c2s v2p0243c1s
v3p0124c2s v3p0419c2s v4p0093c2s
Evans, S.B. v2p0300c1s
v3p0277c1s v3p0350c1s v3p0426c1s
Evans, S.T. v1p1135c2s
v4p0239c1s
Evans, T. v1p0164c2s
v1p0187c2s v1p0188c1s v1p0212c1s
v1p0467c2s v1p0533c2s v1p0796c2s
v1p0826c1s v1p0945c2s v1p1011c1s
v1p1183c1s v2p0257c2s v2p0290c1s
v5p0645c1s
Evans, T.C. v1p0158c2s
v4p0276c2s v6p0202c1s
Evans, T.H. v4p0116c1s
Evans, T.J. v3p0151c1s
Evans, T.S. v5p0058c2s

Evans, T.W. v6p0212c2s
v6p0442c1s
Evans, W.A. v4p0111c2s
Evans, W.E. v5p0472c1s
Evans, W.H. v1p0124c1s
v5p0010c2s v6p0656c1s
Evans, W.P. v5p0140c2s
v6p0464c2s
Evans, W.S. v4p0085c1s
v4p0086c2s v5p0187c2s
Evans, W.W. v1p1248c1s
v2p0466c2s
Evans-Gordon, W. v6p0300c1s
Evans-Jackson, J.E. v5p0584c2s
Evarts, J. v1p0225c2s
v1p0637c2s v1p1150c1s
Evarts, M. v6p0688c1s
Evarts, W.M. v3p0244c2s
Evarts, W.W., jr. v2p0210c1s
Evatt, G.J.H. v6p0708c2s
Eve, A.S. v6p0392c2s
v6p0527c1s
Eve, G.W. v6p0167c2s
v6p0287c2s
Eve, H.W. v5p0130c2s
Eve, Oscar v5p0574c2s
Eveleth, F.H. v2p0059c2s
Evelyn, A. v6p0663c1s
Evelyn, Aldridge v6p0118c1s
Evelyn, E.G. v1p0441c1s
Evelyn, F.W.D' v6p0714c1s
Evelyn, W. v2p0104c1s
Evelyn, W.M. v1p1439c1s
Even, M.Van v5p0366c2s
Everard, H.S.C. v5p0219c2s
v5p0610c1s
Everest, C.M. v4p0344c1s
Everest, C.W. v1p0732c1s
Everest, H.W. v1p0242c1s
v1p0427c1s v2p0081c2s v2p0222c2s
Everest, R. v1p0315c1s
v1p0406c1s v1p0981c2s v1p1352c1s
v1p1353c1s
Everett, A.H. v1p0028c1s
v1p0028c2s v1p0032c2s v1p0091c2s
v1p0105c2s v1p0113c2s v1p0115c1s
v1p0133c1s v1p0164c2s v1p0180c2s
v1p0181c2s v1p0196c2s v1p0197c1s
v1p0202c1s v1p0217c1s v1p0222c1s
v1p0225c2s v1p0232c1s v1p0236c1m
v1p0263c1s v1p0280c2s v1p0318c1s
v1p0322c1s v1p0327c1s v1p0338c2s
v1p0364c2s v1p0391c1s v1p0430c2m
v1p0466c1s v1p0476c2s v1p0483c1s
v1p0486c1s v1p0489c1s v1p0506c1s
v1p0521c1s v1p0531c1s v1p0552c2s
v1p0570c1s v1p0571c2s v1p0572c2s
v1p0585c2s v1p0625c2s v1p0648c2s
v1p0650c2s v1p0667c1m v1p0674c2s
v1p0680c2s v1p0705c2s v1p0742c1s
v1p0754c1s v1p0754c2s v1p0758c2s
v1p0768c1s v1p0784c1s v1p0791c2s
v1p0797c2s v1p0800c2s v1p0849c2s
v1p0868c1s v1p0868c2m v1p0870c2s
v1p0881c2s v1p0895c2m v1p0928c2s
v1p0933c2s v1p0958c1s v1p0966c2s
v1p0976c1s v1p0983c1s v1p1000c2s
v1p1008c1s v1p1026c2m v1p1034c1s
v1p1034c2s v1p1099c2s v1p1129c2s
v1p1133c2s v1p1136c2s v1p1139c1s
v1p1156c2s v1p1175c2s v1p1202c1s
v1p1214c2s v1p1225c2s v1p1229c1s
v1p1233c1s v1p1241c1m v1p1253c2s
v1p1270c1s v1p1283c1s v1p1354c2s
v1p1359c2s v1p1360c2s v1p1378c1s
v1p1386c2s v1p1387c2s v1p1388c2s
Everett, C.C. v1p0062c1s
v1p0129c1s v1p0130c2s v1p0170c1s
v1p0170c2m v1p0305c1s v1p0427c1m
v1p0440c1s v1p0495c2s v1p0527c2s
v1p0528c1s v1p0582c2s v1p0594c1s
v1p0625c2s v1p0685c2s v1p0686c2s
v1p0741c1s v1p0890c2s v1p0958c1s
v1p0980c1s v1p1000c2s v1p1001c1s
v1p1001c2s v1p1094c1s v1p1109c1s
v1p1161c1s v1p1161c2s v1p1295c2s
v1p1301c1s v1p1320c2s v2p0059c1s
v2p0122c1s v2p0174c2s v3p0057c1s
v3p0120c1s v3p0136c1s v3p0143c1s
v3p0190c2s v3p0270c1s v3p0328c1s
v3p0357c2s v3p0360c1s v3p0413c2s
v4p0036c2s v4p0074c2s v4p0076c1s
v4p0076c2s v4p0154c1s v4p0249c1s
v4p0249c2s v4p0300c2s v4p0432c1s
v4p0569c2s v4p0573c1s v5p0115c1s
v5p0257c1s v5p0364c1s v5p0400c1s
v5p0411c1s v5p0480c1s
Everett, E. v1p0003c2s
v1p0004c1s v1p0005c2s v1p0015c1s
v1p0015c2s v1p0022c2s v1p0028c1m
v1p0029c1m v1p0029c2m v1p0030c1s
v1p0031c1s v1p0033c1s v1p0036c2s
v1p0057c2m v1p0062c1s v1p0069c2s
v1p0071c1m v1p0085c1s v1p0113c1s
v1p0152c1m v1p0168c1m v1p0175c2s
v1p0197c1s v1p0230c2s v1p0232c1s
v1p0271c1s v1p0283c1s v1p0294c2s
v1p0295c1s v1p0342c2m v1p0353c1s
v1p0373c2s v1p0381c1s v1p0383c1s
v1p0397c1s v1p0408c2s v1p0413c2s
v1p0416c1s v1p0425c1s v1p0431c1s
v1p0433c1s v1p0474c1m v1p0490c1s
v1p0497c1s v1p0504c2s v1p0513c1s
v1p0518c1s v1p0530c1s v1p0534c2s
v1p0546c1s v1p0551c2m v1p0552c1s
v1p0552c2s v1p0561c2s v1p0566c2s
v1p0572c1s v1p0572c2s v1p0586c2s
v1p0589c2m v1p0592c1s v1p0597c2s
v1p0602c2s v1p0614c1s v1p0625c2s
v1p0666c2s v1p0667c1m v1p0667c2s
v1p0669c2s v1p0674c2m v1p0717c2s
v1p0734c1s v1p0767c1s v1p0791c2s
v1p0812c2s v1p0844c2s v1p0854c1m
v1p0872c2s v1p0884c2s v1p0892c2s
v1p0894c1s v1p0918c1s v1p0921c1s
v1p0925c2s v1p0928c2s v1p0933c2s
v1p0949c2s v1p0973c2s v1p0987c1s
v1p0987c2s v1p0989c2s v1p0996c2s
v1p1023c1s v1p1027c1s v1p1034c1s
v1p1040c2s v1p1052c2s v1p1088c2s
v1p1093c2s v1p1113c2s v1p1124c1s
v1p1128c2s v1p1133c2s v1p1138c2s
v1p1169c2s v1p1183c1s v1p1187c2s
v1p1198c1s v1p1217c2s v1p1224c2s
v1p1246c1s v1p1257c1s v1p1277c1s
v1p1283c1s v1p1292c2s v1p1299c1s
v1p1326c2s v1p1344c2s v1p1348c2s
v1p1349c1s v1p1350c1s v1p1350c2s
v1p1354c2s v1p1356c2s v1p1362c1s
v1p1362c2s v1p1374c2s v1p1378c2s
v1p1383c1s v1p1387c2s v1p1388c1s
v1p1393c2s v1p1395c2m v1p1396c1s
v1p1400c1s v1p1404c1m v1p1412c1s
v1p1429c1s v1p1440c2s v2p0005c2s
v2p0415c2s v2p0429c1s
Everett, E. and Everett, J.
v1p0380c1s
Everett, E. and Kingsley, J.L.
v1p0292c1s
Everett, E.F. v1p0198c1s
v1p0433c1s
Everett, E.P. v5p0223c1s
Everett, H.E. v6p0154c1s
Everett, H.E., Mrs. v1p1123c1s
Everett, H.H. v6p0432c1s
Everett, H.S. v4p0096c1s
v4p0275c1s v4p0394c2s v4p0477c1s
v4p0590c1s
Everett, J. v1p0073c1s
v1p0183c2s v1p0339c2s v1p0407c1s
v1p0818c2s v1p0831c1s v1p1211c1s
Everett, J. and Everett, E.
v1p0380c1s
Everett, J.B. v1p0805c1s
Everett, J.D. v1p0278c2s
v1p0850c2s v1p1293c1m v2p0138c2s
v3p0458c1s v5p0516c1s v6p0258c2s
Everett, J.R. v1p1108c2s
Everett, J.T. v3p0213c1s
v3p0290c1s
Everett, M.T. v5p0195c2s
v5p0386c1s v5p0510c2s
Everett, R. v4p0104c1s
v5p0305c1s v5p0436c2s v5p0606c1s
v6p0178c2s
Everett, R.L. v4p0130c2s
Everett, Ruth v6p0166c2s
v6p0395c1s
Everett, S. v1p0346c2s
Everett, W. v1p0006c1s
v1p0072c1s v1p0190c2s v1p0208c1s
v1p0343c2s v1p0352c1s v1p0682c2s
v1p0684c1s v1p0688c2s v1p1217c2s
v1p1301c1s v3p0084c2s v3p0301c1s
v4p0107c2s v4p0146c2s v4p0245c1s
v4p0263c1s v4p0306c2s v4p0311c1s
v4p0321c2s v4p0337c1s v4p0341c1s
v4p0521c1s v4p0535c2s v4p0577c2s
v4p0624c1s v5p0435c2s v5p0506c1s
v6p0018c1s v6p0131c1s v6p0206c1s
v6p0299c1s v6p0345c1s v6p0362c2s
v6p0583c1s v6p0593c2s
Everett, W.F. v1p0903c1s
Everett, W.G. v5p0239c2s
v5p0337c2s v5p0349c1s v5p0483c1s
Everett, Wm. v3p0164c1s
Everett-Green, E. v4p0258c1s
Everhardt, B.M. and Ellis, J.B.
v5p0223c1s
Everhart, J.E. v1p1390c2s
Everill, H.C. v6p0691c2s
Everitt, G. v4p0158c1s
v4p0160c2s
Everitt, H.C. v6p0441c2s
Evermann, B.W. v2p0272c1s
v3p0045c1s v4p0588c2s v6p0226c2m
v6p0283c1s v6p0524c2s v6p0566c1s
v6p0658c1s
Evers, H. v1p1424c2s
Eversham, Florence v5p0490c2s
Evershed, H. v1p0444c1s
v1p1015c1s v1p1015c2s v1p1016c1s
v2p0143c1s v2p0185c1s v2p0208c1s
v2p0243c1s v2p0400c2m v2p0427c2s
v2p0446c1s v3p0008c2s v3p0103c1s
v3p0219c2s v3p0236c2s v3p0439c2s
Evershed, J. v5p0174c2s
v5p0227c2s
Evershed, J., jr. v4p0556c2m
Evershed, S. v3p0413c2s
Eversley, Lord v6p0191c2s
v6p0445c2s
Everts, T.C. v1p1437c1s
Everts, W.W. v1p0097c2s
v1p1269c2s
Everts, W.W., jr. v3p0084c2s
Every, A. v5p0096c1s
v5p0631c1s
Every, C.A. v2p0250c2s
v2p0356c1s v2p0408c1s v2p0418c1s
Evetts, B. v4p0516c2s
Evetts, B.T.A. v3p0423c2s
Evison, G.H. v5p0004c2s
Evjen, J.O. v6p0031c2s
Evne, Dr.Van v1p1207c2s
Ewait, J.C. v6p0297c2s
Ewald, A.C. v1p0196c2s
v1p0203c1s v1p0398c1s v1p0425c1s
v1p0563c1s v1p0566c2s v1p0585c1s
v1p0690c2s v1p0692c2s v1p0720c2s
v1p0763c1s v1p0807c1s v1p0846c2s
v1p0962c2s v1p0990c2s v1p1012c2s
v1p1024c2s v1p1139c1s v1p1230c2s
v1p1258c2s v1p1264c2s v1p1274c1s
v1p1383c1s v1p1397c2s v1p1417c2s
v2p0049c2s v2p0075c1s v2p0119c2s
v2p0155c1s v2p0212c2s v2p0270c2s
v2p0368c1s v2p0382c1s v2p0466c1s
v2p0471c1s v2p0481c1s v3p0019c1s
v3p0074c2s v3p0105c1s v3p0120c2s
v3p0152c2s v3p0154c2s v3p0155c1s
v3p0231c1s v3p0237c1s v3p0261c2s
v3p0264c1s v4p0240c2s
Ewald, C.F. v1p1326c1s
v1p1329c2m
Ewald, G.H.A.von v1p0582c1s
Ewald, J. v1p1329c2s
Ewan, J. v6p0356c1s
Ewan, J.A. v5p0320c1s
v5p0354c1s v5p0408c2s v5p0544c1s
v6p0103c1s v6p0138c2s v6p0253c1s
Ewan, J.H. v6p0530c1s
Ewan, T. v5p0185c2s
Ewart, C.T. v3p0206c2s
Ewart, G. v5p0630c1s
Ewart, H.C. v2p0022c1s
v2p0112c1s v2p0164c1s v2p0183c1s
v2p0265c2s v2p0267c2s v2p0405c1s
v3p0269c2s v3p0271c2s v3p0472c1s
Ewart, J.C. v2p0154c2s
v3p0030c1s v5p0570c2s
Ewart, J.H. v6p0358c2s
Ewart, J.S. v4p0170c2s
v4p0353c2m v5p0195c1m v5p0466c2s
v6p0095c2s v6p0211c1s v6p0322c2s
Ewart, James C. v6p0633c2s
Ewart, W. v6p0009c2s
Ewbank, H. and Browne, W.H.
v1p1223c1s
Ewbank, T. v1p0029c2s
v1p0083c2s v1p0111c1s v1p0145c2s
v1p0146c1s v1p0158c2s v1p0189c1s
v1p0320c1s v1p0636c1s v1p0636c2s
v1p0956c2s v1p1055c2s v1p1113c1s
v1p1236c1s v1p1249c2s v1p1315c2s
Ewbank, T. and Mott, J.L.. v1p0231c1s
Ewell, A.F. v4p0464c1s
Ewell, A.M. v4p0050c2s
v4p0126c1s v4p0167c1s v4p0193c2s
v4p0321c1s v5p0379c2s v6p0285c2s
v6p0703c2s
Ewell, A.W. v5p0338c1s
v6p0506c1s
Ewell, J.L. v2p0231c1s
v2p0473c1s v3p0377c1s v3p0463c2s
v5p0492c1s v5p0498c1s
Ewell, R.S. v1p0518c2s
v1p1240c1s v1p1346c2s v2p0365c1s
v2p0372c2s
Ewell, R.S. and Kershaw, J.B.
v1p1107c1s
Ewell, R.S. et al. v1p1347c1s
Ewen, R. v4p0043c2s
v4p0044c1m v4p0044c2s v4p0045c1s
v4p0144c1s v4p0199c1s v4p0214c1m
v4p0378c1s v4p0378c2s v5p0007c2s
v5p0046c1s v5p0046c2s v5p0047c1m
v5p0245c1s v5p0245c2s v5p0295c2s
v5p0382c2s v5p0383c2s v5p0487c1s
v5p0584c1s
Ewer, B.C. v6p0012c1s
Ewer, F.C. v1p0188c1s
v1p0551c1s
Ewer, J.H. v1p0775c1s
Ewers, E.P. v5p0288c1s
Ewing, A. v1p0431c1s
v1p1116c2s
Ewing, A.G. v6p0342c1s
Ewing, Anna M. v6p0220c2s
Ewing, C. v1p1012c2s
Ewing, D.B. v1p0023c2s
Ewing, E.C. v5p0380c1s
Ewing, F.A. v1p0882c2s
Ewing, I. v6p0167c1s
Ewing, J. v6p0309c2s
Ewing, J.A. v2p0127c2m
v2p0128c1m v2p0128c2m v2p0272c1s
v2p0394c2m v3p0126c1m v3p0214c2s
v3p0264c1s v3p0384c1s v4p0349c2s
v5p0010c1s v5p0125c2s v5p0367c2s

v5p0482c2s v6p0082c2s v6p0412c1s
Ewing, J.A. and Jenkin, F. v1p1002c2s
Ewing, J.S. v5p0552c2s
Ewing, N. v4p0457c2s
Ewing, N.H. v6p0587c1s
Ewing, Q. v5p0351c2s
Ewing, R.C. v2p0250c2s v2p0251c2s v2p0299c1m v2p0384c2s v2p0451c1s
Ewing, T. v4p0308c1s
Ewing, T. et al. v1p1232c2s
Ewing, W. v6p0475c2s
Ewing, W.G. et al. v5p0114c2s
Ex-Captain of Police v6p0144c1s
Exeter, T.B. v4p0553c2s
Exley, T. v1p1006c1s
Exline, F. v5p0332c2s
Exner, Lt.-Col. v4p0224c1s
Exner, S. v1p0438c1s v3p0142c1s
Expertus and C., A.B. v5p0332c2s
Eyck, H.J.Ten v2p0431c2s
Eycleshymer, A.C. v5p0208c2s
Eykman, P.H. v6p0277c2s
Eykman, R.H. v6p0324c1s
Eyma, L. v1p0339c1s
Eyncourt, E.H.T.D' v5p0643c2s v6p0138c1s
Eyncourt, E.T.D' v1p0693c1s
Eyre, A. v5p0076c2s v5p0202c2s v5p0314c1s v5p0474c1s v5p0532c2s v6p0257c1s v6p0657c1s
Eyre, G.E.B. v1p0908c1s
Eyre, G.F. v6p0009c1s
Eyre, J. v6p0677c1s v6p0698c1s
Eyre, J.H. v1p0163c1s
Eyre, J.O. v5p0031c2s
Eyre, J.R. v3p0222c1s v3p0222c2s v5p0295c2s v6p0078c1s
Eyre, L.L. v2p0193c1s v3p0416c2s
Eyre, Lieut.-Col. v2p0135c1s
Eyre, M. v1p0397c2s v1p0931c1s v1p0940c2s v1p1030c2s v1p1031c1s v1p1152c2s v1p1254c1s v4p0155c2s v4p0256c2s v4p0274c2s v4p0442c1s v4p0588c2s
Eyre, Margaret v6p0709c2s
Eyre, W.H. v3p0229c1s v3p0284c1s v3p0438c1s
Eyre-Todd, G. v3p0031c2s v3p0050c2s v3p0155c2s v3p0224c1s v3p0258c2s v3p0450c1s v4p0039c2s v4p0042c2s v4p0077c1s v5p0024c1s v6p0391c2s
Eyre-Todd, George v5p0019c1s
Eys, W.V. v4p0047c1s
Eyster, Nellie B. v6p0243c1s
Eyster, W.F. v1p0846c2s v4p0158c1s v5p0281c1s
Eytinge, R. v3p0289c1s
Eyton v3p0415c2s
Eyton, R. et al. v4p0170c1s
Eyton, R.H. v1p1006c1s
Eyvie, J. v5p0210c1s
Ezdorf, R.von v6p0027c1s

F., A. v5p0265c1s
F., A.M. v5p0295c1s
F., G.F. v5p0434c2s
F., J.B. v5p0454c1s
v6p0107c1s
Fabeck, L.V.de v4p0626c1s
Faber, A. v1p1239c2s
Faber, A.M. v6p0547c2s
Faber, C. v2p0113c1s
Faber, F.W. v2p0278c2s
Faber, G.L. v3p0154c2s
Faber, G.S. v1p0336c2s
v1p1129c1s
Faber, M.A. v3p0325c2s
Faber, R.S. v5p0453c2s
v6p0441c2s
Faber, W.F. v3p0080c2s
v3p0083c2s v3p0271c2s v3p0300c1s
v3p0302c1s v3p0342c2s v4p0591c2s
Fabian Society v4p0581c1s
Fabian, A. v4p0533c2s
Fabian, H.W. v2p0006c2s
Fabie, A. v1p0297c2s
Fabre, A. v1p0534c1s
Fabre, F. v1p0728c2s
v4p0482c2s
Fabris, C. v5p0618c2s
Fabry, S.L.De v6p0178c1s
Faed, T. v3p0234c2s
Faelten, C. v5p0316c1s
v5p0450c1s
Faelten, Carl v5p0002c1s
v5p0378c2s v5p0450c1m v5p0530c2s
Faerber, A. v5p0610c1s
Fagan, H.G. v4p0291c1s
Fagan, H.S. v1p0036c1s
v1p0434c2s v1p0464c1s v1p0475c1s
v1p0590c2s v1p0631c1s v1p0654c2s
v1p0655c1s v1p0661c1s v1p0713c1s
v1p1196c1s v1p1227c2s v2p0061c2s
v2p0124c2s v2p0168c1s v2p0225c1s
v2p0225c2s v2p0226c1s v2p0227c1s
v2p0228c1s v2p0331c1s v2p0344c1s
v2p0364c2s v2p0429c1s v2p0448c1s
v3p0198c2s v3p0221c1s v3p0222c1s
v3p0222c2s v3p0236c1s v3p0304c2s
v3p0323c2s v4p0310c1s
Fagan, H.S., Rev. v4p0153c2s
Fagan, Henry S. v2p0479c1s
Fagan, L. v2p0233c1s
v3p0471c2s
Fagan, L. et al. v5p0152c2s
Fage, Arthur v6p0087c1s
Fagnani, E. v1p0294c2s
Faguet, E. v5p0044c2s
v6p0181c1s v6p0630c1s
Faguet, Emile v5p0012c2s
Fahie, J.J. v6p0245c2s
Fahlcrantz, D.E. v3p0295c1s
Fahy, F.A. v6p0328c1s
Faija, H. v1p0211c1s
v2p0072c2s v2p0349c2s
Fair, C. v2p0224c2s
Fair, M.C. v6p0578c1s
Fairall, H.H. v4p0096c1s
v4p0109c2s
Fairbairn and Tate v1p0526c1s
Fairbairn, A. v4p0536c1s
v4p0588c1s
Fairbairn, A.M. v1p0254c2s
v1p0255c1s v1p0528c1s v1p0625c2s
v1p1072c2s v1p1093c1s v1p1167c2s
v1p1235c1s v1p1260c1s v1p1402c2s
v2p0082c1s v2p0182c2s v2p0230c2s
v2p0293c2s v2p0366c1s v2p0368c1s
v2p0368c2m v2p0369c1m v2p0376c1m
v3p0013c2s v3p0070c2s v3p0081c1s
v3p0266c2s v3p0349c2s v3p0358c2s
v3p0365c1s v3p0405c2s v3p0427c2s
v4p0042c1s v4p0169c2s v4p0300c2s
v4p0301c1s v4p0353c2s v4p0402c1s
v4p0478c2s v4p0573c1s v4p0597c1s
v5p0023c2s v5p0257c2s v5p0271c2s
v5p0286c2m v5p0311c1m v5p0338c1s
v5p0473c1s v5p0483c2s v5p0514c2s
v5p0611c2s v5p0626c2s v6p0064c1s
v6p0403c2s v6p0609c2s
Fairbairn, A.M. and Martineau, J.
v4p0042c1s
Fairbairn, C. v5p0351c1s
v5p0477c1s
Fairbairn, E. v4p0151c1s
v4p0413c1s
Fairbairn, H. v1p0045c1s
v1p0664c2s v1p0665c2s v1p1210c1s
Fairbairn, H.F. v1p0231c1s
v1p1248c1s
Fairbairn, M.C. v1p0495c1s
Fairbairn, M.L. v5p0207c1s
v6p0536c1s v6p0683c2s
Fairbairn, R.B. v3p0238c1s
Fairbairn, W. v1p0023c2s
v1p0104c1s v1p0145c2s v1p0146c1m
v1p0146c2s v1p0408c1s v1p0522c2s
v1p0523c1m v1p0665c1s v1p0666c1s
v1p0762c2s v1p0826c1m v1p1079c1s
v1p1079c2s v1p1191c2s v1p1246c2m
v1p1247c1s v1p1251c1s v1p1328c2s
v2p0229c1s v2p0419c2s v2p0433c1s
Fairbairn, W. and Tate, T.
v1p1247c1s
Fairbairn, W., Sir v1p0666c1s
v1p1191c2s v2p0419c1s
Fairbanks, A. v3p0171c1s
v4p0262c1s v4p0439c2s v4p0532c1s
v5p0116c1s v5p0121c2s v5p0223c2s
v5p0250c1s v5p0269c1m v5p0454c1s
v5p0641c2s v6p0029c2s v6p0038c2s
Fairbanks, C. v1p0773c1s
v5p0254c2s
Fairbanks, C. and Gooch, F.A.
v4p0246c1s v4p0377c1s
Fairbanks, C.M. v3p0022c2s
v3p0068c1s v3p0208c2s v3p0303c2s
v4p0199c2s v4p0304c2s v4p0319c1s
v4p0523c1s v5p0207c1s v5p0306c1s
Fairbanks, Charlotte v4p0440c1s
Fairbanks, E.R. v1p0461c2s
Fairbanks, G.R. v1p0462c1s
v1p1075c1s v5p0014c2s
Fairbanks, H.F. v6p0003c2s
Fairbanks, H.W. v4p0609c2s
v5p0134c2s v5p0473c2s v5p0528c2s
v5p0580c2s v6p0156c1s v6p0681c1s
v6p0697c2s
Fairbanks, H.W. and Dixon, L.M.
v5p0384c2s
Fairbanks, M.B. v6p0189c1s
Fairbanks, M.B. and Trask, W.B.
v6p0655c1s
Fairbanks, M.M. v4p0118c2s
v4p0468c2s
Fairbanks, R. v1p0461c2s
Fairbanks, W.H. v5p0393c2s
Fairbridge, W.E. v5p0487c2s
Fairbrother, W.H. v5p0028c1s
v6p0211c2s
Fairburn, W.A. v4p0547c2s
Fairchild, A.B. v6p0330c2s
v6p0332c2s
Fairchild, C.G. v1p0389c1s
v1p1223c2s
Fairchild, C.S. v3p0393c1s
v4p0526c2s v5p0382c2s
Fairchild, D. v6p0104c2s
v6p0219c2s v6p0502c2s v6p0598c2s
Fairchild, D.G. v5p0560c1s
v6p0026c1s
Fairchild, E.M. v4p0111c2s
v5p0107c1s v5p0196c1s
Fairchild, F.R. v6p0217c2s
v6p0654c2s
Fairchild, G.M. v5p0154c2s
Fairchild, G.M., jr. v5p0024c1s
v5p0488c2s
Fairchild, G.T. v5p0459c2s
Fairchild, H.L. v1p0142c2s
v1p0352c1s v1p0380c2s v1p0465c1s
v1p0899c1s v2p0015c2s v2p0055c1s
v5p0234c1s v6p0674c2s
Fairchild, J.H. v1p0271c1s
v1p0704c2s v1p0935c2s v1p1097c1s
v1p1149c1s v1p1200c2s v2p0181c1s
v2p0298c1s v2p0298c2s v2p0355c2s
v2p0413c1s v2p0438c1s v3p0090c1s
v3p0129c2s v3p0310c2s v4p0053c2s
v4p0480c1s v5p0484c2s
Fairchild, L. v3p0195c2s
Fairchild, R. v6p0184c2s
Fairchild, S.C. v5p0335c2s
v5p0336c2s v5p0473c1s v6p0371c2s
v6p0704c1s
Fairclough, H.R. v5p0528c2s
Fairfax, F. v1p1087c2s
Fairfax, J.S. v5p0435c1s
Fairfax, L.R. v1p0589c2s
v1p0851c1s v2p0063c2s v2p0371c1s
v3p0254c2s
Fairfax, M. v1p1123c2s
Fairfield, A.R. v2p0405c1s
Fairfield, E.B. v3p0359c2s
v4p0306c1s v4p0482c1s v5p0307c1s
Fairfield, F.G. v1p0105c2s
v1p0210c1s v1p0315c2s v1p0338c1s
v1p0530c1s v1p1019c2s v1p1186c1s
v1p1212c2s v1p1238c2s v1p1260c1s
v1p1376c2s
v2p0060c1s
Fairfield, S. v4p0442c2s
Fairholt, F.W. v1p0134c1s
v1p0167c2s v1p0370c2s v1p0380c2s
v1p0396c2s v1p0397c1s v1p0505c2s
v1p0570c1s v1p0577c2s v1p0651c2s
v1p0764c2s v1p0834c2s v1p0964c1s
v1p1013c2s v1p1039c1s v1p1082c1s
v1p1082c2s v1p1083c1s v1p1097c2s
v1p1131c1s v1p1186c2s v1p1191c1s
v2p0116c2s v2p0248c2s
Fairley, W. v2p0090c2s
Fairlie, J. v4p0350c2s
Fairlie, J.A. v5p0092c1m
v5p0120c1s v5p0128c2s v5p0159c2s
v5p0338c2s v5p0408c1s v5p0456c2s
v5p0526c1s v6p0098c2s v6p0435c1m
v6p0435c2m
Fairlie, R.F. v1p1076c2s
v3p0352c1s
Fairman, C.E. v6p0496c2s
v6p0601c2s v6p0686c2s v6p0696c1s
Fairman, H.C. v4p0412c2s
Fairman, J. v1p1008c1s
Fairman, M.A. v1p0570c1s
v1p1099c1s
Fairman, M.F. v1p0116c2s
Fairman-Ordish, T. v4p0204c2s
Fairthorne, R.F. v1p0237c1s
Fairweather, W. v6p0025c1s
v6p0055c1s
Faith, E.A. and Stebbins, J.
v6p0068c1s
Faith, G.R. v3p0092c1s
Faithful, E. v1p0418c1s
v1p0775c1s v2p0028c1s v4p0087c1s
Faithful, F.E. v1p0357c2s
Faithfull, E. v1p0643c1s
v1p0696c2s v1p0812c2s v1p0904c2s
v1p0918c2s v1p1351c1m v1p1421c1s
v1p1423c1m v1p1424c2s v1p1426c2s
v2p0480c1s v3p0385c2s v3p0469c1s
Faithfull, F.G. v1p0720c1s
v2p0342c1s
Faithfull, F.G., Mrs. v2p0310c2s
v3p0259c1s
Fake, F.L, jr. v6p0256c2s
Falbe, Count de v2p0195c2m
v2p0397c2s
Falcke, Hannah v6p0219c1s
Falconer, A. v1p0693c1s
v1p0779c2s v1p0907c2s v1p1165c2s
Falconer, E. v2p0397c2s
Falconer, H. v1p0793c2s
Falconer, J.W. v4p0417c1s
v6p0517c2s
Falconer, K. v6p0098c1s
v6p0217c2m v6p0591c2s
Falconer, M.W.M. v5p0326c1s
Falconer, R.A. v5p0060c1s
v5p0268c2s v5p0316c2s v6p0064c2s
v6p0340c2s v6p0344c2s
Falconer, T. v1p0349c1s
v1p0947c2s
Falconer, W.L. v3p0031c2s
v3p0409c2s
Fales, I.C. v5p0166c1s
Fales, W.E.S. v6p0097c2s
v6p0120c1s v6p0490c2s
Fales, Winifred v6p0296c1s
Falk, B.B. v6p0342c2s
Falk, H.J. v4p0580c2s
Falke, H.J.von v1p0968c2s
Falke, J. v1p0062c2s
Falke, J.von v3p0158c1s
Falkenau, A. v6p0304c2s
Falkenau, J.T.M. v1p0518c2s
v1p0581c2s
Falkenburg, P. and Zanten, J.H.Van
v5p0391c2s v5p0571c1s
Falkenburg, Paul v5p0225c2s
Falkenhorst, C. v4p0360c2s
Falkiner, C.L. v5p0296c1s
v5p0491c1s v6p0073c1s v6p0292c2s
v6p0379c2s v6p0618c2s
Falkner, F. v1p1258c2s
Falkner, J.M. v4p0370c1s
v5p0517c1s
Falkner, Moya B. v6p0280c2s
Falkner, R. v6p0065c2s
Falkner, R.P. v3p0105c2m
v3p0336c2s v3p0344c2m v4p0288c1s
v4p0458c2s v4p0546c2s v5p0099c2s
v5p0125c2s v5p0133c1s v5p0143c1s
v5p0149c2s v5p0237c2s v5p0301c2s
v5p0485c2s v5p0615c1s v5p0616c2s
v6p0309c1s v6p0506c2s v6p0522c1m
Fall, D. v5p0277c2s
v5p0507c2m
Fall, G.H. v5p0198c1s
Fall, M. v1p0677c1s
v1p0726c2s v1p0851c2s
Fallaize, E. v6p0007c1s
Falle, B. and Humphreys, G.E.
v2p0130c1s
Fallentyre, S.G. v6p0245c2s
Falley, Ada L. v6p0505c1s
Fallon, J. v2p0103c1s
v2p0184c2s v2p0271c2s v2p0311c1s
v2p0332c1s v2p0337c1s v2p0395c2s
v2p0412c2s v2p0442c2s v2p0460c1s
Fallon, J.T. v3p0465c2s
Falloux, Count v1p0898c1s
Fallow, T.M. v3p0084c2s
v3p0334c1m v4p0560c2s
Fallows, A.K. v6p0039c1s
v6p0078c2s v6p0117c1s v6p0136c2m
v6p0621c2s
Fallows, Alice K. v5p0126c2m
v5p0533c2s v6p0417c1s
Falls, D.W.C. v6p0399c1s
v6p0559c2s v6p0589c1s
Falls, F.W. v4p0499c1s
v4p0575c2s
Falls, R.C. v4p0348c2s
Fambri, P. v4p0043c2s
Fancher, E.L. v1p0005c2s
v1p0244c1s v1p0729c2s v1p1363c1s
v3p0206c1s
Fane, C. v4p0402c1s
Fane, E. v5p0070c1s
Fane, V. v3p0243c2s
v3p0463c2s

Fanning, A.M. v4p0149c2s
Fanning, J.T. v4p0613c2s
Fanning, W.J. and Hawkins, R.C. v4p0265c1s
Fanshawe, F. v3p0382c2s
Fansler, P.E. v6p0494c1s
Fanton, C.J.K. v5p0629c1s
Fanton, M.A. v6p0079c1s
Fanton, Mary A. v6p0142c2s v6p0579c2s
Fanu, E.F.Le v2p0109c1s
Fanu, J.S.Le v1p0023c1s v1p0135c1s v1p0563c2s v1p0574c1m v1p0606c2s v1p0770c2s v1p0812c2s v1p1127c1s v1p1294c1s v1p1434c2s v1p1435c2s v2p0212c2s
Fanu, S.Le v1p0202c1s
Far, S.S. v6p0120c2s
Far, Sui Seen v6p0121c1s
Farabee, W.C. v6p0011c1s
Faraday, E.R. v5p0281c1s
Faraday, F.J. v5p0529c2s v6p0153c1s
Faraday, F.J. et al. v4p0596c1s
Faraday, M. v1p0224c1s v1p0271c2s v1p0304c1s v1p0398c2s v1p0399c1m v1p0400c2m v1p0401c1m v1p0463c2s v1p0467c1s v1p0525c2s v1p0541c2s v1p0562c2s v1p0579c2s v1p0748c1s v1p0787c2m v1p0788c1m v1p1002c2s v1p1091c1s v1p1100c2s v1p1163c1s v1p1279c1s v2p0161c2s
Faraday, W. v6p0301c1s
Farber, C.W. v6p0105c1s
Farbstein, D. v5p0307c2s
Fardell, T.G. and Harrison, C. v4p0338c2s
Farelly, M.J. v4p0172c2s
Farey, J. v1p1246c2s
Farey, J., Sen. v1p0885c1s
Farge, C.G.La v4p0527c2s v5p0361c2s v5p0450c1s
Farge, J.La v3p0226c2s v3p0227c2s v3p0419c2s v4p0297c1s v5p0030c1s v5p0303c2s v5p0373c2s v5p0427c2s v5p0450c2s v5p0473c1s v5p0495c1s v5p0500c1s v5p0550c2s v5p0565c2s v5p0632c2s v6p0012c2s v6p0035c2s v6p0052c1s v6p0183c2s v6p0223c2s v6p0228c2s v6p0475c1s v6p0516c1s v6p0531c2s v6p0538c2s v6p0554c1s v6p0622c2s v6p0675c2s
Farge, John La v5p0258c2s v5p0427c1s v5p0575c2s
Fargo, F.F. v2p0152c2s v2p0249c1s v2p0441c1s
Farias, R. v5p0004c1s
Faries, R. v5p0449c1s
Farina, S. v3p0392c2s v4p0408c1s
Farini, A.H.di v4p0380c2s
Faris, R.C. v3p0296c2m v4p0580c2s
Faris, W.W. v1p1059c1s v4p0056c2s
Farish, T.E. v3p0019c2s
Farjeon, B.L. v1p0683c1s v1p0696c1s v1p0767c1s v1p0773c2s v1p1180c1s v1p1182c2s v2p0049c2s v2p0261c1s v2p0267c2s v2p0394c1s v3p0035c1s v3p0294c2s v3p0383c2s v3p0431c2s
Farleigh, E.A. v5p0168c2s v5p0169c1s
Farler, J.P. v3p0004c1s
Farley, A. v1p0490c2s v1p0958c2s
Farley, A.J. v1p1128c1s
Farley, C.A. v1p1031c1s v4p0605c1s
Farley, F.A. v1p0386c1s v1p0608c1s v1p0805c2s v1p1101c1s v1p1393c2s
Farley, J. v1p1147c1s v1p1439c2m v6p0213c1s
Farley, J.L. v1p0151c1s v1p0397c1s v1p1279c1s v1p1331c1s
Farley, J.M. v4p0565c1s
Farley, J.P. v5p0017c2s v5p0200c1m v6p0328c2s
Farley, S. v1p0285c1s v1p1262c1s
Farley, S.E. v1p0433c1s v1p1421c2s
Farley, S.E., Mrs. v1p0843c1s v1p1045c2s
Farlow, A. v5p0114c2s v5p0530c1s
Farlow, A. and Willis, J.B. v5p0114c2s
Farlow, Alfred v6p0122c2m
Farlow, W.G. v1p0152c2s v1p0153c1s v1p0941c2s v1p0945c2s v1p1173c1s v2p0046c1s v3p0051c2s v4p0268c1s v4p0388c1s v5p0223c1s v5p0545c1s v5p0605c1s v6p0576c2s
Farman, A.E. and Nuttall, G.C. v4p0430c2s
Farman, E. v1p1127c2s v5p0067c1s
Farman, E.E. v2p0318c2s
Farmer, A. v5p0099c1s
Farmer, A.A. v1p0462c1s
Farmer, E.Y. v4p0423c2s
Farmer, G. v6p0199c1s
Farmer, J. v1p0151c1s v1p0179c2s v1p0261c1s v1p0275c1s v1p0275c2s v1p0333c1s v1p0572c2s v1p0590c1s v1p0602c2s v1p0846c1m v1p0846c2s v1p0865c1s v1p0911c2s v1p0938c2s v1p1105c1s v1p1407c1s
Farmer, J.B. v4p0146c1s v5p0099c1s v5p0151c2s v6p0098c2s v6p0106c1s
Farmer, M.G. v1p0747c1s
Farmer, S. v2p0117c1s
Farmer, S.S. v1p0301c1s
Farnam, H.W. v1p0863c1s v2p0245c1s v2p0275c2s v3p0171c1s v3p0338c2s v4p0059c1s v4p0059c2s v4p0458c1s v5p0175c2s v5p0321c1s v5p0340c2s v5p0585c1s v6p0322c2s v6p0356c2s
Farnam, H.W. and Villard, H. v4p0563c1s
Farnell, G.L. v5p0362c1s
Farnell, L.R. v3p0164c2s v3p0292c2s v3p0326c2m v3p0381c1s v4p0030c2s v4p0510c2m v6p0273c1s
Farner, J.B. v5p0125c1s
Farney, J. v3p0268c1s
Farnham, C.H. v1p0611c1s v1p0622c1m v1p0767c1s v1p0916c1s v2p0066c1m v2p0067c1s v2p0245c2s v2p0361c1s v3p0286c1s v3p0286c2s v3p0350c2s v3p0371c2s v3p0372c2s v4p0380c1s
Farnham, Edwin v3p0146c2s
Farnham, I.H. v4p0177c1s
Farnham, J.E. v1p0095c2s v1p0192c1s
Farnham, Mrs. v1p0745c2s
Farnham, R.H. v6p0389c2s
Farnham, S. v2p0330c1s
Farnham, S.M. v6p0052c1s
Farnham, T.H. v1p0941c2s v4p0295c2s
Farnham, T.J. v1p1041c1s
Farnol, J. v6p0125c1s
Farnsworth, C.H. v5p0393c2s
Farnsworth, E.C. and Abhedananda, Swami v5p0608c2s
Farnsworth, P.J. v6p0433c1s
Farnsworth, P.T. v6p0011c2s v6p0392c1s v6p0452c1s
Farnum, H.W. v2p0176c1s v2p0408c1s v3p0345c2s
Farquhar, A. v2p0483c1s v5p0227c2s
Farquhar, A.B. v4p0130c2s v4p0144c1s v4p0517c2s v6p0533c2s
Farquhar, A.B. and Farquhar, H. v4p0423c2s
Farquhar, Anna v5p0206c1s v5p0352c2s
Farquhar, E. v5p0028c1s v5p0057c2s v5p0269c1s v6p0271c2s v6p0586c2s
Farquhar, G. v4p0508c2s
Farquhar, G.G. v4p0001c2s v4p0258c1s v4p0352c2s v4p0413c2s v5p0137c2s v5p0214c1s v5p0485c1s
Farquhar, H. v1p1244c1s v4p0141c2s v4p0144c1s v5p0603c2s
Farquhar, H. and Farquhar, A.B. v4p0423c2s
Farquhar, H.R. v4p0577c2s
Farquhar, M. v1p1085c2s
Farquhar, T. v1p0633c2s
Farquharson, C.D. v3p0150c2s v4p0189c2s v4p0196c2s v4p0207c2s v4p0237c1s v4p0287c2s
Farquharson, Dr. v4p0162c1s
Farquharson, H.R. v3p0149c1s v3p0163c1s v3p0431c1s v4p0112c1s
Farquharson, J. v2p0419c2s v5p0423c1s
Farquharson, R. v3p0256c2s v6p0299c1s v6p0360c2s
Farquharson, R.J. v2p0220c1s
Farr, C.C. v4p0588c1s
Farr, C.C. and Milne, J. . v6p0186c1s
Farr, M.B. v3p0056c1s
Farr, W. v1p0083c2s v1p0229c2s v1p0238c1s v1p0259c1s v1p0304c1s v1p0543c2s v1p0546c2s v1p0628c1s v1p0643c1s v1p0873c1s v1p0873c2s v1p1034c1s v1p1078c2s v1p1246c1s v1p1264c1s v1p1285c2s v1p1361c2s
Farr, W.B. v2p0290c2s
Farrah, M. v6p0285c1s v6p0663c1s
Farrah, Mary v6p0101c1s
Farrally, P. v5p0217c1s
Farrand, L. v5p0013c2s v5p0288c2s v6p0053c1s v6p0441c1s v6p0660c1s
Farrand, L. and Cattell, J.McK. v4p0125c2s
Farrand, L. and Warren, H.C. v4p0464c2s
Farrand, M. v5p0157c2s v5p0312c1s v5p0568c2s v5p0574c1s v6p0655c2s v6p0666c2s
Farrand, Max v6p0077c2s v6p0315c2s
Farrand, W. v4p0123c1s v6p0135c2s
Farrand, Wilson v6p0135c1s v6p0136c2s
Farrant, H. v5p0555c1s
Farrant, R. v6p0553c1s
Farrar, A. v3p0256c1s
Farrar, A., jr. v2p0113c2s
Farrar, A.E. v1p1152c1s
Farrar, A.S. v1p0180c2s
Farrar, C.C.S. v1p0309c2s v1p0594c2s
Farrar, E. v2p0160c2s v5p0090c2s v5p0091c1s v5p0241c2s v5p0504c2s
Farrar, E.H. v4p0342c1s
Farrar, F.W. v1p0060c2s v1p0249c1s v1p0391c2s v1p0426c1s v1p0686c2s v1p0998c2m v1p1085c1s v1p1161c2s v2p0001c1s v2p0022c2s v2p0023c2s v2p0044c1m v2p0083c1s v2p0083c2s v2p0124c1s v2p0169c2s v2p0203c2s v2p0236c1s v2p0280c2s v2p0282c2s v2p0351c2s v2p0383c2s v2p0417c1s v2p0432c1s v2p0460c2s v3p0004c1s v3p0007c1s v3p0009c2s v3p0015c1s v3p0015c2s v3p0020c2s v3p0022c1s v3p0025c1s v3p0026c2s v3p0030c1s v3p0037c1s v3p0038c2m v3p0041c1s v3p0050c1s v3p0056c2s v3p0070c1m v3p0077c1s v3p0080c2s v3p0081c1s v3p0081c2s v3p0082c2s v3p0093c1s v3p0106c1s v3p0110c1s v3p0114c1s v3p0141c2s v3p0142c1s v3p0150c1s v3p0151c1s v3p0158c1s v3p0159c2s v3p0166c1s v3p0183c2s v3p0205c1s v3p0208c1s v3p0216c1s v3p0229c1s v3p0234c1s v3p0235c2s v3p0251c1s v3p0260c1s v3p0279c2s v3p0285c1s v3p0300c1m v3p0314c1s v3p0338c2s v3p0349c1s v3p0357c2s v3p0374c1s v3p0385c1s v3p0397c2s v3p0413c2s v3p0427c2s v3p0428c2s v3p0431c2s v3p0432c1s v3p0449c2s v3p0460c1s v3p0461c1m v3p0462c2s v4p0002c1s v4p0042c1s v4p0046c1s v4p0051c1s v4p0068c1s v4p0074c2s v4p0103c2s v4p0109c1s v4p0109c2s v4p0139c2s v4p0218c1s v4p0231c1s v4p0287c1m v4p0300c1s v4p0300c2s v4p0305c2m v4p0325c2s v4p0326c2s v4p0328c2s v4p0339c2s v4p0344c2s v4p0349c1m v4p0420c2s v4p0456c2s v4p0460c1s v4p0477c1s v4p0485c1m v4p0488c2s v4p0497c2s v4p0498c2s v4p0543c2s v4p0548c2s v4p0561c2s v4p0568c1s v4p0613c2s v4p0618c1m v4p0626c2s v5p0069c2s v5p0087c1s v5p0152c2s v5p0281c1s v5p0306c1s v5p0314c2s v5p0377c1s v5p0522c1s v5p0561c2s v5p0576c2s v5p0582c1s v6p0062c2s
Farrar, F.W. and Manning, H.E.C. v3p0255c1s
Farrar, F.W. et al. v3p0084c2s v3p0342c1s v4p0170c1s
Farrar, H.B. v6p0209c1s
Farrar, I.F. v6p0374c1s
Farrar, I.F. and Lane, E.N. v5p0069c2s v5p0334c2s
Farrar, J. v1p0050c2s v1p0070c1m v1p0281c2s v1p0573c1s v1p0732c2s v1p0776c2s v1p0936c1s v1p1100c2s v1p1162c2s v1p1268c2s v1p1310c2s v1p1348c1s v1p1396c2s
Farrar, J.M. v1p0335c1s v1p1343c2s
Farrar, R. v6p0648c2s
Farrar, T. v1p0006c1s v1p0366c1s v1p0445c1s v1p0573c1s v1p1245c1s v1p1264c2s v1p1296c1s v1p1343c2s
Farrell, E. v6p0574c1s
Farrell, H.F.E. v6p0565c1s
Farrell, J.F. v6p0376c2s
Farrell, J.W. v2p0093c2s
Farrell, R.F. v1p0654c1s v1p0661c2s v2p0085c2s v2p0225c1s
Farrell, T.C. v5p0442c2s
Farrell, T.G. v3p0417c1s
Farrelly, M.J. v4p0106c1s v4p0287c2s v4p0297c2s v4p0348c1s v4p0412c1s v6p0006c2s v6p0007c1m v6p0448c2s
Farrelly, P. v6p0242c1s v6p0252c1s
Farren, W. v1p0944c1s v1p1185c1s v1p1185c2s
Farrer, E. v1p0193c2s v2p0066c1s v4p0373c2s v5p0019c2s v6p0096c1m v6p0097c1s v6p0266c1s

Farrer, F.H. v1p0295c2s
Farrer, J.A. v1p0439c2s
v1p0464c1s v1p0803c2s v1p0868c1s
v1p0890c2s v1p0986c1s v1p1042c2s
v1p1059c2s v1p1153c1m v1p1334c2s
v1p1441c2s v2p0014c2s v2p0015c1s
v2p0034c2s v2p0039c1s v2p0061c2s
v2p0160c1s v2p0186c2s v2p0237c1s
v2p0288c2m v2p0304c2s v2p0308c1s
v2p0417c2s v2p0445c2s v2p0465c2m
v2p0466c1s v3p0014c1s v3p0036c2s
v3p0047c2s v3p0050c1m v3p0060c2s
v3p0066c2s v3p0163c2s v3p0176c2s
v3p0225c2s v3p0226c1s v3p0238c1s
v3p0268c2s v3p0283c2s v3p0370c1s
v3p0379c1s v3p0407c2s v3p0428c1s
v3p0432c2s v3p0435c2s v3p0456c2s
v4p0238c2s
Farrer, J.A. and Buxton, S.C.
v1p0657c1s
Farrer, J.A. et al. v1p0657c1s
Farrer, J.C. v2p0143c1s
Farrer, J.S. v3p0224c2s
Farrer, Lord v4p0144c1s
v4p0172c2m v4p0179c2s v4p0247c2s
v4p0382c1s v4p0449c2s v4p0532c1s
v4p0546c2s
Farrer, Lord and Francis, Thos.
v5p0584c1s
Farrer, Lord et al. v4p0476c1s
v4p0596c1s
Farrer, R.J. v6p0249c1s
v6p0354c1s
Farrer, T.C. v3p0352c1s
Farrer, T.H. v1p0301c1s
v1p0449c2s v1p0550c2s v1p0721c1s
v2p0363c2s v3p0181c2s v3p0257c2s
v3p0421c1s v3p0457c2s v4p0563c2s
Farrer, T.H., Sir v5p0203c1s
Farrer, T.H., Sir et al. . v4p0239c1s
Farrer, W. v5p0621c1s
Farrington, C.E. v6p0199c1s
Farrington, F. v5p0061c1s
v5p0384c2s
Farrington, F.L. and Wilson, B.
v5p0328c2s
Farrington, O.C. v3p0029c2s
v4p0288c2s v5p0153c2s v5p0203c1s
v5p0372c1m v5p0385c1s v5p0393c1m
v5p0528c2s v6p0149c1s v6p0412c2m
v6p0437c1s v6p0685c2s
Farrington, S. v1p0483c1s
Farrow, F.R. v3p0237c2s
Farrow, M. v1p0601c2s
Farson, J. v6p0045c1s
v6p0113c1s
Farwell, A. v6p0315c2s
v6p0437c2s
Farwell, C.B. v3p0472c2s
v5p0600c2s
Farwell, E.S. v5p0497c2s
v6p0478c2s v6p0615c2s
Farwell, F.M. v3p0044c1s
Farwell, J.V. v6p0598c1s
Farwell, W. v1p0457c1s
v6p0303c1s
Farwell, W.B. v1p0188c1s
v1p1413c1s v3p0063c1s v3p0067c1s
v3p0079c2m v3p0163c1s v5p0088c2s
Fassett, E.C.B. and Towsend, C.H.
v6p0338c1s
Fassett, F.G. v6p0100c1s
Fassett, J.S. v3p0085c2s
v6p0354c1s
Fassett, J.Sloat v6p0146c2s
Fassig, O.L. v5p0361c1s
Fassin, A.G. v2p0104c2s
v2p0456c1s v2p0482c2s
Fast, R.E. v6p0651c1s
Fath, E.A. v5p0129c2s
Fatima v3p0173c2s
Fatkin, T. v6p0627c1s
Faucher, L. v1p0474c2s
v1p0545c2s
Fauley, W.F. v5p0041c1s
v5p0362c2s
Faulhaber, C. v6p0367c2s
v6p0637c2s
Faulkener, H.W. v4p0379c2s
Faulkner, C.J. and Babcock, J.W.
v4p0595c2s
Faulkner, J.A. v3p0053c1s
v3p0058c2s v3p0082c2s v3p0463c2s
v4p0113c2s v4p0367c2s v4p0398c2s
v4p0488c2s v6p0304c1s v6p0390c1s
v6p0642c1s v6p0692c1s
Faulkner, R.S. v5p0088c2s
Faunce, D.W. v1p0252c2s
v1p0980c1s
Faunce, G. v4p0366c2s
Faunce, W.H.P. v4p0431c1s
v5p0047c2s v5p0288c2s v5p0463c2s
v6p0039c1s v6p0373c2s v6p0428c1m
Faunce, W.H.P. et al. v4p0054c1s
Faunthorpe, J.P. v4p0362c1s
v5p0234c1s
Faure, D.P. v2p0067c1s
Faure-Favier, Louise v6p0704c1s
Fausset, A.R. v3p0041c1s
v3p0357c1s v3p0383c2s
Faust, A.B. v6p0259c2s
v6p0610c2s
Faust, A.J. v1p0205c2s
v1p0503c2s v1p0819c1s v1p0964c1s
v1p0992c2s v1p1274c1s v2p0048c1s
v2p0106c1s v2p0196c2s v2p0254c1s
v2p0260c2s v2p0263c2s v2p0272c2s
v2p0317c1s v2p0333c2s v2p0416c1s
v2p0420c1s v2p0436c1s v2p0466c2s
v3p0364c1s
Faust, A.J., Mrs. v1p1298c1s
Faust, E.D. v1p0007c1s
Faustini, A. v6p0029c1s
Favaro, A. v4p0218c2s
Favenc, E. v4p0038c2s
v4p0366c1s
Favier, A. v5p0347c2s
Faville, J. v3p0209c1s
v3p0249c2s v3p0432c1s
Faville, M.C. v5p0396c2s
v5p0409c1s v5p0527c1s v5p0548c1s
v5p0619c2s
Faville, Malinda C. v5p0413c2s
v5p0522c1s
Favour, L. v1p0561c1s
Favre, C. v6p0266c2s
Fawcett, A. v4p0482c1s
Fawcett, Cicely D. v5p0099c2s
Fawcett, E. v1p0020c1s
v1p0157c2s v1p0189c2s v1p0443c1s
v1p0577c1s v1p0593c1s v1p0704c1s
v1p0755c2s v1p0795c1s v1p0802c1s
v1p0942c2s v1p1055c2s v1p1091c2s
v1p1230c2s v1p1307c2s v1p1405c2s
v1p1416c1s v1p1433c1s v1p1437c1s
v2p0233c1s v2p0252c1s v2p0293c2s
v2p0423c2s v2p0436c2s v2p0441c2s
v3p0057c2s v3p0093c2s v3p0106c1s
v3p0121c1s v3p0312c1s v3p0332c2s
v3p0350c2s v3p0354c1s v3p0362c1s
v3p0400c1s v3p0410c1s v3p0411c1s
v3p0422c1s v3p0470c2s v4p0002c2s
v4p0063c2s v4p0126c2s v4p0160c2s
v4p0194c2s v4p0274c2s v4p0334c2s
v4p0358c2s v4p0392c2s v4p0399c2s
v4p0412c2s v4p0529c1s v4p0603c2s
v4p0615c1s v5p0251c2s v5p0339c2s
v5p0596c1s v6p0179c2s v6p0249c1s
v6p0319c2s v6p0324c1s v6p0464c1s
v6p0540c2s v6p0672c2s
Fawcett, E.D. v4p0249c1s
v4p0273c2s v4p0439c1s v4p0475c1s
v4p0572c2s
Fawcett, Edgar v3p0304c1s
v4p0395c1s v4p0453c2s v5p0084c2s
v5p0210c2s v5p0458c2s v5p0609c1s
v6p0018c2s v6p0630c1s
Fawcett, F. v4p0050c2s
v4p0280c2s v5p0385c2s
Fawcett, H. v1p0015c1s
v1p0185c1s v1p0230c1s v1p0284c2s
v1p0299c1s v1p0299c2s v1p0533c1s
v1p0549c2s v1p0550c1s v1p0550c2s
v1p0607c1s v1p0631c1m v1p0721c1s
v1p0981c1s v1p1026c1s v1p1215c2s
v1p1216c1s v1p1232c2s v1p1285c2s
v1p1356c2s v1p1394c1s v2p0248c1s
Fawcett, H., Mrs. v4p0169c2s
Fawcett, J.F.M. v4p0402c1m
v5p0423c1s v6p0563c1s
Fawcett, M. v6p0217c2s
Fawcett, M.G. v1p0897c2s
v1p1099c1m v1p1214c1s v1p1422c2m
v1p1423c1s v1p1424c1s v2p0477c1s
v2p0477c2s v2p0478c1s v3p0077c2s
v3p0268c2s v3p0468c2s v3p0470c1m
v4p0011c1s v4p0080c1s v4p0240c2s
v4p0398c2s v4p0401c2s v4p0627c2s
v4p0628c2s v4p0630c1m v5p0606c2s
v6p0006c2s v6p0294c2s
Fawcett, M.G. and Dilke, M.M.
v3p0470c1s
Fawcett, M.G. and Hopkins, E.
v2p0178c2s
Fawcett, M.G. and Manning, Cardinal
v3p0268c2s
Fawcett, M.G. et al. v4p0630c1s
Fawcett, M.Y. and Glennie, J.S.S.
v3p0470c1s
Fawcett, P.H. v6p0430c1s
v6p0430c2s
Fawcett, W. v3p0283c2s
v5p0050c1s v5p0274c2s v5p0298c1s
v5p0298c2s v5p0418c2s v5p0506c1s
v5p0526c1s v5p0551c2m v5p0559c1s
v5p0561c1s v6p0082c2s v6p0260c1s
v6p0261c2s v6p0393c1s v6p0509c2s
v6p0515c1s v6p0566c1s v6p0623c2s
v6p0637c1s v6p0637c2s v6p0666c1s
Fawcett, W.L. v2p0242c2s
Fawcett, Waldon v5p0193c2s
v6p0043c2s v6p0687c2s
Fawcette, W.L. v1p0188c1s
v1p0227c2s v1p0282c2s v1p0877c1s
Fawkes, E.M. v5p0500c2s
Fawks, F.A. v2p0019c2s
v2p0208c1s
Faxon, C.E. v4p0061c1s
v4p0134c1s
Faxon, F.W. v5p0440c2s
Faxon, J.L. v4p0002c2s
v6p0616c1s
Faxon, W. and Whorf, E.H.. v6p0641c1s
Fay, A. v1p0752c1s
v1p0885c2s v5p0159c1s
Fay, A.M. v1p0175c1s
Fay, Amy v5p0267c2s
v5p0394c1s v5p0636c1s
Fay, C.D. v3p0091c2s
Fay, C.E. v2p0249c2s
v4p0241c2s v5p0013c2s v6p0433c1s
Fay, C.E. et al. v4p0320c2s
Fay, C.H. v1p0744c2s
v1p0847c1s v1p1056c2s v1p1203c2s
Fay, C.N. v2p0138c1s
Fay, E. v1p1042c2s
Fay, E.W. v4p0003c2s
v4p0007c1s v4p0229c1s v5p0261c2s
v5p0290c2s v5p0454c1s v5p0532c1s
v6p0212c2m v6p0362c2s v6p0503c2s
Fay, Edwin W. v6p0317c2s
Fay, F.H. v5p0210c2s
Fay, G. v1p0720c1s
v1p1145c2s v2p0125c1s v4p0200c2s
v4p0219c1s
Fay, H.W. v3p0439c1s
Fay, J. v5p0224c2s
Fay, J.S. v2p0316c1s
Fay, S.B. v5p0188c1s
Fay, T.S. v1p0104c2s
v1p0114c2s v1p0384c1s v1p1103c2s
Fay, T.S., Mrs. v1p0490c1s
Fayant, F. v6p0009c2s
v6p0037c1s v6p0198c1s v6p0457c2s
v6p0578c1s v6p0693c2s
Faye and Leverrier v1p1014c1s
Faye, C.de v2p0182c2s
Faye, H. and Lapparent, A.de
v2p0319c1s
Faye, H.A.E. v1p0282c1s
v1p1256c2s
Faye, M. v1p0282c1s
v1p0829c2s v2p0096c1s v2p0409c1s
Fayes, H. v5p0638c1s
Fayrer, J. v1p0420c2s
v1p1269c2s v1p1310c2s v2p0139c1s
v2p0218c2s v2p0473c2s v3p0213c1s
v3p0273c1s
Fayrer, J., Sir v3p0014c2s
v3p0397c1m
Fayrer, J., Sir et al. ... v3p0146c1s
Fea, A. v3p0030c1s
v3p0074c2s v3p0095c1s v6p0456c1s
Fearn, R.L. v4p0100c2s
v5p0050c1s
Fearnley, J. v5p0171c1s
v5p0386c1s
Fearon, D.R. v1p0385c2s
v1p1063c1s v1p1422c1s v5p0152c2m
Fearon, J.S. v5p0109c1s
Fearon, J.S. and Allen, E.P.
v5p0111c2s
Feasey, D.H.P. v6p0350c2s
v6p0490c1s v6p0565c2s
Feasey, H.J. v4p0166c2s
v5p0064c2s v5p0322c1s v5p0437c1s
v5p0508c2s
Feasey, H.P. v5p0118c2s
v5p0496c2s v5p0615c1s v6p0423c1s
Feaston, J.T. v1p1061c2s
v1p1201c1s
Feather, A.G. v1p0997c1s
v1p1160c1s v1p1197c2s v1p1286c1s
v1p1361c2s
Featherman, A. v1p0475c1s
Featherstone, A. v1p1001c2s
Featherstone, H.C. v5p0351c2s
Featherstone, W.B. v5p0560c2s
Featherstonehaugh, T. v6p0420c1s
Featherstonhaugh, G.W. ... v1p0507c1s
Febvre, F. v4p0003c1s
Fechet, E.G. v4p0528c1s
Fedchenko, A. v1p0955c1s
Fee, C.S. v6p0567c2s
Fee, J. v2p0151c1s
v2p0345c2s v2p0386c1s
Fee, W.T. v6p0073c1s
v6p0481c2s
Feeling, B. v3p0109c2s
Feeney, C. v5p0352c1s
Feetham, F.B. v4p0232c2s
Feetham, R. v5p0273c2s
Feierabend, A. v2p0383c1s
Feiker, F.M. v6p0197c1s
v6p0540c2s
Feilberg, C.A. v3p0219c2s
Feilberg, H.F. v4p0263c1s
Feilde, M.H. v1p0850c2s
Feilding, W. v2p0173c1s
Feilom, James M. v6p0166c2s
Feinberg, I. v4p0564c2s
Felch, W.F. v2p0124c1s
v5p0038c2s v5p0067c2s
Feldhaus, F.M. v6p0043c2s
Feldman, A. v5p0056c1s
Feldman, W.H. v6p0630c1s
Feldmann, S. v2p0460c2s
Felice, M.de v1p0846c2s
Felix, E.G. v6p0697c1s
Felix, F. v5p0629c2s

Felkin, H.M. v3p0218c1s
Felkin, R.W. v3p0131c1s
v4p0589c1s v5p0540c1s
Felkin, W. v3p0239c2s
Felkins, H.M. v3p0171c2s
Fell, E.F.B. v5p0550c1s
Fell, E.L. v5p0389c2s
Fell, H. v3p0196c2s
v3p0210c2s
Fell, H.G. v6p0074c1s
Fell, J.B. v3p0352c1s
Fell, W. v2p0162c2s
Fell-Smith, C. v4p0494c2s
Fellenberg, W.De v1p0447c2s
v1p0993c2s v1p1396c2s
Fellner, E. v4p0602c2s
Fellom, J.M. v6p0690c1s
Fellowes, A. v2p0030c2s
v2p0051c1s v2p0246c1s v3p0085c1s
v3p0193c2s
Fellowes, E.C. v6p0420c2s
Fellowes, F.W. v1p0955c2m
v3p0022c1s v3p0026c1s v3p0092c2s
v3p0093c1s v3p0422c2s v3p0432c1s
v3p0474c1s
Fellows, A. v6p0004c2s
v6p0069c1s v6p0149c1s v6p0209c2s
v6p0294c1s v6p0304c1m v6p0402c2s
v6p0519c1s v6p0532c1s v6p0675c2s
Fellows, Alfred v6p0183c2s
Fellows, C. v1p0918c2s
Fellows, E.C. v1p0348c2s
Fellows, E.C., Mrs. v2p0206c1s
v2p0317c2s
Fellows, G. v6p0461c1s
Fellows, G.E. v4p0020c1s
v6p0137c1s
Fellows, J.D. v5p0334c1s
Fellows, J.W. v2p0362c2s
v5p0359c2s
Fellows, R. v2p0011c1s
Fellows, S.N. v1p0351c1s
v1p0385c2s v1p0652c1s v1p0926c1s
Fells, B.F. v5p0507c2s
v5p0607c2s
Fells, J.M. v5p0506c1s
Felsburg, D. v6p0599c1s
Felsenthal, B. v1p1279c1s
Felsenthal, E.T. and Romero, M.
v4p0140c1s
Felt, E.P. and Young, D.B.
v6p0362c1s
Felt, J.B. v1p0151c1s
v1p0287c2s v1p0425c1s v1p0590c1s
v1p0707c1s v1p0779c2s v1p0809c2s
v1p0846c1s v1p0896c2s v1p0909c2s
Felter, F.A. v6p0100c1s
Felter, W.L. v6p0704c1s
Felton, C.C. v1p0008c2s
v1p0019c1s v1p0024c1m v1p0027c1s
v1p0045c1s v1p0057c2s v1p0062c1s
v1p0062c2s v1p0107c1s v1p0141c2s
v1p0152c1s v1p0167c2s v1p0190c1s
v1p0228c2s v1p0262c1m v1p0275c1s
v1p0276c1s v1p0300c2s v1p0319c2s
v1p0330c1s v1p0348c1s v1p0350c1m
v1p0377c2s v1p0380c2s v1p0405c2s
v1p0414c1s v1p0415c1s v1p0418c1s
v1p0429c1s v1p0433c1s v1p0446c2s
v1p0468c1s v1p0510c1s v1p0513c2s
v1p0530c1s v1p0552c2s v1p0553c1s
v1p0554c1s v1p0555c1m v1p0559c1s
v1p0573c1s v1p0589c2s v1p0600c2s
v1p0601c1m v1p0615c2s v1p0711c2s
v1p0717c2s v1p0719c1s v1p0753c2s
v1p0768c1m v1p0774c2s v1p0914c1s
v1p0921c1s v1p0946c1s v1p0959c1s
v1p1020c1s v1p1029c2s v1p1131c1s
v1p1148c1s v1p1199c2s v1p1231c1m
v1p1238c1s v1p1281c1s v1p1295c2s
v1p1340c1s v1p1386c1s v1p1400c1m
v1p1400c2s v1p1404c2s v1p1412c1s
v1p1412c2s v1p1425c2s v1p1428c2m
v1p1430c2s v2p0032c2s v2p0244c1s
v2p0259c2s
Felton, C.C. and Bowen, F.
v1p0413c2s
Felton, C.C. and Gray, A.. v1p0437c1s
Felton, C.C. and Palfrey, J.G.
v1p1011c1s
Felton, C.C. and Sparks, J.
v1p0636c2s
Felton, C.E. v4p0459c2s
Felton, E.C. v4p0051c1s
v5p0531c2s
Felton, E.W. v2p0190c1s
v2p0190c2s v2p0244c1s v2p0349c2s
Felton, K. v5p0321c2s
Felton, R.A. v3p0098c2s
Felton, T. v2p0454c2s
Felton, T.C. v1p0886c1s
v3p0154c2s
Felts, P. v1p0248c2s
v1p0495c2s v4p0299c2s
Feltus, B.B. v1p1306c1s
Fendall, P. v1p0859c2s
Fendler, A. v1p1041c1s
Fenely, S.G. v2p0471c2s
Fenimore, C. v1p0298c2s
Fenlon, J.F. v6p0060c2s
v6p0262c2s
Fenn, A.H. v3p0095c2s
Fenn, A.M. v2p0210c1s
v2p0314c1s v2p0427c2m
Fenn, C.H. v5p0438c2s
Fenn, Courtney H. v6p0119c2s
Fenn, E.W. v5p0148c2s
Fenn, G.M. v1p0342c1s
v1p0374c1s v2p0378c1s v2p0439c1s
v3p0107c2s v3p0176c2s v3p0191c1s
v3p0344c1s v3p0440c2s v4p0175c2s
v4p0197c2s v4p0409c1s v4p0558c1s
v5p0100c2s v5p0396c1s v5p0597c1s
v6p0001c1s
Fenn, Geo.M. v4p0387c2s
Fenn, H. and Keeler, A.R.. v1p0939c1s
Fenn, H. and Keeler, R. .. v1p1012c2s
Fenn, W.H. v2p0085c2s
Fenn, W.W. v1p0103c2s
v1p0116c2s v1p0223c2s v1p0365c2s
v1p0439c2s v1p0441c2s v1p0578c1s
v1p0609c1s v1p0764c1s v1p0765c1s
v1p0888c1s v1p0958c1s v1p0959c1s
v1p1107c1s v1p1130c1s v1p1167c1s
v1p1361c1s v1p1378c1s v1p1406c2s
v1p1408c1s v2p0041c1s v2p0049c2s
v2p0111c1s v2p0111c2s v2p0156c2s
v2p0161c1s v2p0177c2s v2p0205c1s
v2p0248c2m v2p0281c1s v3p0022c1s
v3p0113c2s v3p0122c2s v3p0172c2s
v3p0283c2s v3p0311c1s v3p0332c1s
v4p0019c2s v4p0032c1m v4p0083c1s
v4p0120c1s v4p0199c1s v4p0215c2s
v4p0233c2s v4p0246c1s v4p0263c1s
v4p0270c1s v4p0317c1s v4p0319c1m
v4p0319c2m v4p0340c1s v4p0344c2s
v4p0356c1s v4p0404c1s v4p0421c1s
v4p0485c1s v4p0502c2s v4p0517c1s
v4p0550c2s v4p0552c1s v4p0559c1s
v4p0622c2s v4p0635c1s v5p0324c2s
v5p0376c1s v5p0541c1s v6p0367c1s
v6p0417c2s v6p0555c1s v6p0597c2s
Fennel, J.C. v6p0711c1s
Fennell, M. v6p0209c1s
Fennell, W.J. v6p0664c1s
Fenner, C.E. v3p0245c1s
v3p0365c2s
Fenner, E.D., Dr. v1p1437c1s
Fenner, H.K. v3p0281c1s
v4p0374c1s
Fenners, J.M. v4p0155c2s
Fenning, F. v6p0488c1s
Fenollosa, E.F. v4p0106c2s
v4p0296c2s v4p0298c2s v5p0173c2s
v5p0303c2s
Fenton, C.J.K. v4p0073c1s
v4p0127c1s v4p0201c2s v4p0350c2s
v4p0386c1s v4p0528c1s v5p0027c1s
v6p0257c1s
Fenton, D.W. v5p0475c1s
Fenton, D.W., jr. v5p0141c1s
Fenton, E.D. v1p0716c2s
Fenton, F. v1p1016c1s
v3p0002c2s v4p0469c1s
Fenton, F.D. v1p0184c2s
v1p0919c1s
Fenton, H. v1p1385c2s
Fenton, H.J.H. v6p0112c1s
Fenton, I. v1p0221c2s
v1p0750c2s
Fenton, I.D. v1p0083c1s
v1p0439c2s v1p1166c2s v1p1273c1s
v1p1403c1s
Fenton, J. v1p0236c2s
v1p0530c1s v1p0565c1s v1p0651c1s
v1p0690c2s v1p1109c2s v2p0128c2s
v2p0332c1s v2p0352c1s v4p0059c2s
Fenton, J.D. v1p0615c2s
v1p0986c1s
Fenton, V. v5p0233c1s
Fenton, W.H. v4p0058c1s
v4p0145c1s
Fenwick, B. v1p0957c2s
Fenwick, B., Mrs. v5p0416c2s
Fenwick, Ethel A. v5p0634c1s
Fenwick, L. v5p0466c1s
v6p0397c2s
Fenwick, R. v2p0180c1s
Fenwick, T. v1p0146c2s
v1p0666c1s v1p0984c1s
Fenyi, J. v4p0556c2m
v4p0557c1s
Ferd, S.P. v1p0714c1s
v1p1426c2s
Fere, C. v4p0179c2s
v4p0255c2s v4p0284c1s
Fere, C. and Binet, A. ... v3p0206c1s
Fereira, H.W. v2p0002c2s
Feres, A.De v3p0237c1s
Fergus v3p0198c1s
Fergus and Rodwell v1p1159c1s
Ferguson v5p0453c2s
Ferguson, A. v4p0288c1s
Ferguson, A.F. v5p0425c1s
v6p0124c2s
Ferguson, C. v3p0036c1s
v3p0040c2s v3p0296c1s v3p0301c1s
v5p0028c1s v6p0089c1s v6p0170c1s
v6p0263c2s
Ferguson, Chancellor v3p0068c2s
Ferguson, D. v6p0706c1s
Ferguson, E.H. v4p0594c1s
Ferguson, E.M. v6p0642c1s
Ferguson, F.L. v2p0147c1s
Ferguson, H. v1p0123c2s
v3p0042c2s v3p0193c1s v3p0350c1s
Ferguson, H.M. v6p0462c2m
Ferguson, J. v1p0032c2s
v1p0176c1s v1p0230c2s v1p0331c1s
v1p0335c1s v1p0451c1s v1p0621c1s
v1p0685c1s v1p1035c2s v1p1204c2s
v2p0471c1s v4p0108c2s v4p0170c2s
v4p0286c2s v4p0312c2s v4p0397c2s
v5p0127c2s v5p0453c1s v5p0466c1s
v6p0360c2s v6p0577c2s v6p0634c1s
Ferguson, J.C. v6p0119c2s
Ferguson, J.J. v6p0063c2s
Ferguson, J.L. v6p0247c2s
Ferguson, M.C. v6p0611c1s
Ferguson, M.E. v6p0242c1s
Ferguson, M.F. v6p0369c1s
Ferguson, Mr. v1p0269c2s
Ferguson, R. v1p0371c1s
v2p0305c1s v3p0440c1s
Ferguson, R.H. v2p0426c2m
Ferguson, R.M. v4p0318c1s
v6p0233c1s v6p0360c1s v6p0514c2s
v6p0701c2s
Ferguson, R.S. v2p0068c1s
v2p0101c1s v2p0302c1s v2p0327c1s
v2p0375c1s v3p0359c2s v4p0114c2s
v4p0362c1s v5p0094c2s
Ferguson, S. v1p1408c2s
Ferguson, S. et al. v1p0446c1s
Ferguson, S.H. v5p0546c2s
Ferguson, T. v1p0502c2s
Ferguson, T.D. v6p0346c1s
Ferguson, W. v1p0337c2s
v1p0566c1s v2p0136c1s
Ferguson, W.B. v3p0355c2s
v6p0637c2s
Ferguson, W.B.M. v6p0103c1s
v6p0243c1s v6p0393c1s v6p0619c1s
v6p0701c1s
Ferguson, W.L. v4p0057c1s
Ferguson, W.S. v6p0272c1s
Fergusson, A. v2p0146c1s
Fergusson, A.W. and Walker, N.L.
v5p0464c1s
Fergusson, A.W. et al. ... v5p0464c1s
Fergusson, H.A. v5p0010c1s
Fergusson, J. v1p0052c1s
v1p0052c2m v1p0761c2s v1p1144c2s
v2p0261c2s v3p0018c2s v3p0318c2s
v3p0339c2s v4p0088c2s v4p0131c1s
v4p0194c1s v4p0218c2s v4p0237c1s
v4p0372c1s v6p0673c2s
Fergusson, N.A. v3p0099c2s
Fergusson, S.P. v6p0433c2s
Fergusson, W.
v1p0644c1s
Fermor, M. v6p0590c2s
Fermor, O.A. v4p0273c1s
Fernald, B.B. v5p0586c1s
Fernald, C.B. v4p0092c1s
v4p0142c1s v4p0185c1s v4p0222c1s
v4p0428c1s v4p0454c2s v4p0581c2s
v5p0104c2s v5p0325c2s v5p0338c2s
v5p0383c2s v5p0596c2s v5p0644c1s
v6p0344c2s v6p0520c2s
Fernald, C.H. v4p0185c1s
Fernald, Chester B. v6p0078c1s
Fernald, F.A. v2p0015c1s
v2p0021c1s v2p0088c1s v2p0128c2s
v2p0250c2s v2p0402c1s v2p0406c2s
v2p0414c1s v2p0417c1s v2p0418c1s
v2p0429c1s v3p0080c2s v3p0169c1s
v3p0193c2s v3p0207c1s v3p0236c1s
v3p0379c1s v3p0391c2s v3p0423c2s
v3p0450c1s v4p0098c2s v4p0101c1s
v4p0222c1s v4p0602c1s v5p0340c2s
v5p0468c1s
Fernald, G.P. v6p0593c1s
v6p0676c2s v6p0679c1s
Fernald, Grace M. v6p0046c2s
Fernald, H.H. v5p0207c2s
Fernald, J.C. v1p0476c1s
v2p0221c2s v5p0106c1s v6p0225c1s
Fernald, M.C. v3p0264c2s
Fernald, M.L. v5p0035c1s
v6p0067c1s
Fernald, O.M. and Canfield, J.H.
v4p0122c2s
Fernald, R.H. v6p0204c2s
Fernald, W.E. v4p0196c2s
Fernald, W.M. v1p0106c1s
v1p0215c1s v1p0487c1s v1p1000c1s
v1p1060c1s v1p1274c2s
Fernall, C.B. v6p0681c1s
Fernandis, S.C. v6p0447c1s
Fernback, O.H. v5p0094c1s
Fernie, J. v1p0339c2m
Fernie, John v3p0463c1s
Fernow, B. v1p1388c1s
v3p0008c2s v4p0554c2s v6p0564c2s
Fernow, B.E. v3p0158c1m
v3p0435c2m v4p0207c2m v4p0208c1m
v4p0209c1s v4p0233c1s v4p0271c1s
v4p0367c1s v4p0443c2m v4p0552c2s
v4p0583c1s v5p0028c1s v5p0214c1s

v5p0214c2s v5p0351c1s v5p0639c1s v6p0188c1s
Fernow, B.E. and Hersey, Edmund v4p0443c2s
Fernow, C.L. v1p1083c1s
Fernseed, F. v2p0106c1s v2p0106c2s v2p0145c2s v2p0149c1s v2p0213c1m v2p0390c2s v2p0476c1s
Ferrante, G.M. v6p0517c2s
Ferranti, S.C.de and Ince, Francis v3p0132c2s
Ferrar, W.J. v4p0426c2s v4p0590c2s v5p0122c2s v5p0313c1s v5p0342c2s v5p0533c2s v5p0626c2s
Ferrari, G.C. v6p0521c2s
Ferrario, M. v4p0294c2s v5p0075c2s
Ferraris, C.F. v5p0459c2s
Ferraris, M. v6p0332c1s
Ferree, B. v3p0018c1m v3p0018c2m v3p0021c2s v3p0022c1s v3p0070c2s v3p0146c1s v3p0187c2s v3p0292c2s v3p0449c2s v4p0023c2m v4p0024c2m v4p0078c1s v4p0078c2s v4p0092c2m v4p0099c2s v4p0100c2s v4p0116c1s v4p0438c1s v4p0506c1s v5p0097c1s v5p0329c1s v6p0087c1s v6p0501c1s
Ferree, B. and Lamb, C.R.. v5p0467c2s
Ferree, Barr v4p0017c2s v4p0023c2m v4p0030c1s v4p0112c1s v4p0338c1s v5p0025c2s v5p0399c2s
Ferree, C.E. v6p0040c2s
Ferrel, M. v4p0010c2s
Ferrel, W. v1p0099c2m v1p0327c2s v1p0651c1s v1p0829c1m v1p0875c2s v1p0922c2s v1p0936c2s v1p1310c1s v1p1414c1s v2p0090c1s v2p0199c1s v2p0296c2s v2p0313c1s v2p0393c1m v2p0434c1s v2p0475c1s v3p0108c2m v3p0192c2m v3p0196c1s v3p0415c2s v4p0046c1s
Ferrell, C.C. v5p0196c2s
Ferrell, H.J. v6p0706c1s
Ferrell, J.L. v5p0208c1s
Ferrell, L.C. v5p0604c1s v6p0669c2s
Ferrero, C. v4p0365c2s
Ferrero, G. v4p0140c1s v4p0626c2s v4p0627c2s v5p0155c1s v5p0351c2s v5p0392c2s
Ferrero, W. v4p0017c1s v4p0018c1s v4p0030c2s v4p0139c1s v4p0382c1s v4p0555c2s v4p0632c1s v5p0509c2s
Ferrers, Earl v1p0198c2s
Ferrette, Bishop v1p0199c2s v1p0707c2s
Ferri, E. v5p0157c2s
Ferri, J. v1p1000c2s
Ferri, L. v1p0672c2s v4p0118c1s v4p0188c2s v4p0294c2s
Ferriar, J. v1p0810c2s
Ferrier, D. v1p0156c2m v1p0157c1s v2p0073c1s v3p0053c1s
Ferrier, E. v1p0223c1s v1p0417c1s v1p0418c1s v1p0478c1s v1p0568c2s v1p0931c2s v1p1294c2s v1p1392c2s
Ferrier, S.E. v1p0001c2s v1p1169c1s
Ferriere, J.L. v1p0166c2s v1p0205c2s v1p0986c1s v1p1029c2s
Ferries, W.M. v1p1229c2s
Ferrin, C.E. v1p0767c2s
Ferris, A. v4p0523c2s
Ferris, A.A. v1p0404c2s
Ferris, A.C. v3p0063c2s v3p0277c1s
Ferris, A.E. v3p0210c1s v3p0233c2s v3p0413c1s v4p0575c2s
Ferris, A.J. v2p0451c2s
Ferris, Ada E. v4p0321c1s
Ferris, E. v6p0353c2s
Ferris, E.E. v5p0547c2s
Ferris, G.T. v1p0088c2s v1p0263c2s v1p0327c1m v1p0782c1s v1p1068c1s v1p1379c2s v4p0328c1s v4p0555c1s v4p0568c1s v5p0021c1s v5p0137c1s
Ferris, H. v3p0439c2s
Ferris, K.L. v6p0304c2s v6p0675c2s
Ferris, M.L.D. v3p0296c2s
Ferris, Mary L.D. v4p0268c1s
Ferris, S.H. v6p0455c1s
Ferriss, J.H. and Thompson, R.S. v5p0082c1s
Ferriss, W.M. v1p0418c2s v1p0431c2s v2p0091c1s v2p0281c1s v2p0282c2s v2p0342c1s v2p0348c2s v3p0062c2m v3p0086c2s v3p0199c2s v3p0271c2s v3p0331c2s v3p0348c2s v4p0364c1s
Ferriss, W.M. and Finck, H.T. v1p0884c1s
Ferro, A.de v3p0457c1s v3p0467c1s
Ferro, G.v.del v6p0332c1s
Ferro, G.W.del v6p0530c2s
Ferronays, de la v3p0103c2s
Ferry, A.F. v4p0260c1s
Ferry, C.B. v1p1341c2s
Ferry, E.B. v2p0383c2s
Ferry, E.S. v4p0606c1s
Ferry, M.S. v2p0232c2s
Fershaw, J.B.C. v5p0183c1s
Fessenden, G.M. v1p0156c1s
Fessenden, K. v5p0360c1s
Fessenden, R.A. v4p0121c2s v4p0376c2s v5p0185c2s v5p0242c2m v6p0376c2s
Fessenden, S. v1p0745c2s
Fessenden, S.D. and Olmstead, V.H. v4p0179c2s
Fessenden, T.G. v1p0809c1s
Festenberg, D. v5p0083c1s
Festing, E.G. v5p0246c1s v5p0516c2s
Festing, G. v5p0194c2s v5p0211c1s v5p0221c2s v5p0456c2s v5p0546c1s
Fetherstonhaugh, Mrs. v3p0023c1s
Fetherstonhaugh, T. v6p0319c1s v6p0416c2s v6p0623c1s v6p0681c2s
Fetherstonhaugh, V. v6p0471c2s
Fetter, F. v4p0231c1s v4p0432c1s v4p0599c2s
Fetter, F.A. v5p0093c1s v5p0101c2s v5p0121c2s v5p0357c2s v5p0475c1s v5p0485c2s v5p0535c2s v6p0539c1s v6p0634c1s
Feuardent, G.L. v2p0289c1s
Feuchtwanger, L. v1p0101c1s v1p0666c1s v1p0702c2s v1p0732c1s v1p0844c1s v1p0855c1s v1p0920c2s
Feudge, F.R. v1p0173c1s v1p0176c2s v1p0234c2s v1p0314c1s v1p0378c1s v1p0443c1s v1p0565c2s v1p0634c1s v1p0948c1s v1p0975c2s v1p1239c2s v1p1309c1s
Feuillet, O. v1p0696c1s v1p1123c1s v3p0382c2s
Feuling, J.B. v1p0592c1s v1p1364c1s
Feuvre, Amy Le v6p0165c1s
Feval, P. v1p1151c2s v1p1431c1s
Few, W.P. v6p0012c1s v6p0039c2s v6p0184c1s v6p0361c2s v6p0605c1s v6p0605c2s
Fewell, L.R. v1p1281c2s v1p1385c1s
Fewkes, J.W. v1p0681c2s v2p0004c2s v2p0015c2s v2p0403c2s v2p0415c1s v3p0055c2s v3p0063c2s v3p0165c2s v3p0178c2s v3p0273c2m v3p0319c2s v3p0330c1s v3p0375c1m v3p0475c2s v4p0012c1s v4p0094c2s v4p0204c1m v4p0242c1s v4p0429c1s v4p0449c1s v4p0459c1s v4p0531c1s v4p0587c2m v4p0609c2s v5p0172c2s v5p0208c1s v5p0270c1m v5p0270c2m v5p0314c1s v5p0385c2s v5p0405c2s v5p0425c2s v5p0472c1s v5p0561c1s v6p0019c1s v6p0160c2s v6p0296c2m v6p0451c1s v6p0510c1m v6p0523c1s v6p0596c2s v6p0688c2s
Fewkes, J.W. and Stephens, A.M. v4p0587c2m
Fewkes, J.Walter v6p0333c1s
Fewkes, W. v3p0332c1s
Ffennell, M.C. v5p0102c2s v5p0527c2s
Ffoulkes, C.A.J. v4p0589c1s
Ffoulkes, E.S. v1p0197c1s v1p0249c1s v1p0912c2s v1p1116c1s v2p0085c1s
Ffrangdon-Davies, D. v6p0190c1s
Fiala, A. v6p0029c1m
Fiamingo, G. v4p0044c1s v4p0283c1s v4p0294c1s v4p0462c2s v4p0532c2s v4p0535c1s v5p0122c2s v5p0197c1s v5p0429c2s v5p0475c2s v5p0494c1s v5p0536c2s
Fiamingo, G.M. v5p0009c1s v5p0018c1m v5p0092c2s v5p0111c1s v5p0144c1s v5p0158c1s v5p0299c2s v5p0383c1m v5p0429c2s v5p0604c1m v5p0608c1s v6p0441c2s
Fichte, J.G. v1p0067c1s v1p0293c1s v1p0711c2s v1p0999c2s v1p1001c1s v1p1156c1s v2p0099c2s
Fichte, J.H.von v1p0391c2s
Fick, A. v2p0072c1s
Fick, H.H. v6p0252c1s v6p0456c2s
Fick, R. v6p0521c1s
Ficke, C.A. v5p0593c1s v6p0219c2s
Ficklen, Bessie A. v3p0122c2s
Fidgetts, J. v1p1213c2s
Fidlar, C.L. v5p0422c2s
Fidler, F.G. v6p0469c2s
Fidler, G. v4p0520c2s v4p0585c2s v5p0267c2s
Fidler, Gideon v5p0632c1s v5p0642c1s
Field, A. v6p0003c2s v6p0100c1s
Field, A.C. v6p0421c1s
Field, A.D. v1p0228c1s
Field, A.J. v3p0002c2s v3p0036c1s v3p0373c1s v3p0404c2s
Field, B. v2p0014c1s v3p0013c2s v3p0297c1s v3p0311c1s v4p0204c1s
Field, C. v6p0058c1s v6p0564c2s v6p0661c2s
Field, C. and Butler, N.M. v2p0244c2s
Field, C., Major v5p0052c1s v5p0092c2s v6p0072c1s
Field, C.D. v4p0279c2s v4p0307c1s v5p0053c2s v5p0087c2s
Field, C.J. v4p0175c1s
Field, C.L. v4p0306c2s v5p0327c1s
Field, C.W. v1p0622c2s v1p1354c2s v2p0098c1s v2p0433c1s
Field, D. v1p0837c1s v1p1134c1s
Field, D.D. v1p0212c2s v1p0228c1s v1p0650c2s v1p0740c2s v1p0848c2s v1p0915c1s v1p1028c1s v1p1352c2s v2p0077c2s v2p0101c2s v2p0347c2s v3p0090c1m v3p0244c2s v3p0245c1s v3p0416c2s v3p0442c2s v4p0132c2s v4p0307c1s v4p0322c2s v4p0458c2s
Field, D.D. and George, H. v2p0247c2s
Field, D.D. and McCurdy, C.J. v3p0466c2s
Field, D.D. et al. v2p0091c1s
Field, E. v1p0894c2s v1p1216c1s v3p0022c2s v3p0036c1s v3p0067c1s v3p0074c2s v3p0089c2s v3p0201c1s v3p0222c2s v3p0302c2s v3p0347c2s v3p0349c1s v3p0390c1s v3p0412c1s v3p0441c2s v3p0468c2s v4p0028c1s v4p0522c1s v4p0610c1s v5p0130c1s v5p0412c2s
Field, E.D. v4p0050c1s
Field, E.M., Mrs. v4p0409c2s
Field, F. v1p0966c2s v3p0319c2s v5p0056c2s v6p0406c1s
Field, F.A. v6p0098c2s
Field, G.R. v5p0106c2s
Field, G.W. v1p0466c2s v3p0048c1s v3p0192c1s v4p0355c2s v5p0453c2s v6p0381c2s
Field, H.G. v6p0570c1s
Field, H.H. v4p0466c2s v4p0637c2m v5p0131c2s v6p0143c1m v6p0714c2s
Field, H.M. v1p0482c2s v1p0671c1s v1p0690c2s v1p1281c2s v3p0172c2s v3p0216c1m v3p0225c2s v3p0234c1s v3p0246c1m v4p0062c1s v5p0290c2s
Field, J. v3p0233c2s
Field, J.E. v3p0053c2s v4p0105c1s v4p0559c1s v6p0001c2s
Field, J.L. v2p0225c2s
Field, J.M. v1p0969c2s
Field, John E. v5p0617c2s
Field, K. v1p0027c2s v1p0111c2s v1p0170c1s v1p0350c2s v1p0447c1m v1p0454c2s v1p0461c1s v1p0466c2s v1p0521c1s v1p0568c2s v1p0722c2s v1p0733c1s v1p0733c2s v1p1045c2s v1p1109c1m v1p1157c2s v1p1266c1s v2p0465c2s v3p0315c2s v4p0592c2s
Field, Kate v2p0298c2s v3p0007c1s v4p0137c1s
Field, L. v3p0208c1s v4p0139c2s v5p0180c2s
Field, L.C. v2p0236c1s v2p0475c2s
Field, Louise M. v6p0280c1s v6p0543c2s
Field, M. v1p0158c1s v1p0930c2s v1p1272c1s v1p1372c1s v3p0002c2s v3p0021c1s v3p0057c1s v3p0261c1s v3p0278c1s v3p0311c1s v4p0031c2s v4p0093c2s v4p0267c2s v4p0349c1s v4p0399c2s v4p0404c1m v4p0408c1s
Field, M.B. v1p0895c2s
Field, M.D. v4p0285c1s
Field, M.H. v1p1071c2s v3p0178c2s v3p0286c2s v5p0103c2s v5p0112c2s v5p0384c2s
Field, M.H., Mrs. v6p0215c1s
Field, Margaret v4p0308c2s v4p0421c2s v4p0469c1s
Field, Mary H. v2p0344c2s
Field, Michael v3p0341c2s
Field, N. v2p0141c1s
Field, O. v1p0451c2m v1p0950c1s v4p0198c2s
Field, R. v5p0434c2s
Field, R.S. v1p0872c2s v1p0912c1s
Field, S.J. v1p0222c1s
Field, S.W. v1p0248c1s
Field, T. v5p0280c1s
Field, T.P. v3p0345c1s

Field, W.G. v5p0001c2s
v5p0021c1s v5p0189c2s v5p0301c2s
Field, W.H. v6p0319c2s
Field, W.T. v4p0273c1s
v5p0106c2s v6p0307c2s v6p0432c1s
Fielde, A.M. v3p0078c2s
v3p0079c2m v3p0145c1s v4p0106c1s
v4p0106c2s
Fielde, Adele M. v6p0024c2s
Fielden, H.W. v6p0712c2s
Fielden, J.C. v4p0318c1s
Fielder, C.H. v1p1287c2s
v3p0421c2s
Fielder, F.S. v6p0660c2s
Fielding, F. v1p0438c2s
v1p1192c2s v1p1226c1s v1p1358c2s
Fielding, H. v4p0079c2s
v4p0325c1s v4p0390c2s v4p0446c1s
v4p0544c2s v5p0083c1s v5p0084c1m
v5p0202c2s v5p0348c2s v5p0456c2s
v5p0565c2s v6p0047c2s v6p0398c1s
Fielding, Mantle v6p0195c1s
Fielding, W. v2p0150c2s
v3p0136c2s v3p0147c1s
Fielding-Ould, R. v5p0357c1m
v6p0660c1s
Fields, A. v1p0888c2s
v2p0140c1s v2p0265c2s v3p0323c2s
v4p0134c2s v4p0261c1s v4p0551c2s
v4p0569c1s v4p0572c1s v4p0620c2s
v5p0186c1s v5p0235c2s v5p0498c1s
v6p0639c1s
Fields, A., Mrs. v3p0049c2m
v4p0067c2s v6p0070c1s
Fields, Annie v2p0332c1s
v3p0155c1s v5p0381c1s
Fields, Annie, Mrs. v3p0073c2s
v5p0555c2s
Fields, J.T. v1p0081c1s
v1p0148c2s v1p0348c2s v1p0350c2s
v1p0567c1s v1p0733c2s v1p0780c1s
v1p0983c2s v1p0984c1s v1p1054c1s
v1p1220c2s v1p1301c1s v2p0198c1s
Fields, J.T., Mrs. v2p0365c2s
v3p0338c2s v4p0244c1s v5p0121c2s
v5p0533c2s v5p0630c1s
Fiennes, G. v4p0139c1s
v4p0571c2s v5p0244c2s
Fiennes, N., Mrs. v4p0250c1s
v4p0435c2s
Fievez, C. v3p0066c2s
Fife, A. v1p0501c2s
Fife, G.B. v6p0056c1s
v6p0106c2s v6p0169c2s v6p0172c2s
v6p0310c2s v6p0453c1s v6p0459c1s
v6p0518c2s v6p0648c2s v6p0681c2s
v6p0682c1s
Fife, R.W. v6p0624c1s
Fife, W.W. v1p0057c1s
Fifield, S.S. v5p0023c2s
Figgis, J.B. v6p0081c2s
v6p0561c2s
Figgis, J.N. v6p0146c1s
v6p0157c1s v6p0340c2s v6p0571c1s
Figuerola, L. v2p0412c2s
Fike, H.H. v6p0512c1s
Fikel, I.H. v4p0330c2s
Filene, E.A. v6p0705c2s
Filhol, H. v2p0157c1s
Filipino, A. v5p0010c1s
Filipowicz, T. v6p0506c1s
Fillebrown, C.B. et al. .. v5p0530c2s
Fillebrown, T. v4p0153c1s
Fillmore, J.C. v4p0205c2m
v4p0248c1s v4p0281c2s v4p0282c1s
v4p0313c2s v4p0373c1s v4p0388c2s
v4p0389c1m v4p0442c1s v4p0496c2s
v4p0637c2s v5p0088c1s v5p0212c1s
v5p0287c2s v5p0616c1s v6p0230c2s
v6p0231c1s v6p0316c2s v6p0444c2s
v6p0466c2s
Fillmore, M. v1p0094c2s
Fillmore, P.H. v6p0359c2s
v6p0554c2s
Filmer, W. v1p0401c2s
Filon, A. v3p0014c2s
v3p0085c1s v4p0212c2s v4p0491c2s
v4p0500c1s v5p0220c2s v5p0488c2s
v5p0497c2s v6p0077c1s v6p0466c1s
Finberg, A.J. v6p0224c2s
v6p0361c1s v6p0417c2s v6p0553c1s
v6p0620c1s v6p0662c1s
Finch, B.C. v3p0189c1s
v3p0235c2s v4p0124c1s v4p0159c1s
v4p0264c1s v5p0097c2s v5p0208c2s
v6p0057c2s v6p0094c2s v6p0200c1s
v6p0539c2s
Finch, Barbara C. v4p0158c1s
Finch, C. v1p0186c1s
v1p1376c1s
v5p0089c1s
Finch, F.M. v1p0143c1s
v5p0329c2s
Finch, G.B. v2p0228c1s
Finch, J.A. v2p0067c1s
Finch, O. v4p0190c2s
Finch-Hatton, H. v2p0186c2s
Fincham, E.C. v5p0376c1s
v5p0461c2s
Fincham, J. v1p0809c2s
v1p1311c1s
Finck, A.J. v6p0067c2s
Finck, H.T. v1p0114c2s
v1p0138c2s v1p0238c1s v1p0278c2m
v1p0333c2s v1p0517c2s v1p0882c2s
v1p0883c2m v1p1131c1s v1p1160c1s
v1p1210c1s v1p1221c2s v1p1370c2s
v1p1371c2s v1p1380c1m v2p0015c1s
v2p0030c2s v2p0040c2m v2p0060c2s
v2p0173c1s v2p0177c1s v2p0183c2s
v2p0195c2s v2p0200c1s v2p0221c2m
v2p0260c1s v2p0264c1s v2p0280c1s
v2p0283c1s v2p0301c2s v2p0303c1m
v2p0313c1m v2p0319c2s v2p0322c1m
v2p0333c1s v2p0388c2s v2p0389c1s
v2p0429c1s v2p0464c1m v2p0481c1s
v3p0007c1s v3p0062c1s v3p0063c2s
v3p0252c1s v3p0263c2m v3p0290c2s
v3p0310c1s v3p0313c1m v3p0368c2s
v3p0372c2s v3p0374c1s v3p0375c1s
v3p0379c1m v3p0386c1s v3p0403c1s
v3p0448c2s v3p0452c2m v3p0469c1s
v3p0470c1s v3p0474c2m v4p0008c2s
v4p0078c1s v4p0083c2s v4p0084c1s
v4p0213c1s v4p0234c1s v4p0331c1m
v4p0420c2m v4p0494c1s v4p0506c2s
v4p0546c2s v4p0585c1s v4p0608c2s
v5p0004c1s v5p0051c1s v5p0114c1s
v5p0340c2s v5p0349c1s v5p0352c2s
v5p0358c1s v5p0394c2s v5p0395c2s
v5p0422c1s v5p0521c2s v5p0539c1s
v5p0560c1s v5p0564c2s v5p0636c1s
v5p0637c1m v5p0638c1s v5p0644c1m
v6p0134c2s v6p0139c1s v6p0164c1s
v6p0246c2s v6p0254c1s v6p0275c1s
v6p0277c2s v6p0379c1s v6p0388c2s
v6p0392c1m v6p0404c2s v6p0437c2m
v6p0438c1m v6p0438c2m v6p0439c1m
v6p0439c2m v6p0453c1s v6p0468c1s
v6p0468c2s v6p0469c2s v6p0499c1s
v6p0501c2s v6p0575c2s v6p0634c2s
v6p0644c1m v6p0683c1m v6p0711c2s
Finck, H.T. and Ferris, W.M.
v1p0884c1s
Finck, Julia N. v5p0402c2s
Finck, M.E. v2p0314c1s
Finckel, S.D. v1p0777c1s
Findlater, J.H. v5p0055c1s
v5p0072c1s v5p0206c1s v5p0263c2s
v5p0398c2s v5p0424c2s v5p0514c2s
v5p0531c1s v6p0223c1s v6p0462c1s
Findlater, Jane v6p0653c1s
Findlater, Jane H. v5p0415c2s
v5p0533c1s v6p0306c1s v6p0330c1s
v6p0668c1s
Findlater, M. v5p0614c1s
Findlay, A.G. v1p0159c1s
v3p0251c1s
Findlay, E.B. v5p0154c2s
Findlay, F.R.N. v5p0082c1s
Findlay, G. v3p0353c2s
v4p0584c2s
Findlay, G.C. v3p0043c1s
Findlay, G.G. v4p0109c1s
v4p0112c1s v5p0060c1m v5p0137c2s
v5p0378c1s v5p0386c1s v5p0389c1s
v5p0507c2s v6p0037c1s v6p0064c2m
Findlay, J.J. v4p0255c1s
v4p0299c1s v4p0320c2s v4p0460c2s
v5p0179c1s v5p0230c1s v6p0635c1s
Findlay, J.M. v6p0524c2s
Findley, A.I. v4p0292c1s
Findon, B.W. v6p0181c1s
Fine, C. v1p1176c2s
Finelli, L. v1p1197c2s
Fingel, E. v6p0079c1s
Fink, A. v4p0472c1s
Fink, R.A. v1p0847c1s
v1p0946c2s v1p1050c1s v1p1423c2s
Finkelnburg, G.A. v5p0465c1s
v6p0339c2s v6p0449c2s
Finkle, F.C. v5p0622c1s
Finlay v2p0095c1s
Finlay, G. v1p0553c2s
v1p1045c1s
Finlay, J. v6p0649c2s
Finlay, J.D. v1p0026c1s
Finlay, J.R. v4p0493c1s
Finlay, John v5p0131c2s
Finlay, M.E. v5p0054c2s
Finlay, P. v1p1435c2s
v2p0050c2s v2p0083c2s v2p0268c1s
v2p0388c1s v2p0437c2s
Finlay, R. v6p0026c1s
Finlay, T.A. v1p0387c2s
v1p0424c2s v1p1161c2s v2p0133c1s
v2p0423c1s v2p0450c2s v4p0132c1s
v4p0289c1s
Finlay, W.L. v6p0685c2s
Finlayson, A.W. v2p0151c1s
Finlayson, J.C. v2p0215c1s
Finlayson, T.C. v1p0625c1s
v2p0074c1s v2p0083c2s
Finley, E. v1p0338c1s
v1p0625c2s v1p0745c2s v1p1041c2s
v1p1161c2s v1p1432c2s v1p1439c1s
Finley, E.B. v2p0300c1s
v3p0290c1s
Finley, I.B. v6p0364c1s
Finley, J. v4p0044c2s
v5p0460c2s v6p0003c1s v6p0227c2s
v6p0262c1s v6p0275c2s v6p0332c2s
v6p0434c2s v6p0480c2s v6p0515c1s
v6p0603c1s v6p0610c1s v6p0619c1s
Finley, J.H. v4p0096c2s
v4p0103c2s v4p0452c1s v4p0581c1s
v6p0020c1s v6p0280c2s
Finley, J.P. v2p0443c1m
v3p0432c2m v4p0153c2s v4p0523c2s
v5p0275c2s v5p0620c2s v6p0093c2s
Finley, John v6p0330c1s
Finley, R.J. v4p0175c1s
Finley, T. v1p0071c2s
Finley, T.A. v1p0581c1s
v1p1377c2s
Finley, W.H. v6p0143c2s
Finley, W.I. v6p0068c1s
Finley, W.L. v6p0067c2s
v6p0068c2s v6p0276c1s
Finley, W.L. and Bohlman H.T.
v6p0067c1s
Finley, W.Lovell v6p0114c1s
Finn, F. v3p0236c2s
v4p0047c2s v4p0060c2s v4p0567c1s
v6p0235c2s v6p0262c1s
Finn, G.M. v1p0717c1s
Finn, H.M. v1p0525c2s
Finn, J.J. v4p0234c1s
Finn, Mrs. v1p0960c2s
Finn, W.J. v6p0438c2s
Finnegan, J.T. v1p0319c1s
Finnemore, E.P. v5p0640c1s
Finnemore, Emily P. v6p0471c2s
Finnemore, J. v5p0350c1s
v5p0616c2s v6p0013c2s v6p0332c1s
Finney, B.A. v6p0371c2s
Finot, J. v6p0213c1s
v6p0698c2s
Finotti, J.M. v1p0203c1s
v1p0331c1s v1p0683c2s v1p0775c1s
v1p1203c1s
Fiore, P. v4p0288c1s
v5p0437c2s
Fircks, A.V. v1p0473c1s
v1p0515c2s
Firkins, O.N. v6p0380c1s
Firkins, O.W. v6p0505c1s
v6p0505c2s
Firminger, W.K. v4p0318c1s
v4p0599c2s
Firth, C.H. v3p0074c1m
v3p0106c1m v3p0138c1m v3p0139c1s
v3p0188c2s v3p0269c2s v4p0118c1s
v4p0137c2s v4p0141c1m v4p0141c2s
v4p0181c2m v4p0428c1s v4p0434c2s
v5p0102c2s v5p0145c1m v5p0244c1s
v5p0296c1s v5p0363c2s v5p0508c1s
v5p0525c1s v5p0579c1s v6p0048c2s
v6p0159c1m v6p0165c2s v6p0183c2s
v6p0184c1s v6p0206c2s v6p0228c2s
v6p0351c1s v6p0403c1s
Firth, E.C.C. v4p0166c1s
v4p0213c2s v4p0383c2s v4p0628c2s
v5p0351c1s
Firth, J.B. v4p0515c1s
v4p0615c2s v5p0006c1s v5p0251c2s
v6p0072c1s v6p0158c2s v6p0364c2s
v6p0385c1s v6p0415c2s v6p0492c2s
v6p0549c1s v6p0653c1s
Firth, J.D. v4p0316c2s
Firth, J.F.B. v2p0263c2s
Firth, J.F.B., Mrs. v5p0581c2s
Firth, R.H. v6p0408c2s
Firth, W. v6p0603c1s
Fischer, E.S. v6p0050c2s
Fischer, F. v1p0146c1s
Fischer, F.G. v1p0828c2s
Fischer, G.Evelyn v6p0300c2s
Fischer, H.W. v4p0062c1s
v4p0247c2s v4p0264c1s v4p0494c1s
v4p0559c2s v4p0599c1s v4p0622c2m
v5p0064c2s v5p0339c1s
Fischer, J. v2p0295c1s
Fischer, J.B. v6p0625c1s
v6p0709c2s
Fischer, J.F. v5p0284c2s
v6p0314c1m v6p0314c2s v6p0315c1m
v6p0445c2s
Fischer, K. v2p0240c1s
v2p0241c1s v3p0234c2m
Fischer, M. v4p0405c2s
Fischer, T. v4p0272c1s
Fischer, W.E. v4p0456c1s
v4p0527c1s v5p0319c1s
Fish, A. v5p0025c1s
v5p0049c2s v5p0156c2s v5p0262c1s
v5p0267c1s v5p0440c1s v5p0461c2s
v5p0591c1s v5p0632c1s
Fish, Arthur v5p0324c2s
Fish, C.F. v1p1151c2s
Fish, C.R. v6p0144c2s
v6p0377c2s
Fish, D. v4p0151c1s
Fish, G.T. v6p0226c1s
Fish, H.C. v1p1064c2s
v1p1296c2s
Fish, S. v1p0646c2s
Fish, Stuyvesant v6p0189c1s
Fish, W. v5p0556c1s
Fishback, W.M. v3p0094c2s

v3p0346c2s v4p0281c2s v5p0529c2s
Fishback, W.P. v5p0476c2s
Fishberg, M. v6p0344c1m
Fishbough, W. v1p0507c1s
Fishbourne, A. v2p0257c2s
Fisher, A. v5p0187c2m
v5p0238c2s v6p0203c2m v6p0335c2s
Fisher, A., Mrs. v2p0420c1s
Fisher, A.B. v6p0664c1s
Fisher, A.M. v1p0885c2s
v1p1051c2s
Fisher, A.N. v6p0283c1s
Fisher, B. v6p0221c1s
v6p0456c1s
Fisher, C. v4p0028c2s
v4p0299c1s v4p0371c2s v4p0520c1s
v5p0030c1s v5p0079c2s v5p0304c1s
v5p0573c2s v6p0707c2m
Fisher, C.A. and Barbour, E.H.
v6p0091c2s
Fisher, C.S. v6p0458c1s
Fisher, C.T. v1p0835c2s
v1p1291c2s
Fisher, D. v2p0357c1s
v3p0275c2s
Fisher, D.W. v2p0237c1s
v3p0348c2s v4p0102c2s v4p0394c2s
v5p0300c2s v5p0536c1s
Fisher, Dr. v1p0555c2s
Fisher, E. v1p0126c2s
v1p0346c2s v1p0507c1s v1p0686c2s
v1p0687c2s v1p0819c1s v1p0868c2s
v1p0901c1s v1p0926c2s v1p1066c1s
v1p1200c1s v1p1238c2s v1p1263c1s
v1p1410c1s
Fisher, E.B. v1p0773c1s
Fisher, E.T. v1p1089c2s
Fisher, F.C. v1p0332c2s
v1p0334c1s v1p0505c2s v1p0579c1s
v1p0589c2s v1p0611c1s v1p0722c1s
v1p0770c2s v1p0874c1s v1p0923c1s
v1p0927c2s v1p1430c2s v2p0021c2s
v2p0120c2s v3p0069c2s v5p0466c1s
Fisher, F.C. and Reid, C.. v1p1257c2s
Fisher, F.V. v4p0212c2s
v4p0429c1s v4p0481c2s v4p0532c1s
Fisher, G.A. v4p0247c1s
Fisher, G.C. v1p0611c2s
v1p0968c1s v3p0037c1s
Fisher, G.H. v1p0154c1s
v6p0492c1s
Fisher, G.J. v1p0142c2s
v2p0030c1s
Fisher, G.P. v1p0047c2s
v1p0048c1s v1p0071c2s v1p0085c2s
v1p0103c2s v1p0110c1s v1p0118c2m
v1p0126c2s v1p0127c1m v1p0127c2s
v1p0128c1s v1p0129c1s v1p0129c2m
v1p0148c2s v1p0166c1s v1p0180c1s
v1p0210c1s v1p0217c1s v1p0243c1s
v1p0249c1s v1p0307c2s v1p0380c2s
v1p0393c2s v1p0406c2s v1p0443c2s
v1p0520c2s v1p0577c1s v1p0648c2s
v1p0685c1s v1p0688c1s v1p0689c1s
v1p0727c1s v1p0781c2s v1p0810c1s
v1p0847c2s v1p0849c2s v1p0850c1s
v1p0855c2s v1p0940c1s v1p1033c1s
v1p1043c1s v1p1059c1s v1p1064c1s
v1p1066c2s v1p1067c1s v1p1081c2s
v1p1089c2s v1p1097c2s v1p1103c2s
v1p1108c1s v1p1142c2s v1p1188c1s
v1p1200c2m v1p1203c1s v1p1203c2s
v1p1258c1s v1p1260c1s v1p1287c1s
v1p1295c2s v1p1393c2m v1p1410c2s
v1p1428c2s v2p0081c2s v2p0180c2m
v2p0191c1s v2p0268c2s v2p0269c1s
v2p0290c2s v2p0291c1s v2p0389c1s
v2p0479c1s v3p0098c1s v3p0139c1s
v3p0278c1s v3p0313c2s v3p0319c1s
v3p0360c1s v3p0378c1s v4p0057c2s
v4p0129c1s v4p0185c2s v4p0299c1s
v4p0531c2s v4p0556c1s v5p0056c1s
v6p0084c1s v6p0687c2s v6p0690c2s
Fisher, G.P. et al. v1p0496c1s
Fisher, G.T. v1p0643c1s
Fisher, H.A.L. v3p0163c2s
v3p0165c2s v4p0212c2s v4p0258c2s
v4p0462c2s v4p0513c2s v5p0175c1s
v5p0398c1s v6p0288c1s v6p0442c1s
Fisher, H.N. v5p0601c1s
Fisher, H.W. v5p0208c1s
v5p0523c2s
Fisher, I. v4p0059c2s
v4p0287c2s v5p0093c1m v5p0366c1s
v6p0100c1m v6p0146c2s
Fisher, Irving v4p0088c2s
Fisher, J. v2p0227c1s
v2p0248c2s
Fisher, J.A. v2p0253c2s
Fisher, J.B. v1p0486c1s
Fisher, J.C. v1p0312c2s
Fisher, J.F. v1p0567c2s
v4p0246c2s
Fisher, J.H. v1p1075c2s
Fisher, J.K. v1p0054c1s
v1p0556c2s
Fisher, J.R. v1p0453c2s
v4p0328c2s v5p0207c1s v6p0192c1s
v6p0441c2s
Fisher, J.S. v4p0471c2s
v4p0525c1s v4p0546c1s
Fisher, K.B. v2p0289c1s
Fisher, L. v5p0273c1m
v6p0300c1s
Fisher, L.B. v3p0041c2s
Fisher, L.P. v1p1360c1s
Fisher, Lettice v6p0300c1s
Fisher, M.A.E.W. v1p1417c1s
Fisher, M.M. v3p0243c2s
Fisher, M.W. v1p0076c2s
v1p1105c2s v4p0125c1s
Fisher, Mary v5p0513c1s
Fisher, N.H. v1p0434c1s
Fisher, O. v2p0127c1m
v2p0319c1s v2p0434c1s v4p0165c2s
v4p0576c2s v5p0138c2m v6p0186c1s
Fisher, O. et al. v2p0080c2s
Fisher, P. v3p0257c1s
v4p0234c2s
Fisher, R. v1p0192c1s
v1p0193c1m v1p0288c2s v1p0299c1s
v1p0302c2s v1p0430c1s v1p0545c1s
v1p0608c1s v1p1042c2s v1p1044c2s
v1p1057c2s v1p1382c1s v2p0066c1s
Fisher, R.B. v3p0140c1s
Fisher, R.T. v6p0656c1s
Fisher, S. v5p0307c1s
Fisher, S.G. v1p0063c2s
v1p0326c1s v1p0373c1s v1p0397c1s
v1p0538c1s v1p0556c2s v1p0590c2s
v1p0735c1s v1p1078c1s v1p1206c2s
v1p1207c1s v1p1258c2s v1p1349c2s
v2p0002c1s v2p0331c2s v3p0062c1s
v3p0187c2s v3p0442c2s v4p0014c1s
v4p0015c1s v4p0139c2s v4p0275c1m
v4p0433c2s v4p0624c2s v5p0268c1s
v5p0381c1s
Fisher, S.J. v5p0626c2s
Fisher, S.M. v6p0483c1s
Fisher, S.R. v1p0848c1m
v1p1139c1s v2p0176c1s
Fisher, S.W. v1p0388c2s
v1p1046c1s
Fisher, W. v4p0106c1s
v4p0377c2s v4p0378c1s v4p0378c2s
v5p0109c2s v5p0529c2s
Fisher, W.E.G. v4p0091c1s
v4p0122c1s v4p0263c2s v4p0365c2s
v4p0568c2s v4p0571c1s v5p0044c2s
v5p0204c1s v5p0211c2s v5p0382c1s
v5p0470c1s v5p0533c1s v5p0576c1s
Fisher, W.E.Garrett v4p0227c2s
v4p0361c2s
Fisher, W.J. v6p0197c1s
v6p0370c1m v6p0385c2s
Fisher, W.K. v6p0147c2s
v6p0283c1s
Fisher, W.M. v1p0081c2s
v1p0693c1s v1p0718c1s v1p0746c1s
v1p0942c1s v1p1128c1s v1p1200c1s
v1p1380c1s v1p1436c2s v1p1440c2s
Fisher, W.R. v3p0158c1s
v3p0213c1s v4p0207c2m v4p0208c1m
v4p0208c2s v4p0393c1s v5p0210c1s
v5p0368c1s
Fisher, W.W. v2p0468c1s
Fishlake, J.R. v1p0555c1m
Fishwick, H. v2p0247c1s
v6p0368c2m
Fisk et al. v3p0031c1s
Fisk, A.C. v4p0129c1s
v4p0230c1s v4p0524c2s
Fisk, C.B. v3p0170c1s
v3p0252c2s
Fisk, C.G. v6p0570c1s
v6p0671c2s
Fisk, E. v1p0014c1s
v1p0847c1s
Fisk, E.J. v1p0248c1s
v2p0081c1s
Fisk, F.W. v1p0168c1s
v1p1054c2s v1p1064c2s v1p1190c1s
Fisk, G. v1p0239c1s
v1p0283c1s v1p0741c2s v5p0219c1s
Fisk, G.M. v6p0253c2s
v6p0633c2s v6p0655c2s
Fisk, R. v1p0392c1s
v1p0815c2s v1p0848c1s v1p1161c1s
v1p1200c1s v3p0380c2s
Fisk, R., jr. v1p0197c2s
Fisk, S.A. v2p0089c1s
v2p0094c1m v2p0100c2s
Fisk, W. v1p0392c1s
v1p1116c1s v1p1126c1s
Fisk, W.H. v2p0123c2s
Fiske, A.K. v1p0451c1s
v3p0120c1s v3p0292c1s v5p0047c1s
v5p0201c1s v5p0202c1s v5p0241c1s
v6p0047c1s v6p0101c1s
Fiske, A.W. v4p0234c1s
Fiske, B.A. v2p0137c1m
v2p0138c1m v2p0400c2s v2p0454c1s
v3p0134c1s v3p0297c2s v5p0360c1s
Fiske, C. v3p0232c2s
v3p0303c1s
Fiske, C.F. v5p0206c1s
Fiske, D.F. v1p0005c1s
Fiske, D.T. v1p0075c1s
v1p0129c2s v1p0468c2s v1p0521c2s
v1p0527c2s v1p0688c1s v1p0910c1s
v1p1303c2s v5p0116c2s
Fiske, F.S. v1p1229c2s
v4p0078c2s v5p0314c2s
Fiske, G.F. v3p0225c1s
Fiske, G.M. v3p0054c1s
Fiske, H. et al. v5p0292c2s
Fiske, Isabella H. v6p0132c1s
v6p0140c1s v6p0656c1s
Fiske, J. v1p0013c2s
v1p0028c1s v1p0033c1s v1p0066c2m
v1p0210c2s v1p0260c1s v1p0265c1s
v1p0287c2s v1p0297c2s v1p0323c2s
v1p0332c1s v1p0333c2m v1p0390c1s
v1p0431c1s v1p0434c2s v1p0435c1m
v1p0440c1s v1p0464c2s v1p0551c1s
v1p0573c1s v1p0594c1m v1p0637c1s
v1p0723c2m v1p0724c1s v1p0724c2s
v1p0725c1s v1p0742c1s v1p0810c1s
v1p0850c1s v1p0890c2m v1p0891c1s
v1p0891c2m v1p0965c2s v1p0991c1s
v1p0999c1s v1p1058c2s v1p1083c2s
v1p1161c1s v1p1235c2s v1p1238c1s
v1p1273c2s v1p1358c1s v1p1358c2s
v1p1398c2s v1p1433c2s v2p0009c2s
v2p0010c1m v2p0011c1s v2p0098c1s
v2p0103c2s v2p0112c1m v2p0147c1s
v2p0148c1s v2p0173c2s v2p0180c2s
v2p0255c2s v2p0274c1s v2p0275c1s
v2p0278c2s v2p0310c2s v2p0316c1s
v2p0328c2s v2p0399c1s v2p0411c1s
v2p0444c1s v2p0451c2s v2p0452c1s
v2p0452c2m v2p0454c1m v2p0461c2s
v3p0012c1m v3p0020c2s v3p0053c2m
v3p0070c2s v3p0098c2s v3p0113c1s
v3p0144c1s v3p0145c2s v3p0150c2s
v3p0232c1s v3p0375c2s v3p0430c1s
v3p0441c2s v3p0442c1s v3p0442c2m
v3p0474c2s v4p0178c1s v4p0214c1s
v4p0427c1s v4p0478c2s v4p0507c1s
v4p0511c1s v4p0530c2s v4p0605c2s
v5p0024c2s v5p0141c2s v5p0197c2s
v5p0277c1s v5p0374c2s v5p0522c2s
v5p0581c2s v6p0214c2s
Fiske, J. et al. v1p0645c2s
Fiske, J.H. v2p0272c2s
Fiske, J.S. v1p0893c1s
v1p0943c2s v2p0020c1s v2p0266c1s
v2p0328c1s v2p0373c2s v3p0031c2s
v3p0072c2s v3p0204c1s v3p0379c1s
v4p0024c2m v4p0051c2s v4p0189c2s
v4p0294c1s v4p0370c1s v4p0503c1s
v5p0053c1s v5p0299c2m v5p0451c1s
v5p0513c1s v5p0595c2s v6p0230c2s
v6p0330c2m v6p0399c2s
Fiske, John v2p0357c2s
v5p0483c1s v6p0278c2s v6p0418c1s
Fiske, L.R. v4p0482c1s
v5p0037c2s
Fiske, L.R. et al. v3p0371c1s
Fiske, M.M. v5p0003c1s
v6p0612c2s
Fiske, N.W. v1p0803c2s
Fiske, P.S. v6p0377c1s
v6p0530c2s v6p0653c1s
Fiske, R.B. v5p0442c1s
Fiske, S. v4p0293c1s
v5p0632c1s
Fiske, S.R. v1p0414c1s
Fiske, T.S. v6p0136c2m
v6p0406c1s
Fiske, W. v1p0303c1s
v1p0622c1s v2p0337c2s v3p0010c1s
v5p0104c2s
Fiske, W.E. and Collins, W.D.
v5p0185c2s
Fison, H.V. v6p0372c1s
Fison, H.W. v6p0442c2s
v6p0663c2s
Fison, L. v1p0803c1s
v2p0061c1s v2p0155c2m v2p0248c1s
v2p0305c2s v4p0478c1s
Fison, L. and Howitt, A.W.
v2p0115c1s v2p0207c2s v2p0299c2s
Fitch, A. v5p0322c2s
Fitch, A.H. v6p0516c2s
v6p0695c1m
Fitch, A.S. v2p0230c1s
Fitch, C. v3p0458c1s
Fitch, C.E. v1p0500c1s
Fitch, C.H. v2p0072c2s
v2p0156c2s
Fitch, C.L. v5p0622c1s
Fitch, C.W. v2p0166c1s
Fitch, D.C. v5p0547c1s
Fitch, E.T. v1p0130c1s
v1p0406c2s v1p0429c1s v1p0496c1s
v1p0528c2s v1p0564c2s v1p0649c2s
v1p0842c1s v1p0882c2m v1p0884c1s
v1p0947c2s v1p1045c1s v1p1060c1s
v1p1190c1s v1p1200c1s v1p1200c2s
v1p1237c2s v1p1303c2s v1p1406c2s
Fitch, G.H. v2p0080c1s
v3p0063c1s v3p0063c2s v3p0191c2s
v3p0279c2s v3p0374c2s v4p0501c2s
v5p0088c2s v5p0166c2s v6p0093c1s
v6p0165c2s v6p0474c1s v6p0589c1s
Fitch, J. v1p0154c1s
v1p1155c2s v5p0085c1s v5p0179c2s
v5p0360c2s v6p0191c2s v6p0192c1s
Fitch, J., Sir v5p0570c1s

Fitch, J.G. v1p0218c2s
v1p0390c2s v1p0391c2m v1p0392c2s
v1p0392c2s v1p0519c1s v1p1356c2s
v1p1358c1s v1p1422c1s v2p0133c1s
v2p0432c1m v3p0129c1m v3p0468c2s
v4p0169c1s v4p0169c2s v4p0340c2s
v4p0506c1m v4p0506c2s v4p0512c1s
v5p0177c2s v5p0178c1s v5p0346c2s
Fitch, J.L. v3p0075c2s
Fitch, Joshua v6p0089c2s
Fitch, R.G. v4p0068c2s
v5p0072c2s
Fitch, T. v1p0872c1s
Fitch, W.T. v5p0601c2s
v6p0668c1s
Fitchett, W.H. v5p0021c2s
v5p0038c2s v5p0039c1s v5p0066c1s
v5p0066c2s v5p0098c1s v5p0138c2s
v5p0229c2s v5p0274c2s v5p0286c1s
v5p0291c1s v5p0346c2s v5p0377c1s
v5p0385c2s v5p0411c2s v5p0492c1s
v5p0507c2s v5p0625c1s v6p0042c1s
v6p0059c1s v6p0652c2s
Fite, E.D. v6p0098c1s
v6p0527c2s v6p0692c1s
Fite, W. v4p0465c1s
v5p0031c1s v5p0034c2s v5p0134c2s
v5p0436c1s v6p0216c1s v6p0504c1s
Fite, W. and Angell, J.R.. v5p0540c1s
Fithian, E. v1p1141c2s
Fitts, J.F. v1p0209c2s
v1p0335c2s v1p0438c2s v1p0457c2s
v1p0614c2s v1p0626c2s v1p0693c2s
v1p0874c2s v1p0886c1s v1p0889c1s
v1p0904c2s v1p1035c1s v1p1068c1s
v1p1112c1s v1p1385c1s v1p1414c1s
Fitz, E.A. v4p0401c2s
Fitz, G.W. v4p0441c1s
Fitz, H.G. v5p0168c1s
Fitzcook, H. v3p0179c1s
Fitzgerald, A. v4p0141c1s
v4p0311c2s
Fitzgerald, C.C.P. v3p0182c2s
v4p0211c2s v5p0246c2s v5p0303c1s
v5p0619c1s v6p0138c2s v6p0265c2s
v6p0268c2s
Fitzgerald, C.C.Penrose .. v6p0309c2s
Fitzgerald, C.F. v4p0165c1s
Fitzgerald, C.J. et al. .. v4p0609c1s
Fitzgerald, C.L. v1p0018c2s
v2p0288c2s
Fitzgerald, D. v1p0101c2s
v1p0658c1s v1p0661c1s v1p1107c1s
v2p0070c2s v2p0148c2s v2p0304c2s
v2p0467c1s v6p0424c2s
Fitzgerald, D. and Foss, W.E.
v4p0612c2s
Fitzgerald, D.B. v4p0163c1m
v4p0210c2s v4p0420c1s v4p0517c1s
v4p0570c2s v5p0157c2s v6p0183c1s
v6p0394c2s
Fitzgerald, E. v1p0365c2s
v1p1209c1s
Fitzgerald, F.A. v4p0401c2s
v5p0002c2m v5p0594c2s
Fitzgerald, F. v1p0087c2s
v2p0124c2s
Fitzgerald, F.A. v5p0094c1s
Fitzgerald, F.A.J. v4p0089c1s
FitzGerald, F.J. v6p0100c2s
Fitzgerald, G.A. v6p0194c2s
Fitzgerald, G.F. v2p0258c1s
v3p0134c2m v3p0422c1s v4p0187c2s
v5p0184c2s v5p0260c2s v5p0338c1s
Fitzgerald, H.G. v3p0163c2s
Fitzgerald, J. v1p0215c2s
v4p0603c2s v5p0150c1s v6p0361c1s
Fitzgerald, J.A.J. v6p0002c2s
Fitzgerald, J.D. v2p0111c1s
v3p0412c2s v6p0674c1s
Fitzgerald, K.M. v5p0545c1s
Fitzgerald, L. v5p0514c2s
Fitzgerald, Leora A. v6p0607c2s
Fitzgerald, M.F. v5p0063c1s
Fitzgerald, M.M. v5p0268c2s
Fitzgerald, O.P. v4p0397c1s
v6p0675c1s
Fitzgerald, Oscar P. v6p0164c1s
Fitzgerald, P. v1p0005c1s
v1p0110c2s v1p0152c2s v1p0179c1s
v1p0186c1s v1p0281c1s v1p0314c2s
v1p0350c1s v1p0358c1s v1p0366c2s
v1p0459c2s v1p0485c2s v1p0501c1m
v1p0511c1m v1p0520c2s v1p0596c2s
v1p0657c2s v1p0658c1s v1p0667c2s
v1p0694c1m v1p0696c1s v1p0748c1s
v1p0774c1s v1p0837c2s v1p0883c2s
v1p0886c2s v1p0933c2s v1p0950c2s
v1p0971c1s v1p1002c1s v1p1030c1s
v1p1091c1s v1p1107c2s v1p1190c2s
v1p1228c1s v1p1241c2s v1p1253c1m
v1p1277c1s v1p1299c2s v1p1300c1s
v1p1301c1s v1p1362c1s v1p1402c1s
v1p1411c1s v1p1435c1s v2p0002c1m
v2p0049c1s v2p0052c1m v2p0053c2s
v2p0056c1s v2p0057c1s v2p0063c2s
v2p0098c1s v2p0108c1s v2p0171c2s
v2p0178c1s v2p0195c2s v2p0213c2s
v2p0241c1s v2p0241c2s v2p0246c1s
v2p0248c2s v2p0249c1s v2p0264c2s
v2p0265c1s v2p0269c2s v2p0341c2s
v2p0345c1m v2p0354c2m v2p0392c2s
v2p0397c2s v2p0400c1s v2p0402c1s
v2p0416c2s v2p0443c1s v2p0449c2s
v3p0003c1s v3p0038c1m v3p0052c1s
v3p0112c2s v3p0135c2s v3p0181c1s
v3p0257c1s v3p0261c2s v3p0271c2s
v3p0293c2s v3p0296c2s v3p0334c2s
v3p0369c1s v3p0396c1s v3p0402c2s
v3p0433c1s v4p0003c1m v4p0003c2s
v4p0020c2s v4p0024c2s v4p0030c1s
v4p0051c2s v4p0071c1s v4p0120c2s
v4p0155c1m v4p0155c2s v4p0156c1s
v4p0159c2s v4p0285c1s v4p0304c1s
v4p0312c2s v4p0340c1m v4p0341c1s
v4p0394c1s v4p0539c2s v4p0550c2s
v4p0572c1s v4p0574c2s v4p0624c2s
v5p0073c2s v5p0148c2s v5p0161c1s
v5p0309c2s v5p0315c2s v5p0450c2s
v5p0454c2s v5p0510c2s v5p0548c1s
v5p0616c2s v6p0041c1s v6p0077c1s
v6p0173c2s v6p0588c2s v6p0612c2s
v6p0647c2s v6p0655c1s
Fitzgerald, P. and
Hornby, G.P., Sir v3p0182c2s
Fitzgerald, P. and Marshall, F.A.
v3p0109c2s v3p0357c1s
Fitzgerald, P. et al. v4p0003c1s
Fitzgerald, P, Sir v1p1392c2s
Fitzgerald, P.H. v1p0337c2s
v1p0349c1s v1p1174c2s v3p0060c2s
v3p0085c1s v3p0092c1s v3p0109c2s
v3p0123c1s v3p0151c2s v3p0223c2s
v3p0275c1s v3p0306c1s v3p0425c2s
v3p0455c1s
Fitzgerald, Percy v2p0387c2s
v2p0397c2s v2p0400c1s v4p0399c2s
v5p0012c2s v5p0466c1s v5p0612c1s
Fitzgerald, R. v1p1182c2s
Fitzgerald, R.R. v5p0240c1s
Fitzgerald, S.J.A. v3p0319c1s
v3p0326c1s v3p0334c2s v3p0406c1s
v4p0003c1s v4p0210c1s v4p0245c1s
v4p0346c1s v4p0415c1s v5p0491c1s
Fitzgerald, T. v1p0903c1s
Fitzgerald, W. v1p1148c1s
v1p1178c1s
Fitzgerald, W.G. v5p0119c1s
v5p0135c1s v5p0142c2s v5p0312c1s
v5p0318c1s v5p0498c2s v5p0527c2s
v5p0528c2s v5p0553c2s v5p0611c1s
v5p0642c1s v6p0048c2s v6p0060c2s
v6p0169c1s v6p0177c2s v6p0221c1s
v6p0253c2s v6p0277c2s v6p0458c2s
v6p0475c2s v6p0546c2s
Fitzgibbon, J.H. v1p0329c1s
Fitzgibbon, T.F. v6p0627c1s
Fitzgreene v1p1314c1s
Fitzherbert, R.H.C. v5p0069c2s
Fitzherbert, S.W. v5p0225c2s
Fitzhugh, G. v1p0181c2s
v1p0260c1s v1p0419c2s v1p0445c1s
v1p0485c1s v1p0513c2s v1p0599c1s
v1p0668c1s v1p0721c2s v1p0781c1s
v1p0841c2s v1p0842c1s v1p0905c1s
v1p1034c1s v1p1062c2s v1p1206c1m
v1p1208c2s v1p1209c1s v1p1226c1s
v1p1319c1s v1p1373c1s v1p1374c1s
v1p1388c2s v2p0010c1s v2p0053c2s
v2p0167c1m v2p0248c2s v2p0297c1s
v2p0306c2s v2p0309c1m v2p0321c1s
v2p0347c2s v2p0371c2m v2p0461c2s
Fitzhugh, Geo. v1p1374c2s
Fitzhugh, N.M. v2p0026c2s
v3p0433c1s
Fitzjohn, E.M.T. v4p0588c1s
Fitzjohn, S.H. v5p0005c2s
Fitzmaurice, E. v1p0318c2s
v1p0615c1s v1p0721c1s v2p0029c2s
v2p0206c1s v3p0220c2s v3p0242c1s
v3p0369c1s
Fitzmaurice, E., Lord and
Smith, H.H. v2p0247c2s
Fitzmaurice, Edmond, Lord. v6p0159c1s
Fitzmaurice-Kelly, J. v4p0142c2s
v5p0331c1s v5p0442c1s v5p0610c1s
Fitzmaurice-Kelly, James . v4p0159c1s
Fitzpatrick, A. v5p0010c2s
v5p0335c2s v6p0371c1s v6p0467c2s
Fitzpatrick, F. v5p0080c2s
Fitzpatrick, F.A. v4p0234c1s
v5p0406c2s v5p0512c1s v6p0480c2s
v6p0692c1s
Fitzpatrick, F.W. v5p0026c1m
v5p0090c2s v5p0168c2s v5p0323c1m
v5p0428c2s v5p0449c1s v5p0449c2s
v5p0495c1s v5p0621c1s v6p0027c1s
v6p0122c1s v6p0225c2m v6p0567c2s
v6p0634c2s
Fitzpatrick, F.W. and Church, B.C.
v5p0211c1s
Fitzpatrick, H.L. v5p0239c1m
v5p0239c2s
Fitzpatrick, J. v2p0256c1s
Fitzpatrick, J.P. v5p0586c2s
Fitzpatrick, J.W. v6p0348c2s
Fitzpatrick, T. v5p0195c1s
v5p0296c1s
Fitzpatrick, W. v4p0540c1s
Fitzpatrick, W.J. v1p0534c2s
v3p0148c2s
Fitzreimund, P. v5p0048c1s
v6p0394c2s
Fitzroy, A. v2p0206c1s
Fitzroy, R. v1p0099c2s
Fitzsimmons, W.C. v4p0083c2s
Fitzsimon, E. v1p0982c2s
Fitzsimons, S. v1p1161c1s
v2p0274c2s v2p0355c2s v3p0205c1s
v5p0087c1s v5p0198c1s v5p0519c1s
v6p0396c2s v6p0538c1s v6p0547c2s
v6p0576c1s v6p0610c1s
Fitzwilliam, E.C. v5p0485c1s
Fizeau, M.H. v1p0426c1s
Flaccus, L.W. v6p0132c1s
Flagg, A.C. v1p0195c2s
v1p0338c2s v1p0650c1s v1p0918c1s
v1p1077c1s
Flagg, C.N. v5p0030c2s
v5p0031c2s
Flagg, E. v1p0876c1s
v1p1188c2s v4p0024c1s v4p0078c1s
v4p0425c2s v4p0569c1s v6p0024c2s
v6p0453c1s v6p0638c2s
Flagg, E.W. v2p0301c1s
Flagg, Ernest v5p0026c1m
Flagg, I. v4p0118c1s
v6p0672c1s
Flagg, J.H. v4p0515c1s
Flagg, J.S. v5p0023c1s
Flagg, W. v1p0054c2s
v1p0135c2s v1p0136c1s v1p0137c1m
v1p0152c2s v1p0493c1s v1p0723c1s
v1p1201c1s v1p1324c1m
Flagg, W.C. v1p0540c1s
Flagg, W.J. v1p0535c2s
v1p1415c1s
Flaix, E.F.de v3p0033c2s
v3p0243c2s v3p0436c2s
Flaix, E.Fournier de v2p0166c1s
v2p0400c2s v3p0007c2s
Flaix, Fournier de v4p0479c2s
Flamant, A. v2p0423c2s
v3p0313c2s
Flambro, G. v3p0328c1s
v3p0389c1s v3p0460c2s
Flammarion, C. v1p0070c1s
v1p0375c2s v1p0804c1s v1p1014c1s
v1p1202c1s v1p1359c1s v2p0277c2s
v2p0402c1s v2p0417c1s v3p0024c2m
v3p0131c2s v3p0243c1s v3p0269c1s
v3p0269c2s v3p0274c2s v3p0330c2s
v3p0445c2s v4p0083c1s v4p0093c2s
v4p0357c2m v4p0413c2s v4p0440c2s
v5p0035c2s v5p0223c2s v5p0428c1s
v5p0470c1m v5p0609c1s v6p0188c1s
v6p0397c1s v6p0502c1s
Flammarion, Camille v4p0034c1s
Flanagan, Howard v6p0629c1s
Flanagan, J.W. v1p0657c1s
v2p0152c2s v2p0206c1s v2p0226c1s
Flanders, G.F. v1p0232c2s
Flanders, G.T. v1p0060c1s
v1p0082c2s v1p0122c1s v1p0244c1s
v1p0441c1s v1p0496c2s v1p0687c1s
v1p0777c1s v1p0923c2s v1p1271c2s
v1p1355c2s v1p1440c1s v2p0022c1s
v2p0041c2s v2p0098c2s v2p0235c2s
v2p0415c1s v3p0208c1s v3p0284c1s
Flanders, H. v1p0005c2s
v1p0458c2s v1p0538c1s v1p0546c1s
v1p0680c2s v2p0465c1s v3p0117c2s
Flandin, E. v1p0991c1s
Flandin, M. v1p0992c1s
Flandran, C.E. v3p0026c2s
v3p0354c1s v3p0464c1s
Flanigen, J.R. v1p1044c2s
Flanner, H.G. v1p0994c2s
Flannery, G.F. v5p0194c2s
v5p0643c1s
Flannery, J.F., Sir v6p0244c1s
Flather, J.J. v6p0512c2m
Flatt, Prof. v1p0685c1s
Flattely, P.J. v1p0657c2s
Flavell, T. v3p0304c2s
Flaxman, J. v4p0294c1s
Fleay, F.G. v1p1017c2s
v1p1186c1s v1p1186c2s v2p0002c1s
v2p0305c1s v2p0346c1s v2p0404c1s
v2p0437c1s v3p0020c1s v3p0390c1s
v4p0172c1s v4p0519c1s v4p0520c1s
v5p0524c1s v6p0588c2s
Fleay, J.G. v1p1185c1s
Fleeming, A. v6p0001c2s
Fleet, W.Van v3p0195c1s
Fleisberg, O.A. v2p0380c1s
Fleischer, C. v6p0365c2s
Fleischman, C.F. v2p0411c1s
Fleischman, S. v6p0347c1s
Flemer, J.A. v4p0441c1s
v4p0579c1s
Fleming, A. v1p0096c2s
v1p0252c2s v1p0526c2s v1p0952c1s
v3p0124c1s v3p0253c1s v3p0373c1s
v3p0404c2m v3p0459c1s v4p0138c2s
v4p0412c1s v4p0489c2s v5p0627c1s
v6p0287c2s v6p0578c1s
Fleming, B. v6p0303c2s
Fleming, B. et al. v6p0154c1s
Fleming, C.F. v5p0351c1s

v5p0430c1s
Fleming, D.H. v5p0051c1s
v5p0509c2s v6p0159c2s v6p0353c2s
Fleming, E.L. v3p0050c2s
Fleming, G. v3p0098c1s
v3p0201c1s v3p0344c1s v3p0351c2s
v3p0449c1s v3p0469c2s v4p0018c2s
v4p0131c1s v4p0264c1s v5p0271c1s
v6p0298c1s
Fleming, G. and Brown, R.. v1p0055c2s
Fleming, G.R. v4p0288c2s
v4p0384c2s v5p0188c2s v5p0318c2s
v5p0340c1s v6p0152c2s
Fleming, George v4p0207c1s
Fleming, H. v1p1075c1s
v3p0159c1s
Fleming, H.E. v6p0113c1s
Fleming, H.G. v2p0034c2s
Fleming, H.S. v4p0067c2s
v4p0136c1s
Fleming, J. v1p0056c1s
v1p0845c1s
Fleming, J. et al. v3p0222c2s
Fleming, J.A. v3p0132c2s
v4p0176c1m v5p0183c2s v5p0184c2s
v5p0565c2s v5p0571c1s v6p0198c2s
v6p0199c1m v6p0289c1s v6p0636c2m
Fleming, J.C. v2p0065c2s
Fleming, J.F. v6p0287c2s
Fleming, J.H. v4p0116c2s
Fleming, J.M.K., Mrs. v4p0186c1s
Fleming, J.S. v2p0034c1s
Fleming, M., Mrs. v4p0034c2s
Fleming, Margaret v4p0146c2s
v4p0151c2s
Fleming, O. v4p0309c2s
v6p0153c1m v6p0266c2s v6p0271c2s
v6p0383c2s v6p0633c1s v6p0694c2s
Fleming, Owen v6p0408c1s
Fleming, S. v1p0193c1s
v1p0334c1s v1p0508c2s v1p0995c2s
v1p1075c1s v1p1312c1s v3p0430c2s
v4p0085c2s v4p0174c1s
Fleming, T.W. v4p0170c1s
Fleming, W. v1p0700c2s
v1p1076c1s v5p0463c1s v6p0535c1s
Fleming, W.H. v5p0446c1s
Fleming, W.J. v4p0020c2s
Fleming, W.L. v5p0082c1s
v6p0009c2m v6p0010c1s v6p0012c1s
v6p0240c2s v6p0309c1s v6p0312c2s
v6p0390c2s v6p0447c2s v6p0521c1s
v6p0534c1s v6p0606c2s v6p0667c2s
v6p0668c1s
Flemming, A. v1p0104c2s
Fleron, W. v2p0170c1s
v2p0176c1s
Fles, E. v4p0030c1s
v4p0361c2s
Flesche, F.La v4p0217c2s
v4p0363c2s v4p0413c2s v6p0409c1s
Flesher, Helen G. v4p0106c2s
Flesher, T. v4p0373c2s
Fletcher, A.B. v5p0195c1s
v5p0420c2s
Fletcher, A.C. v2p0097c1s
v4p0102c2s v4p0281c2s v4p0282c1m
v4p0282c2s v4p0366c1s v4p0413c2m
v4p0439c2s v4p0584c1s v4p0624c1s
v5p0288c1s v5p0419c2s v5p0510c1s
v5p0631c1s
Fletcher, A.E. v4p0030c2s
v4p0113c1s v5p0409c2s
Fletcher, Alice C. v4p0282c1s
v5p0328c2s v5p0437c1m v6p0485c1s
v6p0613c2s
Fletcher, B. v2p0020c1s
v5p0156c1s v5p0559c1s v6p0027c2s
Fletcher, B., jr. v4p0480c2s
v4p0510c2s
Fletcher, B.F. v4p0023c2s
v4p0025c1s v4p0480c2s v5p0508c1s
v6p0475c2s
Fletcher, B.T. v4p0131c1s
Fletcher, Banister v4p0024c1s
v4p0183c1s
Fletcher, C. v2p0064c1s
v2p0254c1s
Fletcher, C.R.L. v4p0514c2s
Fletcher, Col. v1p0194c2s
v1p1416c2s
Fletcher, D. v1p1017c2s
Fletcher, D.D. v5p0503c2s
Fletcher, D.O. v5p0279c2s
Fletcher, Dudu v1p0466c2s
Fletcher, E. v4p0157c1s
Fletcher, E.A. v6p0217c1s
Fletcher, F. and Benson, A.C.
v6p0382c2s
Fletcher, F.A. v4p0095c2s
Fletcher, F.N. v6p0562c1s
Fletcher, F.V. v5p0095c2s
Fletcher, G. v1p1185c2m
v4p0619c2s
Fletcher, G.R. v5p0023c2s
Fletcher, H.H. v3p0303c2s
Fletcher, H.J. v4p0114c2s
v4p0471c2m v4p0472c1s v4p0580c1s
v4p0582c1s v5p0071c2s
Fletcher, H.M. v1p1314c2s
Fletcher, J. v1p0309c1s
v1p0315c1s v1p0315c2s v1p0317c1s
v1p0384c2s v1p0414c2m v1p0444c1s
v1p0762c1m v1p0764c1s v1p0765c1s
v1p0765c2s v1p0766c1s v1p0766c2s
v1p0801c2s v1p0880c2s v1p0890c2s
v1p0982c1s v1p1024c2s v1p1090c2s
v1p1181c2s v1p1207c1s v1p1260c2s
v1p1391c2s v5p0564c1s
Fletcher, J.B. v3p0124c2s
v3p0155c1s v3p0191c2s v3p0287c1s
v3p0335c1s v3p0475c2s v4p0421c2s
v4p0601c2s v5p0324c1s v5p0613c2s
v6p0101c2s v6p0455c2s
Fletcher, J.C. v1p1224c2s
v3p0411c2s v4p0403c1s v4p0627c1s
Fletcher, J.H. v1p0072c2s
v1p1423c2s
Fletcher, J.M.J. v1p0459c1s
Fletcher, J.S. v3p0382c2s
v4p0002c2s v4p0084c2s v4p0356c1s
v4p0600c1s v5p0318c2s v5p0350c1s
Fletcher, L. v3p0179c1s
v3p0276c1s v3p0280c2s v6p0412c2m
Fletcher, L.A. v5p0532c2s
Fletcher, L.B. v2p0199c1s
v3p0116c2s v5p0339c1s
Fletcher, L.E. v1p0145c2s
v1p1247c2m v6p0507c1s
Fletcher, L.J. v1p0005c1s
v1p0101c1s v1p0520c2s v1p0598c2s
Fletcher, Margaret v6p0704c1s
Fletcher, R. v1p1328c1s
v5p0208c1s
Fletcher, R.C. v6p0191c2s
Fletcher, R.H. v3p0295c1s
v4p0162c2s
Fletcher, R.S. v5p0361c1s
Fletcher, S.W. v6p0243c2m
v6p0485c2s v6p0500c1s v6p0602c2m
v6p0620c2s
Fletcher, S.W. and Massey, W.F.
v6p0087c1s
Fletcher, T. v2p0158c2s
v2p0199c2s
Fletcher, W. v4p0180c1s
v4p0220c2s v4p0347c2s v4p0547c2m
v4p0561c1s
Fletcher, W.A. v3p0204c1s
Fletcher, W.G. v5p0588c2s
Fletcher, W.G.D. v2p0008c2m
v2p0030c2s v2p0052c2s v2p0116c2s
v2p0160c2s v2p0201c1s v2p0204c2s
v2p0212c1s v2p0308c2s v2p0459c2s
v6p0054c1s v6p0592c2m
Fletcher, W.I. v1p0628c2m
v1p1178c2s v2p0051c2s v2p0070c2s
v2p0216c2m v2p0256c1m v3p0011c2s
v3p0049c2s v3p0248c2m v3p0249c1m
v3p0249c2m v3p0338c2s v4p0014c2m
v4p0069c1s v4p0122c2s v4p0134c2s
v4p0329c1m v4p0330c1m v4p0330c2m
v4p0451c2s v5p0016c1m v5p0133c1s
v5p0284c1s v5p0334c1s v5p0335c1s
v5p0336c1s v5p0337c1s v5p0349c1s
v6p0017c1m v6p0087c2s v6p0104c1s
v6p0371c2s
Fletcher, W.I. and Poole, W.F.
v2p0216c2s v2p0336c1s
Fletcher, W.I. and Thwaites, R.G.
v5p0337c1s
Fletcher, W.J. v5p0053c2s
v5p0067c2s v5p0077c2s v5p0209c2s
v5p0401c1s v5p0416c2s v5p0464c2s
v5p0526c2s v5p0545c2s v5p0591c2s
v6p0004c1s v6p0022c2s v6p0100c2s
v6p0201c1s v6p0250c1s v6p0268c2s
v6p0294c2s v6p0301c2s v6p0382c1s
v6p0426c1s v6p0445c1s v6p0445c2s
v6p0483c2s v6p0611c2s v6p0682c1s
Fletcher, W.S. v5p0355c2s
Fletcher, W.Y. v4p0041c1s
v4p0066c1s v4p0066c2s v4p0067c1s
v4p0094c1s v5p0077c2s v5p0498c2s
Fletcher, Wm. v5p0066c1s
Fletcher-Moulton, J. et al.
v4p0239c2s
Fletcher-Vane, F.P. v6p0006c2s
Fleury, A. v5p0105c1s
Fleury, J. v4p0004c2s
v4p0012c2m v4p0182c2s
Fleury, M.de
v5p0289c1s
Flewelling, R.T. v6p0600c1s
Flexner, A. v4p0028c2s
v5p0126c1s v5p0191c1s v5p0484c2s
v5p0517c2s v6p0215c1s v6p0282c1s
v6p0514c2s
Flexner, S. v6p0483c2s
v6p0660c1s
Flexner, S. and Barker, L.F.
v5p0444c2s
Flick, L.F. v6p0660c1s
Flight, W. v1p0745c2s
v1p0828c2s
Flinch, O. v6p0358c2s
Fling, F.M. v3p0384c2s
v5p0266c2s v5p0378c2s v6p0047c2s
v6p0184c2s v6p0292c1s v6p0420c1m
Flinn, J.J. v4p0309c1s
Flint, A. v1p0041c1s
v1p0881c2s v1p1351c1s v1p1360c1s
v3p0030c1s v3p0151c2s v3p0273c1s
v3p0378c2s v3p0394c1s v4p0001c2s
v4p0192c2s v6p0151c2s v6p0587c1s
Flint, A. et al. v3p0350c1s
Flint, A., jr. v1p0380c2s
Flint, A.S. v4p0545c2s
Flint, C.L. v1p0207c2s
Flint, C.R. v5p0085c1s
v5p0093c1s v5p0175c1s v5p0200c1s
v5p0289c1m v5p0423c2s v5p0593c1m
v6p0428c1s v6p0592c1s
Flint, E. v2p0161c1s
v2p0314c1s
Flint, G. v5p0147c2s
v5p0239c2s
Flint, G.E. v5p0253c1s
v6p0151c2s v6p0285c1s
Flint, J. v1p0158c1s
v1p0460c1s v1p1042c1s v5p0304c2s
Flint, J.F. v5p0378c1s
Flint, L.C. v4p0149c1s
Flint, M. v1p0561c1s
v1p0897c1s v1p1127c1s
Flint, M.B. v5p0230c1s
Flint, M.R. v6p0014c1s
Flint, R. v1p0069c1s
v1p0447c1s v1p0640c2s v1p0868c1s
v1p1000c1s v1p1062c1s v1p1307c2s
v2p0088c1s v2p0244c2s v2p0390c2s
v3p0067c1s v3p0357c2s v3p0398c1s
v3p0471c1s v4p0341c2s v4p0533c1s
Flint, T. v1p0031c2s
v1p0084c2s v1p0389c2s v1p0569c2s
v1p0649c1s v1p0770c2s v1p0806c1s
v1p1004c2s
Flint, W. v1p0148c2s
v1p0320c2s v1p0743c1s v3p0248c2s
Flint, W.F. v1p1015c1m
Flintham, L.S. v5p0349c1s
v5p0606c1s
Flood, E. v5p0194c1s
Flood, F.S. v2p0201c1s
v3p0194c1s
Flood, J.C.H. v4p0322c1s
v4p0359c1s v4p0371c2s
Flood, J.H. v2p0143c1s
Flood, N.A. v4p0314c2s
v4p0394c1s v5p0346c2s v5p0409c2s
v5p0461c2s
Flood, N.R. v4p0347c2s
Flood, T.L. v3p0075c1s
v3p0215c1s v3p0295c2s v3p0338c1s
v4p0367c2s v5p0103c2m v5p0202c2s
Flood, T.L. and Barnard, Charles
v4p0179c2s
Flood, T.W. v4p0175c2s
Flood, W.H.G. v4p0142c1s
v6p0180c1s
Flora, C.P. v6p0091c1m
Flora, C.P. and Browing, P.E.
v6p0107c1s
Florance, J.F. v5p0252c1s
Florence, W.J. v3p0453c2s
Florentino, Vincenzo v6p0548c2s
Flores, A. v1p0305c2s
Florian, J.P.C.de v1p0535c1s
Floris, C.L. v3p0427c1s
Flory, J.S. v6p0252c1s
v6p0700c1s
Flourens, E. et al. v3p0301c1s
Flourens, M. v1p1073c1s
v3p0159c2s v3p0369c2s
Flournoy, P.P. v6p0182c2s
Flournoy, T. v5p0441c2s
Flower, B. v6p0582c1s
Flower, B.C. v4p0385c1s
Flower, B.I. v6p0139c1s
Flower, B.O. v3p0150c1s
v3p0209c1s v3p0328c2s v3p0338c2s
v3p0397c2s v3p0398c2s v3p0399c2s
v3p0453c2s v4p0027c2s v4p0099c2m
v4p0101c2s v4p0103c2s v4p0117c2m
v4p0139c2s v4p0148c1s v4p0152c1s
v4p0154c1s v4p0161c2s v4p0162c1s
v4p0181c1s v4p0185c1s v4p0203c1s
v4p0231c1s v4p0255c1s v4p0256c1s
v4p0268c2s v4p0271c2m v4p0275c2m
v4p0294c1s v4p0294c2s v4p0297c2s
v4p0301c1s v4p0316c1s v4p0324c1s
v4p0331c2s v4p0347c2s v4p0360c1s
v4p0370c1m v4p0371c1s v4p0382c2m
v4p0383c2s v4p0396c2s v4p0399c2s
v4p0435c2s v4p0447c2s v4p0448c1s
v4p0449c1s v4p0457c1s v4p0461c1s
v4p0462c1s v4p0464c1s v4p0464c2s
v4p0466c1s v4p0476c2s v4p0478c2s
v4p0479c2s v4p0525c1s v4p0539c2s
v4p0584c1s v4p0590c2s v4p0595c1s
v4p0620c2s v4p0621c1m v4p0622c2s
v4p0629c1s v5p0006c2s v5p0007c2s
v5p0009c2s v5p0019c2s v5p0027c2s
v5p0053c1s v5p0072c2s v5p0078c2s
v5p0121c1m v5p0136c1s v5p0137c2s
v5p0138c1s v5p0143c1s v5p0145c2s
v5p0175c1s v5p0215c1s v5p0236c1s
v5p0253c2m v5p0279c1s v5p0354c1s
v5p0368c1s v5p0392c1s v5p0412c1s
v5p0434c1s v5p0437c1s v5p0468c1s

v5p0470c1s v5p0481c2s v5p0484c2s
v5p0500c1s v5p0513c2s v5p0534c2s
v5p0535c1s v5p0536c1s v5p0537c2s
v5p0543c2s v5p0550c2s v5p0553c2s
v5p0598c1s v5p0599c2s v5p0601c1s
v5p0611c1s v5p0641c2s v6p0003c2s
v6p0019c2s v6p0031c2s v6p0032c2s
v6p0043c2s v6p0052c2s v6p0055c1s
v6p0076c1s v6p0084c1s v6p0095c1s
v6p0103c1s v6p0114c1s v6p0114c2s
v6p0148c1s v6p0148c2m v6p0151c1s
v6p0151c2s v6p0158c1s v6p0165c2s
v6p0169c2m v6p0175c1s v6p0176c2s
v6p0182c2s v6p0193c2s v6p0210c1s
v6p0215c2s v6p0222c2s v6p0239c2m
v6p0245c1s v6p0253c2s v6p0254c1s
v6p0256c2s v6p0279c2s v6p0322c2s
v6p0337c1s v6p0339c2s v6p0345c1s
v6p0357c1s v6p0364c2s v6p0369c1s
v6p0381c1s v6p0381c2s v6p0401c2m
v6p0407c2s v6p0408c1s v6p0409c1s
v6p0417c2s v6p0431c1s v6p0434c2s
v6p0437c2s v6p0463c1s v6p0468c2s
v6p0471c1s v6p0491c2s v6p0494c2s
v6p0495c1m v6p0497c1s v6p0500c2s
v6p0507c2s v6p0508c2s v6p0511c1s
v6p0522c2s v6p0530c2s v6p0534c2s
v6p0536c1s v6p0545c1s v6p0557c2s
v6p0601c1s v6p0609c2s v6p0613c1s
v6p0618c2s v6p0621c1s v6p0634c2m
v6p0641c2s v6p0649c1s v6p0659c1s
v6p0659c2s v6p0662c2s v6p0665c2s
v6p0668c1s v6p0678c1s v6p0683c1s
v6p0683c2s v6p0686c1s v6p0713c2s
Flower, B.O. et al. v4p0464c1s
v5p0263c2s
v5p0443c2s
Flower, E. v5p0178c2s
v5p0457c1s v6p0113c2s v6p0163c1s
v6p0170c1s v6p0201c2m v6p0222c2s
v6p0249c2s v6p0280c2s v6p0287c2s
v6p0310c2s v6p0322c2s v6p0329c2s
v6p0347c1s v6p0407c1s v6p0506c2s
v6p0514c1s v6p0590c2s v6p0621c1s
v6p0621c2s v6p0653c1s v6p0664c1s
v6p0665c1s v6p0672c2s v6p0695c2s
v6p0704c2s
Flower, Elliott v6p0073c2s
v6p0080c2s v6p0103c1s v6p0220c2s
v6p0223c1s v6p0345c2s v6p0398c1s
v6p0684c1s
Flower, F.A. v2p0163c2s
v3p0159c1s v5p0133c1s v5p0548c2s
Flower, J. v6p0618c1s
Flower, J.E. v3p0144c2s
Flower, J.W. v1p0470c2s
v1p0966c1s v1p1255c2s
Flower, L. v1p1181c1s
Flower, Lady v5p0548c2s
Flower, Prof. v1p0960c1s
Flower, R.P. v4p0485c2s
v5p0119c2s v5p0593c2s
Flower, R.P. and Depew, C.M.
v5p0289c1s
Flower, S. v5p0467c2s
Flower, W.C. v1p0966c1s
Flower, W.H. v1p0042c2s
v1p0341c1s v1p0445c1s v1p0791c2s
v1p0793c1s v1p0882c1s v1p0960c1s
v1p1403c1s v2p0013c1s v2p0013c2s
v2p0016c2s v2p0047c1s v2p0147c2s
v2p0149c2s v2p0155c2s v2p0273c1s
v2p0274c1s v2p0274c2s v2p0299c1s
v2p0361c2s v2p0432c2s v2p0471c2s
v3p0292c2m v3p0332c1s v3p0475c2s
v4p0061c2s v4p0271c1s v4p0296c1s
v4p0468c1s v5p0400c1s
Flower, W.W. v6p0623c2s
Flowerden, H. v5p0206c2s
v5p0363c1s
Flowers, R.L. v6p0531c2s
Floy, H. v4p0176c1s
Floy, J. v1p0005c2s
v1p0097c2s v1p0132c1s v1p0165c2s
v1p0189c1s v1p0440c2s v1p0620c1s
v1p0620c2s v1p0689c1s v1p0697c2s
v1p0831c1s v1p0853c2s v1p1237c2s
v1p1399c1s
Floyd, E.F. v5p0034c1s
Floyd, F.W. v2p0014c1s
Floyd, J. v1p0617c2s
Floyd, J.A. v4p0187c2s
v4p0226c1s v4p0635c2s v5p0493c1s
Floyd, J.B. v1p1224c1s
Floyd, J.M. v1p0577c2s
Floyd, M. v4p0437c2s
Floyd, M.R. v2p0450c2s
v3p0112c1s v3p0271c2s
Floyd-Jones, DeLancey v5p0113c1s
Floyer, E.A. v3p0131c1s
v4p0172c2s v4p0557c2s
Floyer, J.K. v5p0335c2s
v6p0079c1s v6p0373c2s
Fluegel, E. v6p0081c2s
Flugel, E. v4p0098c2s
v5p0548c2s
Fluhrer, W.F. v2p0054c2s
Flurscheim, M. v3p0361c2s
v6p0582c1s
Flux, A.H. v6p0096c1s
Flux, A.W. v4p0236c2s
v5p0091c1s v5p0175c2m v5p0245c1s
v5p0248c1s v5p0343c2s v5p0374c2s
v5p0419c1s v5p0526c2s v5p0584c1s
v5p0584c2s v6p0050c1s v6p0096c1s
v6p0266c2s v6p0514c1s v6p0518c1s
v6p0539c1s
Flux, A.W. and Hobson, J.A.
v5p0509c2s
Fly, H. v1p0001c1s
Flynn, C.W. v5p0165c2s
Flynn, J.W. v5p0564c1s
Flynn, Mr. and Mirick, C.M.
v6p0112c1s
Flynn, P.J. v2p0128c2s
v2p0212c2s v2p0213c1s v2p0244c2s
v2p0385c1s v2p0468c1s
Flynt, H.S. v6p0325c1s
v6p0688c1s
Flynt, J. v3p0434c2s
v4p0104c1s v4p0182c2s v4p0223c2s
v4p0296c2s v4p0412c1s v4p0581c2m
v4p0590c2s v5p0072c2s v5p0143c2m
v5p0457c1s v5p0477c2s v5p0481c2s
v5p0566c1s v6p0506c2s v6p0706c1s
Flynt, J. and Walton, F. . v5p0061c2s
v5p0215c2s v5p0282c2s v5p0486c2s
Flynt, Josiah v4p0120c1s
v5p0585c2m
Foa, E. v4p0636c2s
Foard, I. v5p0143c2s
v5p0263c1s
Foard, J.T. v5p0362c2s
v5p0522c1s
Foat, E.W.G. v6p0659c2s
Foat, F.W.G. v5p0565c2s
v6p0273c1s
Fobes, C.S. v5p0048c2s
Focer, M. v1p0676c2s
Focht, D.N. v1p0850c1s
Focht, J.B. v1p1043c1s
Focke, R. v6p0371c2s
Focke, W.O. v2p0344c1s
v2p0413c1s
Fockler, O. v1p0313c1s
v1p0507c1s
Foering, H.A. v6p0406c1s
Foerste, A.F. v3p0223c1s
v4p0185c1s v4p0373c1s v5p0334c1s
v6p0469c2s
Foerster, A.F. v2p0202c2s
Foerster, A.M. v5p0219c2s
Foerster, W. v3p0193c2s
v4p0165c2s
Foerster, W. and Jesse, O.
v4p0120c1s
Foester, W. v2p0025c2s
v2p0064c1s
Fogazzaro, A. v4p0191c1s
v4p0191c2s v4p0352c1s v4p0480c1s
Fogel, P.H. v6p0412c1s
v6p0602c1s
Fogerty, W. v1p0054c1m
Fogg, A.J. v2p0158c2s
Fogg, J.S. v4p0160c1s
Fogg, J.S.H. v3p0026c2s
v3p0051c1s v3p0231c2s v3p0466c2s
v4p0254c2s v4p0312c1s v4p0347c1s
v4p0519c2s v4p0610c2s v5p0356c2s
Fogg, W.P. v1p0185c2s
Fogg-Meade, E. v5p0004c2s
Foggon, J. v2p0037c2s
Fol, H. v2p0287c2m
v3p0118c2s
Foldes, Bela v6p0158c1s
Foley, A.L. v6p0249c1s
Foley, C. v5p0429c1s
v5p0571c1s
Foley, C.A. v4p0195c2s
Foley, G.C. v2p0414c1s
Foley, J.P. v3p0225c2s
v3p0228c1s v3p0343c1s v3p0456c1s
Foley, M.F. v3p0123c1s
v3p0373c2s v6p0395c1s
Foley, R.A. v5p0443c1s
Foley, W.C. v4p0027c2s
v4p0244c2s
Folger, W.C. v1p0273c2s
v1p0464c1s
Folie, F. v4p0409c2s
Folk, J.W. v6p0128c1s
v6p0323c1s v6p0364c1m
Folk, Joseph, W. v6p0191c1s
Folkard, A. v2p0305c1s
v2p0427c2m
Folkard, C.W. v2p0467c1s
v2p0467c2s
Folkes, M. v1p0046c2m
v1p1126c2s v1p1320c2s
Folkestone, H.M. v2p0031c2s
Folkmar, D., Mrs. v5p0511c2s
Folks, H. v4p0064c2s
v4p0103c2s v4p0104c1s v4p0104c2s
v5p0101c2m v5p0102c1s v5p0106c1s
v5p0106c2s v5p0107c1s v5p0344c1s
v5p0406c2s v5p0407c2s v6p0114c2m
v6p0115c1s v6p0175c2s v6p0284c2s
v6p0435c1s v6p0454c2m v6p0518c1s
v6p0660c1s
Folks, R. v6p0463c2s
Follen, C. v1p0009c1s
v1p0052c1s v1p0496c1s v1p0573c1s
v1p0626c1s v1p0730c2s v1p0868c2s
Follet, Miss v1p0071c2s
Follett, C. v6p0271c1s
Follett, C.J. v6p0240c2s
v6p0271c1s
Follett, Chas. v6p0054c2s
Follett, H. v4p0262c2s
Follett, J.B. v4p0083c1s
Follett, L.D. v6p0628c1s
Follett, M.P. v4p0118c1s
Follette, R.M.La v6p0392c2s
Folley, F.J. v6p0584c1s
Follin, M.D.
v6p0021c2s
Folsom, A.A. v3p0326c2s
v6p0432c2s v6p0564c2s
Folsom, C.F. v2p0193c1s
v3p0457c1s v4p0070c2s
Folsom, C.F. et al. v2p0221c2s
Folsom, C.W. v1p0211c2s
Folsom, G. v1p1440c1s
Folsom, J.W. v4p0039c2s
v4p0217c1s v4p0513c1s
Folsom, M.M. v2p0082c2s
Folsom, N.S. v1p0123c2s
v1p0129c2s v1p0464c2s v1p0989c2s
v1p1016c2s v1p1325c2s
Folsom, N.S. and Sears, E.H.
v1p0687c1s
Foltz, C., Mrs. v5p0471c1s
Foltz, F.S. v5p0231c1s
v5p0367c1s v6p0541c2s
Folwell, A.P. v6p0664c2s
Folwell, G.W. v2p0119c2s
Folwell, J.K. v3p0104c1s
Folwell, J.N. v1p1042c1s
Folwell, W.W. v2p0455c2s
v3p0281c1s v3p0336c2s v4p0167c2s
v5p0628c2s
Fonblanque, A. v1p0181c2s
v1p0200c1s v1p0327c1s v1p0407c2s
v1p0442c1s v1p0445c2s v1p0765c2s
v1p0776c2s v1p0786c2s v1p0864c2s
v1p1032c1s v1p1083c1s v1p1087c2s
v1p1216c2s v1p1352c2s v2p0240c1s
Fonblanque, A., jr. v1p0142c2s
v1p0160c1s v1p0200c1s v1p0483c1s
v1p1179c1s v1p1282c1s
Fonblanque, A.de v0p1593c1s
v1p0416c2s v1p0419c2s v1p0617c2s
v1p1012c1s v2p0449c2s v3p0193c1s
Fonblanque, E.B.de v2p0036c2s
Fonblanque, E.M.de v3p0334c2s
Fonblanque, Ethel v3p0467c2s
Fonblanque, L.R.de v3p0213c1s
Fond, F. v4p0571c1s
Fonda, A.I. v4p0378c1s
v5p0045c2s v5p0149c1s
Fonda, J.L. v4p0317c2s
Fondi, E. v6p0072c2s
Fong, W.N. v4p0105c2s
v4p0106c2m v4p0315c2m v6p0118c2s
Fontaine, A.C. v6p0670c2s
Fontaine, C. and Snow, W.B.
v6p0241c1s
Fontaine, E. v2p0321c1s
Fontaine, F.G.De v2p0424c2s
v5p0020c2s
Fontaine, H.La v6p0065c2s
Fontaine, J.A. v6p0045c1s
Fontaine, M.B. v1p1192c1s
Fontaine, M.E. v6p0090c1s
Fontaine, Miss de la v6p0401c2s
Fontaine, W.M. v1p0068c2s
v1p0143c2s v1p0509c2m v1p1373c2m
v1p1401c2m v4p0366c1s
Fontaine, W.W. v1p0734c1s
Fontanes, E. v2p0165c2s
Fontanes, E. and Service, J.
v1p1243c1s
Fontanoy, Marquise de v6p0699c1s
Fontenelle, De v2p0480c2s
Fontenelle, M.de v2p0343c2s
Fontenoy, De v5p0051c1s
Fonvielle, W.de v1p0088c2s
v1p0089c1s v1p0372c2m v1p0399c1s
v1p0501c1s v1p0791c2s v1p0881c2s
v1p0971c1s v1p1074c2s v1p1367c1s
v1p1395c1s v2p0020c2s v2p0340c1s
v5p0271c1s
Fonvielle, Wilfrid de v6p0005c1s
Foord, J. v3p0047c1s
v5p0110c2s v5p0111c1s v5p0111c2s
v5p0323c1s v6p0560c1s
Foos, C.S. v6p0574c2s
Foot, J.I. v1p0985c2s
v1p1094c2s v1p1303c1s
Foot, J.J. v1p0454c2s
v1p0576c2s v1p0990c1s v1p1237c2s
Foot, K.B. v1p0799c2s
v3p0060c1s v3p0102c1s v3p0189c2s
v3p0254c1s
Foot, K.B., Mrs. v3p0314c2s
Foot, L. v1p0638c2s
Foote, A.E. v3p0116c2s
v3p0168c2s v3p0275c2s v4p0367c1m
Foote, A.R. v3p0326c1s
v4p0127c1s v4p0135c1s v4p0143c2s

v4p0234c1s v4p0283c2s v4p0297c1s
v4p0434c1s v5p0383c1s v5p0391c2s
v5p0468c2s v6p0435c2s
Foote, E. v1p0400c2s
v1p0580c1s v1p1268c2s v6p0257c1s
v6p0357c1s v6p0439c1s v6p0712c1s
Foote, E., Mrs. v1p0400c1s
Foote, Elizabeth v6p0552c2s
Foote, F. v6p0074c1s
Foote, H.G. v1p1207c1s
Foote, H.M. v4p0143c1s
Foote, H.W. v1p0076c1s
v1p0155c1s v1p0255c1s v1p0487c2s
v1p0708c1s v1p0756c2s v1p0809c1s
v1p1067c1s v1p1285c2s v1p1310c1s
v1p1340c1s v1p1340c2s v1p1341c1s
v2p0081c1s v2p0267c2s v4p0353c1s
v4p0369c1s v4p0451c1s v4p0494c2s
v6p0325c2s
Foote, H.W. and Penfield, S.L.
v5p0065c2s v5p0123c1s v5p0280c1s
v5p0492c1s v5p0583c2s
Foote, H.W. and Pratt, J.H.
v5p0625c1s
Foote, H.W. and Wells, H.L.
v4p0082c2s v4p0637c1s v5p0087c1s
v5p0499c2s v5p0645c2s
Foote, J.A. v6p0019c2s
Foote, J.V. v6p0441c2s
v6p0691c2s
Foote, K. v1p1306c1s
v2p0342c2s
Foote, K.B. v1p1311c1s
Foote, L.H. v1p0627c1s
v1p1273c2s v4p0106c2s v4p0560c1s
Foote, M.C. v5p0029c1s
v5p0375c1s
Foote, M.H. v1p0188c1s
v1p0491c1s v1p0627c1s v1p1151c1s
v1p1257c2s v2p0089c2s v2p0153c1s
v2p0237c2s v2p0252c2s v2p0286c2m
v2p0287c1s v2p0298c1s v2p0421c2s
v3p0243c1s v3p0354c2s v4p0108c1s
v4p0121c2s v4p0248c2s v4p0361c2s
v4p0414c1s v4p0443c1s v4p0585c2s
v4p0612c2s v5p0274c1s v5p0451c2s
v5p0467c2s v5p0583c2s
Foote, Mary Hallock v6p0076c1s
v6p0200c1s
Foote, S.M. v5p0206c2s
v5p0567c1s v5p0614c2s v6p0035c1s
Foote, T.C. v3p0243c2s
v6p0209c2s
Foote, W.H. v1p0303c1s
Foote, W.M. v4p0010c2s
v4p0324c1s v5p0328c2s v5p0372c1m
Foraker, J.B. v3p0238c1s
v3p0359c1s v3p0420c1s v5p0458c1s
v5p0460c2s v5p0543c2s
Foran, W. v6p0275c2s
Forbes, A. v1p0103c2s
v1p0178c1s v1p0305c2s v1p0328c2s
v1p0460c2s v1p0494c2s v1p0542c2s
v1p0559c2s v1p0651c2s v1p0722c1s
v1p0776c1s v1p0811c2s v1p1134c1s
v1p1137c2s v1p1330c1s v1p1385c1s
v1p1441c2s v2p0028c2s v2p0029c1s
v2p0036c2m v2p0122c1s v2p0135c1s
v2p0165c1s v2p0185c2s v2p0186c1m
v2p0224c1s v2p0252c2s v2p0306c1m
v2p0406c1s v2p0451c2s v2p0465c2m
v2p0476c2s v2p0481c2s v3p0027c2s
v3p0030c2s v3p0039c1s v3p0102c2s
v3p0150c1s v3p0161c1m v3p0162c2s
v3p0180c1m v3p0203c1s v3p0278c2s
v3p0285c1s v3p0311c2s v3p0315c2s
v3p0371c1s v3p0438c2s v3p0454c1s
v3p0454c2s v3p0476c2s v4p0005c1s
v4p0010c1s v4p0013c1s v4p0028c1s
v4p0048c1s v4p0052c1s v4p0127c1s
v4p0130c2s v4p0189c1s v4p0189c2s
v4p0212c1m v4p0232c2s v4p0308c1s
v4p0332c2s v4p0377c1s v4p0391c1m
v4p0393c1m v4p0422c2s v4p0477c2s
v4p0486c1s v4p0494c1s v4p0513c1m
v4p0521c1s v4p0541c2s v4p0554c1s
v4p0610c2s v4p0613c2s v4p0633c2s
v5p0206c2s v5p0398c2s v5p0508c1s
v5p0622c2s v6p0507c2m
Forbes, A., Mrs. v5p0502c2s
Forbes, A.K.H. v5p0055c1s
v5p0519c1s
Forbes, A.K.H., Mrs. v5p0490c2s
Forbes, A.S.C., Mrs. v6p0357c2s
v6p0433c2s
Forbes, Archibald v4p0005c1s
v4p0404c2s v6p0670c1s
Forbes, Athol v5p0432c2s
Forbes, D. v1p0180c1s
v1p0375c2m v1p0507c2m v1p0663c2m
v1p0745c1s v1p0826c1s v1p0900c2s
v1p1113c1s v1p1172c1s v1p1255c2s
v1p1369c1s v1p1377c1s v1p1377c2s
Forbes, E. v1p0509c2m
v1p0882c1s
Forbes, E.H. v4p0185c2s
Forbes, E.H. and Penfield, S.L.
v4p0380c2s
Forbes, E.M. v3p0079c2s
v3p0318c2s v4p0423c1s
Forbes, E.S. v5p0049c1s
Forbes, F.B. v4p0281c1s
v5p0463c2s v6p0239c2s v6p0260c2s
v6p0516c1s
Forbes, F.H. v1p0621c1s
Forbes, Francis B. v6p0312c2s
Forbes, G. v1p0377c1s
v1p0400c2s v1p0557c1s v1p1244c1s
v1p1367c1s v1p1369c1s v2p0126c2s
v2p0137c2s v2p0138c1s v2p0215c1s
v2p0294c1s v3p0133c1s v3p0133c2m
v3p0134c1s v4p0176c2s v4p0403c2m
v4p0455c2s v5p0183c1s v5p0183c2s
v6p0502c1s v6p0531c1s
Forbes, G.M. v3p0129c2s
v6p0341c2s
Forbes, G.W. v6p0448c1s
Forbes, H.C. and Davis, C.H.
v5p0183c2s v5p0184c1s
Forbes, H.O. v1p0049c1s
v1p0135c1s v1p1156c1s v2p0244c2s
v2p0424c2s v3p0301c2s v4p0019c2s
v4p0038c1s v4p0060c2s v4p0098c1s
v4p0228c2s v4p0375c2s v4p0399c1m
v4p0469c1s v4p0624c2s v5p0537c2s
Forbes, H.P. v2p0105c2s
v2p0177c1s v3p0080c2s
Forbes, H.R.P. v5p0282c1s
v5p0555c2s v6p0226c1s v6p0449c1s
Forbes, H.T.S. v5p0433c1s
Forbes, I. v6p0681c2s
Forbes, J. v1p0129c2s
v1p0682c2s v2p0043c2s v2p0215c1s
v3p0042c1s v6p0071c1s v6p0078c2s
Forbes, J.D. v1p0314c2s
v1p0524c1m v1p0792c2s v1p0960c2s
v1p1162c1s
Forbes, J.H. v4p0498c1s
Forbes, J.I. v1p0166c1s
v1p1355c1s
Forbes, J.M. v3p0094c1s
v3p0390c2s v6p0332c2s
Forbes, J.Macbeth v4p0044c1s
Forbes, J.W. v5p0584c2s
Forbes, L. v1p0222c2s
v1p0902c2s
Forbes, M. v5p0132c2s
Forbes, R.B. v1p0613c2s
v1p0746c2s v1p0809c2s v1p1171c2s
v1p1247c1s
Forbes, R.H. v6p0265c1s
Forbes, R.S. v5p0548c2s
Forbes, S.A. v1p0332c2s
v2p0157c1m v3p0246c1m v3p0460c2s
v3p0475c2s
Forbes, S.E.P., Mrs. v4p0428c2s
Forbes, U.A. v1p0460c2s
v2p0373c2s v3p0106c1s v3p0434c2s
v5p0121c1s v5p0130c2s v5p0180c2s
v5p0539c2s v6p0313c2s
Forbes, Urquhart A. v6p0098c2s
Forbes, W.C. v5p0213c1s
Forbes, W.D. v5p0326c1s
v5p0353c2s v6p0355c2s
Forbes-Lindsay, C.H. v6p0476c2s
v6p0477c2s
Forbes-Robertson, F. v5p0379c1s
Forbes-Robertson, J. v4p0066c1s
v4p0387c1s v4p0426c1m
Forbush, T.B. v3p0196c2s
Forbush, W.B. v5p0106c2s
v5p0173c2s v6p0062c1s v6p0095c2s
v6p0341c2s v6p0466c2s
Force, M.F. v1p0141c2s
v1p0484c1s v1p0729c1s v1p0929c1s
v6p0509c1s
Force, M.F. et al. v3p0085c1s
Force, P. v1p0339c2s
v1p0789c1s v1p0946c2s
Forchhammer, G. v1p1173c1m
Forcythe, S. v3p0216c1s
Ford, A. v1p0338c2s
Ford, A.H. v5p0034c1s
v5p0109c2s v5p0188c2s v5p0294c2s
v5p0302c2s v5p0500c2s v5p0501c1m
v5p0501c2m v5p0622c2m v6p0098c2s
v6p0186c2s v6p0198c1s v6p0340c1s
v6p0479c1m v6p0527c2s v6p0585c2s
v6p0612c2s v6p0680c2s
Ford, A.P. v2p0069c1s
v2p0196c1s
Ford, Alex Hume v6p0612c2s
Ford, C. v4p0108c2s
v4p0218c2s v4p0461c1s v5p0284c1s
v5p0484c1m v6p0273c2s v6p0512c2s
v6p0576c1s
Ford, D.B. v1p0685c1s
v1p0686c1s v1p1109c1s v1p1279c1s
Ford, D.E. v1p0802c2s
Ford, D.L. v6p0588c2s
Ford, D.M. v3p0343c2s
Ford, E. v2p0182c2s
v2p0294c2s
Ford, E.E. v1p0574c2s
v2p0302c2s v2p0346c1s
Ford, E.E., Mrs. v1p0062c2s
Ford, E.F., Mrs. v1p0321c2s
v1p0754c2s
Ford, F. v3p0333c2s
v4p0380c2s v4p0538c2s
Ford, F.A. v2p0451c1s
Ford, F.B. v6p0615c1s
Ford, F.L. v4p0025c2s
v4p0483c1s v5p0607c2s v6p0611c2s
Ford, F.W. v2p0081c2s
Ford, Frances G. v6p0516c1s
Ford, G.B. v6p0329c1s
v6p0479c2m v6p0639c2s
Ford, G.R. v6p0023c1s
Ford, G.S. v6p0145c1s
Ford, G.W. v4p0475c2m
Ford, H. v4p0076c1s
v4p0493c2s v5p0554c1s
Ford, H.A. v2p0144c1s
v2p0269c2s
Ford, H.J. v5p0120c2s
v5p0457c2s v5p0583c2s v6p0435c1s
v6p0535c1s v6p0650c2s
Ford, H.T. v6p0435c2s
Ford, Harriet v5p0504c1s
v5p0507c1s
Ford, I.N. v1p0479c2s
v2p0165c2s v3p0053c2s v6p0198c2s
v6p0206c2s v6p0384c1s v6p0479c2s
Ford, J. v1p1334c1s
v4p0383c2s v5p0391c2s v5p0568c2s
Ford, J.D.M. v6p0386c2s
v6p0608c1s
Ford, J.L. v4p0269c1s
v4p0572c1s v4p0588c2s v5p0015c2s
v5p0016c1s v5p0042c2s v5p0067c1s
v5p0148c2s v5p0171c2s v5p0256c2s
v5p0275c2s v5p0279c1s v5p0385c2s
v5p0615c1s v6p0155c1s v6p0181c1m
v6p0407c1s v6p0453c2s v6p0461c2s
v6p0544c2s v6p0601c2m v6p0641c2s
v6p0709c1s
Ford, J.S. v6p0243c1s
Ford, J.T. v3p0416c2s
Ford, Jas.L. v4p0467c1s
Ford, Julia E. v6p0555c2s
Ford, Julia E and Thompson, Kate V.
v6p0711c1s
Ford, L.P. v6p0087c1s
v6p0618c2s
Ford, M. v1p0245c2s
v1p0405c1s v1p0443c2s v1p0599c2s
v1p0711c1s v2p0152c2s
Ford, M.B. v3p0265c1s
v3p0399c1s v4p0425c1s
Ford, M.C. v6p0372c2s
Ford, M.H. v1p0159c1s
v1p0599c2s v1p1219c2s v3p0317c2s
Ford, M.J. v2p0464c2s
Ford, M.K. v6p0106c1s
v6p0223c1s v6p0708c1s
Ford, M.W. v3p0205c1s
v3p0233c1m v3p0369c1s v3p0405c2s
v4p0035c2s v4p0306c2m v4p0522c1s
v4p0575c2s v4p0601c1s v5p0036c2m
v5p0408c1s
Ford, Mary H. v6p0032c2s
v6p0459c2s
Ford, Mary K. v6p0390c1s
Ford, Mrs. Dr. v1p1227c1s
Ford, N.W. v4p0247c1s
Ford, P. v3p0223c1s
v4p0532c2s
Ford, P.L. v2p0335c2s
v3p0003c2s v3p0010c1s v3p0096c2s
v3p0249c1m v3p0249c2s v3p0263c2s
v3p0333c2s v3p0442c2s v4p0155c2s
v4p0160c2s v4p0196c2s v4p0213c1m
v4p0215c1s v4p0226c1s v4p0240c2s
v4p0263c2s v4p0267c2s v4p0299c1m
v4p0310c2s v4p0317c1s v4p0398c2s
v4p0433c1s v4p0433c2s v4p0494c2s
v4p0612c1s v5p0017c1m v5p0029c2s
v5p0163c1s v5p0219c1m v5p0266c1m
v5p0302c1s v5p0555c2s v5p0601c2s
v5p0617c2s v5p0634c2s v6p0684c2s
Ford, P.L. and Bourne, E.G.
v5p0204c1s
Ford, R. v1p0012c1s
v1p0037c1s v1p0052c1s v1p0054c1s
v1p0150c2s v1p0449c1s v1p0521c1s
v1p1228c2m v1p1230c2m v1p1231c1m
v1p1359c1s v1p1383c2s
Ford, R.C. v4p0183c2s
v5p0212c1s v5p0275c2s v5p0339c1s
v5p0351c1s v5p0357c1m
Ford, R.T. v1p0179c1s
v2p0116c1s
Ford, S. v3p0370c2s
v5p0036c1s v6p0002c2s v6p0100c2s
v6p0223c1s v6p0295c2s v6p0300c2s
v6p0333c2s v6p0350c2s v6p0351c2s
v6p0389c2s v6p0464c1s v6p0482c2s
v6p0504c2s v6p0539c1s v6p0582c1s
Ford, S. and Travis, W.J.. v6p0261c2s
Ford, S.Gertrude v6p0112c2s
Ford, S.W. v1p0469c2s
v1p0470c1m v1p1113c1s v1p1280c1s
v1p1325c2s v2p0054c1s v2p0153c2s
v2p0388c1s
Ford, S.W. and Dwight, W.B.
v2p0429c2s
Ford, Sewell v5p0531c2s
v5p0628c1s v5p0634c1s v6p0114c1s
v6p0408c1s v6p0543c2s v6p0645c1s

Ford, T.L. v4p0372c1s
v4p0596c1s v6p0657c2s v6p0707c1s
Ford, W. v5p0336c1s
Ford, W.C. v2p0110c1s
v2p0157c2s v2p0161c1s v2p0168c1s
v2p0231c2s v2p0431c2s v3p0052c1s
v3p0107c2s v3p0162c1s v3p0171c2s
v3p0209c1s v3p0310c1s v3p0363c2s
v3p0450c2m v3p0455c2m v3p0475c2s
v4p0070c1s v4p0084c1s v4p0105c2s
v4p0192c1s v4p0225c1s v4p0230c2s
v4p0246c2s v4p0299c1s v4p0348c2s
v4p0404c1s v4p0438c1s v4p0521c1s
v4p0525c1s v4p0526c1s v4p0526c2s
v4p0564c2s v4p0593c1s v4p0605c2s
v4p0611c2m v4p0612c1s v5p0070c2s
v5p0075c2s v5p0088c2s v5p0102c2s
v5p0128c2s v5p0130c1s v5p0258c2s
v5p0304c1s v5p0321c1s v5p0334c1s
v5p0365c2s v5p0429c1s v5p0443c1s
v5p0542c1s v5p0542c2s v5p0550c1s
v5p0550c2s v5p0567c1s v5p0600c1s
v5p0620c2m v5p0621c1m v5p0627c2s
v5p0640c1m v6p0003c2s v6p0086c1s
v6p0141c1s v6p0185c1s v6p0213c1s
v6p0220c1s v6p0239c1m v6p0239c2s
v6p0278c2s v6p0339c2s v6p0408c2m
v6p0426c1s v6p0487c2s v6p0534c1s
v6p0556c2s v6p0686c2m
Ford, W.E. v6p0045c2s
v6p0184c1s v6p0543c2s
Ford, W.E. and Penfield, S.L.
v5p0087c2m v6p0617c2s
Ford, W.F. v5p0553c2s
v6p0016c2m v6p0051c1s v6p0271c1s
v6p0520c1s
Ford, W.J. v5p0142c2s
v5p0143c1s v6p0157c2s
Forder, A. v5p0442c1s
v6p0344c2s v6p0649c2s
Fordham, E.O. v4p0051c1s
v4p0319c1s
Fordyce, J. v2p0050c1s
v2p0450c2s
Forel, A. v5p0275c2s
v6p0024c1s v6p0024c2s
Forel, F.A. v2p0246c2s
v6p0375c2s v6p0490c2s
Foreman, A. v2p0394c1s
v3p0252c1s
Foreman, G. v6p0465c1m
Foreman, H.G. v6p0480c2s
Foreman, J. v5p0111c1s
v5p0191c1s v5p0444c1s v5p0445c2m
v5p0446c1s v5p0542c1s v5p0542c2m
v6p0492c2m v6p0607c2s
Foreman, R.H. v5p0618c1s
Foresman, R. v5p0393c1s
Forest, E.L.De v1p0829c1s
v1p1293c1s
Forest, Frances De v5p0363c1s
Forest, G.W. v1p0631c1s
Forest, H.P.De v6p0064c2s
Forest, H.S.De v1p0112c1s
Forest, J.De v5p0102c2s
v6p0706c2s
Forest, J.H.De v4p0128c2s
v5p0302c1s v5p0303c1m v6p0163c2s
v6p0335c1m v6p0335c2m v6p0336c1m
v6p0338c2s v6p0369c2s v6p0434c2m
v6p0509c2m v6p0631c2s v6p0663c1m
Forest, J.L.De v6p0115c2s
Forest, J.W.De v1p0199c1s
v1p0204c1s v1p0205c2m v1p0216c2s
v1p0221c1s v1p0258c1s v1p0279c2m
v1p0342c1s v1p0357c1s v1p0368c1s
v1p0467c1s v1p0505c2m v1p0550c2s
v1p0557c2s v1p0601c2s v1p0616c1s
v1p0628c1s v1p0646c2s v1p0649c1s
v1p0668c1s v1p0703c1s v1p0728c2s
v1p0773c2s v1p0795c1s v1p0888c1s
v1p0931c2s v1p0950c2s v1p0952c2s
v1p0964c2s v1p0975c1s v1p1035c1s
v1p1071c1s v1p1225c2s v1p1280c1s
v1p1330c1s v1p1333c1s v1p1335c2s
v1p1345c1s v1p1353c2m v1p1403c1s
v1p1437c1s v4p0401c1m
Forest, K.De v4p0628c1s
v5p0262c2s v5p0454c2s v5p0516c1s
Forest, L. v5p0346c1s
Forest, L.De v5p0264c1s
v5p0404c1s v6p0636c1s
Forest, R.W.De v4p0097c1s
v4p0110c2s v6p0109c2m v6p0454c1s
v6p0638c2m
Forest, V.De v1p0142c1s
Forest, W.E.De v3p0227c2m
Forest, W.H.De v1p0699c2s
Forester, E. v4p0105c2s
v4p0562c1s
Forester, F.B. v6p0440c1s
v6p0544c1s
Forester, G. v6p0008c1s
v6p0604c2s
Forester, J. v1p0196c1s
Forester, M. v5p0555c2m
Forester, T. v1p1273c1s
Forestier, A. v1p0144c2s
Forfar, J. v1p0043c1s
v1p0206c2s v1p0403c1s v1p1154c1s
Forgan, J.B. v5p0046c2s
Forge, A.La v1p0139c2s
v1p0309c2s v1p0471c2s v1p0666c1s
v1p0755c2s v1p0862c2s v1p0887c2s
v1p0951c2s v1p1335c1s
Forgy, E.W. v3p0025c2s
Forlong, J.G.R. v4p0078c1s
v4p0421c1s
Forman, A. v3p0103c2s
v3p0123c2s v3p0232c2s v3p0304c1s
v3p0372c1s v3p0396c1s v4p0106c1s
v4p0402c2s v5p0255c1s
Forman, A.B. v4p0561c1s
Forman, B.R. v1p1346c1s
v3p0259c1s
Forman, E.S. v1p0572c1s
v3p0057c2m
Forman, H.B. v1p0751c1s
v1p1008c1s v1p1106c2s v1p1182c2s
v1p1189c1s v1p1257c1s v2p0063c1s
v2p0159c1s v2p0311c2s v3p0389c2s
v3p0390c1s v5p0488c1s v6p0350c1s
Forman, H.B. and Palgrave, F.T.
v2p0241c1s
Forman, H.Buxton v6p0590c2s
Forman, H.J. v6p0558c2s
Forman, J. v1p0918c1s
v1p1147c1m v6p0562c1s
Forman, J.G. v1p0243c1s
v1p1274c2s
Forman, J.M. v6p0020c1s
v6p0070c1s v6p0101c2s v6p0103c2s
v6p0189c1s v6p0242c1s v6p0330c1s
v6p0346c2s v6p0351c2s v6p0395c2s
v6p0397c2s v6p0434c1m v6p0446c1s
v6p0457c2s v6p0551c2s v6p0682c1s
v6p0688c2s
Forman, Justus Miles v6p0264c2s
Forman, M. v1p0301c2s
Forman, S.E. v6p0128c1s
v6p0129c1s v6p0242c2s v6p0574c2s
Forman, T. v6p0352c2s
Forman, W.H. v2p0108c2s
v2p0197c2s v2p0321c2s v2p0422c1s
Forman, W.J. v6p0174c1s
Formby, H. v1p0883c1s
v1p1094c2s v1p1124c1s v1p1125c2s
v2p0376c1s
Formby, T. v5p0337c1s
Fornance, J. v5p0200c1s
Fornander, A. v4p0251c1s
Fornaro, Carlo de v6p0461c2s
Fornaro, S.de v6p0331c1s
Forney, M.N. v2p0262c1s
v3p0255c1s v4p0115c2s v4p0481c1s
Fornitch, V. v3p0153c1s
Forrest, A.E. v6p0448c1s
Forrest, A.S. v5p0349c1s
Forrest, D.W. v4p0456c1s
Forrest, E.B. v6p0555c1s
Forrest, E.F. v5p0584c2s
v6p0148c1s
Forrest, G. v5p0538c1s
Forrest, G.W. v1p0310c2s
v4p0146c2s v5p0069c1s v5p0157c2s
v6p0091c2s v6p0262c2s v6p0313c2s
Forrest, Gertrude E. v6p0371c1s
Forrest, J. v1p0078c1s
v4p0368c1s v5p0225c1s v5p0591c2s
Forrest, J.D. v4p0379c2s
v5p0471c2s v5p0592c2s
Forrest, L.R.W. v6p0073c1s
Forrest, R.E. v6p0313c2s
v6p0314c1s v6p0314c2s v6p0485c2s
Forrester, A.H. v1p0035c2s
v1p0048c2s v1p0168c1s v1p0231c1s
v1p0318c2s v1p0367c2s v1p0393c2s
v1p0423c1s v1p0452c1s v1p0519c2s
v1p0526c2s v1p0623c2s v1p0713c1s
v1p0730c1s v1p0763c1s v1p0795c1s
v1p0803c1s v1p0861c1s v1p0878c2s
v1p0940c2s v1p0946c1s v1p1005c1s
v1p1064c1s v1p1066c1s v1p1088c2s
v1p1209c2s v1p1212c2s v1p1299c1s
v1p1312c1s v1p1315c2s v1p1364c1s
Forrester, F. v1p0872c1s
Forrester, H. v3p0460c1s
Forrester, Mrs. v1p0583c2s
v1p0626c2s v1p0699c1s v1p0703c2s
v1p0716c2s v1p1070c2s v1p1203c2s
v1p1257c2s v1p1275c1s v2p0462c1s
Forry, S. v1p0578c2s
v1p0579c2s v1p0637c1s v1p0793c2s
v1p0794c1s v1p1073c2m v1p1347c2s
Forshey, C.G. v1p0305c1s
v1p0613c2s v1p0854c2s v1p0876c1s
v1p1075c1s v2p0351c1s
Forshey, Prof. and Bow, J.D.B. De
v1p0073c1s
Forsslund, L. v6p0243c1s
Forstall, E.J. v1p0772c1s
v1p0772c2s
Forstall, W. v6p0248c1s
Forster, E. v5p0187c1s
Forster, E.J. v1p0471c1s
Forster, E.M. v6p0101c1s
v6p0132c1s v6p0187c2s v6p0211c1s
v6p0471c2s v6p0545c1s v6p0619c2s
Forster, E.Morgan v6p0504c1s
Forster, E.N. v6p0011c1s
Forster, H.O.A. v2p0100c1s
v2p0129c1s v4p0238c1s
Forster, H.W. v4p0290c1s
Forster, J. ,............. v1p0255c2s
v1p0319c1s v1p0341c1s v1p0374c1s
v1p0411c2s v1p0466c1s v1p1251c2s
v3p0039c1s v3p0062c2s v3p0247c2s
v3p0377c1s v3p0414c1s v3p0426c1s
v3p0475c2s v4p0155c2s v4p0484c1s
v4p0492c2s v5p0123c2s v5p0331c2s
v5p0510c2s
Forster, J.R. v1p0976c1s
Forster, J.R. and Demidoff, P.
v1p1283c2s
Forster, J.W.L. v4p0414c2s
Forster, M.von v2p0193c2m
Forster, Stephanie v6p0404c2s
Forster, W. v3p0092c2s
Forster, W.E. v1p0169c1s
v1p0571c2s v1p0714c2s v2p0186c2s
v3p0010c1s
Forster, W.J. v3p0409c2s
Forsyth, A.R. v2p0089c1s
v6p0671c1s
Forsyth, Andrew R. v6p0082c2s
Forsyth, D. v6p0173c2s
v6p0707c1s
Forsyth, F.G. v2p0163c1m
Forsyth, G.A. v4p0216c2s
v5p0525c2s
Forsyth, J. v1p0048c1s
v1p0049c2s v1p0124c2s v1p0222c1s
v1p0430c1s v1p0597c1s v1p0624c1s
v1p0639c2s v1p0683c1s v1p0831c1s
v1p0869c2s v1p0872c1s v1p0926c2s
v1p0931c2s v1p1064c1m v1p1089c2s
v1p1128c2s v1p1158c2s v1p1331c2s
v1p1340c1s v1p1356c1s v4p0527c2s
Forsyth, J., jr. v1p0330c1s
v1p1066c2s
Forsyth, J.C. v6p0225c1s
Forsyth, M.I. v4p0311c2s
Forsyth, P. v1p0667c2s
v1p1279c1s
Forsyth, P.J. v5p0145c2s
Forsyth, P.T. v2p0333c1s
v4p0146c1s v5p0115c1s v5p0151c2s
v5p0348c1s v5p0364c1s v6p0043c1s
v6p0065c1s v6p0191c2s v6p0192c1s
v6p0205c2s v6p0215c1s
Forsyth, T.D. v1p1190c1m
Forsyth, T.M. v6p0216c1s
Forsyth, W. v1p0028c2s
v1p0067c1s v1p0168c2s v1p0211c2s
v1p0317c2s v1p0480c2s v1p0560c2s
v1p0611c1s v1p0672c1s v1p0697c2s
v1p0735c1s v1p0753c2s v1p1036c1s
v1p1152c1s v1p1162c1s v1p1263c1s
v1p1267c1s v1p1327c1s v5p0343c2m
Forsythe, C. v3p0358c2s
Forsythe, J. v1p0432c1s
Fort, G.S. v3p0247c1s
v3p0362c2s v4p0296c2s v4p0582c1s
v6p0007c1s
Fort, J.F. v6p0158c1s
Forte, J. v2p0068c1s
v2p0080c1s
Fortebus, T. v5p0355c2s
v5p0411c2s
Forten, C.L. v1p0487c1s
v1p1407c2s
Fortescue, Earl v1p0550c1s
v3p0008c2s v3p0174c1s v3p0221c2s
v3p0255c1s v3p0256c2s
Fortescue, H. v2p0132c2s
Fortescue, J. v4p0192c1s
v6p0007c2s
Fortescue, J.W. v2p0114c2s
v3p0027c2m v3p0226c1s v3p0272c1s
v4p0038c1s v4p0078c1s v4p0119c2s
v4p0141c2s v4p0296c1m v4p0320c2s
v4p0361c2s v4p0476c1s v4p0617c2m
v5p0008c2s v5p0017c1s v5p0092c2s
v5p0243c1s v5p0251c2s v6p0018c1s
v6p0265c2s v6p0271c2s v6p0564c2s
v6p0598c1s v6p0654c1s v6p0655c1s
Fortescue, Lord v5p0116c2s
Fortescue, R. v2p0327c2s
Forth, C.H. v3p0101c1s
Forth, C.J. v6p0406c2s
Fortier, A. v4p0376c2s
v5p0275c1s v6p0387c2s
Fortier, Alcee v4p0342c2m
v4p0409c2s
Fortnum, C.D. v1p0084c2s
v1p0720c1s v1p0941c2s
Fortnum, C.D.E. v1p0053c2s
v1p1039c2s v1p1108c2s v1p1414c2s
v2p0180c1s v2p0349c2s v3p0264c2s
v4p0455c1s v5p0160c2s v5p0201c1s
v5p0262c1s
Fortune, T.T. v4p0538c1s
Fortune, W. v4p0431c2s
Forward, W. v1p0798c1s
Forwood, A.B. v2p0100c1s
v2p0188c2s v2p0443c2s v5p0247c1s
Forwood, W.B. v1p0306c2m
Fosbery, G. v4p0065c2s
v4p0129c2s v4p0224c1s v4p0225c1s
v4p0526c2s v4p0528c1s v4p0575c2s

v5p0290c2s v5p0339c1s v5p0374c2s
Fosbery, G.V. ... v2p0193c2s
Foscolo, U. ... v1p0669c2s
v1p0985c2s
Foscolo, Ugo ... v1p0008c1s
v1p0331c1s
Fosdick, A. ... v4p0402c2s
v4p0633c2s v5p0071c1s v5p0192c1s
v5p0527c2m v5p0581c1s v5p0640c1s
v5p0642c1s
Fosdick, D. ... v1p0124c1s
v1p0626c2s v1p0649c2s v1p0723c2s
v1p0753c1s v1p0933c1s v1p1096c1s
Fosdick, D., jr. ... v1p0404c1s
v1p0944c2s v1p1315c1s
Fosdick, J.W. ... v3p0306c2s
v3p0461c2s v4p0080c1s v4p0145c1s
v4p0211c1s
Fosdick, Lucy H. ... v6p0003c1s
v6p0502c1s
Fosdick, W.W. ... v1p0198c2s
Fosery, G. ... v4p0352c2s
Foshay, M.W. ... v6p0311c2s
Foshay, P.M. ... v3p0326c1s
v5p0368c1s
Foshay, P.M. and Rice, R.R.
v3p0173c2s
Foskett, E. ... v5p0336c2s
Foss, C.D. ... v3p0417c2s
v4p0450c2s v4p0467c1s v6p0257c2s
Foss, E. ... v1p0326c2s
v1p0458c2s v1p0693c1s v1p0870c2s
Foss, G.E. et al. ... v5p0603c1s
Foss, H. ... v6p0692c1s
Foss, Sam Walter ... v6p0375c1s
Foss, W.E. and FitzGerald, D.
v4p0612c2s
Fossati, Dr. ... v1p0643c2s
Fosse, Des and Karth ... v1p0965c2s
Fossman, E.A. ... v2p0259c1s
Fossum, A. ... v5p0182c1s
v6p0594c1s
Fossum, A. et al. ... v4p0186c2s
Foster, A. ... v1p1182c2s
v2p0003c2s v2p0339c1s v5p0422c2s
Foster, A.A. ... v3p0117c1s
Foster, A.E.M. ... v6p0385c2s
v6p0399c1s v6p0442c2s v6p0583c1s
v6p0583c2s v6p0656c1s
Foster, A.G. ... v6p0233c1s
Foster, A.P. ... v1p1337c1s
v4p0129c1s v4p0479c2s
Foster, B. ... v5p0258c2s
v5p0331c1s
Foster, B.B. ... v1p1128c1s
Foster, C. ... v1p0004c2s
v3p0214c1s v4p0377c2s
Foster, C.H. ... v1p0503c1s
v1p0976c2s v1p1016c2s
Foster, C.M. ... v5p0019c1s
Foster, Charles ... v3p0394c2s
Foster, D. ... v1p0483c2s
v2p0240c1s
Foster, E. ... v5p0120c2s
v6p0328c1s v6p0358c1s
Foster, E. and McGamble, E.A.
v6p0644c1s
Foster, E.C. ... v3p0344c2s
v3p0356c2s v4p0294c2s v6p0473c2m
Foster, E.H. ... v5p0442c2s
Foster, E.P. ... v3p0296c2s
Foster, E.W. ... v5p0240c2s
Foster, F. ... v1p0322c1s
v1p0330c1s v5p0070c1s v5p0140c1s
v5p0205c2s
Foster, F.A. ... v1p0140c1s
v1p0370c2s
Foster, F.C. ... v4p0406c1s
Foster, F.F. ... v2p0237c1s
v3p0416c2s
Foster, F.H. ... v1p0426c1s
v1p0559c2s v1p0940c1s v2p0039c1s
v2p0126c2s v2p0133c1s v2p0146c1s
v2p0181c1s v2p0207c1s v2p0222c2s
v2p0387c2s v3p0026c1s v3p0040c2s
v3p0080c2m v3p0096c1s v3p0105c2s
v3p0142c2s v3p0281c1s v3p0428c1s
v4p0053c1s v4p0053c2s v4p0190c2s
v4p0256c1s v4p0300c2s v4p0301c2s
v4p0431c1s v4p0456c2s v4p0573c1s
v4p0583c2s v5p0133c1s v5p0220c1s
v5p0364c1s v5p0378c1s v5p0410c2s
v5p0473c1s v5p0489c2s v6p0089c1s
v6p0480c2s v6p0657c1s
Foster, F.J. ... v4p0234c1s
Foster, F.K. ... v5p0557c2s
v5p0640c2s
Foster, F.K. and McNeill, G.E.
v6p0652c1s
Foster, F.M. ... v3p0468c1s
Foster, F.M., Mrs. ... v3p0095c2s
Foster, F.P. ... v1p1023c2s
v1p1360c2m v6p0627c1s
Foster, F.W. ... v2p0404c1s
Foster, G.B. ... v5p0306c1s
v5p0313c1s v5p0576c2s
Foster, G.C. ... v1p0073c1s
v1p0915c2s v1p1006c2s v1p1074c2s
v2p0170c2s
Foster, G.C. and Glaisher, J.W.L.
v3p0350c2s
Foster, G.E. ... v3p0076c1s
v4p0099c1s v6p0469c1s
Foster, G.F. ... v5p0223c1s
v6p0645c1s
Foster, H. ... v3p0370c2s
Foster, H.D. ... v6p0094c1s
v6p0123c1s v6p0249c2s v6p0293c1s
Foster, H.E. ... v3p0279c2s
v4p0466c1s v5p0435c2s v5p0458c2s
Foster, H.H. ... v5p0532c2s
Foster, H.J. ... v4p0056c1s
v4p0391c2s v6p0012c1s
Foster, H.O.A. ... v1p0543c1s
v2p0255c1s
Foster, H.W. ... v5p0449c1s
Foster, I.F. ... v4p0566c2s
Foster, J. ... v1p0003c1s
v1p0003c2s v1p0006c1s v1p0009c1s
v1p0010c2s v1p0012c2s v1p0013c2m
v1p0018c2s v1p0025c2s v1p0027c1s
v1p0027c2s v1p0028c2s v1p0030c1s
v1p0053c1s v1p0070c1s v1p0075c2s
v1p0078c2s v1p0097c2s v1p0105c1s
v1p0119c1s v1p0121c1s v1p0125c2s
v1p0134c1m v1p0134c2s v1p0140c1s
v1p0144c2s v1p0150c1s v1p0158c2s
v1p0165c1s v1p0165c2s v1p0186c1s
v1p0190c1s v1p0199c2s v1p0207c1s
v1p0208c1s v1p0214c1s v1p0215c1s
v1p0222c2m v1p0231c2s v1p0241c2s
v1p0250c2s v1p0261c2s v1p0274c1m
v1p0289c2s v1p0321c1m v1p0323c2s
v1p0324c2s v1p0345c2s v1p0348c2s
v1p0355c1s v1p0363c1s v1p0370c1s
v1p0372c2s v1p0374c1s v1p0378c1s
v1p0380c2s v1p0383c1s v1p0393c2s
v1p0395c2s v1p0396c1s v1p0402c1s
v1p0408c2m v1p0410c1s v1p0418c2s
v1p0419c2s v1p0446c2s v1p0451c1s
v1p0456c1s v1p0466c1s v1p0472c1m
v1p0480c2s v1p0483c2s v1p0493c2s
v1p0498c2s v1p0502c2s v1p0512c2s
v1p0526c2s v1p0540c1m v1p0541c1s
v1p0543c2s v1p0552c1m v1p0557c1s
v1p0562c2s v1p0567c2s v1p0589c1s
v1p0589c2s v1p0590c2s v1p0591c2m
v1p0592c1m v1p0597c1m v1p0606c2s
v1p0614c2s v1p0618c2s v1p0622c2m
v1p0628c2s v1p0630c1s v1p0630c2s
v1p0631c1s v1p0632c2m v1p0634c2m
v1p0635c1m v1p0635c2s v1p0652c1s
v1p0653c1s v1p0659c2s v1p0660c1s
v1p0670c2s v1p0675c2s v1p0676c2m
v1p0680c1s v1p0683c1s v1p0699c1m
v1p0701c2s v1p0713c2s v1p0740c1s
v1p0740c2s v1p0772c2s v1p0781c1s
v1p0799c1s v1p0800c1s v1p0806c1s
v1p0836c1s v1p0853c1s v1p0859c2s
v1p0867c2s v1p0870c2m v1p0872c2s
v1p0881c1s v1p0901c1s v1p0906c2m
v1p0918c2s v1p0925c1s v1p0929c2s
v1p0934c2s v1p0948c1s v1p0961c2m
v1p0972c1s v1p0992c1s v1p1010c2s
v1p1018c1s v1p1021c1s v1p1023c2s
v1p1029c2s v1p1056c1s v1p1068c2s
v1p1074c1s v1p1102c1s v1p1103c2s
v1p1105c1s v1p1134c1s v1p1139c2s
v1p1146c1s v1p1151c1s v1p1155c1s
v1p1155c2m v1p1165c1m v1p1167c2s
v1p1168c2s v1p1176c1s v1p1205c2s
v1p1211c2s v1p1226c2s v1p1228c2s
v1p1230c1s v1p1242c1s v1p1245c2s
v1p1271c2s v1p1272c2s v1p1286c2s
v1p1296c1s v1p1300c2s v1p1304c2s
v1p1305c2s v1p1306c2s v1p1312c2s
v1p1316c1s v1p1361c1s v1p1361c2s
v1p1381c2m v1p1386c1s v1p1394c1s
v1p1399c2s v1p1406c2s v1p1408c1s
v1p1412c1s v1p1413c2s v1p1419c2s
v1p1435c2s v1p1440c2s v2p0025c1s
v2p0128c2s v2p0144c2s v3p0316c2s
v5p0515c2s
Foster, J.B. ... v1p0093c1s
v5p0635c2s
Foster, J.E. ... v5p0635c2s
Foster, J.E., Mrs. ... v3p0346c1s
Foster, J.F. ... v4p0513c2s
v4p0556c1s
Foster, J.J. ... v2p0206c2s
v2p0290c1s v2p0376c2s v2p0380c2s
v2p0412c1s v3p0300c1s v3p0303c2s
v3p0413c1s v3p0471c2s v4p0372c2s
Foster, J.K. ... v1p0201c2s
Foster, J.M. ... v2p0290c1s
v4p0137c1s v5p0482c1s v5p0518c2s
Foster, J.M. and Butler, W.
v4p0415c1s
Foster, J.McG. ... v3p0341c2s
Foster, J.P. et al. ... v3p0359c1s
Foster, J.P.C. ... v3p0206c1s
v6p0660c2s
Foster, J.W. ... v1p0028c1s
v1p0073c2s v1p0227c2m v1p0267c2s
v1p0279c1s v1p0509c2s v1p0613c2s
v1p0705c2s v1p0876c2m v1p1045c2s
v4p0049c2s v4p0328c1s v5p0122c1s
v5p0326c1s v5p0338c2s v5p0480c2m
v6p0010c1s v6p0016c1s v6p0026c2m
v6p0096c1m v6p0118c1s v6p0118c2s
v6p0119c1s v6p0120c1s v6p0120c2s
v6p0173c1s v6p0186c2s v6p0239c1s
v6p0332c1s v6p0414c2s v6p0606c2s
Foster, J.W. and Bowen, Herbert W.
v6p0550c1s
Foster, J.W. and Whitney, J.D.
v1p0509c1s v1p1271c1s
Foster, J.Y. ... v1p0518c2s
Foster, Julia ... v6p0580c1s
Foster, Julia B. ... v6p0163c2s
Foster, Kate M. ... v5p0402c1s
Foster, M. ... v1p0328c2s
v1p0467c1s v1p1059c1s v1p1308c1s
v1p1358c1s v1p1376c1s v2p0032c1s
v3p0053c1s v3p0436c2s v4p0270c2s
v4p0291c1m v4p0358c1s v4p0363c2s
v4p0442c1s v4p0615c2s v5p0077c1s
v5p0093c2s v5p0171c1s v5p0209c1s
v5p0225c1s v5p0255c2s v5p0276c2s
v5p0343c2s v5p0357c2s v5p0392c2s
v5p0408c1s v5p0481c2s v5p0513c1s
v5p0551c2s v5p0570c2s v5p0605c1s
v6p0007c2s v6p0008c2s v6p0013c1s
v6p0090c1m v6p0178c1s v6p0287c1s
v6p0362c1s v6p0382c1s v6p0428c1s
v6p0552c2s v6p0576c1s v6p0577c1s
v6p0617c1s v6p0622c1s v6p0639c2s
v6p0683c2s v6p0711c2s
Foster, M., jr. ... v1p0881c2s
v1p1261c1s
Foster, M., Sir ... v5p0271c2s
v5p0605c1s
Foster, M.B. ... v3p0185c2s
Foster, M.C. ... v4p0311c1s
Foster, Maximilian ... v6p0100c1s
v6p0301c2s
Foster, Michael, Sir ... v6p0304c2s
Foster, N.B. ... v6p0175c2s
Foster, N.S. ... v2p0141c2s
Foster, P.L.N. ... v3p0009c2s
Foster, P.L.N., jr. ... v3p0412c1s
Foster, P.P. ... v6p0433c1s
v6p0602c2s
Foster, Paul R. ... v6p0298c1s
Foster, R. ... v1p1244c2s
v2p0276c1s v2p0431c1s v3p0303c1s
Foster, R.F. ... v4p0619c2s
v6p0233c2s v6p0311c2s v6p0534c2s
Foster, R.J. ... v6p0359c2s
Foster, R.L. ... v3p0353c1s
v5p0267c1s
Foster, R.S. ... v3p0101c2s
Foster, R.V. ... v2p0045c1s
v2p0081c1s v2p0291c1s v2p0352c2s
v2p0483c1s
Foster, S. ... v1p0024c1s
Foster, T. ... v1p0350c2s
v1p0415c1s v1p0926c1s v1p0979c2s
v1p1154c1s v2p0083c1s v2p0098c1s
v2p0118c1m v2p0147c1s v2p0149c2s
v2p0196c1s v2p0215c1m v2p0283c2s
v2p0297c2s v2p0303c1s v2p0394c1s
v2p0478c2s
Foster, T.B. ... v1p1264c2s
Foster, T.G. and Heath, H.F.
v4p0382c2s v4p0568c2s
Foster, W. ... v4p0148c2s
v4p0417c2s v5p0374c2s v6p0187c1s
v6p0410c2s
Foster, W., Sir ... v5p0588c1s
Foster, W.B. ... v4p0588c2s
v4p0611c1s v5p0283c1s v5p0359c1s
v5p0589c2s v6p0204c1s
Foster, W.E. ... v1p0743c1m
v1p0743c2s v1p1060c1s v1p1085c1m
v1p1088c2s v1p1158c1s v2p0255c2s
v2p0256c1s v2p0257c1s v2p0366c1s
v2p0372c1s v2p0405c2s v2p0444c1s
v3p0010c1s v3p0070c1s v3p0162c1s
v3p0248c2s v3p0249c1m v3p0354c2s
v4p0103c2s v4p0329c2s v4p0463c2s
v4p0536c2s v5p0333c1s v5p0335c1s
v5p0336c2m v5p0341c2s v5p0469c2m
v6p0162c2s v6p0372c2m v6p0373c1m
v6p0643c1s
Foster, W.E. and Dousman, M.E.
v5p0334c1s
Foster, W.E. et al. ... v2p0255c2s
v5p0334c1s
Foster, W.H. ... v1p0094c1s
Foster, W.P. ... v5p0093c2s
v5p0119c2s v5p0158c1s v5p0203c1s
v5p0332c2s v5p0442c2s
Foster, W.T. ... v6p0035c1s
v6p0039c1s v6p0135c1s v6p0135c2s
v6p0197c1s
Foston, H. ... v6p0644c2s
Foston, H.M. ... v4p0191c2s
Fotherby, H.A. ... v6p0376c2s
v6p0680c2s
Fothergill, B. ... v1p0759c1s
Fothergill, G.A. ... v6p0264c2s
Fothergill, G.M. ... v1p0019c2s
v1p0649c1s
Fothergill, J. ... v1p0710c1s
v2p0010c1s v2p0243c2s
Fothergill, J.M. ... v1p0349c1s
v1p0354c1s v1p0465c1s v1p0843c1s
v1p1006c1s v1p1007c1s v1p1179c2s
v1p1210c2s v2p0153c1s v2p0326c1s

v2p0479c2s v3p0433c2s
Fothergill, J.R. v4p0126c1s
Fothergill, Jessie v2p0336c1s
v3p0164c2s
Fothergill, P.A. v2p0106c2s
Fothergill, S. v1p1261c1s
v1p1319c2s v3p0199c2s v5p0557c2s
Fotheringham, D.R. v5p0565c1s
Fotheringham, J.G. v5p0161c2s
v6p0475c2s
Fotheringham, T.F. v3p0066c1s
v3p0365c1s v6p0386c2s
Fottrell, G. v1p0657c1s
v4p0290c1s v6p0254c2s
Foucault, M.L. v1p0376c1s
Fougner, Iver v6p0082c2s
Fouille, A. v4p0244c2s
v5p0220c2s
Fouillee, A. v2p0326c1s
v2p0338c2s v2p0345c1s v2p0424c1s
v3p0136c2s v3p0206c2s v4p0030c1s
v4p0169c1s v4p0253c1s v4p0434c2s
v4p0513c2s v5p0218c2s v5p0313c1s
v5p0411c1s v6p0276c2s v6p0457c1s
v6p0495c2s v6p0539c1s v6p0631c1s
Foulerton, J. v2p0283c2s
v2p0307c2s
Foulger, J.C. v2p0371c2s
v2p0408c1s
Foulk, C.W. and Earhart, R.F.
v6p0671c1s
Foulk, J.S. v1p0691c1s
v1p1042c1s
Foulke, W.D. v3p0086c2s
v4p0117c1m v4p0278c1s v4p0384c1s
v4p0481c1m v4p0537c1s v4p0539c1s
v4p0599c1s v5p0103c1s v5p0422c2s
v5p0545c2s v6p0129c1s v6p0134c1s
v6p0331c1s v6p0550c2s v6p0551c1s
v6p0556c1s
Foulkes, C.J. v6p0183c2s
Foulkes, W.D.J. v4p0324c1s
Fountain v6p0516c1s
Fountain, A. v2p0440c1s
Fountain, L. v1p0103c1s
v1p0296c1s v1p0297c2s v1p0366c2s
v1p0454c1s v1p0459c1s v1p0739c1s
v1p1421c2s
Fountain, Lucy v1p0006c2s
Fountain, P. v6p0071c2s
v6p0096c2s v6p0619c2s v6p0629c1s
Fountain, W.D. v5p0358c2s
Fouque, M. v2p0128c1s
Fouquier, H. v5p0054c2s
v5p0137c1s v5p0645c1s
Fourcaud, L.de v4p0043c1s
v6p0475c1s
Fourcy, C.De v1p0651c1s
Foureau, M.F. v5p0503c2s
Fourier, Baron v1p0589c1s
v1p0725c1s v1p1293c1s v4p0320c2s
Fournier, A. v4p0038c2s
v4p0213c1s v6p0678c2s
Fournier, G.A. v6p0359c1s
Fournier, H. v5p0041c1s
v6p0044c1s v6p0044c2s
Fournier, L.E. v6p0518c1s
Fouse, L.G. v6p0321c2m
v6p0322c1s v6p0322c2s
Fovargue, H.W. v5p0336c2s
Foville, A.de v2p0418c2s
v3p0160c1s v3p0336c2s v3p0408c1s
v4p0212c2s v4p0615c1s v5p0149c2s
v5p0382c2s v6p0347c2s
Fow, J.H. v5p0067c1s
Fowke, F.R. v3p0291c1s
v3p0440c1s v4p0558c2s v5p0483c1s
Fowke, G. v4p0406c1s
v5p0413c2s v6p0019c1s
Fowke, Gerard v4p0072c2s
v5p0527c2s
Fowke, Miss v3p0077c1s
Fowle, F.E., jr. and Abbot, C.G.
v4p0459c2s
Fowle, I.P. v4p0124c2s
v4p0145c1s
Fowle, T.W. v1p0293c1s
v1p0435c1m v1p0550c1s v1p0625c2m
v1p0684c2s v1p0849c2s v1p0873c1s
v1p1031c1s v1p1092c2s v1p1102c2s
v1p1160c2s v1p1176c2s v1p1371c2s
v1p1410c2s v2p0188c1s v4p0109c2s
Fowle, T.W. and Montague, J.S.
v4p0426c2s
Fowle, W.B. v1p0133c2s
v1p0152c1s v1p0506c2s v1p0843c1s
Fowler, A. v1p0457c1s
v1p0708c2s v1p0976c1s v1p1131c2s
v1p1149c2s v1p1273c2s v1p1428c1s
v3p0407c2s v3p0415c1s v4p0167c1s
v4p0330c2s v4p0540c2s v4p0556c2s
v4p0579c1s v5p0173c1s v5p0174c2s
v5p0528c1s v5p0549c1s v5p0549c2s
v5p0560c2s v6p0614c1m
Fowler, C.E. v4p0083c2s
v5p0076c1m v5p0353c2s
Fowler, C.H. v1p0929c1s
v1p1369c2s
Fowler, C.N. v5p0149c2s
v5p0600c2s
Fowler, C.T. v6p0060c1s
Fowler, C.W. v4p0370c1s
Fowler, Canon v5p0171c2s
Fowler, D. v1p0805c1s
v1p1168c2s v1p1183c2s v1p1184c1s
v1p1186c1s
Fowler, D.T. v6p0546c1s
Fowler, D.W. v5p0630c2s
Fowler, E.E. v4p0625c1s
Fowler, E.H. v3p0350c2s
v4p0102c2s v4p0535c2s v5p0531c2s
Fowler, E.T. v4p0144c2s
v4p0348c2s v5p0033c1s v5p0161c1s
v5p0379c1m
Fowler, E.W. v5p0166c2s
v6p0621c1s
Fowler, Ellen T. v6p0244c1s
Fowler, Elliott v6p0354c1s
Fowler, F. v3p0232c1s
v4p0150c2s v4p0368c2s v5p0392c1s
v6p0295c2s v6p0510c1s
Fowler, F. and Caffin, C.H.
v6p0689c1s
Fowler, F. and Sturgis, R.
v6p0570c2s
Fowler, Frank v5p0428c1s
v5p0461c1m v6p0077c2s v6p0086c2s
v6p0510c2s
Fowler, Frank H. v6p0363c1s
Fowler, G.H. v3p0336c1s
Fowler, G.L. v4p0344c2s
v5p0194c2s v5p0383c2s v5p0477c2s
v6p0133c1m v6p0528c1s
Fowler, H. v1p1411c1s
v5p0002c2s v5p0285c2s
Fowler, H., Sir v6p0206c1s
Fowler, H.E., Mrs. v6p0276c1s
Fowler, H.H. v3p0139c1s
Fowler, H.H., Sir v5p0391c2s
Fowler, H.N. v2p0279c2s
v3p0023c2s v3p0170c2s v4p0035c1s
v5p0005c1s v5p0418c1s v5p0436c2s
v5p0537c2s v5p0613c1s v6p0029c2s
v6p0109c1s v6p0195c2s v6p0272c2s
v6p0273c1s v6p0273c2s
Fowler, H.N. and Goodwin, W.W.
v2p0026c2s
Fowler, H.T. v4p0636c1s
v5p0058c1s
Fowler, H.W. v2p0208c2s
v5p0298c2s v5p0475c1s
Fowler, J. v1p0345c2s
v1p0472c1s v1p0864c2s v1p1079c1s
v1p1174c1s v1p1188c2s v1p1264c1s
v2p0180c1s v5p0235c2s
Fowler, J. and Baker, B. . v2p0135c1s
v3p0158c2s
Fowler, J. et al. v2p0143c2s
Fowler, J., jr. v3p0408c2s
Fowler, J.C. v1p0257c2s
v2p0247c2s
Fowler, J.S. v3p0424c2s
Fowler, J.T. v2p0039c1s
v5p0150c1s v6p0480c2s
Fowler, M. v4p0112c1s
Fowler, N.C., jr. v6p0004c2s
Fowler, O. v5p0347c2s
Fowler, R.L. v2p0351c1s
v3p0076c1s v3p0197c1s v3p0260c2s
v3p0437c1s v4p0450c1s v4p0592c2s
Fowler, R.N. v2p0050c1s
Fowler, S. v1p0158c1m
v1p0681c1s v1p1027c2s v1p1348c1s
v1p1352c1s
Fowler, S.P. v1p1418c1s
v2p0331c2s v2p0384c1s v3p0110c2s
Fowler, T. v1p0261c2s
v1p0435c2s v1p0727c1s v5p0196c1s
Fowler, W. v1p0101c2s
v1p0721c1s v2p0218c2s v2p0353c2s
v4p0279c1s
Fowler, W.C. v1p0223c1m
v1p0225c2s v1p0285c1s v1p0292c1s
v1p0641c1s v1p0725c2s v1p0809c1s
v1p0837c1s v1p1348c2s v1p1428c1s
Fowler, W.H. v1p1356c2s
Fowler, W.J. v3p0232c2s
v3p0303c2s v3p0357c1s v4p0620c2s
v5p0410c1s
Fowler, W.S. v1p0982c2m
Fowler, W.W. v1p0892c1s
v3p0045c1m v3p0316c1s v4p0059c2s
v4p0158c1s v4p0241c1s v4p0604c2s
v4p0619c2s v5p0063c2s v6p0067c1s
v6p0206c2s v6p0263c1s
Fox, A. et al. v6p0007c1s
Fox, A.H.L. v1p0435c2s
v1p0469c1s v1p1273c1s
Fox, A.L. v1p0037c1s
v1p0257c1s v1p0262c2s v1p0902c2s
v1p0921c1s v1p0978c1s v1p1173c2s
v1p1272c2s v2p0150c1s v5p0389c1s
Fox, A.S. v6p0647c1s
Fox, A.W. v6p0008c2s
Fox, C. v1p0900c1s
Fox, C., Sir v1p1329c2s
v2p0284c1s
Fox, C.B. v2p0250c1s
Fox, C.F. v6p0583c1s
Fox, C.J. v1p0187c1s
v1p0835c1s
Fox, C.L. v1p0226c2s
Fox, D., Sir v5p0188c2s
Fox, E. v6p0134c2s
v6p0356c2s
Fox, E.B. v4p0356c2s
Fox, E.M. v1p0384c1m
Fox, F. v1p1259c2s
v1p1353c2s v2p0306c1s v2p0420c2s
v5p0594c1s v5p0609c1s v6p0080c1m
v6p0595c1s
Fox, Francis v6p0678c2s
Fox, G.E. v5p0346c1s
v5p0494c2s v6p0548c2s
Fox, G.E. and Joyce, J.G.. v5p0529c1s
Fox, G.H. v2p0254c1s
Fox, G.H., Mrs. v6p0441c1s
Fox, G.L. v4p0338c2s
v6p0574c1s
Fox, G.S. v1p1359c2s
Fox, G.V. v2p0094c2s
v2p0470c2s
Fox, H. v4p0569c1s
v4p0598c1s
Fox, H.E. et al. v4p0113c2s
Fox, H.F. v6p0114c2s
Fox, H.J. v1p0831c1s
v1p0904c2s v1p1013c2s v1p1184c2s
v2p0398c2s
Fox, Hugh F. v6p0115c1s
Fox, J. v4p0075c1s
v4p0113c2s v4p0467c2s v5p0078c2s
Fox, J., jr. v4p0006c2s
v4p0143c1s v4p0210c2s v4p0385c2s
v5p0075c2s v5p0255c2s v5p0315c1s
v5p0359c1s v5p0389c2s v6p0046c2s
v6p0353c1s v6p0381c1s v6p0467c1s
v6p0560c2s v6p0653c1s v6p0697c1s
Fox, J.A. v2p0019c1s
v3p0018c2s v3p0153c2s v3p0187c1s
v4p0025c1s v5p0082c2s
Fox, J.A. and Warren, H.L.
v4p0023c2s
Fox, J.B. v1p0602c1s
v3p0080c2s v3p0346c2s v4p0021c1s
v4p0092c1s v5p0025c1s v5p0056c2s
Fox, J.J. v1p0266c1s
v1p1069c2s v1p1246c1s v1p1376c1s
v5p0055c2s v5p0257c1s v5p0277c1s
v5p0493c1s v6p0123c1s v6p0236c2s
v6p0258c1s v6p0326c1s v6p0428c1s
v6p0428c2s v6p0484c1s v6p0535c1s
v6p0537c1s v6p0547c1s v6p0575c1s
v6p0575c2s v6p0609c2s v6p0617c1s
v6p0642c2s v6p0673c1s
Fox, J.P. v6p0531c2s
Fox, J.W., jr. v3p0008c2s
Fox, James J. v6p0043c1s
v6p0060c2s v6p0104c2s v6p0182c1s
v6p0238c1s v6p0565c1s
Fox, John, jr. v5p0166c2s
v5p0581c1s v6p0031c1s v6p0124c2s
v6p0398c2s
Fox, L.A. v1p0288c2s
v1p0529c1s v2p0235c1s v2p0291c1s
v3p0233c1s v3p0261c2s v3p0359c2s
v3p0424c2s v3p0446c1s v4p0053c1s
v4p0210c1s v4p0542c1s v5p0131c1s
v5p0351c1s v5p0631c1s v6p0055c2s
v6p0484c2s v6p0627c1s
Fox, L.W. v3p0047c2s
v3p0147c2s v4p0193c1s
Fox, N. v1p0472c1s
v1p1069c1s v2p0034c2s v2p0222c2s
v6p0122c2s
Fox, S. v1p0329c2s
v1p1143c1s
Fox, S.N. v3p0209c1s
v4p0041c2s v4p0585c1s v5p0247c2s
Fox, St.G.L. v3p0167c2s
Fox, T. v1p0494c2s
v1p0605c2s
Fox, T.A. v4p0069c1s
Fox, T.B. v1p0038c2s
v1p0200c1s v1p0390c1s v1p0451c1s
v1p0649c1s v1p0707c2s v1p0719c1s
v1p0751c2s v1p0808c2s v1p0977c2s
v1p1054c2s v1p1065c2s v1p1284c2s
v1p1406c2s
Fox, W. v5p0577c2s
v5p0645c2s
Fox, W.A. v4p0537c1s
v5p0527c2s
Fox, W.C. v5p0232c1s
v5p0429c1s
Fox, W.F. v3p0036c1s
Fox, W.J. v1p0027c1s
v1p0170c1s v1p0385c2s v1p0386c1s
v1p0403c2s v1p0595c1s v1p0784c2s
v1p0819c2s v1p1048c2s v1p1054c1s
v1p1162c2s v1p1186c1s v1p1285c1s
v1p1304c2s v1p1384c1s v1p1385c1s
v4p0286c1s
Fox, W.S. v6p0391c2s
Fox, W.W. v4p0268c1s
Fox-Bourne, H.R. v3p0179c2s
v3p0303c2s v3p0307c1s v3p0367c2s
v3p0453c2s
Fox-Bourne, H.R. and Colenso, Harriet
v4p0156c1s

Fox-Bourne, H.R. et al. .. v1p0839c1s
Fox-Davies, G.M. v6p0225c1s
Foxcar, A. v1p0338c1s
Foxcroft, F. v1p0378c2s
v1p0805c1s v3p0358c1s v4p0069c1s
v4p0084c2s v4p0330c2s v4p0385c1s
v4p0555c1s v6p0146c1s v6p0319c2s
v6p0382c1s v6p0518c2s v6p0705c2s
Foxcroft, H.C. v4p0504c1s
v5p0254c2s v5p0416c2s v6p0391c2s
v6p0686c2s
Foxe, S. v4p0467c2s
Foxley, J. v5p0365c1s
Foxton, E. v1p0205c1s
v1p1031c2s v1p1032c1s v1p1202c1s
Foxwell, A. v6p0664c2s
Foxwell, E. v2p0150c2s
v2p0362c2s v2p0364c1s v5p0302c2s
v5p0320c2s v6p0307c2s v6p0330c2s
v6p0334c1s v6p0337c1s v6p0338c1s
Foxwell, H.S. v3p0336c2s
v4p0059c2s v4p0377c2s v4p0378c1m
Foxwell, H.S. and Crump, A.
v4p0237c1s
Foy, P.L. v3p0021c1s
v3p0347c1s v3p0364c2s
Foye, C.H. v5p0429c1s
Foykholm, S. v5p0564c1s
Fradenburgh, A.G. v4p0450c1s
Fradenburgh, J.N. v1p1441c2s
v2p0030c2s v3p0131c1s v4p0173c1s
v4p0310c2s v4p0364c1s v5p0140c2s
v5p0157c2s
Fraenkel, J.E. v4p0230c1s
Fraine, T.W. v5p0547c1s
Fraissinet, A. v4p0440c1s
Fraleck, E.B. v4p0010c2s
Fraley, F. v1p0484c2m
Fraley, J.C. v1p1278c2s
Frame, R. v6p0098c1s
Frames, M.E. v5p0554c2s
Frampton, G. v5p0639c1s
Frampton, G. and Webb, M.. v5p0516c1s
Frampton, L.C. v1p0191c1s
v1p0221c2s
France, A. v5p0312c1s
v5p0451c1s v6p0196c1s
France, Anatole v4p0001c2s
France, C.J. v5p0122c1s
v5p0468c2s v6p0246c1s
France, C.J. and Kline, L.W.
v5p0426c1s
France, C.Q.De v4p0378c1s
France, G.C. v6p0037c2s
France, G.O. v6p0161c2s
France, J.I. v5p0400c2s
France, L.B. v3p0332c2s
France, W.C. v5p0636c2s
v6p0026c2s v6p0145c1m v6p0152c1m
v6p0158c2s v6p0193c2s v6p0213c1s
v6p0228c1s v6p0305c2s v6p0363c1s
v6p0473c1s v6p0483c2s v6p0521c2s
v6p0589c2s v6p0640c2s
Francfort, E. v5p0563c2s
Francheschini, R. v3p0217c1s
Francillon, R.E. v1p0081c2s
v1p0358c1m v1p0374c2s v1p0511c2s
v1p0539c1s v1p0674c1s v1p0734c2s
v1p0941c2s v1p0942c2s v1p1070c2s
v1p1257c2s v1p1259c2s v1p1407c1s
v1p1440c1s v2p0048c1s v2p0232c1s
v4p0475c1s v6p0013c1s v6p0171c1s
v6p0332c2s v6p0365c2s v6p0509c1s
Francis, A.S. v2p0022c1s
v2p0317c2s v6p0417c2s
Francis, B. v1p0365c1s
Francis, C. v1p0046c2s
v1p0402c2s v1p0417c2s v1p0961c2s
v1p1033c1s v1p1081c2s v1p1086c1s
v1p1092c1s v1p1223c1s
Francis, D.R. v6p0388c1s
v6p0563c2m
Francis, E. v1p1371c2s
v2p0177c2s v2p0482c1s v3p0263c1s
Francis, F. v1p0456c1s
v1p1146c1s v1p1383c2s v2p0111c1s
v2p0286c2s v2p0384c1s
Francis, G.G. v1p0587c1s
Francis, H. v3p0103c1s
v3p0195c2s
Francis, H.T. v2p0075c2s
Francis, H.W. v6p0402c1s
Francis, J. v1p0090c2s
v1p1254c2s
Francis, J.B. v1p0145c2s
v1p0271c2s v1p0341c1s v1p0454c2s
v1p0731c1s v1p0985c2s v1p1183c1s
v1p1247c2s v1p1414c1s
Francis, J.W. v1p0298c2s
v1p0605c2s v1p0872c2s v1p0916c2s
Francis, L.E. v3p0389c1s
Francis, M.B. v2p0409c2s
Francis, M.C. v5p0147c1s
v5p0148c1s v5p0148c2s
Francis, M.E. v2p0261c1s
v3p0082c1s v3p0150c1s v3p0210c1m
v3p0284c2s v3p0426c1s v3p0440c2s
v3p0447c2s v4p0226c1s v4p0248c1s
v4p0317c1s v4p0350c1s v4p0412c2s
v4p0419c1s v4p0447c2s v4p0565c2s
v4p0574c1s v4p0578c2s v4p0631c2s
v5p0051c2s v5p0133c2s v5p0166c1s
v5p0170c2s v5p0224c1s v5p0238c2s
v5p0421c2s v5p0426c1s v5p0503c1s
v5p0520c1s v5p0606c1s v6p0122c2s
v6p0153c2s v6p0339c1s v6p0390c2s
v6p0393c2s v6p0394c1s v6p0395c2s
v6p0434c1s v6p0483c2s v6p0492c1s
v6p0593c1s v6p0706c2s
Francis, M.R. v2p0371c1s
Francis, S.M. v6p0189c1s
Francis, T.C. v3p0465c1s
Francis, Thos. and Farrer, Lord
v5p0584c1s
Francis, W. v5p0449c2s
Francis, W.A. et al. v6p0406c1s
Francis, W.H. v6p0655c2s
Francisco, M.E. v6p0222c1s
Francisco, M.J. v4p0135c1s
v4p0387c2m
Franck, F. v1p1316c2s
Franck, L. v4p0124c1s
Franck, L.G. v1p0111c2s
v1p0620c2s v1p1404c2s
Francke, K. v3p0171c2s
v3p0214c2s v3p0261c1s v3p0399c1s
v3p0413c1s v3p0445c1s v4p0013c1s
v4p0223c2s v4p0224c2m v4p0325c2s
v5p0065c1s v5p0230c2s v5p0232c1s
v5p0237c1m v5p0251c1s v5p0254c1s
v5p0258c1m v5p0309c1s v5p0436c2s
v5p0497c1s v5p0518c2s v5p0519c2s
v6p0183c2s v6p0202c1s v6p0252c1s
v6p0252c2s v6p0253c1m v6p0254c1s
v6p0282c1s v6p0283c1s v6p0462c2s
v6p0572c1s
Francke, Kuno v3p0175c2s
v6p0579c2s
Francois, E. v4p0347c1s
Francois, G. v5p0047c1s
v5p0074c1s v5p0536c1s
Francolur, L.B. v1p0505c2s
Frango v5p0165c1s
Frank, A. v2p0363c1s
Frank, E. v5p0050c2s
Frank, F.H.R. v4p0193c2s
Frank, F.H.R. and Phillipi, F.A.
v1p1302c2s
Frank, H. v4p0137c2s
v5p0213c2s v5p0370c1s v6p0243c2s
v6p0339c1s
Frank, Helena v6p0009c2s
Frank, L. v4p0628c1s
Frank, Maude v5p0308c1s
Frank, P. v1p0060c2s
v1p0086c2s v1p0201c2s v1p0215c1s
v1p0676c2s v1p0708c2s
Frank, T. v6p0468c2s
Frank, V.S. v6p0187c1m
Franke, M. v5p0575c1s
Frankel, J. v1p0385c2s
Frankel, L.K. v3p0021c1s
v3p0414c2s v5p0004c1s v6p0109c2s
v6p0284c1s v6p0536c1s
Frankel, L.K. and Smith, E.F.
v3p0134c1s
Frankenburger, D.B. v4p0184c1s
v4p0597c2s v6p0053c1s
Frankenfield, H.C. v5p0318c1m
v6p0670c1s
Frankenthal, A.L. v5p0530c1s
Frankforter, G.B. v6p0015c1s
Frankham, A. v5p0155c1s
Frankland, Dr. v3p0362c1s
Frankland, E. v1p0281c1m
v1p0501c2s v1p0624c2s v1p0747c1s
v1p0881c2m v1p1019c1s v1p1074c2s
v1p1110c2s v1p1239c1s v1p1391c2s
v2p0089c1s v2p0265c1s v2p0287c2s
v2p0406c1s v2p0482c1s v4p0340c2m
v4p0370c2s
Frankland, F. v4p0360c2s
Frankland, F.W. v1p0843c2s
v2p0290c1s
Frankland, G.C. v4p0041c1m
v4p0107c2m v4p0157c1s v4p0331c2s
v4p0370c2s v4p0429c2s v4p0558c1s
v4p0589c1s v4p0613c1s v5p0042c2s
v5p0088c1s v5p0281c1s v5p0376c1s
v5p0435c1m v5p0456c2s v5p0506c1s
v5p0521c2s v5p0534c1s v5p0584c1s
v5p0633c1s v5p0644c1s v6p0009c2s
v6p0046c2s v6p0277c1s v6p0301c1s
v6p0483c1s
Frankland, P. v1p0881c2s
v4p0369c1s v4p0429c2s v5p0622c2s
v6p0585c1s
Frankland, P., Mrs. v4p0369c1s
v5p0343c2s v5p0374c1s v5p0475c1s
Frankland, P.F. v2p0080c2s
v2p0175c2s v2p0265c1s v2p0467c2s
v3p0277c2m v3p0278c1s v3p0380c2s
v3p0422c2s v3p0426c2s v4p0197c1s
v4p0369c1s v5p0104c1s
Frankland, Percy, Mrs. ... v5p0377c2s
Franklin, A. v6p0362c1s
Franklin, B. v1p0027c2s
v1p0243c2s v1p0708c2s v1p0796c2s
v1p0939c2s v1p0965c2s v1p0987c2s
v1p1034c1s v1p1059c2s v1p1094c2s
v1p1275c2s v1p1394c2s v1p1407c1s
v2p0266c1s v2p0367c1s
Franklin, B. et al. v2p0042c1s
Franklin, C.L. v2p0390c1s
v2p0433c2s v2p0477c2s v3p0089c1s
v3p0090c1s v3p0255c2s v3p0269c1s
v3p0348c1s v3p0385c1s v3p0468c1s
v4p0064c1s v4p0210c2s v4p0223c2s
v4p0288c1s v4p0331c2m v4p0375c2s
v4p0475c1s v4p0482c1s v4p0606c1s
v4p0626c1m v4p0628c1s v5p0129c1m
v5p0178c1s v5p0552c2s v6p0139c1s
v6p0252c2s
Franklin, C.L. et al. v5p0129c1s
Franklin, C.Ladd v5p0338c1s
v5p0450c2s
Franklin, E. v1p0648c2s
Franklin, F. v2p0478c1s
v3p0255c2s v3p0347c1s v3p0420c2s
v3p0452c1s v3p0468c1s v4p0377c2s
v5p0149c2s v5p0635c1s v6p0575c2s
Franklin, F. and Newcomb, S.
v2p0347c2s
Franklin, F.S. v6p0704c1s
Franklin, H.C.T. v6p0418c1s
v6p0639c1s
Franklin, H.E. v4p0028c1s
Franklin, I.F. v5p0588c1s
Franklin, J. v3p0272c1s
v3p0361c1s
Franklin, J.B. v2p0181c1s
Franklin, K. v1p0941c2s
Franklin, L. v5p0300c1s
Franklin, N.C. v4p0198c1s
Franklin, R.S. v1p0381c2s
Franklin, S.M. v2p0147c1s
Franklin, S.R. v2p0026c1s
v2p0455c1s
Franklin, V.P. v6p0301c1s
v6p0388c2s
Franklin, Viola P. v6p0547c1s
Franklin, W.B. v2p0306c2s
v2p0386c2s
Franklin, W.D. v6p0452c1s
Franklin, W.M. v3p0233c2s
Franklin, W.S. v5p0037c2s
v5p0242c2s v5p0388c2s v5p0422c2s
v5p0624c1s v6p0198c2s v6p0377c1s
v6p0471c2s v6p0498c2s v6p0576c1s
Franklin, W.S. and Blake, L.I.
v4p0125c1s
Franklin, W.S. and Nichols, E.L.
v3p0132c2s v3p0134c2s v3p0208c1s
v3p0264c1s
Franklyn, C.W. v3p0109c1s
v3p0338c1s v3p0387c1s v3p0411c2s
Franklyn, H.M. v2p0282c2s
Franks, A.W. v1p0167c2s
v1p0203c2s v1p0525c2s v1p0911c1s
v1p0928c1s v1p1242c2s v1p1284c2s
v2p0358c1s v5p0081c2s v5p0470c1s
Franks, A.W. and Black, W.H.
v1p0596c2s
Franks, A.W. and Marchegay, P.
v1p1324c2s
Franks, H. v2p0277c2s
Franks, W.S. v2p0137c1s
Frantz, H. v4p0232c1s
v4p0283c1s v5p0202c1s v5p0224c2s
v5p0251c2s v5p0289c1s v5p0323c1s
v5p0329c2s v5p0386c2s v5p0397c1s
v5p0429c2s v5p0430c2s v5p0431c1s
v5p0431c2s v5p0432c1m v5p0442c2s
v5p0492c1s v5p0498c1s v5p0505c2s
v6p0047c1s v6p0059c2m v6p0073c1s
v6p0079c1s v6p0112c1s v6p0167c2s
v6p0208c2s v6p0245c2s v6p0276c2s
v6p0300c1s v6p0302c1s v6p0471c1s
v6p0480c1s v6p0552c2m v6p0601c2s
v6p0644c1s v6p0713c2s v6p0714c1s
Frantz, Henri v5p0152c1s
v5p0156c2s v5p0367c2s v5p0431c1s
v5p0490c1s
Frantz, J.E. v6p0274c2s
Franz, S.I. v4p0287c2s
v6p0410c2s v6p0433c2s
Franz, S.I. and Griffing, H.
v4p0474c2s
Franz, S.I. and Houston, H.E.
v4p0104c1s
Franzos, K.E. v1p1418c2s
Fraprie, F.R. v6p0091c1s
Fraser and Lovat, J.A. ... v6p0084c2s
Fraser, A. v1p0153c2s
v1p0593c1s v1p0630c2s v1p0941c2s
v1p1182c2s v1p1439c1s v2p0306c1s
v2p0439c2s v3p0451c1s v4p0253c1s
v4p0475c1s
Fraser, A., Mrs. v1p0022c2s
v1p0420c1s v1p0424c2s v1p0518c1s
v1p0579c1s v1p0785c2s v1p0786c2s
v1p0887c1s v1p0942c2s v1p0981c1s
v1p1152c1s v1p1257c1s v1p1339c2s
v2p0082c2s v2p0288c1s v2p0409c2s
v2p0439c1s v3p0067c2s v3p0116c2s
v3p0202c1s v3p0259c2s v3p0336c1s
v3p0356c1s v4p0583c2s v4p0590c2s
Fraser, A.A. v1p0452c2s
Fraser, A.C. v1p0191c1s
v1p0449c2s v1p0675c2s v1p0736c2s

v1p0806c2s v1p1166c2s v1p1286c2s v3p0329c2s v4p0194c1s
Fraser, A.H.L. v2p0218c2s
Fraser, A.T. v2p0117c2s v2p0160c2s v2p0447c1s v3p0416c1s v5p0024c1s
Fraser, A.V. v1p1250c1s
Fraser, B. v6p0691c1s
Fraser, C. v1p0500c1s v1p1247c1s
Fraser, C.A. v4p0381c1s v4p0391c2s v4p0414c2s v4p0510c1s v4p0557c1s v4p0621c1s
Fraser, C.E. v6p0585c1s
Fraser, D. v2p0084c1s v2p0098c2s v2p0236c1s v2p0351c2s v2p0384c2s v2p0391c1s v2p0473c2s
Fraser, D.A. v6p0383c1s
Fraser, D.J. v5p0523c1s
Fraser, Duncan v6p0382c1s
Fraser, F.J. v4p0336c1s
Fraser, G. v1p0664c1s v5p0431c2s v6p0242c1s
Fraser, G.M. v4p0522c1s
Fraser, G.W. v1p1188c2s
Fraser, H. v4p0457c2s v5p0156c2s v5p0633c1s
Fraser, H., Mrs. v6p0440c1s v6p0648c2s
Fraser, J. v1p0563c2s v1p0602c1s v1p1054c1s v2p0336c1s v3p0061c1s v3p0239c2s v3p0243c1s v3p0349c2s v3p0350c2s v5p0039c1s v5p0040c1s v5p0397c1s v6p0041c2m v6p0042c1s v6p0105c2s v6p0451c1s
Fraser, J. and Ruskin, J.. v1p1359c2s
Fraser, J.B. v3p0065c2s v6p0100c1s
Fraser, J.F. v4p0130c2s v4p0144c2s v4p0385c2s v4p0390c2s v4p0618c1s v5p0014c1s v5p0081c2s v5p0084c1s v5p0109c1s v5p0112c1s v5p0122c1s v5p0151c1s v5p0201c2s v5p0272c1s v5p0315c2s v5p0392c2s v5p0396c1s v5p0441c1s v5p0544c1s v5p0596c2s v5p0641c2s v6p0017c1s v6p0593c1s
Fraser, J.G. v5p0227c2s v6p0127c2s v6p0650c2s
Fraser, K. v2p0071c2s
Fraser, M.C. v5p0524c2s v6p0335c1s v6p0336c1s
Fraser, Mary C. v6p0335c1s v6p0335c2s v6p0336c2s v6p0338c2m v6p0339c1s
Fraser, Mr. v1p0806c2s
Fraser, P., jr. v1p0314c2s
Fraser, Prof. v1p0114c1s
Fraser, R.H. v3p0417c1s
Fraser, S. v3p0047c1s
Fraser, T., Sir v6p0107c1s v6p0267c1s
Fraser, T.C. v1p0987c1s v1p1038c1s
Fraser, T.C.B. v1p0270c1s v1p0302c2s
Fraser, W. v1p0337c2s v2p0138c1m
Fraser, W.A. v5p0006c2s v5p0044c2s v5p0083c1s v5p0091c2s v5p0094c1s v5p0135c2s v5p0185c2s v5p0236c2s v5p0241c2s v5p0266c1s v5p0268c2s v5p0269c2s v5p0290c2s v5p0316c2s v5p0341c1s v5p0349c1s v5p0350c2s v5p0356c1s v5p0385c2s v5p0401c2s v5p0456c2s v5p0480c1s v5p0487c1s v5p0506c1s v5p0514c2s v5p0534c1s v5p0550c2s v5p0579c2s v5p0623c2s v6p0002c2s v6p0025c1s v6p0048c2s v6p0100c2s v6p0107c2s v6p0151c2s v6p0174c2s v6p0225c1s v6p0259c1s v6p0262c1s v6p0305c1s v6p0401c1s v6p0420c2s v6p0440c1s v6p0470c2s v6p0523c1s v6p0540c2s v6p0543c2s v6p0577c1s v6p0633c2s v6p0634c2s v6p0656c1s v6p0661c1s
Fraser, W.H. v3p0164c1s v4p0579c2s v5p0088c2s v5p0478c1s
Fraser, W.L. v3p0023c1s v4p0028c2s v4p0101c1s v5p0597c1s v6p0054c2s
Fraser-Corkran, S. v2p0200c1s
Fraser-Lovett, M.H. v4p0551c2s
Fraser-Tytler, C.C. v1p0695c1s
Frather, Julia F.A. v6p0353c1s
Frauenstein, G.M. v2p0026c1s v2p0276c1s
Fray, Gaston v4p0206c1s
Frayser, R.E. v2p0453c2s
Frazar, M.D. v5p0638c2s
Frazer, A.L. v3p0149c2s
Frazer, A.T. v4p0470c2s
Frazer, Hugh, Mrs. v5p0347c2s
Frazer, J.D. v1p0141c1s
Frazer, J.F. v1p0257c2s v1p0491c1s v1p1365c2s v1p1391c2s
Frazer, J.G. v2p0061c1s v2p0151c1s v2p0177c2s v2p0243c2s v2p0277c2s v2p0398c1s v2p0410c2s v4p0017c2s v4p0530c2s v5p0509c1s v5p0583c2s v6p0034c2s v6p0041c2s v6p0221c1s v6p0291c2s
Frazer, P. v1p0484c2s v1p1002c2s v2p0108c2s v2p0173c2s v2p0312c1s v2p0340c1s v2p0464c2s v3p0075c2s v3p0141c2s v3p0444c2s v4p0213c2s v5p0293c2s v6p0182c2s v6p0264c2s v6p0602c2s
Frazer, P., jr. v1p0073c1s v1p0845c1s v1p1059c1s
Frazer, R.W. v5p0561c2s
Frazer, S.C. v4p0548c1s
Frazer, T.R. v4p0531c1s
Frazier, B.W. v2p0030c1s
Frazier, E.L. v1p0074c1s
Fream, W. v2p0162c1s v2p0174c1s v2p0185c1s
Frear, C. v5p0280c2s
Frear, W. v2p0216c2s v6p0231c1s v6p0283c1s
Freas, W.S. v4p0418c1s
Frechette, A.H. v1p1107c2s v2p0383c1s v3p0224c1s v4p0267c1s v4p0304c2s v5p0163c2s v5p0344c2s
Frechette, L. v3p0075c1s v3p0255c2s v3p0359c2s v4p0135c1s v5p0503c2s v6p0691c1s
Frechette, L.H. v4p0087c1s
Fred, W. v5p0153c1s v5p0235c1s v5p0267c2s v5p0304c2s v5p0417c1s v5p0418c2s v5p0431c1m v5p0518c2s v6p0164c2s v6p0167c2s v6p0367c2s
Freddi, Marta v4p0559c2s
Fredenhagen, E.A. v6p0109c1m
Frederic, H. v1p0033c2s v1p0482c2s v1p0858c1s v2p0057c2s v3p0210c1s v3p0287c1s v3p0386c1s v4p0133c1s v4p0430c2s v4p0584c1s v4p0594c2s v5p0415c2s
Frederic, Harold v5p0236c1s
Frederic, J.G. v6p0646c2s
Frederick, G.A. v3p0018c1s
Frederick, J.G. v6p0080c2s
Frederick, J.M.H. v4p0347c2s
Frederick, M.C. v6p0297c2s v6p0315c2s v6p0469c1s v6p0471c1s
Fredericks, A.M. v6p0095c1s v6p0637c2m
Fredericks, B.T. v6p0219c2s v6p0621c2s
Fredericq, L. v3p0379c2s
Fredericq, P. v2p0038c2s v3p0197c2m v4p0050c1m v4p0322c2s v5p0052c2m v6p0057c1m
Fredericq, P. and Laveleye, E.de v2p0038c2s v3p0038c1m
Frederiksen, D.M. v4p0022c1s v4p0044c2s v4p0383c2m
Frederiksen, J.D. v4p0359c1s
Frederiksen, N.C. v2p0093c2s v2p0115c2s v2p0116c1m v2p0317c1s v2p0356c2s v2p0387c1m v2p0387c2s v2p0388c1s v2p0428c1m v2p0430c2s v2p0431c2s v2p0470c2s v4p0230c2s v4p0277c2s v4p0423c2s v5p0217c1s
Frederiksen, N.C. and Bjornson, B. v2p0387c1s
Frederiksen, Prof. v3p0289c1s
Fredet, P. v1p0449c1s v1p0643c1s
Fredsham, G.H. v6p0525c1s
Freebairn, R. v1p0586c2s v1p1029c2s
Freeborn, M.E. v4p0225c1s
Freechette, A.H. v5p0630c2s
Freed, A.T. v1p0209c2s v1p0471c1s
Freedlander and Stillman . v6p0152c2s
Freedlander, J.H. v6p0024c2s v6p0046c1s v6p0304c1s
Freedman, L.M. v5p0434c1s
Freedman, S. v5p0589c2s
Freedman, Samuel v5p0202c1s
Freeland, A. v1p0185c2s v1p0395c2s v1p0397c1s v1p1330c2s
Freeland, E.B. v1p0173c1s v1p0364c2s v1p0594c2s v1p0724c2s v1p1049c1s v1p1108c2s v1p1234c2s
Freeland, F.T. v1p1312c2s
Freeland, J. v6p0126c1s v6p0178c2s v6p0274c1s v6p0590c1s
Freeland, P. v1p0349c2s v1p0835c2s
Freeland, T.A. v4p0303c2s
Freeman, A. v2p0395c1s
Freeman, A.A. v4p0553c2s
Freeman, A.C. v6p0157c1s
Freeman, A.M. v1p1308c2s
Freeman, A.T. v6p0617c1s
Freeman, C. v1p0789c2s v1p1179c1s
Freeman, C.S. v6p0377c1s
Freeman, D. v6p0378c2m v6p0386c2s v6p0695c2s
Freeman, D.R. v6p0214c1s
Freeman, E.A. v1p0020c1s v1p0054c1s v1p0054c2m v1p0056c2s v1p0075c2s v1p0076c2s v1p0080c1s v1p0106c1m v1p0114c2s v1p0150c2s v1p0164c1s v1p0184c2s v1p0220c2m v1p0277c2s v1p0285c2s v1p0326c2s v1p0378c2s v1p0379c1m v1p0379c2s v1p0380c1m v1p0393c1s v1p0403c1s v1p0408c2s v1p0410c2m v1p0411c1m v1p0413c1s v1p0414c1s v1p0416c2s v1p0418c1s v1p0431c1s v1p0436c1s v1p0447c1s v1p0451c2m v1p0483c1s v1p0483c2s v1p0492c2s v1p0503c1s v1p0526c1s v1p0542c2s v1p0547c2s v1p0552c1m v1p0552c2s v1p0553c1m v1p0555c1m v1p0588c1s v1p0593c2m v1p0595c1m v1p0600c1m v1p0601c2s v1p0655c1s v1p0723c2m v1p0750c2s v1p0771c1s v1p0775c1s v1p0781c1s v1p0858c1s v1p0863c2s v1p0869c2m v1p0890c2s v1p0898c1s v1p0926c1m v1p0928c2s v1p0945c2s v1p0953c1s v1p0954c2s v1p0960c2s v1p0973c1s v1p0987c2s v1p1028c2s v1p1048c2s v1p1072c2s v1p1100c1s v1p1121c1s v1p1124c1s v1p1125c1m v1p1125c2s v1p1126c1s v1p1139c1s v1p1194c2s v1p1266c1s v1p1276c2s v1p1330c1s v1p1332c2m v1p1376c1m v2p0006c1s v2p0010c1s v2p0011c1s v2p0012c1s v2p0014c2s v2p0016c1s v2p0019c1s v2p0026c2s v2p0029c2s v2p0053c2s v2p0060c2s v2p0063c2s v2p0068c1s v2p0088c2m v2p0111c1s v2p0141c2s v2p0143c2s v2p0172c1s v2p0186c2s v2p0190c2s v2p0191c2s v2p0204c1s v2p0206c1m v2p0208c2s v2p0209c1s v2p0225c2s v2p0226c1s v2p0249c2s v2p0305c1s v2p0336c1s v2p0374c2s v2p0377c2s v2p0395c2s v2p0440c2s v2p0442c1s v2p0444c1s v2p0447c1s v2p0450c1s v2p0454c1s v2p0455c1s v2p0456c1s v3p0003c2s v3p0010c1s v3p0013c2s v3p0028c1s v3p0046c1s v3p0049c1s v3p0069c2s v3p0070c2s v3p0071c2s v3p0080c2s v3p0081c1s v3p0083c1s v3p0086c1s v3p0087c1s v3p0099c2s v3p0137c1s v3p0137c2s v3p0138c1s v3p0140c2m v3p0144c1s v3p0183c2s v3p0184c1m v3p0184c2s v3p0187c1s v3p0189c2m v3p0202c1m v3p0220c1s v3p0220c2s v3p0225c1s v3p0242c1s v3p0242c2s v3p0253c1s v3p0316c1s v3p0333c1s v3p0365c2s v3p0392c1s v3p0445c1s v4p0025c1s v4p0192c1s v4p0199c2s v4p0214c2s v4p0240c2s v4p0405c1s v4p0449c2s v4p0597c1s
Freeman, E.A. and Mullinger, J.B. v3p0333c1s
Freeman, E.A. and Taylor, I. v3p0392c1s
Freeman, E.A. et al. v2p0373c1s v3p0146c1m
Freeman, Edward A. v4p0476c1s
Freeman, F.C. v3p0389c2s
Freeman, G.A. v3p0014c1s
Freeman, G.E. v3p0164c2s
Freeman, G.S. v6p0283c2s
Freeman, G.W. v4p0453c2s
Freeman, H.A. v5p0164c2s
Freeman, H.E. v6p0592c2s
Freeman, H.E. and Cummings, E.G. v5p0163c1s
Freeman, H.F. v3p0445c2s
Freeman, J.C. v6p0616c1s
Freeman, J.E. v1p0503c1s v6p0126c2s v6p0513c2s
Freeman, J.M. v1p0591c1s v1p1270c2s
Freeman, J.R. v6p0225c1s v6p0225c2m v6p0294c2s v6p0636c1s
Freeman, J.W. v4p0214c2s
Freeman, L.R. v6p0283c1s v6p0329c1s v6p0433c2s v6p0512c2s v6p0648c1s v6p0711c2s
Freeman, M.E.W. v6p0014c1s v6p0090c1s
Freeman, M.L. v3p0447c2s
Freeman, M.S. v3p0342c1s
Freeman, M.W. v4p0254c1s v4p0554c1s v5p0335c1s v6p0165c2s
Freeman, Marilla W. v6p0374c1s
Freeman, Mary E.W. v6p0232c1s v6p0260c2s v6p0304c2s v6p0362c1s v6p0380c2s v6p0387c1s v6p0389c2m v6p0466c1s v6p0500c1s v6p0536c1s v6p0597c2s v6p0607c1s v6p0664c2s
Freeman, Mary E.Wilkins .. v6p0541c2s v6p0586c1s
Freeman, Max v5p0138c2s v5p0548c1s
Freeman, R.A. v5p0238c1s
Freeman, S.H. v2p0138c1s
Freeman, T.J. v5p0365c2s
Freeman, T.J.A. v4p0114c2s v4p0164c1s v4p0331c1s v4p0377c2s v4p0409c1s v4p0411c2m v4p0437c2s v4p0456c2s v4p0500c2s
Freeman, W.T. v4p0016c2s v4p0017c2m v4p0262c2s v4p0394c2s v5p0141c2s v5p0198c1s v5p0629c2s v6p0397c1s

Freemantle, A.L., Sir v4p0433c2s
Freemantle, H.E.S. v6p0007c1s
Freer, A.C. v6p0340c1s
Freer, A.G. v5p0271c2s
v6p0286c1s
Freer, P.C. v4p0099c1s
v4p0566c2s v6p0493c1s v6p0494c2s
Freese, J.G. v1p0619c2s
v1p0620c1s
Freese, J.H. v6p0066c1s
v6p0446c1s v6p0670c2s
Freeth, E. v2p0161c1s
Freeze, J.G. v1p1192c2s
Freiligrath, F. v1p1407c1s
Freire, D. v2p0482c1s
Freitag, J.K. v3p0472c2s
v4p0180c2s v6p0171c2s v6p0701c1s
Freitag, Joseph K. v6p0225c2s
Frelinghuysen, T. v1p0278c1s
Fremantle, A.J.L. v6p0571c1s
Fremantle, C.W. v3p0090c2s
Fremantle, E. v5p0246c2s
Fremantle, E.R. v2p0229c1s
v2p0443c2s v4p0107c1s v4p0395c2s
v6p0141c1s v6p0231c2s v6p0268c2s
v6p0296c2s v6p0309c2s v6p0337c1s
v6p0411c1s v6p0449c1s
Fremantle, H.E.S. v5p0241c1s
v5p0332c2s
Fremantle, W.H. v1p0156c2s
v1p0287c1s v1p0544c1s v1p0634c1s
v1p0650c2s v1p0697c1s v2p0172c2s
v3p0067c1s v3p0175c1s v3p0356c2s
v3p0428c1m v4p0478c1s v5p0536c2s
Fremantle, W.R. v2p0430c1s
Fremont, J.B. v1p1355c1s
v3p0163c1s v6p0102c2s v6p0241c1s
Fremont, J.C. v3p0063c1s
v5p0582c2s
Fremont, Jessie B. v6p0058c2s
Fremy, E. and Valenciennes, A.
v1p0394c1s v1p0881c2s
Fremy, M.E. v1p0664c1s
French, A. v2p0301c1s
v2p0320c1s v2p0383c1s v3p0019c2m
v3p0112c1s v3p0117c2s v3p0123c2s
v3p0147c1s v3p0153c2s v3p0178c1s
v3p0209c2s v3p0222c2s v3p0288c2s
v3p0315c1s v3p0335c1s v3p0355c2s
v3p0359c2s v3p0386c1s v3p0437c2s
v3p0440c2s v3p0447c2s v3p0453c2s
v4p0037c2s v4p0248c2s v4p0274c1s
v4p0303c1s v4p0316c2s v4p0360c1s
v4p0366c1s v4p0463c1s v4p0493c1s
v4p0504c2s v4p0532c1s v4p0536c2s
v4p0580c2s v4p0602c1s v4p0611c1s
v5p0133c2s v5p0197c2s v5p0200c1s
v5p0213c2s v5p0242c2s v5p0254c2s
v5p0300c2s v5p0391c1s v5p0413c1s
v5p0419c2s v5p0437c2s v5p0481c1s
v5p0484c2s v5p0545c2s v6p0154c1s
v6p0488c2s
French, A.D.W. v2p0168c1s
v4p0214c2m
French, A.J. v4p0166c2s
v4p0495c2s
French, Alice v3p0403c2s
v4p0026c2s v4p0195c1m v4p0232c1s
v4p0434c2m v4p0463c2s v4p0538c1s
v4p0550c2s v4p0632c2s v5p0348c1s
v5p0367c1s v5p0402c1s v5p0420c1s
v5p0485c2s v5p0581c1s v5p0586c1s
v5p0623c2s v5p0631c1s v6p0020c1s
v6p0025c1s v6p0060c1s v6p0090c1s
v6p0272c1s
French, Alice W. v5p0376c2s
v5p0531c1s v5p0596c1s
French, Allen v6p0154c1s
French, C. v2p0049c2s
v2p0394c1s v3p0338c1s v5p0496c2s
French, C.F. v4p0489c2s
French, C.W. v3p0170c1s
v3p0189c1s v4p0593c2s v5p0191c2s
v5p0192c1s v5p0511c2m v6p0573c2s
French, D.C. v6p0076c2s
French, E. v4p0011c1s
v4p0114c1s v4p0201c1s v6p0345c1s
French, F. v1p0215c2s
v1p0948c1s v3p0112c1s v3p0471c1s
v4p0398c2s v4p0485c1s v5p0211c2s
v6p0084c1s v6p0582c1s v6p0656c1s
v6p0701c1s
French, F.C. v4p0322c2s
v5p0593c2s v6p0114c1s v6p0537c1s
French, Frank v5p0589c2s
v6p0077c2s v6p0503c1s
French, G. v2p0333c2s
v6p0005c1s
French, G.E. v4p0121c2s
French, G.K. v5p0033c2s
v5p0238c1s v5p0320c1s
French, H. v6p0486c2s
v6p0500c2s v6p0534c1s v6p0568c2s
v6p0594c2s v6p0617c2s v6p0649c1s
v6p0673c2s
French, H.F. v1p0307c2s
French, H.W. v1p0151c2s
v4p0124c1s v5p0039c1s v5p0116c1s
v5p0160c1s v5p0309c1s
French, J. v1p1113c1s
v2p0360c1m v2p0389c2s
French, J.A. v1p0910c2s
v1p1216c2s v1p1262c2s
French, J.B. v2p0073c2s
French, J.D.W. v4p0209c1s
v4p0427c2s
French, J.E. v6p0505c2s
French, J.L. v5p0528c2s
v5p0602c2s v6p0505c2s
French, J.M. v3p0163c1s
v3p0215c2s v3p0267c1s v3p0301c2s
v3p0394c1s v3p0461c1s v4p0094c2s
French, J.P. v1p0727c1s
French, J.R. v2p0152c2s
v2p0335c1s
French, J.S. v6p0406c1s
French, J.W. v1p0246c2s
French, L. v5p0616c1s
French, L.H. v4p0371c1s
v5p0003c2s v5p0264c1s v5p0342c2s
v5p0407c2s v6p0007c2s v6p0110c1s
v6p0355c1s v6p0462c2s v6p0465c2s
v6p0533c1s v6p0627c2s v6p0691c2s
French, Lillie H. v5p0074c1s
v6p0344c2s
French, M. v4p0403c2s
French, M.R. v5p0366c2s
French, S.G. v1p0705c2s
French, V. v2p0055c1s
French, W. v6p0114c2s
v6p0275c2s v6p0494c2s v6p0687c1s
French, W.E.P. v3p0240c1s
v6p0601c1s v6p0604c2s v6p0666c1s
French, W.M.R. v1p0365c1s
v5p0105c2s v6p0034c1s v6p0034c2s
v6p0113c1s
French, W.R. v1p0096c2s
v1p0238c2s v1p0313c2s v1p0496c1s
v1p0598c2m v1p0687c1s v1p0692c2s
v1p0745c1s v1p0767c2s v1p1101c2s
v1p1147c2s v1p1152c1s v1p1440c2s
v2p0041c2s v3p0142c2s
French, Willard v6p0076c2s
v6p0311c1s v6p0493c1s
French-Sheldon, M. v4p0005c1s
v4p0095c1s
Freneau, P. v4p0126c1s
Frenyear, M.G. v3p0118c2s
Frenyear, T.C. v4p0550c1s
Frenzeny, P. v2p0193c1s
Frere, B. v1p0090c2s
v1p0178c2s v1p0706c2s v1p0757c2s
v1p1168c1s v3p0005c1m
Frere, B. et al. v2p0004c1s
Frere, B., Sir v1p0144c2s
v1p0721c2s v2p0004c2s v2p0186c1s
Frere, B.C. v6p0216c1s
Frere, Bartle, Sir v2p0483c2s
Frere, Bartle C. v6p0102c1s
Frere, H.B. v1p1439c1m
v2p0248c1s
Frere, H.B.E., Sir v2p0133c1s
v2p0216c2s v2p0405c1s
Frere, H.Bartle v2p0386c2s
Frere, J.H. v1p0472c1m
v1p1012c2s
Frere, M.E.I. v2p0168c1s
Frere, W.H. v5p0241c2s
Freri, J. v6p0118c2s
Freshe, J. v3p0187c2s
v3p0383c2s
Freshfield, D.W. v1p1361c1s
v2p0009c1m v2p0071c2s v2p0448c2s
v3p0413c2s v4p0093c1s v4p0385c2s
v6p0257c2s v6p0291c1m v6p0433c2s
v6p0561c2m v6p0645c2s v6p0646c1m
Freshfield, E. v1p0183c2s
v1p0764c2s v2p0110c2s v4p0429c1s
v5p0134c1s v5p0300c1s v5p0346c1s
v5p0410c1s v5p0627c1s
Freshfield, E.H. v5p0564c2s
Freshfield, F.H. v5p0140c1s
v6p0586c1s
Freshfield, F.H. and Slater, Edith
v5p0275c2s
Freshfield, F.M. v5p0308c2s
Freshfield, Frances H. ... v5p0071c2s
Fretton, W.G. v2p0105c2s
v4p0137c1s
Fretwell, J. v1p0597c2s
v3p0099c1s v3p0367c1s
Freud, J.R. v5p0120c2s
v5p0507c1s
Freudenthal, J. v4p0054c1s
v4p0542c1s
Freund, E. v2p0049c2s
v3p0171c1s v3p0233c2s v4p0117c2s
v5p0469c1s v6p0355c2s
Freund, E. and Burgess, J.W.
v5p0603c1s
Freund, J.C. v1p0627c1s
v1p0770c1s
Freund, L. and Dexler, H.. v6p0184c1s
Freund, W. v1p0727c2s
Frewen, E. v4p0635c2s
Frewen, M. v2p0182c1s
v2p0281c2s v2p0421c1s v3p0071c1s
v3p0393c1s v3p0443c2s v4p0074c1s
v4p0379c2s v4p0525c1m v4p0526c1s
v4p0596c1s v5p0297c1s v5p0505c2s
v5p0529c2s v6p0006c1s v6p0310c2s
Frewen, M. and Higgins, A.
v4p0377c2s
Frewen, M. et al. v4p0596c1s
Frewen, Moreton v6p0006c1s
v6p0260c1s
Frewer, M. v2p0005c2s
Frey, A.R. v3p0015c1s
v3p0070c1s
Frey, E. v4p0014c1s
Frey, S.L. v1p0858c1s
v1p0876c2s v2p0294c1s v4p0412c2s
Frey, T.C. v6p0600c1s
Freybe v2p0268c2s
Freyhold, B. v1p1276c2s
Freyhold, E. v1p0838c1s
v1p1061c1s
Freytag, G. v4p0345c1s
Fric, Josef et al. v6p0173c1s
Fricke, S. v1p1214c1s
Frid, E.W. v5p0259c1s
Friday, L.F. v6p0117c1s
v6p0154c2s
Fridenberg, S.L. v4p0199c1s
Friedemann, P. v1p0806c2s
Friedenberg, A.M. v6p0627c2s
Friedenwald, H. v4p0131c1m
v5p0134c2m v5p0156c1s v5p0360c2s
Friederichs, H. v4p0288c1s
Friederici, K.M. v1p0375c2s
Friedlaander, I. v6p0040c2s
Friedlaender, V.H. v6p0380c2s
Friedland, F. v4p0007c1s
Friedland, Sofja L. v6p0192c2s
Friedlander, D. v2p0042c2s
Friedlander, I. v6p0277c1s
Friedlander, J.S. v2p0211c2s
v2p0303c1s
Friedlander, M. v3p0230c2s
v4p0004c1s v4p0055c2m v4p0272c1s
v4p0497c1s v6p0364c1s
Friedlander, M.J. v5p0313c2s
Friedlandor, J. v5p0052c1s
Friedman, I.K. v5p0018c2s
v5p0353c1s v6p0180c1s v6p0416c1s
v6p0421c1s
Friedman, L.K. v6p0600c2s
Friedman, L.M. v5p0121c2s
v5p0219c2s v5p0239c1s v5p0323c2s
v5p0362c2s v6p0069c2s v6p0452c1s
v6p0533c2s v6p0653c2s
Friedman, Lee M. v6p0051c1s
Friedmann, M. v4p0302c1s
Friedmann, P. v1p0112c1s
Friedrich, J. v1p1363c2s
Friend, E. v4p0047c2s
v5p0074c1s v5p0129c2s v5p0430c2s
Friend, Emil v5p0431c2s
Friend, H. v2p0014c2s
v2p0117c2s v2p0282c1s v2p0344c1s
v2p0397c2m v4p0105c1s v4p0166c1s
Frierson, E.O. v2p0105c2s
Fries, W.W. v4p0085c1s
v4p0575c2s
Friese, A.E. v2p0356c2s
Friese, R. v2p0415c1s
Frietag, J.K. v6p0412c1s
Frieze, De v5p0621c1s
Frieze, H.S. v1p0786c1s
Frink, H.A. v3p0140c2s
v4p0466c2s v4p0483c1s
Fripp, C.E. v5p0487c2s
v5p0646c2s
Fripp, H. v1p0437c2s
v1p0527c1s v1p0645c1s
Fripp, H.E. v1p0975c2s
Frisbie, E. v2p0095c1s
Frisbie, F.S. v4p0363c1s
Frisbie, L. v1p0868c2s
v1p1279c2s
Frisbie, M.T. v5p0421c1s
Frisby, A. v1p0398c2s
v1p0550c1s v1p0656c1s v2p0330c2s
Frisby, E. v2p0025c2s
v2p0095c1s
Frisby, E. and Brooks, W.R.
v2p0095c1s
Frisby, E. and Sampson, W.T.
v2p0095c2s
Frisby, E. et al. v2p0095c2s
Frissel, E.P. v5p0043c1s
Frissell, H.B. v3p0215c1s
v5p0403c1s v6p0447c2s
v6p0680c1s
Friswell, H. v1p0748c2s
v1p1210c1s
Friswell, J.H. v1p0076c1s
v1p0286c1s v1p0613c2s v1p0742c2s
v1p0756c1s v1p0766c2s v1p0942c2s
v1p0983c2s
Friswell, L.H. v6p0054c2s
Friswell, R.J. v1p0746c2s
v1p1003c2s v1p1110c2s v3p0071c2s
v5p0625c1s
Frith, H. v3p0189c1s
Frith, Miss v3p0279c1s
Frith, W. v4p0401c1s
v4p0425c2s v6p0026c2s v6p0147c2s
v6p0516c1s v6p0517c2s
Frith, W.P. v4p0030c1s

v4p0030c2s v4p0031c1s v4p0166c2s
v4p0276c1s v4p0325c1s v4p0457c1s
Frith, W.P. and Spielmann, M.H.
v4p0004c1s
Fritsch, F.E. v6p0486c1s
Fritsch, G. v4p0174c2s
v4p0175c1s
Fritsch, G.W. v4p0021c1s
Fritts, C.E. v2p0136c1s
v2p0394c2s
Fritts, J.P. v5p0525c1s
Fritz, H. v1p0493c1s
Fritz, J. v5p0211c2s
v5p0298c1s v5p0298c2s
Fritz-Gaertner, R. v1p1113c1s
Fritzenstein, Capt.Von ... v6p0049c2s
Frizell, J.P. v1p0016c2s
v1p0104c2s v1p0270c2s v1p0291c2s
v1p0855c1s v1p1011c2s v1p1110c1s
v1p1328c1s v1p1390c2s v2p0133c1s
v2p0448c2m v3p0438c1s
Frodsham, G.H. v6p0126c1s
v6p0191c1s
Froebeck, C. v1p0019c2s
Froelick, L.D. v6p0674c2s
Froggatt, W.W. v4p0218c2s
Frohman, D. v6p0612c2s
Frohman, Daniel v5p0003c1s
Frohme, K. v2p0177c1s
Frohne, H.W. v6p0235c2s
v6p0316c1s v6p0452c2s
Frohschammer, J. v1p0945c1s
v1p1116c2s v1p1222c1s v1p1260c1s
Froideville, Von v2p0060c1s
v2p0072c2s
Froley, J.W. v6p0657c1s
Fromentin, C. v6p0245c2s
Frommel, G. v4p0283c1s
Fronsac, Count de v5p0486c1s
Froost, L. v1p0856c2s
Frost, A.B. v6p0219c2s
Frost, A.F. v4p0108c2s
v5p0564c1s v5p0641c2s v6p0312c1s
Frost, A.F. and Mayhew, W.H.
v5p0057c2s
Frost, A.J. v1p1127c1s
Frost, A.S. v4p0561c2s
v5p0230c2s
Frost, B. v1p0866c2s
v1p1206c2s v1p1292c2s
Frost, E.A. v4p0323c2s
Frost, E.B. v4p0540c2s
v4p0556c2s v5p0035c1s v5p0174c2s
v5p0644c1s v6p0214c2s v6p0609c1s
Frost, E.W. v6p0115c1s
Frost, H.W. v1p0029c1s
v1p0031c1s v1p0452c1s v1p1241c2s
Frost, J. v1p0211c1s
Frost, J.H.P. v1p0649c2s
Frost, K.T. v6p0078c1s
Frost, M.A. and Caverno, J.H.
v5p0126c2s
Frost, P. v1p0264c2s
Frost, Prof. v1p0043c2s
v1p0372c2s
Frost, R.G. v5p0316c1s
Frost, R.P.B. v2p0404c2s
v2p0480c1s
Frost, S.A. v1p1202c2s
Frost, S.T. v1p0136c1s
v4p0571c1s
Frost, T. v3p0092c1s
v3p0345c1s
Frost, T.G. v3p0025c2s
v3p0091c2s v3p0123c1s
Frost, W.G. v2p0191c1s
v5p0540c2s v5p0541c2s v5p0605c1s
Frost, W.G. and Clapp, C.W.
v2p0092c1s
Frothingham, A.L. v2p0392c2s
v3p0056c1s v5p0495c1s v5p0585c2s
v6p0027c1s
Frothingham, A.L., jr. ... v2p0030c2s
v2p0180c2s v2p0299c1s v2p0429c2s
v3p0018c2s v3p0021c1s v3p0023c1s
v3p0159c1s v3p0224c1s v3p0289c1m
v3p0417c1s v3p0449c1s v4p0022c2s
v4p0024c1s v4p0081c2s v4p0091c2s
v4p0579c1s v4p0603c2s v4p0606c2s
v5p0011c2s v5p0025c1s v5p0465c2s
v5p0495c1s v6p0090c2s
Frothingham, A.L., jr. and
Ward, W.H. v3p0197c2s
Frothingham, A.L., sr. ... v4p0030c2s
Frothingham, E.B. v6p0467c2s
v6p0711c1s
Frothingham, F. v1p0689c2s
v1p1199c1s v1p1341c1s v2p0181c1s
Frothingham, J.P. v5p0519c2s
Frothingham, N.E. v1p0243c1s
v1p0552c2s
Frothingham, N.L. v1p0074c1s
v1p0131c1s v1p0131c2s v1p0167c2s
v1p0172c2s v1p0202c1s v1p0241c2s
v1p0254c2s v1p0346c2s v1p0529c2s
v1p0534c1s v1p0554c2s v1p0555c1s
v1p0558c2m v1p0600c2s v1p0620c1s
v1p0685c1m v1p0687c1s v1p0689c2s
v1p0798c2s v1p0933c1s v1p0939c2s
v1p0980c1s v1p1056c2s v1p1097c2s
v1p1131c2s v1p1156c2s v1p1209c1s
v1p1432c1s v1p1441c2s
Frothingham, O.B. v1p0047c1s
v1p0047c2s v1p0074c1s v1p0103c1s
v1p0120c1s v1p0120c2s v1p0127c1s
v1p0127c2m v1p0150c1s v1p0219c1s
v1p0230c1s v1p0256c1s v1p0264c2s
v1p0420c2m v1p0421c2s v1p0427c1s
v1p0440c2s v1p0495c2s v1p0529c1s
v1p0568c1s v1p0582c1s v1p0613c2s
v1p0685c2s v1p0686c1s v1p0687c1m
v1p0687c2m v1p0688c1s v1p0688c2s
v1p0691c1s v1p0700c1s v1p0732c2s
v1p0741c1s v1p0792c2s v1p0796c2s
v1p0839c2s v1p0848c1s v1p0890c1s
v1p0900c2s v1p0953c1s v1p0972c2m
v1p0992c2s v1p0995c2s v1p1000c1s
v1p1043c2s v1p1057c1s v1p1083c2s
v1p1085c2s v1p1094c2s v1p1109c1s
v1p1111c2s v1p1117c2s v1p1120c1s
v1p1145c2s v1p1182c1s v1p1237c1s
v1p1300c1s v1p1303c1m v1p1325c2s
v1p1341c1s v1p1369c2s v1p1420c1s
v1p1420c2s v1p1424c1s v1p1426c2s
v2p0022c2s v2p0081c2s v2p0100c2s
v2p0115c1s v2p0116c2s v2p0170c2s
v2p0214c2s v2p0224c1s v2p0260c2s
v2p0265c2s v2p0268c2s v2p0297c2s
v2p0335c2s v2p0353c2s v2p0359c1s
v2p0398c2s v2p0416c2s v2p0428c1s
v2p0466c2s v3p0162c2m v3p0348c1s
v3p0456c2s v3p0459c2s v3p0470c1s
Frothingham, O.B. and Chambers, T.W.
v1p0344c2s
Frothingham, O.B. et al. . v2p0460c1s
Frothingham, P.R. v3p0295c1s
Frothingham, R. v1p0033c1s
v1p0609c2s v1p0707c2s v1p0888c2s
Frothingham, W. v1p0069c2s
v1p0383c2s v1p0393c2s v1p0394c1s
v1p0909c2s v1p0915c2s v1p0917c1s
v1p1253c2s
Froud, A.G. v5p0527c1s
Froude, J.A. v1p0012c2s
v1p0020c2s v1p0043c1m v1p0106c2m
v1p0184c2s v1p0185c1s v1p0198c1s
v1p0201c2s v1p0210c1s v1p0225c2s
v1p0250c2s v1p0402c2m v1p0429c2s
v1p0487c1s v1p0538c1s v1p0543c2m
v1p0549c2s v1p0585c1m v1p0590c1s
v1p0591c1s v1p0594c2s v1p0611c1s
v1p0655c2s v1p0657c1m v1p0661c2s
v1p0673c1s v1p0704c1s v1p0706c2s
v1p0722c1s v1p0775c2s v1p0781c1s
v1p0806c2m v1p0823c2s v1p0859c2s
v1p0912c1s v1p0912c2s v1p0948c1s
v1p0954c1s v1p0976c2s v1p1054c2s
v1p1080c1s v1p1087c1s v1p1112c2s
v1p1117c2s v1p1124c2s v1p1133c1s
v1p1142c1s v1p1142c2s v1p1146c2s
v1p1161c2s v1p1170c1s v1p1173c1s
v1p1195c2s v1p1199c2s v1p1212c2s
v1p1296c1s v1p1318c2m v1p1357c2s
v2p0063c1s v2p0069c1s v2p0115c2s
v2p0158c1s v2p0203c2s v2p0204c1s
v2p0268c2s v2p0316c2m v2p0336c1s
v2p0434c2s v3p0403c1s v4p0020c2s
v4p0118c2s v4p0251c1s v4p0511c1s
Froude, J.A. and Newman, F.W.
v1p0210c1s v1p0948c1s
Froude, R.E. v5p0514c2s
Froude, W. v1p0463c1s
v1p1191c2s v1p1192c1s v1p1390c2s
v3p0045c2s
Frousac, Viscount de v4p0596c2s
Frowne, Sadie v6p0628c1s
Fruhr, E.A. v5p0214c2s
Fruit, J.P. v3p0268c2s
v4p0273c1s v5p0455c2s v6p0592c1s
Fry, Agnes and Fry, Edward
v5p0396c2s
Fry, B.S. v1p0177c2s
Fry, B.St.J. v1p0830c2s
v2p0324c2s
Fry, D.P. v2p0015c2s
Fry, E. v1p0463c1s
v1p0810c2s v1p0900c1s v1p0944c2s
v2p0359c2s v3p0208c2s v3p0289c2s
v4p0072c2s v4p0323c2s v4p0498c2s
v4p0546c1s v5p0092c1s v5p0453c2s
v6p0575c2s v6p0644c2s v6p0708c2m
Fry, E.N.L. v4p0091c1s
v4p0213c2s v4p0418c1s
Fry, E.P. v4p0131c2s
Fry, Edward v6p0550c1s
Fry, Edward and Fry, Agnes
v5p0396c2s
Fry, Edward, Sir v5p0130c2s
Fry, F. v1p0125c2s
Fry, G.C. v5p0103c2s
Fry, H. v1p0722c2s
v4p0086c2s v4p0521c1s
Fry, H.B. v4p0229c1s
Fry, J. v1p0875c1s
Fry, J.B. v2p0184c2m
v2p0195c1s v3p0020c2s v3p0031c2s
v3p0179c1s v3p0443c1s v4p0346c2s
v5p0029c1m v5p0375c1s v5p0375c2s
v5p0519c2s v5p0602c2s v5p0626c1s
Fry, J.C. v6p0271c1s
Fry, O.A. v4p0424c2s
v6p0560c1m
Fry, R.E. v5p0030c2s
v5p0053c1s v5p0233c2m v5p0312c1s
v5p0427c2s v5p0529c1s v6p0032c2s
v6p0474c2s
Fry, Roger v6p0636c1s
Fry, Roger E. v6p0695c2s
Fry, T.C. v4p0531c2s
v4p0532c1s y4p0533c1s v4p0623c1s
v5p0340c2s v5p0572c1s v5p0626c2s
v6p0122c2s
Fry, W.S. v6p0317c1s
Fryar, J.R. v5p0194c1s
v6p0712c2s
Fryatt, F.E. v1p0167c2s
v1p0287c1s v1p0707c2s v1p0865c2s
v1p0902c1s v1p1039c2s v2p0069c2s
v2p0475c1s
Frye, H. v6p0184c1s
Frye, Hall v6p0049c1s
v6p0280c1s
Frye, J.A. v4p0121c1s
Frye, P.H. v6p0150c1s
v6p0569c1s v6p0617c1s
Frye, W.P. v3p0186c2s
v3p0318c2s v6p0227c1s v6p0591c1s
v6p0591c2s
Frye, W.P. and Thurman, A.G.
v3p0347c1s
Fryer, A.C. v6p0231c1s
v6p0562c2s
Fryer, C.E. v1p1146c1s
Fryer, E.M. v6p0172c2s
v6p0178c2s
Fryer, Eugenie M. v6p0078c1s
Fryer, F. v6p0088c2s
Fryer, J. v1p0233c2s
v5p0014c2s v6p0120c2s v6p0121c1s
Fryer, W.de B. v1p0064c1s
v1p0213c1s v1p0256c2s v1p0522c1s
v1p0919c2s v1p0962c1s v1p1065c2s
v1p1409c1s
Fryer, W.J. v4p0078c2s
v6p0049c1s
Fryer, W.J., jr. v4p0078c2m
Fryer, W.T., jr. v4p0136c2s
Fryers, A. v3p0019c2s
v3p0157c1s v3p0313c2s v3p0434c2s
Frykholm, S. v5p0156c2s
v5p0235c2s v5p0510c1s v6p0362c1s
Fryksell, A. v2p0420c1s
Fteley, A. v2p0108c2s
Fuchs, J.N.von v1p0526c1s
Fuerst, J. v5p0119c1s
Fuertes, E.A. v2p0373c2s
v5p0277c2s
Fuertes, J.H. v6p0688c2s
Fuertes, L.A. v6p0139c2s
v6p0228c2s v6p0522c1s
Fugitt, C.T. v6p0203c1s
v6p0443c1s
Fuguet, D. v4p0251c2s
v4p0272c1s v4p0341c2s v4p0419c1s
v4p0578c1s
Fuhr, R. v5p0475c1s
Fulano, M. v3p0343c2s
Fulcher, F.A. v4p0060c1s
v4p0060c2m v4p0061c1m v4p0061c2s
v4p0164c1s v4p0368c2s v4p0486c2s
v4p0502c1s v5p0064c1s v5p0148c2s
v5p0440c2s
Fulcher, J.A. v4p0083c2s
Fulcomer, Anna v5p0011c1s
Fulcomer, D., Mrs. v4p0460c2s
Fulda, L. v6p0133c2s
Fullam, W.F. v3p0443c2s
v5p0602c2s v6p0269c1s
Fullard, T.F. v5p0502c2s
v6p0572c2s
Fullarton, J.H. v4p0257c1s
v4p0520c1s
Fullarton, R.W.McL. v4p0266c1s
Fuller, A. v4p0034c2s
v4p0296c1s v4p0494c2s
Fuller, A.A. v4p0383c2s
v6p0174c1s
Fuller, A.B. v1p0494c1s
Fuller, A.M. v4p0498c2s
v5p0242c1s
Fuller, A.W. v4p0621c2s
Fuller, Anna v4p0012c2s
Fuller, B. v2p0073c2s
Fuller, E. v3p0190c2s
v3p0207c1s v3p0389c1s v3p0406c1s
v4p0029c2s v4p0141c1s v4p0160c2s
v4p0408c1s v5p0420c1s v5p0487c2s
v6p0035c2s v6p0069c1s v6p0206c1s
v6p0211c1s v6p0333c2s v6p0380c1s
v6p0610c2s
Fuller, E.D. v5p0335c1s
Fuller, E.Q. v1p0830c1s
v1p0831c1s
Fuller, F. v1p1087c2s
Fuller, F.H. v5p0223c1m
Fuller, F.T. v4p0441c2s
Fuller, G. v1p1209c2s
Fuller, G.F. v6p0640c1s
Fuller, G.W. v4p0199c1s
v4p0502c2s v4p0612c2s v6p0585c2s

v6p0663c2s
Fuller, H. v5p0390c1s
v5p0435c2s v5p0465c1s
Fuller, H.B. v4p0098c1s
v4p0443c1s v4p0618c1s v5p0030c2s
v5p0105c1s v5p0105c2s v5p0163c2s
v5p0186c1s v5p0248c2s v5p0299c2s
v5p0322c1s v5p0379c1s v5p0420c2s
v6p0004c1s v6p0348c2s
Fuller, J.F. v1p0133c1m
v4p0162c1s v4p0276c1s
Fuller, J.R. v1p0800c1s
Fuller, J.W. v6p0352c1s
v6p0486c1s
Fuller, L.D. v6p0084c1s
v6p0257c1s v6p0604c1s
Fuller, M. v2p0442c1s
v2p0465c1s v3p0046c1s v3p0067c1s
v3p0240c2s v3p0338c2s
Fuller, M.K. v5p0170c2s
Fuller, M.L. v5p0507c2s
v6p0186c1s v6p0257c2s
Fuller, M.W. v1p0005c2s
v1p0104c1s v1p0569c1s v2p0064c1s
v2p0234c1s v2p0278c1s v3p0039c1s
v3p0269c2s
Fuller, Mabel B. v5p0071c1s
Fuller, N.E. v4p0361c2s
Fuller, R.H. v3p0196c1s
v6p0233c2s
Fuller, S. v1p0043c2s
v1p0314c1s v1p0514c2s v1p0756c2s
v1p1101c1s v1p1118c2s v1p1237c1s
v2p0044c2s v2p0337c2s v2p0415c1s
v4p0149c2s
Fuller, S.D. v2p0335c2s
Fuller, S.E. v3p0467c2s
Fuller, T.E. v4p0179c1s
Fuller, V.E. v6p0096c1s
Fuller, W. v3p0420c2s
Fuller, W.H. v2p0360c2s
Fuller, Z. v5p0534c2s
Fuller-Maitland, J.A. v4p0048c1s
v5p0609c2s
Fullerton, A. v6p0098c1s
v6p0210c2s v6p0422c1s v6p0457c2s
v6p0460c2s v6p0603c1s
Fullerton, B.M. v1p1361c1s
Fullerton, E.L. v6p0551c2s
v6p0582c1s v6p0700c1s
Fullerton, E.L. and Fullerton, H.B.
v6p0154c1s
Fullerton, Edith L. v6p0247c2s
Fullerton, G. v1p0293c2s
v1p0533c2s v1p0930c2s v1p1257c1s
v1p1438c1s v2p0482c2s
Fullerton, G.S. v2p0016c2s
v2p0097c2s v2p0150c2s v2p0163c2s
v2p0214c2s v2p0221c1s v2p0280c1s
v2p0412c2s v3p0330c1s v4p0434c1s
v4p0439c2s v4p0441c2s v4p0464c2s
v4p0465c2s v5p0220c1s v5p0319c1s
v5p0513c2s v5p0519c2s v5p0542c1m
v5p0580c1s v5p0631c1s
Fullerton, H.B. v6p0301c1s
v6p0577c1s
Fullerton, H.B. and Fullerton, E.L.
v6p0154c1s
Fullerton, J. v1p1295c1s
Fullerton, J.E. v2p0178c2s
v2p0283c2s
Fullerton, J.S. v3p0075c1s
Fullerton, K. v6p0062c2s
v6p0390c1s v6p0509c1s v6p0583c2s
Fullerton, M. v4p0241c1s
Fullerton, W.H. v2p0437c2s
Fullerton, W.L. v6p0022c2s
Fullerton, W.M. v2p0023c1s
v2p0396c2s v3p0012c1s v3p0044c2s
v3p0062c2s v3p0139c1s v4p0064c1s
v4p0160c2s v4p0402c2s v5p0025c1s
v6p0295c2s
Fullom, J.M. v6p0038c1s
v6p0296c1s
Fullonton, J. v2p0034c2s
v2p0099c1s v2p0168c2s v2p0286c1s
Fulmer, H. v6p0462c2s
Fulmer, Harriet v5p0416c2s
Fulmore, Z.T. v6p0102c2s
v6p0414c1s v6p0639c2s v6p0640c1s
Fulton, A.E. v3p0075c2s
Fulton, A.R. v2p0390c2s
v3p0049c2s
Fulton, C.W. v6p0338c2s
Fulton, J. v1p0769c2s
v2p0067c1s v2p0084c1s v3p0040c2s
v4p0122c1s
Fulton, J.S. v5p0416c2s
v6p0417c1s
Fulton, L.D.K. v5p0017c1s
Fulton, R. v1p0494c1s
Fulton, R.B. v6p0192c2s
Fulton, R.L. v4p0472c2s
v5p0643c2s
Fulton, T.C. v4p0227c2s
Fumston, F. v4p0104c2s
Funck-Brentano, F. v3p0243c2s
v4p0352c2s
Funck-Brentano, T. v3p0255c2s
v3p0339c2s
Fung, Yee v3p0079c1s
Funsten, J.B. v6p0315c1s
v6p0546c2s
Funston, E.B. v5p0445c2s
Funston, F. v6p0568c1s
Furbay, H.G. v6p0566c1s
Furber, A. v5p0154c2s
v5p0283c1s v5p0560c2s
Furber, D.L. v3p0329c1s
Furber, E.A. v5p0570c1s
Furber, H.J., jr. v6p0466c2s
Furber, W.C. v6p0464c1s
Furbush, F. v5p0047c2s
v5p0132c2s v5p0211c1s v5p0233c1s
v5p0273c1s v5p0403c1s v5p0409c1s
v5p0417c2s v5p0483c1s
Furbush, Freeman v5p0213c1s
Furey, F.T. v5p0494c1s
Furley, C.G. v2p0304c1s
v3p0361c2s v3p0436c2s
Furley, J. v2p0366c2s
Furlong, C.W. v6p0025c2s
v6p0100c2s v6p0256c1s v6p0430c1s
v6p0492c1s v6p0565c1s v6p0611c1s
v6p0657c1s
Furlong, E.L. v6p0524c2s
v6p0567c1s v6p0589c1s
Furman, G. v1p1400c2s
Furman, H.V.F. v4p0033c1s
Furman, L.S. v4p0202c2s
v4p0308c2s v4p0540c1s v5p0149c1s
v5p0210c2s
Furman, McD. v4p0369c2s
v5p0223c2s v5p0620c2s
Furnell, A.S., Miss v6p0538c1s
Furness, C. v6p0141c1s
Furness, C.E. v4p0167c1s
v4p0588c2s
Furness, Caroline E. v5p0414c1s
Furness, F. v1p0346c1s
Furness, H. v5p0234c2s
Furness, H.H. v3p0388c2m
v4p0519c1m v5p0523c2s v6p0161c1s
Furness, W.E. v2p0120c1s
v2p0142c2s v2p0177c2s v3p0138c1m
Furness, W.H. v1p0052c1s
v1p0128c1m v1p0130c1s v1p0217c1s
v1p0241c2s v1p0333c2s v1p0384c2s
v1p0514c2s v1p0528c2s v1p0625c2s
v1p0684c1s v1p0684c2s v1p0687c1s
v1p0688c1s v1p0703c2s v1p0720c1s
v1p0793c2s v1p0850c1s v1p0900c2s
v1p1363c2s v3p0229c2s v4p0179c1s
Furness, W.R. v6p0587c1s
Furniss, G.L. v4p0449c1s
Furniss, H. v4p0030c2s
v4p0031c2s v4p0045c2s v4p0274c2s
v5p0094c2s v5p0343c2s v6p0487c1s
Furniss, J.J. v1p1233c2s
Furniss, L.E. v1p0144c1s
v1p0366c2s v1p0892c1s
Furnivall, F.J. v1p0223c1s
v2p0271c1s v2p0473c2s v3p0057c1s
v3p0057c2s v3p0075c1m v3p0387c1m
v3p0387c2m v3p0388c2s v4p0356c2s
v4p0517c2s v5p0224c1s v5p0522c1s
v6p0085c1s
Furnivall, F.J. and Morgan, A.
v3p0389c1s
Furnivall, F.J. and Tyler, T.
v3p0154c2s
Furnivall, F.J. et al. ... v2p0058c2s
Furse, C.W. v4p0219c1s
Furse, G.A. v2p0021c2s
v2p0223c2s v2p0259c2s v2p0392c1s
Furse, S.A. v2p0097c1s
Furst, C. v6p0234c2s
Furst, C.B. v4p0159c1s
v5p0103c1s
Furst, I. v2p0299c1s
Furst, S.E. v2p0181c1s
v2p0269c1s
Furtwangler, A. v5p0103c1s
v6p0005c1s v6p0273c1s
Fusco, E. v1p0668c2s
Futrelle, J. v6p0110c2s
v6p0264c2s
Fyfe, A. v1p0267c2s
v1p0501c2s v1p0747c1s
Fyfe, H.C. v5p0211c2s
v5p0492c1s v5p0529c1s v6p0133c2s
v6p0385c1s v6p0454c1s v6p0497c1s
Fyfe, H.H. v4p0006c2s
v4p0117c2s v4p0444c1s v4p0523c1s
v5p0167c2s v5p0191c2s v5p0299c1s
v5p0509c1s v5p0524c1s v5p0575c2s
v6p0003c2s v6p0012c2s v6p0167c2s
v6p0263c1s v6p0394c2s v6p0579c2s
v6p0641c2s v6p0661c1s
Fyfe, Herbert C. v6p0623c1s
Fyfe, J.H. v1p0080c2s
v1p0109c1s v1p0180c2s v1p0315c1s
v1p0353c1s v1p0469c2s v1p0528c1s
v1p0543c2s v1p0740c1s v1p0836c2s
v1p0918c2s v1p1049c1s v1p1216c1s
v1p1318c2s v1p1381c2s v1p1437c2s
Fyfe, J.T. v5p0515c1s
Fyfe, J.W. v6p0245c1s
Fyfe, R.A. v1p0709c1s
Fyfe, W.W. v1p0144c1s
v1p0331c1s v1p0994c2s v1p0995c1s
v1p1188c2s v1p1239c1s
Fyffe, C.A. v1p0641c1s
v2p0247c2m v2p0291c1s v3p0109c1s
v3p0138c1s v3p0162c2s
Fyffe, H.E. v6p0499c1s
Fyffe, J.P. v6p0114c1s
Fyffe, R.E. v6p0366c2s
Fyles, E.E. v6p0228c1s
Fyles, F. v4p0376c2s
Fyles, F.E. v6p0181c2s
Fynes-Clinton, C.F. v1p0244c2s
Fynney, F.B. v3p0476c1s
Fytche, A. v1p0178c1s
Fyte, K. v5p0642c1s
Fyvie, J. v3p0466c2s
v4p0319c1s v4p0350c1s v5p0042c1s
v5p0229c2s v5p0251c1s v5p0259c2s
v5p0370c2s v5p0491c1s v6p0056c2s
v6p0340c1s v6p0344c2s v6p0497c2s

G. v5p0135c1s
G., C.C. v6p0198c2s
G., E.C. v1p0499c2s
v6p0110c1s
G., H.C. v3p0256c1s
G., L.I. and Chambers, E.K.
v6p0159c1s v6p0675c1s
G., S.C. v6p0265c2s
v6p0266c1s
G., W.M. v5p0499c1s
Gabb, W.M. v1p0187c1s
v1p0305c1s v1p0508c2s v1p0509c1s
v1p1148c2m v1p1364c2s
Gabba, C.F. v1p0356c2s
Gabbett, H.S. v5p0232c1s
Gabel, E. v2p0187c1s
v2p0275c1s
Gaboriau, E. v1p0756c1s
Gaboriau, M. v2p0009c2s
Gabriel, Renel v1p0053c1s
Gabrielidis, V. v4p0143c2s
Gade, A.J. v5p0144c2s
Gade, J.A. v6p0596c1s
Gadir, S.A. v6p0313c2s
v6p0315c1s
Gadow, H. v3p0045c1s
v5p0610c1s v6p0471c1s
Gadsby, F. v5p0160c1s
v5p0202c1s v5p0316c2s v5p0366c2s
v5p0424c2s
Gadsby, H.F. v6p0434c2s
v6p0633c2s
Gadsden, J. v1p0284c1s
v1p0461c2s
Gael, A. v6p0355c1s
Gaertner, E. v2p0163c2s
Gaertner, F. v3p0451c1s
Gaertner, R.F. v1p0835c2s
Gaertner, T.L. v4p0385c1s
Gaetke, H. v1p0136c1s
Gaffield, T. v1p0525c2s
v1p0747c1s v6p0258c1s
Gaffney, F.H. v5p0637c2s
v6p0181c2s v6p0703c1s v6p0706c1s
Gaffney, Fannie H. v6p0370c1s
Gaffney, T. v3p0059c1s
Gage, A.E. v5p0224c1m
v5p0316c2s
Gage, G.W. v1p1127c1s
Gage, H.H. v6p0283c1s
Gage, Harriet H. v6p0386c1s
Gage, J. v1p0009c1s
v1p0100c1m v1p0111c2m v1p0172c2s
v1p0173c1s v1p0253c1s v1p0304c2s
v1p0384c2s v1p0608c1s v1p0740c1s
v1p0761c1s v1p1111c1s v1p1122c2m
v1p1227c2s
Gage, J. and Woodward, W.. v1p1129c1s
Gage, K.A. v3p0087c1s
Gage, K.M. v2p0059c1s
Gage, L.J. v2p0106c2s
v4p0101c1s v4p0377c2s v4p0393c2s
v4p0585c2s v5p0105c1s v5p0120c2s
v5p0121c1m v5p0150c1s v5p0604c1m
v6p0162c1s
Gage, M.E.G. v1p0278c2s
Gage, M.F. v5p0597c1s
Gage, M.G. v1p0483c1s
v3p0425c1s
Gage, M.J. v2p0477c1s
Gage, S.H. v1p1016c1s
v2p0203c2s v4p0143c1s v4p0258c2s
v4p0403c1s v4p0441c2s v4p0482c1s
v4p0637c2s v5p0020c2s v5p0165c1s
Gage, S.H. and Gage, S.P.. v2p0370c2s
Gage, S.P. v4p0336c2s
Gage, S.P. and Gage, S.H.. v2p0370c2s
Gage, Susanna P. v5p0399c2s
Gage, W.L. v1p0003c2s
v1p0100c2s v1p0431c2s v1p0856c1s
v1p0927c2s v1p0992c2s v1p1157c1s
v1p1301c1s v1p1322c1s v1p1342c2s
v2p0283c1s
Gager, G.S. v6p0172c2s
Gagliardi, E. v5p0609c2s
Gagliardi, J. v1p0875c1s
Gahan, B. v6p0041c2s
v6p0042c1m
Gahan, C.J. v5p0162c1s
Gai, Hong See v5p0261c2s
Gaidoz, H. and Vigfusson, G.
v2p0319c2s
Gaige, R.C. v6p0503c2s
Gailbraith, H.L.P. v1p0832c1s
Gaillard, D.D. v4p0014c1s
v4p0153c2s
Gaillard, E.M. v4p0036c2s
Gaillard, E.S. v1p1345c1s
Gaillard, E.T. v1p0462c1s
Gaillard, E.W. v5p0335c1s
v6p0371c1s v6p0371c2s v6p0372c2s
v6p0373c1s v6p0374c1s v6p0375c1s
v6p0437c1s v6p0672c1s
Gaillard, J.D. v3p0242c2s
Gailor, T.F. v3p0141c2s
v5p0157c2s v5p0214c2s v5p0500c1s
v6p0484c1s
Gain, W.A. v4p0191c2s
v4p0600c2s
Gaines, A.G. v1p0002c2s
v1p1355c1s
Gaines, A.W. v5p0532c2s
v6p0021c1s v6p0154c2s v6p0365c1s
Gaines, M.W. v6p0414c2m
v6p0594c2m v6p0630c2s
Gaines, Morrell W. v6p0152c1s
Gairdner, C. v4p0038c1s
Gairdner, J. v1p0121c1s
v1p0442c2s v1p0595c1s v1p0708c2s
v1p0850c1s v1p0850c2s v1p0977c2s
v1p1385c1s v2p0142c1s v2p0208c2s
v2p0354c1s v2p0374c1s v3p0074c2s
v3p0106c2s v3p0194c1m v3p0245c1s
v3p0287c2s v3p0360c2m v4p0065c2s
v4p0178c1s v4p0254c2s v4p0382c2s
v4p0508c2s v5p0073c1s v5p0262c1s
v5p0369c1s v5p0491c1s v6p0296c1s
v6p0647c2s v6p0702c2s
Gairdner, J. and Leadam, I.S.
v6p0287c1s
Gairdner, J. and Lloyd, W.W.
v3p0287c2s
Gairdner, J. and Round, J.H.
v2p0015c2s
Gairdner, Prof. v1p0853c1s
Gairdner, S.R. v1p0546c1s
Gairdner, W.T. v1p0607c2s
v1p1427c1s v3p0122c2s
Gairey, J.W. v1p0247c1s
Gairns, J.F. v6p0089c2s
v6p0382c1s v6p0382c2m v6p0432c1s
v6p0432c2s v6p0442c2s
Gaisford, E. v1p0174c2s
v1p0524c2s v1p0549c2s v1p0596c2s
v1p0690c2s v1p1376c2s
Gajani, G. v1p1033c1s
Gak-Tsok-Sin v5p0283c1s
Galbraith, J. v5p0172c2s
Galbraith, J.A. v1p0833c1s
Galbraith, L. v5p0421c1s
Galbraith, W.T. v4p0462c2s
v4p0563c2s
Galbreath, C.B. v5p0336c1s
v5p0336c2s
Galbreath, L.H. v5p0377c1s
Galdemar, A. v4p0074c1s
v4p0126c1s v4p0425c1s v4p0503c1m
Galdos, B.P. v4p0047c2s
v5p0312c1s
Gale, A.G. v6p0566c2s
Gale, Annie G. v4p0372c1s
Gale, C.R. v5p0147c2s
Gale, D.Carroll v6p0664c1s
Gale, E. v1p0681c1s
v6p0038c2s
Gale, E.C. v1p0520c1s
v1p0942c1s v1p1337c2s v1p1420c2s
v3p0171c1s
Gale, E.S. v5p0325c2s
Gale, F. v1p0315c1s
v3p0105c1s v4p0139c1m v4p0604c2s
v5p0143c1s v5p0272c1s
Gale, F. and Selborne, Lord
v3p0465c1s
Gale, F.S. v1p1273c2s
Gale, Fred. v4p0517c1s
v4p0601c1s v4p0604c2s
Gale, G. v1p0497c1s
Gale, H. v3p0198c1s
v3p0293c2s v5p0075c1s v6p0710c2s
Gale, H. and Gale, M.C. .. v6p0117c1s
Gale, H.B. v2p0136c2s
v3p0135c2s v5p0132c1s
Gale, H.G. v6p0444c1s
Gale, Harlow v5p0394c2s
Gale, J.A. v6p0354c1s
Gale, J.B. v3p0268c2s
Gale, J.S. v5p0319c2m
v6p0354c1s
Gale, L.D. v1p1440c1s
Gale, M.C. and Gale, H. .. v6p0117c1s
Gale, M.T. v4p0251c2s
Gale, M.T., Mrs. v1p0575c2s
Gale, N. v4p0249c2s
v4p0405c2s
Gale, Norman v6p0038c2s
Gale, R. v4p0275c1s
Gale, R. and Bell, B. v1p0604c1s
Gale, R. and Passarini, F.
v1p1235c1s
Gale, S. v1p0184c2s
v1p0344c1s
Gale, Z. v6p0235c1s
v6p0261c1s v6p0358c1s v6p0402c2s
v6p0406c2s
Gale, Zona v6p0122c1s
v6p0127c2s v6p0187c2s v6p0189c2s
v6p0296c1s v6p0394c2s v6p0464c1m
v6p0495c1s v6p0622c2s v6p0643c2s
v6p0690c2s
Gale, Zona and Menkey, Jill
v6p0491c2s
Galeatus v5p0032c1s
v5p0252c2s
Gales, R.L. v6p0122c2s
v6p0172c1s v6p0208c1s v6p0480c2s
Gales, S. v1p0037c2s
Galindo, J. v1p0994c1s
Gall, J. v2p0182c2s
Gallagher, C.W. v3p0105c2s
v4p0055c2s
Gallagher, G.F. v6p0604c2s
Gallagher, G.W. v3p0040c2s
v3p0169c2s
Gallagher, H.J. v5p0112c1s
v5p0377c2s
Gallagher, H.P. v2p0254c1s
Gallagher, J.F. v1p0337c1s
Gallagher, T. v5p0182c1s
v5p0203c2s
Gallagher, W. v6p0136c2s
Gallagher, W. et al. v3p0025c2s
Gallagher, W.D. v1p0706c1m
v1p0754c1s v1p0755c2s v1p0938c2s
v1p1397c1s v1p1412c2s
Gallaher, F.M. v3p0346c2s
v4p0207c2s v4p0208c1s
Gallaher, G.M. v5p0474c2s
Gallaher, G.R. v3p0260c2s
v3p0413c2s
Gallaher, W.B. v2p0180c2s
Gallatin, A. v1p0091c1s
v1p0092c1s
Gallatin, A.E. v6p0055c1s
v6p0162c2s v6p0679c2s v6p0695c2s
Gallatin, Albert E. v6p0155c2s
Gallatin, J. v1p0326c1s
v1p1232c1s v1p1359c2s
Gallatly, W. v3p0468c2s
Gallaudet, E.M. v1p0213c1s
v1p0337c1m v2p0113c2s v2p0223c2s
v3p0112c2s v4p0149c2m
Gallaudet, E.M. et al. ... v3p0112c2s
v3p0113c2s
Gallaudet, E.M., Mrs. v4p0072c1s
Gallaudet, T.H. v1p1196c2s
v2p0362c1s
Gallaway, J.C. v1p1103c1s
Galle, J.G. v2p0095c2s
Gallee, J.H. v3p0430c1s
Gallenga, A. v1p0083c2s
v1p0204c1s v1p0331c2s v1p0476c1s
v1p0669c2s v1p0670c2m v1p0671c1s
v1p0671c2m v1p0672c1s v1p0672c2m
v1p0798c2s v1p0800c1m v1p1329c2s
v1p1364c2s v2p0156c1s v2p0232c1s
v3p0159c2s v3p0174c1s v3p0224c1s
v3p0224c2s v3p0225c1s
Gallery, D. v2p0375c1s
Galletly, A. v2p0018c1s
Galletti, Mad. v1p0191c1s
Gallienne, R.L. v3p0020c2s
v3p0029c1s v3p0292c2s v3p0367c2s
v3p0463c2s
Gallienne, R.Le v3p0177c2s
v4p0148c2s v4p0149c2s v4p0153c2s
v4p0240c2s v4p0248c1m v4p0365c2s
v4p0491c1s v4p0549c1s v4p0561c1s
v4p0570c2s v4p0609c2m v4p0630c2s
v5p0012c2s v5p0038c1s v5p0070c1s
v5p0316c2m v5p0317c1s v5p0317c2s
v5p0325c1s v5p0361c2s v5p0446c2s
v5p0553c1s v5p0566c1s v5p0612c2s
v6p0015c2s v6p0043c1s v6p0080c1s
v6p0143c2s v6p0148c1s v6p0160c1s
v6p0164c1s v6p0189c2s v6p0243c1s
v6p0277c1s v6p0286c1s v6p0350c1s
v6p0362c1s v6p0380c2s v6p0388c2s
v6p0466c2s v6p0488c2m v6p0590c1s
v6p0593c2s v6p0595c1s v6p0596c2s
v6p0656c1s v6p0703c2s v6p0707c1s
Gallienne, Richard Le v5p0017c2s
v5p0420c1s
Gallinger, J.G. v2p0194c2s
Gallison, J. v1p0028c2s
v1p0288c1s v1p0433c2s v1p0566c2s
v1p0730c2s v1p0992c1s v1p1053c2s
v1p1354c1s
Gallison, J.C. v5p0219c1s
v5p0642c1s
Gallon, T. v5p0359c1s
Gallop, F.A. v5p0612c2s
Gallou, Tom v5p0264c2s
Gallouedec, L. v5p0359c1s
Galloup, D.P. v1p1288c1s
Galloupe, F.E. v1p0759c2s
v2p0139c1m v3p0408c2s
Galloway, A.A.C. v4p0200c1s
v4p0579c2s
Galloway, B.T. v3p0319c2s
v4p0217c1s v5p0116c1s v6p0008c2s
v6p0077c1s v6p0077c2s v6p0246c2s
v6p0258c2s v6p0679c2s
Galloway, C.B. v6p0280c2s
Galloway, C.B. et al. v6p0391c1s
Galloway, C.E. v6p0655c1s
Galloway, Countess of v2p0477c1s
v3p0184c1s v4p0401c2s v5p0142c2s
Galloway, E. v1p1248c1s
Galloway, G. v3p0362c1s
v6p0216c1s
Galloway, G.D. v5p0462c1s
Galloway, G.N. v2p0238c2s
v2p0385c1s v3p0405c2s
Galloway, M.A.A. v3p0369c2s
v4p0048c1s v6p0072c1s
Galloway, R. v2p0076c1s
v2p0139c2s v2p0424c1s v2p0432c2s
Galloway, R.L. v4p0120c2s
Galloway, T. v1p0827c2s

Galloway, W. v1p0269c1s v1p0844c1s v2p0090c1s v2p0090c2m v2p0093c1s v2p0156c2s v2p0396c2s v3p0092c1s v5p0377c2s

Gallup, A. v4p0471c1s

Gallup, E.S. v1p0262c2s v1p0416c1s

Gallup, E.W. v6p0586c2s

Gallup, F.A. v5p0197c2s v5p0326c1s v5p0326c2m

Gallup, Mrs. v6p0586c2s

Gallwey, H.L. v4p0051c1s

Gallwey, T. v1p1013c2s v2p0054c1s v2p0225c2s v2p0414c2s

Gally, J.W. v1p0133c1s v1p0492c2s v1p0608c2s v1p1182c2s v1p1183c2s v2p0178c1s v6p0569c1s

Galpin, B. v5p0271c2s

Galpin, C. v5p0137c2s

Galpin, F.W. v6p0049c2s v6p0304c2s v6p0534c2s

Galpin, K.T. v6p0387c1s

Galpin, P.G. v6p0277c2s

Galpin, S.A. v3p0213c2s

Galt, A. et al. v4p0177c1s

Galt, A.C. v4p0237c1s v4p0276c1s v4p0610c1s

Galt, G.McF. v5p0370c2s

Galt, J. v1p0034c2s v1p0044c1s v1p0083c1s v1p0228c1s v1p0295c2s v1p0486c1s v1p0503c1s v1p0514c2m v1p0544c1s v1p0831c2s v1p0887c2s v1p0978c2s v1p1154c1s v1p1159c2s v1p1164c2s v1p1172c2s v1p1245c2s v1p1247c1s v1p1401c1m v1p1401c2s

Galt, W. v1p1075c2s v1p1078c1s v3p0352c1s

Galt-Gamble, T.E. v3p0368c2s

Galtier, J. v6p0713c1s

Galton and Watson v1p0442c2s

Galton, A. v3p0058c2s v3p0083c1s v3p0088c2s v3p0119c2s v3p0120c2s v3p0125c2s v3p0328c1s v3p0339c1s v4p0147c1s v4p0197c1s v4p0270c2s v4p0353c2s v4p0603c1s v5p0493c2m v6p0236c2s v6p0312c1s v6p0547c2s

Galton, A. and Taunton, E.L. v6p0547c2s

Galton, C. v4p0077c2m v4p0296c2s

Galton, D. v1p0491c1s v1p0493c2s v1p1079c1m v1p1150c1s v1p1150c2s v2p0185c2s v2p0199c1s v2p0299c2s v2p0385c2s v2p0386c1s v2p0396c1s v2p0419c1s v2p0459c1s v3p0165c1s v3p0192c1s v3p0375c1m v3p0408c2s v3p0448c1s v3p0455c1s v4p0273c2s

Galton, D., Sir v3p0115c1s v3p0352c1s

Galton, Douglas v2p0406c1s

Galton, F. v1p0045c1s v1p0142c2s v1p0155c2s v1p0504c1s v1p0505c1s v1p0557c2s v1p0587c1m v1p0819c2s v1p0820c2m v1p0933c2s v1p1034c2s v1p1036c1m v1p1042c1s v1p1062c2s v1p1163c2s v1p1335c1s v1p1375c2s v2p0016c2m v2p0074c2s v2p0113c2s v2p0119c1s v2p0201c1s v2p0201c2s v2p0207c2m v2p0213c1s v2p0214c2s v2p0282c1s v2p0302c2s v2p0318c1s v2p0340c1m v2p0418c2s v2p0450c1s v2p0457c2s v2p0469c2s v3p0015c2m v3p0027c2s v3p0048c2s v3p0101c2s v3p0146c1s v3p0153c1s v3p0194c2s v3p0204c1s v3p0207c2s v3p0269c1s v3p0274c2s v3p0327c2s v3p0331c2s v3p0423c2s v4p0191c1m v4p0276c1s v4p0364c2s v4p0415c2s v4p0545c2s v4p0546c2s v5p0275c2s v5p0279c1s v5p0447c2s v5p0461c1s v6p0001c2s v6p0212c2m v6p0302c1s v6p0402c2s v6p0486c2s

Galton, F. and Kidd, B. .. v4p0478c2s

Galton, F. and Mahomed, F.A. v2p0100c2s

Galton, F. and Venn, J. .. v3p0015c2s

Galton, F. et al. v2p0418c2s v3p0146c1s v3p0242c2s v4p0320c2s

Galton, G. v4p0274c2s

Galton, J.C. v1p0099c1s v1p0214c2s v1p0256c1s v1p0454c1s v1p0456c1s v1p0456c2s v1p0911c1s v1p0962c2s v1p0966c1m v1p1110c2s v1p1173c1s

Galton, T. et al. v3p0429c2s

Galvin, C.W. v6p0158c1s

Galvin, G.W. v6p0158c1s v6p0517c2s

Galvin, J.L. v3p0170c1s v3p0241c2s

Galwey, T.F. v1p0497c1s v2p0012c2s v2p0121c1s v2p0122c1s v2p0222c1s v2p0226c2s v2p0228c2s v2p0449c2s v3p0162c2s v3p0429c2s

Gambetta, L. v5p0081c1s v5p0131c2s v5p0545c2s

Gambier, Capt. v5p0470c1s

Gambier, J.W. v1p0837c1s v4p0013c2s v4p0087c1s v4p0225c2s v4p0237c1s v4p0243c2s v4p0424c1s v4p0587c1s v5p0173c2s v5p0174c1s v5p0189c1m v5p0243c1s v5p0244c1s v5p0313c1s v5p0502c1s v6p0392c2s v6p0661c1s

Gambier, J.W. and Gundry, R.C. v4p0166c2s

Gambier-Bonsfield, R.W. .. v2p0019c1s v2p0085c1s v3p0018c1m

Gambier-Parry, E. v3p0120c2s v3p0312c1s

Gamble, E.A.M. v5p0533c1s v5p0624c1s

Gamble, G. v5p0419c2s

Gamble, George v5p0575c1s

Gamble, J. v6p0126c1s v6p0636c1m

Gamble, J.G. v1p0307c1s

Gamble, S.G. v2p0060c1s

Gamble, S.W. v5p0509c1s

Gamble, W.M. v5p0350c1s v5p0489c2s

Gambold, J. v1p1398c2s

Gamewell, M.P. v6p0119c2s

Gamewell, Mary P. v6p0117c2s

Gamgee, A. v1p1101c2s v2p0032c1s v2p0394c1s v4p0263c1s

Gamgee, J. v1p1325c1s v3p0090c2s

Gammell, F.H. v6p0395c2s

Gammell, W. v1p0169c1s v1p0205c1s v1p0861c2s v1p1089c1s v1p1385c2s v1p1412c1m

Gandhi, V.R. v4p0374c2m v5p0301c2s

Gandhi, V.R. et al. v4p0374c2s

Gandolfo, E. v3p0018c1s

Gandy, J.R. v2p0169c2s v2p0291c2s

Gane, W.L. v1p0038c2s v1p0359c1s v1p0837c2s

Ganem, H. v2p0410c1s

Ganett, H. v4p0410c2s

Ganett, S.M. v6p0680c1s

Ganle, J. v6p0376c1s

Ganley, M. v5p0097c1s

Ganly, W. v3p0137c1s

Gann, Dr. v5p0389c1s

Gann, T. v5p0288c2s

Gann, Thomas v5p0367c1s

Gannet, D. v3p0050c1s

Gannet, E. v5p0451c2s

Gannett, A. v1p0371c1s v1p0846c1s

Gannett, A.M. v3p0390c1s v3p0411c1s

Gannett, E.S. v1p0006c1s v1p0043c2s v1p0129c2s v1p0178c2s v1p0244c2s v1p0557c2s v1p0573c1s v1p0706c1s v1p0832c1s v1p0925c1s v1p0983c1s v1p1043c2s v1p1044c1s v1p1064c2s v1p1067c2s v1p1091c1s v1p1094c1m v1p1095c1s v1p1095c2s v1p1292c2s v1p1310c1s v1p1340c2m v1p1341c1s v1p1384c1s

Gannett, H. v1p0030c2s v1p0212c1s v1p0279c1s v1p0279c2s v1p1045c2s v2p0299c2s v2p0308c2s v2p0352c1s v2p0441c1s v2p0450c2s v2p0454c2s v2p0455c1m v3p0270c2s v3p0353c2m v3p0444c1s v3p0458c2s v4p0281c2s v4p0360c1s v4p0453c1s v4p0594c2s v4p0596c2m v5p0010c2s v5p0133c1s v5p0214c1s v5p0256c1s v5p0481c2s v5p0550c1s v5p0580c1s v5p0621c1s v6p0106c2s v6p0426c2s v6p0433c2s v6p0492c2s v6p0493c1s v6p0656c1s v6p0668c1s v6p0692c2s

Gannett, H.C. v4p0222c1s

Gannett, J.M. v3p0276c2s

Gannett, S.E. v5p0421c1s

Gannett, S.S. v4p0091c1s

Gannett, W.C. v1p0259c2s v1p0487c1s v1p0865c1s v1p1137c1s v2p0181c1s v2p0307c2s v4p0119c1s v6p0639c1s

Gannon, F.A. v6p0685c2s

Gannon, H. v2p0247c1s

Gannon, J.H., jr. v6p0598c2s

Ganong, W.F. v2p0261c1s v3p0372c1s v3p0441c2s v4p0322c1s v4p0566c2s v5p0073c1s v5p0073c2s v5p0533c2s v6p0188c1s v6p0357c1s v6p0502c2m v6p0503c1s v6p0601c2m

Ganong, W.F. and Hayes, E. v6p0386c1s

Gans, C. v5p0187c2s v5p0432c1s v6p0185c1s v6p0237c2s v6p0241c2s v6p0479c1s

Gans, D. v1p0081c2s v1p0119c2s v1p0120c1s v1p0138c1s v1p0252c2s v1p0292c2s v1p0598c2m v1p0640c2s v1p0645c2s v1p0646c1s v1p0687c2s v1p0732c1s v1p0847c1s v1p0900c2s v1p1086c1s v1p1308c1s v1p1328c2s

Gans, H.S. v6p0453c1s

Ganse, H.D. v1p0096c1s v2p0225c1s

Ganse, H.G. v5p0117c1s

Ganss, H.G. v4p0494c1s v5p0351c1s v5p0386c2s

Gante, Pedro de v1p0891c2s

Ganthony, R. v4p0246c2s

Gantt, E.W. v4p0464c2s

Gantt, H.L. v4p0217c2s v4p0548c1s v6p0073c2s v6p0355c2m v6p0682c2s

Gantt, H.L. and Maury, D.H., jr. v2p0457c2s

Gantt, T.T. v1p0453c2s

Ganucci, R. and Nesbitt, A. v1p0674c1s

Ganz, A.F. v6p0198c1s

Garay, F.de v2p0287c1s

Garbe, R. v4p0379c1s v4p0439c1m v5p0202c1s v5p0585c2s

Garber, J.P. v4p0566c1s v6p0134c1s

Garbett, C.F. v5p0116c2s v5p0332c1s

Garbett, E. v1p0189c1s v1p0625c2s v1p0709c1s v1p0848c1s

Garbett, E.L. v2p0006c1s v2p0159c1s v2p0364c1s v2p0426c1s

Garbett, H. v6p0558c1s

Garcia, F. and Cockerell, J.D.A. v5p0253c1s

Garcia, M. v4p0142c2s v5p0530c2s

Garcke, E. v5p0184c1s

Garczynski, E.R. v2p0023c1s

Garczynski, R.E. v1p1148c1s

Gard, W.E. v1p0920c2s

Garde, P.C.de la v1p0195c1s

Garden, F. v1p1045c1s

Garden, J. v1p1256c1s

Garden, W. v5p0589c2s

Gardener, C. v4p0452c1s v4p0478c1s v5p0029c1s

Gardener, H.H. v3p0119c1s v3p0324c1s v3p0469c1s v4p0168c2s v4p0185c1s v4p0197c2s v4p0255c1s v4p0296c2s v4p0373c1s v4p0619c1s v4p0629c2s v5p0051c2s

Gardette, C.D. v1p0709c1s v1p0851c2s v1p0866c2s v1p0993c2s v1p1272c1s

Gardiner, B. v3p0023c1s v3p0166c1s v3p0411c1s

Gardiner, B.M. v2p0165c1s v2p0306c1s v3p0347c2s

Gardiner, C.A. v2p0361c2s v5p0019c2s v5p0199c2s

Gardiner, C.A. et al. v2p0309c1s

Gardiner, E. v5p0249c1s

Gardiner, E.G. v4p0147c2s v6p0102c1s

Gardiner, E.J. v3p0475c1s

Gardiner, E.N. v6p0347c2s v6p0478c1s v6p0709c1s

Gardiner, F. v1p0121c1s v1p0122c2s v1p0123c1s v1p0127c1s v1p0130c1s v1p0131c1s v1p0246c2s v1p0318c2s v1p0333c2s v1p0467c1s v1p0621c2s v1p0685c1s v1p0686c1s v1p1140c2s v1p1301c2s v1p1302c1s v2p0042c2m v2p0043c2s v2p0044c1s v2p0254c2s v3p0042c1s v3p0042c2s v3p0043c1s v3p0043c2s v3p0117c1s v5p0179c2s

Gardiner, F., jr. v2p0307c1s

Gardiner, F.H. v5p0174c2s

Gardiner, F.J. v5p0271c2s

Gardiner, Fanny H. v5p0543c1s

Gardiner, G.W. v2p0382c1s

Gardiner, H.K. v6p0521c2s

Gardiner, H.N. v2p0266c2s v3p0379c1s v5p0180c1s v5p0187c2s v6p0017c2s v6p0642c2s

Gardiner, H.S. v3p0225c1s

Gardiner, J. v2p0008c2s v4p0011c1s

Gardiner, J.B. v1p1144c1s

Gardiner, J.E. v1p1192c1s

Gardiner, J.H. v5p0056c1s v6p0060c2s v6p0064c2s v6p0281c2s

Gardiner, J.S. v1p0295c2s v1p0725c2s v5p0298c1s v5p0498c1s v6p0149c2m v6p0396c1s v6p0488c2s v6p0585c2s

Gardiner, J.S. and Schwarz, E.H.L. v6p0149c2s

Gardiner, J.S.J. v1p1286c2s

Gardiner, J.Stanley v6p0107c2s v6p0315c2s

Gardiner, J.W. v2p0306c1s v2p0474c2s

Gardiner, L. v3p0463c2s

Gardiner, Linda v3p0268c2s v4p0310c1s

Gardiner, Margaret D. v6p0484c1s

Gardiner, O.C. v1p0443c1s v1p0625c2s v1p0655c1s

Gardiner, R.K. v6p0344c2s v6p0543c1s

Gardiner, Ruth K. v6p0400c2s
Gardiner, Ruth K., Mrs. .. v6p0299c2s
v6p0667c1s
Gardiner, S.R. v1p0085c1s
v1p0352c1s v1p0676c1s v1p0676c2s
v1p0809c2s v1p1081c2s v1p1219c1s
v2p0031c1s v2p0108c2s v2p0117c2s
v2p0191c2s v2p0195c1s v2p0204c1s
v2p0226c1s v2p0270c1s v2p0364c2s
v2p0401c1s v3p0099c1s v3p0138c1s
v3p0174c1s v3p0187c1s v3p0188c1s
v3p0316c2s v3p0343c1s v3p0420c2s
v3p0453c2s v4p0097c2s v4p0141c1s
v4p0362c1s v5p0066c1s v5p0102c2s
v5p0133c2s v5p0145c1m v5p0440c2s
Gardiner, S.R. and Lecky, W.E.H.
v2p0226c1s
Gardiner, S.R. and Wright, W.A.
v2p0416c1s
Gardiner, S.R. et al. v2p0416c1s
Gardiner, T. v6p0191c2s
v6p0193c2s
Gardiner, T.J. v6p0351c1s
Gardiner, T.J.G. v6p0357c2s
Gardiner, W. v3p0333c2s
Gardiner, W.H. v1p0298c2m
v1p0449c1s v1p0918c1s v1p1410c1s
v2p0112c1s
Gardiner, W.M. v6p0044c1s
Gardner, A. v2p0239c2s
Gardner, A.B. v1p0033c2m
v1p0805c1s v1p1342c1s v2p0012c1s
v2p0061c1s v2p0062c2s v2p0310c1s
v2p0470c2s v3p0447c1s
Gardner, A.H. v6p0441c2s
Gardner, A.K. v1p0817c1s
v1p1005c1s
Gardner, A.P. v4p0143c2s
v5p0460c2s
Gardner, Alice v3p0233c1s
v6p0306c2s
Gardner, C. v1p0362c1s
v1p0951c2s
Gardner, C.T. v2p0078c2s
v2p0079c1s
Gardner, Col. v1p1342c1s
Gardner, D. v1p0696c2s
v1p0946c1s v1p1410c1s v1p1412c2s
v2p0306c1s
Gardner, D.P. v1p0061c1s
v1p0319c2s
Gardner, E. v5p0036c2s
v5p0142c2s v5p0608c1s
Gardner, E.A. v2p0307c2s
v3p0017c2s v3p0025c1s v3p0052c2s
v3p0108c2s v3p0216c2s v3p0217c1s
v3p0219c1s v3p0382c2s v3p0447c2s
v4p0023c1m v4p0324c2s v4p0422c2s
v4p0423c1s v4p0458c1s v4p0510c2m
v5p0272c1s v6p0038c2s v6p0636c1s
Gardner, E.A. and Schultz, R.W.
v4p0186c2s
Gardner, E.A. et al. v3p0108c2s
v3p0273c2s v4p0364c1s
Gardner, E.C. v4p0024c1s
v4p0024c2s v4p0073c1s v4p0265c1s
v4p0387c1s v4p0506c1s v5p0026c1s
v5p0026c2s v5p0508c1s
Gardner, E.G. v4p0197c1s
v5p0152c2m v5p0153c1s v5p0166c1s
v5p0253c2s v5p0268c2s v5p0348c2s
v5p0455c1s v5p0455c2s v5p0578c1s
v6p0104c2s v6p0164c1m
Gardner, E.J. v1p1138c2s
Gardner, E.S. v5p0381c1s
v5p0406c1s
Gardner, F. v1p0727c2s
v6p0127c2s v6p0495c1s
Gardner, F. et al. v4p0239c2s
Gardner, F.D. v6p0602c2s
Gardner, F.Q.C. v6p0254c2s
Gardner, G.C. v3p0433c2s
v4p0024c1s v4p0024c2s v5p0026c1s
Gardner, G.E. v4p0184c2s
v5p0636c2s
Gardner, G.W. v1p0121c1s
v1p1093c1s
Gardner, H.B. v3p0292c1s
v3p0421c1s v6p0188c2s
Gardner, H.D. v1p0266c1s
v1p1312c1s v3p0088c2s
Gardner, H.G. v6p0243c2s
Gardner, H.H. v3p0217c2s
Gardner, I.M. v3p0197c2s
v3p0356c2s v3p0358c2s v4p0597c2s
Gardner, Ida M. v5p0561c2s
Gardner, J. v1p0271c1m
v1p0271c2m v4p0304c2s v5p0360c2s
Gardner, J.S. v1p0056c1s
v1p0154c2s v1p0214c2s v1p0291c2s
v1p0321c2s v1p0420c1m v1p0470c2s
v1p0960c1s v2p0001c1s v2p0007c2s
v2p0073c2s v2p0149c1s v2p0159c1s
v2p0340c2s v2p0345c2s v3p0056c1s
v3p0100c2s v3p0136c2s v3p0223c1s
v4p0179c2s v4p0292c1s v4p0437c2s
v5p0255c1s v5p0298c2s v5p0328c2s
v5p0371c2s v5p0529c1s v6p0083c2s
v6p0186c1s v6p0365c1s v6p0427c1s
Gardner, J.S. and
Jukes-Browne, A.J. v3p0309c2s
Gardner, J.S. et al. v2p0423c2s
Gardner, J.T. v1p1296c1m
Gardner, L.L. v4p0597c2s
Gardner, M. v5p0036c2s
v6p0272c2s
Gardner, Monica M. v6p0354c2s
Gardner, P. v1p0051c2s
v1p0338c1s v1p0555c2s v1p0889c1s
v2p0021c1s v2p0091c2s v2p0170c1s
v2p0190c1s v2p0206c1s v2p0409c2s
v3p0021c1s v3p0048c1s v3p0142c1s
v3p0199c2s v3p0217c1s v3p0294c2s
v3p0326c1s v3p0357c1s v3p0377c1s
v3p0447c1s v4p0077c1s v4p0082c1s
v4p0245c1s v4p0288c2s v4p0326c1s
v4p0403c1s v4p0451c2s v4p0548c2s
v5p0249c2s v5p0429c1s v5p0591c1s
v5p0604c2s v6p0177c1s v6p0383c1s
v6p0391c1s v6p0548c1s v6p0675c1s
Gardner, P. and Imhoof-Blumer, F.
v3p0324c2s
Gardner, S. v5p0552c1s
Gardner, S.A. v2p0249c1s
v2p0389c2s v2p0437c2s
Gardner, S.M.H. v4p0197c2s
Gardner, T.M. v6p0004c1s
v6p0100c2s
Gardner, W.B. v4p0631c1m
Gardner, W.H. v1p0227c1s
v1p0320c2s v1p0811c2s v3p0296c2s
v4p0069c2s v4p0497c2s v4p0624c1s
v5p0546c2s
Gardwell, G. v1p0713c1s
Gardyne, A. v3p0306c2s
Garel, E. v2p0003c1m
v2p0090c2s v2p0096c2s v2p0120c1s
v2p0142c1s v2p0187c1m v3p0181c2s
Garella, N. v1p0963c1s
Garfield, H.A. v5p0134c1s
v5p0134c2s v6p0151c1s
Garfield, J.A. v1p0212c1s
v1p0291c1s v1p0325c1m v1p0453c1s
v1p1232c2s v1p1342c1s v3p0167c1m
Garfield, J.R. et al. v6p0309c1s
Garfit, A. v1p0108c1s
Garforth, W.E. v5p0377c2s
Garibaldi, R. v5p0300c2s
v6p0048c1s v6p0254c1s
Gariel, C.M. v1p0759c1s
v1p1143c2s
Garis, F.de v5p0067c1s
Garland, A.H. v5p0318c1s
Garland, Abbie N. v5p0423c1s
Garland, B. v4p0451c1s
Garland, C.H. v4p0329c2s
v5p0166c2s v5p0332c2s v5p0461c1s
v5p0571c1s v5p0636c1s
Garland, C.H. et al. v4p0408c2s
Garland, C.M. v6p0197c1s
Garland, H. v3p0052c2s
v3p0122c1s v3p0144c2s v3p0149c1s
v3p0170c1s v3p0195c1s v3p0203c2s
v3p0206c2s v3p0341c2s v3p0359c2s
v3p0405c2s v3p0425c2s v3p0440c2m
v4p0015c1s v4p0030c2s v4p0034c2s
v4p0190c1s v4p0195c1s v4p0197c2s
v4p0198c2s v4p0234c2s v4p0262c1s
v4p0268c2s v4p0292c1s v4p0309c2s
v4p0412c2s v4p0464c1s v4p0484c2s
v4p0500c2s v4p0542c2s v4p0564c2s
v4p0617c1m v4p0617c2s v4p0626c2s
v5p0041c2s v5p0043c1s v5p0141c2s
v5p0150c1s v5p0169c2s v5p0229c2s
v5p0234c1s v5p0238c2s v5p0239c2s
v5p0242c1m v5p0242c2s v5p0262c2s
v5p0287c2s v5p0318c1s v5p0318c2m
v5p0440c1s v5p0489c2s v5p0606c1m
v5p0645c1s v6p0223c1s v6p0225c2s
v6p0291c2s v6p0317c1s v6p0459c2s
v6p0596c1s v6p0663c1s
Garland, H. and Campbell, P.H.
v5p0491c1s
Garland, H. and Schindler, S.
v4p0464c2s
Garland, H. et al. v4p0030c2s
v4p0464c1s v5p0263c2s
v6p0055c1s v6p0461c2s
Garland, Hamlin v5p0182c2s
v5p0238c2s v5p0431c2s v5p0585c1s
v5p0585c2s v6p0674c2s
Garland, L.C. v1p0071c1s
v1p1014c2s
Garland, L.W. v5p0151c1s
v5p0490c1s
Garland, M.J. v4p0037c1s
Garland, R.A. v4p0362c1s
Garland, V. v6p0092c1s
Garland, Virginia v6p0068c1s
v6p0071c1s v6p0123c2s v6p0400c1s
v6p0423c1s v6p0470c2s v6p0504c1s
v6p0701c1s
Garland, W. v5p0222c1s
Garlanda, F. v3p0140c1s
v3p0224c1s
Garman, C.E. v2p0202c2s
Garman, H. v4p0093c2s
v4p0204c2s v4p0524c1s
Garman, S. v2p0059c2s
v2p0399c1s v3p0014c1s v3p0194c2s
v3p0246c1m v4p0124c2s v4p0394c2s
Garman, S.W. v1p0492c1s
Garmo, C.De v3p0194c2s
v3p0236c2s v3p0306c2s v3p0325c1s
v4p0169c2s v4p0187c2s v4p0255c1s
v4p0512c1s v4p0554c1m v4p0622c1s
v5p0176c2s v5p0177c1s v5p0179c1s
v5p0512c1s v5p0520c1s v6p0366c1s
v6p0704c1s
Garmo, C.De et al. v5p0127c1s
Garneau, H. v5p0222c2s
Garner, J.M. v6p0460c1s
Garner, J.W. v5p0380c2s
v6p0009c2s v6p0252c1s v6p0254c2s
v6p0284c2s v6p0348c1s v6p0391c1s
v6p0411c1s v6p0659c1s v6p0667c1s
Garner, R. v1p1326c2s
Garner, R.L. v3p0285c2s
v4p0232c2s v4p0379c1m v4p0541c1s
v6p0118c1s
Garnet, H. v5p0194c2s
Garnet, J. v1p0752c2s
Garnett, C. and Garnett, E.
v5p0582c1s
Garnett, C., Mrs. v1p1164c2s
v2p0008c1s v2p0026c2s v2p0049c2s
v2p0171c2s v2p0201c1s v2p0254c1s
v2p0298c1s v2p0308c1m v2p0384c2m
v2p0395c2s v2p0458c1m v2p0464c2s
v2p0482c1s v3p0005c2s v3p0153c1s
v3p0155c2s v3p0257c2s v3p0411c2s
v5p0259c2s
Garnett, Dr. v4p0293c2s
Garnett, E. v4p0299c1s
v4p0331c2s v5p0141c1s v5p0144c1s
v5p0240c2s v5p0413c1s v6p0179c2s
v6p0301c2s v6p0339c1s v6p0342c2s
v6p0364c2s v6p0461c2s
Garnett, E. and Garnett, C.
v5p0582c1s
Garnett, E., Mrs. v4p0092c2s
Garnett, E.E. v5p0341c1s
v5p0533c1s
Garnett, E.M. v3p0368c1s
Garnett, F.E. v6p0354c2s
Garnett, G. v5p0077c2s
Garnett, H. v5p0103c2s
v5p0529c1s v5p0599c2s v5p0601c1s
Garnett, J.M. v1p0390c2s
v1p1223c1s v1p1288c1s v2p0461c2s
v3p0140c1s v3p0171c1s v4p0040c2s
v4p0051c2s
Garnett, K.P. v4p0066c2s
Garnett, L. v5p0505c2s
Garnett, L.A. v1p0533c1s
v1p1198c2s v4p0230c2s v4p0378c2s
Garnett, L.J. v5p0383c2s
Garnett, L.M. v5p0637c2s
Garnett, L.M.J. v4p0558c2s
v4p0629c1s v5p0028c2s v5p0249c2s
v5p0256c1s v5p0359c2s v5p0444c2s
v5p0445c1s v5p0560c1s v6p0613c1s
Garnett, Lucy M.J. v5p0253c1s
Garnett, M.R.H. v1p1354c2s
Garnett, Mrs. v5p0596c1s
Garnett, R. v1p0165c1s
v1p0399c2s v1p0628c2s v1p0742c2s
v1p0979c1s v1p1067c1s v1p1189c2m
v1p1376c2s v1p1382c1s v2p0057c1m
v2p0070c2s v2p0255c2s v2p0420c1s
v3p0055c2s v3p0140c2s v3p0449c2s
v4p0010c1m v4p0025c2s v4p0049c1s
v4p0063c2s v4p0067c1s v4p0073c2s
v4p0074c1s v4p0090c1s v4p0118c1s
v4p0181c2s v4p0262c1s v4p0424c2s
v4p0430c2m v4p0519c1s v4p0520c1s
v5p0013c1s v5p0097c1s v5p0142c1s
v5p0250c2s v5p0253c1s v5p0357c1s
v5p0429c2s v5p0466c1s v5p0525c1s
v6p0041c1s v6p0075c2s v6p0084c2s
v6p0101c1s v6p0101c2s v6p0157c1s
v6p0174c2s v6p0184c2s v6p0196c1s
v6p0202c2s v6p0203c1s v6p0240c1s
v6p0276c2s v6p0289c1s v6p0313c1s
v6p0344c2s v6p0389c2s v6p0418c1s
v6p0461c1s v6p0478c2s v6p0510c2s
v6p0648c1s v6p0709c1s
Garnett, T.S., jr. v2p0306c1s
Garnett, W. v1p0813c2s
v2p0281c2s v3p0445c1s v5p0458c1s
Garnier, E. v3p0386c1s
Garnier, J.H. v2p0168c2s
Garnier, R.M. v4p0007c2s
v4p0220c1s
Garnsey, E.E. v5p0392c2s
Garnsey, J.H. v5p0311c1s
Garo, C. v5p0028c2s
Garollo, G. v5p0110c1s
v5p0528c1s
Garoutte, M.E. v6p0456c1s
Garozynski, E. v6p0076c1s
Garrard, C.C. v6p0449c1s
v6p0496c1s
Garrat, S. v3p0043c2s
Garratt, A.V. v5p0622c1s
Garraway, J. v5p0517c2s
Garrett, A.B. v1p0366c1s
v1p1426c2s
Garrett, A.B., Mrs. v1p0038c2s
v1p0177c1s v1p0343c2s

Garrett, A.H. v6p0156c1s
Garrett, C.H. v6p0004c1s
v6p0592c2s v6p0633c2s
Garrett, E. v1p0606c1s
v2p0013c1s v2p0026c2s v2p0077c2s
v2p0241c2s v2p0266c1s v2p0300c2s
v2p0366c2s v3p0205c1s v3p0250c2s
v3p0412c1s v5p0085c1s
Garrett, E.H. v5p0365c1s
Garrett, Edward v3p0272c1s
Garrett, F.E. v4p0005c2s
v5p0007c1s v5p0320c1s v6p0542c1m
Garrett, F.Edmund v5p0586c2s
Garrett, G. v2p0080c1s
Garrett, G.W. v1p0111c1s
v1p0812c2s
Garrett, L.B. v6p0506c1s
Garrett, M.G. v1p1179c2s
Garrett, P.C. v4p0281c2s
v5p0439c1s
Garrett, R. v1p1078c1s
v6p0684c2s
Garrett, S., Mrs. v5p0451c1s
Garrett, T.H. v1p0844c1m
v1p1179c2s
Garrett, T.H. and Booth, J.C.
v1p0624c2s v1p0939c1s
Garrett, W. v5p0298c1s
v5p0492c2s
Garrett, W.R. v2p0411c2s
v3p0424c2s
Garrettson, F. v1p1325c2s
Garrigues, G. v1p0274c1s
v1p0351c2s v2p0181c2s v2p0201c2s
v3p0388c2s
Garrigues, H.J. v4p0058c2s
Garriott, E.B. v5p0276c2s
v5p0626c1m
Garrison, C.G. v4p0157c2s
v5p0093c2s
Garrison, F.J. v1p0501c1s
Garrison, F.J. and Garrison, W.P.
v2p0171c2s
Garrison, F.L. v2p0067c2s
v2p0229c1s v2p0419c2m v3p0009c1s
v3p0223c1s v3p0320c1s v3p0430c2s
v4p0027c2s v4p0291c2s v5p0214c1s
v6p0118c2s v6p0419c1s v6p0570c1s
Garrison, G.P. v4p0050c2s
v4p0127c2s v5p0373c1s v6p0085c2s
v6p0628c1s v6p0640c1m v6p0671c2s
Garrison, J.D. v4p0538c2s
v5p0238c1s v5p0459c2s
Garrison, J.F. v1p0021c1s
v1p0189c1s v1p0249c1s v1p0333c2s
v1p0529c1s v1p0848c1s v1p0933c2m
v2p0423c2s v3p0148c2s v3p0258c2s
v3p0349c2s
Garrison, J.H. v2p0083c2s
Garrison, J.S. v1p1109c1s
Garrison, L.M. v3p0190c1s
v3p0444c1s
Garrison, L.McK. v3p0267c2s
v4p0245c1s v4p0249c2s v4p0250c1s
v5p0038c1s v5p0147c2s
Garrison, O.G. v1p0511c2s
Garrison, S.C. v3p0170c1s
v4p0515c2s
Garrison, T. v5p0203c1s
v5p0538c2s v6p0583c1s v6p0703c2s
Garrison, W.H. v4p0620c1s
Garrison, W.L. v3p0296c2s
v4p0022c2s v4p0160c1s
Garrison, W.L. et al. v5p0530c2s
v6p0712c2s
Garrison, W.L., jr. v4p0007c1s
v4p0152c2s
Garrison, W.P. v1p0034c2s
v1p0059c2s v1p0116c2s v1p0158c1s
v1p0175c1s v1p0178c2s v1p0194c1s
v1p0237c2s v1p0265c2s v1p0298c1s
v1p0299c1s v1p0299c2s v1p0501c1s
v1p0521c2s v1p0540c2s v1p0627c2s
v1p0635c2s v1p0642c2s v1p0668c2s
v1p0743c1s v1p0774c1s v1p0790c2s
v1p0809c1s v1p0901c1s v1p0922c2m
v1p0942c2s v1p0996c2s v1p0997c1s
v1p1045c2s v1p1048c1s v1p1069c2m
v1p1096c2s v1p1107c2s v1p1129c2s
v1p1133c2s v1p1148c2s v1p1216c1s
v1p1218c2s v1p1243c1s v1p1276c1s
v1p1399c2s v1p1412c1s v1p1414c2s
v1p1428c2s v2p0031c1s v2p0053c2s
v2p0054c1s v2p0055c1s v2p0074c2s
v2p0077c1s v2p0088c1s v2p0099c2s
v2p0106c1s v2p0197c1s v2p0205c1s
v2p0251c2s v2p0299c2s v2p0353c1s
v3p0010c1s v3p0040c2s v3p0056c2m
v3p0121c1s v3p0139c1s v3p0139c2s
v3p0304c1s v3p0337c2s v3p0368c1s
v3p0384c2s v3p0445c1s v3p0470c1s
v4p0183c1s v4p0183c2s v4p0201c2s
v4p0202c2s v4p0246c1s v4p0249c1s
v4p0251c1s v4p0257c2s v4p0261c1s
v4p0298c2s v4p0330c1s v4p0345c1s
v4p0387c1s v4p0469c2s v4p0515c1s
v4p0517c2s v4p0538c1s v4p0541c1s
v4p0549c2s v4p0550c1s v4p0584c1s
v4p0584c2s v4p0595c1s v4p0596c2s
v4p0608c2s v5p0088c1s v5p0140c1s
v5p0141c1s v5p0157c1s v5p0254c2s
v5p0354c1s v5p0597c2s v5p0612c1s
v6p0001c2s v6p0052c1s v6p0089c2s
v6p0227c2s v6p0259c2m v6p0293c1s
v6p0312c1s v6p0361c1s v6p0363c1s
v6p0401c1s v6p0442c2s v6p0510c2s
v6p0523c1s v6p0553c1m v6p0605c1s
v6p0649c1s v6p0690c2s
Garrison, W.P. and Garrison, F.J.
v2p0171c2s
Garrison, W.P. and Godkin, E.L.
v1p0540c2m
Garrod, A.B. v1p0019c2s
Garrod, A.H. v1p0041c1s
v1p0200c1s v1p0407c1s v1p0434c1s
v1p0579c1s v1p0604c1s v1p0907c1s
v1p1055c2s v1p1065c1s v1p1236c1s
v1p1304c2s
Garrod, H.B. v2p0037c1s
v2p0479c1s v3p0008c1s v3p0057c2s
v3p0387c1s v3p0425c1s
Garrod, H.C. v5p0118c2s
v5p0332c1s v5p0434c2s
Garrod, H.W. v6p0122c1s
v6p0537c1s
Garrold, R.P. v6p0473c1s
Garron, K. v6p0081c2s
Garrot, H.G. v5p0048c2s
Garrucci, R. v1p0167c1s
v1p0441c2s v1p0962c2s v1p1178c1s
Garry, J. v5p0261c1s
v5p0349c2s v6p0069c1s v6p0286c1s
Garry, Jaye v5p0215c2s
Garshin v5p0215c2s
Garshin, V. v3p0159c1m
v5p0152c1s
Garshine, M. v3p0356c1s
Garskine, V. v4p0611c1s
Garson, J. v4p0236c2s
Garson, J.G. v2p0073c1s
v2p0106c1m v2p0249c2s v2p0440c2s
Garson, J.G. and Mortimer, J.R.
v4p0046c2s
Garstang, A.H. v6p0388c2s
Garstang, John v6p0058c1s
Garstang, W. v4p0110c2s
v4p0309c1s v4p0377c1s v4p0586c2s
v6p0226c2s
Garstin, N. v2p0275c1s
v3p0188c1s v4p0086c2s v5p0144c2s
v5p0166c2s v5p0213c2s v5p0566c2s
Garstin, W. v5p0181c2s
Garstin, W.E. v6p0457c2s
Garston, N. v5p0012c2s
Garth, R. v4p0278c2s
Gartner, E. v2p0112c1s
Gartner, F. v3p0277c2s
Garver, J.A. v1p0810c1s
Garver, M.M. v1p0907c1m
Garver, W.L. v4p0214c1s
v6p0601c1s
Garvey, I. v3p0282c1s
v3p0284c1s v4p0386c2s v4p0552c1s
v5p0166c1s v5p0607c2s
Garvey, M.A. v1p0391c1s
v3p0128c1s
Garvey, T. v4p0350c2s
v5p0054c2s
Garvie, A.F. v5p0003c2s
v5p0264c1s v6p0043c1s v6p0123c2s
v6p0145c2s v6p0341c1s v6p0341c2s
v6p0342c1s v6p0536c1s v6p0537c2s
v6p0674c1s
Garvin, Ethel v6p0520c2s
Garvin, F.C. v6p0076c1s
Garvin, J.L. v4p0315c2s
v5p0598c1s v6p0266c2s v6p0294c1s
v6p0633c1s
Garvin, L. v5p0433c2s
v5p0435c2s v5p0598c1s
Garvin, L.F.C. v6p0081c1m
v6p0128c2s v6p0146c1s v6p0355c2s
v6p0615c1s v6p0659c2s
Garvin, Lucius F.C. v6p0542c1s
Garwood, E.J. v6p0257c2s
Gary, G. v3p0248c1s
v3p0376c2s v3p0466c1s v4p0471c2s
Gary, J.A. v5p0461c2s
Gary, J.E. v4p0017c1s
Gascoigne, R.F.T. v2p0242c2s
Gaskell, A.F. v5p0537c1s
Gaskell, C.M. v1p0971c1s
v1p1405c1s v2p0090c2s v2p0104c2s
v2p0142c1s v2p0247c2s v2p0482c1s
v3p0274c1s v3p0381c1s v4p0119c1s
v4p0257c1s v4p0617c1s v6p0544c2s
Gaskell, C.M., Lady v2p0395c2s
v3p0469c2s v4p0205c2s
Gaskell, E.C. v1p0309c2s
v1p0311c2m v1p0324c2s v1p0332c2s
v1p0360c2s v1p0579c1s v1p0612c2s
v1p0758c1s v1p0796c1s v1p0797c1s
v1p0874c1s v1p0887c1s v1p0887c2s
v1p0926c2s v1p0940c2s v1p1188c1s
v1p1202c2s v1p1397c2s v1p1418c2s
Gaskell, G.V. v2p0447c1s
v3p0411c1s
Gaskell, W.H. v2p0309c2s
v3p0300c1s
Gaskins, V.M. v4p0032c1s
Gasler, M. v5p0307c2s
v5p0484c1s
Gasparin, Countess de v1p0190c2s
v1p0377c1s
Gasparis, A.de v6p0320c2s
Gaspey, T. v1p0673c2s
v1p1188c2s v1p1212c1s
Gasquet, A. v6p0286c1s
Gasquet, F.A. v2p0003c1s
v3p0462c2s v4p0053c1s v4p0247c1s
v4p0377c1s v5p0042c2s v5p0060c2s
v5p0177c2s v5p0423c1s v5p0511c1s
v6p0014c2s v6p0189c2s v6p0219c1s
v6p0274c1s v6p0514c2s
Gasquet, J.R. v2p0180c2s
v2p0222c1s v3p0016c1s v3p0148c2s
v3p0206c1s v3p0270c2m v3p0422c1s
v4p0045c1s v4p0056c1s v4p0128c2s
v4p0343c1s
Gasquoine, C.P. v5p0040c2s
v5p0513c1s v5p0641c2s
Gassiot, J.P. v1p0164c2s
Gasson, T.I. v6p0538c1s
Gast, C.E. v1p0519c2s
Gast, F.A. v1p0120c2s
v1p0581c1m v1p0581c2s v1p0691c1s
v1p0794c1s v1p0874c1s v1p1057c1s
v1p1177c1s v1p1203c2s v1p1221c2s
v1p1222c1s v1p1237c1s v1p1279c2s
v1p1417c1s v2p0025c2s v2p0030c2s
v2p0043c1m v3p0242c2s v4p0253c1s
v4p0561c2s v5p0060c2s v5p0503c2s
v5p0576c2s v6p0061c2m v6p0062c1s
v6p0065c1m v6p0519c2s
Gast, F.A. et al. v6p0376c1s
Gaster, Leon v6p0197c2s
Gaster, M. v4p0193c2s
v4p0261c1s v4p0350c1s v5p0106c1s
v5p0174c1s v5p0308c1s v5p0645c2m
v6p0343c2s v6p0411c2s v6p0648c2s
Gaston, C.R. v6p0130c1s
Gaston, E.B. v6p0218c1s
Gaston, E.P. v5p0459c2s
Gaston, J. v1p1225c2s
Gaston, W. v1p1049c1s
v1p1262c2s
Gastrow, J. v4p0309c2s
Gatacre, W., Sir v5p0420c2s
Gatchell, C. v3p0280c1s
Gatchell, G.W. v6p0223c2s
Gately, S.L. and Kletzsch, A.P.
v2p0419c1s
Gates, B.F. v6p0688c2s
Gates, C.F. v4p0470c1s
v6p0162c2s
Gates, C.H. v1p0892c1s
Gates, D.A. v6p0634c1s
Gates, E. v4p0365c2s
v5p0185c2s v6p0513c1s
Gates, E.P. v6p0365c1s
Gates, Eleanor v6p0086c2s
v6p0256c2s v6p0257c1s v6p0541c1s
v6p0611c2s v6p0711c1s
Gates, F.T. v6p0601c1s
Gates, G.A. v4p0333c2s
Gates, H.W. v6p0341c2s
v6p0626c2m
Gates, L.F. v3p0340c1s
v4p0184c2s v4p0562c1s v4p0570c1s
v5p0127c2s v5p0192c2s v5p0256c1s
v5p0282c1s v5p0505c1s v5p0625c2s
v6p0532c1s
Gates, M.E. v1p0072c1s
v2p0219c1s v3p0242c2s v4p0532c2s
Gates, M.E. and Northrop, C.
v4p0122c2s
Gates, M.E., Mrs. v4p0201c1s
Gates, N.J. v1p0454c1s
Gates, O.H. v4p0001c2s
v4p0054c2m v4p0573c1s v5p0058c1s
Gates, P.W. v6p0013c1s
Gates, S. v1p0569c2s
Gates, S.F. v1p1397c1s
Gates, S.L. v6p0496c2s
Gates, S.Y. v3p0288c1s
Gates, W.A. v6p0109c1s
v6p0420c1s
Gates, W.F. v4p0417c1s
v4p0442c1s v4p0605c1s v5p0394c1s
v5p0423c2s
Gath, G. v1p0830c1s
Gathorne-Hardy, A.E. v2p0021c1s
v2p0114c2s
Gatke, H. v1p0136c1s
Gatley, J. v3p0101c1s
Gatliff, C. v1p0373c2s
Gatschet, A.S. v1p0636c2s
v1p0637c1s v2p0083c2s v2p0219c1s
v2p0219c2s v2p0220c1m v2p0241c1s
v2p0242c2s v2p0243c2s v2p0249c2s
v2p0281c1s v2p0325c2s v2p0359c1s
v2p0482c2s v4p0072c1s v4p0205c2s
v4p0363c2s v4p0366c1s v4p0368c2s
v4p0586c1s v4p0619c2s v5p0097c1s
v5p0287c2s v5p0406c1s v5p0434c2s
v6p0104c1s
Gattie, A.W. v6p0191c2s
Gattie, G.B. v2p0308c2s
Gattie, W. v3p0107c2s
v3p0360c1s

Gattie, W.M. v3p0020c1s
v3p0251c1s v3p0355c1s
Gattie, Walter M. v4p0286c2s
Gatty, C.T. v2p0193c2s
v5p0278c1s
Gatty, R.A. v5p0210c2s
v6p0449c1s v6p0515c1s v6p0554c2s
v6p0581c1s v6p0620c1s v6p0701c1s
Gatty, Reginald, A. v6p0524c1s
Gatty, Victor H. v6p0058c1s
Gaudard, J. v1p0051c1s
v1p0471c1s v2p0460c1s
Gaudier, A. v5p0521c1s
Gaudin, D.H. v4p0476c2s
Gaudini, Conte v4p0197c1s
Gaudry, A. v2p0327c1s
v4p0018c1s v5p0641c2s
Gaul, G. v4p0296c1s
v4p0403c2s
Gaule, J. v4p0009c2s
Gaullieur, H. v4p0515c1s
Gault, F.B. v5p0028c1s
v5p0228c2s v6p0509c2s
Gault, J.W. v5p0558c2s
Gault, Paul v4p0587c1s
Gault, R.H. v6p0535c1s
v6p0544c1s
Gault, T.T. v1p0259c1s
Gaulter, J. v1p0808c1s
Gaultier, P. v5p0238c2s
Gaunt, M. v3p0082c1s
v3p0168c2s v4p0072c1s v4p0155c1s
v4p0341c2s v4p0342c1s
Gaunt, Mary v6p0597c1s
Gauss, E.F.L. v4p0092c1s
v5p0396c2s
Gauss, H.G. v6p0340c2s
Gauss, R. v3p0168c1s
Gaussen, P.C. v2p0415c1s
Gausser, A.H. v6p0054c2s
Gautier, A. v1p0518c1s
v1p0903c2s v1p1143c2s
Gautier, E. v4p0261c1s
v4p0610c1s v5p0492c2s
Gautier, F. v1p0664c1s
v1p1251c1m v2p0383c2s v3p0090c2s
v4p0490c2s v5p0595c2s
Gautier, J. v3p0385c2s
Gautier, Judith v6p0390c2s
Gautier, L. v5p0052c1s
Gautier, P.W. v1p1297c2s
Gautier, T. v1p0062c2s
v1p0428c2s v1p0497c1s v1p0596c1s
v1p0731c1s v1p0762c2s v1p0871c2s
v1p0895c2s v1p1104c2s v1p1413c2s
Gauvain, A. v3p0160c1s
Gavanescul, T. v4p0012c2s
Gave, A. v3p0030c2s
v3p0377c2s
Gave, P. v4p0561c2s
Gavel, E. v2p0124c2s
v2p0400c2s
Gavey, J. v1p0150c2s
v1p1291c1s v5p0571c1s
Gavin, M. v1p0381c1s
v1p0528c1s v1p0640c2m v1p1116c1s
Gaw, C. v6p0256c1s
Gawler, J.C. v3p0005c1s
Gawne, J. v4p0031c2s
Gay, D.F. v5p0151c1s
v5p0525c1s
Gay, E.F. v1p1077c2s
v6p0008c1s v6p0189c1s v6p0206c1s
v6p0304c1s
Gay, E.J. v4p0281c2s
Gay, F.B. v6p0372c2s
Gay, F.L. v1p0503c2s
v3p0259c2s
Gay, G.E. v5p0413c2s
v5p0512c1s v6p0190c1s v6p0290c1s
Gay, M. v2p0364c1s
Gay, Mary R. v6p0479c1s
Gay, S. v1p0928c2s
Gay, S.H. v1p0227c2s
v1p1019c1s v1p1438c1s v2p0161c2s
v2p0230c1s v2p0453c2s
Gay, S.M. v4p0527c2s
Gay, S.M. and Russell, F.E.
v4p0564c2s
Gay, W.R. v6p0397c1s
Gay, Walter
v6p0034c1s
Gayangos, P.de
v1p0449c1s
Gayarre, C. v1p0180c2s
v1p0487c1s v1p0772c2s v1p0815c2s
v1p1097c2s v1p1224c1s v1p1315c1s
v2p0037c1s v2p0114c1s v2p0232c1s
v2p0246c1s v2p0267c1m v2p0278c2s
v2p0315c2s v2p0318c2s v2p0328c2s
v2p0366c2s v2p0394c1s v3p0034c2s
v3p0068c2s v3p0414c2s v3p0446c2s
Gaye, A. v1p0144c2s
v1p0877c2s v3p0061c2s v3p0087c1s
v3p0170c2s v3p0184c1s v3p0193c2s
v3p0244c1s v3p0305c1s v3p0388c2m
v3p0389c1s v3p0391c2s v3p0417c1s
v3p0426c1s v3p0430c2s v3p0462c1s
v4p0114c2s v4p0409c1s v4p0516c1s
v4p0575c2s v5p0249c1s
Gaye, S. v1p0880c2s
v5p0291c1s
Gayley, C.M. v2p0007c1s
v2p0428c1s v4p0184c1s v6p0258c1s
v6p0379c2s v6p0420c1m v6p0505c2s
Gayley, C.M. and Browne, D.H.
v3p0312c1s
Gayley, C.M. and Lang, Ossian
v6p0193c2s
Gaylord, Harriet v6p0621c1s
Gaylord, T.P. v5p0013c2s
Gaylord, W. v1p0718c1s
Gaylord, W.R. v6p0405c2s
Gaynor, W.C. v3p0066c2s
v4p0087c2s v4p0354c1s v4p0499c1s
v5p0385c2s v6p0045c1s
Gaynor, W.J. v4p0116c1s
v5p0408c1s v6p0453c1m v6p0658c2s
Gear, H.B. v6p0198c1s
Gear, H.L. v2p0412c2s
Gearcy, C. v1p0461c1s
Geare, B.I. v6p0591c2s
Geare, R. v6p0338c2s
Geare, R.I. v3p0277c1s
v5p0564c2s v6p0053c1s v6p0107c2s
v6p0203c2s v6p0210c2s v6p0228c1s
v6p0337c2s v6p0354c2s v6p0470c1s
v6p0491c1m v6p0509c1m v6p0511c2s
v6p0629c2s v6p0668c2s
Geary, G. v1p1331c1s
Geary, H. v1p0493c2s
Geary, T.J. v6p0120c1s
Geary, T.J. and Ingersoll, R.G.
v4p0106c1s
Gebhardt, C. v6p0358c1s
v6p0532c2s
Geddes, G. v1p0943c1s
Geddes, J., jr. v6p0609c2s
Geddes, J.D. v6p0496c2s
Geddes, McVail v3p0445c2s
Geddes, P. v2p0080c1s
v4p0598c1s v5p0151c2s v5p0193c2s
v5p0228c2s v5p0235c1s v5p0358c1s
v5p0430c2s v5p0500c2s v5p0611c1s
v6p0128c2s v6p0129c1s v6p0399c1s
v6p0576c1s
Geddes, P. and Thomson, J.A.
v4p0429c2s
Geddes, W.D. v1p0601c1s
v3p0262c1s
Geddes, W.D. and Blackie, J.S.
v1p0601c1s
Geddie, J. v4p0537c1s
v5p0148c2s v5p0157c2s v5p0528c1s
Geden, A.S. v5p0286c2s
v5p0411c2s
Gedge, C.J. v3p0451c2s
Gedney, F.G. v1p1013c2s
v3p0337c2s
Gee, A.A. v3p0276c2s
Gee, C.A. v1p0452c2s
Gee, R. v5p0331c2s
Gee, W.M. v2p0185c2s
Geelmuyden, H. et al. v2p0090c1s
Geer, A.B. v6p0534c2s
Geer, C.M. v6p0353c2s
v6p0599c2s
Geer, H.B. v6p0339c2s
v6p0432c2s v6p0678c1s
Geer, W.C. v6p0112c1s
Geere, Frank v6p0317c2s
Geere, H.V. v5p0043c1s
v5p0076c2s
Geere, V. v6p0359c2s
v6p0458c1s
Geetruyn, E.van v2p0294c2s
Geffcken, F.H. v3p0154c1s
v3p0163c2s v3p0171c1m v3p0171c2m
v3p0217c2s v3p0224c2s v3p0369c2s
v3p0370c2s v3p0464c2s v4p0051c2s
v4p0166c2s v4p0189c2s v4p0211c1s
v4p0224c1s v4p0224c2s v4p0237c1s
v4p0326c2s v4p0533c2s
Geffcken, H. v2p0176c2m
v3p0082c2s v4p0190c1s v4p0395c2s
v4p0492c2s
Geffroy, G. v6p0416c1s
v6p0713c1s
Gehring, A. v4p0029c2s
v5p0201c2s v6p0438c1s
Geijer, E.G. v2p0261c1s
Geikie, A. v1p0050c2s
v1p0051c1s v1p0164c1s v1p0193c1s
v1p0197c1s v1p0201c1s v1p0209c1s
v1p0269c1s v1p0279c2s v1p0349c2s
v1p0402c1s v1p0431c1s v1p0434c2s
v1p0506c1s v1p0506c2s v1p0507c2s
v1p0508c1s v1p0509c1s v1p0509c2m
v1p0514c1s v1p0519c1s v1p0524c1s
v1p0565c2s v1p0621c2s v1p0668c1s
v1p0707c2s v1p0728c2s v1p0749c2s
v1p0760c1s v1p0779c1s v1p0855c1s
v1p0880c2s v1p0926c2s v1p0929c2s
v1p0948c2s v1p0960c2s v1p0995c1m
v1p1113c1m v1p1191c1s v1p1240c2s
v1p1360c1s v1p1370c1s v1p1435c1s
v1p1437c1s v2p0027c1s v2p0038c2s
v2p0053c2s v2p0102c2s v2p0108c2m
v2p0173c2s v2p0174c1s v2p0177c2s
v2p0262c2s v2p0284c2s v2p0314c1s
v2p0373c2s v2p0387c2m v2p0463c1m
v2p0482c1s v3p0055c1s v3p0111c1s
v3p0126c1s v3p0196c1s v3p0348c2s
v4p0222c2s v4p0223c1s v5p0513c2m
v5p0614c1s v6p0166c1s v6p0360c1s
v6p0377c1s v6p0403c2s v6p0417c2s
v6p0427c1s v6p0488c2s v6p0543c2s
v6p0549c1s
Geikie, A., Sir v4p0504c2s
Geikie, A.C. v1p0195c1s
v1p0416c2s v1p0910c1s
Geikie, Archibald v2p0060c1s
v6p0070c1s v6p0301c1s v6p0624c1s
Geikie, C. v1p0082c1s
v1p0394c2s v3p0308c1s
Geikie, E. v2p0094c1s
Geikie, J. v1p0227c1s
v1p0582c1s v1p0622c1s v2p0173c2s
v2p0193c1s v2p0224c1s v2p0379c2s
v3p0173c2s v5p0124c1s v5p0250c2s
v5p0389c2s
Geisberg, L. v5p0496c2s
Geise, E.F. v1p0778c1m
v1p1432c2s
Geisler, J.S. v5p0081c1s
Geist, P.von v1p1139c2s
Geistweit, W.H. v6p0419c2s
Geisy, S.H. v3p0081c1s
Gekeler, A.G. v5p0236c1s
v5p0536c1s v5p0536c2m
Gekeler, H.S. v5p0037c2s
Geldart, E.M. v1p0127c1s
v1p0359c1s v1p0553c1s v2p0458c1s
Geldart, W.M. v6p0622c1s
Gelder, W.de v5p0184c1s
Geldner, K. v3p0048c2s
Gell, E.L. v4p0226c2s
Gell, F. v1p0339c1s
v1p1380c2s
Gell, P.L. v2p0191c2s
Gell, P.L. and West, A. .. v5p0471c2s
Gellender, E.E. v5p0046c1s
v6p0267c1s
Gelling, B.R. v6p0042c1s
Gemunder, G. v1p1372c2s
Genet, E.C. v1p0463c1s
Genet, G.C. v1p0105c2s
v4p0403c1s
Gennadius, J. v4p0021c1s
v4p0186c1s v4p0241c1s v4p0241c2m
v4p0413c1s v5p0086c1s v5p0142c2s
v5p0248c2s v5p0249c1s v5p0249c2s
Gennings, J. v4p0340c1s
v5p0002c1s v5p0345c2s
Genone, H. v4p0328c2s
v4p0534c1s v4p0542c1s
Genone, T. v4p0333c2s
v5p0507c2s
Gent, G.W. v4p0112c1s
Genth, F.A. v1p0826c1s
v1p0828c2s v1p0844c2m v1p0845c1s
v1p0927c2s v3p0280c2s v4p0372c1s
Genth, F.A. and Penfield, S.L.
v3p0242c2s
Genthe, A. v5p0448c2s
Genthe, K.W. v6p0576c2s
Genthe, M.K. v6p0252c2s
v6p0704c1s
Genthe, Martha K. v5p0228c2s
v6p0250c2s
Gentry, Parma v5p0317c2s
Gentry, T.C. v1p0462c2s
Gentry, T.G. v1p1232c1s
Genung, A.O. et al. v5p0610c1s
Genung, C.H. v3p0176c1s
v3p0207c1s v4p0223c2s v4p0549c2s
v5p0064c2s v5p0237c1s v5p0497c2s
v5p0559c1s v6p0092c1s
Genung, G.F. v2p0139c1s
v3p0229c1s v3p0371c1s v3p0404c2s
v4p0030c2s v4p0300c1s v4p0431c1s
v4p0585c2s v5p0307c1s v5p0441c2s
Genung, J.F. v3p0028c2s
v3p0042c1s v3p0189c1s v3p0253c1s
v3p0302c1s v3p0361c2s v4p0055c2s
v4p0183c2s v4p0483c1s v5p0060c2s
Genung, N.H. v4p0219c1s
Geoffrey, C.P. v4p0478c2s
Geofroy, G.De v6p0048c2s
Geoghegan, E. v3p0404c1s
v3p0444c2s
Geoghegan, M. v2p0239c2s
v5p0529c1s
Geoghegan, Mary v4p0299c1s
v5p0322c2s v6p0202c2s
Geoghegan, R.H. v6p0092c1s
George, A.C. v1p0128c2s
v1p0688c1s v1p0830c1s v1p1047c1s
v2p0025c1s v2p0085c2s v2p0380c2s
George, A.E. v4p0108c2s
George, A.G. v2p0286c1s
George, A.J. v4p0118c1s
v5p0242c2s v6p0172c1s
George, C.E. v2p0179c2s
v3p0314c1s v5p0441c2s
George, D.L. v6p0191c1s
George, E. v5p0026c1s
George, E.A. v5p0108c1s
v5p0628c2s
George, H. v1p0398c1s

v1p0398c1s v1p0703c2s v1p0956c2s
v1p1027c1s v1p1285c1s v1p1285c2s
v2p0136c1s v2p0151c2s v2p0174c2s
v2p0224c2m v2p0225c2s v2p0346c2s
v2p0454c1s v3p0027c1s v3p0170c1s
v3p0221c2s v3p0238c2s v3p0252c2s
v3p0412c2s v4p0591c1s
George, H. and Atkinson, E.
v3p0241c2s v3p0421c1s
George, H. and Field, D.D.
v2p0247c2s
George, H. and Hyndman, H.
v2p0370c1s
George, H. and Hyndman, H.M.
v2p0407c2s
George, H. et al. v3p0421c1s
George, H., jr. v4p0540c1s
v6p0016c2s
George, H., jr. et al. ... v6p0055c1s
George, H.B. v3p0419c1s
v5p0398c1s
George, H.T. v5p0041c2s
v5p0279c1s v5p0455c2s v6p0695c1s
George, H.W. v4p0158c2s
George, Henry v2p0325c1s
George, J. v1p0102c2s
George, J.E. v5p0105c1m
v5p0124c1s v5p0557c2s
George, J.H. v3p0001c1s
George, Prince of Cumberland
v1p0884c2s
George, Prince of Wales .. v2p0031c1s
George, R.D. v6p0196c1s
v6p0412c1s v6p0419c1s
George, S.A. v4p0390c2s
George, W. v3p0075c1s
George, W. and Ingram, J.H.
v2p0075c2s
George, W.S. v1p1211c2s
Georgeson, C.C. v6p0010c2s
Georgi, K. v4p0271c1s
Geppert, Mrs. v5p0347c1s
Gerahty, G.M. v3p0262c1s
v3p0268c2s v3p0323c1s
Geraland, G. v5p0173c1s
Gerald, C.F. v5p0342c1s
Gerald, F. v4p0232c2s
v4p0325c1s
Gerald, G.B. v3p0071c2s
Gerald, J. v3p0419c2s
Gerard, A.N. v4p0203c2s
Gerard, D. v3p0068c1s
v3p0314c2s v4p0028c2s v4p0178c2s
v4p0414c1s v4p0431c1s v4p0590c1s
v6p0375c2s
Gerard, E. v3p0185c2s
v3p0340c1s v3p0435c1s v4p0207c2s
v5p0259c1s v5p0465c1s v6p0610c2s
Gerard, E.D. v2p0304c1s
Gerard, F. v1p0066c1s
v2p0040c2s v5p0487c1s
Gerard, F.A. v4p0163c1s
v4p0483c1s
Gerard, J. v1p0011c1m
v1p0027c1s v1p0106c1s v1p0247c1s
v1p0594c2s v1p0692c2s v1p0751c1s
v1p1234c2s v1p1409c2s v2p0130c2s
v2p0336c1s v2p0361c1s v3p0008c2s
v3p0013c2s v3p0045c2s v3p0069c1s
v3p0104c1s v3p0137c1s v3p0143c2s
v3p0145c2m v3p0147c2s v3p0217c2s
v3p0265c2s v3p0297c1s v3p0333c2s
v4p0007c1s v4p0190c2s v4p0191c1m
v4p0244c2s v5p0097c2s v5p0252c2m
v5p0305c1m v6p0131c1s v6p0211c1s
v6p0240c1s v6p0340c2s v6p0482c1s
v6p0576c1s v6p0702c1s
Gerard, J.N. v4p0049c2m
v4p0069c2s v4p0078c2s v4p0087c1s
v4p0090c1s v4p0111c1m v4p0146c1m
v4p0186c2s v4p0203c2m v4p0204c1s
v4p0219c2m v4p0227c1s v4p0242c2m
v4p0266c2s v4p0291c1m v4p0393c1m
v4p0416c1m v4p0435c1s v4p0491c2s
v4p0504c1s v4p0531c2s v4p0586c2s
v4p0613c1m v4p0623c2s v5p0287c2s
v6p0230c1s
Gerard, J.W. v2p0050c2s
v2p0121c2s v2p0130c1s v2p0168c1s
v2p0200c2s v2p0211c1s v2p0266c2s
v2p0313c2s v3p0159c1s v3p0189c1s
v3p0304c1s v3p0415c1s v3p0441c2s
v4p0083c1s v4p0310c2s
Gerard, John v6p0241c2s
Gerard, L. v5p0182c2s
Gerard, M. v3p0036c2m
Gerard, P. v1p0653c2s
Gerard, S. v1p0023c1s
Gerard, S.L. v5p0146c2s
Gerard, W.R. v4p0446c1s
v6p0317c1s v6p0632c2s
Geraud, J. v1p0850c1s
Gerber, A. v4p0590c1s
Gerber, E.R. v6p0532c1s
Gerberding, G.H. v3p0261c1s
v3p0440c1s
Gerdes, F.H. v1p0913c1s
v1p1345c2s
Gere, A.R. v1p0238c1s
v1p1339c2s
Gerhard, A.S. v2p0166c2s
Gerhard, C.S. v1p0048c1s
v1p0296c2s v1p0495c2s v2p0081c1s
v2p0132c2s v3p0357c1s v4p0149c2s
v5p0055c2s v5p0305c2s
Gerhard, F. v1p0982c1s
Gerhard, W.P. v2p0122c2s
v2p0396c2s v2p0467c1s v4p0047c2s
v4p0160c1s v4p0200c1s v4p0220c2m
v4p0274c1s v4p0473c1s v4p0502c2s
v4p0572c2m v5p0049c2s v5p0207c2s
v5p0226c1s v5p0226c2s v5p0455c1m
v5p0478c1s v5p0507c2s v5p0508c1m
v5p0521c2s v5p0576c1m v6p0054c1s
v6p0248c1s v6p0298c1m v6p0401c2s
v6p0569c2s v6p0573c1s v6p0574c1s
v6p0641c2m v6p0688c1s v6p0688c2m
Gerhard, Wm.Paul v2p0396c2s
Gerhardt, K. et al. v2p0184c2s
Gerhardt, P. v1p0619c2s
Gerhart, E.V. v1p0003c1s
v1p0043c2s v1p0096c1m v1p0121c1s
v1p0122c1s v1p0122c2s v1p0129c1s
v1p0197c1s v1p0241c2s v1p0253c2s
v1p0255c2s v1p0276c1s v1p0276c2s
v1p0313c2s v1p0375c1s v1p0386c1s
v1p0426c1s v1p0442c1s v1p0514c2m
v1p0527c2s v1p0613c1s v1p0620c2m
v1p0726c1s v1p0760c2s v1p0794c2s
v1p0847c1s v1p0966c1m v1p0999c2s
v1p1001c1s v1p1062c1s v1p1092c2s
v1p1097c2s v1p1103c2s v1p1140c2s
v1p1157c1s v1p1157c2s v1p1216c2s
v1p1245c1s v1p1302c1s v1p1302c2s
v1p1303c1m v1p1304c1s v1p1338c2s
v1p1342c2s v2p0041c2s v2p0042c1s
v2p0221c1s v2p0235c1s v2p0290c2s
v2p0291c2s v2p0367c2s v2p0408c2s
v2p0438c1s v3p0064c1s v3p0070c2s
v3p0080c2s v3p0163c1s v3p0357c2s
v3p0427c2s v4p0077c2s v4p0193c2s
v4p0232c2s v4p0301c1s v4p0322c2s
v4p0456c2s v4p0478c2m v4p0632c2s
v5p0055c2s v5p0059c1s v5p0114c1s
v5p0514c1s v6p0531c2s
Gerhart, E.V. et al. v3p0300c1s
Gerhart, R.L. v1p0123c2s
v1p0404c2s v1p0689c2s v1p1086c2s
v1p1294c2s v1p1429c2s v2p0027c2s
v4p0190c2s
Gerini, G.E. v4p0416c2s
v5p0112c1s v5p0527c2s v6p0118c1s
v6p0119c1s v6p0119c2s v6p0470c2s
v6p0593c1s
Gerish, W.B. v5p0104c2s
v6p0022c2s
Gerlache, Capt. v5p0022c1s
Gerland, E. v2p0138c1s
Gerland, G. v5p0456c2s
Germain, E. v4p0078c2s
Germain, Eugene v5p0430c1s
German, F. v5p0211c1s
German, J.F. v4p0414c2s
Germanicus v5p0040c1s
v5p0232c1s v5p0631c2s
Germann, G.B. v5p0204c1s
v5p0513c2s v6p0672c1s
Germano, P. v3p0231c1s
Germano, Padre v4p0431c1s
Germanus, Padre v4p0303c2s
Gerner, H. v1p0978c1s
Gerner, R. v1p0008c2s
v1p0408c1s
Gerome, J.L. v6p0034c1s
Gerothwohl, M.A. v6p0042c2m
v6p0048c1s v6p0090c2s v6p0150c1s
v6p0179c1s v6p0238c1s v6p0241c2s
v6p0394c2m v6p0557c1s v6p0570c2s
Gerould, G.H. v5p0318c1s
v5p0573c2s v6p0513c2s
Gerould, J.F. v5p0077c2s
Gerould, J.H. v5p0268c2s
v6p0019c1s v6p0713c2s
Gerould, J.T. v5p0333c2s
v6p0375c1s
Gerould, S.L. v3p0236c1s
Gerould, W. v3p0243c2s
v3p0378c1s
Gerrard, E.A. v6p0316c1s
Gerrard, T.J. v6p0024c2s
v6p0123c1s
Gerrare, W. v5p0253c1s
v5p0276c2s v5p0527c1s v6p0398c2s
v6p0593c1s
Gerrell, G. v5p0376c2s
Gerrie, J.P. v6p0096c1s
v6p0097c1s v6p0126c2s v6p0519c1s
Gerrier, Edith v4p0069c1s
Gerring, K. v4p0145c2s
Gerry, E.T. v2p0077c2s
v3p0067c2s v3p0133c2s v4p0202c2s
Gerry, M.S. v6p0070c2s
Gerry, S.L. v3p0051c1s
v3p0332c1s
Gersdorff, Countess v6p0251c1s
Gerstaecker, F. v1p0518c1s
v5p0232c1s
Gersteau, L. v1p1420c1s
Gersth, R. v1p0237c1s
Gerstner, F.A.de v1p1076c2s
Gerstner, F.A.von v1p0094c2s
v1p1076c2m v1p1077c1s v1p1077c2s
v1p1249c2s v1p1351c1s
Gervans, J.G. v1p0490c2s
Gervex, H. and Stevens, A.
v3p0306c1s v3p0320c1s
Gerwig, G.W. v5p0421c2s
v6p0514c1s
Gesell, A.L. v6p0279c2s
v6p0339c1s v6p0630c1s
Gesenius, F.H.W. v1p0581c2s
Gesner, A. v1p0268c2s
Gess, W.F. v1p0074c2s
v4p0196c2s v4p0300c2s
Gessner, F.B. v4p0207c1s
v4p0248c2s v6p0173c1s v6p0507c1s
Gessner, F.B. and Edwards, E.J.
v4p0347c2s
Gessner, F.M. v3p0174c2s
Gest, E. v1p0939c1s
Gest, J.H. v2p0219c2s
v4p0102c1s
Gestel, J.T.van v4p0068c1s
v4p0313c1s v4p0576c2s v5p0172c1s
Gether, A.E. v4p0523c1s
Getman, F.H. v5p0195c2s
v6p0325c2s
Gettemy, C.F. v6p0541c1s
Gettrau, Baroness von v3p0293c2s
Getty, R.A. v5p0389c1s
Gevaert, F.A. v4p0388c2s
Geyelin, E. v1p1392c1m
Geyer, W.E. v1p0459c1s
Geyern, D.von v3p0014c2s
Geyger, A. v1p0923c2s
Geymonat, P. v3p0225c1s
Geyt, A.B.Le v1p0025c1s
v1p0520c1s v1p1215c1s v1p1292c1s
v1p1313c2s v1p1411c1s v1p1423c1s
v1p1427c1s
Ghait, A.Le v4p0050c1s
Ghani, M.A. v5p0535c1s
Ghent, W.J. v5p0535c2s
v5p0641c1s v6p0158c2s v6p0222c2m
v6p0263c2s v6p0601c2s v6p0711c2s
Ghequier, A.de v3p0198c1s
v3p0230c1s
Ghequier, T.B. v1p0089c2s
v1p1326c1s v2p0019c1s v2p0329c1s
Ghose, J.N. v4p0391c1s
Ghose, Manomohan v4p0279c2s
Ghosh, A.H. v5p0284c1s
Ghosh, A.S. v5p0285c1s
v5p0529c2s v5p0580c1s v5p0589c1s
Ghosh, A.S.K. v5p0113c2s
v6p0644c2s
Ghosh, A.Sarath Kumar..... v6p0354c1s
Ghosh, Nanda Lal v2p0218c2s
Ghosn-el-Howie v6p0579c2s
v6p0593c2m
Ghulamus-Saqlan v4p0390c1s
Giacosa, G. v5p0299c2s
Giacosa, P. v4p0363c1s
Giard, Prof. v3p0240c2s
Gibb, A.N. v6p0613c1s
Gibb, D., Sir v1p1255c2s
Gibb, E.G.W. v2p0324c2s
Gibb, G.D., Sir v1p0212c1s
v1p0767c2s
Gibb, J. v1p0127c1s
v1p0138c2s v1p0517c1s v1p0583c2s
v1p1061c1s v1p1128c2s v1p1338c1s
v1p1384c1s v2p0016c1s v2p0024c2s
v2p0115c2s v2p0257c2s v2p0258c2s
v2p0300c2s v4p0186c1s v4p0330c2s
v4p0468c1s v5p0196c1s
Gibb, J.B. v6p0322c1s
Gibb, S.J. v6p0078c2s
Gibberd, V. v5p0177c1s
Gibbes, L.R. v1p0327c2s
v1p0463c1s v1p0813c2s v1p0936c1s
Gibbings, A.H. v5p0183c1m
Gibbins, C.M. v1p0474c1s
Gibbins, H.J. v4p0432c1s
v6p0064c2m
Gibbins, H.de B. v3p0044c2s
v3p0046c2s v3p0127c2s v3p0175c2s
v3p0197c1s v3p0363c2s
v4p0487c2s
Gibbon, C. v1p0023c1s
v1p0361c1s v1p0579c1s v1p0627c1m
v1p0943c1s v1p1070c2s v2p0062c2s
v2p0102c2s v2p0199c1s v2p0267c2s
v2p0272c2s v2p0321c2s v3p0024c1s
v3p0047c2s v3p0149c1s v3p0266c1s
Gibbon, F.P. v5p0253c1s
v5p0529c1s
Gibbon, G. v3p0394c2s
v5p0130c1s v5p0213c2s
Gibbon, J. v1p0327c1s
v1p0636c1s v1p0666c2s v1p1113c1s
v1p1113c2s v1p1201c2s v1p1202c2s
v2p0017c2s v3p0172c1s v4p0592c1s
v4p0617c2s v4p0630c1s v5p0029c1s
v5p0472c1s v5p0529c1s v5p0618c1s
v6p0025c2s
Gibbon, J. and Wood, C.E.S.
v5p0288c2s
Gibbon, J.H. v1p0037c1s
v1p0272c2s v1p0273c1s v1p0860c1s

v1p1147c1s v1p1208c1s
Gibbon, P. v6p0306c2s
v6p0368c2s v6p0398c1s v6p0556c1s
v6p0557c2s v6p0559c1s v6p0581c1m
v6p0652c2s v6p0682c1s v6p0702c1s
Gibboney, D.C. v6p0535c1s
Gibbons, A.St.H. v5p0362c2s
v6p0006c1m
Gibbons, A.St.H. and Quicke, F.C.
v5p0362c2s
Gibbons, C. v2p0168c2s
Gibbons, C.H. v4p0327c1s
v4p0604c1s
Gibbons, Cardinal v2p0478c2s
v3p0238c2s v3p0458c2s
Gibbons, Cardinal et al. . v3p0119c1s
Gibbons, H. v1p1148c2s
v1p1240c2s
Gibbons, H.de B. v3p0006c2s
v5p0570c1s
Gibbons, H.J. v4p0154c2s
v5p0392c1s v6p0492c1s
Gibbons, J. v1p0695c2s
v1p0696c1s v1p0806c2s v1p0871c2s
v2p0297c2s v2p0351c2s v2p0368c2s
v3p0011c1s v3p0379c2s v3p0395c2s
v4p0310c1s v4p0382c1s v4p0456c1s
v4p0489c1s v4p0566c1s v5p0484c1s
v6p0368c1s
Gibbons, J. et al. v1p0645c2s
v3p0378c2s
Gibbons, J., Cardinal v5p0492c2s
v6p0390c2s v6p0703c2s
Gibbons, J.C. v4p0430c2s
v4p0601c1s
Gibbons, J.H. v5p0323c1s
v6p0445c2s
Gibbons, J.M. v6p0569c1s
Gibbons, J.S. v1p0263c2s
v1p1278c1s v1p1349c1s v1p1351c2m
v5p0579c1s
Gibbons, John v4p0287c2s
Gibbons, M. v1p0892c2s
Gibbons, O. v4p0381c1s
Gibbons, P.E. v1p0373c1s
v1p0444c2s v1p0844c1s v1p0968c1s
v1p1170c2s v2p0005c2s
Gibbons, T. v3p0089c2s
v3p0155c1s
Gibbons, T. et al. v1p0100c1s
Gibbons, W.F. v4p0269c2s
v4p0372c1s v5p0074c2s v5p0096c1s
v5p0517c2s v5p0583c2s v5p0606c1s
Gibbons, W.P. v1p0188c2s
Gibbs, A. v5p0344c2s
Gibbs, A.E. v3p0247c1s
Gibbs, A.S. v1p0163c2s
v1p0383c2m v1p0530c1s v1p0531c1s
v1p1437c2s
Gibbs, Arch. v5p0012c2s
Gibbs, D. v6p0494c2s
Gibbs, E.J. v4p0339c1s
v4p0490c1s
Gibbs, G. v1p0280c2s
v1p0368c2s v1p1419c1s v4p0030c2s
v5p0134c1s v5p0156c1s v5p0310c1m
v6p0388c1s
Gibbs, G. and Gibbs, W.E.. v2p0137c2s
Gibbs, G.S. v6p0010c2s
v6p0712c2s
Gibbs, George v6p0382c2s
Gibbs, H. v6p0344c2s
Gibbs, H.C. v3p0044c2s
v4p0144c1s v5p0284c2s v5p0285c1s
Gibbs, H.H. v1p0133c2s
v2p0046c1s v2p0182c1s v2p0353c2s
v3p0107c2s v3p0281c2s v3p0393c1s
v4p0524c1s
Gibbs, H.H. and Bacon, H.. v4p0524c1s
Gibbs, H.J. v2p0273c1s
Gibbs, J. v3p0017c2s
Gibbs, J.C. v1p0017c1s
Gibbs, J.D. v2p0137c2s
Gibbs, J.S. v2p0475c2s
Gibbs, J.W. v1p0065c1s
v1p0118c2s v1p0120c2s v1p0204c1s
v1p0416c1s v1p0417c1s v1p0419c1s
v1p0554c2m v1p0582c1s v1p0651c1s
v1p0727c2s v1p0980c2s v1p0999c1s
v1p1115c1s v1p1139c2s v1p1219c2s
v1p1296c2s v1p1362c2s v2p0007c2s
v2p0258c1s v2p0258c2s v2p0367c2s
v3p0092c2s v3p0250c2m v3p0356c2s
v5p0410c1s v6p0251c1s
Gibbs, J.W. and Tait, P.G.
v3p0350c2s
Gibbs, J.W.M. v2p0182c2s
Gibbs, L. v6p0196c1s
Gibbs, M. v4p0060c2s
v4p0061c2s
Gibbs, M.I. v4p0278c2s
Gibbs, Mary V. v3p0234c1s
Gibbs, P. v5p0138c2s
Gibbs, R.E. v6p0497c2s
Gibbs, W. v1p0004c1s
v1p0149c1s v1p0224c2m v1p0945c1s
v1p1016c2s v1p1268c2s v3p0142c1s
v5p0015c1s
Gibbs, W.A. v1p0102c2s
v3p0123c2s v3p0414c1s v4p0339c2s
Gibbs, W.E. v3p0068c2s
Gibbs, W.E. and Gibbs, G.. v2p0137c2s
Giberne, A. v2p0127c1s
v2p0344c1s v2p0425c2s v3p0209c2s
v3p0333c2s v4p0157c1s
Giberne, Agnes v4p0597c1s
v5p0076c1s
Giberson, N.S. v2p0211c2s
Gibert, A.T. v4p0030c2s
v5p0145c2s v5p0196c2s
Gibier, P. v3p0098c1s
v3p0205c2s v3p0237c2s v4p0441c2s
Gibney, R. v3p0339c1s
Gibney, R.D. v1p0609c2s
v3p0126c2s
Gibney, S. v1p0442c2s
v1p0570c2s v2p0194c2s v4p0262c2s
Gibney, V.P. v6p0386c2s
Gibney, Wm. v2p0468c1s
Gibside, N. v6p0254c1s
Gibson, A.E. v5p0009c1s
v6p0394c1s v6p0423c2s v6p0458c2s
v6p0587c1s
Gibson, A.H. v4p0037c1s
v6p0204c1s v6p0661c1s
Gibson, B. v5p0159c1s
Gibson, C. v5p0413c2s
Gibson, C.B. v1p0403c1s
v1p1064c2s v1p1081c2s v1p1235c2s
Gibson, C.D. v5p0181c2s
v5p0408c1s
Gibson, C.H. v1p1419c1s
Gibson, Com. v1p0599c1s
Gibson, E. v5p0001c2s
v5p0019c1s v5p0262c2s v5p0283c1s
v5p0337c2s v5p0340c2s v5p0347c1s
v5p0351c2s v5p0369c2s v5p0406c2s
v5p0517c1s
Gibson, E.J. v4p0612c2s
v5p0480c2s
Gibson, E.R. v6p0595c2s
Gibson, F. v1p0740c1s
v2p0096c2m v3p0094c2s
Gibson, F.V. v5p0044c1s
v5p0589c2s
Gibson, G.H. v6p0198c1m
v6p0198c2s
Gibson, G.R. v1p0058c1s
v1p0094c1s v1p0284c1s v1p0849c1s
v1p1038c2s v1p1044c2s v1p1076c2s
v1p1085c2s v1p1099c1s v1p1153c2s
v1p1198c1s v1p1198c2s v1p1199c1s
v1p1319c2s v1p1360c1s v2p0298c2s
v2p0320c2s v2p0465c1s v3p0033c1s
v4p0199c1s
Gibson, H. v2p0004c1m
v2p0271c1s v2p0292c1s v2p0460c2s
v2p0482c2s v3p0008c1s v3p0037c2s
v3p0428c2m
Gibson, H.G. v6p0707c2s
Gibson, H.S. v6p0352c1s
Gibson, J. v1p0943c2s
v1p1147c1s v2p0157c2s v4p0337c1s
Gibson, J. and Macoun, J.. v1p0617c2s
Gibson, J.A. v5p0134c2m
v5p0594c1s v5p0632c2s v6p0098c2s
v6p0374c1s v6p0569c1s
Gibson, J.B. v1p0711c2s
v2p0214c2s v2p0283c1s v2p0285c1s
v2p0307c2s v2p0358c1s v2p0378c2s
v5p0279c1s
Gibson, J.M. v1p0047c2s
v2p0081c2s v2p0235c1s v2p0351c2s
v3p0404c2s v4p0103c1s v4p0284c1s
v4p0331c1s v4p0418c1s v5p0060c1s
Gibson, J.R., jr. v3p0037c2s
Gibson, J.S. v5p0273c1s
v5p0419c2s
Gibson, L.C. v4p0048c2s
Gibson, L.H. v5p0026c1s
v5p0430c2s v6p0028c1s v6p0028c2m
v6p0106c2s
Gibson, M.B. v4p0110c1s
v4p0253c2s v4p0270c1s v5p0505c2s
Gibson, M.F. v4p0411c1s
Gibson, P. v6p0669c2s
Gibson, R. v5p0081c2s
Gibson, R.L. v1p0856c2s
v1p0897c1s
Gibson, R.M. v5p0238c2s
Gibson, R.R. v5p0160c2s
Gibson, R.W. v2p0008c1s
v2p0019c1s v2p0020c1s v4p0024c2s
v4p0025c1s v4p0043c2s v4p0092c1s
Gibson, Ruth v5p0540c1s
Gibson, S. v6p0074c1s
Gibson, Strickland v6p0074c1s
Gibson, T.E. v1p0143c2s
v1p0181c1s v1p0720c2s
Gibson, T.H. v1p0019c2s
Gibson, T.W. v4p0010c2s
Gibson, W. v1p0919c2s
v1p0991c1s v1p1122c2s v1p1194c2s
v1p1255c2s v1p1352c1s v2p0420c2s
v4p0211c2s v4p0242c2s v5p0492c2s
v6p0422c1s v6p0437c1s v6p0451c2s
v6p0689c2s
Gibson, W.H. v1p0082c2s
v1p0114c1s v1p1213c2s v1p1240c1s
v2p0002c1s v2p0053c1s v2p0222c2s
v2p0307c1s v2p0344c1s v2p0345c1s
v2p0476c1m v2p0479c1s v3p0045c2s
v3p0046c1s v3p0061c2s v3p0167c1s
v3p0278c1s v3p0305c2s v3p0465c2s
v4p0021c1s v4p0069c2s v4p0101c1s
v4p0142c2s v4p0159c2s v4p0203c2s
v4p0204c1s v4p0263c2s v4p0359c2s
v4p0388c1m v4p0583c1s v5p0423c1s
Gibson, W.J. v5p0210c1s
Gibson, W.L. v1p1230c1s
Gibson, W.R.B. v5p0328c2s
v6p0514c1s v6p0598c1s
Gibson, W.S. v1p0946c1s
v1p1325c1s v2p0063c2s
Gibson, W.T. v1p0207c2s
Gibson, W.W. v5p0608c1s
v6p0310c2s
Gibson, Willis v5p0369c2s
v6p0030c2s
Gibson, Winifred v6p0614c1s
Giddings, F. v5p0537c1s
v6p0017c2s
Giddings, F.H. v3p0067c1m
v3p0067c2s v3p0095c1s v3p0218c2s
v3p0297c1s v3p0337c1s v3p0345c2s
v3p0352c1s v3p0398c2s v3p0399c2m
v3p0452c2s v4p0152c1s v4p0350c2s
v4p0351c1s v4p0532c2s v4p0535c1s
v4p0535c2s v5p0102c1s v5p0175c1s
v5p0196c1s v5p0248c2s v5p0281c1s
v5p0357c2s v5p0459c1s v5p0470c1s
v5p0471c1s v5p0537c1m v5p0583c1s
v6p0085c2s v6p0161c1s v6p0214c2s
v6p0223c2s v6p0262c1s v6p0263c1s
v6p0317c2s v6p0526c1s v6p0599c2s
v6p0601c1s v6p0602c1m v6p0607c1s
v6p0610c1m v6p0622c2s
Giddings, H.A. v3p0013c2s
v3p0296c2s v4p0443c1s v4p0482c2m
v4p0523c2s v5p0182c2s v5p0399c2s
v5p0528c2s
Giddings, T.H. v5p0386c1s
Gide, C. v3p0336c2s
v3p0421c1s v4p0008c1s v4p0132c2s
v4p0504c2s v4p0553c1s v5p0136c1m
Gidley, W.S. v5p0176c2s
Gidney, C.M. v5p0508c1s
Gielgud, A. v1p0332c1s
v1p1024c1s v1p1331c2s v3p0069c1s
v3p0103c2s v3p0336c1m
Giering, E.T. v6p0698c2s
Gies, W.J. v6p0067c1s
v6p0409c1s
Giese, E.F. v1p0097c1s
Giese, M. v4p0196c1s
Gieseler, E.A. v2p0440c2s
v3p0034c2s v3p0251c1s v3p0272c2s
v3p0430c1s
Giesy, S.H. v1p0005c1s
v1p0096c2s v1p0243c2s v1p0613c2s
v1p0686c1s v1p0689c1s v1p1088c1s
v1p1152c1s v1p1200c2s v3p0016c1s
v3p0175c1s v4p0300c2m
Giffard-Ruffe, H. v5p0461c2s
Giffen, R. v1p0018c1s
v1p0067c2s v1p0086c2s v1p0133c2s
v1p0453c1s v1p0545c2s v1p0721c2s
v1p1049c2s v1p1077c2s v1p1198c1s
v1p1285c1s v1p1365c1s v2p0005c2s
v2p0215c2s v2p0225c1s v2p0245c2s
v2p0353c2s v2p0418c2m v2p0444c1s
v3p0044c2s v3p0067c1m v3p0180c2s
v3p0185c1s v3p0210c2s v3p0271c1s
v3p0285c2s v3p0343c2s v3p0345c2s
v3p0393c2s v3p0452c1m v4p0377c2s
v4p0546c2s v5p0245c2s v5p0248c1s
v5p0282c1s v5p0285c2s v5p0382c2s
v5p0383c1s v5p0469c1s v5p0550c2s
v5p0587c2s v5p0588c2s v5p0627c2s
v6p0083c1s v6p0205c2s v6p0224c1s
v6p0266c2m v6p0268c1s v6p0690c1s
Giffen, R. and Newmarch, W.
v1p0545c1s
Giffen, R. et al. v6p0310c1s
Giffen, R., Sir v5p0244c1s
v5p0248c1s v5p0550c1s
Giffert, A.C. v5p0279c2s
Giffin, C.M. v6p0381c1s
Giffin, W.M. et al. v3p0422c1s
Giffiths, A. v2p0311c1s
v6p0271c2s
Giffiths, L.M. v3p0269c2s
Gifford, E.H. v4p0057c1s
v4p0277c1s v4p0300c2s v5p0201c2s
Gifford, F.E. v6p0247c1s
v6p0581c1s
Gifford, G.R. v1p1326c1s
Gifford, J. v4p0207c2m
v4p0208c1s v4p0281c2s v4p0291c2s
v4p0442c1s v5p0214c2m v5p0507c2s
v6p0229c1s v6p0233c2s
Gifford, J.W. v4p0440c2s
v4p0487c1s
Gifford, L.J.K., Mrs. v1p0248c1s
v1p0810c1s v1p1270c2s
Gifford, M.W. v5p0114c2s
Gifford, O.P. v4p0102c1s
Gifford, O.P. et al. v4p0054c1s
Gifford, W. v1p0311c1s
v1p0383c1s v1p0467c2s v1p0602c2s

v1p1168c2m v1p1169c2s v1p1430c2s
v5p0115c1s
Gifford, W.L.R. v3p0121c1s
v4p0154c2s
Gifoon, Ali Effendi v4p0537c2s
Gift, F. v1p0851c2s
Gift, G.W. v2p0021c2s
Gift, T. v1p0077c2s
v1p0098c1s v1p0441c2s v1p0564c2s
v1p0626c2s v1p0668c1s v1p0887c1s
v1p0887c2s v1p1314c2s v1p1327c1s
v1p1335c1s v1p1375c2s v2p0008c1s
v2p0460c2s v2p0471c2s
Giglinger, G. v6p0176c1s
Giglioli, C.H.D.Stocker .. v3p0439c1s
Giglioli, H.H. v1p0911c1s
v2p0471c2s v2p0483c2s v3p0305c1m
v4p0424c2s v4p0556c1s
Giglioli, I. v4p0513c1s
v5p0152c2s v5p0165c1s v5p0292c1s
Giglioli, J. v2p0169c2s
v2p0396c1s
Gignilliat, L.R. v6p0445c2s
Gigot, A. v2p0329c1s
Gihon, A.L. v1p0083c2s
v1p0196c1s v1p0198c1s v1p0752c1s
v1p0785c2s
Gilard, L. v3p0159c2s
v3p0161c2s
Gilbart, J.W. v1p0090c2s
v1p0095c1s v1p0283c1m v1p0325c2m
v1p0545c2s v1p1123c2s v1p1166c1s
Gilbert, A.N. v1p0682c1s
Gilbert, B. v6p0264c1s
Gilbert, B.L. v3p0353c2s
v4p0471c2s
Gilbert, C. v4p0296c1s
Gilbert, C.B. v4p0170c2s
v4p0255c1s v4p0505c2s v4p0554c1s
v5p0264c2s v5p0360c2s v5p0569c2s
v6p0290c1s v6p0371c2s v6p0522c2s
Gilbert, C.B. et al. v5p0471c2s
Gilbert, C.C. v2p0054c2s
Gilbert, C.H. and Jordan, D.S.
v1p1146c1s
Gilbert, D.M. v1p0043c2s
v2p0479c1s v3p0082c2s v5p0351c1s
Gilbert, F. v1p0027c2s
v1p0227c2m v1p0228c1s v1p0235c2s
v1p0282c2s v1p0384c1s v1p0397c1s
v1p0426c2s v1p0636c1s v1p0871c1s
v1p1352c2s v2p0452c2s
Gilbert, F.M. v5p0143c1s
Gilbert, G.A. v5p0350c2s
Gilbert, G.H. v3p0043c1s
v4p0057c2s v4p0058c1s v4p0573c1s
v4p0628c2s v5p0024c1s v5p0059c1s
v5p0115c2s v5p0158c2s v5p0241c2s
v5p0306c2s v5p0436c2s v6p0122c1s
v6p0169c1s v6p0293c1s v6p0341c2m
v6p0342c1s v6p0590c1s
Gilbert, G.K. v1p0148c1s
v1p0279c1s v1p0523c2s v1p0551c1s
v1p0812c2s v1p1147c1s v2p0051c1s
v2p0114c2s v2p0128c1s v2p0173c2s
v2p0390c2s v3p0169c1m v3p0240c1s
v3p0359c1s v4p0272c1s v4p0486c1s
v5p0385c1s v5p0424c1s v5p0488c1s
v5p0580c1s v5p0603c1s v6p0217c2s
v6p0486c2s v6p0512c1m v6p0568c1s
v6p0576c2s v6p0582c2s
Gilbert, G.K. et al. v2p0035c1s
Gilbert, G.N. v1p0509c1s
Gilbert, H. v5p0139c2s
v5p0326c1s v5p0635c2s v6p0362c2s
Gilbert, H.F. v5p0212c1s
Gilbert, J. v1p0058c1s
v1p0075c1s v1p0254c2s v1p1313c1s
v2p0027c2s v5p0206c1s
Gilbert, J. et al. v2p0123c1s
Gilbert, J.A. and Patrick, G.T.W.
v4p0529c2s
Gilbert, J.H. v1p1364c2s
v2p0005c1s v2p0080c1s v3p0306c1s
Gilbert, J.H. and Lawes, J.B.
v1p1404c1s
Gilbert, J.W. v6p0547c1s
v6p0547c2m
Gilbert, L. v5p0206c1s
Gilbert, L.M. v1p1131c2s
Gilbert, R. v1p0398c2s
v2p0316c2s
Gilbert, R.D. and Gooch, F.A.
v6p0019c1s v6p0713c1s
Gilbert, R.M. v5p0322c2m
v5p0524c2s
Gilbert, S. v1p0152c1s
v1p0228c1s v2p0323c2s v2p0428c1s
v2p0452c2s v6p0456c1s
Gilbert, S. and Muller, M.
v4p0479c1s
Gilbert, S.K. v2p0246c2s
Gilbert, W. v1p0039c1s
v1p0185c1s v1p0218c2s v1p0297c1s
v1p0317c1s v1p0337c1s v1p0347c2s
v1p0373c2s v1p0554c1s v1p0592c1s
v1p0606c1s v1p0623c2s v1p0644c2s
v1p0690c2m v1p0722c1s v1p0766c1s
v1p0816c2s v1p0904c2s v1p0913c2s
v1p0984c1s v1p0997c2s v1p1030c2s
v1p1042c1s v1p1064c1s v1p1138c2s
v1p1139c1s v1p1292c1s v1p1305c1s
v1p1371c2m v1p1425c1s v1p1431c2m
Gilbert, W.M. v4p0253c1s
v4p0437c2s v4p0494c1s v5p0041c2s
v5p0233c1s v5p0309c2s v6p0258c1s
v6p0578c2s
Gilbert, W.S. v1p0454c1s
v1p0765c2s v1p1315c1s
Gilbertson, A. v4p0188c1s
v4p0516c2s
Gilbertson, E. v5p0404c2s
Gilbertson, F.W. v6p0692c1s
Gilbey, W. v6p0044c1s
v6p0297c1s
Gilbraith, A. v6p0189c2s
Gilbraith, A.S. v6p0279c2s
Gilburt, J. v2p0256c2s
v5p0070c1s v5p0332c2s v5p0333c1s
Gilchrist, A. v1p1269c2s
v2p0152c1s
Gilchrist, A.G. v5p0480c1s
Gilchrist, B.B. v6p0440c2s
v6p0695c1s
Gilchrist, G. v4p0492c1s
v5p0629c2s
Gilchrist, H.H. v5p0497c2s
Gilchrist, H.M. v4p0551c1s
Gilchrist, I. v4p0575c2s
Gilchrist, J.C. v5p0591c1s
Gilchrist, J.G. v2p0075c1s
v5p0547c2s
Gilchrist, Murray v6p0219c1s
Gilchrist, R.M. v5p0411c2s
v6p0057c2s v6p0109c2s v6p0358c1s
v6p0680c2s
Gildea, W. v3p0431c1s
v4p0277c2s
Gildea, W.L. v5p0080c1s
v5p0283c2s
Gilder, J.B. v1p0150c1s
v3p0410c1s v4p0046c2s v4p0427c1s
v4p0456c1s v5p0013c1s v5p0079c1s
v5p0237c1s v5p0267c2s v5p0385c1s
v5p0398c1s v5p0407c1s v5p0432c2s
v5p0446c2s v5p0496c1s v5p0551c2s
v5p0553c2s v5p0554c1s v6p0284c1m
v6p0301c1s v6p0339c2s
Gilder, J.B. and Gilder, J.L.
v5p0071c1s
Gilder, J.L. v3p0049c2s
v3p0232c2s v3p0292c1s v4p0198c2s
v4p0221c1s v4p0246c2s v4p0248c1s
v4p0261c1s v4p0328c1s v4p0408c2s
v5p0002c1s v5p0078c1s v5p0079c2s
v5p0084c1s v5p0161c1s v5p0164c1s
v5p0186c1s v5p0206c1s v5p0206c2s
v5p0209c2s v5p0233c2s v5p0274c2m
v5p0352c1s v5p0376c1s v5p0387c2s
v5p0398c1s v5p0416c1s v5p0509c1s
v5p0548c2s v5p0574c2s v5p0575c1m
v5p0578c1s v5p0582c1s v5p0616c2s
v6p0059c2s
Gilder, J.L. and Gilder, J.B.
v5p0071c1s
Gilder, Jeannette L. v5p0227c1s
v5p0456c1s v6p0066c2s v6p0084c1s
v6p0088c2s v6p0147c2s v6p0179c1s
v6p0183c2s v6p0213c1s v6p0213c2s
v6p0228c1s v6p0262c1s v6p0263c1s
v6p0293c1s v6p0295c1s v6p0302c1s
v6p0304c2s v6p0361c1s v6p0361c2s
v6p0369c1s v6p0379c1s v6p0394c2s
v6p0469c1s v6p0504c2s v6p0531c1s
v6p0544c1s v6p0555c1s v6p0594c1s
v6p0610c1s v6p0618c1s v6p0619c1s
v6p0634c2s v6p0682c1s v6p0683c1s
v6p0684c1s v6p0697c2s v6p0702c2s
v6p0705c2m
Gilder, Joseph B. v5p0446c2s
Gilder, R.W. v1p0166c2s
v1p0445c1s v1p0738c1s v1p1253c1s
v3p0011c2s v3p0091c2s v3p0253c2s
v3p0306c2s v4p0299c1s v4p0624c1s
v5p0040c2s v5p0063c2s v5p0115c2s
v5p0308c2s v5p0339c2s v5p0639c2s
v6p0033c1s v6p0085c1s v6p0086c2s
v6p0122c1s v6p0131c1s v6p0166c1s
v6p0295c1s v6p0339c2s v6p0351c2s
v6p0365c1s v6p0389c1m v6p0451c2s
v6p0585c1s v6p0589c2s v6p0630c1s
v6p0643c1s v6p0653c1s v6p0695c2s
Gilder, W.H. v1p0425c1s
v3p0019c1s v3p0197c2s v3p0207c1s
v3p0392c2s v4p0349c2s
Gildersleeve, B.L. v1p0008c2s
v1p0047c2s v1p0262c1s v1p0262c2s
v1p0275c2s v1p0323c2s v1p0553c1s
v1p0603c2s v1p0698c1s v1p0813c2s
v1p0998c2s v1p1016c2s v1p1217c2s
v1p1221c1s v1p1358c1s v1p1366c2s
v1p1435c1s v2p0021c1s v2p0026c2s
v2p0088c1m v2p0144c1s v2p0176c2s
v2p0177c1s v2p0184c2s v2p0190c2s
v2p0191c1m v2p0249c1s v2p0268c2s
v2p0342c1s v2p0354c1s v2p0373c1s
v2p0395c1s v3p0022c2m v3p0087c1s
v3p0158c1s v3p0184c2s v3p0199c2s
v3p0243c2s v3p0295c2s v4p0118c1s
v4p0189c2s v4p0448c1s v4p0538c1s
v5p0249c1s v5p0439c1s v6p0273c2s
v6p0469c1s
Gildersleeve, B.L. and
McDaniels, J.H. v4p0241c1s
Gildersleeve, B.L. and
Miller, C.W.E. v6p0680c2s
Gildersleeve, B.L. and Smith, R.H.
v4p0128c1s
Gildersome-Dickenson, C.E.
v4p0621c2s
Gile, M.A. v3p0213c2s
Gilebs, G.S. v2p0457c1s
Gilenthea, R.T. v6p0127c2s
Giles, C. et al. v1p0645c2s
Giles, E. v4p0174c1s
v4p0257c1s
Giles, E.A. v2p0411c1s
Giles, E.O. v5p0164c2s
Giles, H. v1p0085c1s
v1p0085c2s v1p0105c2s v1p0189c1s
v1p0211c2s v1p0253c1s v1p0345c1s
v1p0362c1s v1p0381c1m v1p0382c2s
v1p0406c1s v1p0425c2s v1p0495c2s
v1p0523c1s v1p0558c2s v1p0594c2s
v1p0602c1s v1p0654c2s v1p0656c2s
v1p0908c1s v1p1064c1s v1p1168c1s
v1p1178c1s v1p1185c1s v1p1234c2s
v2p0235c2s
Giles, H.A. v1p0232c1s
v1p0233c1s v1p0234c1s v1p0235c2m
v1p0236c1s v1p0443c1s v1p0825c1s
v1p1014c1s v1p1238c1s v4p0106c1s
v4p0106c2m v5p0113c1s v5p0132c2s
v6p0118c2s v6p0120c2s v6p0121c1s
v6p0231c2s v6p0332c2s v6p0334c2s
v6p0476c1s
Giles, L. v6p0118c1s
v6p0240c1s
Giles, M.F. v6p0036c1s
Giles, O., Mrs. v6p0177c2s
Giles, P. v2p0299c2s
v3p0184c1s v4p0026c2s v4p0435c1s
Giles, W.A. v6p0356c2s
v6p0450c1s v6p0599c2s
Giles, W.A. et al. v5p0592c2s
Gilfillan, G. v1p0017c2s
v1p0022c2s v1p0037c2s v1p0060c2s
v1p0105c1s v1p0120c2s v1p0132c2s
v1p0140c1s v1p0148c1s v1p0168c1s
v1p0168c2s v1p0170c1s v1p0177c2s
v1p0181c2m v1p0287c1s v1p0311c1s
v1p0319c1s v1p0332c1s v1p0335c2s
v1p0376c2s v1p0405c1s v1p0447c2s
v1p0470c2s v1p0568c2s v1p0584c1s
v1p0602c1s v1p0616c1m v1p0677c1m
v1p0712c2s v1p0733c2s v1p0738c2s
v1p0780c1s v1p0781c1s v1p0842c1s
v1p0849c1s v1p0858c1s v1p0864c1s
v1p0866c2s v1p0893c2m v1p0920c2s
v1p0937c1s v1p0946c1s v1p0990c2s
v1p1022c2s v1p1111c2s v1p1162c1s
v1p1184c2s v1p1185c1s v1p1189c1s
v1p1190c2s v1p1253c1s v1p1294c2s
v1p1307c1s v1p1367c1s v1p1385c2s
v1p1413c1s v1p1429c2s v1p1438c1s
v2p0168c1s
Gilfillan, J.A. v2p0292c1s
Gilfillan, L. v4p0590c1s
Gilfillan, R. v1p1020c2s
Gilhan, L. v6p0106c1s
Gilkes, A.H. v5p0037c1s
v6p0194c1s
Gilkeson, A. v2p0407c2s
Gill, A.H. v6p0474c2s
Gill, A.K. v5p0396c1s
v5p0398c2s
Gill, C.H. v3p0414c1s
Gill, C.R. v5p0148c1s
Gill, D. v2p0417c2s
v3p0024c2s
Gill, E.M. v5p0256c1s
Gill, E.S. v6p0496c1s
Gill, E.W.B. v6p0681c2s
Gill, F. v5p0441c2s
Gill, F.H. v6p0074c1s
Gill, F.N.G. v5p0043c1s
v5p0559c2s v6p0047c1s v6p0624c1s
Gill, H.V. v5p0227c1s
v5p0530c2s
Gill, J.H. v1p0403c2s
Gill, J.R. v6p0166c2s
Gill, J.T. v1p0933c2s
Gill, M. v6p0180c2s
Gill, R.C. v3p0109c2s
v3p0418c2s v4p0631c2s
Gill, T. v1p0042c1s
v1p0057c2s v1p0213c2s v1p0435c1s
v1p0437c2s v1p0456c1s v1p0456c2m
v1p0663c2s v1p0691c2s v1p0737c1s
v1p0791c2s v1p0792c1s v1p0793c2s
v1p0800c2s v1p0820c2s v1p0960c1s
v1p1250c2s v1p1368c1s v1p1403c1s
v2p0070c2s v2p0157c1s v3p0107c2s
v3p0379c2s v3p0383c1s v4p0048c1s
v4p0071c2s v4p0201c1s v4p0270c2s
v4p0327c1s v4p0422c1s v4p0603c1s
v4p0637c2s v5p0049c2s v5p0136c2m
v6p0029c2s v6p0172c1s v6p0195c1s
v6p0227c1m v6p0297c2s v6p0396c2m
v6p0585c2s v6p0589c1s v6p0694c1s

v6p0698c1s
Gill, T. and Langley, S.P. v4p0232c1s
Gill, T.H. v1p0111c2s v1p0358c1s v1p0642c2m v1p0782c1s v1p0841c2s v1p1393c1m v1p1398c2s v2p0221c2m v2p0468c1s
Gill, T.K. v1p1398c2s
Gill, T.P. v2p0001c2s v2p0125c1s v2p0227c2s v2p0470c2s v3p0096c2s v3p0115c2s v3p0321c2s
Gill, Theo. v6p0570c2s
Gill, W. v2p0383c2s
Gill, W.A. v3p0246c1m v3p0295c1s v5p0122c2s v6p0242c1s
Gill, W.F. v5p0437c2s v5p0455c1s
Gill, W.I. v1p0651c1s v3p0080c2s v3p0107c1s v3p0148c2s v3p0435c1s
Gill, W.J. v1p0234c2s v1p0992c1s
Gill, W.L. v6p0573c2s
Gill, W.T. and Law, O.P. . v6p0042c1s
Gill, W.W. v1p0871c1s v1p0962c2s v1p1227c2s v2p0102c2s v2p0117c1s v2p0125c1s v2p0311c1s v2p0348c2s
Gillaphin, H.T. v5p0537c2s
Gillard, P.A. v5p0359c2s
Gillen, F.J. and Spencer, B. v5p0193c2s v5p0583c1s
Gilleran, T. v4p0489c1s
Gillespie, A. v5p0017c2s v5p0566c2s
Gillespie, C.B. v3p0092c1s v3p0280c2s
Gillespie, D.H.M. and Walker, C.F. v5p0295c1s
Gillespie, E.D. v5p0443c1s
Gillespie, F. v4p0235c2s
Gillespie, W.H. v1p0592c2s v1p0964c1s
Gillespie, W.M. v1p0435c2s v1p0811c1m v1p1110c2s
Gillett, A.L. v5p0280c2s v6p0123c1s v6p0168c2s v6p0197c1s v6p0419c1s
Gillett, C.R. v2p0009c1s v2p0354c2s v3p0130c2s v3p0333c1s v4p0073c1s v4p0172c2s v4p0330c1s
Gillett, E. v1p0750c2s v1p0789c2s v1p0846c2s v1p1437c2s
Gillett, E.H. v1p0006c1s v1p0034c2s v1p0076c2s v1p0223c1s v1p0240c1s v1p0242c2s v1p0292c1s v1p0393c2s v1p0466c1s v1p0603c1s v1p0614c2s v1p0618c1m v1p0680c1s v1p0729c2s v1p0811c2s v1p0842c1s v1p0870c1s v1p0964c2s v1p1032c2s v1p1046c1m v1p1047c1s v1p1068c1s v1p1103c1m v1p1108c1s v1p1214c1s v1p1279c2s v1p1340c1s v1p1402c2s v1p1404c2m v1p1409c1s v1p1416c2s v1p1436c1s v2p0289c2s v2p0352c2s v2p0448c1s v2p0470c1s
Gillett, P.G. v3p0112c2m
Gillette, A.D. and McAndrew, S. v4p0132c1s
Gillette, A.D. and McAndrew, W.S. v4p0085c1s
Gillette, C.E. v6p0666c1s
Gillette, E. v5p0318c1s
Gillette, G.W. v6p0086c2m
Gillette, J.M. v5p0148c2s
Gillette, King C. v6p0708c2s
Gillette, W. v5p0272c2s
Gillette, W.H. and Burnett, F.H. v2p0146c2s
Gilley, F.M. v6p0141c2s
Gillham, R. v3p0062c1s v4p0173c2s
Gilliam, E.W. v2p0079c2s v2p0082c1s v2p0308c2s v2p0309c1s v2p0353c1s v3p0158c2s v3p0374c1s v3p0386c1s
Gilliams, E.L. v4p0118c1s v4p0494c2s v4p0611c2s
Gilliat-Smith, F.E. v4p0095c1s v4p0110c2s v4p0164c1s v4p0418c1s v4p0574c1s
Gillie, E.A. v5p0419c2s v6p0388c2s
Gillies, C.L. v1p0841c2s
Gillies, J. v1p0001c2s v1p0773c2s v1p0992c2s v1p0993c1s
Gillies, M. v1p0599c2s v1p0715c1s
Gillies, M.L. v1p0439c1s v1p0703c1s v1p0774c1s v1p0988c1s v1p1362c2s
Gillies, R.P. v1p0068c2s v1p0469c2s v1p0515c1s v1p0530c2s v1p0531c1s v1p0558c2m v1p0603c2m v1p0608c2s v1p0642c1s v1p0712c1m v1p0720c1m v1p0724c2s v1p0798c2s v1p0864c2s v1p0879c2m v1p0938c1m v1p0951c1s v1p1011c1s v1p1073c1s v1p1084c1s v1p1084c2s v1p1138c1s v1p1156c2m v1p1157c1s v1p1160c1s v1p1169c1s v1p1274c2s
Gilliland, M.S. v4p0096c1s v4p0421c1s v4p0447c1s v4p0628c2s
Gilliland, M.S. et al. ... v4p0253c1s
Gillilau, J.D. v5p0387c1s
Gillingham, H.P. v1p1188c2s
Gillington, Alice E. v6p0256c2s
Gillington, M.C. v4p0500c1s v4p0542c1s
Gillis, C.J. v4p0280c2s
Gillis, J.L. v6p0615c1s
Gillis, J.M. v5p0254c1s v6p0008c1s
Gillis, R.P. v1p0257c1s
Gilliss, J.M. v1p0230c2s v1p0281c2s v1p0376c1s
Gilliss, J.R. v1p0956c2s
Gillman, J.V. v5p0449c2s v5p0637c2s v6p0596c1s
Gillmor, H.G v5p0582c2s v6p0054c2m
Gillmore, E.W. v5p0350c2s
Gillmore, I.H. v6p0466c2s v6p0619c2s
Gillmore, Inez H. v6p0084c1s v6p0603c1s
Gillmore, J.C. v5p0445c1s v5p0446c1s
Gillmore, P. v2p0259c2s v3p0119c2s
Gillmore, Q.A. v1p0174c2s v1p0211c1s v1p0221c1s v1p0366c1s v1p1110c1s v2p0373c2s
Gillott, T. v1p1127c1s v1p1249c1s v2p0419c2s
Gillpatrick, W. v6p0414c2s
Gills, J.L. v3p0382c1s
Gillson, H.L. v5p0089c2s
Gillson, Wm.E. v2p0087c2s
Gilman, A. v1p0384c1s v1p0417c2s v1p0420c2s v1p0533c2s v1p0569c1s v1p0931c1s v1p1146c1s v1p1434c1s v2p0020c1s v3p0468c2m v4p0422c2s v4p0470c1s v6p0193c1s v6p0542c1s v6p0573c1s
Gilman, A.D. v1p0053c2s v1p0723c1s
Gilman, B. v4p0194c2s v5p0380c2s v5p0384c1s v5p0598c1s v6p0471c2s v6p0480c1s v6p0585c1s v6p0680c2s
Gilman, B., Mrs. v6p0072c2s
Gilman, B.I. v4p0106c2s v4p0389c2s v4p0414c1s v4p0421c1s v4p0447c1s v4p0465c1s v5p0005c1s
Gilman, C. v1p0339c1s
Gilman, C.R. v1p0835c2s
Gilman, Charlotte P. v5p0645c1s v6p0071c1s v6p0116c1s v6p0178c2m v6p0182c1m v6p0295c1s v6p0295c2s v6p0423c2s v6p0620c1s v6p0630c1s v6p0673c2s v6p0691c1s v6p0703c1s v6p0705c2s v6p0706c1s
Gilman, D.C. v1p0010c2m v1p0014c2s v1p0034c1s v1p0051c1s v1p0114c1s v1p0188c2s v1p0275c1s v1p0292c1s v1p0303c1s v1p0341c1s v1p0384c1s v1p0384c2s v1p0389c2m v1p0506c1m v1p0613c2s v1p0679c2s v1p0744c2s v1p0796c2s v1p0923c1s v1p0927c2s v1p0989c2s v1p1109c1m v1p1158c1s v1p1158c2s v1p1163c2s v1p1264c1s v1p1356c1s v1p1394c1s v1p1436c1m v2p0010c2m v2p0040c1s v2p0092c2m v2p0130c2s v2p0131c1s v2p0195c2s v2p0237c2s v2p0407c2s v2p0442c1s v2p0455c2s v2p0456c1s v3p0030c1s v3p0074c1s v3p0091c2s v3p0137c1s v3p0169c1m v3p0231c2s v3p0386c1s v3p0389c1s v4p0071c1s v4p0123c2s v4p0170c2m v4p0228c1s v5p0003c2s v5p0152c1s v5p0178c2s v5p0437c1s v5p0581c2s v5p0643c2s v6p0002c1s v6p0064c2s v6p0074c2s v6p0102c1m v6p0213c2s v6p0361c2s v6p0471c1s v6p0572c2s v6p0576c1s v6p0600c2s v6p0671c1s v6p0696c1s
Gilman, D.C. and Remsen, I. v6p0344c2s
Gilman, E. v5p0499c2s
Gilman, E.H. v6p0124c1s v6p0352c2s
Gilman, E.S. v5p0166c2s
Gilman, E.W. v1p0031c1s v1p0118c2m v1p0253c1s v1p0313c2m v1p0619c2s v1p0930c2s v1p1064c2s v1p1270c1s v1p1396c1s v3p0096c1s v3p0097c1s
Gilman, Elisabeth v5p0274c1s
Gilman, Eliz.H. v6p0124c2s v6p0295c2s
Gilman, F. v2p0425c2m v3p0346c1s
Gilman, F.G. v5p0317c1s
Gilman, J. v1p0274c1s
Gilman, J.B. v3p0234c1s v3p0275c1s
Gilman, L. v6p0392c1m v6p0404c2s v6p0437c2s v6p0620c2s v6p0683c1s
Gilman, Lawrence v6p0142c1s v6p0167c1s v6p0438c1s v6p0451c2s
Gilman, Leonie v6p0411c1s
Gilman, M.R.F. v3p0164c2s v3p0449c1s v5p0269c1s
Gilman, M.R.F., Mrs. v3p0433c2s
Gilman, N.P. v1p0426c2s v1p0434c1s v1p0434c2s v1p1275c2s v1p1304c1s v1p1341c1s v1p1353c2s v2p0220c1s v2p0324c1s v2p0356c2s v3p0012c1s v3p0035c2s v3p0038c2s v3p0091c1s v3p0128c2s v3p0214c2s v3p0296c2s v3p0345c2m v3p0398c2m v3p0446c1s v3p0449c2s v4p0152c1s v4p0448c1s v4p0461c1m v4p0531c2s v4p0620c1s v5p0053c1s v5p0136c1s v5p0194c2s v5p0535c2s
Gilman, N.P. and Toy, C.H. v5p0197c2s
Gilman, S. v1p0169c2m v1p0208c2s v1p0264c2s v1p0330c1s v1p0342c2s v1p0415c1s v1p0560c1s v1p0692c1s v1p0843c1s v1p0982c2s v1p0989c2s v1p1038c2s v1p1070c2s v1p1095c1s v1p1098c1s v1p1102c1s v1p1235c2s v1p1350c1s
Gilman, S.C. v4p0413c1s
Gilman, S.H. v1p1247c1s
Gilman, Sophia B. v5p0465c1s
Gilman, T. v4p0043c2s v4p0191c1s v4p0255c2s v6p0014c1s v6p0130c2s
Gilman, W. v3p0012c1s v3p0371c2s v4p0368c1s v4p0497c2s
Gilman, W.S. v1p0387c2s
Gilman, W.S., jr. v1p0077c1m v2p0129c2s
Gilmer, Eliz.M. v6p0155c1s
Gilmore, C.W. v6p0051c2m
Gilmore, D. v4p0077c2s
Gilmore, D.C. v3p0348c1s
Gilmore, E.A. v6p0321c1s v6p0516c1s
Gilmore, G.W. v3p0141c2s v4p0053c1s v4p0149c1s v5p0379c2s v6p0062c2s v6p0065c1s
Gilmore, J. v1p1082c1m v3p0024c1s v3p0107c1s v3p0384c2s v6p0400c2s
Gilmore, J.E. v4p0033c1s v4p0040c2s v4p0561c1s
Gilmore, J.H. v1p1186c2s v2p0058c2s v4p0343c2s v6p0079c1s
Gilmore, J.R. v1p0005c1s v1p0035c1s v1p0362c1s v1p0693c2s v1p0823c2s v1p1224c1s v1p1294c2s v1p1346c2s v2p0117c1s v2p0167c2s v2p0308c2s v2p0374c1s v2p0395c2s v2p0411c2s v3p0014c2s v3p0312c1s v3p0443c1s v3p0466c2s v4p0220c1s v4p0401c2s v5p0086c1s v5p0187c1s v5p0512c1s
Gilmore, James v5p0495c2s
Gilmore, M.S. v5p0311c2s v6p0346c2s
Gilmore, Q.A. v2p0333c2s
Gilmour, A.P. v6p0269c2s v6p0654c2s v6p0656c2s v6p0665c2s
Gilmour, G. v5p0338c1s
Gilmour, J. v2p0003c2s
Gilmour, J.H. v3p0196c2s
Gilmour, R. v3p0378c2s
Gilpatrick, M.S. v6p0391c2s v6p0682c1s
Gilpin, A. v6p0311c2s
Gilpin, H.D. v1p0986c1s
Gilpin, T. v1p0848c2s v4p0481c1s
Gilpin, T.E. v6p0226c1s
Gilpin, V. v6p0229c1s
Gilpin, W. v1p0628c1s v2p0454c1s
Gilray, T. v1p0163c2s
Gilroy, F. v6p0407c1s
Gilroy, T.F. v4p0401c1s
Gilsa, Baroness Von v5p0094c2s
Gilson, F.H. v5p0394c2s
Gilson, H.R. v6p0623c1s
Gilson, J.P. v4p0328c1s v5p0433c1s v5p0631c2s
Gilson, R.R. v5p0342c1s v5p0355c1s v5p0555c2s v6p0001c2s v6p0036c1s v6p0201c1s v6p0214c1s v6p0220c2s v6p0264c1s v6p0307c2s v6p0380c2s v6p0381c1s v6p0431c2s v6p0466c1s v6p0505c1s v6p0615c1s v6p0651c1s v6p0700c1s v6p0710c2s
Giltner, L. v5p0003c1s
Giltner, L.G. v5p0085c2s v5p0315c1s v5p0517c1s v6p0045c1s v6p0055c2s v6p0107c2s v6p0184c1s v6p0218c2s v6p0221c1s v6p0297c1s v6p0405c2s v6p0536c1s v6p0541c2s v6p0611c2s
Giltner, L.G. and Petrie, C.G. v6p0694c2s
Ginaodh, D. v4p0141c1s
Ginders, H.I. v6p0100c1s
Gindriez, C. v1p0968c2s v1p0970c2m

Ginger, M.C. v6p0330c2s
Gingrich, C.S. v6p0393c1s
v6p0417c2m
Ginn, E. v6p0573c1s
Ginsburg, B. v6p0591c2s
Ginsburg, B.W. v4p0100c1s
v5p0526c2s v6p0384c2s
Ginsburg, C.D. v1p0119c1s
v2p0042c2s v2p0043c1s v2p0043c2s
Ginsburg, G.D. v2p0398c2s
Ginty, E.B. v4p0088c1s
Ginwalla, N.S. v3p0211c1s
Ginzberg, L. v6p0021c2s
v6p0249c2s v6p0251c1s
Gioberti, V. v1p0976c2s
Gioskov, E. v6p0008c2s
v6p0238c1s
Giovannoli, H. v6p0087c2s
Girard, A.C. v5p0489c1s
Girard, Anatole v6p0220c1s
Girard, M. v1p0324c1s
v6p0153c1s
Girard, P. v1p0147c1s
v1p0198c1s v1p0243c2s v1p0353c2s
v1p0393c1s v1p0419c1s v1p0422c1s
v1p0638c1s v1p0640c1s v1p0697c1s
v1p0713c1s v1p0714c1s v1p0784c2s
v1p0797c1s v1p0912c2s v1p0963c1s
v1p0963c2s v1p1058c1s v1p1067c2s
v1p1117c2s v1p1215c2s v1p1348c2s
v1p1349c2s v1p1399c2s
Girardeau, C.M. v4p0617c2s
v5p0464c1s v5p0490c2s
Girardeaux, J.L. v4p0573c1s
Girardin, J.P.L. v1p0785c2s
Girardin, Mme.de v1p1427c1s
Giraud, P. v1p0448c2s
Giraud, T.E. v1p0052c2s
Girault, M.L. v6p0012c2s
Gird, Richard v6p0056c2s
Girdlestone, E. v1p0015c1m
v1p0251c1s v1p0721c2s
Girdlestone, R.B. v1p0691c2s
v1p1141c1s v5p0507c1s
Girdner, J.H. v4p0116c2s
v5p0134c2s v5p0232c1s v5p0277c2s
v5p0291c2s v5p0412c2m v5p0440c1s
v6p0121c2s v6p0199c1s v6p0247c2s
v6p0396c2s v6p0408c2s
Girdner, J.H. et al. v5p0259c2s
Girdner, J.M. v6p0231c1s
Girm-Hochberg, T. v5p0389c2s
v5p0637c2s
Girod, L. v5p0492c2s
Girod, W. v5p0195c1s
v5p0311c1s
Girouard, P., Sir v6p0006c1s
Girtin, T. v1p0904c2s
Girty, G.H. v5p0160c1s
v6p0489c1s v6p0657c1s
Gisborne, F.A.W. v6p0025c1s
v6p0633c2s
Gisborne, F.H. v3p0066c2s
Gissing, A. v4p0052c2s
v5p0331c2s
Gissing, G. v2p0339c2s
v3p0247c2s v3p0250c2s v3p0300c1s
v4p0088c2s v4p0127c2s v4p0149c1s
v4p0195c2s v4p0240c2s v4p0262c2s
v4p0276c2s v4p0286c1s v4p0337c2s
v4p0342c2s v4p0370c1s v4p0388c1s
v4p0418c2s v4p0437c1s v4p0448c2s
v4p0589c1s v5p0036c1s v5p0159c2s
v5p0186c1s v5p0272c1s v5p0295c1s
v5p0338c1s v5p0421c1s v5p0458c2s
v5p0516c1s v5p0545c2s v6p0043c1s
v6p0173c1s v6p0561c2s
Gissing, George v4p0527c1s
Gissler, C.F. v1p0299c2s
v2p0105c2s v2p0230c2s
Gist, M. v1p0295c2s
Gist, W.W. v3p0343c1s
v4p0293c1s v5p0279c1s
Githens, A.M. v5p0025c2s
Gitterman, J.M. v4p0401c1s
Gittermann, J.M. v4p0119c2s
v4p0400c2s
Gittings, E.B. v3p0194c1s
Gittings, Ella B. v4p0091c2s
Gittings, L. v4p0490c2s
v4p0543c1s
Gitzycki, G.von v2p0117c1s
Giuliano, C. v3p0230c2s
Giuseppi, M.S. v5p0404c2s
v6p0411c1s
Giusti, G. v1p1151c1s
Givens, Helen W. v6p0324c2s
Givens, L.M. v1p1245c1s
Givens, W.R. v6p0274c1s
v6p0365c1s v6p0609c1s v6p0684c1s
Givskov, E. v6p0253c2s
Givskov, Erik v6p0057c1s
Gizycki, G.von v2p0147c1s
v3p0250c2s v4p0111c2s v4p0149c2s
v4p0154c1s v4p0187c2s v4p0394c2s
Gjers, J. v1p1249c1s
Gladden, E.W. v4p0534c1s
Gladden, G. v4p0021c2s
v4p0137c1s v5p0532c1s
Gladden, W. v1p0147c1s
v1p0394c1s v1p0602c2s v1p0672c2s
v1p0741c2s v1p1304c1s v2p0003c2s
v2p0013c1s v2p0022c2s v2p0053c2s
v2p0081c1s v2p0081c2m v2p0120c1s
v2p0132c1s v2p0170c2s v2p0244c2m
v2p0245c1s v2p0297c2s v2p0331c2s
v2p0407c1m v2p0408c1s v2p0468c2s
v3p0114c2s v3p0127c1s v3p0149c2s
v3p0194c2s v3p0341c1s v3p0397c2m
v3p0398c1s v3p0398c2s v3p0414c1s
v4p0011c1s v4p0015c1s v4p0067c1s
v4p0097c1s v4p0111c2s v4p0112c1s
v4p0116c2s v4p0134c2s v4p0135c2s
v4p0191c1s v4p0283c1s v4p0351c2s
v4p0455c2s v4p0461c1s v4p0467c1s
v4p0478c1m v4p0530c2s v4p0531c2s
v4p0532c2m v5p0018c1s v5p0115c1s
v5p0131c1s v5p0192c2s v5p0289c1s
v5p0310c1s v5p0440c1s v5p0471c2m
v5p0484c1s v5p0536c1s v5p0536c2s
v5p0543c2s v5p0603c1s v6p0013c1s
v6p0122c2s v6p0546c1s
Gladden, W. et al. v2p0205c1s
v3p0083c2s
Gladden, Washington v6p0084c1s
v6p0125c1s v6p0546c1s
Gladdish, W.L. v5p0307c1s
Gladhill, J.T. v3p0374c2s
v4p0154c1s v4p0190c2s v5p0236c2s
v5p0463c2s
Gladish, W.L. v5p0221c1s
v5p0520c2s v6p0061c2s v6p0526c1s
Gladstone, A. v6p0041c1s
v6p0147c2s
Gladstone, F.M. v4p0228c1s
Gladstone, H.J. v3p0211c2s
v4p0428c1s
Gladstone, J.H. v1p0322c1s
v1p0443c2s v1p0748c2s v1p1015c1s
v1p1268c2s v2p0076c2s v2p0132c1s
v2p0138c2s v2p0258c2s v2p0367c2m
v2p0446c1s v3p0380c1s v3p0380c2s
v3p0422c2s v4p0026c1s v5p0054c2s
v5p0104c1s v5p0136c2s v5p0222c1s
v5p0371c2s
Gladstone, J.H. and Tribe, A.
v2p0137c2s
Gladstone, Mary v2p0008c1s
Gladstone, T.M. v3p0013c1s
v3p0062c1s
Gladstone, W.E. v1p0004c1s
v1p0019c1s v1p0081c2s v1p0105c2s
v1p0150c2s v1p0251c1s v1p0278c2s
v1p0288c1s v1p0308c2s v1p0379c1s
v1p0394c2s v1p0395c2s v1p0398c2s
v1p0408c2s v1p0413c2s v1p0432c1s
v1p0483c1s v1p0486c2s v1p0549c2s
v1p0551c2s v1p0552c1s v1p0552c2s
v1p0600c1m v1p0600c2m v1p0601c1m
v1p0663c1s v1p0685c2s v1p0737c2s
v1p0741c2s v1p0781c1s v1p0863c2s
v1p0938c1s v1p0941c2s v1p0942c1s
v1p0944c1s v1p0979c2s v1p1053c2s
v1p1076c2s v1p1081c1s v1p1090c1s
v1p1092c2s v1p1097c2s v1p1109c2s
v1p1134c1s v1p1135c1m v1p1294c2s
v1p1330c1m v1p1333c2s v1p1341c2s
v1p1360c2s v1p1370c1s v1p1406c1s
v2p0106c2m v2p0172c2s v2p0369c1s
v2p0371c1s v2p0395c1s v3p0016c1s
v3p0025c1s v3p0035c1s v3p0040c2s
v3p0041c1m v3p0042c1s v3p0049c1s
v3p0054c2s v3p0081c1s v3p0081c2s
v3p0083c1m v3p0083c2s v3p0104c1s
v3p0135c1s v3p0138c1s v3p0138c2s
v3p0141c1s v3p0158c2s v3p0162c1s
v3p0165c2s v3p0166c1s v3p0181c2s
v3p0182c2s v3p0183c1m v3p0184c2s
v3p0185c2s v3p0194c2s v3p0197c2s
v3p0199c2m v3p0205c2s v3p0219c2s
v3p0220c1m v3p0220c2s v3p0222c1m
v3p0225c1s v3p0225c2s v3p0245c2s
v3p0273c2s v3p0289c1s v3p0292c2s
v3p0310c1s v3p0340c1s v3p0360c2s
v3p0402c2s v3p0425c1s v3p0454c2s
v3p0458c1s v4p0027c1s v4p0028c2s
v4p0041c2s v4p0052c1s v4p0081c1m
v4p0147c1s v4p0189c1s v4p0189c2s
v4p0218c1s v4p0254c1s v4p0255c2s
v4p0261c2s v4p0263c1s v4p0329c2s
v4p0352c2s v4p0413c1s v4p0448c2s
v4p0505c1s v4p0520c2s v4p0548c2s
v4p0557c1s v4p0603c1s v5p0173c2s
v5p0268c2s
Gladstone, W.E. and Blaine, J.G.
v3p0162c2s
Gladstone, W.E. and Lecky, W.E.H.
v3p0210c2s
Gladstone, W.E. and Morley, J.
v4p0028c1s
Gladstone, W.E. et al. ... v3p0119c1s
v3p0454c2s v4p0027c2s
Gladstonian M.P., A. v3p0182c2s
Glagg, P.J. v4p0021c1s
Glaisher, J. v1p0008c1s
v1p0073c2s v1p0088c2m v1p0089c1m
v1p0266c1s v1p1293c1s v2p0032c1s
v2p0192c1s v2p0406c2s
Glaisher, J.W.L. v1p0339c2s
v1p0810c2s v2p0280c1m v2p0405c2m
v5p0157c2s
Glaisher, J.W.L. and Foster, G.C.
v3p0350c2s
Glamis, Cecelia, Lady v5p0235c1s
Glancey, M.F. v6p0191c1s
Glangeaud, P. v5p0064c1s
Glanville, E. v6p0069c2s
Glanville, F.B. v1p0012c2s
Glanville, W.E. v4p0323c1s
v5p0327c2s
Glardon, A. v3p0359c2s
Glardon, M.A. v3p0119c2s
Glascock, J.L. v4p0152c2s
Glascock, M.W. v2p0199c2s
v3p0036c2s v4p0590c1s
Glase, A.E. v5p0174c1s
v5p0348c2s v5p0388c1s
Glaser, L. v2p0015c1s
Glaser, O.C. v6p0045c1s
v6p0047c1s v6p0713c2s
Glasgow, A.G. v5p0226c2s
Glasgow, E. v5p0055c1s
v5p0220c1s v5p0456c2s
Glasgow, James. v6p0051c2s
Glasgow, W.A. v6p0483c2s
Glashaw, J.C. v2p0319c1s
Glaspell, S.K. v6p0045c2s
v6p0232c1s v6p0240c1s v6p0311c1s
v6p0397c2s
Glaspell, Susan K. v6p0301c1s
Glass, G.H. v1p0491c1s
v1p1150c1s
Glass, H.A. v4p0049c1s
v4p0112c1s v4p0567c1s v5p0047c2s
Glass, M. v6p0245c2s
Glass, M. and Johnston, H.M.
v6p0058c1s
Glass, Montague v6p0103c1s
Glassco, H.B. v5p0339c2s
Glassel, W.T. v1p0221c1s
Glassford, W.A. v5p0005c1s
v5p0044c1s v5p0460c1s v6p0693c1s
Glasson, W.H. v5p0572c2s
v6p0137c1s v6p0391c1s v6p0447c2s
v6p0488c1m v6p0529c2s v6p0533c2s
v6p0663c1s
Glauding, W.M.B. v4p0372c2s
Glave, E.J. v3p0096c1m
v3p0151c2s v3p0395c1s v4p0005c2s
v4p0009c1s v4p0228c1s v4p0409c2s
v5p0005c2s v5p0132c2s
Glazebrook, H. v4p0432c2s
Glazebrook, R.T. v2p0098c1s
v2p0322c2s v5p0330c2s v5p0399c2s
v5p0426c1s v5p0449c1s v5p0498c1s
v5p0554c1s v5p0561c1s v6p0256c1s
v6p0258c2s v6p0468c2s
Glazier, W.B. v1p0732c2s
Gleadell, W.H. v3p0051c2s
v3p0358c2s v4p0043c1s v4p0106c1s
v4p0343c2s v4p0501c2s v4p0636c1s
v4p0637c1s v6p0160c2s
Gleason, A. and Gleason, E.
v4p0523c2s
Gleason, A.H. v6p0044c1s
v6p0044c2s v6p0124c2s v6p0298c2s
v6p0360c1s v6p0422c2s v6p0450c2s
v6p0507c2s v6p0527c2s v6p0554c1s
v6p0562c1s v6p0633c2s
Gleason, A.W. v6p0209c1s
Gleason, Arthur H. v6p0104c1s
v6p0189c1s v6p0599c1s
Gleason, C.W. v4p0123c1s
Gleason, Caroline F. v6p0499c1s
Gleason, E. and Gleason, A.
v4p0523c2s
Gleason, H.W. v5p0202c2s
v5p0449c1s v5p0455c1s
Gleason, W.W. v4p0597c1s
Gledhill, E. v1p0825c2s
Gledhill, H.R. v3p0190c2s
Gledstone, J.P. v1p1406c2s
Gleed, C.S. v4p0035c1s
v4p0428c2s v4p0526c2s v4p0617c1m
v4p0636c2s v5p0223c1s v5p0313c2m
v5p0552c1s
Gleed, C.S. et al. v6p0100c2s
Gleed, J.W. v3p0289c1m
v3p0460c2s v4p0308c1s v4p0401c1s
Gleeson, J.M. v6p0022c1s
v6p0182c2s v6p0246c1s v6p0472c2s
v6p0512c2s
Gleeson, J.M. and Knight, C.R.
v6p0246c1s
Gleeson, M. and Knight, C.R.
v6p0368c1s
Glegg, A.T. v5p0641c1s
Glehn, M.von v3p0201c2s
Glehn, O.von v5p0156c2s
Gleichen, Count v3p0304c2s
v4p0586c2s
Gleichen, Gen. v5p0244c1s
Gleig, A. v6p0597c2s
Gleig, A.C. v4p0246c2s
Gleig, C. v4p0238c1s
v4p0287c1s v5p0405c2s v6p0032c1s
Gleig, G.K. v1p0785c2s
Gleig, G.R. v1p0030c1s
v1p0059c2s v1p0162c1s v1p0176c2s
v1p0215c1s v1p0224c1s v1p0341c1s

v1p0542c2s v1p0543c2s v1p0624c2s
v1p0629c1s v1p0673c1s v1p0838c1m
v1p0841c1s v1p1066c1s v1p1066c2s
v1p1101c2s v1p1166c2s v1p1218c2s
v1p1230c1s v1p1263c1m v1p1303c2s
v1p1337c2s v2p0185c2s
Glen, C.V. v5p0390c1s
Glen, C.Y. v5p0586c1s
Glen, Catherine Y. v6p0701c2s
Glen, F.W. v4p0085c1s
Glendon, G. v6p0111c1s
v6p0225c1s
Glenelg, P. v4p0269c1s
Glenesk, A. v5p0347c1s
Glenn, D.C. v1p0853c2s
Glenn, E.F. v3p0278c2s
v3p0281c2s
Glenn, G.P. v6p0575c1s
Glenn, J. v4p0064c1s
Glenn, J.M. v5p0102c1s
Glenn, J.M. et al. v4p0081c1s
Glenn, J.W. v1p1019c1s
Glenn, L.C. v4p0147c2s
v5p0541c1m
Glenn, S.F. v1p0133c1s
v1p0306c2s v1p1195c2s
Glenn, T.A. v3p0203c2s
v3p0315c2s
Glenn, W. v3p0082c1s
Glennie, J.S.S. v1p0065c1s
v1p0590c2s v1p0594c2s v1p0784c2s
v1p1165c1s v2p0288c2s v2p0385c1s
v3p0023c1s v3p0434c2s v4p0517c2s
v5p0417c1s
Glennie, J.S.S. and Blackley, W.L.
v1p0898c1s
Glennie, J.S.S. and Fawcett, M.Y.
v3p0470c1s
Glenny-Crory, W. v4p0290c1s
v4p0290c2s v4p0430c2s
Glenton, E. v5p0229c2s
Glessner, R.W. v6p0255c1s
Glidden, C.H. v4p0325c2s
v5p0643c1s
Glidden, C.J. v6p0044c2s
Glidden, M.M. v5p0316c1s
Glidden, Minnie M. v5p0178c2s
Gliddon, W.A. v1p0635c2m
Glieg, G.R. v2p0470c1s
Glines, J. v1p0425c1s
v1p0846c1s
Gloag, P.J. v3p0001c1s
v3p0043c2s v3p0112c2s v3p0208c1s
v3p0229c1m v3p0229c2s v3p0231c1s
v3p0233c2s v3p0255c2s v3p0348c1s
v3p0355c2s v3p0360c1s v3p0466c1s
v4p0301c1s v4p0352c1s v4p0380c1s
v4p0384c1s v4p0490c1s v4p0601c2s
v5p0059c1s
Gloag, W.M. v5p0143c2s
Glogau, G. v1p1061c2s
Glouvet, J.de v4p0454c2s
Glover, A.K. v2p0221c2s
v4p0013c1s v5p0016c2s v5p0060c2s
v5p0113c1s v5p0307c1s v5p0307c2s
v6p0515c1s
Glover, A.K., Rev. v5p0307c2s
Glover, C.H. v1p1188c1s
Glover, E.C. v3p0172c2s
Glover, F. v4p0091c1s
Glover, G. v1p0501c2s
v3p0168c1s
Glover, J. v2p0442c2s
v5p0619c1s v6p0649c2s
Glover, J.R. v4p0392c2s
Glover, L.B. v6p0181c2s
Glover, Marguerite v6p0336c2s
Glover, S.E. v3p0058c1s
Glover, T. v1p0307c1s
Gluckenberger, B. v5p0002c1s
Glumen, F.B.von v2p0286c2s
Glunicke, G.J.R. v6p0354c2s
Glyde, T. v2p0223c2s
Glyn, C. v4p0161c2s
Glyn, Coralie v4p0407c2s
Glyn, E.C. v4p0171c2s
v5p0180c1s
Glyn, S.C.C. v4p0505c1s
Glyndon, H. v1p0245c2s
Glynne, S. v5p0171c2s
Gmeiner, J. v2p0059c2s
v2p0380c2s v2p0415c1s v3p0114c2s
v3p0175c2s v3p0364c1s v3p0364c2s
v3p0428c2s
Gmelin, L. v5p0026c1s
Gneist, R. v2p0040c2s
v2p0302c1s v2p0358c1s
Gnoli, U. v6p0409c1s
Gnoli, U. et al. v6p0648c1s
Goad, T.W. v3p0176c1s
v3p0393c2s
Goadby, E. v1p0138c2s
v1p0263c2s v1p0544c2s v1p0732c2s
v1p0736c1s v1p1112c1s v1p1260c1s
v4p0232c2s
Goadby, H. v1p0041c1s
v1p1048c1s
Gobel, M. v1p0941c2s
v1p1359c1s
Godalming v5p0491c1s
Godard, G.S. v6p0615c1s
Godard, J.C. v6p0141c2s
Godard, J.G. v4p0564c2s
v6p0058c1s v6p0187c2s v6p0267c1s
v6p0310c1m v6p0370c1s
Godbey, A.H. v6p0063c1s
v6p0128c1s v6p0277c1s v6p0279c1m
v6p0355c1s v6p0475c2s v6p0592c2s
Goddard, A. v3p0151c2s
v4p0352c2s v5p0048c1s
Goddard, A.E. v4p0559c2s
v5p0056c2s v5p0636c2s
Goddard, A.F. v2p0224c1s
Goddard, D. v6p0431c1s
v6p0585c1s
Goddard, E. v3p0410c2s
v6p0589c1s
Goddard, E.C. v4p0223c1s
v5p0374c1m
Goddard, E.H. v4p0134c2s
v5p0632c2s v6p0027c1s
Goddard, E.N. v2p0155c1s
v2p0256c1s
Goddard, F.B. v2p0110c2s
v3p0130c2s
Goddard, G.F. v1p0557c2s
v1p1012c2s
Goddard, H.C. v6p0610c2s
Goddard, H.H. v5p0202c1s
v6p0252c1s
Goddard, H.P. v1p0334c1s
v3p0387c2s v4p0263c2s v5p0128c2s
v6p0255c2s
Goddard, J. v1p0365c1s
v1p0539c1s v1p0606c1s v1p0693c1s
v1p0930c2s v1p0937c2s v1p0940c2s
v1p0942c1s v1p1204c2s v4p0229c1s
v4p0559c2s v4p0625c2s v6p0020c1s
v6p0043c1s v6p0062c1s v6p0062c2s
v6p0165c2s v6p0189c2s v6p0192c2s
v6p0238c2s v6p0402c1s v6p0603c1s
Goddard, J. and Weber, C.. v1p0246c1s
Goddard, M.Le Baron v1p0733c1s
v1p1030c1s
Goddard, P.E. v6p0361c1s
v6p0362c1s
Goddard, W. v4p0527c1s
v5p0140c1s v5p0338c1s v5p0363c2s
v5p0483c1s v6p0175c1s v6p0621c1s
Goddard, W.G. v1p0169c2s
v1p0797c1s
Godden, G.M. v4p0357c1s
v4p0385c2s v5p0001c2s v5p0286c1s
Godden, Gertrude M. v4p0280c1s
Godding, W.W. et al. v2p0150c2s
Goden, H.von v5p0054c1s
Godet, F. v1p0129c1s
v1p0794c2s v2p0017c1s v4p0057c1s
v4p0301c1s v4p0431c1s
Godet, F. and Plumptre, E.H.
v2p0478c1s
Godet, M. v2p0154c1s
Godfernaux, A. v5p0169c1s
Godfrey, A.H. v5p0097c2s
v5p0150c2m v5p0151c1m v5p0215c2s
v5p0271c1s v5p0406c1s v5p0458c1s
Godfrey, C. v6p0251c1s
Godfrey, C.E. v6p0088c2s
Godfrey, E. v4p0040c1s
Godfrey, E.S. v4p0145c1s
v5p0098c2s
Godfrey, Eliz. v6p0056c1s
Godfrey, G.W., Mrs. v1p0076c2s
v1p0105c2s v2p0161c2s v2p0239c2s
v2p0301c1s v2p0360c1s v2p0456c1s
Godfrey, H. v5p0316c2s
v5p0390c1s v6p0128c2s v6p0585c1s
v6p0687c2s
Godfrey, H.H. v5p0324c1s
v5p0406c1s v5p0583c1s
Godfrey, J.E. v1p0204c2s
v1p0637c1s v1p0988c1s v1p1143c1s
Godfrey, M.R. v1p0359c1s
Godfrey, T. v6p0378c2s
Godfrey, Winona v5p0425c2s
Godkin, C.S. v2p0201c2s
Godkin, E.L. v1p0009c2s
v1p0011c1s v1p0017c2m v1p0018c1m
v1p0032c1m v1p0043c2m v1p0050c2s
v1p0058c1s v1p0058c2s v1p0064c2s
v1p0067c2s v1p0076c2s v1p0084c1s
v1p0090c2s v1p0092c1s v1p0092c2m
v1p0097c2m v1p0099c2s v1p0103c2s
v1p0110c1s v1p0119c2s v1p0133c2s
v1p0144c1s v1p0145c1s v1p0147c2s
v1p0148c2s v1p0155c2s v1p0168c1s
v1p0177c2s v1p0179c2s v1p0180c2s
v1p0183c2s v1p0184c1s v1p0185c1s
v1p0187c1s v1p0193c1s v1p0198c1m
v1p0198c2m v1p0201c2m v1p0205c1s
v1p0208c2m v1p0209c2s v1p0219c1s
v1p0231c2s v1p0235c1m v1p0235c2s
v1p0237c1s v1p0248c1m v1p0253c2s
v1p0255c1s v1p0257c1s v1p0258c1m
v1p0258c2m v1p0259c1m v1p0264c1s
v1p0264c2s v1p0269c2s v1p0271c1s
v1p0275c1s v1p0275c2s v1p0276c1m
v1p0276c2s v1p0282c1s v1p0284c1s
v1p0285c2m v1p0286c1m v1p0287c1s
v1p0289c2s v1p0291c2m v1p0296c1s
v1p0299c1s v1p0299c2s v1p0300c2m
v1p0301c1s v1p0304c1s v1p0308c1s
v1p0313c2m v1p0314c1s v1p0317c1s
v1p0322c2s v1p0323c1s v1p0323c2m
v1p0325c1s v1p0325c2m v1p0326c1m
v1p0326c2s v1p0327c1s v1p0335c1s
v1p0342c2s v1p0343c1m v1p0344c2s
v1p0351c1s v1p0353c1s v1p0353c2m
v1p0379c1m v1p0379c2m v1p0380c1m
v1p0382c2s v1p0384c2m v1p0385c2s
v1p0387c2s v1p0393c1s v1p0397c1m
v1p0398c1s v1p0406c1s v1p0406c2s
v1p0417c1s v1p0433c2s v1p0437c2s
v1p0442c2s v1p0444c2s v1p0445c2s
v1p0447c1s v1p0448c2m v1p0451c2s
v1p0453c1m v1p0458c1s v1p0461c2s
v1p0467c1s v1p0467c2m v1p0477c2m
v1p0478c1m v1p0478c2m v1p0479c1s
v1p0479c2s v1p0480c1s v1p0480c2m
v1p0481c1m v1p0481c2s v1p0486c2s
v1p0487c1s v1p0489c1s v1p0494c1s
v1p0498c2s v1p0500c1m v1p0504c2m
v1p0515c2s v1p0525c1s v1p0538c1m
v1p0540c1m v1p0540c2m v1p0543c1s
v1p0545c1s v1p0546c2s v1p0547c1s
v1p0549c2s v1p0550c1s v1p0553c2s
v1p0556c1s v1p0569c1s v1p0571c1s
v1p0572c2s v1p0576c1m v1p0584c2s
v1p0601c2s v1p0604c2s v1p0605c1s
v1p0610c1s v1p0613c2s v1p0618c1s
v1p0626c1s v1p0628c1m v1p0637c2m
v1p0640c1s v1p0649c2s v1p0650c1s
v1p0650c2m v1p0654c2s v1p0656c1s
v1p0656c2s v1p0657c1m v1p0657c2m
v1p0658c1s v1p0658c2s v1p0659c1s
v1p0660c2s v1p0661c2s v1p0672c2s
v1p0693c2m v1p0696c1s v1p0696c2m
v1p0698c1s v1p0710c1s v1p0713c2m
v1p0714c2m v1p0715c1m v1p0720c2s
v1p0721c1m v1p0721c2s v1p0735c1m
v1p0737c2s v1p0740c2s v1p0741c1s
v1p0741c2s v1p0757c1s v1p0758c1s
v1p0767c1s v1p0772c1s v1p0772c2m
v1p0778c2s v1p0779c1s v1p0784c2s
v1p0789c2s v1p0797c2s v1p0802c1s
v1p0819c2s v1p0830c2s v1p0832c1s
v1p0833c2s v1p0847c2s v1p0848c2s
v1p0860c1s v1p0860c2s v1p0861c1s
v1p0865c1s v1p0869c1s v1p0869c2s
v1p0873c1s v1p0880c2m v1p0886c1s
v1p0896c1m v1p0897c2m v1p0905c1m
v1p0905c2m v1p0906c1s v1p0906c2s
v1p0913c2s v1p0914c1m v1p0917c2s
v1p0922c1s v1p0924c2s v1p0931c1s
v1p0937c1s v1p0944c2s v1p0945c2s
v1p0946c1s v1p0950c1s v1p0962c1s
v1p0963c2m v1p0964c2s v1p0965c1s
v1p0965c2s v1p0967c1s v1p0968c2s
v1p0974c2m v1p0976c2s v1p0983c1m
v1p0984c1s v1p0993c2s v1p0997c1s
v1p0998c2s v1p1013c1m v1p1018c1s
v1p1025c1s v1p1026c1m v1p1026c2s
v1p1027c2s v1p1028c1m v1p1028c2m
v1p1029c1s v1p1030c1s v1p1032c2s
v1p1034c2s v1p1035c2s v1p1039c1s
v1p1048c1m v1p1048c2m v1p1049c2s
v1p1052c2s v1p1055c1s v1p1057c2m
v1p1060c2s v1p1061c1m v1p1064c2s
v1p1066c1s v1p1074c1m v1p1078c2s
v1p1080c2s v1p1083c2s v1p1087c1m
v1p1099c2s v1p1100c1m v1p1101c1m
v1p1102c2s v1p1104c2s v1p1106c1s
v1p1106c2s v1p1108c2s v1p1109c2s
v1p1110c2s v1p1115c1s v1p1115c2s
v1p1117c1s v1p1131c1s v1p1135c2s
v1p1145c2m v1p1148c1m v1p1148c2s
v1p1149c2s v1p1159c2s v1p1161c1s
v1p1163c2s v1p1179c2m v1p1182c1m
v1p1197c1s v1p1198c1m v1p1198c2m
v1p1199c1m v1p1204c2s v1p1214c1m
v1p1215c1m v1p1215c2s v1p1216c1s
v1p1217c2s v1p1223c2s v1p1224c1m
v1p1225c1s v1p1225c2m v1p1228c1s
v1p1228c2s v1p1229c2s v1p1230c1m
v1p1232c1m v1p1232c2m v1p1234c2s
v1p1235c2s v1p1242c2s v1p1245c1m
v1p1253c2m v1p1261c1m v1p1261c2s
v1p1264c2m v1p1265c1s v1p1267c1m
v1p1272c1m v1p1281c2s v1p1282c1m
v1p1283c1m v1p1283c2m v1p1285c2m
v1p1290c2s v1p1292c1s v1p1292c2m
v1p1303c1s v1p1305c2s v1p1311c1m
v1p1323c1s v1p1323c2m v1p1330c1m
v1p1331c1m v1p1332c1s v1p1332c2m
v1p1334c2m v1p1336c2s v1p1342c1s
v1p1344c1s v1p1345c1s v1p1348c1s
v1p1349c1s v1p1353c1m v1p1354c1s
v1p1355c1s v1p1357c1s v1p1357c2m
v1p1363c1m v1p1374c2s v1p1378c1s
v1p1378c2m v1p1379c2m v1p1380c1s
v1p1382c1s v1p1383c2s v1p1385c1s
v1p1401c2s v1p1407c2s v1p1419c2s
v1p1420c1m v1p1420c2m v1p1421c1s
v1p1421c2s v1p1424c1s v1p1425c1m
v1p1425c2s v1p1426c1m v1p1426c2s
v1p1436c1m v2p0018c1s v2p0024c1s
v2p0034c1s v2p0038c2s v2p0049c1m
v2p0051c1s v2p0072c1s v2p0073c1s
v2p0075c2s v2p0079c2m v2p0084c1s
v2p0086c1s v2p0086c2m v2p0087c1m

v2p0089c1s v2p0091c1s v2p0092c2m
v2p0093c1s v2p0099c1s v2p0101c2s
v2p0103c2s v2p0115c1s v2p0121c1s
v2p0125c1s v2p0130c2s v2p0134c1m
v2p0134c2s v2p0151c2s v2p0164c2m
v2p0165c1s v2p0167c2s v2p0168c1s
v2p0170c2s v2p0171c1s v2p0176c1s
v2p0176c2m v2p0179c2s v2p0183c1s
v2p0184c1s v2p0187c2m v2p0188c2m
v2p0189c1s v2p0193c1m v2p0193c2s
v2p0206c1s v2p0207c1s v2p0207c2m
v2p0208c1s v2p0224c1s v2p0224c2m
v2p0225c1s v2p0225c2m v2p0226c1s
v2p0227c1s v2p0227c2s v2p0228c2m
v2p0238c2s v2p0241c2s v2p0242c2s
v2p0243c2m v2p0245c2s v2p0248c1s
v2p0248c2s v2p0255c1s v2p0263c2s
v2p0267c2m v2p0282c2s v2p0286c2s
v2p0290c2s v2p0294c1s v2p0298c1s
v2p0306c2s v2p0312c2s v2p0314c1s
v2p0319c2s v2p0323c2s v2p0327c2s
v2p0329c2s v2p0331c1m v2p0337c1s
v2p0348c2s v2p0349c1s v2p0349c2s
v2p0353c2m v2p0355c1s v2p0362c2s
v2p0365c2s v2p0370c2s v2p0384c1s
v2p0400c2s v2p0403c1s v2p0411c1m
v2p0412c1s v2p0413c1s v2p0420c2m
v2p0422c2s v2p0423c1m v2p0432c2s
v2p0433c1m v2p0434c1s v2p0437c1s
v2p0451c2s v2p0452c2m v2p0453c2s
v2p0454c1s v2p0454c2m v2p0455c2s
v2p0465c1s v2p0471c1s v2p0472c1s
v2p0473c1s v2p0477c2s v2p0478c1s
v3p0005c1s v3p0013c1m v3p0017c1s
v3p0025c2s v3p0031c2s v3p0034c2m
v3p0037c2s v3p0046c2s v3p0047c1s
v3p0052c1m v3p0078c1m v3p0085c2m
v3p0086c2s v3p0088c1m v3p0088c2s
v3p0091c2s v3p0093c1s v3p0099c1s
v3p0100c1m v3p0102c2s v3p0103c2s
v3p0105c1s v3p0114c1s v3p0115c2s
v3p0116c2s v3p0142c1s v3p0146c1s
v3p0149c2s v3p0152c1s v3p0157c1s
v3p0161c2s v3p0165c1s v3p0172c1s
v3p0174c1m v3p0179c1s v3p0185c2s
v3p0199c1s v3p0208c2s v3p0209c1m
v3p0214c2s v3p0220c2s v3p0224c1s
v3p0225c2m v3p0232c2s v3p0233c1s
v3p0237c1s v3p0237c2s v3p0238c2s
v3p0241c1s v3p0248c1s v3p0271c1s
v3p0273c2s v3p0285c2s v3p0291c2s
v3p0299c1m v3p0302c2m v3p0303c1s
v3p0304c1s v3p0306c2s v3p0310c1s
v3p0312c2s v3p0322c1m v3p0324c2s
v3p0325c1s v3p0332c2s v3p0336c2s
v3p0337c2m v3p0345c2s v3p0349c1m
v3p0353c2s v3p0362c2s v3p0368c2s
v3p0369c2s v3p0371c1s v3p0374c1s
v3p0397c2s v3p0399c1m v3p0399c2s
v3p0401c2s v3p0406c2s v3p0412c2s
v3p0414c2s v3p0415c2s v3p0419c2m
v3p0420c1s v3p0425c2s v3p0430c2s
v3p0434c1m v3p0443c2m v3p0444c1s
v3p0449c1s v3p0462c1s v3p0469c1s
v4p0006c1s v4p0013c1s v4p0017c1s
v4p0027c1m v4p0035c2m v4p0042c1s
v4p0049c2s v4p0059c2s v4p0069c1s
v4p0090c2s v4p0095c1s v4p0104c2s
v4p0106c1s v4p0107c2s v4p0115c1s
v4p0131c1s v4p0137c2m v4p0144c1s
v4p0152c1s v4p0156c2s v4p0168c2s
v4p0172c2s v4p0174c1s v4p0177c2s
v4p0180c2s v4p0183c1s v4p0183c2s
v4p0189c2s v4p0192c2s v4p0199c1s
v4p0206c2m v4p0207c1s v4p0216c2s
v4p0224c2s v4p0227c2m v4p0230c2s
v4p0237c2s v4p0238c2s v4p0250c2s
v4p0251c1m v4p0266c1s v4p0273c2s
v4p0274c1s v4p0275c1s v4p0275c2s
v4p0277c2s v4p0288c1s v4p0289c2s
v4p0290c1s v4p0302c1s v4p0305c1s
v4p0310c2s v4p0326c2s v4p0328c2s
v4p0346c1m v4p0362c1s v4p0377c2s
v4p0379c2m v4p0395c2s v4p0400c1s
v4p0402c2s v4p0423c2s v4p0430c2s
v4p0436c1s v4p0449c2s v4p0450c2s
v4p0454c2s v4p0460c1s v4p0462c2s
v4p0468c2m v4p0483c2s v4p0491c2s
v4p0495c2s v4p0501c1m v4p0514c2s
v4p0515c1s v4p0524c2s v4p0525c2s
v4p0531c2s v4p0534c1m v4p0553c2s
v4p0556c1s v4p0562c2s v4p0563c1s
v4p0582c1s v4p0591c1s v4p0595c1m
v4p0595c2s v4p0596c1s v4p0600c1s
v4p0602c1m v4p0610c1s v4p0611c1s
v4p0626c1s v5p0004c2s v5p0040c1s
v5p0089c2s v5p0100c2s v5p0111c1s
v5p0115c1s v5p0119c2s v5p0120c2m
v5p0122c2m v5p0128c1s v5p0128c2s
v5p0131c2s v5p0132c1s v5p0133c1s
v5p0142c2m v5p0143c2s v5p0145c2s
v5p0150c1s v5p0158c1s v5p0158c2s
v5p0163c2s v5p0168c2s v5p0177c1s
v5p0190c2s v5p0191c2m v5p0198c2m
v5p0210c1s v5p0217c2s v5p0220c2s
v5p0247c2s v5p0258c2s v5p0265c1s
v5p0277c1s v5p0281c1s v5p0300c2s
v5p0326c2s v5p0330c1s v5p0341c1s
v5p0345c2s v5p0375c1m v5p0399c2s
v5p0413c1s v5p0417c1s v5p0422c2s
v5p0432c2s v5p0443c2s v5p0446c1s
v5p0457c2s v5p0471c2s v5p0489c2s
v5p0507c2s v5p0513c1s v5p0516c2s
v5p0543c1s v5p0600c1s v5p0617c2s
v5p0618c1m v5p0618c2s v5p0620c1s
v5p0625c1s
Godkin, E.L. and Almy, C., jr.
v1p0195c1s v1p0457c2s
Godkin, E.L. and Clark, E.P.
v3p0036c1s
Godkin, E.L. and Garrison, W.P.
v1p0540c2m
Godkin, E.L. and Hewitt, A.S.
v1p0871c1s
Godkin, E.L. and Holland, H.W.
v1p0199c2s v1p0960c1s
Godkin, E.L. and Laugel, A.
v1p0481c1s
Godkin, E.L. and Macvane, S.M.
v4p0602c1s
Godkin, E.L. and Pomeroy, J.N.
v1p0322c2s v1p1375c1s
Godkin, E.L. and Sedgwick, A.G.
v1p0504c2s v2p0414c1s v2p0420c2s
Godkin, E.L. and White, H.
v2p0068c1s
Godkin, E.L. and Wright, C.
v1p0839c1s
Godkin, G.G. v5p0263c1s
Godkin, G.S. v1p0328c1s
v2p0011c2s v2p0012c2s v2p0040c2s
v2p0171c2s v2p0246c2s v2p0304c1s
v3p0071c1s v3p0124c1s v3p0225c1s
v4p0445c1s v5p0202c1s v6p0543c1s
Godkin, J. v1p0448c2s
v1p0653c1m v1p0653c2m v1p0657c2s
v1p0659c1s
Godl, F. v3p0171c1s
Godley, A.D. v4p0420c1s
v5p0074c2s v5p0190c1s v5p0426c2s
v5p0614c2s v6p0032c2s
Godley, A.D. and Smith, J.G.
v5p0426c1s
Godley, E.C. v5p0548c1s
v5p0573c2s v5p0634c2s v6p0078c1s
v6p0115c2s v6p0183c2s v6p0427c1s
v6p0588c1s
Godley, Eveline v6p0054c1s
Godley, Eveline C. v5p0497c2s
v6p0181c1m
Godman, Dr. v1p1017c1s
Godman, Inez A. v6p0467c2s
Godman, J.D. v1p0106c1m
Godman, W.D. v1p0254c1s
Godowsky, Leopold v5p0394c1s
Godsall, M.B. v4p0183c1s
v4p0492c2s
Godsby, H.F. v6p0223c2s
Godsell, D.A. v5p0015c1s
Godson, Josepha B. v6p0219c2s
Godwin, E.W. v1p1144c2s
v2p0061c1s v2p0190c1s
Godwin, G. v1p0808c1s
v2p0123c1s
Godwin, G.N. v5p0467c1s
Godwin, H. v1p0360c2s
Godwin, J.H. v1p0128c2s
v2p0034c2s v2p0044c2s
Godwin, P. v1p0024c1s
v1p0026c2s v1p0029c1s v1p0031c1s
v1p0034c2s v1p0043c1s v1p0081c1s
v1p0172c2s v1p0212c1s v1p0286c1s
v1p0287c2s v1p0322c1s v1p0332c1s
v1p0334c2s v1p0349c2s v1p0380c1s
v1p0405c1s v1p0430c1s v1p0430c2s
v1p0533c2s v1p0572c1s v1p0588c1s
v1p0711c1s v1p0720c1s v1p0793c2s
v1p0862c2s v1p0877c2s v1p0916c2s
v1p0956c2s v1p0963c1s v1p0964c2s
v1p0976c1s v1p1009c1s v1p1116c1s
v1p1175c1s v1p1208c1s v1p1350c2m
v1p1352c1s v1p1354c1s v1p1366c1s
v1p1370c2s v4p0144c2s
Godwin-Austen, H.H. v1p1256c1m
v2p0319c2s
Goebel, H. and Antrim, E.. v5p0597c1s
Goebel, J. v3p0251c2s
Goebel, K. v5p0503c1s
v6p0502c2s
Goegg, G. v6p0595c1s
Goeje, M.J.de v3p0087c2s
Goepp, C. v1p0589c1s
v1p0833c1s v2p0240c2s
Goepp, P.H. v4p0561c1s
v6p0439c1s
Goerwitz, E.F. v5p0266c2s
v5p0379c2s v6p0156c2s v6p0260c1s
Goes, E. v5p0377c1s
Goeschel, C.F. v1p0626c1s
v2p0215c1s v2p0215c2s v2p0410c2s
Goeschel, K.F. v3p0209c1s
Goessmann, C.A. v1p0163c2s
v1p0225c1s v1p0844c2s v1p1146c2s
Goethe, J.W.v. v1p0458c1s
v2p0213c1s
Goethe, J.W.von v1p0669c1s
v1p0725c1s
Goettsch, C. v6p0323c2s
Goetz, H.A. v3p0059c1s
v4p0078c1s
Goetz, P.B. v4p0309c1s
Goetz, V. v1p1135c1s
Goetz, Vera v1p0207c1s
Goff, E.S. v2p0093c2s
v2p0158c2s v4p0285c2s v4p0445c1s
v4p0447c2s v4p0552c2s v5p0561c1s
Goff, J.W. v4p0042c2s
Goff, W. v3p0415c1s
v4p0556c2s
Goffic, C.Le v5p0338c2s
Goffin, R.J.R. v5p0086c2s
Gofton, J.E. v6p0515c2s
Goggin, J.M. v2p0077c1s
Gogol, N. v1p1138c1s
Gogol, N.V. v3p0272c1s
Goh, D. v4p0298c2s
Goh, Daigoro v3p0227c1s
v4p0298c2s
Gohier, U. v5p0019c2s
v5p0218c1s v5p0218c2s v5p0374c2s
v5p0493c1s v5p0594c2s v6p0236c2s
v6p0237c2s v6p0488c1s v6p0538c2s
v6p0555c2s
Gohier, Urbain v6p0236c2m
Gohre, P. v5p0399c2s
Going, C.B. v3p0457c2s
v4p0202c2m v4p0403c2s v4p0617c2s
v5p0008c1s v5p0188c1s v5p0201c1s
v5p0321c2s v5p0557c1s v6p0088c2s
Goiran, G. v4p0294c1s
Gokhale, G.K. v6p0314c2s
Golay, J. v6p0295c2s
Gold, E. v4p0079c1s
v4p0463c1s
Golden, A.L. v5p0478c2s
Goldenson, S.H. v6p0600c1s
Goldenweiser, E.A. v6p0343c2s
Golder, F.A. v6p0011c2s
v6p0353c2s
Goldie, C. v3p0021c1s
Goldie, F. v1p0110c2s
v1p0302c1m v1p0629c2s v1p0824c2s
v1p0953c2s v1p1013c1s v1p1092c1s
v1p1119c1s v1p1138c2s v2p0165c1s
v2p0217c1s v3p0009c1s v3p0021c2s
v3p0228c2s v3p0270c1s v4p0030c2s
v6p0242c1s
Goldie, G. v1p0043c1s
v1p0728c1s v1p0967c1s v1p1144c1s
v1p1144c2s v1p1317c2s v1p1437c2m
v2p0168c1s v2p0375c1s
Goldie, G. and Shaw, G.B.. v2p0070c1s
Goldie, G.T. v4p0001c2s
v4p0005c2s v5p0005c2s v6p0159c2s
v6p0183c2s v6p0250c2s
Goldie, M.H.G. v5p0157c1s
Golding, L. v5p0007c2s
v5p0068c1s v6p0358c2s
Golding, L.T. v5p0120c1s
Golding, Lewis v6p0054c1s
Goldman, C.S. v6p0006c1s
Goldmann, Agnes v5p0586c2s
Goldmark, H. v1p0400c2s
Goldmark, J.C. v6p0115c1m
v6p0117c1s v6p0294c1s
Goldmark, Josephine C. ... v6p0708c1s
Goldring, W. v3p0435c2s
v4p0483c2s
Goldschmidt, J. v4p0228c1s
Goldschmidt, M. v1p0889c1s
v1p1126c2s
Goldschmidt, M.A. v2p0406c2s
Goldschmidt, V. and Nicoll, W.
v6p0610c2s
Goldschmied, P. v6p0086c2s
Goldsmid, F. v2p0003c2s
v4p0559c1s
Goldsmid, F., Sir v3p0327c2s
Goldsmid, F.G. v4p0215c1s
Goldsmid, F.H. v1p1376c1s
Goldsmid, F.I. v5p0226c1s
Goldsmid, F.J. v2p0098c2s
v3p0055c2s v3p0211c1s v3p0234c2s
v4p0283c1s v4p0435c2s v4p0474c1s
v5p0533c2s
Goldsmid, F.J., Sir v2p0025c1s
v2p0134c2s v2p0168c1s v2p0323c2s
v2p0403c2s
Goldsmid, J. v2p0218c1s
v3p0010c1s
Goldsmid, J., Sir v2p0133c2s
v2p0230c2s
Goldsmith, E. v6p0305c1s
v6p0566c2s
Goldsmith, H.C. v3p0301c1s
Goldsmith, H.J. v1p0683c1s
Goldsmith, I. v2p0381c1s
Goldsmith, M. v3p0108c2s
Goldsmith, O. v1p0346c1s
v1p0385c2s v1p1322c2s v2p0399c1s
Goldstein, J. v6p0457c1s
Goldstein, V. v6p0702c2s
Goldstraw, W. v2p0019c2s
v2p0141c1m
Goldthwaite, K. v6p0612c1s
Goldthwaite, L.A. et al. . v6p0635c1s
Goldthwaite, V. v6p0428c2s
Goldziher, I. v6p0285c2s
Goldzihers, I. v2p0283c1s
Goler, G.W. v6p0417c1s

Goll, H. v1p1127c2s
Gollancz, H. v5p0521c1s
v5p0530c1s
Gollancz, Hermann v4p0314c1s
Gollancz, I. v6p0264c2s
v6p0594c1s
Gollancz, I. and Jacobs, J.
v3p0463c2s
Gollmer, C.A. v2p0429c1s
Golsworthy, A. v5p0077c2s
v5p0346c2s v5p0623c2s
Goltz, Gen.Von der v6p0654c2s
Goltz, Von der v5p0375c1s
v5p0516c1s
Golwald, L.A.
v3p0427c2s
Gomme, Alice B. v6p0072c1s
Gomme, C.L. v2p0353c2s
v6p0375c2s
Gomme, G. v6p0385c1s
Gomme, G.L. v1p0085c1s
v1p0408c2s v1p0588c1s v1p0744c1s
v1p1133c2s v1p1216c2s v1p1326c1s
v2p0005c2s v2p0060c2s v2p0082c2s
v2p0097c1s v2p0103c2s v2p0142c1m
v2p0143c1s v2p0155c1s v2p0160c2s
v2p0184c1s v2p0187c1s v2p0208c2s
v2p0247c1s v2p0248c1s v2p0264c1s
v2p0294c2s v2p0302c1s v2p0317c1s
v2p0372c1s v2p0412c1s v2p0439c1s
v2p0461c1s v3p0082c1s v3p0319c1s
v4p0058c1s v4p0066c2s v4p0205c1s
v4p0257c1s v4p0286c2s v4p0312c2s
v4p0338c2s v4p0414c2s v5p0192c2s
v5p0212c1s v5p0346c2s v5p0357c2s
v5p0559c1s
Gomme, J.L. v1p1331c1s
Gomme, L. v4p0338c1s
v5p0490c1s v6p0383c1s v6p0383c2s
v6p0479c2s v6p0711c2s
Gompers, G. v6p0115c1s
Gompers, S. v3p0434c1s
v4p0314c2s v5p0557c2s v6p0026c1s
Gompers, S. et al. v4p0553c2s
Gompf, E.J. v4p0178c1s
Gompf, Emma J. v6p0177c1s
Goncher, J.F. v5p0289c1s
Gondy, H. v5p0351c1s
Gonin, L. v1p1019c1s
Gonner, E.C.K. v3p0028c1s
v3p0074c2s v3p0138c1s v3p0360c2s
v4p0044c1s v4p0158c2s v4p0571c1s
Gontaut-Biron, Raoul de .. v6p0297c2s
Gontz, T. v5p0288c2s
v5p0451c1s
Gonzales, Jose v6p0173c1s
Gooch, C. v1p0313c1s
Gooch, Dr. v1p0295c1s
v1p1013c2s v1p1070c1s v1p1210c1s
Gooch, F.A. v4p0316c1s
v5p0382c1s v6p0514c1s
Gooch, F.A. and Austin, M.
v5p0017c2s v5p0359c2m v5p0426c2s
Gooch, F.A. and Baldwin, DeF.
v5p0002c2s
Gooch, F.A. and Blake, J.C.
v6p0083c2s
Gooch, F.A. and Browning, P.E.
v3p0021c1s v3p0219c1s v4p0288c2s
Gooch, F.A. and Clemons, C.F.
v4p0514c1s
Gooch, F.A. and Curtis, R.W.
v6p0278c2s
Gooch, F.A. and Danner, E.W.
v3p0015c2s v4p0454c2s
Gooch, F.A. and Ensign, J.R.
v3p0056c1s
Gooch, F.A. and Evans, P.S., jr.
v4p0514c1s
Gooch, F.A. and Fairbanks, C.
v4p0246c1s v4p0377c1s
Gooch, F.A. and Gilbert, R.D.
v6p0019c1s v6p0713c1s
Gooch, F.A. and Gruener, H.W.
v3p0015c2s v4p0405c1s
Gooch, F.A. and Hart, T.S.
v3p0340c2s
Gooch, F.A. and Havens, F.S.
v4p0012c2s v5p0113c2s
Gooch, F.A. and Hodge, B.. v4p0028c2s
Gooch, F.A. and Jones, L.C.
v5p0071c2s
Gooch, F.A. and Krieder, D.A.
v4p0107c2s
Gooch, F.A. and McClenahan, F.M.
v6p0121c2s
Gooch, F.A. and Mar, F.W.. v3p0080c1s
Gooch, F.A. and Medway, H.E.
v6p0552c2s
Gooch, F.A. and Morgan, W.C.
v4p0568c1s
Gooch, F.A. and Morley, F.H.
v5p0237c2s
Gooch, F.A. and Morris, J.C.
v5p0030c1s
Gooch, F.A. and Moseley, H.P.
v4p0028c2s
Gooch, F.A. and Norton, J.T., jr.
v5p0382c1s
Gooch, F.A. and Peirce, A.W.
v4p0514c1m
Gooch, F.A. and Peters, C.A.
v5p0254c2s v5p0426c1s v5p0571c2s
Gooch, F.A. and Phelps, I.K.
v4p0028c2s v4p0089c1s
Gooch, F.A. and Phelps, M.A.
v6p0032c2s
Gooch, F.A. and Phinney, J.I.
v4p0494c1s
Gooch, F.A. and Pulman, O.S., jr.
v5p0382c1s
Gooch, F.A. and Reynolds, W.G.
v4p0514c1s
Gooch, F.A. and Scoville, W.S.
v4p0514c1s
Gooch, F.A. and Smith, C.G.
v3p0080c1s
Gooch, F.A. and Stookey, L.B.
v6p0674c1s
Gooch, F.A. and Walker, C.F.
v5p0295c1s
Gooch, G.P. v5p0040c1s
v5p0178c2s v6p0399c1s v6p0665c1s
Gooch, J.M. v1p1360c1s
Gooch, R. v1p0612c2s
Gooch, T.S. v2p0457c2s
v3p0354c1s v3p0447c1s
Gooch, W.D. v2p0004c2s
v2p0421c1m
Good, A. v3p0047c2s
v3p0473c1s
Good, A. and Anderson, W.. v3p0100c2s
Good, E.L. v5p0033c1s
v5p0268c1s
Good, J.H. v1p0619c2s
Good, J.I. v4p0020c2s
v4p0224c1s v4p0477c1s v4p0637c2s
v5p0482c1s v6p0535c2s
Good, J.I. and Drury, J.B.
v5p0482c1s
Good, J.I. et al. v3p0356c2s
Good, J.M. v5p0612c1s
v6p0373c1s v6p0611c2s
Good, J.W. v5p0088c2s
Good, Jessie M. v6p0247c1s
Good, T. v6p0133c1s
v6p0328c2s v6p0356c2s v6p0601c1s
v6p0652c1s v6p0708c2s
Goodale, B.N. v4p0333c1s
v4p0356c2s
Goodale, D. v6p0183c1s
Goodale, D.H.R. v3p0101c2s
v4p0219c2s v4p0485c2s
Goodale, D.H.R., Mrs. v2p0361c2s
Goodale, D.R. v3p0040c2s
v3p0209c2s v4p0119c2s v4p0146c1s
v4p0286c1s v4p0598c2s v5p0041c2s
v5p0422c1s v6p0697c1s
Goodale, Dora Read v6p0014c1s
Goodale, E. v1p0038c2s
v3p0034c1s v3p0189c1s v3p0213c1s
v3p0213c2s v3p0214c1m v3p0329c1s
Goodale, G.L. v1p0519c1s
v1p1326c2s v2p0080c1s v3p0051c2s
v3p0071c2s v3p0125c2s v3p0179c2s
v3p0290c2s v3p0347c2m v3p0435c2s
v3p0447c2s v4p0087c1s v4p0208c2s
v4p0235c1s v4p0400c1s v5p0529c2s
v6p0146c2s v6p0233c1s
Goodale, J.H. v2p0311c1s
Goodale, R.L. v6p0197c1s
Goodale, W.H. v4p0116c1m
v4p0430c2s
Goodale-Eastman, E. v4p0281c2s
Goodall, J. v1p0371c1s
v1p1360c1s
Goodard, H.C. v6p0136c1s
Goodard, Warren v6p0404c2s
Goodbody, F.G.W. v2p0444c2s
Goodbrand, R. v1p0134c1s
Goodby, E. and Asquith, H.H.
v3p0031c1s
Goodchild, C.W. v3p0329c2s
Goodchild, F.M. v4p0438c2s
v4p0559c2s
Goodchild, T. v1p0246c1s
Goode, A. v4p0350c1s
Goode, G.B. v1p0115c1s
v1p0449c2s v1p0456c2s v1p0457c1s
v1p0820c1s v2p0073c2s v2p0157c2s
v2p0194c2s v3p0030c1s v3p0030c2s
v3p0153c2s v3p0390c2s v3p0444c2s
v4p0009c2s v4p0165c2s v4p0388c1m
v4p0445c2s v4p0484c2s v4p0508c1m
v4p0530c2s v5p0533c2s
Goode, G.B. and Bean, T.H.
v1p0456c2s v1p0457c1s
Goode, H. v1p0449c1s
Goode, J. v5p0132c1s
v5p0255c1s v5p0613c1s v6p0197c1s
Goode, J.P. v6p0400c1s
Goode, M.M. v2p0151c2s
v2p0474c1s
Goode, R. v1p0541c2s
Goode, R.U. v3p0110c2s
v3p0318c2s v5p0065c1s v5p0278c2s
v5p0384c1s
Goode, Richard U. v4p0423c2s
Goode, W.A.M. v5p0544c1s
Goode, W.A.M. and Graham, G.E.
v5p0100c1s
Goode, W.H. v1p0329c1s
v1p0526c1s
Goodell, A.C., jr. v2p0279c2s
v2p0393c2s v3p0457c2s v4p0270c2s
Goodell, C.L. v1p0439c2s
v1p1210c1s v6p0513c2s
Goodell, D.H. and Upton, S.
v3p0423c2s
Goodell, H.H. v3p0271c1s
Goodell, Margaret P. v5p0530c2s
Goodell, T.D. v4p0597c1s
v5p0164c1s v5p0250c1m v5p0577c2s
Goodell, W. v1p0294c1s
v1p0643c2s
Goodenough, A. v6p0154c1s
Goodenough, J.G. v1p0547c2s
Goodenough, W.H. v4p0609c1s
Goodenow, S.B. v1p0253c1s
v1p0253c2s v1p0254c2s v1p0290c1m
v1p0626c1s v1p1061c2s v1p1175c2s
v1p1222c1s v3p0040c1s v4p0149c2s
v4p0352c1s
Goodenow, W.S.B. v1p1423c2s
Gooderham, C.H. v4p0381c2s
Goodfellow, B. v1p0145c2s
Goodfellow, E. v3p0287c1s
Goodfellow, G.E. v3p0126c1s
Goodhart, R.E., Mrs. v5p0234c2s
Goodhow, F.J. v5p0119c2s
Goodhue, B.G. v5p0474c1s
v5p0504c2s v5p0612c1s v6p0187c2s
Goodhue, E.W. v6p0076c2s
Goodhue, H.E. v6p0126c2s
v6p0612c2s
Goodhue, J.A. v1p0124c1s
Goodhue, S. v4p0269c1s
v4p0417c2s v4p0456c1s
Goodhugh, W. v1p0117c2s
v1p0121c1s v1p0129c2s v1p0980c1s
Goodier, A. v6p0304c2s
v6p0307c1s v6p0340c2s
Goodier, Alban v5p0633c2s
Gooding, W.L. v1p0770c2s
v4p0432c2s v4p0464c2s
Goodknight, J.L. v2p0382c1s
Goodlet, I. v3p0388c2s
v4p0519c1m
Goodloe, A.C. v5p0301c1s
v5p0481c1s
Goodloe, Abbe C. v4p0123c2s
v5p0491c2s v5p0625c1s
Goodloe, C. v6p0057c1s
Goodloe, Carter v6p0179c2s
v6p0215c2s
Goodloe, D.R. v3p0149c2s
v3p0289c1s
Goodloe, E. v6p0307c1s
Goodloe, H.H. v1p0905c2s
Goodman, A.T. v2p0200c1s
Goodman, E.J. v2p0271c1s
v3p0233c2s v3p0376c1s v3p0470c2s
v4p0272c1s v4p0391c1s v4p0446c2s
Goodman, G.D. v5p0614c2s
Goodman, H.M. v3p0071c2s
v3p0143c1s
Goodman, Inez A. v6p0178c2s
Goodman, J. v6p0615c1s
Goodman, J.D. v1p0059c1s
Goodman, J.T. v6p0407c2s
Goodman, J.Y. v4p0473c1s
Goodman, N. and Norgate, F.
v2p0416c1s
Goodman, R.J. and Browning, P.E.
v4p0600c1s
Goodman, W. v2p0032c1s
v2p0299c1s v2p0413c1s v3p0021c1s
v5p0033c1s
Goodnow, A.W. v1p0688c1s
v4p0186c2s v4p0302c1s
Goodnow, F.J. v2p0003c1s
v2p0110c1s v2p0126c1s v2p0131c1s
v2p0150c1s v2p0452c2s v3p0072c2s
v3p0255c1m v3p0348c1s v4p0115c1s
v4p0353c1s v4p0472c2s v4p0552c2s
v5p0120c1s v5p0584c2s v6p0324c2s
v6p0363c2s v6p0435c2s v6p0452c1s
Goodnow, I.T. v2p0071c2m
v2p0089c1s
Goodrich, A. v2p0157c1s
v2p0235c2s v4p0161c1s v5p0082c1s
v5p0154c2s v5p0304c2s v5p0354c2s
v5p0553c2s v5p0566c1s v6p0003c1s
v6p0009c1s v6p0044c1s v6p0048c2s
v6p0052c1s v6p0075c2s v6p0095c1s
v6p0116c1s v6p0145c1s v6p0172c2s
v6p0198c1s v6p0205c1s v6p0228c2s
v6p0260c1s v6p0294c2s v6p0363c2s
v6p0591c1s v6p0591c2m
Goodrich, A. and Cunniff, M.G.
v5p0407c2s
Goodrich, A.L. v5p0192c1s
v5p0266c2s
Goodrich, Arthur et al. .. v6p0379c1s
Goodrich, C.A. v1p0215c2s
v1p0318c2s v1p0421c2s v1p0593c2s
v1p0990c2s v1p1042c1s v1p1064c1s
v1p1211c1s v1p1357c1s v1p1396c1s
v1p1410c1s v1p1436c1s
Goodrich, C.E. v1p1265c2s

Goodrich, C.F. v3p0186c2s v4p0395c2s v5p0517c1s v6p0445c1s v6p0668c2s v6p0700c2s
Goodrich, C.J. v6p0623c2s
Goodrich, E.P. v6p0143c1s
Goodrich, E.S. v4p0420c1s
Goodrich, E.S. and Major, C.I.F. v4p0584c2s
Goodrich, F.B. v3p0462c1s
Goodrich, F.M. v6p0279c1s v6p0352c1s
Goodrich, F.P. v4p0270c2s
Goodrich, Frank v4p0532c2s
Goodrich, H.B. v5p0318c1s
Goodrich, H.G. and Corbin, E.A. v1p0146c1s
Goodrich, H.H. v1p0942c2s
Goodrich, H.P. v1p0050c1s v1p0490c2s
Goodrich, H.S. v3p0241c2s
Goodrich, J.A. v6p0712c1s
Goodrich, J.K. v1p0458c2s v3p0006c2m v3p0227c2s v5p0109c2s v5p0113c1s v5p0258c2s v5p0303c1m v5p0541c2s v6p0338c1s
Goodrich, J.T. v6p0338c2s
Goodrich, L. v4p0038c2s
Goodrich, L.C. v2p0017c2s v2p0271c1s v2p0405c1s
Goodrich, M. v1p0096c2s v1p0130c1s v1p0130c2s v1p0426c1s v1p0528c1s v1p0684c2s v1p0688c1s v1p1087c1s v1p1203c1s v1p1355c2m v3p0042c2s v3p0166c1s
Goodrich, M.H. v4p0277c1s
Goodrich, S.F. v3p0102c1s v4p0197c1s
Goodrich, S.F. and Thomas, E.M. v3p0207c1s
Goodrich, S.G. v1p0390c1s v1p0794c2s
Goodrich, W.F. v5p0482c2s v6p0244c1s
Goodrich, W.H. v1p1043c2s
Goodrich, W.W. v5p0543c2s
Goodrich-Freer, A. v5p0079c2s v5p0257c1s v5p0261c1m v5p0470c1s v6p0293c2s v6p0343c1s v6p0618c2s
Goodrick, A.T.S. v1p0518c1s v6p0239c1s v6p0254c2s v6p0472c2s v6p0627c2s v6p0670c2s
Goodridge, B.A. v4p0087c1s v4p0444c1s
Goodsell, D.A. v3p0108c1s v3p0194c2s v4p0282c2s v4p0436c2s v4p0617c1s v4p0620c1s v6p0513c1s
Goodsell, D.A. et al. v3p0073c2s
Goodson, A.J. v4p0565c2s
Goodspeed, A.W. v4p0487c1s v5p0492c1s v6p0350c2s
Goodspeed, C. v1p0038c2s v1p0681c1s v6p0259c1s
Goodspeed, C.E. v6p0075c1s
Goodspeed, C.S. v6p0699c2s
Goodspeed, E.J. v5p0003c2s v5p0041c2s v5p0059c1m v5p0269c1m v5p0305c1s v5p0428c2s v5p0430c1s v5p0463c1s v6p0063c1s v6p0063c2m v6p0064c1s v6p0073c2s v6p0273c1s v6p0361c2m v6p0403c2s v6p0639c2s v6p0647c2s
Goodspeed, E.T. v6p0359c2s v6p0473c2s
Goodspeed, F.J. v6p0471c1s
Goodspeed, F.L. v6p0519c1s
Goodspeed, G.S. v4p0085c1s v4p0100c1s v4p0193c1s v4p0280c2s v4p0300c2s v4p0479c2s v5p0035c1s v5p0037c2s v5p0057c1s v5p0106c2s v5p0279c1s v5p0371c1m v5p0441c1s v5p0495c2s v6p0186c1s v6p0272c2s v6p0292c1s v6p0548c2s
Goodwillie, J.M. v4p0353c2s
Goodwin, A.H. v6p0154c1s v6p0499c2s v6p0507c2s v6p0591c1s v6p0596c1s v6p0638c2s
Goodwin, C. v4p0158c2s
Goodwin, C.A. v4p0256c2s
Goodwin, C.C. v1p0871c2m v5p0237c2s v5p0378c1s v5p0387c1s
Goodwin, C.J. v3p0016c1s v4p0614c1s v5p0495c1s v6p0101c2s
Goodwin, C.T. v4p0448c1s
Goodwin, C.W. v1p0300c1s v1p1150c1s
Goodwin, D. v3p0466c1s v6p0442c2s
Goodwin, D.C. v2p0052c1s v2p0402c1s
Goodwin, D.R. v1p0122c1s v1p0122c2s v1p0127c1s v1p0241c1s v1p0359c1s v1p0416c1s v1p0416c2m v1p0441c2s v1p0618c1s v1p0641c2s v1p0648c1s v1p0723c2s v1p0741c2s v1p0783c1s v1p0792c2s v1p0796c2m v1p1073c2m v1p1097c2s v1p1101c2s v1p1238c2s v2p0044c1s v3p0192c2s v3p0404c2s
Goodwin, Dr. v1p0640c1s
Goodwin, E. v5p0083c2s
Goodwin, E.B. v5p0565c1s v6p0279c2s v6p0285c2s
Goodwin, E.J. v4p0170c1s v4p0174c1m v4p0257c1m v4p0321c2s v4p0463c2s v5p0470c1s v6p0002c1s v6p0136c1s v6p0136c2s v6p0452c2s v6p0454c2s
Goodwin, E.L. v2p0478c1s
Goodwin, E.R. v5p0544c1s v5p0621c1s v5p0629c1s v5p0634c2s v5p0637c2m
Goodwin, E.S. v1p0016c2s
Goodwin, F. v4p0253c2s
Goodwin, F.P. v6p0464c2s
Goodwin, G. v4p0037c1s v4p0075c2s v4p0492c1s v6p0233c2s
Goodwin, G.D. v5p0233c2s v5p0325c2s v6p0419c2s
Goodwin, G.E. v5p0209c1s
Goodwin, G.S. v6p0073c2m
Goodwin, H. v1p0252c1s v1p0272c2s v1p0527c2s v1p0545c2s v1p0794c1s v1p0860c1s v1p0901c1s v2p0015c1s v2p0017c2m v2p0022c1s v2p0082c2s v2p0097c2s v2p0251c1s v2p0258c1s v2p0307c2s v2p0451c1s v2p0462c1s v2p0472c1s v3p0037c2s v3p0038c1s v3p0083c1s v3p0084c1s v3p0111c1s v3p0365c2s v3p0429c1s v3p0459c1s v4p0128c1s v4p0402c1s
Goodwin, H. and Romanes, G.J. v2p0280c1s
Goodwin, H.B. v3p0181c2s v3p0182c1s v5p0145c1s v5p0151c1s v6p0623c1s
Goodwin, H.D. v4p0439c2s
Goodwin, H.M. v1p0180c1m v1p0229c1s v1p0426c2s v1p0685c1s v1p0901c1s v1p1303c2s v2p0041c2s v2p0099c2s v2p0478c1s v3p0091c1s v3p0297c1s v3p0416c1s v3p0472c1s
Goodwin, Inez J. v6p0705c2s
Goodwin, J. v1p0137c2s v1p0909c1s v1p1195c1s
Goodwin, J.M. v5p0468c2s v5p0534c1s v5p0534c2s
Goodwin, J.O. v1p1361c1s
Goodwin, L.S. v4p0004c2s v6p0437c1s
Goodwin, M.B. v2p0035c1s v4p0216c1s v5p0021c2s
Goodwin, M.C. v4p0209c2s v4p0234c1s
Goodwin, M.W. v4p0247c1s v5p0234c1s v6p0235c2s v6p0628c1s
Goodwin, Prof. v1p0259c2s
Goodwin, R. v3p0306c2s
Goodwin, T.A. v4p0055c2s v4p0367c2s
Goodwin, W. v1p1085c1s v1p1262c2s
Goodwin, W.H., jr. v3p0190c1s
Goodwin, W.I. v3p0293c1s
Goodwin, W.L. et al. v2p0364c1s
Goodwin, W.R. v1p0398c1s v1p0978c1s v2p0371c2s v3p0132c1s
Goodwin, W.W. v1p0072c2s v1p0075c2s v1p0552c2s v1p0554c2s v1p0555c2s v1p0889c1m v1p1018c2s v1p1221c1s v1p1327c1s v2p0410c1s v2p0442c1s v2p0447c2m v3p0456c1s v4p0026c2s v4p0118c1s v4p0183c2s v4p0505c2s v5p0257c1s v6p0196c1s v6p0273c1s v6p0288c2s
Goodwin, W.W. and Adams, C.F. v4p0170c1s
Goodwin, W.W. and Fowler, H.N. v2p0026c2s
Goodyear, C. v6p0381c1s v6p0508c1s
Goodyear, W.H. v1p0054c1s v1p0213c2s v1p0531c1s v2p0075c2s v3p0108c2s v3p0259c1s v4p0019c2s v4p0024c1m v4p0024c2s v4p0241c2s v4p0288c2s v4p0342c2s v4p0405c1s v4p0417c2s v4p0436c2s v5p0026c2s v5p0035c2s v5p0129c2s v5p0193c2s v5p0270c2s v5p0300c2s v5p0452c1s v5p0591c1s v6p0027c2m v6p0159c1s v6p0236c2s v6p0365c2s v6p0676c2s
Goodyear, W.M. v4p0405c1s
Googins, G.E. v6p0651c1s
Gookin, F.E. v2p0419c1s
Gookin, F.W. v3p0227c1s v4p0298c2s v5p0046c2s v5p0051c1s v5p0122c1s v5p0499c2m v6p0285c1s v6p0332c1s v6p0336c1s v6p0337c2s v6p0425c1s v6p0634c2s
Goold, N. v6p0351c2s
Goold, W. v1p0442c1s v1p0965c2s
Goose, E. v6p0246c2s
Gopalacharlu, S.E. v4p0258c1s
Goppelsroder, F. v1p0959c2s
Gorby, S.S. v4p0220c2s
Gorceix, M.H. v2p0117c2s
Gordon, A. v1p0098c2m v1p0166c1s v1p0215c1s v1p0217c1s v1p0249c2s v1p0728c1s v1p0937c1s v1p1069c1m v1p1070c1s v1p1180c1s v1p1227c2s v2p0108c1s v2p0155c2s v2p0303c1s v2p0360c2s v2p0432c1s v3p0154c1s v3p0154c2s v3p0237c1s v3p0307c1s v3p0377c2s v3p0381c1m v3p0394c1s v3p0435c2s v4p0146c1s v4p0154c1s v4p0157c1s v4p0197c1s v4p0207c1s v4p0221c1s v4p0276c2s v4p0317c1s v4p0331c2s v4p0361c1s v4p0448c1s v4p0469c1s v4p0474c1s v4p0552c1s v6p0058c1s
Gordon, A.C. v3p0155c1s v3p0328c1s v3p0332c2s v3p0402c2s v6p0013c2s
Gordon, A.D. v1p1264c1s
Gordon, A.J. v1p0060c2s v1p0097c1s v1p0421c2s v1p0853c1s v4p0234c1s v4p0362c2s v4p0427c2s v5p0066c1s v5p0102c2s v5p0209c1s v5p0253c1s v5p0318c2s v5p0339c2s
Gordon, A.J. and Child, A.B. v3p0283c1s
Gordon, A.M. v3p0113c1s v3p0133c2s v4p0627c1m
Gordon, A.M.R. v4p0052c1s v4p0585c1m v4p0636c2s
Gordon, A.R. v2p0213c2s v6p0062c2s v6p0339c2s v6p0691c2s
Gordon, Alex. v4p0158c1s v4p0240c2s v5p0595c2s
Gordon, Alex R. v6p0061c2s
Gordon, C. v1p0341c1s v1p0505c2s v1p0774c1s v2p0215c1s v3p0006c2s
Gordon, C.C. v1p0423c1s v1p0649c2s
Gordon, C.D. v4p0213c2s
Gordon, C.E. v6p0149c2s
Gordon, C.G. v3p0401c1s
Gordon, C.G., Gen. v5p0176c1s
Gordon, C.H. v3p0236c1s v3p0251c2s v5p0241c2s
Gordon, C.H. and Graton, L.C. v6p0451c1s
Gordon, C.T. v6p0711c2s
Gordon, Craig v6p0243c1s
Gordon, D.E. v6p0092c2m
Gordon, D.M. v1p0164c2s v1p1416c1s
Gordon, E. v5p0043c2s
Gordon, E.C. v1p1374c1s
Gordon, F. v1p0874c2s v1p1128c2s v2p0440c1s
Gordon, F.C. v4p0078c2s v4p0162c2s
Gordon, G. v1p0180c1s v1p0635c1s v1p0823c2s v1p1390c2s v5p0423c1s v5p0479c1s
Gordon, G.A. v2p0351c2s v3p0061c2s v3p0281c1s v4p0097c2s v4p0144c2s v4p0417c2s v4p0434c1s v4p0550c2s v4p0595c1s v4p0635c2s v5p0014c2s v5p0206c1s v5p0225c2s v5p0442c1s v5p0461c1s v5p0541c1s v5p0578c1s v6p0202c1s v6p0450c1s v6p0697c2s
Gordon, G.B. v5p0136c2s v5p0269c2s
Gordon, G.E. v3p0045c1s v3p0107c2s
Gordon, G.P. v4p0338c2s v6p0021c2s v6p0220c2s v6p0573c2s
Gordon, G.W. v3p0087c2s v5p0296c2s
Gordon, Gerald P. v6p0034c2s
Gordon, H. v3p0271c2s v4p0134c1s v5p0248c2s v6p0157c2m
Gordon, H.C. v5p0345c2s v5p0453c1s
Gordon, H.D. v4p0471c1s
Gordon, J. v1p0074c2s v1p0104c2s v1p0370c1s v1p1398c2s v2p0445c2s v3p0413c2s v4p0382c2s v4p0616c1s
Gordon, J.B. v1p0862c1s v3p0441c1s v6p0255c1s v6p0668c1s
Gordon, J.C.H. and Aberdeen, Earl of v2p0187c2s
Gordon, J.E.H. v2p0136c2s v3p0132c2s v4p0176c1s
Gordon, J.E.H., Mrs. v4p0537c2s
Gordon, J.H. v6p0042c1s
Gordon, J.J.H. v3p0211c2s
Gordon, J.O. v2p0200c2s
Gordon, J.P. v6p0024c1s
Gordon, J.S. v5p0432c1s
Gordon, J.T. v1p0458c2s v1p0540c1s v1p1156c1s
Gordon, K. v6p0212c1s v6p0704c1s
Gordon, Kate v6p0408c1s
Gordon, L.S., Sir v3p0120c1s
Gordon, M. v5p0466c1s
Gordon, M.L. v2p0059c2m v2p0369c1s
Gordon, M.L. and Carus, P. v5p0081c2s
Gordon, M.M.O. v5p0324c1s
Gordon, Margery v6p0142c2s
Gordon, P. v4p0625c1s v5p0236c1s

Gordon, Pelham v5p0169c2s
Gordon, Q. v4p0207c1s
v4p0551c1s v5p0565c2s
Gordon, R. v1p0497c2s
v3p0368c2s v3p0391c2s v4p0471c2s
v6p0405c2m
Gordon, R.H. v6p0681c1s
Gordon, S. v5p0583c2s
v6p0544c2s v6p0590c2s
Gordon, S.B. v4p0424c2s
v5p0511c2s
Gordon, S.B. and Willey, D.A.
v5p0009c2s
Gordon, S.D. v5p0246c2m
v5p0374c2s v5p0503c2s v5p0517c1s
v5p0526c2s v5p0532c2s v5p0645c2m
v6p0411c1s
Gordon, T.E. v5p0001c1s
v5p0441c1s
Gordon, T.F. v1p0091c1s
v2p0473c1s
Gordon, W. v2p0121c1s
v2p0182c2s v2p0221c1s v2p0244c1s
v2p0269c2s v2p0270c1s v2p0345c1s
v2p0366c1s
Gordon, W.E. v6p0012c2s
v6p0308c2m v6p0309c1s
Gordon, W.F. v2p0320c2s
v2p0451c1s
Gordon, W.G. v3p0168c2s
Gordon, W.I. v2p0235c2s
Gordon, W.J. v2p0021c2s
v2p0066c2s v2p0101c2s v2p0259c1s
v2p0263c1s v2p0264c2s v2p0350c1s
v2p0387c1s v2p0399c2s v2p0409c1s
v3p0104c2s v3p0151c1s v3p0158c2s
v3p0174c2s v3p0182c1s v3p0223c2s
v3p0250c2s v3p0256c1s v3p0256c2s
v3p0285c1s v3p0336c2s v3p0344c1m
v3p0351c2s v3p0352c2s v3p0383c1s
v3p0391c1s v3p0397c1s v3p0421c2s
v3p0426c2m v3p0435c1s v4p0228c2s
v4p0264c1m v4p0419c2s v4p0424c2s
v4p0443c2s v4p0634c2s
Gordon, W.T. v3p0371c2s
Gordon-Cumming, C. v1p0678c1s
Gordon-Cumming, C.F. v1p0812c2s
v1p0876c1s v1p1179c1s v1p1377c1s
v1p1404c2s v2p0007c2s v2p0063c2s
v2p0113c2s v2p0273c2s v2p0297c2s
v3p0047c2s v3p0049c1s v3p0068c2s
v3p0072c2m v3p0078c2s v3p0126c1s
v3p0273c1s v3p0467c1s v3p0474c1s
v4p0020c2s v4p0064c1s v5p0098c2s
Gordon-Cumming, C.F. and
Middleton, Lady v3p0467c1s
Gordy, J.P. v2p0053c2s
v2p0147c1s v2p0285c1s v3p0052c1s
v3p0115c2s v3p0348c2s v3p0429c2s
v4p0050c1s v4p0465c1s v6p0476c2s
Gore, A. v1p0030c1s
Gore, C. v4p0461c2s
v4p0515c2s v4p0532c1s v5p0117c1s
v6p0189c2s
Gore, C.F. v1p0414c1s
v1p1009c2s
Gore, C.F., Mrs. v1p0919c1s
v1p1367c1s
Gore, C.G.F. v1p0141c1s
Gore, C.G.F., Mrs. v1p0218c1s
Gore, G. v1p0401c2m
v1p1431c2s v2p0090c2s v2p0103c2s
v2p0390c2s v2p0424c1s v2p0438c1s
v2p0463c1s v4p0507c2s v6p0145c2s
v6p0428c2s
v6p0672c2s
Gore, H. v1p0501c2s
Gore, J.E. v2p0070c1s
v3p0125c2s v3p0276c1s v3p0279c1s
v3p0286c2s v3p0407c1m v3p0407c2m
v4p0010c2s v4p0011c2s v4p0034c1s
v4p0046c1m v4p0219c2s v4p0235c1s
v4p0306c2s v4p0370c2s v4p0454c1s
v4p0528c1s v4p0535c2s v4p0545c1s
v4p0545c2s v4p0556c1s v4p0556c2s
v4p0557c1s v4p0567c2s v4p0597c1s
v5p0185c1s v5p0195c2s v5p0264c1s
v5p0273c2s v5p0338c1s v5p0372c2s
v5p0402c1s v5p0549c1m v5p0549c2m
v5p0550c1s v6p0005c1s v6p0009c1s
v6p0037c2s v6p0104c1s v6p0152c1s
v6p0294c1s v6p0308c1s v6p0446c1s
v6p0614c1m v6p0614c2m
Gore, J.Ellard v5p0549c1s
v5p0561c1s
Gore, J.H. v3p0030c2s
v3p0113c1s v3p0276c2s v3p0290c2s
v3p0380c2s v3p0442c2s v4p0123c1s
v4p0165c2m v4p0228c2s v4p0243c1s
v4p0260c2s v4p0316c1s v4p0318c2s
v4p0329c2s v4p0355c2s v4p0431c2s
v4p0452c1m v4p0461c1s v5p0092c1s
v5p0102c1s v5p0172c1s v5p0231c1s
v5p0232c2s v5p0366c1s v5p0372c2s
v5p0400c1s v5p0421c2s v5p0487c1s
v5p0598c2s v5p0600c1s v5p0625c1s
v6p0714c2s
Gore, J.W. and Venable, F.P.
v2p0438c2s
Gore, L. v1p0043c2s
v1p1088c1s
Gore, Mrs. v1p0001c2s
v1p0108c2s v1p0308c1s v1p0617c2s
v1p1280c1s v1p1293c2s
Gore, R.T. v1p0835c1s
Gore, S.W. v4p0139c1s
Gore-Booth, E. v5p0474c2s
Gore-Browne, W. v3p0180c1s
Gorgas, W.C., Col. v6p0476c1s
Gorges, G.H. v5p0397c1s
Gorges, M. v5p0297c2s
Gorges, Mary v5p0082c2s
v5p0296c1m v5p0595c1s v6p0327c2s
v6p0648c2s
Gorges, Mrs. v6p0352c1s
Gorgon, W.J. v4p0610c2s
Gorham, D.B. v1p0307c2s
Gorham, G. v2p0405c2s
v2p0474c2s
Gorham, G.E. v5p0201c2s
Gorham, H.S. v6p0262c1s
Gorham, J. v1p0701c2s
v2p0150c2s
Gorham, T.A. v1p1316c2s
Gorham, W.A. v5p0317c2s
Gorky, M. v5p0160c1s
v5p0357c1s v5p0569c1s v6p0111c2s
v6p0351c1s v6p0375c2s v6p0396c2s
Gorky, Maxim v6p0014c2s
v6p0117c1s v6p0142c2s v6p0144c1s
v6p0400c2s v6p0423c1s v6p0431c2s
v6p0452c2s v6p0457c2s v6p0492c2s
v6p0532c1s v6p0598c2s v6p0603c2s
v6p0625c1s
Gorle, J. v1p0888c2s
Gorman, L. v5p0258c2s
v6p0574c2s
Gorman, M.W. v5p0010c2s
v5p0629c2s
Gorman, S.B. v3p0297c1s
Gorman, T.P. v3p0066c1s
v4p0411c2s v4p0424c2s
Gornalle, R. v5p0590c1s
Gorren, A. v4p0212c1s
v4p0221c2s v4p0305c2s v4p0313c2s
v4p0626c2s v5p0144c1s v5p0627c2s
v6p0694c1s
Gorren, Aline v5p0016c2s
v5p0221c1s v5p0536c2s
Gorrie, J. v1p0452c2s
v1p0579c2s
Gorringe, H.H. v1p0380c1s
v1p0642c2s v1p0650c2s v1p0738c1s
v1p1329c2m v2p0454c1s
Gorst, H.E. v5p0177c1s
v6p0143c2s v6p0201c2s v6p0269c2s
v6p0270c1s v6p0274c2s v6p0437c2m
v6p0438c1s v6p0438c2s v6p0439c2s
v6p0468c1s v6p0634c2s v6p0678c2s
v6p0683c1s v6p0712c1s
Gorst, Harold v5p0110c1s
Gorst, Harold E. v6p0089c2s
Gorst, J. v4p0017c2s
v6p0191c2s
Gorst, J., Sir v5p0178c2s
v6p0600c1s
Gorst, J.E. v1p0918c2s
v2p0186c1s v3p0181c1s v4p0170c1m
v4p0239c2s v4p0532c2s v5p0511c2s
v6p0108c1s v6p0117c1s v6p0498c1s
v6p0600c1s
Gorton and Ralph v3p0046c2s
Gorton, D.A. v1p0016c2s
v1p0073c2s v1p0204c2s v1p0258c2s
v1p0343c1s v1p0356c1s v1p0356c2s
v1p0359c2s v1p0427c1m v1p0537c2s
v1p0578c2s v1p0619c1s v1p0643c2s
v1p0646c2s v1p0714c1s v1p0714c2s
v1p0745c2s v1p0747c2s v1p0793c2s
v1p0802c1s v1p0802c2s v1p0805c1s
v1p0812c1s v1p0820c1s v1p0843c2s
v1p0865c2s v1p0898c1s v1p0898c2s
v1p1006c1s v1p1174c1m v1p1271c1s
v1p1319c1s v1p1352c2s v4p0580c2s
Gorton, D.A. et al. v1p0356c1s
Gorton, E. v4p0285c1s
Gorton, J. v1p0700c1s
Goschen, C.J. v2p0182c1s
Goschen, G.J. v1p0625c1s
v2p0142c2s v2p0190c2s v3p0210c2s
Goschen, Viscount v6p0108c1s
Goshorn, A.T. v4p0100c2s
Goshorn, A.T. et al. v4p0101c1s
Gosling, A. v4p0094c2s
Gosman, A. v1p0641c2s
v1p0690c1s v3p0143c1s
Gosnell, R.E. v4p0009c1s
v4p0073c2s
Gosow, B.F. v3p0405c1s
Goss, C.F. v3p0288c2s
v4p0387c1s v6p0478c2s
Goss, E.H. v1p0110c2s
v1p0571c2s v1p0808c2s v1p0998c1s
v2p0039c1m v2p0112c1s v2p0295c1s
v2p0342c1s v2p0371c1s v3p0038c1s
v3p0123c1s v3p0272c1s
Goss, E.S. v4p0121c1s
Goss, O.W. v2p0246c2s
Goss, W.F.M. v4p0467c2s
v6p0615c1s
Goss, W.H. v1p1255c2s
v2p0018c1s v3p0230c2s
Goss, W.L. v2p0060c2m
v2p0270c1s v2p0335c1s v2p0453c2s
Gossan, N.J. v3p0212c2s
Gosse, E. v2p0183c2s
v2p0232c2s v2p0237c2s v2p0364c2s
v2p0402c1s v3p0007c1s v3p0011c2s
v3p0020c2s v3p0028c2m v3p0057c1s
v3p0100c1s v3p0106c1s v3p0114c2s
v3p0140c2s v3p0152c1s v3p0154c2s
v3p0177c1s v3p0206c2s v3p0207c1s
v3p0232c1s v3p0237c1s v3p0253c1s
v3p0253c2m v3p0335c1s v3p0335c2m
v3p0340c1s v3p0355c2s v3p0396c1s
v3p0399c1s v3p0409c2s v3p0424c2s
v3p0434c2s v3p0449c2s v4p0001c1s
v4p0011c2s v4p0021c2s v4p0042c1s
v4p0051c1s v4p0153c2s v4p0159c1s
v4p0260c2s v4p0320c1s v4p0334c2s
v4p0335c1s v4p0344c1s v4p0351c1s
v4p0395c1s v4p0408c2s v4p0430c1s
v4p0437c1s v4p0446c1s v4p0492c1s
v4p0510c2m v4p0523c1s v4p0549c2s
v4p0577c2s v4p0587c2s v4p0620c2s
v4p0629c1s v5p0050c2s v5p0076c1s
v5p0080c1s v5p0083c1s v5p0094c2s
v5p0142c1s v5p0163c2s v5p0192c2m
v5p0200c2s v5p0204c2s v5p0221c1m
v5p0254c2s v5p0255c2s v5p0261c1s
v5p0270c2s v5p0341c2s v5p0377c1s
v5p0411c2s v5p0414c2s v5p0435c2m
v5p0446c2s v5p0500c2s v5p0510c2s
v5p0528c2s v5p0553c1s v5p0562c1s
v5p0573c1s v5p0609c1s v5p0610c1s
v5p0630c1s v6p0002c1s v6p0047c1s
v6p0074c2s v6p0172c1m v6p0181c1s
v6p0209c2s v6p0218c2s v6p0305c2s
v6p0307c1s v6p0309c2s v6p0325c2s
v6p0420c1s v6p0471c2s v6p0484c1s
v6p0526c2s v6p0531c1s v6p0629c1s
v6p0679c1s
Gosse, E. and Edmundson, G.
v2p0289c2s
Gosse, E. and Paul, H. ... v4p0569c1s
Gosse, E. et al. v6p0183c1s
Gosse, E.M. v4p0079c1s
Gosse, E.W. v1p0426c1s
v1p0551c2s v1p0621c1s v1p0760c1s
v1p0930c1m v1p0937c2s v1p0951c1s
v1p0998c1s v1p1311c1s v1p1396c1s
v2p0037c2s v2p0058c2s v2p0085c1s
v2p0106c1s v2p0113c1s v2p0120c1s
v2p0205c2s v2p0230c1s v2p0241c2s
v2p0263c1s v2p0329c2s v2p0378c2s
v2p0392c2m v4p0142c1s v4p0510c2s
v4p0575c1s
Gosse, Edmund v5p0018c2s
v5p0020c1s v5p0357c2s v6p0066c2s
v6p0425c2s
Gosse, Ellen v4p0626c1s
Gosse, P.H. v1p0041c2m
v1p0333c1s v1p0527c2s v1p0675c2s
v1p0899c2s v1p1189c1s v1p1239c1s
v1p1379c2s v3p0377c2s
Gosselin, J. v1p0368c1s
Gossip, A.J. v4p0259c1s
Gossip, G.H. and Matheson, F.J.
v5p0543c1s
Gossip, G.H.D. v3p0028c1s
v3p0104c2s v3p0162c2s v4p0237c2s
v4p0601c2s v5p0147c2s
Gossip, R. v2p0043c2s
Gostick, J. v1p0289c1s
Gotch, F. v5p0182c2s
v5p0278c1s
Gotch, F.W. v1p0096c1s
v1p0189c1s
Gotch, Francis v6p0082c2s
Gotch, Fs. v5p0392c2s
v5p0404c2s
Gotch, J.A. v6p0244c2s
Gothard, E.von v4p0541c1s
Goto, S. v6p0234c1s
Gottberg, O.von v6p0100c2s
Gottheil, G. v1p0690c1s
v2p0238c2s v3p0229c2s v4p0400c2s
v6p0343c1m
Gottheil, J.H. v5p0543c1s
Gottheil, R. v4p0302c1s
v5p0050c2s v5p0301c2s v5p0645c2m
v6p0285c2s v6p0343c2s v6p0352c2s
v6p0566c2s
Gottheil, R.J.H. v2p0011c2s
v3p0011c2s v5p0319c2s v6p0065c1s
v6p0320c1s v6p0343c1s v6p0608c1s
v6p0713c1s
Gottheil, Richard v5p0307c2s
Gotthels, J. v1p0139c1s
Gotthilf, O. v4p0615c2s
Gottingen, L.vomB. v4p0379c2s
Gottsberger, F. v4p0334c1s
Gottschalk, L.G. v5p0089c2s
v5p0096c2s
Gottsche, C. v2p0233c2s
v2p0463c1s
Gotwald, F.G. v5p0114c2s
Gotwald, L.A. v1p0407c2s
v1p0580c2s v1p0731c2s v1p0847c1s
v1p0865c1s v1p1042c2s v1p1348c1s

v4p0301c1s v4p0345c1s
Gotz, J. v2p0413c2s
Goucher, J.F. v6p0125c1s
v6p0498c1s v6p0519c2s
Goucher, J.F. et al. v5p0636c2s
Goudie, G. v4p0442c1s
v4p0520c2s
Goudiss, C.H. v6p0262c1s
Goudy, F.C. v6p0329c1s
Goudy, H. v4p0044c2s
v4p0213c2s v5p0093c2s v6p0662c2s
Gougar, H.M. v4p0333c2s
v4p0334c1s
Gougar, Helen M. v6p0120c1s
v6p0492c2s
Gouge, W.M. v1p0093c2s
v1p0095c1s v1p0283c2s
Gough, A.B. v6p0440c2s
Gough, C.J.S. v5p0284c2s
Gough, G.W. v6p0678c2s
v6p0682c2s
Gough, H. v2p0185c1s
v4p0066c2s v4p0254c2s v5p0005c1s
Gough, Hugh v5p0002c1s
Gough, J.B. v1p0435c2s
v1p0564c1s v1p0792c2s v1p1215c1s
v4p0162c2s
Gough, R. v1p0099c2s
v1p0200c1s v1p0336c2s v1p0404c2s
v1p0464c2s v1p0604c1s v1p0768c2s
v1p0865c1s v1p0874c1m v1p0937c2s
v1p0967c2s v1p1114c2m v1p1121c2s
v1p1129c1s v1p1146c1m v1p1173c2s
v1p1263c2s
Gouinlock, W.C. v3p0030c2s
Goulaeff, E.E. v1p1138c1s
v1p1435c1s
Goulburn, E.M. v1p1217c2s
Goulburn, M. v1p0976c2s
Gould, A. v1p0460c2s
v1p1254c1s
Gould, A.A. v1p0086c2s
v1p0898c2s v1p0899c1s
Gould, A.W. v3p0105c1s
v3p0128c1s v3p0359c2s
Gould, B.A. v1p0070c2s
v1p0281c2s v1p0370c1s v1p0400c1s
v1p0768c2s v1p0936c1s v1p1244c1s
v1p1268c1s v1p1268c2s v1p1293c1s
v2p0018c1s v2p0095c1s v2p0417c2s
v2p0434c1s
Gould, B.A., jr. v1p0069c2s
v1p0498c1s v1p0588c2s v1p1064c1s
v1p1356c1s
Gould, C. v1p1349c1s
Gould, C.H. v6p0427c1s
Gould, C.N. v5p0142c2s
v5p0288c1s v5p0313c2s v5p0402c1s
v6p0332c2s
Gould, E. v2p0147c1s
v3p0141c2s v4p0057c2s v5p0304c2s
v6p0001c2s v6p0060c1s
Gould, E.B. v1p1125c2s
Gould, E.P. v1p0129c1s
v1p0130c2s v1p0496c1s v1p0646c1s
v1p0689c1s v1p1152c1s v2p0046c1s
v2p0068c2s v2p0140c1s v2p0207c2s
v2p0269c2s v2p0317c2s v2p0403c2s
v2p0406c1s v2p0469c1s v3p0002c2s
v3p0043c1s v3p0059c2s v3p0062c1s
v3p0067c1s v3p0075c2s v3p0079c1s
v3p0084c2s v3p0096c1s v3p0199c1s
v3p0272c2s v3p0295c2s v3p0309c1s
v3p0335c1s v3p0354c1s v3p0359c2s
v3p0362c2s v3p0409c2s v3p0462c2s
v3p0467c2s v4p0003c2s v4p0056c2s
v4p0130c2s v4p0234c1s v4p0502c1s
v4p0626c2s v5p0012c1s v5p0079c2s
v5p0166c1s v5p0301c1s v5p0384c2s
v5p0436c1s
Gould, E.R.L. v2p0184c1s
v2p0262c1s v2p0280c1s v2p0335c1s
v2p0335c2s v3p0321c1s v4p0022c2s
v4p0266c2s v4p0315c1m v4p0334c1m
v4p0530c1s v4p0546c2s v4p0568c1s
v4p0581c2s v4p0591c1s v5p0120c2s
v5p0268c2s v5p0273c1m v6p0300c1s
Gould, E.S. v1p0031c2s
v1p0032c1s v1p0051c1s v1p0162c1s
v1p0253c1s v1p0318c1s v1p0523c1s
v1p0895c1s v1p0917c1s v1p1101c1s
v1p1185c1s v1p1259c1m v1p1382c1s
v2p0018c2s v2p0111c1s v2p0196c1s
v2p0421c1s v2p0440c2s v2p0464c2s
v4p0142c2s v5p0147c2s v5p0559c2s
v6p0406c1s v6p0413c2s
Gould, Eliz.P. v6p0697c1s
Gould, F.B. v4p0311c1s
Gould, F.C. v2p0383c2s
v2p0415c2s v3p0104c1s v5p0156c2s
Gould, F.H. v6p0430c2s
Gould, F.H.C. v6p0068c1s
Gould, F.J. v5p0195c2s
Gould, G.M. v3p0209c1s
v3p0273c1s v4p0075c2s v4p0140c2s
v4p0161c2s v4p0167c2s v4p0271c2s
v4p0275c2s v5p0106c1s v6p0014c1s
v6p0070c2s v6p0172c2s v6p0217c1m
v6p0285c1s v6p0319c1s
Gould, G.P. v1p0263c2s
Gould, Geo.J. v6p0507c2s
Gould, J.H. v3p0309c2s
v3p0409c1s
Gould, J.S. v1p0207c2s
Gould, L.A. v6p0063c1s
Gould, L.J. v3p0093c2s
Gould, S.B. v1p0081c2s
v1p0174c1s v1p0323c1s v1p0555c2s
v1p0582c1s v1p0587c2s v1p0610c2s
v1p0622c2s v1p0701c2s v1p0836c2s
v1p0837c2s v1p0857c1s v1p0921c1s
v1p0951c1s v1p1104c1s v1p1136c2s
v1p1278c1s v1p1307c2s v1p1405c2s
v1p1411c1s v1p1426c2s v2p0178c2s
v2p0232c2s v2p0295c2s v2p0302c1s
v3p0020c1s v3p0159c1s v3p0166c1s
v3p0291c2s v3p0292c1s v3p0305c2s
v3p0356c1s v3p0384c2s v3p0411c1s
v3p0411c2s v4p0138c2s v4p0143c1s
v4p0147c2s v4p0386c1s v6p0466c1s
Gould, S.Baring v3p0231c1s
v5p0279c1s
Gould, W. v1p0712c2s
Gould, W.E. v1p0093c2s
Goulding, F. v5p0342c1s
Goulding, F.R. v1p0042c1s
v1p0724c1s v1p1059c2s v1p1365c1s
Goulee, P.M., Mrs. v4p0081c1s
Gouley, J.W.S. v4p0586c2s
Gounod, C.F. v4p0233c1s
Gour, H.S. v3p0268c2s
Gouraud, A.H. v4p0256c1s
v4p0517c1s
v5p0208c2s
Gouraud, Col. v3p0330c1s
Gourcq, J.Du v4p0034c1m
Gourdin, F.P. v1p0815c2s
v1p0963c2s
Gourlay, C. v6p0038c2s
Gourlay, H. v4p0314c1s
Gourlay, R. v4p0086c2s
v4p0626c2s v5p0125c2s v5p0153c1s
v5p0155c2s v5p0191c1s v5p0251c1s
v5p0276c2s v5p0534c1s v5p0598c1s
Gourlay, Reginald v6p0275c1s
Gournay, P.F.de v2p0055c2s
v2p0107c1s v2p0165c1s v2p0210c2s
v2p0244c2s v2p0375c2s v2p0402c1s
v3p0052c1s v3p0163c2s v3p0198c1s
v4p0397c1s
Gouvy, M.A. v3p0107c2s
Govan, A. v1p1402c2s
Gove, A. v3p0379c1s
v4p0393c2s v5p0511c2s v6p0574c2s
Gove, A. et al. v5p0471c2s
Gove, A., Lady v5p0468c1s
Gove, Aaron v5p0512c1s
Gove, Agnes v5p0380c2s
Gove, G. v1p1164c1s
Gove, H. v5p0209c1s
Gove, J.F. v6p0613c2s
Gove, J.H. v3p0015c1s
Gover, R.M. v3p0117c2s
Govett, E. v6p0475c1s
Govin, A. v5p0258c1s
Gow, G.B. v2p0431c1s
v5p0200c1s
Gow, G.C. v6p0708c2s
Gow, Geo.C. v6p0438c2s
Gow, J. v2p0344c2s
Gowan, W.E. v4p0105c1s
v5p0111c1s v5p0383c1s
Gowen, H.H. v4p0086c2s
v4p0250c2m v4p0500c2s v4p0600c1s
v5p0073c1s v5p0081c2s v5p0201c1s
v5p0259c1s
Gowen, J.E. v1p0357c1s
Gower and Monson v6p0187c2s
Gower, E. v4p0207c1s
v4p0362c2s
Gower, F.Leveson v5p0086c1s
Gower, G.L. v5p0243c1s
v5p0283c1s
Gower, R. v1p0705c2s
v1p0711c1s v2p0397c1s v4p0355c2s
Gower, R., Lord v1p1186c1s
Gower, R.S. v5p0171c2s
v6p0054c2s
Gowers, W.R. v4p0606c1s
v6p0220c2s
Gowing, A., Mrs. v3p0387c2s
v3p0388c2s
Gowing, E.A. v3p0092c2s
v3p0110c2s v3p0234c2s v3p0235c1s
v4p0063c2s v4p0080c2s v4p0158c2s
v4p0191c2s v4p0243c1s v4p0247c1s
v4p0353c2s v4p0430c2s v4p0495c1s
v4p0529c1s v4p0542c1s v4p0543c2s
Gowing, Grace G. v6p0604c2s
Gowland, W. v4p0074c2s
v4p0133c2s v4p0297c1s v5p0302c2s
v5p0371c2m v5p0494c2s v6p0619c1s
Gowrdin, F.P. v1p0725c2s
Gozlan, L. v1p1392c1s
v1p1392c2s
Gozzaldi, M. v3p0204c2s
Graaff, A.S.Van de v4p0396c2s
Grabau, A.W. v6p0132c2s
v6p0158c2s v6p0248c2s v6p0250c2s
v6p0251c1s
Grabau, A.W. and Kemp, J.F.
v6p0250c2s
Grabil, E.V. v4p0127c1s
v4p0423c2s
Grabo, C.H. v6p0026c2s
v6p0209c1s v6p0440c2s v6p0612c2m
v6p0641c2s
Grace, A. v1p1251c2s
Grace, F.W. v1p1353c2s
Grace, P.C. v1p0843c1s
Grace, W.G. v3p0105c1s
v4p0139c1s v5p0143c1s
Grace, W.G. and Brownlee, W.M.
v3p0104c2s
Grace, W.R. v2p0086c1s
Grace, W.R. et al. v2p0089c1s
Gracey, J.T. v1p0632c2s
v1p1287c1s v2p0292c1s v6p0525c2s
Gracey, L.L. v4p0571c2s
Gracey, L.R. v4p0539c2s
Gracey, W.T. v5p0113c1s
Gracy, S.L. v4p0106c2s
Grad, M.C. v1p0876c1s
v1p1246c2s
Gradenwitz, A. v6p0134c2s
v6p0198c1s v6p0199c1s v6p0248c1s
v6p0376c2s v6p0496c2s v6p0636c1s
v6p0637c1s
Gradle, H. v2p0175c2s
Gradwell, R. v2p0247c1s
Gradwohl, M. v5p0567c2s
Grady, H.W. v1p0306c1s
v2p0308c2s v3p0401c2s
Grady, S.G. v1p0219c1s
v1p1031c1s
Grady, S.O. v3p0354c2s
Graebner, A. v3p0283c2s
Graefe, A.von v1p1375c1s
Graeff, I.E. v1p0246c1s
v1p0254c1s v1p0293c1s v1p0379c1s
v1p0381c1m v1p0639c1s v1p0642c1s
v1p0686c2s v1p0900c2s v1p0980c1s
v1p1054c2s v1p1058c2s v1p1263c2s
v1p1294c1s v1p1356c1s v2p0081c1s
v2p0108c1s v3p0042c1s v3p0044c2s
v3p0084c2s v3p0229c1s v5p0114c1s
Graeff, J. v1p1314c2s
Graeff, J.E. v1p1096c2s
v2p0235c2s v2p0414c2s v2p0415c1s
Graeff, Virginia E. v6p0370c1s
Graeme, A.M.S. v2p0108c1s
Graeme, J. v3p0246c1s
Graeme, L. v4p0497c2s
Graeme, R. v3p0003c1s
Graetz, H. v4p0306c1s
Graetz, V. v6p0410c2s
Graf, A. v5p0486c2s
Graf, Arturo v5p0328c2s
Graff, F. v1p1248c1s
Graff, L.von v4p0637c2s
Graffenried, C.de v3p0170c2s
v4p0169c1s v4p0262c1s v4p0532c1s
v4p0626c1s v4p0630c1m v5p0052c2s
v6p0057c1s v6p0057c2s
Graffenried, C.de and
Willoughby, W.F. v3p0077c2s
Grafton, A.B. v6p0357c2s
Grafton, C.C. v3p0362c1s
v6p0544c2m
Grafton, G. v1p0833c2s
v1p1224c2s
Grafton, M.E. v2p0145c2s
Grafton, Mary E. v2p0421c2s
Graham, A. v1p0707c1s
v3p0303c2s v3p0367c1s
Graham, A.A. v1p0142c1s
v1p0639c1s v1p0675c1s v1p0797c2s
v1p1075c2s v1p1190c2s v1p1371c2s
v1p1379c1s v2p0094c2s v2p0320c1s
v2p0395c2s v2p0418c1s v3p0307c2s
Graham, A.J. v1p0426c1s
Graham, A.S. and Woodhull, Anna M.W.
v6p0696c2s
Graham, C. v1p0108c1s
v1p0192c1s v1p0449c1s v1p1292c2s
v3p0054c1s
Graham, C.G.C. v5p0566c2s
Graham, C.I. v6p0534c1s
Graham, C.K. v1p0211c1s
v1p0272c1s
Graham, C.M. v5p0179c1s
v5p0325c2s
Graham, D. v2p0279c2s
v4p0360c1m
Graham, D.S. v3p0195c2s
v4p0565c2s
Graham, E. v5p0069c2s
v5p0333c1s
Graham, E.K. v6p0137c2s
v6p0346c1s
Graham, E.M. v6p0109c2s
v6p0441c1s
Graham, E.P. v6p0333c2s
Graham, F. v6p0123c2s
Graham, G., Sir v3p0177c2s
Graham, G.C. v3p0021c1s
Graham, G.C.Cunninghame .. v5p0241c2s
Graham, G.E. and Goode, W.A.M.
v5p0100c1s
Graham, G.L. v6p0689c1s

Graham, H. v1p0699c2s v2p0434c1s v3p0168c1s v3p0175c1s v3p0207c2s v3p0213c1s v3p0218c2s v3p0258c2s v3p0305c2s v3p0346c1s v4p0129c2s
Graham, H.G. v1p1133c1s v4p0509c1s
Graham, H.L. v4p0060c1s v5p0062c2m v5p0252c1s v6p0534c2s
Graham, H.W. v6p0102c2s v6p0690c2s
Graham, Harry v6p0052c2s
Graham, Henry v4p0229c1s
Graham, J. v1p0323c1s v1p1216c2s v3p0201c1s v3p0295c2s v3p0331c2s v4p0233c2s v4p0515c2s v6p0095c1s v6p0165c2s v6p0523c1s v6p0680c2s
Graham, J.A. v6p0177c2m v6p0178c1m v6p0417c2s v6p0447c1s
Graham, J.B. v6p0191c1s
Graham, J.C. v3p0374c2s v4p0225c1s v4p0599c2s
Graham, J.E. v3p0129c1s v4p0171c1s v5p0568c1s v5p0573c1s v5p0588c1s v6p0193c2s
Graham, J.H. v6p0624c2s
Graham, J.Whidden v4p0565c1s
Graham, K.A. v6p0043c1s v6p0200c2s
Graham, M. v1p0168c1s v3p0081c2s v3p0366c1s v3p0473c2s
Graham, M.C. v4p0010c1s v4p0207c1s v4p0273c2s v4p0625c1s v5p0036c1s v6p0217c1s v6p0400c2s
Graham, M.G. v6p0702c1s
Graham, Maj. v2p0288c2s
Graham, Marquis of v6p0083c1m
Graham, Mary v2p0385c1s v5p0165c1s
Graham, N.C. v6p0241c1s v6p0392c1s
Graham, N.D.S. v5p0567c2s
Graham, O. v5p0064c1s
Graham, P. v3p0340c1s
Graham, P.A. v2p0381c2s v2p0428c2s v3p0091c1s v3p0207c2s v3p0425c1s v4p0008c1m v4p0037c1s v4p0066c1s v4p0110c2s v4p0202c1s v4p0244c2s v4p0299c1s v4p0318c1s v4p0422c2s v4p0447c2s v4p0585c2s v5p0043c1s v5p0094c2s v5p0139c2s v5p0194c1s v5p0414c1s v5p0512c2s v5p0515c2s v5p0611c1s
Graham, Prof. v3p0054c1s
Graham, R. v1p0045c1s v1p0684c2s v1p0769c1s v1p1001c2s v1p1003c2s v1p1292c1s v1p1367c1s v3p0023c1s v3p0141c2s v4p0121c2s v4p0500c2s v5p0425c1s v5p0608c2s
Graham, R., Miss v6p0396c2s v6p0424c2s
Graham, R.B.C. v4p0023c1s v4p0296c2s v4p0300c1s v4p0383c1s v4p0486c1s v4p0500c2s v4p0505c1s v4p0508c2s v5p0008c1s v5p0023c2s v5p0024c2s v5p0078c1s v5p0100c1s v5p0127c2s v5p0255c2s v5p0430c1s v5p0492c2s v5p0509c2s v5p0528c2s v5p0534c1s v5p0541c1m v5p0583c2s v5p0585c2s v5p0606c1s v5p0610c1s v6p0012c1s v6p0025c2s v6p0026c1s v6p0077c1s v6p0094c1s v6p0107c1s v6p0202c2s v6p0218c2s v6p0220c2s v6p0235c1s v6p0275c2s v6p0301c2s v6p0362c1s v6p0414c2s v6p0421c2s v6p0430c1m v6p0467c1s v6p0594c1s v6p0619c1s v6p0623c2s v6p0632c2s v6p0698c2s v6p0712c2s
Graham, R.B.Cunninghame .. v3p0207c2s v3p0472c1s v6p0111c2s v6p0306c2s
Graham, R.C. v3p0248c1s v4p0579c1s v6p0647c2s
Graham, R.H. v3p0303c2s
Graham, R.P.D. v6p0521c1s
Graham, S.L. v1p0096c1s v1p0594c2s
Graham, T. v1p0036c1s v1p0426c1s v1p0455c1s v1p0502c2s v1p0619c1s v1p0751c2s v3p0425c1s
Graham, T.H. v5p0099c1s
Graham, T.H.B. v3p0147c1s v3p0216c1s v4p0034c1s v4p0049c1s v4p0073c2m v4p0143c1m v4p0162c2s v4p0351c1m v4p0375c2s v4p0415c2s v4p0559c1s v4p0576c1s v5p0169c2s v5p0173c2m v5p0193c1s v5p0207c2s v5p0259c2s v5p0442c2s
Graham, Thomas H.B. v4p0073c2s v4p0091c1s v5p0609c1s
Graham, W. v2p0382c1s v3p0399c1s v4p0081c2s v4p0119c1s v4p0122c2s v4p0212c1s v4p0309c1s v4p0323c1s v4p0370c1s v4p0414c1s v4p0455c1s v4p0520c1s v5p0381c2s v5p0503c2s v5p0606c1s
Graham, W.W. v2p0203c1s
Graham, William v4p0516c1s
Grahame, A.B.C. v4p0409c1s
Grahame, F. v1p1155c2s
Grahame, F., Mrs. v1p0374c2s
Grahame, F.R. v1p1384c1s
Grahame, G. v3p0320c1s v4p0243c2s
Grahame, George v4p0118c1s v5p0159c1s
Grahame, J. v5p0525c2s
Grahame, J.B. v6p0627c2s
Grahame, K. v4p0276c1s v4p0349c2s v5p0201c2s v5p0301c1s v5p0503c2s
Grahame, Kenneth v4p0588c1s
Grahame, R. v1p0609c2s v1p0770c2s
Grahame, T.L. v5p0077c1m
Grain, F.K. v6p0248c2s
Grain, R.C. v3p0312c2s v3p0356c1s
Grainger, A. v6p0042c1s
Gram, J.S. v2p0204c2s v2p0380c1s v2p0387c2s v2p0409c2m
Grammer, G.C. v1p1207c2s
Granberry, J.C. v1p0427c1s v1p1201c1s
Grand, P. v6p0148c1s
Grand, S. v3p0226c1s v3p0234c1s v4p0189c1s v4p0226c2s v4p0352c1s v4p0626c2s v5p0191c2s
Grand, Sarah v4p0067c2s v4p0377c1s v4p0590c1s v4p0634c1s v5p0363c1s v5p0628c1s
Grandgent, C.H. v3p0141c1s v4p0215c1s v6p0072c1s v6p0241c2s v6p0363c1s v6p0423c1s
Grandgent, C.H. et al. ... v4p0320c2s
Graneisen, C.L. v1p0597c2s
Granet, E.J. v4p0031c2s
Granfelt, A.A. v6p0224c2s v6p0371c1s
Grange, A. v4p0312c2s
Grange, A.D. v6p0009c1s
Grange, A.M. v2p0230c1s v3p0364c2s v4p0097c2s v4p0221c1s v5p0117c2s
Grange, A.W. v4p0485c1s
Grange, E.A.A. v5p0270c2s
Granger, A.C. v5p0336c1s
Granger, A.H. v6p0055c2s
Granger, A.O. v3p0208c1s
Granger, A.O., Mrs. v6p0115c1s v6p0706c1s
Granger, E. v5p0288c1s v6p0256c1s v6p0295c1s v6p0437c1s
Granger, F. v1p0207c1s v4p0026c2s v5p0386c1s v6p0142c1s v6p0240c1s
Granger, J.H. v1p0848c1s
Granger, J.N. v1p1149c2s
Granger, L.T. v6p0538c2s
Granger, W.N. v1p0423c1s v1p1063c1s
Grannan, C.J. v5p0486c2s
Grannan, C.P. v4p0057c2m v6p0060c1s v6p0060c2s v6p0065c1s
Grannis, H. v6p0033c1s
Granniss, G.W. v5p0242c1s
Granrud, J.E. v5p0119c1s
Grant, A. v1p1329c1s v2p0070c1s v4p0073c2s v4p0199c2s v4p0256c1s v4p0366c1s v4p0400c1s v4p0539c2s v6p0289c1s v6p0603c2s
Grant, A., Sir v1p0868c1s v1p1422c2s
Grant, A.H. v2p0242c2s v2p0457c2s v4p0298c2s v4p0348c1s v6p0349c1s
Grant, A.R. v1p0435c2s
Grant, Arthur v4p0448c1s
Grant, B. v1p0119c1s v1p0121c1s v1p0646c1s v1p0972c2s
Grant, B.R. v1p1247c1s
Grant, C. v1p0446c2s v1p0583c1s v1p0633c2s v1p0690c2s v1p1184c1s v2p0061c2s v2p0231c1s v2p0241c2s
Grant, C.C. v2p0202c2s v3p0107c1s v3p0323c2m
Grant, C.E. v2p0054c1s
Grant, C.R. and Stanton, E.C. v5p0484c2s
Grant, E.C. v4p0344c2s
Grant, F. v3p0368c1s
Grant, F.D. v2p0184c2s v5p0242c1s
Grant, F.E. v6p0641c1s
Grant, F.J. v3p0383c2s
Grant, Frederick D. v4p0328c1s
Grant, G. v1p0446c1s v3p0035c1s v5p0012c1s v5p0581c2s
Grant, G.A. v6p0562c2s
Grant, G.B. v1p0185c2s v3p0135c2s v3p0168c1m
Grant, G.H. v6p0620c1s
Grant, G.J.F. v4p0059c2s v5p0383c1s v6p0157c2s
Grant, G.J.Forsyth v5p0284c2s
Grant, G.M. v1p0194c1s v1p0235c1s v1p0610c1s v1p1095c1s v1p1103c2s v1p1399c2s v1p1416c1s v2p0056c2m v2p0066c1s v2p0091c1s v3p0170c1s v3p0179c2s v3p0181c1s v3p0241c1s v3p0304c2s v3p0345c2s v3p0441c1s v4p0085c1s v4p0086c1s v4p0227c2s v4p0479c2s v4p0598c1s v5p0408c2s v6p0642c2s
Grant, H.A. v1p0524c2s
Grant, Helen L. v6p0068c2s
Grant, I. v3p0054c2s v3p0247c1s v3p0250c1s v3p0457c2s
Grant, J. v1p0171c1s v1p0351c1s v1p0439c2s v1p0519c1s v1p0585c2s v1p0709c1s v1p0909c1s v1p0914c2s v1p1217c2s v1p1221c1s v1p1339c2s v1p1367c1s v1p1397c1s v2p0094c2s v3p0398c2s
Grant, J.A. v1p1370c2s
Grant, J.C. v4p0321c2s v5p0234c1s
Grant, J.M. v2p0369c2s
Grant, Jean v5p0511c1s
Grant, L. v6p0386c1s v6p0684c1s
Grant, M. v4p0381c2s
Grant, M.H. v5p0011c2s
Grant, M.M. v1p0951c2s
Grant, O. v3p0158c1s
Grant, P. v2p0205c2s
Grant, P.S. v5p0379c2s v6p0228c1s v6p0531c1s v6p0595c2s
Grant, R. v1p0827c2s v2p0030c1s v3p0005c2s v3p0051c1s v3p0147c2s v3p0407c1s v3p0420c2s v3p0439c2s v4p0040c2s v4p0081c2s v4p0101c2s v4p0276c2s v4p0336c1s v4p0361c1s v4p0407c1s v4p0415c1s v4p0476c2s v4p0483c2s v5p0208c1s v5p0257c1s v6p0289c2s v6p0364c1s v6p0664c2s
Grant, R.B. v6p0652c2s
Grant, Robert v5p0082c1s v5p0475c1s v5p0517c2s
Grant, T. v5p0282c1s
Grant, T.B. v4p0290c1s v4p0291c2s v4p0553c1s v4p0596c2m
Grant, U.S. v2p0075c2s v2p0314c1s v2p0349c2s v2p0400c2s v2p0460c1s v2p0474c1s v3p0343c1s
Grant, W. v4p0062c2s v4p0631c2s
Grant, W.G. v5p0029c2s
Grant, W.H. v1p0563c2s v1p0916c1s v1p1110c2m v1p1111c1m
Grant, W.J.A. v2p0109c1s
Grant, W.L. v6p0467c2s
Grant-Duff, A.J. v2p0212c2s
Grant-Duff, M.E. v1p0067c2s v3p0021c1s v4p0153c2s v6p0255c2s v6p0288c2s v6p0293c1s v6p0314c1s v6p0351c1s v6p0630c2s v6p0645c1s
Grantham, W. v5p0119c1s
Grantoff, Otto v6p0701c1s
Granton, P. v1p1427c1s
Granville, H. v4p0015c2s v5p0075c2s
Granville, H.S. v5p0082c1s
Granville, J.M. v1p0156c2s v1p0365c2s v1p0456c1s v1p0644c1s v1p1200c2s v1p1432c2s v2p0055c1s v2p0122c1s v2p0123c2s v2p0290c1s v2p0405c2s v3p0123c1s
Granville, J.Mortimer v2p0420c2s
Granville, M. v2p0480c2s v4p0233c1s
Granville, V. v6p0419c1s v6p0594c1s v6p0710c2s
Granville, Vera v5p0251c2s
Grape, J., jr. v2p0152c1s
Grasset, A. v6p0075c2s
Grassi, G.B. v5p0357c1s
Grassman, H. v4p0223c1s
Gratacap, L.P. v1p0621c2s v2p0073c1s v2p0088c1s v2p0102c1s v2p0274c2m v2p0286c2m v2p0323c2s v2p0327c1s v2p0446c1s v2p0457c1s v2p0483c1s v3p0010c2s v3p0141c1s v3p0169c2s v3p0266c1s v4p0094c2s v4p0135c2s v4p0196c1s v4p0210c1s v4p0476c2s v5p0215c1s v5p0254c2s v5p0393c1m v6p0189c2s v6p0412c2s
Graton, L.C. and Gordon, C.H. v6p0451c1s
Graton, L.C. and Schaller, W.T. v6p0523c2s
Grattan, E.A. v1p0109c2s v1p0415c1s v1p0652c2s v1p0659c2s v1p0661c2s
Grattan, H.P. v2p0063c1s v2p0083c1s
Grattan, T.C. v1p0171c2s v1p0370c2s v1p0662c1s v1p0703c2s v1p0809c2s v1p0888c2s
Gratz, F. v5p0317c1s
Gratz, H. v5p0115c1s
Gratz, R.J. v3p0057c1s
Gratz, S. v2p0062c2s
Grave, C. v5p0021c2s v5p0051c2s v6p0226c2s
Graves, A. v1p0815c2s v5p0074c2s
Graves, A.P. v1p0949c2s

v1p1240c1s v1p1378c2s v2p0228c2s
v4p0511c1s v5p0168c1s v5p0359c2s
v5p0564c1s v5p0573c1s v6p0498c1s
Graves, A.S. v3p0460c1s
Graves, C. v5p0606c1s
v6p0161c2s
Graves, C.A. v4p0190c2s
Graves, C.H. v6p0340c1s
Graves, C.L. v3p0293c1s
v4p0351c1s v6p0345c1s v6p0360c2s
v6p0385c1s v6p0437c2s v6p0438c1m
v6p0438c2m v6p0439c1s v6p0543c2s
v6p0546c2s v6p0617c1s v6p0618c1s
v6p0634c2s v6p0649c2s
Graves, C.M. v6p0333c2s
v6p0366c1s v6p0504c2s v6p0508c1s
v6p0644c1s
Graves, Col. v5p0354c2s
Graves, Dr. v1p1317c1s
Graves, E.O. v1p0259c1s
Graves, Elma v5p0391c1s
Graves, F. v5p0242c2s
v6p0683c1s
Graves, F.B. v1p0799c1s
v6p0371c1s
Graves, F.J. v5p0588c1s
v6p0534c1s v6p0654c2s
Graves, F.P. v5p0605c1s
v6p0137c1s v6p0194c1s v6p0473c1s
v6p0479c2s v6p0574c2s
Graves, G.E. v1p1400c1s
Graves, G.M. v2p0242c2s
Graves, H. v4p0268c2s
v5p0061c1s v5p0547c1s
Graves, H.C. v1p0111c2s
v5p0460c1s
Graves, H.S. v5p0213c1s
v5p0214c1s
Graves, J. v1p0795c2s
Graves, J.H. v6p0130c2s
Graves, J.T. v6p0446c2s
Graves, J.T. and Bois, W.E.B.Du
v6p0039c2s
Graves, L. v3p0299c1s
Graves, P.P. v5p0593c2s
v6p0282c2s
Graves, R.E. v2p0354c2s
v4p0293c1s
Graves, R.H. v1p0173c2s
v1p0233c2s v1p0236c2s v1p0289c2s
v1p1284c2s v6p0057c2s v6p0301c2s
v6p0482c1s
Graves, R.P. v3p0188c2s
Graves, R.S. v6p0511c1s
Graves, R.W. v2p0032c1s
v2p0203c2s
Graves, Ralph H. v6p0281c1s
Graves, S. v1p0977c2s
v1p1042c1s v1p1065c1s v2p0027c2s
v2p0067c1s v2p0359c1s
Graves, W.C. v6p0113c1s
Gravier, G. v2p0250c1s
Grawitz, G. v2p0072c2s
Gray, A. v1p0009c1s
v1p0013c2s v1p0021c2s v1p0026c1s
v1p0029c1s v1p0133c1s v1p0150c1s
v1p0152c2m v1p0153c1m v1p0196c1s
v1p0196c2s v1p0213c2s v1p0225c1s
v1p0265c2s v1p0313c1s v1p0333c1m
v1p0333c2m v1p0360c1s v1p0390c2s
v1p0434c1s v1p0449c2s v1p0468c1m
v1p0507c2s v1p0515c2s v1p0536c1s
v1p0602c2m v1p0627c1s v1p0645c2m
v1p0678c1s v1p0779c1s v1p0803c2s
v1p0872c2s v1p0899c2s v1p0918c2s
v1p0951c2s v1p1007c2s v1p1014c2m
v1p1015c1m v1p1015c2s v1p1016c1s
v1p1022c1s v1p1127c2s v1p1138c1s
v1p1149c1s v1p1174c2s v1p1178c2s
v1p1233c1m v1p1266c1s v1p1316c2s
v1p1324c1s v1p1364c2s v1p1380c1s
v1p1396c2s v1p1410c1s v1p1434c2s
v2p0004c2m v2p0031c1s v2p0040c1m
v2p0053c1m v2p0112c1s v2p0141c1s
v2p0159c1s v2p0159c2m v2p0170c2m
v2p0200c1s v2p0222c2s v2p0234c1s
v2p0237c1s v2p0238c2s v2p0246c2s
v2p0267c1s v2p0272c1s v2p0296c1s
v2p0307c1m v2p0316c1s v2p0336c1s
v2p0380c1s v2p0447c2s v2p0448c1s
v3p0048c1s v3p0111c1s v3p0121c1s
v3p0134c1s v3p0422c2s v3p0466c2s
v4p0165c1s v4p0175c1s v4p0177c1m
v4p0201c2s v4p0243c2s v4p0309c2s
v5p0153c2s v5p0314c2m v5p0356c1m
v5p0367c1s v5p0372c1s v5p0486c1s
v5p0489c2s
Gray, A. and Ernst, C.W. . v2p0112c2s
Gray, A. and Felton, C.C.. v1p0437c1s
Gray, A. and Treadwell, D.
v1p1233c1s v1p1303c2s
Gray, A. and Trumbull, J.H.
v1p0065c1s
Gray, A. and Vincent, C.E.H.
v3p0274c2s
Gray, A.M. v1p1292c2s
Gray, A.R. v6p0042c2s
v6p0187c1s
Gray, Asa v2p0344c1s
Gray, C.A. v5p0612c2s
Gray, C.B. v1p1310c2s
v4p0366c1s
Gray, C.D. v5p0058c2s
v5p0462c2s
Gray, Clarke v6p0103c1s
Gray, D. v1p0066c2s
v1p0638c2s v1p1375c2s v5p0075c2s
v5p0082c1s v5p0146c1s v5p0216c1s
v5p0224c2s v5p0262c2s v5p0366c2s
v6p0024c1s v6p0080c1s v6p0124c1s
v6p0187c2s v6p0236c1s v6p0330c1s
v6p0493c1s v6p0507c2s v6p0535c2s
v6p0647c2s
Gray, David v5p0096c1s
v5p0145c2s v5p0432c1s v6p0417c2s
Gray, E. v1p0006c1s
v1p0463c1s v1p0883c2s v4p0081c1s
v4p0566c1s v4p0567c1s v5p0177c2s
Gray, E.C. v1p0321c1s
v1p0536c1s v1p1219c2s
Gray, E.F. v6p0175c1s
v6p0511c2s
Gray, E.M. v6p0660c2s
Gray, E.P. v2p0064c1s
v2p0236c1s v2p0250c2s v3p0040c1s
Gray, Earl v4p0580c2s
Gray, Elizabeth F. v6p0551c2s
v6p0712c2s
Gray, F. v4p0124c1s
Gray, F.C. v1p0033c1s
v1p0211c2s v1p0403c1s v1p0429c2s
v1p0680c1s v1p0783c1s v1p1323c1s
Gray, F.J. v6p0169c2s
v6p0201c1s
Gray, F.M. v1p1067c1s
v1p1127c1s v1p1434c1s
Gray, F.T. v1p0847c1s
Gray, G. v4p0014c1s
Gray, G.A. v6p0294c2s
Gray, G.B. v5p0055c2s
v5p0058c1s v5p0307c2s v5p0645c2s
v6p0445c2s
Gray, G.D. v6p0534c2s
Gray, G.F. v6p0419c2s
Gray, G.H. v1p1167c2s
v1p1276c1s
Gray, G.J. v2p0155c2s
v2p0473c1s
Gray, G.W. v2p0009c2s
Gray, G.Z. v1p0264c1s
Gray, H. v3p0150c1s
Gray, H.D. v5p0523c1s
v5p0612c1s
Gray, H.St.George v6p0055c1s
v6p0215c1s
Gray, J. v2p0155c1s
v2p0450c2s v3p0123c2s v4p0070c1s
v5p0342c1s v6p0167c1s v6p0365c1s
v6p0391c2s v6p0572c1s
Gray, J., Mrs. v1p1263c2s
Gray, J.A. v4p0004c2s
v4p0005c1s v4p0521c1s
Gray, J.B.M. v1p1221c1s
Gray, J.C. v1p0031c2s
v1p0033c1s v1p0115c2s v1p0228c2s
v1p0262c1s v1p0270c1s v1p0276c1s
v1p0331c1s v1p0343c2s v1p0372c2s
v1p0468c1s v1p0605c2s v1p0910c2s
v1p0946c1s v1p0950c2s v1p0953c1s
v1p1284c1s v1p1322c1s v1p1324c1s
v6p0256c1s
Gray, J.C. et al. v5p0496c2s
Gray, J.C., jr. v1p0309c1s
Gray, J.E. v1p0983c2s
v1p0984c1s v1p1254c1s v1p1366c2s
Gray, J.G. v4p0315c2s
Gray, J.H. v1p0018c1s
v3p0065c1s v3p0398c2s v4p0114c2s
v5p0105c1s v5p0226c2m v5p0365c1s
v5p0391c2s v5p0556c2s v6p0084c1s
Gray, J.J. v5p0379c2s
Gray, J.M. v1p0146c2s
v1p0327c1s v1p0605c1s v1p0979c1s
v1p1246c2s v2p0007c2s v2p0041c1s
v2p0053c2s v2p0058c1s v2p0247c1s
v2p0253c2s v2p0270c1s v2p0271c1s
v2p0278c1s v2p0332c2s v2p0341c2s
v2p0368c1s v2p0378c2s v2p0392c1s
v3p0057c1s v3p0174c1s v3p0194c2s
v3p0342c2s v3p0389c1s v4p0075c2m
v4p0080c1s v4p0146c2s v4p0168c1s
v4p0178c1s v4p0198c2s v4p0210c1s
v4p0254c2s v4p0308c2s v4p0309c2s
v4p0480c1s v4p0482c1s v4p0510c1s
v4p0530c1s v4p0564c1m v4p0611c1s
v4p0615c2s v5p0329c2s
Gray, J.P. v6p0039c2s
Gray, J.T. v1p0039c1s
v1p0121c2s
Gray, L.F. v4p0069c1s
Gray, L.H. v5p0289c1s
v6p0079c1s
Gray, L.H. and Schuyler, M., jr.
v5p0264c1s
Gray, L.M. v2p0367c1s
v2p0476c1s v3p0379c1s
Gray, M. v2p0405c2s
v3p0102c2s v3p0300c2s v3p0359c1s
v3p0375c2s v3p0393c2s v4p0458c2s
v4p0552c2s v4p0629c1s v5p0215c2s
Gray, M.D. v5p0495c1s
v6p0548c2s
Gray, M.I. v6p0571c2s
v6p0705c2s
Gray, M.R. v6p0563c1s
v6p0703c1s
Gray, Minna v5p0346c1s
Gray, Mrs. v1p0245c1s
v1p1106c1s v1p1203c2s
Gray, Oliver v6p0290c2s
Gray, P.L. v4p0127c2s
Gray, R. v1p0136c1s
v1p0544c1s v1p0693c1s v1p0705c2s
v1p0908c1s v1p0967c1s v1p1020c1s
v1p1358c2s v2p0472c2s v6p0642c1s
Gray, S. v3p0020c1s
Gray, Stephen v4p0097c2s
Gray, T. v1p0285c2s
v1p0312c2s v1p0401c2s v1p0538c1s
v1p0623c1s v1p0795c1s v1p0820c2s
v1p0897c1s v1p1328c2s v3p0409c1s
v4p0219c1s v4p0455c2s v4p0571c1s
v5p0184c2s
Gray, T.C. v1p0509c2s
Gray, W. v1p0439c1s
v1p1293c2s
Gray, W.A. v2p0125c2s
Gray, W.C. v2p0148c1s
Gray, W.D. v6p0499c2s
v6p0653c1s
Gray, W.E. v6p0511c2s
Gray, W.Forbes v5p0222c1s
Gray, W.I. v3p0211c2s
Gray, W.J. v1p1207c2s
Gray, W.M. v4p0144c1s
v5p0424c2s
Graybill, J.E. v2p0383c2s
v2p0480c1s
Graycroft, J.H. v6p0402c2s
Graydon, N.A. v2p0129c2s
Graydon, W.M. v4p0276c2s
Grayson, A.J. v1p0674c2s
v1p0833c2s v1p1324c2s
Grayson, D. v6p0146c2s
Grayson, F.W. v2p0452c2s
Grayson, G. v5p0046c2s
Grayson, H. v6p0118c1s
Grayson, J.R. v6p0220c1s
Grayson, J.W. v1p0772c2s
Grayson, P. v6p0606c2s
Grayson, W.A. v1p0537c2s
Grayson, W.J. v1p0029c1s
v1p0675c1s v1p0823c2s v1p1001c1s
v2p0104c2s v2p0380c1s
Grayson, W.S. v1p0085c2s
v1p0793c2s v1p0843c2s v2p0067c2s
v2p0255c1s v2p0405c1s
Graziani, A. v4p0347c2s
Greaney, J.J. v6p0228c1s
Greard, M. v2p0119c1s
Greathead, J.H. v3p0457c2s
Greathed, E.A. v6p0044c1s
Greatheed, S. v1p0546c2s
Greathouse, C.H. v6p0247c2s
Greatorex, E. v1p0444c2s
v2p0100c2m v2p0146c2s
Greaves, C. v1p0432c2s
v1p1390c1s
Greaves, G. v2p0275c1s
Greble, G.P. v5p0240c1s
Greck, E. v5p0384c1s
v5p0640c1s
Greef, G.De v6p0602c1s
Greeley, A. v2p0057c1s
Greeley, A.P. v5p0294c2s
Greeley, C. v3p0441c2s
v4p0323c1s v4p0466c1s v4p0467c1s
v4p0532c2s v6p0513c1s
Greeley, C.D. v2p0386c2s
Greeley, C.De V. v3p0405c1s
Greeley, H. v1p0228c1s
v1p0282c2s v1p0291c2s v1p0299c1s
v1p0300c1s v1p0325c1s v1p0453c1s
v1p0486c1s v1p0711c2s v1p0898c1s
v1p1013c2s v1p1048c2s v1p1057c1m
v1p1067c2s v1p1110c2s v1p1183c1s
v1p1215c1s v1p1223c2s v1p1238c1s
v1p1283c1s v1p1283c2s v1p1344c1s
v1p1344c2s v1p1345c2s v1p1382c1s
v1p1399c2s v1p1400c2m v3p0251c2s
Greeley, N. v3p0200c1s
Greeley, S.S. v6p0281c2s
Greely, A.W. v2p0020c1s
v2p0020c2m v2p0192c2s v2p0468c2s
v3p0007c2s v3p0019c1s v3p0147c1s
v3p0169c1m v3p0237c1s v3p0283c1s
v3p0295c2s v3p0307c1s v3p0353c2s
v3p0414c2s v3p0466c1s v4p0008c2s
v4p0019c2m v4p0025c2m v4p0049c2s
v4p0068c1s v4p0115c2s v4p0124c1s
v4p0299c1s v4p0392c1s v4p0404c1s
v4p0473c1s v4p0550c2s v5p0010c2s
v5p0027c1s v5p0044c1s v5p0155c1s
v5p0228c2s v5p0272c2s v5p0276c2s
v5p0397c2s v5p0448c1s v5p0456c2s
v5p0528c1s v5p0591c2s v6p0023c2s
v6p0066c2s v6p0111c2s v6p0175c1s
v6p0250c1s v6p0378c1s v6p0557c1s
v6p0594c1s
Greely, A.W. and Hayden, E.

v3p0047c2s
Green, A.C. v6p0133c1s
Green, A.F.U. v6p0665c2s
v6p0686c1s
Green, A.G. v5p0289c1s
Green, A.H. v1p0269c1s
v1p0509c2m v2p0090c2s v2p0127c1m
v2p0127c2s v2p0174c1s v2p0229c2s
v3p0451c2s v4p0222c2s v4p0385c2s
v4p0508c2s
Green, A.H., Mrs. v4p0565c2s
Green, A.J. v6p0503c1s
Green, A.K. v3p0294c2s
v3p0463c2s
Green, A.L. v5p0093c2s
Green, A.S. v4p0244c1s
v5p0068c1s v5p0083c2s v5p0172c1s
v5p0191c1s v5p0635c2s
Green, A.S., Mrs. v5p0068c1s
Green, A.W. v1p1240c2s
Green, Alice S. v4p0244c1s
v6p0392c1s
Green, Anna K. v6p0703c1s
Green, B. v1p0392c2s
v1p1096c1s
Green, B.E. v5p0626c1s
Green, B.H. v6p0687c1s
Green, B.L. v1p0598c1s
Green, B.R. v5p0133c1m
v5p0334c1s v6p0374c2s
Green, B.T. v1p0286c2s
Green, C.E. v3p0074c1s
v3p0106c1s v5p0033c1s
Green, C.M. v1p0852c1s
Green, D. v1p0118c1s
v1p0244c2s v1p0772c2s v1p0825c1s
Green, D.H. v5p0484c1s
Green, D.I. v3p0218c1s
v4p0097c1s v4p0135c2s v4p0599c2s
v5p0607c1s v6p0512c1s
Green, D.M. v1p1110c1s
Green, E. v1p1008c1s
v2p0070c1s v4p0254c2s v5p0087c2s
v5p0262c2s v5p0265c2s
Green, E., Mrs. v1p0319c1s
Green, E.B. v5p0336c1s
Green, E.E. v4p0263c1s
v4p0535c2s
Green, E.L. v6p0296c1s
Green, E.M. v4p0149c1s
v4p0189c1s v5p0007c1s v5p0009c1s
v5p0100c2s
Green, E.M., Mrs. v6p0641c2s
Green, F. v5p0644c1s
v6p0281c2s
Green, F.B. v2p0427c1s
Green, F.G. v4p0165c1s
v4p0244c1s v4p0504c2s v4p0538c2s
Green, F.K. v6p0407c1s
v6p0428c1s
Green, F.L. v5p0093c2s
v5p0188c1s v5p0612c1s
Green, F.M. v1p0230c1s
v1p0768c2s v1p1096c1s v1p1270c1s
v2p0291c2s v3p0342c1s
Green, F.W.E. and Bousfield, E.G.P.
v6p0305c2s
Green, G. v1p1309c2s
v4p0148c2s
Green, G.A. v2p0159c2s
Green, G.C. v3p0143c2s
Green, G.R. v4p0542c1s
Green, G.S., jr. v1p0160c2s
Green, G.W. v1p0144c1s
v1p0275c2s v1p1077c2s v2p0050c1m
v2p0071c2m v2p0087c1s v2p0415c2s
v4p0119c1s v4p0429c1s
Green, H. v3p0186c1s
v4p0120c2s
Green, H.E. v3p0249c2s
v3p0332c1s v3p0408c1s v4p0092c1s
Green, H.J. v4p0577c2s
Green, H.K. v1p1309c1s
Green, H.R., Sir v2p0217c1s
Green, H.S. v5p0237c1s
Green, H.W. v1p1294c1s
Green, I. v2p0058c1s
Green, J.A. v5p0104c2s
Green, J.B. v1p0563c2s
v1p1165c2s v1p1341c2s v3p0364c1s
Green, J.C. v5p0384c1s
Green, J.D. v1p0126c2s
Green, J.F. v3p0250c2s
Green, J.H. v4p0179c2s
Green, J.M. v5p0406c1s
Green, J.O. v4p0151c1s
Green, J.R. v1p0343c2s
v1p0476c1s v1p0953c2s v2p0047c2s
v2p0360c1s v3p0358c2s v4p0446c1s
v5p0099c1s v5p0426c2s v5p0644c1s
v6p0077c2s v6p0078c2s v6p0479c1s
v6p0617c2s
Green, J.T. v3p0406c1s
Green, L.D. v5p0410c2s
Green, M. v4p0378c2s
Green, M.A. v1p1174c1s
v3p0054c1s v3p0078c2s v3p0296c2s
v4p0132c2s v4p0622c2s
Green, N. v2p0152c2s
v2p0181c1s v2p0433c1s v3p0107c2s
v3p0423c1s
Green, N.E. v2p0402c1s
Green, O.M. v6p0346c2s
v6p0480c1s
Green, P. v4p0431c2s
Green, R. v1p0751c2s
v1p1319c1s v4p0295c1s
v5p0372c2s
Green, R.M. v6p0193c1s
Green, S.A. v1p0483c2s
v1p0556c1s v1p0981c1s v2p0192c2s
v3p0060c1s v3p0072c1s v3p0186c1m
v4p0317c2s v4p0455c2s v5p0251c1s
v5p0343c2s v6p0275c1s
Green, S.G. v2p0435c1s
v3p0396c1s
Green, S.M. and Rockwood, G.I.
v4p0547c2s
Green, S.S. v1p0149c2s
v1p0451c1s v1p0742c1s v1p0743c1s
v1p0743c2s v1p1062c2s v2p0255c2m
v2p0256c1s v2p0358c2s v2p0425c2s
v2p0426c1s v3p0249c1m v3p0249c2s
v3p0471c2s v4p0329c1s v5p0334c2m
Green, S.S. et al. v2p0255c2s
Green, T. v1p0071c2s
v2p0092c2s v2p0098c2s
Green, T.H. v1p0434c1s
v1p0436c2s v1p0556c1s v1p0582c2s
v1p1235c1s v2p0274c1s
Green, T.L. v6p0424c2s
Green, W. v1p0186c2s
v1p1350c1s v1p1387c1s v5p0516c1s
Green, W.A.
v6p0215c2s
v6p0684c1s
Green, W.C. v3p0199c2s
v3p0207c2s v3p0371c2s v5p0063c1s
v5p0152c2s v5p0278c2s v5p0315c1s
v6p0172c1s v6p0212c2s v6p0250c1s
v6p0684c2s
Green, W.D. v5p0017c1s
Green, W.H. v1p0018c2s
v1p0119c2s v1p0120c1s v1p0121c2s
v1p0122c1m v1p0122c2s v1p0123c1m
v1p0124c1s v1p0124c2m v1p0125c1m
v1p0125c2m v1p0131c1s v1p0378c1s
v1p0396c1m v1p0554c2s v1p0590c1s
v1p0628c2s v1p0681c1s v1p0684c2s
v1p0689c2s v1p0923c2s v1p0933c2s
v1p0975c2s v1p0985c1s v1p0999c1s
v1p1056c1m v1p1056c2m v1p1150c2s
v1p1312c2s v1p1338c2s v1p1434c1s
v1p1436c2s v2p0025c2s v2p0042c2s
v2p0043c1s v2p0043c2s v2p0199c2s
v2p0336c2s v2p0356c2s v3p0042c1s
v3p0082c1s v4p0055c1m v4p0057c2s
v4p0541c2s v4p0561c2s v5p0056c1s
v5p0057c2s
Green, W.H. and Briggs, C.A.
v2p0042c1s
Green, W.H. et al. v5p0055c1s
Green, W.S. v4p0292c2s
v6p0065c2s
v6p0531c2s
v6p0562c1s
Green, Will.S. v4p0155c2s
Greenawalt, S.A. v6p0390c1s
Greenbough, J.G. v6p0126c1s
Greene, A. v4p0031c1s
Greene, A.C. v2p0066c2s
Greene, A.R. v2p0312c1s
v4p0308c1s
Greene, A.S. v2p0419c1s
Greene, B.A. v4p0566c2s
Greene, B.E. v4p0175c2s
v4p0176c1s
Greene, B.R. v1p0902c2s
v1p1191c2s
Greene, C.A. v2p0056c2s
Greene, C.E. v2p0467c1s
Greene, C.G., jr. v1p0478c2s
v1p0488c1s v1p0515c2s v1p0653c2s
v1p1331c1s
Greene, C.M. v4p0038c2s
v5p0087c2s v6p0330c1s v6p0359c2s
v6p0452c1s
Greene, C.S. v3p0165c1s
v3p0374c2s v3p0390c1s v4p0194c2s
v4p0292c2s v4p0365c1s v4p0463c2s
v4p0470c1s v4p0486c1s v4p0492c1s
v4p0501c2m v4p0554c1s v5p0088c2s
v5p0124c1s v5p0260c1s v5p0370c1s
v5p0605c1s v5p0644c2s v6p0409c2s
Greene, C.S. and Boeringer, P.N.
v4p0083c1s
Greene, D. v1p0070c1s
v1p1315c2s
Greene, D.C. v3p0226c2s
v3p0227c1s v3p0298c2s v4p0106c2s
v5p0303c1s
Greene, D.M. v1p1170c2s
v1p1182c2s v1p1246c1s v1p1246c2s
v1p1249c2s
Greene, E. v5p0541c1m
Greene, E.L. v1p0153c1s
v1p0279c1s v1p0279c2s v1p0463c1s
v1p0666c2s v1p0912c2s v1p1013c2s
v1p1113c2s v1p1435c2s v4p0392c1s
v6p0077c1m v6p0077c2m v6p0362c2s
v6p0374c1s
Greene, E.V. v1p1330c1s
Greene, F.L.
v4p0533c1s
Greene, F.V. v1p0087c2s
v1p0394c2s v1p0470c1s v1p0757c2s
v1p1346c1s v2p0078c1s v2p0133c2s
v2p0240c1s v2p0270c1s v2p0337c1s
v2p0349c1s v2p0453c2s v3p0089c2s
v4p0370c2s v4p0400c1s v5p0360c1s
v5p0598c2s v5p0618c1s v6p0557c1s
Greene, G.F. v4p0109c2s
v5p0436c1s
Greene, G.W. v1p0006c1m
v1p0033c1m v1p0033c2s v1p0110c1s
v1p0144c1s v1p0206c1s v1p0220c2s
v1p0231c2s v1p0273c2s v1p0298c2s
v1p0331c2s v1p0390c1s v1p0466c2m
v1p0556c2m v1p0559c2s v1p0565c2s
v1p0585c2s v1p0593c2s v1p0667c2s
v1p0668c2s v1p0669c1s v1p0671c1s
v1p0671c2s v1p0694c2s v1p0701c2s
v1p0712c1s v1p0717c2s v1p0743c1s
v1p0783c1s v1p0798c2s v1p0964c2s
v1p0995c1s v1p1010c1s v1p1066c2s
v1p1089c2s v1p1125c2s v1p1126c1s
v1p1151c2s v1p1307c2s v1p1350c2s
v2p0075c1s v2p0101c2s v2p0148c1s
v2p0249c1s v2p0255c1s v2p0267c2s
Greene, H.A. v5p0290c1s
Greene, H.B. v5p0013c2s
Greene, H.C. v5p0629c2s
v6p0196c1s
Greene, H.I. v4p0145c2s
v6p0698c1s
Greene, H.V. v6p0536c1s
Greene, H.W. v4p0527c2s
v4p0607c1s
Greene, J. v2p0249c1s
v2p0257c2s v4p0183c2s
Greene, J.B. v2p0034c2s
Greene, J.D. v6p0282c1s
v6p0317c1s v6p0622c2s
Greene, J.E. v4p0281c2s
Greene, J.H. v1p1400c1s
Greene, J.L. v2p0223c1s
v4p0059c1s v5p0149c1s
Greene, J.L. et al. v4p0286c2s
Greene, J.M. v1p1101c1s
Greene, J.R. v1p0215c2s
v1p1213c1s
Greene, J.W. v4p0322c2s
v4p0325c2s
Greene, L.D. v5p0399c1s
Greene, M.A. v3p0344c2s
v4p0630c1s v5p0204c2s v5p0250c1s
Greene, M.L. v6p0571c2s
Greene, M.S. v5p0151c1s
Greene, M.W. v3p0185c1s
Greene, Mary A. v6p0165c2s
Greene, N. v1p1032c1s
Greene, R. v4p0093c1s
v6p0672c2s v6p0710c2s
Greene, R.A. v3p0011c1s
Greene, R.F. v5p0456c1s
Greene, R.G. v1p0052c2s
Greene, R.H. v3p0056c2s
v3p0091c2s v3p0093c1s v3p0344c1s
v3p0444c2s v3p0464c2s v3p0474c1s
v6p0274c1s
Greene, Richard v4p0285c1s
Greene, S. v5p0139c1s
Greene, S.D. v4p0379c1s
v4p0403c2s v5p0185c1s
Greene, S.D. and Colston, R.E.
v2p0295c1s
Greene, S.G. v3p0041c2s
Greene, S.P.M. v3p0376c2s
Greene, S.P.McL. v3p0003c2s
v3p0164c2s
Greene, S.S. v1p0385c2s
v1p0935c2s v1p1085c1s
Greene, T.A. v1p1158c2s
Greene, T.L. v3p0148c1s
v3p0157c1s v3p0238c2s v3p0352c1m
v3p0353c1m v3p0353c2m v3p0444c2s
v4p0043c2s v4p0044c1s v4p0134c2s
v4p0195c1s v4p0203c1s v4p0230c2s
v4p0288c1m v4p0292c1s v4p0458c1s
v4p0470c2m v4p0471c1m v4p0471c2s
v4p0472c1m v4p0472c2s v4p0474c2s
v4p0526c2s v4p0550c1s v4p0553c1s
v4p0553c2m v4p0609c1s v4p0617c1s
Greene, T.W. v1p1253c2s
v4p0310c2s v4p0542c2s
Greene, V. v5p0278c2s
Greene, W. v1p0819c2s
v1p1297c2s
Greene, W.A. v2p0328c2s
v2p0372c1s v3p0123c2s v3p0296c1s
Greene, W.B. v2p0209c2s
v5p0114c1s v6p0162c1s
Greene, W.B., jr. v3p0080c2s
v4p0109c1m v4p0109c2s v4p0382c1s
v4p0475c1s v4p0478c2s v5p0023c2s
v5p0052c2s v5p0114c1s v5p0115c1m
v5p0483c2m v5p0576c2m v6p0309c2s
v6p0420c2s v6p0536c2s
Greene, W.H. v1p0955c1s
v5p0055c2s v5p0338c2m

Greene, W.H. and Hooker, S.C.
v3p0040c1s v3p0242c2s v3p0247c1s
Greene, W.H. and Wahl, W.H.
v4p0353c1s v4p0366c2s
Greene, W.S. v6p0425c2s
Greene, W.T. v1p0358c2s
v1p0520c1s v1p0527c2s v1p0609c1s
v1p0701c2s v1p0956c2s v1p0986c1s
v1p1128c1s v1p1312c1s v3p0045c1s
v4p0061c2s v4p0343c1s v5p0063c1s
v5p0063c2s v5p0064c1s
Greene, W.U. v2p0080c1s
Greener, R.T. v1p0904c2s
v1p0905c2s v4p0397c1s
Greener, W.O. v4p0027c2s
Greener, W.W. v2p0193c2s
Greenfield, H. v1p0025c1s
Greenhalge, F.T. v4p0233c2s
v4p0450c2s
Greenhill, A.G. v3p0031c1s
v3p0186c2s v3p0404c1s v3p0444c2s
v4p0173c2m v4p0204c2s v4p0363c1s
v4p0616c1s v5p0582c2m
Greenhill, A.G. et al. ... v3p0459c1s
Greenhill, W.A. v2p0044c2s
v2p0058c2s v3p0302c1m
Greenhod, E. v2p0028c1s
Greenhood, J.M. v6p0574c1s
Greenhough, W.H. v5p0335c1s
Greenhow, E.H. v1p0578c2s
Greenhow, H.M. v3p0233c2s
Greenhow, R. v1p0441c2s
v1p0833c2s v1p0854c2s
Greenidge, A.H.J. v4p0582c2s
v6p0402c2s v6p0662c2s
Greening, E.O. v6p0148c1s
Greenland, C.F. v6p0491c1s
Greenland, E.J. v1p0959c1s
Greenland, W.K. v6p0114c2s
Greenlaw, E.A. v5p0367c2s
Greenlaw, G. v2p0200c2s
v2p0406c2s
Greenlaw, L.H. v5p0076c1s
v5p0232c1s v5p0506c1s v5p0633c2s
Greenleaf, C. v1p1288c1s
Greenleaf, C.R. v5p0159c1s
Greenleaf, E. v3p0203c1s
v3p0355c1s
Greenleaf, J. v1p0975c2s
Greenleaf, J.L. v2p0459c1s
v4p0048c1s v4p0375c1s v4p0623c2s
v5p0210c2s
Greenleaf, K.V. v4p0498c2s
Greenleaf, M. v6p0217c1s
Greenleaf, R.W. v4p0249c2s
Greenleaf, T. v5p0532c1s
Greenleaf, W.L. v4p0370c2s
Greenlee, C.E. v6p0190c1s
Greenlee, L. v4p0208c2s
v4p0416c1s v4p0602c2s v6p0124c1s
Greenlee, Lennie v6p0229c2s
Greenman, M.J. v3p0250c2s
v4p0331c1s
Greenough, E.P. v3p0461c2s
Greenough, H. v1p0053c2m
v1p0062c1s v1p0425c2s v1p0831c2s
v4p0011c2s
Greenough, H.S. v2p0211c2s
Greenough, J.B. v1p0140c1s
v1p0724c2s v1p0945c1s v3p0363c2s
v4p0249c1s
Greenough, J.C. v3p0378c1s
Greenough, J.J. v4p0169c1s
v4p0183c2s v4p0249c1s
Greenough, R.S. v1p1387c2s
Greenough, R.S., Mrs. v1p0307c2s
v1p0923c1s v1p1069c1s
Greenough, W.W. v1p0742c2s
v1p0743c1s v1p0857c1s
Greenslade, S.K. v6p0371c1s
Greenslet, F. v5p0103c1s
v5p0167c2s v5p0331c1s v5p0456c1s
v5p0472c2s v5p0573c1s v6p0041c1s
v6p0066c2s v6p0085c1s v6p0155c2s
v6p0461c1s v6p0505c2s v6p0549c1s
v6p0565c1s v6p0617c1s v6p0629c2s
v6p0692c1s
Greenstone, J.H. v6p0343c1s
Greenstreet, J. v2p0124c2s
v3p0046c2m v4p0082c1s
Greenstreet, W.J. v4p0171c2s
Greenwald, E. v1p0097c2s
v1p0125c1s v1p0432c2s
Greenway, E.M. v1p0807c2s
Greenwell, D. v1p0203c1s
v1p0405c2s v1p0599c1s v1p0697c1s
v1p0773c2s v1p1017c2s v1p1205c2s
Greenwell, T.W. v1p0394c2s
Greenwell, W. v3p0020c1s
v3p0452c1s v5p0078c1s v6p0690c1s
Greenwood, C.C. v6p0255c2s
Greenwood, F. v1p0535c2s
v1p0799c2s v1p0976c1s v3p0098c2s
v3p0140c2s v3p0144c1s v3p0171c1s
v3p0171c2s v3p0177c1s v3p0179c2s
v3p0181c2m v3p0183c1s v3p0238c2s
v3p0302c2s v3p0303c1s v3p0321c2s
v3p0338c2s v3p0439c2s v3p0454c1s
v3p0471c2s v4p0011c1s v4p0027c2s
v4p0048c1s v4p0161c2m v4p0189c2s
v4p0213c2s v4p0214c1s v4p0221c2s
v4p0238c2m v4p0239c1s v4p0239c2s
v4p0240c1m v4p0253c1s v4p0289c2s
v4p0394c1s v4p0428c2s v4p0461c1s
v4p0491c2s v4p0584c2s v5p0019c2m
v5p0050c2s v5p0110c2s v5p0189c1s
v5p0191c1s v5p0197c1s v5p0311c1s
v5p0352c2s v5p0410c1s v5p0457c2s
v5p0471c2s v5p0520c1s v5p0631c2s
v6p0006c2s v6p0024c1s v6p0119c1s
v6p0192c1s v6p0267c1m v6p0483c2m
Greenwood, F. et al. v3p0241c2s
Greenwood, F.W.P. v1p0006c1s
v1p0009c2s v1p0032c2s v1p0037c2s
v1p0073c2s v1p0087c1s v1p0124c1s
v1p0126c2s v1p0140c2s v1p0149c1s
v1p0162c2s v1p0229c1s v1p0243c1s
v1p0322c2s v1p0330c1s v1p0348c1s
v1p0390c1s v1p0444c2s v1p0448c1s
v1p0449c1s v1p0537c1s v1p0560c1s
v1p0578c1s v1p0581c1m v1p0591c1s
v1p0620c1s v1p0704c1s v1p0719c1s
v1p0731c1s v1p0754c1s v1p0775c1m
v1p0788c2s v1p0805c2s v1p0813c2s
v1p0843c1s v1p0853c1s v1p0867c2s
v1p0933c1s v1p1010c1s v1p1011c1s
v1p1025c1s v1p1052c2s v1p1086c2s
v1p1089c1s v1p1091c1s v1p1096c1s
v1p1114c1s v1p1127c2s v1p1141c2s
v1p1169c1s v1p1175c2s v1p1207c2s
v1p1262c1s v1p1309c2s v1p1341c1m
v1p1371c2s v1p1419c1s v1p1425c2s
v1p1430c1s
Greenwood, G. v1p1376c1s
v4p0198c2s v4p0542c2s v5p0455c2s
Greenwood, G.F. v4p0552c2s
Greenwood, G.G. v4p0051c2s
v4p0269c1s v4p0270c2s v4p0573c1s
v6p0046c2s v6p0586c1s v6p0587c2s
v6p0588c1s v6p0637c1s
Greenwood, Grace v1p0751c2s
Greenwood, H. v2p0102c2s
v2p0252c2s v4p0319c1s
Greenwood, H.R. v2p0374c1s
Greenwood, I.J. v1p0034c1s
v1p0154c2s v1p1388c1s v1p1388c2m
v1p1412c2s v2p0063c1s v3p0008c2s
v3p0371c2s v4p0052c1s v4p0071c2s
v4p0342c1s v4p0361c2s v4p0418c1s
v4p0615c2s v5p0066c2s v5p0310c1s
v5p0324c2s v5p0510c2s v5p0554c1s
v5p0625c1s
Greenwood, I.T. v1p0503c1s
v6p0360c2s
Greenwood, J. v1p0179c2s
v1p0373c1s v1p0414c1s v1p0433c1s
v1p0542c2s v1p0592c2s v1p0762c1s
v1p0763c1s v1p0763c2s v1p0764c1m
v1p0765c1s v1p0766c1s v1p0861c1s
v1p0878c2s v1p0883c1s v1p0947c2s
v1p0982c1m v1p1040c1s v1p1074c2s
v1p1085c1s v1p1222c1s
Greenwood, J.M. v2p0077c2s
v2p0204c1s v2p0304c2s v3p0268c1s
v3p0299c1s v3p0306c2s v3p0404c1s
v4p0071c2s v4p0103c1s v4p0360c2s
v4p0505c2s v5p0028c1s v5p0122c1s
v5p0400c2s v5p0511c1s v5p0512c1m
v6p0004c2s v6p0194c2s v6p0207c2s
v6p0278c1s v6p0622c2s v6p0635c1m
v6p0673c2s
Greenwood, J.M. et al. ... v5p0471c2s
Greenwood, James M. v6p0199c2s
Greenwood, L. v1p0895c2s
Greenwood, M. v5p0327c1s
v5p0637c2s v6p0592c1s
Greenwood, Maj. v5p0103c1s
Greenwood, P. v4p0117c2s
Greenwood, T. v2p0467c1s
v3p0252c1s v4p0388c1s
Greenwood, W. v5p0246c1s
Greer, D.H. v2p0407c2s
Greer, F.A. v4p0145c1s
v4p0322c2s
Greer, H. v2p0137c2s
Greer, H.H. v6p0069c1s
v6p0393c2s
Greer, J.H. v3p0187c1s
Greer, S. v4p0058c2s
v4p0589c1s
Greer, T. v5p0163c2s
Greeves, F. v1p0123c1s
Greeves, J. v1p0830c2s
Greg, L. v1p0064c1s
v2p0005c1s
Greg, L.L. v4p0254c1s
Greg, P. v1p0065c2s
v1p0372c1s v1p0563c2s v1p1431c2s
v2p0011c2m v2p0208c2s v2p0277c2s
v2p0306c1s v2p0330c2s v2p0331c2s
v2p0334c2s v2p0370c1s v2p0420c2s
v2p0480c1s v3p0209c1s
Greg, P. and Kebbel, T.E.. v2p0144c2s
Greg, R.P. v2p0158c2s
v2p0242c2s v2p0281c2m v5p0221c2s
v5p0224c1s v5p0563c2s
Greg, T.T. v1p1428c2s
v2p0127c1s v2p0283c1s v3p0060c1s
Greg, W.R. v1p0059c2s
v1p0060c2m v1p0068c1s v1p0128c1s
v1p0165c2s v1p0239c2s v1p0285c2s
v1p0302c2m v1p0355c1s v1p0409c1s
v1p0430c1m v1p0477c2s v1p0479c1s
v1p0480c2s v1p0515c2s v1p0545c2m
v1p0546c1s v1p0546c2s v1p0594c1s
v1p0639c2s v1p0652c1s v1p0714c1m
v1p0714c2s v1p0715c1m v1p0745c1s
v1p0778c2s v1p0798c1s v1p0805c1s
v1p0893c1s v1p1087c2s v1p1113c1m
v1p1215c2s v1p1218c1s v1p1245c2s
v1p1261c1s v1p1261c2s v1p1265c1s
v1p1367c1s v1p1431c1s v2p0172c1s
Greg, W.R. et al. v1p0406c1s
Greg, W.W. v5p0435c1s
v6p0046c2s v6p0138c1s v6p0252c1s
v6p0504c1s v6p0587c1s v6p0588c1s
v6p0650c2s
Gregan, T.J. v1p0322c1s
Gregg, A.S. v3p0253c1s
Gregg, E.R. et al. v4p0138c1s
Gregg, F.J. v5p0086c1s
v5p0497c2s v5p0553c2s v6p0684c2s
Gregg, F.L. v5p0253c1s
Gregg, F.T. v5p0051c2s
Gregg, J. v1p0339c2s
v1p1001c1s
Gregg, J.B. v1p0189c2s
v2p0027c2s
Gregg, R.E. v4p0550c2s
Gregg, T.A. v6p0391c2s
Gregg, W. v1p1014c2s
v1p1225c2s
Gregmore, H. v6p0024c2s
v6p0291c2s
Grego, J. v2p0136c1s
v2p0264c1s v2p0329c1s v4p0029c2m
v4p0031c1s v4p0083c1s v4p0259c2s
v4p0341c2s v4p0342c1s v4p0453c1s
v5p0048c1s v5p0233c2s
Gregoire, M. v2p0215c2s
Gregor, L.R. v6p0654c1s
Gregor, W. v2p0310c1s
v4p0205c1s v4p0508c2s v4p0511c1s
v4p0616c2s
Gregorovius, F. v1p0046c2s
v6p0075c2s
Gregory, A. v4p0291c2s
v4p0311c1s v5p0296c2s v5p0476c1s
v6p0366c2s v6p0565c1s
Gregory, A., Lady v2p0350c1s
v2p0410c2s
Gregory, A.C. v4p0038c2s
Gregory, Augusta v5p0204c2s
v5p0296c1s v6p0222c2s v6p0282c2s
v6p0328c1s
Gregory, B. v6p0018c2s
v6p0648c2s
Gregory, C.H. v1p0445c1s
Gregory, C.M. v6p0249c1s
Gregory, C.N. v1p0616c1s
v5p0328c1s v5p0329c2s v6p0171c1s
v6p0550c1s
Gregory, C.P. v1p0076c1s
v1p0778c1s
Gregory, C.R. v1p0517c2s
v1p1089c1s v1p1093c2s v1p1312c2s
v2p0191c1s v2p0361c2s v5p0059c2s
v5p0060c2s v5p0114c2s v5p0232c1s
v5p0428c2s v5p0625c1s v6p0063c1s
v6p0190c1s v6p0355c2s v6p0693c1s
Gregory, Canon v2p0131c1s
Gregory, D.S. v1p0128c2m
v1p0379c1s v1p0839c2s v1p0978c1s
v1p1043c2s v1p1301c1s v2p0044c2s
v2p0132c2s v2p0275c2s v4p0188c1s
v5p0087c1s v5p0447c1s v5p0545c2s
Gregory, D.S. and Bissell, E.C.
v2p0045c1s v2p0082c1s
Gregory, E. v5p0276c2s
v5p0409c1s v5p0430c2s v5p0604c2s
v5p0637c2s v6p0005c2s v6p0600c2s
v6p0680c2s v6p0690c1s
Gregory, E.C. v5p0459c1s
Gregory, E.L. v4p0155c1s
v4p0601c1s
Gregory, E.S. v1p1100c1s
Gregory, E.W. v5p0268c2s
Gregory, F.A. v5p0354c2s
Gregory, H.E. v5p0018c2s
v5p0571c2s
Gregory, J.E. v4p0341c2s
Gregory, J.J.H. v1p0638c2s
Gregory, J.M. v1p0391c2s
v1p0392c1s v2p0086c2s v2p0312c2s
v4p0476c2s v5p0179c1s
Gregory, J.N. v1p0276c2s
Gregory, J.R. v2p0285c2s
v3p0039c2s v3p0166c1s v3p0175c2s
v3p0229c2s v3p0264c1s v3p0279c1s
v3p0309c2s v3p0357c2m v3p0438c1s
v4p0367c1s v5p0027c2s
Gregory, J.S. v6p0546c2s
Gregory, J.W. v4p0005c1s
v4p0005c2s v4p0012c1s v4p0025c2s
v4p0223c1s v4p0310c1s v4p0350c2s
v4p0406c1s v4p0571c2s v4p0574c2s
v4p0588c2s v5p0022c1s v5p0137c1s
v5p0173c1s v5p0228c2s v5p0229c1s
v6p0023c1m v6p0041c2s
Gregory, J.W. and

Johnston-Lavis, H.J. .. v4p0185c2s
Gregory, M. v6p0507c2s
Gregory, R. v2p0084c2s
v2p0107c1s v2p0130c2s v2p0131c1s
v3p0101c1s v3p0128c2s v3p0129c1s
v3p0141c2s v3p0240c1s v4p0092c2s
v4p0112c1s v4p0479c2s
Gregory, R. and Stanley, E.L.
v3p0129c1s
Gregory, R. et al. v4p0239c1s
Gregory, R.A. v3p0094c1s
v3p0133c2s v3p0271c1s v3p0331c1s
v3p0446c1s v4p0034c1s v4p0037c2s
v4p0047c2s v4p0099c1s v4p0406c1s
v4p0434c2s v4p0451c1s v4p0540c2s
v4p0566c2m v4p0601c1s v5p0363c1s
v5p0448c2s v6p0038c1s v6p0609c1s
v6p0614c2s
Gregory, R.R.C. v5p0178c1s
v5p0254c1s
Gregory, S. v1p1006c1s
v1p1421c1s
Gregory, W. v1p0014c2s
v1p0824c2s v2p0024c2s v5p0047c2s
Gregory, W., Sir v3p0310c1s
Gregory, W.A. v3p0134c2s
Gregory, W.D. v5p0582c2s
v6p0529c2s
Gregory, W.H. v2p0017c2s
v2p0133c2s v2p0410c1s v3p0212c1s
Gregory, W.H., Sir v2p0217c2s
Gregory, W.K. v6p0277c2s
v6p0509c1s
Gregory-Flesher, H. v4p0085c2s
Gregory-Flesher, H.E. v4p0371c1s
Gregory-Flesher, H.E., Mrs.
v6p0629c2s
Gregory-Flesher, Helen ... v6p0337c2s
v6p0338c1s
Gregory-Flesher, Helen E.. v6p0009c1s
Gregson, A.K. v6p0421c2s
v6p0589c1s
Gregson, C.W. v6p0589c1s
Gregson, W. v4p0344c2s
Greig, D. v2p0450c2s
Greig, Edvard v5p0390c1s
Greig, G. v2p0162c2s
Greig, J. v6p0054c2s
v6p0258c2s v6p0553c1s
Grein, J.T. v2p0210c2s
Greiner, T. v4p0234c2s
v4p0292c2s v4p0414c1s
Grendon, F. v6p0639c1s
Grenell, J. v6p0306c1s
Grenet, L. and Charpy, G.. v6p0328c2s
Grenfell, A. v6p0196c1s
Grenfell, B.P. v4p0424c2s
v5p0306c2s
Grenfell, B.P. and Hunt, A.S.
v5p0430c1s
Grenfell, G. v6p0144c1s
Grenfell, H. v5p0319c1s
v5p0376c2s
Grenfell, H.R. v1p0094c2s
v1p1040c1s v2p0096c2s v2p0294c2s
v5p0045c1s
Grenfell, M. v5p0415c2s
Grenfell, W. v3p0307c1s
Grenfell, W.H. v3p0368c1s
v4p0064c2s v4p0227c1s v4p0420c1s
v4p0486c2s v4p0635c1s v5p0050c2s
v5p0067c2s v5p0567c2s v5p0594c2s
Grenfell, W.T. v5p0321c2s
v6p0226c2s v6p0301c1s v6p0357c2s
v6p0365c2s
Grenier, T. v6p0675c2s
Grensted, F. v2p0096c1s
Grenville-Murray, E.C. ... v4p0201c2s
v4p0496c2s
Gresham, J.C. v4p0584c2s
v5p0573c2s
Gresley, R. v6p0360c2s
Greswell, W. v2p0004c2m
v2p0014c2s v2p0067c1s v2p0093c1s
v2p0140c2s v2p0168c1s v3p0005c1s
v3p0067c1s v3p0092c2s v3p0177c1s
v3p0181c1s v3p0209c1s v3p0350c2m
v3p0400c1s v3p0472c1s v4p0006c1m
v4p0359c1s v4p0402c1s v4p0428c2s
v4p0448c2s v4p0468c2s v4p0536c1s
v4p0632c1s v5p0006c2s v5p0007c1s
v5p0012c1s v5p0048c2s v5p0068c1s
v5p0192c2s v5p0588c2s v6p0006c2m
v6p0054c1s v6p0138c2s
Greswell, W.H. v3p0335c2s
Greswell, W.P. v4p0236c2s
Greswell, Wm. v3p0091c1s
v4p0061c1s
Gret, P. v6p0585c1s
Greth, J.C.W. v6p0688c1s
Gretillat, A. v3p0365c1s
v3p0418c1m v4p0215c1s
Gretton, G.LeM. v2p0028c2s
Gretton, J.G. v6p0662c1s
Greusel, J.H. v3p0306c1s
Greven, H.B. v3p0198c2s
v3p0285c2s v4p0260c1s
Greville, E. v6p0589c2s
Greville, H. v1p0361c1s
v2p0167c2s v2p0261c1s
Greville, L. v5p0118c2s
Greville, V. v4p0079c2s
v4p0356c2s v4p0516c1s v4p0627c1s
Greville, V., Lady v2p0349c1s
Greville, V., Mrs. v4p0222c1s
Greville, Violet v4p0162c1s
Greville, Violet, Lady ... v6p0300c1s
v6p0585c1s
Greville-Nugent, E. v6p0328c1s
Grevstad, N. v3p0102c2s
v4p0137c1s
Grew, E.S. v4p0173c1s
v4p0288c1s v4p0512c1s v4p0514c2s
v4p0565c2s v5p0085c1s v5p0239c2s
Grew, J.C. v6p0049c1s
v6p0305c2s
Grew, M. v1p0242c2s
Grew, M.S. v5p0201c1s
Grey, A. v2p0370c1s
v4p0222c1s
Grey, A. et al. v2p0370c1s
Grey, C.E., Sir and Scott, W., Sir
v1p0191c2s
Grey, E. v5p0025c2s
v5p0587c2s v6p0093c1s v6p0269c2s
v6p0271c1s
Grey, Earl v1p0012c2m
v1p0544c1s v1p0561c1s v2p0208c2s
v2p0224c2s v2p0226c1s v3p0005c1s
v3p0183c1s v3p0221c2s v3p0321c2s
v3p0431c1s v4p0193c2s v4p0214c1s
v4p0462c2s v5p0586c2s
Grey, Earl et al. v4p0476c1s
Grey, Edward v4p0201c1s
Grey, Elmer v5p0026c1s
Grey, F.W. v2p0358c1s
v3p0175c2s v4p0152c1s v4p0469c1s
v4p0593c2s v5p0002c1s v5p0233c2s
v5p0483c1s v6p0097c1s
Grey, G. v2p0086c2s
v2p0150c1s v5p0313c1s v5p0490c2s
Grey, G., Sir v1p0338c2s
v1p0877c1s
Grey, H. v1p0630c2s
v6p0121c1s
Grey, H.M. v5p0006c1s
v5p0387c1m
Grey, H.W. v5p0105c2s
Grey, Helen v6p0378c1s
Grey, J.A. v4p0200c1s
Grey, J.C. v1p0808c2s
Grey, K.M. v1p0404c2s
Grey, Lemon v6p0328c1s
Grey, M.G. v1p0673c2s
v1p0819c2s v1p1216c2s v1p1300c2s
v1p1421c1s v2p0297c2s
Grey, M.G. and Newman, F.W.
v1p0427c1s
Grey, Mrs. v3p0468c2s
Grey, Oliver v6p0020c1s
Grey, R. v5p0038c2s
Grey, S. v2p0028c1s
Grey, T.G. v1p0527c2s
Grey, W. v4p0421c1s
v5p0492c1s
Grey, W.E. v4p0560c1s
Grey, W.M. v5p0149c1s
v5p0245c1s
Grey-Egerton, H., Lady and
Sykes, J., Lady v4p0594c2s
Gribayedoff, V. v3p0305c2s
v3p0332c1s v3p0448c2s v4p0496c1s
v4p0522c2s v4p0610c2s v5p0552c2s
Gribble, F. v4p0203c1s
v4p0204c2s v4p0313c2s v4p0385c2s
v4p0588c1s v5p0013c2s v5p0193c2s
v5p0251c1s v5p0312c1s v5p0466c1s
v6p0009c1s v6p0072c1s v6p0184c1s
v6p0283c2m v6p0391c1m v6p0417c2s
v6p0455c2s v6p0563c1s v6p0569c1m
v6p0610c1s v6p0616c2s v6p0624c1s
v6p0648c2s v6p0713c1s
Gribble, Francis v5p0623c2s
v6p0150c1s
Gribble, H.A.K. v2p0057c2s
Gribble, J.B. v1p0307c2m
v2p0029c1s
Gribble, J.D.B. v5p0613c2s
Gribble, N. v3p0183c2s
v3p0357c2s v3p0401c1s
Gribble, R. v6p0433c2s
Gribble, T.G. v3p0354c2s
v4p0250c2s v4p0257c2s
Gridley, A.D. v1p0211c1s
v1p0253c1s v1p0409c2s v1p0709c2s
v1p0723c1m v1p0842c1s v1p1009c1s
v1p1082c2s
Griebel, J.D. v1p0248c2s
Grieg, E. v4p0506c2s
v5p0609c2s v6p0440c1s
Grieg, W.W. v6p0586c2s
Grier, J.A. v1p0859c1s
v1p1100c2s v3p0393c2s v3p0459c1s
Grier, L. v5p0427c2s
Grier, R.M. v4p0577c2s
Grier, R.M. et al. v4p0120c2s
v4p0553c1s
Grier, S.C. v5p0154c2s
v5p0240c1s v5p0437c2s v5p0556c1s
v5p0619c2s v6p0279c1s
Grierson, E. v6p0083c2s
Grierson, Eliz. v6p0205c2s
Grierson, F. v5p0009c1s
v5p0228c1s v6p0016c1s v6p0032c1s
v6p0075c1s v6p0184c1s v6p0221c2s
v6p0396c2s v6p0677c1s
Grierson, F.W. v4p0340c2m
Grierson, G.A. v3p0318c1s
v3p0450c1s v6p0314c1s
Grierson, J.M. v2p0428c1s
Grierson, P.J.H. v4p0151c1s
v4p0322c2s v6p0211c1s
Grierson, T.B. v4p0292c1s
v6p0328c2s
Griesemer, F.A. v1p0213c1s
v1p0214c2s v1p1287c2s
Grieve, A.J. v5p0066c2s
Grieve, R. v4p0315c1s
v4p0463c2s v5p0270c2s v6p0542c1s
Griffen, A.M. v4p0150c1s
Griffes, J.H. v4p0201c1s
Griffin, A. v3p0346c1s
v4p0244c1s v5p0147c1s
Griffin, A.P.C. v2p0203c2s
v2p0299c2s
Griffin, C.L. v5p0353c2s
Griffin, C.S. v5p0559c2s
v6p0624c2s
Griffin, D. v1p1031c1s
Griffin, E. v3p0133c1s
v3p0382c2s v4p0175c2s v5p0604c1s
Griffin, E.H. v1p1412c1s
v3p0245c2s v3p0445c1s v5p0446c2s
v5p0470c2s v6p0057c2s v6p0444c1s
v6p0490c1s v6p0642c1s
Griffin, F.W. v3p0414c2s
Griffin, G. v1p0598c2s
v1p1121c1s v1p1260c2s
Griffin, G.B. v2p0224c1s
v6p0395c2s
Griffin, G.H. v1p1140c2s
v2p0303c1s
Griffin, H.A. v2p0117c1m
Griffin, H.H. v4p0521c1s
Griffin, H.L. v5p0614c2s
Griffin, J.C. v5p0281c2s
Griffin, J.J. v1p0495c1s
v6p0002c2s v6p0040c1s v6p0325c2s
Griffin, J.T. v6p0573c2s
Griffin, L. v1p0630c1s
v1p0631c1s v3p0211c1s v3p0212c1m
v4p0001c2s v4p0033c1s v4p0051c1s
v4p0107c1s v4p0279c1s v4p0308c2m
v4p0350c1s v4p0415c1s v4p0436c1s
v5p0284c2s v5p0285c2s v5p0287c1s
v5p0313c1s v5p0398c2s v5p0441c1s
v5p0479c2s v5p0529c1s v6p0006c2s
Griffin, L., Sir v2p0193c2s
v2p0218c1m v2p0380c2s v2p0454c1m
v3p0003c2s v3p0058c2s v4p0001c2s
v5p0341c2s
Griffin, L., Sir and Blunt, W.S.
v2p0217c2s
Griffin, L., Sir and Hanna, H.B.
v5p0005c1s
Griffin, L.F. v3p0099c1s
v4p0316c1s
Griffin, L.H.
v4p0279c2s
Griffin, L.H., Sir v4p0280c2s
Griffin, L.R. v3p0147c1m
Griffin, Lepel v4p0280c1s
Griffin, Lilian B. v6p0618c2s
Griffin, M. v3p0239c2s
Griffin, M.A. v6p0446c1s
Griffin, M.F. v1p0192c2s
Griffin, M.I. v1p0278c1s
Griffin, M.I.J. v6p0052c2s
v6p0141c2s v6p0213c2s v6p0296c2s
v6p0345c2s
Griffin, M.J. v1p0193c1s
v1p0610c1s v1p0683c2s v1p0781c2s
v1p0912c1s v1p0923c1s v3p0015c2s
v3p0262c1m v3p0444c1s v4p0085c2s
v4p0086c1s v4p0427c2s v5p0513c1s
Griffin, M.K. v6p0446c2s
Griffin, M.L. v3p0045c1s
v3p0167c1s v3p0242c1s v3p0387c2s
Griffin, N.H. v1p0496c2s
Griffin, P. v5p0269c2s
Griffin, P. et al. v5p0572c2s
Griffin, R. v2p0480c1s
Griffin, R.A. v2p0437c2s
v2p0447c2s v3p0115c1s v3p0248c1s
v3p0283c1s v3p0418c1s
Griffin, S. v3p0040c2s
Griffin, S.B. v2p0295c2s
Griffin, S.P. v1p1249c2s
Griffin, U. v6p0098c1s
Griffin, W. v2p0065c2s
v2p0066c1s v3p0065c1s v4p0171c1s
Griffin, W.H. v5p0458c2s
v6p0085c1m v6p0179c1s
Griffin, W.M. v5p0128c1s
Griffin, Zaidee v6p0223c1s
Griffing, H. v4p0036c2s
v4p0317c2s v4p0421c1s v4p0435c1s
v4p0465c1s v4p0528c2s
Griffing, H. and Franz, S.I.
v4p0474c2s

Griffis, H.L. and Shepard, J.H.
v3p0075c2s
Griffis, W.E. v1p0302c1s
v1p0678c1m v1p0678c2m v1p0679c1m
v1p0679c2s v1p0890c2s v1p1039c1s
v1p1052c1s v1p1113c1s v1p1152c2s
v1p1314c2s v2p0103c1m v2p0233c2m
v2p0336c1s v3p0100c2s v3p0225c2s
v3p0226c2m v3p0227c1m v3p0227c2m
v3p0300c2s v3p0378c1s v3p0446c1s
v3p0464c2s v4p0014c2s v4p0016c2s
v4p0055c2s v4p0070c1s v4p0105c1s
v4p0105c2s v4p0133c2m v4p0134c1s
v4p0166c1s v4p0201c2s v4p0248c2s
v4p0260c1m v4p0260c2s v4p0296c2m
v4p0297c1s v4p0298c1s v4p0328c1s
v4p0398c2s v4p0416c2s v4p0521c1s
v4p0591c2s v4p0596c2s v4p0634c1s
v5p0052c2s v5p0064c2s v5p0108c2s
v5p0109c1s v5p0110c2s v5p0111c1s
v5p0112c1s v5p0113c1s v5p0172c1s
v5p0173c2s v5p0199c1s v5p0258c2s
v5p0266c2s v5p0302c2s v5p0303c2s
v5p0329c1s v5p0332c1s v5p0374c2s
v5p0406c1s v5p0427c1s v5p0431c1s
v5p0451c2s v5p0510c2s v5p0543c1s
v5p0560c1s v5p0564c2s v5p0592c1s
v5p0602c2s v5p0631c1m v5p0641c2s
v5p0643c2s v6p0024c2s v6p0119c1s
v6p0186c2s v6p0332c1s v6p0334c2m
v6p0335c1m v6p0336c1m v6p0336c2m
v6p0337c1s v6p0337c2m v6p0338c2m
v6p0350c2s v6p0351c1s v6p0354c1s
v6p0354c2s v6p0366c1s v6p0408c2s
v6p0500c1s v6p0538c2m v6p0556c1m
v6p0560c1s v6p0560c2s v6p0562c1s
v6p0624c2s
Griffis, W.F. v6p0334c2s
Griffiss, R.L. v6p0309c1s
Griffith, A. v1p0590c1s
v6p0266c1s
Griffith, A.F. and Tomlinson, C.
v3p0251c1s
Griffith, A.H. v5p0586c1s
Griffith, A.L. v6p0002c2s
Griffith, D. v5p0393c1s
Griffith, E.C. v6p0606c2s
Griffith, E.K. v3p0473c1s
Griffith, F.L. v3p0087c2s
v3p0131c1s v3p0132c1s v3p0420c2s
Griffith, G. v1p0272c1s
v1p1122c1s v1p1404c1s v2p0032c1s
v5p0106c2s
Griffith, G.B. v1p0110c2s
v1p0207c1s v1p0213c1s v1p0340c1s
v1p0378c2s v1p0465c1s v1p0468c1s
v1p0625c1s v1p0768c1s v1p1039c2s
v1p1388c2s v1p1407c2s v2p0104c2s
v2p0253c2s v2p0277c1s v2p0299c1s
v2p0311c1s v2p0467c1s
Griffith, G.F.X. v4p0586c1s
Griffith, H.S. v6p0312c1s
v6p0423c1s
Griffith, M. v1p0567c1s
Griffith, M.D. v5p0367c1s
v5p0643c2s
Griffith, S.S. and Mario, J.W.
v1p0880c1s
Griffith, T.B. v4p0568c1s
Griffith, T.M. v1p0161c1s
v1p0356c1s v1p0848c2s v4p0622c1s
Griffith, V.P. v1p0220c2s
Griffith, W. v2p0033c2s
v2p0034c1s v5p0124c1s v5p0148c2s
v6p0132c2s v6p0452c2s v6p0646c2s
v6p0712c2s
Griffith, W.H. v5p0013c2s
v5p0274c2s v6p0312c1s
Griffith, W.L. v6p0095c2s
Griffith-Boscawen, A. v4p0577c2s
v4p0608c2s v4p0609c1s
Griffith-Boscawen, A. and
Webster, R.E. v4p0609c1s
Griffith-Jones, E. v5p0396c1s
Griffiths, A. v1p0184c1s
v1p0301c2s v1p0520c2s v1p0539c2s
v1p1180c2s v2p0067c2s v2p0211c1s
v3p0147c1s v3p0164c1s v3p0325c2s
v4p0060c2s v4p0062c1s v4p0137c1s
v4p0140c1s v4p0172c1s v4p0173c1s
v4p0207c1s v4p0235c2s v4p0236c1s
v4p0236c2s v4p0344c2s v4p0356c1s
v4p0361c2s v4p0433c1s v4p0442c2s
v4p0460c1s v4p0537c1s v4p0539c1s
v4p0610c1s v5p0028c2s v5p0078c1s
v5p0127c2s v5p0135c2s v5p0153c1s
v5p0180c2s v5p0181c2s v5p0243c2m
v5p0244c1m v5p0248c1s v5p0272c1s
v5p0283c1s v5p0293c1m v5p0315c2s
v5p0317c2s v5p0346c2s v5p0375c1s
v5p0467c1m v5p0537c2s v5p0539c2s
v5p0587c2s v5p0588c1s v6p0007c2s
v6p0099c1s v6p0256c1s v6p0265c2s
v6p0271c2s v6p0367c2s v6p0464c2s
Griffiths, A.L. v6p0494c1s
Griffiths, Arthur v2p0350c1s
Griffiths, E.B. v6p0082c2s
Griffiths, E.H. v4p0310c2s
Griffiths, E.M. v5p0511c2s
Griffiths, G.S. v3p0015c1m
Griffiths, L.M. v3p0037c1s
v3p0269c2s v3p0387c2s v3p0388c1s
v3p0388c2s v4p0358c1s v4p0519c1s
Griffiths, Mrs. v1p0107c1s
Griffiths, R.J. v3p0094c1s
Griffs, W.E. v3p0079c1s
v3p0226c2s
Griggs, E.H. v4p0148c1s
v5p0196c1s
Griggs, G.K. v2p0462c1s
v3p0154c2s
Griggs, H. v5p0394c2s
Griggs, J.C. v4p0107c2s
v4p0417c1s
Griggs, J.F. v6p0118c1s
Griggs, J.S., jr. and Davis, C.H.
v4p0180c1s
Griggs, J.W. v5p0328c1s
Griggs, L. v1p0471c1s
Griggs, Robert F. v6p0086c2s
Grignon, A. v1p0556c1s
Grigsby, H.B. v1p1082c2s
Grigsby, W.E. v1p0679c2s
v4p0145c2s v4p0172c2s
Grim, I.S. v6p0323c1s
v6p0632c2s
Grimble, A. v5p0505c2m
v5p0514c2s v6p0565c2s
Grimblecom, C.E. v4p0079c1s
Grimes, C.H.D. v6p0184c2s
Grimke, A.H. v3p0001c2s
v3p0015c2s v3p0389c2s v6p0447c2m
Grimke, C.F. v4p0621c1s
Grimley, W.H. v4p0280c2s
v5p0181c1s
Grimm, C.W. v4p0444c2s
v5p0256c1s
Grimm, G.W. v2p0046c2s
Grimm, H. v1p0834c2s
v1p1082c2s v1p1366c2s
Grimshaw, B. v6p0421c1s
v6p0455c1m
Grimshaw, P.H. v5p0292c1s
v5p0388c2s v5p0430c1s
Grimshaw, R. v1p0367c1s
v1p0493c1s v1p0495c1s v1p1154c1s
v2p0039c2s v2p0220c1s v2p0262c1s
v2p0287c2s v2p0289c1s v2p0419c1s
v3p0048c2s v3p0100c1s v3p0102c1s
v4p0180c2s v4p0403c2s v4p0455c2s
v5p0556c1s v6p0276c2s
Grimshaw, R. and Ware, L.S.
v2p0424c1s
Grimsley, G.P. v4p0372c1s
Grimthorpe, Baron v4p0157c2s
Grimthorpe, Lord v3p0083c2s
v3p0269c1s v4p0025c1m
Grindon, L.H. v1p0119c1s
v1p0462c2s
Grindriez, C. v1p0284c2s
Grindrod, C. v2p0019c1s
Grindrod, Charles v2p0035c1s
Grinfield, E.W. v1p0120c2s
Grinling, C.H. v6p0528c1s
v6p0529c2m
Grinnell, C.E. v1p0121c2s
v1p0208c1s v1p0521c2s v1p0690c1s
v1p0849c2s v1p1089c2s v1p1176c2s
v1p1276c1s v2p0045c2s v2p0193c1s
v2p0228c2s v2p0233c1s v2p0251c2s
v2p0322c2s v5p0075c1s v5p0166c2s
v5p0392c2s v6p0572c2s
Grinnell, E. v4p0282c2s
v6p0056c2s v6p0068c2s v6p0302c2s
Grinnell, E. and Grinnell, J.
v6p0067c2s v6p0068c1s v6p0261c2s
v6p0303c1s v6p0378c1s v6p0612c1s
v6p0644c2s
Grinnell, F.W. v6p0166c2s
v6p0175c1s
Grinnell, G.B. v1p0317c2s
v1p0804c2s v2p0406c2s v4p0063c1s
v4p0078c1s v4p0102c2s v4p0228c2s
v4p0431c2m v4p0557c1s v4p0636c1s
v5p0065c2s v5p0067c1s v5p0225c1s
v5p0234c1s v5p0288c2m v5p0342c2s
v5p0384c1s v5p0472c2s v5p0504c2s
v6p0023c2s v6p0112c2m v6p0316c1m
v6p0510c2s
Grinnell, G.B. and Dana, E.S.
v1p0718c2s
Grinnell, J. and Grinnell, E.
v6p0067c2s v6p0068c1s v6p0261c2s
v6p0303c1s v6p0378c1s v6p0612c1s
v6p0644c2s
Grinnell, W.M. v5p0062c1s
Grinnell, W.Morton v6p0528c2s
Grinsted, T.I. v1p0527c1s
Grinsted, T.P. v1p0005c1s
v1p0095c2s v1p0116c2s v1p0362c1s
v1p0445c1s v1p0458c2s v1p0703c2s
v1p0766c1s v1p0784c2s v1p0943c1s
v1p1368c2s v1p1438c1s
Grinten, A.J.van der v6p0186c1s
Grisbrook, E.O. v6p0097c1s
Griscom, I.M. v6p0146c1s
Griscom, I.W. v6p0329c1s
Griscom, J. v1p0390c1s
v1p0720c2s
Griscom, L.W. v6p0447c1s
Griscom, W.W. v1p0399c2s
Grissell, T. v1p1402c1s
Grissen, C. v4p0522c1s
Grissom, A.C. v3p0247c2s
v3p0371c2s v4p0460c2s
Griswold, A.L. v4p0099c1s
v4p0180c2s
Griswold, A.V. v1p0421c1s
Griswold, C. v1p1263c1s
Griswold, H.T. v1p1043c1s
v4p0523c2s
Griswold, L. v4p0223c1s
v6p0071c2s
Griswold, Latta v6p0083c2s
Griswold, M.A. v3p0254c1s
Griswold, R.W. v1p0076c1s
v1p0200c1s v1p0200c2s v1p0950c1s
Griswold, S.G.V. v5p0170c2s
Griswold, W.M. v1p0610c2s
v1p1276c2s v1p1357c1s v2p0028c1s
v2p0102c2s v2p0177c1s v2p0216c2s
v2p0233c1s v2p0461c2s v3p0050c1s
v3p0097c2s v3p0417c2s v4p0448c1s
v4p0530c1s v5p0205c2s
Griswold, W.R. v1p0298c2m
v1p1047c2s
Gritten, W.G.H. v6p0665c2s
Groat, G.G. v5p0015c2s
v6p0196c2s
Groce, B. v4p0183c2s
v4p0184c2s
Groebel, K. v4p0070c1s
Groesbeck, H.J. v1p1011c1s
Groff, A. v3p0057c1s
v4p0048c2s v4p0076c2s
Groff, Alice v5p0635c1s
Groff, G.G. v3p0231c2s
v3p0375c1s v4p0262c2s v5p0460c1s
v5p0460c2s v5p0591c2s v6p0509c2s
Groff, L.A. v6p0360c2s
Grogan, E.S. v5p0008c1s
v5p0487c2s v6p0378c1s v6p0542c1m
Grogan, W.E. v5p0159c1s
v5p0488c2s v5p0606c2s v6p0387c1s
Grohman, W.A.B. v1p0216c1s
v1p1214c1s v1p1239c2s v1p1337c2s
v2p0056c2s v2p0180c2s v5p0225c1s
v6p0230c2s v6p0246c1s v6p0285c1s
Grohman, W.A.Baillie v2p0295c2s
Grohman, W.B. v1p0208c1s
Gromort, G. v6p0479c2s
v6p0480c1s v6p0650c2s v6p0651c1s
Gron, N. v5p0217c1s
v5p0600c1s
Gronau, G. v5p0330c1s
Groneman, H.J.H. v2p0028c2s
v2p0285c2s
Gronkowski, C. v6p0157c2s
v6p0362c1s
Gronkowski, Camille v6p0201c2s
v6p0479c2m
v6p0516c2s
Gronkowski, Camille and
Perigord, Louis de, Count
v6p0424c2s
v6p0479c2s
Gronlund, L. v3p0296c2s
v3p0397c2s
Gronlund, L. and Takahashi, K.T.
v5p0537c1s
Gronow, H. v6p0323c2s
Groom, P. v4p0185c2s
v5p0510c2s
Groome, F.H. v3p0154c2s
v3p0157c1s v3p0173c1s
v3p0185c2s
Groome, W.W. v4p0555c1s
Groot, G.A. v5p0382c2s
Groot, H.De v1p0187c1s
v1p0188c1m v1p0287c1s v1p0360c2s
v1p0532c2s v1p0845c2s v1p0875c2s
v1p1197c2s v2p0064c2s v2p0482c2s
v3p0063c2s
Gropallo, L. v6p0331c1s
Gros, J. v6p0524c2s
Gros, M. v2p0370c2s
Grosart, A.B. v2p0062c2s
v2p0110c2s v2p0201c1s v2p0417c1s
v2p0449c1s
Grose, F. v1p0469c1s
v1p1240c2s
Groser, W.P. v6p0048c1s
v6p0235c2s v6p0267c2s v6p0310c1s
Grosh, A.B. v2p0070c2s
Grosjean, K. v3p0119c2s
Groso, F. v3p0251c2s
Gross, A.E. v6p0559c2s
Gross, C. v2p0202c1s
v2p0264c2s v3p0055c2s v3p0085c1s
v3p0230c2s v3p0256c2m v4p0122c2s
v4p0134c2s v4p0181c1s v4p0244c1s
v5p0044c1s v5p0345c1s v5p0481c1s
v5p0605c1s v6p0325c1s v6p0499c2s
Gross, J.B. v1p0769c1s
v1p0818c2s
Gross, M. v1p0015c1s
v6p0492c2s
Gross, R.J. v6p0558c1s
Grossart, A.B. v5p0140c2s
Grosscup, P.S. v6p0150c2s

v6p0151c1m v6p0659c1s
Grosscup, P.S. and Davis, C.K. v4p0553c2s
Grosse, E. v4p0255c1s v4p0553c2s
Grosse, F. v5p0370c2s
Grosse, J. v1p1104c1s
Grosser, H.S. v6p0113c2m
Grosser, Hugo S. v6p0436c1s
Grossetete-Thierry, M. ... v4p0097c1s
Grossi, V. v4p0294c1s
Grossman, E.B. v4p0068c1s
Grossman, Edith S. v6p0653c1s
Grossman, R. v4p0522c1s
Grossmann, K. v4p0195c2s v4p0273c1s
Grossmann, K. and Lomas, J. v4p0273c1s
Grossmith, G. v5p0560c1s
Grossmith, G., jr. v2p0344c2s
Grosvenor, A. v4p0528c1s v5p0531c1s
Grosvenor, C.H. v5p0403c2s v5p0603c2s v6p0458c2s
Grosvenor, C.H. and Wheeler, J. v4p0602c1s
Grosvenor, D. v1p0528c1s
Grosvenor, E.A. v4p0228c2s v4p0241c2s v5p0134c1s v5p0501c2s v5p0527c2s v6p0557c1s v6p0686c1s
Grosvenor, G. v3p0105c1s v6p0353c1s
Grosvenor, G.H. v5p0011c1s v5p0015c1s v5p0022c1s v5p0022c2s v5p0027c1s v5p0285c2s v6p0250c2s v6p0320c1s v6p0476c1s v6p0477c1s v6p0536c1s v6p0606c1s v6p0670c1s v6p0688c1s
Grosvenor, L. v1p0074c2s v1p0666c1s
Grosvenor, M. v1p0426c2s v1p0868c1s
Grosvenor, W.M. v1p0198c2s v1p0286c1s v1p1075c2m v1p1087c1m v3p0416c2s v4p0619c1s
Groszmann, M.P.E. v5p0106c2s v5p0231c1s v5p0569c1s v6p0115c2s
Groszmann, N.P.E. v5p0106c1s
Grote, A.R. v1p0029c1s v1p0181c1m v1p0307c2s v1p0523c2s v1p0644c2s v1p0793c2s v1p0926c2s v1p1039c1s v2p0132c2s v2p0299c2m v3p0195c2s v5p0085c2s
Grote, G. v1p0403c2s v1p0496c1s v1p0553c1s v1p0555c1s v1p0732c2s v1p1308c1s
Grote, J. v1p0810c2s v1p0863c1s v1p0976c2s
Grote, Prof. v4p0404c1s v4p0578c2s
Groth, P. v6p0460c2s
Grothe, A. v1p1286c1m
Grothe, H. v2p0432c2s
Grotjan, P.A. v4p0617c2s
Groussac, P. v4p0256c1s
Grousset, P. v4p0127c1s v4p0324c2s
Grout, A.J. v6p0582c1s
Grout, C.L. v6p0117c1s
Grout, C.M. v1p0192c1s
Grout, E.M. v5p0226c2s v5p0391c2s
Grout, H.M. v1p1227c2s v1p1401c2s
Grout, L. v1p0229c1s v1p1302c2s v1p1441c2s v2p0309c1s
Grove, A. v6p0207c1s
Grove, A. and Ellis, H. .. v6p0703c2s
Grove, A., Lady v6p0703c1s
Grove, Agnes v5p0201c1s v5p0638c1s
Grove, F.C. v1p1368c2s
Grove, G. v1p0127c2s v1p0161c1s v1p0347c1s v1p0993c2s v1p1284c1s v1p1295c2s v3p0091c1s
Grove, Lady v6p0298c2s
Grove, W. v1p1390c1s
Grove, W.R. v1p0304c1s v3p0015c1s
Grover, G.F. v1p0455c1s
Grover, J.W. v1p1075c2s v1p1077c2s v2p0362c2s
Grover, O.D. v5p0498c2s v6p0034c1s
Groves, C.W. v4p0257c1s
Groves, J.P. v3p0357c1s
Groves, S. v4p0609c1s
Grower, G.G. v2p0060c2s v2p0138c2s
Growoll, A. v3p0070c1s v4p0092c1s v4p0102c1s v6p0075c1s v6p0239c1s
Grubb, E. v4p0192c1s v4p0344c1s v5p0474c1s
Grubb, E.B. v1p1264c2s v4p0043c1s
Grubb, H. v2p0145c2s v2p0319c1s v2p0433c2s v3p0407c2s v4p0568c1s
Grubb, H., Sir v3p0423c2m
Grubb, S.F. v1p1184c1s
Grubbs, I.B. v2p0044c2s v2p0045c1s v2p0255c1s v2p0358c1s
Grubhofer, T. v5p0431c2s
Gruchy, G.F.B.de v3p0073c1s
Grudzinski, Anna v6p0115c2s
Grueber, E. v4p0261c1m
Gruenberg, E. v5p0612c2s
Gruener, H. v4p0405c1s v4p0564c1s
Gruener, H.W. and Gooch, F.A. v3p0015c2s v4p0405c1s
Grugan, F.C. v5p0183c2s
Gruhl, Edwin F. and Robinson, Edgar E. v6p0529c1s
Grumbine, J.C.F. v3p0111c1s v4p0148c1s v4p0447c1s v4p0478c1s v4p0480c1s v4p0609c2s
Grummann, P.H. v6p0283c1s v6p0623c2s
Grump, C.G. v3p0075c1s
Grun, W.H. v1p0126c1s
Grunbaum, A.S. v5p0042c2s
Grunbaum, M. v1p1281c2s
Grunbaum, N. v1p0892c1s
Grund, F.J. v1p0244c2s v1p0510c1s v1p0515c1s v1p1283c1s
Grund, J.P. v5p0064c2s v5p0320c1s v5p0389c1s
Grundemann, R. v2p0292c1s
Grundy, C.H. v1p1179c1s
Grundy, E.L. v4p0421c2s
Grundy, F. v4p0420c1s
Grundy, S. v2p0122c2s v2p0123c1m v2p0344c2s
Grundy, S. and Jones, H.A. v3p0122c1s
Gruneisen, C.L. v1p0363c2s
Gruner, L. v2p0103c2s
Gruner, M.L. v1p0664c1s v2p0229c1s
Grunow, W. v1p0207c1s
Grunsky, C.E. v5p0088c1s v6p0477c2s
Grunwaldt, E.M. v6p0556c1s
Grunwedel, A. v5p0084c1s
Gruppe, C.P., Mrs. v6p0071c1s
Gruss, Dr. v1p1268c2s
Gruver, O.H. v5p0351c1s
Gruyther, C.M.De v6p0569c2s
Grylls, J.W. v1p0698c2s v1p0952c1s v1p0983c2s
Gryzanovski, E. v1p0287c1s v1p0478c2s v1p0671c2s v1p0672c2m v1p0673c1m v1p0673c2s v1p0714c2s v1p0884c2s v1p0898c1s v1p0964c2s v1p1033c1s v1p1061c1m v1p1100c1s v1p1116c2s v1p1160c1s v1p1214c2s v1p1363c1s v1p1380c1s v1p1424c1s
Gryzanovski, E.G.F. v6p0135c1s v6p0615c1s
Gsell, P. v4p0276c1s v4p0390c1s v4p0421c2s
Guarini, E. v6p0014c1s v6p0177c2s v6p0197c2s v6p0198c2s v6p0199c1s v6p0304c2s v6p0354c2s
Guarini, Emile v6p0275c2s v6p0490c1s
Guarini, G.B. v5p0231c2s
Guastavino, R. v4p0102c1s v4p0131c1s
Gubbins, J.A. v3p0258c1s
Gubernatis, A. v1p0671c1s
Gubernatis, A.de v1p0672c1s v1p0672c2s v1p0673c2s v1p0834c2s v1p0964c2s v1p1358c1s v2p0230c2m v3p0131c2s v6p0332c1s
Guchen, Father v1p1396c2s
Gudeman, A. v3p0335c1s v4p0561c2s
Gudemann, M. v4p0306c1s
Gudger, E.W. v6p0276c1s
Gue, B.F. v5p0079c1s
Guebhard, A. v2p0463c2s
Guelt, A. v1p0199c2s
Guenther, T. v6p0233c1s
Guenyveau, A. v1p0141c1s
Guerber, H.A. v5p0487c1s
Guerin, E. v1p1079c1s
Guerin, H. v5p0298c1s
Guerin, M.de v4p0094c2s
Guerin, T. v1p0086c2s
Guerlac, O. v5p0168c2m v5p0189c1s v5p0201c1s v5p0216c2m v5p0217c2s v5p0218c2s v5p0508c2s v6p0059c1s v6p0140c1s v6p0237c2s v6p0238c1s v6p0242c2s v6p0339c1s v6p0485c1s v6p0683c2s
Guerlac, O.G. v6p0002c1s
Guerlac, Othon v5p0104c1s
Guernsey, A.H. v1p0010c1m v1p0010c2m v1p0011c1s v1p0018c1s v1p0018c2s v1p0019c1s v1p0035c1s v1p0037c2s v1p0054c2s v1p0055c1s v1p0056c2s v1p0078c1s v1p0091c2s v1p0098c1s v1p0107c2s v1p0148c2s v1p0162c2s v1p0188c1s v1p0196c1s v1p0197c1m v1p0201c2s v1p0203c2s v1p0211c2s v1p0230c2s v1p0258c1s v1p0334c2s v1p0335c1s v1p0370c2s v1p0379c1s v1p0402c1s v1p0424c2s v1p0452c1s v1p0485c1s v1p0532c2s v1p0559c1s v1p0576c1s v1p0591c2m v1p0597c1m v1p0597c2s v1p0666c2s v1p0677c2s v1p0678c1s v1p0678c2s v1p0680c2s v1p0690c1s v1p0698c1s v1p0712c2s v1p0722c2m v1p0734c1s v1p0749c2s v1p0762c1s v1p0782c1s v1p0806c2s v1p0832c2s v1p0837c2s v1p0879c1s v1p0919c2s v1p0922c2s v1p0966c2s v1p0993c1s v1p1012c1s v1p1111c1s v1p1121c1s v1p1136c2s v1p1137c1s v1p1145c1s v1p1180c1s v1p1190c2s v1p1191c2m v1p1194c1m v1p1224c2s v1p1238c2s v1p1252c2s v1p1274c1s v1p1398c2s v1p1399c2s v1p1435c1s
Guernsey, C.F. v1p0273c2s v1p0674c2s v1p0942c1s v1p1087c2s v1p1417c2s v3p0332c2s v3p0411c1s v3p0449c1s v3p0456c2s
Guernsey, C.W. v1p0623c1s v1p1017c1s
Guernsey, F.R. v1p0905c2s v6p0414c2s
Guernsey, J. v1p0290c1s v1p1010c1s
Guernsey, L.E. v1p0851c2m v1p1067c1s
Guernsey, R.S. v1p0734c2s v4p0392c2s v6p0538c2s v6p0692c1s
Guerra, Rosa de v6p0091c1s
Guerrero, E.A.P. v4p0403c2s
Guerry, W.A. v5p0055c2s v5p0420c1s v5p0555c2s v6p0428c2s
Guertin, F. v4p0485c1s v4p0619c1s
Guertin, F.I. v4p0625c1s
Guertin, F.L. v4p0040c2s v4p0351c2s v4p0366c1s
Guertin, Florence v4p0635c1s
Guerville, A.B.de v4p0298c1s v4p0476c1s
Guest, A. v3p0239c2s v3p0272c2s v3p0410c1s v5p0552c1s
Guest, A.R. and McKillop, A. v5p0314c1s
Guest, G.H. v1p1434c1s
Guest, I. v6p0266c1s
Guest, J. v2p0379c1s
Guffin, J.C. v5p0179c1s
Guffin, R. v1p0921c2s
Guggenberger, L.S. v3p0120c1s
Guggenheimer, A. v6p0496c2s
Guial, E.L. v1p0906c1s
Guicestre, G. v3p0018c1s
Guichainville, LeMetayer de v3p0070c2s
Guider, A. v1p0966c2s
Guieysse, M.P. v5p0034c1s
Guilbert, A.B. v3p0003c1s
Guild, C. v5p0405c2s
Guild, C., jr. v3p0337c1s v5p0496c1s v6p0609c1s
Guild, E.C. v1p0599c2s
Guild, E.P. v3p0002c2s v3p0082c1s v3p0103c2s v3p0272c1s v3p0295c2s
Guild, E.W. v2p0240c2s
Guild, F.N. v6p0681c1s
Guild, G. v5p0240c2s
Guild, H.R. v5p0150c1s
Guild, I.T. v6p0028c1s
Guild, M.P. v5p0079c2s v5p0581c1s
Guild, Mary v5p0347c2s
Guild, R.A. v1p0132c2s v1p0169c2m v2p0191c2s v2p0256c1s v2p0275c2s v3p0056c2s v3p0121c2s v3p0190c1s v3p0230c2s v5p0512c2s
Guild, W. v5p0403c2s
Guilds, M. v5p0182c1s
Guilford, C.C. v5p0395c1s
Guillaume, C.E. v5p0449c2s v5p0551c2s v6p0325c1s
Guillaume, E. v4p0082c1s
Guillaume, H. v4p0436c2s
Guillemard, A.C. v2p0162c1s
Guillemard, A.G. v2p0110c2s v2p0116c1s v2p0156c1s v2p0162c1m v2p0198c1s v2p0271c2s v2p0312c1s v2p0316c2m v2p0428c1s
Guillemard, F.H. v3p0383c1m
Guillemard, F.H.H. v3p0109c1s v4p0058c2s v4p0180c1s
Guillemin, A. v1p1243c2s v4p0445c1s
Guillemot, M. v6p0479c2s
Guillet, C. v5p0480c1s v6p0382c1s v6p0444c1s
Guillow, L.E. v5p0430c1s
Guilmant, A. v5p0423c2s
Guimard, H. v6p0033c2s
Guinee, W.B. v1p0785c1s v1p0862c2s v1p1127c1s v1p1279c2s v2p0430c1s
Guiney, L.E. v3p0037c1s
Guiney, L.I. v2p0118c1s v2p0212c1s v2p0436c1s v3p0061c2s v3p0074c1s v3p0110c2s v3p0261c2s

v3p0266c1s v3p0322c1s v3p0333c2s
v3p0340c1s v3p0353c2s v3p0448c1s
v4p0195c2s v4p0251c2s v4p0417c2s
v4p0502c1s v4p0601c1m v5p0051c1s
v5p0201c1s v5p0206c2s v5p0220c1s
v5p0364c1s v5p0418c1s v5p0428c2s
v6p0278c2s v6p0345c1s
Guiney, Louise I. v6p0048c1s
v6p0115c2s v6p0194c2s v6p0209c1s
v6p0381c1s
Guinn, J.M. v3p0375c1s
v6p0260c2s
Guinnipp, Gen. v1p0570c2s
Guipon, L. v6p0362c1s
Guise, R.E. v5p0406c1s
Guise-Tucker, W. v5p0028c2s
Guizot, F. v1p0241c2m
v1p0387c2s v1p0441c1s v1p0478c2s
v1p0546c2s v1p0907c2s v1p1094c1s
Guizot, M. v1p0480c2s
v1p1222c1s
Gulbrandson, A. v1p0104c2s
Gulesian, M.H. v5p0028c2m
Gulick, A.W. v4p0250c2s
Gulick, H.L. v6p0540c2s
Gulick, J.T. v1p1233c1s
v3p0106c2s v3p0145c1m v3p0145c2s
v4p0108c2s
v6p0608c2s
Gulick, L. v4p0434c2s
v5p0225c1s v5p0393c1s
Gulick, L.H. v1p1030c1s
v6p0284c2m
Gulick, Luther H. v6p0246c2s
Gulick, S.L. v6p0421c2m
Gulick, W.B. v1p0873c2s
Gull, C.G. v5p0375c2s
Gull, W., Sir et al. v1p0934c1s
Gull, W.W. v1p0019c2s
Gulland, J.W. v6p0578c1s
Gullick, T.J. v4p0029c2s
Gullifer, H. v1p0047c2s
v2p0315c1s v3p0272c1s
Gullifer, Helena v3p0392c2s
Gulliver, F.P. v5p0171c1s
v6p0250c2s
Gulliver, G. v1p0882c1s
v1p1083c1s
Gulliver, J.H. v1p0365c2s
v2p0082c2s v3p0175c1s v3p0176c1s
v3p0389c2s v4p0177c2s v5p0558c2s
v5p0572c1s
Gulliver, J.H. and Ritchie, E.
v4p0154c1s
Gulliver, J.P. v1p0868c1s
v1p0930c1s v1p1007c1s v1p1119c2s
v1p1254c2s v1p1366c2s v3p0229c1s
v3p0282c2s v3p0423c2s
Gulliver, J.P. et al. v2p0481c2s
Gully, W.C. v5p0264c1s
Gulston, A. v6p0301c6s
Gumbel, Prof. v1p1223c1s
Gumbleton, H.A. v3p0304c1s
Gumley, N.W. v2p0188c1s
v2p0189c2s
Gumm, C.C. v6p0448c1s
Gummere, A.M. v2p0061c2s
v2p0360c2s v5p0222c1s v5p0426c1s
v5p0474c1s v6p0383c1s
Gummere, F.B. v2p0040c1s
v2p0125c2s v2p0143c2s v2p0145c1s
v4p0184c1s v6p0380c1s v6p0470c2s
v6p0505c2s
Gummested, L.M. v6p0438c1s
Gump, W.E. v3p0422c2s
Gumpach, J.von v1p0849c2s
Gumpel, C.G. v4p0532c2s
v5p0113c2s v5p0453c1s v5p0506c1s
Gumplowicz, L. v6p0685c2s
Gun, Col. v5p0423c1s
Gunckel, J.E. v4p0267c1s
Gunckel, L.B. v5p0425c2s
Gunckel, L.W. v4p0486c2s
v5p0255c1s v5p0369c2s v5p0428c1m
v5p0505c1s
Gundry, A.W. v1p0427c1s
v2p0147c1s
Gundry, R.C. v5p0112c2s
Gundry, R.C. and Gambier, J.W.
v4p0166c2s
Gundry, R.S. v2p0052c2s
v2p0078c2s v2p0103c1s v2p0382c1s
v2p0442c2s v3p0078c2m v3p0079c1s
v3p0210c2s v3p0392c2s v3p0428c2m
v3p0433c1s v4p0070c1s v4p0077c2m
v4p0105c1m v4p0105c2s v4p0133c2s
v4p0183c1s v4p0209c2s v4p0262c2s
v4p0297c1s v4p0328c1s v4p0374c1s
v4p0433c1s v4p0452c2s v4p0495c2s
v4p0522c2s v5p0108c2s v5p0110c2s
v5p0112c1m v5p0438c2s v5p0529c1s
v6p0211c1s v6p0471c2s v6p0508c2s
Gundry, S.R. v4p0017c1s
Gundy, A.A. v4p0396c2s
Gunkel, H. v5p0057c1s
v5p0254c1s v6p0062c1m v6p0063c1s
Gunlogsen, A. v4p0601c1s
Gunlogsen, A.H. v2p0214c1m
v4p0168c1s v4p0273c1s v4p0528c1s
v6p0301c1s
Gunn, C.H.
v1p0680c2s
Gunn, G.D. v5p0075c1s
Gunn, G.W. v6p0458c2s
Gunn, J.H. v2p0214c2s
v2p0476c1s
Gunn, J.N. v5p0138c2s
Gunn, M.S. v5p0135c1s
v5p0434c1s
Gunnery, C.S. v5p0313c1s
Gunning, W.D. v1p0181c2s
v1p0919c2s v1p1015c1s v1p1055c1s
v2p0159c2s v4p0003c2s v4p0308c2s
v4p0479c1s v4p0511c1s v4p0578c2s
Gunnison, A. v6p0698c2s
Gunnison, C.A. v5p0510c2s
Gunnison, H.F. v3p0009c1s
Gunsaulus, F.W. v4p0143c1s
v4p0300c2s v4p0415c2s v5p0028c2s
v6p0239c2s v6p0330c2s
Gunsaulus, G.W. v1p0071c2s
v1p1022c1s
Gunsberg, I. v4p0099c1m
v4p0099c2m
Gunter, A. v2p0030c1s
v2p0216c2s v2p0340c2s
Gunter, A.C. v5p0040c2s
Gunther, A. v1p0039c2s
v1p0456c1s v1p0456c2m v1p0499c2s
v1p0960c2s v1p1213c1s v1p1317c1s
v2p0399c1s v3p0045c1s
Gunther, R.T. v5p0447c1s
v5p0606c1s v6p0441c2m
Gunthorp, Pauline v6p0136c2s
Gunthorpe, G.J., Mrs. v1p0098c1s
v1p0940c1s
Gunton, G. v2p0135c2s
v3p0170c1s v3p0239c1s v3p0398c2s
v3p0437c1m v4p0044c2s v4p0315c2s
v4p0378c2s v4p0462c1s v4p0462c2s
v5p0018c1s v5p0018c2s v5p0039c1s
v5p0093c1s v5p0138c1s v5p0150c1s
v5p0158c1s v5p0175c1s v5p0175c2s
v5p0209c2s v5p0293c1s v5p0320c2s
v5p0351c2s v5p0392c1s v5p0434c1s
v5p0465c2s v5p0496c1s v5p0540c2s
v5p0550c1s v5p0557c1m v5p0567c1s
v5p0584c2s v5p0592c1s v5p0610c2s
v5p0617c1s
Gunton, G. and Dowd, J. .. v5p0320c2s
Gunton, G. et al. v4p0462c2s
Gunton, George v4p0524c2s
Gunton, George and Commons, J.R.
v4p0152c1s
Gunton, R.J. v2p0139c1s
Guppy, E.L. v3p0334c2s
Guppy, H.B. v1p0233c2s
v2p0047c2s v2p0063c2s v2p0102c2s
v2p0373c2s v2p0409c1m v3p0235c1s
v4p0133c2s
Guppy, H.B. et al. v3p0100c2s
Guppy, T.R. v1p1191c2s
Gupta, A. v3p0354c1s
Gupta, S.N. v4p0258c1s
Guptill, A.B. v3p0307c2s
v3p0474c2s
Guptill, E.L. v4p0391c2s
Guptill, T.H. v6p0149c1s
Guptra, K.P. v3p0196c2s
Guraini, Emile v6p0230c2s
Gurley, G.D. v4p0032c2s
Gurley, R.R. v6p0227c1s
Gurlitt, C. v4p0457c1s
Gurlt, A. v1p0663c1s
Gurnell, L. v5p0234c1s
Gurnell, Leslie v5p0379c1s
Gurnell, R. v4p0197c2s
Gurney, A. v1p0479c1s
v1p1371c1s
Gurney, D. v1p0608c1s
v1p0738c2s
Gurney, E. v1p0106c1s
v1p0353c2s v1p0745c1s v1p0861c2s
v1p0882c2m v1p0884c2s v1p1086c1s
v1p1376c2s v2p0195c1s v2p0211c1s
v2p0213c2s v2p0302c2s v2p0303c1s
v2p0358c1s v2p0368c2s v2p0420c2s
v2p0457c1m v2p0462c2s v2p0464c1s
v3p0105c2s v3p0206c1s v3p0423c1s
v3p0429c2s
Gurney, E. and James, W. . v2p0140c2s
Gurney, E. and Myers, F.W.H.
v2p0017c2m v2p0284c1s v2p0284c2s
v2p0338c1s v2p0440c1m v2p0445c1s
Gurney, E. and Myers, W.H.
v2p0474c1s
Gurney, E. et al. v2p0440c1s
Gurney, E.W. v1p0060c1s
v1p1143c1s
Gurney, H. v1p0103c2s
v1p0203c2s v1p0427c1s v1p1065c2s
Gurney, H.P. and Irving, A.
v3p0380c1s
Gurney, J.H. v1p0412c2s
v1p0588c1s
Gurney, J.J. v1p0130c2s
Gurney, S.G. v2p0034c2s
v2p0367c2s
Gurney, Sybella et al. ... v6p0214c1s
Gurowski, A.de v1p1209c1s
Gurteen, S.H. v4p0097c1s
Gurton, E.B. v3p0231c2s
Gurtt, A. v1p1291c1s
Guss, A.L. v2p0268c2s
v2p0369c2s
Gussfeldt, P. v1p0025c1s
Gustafson, A. v1p0922c1s
v1p1136c1s v3p0346c1s v4p0009c2s
v4p0162c1s
Gustafson, A.C.J. v1p0010c1s
v1p0536c2s
Gustafson, Axel v4p0333c2s
Gustafson, J.B. v2p0296c1s
Gustafson, Z.B. v1p0168c1s
v1p0702c2s v2p0040c2s v2p0242c2s
v2p0247c1s v2p0249c2s v2p0380c1s
Gustavino, R. v3p0090c1s
Gutch, E. v4p0442c2s
Gutch, J.M. v1p0051c2s
v1p1112c1s
Guth, W.W. v6p0571c1s
Guthe, K.E. v5p0185c1s
Guthrie, A. v1p0146c1s
Guthrie, C.C. v6p0285c1s
Guthrie, C.C. and Stewart, G.N.
v6p0456c1s
Guthrie, C.J. v5p0143c1s
Guthrie, D.K. v2p0129c1s
v2p0164c1s
Guthrie, E.E. v3p0270c1s
v4p0310c2s
Guthrie, E.G. v6p0627c1s
Guthrie, F. v1p0217c2s
v2p0458c2s v3p0072c1s v3p0380c2s
v4p0441c2s v4p0507c2s
Guthrie, F. et al. v3p0045c2s
Guthrie, F.A. v2p0403c2s
v3p0293c2s v3p0427c1s v4p0520c2s
v4p0531c1s
Guthrie, H. v3p0341c1s
Guthrie, J.A. v5p0314c1s
Guthrie, J.J. v6p0074c2s
Guthrie, J.W. v5p0322c1s
v6p0246c2s v6p0301c2s v6p0464c2s
Guthrie, K. v5p0382c1s
Guthrie, T. v1p0383c2s
v1p0415c1s v1p0909c1s v1p0966c1s
v1p0971c1s v1p1064c1s v1p1074c2m
v1p1094c2s
Guthrie, W.N. v5p0011c2s
v5p0029c2s v5p0031c1s v5p0066c1s
v5p0098c2s v5p0125c2s v5p0209c2s
v5p0258c1s v5p0331c1s v5p0342c1s
v5p0355c2s v5p0385c2s v5p0441c2s
v5p0455c2s v5p0519c2s v5p0644c1s
v6p0140c2s v6p0260c1s v6p0575c2s
v6p0656c2s
Guthrie, W.N. and Young, J.W.
v5p0370c2s
Guthrie-Smith, N. v4p0438c1s
Gutode, L. v3p0462c1s
Gutridge, A.W. v6p0109c1s
v6p0420c1s
Gutzkow, K. v1p1051c1s
v2p0456c2s v4p0598c2s
Guy, C. v5p0217c1s
Guy, G.H. v4p0032c2s
v5p0185c1m v5p0575c2s v6p0199c2s
v6p0224c1s
Guy, H.H. v5p0302c2s
Guy, W. v6p0360c2s
Guy, W.A. v1p0082c2s
v1p0285c2s v1p0351c2s v1p0407c1s
v1p0436c1s v1p0543c1s v1p0578c1s
v1p0578c2s v1p0605c2s v1p0610c1m
v1p0643c2s v1p0745c1s v1p0753c2s
v1p0873c2s v1p0933c2s v1p1161c2s
v1p1174c1s v1p1215c1s v1p1245c2s
v1p1246c1s v1p1285c1s v1p1293c1s
v1p1376c1s v1p1394c2s v2p0405c2m
v2p0418c2s
Guy, W.H. v1p0295c1s
Guyau, M. v2p0022c2s
v2p0389c1s
Guye, G.E. v6p0498c1m
Guyer, Michael F. v6p0444c2s
Guyon, F.T. v5p0501c2s
Guyon, G. v1p1441c2s
Guyot, A. v1p0207c2s
Guyot, A.H. v1p0048c1s
Guyot, Y. v1p0498c2s
v2p0329c1s v3p0052c1s v3p0160c1s
v4p0212c2s v5p0168c2m v5p0217c1s
v5p0588c2s v6p0108c1s v6p0236c2s
v6p0254c2s v6p0265c1s v6p0557c1s
v6p0624c1s v6p0624c2s
Guyot, Y. et al. v4p0557c2s
v6p0108c1s v6p0633c1s
Guyot, Yves v2p0165c2s
v4p0533c2s
Guyot-Daubes, M. v4p0549c2s
Guzzi, P. v1p1390c2s
Gwaines, Tresham v5p0238c2s
Gwatkin, H.M. v5p0059c1s
v5p0162c1s v5p0297c2s
Gwillim, G.H. v4p0053c2s
v4p0099c2s
Gwillim, G.H. and Yule, H.W.
v5p0083c2s
Gwillim, J.C. v4p0075c1s

Gwilt v2p0342c2s
Gwin, J.M. v6p0363c2s
Gwin, W.M. v3p0400c2s
Gwin, W.M. and Coleman, E.G.
v3p0187c1s
Gwyllym, St.John v2p0269c1s
Gwynfe, B. v4p0376c1s
Gwynn, C.W. v5p0540c1s
Gwynn, G. v6p0495c1s
Gwynn, S. v4p0010c1s
v4p0542c2s v4p0549c1s v5p0144c2s
v5p0145c2s v5p0165c2s v5p0205c1s
v5p0234c1s v5p0254c2s v5p0295c2m
v5p0297c1s v5p0297c2m v5p0331c1s
v5p0352c1s v5p0387c2s v5p0397c2m
v5p0430c1s v5p0435c2s v5p0446c2s
v5p0451c1s v5p0455c1s v5p0507c1s
v5p0514c2s v5p0520c1s v5p0553c1s
v5p0573c1s v5p0634c2s v5p0636c2s
v6p0090c2s v6p0106c2s v6p0178c2s
v6p0205c1s v6p0227c1s v6p0227c2s
v6p0274c2s v6p0289c1s v6p0303c1s
v6p0326c1s v6p0326c2s v6p0327c2s
v6p0328c1m v6p0328c2s v6p0344c2s
v6p0352c1s v6p0365c1s v6p0442c1s
v6p0562c2s v6p0589c2s v6p0641c2s
v6p0658c1s v6p0670c2s
Gwynn, S.L. v3p0389c1s
v4p0519c1s
Gwynn, Stephen v5p0557c2s
v5p0589c2s v6p0289c1s
Gwynne, G. v1p1265c2s
Gwynne, G. and Young, J. . v1p1265c1s
Gwynne, H.A. v4p0147c2s
Gwyther, G. v1p0500c2s
v1p0902c1s v1p1063c2s v1p1141c2s
v1p1170c2s v1p1308c2s
Gyl, J.A.M. v6p0088c2s
v6p0516c2s
Gyles, Lena v4p0007c1s
Gymer, Rose C. v6p0116c2s
Gyorgy, B. v3p0204c2s
Gyp v5p0378c2s
v5p0510c2s

H. v5p0289c2s
H., A. v6p0049c1s
H., A.C. v5p0049c1s
v5p0197c2s v5p0404c1s v6p0021c1s
v6p0312c2s v6p0315c1s
H., A.D. v6p0193c2s
H., A.R. v6p0037c2s
H., C.H. v6p0157c1s
H., E. v5p0481c1s
H., E.J. v4p0309c1s
H., F.W. v6p0214c1s
H., G.P. v6p0527c2s
H., H. v5p0626c1s
v6p0157c1s
H., H.W. v5p0014c2s
H., J.T. v6p0011c2s
H., L. v6p0048c2s
H., L.H. v5p0428c2s
H., R.T. v6p0679c2s
H., S.A. v1p0617c1s
H., V.C. v6p0706c1s
H., W.A. v6p0029c1s
H., W.E. v4p0480c1s
Haack, R. v5p0232c1m
v5p0526c1s
Haacke, W. v4p0061c1s
v5p0299c1s v5p0389c2s
Haan, W.G. and Harts, W.W.
v6p0568c2s
Haarklow, Johannes v5p0083c1s
Haas, J.de v3p0218c1s
Haast, J. v1p0918c2s
Haast, J.Van v2p0174c1s
Haast, J.von v1p0919c1s
v2p0159c1s
Habberton, J. v1p0725c2s
v1p0887c2s v1p0929c2s v1p1274c1s
v2p0059c1s v2p0066c2s v3p0007c2s
v3p0008c2s v3p0025c1s v3p0059c2s
v3p0121c2s v3p0135c2s v3p0142c1s
v3p0149c1s v3p0269c1s v3p0274c2s
v3p0312c1s v3p0330c1s v3p0398c1m
v3p0401c2s v3p0461c2s v4p0080c2s
v4p0190c2s v4p0532c2s v4p0619c1s
Habberton, J.H. v2p0030c1s
Haberlandt, G. v3p0289c2s
Habersham, A.W. v1p0677c2s
Habersham, H.S. v4p0571c2s
Habershon, S.O. et al. ... v1p0934c1s
Haccius, G. v3p0195c1s
Hack, C.A. v4p0245c1s
Hackel, E. v1p1105c1s
Hacker, B.M. v5p0460c2s
Hacker, T.J. v5p0174c1s
Hackett, Anna S. v4p0400c1s
Hackett, C. v6p0685c1s
Hackett, C.W. et al. v4p0384c1s
Hackett, F.H. v6p0568c2s
Hackett, F.W. v1p0564c2s
v2p0039c1s v2p0350c1s v2p0444c1s
v4p0046c2s v4p0071c2s v4p0240c2s
v4p0377c2s v4p0574c2s v4p0623c1s
v5p0134c2s v5p0488c2s v6p0404c2s
Hackett, H.B. v1p0122c2s
v1p0123c1s v1p0128c1s v1p0130c1m
v1p0686c2s v1p0688c2s v1p0689c1s
v1p0903c1s v1p0960c2s v1p0961c1s
v1p0961c2s v1p0980c2s v1p0998c1s
v1p1018c2s v1p1056c1s v1p1066c2s
v1p1260c1s
Hackett, K. v4p0037c1s
v4p0388c2m v4p0415c1s v4p0527c1m
v4p0527c2m v4p0607c1m v5p0422c1s
v5p0530c2s v5p0614c1m v6p0437c2s
v6p0604c1s
Hackett, Karleton v5p0530c2s
Hackett, O. v1p1439c1s
v4p0001c1s v4p0165c2s v4p0401c1s
v4p0458c2s v4p0513c2s
Hackett, W.B. v1p0648c2s
Hackett, W.H. v2p0237c1s
v2p0311c2s
Hackett, W.H.Y. v1p0680c1s
Hackley, C.W. v1p0003c2s
v1p0070c2s v1p0761c1s v1p1356c2m
v1p1357c1s
Hackner, W. v3p0398c2s
Hadaway, W.S. v4p0174c2s
Haddan, J.L. v1p1321c1s
v3p0412c1s v3p0438c2s
Hadden, A. v5p0253c2s
Hadden, C. v3p0432c2s
Hadden, D.E. v4p0540c2s
v5p0561c1s v6p0041c1s v6p0625c2s
v6p0626c1s
Hadden, J.C. v3p0064c1s
v3p0117c1s v3p0206c1s v3p0237c2s
v3p0261c1s v3p0293c1m v3p0293c2s
v3p0296c2s v3p0348c1s v3p0381c2s
v3p0394c2s v4p0037c1s v4p0078c1s
v4p0163c2s v4p0198c1s v4p0233c1s
v4p0259c2s v4p0358c2s v4p0364c2s
v4p0388c2m v4p0389c1m v4p0425c1s
v4p0442c1s v4p0444c2s v4p0445c1s
v4p0463c2s v4p0476c1s v4p0494c2s
v4p0510c1s v4p0549c1s v5p0080c1s
v5p0110c2s v5p0113c2s v5p0253c2m
v5p0278c1s v5p0323c1s v5p0369c2s
v5p0388c1s v5p0393c1s v5p0394c2s
v5p0395c2m v5p0399c2s v5p0423c2s
v5p0470c1s v5p0491c1s v5p0533c1s
v5p0539c1s v5p0578c1s v5p0609c2m
v5p0616c1s v6p0059c1s v6p0060c2s
v6p0161c2s v6p0345c1s v6p0437c2s
v6p0468c1s v6p0545c2s v6p0552c2s
v6p0702c2s
Hadden, J.E. v5p0236c2s
Hadden, R.H. v1p0219c1s
v1p0765c1s
Hadden, R.V. v3p0324c2s
Hadden, T.C. v4p0620c2s
Haddo, G. v4p0134c1s
Haddock, C.B. v1p0392c2s
v1p0753c2s v1p1065c1s v1p1057c1s
v1p1085c1s
Haddock, F.C. v3p0080c2s
v3p0101c2s v4p0130c1s
Haddock, R. v2p0153c2s
Haddon, A.C. v2p0157c2s
v3p0211c2s v3p0319c2s v3p0433c1m
v4p0030c2s v4p0205c1s v4p0289c1s
v4p0290c2s v4p0579c2s v4p0584c2s
v4p0631c1s v5p0022c2s v5p0023c1s
v5p0031c2s v5p0405c2s v5p0420c2s
v5p0508c2s v5p0536c2s v5p0583c1s
v6p0018c2s v6p0023c2s v6p0082c1s
v6p0167c2s v6p0204c2s v6p0212c1s
v6p0400c1s v6p0409c2s v6p0576c2s
v6p0622c1s v6p0626c1s v6p0650c2s
Haddon, A.C. et al. v4p0095c1s
Haddon, A.L. v4p0161c1s
Haddon, Alfred C. v5p0039c2s
Haddon, C. v2p0251c2s
Haddon, J.C. v4p0048c1s
Haddon, J.G. v6p0461c2s
Haddon, L.C. v6p0688c1s
Haddon, R. v3p0280c2s
Haddon, T.W. v4p0127c1s
v4p0340c2s
Haddow, R. v6p0262c1s
Hadduck, C.B. v1p0264c2s
v1p0711c1s v1p0848c1s v1p0867c2s
Haden, F.S. v3p0141c1m
v3p0142c2s v3p0317c2m v5p0155c1s
Haden, S. v2p0287c1s
Hadermann, J.R. v1p0609c1s
v1p0856c2s
Hadfield, R.A. v4p0270c1s
Hadland, S. v3p0422c1s
Hadley, A. v2p0348c2s
Hadley, A.T. v2p0097c1s
v2p0130c1s v2p0362c2m v2p0363c1m
v3p0099c1s v3p0215c1s v3p0218c2m
v3p0348c2s v3p0352c1s v3p0352c2m
v3p0353c1m v3p0353c2m v3p0409c1s
v3p0423c1s v3p0435c1s v3p0437c1s
v3p0461c2s v3p0471c2s v4p0167c2m
v4p0188c1s v4p0233c1s v4p0233c2s
v4p0287c2s v4p0450c1m v4p0458c1s
v4p0461c1s v4p0533c1s v4p0533c2s
v4p0627c2s v4p0635c1s v5p0163c1s
v5p0175c2s v5p0177c2s v5p0178c2m
v5p0198c2m v5p0289c1s v5p0457c1m
v5p0526c2s v5p0592c2s v5p0616c2s
v6p0002c1s v6p0059c2s v6p0135c1s
v6p0137c2s v6p0145c2s v6p0190c1s
v6p0192c2m v6p0193c1s v6p0507c1s
v6p0518c2s v6p0522c1s v6p0522c2s
v6p0540c1s v6p0581c2s v6p0672c1s
v6p0710c2s
Hadley, A.T. and Abbott, L.
v5p0177c1s
Hadley, A.T. and Harrison, C.C.
v5p0127c1s
Hadley, A.T. and Summer, W.G.
v2p0100c2s
Hadley, A.T. and Turrell, G.G.
v4p0167c2s
Hadley, Arthur T. v6p0272c2s
Hadley, C. v6p0316c1s
Hadley, D.B. v5p0079c1s
Hadley, D.R. v6p0278c1s
Hadley, F.A. v6p0695c2s
Hadley, H. v6p0125c2s
Hadley, J. v1p0040c1s
v1p0208c1s v1p0416c2s v1p0417c1s
v1p0513c2s v1p0552c1s v1p0554c1s
v1p0555c2s v1p0891c1s v1p0999c1s
v1p1020c1s v1p1180c2s v1p1184c2s
v1p1187c2s v1p1295c2s v1p1309c1s
Hadley, J.B. v5p0202c1s
Hadley, J.C. v3p0043c2s
Hadley, L.M. v5p0032c1s
v6p0627c2s
Hadley, M.H. v6p0277c1s
Hadley, Minnie E. v6p0032c1s
Hadley, P.B. v6p0497c2s
Hadley, Phil.B. v6p0214c2s
Hadley, S.M. v6p0614c1s
Hadley, S.P. and Hill, M.. v5p0350c1s
Hadley, W.T. v5p0303c2s
Hadlow, J.B. v6p0612c2s
Hadman, E.F. v3p0218c1s
Hadow, W.H. v5p0075c1m
Hadwen, E. v5p0234c1s
v6p0299c2s
Hadzsits, G.D. v6p0211c2s
v6p0504c2m
Hadzsits, Irma v5p0202c2s
Hadzsits, W.D. v6p0143c1s
Haeber, F. v2p0205c2s
Haeckel, E. v1p0102c2s
v1p0434c1s v1p0435c1s v1p0618c1m
v1p1059c1s v2p0112c2s v2p0362c1s
v4p0185c2s v4p0191c1s v4p0229c2s
v4p0255c2s v4p0270c2s v4p0379c1s
v4p0441c1m v4p0606c2s
Haeckel, E. et al. v4p0095c1s
Haeffer, J.F.X. v2p0415c1m
Haertel, M.H. v6p0323c2s
Haeselbarth, A.C. v6p0161c1s
v6p0510c1s
Hafer, L.B. v6p0420c2s
Haff, H. v5p0643c1s
Haffkine, W.M. v4p0108c1s
v5p0291c1s
Hag, Sahib el- v2p0134c1s
Hagadorn, C.B. v5p0309c2s
v5p0375c2s
Hagadorn, F.A. v4p0223c1s
v4p0356c1s
Hagadorn, F.L. v3p0391c1s
Hagaman, F.F. v6p0169c1s
Hagan, F.J. v3p0113c2s
v4p0047c1s v5p0388c1s v5p0485c2s
v5p0596c1s
Hagany, J.B. v1p0422c2s
v1p1211c2s v1p1398c2s v1p1399c1s
Hagar, D.B. v3p0360c2s
Hagar, G.J. v2p0329c1s
v2p0444c2s v3p0301c2s v3p0303c1s
v6p0015c2s
Hagar, H. v3p0184c2s
Hagar, S. v5p0050c2s
v5p0374c1s
Hagarty, E.W. v5p0421c2s
Hageman, S.A. v5p0450c1s
Hagemann, G.A. v3p0013c2s
Hagen, G. v1p1390c1s
Hagen, H.A. v1p0044c2s
v1p0148c2m v1p0645c1m v1p0702c2s
v1p0742c1s v1p0743c1s v1p0882c1s
v2p0016c1s v2p0192c2s v2p0256c1s
v2p0294c2s v2p0415c2s
Hagen, J. v2p0152c1s
Hagen, J.G. v2p0014c1s
v2p0129c2s v2p0254c2s
Hagen, L. v5p0033c1s
Hagen, W.E. v1p0533c1s
v1p0999c1s
Hagenau, M. v5p0338c2s
Hagenbach, Dr. v1p0571c2s
v1p1157c1s
Hagenbach, K.A. v1p1000c1s
v1p1304c1s
Hagenbach, K.R. v1p0348c1s
v1p0883c1s
Hager, A.D. v1p0300c1s
v1p0844c1s v1p1271c1s
Hager, C.F., jr. v3p0409c2s
Hager, C.W. v6p0095c2s
Hager, G.J. v2p0238c2s
Hager, H. and Rhys, J. ... v2p0249c1s
Hager, J.H. v3p0125c2s
v3p0267c2s v3p0268c1s v3p0325c1s
v6p0384c1s
Hager, J.S. v2p0118c2s
Hager, S. v6p0490c1s
Hagerman, H.J. v6p0556c2s
Hagerty, T.F. v4p0362c2s
Hagerty, T.J. v5p0480c1s
Hagey, J.C. v1p0769c2s
Haggard, A. v3p0444c1s
v4p0085c2s v4p0381c2s v6p0563c1s
Haggard, A.H. v2p0111c2s
v2p0217c2s
Haggard, Andrew v6p0389c1s
Haggard, F.T. v2p0362c2s
Haggard, H.R. v2p0234c2s
v2p0265c1s v3p0008c2s v3p0108c2s
v3p0151c2s v3p0176c1s v3p0187c2m
v3p0228c2s v3p0264c2s v3p0417c1s
v5p0203c1s v5p0413c1s v5p0559c1s
v5p0563c1s v6p0206c2s v6p0349c1s
Haggard, H.R. and Lang, A.
v3p0472c2s
Haggard, H.Rider v6p0153c2s
v6p0187c1s
Haggard, H.Rider et al. .. v4p0133c1s
Haggerston, W.J. v2p0310c1s
v2p0439c1s
Hagood, J. v3p0328c2s
Hagood, L.M. v3p0299c1s
Haguch v5p0246c1s
v5p0291c2s v5p0502c1s
Hague, A. v2p0318c2s
v2p0426c2s v3p0010c2s v3p0172c1s
v3p0184c2s v3p0247c2s v3p0381c1s
v3p0474c2s v4p0486c2s v4p0635c2s
v6p0711c1s
Hague, A. and Iddings, J.P.
v2p0463c1m
Hague, Arnold v5p0614c1s
Hague, C.A. v4p0008c2s
v4p0221c1m v4p0467c1s v4p0547c1s
v5p0551c1m v6p0523c1s
Hague, G. v1p0486c1s
v2p0106c2s v6p0050c2s
Hague, J. v4p0086c1s
v4p0414c2s

Hague, J.B. v1p0600c1s
Hague, J.D. v1p0301c2s
v1p0560c1s v1p1407c1s v2p0112c2s
v2p0385c1s v2p0402c2s v2p0411c2s
v4p0372c2s v4p0524c1s v6p0101c2s
v6p0210c1s v6p0330c1s v6p0339c1s
v6p0351c2s
Hague, W. v1p0179c1s
v1p0461c2s v2p0312c1s v2p0334c2s
Hahn, C.C. v1p1295c1s
v6p0690c1s
Hahn, C.W. v6p0066c2s
Hahn, I. v1p0146c1s
Hahn, M. v5p0526c1s
Hahn, Prof. v1p0119c2s
Hahn, R.D. v4p0338c1s
Hahn-Hahn, I. v2p0421c2s
Haig, A. v6p0634c2s
Haig, Alex. v6p0497c2s
Haig, H.A. v6p0106c1s
v6p0520c2s
Haig, J.C. v5p0391c1s
v5p0419c1s
Haig, W. v5p0285c1s
Haigh, D.H. and Sharpe, F.
v1p0272c1s
Haigh, W.M. v1p1041c2s
Haight, A.S. v5p0284c1s
Haight, B.I. v1p1380c1s
Haight, C. v1p0193c2s
v1p0943c1s
Haight, C.S. v4p0517c1s
Haight, E.H. v5p0573c1s
v6p0679c2s
Haight, Eliz.H. v6p0296c2s
Haight, G.W. v2p0373c1s
Haighton, E.A. v2p0126c1s
Hail, A.D. v2p0022c1s
Hail, J.B. v2p0044c2s
Haile, M. v6p0404c1s
v6p0419c1s
Haill, C.H. v1p0001c2s
Haill, F.E. v5p0617c2s
v6p0305c2s
Hailliday, G. v6p0688c2s
Hailmann, W.N. v2p0131c2s
v2p0132c1s v2p0168c2m v2p0297c1s
v2p0432c1m v4p0282c1s
Hailstone, S. v1p0776c2s
Hain, J.P. v3p0318c2s
Hain, S.S. v6p0093c1s
Haine, F.H. v6p0498c1s
Haine, F.W. v3p0094c2s
v4p0462c2s
Haines, A.M. v1p0565c1s
v1p0576c2s v3p0363c2s v4p0251c2s
Haines, Alice C. v6p0175c1s
Haines, C.R. v3p0177c2s
v5p0240c1s
Haines, C.W. v5p0173c1s
Haines, E.M. v1p1318c1s
Haines, H. v3p0013c2s
v3p0024c1s v3p0089c2s v3p0157c1s
v3p0272c1s v3p0344c2s v6p0159c1s
Haines, H.B. v6p0045c1s
Haines, H.E. v5p0016c1s
Haines, H.R. v1p0209c2s
v1p0887c2s v1p1263c2s
Haines, Harry B. v6p0044c2s
Haines, Helen v6p0158c1s
v6p0293c2s v6p0661c2s
Haines, Helen E. v6p0371c1s
v6p0373c1s
Haines, M.E. v4p0423c2s
Haines, M.G. v5p0203c1s
Haines, R. v1p0997c2s
v1p1390c1s v2p0200c2s v2p0288c2s
v2p0467c1s v3p0223c1s v3p0243c1s
v3p0456c2m
Haines, R.B., jr. v4p0221c1s
Haines, T. v1p0144c1s
Haines, T.H. v6p0005c2s
v6p0607c1s
Haines, T.H. and Davies, A.E.
v6p0534c1s
Haines, T.H. and Williams, J.C.
v6p0680c2s
Haines, T.J. v6p0058c1s
Haines, W. v5p0383c2s
Hains, A.J. v6p0255c1s
Hains, P.C. v5p0124c2s
v5p0294c1s v6p0477c1s v6p0477c2s
Hains, T.J. v5p0475c1s
v5p0524c1s v6p0203c2s v6p0351c2s
v6p0397c2s v6p0580c1s v6p0646c1s
v6p0692c2s
Haite, G.C. v4p0511c2s
Haithcox, H.C. v1p0252c2s
v2p0214c1s v4p0170c2s
Hake, A.E. v1p0150c2s
v1p1213c2s v2p0052c2s v4p0044c2s
v4p0070c1s v4p0124c1s v4p0126c1s
v4p0265c2s v4p0320c2s
Hake, A.E. and Wesslau, O.E.
v3p0420c1s
Hake, C.G. v3p0109c1s
Hake, H.W. and Kingzett, C.T.
v2p0341c1s
Hake, T.G. v1p0142c1s
v2p0123c2s v4p0231c2s
Hake, T.St.E. v3p0031c2s
v3p0176c2s v3p0209c2s v3p0246c1s
v3p0275c1s v3p0311c2s v4p0303c2s
v4p0391c2s v4p0412c1s v4p0625c1s
v5p0226c1s v5p0411c2s v5p0517c1s
v5p0526c1s v5p0616c1s v6p0633c2s
Halbert, A. v1p0358c2s
Halbert, C.A. v1p0608c2s
v1p0767c1s
Halbert, H.L. v4p0107c2s
Halbert, H.S. v2p0080c1s
Halbherr, F. v3p0104c2s
v3p0183c2s v3p0217c1s v3p0255c1s
v3p0338c1m v4p0139c1s v4p0294c1s
v4p0523c1s v5p0142c2m v5p0240c2s
v5p0463c1s
Haldane, A., Capt. v5p0465c1s
v5p0588c1s
Haldane, E.S. v5p0068c1s
v5p0261c1s
Haldane, Elizabeth S. v4p0628c1s
Haldane, J. v5p0613c2s
Haldane, J.S. v2p0257c2s
v2p0339c2s v5p0351c1s v5p0564c1s
Haldane, R.B. v1p0582c2s
v2p0240c2s v2p0241c1s v3p0131c2s
v3p0182c2s v3p0193c1s v3p0238c2s
v3p0248c1m v3p0470c1s v4p0253c1s
v4p0266c1s v4p0508c2s v5p0024c1s
v5p0231c1m v6p0357c1s
Haldane, R.B. et al. v6p0191c2s
Haldar, H. v4p0242c1s
v4p0253c1s v5p0001c2s
Haldeman, S.S. v1p0032c1s
v1p0061c1s v1p0416c2s v1p0664c1s
v1p0703c2s v1p1159c2s v1p1238c1s
v1p1440c2s
Hale, A. v2p0384c1s
v2p0421c1s v3p0474c1s
Hale, A.G.R. v5p0555c2s
Hale, A.M. v4p0451c2s
Hale, A.S. v1p0096c2s
v1p0700c1s
Hale, Annie R. v6p0434c2s
Hale, B. v1p0899c2s
v5p0520c2s
Hale, C. v1p0173c1s
v1p0258c1s v1p0339c1s v1p0395c2s
v1p0396c1s v1p1212c1s v1p1285c1s
v1p1348c2s v5p0426c2s v5p0445c1s
Hale, C.R. v1p0018c1s
v1p0239c1s v1p0421c2s v1p0642c2s
v1p0877c2s v1p1134c2m v1p1136c1s
v2p0081c1s v3p0082c2s v3p0276c2s
Hale, C.S. v1p0017c2s
v1p0018c1s v1p0856c2s
Hale, D. v4p0459c2s
Hale, D., jr. v1p0454c2s
Hale, E. v1p0187c1s
v1p0225c1s v1p0295c1m v1p0450c1s
v1p0598c1s v1p0744c2s v1p0816c2m
v1p0976c1s v1p1007c1s v1p1436c2s
v4p0484c1s v6p0689c1s
Hale, E., jr. v1p0026c2s
v1p0173c2s v1p0457c2s v1p1348c1s
Hale, E.A. v1p1305c1s
Hale, E.D. v2p0067c1s
Hale, E.E. v1p0017c2s
v1p0024c1s v1p0028c2s v1p0033c1m
v1p0045c1s v1p0048c2s v1p0060c2s
v1p0066c2s v1p0083c1s v1p0084c2s
v1p0118c2s v1p0128c1s v1p0151c2s
v1p0160c2s v1p0188c1m v1p0209c2m
v1p0220c2s v1p0238c2s v1p0245c1s
v1p0248c2s v1p0249c1s v1p0255c1s
v1p0258c1m v1p0258c2m v1p0259c1s
v1p0273c2s v1p0275c2s v1p0289c1s
v1p0301c1m v1p0303c2s v1p0316c2s
v1p0324c2s v1p0334c2s v1p0351c1s
v1p0386c1s v1p0411c1s v1p0412c2s
v1p0416c2s v1p0433c1m v1p0436c1s
v1p0484c1s v1p0485c1s v1p0487c1s
v1p0492c2s v1p0494c1s v1p0499c2s
v1p0504c2s v1p0537c2s v1p0566c1s
v1p0570c2s v1p0576c1s v1p0609c1s
v1p0623c1s v1p0678c2m v1p0687c1s
v1p0695c1s v1p0697c2s v1p0715c1s
v1p0730c1s v1p0753c1s v1p0757c2s
v1p0766c2s v1p0768c1s v1p0770c2s
v1p0786c1s v1p0795c1s v1p0809c1s
v1p0811c1s v1p0820c2s v1p0839c1s
v1p0856c2s v1p0861c1s v1p0886c2s
v1p0889c1s v1p0909c2m v1p0921c1s
v1p0927c1s v1p0960c2s v1p0976c2s
v1p0982c2s v1p0996c2s v1p0998c1s
v1p1018c1s v1p1064c2s v1p1109c1m
v1p1123c2s v1p1200c1s v1p1208c1s
v1p1209c2s v1p1215c1s v1p1232c1s
v1p1267c1s v1p1285c2m v1p1289c2s
v1p1292c1s v1p1294c1s v1p1299c1s
v1p1336c1s v1p1340c1s v1p1340c2s
v1p1342c1s v1p1344c1s v1p1344c2s
v1p1349c2s v1p1350c1m v1p1355c1s
v1p1358c2s v1p1396c2s v1p1402c1s
v1p1425c2s v1p1429c1s v1p1431c2s
v2p0010c1s v2p0011c2s v2p0028c1s
v2p0039c1s v2p0076c1s v2p0078c1s
v2p0093c1s v2p0094c2s v2p0114c2s
v2p0118c1s v2p0131c1s v2p0155c1s
v2p0234c2s v2p0237c2s v2p0254c2s
v2p0310c2s v2p0322c1s v2p0327c2s
v2p0388c1s v2p0400c1s v2p0407c1s
v2p0451c2s v2p0455c1s v3p0010c2m
v3p0011c1s v3p0038c2s v3p0049c2m
v3p0051c1s v3p0051c2s v3p0053c2s
v3p0066c2s v3p0075c2s v3p0081c2s
v3p0085c2s v3p0087c1s v3p0089c1s
v3p0099c2s v3p0102c1s v3p0102c2m
v3p0128c1s v3p0128c2s v3p0136c1s
v3p0136c2m v3p0149c1s v3p0158c1s
v3p0162c1s v3p0164c1s v3p0166c2s
v3p0188c1m v3p0190c2s v3p0199c1s
v3p0205c1s v3p0217c2s v3p0236c2s
v3p0259c2s v3p0263c2s v3p0271c1s
v3p0281c1s v3p0291c1s v3p0294c1s
v3p0298c2s v3p0300c1s v3p0300c2s
v3p0309c2s v3p0332c2s v3p0337c1s
v3p0341c2s v3p0346c2s v3p0348c2s
v3p0368c1s v3p0397c2s v3p0414c1s
v3p0417c1s v3p0422c2s v3p0423c1s
v3p0431c2s v3p0432c1s v3p0441c2s
v3p0442c1s v3p0458c2s v3p0469c2s
v3p0470c2s v4p0013c2s v4p0015c2s
v4p0022c2s v4p0037c1m v4p0071c1s
v4p0081c2s v4p0096c1s v4p0096c2s
v4p0097c1s v4p0098c2m v4p0115c1s
v4p0128c2s v4p0132c2s v4p0169c1s
v4p0170c2m v4p0190c1s v4p0216c1s
v4p0229c1s v4p0232c1s v4p0245c2s
v4p0249c1s v4p0249c2s v4p0254c1s
v4p0260c2m v4p0261c1s v4p0261c2s
v4p0274c1s v4p0275c1s v4p0275c2s
v4p0282c1s v4p0294c1s v4p0299c1s
v4p0301c2s v4p0315c2s v4p0342c1s
v4p0350c2s v4p0351c2s v4p0372c2s
v4p0398c2s v4p0414c1s v4p0431c1m
v4p0431c2s v4p0432c1s v4p0450c2s
v4p0455c2s v4p0461c1s v4p0474c2s
v4p0483c2s v4p0505c2s v4p0554c2s
v4p0555c1s v4p0568c2s v4p0580c2s
v4p0584c1s v4p0594c2s v4p0619c1s
v4p0628c1s v4p0636c1s v5p0072c1s
v5p0072c2s v5p0157c1s v5p0187c1s
v5p0191c2s v5p0197c1s v5p0219c1s
v5p0254c1s v5p0350c1m v5p0359c1s
v5p0364c1s v5p0409c2s v5p0410c2s
v5p0437c2m v5p0555c1s v6p0076c2s
v6p0108c2s v6p0123c2s v6p0145c1s
v6p0185c1s v6p0278c1s v6p0282c1s
v6p0350c1s v6p0405c1s v6p0454c2s
v6p0465c1s v6p0492c2s v6p0504c2s
v6p0537c1s v6p0542c1s v6p0633c2s
v6p0677c1s v6p0687c2s
Hale, E.E. and Allen, J.H.
v1p1352c2s
Hale, E.E. and Briggs, G.W.
v1p1009c1s v1p1380c2s
Hale, E.E. and Choate, J.H.
v3p0009c1s
Hale, E.E. and Savage, M.J.
v3p0385c2s
Hale, E.E. et al. v2p0233c1s
v3p0051c1s v3p0083c2s v3p0454c2s
v4p0500c2s
Hale, E.E., jr. v4p0004c2s
v4p0025c1s v4p0030c1s v4p0183c2s
v4p0184c1s v4p0220c1s v4p0241c2s
v4p0334c2s v4p0368c2m v4p0405c2s
v4p0430c1m v4p0448c1m v4p0475c1s
v4p0500c2s v4p0518c2s v4p0519c1s
v4p0570c1s v4p0606c1s v5p0014c1s
v5p0098c1s v5p0161c1s v5p0167c1s
v5p0221c1s v5p0227c1s v5p0258c1s
v5p0264c2s v5p0273c2s v5p0317c2s
v5p0341c2s v5p0454c2m v5p0462c2s
v5p0495c1s v5p0497c2m v5p0524c2s
v5p0585c1s v6p0159c1s v6p0168c2s
v6p0228c1s v6p0301c1s v6p0588c1m
v6p0678c2s
Hale, E.M.
v3p0342c2s
Hale, Ellen D. v5p0413c1s
Hale, Ellen Day v5p0070c2s
Hale, G.E. v3p0403c2s
v3p0415c2m v4p0100c2s v4p0440c1s
v4p0540c2s v4p0541c1s v4p0556c2m
v4p0557c1s v5p0314c2s v5p0549c2s
v6p0614c2s v6p0625c2s
Hale, G.E. and Crew, H. .. v4p0557c1s
Hale, G.E. and Douglass, A.E.
v5p0549c2s
Hale, H. v1p0837c2s
v2p0024c1s v2p0048c2s v2p0193c1s
v2p0212c1s v2p0217c2s v2p0219c1s
v2p0229c2s v2p0237c2s v2p0249c1s
v2p0249c2m v2p0277c2s v2p0361c2s
v3p0023c1s v3p0045c1s v3p0055c1s
v3p0066c1s v3p0242c1s v3p0242c2m
v3p0332c1s v3p0351c2s v4p0001c2s
v4p0020c1s v4p0259c2s v4p0270c1s
v4p0304c1s v4p0312c1s v4p0320c1m
v4p0351c2s v4p0588c2s v4p0623c1m
v5p0027c2s v5p0234c2s v5p0599c2s
v5p0617c2s v6p0087c2s v6p0289c2s
v6p0383c1s v6p0500c1s
Hale, H.C. v4p0034c2s
Hale, H.D. v5p0257c1s
Hale, H.P. and Naville, E.
v6p0642c1s
Hale, Horatio v2p0322c1s

v4p0205c1s
Hale, I. v4p0175c1s
v4p0175c2s
Hale, J.G. v1p0096c2m
v1p0123c1s v1p0620c1s v1p0684c1s
v1p1398c2s
Hale, J.H. v6p0099c2s
v6p0485c2s
Hale, K. v5p0003c1s
v6p0010c2s v6p0596c1s
Hale, L. v1p1156c1s
v1p1157c1s v1p1281c1s v2p0165c1s
v3p0180c1s v3p0347c2s v3p0454c2s
v4p0235c2m v4p0625c2s v5p0230c2s
v5p0243c2s v5p0244c1s v5p0244c2s
v5p0245c1s v5p0298c1s v5p0588c2s
v5p0616c2s v5p0618c1s v6p0685c1s
Hale, L., Col. v3p0171c1s
Hale, L.A. v1p0838c2s
v1p0839c1s
Hale, L.G. v6p0568c2s
Hale, L.P. v1p0142c1s
v1p0211c1s v1p0336c2s v1p0390c1s
v1p0447c2s v1p0565c1s v1p0683c1s
v1p0885c2s v1p0904c2s v1p0942c1s
v1p0959c2s v1p0961c2s v1p1071c1s
v1p1335c1s v1p1335c2s
Hale, L.P. and Bynner, E.L.
v3p0440c2s
Hale, Lilian W. v5p0638c2s
Hale, Lonsdale v4p0625c2s
Hale, Louisa C. v6p0156c2s
Hale, Louise C. v5p0193c1s
v6p0289c2s v6p0352c1s v6p0432c1s
v6p0676c1s v6p0676c2s
Hale, M. v1p1048c1s
v1p1305c2s v4p0257c2s v4p0595c1s
v4p0630c1s
Hale, M.E. v5p0066c2s
v5p0257c2s
Hale, M.Gordon v4p0561c2s
Hale, M.W. v1p0442c1s
Hale, Miss v1p0076c1s
Hale, N. v1p0034c2s
v1p0092c1s v1p0151c2s v1p0154c1m
v1p0292c1s v1p0366c1s v1p0437c1s
v1p0461c2s v1p0506c1m v1p0532c1s
v1p0636c2s v1p0637c2s v1p0677c2s
v1p0678c1s v1p0683c2s v1p0798c1s
v1p0809c1s v1p0833c1s v1p0921c2s
v1p0927c1s v1p1076c2s v1p1077c1m
v1p1078c2s v1p1227c1s v1p1350c2s
Hale, P. v1p1318c1s
Hale, R. v1p0188c2s
Hale, R.B. v4p0019c2s
v4p0097c2s v4p0187c1s v4p0206c1s
v4p0369c2s v4p0439c1s v4p0598c2s
Hale, R.S. v1p0566c1m
v5p0182c2s v5p0550c2m v6p0072c2s
v6p0598c2s
Hale, R.W. v6p0182c1s
v6p0278c1s v6p0312c1s v6p0404c1s
v6p0663c1s
Hale, S. v1p0108c1s
v1p0192c2s v1p0294c1s v1p0345c2s
v1p0416c1s v1p1033c1s v3p0201c2s
Hale, S.J. v1p0024c1s
v1p0889c2s v1p0983c1s v1p1419c2s
v3p0239c2s
Hale, S.J., Mrs. v1p0082c1s
v1p0357c2s v1p0359c2s v1p0426c2s
v1p0447c2s v1p0469c2s v1p0697c2s
v1p0908c2s
Hale, T. v5p0207c2s
Hale, W. v3p0195c1s
v5p0048c1s v5p0061c1s v5p0406c1s
v5p0524c1s v5p0541c2s v6p0012c2s
v6p0044c1s v6p0161c2s v6p0634c1s
Hale, W.A. v1p1423c1s
Hale, W.B. v4p0045c2s
v4p0113c1s v4p0194c1s v4p0369c2s
v4p0384c2s v4p0479c2s v4p0532c1s
v4p0617c2s v6p0492c1s
Hale, W.G. v2p0136c1s
v3p0087c1s v3p0243c2m v3p0425c1s
v4p0015c2s v4p0321c2m v5p0326c2s
v6p0105c1s v6p0130c1s v6p0630c2s
Hale, W.G. and Wheeler, B.I.
v2p0430c1s
Hale, W.H. v4p0014c1s
Hale, W.P. v3p0332c2s
Hale, W.S. v4p0423c2m
Hale, W.T. v4p0480c2s
Hale, Wm.H. v4p0377c2s
Halen, H.A. v4p0270c1s
Hales, A.G. v5p0619c1s
Hales, F. v6p0654c1s
Hales, F.N. v6p0709c2s
Hales, H.M.A. v6p0439c2s
Hales, J.W. v1p0416c1s
v1p0418c1s v1p1123c2s v1p1184c2s
v1p1259c2s v1p1260c1s v2p0075c2s
v2p0111c2s v2p0195c1s v2p0201c1s
v2p0210c1s v2p0243c1s v2p0398c1s
v2p0457c1s v3p0075c1m v3p0076c2s
v3p0140c2s v3p0262c1s v3p0279c2s
v3p0290c1s v3p0321c2s v3p0332c2s
v3p0388c1s v3p0388c2s v4p0173c2s
v4p0343c1s v4p0371c2s v4p0517c1m
v4p0518c1s v4p0570c1s v5p0103c1s

v5p0523c2s v5p0630c1s v6p0110c2s
v6p0229c2s v6p0587c2s v6p0588c1s
Hales, S. v5p0584c1s
Halevy, L. v1p1328c1s
v3p0164c1s v3p0259c2s v3p0438c2s
v4p0426c1s v5p0596c1s
Haley, C.S. v6p0671c2s
Haley, T.P. v1p1354c1s
Haley, W.D. v1p0218c1s
v1p0693c2s v1p1388c2s
Halfield, E.F. v1p1178c2s
Halford, G. v4p0355c2s
v5p0609c2s
Halford, H. v1p1408c2s
Halhed, W.B. v1p0303c1s
Haliburton, H. v3p0335c1s
v3p0462c1s v3p0462c2s v4p0574c2s
Haliburton, R.G. v1p0192c2s
v1p0441c2s v1p0600c1s v1p0926c2s
v1p1106c1s v1p1213c2s v2p0316c1s
v2p0345c1s v2p0350c1s v4p0468c1s
v5p0503c1s
Haliburton, T.C. v1p0108c2s
v1p0371c1s v1p0438c2s v1p0940c2s
v1p1148c1s v1p1174c1s
Halid, H. v6p0470c1s
Halifax, C.L., Viscount .. v4p0113c2s
Halifax, Earl v4p0482c2s
Halifax, G.R. v6p0231c1s
v6p0272c1s v6p0309c1s v6p0665c2m
Halifax, Guy R. v6p0522c1s
Halifax, Lord v4p0113c2s
Halifax, M.C. v2p0295c1s
Halifax, Viscount v5p0493c1s
v6p0125c2s
Halifax, Viscount and C.L.W.
v5p0117c1s
Halifax, Viscount et al. . v6p0191c2s
Halim Pasha, Prince v2p0133c2s
v2p0410c1s
Halitvock, K.O. v5p0301c1s
Halkett, C.C. v4p0173c1s
v4p0198c1s
Halkett, G.R. v2p0368c1s
v2p0392c1s v4p0029c1s v4p0030c2s
v4p0227c2s v4p0430c2s v4p0438c2s
v4p0494c1m
Halkett, P.A. v3p0408c2s
Halkett, V.M.C. v6p0140c2s
Hall, A. v1p0070c2s
v1p0223c1s v1p0226c2s v1p0444c2s
v1p1003c2s v1p1014c1s v1p1178c2s
v1p1202c1s v1p1214c1s v1p1228c1s
v2p0014c1s v2p0026c1s v2p0250c2s
v2p0404c1s v2p0409c1s v2p0417c2m
v2p0456c2s v3p0002c1s v3p0109c2s
v3p0273c1s v3p0451c2s v4p0091c2s
v4p0484c1s v5p0035c2s v5p0240c2s
v5p0430c1s v6p0037c2s v6p0038c1s
v6p0111c1s v6p0174c1s v6p0218c2s
v6p0427c2s v6p0542c1s
Hall, A. et al. v2p0095c2s
Hall, A., jr. v5p0602c2s
Hall, A.C. v1p0141c2s
v1p0256c2s v1p1039c2s v5p0150c2s
v5p0564c2s v6p0013c2s
Hall, A.C.A. v1p0284c2s
v2p0113c2s v3p0056c2s
Hall, A.D. v3p0141c2s
v6p0008c2m v6p0220c1s
Hall, A.F. and Hall, S.C.
v1p0867c1s
Hall, A.H. v3p0165c1s
v3p0385c2s v5p0151c1s v5p0634c1s
Hall, A.M. v1p0656c2s
Hall, A.N. v5p0095c2s
Hall, A.O. v1p0026c2s
v1p0316c1s v1p0918c1s v1p1257c1s
v4p0045c2s v4p0063c2s v4p0077c1s
v4p0141c2s v4p0146c2s v4p0179c1s
v4p0190c1s v4p0225c1s v4p0233c2s
v4p0246c2s v4p0259c2s v4p0347c2s
v4p0401c1s v4p0409c1s v4p0432c2s
v4p0457c1s v4p0558c2s v4p0576c2s
v4p0583c2s v4p0600c1s v5p0154c1s
v5p0166c2s v5p0290c2s v5p0366c2s
v5p0398c2s v5p0515c1s v5p0529c2s
v5p0533c2s v5p0584c1s v5p0607c2s
v5p0639c1s
Hall, A.S. v5p0207c1s
Hall, A.W. v2p0339c2s
v2p0355c2s
v3p0330c1s
Hall, Adelaide S. v5p0297c1s
Hall, Asaph v5p0453c1s
v6p0201c1s v6p0469c1s
Hall, B. v1p0479c1s
v1p0815c1s v4p0096c2m v4p0431c1s
v4p0564c2m v5p0010c1s v5p0026c1s
v5p0107c1s v5p0274c1s v5p0301c1s
v5p0324c1s v5p0468c1s
Hall, B. and Crosby, E.H.. v5p0506c1s
Hall, B. et al. v5p0567c2s
v6p0055c1s v6p0310c2s
Hall, B.F. v1p0689c1s
v6p0443c1s
Hall, B.H. v1p1367c1s
v1p1402c2s
Hall, B.R. v1p0392c2s
Hall, Bolton v4p0533c2s

Hall, C. v1p0961c1s
Hall, C.A.K. v4p0211c2s
Hall, C.B. v1p0092c2s
v1p0817c1s v3p0356c1s v4p0350c1s
v4p0369c1s v4p0370c2m v5p0356c2s
v5p0375c2s
Hall, C.C. v3p0152c2s
v5p0127c2s v6p0002c1s v6p0021c1s
v6p0484c1s v6p0537c1s v6p0537c2s
v6p0643c1s
Hall, C.E. v2p0093c1s
v6p0210c2s
Hall, C.G. v6p0255c1s
Hall, C.H. v1p0330c2s
v1p0495c2s v2p0483c2s v3p0192c1s
v3p0277c1s
Hall, C.N. v5p0133c2s
v5p0139c2s v5p0203c1s v5p0405c1s
Hall, C.P. v3p0442c2s
Hall, C.S. v1p0134c2s
Hall, C.S. and McCurdy, C.J.
v3p0322c1s
Hall, C.W. v4p0317c2s
v5p0083c1s v5p0108c2s v5p0112c1s
v5p0202c1s v5p0215c2s v5p0314c2s
v5p0349c1s v5p0373c1s v5p0545c1s
v5p0574c1s v6p0329c2s
Hall, C.W. and Peckham, S.F.
v1p0751c1s
Hall, D. v2p0082c2s
v6p0670c2s
Hall, D.B. v6p0370c2s
v6p0371c2s
Hall, D.P. v5p0003c2s
Hall, E. v1p0153c1s
v1p1062c1m v1p1062c2s v2p0173c2s
Hall, E.B. v1p0001c2s
v1p0006c1s v1p0096c1s v1p0198c2s
v1p0223c2s v1p0285c1s v1p0357c2m
v1p0460c1s v1p0535c1s v1p0563c2s
v1p0610c1s v1p0686c2s v1p0687c1s
v1p0698c1s v1p0779c1s v1p0805c2s
v1p0818c1s v1p0940c2s v1p0944c2s
v1p0982c2s v1p1043c2s v1p1050c1s
v1p1089c1s v1p1094c2s v1p1101c1s
v1p1127c2s v1p1159c2s v1p1315c2s
v1p1341c1s v1p1386c1s v1p1429c1s
v1p1438c2s
Hall, E.C. v5p0038c2s
v5p0406c1s v5p0505c2s
Hall, E.E. v2p0432c1s
Hall, E.E. and Bacon, L. . v1p0910c1s
Hall, E.F. v1p0305c1s
v1p0671c1s v2p0087c1s
Hall, E.H. v1p0117c1s
v1p0233c2s v1p0399c1m v1p0499c1s
v1p0679c1m v1p0696c2s v1p0788c1s
v1p0853c1s v1p0980c1s v1p1063c1s
v1p1151c2s v1p1325c2s v2p0091c1s
v2p0138c1s v2p0272c1s v2p0332c1s
v3p0064c2s v3p0264c1s v3p0301c1s
v3p0303c2s v3p0331c2s v4p0301c1s
v4p0417c2s v4p0441c2m v4p0480c2s
v4p0591c2s v5p0010c1s v5p0126c1m
v5p0126c2s v5p0450c2s v6p0039c2m
v6p0111c2s v6p0135c1s v6p0139c1s
v6p0251c2s v6p0333c2s v6p0475c2s
v6p0498c1s v6p0641c1s v6p0643c1s
v6p0668c1s v6p0669c2s v6p0687c2s
Hall, E.H. et al.
v6p0406c1s
Hall, E.J. v1p0083c1s
v1p1131c2s
Hall, E.L. v4p0110c2s
v4p0123c1s v4p0576c2s
Hall, E.M. v2p0221c1s
Hall, E.P. v1p1417c2s
Hall, E.T. and Peek, F. .. v4p0115c2s
Hall, E.V. v6p0125c2s
Hall, E.Van C. v5p0258c2s
Hall, E.W. v1p0273c1s
v1p0518c1s v1p0743c2s v6p0131c1s
Hall, Edith H. v6p0272c1s
Hall, Edwin H. v6p0576c1s
Hall, Eliza C. v6p0629c1s
v6p0663c1s
Hall, F. v1p0090c2s
v1p0098c2s v1p0273c2s v1p0417c1m
v1p0522c2s v1p0592c1s v1p0630c2s
v1p0633c1s v1p0633c2s v1p0712c2s
v1p0738c2m v1p0858c1s v1p1055c2s
v1p1192c2s v2p0036c2s v2p0108c2s
v2p0144c1s v2p0144c2s v2p0194c1s
v2p0421c1s v3p0012c1s v3p0139c2m
v3p0140c2s v3p0329c2s v3p0357c1s
v3p0400c1s v4p0004c1s v4p0014c1s
v4p0016c1s v4p0155c2s v4p0247c2s
v4p0283c2s v4p0284c1s v4p0327c1s
v4p0375c1s v4p0482c1s v4p0508c1s
v4p0516c1s v4p0529c1s v4p0621c2s
v5p0023c2s v5p0166c1s v5p0213c2s
v5p0294c2s v5p0421c1s v5p0442c2s
v5p0453c1s
Hall, F.A. v6p0005c1s
Hall, F.E. v1p0109c1s
v1p0417c1s v1p0963c1s
Hall, F.H. v5p0360c1s
Hall, F.M.Howe v4p0068c1s
v4p0267c2s
Hall, F.S. v6p0318c2s

v6p0439c1s v6p0452c1s v6p0573c2s
Hall, Fitzedward v3p0114c2s
v3p0302c1s v3p0432c2s v4p0201c2s
Hall, Florence Howe and Howe, M.
v6p0081c2s
Hall, G. v1p0621c1s
v4p0107c1s v4p0159c2s v4p0269c2s
v4p0424c1s v4p0485c1s v4p0603c1s
Hall, G. and Motoro, Y. .. v3p0115c2s
Hall, G.A. v6p0115c1s
Hall, G.R. v3p0192c1s
v3p0472c1s v3p0472c2s
Hall, G.S. v1p0009c1s
v1p0162c2m v1p0297c2s v1p0343c1s
v1p0427c1s v1p0517c2s v1p0518c1s
v1p0541c1s v1p0582c2m v1p0620c2m
v1p0690c2s v1p0726c1s v1p0732c2s
v1p0736c2s v1p0758c2s v1p0770c2s
v1p0810c2s v1p0907c1s v1p0935c2s
v1p0993c2m v1p1000c2s v1p1001c2s
v1p1007c1s v1p1029c2s v1p1162c1s
v1p1228c1s v1p1238c1s v1p1376c2s
v1p1411c2s v2p0078c1m v2p0122c1s
v2p0130c2s v2p0132c1s v2p0149c1s
v2p0201c2s v2p0337c1s v2p0358c1m
v2p0388c1s v2p0432c1s v2p0440c1s
v2p0474c1s v3p0077c2m v3p0087c1s
v3p0128c2s v3p0215c2s v3p0411c1s
v3p0422c1s v3p0475c1s v4p0103c1s
v4p0169c2s v4p0170c2s v4p0196c2s
v4p0381c2s v4p0461c1m v4p0465c1s
v4p0466c1s v4p0481c2s v4p0505c1s
v4p0566c1s v4p0566c2s v5p0004c1s
v5p0019c1s v5p0106c1s v5p0204c1s
v5p0233c2s v5p0316c1s v5p0447c1s
v5p0511c1s v6p0117c1s v6p0132c1s
v6p0134c2s v6p0193c2m v6p0410c2s
v6p0521c1s v6p0521c2s v6p0540c1s
Hall, G.S. and Allin, A. . v5p0327c1s
v5p0579c2s
Hall, G.S. and Browne, C.E.
v6p0117c2s
Hall, G.S. and Donaldson, H.H.
v2p0299c2s
Hall, G.S. and Ellis, A.C.
v4p0103c1s v4p0158c2s
Hall, G.S. and Hartwell, E.M.
v2p0045c2s
Hall, G.S. and Jastrow, J.
v2p0372c1s
Hall, G.S. and Motoro, Y.. v3p0394c2s
Hall, G.S. and Smith, J.L.
v6p0161c2s
Hall, G.S. and Smith, T.L.
v6p0137c1s v6p0323c1s v6p0376c2s
Hall, G.S. and Smith, Theodate L.
v6p0053c1s v6p0592c2s
Hall, G.S. et al. v2p0132c1s
v4p0168c2s
v5p0558c1s
Hall, G.Stanley v5p0179c2s
v5p0369c1s v5p0470c2m v5p0519c1s
v6p0078c1s v6p0116c2s v6p0194c1s
v6p0221c2s v6p0290c2s v6p0292c2s
v6p0427c2s v6p0447c2s v6p0459c1s
v6p0486c1m v6p0497c2s v6p0516c1s
v6p0635c1s v6p0665c1s v6p0665c2s
v6p0712c1s
Hall, G.Stanley and Saunders, F.H.
v5p0452c2s
Hall, Gertrude v4p0321c2s
v4p0429c2s v4p0575c2s
Hall, H. v1p0033c1s
v1p0034c1m v1p0154c2s v1p0349c1s
v1p0805c1s v1p0917c2s v1p1014c2s
v1p1203c1s v1p1310c1s v1p1367c2m
v2p0008c1s v2p0012c1s v2p0021c2s
v2p0076c2s v2p0096c2s v2p0121c1s
v2p0139c1s v2p0144c2s v2p0215c2s
v2p0251c2s v2p0281c2s v2p0282c1s
v2p0283c2s v2p0295c1s v2p0373c2s
v2p0436c2s v3p0016c2s v3p0110c2s
v3p0222c1s v3p0324c2s v3p0391c1s
v3p0427c1s v3p0457c2s v3p0467c1s
v4p0049c1s v4p0097c2s v4p0432c1s
v4p0463c1s v5p0037c1s v5p0103c1s
v5p0161c1s v5p0492c2s v5p0551c2s
v6p0476c2s
Hall, H.B. v1p0015c2s
v1p0029c1s v1p0062c1s v1p0072c2s
v1p0160c1s v1p0718c2s v1p0753c2s
v1p0762c2s v1p0915c2s
Hall, H.C. v5p0183c1s
Hall, H.D. v3p0188c1s
Hall, H.F. v5p0296c1s
v6p0291c2s v6p0391c2s v6p0442c1s
Hall, H.H. v2p0053c2s
v3p0050c2s v3p0151c1s v3p0271c1s
v5p0388c1s
Hall, H.J. v6p0508c1s
Hall, H.J., Mrs. v6p0481c1s
v6p0573c2s v6p0656c2s
Hall, H.R. v1p1307c2s
v5p0396c2s v6p0157c1s v6p0272c2s
v6p0351c1s v6p0357c2s v6p0458c1s
v6p0642c1s
Hall, H.S. v6p0264c2s
v6p0450c2s v6p0701c1s
Hall, H.W. v1p0570c1s
v1p1421c2s
Hall, Herman J., Mrs. v6p0331c1s
v6p0630c1s
Hall, Hubert v6p0268c1s
v6p0501c1s
Hall, I.H. v1p0328c2s
v3p0042c2m v3p0187c2s v3p0346c2s
v3p0418c2m v4p0389c2s v4p0437c1s
Hall, J. v1p0049c2s
v1p0119c1s v1p0160c1s v1p0253c1s
v1p0282c2s v1p0283c2s v1p0387c2s
v1p0469c2s v1p0493c1s v1p0509c1s
v1p0509c2s v1p0718c1s v1p0750c1s
v1p0756c2s v1p0834c1s v1p0847c2s
v1p0852c1s v1p0854c2s v1p0935c2s
v1p0954c2s v1p1000c1s v1p1037c1s
v1p1050c2s v1p1149c2s v1p1159c1s
v1p1198c1s v1p1270c1s v1p1271c1s
v1p1363c2s v1p1367c2s v1p1416c2s
v1p1432c2s v1p1439c2s v2p0054c1s
v2p0085c1s v2p0313c2s v2p0353c1s
v3p0011c2s v3p0012c2s v3p0096c1s
Hall, J. and Alexander, J.W.
v1p0935c2s
Hall, J. and Depew, C. ... v3p0449c1s
Hall, J.A. v3p0204c2s
v4p0470c2s v5p0409c1s v6p0567c1s
Hall, J.C. v3p0012c1s
v3p0296c1s v3p0391c1s v5p0195c2s
v6p0324c1s v6p0357c1s
Hall, J.E. v5p0142c2s
Hall, J.G. v1p0314c1s
v1p0759c2s v3p0343c1s
Hall, J.G., jr. v2p0328c1s
v3p0118c2s v3p0285c1s v3p0319c1s
v3p0341c2s v3p0456c1s
Hall, J.J. v1p0828c2s
v1p0829c2s v1p1002c2s v1p1081c1m
Hall, J.L. v6p0415c2s
Hall, J.N. v3p0014c2s
v4p0232c2s v4p0633c1s
Hall, J.P. v4p0615c2s
v6p0364c2s
Hall, J.W. v1p0140c1s
v5p0056c2s v5p0413c2s
Hall, J.W.D. v2p0229c2s
v2p0431c1s v3p0420c2s
Hall, Kate M. v5p0088c2s
Hall, L. v1p0957c1s
v2p0176c1s v3p0006c1s v3p0355c2s
v6p0605c2s
Hall, L.C. v6p0636c2s
Hall, L.J. v1p0159c2s
v1p0612c1s v1p0698c1s v1p1420c2s
v1p1421c1s v1p1423c1s
Hall, L.J., Mrs. v1p0308c2s
v1p0367c2s v1p1201c1s
Hall, L.M. v2p0178c2s
v2p0221c1s v2p0340c2s v2p0434c2s
v2p0478c1m v3p0102c2s v3p0468c2s
Hall, M. v1p1268c1s
v1p1440c2s v3p0415c1s v6p0166c1s
Hall, M.E. v5p0419c2s
Hall, M.R., Mrs. v1p0229c2s
v1p0854c1s v1p1089c1s v1p1434c1s
Hall, Mary M. v5p0283c2s
Hall, N. v1p0699c1s
v1p0714c1s v1p1352c1s v3p0306c1s
v4p0244c2s v4p0246c1s v5p0254c2s
Hall, N. and Shuttleworth, H.C.
v4p0572c1s
Hall, N.M. v4p0247c1s
v5p0069c2s v5p0334c1s v6p0295c1s
v6p0686c2s
Hall, N.W. v4p0015c1s
Hall, Newman v4p0543c2s
Hall, O. v4p0038c1s
v4p0095c1s v4p0203c1s v4p0395c2s
v5p0115c2s v5p0281c1s v5p0313c2s
v5p0386c2s v5p0411c2s v5p0442c2s
v5p0506c2s
Hall, Owen v4p0341c1s
Hall, P.F. v3p0057c2s
v4p0275c1s v5p0280c2m v5p0581c1s
v6p0309c1m v6p0520c2s
Hall, P.F. et al. v6p0309c1s
Hall, R. v1p0497c1s
v5p0416c1s v5p0440c2s v5p0642c1s
Hall, R.C. v3p0191c2s
Hall, R.H. v5p0626c2s
Hall, R.N. v6p0713c1m
Hall, Ruth v5p0205c2s
v5p0206c1s v5p0313c1s v5p0605c2s
Hall, S. v5p0537c1s
Hall, S.C. v1p0049c1s
v1p0274c1s v1p0311c1s v1p0324c1s
v1p0403c2s v1p0584c1s v1p0596c1s
v1p0602c1s v1p0602c2s v1p0616c1s
v1p0656c1s v1p0719c1s v1p0722c1s
v1p0864c1s v1p0866c2s v1p0870c1s
v1p0871c1s v1p0944c1m v1p1114c1s
v1p1210c2s v1p1211c1s v1p1211c2s
v1p1413c1s v1p1429c2s
Hall, S.C. and Hall, A.F.
v1p0867c1s
Hall, S.C. and Hall, S.C., Mrs.
v1p0155c1s v1p0191c2s v1p0383c1s
v1p0602c2s v1p0707c1s v1p0722c2m
v1p0855c2s v1p0870c2s v1p1226c1s
v1p1298c2s v1p1381c2s
Hall, S.C. and Jewitt, L.. v1p0414c2s
Hall, S.C., Mr. and
Hall, S.C., Mrs. v1p0602c2s
v1p0707c1s v1p0855c2s
v1p0870c2s
v1p1298c2s
v1p1381c2s
Hall, S.C., Mrs. v1p0002c2s
v1p0116c1s v1p0150c1s v1p0177c2s
v1p0192c1s v1p0209c2m v1p0222c2s
v1p0226c1s v1p0265c1s v1p0310c1s
v1p0311c1s v1p0332c2s v1p0368c1s
v1p0383c1m v1p0414c1s v1p0446c1s
v1p0542c1s v1p0564c1s v1p0583c2s
v1p0596c1s v1p0624c2s v1p0660c1s
v1p0674c1s v1p0726c1s v1p0756c1s
v1p0774c2s v1p0776c1s v1p0806c1m
v1p0807c2s v1p0859c1s v1p0870c2s
v1p0906c1s v1p0940c1s v1p0940c2s
v1p0987c1s v1p1010c2s v1p1035c2s
v1p1084c2s v1p1088c1s v1p1173c2s
v1p1258c1s v1p1281c1s v1p1294c1s
v1p1335c2s v1p1393c1s v1p1418c2s
v2p0388c2s
Hall, S.C., Mrs. and Hall, S.C.
v1p0155c1s v1p0191c2s v1p0383c1s
v1p0722c2s v1p1226c1s
Hall, S.C., Mrs. and
Hall, S.C., Mr. v1p0602c2s
v1p0707c1s v1p0855c2s v1p0870c2s
v1p1298c2s v1p1381c2s
Hall, S.M. v6p0090c2s
v6p0139c2s v6p0157c1s v6p0229c2s
v6p0260c2s v6p0263c2s v6p0424c1s
v6p0465c2s v6p0515c1s v6p0649c2m
Hall, S.R. v1p1159c1s
v1p1288c1s
Hall, S.T. v1p0541c2s
Hall, Sharlot M. v6p0030c1s
v6p0091c1s v6p0171c2s v6p0233c2s
v6p0243c2s v6p0570c1s v6p0670c1s
Hall, T.B. v1p1238c1s
v2p0415c1s
Hall, T.C. v4p0300c2s
v4p0475c1s v6p0043c1s v6p0212c1s
v6p0519c1s v6p0600c2s
Hall, T.C. et al. v4p0054c1s
Hall, T.H. v2p0331c1s
Hall, T.M. v1p0008c1s
Hall, T.O. v2p0460c1s
Hall, T.P. v4p0539c1s
Hall, T.W. v4p0308c1s
v6p0441c1s
Hall, U.S. v4p0278c1s
Hall, V. v3p0040c1s
v4p0002c1s
Hall, W. v1p0303c1s
v1p0425c1s v1p0535c2s v1p1110c1s
v1p1209c2s v1p1306c2s v2p0244c1s
v2p0280c2s v2p0354c1s v3p0099c1s
v4p0133c2s
Hall, W.B., jr. v5p0628c2s
Hall, W.D. v6p0203c1s
v6p0218c2s
Hall, W.E. v1p0041c2s
v1p0204c1s v1p0650c2s v1p0793c1s
v4p0175c1s
Hall, W.H. v1p0972c1s
v3p0063c1s
v3p0223c2s
Hall, W.H.B. v3p0320c2s
Hall, W.K. v1p0146c1s
Hall, W.P. v4p0093c1s
v4p0497c2s
Hall, W.S. v4p0031c1s
v4p0268c2s
Hall, W.T. v1p1346c2s
Hall, Walter and Kemble, E.W.
v6p0076c2s
Hall, Wm.H. v4p0083c2s
Hall-Brown, Lucy v5p0211c1s
Hallam, A. v2p0397c1s
Hallam, E. v5p0396c1s
Hallam, Florence M. and
Phinney, Emma D. v4p0161c2s
Hallam, H. v1p0040c1s
v1p0368c2s v1p0410c2s v1p0411c2s
v1p0475c1s v1p0776c1s v5p0308c2s
Hallam, J. v2p0255c2s
v2p0256c1s
Hallam, O.B. v3p0444c1s
Hallam, R.A. v1p0170c1s
v1p0247c1s v1p0422c1m v1p0422c2s
v1p0485c2s v1p0496c1s v1p1342c2s
Hallard, A. v5p0003c2s
v6p0108c2s v6p0539c1s
Hallays, A. v6p0480c1s
Hallberg, L.G. v1p0227c2s
Halle, G. v4p0231c1s
v4p0372c2s
Halleck, C. v1p0760c1s
v1p0909c1s
Halleck, R.P. v4p0586c1s
v6p0290c1s v6p0581c2s
Halleck, R.R. v6p0192c2s
Halleck, Reuben P. v6p0078c2s
Hallen, A.W.C. v3p0381c1s
v4p0423c1s
Hallenbeck, V. v4p0018c2s
Haller, G.O. v5p0507c2s
Hallet, C. v6p0231c1s

Hallet, E. v2p0289c2s
Hallett, C. v6p0020c2s
Hallett, C.C. v6p0070c2s
Hallett, H. v2p0061c2s
v5p0523c1s
Hallett, H.S. v2p0220c1s
v2p0399c1s v3p0023c2s v3p0060c2m
v3p0391c2m v3p0475c2s v4p0106c1s
v4p0127c1s v4p0318c1s v4p0617c2s
v5p0084c1m v5p0109c1s v5p0110c1s
v5p0111c1s v5p0111c2s v5p0319c2s
v5p0502c1s
Hallett, J.H. v2p0103c2s
Hallett, W.H. v5p0523c2s
v6p0588c1s
Hallewell, C.M.G. v6p0657c2s
Halley, Dr. v1p0978c1s
Halley, G. v2p0107c2s
v2p0199c1s
Halley, R. v1p0132c1s
v1p0355c2m v1p0601c1s v1p1097c2s
v1p1211c1s v1p1296c2s v1p1411c2s
v1p1413c2s
Halliburton, W.D. v3p0047c2s
v4p0064c1s v4p0088c2s v4p0288c2s
v4p0346c1s v4p0434c2s v4p0462c2s
v5p0067c1s v5p0371c1s v5p0505c2s
v6p0111c2s
v6p0498c2s
Halliday, A. v1p0433c1s
Halliday, A.J. v3p0108c1s
v4p0201c1s v4p0327c2s v4p0373c2s
v4p0527c1s
Halliday, Carl and Brown, J.T., jr.
v6p0284c1s
Halliday, E.M. v4p0042c2s
v4p0310c2s v4p0611c2s
Halliday, R.F. v6p0396c1s
Halliday, R.T. v6p0276c1s
v6p0313c2s
Halliday-Antona, A. v5p0460c2s
Halliday-Antona, Annetta . v6p0558c2s
Hallidie, A.S. v3p0020c1s
v3p0144c1s v3p0239c1s v3p0374c1s
v4p0122c1s v6p0699c2s
Halliwell, J.O. v1p0393c2s
v1p0425c1s v1p0683c1s v1p1185c2s
Halliwell, M.M. v5p0238c2s
Halliwell-Phillipps, J.O.. v2p0398c1s
v3p0236c2s
Hallock, A. v5p0015c1s
Hallock, A.McC. v4p0181c1s
Hallock, C. v1p0006c2s
v1p0715c2s v1p0909c1s v1p1088c1s
v1p1140c1s v3p0007c1m v4p0052c1s
v4p0163c2s v5p0320c1s v5p0547c1s
v6p0072c1s v6p0245c1s v6p0316c1s
v6p0317c1s v6p0566c1s
Hallock, E.J. v2p0025c1s
v2p0204c2s
Hallock, E.S. v6p0127c2s
Hallock, G.W. v4p0041c2s
v4p0502c2s
Hallock, M. v6p0523c1s
Hallock, Mary v6p0543c1m
Hallock, P.F. v4p0461c1s
Hallock, R.T. v1p1328c2s
Hallock, W. v3p0075c2s
v3p0156c1s v3p0252c2s v3p0400c1s
v4p0042c2s v4p0065c2s v4p0616c2s
v5p0610c1s
Hallock, W.H. v1p0678c2s
Hallock, William v5p0545c1s
Hallopeau, L.A. and Poisson, A.
v4p0482c2s
Hallowell, A. v2p0078c1s
Hallowell, E. v6p0070c2s
Hallowell, E.A. v6p0488c2s
Hallowell, E.M. v4p0019c1s
Hallowell, Eleanor A. v6p0081c2s
v6p0289c2s v6p0344c1s
Hallowell, F.B. v3p0233c1s
Hallowell, J.D. v6p0257c1s
Hallowell, J.K. v2p0094c1s
v2p0102c1s v2p0193c2s
Hallowell, J.M. v3p0025c2s
v3p0190c1s
Hallowell, R.P. v1p1069c2s
Hallowell, S.C. v1p0942c1s
Hallowell, S.C., Mrs. v1p1094c2s
Hallsett, V.C. v6p0084c2s
Hallward, R. v2p0379c2s
Halm, F. v1p0191c1s
Halm, J. v5p0549c2s
v5p0561c1s v6p0626c1s
Halortie, Baron de v2p0424c1s
Halpin, J. v3p0250c1s
v3p0423c2s v4p0333c2s
Halpine, C.D. v1p1020c1s
Halpine, C.G. v1p1235c2s
Halse, G. v1p0338c1s
v2p0062c2s
Halsey, C., Mrs. v1p0004c2s
v1p0717c2s
Halsey, C.H. v1p1107c2s
v1p1160c1s
Halsey, C.H., Mrs. v1p0556c2s
v1p0712c1s
Halsey, E. v5p0299c2s
Halsey, E.G. v1p0006c2s
v1p0403c1s v1p0800c1s
Halsey, F.A. v4p0314c2m
v4p0457c1s v4p0559c2s v6p0413c2s
Halsey, F.A. et al. v6p0413c2s
Halsey, F.W. v5p0016c1s
v5p0038c1s v5p0071c1s v5p0145c1s
v5p0147c2s v5p0160c1s v5p0420c1s
v5p0620c2s v6p0091c1s v6p0423c2s
v6p0444c2s
Halsey, J.J. v2p0011c2s
v2p0144c1m v2p0313c2s v3p0011c2s
v3p0149c1s v3p0154c2s v3p0228c1s
v3p0236c1s v3p0268c2m v3p0291c2s
v3p0304c2s v3p0308c2s v3p0348c1s
v3p0446c2s v3p0449c2s v3p0456c1s
v4p0038c2s v4p0167c1s v4p0323c1s
v4p0332c2s v4p0443c1s v4p0605c2s
v4p0620c1s v5p0189c2s v5p0242c1s
v5p0281c1s v5p0329c1s v5p0416c1s
v5p0544c1s v5p0600c1s v6p0180c1s
v6p0287c1s v6p0310c1s v6p0369c2s
v6p0530c2s v6p0534c1s v6p0539c2s
Halsey, L.J. v1p0751c1s
Halsey, L.R. v3p0249c2s
v3p0253c2s
Halsey, L.R.J. v1p1304c1s
Halsey, R.T.H. v6p0541c1s
Halstead, A. v4p0402c2s
v5p0354c1s v5p0413c1s v5p0548c1s
v6p0151c2s
v6p0666c2s
Halstead, M. v2p0394c1s
v3p0046c1s v3p0085c1s v3p0179c1s
v3p0184c2s v3p0299c2s v3p0402c1s
v3p0441c2s v3p0442c2s v3p0443c2s
v4p0063c2s v4p0074c2s v4p0100c1s
v4p0101c1s v4p0119c1s v4p0142c1s
v4p0212c1s v4p0220c1s v4p0222c1m
v4p0246c2s v4p0247c1s v4p0305c2s
v4p0347c2s v4p0373c1s v4p0377c1s
v4p0418c2s v4p0437c2s v4p0449c2s
v4p0525c1s v4p0595c2m v5p0259c2s
v5p0525c2s v5p0598c2s v5p0612c1s
v6p0273c2s v6p0464c2s
Halstead, M. et al. v3p0138c1s
Halstead, Murat v4p0062c1s
v5p0126c1s
v5p0203c1s
v5p0322c2s
Halstead, Murat and Chamberlin, H.B.
v3p0460c1s
Halstead, R. v4p0127c2s
v4p0608c1s
v5p0136c1s
Halstead, W.R. v4p0439c2s
Halsted, B. v1p0494c2s
Halsted, B.A. v3p0202c2s
Halsted, B.D. v1p0021c2s
v1p0139c2s v1p0494c2s v1p1016c1s
v2p0169c2s v2p0261c2s v2p0344c1s
v2p0370c2s v2p0399c1s v2p0471c2s
v3p0019c2s v3p0051c2s v3p0063c1m
v3p0147c1s v3p0156c1m v3p0199c1s
v3p0333c2s v3p0334c1m v3p0341c2s
v3p0384c1s v3p0459c1s v4p0007c2s
v4p0021c2m v4p0069c2s v4p0135c2s
v4p0150c1s v4p0198c2s v4p0202c2s
v4p0204c1s v4p0217c1s v4p0219c2s
v4p0331c1s v4p0440c2s v4p0445c2s
v4p0446c1s v4p0583c2s v4p0601c1s
v4p0631c1s v5p0073c1s v5p0453c2s
v5p0454c1s v5p0548c2s
Halsted, Byron D. v4p0449c1s
Halsted, C. v5p0154c1s
Halsted, E. v4p0267c1s
Halsted, Elinor v4p0355c1s
Halsted, G.B. v1p0021c2s
v1p0760c1s v1p0760c2s v1p0761c1m
v1p0875c2s v1p1087c2s v2p0115c2s
v4p0223c1m v4p0409c1s v4p0566c2s
v5p0013c2s v5p0098c2s v5p0158c2s
v5p0229c2m v5p0320c2s v5p0337c1s
v5p0513c2s v5p0564c2s v6p0015c1s
v6p0066c2s v6p0251c1m
v6p0381c2m
Halsted, G.B. and Monck, W.H.S.
v5p0229c2s
Halsted, L.B. v4p0116c1s
v5p0114c1s
v5p0292c1s
Halsted, N.O. v6p0123c2s
Halsted, S.D. v2p0028c1s
v2p0063c1s v2p0208c2s
v2p0280c2s
v3p0282c1s
Halton, E.B. v5p0450c2s
v6p0033c1s v6p0052c1s v6p0150c2s
v6p0165c2s v6p0598c2s
v6p0612c1s
v6p0712c1m
Halton, E.H. v6p0425c2s
Halton, L.G. v6p0184c2s
Haltzoper, E.C. v6p0612c1s
Haly, E.J. v4p0434c1s
Haly, G. v1p1108c1s
Haly, G.T. v3p0154c1s
Ham, A. v4p0548c1s
Ham, C. v3p0266c2s
Ham, C.H. v2p0275c2s
Ham, G.H. v4p0353c2s
Ham, J.R. v2p0122c1s
v3p0121c2m
Ham, W.C. v5p0403c2s
Hamberg, N.P. v1p1382c1s
Hamberger, J. v1p0083c1s
Hambidge, J. v5p0121c2s
Hamblen, Emily S. v5p0316c1s
Hamblen, H.E. v5p0188c1s
v5p0343c2s v5p0344c1s v5p0476c2s
v5p0478c1s v6p0204c1s v6p0528c2s
v6p0529c2s
v6p0530c2s
Hambleton, G.W. v3p0097c2s
v3p0098c1m
v3p0331c1m
Hamblin, D. v1p0099c2s
v1p1112c2s
Hambry, H.E. v2p0162c1s
Hamburger, A. v5p0574c2s
Hamel, F. v6p0685c2s
Hamel, J. v3p0422c2s
Hamel, Maurice v3p0124c2s
Hamer, F.E. v5p0054c2s
v5p0171c2s v5p0180c1s
v5p0312c1s
v5p0342c1s
Hamer, J. v4p0517c1s
v4p0519c1s
v5p0581c2s
Hamer, J.H. v3p0435c1s
Hamer, J.W. v6p0322c1s
Hamer, W.H. v5p0158c2s
Hamersley, J.W. v1p1243c1s
Hamersly, L.R. v1p0471c2s
Hamerton, G. v3p0161c1s
Hamerton, Mrs. v1p0813c2s
Hamerton, P.G. v1p0009c1s
v1p0026c1m v1p0041c2s v1p0059c1s
v1p0061c2m v1p0062c2s v1p0063c2s
v1p0064c1s v1p0064c2s v1p0066c1s
v1p0186c1s v1p0196c2s v1p0293c2s
v1p0334c2s v1p0341c2s v1p0353c2s
v1p0357c1s v1p0358c2s v1p0361c1m
v1p0373c1s v1p0425c2m v1p0428c2m
v1p0454c1s v1p0474c2s v1p0495c1s
v1p0511c1s v1p0521c1s v1p0538c2s
v1p0541c2s v1p0561c1s v1p0564c2s
v1p0616c1s v1p0616c2s v1p0650c1s
v1p0675c2s v1p0724c1s v1p0724c2s
v1p0736c2s v1p0738c1s v1p0803c1s
v1p0839c2s v1p0881c1s v1p0897c1s
v1p0914c2s v1p0935c2s v1p0957c2s
v1p0958c1m v1p0958c2m v1p0959c1s
v1p0959c2m v1p0962c1s v1p0968c2s
v1p0969c2s v1p1003c1s v1p1041c1s
v1p1045c2s v1p1059c1s v1p1104c2s
v1p1131c1m v1p1177c2s v1p1216c1s
v1p1256c1s v1p1277c2s v1p1311c1s
v1p1313c1s v1p1333c2s v1p1339c2s
v1p1358c1s v1p1434c2m v2p0012c2s
v2p0022c2s v2p0030c1s v2p0063c2s
v2p0092c1s v2p0111c2s v2p0135c1s
v2p0143c1s v2p0146c2s v2p0156c1s
v2p0167c2s v2p0215c1s v2p0248c2m
v2p0289c1s v2p0302c1s v2p0324c2s
v2p0329c1s v2p0334c2s v2p0341c2s
v2p0380c1s v2p0382c2s v2p0387c1s
v2p0461c1s v3p0050c1s v3p0097c2s
v3p0131c2s v3p0139c1s v3p0142c2s
v3p0153c1s v3p0160c1s v3p0161c1s
v3p0163c2s v3p0187c2s v3p0253c2s
v3p0255c2s v3p0287c2s v3p0317c2m
v3p0322c2s v3p0325c2s v3p0354c2s
v3p0358c2s v3p0435c2s v3p0438c2s
v4p0024c1s v4p0024c2s v4p0029c2s
v4p0030c2s v4p0071c2s v4p0098c2s
v4p0120c1s v4p0153c2s v4p0164c1s
v4p0187c1s v4p0201c2s v4p0207c1s
v4p0215c2s v4p0222c1s v4p0320c2s
v4p0327c1s v4p0353c1s v4p0364c1s
v4p0386c2s v4p0425c1s v4p0468c1s
v4p0480c1s v4p0562c2s v4p0604c1s
Hamerton, P.G., Mrs. v5p0218c2s
v5p0607c1s v6p0241c2s
Hamerton, P.S. v3p0339c2s
Hames, F.E. v5p0274c2s
Hames, P.H. v4p0171c1s
Hamey, G.L. v3p0360c1s
Hamill, I.M. v5p0065c1s
v5p0086c1s v6p0524c2s v6p0555c2s
Hamill, Isabel M. v5p0055c1s
v5p0365c2s v6p0106c2s
Hamill, S.M. v1p1159c1s
v4p0175c1s
Hamilton, A. v1p0013c1s
v1p0331c1s v1p0530c1s v1p0543c2s
v1p0632c2s v1p0918c2s v1p1151c1s
v1p1156c2s v1p1176c1s v1p1348c1s
v1p1428c2s v2p0059c1s v2p0103c2s
v2p0444c2m v3p0038c2s v3p0043c2s
v3p0353c1s v3p0418c2s v4p0192c1s
v5p0242c1s v6p0005c2m v6p0091c1s
v6p0162c2s v6p0317c2s v6p0470c1s
v6p0509c2s
Hamilton, A.B. v4p0246c2s
v6p0119c1s
Hamilton, A.F. v6p0607c2s
Hamilton, A.H.A. v1p0387c1s
v1p1069c2s v1p1070c1m v1p1070c2m
v1p1258c2s v2p0293c2s

Hamilton, A.K. v2p0378c1s
Hamilton, A.L. v3p0326c2s
Hamilton, A.M. v1p1266c1s
 v3p0195c1s v3p0405c1s v4p0530c1s
 v4p0624c1s v5p0291c2s v5p0508c1s
 v5p0592c1s v6p0464c1s v6p0518c1s
Hamilton, A.McL. v1p0346c2s
 v4p0555c2s
Hamilton, B. v2p0082c2s
 v4p0030c1s
Hamilton, B.G. v5p0548c1s
Hamilton, C. v6p0388c1s
 v6p0457c2s v6p0461c2s v6p0541c1s
 v6p0548c2s
Hamilton, C.A., Mrs. v1p1433c1s
Hamilton, C.F. v5p0243c1s
 v5p0501c1s v6p0097c2s
Hamilton, C.J. v2p0087c2s
 v2p0408c2s v3p0059c2s v3p0080c1s
 v3p0241c2s v3p0328c1s v4p0261c1s
 v4p0353c1s v4p0437c1s v4p0625c2s
 v5p0052c1s v5p0104c2s v6p0165c2s
 v6p0424c2s v6p0431c1s
Hamilton, C.M. v5p0624c2s
 v6p0085c1s v6p0302c1s
Hamilton, C.V., Mrs. v1p0367c2s
 v1p0785c2s v1p1151c1s
Hamilton, Clara E. v6p0543c2s
Hamilton, D.A. v3p0038c2s
Hamilton, D.H. v1p0702c2s
Hamilton, Dr. v1p0566c2s
Hamilton, E. v1p1177c2s
 v2p0308c1s v3p0045c2s v5p0010c2s
 v5p0243c1s v5p0510c1s
Hamilton, E., Sir v1p0391c1s
Hamilton, E.A. v4p0037c2s
Hamilton, E.B. v2p0165c1s
 v2p0167c2s v2p0168c1s v2p0329c2s
 v3p0296c1s v4p0002c1s
Hamilton, E.E. v1p0468c2s
 v1p1324c2s
Hamilton, E.J. v1p0869c1s
 v6p0211c2s v6p0278c1s v6p0338c1s
 v6p0648c2s
Hamilton, E.L. v4p0354c1s
Hamilton, E.M. v5p0354c2s
Hamilton, E.W., Sir v5p0235c1s
Hamilton, Ernest v5p0434c1s
 v5p0442c2s v5p0476c1s
Hamilton, F. v6p0545c2s
Hamilton, F.A. v4p0082c1s
 v4p0512c2s
Hamilton, F.H. v2p0282c1s
 v2p0396c2s
Hamilton, F.N. v6p0593c1s
Hamilton, F.W. v4p0467c1s
 v5p0101c2s
Hamilton, F.W. et al. v4p0275c1s
Hamilton, Frederic and Hichens, R.
 v5p0590c2s
Hamilton, G. v1p0079c1s
 v3p0232c1m v3p0364c1s v4p0013c2s
 v4p0238c1s v4p0410c2s
Hamilton, G. and Rawson, R.W.
 v4p0410c2s
Hamilton, G.A. v4p0585c2s
Hamilton, H. v4p0108c1s
 v6p0396c1s
Hamilton, H.R. v1p0065c1s
 v1p1129c1s
Hamilton, J. v1p0119c1s
 v1p0120c1m v1p0209c2m v1p0358c1s
 v1p0423c2m v1p0655c1s v1p0749c2s
 v1p0781c2s v1p0819c1s v1p0843c2s
 v1p1015c2s v1p1139c2s v1p1199c2s
 v1p1219c1s v1p1269c2s v1p1416c2s
 v4p0530c2s
Hamilton, J. and Strachey, E.
 v1p0657c2s
Hamilton, J.A. v1p0403c2s
 v1p0449c2s v1p1048c1s v1p1267c1s
 v2p0192c1s v2p0273c1s v2p0287c1s
 v3p0036c2s v3p0273c2s v3p0333c1s
 v4p0001c2s v4p0152c1s v4p0173c2s
 v4p0304c2s v4p0423c1s v4p0444c1s
 v4p0581c1s v5p0020c2s v5p0085c2s
Hamilton, J.B. v3p0474c1s
Hamilton, J.B. et al. v2p0080c2s
Hamilton, J.C. v3p0395c2s
 v4p0075c1s v4p0281c2s v4p0400c1s
Hamilton, J.G.DeR. v6p0175c1s
Hamilton, J.H. v4p0322c1s
 v5p0120c2s v5p0509c2m v5p0565c1s
 v5p0568c2s v5p0622c2s
Hamilton, J.J.H. v3p0422c1s
 v4p0123c1s
Hamilton, J.P. v6p0003c2s
Hamilton, J.Perrine v6p0070c2s
Hamilton, J.R. v1p0786c2s
 v1p1374c1s
Hamilton, J.S. v6p0173c1s
Hamilton, J.T. v4p0009c1s
 v4p0382c2s
Hamilton, J.W. v3p0148c2s
 v5p0354c1s
Hamilton, Jack v6p0632c1s
Hamilton, K.W. v1p0931c2s
 v2p0309c1s v6p0045c2s v6p0423c1s
Hamilton, L. v3p0209c2s
 v4p0441c1s
Hamilton, L.McL. v6p0347c2s
 v6p0416c2s v6p0464c2m v6p0478c1s
Hamilton, M. v1p0377c1s
 v3p0341c1s v4p0120c1s v4p0395c2s
 v6p0022c2s v6p0639c1s
Hamilton, M.A.B. v2p0032c1s
 v2p0052c2s
Hamilton, M.C. v2p0331c1s
Hamilton, Major v1p0770c2s
Hamilton, N.A. v5p0121c1s
Hamilton, N.D. v5p0324c1s
Hamilton, P.G. v3p0329c1s
Hamilton, P.G.C., Sir v3p0086c1s
Hamilton, P.J. v6p0365c1s
Hamilton, P.S. v1p0543c2s
Hamilton, P.St.C. v6p0229c1s
Hamilton, Prof. v1p0070c2s
 v1p0321c2s
Hamilton, R. v2p0132c1s
 v2p0141c2s v3p0129c1s v3p0129c2s
 v4p0575c2s
Hamilton, R.G.C., Sir v4p0378c2s
Hamilton, R.J. v5p0200c2s
Hamilton, R.S. v1p1215c1s
Hamilton, R.V. v4p0182c1s
 v5p0270c1s
Hamilton, R.V. and Martin, R.B.
 v5p0364c1s
Hamilton, R.W. v1p0384c2s
 v1p0449c1s
Hamilton, S. v1p1349c2s
Hamilton, S.A. v6p0605c2s
Hamilton, S.D. v6p0657c1s
Hamilton, S.M. v5p0620c2s
Hamilton, S.M. and Ormond, A.T.
 v4p0346c2s
Hamilton, T. v1p0656c2s
Hamilton, T.C. v4p0010c2s
Hamilton, T.H. v3p0393c2s
Hamilton, W. v1p0146c1m
 v1p0273c1s v1p0437c1s v1p0469c1s
 v1p0551c2s v1p0653c2s v1p0807c2s
 v1p0830c1s v1p0966c1s v1p1392c1s
 v2p0052c1s v2p0225c1s v2p0346c1s
 v2p0347c1s v4p0122c2s
Hamilton, W., Sir v1p0262c1s
 v1p0293c1s v1p0309c2s v1p0323c1s
 v1p0329c2s v1p0337c1s v1p0387c2s
 v1p0422c2s v1p0760c2s v1p0811c1s
 v1p0817c1s v1p0826c2s v1p0954c1s
 v1p0989c1s v1p1001c2s v1p1002c1s
 v1p1029c2s v1p1177c2s v1p1356c2s
 v1p1357c1s
Hamilton, W.A.B. v2p0071c2s
 v3p0180c2s
Hamilton, W.D. v5p0321c2s
 v6p0240c2s
Hamilton, W.E. v2p0147c1s
Hamilton, W.H. v6p0241c1s
Hamilton, W.J. v1p0466c2s
Hamilton, W.L. v6p0431c1m
Hamilton, W.R. v3p0063c1s
 v3p0066c2s v3p0125c2s v3p0278c2m
 v3p0279c1m v3p0288c1s v3p0361c2s
 v3p0411c1s v4p0274c1s v4p0370c1m
 v4p0370c2m v4p0396c1m v4p0398c1s
 v4p0491c1s v4p0527c2s v4p0552c1s
 v4p0591c2s v5p0043c2s v5p0375c2s
 v5p0410c2s v6p0666c1m
Hamilton, Z.M. v5p0227c2s
Hamilton-Gordon, J.C. and
 Aberdeen, Earl of v2p0318c2s
Hamilton-Knight, F. v3p0367c1s
Hamist, A.J. v2p0376c2s
Hamitt, C.H. v3p0139c1s
Hamley, C. v1p1389c2s
 v2p0142c1s
Hamley, E. v2p0185c2s
Hamley, E., Sir v2p0432c2s
 v3p0181c1m
 v3p0256c1s
Hamley, E.B. v1p0716c2s
 v1p0732c1s v1p0735c2s v1p1133c2s
 v1p1184c2s v1p1202c1s
Hamley, E.C. v4p0011c2s
 v4p0077c1s
Hamley, W.G. v2p0275c1s
Hamlin, A.C. v1p0349c1s
 v1p0405c1s v1p1146c2s
Hamlin, A.D.F. v3p0050c2s
 v3p0122c2s v3p0386c2s v4p0023c2s
 v4p0024c2s v4p0025c1s v4p0480c2s
 v5p0025c2s v5p0026c2s v5p0082c2s
 v5p0156c2s v5p0216c2s v5p0299c2s
 v5p0424c1s v5p0494c1s v5p0594c2s
 v6p0028c1m v6p0033c2s v6p0084c1s
 v6p0128c1s v6p0136c1s v6p0374c1s
 v6p0374c2s
Hamlin, A.D.F. and Lamb, F.S.
 v5p0025c2s
Hamlin, A.J. v4p0288c1s
 v5p0292c2s
Hamlin, Alice J. v4p0036c2s
Hamlin, C. v1p0013c1s
 v1p0580c2s v1p0963c2s v1p0999c2s
 v1p1209c1s v2p0292c1s v2p0381c1s
 v2p0449c1s v3p0010c2m v3p0215c1s
 v3p0230c2s v3p0283c1s v3p0313c1s
 v3p0346c2s v3p0369c2s v3p0372c2s
 v3p0387c1s v3p0412c1s v3p0427c2s
 v3p0438c1s v4p0014c1s v4p0027c1s
 v4p0350c1s v4p0586c2s v5p0594c2s
 v6p0460c2s
Hamlin, C.E. v1p1160c2s
Hamlin, C.H. v4p0219c1s
 v5p0400c2s
Hamlin, C.S. v4p0563c1s
 v5p0382c2s v6p0515c2s
Hamlin, Cyrus v4p0027c2s
Hamlin, E.S. v1p0222c1s
Hamlin, E.W. v4p0037c1s
Hamlin, J.H. v6p0171c2s
 v6p0594c1s
Hamlin, L. v5p0222c1s
Hamlin, L.A. v6p0113c2s
Hamlin, S.D. v3p0354c1s
Hamlin, T.S. v2p0100c2s
 v4p0053c2s v4p0612c1s v5p0118c2s
 v5p0142c1s v5p0618c2s v6p0064c2s
Hamlin, T.S. et al. v5p0274c2s
Hamm, G.L. v3p0284c2s
Hamm, M. v3p0061c1s
Hamm, M.A. v4p0072c2s
 v4p0297c1s v5p0108c2s v5p0111c2s
 v5p0444c1s v5p0481c1s v6p0045c2s
 v6p0094c2s v6p0103c2s v6p0349c1s
 v6p0437c1s
Hamm, M.A. et al. v4p0629c2s
Hamm, Margherita A. v6p0710c2s
Hamm, W. v1p0271c1s
Hamm, W.C. v3p0172c1s
 v5p0188c2s v5p0464c2s
Hamma, M.W. v2p0251c2s
Hammar, W.J. v6p0312c1s
Hammat, E.S. v6p0596c2s
Hammatt, A. v1p0388c2s
Hammatt, E.S. v5p0214c2s
Hammatt, M.L. v6p0228c1s
Hammell, G.M. v4p0194c1s
 v4p0226c2s v4p0247c2s v4p0631c2s
 v5p0546c2s v5p0610c1s v6p0389c1s
 v6p0483c2s
Hammell, G.W. v5p0642c2s
Hammer, D. v6p0530c2s
Hammer, K.V. v5p0392c1s
Hammer, S.C. and Nyhuus, Haakon
 v6p0679c1s
Hammer, W.J. v5p0586c1s
 v6p0003c1s v6p0199c1s v6p0507c2s
 v6p0527c1s v6p0582c2s
Hammerstein, O. v5p0255c1s
Hammerstein, Oscar v6p0181c1s
Hammerton, C. v4p0409c2s
 v4p0501c2s
Hammerton, C.R. v3p0216c2s
 v3p0416c2s v4p0108c1s v4p0363c1s
Hammerton, J.A. v5p0043c1s
 v5p0086c2s v5p0311c1s v5p0435c2s
 v6p0165c2s v6p0617c2s v6p0632c2s
Hammett, A. v1p0652c2m
Hammick, J.T. v1p0315c2s
 v1p1245c2s
 v1p1246c1s
Hammill, F. v4p0315c1s
Hammill, F. and Mahon, J.L.
 v3p0434c2s
Hammond et al. v1p1360c1s
Hammond, A. v1p0108c2s
Hammond, A.D. v1p0603c2s
Hammond, C. v1p0003c2s
 v1p0262c1s v1p0285c1s v1p0404c2s
 v1p0731c1s v1p0862c2s
Hammond, C.E. v2p0224c2s
Hammond, C.F. v4p0201c2s
Hammond, C.M. v3p0029c1s
 v3p0250c2s v3p0253c2s v3p0257c2s
Hammond, E.G. v1p1347c2s
Hammond, E.P. v6p0111c1s
Hammond, Ella M. v5p0361c2s
Hammond, F. v6p0670c1s
Hammond, F.S. v5p0255c1s
 v6p0466c1s v6p0541c2s
Hammond, G.N. v1p0760c2s
Hammond, H.E. v6p0359c1s
Hammond, I.W. v2p0073c1s
 v2p0405c1s v3p0167c2s
Hammond, J.B. v4p0262c1s
Hammond, J.C. v6p0197c1s
Hammond, J.H. v1p1223c2m
 v5p0006c1s v5p0238c1s v5p0587c1s
 v6p0260c2s v6p0654c1s v6p0654c2s
Hammond, J.Hays v6p0186c2s
 v6p0336c2s
Hammond, J.L. v6p0235c2s
 v6p0270c1s
Hammond, J.W. v3p0395c2s
 v4p0068c2s
Hammond, L. v6p0294c2s
Hammond, L.H. v6p0448c2s
 v6p0605c1s v6p0623c2s
Hammond, M.B. v4p0115c2s
 v5p0139c1m v5p0457c1s v5p0630c1s
 v5p0638c1s v6p0143c2s
Hammond, M.M. v4p0084c2s
 v5p0089c1s v5p0638c1s
Hammond, N.H. v5p0589c1s
Hammond, O.G. v5p0397c2s
 v6p0057c1s v6p0345c2s v6p0387c2s
Hammond, P.F. v1p1211c1s
Hammond, R. v5p0183c1s

Hammond, W. v4p0188c1s
v4p0446c1s
Hammond, W.A. v1p0045c2s
v1p0210c1s v1p0237c2s v1p0643c1m
v1p0644c1s v1p0843c2s v1p0850c1s
v1p0907c1s v1p1023c1s v1p1204c2s
v1p1238c2s v1p1314c1s v2p0054c1s
v2p0096c1s v2p0107c1s v2p0129c1s
v2p0195c1s v2p0215c1s v2p0222c1s
v2p0243c2s v2p0269c2s v2p0289c2s
v2p0309c2s v2p0478c1s v3p0053c1s
v3p0118c1s v3p0135c1s v3p0207c1s
v3p0216c2s v3p0359c2s v3p0415c1s
v4p0071c2s v4p0271c1s v4p0286c1s
v4p0441c2s v4p0606c1s v5p0028c1s
v5p0447c1s v6p0273c2s v6p0383c1s
v6p0533c1s
Hammond, W.A. et al. v1p0500c1s
v2p0171c1s v2p0477c2s
v3p0123c1s
Hammond, W.F. v3p0347c2s
Hammond, W.G. v1p0734c2s
v3p0027c1s v3p0094c2s v4p0322c2s
v4p0323c2s
Hammond, W.J. v3p0053c2s
v3p0395c2s
Hammond-Spencer, H.C. v6p0678c2s
Hamner, T.F. v2p0214c1s
Hamon, A. and Hamon, H. .. v6p0237c2s
Hamon, H. and Hamon, A. .. v6p0237c2s
Hampden, J. v2p0127c1s
Hampden, Viscount v2p0225c2s
Hamper, W. v1p0161c1s
v1p0433c2s v1p0567c2s v1p0948c1s
v1p1010c2s v1p1413c2s
Hamper, W. and Douce, H.F.
v1p1132c1s
Hampole, Richard of v1p0124c2s
Hampson, J.M.C. v5p0330c2s
Hampson, J.N. v5p0248c1s
Hampton, C.E. v6p0666c1s
Hampton, E.L. v6p0540c2s
Hampton, I. v4p0409c2s
Hampton, J. v6p0478c2s
Hampton, K.P. v5p0306c1s
Hampton, W. v1p1226c1s
v1p1346c2s v2p0098c1s v3p0039c1s
v4p0471c2s
Hampton, W. et al. v4p0553c2s
Hampton, Wade v3p0299c1s
v3p0299c2s
Hanaway, E.S., Miss v3p0078c1s
Hanbury, B. v1p0736c2s
Hanbury, D.T. v5p0076c2s
v6p0097c2s
Hanbury, R.W. v1p0553c2s
v3p0179c2s v4p0235c2s
Hanbury, R.W. et al. v4p0290c1s
Hanbury-Williams, C. v5p0360c1s
v5p0633c1s v6p0097c1s v6p0227c1s
v6p0354c1s v6p0399c1s v6p0571c1s
v6p0674c1s
Hance, J.L. v1p0478c2s
v1p0752c2s v1p0832c1s
Hanchett, H. v5p0450c1s
Hanchett, H.C., Dr. v5p0395c2s
Hanchett, H.G. v4p0389c2s
v4p0456c1s v6p0136c1s v6p0438c1s
Hanckel, T.M. v1p1225c2s
Hancock, A. v2p0163c1m
Hancock, A.B. v4p0322c1s
Hancock, A.E. v6p0013c1s
v6p0049c1s v6p0127c1s v6p0281c1s
v6p0463c1s v6p0504c2s v6p0623c2s
Hancock, C. v4p0244c1s
v4p0370c1s v4p0387c1s v4p0533c2s
v4p0632c2s
Hancock, E.L. v6p0357c2s
Hancock, Ernest L. v6p0140c2s
Hancock, H. v5p0149c1s
Hancock, H.I. v6p0344c1s
v6p0570c1s
Hancock, H.J.B. v1p1312c1s
Hancock, J. v2p0202c2s
Hancock, J.A. v4p0104c2s
v4p0247c1s v4p0384c2s v5p0107c2s
v6p0503c2s
v6p0707c2s
Hancock, J.D. v4p0378c1s
Hancock, J.L. v4p0337c2s
v4p0417c2s v4p0451c1s v4p0587c2s
v6p0157c2s
Hancock, L.T. v6p0303c1s
Hancock, La T. v6p0101c1s
Hancock, La Touche v6p0505c2s
v6p0677c2s
Hancock, M. v5p0168c1s
Hancock, M.G. v4p0385c2s
Hancock, M.S. v4p0052c2s
v4p0331c2s v4p0365c2s v4p0438c1s
v4p0620c1s v5p0279c1s v5p0561c2s
v6p0388c1s
Hancock, Mary S. v4p0391c1s
v4p0529c1s
Hancock, N. v1p0657c1s
Hancock, O. v4p0461c1s
Hancock, Prof. v1p0982c1s
Hancock, S.J. v1p1183c1s
Hancock, T. v2p0195c1s
v2p0378c2s
Hancock, W.N. v1p0388c1s
Hancock, W.P. v6p0198c1s
v6p0512c2s v6p0661c1s
Hancock, W.S. v1p0518c2s
Hand, A.H. v1p0688c1s
v2p0085c2s
Hand, G.R. v2p0017c2s
v2p0082c2s v2p0145c2s v2p0180c2m
v2p0205c2s
Hand, S. et al. v1p0198c2s
Handasyd, T.B. v1p1121c1s
Handi, Kad v2p0445c2s
Handiboe, J. v5p0464c2s
v6p0621c2s
Handley, F. v4p0052c1s
v4p0578c2s
Handley, H. v2p0084c2s
v2p0290c2s v6p0125c2s
Handley, L.DeB. v6p0629c1s
Handly, J.M. v6p0307c1s
Handly, M.W. v5p0398c2s
Hands, A. v6p0377c1s
Hands, T. v2p0169c1s
Handy, M.P. v1p1313c2m
v2p0238c2s v3p0456c1s v4p0082c1s
v4p0100c1s v4p0606c1s v5p0224c1s
v5p0430c2s
Handy, M.P., Mrs. v4p0100c2s
Handy, S.M. v3p0298c2s
v5p0541c2s
Handy, W.J. v6p0092c2s
v6p0093c1m
Handy, W.M. v5p0542c1s
Handy, W.M. et al. v5p0158c2s
Handyside, H. v1p1076c2s
Haney, J.D. v6p0290c1s
Haney, J.P. v5p0156c1s
v5p0512c1s v6p0036c1s
v6p0399c2s
Haney, L.H. v6p0135c1s
Hanford, G.B. v4p0424c2s
Hanford, R.W. v1p0595c1s
Hank, H.C. v6p0103c1s
Hankey, H.A. v6p0125c1s
Hankey, T. v1p0095c1m
v1p0352c2s
Hankin, E.H. v3p0118c1s
v3p0425c2s v4p0107c2s
v5p0055c1s
v6p0423c2m
Hankin, J.E.C. v5p0045c2s
Hankin, Mrs. v1p1252c1s
Hankin, S.J.E.C. v4p0328c1s
v4p0560c1s
Hankin, St.J. v5p0523c2s
v6p0612c2s
Hankin, St.J.E.C. v4p0136c1s
v4p0140c1s v5p0067c2s v5p0092c2s
v5p0397c1s v5p0413c1s
Hankins, F. v3p0223c2s
Hanks, H.G. v1p0150c1s
v2p0118c1s v2p0182c1s v3p0317c1s
v5p0237c2s
Hanly, J.F. v6p0321c1s
Hanna, C.A. and Thomas, L.A.
v4p0433c2s
Hanna, H.B. v4p0107c1s
v5p0001c1s v5p0284c1s
Hanna, H.B. and Griffin, L., Sir
v5p0005c1s
Hanna, H.S. et al. v6p0378c2s
v6p0480c2s
Hanna, J.R. v5p0341c2s
Hanna, J.W. v2p0161c2s
v2p0425c1s
Hanna, M.A. v5p0526c2m
v6p0026c1s v6p0393c2m
Hanna, M.C. v6p0652c1s
Hanna, M.E. v6p0160c1m
v6p0160c2m
Hanna, N.D. v5p0360c2m
Hanna, Robert v4p0579c2s
Hanna, T.A.H. v2p0371c1s
Hanna, Tacie M. v6p0139c2s
Hanna, W. v1p0685c1s
Hanna, W.T.C. v3p0069c1s
Hannaford, E. v1p1256c1m
Hannaford, Samuel v5p0025c2s
Hannah, A.L. v4p0207c1s
Hannah, G. v1p1387c1s
Hannah, J. v1p0264c1s
v1p0794c2s v1p0850c1s v1p1161c2s
Hannam, F.W. v3p0377c1s
Hannan, C. v2p0394c1s
v5p0272c1s v5p0382c1s
Hannan, Chas. v3p0078c1s
Hannan, T. v4p0452c2s
v4p0478c1s
Hannath, E. v6p0533c1s
Hannay, A. v2p0099c1s
Hannay, D. v2p0378c2s
v3p0381c2s v4p0072c1s v4p0078c2s
v4p0090c1s v4p0133c2s v4p0196c2s
v4p0234c1s v4p0238c1m v4p0348c2s
v4p0354c1s v4p0363c2s v4p0516c1s
v4p0521c2s v4p0560c2s v5p0100c1s
v5p0166c2s v5p0189c2s v5p0216c2s
v5p0233c1s v5p0243c1s v5p0246c1s
v5p0250c2s v5p0398c1s v5p0404c1s
v5p0411c1s v5p0456c2s v5p0543c1s
v5p0625c1s v6p0077c2s v6p0187c1s
v6p0441c2m v6p0442c1s v6p0448c2s
v6p0449c1s v6p0608c1s v6p0712c2s
Hannay, David v4p0237c2s
v4p0356c1s v4p0395c2s
Hannay, J. v1p0098c2s
v1p0140c2s v1p0384c1s v1p0398c2s
v1p0419c1s v1p0421c1s v1p0603c1s
v1p0682c1s v1p0775c2s v1p0804c1s
v1p0849c1s v1p0985c1s v1p1152c1s
v1p1167c1s v1p1230c1s v1p1279c1s
v1p1298c2s v1p1337c2s v3p0260c2s
v5p0405c1s v6p0461c1s v6p0523c1s
v6p0525c1s v6p0685c1m
Hannay, J.B. v1p0348c2m
v1p1218c2s
Hannay, J.C. v6p0245c1s
Hannay, J.O. v6p0245c1s
Hannay, R. v1p0309c2s
Hannay, R.C.F. v1p0394c1s
Hanne, J.R. v1p0514c2s
Hannigan, D.F. v2p0297c1s
v3p0168c2s v3p0201c2s v3p0221c1s
v3p0246c2s v3p0308c1s v3p0382c1s
v4p0005c2s v4p0028c1s v4p0037c2s
v4p0080c1m v4p0188c2s v4p0198c1s
v4p0202c1s v4p0248c1m v4p0335c2s
v4p0376c1s v4p0377c1s v4p0408c1s
v4p0408c2s v4p0489c2s v4p0509c2s
v4p0560c1s v4p0614c1s v5p0080c2s
v5p0104c2s v5p0145c1s v5p0172c2s
v5p0177c1s v5p0207c1s v5p0217c2s
v5p0387c2s v5p0415c2s v5p0433c2s
v5p0532c1s v5p0562c2s v6p0284c1s
Hannigan, D.F. and Martyn, E.
v3p0469c2s
Hanning, D. v1p0497c1s
Hannon, J.W. v5p0421c1s
Hannus, H. v6p0028c2m
Hanotaux, G. v5p0430c2s
Hanrod, H.D. v2p0090c1s
Hanry, G.V. v5p0460c2s
Hanry, J. v1p0398c2s
Hansard, A.C. v5p0032c2s
v5p0124c2s
Hansard, W. v1p1171c2s
v1p1172c1s
Hansbrough, H.C. v4p0275c2s
v6p0329c1s
Hansbrough, H.C. et al. .. v4p0129c1s
v4p0230c2s
v4p0525c1s
Hanscom, A.E. v5p0389c1s
v6p0641c1s
Hanscom, A.L. v3p0253c1s
Hanscom, Adelaide v6p0497c2s
Hanscom, B. v6p0090c1s
v6p0229c2s
Hanscom, Beatrice v6p0259c2s
v6p0594c1s
Hanscom, E.D. v5p0638c2s
Hanscom, Eliz.D. v6p0135c2s
Hansell, C. v5p0478c1s
Hansen, A.M. and Touche, T.D.La
v4p0317c1s
Hansen, A.M. et al. v2p0435c2s
Hansen, G. v5p0098c2s
Hansen, J. v5p0054c2s
Hansen, M.C. v2p0361c1s
Hansen, M.G. v1p0328c1s
v2p0097c1s v2p0099c1s v2p0192c2s
v3p0379c1s v3p0428c1s v3p0447c1s
v4p0109c2s v4p0286c1s v4p0467c1s
Hanshew, T.W. v6p0397c2s
v6p0689c2s
Hansoldt, H. v3p0209c1s
Hanson, A.J. v1p0235c1s
v2p0298c2s v2p0456c2s v4p0106c1s
Hanson, Burton v6p0058c1s
Hanson, C. v4p0031c2s
Hanson, C.L. v6p0207c1s
Hanson, E.S. v6p0143c1s
Hanson, H.N. v4p0231c1s
Hanson, I.W. v5p0630c2s
Hanson, J.C.M. v6p0104c1m
Hanson, J.H. v1p0841c2s
v1p0842c2s v1p1021c1s v1p1411c2m
Hanson, J.M. v5p0451c2s
Hanson, J.S. v6p0443c1s
Hanson, J.T. v2p0240c1s
v2p0277c1s v2p0334c1s v2p0362c2s
v2p0420c2s
Hanson, J.W. v2p0105c2s
Hanson, M.G. v1p0499c2s
Hanssen, F. v3p0243c2s
Hansteen, C. v1p0077c1s
Hansteen, Prof. v2p0401c2s
Hanus, P. v6p0196c2s
Hanus, P.H. v4p0122c2s
v4p0126c2s v4p0137c1s v4p0171c2s
v4p0249c2s v4p0512c2m v4p0554c2s
v5p0126c1s v5p0176c2s v5p0182c2s
v5p0264c2s v5p0366c1s v5p0511c1s
v5p0517c2s v5p0518c1m v6p0192c2s
v6p0290c1s v6p0291c1s v6p0435c1s
v6p0537c1s v6p0635c2s
Hanway, D. v5p0075c2s
Hapgood, H. v3p0207c1s
v4p0554c1s v5p0165c1s
v5p0232c2m

v5p0307c2s v5p0308c1s v5p0497c1s
v5p0548c1s v5p0616c2s v5p0646c2s
v6p0343c2s v6p0450c2s
Hapgood, H. and Maurice, A.B.
v6p0456c1s
Hapgood, H.J. v6p0137c1m
v6p0410c1s
Hapgood, I.F. v2p0381c2m
v2p0432c1s v2p0442c2s v3p0370c1s
v3p0370c2s v3p0372c2s v3p0373c2s
v3p0431c2s v3p0432c1m v4p0010c1s
v4p0159c2s v4p0310c2s v4p0313c1m
v4p0313c2s v4p0327c1s v4p0481c1s
v4p0495c2m v4p0496c1m v4p0496c2s
v4p0497c1s v4p0499c2s v4p0522c2s
v4p0548c2s v4p0578c2s v4p0586c2s
v4p0589c1s v4p0607c1m v5p0138c2s
v5p0442c1s v5p0502c2m v5p0505c1s
v6p0179c2m v6p0527c2s
v6p0702c1s
Hapgood, I.J. v4p0217c2s
Hapgood, Isabel F. v4p0495c2s
v4p0496c2s v6p0246c2s v6p0457c1s
v6p0555c2s v6p0556c2s v6p0557c1m
v6p0557c2s v6p0558c1m v6p0558c2m
v6p0559c1s
v6p0593c1s
Hapgood, L.F. v5p0581c2s
Hapgood, N. v3p0002c1s
v3p0057c1s v3p0068c2s v3p0122c1s
v3p0132c1s v3p0265c1s v3p0355c1s
v3p0432c1s v3p0475c2s v4p0021c1s
v4p0042c1s v4p0143c1s v4p0296c1s
v4p0461c2s v5p0003c1s v5p0031c2s
v5p0167c2m v5p0222c1s v5p0222c2s
v5p0234c2s v5p0339c1s v5p0386c2s
v5p0454c1s v5p0485c2s v5p0497c1s
v5p0575c2s v5p0576c1s v5p0620c2s
v5p0632c1s v6p0145c2s v6p0258c1s
v6p0275c1s
Hapgood, Norman v5p0608c1s
Hapgood, U. v6p0566c2s
Hapley, H. v2p0315c1s
Happel, J. v3p0060c1s
Happer, A.P. v1p0853c2s
v3p0078c2s v3p0079c1s v3p0227c1s
v4p0128c2s
v4p0415c1s
Haras, S. v4p0493c1s
Haraszthy, A. v1p0188c2m
v1p1415c2s
Harbaugh, H. v1p0024c1s
v1p0112c1s v1p0120c1s v1p0206c2m
v1p0230c1s v1p0238c2s v1p0242c1s
v1p0244c1s v1p0254c2s v1p0285c1s
v1p0289c1s v1p0323c2s v1p0336c1s
v1p0440c1s v1p0468c2s v1p0581c1s
v1p0583c1m v1p0599c2s v1p0620c1s
v1p0686c2s v1p0688c1s v1p0752c1s
v1p0756c2s v1p0778c1s v1p0823c2s
v1p0847c1s v1p1040c2s v1p1090c2s
v1p1120c1s v1p1149c2s v1p1158c2s
v1p1278c1s v1p1424c1s v1p1432c2s
v1p1433c1s
Harbaugh, Linn v6p0239c2s
Harben, W.N. v3p0090c1s
v3p0192c1s v4p0361c1s v4p0500c1s
v4p0619c2s v5p0135c2s v5p0206c2s
v5p0308c2s v5p0500c1s v5p0577c2s
v6p0223c2s v6p0433c2s v6p0525c2s
v6p0662c2s
Harbert, E.B. v1p1214c1s
Harberton, F.W. v1p1424c1s
v2p0124c1s
Harboe, P. v6p0079c2s
v6p0164c1s
Harboe, Paul v6p0020c1m
v6p0225c1s
Harbord, J.G. v5p0290c1s
Harbourne, J.W. v5p0206c1s
Harby, I. v6p0699c2s
Harby, L.C. v2p0234c2s
v3p0276c2s v3p0295c1s v3p0300c2s
v3p0425c2s
v4p0223c1s
Harcolm, A.M. v5p0473c2s
Harcourt, A. v1p1066c1s
v3p0240c1s v3p0433c2s v4p0438c2m
v4p0493c1s v5p0284c2s
v5p0583c2s
Harcourt, A.F.P. v6p0265c1s
Harcourt, A.F.P. and Waters, W.G.
v6p0679c1s
Harcourt, A.V. v1p0501c2m
v3p0167c2s
Harcourt, Betty v6p0617c2s
Harcourt, C. v5p0373c1s
Harcourt, C.E. v6p0501c1s
Harcourt, Carmen v5p0155c2s
Harcourt, L.F. v1p0408c1s
Harcourt, L.V. v1p0409c1s
Harcourt, L.W.V. v5p0137c2s
Harcourt, L.W.Vernon v6p0609c1s
Harcourt, T.A. v1p0027c1s
v1p0083c2s v1p0190c2s v1p0303c2s
v1p0319c2s v1p0626c2s v1p0675c2s
v1p0693c2s v1p0735c2s v1p0756c1s
v1p0819c1s v1p0890c2s
Harcourt, V. v2p0258c2s
Hard, A.S. v6p0096c2s
Hard, O.W. v3p0159c2s
v3p0332c1s
Hard, W. v6p0056c1s
v6p0113c1s v6p0114c1s v6p0601c2s
v6p0618c1s v6p0697c1s
Hardacre, E.C. v1p0265c1s
v1p0397c2s
Hardaker, M.A. v1p1094c2s
v1p1182c1m v2p0408c2s v2p0477c1s
Hardcastle, M. v1p1339c2s
v1p1394c1s
Hardee, W.J. v1p0881c1s
v1p0991c1s
Harden, A. v6p0651c1s
Harden, E.W. v5p0360c1s
Harden, M. v6p0254c2s
Harden, W.N. v4p0277c1s
Harder, J.F. v5p0119c2s
v6p0028c1s
Harder, W.C. v6p0345c1s
Hardie, F.H. v5p0373c1s
Hardie, J.K. v4p0239c1s
v4p0315c2s v5p0246c1s v6p0270c2s
v6p0355c2s v6p0356c1s v6p0356c2s
v6p0665c1s
Hardie, J.K. and Whetstone, F.J.
v4p0214c1s
Hardie, J.K. et al. v5p0332c1s
Hardie, J.Keir v4p0315c2s
Hardie, K. v4p0112c1s
v4p0314c2s
Hardie, M. v5p0239c1s
v6p0032c2s v6p0039c1s
Hardie, M.B. v4p0229c1s
v5p0255c2s v5p0486c2s
Hardie, Martin v6p0041c1s
Hardie, R.P. v4p0026c2s
v4p0446c2s v6p0091c2s
Hardie, T.K. v6p0601c2s
Hardie, V. v6p0020c2s
Hardin, E.E. v4p0370c2s
v4p0401c1s v5p0029c2s
Hardin, J.J. v1p0033c2s
Hardin, M.D. v5p0038c1s
Harding, A.C. v2p0141c2s
Harding, B.F. v5p0290c2s
Harding, C. v2p0434c1s
v3p0410c2s v4p0218c2s v6p0701c1s
Harding, C.H. v1p0387c2s
v1p0968c1s
Harding, C.W. v2p0469c1s
Harding, E. v1p1020c2s
v6p0386c1s
Harding, E.J. v2p0075c2s
v2p0260c2s v3p0151c2s v3p0207c1s
v3p0325c2s v3p0335c2s
Harding, E.L. v3p0152c1s
Harding, F. v6p0025c1s
v6p0327c2s v6p0503c2s
Harding, Freeman v6p0058c1s
v6p0138c1s
Harding, G. v1p0484c2s
Harding, G.E. v1p0195c2s
v3p0409c1s v4p0177c2s
Harding, H.A. v6p0046c2s
Harding, H.A. and Stewart, F.C.
v6p0090c2s
Harding, J.C. v1p0740c1s
Harding, J.N.M. v1p1075c2s
Harding, J.W. v1p0406c2s
v6p0172c2s
v6p0453c1s
Harding, L.A. v4p0369c2s
Harding, Mary v5p0145c2s
v5p0426c2s
v6p0665c2s
Harding, R.B. v1p0745c2s
v1p1055c2s
v1p1258c1s
Harding, S.B. v4p0563c2s
Harding, S.L. v3p0044c1s
Harding, W. v1p1080c2s
Harding, W.F. v4p0281c2s
Harding, W.P.G. v5p0207c1s
Hardinge, A. v4p0284c1s
Hardinge, E.M. v4p0158c2s
v4p0370c2s
v4p0532c1s
Hardinge, W.H. v3p0292c2s
Hardinge, W.M. v1p0045c1s
v1p0246c2s v1p0489c2s v1p0554c1s
v3p0098c1s v3p0208c1m v3p0315c2s
v3p0367c2s v4p0305c2s v4p0361c2s
v4p0492c1s v4p0613c2s
Hardinge, Wm.M. v4p0492c1s
Hardman, E. v2p0424c1s
Hardman, E.T. v1p0073c2s
v2p0027c2s
Hardman, F. v1p0551c1s
Hardman, F.W. v4p0186c2s
Hardman, H.F. v4p0028c1s
Hardman, J.E. v5p0378c1s
Hardman, W. v1p1282c2s
v2p0124c2s
Hardt, C.R. v6p0051c1s
Hardwiche, H.J. v3p0145c2s
Hardwick, A.A. v6p0592c1s
Hardwick, C. v2p0023c1s
v2p0172c2s
Hardwick, C.A. v6p0532c2s
Hardwick, J.W. v5p0319c2s
v5p0603c1s v5p0629c1s
Hardwick, T. v1p1124c2s
v1p1368c2s
Hardwick, W. v2p0375c1s
Hardwicke, W. v1p0647c2s
v1p1376c1s
Hardwicke, W.W. v3p0090c2s
v3p0113c1s
Hardy, A.E.G. v3p0122c2s
Hardy, A.E.Gathorne v2p0170c1s
v2p0355c1s
Hardy, A.L. v2p0362c1s
v3p0292c1s v3p0385c2s v3p0447c2s
Hardy, A.S. v1p1316c1s
v2p0429c1s v3p0016c2s v3p0106c1s
v3p0151c2s v3p0208c2s v3p0225c2s
v3p0226c2m v3p0271c2s v3p0322c2s
v4p0101c2s v4p0116c2s v4p0344c2s
v4p0478c1s v5p0417c1s v6p0291c2s
Hardy, C.A. v4p0333c1s
Hardy, C.C. v4p0552c1s
Hardy, D., Lady v3p0118c2s
v3p0194c1s v3p0228c1s
Hardy, E.A. v6p0370c2s
v6p0467c2s
Hardy, E.G. v3p0365c2m
Hardy, E.I. v3p0177c2s
v3p0323c2s
Hardy, E.J. v1p0967c2s
v2p0010c1s v3p0020c1s v3p0058c1s
v3p0061c1s v3p0120c1s v3p0127c1s
v3p0269c2s v3p0270c1s v4p0117c1s
v4p0157c1s v4p0263c2s v4p0292c2s
v4p0322c2s v4p0351c1s v4p0382c1s
v4p0428c2s v4p0479c1s v4p0536c1s
v4p0571c2s v5p0029c1s v5p0101c1s
v5p0243c1s v5p0362c2s v5p0375c1s
v5p0481c1s v5p0489c2s v5p0538c1m
v5p0562c1s v5p0569c2s v5p0582c1s
v5p0623c1s v6p0118c1s v6p0120c2m
Hardy, E.J., Rev. v5p0481c1s
Hardy, E.L. v5p0217c2s
v5p0351c2s
Hardy, F. v2p0223c2s
Hardy, F.H. v4p0457c2s
v4p0511c2s v4p0526c1s v4p0596c1m
v5p0001c2s v5p0517c1s v5p0603c2s
Hardy, G. v1p0451c2s
Hardy, G.E. v3p0249c2s
v3p0253c2s v4p0387c1s
Hardy, G.F. v4p0172c2s
Hardy, H. v1p0526c2s
v4p0133c1s
Hardy, I.D. v1p0279c1s
v1p0623c2s v1p0919c2s v1p1147c1s
v1p1148c2m v1p1196c1s v2p0048c2s
v2p0327c2s v2p0372c2s v3p0157c2s
v3p0291c2s v4p0626c2s
Hardy, Iza D. v3p0300c1s
Hardy, J. v4p0142c2s
v4p0611c1s
Hardy, J.F. v1p0025c1s
v1p0465c2s
Hardy, J.J. v4p0360c2s
Hardy, J.K. v6p0356c2s
Hardy, L. v4p0414c2s
v4p0623c2s v5p0004c1s v5p0067c2s
v5p0202c2s v5p0348c1s v5p0390c2s
Hardy, Lady v1p0496c2s
v1p0732c2s v2p0397c2s
Hardy, Lucy v5p0530c2s
Hardy, M. v6p0179c2s
v6p0594c1s
Hardy, M., Col. v6p0157c2s
Hardy, R. v1p0617c2s
Hardy, S.E.M. v4p0067c2s
v4p0310c1s v4p0358c1s v5p0315c1s
v5p0328c2s v5p0404c2s
Hardy, S.M. v4p0378c2s
v4p0458c1s
Hardy, S.McL. v4p0377c2s
v4p0458c1s
Hardy, Sallie E.M. v4p0358c1s
v5p0014c1s v5p0041c2s v5p0073c2s
v5p0078c1s v5p0086c2s v5p0088c2s
v5p0095c2s v5p0250c1s v5p0262c1m
v5p0276c2s v5p0304c1s v5p0314c2s
v5p0330c1s v5p0344c2s v5p0363c2m
v5p0365c1m v5p0378c2s v5p0437c1s
v5p0439c1s v5p0470c1s v5p0478c2m
v5p0491c1m v5p0515c1s v5p0518c2m
v5p0557c2s v5p0569c1s v5p0594c1m
v5p0596c2s v5p0604c1s v5p0606c1s
v5p0620c2s v5p0630c1s
v5p0633c2m
v5p0642c2s
Hardy, T. v1p0356c1s
v1p0443c2s v1p0569c2s v1p0725c1s
v1p0959c2s v1p1102c1s v1p1328c1s
v2p0035c1s v2p0122c1s v2p0249c2s
v2p0440c1s v2p0449c2s v2p0479c1s
v3p0151c2s v3p0152c1m v3p0153c2s
v3p0240c1s v3p0278c1s v3p0312c2s
v3p0453c1s v3p0460c1s v3p0471c1s
v4p0091c2s v4p0198c1s v4p0252c1s
v4p0306c1s v4p0360c1s v4p0527c1s
v5p0101c1s v5p0115c2s v5p0193c2s
v5p0374c1s v5p0540c1s v6p0087c1s
v6p0653c2s

Hardy, T.D. v1p0693c1s
Hardy, T.H. v1p0639c1s
Hardy, T.J. v5p0183c1s
Hardy, Thomas v3p0157c2s
v4p0581c2s
v6p0127c1s
Hardy, W. v1p1106c1s
Hardy, W.B. v5p0450c1s
Hardy, W.J. v2p0212c1m
v3p0098c2s v3p0189c1s v3p0198c1s
v3p0204c2s v3p0226c1s v3p0273c2s
v3p0403c1s v4p0067c1m v4p0201c2s
v4p0487c2s v4p0587c1s v5p0071c1s
v5p0118c2s v5p0186c1s v5p0295c2s
v5p0557c2s
v5p0581c2s
Hardy, W.S. v4p0340c1s
Hardy, W.T. v4p0617c1s
Hare, A.J.C. v1p0672c1s
v1p0766c2s v1p0775c2s v1p1125c1s
v1p1155c1s v1p1230c2s v1p1243c1s
v2p0166c1s v2p0205c1s v2p0327c1s
v2p0401c2s v2p0429c2s v3p0320c2s
v4p0549c2s v5p0345c2s v5p0417c1s
v5p0495c2s v5p0528c2s
Hare, A.K. v3p0294c2s
Hare, A.T. v3p0251c1s
Hare, C. v4p0426c2s
v5p0432c2s v6p0680c2s
Hare, Christopher v5p0304c2s
Hare, G.E. v3p0043c1s
v3p0324c1s
Hare, J. v1p0258c1s
Hare, J.A. v6p0623c2s
Hare, K. v3p0186c1s
v4p0571c2s
Hare, R. v1p0093c2s
v1p0141c2s v1p0143c1m v1p0224c1s
v1p0273c1s v1p0400c1m v1p0400c2s
v1p0454c2s v1p0498c2m v1p0541c2s
v1p0579c2s v1p0619c1s v1p0749c1m
v1p0755c2s v1p0892c2s v1p1233c1m
v1p1240c1s v1p1256c2m v1p1316c2m
v1p1390c1s v1p1391c2m v2p0370c1s
Hare, T. v1p0398c2s
v1p0425c2s v1p0549c2s v1p0635c1s
v1p0763c1s v1p0848c2m v1p0974c1s
v1p1056c1s v1p1099c1m v1p1099c2m
v1p1285c2s
Hare, W.E. v6p0148c1s
Harford, C.J. v1p0409c1m
Harford, F.K. v4p0182c1s
Harford, G. v6p0065c1s
Harford-Battersby, C.F. .. v5p0061c2s
Harg, J.M. v6p0625c2s
Harger, C.M. v3p0253c1s
v4p0026c1s v4p0092c2s v4p0205c2s
v5p0313c2s v5p0380c2s v5p0418c2m
v5p0625c2m v6p0056c2s v6p0081c1s
v6p0105c1s v6p0154c2s v6p0219c2s
v6p0229c1s v6p0233c1m v6p0282c2s
v6p0316c1s v6p0317c1s v6p0349c1m
v6p0382c2s v6p0416c1s v6p0432c1s
v6p0448c2s v6p0465c1m v6p0513c1m
v6p0590c1s v6p0602c2s v6p0607c1s
v6p0656c2s v6p0692c2s v6p0693c2s
Harger, O. v1p0470c2s
Hargis, T.F. v2p0240c1s
v2p0251c1s
Hargitt, C.W. v5p0295c1s
v6p0066c2s v6p0067c1s v6p0325c1s
v6p0706c2s
Hargitt, C.W. and Osborn, H.L.
v4p0435c1s
Hargrave, H. v1p1148c1s
v1p1148c2s v1p1363c2s
Hargrave, M. v4p0089c1s
v4p0195c2s v4p0207c1s v4p0254c2s
v4p0294c1s v4p0295c1s v4p0460c2s
v4p0473c2s v4p0630c2s v6p0675c1s
Hargrave, Mary v4p0506c2s
Hargrave, W. v1p1210c2s
Hargreave, H. v1p0966c2s
Hargreaves, J. v1p0665c1s
Hargreaves, J.G. v1p0375c1s
Hargrove, C. v1p0140c2s
v1p1186c2s v1p1306c1s
Hargrove, E.T. v4p0573c2s
v5p0465c2s v5p0577c1s
Hargrove, H.H. v5p0320c2s
Hargrove, R.K. v6p0674c2s
Haring, H.A. v5p0626c2s
Haring, J.S. v4p0588c1s
Harington, H.B. v4p0107c1s
v4p0214c2s
Harischandra, N. v6p0536c1s
Hark, J. v2p0049c2s
Hark, J.M. v2p0027c2s
v2p0265c2s v2p0297c2s v3p0145c2s
v3p0199c1s v5p0332c2s
Harkavy, A. v5p0503c1s
Harkavy, A. and Margoliouth, D.S.
v5p0503c1s v5p0518c2s
Harker, A. v2p0046c2s
v4p0125c1s v4p0366c2s v4p0437c2m
v4p0486c2m v5p0491c2s
Harker, B.J. v4p0235c1s
Harker, C.R. v3p0360c1s
Harker, J.A. v6p0260c1s
Harker, L.A. v5p0035c2s
v5p0131c2s v5p0164c2s v5p0233c2s
v5p0349c2s v5p0507c2s v6p0142c2s
v6p0249c2s v6p0597c2s
Harker, L.Allen v6p0555c1s
v6p0673c2s
Harkey, S.L. v1p0285c2s
v1p1139c2s
Harkey, S.W. v1p0095c2s
v1p0119c2s v1p0700c1s v1p0778c1s
v1p0778c2s v1p0852c1s v1p1099c1s
v2p0071c1s v2p0470c1s
Harkins, C. v4p0026c2s
Harkins, E.A. v6p0391c2s
Harkins, E.F. v6p0004c1s
v6p0046c1s v6p0053c2s v6p0057c2s
v6p0072c2s v6p0177c1s v6p0195c2s
v6p0229c2s v6p0235c2s v6p0280c1s
v6p0280c2s v6p0383c1s v6p0386c2s
Harkins, T.F. v1p1202c1s
Harkness, A. v1p0551c2s
Harkness, A.G. v6p0679c2s
Harkness, A.H. and Cumberland, B.
v5p0605c1s
Harkness, J. v1p0048c1s
Harkness, M.E. v1p1423c1s
v2p0245c1s v2p0264c1s v2p0363c2m
v2p0477c1s
Harkness, R. v1p0312c1s
Harkness, W. v1p0281c2s
v1p1268c1s v1p1292c1s v2p0459c1s
v3p0127c1s v3p0459c1s v4p0440c1s
v4p0535c2m v5p0417c1s
Harkness, W. and Rucker, A.W.
v3p0264c1s
Harlan, A.J. v6p0666c2s
Harlan, J.M. v5p0632c1s
Harlan, J.S. v6p0509c2s
Harland, H. v3p0241c2s
v3p0410c2s v4p0053c1s v4p0163c2s
v5p0051c1s v5p0301c2s v5p0517c1s
v6p0440c1s
Harland, J. v1p0266c1s
Harland, M. v1p0518c2s
v3p0281c1s v3p0469c1s v4p0628c1s
v4p0629c1s v5p0008c2s v5p0379c1s
Harland, M. et al. v3p0202c2s
v3p0269c1s v3p0454c2s v4p0270c1s
Harland, Marion v1p1296c1s
v6p0123c2s v6p0219c1s v6p0585c1s
v6p0645c1s
v6p0685c2s
Harley, B. v1p1243c1s
Harley, C.De v2p0079c1s
Harley, G. v1p0045c1s
v3p0007c2s v3p0123c1s v3p0265c2s
v4p0095c2s
Harley, H.L. v6p0143c1s
Harley, J.H. v5p0535c1s
v6p0212c1s
Harley, L.R. v4p0044c1s
v4p0047c2s v4p0116c2s v4p0215c2s
v4p0233c1s v4p0257c1s v4p0259c1s
v4p0351c1s v4p0393c2s v4p0403c1s
v4p0434c1m v4p0453c1s v4p0470c1s
v4p0476c1s v4p0481c1s v4p0594c2s
v5p0337c1s v5p0399c2s v5p0439c2s
v5p0440c1s
Harley, Lucy v5p0216c1s
Harley, Mrs. v1p0308c2s
Harley, W.S. v4p0116c1s
Harlez, C.de v2p0249c2s
v3p0059c1m v3p0079c1s v3p0229c1s
v4p0057c2s v4p0078c1s v4p0105c2s
v4p0106c2s v4p0284c1s v4p0353c1s
v4p0507c1s v5p0325c1s
Harlez, C.de and West, E.W.
v3p0029c1s
Harlez, Ch.de v3p0042c1s
Harlin, T. v1p0214c1s
Harlin, W. v1p0347c1s
Harling, E. v5p0219c2s
v5p0452c2s v5p0481c1s
v5p0516c2s
Harlow, C.H. v2p0191c1s
v4p0104c2s
Harlow, Edward v4p0333c1s
Harlow, J.H. v1p1065c2s
Harlow, W.B. v3p0092c2s
v3p0146c1s
v3p0415c1s
Harlow, W.T. v1p1379c1s
Harlowe, B. v5p0115c2s
v5p0534c2s
Harlowe, P. v6p0629c1s
Harman, E.A. v5p0226c2s
Harman, Elizabeth v5p0213c2s
Harman, H.A. v2p0254c2s
Harman, H.M. v1p0122c2s
v1p0125c1s v1p0125c2s v1p0131c1s
v1p0825c1s v1p0979c1s v1p1303c2s
v2p0237c1s v2p0327c1s v3p0041c2m
v3p0284c1s v3p0313c1s v3p0418c2s
v3p0420c2s
v4p0056c2s
Harman, J.A. v4p0087c1s
v4p0250c2s
Harman, M.L. v4p0094c2s
Harmer, E.G. v3p0206c1s
v3p0345c1s
Harmer, T. v1p0660c1s
v1p1129c1s
Harmon, G.M. v1p0252c2s
v1p1215c1s v1p1356c1s v2p0211c1s
v2p0455c2s v3p0229c2s v3p0282c1s
v3p0324c1s v3p0359c2s v4p0056c2s
v5p0442c1s
Harmon, H.M. v1p0527c1s
v1p0867c2s v5p0028c1s
Harmon, J. v6p0155c1s
Harmon, O.E. v4p0165c2s
v4p0424c2s v4p0588c1s v5p0248c2s
v5p0522c1s
Harms, F. v1p1160c1s
Harmsworth, A. v6p0044c2s
Harmsworth, A.C. v4p0025c1s
v4p0295c2s
Harmsworth, Alfred C.W. .. v6p0456c1s
Harnack, A. v1p0241c2s
v1p1123c2s v2p0085c2s v2p0302c1s
v4p0377c1s v5p0114c2s v6p0292c2s
v6p0699c1s
Harnack, A. and Ward, H., Mrs.
v4p0021c1s
Harnack, Adolf v5p0306c2s
Harnack, O. v3p0175c2s
Harnaker, W.D. v4p0363c1s
Harned, M. v5p0230c2s
v6p0279c2s
Harness, A. v1p1441c2s
Harney, G.J. v1p1100c1s
v2p0210c2s v4p0182c1s
v4p0318c1s
v4p0333c1s
Harney, G.L. v3p0442c1s
Harney, W.W. v1p0356c1s
v1p0608c2s v1p0703c2s v1p0706c1s
v1p1172c2s v1p1226c1s v1p1311c1s
v1p1408c1s v2p0086c2s v2p0159c2s
v2p0322c2s v2p0473c2s
Harnsworth, A. v5p0409c2s
Harold, John v5p0384c1s
Harpe, J.F.de la v1p0057c2s
Harpe, La v1p1263c1s
Harpel, M.S. v5p0423c1s
Harper, A. v4p0023c1s
v5p0220c1s
Harper, A.M. v1p0904c2s
Harper, A.P. v4p0401c2s
Harper, C.G. v5p0248c2s
v5p0344c2s v5p0439c1s v5p0527c2s
Harper, C.M. v6p0532c1s
Harper, Chancellor v1p1208c2s
Harper, D.N. and Penfield, S.L.
v2p0041c1s v2p0364c2s
Harper, D.N. and Penfield, S.N.
v2p0201c1s
Harper, E.B. and Litchfield, G.A.
v4p0286c2s
Harper, E.J. v6p0385c1s
Harper, E.T. v4p0302c1s
v5p0307c2s v5p0308c1s
Harper, F.A.B. v1p0913c2s
Harper, G.M. v4p0147c1s
v6p0241c2s v6p0302c1s v6p0428c2s
v6p0545c2s v6p0670c1s
Harper, G.McL. v5p0044c2s
v5p0084c1s v5p0221c1s v5p0504c1s
v6p0516c2s
Harper, H.A. v3p0040c1s
v3p0146c2s v3p0166c1s v3p0241c2s
v3p0374c1s v4p0404c2s v4p0438c2s
v6p0505c1s
Harper, H.W. v6p0640c1s
Harper, I.H. v5p0349c1s
v5p0637c2s v6p0023c2s v6p0219c1s
v6p0704c1s v6p0705c2m
Harper, Ida H. v5p0202c1s
v6p0023c2s v6p0134c1s v6p0402c1s
v6p0591c1s v6p0613c2m v6p0704c2s
Harper, J. v5p0038c2s
Harper, J.B. v1p1295c2s
v6p0183c1s
Harper, J.M. v5p0090c1s
Harper, Janet v4p0492c1s
Harper, L. v1p0174c2s
v1p1128c2s
Harper, L.A. v5p0069c2s
Harper, R. v1p0199c1s
v1p1105c1s v6p0435c1s v6p0572c1s
Harper, R.F. v4p0033c2s
v4p0040c2s v5p0402c1s v6p0037c1s
v6p0046c1m v6p0069c1s
Harper, R.M. v6p0303c1s
v6p0358c2s
Harper, Ruth v1p0035c1s
Harper, S.B. v1p0260c1s
v1p0487c2s v1p1276c2s
Harper, S.B.A. v1p0247c2s
v1p0964c1s v1p1117c2s v1p1187c1s
v1p1203c1s
Harper, S.N. v6p0558c1s
Harper, T. v1p0208c2s
v1p0219c2s v1p0285c1s v1p0407c1s
v1p0868c2s v2p0181c1s v2p0271c1s
v2p0381c2s v2p0479c2s
Harper, V. v6p0025c1s
v6p0230c1s v6p0471c2s v6p0474c1s
v6p0494c1s v6p0581c1s
Harper, Vincent and
Cameron, Agnes D. v6p0082c1s

Harper, W. v1p0561c1s v6p0529c2s
Harper, W.R. v4p0019c2s v4p0054c2s v4p0055c1m v4p0055c2s v4p0056c2s v4p0082c2s v4p0098c2s v4p0123c2s v4p0138c2s v4p0148c2s v4p0151c2m v4p0168c1s v4p0194c1s v4p0230c2s v4p0300c2s v4p0341c1s v4p0352c1s v4p0384c1s v4p0430c2s v4p0462c1m v4p0537c1s v4p0586c1s v5p0056c2s v5p0057c1s v5p0058c2s v5p0127c1s v5p0299c1s v5p0308c1m v5p0576c2s v5p0604c2s v6p0061c1s v6p0062c2m v6p0136c1m v6p0192c2s v6p0194c1s v6p0290c1s v6p0373c2s v6p0519c1s v6p0538c1s v6p0643c1s v6p0671c1s
Harper, W.R. and Barrows, J.H. v4p0100c1s
Harper, W.R. et al. v3p0091c2s
Harper, W.St.J. v6p0125c1s
Harpham, F.E. v5p0503c1s v6p0020c2s
Harraden, B. v3p0001c2s v3p0025c1s v3p0115c1s v3p0461c2s v4p0034c2s v4p0060c1s v4p0083c2s v4p0233c2s v4p0248c2s v4p0257c2s v4p0273c2s v4p0360c2s v5p0088c2s v5p0233c1s
Harraden, Beatrice v5p0256c1s v5p0340c1s v5p0416c2s
Harrah, C.J. v4p0315c2s v4p0563c1s
Harrassowitz, O. v2p0052c1s
Harrell, C.E. v5p0113c1s
Harrell, Carrie Elizabeth. v5p0043c2s
Harrell, H. v5p0636c1s
Harries, A. and Lawrence, H.N. v3p0133c2s
Harries, H. v3p0156c2s v3p0276c2s v3p0458c2s v3p0465c1s v4p0036c1s v5p0554c2s
Harriman, F.P. v3p0124c2s
Harriman, F.W. v3p0281c1s
Harriman, H.M. v5p0239c1s
Harriman, K.E. v6p0127c2s v6p0132c1s v6p0147c2s v6p0155c1s v6p0289c2s v6p0358c1s v6p0562c1s v6p0620c2s
Harriman, Karl E. v6p0198c1s v6p0352c1s v6p0475c1s v6p0689c2s
Harriman, Karl Edwin v6p0117c1s
Harriman, M.A. v5p0287c2s
Harriman, Mary A. v5p0288c1s
Harriman, N.H. v5p0445c2s
Harriman, R.E. v5p0598c1s
Harriman, W. v1p1386c2s v2p0037c2s v2p0067c2s v2p0097c2s v2p0241c1m v2p0466c1s v2p0479c1s
Harrington, A. v5p0020c1s
Harrington, B.J. v1p0760c1s v3p0009c2s v6p0019c1s v6p0075c2s v6p0091c2s v6p0415c1s
Harrington, C. v3p0082c1s v6p0231c2s
Harrington, C.S. v2p0030c1s v6p0527c2s
Harrington, Dr. v1p0275c1s v1p0776c1s
Harrington, Emily v6p0299c2s
Harrington, G.S. v6p0076c2s
Harrington, H.E. v1p1208c1s
Harrington, H.F. v1p0183c2s v1p0208c2s v1p0229c1s v1p0283c1s v1p0288c1s v1p0959c2s v1p1131c2s v1p1226c1s v1p1270c1s v1p1387c2s
Harrington, H.T. v2p0345c2s
Harrington, J. v1p0497c2s v6p0511c1s
Harrington, J., jr. v1p0884c2s
Harrington, J.W. v5p0275c1s v5p0406c2s v5p0424c2s v5p0449c2s
Harrington, James and Dwight, T.W. v3p0443c2s
Harrington, K.P. v4p0123c2s v5p0162c1s v6p0378c2s v6p0413c1s
Harrington, M. v1p0236c2s
Harrington, M.H. v5p0460c1s
Harrington, M.R. v5p0001c2s v6p0164c2s v6p0591c1s
Harrington, M.W. v1p1244c2s v2p0025c2m v2p0026c1m v2p0230c2s v2p0340c2s v2p0373c2s v2p0441c2s v4p0615c2m v5p0460c1s v5p0562c1s v6p0690c2s
Harrington, N.R. v5p0458c1s
Harrington, W.E. v4p0366c2s v5p0184c2s v5p0476c1s v6p0527c2s
Harris, A. v1p0360c1s v1p0423c1s v1p0948c1s v1p1001c1s v1p1083c2s v1p1157c1s v1p1216c2s v2p0023c2s v2p0124c2s v2p0220c2m v2p0225c2s v2p0226c2m v2p0481c1s v3p0022c1s v3p0171c2s v3p0214c2s v3p0215c1m v4p0544c2s v6p0443c2s v6p0523c2s
Harris, A., Sir v4p0415c1s
Harris, A.B. v1p0081c1s v1p0166c2s v1p0575c2s v1p0779c2s v1p0952c1s v1p0993c2s v1p1145c2s
Harris, A.I. v4p0149c1s
Harris, A.L. v3p0425c2s v4p0473c1s v5p0494c2s v5p0563c1s v6p0366c2s
Harris, A.W. v4p0195c1s
Harris, C. v1p1245c1s v2p0312c1s v5p0258c1s v6p0466c2s
Harris, C.A. v5p0031c2s v5p0148c1s
Harris, C.C. v1p0600c2s
Harris, C.P. v1p0211c2s
Harris, C.X. v2p0242c2s
Harris, D.F. v2p0221c1s
Harris, D.L. v1p0258c1s v1p0880c2s
Harris, D.M. v2p0044c1s v2p0235c1s
Harris, E. v1p0579c1s v1p0778c1s v1p1355c1s v5p0071c1s v5p0228c1s v6p0582c1s
Harris, E. and Simmons, L.M. v4p0171c1s
Harris, E.A. v1p0161c2s
Harris, E.D. v1p1363c1s v2p0289c2s v2p0379c2s v2p0422c2s v2p0436c1s v3p0196c1s v3p0436c2s v4p0158c2s v4p0545c1s v5p0347c1s
Harris, E.G. v4p0467c1s
Harris, E.L. v5p0123c1s v5p0160c1s v6p0141c1s
Harris, E.L. et al. v6p0039c1s
Harris, E.P. v4p0004c1s
Harris, Edna v5p0411c1s
Harris, F. v2p0078c1s v2p0226c1s v3p0085c1s v3p0284c1s v3p0286c2s v3p0390c1s v3p0436c2s v4p0174c1s v4p0461c1s v4p0552c1s v5p0289c1s v5p0524c1s
Harris, F.A. v1p1314c2s
Harris, F.B. v1p0678c1s v3p0254c1s v3p0283c1s v3p0467c2s v4p0298c2s
Harris, F.L. v2p0469c2s
Harris, F.R. v4p0006c1s
Harris, Frank v5p0219c2s v5p0220c1s
Harris, G. v1p0412c2s v1p0646c2s v1p0648c1s v1p0767c2s v1p0868c1s v1p1073c1s v1p1433c1s v2p0041c2s v2p0081c1s v2p0121c1s v2p0142c1m v2p0196c2s v2p0343c2s v3p0043c2s v3p0054c2s v3p0081c1s v3p0143c1s v3p0175c1s v3p0178c2s v3p0194c2s v3p0244c1s v3p0389c2s v3p0464c2s v5p0158c1s v5p0176c2s v5p0280c1s v6p0018c2s v6p0137c1s v6p0194c1s
Harris, G. and Hyde, W.DeW. v6p0135c2s
Harris, G. et al. v5p0576c2s
Harris, G.D. v4p0185c1s v4p0570c2s
Harris, G.D. and Dumble, D.T. v4p0219c1s
Harris, G.F. v1p0349c1s
Harris, G.H. v6p0107c2s
Harris, G.W. v3p0048c2s v3p0055c2s v3p0101c1m v3p0319c2s v5p0333c2s v6p0227c2s v6p0338c2s v6p0398c2s v6p0503c2s v6p0564c2s v6p0620c2s
Harris, H. v3p0092c1s
Harris, H.E. v6p0697c2s
Harris, H.F. v6p0176c1s v6p0176c2s
Harris, H.F. et al. v5p0163c2s
Harris, H.G. v3p0192c2s
Harris, H.J. v6p0114c2s
Harris, H.K. v5p0597c1s v6p0036c1s
Harris, H.M. v6p0485c1s
Harris, H.P. v4p0088c1s v5p0345c2s
Harris, H.P. and Beachcroft, R.M. v4p0338c2s
Harris, H.S.F. v5p0538c1s
Harris, H.S.T. v5p0162c2s
Harris, Hal v5p0017c1s
Harris, I. v3p0040c2s v4p0312c2s v4p0360c1s v5p0645c1s
Harris, I.G. and Johnston, A.S. v1p1347c1s
Harris, I.H., Mrs. v6p0564c1s
Harris, J. v1p0678c2s v1p1214c2s v3p0323c1s v3p0365c2s
Harris, J.A. v1p0259c1s v1p0335c2s v1p0531c1s v2p0038c2s v2p0042c2s v5p0141c2s v6p0094c1s v6p0255c1s v6p0440c1s v6p0608c2m
Harris, J.Arthur v6p0582c1s
Harris, J.C. v1p1339c1s v2p0026c2s v2p0033c1m v2p0167c1s v2p0361c2s v2p0432c1s v2p0447c1s v2p0451c1s v3p0012c2s v3p0027c1s v3p0029c2s v3p0030c2s v3p0097c1s v3p0254c1s v3p0311c1s v3p0402c1s v4p0040c2m v4p0050c2s v4p0065c2s v4p0124c1s v4p0126c2s v4p0210c2s v4p0267c2s v4p0321c2s v4p0511c1s v5p0116c1s v5p0158c2s v5p0210c2s v5p0274c2s v5p0379c1s v5p0496c2s v5p0500c1s v5p0507c2m v6p0025c1s
Harris, J.C. et al. v2p0309c1s
Harris, J.G. v1p1227c2s
Harris, J.H. v4p0321c2s v5p0121c2m v5p0182c2m v5p0249c2m v5p0326c1s v5p0561c2m v6p0055c1s v6p0175c1s v6p0207c1s
Harris, J.J. v6p0148c1s
Harris, J.M. v1p0186c2s v6p0027c2s
Harris, J.R. v2p0043c2s v2p0044c1s v2p0240c1s v2p0327c2s v2p0420c2s v3p0034c1s v3p0042c2m v3p0195c1s v3p0401c1s v4p0056c2m v4p0057c1s v4p0155c1s v4p0437c1s v4p0561c2s v4p0564c1s v5p0058c2m v5p0060c1m v5p0193c2s v5p0253c1s v5p0311c2s v5p0490c2s v5p0581c2s v5p0590c2s v5p0610c1s v6p0059c2s v6p0063c2s v6p0064c1m v6p0064c2s v6p0157c1s v6p0339c2s v6p0639c2s
Harris, J.Rendel v4p0564c1s v5p0240c2s
Harris, J.S. v4p0120c2s
Harris, J.T. v1p0884c2s v1p1140c2s
Harris, J.W. v6p0637c1s
Harris, K. v6p0041c1s v6p0239c1s
Harris, L. v5p0324c1s
Harris, L.H. v4p0390c2s
Harris, L.H., Mrs. v6p0014c1s v6p0220c2s v6p0222c2s v6p0223c1s v6p0288c2s v6p0397c2s v6p0434c2s v6p0454c1s v6p0459c2s v6p0461c2s v6p0465c2s v6p0564c1s v6p0584c1s v6p0605c1s v6p0606c2m v6p0684c1s v6p0703c1s
Harris, L.I. v6p0084c1s
Harris, L.M. v1p0826c2s v1p1407c2s
Harris, L.O. v4p0399c2s v6p0422c1s
Harris, Lord v2p0065c1s v2p0091c1s v2p0107c1m v5p0142c2s
Harris, M. v5p0129c1s v5p0162c2s v5p0632c2s v6p0176c1s v6p0201c1s v6p0311c1s v6p0407c1s v6p0551c2s v6p0581c1s v6p0697c2s
Harris, M.A. v5p0585c1s
Harris, M.B. v5p0333c2s
Harris, M.C. v1p0141c2s v4p0408c2s v4p0447c1s v4p0539c2s v5p0159c2s
Harris, M.D. v4p0503c2s v5p0024c2s v6p0704c1s
Harris, M.H. v4p0302c1s v4p0306c1s v4p0591c2s v6p0109c2s
Harris, M.K. v3p0345c2s v3p0394c2s
Harris, M.M. v6p0189c1s
Harris, Mamie B.S. v6p0410c1s
Harris, Mary Dormer v6p0426c2s
Harris, May v6p0645c2s
Harris, N.D. v6p0600c2s v6p0622c1s
Harris, N.H. v1p0557c2s
Harris, R. v1p0613c2s
Harris, R.A. v5p0222c1s v6p0445c2s v6p0459c2s v6p0625c2s v6p0646c1m
Harris, R.H. v6p0402c2s
Harris, R.O. v5p0467c1s
Harris, R.P. v4p0134c1s
Harris, S. v1p0002c2s v1p0239c2s v1p0240c2m v1p0243c2s v1p0347c1s v1p0447c2s v1p0496c1s v1p0563c2s v1p0641c2m v1p0686c2m v1p0712c2s v1p0714c1s v1p0773c1s v1p0840c1m v1p1064c2s v1p1161c2s v1p1176c2s v1p1180c1s v1p1302c2s v1p1422c1s v2p0437c2s v3p0010c2s v3p0041c2s v4p0169c2s
Harris, S.H. v6p0270c2s
Harris, T. v3p0360c1s
Harris, T.B. v4p0551c1s
Harris, T.R. v4p0284c1s
Harris, T.S. v5p0122c2s
Harris, T.W. v1p0006c2s v1p0030c2s v1p0696c1s v1p1000c2s v4p0214c1s v4p0332c2s v4p0552c2s
Harris, W. v1p0137c2s v1p0631c1s v1p1122c2s v1p1152c1s v6p0058c2s
Harris, W.B. .... v3p0287c1s v3p0390c2s v4p0002c1s •v4p0027c1m v4p0027c2s v4p0036c1s v4p0040c1s v4p0105c2s v4p0248c2s v4p0313c2m v4p0352c1s v4p0383c1m v4p0387c1s v4p0562c1s v4p0576c2s v4p0614c2s v4p0635c1s v4p0635c2s v5p0010c1s v5p0236c1s v5p0249c1s v5p0358c2s v5p0387c1m v5p0388c1s v6p0250c1s v6p0429c2m v6p0430c1m v6p0531c1s v6p0544c2s
Harris, W.C. v2p0157c1s v5p0208c1s v5p0210c2s v5p0591c2m

v6p0053c2s v6p0226c1s v6p0226c2s v6p0227c1m v6p0227c2m v6p0229c2s v6p0264c2s v6p0657c2s v6p0658c1m
Harris, W.H. v5p0102c2s
Harris, W.I. v3p0035c1s
Harris, W.J. v2p0225c2s v2p0356c2s v3p0006c2s v4p0466c2s v4p0615c1s
Harris, W.J. and Lake, K.A. v6p0271c2s
Harris, W.L. v1p0906c2s v6p0027c2s v6p0436c2s
Harris, W.N. v6p0358c2s
Harris, W.R. v1p0428c1s v1p1278c2s
Harris, W.S. v1p0400c2s v1p0749c1m
Harris, W.T. v1p0014c2s v1p0061c2s v1p0108c1s v1p0108c2s v1p0117c1s v1p0148c2s v1p0202c1s v1p0277c1s v1p0304c1s v1p0304c2s v1p0323c1s v1p0330c2s v1p0385c1m v1p0385c2s v1p0386c1s v1p0389c2m v1p0391c2m v1p0392c1m v1p0446c1s v1p0529c1s v1p0582c2m v1p0702c2s v1p0714c1s v1p0724c2s v1p0727c1s v1p0820c1s v1p0834c2m v1p0837c1s v1p0882c2s v1p0924c2s v1p0964c1s v1p0993c2s v1p1000c1s v1p1000c2m v1p1001c2m v1p1037c2s v1p1051c2s v1p1083c1s v1p1085c1s v1p1092c2s v1p1097c1s v1p1159c1s v1p1215c1s v1p1234c1s v1p1235c1s v1p1244c2s v1p1262c2s v1p1297c2s v1p1324c2s v1p1410c1s v1p1429c2s v2p0087c2s v2p0088c1s v2p0130c2m v2p0131c1s v2p0131c2s v2p0139c2s v2p0140c1s v2p0143c2s v2p0175c2s v2p0200c1s v2p0220c2s v2p0240c2s v2p0241c1s v2p0244c2s v2p0297c1s v2p0334c1s v2p0339c2s v2p0358c1s v2p0407c1s v2p0432c1s v3p0038c2s v3p0049c2s v3p0128c2s v3p0130c1s v3p0136c1s v3p0170c1s v3p0175c2s v3p0241c1m v3p0249c1s v3p0267c1s v3p0296c2s v3p0330c1s v3p0334c1s v3p0348c1m v3p0378c2m v3p0379c1s v3p0380c1s v3p0398c1s v3p0475c1s v4p0137c1s v4p0169c1m v4p0170c1s v4p0170c2s v4p0178c2s v4p0191c2s v4p0255c1m v4p0287c1m v4p0288c2s v4p0308c1s v4p0353c2s v4p0382c1s v4p0397c1s v4p0437c1s v4p0506c1s v4p0512c1s v4p0512c2s v4p0554c1s v5p0030c1s v5p0126c1s v5p0177c2s v5p0178c2s v5p0179c2m v5p0268c2s v5p0320c2s v5p0326c2s v5p0341c1s v5p0413c2s v5p0431c2s v5p0489c1s v5p0511c1s v5p0512c1s v5p0512c2s v5p0536c2s v5p0540c2s v5p0635c2s v6p0193c2s v6p0250c2s v6p0317c2s v6p0431c1m v6p0506c2s v6p0538c1s v6p0542c2s v6p0573c2s v6p0599c2s v6p0605c1s v6p0610c1s
Harris, W.T. and Cockerell, T.D.A. v5p0177c2s
Harris, W.T. and Talbot, E., Mrs. v3p0398c1s
Harris, W.T. et al. v2p0328c1s v4p0554c1s v4p0598c1s
Harris, Wm.T. v3p0358c1s
Harrison, A. v1p0517c1s v1p0750c1s v1p1144c1s v5p0201c1s v6p0065c1s v6p0257c1s v6p0607c2s v6p0612c2s
Harrison, A.A. v2p0267c1s v4p0182c2s
Harrison, A.B. v1p0311c2s
Harrison, A.F. v6p0059c1s v6p0429c2s v6p0600c2s
Harrison, A.J. v3p0081c1s v3p0088c1s v3p0162c2s
Harrison, A.S. v1p0007c1s v1p0238c1s
Harrison, A.T. v1p1426c2s
Harrison, B. v2p0025c1s v2p0146c2s v3p0234c1s v4p0102c1s v4p0524c2s v5p0150c1s v5p0218c2s v5p0331c2s v5p0363c1s v5p0504c1s v5p0598c2s
Harrison, B., Mrs. v3p0013c2s v4p0148c1s v4p0186c2s v4p0366c1s v4p0484c2s v4p0559c2s v4p0619c1s v5p0040c2s v5p0276c1s v5p0379c2s v5p0415c2s v5p0591c1s v5p0633c2s v5p0635c2s v6p0051c2s v6p0182c2s v6p0601c2s
Harrison, B. et al. v4p0270c1s
Harrison, B.E. v2p0113c1s
Harrison, B.F. v1p0621c2s v1p1081c1s
Harrison, B.H. v4p0177c2s
Harrison, B.L. v4p0074c1s v4p0440c2s
Harrison, Birge v3p0021c2s
Harrison, Burton, Mrs. ... v3p0111c2s v4p0210c1s v4p0402c2s v4p0413c2s v5p0239c2s v5p0262c1s v5p0634c2s
Harrison, C. v3p0184c2s v3p0243c2s v3p0350c2s v3p0355c2s v3p0425c1s v4p0006c1s v4p0245c2s v4p0340c2s
Harrison, C. and Fardell, T.G. v4p0338c2s
Harrison, C.C. v1p0439c2m v1p1142c2s v2p0077c2s v2p0108c2s v2p0130c1s v2p0208c2s v2p0453c2s v3p0061c2s v3p0102c2s v3p0325c2s v3p0455c2m v3p0461c1s v3p0464c2s v3p0469c2s v4p0040c2s v4p0221c1s v4p0380c1s v4p0494c2s v4p0571c2s v4p0624c1s v5p0314c2s
Harrison, C.C. and Hadley, A.T. v5p0127c1s
Harrison, C.H. v6p0534c1s
Harrison, Carter H. v6p0304c1s
Harrison, E.B. v4p0384c2s v4p0418c2s v4p0629c2s v5p0425c1s v6p0480c1s v6p0630c2s v6p0702c2s
Harrison, E.W. v1p1219c1s
Harrison, F. v1p0010c1s v1p0081c2s v1p0138c2s v1p0148c1s v1p0247c2s v1p0285c2m v1p0299c1s v1p0313c2s v1p0314c1s v1p0320c1s v1p0323c1s v1p0355c1s v1p0445c2s v1p0472c2s v1p0478c1s v1p0478c2s v1p0479c2s v1p0481c1s v1p0490c2s v1p0544c2s v1p0545c1m v1p0549c2s v1p0639c2s v1p0642c2s v1p0665c2s v1p0699c2s v1p0729c1s v1p0730c2s v1p0740c1s v1p0814c1s v1p0826c2s v1p0859c2s v1p0936c1s v1p0964c1s v1p0973c2s v1p0977c2s v1p0985c1s v1p1002c1s v1p1025c2s v1p1037c2m v1p1040c2s v1p1053c2s v1p1160c2s v1p1221c2s v1p1227c2s v1p1263c1s v1p1319c2s v1p1320c1s v1p1331c2s v1p1430c2s v2p0005c1s v2p0068c2s v2p0097c2s v2p0135c2s v2p0164c2s v2p0170c2s v2p0174c2s v2p0175c1s v2p0187c1s v2p0189c2s v2p0245c1s v2p0263c2s v2p0267c1s v2p0285c1s v2p0305c1m v2p0315c1s v2p0350c1s v2p0368c2s v2p0369c1s v2p0445c2s v3p0006c1s v3p0035c2s v3p0054c1s v3p0059c1m v3p0068c2s v3p0081c1s v3p0130c1s v3p0134c2m v3p0139c1s v3p0144c1s v3p0146c1m v3p0158c1s v3p0160c2s v3p0161c1m v3p0204c1s v3p0220c1s v3p0220c2s v3p0221c1s v3p0248c1s v3p0256c1m v3p0260c2s v3p0274c1s v3p0317c2s v3p0320c2s v3p0322c1s v3p0332c1s v3p0338c1s v3p0340c1s v3p0367c1s v3p0367c2s v3p0371c2s v3p0412c2s v3p0428c2s v3p0434c2s v3p0439c2s v3p0441c2s v3p0469c1s v3p0471c1s v4p0028c1s v4p0029c1s v4p0074c1s v4p0090c1s v4p0130c2m v4p0155c1s v4p0157c1s v4p0160c2s v4p0177c2s v4p0184c2s v4p0189c2s v4p0199c2s v4p0225c2s v4p0259c1s v4p0261c2s v4p0270c2s v4p0311c2s v4p0338c1s v4p0339c1s v4p0346c2s v4p0351c1s v4p0351c2s v4p0371c1s v4p0387c2s v4p0388c1s v4p0394c1s v4p0425c1s v4p0448c2s v4p0454c1m v4p0483c2s v4p0489c2s v4p0490c2s v4p0494c2s v4p0561c1s v4p0571c1s v4p0584c2s v4p0615c2s v4p0627c2s v5p0014c2s v5p0026c1s v5p0115c1s v5p0144c2s v5p0145c1s v5p0186c1s v5p0210c1s v5p0220c1s v5p0222c2s v5p0233c1s v5p0264c1s v5p0314c1s v5p0323c2s v5p0345c2s v5p0352c2s v5p0457c2s v5p0461c1s v5p0558c1s v5p0602c1s v6p0018c1s v6p0107c1s v6p0134c2s v6p0206c2s v6p0243c1s v6p0245c2s v6p0255c2s v6p0456c2s v6p0555c1s v6p0616c2s v6p0639c1s v6p0643c1s v6p0644c2s v6p0656c2s
Harrison, F. et al. v4p0289c2s
Harrison, F., Mrs. v4p0148c2s v4p0631c2s v6p0178c2s v6p0206c2s v6p0264c1s v6p0584c2s v6p0703c1m
Harrison, F.B. v2p0145c2s v2p0226c1s v3p0072c1s v3p0425c1s v4p0022c2s v4p0200c2s v5p0515c2s v6p0332c2s
Harrison, F.Bayford v5p0310c1s
Harrison, F.C. v3p0369c1s v4p0230c2s v4p0279c1s v4p0280c2m v4p0494c2s v4p0525c1s
Harrison, Frederic v4p0495c1s
Harrison, G. v1p0727c1s
Harrison, G.B. v4p0629c1s
Harrison, G.F. v2p0275c1s
Harrison, G.F.E. v5p0538c1s
Harrison, G.H. et al. v2p0328c1s
Harrison, H. v2p0148c2s v2p0343c2s v3p0114c1s v4p0151c1s
Harrison, H.L. v1p0442c1s v3p0211c2s
Harrison, Hall v3p0194c1s
Harrison, J. v1p0145c2s v1p0146c1s v1p0269c1s v1p0759c2s v3p0439c2s v5p0392c1s
Harrison, J., jr. v1p0978c2s
Harrison, J.A. v1p0103c1s v1p0113c2s v1p0182c2s v1p0225c2s v1p0583c1s v1p0680c1s v1p0886c1s v1p1126c1s v1p1155c1s v1p1169c2s v1p1274c1s v1p1284c1s v1p1371c1s v2p0006c2s v2p0040c1s v2p0092c2s v2p0094c1s v2p0107c1s v2p0343c1s v2p0359c1s v2p0377c2s v2p0385c2s v2p0400c1s v2p0458c2s v3p0103c1s v3p0138c2s v3p0224c2m v3p0258c1s v3p0259c1s v3p0317c2s v3p0331c1s v3p0366c2s v3p0390c1s v3p0429c1s v4p0376c2s v5p0002c1s v5p0210c2s v5p0216c2s v5p0221c2s v5p0275c1s v5p0322c2s v5p0382c1s v5p0455c2s v5p0465c1s v5p0521c1s v5p0632c1s v6p0332c1s v6p0441c1s v6p0505c1s
Harrison, J.A. and Brainerd, E. v2p0033c1s
Harrison, J.B. v1p0830c1s v1p0944c2s v1p1400c2s v2p0314c1s v3p0149c1s v3p0213c1s v3p0213c2s v4p0207c2s v4p0209c1m
Harrison, J.C. v2p0088c1s v2p0406c1s v5p0287c1s v5p0529c2s
Harrison, J.E. v2p0392c2s v3p0017c2s v3p0199c2s v3p0233c1s v3p0428c1s v3p0447c2s v4p0002c2s v4p0029c2s v4p0030c2s v4p0093c2s v4p0152c1s v4p0185c2s v4p0197c2s v4p0242c2s v4p0253c2s v4p0404c2s v4p0425c1s v4p0435c2s v4p0510c2s v4p0528c1s v6p0219c1s
Harrison, J.J. v5p0006c1s
Harrison, J.L. v4p0330c1s v5p0016c1s v5p0334c2s v5p0336c2s v6p0370c2m
Harrison, J.O. v2p0088c1s
Harrison, J.P. v1p0374c2s v1p0378c2s v1p0590c1m v2p0260c2s v2p0386c1s v2p0401c1s
Harrison, J.W. v1p0883c1s
Harrison, J.W.D. v2p0363c2s
Harrison, Ja.A. v5p0237c1s
Harrison, Jane E. v5p0429c1s
Harrison, L. v3p0031c1s v3p0132c1s
Harrison, L. et al. v3p0097c1s
Harrison, M. v2p0112c1s v2p0139c2s v2p0194c1s v2p0365c1s v2p0441c2s v2p0442c1s v2p0443c2s v2p0461c1s v2p0471c1s v3p0073c2s v3p0077c1s v3p0135c1s v3p0162c1m v3p0191c1s v3p0192c1s v3p0229c1s v3p0232c1s v3p0256c2s v3p0257c2m v3p0324c1s v3p0325c2s v3p0455c1s v4p0132c1s v4p0185c2s v4p0300c2s v4p0620c2s
Harrison, M.M. v4p0196c1s
Harrison, N. v6p0358c1s
Harrison, Norvell v6p0572c1s
Harrison, Prof. v1p0554c2s
Harrison, R. v1p0108c2s v1p0495c2s v1p0628c2s v1p0743c2s v1p1367c2s v2p0105c1s v2p0143c2s v2p0315c2s v2p0354c1s v4p0610c2s v5p0438c2s v5p0466c2s v6p0268c1s v6p0310c1s
Harrison, R.C. v3p0207c1s
Harrison, S.F. v3p0003c2s v3p0210c1s v3p0259c1s v4p0215c2s v5p0534c2s v6p0145c2s v6p0655c2s
Harrison, T. v4p0316c2s
Harrison, T.B. v4p0121c1s
Harrison, T.S. v5p0181c2s
Harrison, Theodosia v5p0530c2s
Harrison, V.B. v3p0310c1s
Harrison, W. v1p0288c2s v2p0243c1s v4p0120c1s v4p0362c2s v4p0633c1s v5p0346c2s v5p0604c2s v6p0008c1s v6p0141c2s v6p0292c2s
Harrison, W., Mrs. and Malet, Lucas v3p0326c2s
Harrison, W.G. v1p0918c2s
Harrison, W.H. v1p0143c1s v1p0583c2s v1p1038c1s v4p0295c2s
Harrison, W.J. v2p0117c2s v2p0173c2m v2p0174c1s v2p0249c2s v2p0275c1s v2p0364c2s v2p0390c2s v3p0402c2s
Harrisse, H. v1p0475c1s v1p0654c2s v1p1280c1s v5p0086c2m
Harrity, W.F. v4p0595c2s
Harrod, H. v1p0207c2s v1p0605c2s v1p1402c1s v1p1434c2s
Harrod, H.D. v2p0126c1s v2p0206c1s v2p0264c1s v2p0348c2s v5p0104c2s
Harrold, J.B. v5p0337c2s v6p0556c2s
Harrold, P.J. v2p0255c1s
Harroun, G.K. v5p0148c1s
Harrow, G. v6p0083c2s
Harrower, C.S. v3p0101c1s
Harrower, G.H. v3p0357c1s
Harrower, H.D. v2p0299c2s
Harrower, Prof. v4p0134c1s

Harry, J.E. v4p0026c2s
Harry, J.W. v6p0404c2s
Harry, P. v6p0217c1s
Harsha, W.J. v2p0112c2s
v2p0219c1m v2p0219c2s v3p0214c1s
Harsha, W.W. v3p0281c2s
Harshaw, W.R. v5p0336c1s
Harshberger, J. v4p0202c2s
Harshberger, J.W. v4p0060c1s
v4p0069c2s v4p0134c1s v4p0281c1s
v4p0445c1s v4p0445c2s v4p0467c1s
v5p0099c2s v5p0151c2s v5p0197c2s
v5p0226c1s v5p0400c1s v5p0459c2s
v6p0077c2s v6p0229c1s v6p0570c1s
Harson, M.J. v6p0085c2s
Hart, A.B. v2p0197c1s
v3p0025c2s v3p0065c2s v3p0076c1s
v3p0085c2s v3p0086c1s v3p0086c2s
v3p0197c2s v3p0198c2s v3p0202c1s
v3p0241c2s v3p0356c2s v3p0362c1s
v3p0391c1s v3p0401c2s v3p0433c2s
v4p0014c1s v4p0014c2m v4p0035c2s
v4p0063c2s v4p0095c1s v4p0122c2s
v4p0158c2s v4p0211c1s v4p0234c1s
v4p0241c1s v4p0259c1s v4p0380c2s
v4p0382c1s v4p0385c2s v4p0406c2s
v4p0450c2s v4p0476c2s v4p0502c1s
v4p0555c1s v4p0560c2s v4p0566c1s
v4p0580c1s v4p0584c1s v4p0595c2s
v4p0598c1s v5p0148c1s v5p0209c2s
v5p0256c2s v5p0257c1m v5p0266c1m
v5p0380c2s v5p0384c1s v5p0521c2s
v5p0574c1s v5p0599c2s v5p0601c2s
v5p0603c1s v6p0294c2s v6p0447c1s
v6p0448c2s v6p0605c2s
Hart, A.B. et al. v5p0179c2s
Hart, A.M. v4p0298c1s
Hart, A.N. v1p0872c2s
Hart, A.W. v2p0236c2s
v2p0353c2s v2p0379c1s v2p0389c1s
v2p0424c2s
Hart, B. v1p0035c1s
v1p0458c1s v1p0538c1s v1p0853c1s
v1p0928c1s v1p0928c2m v2p0003c1s
v2p0034c2s v3p0061c1s v3p0401c2s
v5p0189c2s
Hart, Burdett v2p0038c2s
Hart, C.F. v1p0949c1s
Hart, C.H. v1p0566c1s
v1p0731c1s v1p0873c1s v1p0924c1s
v1p1047c2s v1p1406c1s v2p0019c2s
v2p0102c1s v2p0466c2s v3p0162c1s
v3p0456c1s v4p0456c1s v4p0611c2m
v4p0612c1s v5p0079c1s v5p0219c1s
v5p0264c1s v5p0304c1s v5p0310c2m
v5p0337c2m v5p0529c1s v5p0557c2s
v6p0167c2s v6p0239c2m v6p0419c1s
v6p0622c1m v6p0658c2s v6p0705c1s
v6p0712c1s
Hart, D. v3p0341c2s
v4p0091c1s
Hart, D.A. v4p0096c1s
v5p0420c1s v5p0463c1s
Hart, D.M. v4p0349c1s
Hart, E. v1p0606c1s
v1p0641c2s v1p0944c1s v1p0981c1s
v2p0199c1s v2p0226c1s v2p0287c1s
v3p0192c2s v4p0107c2m v4p0108c1m
v4p0271c2m v4p0296c2s v4p0297c2s
v4p0298c1s v4p0396c1s v4p0455c1m
v4p0468c2s v4p0540c1s v4p0606c2s
Hart, E., Mrs. v3p0102c1s
v4p0297c1s v6p0531c1s
Hart, E.A. v1p0235c1s
Hart, E.J. v2p0398c2s
v4p0425c2s
Hart, E.L.de v4p0521c1s
Hart, E.L.De v4p0192c2s
v5p0135c1s
Hart, E.M. v6p0472c1s
Hart, E.S. v2p0375c1s
Hart, F. v4p0363c1s
v5p0139c1s v5p0472c1s
Hart, F.J. v6p0177c2s
Hart, F.S. and Hunking, A.W.
v2p0470c1s
Hart, G.A. v1p1078c2s
Hart, G.G. v3p0356c1s
Hart, H.A. v1p0286c1s
Hart, H.H. v3p0105c2s
v4p0275c1s v5p0106c1s
Hart, H.M. v2p0132c1s
v6p0227c2s
Hart, I.W. v5p0324c1s
Hart, J., sr. v4p0109c1s
Hart, J.A. v5p0060c1s
Hart, J.C. v1p0289c2s
v1p0291c1m v1p1140c1s
Hart, J.E. v1p0664c1s
Hart, J.G. v6p0207c1s
Hart, J.H. v5p0356c1s
v6p0301c1s v6p0535c2s
Hart, J.H.A. v6p0058c1s
v6p0495c2s v6p0579c1s v6p0656c1s
Hart, J.M. v1p0114c2m
v1p0183c1s v1p0219c2s v1p0276c2s
v1p0303c2s v1p0386c1s v1p0391c2s
v1p0436c2s v1p0477c1s v1p0513c2s
v1p0518c1s v1p0531c1s v1p0531c2s
v1p0920c1s v1p0996c2s v1p0997c1m
v1p1026c1s v1p1127c1s v1p1184c2s
v1p1267c1s v1p1370c2m v2p0063c1s
v2p0072c2s v2p0143c2s v3p0022c2s
v3p0101c1s v3p0336c1s v3p0360c1s
v4p0184c1m v4p0184c2m v4p0243c1s
v6p0135c1s v6p0259c2s v6p0587c2s
Hart, J.N.De v2p0300c1s
Hart, J.S. v1p0040c1s
v1p0074c2s v1p0118c1s v1p0127c2s
v1p0285c1s v1p0415c2s v1p0416c1s
v1p0796c2s v1p0911c2s v1p1063c1s
v1p1159c1s v1p1186c1s v1p1187c2s
v1p1288c1s
Hart, J.W.T. v6p0581c2s
Hart, Jos.H. v6p0209c1s
Hart, K. v3p0388c2s
Hart, L. v1p0110c2s
v1p0264c2s v1p0291c1s v1p0938c2s
v1p1096c1s v1p1200c1s v5p0102c2s
v5p0393c1s
Hart, L.W. v5p0350c1s
Hart, Lavinia v5p0082c1s
v5p0276c2s v5p0340c1s v5p0404c2s
v5p0547c2s v5p0630c2s v5p0638c2s
v6p0155c1s v6p0176c2s v6p0388c1s
v6p0397c1s v6p0648c1s v6p0703c2s
Hart, M. v5p0276c2s
Hart, Mabel v5p0100c2s
Hart, P. v5p0186c2s
v5p0316c2s v5p0438c1s v5p0490c2s
Hart, P.W. v5p0374c1s
v5p0469c2s v5p0555c2m v5p0564c2s
v5p0596c2s v5p0644c2s v6p0001c2s
v6p0091c1s v6p0636c1s
Hart, Phoebe v5p0383c2s
v5p0518c1s
Hart, R. v3p0116c2s
v5p0111c2s
Hart, R., Sir v5p0108c2m
v5p0110c1s
v5p0438c2m
Hart, R.E.S. v4p0637c1s
v5p0331c2s v5p0612c1s
Hart, R.W. v5p0512c2s
Hart, Robert, Sir v5p0109c1s
Hart, Rollin L. v6p0450c2s
Hart, S. v1p0580c2s
v1p0603c2s v1p0700c2s v1p0992c1s
v2p0406c2s v2p0420c1s v3p0192c1s
v3p0207c1s v3p0436c1s v6p0052c1s
Hart, S.C. v4p0102c2s
v6p0207c1s
Hart, S.K. v4p0149c2s
Hart, Sophie v4p0089c1s
v5p0312c1s
Hart, T.A.A. v6p0062c1s
Hart, T.N. v5p0072c2s
Hart, T.N. et al. v3p0085c2s
Hart, T.S. and Gooch, F.A.
v3p0340c2s
Hart, W. v4p0374c1s
Hart, W.E. v4p0283c1s
v4p0316c1s v4p0317c1s v4p0382c1s
v4p0471c1s v4p0607c2s
v4p0614c2s
Hart, W.G. v5p0592c1s
v6p0658c2s
Hart, W.H. v1p0786c2s
Hart, W.M. v6p0283c2s
Hart, W.W.De v5p0209c1s
Hart-Davies, T. v6p0045c1s
v6p0351c1s
Hart-Davis, H.V. v5p0344c2s
Harte, B. v1p0288c1s
v4p0154c2s v4p0635c1s v5p0195c1s
v5p0301c1s v5p0325c2s v5p0482c2s
v5p0556c1s v5p0619c2s
Harte, Bret v1p0013c2s
v1p0277c2s v1p0287c2s v1p0311c1s
v1p0362c1s v1p0422c2s v1p0465c2s
v1p0466c2s v1p0490c2s v1p0496c1s
v1p0505c2s v1p0514c2s v1p0542c2s
v1p0550c2s v1p0580c2s v1p0583c2s
v1p0602c1s v1p0609c2s v1p0623c2s
v1p0624c1s v1p0627c2s v1p0735c1s
v1p0776c1s v1p0776c2s v1p0786c2s
v1p0837c2s v1p0863c2s v1p0877c1s
v1p0878c2s v1p0952c1s v1p0956c1s
v1p0986c2s v1p0994c2s v1p1035c2s
v1p1051c1s v1p1123c1s v1p1294c2s
v1p1317c2s v1p1328c2m v1p1339c1s
v1p1383c2s v2p0017c1s v2p0163c2s
v2p0215c2s v2p0252c2s v2p0265c2s
v2p0400c2s v3p0104c2s v3p0122c2s
v3p0153c2s v3p0260c1s v4p0130c1s
v4p0284c2s v4p0304c1s v4p0477c1s
v4p0500c1s v4p0520c2s v5p0004c2s
v5p0024c1s v5p0063c2s v5p0239c2s
v5p0262c2s v5p0340c1s v5p0370c2s
v5p0434c2s v5p0555c1s v5p0590c1s
v6p0285c2s v6p0389c2s v6p0472c1s
v6p0519c2s v6p0638c2s
Harte, C. v1p0943c1s
Harte, F.B. v1p0169c2s
v1p0245c2s v2p0050c1s v3p0375c2s
v4p0253c2s v5p0127c2s
Harte, F.Bret v4p0636c1s
Harte, W. v3p0065c1s
Harte, W.B. v3p0003c1s
v3p0065c1m v3p0065c2m v3p0066c1s
v3p0315c1s v4p0068c2s v4p0160c2s
v4p0225c2s v4p0292c2s v4p0303c2s
v4p0335c1s v4p0553c1s v4p0620c2s
v5p0520c1s
Harter, Eugene W. v6p0041c1s
v6p0657c2s
Harter, M.D. v3p0032c2s
v4p0044c1s v4p0378c1s
v4p0378c2s v4p0449c2s
v4p0524c2s
Harter, M.D. et al. v4p0524c2s
v4p0526c1s
Harter, N. and Bryan, W.L.
v5p0570c2m
Hartes, J.O. v5p0555c2s
Hartier, M. v4p0190c1s
Hartier, Mary v4p0276c2s
v4p0604c2m v5p0308c2s v5p0364c2s
v5p0626c1s
Hartier, O. v4p0637c1s
Harting, H. v4p0069c1s
Harting, J.E. v1p0340c2s
v1p1419c1s v4p0060c2s v4p0194c1s
v5p0517c1s
Harting, J.E. and Newton, A.
v4p0037c1s
Harting, J.E. et al. v4p0030c2s
Hartland, E. v5p0359c1s
Hartland, E.S. v3p0157c1s
v3p0325c1s v4p0143c1s v4p0205c2m
v4p0206c1m v4p0229c1s v4p0356c2s
v4p0357c1s v4p0433c1s v4p0443c2s
v4p0470c2s v4p0527c1m v4p0583c1s
v5p0007c1m v5p0039c1s v5p0053c1s
v5p0099c1s v5p0244c2s v5p0291c2s
v5p0583c1s v6p0180c1s v6p0402c2s
v6p0537c1s v6p0664c1s
Hartland, F.S. v6p0618c2s
Hartland, J.C. v6p0334c2s
Hartland, M.E. v5p0391c1s
Hartley, A. v5p0448c2s
v5p0531c2s
Hartley, B., Mrs. v1p0561c1s
Hartley, C.A. v1p0332c1s
v2p0221c2s
v2p0308c1s
Hartley, C.A., Sir v1p0332c1s
Hartley, C.G. v5p0638c2s
v6p0263c1s
Hartley, E.L. v6p0665c1s
Hartley, G. v1p1190c1m
Hartley, G.W. v3p0373c1s
v3p0374c1s v3p0381c1s v3p0391c1s
v4p0151c1s v4p0198c2s v4p0528c1s
v5p0225c1s v5p0261c1s v5p0466c2s
v6p0223c2s v6p0232c2s
v6p0566c1m
Hartley, I.S. v1p0688c1s
v2p0396c2s v3p0097c1s v3p0347c2s
v3p0404c2s
Hartley, J.W. v3p0190c1s
Hartley, M. v6p0164c2s
Hartley, N. v5p0054c2s
Hartley, N.N. v4p0411c2s
Hartley, N.W. v4p0540c2s
Hartley, R. v5p0260c1s
Hartley, S. v2p0196c1s
Hartley, W.N. v1p0017c1m
v1p0619c1s v1p0621c2m v1p0844c2s
v1p1366c1s v2p0076c1s v2p0373c2s
v3p0118c2s v3p0151c1s v3p0316c2s
v3p0395c1s v3p0415c2s
Hartlib, S. v1p0014c2s
Hartman, C.S. v4p0521c2s
Hartman, C.V. v4p0385c1s
Hartman, C.Z. v6p0274c2s
Hartman, E.T. v6p0651c1s
Hartman, F. v1p0619c2s
Hartman, J. v4p0063c2s
Hartman, J.E. v5p0263c1s
v6p0341c1s
Hartman, J.M. v2p0169c2s
v3p0107c1s v4p0217c2s
Hartman, John M. v3p0047c1s
Hartman, L. v6p0440c1s
Hartmann, C. v4p0578c1s
Hartmann, C.S. v2p0123c1s
v3p0224c2s
v3p0376c2s
Hartmann, E.von v1p0333c2s
v1p1001c2s
Hartmann, J.E. v6p0288c1s
Hartmann, M. v6p0342c2s
Hartmann, R. v2p0017c1s
Hartmann, S. v5p0633c2s
v6p0496c2s v6p0497c1s v6p0566c2s
v6p0579c2s v6p0581c1s
Hartmann, Sadakichi v6p0280c1s
Hartmann, W. v6p0572c1s
Hartnell, E.S. v6p0426c2s
Hartness, E. v1p0714c1s
v1p0993c2s
Hartog, C. v4p0174c1s
v4p0449c1s v4p0463c1s
Hartog, M. v4p0481c2s
v5p0369c2s v5p0416c1s
Hartog, M. and Romanes, G.J.
v4p0514c1s
Hartog, M.M. v2p0257c1s
Hartog, P.J. v3p0327c1s

v5p0447c1s v6p0040c1s v6p0623c1s
Harton, Robert v4p0481c2s
Harton, Robert, Sir v4p0012c2m
Hartoz, M. v6p0106c1s
Hartpence, W.R. v3p0042c2s v4p0056c2s
Hartranft, C.D. v4p0534c2s v6p0065c2s v6p0080c1s
Hartranft, J.F. v2p0389c1s
Hartridge, C.W. v6p0618c1s
Harts, W.W. v6p0234c1s v6p0493c2s
Harts, W.W. and Haan, W.G. v6p0568c2s
Hartsell, J.C. v4p0170c1s
Hartshorne, A. v4p0172c1s v4p0292c1s v6p0110c2s v6p0170c2s v6p0511c2s v6p0524c1s
Hartshorne, A.C. v6p0009c1s v6p0234c1s v6p0336c2s v6p0349c1s v6p0355c1s v6p0648c2s
Hartshorne, B.F. v1p0173c2s v1p0214c1m
Hartshorne, C.H. v1p0845c1s v1p0947c2s v1p1115c1s v6p0209c1s
Hartshorne, H. v1p0323c1s v1p0484c2s v1p1233c2s v1p1371c1s v2p0001c2s v2p0283c1s v2p0340c2s v2p0424c1s v2p0457c1s v3p0336c1s
Hartshorne, R. v4p0136c1s
Hartswick, J.B. v5p0239c2s
Hartt, Amry B. v6p0055c2s
Hartt, C.F. v1p0026c2m v1p0135c1s v1p0158c1m v1p0158c2m v1p0508c1s v1p0508c2s v1p0638c2s v1p0644c2s v1p0799c1s v1p1039c1s v1p1359c1s
Hartt, H.A. v3p0123c1s v4p0009c2m v4p0542c1s
Hartt, I.W. v4p0016c1s
Hartt, J.K. v6p0413c1s
Hartt, L.L. v1p0327c2s
Hartt, M.B. v5p0081c2s v5p0309c1s v5p0410c1s v6p0277c1s
Hartt, Mary B. v5p0082c1s v6p0581c1s
Hartt, R.L. v5p0013c2s v5p0082c1s v5p0120c1s v5p0190c2s v5p0274c2s v5p0295c1s v5p0351c1s v5p0384c2s v5p0387c1s v5p0405c1s v5p0405c2m v5p0410c1m v5p0418c2s v6p0004c2s v6p0379c2s v6p0395c2s
Hartt, Rollin L. v6p0076c2s
Hartwell, C. v1p1081c1s
Hartwell, C.S. v6p0190c2s v6p0401c2s
Hartwell, E.M. v2p0013c1s v4p0020c1s v5p0119c2s
Hartwell, E.M. and Hall, G.S. v2p0045c2s
Hartwell, E.S. v6p0120c2s
Hartwell, E.W. v6p0423c1s
Hartwell, J.B. and Browning, P.E. v5p0411c1s
Hartwell, M.A. v5p0236c2s v6p0478c1s
Hartwell, R.W. v5p0585c1s
Hartwell, S.O. v5p0265c1s
Hartwick, C. v2p0361c2s
Hartwig, G. v4p0474c1s
Hartwig, O. v4p0354c2s
Hartwig, P. v4p0254c2s
Hartzel, J.S. v2p0339c1s
Hartzell, J.C. v1p0905c2s
Hartzell, J.C., jr. v4p0222c2s
Hartzell, J.H. v1p0420c1s v1p0505c1s
Hartzenbusch, J.E. v1p0155c1s
Harven, W.N. v4p0216c1s
Harvey, A. v1p0004c1s v1p0192c2s v1p0213c1s v1p0790c2s v1p0910c2m v1p1324c1s v1p1435c2s v2p0074c1s v2p0305c2s v2p0383c1s v2p0427c1s v4p0125c2s v4p0130c2s v4p0313c2s v4p0441c1s v4p0508c1s v4p0630c2s
Harvey, A.S. v1p0268c1s v1p0981c1s v1p1327c2s v5p0150c1s
Harvey, Alex. v5p0180c2s
Harvey, C. v2p0276c2s v2p0327c1s v5p0505c2s v5p0552c1s v6p0422c2s
Harvey, C.A. v3p0112c1s
Harvey, C.H. v6p0032c1s
Harvey, C.M. v4p0129c1s v5p0349c1s v5p0380c2s v5p0418c2s v5p0486c1s v6p0260c1s v6p0316c2s v6p0317c1s v6p0387c2s v6p0464c2s v6p0499c2m v6p0534c2s v6p0540c1s v6p0551c1s v6p0607c1s v6p0690c1s
Harvey, C.N. v6p0476c1s
Harvey, C.T. v3p0277c2s v3p0305c1s
Harvey, C.W. v6p0190c1s v6p0398c2s v6p0537c2s
Harvey, Charles M. v6p0315c1s
Harvey, E.B. v2p0103c1s
Harvey, E.E. v6p0054c2s
Harvey, E.L. v1p1114c1s
Harvey, F. v6p0253c2s
Harvey, F. and Edgcumbe, R. v2p0063c1s
Harvey, F.H. v6p0428c2s
Harvey, F.L. v4p0526c2s
Harvey, G. v1p0143c1s v1p1353c1s v6p0265c1s v6p0666c1s
Harvey, G.M. v6p0515c1s
Harvey, G.U. v6p0445c1s
Harvey, G.Upton v6p0039c2s
Harvey, H. v2p0034c2s
Harvey, H.E. v4p0625c2s v5p0513c1s v5p0638c1s
Harvey, J. v4p0328c2s v5p0409c1s v5p0517c1s
Harvey, J.C. v4p0043c2s v4p0075c1s v4p0372c2s v4p0423c1s v4p0447c1s
Harvey, J.L. v5p0204c1s
Harvey, L. v3p0018c1s v3p0447c2s
Harvey, L.C. v4p0027c2s v4p0247c1s
Harvey, M. v5p0408c2s
Harvey, Mrs. v5p0430c1s
Harvey, O.J. v2p0279c1s
Harvey, R.S. v3p0310c1s
Harvey, Seth v5p0028c1s
Harvey, W. v4p0287c1m
Harvey, W.F. v6p0125c1s v6p0404c1s
Harvey, W.H. v4p0378c1s v4p0524c2s v5p0424c2s
Harvie, E.F. v6p0006c2s v6p0220c1s
Harward, L. v6p0260c2s v6p0411c1s
Harwood, A.A. v1p0442c2s
Harwood, C. v6p0088c2s v6p0174c1s v6p0455c2s v6p0533c2s
Harwood, Charlotte v6p0124c1s
Harwood, E. v1p0048c1s v1p0527c1s v1p0799c2s v1p0994c1s v1p1120c1s v1p1121c2s v1p1253c1s v1p1311c1s
Harwood, Edith v5p0073c2s
Harwood, F. v4p0052c1s v6p0245c2s
Harwood, Henry and Angell, F. v5p0369c2s
Harwood, J. v1p0023c1s v1p0338c2s v1p0352c2s v1p0500c2s v1p1173c2s v1p1174c1s v1p1403c1s
Harwood, J.B. v1p0469c2s v1p0583c2s v1p0716c2s v1p1438c2s v2p0321c2s
Harwood, J.G. v1p0542c1s v1p1176c1s
Harwood, M. v5p0222c2s
Harwood, M.S. v6p0088c1s
Harwood, P.L. v6p0571c2s
Harwood, W.H. v5p0123c2s v6p0371c1s
Harwood, W.S. v4p0031c1s v4p0195c1s v4p0365c1s v4p0440c1s v4p0528c2s v4p0629c2s v5p0065c1s v5p0090c2s v5p0103c2s v5p0136c1s v5p0378c1s v5p0378c2s v5p0388c2s v5p0420c1s v5p0443c2s v5p0491c1s v5p0518c2s v5p0532c2s v5p0570c2s v5p0627c2s v5p0644c2s v6p0008c2s v6p0009c1s v6p0088c1s v6p0092c2s v6p0096c1s v6p0097c1s v6p0120c1s v6p0149c2s v6p0220c1s v6p0226c2s v6p0321c1s v6p0337c2s v6p0367c2s v6p0401c1s v6p0451c2s v6p0474c1s v6p0502c2s v6p0594c2s v6p0671c1s
Harwood, W.S. and Crissey, F. v5p0223c2s
Hasbach, W. v3p0127c2s v5p0533c1s
Hasbrouck, E.M. v4p0093c2s v4p0364c1s
Hasbrouck, J.L. v4p0372c1s
Hasbrouck, M. v4p0299c2s
Hascall, J. v1p0646c1s
Haselfoot, F.W. v5p0233c2s
Hasell, E.J. v1p0170c2s v1p0186c1s v1p0429c2s v1p0530c2s v2p0064c1s v3p0312c1s
Hasenclever, R. v1p0947c1s v1p1266c2s
Hashiguchi, J. v6p0336c1s v6p0336c2s
Hashiguchi, Jihei v6p0335c2s
Haskell, B.G. v6p0350c1s
Haskell, E.B. v6p0661c1s
Haskell, E.M. v4p0103c2s
Haskell, E.M. and Bolton, T.L. v5p0034c2s v5p0319c1s
Haskell, F.W. v6p0528c1s
Haskell, H.J. v6p0016c2s v6p0292c2s v6p0378c1s v6p0441c1s v6p0495c2s v6p0626c2s
Haskell, M.A. v5p0402c2s v5p0583c1s
Haskell, Mabel P. v4p0234c1s v6p0321c1s
Haskell, Mary E. v6p0215c1s
Haskell, R.B. v3p0210c2s
Haskell, R.C. v1p0812c2s
Haskell, W.G. v4p0309c1s
Haskin, W.L. v5p0032c1s
Haskins, C.C. v2p0460c1s
Haskins, C.D. v5p0248c2s v6p0197c2s v6p0199c1s
Haskins, C.H. v4p0214c1s v4p0584c1s v4p0601c1s v5p0266c2s v5p0368c1s v5p0609c1s v6p0320c1m v6p0348c1s v6p0478c2s v6p0480c1s v6p0675c1s
Haskins, D.G. v1p0351c1s v2p0140c1s v5p0154c1s
Haskins, E.F. v6p0038c2s v6p0108c1s v6p0184c2s v6p0598c1s v6p0698c1s
Haskins, J.R. v1p0512c1s v1p0889c2s
Haskins, R.W. v1p0612c2s v1p0718c2s v1p0927c2s v1p1014c1s v1p1359c1s
Haskins, T.H. v4p0202c2s v4p0207c2s v4p0208c2s
Haskins, T.W. v2p0083c2s v4p0116c2s
Haslam, A.S. v5p0132c1s
Haslam, E. v2p0148c2s
Haslam, W. v1p0427c1s v1p0434c1s v1p1360c2s v1p1377c2s
Haslam, W. et al. v1p0356c1s
Haslehurst, E.W. v5p0498c2s
Haslett, W.C. v6p0359c2s
Haslett, W.T.H. v4p0034c2s
Haslewood, F. v3p0307c2s
Hasluck, E.W. v6p0320c1s
Hasluck, F.W. v6p0163c1m v6p0505c1s
Hasluck, P.N. v3p0439c1s
Hass, F.W. v6p0125c2s v6p0571c1s
Hass-Karl, G.C.H. v6p0647c2s
Hassall, A. v3p0442c2s v4p0355c1s
Hassam, J.T. v1p0151c2s v1p0205c1s v1p0223c2s v1p0591c1s v2p0076c1m v2p0122c1s v2p0172c2s v2p0197c1s v2p0355c2s v3p0075c2s v3p0190c2s v4p0257c2s v5p0127c2s
Hassard, C. v6p0384c2s v6p0417c1s
Hassard, J.R.G. v1p0042c1s v1p0062c1s v1p0192c2s v1p0195c1s v1p0219c1s v1p0257c1s v1p0263c2s v1p0281c1s v1p0285c2s v1p0321c2s v1p0350c2s v1p0432c1s v1p0458c1s v1p0594c2s v1p0683c2s v1p0812c2s v1p0872c1s v1p0888c1s v1p0891c1s v1p0916c1s v1p0917c1s v1p1012c2s v1p1048c2s v1p1098c1s v1p1109c1s v1p1115c2s v1p1117c1s v1p1117c2m v1p1119c1s v1p1134c2s v1p1136c1s v1p1180c1s v1p1231c2s v1p1240c1s v1p1306c2s v1p1312c1s v1p1349c2s v1p1410c1s v2p0058c1s v2p0175c1s v2p0260c1s v2p0267c1s v2p0375c2s v2p0450c2s v2p0464c1s v3p0063c1s
Hasse, A.R. v4p0329c1s v4p0329c2s v4p0341c2s v5p0097c1s v5p0471c1s v5p0602c2s v6p0462c1s v6p0522c1m v6p0522c2s
Hasse, Adelaide R. v6p0104c1s
Hasselberg, B. v4p0420c1s v4p0540c2s
Hassenfratz, M. v1p0160c2s
Hassert, K. v4p0380c1s
Hassett, M.F. v6p0069c1s
Hassett, M.M. v6p0104c1s v6p0478c1s
Hasskarl, G.C.H. v3p0347c2s v3p0371c2s
Hassler, F.R. v1p0269c2s
Hassler, F.W.B. v1p1347c2s
Hassler, H.E. v6p0373c1s
Hassler, Harriet E. v6p0619c1s v6p0619c2s
Hassler, J.P. v3p0237c2s
Hassles, H.E. v6p0509c2s
Hasson, C.A. v5p0360c1s
Hasson, W.F.C. v4p0501c2s
Hastam, J.H. v4p0459c1s
Haste, R.A. v6p0395c2s v6p0460c2s
Hasted, J.O. v3p0223c2s
Hastie, A.H. v4p0187c1s v5p0571c1s
Hastie, B. v2p0246c1s v3p0453c1s
Hastie, G. v4p0200c2s
Hastie, W. v3p0358c2s
Hastings, A. v5p0587c1s
Hastings, C. v3p0331c1s v4p0048c2s
Hastings, C.H. v5p0537c1s v5p0638c2s v6p0373c2s
Hastings, C.S. v1p0525c2s v1p1267c2s v1p1268c2s v2p0094c2s v2p0318c2s v2p0424c2m v2p0433c2m v2p0459c1s v3p0001c1s v3p0357c1s v3p0423c1s v5p0571c2s v6p0216c2m
Hastings, D.L. v5p0421c1s

v6p0232c1s v6p0378c2s
Hastings, E.B. v5p0147c1s
v5p0619c1s
Hastings, F. v1p1236c2s
v2p0102c1s v2p0271c2s v2p0414c2s
v2p0425c2s v2p0436c1s v3p0075c1s
v3p0237c1s v3p0372c2s v5p0039c2s
Hastings, G.H. v1p0120c2s
Hastings, H. v2p0002c2s
Hastings, H.R. v6p0504c2s
Hastings, J. v6p0028c1s
Hastings, M.V. v1p0761c1s
Hastings, S. v6p0431c1s
Hastings, S.H. v3p0442c2s
Hastings, T. v1p0882c2m
v1p0883c1m v4p0024c1s v4p0078c1s
v5p0026c1s
Hastings, T. and Bacon, L.
v1p0882c2s v1p0883c2s
Hastings, T.S. v3p0413c2s
Hastings, Wilhelmina v6p0117c1s
Hasty, L.H. v1p1243c2s
Haswell, C.H. v1p0037c1s
v1p0146c2s v1p0211c1s v1p0287c2s
v1p0455c1s v1p0551c1s v1p0570c2s
v1p0751c1s v1p0873c2s v1p0901c2s
v1p1065c1s v1p1197c1s v1p1261c1s
v1p1328c2s v5p0362c1s v5p0551c1s
Hatch, E. v1p0250c2s
v2p0084c1s v2p0129c1s v2p0145c2s
v2p0442c1s v3p0275c2s v3p0380c1s
v4p0252c1s
Hatch, E.A. v5p0612c1s
Hatch, E.D.W., Mrs. v2p0365c1s
v3p0103c2s v3p0286c1s
Hatch, E.E. v4p0355c1s
v5p0621c2s v6p0571c1s
Hatch, E.F.G. v6p0665c1s
Hatch, E.W. v4p0301c2s
Hatch, F.H. v3p0107c1s
v4p0068c1s v5p0007c2s v5p0136c2s
Hatch, G.B. v6p0490c1s
Hatch, H.R. v4p0056c2s
v5p0058c1s
Hatch, J.L. v1p0687c1s
v1p1270c1s
Hatch, J.M. v1p0573c2s
Hatch, J.N. v5p0298c1s
Hatch, M.D. v4p0032c2s
v5p0339c1s
Hatch, M.R.P. v2p0312c1s
v3p0184c2s v3p0266c2s v3p0308c2s
v5p0120c1s v6p0282c1s
Hatch, Mary R.P. v6p0165c2s
v6p0360c1s v6p0563c1s v6p0618c2s
Hatch, R. et al. v2p0245c1s
Hatch, R.P. v3p0141c1s
Hatch, W.E. v6p0290c1s
Hatchard, M.L. and Bigg, A.H.
v3p0429c2s
Hatcher, J.B. v4p0094c2s
v4p0156c1s v4p0156c2s v4p0210c1s
v4p0321c1s v4p0563c1s v5p0093c1s
v5p0215c1s v5p0435c1m v5p0518c2s
v6p0107c1s v6p0234c2s v6p0347c2s
v6p0483c1s v6p0677c2s
Hatchett-Jackson, E. v4p0081c1s
Hatfield, C.A.P. v5p0098c1s
Hatfield, E.D. v4p0090c1s
Hatfield, E.F. v1p0398c1s
v1p0688c2s v1p1046c1s v1p1047c2s
v2p0065c2s
Hatfield, F.D. v4p0111c1s
Hatfield, G. v3p0044c2m
v3p0099c1s v3p0106c2s
Hatfield, H.R. v5p0592c2s
Hatfield, J.T. v4p0146c1s
v4p0386c2s v4p0620c2s v5p0237c1m
v5p0605c2s v5p0629c2s v6p0287c2s
v6p0434c2m
Hatfield, James Taft v5p0393c1s
Hatfield, L.H. v4p0135c1s
Hatfield, O.P. v2p0055c2s
Hatfield, R.G. v1p0053c1s
v1p0097c2s v1p0913c2s
Hatfield, T.D. v4p0033c1s
v4p0040c1s v4p0049c2m v4p0060c2s
v4p0087c1m v4p0087c2s v4p0090c1m
v4p0111c1m v4p0203c1s v4p0204c1s
v4p0242c2m v4p0248c1s v4p0269c2s
v4p0319c1s v4p0416c1m v4p0416c2s
v4p0483c2s v4p0486c1s v4p0486c2s
v4p0491c2m v4p0605c1m v5p0487c2s
Hathaway, A.J., Mrs. v2p0388c2s
Hathaway, A.S. v4p0223c1s
v5p0229c1s
Hathaway, B. v1p1416c1s
v4p0398c1s
Hathaway, E.J. v4p0138c1s
Hathaway, F.P. v1p0149c1s
Hathaway, Jo v5p0283c1s
Hathaway, W.E. v5p0277c2s
Hathaway, W.F. v6p0096c1s
Hatherly, A.G. v3p0293c1s
Hatherly, S.G. v1p0883c1s
v3p0099c2s v4p0242c1s
Hatheway, J.R. v6p0494c2s
Hathway, C. v1p0083c1s
Hatson, C.W. v1p0148c1s
v1p0744c2s
Hatt, W.K. v5p0389c1s
v6p0515c2s
Hatton, Bessie v6p0384c2s
Hatton, H. v1p0291c2s
v1p1174c2s
Hatton, H.F. v2p0029c1s
v4p0038c1s
Hatton, J. v1p0067c2s
v1p0073c1s v1p0133c1m v1p0166c2s
v1p0167c2s v1p0193c1s v1p0194c2s
v1p0235c1s v1p0246c1s v1p0267c1s
v1p0341c2s v1p0362c1s v1p0365c2s
v1p0413c2m v1p0445c2s v1p0486c2s
v1p0520c1s v1p0606c1s v1p0696c2s
v1p0702c1s v1p0710c1s v1p0737c1s
v1p0763c2m v1p0819c1s v1p0952c2s
v1p1057c1s v1p1065c2s v1p1182c2s
v1p1198c1s v1p1259c2s v1p1293c2s
v1p1351c1s v1p1371c2s v2p0010c2s
v2p0024c1s v2p0048c1s v2p0052c2m
v2p0090c1s v2p0113c1s v2p0120c1s
v2p0153c2s v2p0197c1s v2p0197c2s
v2p0207c1s v2p0210c2s v2p0229c2s
v2p0230c1s v2p0238c2s v2p0242c2s
v2p0253c2s v2p0262c2s v2p0263c2s
v2p0265c1s v2p0295c2s v2p0314c1s
v2p0359c2s v2p0436c2s v2p0481c2s
v3p0046c1s v3p0089c1s v3p0246c1m
v3p0254c2s v3p0266c1s v4p0062c1s
v4p0087c1s v4p0121c1s v4p0159c2s
v4p0293c1s v4p0389c2s v4p0390c1s
v4p0438c1s v4p0442c1s v4p0541c2s
v4p0548c2s v4p0569c2s v4p0578c1s
v4p0579c1s
Hatton-Luck, J.W. and
Macdonald, J.R. v3p0399c1s
Hattori, Y. v6p0334c2s
Hatzel, E. v1p0280c2s
Hau, A. v3p0191c1s
v3p0352c1s
Hauer, F.von v1p0550c2s
Hauff, W. v1p0371c1s
Haug, H. v1p0498c1s
Haug, J. v1p0538c2s
v1p1192c1s
Haughton, B. v1p1078c1s
Haughton, E. v5p0606c2s
Haughton, G.D. v1p0071c2s
v1p0124c2s v1p0248c1s v1p1263c2s
v1p1270c1s
Haughton, H.D. v1p0138c1s
Haughton, J. v1p0245c1s
v1p0969c1s v3p0238c1s
Haughton, S. v1p0375c1s
v1p0375c2s v1p0381c2s v1p0509c2s
v1p0579c1s v1p0881c2m v2p0127c2s
v2p0173c2s v2p0441c2s
Haughton, S. and Reynolds, J.E.
v1p1390c1s
Haultain, A. v4p0067c2s
v4p0085c2s v4p0086c2s v4p0362c1s
v4p0474c2s v4p0534c2s v5p0091c1s
v5p0239c1s v5p0536c1s v6p0097c2s
v6p0261c1s v6p0633c1s v6p0684c1s
Haultain, T.A. v3p0154c1s
v5p0154c2s v5p0421c2s v6p0160c1s
v6p0306c2s v6p0580c1s
Haunay, J. v1p0165c1s
Haupt, H. v1p0161c1s
v1p0161c2s v1p0162c1s v1p1076c2s
v1p1078c1m v1p1079c1s v1p1427c1s
v3p0223c1s v4p0008c2s v4p0530c1s
v5p0010c1s v5p0149c1s v5p0206c2s
v5p0380c2s
Haupt, L.M. v1p0583c2s
v1p0982c1s v1p1011c2s v1p1212c1s
v1p1260c2s v3p0066c1s v3p0153c2s
v3p0166c2s v3p0189c2s v3p0230c1s
v3p0329c1s v3p0349c1m v3p0352c2s
v3p0354c2s v3p0362c2s v3p0430c1s
v3p0442c2s v4p0087c1m v4p0115c2s
v4p0116c1s v4p0353c1s v4p0438c1s
v4p0471c2s v4p0485c2s v4p0614c1m
v5p0130c1s v5p0294c1s v5p0380c2s
v5p0410c2s v5p0550c2s v6p0324c2s
v6p0342c2s v6p0422c1s v6p0452c2s
v6p0660c2s v6p0688c2m v6p0689c1s
Haupt, L.M. and Meerten, H.v.
v6p0422c1s
Haupt, L.M. and Turtle, T.
v3p0371c1s
Haupt, Lewis M. v3p0324c2s
Haupt, P. v2p0030c2s
v2p0315c1s v3p0019c2s v3p0125c2s
v5p0332c1s v6p0061c1s v6p0062c1s
v6p0062c2s v6p0533c2s
Haupt, Paul v6p0253c1s
Hauptmann, C. v5p0194c1s
Hauptmann, G. v4p0247c1s
v5p0562c1s v6p0200c1s
Haupton, W. v1p1343c2s
Hauptvogel, R. v6p0070c2s
Hauranne, E.Duvergier de . v1p0152c2s
Haurean, B. v1p0388c1s
v1p1158c2s
Hauser, H. v5p0482c1s
Hauser, I.L. v5p0285c1s
Hausknecht, E. v3p0226c2s
v3p0388c1s
Hausmann, J.F.L. v1p1155c1s
Hausmann, Prof. v1p0428c2s
v1p1363c1s
Haussonville, Count d' ... v5p0638c1s
Haussonville, M.d' v2p0452c2s
Hautreux, A. v4p0036c1s
Havard, H. v4p0295c2s
Havard, V. v1p1221c2s
v2p0287c1s v4p0443c1s v6p0398c2s
Havelaar, M. v1p0373c1s
Havell, E.B. v6p0314c2s
v6p0315c1s v6p0631c1m
Havell, H.L. v3p0019c2s
v3p0326c2s v3p0413c2s v6p0565c1s
Havelock, H. v5p0138c2s
v6p0559c2s
Havelock, H., Sir v1p0543c1s
Havelock, H.M. v1p0379c1s
v1p0634c2s
Havelock-Allan, H., Sir .. v5p0246c1s
v5p0375c2s
Haven, A.B. v1p0203c1s
v1p0245c2s v1p0628c1s v1p0738c1s
v1p0799c2s v1p1257c2s
Haven, A.R. v3p0275c1s
Haven, C.C. v1p0284c1s
v1p0486c1s v1p0599c2s v1p0600c1s
v1p1057c1s
v1p1319c1s
Haven, E.O. v1p0227c2s
v1p0261c1s v1p0333c2s v1p0389c2s
v1p0551c1s v1p0646c2s v1p0816c2s
v1p0830c2s v1p0992c1s v1p1104c1s
v1p1342c2s
Haven, G. v1p0096c1s
v1p0646c1s v1p0741c1m v1p0832c2s
v1p1132c2s v1p1343c1s v1p1352c2s
v1p1398c2s v1p1404c2s v1p1429c2s
Haven, G.De v3p0277c1s
Haven, H.P. v1p0208c2s
v1p1403c1s
Haven, J. v1p0293c1s
v1p0568c1m v1p0820c2s v1p0839c2s
v1p0850c2s v1p1043c2s v1p1200c2s
Haven, K.M. v1p1108c2s
v2p0194c1s v2p0387c1s
Haven, N. v1p0729c2s
v1p0730c2s v1p1404c1s
Haven, N.A. v1p1348c1s
Haven, S.F. v1p0743c1s
v1p0811c1s v1p1033c2s
Haven, T. v6p0058c1s
Havens, A.W. v6p0027c1s
Havens, C. v1p0770c2s
Havens, C.E. v1p0027c2s
v1p0625c1s v1p0704c1s v1p1022c1s
v1p1054c1s v1p1295c2s
Havens, F.S. v5p0014c1m
v5p0411c1s
Havens, F.S. and Gooch, F.A.
v4p0012c2s v5p0113c2s
Havens, F.S. and Way, A.F.
v5p0277c2s v5p0298c1s
Havens, M.A. v6p0359c2s
Haverfield, F. v3p0055c1s
v3p0076c1s v3p0109c1s v3p0199c2s
v3p0243c2s v3p0252c1s v3p0300c1s
v3p0314c1s v4p0089c1s v4p0099c2s
v4p0109c1s v4p0245c1s v4p0489c1s
v4p0523c2s v5p0492c2s v5p0494c2s
v6p0424c2s v6p0547c1m v6p0594c1s
Haverfield, F.J. v6p0469c2s
Haverfield, T.F. v2p0242c2s
Havergal, F.R. v1p1270c2s
v1p1309c1s v2p0203c1s
Havernick, H.A.C. v1p0125c1s
v1p0438c2s
Haverstik, L. v1p1343c2s
Havesty, M. v1p0654c2s
Havet, J. v5p0218c1s
Haviland, A. v2p0199c1s
v2p0393c2s v3p0118c2s
Haviland, C.T. v1p1160c2s
v5p0149c2s
Haviland, Dr. v1p0165c2s
Havilland, S.de v3p0112c1s
v3p0238c1s v3p0275c1s v3p0411c2s
v3p0424c1s v4p0571c2s
Haward, V. v5p0507c2s
Haward, W. v1p0934c2s
Hawcroft, J.M. v1p1210c2s
Haweis, H.R. v1p0107c2s
v1p0108c1s v1p0109c1s v1p0110c2m
v1p0200c2s v1p0238c1s v1p0250c2s
v1p0347c1s v1p0527c1s v1p0569c2s
v1p0576c1s v1p0692c2s v1p0752c1s
v1p0761c1s v1p0774c2s v1p0777c1s
v1p0820c1s v1p0868c2s v1p0882c1m
v1p0882c2m v1p0883c2m v1p0906c2s
v1p0957c1s v1p1007c2s v1p1041c2s
v1p1055c1s v1p1144c1s v1p1160c1s
v1p1222c1s v1p1258c2s v1p1260c2s
v1p1372c2m v1p1379c2s v1p1380c1s
v2p0032c1s v2p0053c2s v2p0058c1s
v2p0070c2s v2p0079c1s v2p0100c1s
v2p0125c1s v2p0127c1s v2p0135c1s
v2p0171c1s v2p0190c1s v2p0191c2s
v2p0205c2s v2p0260c1m v2p0299c1s
v2p0366c1m v2p0377c2s v2p0404c1s
v2p0422c1s v2p0425c2s v2p0454c1s
v2p0464c1s v2p0470c1s v3p0038c1s

v3p0055c2s v3p0135c1s v3p0252c1s v3p0313c2s v3p0349c1s v3p0466c2s v4p0042c2s v4p0050c2s v4p0112c2s v4p0140c2s v4p0179c1s v4p0225c2s v4p0294c2s v4p0361c2s v4p0382c1s v4p0382c2s v4p0383c1s v4p0388c2s v4p0390c1s v4p0424c1s v4p0436c1s v4p0467c1s v4p0494c1s v4p0499c2s v4p0539c2s v4p0542c1s v4p0543c2s v4p0572c1s v5p0030c2s v5p0226c1s v5p0302c1s v5p0387c1s v5p0395c1s v5p0480c2s v5p0595c1s v5p0612c2s
Haweis, H.R., Mrs. v2p0263c2s v3p0324c2s
Haweis, M.A. v4p0110c1s
Haweis, M.E. v1p0088c2s v1p0105c2s v1p0223c1s v1p0366c2s v2p0075c2s v2p0089c2s v2p0093c2s v2p0114c1s v2p0123c2s v3p0122c2s v3p0230c2s v3p0471c2s v4p0001c1s v4p0092c2s v4p0148c2s v4p0629c2s v5p0520c2s
Haweis, Mrs. v1p0366c2s v4p0626c1s
Hawes, Alex.G. v6p0084c2s
Hawes, C.P. v1p0359c2s v1p0420c2s v1p1322c1s
Hawes, E.S. v4p0512c2s
Hawes, G.R. v5p0327c2s
Hawes, G.W. v1p0292c2s v1p0540c1s v1p0664c2s v1p0911c1m v1p1113c1s
Hawes, J. v1p0447c2s v1p0847c1s v1p1288c1s
Hawes, J.W. v1p0158c1s v4p0072c1s
Hawes, M. v3p0067c1s
Hawes, P. v4p0001c1s
Hawes, W. v3p0139c1s v3p0146c2s v3p0183c2s v3p0251c2s v3p0352c1s v3p0397c1s
Hawke, J. v4p0219c1s
Hawke, M. v4p0419c2s
Hawker, M. v4p0193c2s v4p0273c2s
Hawker, M.E. v4p0634c1s
Hawker, M.P. v2p0444c1s v3p0073c2s
Hawker, T.G.L. v4p0251c1s
Hawkes, A. v6p0447c1s
Hawkes, C. v5p0396c1s v6p0153c2s v6p0386c2s v6p0466c1s v6p0631c2s v6p0694c1s
Hawkes, Clarence v6p0165c2s v6p0622c2s
Hawkes, E.E. v6p0044c2s
Hawkes, G. v5p0198c1m v5p0236c2s v5p0563c2s v5p0567c2s
Hawkes, Gilbert v5p0563c2s
Hawkes, N.M. v3p0054c2s v3p0137c1s v3p0223c2s v3p0349c2s
Hawkesworth, A.S. v6p0407c1s
Hawkins, A.H. v4p0252c1s v5p0165c1s v5p0316c2s v5p0386c2s v6p0179c2s v6p0325c1s v6p0694c1s
Hawkins, A.Hope v4p0033c1s v4p0137c1s v4p0139c2s v4p0145c1s v4p0282c2s v4p0343c1s v4p0604c1s v4p0607c2s v5p0233c1s v5p0387c2s v5p0415c2s v5p0597c2s
Hawkins, A.S. v6p0039c1s
Hawkins, Anthony H. v6p0420c2s
Hawkins, B.W. v3p0179c1s v3p0422c1s
Hawkins, C.A. v6p0044c1s
Hawkins, C.C. v3p0021c1s
Hawkins, C.H. v1p0364c1s v1p1379c2s
Hawkins, C.J. v5p0369c2s v6p0215c1s v6p0691c2s
Hawkins, D.A. v1p0040c1s v1p0385c1s
Hawkins, E. v1p0272c1s v1p0272c2m
Hawkins, F. v2p0059c1s v2p0087c1s v2p0094c2m v2p0230c1s v2p0252c2s v2p0299c1s v2p0398c1s v2p0401c2s v2p0435c1s v3p0037c2s v3p0089c2s v3p0124c2s v3p0388c1s v3p0401c1s v4p0050c2s v4p0126c1s v4p0242c2s v4p0293c1s v4p0294c1s v4p0338c2s v4p0339c1s v4p0355c2s v4p0417c2s v4p0425c2s v4p0438c2s v4p0486c1s v4p0499c2s v4p0518c1m v4p0607c1m v5p0426c1s
Hawkins, H. et al. v4p0139c2s
Hawkins, H.S. v5p0290c1s
Hawkins, J. v1p0689c1s v1p1353c2s v2p0199c2s v2p0221c1s v2p0291c2s v2p0299c2s v3p0094c2s v3p0230c1s v4p0578c1s
Hawkins, J.D. v3p0281c1s v3p0394c1s
Hawkins, J.I. v1p0211c1s
Hawkins, J.M. v1p0698c2s
Hawkins, J.T. v4p0128c1s v4p0347c2s v4p0470c1s
Hawkins, John v4p0205c1s
Hawkins, R.C. v3p0058c1s v4p0090c2s v6p0554c2s v6p0559c2s
Hawkins, R.C. and Fanning, W.J. v4p0265c1s
Hawkins, W. v1p1209c2s
Hawkins, W.T. v2p0304c1s
Hawks, F.L. v1p0247c2s v1p0422c1m v1p0567c2s v1p0680c1m v1p0923c1s v1p1252c1s v1p1373c2s
Hawks, J.S. v1p0032c1s
Hawksford, C.M. v1p0693c2s v2p0234c2s v2p0280c2s
Hawkshaw, J. v1p1365c1s
Hawkshaw, J., Sir v1p0408c1m
Hawkshaw, J.C. v1p1110c1m
Hawksley, J.M.A. v5p0638c2s
Hawksley, W.C., Mrs. v4p0327c1s v5p0418c1s
Hawksley, W.M.A., Mrs. ... v4p0516c2s v4p0630c2s
Hawkwood, J. v5p0139c2s v5p0176c1s v5p0214c2s v5p0272c1s v5p0358c2s v5p0456c1s
Hawley, A.T. v2p0446c2s
Hawley, B. v1p0126c2s v1p0127c1s v1p0389c2s v1p0830c2s v1p0882c2s v1p1028c1s
Hawley, C.E. v1p1071c2m
Hawley, E. v5p0114c2s
Hawley, E.B. v1p0059c2s
Hawley, E.H. v5p0210c1s v6p0210c1s v6p0228c1s
Hawley, F.B. v1p0198c2s v1p0963c2s v1p1026c2s v2p0430c2s v3p0026c1s v3p0345c2s v3p0452c2s v4p0088c1s v4p0354c2s v4p0359c2s v4p0461c1s v5p0467c2m v6p0189c1s v6p0372c2s
Hawley, F.M. v6p0111c1s v6p0227c2s
Hawley, G. v5p0173c1s
Hawley, H.A. v3p0048c1s
Hawley, J.R. v3p0146c2s v4p0248c2s
Hawley, M.E. v6p0371c1s v6p0629c2s
Hawley, R.N. v6p0029c1s
Hawley, S. v6p0077c1s v6p0154c1s v6p0512c1s v6p0602c2s v6p0629c1s
Hawley, S.E. v4p0518c2s
Hawley, W.A. v5p0567c2s v5p0568c2s
Hawley, W.L. v5p0350c1s v5p0403c2s v5p0406c2s v5p0409c1s v5p0464c2s v5p0545c1s v5p0566c1s v5p0566c2s v5p0621c2s v6p0435c2s v6p0453c1s
Hawn, H.G. v4p0178c2s v4p0527c2s v5p0614c1s
Hawnsley, H.D. v3p0277c1s
Haworth, E. v2p0173c2m v2p0472c2s v4p0120c2s v4p0362c2s
Haworth, P.L. v5p0467c2s v6p0235c2s v6p0240c1s
Haworth, R.L. v6p0447c2s
Hawson, F.E. v6p0229c2s v6p0569c1s
Hawtayne, G.H. v4p0251c1s v4p0612c1s
Hawthorne, F.W. v6p0651c2s
Hawthorne, H. v5p0440c2s v5p0644c2s v6p0625c2s v6p0680c1s
Hawthorne, H.C. v5p0032c2s v5p0294c1s
Hawthorne, H.L. v5p0124c2s v5p0444c1s
Hawthorne, Hildegarde v5p0577c2s
Hawthorne, J. v1p0082c1s v1p0160c1s v1p0167c1s v1p0185c2s v1p0188c2s v1p0197c2s v1p0308c1s v1p0357c1s v1p0370c1s v1p0500c1s v1p0501c1s v1p0697c1s v1p0707c1s v1p0764c2s v1p0766c1s v1p0877c1s v1p0878c2s v1p0879c2s v1p0908c1s v1p0935c1s v1p0981c1s v1p1008c2s v1p1011c2s v1p1051c1s v1p1127c2s v1p1132c1s v1p1154c2m v1p1174c1s v1p1277c1s v1p1300c2s v1p1313c2s v2p0005c1s v2p0011c1m v2p0012c2s v2p0027c1s v2p0030c1s v2p0037c1s v2p0077c2s v2p0093c1s v2p0110c2s v2p0112c2s v2p0120c1s v2p0126c1s v2p0139c2s v2p0155c1s v2p0198c1m v2p0241c2s v2p0267c2s v2p0291c2s v2p0304c1s v2p0340c2s v2p0355c2s v2p0366c1s v2p0384c1s v2p0395c2s v2p0422c1s v2p0446c2s v2p0472c1s v3p0039c1s v3p0048c1s v3p0068c2s v3p0118c1s v3p0119c2s v3p0148c2s v3p0191c2s v3p0236c1s v3p0279c2s v3p0294c1s v3p0308c1s v3p0315c1s v3p0335c1s v3p0363c2s v3p0384c2s v3p0394c1s v3p0398c2s v3p0428c2s v3p0455c1s v4p0036c1s v4p0058c2s v4p0100c2s v4p0101c1s v4p0138c2s v4p0198c1s v4p0206c1s v4p0231c1s v4p0260c1s v4p0260c2s v4p0262c2s v4p0306c2s v4p0341c2s v4p0374c1s v4p0460c2s v4p0542c2s v4p0609c1s v4p0612c1s v4p0631c2s v5p0199c2s v5p0301c2m v5p0471c2s v5p0490c1s v5p0530c2s v5p0591c1s v5p0628c2s v6p0075c1s v6p0208c1s v6p0283c2m v6p0284c2s v6p0285c1s v6p0312c2s v6p0346c2s v6p0366c2s v6p0417c2s v6p0471c2s v6p0662c2s
Hawthorne, J. and Emerson, E.W v6p0202c2s
Hawthorne, J. and Payne, W.M. v6p0088c2s
Hawthorne, J. and Savage, M.J. v3p0405c1s
Hawthorne, J. and Wharton, A.H. v3p0463c2s
Hawthorne, Julian v4p0435c2s v5p0082c1s v5p0182c1s v5p0284c2s v5p0285c1m v5p0286c2m v5p0419c1s v6p0200c1s v6p0283c2s v6p0388c2s
Hawthorne, N. v1p0005c2s v1p0013c2s v1p0065c2s v1p0075c2s v1p0085c1s v1p0095c2s v1p0135c1s v1p0152c2m v1p0179c1s v1p0210c1s v1p0245c1s v1p0256c2s v1p0333c1s v1p0394c1s v1p0414c1s v1p0447c1s v1p0449c2s v1p0461c1s v1p0466c1s v1p0473c1s v1p0610c1s v1p0649c1s v1p0670c2s v1p0732c2s v1p0766c1s v1p0953c2s v1p0969c2s v1p1011c1s v1p1040c2s v1p1054c1s v1p1155c2s v1p1178c1s v1p1183c2s v1p1213c2s v1p1298c2s v1p1344c2s v1p1387c1s v1p1408c2s v2p0013c1s v5p0232c2s v5p0258c1s
Hawthorne, N., Mrs. v1p0915c1s
Hawtrey, C. v6p0642c1s
Hawtrey, R.G. v5p0512c1s v5p0619c1s
Haxthausen, Baron v1p0679c2s
Hay, A. v1p0570c2s
Hay, A., Lady v1p0800c1s
Hay, C. v1p1121c2s v5p0426c2s
Hay, C.A. v1p0126c1s v1p0285c2s v1p0769c1s v1p0847c1s v3p0261c1m
Hay, C.E. v2p0290c2s v3p0084c1s v5p0135c1s v5p0348c1s v5p0485c2s v6p0123c2s
Hay, C.G. v6p0300c1s
Hay, C.G. and Hodge, H. .. v5p0583c1s
Hay, E. v2p0473c1s v5p0380c2s
Hay, E.F. v4p0001c1s
Hay, E.G. v6p0096c2s
Hay, F. v6p0355c1s
Hay, G. v2p0033c1s v3p0090c1s
Hay, G.N. v5p0433c1s
Hay, G.U. v6p0097c2s
Hay, H.C. v4p0053c1s v4p0132c2s v4p0559c2s v5p0198c2s v5p0201c2s v5p0337c2s v5p0354c1s v5p0560c2s v6p0008c1s v6p0061c1s v6p0115c2s v6p0145c2s v6p0186c2s v6p0334c2s v6p0397c2s v6p0451c1s v6p0513c1s v6p0527c1m v6p0576c1m v6p0611c1s v6p0621c2s
Hay, H.C. and Wright, T.F. v5p0057c2s
Hay, J. v1p0087c1s v1p0142c2s v1p0332c1s v1p0404c1s v1p0424c1s v1p0692c1s v1p0872c1s v1p0876c2s v1p1228c2s v3p0251c2s v4p0178c1s v5p0420c1m v6p0071c1s v6p0112c2s v6p0277c2s v6p0616c1s
Hay, J. and Nicolay, J.G.. v2p0259c1s v3p0251c2s
Hay, J.C.D. v5p0050c1s
Hay, J.H.D. v3p0038c2s v3p0048c1m v3p0333c1s
Hay, J.H.Drummond v3p0288c2s
Hay, J.M. v6p0362c1s
Hay, John v6p0239c1s v6p0451c2s
Hay, M.C. v1p0181c2s v1p0446c1s v1p0609c1s v1p0703c1s v1p0930c2s v1p1339c1s v1p1397c2s
Hay, O.P. v3p0009c2s v3p0012c2s v3p0173c2s v3p0271c1s v5p0050c1s v5p0103c2s v5p0173c1s v5p0208c2m v5p0233c2s v5p0278c2s v5p0509c2s v5p0567c2s v5p0610c1s v6p0017c2s v6p0234c2s v6p0662c1s v6p0677c2s
Hay, O.P. and Hay, W.P. .. v3p0053c1s
Hay, P.D. v1p1225c2s v2p0069c1s v2p0276c2s
Hay, R. v3p0234c1s
Hay, T.W.L. v1p1380c2s
Hay, W. v1p0243c1s v1p0554c1s
Hay, W.D. v2p0311c1s v2p0422c1s v3p0304c2s
Hay, W.P. and Hay, O.P. .. v3p0053c1s
Hay-Hunter, P. v4p0155c1s
Hayard, P.B. et al. v3p0277c2s
Hayashi, Baron v5p0303c1s
Haycraft, J.B. v4p0016c2s v4p0516c2s
Haycraft, T.N. v5p0012c2s
Haycraft, W.T. v1p0146c1s

v1p1246c2s
Haycroft, J.B. v2p0253c2s
Hayden, A. v4p0066c2s
v4p0306c2s v4p0347c2s v4p0410c1s
Hayden, A.S. v1p0871c1s
Hayden, C.A. v6p0439c2s
Hayden, C.B. v1p0622c1s
Hayden, E. v2p0127c2s
v2p0128c1s v2p0314c1s v3p0108c2s
v3p0410c2m v4p0551c1s
Hayden, E. and Dutton, C.E.
v3p0126c1m
Hayden, E. and Greely, A.W.
v3p0047c2s
Hayden, E.A. v6p0410c1s
Hayden, E.G. v6p0099c2s
Hayden, Eleanor G. v5p0051c2s
v5p0640c1s
Hayden, F.V. v1p0268c1s
v1p0279c2s v1p0329c1s v1p0508c2m
v1p0509c1s v1p0509c2s v1p0519c1s
v1p0571c1s v1p0749c1s v1p0796c1s
v1p0863c2s v1p0903c2s v1p1112c2s
v1p1113c2m v1p1240c2s v1p1296c1s
v1p1437c1m v2p0455c1s
Hayden, F.V. and Meek, F.B.
v1p0508c2m v1p0903c2m
Hayden, H., jr. v4p0176c2s
Hayden, H.E. v1p0865c1s
v1p1107c2s v1p1344c1s v2p0145c1s
v3p0011c1s v3p0128c1s v3p0208c1s
v3p0252c1s v3p0450c2s v4p0612c1s
Hayden, H.H. v1p0106c2s
Hayden, M. v3p0073c1s
v4p0096c1s v4p0360c1s
Hayden, M.P. v1p0689c2s
v1p1141c1s
Hayden, N.W.J. v5p0145c2s
Hayden, P.C. v4p0388c2s
Hayden, P.J. v3p0178c1s
Hayden, W. v2p0408c2s
v3p0241c1s
Hayden, W.B. v1p0356c2s
Hayden, W.M. v6p0571c2s
Hayden, W.R. v4p0187c2s
Haydn, H.M. v6p0121c2s
Haydon, A.G. v4p0393c2s
Haydon, B.R. v1p1171c1s
Haydon, D.M. v2p0148c1s
Haydon, R.S. v3p0332c2s
v3p0377c1s
Haydon, T.C. v6p0028c2m
Hayes, A. v3p0468c2m
Hayes, A.A. v1p0665c1s
v1p0737c1s v1p1179c2s v1p1390c1s
v1p1390c2s v1p1440c1s v2p0078c2s
v2p0116c1s v2p0129c1s v2p0311c2s
v2p0321c2s v2p0332c1s v2p0411c2s
v2p0449c2s v3p0025c1s v3p0078c2s
v3p0243c1s v4p0593c2s
Hayes, A.A., jr. v1p0227c1s
v1p0231c2s v1p0235c2s v1p0279c1m
v1p0279c2m v1p0380c1s v1p0795c1s
v1p1009c2s v1p1011c1s v1p1123c1s
v1p1151c1s v1p1280c1s v1p1342c2s
v1p1347c1s
Hayes, A.L. v1p0146c1s
v1p0257c2s v1p0987c2s v1p1227c2s
Hayes, C.W. v2p0198c2s
v4p0636c2s v5p0410c2s
Hayes, C.W. and Willis, B.
v4p0021c2s
Hayes, C.Willard v5p0410c2m
Hayes, D.A. v5p0557c2s
v6p0064c2s v6p0258c2s v6p0341c2s
Hayes, E. v6p0140c2s
Hayes, E. and Ganong, W.F.
v6p0386c1s
Hayes, E.Cary v6p0602c1s
Hayes, E.S.P. v6p0018c1s
Hayes, F.B. v5p0303c2s
v5p0406c2s
Hayes, G.E. v1p0509c1s
v1p0917c2s
Hayes, H. v4p0263c2s
Hayes, H.V. and Trowbridge, J.
v2p0170c2s v2p0340c1s
Hayes, Harriet H. v5p0105c2s
Hayes, I.I. v1p0055c2s
v1p0357c2s v1p0425c1s v1p0524c1s
v1p0527c2s v1p0557c1m v1p0562c1s
v1p0927c2m v1p1335c1s v1p1339c1s
Hayes, J. v1p0078c1s
v1p0188c1s v1p0188c2s v1p0427c1s
v1p0444c2m v1p0527c1s v1p0640c1s
v1p0714c2s v1p0721c1s v1p1063c1s
v1p1151c1s v4p0403c2s v4p0609c2s
Hayes, J.A. v4p0271c2s
v5p0060c1s v5p0305c2s
Hayes, J.H. v1p0428c1s
Hayes, J.N. v6p0486c1s
Hayes, J.R. v5p0192c2s
v6p0124c2s v6p0359c2s v6p0586c2s
v6p0640c2m
Hayes, P.J. v6p0402c1s
Hayes, S.D. v1p0892c2s
Hayes, S.P. v6p0005c2s
v6p0541c2s
Hayes, W.H. v6p0158c1s
Hayford, E.D. v6p0391c1s
Hayford, J.F. v5p0035c1s
v5p0228c1s v6p0039c2s v6p0106c2s
v6p0296c1s
v6p0666c2s
Haygood, A.G. v3p0401c2s
v4p0396c2s
Haygood, A.G. et al. v4p0166c1s
Hayhurts, L.W. v4p0149c2s
Hayler, G.W. v5p0026c2m
v5p0388c1s v6p0431c1s
Hayley, H.W. v5p0054c1s
Hayley, R.M. v1p1134c2s
Hayllar, Florence v6p0116c1s
v6p0173c1s
Hayllar, J.C. v4p0106c2s
Hayman, H. v1p0598c2s
v1p0600c1s v1p0619c2s v1p0731c2s
v1p0776c1s v1p1109c2s v1p1278c1s
v2p0005c1s v2p0021c1s v2p0044c2s
v2p0119c1s v2p0206c2s v2p0232c1s
v2p0251c2s v2p0259c1s v2p0297c2s
v2p0326c1s v2p0349c2s v2p0377c1s
v2p0382c1s v2p0388c1s v2p0395c1s
v2p0429c2s v2p0432c1s v3p0019c2s
v3p0043c1m v3p0043c2s v3p0061c2m
v3p0086c2s v3p0147c1s v3p0297c2s
v3p0302c2m v3p0317c1s v3p0366c1s
v3p0389c1s v4p0055c1m v4p0081c2m
v4p0181c2s v4p0328c1s v4p0358c2s
v4p0458c2s v4p0506c2s v4p0567c2m
v5p0043c1s v5p0055c2s v5p0056c1s
v5p0084c2s v5p0162c1s v5p0193c2s
v5p0233c2s v5p0311c1s v5p0499c2s
v6p0030c1s v6p0060c2s v6p0104c2s
v6p0122c2s v6p0396c2s v6p0504c2s
Hayman, H.P. v1p0364c1s
Hayman, P. v3p0109c2s
Hayman, S. v1p0551c1s
v1p0752c1s
Hayne, P.H. v1p0332c1s
v1p0491c1s v1p0782c2s v1p0856c2s
v1p1223c2s v1p1375c2s v2p0075c1s
v2p0098c1s v2p0172c1s v2p0242c2s
v2p0249c2s v2p0431c2s v2p0464c1s
Hayne, R.Y. v1p0754c1s
v2p0240c1s
Hayne, W.H. v2p0028c1s
v2p0059c1s v2p0157c2s v2p0175c1s
v2p0353c2s v2p0367c1s v3p0242c2s
v4p0251c2s v6p0580c1s
Haynes, D.C. v1p0536c2s
v1p1059c2s
Haynes, E.C. v4p0635c2s
Haynes, E.J. v3p0051c1s
v3p0342c1s
Haynes, E.S.P. v6p0032c1s
v6p0094c2m v6p0176c2s v6p0278c2s
v6p0473c1m v6p0678c2s
Haynes, F.E. v4p0453c1s
Haynes, G.C. v1p0576c2s
Haynes, G.H. v4p0312c2s
v4p0359c2s v4p0481c1s v5p0319c1m
v5p0485c2s v5p0559c1s v6p0487c1s
v6p0632c1s
Haynes, G.N. v6p0583c1s
Haynes, H.P. v1p0377c1s
v1p0625c1s v1p1425c2s
Haynes, H.W. v1p0793c2s
v2p0008c2s v2p0352c1s v3p0023c1s
v3p0139c2m v3p0241c1s v3p0394c2s
v4p0126c1s v4p0249c1s v4p0422c1s
v4p0437c2s v4p0456c2s v4p0561c1s
v5p0014c2s
Haynes, J. v4p0225c1s
v4p0484c2s v4p0515c1s v5p0175c2s
Haynes, J.A. v6p0077c1s
Haynes, J.C. v6p0439c1s
Haynes, L. v3p0120c2s
v3p0243c1s
Haynes, M.A. v1p0896c2s
Haynes, M.F. v4p0543c2s
Haynes, M.S. v3p0056c1s
Haynes, N.S. v2p0206c1s
Haynes, S. v5p0539c2s
Haynes, T.H. v6p0041c2s
Haynie, H. v2p0319c1s
v4p0586c2s v5p0218c1s v5p0432c1m
v5p0633c1s
Haynie, J.H. v1p0059c2s
v1p0068c2s v5p0532c1s
Hays, A.M. v4p0190c2s
Hays, C.W. and Campbell, M.R.
v4p0021c2s
Hays, E.O. v4p0588c1s
Hays, F.C. v5p0110c2s
Hays, G.P. v3p0084c2s
Hays, G.S. v5p0440c2s
Hays, H.M. v6p0305c2s
Hays, J.W. v3p0015c1s
v4p0026c1s
Hays, W.J. v1p0042c1s
v1p0340c2s
Hays, W.M. v6p0219c2s
v6p0665c2s
Hayter, A. v2p0185c2s
Hayter, A.D. v1p0543c1s
Hayter, A.D., Sir v3p0222c2s
Hayter, H. v1p0161c1s
Hayter, H.H. v1p1370c1s
Hayter, R. v5p0544c1m
Haythornthwaite, F. v2p0216c2s
Hayward, A. v1p0007c2s
v1p0018c2s v1p0032c1s v1p0191c2s
v1p0196c2s v1p0227c1s v1p0297c2s
v1p0352c2s v1p0371c1s v1p0383c1s
v1p0483c1s v1p0489c2s v1p0503c1s
v1p0505c2s v1p0565c1s v1p0593c2s
v1p0594c2s v1p0597c1s v1p0699c1s
v1p0731c2m v1p0734c2s v1p0757c2s
v1p0800c1s v1p0945c2s v1p0946c1s
v1p0968c1s v1p0970c1s v1p1106c1s
v1p1146c2m v1p1154c1s v1p1229c1s
v1p1405c2s
Hayward, A.L. v4p0329c1s
Hayward, A.W. v3p0463c1s
Hayward, C. v1p0184c1s
Hayward, C.A. v5p0636c1s
Hayward, E.F. v2p0260c2s
v2p0465c2s v2p0474c2s v2p0475c1s
v3p0061c2s v3p0089c1s v3p0341c2s
v3p0441c1s v3p0442c2s v4p0398c2s
Hayward, F. v5p0610c2s
Hayward, F.H. v5p0528c2s
Hayward, G. v1p0237c2s
v1p0899c1s
Hayward, J. v1p1238c1s
Hayward, J.W. v1p0607c2s
v4p0131c1s
Hayward, L. v5p0172c1s
v5p0616c2s
Hayward, R. v3p0350c2s
Hayward, R.B. v2p0280c1s
Hayward, R.B. et al. v3p0444c2s
Hayward, R.H. v2p0291c1s
v2p0370c1s
Hayward, S. v1p0314c1s
v2p0178c2s v4p0091c2s v4p0445c2s
Hayward, T.B. v4p0111c2s
Hayward, T.E. v6p0376c2m
Hayward, T.E. and Waters, A.C.
v5p0459c2s
Hayward, W. v5p0436c2s
Hayward, W.H.B. v6p0092c2s
Haywarde, R. v1p1417c1s
Haywood, J. v2p0127c1s
v2p0409c1s v3p0125c2s
Haywood, M.D. v6p0686c2s
Haywood, P.D. v2p0006c2s
Haywood, S.H. v1p1161c1s
Hazard, B. v2p0086c2s
Hazard, C. v2p0025c1s
v3p0288c1s v4p0562c1s v5p0267c1s
Hazard, E. v1p1246c2s
Hazard, J. v5p0463c2s
Hazard, J.P. v2p0306c1s
v2p0411c2s
Hazard, R. v2p0407c1s
v2p0424c2s
Hazard, R. and Spahr, C.B.
v4p0059c1s
Hazard, R.G. v1p0041c2s
v1p0860c2s v2p0274c1m
Hazard, R.M. v1p1349c1s
Hazard, W.H. v4p0055c1s
v5p0060c2s v5p0307c1s
Hazell, A.P. v5p0383c1s
Hazeltine, H.D. v6p0245c1s
v6p0343c2s
Hazeltine, M.E. v4p0329c2s
v5p0334c1m v5p0355c2s v5p0560c2s
v6p0371c2s v6p0372c1s
Hazeltine, M.W. v1p0421c1s
v1p0600c2s v1p1071c1s v1p1137c1s
v1p1178c1s v1p1294c2s v3p0138c1s
v3p0144c2s v3p0469c1s v4p0142c2m
v4p0235c2s v4p0401c1s v4p0405c2s
v4p0591c2s v5p0122c1s v5p0148c1s
v5p0294c1s v5p0454c2s v5p0481c2s
v5p0601c1s v6p0102c1s v6p0565c2s
v6p0677c1s
Hazeltine, M.W. et al. ... v4p0129c1s
Hazeltine, Mary E. et al.. v6p0532c2s
Hazeltine, Mayo W. v6p0205c1s
Hazen, A. v4p0612c2s
v5p0490c1s v5p0622c1s
Hazen, A.P. v6p0535c2s
Hazen, C. and Manderson, F.
v5p0015c1s
Hazen, C.D. v5p0140c1s
Hazen, H.A. v1p0099c2m
v1p0289c2s v1p0290c1s v1p0577c1s
v1p0911c2s v2p0006c1s v2p0087c2s
v2p0092c1s v2p0213c1m v2p0358c2s
v2p0364c1s v2p0426c1s v2p0438c2s
v2p0443c1s v3p0007c1s v3p0031c1s
v3p0044c1s v3p0090c2s v3p0108c2m
v3p0127c2s v3p0276c1s v3p0353c2m
v3p0410c2m v3p0416c1s v3p0430c1s
v3p0432c2m v3p0458c2m v3p0465c1m
v4p0036c1s v4p0119c2s v5p0624c1s
Hazen, H.A. and Merriman, M.
v4p0381c1s
Hazen, M.B. v2p0402c2s
Hazen, M.W. v3p0416c2s
Hazen, W.B. v1p1296c1s
v1p1316c2s
Hazewell, C.C. v1p0014c2s
v1p0033c2s v1p0068c2s v1p0220c2s
v1p0316c2s v1p0322c1s v1p0335c1s
v1p0411c1m v1p0431c1s v1p0510c2s

v1p0567c2s v1p0585c1s v1p0629c1s
v1p0671c1s v1p0708c2s v1p0833c1m
v1p0838c1s v1p0862c2s v1p0895c2s
v1p0902c1s v1p0923c1s v1p0983c1s
v1p1061c1s v1p1087c1s v1p1099c2s
v1p1137c1s v1p1206c2s v1p1229c2s
v1p1232c1s v1p1320c2s v1p1323c1s
v1p1343c1s v1p1344c1s v1p1350c1s
v1p1352c1s v1p1384c1s
Hazleton, G.W. v3p0150c2s
Hazleton, H.I. v5p0525c1s
Hazlett, D.M. v6p0476c1s
Hazlitt, W. v1p0051c1s
v1p0177c2s v1p0183c2s v1p0274c1m
v1p0341c1s v1p0364c1s v1p0451c1s
v1p0616c2s v1p0990c2s v1p1104c2s
v1p1127c1s v1p1171c1s v1p1189c2s
v1p1202c1s v1p1235c1s v1p1279c1s
v1p1383c1s
Hazlitt, W.C. v2p0030c1s
v2p0051c2s v2p0091c2s v2p0121c1s
v2p0146c1s v2p0151c2s v2p0198c2s
v2p0206c2s v2p0341c1s v2p0355c1s
v2p0427c1s v2p0458c2s v3p0122c1s
v3p0240c2s v3p0300c1s v3p0448c1s
v4p0037c1s v4p0039c2s v4p0066c2s
v4p0251c2s v5p0259c2s v6p0200c2s
v6p0287c1s v6p0330c2s
Hazzard, J.R.G. v1p0032c2s
v1p1417c1s
Hazzard, R.G. v1p0714c1s
Hazzledine, G.D. v6p0283c1s
Head, A.P. v6p0328c2s
Head, A.P. and Head, J. .. v5p0298c2s
Head, B.V. v2p0091c2m
Head, E. v1p0382c2s
v1p1115c1s v1p1230c2s
Head, E., Sir v1p1041c1s
v1p1178c2s
Head, E.W. v1p1016c2s
v1p1055c2s
Head, F. v5p0194c2s
Head, F.B. v1p0547c1s
Head, F.B., Sir v1p0162c1s
v1p0192c1s v1p0192c2s v1p0193c2s
v1p0219c1s v1p0303c1s v1p0359c1s
v1p0415c2s v1p0545c2s v1p0636c1s
v1p0659c2s v1p0765c1s v1p0767c1s
v1p0844c1s v1p0845c2s v1p1031c1s
v1p1031c2m v1p1038c2s v1p1051c2s
v1p1077c1s v1p1077c2s v1p1087c2s
v1p1289c2s v1p1392c2s
Head, F.H. v1p0637c2s
v1p1147c1s v4p0100c1s v4p0100c2s
v4p0102c1s v4p0299c1s v4p0377c2s
v4p0526c1s v6p0003c2s
v6p0366c1s
Head, J. v1p0146c1s
v2p0419c2s
Head, J. and Head, A.P. .. v5p0298c2s
Head, J.M. v6p0435c1s
Head, K. v5p0078c1s
Head, P.R. v2p0342c2s
Head, R.E. v5p0321c2s
v6p0201c2s
Headden, W.P. v3p0046c2s
v3p0093c1s v3p0330c1s v3p0419c2s
v4p0011c1s v4p0309c2s v4p0545c1s
v4p0586c2s v5p0580c2s v6p0091c2s
v6p0527c2s v6p0594c2s
Headington, N. v1p0946c2s
Headlam, A.C. v5p0118c1s
Headlam, Cecil v6p0703c2s
Headlam, J. v6p0294c1s
Headlam, J.E.W. v5p0252c2s
Headlam, J.W. v4p0189c2s
v4p0285c2s v5p0590c1s
Headlam, S.D. v3p0399c1s
Headlam, W. v6p0005c1s
v6p0273c1s
Headlam, W. et al. v4p0256c1s
Headland, I.T. v4p0328c2s
v5p0051c1s v5p0109c2s v5p0110c2m
v5p0111c2m v5p0112c1s v5p0113c1s
v5p0302c1s v5p0341c2s
Headland, T. v5p0112c2s
Headlee, T.J. v6p0256c2s
Headley, F.W. v4p0060c1s
v4p0202c1s v5p0051c2s v5p0632c2s
Headley, I. v1p0818c2s
Headley, J.T. v1p0021c1s
v1p0025c2s v1p0033c1s v1p0037c2s
v1p0087c2s v1p0098c1s v1p0154c1s
v1p0172c1m v1p0176c2s v1p0187c2s
v1p0196c2s v1p0208c1s v1p0216c1s
v1p0275c1s v1p0319c1s v1p0332c1s
v1p0338c2s v1p0346c2s v1p0430c1s
v1p0461c2s v1p0464c1s v1p0475c2s
v1p0556c2s v1p0636c1s v1p0695c1s
v1p0725c1s v1p0772c1s v1p0777c1s
v1p0809c2s v1p0834c1s v1p0871c1s
v1p0877c1s v1p0880c2s v1p0895c1s
v1p0909c1s v1p0962c2s v1p0965c1m
v1p0996c2s v1p1014c1s v1p1030c1s
v1p1053c1s v1p1124c2s v1p1191c1s
v1p1195c1s v1p1387c2s v1p1392c1s
v2p0012c1s v2p0020c2s v2p0053c2s
v2p0219c1s
Headley, P.C., jr. v3p0330c2s
Headley, R. v4p0401c2s
Heald, F.D. v6p0445c2s
v6p0651c1s
Heales, A. v1p1178c1s
Healey, F.P. v1p0849c2s
Healey, S. v1p0882c2s
Healey, T.M. v2p0450c2s
Healy, A.A. v4p0563c2s
Healy, C. v6p0333c2s
Healy, C.A. v5p0168c2s
v5p0169c1s
Healy, G.P.A. v3p0106c2s
v3p0339c2s v4p0137c1s
Healy, J. v1p0089c2s
v1p0100c2s v1p0707c1s v1p0771c1m
v1p1294c2s v2p0225c2s v3p0445c1s
Healy, J.B. v4p0126c1s
Healy, M. v1p0885c2s
Healy, P.J. v2p0079c2s
v6p0449c1s
Healy, Patrick J. v6p0025c1s
Healy, T.L. v5p0115c1s
v5p0165c1s
Healy, T.M. v2p0206c1s
v2p0224c2s v2p0226c2m v3p0221c1s
v3p0322c1s v4p0290c1m v4p0290c2s
Heap, D.P. v2p0136c2s
v2p0258c2s v4p0046c2s v5p0002c2s
Heap, J.P. v6p0447c2s
Heaphy, T. v1p0205c2s
v1p1125c2s
Heard, A. v2p0220c1s
Heard, A. et al. v4p0133c2s
Heard, A.F. v3p0370c1m
Heard, Dwight B. v6p0030c1s
Heard, F.F. v1p0882c2s
v1p0884c2s
Heard, I.V.D. v3p0194c1s
v3p0281c2s
Heard, J. v2p0159c1s
v2p0398c2s v3p0035c2s v3p0155c2s
v4p0515c2s v6p0293c2s
Heard, J., jr. v2p0409c2s
v3p0073c2s v3p0079c2s v3p0161c1s
v3p0189c1s v3p0232c1s v3p0276c1s
v3p0371c1s v3p0374c2s v3p0396c2s
v3p0426c2s v4p0010c2s v4p0088c2s
v4p0093c1s v4p0310c2s v4p0349c1s
v4p0362c1s v4p0546c1s v5p0047c2s
Heard, J.B. v1p0630c1s
v1p0633c2s v3p0428c1s v5p0396c2s
Heard, J.T. v2p0199c1s
Heard, M. v6p0243c1s
Heard, S., jr. v2p0327c2s
Heard, S.T. v4p0195c2s
v5p0203c2s
Hearn, C.W. v5p0448c1s
Hearn, D. v1p0760c1s
Hearn, L. v2p0063c1s
v2p0312c1s v3p0069c1s v3p0080c1s
v3p0112c1s v3p0172c1s v3p0178c2s
v3p0188c1s v3p0226c2s v3p0227c2s
v3p0234c2s v3p0237c1s v3p0244c1s
v3p0268c1s v3p0270c1s v3p0271c2s
v3p0339c2s v3p0390c2s v3p0460c2m
v3p0474c2s v4p0105c1s v4p0164c2s
v4p0296c2s v4p0297c1m v4p0297c2m
v4p0298c1s v4p0298c2m v4p0313c2s
v4p0336c2s v4p0476c1s v4p0624c2s
v5p0301c1s v5p0411c2s v6p0181c2s
v6p0335c2s v6p0369c1s v6p0548c2s
v6p0610c1s v6p0619c2m v6p0620c1s
v6p0664c1s
Hearnshaw, F.J.C. v6p0293c1s
Hearst, Phoebe v6p0026c2s
Hearst, W.R. v3p0232c2s
Heaslip, C.T. v6p0039c1m
v6p0243c1s v6p0453c2s
Heath, A. v1p0938c1s
Heath, C.K. v4p0622c1s
Heath, D. v4p0135c2s
Heath, D.D. v1p0467c1s
v1p0812c1s
Heath, D.I. v1p0793c2s
v1p0820c2s v1p0856c1s
Heath, E.G. v4p0069c1s
Heath, E.R. v2p0119c1s
v2p0219c2s v2p0337c1m
Heath, F. v1p0904c2s
Heath, F.E. v1p0155c2s
Heath, F.G. v2p0030c1s
v2p0117c2s v2p0162c2s v2p0252c1s
v2p0264c1s v2p0330c1s v3p0141c1s
v3p0210c2s
Heath, G. v3p0475c1s
Heath, G. and Crump, W.B.. v4p0507c2s
Heath, H. v2p0055c2s
Heath, H.F. and Foster, T.G.
v4p0382c2s v4p0568c2s
Heath, I.D. v2p0324c1s
Heath, J.St.G. v6p0089c2s
v6p0328c2s v6p0675c2s
Heath, K. v2p0300c2s
Heath, Kate v2p0317c1s
v6p0030c1s
Heath, Maud v6p0604c2s
Heath, Maud E. v6p0677c2s
Heath, N.B. v3p0089c1s
Heath, P.S. v5p0120c2s
v5p0356c2s v5p0603c2s
Heath, R. v1p1072c1s
v2p0013c1s v2p0052c2s v2p0055c2s
v2p0073c1s v2p0166c1s v2p0289c1s
v2p0329c2m v2p0344c1s v2p0349c1s
v2p0369c2s v2p0380c1s v2p0401c1m
v2p0422c1s v3p0012c2s v3p0035c2s
v3p0055c2s v3p0073c2s v3p0075c1s
v3p0142c1s v3p0159c2s v3p0160c2s
v3p0244c1m v3p0269c2s v3p0279c2s
v3p0367c2s v3p0431c2s v4p0007c2m
v4p0016c2s v4p0079c1s v4p0090c2s
v4p0136c1m v4p0152c2s v4p0162c1s
v4p0213c1s v4p0240c1s v4p0252c1m
v4p0259c2s v4p0345c1s v4p0382c2s
v4p0392c2s v4p0455c1s v4p0521c2s
v5p0033c2s v5p0083c1s v5p0158c2s
v5p0197c2s v5p0469c1s v5p0469c2s
v5p0535c1s v6p0152c1s v6p0236c2m
Heath, Richard v5p0236c2s
Heath, S. v5p0061c2s
Heath, S.R. v2p0473c1s
v5p0615c1s
Heath, Sallie R. v6p0093c2s
Heath, Sarah R. v5p0628c1s
Heath, T.E. v6p0614c1m
Heath, W.J.W. v1p1326c2s
Heathcote, A.M. v2p0279c2s
v3p0110c2s v3p0458c1s
Heathcote, C. v6p0087c1s
Heathcote, Charles v6p0086c2s
Heathcote, E. v5p0504c2s
Heathcote, J.M. v4p0569c1s
Heathcote, J.N. v5p0504c2s
Heather, W.M. v2p0244c1s
Heather-Bigg, A. v4p0262c1s
Heather-Bigg, Ada v3p0174c2s
Heatland, E.S. v6p0603c2s
Heatley, D.P. v5p0128c2s
Heaton, C. v3p0088c2s
Heaton, C.W. v1p0142c2s
v1p0955c2s v1p0957c2s v2p0160c2s
v2p0265c1s v3p0318c1s
Heaton, E. v4p0124c2s
v4p0418c2s v5p0178c2s v5p0187c1s
Heaton, E.M. v3p0310c1s
Heaton, E.P. v5p0595c1s
Heaton, H.A. v5p0229c2s
v5p0279c2s
Heaton, J.A. v3p0037c1m
Heaton, J.H. v3p0340c1m
v4p0036c1s v4p0157c2s v4p0163c2s
v4p0357c1s v4p0454c1m v4p0567c1s
v4p0567c2s v4p0582c1s v5p0248c1s
v5p0461c1s v5p0461c2m v5p0570c2m
v6p0008c2s v6p0270c2s v6p0479c1m
v6p0507c1s v6p0511c1m
Heaton, J.Henniker v4p0454c1s
Heaton, J.L. v3p0235c2s
v3p0448c2s v5p0203c1s
Heaton, M.M. v1p0319c1s
v1p0784c2s v1p0880c1s v1p1242c2s
v1p1306c2s v1p1365c1s v2p0069c1s
v2p0125c1s v2p0474c2s
Heaton, T.L. v6p0600c1s
Heaven, L.P. v2p0075c2s
v2p0261c1s v2p0354c1s v2p0386c1s
v3p0074c2s v3p0411c1s v3p0450c2s
Heaven, Louise P. v2p0287c1s
Heavens, F.J. v6p0504c2s
Heaviside, J.C. v1p0022c2s
Heaviside, O. v4p0177c1s
v6p0204c1s v6p0365c2s v6p0604c2s
Heawood, E. v4p0005c1s
v4p0005c2s v5p0005c2s v5p0006c1s
v5p0008c1s v5p0039c2s v5p0567c2s
v6p0258c1s v6p0683c2s
Hebberd, R.W. v5p0013c1s
v6p0109c2s v6p0321c1s v6p0452c1s
Hebberd, S.S. v1p0002c2s
v1p0047c2s v1p0173c2s v1p0198c1s
v1p0241c2s v1p0244c1s v1p0424c1s
v1p0434c1s v1p0559c2s v1p0581c1s
v1p0625c2s v1p0688c2s v1p0816c1s
v1p0858c1m v1p0957c1s v1p1017c1s
v1p1026c1s v1p1066c2s v1p1089c1s
v1p1162c1s v1p1260c1s v1p1355c1m
v1p1355c2m v2p0027c2s v2p0134c2s
v2p0146c1s v2p0236c1s v2p0324c1s
v2p0333c1s v2p0339c2s v2p0357c1s
v2p0435c2s v2p0439c1s v2p0440c1s
v2p0460c1s
Hebditch, E. v2p0039c2s
Hebeler, B. v1p1061c1s
Heber, R. v1p0096c2s
v1p0158c2s v1p0182c2s v1p0261c2s
v1p0310c2s v1p0517c2s v1p0552c1s
v1p0563c2s v1p0841c2s v1p0992c1s
v1p1010c2s v1p1134c1s v1p1136c1s
v1p1168c1s v1p1399c1s v1p1405c2s
Hebermann, C.G. v4p0169c2m
v4p0598c2s
Heck, L. v4p0379c1s
Heck, W.H. v6p0128c1s
v6p0194c2s v6p0249c2s v6p0581c2s
v6p0605c1s
Hecker, I.T. v1p0217c1s
v1p0286c1s v1p0386c1s v1p0481c1s
v1p0492c2s v1p0582c1s v1p0648c2s
v1p0671c2s v1p0672c2s v1p0741c2s
v1p1059c1s v1p1083c2s v1p1086c1s
v1p1116c1s v1p1117c2s v1p1120c1s

v1p1135c2s v1p1159c2m v1p1161c2s v1p1215c2s v1p1321c1s v1p1354c1s v2p0231c2s v2p0268c2s v2p0349c1s v2p0357c2s v2p0358c2s v2p0375c2s v2p0388c2m v3p0020c2s v3p0058c1m v3p0136c1s v3p0172c2s v3p0191c1s v3p0247c1m
Hecker, I.T. and Hewit, A.F. v1p0711c2s
Heckert, C.G. v6p0194c2s
Heckethorn, C.W. v5p0164c1s v5p0345c2s v5p0346c1s v5p0346c2s v5p0567c2s
Heckewelder, J. v2p0320c1s
Heckman, W. v5p0031c2s
Heclis, J.L. v1p0334c1s
Hector, A.F. v1p0586c1s v1p1405c1s v1p1428c1s v2p0003c1s v2p0457c1s v4p0210c1s v4p0386c1s
Hector, J. v1p0164c1m v1p0856c1s v1p1256c1s v2p0463c1s v3p0304c2s
Hedberg, T. v5p0196c2s
Hedbrooke, A. v2p0100c2s
Heddie, E. v3p0271c1s
Heddle, E.F. v5p0277c1s v5p0431c2s v6p0581c2s v6p0653c1s
Heddle, Ethel F. v5p0413c2s v6p0242c2s v6p0534c1s
Heddle, M.F. v1p0948c2s v2p0005c1s
Hedenberg, W.L. v4p0516c2s
Hedge, F.H. v1p0038c1s v1p0125c1s v1p0128c1s v1p0166c1s v1p0217c1s v1p0248c1s v1p0253c1s v1p0260c1s v1p0260c2s v1p0274c1s v1p0368c2s v1p0370c1s v1p0380c2s v1p0405c2s v1p0426c1s v1p0429c2s v1p0431c2s v1p0433c1s v1p0440c1s v1p0441c1s v1p0450c1s v1p0513c2s v1p0514c1s v1p0520c1s v1p0530c2s v1p0537c2s v1p0594c1s v1p0640c2s v1p0686c1s v1p0736c2s v1p0898c2s v1p0923c1s v1p0945c1s v1p0980c2s v1p1005c1s v1p1064c2s v1p1086c1s v1p1094c1m v1p1119c2s v1p1156c2s v1p1160c1s v1p1217c1s v1p1222c1s v1p1274c2s v1p1301c1m v1p1322c1s v1p1326c1s v1p1328c2s v1p1340c1s v1p1358c1s v2p0029c2s v2p0037c2s v2p0051c1s v2p0069c1s v2p0083c2s v2p0087c2s v2p0147c1s v2p0268c2s v2p0297c2s v2p0377c1s v2p0483c1s v3p0025c1s v3p0135c2s v3p0151c2s v3p0250c2s v3p0284c2s v3p0297c2s v3p0418c2s
Hedge, F.H. and Abbot, E.. v1p1302c2s
Hedge, F.H. et al. v1p0645c2s
Hedge, J.G. v1p0732c1s
Hedge, J.H. v1p1050c2s
Hedge, L. v1p0485c2s
Hedge, R.H. v1p0405c2s
Hedge, T. v4p0283c1s
Hedgecock, G.G. v6p0542c1s
Hedgepeth, V.W.B. v6p0030c1s v6p0290c1s v6p0609c1s
Hedger, Caroline v6p0113c2s
Hedges, K. v2p0136c2m v4p0215c2s v6p0377c1m
Hedges, M.B. v3p0361c1s
Hedges, S.B. v4p0374c1s v4p0442c1s v4p0452c1s
Hedin, D.S. v6p0286c1s
Hedin, S. v4p0390c1s v4p0587c1s v5p0034c1m v5p0496c1s v6p0036c2m v6p0355c1s v6p0645c2s
Hedin, Sven v6p0036c1s v6p0069c2s
Hedley, C. v4p0038c1s v4p0270c2s v5p0037c2s
Hedley, J. v1p0193c1s v3p0107c2s v3p0245c1s v3p0432c2s v5p0045c2s v6p0117c2s v6p0185c1s
Hedley, J.C. v1p1306c2s v3p0040c2s v5p0513c1s v6p0368c1s
Hedley, J.C. and Paul, H.. v5p0289c1s
Hedley, J.E. v2p0349c2s
Hedrick, E.R. v6p0091c2s
Hedrick, H.B. v6p0413c2s
Hedrick, N.P. v5p0430c1s
Hedrick, P.L. v6p0648c2s
Heeghway, T. v2p0211c2s
Heenan, T.E. v6p0198c2s
Heermance, E.L. v6p0153c2s
Heermance, T.W. v4p0035c1s v4p0186c2s v5p0194c2s v6p0149c2s
Heermance, T.W. and Lord, G.D. v5p0137c2s
Heermance, T.W. and Richardson, R.B. v5p0194c2s
Heermans, F. v4p0473c2s v5p0626c2s
Heermans, J.W. v6p0380c1s
Hefelbower, S.G. v5p0503c2s v5p0577c1s v6p0040c2s
Hefelbower, S.G. and Kirn, O. v5p0165c1s
Hefele, C.J. v1p1206c2s
Hefele, Dr.von v1p1372c1s
Hefferman, M.P. v6p0103c1s
Heffernan, M.P. v5p0507c2s
Heffner, W.C. v6p0600c1s
Heg, J.E. v4p0285c1s
Hegan, A.C. v5p0021c2s v6p0388c2s v6p0695c1s
Hegedus, A., jr. v5p0186c1s v5p0309c2s v5p0442c1s v6p0303c2s
Hegedus, Alexander, jr. .. v6p0042c2s v6p0345c2s
Hegel, G.W.F. v1p0057c2s v1p0061c2s v1p0063c2m v1p0144c2s v1p0237c1s v1p1017c1s v1p1237c1s v1p1277c2s v2p0368c1s v2p0368c2s v2p0369c1s v3p0358c1s
Hegeler, E.C. v4p0214c1s v4p0247c2s v4p0262c1s v4p0345c1s v4p0478c2m v4p0537c2s
Hegeler, E.C. et al. v4p0188c1s
Heggem, C.O. v4p0008c2s v4p0210c1s v6p0615c2s
Hegner, H.F. v4p0269c1s v5p0536c1s
Heiberg, J.L. v2p0212c1s
Heidborn, A. v6p0431c2s
Heidel, W.A. v3p0384c2s v4p0039c2s v5p0179c2s v5p0371c2s v6p0209c2s v6p0273c1s v6p0496c1s
Heidelbach, A.S. v4p0230c2s
Heideloff, C. v1p0495c1s
Heideloff, Prof. v1p0305c2s v1p0495c1s
Heidenhain, R. v1p0620c2s
Heighway, T. v2p0317c2s
Heilborn, E. v5p0230c2m v6p0252c1m
Heilig, S. v5p0044c1s v5p0508c2s v6p0013c2s v6p0044c2s v6p0224c2s v6p0304c1s v6p0570c1s
Heilman, L. v1p0847c2s
Heilman, L.M. v1p0731c2s v2p0034c2s v4p0345c2s
Heilmeyer, A. v6p0579c2s
Heilprin, A. v2p0112c1s v2p0173c1s v2p0439c2s v2p0458c1s v3p0047c1s v3p0185c1s v3p0207c1s v3p0290c1m v3p0372c1s v4p0025c1m v4p0025c2s v4p0065c1s v4p0147c2s v4p0192c2s v4p0203c1s v4p0227c1s v4p0271c1s v4p0417c2s v4p0507c2s v5p0010c2s v5p0022c2s v5p0154c2s v5p0318c1m v5p0318c2s v5p0413c1s v5p0503c2s v5p0605c1s v6p0100c2s v6p0276c1s v6p0403c2s v6p0433c1s v6p0486c1s v6p0486c2m v6p0487c1m v6p0681c1s
Heilprin, Angelo v6p0023c1s
Heilprin, L. v3p0197c1s v4p0221c1s v4p0473c2s v5p0043c2s
Heilprin, M. v1p0020c2s v1p0025c2s v1p0058c1s v1p0067c2s v1p0069c2s v1p0079c2s v1p0080c1s v1p0080c2m v1p0121c2s v1p0123c1s v1p0145c1s v1p0154c1s v1p0175c2s v1p0220c2s v1p0271c1s v1p0328c2s v1p0348c1s v1p0379c2s v1p0396c1s v1p0397c1s v1p0473c2s v1p0474c2s v1p0476c1s v1p0477c1s v1p0477c2m v1p0478c1s v1p0478c2s v1p0480c1m v1p0480c2s v1p0503c2s v1p0516c1s v1p0517c2s v1p0601c1s v1p0615c1s v1p0615c2s v1p0691c1m v1p0788c2s v1p0831c2s v1p0863c2s v1p0892c1s v1p0894c2s v1p0951c1s v1p0957c1s v1p0963c2s v1p0967c1s v1p0980c2s v1p0992c1s v1p1023c2s v1p1037c1s v1p1045c1s v1p1073c1s v1p1096c2s v1p1133c2s v1p1135c2m v1p1138c2s v1p1180c1s v1p1190c1s v1p1209c1s v1p1230c1s v1p1234c2s v1p1305c2s v1p1314c1m v1p1330c1m v1p1332c2s v1p1346c2s v1p1370c1s v1p1382c2s v1p1412c2s v2p0007c2s v2p0029c2m v2p0032c1s v2p0042c2s v2p0043c1s v2p0043c2s v2p0044c2s v2p0048c1s v2p0060c2s v2p0071c1s v2p0108c1s v2p0110c2s v2p0116c1s v2p0130c1s v2p0135c1s v2p0156c1s v2p0164c2s v2p0166c1s v2p0166c2m v2p0170c1s v2p0176c2s v2p0177c1s v2p0202c1s v2p0204c1s v2p0211c2s v2p0231c2s v2p0237c1s v2p0240c1s v2p0272c1m v2p0286c1s v2p0316c2s v2p0337c2s v2p0347c1s v2p0359c2s v2p0379c1s v2p0380c2m v2p0381c1s v2p0405c1s v2p0412c2m v2p0420c1s v2p0442c2s v2p0460c2s v2p0474c2s v3p0059c2s v3p0230c1m
Heim, A. v3p0377c1s
Heim, M. v5p0021c2s
Heimburg, H. v5p0499c2s
Heimburg, W. v3p0315c1s
Heimercheidt, A. v1p0471c1s
Heincke, F. v1p0456c2s
Heindel, R.L. v6p0699c2s
Heine, H. v1p0133c2s v1p1320c1s v1p1417c2s v2p0300c2s v5p0581c1s
Heineman, H. v1p0618c2s
Heinemann, A.H. v4p0354c2s v4p0467c2s v4p0514c2s v5p0288c2s
Heinemann, W. v2p0181c2s v2p0277c1s v2p0447c2s v4p0466c2s
Heiner, E. v1p0254c1s v1p0814c1s
Heinig, A. v6p0141c1s
Heinigke, O. v5p0026c1s v6p0084c1s v6p0258c2s
Heinrichs, E.H. v4p0004c1s
Heinrichs, H. v3p0428c2s
Heins, E. v3p0411c2s
Heins, Edward v4p0588c2s
Heinze, J.O., jr. v6p0546c2s
Heinzle, J.U. v3p0262c2s
Heis, E. v1p0077c2s
Heiskell, J.B. v2p0250c2s v3p0113c1s
Heisler, C.W. v4p0300c1s v4p0429c2s v5p0126c2s v5p0177c1s v5p0177c2s v6p0065c1s v6p0666c2s
Heisler, D.Y. v1p0048c1s v1p0096c2s v1p0252c2s v1p0253c2s v1p0276c1s v1p0351c2s v1p0357c2s v1p0536c2s v1p0538c2s v1p0570c1s v1p0625c2s v1p0641c2s v1p0756c2s v1p0900c2s v1p1043c2s v1p1097c2s v1p1101c1s v1p1432c2s v1p1433c1s v2p0213c1s v2p0235c1s
Heistand, H.O.S. v6p0522c2s
Heister, J.E. v1p0847c1s
Heitz, John v4p0580c1s
Heizman, C.L. v5p0375c2s v5p0507c2s
Helbig, F. v4p0206c1s
Helburn, J.W. v6p0008c2s v6p0182c2s v6p0233c2s v6p0534c1s v6p0568c2s
Heldenbrand, W. v1p0162c1s v2p0055c2s
Hele-Shaw, H.S. v3p0164c2s v5p0621c2s v6p0545c1s
Hele-Shaw, Prof. v5p0041c1s
Helfenstein, E. v1p0505c1s
Helfenstein, J. v1p1357c1s
Helfenstein, S., jr. v1p0247c1s v1p0485c2s
Helffrich, W.A. v3p0043c2s
Heliot, Claire v6p0378c1s
Hellams, T.B.R. v6p0403c1s
Hellems, B.R. v6p0277c1s
Hellems, F.B.R. v5p0472c2s v6p0209c2s v6p0212c2s v6p0273c2m v6p0344c2s
Heller, A.J. v4p0036c2s v4p0054c2s v4p0300c1s v5p0033c2s
Heller, C. v6p0616c1s
Heller, H.H. v6p0004c2s
Heller, Harriet H. v4p0466c1s
Heller, O. v3p0171c1s v3p0206c2s v4p0320c1s v6p0058c2s
Heller, Otto v6p0253c1s
Hellier, B. v3p0229c2s
Hellier, C.E. and Allen, C.L. v4p0131c2s
Hellig, S. v6p0183c2s
Hellig, S. and Dewey, S. . v6p0302c2s
Hellings, Emma L. v6p0552c1s
Helliwell, M.M. v4p0207c1s v5p0283c1s v6p0704c2s
Helliwell, M.McL. v6p0096c2s v6p0161c2s
Hellman, G.S. v5p0020c2s v5p0412c1s v6p0054c2s v6p0140c1s v6p0407c1s v6p0486c1s v6p0706c2s
Hello, E. v1p1284c2s
Hellthaler, Andrew v6p0203c1s
Hellwald, F.von v1p1162c1s
Hellyer, J.S. v2p0122c2s
Helm, B. v2p0291c2s
Helm, E. v4p0136c1s v4p0279c1s v4p0279c2s v4p0553c2s v6p0153c1m
Helm, E.T. v5p0339c2s
Helm, J.C. v4p0050c2s
Helm, J.I. v1p1082c2s v1p1402c2s
Helm, N.W. v6p0085c1s v6p0331c2s v6p0455c2s
Helm, W.H. v6p0480c1s
Helmer, F.T. v6p0425c2s
Helmholtz, H. v1p0400c2m v1p0443c2s v1p0510c1m v1p0518c1s v1p1222c2s v1p1336c2m
Helmholtz, H.L.F. v1p0467c1s v2p0280c1s
Helmholtz, R.von v4p0311c2s
Helmick, M.A. v5p0033c2s
Helmore, M.C. v2p0354c1s
Helmsley, W.B. v2p0155c2s v3p0344c1s
Helps, A. v1p0296c1m v1p0406c1s v1p0425c1s v1p0477c2s v1p0538c2s v1p0708c2s v1p0777c1s v1p1086c1s v1p1258c2s v1p1308c1s v1p1384c1s v1p1429c1s
Helps, E.A. v1p0608c1s
Helwig, J.B. v1p0276c1s
Hemans, C.J. v1p0205c2s v1p1125c1s
Hemans, F. v1p0346c2s v1p0448c1s v1p1220c1s

Hemans, F., Mrs. v1p0553c1s
v1p1220c2s v1p1308c1s
Hemans, H.W. v1p0477c2s
v1p0896c1s v1p1060c2s
Hemenway, F.D. v1p1415c2s
Hemenway, M. v5p0419c1s
Hemenway, R.F. v4p0201c1s
v4p0513c2s
Hemery, F.H. v1p1162c2s
Hemery, Gertrude v4p0148c2s
Heming, A. v6p0098c1s
Heming, A.H.H. v4p0087c1s
v4p0292c2s
Heming, H. v1p0405c2s
Heming, W. v6p0642c1s
Hemingham, L. v4p0162c1s
Hemingway, A. v6p0365c1s
Hemment, J.C. v5p0642c2s
Hemmeter, J.C. v4p0483c1s
Hemming, A.W.L., Sir v6p0144c1s
Hemming, G.W. v2p0065c1s
v4p0082c2s
Hemming, V. v6p0222c1s
Hemphill, J.C. v4p0524c2s
Hemphill, J.C. et al. v4p0524c2s
Hemphill, R.I. v4p0538c2s
Hempl, C. v5p0072c1s
Hempl, G. v3p0170c2s
v4p0014c1s v4p0183c1s v4p0621c2s
v5p0126c2s v5p0127c1s v5p0249c1s
v5p0523c1s
Hempl, Geo. v4p0568c2s
Hempstead, E.A. v4p0129c1s
Hempstead, H.E. v1p0784c1s
Hems, H.T., jr. v5p0337c2s
Hemsen, Prof. v1p0980c1s
Hemsley, W.B. v2p0053c1s
v2p0073c2s v3p0051c2s v3p0224c1s
v3p0235c1s v4p0069c2s v4p0202c2s
v4p0218c2s v4p0293c2s v4p0445c2s
v4p0513c1s v4p0584c1s v5p0038c2s
v6p0632c1s
Hemstreet, C. v6p0453c1s
Hemstreet, C.M. v6p0454c1s
v6p0686c2s
Hemstreet, W. v6p0008c1s
v6p0105c1m v6p0160c1s v6p0175c1s
v6p0309c2s v6p0446c2s v6p0516c1s
v6p0624c1s v6p0651c1s
Henck, J.B. v1p0051c1s
v1p0966c1s
Henderson, A. v2p0032c1s
v3p0250c2s v6p0163c2s v6p0283c1s
v6p0305c2s v6p0394c1m v6p0495c1s
v6p0552c2s v6p0589c2s v6p0600c1s
Henderson, A.H. v6p0005c2s
v6p0167c2s v6p0204c1s v6p0230c2s
v6p0257c1s v6p0311c1s v6p0361c2s
v6p0365c2s v6p0412c1s v6p0432c2s
v6p0433c2s v6p0440c2s v6p0466c2s
v6p0554c2s v6p0586c1s v6p0602c2s
Henderson, A.M. v1p0977c2s
Henderson, Archibald v6p0222c2s
Henderson, B.W. v5p0371c2s
v5p0537c1s v6p0449c1s v6p0548c2s
Henderson, C.G. v5p0483c2s
Henderson, C.H. v3p0040c1s
v3p0075c2s v3p0174c2m v3p0267c1s
v3p0279c1s v3p0404c1s v3p0445c1s
v4p0168c2s v4p0169c1s v4p0228c1s
v4p0354c1s v4p0368c2s v4p0598c1s
v5p0179c1s v5p0199c2s v5p0328c1s
v5p0360c2s v5p0449c2s v5p0644c1s
v6p0509c2s v6p0535c1s
Henderson, C.R. v2p0333c2s
v4p0033c2s v4p0080c2s v4p0097c1s
v4p0103c2s v4p0152c1s v4p0374c1s
v4p0428c2s v4p0452c1s v4p0452c2s
v4p0513c1s v4p0533c1s v4p0534c2s
v4p0535c1m v4p0573c1s v4p0633c1s
v5p0100c2s v5p0289c1s v5p0306c1s
v5p0443c2s v5p0459c1s v5p0466c2s
v5p0471c2s v5p0535c1s v5p0535c2s
v5p0536c1s v6p0109c2m v6p0125c1s
v6p0135c2s v6p0238c1s v6p0322c2s
v6p0348c2s v6p0538c1s
Henderson, C.R. et al. ... v5p0592c2s
Henderson, D.B. v6p0666c2s
Henderson, D.M., jr. v6p0664c2s
Henderson, E. v1p0096c1s
v1p0529c2s
Henderson, E.E. v6p0695c2s
Henderson, E.F. v5p0319c2s
v6p0110c1s
Henderson, E.J. v6p0564c1s
Henderson, E.Y.W. v3p0065c2s
Henderson, F.B. v5p0008c1s
Henderson, G.C. v6p0707c1s
Henderson, G.F.R. v4p0284c1s
v4p0584c2s v5p0290c1s v5p0375c1s
v5p0398c1s v5p0565c2s v6p0319c1s
Henderson, G.G. v5p0160c1s
Henderson, G.R. v3p0373c1s
v5p0202c2s
Henderson, H. v3p0018c1s
v3p0395c1s
Henderson, H.B. v6p0314c2s
Henderson, H.C. v6p0078c2s
Henderson, H.W. v6p0150c1s
Henderson, Helen W. v6p0263c2s
v6p0487c2s
Henderson, I.I. v2p0309c1s
Henderson, J. v1p0752c1s
v1p1079c1s v1p1251c1s v1p1341c2s
v5p0338c1s v5p0634c2s v6p0139c2s
v6p0257c2s v6p0522c1s
Henderson, J. et al. v3p0470c1s
Henderson, J.A. v1p1248c1m
v1p1249c2s
Henderson, J.C. v4p0524c2s
Henderson, J.G. v1p0174c1s
v1p1018c1s v1p1084c1s
Henderson, J.H. v5p0191c1s
v5p0357c2s v6p0025c2s
Henderson, J.R. v2p0268c1s
v6p0386c2s
Henderson, J.R.A. v2p0151c2s
Henderson, J.S. v1p0138c2m
v1p0582c2m v1p0723c2s v1p0826c1s
v1p1075c1s v1p1085c2m v1p1156c1m
v6p0077c1s v6p0286c1s v6p0578c1s
Henderson, J.Scot v4p0044c1s
Henderson, J.T.A. v2p0027c2s
Henderson, Junius v6p0699c1s
Henderson, K. v6p0182c2s
Henderson, Louise C. v5p0081c1s
v5p0258c1s v5p0590c2s v5p0628c1s
Henderson, M.E. v6p0107c2s
v6p0179c1s v6p0504c2s
Henderson, M.Sturge, Mrs.. v6p0411c2s
Henderson, P. v1p0462c2s
Henderson, P.A.W. v3p0184c2s
v4p0227c2s v4p0419c2s v5p0209c2s
v6p0105c2s v6p0130c1s v6p0263c2s
Henderson, R. v2p0083c1s
v2p0183c2s v2p0234c2s v2p0292c1s
v2p0450c2s v5p0107c2s
Henderson, R.C. v5p0135c1s
v5p0293c2s v6p0639c2s
Henderson, T.F. v5p0102c2s
v6p0088c2s
Henderson, T.F. et al. ... v3p0044c2s
Henderson, V. v5p0088c2s
v6p0093c2s v6p0366c1s v6p0671c2m
Henderson, W. v1p0792c2s
v3p0141c2s
Henderson, W.A. v6p0587c1s
Henderson, W.C. v5p0320c1s
Henderson, W.C. et al. ... v6p0225c1s
Henderson, W.D. v1p0094c1s
v1p0250c1s
Henderson, W.G. v6p0439c2s
Henderson, W.J. v2p0267c1s
v3p0257c2s v3p0303c2s v3p0405c2s
v3p0473c2s v4p0391c2s v4p0562c2s
v4p0572c2s v4p0634c2m v5p0213c1s
v5p0401c2s v5p0575c2s v5p0619c1s
v5p0642c2m v5p0643c1s v6p0134c1s
v6p0227c1s v6p0438c2m v6p0468c1s
v6p0469c2s v6p0498c2s v6p0562c2s
v6p0595c2s v6p0644c1s v6p0683c1s
v6p0710c1s
Henderson, W.M. v1p0145c2s
v1p0146c2m v1p0280c2m v1p0408c1s
v1p1065c1m v1p1065c2s v1p1392c1s
v2p0419c2s v3p0137c1s v4p0547c1s
Henderson, W.O. v4p0585c1s
Henderson, W.P. and Cushman, J.A.
v6p0026c2s v6p0542c1s
Henderson, W.T. v5p0526c2s
v6p0142c2s
Henderson, Y. v6p0566c1s
Hendren, S.R. v4p0282c2s
Hendrick, A.C. v1p0554c1s
Hendrick, B.J. v5p0262c1s
v5p0340c1m v6p0066c1s v6p0068c2s
v6p0077c2s v6p0087c1s v6p0262c2s
v6p0308c1s v6p0321c2s v6p0322c2s
v6p0343c2s v6p0388c1s v6p0453c1s
v6p0623c1s v6p0638c1s v6p0638c2s
v6p0652c2s v6p0662c1s v6p0676c1s
v6p0710c2s
Hendrick, Burton J. v6p0037c2s
Hendrick, E. v6p0183c1s
Hendrick, J.R. v3p0299c2s
Hendrick, J.T. v1p0283c2s
Hendrick, R.J. v4p0635c1s
Hendrick, W. v4p0575c2s
Hendrick, W.J. v6p0669c2s
Hendrick, W.J. et al. v6p0169c2s
Hendricks, A. v4p0281c2s
v4p0582c2s v5p0078c1s v5p0323c1s
v5p0344c1s v5p0458c1s v5p0572c2s
v5p0629c1s
Hendricks, H. v4p0535c2s
Hendricks, J.C. v4p0636c1s
Hendricks, J.E. v1p0463c1s
v1p1067c1s v2p0047c1s v2p0127c2s
v2p0414c2s
Hendricks, T.A. v1p1101c2s
v1p1353c1s
Hendrickson, G.L. v4p0114c1s
v4p0489c1s v5p0002c1s v5p0270c2m
v6p0127c1s v6p0127c2s v6p0489c1s
v6p0623c1s
Hendrickson, L.R. v1p1295c1s
Hendriks, F. v1p0043c2s
v1p0550c2s v1p0631c1s v1p1230c1s
v1p1274c2s
v1p1285c2s
v1p1376c1s
Hendrix, E.R. v5p0067c2s
v5p0075c2s v5p0372c2s v5p0625c2s
v6p0341c2s
Hendrix, H. v5p0382c1s
Hendrix, J.C. v4p0526c1s
v4p0566c1s
Hendry, G. v5p0525c2s
Hendry, H. v4p0090c2s
v4p0178c2s v4p0575c2s v5p0049c2s
v5p0425c2s v5p0629c2s
Hendry, J. v2p0323c2s
Heneage, E. v4p0210c2s
Heneboy, R. v6p0245c1m
Henebry, R. v6p0328c1s
Heness, T. et al. v3p0242c2s
Henessey, P. v1p1116c2s
Henfrey, A. v1p1015c2s
Henfrey, H.W. v2p0051c2s
v2p0383c1s
Hengiston, J.H. v1p0226c1s
Hengiston, J.W. v1p0089c2s
v1p0611c1s v1p0856c2s v1p0916c2s
v1p0939c1s v1p0988c1s v1p0996c2s
v1p1039c1s v1p1389c1s
Hengstenberg, E.W. v1p0122c2s
v1p0124c2s v1p0226c1s v1p1267c2s
Hengstler, L.T. v6p0324c2s
Henham, E.G. v5p0150c1s
v5p0222c2s v5p0267c2s v5p0275c2s
v5p0276c1s v5p0410c1s v5p0578c1s
v6p0465c2s v6p0663c2s
Henkel, D.M. v1p0599c2s
Henkle, W.D. v1p0819c1s
Henley, J. v6p0289c2s
Henley, S.H. v6p0002c2s
Henley, T.C. v1p0105c2s
Henley, W.E. v1p0186c1s
v1p0456c1s v1p0606c1s v1p0736c1s
v1p0942c1s v1p1382c2s v2p0002c1s
v2p0210c2s v2p0248c2s v2p0385c1s
v3p0243c2s v4p0042c2s v4p0364c2s
v5p0079c1s v5p0084c1s v5p0190c1s
v5p0194c1s v5p0255c2s v5p0259c1s
v5p0361c2s v5p0376c2s v5p0415c2s
v5p0446c2s v5p0517c1s v5p0552c2s
v5p0581c1s
Henley, W.E. and Stevenson, R.L.
v4p0346c2s
Henley, W.E. et al. v4p0239c2s
Henly, M. v1p0571c2s
Henman, W. v2p0209c1s
Henman, Wm. v6p0677c1s
Henn, A.B. v5p0186c1s
v5p0422c2s
Henn, A.W. v6p0619c1s
Henn, W. v4p0203c1s
v4p0634c2s
Henne, H.M. v5p0203c2s
v5p0326c1s v5p0590c2s v5p0596c2s
Henne, H.Meyer v5p0170c1s
Henneberry, K.M. v4p0330c1s
Hennel, W.U. v6p0617c1s
Hennell, Sara and Bray, Caroline
v6p0200c2s
Henneman, J.B. v4p0184c1s
v4p0605c2s v5p0049c1s v5p0078c1s
v5p0157c1s v5p0170c1s v5p0192c1s
v5p0341c2s v5p0522c2s v5p0572c2s
v6p0072c1s v6p0276c2s v6p0361c2s
v6p0380c1s v6p0461c1s v6p0585c2s
v6p0606c2s
Henneman, J.B. and Bose, W.P.Du
v6p0218c1s
Hennequin, A. v3p0122c1m
v3p0334c2s v4p0215c1s v4p0587c2s
v5p0282c2s
Hennessy et al. v1p0831c2s
Hennessy, H. v1p0265c1s
v1p0375c2s v1p0376c1s v1p0668c2s
v1p0737c1s v1p1390c2s
Hennessy, H. et al. v1p0627c2s
Hennessy, J.P. v1p1081c2s
v2p0224c2s v2p0228c2s v3p0199c1s
Hennessy, J.P., Sir v3p0004c2m
v3p0079c1s v3p0183c1s
Hennessy, M. v3p0130c1s
v4p0182c1s v4p0183c2s v4p0242c2s
v4p0328c2s
Hennessy, P. v3p0005c1s
Henniker, A., Mrs. v4p0041c1s
v4p0071c2s
Henniker, F. v4p0420c2s
Henniker, H.J. v6p0636c1s
Henniker, Mrs. v5p0578c2s
Henniker, R. v2p0249c1s
Henniker-Heaton, J. v2p0350c2s
v3p0027c2s
Hennin, G.de v2p0449c1s
v3p0284c2s v3p0438c2s
Henning, A.S. v2p0080c2s
Henning, B.S. v4p0473c2s
Henning, C.L. v6p0289c2s
Henning, G.C. v4p0571c1s
v5p0188c2s
Henning, G.W. v1p0119c1s
Henning, H.M. v3p0041c2s
Henning, S. v3p0346c2s
Hennings, K. v3p0153c2s
Henook-Makhewe-Kelenaka .. v5p0528c1s

Henrard, P. v1p0356c1s
Henri, C. and Henri, V. .. v5p0480c2s
Henri, V. and Henri, C. .. v5p0480c2s
Henrici, O. v2p0174c1m
v2p0280c1m v3p0165c2s v3p0382c1s
v5p0570c1s
Henrick, B.J. v6p0056c1s
Henriksen, M.E. v6p0066c2s
v6p0274c1s
Henriques, A. v4p0171c1s
Henriques, A.G. v5p0565c1s
Henriques, A.G. et al. ... v1p0934c1s
Henriques, E.N. v5p0032c2s
Henriques, H.S. v4p0379c2s
Henriques, H.S.Q. v5p0307c2s
v6p0343c1s v6p0343c2m
Henrivaux, J. v5p0235c2s
Henrotin, E.M. v2p0112c2s
v4p0100c2s v4p0102c1s v4p0630c2s
v6p0176c2s v6p0706c1s
Henrotin, Ellen M. v5p0108c1s
v5p0637c1s v5p0638c2m v6p0581c2s
Henry, A. v5p0039c1s
v5p0179c1s v5p0360c2s v5p0425c2s
v6p0042c1s v6p0207c1s v6p0235c1s
v6p0340c1s v6p0454c2s v6p0622c1s
v6p0649c2s v6p0714c2s
Henry, A.J. v6p0690c1s
Henry, A.S. v6p0026c2s
v6p0032c1s v6p0085c1s v6p0228c1s
v6p0284c2s v6p0552c1s
Henry, Alice v6p0026c1s
v6p0257c1s v6p0705c1s
Henry, Arthur v5p0280c2s
Henry, B.C. v4p0389c2s
v5p0394c2s
Henry, Bertram C. v5p0134c1s
v5p0395c1s
Henry, C. v1p0529c1s
v4p0411c1s v4p0530c1s
Henry, C.S. v1p0594c2s
v1p0646c2s v1p0732c2s v1p0769c1s
v1p0775c1s v1p0812c2s v1p0819c2s
v1p0838c2s v1p0868c2s v1p1054c2s
v1p1345c2s v1p1346c1s v1p1348c1s
v1p1351c1s
Henry, D.F. v1p1390c1s
Henry, Dr. v1p1346c2s
Henry, E. and Robinson, J.B.
v3p0059c2s
Henry, E.M. v3p0172c2s
v3p0243c1s v3p0294c2s v3p0324c1s
v4p0523c2s
Henry, F.A. v1p0003c1s
v1p0241c1s v1p0309c2s v1p0454c1s
v1p0594c1s v1p0625c2s v1p0652c1s
v1p0702c1s v1p1000c2s v1p1051c1s
v1p1325c2s v2p0041c2s v2p0369c2s
v3p0437c2s v5p0196c1s
Henry, F.K. v4p0212c2s
Henry, F.P. v6p0500c2s
Henry, G.C. v4p0372c2s
v6p0344c2s
Henry, G.G. v6p0126c2s
Henry, G.L. v1p0358c1s
v1p0931c2s
Henry, G.V. v5p0128c1s
Henry, G.V., Mrs. v5p0460c1s
v5p0507c1s
Henry, H.F. v4p0088c1s
v4p0313c2s
Henry, H.T. v4p0052c1s
v4p0233c1s v4p0263c1s v4p0271c2s
v4p0388c2s v5p0142c1s v5p0439c2s
v6p0612c1s
Henry, Hugh v5p0039c2s
v5p0406c1s
Henry, J. v1p0164c2s
v1p0174c2s v1p0269c2s v1p0278c2s
v1p0381c2s v1p0392c2s v1p0401c1s
v1p0467c1s v1p0749c1s v1p0799c1s
v1p1162c1s v1p1212c1m v6p0274c1s
Henry, J.A. v1p1160c1s
Henry, J.C. v2p0138c2s
Henry, J.K. v4p0538c1s
Henry, J.R. v6p0413c1m
Henry, J.R. and Herschel, A.S.
v6p0413c1s
Henry, J.S. v6p0244c2s
Henry, John R. v6p0524c1s
Henry, K.D. v5p0233c1s
v6p0613c1s
Henry, K.O. v5p0548c1s
Henry, M.A. v5p0262c1s
Henry, M.H. v3p0273c1s
Henry, M.L. v2p0057c2s
v2p0175c1s v2p0197c2s v2p0266c1s
v2p0281c1s v2p0283c2s v2p0436c1s
Henry, M.P. v3p0452c1s
Henry, N.B. et al. v3p0422c1s
Henry, O. v5p0230c1s
v5p0628c2s v6p0094c1s v6p0153c2s
v6p0174c1s v6p0179c1s v6p0179c2s
v6p0212c1s v6p0235c2s v6p0275c2s
v6p0279c1s v6p0290c2s v6p0294c1s
v6p0298c2s v6p0402c1s v6p0421c1s
v6p0496c1s v6p0500c1s v6p0531c2s
v6p0540c2s v6p0554c2s v6p0581c1s
v6p0637c1s v6p0638c1s v6p0648c2s
v6p0657c1s v6p0665c2s
Henry, P. v3p0228c1s
v6p0629c2s
Henry, P. and Henry, P. .. v2p0340c1m
Henry, P.E. v1p1126c1s
Henry, Rene v6p0042c2s
Henry, S. v4p0148c1s
v4p0214c2s
Henry, S.M.I., Mrs. et al.
v3p0148c1s
Henry, S.O. v3p0223c2s
v3p0353c2s
Henry, T. v1p0897c1s
Henry, W. v1p1050c1s
v2p0397c1s
Henry, W.A. v1p1315c1s
Henry, W.E. v5p0334c2s
v5p0335c2s v6p0374c2s
Henry, W.H. v6p0287c1s
Henry, W.W. v1p0261c1s
v1p0585c2m v1p1211c1s v3p0396c1s
v4p0605c2s v5p0620c2s v5p0621c1s
Henry-Ruffin, M.E. v4p0028c1s
v4p0488c1s v5p0258c1s
Henschel, C.A. v1p0956c1s
v1p1397c1s
Henschel, G. v5p0075c1s
Hensel, E.P. v6p0490c2s
Hensel, L. v4p0352c2s
Hensel, O. v2p0260c1s
v3p0334c1s v4p0269c2s
Hensel, Octavia v5p0393c2s
Hensel, S.T. v6p0375c2s
Hensel, W.U. v3p0046c2s
Henser, H.J. v3p0302c1s
Henshall, J.A. v2p0036c1s
v5p0049c1s v6p0053c2m v6p0227c2s
v6p0264c2s
Henshall, J.A., Dr. v5p0209c1s
Henshaw, D. v1p0333c1s
Henshaw, H. v6p0638c2s
Henshaw, H.E. v2p0201c1s
Henshaw, H.W. v2p0403c2s
v3p0063c1s v3p0213c2s v3p0282c2s
v6p0317c1s
Henshaw, J.P.K. v1p0841c2s
Henshaw, J.W. v6p0082c2s
v6p0227c2s v6p0546c2m
Henshaw, M. v4p0331c2s
Henshaw, S. v4p0021c2s
v6p0304c2s
Henshaw, S.E. v1p0235c1s
v1p0293c2s v1p0298c1s v1p0339c2s
v1p0839c2s v1p1421c1s
Henshaw, W.H. v2p0014c2s
Hensley, A. and Irwin, M.M.
v5p0537c1s
Hensley, W.B. v3p0238c1s
Henslow, G. v1p0434c2s
v1p0452c2s v1p1014c2s v1p1015c1m
v1p1015c2s v2p0015c1s v2p0252c1m
v2p0398c2s v2p0474c2s v4p0077c2s
v4p0255c2s v4p0540c1s v4p0600c2s
v5p0514c2s v5p0608c1s v6p0165c2s
Henslow, G. and Bastin, S.L.
v6p0229c2s
Hensman, H. v5p0597c1s
v6p0242c1s v6p0252c2s
Hensoldt, H. v3p0026c1s
v3p0072c2s v3p0089c2s v3p0295c2s
v3p0297c1s v3p0380c2s v4p0071c2s
v4p0349c1s v4p0424c1s v4p0487c2s
v4p0576c1s
Henson, C.H. v6p0342c1s
Henson, H. v5p0315c1s
v5p0489c2s v6p0060c2s v6p0693c2s
Henson, H.H. v5p0117c2s
v5p0132c1s v5p0381c1s v5p0561c2s
v6p0123c2s v6p0126c1s v6p0187c2s
v6p0369c1s v6p0508c2s v6p0531c2s
v6p0536c2s
Henson, P.S. v4p0568c1s
Henson, W.S. v1p0017c1s
Henszey, J.W. v6p0318c2s
Hent, W.H. v5p0494c1s
Henton, G.M. v5p0097c1s
Hentschel, C. v5p0467c2s
Hentschel, E. v1p0365c1m
v1p1201c1s
Henty, C.G. v2p0324c2s
Henty, E.A. v3p0282c1s
Henty, G.A. v1p0067c1s
v1p0443c2s v1p0634c2s v1p1011c2s
v5p0582c2s
Henty, W. v2p0397c1s
Hentz, C.L. v1p1371c2s
Hentz, C.L., Mrs. v1p0076c2s
v1p0106c1s v1p0151c1s v1p0974c2s
Hentz, H. et al. v4p0081c1s
Henzel, C.B. v1p1411c1s
Hepburn, A. et al. v4p0525c1s
Hepburn, A.B. v2p0387c1s
v4p0043c2s v4p0066c1s v4p0393c2s
v6p0156c2s v6p0425c1s
Hepburn, A.P. v4p0143c2s
Hepburn, A.P. and Homer, C.C.
v4p0143c2s
Hepburn, C.H. v4p0027c2s
v4p0090c1s v4p0544c2s
Hepburn, D.H. v4p0090c1s
Hepburn, G.G. v1p0167c1s
v1p0207c2s v1p1111c2s v4p0177c2s
Hepburn, W. v6p0322c2s
Hepburn, W.B. v6p0233c1s
Heppe, H. v1p0189c2s
v1p0514c2s v1p0589c1s v1p0778c2s
v1p0818c1s
Heppel, G. v4p0361c1s
Hepper, L.L. v6p0035c1s
Hepple, M. v1p1425c2s
Hepson, H.H. v5p0305c1s
Hepworth, G. v3p0337c2s
Hepworth, G.H. v1p1341c2s
v3p0330c2s v4p0226c2s v4p0534c1s
Hepworth, M. v3p0343c2s
Hepworth, T.C. v3p0330c2s
v4p0139c2s v4p0440c2s v5p0010c1s
v5p0050c2s v5p0065c2s v5p0160c2s
v5p0227c2s v5p0355c2s v5p0448c1m
v6p0035c1s v6p0219c1s v6p0405c2s
v6p0498c2s
Hepworth-Dixon, M. v4p0380c1s
Herapath, J. v1p0759c2s
v1p1076c1s
Herapath, T.J. and Herapath, W.
v1p0336c2s
Herapath, W. and Herapath, T.J.
v1p0336c2s
Heraud, E. v1p0983c2s
Heraud, J.A. v1p0021c1s
v1p0155c1s v1p0368c2s v1p0710c1s
v1p1185c2s v1p1186c2s v1p1219c2s
Herbart, J.F. v1p0811c1s
v1p1062c1m
Herben, S.J. v5p0472c1s
v5p0595c2s v6p0195c1s
Herbermann, C.G. v2p0088c1s
v2p0173c1s v3p0110c2s v3p0356c2s
v3p0364c1s v3p0364c2s v3p0365c1s
v4p0040c2s v4p0306c1s v6p0286c2s
v6p0683c2s
Herbert and Hodgson v1p0591c2s
Herbert, A. v1p0192c2s
v2p0132c2s v2p0329c1s v2p0348c1m
v3p0008c1s v3p0146c1s v3p0158c1s
v3p0222c1s v3p0301c1s v3p0399c2s
v4p0165c1s v4p0233c1s v4p0239c1s
v5p0035c1s v5p0176c2s v5p0376c2s
v5p0488c1s v5p0579c1s v5p0589c1s
v6p0205c1s v6p0229c1s v6p0252c2s
Herbert, A. and Wager, H.. v4p0008c2s
Herbert, A. and Wager, N.. v3p0007c1s
Herbert, A. et al. v3p0146c1s
Herbert, A., Hon. v4p0590c2s
Herbert, A.J. v2p0311c2s
v2p0466c2s
Herbert, A.K. v4p0132c1m
v4p0156c1s v5p0135c2s v6p0352c2s
Herbert, C. v5p0013c2s
v5p0044c1s v5p0558c2s v6p0385c2s
Herbert, Col. v4p0279c2s
Herbert, E. v1p0270c2s
v1p0511c1s v1p0556c2s v1p0557c1s
v1p0753c2s v1p1242c2s v1p1299c1s
v1p1309c2s
Herbert, F.W.von v6p0087c1m
Herbert, G. v1p0176c1s
Herbert, G.F. v5p0244c1s
v6p0305c1s
Herbert, G.N. v5p0557c1s
Herbert, H. v2p0004c2s
Herbert, H.A. v4p0107c1s
v4p0184c2s v4p0265c2s v4p0266c1s
v4p0283c2s v4p0395c2m v4p0475c2s
v4p0500c1s v5p0403c2s v5p0480c2s
v5p0543c2s v5p0602c2s v5p0603c1s
Herbert, H.A. and Donnelly, T.
v4p0243c2s
Herbert, H.W. v1p0088c1s
v1p0136c2s v1p0168c1s v1p0432c2s
v1p0442c1s v1p0457c1s v1p0499c1s
v1p0556c1s v1p0558c1s v1p0692c1s
v1p0726c1s v1p0806c1s v1p0807c1s
v1p0887c2s v1p0896c2s v1p0949c2s
v1p0953c2s v1p1069c1s v1p1071c1s
v1p1081c2s v1p1121c1s v1p1133c1s
v1p1221c1s v1p1427c2s v1p1428c1s
Herbert, J.A. v5p0262c1s
v6p0013c2s
Herbert, J.B. v5p0411c2s
Herbert, J.W. v5p0003c1s
v5p0548c1s
Herbert, K. v6p0148c1s
Herbert, L. v1p0246c2s
v5p0620c2s
Herbert, Lady v1p0021c2s
v1p0449c1s v1p0834c2s v1p1229c1s
v2p0052c2s v2p0104c2s v2p0377c2s
v3p0395c1s
Herbert, M.E. v1p0345c2s
v1p1401c2s v3p0264c2s v4p0268c1s
v4p0488c1s v4p0496c2m v5p0489c2s
Herbert, P. v6p0090c1s
v6p0147c2s
Herbert, St.L. v2p0186c1s
Herbert, W. v1p0836c2s
Herbert, W.J. v6p0661c2s
Herbert, W.V. v6p0504c1s
Herbert of Lea, Lady v3p0109c1s
Herbertson, A.G. v5p0282c1s
Herbertson, A.G. and Kerr, E.T.

v6p0516c1s
Herbertson, A.J. v4p0403c1s
v5p0467c2s v5p0478c1s v6p0006c2s
v6p0082c1m v6p0186c2s v6p0250c2s
v6p0395c2s v6p0530c2s
Herbertson, J.L. v6p0597c2s
Herbertson, M. v3p0319c2s
Herbin, J. v4p0162c2s
Herbin, J.F. v5p0003c1s
Herbst, O. v1p1430c1s
Herczeg, F. v6p0303c2s
Herdan, B. v3p0165c1s
Herder, J.G. v1p0123c2s
v1p0600c1s v1p0684c2s v1p0687c2s
Herdman, H.H., jr. v5p0591c1s
Herdman, J.O. v4p0526c2s
Herdman, W.A. v2p0024c2s
v2p0123c2s v2p0213c2s v2p0448c1s
v3p0403c2s v3p0438c1s v5p0039c2s
v5p0062c2s v5p0397c2m v6p0485c2s
Hereford, B. v2p0043c1s
Hereford, J. v5p0457c2s
v6p0191c2s
Heresh, J.C. v2p0396c1s
Hereward, L. v4p0116c2s
Herfner, I. v1p0824c2s
Herford, B. v1p0261c2s
v1p0405c1s v1p0410c2s v1p1094c1s
v1p1098c2s v1p1270c1s v2p0200c1s
v2p0351c1s v2p0444c2s v3p0084c2s
v4p0328c2s v4p0480c1s v4p0488c1s
v4p0488c2s v4p0527c2s v6p0073c2s
Herford, C.H. v2p0037c1s
v2p0092c1s v2p0105c2s v2p0176c1s
v2p0277c1s v2p0387c2s v3p0075c1s
v3p0140c1s v3p0186c1s v3p0204c2s
v3p0206c2m v3p0389c2s v3p0390c1s
v4p0184c1s v4p0272c1m v4p0519c1s
v5p0278c1s
Herford, C.H. and Palgrave, F.T.
v3p0075c1s
Herford, C.H. et al. v4p0340c2s
Herford, I.S.A. v3p0093c2s
v3p0232c1s v3p0244c1s v3p0295c1m
v3p0325c2s v3p0431c2s v4p0160c2s
v5p0517c2s v5p0634c1s v6p0541c1s
Herford, J.S.A. v3p0466c1s
v4p0236c1s
Herford, L.S.A. v4p0370c1s
Herford, O. v6p0285c1s
Herford, R.T. v4p0229c1s
Herford, W.H. v1p0355c1s
v1p1422c2s
Hergesell, H. v5p0044c1s
Hericourt, M. v2p0303c1s
Hering, C. v3p0133c2s
v3p0134c1s v3p0320c1m v3p0474c1s
v4p0177c1s v4p0455c2s v6p0054c1s
Hering, Carl v3p0289c2s
Hering, D.W. v4p0441c2m
v5p0492c1s v6p0135c2s
Hering, E. v4p0364c2s
v4p0397c2s v5p0404c2s
Hering, F.F. v3p0172c1s
Hering, H.A. v4p0139c1s
v5p0074c2s v5p0098c1s v5p0155c1s
v5p0294c2s v5p0365c2s
Hering, M.G. v5p0122c2s
v6p0131c2s v6p0707c2m
Hering, R. v2p0396c1s
v2p0468c1s v3p0329c1s v4p0516c2s
v4p0613c1s v4p0613c2m v5p0042c2s
v5p0225c2s v5p0521c1s v5p0521c2s
Hering, R. and Clarke, T.C.
v1p0161c1s
Heriot, E. v1p0221c1m
v1p1051c2s v1p1174c1s v1p1223c2s
v1p1224c2s v1p1334c1s
Herisson, J.L. and Miller, F.T.
v6p0278c1s
Herkless, J. v5p0099c1s
Herkless, W.R. v4p0095c1s
Herkomer, H. v2p0478c2s
v4p0255c2s v4p0406c1s v4p0544c1s
v5p0187c2s
Herkomer, H.von v6p0367c2s
v6p0510c2s v6p0620c1s
Herlihy, J. v4p0169c2s
v4p0240c1s v5p0247c1s v5p0296c2s
v6p0280c1s v6p0299c1s
Herman, H. v1p1210c1s
v2p0026c2s v3p0269c2s v4p0342c1s
v4p0544c1s
Herman, H. and Murray, D.C.
v3p0312c2s v3p0466c1s
Herman, H. and Murray, D.Christie
v4p0624c2s
Hermann, A. v4p0223c1s
Hermann, F. v1p0614c1s
Hermann, L. v1p0040c2s
Hermans, W.S.H. v5p0037c2s
Hermant, J. v4p0100c2m
Hermeline, Abbe v6p0238c1s
Hern, F.
v2p0115c2s
Herndon, E.W. v2p0043c2s
v2p0083c2s v2p0084c2s v2p0108c2s
v2p0150c2s v2p0169c2s v2p0221c1s
v2p0221c2s v2p0297c2s v2p0432c2s
v2p0475c2s v3p0033c2m v3p0084c1s
v3p0086c1s v3p0313c2s v3p0359c1s
Herndon, Emily v4p0268c2s
Herne, F.S. v2p0256c2s
Herne, J.A. v4p0413c2s
v5p0167c1s
Herney, M. v3p0341c2s
Heroe, G. v6p0236c2s
Herold, A.F. v5p0023c1s
Heron, A. v2p0071c2s
v4p0017c2s
Heron, E. v1p0603c2s
v1p1288c2s
Heron, E. and Heron, H. .. v5p0159c1s
v5p0163c1s v5p0396c2s v5p0404c2s
v5p0421c1s v5p0534c1s v5p0562c2s
v5p0642c1s
Heron, G.A. v3p0237c2s
Heron, H. v4p0502c1s
Heron, H. and Heron, E. .. v5p0159c1s
v5p0163c1s v5p0396c2s v5p0404c2s
v5p0421c1s v5p0534c1s v5p0562c2s
v5p0642c1s
Heron, M. v1p1336c2s
v2p0139c2s v2p0343c2s
Heron-Allen, E. v3p0079c2s
v3p0294c1s v4p0605c1s
Heron-Maxwell, B. v6p0459c1s
Herrald, D.B. v3p0120c1s
Herran, T.D. v6p0477c1s
Herrera, A.L. v5p0404c2s
v5p0413c1s v5p0514c1s
Herreshoff, G. v6p0456c1s
v6p0650c1s
Herreshoff, J.B.F. v6p0111c2s
v6p0112c1s
Herreshoff, L. v3p0473c2m
Herrick, A. v4p0032c2s
Herrick, A.B. v5p0183c2s
Herrick, A.E. v5p0273c2s
v5p0355c1s v5p0424c2s v5p0567c2s
Herrick, A.H. v5p0556c1s
Herrick, B.F. v3p0234c2s
v4p0365c1s v4p0585c1s v6p0296c1s
v6p0534c2s v6p0545c1s
Herrick, B.F., Miss v5p0088c1s
Herrick, Bertha F. v6p0092c2s
v6p0093c2s v6p0229c2s
Herrick, C. v6p0002c1s
v6p0658c2s
Herrick, C.A. v5p0601c2s
v6p0141c1m v6p0190c1s v6p0250c2s
v6p0459c2s v6p0635c1s
Herrick, C.J. v6p0015c1s
v6p0015c2s v6p0067c1s v6p0227c1s
Herrick, C.Judson v6p0015c2s
Herrick, C.L. v1p0420c1s
v2p0118c1s v3p0072c1s v3p0073c2s
v3p0380c1s v4p0130c1s v4p0462c1s
v5p0369c2s v5p0470c2s v6p0405c2s
v6p0418c2s v6p0658c2s
Herrick, C.T. v5p0165c2s
v5p0434c2s v5p0519c2s v6p0039c1s
v6p0039c2s v6p0246c1s v6p0299c2s
v6p0397c2s v6p0702c2s
Herrick, E.C. v1p0077c1s
v1p0292c1s v1p0589c1s v1p0827c1m
v1p0827c2s
Herrick, Elizabeth v6p0103c1s
Herrick, F.H. v3p0030c2s
v3p0382c2s v4p0060c1s v4p0245c2s
v4p0256c2s v4p0337c1s v4p0511c1s
v5p0064c1m v5p0180c2s v5p0256c1s
v6p0068c2s v6p0114c1s v6p0382c1s
v6p0497c2s v6p0642c1m
Herrick, G.F. v1p0241c1s
v1p0294c2s v1p0379c1s v1p0440c2s
v1p0857c2s v1p0858c1s v1p1056c1s
v1p1059c2s v1p1148c1s v2p0045c1s
v3p0081c1s
Herrick, H.N. v4p0051c1s
Herrick, H.W. v1p0113c1s
v1p1244c2s v2p0418c1s
Herrick, I.A. v4p0164c1s
v4p0522c1s
Herrick, J.C. v6p0464c1s
Herrick, J.R. v1p0391c2s
v1p0568c1s v1p0797c2s v1p0869c1s
v1p0907c1s v1p1302c2s
Herrick, N.J. v4p0304c2s
Herrick, R. v4p0100c1s
v4p0578c1s v5p0440c1s v5p0458c1s
v5p0467c2s v5p0483c1s v6p0141c2s
v6p0203c2s v6p0543c1s v6p0593c1s
Herrick, R.W. v3p0164c1s
v4p0183c1s v4p0184c1s v4p0343c1s
v4p0458c1s v4p0469c2s
Herrick, S.B. v1p0044c1s
v1p0107c1s v1p0301c1s v1p0449c1s
v1p0462c2s v1p0511c2s v1p0645c2s
v1p0693c2s v1p0711c1s v1p0745c1s
v1p0757c1s v1p0899c1s v1p1012c1s
v1p1015c1s v1p1015c2s v1p1029c2s
v1p1172c1s v1p1219c2s v1p1239c1s
v2p0322c2s v3p0152c2s v3p0231c2s
v3p0290c1s v3p0333c1s v3p0334c1s
Herrick, S.B. and Hughes, M.W.
v3p0401c2s
Herrick, S.B., Mrs. v1p0021c1s
v1p0107c1s v1p0156c2s v1p0160c1s
v1p0301c1s v1p0511c2s v1p0610c2s
v1p0619c1s v1p0632c1s v1p0633c1s
Herrick, S.B., Sir v1p1171c2s
Herrick, S.E. v3p0322c2s
Herridge, W.T. v3p0037c2s
v3p0056c2s v3p0080c2s v3p0107c2s
Herries, V. v3p0428c2s
Herring, A. v1p0665c1s
Herring, C. v2p0126c2s
Herring, F.E. v4p0009c1s
Herring, G. v3p0205c2s
Herring, R. v1p0362c2s
v1p0997c1s
Herringham, C.J. v6p0512c1s
Herrington, A. v5p0151c2s
v6p0469c2s
Herriott, F.I. v4p0059c2s
v4p0233c1s
Herrle, G. v4p0082c1s
Herrmann, A. v3p0263c2s
v4p0062c2s v4p0529c2s
Herrmann, C. v4p0396c1s
Herron, E.K. v5p0168c1s
v5p0339c1s v5p0532c2s
Herron, G.D. v4p0109c2s
v4p0113c1s v4p0193c2s v4p0532c2s
v5p0306c2s v5p0470c1s v5p0598c1s
Herschel, A.S. v1p0077c1s
v1p0327c2s v1p0459c1s v1p0467c1s
v1p0497c1s v1p0606c1s v1p0827c1m
v1p1068c2s v1p1112c2s v1p1234c1s
v1p1244c2s v1p1369c1s v1p1394c2s
v1p1414c1s v2p0028c1s v2p0138c1s
v2p0412c2m v3p0155c2s v4p0037c2s
v4p0326c2s v4p0367c1s v5p0372c1s
v5p0441c1s v6p0524c1s v6p0627c1s
Herschel, A.S. and Henry, J.R.
v6p0413c1s
Herschel, C. v1p0086c2s
v1p0377c1s v1p0618c2s v1p1110c1s
v1p1390c1s v1p1390c2m v3p0147c1s
v4p0586c2s v5p0622c1s
Herschel, J. v1p0375c2m
v1p0505c2s v1p0986c1s v2p0003c1s
v2p0095c1s v2p0180c1s
Herschel, J. et al. v2p0015c1s
Herschel, J., Sir v1p1377c1s
Herschel, J.F. v1p1377c1s
Herschel, J.F.W. v1p0600c2s
v1p0746c2s v1p0815c1s v1p0829c1s
v1p1267c2s v1p1394c2s v2p0426c2s
Herschel, J.F.W., Sir v1p0070c2s
v1p0074c1s v1p0210c1s v1p0281c2s
v1p0305c1s v1p0331c2s v1p0376c2s
v1p0467c1s v1p0613c2s v1p0639c2s
v1p0788c2s v1p0936c2s v1p1053c2s
v1p1404c2s v2p0303c2s v2p0455c2s
v3p0407c1s
Hersee, H. v2p0322c1s
v2p0372c2s
Hersey, E. v4p0443c2s
Hersey, Edmund and Fernow, B.E.
v4p0443c2s
Hersey, H.E. v3p0057c1s
v3p0146c2s v5p0018c1s v5p0126c1s
v6p0702c2s
Hersey, I.C. v6p0110c1s
Hersey, M.L. v5p0135c2s
Hershey, A.S. v4p0142c2s
v5p0147c2s v6p0560c2s
Hershey, Amos S. v6p0277c2s
v6p0324c2s
Hershey, O.F. v4p0213c2s
v4p0535c2s v5p0351c2s
Hershey, O.H. v4p0526c2s
v5p0210c2s v5p0474c1s v6p0157c1s
v6p0353c1m
Hershey, S.R. v4p0037c2s
Herter, C.A. v3p0206c2s
v6p0046c2s
Hertford, Emily M. v5p0102c2s
Hertford, Marquis of v2p0185c2s
Herts, A.M. v6p0438c2s
Hertwig, J.G. v1p1063c1s
v4p0480c1s v4p0596c2s
Hertwig, O. v4p0541c2s
Hertz, F. v4p0559c1s
Hertz, H. v1p0708c1s
v3p0133c2m v3p0250c2s
Herve, A. v3p0372c1s
Hervey, A. v4p0249c2s
v6p0255c1s
Hervey, A.B. v5p0321c1s
v5p0479c2s
Hervey, C. v1p0059c2s
v1p0086c1s v1p0116c2s v1p0274c2s
v1p0363c1m v1p0488c1s v1p0512c1s
v1p0564c1s v1p0566c1s v1p0728c2s
v1p0808c1s v1p0930c2s v1p0968c1m
v1p1033c1s v1p1073c2s v1p1086c2s
v1p1129c2s v1p1280c2s v2p0002c1m
v2p0030c1s v2p0031c1s v2p0032c2s
v2p0037c1m v2p0055c2s v2p0094c2s
v2p0118c2s v2p0122c1s v2p0157c1s
v2p0159c1s v2p0176c1s v2p0181c2s
v2p0194c1s v2p0233c1s v2p0241c2s
v2p0247c1s v2p0263c2s v2p0272c2m
v2p0282c2s v2p0283c2s v2p0315c1s
v2p0323c2s v2p0329c1s v2p0329c2m
v2p0345c1s v2p0350c2s v2p0362c1s
v2p0368c1s v2p0396c2s v2p0405c2s

v2p0416c2s v2p0421c2s v2p0436c2s
v2p0457c1s v2p0457c2s v2p0458c1s
v2p0463c2s v2p0465c1s v3p0044c1s
v3p0116c2m v3p0202c2s v3p0203c1s
v3p0254c1s v3p0267c2s v3p0296c1s
v3p0314c2s v3p0316c2s v3p0320c1s
v3p0336c1s v3p0351c2s v3p0406c1s
v3p0432c2s v3p0449c2s v3p0454c1s
v4p0028c2s
Hervey, C.M. v5p0158c2s
Hervey, Charles v3p0243c1s
v4p0425c2s v4p0505c1s v4p0580c1s
Hervey, Charline W. v6p0187c1s
Hervey, D.E. v2p0213c1s
v3p0084c1s v3p0260c1s v3p0293c2s
v4p0245c2s v4p0408c2s
Hervey, E.D. v1p0371c1s
Hervey, E.L. v1p0147c2s
v1p0413c2s v1p0761c1s v1p1309c2s
Hervey, F.L. and Oliver, J.E.
v3p0012c2s
Hervey, F.R.J. v1p0510c1s
Hervey, G.N. v1p1240c2s
Hervey, G.W. v1p0883c1s
Hervey, H. v5p0251c2s
v5p0355c2s
Hervey, R.K. v3p0002c2s
v3p0207c1s v3p0375c2s v3p0406c2m
v3p0440c2s
Hervey, T.K. v1p0218c2s
Hervey, T.K., Mrs. v1p1370c1s
Hervey, W.L. v4p0512c2s
v4p0557c2s v4p0566c1s v5p0179c2s
v6p0135c2s v6p0162c1s v6p0189c2s
v6p0191c1s v6p0199c2s v6p0290c2s
v6p0305c1s v6p0318c1s v6p0410c1s
v6p0537c2s v6p0574c1s v6p0671c1s
Herz, N. v5p0174c1s
Herzberg, H. v4p0450c1s
Herzberg, O. v5p0004c2s
v5p0169c2s
Herzfeld, A.G. v4p0506c1s
v5p0169c2s v5p0191c1s
Herzfeld, Elsa G. v6p0638c1m
Herzl, T. v5p0645c2s
Herzog, C. v2p0087c1s
v2p0363c1s v2p0433c1s
Herzog, E. v1p0940c1s
v3p0311c1s
Herzog, J.J. v1p0242c2s
v1p0769c1s v1p1363c2s
Herzog, Prof. v1p0131c1s
v1p0423c2s
Herzon, A. v1p0952c2s
Hesekiel, G. v5p0365c2s
Heseltine, J.P. v4p0230c2m
v4p0280c2s
Hesford, H. v5p0253c1s
v5p0283c1s
Hesketh, E. v6p0378c2s
Hess, C.D. v5p0421c2s
Hess, F. v2p0459c1s
Hess, F.L. v6p0647c2m
Hess, Frances H., Mrs. ... v6p0480c1s
Hess, Frank L. v6p0395c1s
Hess, H. v6p0152c1s
v6p0392c2s v6p0682c2m
Hess, J.S. v1p1296c2s
v2p0295c2s v2p0348c1s
Hess, J.W. v5p0538c1s
Hess, P. v1p0374c2s
Hesse-Kaye, E. v3p0127c1s
v3p0391c2s v3p0394c2s
Hesse-Wartegg, E.von v2p0448c1s
v3p0113c2s v5p0132c2s v6p0339c1s
Hesselrigge, S. v6p0046c1s
v6p0586c1s
Hessels, J.H. v2p0054c1s
v2p0145c2s v2p0326c2m v2p0354c2s
v3p0344c1s
Hessels, J.H. et al. v2p0145c2s
Hessey, E. v6p0410c1s
v6p0524c2s
Hessey, J.A. v1p0251c1s
v3p0341c2s
Hester, F. v2p0151c1s
Heston, A.M. v6p0039c2s
Heth, H. and Hood, J.B. .. v1p0518c2s
Hetherington, C.W. v6p0039c1s
Hetherington, H.F. v5p0312c1s
v5p0433c2s
Hetherington, Helen F. ... v5p0014c1s
Hetherington, J. v4p0174c2s
Hetherington, J.N. v1p0465c2s
v1p1184c2s
Hetherington, W.M. v1p0274c1s
Hetrick, J.T. v6p0454c1s
Hetrick, W.H. v6p0419c1s
Hetterson, S.L. v5p0481c1s
Hetzel, H.W. v5p0360c2s
Heugh, H. v1p0240c2s
Heuglin, M.T.von v1p1238c2s
Heumann, K. v1p0459c1s
Heureux, J.L' v2p0241c2s
Heusch, W.de v5p0129c2s
Heuser, H.J. v2p0022c2s
v2p0048c1s v2p0293c2s
Heuton, S.H. v6p0350c2s
Heuvel, J.A. v1p0576c2s
v1p0638c1s v1p1237c1s
Heuvel, J.C.V. v1p0107c1s
Heward, E.V. v5p0130c1s
v5p0186c2s v5p0581c2s v6p0347c2s
v6p0411c1s v6p0648c2s v6p0677c1s
Hewart, B. v5p0123c2s
v5p0615c2s
Hewat, A. v3p0217c2m
v4p0286c2s v5p0071c2s
Hewes, F.W. v3p0322c2s
v3p0337c1s v4p0595c1s v5p0600c2s
v5p0601c1s v6p0090c1s v6p0308c2s
v6p0682c1s
Hewes, O.K. v6p0629c2s
Hewetson, W.T. v5p0403c2s
Hewett, E.L. v6p0292c1s
v6p0475c1s v6p0486c1s
Hewett, Edgar L. v6p0190c2s
Hewett, Grace L. v6p0585c1s
Hewett, H. v2p0056c2s
Hewett, S.C. v4p0072c2s
Hewett, W.J. v6p0545c2s
Hewett, W.T. v2p0176c1s
v2p0181c1s v2p0293c2s v2p0322c2s
v2p0456c1s v3p0091c2s v3p0171c2s
v3p0176c1s v3p0377c1s v5p0605c2s
v6p0518c2s
Hewett, W.Y. v3p0300c1s
Hewill, J.N.B. v4p0537c2s
Hewins, C.M. v1p0370c2s
v2p0077c2s v2p0256c1s v3p0049c1s
v3p0249c1s v3p0249c2s v3p0469c2s
v4p0129c2s v4p0249c1s v4p0330c1s
v5p0106c2m v5p0334c1s v5p0334c2s
v5p0606c2s v6p0116c1s v6p0145c1s
v6p0375c1s
Hewins, Caroline M. v6p0374c2s
Hewins, W.A.S. v4p0167c1s
v4p0340c2s v4p0581c1s v5p0175c2s
v5p0615c2s v6p0252c1s v6p0271c2s
Hewit, A. v1p0294c1s
Hewit, A.F. v1p0019c1s
v1p0089c2s v1p0097c1s v1p0098c1s
v1p0117c2s v1p0120c2s v1p0121c2s
v1p0171c1s v1p0238c2s v1p0242c1m
v1p0244c1s v1p0255c2s v1p0267c1s
v1p0286c1s v1p0288c2s v1p0293c1m
v1p0339c2s v1p0355c1s v1p0356c2m
v1p0358c1s v1p0386c1s v1p0421c2s
v1p0438c1m v1p0440c2s v1p0477c2s
v1p0493c2s v1p0495c2s v1p0536c2s
v1p0620c2s v1p0640c2s v1p0641c2s
v1p0646c1s v1p0655c2s v1p0673c2s
v1p0682c2s v1p0686c2s v1p0700c1s
v1p0741c1s v1p0745c2m v1p0771c1s
v1p0791c1s v1p0808c2s v1p0869c2s
v1p0896c2s v1p0917c1s v1p0920c2s
v1p0943c2s v1p0954c1s v1p0955c2s
v1p0994c1s v1p0999c1s v1p1001c1s
v1p1013c1m v1p1032c2s v1p1033c1m
v1p1037c2s v1p1057c2s v1p1063c1s
v1p1084c2s v1p1085c2s v1p1086c1m
v1p1097c1s v1p1106c1s v1p1115c1s
v1p1116c1m v1p1117c2s v1p1118c2m
v1p1119c1s v1p1119c2m v1p1120c2s
v1p1121c1s v1p1135c1s v1p1139c2s
v1p1156c2s v1p1157c2s v1p1158c1s
v1p1255c1s v1p1269c2s v1p1277c2s
v1p1306c2s v1p1358c1s v1p1363c1s
v1p1421c1s v1p1432c1m v2p0042c2s
v2p0068c2s v2p0088c2s v2p0099c1s
v2p0110c2s v2p0120c1s v2p0146c1s
v2p0198c1s v2p0234c2m v2p0270c1s
v2p0277c1s v2p0277c2s v2p0308c2s
v2p0323c2s v2p0328c1s v2p0328c2m
v2p0365c1s v2p0375c2m v2p0376c1s
v2p0376c2s v2p0382c2s v2p0389c1s
v2p0435c2s v2p0482c2s v3p0005c2s
v3p0042c2s v3p0064c1s v3p0081c1s
v3p0081c2s v3p0127c2s v3p0141c2s
v3p0150c1s v3p0204c1s v3p0215c2s
v3p0302c1s v3p0314c2s v3p0339c1s
v3p0342c2s v3p0345c1s v3p0363c2s
v3p0364c1s v3p0364c2s v3p0378c2s
v3p0379c2s v3p0380c2s v3p0416c1s
v4p0056c2s v4p0074c1s v4p0112c2s
v4p0158c2s v4p0185c2s v4p0229c1s
v4p0274c1s v4p0300c1s v4p0300c2s
v4p0326c2s v4p0333c2s v4p0354c1s
v4p0384c1s v4p0479c1m v4p0482c1s
v4p0488c1m v4p0488c2m v4p0489c1m
v4p0526c2s v4p0558c1s v4p0573c1s
Hewit, A.F. and Hecker, I.T.
v1p0711c2s
Hewit, A.S.
v1p0665c1s
Hewitt, A. v5p0105c2s
v6p0133c2s v6p0377c1s v6p0452c1s
v6p0546c2s
Hewitt, A.S. v1p0663c1s
v1p0663c2s v1p0845c2s v2p0128c2s
v2p0229c1s
Hewitt, A.S. and Godkin, E.L.
v1p0871c1s
Hewitt, C. v4p0175c2s
Hewitt, C.C. v5p0599c1s
Hewitt, C.E. v3p0323c1s
Hewitt, C.N. v3p0192c1s
Hewitt, E.C. v1p0450c2s
v2p0315c2s v5p0635c1s v5p0635c2s
Hewitt, E.L. v6p0015c1m
v6p0607c1s
Hewitt, E.T. v5p0419c2s
Hewitt, H. v3p0220c1s
v3p0315c1s v5p0028c2s
Hewitt, J. v1p0059c1s
v2p0021c2s
Hewitt, J.F. v3p0080c1s
v3p0220c2s v3p0450c1s v4p0014c1s
v4p0022c1s v4p0045c2s v4p0258c1m
v4p0298c2s v4p0376c2s v4p0475c2s
v4p0577c1s v5p0088c1s v5p0098c2s
v5p0116c1s v5p0145c2s v5p0180c2s
v5p0533c2s v5p0563c2s v5p0624c2s
v6p0408c2s
Hewitt, J.N.B. v3p0142c2s
v3p0223c2s v6p0470c1s
Hewitt, J.N.B. and Thomas, C.
v6p0275c2s v6p0709c2s
Hewitt, J.S. v4p0026c2s
Hewitt, L.E. v6p0166c2s
Hewitt, M.E. v1p0160c2s
v1p0166c1s v1p0228c2s
Hewitt, M.E., Mrs. v1p0735c1s
Hewitt, N. v1p0686c2s
v1p1378c1s v1p1415c2s
Hewitt, N.H. v1p1200c2s
Hewitt, R.L. v6p0093c1s
Hewitt, W. v1p1114c2s
v4p0082c1s v4p0624c2s v5p0004c2s
v5p0086c2s v5p0108c1s
Hewitt, W.G. v4p0040c1s
Hewitt, W.T. v1p0740c2s
v3p0253c2s
Hewlett, E.G.W. v3p0215c2s
v3p0338c1s
Hewlett, G. v6p0228c1s
Hewlett, H.G. v1p0060c2s
v1p0088c1s v1p0140c2s v1p0583c1s
v1p0705c2s v1p0722c2s v1p0759c1s
v1p0873c1m v1p1020c2s v1p1041c1s
v1p1051c2s v1p1054c1s v1p1098c1s
v1p1220c1s v1p1220c2s v1p1286c2s
v1p1333c2s v2p0241c1s v2p0427c2m
v3p0074c1s v3p0125c2s v3p0158c1s
v3p0189c2s v3p0253c1s v3p0288c2s
v3p0453c2s v5p0186c1s v5p0193c1s
Hewlett, J. v1p0009c1s
v1p0138c2s v1p0438c1s v1p0455c2s
v1p0458c2s v1p0710c1s v1p0745c1s
v1p0994c2s v1p1091c1s v1p1251c2s
v1p1318c1s v1p1408c2s
Hewlett, M. v3p0052c2s
v3p0225c1s v3p0288c2s v4p0064c2s
v4p0070c1s v4p0369c1m v5p0020c1s
v5p0170c2s v5p0232c2s v5p0254c1s
v5p0260c1s v5p0311c2s v5p0355c1s
v5p0371c1s v5p0516c1s v6p0088c1s
v6p0231c1s v6p0608c1s v6p0681c2s
Hewlett, M.H. v2p0366c2s
Hewlett, R.J. v6p0368c2s
Hewlett, R.T. v5p0609c1s
v6p0030c2s v6p0047c1s v6p0098c2s
v6p0501c2s v6p0569c2s v6p0595c1s
v6p0597c2s v6p0657c2s v6p0663c2s
v6p0688c1s
Hews, M.C. v6p0019c2s
Hewson, E. v1p0725c2s
Hewson, E.W. v6p0335c2s
Hewson, Ernest W. v6p0244c1s
Hewson, F. v1p1311c2s
Hewson, M.B. v1p0195c1s
v1p0539c2s v1p0913c1s
Hexamer, C.A. v4p0228c1s
v5p0002c2s v6p0321c2s
Hexamer, C.J. v2p0126c1s
v2p0156c2m v2p0157c1s v2p0289c1m
v2p0437c1s v4p0200c1s v4p0572c1s
v4p0632c2s v5p0208c1s
Heydecker, W.A. v2p0040c2s
v2p0131c2s v2p0165c2s v2p0234c2s
Heydemann, C.H. v5p0321c2s
v5p0491c1s
Heyden, H.E. v1p1345c1s
Heydenfeldt, S. v1p1205c1s
Heydenreich, L.W. v1p0117c2s
v1p0245c2s v1p0676c1s v1p0980c1s
v1p1304c1s
Heydrick, B.A. v5p0352c1s
v6p0171c1s v6p0207c2s v6p0216c2s
v6p0352c2s v6p0442c2s v6p0539c2s
v6p0611c1s v6p0623c1s v6p0677c2s
Heyer, J.F. v3p0093c1s
Heyer, R.G. v1p0228c2s
Heygate, C.B. v4p0617c2s
Heyking, E.von v5p0438c2s
v6p0274c2s v6p0410c2s
Heyl, H.R. v2p0137c1s
Heyl, P.R. v5p0624c2s
v6p0406c2s v6p0411c1s
Heyler, E.O. v4p0416c1s
Heymann, M. v5p0106c1s
Heyn, E. v5p0078c2s
v6p0412c1s
Heyn, E.C. v6p0279c2s
v6p0297c1s
Heyn, E.T. v4p0107c2s
v4p0504c1s v6p0699c1s
Heys, W. v2p0465c2s
Heyse, P. v1p0108c2s
v1p0407c1s v1p0767c1s v1p0887c2s

v1p1072c1s v3p0082c1s v3p0135c2s v3p0367c2s v3p0411c2s v4p0616c1s
Heyse, Paul v4p0262c2s v5p0283c1s
Heysinger, I.W. v6p0232c2s
Heyward, T. v2p0061c2s
Heywood, A., jr. v2p0214c1s
Heywood, Alice and Vortriede, Helen A. ... v6p0598c1s
Heywood, H. v6p0120c2s v6p0523c1s
Heywood, J. v1p0158c2s v1p0190c1s v1p0636c1s v2p0167c1s v2p0176c1s v2p0429c1s v2p0434c1s
Heywood, J.C. v1p1348c1s
Heywood, J.H. v1p0336c1s v1p1207c2s v1p1292c2s v3p0135c1s
Heywood, W. v6p0275c2s
Hiatt, C. v5p0074c2s v5p0238c2s v5p0385c1s v5p0432c2s v5p0470c1s v5p0509c1s v6p0692c1s
Hiatt, C.T.J. v3p0152c1s v3p0168c2s v3p0333c1s v4p0564c1s v5p0224c2s v5p0461c2s
Hibbard, A. v6p0450c2s
Hibbard, B.H. v6p0315c1s
Hibbard, F.G. v1p0045c2s v1p0074c1s v1p0124c1s v1p0131c1s v1p0344c2s v1p0601c2s v1p0641c1m
Hibbard, G. v5p0033c2s v5p0163c1s v5p0340c1s v5p0470c1s v5p0487c1s v5p0490c2s v5p0547c1s v5p0577c2s v5p0608c2s v5p0634c1s v6p0012c2s v6p0034c1s v6p0217c1s v6p0243c1s v6p0261c1s v6p0264c1s v6p0287c2m v6p0288c2s v6p0289c1s v6p0346c1s v6p0359c1s v6p0368c2s v6p0389c2s v6p0429c2s v6p0440c2s v6p0467c1s v6p0540c1s v6p0541c1s v6p0562c1s v6p0619c2s v6p0689c2s
Hibbard, G.A. v2p0214c2s v3p0023c1s v3p0110c2s v3p0113c2s v3p0121c2s v3p0137c1s v3p0164c2s v3p0178c1s v3p0210c1s v3p0271c2s v3p0467c2s v3p0473c1s v4p0091c2s v4p0165c2s v4p0222c1s v4p0326c2s v4p0373c2s v4p0414c1s v4p0473c1s v4p0491c1s v4p0556c1s v4p0572c2m v4p0606c2s v4p0619c2s v5p0555c1s
Hibbard, G.S. v3p0085c2s
Hibbard, George v5p0364c2s v5p0366c2s v6p0007c2s
Hibbard, Grace v6p0586c1s
Hibbard, J.D. v6p0468c1s
Hibbard, S. v1p0375c2s v1p0745c1s
Hibben, J.C. v5p0604c2s
Hibben, J.G. v4p0036c2s v4p0039c2s v4p0188c1s v4p0459c1s v4p0515c1s v4p0589c1s v5p0024c1s v5p0290c2s v5p0376c1s v5p0480c1s v5p0495c1s v6p0204c1s
Hibben, J.S. v6p0496c1s
Hibberd, E.L. v4p0229c2s v4p0445c1s
Hibberd, S. v1p0049c1s v1p0107c1s v1p0136c1s v1p0136c2s v1p0139c2s v1p0152c2s v1p0214c2s v1p0491c2s v1p0492c1s v1p0573c2s v1p0581c1s v1p0645c1s v1p0646c2s v1p0717c1s v1p0804c2s v1p0946c1s v1p0947c2s v1p0962c1s v1p0975c1s v1p1068c2s v1p1099c2s v1p1112c1s v1p1141c2s v1p1172c2s v1p1198c1s v1p1232c1s v1p1239c1s v1p1361c2s v1p1441c1s v3p0165c1s v3p0340c2s
Hibberd, S.S. v1p0948c1s
Hibbert, A. v3p0167c1s
Hibbert, H.G. v4p0260c1s
Hibbert, W.G. v2p0038c1s
Hibbs, R.A. v6p0116c1s
Hibshman, H.H.W. v1p0649c1s v4p0261c1s
Hice, R.H. v4p0048c2s v4p0411c2s
Hichborn, A. v1p0140c2s
Hichborn, C.S. v3p0066c2s
Hichborn, P. v4p0521c2s v5p0558c2s
Hichens, R. v4p0167c1s v4p0352c2s v5p0066c2s v6p0171c2s
Hichens, R. and Hamilton, Frederic v5p0590c2s
Hichens, R.S. v3p0056c1s v3p0259c2s
Hichens, Robert v5p0359c1s
Hickcox, J.H. v1p0272c2s
Hickey, E.H. v2p0241c1s v2p0273c1s v3p0044c2s v3p0109c2s v3p0245c1s v3p0267c2s v3p0337c2s
Hickling, H. v5p0216c1s v5p0269c2s
Hickman, W.A. v6p0024c1s v6p0261c2s v6p0472c1s
Hickman, W.H. v6p0111c1s v6p0190c2s
Hickok, H.R. v6p0416c2s
Hickok, L.P. v1p0252c1s v1p0275c2s v1p0348c2s v1p0434c2s v1p0467c1s v1p0527c2s v1p0528c1s v1p0598c2s v1p0613c2s v1p0964c1s v1p0989c2s v1p1000c1m v1p1090c1s v1p1097c2s v1p1101c1s v1p1104c2s v1p1200c2s v1p1293c2s v1p1302c1m v1p1303c2s v2p0257c2s v2p0394c2s
Hickox, C. v1p0692c2s v1p0837c1s v1p1008c2s v1p1048c1s v1p1066c1s v1p1123c1s v1p1157c2s v1p1193c1s v1p1388c2s v2p0283c2s
Hicks, B.M. v5p0101c1s
Hicks, E.L. v2p0190c2s v2p0305c1s v3p0016c1s v3p0206c2s v3p0217c1m v3p0233c1s v3p0371c2s v3p0428c1s v4p0094c2s v4p0285c2m v4p0355c1s v4p0533c2s v5p0572c1s v6p0142c1s
Hicks, F.C. v4p0157c1s v4p0580c2s v6p0176c2s v6p0373c2s v6p0402c1s
Hicks, F.C. and Williams, H. v5p0588c2s
Hicks, G. v1p1063c1s
Hicks, G.D. v6p0004c1s v6p0349c2s
Hicks, G.H. v4p0069c2s
Hicks, H. v1p1112c2s v2p0274c1s v3p0265c2s v4p0018c1s v5p0358c1s v6p0656c1s
Hicks, H.A. v4p0140c2s
Hicks, J.A. v1p1367c1s
Hicks, J.B. v1p0021c2s v1p1378c2s
Hicks, L.E. v1p0939c1s v1p0993c2s v1p1163c2s v1p1301c2s v2p0099c2s v2p0274c2s v2p0358c2s v4p0343c1s
Hicks, M. v1p1294c1s
Hicks, M.D. v4p0029c2s
Hicks, M.R. and Barry, M.N. v6p0304c1s v6p0705c1s
Hicks, R.B. v1p1374c1s
Hicks, R.D. v3p0019c2s
Hicks, T. v2p0357c2m
Hicks, W.E. v4p0619c2s v5p0061c1s v6p0180c2s
Hicks, W.L. v4p0569c1s
Hicks, W.M. v4p0441c2s
Hickson, M. v2p0226c1s v3p0154c2s v3p0220c2s v3p0335c1s v3p0438c1s
Hickson, M.M. v5p0010c2s v5p0040c2s v5p0349c2s v5p0435c2s v5p0533c2s v5p0570c2s v5p0596c1s v6p0014c1s
Hickson, Mary v3p0220c1m
Hickson, Miss v2p0073c1s
Hickson, S.J. v2p0371c1s v2p0394c2s v4p0121c2m v4p0420c1s v4p0511c1s v4p0637c2s
Hickson, S.J. and Lowne, B.T. v2p0150c2s
Hickson, W.E. v1p0567c2s v1p0715c1s v1p0763c1m v1p0764c2s v1p0880c2s v1p0914c2s v1p0973c1s v1p1034c2s v1p1050c2s v1p1075c2s v1p1158c2s v1p1402c2s
Hickson, W.S. v1p1031c1s
Hidden, W.B. v4p0599c1s
Hidden, W.E. v1p0828c1m v1p0828c2s v1p0844c2s v2p0196c1s v2p0285c2s v2p0290c1s v3p0128c1s v3p0275c2s v3p0276c1s v4p0347c2s v4p0587c2s v5p0259c2s v5p0546c1s v6p0418c2s
Hidden, W.E. and Hillebrand, W.F. v4p0493c1s
Hidden, W.E. and Judd, J.W. v5p0499c2s
Hidden, W.E. and Mackintosh, J.B. v3p0026c2s v3p0338c1m v3p0414c2s v3p0475c1s
Hidden, W.E. and Penfield, S.L. v3p0188c2s
Hidden, W.E. and Pratt, J.H. v5p0487c2m v5p0645c2s
Hidden, W.E. and Washington, H.S. v3p0280c2s
Hiestand, E.M. v1p0495c1s v1p0914c1s v1p1282c2s v2p0457c1s
Hiestand, Sarah W. v6p0207c2s
Hiester, A.V. v6p0370c1s
Higashi, K. v6p0337c2s
Higashi, K. and Leonard, H.F. v6p0344c1s v6p0709c1s
Higashi, Katsukuma v6p0344c1s
Higbee, E.E. v1p0048c1s v1p0061c2s v1p0241c1s v1p0242c2s v1p0248c2s v1p0417c2s v1p0520c2s v1p0594c1s v1p0624c1s v1p0686c1s v1p0687c2s v1p0733c2s v1p0990c1s v1p1089c1s v1p1102c2s v1p1121c2s v1p1140c2s v1p1325c2s v5p0511c2s
Higbee, J.M. v1p0139c2s v1p0624c1s v1p0649c2s v1p1247c1s
Higgin, G. v1p1390c1s v2p0080c2s v2p0412c2s
Higgin, L. v2p0308c2s v3p0093c1s v4p0028c2s v4p0047c2s v4p0396c1s v6p0012c1s v6p0607c2s
Higginbottom, F.J. v5p0272c1s v5p0433c1s
Higginbottom, J. v1p1280c1s
Higgins, A. v3p0361c1s v4p0510c1s v5p0210c1s v5p0249c2s v5p0489c1s v6p0164c1s v6p0385c1s v6p0647c2s
Higgins, A. and Frewen, M. v4p0377c2s
Higgins, A.F. v1p0082c2s v3p0035c2s v4p0423c2s
Higgins, A.P. v5p0187c2s
Higgins, E.A. v3p0378c1s
Higgins, E.E. v5p0183c2s v5p0391c2s v5p0556c2s v5p0586c1s
Higgins, F.C. v4p0451c1s
Higgins, H. v5p0562c2s v6p0689c2m v6p0692c1s
Higgins, H.B. v5p0039c1s v6p0391c2s v6p0667c1s
Higgins, H.H. v1p0042c2s v1p0757c1s v2p0062c2s v2p0073c2s v2p0289c1s v4p0036c2s
Higgins, J.C. v2p0121c1s
Higgins, K.C. v3p0446c1s
Higgins, L.P. v4p0098c2s v4p0164c2s
Higgins, M.J. v1p0391c1s v1p0391c2s v1p0834c1s
Higgins, M.P. v5p0353c2s v5p0367c2s v6p0392c2s
Higgins, P.J. v1p1366c2s v2p0423c1s
Higgins, R.C. v1p0905c1s v1p0905c2s v1p1002c2s
Higgins, R.J. v2p0185c2s
Higgins, R.T. v3p0179c2s v3p0180c1m
Higgins, R.T., Col. v2p0463c2s
Higgins, S.A. v4p0203c1s v4p0503c1s
Higgins, S.E.A. v4p0423c1s
Higgins, T.W.E. and Rhys, J. v4p0200c2s
Higgins, W.M. v1p1390c2s
Higginson, A.H. v6p0055c1s v6p0068c1s v6p0163c2s v6p0177c2s v6p0183c2s
Higginson, E. v1p0129c1s v3p0113c1s v4p0276c1s v4p0321c1s v4p0386c2s v4p0449c1s v4p0562c1s v5p0595c2s v6p0707c1s
Higginson, G.W. v4p0235c2s
Higginson, H. v1p0885c1s
Higginson, H.L. et al. ... v5p0524c2s
Higginson, M.T. v6p0386c1s
Higginson, M.W. v6p0132c2s v6p0178c2s v6p0381c1s
Higginson, Margaret Waldo. v6p0117c2s
Higginson, T.W. v1p0008c2s v1p0032c1s v1p0038c1s v1p0049c1s v1p0136c1s v1p0179c2s v1p0201c2s v1p0203c2s v1p0229c1s v1p0229c2s v1p0230c1s v1p0276c1m v1p0308c2s v1p0323c2s v1p0339c2s v1p0343c2s v1p0403c2m v1p0446c2s v1p0451c1s v1p0463c1s v1p0501c1s v1p0523c1s v1p0531c1s v1p0564c1s v1p0575c2s v1p0600c2s v1p0620c1s v1p0625c2s v1p0662c1s v1p0676c1s v1p0706c1s v1p0733c2s v1p0741c1s v1p0749c2s v1p0785c1s v1p0790c2s v1p0792c2s v1p0802c1m v1p0805c1s v1p0823c2s v1p0838c2s v1p0846c2s v1p0864c2s v1p0891c1s v1p0892c2s v1p0900c2s v1p0905c1s v1p0910c1s v1p0972c2m v1p1005c1s v1p1018c2s v1p1019c2s v1p1036c2s v1p1059c2m v1p1095c2s v1p1105c2s v1p1151c1s v1p1157c2m v1p1170c1s v1p1208c1m v1p1208c2s v1p1213c2s v1p1225c1s v1p1267c1s v1p1272c2s v1p1313c2s v1p1344c2s v1p1345c1s v1p1346c1s v1p1347c2m v1p1373c2s v1p1374c1s v1p1386c2s v1p1406c2s v1p1409c2s v1p1421c2s v1p1422c2s v2p0009c2s v2p0010c1m v2p0010c2m v2p0011c1m v2p0011c2s v2p0012c1s v2p0066c1s v2p0131c1s v2p0139c2s v2p0140c1s v2p0158c2s v2p0171c2m v2p0184c2s v2p0219c1m v2p0232c1m v2p0260c1s v2p0265c2s v2p0295c2s v2p0308c1s v2p0316c1s v2p0339c1s v2p0346c1s v2p0353c1s v2p0384c1s v2p0404c2s v2p0413c1s v2p0413c2s v2p0454c1m v2p0463c2s v2p0465c2s v2p0470c2s v2p0472c1s v2p0474c2s v2p0477c2s v3p0031c2s v3p0109c2s v3p0117c2s v3p0136c1s v3p0191c2s v3p0200c2s v3p0242c2s v3p0249c1m v3p0249c2s v3p0253c1s v3p0259c2s v3p0266c2s v3p0305c2s v3p0329c2s v3p0335c1s v3p0351c1s v3p0437c2s v3p0470c1s v3p0472c2s v4p0009c2s v4p0113c1s v4p0216c2s v4p0257c1s v4p0309c1s v4p0335c1s v4p0343c2s v4p0363c2s v4p0448c2m v4p0489c2s v4p0505c1s v4p0529c1s v4p0551c2s v4p0620c1s v4p0620c2s v5p0014c2s v5p0023c1s v5p0079c2s v5p0172c1s v5p0190c2s v5p0202c1s

v5p0237c1s v5p0264c2s v5p0268c1s
v5p0341c1s v5p0345c2s v5p0402c2s
v5p0403c1s v5p0431c2s v5p0432c2s
v5p0471c2s v5p0482c1s v5p0633c2s
v6p0014c2s v6p0021c1s v6p0029c2s
v6p0040c2s v6p0043c1s v6p0047c1s
v6p0053c1s v6p0075c1s v6p0076c2s
v6p0085c1m v6p0090c1s v6p0147c2s
v6p0155c1s v6p0161c1s v6p0202c2s
v6p0207c2s v6p0248c1s v6p0250c1s
v6p0282c1s v6p0284c1s v6p0292c2s
v6p0366c1s v6p0369c1s v6p0379c2s
v6p0386c1s v6p0389c1s v6p0390c2s
v6p0438c2s v6p0446c2s v6p0473c1s
v6p0504c2s v6p0547c1s v6p0619c1s
v6p0653c2s v6p0678c2s v6p0697c1s
v6p0707c2s
Higginson, T.W. and
Jaques, F.W., Mrs. v4p0593c2s
Higginson, T.W. and Lothrop, S.K.
v5p0257c1s
Higginson, T.W. et al. ... v3p0138c1s
v5p0179c2s
v6p0074c2s
Higgs, H. v3p0067c1s
v3p0247c1s v4p0088c1s v4p0632c2s
v5p0134c2s v5p0641c1s
Higgs, M. v6p0653c2s
Higgs, Mary v6p0399c1s
v6p0601c2s
Higgs, P. v2p0136c2s
v3p0132c2s
Higgs, R.W. v2p0413c2s
Higgs, W. v3p0038c2s
v3p0089c1s v3p0143c1s v3p0334c2s
v3p0357c2s v3p0425c1s v3p0429c2s
v3p0454c2s v5p0088c1s
High, J.L. v2p0251c2s
v4p0576c2s v4p0609c2s
Higham, C. v5p0563c2s
Higham, Chas. v5p0125c2s
Higham, Mary R. v6p0307c1s
Highland, T.H. v6p0327c1s
Highley, S. v3p0263c2s
v3p0330c2s
Hight, L.L. v5p0316c1s
Highton, H. v1p0498c1s
v1p1291c1s v2p0076c1s v2p0138c2s
v3p0166c2s v3p0423c1s
Highton, H.E. v5p0557c1s
Higley, E.H. v2p0358c1s
Higley, W.K. v1p0983c1s
v1p1015c2s
Hilber, V. v3p0382c2s
Hilbert, D. v6p0383c1s
Hilbert, W.F. v6p0318c1s
Hilburn, W. v6p0322c2s
Hilcken, G.F. v5p0335c2s
Hildane, E. v4p0103c2s
v4p0370c1s
Hildebrand, F. v2p0344c1s
Hildebrandsson, H. v3p0027c1s
Hildebrandt, Vice-Admiral. v6p0631c2s
Hildebrant, A. v1p1249c1s
Hildeburn, C.H. v1p0997c1s
Hildeburn, C.R. v1p0603c1s
v1p1192c2s v1p1242c2s v2p0383c1s
v3p0329c1s v4p0108c1s v4p0172c1s
v4p0438c1s v4p0459c1s v5p0439c2s
Hildegarde, H.T. v3p0180c1s
Hildenbrand, W. v1p0184c1s
Hilder, F.F. v2p0300c1s
v2p0429c2s v5p0287c2s v5p0443c2m
v5p0444c2s v5p0445c1s v5p0586c2s
Hilditch, J.B. v4p0484c1s
Hildreth, C. v6p0586c2s
Hildreth, C.L. v2p0148c2s
v3p0335c2s v4p0158c1s v4p0409c1s
Hildreth, M.A. v5p0444c2s
Hildreth, R. v1p0591c1s
v1p1049c2s v1p1207c2s v1p1242c2s
v1p1330c2s v1p1332c2s
Hildreth, S.P. v1p0141c2s
v1p0268c2s v1p0829c1s v1p0938c2s
Hildreth, T.F. v5p0604c1s
Hildt, J.C. v6p0556c2s
Hildyard, A.D. v3p0448c2s
Hildyard, D'A. v4p0497c1s
Hildyard, G. v2p0164c2s
Hildyard, H. v5p0375c1s
Hildyard, H.J.T. v3p0171c1s
Hileman, A. v6p0230c1s
Hiley, F.E. v6p0105c2s
Hilgard, E.W. v1p0017c2s
v1p0367c1s v1p0459c1s v1p0508c2m
v1p0509c1m v1p0509c2s v1p0523c2s
v1p0562c1s v1p0749c1s v1p0772c2m
v1p0834c1s v1p0854c1m v1p0854c2m
v1p0976c1s v1p1218c1m v1p1379c2s
v2p0038c1s v2p0185c1s v2p0435c2m
v3p0217c1s v4p0010c2m v4p0083c2s
v4p0153c2s v4p0192c2s v4p0317c1s
v4p0548c2s v5p0227c2s v6p0025c2s
v6p0029c2s v6p0216c1s v6p0264c1s
v6p0422c1s v6p0433c1s v6p0546c1s
v6p0602c2m
Hilgard, J.E. v1p0326c2s
v1p0562c1s v1p0787c2s v1p0815c1s
v1p1034c1s v1p1310c1s v1p1367c1s
Hilgard, J.E. and Bache, A.D.
v1p0788c2s
Hilgard, T.C. v1p0642c1s
v1p1368c2s v2p0299c2s
Hilgenfeld, A. v2p0339c1s
Hill et al. v3p0031c1s
Hill, A. v1p0023c2m
v1p0831c2s v1p1390c2s v1p1418c2s
v2p0202c2s v2p0220c2s v4p0338c1s
v6p0067c2s v6p0522c2s
Hill, A.A. v5p0010c1s
v5p0318c1m v6p0480c2s v6p0486c1s
v6p0524c1s v6p0567c2s v6p0568c1s
Hill, A.C. v3p0130c1s
v4p0153c1s v4p0506c1s v6p0517c2s
Hill, A.E. v1p0979c1s
Hill, A.G. v2p0315c2s
v4p0333c1s v4p0417c1s v4p0492c2s
v5p0367c2s v5p0423c2s v6p0607c2s
Hill, A.H. v1p0836c2s
v1p0981c2s v1p1040c1s
Hill, A.H., jr. v1p0636c1s
Hill, A.J. v2p0299c2s
v3p0010c1s v3p0283c2s
Hill, A.L. v3p0410c1s
v4p0103c1s v5p0405c1s v5p0512c1s
v5p0643c2s
Hill, A.P. v1p0518c2s
Hill, A.R. and Watanabe, R.
v4p0515c1s
Hill, A.R. and Watanbe, R.
v4p0388c1s
Hill, A.S. v1p0285c2s
v1p0558c2s v1p0719c2s v1p1065c2s
v1p1253c1s v1p1275c1s v1p1275c2s
v1p1344c2s v1p1352c2s v2p0065c2s
v2p0071c2s v2p0144c1s v3p0139c2s
v3p0140c1m
Hill, A.S. and Withey, E.A.
v5p0192c1s
Hill, A.W.S. v4p0049c2s
Hill, Alex. v6p0177c2s
Hill, B. v1p0295c1s
v1p0349c2s v1p0606c1s
Hill, B.D. v1p0301c1s
v1p0347c1s v1p1366c1s
Hill, B.F. v6p0411c1s
Hill, Ben v3p0196c1s
Hill, C. v2p0382c1s
v3p0415c2s v5p0561c2m
Hill, C.B. v4p0577c1s
Hill, C.H. v1p0504c1s
v1p0524c2s v1p0808c1s v1p0985c1s
v1p1012c2s
Hill, C.L. v6p0176c2s
v6p0402c1s
Hill, C.M. v5p0193c1s
v6p0295c1s
Hill, C.S. v4p0303c1s
Hill, D. v2p0079c1s
v2p0152c2s v2p0292c1s
Hill, D.B. v1p0807c1s
v4p0363c1s v5p0158c2s v5p0330c1s
Hill, D.G. v4p0150c2s
Hill, D.H. v1p0228c1s
v1p0310c2s v1p0389c1s v1p0643c2s
v1p0833c1s v1p0967c1s v1p1028c2s
v1p1205c1s v1p1223c2s v1p1387c1s
v2p0052c2s v2p0335c1s v2p0411c2s
v3p0076c2s v3p0401c2s v4p0295c2s
Hill, D.H. and Porter, F.J.
v2p0170c1s
Hill, D.H., jr. v4p0128c2s
v4p0269c1s v4p0408c1s
Hill, D.J. v2p0054c2s
v2p0149c2s v2p0150c1s v2p0235c2s
v2p0244c1s v2p0323c1s v2p0333c1s
v2p0336c2s v2p0358c2s v2p0371c1s
v3p0357c2s v3p0445c1s v3p0469c1s
v4p0029c1s v4p0169c2s v4p0287c2s
v4p0464c1s v5p0543c1s v5p0603c1s
v6p0014c2s
Hill, D.S. v6p0523c1s
Hill, Dr. v1p0736c1s
Hill, E. v1p0315c2s
v2p0107c2s v2p0127c1s v5p0145c2s
v5p0307c1s v6p0134c2s
Hill, E.A. v4p0026c1m
v4p0304c2s v6p0291c1s
Hill, E.B. v1p0643c2s
v4p0311c1s v5p0394c2s
Hill, E.E. v5p0535c2s
v5p0569c2s v6p0574c2s
Hill, E.F. v4p0443c2s
Hill, E.J. v2p0344c1s
v4p0064c1s v4p0069c2s v4p0100c1s
v4p0145c1s v4p0202c2s v4p0208c1s
v4p0209c1s v4p0271c1s v4p0410c1s
v4p0416c2s v4p0422c2s v4p0458c2s
v4p0491c2s v4p0498c1s v4p0631c2s
v5p0451c2s v6p0593c1s
Hill, Emily v5p0534c2s
Hill, F. v1p0230c1s
Hill, F.A. v3p0091c1s
v4p0360c2s v5p0264c2s
Hill, F.C. v1p0668c1s
v2p0163c2s
Hill, F.D. v6p0294c2s
Hill, F.H. v1p0046c2s
v1p0166c2s v1p0442c1s v2p0189c1s
v2p0189c2s v2p0225c2s v2p0226c1s
v2p0330c1s v2p0407c2s v3p0137c2s
v3p0138c2s v3p0199c1s v3p0202c1s
v3p0221c1s v3p0321c2m v4p0190c2s
v4p0240c2s v4p0293c1s v4p0604c1s
v6p0486c2s v6p0501c1s
Hill, F.H. and O'Connor, T.P.
v4p0289c2s
Hill, F.J. v4p0583c1s
Hill, F.P. v3p0122c2s
v4p0329c2s v4p0330c1s v5p0334c1s
v5p0335c1s v5p0336c2s v6p0371c2s
Hill, F.T. v6p0084c2s
v6p0089c1s v6p0128c1s v6p0345c1s
v6p0363c2s v6p0365c1s v6p0377c2s
v6p0669c2s
Hill, Frank H. v4p0152c1s
v4p0155c2s
Hill, Frank P. v6p0372c2s
Hill, G. v1p0075c1s
v1p0177c1s v1p0269c2s v1p0340c1s
v1p0345c2s v1p0347c2s v1p0569c1s
v1p0573c2s v1p0645c2s v1p0646c1s
v1p0785c1s v1p0794c2s v1p0868c1s
v1p0983c1s v1p1013c2s v1p1023c2s
v1p1058c2s v1p1064c2s v1p1141c1s
v1p1151c1s v1p1161c1s v1p1161c2s
v1p1300c2s v1p1320c1s v1p1355c2s
v2p0455c2s v4p0023c1s v4p0023c2s
v4p0078c1s v4p0180c1m v4p0366c2s
v5p0014c1s v5p0095c1s v5p0097c2s
v5p0162c1s v5p0186c2s v5p0239c2s
v5p0252c1s v5p0357c2s v5p0373c1s
v5p0397c2s v5p0531c2s v6p0131c2s
v6p0143c1s v6p0206c1s v6p0272c1s
v6p0464c1s
Hill, G.A. v4p0037c2s
v4p0126c2s v5p0401c1s v6p0146c1s
v6p0367c2s v6p0653c2s
Hill, G.B. v3p0051c2s
v3p0205c1s v3p0231c2m v4p0039c2s
v4p0304c1s v4p0492c1s v5p0564c1s
Hill, G.C. v3p0155c2s
v4p0230c2s v4p0526c1s v4p0526c2s
Hill, G.E. v6p0585c1s
Hill, G.F. v4p0121c2m
v4p0345c2s v4p0363c1s v4p0444c2s
v4p0510c2s v5p0368c1s v6p0342c1m
v6p0590c1s v6p0643c2s
Hill, G.W. v1p0375c1s
v3p0125c2s v4p0034c1s v4p0281c1s
v4p0592c1s v5p0009c2s v5p0598c2s
Hill, George v4p0252c2s
v4p0411c1s
Hill, H. v4p0015c1s
v4p0095c1s v4p0253c2s v4p0259c2s
v4p0458c1s v4p0512c2s v4p0585c1s
v4p0599c2s v5p0440c2s v5p0629c1s
Hill, H.A. v1p0102c1s
v1p0180c2m v1p0235c1s v1p0455c1s
v1p0620c1s v1p0736c1s v1p0902c2s
v1p1041c1s v1p1147c1s v1p1192c2s
v1p1249c2s v1p1283c2s v1p1402c1s
v1p1438c1s v2p0107c2s v2p0291c2s
v2p0339c1s v3p0010c2s v3p0109c2s
v3p0270c2s v3p0463c2s v4p0069c1s
v4p0398c2s v4p0420c2s v4p0516c2s
v4p0624c1s v5p0089c2s
Hill, H.D. and Whitehead, J.B.
v6p0583c1s
Hill, H.F. v4p0212c2s
Hill, H.J.T. v5p0212c1s
v5p0379c2s
Hill, Headon v4p0258c2s
Hill, J. v2p0002c2s
v2p0305c2s v2p0384c1s v2p0467c2s
v6p0219c1s
Hill, J.A. v1p1291c2s
v4p0277c2s v4p0278c1s v4p0564c2s
v5p0158c2s v5p0188c1s v5p0283c2s
v5p0308c2s v5p0374c2s v5p0438c2s
v5p0456c2s v5p0494c2s v5p0596c2s
v5p0616c1s
Hill, J.Arthur v6p0521c1s
Hill, J.B. v2p0342c2s
Hill, J.C. v5p0118c1s
Hill, J.H. v6p0371c2s
Hill, J.J. v5p0593c1s
v6p0220c1s
Hill, J.L. v4p0108c2s
Hill, J.M. v1p0981c1s
v1p1431c1s
Hill, J.P. v6p0073c1s
v6p0366c2s v6p0384c1s v6p0500c1s
Hill, J.S. v4p0340c2s
Hill, J.W. v1p0161c1s
v1p0759c1s v1p1212c2s v1p1247c1m
v1p1247c2s v1p1248c1s v1p1361c2s
v2p0090c1s v2p0144c1s v2p0359c2m
v2p0419c1m v6p0143c2s v6p0224c1s
Hill, James J. v6p0470c1s
Hill, Joanna M. v4p0104c1s
Hill, Lucy B. v4p0174c1s
Hill, M. v3p0146c2s
v3p0309c2s v3p0406c2s v4p0335c1s
v4p0414c1s v5p0548c2s v5p0594c1s
v6p0079c1s v6p0193c1s v6p0194c1s
v6p0243c2s v6p0291c2s
Hill, M. and Hadley, S.P.. v5p0350c1s
Hill, M.D. v4p0094c1s
Hill, M.K. v6p0085c1s

v6p0589c1s v6p0590c1m v6p0597c2s
v6p0662c2s
Hill, Mabel v6p0341c1s
Hill, Marion v5p0036c1s
v5p0420c2s v6p0166c1s v6p0280c1s
Hill, N. v2p0212c2s
v4p0338c1s
Hill, N.N., jr. v1p1400c2s
v2p0062c1s v2p0106c1s
Hill, N.P. v2p0114c1s
v2p0181c2s
Hill, N.P. et al. v2p0403c1s
Hill, O. v1p0218c2s
v1p0219c1s v1p0284c2s v1p0305c2s
v1p0607c1s v1p0722c1s v1p0765c1s
v1p1030c2m v1p1031c1s v2p0366c2s
v3p0257c1s v3p0321c1s v3p0338c2m
v4p0452c1s v5p0433c1s
Hill, O. et al. v2p0264c1s
v2p0349c1s
Hill, O.T. v1p0526c1s
v1p0620c1s v1p0836c2s v1p0852c1s
v1p0860c1s
Hill, O'D.T. v1p0442c1s
Hill, Octavia v6p0443c2s
Hill, R. v1p0347c2s
v1p0645c2s v1p0668c2s v1p1037c2s
v1p1196c2s v1p1209c2s
Hill, R.D. v2p0101c1s
Hill, R.G. v5p0061c1s
v5p0375c1s
Hill, R.H.E. v6p0291c1s
v6p0697c2s
Hill, R.J. v5p0460c1s
Hill, R.S. v3p0258c2s
v4p0486c2s
Hill, R.T. v3p0019c2s
v3p0104c2s v3p0169c1s v3p0169c2m
v3p0177c1s v3p0315c1s v3p0425c2s
v3p0426c1s v4p0016c1s v4p0026c1s
v4p0031c2m v4p0126c1s v4p0139c1s
v4p0142c2s v4p0292c1m v4p0368c1s
v4p0423c2s v4p0539c2s v5p0023c1s
v5p0124c2s v5p0146c2m v5p0301c2s
v5p0312c2s v5p0460c2s v5p0489c1s
v5p0574c1s v6p0016c1m v6p0029c2s
v6p0433c1s v6p0465c1s v6p0487c1s
v6p0681c1s v6p0681c2s
Hill, R.T. and Penrose, R.A.F., jr.
v3p0104c2s
Hill, R.W. v1p1094c2s
Hill, Robert T. v5p0460c2s
Hill, S.A. v1p1268c2s
v2p0468c2s v3p0067c1s v3p0187c2s
v3p0250c2s v3p0424c1s
Hill, S.M. v4p0197c1s
v4p0426c2s v5p0293c2s
Hill, S.P. v1p0392c1s
Hill, T. v1p0004c2s
v1p0013c2s v1p0047c2s v1p0055c1s
v1p0123c1s v1p0134c2s v1p0163c1s
v1p0216c1s v1p0224c2s v1p0276c1s
v1p0312c2s v1p0313c1s v1p0333c1s
v1p0348c1s v1p0403c2s v1p0424c1s
v1p0427c1s v1p0452c2s v1p0455c2s
v1p0468c2s v1p0510c1m v1p0598c2s
v1p0613c1s v1p0641c2m v1p0710c1s
v1p0711c2s v1p0730c1s v1p0745c2s
v1p0810c2s v1p0811c1m v1p0815c2s
v1p0820c2s v1p0855c1s v1p0875c2s
v1p0881c2s v1p0882c1s v1p0882c2s
v1p0899c1s v1p0901c1s v1p0919c2s
v1p0925c2s v1p0936c1s v1p0947c2s
v1p0979c2s v1p1002c1s v1p1006c2s
v1p1046c1s v1p1086c1m v1p1092c2s
v1p1161c1s v1p1221c1s v1p1238c1s
v1p1252c1s v1p1262c2s v1p1270c2s
v1p1278c1m v1p1302c1s v1p1303c1m
v1p1303c2s v1p1313c1s v1p1336c2s
v1p1340c1m v1p1341c2s v1p1406c2s
v1p1407c1s v1p1428c1s v1p1432c2s
v2p0004c2s v2p0037c2s v2p0044c2s
v2p0071c2s v2p0099c2s v2p0147c1s
v2p0221c1m v2p0262c2s v2p0274c1s
v2p0308c2s v2p0339c1s v2p0366c1s
v2p0437c1s v2p0455c2s v2p0456c1s
v3p0049c2s v3p0104c1s v3p0111c1s
v3p0229c1s v3p0265c2s v3p0322c1s
v3p0404c1s v3p0435c2s
Hill, T.L. v1p0129c1s
Hill, T.P. and Abbot, J.B.
v1p0816c2s v1p0911c2s
Hill, W. v1p1221c2s
v1p1333c2s v4p0007c2s v4p0014c1s
v4p0462c2s v4p0472c2s v4p0563c2s
v4p0564c1m v4p0607c2s v5p0556c2s
v6p0009c1s v6p0105c1s v6p0528c2s
Hill, W.B. v2p0309c1s
v2p0451c1s v3p0034c1s v3p0103c1s
v3p0416c2s v4p0223c2s v4p0317c2s
v4p0534c2s v5p0307c1s v6p0447c2s
Hill, W.H. v1p0625c2s
v1p0643c2s v1p1055c2s v1p1181c2s
v1p1221c2s v2p0215c1s v2p0241c1s
v3p0385c1s v4p0130c1s
Hill, W.K. v4p0170c2s
v5p0177c2m v5p0178c2s v5p0179c1s
v5p0179c2s v6p0192c1s v6p0205c2s
v6p0702c2s
Hill, W.L. v1p0840c2s
v1p1257c2s
Hill, W.N. v1p0401c1m
Hill, W.S. v1p0623c1s
Hill, Will v4p0110c1s
v4p0333c1s v4p0527c1s v4p0578c1m
Hill-Burton, M.R. v5p0303c2s
v5p0448c1s
Hill-Climo v6p0209c1s
v6p0408c2s v6p0654c2s
Hill-Climo, W. v4p0235c2s
v4p0278c2s v5p0029c1m v5p0029c2m
v5p0133c2s v5p0284c2s v5p0538c1s
v5p0604c2s v6p0031c1m v6p0031c2s
v6p0569c2s
Hill-Tout, C. v6p0141c2s
v6p0316c2m v6p0565c2s
Hillard, G.S. v1p0152c1s
v1p0172c1s v1p0184c1s v1p0262c1s
v1p0273c2s v1p0298c2s v1p0312c2s
v1p0373c2s v1p0418c2s v1p0433c1s
v1p0433c2s v1p0496c2s v1p0506c1s
v1p0530c2s v1p0557c1s v1p0575c2s
v1p0582c1s v1p0735c1s v1p0774c2s
v1p0804c2s v1p0805c2s v1p0832c2s
v1p0841c2s v1p1033c2s v1p1047c2s
v1p1052c2s v1p1056c1s v1p1065c2s
v1p1085c2s v1p1126c2s v1p1158c1s
v1p1207c2s v1p1211c1s v1p1231c1s
v1p1253c1s
Hillard, G.S. and Palfrey, J.G.
v1p0285c1s
Hillard, K. v1p0026c1s
v1p0090c1s v1p0106c2m v1p0369c2s
v1p0583c1m v1p0611c2s v1p0695c1s
v1p0837c2s v1p0851c2s v1p0886c1m
v1p0887c2s v1p0917c1s v1p0942c1s
v1p1085c2s v1p1127c1s v1p1186c2m
v2p0048c2s v2p0150c1s v2p0377c2s
v3p0046c2s v3p0126c2s v3p0263c2s
v4p0251c2s
Hillard, P.S. v6p0032c1s
Hillard, W. v1p1175c2s
Hilleary, J.E. v2p0039c2s
Hillebrand, H.L. v6p0296c1s
Hillebrand, K. v1p0138c2s
v1p0324c2s v1p0397c2s v1p0413c1s
v1p0413c2s v1p0474c2s v1p0477c2s
v1p0488c2s v1p0516c1s v1p0516c2s
v1p0517c2s v1p0561c2s v1p0587c1s
v1p0672c2s v1p0831c2s v1p0897c2s
v1p1013c1s v1p1157c1s v1p1369c2s
v1p1414c1s v2p0317c2s
Hillebrand, W.F. v2p0262c2s
v3p0115c2s v3p0445c2s v3p0446c1s
v4p0083c1s v4p0140c2s v4p0637c1s
v5p0382c1s v5p0607c1s v6p0403c2s
v6p0411c1s v6p0418c2s
Hillebrand, W.F. and Cross, W.
v2p0342c1s v2p0429c2s v2p0483c1s
Hillebrand, W.F. and Dana, E.S.
v3p0440c1s
Hillebrand, W.F. and Hidden, W.E.
v4p0493c1s
Hillebrand, W.F. and Lindgren, W.
v6p0030c1s
Hillebrand, W.F. and Penfield, S.S.
v6p0014c1s
Hillebrand, W.F. and Ransome, F.L.
v5p0095c1s
Hillebrand, W.F. and Schaller, W.T.
v6p0365c1s
Hillebrand, W.F. and
Washington, H.S. v3p0099c2s
Hillebrand, W.F. et al. .. v5p0062c2s
v5p0496c2s
Hillegas, H.C. v5p0007c1m
v5p0320c1s v5p0465c1s v5p0627c1s
Hillel, B. v2p0369c1s
Hillel, F. v3p0326c1s
v3p0340c2s v3p0472c1s
Hiller, A. v5p0351c1s
Hiller, F. v1p0226c1s
v1p0819c2s v1p1128c2s
Hiller, G.L. v2p0110c2s
Hiller, H.C. v4p0185c2s
v4p0191c2s
Hiller, H.M. v5p0071c2s
Hillern, W.von v1p0590c1s
Hilles, A.E.U. v4p0626c1s
Hilles, C.D. v6p0535c2s
Hillhouse, J.A. v1p0755c1s
Hillhouse, W. v1p0556c2s
v3p0257c1s
Hilliard, C.D. v5p0141c2s
Hilliard, Caroline E. v3p0396c2s
Hilliard, H.W. v1p1348c1s
v1p1395c2s
Hilliard, J.N. v4p0198c2s
v5p0209c1s v5p0234c1s
Hilliard, S.H. v3p0359c1s
Hillier, A. v5p0006c2s
v5p0007c1s v5p0080c2s v6p0660c1s
Hillier, A.C. v5p0632c1s
Hillier, A.P. v5p0013c2s
Hillier, A.P. and Murray, W.
v5p0362c2s
Hillier, G.L. v3p0108c1s
v5p0150c2s v5p0151c1s
Hillier, W.C. v6p0354c1s
Hilliers, A. v6p0595c2s
v6p0626c2s
Hillis, N.D. v5p0306c1s
v5p0456c1s v5p0472c1s v5p0473c1s
v5p0481c2s v6p0288c1s v6p0523c1s
Hillman, H. v5p0110c2s
Hillman, H.W. v6p0199c1s
Hillman, J.W. v5p0444c1s
Hillman, S.D. v1p0071c1s
v1p0527c2s v1p0613c2s v1p0727c2s
v1p0792c2s v1p0830c1s v1p0874c1s
v1p1299c2s v1p1320c1s v2p0257c2s
v3p0199c2s v3p0258c1s v5p0577c1s
Hillquit, M. et al. v6p0600c2s
Hills, A. v6p0371c2s
Hills, A.F. v5p0467c2s
v5p0575c1s v6p0641c1s
Hills, C.H.T. v6p0380c2s
Hills, Caroline M. v5p0113c2s
Hills, Christine D.F. v6p0176c1s
Hills, Cora B. v5p0354c2s
Hills, E.C. v5p0148c2s
Hills, E.H. v6p0323c2s
Hills, F.L. v5p0470c1s
Hills, G.H. v1p1363c1s
Hills, G.M. v1p1280c2s
Hills, H.F. v5p0023c2s
v5p0074c1s v5p0345c1s
Hills, J.C. v2p0179c1s
Hills, K.F. v4p0603c2s
v5p0120c1s v5p0262c2s v5p0279c2s
v6p0319c2s v6p0672c2s
Hills, R.E. v2p0435c1s
Hills, W.H. v3p0100c1s
v3p0128c1s v3p0303c1s v3p0392c2s
v3p0473c1s v4p0330c1s v4p0408c1s
v4p0469c2s v4p0522c1s v4p0589c1s
v5p0040c2s v5p0132c1s v5p0360c2s
Hills, W.S. v4p0257c2s
Hillyar, J.M. v2p0080c2s
v2p0273c1s
Hillyer, S.G. v5p0155c2s
v6p0125c2s
Hillyer, V. v5p0094c1s
Hillyer, V.M. v6p0401c2s
v6p0571c2s
Hillyer, W.H. v5p0339c2s
v5p0341c2s
Hillyer, W.S. v4p0117c2s
Hilprecht, H.V. v3p0131c1s
v5p0042c1s
Hilton, E. v4p0419c1s
v6p0150c2s
Hilton, G.H. v1p0735c1s
Hilton, H. v6p0160c1s
Hilton, H. and Sanderson, J.B.
v6p0286c2s
Hilton, H.H. v5p0239c1s
Hilton, J. v3p0082c1s
v4p0110c2s v5p0155c2s
Hilton, J.D. v5p0031c1s
v5p0067c2s v5p0168c1s v5p0346c2s
v5p0381c1s v5p0414c2s v5p0474c1s
v5p0531c2s v6p0434c1s
Hilton, W.A. v6p0368c2s
Hilty, J.K. v4p0226c2s
Hilyard, E.W. v2p0006c1s
Hilyard, H.A. v4p0404c1s
Himes et al. v1p0387c2s
Himes, C.F. v1p0382c1s
v1p1003c1s v1p1375c1s v2p0002c1s
v2p0124c1s v3p0330c2s v3p0409c2s
v4p0192c2s v5p0448c2m
Himes, J.A. v1p1430c1s
v2p0014c1s v2p0087c1s v2p0289c2s
v2p0398c2s v6p0137c1s
Himmelwright, A.L.A. v4p0078c1s
v4p0200c1s
Hinchliffe, H.J. v1p0203c2s
v1p1234c2s
Hinchman, L. v1p0596c2s
Hinckledeyn, C. v3p0018c1s
Hinckley, C.T. v1p0065c1s
v1p0065c2s v1p0171c2s v1p0186c2s
v1p0348c2s v1p0374c1s v1p0407c1s
v1p0419c2m v1p0725c1s v1p0965c2s
v1p1197c2m v1p1337c1s
Hinckley, H.B. v5p0495c1s
Hinckley, H.V. v4p0292c2s
v4p0590c2s
Hinckley, M.H. v1p0308c2s
Hinckley, Mary v2p0446c1m
Hinckley, W. v4p0243c1s
v4p0277c1s v4p0462c1s v4p0603c1s
Hincks, Dr. v1p0395c1s
v1p1151c1s
Hincks, E. v1p0054c2s
v1p0069c2s v1p0084c1s v1p0246c2s
v1p0395c2s v1p0831c1s v1p0923c1s
Hincks, E. and Parker, F.. v1p0246c2s
Hincks, E.Y. v2p0470c1s
v3p0042c2s v3p0081c2m v3p0282c1s
v4p0021c1s v4p0431c1s v4p0561c2s
v5p0060c1m v6p0598c2s
Hincks, F. v1p0091c2s
v1p0194c1s
Hincks, F., Sir v1p0192c1m
v1p0192c2s v1p0193c2s v1p0284c2s
Hincks, M.A. v6p0164c1m
v6p0334c2s
Hincks, T. v1p0041c1s

v1p0817c2m v1p1018c2s v1p1029c2s
v1p1441c2s v2p0483c2s
Hincks, W. v1p0041c2s
v1p0109c2s v1p0135c2s v1p0137c1s
v1p0153c1s v1p0164c2s v1p0184c2s
v1p0193c2s v1p0214c1s v1p0262c2s
v1p0297c1s v1p0382c2s v1p0406c2s
v1p0493c1s v1p0499c2s v1p0504c1s
v1p0536c2s v1p0575c1s v1p0618c2s
v1p0642c1m v1p0649c1s v1p0859c1s
v1p0899c1m v1p1015c2s v1p1016c1s
v1p1026c1s v1p1050c2s v1p1088c1s
v1p1177c2s v1p1233c1s v1p1364c2s
Hind, A.M. v6p0545c2s
Hind, C.L. v3p0126c2s
v3p0239c2s v3p0270c1s v3p0322c1s
v3p0431c2s v4p0245c2s v4p0455c1s
Hind, C.Lewis v3p0256c1s
Hind, G.L. v6p0545c2s
Hind, H.Y. v1p0068c2s
v1p0164c1m v1p0375c2s v1p0494c1s
v1p0523c2s v1p0909c1s v1p0931c1s
v3p0176c2s v3p0236c2s
Hind, J.R. v1p0070c2s
v1p0071c1s v1p0281c2s v1p0282c1s
v1p0382c1s v1p0387c2s v1p0589c1s
v1p1014c1s v1p1267c2s v1p1367c1s
v1p1379c1s v2p0095c2s
Hind, L. v3p0057c1s
v4p0134c2s v4p0366c1s v4p0498c2s
v5p0524c1s
Hind, P.A.A. v4p0001c2s
Hinde, G.J. v3p0415c1s
Hinde, S.L. v4p0128c2s
Hinde, S.L., Mrs. v6p0378c2s
v6p0398c1s
Hindenburg, A. v5p0127c2s
v5p0135c1s v6p0147c1s v6p0565c1s
Hinderer, J. v1p0702c2s
Hindlip, Lord v6p0006c1s
Hinds, J.I.D. v2p0014c2s
v2p0090c1s v2p0437c1s v2p0442c1s
v4p0183c2s v5p0249c2s
Hindsale, B.A. v2p0460c1s
Hindsley, T. v2p0028c2s
Hine, C.D. v4p0592c1s
v5p0477c1s v6p0528c1s
Hine, C.DeL. v5p0240c2s
v5p0476c2s v5p0477c2s v5p0585c2s
Hine, L.A. v1p0721c2s
Hine, L.W. v6p0316c1s
Hine, T.C. v2p0073c1s
v2p0476c2s
Hines, C.F. v6p0496c2s
Hines, D. v5p0151c1s
Hines, H.K. v4p0416c2s
Hines, J.A. v1p0842c2s
v1p1294c2s
Hines, L.S. v3p0031c1s
v3p0138c2s v3p0140c2s
Hines, T.A. v5p0348c1s
Hines, T.H. v2p0298c1s
v2p0316c2s v3p0288c1s
Hines, W.D. v5p0204c1s
v6p0324c2s v6p0529c1s
Hingeley, J.B. v6p0413c1s
Hinke, W.J. v5p0424c2s
v6p0061c2s v6p0379c1s
Hinkley, W.H. v4p0056c1s
v5p0058c1s v5p0114c2s v5p0546c2s
v5p0577c2s v6p0611c1s
Hinks, A.R. v5p0035c1s
v6p0210c2m v6p0403c1s v6p0619c1s
v6p0625c2s
Hinkson, H.A. v4p0289c1s
v4p0589c1s v5p0104c2s v5p0131c2s
v5p0322c1s v5p0349c2s v5p0365c2s
v5p0396c1s v5p0566c1s v6p0183c1s
Hinkson, K. v4p0634c1s
Hinkson, K.T. v4p0179c1s
v4p0291c2s v4p0303c2s v4p0308c2s
v4p0469c2s v4p0492c1s v4p0493c2s
v5p0048c1s v5p0373c2s
Hinkson, Katharine v4p0339c1s
Hinkson, Katharine T. v6p0367c1s
Hinkson, Katharine Tynan . v6p0711c2s
Hinman, C.W. v1p0501c2s
Hinman, E.L. v6p0647c1s
Hinman, G.W. v4p0224c2s
v4p0327c1s v4p0423c2s v4p0462c2s
Hinman, M.W. v2p0206c1s
Hinman, R. v2p0299c2s
Hinrichs, A. v4p0071c2s
Hinrichs, F.W. v6p0454c1s
Hinrichs, G. v1p0749c2s
v1p0827c1s v1p0903c2s v1p1014c1s
Hinsdale, B.A. v1p0127c2m
v1p0307c2s v1p0497c2s v1p0640c2s
v1p0839c2s v1p0940c1s v1p0964c2m
v1p1043c1s v1p1120c2s v1p1161c1s
v1p1363c1s v2p0099c1s v2p0108c2s
v2p0130c2s v2p0171c1s v2p0405c1s
v2p0411c1s v2p0451c2s v2p0453c2s
v3p0010c1s v3p0067c2s v3p0096c2s
v3p0129c2s v3p0313c2s v3p0362c2s
v3p0378c1s v3p0421c2s v4p0013c1s
v4p0122c2s v4p0170c1s v4p0171c1m
v4p0171c2s v4p0249c1s v4p0332c2s
v4p0365c1s v4p0369c1s v4p0375c1s
v4p0505c2s v4p0506c1s v4p0512c2s
v4p0597c2m v5p0016c1s v5p0088c1s
v5p0172c1s v5p0178c2m v5p0179c1s
v5p0179c2s v5p0305c1s v5p0315c1s
v5p0414c1m v5p0474c1s v5p0511c2s
v5p0512c1s v5p0521c2s v5p0558c1s
v5p0613c1s v5p0620c2s v5p0621c1s
v5p0627c1s v5p0645c2s
Hinsdale, B.A. et al. v3p0146c1s
v4p0123c1s
v5p0127c1s
Hinsdale, B.O. v3p0129c2s
Hinsdale, E.C. v5p0636c2s
Hinsdale, E.D. v5p0062c1s
Hinsdale, L.F. v3p0190c1s
v4p0342c2s v5p0142c1s
Hinsdale, W.B. v6p0409c1s
Hinton, A.H. v5p0563c1s
v6p0497c1s
Hinton, C.H. v1p0471c2s
v5p0644c1s v6p0235c2s v6p0472c2s
Hinton, J. v1p0374c1s
v1p0869c1s v1p1096c1s v1p1336c2s
Hinton, L.J. v1p0342c2s
v1p0409c2s
Hinton, M.B. v5p0474c2s
v6p0491c1s
Hinton, Mary H. v6p0291c2s
Hinton, R.J. v1p0017c2s
v1p0068c1s v1p0163c1s v1p0219c1s
v1p0234c1s v1p0299c1s v1p0638c1s
v1p0714c2s v1p0844c1s v1p1216c1s
v1p1319c2s v2p0245c2s v3p0118c1s
v3p0460c1s v4p0026c1s v4p0080c1s
v4p0292c2s v4p0438c2s v4p0449c2s
v4p0596c2s v5p0148c1m v5p0288c1s
v5p0313c2s v5p0601c1s
Hinton, R.J., Col. v4p0075c1s
Hinueber, C.von v6p0640c1s
Hioki, Eki v6p0334c1m
Hipkins, A.J. v2p0195c2s
v3p0293c2s v3p0332c1s v5p0395c2s
Hipkins, A.S. v4p0444c2s
Hippisley, A.J., Mrs. v1p0445c1s
v1p0458c1s
Hippisley, J. v2p0359c2s
Hippisley, R.L. v5p0185c1s
Hipschutz, A. v5p0002c2s
Hipwell, H.H. v6p0641c2s
Hipwell, J.W. v5p0036c2s
v5p0105c1s
Hirai, K. v4p0560c2s
Hirai, K.M. v4p0298c1s
Hird, Frank v6p0084c2s
Hirm, M. v2p0402c1s
Hirn, G.A. v1p1247c1s
Hirn, G.A. et al. v1p1248c1s
Hirn, Y. v5p0031c1s
Hirsch, E.G. v2p0022c1s
v3p0230c1s v4p0100c1s v4p0302c1s
v4p0597c2s
Hirsch, Emil G. v6p0114c2s
Hirsch, L. v4p0245c1s
Hirsch, M.de v3p0230c2s
v3p0329c1s
Hirsch, S.A. v4p0258c1s
v4p0302c1s v4p0437c2s v4p0482c2s
v5p0042c2s v5p0058c1s v5p0260c2s
v5p0308c1s
Hirsch, W. v4p0272c1s
v5p0228c1s
Hirschfeld, G. v1p0941c2s
v2p0336c1s v2p0392c2s
Hirschfeld, G. et al. v3p0297c2s
Hirschfeld, H. v4p0224c2s
v4p0293c2s v4p0302c1s v5p0381c2m
v5p0384c2s v6p0426c2s
Hirschfeld, H., Dr. v6p0249c2s
Hirschfeld, J. v4p0429c1s
v5p0163c2s v5p0293c2s
Hirschler, D. v4p0438c2s
Hirshberg, L.K. v6p0408c2s
Hirst, A. v4p0027c2s
Hirst, A.C. v6p0413c1s
Hirst, Dr. v1p0510c1s
Hirst, F.W. v5p0040c1s
v5p0119c2s v5p0234c2m v5p0245c2s
v5p0557c1s v5p0594c2s v6p0277c2s
v6p0299c1s v6p0324c1s v6p0353c2s
Hirst, F.W. and Ball, S. . v5p0536c2s
Hirst, Francis W. v6p0349c1s
Hirst, Frank W. v6p0267c1s
Hirst, G.M. v6p0465c1s
Hirst, H.B. v1p0494c1s
Hirst, J. v2p0139c1s
v3p0087c1s v3p0104c2m v3p0183c2s
v3p0201c2s v3p0251c2s v3p0358c2s
v3p0366c2s v3p0390c2s v3p0418c1s
v3p0441c1s v3p0469c1s v4p0283c1s
Hirst, J. and Cox, J.C. .. v3p0155c1s
Hirst, J. et al. v4p0012c1s
Hirst, J.F. v1p1056c2s
Hirst, Joseph v3p0475c2s
Hirth, F. v6p0118c1s
v6p0142c1s
Hirzel, L. v1p0123c2s
His, W. v5p0350c2s
v5p0577c2s
Hisa, M. v4p0107c1s
Hisa, Michitaro v4p0463c1s
Hise, C.R.Van v2p0207c2s
v2p0287c1s v3p0116c1s v3p0200c2s
v3p0412c1s v4p0291c2s v4p0456c2s
v4p0624c2s v5p0423c1s v5p0491c2s
v6p0251c1s
Hise, C.R.Van and Pumpelly, R.
v4p0270c1s
Hislam, P.A. v6p0668c2m
Hiss, H. v4p0359c1s
v4p0370c2s v5p0216c1m v5p0239c1s
v5p0276c1s v5p0583c2s
Hiss, P.H. v6p0663c2s
Historicus v6p0223c2s
v6p0476c2s
Hitch, E.E. v6p0462c1s
Hitchborn, P. v4p0521c1s
Hitchcock, A.M. v5p0192c2s
Hitchcock, A.N. v6p0142c2s
Hitchcock, A.P. v2p0213c1s
Hitchcock, A.S. v5p0453c2s
v6p0502c2s v6p0569c1s
Hitchcock, B.A. v6p0482c1s
Hitchcock, C. v1p0847c1s
Hitchcock, C.C. v6p0690c1s
Hitchcock, C.F. v4p0129c2s
Hitchcock, C.H. v1p0267c2s
v1p0375c1s v1p0507c2s v1p0509c2s
v1p0626c2s v1p0745c1s v1p0909c1s
v1p0911c2m v1p1112c2s v1p1302c1s
v2p0108c2s v2p0214c1s v2p0248c2s
v2p0316c1s v3p0207c1s v3p0236c1s
v3p0265c1s v5p0162c2s v5p0410c1s
v6p0242c2s v6p0351c1s v6p0463c2s
v6p0681c2s
Hitchcock, D.H. v1p0968c2s
Hitchcock, E. v1p0155c1s
v1p0225c2s v1p0268c1s v1p0268c2s
v1p0313c1s v1p0342c1s v1p0367c1s
v1p0375c2s v1p0465c2s v1p0466c1m
v1p0470c1s v1p0507c1m v1p0507c2s
v1p0509c1s v1p0528c2s v1p0578c2s
v1p0580c1s v1p0717c2s v1p0767c2s
v1p0809c1s v1p0827c2s v1p0900c2s
v1p0901c1s v1p0999c1s v1p1105c1s
v1p1262c2s v1p1301c2s v1p1415c1m
v2p0027c1s v4p0020c1s
Hitchcock, E., jr. v1p0470c1s
v1p0792c2s v3p0473c1s v4p0015c1s
v4p0441c1s
Hitchcock, E.A. v6p0329c2s
Hitchcock, F.H. v6p0015c1m
Hitchcock, G. v3p0051c2s
v3p0198c2s
Hitchcock, H. v1p0213c2s
v1p0328c2s v2p0276c2s
Hitchcock, J.R.W. v1p0573c1s
Hitchcock, R. v1p0815c1s
v2p0023c1s v2p0119c2s v2p0385c2s
v2p0393c1s v3p0089c1s v3p0239c2s
v3p0353c1s v3p0450c2s v4p0105c1s
v4p0297c2s v4p0440c1m v5p0177c1s
v6p0244c2s v6p0422c2s v6p0618c1s
Hitchcock, R.C. v3p0055c2s
Hitchcock, R.D. v1p0235c2s
v1p0398c1s v1p0421c2s v1p1441c2s
v2p0436c2s
Hitchcock, R.D. et al. ... v2p0353c1s
Hitchcock, T. v1p0843c1s
v1p1338c2s v5p0281c2s
Hitchens, J.H. v2p0477c1s
Hitchins, M. v1p0210c2s
v1p1122c2s
Hitchler, T. v5p0332c2s
v6p0354c2s v6p0371c2s v6p0372c1s
Hitchman, F. v1p0988c1s
v2p0125c2s v2p0164c2s v3p0036c2s
v3p0062c2s v3p0174c1s
Hitchman, J.F. v1p0134c1s
v1p0255c2s
Hite, C.E. v4p0316c1s
Hite, L.F. v4p0559c2s
v5p0349c1s v6p0522c1s v6p0554c1s
v6p0628c2s
Hittel, F. v3p0052c2s
Hittell, C.H. v6p0092c1s
v6p0656c1s
Hittell, J.S. v1p0187c1s
v1p0260c1s v1p0323c1s v1p0530c2s
v1p0710c1s v1p0749c2s v1p0845c2s
v1p1002c2s v1p1237c1s v1p1246c2s
v1p1321c1s v1p1419c2s v2p0079c2s
v3p0017c2s v3p0053c2s v3p0063c1s
v3p0063c2s v3p0065c2s v3p0176c1s
v3p0317c1s v3p0327c2s v3p0456c1s
v4p0489c1s v4p0544c2s v6p0093c2s
Hittell, T.H. v2p0009c2s
v2p0064c1s v4p0256c2s v6p0066c1s
v6p0092c2m v6p0414c2s
Hitz, J. v2p0205c2s
v2p0466c2s v6p0350c1s
Hitzig, E. v6p0708c2s
Hjaltalin, J.A. v1p0206c1s
Hjaltalin, Jon A. v1p0041c1s
Hjarne, H. v4p0418c1s
Ho, Yow v5p0109c2s
v5p0112c1s v5p0112c2m
Hoadley, B.J. v6p0088c1s
Hoadley, G. v3p0090c1s
Hoadley, G.A. v6p0471c1s
Hoadley, J.C. v1p0146c2s
v1p1248c1s v2p0344c2m v2p0467c2s

Hoadly, C.J. v1p0292c1s
v1p0337c2s v1p0372c1s v1p0422c1s
Hoadly, G. v3p0031c2s
v3p0346c2s
Hoads, S.N. v2p0108c2s
Hoag, E.B. v6p0296c2s
Hoagland, N. v3p0432c2s
Hoague, I.T. v1p0437c2m
v1p0699c2s v1p0735c1s
Hoar, G.F. v1p0048c2s
v1p0259c1s v1p0291c1s v1p0389c2s
v1p1267c1s v3p0132c1s v3p0349c2s
v3p0359c1s v4p0556c1s v4p0630c1s
v5p0047c2s v5p0135c1s v5p0257c1s
v5p0422c2m v5p0445c1s v5p0445c2s
v5p0457c2s v5p0485c2s v5p0519c2s
v5p0525c2s v5p0550c1s v5p0603c1s
v5p0603c2s v5p0624c2s v6p0018c2s
v6p0301c1s v6p0347c1s v6p0491c1s
v6p0524c1s v6p0583c2s v6p0697c2m
Hoar, G.F. and Bayard, T.F.
v4p0595c2s
Hoar, G.F. and McCrary, G.W.
v1p1077c2s
Hoar, G.F. and Roe, A.S. . v6p0325c1s
v6p0707c1s
Hoar, S. v5p0568c1s
Hoare, A. v4p0338c2s
Hoare, A.F. v5p0614c2s
Hoare, E.B. v3p0044c2s
v3p0304c2s
Hoare, H.E. v2p0107c2s
Hoare, H.N.H. v6p0109c2s
Hoare, H.W. v1p0123c1s
v2p0204c1s v2p0263c1s v2p0331c2s
v2p0334c2s v5p0055c2m v6p0060c2s
v6p0104c1s
Hoare, J.D. v6p0184c2s
v6p0294c2s
Hoare, J.N. v1p0394c2s
Hoare, M.A. v1p0378c2s
Hoare, Mrs. v1p0302c1s
v1p0331c1s v1p0443c1s v1p0655c1s
Hoare, R. v5p0627c2s
Hoare, R.C., Sir v1p0100c1s
v1p0218c2s v1p0567c2s v1p0874c1s
Hoare, R.H. v1p0497c1s
Hoatson, J. v5p0201c1s
v5p0611c2s v6p0545c2s
Hoban, P.J. v6p0147c1s
Hobart, A.S. v2p0414c1s
Hobart, C. v1p0901c2s
v4p0323c2s v5p0572c2s
Hobart, C.W. v3p0069c2s
v3p0071c1s v3p0137c1s v3p0313c2s
v3p0343c1s v3p0379c1s v3p0435c2s
v3p0465c2s v4p0001c1s v4p0041c2s
v4p0051c1s v4p0077c2s
Hobart, D.J.H. v5p0510c1s
Hobart, E. v6p0504c2s
Hobart, E.L. v3p0112c2s
Hobart, Ethel v6p0352c1s
Hobart, F. v4p0522c2s
Hobart, H.R. v1p0227c2s
v1p0228c1s
Hobart, J.F. v4p0424c2s
Hobart, J.H. v1p0422c1s
v4p0504c1s
Hobart, L.S. v1p0848c1s
Hobart, Lord v1p0017c2s
v1p0091c2s v1p0142c2s v1p0270c1s
v1p0398c1s v1p0474c2s v1p0545c1s
v1p0545c2s v1p0650c1s v1p0651c1s
v1p0801c1s v1p0973c2s v1p1385c1s
v1p1431c2s
Hobart, Richard B. v6p0313c2s
Hobart-Hampden, Albina ... v5p0641c1s
Hobbe, W.H. v6p0160c1s
Hobbes, J.O. v5p0315c1s
Hobbins, A.R. v2p0317c1s
Hobbs, A.I. v1p0292c2s
v1p0296c2s v1p0598c2s v1p0773c2s
v2p0082c1s v2p0240c1s
Hobbs, C.A. v4p0085c1s
Hobbs, C.W. v5p0290c1s
Hobbs, E.W. v6p0293c2s
Hobbs, G. v1p0595c2s
Hobbs, G.W. v3p0087c2s
Hobbs, J.F. v5p0039c2s
v6p0298c1s
Hobbs, J.P. v5p0313c2s
Hobbs, M.C. v3p0436c1s
Hobbs, R.G. v4p0573c1s
Hobbs, W.B. v4p0564c1s
Hobbs, W.H. v3p0363c1s
v4p0068c1s v4p0085c1s v4p0562c1s
v4p0581c2s v5p0030c2s v5p0160c2s
v5p0223c1s v5p0229c1s v5p0238c2s
v5p0280c1s v6p0301c1s v6p0450c1s
v6p0498c2s v6p0582c2s v6p0674c2s
Hoben, A. v6p0341c2s
v6p0475c2s
Hoben, T.A. v5p0428c2s
v6p0340c2s v6p0404c1s
Hobhouse, A. v1p1424c2s
v2p0218c1s v2p0263c1s v3p0346c2s
Hobhouse, A., Sir v1p0010c1s
v2p0264c1s
Hobhouse, C.E. v6p0265c2s
Hobhouse, E. v5p0171c2s
v5p0638c2s
Hobhouse, Emily v5p0131c2s
Hobhouse, H. v3p0256c2s
Hobhouse, J.C. v3p0256c2s
Hobhouse, L.T. v3p0072c2s
v3p0214c2m v5p0126c1m v5p0131c2s
v6p0278c2s v6p0632c2s
Hobhouse, Lord v2p0247c2s
v4p0052c2m v4p0266c1s v4p0338c2s
v5p0099c2s v5p0595c2s
Hobhouse, Lord et al. v4p0557c2s
Hobhouse, O. v2p0218c1s
Hobkirk, C.P. v1p1112c1s
Hobley, C.W. v4p0005c1s
v4p0586c1s v5p0314c1s v5p0364c2s
v6p0052c1s
Hoblit, O.B. v5p0213c1s
Hobman, J.B. v5p0100c2s
v6p0171c1s v6p0256c2s
Hobson, Anne v6p0153c1s
Hobson, B.L. v4p0109c2s
v5p0301c2s v5p0397c1m v5p0576c1s
Hobson, E. v6p0083c2s
Hobson, J. v4p0157c1s
Hobson, J.A. v3p0131c2s
v3p0137c2s v3p0343c2s v3p0358c2s
v4p0097c1s v4p0168c2s v4p0268c2s
v4p0347c2s v4p0455c2s v4p0532c1s
v4p0591c1m v4p0599c1s v4p0608c1s
v5p0006c2s v5p0007c2s v5p0047c2s
v5p0220c1s v5p0229c2s v5p0357c2s
v5p0536c2s v6p0026c1s v6p0097c2s
v6p0170c1s v6p0176c1m v6p0184c1s
v6p0203c2s v6p0240c1m v6p0246c1s
v6p0266c2s v6p0299c1s v6p0310c1m
v6p0324c1s v6p0417c2s v6p0425c2s
v6p0446c2s v6p0463c2s v6p0520c1s
v6p0555c1s v6p0658c2s
Hobson, J.A. and Flux, A.W.
v5p0509c2s
Hobson, J.A. and Hosken, W.
v5p0588c2s
Hobson, J.M. v4p0554c2s
Hobson, J.P. v6p0075c1s
Hobson, R.P. v5p0371c1m
v6p0324c1s v6p0445c2s v6p0580c1s
v6p0668c2s
Hobson, S.G. and Macrosty, H.W.
v5p0552c1s
Hoch, E. v4p0100c1s
Hoch, E.S. v4p0634c2s
v5p0105c1s v5p0553c2s v6p0563c2m
v6p0564c1m
Hochdoerfer, F.R. v4p0345c1s
Hochheimer, L. v2p0472c1s
Hochstetter, C. v1p1265c2s
Hocker, E.W. v5p0607c1s
Hockin, C. v1p1024c2s
Hocking, S.K. v3p0360c1s
v4p0414c1s v5p0267c2s
Hocking, T.C. v6p0613c2s
Hodden, F.H. v6p0244c2s
Hodder, A. v4p0382c1s
v4p0585c2s v5p0018c1s v5p0193c1s
v6p0340c1s v6p0453c2s
Hodder, A.L. v4p0316c2s
v4p0382c1s v4p0405c2s v4p0599c1s
Hodder, E. v2p0049c2s
Hodder, F.H. v5p0086c2s
v5p0166c2s v5p0315c1s v5p0384c1s
v6p0016c2s v6p0094c2s v6p0140c1m
v6p0387c2m v6p0666c2s v6p0667c2s
v6p0683c2s v6p0697c1s
Hodder, G. v1p0534c1s
v1p0776c1s v1p1298c2s
Hodder, R. v5p0250c2s
v5p0456c1s
Hodder-Williams, J.E. v5p0113c2s
v5p0141c1s
Hoddern, L.H. v6p0071c2s
Hoddick et al. v4p0020c2s
Hodell, C.W. v4p0184c1s
v4p0518c2s v5p0080c1s v5p0116c1s
v5p0366c2s v5p0418c2s v5p0522c2s
v5p0532c2s v5p0573c1s v6p0132c1s
v6p0136c2s
Hodern, L.H. v6p0280c1s
Hodgdon, F.W. v6p0384c1s
Hodge, A.A. v1p1046c2s
v1p1091c2s v1p1147c2s v2p0098c1s
v2p0235c2s v2p0352c2s v2p0367c2m
v2p0417c1s v2p0475c1s v2p0475c2s
v3p0175c1s v3p0378c2s
Hodge, A.A. and Kidder, F.A.
v2p0297c2s
Hodge, A.A. and Warfield, B.B.
v1p0645c2s
Hodge, A.A. et al. v2p0438c1s
Hodge, B. and Gooch, F.A.. v4p0028c2s
Hodge, C. v1p0004c2s
v1p0020c2s v1p0030c2s v1p0047c1s
v1p0048c1m v1p0074c2m v1p0099c1m
v1p0118c1s v1p0125c1s v1p0126c1s
v1p0129c2m v1p0132c1s v1p0159c2s
v1p0180c1m v1p0244c2s v1p0247c2s
v1p0248c2m v1p0252c1s v1p0252c2m
v1p0309c2s v1p0334c2s v1p0353c2s
v1p0391c2s v1p0392c1s v1p0393c1m
v1p0398c1m v1p0404c2s v1p0408c2s
v1p0441c1s v1p0485c2s v1p0517c1s
v1p0528c2s v1p0613c1s v1p0626c2s
v1p0641c1s v1p0645c2s v1p0646c1s
v1p0700c1s v1p0750c1s v1p0756c2s
v1p0775c1s v1p0794c1m v1p0803c1s
v1p0846c1m v1p0847c1s v1p0909c2s
v1p0912c1s v1p0954c1s v1p0972c1s
v1p1043c2s v1p1046c1m v1p1046c2m
v1p1047c1m v1p1047c2s v1p1059c1s
v1p1088c2s v1p1091c1s v1p1093c1s
v1p1099c2s v1p1118c1s v1p1142c2s
v1p1165c2s v1p1175c2s v1p1200c1s
v1p1200c2m v1p1206c1s v1p1206c2s
v1p1207c1s v1p1207c2s v1p1208c2s
v1p1260c1s v1p1270c1m v1p1287c1s
v1p1302c1s v1p1303c2s v1p1321c1s
v1p1342c2s v1p1352c2s v1p1378c1s
v1p1401c1s v2p0010c2s v2p0082c2s
Hodge, C. and Alexander, A.
v1p0003c1s
Hodge, C. and Alexander, J.A.
v1p1140c1s v1p1165c1s
Hodge, C. and Hope, M.B. . v1p0454c2s
Hodge, C.F. v3p0070c1s
v3p0167c1s v3p0356c2s v3p0404c2s
v4p0443c1s v4p0606c2s v5p0011c2s
v5p0400c2s v6p0066c2s v6p0128c1s
v6p0275c1s
Hodge, C.F. and Aikins, H.A.
v4p0463c1s
Hodge, C.W. v1p0118c2s
v4p0308c2s v4p0382c1s v5p0114c2s
v5p0279c1s v6p0544c2s v6p0642c2s
Hodge, C.W. and Tawney, G.A.
v5p0166c1s
Hodge, C.W., jr. v4p0439c2s
Hodge, D.M. v1p0426c2s
v1p0434c1s v1p1096c1s v1p1132c2s
v2p0043c1s v2p0147c1s v2p0149c1s
v2p0235c1s v3p0040c2s
Hodge, F.W. v4p0070c1s
v5p0002c2s v5p0137c2s v5p0371c1m
v6p0349c2s
Hodge, G.B. v1p1191c1s
v1p1345c1s v5p0334c1s v5p0644c2s
Hodge, G.F. v6p0135c2s
Hodge, G.S. v6p0066c2s
Hodge, G.W. v1p0138c1s
v1p0255c1s v2p0084c1s v3p0084c2m
Hodge, H. v5p0085c2s
v5p0569c2s v6p0495c1s v6p0587c2s
Hodge, H. and Abbey, E.A.. v6p0587c2s
Hodge, H. and Bridges, R.. v6p0350c2s
Hodge, H. and Hay, C.G. .. v5p0583c1s
Hodge, H.H. v6p0613c1s
Hodge, Harold v5p0328c2s
Hodge, Helen H. v6p0405c1m
Hodge, J.B. v5p0495c1s
v6p0535c2s v6p0714c1s
Hodge, J.M. v6p0243c2s
Hodge, R.M. v3p0157c1s
v3p0157c2s
Hodge, S.C. v4p0056c2s
Hodge, S.R. v5p0265c1s
Hodge, T. v2p0158c1s
v2p0441c2s v3p0264c2s
Hodge, W.B. v1p1192c2s
v1p1384c2m
Hodge, W.H. v1p0218c2s
v1p0820c1s v5p0540c1s
Hodge, W.L. v1p0273c1s
v1p0913c1s v3p0249c2s v4p0287c2s
Hodge, W.S. v1p0649c2s
Hodgen, J.T. et al. v1p0500c1s
Hodgens, E. v5p0242c2s
v5p0440c2s
Hodgens, S. v5p0501c2s
Hodges, A.D. v4p0566c2s
v5p0224c2s v5p0632c1s v6p0546c2s
Hodges, A.D., jr. v3p0353c2s
v5p0019c1s v6p0407c2s v6p0569c2s
Hodges, C.B. v6p0009c1s
Hodges, C.C. v3p0076c2s
v3p0325c2s v4p0186c2s
Hodges, D.G. v6p0107c1s
Hodges, Dr. v1p0947c2s
Hodges, E. v1p1192c2s
v5p0043c1s
Hodges, E.R. v4p0313c1s
Hodges, Elizabeth v5p0094c1s
v5p0504c2s
Hodges, G. v4p0110c1s
v4p0113c2s v4p0185c2s v4p0478c2s
v6p0137c2s v6p0537c1s v6p0613c1m
v6p0652c1s
Hodges, H. v1p0512c2s
v4p0306c1s v6p0309c2s
Hodges, J. v3p0094c1s
Hodges, K. v2p0094c1s
Hodges, N.D.C. v1p0498c2s
v1p0858c2m v4p0332c1s v6p0075c1s
v6p0372c1s
Hodges, N.D.C. et al. v3p0251c1s
v6p0371c1s
Hodges, S. v1p1409c2s
v2p0462c1s v3p0203c1s v4p0032c1m
v4p0147c2s v4p0155c2s v4p0346c1s
v4p0509c1s v4p0560c2s v4p0619c1s
v4p0634c1s v5p0127c2s
Hodges, W.C. v5p0061c1s
Hodges, W.R. v4p0499c1s

Hodgetts, E.A.B. v2p0281c1s v2p0337c2s v2p0381c1s v2p0381c2m v2p0401c2s v3p0061c2s v5p0365c1s
Hodgetts, F. v2p0021c2s
Hodgetts, J.F. v2p0082c1s v2p0326c1s v2p0387c1s v3p0422c2s
Hodgins, G.G. v5p0173c1s
Hodgins, G.S. v5p0061c1s v5p0185c1s v5p0476c2s
Hodgins, J.G. v1p0386c2s
Hodgins, T. v1p0194c1s v1p0320c2s v1p0342c1s v1p0974c2m v1p1053c2s v4p0086c1s v4p0212c2s v4p0262c1s v4p0597c1s v5p0090c1s v5p0090c2s v6p0097c2m
Hodgkill, T. v3p0318c1s
Hodgkin, A.T. v5p0181c2s
Hodgkin, Dr. v1p0427c2s
Hodgkin, H. v3p0136c1s v5p0006c1s v5p0439c2s
Hodgkin, H. and Buxton, S. v4p0586c1s
Hodgkin, J.B. v5p0105c2s
Hodgkin, J.E. v2p0268c2s
Hodgkin, L.V. and Browne, H.M. v3p0051c2s v3p0130c2s
Hodgkin, T. v1p0196c1s v1p0700c2s v2p0328c1s v2p0382c1s v2p0462c1s v3p0109c1s v3p0318c1s v3p0403c1s v3p0414c2s v3p0451c1s v5p0144c2s v5p0436c2s v5p0495c1s v5p0577c1s v6p0543c1s
Hodgkins, J.G. v1p0192c1s v1p0917c2s
Hodgkins, L.M. v4p0616c2s
Hodgkins, T. v6p0010c1m
Hodgkinson, A. v2p0425c1s v4p0125c1s
Hodgkinson, E. v1p1010c2s
Hodgman, H.M. v5p0177c1s
Hodgskin, J.B. v1p0008c1s v1p0069c1s v1p0092c2m v1p0093c1s v1p0094c2s v1p0154c2s v1p0180c2s v1p0192c2s v1p0212c1s v1p0269c2s v1p0273c1s v1p0304c1s v1p0306c1s v1p0320c1s v1p0325c2m v1p0326c1m v1p0397c1s v1p0424c1s v1p0431c2s v1p0467c2s v1p0477c2s v1p0478c1s v1p0480c1s v1p0494c1m v1p0533c1s v1p0579c1s v1p0647c2m v1p0714c2s v1p0722c1s v1p0735c1m v1p0801c1s v1p0861c1m v1p0898c2s v1p0900c2s v1p1026c1s v1p1026c2s v1p1049c2s v1p1061c1s v1p1076c1s v1p1078c2s v1p1079c1m v1p1079c2s v1p1080c1s v1p1100c1s v1p1192c1s v1p1232c1s v1p1232c2m v1p1234c1s v1p1234c2s v1p1261c1s v1p1310c2s v1p1323c1s v1p1344c1s v1p1359c2m v1p1394c1s v1p1399c2s
Hodgson and Herbert v1p0591c2s
Hodgson, A. v2p0445c2s
Hodgson, C.C. v2p0288c1s
Hodgson, E. and Eaton, F.A. v3p0313c1s
Hodgson, E.J. v5p0587c1s
Hodgson, F. v1p0731c2s
Hodgson, F.C. v5p0384c1s v5p0422c2s v5p0504c1s v5p0617c1s v6p0407c2s
Hodgson, F.T. v4p0164c1s v4p0291c1s
Hodgson, G. v5p0421c1s v6p0635c1s
Hodgson, H. v6p0206c1s v6p0277c2s v6p0323c2s v6p0324c1s v6p0485c1s
Hodgson, H.M. v6p0253c2s
Hodgson, J. v1p0303c1s
Hodgson, J.C. v1p0546c1s v1p1133c2s
Hodgson, J.E. v3p0167c1s v4p0029c1s v4p0031c1s v4p0031c2s v4p0124c2s v4p0301c1m v4p0319c2s v4p0474c2s v4p0528c2s
Hodgson, J.E. and Eaton, F. v3p0306c1s v3p0475c2s
Hodgson, J.E. and Eaton, F.A. v3p0034c2s v3p0073c1s v3p0166c1s v3p0191c2s v3p0289c1s v3p0303c2s v3p0328c1s v3p0413c1s v4p0202c1s v4p0493c1s v4p0493c2s v4p0531c2s v4p0587c1s
Hodgson, J.E. and Eaton, Fred. v3p0102c1s
Hodgson, J.E. and Eaton, Fred.A. v3p0165c2s v3p0360c1s v3p0368c1s
Hodgson, J.T. v4p0492c2s
Hodgson, M. v6p0278c2s v6p0448c2s
Hodgson, R. v2p0154c1s v2p0339c1s v2p0366c1s v3p0172c1s v3p0348c1s v3p0405c1s v4p0218c1s v4p0457c1s v4p0567c2s v6p0490c1s
Hodgson, R., jr. v1p0556c1s v1p1235c1s
Hodgson, S.H. v1p0208c2s v1p0271c2s v1p0702c1s v1p0760c2s v1p0826c2s v1p0875c2s v1p0999c2s v1p1062c1s v1p1161c1s v1p1228c1s v1p1311c2s v1p1410c2s v2p0117c1s v2p0167c1s v2p0203c2s v2p0285c1s v2p0339c1s v2p0339c2m v2p0340c2s v2p0358c1s v3p0330c1s v3p0348c2s v4p0130c1s v5p0101c1s v5p0470c2s
Hodgson, S.H. and Main, A. v1p0271c2s
Hodgson, S.H. et al. v5p0580c1s
Hodgson, T.H. v3p0464c1s
Hodgson, W. v2p0109c2s v3p0148c1s
Hodgson, W.B. v1p0384c2s v1p1422c1s v6p0197c1s
Hodgson, W.B., Mrs. v1p0572c1s
Hodgson, W.E. v2p0440c1s v3p0114c2s v3p0264c1s v3p0322c2s v3p0381c1s v3p0398c2s v3p0405c2s v3p0428c1s v4p0007c1s v4p0037c2s v4p0087c1s v4p0152c1s v4p0188c2s v4p0191c1s v4p0198c1s v4p0364c2s v4p0429c1s v4p0457c2m v4p0478c2s v4p0482c2s v4p0500c2s v4p0585c1s v5p0474c2s v5p0484c1s v5p0592c1s v6p0471c2s v6p0488c1s v6p0566c1m v6p0657c2s v6p0658c1s v6p0696c1s
Hodgson, W.Earl v2p0391c1s
Hodgson, W.H. v6p0674c1s
Hodson, C.E. v3p0037c1s v3p0064c1m v3p0108c1s v3p0232c2s v3p0277c1m v3p0373c2s v3p0374c2s v4p0578c2s
Hodson, C.G. v1p0011c2s
Hodson, J. v1p0676c1s v3p0179c1s
Hodson, J.C. v5p0205c1s
Hodson, J.S. v2p0145c1s
Hodson, R.E. v2p0122c2s v5p0163c1s
Hodson, T.C. v6p0399c1s
Hoe, R. v5p0450c2s
Hoeber, A. v4p0074c1s v5p0096c1s v5p0280c1s v5p0419c2s v5p0462c1s v5p0516c1s v5p0530c1s v5p0552c1s v5p0552c2s v6p0167c1s v6p0241c1s v6p0301c2s v6p0518c1s v6p0531c1s
Hoebner, A. v6p0570c2s
Hoeck, L.G. v4p0541c1s v6p0060c2s
Hoecken, C. v1p1039c1s
Hoedemaher, P.J. v2p0205c1s
Hoeffer, J.F.X. v1p1237c1s
Hoehle, C. v2p0392c2s
Hoeing, C. v5p0573c2s
Hoek, H. v6p0072c2s
Hoenig, F. v5p0007c2s v5p0076c2s v5p0587c1s
Hoenig, Major v6p0205c1s
Hoenig, W. v2p0177c1s
Hoernle, R.F.A. v6p0513c1s
Hoes, R.R. v3p0300c2s v3p0426c1s
Hoey, C. v1p0023c1s v1p0558c2s v1p1054c1s v1p1071c1s v2p0267c2s
Hoey, C., Mrs. v1p0143c1s v1p0169c2s v1p0534c1s v1p1071c2s v1p1310c2s v2p0361c1s v2p0395c2s
Hoey, D.G. v3p0448c1s
Hoey, J.C. v1p0979c1s
Hofer, E. v4p0416c2m v4p0581c2s v5p0130c2s
Hofer, Mari R. v5p0274c1s
Hoff, A.B. v4p0521c2s
Hoff, J.H.van't v5p0104c1s
Hoff, J.R. v5p0271c2s
Hoff, J.V.van't v6p0497c2s
Hoff, J.Van R. v5p0342c1s
Hoff, K.A.E.von v1p0828c2s
Hoffding, H. v3p0143c1s v3p0459c2s v4p0575c1s v4p0616c2s v6p0019c1s v6p0495c2s v6p0521c2s v6p0602c1s
Hoffer, F. v1p1379c2s
Hoffer, J. v2p0076c2s
Hofflund, R.W. v6p0654c1s
Hoffman, A.S. v6p0111c1s v6p0484c1s v6p0597c1s
Hoffman, A.W. v1p0371c2s
Hoffman, Adolf v5p0508c2s
Hoffman, C.F. v1p0520c1s v1p0642c2s v1p0736c2s v1p0853c2s v1p0921c2s v1p1178c1s v1p1319c1s v1p1335c1s v6p0315c2s
Hoffman, E.F. v1p0925c1s v1p1028c1s v1p1050c2s
Hoffman, E.I. v4p0635c1s v5p0004c1s v5p0564c1s
Hoffman, E.T. v5p0206c2s v5p0539c1s
Hoffman, E.T.A. v1p0334c1s v1p0359c1s v1p0402c2s v1p0809c2s v1p1145c1s
Hoffman, F. v1p0362c1s v1p0397c1s v1p0858c1s
Hoffman, F.K. v6p0389c2s v6p0581c1s
Hoffman, F.L. v4p0396c2s v4p0397c1m v4p0555c2m v5p0461c1s v6p0106c2s v6p0167c1s v6p0322c1s v6p0355c2s v6p0680c2s
Hoffman, F.M. v4p0433c1s
Hoffman, F.S. v1p0038c1s v5p0391c1s v5p0577c1s v6p0309c2s
Hoffman, G.C. v6p0603c2s
Hoffman, G.D. v4p0252c2s
Hoffman, Hal v6p0532c1s
Hoffman, J. v4p0548c2s
Hoffman, J.M. v2p0265c1s v3p0310c2s
Hoffman, J.N. v1p0778c1m
Hoffman, K. v5p0240c2s v5p0271c2s v5p0330c2s v5p0407c1s v6p0165c2s v6p0175c2s v6p0251c2s v6p0505c1s v6p0555c1s
Hoffman, M. v1p1109c1s
Hoffman, M.L. v1p0114c2s
Hoffman, Prof. v6p0145c1s
Hoffman, W. v1p0005c1s v1p0454c1m v1p0701c2s v1p1144c2s
Hoffman, W.B. v4p0553c1s
Hoffman, W.C. v1p0336c1s
Hoffman, W.J. v1p0058c1s v1p0636c2s v1p0908c1s v1p1334c1s v1p1364c2s v4p0063c2s v4p0205c2s v4p0282c2m v4p0433c2s v4p0455c1s v4p0558c2s
Hoffman, W.N. v6p0315c2s
Hoffmann, D.O.N. v5p0082c1s
Hoffmann, E. v5p0391c1s
Hoffmann, E.A. v1p0357c1s v1p0485c2s v1p1313c1s
Hoffmann, F. v1p1079c2s v1p1356c1s v2p0336c1s v3p0051c2s v4p0504c2s
Hoffmann, H. v1p0707c2s v1p0732c1s v5p0566c2s
Hoffmann, J. v4p0442c1s
Hoffmann, M. v1p0138c1s
Hoffmann, Prof. v5p0133c1s
Hoffmann, S.V. and Searing, L. v3p0125c2s
Hoffmeister, G.B. v3p0118c1s v3p0351c2s
Hoffmeyer, N. v1p0557c1s
Hoffnung, A. v4p0251c1s
Hoffsten, E.G. v6p0589c2s
Hofland, B. v1p1266c1s
Hofland, B., Mrs. v1p0282c1s
Hofland, F.R. v1p0453c2s
Hofland, Mrs. v1p1323c2s
Hofling, Prof. v1p0756c2s
Hofmann, A.W. v1p0224c1m v2p0076c2s
Hofmann, Dr. v1p0990c1s
Hofmeyer, A. v5p0006c1s v6p0203c1s v6p0713c1s
Hoftman, Zur See v6p0287c1s
Hogan, E. v1p1225c2s v1p1265c1s v3p0017c2s v3p0092c1s v3p0093c2s v3p0114c1s v3p0152c2s v3p0154c2s v3p0203c2s v3p0223c1s v3p0312c1s v3p0419c1s v3p0462c1s v3p0473c1s v4p0023c1s v4p0047c1s v4p0261c1s v6p0398c2s v6p0414c2s v6p0417c2s
Hogan, Elodie v6p0116c2s v6p0407c1s v6p0568c1s
Hogan, F.J. v6p0625c1s
Hogan, J. v4p0348c1s v5p0218c1s v5p0379c1s v5p0439c2s v5p0513c1s
Hogan, J.F. v2p0365c1s v3p0221c2s v3p0427c1s v4p0038c1s v4p0038c2s v4p0085c1s v4p0135c2s v4p0198c2s v4p0237c1s v4p0362c1s v4p0427c2s v4p0452c2s v4p0536c1s v5p0039c1s v5p0069c2s v5p0215c1s v5p0497c1s v5p0559c1s v6p0282c2s
Hogan, J.G. v5p0549c2s
Hogan, L.E. v4p0370c2m v5p0106c1s
Hogan, P.T. v1p0609c2s
Hogane, J.T. v2p0460c1s
Hogar, Stansbury v4p0369c1s
Hogarth, D.C. v6p0491c2s
Hogarth, D.G. v3p0008c1s v3p0016c1s v3p0108c2s v3p0217c1s v3p0262c2s v4p0145c1s v4p0153c2s v4p0173c1m v4p0396c1s v4p0441c1s v5p0142c2s v5p0462c1s v5p0645c2s v6p0027c1s v6p0047c1s v6p0118c1s v6p0157c1m v6p0163c1s v6p0187c1s v6p0295c2s v6p0353c2s v6p0390c2s v6p0409c1s v6p0444c1s v6p0457c2s v6p0459c1s v6p0712c2m
Hogarth, D.G. and Munro, J.A.R. v3p0023c2s
Hogarth, D.G. and Sayce, A.H. v4p0172c1s
Hogarth, D.G. et al. v4p0172c1s v6p0444c2s
Hogarth, G. v1p0105c2s v1p0108c1s v1p0261c1s v1p0479c2s v1p0771c2s v1p0858c2s v1p1023c1s
Hogarth, J.E. v4p0151c2s v4p0287c1s v4p0555c1s v5p0228c2s v5p0637c2s v6p0281c1s
Hogarth, W.D. v3p0108c2s

Hogben, J. v2p0009c2s
v2p0435c1s v3p0472c1s v5p0640c2s
Hoge, A. v3p0184c2s
v3p0451c2s
Hoge, M.D. and Kemper, W.H.
v1p0675c1s
Hogg, E.F. v5p0107c2s
v5p0108c1s v5p0223c1s
Hogg, E.F. and Innes, A.D.
v5p0178c1s
Hogg, H. v1p0105c1s
Hogg, H.W. v4p0013c1s
v5p0053c2s v5p0057c2s v5p0152c1s
v5p0174c1s v5p0194c1s
Hogg, J. v1p0076c2s
v1p0098c1s v1p0150c1s v1p0183c1s
v1p0260c2s v1p0278c2s v1p0312c2s
v1p0357c1s v1p0365c2s v1p0394c1s
v1p0397c1s v1p0397c2s v1p0435c2s
v1p0439c2m v1p0519c2s v1p0583c2s
v1p0642c1s v1p0643c1s v1p0644c2s
v1p0731c2s v1p0773c2s v1p0844c1s
v1p0851c1s v1p0877c1s v1p0889c2s
v1p1168c2s v1p1190c1s v1p1222c1s
v1p1239c1s v1p1259c2s v1p1308c2s
v1p1328c1s v1p1334c1s v1p1417c2s
v2p0022c2s v2p0093c2s v2p0206c2s
v3p0115c2s v3p0196c1s v3p0280c2s
v3p0362c1s
Hogg, J. et al. v1p0214c2s
Hogg, J.E. v6p0360c1s
v6p0360c2m v6p0366c2s
Hogg, L.M. v1p0115c1s
v1p0671c2s v1p0673c1s v1p1117c1s
Hogg, Q. v5p0458c1s
Hogg, W. v4p0557c2s
v5p0139c1s v5p0385c1s
Hogg, W.A. v1p1127c2s
Hoggan, F.E. v2p0217c2s
v2p0477c1s
Hoggan, G. v1p1376c1s
v2p0477c1s
Hoggson, W.J. v6p0051c1s
Hogue, A. v6p0363c1s
Hogue, Addison v5p0269c1s
v6p0523c1s
Hogue, O.D. v5p0201c1s
Hohler, V. v5p0262c1s
Hohlfeld, A.R. v6p0259c2s
Hohnested, G.S. v6p0364c1s
Hohoff, W. v1p0897c2s
Hoisington, H.R. v1p0634c1s
Hoke, H.M. v3p0360c1s
v3p0391c1m v4p0096c1s v4p0335c1s
v4p0428c2s v4p0466c2s v4p0512c2s
v5p0576c1s v5p0590c2s v5p0615c1s
v6p0212c2s v6p0540c2s v6p0682c1s
Hoke, N.C. v4p0406c2s
Holabird, S.B. v4p0051c2s
v4p0161c2s v4p0189c2s v4p0222c1s
v4p0247c1s v4p0392c1s v4p0490c1s
v4p0602c1s v5p0029c1s v5p0029c2s
v5p0586c1s
Holaday, J.M. v3p0090c1s
Holaind, R.I. v5p0593c2s
Holbeach, H. v1p0056c2s
v1p0105c2s v1p0144c2s v1p0333c1s
v1p0354c2s v1p0373c2s v1p0414c2s
v1p0446c2s v1p0451c1s v1p0569c2s
v1p0584c1s v1p0741c2s v1p0775c2s
v1p0782c2s v1p0824c1s v1p0839c2s
v1p0868c1s v1p0869c1s v1p0869c2s
v1p1108c1s v1p1164c1s v1p1176c2s
v1p1193c1s v1p1252c1m v1p1321c1s
v1p1422c2s
Holber, A. v5p0121c2s
v6p0403c1s v6p0442c2s
Holberton, W. v3p0154c2s
v3p0436c2s v4p0089c2s
Holborn, A. v2p0368c2s
Holborn, L. and Day, A.L.. v5p0226c2s
v5p0237c2s v5p0371c2m
Holbrook, B.H. v4p0170c2s
Holbrook, C. v5p0201c1s
Holbrook, E.St.G. v6p0560c1s
Holbrook, J.C. v1p0594c2s
v1p0601c1s v1p1103c1s
Holbrook, J.S. v5p0337c1s
Holbrook, M.L. v4p0033c2s
Holbrook, R. v5p0127c1s
v6p0289c2s
Holbrook, R.H. v4p0170c2s
Holbrook, R.T. v6p0479c1s
v6p0679c2s
Holbrook, R.W. v6p0275c1s
Holbrook, W.A. v6p0105c1s
Holbrook, Z.S. v4p0116c2s
v4p0150c1s v4p0230c1s v4p0283c1s
v4p0430c1s v4p0534c2s v4p0535c1s
v4p0535c2s v5p0105c1s v5p0115c1s
v5p0120c2s v5p0265c2s v5p0445c1s
v5p0458c2m v5p0592c2s
Holck, L.G. v4p0300c1s
v6p0364c1s
Holcomb, S.W. v4p0609c2s
Holcomb, W.P. v2p0052c2s
v2p0335c1s
Holcombe, A.N. v6p0263c1s
v6p0637c1s
Holcombe, A.R. v6p0447c2s
v6p0448c1s
Holcombe, C. v4p0328c1s
v6p0118c1s v6p0119c1m v6p0120c1m
v6p0421c2s v6p0468c2s v6p0561c1s
Holcombe, Emily S.G. v6p0563c2s
Holcombe, J.P. v1p1208c1s
Holcombe, N.J. v3p0363c2s
Holcombe, S.B. v2p0058c2s
Holcombe, W.H. v1p1016c1s
v2p0304c1s v2p0309c1s v2p0401c2s
v2p0411c1s
Holdane, R.S. v5p0391c1s
Holden, A. v5p0222c2s
v5p0236c2s
Holden, A.P. v2p0469c1s
Holden, Col. v6p0201c1s
Holden, E. v1p0200c2s
v1p0298c1s v1p1311c1s v1p1343c2m
v6p0618c2s
Holden, E.L. and Hutchins, C.C.
v3p0334c1s
Holden, E.S. v1p0071c1s
v1p0257c1s v1p0281c2s v1p0588c2s
v1p0592c1s v1p0743c1s v1p0744c2s
v1p0749c1s v1p0808c1s v1p0903c2m
v1p0936c1s v1p0962c2s v1p0992c1s
v1p1243c2s v1p1244c1s v1p1267c2s
v1p1269c1s v1p1291c2s v1p1292c1s
v1p1312c1s v1p1395c1s v1p1397c1s
v2p0025c1s v2p0026c1s v2p0028c2s
v2p0073c1s v2p0080c1s v2p0083c1m
v2p0113c1s v2p0129c2s v2p0202c1m
v2p0249c1s v2p0257c2m v2p0308c1s
v2p0340c1s v2p0345c1s v2p0386c2m
v2p0417c2s v2p0433c2s v2p0441c2s
v2p0443c1s v2p0452c1s v2p0455c2s
v3p0024c2s v3p0031c2s v3p0069c1s
v3p0126c1m v3p0250c1m v3p0286c2s
v3p0298c2s v3p0330c2s v3p0407c1s
v3p0407c2m v3p0423c1s v3p0460c2s
v4p0034c1s v4p0037c2s v4p0040c1s
v4p0137c2s v4p0159c2s v4p0166c1s
v4p0167c1s v4p0330c2s v4p0357c2m
v4p0358c1s v4p0381c1m v4p0396c1s
v4p0562c2s v4p0598c2s v5p0035c1s
v5p0044c1s v5p0113c1s v5p0173c1s
v5p0212c2s v5p0267c2s v5p0269c2s
v5p0333c2s v5p0337c1s v5p0362c1s
v5p0363c1s v5p0369c2s v5p0417c1s
v5p0458c1s v5p0467c2s v5p0549c1s
v6p0038c1s v6p0046c2s v6p0148c2s
v6p0228c2s v6p0245c2s v6p0427c1s
v6p0518c2s v6p0536c2s v6p0576c2s
v6p0613c2s v6p0666c1m v6p0693c1s
Holden, E.S. and Keyser, F.
v2p0283c2s
Holden, E.S. and Schur, W.
v2p0283c2s
Holden, E.S. and Seeliger, H.
v2p0417c1s
Holden, F.C. v6p0020c2s
Holden, G.H. v1p0575c2s
Holden, H.M., Mrs. v2p0027c1s
Holden, J. v2p0475c1s
v5p0442c2s v6p0382c1s
Holden, J.A. v6p0567c2s
Holden, J.B. v1p0046c1s
v1p0368c2s v1p1255c2s
Holden, J.E. v6p0377c2s
Holden, M.E. v4p0464c1s
Holden, P.G. v6p0149c2s
Holden, R. v3p0007c2s
v3p0046c2s v3p0180c1s v3p0361c2s
v4p0225c2s v4p0392c2s v5p0531c2s
Holden, R. and Douce, F. . v1p0464c2s
v1p1307c2s
Holden, R.M. v6p0110c2s
v6p0416c2s
Holden, R.McK. v6p0290c2s
Holden, S.O. v5p0073c1s
Holden, S.S. v2p0089c2s
Holden, W. v3p0405c2s
Holder, C.F. v1p1241c1s
v2p0015c1m v2p0071c1s v2p0106c1s
v2p0137c2s v2p0156c2s v2p0157c2s
v2p0261c2s v2p0289c2s v2p0340c1s
v2p0393c1s v2p0399c1m v2p0429c1s
v2p0449c1s v2p0472c2s v3p0154c1s
v3p0167c1s v3p0213c2s v3p0382c2s
v3p0392c1s v4p0083c1s v4p0201c1s
v5p0020c2s v5p0112c2m v5p0113c2s
v5p0208c2s v5p0372c2s v5p0418c1s
v5p0442c1s v5p0516c2s v5p0524c1s
v5p0534c1s v5p0546c1s v5p0547c2s
v5p0594c1s v5p0595c1s v6p0023c2s
v6p0025c2s v6p0053c2s v6p0092c2s
v6p0093c1m v6p0093c2m v6p0104c1s
v6p0129c2s v6p0149c2s v6p0155c2s
v6p0171c1s v6p0177c2s v6p0226c1m
v6p0227c1m v6p0227c2s v6p0230c1s
v6p0264c2s v6p0293c2s v6p0304c1s
v6p0433c1s v6p0482c1m v6p0509c1s
v6p0524c2s v6p0606c1s v6p0607c1s
v6p0629c2s v6p0631c2s v6p0660c2s
v6p0692c2s
Holder, F.W. v6p0041c2s
Holder, H.L. v4p0615c2s
Holder, J.B. v1p0462c1s
v2p0011c2s v4p0511c2s
Holder, J.B. and Allen, J.A.
v2p0471c2s
Holder, Lady v6p0042c2s
Holder, R. v5p0361c1s
Holderness, T.W. v6p0313c2s
Holdich, H.H. v1p0951c2s
Holdich, J. v1p0830c2s
v1p1027c1s v1p1362c2s
Holdich, N.H. v1p0076c2s
Holdich, Prof. v1p0723c1s
Holdich, T. v6p0036c2s
v6p0313c2s
Holdich, T., Sir v5p0228c2s
Holdich, T.H. v1p0798c2s
v3p0169c1s v4p0307c2s v4p0350c2s
v5p0005c1s v5p0006c1s v5p0286c1s
v5p0332c1s v5p0343c2s v5p0375c1s
v5p0441c2s v5p0563c2s v5p0579c2s
v5p0580c2s v5p0582c2s v6p0005c2s
v6p0010c1s v6p0011c2s v6p0020c1s
v6p0082c1s v6p0186c2s v6p0250c1m
v6p0313c2s v6p0459c1s v6p0526c1s
v6p0627c2s
Holdich, T.H., Sir v5p0034c1s
v5p0265c2s
Holdich, T.R. v5p0034c1s
Holding, E.E. v3p0112c1s
Holdish, H.H. v2p0250c2s
Holdsworth, A.E. v2p0423c1s
v3p0150c1s v3p0445c2s v4p0619c1s
v5p0237c1s
Holdsworth, W.S. v6p0403c2s
v6p0651c2s v6p0711c1s
Hole, C. v1p0096c2s
Hole, H. v3p0429c2s
Hole, S.R. v5p0563c1s
Holford, C.N. v2p0312c2s
Holgate, C.W. v2p0028c1s
v2p0256c2s
Holgate, H. v5p0317c1s
Holiday, H. v4p0162c1s
v4p0631c1s v6p0294c1s
Holingshead, J. v1p0307c1s
v1p0982c1s v1p1107c2s
Holl, H. v1p0133c1s
Holland, A.L. v6p0672c2s
Holland, B. v2p0078c1s
v2p0345c1s v4p0108c2s v4p0354c1s
v4p0548c2s v4p0562c1s v4p0581c1s
v5p0117c2s v5p0296c1s v5p0296c2s
v5p0297c1m v5p0309c2s v5p0419c1s
v5p0420c2s
Holland, B.H. v3p0073c2s
Holland, C. v4p0043c2s
v4p0135c2s v4p0348c2s v4p0392c2s
v4p0438c1s v5p0256c1s v5p0326c1s
v5p0447c2s v5p0465c2s v5p0625c2s
v6p0034c2s v6p0108c2s v6p0220c2s
v6p0289c2s v6p0480c1s v6p0581c2s
v6p0697c1s
Holland, C.B. and Cooper, A.
v1p1250c2m
Holland, Clive v5p0431c2s
v5p0643c1s v6p0075c1s v6p0480c1s
v6p0499c1s v6p0663c2s
Holland, E.G. v1p0247c2s
v1p0289c2s v1p0446c2s v1p1186c2s
Holland, E.H. v6p0709c2m
Holland, E.W. v1p1200c2s
Holland, F. v1p0366c1s
Holland, F.C. v5p0007c2s
Holland, F.H. v4p0154c1s
v4p0386c1s v4p0409c1s
Holland, F.M. v1p0120c1s
v1p0184c2s v1p0319c1s v1p0641c1s
v1p0996c2s v4p0064c2s v4p0082c1s
v4p0102c1s v4p0125c2s v4p0128c1s
v4p0155c1s v4p0160c1s v4p0170c2s
v4p0178c2s v4p0188c1s v4p0188c2s
v4p0196c1s v4p0244c2s v4p0358c2s
v4p0396c2s v4p0461c2s v4p0478c1s
v4p0481c1s v4p0533c1s v4p0553c2s
v4p0607c1s v4p0628c2s v4p0633c2s
Holland, F.W. v1p0106c2s
v1p0118c1s v1p0150c2s v1p0185c1s
v1p0198c2s v1p0294c1m v1p0312c1s
v1p0316c2s v1p0329c2s v1p0362c1s
v1p0396c1s v1p0414c1s v1p0554c1s
v1p0682c2s v1p0710c1s v1p0777c2s
v1p0879c1s v1p0880c1s v1p0961c1s
v1p1052c2s v1p1056c2s v1p1112c2s
v1p1147c1s v1p1193c2s v1p1212c2s
v1p1253c2s v1p1278c2s v1p1419c1s
v2p0108c1s v2p0250c1s v3p0105c1s
v3p0235c1s
Holland, H., Sir v1p0071c1s
v1p0074c1s v1p0078c2s v1p0184c2s
v1p0225c1s v1p0301c2s v1p0329c2s
v1p0365c2s v1p0613c2s v1p0745c1s
v1p0767c2s v1p0792c2s v1p0793c2s
v1p0900c2m v1p1006c1s v1p1124c1s
v1p1172c1s v1p1209c1s
Holland, H.E. v3p0250c1s
Holland, H.L. v1p0897c2s
Holland, H.S. v3p0218c1s
v3p0252c1s v4p0039c1s v4p0111c2s
v4p0112c1s v4p0193c2s v4p0273c2s
v4p0314c1s v5p0120c1s
Holland, H.S. and Carter, J.
v6p0141c1s v6p0428c2s
Holland, H.S. et al. v4p0170c1s

Holland, H.S., Sir v1p0073c1s
Holland, H.W. v1p0202c2s
v1p0333c2s v1p0405c2s v1p0406c2s
v1p0458c2s v1p0486c1s v1p0630c1s
v1p0729c2m v1p0999c2s v1p1000c1s
v1p1001c1s v1p1009c2s v1p1019c1s
v1p1053c2s v1p1074c2s v1p1153c2s
v1p1161c1s v1p1179c2s v1p1305c1s
v1p1346c1s v2p0104c1s v2p0162c1s
v2p0169c1s v2p0201c2s v2p0356c2s
v3p0061c2s v3p0335c1s
Holland, H.W. and Godkin, E.L.
v1p0199c2s v1p0960c1s
Holland, J. v1p0499c1s
v1p0855c2s v1p1105c2s v1p1312c2s
Holland, J.E. v1p1088c2s
Holland, J.G. v1p0065c1s
v1p0229c2s v1p0837c2s v1p0920c2s
v1p1180c2s v1p1418c2s
Holland, J.H. v5p0149c2s
Holland, J.L. v1p1090c1s
Holland, J.P. v4p0004c2s
v4p0100c2s v4p0204c2s v5p0558c2m
v6p0043c2s v6p0044c1s
Holland, J.R. v2p0227c1s
Holland, J.R. et al. v1p0380c1s
Holland, L. v4p0412c1s
v5p0419c1s v5p0542c2s v6p0501c1s
Holland, L.R. v3p0065c1s
v6p0593c1s
Holland, M. v4p0082c1s
v4p0374c1s
Holland, Maj. v1p0850c2s
Holland, N.M. v5p0297c1s
Holland, Olive v6p0427c1s
Holland, P. v5p0017c1s
v5p0290c1s v5p0524c2s v5p0618c2s
Holland, P.H. v1p0314c2s
v3p0280c1s
Holland, R. and Burrows, H.W.
v4p0207c1s
Holland, R.A. v1p1189c2s
v2p0215c1s v2p0339c1s v2p0366c1s
Holland, R.A., jr. v4p0437c1s
Holland, R.S. v6p0407c1s
v6p0627c1s
Holland, S. v6p0298c1s
v6p0685c1s
Holland, S. and Stewart, I.
v6p0462c2s
Holland, S.C. v1p0016c2s
v6p0185c2s
Holland, S.L. v3p0017c1s
v4p0322c2s v5p0312c2s
Holland, T.E. v1p0954c1s
v2p0423c2s v3p0049c1s v3p0316c2s
v4p0106c2s v4p0107c1s v4p0246c1s
v4p0287c2s v5p0067c1s v5p0437c2s
v6p0449c2s v6p0676c1s
Holland, T.E. and Rashdall, H.
v3p0316c2s
Holland, T.H. v3p0207c1s
v6p0185c2s
Holland, T.W. v1p0682c1s
Holland, W., Sir v1p0817c2s
Holland, W.H. v1p0935c1s
Holland, W.J. v3p0419c1s
v5p0095c1s v5p0622c1s v6p0055c1s
v6p0174c2s v6p0214c2s v6p0320c2s
v6p0437c1s
Holland, W.J. et al. v6p0102c1s
Holland, W.M. v1p0641c1s
Holland, W.W. v1p0982c2s
Holland, W.W. et al. v1p0204c2s
Hollander, B. v3p0053c1s
v4p0541c1s v6p0079c2s v6p0320c1s
Hollander, J.H. v4p0114c1s
v4p0481c1s v4p0483c2s v5p0009c1s
v5p0015c2m v5p0044c2s v5p0077c1s
v5p0199c1s v5p0289c1s v5p0460c1m
v5p0568c2s v5p0584c2s v6p0009c1s
v6p0016c1m v6p0176c1s v6p0356c2s
v6p0411c2s v6p0506c2s v6p0510c1m
v6p0540c1s v6p0667c1s
v6p0674c1s
Hollands, E.H. v6p0145c2s
Hollands, S.H. v5p0368c1s
Hollaner, O. v1p1248c1s
Hollerith, H. v3p0444c1s
Holleway-Calthrop, H.C. .. v2p0402c1s
Holley, A.L. v1p0116c1s
v1p0273c1s v1p0664c2m v1p0665c2s
v1p1251c1m v1p1251c2s
Holley, A.S. v1p1251c2s
Holley, G.W. v1p0424c1s
v1p0919c2s v2p0180c1s v2p0314c1s
Holley, H. v1p1018c1s
Holley, M. v3p0001c1s
v4p0052c2s v4p0305c1s v6p0177c1s
v6p0395c2s
Holley, Marietta v6p0362c2s
Hollick, A. v5p0015c1s
v5p0073c1s v5p0214c1s v5p0402c1s
v6p0014c1s v6p0540c1s
Hollick, A. and Jeffrey, E.C.
v6p0157c1s
Hollick, A. and Mercer, H.C.
v5p0358c1s
Hollidan, C. v6p0447c2s
Holliday, C. v6p0606c2s
Holliday, W.A. v2p0245c1s
v4p0194c1s
Hollingshead, J. v1p0047c1s
v1p0367c1s v1p0760c1s v1p0763c2s
v1p0938c1s v2p0002c2s v2p0113c2s
v2p0263c2s v2p0280c1s v2p0338c1s
v2p0416c2s v4p0544c1s v4p0601c1s
v5p0129c2s v6p0359c2s
Hollingsworth, C.E. v6p0150c1s
Hollingsworth, C.M. v2p0396c2s
Hollins, J. v5p0506c2s
Hollinsworth, V.M. v2p0423c2s
Hollis, A.P. v5p0265c1s
v5p0525c1s
Hollis, G.F. v5p0007c2s
Hollis, I.N. v4p0249c1s
v4p0323c2s v5p0134c1s v5p0257c1s
v5p0401c1s v5p0507c1s v5p0543c2s
v5p0602c2m v6p0039c1s v6p0231c2s
v6p0282c1s
Hollis, I.N. et al. v4p0180c1s
v4p0395c2s
Hollis, W.A. v5p0418c2s
Hollister, C.E. v2p0278c1s
Hollister, E. v1p0624c1s
Hollister, G.B. v6p0010c2s
Hollister, G.H. v1p0768c1s
v1p1252c1s v1p1281c1s
Hollister, H.A. v6p0600c1s
Hollister, H.C. v6p0657c2s
Hollister, H.E. v6p0712c2s
Hollister, W.C. v6p0529c2s
Hollond, E.W. v1p0765c1s
v1p1031c1m v1p1361c1s
Hollond, H.W. v1p0766c1s
Hollond, J.R. v2p0275c2s
Holloway, C.M. v3p0302c1s
Holloway, E. v4p0140c2s
Holloway, G. v3p0163c1s
v3p0221c2s v4p0412c1s
Holloway, G.T. v4p0573c2s
v5p0002c2s v5p0442c2s
Holloway, H.C. v1p1237c2s
v4p0456c2s
Holloway, I.P. v2p0281c2s
Holloway, J. v1p0826c1s
Holloway, J.E., Mrs. v4p0352c2s
Holloway, J.F. v2p0419c2s
v3p0165c2s v4p0180c1s v4p0180c2s
v4p0216c1s v4p0547c1s
Holloway, L.C. v2p0162c1s
Holloway, W. v4p0449c2s
v6p0672c2s v6p0703c2s
Holloway, W.R. and Wyeth, J.A.
v3p0064c2s v3p0095c2s
Hollowell, J.H. v1p0323c2s
v1p1381c1s v2p0009c1s v2p0033c1s
v2p0124c2s v2p0151c2s v2p0202c2s
v2p0435c1s v3p0076c1s v3p0096c2s
v5p0178c2s v6p0036c1s v6p0081c2s
v6p0495c1s
Holls, F.W. v3p0451c2s
v4p0224c1s v4p0265c1s v5p0329c2s
v5p0437c2s v6p0202c1s v6p0274c2s
Hollway, J. v1p0493c2s
v1p1266c2s
Hollway-Calthrop, H.C. ... v2p0337c2s
Holly, Flora M. v5p0355c2s
v5p0520c1s v5p0631c1s
Holly, H.H. v1p0373c2s
Holly, J.T. v1p0104c2s
v1p1140c2s v5p0403c1s
Hollyday, G.T. v1p1311c1s
v2p0205c2s
Hollyday, L. v1p1345c1s
Holm, E. v3p0147c2s
Holm, J. v3p0090c1s
Holm, N. v1p0805c1s
Holm, Saxe v1p0365c1s
v1p0397c2s v1p0425c2s v1p0444c1s
v1p0471c2s v1p0609c1s v1p0692c2s
v1p0888c2s v1p0942c2s v1p1273c1s
v1p1408c1s v2p0152c2s
Holm, T. v4p0145c1s
v4p0145c2s v5p0151c1s v5p0194c2s
v5p0456c2s v6p0020c1s v6p0106c1s
v6p0159c2s v6p0163c1s v6p0469c2s
v6p0656c2s
Holman, A. v4p0417c1s
Holman, C.V. et al. v6p0667c1s
Holman, D.E. v3p0261c1s
Holman, D.S. v1p0075c2s
v1p1002c2s
Holman, E.E. v6p0154c1s
v6p0581c1s
Holman, H. v4p0609c1s
Holman, L.A. v6p0538c2s
Holman, S.A. v1p0248c2s
v1p1060c1s
Holman, S.W. v2p0168c2s
v2p0438c2s v6p0357c1s
Holman, W.S. v2p0358c2s
Holmden, W. v4p0024c2s
v4p0029c2m v4p0030c1m
Holme, C. v4p0455c1s
v5p0226c1s v5p0302c1s v5p0303c2s
v5p0462c1s v5p0639c1s v6p0338c1s
Holme, F. v5p0168c1s
Holme, G. v4p0002c1s
v4p0039c1m v4p0046c1s v4p0066c1s
v4p0080c1s v4p0127c2s v4p0196c1s
v4p0282c2s v4p0341c1s v4p0375c2s
v4p0389c1s v4p0469c1s v4p0509c2s
v4p0548c1s v4p0580c1s v4p0608c2s
v6p0146c2s
Holme, H. v1p0144c1s
Holme, M. v1p1327c2s
Holme, Myra v2p0342c2s
Holme, R. v2p0441c1s
Holmes, A. v1p0122c2s
v1p0955c1s v1p1350c2s v5p0416c1s
Holmes, A.G. v5p0170c2m
v6p0183c1s
Holmes, A.H. v5p0367c1s
Holmes, A.M. v4p0185c1s
v4p0255c1s
Holmes, B. v5p0474c1s
Holmes, C. v6p0024c2s
Holmes, C.I. v5p0386c2s
Holmes, C.J. v5p0113c1s
v5p0473c1s v6p0538c2s v6p0679c2s
Holmes, Clara H. v5p0205c1s
v5p0263c2s
Holmes, D. v1p1161c1s
Holmes, D., Mrs. v1p0116c2s
Holmes, D., jr. v1p0074c1s
v1p0996c1s
Holmes, E. v3p0354c1s
v5p0008c2s v5p0337c2s v5p0613c1s
Holmes, E.A. et al. v5p0106c2s
Holmes, E.E. v1p1106c1s
Holmes, E.K. v6p0087c2s
Holmes, E.M. v2p0252c1s
v5p0073c1s
Holmes, E.R. v4p0145c1s
v4p0181c1s v5p0228c2s
Holmes, Ethel v6p0013c1s
Holmes, F.H. v1p0748c1s
v3p0132c2s
Holmes, F.M. v2p0256c1s
v3p0105c1s v3p0434c1s v4p0063c1s
v4p0201c1s v4p0547c2s
Holmes, F.S. v1p0221c1s
v4p0617c1s v6p0050c1s
Holmes, G. v1p0061c2s
v1p1160c2s v2p0066c2s v3p0067c2s
v3p0282c1s v3p0342c1s v3p0413c2s
v4p0518c2s v5p0611c2s v6p0003c2s
v6p0358c1s
Holmes, G.F. v1p0069c2s
v1p0184c2s v1p0340c1s v1p0417c1s
v1p0532c1s v1p0533c1s v1p0639c1s
v1p0692c1s v1p0704c2s v1p0739c1s
v1p0741c2s v1p0999c2s v1p1056c2s
v1p1157c1s v1p1194c2s v1p1199c1s
v1p1206c2m v1p1337c1s v2p0005c1s
v2p0096c1s v2p0120c1s v2p0128c2s
v2p0249c1s v2p0289c2s v2p0339c1s
Holmes, G.K. v3p0029c1s
v3p0101c1s v3p0289c1s v4p0008c1s
v4p0157c1s v4p0315c2s v4p0383c2m
v4p0538c1s v4p0568c2s v4p0599c1s
v4p0615c1m v5p0468c2s v5p0598c2s
Holmes, H.M. v6p0251c2s
Holmes, I.M. v3p0256c2s
Holmes, J. v1p0165c1m
Holmes, J.A. v1p0229c2s
Holmes, J.B. v1p0471c2s
v1p0921c2s v1p1123c1s v4p0098c1s
Holmes, J.H. v3p0260c1s
v5p0316c1s
Holmes, J.T. v4p0323c1s
Holmes, L.M. v5p0635c1s
Holmes, M.E. v4p0222c2s
v4p0505c1s
Holmes, M.J. v4p0254c2s
v4p0386c1s
Holmes, M.S. v4p0519c2s
Holmes, N.J. v1p1290c2s
Holmes, O.W. v1p0024c1s
v1p0045c2s v1p0051c2s v1p0060c1s
v1p0065c2s v1p0081c2s v1p0088c1s
v1p0315c1s v1p0346c2s v1p0361c1s
v1p0393c2s v1p0431c2s v1p0433c1s
v1p0455c2s v1p0462c1s v1p0560c1s
v1p0609c2s v1p0610c1s v1p0746c1s
v1p0886c1s v1p0898c2s v1p0939c2s
v1p0947c2s v1p1003c2s v1p1019c2s
v1p1054c2m v1p1064c1s v1p1252c2m
v1p1353c2s v1p1378c2s v1p1434c2m
v2p0017c1s v2p0026c2s v2p0029c2s
v2p0038c1s v2p0062c1s v2p0148c1s
v2p0158c2s v2p0178c2s v2p0205c2s
v2p0230c1s v2p0243c1s v2p0265c2s
v2p0267c2s v2p0271c2s v2p0310c1s
v2p0334c2s v2p0422c1s v3p0056c1s
v3p0061c2s v3p0144c2m v3p0260c1m
v3p0315c2s v3p0420c2s v4p0118c2s
v4p0620c2s v5p0327c2s
Holmes, O.W. and Crawford, F.M.
v3p0442c1s
Holmes, O.W. et al. v2p0029c2s
v3p0190c2s
Holmes, O.W., jr. v1p0729c2s
v1p1016c2s v1p1037c2s v1p1324c2s
v2p0251c2s v4p0186c1s v4p0535c2s
Holmes, R. v2p0290c1s
v4p0579c2s
Holmes, R.R. v4p0338c2s
v5p0632c2s v6p0419c1s v6p0700c2s

Holmes, R.W.A. v2p0227c2s
v2p0228c1s
Holmes, S. v1p1191c2s
v4p0275c2s v5p0625c1s
Holmes, S.J. v5p0122c1s
v6p0325c1s
Holmes, S.T. v4p0181c2s
Holmes, T. v4p0025c1s
v4p0137c1s v4p0158c2s v5p0170c1s
v5p0270c1s v5p0289c2s v5p0313c1s
v6p0637c2s
Holmes, T.DeB. v4p0145c2s
Holmes, T.R. v4p0216c2s
v4p0280c1s v6p0130c1s
Holmes, T.R.E. v1p1384c1s
v2p0204c2s v2p0305c2s v3p0109c2s
v3p0130c1s v4p0259c2s
Holmes, T.V. v1p0140c1s
v5p0163c1s
Holmes, Thomas v5p0143c1s
Holmes, W.H. v1p0523c2s
v1p0936c1s v1p1437c1s v2p0010c1s
v2p0286c2m v2p0295c1s v2p0299c2s
v2p0337c1s v2p0352c1s v2p0436c1s
v4p0368c1s v4p0422c1s v4p0457c1s
v5p0082c1s v5p0136c2s v5p0358c1s
v5p0358c2s v5p0417c1s v5p0462c1s
v6p0008c1s v6p0023c2s v6p0302c2s
v6p0339c2s v6p0432c2s v6p0526c1s
Holmes, W.H. and Dorsey, G.A.
v5p0532c1s v5p0583c2s
Holmes, W.P.B. v6p0522c2s
Holmes-Forbes, A.W. v4p0121c2s
v4p0147c2s
Holmested, G.S. v1p0721c2m
v1p0722c1s
Holms, G. v5p0539c2s
Holms, J. v1p0542c2s
v1p0974c2s v5p0559c1s
Holms, J.D. v3p0165c2s
v3p0248c1s v3p0321c2s v3p0322c1s
v4p0238c2s v5p0248c1s v5p0464c1s
v6p0271c1s
Holms, P. v5p0055c1s
Holms, P.G. v5p0237c2s
Holms, W.L. v5p0150c2s
Holmstrem, V. v5p0034c1s
v5p0501c1s
Holmstrem, V. and Ookhtomsky, Prince
v5p0247c1s
Holoran, G.H. v5p0511c1s
Holroyd, C. v3p0472c2s
Holroyd, J. v1p1296c1s
Holst, H.E.von v4p0597c1s
v6p0216c1s v6p0484c1s
Holst, H.von v1p0007c1s
v1p0059c2s v1p0379c2s v1p0477c2s
v1p0485c2s v1p0498c2s v1p0516c1s
v1p0675c2s v1p0849c2s v1p0894c2s
v2p0229c2s v4p0170c1s v4p0514c2m
v4p0525c2s v4p0553c1s v4p0574c1s
Holst, H.von et al. v1p0927c1s
Holt, A. v6p0355c2s
Holt, A. and Leigh, J.G. . v6p0359c2s
Holt, B.W. v5p0567c2s
v5p0593c1s
Holt, C.L. v3p0133c1s
Holt, C.S. v1p0279c1s
v1p0537c1s
Holt, E. v1p0601c1s
v1p0846c1s v1p1355c2s
Holt, E.B. v6p0522c1s
Holt, E.E. v3p0047c2s
Holt, E.W.L. v4p0200c2s
Holt, Eliot v2p0475c2s
Holt, G.C. v4p0346c1s
v4p0375c2s v4p0427c1s v4p0616c1s
v6p0051c1s v6p0294c2s
Holt, G.S. v6p0290c1s
Holt, H. v1p0556c2s
v1p1235c2s v2p0102c2s v3p0050c1m
v3p0100c1m v3p0253c1m v4p0017c1s
v4p0532c1s v6p0019c2s v6p0141c2s
v6p0379c2s v6p0523c1s v6p0609c2s
v6p0610c1s
Holt, H.E. v2p0303c1s
Holt, H.J. v6p0620c1s
Holt, J. and Speed, J. ... v3p0416c2s
Holt, J.R. v4p0357c2m
Holt, J.S. v1p0014c1s
v1p1236c1s v1p1351c1s
Holt, L.E. v4p0020c2s
v6p0546c1s
Holt, R.B. v4p0566c1s
v4p0586c1s v5p0363c1s
Holt, Rosa B. v4p0607c1s
Holt, Rosa R. v4p0440c2s
Holt, W. v6p0070c2m
Holterhoff, E., jr. v1p0137c1s
Holton, I.F. v1p0792c2s
v1p0900c2s
Holton, S.H.D. v6p0543c1s
Holtz, F.L. v5p0400c2s
Holtzapfel, J.J. v4p0502c1s
Holtzapffel, C. v1p0503c1s
v1p0799c1s
Holtzclaw, W.H. v6p0448c2s
Holtzendorff, F.von v1p0516c2s
v1p0881c1s v1p1060c2m
Holtzmann, H. v4p0047c2s
Holtzmeyer, G. v3p0202c2s
Holtzoper, E.C. v6p0154c1m
v6p0174c1s v6p0179c1s v6p0247c1s
v6p0278c1s v6p0285c2s v6p0298c2m
v6p0300c1s v6p0676c2s v6p0688c2s
v6p0700c2s
Holub, E. v2p0004c2s
Holway, D.N. v4p0286c2s
Holyoake, E.A. v4p0627c1s
v4p0629c1s
Holyoake, G.J. v1p0029c2s
v1p0299c1s v1p0299c2s v1p0640c1s
v1p1028c2m v1p1215c2s v1p1216c1s
v1p1245c1s v2p0101c2s v2p0145c2s
v2p0451c2s v3p0024c1s v3p0099c1m
v4p0141c1s v4p0382c1s v4p0479c1s
v4p0513c1m v4p0575c1s v5p0018c1s
v5p0177c1s v6p0148c1s v6p0466c1s
v6p0705c1s
Holyoake, G.J. and Millerand, M.
v3p0099c1s
Holyoake, G.J. et al. v4p0557c2s
Holyoake, M.Q. v4p0320c1s
v4p0356c1s v4p0564c2m v5p0161c1s
v5p0371c1s v5p0428c1m
Holyoake, Maltus Q. v5p0324c1s
Homans, J.S. v1p0647c2s
v1p0936c1s
Homans, L.S. v1p0325c2s
v1p1349c1s
Homans, S. v1p0647c1s
v1p0647c2m v1p1351c1s v2p0091c2s
v3p0217c2s v4p0261c1s v5p0292c2s
Homans, S. et al. v4p0286c2s
Home, A.D. v2p0162c2s
Home, B. v6p0700c2s
Home, C. v1p0163c2s
Home, R. v1p1282c1s
Home, R.D. v6p0544c2s
Homer, A.N. v3p0157c2s
v3p0351c1s
Homer, C.C. and Hepburn, A.P.
v4p0143c2s
Homer, C.W. v1p0329c1s
Homer, E.B. v5p0026c1s
v5p0469c2s v6p0520c2s
Homer, F. v1p0965c2s
Homer, M. v6p0338c1s
Homer, Sarah S. v4p0588c2s
Homersham, W.C. v1p0174c1s
v1p0288c1s
Homes, A. v1p1331c1s
Homes, H. v1p1415c2s
v2p0475c1s
Homes, H.A. v1p0149c1s
v1p0294c2s v1p0743c1m v1p0743c2m
v1p0815c2s v2p0070c2s v2p0255c2m
v2p0313c2s v2p0420c1s
Homfray, F.A. v5p0623c2s
Hompes, M. v4p0221c1s
Honan, M.B. v1p0672c1s
v1p0800c2s
Honda, K. and Shimizu, S.. v5p0557c2s
Hone, N. v4p0601c1s
Hone, P. v1p0282c2s
Honey, S.R. v3p0360c2s
Honeyman, J. v2p0072c1s
v6p0262c1s v6p0673c2m
Honeyman, M.F. v4p0052c1s
Honinghaus, J.V. v1p1121c1s
Honnywill, W.K. v4p0227c2s
v4p0268c1s
Honore, J. v4p0457c2s
Honson, J.M.P. v6p0546c1s
Hontum-Schindler, A. v2p0336c2s
Hood, A. v2p0290c1s
v5p0420c2m v5p0421c1s
Hood, A.N. v5p0180c1s
v6p0394c2s
Hood, A.N. and Bridport, V.
v5p0076c2s
Hood, C. v1p0664c1s
Hood, C.H. v3p0035c2s
Hood, C.N. v4p0267c1s
v4p0437c1s v5p0150c1s
Hood, C.W. v3p0449c1s
Hood, E.K. v6p0674c2s
Hood, E.P. v2p0009c1s
v2p0056c1s v2p0090c2s v2p0117c2s
v2p0196c2s v2p0207c1s v2p0250c2m
v2p0264c2s v2p0372c2s v2p0374c2s
v2p0386c2s v2p0390c1s v2p0406c1s
Hood, F. v5p0496c2s
v5p0526c2s v5p0642c1s
Hood, G. v1p1066c2s
Hood, G.P.J. v5p0195c2s
Hood, J.B. and Heth, H. .. v1p0518c2s
Hood, J.E. v1p0565c1s
v1p1113c2s
Hood, J.V. v5p0422c1s
Hood, J.W. v6p0447c1s
Hood, L. v1p0689c2s
Hood, M.A. v6p0300c1s
Hood, N.G. v5p0571c2s
Hood, T. v1p0002c2s
v1p0027c2s v1p0144c1s v1p0189c2s
v1p0202c2s v1p0208c2s v1p0229c1s
v1p0289c1s v1p0335c2s v1p0340c2s
v1p0350c1s v1p0439c1s v1p0441c2s
v1p0491c1s v1p0609c1s v1p0675c2s
v1p0878c2m v1p0885c2s v1p0889c1s
v1p0892c1s v1p0913c2s v1p0942c2s
v1p0951c2s v1p0955c1s v1p0964c1s
v1p1007c2s v1p1017c2s v1p1024c1s
v1p1049c1s v1p1102c1s v1p1105c2s
v1p1145c1s v1p1145c2s v1p1151c1s
v1p1159c2s v1p1185c2s v1p1188c2s
v1p1219c2s v1p1239c2s v1p1240c1s
v1p1241c2s v1p1339c2s v1p1368c1s
v1p1433c1s
Hood, T.E. v1p1415c1s
Hood, Tom v1p0330c1s
Hook, A. v6p0312c1s
v6p0355c1s v6p0360c2s v6p0482c2s
v6p0538c2s v6p0541c2s v6p0634c1m
v6p0665c1s
Hook, B. v2p0047c1s
v2p0153c1s v2p0393c1s
Hook, T. v1p0277c1s
v1p0521c2s v1p0563c2s v1p0765c1s
v1p1041c1s v1p1136c2s
Hook, T.E. v1p0036c1s
v1p0074c1s v1p0259c2s v1p0446c1s
v1p0885c2s v1p1016c1s v1p1044c2s
Hooke, R. v3p0333c2s
Hocker, B.R. v6p0142c2s
Hooker, C.E. v2p0238c1s
Hooker, E. v1p0848c1s
v1p0884c2s v4p0263c1s
Hooker, E.G. v5p0370c2s
Hooker, E.T. v2p0152c2s
Hooker, E.W. v1p0038c1s
v1p0076c2s v1p0689c1s v1p0847c2s
Hooker, G.E. v5p0475c1s
v5p0556c1s v6p0252c2s
Hooker, H. v1p0002c1s
v1p0868c1s
Hooker, H.B. v1p0648c2s
Hooker, H.E. v4p0385c1s
v5p0389c1s
Hooker, I.B. v1p0351c1s
v1p1424c2s
Hooker, J. v1p1420c1s
Hooker, J.D. v1p0153c1s
v1p0524c1s v1p1014c2s v1p1016c1s
v1p1113c1s v1p1233c1s v1p1364c1s
v1p1364c2s
Hooker, J.D., Sir v1p0926c2s
v5p0153c2s
Hooker, J.E. v3p0149c1s
Hooker, L. v1p0280c1s
Hooker, O.E. v6p0400c2s
Hooker, R.H. v4p0094c2s
v4p0120c2s v5p0363c1s v6p0463c2s
Hooker, S.C. v3p0329c1s
v3p0457c1s v3p0457c2s v4p0199c1s
v5p0621c2s
Hooker, S.C. and Greene, W.H.
v3p0040c1s
v3p0242c2s
v3p0247c1s
Hooker, S.H. v5p0423c2s
Hooker, Susan H. v6p0573c2s
Hooker, W. v1p0354c1s
v1p0643c2s v1p0816c2s v1p0817c1s
v1p0930c2s v1p1063c1s
Hooker, W.E. v6p0418c1s
Hookham, G. v6p0573c2m
Hoole, C. v1p0262c2s
v1p0353c2s v1p0727c1s v1p1158c1s
Hoole, E. v1p0630c1s
v1p1143c2s v1p1318c1s v3p0125c1s
Hoole, E. et al. v2p0264c1s
Hooper, A. v1p1426c1s
v5p0396c1s
Hooper, C.E. v5p0158c1s
Hooper, C.L. v2p0368c1s
Hooper, D. v3p0422c1s
Hooper, E.W. and Brimmer, M.
v4p0204c2s
Hooper, F.W. v4p0074c2s
Hooper, G. v1p0316c2s
v3p0401c1s v3p0414c1s
Hooper, G.F. v2p0238c2s
v3p0326c2s v3p0375c1s
Hooper, G.K. v5p0550c2s
Hooper, G.N. v3p0069c1m
v3p0412c1s
Hooper, H. v6p0534c2s
Hooper, H.O. v4p0084c1s
Hooper, I. v4p0157c2s
v4p0393c2s
Hooper, I.H. v1p0740c2s
Hooper, J. v2p0343c2s
v2p0435c1s v4p0016c2s v4p0068c1s
v4p0246c1s v4p0256c2s
Hooper, J.R. v2p0095c2s
v2p0404c2s v2p0417c2s
Hooper, James v5p0531c2s
v5p0562c1s
Hooper, L.H. v1p0034c2s
v1p0100c2s v1p0143c1s v1p0171c2s
v1p0181c1s v1p0361c1s v1p0366c2s
v1p0371c2s v1p0429c1s v1p0489c2s
v1p0526c2s v1p0611c2m v1p0643c1s
v1p0758c1s v1p0818c1s v1p0848c2s
v1p0872c2s v1p0886c1s v1p0886c2s
v1p0888c2s v1p0890c1s v1p0913c2s
v1p0944c1s v1p0949c1s v1p0959c2s
v1p0967c2s v1p0968c1m v1p0969c1m

v1p0969c2m v1p0970c1m v1p0970c2m v1p0971c1m v1p0971c2m v1p1003c1s v1p1106c2s v1p1113c2s v1p1141c1s v1p1179c2s v1p1213c2s v1p1242c2s v1p1258c1s v1p1280c2s v1p1282c2s v1p1336c1s v1p1339c1s v2p0385c1s v4p0031c1s v4p0425c1s
Hooper, N.S. v5p0613c2s
Hooper, R. v2p0017c1s v4p0228c1s
Hooper, S. v1p0325c1s v1p1232c1s
Hooper, W. v1p1245c2s v5p0237c2s
Hooper, W.DeM. v2p0204c2s
Hooper, W.P. v4p0490c2s
Hooper, W.R. v1p0139c2s v1p0185c1s v1p0453c1s v1p0905c1m v1p1038c2s v1p1062c2s v1p1343c1s v1p1354c2s v1p1388c2s v1p1389c1s v1p1428c2s
Hooper, W.S. v1p0588c1s
Hooppell, R.E. v3p0271c2s
Hoops, J. v4p0312c1s
Hoorveg, J.L. v1p0017c1s
Hoose, J.H. v2p0221c1s v2p0432c1s v6p0308c2s
Hooton, C. v1p1297c2s v1p1375c2s
Hooton, H. v4p0524c1s
Hooton, M. v5p0200c1s
Hoover, H.C. v6p0419c1s
Hope, A. v2p0039c2s v3p0230c2s v3p0294c2s v3p0370c1s v3p0425c2s v4p0033c1s v4p0072c2s v4p0110c2s v4p0143c1s v4p0150c2s v4p0178c2s v4p0192c2s v4p0207c1s v4p0274c2s v4p0317c1s v4p0327c2s v4p0344c1s v4p0352c1s v4p0407c2s v4p0439c1s v4p0441c1s v4p0444c2s v4p0461c2s v4p0512c2m v4p0544c1s v4p0575c2s v4p0619c1s v5p0131c2s v5p0591c1s v6p0543c2s
Hope, A.J.B.B. v1p1433c1s
Hope, Altruist v5p0188c1s
Hope, Anthony v5p0449c1s v5p0500c1s
Hope, C. v1p0037c1s v5p0013c1s v5p0522c1s v5p0524c1s
Hope, E. v5p0316c1s v5p0377c1s v5p0446c2s
Hope, E.R. v2p0197c2s
Hope, E.S. v6p0150c2s
Hope, F. v5p0397c2s v6p0067c1s v6p0628c1s
Hope, J.B. v1p0218c2s
Hope, J.C. v1p0504c2s v1p0812c1s
Hope, Lady v1p0271c2s v1p0934c2s
Hope, M. v1p0896c2s
Hope, M.B. v1p0105c2s v1p0112c2s v1p0179c1s v1p0242c2s v1p0416c2s v1p0507c1s v1p0593c1s v1p0791c1s v1p0852c1s v1p1046c2s v1p1073c1s v1p1073c2s v5p0305c1s
Hope, M.B. and Hodge, C. . v1p0454c2s
Hope, N. v2p0324c1s
Hope, R.C. v2p0268c1s v2p0387c2s v3p0084c2s v3p0177c1m v3p0376c2s v3p0459c2s v4p0113c2s v4p0616c2m v5p0296c1s
Hope, S. v2p0060c2s v2p0213c2s v2p0298c1s
Hope, T.C., Sir v3p0212c2s v3p0352c1s
Hope, W. v3p0386c2s v6p0445c1s
Hope, W., Mrs. v4p0567c2s
Hope, W.H.S. v3p0069c2s v3p0237c1s v3p0292c1s
Hope, W.H.St.J. v3p0262c2s v3p0392c2m v4p0523c2m v5p0262c2s
Hope, W.H.St.John v5p0235c2s v5p0319c1s v6p0184c2s v6p0383c2s v6p0579c2s v6p0594c1s
Hope-Robertson, C. v1p0181c1s
Hopgood, J. v1p0250c1s
Hopkins, A. v1p1412c1s v5p0206c1s v5p0460c2s v6p0052c1s
Hopkins, A.F. v1p1241c1s v1p1348c1s
Hopkins, A.G. v1p0727c2s v2p0088c1s v2p0377c1s v2p0440c2s v3p0007c1s v3p0233c2s v3p0294c1s v3p0467c2s v4p0589c2s v5p0260c1s v5p0322c1s v5p0349c2s v5p0434c2s v5p0519c2s v5p0628c1s
Hopkins, A.H. v4p0330c2s v6p0373c2s v6p0437c1s
Hopkins, A.H. et al. v6p0017c1s
Hopkins, A.J. v2p0341c1s v5p0460c2s v5p0567c1s
Hopkins, A.T. v5p0092c1s
Hopkins, B.F. v1p1170c2s
Hopkins, B.J. v2p0095c1s v2p0386c2s
Hopkins, C.G. v6p0602c2s
Hopkins, C.T. v1p0356c2s v1p0497c1s v1p0937c2s v1p0947c1s v1p1238c1s v2p0148c2s v2p0452c1s v4p0084c1s v4p0129c1s v4p0356c1s v6p0093c2s v6p0567c2s v6p0591c2s
Hopkins, Canon v2p0004c1s v2p0292c1s v3p0147c2s
Hopkins, D. v2p0407c2s
Hopkins, E. v1p0278c1s v1p0643c1s v1p0645c2s v1p0755c2s v1p1015c1s v1p1069c1s v2p0043c2s v2p0191c1s v2p0367c1s v2p0405c1s v2p0409c1s v3p0462c2s
Hopkins, E. and Fawcett, M.G. v2p0178c2s
Hopkins, E.A. v1p0725c2m v1p0966c2m v1p0967c1m
Hopkins, E.D. v4p0545c1s
Hopkins, E.J. and Rimbault, E.F. v1p0947c2s
Hopkins, E.M. v3p0344c1s
Hopkins, E.W. v2p0372c2s v4p0158c1s v4p0218c1s v4p0244c1s v4p0261c1s v4p0601c1s v5p0055c1s v5p0069c1m v5p0156c1s v5p0233c2s v5p0237c1s v5p0285c1s v5p0285c2m v5p0324c1s v5p0453c1s v5p0508c1m v6p0017c2m v6p0038c2s v6p0569c2s v6p0645c2m
Hopkins, Ellice v1p0044c1s
Hopkins, F.M. v4p0067c2s
Hopkins, Florence M. v6p0375c1s
Hopkins, G. v5p0236c2s
Hopkins, G. et al. v2p0426c2s
Hopkins, G.F. v1p1309c1s
Hopkins, G.G. v5p0456c2s
Hopkins, G.S. v4p0500c1s
Hopkins, H. v6p0498c1s
Hopkins, I.E. v1p0627c2s
Hopkins, I.T. v1p0210c1s v1p0213c1s v1p0519c2s v1p0905c2s v1p0942c2s
Hopkins, J. v3p0328c2s v3p0383c2s
Hopkins, J.A. v5p0332c2s
Hopkins, J.B. v1p0355c1s v1p0562c1s v1p0606c1s v1p0741c2s v1p0790c2s v1p0851c1s v1p0914c2s v1p0952c1s v1p1344c1s v2p0024c2s v2p0055c2s v2p0060c2s v2p0071c1s v2p0105c1s v2p0107c1s v2p0113c1s v2p0155c2s v2p0170c2s v2p0208c2s v2p0221c2s v2p0225c2s v2p0259c1s v2p0259c2s v2p0330c1s v2p0342c1s v2p0349c1s v2p0356c1s v2p0361c1s v2p0366c1s v2p0408c1s v2p0423c1s v2p0471c2s v3p0070c1s v3p0135c2s v3p0245c1s v3p0343c2s v4p0081c2s
Hopkins, J.C. v4p0001c2m v4p0006c1s v4p0071c1s v4p0085c1s v4p0085c2s v4p0086c2m v4p0095c1s v4p0105c2s v4p0112c2s v4p0227c1s v4p0239c2s v4p0266c1s v4p0297c2s v4p0483c1s v4p0491c1s v4p0500c1s v4p0514c2s v4p0530c1s v4p0591c2s v5p0006c1s v5p0007c2s v5p0090c1s v5p0090c2s v5p0180c1s v5p0428c2s v5p0586c2s v5p0611c1s
Hopkins, J.D. v1p0323c2s
Hopkins, J.E. v1p0746c1s
Hopkins, J.F. v4p0456c1s
Hopkins, J.G. v4p0085c2s
Hopkins, J.H. v1p0124c1s v1p0329c1s v1p0422c1m v1p0731c2s v1p1109c1s v1p1266c1s v2p0047c2s v2p0067c1s v2p0084c1s v2p0084c2s v2p0357c1m v2p0360c1s v3p0049c2s v3p0084c2s v3p0205c2s v3p0254c1s v3p0284c2s v3p0319c1s v3p0319c2s v3p0327c1s v3p0328c1s v3p0356c2s v3p0461c1s
Hopkins, J.H. et al. v3p0084c1s v3p0205c2s
Hopkins, J.H., jr. v1p0275c2s v1p0336c1s v1p0485c2s v1p1134c2s
Hopkins, J.L. v3p0316c2s
Hopkins, J.S. v4p0333c2s v4p0525c2s v5p0413c1s
Hopkins, Julia A. v6p0394c1s
Hopkins, L.C. v6p0301c1s
Hopkins, L.P. v1p0991c1s v2p0358c1s v2p0358c2s v4p0507c1s
Hopkins, Louise M. v5p0585c1s
Hopkins, M. v1p0110c1s v1p0241c1s v1p0290c1s v1p0305c1s v1p0440c1s v1p0528c1s v1p0536c2s v1p0575c1s v1p0711c1s v1p0868c2s v1p0889c2s v1p0948c2s v1p1055c1s v1p1336c2s v2p0021c1s v2p0250c2s v2p0251c1s v2p0322c2s v2p0336c2s
Hopkins, Miss v1p0851c1s v1p0873c2s
Hopkins, N.M. v6p0620c1s
Hopkins, S. v1p0122c2s v1p0123c1s v1p0305c1s v1p0343c2s
Hopkins, S.F. v1p0084c1s v1p0596c2s v1p0733c1s v1p0763c2s v1p0785c2s v1p1409c1s
Hopkins, S.M. v1p0085c2s v1p0361c1s v1p0421c2s v1p0903c1s v2p0172c2s v2p0352c2s
Hopkins, T. v1p0575c1s v1p0884c2s v1p1017c2s v1p1052c2s v1p1300c2s v1p1361c2s v2p0209c2s v2p0291c2s v2p0365c2s v2p0449c2s v2p0479c1s v3p0015c1s v3p0069c1s v3p0207c2s v3p0210c2s v3p0333c1s v3p0367c1s v3p0435c2s v3p0436c1s v4p0058c1s v4p0092c1s v4p0124c1s v4p0399c2s v4p0418c2s v4p0453c2s v4p0459c2s v4p0564c2s v4p0605c1s v4p0634c1s v5p0033c2s v5p0129c2s v5p0210c2s v5p0218c1s v5p0227c1s v5p0365c2s v5p0379c1s v5p0466c2s v5p0483c1s v5p0508c2s v5p0566c1s v5p0567c2s v6p0075c2s v6p0155c2s v6p0681c2s
Hopkins, T.C. v4p0038c1s v4p0042c1s v5p0204c2s v5p0314c1s v5p0558c2s
Hopkins, T.M. v4p0007c2s v5p0093c2s v5p0100c2s v5p0117c1s v5p0122c1s v5p0138c1s v5p0205c2s v5p0325c1s
Hopkins, T.W. v1p0692c2s
Hopkins, Tighe v4p0439c2s v5p0509c2s
Hopkins, U.N. v6p0155c1s
Hopkins, W. v1p0376c1s v1p0746c1s v5p0016c2m v5p0104c2s v5p0153c1s v5p0189c1s v5p0284c2s v5p0285c1s v5p0286c2s v5p0390c2s v5p0417c2s v5p0443c1s v5p0453c1s v5p0469c2s v5p0577c2s v5p0612c1s v5p0624c1s v6p0565c1s
Hopkins, W.H. v5p0641c1s
Hopkins, W.J. v4p0176c1s v5p0185c1s v6p0123c2s v6p0129c2s v6p0165c2s v6p0218c2s v6p0465c2s
Hopkins, W.R. v1p1170c2s v2p0310c2s v4p0119c1s v6p0688c2s
Hopkins, W.W. v3p0229c2s
Hopkinson, A. v5p0272c2s
Hopkinson, A. and Bowley, A.L. v5p0615c2s
Hopkinson, A.W. v6p0098c2s
Hopkinson, C.A. v1p0436c2s v1p0878c2s v1p1336c1s v1p1339c1s
Hopkinson, C.A., Mrs. ... v1p1071c2s
Hopkinson, E. and Hopkinson, J. v2p0126c2s
Hopkinson, E. and Siemens, A. v3p0134c1s
Hopkinson, F. v1p0102c2s
Hopkinson, H.C.B. v5p0089c1s v5p0540c1s
Hopkinson, H.M. v2p0045c1s
Hopkinson, J. v1p0399c1s v1p1099c2s v1p1257c1s v1p1359c2s v2p0136c2s v3p0207c1s v3p0264c1s v3p0357c1s v4p0180c2s v4p0360c2s
Hopkinson, J. and Hopkinson, E. v2p0126c2s
Hopkinson, J.H. and Baker-Penoyre, J. v6p0409c2s
Hopkinson, W.F. v3p0035c1s
Hopley, C.C. v1p0436c1s v2p0261c2s v2p0337c1s v2p0406c2s
Hopley, C.E. v1p1183c1s
Hopley, H. v2p0017c2s v2p0348c2s v2p0377c2s v2p0410c1s v2p0426c1s v2p0461c2s
Hopp, J. v6p0084c1s v6p0181c1s
Hoppell, R.E. v4p0487c2s
Hopper, J. v6p0078c1s v6p0094c1s v6p0140c2s v6p0144c1s v6p0217c2s v6p0347c1s v6p0347c2s v6p0394c1s v6p0482c2s v6p0483c1s v6p0501c1s v6p0603c2s
Hopper, James v5p0215c2s v6p0105c2s v6p0567c2s v6p0622c1s
Hopper, N. v4p0413c2s v4p0418c1s v4p0475c2s v5p0012c2s v5p0115c2m v5p0153c1s v5p0325c2s v5p0452c1s
Hopper, Nora v5p0474c2s v5p0590c2s
Hopper, W.R. v1p1261c2s
Hoppin, A. v4p0011c1s
Hoppin, F.L.V. v3p0018c1s v4p0023c2s
Hoppin, G.M. v1p0006c2s
Hoppin, J.C. v4p0463c2s v5p0027c2s
Hoppin, J.M. v1p0062c2s v1p0063c2s v1p0107c2s v1p0180c1s v1p0207c1s v1p0248c2s v1p0252c2s v1p0255c2s v1p0274c2s v1p0418c1s v1p0458c2s v1p0496c1s v1p0513c2s v1p0536c2s v1p0552c1s v1p0567c2s v1p0572c2s v1p0684c1s v1p0697c1s v1p0729c1s v1p0812c2s v1p0857c2s v1p0955c1s v1p1043c1m v1p1043c2s v1p1044c1s v1p1084c2s v1p1085c1s v1p1157c1s v1p1171c1s v1p1306c1s v1p1357c1s v1p1433c1s v2p0022c2s v2p0130c2s v3p0021c2m v3p0022c1s v3p0242c1s v3p0292c1s
Hoppin, Joseph C. v6p0477c2s
Hoppin, W.J. v1p0062c2s v1p1036c1s

Hopps, J.P. v1p0072c1s
v1p0392c1s v1p0529c2s v1p0684c2s
v1p0695c1s v2p0043c2s v2p0451c2s
v3p0305c2s v5p0417c1s
Hoppus, M.M.A. v2p0051c2s
Hopson, G.B. v2p0290c2s
Hopwood, C.H. et al. v4p0139c2s
Hopwood, J. v5p0092c2s
v5p0161c2s
Horace v3p0087c2s
Horack, F.A. v6p0621c2s
Horan, F.S. v4p0035c2s
Hordeen, L.H. v6p0203c1s
Horden, F.S. v4p0138c2s
Horder, P.M. v4p0025c1s
Horder, W.G. v2p0235c1s
v2p0342c1s v3p0035c1s v3p0173c1s
v3p0206c1m v3p0313c1s v3p0318c1s
v3p0354c2s v3p0395c1s v3p0468c1s
v4p0490c1s v5p0022c2s v6p0305c1s
Horder, W.Garrett v6p0391c2s
Hordern, L.H. v6p0004c1s
v6p0041c2s v6p0138c2s v6p0268c2s
v6p0309c2s v6p0310c1m
Hordern, L.R. v6p0138c2s
Hordern, P. v1p0173c2s
v1p0178c1s v1p0388c1s v3p0031c2s
v3p0059c1s v3p0060c2s v3p0217c1s
v3p0379c2s v3p0391c2s v3p0441c1s
v4p0079c2m v4p0278c2s v4p0281c1s
Hordern, R.N. v6p0097c1s
Hore, E.C. v2p0430c2s
v4p0005c2s
Hore, H.F. v1p1146c2s
Hore, S.C. v3p0447c1s
Horgan, Mary H.B. v6p0563c1s
Horing, C. v6p0678c1s
Hormell, W.G. v5p0430c1s
Horn, C.H. v5p0191c1s
Horn, E.F. v3p0261c1s
Horn, E.F.B. v4p0162c2s
Horn, E.T. v1p0777c2s
v2p0269c1s v2p0434c2s v3p0094c2s
v5p0641c2s
Horn, F. v5p0253c1s
Horn, G.H. v2p0252c2s
Horn, H. v1p0997c2s
Horn, J. v3p0258c2s
Horn, R.T. v2p0027c1s
v2p0074c2s v2p0293c1s v2p0319c1s
v2p0390c1s
Horn, R.T.van v2p0257c2s
v2p0258c1s
Horn, T.N. v5p0571c2s
Horn, W.A. v5p0039c1s
Horn, W.O.Von v1p0934c1s
Hornaday, J.P. v6p0631c1s
Hornaday, W.T. v1p0138c2s
v2p0138c2s v3p0010c2s v3p0014c1s
v3p0036c2s v3p0059c1s v3p0067c1s
v3p0103c1s v3p0449c1s v5p0021c1s
v5p0063c1s v5p0646c1s v6p0022c1s
v6p0284c2s v6p0658c2s v6p0685c2s
Hornaday, W.T. and Phillips, J.M.
v6p0433c1s
Hornbeck, S.K. v6p0542c2s
Hornblow, A. v4p0104c1s
v4p0161c1m v4p0305c2s v4p0408c2s
v4p0415c1s v4p0446c2s v4p0458c1s
v4p0486c1s v4p0544c1s v4p0637c1s
v5p0152c1s v5p0240c2s v5p0582c1s
v6p0527c1s
Hornblower, L. v1p0455c2s
Hornblower, W.B. v1p0447c1s
v4p0323c1s v6p0102c2s
Hornbrook, A.R. v4p0409c1s
Hornbrooke, F.B. v1p0248c1s
v1p0675c1s v2p0297c2s v2p0304c2s
v2p0311c2s v2p0351c2s v2p0368c1s
v2p0369c2s v4p0076c2m v4p0163c2s
v4p0448c1s
Hornbrooke, F.H. v3p0057c2s
Hornby, G.P. v4p0604c1m
Hornby, G.P., Sir v3p0182c1s
v3p0182c2s v4p0604c1s
Hornby, G.P., Sir and Fitzgerald, P.
v3p0182c2s
Horne, Alice M. v5p0606c1s
Horne, C.S. v5p0145c1s
v6p0191c2s v6p0319c1s
Horne, C.Van v5p0406c2s
Horne, D.Van v1p0910c1s
v1p1203c2s v3p0029c2s
Horne, H.H. v6p0698c2m
Horne, H.P. v3p0072c1s
v4p0340c1s v4p0368c2s v4p0374c1s
v4p0383c2s v5p0156c1s v5p0354c2s
v5p0427c2s v5p0597c1s v5p0610c1s
v5p0615c1s v6p0077c2s
Horne, Herbert P. v5p0399c1s
Horne, J. v5p0229c1s
Horne, J. and Peach, B.N.. v2p0174c1s
Horne, P. v6p0207c1s
Horne, R. v1p0917c1s
Horne, R.A. v2p0182c2s
Horne, R.H. v1p0068c2s
v1p0078c1s v1p0079c2s v1p0081c1s
v1p0170c1m v1p0178c1s v1p0223c1m
v1p0257c2s v1p0301c2s v1p0328c2s
v1p0347c2s v1p0363c1s v1p0430c1s
v1p0437c2s v1p0439c1m v1p0446c2s
v1p0469c1s v1p0653c1s v1p0656c2s
v1p0680c1s v1p0708c1s v1p0761c2s
v1p0801c2s v1p0856c1s v1p0898c2s
v1p0906c2s v1p0918c2s v1p0994c2s
v1p1189c2s v1p1221c1s v1p1222c1s
v1p1233c1s v1p1269c2s v1p1320c2s
v2p0088c2s v2p0250c1s v2p0409c1s
v3p0030c1s
Horne, R.H. and Browning, E.B.
v1p1061c2s
Hornell, J. v4p0209c2s
v4p0607c1s
Hornell, T. v4p0061c1s
Horner, B. v4p0417c1s
Horner, C. v6p0079c1s
Horner, F. v1p0091c1s
v1p0302c1s v1p0384c1s v1p0406c1s
v1p0771c2s v1p0784c1s v1p1025c2s
v1p1197c1s v1p1232c1s v1p1253c2s
Horner, I. v1p0124c2s
Horner, J. v1p0684c2s
v1p0762c2s v1p0891c1s v1p0935c1s
v1p1081c2s v1p1385c1s v3p0082c1s
v3p0371c1s v4p0256c2s v4p0298c2s
v4p0467c1s v4p0503c2s v4p0515c1s
v4p0576c2s v5p0016c1s v5p0068c2s
v5p0141c2m v5p0215c2s v5p0267c2s
v5p0353c1m v5p0389c1s v5p0431c1m
v5p0641c1m v6p0156c1s v6p0235c1s
v6p0254c1s v6p0272c1s v6p0294c1s
v6p0362c2s v6p0375c2s v6p0392c2m
v6p0393c1m
Horner, J.S. v5p0144c2s
v5p0181c1s v5p0412c1s v5p0540c1s
Horner, J.Stuart v5p0181c1s
Horner, Joseph v6p0156c1s
v6p0274c2s v6p0304c2s v6p0392c2s
v6p0408c1s v6p0502c1s
Horner, L. v1p0267c2s
Horner, L.F. v4p0485c2s
Horney, G.P. v4p0635c1s
Hornibrook, J.L. v4p0009c1s
v4p0155c2s v5p0309c2s v5p0518c1s
v6p0401c1s
Horning, L.E. v4p0051c2s
v5p0091c2s v6p0588c2s
Hornor, W.M. v5p0354c2s
v5p0436c1s
Hornsby, W. v4p0105c2s
Hornsby, W.J. v6p0092c1s
Hornsby, W.L. v5p0110c2s
Hornsey, J.F. v6p0473c1s
Hornung, A. v6p0430c1s
Hornung, E.W. v3p0405c1s
v3p0413c1s v4p0006c2s v4p0080c2s
v4p0233c1s v4p0310c1s v4p0490c1s
v4p0576c1s v4p0590c1s v5p0074c1s
v5p0311c2s v5p0326c1s v5p0396c1s
v5p0412c2s v5p0419c2s v5p0521c2m
v5p0581c1s v5p0612c1s v5p0642c1s
v6p0125c1s v6p0586c1s
Hornyold, V. v1p0803c2s
v1p0808c2s
Horowitz, J. v4p0269c2s
Horr, G.E., jr. v3p0080c2s
Horr, N.T. v3p0068c1s
Horry, P.T. v1p0038c2s
v1p0893c1s
Horsbrugh, E.B. v1p0309c2s
Horseley, J.W. v2p0124c2s
Horsfall, T.C. v2p0022c2s
v2p0297c2s v5p0177c2s v6p0190c2s
Horsfall, T.C. et al. v4p0557c2s
Horsfall, T.G. v6p0300c1s
Horsfell, T.C. v6p0284c2s
Horsfield, H.K. v3p0165c1s
v4p0379c1s v4p0419c1s
Horsfield, M.M. v3p0362c1s
Horsfield, R.W. v1p0830c1s
Horsfield, T. v1p0093c1s
Horsford, C. v5p0525c1s
v5p0612c2s
Horsford, Cornelia v5p0172c1s
Horsford, E.H. v4p0416c2s
Horsford, E.N. v1p0301c2s
v1p0398c2s v1p0462c1s v1p0825c2s
v2p0220c1s
Horsford, F.H. v4p0332c1m
Horsley, G.C. v6p0167c2m
Horsley, J.H. v4p0052c2s
Horsley, J.W. v1p1204c2s
v1p1266c1s v1p1305c1s v2p0355c1m
v3p0074c1s v3p0077c1s v4p0451c2s
Horsley, Maud v6p0073c1s
Horsley, R. v4p0149c1s
v4p0222c1s v4p0257c2s v5p0159c1s
Horsley, V. v2p0054c2s
v2p0299c2s v2p0474c1m v3p0290c2s
v4p0461c2s
Horsley, V. and Beevor, C.E.
v3p0285c2s
Horsley, V. and Ruffer, M.A.
v4p0606c2s
Horsley, Victor v6p0107c1s
Horst, A.L. v6p0528c2s
Hort, F.J.A. v1p0864c1s
Hort, F.J.A. and Sanday, W.
v3p0385c1s
Hort, W.P. v1p1226c1s
v1p1436c2s
Horteloup, M. v6p0086c2s
Horter, J.C. v6p0554c1s
Horton, A. v3p0263c2s
Horton, A.H. v3p0054c1s
Horton, D. v4p0279c1s
v4p0525c2s
Horton, E.A. v1p0241c2s
v1p0440c1s v1p1302c1s v1p1340c2s
v2p0074c2s v2p0426c1s
Horton, G. v4p0413c2m
v5p0036c2s v5p0268c1s
Horton, H.G. v2p0096c2s
v2p0128c2s
Horton, R.F. v3p0096c2s
v4p0031c1s v4p0103c1s v4p0149c1s
v4p0261c2s v4p0303c2s v4p0336c2s
v4p0506c1s v4p0603c1s v4p0630c2s
v5p0151c2s v5p0220c1s v5p0271c2s
v5p0435c1s v5p0492c2s v5p0500c1s
v5p0559c1s v6p0218c1s v6p0513c1s
Horton, R.F., Rev. v3p0355c1s
Horton, S.B. v2p0081c2s
Horton, S.D. v1p1099c1s
v1p1199c1s v2p0046c1s v2p0403c1s
Horton, S.D. et al. v2p0034c1s
Horton, Thaddeus, Mrs. ... v6p0451c2s
Horton-Smith, L. v4p0253c1s
v4p0312c1s v4p0576c1s v5p0257c2s
Horton-Smith, R.J. v4p0504c1s
Horwell, H.W. v5p0284c1s
Horwill, H.W. v3p0306c1s
v4p0053c1s v5p0126c2s v5p0177c2s
v5p0311c1s v5p0484c2s v5p0588c2s
v6p0060c2s v6p0078c1s v6p0190c2s
v6p0204c2s v6p0283c2s v6p0302c1s
v6p0369c1s v6p0384c1s v6p0389c1s
v6p0429c1s v6p0463c2s v6p0473c1m
v6p0529c2s v6p0647c1s v6p0678c1s
Horwitz, S.G. v4p0563c1s
v4p0580c2s
Horwood, A.M. v5p0085c2s
v5p0283c1s v5p0404c1s
Hose, C. v4p0045c2s
v4p0068c1m v5p0071c2s
Hosea, L.M. v2p0332c2s
Hosegood, T.P. v2p0163c2s
Hosford, A.P. v6p0458c2s
Hosford, B. v1p0806c1s
Hosford, B.F. v1p0117c1s
v1p0131c2s v1p0507c2s v1p1302c1s
Hoshi, T. v5p0303c1s
Hosic, A. v6p0004c2s
Hosie, A. v1p1269c1s
Hosken, E. v1p0296c1s
v1p0353c2s
Hosken, W. v5p0007c1s
v5p0588c2s
Hosken, W. and Hobson, J.A.
v5p0588c2s
Hoskier, F.H. v5p0032c2s
Hoskin, M. v5p0112c2s
Hosking, Prof. v1p0327c1s
Hosking, W. v1p0957c1s
v1p1366c1m
Hoskins, F.D. v1p0433c2s
v1p0441c2s v1p0981c2s v2p0120c2s
Hoskins, F.E. v6p0289c2s
Hoskins, J. v1p1422c1s
v1p1426c1s
Hoskins, J.R. v2p0366c1s
v2p0416c1s
Hoskins, J.T. v1p1237c2s
v1p1425c2s
Hoskins, L.M. v1p0024c2s
v2p0094c2s v4p0486c2s
Hoskins, T.H. v4p0099c1s
v4p0178c2s v4p0217c1m v4p0233c2s
v4p0281c1s v4p0354c2s v4p0416c1s
v4p0432c2s v4p0463c2s v4p0535c2s
v4p0631c2s
Hoskyns, C.W. v1p0721c1s
v3p0006c2s
Hoskyns-Abrahall, J. v2p0457c1s
Hosmer, G.H. v2p0235c1s
Hosmer, G.W. v1p0437c2s
v1p0452c2s v1p0697c2s v1p0709c1s
v1p0824c2s v1p0977c2s v1p1058c2s
v1p1064c2s
Hosmer, G.W. and Ellis, R.
v1p1174c1s
Hosmer, J.K. v1p0069c1s
v1p0276c2s v1p0363c2m v1p0446c1s
v1p0516c2s v1p0573c2s v1p0583c1s
v1p0776c2s v1p0869c1s v1p1152c1s
v1p1263c1s v1p1318c1s v2p0002c2s
v3p0005c2s v3p0097c2s v3p0108c1s
v3p0191c1s v3p0248c2s v3p0447c1s
v5p0015c2s v5p0334c1s v5p0380c2s
v5p0415c1s v6p0369c2m v6p0373c1s
v6p0422c1s
Hosmer, J.K. and Allen, W.F.
v1p0924c2s v3p0047c1s
Hosmer, K. v5p0639c1s
Hosmer, M. v1p0359c2s
v1p0442c2s v1p0491c2s v1p0519c1s
v1p0807c1s v1p1052c1s v1p1313c1s
v1p1327c1s v1p1369c2s v2p0060c2s
Hosmer, S.D. v1p0638c1s
v1p0892c2s

Hosmer, W. v1p0310c1s
Hosmer, W.C. v1p0752c1s
v1p0989c2s
Hosmer, W.H.C. v1p0030c2s
Hoss, E.E. v4p0118c1s
Hoste, C.D. v5p0343c1s
Hoste, J.W. v4p0170c2s
Hoste, M.R. v5p0125c2s
v5p0304c1s
Hostetter, A.B. v5p0335c2s
Hotchkin, W.R. et al. v6p0170c2s
Hotchkiss, F. v5p0094c2s
Hotchkiss, J. v1p1374c1s
v3p0450c2s v3p0460c2s
Hotchkiss, J.E. v5p0259c2s
Hotchkiss, J.S. v5p0491c1s
Hotchkiss, S.M. v3p0434c1s
v4p0390c2s
Hotchkiss, T.W., jr. v4p0459c1m
Hotchkiss, V.R. v1p0176c1s
v1p1191c1s
Hotchkiss, W.H. v4p0051c2s
v4p0078c1s v4p0115c1s v4p0249c1s
v5p0046c2s v5p0047c1s v5p0082c1s
v5p0465c2s
Hotchkiss, W.L. v6p0059c1s
Hotchkiss, Willard E. v6p0113c2s
Hotowetz, R. v6p0624c1s
Hotz, A. v5p0441c1s
Houdetot, A.D' v1p0771c2s
Hough, C.A. v4p0122c1s
Hough, E. v3p0475c1s
v5p0209c1s v5p0227c2s v5p0271c1s
v5p0453c1s v5p0463c1s v5p0586c1s
v5p0624c2s v5p0625c2m v5p0626c1s
v6p0075c2s v6p0139c2s v6p0159c1s
v6p0227c2s v6p0256c2s v6p0292c1s
v6p0300c2s v6p0351c2s v6p0618c2s
v6p0654c1s v6p0692c2s v6p0701c1s
Hough, Emerson v6p0450c1s
Hough, F.B. v1p0272c1s
v1p1348c2s v2p0162c2m v2p0418c2s
v2p0479c1m
Hough, G.W. v1p0099c2s
v1p0246c1s v1p0498c1s v1p1244c1s
v2p0083c1m v2p0239c2s v2p0319c1m
v4p0110c2s v4p0186c1s v4p0306c2m
v4p0307c1s v5p0312c2s v5p0549c2s
v6p0348c1m
Hough, G.W. and Johnson, H.A.
v3p0112c2s
Hough, H. v4p0597c1s
Hough, J. v1p0714c1s
Hough, J.S. v1p0258c1s
v1p0997c2s v1p1015c1s
Hough, L. v1p0592c2s
v1p0762c2s v1p1237c1s v1p1431c2s
Hough, L.H. v6p0040c1s
Hough, O. v4p0260c2s
v4p0265c2s v5p0144c1s v6p0039c2s
Hough, R.B. v4p0217c1s
Hough, R.H. v6p0688c1s
Hough, T. and Sedgwick, W.T.
v6p0498c2s
Hough, W. v3p0015c1s
v3p0096c1s v3p0323c1s v5p0319c2s
v5p0338c2s v5p0373c2s v5p0579c2s
v6p0023c2s v6p0030c1s v6p0491c1s
v6p0523c1s v6p0593c2s v6p0683c1s
Hough, W.S. v3p0234c2s
v4p0446c2s
Houghton, A. v5p0155c2s
v5p0355c1s v5p0542c1s
Houghton, A.B. v2p0058c2s
v2p0321c2s v3p0224c2s v3p0398c2s
Houghton, A.E. v5p0542c2s
v6p0184c2s
Houghton, B. v1p0634c1s
Houghton, E.L. v3p0042c2s
v3p0081c1s v3p0229c2m
Houghton, F. v3p0231c1s
v3p0452c1s v5p0051c2s
Houghton, G. v1p1150c1s
v2p0276c2s v2p0466c2s
Houghton, G.F. v1p1307c1s
Houghton, J.F. v1p1119c2s
Houghton, L.S. v1p0461c2s
v1p0462c1s v1p0607c2s v1p0862c2s
v1p0966c2s v2p0092c2s v2p0170c1s
v2p0308c2s v2p0408c2s v3p0073c2s
v3p0149c2s v4p0212c2s v5p0029c2s
v6p0030c2s v6p0046c1s v6p0160c1s
v6p0330c2s
Houghton, L.S., Mrs. v2p0012c2s
Houghton, Lord v1p0067c1s
v1p0607c2m v1p0625c1s v1p0818c1s
v1p1211c2s v1p1276c1m v1p1409c1s
v4p0166c1s v4p0291c1s
Houghton, Louise S. v6p0561c2s
Houghton, P. v4p0164c2m
Houghton, R.C. v2p0416c1s
v3p0031c2s v3p0057c1s v3p0191c2s
v3p0431c2s v4p0543c2s
Houghton, W. v1p0184c1s
v1p0456c1s v1p0456c2s v1p0579c1s
v1p0645c1s v1p0734c1m v1p1029c1s
v1p1029c2s v1p1132c1s v1p1146c1s
v1p1172c2s v1p1254c1s v1p1334c1s
v1p1391c2s v2p0021c1s v2p0041c2s
v2p0105c1s v2p0157c2s v2p0204c1s
v2p0307c1s v2p0310c1s v2p0334c2s
v2p0418c1s
Houghton, W.A. v6p0363c1s
Houk, A.H. v6p0264c1s
Houldsworth, W.H. v4p0059c1s
v4p0280c1s v4p0580c2s
Hourwich, I.A. v3p0230c2s
v4p0008c1s v4p0135c1s v4p0192c2s
v4p0461c1s v4p0495c2s v4p0496c1s
v5p0502c1s v6p0008c1s v6p0224c2s
v6p0343c1s v6p0514c1s v6p0556c2s
v6p0558c1m v6p0558c2m v6p0559c1s
v6p0659c1s
Housden, J.A.J. v3p0034c1s
v4p0454c1s v6p0511c2s
House, E. v1p0196c1s
v1p0452c1s
House, E.H. v1p0202c1s
v1p0341c2s v1p0678c2s v1p0679c1m
v1p0679c2m v1p0732c2s v1p0755c2s
v1p0837c2s v1p0969c1s v1p1197c1s
v1p1408c2s v3p0224c1s v3p0227c1s
v3p0227c2m v3p0354c2m v3p0371c2s
v3p0452c2s v3p0474c2s v5p0071c2s
House, R.T. v6p0154c2s
Housel, L.Van v1p0376c2s
Housley, S.J. v5p0067c2s
Housman, A.E. v3p0003c2s
v4p0537c1s v5p0282c2s v6p0305c2s
Housman, L. v4p0063c2s
v4p0242c2s v4p0265c2s v5p0113c1s
v5p0222c1s v5p0224c2s v5p0300c1s
v5p0349c2s v5p0389c2s v5p0399c1s
v5p0452c1s v5p0555c2s v5p0633c1s
v6p0011c2s v6p0161c1s v6p0168c1s
v6p0279c1s v6p0300c2s v6p0619c1s
Houssay, F. v4p0511c1s
Houssaye, A. v1p0189c2s
v1p1320c2s v2p0421c2s v3p0293c2s
Houssaye, F. v4p0018c2s
Houssaye, H. v1p1125c1s
v4p0002c1s v4p0392c2s v5p0221c1s
Houston and Thomson v1p0426c1s
v1p0835c1s
Houston, A. and Darlington, T.
v4p0112c2s
Houston, A.C. v4p0015c2s
v4p0138c2s v4p0152c1s v4p0194c2s
v4p0592c1s v4p0593c1s
Houston, D. v2p0467c2s
Houston, D.F. v6p0152c2s
Houston, E.J. v1p0348c2s
v1p0579c2s v1p0639c2s v1p0748c1s
v2p0137c2s v2p0356c1s v2p0429c2s
v2p0433c1m v2p0433c2m v3p0002c2s
v3p0095c1s v3p0132c2s v3p0133c1s
v3p0178c2s v3p0353c2m v3p0423c1s
v4p0094c2m v4p0208c2s v4p0349c2m
v5p0185c1m v6p0221c1s v6p0239c1s
v6p0239c2s
Houston, E.J. and Delambre, J.B.J.
v4p0136c1s
Houston, E.J. and Frankl., J.
v3p0423c1s
Houston, E.J. and Kennelly, A.E.
v4p0175c1s v4p0487c1s
Houston, E.J. and Thomson, E.
v1p0374c1s v1p0398c2s v1p0399c2m
v1p0400c1s v1p0401c1s v2p0137c2s
Houston, E.S. v4p0385c1s
v5p0148c1s
Houston, Edwin J. v6p0199c1s
Houston, H.E. and Franz, S.I.
v4p0104c1s
Houston, H.S. v5p0078c2s
v5p0082c1s v5p0530c2s v6p0520c2s
Houston, N.P. v1p0901c2s
Houston, S. v6p0639c2s
Houston, T.J. v5p0233c1s
Houstoun, Mrs. v3p0382c2s
v3p0390c1s v3p0405c2s v3p0467c2s
Houts, L.M. v6p0535c2s
Houtum-Schindler, A. v2p0284c1s
v2p0321c2s v2p0409c1s v4p0348c2s
v4p0436c1m
Houx, J.H. v2p0250c2s
v2p0384c2s
Houzeau, J.C. v3p0024c2s
v3p0404c1s
Hovelacque, A. v2p0249c1s
Hovelaque, E. v4p0091c1s
Hovey, A. v1p0058c1s
v1p0096c1s v1p0096c2m v1p0097c2s
v1p0127c2s v1p0240c2s v1p0254c2s
v1p0255c1s v1p0393c2s v1p0538c1s
v1p0592c2s v1p0688c2s v1p0712c1s
v1p0769c1s v1p0850c1s v1p0948c1s
v1p1053c2s v1p1093c1s v1p1101c1s
v1p1244c2s v1p1262c1s v1p1302c2s
v1p1421c2s v2p0221c1s v2p0222c2s
v3p0465c2m v5p0306c2s v6p0062c1s
Hovey, A. and Cook, J. ... v5p0432c2s
Hovey, A. et al. v2p0437c2s
Hovey, C. v5p0259c1s
v5p0446c2s
Hovey, C.C. v6p0694c2s
Hovey, E.C. v4p0101c2s
v4p0330c1s v4p0330c2s v4p0359c2s
Hovey, E.O. v3p0100c2s
v3p0174c2s v3p0435c1s v4p0099c1s
v5p0002c2s v5p0393c1s v6p0015c1s
v6p0015c2m v6p0105c1s v6p0250c2m
v6p0274c1s v6p0403c2s v6p0451c2s
v6p0486c2m v6p0487c1m v6p0558c2s
v6p0565c1m v6p0593c2s
Hovey, Ester L. v5p0579c2s
Hovey, H.C. v1p0209c1m
v1p0268c1s v1p0565c1s v1p0792c1s
v1p1072c2s v2p0273c2s v2p0481c1s
v3p0147c2s v3p0372c2s v4p0351c2s
Hovey, R. v4p0349c1m
v4p0428c2s v4p0562c2s v5p0008c2s
v5p0349c1s v5p0349c2s v5p0539c1s
v5p0547c2s
Hovey, S. v1p0045c2s
v1p1143c1s
Hovey, W.A. v1p0299c1s
Hovie, C.DeF. v5p0428c2s
Hovykaas, I. v1p0685c2s
How, F.D. v5p0107c1s
v5p0108c1s v5p0152c2s v5p0153c1s
v5p0233c2s v5p0272c1s v5p0273c2s
v5p0310c1s v5p0328c2s v5p0353c2s
v5p0413c2s v5p0479c2s v5p0519c2s
v5p0630c2s v5p0641c2s v5p0644c2s
v6p0139c1s
How, F.Douglas v6p0565c2s
How, H. v1p0939c1s
v1p1189c1s
How, W. et al. v4p0111c2s
How, W.W. v4p0271c2s
How, W.W. et al. v4p0553c1s
Howard, A.A. v3p0449c1s
v6p0564c1s
Howard, A.D. v6p0540c2s
Howard, A.J. v5p0289c1s
Howard, A.W. v4p0503c1s
Howard, A.W.H. v1p0628c1s
Howard, B. v2p0313c1s
v3p0308c2s v5p0548c1s
Howard, B.E. v4p0036c2s
v6p0254c1s v6p0255c1s v6p0347c1s
v6p0348c1s
Howard, B.F. v2p0258c2s
Howard, B.W. v2p0041c1s
v3p0432c2s v5p0356c2s v5p0361c2s
Howard, Blanche W. v5p0412c2s
v5p0575c1s
Howard, Bronson v6p0625c1s
Howard, Burt E. v6p0013c2s
Howard, C. v3p0032c1s
v3p0058c2m v3p0060c2m v3p0063c2s
v3p0069c2s v3p0109c2s v3p0151c1s
v3p0188c2s v3p0195c1s v3p0223c2s
v3p0232c1s v3p0242c1s v3p0275c1s
v3p0328c2s v3p0357c1s v4p0140c2s
v4p0398c1s v6p0025c2s v6p0176c1s
v6p0263c2s v6p0320c2s v6p0646c2s
v6p0700c2s
Howard, C., Lady v1p1016c1s
Howard, C.B. v6p0201c2s
v6p0681c1s
Howard, C.H. v5p0461c2s
Howard, C.H.C. v3p0103c2s
v3p0456c1s
Howard, C.P. v1p0812c1s
v2p0433c2s v4p0545c1s v5p0174c2s
v6p0187c2s
Howard, Chapin v6p0213c2s
Howard, Chas., Mrs. v6p0246c2s
Howard, Clifford v6p0687c1s
Howard, D.S. v1p0098c1m
v1p0329c2s v1p0366c1s v1p0570c2s
v1p0854c1s v1p0854c2s v1p1110c2s
Howard, E. v1p0828c2s
v1p1032c1s v1p1436c2s v2p0310c2s
Howard, E.D. v6p0253c1s
v6p0708c1s
Howard, E.E. v5p0312c1s
Howard, E.F. v5p0544c2s
Howard, E.G. v3p0174c2s
v3p0461c1s
Howard, E.V. v4p0578c1m
Howard, Earl Dean v6p0253c1s
Howard, Emma S. v6p0705c2s
Howard, Ernest v6p0322c1s
Howard, F. v4p0487c2s
Howard, F.E. v5p0530c2s
Howard, F.G. v2p0036c1s
Howard, F.H. v4p0459c1s
v5p0034c2s v5p0087c1s v5p0408c1s
v5p0466c1s
Howard, F.K. v1p1344c1s
Howard, F.W. v4p0314c1s
v4p0430c1s v4p0463c1s v4p0489c1s
v5p0293c1s v5p0536c1s
Howard, G. v1p0218c2s
v4p0592c1s v5p0281c2s v6p0315c2s
Howard, G.E. v3p0014c1s
v3p0445c1s v4p0134c2s v5p0190c1s
v5p0267c1s v6p0206c1s v6p0485c1s
Howard, H. v1p0021c1s
v1p0161c1s v1p0464c2s v1p1132c1s
v3p0150c1s v3p0285c2s v3p0296c1s
v4p0142c2m
Howard, H.M. v4p0132c1s
v4p0561c2s
Howard, H.N. v6p0442c2m
Howard, H.S. v4p0341c1s
Howard, Ince v6p0430c1s

Howard, J. v1p1079c2s
v2p0005c2s v2p0100c1s v2p0248c1s
v4p0527c2m v4p0629c1s
Howard, J., jr. v1p0361c2s
v3p0132c1s
Howard, J.A. v1p0054c1s
v1p1324c1s
Howard, J.D. v1p0542c1s
v1p0594c2s v1p0866c2s v1p1413c1s
Howard, J.E. v3p0054c1s
v3p0270c2s v3p0295c1s v3p0471c1s
v6p0106c2m v6p0143c1s
Howard, J.G. v5p0026c2s
v6p0093c2s
Howard, J.M. v2p0122c1s
v2p0338c1s
Howard, J.Q. v1p0031c1s
v1p0804c2s v1p0965c2s v1p1048c2s
v2p0320c1s v2p0406c1s v3p0150c2s
v3p0310c2s
Howard, J.R. v5p0503c1s
Howard, J.R. et al. v4p0551c2s
Howard, J.T. v5p0001c1s
Howard, J.W. v5p0556c2s
Howard, L. v4p0517c2s
v5p0112c1s
Howard, L.C. v6p0400c2s
v6p0612c1s
Howard, L.O. v5p0206c2s
v5p0210c1s v5p0292c1m v5p0317c2s
v5p0350c2s v5p0357c1s v5p0388c2m
v5p0507c1s v5p0546c1s v5p0596c2s
v6p0152c2m v6p0320c2m v6p0396c1s
v6p0431c2m v6p0585c2s v6p0711c1m
Howard, L.O. and Weeks, H.C.
v6p0431c2s
Howard, M. v5p0416c2s
Howard, M., Lady v5p0163c2s
v5p0361c2s
Howard, M.L.M. v4p0166c2s
Howard, M.M. v1p0073c1s
v1p0837c2s
Howard, M.W. et al. v5p0382c2s
Howard, McH. v1p1107c1s
v1p1142c1s
Howard, Marion v5p0435c2s
Howard, O. v3p0363c1s
Howard, O.O. v1p0073c1s
v1p0222c2s v1p0518c2s v1p0919c2s
v1p1382c2s v2p0167c1s v3p0026c1s
v3p0089c2s v3p0106c2s v3p0203c1s
v3p0214c1m v3p0333c1s v4p0028c1s
v4p0137c2s v4p0579c1s v5p0006c1s
v5p0007c1s v5p0029c2s v5p0100c1s
v5p0148c2m v5p0328c1s v5p0440c1s
v5p0599c1m v6p0119c2s v6p0161c2s
v6p0378c1m
Howard, O.O. and Pleasanton, A.
v2p0074c1s
Howard, O.O. et al. v5p0541c2s
Howard, O.R. v1p0830c2s
v1p1399c1s
Howard, P.F. v1p0153c2s
Howard, R.B. v3p0324c2s
Howard, R.H. v1p0179c1s
v1p0693c1s v1p0840c2s v1p0907c2s
v1p1200c1s v3p0205c1s v3p0460c1s
v4p0113c1s
Howard, R.H. et al. v3p0250c1s
Howard, R.S. v1p1159c2s
Howard, R.W. v1p0785c1s
Howard, S.E. v6p0247c1s
Howard, S.H. v6p0311c2s
Howard, S.O. v6p0431c2s
Howard, T.D. v1p0313c1s
v3p0094c2s v3p0135c2s
Howard, V.E., Mrs. v1p0339c1s
v1p0837c1s
Howard, W. v4p0073c1s
v4p0431c2s v4p0485c2s v4p0523c1s
Howard, W. et al. v4p0314c2s
Howard, W.G. v1p0120c1s
v1p0404c1m v4p0558c2s
Howard, W.L. v3p0007c1s
v3p0357c1s v5p0037c1s v6p0174c2s
v6p0311c2s v6p0430c2s v6p0504c2s
v6p0663c1s
Howard, W.Lee v6p0290c1s
Howard, W.S. v6p0011c2m
v6p0046c1s v6p0080c2s v6p0110c2s
v6p0180c1s v6p0234c2s v6p0278c2s
v6p0319c2s v6p0364c2s v6p0473c2s
v6p0541c2s v6p0589c1s v6p0632c2s
v6p0698c2s v6p0709c2s
Howard, W.W. v2p0008c2s
v3p0159c2s v3p0207c1s v3p0278c1s
v5p0148c1m v5p0301c2s v5p0608c2s
Howard-Flanders, W. v6p0385c2s
v6p0686c1s
Howard-Smith, S. v5p0551c2s
v6p0147c2s
Howarth, Anna v5p0068c1s
Howarth, E. v3p0186c1s
Howarth, H. v4p0023c1s
Howarth, H.H. v2p0014c2s
Howarth, M. v4p0407c2s
v5p0315c1s
Howarth, Mary v5p0168c2s
v6p0195c1s
Howarth, O. v3p0044c1s
v4p0036c1s v4p0040c1s v4p0145c1s
Howarth, O.H. v4p0452c2s
v4p0523c2s v4p0527c1s
Howarth, O.J.R. v6p0326c2s
Howarth, O.W. v1p0982c1s
v4p0270c1s
Howarth, W. v2p0088c2s
Howatt, J.R. v3p0263c2s
v3p0445c2s v3p0446c1s v4p0076c2s
Howden, C.R.A. v5p0515c2s
Howden, F.A. v5p0262c2s
Howden, J. v2p0169c1s
Howe, A.F. v6p0407c2s
Howe, C.D. v6p0656c1s
Howe, C.E. v5p0444c1s
Howe, C.S. v6p0015c1s
v6p0015c2s v6p0635c2s
Howe, E. v6p0184c2s
v6p0486c2s v6p0565c1s
Howe, E. and Browning, P.E.
v5p0560c1s
Howe, E.F. v1p0290c2s
v4p0434c2s v4p0457c2s v6p0491c1s
Howe, E.J. v2p0155c2s
v2p0467c1s
Howe, E.L. v6p0038c2s
Howe, E.M. v5p0511c2s
v6p0605c1s
Howe, E.W. v3p0303c1s
v4p0617c2s
Howe, F., jr. v6p0105c1s
Howe, F.C. v4p0224c2s
v4p0277c2s v4p0423c2s v4p0622c2s
v5p0323c1s v5p0568c1s v5p0568c2s
v6p0131c1m v6p0188c2s v6p0230c2s
v6p0258c1s v6p0384c2s v6p0436c1s
v6p0519c2s v6p0563c2s v6p0669c2s
v6p0692c2s
Howe, F.M. v6p0349c2s
Howe, G. v1p0121c2s
v1p0404c1s v1p1035c2s v3p0395c1s
Howe, H.A. v2p0095c1s
v2p0129c2s v2p0262c2s v2p0480c1s
v4p0034c1s v4p0175c1s v4p0186c1m
v4p0568c1s v5p0035c1s v5p0035c2m
v6p0186c1s v6p0245c2s v6p0397c1s
Howe, H.C. v4p0033c2s
v6p0158c2s
Howe, H.J. v5p0451c1s
Howe, H.M. v4p0548c1s
v6p0013c1s v6p0328c2m v6p0412c1s
v6p0635c2s
Howe, J. v1p0773c2s
Howe, J.B. v1p0092c1s
v1p0435c2s v1p1054c1s
Howe, J.C. and McKay, T.C.
v5p0184c1s
Howe, J.D. v6p0488c2s
Howe, J.F. v1p0422c1s
Howe, J.I. v1p1010c2s
Howe, J.L. v3p0380c1s
v4p0507c2s v5p0083c1s v5p0261c2s
v5p0309c2s v5p0371c2s v5p0440c2s
v6p0111c2s v6p0497c1s
Howe, J.L. and Campbell, H.D.
v4p0102c2s v6p0412c2s
Howe, J.L. et al. v4p0014c1s
Howe, J.S. et al. v6p0312c2s
Howe, J.W. v1p0248c2s
v1p0322c2s v1p0369c2s v1p0528c2s
v1p0571c2s v1p0702c2s v1p0779c2s
v1p1244c2s v1p1426c1s v2p0012c1s
v2p0037c1s v2p0056c1s v2p0069c1s
v2p0198c1s v2p0244c2s v2p0257c2s
v2p0265c2s v2p0410c1s v2p0477c1s
v3p0015c2s v3p0122c2s v3p0285c2s
v3p0468c1s v3p0468c2s v3p0469c2s
v4p0166c2s v4p0210c2s v4p0629c2s
v5p0137c2s v6p0202c1s
Howe, J.W. et al. v3p0454c2s
Howe, J.W., Mrs. v1p1399c2s
v2p0131c1s
Howe, Julia W. v6p0706c1s
Howe, Julia Ward v6p0124c1s
v6p0376c1s
Howe, L. v4p0028c2s
v4p0193c1s
Howe, L.C. v4p0441c1s
v5p0350c2s v5p0628c1s v6p0113c2s
Howe, L.D. and Duffie, C.D.
v6p0071c1s
Howe, L.McH. v6p0570c2s
Howe, L.S. v5p0177c1s
Howe, M. v3p0265c1s
v3p0412c2s v6p0214c1s v6p0400c2s
v6p0508c2s v6p0548c1s
Howe, M. and Hall, Florence Howe
v6p0081c2s
Howe, M.A. v1p0159c1s
Howe, M.A.D. v5p0071c1s
v5p0080c2s v5p0135c2s v5p0167c1s
v5p0187c1s v5p0254c2s v5p0432c2s
v5p0455c1s v6p0404c2s
Howe, M.A.DeW. v3p0388c2s
v4p0198c2s v5p0259c1s v5p0268c1s
v5p0272c1s v5p0274c2s v5p0276c1s
v5p0299c1s v5p0347c1s v5p0350c1s
v5p0464c1s v5p0629c2s v5p0630c1s
v5p0632c1s v6p0076c1s v6p0076c2s
v6p0077c1s v6p0147c2s v6p0169c1s
v6p0379c1s v6p0697c1s
Howe, M.A.DeW., jr. v3p0119c2s
Howe, Maud v3p0203c2s
v6p0019c1s v6p0047c1s v6p0301c1s
Howe, R.H. v4p0252c2s
Howe, R.H., jr. v6p0070c1s
v6p0375c2s
Howe, S. v5p0346c1s
v6p0027c2s v6p0028c2m v6p0079c2s
v6p0156c1s v6p0203c2s v6p0258c2s
v6p0299c2m v6p0413c2s v6p0470c2s
v6p0554c2s v6p0623c2s v6p0684c1s
Howe, S.G. v1p0142c1m
v1p0162c2m v1p0554c2s v1p0643c1s
v1p0644c1s v1p0724c2s
Howe, S.H. v6p0642c2s
Howe, T.O. v1p0556c1s
v1p0698c1s v1p1048c1s
Howe, W. v5p0473c2s
Howe, W.D. v6p0588c1s
Howe, W.F. v5p0392c2s
Howe, W.H. v5p0614c2s
Howe, W.T. v1p0300c2s
Howe, W.W. v3p0086c1s
v3p0302c2s v5p0600c1s v5p0602c1s
v5p0603c1s v6p0548c2s
Howe, W.W. and Andrews, E.B.
v5p0592c2s
Howe, W.W. et al. v5p0592c1s
Howe, Z.H. v1p0626c1s
v1p1328c1s
Howell and Ward v3p0276c1s
Howell, B.E. v5p0041c2s
v5p0547c2s
Howell, C. v4p0036c1s
v4p0233c2s v4p0593c1s
Howell, C.F. v4p0431c1s
Howell, D.J. v5p0092c2s
Howell, E.B. v3p0214c2s
v4p0143c2s v4p0446c2s v4p0473c2s
Howell, E.C. v4p0619c2s
Howell, E.E. v2p0293c1s
v3p0276c1m v4p0366c2m v4p0367c1m
Howell, E.J. v4p0368c2s
Howell, E.K. v5p0179c1s
Howell, F. v1p1419c2s
Howell, G. v1p0048c2s
v1p0650c1s v1p1261c2s v1p1288c2s
v1p1319c2m v1p1431c1s v2p0348c2s
v2p0444c2m v3p0239c1s v3p0397c2s
v3p0413c1s v3p0434c1m v3p0434c2s
v4p0314c1s
Howell, G. and Potter, G.. v1p0379c1s
Howell, G.R. v1p0030c1s
v1p0880c2s
Howell, Geo. v3p0434c1s
v3p0452c1s
Howell, H.S. v3p0035c2s
v4p0047c1s v4p0178c2s v4p0251c1s
v4p0425c2s
Howell, J.W. v2p0137c1s
v4p0174c2s
Howell, M.A., jr. v1p0499c1s
v1p0718c2s
Howell, P. v5p0040c1s
Howell, R.B.C. v1p0310c1s
Howell, S. v1p0594c2s
v1p1182c2s
Howell, T.J. v2p0162c1s
Howell, W. v5p0639c2s
Howell, W.B.L. v4p0246c2s
Howell, W.H. v2p0049c2s
v5p0062c1s v5p0518c2s v6p0592c1s
Howells, A.T. v1p0308c2s
v1p0455c2s v1p1102c1s
Howells, J.M. v5p0175c1s
Howells, M. v6p0643c1s
Howells, W.C. v1p0191c1s
v1p0732c2s
Howells, W.D. v1p0021c1s
v1p0071c1s v1p0083c2s v1p0162c2s
v1p0181c2s v1p0199c1s v1p0216c1s
v1p0256c2s v1p0263c2s v1p0281c1s
v1p0295c1s v1p0300c2s v1p0308c1s
v1p0326c2s v1p0331c2s v1p0335c2s
v1p0353c1s v1p0357c1s v1p0365c1s
v1p0446c2s v1p0449c2s v1p0467c2s
v1p0505c2s v1p0520c2s v1p0523c2s
v1p0534c2s v1p0586c2s v1p0669c2s
v1p0672c1s v1p0716c2s v1p0768c1s
v1p0772c1s v1p0797c2s v1p0801c2s
v1p0870c1s v1p0879c2s v1p0892c2s
v1p0920c1s v1p0924c1s v1p0943c1s
v1p0952c1s v1p0957c1s v1p0973c1s
v1p0974c2s v1p0995c1s v1p0997c1s
v1p1029c2s v1p1053c1s v1p1126c1s
v1p1183c1s v1p1263c2s v1p1315c2s
v1p1339c2s v1p1366c1s v1p1396c2s
v2p0088c2s v2p0139c1s v2p0159c2s
v2p0171c2s v2p0220c1s v2p0233c1s
v2p0254c1s v2p0254c2s v2p0290c2s
v2p0293c2s v2p0300c2s v2p0314c1s
v2p0347c1s v2p0349c2s v2p0367c2s
v2p0373c1s v2p0402c1s v2p0477c1s
v3p0014c2s v3p0016c2s v3p0117c2s
v3p0155c1s v3p0209c1s v3p0251c2s
v3p0308c2m v3p0386c2s v3p0418c1s
v4p0068c2s v4p0073c1s v4p0075c1s
v4p0101c2s v4p0114c2s v4p0136c2s
v4p0161c2s v4p0186c1s v4p0190c1s

v4p0226c2s v4p0260c2s v4p0327c2m
v4p0328c2s v4p0334c2s v4p0341c1s
v4p0360c1s v4p0398c2s v4p0400c1s
v4p0400c2s v4p0414c2s v4p0429c1s
v4p0433c1s v4p0447c2s v4p0458c1s
v4p0492c2s v4p0515c1s v4p0534c2s
v4p0535c2s v4p0550c2s v4p0582c2s
v4p0591c1s v4p0593c1s v4p0633c1s
v5p0016c2m v5p0036c1s v5p0053c1s
v5p0089c1s v5p0100c1s v5p0104c2s
v5p0122c2s v5p0132c2s v5p0161c2s
v5p0167c1s v5p0167c2s v5p0203c2s
v5p0205c2m v5p0206c1s v5p0275c2s
v5p0287c2s v5p0317c2s v5p0334c2s
v5p0350c1s v5p0355c2s v5p0415c2s
v5p0428c1s v5p0456c1s v5p0473c1s
v5p0527c2s v5p0553c2s v5p0554c1s
v5p0555c1s v5p0576c1s v5p0620c1s
v5p0625c2s v6p0004c1s v6p0007c2s
v6p0017c2s v6p0018c2m v6p0053c2s
v6p0080c1s v6p0112c2s v6p0114c1s
v6p0156c1s v6p0184c1s v6p0184c2s
v6p0189c2s v6p0196c1s v6p0200c2s
v6p0205c1s v6p0207c2s v6p0208c1s
v6p0215c2s v6p0231c1s v6p0284c1m
v6p0287c1s v6p0291c2s v6p0305c2s
v6p0333c1s v6p0350c2s v6p0385c2s
v6p0431c2s v6p0459c2s v6p0472c2s
v6p0504c2s v6p0603c2s v6p0606c2s
v6p0644c2s v6p0686c2s v6p0709c2s
v6p0713c1s
Howells, W.D. et al. v6p0461c2s
Howerth, I.W. v4p0121c2s
v4p0294c1s v4p0415c2s v4p0461c1s
v4p0535c1m v5p0022c2s v5p0277c1s
v5p0483c1s v5p0535c2s v5p0536c1s
v6p0129c1s v6p0189c2s v6p0486c1s
Howerth, Ira W. v6p0318c1s
v6p0600c1s v6p0684c2s
Howerth, J.W. v6p0190c1m
Howerth, T.W. v5p0177c2s
Howes, C.A. v5p0509c1s
Howes, D.J. v6p0035c2s
Howes, F. v1p1192c2s
Howes, G.B. v5p0153c2s
v5p0432c2s v5p0529c2s v5p0532c1s
v5p0590c2s v5p0639c2m v6p0430c2s
Howes, H. v1p0921c1s
v1p1124c1s
Howes, O. v1p0724c1s
v3p0178c1s
Howes, O., jr. v1p0018c1s
v1p1173c2s v3p0012c1s
Howes, S.B. and Weston, S.
v1p0272c1s v1p0554c1s
Howes, S.O. v6p0681c2s
Howgate, H.W. v1p0055c1s
v1p0055c2s v2p0004c1s v2p0020c2m
v2p0347c1s
Howgrave, W. v6p0634c1s
Howgrave, W.G. v1p0218c2s
v1p0981c2s
Howgrave, W.S. v1p1044c2s
Howle, D. v5p0395c2s
Howie, J.M. v3p0300c1s
Howie, Muir, Dr. v2p0442c1s
Howison, C.H. v6p0306c2s
Howison, G. v1p0323c2s
v1p0685c2s v4p0191c1s
Howison, G.H. v1p0811c1s
v2p0176c1s v2p0211c2s v2p0339c2s
v2p0346c2s v2p0389c2s v3p0171c1s
v4p0338c1s v4p0464c2s v4p0506c2s
v5p0236c1s v6p0104c1s v6p0495c2s
Howison, R.R. v1p0485c2s
Howison, W. v1p1135c1s
Howitt, A.M. v1p0880c1s
Howitt, A.W. v1p0149c2s
v2p0029c1m v2p0244c2m v3p0027c1s
v3p0027c2s v3p0117c2s v3p0275c1s
v6p0042c1s
Howitt, A.W. and Fison, L.
v2p0115c1s v2p0207c2s v2p0299c2s
Howitt, M. v1p0080c2s
v1p0098c1s v1p0108c2s v1p0162c2s
v1p0179c2s v1p0230c1s v1p0327c1s
v1p0361c2s v1p0501c1s v1p0616c1s
v1p0618c1s v1p0677c1s v1p0697c1s
v1p0756c1s v1p0774c1s v1p0774c2s
v1p0879c2s v1p0938c1s v1p0951c2s
v1p0958c1s v1p1044c1s v1p1109c1s
v1p1202c1s v1p1269c2s v1p1274c2s
v1p1318c2s v1p1334c1s v1p1428c1s
v1p1433c2s v2p0065c1s v2p0210c1s
v2p0377c2m v2p0459c2s v4p0046c2s
v4p0047c2s v4p0052c2s v4p0098c1s
v4p0221c1s v4p0285c1s v4p0342c1s
v5p0541c2s
Howitt, Margaret v1p1337c2s
v3p0036c1s v3p0074c2s v3p0274c2s
v4p0375c2s
Howitt, Mary v1p0037c1s
v1p0040c2s v1p0088c2s
Howitt, R. v1p0668c1s
Howitt, W. v1p0049c1s
v1p0076c1s v1p0088c1s v1p0102c2s
v1p0116c2s v1p0299c1s v1p0339c1s
v1p0353c2s v1p0383c1s v1p0387c1s
v1p0406c1s v1p0409c2s v1p0413c1s
v1p0414c2s v1p0447c1s v1p0460c2s
v1p0472c1s v1p0487c2m v1p0499c2s
v1p0514c2s v1p0520c2s v1p0525c1s
v1p0542c1s v1p0548c2s v1p0574c1m
v1p0633c2s v1p0655c1s v1p0656c2s
v1p0659c2s v1p0668c1s v1p0677c2s
v1p0698c2m v1p0714c2s v1p0718c2s
v1p0799c1s v1p0811c2s v1p0813c2s
v1p0814c1s v1p0818c2s v1p0831c2s
v1p0834c2s v1p0869c2s v1p0920c1s
v1p0933c1s v1p0937c1m v1p0937c2m
v1p0983c1s v1p0988c2s v1p1020c1s
v1p1030c2s v1p1069c1s v1p1069c2s
v1p1080c1s v1p1111c1s v1p1178c1s
v1p1256c1s v1p1266c2s v1p1285c1s
v1p1389c1s v1p1407c2m
Howitz, D. v2p0162c1s
Howland, A.E. v5p0452c2m
Howland, C. v1p0703c2s
v1p0770c1s v1p0933c2s
Howland, C.G. v1p1095c2s
v1p1338c2s
Howland, C.P. v5p0174c2s
Howland, Cora R. v6p0641c2s
Howland, D.B. v5p0477c1s
v6p0501c1s
Howland, E. v1p0042c1s
v1p0093c2s v1p0132c2m v1p0148c2s
v1p0149c1s v1p0162c1s v1p0187c1s
v1p0225c2s v1p0258c2s v1p0296c2s
v1p0497c1s v1p0561c2s v1p0638c1s
v1p0678c1s v1p0724c1s v1p0743c2m
v1p0863c1s v1p0982c1s v1p1077c1s
v1p1078c1s v1p1080c2s v1p1199c2s
v1p1216c1s v1p1317c2s v2p0152c2s
v2p0193c1s
Howland, G. v1p0390c1s
Howland, H.A. v3p0347c2s
Howland, H.C. v6p0599c1s
Howland, H.E. v4p0231c2s
v4p0580c1s v4p0635c1s v5p0328c1s
v5p0643c2s
Howland, H.F. v4p0359c2s
Howland, H.H. v6p0316c1s
Howland, H.J. v6p0004c1s
v6p0161c1s v6p0579c1s v6p0709c1s
Howland, H.R. v6p0018c1s
v6p0676c2s
Howland, H.S. v6p0701c2s
Howland, I. v4p0627c2s
Howland, M. v1p0107c1s
v1p0177c1s v1p0299c2s v1p0461c1s
v1p0462c2s v1p0540c1s v1p0696c1s
v1p0744c2s v1p0885c1s v1p0921c1s
v1p0971c2s v1p0997c2s v1p1040c1s
v1p1440c2s v2p0179c2s v2p0245c1s
v2p0443c2s
Howland, M.H. v1p1420c2s
Howland, Marie v6p0335c1s
Howland, O.A. v4p0031c1s
v4p0085c2s v4p0086c2s v4p0574c2s
v5p0091c2s
Howland, R.H. v5p0393c2s
Howland, S.W. v3p0175c1s
v5p0358c2s v6p0213c2s v6p0342c1s
v6p0657c1s
Howland, W. and Thayer, W.S.
v1p0774c2s
Howlett, C.A.S. v5p0002c2s
Howlett, E. v4p0045c1s
v4p0079c2s v4p0357c1s
Howlett, England v3p0060c1s
Howlett, F. v1p0257c2s
v1p1269c1s
Howlett, J.A. v4p0053c2s
v4p0055c1s v4p0056c1s v4p0057c2m
v5p0057c1s v5p0057c2s v5p0058c2s
v5p0470c1s v6p0064c1s v6p0302c2s
Howlett, J.H. v3p0038c2s
Howlett, L.G. v6p0156c1s
Howley, B. v3p0359c2s
Howley, J. v6p0065c2s
Howley, J.F.W. v3p0206c1s
v3p0471c1s v6p0308c1s v6p0355c1s
Howley, M.F. v2p0311c1s
v3p0062c1s
Howley, R. v3p0301c1m
Howman, K. v1p0729c2s
Howorth, H. v4p0388c1s
Howorth, H., Sir v4p0020c1s
Howorth, H.H. v1p0050c2s
v1p0066c2s v1p0087c2s v1p0113c2s
v1p0204c2s v1p0333c2s v1p0449c2s
v1p0516c1s v1p0701c2s v1p0702c2s
v1p0709c2m v1p0924c2m v1p1073c2s
v1p1154c1m v1p1209c1s v1p1337c1s
v2p0040c1s v2p0056c2m v2p0094c1s
v2p0111c2s v2p0147c2s v2p0166c2s
v2p0176c2s v2p0211c2s v2p0228c2s
v2p0272c1s v2p0295c1s v2p0316c2s
v2p0374c2s v2p0404c2s v2p0428c1s
v2p0457c2s v3p0059c2s v3p0130c2s
v3p0217c1s v3p0233c1s v3p0265c1s
v3p0391c2s v4p0040c2s v4p0054c1s
v4p0093c2s v4p0187c1m v4p0244c2m
v4p0272c2s v4p0388c1s v4p0435c2s
v4p0515c2s v5p0020c1s v5p0042c1s
v5p0228c2s v5p0287c1s v5p0437c2s
v5p0625c2s v6p0592c1s
Howorth, H.H. and Wallace, A.R.
v4p0317c1s
Howorth, H.H. et al. v3p0438c1s
Howorth, H.W. v1p0280c2s
Howra, Prince v1p0305c1s
Howse, E.S. v1p0407c2s
v1p0708c2s v2p0115c2s
Howson, E.W. v4p0271c2s
Howson, H. v1p0160c2s
v1p0444c1s v1p0622c1s v1p0978c1s
Howson, J.S. v1p0038c1s
v1p0127c1s v1p0226c2m v1p0239c1s
v1p0274c2s v1p0340c1s v1p0681c2s
v1p0696c1s v1p0817c2s v1p0900c2s
v1p0977c2s v1p0980c1s v1p0980c2m
v1p0994c1s v1p1312c1s v2p0007c2s
Howson, R. v1p0665c2m
v2p0461c1s
Howton, A. v4p0271c2s
Hoxie, G.L. v6p0432c2s
Hoxie, R.F. v4p0059c1s
v4p0482c2s v4p0525c1s v5p0175c1s
v6p0222c2s v6p0292c1s v6p0516c1s
v6p0632c2s v6p0666c2s v6p0674c1s
Hoxie, R.H. v6p0169c2s
Hoxie, S. v3p0070c2s
v3p0198c2s
Hoy, P.R. v1p0810c1s
Hoy, W.A. v6p0128c1s
Hoyle, E.D. v5p0032c1s
Hoyle, J.C. v4p0156c2s
Hoyle, W.E. v4p0154c2s
v4p0508c1s v5p0350c2s
Hoyt, A.H. v1p0216c2s
v1p0586c1s v1p0593c2s v1p1018c1s
v2p0094c1s
Hoyt, A.J. v2p0418c2s
Hoyt, A.M. v1p0519c2s
Hoyt, A.W. v1p0279c1s
Hoyt, C.S. v4p0275c1s
Hoyt, D.W. v1p1241c1s
v1p1398c1s v1p1412c1s v2p0202c2s
v6p0283c2s
Hoyt, E. v5p0638c2s
v6p0201c1s v6p0308c1s v6p0381c1s
v6p0440c1s v6p0441c2s v6p0625c1s
v6p0674c2s v6p0703c1s
Hoyt, Eleanor v5p0061c1s
v6p0534c1s
Hoyt, F.T. v6p0619c1s
Hoyt, F.W. v6p0028c1s
v6p0618c2s v6p0687c1s
Hoyt, H.M. v6p0094c1s
Hoyt, H.W. v5p0136c1s
Hoyt, J.C. v1p0197c1s
v1p0789c2s
Hoyt, J.G. v1p0001c1s
v1p0016c1s v1p0436c1s v1p0998c2s
Hoyt, J.M. v1p0850c1s
v2p0437c1s
Hoyt, J.R. v6p0458c2s
Hoyt, J.W. v2p0455c2s
v5p0400c1s v5p0605c1s
Hoyt, J.W. et al. v5p0388c2s
Hoyt, L.W. v3p0395c2s
Hoyt, N. v2p0043c2s
Hoyt, R. v1p0718c1s
Hoyt, W. v2p0236c1s
v2p0251c1s v2p0307c1s v2p0350c1s
v2p0437c1s v4p0466c2s v4p0467c1s
Hoyt, W.A. v4p0395c1s
Hoyt, W.C. v1p0915c2s
v1p1067c1s v1p1398c2s
Hoyt, W.E. v3p0121c2s
Hoyt, W.S., Mrs. v4p0066c1s
Hoyt, Wayland v4p0543c2s
Hozier, H.M. v1p0430c1s
v2p0185c2s v2p0186c2s v2p0261c2s
v3p0094c1s v3p0139c1s v3p0179c2s
v6p0636c1s
Hrdlicka, A. v5p0195c1s
v5p0401c1s v5p0427c2s v6p0024c2s
v6p0045c2s v6p0073c1s v6p0114c1s
v6p0156c1s v6p0317c1s v6p0361c2s
v6p0397c1s v6p0414c1s v6p0479c1s
v6p0500c1s v6p0577c2s
Hrdlicka, Ales v5p0069c1s
Huband, W.G. v1p0388c1s
Hubback, C.A. v1p1253c2s
Hubbard, A.J. and Hubbard, G.
v6p0397c1s
Hubbard, B. v2p0287c2m
v2p0300c1s v3p0240c1s v4p0207c2s
Hubbard, C.L. v6p0285c2s
v6p0677c1s
Hubbard, C.M. v4p0535c1s
v5p0102c1s
Hubbard, C.W. v6p0691c2s
Hubbard, D.G. v1p0037c2s
v1p0786c1s v2p0303c2s v3p0476c1s
Hubbard, E. v1p0061c1s
v4p0015c1s v4p0279c1s v4p0525c1s
v4p0582c1s v5p0050c2s v5p0105c2s
v5p0173c2s v6p0141c2s v6p0256c2s
v6p0284c2s v6p0472c1s v6p0537c1s
v6p0659c1s v6p0695c2s
Hubbard, E.W. v4p0506c2s
v4p0521c1s v5p0626c1s
Hubbard, E.W., Mrs. v4p0608c2s
Hubbard, Elbert v6p0463c1s
v6p0584c2s v6p0649c1s
Hubbard, F.M. v1p0084c1s

v1p0106c2s v1p0334c2s v1p0394c2s
v1p0573c2s v1p0588c2s v1p0723c1s
v1p0927c2s v1p1217c2s v1p1287c2s
Hubbard, G. v5p0098c2s
Hubbard, G. and Hubbard, A.J.
v6p0397c1s
Hubbard, G.B. v3p0271c1s
Hubbard, G.C. v2p0433c1s
Hubbard, G.D. v6p0182c2s
v6p0250c1s
Hubbard, G.G. v1p0676c1s
v1p1038c2s v1p1076c2s v1p1291c1s
v2p0093c2s v2p0098c2s v2p0102c2s
v2p0224c1s v2p0284c1s v2p0380c2s
v2p0423c2s v3p0004c2s v3p0112c2s
v3p0352c2s v3p0402c1s v4p0002c1s
v4p0005c1s v4p0005c2s v4p0006c1m
v4p0008c2s v4p0013c1s v4p0117c2s
v4p0127c1m v4p0496c1s v4p0538c2s
v4p0612c2s v5p0228c2s
Hubbard, G.G. and Baker, M.
v5p0228c2s
Hubbard, G.H. v2p0305c1s
v2p0434c1s v3p0238c2s v3p0295c2s
v3p0341c1s v3p0356c2s v3p0399c1s
v3p0403c2m v3p0412c2s v4p0610c1s
v5p0628c1s v6p0064c1s v6p0089c1s
v6p0189c1s v6p0455c2s
Hubbard, H. v6p0436c2s
Hubbard, H.G. v2p0273c2s
v4p0232c2s
Hubbard, H.W. v2p0282c2s
v2p0346c2s v3p0200c1s v4p0149c2s
Hubbard, J.G. v1p0414c1s
v2p0084c1s v2p0216c2s v3p0118c2s
Hubbard, J.M. v1p0144c2s
v1p0150c2s v1p0451c1m v1p0452c2s
v2p0001c2s v2p0070c2s v2p0098c2m
v2p0194c2s v2p0240c1s v2p0255c2s
v2p0396c1s v2p0448c1s v3p0004c2m
v3p0005c1s v3p0066c2s v3p0131c1s
v3p0136c2s v3p0189c1s v3p0249c1s
v3p0391c2s v3p0395c2s v4p0005c1s
v4p0006c2m v4p0033c1s v4p0068c2s
v4p0078c2s v4p0179c1s v4p0347c1s
v4p0359c1s v4p0496c1s v4p0537c2s
v5p0071c2s v5p0111c2s v5p0187c1s
v5p0530c1s v5p0593c2s v6p0075c2s
v6p0144c1s v6p0494c1s v6p0664c1s
Hubbard, James M. v3p0379c1s
Hubbard, L., jr. v5p0004c1s
v5p0123c2s v5p0139c2s v5p0209c1s
v5p0209c2s v5p0243c1s v5p0279c2s
v5p0347c1s v5p0374c1s v5p0380c2s
v5p0451c2s v5p0527c1s v5p0547c1s
v5p0578c2s v6p0051c2s v6p0099c1m
v6p0132c2s v6p0154c1s v6p0227c1s
v6p0227c2m v6p0244c2s v6p0316c1s
v6p0422c1s v6p0427c2s v6p0428c1s
v6p0464c2s v6p0599c1s v6p0653c1s
v6p0706c2s v6p0713c2s
Hubbard, L.F. v3p0281c2s
Hubbard, L.L. and Koenig, G.A.
v4p0455c2s
Hubbard, Leonidas, jr., Mrs.
v6p0357c2s
Hubbard, M.B. v6p0357c2s
Hubbard, N.M. and Aldrich, Charles
v2p0363c2s
Hubbard, N.W. v2p0332c2s
Hubbard, O.P. v1p1406c2s
v2p0112c1s v3p0117c2s v3p0245c1s
v3p0435c2s
Hubbard, P. v1p1177c2s
Hubbard, R.B. v1p0385c2s
Hubbard, R.D. v3p0227c2s
Hubbard, S. v2p0262c2s
Hubbard, S., jr. v6p0274c2s
Hubbard, S.A. v1p0614c2s
v2p0046c2s v2p0047c2s v2p0068c2s
v2p0069c1s v2p0121c2s v2p0169c1s
v2p0195c1s v2p0232c1s v2p0253c2s
v2p0269c2s v2p0271c2s v2p0324c1s
v2p0337c2s v2p0361c2s v2p0380c1s
v2p0381c1s v2p0381c2s v2p0439c1m
v3p0068c2s v3p0175c2s v3p0432c1s
v4p0028c2s v4p0061c1s v4p0077c2s
v4p0150c2s v4p0417c2s v4p0419c1s
v5p0038c1s
Hubbard, S.F. v4p0580c2s
Hubbard, S.H. v3p0418c1s
Hubbard, S.W. v3p0331c2s
Hubbard, T.M. v1p0901c1s
Hubbard, W. v3p0056c1s
v3p0263c2s v5p0220c2s v5p0484c2s
Hubbard, W.F. v3p0007c2s
v3p0243c1s
Hubbard, W.J. v1p1388c1s
Hubbard, W.L. v5p0131c2s
Hubbell, C.B. v5p0179c1s
v6p0127c1s v6p0323c1s
Hubbell, C.G. v5p0058c1s
v5p0058c2s v5p0503c2s v6p0307c2s
Hubbell, Chas.B. v4p0051c2s
Hubbell, F.L. v1p0302c1s
Hubbell, H.W. v4p0215c1s
v5p0601c2s
Hubbell, W.W. v1p1218c1s
Hubbenet, ... v3p0383c2s
Hubbert, W.E. v1p0778c1s
Huber, C.C. v6p0037c1s
Huber, E. v2p0182c2s
v5p0440c1s
Huber, G.C. v6p0449c2s
Huber, J. v1p0517c2s
Huber, J.B. v5p0114c2s
v6p0501c2s
Huberich, C.H. v6p0120c2s
v6p0483c2s
Hubert et al. v4p0020c2s
Hubert, P.G. v5p0394c2s
v5p0449c1s
Hubert, P.G., jr. v1p0916c2s
v2p0002c2s v2p0224c1s v2p0464c1s
v3p0230c2s v3p0330c1s v3p0369c1s
v3p0372c1s v3p0451c2s v4p0058c2s
v4p0082c1s v4p0085c1s v4p0179c2s
v4p0225c1s v4p0405c2s v4p0568c2s
v5p0027c1s v5p0159c2s v5p0170c1s
v5p0174c1s v5p0201c1s v5p0578c2s
v5p0602c1s v5p0615c2s v5p0616c2s
v6p0054c2s v6p0225c1s v6p0252c2s
Hubertz, J.R. v1p0623c1s
v1p0643c2s
Hubner, C.W. v1p0073c1s
Hubner, E. v5p0355c1s
Hubrecht, A.A.W. v1p1266c2s
v2p0354c1s v5p0528c1s v6p0440c1s
v6p0657c2s
Huchon, R. v6p0155c2s
Huck, O. v5p0326c1s
Huckel, E.W. v6p0110c1s
Hudd, A.E. v3p0131c1s
Huddart, J. v2p0149c1s
v2p0149c2s
Huddilston, J.H. v5p0121c2s
v5p0539c2s
Huddleston, E.H. v3p0123c1s
v3p0345c1s
Huddleston, K. v4p0124c2s
Hudgins, M.S. v1p0523c1s
Hudleston, F.J. v3p0333c2s
v4p0145c2s v4p0326c1s
Hudnall, W.D., Mrs. v6p0179c1s
Hudson, A. v4p0280c1s
Hudson, A.J.M. v1p1326c1s
Hudson, A.S. v3p0077c1s
Hudson, A.T.M. v1p1084c1s
Hudson, B.K. v5p0495c2s
v5p0565c2s
Hudson, C. v1p0110c1s
v1p0175c2s v1p0302c2s v1p0361c2s
v1p0593c1s v1p0808c2s v1p0925c1s
v1p1057c2s v1p1318c1s
Hudson, C.B. v4p0200c2s
v4p0201c1s v4p0593c1s
Hudson, C.H. v2p0364c1s
Hudson, C.T. v3p0297c1s
v3p0367c2s
Hudson, E. v4p0592c1s
Hudson, E.D. v1p0082c2s
Hudson, E.H. v3p0162c2s
v5p0276c2s v5p0288c1s v6p0633c2s
Hudson, F. v1p0033c1s
v1p0287c2s v2p0135c2s v3p0123c2s
Hudson, F.M. v5p0194c2s
Hudson, G.A. v1p0328c1s
Hudson, G.H. v4p0102c2s
v4p0541c2s
Hudson, H. v3p0352c2s
v5p0243c2s v5p0276c2s v6p0433c2s
Hudson, H.B. v3p0240c1s
v4p0463c1s v5p0399c2s
Hudson, H.N. v1p0069c1s
v1p0086c2s v1p0384c2s v1p0568c2s
v1p0781c2s v1p0782c1s v1p0867c2s
v1p1184c2m v2p0202c2s v2p0469c2s
Hudson, H.P. v6p0607c2s
Hudson, H.R. v1p0287c2s
v1p0335c2s v1p0534c1s v1p0851c2s
v3p0323c2s
Hudson, J. v3p0206c1s
v4p0153c2s v5p0164c2m v5p0380c2s
v6p0123c2s v6p0243c1s v6p0664c2s
v6p0696c2s
Hudson, J.F. v3p0089c1s
v3p0285c2s
Hudson, J.H. v5p0232c2s
Hudson, J.K. v6p0134c2s
Hudson, J.K., Mrs. v5p0013c2s
v5p0021c2s v5p0242c1s v5p0421c1s
v5p0548c1s v5p0578c1s
Hudson, J.R., Mrs. v5p0041c2s
Hudson, J.W. v4p0451c2s
v5p0617c2s v6p0568c2s
Hudson, P. v5p0578c2s
Hudson, R. v1p0659c2s
v1p0746c2s v1p0944c1s v1p0995c1s
v1p1077c1s v1p1418c2s v3p0170c2s
v3p0171c2s v3p0408c1s v4p0224c2s
v4p0546c1s v5p0348c2s
Hudson, T.J. v5p0281c1s
v5p0543c1s
Hudson, U. v6p0037c1s
v6p0129c2s v6p0423c1s
Hudson, W. v4p0498c2s
v5p0068c1s
Hudson, W.H. v2p0047c2s
v2p0078c1s v2p0107c1s v2p0151c1s
v2p0211c2s v2p0332c2m v2p0359c2s
v2p0414c2s v3p0002c2s v3p0045c1m
v3p0070c2s v3p0073c2s v3p0109c2s
v3p0122c1m v3p0203c2m v3p0257c1s
v3p0292c2s v3p0306c1s v3p0318c2s
v3p0376c1s v3p0384c1s v3p0392c1s
v3p0406c2m v3p0419c1s v4p0001c1s
v4p0060c1s v4p0141c2s v4p0160c2s
v4p0184c2s v4p0188c2s v4p0267c2s
v4p0430c1s v4p0448c1s v4p0474c1s
v4p0482c1s v4p0507c1s v4p0513c2s
v4p0515c2s v4p0518c2s v4p0531c1s
v4p0541c1m v4p0606c1s v4p0633c2s
v5p0005c1s v5p0011c1s v5p0041c1s
v5p0042c2s v5p0063c1s v5p0063c2m
v5p0075c1s v5p0124c2s v5p0160c1s
v5p0166c2s v5p0211c2s v5p0214c1s
v5p0300c2s v5p0344c2s v5p0395c2s
v5p0405c2s v5p0426c1s v5p0433c2s
v5p0509c2s v5p0545c2s v5p0547c2s
v5p0560c2s v5p0609c2s v5p0632c1m
v5p0635c1s v6p0068c2s v6p0162c1s
v6p0271c2s v6p0582c2s v6p0584c1s
v6p0590c2s v6p0603c2s v6p0610c1s
v6p0659c2s
Hudson, W.H.H. v3p0147c2s
v4p0361c1s
Hudspeth, J. v4p0072c2s
v5p0481c2s
Hudworth, G. v5p0554c1s
Huebner, G.G. v6p0308c1s
Huebner, S. v6p0141c1s
v6p0271c2s v6p0319c2s v6p0321c2s
v6p0322c2m v6p0529c2s v6p0634c1s
Hueffer, F. v1p0115c2s
v1p0138c2s v1p0150c2s v1p0238c1s
v1p0459c1s v1p0669c2s v1p0884c2s
v1p0459c1s v1p0669c2s v1p0884c2s
v1p0943c2s v1p0995c1s v1p1160c1m
v1p1197c1s v1p1327c1m v1p1379c2m
Hueffer, F.M. v4p0492c1s
v5p0310c1s v5p0376c1s v5p0388c2s
v5p0497c1s v6p0052c2s v6p0173c2s
v6p0214c1s v6p0228c2s v6p0465c2s
v6p0552c1s v6p0677c2s
Hueppe, F. v5p0162c2s
Huet, A. v4p0403c1s
Huet, A.B. v1p1290c1s
Huey, E.B. v5p0479c2s
Huey, R. v6p0552c1s
Huff, L.J. v3p0175c2s
v3p0176c1s v3p0243c1s v3p0379c1s
Huffcut, E.W. v3p0140c1s
v3p0218c2s v3p0284c1s v3p0421c2s
v4p0182c1s v4p0307c1s v4p0323c1s
v4p0550c1s v5p0138c1s v6p0659c1s
Huffcut, Ernest W. v6p0176c2s
Huffman, Bert v6p0009c1s
Hufford, R.W. v3p0229c1s
v4p0045c1s
Hug, Prof. v1p0554c2s
v1p0961c1s
Hugel, A.von v4p0047c1s
Hugel, Baron von v6p0061c2s
Hugel, Carl von v2p0286c1s
Hugel, F.von v4p0053c1s
v4p0111c2s v6p0216c1s v6p0383c1s
Hugessen, E.H.K. v1p0607c1s
Huggins, E.L. v2p0219c2s
v3p0396c2s v4p0063c1s
Huggins, Lady and Huggins, W., Sir
v5p0549c2s
Huggins, Marg.L. v4p0033c2s
Huggins, S. v2p0020c1s
Huggins, W. v1p0562c1s
v1p0726c1s v1p0804c1s v1p0903c2m
v1p1233c2m v1p1234c1s v1p1244c1m
v2p0095c1m v2p0095c2s v2p0413c2s
v2p0417c1s v2p0424c2m v2p0425c1m
v2p0461c1m v3p0024c2s v3p0108c2s
v3p0298c2s v4p0037c2s v4p0540c2s
v5p0035c2s
Huggins, W. and Huggins, W., Mrs.
v4p0037c2s
Huggins, W. and Miller, W.A.
v1p1244c1s
Huggins, W. and Pickering, W.H.
v2p0425c1s
Huggins, W. et al. v3p0298c2s
v4p0037c2s
Huggins, W., Mrs v3p0108c2s
Huggins, W., Mrs. and Huggins, W.
v4p0037c2s
Huggins, W., Sir and Huggins, Lady
v5p0549c2s
Hugh, D.D. v5p0177c1s
Hughes, A. v3p0463c1s
v6p0269c1s v6p0462c2s
Hughes, A. and Crump, C.G.
v4p0143c2s
Hughes, A. et al. v5p0125c1s
Hughes, A.E. v5p0134c2s
v5p0331c2s
Hughes, A.M.D. v5p0452c2s
v6p0526c2s
Hughes, B.F. v4p0287c2s
Hughes, C. v6p0221c1s
Hughes, C.H. v3p0182c1s
Hughes, D.E. v1p0401c2s
v1p0639c2s v1p0788c1s v1p0858c2s
v2p0136c2s v2p0229c1s v2p0272c1m

v2p0419c2s
Hughes, E. v4p0620c1s
v5p0259c2s v6p0304c1s
Hughes, E.C. v6p0573c1s
Hughes, E.H. v6p0060c1s
Hughes, E.P. v5p0177c2s
Hughes, G.M. v6p0135c1s
Hughes, G.W. v1p0109c2s
v1p0300c1s v1p1248c1s v1p1312c2s
Hughes, H. v1p0714c1s
v4p0362c2s
Hughes, H.P. v3p0040c1s
v3p0129c1s v3p0166c2s v3p0181c1s
v4p0109c2s v5p0097c1s v5p0197c2s
Hughes, H.P. and Ball, W.E.
v4p0589c2s
Hughes, H.P. et al. v3p0342c1s
v3p0458c2s
Hughes, H.P., Mrs. v5p0150c2s
Hughes, H.Price v3p0460c1s
Hughes, H.W. v2p0361c1s
Hughes, I.J. v6p0475c1s
Hughes, J. v1p0098c2s
v1p0787c1s v1p1425c1s v2p0271c2s
v2p0376c1s v6p0400c1s
Hughes, J.C. v2p0219c1s
Hughes, J.H. v6p0648c1s
Hughes, J.J. v6p0429c2s
Hughes, J.L. v2p0204c1s
v3p0355c1s v4p0046c1s v4p0216c1s
v4p0255c1s v4p0260c2s v4p0311c1s
v4p0446c2s v4p0630c1s v5p0161c1s
v5p0582c2s v6p0351c2s v6p0575c1s
Hughes, J.S. v6p0291c2s
v6p0590c1s
Hughes, K. v6p0358c2s
Hughes, M.C. v5p0623c1s
Hughes, M.E. v6p0396c1s
Hughes, M.W. v4p0607c1s
Hughes, M.W. and Herrick, S.B.
v3p0401c2s
Hughes, Margaret v6p0184c1s
Hughes, P. v6p0428c1s
Hughes, Percy v6p0582c2s
Hughes, Prof. v1p0835c1s
Hughes, R. v4p0076c1s
v4p0111c1s v4p0127c2s v4p0249c1s
v4p0291c2s v4p0309c2s v4p0635c1s
v5p0013c2s v5p0020c1s v5p0094c2s
v5p0131c2s v5p0636c2s v6p0013c2s
v6p0099c1s v6p0108c1s v6p0433c2s
v6p0589c2s
Hughes, R.E. v5p0177c2s
Hughes, R.P. v5p0098c1s
v5p0531c1s
Hughes, R.W. v3p0269c2s
Hughes, Rupert v5p0028c2s
v5p0050c1s v5p0448c2s v6p0075c2s
Hughes, S.E. v1p0018c1s
v1p1346c1s
Hughes, S.L. v2p0247c1s
Hughes, S.P. v2p0021c2s
Hughes, T. v1p0114c2s
v1p0134c2s v1p0217c1s v1p0251c2s
v1p0270c1s v1p0303c1s v1p0387c1s
v1p0408c2s v1p0483c2m v1p0595c2s
v1p0631c2s v1p0668c1s v1p0671c1s
v1p0687c1s v1p0696c2s v1p0713c2s
v1p0761c2m v1p0805c1s v1p0810c1s
v1p0919c2s v1p0922c1s v1p0953c2s
v1p0968c2s v1p1063c1s v1p1214c2s
v1p1225c1s v1p1243c1s v1p1287c1s
v1p1307c2s v1p1315c1s v1p1319c2s
v1p1341c2s v1p1345c2s v1p1346c1s
v1p1356c2s v1p1378c1s v1p1392c2s
v1p1400c2s v1p1431c1s v2p0101c2s
v2p0191c1s v2p0196c1s v2p0255c1s
v2p0267c2s v2p0444c2s v2p0480c2s
v3p0099c1s v3p0174c1s v3p0234c2s
v3p0283c2s v3p0473c2s v4p0020c1s
v4p0171c2s v4p0191c2s v4p0281c2s
v4p0294c1s v4p0299c2s v4p0361c2s
v4p0396c1s v4p0432c2s v4p0465c1s
v4p0490c1s v4p0508c1s v5p0380c1s
v5p0542c2s v6p0693c1s
Hughes, T. and Rawlins, W.D.
v1p0031c1s
v1p0303c1s
v1p0573c1s
Hughes, T. and Warner, H.L.
v3p0368c2s
Hughes, T.H. v5p0565c2s
Hughes, T.J. v4p0368c2s
Hughes, T.L. v4p0505c1s
Hughes, T.M. v1p0786c1s
v2p0273c2s v5p0027c2s
Hughes, T.McK. v1p0209c1s
v1p0508c1s v2p0128c2s v2p0420c1s
v4p0227c1s v5p0614c1s
Hughes, T.P. v2p0006c1s
v3p0237c2s v3p0284c1s v3p0284c2s
v4p0005c1s v4p0293c2s v4p0544c1s
v6p0431c2s
Hughes, T.W.H. and King, W.
v5p0238c2s v5p0285c2s
Hughes, Thomas v4p0418c1s
Hughes, W. v2p0153c2s
v3p0308c2s v6p0314c1m
Hughes, W.,Mrs. v2p0403c2s
Hughes, W.E. and Sharp, B.
v4p0025c1s
Hughes, W.M. v4p0053c1s
v4p0148c1s
Hughes, W.S. v3p0134c1s
v3p0413c2s v3p0433c1s
Hughes-Games, S.H.W. v5p0079c1s
Hughes-Hallett, H.H. v5p0049c2s
Hughson, S.C. v3p0268c1s
v4p0356c1s v4p0444c2s v5p0095c1s
v5p0452c1m
Hugi, J.F. v1p0524c1s
Hugill, J.S. v4p0137c1s
Hugo, C. v1p0611c2s
Hugo, T. v1p1010c1s
Hugo, V. v1p0181c2s
v1p0420c2s v1p0770c1s v1p0795c1s
v2p0266c2s v4p0118c1s v4p0429c1s
v4p0430c1s v5p0163c2s v5p0522c1s
Hugo, Victor v4p0335c2s
Hugo, Victor and Meetkerke, C.E.
v4p0193c1s
Hugunin, H.M. v4p0041c1s
v4p0518c1s
Huidekoper, F. v1p1309c2s
Huidekoper, F.L. v4p0613c2s
v5p0098c1s v5p0304c2s v5p0398c1s
v6p0041c1s v6p0187c2s v6p0442c1s
v6p0668c1s v6p0678c2s
Huiginn, E.J.V. v3p0013c1s
v3p0163c1s v3p0262c2s v3p0364c1m
Huish, M. v1p1079c1s
Huish, M.B. v3p0021c1s
v3p0226c2m v4p0316c2s v4p0421c2s
v4p0621c2s v5p0113c2s v5p0566c2s
Huizinga, A.H. v3p0012c2s
v3p0384c2s v4p0313c2s v4p0373c1s
v5p0056c2s v5p0060c1s
Huizinga, A.W. v4p0056c1s
v4p0109c1s
Hulbert, A.B. v5p0113c1s
v5p0303c1s v5p0474c2s v6p0037c2s
v6p0078c2s v6p0098c1s v6p0130c2s
v6p0286c2s v6p0388c1s v6p0524c1s
v6p0530c2s v6p0545c1s v6p0584c2s
v6p0686c2m v6p0712c2s
Hulbert, C.B. v5p0236c2s
Hulbert, E.B. v6p0057c1s
Hulbert, E.J. v5p0264c1s
Hulbert, H.B. v5p0111c1s
v5p0319c2m v6p0354c1m v6p0400c1s
v6p0525c1s
Hulbert, H.R. v6p0594c1s
Hulbert, H.W. v2p0230c1s
v2p0426c1s v3p0043c2s v4p0374c2s
v5p0299c1s v6p0126c2s v6p0170c2s
Hulbert, W.D. v5p0051c2s
v5p0156c2s v5p0304c1s v5p0347c2s
v5p0459c2s v6p0304c1s v6p0359c1s
v6p0389c2m v6p0391c1s v6p0472c1s
v6p0631c1s v6p0658c1s v6p0672c2s
Hulbert, W.H. v2p0089c1s
Hulburd, C.T. v1p1389c1s
Hulbut, H.W. v3p0129c1s
Hulerich, C.H. v6p0676c1s
Huling, Caroline A. v6p0621c2s
Huling, E.P. v6p0280c1s
Huling, Ellen P. v6p0562c2s
Huling, J.B. v1p0149c1s
Huling, R.G. v2p0030c2s
v2p0191c2s v2p0470c2s v3p0195c2m
v3p0203c2s v3p0360c2s v4p0086c2s
v4p0188c2s v4p0234c1s v4p0257c1s
v4p0259c1s v4p0398c2m v4p0627c2s
v5p0264c2s v5p0405c2m v5p0569c2m
v6p0291c1s
Huling, R.G. and Schurman, J.G.
v4p0512c1s
Huling, R.G. et al. v4p0512c2s
v5p0265c1s
Hulk, A.H. v2p0202c2s
Hull, A.J. v6p0484c1s
Hull, A.L. v1p1124c1s
Hull, C.H. v3p0044c2s
v3p0070c1m v3p0136c1s v3p0178c2s
v3p0348c1s v3p0397c2s v3p0421c1s
v4p0224c2s v4p0235c1s v4p0336c2s
v4p0437c2m v4p0497c1s v4p0565c1s
v5p0442c2s v5p0563c1s v6p0696c1s
Hull, E. v1p0103c2s
v1p0332c1s v1p0344c2s v1p0558c2s
v1p0615c1s v2p0090c1s v2p0090c2m
v2p0127c2s v2p0229c1s v2p0252c1s
v2p0434c1s v2p0467c2s v2p0468c1s
v5p0153c1s v5p0417c2s
Hull, E.R. v4p0112c1s
v4p0351c1s v5p0278c1s
Hull, Eleanor v5p0296c2s
v6p0169c1s
Hull, F.P. v5p0624c2s
Hull, G.H. v4p0291c2s
v5p0298c1m v5p0451c1s v6p0472c2s
Hull, G.H.S. v2p0101c1s
v2p0118c2s v2p0325c1s
Hull, G.S. v1p0735c1s
v6p0290c1s
Hull, J. v3p0222c2m
Hull, J.A.T. v5p0599c1m
Hull, J.H. v3p0349c1s
Hull, L.C. v4p0033c2s
v5p0512c2s v6p0207c1s v6p0363c1s
Hull, N.V. v1p1139c1s
Hull, S.E. v1p0337c1s
Hull, W. v1p0257c2s
v1p0258c2s v1p0280c1s v1p0373c1s
v1p0435c1s v1p0572c2s v1p0581c1s
v1p0687c2s v1p0778c1m v1p0848c1s
v1p0945c2s v1p1064c2s v1p1070c2s
v2p0061c1s v2p0120c1s v2p0136c1s
v2p0269c1s v2p0277c1s v2p0304c1s
v2p0447c2s v3p0139c2s v3p0240c1s
v3p0441c2s v4p0057c1s v4p0249c1s
v4p0372c2s v4p0550c2s v5p0234c1s
v5p0350c2s
Hull, W.E. v2p0292c1s
v4p0249c1s v4p0456c1s v5p0202c1s
Hull, W.I. v5p0107c2s
v5p0230c1s
Hullah, J. v1p0397c2s
v1p0527c1s v1p0584c1s v1p0834c1s
v1p0885c1s v1p1220c1s v1p1376c2s
Hullah, M.E. v2p0045c2s
v2p0168c2s v3p0192c1s
Hulley, L. v6p0192c2s
v6p0390c1s
Hulme, E. v1p1014c2s
Hulme, E.W. v4p0228c1s
v4p0430c1s v5p0435c1m v6p0483c2s
Hulme, F.E. v1p0949c1m
v3p0051c2s v3p0216c2s v3p0314c2s
v3p0422c1s
Hulme, W.H. v6p0069c2s
Hulme, W.R. v6p0542c1s
Hulme-Beaman, A. v3p0050c2s
v3p0059c2s v3p0262c2s v3p0286c2s
v3p0385c2s
Hulme-Reaman, E. v6p0395c2s
Hulner, J. v6p0478c2s
Hulst, N.P. v4p0292c1s
Hulton, Costanza v6p0353c2s
Humber, H. v1p0200c2s
Humbert, A.C. v5p0007c2s
v5p0081c2s v5p0448c1s
Humboldt, A. v1p0375c1s
v1p0579c2s v1p0668c2s v1p1377c2s
Humboldt, A.von v1p0029c2s
v1p0199c2s v1p0377c1s v1p0532c2s
v1p0725c2s
Hume and Nasmyth v1p0997c2s
Hume, A. v5p0366c1s
Hume, B. v5p0411c1s
Hume, D. v1p0558c1s
Hume, E. v6p0600c2s
Hume, F. v3p0345c1s
v4p0242c2s v4p0295c2s v4p0299c2s
v4p0473c1s
Hume, F.C. v5p0562c2s
Hume, J. v1p0791c1s
Hume, J.C. v5p0497c1s
Hume, J.F. v1p0698c1s
v1p1100c1s v1p1245c1s v2p0110c1s
v2p0224c1s v2p0370c2m v2p0413c2s
v2p0420c2s v3p0253c1s v4p0424c2s
v4p0514c2s v4p0526c2s v4p0593c1s
v4p0623c1s
Hume, M. v5p0236c2s
v5p0330c1s v5p0543c1m v6p0200c2s
Hume, M.A.S. v3p0039c1s
v4p0051c2s v4p0097c2s v4p0164c2s
v4p0181c2s v4p0435c1s v4p0438c2m
v4p0539c2s v5p0219c2s v6p0488c2s
v6p0608c1s
Hume, Martin A.S. v5p0355c1s
Hume, W.F. v4p0041c2s
v4p0196c1s v4p0204c2s v4p0410c2s
v5p0414c1s v6p0457c2s
Hume, W.H. v2p0165c1s
Humes, A.L. v6p0324c2s
Hummel, J.J. v3p0125c1s
Humpal-Zeman, J., Mrs. ... v4p0268c2s
Humphrey, A. v3p0095c2s
Humphrey, A.P. v2p0092c2s
v5p0104c1s
Humphrey, C.A. v1p0253c2s
Humphrey, E.P. v2p0299c2s
v2p0352c2s
Humphrey, E.P. and McGill, A.T.
v1p1046c1s
Humphrey, F.P. v3p0102c2s
v4p0019c1s v4p0126c2s
v4p0251c2s
Humphrey, G.H. v2p0279c1s
Humphrey, G.R. v2p0256c2s
v4p0474c2s
Humphrey, H. v1p0005c2s
v1p0034c2s v1p0119c2s v1p0148c1s
v1p0393c1s v1p0522c2s v1p0847c1s
v1p0878c2s v1p1064c1s v1p1158c1s
v1p1395c2s v1p1428c1s
Humphrey, H.A. v6p0248c1s
Humphrey, H.P. v6p0595c1s
Humphrey, H.T. v3p0146c1s
Humphrey, J.E. v4p0043c2s
v4p0069c2s v4p0094c1s v4p0217c2s
v5p0150c1s
Humphrey, L.M. v1p0792c2s
Humphrey, Mary v6p0113c2s
Humphrey, Mrs. v4p0185c1s
v4p0189c1s
Humphrey, O.M. v4p0153c1s
Humphrey, R.L. v5p0099c1s

v6p0106c2s
Humphrey, W. v2p0180c2s
v2p0205c2s v2p0235c1s v2p0277c1s
v2p0354c1s v2p0382c2m v3p0083c2s
v3p0147c1s v3p0210c1s v3p0210c2s
v3p0229c1s v3p0258c2s v3p0274c2s
v3p0435c1s v4p0129c2s v5p0494c1s
Humphrey, W.E. v6p0591c2s
Humphrey, Z.M. v1p0099c1s
v1p1210c2s
Humphreys, A.A. v1p0615c1s
v1p0814c2s
Humphreys, A.A. and Abbot, H.L.
v1p0854c2s
Humphreys, A.C. v6p0204c1m
Humphreys, A.L. v3p0190c2s
v4p0316c2s
Humphreys, A.W. v1p0664c2s
Humphreys, B.G. v1p0485c2s
v2p0166c2s
Humphreys, C.A. v2p0267c2s
Humphreys, C.J.R. v4p0175c1s
v4p0220c2m
Humphreys, D. v2p0228c2s
Humphreys, E.B. v1p0415c2s
Humphreys, E.R. v1p0057c2s
v1p0262c1s v1p0556c1s v1p0999c1s
v3p0243c2s
Humphreys, F.L. v6p0299c2s
Humphreys, G.E. v2p0239c2s
Humphreys, G.E. and Falle, B.
v2p0130c1s
Humphreys, H.N. v1p0107c1m
v1p0108c2m v1p0272c1m v1p0272c2m
v1p0323c1s v1p0463c2s v1p0645c1s
v1p0692c1s v1p0815c2s v1p0875c1m
v1p0922c1s v1p1014c2s v1p1016c1s
v1p1037c1s v1p1108c2s
Humphreys, J. v1p0271c2s
v1p0488c1s v1p0510c2s v1p0707c2s
v1p1217c1s v3p0034c2s v3p0140c2s
v4p0228c1s v5p0067c2s v6p0011c1s
Humphreys, J.T.C. v2p0226c2m
v4p0289c1s
Humphreys, Jennett and Skeat, W.W.
v4p0098c1s
Humphreys, L.G. v3p0271c1s
Humphreys, M.G. v2p0114c2s
v2p0315c2s v2p0447c2s v3p0242c1s
v3p0396c2s v4p0210c2s v4p0630c2m
v5p0015c1s v5p0230c1s v5p0303c1s
v5p0303c2s v5p0584c2s v6p0536c1s
Humphreys, M.L. v1p0397c2s
Humphreys, M.W. v3p0006c1s
Humphreys, Mary G. v4p0632c2s
v6p0300c2s
Humphreys, N.A. v1p0338c2s
v2p0257c2s v2p0299c1s v3p0137c2s
v3p0216c2s v3p0288c2s
Humphreys, N.A. and Milnes, A.
v5p0533c1s
Humphreys, P.W. v6p0249c1s
v6p0496c2s
Humphreys, W.M. v2p0148c1s
Humphries, H.H. v5p0460c1s
Humphris, D.J. v3p0386c2s
Humphry, H.M. v2p0247c2s
Humphry, H.P. v6p0163c1s
Humphry, Mrs. v3p0111c2s
v3p0257c2s v4p0058c2s
Humphry, Prof. v3p0072c1s
Humphry, W.G. v1p0118c2s
v1p0126c1s v1p0239c2s v1p0503c1s
v1p0644c2s v1p0978c1s
Humpidge, T.S. v2p0284c2s
Humpstone, J. v6p0341c2s
Hundley, D.R. v1p0284c1s
v1p0298c1s
Huneker, J. v5p0114c1s
v5p0393c1s v5p0615c2s v6p0283c1s
v6p0305c2s v6p0394c2s v6p0405c1s
v6p0620c2s v6p0622c1s v6p0630c1s
Huneker, J.G. v5p0361c1s
v5p0616c1s
Hungerford, E. v1p0173c1s
v1p0523c2s v1p0556c2s v2p0018c1s
v2p0131c2s v2p0213c2s v2p0261c2s
v2p0266c1s v2p0351c2s v2p0386c1s
v2p0390c2s v2p0406c2s v2p0415c1s
v3p0016c2s v3p0084c1s v3p0341c2s
v3p0415c1s
Hungerford, J. v1p0737c2s
v1p1045c2s
Hungerford, M.C. v2p0197c2s
v4p0516c1s
Hungerford, M.H., Mrs. ... v4p0598c2s
Hungerford, Mrs. v3p0412c1s
v4p0437c1s v4p0453c2s
Hungerford, S.S. v1p0154c1s
Hungerford, T. v5p0250c1s
v5p0285c2s
Hunking, A.W. and Hart, F.S.
v2p0470c1s
Hunner, G.L. v6p0390c1s
Hunnewell, F.A. v6p0669c1s
Hunnewell, H.H. v4p0483c2s
v4p0616c2s
Hunnewell, J.F. v1p0221c1m
v3p0074c2s v5p0276c1s
Hunnybun, W.M. v4p0190c1s
Hunt, A. v1p0788c1s
v5p0623c1s
Hunt, A.E. v4p0012c2s
v4p0177c1s v5p0014c1s v5p0392c2s
Hunt, A.F. v1p0105c1s
v1p0538c2s v1p1012c2s
Hunt, A.H. v6p0498c2s
Hunt, A.R. v2p0393c2s
v6p0351c1s v6p0653c1s
Hunt, A.S. and Grenfel, B.P.
v5p0430c1s
Hunt, A.W. v1p0958c2s
v1p1333c2s v3p0242c1s v3p0438c2s
Hunt, A.W., Mrs. v1p0732c1s
v3p0240c1s v4p0386c2s
Hunt, Alice K. v5p0343c2s
Hunt, B.G. v5p0092c1s
v5p0373c1s
Hunt, B.P. v1p0676c1s
Hunt, C.J. v6p0496c1s
Hunt, C.L. v5p0106c2s
v6p0055c2s v6p0178c2s v6p0212c1s
v6p0376c1m v6p0381c1s v6p0498c1s
v6p0703c1s
Hunt, C.W. v5p0334c2s
v6p0116c2s v6p0370c2s v6p0371c2m
Hunt, C.W. and Moore, E.L.
v5p0335c1s
Hunt, Clara W. v6p0116c2s
Hunt, D. v2p0282c1s
Hunt, D.R.C. v6p0356c1s
Hunt, E. v1p1342c1s
Hunt, E.B. v1p0030c2s
v1p0271c2s v1p0326c2s v1p0461c2s
v1p0462c1s v1p0467c1s v1p0628c1s
v1p0641c2s v1p0706c2s v1p0747c1s
v1p0798c2s v1p0917c2s v1p0936c2s
v1p0947c2s v1p0989c1s v1p1164c1s
v1p1222c2s v1p1386c1s v6p0076c2s
Hunt, E.M. v1p0902c2s
v1p1401c2s v2p0198c2s v2p0382c1s
v4p0122c2s
Hunt, Eleanor v6p0441c2s
Hunt, F. v1p0035c1s
v1p0092c1s v1p0180c1m v1p0220c2s
v1p0269c2m v1p0282c2s v1p0283c2m
v1p0339c1s v1p0474c1s v1p0968c1s
v1p1245c1s v1p1249c1s v1p1429c1s
v2p0146c1s
Hunt, F.A. v6p0013c1s
v6p0029c1s v6p0381c2s v6p0531c2s
Hunt, F.J. v6p0154c1s
Hunt, F.L. v1p0195c1s
Hunt, F.W. v6p0011c1s
v6p0571c1s
Hunt, Fred A. v6p0598c2s
Hunt, G. v3p0308c2s
v3p0326c1s v3p0402c1s v4p0403c1s
v4p0411c1s v4p0611c2s v5p0003c2s
v5p0134c2s v5p0355c1s v5p0418c1m
v6p0128c1s v6p0146c2s v6p0248c1s
v6p0312c1s v6p0444c1s
Hunt, G.E. v6p0316c1s
v6p0554c2s
Hunt, G.H. v2p0344c2s
Hunt, G.P. and Skeel, T. . v1p1249c1s
Hunt, H. v1p0430c1s
v1p0502c2s v2p0479c1s
Hunt, H.E. v5p0105c2s
Hunt, H.J. v2p0177c2m
v3p0172c1s v5p0032c2s
Hunt, J. v1p0045c1s
v1p0045c2m v1p0118c2s v1p0157c1s
v1p0180c2s v1p0207c2s v1p0241c2s
v1p0242c2s v1p0277c1s v1p0312c1s
v1p0419c1s v1p0481c2s v1p0515c1s
v1p0586c2s v1p0595c2s v1p0614c1m
v1p0912c1s v1p0940c1s v1p1058c2s
v1p1067c2s v1p1083c2s v1p1100c1s
v1p1109c2s v1p1115c2s v1p1182c2s
v1p1303c1s v1p1304c1m v1p1312c2s
v1p1314c2s v2p0084c2s v2p0104c2s
v2p0153c1s
Hunt, J., jr. v1p0297c2s
Hunt, J.G. v1p1012c1s
Hunt, J.H.L. v1p0418c2s
v1p1328c1s v1p1417c1s
Hunt, L. v1p0057c1s
v1p0219c2s v1p0497c2s v1p0520c2s
v1p0531c2s v1p0751c1s v1p0796c1s
v1p0934c2s v1p1191c1s v1p1202c1s
v1p1247c2s v1p1282c2s v1p1317c1s
v1p1326c1s v1p1417c1s v1p1440c2s
v2p0316c1s v4p0335c1s v5p0079c2s
v6p0107c2s
Hunt, L.B. v6p0183c1m
v6p0706c2s
Hunt, L.L. v2p0296c1s
Hunt, L.R. v5p0177c1s
Hunt, Leigh v1p0008c2s
Hunt, M. v1p0753c2s
v1p0870c1s v1p1108c1s v2p0008c2s
v2p0055c1s v2p0075c2s v2p0242c1s
v2p0275c2s v2p0323c2s v2p0379c1s
v2p0401c2s v2p0443c2s v2p0448c1s
v3p0025c1s v3p0031c2s v3p0034c1s
v3p0052c1s v3p0122c2m v3p0130c2s
v3p0251c2s v3p0293c2s v3p0355c1s
v3p0363c2s v3p0386c2s v3p0416c2s
v3p0436c1s v4p0200c2s v4p0213c2s
v4p0235c1s v4p0325c1s v4p0375c2s
v4p0386c2s v4p0584c1s v4p0598c2s
v5p0504c2s v6p0024c2s v6p0028c2m
Hunt, M.H. v4p0568c1s
v5p0571c2m v6p0637c2s
Hunt, Margaret v2p0466c1s
v2p0472c1s v4p0343c1s
Hunt, R. v1p0070c2s
v1p0267c2s v1p0268c1s v1p0278c2s
v1p0401c1s v1p0401c2s v1p0463c2s
v1p0508c1s v1p0547c1s v1p0619c1s
v1p0621c2s v1p0663c1s v1p0746c2m
v1p0747c1s v1p0747c2s v1p0786c2s
v1p0813c1s v1p0845c2m v1p1003c2s
v1p1014c2s v1p1213c2s v1p1244c1s
v1p1267c2s v1p1268c1s v1p1291c1s
v2p0090c2s v2p0181c2s v2p0229c2s
v3p0280c1s v3p0409c1s v4p0047c2s
v5p0401c1s
Hunt, R.D. v4p0083c2s
v5p0088c1s v5p0605c1s v6p0242c1s
v6p0557c2s
Hunt, R.M. v1p0052c2s
Hunt, R.W. v1p0116c1s
v1p1250c2s v3p0409c1s v4p0624c2s
v5p0298c1s v5p0353c2s v5p0368c2s
v5p0478c1s v6p0325c1s
Hunt, S. v1p0994c1s
v2p0199c2s v3p0276c2m
Hunt, S.B. v1p0155c2s
v1p0237c2s v1p0282c1s v1p0338c1s
v1p0351c2s v1p0816c2s v1p0904c2s
v1p1209c1s v1p1319c2s
Hunt, S.F. et al. v5p0592c1s
Hunt, S.P. v6p0004c2s
Hunt, T. v1p0571c1s
v1p0714c2s v1p0773c2s v1p1083c1s
v1p1189c1s v2p0289c2s v2p0371c2s
v3p0377c1s
Hunt, T.H. v5p0546c1s
Hunt, T.J.de la v4p0035c2s
Hunt, T.S. v1p0025c1s
v1p0035c1s v1p0048c1s v1p0073c2s
v1p0139c1s v1p0158c2s v1p0190c1s
v1p0193c1s v1p0224c1m v1p0224c2s
v1p0225c1s v1p0225c2m v1p0228c1s
v1p0299c2s v1p0375c1s v1p0507c2s
v1p0508c1m v1p0508c2s v1p0509c1s
v1p0509c2m v1p0540c1s v1p0619c1s
v1p0665c1s v1p0750c1s v1p0809c1s
v1p0826c1m v1p0844c1s v1p0844c2s
v1p0845c1s v1p0855c1s v1p0909c2s
v1p0939c1s v1p0943c2s v1p1112c2m
v1p1113c1m v1p1147c1s v1p1367c2s
v1p1376c2s v1p1389c2s v1p1391c1s
v2p0006c2s v2p0009c1s v2p0072c1s
v2p0076c2s v2p0108c2s v2p0174c1s
v2p0307c1s v2p0374c1s v2p0390c2s
v3p0075c2s v3p0419c1s
Hunt, T.S. and Logan, W.E.
v1p0751c1s
Hunt, T.W. v1p0040c1s
v1p0426c2s v2p0003c2s v2p0119c1s
v2p0144c1m v2p0144c2m v2p0414c1s
v3p0020c2s v3p0040c2s v3p0106c1s
v3p0122c1s v3p0140c1s v3p0141c1s
v3p0144c1s v3p0329c2s v3p0342c1s
v4p0075c2s v4p0183c2s v4p0343c2s
v4p0619c2s v4p0632c1s v5p0030c1s
v5p0125c2s v5p0314c1s v5p0341c2s
v5p0463c2s v5p0569c1s v5p0573c1m
v6p0208c2m v6p0211c2s v6p0379c2s
Hunt, V. v4p0051c1s
v4p0179c2s v4p0570c2s v5p0266c1s
Hunt, W. v1p0411c1s
v4p0181c1s v6p0292c2s
Hunt, W.E. v2p0303c2s
v4p0203c1s v5p0419c2s
Hunt, W.F. and Kraus, E.H.
v6p0624c2s
Hunt, W.G. v1p0093c2s
v1p0265c2s
Hunt, W.G.F. v5p0369c2s
v5p0467c1s
Hunt, W.H. v1p0066c1s
v1p0300c2s v2p0352c2s v3p0023c1s
v3p0229c1s v3p0246c1m v3p0376c2s
v4p0161c1s v5p0107c2s v5p0153c1s
v5p0253c2s v5p0460c1s v6p0510c1s
v6p0598c2s
Hunt, W.Holman v3p0021c2s
v5p0483c1s
Hunt, W.S. v4p0274c2s
v4p0293c1s
Hunt, W.W. v4p0082c1s
v4p0110c1s v4p0173c1s v4p0338c1s
v4p0491c1s
Hunt, Wray W. v5p0197c1s
Hunter, A. v1p0328c1s
v1p0354c2s v1p0365c1s v1p0407c1s
v1p0628c2s v1p0826c1s v2p0091c1s
v2p0399c1s v3p0053c2s v3p0099c1s
v3p0205c1s v3p0405c1s v4p0110c1s
v4p0157c1s v5p0601c2s v6p0482c1s
Hunter, A.F. v4p0610c1s
Hunter, A.S. v5p0606c2s
Hunter, A.T. v5p0375c1s
v5p0614c2s v6p0681c2s
Hunter, Alex. v6p0132c1s
Hunter, Anna F. v5p0509c2s

Hunter, C.H. ... v5p0033c1s
Hunter, C.L. ... v1p0927c2s
Hunter, D. ... v5p0576c1s v6p0045c2s v6p0387c2s
Hunter, Dulany ... v5p0589c2s v6p0163c2s v6p0340c1s v6p0492c1s
Hunter, E. ... v6p0416c2s
Hunter, F.M. ... v1p1217c2s
Hunter, G.L. ... v6p0244c2s v6p0554c1s v6p0554c2s
Hunter, G.M. ... v3p0368c1s
Hunter, H. ... v3p0037c2s v3p0339c1s v3p0381c2s
Hunter, H.C. ... v5p0317c2s
Hunter, H.E. ... v2p0110c1s
Hunter, J. ... v1p0107c1s v1p0110c2s v1p0190c1s v1p0223c1s v1p0398c1s v1p0563c1s v1p0667c2s v1p0760c1s v1p0779c2s v1p0807c1s v1p0965c2s v1p1114c1s v1p1130c1s v1p1375c1s v1p1402c2s v2p0068c2s v4p0612c1s v6p0332c1s
Hunter, J.H. ... v1p0142c1s v2p0166c2s
Hunter, J.R. ... v4p0043c1s v6p0604c2s
Hunter, J.T. ... v3p0068c2s
Hunter, K.D. ... v6p0236c2s v6p0241c2s
Hunter, K.M. ... v5p0453c1s
Hunter, M.S. ... v4p0027c2s
Hunter, M.T. ... v5p0276c1s v6p0303c2s
Hunter, M.Van B. ... v6p0694c2s
Hunter, Mrs. ... v3p0309c1s
Hunter, P.H. ... v4p0303c1s
Hunter, P.S. ... v2p0047c1s
Hunter, R. ... v2p0034c2s v2p0075c2s v2p0096c2s v2p0216c2s v2p0263c1s v2p0330c1s v3p0073c2s v3p0255c2s v3p0256c2s v4p0333c1s v5p0134c2s v5p0190c2s v5p0421c2s v5p0425c2s v6p0115c1s v6p0153c2s v6p0277c2s v6p0347c2s v6p0585c1s v6p0619c1s v6p0651c2s v6p0702c2s
Hunter, R., Sir ... v6p0228c1s v6p0375c1s
Hunter, R.M.T. ... v1p1345c2s v1p1346c1m v1p1388c1s v2p0370c2s v2p0405c2s
Hunter, R.S. ... v1p0089c2s
Hunter, R.V. ... v4p0111c2s
Hunter, Robert ... v6p0117c1m
Hunter, S.J. ... v6p0021c1s v6p0290c2s
Hunter, T. ... v2p0315c2s
Hunter, T. et al. ... v2p0132c1s
Hunter, W. ... v1p0209c1s v5p0346c2s v5p0622c2s v6p0314c2s
Hunter, W., Sir ... v3p0212c2s
Hunter, W.A. ... v1p0559c1s v1p0714c1s v1p1031c1s v4p0237c2s v4p0418c2s v4p0472c2s v4p0566c1s
Hunter, W.H. ... v5p0410c2s v5p0429c1s v5p0526c1m
Hunter, W.R. ... v5p0105c1s
Hunter, W.W. ... v1p0629c1s v1p1081c1s v2p0203c1s v3p0020c2s v3p0027c1s v3p0210c2s v3p0211c2m v3p0212c1m v3p0311c2s v4p0280c2s v6p0315c1s
Hunter, W.W. and Lockyer, J.N. v1p0443c1s v1p1269c1s
Hunter, W.W. et al. ... v3p0130c1s
Hunter, W.W., Sir ... v3p0204c1s v3p0212c2s v3p0283c1s v3p0358c1s v4p0280c1s
Hunter-Blair, D., Sir ... v5p0586c1s
Hunter-Blair, D.O. ... v6p0548c1s
Hunter-Blair, O. ... v3p0114c1s
Hunting, H.G. ... v6p0629c1s
Hunting, J.D. ... v3p0415c1s v3p0431c2s v4p0160c2s v4p0304c2s
Hunting, W. ... v5p0594c1s
Huntingford, E.W. ... v5p0076c1s v5p0156c1s
Huntington, A.J. ... v1p0072c1s v1p0075c2s
Huntington, A.K. ... v1p1251c1s
Huntington, A.M. ... v4p0114c1s v5p0038c1s v5p0224c1s v5p0495c2s
Huntington, A.O. ... v6p0225c1s v6p0500c1s
Huntington, A.T. ... v6p0084c1s
Huntington, Agnes ... v6p0502c2s
Huntington, C. ... v1p0568c1s
Huntington, C.A. ... v4p0282c2s
Huntington, C.M. ... v4p0297c2s v4p0305c1s v4p0626c2s
Huntington, C.P. ... v1p0956c2s v3p0352c1s v3p0395c1s
Huntington, D. ... v1p0417c1s
Huntington, D.F. ... v1p0821c1s
Huntington, D.W. ... v5p0473c2s v6p0223c2s
Huntington, D.W. and Black, A. v3p0330c2s
Huntington, Dwight W. ... v6p0275c1s
Huntington, E. ... v6p0212c2m v6p0544c2s v6p0596c1s v6p0645c2s v6p0661c1s
Huntington, E.A. ... v1p0119c1s v6p0492c1s
Huntington, E.M. ... v1p0939c1s
Huntington, E.S. ... v3p0429c2s
Huntington, Ellsworth ... v6p0349c2s
Huntington, F.C. ... v3p0256c1s
Huntington, F.D. ... v1p0007c1s v1p0043c2s v1p0054c2s v1p0229c2s v1p0239c1s v1p0254c2s v1p0275c2s v1p0360c2s v1p0493c1s v1p0500c1s v1p0620c1s v1p0676c2s v1p0697c2s v1p0714c2s v1p0754c1s v1p0807c2s v1p0915c1s v1p0931c2s v1p0960c2s v1p0987c2s v1p1009c1s v1p1042c2s v1p1104c1s v1p1132c1s v1p1175c2s v1p1236c2s v1p1272c1s v1p1288c2s v1p1425c1s v2p0131c2s v2p0225c1s v2p0245c1s v2p0348c1s v2p0360c1s v3p0128c1s v3p0245c1s v3p0397c2m v3p0399c1s v4p0136c2s v4p0553c2s
Huntington, F.D. et al. .. v3p0084c1s v3p0217c2s
Huntington, G. ... v2p0198c1s v2p0439c1s v3p0083c1s v3p0162c1s v3p0200c1s v3p0245c2s v3p0266c1s v3p0298c1s v3p0463c2s v4p0139c2s
Huntington, G.S. ... v5p0018c2s v5p0387c2s
Huntington, H. ... v4p0296c2s v5p0435c1s
Huntington, H.A. ... v1p0256c1s v1p0610c1s v1p0676c2s v1p1019c2s v2p0073c1s v2p0153c1s
Huntington, H.F. ... v4p0360c1s v5p0151c1s v5p0230c1s
Huntington, H.G. ... v5p0458c1s
Huntington, H.L. ... v6p0390c1s
Huntington, H.S. ... v1p0648c2s v1p1157c2s
Huntington, H.W. ... v5p0073c1s v5p0083c1m v5p0127c2s v5p0164c2m v5p0502c2s v5p0634c2s
Huntington, Harriet L. ... v6p0701c2s
Huntington, Helen F. ... v5p0096c2s v5p0282c2s v5p0355c1s v5p0356c1s v5p0423c1s
Huntington, J. ... v1p0024c1s v1p0617c1s v2p0342c1s
Huntington, J.H. ... v2p0102c1s
Huntington, J.O.S. ... v3p0424c1s v4p0438c2s
Huntington, J.T. ... v2p0145c2s v2p0434c1s
Huntington, J.V. ... v2p0107c2s
Huntington, M.C. ... v5p0024c1s v5p0378c1s v5p0644c1s v6p0036c1s v6p0448c2s
Huntington, O.W. ... v2p0108c2s v3p0276c1m
Huntington, O.W. and Kunz, G.F. v4p0089c1s v4p0154c2s
Huntington, S. ... v1p1329c2s
Huntington, T.F. ... v4p0122c2s v4p0354c1s v5p0081c2s v5p0192c1s v5p0193c1s v5p0256c1s v6p0366c2s
Huntington, T.H. ... v5p0167c2s
Huntington, W.H. ... v5p0574c1s
Huntington, W.R. ... v1p0284c2s v2p0096c2s v3p0094c2s
Huntley, G.N. ... v3p0192c2s
Huntley, H.V. ... v1p0498c2s
Huntley, Marquis of ... v2p0129c1s
Hunton, C.H. ... v4p0072c1s v4p0517c2s
Huntoon, B.B. ... v2p0049c2s
Huntoon, D.Y.V. ... v3p0279c2s
Huntsman, Mary F. ... v6p0706c2s
Hupfeld, Dr. ... v1p0977c2s
Hupfeld, H. ... v1p1027c2s v1p1234c2m
Hurd, A. ... v6p0020c2s v6p0181c2s
Hurd, A.D. ... v4p0155c1s
Hurd, A.S. ... v5p0077c1s v5p0077c2s v5p0086c2s v5p0124c1s v5p0206c2s v5p0245c1s v5p0246c2m v5p0401c1s v5p0557c1s v5p0588c2s v6p0054c1s v6p0101c2s v6p0172c2s v6p0204c1s v6p0237c2s v6p0254c2m v6p0267c2s v6p0268c1m v6p0268c2m v6p0269c1m v6p0334c1s v6p0336c1m v6p0337c1s v6p0445c1m v6p0529c2s v6p0530c1s v6p0556c1s v6p0557c2m v6p0560c2s v6p0580c1m v6p0623c1m v6p0650c1s v6p0654c1s v6p0661c1s v6p0668c2s v6p0685c2s v6p0686c1m v6p0699c1s
Hurd, A.S. and Robertson, E. v5p0368c2s
Hurd, A.S. and White, A. . v6p0555c2s
Hurd, Annie G. ... v5p0566c1s
Hurd, C.E. ... v1p0914c1s v3p0021c2s v3p0101c2s v3p0208c2s v5p0382c1s v5p0443c1s
Hurd, C.E. and Chamberlin, J.E. v3p0167c1s
Hurd, C.O. ... v2p0345c2s
Hurd, E. ... v1p1285c1s
Hurd, F.H. ... v4p0283c2s
Hurd, H.B. ... v3p0241c2s v6p0348c2s
Hurd, H.M. ... v5p0271c2s v6p0408c2s
Hurd, J.C. ... v1p0109c1s v1p0294c2s v1p0808c2s v1p1245c1s v1p1267c1s
Hurd, P.A. ... v4p0133c1s v4p0182c2s v4p0402c1s
Hurd, P.C. ... v4p0402c1s
Hurd, P.H. ... v5p0245c2s
Hurd, P.R. ... v2p0081c1s v2p0099c2s
Hurd, R.M. ... v3p0048c1s v3p0474c1s v6p0128c1m
Hurd, W. and Poole, E. ... v6p0621c1s
Hurkson, H.A. ... v5p0350c1s
Hurlbert, G.C. ... v3p0318c2s
Hurlbert, H.W. ... v2p0214c2s
Hurlbert, W.H. ... v2p0165c2s v2p0231c1s v2p0349c1s v2p0454c2s v3p0066c1s v3p0161c1s v3p0161c2s v3p0355c2s
Hurlburt, A.C. ... v4p0348c2s
Hurlburt, B.S. ... v3p0140c1s
Hurlburt, E.B. ... v4p0012c2s
Hurlburt, E.B. and Wells, H.L. v4p0016c1s
Hurlburt, T. ... v1p0793c1s
Hurlbut, B.S. ... v4p0183c2s
Hurlbut, E.A. ... v6p0683c1s
Hurlbut, E.J. ... v6p0706c2s
Hurlbut, E.W. ... v6p0555c1s
Hurlbut, G.C. ... v1p0697c1s v1p0896c1s
Hurlbut, H.H. ... v2p0250c1m v3p0245c2s
Hurlbut, H.W. ... v1p1230c2s
Hurlbut, J.L. ... v5p0253c1s
Hurlbut, M.L. ... v1p0002c2s v1p0433c2s v1p0805c2s v1p0848c1s v1p1168c1s
Hurlbut, S.A. ... v1p0376c1s
Hurlbut, W.H. ... v1p0099c2s v1p0142c1s v1p0477c1s v1p0489c1s v1p0556c1s v1p0583c1s v1p0623c1s v1p0709c1s v1p0774c2s v1p1022c2s v1p1212c1s
Hurley, E.G. ... v6p0501c2m
Hurley, P. ... v4p0291c1s v4p0411c2s
Hurley, T.D. ... v5p0102c1s v6p0348c2s
Hurlin, W. ... v1p0038c2s v1p0764c1s v1p0853c1s v1p0979c2s v2p0263c1s v3p0256c2s
Hurling, R.G. ... v2p0466c1s
Hurll, E.M. ... v4p0085c1s v5p0450c2s v6p0114c1s v6p0499c1s
Hurll, E.M. and Carson, H. v4p0335c2s
Hurll, M.M. ... v5p0402c2s
Hurlston, A. ... v2p0422c1s
Hurrell, J.D. ... v3p0362c1s
Hurry, A. ... v5p0155c2s
Hurst, Ben ... v6p0008c1s v6p0159c1s v6p0584c2s v6p0622c1s
Hurst, C. ... v6p0615c2m
Hurst, C.C. ... v5p0423c1s
Hurst, C.H. ... v4p0023c1s v4p0255c1s v4p0255c2s v4p0326c2s
Hurst, G. ... v2p0037c2m v2p0061c1s
Hurst, G.H.J. ... v5p0366c1s
Hurst, G.P. ... v4p0577c1s v5p0203c2s
Hurst, H. ... v1p1292c1s
Hurst, H.S. ... v1p0433c1s
Hurst, J.F. ... v1p0113c2s v1p0166c1s v1p0254c1s v1p0290c2s v1p0432c1s v1p0772c1s v1p0890c1s v1p1177c1s v1p1303c1s v1p1306c1s v1p1357c1s v2p0331c2s v2p0336c1s v3p0008c2s v3p0025c2s v3p0030c2s v3p0035c2s v3p0062c2s v3p0176c1s v3p0195c2s v3p0196c2s v3p0205c2s v3p0211c2s v3p0212c1m v3p0213c1s v3p0237c1s v3p0283c1s v3p0284c1s v3p0313c1s v3p0374c1s v3p0423c2s v3p0432c1s v4p0097c2s v4p0113c1s v5p0117c1s v5p0132c1s v5p0139c2s v5p0630c1s
Hurst, J.L. ... v4p0309c1s v4p0502c1s v4p0520c1s v5p0092c1s v5p0331c1s
Hurst, J.R. ... v1p0597c2s
Hurton, W. ... v1p0037c1s
Hurtubis, F., jr. ... v5p0634c2s
Hurtzig, A.C. ... v2p0342c1s
Hurwitz, H. ... v2p0237c1s
Hus, H. v6p0682c1s
Husband, E.B. ... v5p0068c1s v5p0246c1s v5p0587c1s v6p0271c1s
Husband, M.G. ... v5p0446c2s
Husband, Mary G. ... v4p0164c1s
Husband, T.F. ... v4p0506c2s
Huse, C.E. ... v3p0311c1s v4p0035c1s
Huse, Carolyn E. ... v5p0394c2s

Huse, H.A. v5p0384c2s
Huse, H.P. v4p0203c1s
v5p0508c2s
Husik, I. v6p0029c2m
v6p0147c1s
Huskison, F. v3p0185c1s
Huson, W.H. v4p0382c1s
v4p0531c1s
Huss, G.M. v5p0273c2s
Hussain, Mushtak v4p0376c2s
Hussey, C. v4p0469c2s
Hussey, C.C. v4p0621c1s
Hussey, E.F. v6p0375c2s
Hussey, Ethel F. v6p0188c1m
Hussey, G.B. v3p0106c2s
v3p0193c2s v3p0334c2s v4p0446c2s
Hussey, J. v1p0079c1s
Hussey, Lizzie T. v5p0178c1s
Hussey, S.M. v3p0220c2m
Hussey, T.W.H. v2p0306c1s
Hussey, W.J. v4p0126c2m
v5p0129c2s v5p0549c1s
Husson, M. v1p0969c1s
Hussy, A. v6p0221c1s
Huston, C. v1p0146c2s
v1p0664c2s
Huston, C.W. v1p1186c1s
Huston, P.G. v6p0233c1s
Hutcher, J.B. v4p0577c2s
Hutcheson, D. v2p0112c2s
Hutcheson, J.C. v1p0029c2s
v1p0032c2s v1p0144c1s v1p0406c1s
v1p0458c1s v1p0802c2s v1p0915c1s
v1p0917c2s v1p1048c1s v1p1239c2s
v1p1354c2s v1p1435c1s v1p1438c2s
Hutcheson, R. v1p1175c2s
v5p0544c2s v6p0120c1s
Hutcheson, T. v2p0383c1s
v2p0391c1s
Hutcheson, W. v1p0318c1s
Hutchings, J. v1p1173c2s
Hutchings, S. v3p0389c1s
v4p0301c1s
Hutchins, B.L. v5p0615c1s
v5p0615c2s v6p0387c2s v6p0704c2m
Hutchins, C.C. v3p0275c2s
v3p0351c2s v3p0403c2m v4p0008c2s
v4p0020c1s v4p0062c2s v4p0252c2s
v5p0227c1s v5p0481c2s v6p0078c2s
v6p0585c2s
Hutchins, C.C. and Holden, E.L.
v3p0334c1s
Hutchins, C.C. and Pearsons, J.C.
v6p0009c2s
Hutchins, C.C. and Robinson, F.C.
v4p0141c2s
Hutchins, C.C. and Trowbridge, J.
v3p0415c1s
Hutchins, C.J. v1p0453c2s
v1p0982c2s
Hutchins, D.E. v3p0287c1s
v5p0214c2s v6p0132c2s v6p0212c2s
v6p0531c1s
Hutchins, E.R. v5p0566c2s
Hutchins, F.A. v4p0330c1s
v4p0624c2s v5p0335c2m v5p0336c2s
Hutchins, G.H. v6p0316c1s
Hutchins, G.P. and Browning, P.E.
v5p0575c1s
Hutchins, H. v4p0512c1s
v4p0610c2s
Hutchins, H.B. v3p0101c1s
Hutchins, J. v2p0243c1s
v2p0451c1s v3p0096c2s v3p0283c2s
v3p0440c2s v4p0592c2s
Hutchins, M. v4p0553c1s
Hutchins, P.A. v6p0574c1s
Hutchins, S. v1p0380c2s
v2p0044c2s
Hutchins, W. v6p0298c2s
v6p0695c1s
Hutchins, W.F. and Sherman, S.O.
v6p0365c1s
Hutchins, W.W. v4p0390c1s
Hutchins, Weston F. and
Sherman, Stephen O. ... v6p0405c1s
Hutchinson, A. v4p0411c1s
Hutchinson, B.P. v3p0461c2s
Hutchinson, C.C. v5p0350c2s
Hutchinson, C.T. v5p0183c1s
Hutchinson, E. v1p0528c1s
v1p1301c2s v3p0004c1m v3p0305c2s
Hutchinson, E.M. v3p0327c2s
Hutchinson, E.S. v2p0327c2s
Hutchinson, F.W.W. v6p0230c1s
Hutchinson, G. v4p0069c2s
Hutchinson, G.T. v6p0542c2s
Hutchinson, H. v3p0047c1s
v3p0063c2s v3p0099c1s v3p0105c1s
v3p0107c2s v3p0203c1s v3p0322c2s
v3p0419c2s v3p0426c2s v3p0450c2s
v4p0139c1s v4p0222c1s v4p0231c2s
v4p0244c2s v4p0418c2m v4p0460c2s
v4p0605c2s v5p0193c1s v5p0239c1m
v5p0413c1s v5p0505c2s v5p0554c2s
v5p0578c1s v6p0181c1s v6p0261c1s
v6p0261c2s v6p0692c1s
Hutchinson, H.D. v5p0501c2s
Hutchinson, H.E.M. v6p0347c1s
Hutchinson, H.G. v3p0177c1s
v3p0309c2s v4p0042c2s v4p0061c1s
v4p0061c2s v4p0193c2s v4p0231c2m
v5p0086c2s v5p0143c1s v5p0168c1m
v5p0233c1s v5p0340c1s v5p0404c1s
v5p0455c1s v5p0494c2s v5p0547c1s
v6p0014c2s v6p0232c2s v6p0242c2s
Hutchinson, H.N. v3p0328c2s
v3p0451c2m v4p0125c1s v4p0166c1s
v4p0227c1s v4p0511c1s v4p0633c1s
v5p0013c2s
Hutchinson, Horace G. v6p0153c2s
Hutchinson, J. v1p0321c1s
v1p0578c2s v1p1100c2s v2p0064c1s
v2p0400c2s v2p0406c2s v4p0135c1s
v4p0181c1s v6p0480c2s
Hutchinson, J. and Pearson, K.
v2p0042c1s
Hutchinson, J.C. v2p0463c2s
Hutchinson, J.D. v2p0480c1s
Hutchinson, J.G. v6p0355c1s
v6p0652c1s
Hutchinson, J.R. v5p0250c2s
Hutchinson, L. v4p0008c1s
v6p0080c1s v6p0093c2s v6p0383c1s
Hutchinson, M. v2p0062c1s
Hutchinson, M.H. v6p0007c2s
Hutchinson, M.T. v6p0678c2s
Hutchinson, Mrs. v1p0144c2s
v2p0177c2s
Hutchinson, N.M. v1p0696c2s
v1p0773c2s v1p1421c1s
Hutchinson, R. v2p0104c1s
Hutchinson, R.F. v2p0435c2s
v3p0088c2s v3p0134c2s
Hutchinson, T. v1p0452c1s
v4p0085c1s v4p0122c1m v4p0138c1s
v4p0163c2s v4p0184c1s v4p0184c2s
v4p0234c2s v4p0243c1s v4p0299c1s
v4p0312c1s v4p0325c1s v4p0337c1m
v4p0348c1s v4p0509c2s v4p0520c2s
v4p0632c1m v6p0135c1s v6p0359c2s
Hutchinson, T.J. v1p0992c2s
v1p0993c1s v3p0395c2s
Hutchinson, T.N. v1p1131c2s
Hutchinson, T.V. v4p0269c1s
Hutchinson, W. v1p0409c1s
v3p0053c1s v3p0192c2s v4p0048c2s
v4p0149c2s v4p0191c1s v4p0232c1s
v4p0286c1s v4p0331c1s v5p0020c1s
v5p0021c1s v5p0067c2s v5p0092c1s
v5p0140c1s v5p0162c2s v5p0198c1s
v5p0427c2s v5p0455c1s v5p0463c1s
v6p0177c2m v6p0178c1s v6p0402c1s
v6p0470c1s v6p0503c2s
Hutchinson, W.B. v5p0396c1s
Hutchinson, W.E. v6p0318c2s
Hutchinson, W.F. v3p0034c1s
v3p0314c1s v3p0436c1s
Hutchinson, W.G. v5p0171c2s
v6p0003c2s v6p0650c2s
Hutchinson, W.N. v1p0665c2s
v2p0003c1s v2p0443c2s v3p0395c1s
Hutchinson, W.Q. v6p0056c1s
Hutchinson, W.S. v2p0213c2s
v2p0447c2s v3p0078c1s v3p0210c1s
v3p0267c1s v3p0283c2s v3p0416c1s
v3p0430c2s v4p0012c2s v4p0165c2s
v4p0247c2s v4p0412c1s
Hutchinson, W.Z. v4p0049c1s
Hutchinson, Woods v6p0173c2s
v6p0402c1s
Hutchison, G. v1p0565c1s
v1p1080c2s v1p1240c1s
Hutchison, J. v1p0818c1s
v1p1294c2s v3p0229c1s
Hutchison, J. and Laurie, S.S.
v2p0455c2s
Hutchison, P.A. v6p0108c2s
Hutchison, W.E. v6p0447c2s
Huth, A.H. et al. v5p0152c2s
Hutson, C.W. v1p0430c1s
v1p0514c2s v1p0598c1s v1p0983c1s
v1p1121c2s v1p1220c1s v4p0571c1s
v5p0054c1s v5p0144c2s v6p0285c1s
Hutson, G.W. v1p1277c2s
Hutt, A.G. v2p0250c1s
Hutt, F.W. v6p0562c1s
Hutten, Baroness von v6p0002c2s
v6p0351c2s
Hutten, Bettina von v6p0179c1s
v6p0471c2s v6p0595c2s v6p0643c2s
v6p0653c1s v6p0698c1s
Hutten, T.C. v5p0586c2s
Hutter, E.W. v1p0315c2s
v1p0320c1s v1p1042c1s
Hutton, A. v4p0265c1s
v6p0244c2s
Hutton, A.W. v3p0418c1s
v4p0187c2s v4p0415c1s v4p0560c2s
v5p0070c1s v5p0262c2s v5p0336c1s
v6p0123c1s v6p0369c2s v6p0383c2s
Hutton, B. v3p0202c2s
v3p0231c1s v3p0473c1s
Hutton, C. v1p0151c1s
Hutton, E. v5p0340c1s
v5p0490c2s v5p0598c1s v6p0022c2s
v6p0149c2s v6p0331c1s v6p0483c2s
v6p0512c2s v6p0565c1s v6p0585c1s
v6p0592c1s v6p0607c2s v6p0611c1s
v6p0650c1s v6p0664c1s v6p0676c2m
Hutton, E.T.H. v4p0284c1s
v5p0290c1s v5p0389c2s v5p0425c1s
v6p0042c1s
Hutton, F.R. v4p0180c2s
v4p0217c1s v4p0360c2s v4p0547c2s
v5p0353c1s v5p0551c1m
Hutton, F.W. v6p0023c2s
v6p0214c1s v6p0288c1s v6p0354c2s
Hutton, G.C. v2p0084c1s
Hutton, H. v1p1300c1s
Hutton, H.D. v1p0657c2s
v1p0661c1s v1p1357c2s
Hutton, J. v1p0010c1s
v1p0153c2s v1p0186c1s v1p0441c2s
v1p0443c2s v1p0459c1s v1p0482c2s
v1p0599c1s v1p0618c1s v1p0633c1s
v1p0634c2m v1p0766c1s v1p0915c1s
v1p1124c1s v1p1134c2s v1p1336c2s
v2p0024c1s v2p0105c1s v2p0166c1s
v2p0217c1s v2p0218c2s v3p0054c1s
v3p0096c2s v3p0103c1s v3p0138c2s
v3p0212c1s v3p0228c2s v3p0381c1s
v3p0381c2s v3p0391c1s v4p0041c2s
v5p0458c2m
Hutton, J.A. v6p0082c2s
v6p0218c1s
Hutton, James v3p0446c2s
v4p0549c2s
Hutton, L. v2p0122c2s
v2p0333c2s v3p0002c2s v3p0060c2s
v3p0092c1s v3p0113c2s v3p0128c1s
v3p0188c2s v3p0270c1s v3p0281c2s
v3p0298c2s v3p0387c2s v4p0079c1s
v4p0150c1s v4p0202c2s v4p0234c1m
v4p0293c2s v4p0602c2s v5p0003c1s
v5p0066c1s v5p0161c1s v5p0495c2s
v5p0630c2s v6p0620c1s
Hutton, Laurence v4p0067c1s
v6p0379c1s
Hutton, M. v5p0249c2s
Hutton, M.H. v2p0062c1s
v2p0405c2s v3p0415c2s
Hutton, N.H. v1p0455c2s
Hutton, R.H. v1p0072c1s
v1p0086c2s v1p0201c1s v1p0242c2s
v1p0478c1s v1p0688c1s v1p0726c2s
v1p0868c1s v1p0869c1s v1p0979c2s
v1p0980c1s v1p1238c2s v1p1294c2s
v1p1308c1s v2p0022c1s v2p0090c1s
v2p0174c2s v2p0280c2s v2p0285c1s
v2p0311c2m v2p0462c2s v3p0057c1s
v3p0143c1s v3p0265c2s v3p0302c1s
v4p0227c1s v4p0270c2s v4p0480c2s
v4p0611c1s
Hutton, R.H. and Cyon, E.De
v2p0462c1s
Hutton, R.H. et al. v1p1221c2s
Hutton, S.K. v2p0267c2s
v3p0164c2s v3p0386c2s
Hutton, W.B. v4p0078c1s
Hutton, W.E. v6p0136c2s
Hutton, W.H. v3p0287c2s
v4p0097c2s v4p0322c1s v4p0382c2s
v5p0139c1s v5p0141c1s v5p0558c1s
v6p0121c1s v6p0142c2s v6p0210c1s
v6p0247c2s v6p0590c2s v6p0622c1s
v6p0622c2s
Huvetys, P. v2p0131c2s
Huxley, H. v5p0039c2s
Huxley, H.M. v6p0630c2s
Huxley, L. v5p0277c1m
v6p0680c2s v6p0689c2s
Huxley, T. v3p0422c2s
v4p0007c1s
Huxley, T.D. v1p0538c1s
Huxley, T.H. v1p0041c2m
v1p0042c2s v1p0045c2s v1p0134c1m
v1p0134c2m v1p0135c1s v1p0214c2m
v1p0215c1s v1p0267c2s v1p0280c2s
v1p0301c1s v1p0323c1s v1p0333c1m
v1p0345c2s v1p0390c1s v1p0418c1s
v1p0427c2s v1p0434c2s v1p0435c1s
v1p0504c1s v1p0545c1s v1p0565c1s
v1p0573c1s v1p0579c1s v1p0588c2s
v1p0745c2s v1p0746c1s v1p0794c1s
v1p0899c2s v1p0900c2s v1p0960c1m
v1p1005c1s v1p1007c1m v1p1037c2s
v1p1050c1s v1p1059c1s v1p1099c2s
v1p1160c2s v1p1163c1s v1p1164c1s
v1p1171c2s v1p1172c1s v1p1177c2m
v1p1232c2s v1p1233c1m v1p1244c2s
v1p1288c2s v1p1325c1s v1p1356c2s
v1p1357c2s v1p1436c2s v1p1439c1s
v2p0106c2s v2p0112c1s v2p0130c2s
v2p0135c1s v2p0158c1s v2p0172c2m
v2p0280c1s v2p0282c1s v2p0297c2s
v2p0325c2s v2p0327c1s v2p0384c1s
v2p0389c1s v2p0390c1s v2p0437c2s
v2p0456c2s v3p0023c1s v3p0040c2s
v3p0067c2s v3p0082c2s v3p0100c2s
v3p0114c2m v3p0142c1s v3p0166c1m
v3p0170c1s v3p0174c2s v3p0178c1s
v3p0190c2s v3p0215c1s v3p0267c2s
v3p0271c1s v3p0274c1s v3p0282c1s
v3p0342c2s v3p0345c2s v3p0355c2m
v3p0361c2s v3p0368c1s v3p0379c2m
v3p0380c1s v3p0413c1s v4p0042c1s
v4p0058c1s v4p0190c2s v4p0191c2s
v4p0454c1s v4p0588c2s v5p0022c2s
v6p0005c2s

Huxley, T.H. and Drummond, H. v2p0106c2s
Huxley, T.H. and Pasteur, L. v3p0205c2s
Huxley, T.H. et al. v3p0005c2s v4p0570c1s v5p0153c2s
Huyette, J.N. v5p0292c1s v5p0369c2s
Huyghue, S.D. v1p0194c2s v1p0195c1s
Huyshe, W. v4p0348c1s v5p0249c1s v5p0420c2s v5p0516c1s v5p0594c2m
Huyssoon, P.V. v2p0036c2s v2p0104c2s
Hyacinth, S. v1p0058c1s v1p0078c1s v1p0136c1s v1p0138c1s v1p0188c1m v1p0636c2s v1p0927c2s v1p1011c1s v1p1140c2s v1p1188c1s v1p1204c2s v1p1297c2s v1p1315c1s
Hyacinthe, Pere v1p0714c2s
Hyams, W. v5p0633c2s
Hyamson, A.M. v5p0154c1s v5p0371c1s v5p0453c2s v6p0111c1s v6p0330c2s v6p0511c1s
Hyamson, M. v4p0306c1s v5p0307c1s
Hyatt, A. v1p0279c2s v1p0699c1s v1p0875c1s v1p1113c1s v1p1239c1s v2p0072c2s v2p0073c1s v2p0250c1s v2p0307c1s v2p0343c2s v2p0442c1s v3p0321c1s v4p0096c1s v4p0441c1s v4p0506c2s v4p0566c2s v5p0150c2s
Hyatt, A. and Arms, J.M. . v4p0366c2s
Hyatt, C.R. v2p0444c2s
Hyatt, J.T. v4p0503c1s
Hyatt, S.P. v6p0006c2s
Hyatt, W.H. v2p0326c1s
Hyde, A. v1p1182c1s v1p1183c1s
Hyde, A.B. v1p0331c1s v1p0725c1s v1p1150c2s v2p0056c2s v2p0249c2s v3p0041c2s v3p0147c2s v4p0028c1s v4p0035c2s v4p0041c2s v4p0241c1s v4p0262c1s v4p0505c1s v5p0022c2s v5p0167c2s v5p0630c2s v6p0086c2s v6p0586c1s v6p0635c1s
Hyde, A.E. v6p0451c1s v6p0607c1s
Hyde, A.G. v4p0024c2m v4p0084c2s v4p0399c2s v5p0041c2s v5p0405c1s v5p0467c1s v6p0330c1s v6p0451c2s v6p0483c1s v6p0677c1s
Hyde, A.H. v5p0121c1s v5p0280c2s
Hyde, A.M. v5p0485c1s v5p0607c1s
Hyde, A.S. v6p0035c1s
Hyde, C.C. v5p0019c2s v6p0008c1s v6p0010c1s v6p0020c2s v6p0477c2s v6p0655c2s
Hyde, C.E. v5p0362c1s
Hyde, C.H. v4p0585c2s
Hyde, C.M. v1p0595c1s
Hyde, D. v3p0222c2s
Hyde, D. and Synge, J.M. . v6p0328c1s
Hyde, Douglas v6p0662c2s
Hyde, Douglas and McCarter, H. v6p0327c2s
Hyde, E.W. v1p0051c1s v1p0377c1s v1p1080c2s v3p0008c1s
Hyde, F.A. v6p0044c1s
Hyde, G. v3p0439c2s v5p0092c2s
Hyde, G.M. v3p0437c1s v4p0070c2s v4p0075c2s v4p0475c1s v4p0566c1s v4p0572c2s v5p0093c1s v5p0212c1s v5p0218c2s v5p0234c2s v5p0235c1s v5p0274c2s v5p0438c1s v5p0451c2s v5p0582c1s
Hyde, G.W. and Smith, W.J. v3p0071c2s
Hyde, H. v1p1290c1s v3p0422c2s v5p0317c1s v6p0490c2s
Hyde, H.D. v1p0327c1m
Hyde, H.M. v6p0003c1s v6p0420c2s
Hyde, I.H. v3p0192c2s
Hyde, J. v4p0222c1s v5p0054c2s v5p0133c2s v5p0148c1s v5p0166c2m v5p0186c1s v5p0190c2s v5p0201c2s v5p0391c1s v5p0399c1s v5p0438c1m v5p0444c1s v5p0621c2s v5p0627c2s v6p0060c2s v6p0360c1s v6p0485c2m
Hyde, J.C. v5p0505c1s
Hyde, J.M. v1p1191c2s v6p0132c2s
Hyde, J.N. v1p1436c1s v2p0118c2s v5p0533c1s v6p0619c1s
Hyde, J.T. v1p0977c2s
Hyde, John v5p0644c2s
Hyde, S. v1p0745c1s v1p1014c1s v1p1051c1s v1p1071c1s v1p1323c1s v1p1435c2s
Hyde, T.A. v3p0056c1s v5p0376c2s
Hyde, V.D................. v6p0697c2s
Hyde, W. and Leuba, J.H. . v6p0279c1s
Hyde, W.B. v1p1321c2s
Hyde, W.D. v2p0146c1s v2p0180c2s v3p0091c2m v3p0331c2s v4p0170c1s v4p0420c2s v4p0443c1s v4p0466c2s v6p0450c1s
Hyde, W.D. and Atkinson, E. v4p0398c2s
Hyde, W.DeW. v3p0128c2s v3p0146c1s v3p0175c2s v3p0374c1s v4p0103c2s v4p0113c2s v4p0123c2s v5p0002c1s v5p0094c1s v5p0118c1s v5p0186c1s v5p0201c2s v5p0532c2s v5p0576c2s v5p0577c1s v5p0595c2s v6p0030c1s v6p0123c1s v6p0135c1s v6p0135c2s v6p0156c2s v6p0192c2s v6p0193c1s v6p0212c1s v6p0441c1s v6p0447c1s v6p0519c2s v6p0642c2s
Hyde, W.DeW. and Harris, G. v6p0135c2s
Hyde, W.DeW. et al. v3p0091c2s
Hyde, W.DeWitt v6p0296c1s
Hyde, W.L. v2p0099c2s
Hyde, W.W. v5p0031c1s
Hylan, J.B. v4p0036c2s
Hylan, J.P. v6p0040c2s v6p0399c2s
Hyland-MacGrath, T.J. v3p0335c1s
Hylande-MacGrath, T.J. ... v3p0337c2s
Hymers, M.E.S. v6p0223c2s
Hyndham, G. v3p0199c2s
Hyndman, H. and George, H. v2p0370c1s
Hyndman, H.H.F. v6p0369c2s
Hyndman, H.M. v1p0078c1s v1p0209c2s v1p0629c1s v1p0631c1s v1p0658c2s v1p1104c1s v1p1353c1s v2p0142c1s v2p0143c1m v2p0189c1s v2p0371c2s v2p0407c2s v2p0408c1m v2p0479c2s v3p0131c2s v3p0141c1s v3p0398c1s v3p0446c2s v3p0458c1s v4p0100c1s v5p0229c2s v5p0285c1s
Hyndman, H.M. and George, H v2p0407c2s
Hynds, A. v2p0209c2s
Hyne, C. v5p0170c2s v5p0339c2s v5p0390c1s v5p0506c1s
Hyne, C.J.C. v4p0199c2s v4p0278c1s v4p0305c2s v4p0311c1s v4p0320c2s v4p0342c1s v4p0364c2s v5p0466c1s v5p0485c2s v5p0586c1s
Hyne, C.J.Cutcliffe v4p0255c2s v4p0429c1s v4p0584c1s v4p0618c2s v5p0043c1s v5p0485c1s
Hynes, S.B., Mrs. v1p1401c1s
Hynes, W.J. v6p0503c1s
Hypes, O.T. v6p0611c2s
Hyskell, C.M. v6p0076c1s v6p0142c1s v6p0434c1s v6p0509c2s
Hyskins, S.F. v1p1337c1s
Hyslop, J. v4p0172c1s v5p0401c2s v6p0710c1s
Hyslop, J.H. v2p0147c1s v2p0358c2s v3p0032c1s v3p0044c2m v3p0105c1s v3p0111c1s v3p0127c1s v3p0143c1s v3p0145c2m v3p0192c1s v3p0320c2s v3p0348c2s v3p0391c1s v3p0402c2s v3p0451c1m v3p0452c2s v4p0097c1s v4p0188c2s v4p0210c1s v4p0214c1m v4p0284c2s v4p0315c1s v4p0315c2s v4p0338c1s v4p0455c1s v4p0464c2s v4p0482c1s v4p0506c2s v4p0532c1s v4p0539c1s v4p0622c1s v5p0119c2s v5p0179c1s v5p0211c1s v5p0280c2s v5p0281c1m v5p0313c2s v5p0337c2m v5p0397c1s v5p0404c2s v5p0425c2s v5p0436c2s v5p0470c1m v5p0546c2m v5p0571c1s v5p0606c1s v6p0066c2s v6p0166c2s v6p0309c1s v6p0310c2s v6p0349c2s v6p0495c2s v6p0496c1s v6p0576c1s v6p0643c2s v6p0670c2s
Hyvernat, H. v4p0027c1s v6p0051c2m v6p0285c2s v6p0365c2s v6p0470c1s

Ian-Ruban, W. v6p0558c2s
Ian-Ruban, Wanda v6p0561c1s
I'Anson, J.C. v6p0393c2s
Iasigi, N. v5p0438c1s
Ibbetson, W.J. v2p0135c2s
Ibbs, Edith A. v6p0073c2s
Iberti, C. v6p0623c2s
Ibsen, H. v2p0435c2s
v3p0240c1s
v5p0420c2s
v6p0048c1s
v6p0562c1s
Ibsen, M. v6p0387c2s
Ichihara, M. v3p0227c1s
v4p0297c2s
Iddesleigh, Earl of v2p0365c2s
v4p0407c1s v4p0456c1s v5p0038c2s
Iddesleigh, Lord v6p0054c2s
v6p0402c2s
Iddesleigh, W.S.N. v6p0041c1s
Iddings, D.W. v6p0097c1s
Iddings, J.P. v2p0094c2s
v2p0173c2s v2p0214c2s v2p0322c2s
v3p0254c1s v3p0350c2s
Iddings, J.P. and Barus, C.
v4p0174c2s
Iddings, J.P. and Cross, W.
v2p0008c1s
Iddings, J.P. and Hague, A.
v2p0463c1m
Iddings, J.P. and Penfield, S.L.
v3p0150c2s
Iddings, L.M. v4p0125c1s
Iddings, S.M. v5p0589c1s
Ide, A.L.B. v5p0383c1s
Ide, F.O. v6p0116c1s
Ide, G.B. v1p0112c1s
Ide, H.C. v4p0116c1s
v5p0506c2m v6p0492c2s
Ide, K.K. v5p0202c1s
v5p0535c2s
Idle, T.W. v5p0390c2s
Ierson, H. v1p0840c1s
Iglehart, F.C. v4p0500c2s
v4p0557c2s v4p0636c1s
Ignota v5p0190c2m
v6p0555c2s
Ignotus v5p0173c2s
v5p0302c1s v5p0541c1m v6p0253c2s
v6p0266c1s v6p0668c1s
Ihering, H.v. v4p0376c2s
Ihering, H.von v5p0404c2s
Ihlseng, M.C. v1p1222c2s
v1p1427c1s v4p0524c1s v4p0547c2s
Ihmels, L. v6p0348c2s
Iken, M. v3p0471c2s
Ilbert, C.P. v4p0279c2s
v4p0325c2s v4p0548c2s v6p0481c2m
Ilbert, L. v5p0273c2s
Iles, C.M. v6p0566c1s
Iles, G. v1p0295c2s
v1p0299c1s v1p0434c2s v1p0435c1s
v1p0467c1s v1p0587c1s v1p0875c2s
v2p0156c2s v2p0208c1s v2p0223c1s
v2p0354c1s v2p0363c2s v2p0369c1s
v3p0065c1s v3p0095c1s v3p0169c2s
v3p0218c1s v3p0274c2s v3p0365c1s
v3p0437c1s v4p0067c1s v4p0082c1s
v4p0335c1s v4p0461c1s v4p0508c1s
v5p0070c1s v5p0234c1s v5p0334c1s
v5p0335c2s v5p0341c2s v5p0342c1s
v5p0469c2s v6p0017c1s v6p0047c1s
v6p0198c2s v6p0225c2s v6p0609c2s
v6p0610c1s
Iles, G. et al. v6p0017c1s
Iles, Geo. v6p0098c1s
v6p0366c1s
Ilex, A. v1p0703c1s
Ilgenfritz, A. v1p0848c2s
v1p1088c1s v1p1401c2s
v2p0276c2s
Iliff, E. and Waterbury, L.
v4p0577c1s
Ilowizi, H. v5p0041c2s
v5p0255c1s
Ilch, I. v2p0236c2s
Illingworth, J.R. v5p0571c2s
Illingworth, W. v1p0206c2s
v1p0585c1s
Illmer, L. v6p0285c2s
Illsley, C.E. v1p0599c2m
v2p0019c1s v2p0055c2s
Illyne, Mary v6p0512c1s
v6p0559c2s
Ilsley, M. v6p0288c2s
v6p0396c1s v6p0554c2s
Ilsley, S. v6p0210c2s
Image, D.M. v5p0442c2s
Image, S. v4p0150c2s
v4p0348c1s v6p0079c2s v6p0187c1s
v6p0218c1s
Image, Selwyn v5p0044c1s
v6p0090c1s v6p0163c1s
Imber, N.H. v4p0302c2s
v4p0389c1m v5p0232c2s
Imbert, H. v5p0565c1s
Imboden, J.D. v1p0518c2s
v1p0734c1m v2p0232c2s v2p0275c1s
v2p0400c1s
Imbrie, W. v3p0227c1s
Imbrie, W.M.K. v2p0235c1s
Imhoof-Blumer, F. and Gardner, P.
v3p0324c2s
Immler, F.O. and Cornwall, A.L.
v4p0629c1s
Imperialist, An v4p0582c1s
Impey, F. v4p0578c2s
Imray, J. v1p0862c1s
Ince, Francis and Ferranti, S.C.de
v3p0132c2s
Ince, H. v6p0005c1s
v6p0027c2s
Incledon, B. v1p1010c2s
Indigo, J. v2p0218c2s
Indy, Vincent D' v5p0042c1s
v6p0438c1s
Ingall, H. v3p0476c1s
Ingalls, E. v3p0468c1s
Ingalls, J.J. v2p0058c1s
v2p0131c2s v3p0337c1s v3p0345c2s
v3p0470c1s v4p0101c2s v4p0308c1s
v5p0420c1s v5p0422c2s
Ingalls, J.K. v1p1394c1s
v1p1430c2s
Ingalls, J.M. and Chester, J.
v5p0252c2s
Ingalls, M.E. v4p0471c2s
v5p0603c2s
Ingalls, W.R. v4p0526c2s
Ingals, E.F. v4p0100c1s
Inge, W.R. v4p0112c2s
v5p0244c2s v5p0313c1s v5p0386c1s
v5p0404c2s v6p0399c1s
Ingelow, J. v1p0071c1s
v1p0168c1s v1p0266c2s v1p0360c1s
v1p0446c1s v1p0590c1s v1p0627c2s
v1p0728c2s v1p0801c1s v1p0803c2s
v1p0924c2s v1p0938c1s v1p1087c1s
v1p1151c2s v1p1155c2s v1p1335c2s
v2p0129c2s v2p0182c2s v3p0014c2s
v3p0092c2s v3p0258c2s v3p0385c1s
Ingelow, Jean v4p0385c1s
Ingen, W.B.Van v5p0303c2m
Inger, A.S. v5p0422c1s
Ingersleben, E.von v1p0423c2s
Ingersoll, A.J. v5p0563c1s
Ingersoll, C.A. v4p0142c1s
Ingersoll, C.J. v1p0027c2s
v1p0148c2s v1p0304c1s
Ingersoll, E. v1p0135c1s
v1p0137c1s v1p0139c2s v1p0174c1s
v1p0186c2s v1p0195c2s v1p0207c2s
v1p0344c2s v1p0451c2s v1p0646c2s
v1p0732c2s v1p0767c1s v1p0842c2s
v1p0859c1s v1p0879c2s v1p0984c1s
v1p1113c1s v1p1113c2s v1p1151c1s
v1p1191c1s v1p1213c1s v1p1244c1s
v1p1273c2s v2p0004c2s v2p0010c2s
v2p0056c2s v2p0090c2s v2p0094c1m
v2p0110c2s v2p0152c2s v2p0157c1s
v2p0159c2s v2p0193c2s v2p0202c2s
v2p0208c1s v2p0219c2s v2p0232c1s
v2p0262c2s v2p0268c1s v2p0290c2s
v2p0302c2s v2p0323c1s v2p0333c2m
v2p0365c1m v2p0367c1s v2p0374c2s
v2p0384c2s v2p0385c2s v2p0387c1s
v2p0457c2s v2p0464c1s v2p0465c1s
v2p0467c1m v3p0046c1s v3p0066c1s
v3p0082c1s v3p0093c1m v3p0103c1s
v3p0137c1s v3p0189c2s v3p0234c2s
v3p0286c2s v3p0290c1m v3p0290c2s
v3p0307c2s v3p0386c2s v3p0405c1s
v3p0405c2s v3p0428c1s v4p0048c2s
v4p0058c2s v4p0145c2s v4p0174c1s
v4p0199c2s v4p0282c1s v4p0363c2s
v4p0543c2s v4p0587c2s v4p0637c2s
v5p0001c1s v5p0063c1m v5p0063c2s
v5p0358c1s v5p0361c1s v5p0407c1s
v5p0424c1s v6p0068c1s v6p0171c2s
v6p0502c2s
Ingersoll, Ernest v2p0395c1s
Ingersoll, F.R. v1p1212c1s
Ingersoll, H.M. v4p0332c1s
Ingersoll, I.D. v2p0353c1s
Ingersoll, J. v4p0432c2s
v5p0012c2s v5p0130c2s v5p0268c1s
v5p0362c2s
Ingersoll, J.R. v1p0484c2s
Ingersoll, L.D. v1p0624c1s
v1p1084c2s v1p1177c1s v1p1296c1s
v1p1403c1s
Ingersoll, R.G. v1p0240c2s
v2p0259c1s v2p0481c1s v3p0005c2s
v3p0021c1s v3p0029c1s v3p0081c1s
v3p0105c1s v3p0119c1s v3p0175c1s
v3p0205c2s v3p0216c1m v3p0238c2s
v3p0329c1s v3p0364c2s v3p0432c1s
v3p0442c1s v4p0421c1s v4p0480c2s
v5p0009c1s
Ingersoll, R.G. and Black, J.S.
v1p0240c2s
Ingersoll, R.G. and Geary, T.J.
v4p0106c1s
Ingersoll, R.G. et al. ... v5p0115c2s
Ingersoll, W.H. v2p0236c1s
v3p0229c2s
Ingersoll, Will E. v6p0397c2s
Ingham, J.H. v2p0205c2s
v5p0503c2s
Ingham, J.W. v6p0241c2s
v6p0242c1s v6p0487c2s
Ingham, S.D. v1p0325c2s
Ingle, E. v2p0105c1m
v2p0211c2s v2p0248c1s v2p0262c1s
v2p0279c1m v2p0330c1s v2p0373c2s
v2p0444c1s v2p0461c2m v2p0462c1s
v2p0476c1s v3p0405c2s v4p0397c1s
v4p0402c2s
Ingle, Edward v2p0330c1s
Ingleby, C.M. v1p0303c1s
v1p0492c1s v1p1081c1s v1p1368c1s
v2p0112c2s v2p0242c2s v2p0295c2s
Ingleby, H. v3p0295c2s
v3p0451c1s
Inglehart, F.C. v4p0367c2s
v4p0620c2s
Inglehart, W. v4p0101c1s
v4p0102c1m
Inglis, D. v1p0163c2s
v1p0923c1s v1p1055c1s v1p1070c1s
Inglis, F. v1p0331c1s
v1p0363c2s v1p1241c1s
Inglis, G. v1p0869c1s
Inglis, H.D. v1p0082c2s
v1p0310c1s v1p1337c2s
Inglis, H.S. v4p0292c2s
Inglis, J. v1p1227c1m
v2p0311c2s v2p0348c2s v3p0432c2s
v4p0399c2s
Inglis, J.G. v5p0057c1s
Inglis, W. v6p0160c2s
v6p0261c1s v6p0477c1s
Inglis, W.M. v4p0141c2s
v4p0437c1s
Inglis, W.O. v5p0327c2s
v6p0415c1s
Ingold, F. v6p0179c2s
Ingpen, R.E. v4p0048c1s
Ingpen, Roger v5p0088c2s
Ingraham, A. v1p0416c1s
v1p1070c1s v1p1283c1s v1p1283c2s
Ingraham, A.F.W. v5p0119c2s
Ingraham, D.G. v1p0551c1s
Ingraham, G.H. v6p0027c1s
Ingraham, J.A. v1p0065c2s
Ingraham, J.H. v1p0196c1s
v1p0755c2s v1p0841c1s v1p0889c2s
v1p0950c2s v1p1175c2s v1p1401c2s
Ingraham, R.S. v5p0223c2s
Ingram, A.E. v6p0358c2s
Ingram, B. v6p0040c1s
Ingram, B. and Burgess, A.F.
v6p0526c2s
Ingram, D. v2p0316c1s
Ingram, E.E. and Bemis, F.W.
v6p0436c1s
Ingram, E.V. v4p0335c1s
Ingram, F.F. v6p0377c1s
Ingram, G.S. v2p0265c2s
Imgram, H.B. v4p0064c2s
Ingram, J.D. v3p0220c1s
Ingram, J.H. v1p0183c2s
v1p0345c1s v1p0796c1s v1p1019c2m
v2p0075c2s v2p0345c2s v3p0056c2s
v5p0438c2s
Ingram, J.H. and George, W.
v2p0075c2s
Ingram, J.H. et al. v4p0075c2s
Ingram, J.K. v1p1026c2s
Ingram, J.N. v3p0191c2s
v3p0304c2s v4p0470c1m
Ingram, John H. v4p0356c1s
Ingram, T.D. v3p0222c1s
Ingram, W.C. v5p0442c1s
Ingram, W.H. v6p0213c1s
v6p0236c2s
Ingres, M. v6p0423c2s
Inkersley v5p0148c2s
Inkersley, A. v3p0304c2s
v4p0016c2s v4p0047c1s v4p0073c2s
v4p0083c2s v4p0098c2s v4p0219c2s
v4p0220c1s v4p0241c2s v4p0368c2m
v4p0419c2s v4p0420c2s v4p0467c1s
v4p0477c2s v4p0499c2s v4p0502c1m
v4p0571c2s v4p0634c2s v5p0047c2s
v5p0233c2s v5p0239c1s v5p0367c1s
v5p0424c2s v5p0507c1s v6p0010c2s
v6p0043c1s v6p0104c1s v6p0365c2s
v6p0382c2s v6p0395c2s v6p0414c2s
v6p0455c1s v6p0465c1s v6p0466c1s
v6p0491c1s v6p0566c2s v6p0677c1s
Inkersley, A. and Brommage, W.H.
v4p0226c1s
Inkersley, Arthur v5p0478c2s
v6p0030c1s v6p0085c2s v6p0093c1s
v6p0106c1s v6p0124c2s
Inkster, L. v5p0333c2s
Inman, G. v2p0012c1s
Inman, H. v2p0351c2s
v2p0421c2s v4p0308c1s v5p0506c1s
Inman, J. v1p0988c2s
v1p1220c1s v1p1252c2s v1p1439c2s
Innes, A. v5p0296c1s
Innes, A.D. v4p0466c2s
Innes, A.D. and Hogg, E.F.
v5p0178c1s
Innes, A.N. v6p0405c2s
Innes, A.T. v1p0091c2s
v1p0247c1s v1p0252c2s v1p0427c1s
v1p0524c2s v1p0689c1m v1p0783c2s

v1p1013c1s v1p1046c1s v1p1047c2s v1p1109c2s v1p1116c1s v1p1165c2m v1p1168c1s v1p1243c1s v1p1338c2s v2p0065c1s v2p0085c2s v2p0391c1s v2p0392c1s v3p0083c1s v3p0104c1s v3p0206c1s v3p0381c1s v3p0423c1m v4p0076c1s v4p0457c1s v4p0509c1s v6p0206c2s
Innes, A.Taylor v6p0577c2s
Innes, E.R. v2p0277c2s v2p0427c2s
Innes, H. v1p0657c1s
Innes, J. v5p0097c2s v5p0635c1s v6p0086c2s v6p0474c1s
Innes, J.M'L. v5p0285c2s v5p0490c2s
Innes, L.C. v4p0131c2s v5p0285c1s v6p0312c2s v6p0486c2s
Innes, M.G.M. v5p0302c1s
Innes, R.T.A. v5p0294c1s
Innes, T. v6p0209c1s v6p0681c2s
Inness, J.H. v1p0231c1s
Innis, G.S. v5p0293c1s
Innis, T. v3p0006c1s
Inouye, J. v5p0303c1s
Insley, E. v5p0098c1s v5p0430c2s v6p0516c1s
Internat v6p0699c2s
Inwards, R. v4p0615c2s
Inwin, J. v3p0070c2s
Ion, T.P. v5p0587c1s v5p0595c1s
Ipsen, A. v4p0147c1m v5p0152c2m v6p0164c1m
Irby, A.P. v1p0151c1s v1p1133c2s v5p0379c1s v5p0412c1s v6p0330c1s
Irby, A.P. and Mackenzie, G.M. v1p0174c2s v1p1180c1s v1p1331c2s
Irby, P. v3p0050c2s
Iredell, F.W. v3p0408c2s
Iredell, Harriet v5p0479c2s
Ireland, A. v2p0068c2s v2p0113c1s v2p0140c1s v2p0391c2s v5p0006c2s v5p0109c1s v5p0128c1s v5p0128c2m v5p0245c2s v6p0088c2s v6p0138c2m v6p0296c1s v6p0317c2s v6p0339c1s v6p0396c1s v6p0492c2s v6p0494c2s v6p0570c2s v6p0620c1s
Ireland, A. and Siclen, G.W.Van v5p0587c1s
Ireland, A.E. v3p0057c1s v3p0389c2s v4p0155c2s
Ireland, A.I. v4p0177c2s
Ireland, Alleyne v5p0246c1s
Ireland, E.A. v5p0276c1s v6p0539c1s
Ireland, E.N. v6p0274c2s
Ireland, E.N. and Park, F. v3p0152c1s
Ireland, Ethel v3p0366c1s
Ireland, F.G. v1p0570c1s v3p0268c1s v4p0321c2s v4p0570c2s
Ireland, J. v2p0436c1s v3p0084c2s v3p0271c2s v4p0500c2s v5p0347c2s v5p0459c1s v5p0557c2s
Ireland, J. et al. v6p0368c1s
Ireland, John v5p0603c1s
Ireland, M.E. v1p0341c1s v4p0354c2s
Ireland, Mrs. v4p0216c2s
Ireland, R.R. v6p0305c2s
Ireland, W.A. v5p0244c2s v5p0320c2s v5p0591c1s
Ireland, W.W. v4p0133c2s v5p0157c1s
Ireton, F.G. v2p0105c2s v2p0239c1s v2p0282c2s
Iris, F.M. v6p0053c2s v6p0227c2s
Irish, C.W. v2p0009c2s v2p0375c1s v2p0417c2s v2p0425c1s v3p0127c1s v6p0141c2s
Irish, J.P. v3p0420c2s v4p0083c1s v4p0526c1s v6p0265c1s v6p0515c2s
Irish, W.N. v1p0320c1s
Irizar, J. v6p0023c1s
Irland, F. v4p0542c2s v5p0050c2s v5p0077c1s v5p0377c2s v5p0424c2s v5p0466c2s v5p0534c1s v6p0394c1s v6p0658c1s v6p0709c2m
Irons, D. v4p0179c1m v4p0179c2m v4p0259c1s v5p0187c1s v5p0187c2s v5p0519c1s v6p0212c1s
Irons, G. v2p0056c1s
Irons, M. v2p0245c1s
Irons, W.J. v1p1083c2s v1p1338c2s v2p0087c1m
Irvin, C. v6p0619c2s
Irvine, A.F. v6p0672c1s
Irvine, Alex.F. v6p0126c2s v6p0357c1s
Irvine, J. v5p0238c1s
Irvine, J.H. v6p0481c2s
Irvine, J.T. v3p0328c1s
Irvine, J.W. v4p0571c2s
Irvine, L.H. v6p0568c2s
Irvine, R. et al. v3p0100c1s
Irvine, W. v4p0523c2s
Irving, A. v2p0179c2s v3p0457c1s v4p0320c1s
Irving, A. and Gurney, H.P. v3p0380c1s
Irving, A.P. v5p0269c1s
Irving, D. v2p0352c2s
Irving, E. v1p0996c1s v1p1030c2s v1p1170c1s v1p1237c2s
Irving, E.A. v3p0003c2s v4p0245c1s v4p0374c1s v4p0377c1s v4p0444c1s v5p0110c2s v5p0113c2s v5p0260c2s v5p0357c1s v5p0536c2s v5p0594c1s
Irving, F.F. v3p0418c1s v4p0190c1s v5p0565c1s
Irving, G. v4p0370c1s
Irving, G.A. v6p0429c1s v6p0429c2s
Irving, H. v1p0035c2s v1p1183c1s v1p1184c2s v1p1185c2s v2p0002c1s v2p0010c2s v2p0123c1s v2p0372c1s v2p0398c1s v2p0416c2s v3p0002c1s v3p0175c2s v3p0223c2s v3p0427c1s v4p0002c2m v4p0293c1s v4p0544c1s v5p0575c2s v6p0391c2s
Irving, H., Sir v4p0572c1s
Irving, H.B. v5p0003c1s v5p0024c2s v6p0003c1s v6p0127c1s v6p0261c2s v6p0612c2s
Irving, Henry et al. v3p0406c1s
Irving, J.T. v1p0345c2s v1p0693c1s v1p0935c1s
Irving, L. v4p0013c2s v4p0014c2s v4p0384c2s v4p0408c1s v4p0408c2s v4p0611c2m
Irving, L.R. v6p0586c1s
Irving, M. v5p0602c2s v6p0493c1s v6p0494c2s v6p0682c1s
Irving, Minna v5p0256c1s v5p0295c1s v5p0356c2s
Irving, P.M. v1p0667c1s
Irving, R. v1p0300c1s v1p1152c2s v1p1271c1s
Irving, R.D. v1p1113c1s v1p1417c1m v2p0018c2s v2p0207c2s v2p0229c2s v3p0205c1s
Irving, W. v1p0001c2s v1p0022c1m v1p0028c1s v1p0114c2s v1p0207c2s v1p0312c2s v1p0407c1s v1p0735c1s v1p0854c1s v1p0857c2s v1p0928c2s v1p1209c2s v1p1229c1s v1p1434c1s v5p0495c1s
Irving, W.F. v5p0366c2s
Irvins, W.M. v1p0699c2s
Irwell, L. v4p0085c1s v4p0086c1s v4p0086c2m v4p0191c2s v4p0237c1s v4p0247c2s v4p0271c1s v4p0314c1s v4p0369c1s v4p0384c1s v4p0416c1s v4p0462c2s v4p0526c2s v4p0563c2s v4p0580c2s v4p0581c1s v5p0119c1s v5p0291c1s v5p0548c2s v5p0559c2s v5p0560c1s v5p0618c1s v6p0071c1s v6p0216c2s v6p0237c2s v6p0299c1m v6p0348c1s
Irwell, Lawrence v4p0236c2s
Irwin, A. v1p0477c1s v3p0028c1s v6p0239c2s
Irwin, E.P. v6p0072c2s v6p0088c1s v6p0134c1s v6p0142c1s v6p0474c1s v6p0568c1s v6p0568c2s
Irwin, F. v6p0067c2s
Irwin, G.A. v5p0118c2s
Irwin, G.F. v6p0254c2s
Irwin, H.M. v2p0034c2s v2p0041c2s v2p0186c1s v2p0199c2m v2p0237c1s v2p0299c1s v2p0382c1s v2p0408c1s v4p0523c1s
Irwin, J. v1p0673c2s v1p1118c1s
Irwin, J.N. v4p0026c2s v4p0289c1s v4p0292c2s
Irwin, J.N.H. v6p0072c2s
Irwin, J.O. v1p1186c2s
Irwin, M.H. v5p0269c1s v5p0554c2s
Irwin, M.M. v6p0176c2s
Irwin, M.M. and Hensley, A. v5p0537c1s
Irwin, May v5p0547c2s
Irwin, R.B. v1p0444c2s v1p0540c2s v1p0839c1s v1p1176c1s
Irwin, R.J.J. v5p0579c1s
Irwin, S.T. v5p0140c2s v6p0026c2s v6p0155c2s v6p0284c2s v6p0359c2s v6p0575c1s
Irwin, T. v1p0046c1s v1p0184c2s v1p0208c1s v1p0394c1s v1p0403c1s v1p0442c2s v1p0530c2s v1p0626c1s v1p0726c2s v1p0774c1s v1p0891c1s v1p0928c2s v1p0934c2s v1p0949c2s v1p0990c2s v1p1055c1s v1p1301c1s
Irwin, T.C. v2p0336c2s
Irwin, W. v2p0192c1s v2p0225c1s v3p0007c2s v6p0121c1s v6p0282c2s v6p0487c1s v6p0567c2s v6p0613c1s v6p0622c2s
Irwin, W. and Burgess, G.. v6p0536c1s
Irwin, W.G. v5p0125c2m v5p0360c1s v5p0399c2s v5p0443c2s v5p0446c1s v5p0543c1s v6p0081c2s v6p0133c1s
Irwin, Wallace v6p0379c1s
Isaac, T.S. v1p1076c2s
Isaacs, A.S. v3p0224c1s v3p0232c2s v3p0264c1s v3p0351c1s v3p0378c2s v3p0389c2s v4p0301c2m v5p0311c2s v5p0566c1s v6p0343c2s v6p0630c1s
Isaacs, Abram, S. v3p0233c1s
Isaacs, Dr. v1p0519c1s
Isaacs, E.J. v6p0286c2s
Isaacs, I.H. v4p0301c2s
Isaacs, L.H. v4p0431c2s
Isaacs, L.M. v5p0113c2s v5p0560c1s v5p0609c2s v6p0256c1s v6p0438c2s v6p0439c1s v6p0468c1s
Isaacs, M.S. v4p0258c1s
Isaacson, A. v4p0228c2s v4p0528c1s v5p0142c1s v5p0232c2s v5p0291c2s
Isabell, J. v2p0330c1s v5p0208c2s v6p0021c1s v6p0056c2s v6p0144c1s v6p0150c1s v6p0221c1s v6p0226c2s v6p0227c2s v6p0434c2s
Isabell, John v6p0056c2s v6p0418c1s
Isbister, A.K. v1p0508c2s v1p0611c1s v3p0098c2s v3p0203c2s
Isborne, W.H. v6p0630c1s
Ischikawa, C. and Weismann, A. v3p0209c2s
Ise, J.T. v3p0441c1s
Iselin, J.F. v2p0389c2m v5p0131c1s v5p0289c2s
Isemonger, E.E. v4p0524c1s
Isgrigg, J.E. v6p0177c1s
Ishak, Ibn v4p0293c2s
Isham, E.S. v1p1099c2s
Isham, G.S. v5p0538c1s
Isham, N.M. v6p0084c2s
Isherwood v3p0349c2s v3p0408c2s
Isherwood, B.F. v1p0145c2m v1p0146c2s v1p0269c2m v1p0580c2s v1p0664c1s v1p0956c2s v1p1012c1s v1p1170c2m v1p1246c2m v1p1247c1m v1p1247c2s v1p1248c1s v1p1248c2s v1p1249c1m v1p1249c2m v1p1250c1m v1p1362c2s v1p1390c1m v2p0090c1s v2p0119c2s v2p0336c1s v2p0386c2s v2p0419c1s v5p0617c2s
Isherwood, E. v3p0047c2s
Ismay, H. v6p0388c1s v6p0441c1s v6p0707c1s
Isom, M.F. v6p0470c1s
Israels, C.H. v5p0023c2s v6p0027c1s v6p0027c2s v6p0546c2s v6p0600c2s
Istria, Countess d' v1p1209c1s
Istria, D.d' v1p0489c1m v1p0554c1m v1p1377c2s
Istria, Dora d' v1p1421c2s v1p1425c1s v2p0129c1s
Italian, An v6p0331c2s
Itier, J. v1p0233c1s v1p0236c1s
Ito, H. v6p0334c2s v6p0652c1s
Ittner, A. v6p0025c2s
Iturbide, A.De v4p0368c2s v5p0373c2s
Iurs, G.McE. v6p0420c1s
Iurs, Grace McE. v6p0375c2s v6p0420c1s v6p0441c1s v6p0525c2s v6p0694c2s
Ivan, E. v6p0144c1s
Ivanovich v6p0331c2s v6p0406c2s
Ivanovitch v6p0560c1s v6p0711c1s
Ivens, A.H. v4p0207c1s
Iverach, J. v2p0352c2s v2p0437c2s v4p0082c2s v4p0109c2s v4p0516c1s v4p0541c2m v5p0115c1s v5p0196c1s v5p0198c1s v5p0236c2s v5p0249c2s v5p0277c1s v5p0313c2s v5p0319c1s v5p0369c1s v5p0470c2s v5p0481c2s v5p0483c2m v6p0307c1s v6p0358c1s v6p0496c1s v6p0610c2s v6p0673c1s
Ivers, Grace McE. v6p0171c1s
Ives, A.E. v3p0202c2s v3p0468c1s
Ives, B. v3p0453c2s v4p0065c2s v4p0066c1s v4p0593c1s
Ives, C.A. et al. v2p0355c1s
Ives, F.E. v2p0340c1m v3p0080c1s v3p0193c2s v3p0251c2s v3p0263c2s v3p0330c2m v3p0331c1s v4p0253c2m v4p0440c2m v5p0447c2s v5p0456c2s v6p0415c2m v6p0497c1s v6p0497c2m
Ives, G. v5p0467c1s
Ives, G.B. v6p0184c1m
Ives, H. v6p0070c1s
Ives, H.C. v6p0563c2s

Ives, H.E. v6p0497c1s
Ives, J.C. v1p0279c2s
Ives, J.M. v5p0017c1s
v5p0133c2s
Ives, J.S. v6p0308c2s
Ives, L.H. v5p0151c1s
v5p0460c1s
Ives, P. v5p0626c2s
Ives, T.C. v4p0277c2s
Ivins, W.M. v1p0729c1s
v2p0086c1s v3p0292c1s v4p0405c2s
Ivins, W.M., jr. v6p0556c1s
v6p0606c1s
Ivis, F.M. v6p0439c2s
Ivory, W. v1p0748c1s
v1p1203c2s
Iwaji, Okamoto v6p0369c2s
Iwan-Muller, E. v6p0542c1s
Iwan-Muller, E.B. v4p0582c1s
v5p0007c2s v5p0376c2s v5p0588c2s
v6p0048c1s v6p0270c2s v6p0418c1s
v6p0542c1s v6p0665c2s
Iwasaki, C. v5p0146c2s
Iyenaga, J. v6p0186c1s
Iyenaga, T. v3p0226c2s
v6p0334c1s v6p0334c2s v6p0336c1s
v6p0560c2s
Izawa, H. v4p0165c1s

J., D.M. ... v5p0355c1s
J., G. ... v6p0338c1s
Jacassy, A.F. ... v2p0240c1s
v3p0070c1s v3p0287c2s v3p0298c1m
v3p0436c2s
Jacberns, R. ... v5p0151c2s
v5p0164c1s v5p0342c2s v5p0544c2s
Jaccaci, A.F. ... v4p0189c1s
v4p0484c1s v4p0498c1s v4p0539c2s
v4p0604c1s v5p0612c1s v6p0486c2s
Jaccard, A. ... v5p0034c2s
v5p0065c2s v5p0442c2s
Jack, A.A. ... v6p0262c1s
Jack, A.E. ... v5p0573c1s
Jack, E. ... v2p0162c1m
Jack, Edward ... v4p0351c1s
Jack, Flint ... v1p1200c1s
Jack, J. ... v1p0145c2s
Jack, J.G. ... v4p0022c2s
v4p0045c2s v4p0060c1s v4p0089c1s
v4p0190c2s v4p0202c2s v4p0204c1m
v4p0217c1s v4p0225c1s v4p0251c2s
v4p0255c1s v4p0260c2s v4p0262c2s
v4p0264c1s v4p0265c1s v4p0308c1s
v4p0327c1s v4p0349c2s v4p0425c1s
v4p0445c2s v4p0452c2s v4p0491c2s
v4p0522c1m v4p0583c1m v4p0623c1s
v5p0398c2s v5p0547c2s v5p0590c1s
v5p0632c1s
Jack, L.A. ... v1p0195c1s
Jack, Prof. ... v3p0459c2s
Jack, R.L. ... v6p0589c1s
Jack, R.Lockhart. ... v6p0119c2s
Jack, W. ... v1p0385c1s
v1p0497c2s v1p1006c2m v1p1357c2s
v1p1370c2s v2p0456c1s v5p0524c2s
Jack, W.B. ... v1p1397c1s
Jackberns, R. ... v5p0390c1m
Jacker, E. ... v1p0022c1s
v1p0327c1s v1p0329c1s v1p0636c2s
v1p0637c1s v1p0638c1s v1p0726c1s
v1p0853c1s v2p0217c2s v2p0249c1s
v2p0274c2s v2p0473c1s
Jackman, J.S. ... v2p0302c1s
Jackman, J.S. and Watkins, S.R.
v2p0299c2s
Jackman, N.S. ... v4p0135c1s
Jackman, W. ... v5p0512c1s
Jackman, W.S. ... v4p0026c2s
v4p0395c1s v4p0554c1s v5p0241c2s
v5p0391c1s v5p0512c1s v5p0512c2s
v6p0067c1s v6p0320c2s v6p0406c1s
v6p0444c2s v6p0480c2s
Jackol, J. ... v6p0224c2s
Jacks, L.P. ... v4p0310c2s
v5p0500c2s v6p0125c1s
Jackson and Ott ... v1p0533c1s
Jackson, A. ... v1p0975c1s
Jackson, A.A. ... v2p0082c2s
Jackson, A.B. ... v5p0413c2s
Jackson, A.C. ... v6p0010c2s
Jackson, A.M. ... v4p0154c2s
Jackson, A.V.W. ... v2p0372c2s
v4p0015c1s v4p0040c1s v4p0147c2s
v4p0158c1s v4p0218c1s v4p0246c1s
v4p0637c2s v5p0390c2s v5p0423c2s
v5p0424c1s v5p0433c2s v5p0508c1s
v5p0522c2s v6p0072c2s v6p0225c2s
v6p0320c1s v6p0489c2m
Jackson, A.V.Williams ... v6p0164c2s
Jackson, A.W. ... v1p0258c2s
v1p0687c2s v2p0374c1s v3p0063c1s
v3p0148c2s v4p0358c2s v5p0155c1s
v5p0264c2s v5p0364c1m
Jackson, Arabelle H. ... v6p0116c2s
Jackson, B. ... v1p1141c1s
v6p0491c1s
Jackson, B.D. ... v2p0051c2s
Jackson, Birdsall ... v6p0424c2s
Jackson, C. ... v2p0060c2s
v2p0145c2s v2p0300c2s v6p0299c2s
v6p0549c2s v6p0637c2s
Jackson, C., jr. ... v1p0762c2s
Jackson, C.C. ... v3p0232c1s
v3p0267c2s
Jackson, C.C., Lady ... v1p0105c1s
Jackson, C.J. ... v5p0547c1s
Jackson, C.L. ... v4p0132c1s
Jackson, C.N. ... v2p0317c1s
Jackson, C.N., Mrs. ... v4p0406c1s
Jackson, C.T. ... v1p0225c1s
v1p0300c1s v1p0405c2s v1p0432c2s
v1p0509c1s v1p0789c2s v1p0809c1s
v1p0828c1s v1p1290c1s v5p0036c1s
v5p0267c2s v6p0080c2s
Jackson, C.T. and Alger, F.
v1p0931c1s
Jackson, Cyril ... v6p0192c1s
Jackson, D.C. ... v4p0175c2m
v4p0176c1s v5p0172c2s v5p0183c2s
v6p0198c2s v6p0204c2s v6p0406c2s
Jackson, D.C. and Jackson, W.B.
v6p0197c2s
Jackson, D.D. ... v6p0173c1s
Jackson, E. ... v1p0213c2s
v1p1322c1s v5p0426c1s
Jackson, E.C. ... v4p0199c1s
v5p0341c2s
Jackson, E.E. ... v6p0079c2m
Jackson, E.H. ... v5p0125c2s
v6p0197c1s
Jackson, E.P. ... v4p0381c2s
v4p0429c2s v5p0440c1s
Jackson, E.W. ... v4p0455c1s
v4p0614c2s
Jackson, F. ... v1p0742c2s
Jackson, F.G. ... v4p0295c2s
Jackson, F.G. et al. ... v5p0219c2s
Jackson, F.H. ... v5p0446c1s
v6p0271c1s v6p0609c2m
Jackson, F.H. et al. ... v5p0430c2s
Jackson, F.N. ... v6p0124c2s
Jackson, F.W. ... v6p0199c1s
Jackson, Fanny R. ... v6p0489c1s
Jackson, G. ... v5p0311c2s
v5p0348c2s v6p0484c2s
Jackson, G.A. ... v1p0359c2s
v1p0506c1s v1p0567c2s v2p0028c1s
v3p0076c1s v3p0241c1s v3p0283c1s
v3p0289c1s v3p0341c2s v3p0427c2m
Jackson, G.F. ... v1p0280c1s
v1p0303c2s
Jackson, G.M. ... v5p0326c2s
Jackson, G.R. ... v1p0927c2s
Jackson, Geo. ... v5p0232c2s
Jackson, H. ... v1p0025c1s
v1p1172c2s v5p0447c2s
Jackson, H.H. ... v1p0140c2s
v1p0279c1m v1p0279c2m v1p0471c2s
v1p0500c2s v1p0513c2s v1p0638c1s
v1p0703c2s v1p0756c1s v1p1030c1s
v1p1051c1s v1p1365c2s v1p1380c1s
v2p0018c1s v2p0028c1s v2p0041c1s
v2p0062c1s v2p0064c1s v2p0064c2s
v2p0067c2s v2p0077c1s v2p0094c1m
v2p0130c1s v2p0166c1s v2p0219c2s
v2p0239c2s v2p0261c1s v2p0266c1s
v2p0286c2s v2p0298c2s v2p0304c2s
v2p0318c2m v2p0323c1s v2p0354c1s
v2p0359c1m v5p0301c1s
Jackson, H.H. et al. ... v2p0205c1s
Jackson, H.H., Mrs. ... v1p0114c1s
v1p0732c2s
Jackson, H.M. ... v1p0088c1s
v1p0245c2s v1p0887c2s v1p1201c1s
v1p1438c1s
Jackson, H.R. ... v1p0675c1s
Jackson, H.W. ... v2p0166c2s
Jackson, J. ... v1p0203c2s
v2p0206c2s v3p0129c1s v3p0243c2s
v4p0238c2s v4p0247c1s
Jackson, J.C. ... v2p0050c1s
v4p0300c1s v5p0116c2s
Jackson, J.E. ... v1p0612c2s
v2p0374c1s
Jackson, J.E. and Nichols, J.G.
v1p0616c1s v1p0651c2s
Jackson, J.F. ... v1p0008c1s
v1p0034c1s
Jackson, J.H. ... v2p0309c2s
v3p0232c1s v4p0171c1s v4p0479c2s
Jackson, J.M. ... v6p0301c1s
Jackson, J.P. ... v3p0135c1s
v3p0305c1s v5p0184c1s
Jackson, J.R. ... v1p0095c2s
v1p0098c2s v1p0153c1s v1p0184c1s
v1p0270c2m v1p0271c1s v1p0299c2s
v1p0327c2s v1p0362c2s v1p0429c1s
v1p0452c1s v1p0493c1s v1p0537c2s
v1p0598c1s v1p0602c2s v1p0744c1s
v1p0796c1s v1p0919c1s v1p0965c2s
v1p1015c2s v1p1039c2s v1p1081c1s
v1p1141c2s v1p1198c1s v1p1260c1s
v1p1265c1m v1p1266c2s v1p1287c2s
v1p1311c1s v1p1364c1s v1p1382c1s
v1p1404c1s v2p0053c2s v2p0145c1s
v3p0044c2s v3p0271c2s v3p0333c2s
v4p0446c1s v5p0073c1s v5p0287c1s
Jackson, J.W. ... v1p0066c2s
v1p0073c1s v1p0287c1s v1p0347c1s
v1p0382c2s v1p0427c2s v1p0472c1s
v1p0478c1s v1p0652c2s v1p0659c2s
v1p0692c1s v1p0786c2s v1p0857c1s
v1p0964c1s v1p1004c2m v1p1037c2s
v1p1073c2s v1p1211c1s v1p1217c2s
v1p1218c1s v1p1238c1m v1p1274c2s
v1p1330c1s
Jackson, James ... v4p0376c1s
Jackson, K.J. et al. ... v2p0477c2s
Jackson, L. ... v4p0247c2s
v4p0276c2s v4p0277c1s v4p0486c1s
v6p0457c1s
Jackson, L.D. ... v2p0281c2s
v2p0419c2s
Jackson, L.H. ... v6p0615c2m
Jackson, L.S., Sir ... v2p0039c2s
Jackson, L.W. ... v5p0628c2s
Jackson, Lady ... v1p0737c1s
v1p1114c1s v2p0375c1s v3p0272c1s
Jackson, M. ... v4p0226c1s
v4p0532c2s v4p0631c1s
Jackson, M.P. ... v2p0194c1s
v4p0027c2s v4p0089c2s v4p0148c2s
v4p0195c2s v4p0233c2s v4p0255c2s
v4p0264c1s v4p0399c1s v4p0623c1s
Jackson, M.P. and McNab, P.
v4p0029c1s
Jackson, M.P. and Slade, R.J.
v4p0029c1s
Jackson, N.L. ... v5p0547c1s
v5p0573c1s
Jackson, O.E. ... v3p0360c1s
Jackson, P.H. ... v2p0097c2s
v2p0229c1s
Jackson, P.R. ... v1p0876c1s
Jackson, R. ... v2p0209c1s
v2p0344c2s
Jackson, R.C. ... v5p0012c1s
Jackson, R.F. ... v2p0369c1s
Jackson, R.R. ... v1p0628c2s
Jackson, R.S. ... v4p0009c2s
Jackson, R.T. ... v2p0244c2s
v3p0325c2m v6p0056c1s
Jackson, R.W. ... v5p0450c2s
v5p0534c2s
Jackson, S. ... v1p0830c2s
v2p0006c2s v3p0007c1m v3p0008c1s
v3p0055c1s v3p0128c2s v3p0383c1s
v4p0048c1s v4p0187c1s v6p0010c1s
Jackson, S.M. ... v2p0337c2s
v4p0267c2s v4p0438c2s v4p0479c1s
v5p0163c2s v5p0390c2s v5p0436c1s
Jackson, T. ... v1p0169c2s
Jackson, T.G. ... v4p0025c1s
v4p0072c1s v4p0419c2s v6p0028c2m
Jackson, T.J. ... v3p0073c1s
Jackson, T.J. et al. ... v1p1347c1s
Jackson, T.S. ... v5p0526c2s
Jackson, T.W. ... v2p0473c2s
Jackson, U.A. ... v1p1419c2m
Jackson, W. ... v4p0602c2s
v4p0609c2s
Jackson, W.B. and Jackson, D.C.
v6p0197c2s
Jackson, W.H. ... v1p0279c2s
Jackson, W.W. ... v4p0200c1s
v5p0207c2s
Jacob, A. ... v1p1382c1s
v1p1391c2s
Jacob, B. ... v5p0199c1s
Jacob, E. ... v1p1121c2s
Jacob, E.H. ... v2p0459c1s
Jacob, G.A. ... v1p0848c1s
v4p0021c2s v4p0502c2s v4p0601c1s
Jacob, K. ... v2p0069c2s
v2p0176c2s v2p0341c2s v2p0381c1s
v2p0428c1s
Jacob, S.S. ... v2p0070c1s
Jacob, Son of Aaron ... v6p0567c1s
Jacob, T.E. ... v6p0299c1s
v6p0657c2s
Jacob, Violet ... v6p0415c2s
v6p0687c2s
Jacob, W.H. ... v2p0475c1s
Jacobi, A. ... v2p0318c1s
v6p0417c1s v6p0660c1s
Jacobi, C.T. ... v6p0307c2s
v6p0517c1m
Jacobi, J.S. ... v1p0948c2s
Jacobi, M.P. ... v1p1426c1s
v2p0132c1m v2p0222c1s v2p0477c1s
v3p0348c1s v3p0468c2s v4p0630c1s
Jacobs, C.P. ... v2p0343c2s
v3p0231c1s
Jacobs, C.W. ... v5p0577c1s
Jacobs, E. ... v6p0082c2s
v6p0133c1s v6p0149c1s v6p0418c2m
v6p0688c1s
Jacobs, E.H. ... v6p0105c2s
v6p0473c2s
Jacobs, G.M. ... v5p0047c1s
v5p0480c1s v6p0394c2s
Jacobs, H.E. ... v1p0225c2m
v1p0288c2s v1p0296c2s v1p0848c1s
v1p1089c1s v1p1139c1s v1p1140c1s
v4p0345c1s v5p0369c1s
Jacobs, H.H. ... v6p0672c1s
v6p0701c2s
Jacobs, H.W. ... v6p0528c2s
Jacobs, J. ... v1p0511c2s
v1p0529c1s v1p0668c2s v1p0691c1s
v2p0236c2s v2p0237c1s v2p0358c1s
v3p0038c2s v3p0342c2s v4p0103c1s
v4p0182c1s v4p0204c2s v4p0301c2s
v4p0302c1s v4p0302c2m v4p0478c2s
v4p0480c2s v4p0513c2s v4p0539c2s
v4p0549c1s v4p0569c1s v5p0001c1s
v5p0155c1s v5p0174c1s v5p0193c1s
v5p0236c1s v5p0307c2s v5p0308c1s
v5p0310c1s v5p0364c1s v5p0435c2s
v5p0630c1s
Jacobs, J. and Gollancz, I.
v3p0463c2s
Jacobs, J. and Neubauer, A.
v3p0233c1s
Jacobs, J. and Nutt, A. ... v4p0155c2s
v4p0361c1s
Jacobs, J. and Spielman, I.
v3p0230c1s
Jacobs, J. et al. ... v3p0050c2s
Jacobs, J.M. ... v6p0618c2s
Jacobs, M. ... v1p0134c2s
v1p0507c1s v1p0518c2s v1p0795c1m
v1p0829c1s v1p0829c2s v1p1303c2s
Jacobs, M.W. ... v1p0897c2s
v1p0900c1s
Jacobs, W.B. ... v4p0192c1s
v4p0512c2s v4p0566c1s v5p0518c1s
v6p0581c2s
Jacobs, W.B. et al. ... v5p0511c1s

Jacobs, W.W. v4p0062c2s
v4p0107c2s v4p0131c1s v4p0156c2s
v4p0343c1s v4p0588c1s v5p0004c1s
v5p0093c2s v5p0149c1s v5p0162c2s
v5p0202c1s v5p0238c2s v5p0322c1s
v5p0365c2s v5p0381c1s v5p0474c2s
v5p0479c1s v6p0020c2s v6p0108c2s
v6p0146c1s v6p0176c1s v6p0235c2s
v6p0287c2s v6p0292c1s v6p0388c2s
v6p0425c2s
Jacobsen, E.P. v4p0294c1s
Jacobsen, Sara v6p0075c1s
Jacobson, P.N. v3p0044c1s
Jacobson, S.L. v5p0053c1s
v5p0137c2s v5p0332c2s v5p0394c1s
Jacobus, C. v6p0428c1s
Jacobus, D.L. v6p0081c2s
v6p0699c2s
Jacobus, D.S. v5p0338c1s
v6p0204c2s
Jacobus, M.W. v1p0122c2s
v1p0287c2s v1p1047c1s v4p0057c2m
v5p0059c2m v5p0558c1s v6p0061c1s
v6p0063c1s v6p0064c1s v6p0341c2s
v6p0513c2s
Jacobus, Marion C. v6p0243c1s
Jacobus, R.P. v4p0046c1s
v4p0070c1s v4p0172c1s v4p0430c1s
v4p0462c1s
Jacoby, Dr. v1p0907c1s
Jacoby, H. v4p0232c1s
v4p0322c1s v4p0440c1s v4p0497c1s
v4p0616c1s v5p0035c1s v5p0448c1s
v5p0456c2s v5p0560c2s v5p0561c1s
v6p0365c2s
Jacoby, H.S. v6p0081c1s
Jacoby, J.C. v2p0235c2s
v5p0056c1s v5p0281c1s
Jacoby, L.S. v1p1399c1s
Jacounchikoff, Marie v5p0193c1s
Jacox, F. v1p0112c1s
v1p0145c1s v1p0154c1s v1p0228c2s
v1p0230c1s v1p0296c2s v1p0317c1s
v1p0324c2s v1p0346c1s v1p0352c2s
v1p0372c1s v1p0453c2s v1p0469c1s
v1p0493c2s v1p0497c2s v1p0521c1s
v1p0539c1s v1p0551c1s v1p0569c2s
v1p0574c2s v1p0621c1s v1p0696c1s
v1p0733c1s v1p0755c2s v1p0756c1s
v1p0774c1s v1p0812c1s v1p0816c2s
v1p0852c1s v1p0879c1s v1p0913c2s
v1p0918c2s v1p1049c1s v1p1085c2s
v1p1096c1s v1p1190c2s v1p1220c2s
v1p1221c1s v1p1246c1s v1p1280c2s
v1p1299c2s v1p1305c2s v1p1314c2m
v1p1316c1s v1p1358c1s v1p1363c1s
v1p1376c2s v1p1404c1s v1p1406c1s
v1p1418c2s v1p1440c1s
Jacquemont, S. v1p0810c1s
Jacques, D.H. v1p0142c2s
v1p0891c2s v1p0892c1s
Jacques, D.R. v1p0514c2s
v1p0539c1s v1p0648c1s v1p0821c1m
v1p0823c2s
Jacques, J. v5p0580c2s
v6p0648c1s
Jacques, M.J. v4p0092c2s
Jacques, W.W. v1p0004c2s
v1p1222c2s v2p0019c1s v2p0137c1s
v2p0433c1m v4p0176c2s
Jadwin, E. v6p0204c1s
Jadwin, M. v5p0368c2s
Jadwin, M. et al. v5p0423c2s
Jaeger, A. v2p0042c2s
Jaeger, H. v2p0317c1m
v3p0307c2m v4p0407c2s
Jaeger, L. v2p0215c1s
v2p0353c2s
Jaffray, E. v6p0052c1s
Jaffray, W. v1p1005c1s
Jagemann, H.C.G.von v3p0140c2s
Jaggar, T.A. v5p0155c2s
v5p0232c2s v6p0403c2s v6p0486c2m
v6p0677c2s
Jaggar, T.A., jr. v5p0374c1m
Jaggard, W. v6p0332c2s
Jago, F.V. v1p0723c1s
Jago, W. v2p0073c1s
v2p0076c2m v2p0108c2s v3p0054c1s
v6p0143c2s
v6p0229c2s
Jagow, E.von v5p0221c2s
v5p0562c1s
Jahns, R. v2p0268c1s
Jailer, T.F. v3p0313c2s
James, A.C. v5p0258c2s
James, B.B. v5p0320c2s
James, B.F.H. v6p0014c2s
James, B.W. v4p0443c1s
James, C. v5p0298c1s
James, C.P. v1p0731c2s
James, C.T. v1p0306c1s
v1p0306c2s v1p0307c1s
James, C.T.C. v3p0030c1s
v4p0258c2s v4p0273c2s
James, C.W. v5p0393c2s
v6p0228c1s v6p0438c1s
James, D.R. v1p0486c2s
James, E. v1p0919c1s
v1p1098c1s v5p0186c2s
James, E.J. v2p0001c2s
v2p0079c2s v2p0088c1s v2p0119c2s
v2p0131c2s v2p0172c1s v2p0231c2s
v2p0251c1s v2p0347c2m v2p0363c1s
v3p0013c1s v3p0036c1s v3p0066c1s
v3p0087c1s v3p0119c2s v3p0168c1s
v3p0215c1s v3p0246c1s v3p0351c2s
v3p0353c1m v3p0378c1s v3p0399c1s
v3p0408c1s v3p0418c1s v3p0421c1s
v4p0077c1s v4p0213c1s v4p0277c2s
v4p0449c2s v4p0531c2s v4p0593c1s
v4p0598c1m v5p0054c1m v5p0119c2m
v5p0175c2s v5p0254c2s v5p0338c2s
v5p0399c2s v5p0430c2s v5p0485c2s
v5p0556c2m v6p0191c1s v6p0366c2s
v6p0652c2s v6p0671c1m v6p0671c2s
James, E.J. and Taussig, F.W.
v2p0418c1s
James, E.J. et al. v2p0403c1s
James, E.L. v2p0176c1s
v3p0445c1s
James, E.W. v4p0406c1s
James, Elizabeth M. v6p0339c2s
James, F. v2p0290c2s
James, G.B. v4p0209c2s
James, G.M. v4p0140c2s
James, G.O. v6p0506c1s
v6p0647c1s
James, G.P.R. v1p0061c1s
v1p0105c1s v1p0137c2s v1p0149c2s
v1p0799c2s v1p0950c2s v1p1258c1s
James, G.W. v1p1361c1s
v5p0041c2s v5p0049c1m v5p0288c1s
v5p0462c1s v5p0534c1s v5p0544c2s
v5p0547c1s v6p0070c1s v6p0085c1s
v6p0092c2s v6p0295c2s v6p0315c1s
v6p0325c1s v6p0350c1s v6p0421c1s
v6p0430c2s v6p0561c2s v6p0567c2s
v6p0633c2s v6p0682c2s
James, G.Wharton v6p0264c1s
James, H. v1p0074c2s
v1p0201c1s v1p0201c2s v1p0313c1s
v1p0441c1s v1p0568c1s v1p0582c2s
v1p0802c1s v1p0802c2s v1p0901c1s
v1p1094c2s v1p1096c1s v1p1161c1s
v1p1238c1m v1p1274c2m v1p1308c1s
v1p1420c2s v2p0022c1s v2p0029c2s
v2p0053c1s v2p0125c2s v2p0155c1s
v2p0165c2s v2p0174c2s v2p0215c2s
v2p0246c1s v2p0264c2s v2p0310c2s
v2p0354c1s v2p0420c1s v2p0443c2s
v2p0447c1s v2p0448c2s v3p0005c2s
v3p0014c2s v3p0023c1s v3p0024c1s
v3p0073c2s v3p0100c1s v3p0106c1s
v3p0111c2s v3p0135c2s v3p0177c1s
v3p0206c2s v3p0248c1s v3p0255c2s
v3p0257c2s v3p0259c1s v3p0269c1s
v3p0271c2s v3p0323c1s v3p0349c2s
v3p0360c1s v3p0375c2s v3p0400c1s
v3p0409c2s v3p0434c2s v3p0439c1s
v3p0449c1s v4p0042c1s v4p0122c2s
v4p0135c1s v4p0163c2s v4p0202c1s
v4p0228c1s v4p0299c2s v4p0309c2s
v4p0327c2s v4p0341c2s v4p0343c2s
v4p0369c2s v4p0405c2s v4p0412c2s
v4p0460c1s v4p0610c2s v4p0619c1s
v5p0052c2s v5p0078c1s v5p0205c2s
v5p0221c1s v5p0248c2s v5p0256c1s
v5p0366c2s v5p0379c1s v5p0497c2s
v5p0520c1s v5p0553c1s v5p0596c1s
v5p0627c2s v6p0014c1s v6p0022c2s
v6p0049c1m v6p0076c1s v6p0083c2s
v6p0232c2s v6p0301c2s v6p0450c1s
v6p0452c1s v6p0453c2m v6p0456c1s
v6p0491c2s v6p0543c2s v6p0569c1s
v6p0686c2s v6p0713c1s
James, H. et al. v3p0106c1s
v4p0174c1s
James, H., jr. v1p0006c2s
v1p0009c2s v1p0010c1s v1p0019c1s
v1p0020c1s v1p0030c1m v1p0035c1s
v1p0045c1s v1p0089c2s v1p0090c1s
v1p0103c1s v1p0116c2s v1p0156c1s
v1p0170c1s v1p0170c2s v1p0194c1s
v1p0216c2s v1p0225c2s v1p0226c2s
v1p0286c1s v1p0289c1s v1p0312c2s
v1p0318c1s v1p0318c2s v1p0329c1s
v1p0335c2s v1p0341c1s v1p0341c2s
v1p0347c2s v1p0349c2s v1p0350c2s
v1p0361c2s v1p0369c2s v1p0371c2s
v1p0408c2s v1p0409c2s v1p0414c2m
v1p0415c1s v1p0420c2s v1p0423c1s
v1p0429c1s v1p0431c2s v1p0451c1s
v1p0471c2s v1p0479c2s v1p0480c2s
v1p0489c2s v1p0490c1s v1p0496c2s
v1p0503c1s v1p0503c2s v1p0506c1s
v1p0511c1s v1p0511c2m v1p0512c1m
v1p0520c1s v1p0530c1s v1p0531c2s
v1p0536c1s v1p0560c2m v1p0573c2s
v1p0575c2s v1p0593c2s v1p0610c2s
v1p0612c1m v1p0650c1s v1p0668c1s
v1p0673c1s v1p0683c2s v1p0709c1s
v1p0714c2s v1p0716c1s v1p0726c2s
v1p0743c1s v1p0744c1s v1p0748c1s
v1p0757c2s v1p0763c2m v1p0765c2s
v1p0766c1m v1p0768c2s v1p0784c2s
v1p0786c1s v1p0809c2s v1p0813c1s
v1p0873c1s v1p0875c1s v1p0886c1s
v1p0887c1s v1p0913c1s v1p0919c2s
v1p0926c1s v1p0950c1s v1p0977c2s
v1p0979c2s v1p0988c2s v1p1008c2m
v1p1032c1s v1p1036c1s v1p1053c2s
v1p1068c2s v1p1070c2s v1p1084c1s
v1p1092c1s v1p1113c2s v1p1123c1s
v1p1125c2s v1p1126c1m v1p1137c2s
v1p1140c1s v1p1143c1m v1p1151c2s
v1p1168c1s v1p1218c1s v1p1255c1s
v1p1257c2s v1p1258c1s v1p1275c1m
v1p1276c1m v1p1286c1s v1p1295c1s
v1p1295c2s v1p1300c1s v1p1301c1s
v1p1317c2m v1p1323c1s v1p1351c1s
v1p1387c1s v1p1389c1s v1p1389c2s
v1p1407c1s v1p1424c2s v2p0068c2s
v2p0111c1s v2p0112c2m v2p0140c1s
v2p0346c2s v2p0385c1s v2p0402c1s
v2p0458c2s
James, H., sr. v6p0202c1s
James, H.A. v2p0416c2s
v3p0101c2s
James, H.E.M. v4p0279c2s
v4p0280c2s
James, H.K. v2p0057c2s
v2p0168c2s v2p0192c2s v2p0209c2s
v2p0330c1s
James, H.P. v2p0256c2s
v2p0313c1s v2p0365c2s v4p0329c2s
v5p0335c1s v5p0336c2s
James, H.W. v1p0723c1s
James, Henry v4p0602c2s
v5p0196c2s v5p0582c2s v5p0632c2s
v6p0208c1s v6p0228c2s
James, Henry, 2d v5p0257c1s
James, I. v1p0467c2s
v1p1207c2s v3p0111c2s
James, I., Mrs. v1p0049c1s
v1p0101c1s v1p0153c1s v1p0498c1s
v1p0927c1s v1p1015c1m
James, J. v6p0238c1s
James, J.A. v1p0847c2s
v1p1057c2s v1p1237c2s v4p0282c1s
v4p0282c2s v5p0295c1s
James, J.A. and Cunningham, Dr.
v1p0027c2s
James, J.B. v1p0246c2s
v4p0026c1s
James, J.D. v1p1158c2s
James, J.F. v1p0042c2s
v1p0188c1s v1p1329c1s v2p0010c1s
v2p0016c1s v2p0086c1s v2p0094c1s
v2p0120c2s v2p0202c2s v2p0245c2s
v2p0343c1m v3p0167c2s v3p0310c2s
v3p0337c2s v4p0196c1s v4p0417c1s
v4p0542c2s
James, J.G. v6p0482c2s
v6p0541c2s
James, J.H. v4p0370c2s
James, Jos.F. v3p0279c1s
James, L. v5p0390c2s
v6p0558c2s v6p0636c1s
James, L.G. v3p0068c2s
v3p0079c1s v3p0399c2s v4p0007c2s
v4p0012c2s v4p0188c1s v4p0398c2s
James, M. v1p1219c1s
James, M.B. v5p0036c2s
James, M.E. v5p0554c1s
James, M.R. v4p0510c1s
v5p0306c2s
James, M.S.R. v4p0329c1s
v4p0339c2s v4p0627c1s v5p0333c1s
v5p0636c1s v6p0100c2s v6p0370c2s
v6p0704c1s
James, Mabel H. v6p0092c2s
James, P. v5p0416c2s
James, S. v1p0272c2s
James, S.B. v1p0264c2s
v1p0753c2s v2p0381c2s
James, S.J. v5p0322c2s
James, S.R. v3p0143c2s
James, T. v1p0107c1s
v1p0463c1s v1p0499c2s v1p0715c1s
James, T.C. v4p0572c1s
James, T.L. v3p0264c1s
v3p0340c1s v3p0371c2s v3p0459c2s
v4p0257c1s v4p0350c1s v4p0454c1m
v4p0544c2s v5p0045c2s v5p0046c2s
v5p0185c2s v5p0468c2s v6p0511c1s
v6p0669c2s
James, Thos.L. v4p0636c1s
James, V.S. v5p0507c1s
James, W. v1p0009c1s
v1p0036c2s v1p0042c2s v1p0045c2s
v1p0069c1s v1p0082c1s v1p0156c2s
v1p0265c1s v1p0427c1s v1p0435c1s
v1p0496c2s v1p0551c1s v1p0623c1s
v1p0648c2s v1p0649c1s v1p0817c1s
v1p0820c2s v1p0843c1s v1p0843c2m
v1p0993c2s v1p1002c1s v1p1007c1s
v1p1062c1s v1p1084c1s v1p1176c1s
v1p1209c2s v1p1228c1s v1p1235c1s
v1p1300c2s v1p1360c1s v1p1376c1s
v1p1426c1s v1p1433c2s v2p0091c1s
v2p0152c1s v2p0200c1s v2p0224c1s
v2p0358c1s v2p0365c1s v2p0378c2s
v3p0037c1s v3p0038c1s v3p0111c1s
v3p0187c2s v3p0190c2s v3p0217c2m
v3p0287c1s v3p0341c2s v3p0384c2s
v3p0402c2s v3p0430c2s v4p0050c1s
v4p0179c1s v4p0283c1s v4p0331c1s
v4p0372c1s v4p0421c1s v4p0464c1m
v4p0465c1s v4p0481c2s v4p0574c1s

v4p0575c1s v4p0622c1m v5p0008c2m
v5p0103c2s v5p0396c2s v5p0471c1s
v6p0003c1s v6p0039c2s v6p0081c2s
v6p0181c2s v6p0282c1s v6p0302c2m
v6p0399c1s v6p0485c1s v6p0495c2s
v6p0609c2m v6p0613c1s v6p0622c2s
James, W. and Gurney, E. . v2p0140c2s
James, W. and Ward, J. ... v3p0147c1s
James, W. et al. v5p0524c2s
James, W.B. v6p0409c1s
James, W.C. v1p1424c1s
v5p0098c1s
James, W.E. v1p1333c1s
James, W.H. v1p0219c1s
v1p0356c1s v3p0159c2s v4p0106c2s
v4p0433c2s v4p0499c2s v4p0552c1s
v4p0576c2s v5p0244c1s v5p0397c2s
v5p0624c1s v5p0625c1s v6p0060c1s
v6p0702c2s
James, W.J. v3p0015c2s
James, W.P. v5p0206c1s
v6p0468c1s
James, W.T. v4p0041c1s
v4p0414c2s v4p0621c2s v5p0075c2s
v5p0254c1s
James, William v5p0349c1m
v5p0483c1s v6p0165c2s v6p0353c1s
Jameson, A. v1p0714c1s
Jameson, A.E. v5p0539c1s
Jameson, C.D. v3p0054c1s
Jameson, C.D. and Remley, H.
v3p0071c2s
Jameson, E.M. v5p0077c2s
Jameson, E.O. v4p0363c2s
Jameson, H.L. v6p0485c2s
Jameson, H.W. v1p1085c2s
Jameson, J.A. v2p0087c1s
v2p0348c1s v2p0414c1s v2p0418c1s
v3p0105c1s v3p0402c2s
Jameson, J.A. and Woolsey, T.D.
v2p0119c2s
Jameson, J.F. v2p0129c1s
v2p0265c1s v2p0295c2s v2p0313c2s
v2p0418c1s v3p0055c2s v3p0197c1s
v3p0197c2s v3p0260c1s v3p0383c1s
v3p0452c1s v4p0544c2s v4p0592c2s
v4p0607c2s v5p0135c1s v6p0094c2s
v6p0210c2s v6p0292c1s v6p0344c2s
v6p0563c1s v6p0670c2s
Jameson, L.H. v1p0825c1s
Jameson, Mrs. v1p0949c1s
Jameson, W. v1p0365c1s
v2p0024c2s
Jametel, M. v2p0157c1s
Jamieson, A. v2p0055c1s
v2p0137c1s v6p0701c1s
Jamieson, Andrew v6p0014c1s
Jamieson, G. v4p0525c1s
Jamieson, G.S. and Penfield, S.L.
v6p0663c1s
Jamieson, H. v5p0635c1s
Jamieson, J. v2p0031c1s
v4p0012c2s v6p0382c1s v6p0435c2s
Jamieson, M.M. v5p0304c1s
Jamieson, T. v4p0491c1s
Jamin, G. v4p0345c2s
Jamin, J. v1p0008c1s
v1p0399c1s v1p1014c2s v1p1239c1s
v2p0172c1s
Jamin, J. and Bertrand, A.
v1p0502c1s
Jamison, C.V., Mrs. v4p0523c2s
Jamison, R. v4p0073c1s
v4p0176c1s v4p0586c2s
Jamrach, A.E. v1p0135c1s
Jamshad v4p0307c2s
Jane, F.T. v3p0313c2s
v4p0339c2s v4p0395c2s v4p0579c2m
v5p0111c2s v5p0356c2s v5p0401c2s
v5p0516c2s v5p0543c2m v5p0582c2m
v5p0598c2s v5p0619c1s v6p0163c1s
v6p0226c2s v6p0268c2m v6p0296c2s
v6p0541c1s
Jane, Fred.T. v5p0085c2s
Janes, E. v1p0121c2s
v1p0646c1s v1p0883c1s v1p1102c1s
v2p0328c1s v2p0358c2s v3p0119c1s
Janes, E.S. v1p0252c2s
v1p0384c2s v1p0848c1s
Janes, F.O. v6p0163c2s
Janes, L.G. v1p0286c2s
v1p1005c1s v3p0165c2s v3p0357c2s
v4p0060c1s v4p0074c2s v4p0117c2s
v4p0171c1s v4p0233c1s v4p0450c2s
v4p0479c2s v4p0500c2s v4p0508c1s
v4p0535c1s v4p0541c2s v4p0610c1s
v5p0240c2s v5p0484c1s
Janes, M.P. v2p0338c2s
Janes, S.H. v1p0509c2s
v1p1233c2s
Janet, C. v5p0430c1s
Janet, P. v1p0351c2s
v1p0452c2s v1p0476c1s v1p0487c1s
v1p0623c1s v1p1236c2s v2p0156c1s
v2p0415c1s v3p0348c2s v6p0410c2s
Janeway, H.M. v4p0600c1s
Janeway, T.C. v6p0279c1s
Janin, J. v1p1030c1s
v1p1240c1s
Janion, R.G. v3p0445c1s
Jannaris, A.N. v4p0341c2s
v4p0376c1s v4p0519c2s v5p0058c2s
v6p0063c1s v6p0344c2m v6p0503c2s
Jannasch, P. and Locke, J.
v4p0579c1s
Jannet, C. v4p0489c1s
v4p0532c2s
Janney, J.J. v2p0033c1s
v3p0279c1s
Janoyer, M. v1p0665c1s
v1p1266c2s
Jansen, K. v2p0482c2s
Jansen, W.A. v5p0155c1s
Janson, F.H. v1p0736c1s
Janson, K. v1p0139c1s
v1p0566c1s v2p0133c1s v2p0193c1s
v2p0197c2s v2p0387c1s v2p0476c2s
v3p0307c1s
Janssen, Dr. v1p0050c2s
Janssen, J. v1p1267c2s
v2p0283c2s v3p0403c2s v5p0453c2s
Janssen, J.C. v2p0026c1s
Janssen, M. v1p0381c2s
Janssens, F. v3p0293c1s
v3p0299c1s v4p0489c1s
Januaris, A.N. v3p0184c1s
v4p0241c2s
Janvier, C.A. v4p0463c1s
v4p0580c1s v5p0020c2s
Janvier, H.A. and Smith, Oberlin
v6p0134c2s
Janvier, J.A. v6p0296c1s
Janvier, T.A. v1p0627c1s
v2p0026c2s v2p0073c1s v2p0094c1m
v2p0253c1s v2p0266c2s v2p0269c2s
v2p0286c2s v2p0287c1s v2p0296c1m
v2p0315c1s v2p0323c2s v2p0328c1s
v2p0374c1s v2p0439c2s v3p0025c1s
v3p0077c2s v3p0141c2s v3p0210c1s
v3p0276c2m v3p0277c1s v3p0372c2s
v3p0374c1s v3p0440c2s v3p0446c1s
v4p0034c2s v4p0110c2s v4p0126c1s
v4p0172c1s v4p0200c2s v4p0276c1s
v4p0277c1s v4p0336c2s v4p0400c1m
v4p0400c2m v4p0401c1s v4p0429c2s
v4p0460c1s v4p0463c1s v4p0482c2s
v4p0483c2s v4p0490c2s v4p0511c2s
v4p0529c1s v4p0540c1s v5p0155c2s
v5p0171c1s v5p0214c2s v5p0469c2s
v5p0516c2s v5p0629c2s v5p0641c2s
v6p0080c2s v6p0110c2s v6p0145c2s
v6p0196c2s v6p0284c2s v6p0301c2s
v6p0414c1s v6p0415c1s v6p0452c1s
v6p0523c2s v6p0534c1s v6p0552c1s
v6p0562c1s v6p0570c1s
Janvrin, M. v1p1175c2s
Janvrin, M.W. v1p0879c1s
v1p1315c2s v1p1407c2s
Japhson, H.L. v1p0652c2s
Japp, A.H. v1p0018c2s
v1p0215c1s v1p0321c1s v1p0463c1s
v1p0583c1s v1p0602c2s v1p0705c2s
v1p0719c2s v1p0766c1s v1p0952c2m
v1p1022c2s v1p1290c2s v1p1368c1s
v1p1414c1s v2p0022c1m v2p0046c1s
v2p0061c1s v2p0085c2s v2p0116c1s
v2p0140c1s v2p0153c2s v2p0181c2s
v2p0194c1s v2p0200c1s v2p0265c2s
v2p0293c2m v2p0327c2s v2p0335c1s
v2p0397c2s v2p0481c2s v3p0115c1s
v3p0142c1s v3p0188c2s v3p0189c2s
v3p0193c1s v3p0247c2s v3p0288c1s
v3p0324c2s v3p0344c2s v3p0351c1s
v3p0353c2s v3p0373c2m v3p0381c2s
v3p0472c1s v4p0065c2s v4p0073c1s
v4p0098c2s v4p0131c2s v4p0133c2s
v4p0215c2s v4p0226c2s v4p0298c2s
v4p0332c2s v4p0355c2s v4p0375c2s
v4p0420c1s v4p0458c2s v4p0509c2s
v4p0536c2s v4p0549c1s v4p0598c2s
v4p0601c2s v4p0605c1s v4p0630c2s
v5p0043c2s v5p0063c2s v5p0151c2s
v5p0153c2s v5p0411c2s v5p0532c1s
v5p0533c1s v5p0639c1s v6p0067c1s
v6p0067c2s v6p0161c1s v6p0163c1s
v6p0432c2s v6p0576c1s
Japp, Alex.H. v4p0016c1s
Japp, J.H. v2p0372c1s
Jaques, D.R. v1p0647c2s
Jaques, E.T. v5p0047c1s
Jaques, F.W., Mrs. and
Higginson, T.W. v4p0593c2s
Jaques, H. v2p0100c2s
Jaques, Herbert v5p0547c2s
Jaques, M. v3p0102c2s
Jaques, W.H. v4p0027c2s
v4p0416c2s v4p0610c2s v5p0124c2s
v5p0583c1s v5p0602c2s v6p0045c2s
Jaques, W.K. v6p0408c1s
Jaquet, R.G. v3p0429c2s
Jaquith, A. v1p0268c1s
Jaquith, W.L. v3p0049c2s
Jarboc, K. v6p0069c1s
Jarboe, K. v4p0209c2s
v5p0258c2s v5p0338c1s v5p0381c1s
v6p0069c1s v6p0291c2s v6p0434c1s
v6p0544c1s
Jarboe, Kathryn v5p0165c2s
v6p0544c1s
Jarchow, H.N. v4p0207c2s
Jardine, D. v1p0563c1s
Jardine, J. v4p0307c1s
v5p0081c2s v5p0084c1s v5p0110c1s
v5p0120c2s v5p0146c2s v5p0181c1s
v5p0284c2m v5p0285c2s v5p0286c2s
v5p0287c1s v6p0099c1s v6p0249c1s
Jardine, J., Sir v5p0071c2s
Jardine, J.P. v1p0947c2s
Jardine, Justice v4p0079c2s
Jardine, W. v1p1146c2s
v6p0710c1s
Jarlson, A. v6p0628c2s
Jarmain, G. v1p1428c2s
Jarnette, E.M.De v2p0106c1s
v6p0301c1s
Jarnigan, T.R. v5p0302c2s
Jarotsky, T.von v5p0375c1s
Jarrell, M.W. v5p0262c2s
v6p0201c1s
Jarrett, H.S. v2p0218c2s
v2p0373c1s v5p0350c2s
Jarrett, J. v4p0213c2s
v4p0462c1s
Jarrold, E. v4p0536c2s
Jarves, H.D. v1p0504c1s
v1p1435c1s
Jarves, J.J. v1p0062c1m
v1p0063c1s v1p0063c2s v1p0368c1s
v1p0427c1s v1p0445c1s v1p0599c1s
v1p0669c1s v1p0672c1s v1p0805c1s
v1p0959c1s v1p0969c2s v1p0970c2s
v1p0993c2s v1p1029c2s v1p1052c1s
v1p1125c2s v1p1149c2m v1p1171c2s
v1p1342c1s v2p0177c2s v2p0180c1s
v2p0458c2s
Jarvis A. v2p0374c1s
Jarvis, A.W. v4p0110c1s
v4p0231c1s v4p0624c1s v5p0345c1s
v5p0345c2s v5p0367c1s v6p0124c1s
v6p0565c1s
Jarvis, A.W. and Cambray, P.G.
v6p0383c2s v6p0385c1s
Jarvis, A.W. and Turtle, R.
v6p0083c1s
Jarvis, D. v1p0525c2s
Jarvis, E. v1p0448c1s
v1p0578c2s v1p0625c2s v1p0644c1s
v1p0644c2s v1p0706c1s v1p0745c2s
v1p0809c2m v1p1007c2s v1p1285c1s
v1p1346c2s v2p0097c2s v2p0152c2s
Jarvis, J.B. v6p0171c1s
Jarvis, M.C.H. v6p0189c1s
Jarvis, N.S. v6p0240c1s
v6p0424c1s v6p0442c1s
Jarvis, S. v4p0191c1m
v4p0331c1s v5p0031c1s v5p0358c1s
v5p0635c2s v6p0389c1s
Jarvis, S.F. v1p0679c2s
v1p0964c2s v1p1050c1s
Jarvis, S.M. v1p0192c2s
Jarvis, T.S. v4p0196c2s
Jarvis, W. v6p0657c2s
Jasmin, J. v1p1257c2s
Jast, L.S. v5p0097c1s
v5p0333c1s v5p0336c1s v6p0104c1s
v6p0370c2s v6p0374c2s
Jastrow, H. v5p0165c2s
v5p0293c1s
Jastrow, J. v2p0005c1s
v2p0054c2s v2p0077c2s v2p0247c1s
v2p0249c1s v2p0265c2s v2p0272c1s
v2p0358c1s v2p0362c2s v2p0390c1s
v2p0412c2s v2p0415c1s v2p0439c2s
v3p0012c2s v3p0016c2s v3p0047c1s
v3p0077c2s v3p0113c1s v3p0147c2s
v3p0274c1s v3p0274c2m v3p0348c1m
v3p0348c2m v3p0405c1m v3p0407c1s
v4p0017c2s v4p0071c2s v4p0218c1s
v4p0271c2m v4p0272c1s v4p0273c2s
v4p0365c1s v4p0379c1s v4p0385c2s
v4p0464c1s v4p0464c2m v4p0465c1m
v4p0529c2s v4p0537c2s v4p0637c1s
v5p0075c1s v5p0128c2s v5p0204c1s
v5p0344c1s v5p0417c1s v5p0470c2s
v5p0471c1m v5p0571c1s v5p0613c1s
v6p0002c1s v6p0004c2s v6p0021c1s
v6p0057c2s v6p0102c1s v6p0145c2s
v6p0190c1s v6p0203c2s v6p0350c1m
v6p0434c2s v6p0609c1s v6p0617c1m
v6p0623c1s v6p0650c1s
Jastrow, J. and Hall, G.S.
v2p0372c1s
Jastrow, J. et al. v6p0102c1s
Jastrow, Joseph v4p0349c2s
v4p0366c1s v6p0137c2s
Jastrow, M. v1p1186c2s
v2p0236c2s v2p0239c1s v4p0033c2s
v4p0040c2s v4p0053c2s v5p0056c2s
v5p0484c1s v5p0503c1s v5p0507c1s
v5p0579c2s v6p0646c2s
Jastrow, M. and Kelsey, F.W.
v4p0634c1s
Jastrow, M., jr. v2p0284c2s
v3p0049c2s v3p0057c2s v3p0107c2s
v3p0388c1s v4p0417c1s v4p0033c2s
v4p0055c1s v4p0172c1s v4p0302c2s
v4p0349c1s v4p0422c2s v4p0479c1s
v4p0515c1s v4p0567c2s v5p0042c1s
v5p0057c1s v5p0141c2s v5p0181c2s
v5p0257c2s v5p0412c2s v6p0156c2s

v6p0344c1s v6p0370c2s v6p0446c1s
Jastrow, Morris v6p0045c2s
v6p0046c1s
Jastrow, Morris, jr. v6p0583c1s
Javage, M.J. v4p0200c1s
Jay, A.O. v4p0338c2s
Jay, E.S. v1p0924c1s
v1p1327c2s
Jay, F. v4p0261c1s
Jay, H. v1p1257c1s
Jay, J. v1p0259c1s
v1p0876c1s v1p1117c2s v1p1344c2s
v1p1348c2s v1p1353c1s v1p1387c2s
v2p0459c2s v3p0128c2s v3p0287c1s
Jay, R. v6p0326c1s
Jayare and Almar, J. v6p0558c2s
Jaycox, W.A. v4p0357c1s
Jayne, Eliz.T. v6p0567c1s
Jayne, F.J. v4p0331c1s
Jayne, H. v5p0096c2s
v6p0629c1s
Jayne, M. v6p0209c1s
Jaynes, A.A. v6p0152c2s
v6p0410c1s
Jaynes, E.S. v6p0671c1s
Jayram, A. v1p1164c1s
Jeaffreson, H.H. v3p0295c1s
Jeaffreson, J.C. v1p0591c2s
v2p0063c1m v2p0120c2s v2p0239c1s
v2p0251c2s v2p0338c2s v2p0399c2m
Jeaffreson, J.C. and Timmins, S.
v2p0063c1s
Jeanniot, G. v5p0275c1s
Jeans, A. v6p0303c2s
Jeans, J. v1p0471c1s
v5p0115c2s
Jeans, J.H. v6p0526c2s
Jeans, J.H. and White, W.H.
v6p0623c1s
Jeans, J.S. v1p0087c1s
v1p0267c2s v1p0665c1s v1p0966c2s
v1p1438c1s v2p0245c1s v2p0362c2s
v2p0418c2s v3p0006c2s v3p0257c1s
v3p0318c2m v3p0352c2s v4p0101c1s
v4p0315c1s v4p0472c1s v4p0472c2s
v4p0521c1s v4p0553c1m v4p0563c1s
v4p0563c2s v5p0066c2s v5p0289c2s
v5p0298c1s v5p0298c2m v5p0557c1s
Jeans, W.T. v4p0292c1s
Jebb, A., Mrs. v2p0132c2s
v2p0275c2s
Jebb, C. v5p0304c1s
v5p0331c2s v5p0459c2s v6p0368c2m
Jebb, E.L. v2p0196c1s
v2p0228c2s v4p0031c1s v4p0261c2s
Jebb, H.H. v5p0568c1s
v6p0207c1s
Jebb, J.G., Mrs. v4p0004c1s
Jebb, L. v6p0045c2s
v6p0186c2s v6p0411c2s v6p0630c2s
v6p0661c1s
Jebb, Louisa v6p0025c2s
v6p0647c1s
Jebb, R. v5p0091c1s
Jebb, R.C. v1p0051c2s
v1p0429c2s v1p0553c2s v1p1221c1s
v1p1295c1s v2p0021c1s v2p0025c1s
v2p0026c2s v2p0203c2s v2p0214c2s
v2p0353c2s v2p0358c2s v2p0446c2s
v2p0447c2s v3p0114c1s v3p0184c2s
v3p0199c2s v3p0208c1s v3p0332c2s
v3p0430c2s v4p0118c1s v4p0242c1s
v4p0403c1s v6p0082c1s v6p0672c1m
Jeff, W.E. v1p0386c1s
Jeffcott, J.M. v1p0795c2s
Jefferies, R. v1p0015c2s
v1p0016c1s v1p0444c1s v1p0444c2m
v1p0451c2s v1p0693c2s v1p0709c2s
v1p0715c1s v1p0715c2s v1p0862c1s
v1p1079c1s v1p1192c2s v2p0047c1s
v2p0048c1s v2p0056c1s v2p0104c1s
v2p0154c1s v2p0155c1s v2p0160c1s
v2p0166c1s v2p0208c2s v2p0243c1s
v2p0264c2s v2p0307c2s v2p0318c2s
v2p0393c1s v2p0415c2s v2p0424c2m
v2p0434c2s v2p0451c1s v2p0462c1s
v3p0113c2s v3p0233c2s v3p0294c2s
v3p0297c2s v3p0414c2m v3p0415c2s
v3p0461c2s v3p0466c1s v4p0165c2s
v4p0198c2s v4p0319c1s v4p0319c2s
v4p0395c1s v4p0543c1s v4p0556c1s
v4p0602c2s v4p0604c2s
Jeffers, E.T. v2p0132c2s
Jeffers, W.M. v1p1246c2s
Jeffers, W.N. v1p0455c1s
v1p1107c2s
Jefferson, J. v1p1255c1s
v4p0068c1s v6p0309c2s
Jefferson, M.S. v6p0408c1s
Jefferson, M.S.W. v5p0579c2m
Jefferson, O.R. v4p0396c2s
v4p0538c2s
Jefferson, T. v1p0978c2s
v1p1147c1s
Jeffersonian, A. v6p0426c1s
Jeffery, C.E. v4p0569c1s
v5p0373c2s v5p0612c1s
Jeffery, F. v6p0088c1s
v6p0350c2s v6p0628c1s
Jeffery, J.C. v3p0310c1s
Jeffery, R. v1p0397c2s
Jeffery, W. v5p0039c1s
v6p0291c2s v6p0510c2s
Jeffery, W. and Becke, L.. v4p0210c1s
v5p0039c2s v5p0250c2s v5p0566c2s
Jeffray, R.J. v2p0361c1s
Jeffree, F. v3p0230c2s
Jeffrey, A. v2p0310c2s
Jeffrey, E.C. v6p0430c2s
Jeffrey, E.C. and Hollick, A.
v6p0157c1s
Jeffrey, F. v1p0003c2s
v1p0021c1m v1p0022c2s v1p0027c1s
v1p0059c1s v1p0072c2s v1p0084c1s
v1p0087c1m v1p0098c2s v1p0099c1s
v1p0101c1s v1p0105c1s v1p0105c2s
v1p0106c1s v1p0113c1s v1p0154c1s
v1p0165c2m v1p0179c1s v1p0181c2s
v1p0182c1m v1p0182c2m v1p0183c1m
v1p0191c2m v1p0193c2s v1p0219c2s
v1p0225c2s v1p0231c2s v1p0233c2s
v1p0270c1m v1p0277c1s v1p0280c2m
v1p0310c2m v1p0311c1m v1p0318c1s
v1p0323c2s v1p0324c2m v1p0330c2s
v1p0341c1s v1p0342c1s v1p0356c2s
v1p0368c1s v1p0375c2s v1p0383c1m
v1p0395c1s v1p0395c2s v1p0408c2s
v1p0410c1s v1p0414c1s v1p0417c2s
v1p0418c1s v1p0418c2s v1p0430c2s
v1p0443c2s v1p0467c2s v1p0472c1s
v1p0475c1s v1p0475c2m v1p0476c1s
v1p0483c2s v1p0484c1s v1p0484c2s
v1p0485c1s v1p0489c2s v1p0508c1s
v1p0513c1s v1p0531c2s v1p0539c1s
v1p0544c2s v1p0546c2s v1p0548c1m
v1p0559c1s v1p0566c2s v1p0567c2s
v1p0568c1s v1p0577c1s v1p0578c1s
v1p0581c1s v1p0584c2s v1p0590c2s
v1p0596c1s v1p0596c2s v1p0616c2s
v1p0618c1s v1p0631c2s v1p0632c2m
v1p0634c2s v1p0656c1s v1p0667c1m
v1p0667c2s v1p0676c2s v1p0694c1s
v1p0695c1s v1p0704c1s v1p0707c2s
v1p0712c1s v1p0725c2s v1p0736c1s
v1p0738c2s v1p0749c1m v1p0754c1s
v1p0759c1s v1p0760c2s v1p0768c2s
v1p0776c1s v1p0783c2s v1p0801c2s
v1p0840c1s v1p0859c2s v1p0863c1s
v1p0864c1s v1p0866c2s v1p0867c1m
v1p0868c2s v1p0870c2s v1p0902c1s
v1p0902c2s v1p0932c2s v1p0948c2s
v1p0958c2s v1p0961c2s v1p0966c2s
v1p0970c1s v1p0973c2s v1p0986c1s
v1p0987c1s v1p0989c1s v1p0989c2s
v1p1004c2s v1p1021c2m v1p1050c1m
v1p1052c2s v1p1054c1m v1p1069c2m
v1p1092c1m v1p1106c2s v1p1114c1s
v1p1116c2s v1p1118c1s v1p1136c1s
v1p1140c1s v1p1167c1s v1p1168c2s
v1p1169c1m v1p1169c2m v1p1170c2s
v1p1183c2s v1p1184c1s v1p1185c1s
v1p1190c2s v1p1201c1s v1p1205c2s
v1p1210c2s v1p1213c1s v1p1221c2s
v1p1226c2m v1p1227c1m v1p1241c1s
v1p1241c2m v1p1253c2m v1p1275c2s
v1p1277c1s v1p1281c2s v1p1284c2s
v1p1294c1s v1p1301c1s v1p1303c2s
v1p1360c1s v1p1364c1s v1p1372c2s
v1p1373c1s v1p1383c1s v1p1385c2s
v1p1410c1s v1p1413c1m v1p1430c1m
v1p1430c2m
Jeffrey, F and Brougham, H.
v1p0395c1s
Jeffrey, F. and Scott, W., Sir
v1p0851c1s
Jeffrey, R. v1p1046c1s
v1p1047c2s
Jeffrey, R.T. v1p0282c2s
Jeffrey, W. v6p0562c2s
Jeffrey, W.H. v4p0275c1s
v4p0275c2s v4p0610c1m
Jeffreys, E.C. v1p0924c2s
Jeffreys, J.G. v1p0156c1s
v1p0340c1m v1p0366c1s v1p0707c1s
v1p1152c1s v1p1340c1s v2p0073c2s
v2p0315c1s
Jeffreys, J.L. v5p0029c1s
Jeffreys, M.E. v6p0298c2s
Jeffries, B.J. v2p0032c2s
v2p0093c2m
Jeffries, B.Joy v2p0462c1s
Jeffries, R. v1p1109c1s
v1p1276c1s v1p1423c2s v2p0249c2s
v2p0461c1s v2p0475c1m v2p0475c2s
v3p0400c1s
Jehl, F. v2p0136c2s
Jeitteles, L.H. v1p0340c2s
Jekyll, A. v4p0104c2s
Jekyll, G. v4p0150c2s
Jekyll, J. v6p0638c1s
Jelf, E.A. v4p0440c1s
Jelf, W.E. v1p0428c1s
Jellett, H. v2p0084c2s
Jellett, J.H. v1p0250c1s
Jellicoe, C. v1p0090c2s
Jelliffe, H.L. v4p0511c2s
Jelliffe, Helena L. v5p0054c1s
Jelliffe, S.E. v5p0124c2s
v5p0292c1s v5p0546c1s
Jellinek, G. v5p0108c2s
v6p0481c2s
Jelly, A.C. v6p0115c2s
Jenckes, T.A. v1p0259c1s
Jendwine, H.S. v5p0032c2s
Jenifer, G.D. v6p0662c1s
Jenifer, W.H. v1p0087c2s
Jenisen, Madge C. v6p0035c2s
Jenison, M.C. v6p0302c1s
v6p0562c1s
Jenison, M.G. v6p0302c2s
Jenkin, C., Mrs. v1p0942c2s
Jenkin, F. v1p0184c1s
v1p0401c1s v1p1195c2s v1p1288c2s
v1p1291c1s v2p0209c1s v2p0434c1m
v3p0423c1s v3p0423c2s
Jenkin, F., Mrs. v2p0108c1s
Jenkin, F. and Bell, G.J.. v2p0402c1s
Jenkin, F. and Ewing, J.A.
v1p1002c2s
Jenkin, T.W. v1p0165c2s
Jenkins, Anna S. v5p0585c2s
Jenkins, C.C. v4p0598c2s
Jenkins, C.E. v4p0100c1m
Jenkins, C.F. v4p0118c2s
v5p0448c2s v6p0406c1s
Jenkins, C.W. v2p0176c2s
Jenkins, Cora W. v6p0439c1s
Jenkins, E. v1p0138c2s
v1p0250c1s v1p0298c1s v1p0406c1s
v1p0545c1s v1p0885c2m v1p1336c1s
v2p0005c2s
Jenkins, E.E. v5p0032c1s
Jenkins, E.F. v6p0116c2s
v6p0117c2s v6p0481c2s
Jenkins, F.L. v6p0424c1s
Jenkins, F.L. and Moira, G.E.
v5p0156c1s
Jenkins, H. v1p0192c1s
Jenkins, H.C. v4p0589c1s
Jenkins, H.D. v1p0025c2s
v1p0037c1s v1p0082c1s v1p0184c1s
v1p0227c2s v1p0258c2s v1p0327c1s
v1p0348c1s v1p0381c1s v1p0546c1s
v1p0673c2s v1p0776c2s v1p0818c2s
v1p1080c1s v1p1313c2s v1p1325c2s
v3p0378c1s v5p0351c2s
Jenkins, H.M. v1p0157c2s
v1p0497c1s v1p1405c2s v2p0045c2s
v2p0068c1s v2p0115c1s v2p0115c2s
v2p0136c1s v2p0164c1s v2p0171c1m
v2p0173c1s v2p0184c1s v2p0194c1m
v2p0195c2s v2p0214c2s v2p0238c2s
v2p0253c1s v2p0259c1s v2p0279c2s
v2p0295c2s v2p0331c2s v2p0335c1m
v2p0335c2m v2p0348c1s v2p0360c2s
v2p0370c2s v2p0371c1s v2p0422c2s
v2p0431c2m v2p0461c2s v2p0464c2s
v2p0468c1s v2p0469c2s v3p0053c2s
v3p0109c1s v3p0291c2s v3p0326c1s
v4p0433c2s v4p0599c2s v5p0339c2s
v5p0439c2m
Jenkins, H.W. v1p0030c1s
v2p0372c1s
Jenkins, J. v5p0068c1s
Jenkins, J.F. v1p0606c1s
Jenkins, J.G. v6p0042c1s
Jenkins, J.J. v5p0592c2s
Jenkins, J.M. v2p0163c2s
Jenkins, J.S. v5p0147c2s
Jenkins, M. v6p0004c2s
Jenkins, M.C. v1p0189c1s
v1p0799c2s v1p0807c2s v1p0903c1s
Jenkins, M.G. v4p0247c2s
Jenkins, N.C. v1p1126c1s
Jenkins, O.B. v5p0057c1s
v5p0095c1s v6p0279c1s
Jenkins, R.C. v1p0240c1s
v1p0252c1s v4p0112c2s
Jenkins, Rhys v4p0580c2s
Jenkins, S. v3p0228c1s
v4p0025c2s v4p0163c1s
Jenkins, S.P., Mrs. v1p0174c1s
Jenkins, T. v6p0241c1s
Jenkins, T.A. v6p0479c1s
Jenkins, T.J. v2p0269c1s
v2p0357c1s v2p0375c2s v3p0316c2s
v3p0378c2s v4p0312c2s
Jenkins, W. v6p0045c2s
v6p0099c2s v6p0169c2s v6p0307c2s
v6p0569c2s
Jenkins, W.G. v3p0112c2m
Jenkins, W.M. v2p0335c1s
Jenkins, W.T. v4p0468c2s
Jenkinson, A. v4p0076c2s
v4p0082c2s v4p0361c1s
Jenkinson, A.J. v6p0143c2s
v6p0506c2s
Jenkinson, E.F. v4p0342c1s
Jenkinson, J.H. v5p0561c1s
Jenkinson, S.H. v6p0280c1s
Jenks, A. v3p0375c2s
Jenks, A.E. v3p0474c1s
v5p0194c2s v5p0288c1s v6p0055c1s
v6p0188c2s v6p0224c1s v6p0492c2s
v6p0493c1s
Jenks, E. v3p0235c1s
v4p0182c2s v4p0269c2s v4p0318c2m
v4p0364c1s v4p0396c1s v5p0034c2s
v5p0139c2s v5p0223c2s v5p0485c2s
v6p0144c2s v6p0277c1s v6p0360c1s

v6p0395c1s v6p0650c2s
Jenks, E.A. v5p0576c2s
Jenks, E.P. v5p0150c2m
Jenks, F. v1p0132c2s
v1p0528c1s v1p0641c1s
Jenks, F.H. v3p0293c2s
v4p0359c2s
Jenks, G.B., Mrs. v4p0168c1s
Jenks, G.C. v6p0174c1s
Jenks, H.F. v1p0118c2m
v1p0337c1s v1p0567c2s v1p0685c2s
v1p0724c2s v1p0879c2s v1p1094c2s
v1p1354c1s v1p1380c2s v1p1427c2s
v4p0069c1s
Jenks, J. v4p0585c2s
Jenks, J.W. v1p0283c1s
v1p0395c2s v1p1278c2s v3p0127c2s
v3p0241c2s v3p0277c2s v3p0362c2s
v3p0376c1s v3p0462c1s v4p0072c2s
v4p0171c2s v4p0178c1s v4p0182c1s
v4p0379c2s v4p0429c1s v4p0450c2s
v4p0461c1s v4p0466c1s v4p0481c1s
v4p0526c1s v4p0581c1s v4p0584c1s
v5p0217c1s v5p0230c1s v5p0391c2s
v5p0465c1s v5p0584c2s v5p0592c2m
v5p0593c1m v5p0640c2s v6p0013c1s
v6p0119c2s v6p0138c2s v6p0162c1s
v6p0186c2s v6p0196c1s v6p0470c1s
v6p0493c1s v6p0494c1m v6p0659c1s
Jenks, J.W. et al. v4p0524c2s
Jenks, Jeremiah W. v6p0118c2s
v6p0121c1s v6p0193c2s
Jenks, P.E. v5p0076c2s
v5p0217c1s v5p0228c1s v5p0490c1s
Jenks, Prof. v3p0434c1s
Jenks, S.H. v1p1403c1s
Jenks, T. v4p0384c1s
v5p0036c1s v5p0107c2s v5p0156c1s
v5p0275c2s v5p0433c2s v5p0450c2s
v6p0015c2s v6p0143c1s v6p0217c2s
v6p0303c1s v6p0348c1s v6p0405c2s
v6p0495c1s v6p0535c2s v6p0584c1s
v6p0683c2s
Jenks, Tudor v5p0597c2s
v6p0641c1s
Jenks, W. v1p0681c2s
v1p0809c2m v1p0909c2s v1p0910c2m
Jenkyn, T.W. v1p0599c1s
Jenkyns, E. v2p0395c2s
Jenla, H. v1p1192c2m
Jenne, F., Mrs. v2p0077c2s
Jenne, Lady v6p0194c2s
Jenner, A.B. v6p0123c2s
Jenner, A.J.B. v6p0123c2s
v6p0187c1s
Jenner, A.J.Baden v6p0099c2s
v6p0240c1s
Jenner, D., Rev. v6p0641c1s
Jenner, G. v1p1422c2s
v5p0167c1s
Jenner, H. v6p0362c2s
Jenner-Fust, H. v6p0384c2s
v6p0650c1s
Jenness, G.H. v2p0063c1s
v2p0452c1s
Jenness, T.R. v1p0638c2s
Jenney, A.M. v5p0419c2s
Jenney, S.G. v3p0025c2s
Jenney, W.L.B. v2p0396c2s
v5p0082c2s v5p0628c2s
Jenney, W.P. v1p0509c1s
v1p1297c1s
Jennings, A.S. v5p0340c1s
v6p0159c2s
Jennings, A.V. v4p0093c2s
v5p0001c2s v5p0034c2s v5p0312c1s
v5p0381c1s v5p0519c1s
Jennings, C.E. v3p0047c2s
v3p0435c1s
Jennings, C.P. v1p0685c2s
Jennings, E.W. v5p0273c2s
Jennings, H. v1p0437c2s
v1p0573c2s v1p0750c2s
Jennings, H.J. v4p0273c2s
v4p0293c1s v4p0518c1m v4p0550c1s
v4p0570c1s
Jennings, H.S. v5p0290c2s
v5p0469c1s
v6p0019c1s
Jennings, I. v1p0131c2s
Jennings, Janet v6p0696c2s
Jennings, K.V. v1p1362c2s
Jennings, L.J. v1p0196c1s
v1p0327c2s v1p0354c2s v1p0602c2s
v1p1069c1s v1p1353c1s v2p0184c2s
v3p0116c1s v3p0139c1s v3p0162c2s
v3p0179c2s v3p0231c1s v3p0311c2s
v3p0321c1s v3p0347c1s v3p0348c2s
v3p0420c1s v3p0434c1s
Jennings, M.E. v4p0273c1s
Jennings, P. v4p0076c1s
v4p0213c1s
Jennings, Pauline v5p0395c2s
v5p0565c1s
Jennings, R. v2p0194c1s
Jennings, Rufus P. v6p0092c1s
Jennings, W. v6p0071c1s
Jennings, W.J. v4p0023c2s
Jennings, W.N. v6p0496c2s
v6p0681c2s
Jennings-Bramly, W. v5p0531c1s
Jennison, E.M. v6p0231c1s
Jennison, M.G. v5p0158c2s
Jensen, C. v4p0484c2s
Jensen, M.E. v6p0461c1s
Jensen, Martin E. v6p0436c1s
Jensen, O. v6p0490c2s
Jensen, P. v1p0146c2s
Jenson, P. v4p0259c1s
Jenvier, T.A. v1p0055c2s
Jephson, A.J.M. v3p0004c2s
v3p0299c2s v4p0545c1s v5p0008c1s
Jephson, A.M. v3p0136c2s
v3p0406c2s
Jephson, H. v2p0227c2s
v4p0174c1s v4p0243c2s v4p0289c2s
v4p0290c1s v5p0154c2s
Jephson, H.J. v4p0087c1s
Jephson, Lady v4p0086c2s
Jephson, P.P. v6p0656c2s
Jephson, R.M. v1p0198c2s
v1p0773c1s
Jepp, A.H. v6p0656c2s
Jeppe, F. v4p0231c1s
v4p0637c2s
Jepson, B. v6p0438c1s
Jepson, E. v5p0083c2s
v5p0348c1s v6p0158c1s v6p0201c1s
v6p0517c1s v6p0526c1s
Jepson, E. and Blames, D.. v5p0534c1s
Jepson, E. and Nesbit, E.. v5p0308c2s
Jepson, E.A. v4p0384c1s
Jepson, G.E. v6p0283c2s
Jepson, R.M. v1p0577c2s
Jepson, W.L. v6p0463c1s
Jerdan, C. v3p0041c1s
v3p0084c1s v3p0349c1s
Jerdan, S.S. v1p1429c1s
Jerdan, W. v1p0100c1s
v1p0592c2s v1p0648c1s v1p0693c2s
v1p1106c2s v1p1209c2s v1p1213c2s
v1p1306c2s v1p1384c1s
Jeremiah, J. v1p0077c1s
v1p0157c2s
Jericho, C.R. v1p0580c2s
Jerir, Mohammadibn v6p0630c2s
Jermain, F.D. v5p0336c1s
Jernegan, P.F. v4p0058c1s
v4p0194c1s
Jernigan, T.R. v4p0593c2s
v5p0109c1s
Jerningham, C.E. v1p0800c1s
Jerningham, E. v1p0393c2s
v1p0411c1s
Jerningham, H.E.H. v4p0361c2s
v5p0221c1s
Jerningham, Mrs. v3p0339c1s
Jeroloman, A.J. v5p0330c2s
Jerome, C.T. v1p0788c1s
v1p1387c2s v2p0067c2s v2p0269c2s
v3p0067c2s
Jerome, F.B. v6p0047c2s
Jerome, H.J. v4p0311c1s
Jerome, Hattie L. v5p0512c2s
Jerome, J.K. v3p0088c2s
v3p0144c2s v3p0258c1s v3p0309c1s
v3p0323c1s v3p0421c2s v4p0107c2s
v4p0327c2s v4p0360c2s v4p0389c2s
v4p0391c2s v4p0408c2s v4p0477c2s
v4p0626c2s v5p0216c1s v5p0300c2s
v5p0331c2s v5p0460c2s v5p0563c1s
v6p0303c1s v6p0495c2s
Jerome, J.T. v2p0281c1s
Jerome, Jerome K. v5p0636c1s
Jerome, L.B. v6p0462c1s
Jerome, Lucy B. v5p0354c2s
v6p0541c1s v6p0590c2s v6p0628c1s
v6p0704c1s
Jerome, P. v1p0702c1s
Jerome, S. v4p0512c2s
Jerome, St. v2p1422c1s
Jerome, T.S. v4p0130c2s
Jerram, C.S. v3p0302c1s
Jerrold, B. v1p0167c2s
v1p0169c2s v1p0240c2s v1p0349c2s
v1p0350c2s v1p0361c1s v1p0390c2s
v1p0469c1s v1p0621c1s v1p0968c1s
v1p0968c2s v1p0971c2s v1p1059c1s
v1p1322c2s v1p1382c1s v1p1403c1s
v1p1432c1s v2p0358c2s
Jerrold, D. v1p0087c1s
v1p0446c2s v1p0505c2s v1p0738c2s
v1p0869c2s v1p0878c1m v1p1123c1s
v1p1143c2s
Jerrold, E. v1p0148c2s
v1p0365c1s v1p0371c2s v1p0490c1s
v1p0503c1s v1p0564c2s v1p0887c2s
v1p0926c1s v2p0167c2s v2p0416c2s
v2p0451c1s v3p0178c1s
Jerrold, E.D. v1p0088c1s
Jerrold, L. v6p0154c2s
v6p0169c1s v6p0237c1s v6p0237c2s
v6p0242c1s v6p0426c1s v6p0556c1s
v6p0600c2s
Jerrold, Laurence v6p0130c2s
Jerrold, W. v5p0145c1s
v6p0202c2s v6p0360c2s
Jerrold, W.B. v1p0419c2s
v1p1334c2s
Jersey, Countess of v2p0059c2s
v2p0438c2s v3p0469c2s v3p0470c1m
v4p0298c1s v4p0398c1s v4p0501c1s
v5p0570c2s v6p0109c2s v6p0208c1s
v6p0305c1s v6p0354c1s
Jersey, M.E. v2p0478c1s
v3p0196c2s v3p0244c1s v5p0424c2s
v5p0629c2s
Jersey, M.E., Countess of. v6p0117c2s
Jervey, H. v6p0394c2s
Jervey, J.P. v6p0666c1s
Jervis, A.N. v4p0048c1s
v6p0043c2s
Jervis, Arthur N. v6p0044c1s
Jervis, J.B. v1p0424c1m
v1p0611c1s v1p0918c1s v1p1079c2s
Jervis, L. v5p0283c1s
v5p0452c2s v5p0520c2m v5p0530c1s
Jervis, W.P. v3p0266c2s
v3p0267c1s v3p0439c1s
Jervis-Smith v5p0448c2s
Jervis-Smith, F. v5p0252c2s
Jervois, W.F.D., Sir v3p0182c1s
Jess, F.B. v4p0201c1s
Jesse, E. v1p0022c2s
v1p0039c1s v1p0041c2s v1p0042c2s
v1p0107c1s v1p0107c2s v1p0115c1s
v1p0135c1s v1p0311c1s v1p0313c1s
v1p0320c2s v1p0323c1s v1p0340c2s
v1p0428c1s v1p0527c1s v1p0542c1m
v1p0588c2s v1p0646c2s v1p0647c1s
v1p0674c2s v1p0678c1s v1p0701c2s
v1p0789c1s v1p0814c1s v1p0837c2s
v1p0934c1s v1p1011c1s v1p1083c1s
v1p1084c1s v1p1112c1s v1p1146c1s
v1p1190c1s v1p1255c1s v1p1273c2m
v1p1294c2s v1p1298c2s v1p1335c1s
v1p1383c2s v1p1389c1s v1p1392c2s
v1p1397c2s v1p1404c1s
Jesse, O. v3p0088c2s
Jesse, O. and Foerster, W.
v4p0120c1s
Jesse, R.H. v4p0123c1s
v4p0512c2s v5p0550c1s v5p0605c1s
v6p0252c2s
Jessen, B.B. v6p0002c1s
Jessen, J. v5p0370c1s
Jessop, A. v3p0073c2s
Jessop, E.M. v4p0018c1s
v4p0437c2s v4p0623c2s v5p0566c2s
v5p0633c1m v6p0194c2s
Jessop, F.W. v6p0618c1s
Jessop, G.H. v1p0595c1s
v1p0773c1s v1p1278c1s v1p1313c2s
v3p0101c2s v3p0118c2s v3p0135c2s
v3p0240c2s v3p0243c1s v3p0311c2s
v3p0362c1s v3p0440c2s v4p0161c2s
Jessop, G.H. and Matthews, B.
v3p0312c2s
Jessop, G.L. v5p0143c1s
Jessopp, A. v2p0005c2s
v2p0010c1s v2p0018c1s v2p0048c2s
v2p0065c1s v2p0084c1s v2p0100c2s
v2p0141c2s v2p0143c1m v2p0168c2s
v2p0247c2s v2p0254c2s v2p0294c2s
v2p0301c2m v2p0315c2s v2p0334c1s
v2p0427c1s v2p0427c2s v3p0009c1s
v3p0044c2s v3p0045c2s v3p0049c2s
v3p0055c2s v3p0060c2s v3p0074c1s
v3p0083c1s v3p0083c2s v3p0084c1s
v3p0102c2m v3p0121c1s v3p0138c2s
v3p0139c1s v3p0141c1m v3p0196c1s
v3p0197c2s v3p0241c1s v3p0291c1s
v3p0307c1s v3p0336c2s v3p0349c1s
v3p0354c1s v3p0356c1s v3p0384c1s
v3p0386c1s v3p0397c1s v3p0455c1s
v3p0464c1s v4p0068c1s v4p0079c1s
v4p0091c2s v4p0092c2m v4p0112c1s
v4p0112c2m v4p0120c1s v4p0244c2s
v4p0277c2s v4p0358c1s v4p0409c1s
v4p0426c2s v4p0488c1m v4p0527c1s
v4p0559c1s v4p0599c1s v4p0622c2s
v5p0025c1s v5p0118c1s v5p0122c2s
v5p0182c1s v5p0190c2s v5p0191c1s
v5p0323c1s v5p0382c1s v5p0418c2s
v5p0432c2s v5p0612c1s v6p0154c1s
Jessopp, G.H. and Matthews, B.
v3p0075c2s
Jessup, H.H. v1p0733c1s
v2p0025c1s v2p0429c2m v3p0184c1s
v3p0283c1s v4p0374c2s v5p0042c1s
Jessup, R.J. v4p0388c2s
Jeter, J.B. v1p0097c1s
Jeula, H. v1p1264c2s
Jeune, F.H. v5p0140c2s
Jeune, F.H., Sir v4p0323c1s
Jeune, Lady v4p0071c2s
v4p0131c2s v4p0148c2s v4p0156c1s
v4p0215c2s v4p0340c1m v5p0193c2s
v6p0194c2s
Jeune, M. v2p0477c2s
v3p0077c2m v3p0198c1s v3p0416c2s
v4p0140c2s v4p0162c1s v4p0182c2s
v4p0451c2s v4p0516c1s v4p0628c2s
v4p0629c2s v5p0101c1s v5p0570c2s
v5p0610c2s v6p0083c1s
Jeune, M. et al. v4p0582c2s
Jeune, M., Lady v4p0522c1s
v5p0076c1s
Jeune, Mary v3p0050c1s
v3p0158c2s v3p0338c2m v3p0469c1s

v4p0158c2s
Jeune, Mary, Mrs. v3p0469c2s
Jeune, Mrs. and Walker, W.J.
v3p0468c1s
Jevons, F.B. v3p0199c2s
v4p0035c2s v4p0242c1m v4p0292c1s
v4p0391c2s v4p0608c1s v5p0483c2s
v5p0583c2s v6p0537c2s
Jevons, M.A. v1p0441c1s
Jevons, S. v1p0532c2s
v1p1070c1s
Jevons, S. et al. v1p0839c2s
Jevons, T.E. v3p0337c1s
Jevons, Thos.E. v4p0379c2s
Jevons, W. v1p0692c2s
v1p0815c1s v1p1293c2s
Jevons, W.S. v1p0035c2s
v1p0133c2s v1p0197c2s v1p0237c2s
v1p0272c2s v1p0287c2s v1p0311c2s
v1p0321c1s v1p0325c2s v1p0333c2s
v1p0346c1s v1p0434c1s v1p0435c2s
v1p0510c1s v1p0532c2s v1p0587c1s
v1p0621c1s v1p0639c2s v1p0718c2s
v1p0721c1s v1p0736c1s v1p0743c2s
v1p0752c1s v1p0761c1s v1p0811c1s
v1p0839c2s v1p0861c1m v1p0868c2s
v1p0881c2m v1p0933c2s v1p0963c2s
v1p0967c1s v1p1026c1s v1p1026c2m
v1p1038c1s v1p1049c2s v1p1162c1s
v1p1164c1s v1p1198c2m v1p1269c1s
v1p1290c2s v1p1360c2s v2p0288c2s
v2p0300c2s v2p0347c2s v2p0426c2s
v2p0477c2s
Jewell, E.C. v5p0642c2s
Jewell, F.S. v1p1288c2s
v2p0081c2s v2p0215c2s v3p0330c1s
v3p0342c1s
Jewell, J. v3p0422c2s
Jewell, J.R. v6p0182c1s
v6p0444c2s
Jewell, J.S. v1p0228c1s
v1p0420c2s v1p0467c1s v1p0792c2s
v1p1007c1s v1p1062c1s v1p1238c1s
Jewell, J.S. et al. v2p0221c2s
Jewell, L.E. v4p0410c1s
Jewell, T.F. v1p1222c2s
v2p0393c1s v4p0395c2s
Jewett, C. v5p0448c2s
Jewett, C.C. v1p0148c2s
v1p0373c1s
Jewett, E.D. v5p0611c2s
Jewett, E.H. v2p0102c1s
v2p0475c2m
Jewett, F.R. v6p0086c2s
Jewett, G.B. v1p0125c2s
v1p0126c1s v2p0013c2s
Jewett, H.J. v1p1297c1s
Jewett, I.A. v1p1400c1s
Jewett, J.A. v1p0958c2s
Jewett, J.H. v6p0469c1s
Jewett, J.L. v1p0618c1s
v1p0777c1s v1p0985c2s v1p1058c2s
Jewett, L. v5p0170c2s
Jewett, S. v6p0331c2s
v6p0662c1s
Jewett, S.O. v1p0038c2s
v1p0138c2s v1p0340c1m v1p0770c2s
v1p1011c2s v1p1036c2s v1p1110c2s
v1p1371c1s v2p0125c1s v2p0152c2m
v2p0196c2s v2p0205c1s v2p0243c1s
v2p0248c2s v2p0278c1m v2p0279c2s
v2p0322c1s v2p0442c2s v2p0449c2s
v3p0061c2s v3p0103c1s v3p0137c2s
v3p0147c2s v3p0148c1s v3p0176c1s
v3p0209c2s v3p0231c1s v3p0242c1s
v3p0245c1s v3p0254c1s v3p0260c2s
v3p0274c2s v3p0282c1m v3p0283c2s
v3p0297c1s v3p0300c1s v3p0351c1s
v3p0419c1s v3p0433c2s v3p0462c2s
v3p0466c1s v4p0010c2s v4p0011c2s
v4p0052c1s v4p0052c2s v4p0136c2s
v4p0150c2s v4p0194c1s v4p0202c1s
v4p0244c1s v4p0257c2s v4p0268c2s
v4p0331c1s v4p0397c2s v4p0414c2s
v4p0429c2s v4p0512c1s v4p0610c2s
v5p0069c1s v5p0071c2s v5p0135c2s
v5p0171c2s v5p0186c2s v5p0213c2s
v5p0243c1s v5p0269c2s v5p0324c1s
v5p0363c2s v5p0474c2s v5p0583c1s
Jewett, Sarah O. v5p0416c2s
v5p0628c2s v6p0596c1s v6p0611c2s
v6p0612c1s
Jewett, Sarah Orne v6p0485c2s
Jewett, Sophie v6p0220c2s
Jewitt, J. v2p0073c1s
Jewitt, L. v1p0062c2s
v1p0088c1m v1p0102c1s v1p0110c2m
v1p0133c2s v1p0143c1s v1p0157c2s
v1p0163c1s v1p0167c1s v1p0171c2s
v1p0210c2m v1p0234c2m v1p0298c1s
v1p0304c1s v1p0320c1m v1p0321c1s
v1p0345c1s v1p0360c2s v1p0362c1s
v1p0439c2s v1p0440c1s v1p0449c1s
v1p0453c2s v1p0460c2s v1p0462c2s
v1p0494c1s v1p0494c2s v1p0541c2s
v1p0597c1s v1p0605c1s v1p0661c2s
v1p0694c2s v1p0734c2s v1p0776c1s
v1p0824c2s v1p0876c1s v1p0882c1s
v1p0962c1s v1p1010c2s v1p1039c1s
v1p1039c2m v1p1045c1s v1p1113c1s
v1p1164c2s v1p1178c1s v1p1196c2s
v1p1255c2s v1p1311c1s v1p1313c2s
v1p1314c2s v1p1367c2s v1p1380c1s
v1p1396c2s v1p1433c2s v1p1437c2s
v2p0002c2s v2p0007c2s v2p0019c2s
v2p0037c2s v2p0052c2s v2p0053c2s
v2p0055c2s v2p0056c2s v2p0062c1s
v2p0073c2s v2p0085c1s v2p0103c2s
v2p0104c1s v2p0105c2s v2p0108c2m
v2p0116c1s v2p0119c2s v2p0124c1s
v2p0181c1s v2p0196c2s v2p0201c1m
v2p0207c2s v2p0270c2s v2p0275c1s
v2p0277c1s v2p0278c2s v2p0282c2m
v2p0301c2s v2p0312c2s v2p0342c2s
v2p0348c2s v2p0351c1m v2p0367c2s
v2p0374c2s v2p0393c2s v2p0416c2s
v2p0461c2s v2p0469c2s v4p0162c1s
v4p0574c2s v5p0514c2s
Jewitt, L. and Bateman, T.
v1p1039c2s
Jewitt, L. and Briggs, J.J.
v1p0409c1s v1p0708c1s
Jewitt, L. and Hall, S.C.. v1p0414c2s
Jewitt, L. and Pears, S.A.
v1p1311c1s
Jewitt, L. and Watts, A.M.H.
v1p1397c2s
Jewitt, W.H. v5p0114c1s
v5p0427c1s
Jewsbury, G.E. v1p0871c1s
Jex-Blake, S. v1p1421c1s
v2p0477c1s v3p0469c2s v4p0628c2s
Jex-Blake, T.W. v1p0251c2s
Jeyes, S.H. v3p0208c2s
v5p0037c1s v6p0107c2s
Jillson, B.C. v1p1041c2s
Jillson, C. v2p0382c1s
v3p0017c1s
Jillson, D. v2p0460c1s
v5p0625c1s
Jillson, H.L. v4p0550c1s
v5p0251c2s v5p0606c2s
Jilson, H.L. v5p0216c1s
Jilson, W.E. v3p0140c1s
Jim v6p0501c2s
Jitta, J. v4p0044c2s
Joachim, H.H. v6p0001c2s
v6p0659c2s
Joass, J.J. v5p0225c2s
Job, H.K. v6p0067c2s
v6p0068c1m v6p0162c2s v6p0195c2s
v6p0229c1m v6p0236c1s v6p0283c2s
v6p0464c1s v6p0472c2s v6p0487c1s
v6p0496c2m v6p0513c1s v6p0524c1s
v6p0698c1s
Job, H.R. v6p0688c1s
Job, R. v5p0476c1s
v6p0475c1s v6p0529c2s v6p0616c2s
Job, T. v1p0787c2s
Jobbins, W.E.H. v2p0057c2s
Jobs, H.K. v6p0289c1s
Jobson, D.W. v1p0267c1s
Jobson, Dr. v1p0078c1s
Jobson, W. v1p1398c1s
Jocelyn, J.R.J. v5p0124c2m
Jocelyn, L.P. v5p0449c1s
Jocelyn, R. v1p0245c2s
v1p0621c1s
Jocelyn, R., Mrs. v3p0122c2s
Jocelyn, S.P. v5p0011c1s
Jochelson, W. v6p0354c2s
v6p0712c2s
Jock, Edward v4p0499c1s
Jocobi, M.P. v3p0030c1s
v3p0242c2s
Jocobs, J. v3p0044c1s
Jocobus, M.W. v3p0102c2s
Jodl, F. v3p0287c2s
v4p0093c1s v4p0188c2s v4p0226c2s
v4p0439c1s v4p0478c1s v5p0237c1s
v5p0313c2s
Joel, J.E. v3p0269c1s
v5p0055c1s v5p0118c1s v6p0304c1s
v6p0356c1s
Joerns, W.G. v6p0030c2s
v6p0436c1s v6p0529c1s v6p0535c2s
v6p0546c1s v6p0654c1m
Joffe, J.A. v5p0502c2s
Johannesburg Resident v4p0582c1s
Johannis, P. v1p0388c1s
Johansen, Peter v6p0039c2s
John, A. v6p0020c1s
John, D.C. v2p0249c1s
John, E. v1p0533c2s
v1p0786c2s v1p0952c2s
John, H.F. v6p0045c2s
John, J.P.D. v3p0098c1s
John, V. v2p0418c2s
John-Brenon, F.S. v1p0197c1s
Johnes, W. v5p0087c1s
Johnes, Winifred v4p0123c2s
Johns, A.E. v1p0511c2s
Johns, B.G. v1p0497c1s
v1p1179c1s v2p0032c1s v2p0049c2s
v2p0123c2s v2p0180c1s v2p0395c2s
v2p0456c1s v3p0026c2s v3p0061c2s
v3p0116c2s v3p0119c2s v3p0156c1s
v3p0365c2s v3p0392c2s v3p0397c1s
v3p0432c1s v3p0458c2s v4p0124c2s
v4p0285c2s v4p0299c1s v4p0491c2s
v4p0515c2s v4p0585c1s v4p0631c2s
v5p0386c2s
Johns, C. v6p0596c2s
Johns, C.H.W. v4p0033c2s
v5p0028c1s v5p0035c1s v6p0330c2s
v6p0339c2s v6p0561c2s
Johns, E.G. v5p0593c1s
v5p0601c1s
Johns, E.N. v2p0071c1s
v2p0196c2s
Johns, J. v1p0952c2s
v1p1149c1s v1p1412c2s
Johns, R. v1p0111c2s
v1p0349c1s v1p0357c1s v1p0755c2s
v1p0791c1s v1p0791c2s v1p0801c1s
v1p0878c1s v1p1417c2s
Johnson et al. v1p0825c2s
Johnson, A. v4p0097c1s
v4p0346c2s v5p0102c1s v5p0204c2m
v5p0459c1s v6p0109c2s v6p0128c2s
v6p0168c2m v6p0188c2s v6p0482c1s
Johnson, A. et al. v4p0097c1s
Johnson, A., Mrs. v2p0002c2s
Johnson, A.A. v4p0117c2s
v4p0176c1s v4p0256c1s v4p0546c2s
Johnson, A.B. v1p0091c2s
v1p0094c2s v1p0095c1s v1p0304c1m
v1p0448c1s v1p0533c1s v1p0570c1s
v1p0587c2s v1p0647c2s v1p0795c1s
v1p0860c2s v1p0999c2s v1p1153c1s
v1p1267c1s v1p1308c2s v1p1354c2s
v1p1360c1s v1p1369c1s v2p0027c1s
v2p0256c1s v3p0192c2s v3p0291c1s
v3p0392c2s v3p0401c2s v3p0415c1s
v5p0111c2s
Johnson, A.C. v6p0425c2s
v6p0623c1s
Johnson, A.E. v3p0129c1s
Johnson, A.H. v5p0130c2s
Johnson, A.L. v1p0076c2s
v1p0851c1s v1p0950c1s v1p1257c2s
Johnson, A.N. v1p0884c2s
Johnson, A.S. v1p0835c2s
v1p0935c2s v6p0356c2s v6p0484c1s
v6p0539c1s v6p0682c2s
Johnson, A.T. v6p0227c2m
v6p0607c1s v6p0658c1m
Johnson, Alfred S. v6p0188c1s
Johnson, B. v6p0303c1s
Johnson, B.T. v1p0807c2s
v1p1245c1s v2p0091c2s v2p0168c2s
v2p0279c1m v2p0475c1s
Johnson, C. v4p0194c2s
v4p0372c2s v5p0018c1s v5p0084c2s
v5p0107c1s v5p0190c2s v5p0191c2s
v5p0217c2s v5p0218c2s v5p0275c1s
v5p0296c2s v5p0315c2s v5p0322c1s
v5p0376c2s v5p0378c2s v5p0389c1s
v5p0400c2s v5p0409c2s v5p0532c1s
v6p0030c2s v6p0071c2s v6p0134c1s
v6p0250c1s v6p0250c2s v6p0251c2s
v6p0299c2s v6p0320c2s v6p0325c2s
v6p0333c2s v6p0350c2s v6p0387c2s
v6p0419c2s v6p0422c1m v6p0450c2s
v6p0459c2s v6p0473c2s v6p0490c2s
v6p0532c2s v6p0571c2s v6p0597c2s
v6p0662c1s v6p0691c1s v6p0693c1s
v6p0693c2s v6p0696c2s
Johnson, C. et al. v5p0125c1s
Johnson, C.B. v2p0405c1s
Johnson, C.C. v6p0573c2s
v6p0575c1s
Johnson, C.F. v1p0162c1s
v1p0212c1s v2p0092c1s v2p0190c1s
v2p0398c1s v2p0479c2s v3p0389c2s
v4p0485c2s
Johnson, C.F., jr. v1p0942c2s
v2p0454c1s
Johnson, C.H. v6p0660c1s
Johnson, C.M. v5p0246c2s
v5p0401c1s v5p0401c2s v6p0268c2s
v6p0445c1m
Johnson, C.N. v4p0011c1s
v4p0417c2s v5p0467c2s
Johnson, C.P. v3p0035c2s
v3p0117c1s v3p0397c1s v3p0426c1m
v4p0155c1s v4p0200c2s v4p0571c1s
v4p0571c2s v4p0610c2s
Johnson, C.Ross v6p0604c2s
Johnson, C.S. v2p0238c1s
v4p0011c2s v4p0032c1s v4p0070c1s
v4p0081c2s v4p0088c1s v4p0132c1s
v4p0153c2s v4p0225c1s v4p0243c2s
v4p0254c1s v4p0313c1s v4p0350c2s
v4p0361c2s v4p0367c2s v4p0371c1s
v4p0398c1s v4p0400c2s v4p0506c2s
v4p0548c1s v4p0550c1s v4p0575c1s
v4p0613c1s
Johnson, C.W.L. v4p0307c1s
v6p0609c2s
Johnson, Catherine B. v5p0264c1s
Johnson, Claude v6p0044c2s
Johnson, Clifton v4p0622c2s
v4p0624c1s v5p0048c1s v6p0153c1m
v6p0176c1s v6p0279c2s v6p0429c2s
v6p0430c2s v6p0464c2s v6p0573c1s
v6p0627c1s v6p0638c2s
Johnson, Col. v1p1410c1s
v1p1436c2s
Johnson, D.H. v1p0166c2s

v1p0951c2s
Johnson, D.N. v2p0087c1s
v2p0174c2s v2p0248c1s v2p0328c1s
v2p0468c2s v3p0170c1s v3p0452c1s
Johnson, D.W. v6p0173c1s
v6p0180c2s v6p0451c1s v6p0544c2s
v6p0650c1s
Johnson, E. v1p0290c2s
v1p0291c1s v1p0807c2s v1p1240c1s
v1p1388c2s v2p0356c1s v3p0018c1s
v3p0198c2s v3p0434c1s v4p0024c1s
v4p0404c1s v5p0362c2s v5p0636c2s
v6p0348c1s v6p0350c2s
Johnson, E.B. v5p0168c1s
Johnson, E.D. v6p0451c2s
Johnson, E.E. v1p0753c2s
v1p1430c1s
Johnson, E.F. v1p0195c2s
v1p0824c1s v1p0876c2s v6p0345c1s
v6p0477c1s
Johnson, E.G. v3p0044c2s
v3p0054c2s v3p0076c2s v3p0135c2s
v3p0138c1s v3p0152c1s v3p0198c2s
v3p0200c1s v3p0201c2s v3p0240c2s
v3p0258c1s v3p0268c1s v3p0426c1s
v4p0028c1s v4p0046c1s v4p0122c1s
v4p0259c2s v4p0261c1s v4p0268c2s
v4p0292c1s v4p0302c2s v4p0332c2s
v4p0333c1s v4p0337c1s v4p0395c2s
v4p0421c1s v4p0480c2s v4p0484c2s
v4p0492c1s v4p0499c2s v4p0520c2s
v4p0561c1s v4p0576c2s v5p0027c1s
v5p0065c1m v5p0079c1s v5p0084c1s
v5p0084c2s v5p0110c2s v5p0145c1s
v5p0164c1s v5p0171c1s v5p0197c1s
v5p0217c1s v5p0275c1s v5p0285c2s
v5p0320c1s v5p0330c2s v5p0352c1s
v5p0364c1s v5p0390c2s v5p0398c2s
v5p0404c1s v5p0425c1s v5p0433c2s
v5p0435c2s v5p0491c2s v5p0513c1s
v5p0519c1s v5p0547c1s v5p0553c2s
Johnson, E.H. v2p0085c2s
v3p0026c1s v3p0082c1s v3p0118c1s
v3p0123c2s v3p0133c1s v3p0244c1s
v3p0413c1s v4p0229c1s v4p0261c1s
v5p0134c1s v5p0280c1s v6p0632c2s
v6p0634c1s
Johnson, E.H. et al. v3p0283c1s
Johnson, E.J. v1p0787c2s
Johnson, E.L. v5p0139c1s
Johnson, E.M. v1p0979c2s
v6p0209c1s
Johnson, E.M., jr. v6p0519c1s
Johnson, E.P. v2p0098c1s
v2p0113c1s v3p0361c2s v4p0087c2s
v4p0381c1s
Johnson, E.R. v2p0289c2s
v4p0403c2s v4p0407c1s v4p0470c2s
v4p0472c1s v4p0485c1s v4p0565c1s
v4p0593c1s v5p0294c1s v5p0410c1m
v5p0477c2s v6p0324c1m v6p0324c2s
v6p0330c2s v6p0476c2s v6p0477c2m
Johnson, E.S. v3p0342c1s
v5p0016c1s v6p0207c1s v6p0698c1s
v6p0702c1s v6p0712c1s
Johnson, E.T. v3p0054c1s
v3p0060c1s v3p0101c1s v3p0102c1s
v3p0259c1s v3p0446c1s
Johnson, E.W. v1p0031c2s
Johnson, Ella H. v5p0248c2s
Johnson, Ellen C. v5p0525c1s
Johnson, Emery R. v6p0324c1s
Johnson, F. v1p0115c2s
v1p0689c1s v1p0772c1s v1p0993c2s
v1p1049c1m v1p1138c1s v1p1155c1s
v1p1411c2s v2p0013c1s v2p0110c1s
v2p0213c1s v2p0307c2s v6p0341c2s
v6p0705c1s
Johnson, F.B. v2p0128c2s
Johnson, F.C. v5p0309c2s
Johnson, F.C.O. v4p0062c1s
Johnson, F.H. v1p0959c1s
v2p0099c2s v2p0149c1m v2p0149c2m
v2p0222c2s v2p0350c1s v2p0366c1s
v2p0371c1m v2p0447c2s v3p0016c1s
v3p0026c1s v3p0103c2s v3p0104c1s
v3p0145c1s v3p0272c2s v3p0355c2s
v3p0373c2s v3p0427c1s v3p0437c2s
v3p0440c2s
Johnson, F.K. v5p0435c2s
v6p0518c1s v6p0664c2s v6p0696c2s
Johnson, F.M. v3p0128c1s
v3p0199c1s
Johnson, F.P. v1p0053c1s
v1p0073c1s
Johnson, F.S. v6p0166c1s
Johnson, G. v5p0094c2s
v5p0140c1s v5p0166c1s v5p0519c2s
v6p0301c2s
Johnson, G.E. v4p0196c2m
v4p0219c2s v4p0446c2s v5p0454c2s
v5p0570c2s
Johnson, G.H. v2p0085c1s
v2p0438c1s v4p0554c2s
Johnson, G.J. v1p0174c2s
Johnson, G.L. v4p0420c2s
v5p0422c2s
Johnson, G.S. v1p1390c2m
v3p0456c2s
Johnson, G.W. v1p0694c2s
Johnson, George v6p0199c1s
Johnson, H. v2p0042c2s
v2p0145c1s v2p0152c1s v2p0475c2s
v3p0073c1s v3p0076c2s v3p0204c2s
v3p0415c2s v4p0267c2s v6p0064c2s
v6p0290c2s
Johnson, H.A. and Hough, G.W.
v3p0112c2s
Johnson, H.B. v6p0055c2s
Johnson, H.G. v1p1400c1s
Johnson, H.H. v5p0425c1s
Johnson, H.Luttmann v5p0173c1s
Johnson, H.M. v1p0173c1s
v1p0557c2s v1p0679c2s v1p1086c1s
v3p0353c2s
Johnson, H.P. v6p0022c2s
Johnson, H.R. v3p0238c2s
Johnson, H.S. v6p0300c2s
Johnson, H.T. v4p0608c2s
Johnson, H.W. v6p0290c2s
Johnson, Helen K. v2p0409c2s
Johnson, Hugh S. v6p0060c1s
Johnson, I.E. v3p0203c1s
Johnson, J. v1p0167c2s
v1p0916c2s v1p1047c2s v1p1306c2s
v1p1310c2s v2p0054c1s v2p0279c1s
v2p0408c2m v2p0425c2s v2p0442c2s
v6p0096c2s v6p0226c1s v6p0227c1s
v6p0599c1s v6p0656c1s v6p0661c1s
Johnson, J., jr. v3p0052c2s
v3p0378c2s v6p0623c2s
Johnson, J.A. v1p0016c1s
v1p0106c2s v1p0328c1s v1p0733c1s
v1p0949c2s v1p1035c2s v1p1278c2m
v1p1396c2s v2p0166c1s v2p0327c1s
Johnson, J.B. v1p1055c2s
v2p0373c2s v2p0415c1s v4p0146c2s
v5p0383c1s v5p0507c2s v6p0373c1s
v6p0671c1s
Johnson, J.C. v3p0307c1s
v4p0079c1s v4p0166c1s v4p0389c1s
v5p0268c2s v5p0385c2s
Johnson, J.E. v1p0234c1s
v1p0236c1s v1p0236c2s v1p0358c1s
v1p0792c1s v1p0861c2m v1p0862c1s
v1p1280c1s v1p1317c1s v1p1321c1s
v2p0186c2s v2p0224c2s v5p0638c1s
Johnson, J.F. v1p1218c1s
v4p0526c1s v5p0120c2s v5p0121c1s
v5p0149c2s v5p0382c2s v5p0584c1s
v6p0516c1s
Johnson, J.G. v6p0387c2s
v6p0523c2s
Johnson, J.H. v1p0329c2s
v1p0978c2s
Johnson, J.K. v5p0050c2s
Johnson, J.M. v1p0528c2s
v1p1222c2s
Johnson, J.O. v1p0248c1s
v2p0210c2s v2p0381c2s
Johnson, J.W. v2p0461c2s
v5p0423c2s v5p0625c2s v6p0448c1s
Johnson, K.L. v4p0409c1s
Johnson, L. v1p0745c2s
v1p1232c2s v3p0020c2s v3p0022c2m
v3p0030c1s v3p0152c1s v3p0237c1m
v3p0275c1s v3p0288c2s v3p0302c1s
v3p0316c1s v3p0318c1s v3p0426c1s
v4p0051c1s v4p0063c2s v4p0089c2s
v4p0148c2s v4p0157c2s v4p0232c2s
v4p0263c2s v4p0274c2s v4p0311c2s
v4p0353c2s v4p0365c2s v4p0430c1s
v4p0479c1s v4p0483c2s v4p0492c1s
v4p0549c1s v4p0549c2m v4p0569c2s
v4p0585c1s v4p0610c2s v4p0623c2s
v4p0635c1s v5p0086c1s v5p0121c2s
v5p0141c1s v5p0255c2s v5p0433c2s
v5p0435c2s v5p0581c1s v6p0327c1s
Johnson, L.C. v1p0012c1s
v1p0262c2s v1p0898c2s v1p0901c1s
v1p1037c2s v3p0155c2s v3p0178c2s
v4p0009c1s v4p0203c1s
Johnson, L.H. v5p0049c1s
v6p0043c2s
Johnson, L.J. v6p0282c1s
Johnson, L.M. v1p1078c1s
Johnson, L.W. v1p1348c2s
Johnson, M.C. v4p0058c2s
Johnson, M.E.W. v3p0042c1s
Johnson, M.H. v6p0373c1s
Johnson, M.L. v4p0320c1s
v5p0374c1s v6p0098c2m v6p0133c2s
v6p0644c2s
Johnson, M.M. v5p0517c1s
Johnson, M.R. v6p0407c1s
Johnson, Margaret v6p0183c2s
Johnson, N.C. v5p0265c1s
Johnson, O. v1p0274c2s
v2p0074c1s v2p0171c2s v2p0297c1s
v2p0324c1s v2p0358c2s v3p0015c2s
v3p0347c2s v6p0378c1s
Johnson, O.B. v1p0137c1s
Johnson, R. v1p1085c2s
v1p1343c2s v2p0092c2s v2p0175c1s
v2p0184c2s v2p0451c2s v3p0108c1s
v3p0337c1s v5p0341c1s v5p0628c2s
Johnson, R. et al. v2p0150c2s
Johnson, R.A. .... v1p029[illegible]c1s
v1p0676c1m v1p1285c1s v6p026[illegible]c1s
v6p0265c2s
Johnson, R.A. and Richards, O.W.
v5p0426c1s
Johnson, R.B. v4p0272c1s
v4p0273c1s v4p0346c2s v4p0516c1s
v4p0622c1s v5p0190c1s v5p0192c2s
v6p0206c1m v6p0270c2s v6p0382c1s
Johnson, R.F. v3p0022c2m
Johnson, R.H. v5p0222c1s
v5p0301c1s v5p0534c1s v6p0658c1s
Johnson, R.M. v1p0371c1s
v1p0905c1s v1p1096c2s v1p1270c1m
v3p0030c1s
Johnson, R.U. v3p0100c1s
v4p0207c2s v5p0272c1s v5p0349c2s
Johnson, Rossiter v6p0195c2s
Johnson, S. v1p0137c2s
v1p0342c2s v1p0392c2s v1p0486c1s
v1p0486c2s v1p0529c1s v1p0533c1s
v1p0680c2s v1p0715c1s v1p0746c1s
v1p0900c1s v1p0964c1s v1p1093c2s
v1p1094c1s v1p1095c2s v1p1237c2m
v1p1250c1s v1p1271c2s v1p1273c1s
v1p1321c1s v1p1353c2s v2p0258c1s
v5p0155c2s v6p0646c2s
Johnson, S. and Clarke, J.F.
v1p0130c2s
Johnson, S.E. v5p0512c2s
v5p0528c2s v5p0593c2s v5p0608c2s
Johnson, S.E.A. v5p0379c2s
Johnson, S.G., Sir v6p0300c2s
Johnson, S.L. v1p0428c1s
v4p0526c2s v4p0618c2s
Johnson, S.M. v6p0153c1s
v6p0313c1s
Johnson, S.W. v1p0014c2s
v1p0015c1s v1p0923c2m v1p0955c1s
v1p0955c2s v1p1238c2s v1p1265c1s
v2p0003c1s
Johnson, Stanley v6p0155c1s
Johnson, T. v1p0037c1s
v1p0177c1s v1p0480c2s v1p0712c2s
v1p0914c1s v2p0040c1s v2p0120c1s
v2p0136c2s v2p0258c1s v2p0299c2s
v2p0329c1s v2p0391c2s v3p0050c1m
v3p0198c2s v3p0246c2s v3p0352c2s
v4p0010c2s v4p0505c1s v4p0577c1s
v6p0005c1s
Johnson, Theodore v3p0372c1s
v3p0395c1s v3p0462c1s
Johnson, V.E. v4p0004c2s
v4p0010c1s v4p0180c1s
Johnson, V.W. v1p0089c2s
v1p0223c2s v1p0378c2s v1p0627c1s
v1p0798c2s v1p1083c1s v3p0425c2s
v3p0453c1s
Johnson, W. v1p0066c2s
v1p0289c1s v1p0384c2s v1p1049c2s
v3p0054c1s v5p0522c1s v6p0240c2s
v6p0558c2s
Johnson, W.A. v4p0096c2s
v6p0201c1s v6p0226c1s v6p0497c2s
Johnson, W.B. v1p1104c1s
v1p1248c1s v5p0613c1s
Johnson, W.C. v4p0403c2s
v6p0197c2s v6p0589c2s
Johnson, W.D. v3p0432c2s
Johnson, W.D. and McGee, W.J.
v4p0515c2s
Johnson, W.E. v4p0083c1s
v6p0637c2s
Johnson, W.F. v6p0476c1s
v6p0683c1s
Johnson, W.H. v1p0663c1m
v3p0092c1s v3p0214c1s v4p0321c2s
v4p0330c2s v4p0605c2m v5p0029c2s
v5p0126c2s v5p0191c2s v5p0192c1s
v5p0209c1s v5p0281c1s v5p0369c1s
v5p0427c2s v5p0436c1s v5p0493c1s
v5p0567c1s v5p0586c1s v6p0039c1s
v6p0070c1s v6p0111c1s v6p0127c1s
v6p0130c1s v6p0208c1s v6p0283c2s
v6p0289c2s v6p0304c1s v6p0389c1s
v6p0449c1s v6p0645c2s v6p0674c1s
v6p0679c1s v6p0686c2s
Johnson, W.K. v4p0092c2s
v5p0194c1s v5p0331c1s
Johnson, W.O. v1p0033c1s
v1p0316c2s v1p0408c2s v1p0472c1s
v1p0473c1s v1p0594c1s v1p0817c1s
v1p1350c1s
Johnson, W.P. v4p0201c2s
v4p0337c2s
Johnson, W.R. v1p0045c1s
v1p0174c2s v1p0268c1s v1p0268c2s
v1p0365c1s v1p0391c2s v1p0467c1s
v1p0493c2s v1p0579c2s v1p0664c2s
v1p0666c1s v1p0844c1s v1p1128c2s
v1p1233c1s v1p1236c2s v1p1247c1m
v1p1247c2s v6p0258c1s
Johnson, W.S. v5p0123c2s
v5p0463c1s v6p0099c1s v6p0361c2s
Johnson, W.W. v1p1268c1s
v3p0250c2s
Johnson-Browne, E.F. v5p0322c1s
Johnston, A. v2p0099c2s
v2p0100c2s v2p0310c2s v2p0452c1s
v3p0011c2s v3p0098c2s v3p0157c1s
v3p0178c1s v3p0244c2s v3p0442c1s
v6p0010c1s
Johnston, A. and Buxton, E.N.

v3p0252c2s
Johnston, A.A. v5p0053c1m
v5p0094c2s v5p0123c2s v6p0057c2s
v6p0131c2s
Johnston, A.A.F. v5p0138c1s
v5p0612c2s v6p0559c1s
Johnston, A.C. v5p0423c1s
Johnston, A.F. v5p0085c2s
v6p0051c2s
Johnston, A.J. v2p0469c2s
Johnston, A.K. v1p0562c1s
Johnston, A.S. and Harris, I.G.
v1p1347c1s
Johnston, C. v1p1344c2s
v3p0431c2s v3p0438c1s v4p0033c1s
v4p0040c2s v4p0051c1s v4p0148c1s
v4p0281c1s v4p0379c1s v4p0473c1s
v4p0530c1s v4p0598c2s v4p0618c1s
v4p0635c2s v5p0015c2s v5p0016c2s
v5p0017c1s v5p0018c2s v5p0111c1s
v5p0111c2s v5p0219c1s v5p0257c2s
v5p0286c1s v5p0299c1s v5p0320c1s
v5p0325c1s v5p0390c2s v5p0411c2s
v5p0444c2s v5p0502c1s v5p0524c1s
v5p0582c1m v6p0173c1s v6p0301c2s
v6p0326c2s v6p0355c1s v6p0367c2s
v6p0392c1s v6p0559c1s v6p0559c2s
v6p0584c2s v6p0672c2s v6p0675c2s
v6p0678c1s v6p0702c1s v6p0711c1s
Johnston, C.C. and Lea, M.C.
v4p0632c2s
Johnston, C.L. v2p0381c1s
Johnston, C.N. v5p0009c2s
Johnston, Charles v5p0286c1s
v5p0359c1s
Johnston, D. v5p0228c1s
v6p0085c1s v6p0152c2s v6p0399c2s
v6p0577c2s
Johnston, D.V.R. v3p0049c2s
Johnston, D.V.R. and Poole, R.B.
v4p0066c2s
Johnston, E. v6p0094c1s
Johnston, E.B. v2p0212c1s
v2p0350c1s v2p0466c2s v6p0034c1s
v6p0543c1s
Johnston, E.S. v4p0633c1s
Johnston, F. v4p0487c2s
Johnston, F.C. v6p0014c2s
Johnston, G. v3p0154c2s
Johnston, G.H. v1p0258c1s
v1p0344c2s v1p1292c2s v1p1415c1s
v1p1420c2s v1p1422c1s
Johnston, G.R. v5p0496c1s
Johnston, G.W. v6p0272c1s
v6p0573c2s v6p0663c1s
Johnston, H. v2p0312c2s
v4p0315c1s v4p0315c2s v4p0508c1s
v6p0524c1s v6p0613c2s v6p0664c1m
Johnston, H.A. v4p0130c1s
Johnston, H.H. v2p0004c1s
v3p0004c1m v3p0004c2s v3p0005c1m
v3p0066c2s v3p0282c2m v3p0309c1s
v3p0407c1s v4p0005c1m v4p0065c1s
v5p0418c2s v6p0006c2s v6p0007c2s
v6p0051c2m v6p0246c1s v6p0254c2s
v6p0267c1s v6p0370c1s v6p0404c2s
v6p0524c1s v6p0558c2s
Johnston, H.H. and Williams, R.C.
v3p0004c1s
Johnston, H.H. et al. v3p0004c1s
Johnston, H.H., Sir v5p0503c2s
v6p0006c1s
Johnston, H.M. v6p0262c1s
Johnston, H.M. and Glass, M.
v6p0058c1s
Johnston, H.McB. v6p0305c1s
v6p0347c2s v6p0483c1s
Johnston, H.P. v1p0090c1s
v1p0303c2s v1p0447c1s v1p0566c1s
v1p0818c1s v1p1256c1s v2p0012c1m
v2p0022c1s v2p0161c2s v2p0166c1s
v2p0194c2s v2p0240c2s v2p0313c1s
v2p0354c2s v2p0374c1s v2p0383c1s
v2p0430c2s v2p0457c2s v2p0466c2s
v4p0015c2s v4p0579c2s
Johnston, H.W. v5p0326c2s
v6p0363c1s
Johnston, Harry v6p0370c1s
Johnston, Henry v3p0174c1s
Johnston, J. v1p0073c2s
v1p0507c2s v1p0789c2s v1p0985c2s
v2p0131c2s v2p0217c1s v2p0292c1s
v2p0382c1s v4p0006c2s v4p0237c1s
v5p0143c2s v5p0312c2s v5p0488c1s
v6p0204c2s v6p0219c2s v6p0563c1s
Johnston, J.B. v6p0071c1s
v6p0582c2s
Johnston, J.C.R. v6p0428c2s
Johnston, J.D. v1p0856c2s
Johnston, J.E. v1p0175c1s
v1p0795c2s v1p1180c2s v1p1347c1s
v2p0299c2s v2p0395c2s v2p0400c1s
v3p0026c1s v3p0386c1s
Johnston, J.F.W. v1p0844c2s
v1p1155c1s
Johnston, J.H. v6p0245c2s
Johnston, J.K. v1p1324c2s
Johnston, J.O. v5p0576c2s
Johnston, J.S. v1p0045c2s
v5p0315c1s
Johnston, J.W. v1p0389c2s
v1p1373c2s v2p0093c2s v2p0308c1s
v2p0358c2s v2p0375c2s v2p0452c1s
v3p0011c1s v3p0030c1s v5p0081c1s
v5p0305c2s v5p0372c2s
Johnston, J.W. and Cable, G.W.
v2p0411c1s
Johnston, James v6p0325c1s
Johnston, K. v1p0966c2s
Johnston, K., jr. v1p0922c2s
Johnston, K.L. v5p0130c1s
v5p0188c1s v5p0455c2s
Johnston, L. v1p0717c1s
v4p0111c2s v4p0424c1s v4p0589c2s
v5p0463c1s v5p0463c2s v6p0020c2s
v6p0121c2s v6p0361c2s v6p0424c2s
v6p0478c1s v6p0513c2s v6p0538c1s
Johnston, Lucian v6p0178c2s
Johnston, M. v5p0038c1s
v5p0581c1s v6p0040c2s
Johnston, M.C. v4p0439c2s
Johnston, M.F. v5p0135c2s
v6p0052c2s v6p0127c2s v6p0209c1s
v6p0462c2m v6p0564c2s
Johnston, M.F., Mrs. v6p0035c2s
Johnston, Mary v5p0282c1s
v6p0596c1s
Johnston, Prof. v1p0211c2s
v1p1132c1s
Johnston, R. v3p0142c2s
Johnston, R.H. v2p0282c1s
Johnston, R.L.N. v6p0429c2s
Johnston, R.M. v1p0110c1s
v1p1067c2s v1p1159c2s v1p1414c1s
v2p0056c1s v2p0118c1s v2p0168c2s
v2p0175c1s v2p0176c1s v2p0181c2s
v2p0208c1s v2p0212c2s v2p0232c2s
v2p0238c1s v2p0243c1s v2p0290c2s
v2p0339c1s v2p0339c2s v2p0397c1s
v2p0398c2s v2p0436c1s v3p0064c2s
v3p0093c2s v3p0136c2s v3p0147c1s
v3p0222c2s v3p0269c2s v3p0284c1s
v3p0284c2s v3p0287c2s v3p0291c1m
v3p0310c2s v3p0311c1s v3p0349c2s
v3p0362c1s v3p0384c2s v3p0413c1s
v3p0416c2s v3p0435c2s v3p0465c1s
v4p0038c1s v4p0040c2s v4p0223c2s
v4p0293c1m v4p0386c1m v4p0412c2s
v4p0432c1s v4p0572c2s v4p0588c2s
v5p0024c2s v5p0100c2s v5p0378c2s
v5p0425c1s v6p0058c2s v6p0228c1s
v6p0292c1s v6p0292c2s v6p0441c2s
v6p0448c2s v6p0536c1s v6p0652c2s
v6p0685c1s
Johnston, R.W. v5p0121c1s
v5p0570c2s
Johnston, T. v1p1127c2s
Johnston, T.P. v1p0280c1s
Johnston, T.S. v1p0119c2s
v1p0852c1s
Johnston, W. v3p0053c1s
v5p0483c2s v6p0610c2s
Johnston, W.C. v1p1436c1s
Johnston, W.D. v5p0060c2s
v5p0252c2s v5p0546c2s v6p0065c2s
v6p0073c2s v6p0373c2s v6p0374c2s
Johnston, W.H. v3p0015c1s
v5p0290c1m v6p0495c1s
Johnston, W.H., jr. v3p0371c2s
Johnston, W.J. v3p0092c1s
v6p0327c1s
Johnston, W.P. v1p1347c2s
v2p0238c1s v2p0309c1s v2p0400c2s
v2p0456c1s
Johnston, W.P., Mrs. v4p0396c2s
Johnston, W.R. and Wells, H.L.
v4p0016c2s
Johnston, W.W. v5p0153c2s
Johnston-Lavis, H.J. v1p1377c1s
v2p0128c1s v2p0128c2s v2p0394c2s
v2p0463c1m v3p0142c2s v3p0384c1s
v4p0486c2s v4p0536c2s v4p0603c2s
v5p0229c1s
Johnston-Lavis, H.J. and
Gregory, J.W. v4p0185c2s
Johnstone, A. v3p0354c2s
Johnstone, C. v3p0182c1s
v4p0460c1s
Johnstone, C.E. v3p0344c2s
Johnstone, C.L. v2p0381c2s
Johnstone, D.C. v5p0286c1s
Johnstone, D.L. v3p0294c2s
v4p0590c1s v5p0194c1s v5p0319c1s
v5p0348c1s
Johnstone, E. v1p0211c2s
Johnstone, E.R. v6p0115c2s
v6p0221c2s
Johnstone, Elizabeth M. .. v4p0543c1s
Johnstone, G. v5p0033c2s
Johnstone, H. v5p0202c1s
Johnstone, H.M. v5p0044c1s
v5p0365c1s v6p0654c2s
Johnstone, H.T. v5p0144c1s
Johnstone, J. v2p0382c1s
v6p0226c2s
Johnstone, J., Sir v3p0266c1s
Johnstone, L. v3p0219c1s
Johnstone, Mrs. v1p0141c1s
v1p0787c1s v1p0921c2s v1p1280c2s
v1p1372c2s v1p1402c2s
Johnstone, R. v3p0043c2s
Johnstone, R.M. v1p0878c1s
Johnstone, T.B. v2p0381c1s
Johnstone, W.A. v5p0109c1s
v5p0359c2s
Johnstone, W.H. v4p0632c1s
Johonnot, A. v1p0694c2s
Johonnot, J. v3p0283c2s
Johow, F. v2p0121c2s
Joigny, A. v4p0088c2s
Jokai, M. v1p1209c2s
v2p0456c2s v5p0317c1s
Jokai, Maurus v4p0321c1s
Joliet, C. v1p1061c2s
Joline, A.H. v6p0043c2m
Joline, Adrian H. v6p0674c1s
Jolley, A.M. v4p0228c2s
Jolliffe, P. v6p0597c2s
v6p0681c1s
Jolly, W. v1p0372c1m
v1p0391c2s v1p0404c1s v1p0758c2s
v1p0950c1s v1p1288c1s v1p1412c1s
v2p0132c2s v2p0202c2s v2p0290c1s
v3p0034c1s v3p0294c2s v4p0337c1s
v6p0260c2s
Jolly, Wm. v3p0191c2s
Joly, J. v2p0136c1s
v2p0199c1s v2p0282c2s v2p0462c2s
v4p0440c2s v6p0362c2s v6p0497c1s
Joly, N. v1p0454c2s
v1p1327c1s v1p1390c1s
Jonas, A.C. v6p0298c1s
v6p0697c1s
Jonas, J.D.E. v5p0517c2s
Joncieres, Victorin v5p0365c2s
Jone, W. v6p0501c2s
Jones, A. v1p0109c2s
v1p0400c2s v1p0768c2s v1p1256c2s
v1p1358c2s v1p1386c1s v2p0332c1s
v3p0056c2s v6p0071c2s v6p0280c1s
Jones, A.B. v2p0043c1s
v2p0180c2s
Jones, A.C. v1p0146c1s
v1p0621c2s v1p1075c1s v1p1289c2s
v4p0606c2s
Jones, A.L. v6p0148c1s
Jones, A.M. v6p0129c1s
Jones, A.S. v1p1417c2s
v2p0396c1s v2p0436c2s v4p0484c1s
v6p0592c1s
Jones, A.T. v1p0942c2s
Jones, A.W. v5p0245c1s
Jones, Alice I. v5p0087c2s
Jones, Alma B. v3p0413c2s
Jones, B. v1p1007c1s
v3p0099c1s v4p0092c1s v4p0132c2s
v4p0336c1s v4p0461c1s v5p0064c1s
v5p0225c2s v5p0339c1s v5p0348c1s
v5p0432c2s
Jones, B.D. v2p0159c2s
Jones, B.F. v2p0212c2s
Jones, Beatrix v6p0367c2s
Jones, Bernard v5p0164c2s
Jones, C. v4p0440c1s
v5p0448c2s v6p0497c1s
Jones, C.A. v1p0802c1s
v1p1347c2s
Jones, C.A.R. v2p0284c1s
Jones, C.C. v2p0359c1s
Jones, C.C., jr. v1p0030c2s
v1p0450c2s v1p0512c1s v1p1343c1s
v1p1346c2s v2p0057c2s v2p0116c2s
v2p0193c2s v2p0206c2s v2p0270c1s
v2p0309c1s v2p0400c1s v2p0443c1s
v3p0064c2s v3p0095c2s v3p0113c1s
v3p0170c2s v3p0187c1s v3p0188c1s
v3p0205c1s v3p0376c1s v4p0411c1s
Jones, C.E. v1p0956c1s
Jones, C.H. v1p0451c1s
v1p0916c2s v1p1205c2s v1p1331c1s
v4p0337c2s v5p0344c1s v5p0374c2s
v5p0476c1s v6p0070c2s v6p0105c1s
Jones, C.H.W. v6p0019c1s
v6p0092c1s
Jones, C.J. v6p0086c2s
Jones, C.L. v6p0394c1s
Jones, C.P. v3p0047c2s
Jones, C.S. v5p0273c1s
v6p0683c2s
Jones, C.W. v3p0232c2s
Jones, Charlotte R. v5p0324c2s
Jones, Chester L. v6p0436c2s
Jones, D.A. v4p0322c2s
v4p0471c2s
Jones, D.M. v5p0072c1s
v5p0099c1s v5p0559c1s v6p0110c1s
v6p0167c1s v6p0259c2s v6p0306c1s
v6p0704c2s
Jones, D.R. v1p0045c2s
v1p0795c2s v1p1345c2s v2p0263c2s
Jones, Dora M. v5p0050c1s
v5p0625c2s v6p0483c1s
Jones, E. v1p0636c2s
v2p0280c2s v4p0098c1s v4p0298c2s
Jones, E.A. v6p0500c2s
Jones, E.C. v1p0407c2s
v1p1043c2s v1p1417c2s
Jones, E.D. v1p0236c1s
v1p1287c2s v5p0101c2s v5p0217c2s
v5p0465c2s v5p0542c2s v5p0615c1s

v6p0190c1s v6p0295c1s v6p0318c2s v6p0399c2s
Jones, E.E.C. v4p0253c1s v4p0338c1s v5p0038c1s v5p0344c2s v5p0619c2s
Jones, E.E.Constance v6p0286c1s v6p0427c2s
Jones, E.F. v1p0695c1s v5p0564c2s
Jones, E.J. v6p0643c2s
Jones, E.L. v6p0104c1s
Jones, E.N. v2p0475c2s
Jones, E.R. v1p1400c2s v6p0302c1s
Jones, E.S. v5p0531c1s
Jones, E.W. v1p0234c1s v1p1311c2s v1p1398c1s
Jones, Emma S. v5p0213c2s
Jones, F. v5p0039c1s
Jones, F.A. v5p0250c2s v6p0691c1s
Jones, F.H. v2p0082c1s
Jones, F.L. v6p0574c1s
Jones, F.N. v4p0069c1s v4p0281c2s
Jones, F.R. v4p0129c2s v4p0565c1s v5p0150c1s v5p0186c2s v5p0304c1s v5p0363c2s v5p0503c1s v6p0110c2s v6p0264c2s v6p0274c2s v6p0393c1s v6p0507c2s v6p0632c1s v6p0683c2s v6p0694c2s
Jones, F.S. v5p0589c2s
Jones, F.T. v1p0060c1s
Jones, F.W. v5p0423c2s v6p0636c2s
Jones, G. v1p0349c2s v1p1440c2m v6p0166c1s v6p0289c2s v6p0555c1s v6p0577c2s v6p0677c2s v6p0705c1s
Jones, G.C. v1p0944c2s
Jones, G.F. v5p0121c1s
Jones, G.H. v4p0237c2s
Jones, G.L. v6p0702c1s
Jones, G.M. v3p0098c1s v4p0329c1s v4p0329c2s v6p0370c2s
Jones, G.R. v4p0070c2s
Jones, G.S. v1p0633c1m v1p0637c2s v1p0890c2s v1p1309c1s v1p1440c1s v2p0071c2s v3p0246c2s v3p0423c1s v3p0423c2s v5p0363c1s v5p0370c2s
Jones, G.W. v3p0352c2s v3p0353c1s v5p0288c2s
Jones, H. v1p0117c1s v1p0160c1s v1p0165c2s v1p0320c1m v1p0482c1s v1p0529c1s v1p0809c2s v1p1030c2s v1p1087c1s v1p1172c2s v1p1431c2s v2p0006c1s v2p0063c2s v2p0066c1s v2p0074c2s v2p0119c2s v2p0120c2s v2p0121c1s v2p0123c2s v2p0128c2s v2p0133c1s v2p0146c2s v2p0152c2s v2p0161c1s v2p0209c2s v2p0236c1s v2p0263c1s v2p0296c1s v2p0310c1s v2p0345c2s v2p0366c2s v2p0372c2s v2p0402c1s v2p0407c1s v2p0407c2s v2p0429c1s v2p0443c1s v2p0467c1s v2p0475c2s v2p0480c1s v3p0006c2s v3p0071c2s v3p0080c2s v3p0088c1s v3p0091c2s v3p0118c1s v3p0173c2s v3p0229c2s v3p0257c1s v3p0307c2s v3p0329c1s v3p0385c1s v3p0397c1s v4p0049c2s v4p0076c1s v4p0088c2s v4p0113c2s v4p0149c1s v4p0188c1s v4p0195c1s v4p0238c1s v4p0273c1s v4p0313c2s v4p0314c1s v4p0342c2s v4p0382c1s v4p0409c2s v4p0423c1s v4p0439c2s v4p0580c1s v4p0619c2s v4p0633c1s v5p0146c1s v5p0198c2s v5p0628c2s v6p0048c1s v6p0412c1s v6p0532c2s v6p0537c1s v6p0600c1s
Jones, H., Mrs. v1p0925c2s v3p0299c2s
Jones, H., Prof. v6p0271c1s
Jones, H.A. v2p0123c1s v2p0345c1s v2p0436c2s v3p0153c2s v3p0334c2s v4p0053c2s v4p0088c1s v4p0160c2m v4p0237c1s v4p0369c2s v5p0167c1s v6p0180c2m v6p0181c1s
Jones, H.A. and Grundy, S. v3p0122c1s
Jones, H.A. and Tree, H.B. v3p0002c2s v3p0406c1s
Jones, H.C. v4p0099c1s v5p0104c1s v5p0205c1s v5p0330c2s v5p0479c1s v5p0513c1s v6p0112c1s v6p0471c2s
Jones, H.D. v6p0603c2s
Jones, H.F. v6p0210c2s
Jones, H.G. v1p0097c2s v1p0704c2s v2p0298c1s v4p0424c2s v4p0484c2s
Jones, H.K. v1p0625c2s v1p0999c2s v1p1187c1s v1p1366c2s v2p0351c2s
Jones, H.L. v1p0387c2s v6p0092c2s v6p0222c1s v6p0299c2s v6p0421c1s v6p0422c2s v6p0438c2s v6p0656c1s
Jones, H.O. v5p0314c1s
Jones, H.R. v4p0284c1s
Jones, H.S. v4p0099c2s v4p0600c2s v5p0238c2s v6p0034c1s v6p0549c2s
Jones, Harry v6p0271c2s
Jones, Harry, Rev. v4p0505c2s
Jones, Helen L. v6p0233c1s v6p0466c1s v6p0499c2s v6p0593c2s v6p0633c2s
Jones, I. v2p0424c2s
Jones, I.E. v5p0628c1s
Jones, I.W. v6p0070c1s
Jones, J. v1p0003c1s v1p0037c2s v1p0071c2m v1p0130c2s v1p0224c2s v1p0436c1s v1p0502c1s v1p0666c1s v1p0682c2s v1p0715c1s v1p0802c2s v1p0876c2s v1p0966c1s v1p1120c1s v1p1142c2s v1p1174c2s v1p1252c1s v2p0229c2s v2p0296c2s v3p0294c2s v6p0602c2s
Jones, J. and Cooper, S. . v1p1343c2s
Jones, J.A.K. v5p0603c1s
Jones, J.B. v3p0210c1s v3p0248c1s
Jones, J.C. v1p0619c2s v5p0126c2s
Jones, J.E. v4p0344c2s
Jones, J.G. v1p0538c1s
Jones, J.H. v1p0426c2s v1p0603c1s v1p0633c1s v1p0714c2s v1p1258c2s v2p0245c1s v3p0415c2s v4p0144c1s v5p0181c2s
Jones, J.K. and Allison, W.B. v5p0464c2s
Jones, J.K. and Roots, L.S. v3p0087c2s
Jones, J.L. v5p0274c2s v6p0419c2m v6p0677c1s
Jones, J.L., Mrs. v1p0450c2s
Jones, J.M. v1p0115c1s
Jones, J.P. v2p0292c1s v2p0293c1m v2p0323c2s v2p0361c2s v3p0196c2s v4p0526c1s v5p0060c1s v5p0265c2s v5p0284c2s
Jones, J.W. v1p0037c2s v1p0048c2s v1p0165c1s v1p0288c1s v1p0734c1s v1p0743c1s v1p0744c1s v1p0745c1s v1p0745c2s v1p1226c1s v1p1346c1m v1p1347c1s v2p0098c1s v2p0113c1s v2p0252c2s v2p0372c2s v2p0453c1s v2p0453c2s v2p0461c2s v3p0225c2s v4p0324c2s v4p0509c2s v5p0301c1s v5p0329c1s v5p0377c2s
Jones, K.A. v5p0606c2s
Jones, K.E. v6p0017c1s
Jones, L. v2p0367c1s v6p0068c2s
Jones, L.A. v1p0042c1s v1p0274c2s v1p0646c2s v1p0724c1s v1p1027c1s v1p1394c1s v2p0027c2m v2p0363c2s v2p0420c2s v3p0026c2s v3p0216c1s v4p0239c1s v4p0323c2s v5p0326c1s v5p0337c1s v5p0586c1s v6p0294c2s v6p0360c2s
Jones, L.A.A. v4p0266c1s v5p0272c1s v6p0267c2s
Jones, L.A.A. et al. v4p0290c1s
Jones, L.C. v1p0188c1s v1p0927c2s v1p1150c1m v1p1204c1s v1p1401c2s v2p0207c1s v2p0316c1s v2p0361c1s v5p0071c2m v5p0094c1s
Jones, L.C. and Browning, P.E. v4p0082c1s
Jones, L.C. and Gooch, F.A. v5p0071c2s
Jones, L.E. v1p0743c2s v2p0070c2s
Jones, L.G. v4p0115c2s
Jones, L.H. v4p0466c1s v4p0466c2s v5p0525c1s
Jones, L.M. v1p0276c1s
Jones, L.R. v4p0454c2m
Jones, M. v5p0118c1s v6p0358c1s
Jones, M.A. v1p1307c2s
Jones, M.B. v6p0683c2s
Jones, M.C. v4p0064c1s v4p0164c2s v4p0466c2s v4p0629c1s v5p0193c1s
Jones, M.E. v4p0271c1s
Jones, M.H. v3p0214c2s
Jones, M.M. v1p0303c1s v1p0823c1s v1p0877c2s v1p0950c2s
Jones, Marian E. v5p0498c1s v5p0498c2s
Jones, Mary C. v3p0309c1s v6p0281c2s
Jones, N. v3p0012c2s v4p0609c1s
Jones, N.W. v6p0176c2s v6p0402c1s
Jones, O. v5p0333c2s
Jones, O.S. v4p0035c2s v4p0419c2s v4p0504c2s
Jones, P.B. v5p0322c1s
Jones, P.Burne v5p0310c1s
Jones, P.C. v4p0250c2s
Jones, P.F. v6p0326c1s v6p0327c2s
Jones, P.L. v2p0042c1s v2p0068c2s v2p0297c1s v3p0440c1s
Jones, Plummer F. v6p0333c2s
Jones, R. v3p0272c2s v4p0040c2s v4p0116c1s v4p0419c2m v5p0523c1s v6p0006c2m v6p0079c2s v6p0168c2s v6p0207c1s v6p0383c2s v6p0418c2s
Jones, R., Mrs. v1p0815c1s
Jones, R.C. v1p1278c1s
Jones, R.D. v3p0260c1s v4p0223c1s v4p0223c2s
Jones, R.E. v5p0126c1s v5p0127c1s v5p0281c2s v5p0511c1s v5p0620c2s v6p0452c1s
Jones, R.G. v1p0119c2s
Jones, R.H. v5p0033c2s
Jones, R.S. v4p0588c1s
Jones, R.W. v5p0126c1s
Jones, S. v1p0221c1m v1p0823c2s v1p1145c2s v2p0351c1s v5p0435c2s
Jones, S.A. v3p0429c1s
Jones, S.C. v6p0100c2s
Jones, S.M. v5p0119c2s v5p0641c1s v6p0210c1s v6p0216c1s v6p0263c1s v6p0459c1s
Jones, T. v1p0149c2s v2p0236c1s
Jones, T.C. v2p0265c1s
Jones, T.E. v3p0062c1s v3p0436c1s
Jones, T.H. v1p0817c1s
Jones, T.I. v6p0133c2s v6p0419c1s v6p0554c1s
Jones, T.J. v2p0433c1s v6p0447c2s
Jones, T.P. v1p0038c2s v1p0082c1m v1p0257c2s v1p0463c1s v1p0578c1s v1p0679c2s v1p0815c2s v1p0978c2s v1p0991c1m v1p1233c1s v1p1319c2s v1p1363c1s
Jones, T.R. v1p0348c2s v1p0508c1s v4p0352c1s v4p0446c1s v5p0554c2s
Jones, W. v1p0001c1s v1p0042c1s v1p0102c2s v1p0347c2s v1p0362c2s v1p0578c2s v1p0609c2s v1p0618c2s v1p0710c2s v1p0739c1s v1p0786c2s v1p0823c2s v1p0849c2s v1p0887c1s v2p0412c1s v3p0223c2s v3p0229c2s v3p0377c1s v3p0464c1s v5p0507c1s v6p0012c2s
Jones, W., Mrs. v2p0132c1s
Jones, W.A. v1p0229c1s v1p0280c1s v1p0318c1s v1p0330c1s v1p0438c1s v1p0448c1s v1p0505c1s v1p0695c1s v1p0739c1s v1p0748c2s v1p0753c2s v1p0767c1s v1p0933c1s v1p1006c1s v4p0373c1s v5p0323c1s v5p0445c2s v6p0316c2s
Jones, W.A. and Kennan, G. v6p0613c1s
Jones, W.B. v1p0155c2s v1p0653c1m v1p0655c2s v1p0657c2m v1p0660c1s v1p0661c1s v2p0248c1s
Jones, W.C. v3p0099c1s v3p0234c2s v4p0567c2s v5p0088c2m v6p0058c1s v6p0092c2s
Jones, W.F.D. v4p0530c2s
Jones, W.H. v2p0146c2s v2p0160c2s
Jones, W.H.H. v1p0930c2s
Jones, W.H.R. v2p0275c2s
Jones, W.L. v6p0653c1s v6p0683c2s
Jones, W.M. v4p0262c1s v5p0158c2s v5p0500c2s v5p0589c2s
Jones, W.W. v2p0374c1s
Jones, William v4p0456c1s
Jones-Davies, W. v6p0122c1s
Jonge, I.W.De v4p0120c1s
Jonglet, A. v1p0016c2s
Jonson, G.C.Ashton and Norman, H. v6p0385c1s v6p0618c1s
Jonson, M.L. v6p0200c2s
Jonveaux, E. v1p0067c2s v1p1333c2s v1p1361c2s
Joor, H. v6p0055c2s v6p0141c2s v6p0256c1s v6p0340c2s v6p0451c2s
Jope, Dr. v2p0054c2s v2p0283c1s
Jope-Slade, R. v4p0174c2s v4p0634c2s v5p0216c1s
Jopling, C.M. v1p1256c1s
Jopling, R.T. v1p0316c2s
Jordan, A. v4p0317c1s v6p0260c1s
Jordan, C. v3p0173c2s
Jordan, C.B. v6p0125c1s
Jordan, D. v4p0191c2s
Jordan, D.S. v1p0279c1s v1p0332c2s v1p0456c1s v1p0986c2s v1p1015c2s v1p1146c1s v1p1173c1s v1p1312c2s v2p0006c1s v2p0015c1s v2p0046c2s v2p0112c1m v2p0149c2s v2p0157c1s v2p0212c2s v2p0258c1s v2p0344c1s v2p0346c2s v2p0362c1s v3p0006c1s v3p0014c1s v3p0014c2s v3p0082c2s v3p0092c2s v3p0111c1s

v3p0145c1s v3p0310c1s v3p0380c2s
v3p0421c1s v3p0444c2s v4p0007c1s
v4p0016c2s v4p0045c2s v4p0060c1s
v4p0064c2s v4p0148c1s v4p0168c2s
v4p0178c2s v4p0191c2s v4p0200c2s
v4p0201c1s v4p0255c2s v4p0326c1s
v4p0327c2s v4p0379c1s v4p0381c2s
v4p0395c1s v4p0507c1m v4p0544c2s
v4p0561c1s v4p0568c1s v4p0577c2s
v4p0635c2m v5p0008c2s v5p0010c2s
v5p0024c2s v5p0051c1s v5p0063c1s
v5p0088c1s v5p0126c2s v5p0169c2s
v5p0179c1s v5p0198c1s v5p0198c2s
v5p0208c2m v5p0209c1s v5p0255c2s
v5p0263c1s v5p0267c1s v5p0281c1s
v5p0377c1s v5p0391c1s v5p0404c1s
v5p0426c1s v5p0475c2s v5p0513c2s
v5p0514c2s v5p0522c1s v5p0534c1s
v5p0591c2s v5p0593c2s v5p0596c2s
v5p0604c2s v5p0646c2s v6p0010c2s
v6p0134c2s v6p0135c2s v6p0139c1s
v6p0139c2s v6p0186c1s v6p0191c1s
v6p0211c2s v6p0225c1s v6p0226c2m
v6p0227c1m v6p0227c2s v6p0230c2s
v6p0283c1s v6p0290c1s v6p0306c2s
v6p0352c1s v6p0381c2s v6p0471c1s
v6p0498c1s v6p0565c2s v6p0566c1s
v6p0567c2s v6p0572c2s v6p0580c2s
v6p0594c1s v6p0608c2m v6p0609c2s
v6p0613c1m v6p0658c1m v6p0671c1s
v6p0671c2s v6p0672c1m v6p0673c1s
v6p0675c1s v6p0704c1s v6p0713c2m
Jordan, D.S. and Clark, G.A.
v5p0517c1s v6p0072c1s
Jordan, D.S. and Copeland, H.E.
v1p1149c2s
Jordan, D.S. and Gilbert, C.H.
v1p1146c1s
Jordan, D.S. and Kellogg, V.L.
v6p0567c1s v6p0662c2s
Jordan, D.S. et al. v5p0126c1s
v5p0445c1s
Jordan, D.Starr v6p0337c2s
v6p0567c2s v6p0684c2s
Jordan, E. v6p0004c1s
v6p0226c1s v6p0353c1s v6p0388c1s
v6p0504c1s v6p0595c1s v6p0627c2s
v6p0675c1s
Jordan, E.G. v4p0305c2s
v4p0497c1s v4p0628c2s v5p0563c1s
v5p0614c1s v6p0469c2s
Jordan, E.O. v5p0062c1s
v5p0105c1s v5p0193c2s v5p0205c1s
v5p0644c1s v6p0047c1s v6p0305c1s
v6p0601c2s
Jordan, E.O. and Richards, E.H.
v3p0306c1s
Jordan, E.O. et al. v6p0102c1s
Jordan, F. v1p0893c2s
v4p0556c1s
Jordan, G. v1p0471c1s
Jordan, H. v5p0073c2s
Jordan, J. and Biddle, T.. v1p0240c2s
Jordan, J.N. v2p0079c1s
v2p0448c1s
Jordan, J.W. v1p1092c1s
v2p0200c1s v2p0415c2s v3p0040c1s
v4p0048c2s v5p0055c1s v5p0134c2m
v5p0219c1s v5p0271c2s v5p0439c2m
v5p0443c1s v5p0639c2s v6p0095c1s
v6p0316c2s v6p0393c1s v6p0588c2s
Jordan, K. v4p0034c2s
v4p0312c1s v4p0491c1s v5p0163c1s
v5p0203c2s v6p0382c2s
Jordan, Kate v6p0358c2s
v6p0359c1s v6p0662c2s
Jordan, L.H. v3p0112c1s
v6p0646c2s
Jordan, M. v1p0826c1m
Jordan, M.A. v3p0396c2s
v4p0566c1s v4p0627c2s v5p0636c2s
v6p0192c2s v6p0207c1m
Jordan, M.E. v4p0253c1s
Jordan, Mary A. v5p0520c2s
v6p0706c1s
Jordan, S. v1p0203c1s
v5p0529c1s
Jordan, S.S. v1p0851c1s
Jordan, T. v1p0105c2s
v1p0334c2s v1p1218c2s v1p1346c2s
v2p0400c2s v2p0452c2s v3p0107c1s
v3p0390c2s
Jordan, T.J. v3p0071c1s
v3p0429c1s v3p0443c1s
Jordan, T.W. v6p0134c2s
v6p0518c2s
Jordan, W. v3p0079c2s
Jordan, W.G. v4p0221c2s
v4p0365c1s v5p0056c2s v5p0058c2s
v6p0165c2s
Jordan, W.L. v3p0446c2s
Jordan, W.T. v6p0168c1s
Jorgensen, A.D. v5p0510c2s
Joseph, D. v2p0218c2s
Joseph, Frances A. v4p0301c2s
Joseph, G.A. v5p0100c1s
Joseph, H.W.B. v6p0302c2s
Joseph, M. v4p0456c2s
v5p0308c1s v5p0484c1s v5p0495c2s
Joseph, Maria G.G.Q.De ... v6p0224c1s
Josephson, A.G.S. v4p0058c1s
v4p0154c2s v5p0333c1s v6p0017c1s
v6p0065c2m v6p0276c2s v6p0373c2s
v6p0374c2m
Josephson, J. v6p0534c2s
v6p0643c2s
Josephson, Julien v6p0397c1s
v6p0539c2s v6p0569c2s
Josephus v4p0302c2s
Joslin, B.F. v1p0282c1s
v1p0401c1s
Joslin, B.S. v1p0077c1s
Joslin, L.B. v6p0106c1s
v6p0325c2s
Joslyn, E. v4p0375c1s
Joslyn, R.W. v4p0564c2s
v5p0327c2s
Jost, J.M. v2p0241c1s
Joubert, C. v6p0556c2s
v6p0559c2s
Joubert, F. v1p1003c1s
Joubin, L. v6p0168c1s
v6p0426c1s
Jouffroy, T.L. v5p0018c1s
Joule, B.St.J.B. v1p0749c1s
Joule, J.P. v1p0401c1s
v2p0046c1s
Jourdain, E.F. v4p0147c1m
Jourdain, F. v2p0024c2s
v6p0527c2s
Jourdain, Ph.E.B. v6p0145c2s
Jourdan, F. v1p0436c1s
v1p0532c1s
Jousselin, Stephane v6p0241c2s
Jouy, P.L. v3p0100c2s
Jowett, B. v3p0037c1s
Jowett, F.W. v6p0539c2s
Joy, C.A. v1p0230c2s
v1p0437c1s v1p0526c1s v1p0527c1s
v1p0828c2s v1p0966c2s v1p1162c1s
v1p1418c2s
Joy, C.E. v2p0208c2s
Joy, C.H. v6p0710c2s
Joy, J.R. v4p0242c1s
v5p0311c2s
Joy, V.H. v1p0175c1s
Joyce, F. v2p0301c2s
Joyce, G.H. v5p0005c1s
v5p0154c2s v5p0203c2s v5p0386c1s
Joyce, J. v5p0278c2s
Joyce, J.A. v4p0080c1s
Joyce, J.G. v1p1197c1s
v1p1411c1s v1p1414c1s v2p0141c2s
Joyce, J.G. and Fox, G.E.. v5p0529c1s
Joyce, M. v5p0502c2s
Joyce, P.W. v1p0660c1s
v1p1235c2s v2p0471c1s
Joyce, R.D. v1p0877c1s
Joye, D. v6p0237c2s
Joynes, E.S. v1p0389c2s
v1p1223c2s v2p0131c2s v6p0296c1s
Joynes, E.S. and Allinson, F.G.
v6p0296c1s
Joynes, J.L. v2p0223c2s
v2p0466c2s
Judah, H.R., jr. v6p0569c2s
Judah, M.J. v4p0004c1s
v4p0575c2s
Judd, A.M. v4p0012c2s
v4p0062c2s v4p0089c2s v4p0625c1s
v5p0154c1s v5p0250c2s
Judd, C.H. v5p0062c1m
v5p0279c2s v5p0422c2s v5p0447c1s
v5p0642c2s
Judd, H. v1p0484c1s
Judd, H.M. v6p0089c1s
Judd, J.W. v1p0507c2s
v1p0762c1s v1p0960c1s v1p1296c2s
v2p0090c2s v2p0174c1s v2p0239c2s
v2p0269c2s v2p0462c2s v3p0107c1s
v3p0169c2m v3p0238c1s v3p0363c1s
v3p0451c1s v4p0095c1s v4p0356c1s
v4p0367c1s v5p0478c1s
Judd, J.W. and Hidden, W.E.
v5p0499c2s
Judd, J.W. et al. v4p0095c1s
Judd, S. v1p0118c1s
v1p0292c2s v1p0565c1s v1p0603c1s
v1p0638c2s v1p1262c2s
Judd, S.C. v2p0357c1s
v3p0347c1s
Judd, S.D. v5p0063c1s
v5p0097c1s v5p0292c1s v5p0424c1s
Judge, E.S. v5p0092c1s
Judge, Emily S. v4p0046c1s
Judge, Emily S. et al. ... v4p0557c2s
Judge, M.H. v4p0557c2s
v5p0561c2s v6p0218c2s v6p0269c1s
Judge, M.H. et al. v4p0557c2s
Judge, W.Q. v4p0063c2s
Judius v5p0456c1s
Judkins, T.C. v1p0928c2s
Judson, A.M. v1p0404c1s
Judson, E. v1p1153c1s
Judson, E.C., Mrs. v1p1111c1s
Judson, F.N. v5p0380c2s
v6p0151c1s
Judson, H.P. v2p0204c1s
v4p0004c1s v4p0063c1s v4p0081c1s
v4p0100c1s v4p0115c1m v4p0251c2s
v4p0317c2s v4p0325c2s v4p0481c2s
v4p0592c2s v4p0594c2s v4p0596c2s
v5p0128c2s v5p0231c2s v5p0306c2s
v5p0591c2s v5p0600c1s v6p0048c1s
v6p0113c2s v6p0392c2s v6p0557c2s
v6p0671c2s
Judson, H.P. et al. v4p0123c1s
Judson, J.A. v1p1287c1s
v1p1390c1s
Judson, W.L. v5p0159c1s
Judson, W.V. v6p0693c1s
Juhl, T. v5p0459c1s
Jukes, A. v1p1101c1s
Jukes-Browne, A.J. v3p0309c2s
v3p0414c2s v4p0088c1s v4p0183c1s
v4p0407c1s v4p0410c2s
Jukes-Browne, A.J. and Gardner, J.S.
v3p0309c2s
Julian, E.B. v6p0229c1s
Julian, F.E. v6p0097c2s
Julian, G.H. v1p0343c1s
Julian, G.R. v2p0229c2s
Julian, G.W. v1p0089c1s
v1p0540c2s v1p0722c1s v1p1090c2s
v1p1100c1s v1p1264c2s v2p0001c1s
v2p0016c2s v2p0099c1s v2p0248c2m
v2p0358c2s v2p0362c2s v2p0363c1s
v2p0405c1s v2p0454c2s v3p0047c1s
v3p0302c2m v3p0437c2s v3p0459c1s
v4p0246c1s v4p0468c2s v4p0520c2s
v4p0529c2s v4p0594c1m v4p0594c2s
v4p0596c2s v5p0485c2s v5p0552c2s
v5p0601c2s
Julian, G.W. and Ridpath, J.C.
v5p0600c2s
Julian, M. v2p0063c2s
Julien, A.A. v2p0060c1s
v5p0554c2s
Julien, A.A. and Bolton, H.C.
v2p0036c2s v2p0403c2s
Julihu, C.E. v5p0129c1s
Julius v6p0557c2s
Julliard, E. v3p0438c2s
June, J. v3p0118c1s
v3p0202c2s
June, Jenny v3p0261c1s
Jung, Salar v3p0144c2m
Jung, W.de v6p0093c1s
Jung-Stilling, J.H. v1p0446c1s
Junge, F.E. v6p0248c1s
Junghaendel, H.M. v5p0271c2s
Junkin, G. v1p0978c1s
Junkin, M. v1p0289c1s
v1p0574c1s
Junod, H.A. v6p0053c2s
Jurado, A.R. v5p0445c2s
v6p0493c2s
Jurado, A.R.Y. v6p0493c2s
Jurgens, A. v3p0311c2s
Jurgensen, Miss v1p0940c1s
Jusserand, J. v5p0496c1s
Jusserand, J.A.A.J. v6p0350c1s
Jusserand, J.J. v3p0094c1s
v3p0139c1s v3p0245c1s v3p0387c1s
v4p0098c1s v4p0160c2s v4p0182c1s
v4p0508c2s v5p0192c2s v5p0572c2s
v6p0407c2s
Just, C.F. et al. v6p0268c1s
Justi, H. v5p0045c2s
v6p0100c1s v6p0133c1s
Jutten, D.B. v3p0432c1s
Juvenet, J. v3p0354c1s

K., C.G. v6p0157c2s
K., H.B.S. v6p0175c2s
K., J.M. v5p0281c2s
Kaan, F.W. v3p0333c1s
Kabbadias, P. v5p0516c1s
Kader, Abd-el v1p0604c2s
Kaeder, M. v1p0111c2s
Kaempffert, W. v6p0403c1s v6p0427c2s
Kaempffert, W.B. v6p0320c2s v6p0427c2s v6p0576c1s v6p0614c1s v6p0626c1s
Kaempffert, W.B. and Larkin, E.L. v6p0187c2s
Kaftan, J. v5p0040c2s
Kahn, I. v5p0110c1s
Kahn, Julius v6p0143c1s
Kahn, R.W. v3p0468c2s
Kahnis, K.F.A. v1p0001c1s v1p1312c2s v2p0028c1s v2p0334c2s
Kaime, G.S. v1p0776c2m
Kain, J.H. v1p0617c2s v1p0876c1s
Kain, L. v5p0337c2s
Kaines, J. v1p0045c1s v1p0287c1s
Kains, M.G. v5p0222c2s v5p0458c1s v6p0229c2s v6p0288c1s
Kains-Johnson, G. v6p0660c2s
Kaiser, C.S. v6p0209c2s
Kakuzo, Okakura v6p0033c1s
Kalb, C.De v3p0219c2s v3p0319c2s v3p0327c2s v4p0072c1s v4p0104c2s v4p0168c1s v4p0404c1s v4p0436c2s v4p0470c2s v4p0472c2m v5p0024c2s v5p0373c1s v6p0161c1s v6p0184c2s v6p0414c2m v6p0434c1s v6p0477c1s v6p0595c2m v6p0650c1s
Kales, A.M. v6p0232c2s
Kales, M.A. v6p0146c2s
Kalisch, Alfr. v5p0500c1s
Kalisch, L. v1p1300c1s
Kallock, S.K. v1p0976c2s v1p1064c2s
Kalmbach, C.L. v1p0924c1m
Kalopothakes, D. v4p0130c2s v4p0144c2s v4p0241c1s v4p0413c2s v5p0142c2m v6p0169c2s v6p0466c2s
Kalor, Mary F. v4p0281c2s
Kalussowski, H.D. v1p1025c1s v1p1209c1s
Kalussowski, H.H. v1p1024c1s
Kame, G.B. v1p1203c2s
Kamphaussen, A. v5p0357c1s
Kane, H.H. v2p0197c2s
Kane, J.K. v1p0484c2s
Kane, P. v1p0236c2s v1p0637c2s v1p0638c1s v1p1088c1s v1p1382c2s
Kaneko, K. v3p0226c2s v6p0186c1s v6p0186c2s v6p0334c1s v6p0334c2s v6p0335c2m v6p0336c1s v6p0337c1s v6p0337c2s v6p0338c2s v6p0560c1m
Kaneko, N.T. v1p0875c1s
Kang, Yeu Wei v5p0111c2s v6p0119c1s
Kanold, H.F.W. v6p0523c1s
Kant, A.B. v4p0117c2s
Kant, B.A. v4p0310c2s
Kant, I. v1p0045c1s v1p0595c1s v1p0779c1s v1p1177c2s
Kanthack, A.A. v4p0041c1s v4p0430c2s v5p0043c1s
Kapadia, J.P. v5p0207c2s
Kaplan, B.M. v6p0025c1s
Kapp, E. v1p1001c2s
Kapp, F. v1p0080c2s v1p0138c1s v1p0138c2s v1p0379c2s v1p0477c2s v1p0478c1m v1p0478c2s v1p0516c1s v1p0516c2s v1p0517c1s v1p0625c2s v1p0990c1s v1p1060c1m v1p1060c2m v1p1061c1m v1p1117c1s v1p1150c2s v1p1215c2s v1p1251c2s v1p1292c1s v1p1313c2s v1p1438c1s v2p0048c1m v2p0176c1s v2p0176c2m v2p0177c1m v2p0180c2s v2p0195c2s v2p0202c1s v2p0250c1m v2p0269c1s v2p0276c1s v2p0357c2m v2p0358c1m v2p0362c2m v2p0363c2s v2p0446c1s
Kapp, G. v1p0612c1s v3p0133c1s v4p0177c1s
Kapp, Gisbert v6p0415c2s
Kappler, A. v3p0285c2s
Kapteyn, J.C. v6p0613c2s
Karageorgevitch, B. v4p0047c1s v4p0146c1s v4p0431c2s v4p0468c1s v4p0506c2s v4p0622c1s v5p0159c2s v5p0473c1s v5p0607c1s v6p0059c2s v6p0102c2s v6p0152c2s v6p0235c1s v6p0546c1s v6p0595c1s
Karageorgevitch, B., Prince v5p0289c2s v5p0609c2s v6p0053c1s
Karageorgevitch, P. v6p0480c1s
Karageorgevitch, Prince .. v5p0023c1s
Karan, A.K. v6p0430c1s
Karapetoff, W. v6p0376c2s
Karcher, T. v1p0334c2s
Kargl, L. v1p0463c2s
Karib, R.B. v4p0436c1s
Karkaria, R.P. v5p0010c2s v6p0130c2s
Karkavitsas, A.D. v4p0034c2s
Karl, J. v4p0001c1s
Karnes, J.V.C. v2p0086c2s
Karns, T.C. v6p0302c2s
Karples, G. v3p0193c1s
Karr, B. v3p0341c1s v5p0184c2s
Karr, H.S. v6p0356c2s v6p0460c2s
Karr, L. v6p0032c2s v6p0452c1s
Karr, W.S. v2p0218c2s
Karr, W.S.S. v2p0170c2s
Karsten, G. v2p0426c2s
Karsten, G.E. v6p0288c1s
Karth and Fosse, Des v1p0965c2s
Kasasis, N. v1p0553c1s
Kasebier, G. v4p0138c2s v4p0406c1s
Kassel, C. v6p0090c2s v6p0396c2s v6p0638c1s
Kasson, F.A. v3p0190c1s
Kasson, F.H. v3p0053c1s v3p0200c2s v3p0207c1s v3p0266c2s v3p0448c2s v4p0101c1m v4p0171c2s v4p0263c1s v4p0589c1s v5p0176c2s v5p0178c2s v5p0179c1s v5p0179c2s v5p0256c2s v5p0258c2s v5p0316c1s v5p0413c2m v5p0488c1s
Kasson, J.A. v1p0862c2m v2p0048c1s v2p0086c2s v2p0098c2s v3p0420c2s v3p0464c1s v4p0128c2s v5p0242c2s v5p0354c1s v5p0480c1s
Kastle, J.H. and Loevenhart, A.S. v6p0325c2s
Katanoff, N. v5p0595c1s
Kataoka, M. v4p0503c2s
Katayama, Sen v4p0271c1s
Kate, H.F.C.Ten v1p0166c1m
Kate, H.Ten v4p0099c1s v4p0328c1s
Kathman, J.C. v2p0267c1s
Katscher, L. v1p0037c1s v1p0369c2s v2p0054c1s v2p0384c2s v2p0430c1s v2p0449c2s v3p0170c2s v3p0256c2s v4p0105c2s v4p0269c2m v4p0326c1s v4p0390c1s v4p0501c1s v4p0586c2s v5p0260c2s v5p0276c1m v5p0457c1s v5p0467c2m v6p0303c1m v6p0356c1s v6p0356c2s v6p0437c1s v6p0528c1s v6p0601c1s v6p0650c1s
Katte, A.G. v3p0462c1s
Katterus, D. v1p0849c2s
Kauffman, J.C. v1p0599c2s
Kaufman, E.B. v4p0215c2s v4p0247c1s v6p0103c1s v6p0167c1s v6p0342c2s v6p0550c1s
Kaufman, Emma B. v6p0511c2s
Kaufman, H.P. v2p0239c1s
Kaufman, Jessie v5p0258c2s v5p0401c1s
Kaufman, M. v4p0303c1s v4p0495c1s v5p0308c2s
Kaufman, M.S. v5p0325c2s
Kaufman, W.P. v6p0276c1s
Kaufmann, D. v4p0040c2s v4p0053c1s v4p0151c2s v4p0189c1s v4p0284c2s v4p0301c2s v4p0302c1s v4p0393c1s v5p0010c2s v5p0014c1s v5p0260c2s v5p0304c1s v5p0362c2s v5p0368c2s v5p0371c1s v5p0428c2s v5p0460c1s v5p0497c2s v5p0565c1s v5p0566c1s v5p0645c2s
Kaufmann, M. v1p0922c1m v1p1136c1s v2p0030c2s v2p0097c1m v2p0101c2s v2p0163c2s v2p0210c1s v2p0223c2s v2p0242c2s v2p0243c1m v2p0245c1s v2p0247c1m v2p0250c1s v2p0277c1s v2p0278c2s v2p0297c2s v2p0298c1s v2p0314c2s v2p0328c2s v2p0357c2s v2p0383c2s v2p0407c1s v2p0407c2m v2p0408c1m v2p0457c1s v3p0175c2s v3p0396c1s v3p0398c2m v3p0399c1s v3p0446c2s v4p0039c1s v4p0408c2s v4p0533c2s v4p0534c1s v5p0058c1m v6p0008c1s v6p0062c1s v6p0063c1s v6p0277c1s v6p0339c2s v6p0482c1s
Kaukel, A.J. v6p0222c2s
Kautz, A. et al. v2p0312c1s
Kautz, A.V. v1p1081c1s v2p0287c1s v3p0441c2s v5p0290c2s v5p0375c1s
Kautzsch, E. v2p0327c1s
Kavana, R.M. v5p0192c2s v6p0207c2s
Kavanagh, E. v5p0120c1s v5p0409c1s
Kavanagh, F.E. v4p0484c1s
Kavanagh, J. v1p0043c1s v1p0181c2s v1p0481c1s v1p0482c2m v1p0504c2s v1p0672c1s v1p0738c2s v1p0772c1s v1p0841c1s v1p0842c2s v1p0886c2s v1p0923c1s v1p1125c2s v1p1257c2s v4p0120c1s v4p0272c1s v4p0618c1s
Kavanagh, J.M. v2p0061c1s
Kavanagh, J.W. v1p0657c1s v1p0866c2s
Kavanagh, M. v6p0579c1s
Kavanagh, R. v3p0440c1s
Kavanaugh, W.B. v6p0603c1s
Kaw, Hong Ben v3p0079c2s
Kawaguchi, E. v6p0369c2s v6p0646c1s
Kawakami, K.K. v6p0118c1s v6p0337c2m v6p0354c1s v6p0398c2s
Kawelin, W. v4p0188c2s
Kay, C. v4p0199c2s
Kay, C.A.De v1p0184c2s v1p0679c2s v1p0796c2s
Kay, C.De v1p0100c2s v1p0397c2s v1p1387c1s v2p0072c2s v2p0210c1s v2p0227c1s v2p0228c1m v2p0456c2s v2p0477c1s v3p0054c1s v3p0058c2s v3p0123c1s v3p0148c1s v3p0184c1s v3p0219c2s v3p0220c1m v3p0221c2m v3p0222c1s v3p0222c2m v3p0242c1s v3p0279c2s v3p0335c2s v3p0368c1s v3p0392c1s v3p0469c1s v4p0031c1s v4p0033c1s v4p0118c1s v4p0196c2s v4p0217c2s v4p0243c2s v4p0310c1s v4p0382c2s v4p0386c2s v4p0387c1s v4p0569c1s v4p0622c2s v5p0030c2m v5p0033c1s v5p0054c1s v5p0065c1s v5p0356c1s v5p0361c2s v5p0365c1s v5p0377c2s v5p0406c2s v5p0407c2s v5p0433c2s v5p0462c1s v5p0475c2s v5p0497c2s v5p0547c1s v5p0574c1s v5p0597c1s v5p0614c2s v6p0030c2s v6p0100c1s v6p0109c1s v6p0126c2s v6p0143c1m v6p0154c1s v6p0187c1s v6p0248c1s v6p0300c1s v6p0412c1m v6p0452c1s v6p0453c1s v6p0486c2s v6p0649c2s v6p0677c1s
Kay, Charles De v6p0674c2s
Kay, D. v2p0029c2s
Kay, E.De v1p1364c1s
Kay, H.C. v2p0007c2s v2p0134c2s v2p0338c1s
Kay, J.I. v5p0159c2s
Kay, J.T. v2p0088c1s v2p0105c1s v2p0260c2s v3p0396c2s v4p0092c1s v4p0118c1s v4p0428c1s v4p0517c2s v5p0426c1s
Kay, J.W. v4p0011c1s
Kay-Robinson, E. v2p0443c1s
Kaye, J.B. v4p0204c1s
Kaye, J.W. v1p0178c2s v1p0292c2s v1p0303c2s v1p0404c2m v1p0731c1s v1p0755c2s v1p0790c2s v1p0805c2s v1p0826c2s v1p0906c1s v1p0920c2s v1p1039c2s v1p1314c2s v1p1413c1s
Kaye, P.L. v5p0015c1s v6p0510c1s
Kayl, W.J. v5p0294c2s
Kays, T. v2p0050c2s
Kayser, H. v4p0126c2s v5p0275c1s
Kayserling, M. v4p0066c1s v5p0023c1s v5p0260c2s v5p0308c1s v5p0322c2s
Kayserling, M. and Adler, E.N. v5p0041c1s
Kaztauskis, A. v6p0380c1s
Keach, S.B. v1p1209c2s
Keady, W.G. v2p0139c1s
Kean, C. v1p0918c2s
Kean, J.R. v6p0160c1s
Kean, R.G.H. v1p0262c1s
Keane, A.H. v1p0009c2s v1p0018c2s v1p0026c1s v1p0078c2s v1p0079c2s v1p0427c2m v1p0454c2s v1p0639c1s v1p0724c1s v1p0724c2s v1p1148c1s v1p1154c2s v1p1287c2s v1p1331c1s v1p1333c2s v2p0003c2s v2p0004c1m v2p0004c2s v2p0006c1s v2p0010c2s v2p0011c1s v2p0016c2s v2p0025c1s v2p0033c1s v2p0039c2s v2p0098c2m v2p0103c1m v2p0147c2m v2p0169c1s v2p0193c1s v2p0218c2s v2p0219c1m v2p0228c2s v2p0240c1s v2p0242c2s v2p0244c2m v2p0249c1s v2p0249c2s v2p0279c1s v2p0286c2s v2p0297c1s v2p0326c1s v2p0336c2s v2p0361c2s v2p0377c1s v2p0381c2s v2p0394c2s v2p0406c2s v2p0410c1m v2p0410c2s v2p0421c1s v3p0096c1s v3p0142c2s v3p0273c2s v3p0342c2s v3p0350c2s v3p0395c1s v3p0397c2s v4p0013c2s v4p0041c2s v4p0296c2s v4p0359c1s v4p0522c2s v4p0576c1s v5p0099c2s v6p0053c2s v6p0061c2s v6p0196c2s v6p0259c1s v6p0316c2s v6p0542c2s v6p0713c1s
Keane, J. v6p0234c1s
Keane, J., Sir v6p0337c2s
Keane, J.F. v2p0011c2s v2p0283c2s
Keane, J.J. v1p0241c1s v1p0243c2s v1p0580c2s v2p0482c2s v3p0084c2s v3p0100c2s v3p0193c1s v3p0246c2s v3p0247c1m v3p0259c1s v3p0364c1m v3p0365c1m v3p0377c2s v3p0412c1s v3p0445c1s v5p0014c2s

v6p0484c2s
Keane, J.J. and O'Bryne, M.C.
v2p0375c2s
Keane, R.N. v2p0369c1s
Kearley, H.E. v4p0493c2s
Kearney, J.W. v1p1349c1s
Kearney, L.F. v3p0175c1s
Kearney, T.H. v6p0531c2s
Kearney, T.H., jr. v4p0235c1s
Kearns, D. v5p0365c2s
Kearns, W.E. v5p0321c1s
Kearsley, E. v1p0191c1s
v1p1300c2s
Kearton, R. v5p0064c1s
Keary, A. v1p0204c2s
v1p0361c2s v1p1132c1s
Keary, C.F. v1p0217c2s
v1p0338c1s v1p0601c1s v1p0890c2s
v1p0891c2s v1p1001c1s v1p1096c1s
v1p1114c1s v1p1221c2s v1p1263c1s
v2p0091c2s v2p0175c2s v2p0343c1s
v2p0379c1s v3p0207c2s v4p0031c2s
v4p0210c1s v4p0279c2s v5p0282c1s
v5p0442c2s v5p0609c2s v6p0032c2s
v6p0158c2m v6p0223c1s v6p0379c2s
v6p0495c1s v6p0505c2s v6p0622c2s
v6p0628c1s
Keary, C.K. v2p0091c2s
Keary, E. v1p0536c1s
v1p0756c1s v3p0263c1s
Keary, H.D. v3p0109c1s
Keasbey, A.Q. v3p0034c2s
v3p0443c2s
Keasbey, H.G. v5p0445c1s
Keasbey, L.M. v4p0167c2s
v4p0379c2s v4p0403c2s v4p0526c1s
v5p0122c1s v5p0175c1s v5p0198c1s
v5p0228c2s v5p0294c1s v5p0410c2s
v5p0537c1s v6p0148c1s v6p0397c1s
v6p0674c1s
Keate, G. v1p1121c2s
Keating, F.L.C. v6p0452c2s
Keating, J. v6p0056c1s
v6p0464c1s v6p0584c2s v6p0595c2s
Keating, J.F. v6p0467c1s
Keating, J.M. v2p0308c2s
Keating, O. v2p0360c1s
Keatinge, A. v4p0391c1s
Keatinge, M., Mrs. v6p0663c1s
Keatinge, Mary A. v6p0474c1s
Keatinge, O. v2p0131c1s
v2p0145c1s v2p0300c2s v2p0357c1s
v2p0367c2s v2p0387c2s
Keatley, J. v4p0009c2s
Keatley, J.H. v3p0007c1m
v3p0176c2s
Keats, G. v5p0364c2s
v5p0421c1s
Keats, T.W. v1p1266c2s
Keay, F.E. v4p0132c1s
v4p0219c1s v5p0160c2s v5p0168c2s
v5p0405c1s
Keay, J.S. v2p0218c2s
Keay, J.S. and Amos, S. .. v2p0135c1s
Keays, H.A. v5p0360c2s
Kebbel, T.E. v1p0043c1s
v1p0077c2s v1p0355c1s v1p0397c2s
v1p0414c2s v1p0512c1s v1p0550c1m
v1p0727c2s v1p0791c1s v1p0976c1s
v1p0992c2s v1p1032c2s v1p1235c2s
v1p1308c1s v2p0028c2m v2p0036c2s
v2p0066c2s v2p0105c1s v2p0108c1s
v2p0116c1s v2p0174c2m v2p0187c1s
v2p0208c2m v2p0269c2s v2p0288c1s
v2p0331c2m v2p0334c2s v2p0343c1s
v2p0354c1s v2p0394c2s v2p0401c1s
v2p0415c2s v2p0443c2s v2p0470c1s
v3p0036c2s v3p0055c2s v3p0114c2s
v3p0129c1s v3p0138c1s v3p0138c2s
v3p0183c1s v3p0202c1s v3p0307c1s
v3p0316c1s v3p0322c2m v3p0329c1s
v3p0385c1s v3p0391c1s v3p0433c1s
v3p0474c2s v4p0181c2s v4p0184c2s
v4p0219c1s v4p0239c1s v4p0316c1s
v4p0444c2s v4p0470c1s v4p0521c2s
v4p0543c1s v4p0617c1s v4p0629c2s
v4p0635c2s v5p0083c2s v5p0113c2s
v5p0117c1s v5p0136c1s v5p0139c2m
v5p0189c1s v5p0206c2s v5p0272c1s
v5p0434c2s v5p0611c2s v6p0178c1s
v6p0205c1s v6p0269c2s v6p0395c1s
v6p0501c1s
Kebbel, T.E. and Greg, P.. v2p0144c2s
Kebbel, T.E. and Munro, H.A.J.
v1p0727c2s
Kebbel, T.H. v2p0164c1s
v2p0316c1s
Kebbel, T.S. v4p0429c1s
Kebler, L.E.A. v4p0398c1s
Kebler, L.F. v4p0010c2s
v4p0049c1s v4p0068c1s v6p0124c2s
Kechie, J. v5p0034c2s
Kechie, W.J. v5p0150c1s
v5p0292c2s v5p0611c2s
Kechil, J. v4p0556c1s
Keddell, E.A. v6p0108c1s
v6p0121c1s v6p0608c2s
Keddell, Emmie A. v5p0578c2s
Keddie, H. v1p0160c2s
v1p1266c1s v3p0123c2s
Kedney, J.S. v3p0080c2s
v3p0186c2s
Kedzie, A.S. v1p0228c1s
Kedzie, R.C. v3p0007c2s
Kedzie, W.K. v2p0290c1s
Keeble, F.W. v5p0481c1s
Keech, E.E. v6p0329c1s
v6p0469c1s
Keedy, J.L. v6p0626c2s
Keefe, T. v1p1094c1s
Keefer, S. v1p0161c1s
Keefer, T.C. v1p0621c1s
Keegan, M. v5p0636c1s
Keegan, P.O. v6p0045c1s
Keegan, P.Q. v1p0046c2s
v1p0106c2s v1p0274c2s v1p0320c2s
v1p0360c2s v1p0364c1s v1p0502c2s
v1p0602c2s v1p0871c2s v1p1127c1s
v2p0014c1s v2p0225c1s v2p0260c2s
v2p0323c2s v5p0211c1s v5p0211c2s
v5p0329c1s
Keegan, Q. v1p0753c2s
v1p1069c1s
Keegan, R.L. v4p0589c1s
Keeler, A.R. and Fenn, H.. v1p0939c1s
Keeler, B.C. v3p0168c1s
v3p0422c2s
Keeler, C. v6p0433c1s
v6p0435c1s v6p0567c1s v6p0568c1s
v6p0631c1s
Keeler, C.A. v5p0088c2s
v6p0068c1s v6p0350c1s
Keeler, George v5p0461c2s
Keeler, H. v6p0039c1s
Keeler, J.E. v2p0362c1s
v2p0374c2s v3p0298c2s v3p0403c2s
v4p0396c1m v4p0445c1s v4p0503c2m
v4p0540c2m v5p0035c2s v6p0038c1s
Keeler, J.S. v4p0540c2s
Keeler, R. v1p0169c1s
v1p0235c1s v1p0235c2s v1p0289c1s
v1p0431c2s v1p0478c2s v1p0504c1s
v1p0540c2s v1p0606c2s v1p0737c1s
v1p0849c1s v1p1148c2s v1p1175c1s
v1p1202c2s v1p1389c1s
Keeler, R. and Fenn, H. .. v1p1012c2s
Keeler, R. and Waud, A.R.. v1p0102c2s
v1p0148c1s v1p0227c2s v1p0580c2s
v1p0792c1s v1p0819c2s v1p0854c1s
v1p0897c1s v1p0913c1m v1p1144c1s
v1p1223c2s v1p1369c2s
Keeley, L. v4p0284c1s
Keeley, L.E. v4p0162c2m
v4p0177c2s v4p0284c1s
Keeling, A.E. v5p0122c1s
v5p0397c2s
Keeling, E.D. v2p0318c1s
v4p0065c1s v4p0160c1s v4p0442c1m
v5p0065c1s
Keeling, E.D'E. v4p0470c1s
v5p0295c2s
Keeling, E.D'Esterre v4p0414c1s
Keely, G.W. v1p0463c1s
Keely, J.E.W. v4p0603c2s
Keely, J.W. v3p0157c2s
Keely, R.N., jr. v4p0384c1s
v4p0403c2s
Keen, A. v2p0480c2s
Keen, Adelaide v5p0001c1s
Keen, E.H. v5p0441c1s
v5p0455c1s v6p0513c2s v6p0628c1s
Keen, G.B. v1p0713c2s
v2p0244c2s v3p0029c1s
Keen, H. v4p0110c2s
v4p0256c1s
Keen, J. v1p0226c2s
v1p0244c2s v1p0374c1s
Keen, J.H. v6p0082c2s
v6p0277c2s v6p0443c2s v6p0650c2s
Keen, W.W. v2p0462c2s
v3p0416c2s v4p0300c1s v4p0487c1s
v4p0606c2s v5p0305c2s v6p0408c2s
Keene, A. v1p0035c2s
v6p0352c2s v6p0675c2s
Keene, A.G. v6p0596c1s
Keene, A.H. v2p0004c1s
Keene, F. v4p0264c1s
v4p0451c1s
Keene, Florence R. v6p0561c1s
Keene, H.G. v2p0089c2s
v2p0125c2s v2p0217c2s v2p0218c2s
v2p0219c1s v2p0251c2s v2p0478c1s
v3p0073c1s v3p0096c1s v3p0118c2s
v3p0124c1s v3p0199c1s v3p0200c1s
v3p0211c2s v3p0225c2s v3p0269c1s
v3p0272c1s v3p0312c1s v3p0325c1s
v3p0326c2s v3p0347c2s v3p0355c2s
v3p0369c2s v3p0463c1s v4p0087c2s
v4p0249c2s v4p0261c2s v4p0361c2s
v4p0384c1s v4p0533c1m v5p0031c2s
v5p0217c2s v5p0285c2s v5p0286c1m
v5p0579c2s v5p0622c2s
Keene, J.B. v5p0260c2m
v5p0486c2s v5p0563c2s v5p0578c2s
v6p0156c2s v6p0215c1s v6p0259c1s
v6p0285c2s v6p0375c2s v6p0527c1s
Keene, J.H. v1p0608c2s
v4p0273c1s v4p0382c2s v4p0404c2s
v5p0209c1m
Keene, J.J. v3p0336c2s
Keene, R. v3p0288c1s
Keener, W.A. v4p0325c1s
Keeney, G.D. v1p1141c2s
Keep, A.P.P. v5p0559c1s
Keep, E.A. v2p0405c2s
Keep, H.E. v4p0154c1s
v5p0227c2s v6p0172c1s v6p0281c2s
Keep, J. v3p0145c2s
Keep, J.R. v1p0337c1s
v1p1196c2s
Keep, R.P. v1p0326c2s
v1p0388c1s v1p0428c1s v1p0564c1s
v1p1401c2s v2p0190c1s v2p0474c2s
v3p0091c1s v3p0199c2s v3p0267c1s
v4p0144c2s v5p0150c1s v5p0249c1s
v5p0372c1s v5p0579c1s v6p0078c1s
v6p0089c2s v6p0162c2s
Keer, A.M. v3p0025c1s
Keer, W.B. v1p0429c1s
v1p0634c2s v2p0323c2s v2p0337c1s
Keese, G.P. v2p0038c1m
v5p0136c1s
Keese, W.L. v1p0704c2s
v2p0195c2s v2p0204c2s
Keesling, A.L. v6p0266c1s
Keeton, A.E. v5p0235c2s
v5p0251c1s v5p0422c1s v5p0499c2s
v5p0593c2s v6p0059c1s v6p0121c2s
v6p0142c2s v6p0258c2s v6p0433c2s
v6p0438c1s v6p0439c1s v6p0457c1s
v6p0544c1s v6p0554c1s v6p0558c2s
v6p0572c1s v6p0620c2s v6p0634c2m
Keffer, C.A. v4p0070c2s
v4p0099c2s v4p0208c1s v4p0387c1s
v4p0443c2s v4p0444c1m v4p0583c2s
v5p0451c2s
Keffer, C.H. v4p0092c1s
v4p0136c1s
Keffer, J.C. v2p0212c1s
Kegan, P.Q. v1p0863c1s
v2p0223c1m
Kehelpannala, T.B.P. v4p0308c1s
Kehof, J.J. v4p0503c2s
Keidel, G.C. v6p0005c2s
Keifer, J.W. v3p0289c1s
v6p0539c2s v6p0586c2m
Keiffer, J. v3p0162c1s
Keiffer, M. v2p0371c1s
Keightley, F. v1p0451c2s
Keightley, F.C. v5p0133c2s
Keightley, T. v1p1235c2s
Keil, C.A.G. v1p1222c1s
Keil, C.F. v3p0043c2s
Keil, K.F. v1p0123c1s
Keiley, B.J. v1p0670c1s
v1p1032c2s
Keiley, C.R. v6p0333c2s
Keim, De B.R. v1p0760c1s
v1p0784c2s v1p0854c2s
v1p0903c1s
v1p1345c2s
Keim, H.M. v1p1085c2s
Keiper, F. v5p0614c2s
Keirstead, W.C. v6p0544c2m
Keiser, E.H. and Breed, M.B.
v4p0011c2s
v4p0349c2s
Keiser, J.R. v1p0121c1s
v1p0528c2s
Keister, G. v4p0024c1s
Keith, A. v4p0021c1s
v4p0105c1s v4p0232c2s v4p0352c1s
v4p0415c2s v4p0444c2s v5p0172c2m
Keith, A. and Darton, N.H.
v5p0204c2s
Keith, A.C., Mrs. v2p0327c1s
Keith, A.Y. v5p0165c2s
v5p0405c2s
Keith, B.F. v5p0608c1s
Keith, C.P. v3p0008c2s
v5p0632c1s
Keith, E. v2p0051c1s
v2p0069c1s v2p0094c2s v2p0327c2m
v3p0429c2s v4p0380c1s
Keith, G.S. v5p0488c1s
Keith, H.P. v6p0390c1s
Keith, J. v3p0137c2s
v3p0441c2s v3p0442c1s
Keith, J.B. v3p0286c2s
Keith, L. v1p1157c2s
v3p0183c2s v3p0385c1s v3p0440c1s
v5p0282c1s v5p0590c2s v5p0613c2s
v6p0358c1s
Keith, M.R. v3p0266c2s
Keith, Mercia A. v5p0630c2s
Keith, N.S. v2p0138c2s
Keith, Nellie v4p0548c2s
Keith, W.S. v6p0149c1s
Keiting, C. v6p0070c2s
Kekewich, G.W. v6p0191c1m
v6p0191c2s
Kekule, A. v1p0225c2s
Kelbourn, P.K. v1p1021c1s
Kelby, W. v1p0272c1s
v1p1310c1s v1p1349c2s
Kelekian, D. v4p0001c1s
Kelker, L.R. v5p0443c1s
v6p0492c1s
Kell, J.M. v2p0006c2s
Kellam, F.B. v6p0321c2s

Kelland, P. v1p1244c1s
Kelland, Prof. v1p0144c2s
Kellar, F.A. v5p0143c1s v6p0157c2s
Kellar, H. v4p0282c1s v4p0349c1m v6p0702c1s
Kellar, J.W. v4p0305c1s
Keller, A.D. v6p0295c2s
Keller, A.G. v5p0230c1s v5p0289c1s v5p0299c2s v5p0321c2s v5p0537c1s v6p0074c2s v6p0080c1s v6p0138c2m v6p0164c1s v6p0443c2s v6p0510c2s v6p0602c1s
Keller, C. v6p0631c1s
Keller, E. v6p0357c1s
Keller, E.R. v4p0624c2s v5p0172c2s
Keller, E.R. and Kidwell, E. v3p0167c2s
Keller, F. v2p0185c1s
Keller, F.A. v6p0605c2s
Keller, G. v5p0612c1s v6p0380c2s
Keller, H. v2p0385c2s
Keller, H.F. v3p0116c2s v3p0237c2s v4p0133c1s v4p0366c2s v5p0211c2s v6p0040c1s
Keller, H.F. and Maas, P.. v4p0555c2s v5p0160c2s
Keller, Helen v6p0070c2s v6p0071c1s v6p0135c2s v6p0279c1s v6p0350c1s
Keller, J.E. v2p0279c2s v3p0250c1s
Keller, J.W. v5p0392c1s
Keller, L. v2p0115c2s
Keller, P.G.W. v6p0574c1s
Keller, W.H. v6p0363c2s
Kellerman, K.F. and Beckwith, T.D. v6p0046c2s
Kellerman, W.A. v5p0073c1s
Kellerman, W.A., Mrs. v3p0145c2s v4p0540c1s
Kellet, I. v6p0238c1s
Kellett, E.E. v5p0316c2s v6p0301c1s v6p0431c2s v6p0484c1s
Kelley, A.M. v1p0288c2s
Kelley, D.C. v2p0238c2s
Kelley, E. v4p0232c1m v5p0342c1s v5p0430c1s v5p0596c1s v6p0215c2s v6p0397c2s v6p0407c1s
Kelley, E. et al. v2p0091c1s
Kelley, E.E. v5p0419c2s
Kelley, E.S. v4p0040c2s v4p0608c2s
Kelley, F. v2p0477c2s v2p0478c2s v5p0106c1s v5p0134c2s v5p0275c2s v6p0078c2s v6p0115c1m v6p0117c2s v6p0124c1s v6p0321c1s v6p0367c2s v6p0523c2s v6p0585c1s v6p0652c2s v6p0703c2s
Kelley, F.B. v5p0120c2s
Kelley, F.M. v1p0075c1s
Kelley, F.W. v4p0115c2s
Kelley, Florence v4p0071c1s v5p0134c2s v5p0181c2s v5p0321c1s v6p0115c1s
Kelley, G.C. v4p0199c1s
Kelley, J.D.J. v1p1151c1s v1p1280c1s v3p0409c1s v3p0474c1s v4p0511c1s v4p0558c1s v6p0616c1s
Kelley, J.H. v5p0137c1s
Kelley, J.J. v1p0155c2s
Kelley, M. v6p0124c2s
Kelley, M.E. v3p0420c2s
Kelley, M.E.J. v4p0463c2s v5p0557c2s v5p0572c1s v5p0598c1s v5p0637c1s
Kelley, M.S. v6p0050c1s
Kelley, R.J. v2p0227c2s
Kelley, R.L. v6p0116c2s
Kelley, T.L. v2p0252c1s
Kelley, W.D. v1p0133c2s v3p0296c2s v3p0346c2s v3p0360c1s v3p0416c2s v4p0538c2s
Kelley, W.D. et al. v1p1232c2s
Kelley, W.J. v3p0016c2s
Kelley, W.V. v2p0112c2s v2p0474c1s v3p0329c2s
Kellicott, D.S. v5p0167c1s
Kellner, M. v6p0343c2s
Kellner, M.L. v3p0114c2s
Kelloe, Frances A. v5p0143c1s v5p0636c1s
Kellogg, A. v1p1015c1s
Kellogg, A.C. v4p0460c2s
Kellogg, A.E. v4p0474c2s
Kellogg, A.H. v2p0133c2s v2p0343c1s v3p0131c1s
Kellogg, A.M. v6p0247c2s
Kellogg, A.P. v6p0309c1s
Kellogg, A.W. v5p0075c1s v5p0637c2s v6p0076c2s v6p0110c1s
Kellogg, Alice M. v6p0095c1s
Kellogg, B. v4p0184c2s
Kellogg, C.D. v2p0077c1s v4p0097c1s
Kellogg, C.L. v1p0679c2s v1p0940c2s v2p0403c2s
Kellogg, C.P. v5p0399c2s
Kellogg, D.O. v1p0195c2s v1p0704c2s v1p0714c2s v1p0981c2s v1p1327c2s v2p0011c1s v2p0011c2s v2p0013c1s v2p0074c2m v2p0114c2s v2p0131c1s v2p0263c1s v2p0299c2s v2p0333c2m v2p0349c1m v2p0355c1s v2p0356c2m v2p0364c2s v2p0382c2s v2p0399c1s v2p0413c2s v2p0475c2s v3p0074c1s v3p0114c2s v3p0129c2s v3p0132c1s v3p0156c1s v3p0163c1s v3p0213c2s v3p0231c2s v3p0238c2s v3p0243c1s v3p0253c2s v3p0261c1s v3p0296c1s v3p0329c1s v3p0336c2s v3p0338c2s v3p0347c1s v3p0349c2s v3p0399c1s v3p0414c2s v3p0462c1s v5p0632c1s
Kellogg, D.S. v6p0108c2s
Kellogg, E. v1p0254c2s v1p0713c1s
Kellogg, E.L. v4p0201c2s v4p0429c1s v5p0481c2s v5p0591c2s
Kellogg, Eva D. v2p0131c1s
Kellogg, F.A. v4p0323c2s
Kellogg, F.E. v4p0163c1s v5p0170c2s v5p0357c2s v6p0183c1s v6p0396c1s
Kellogg, G.D. v5p0299c2s v5p0610c1s
Kellogg, G.M. v1p0333c2s v1p0432c2s v1p0469c2s v1p0745c1s v1p1054c2s v1p1176c2s v1p1391c1s
Kellogg, J. v4p0131c2s
Kellogg, J.A. et al. v4p0315c1s
Kellogg, J.H. v1p0857c2s v4p0602c2s
Kellogg, J.L. v3p0071c2s
Kellogg, J.W. v5p0184c2s
Kellogg, M. v1p0536c2s v1p1357c2s v2p0029c2s v2p0156c1s v2p0454c1s v2p0470c2s v6p0361c1s v6p0363c1s
Kellogg, M. and Tetlow, J. v4p0122c2s
Kellogg, M.D. v5p0558c2s v6p0086c1s v6p0306c2s v6p0437c2s
Kellogg, P.U. v6p0318c1s v6p0451c2s
Kellogg, S.G. v6p0088c2s
Kellogg, S.H. v1p0173c2s v1p0242c2s v1p0690c2s v2p0003c1s v2p0059c2m v2p0083c2s v2p0148c1s v2p0203c2s v2p0235c2s v2p0251c2s v2p0291c2s v2p0299c2s v2p0301c2s v2p0355c2s v2p0368c2s v2p0475c1s v3p0104c1s v3p0142c2s v3p0279c2s v3p0342c2s v3p0358c1s v3p0436c1s v4p0451c1s
Kellogg, S.W. v1p0076c2s v1p0287c1s v1p0586c1s v1p0607c2s v1p0755c2s v1p0756c2s v1p0803c1s v1p0875c2s v1p0878c2s v1p1025c1s v1p1361c1s v1p1404c2s
Kellogg, T.H. v3p0140c1s v3p0330c1s
Kellogg, V.L. v4p0327c1m v4p0470c1s v5p0270c2s v5p0507c1s v6p0034c2s v6p0088c1s v6p0106c1s v6p0320c2m v6p0402c1s v6p0406c2s v6p0477c2s v6p0567c1s v6p0675c1m
Kellogg, V.L. and Jordan, D.S. v6p0567c1s v6p0662c2s
Kellogg, W.L. and Bell, R.G. v6p0594c2s
Kellogg, W.P. v6p0275c1s
Kellor, F.A. v5p0402c2s v5p0449c1s v5p0521c2s v5p0636c2m v6p0202c2s v6p0257c1s v6p0323c1s
Kellor, Frances A. v5p0034c2s v5p0143c2m
Kellor, Frances A. and Nibecker, F.H. v5p0454c2s
Kelly and Paratt v6p0413c1s
Kelly, A. v3p0036c2s v5p0382c1s v6p0454c1s v6p0704c1s
Kelly, A.B. v1p0995c2s
Kelly, Arthur v6p0150c1s
Kelly, B. v5p0116c2s v5p0310c1s v5p0528c2s
Kelly, E. v2p0148c2s v2p0167c2s v2p0363c2s v3p0462c1s v4p0124c2s v4p0438c2s v5p0119c2s v5p0543c1s v6p0435c1s
Kelly, E.L. v5p0318c2s
Kelly, E.P. v6p0305c1s
Kelly, E.W. v5p0271c1s
Kelly, Ellen v5p0394c1s
Kelly, F. v2p0077c2s v6p0114c1s v6p0487c2s
Kelly, F.F. v6p0400c1s v6p0706c2s
Kelly, Florence F. v6p0153c2s v6p0321c2s v6p0454c2s v6p0455c1m
Kelly, G.B. et al. v5p0179c1s
Kelly, H.B. v5p0412c2s
Kelly, J. v2p0050c2s v2p0080c2s v2p0236c1s v2p0328c2s v2p0413c1s v3p0276c2s v3p0376c2s
Kelly, J.D.J. v2p0481c1s
Kelly, J.F. v5p0485c1s
Kelly, J.G. v1p0442c1s v1p1184c1s v2p0399c1s
Kelly, J.J. v1p0534c2s
Kelly, James Fitzmaurice . v4p0408c1s
Kelly, John v5p0505c2s
Kelly, M. v6p0292c1s v6p0311c1s v6p0330c1s v6p0353c1s v6p0360c1s v6p0380c2s v6p0388c1s v6p0430c2s v6p0483c1s v6p0695c1s
Kelly, M.A. v6p0441c1s
Kelly, M.E.J. v4p0628c2s
Kelly, M.J. v1p0203c2s v1p0735c2s v5p0609c2s
Kelly, M.T. v2p0171c1s v2p0416c1s v4p0077c1s v4p0243c1s
Kelly, Myra v6p0380c1s v6p0604c2s v6p0613c2s v6p0650c2s
Kelly, R.J. v2p0101c2s v2p0224c2s v2p0227c2s v2p0379c1s
Kelly, R.M. v2p0474c2s
Kelly, R.T. v5p0051c2s v5p0180c2m v5p0181c1s v5p0181c2s v5p0559c1s
Kelly, T. v4p0607c1s
Kelly, T.L. v3p0069c1s v3p0261c2s v3p0453c2s
Kelly, W. v2p0253c1s v2p0270c2s v2p0292c1s v2p0343c2s v3p0437c2s v5p0368c2s v6p0060c1s v6p0482c2s v6p0592c2s
Kelly, W., jr. v5p0020c2s
Kelly, W.C. v1p0977c1s
Kelly, W.D. v2p0167c1s v2p0347c2s v2p0371c1s v3p0465c2s
Kelly, W.H. v6p0266c1s v6p0509c1s
Kelper, L.R. v6p0086c1s
Kelsall, T.F. v1p0106c2s
Kelsey, A. v6p0128c1s v6p0435c2s
Kelsey, A.W. v1p0926c2s
Kelsey, Albert v5p0026c1s
Kelsey, C. v5p0106c1s v5p0107c1s v5p0313c1s v6p0446c2s v6p0447c2s v6p0448c1s v6p0491c2s
Kelsey, C.H. v6p0176c2s
Kelsey, C.H. et al. v4p0286c2s
Kelsey, F. v6p0130c1s
Kelsey, F.W. v2p0166c1s v2p0167c1s v2p0338c1s v2p0418c1s v3p0164c2s v4p0122c2s v4p0257c1s v4p0321c2s v4p0369c1s v4p0523c1s v4p0566c1s v5p0121c2s v5p0326c2s v5p0432c2s v5p0605c1s v6p0026c2s v6p0076c1s v6p0362c2m v6p0415c2s v6p0508c1s
Kelsey, F.W. and Jastrow, M. v4p0634c1s
Kelsey, G.W. v4p0456c1s
Kelsey, J.S. v4p0167c2s
Kelsey, L.D. v5p0259c2s
Kelso, H.A. v5p0438c1s
Kelso, H.A., jr. v4p0442c1s v4p0566c2s v5p0450c1s
Kelso, J.A. v5p0185c2s
Kelso, J.A. and Smith, J.M.P. v6p0598c1s
Kelso, J.J. v4p0104c1s v5p0107c1s v6p0098c1s v6p0109c1s v6p0157c2s
Kelso, T.L. v4p0329c2s
Kelso, T.L., Miss and Wing, J.N. v5p0542c1s
Keltie, J.S. v2p0191c2s v3p0004c1m v3p0005c1m v3p0169c1m v3p0406c2s v5p0200c1s v5p0228c2s v5p0245c2s v6p0036c1s v6p0506c1s
Keltie, J.Scott v6p0023c1s
Kelton, J.C. v3p0279c1s
Kelton, M.E. v5p0228c2s
Kelvin v5p0607c2s
Kelvin et al. v5p0492c1s
Kelvin, K. v1p0457c2s
Kelvin, Lord v4p0165c2s v4p0180c1s v4p0293c2s v4p0305c1s v5p0172c2s v5p0424c2s v6p0618c2s
Kelvin, Lord et al. v4p0177c1s v4p0487c1s
Kelvin, W. v4p0204c1s
Kemball, A.B. v2p0336c2s
Kemball, A.B., Gen.Sir ... v4p0005c1s
Kemble, D. v4p0437c1s
Kemble, E. v4p0521c2s
Kemble, E. et al. v4p0081c1s v4p0564c1s
Kemble, E.W. v5p0273c2s v6p0166c2s v6p0596c1s
Kemble, E.W. and Hall, Walter v6p0076c2s
Kemble, F. v3p0367c1s
Kemble, F.A. v1p0364c1s v1p0782c1s v1p1185c1s v1p1185c2m v1p1186c1s
Kemble, Fanny v2p0385c1s v2p0398c1s
Kemble, J.M. v1p0040c1s v1p0598c2s v1p1132c1m v1p1178c1s v1p1359c1s
Kemble, J.R. v5p0465c2s v5p0500c2s
Kemble, S. v3p0303c2s

Kemeny, E. v6p0112c2s
Kemeys, E. v5p0329c2s
Kemmerer, E.W. v6p0260c2m v6p0493c2s v6p0494c1s v6p0516c1s v6p0620c1s
Kemp, A.F. v1p1392c1s
Kemp, D. v2p0419c1s v2p0481c1s v2p0481c2m v4p0634c2s v5p0317c1s
Kemp, E. v6p0573c1s
Kemp, E.G. v5p0539c1s
Kemp, J.F. v3p0101c2s v3p0117c2s v3p0118c1s v3p0326c2s v3p0339c2m v3p0367c1s v4p0327c2s v4p0519c2s v5p0122c1s v5p0479c1s v6p0004c1s v6p0186c1m v6p0412c1s v6p0452c2s v6p0514c1s v6p0681c1s
Kemp, J.F. and Darton, N.H. v4p0155c2s
Kemp, J.F. and Grabau, A.W. v6p0250c2s
Kemp, J.T. v3p0072c2s v4p0292c1s
Kemp, O. v5p0209c2s
Kemp, R.W. v6p0456c1s
Kemp-Welch, A. v6p0498c2s
Kemp-Welch, Alice v5p0186c1s v6p0247c2s v6p0439c1s
Kemp-Welch, W. v6p0055c1s v6p0703c2s
Kempe, A.B. v1p0751c1s v1p0798c2s v1p1258c2s v3p0429c2s
Kempe, A.J. v1p0598c1s v1p1115c1s v1p1122c2s v1p1190c1s v1p1402c1s
Kempe, J. v1p0561c1s v1p1121c2s v2p0231c1s
Kemper, W.H. v1p1010c2s v1p1237c2s
Kemper, W.H. and Hoge, M.D. v1p0675c1s
Kempin, Emily v3p0206c1s
Kempt, R. v1p0383c2s v2p0130c1s
Kempton, H.S. v6p0523c1s
Kempton, R.C. v5p0538c1s
Kempton, W.D. v5p0123c2s
Kemys, E., jr. v3p0416c1s
Kenaston, C.A. v4p0085c2s
Kenaston, G.P. v2p0232c2s
Kendal, C. v1p0245c2s v1p0575c2s
Kendal, J. v5p0051c2s v5p0341c2s v5p0441c2s v5p0475c2s v5p0493c1s v5p0598c2s v6p0196c1s v6p0421c2s
Kendal, M. v6p0066c1s
Kendal, Madge v6p0612c2s
Kendal, Mrs. v3p0122c2s
Kendall, A. v1p0674c2m
Kendall, E.K. v1p0904c2s
Kendall, E.O. v1p0281c2s
Kendall, F.H. v6p0662c1s
Kendall, G.W. v1p0833c1s
Kendall, H. v1p1147c1s v2p0200c1s v2p0368c1s
Kendall, H.L. v1p0687c2s
Kendall, J. v4p0572c2s v4p0614c2s
Kendall, J.F. v1p0314c1s v1p0966c2s
Kendall, M. v2p0035c1s v3p0034c1s v3p0052c1s v3p0150c1s v3p0150c2s v3p0233c1s v3p0250c1s v3p0461c1s v4p0050c2s v4p0097c1s v4p0161c2s v4p0341c1s v4p0551c1s v4p0557c2s v5p0033c2s v5p0059c1s v5p0149c1s v5p0256c1s v5p0441c2s v5p0596c2s
Kendall, M.A. v5p0152c2s
Kendall, Margaret C. v5p0220c2s
Kendall, May v6p0697c1s
Kendall, O.H. v1p0842c1s
Kendall, R.R. v5p0627c1s
Kendall, S.A. v1p0360c1s
Kendall, S.C. v1p0155c2s v4p0625c1s v6p0386c1s v6p0467c1s
Kendall, W. v6p0420c2s
Kendall, W.A. v1p0048c1s v1p0356c1s v1p0652c1s v1p1308c1s
Kendell, B. v5p0064c2s v5p0079c1s v5p0127c2s v5p0250c1s v5p0294c1s
Kendrick, A. v4p0349c2s
Kendrick, A.C. v1p0096c1m v1p0118c2s v1p0685c2s v1p0724c1s v1p0867c2s v1p0980c1s v1p1217c2s v1p1412c1s v2p0403c2s v3p0229c1s v3p0404c2s
Kendrick, C. v2p0180c2s v3p0324c1s
Kendrick, F. v6p0399c2s
Kendrick, J. v1p0409c1s
Kendrick, J.K. v1p0430c1s
Kendrick, J.M. v1p0208c2s
Kendrick, J.R. v2p0131c1s v3p0143c1s v3p0266c2s v3p0378c2s v3p0443c1s
Kendrick, W. v5p0054c2s v5p0342c2s v5p0438c1s v5p0644c1s
Kenealy, A. v3p0097c1s v3p0289c2s v3p0470c2s v4p0630c1s v5p0379c1s v5p0635c1m v6p0151c2s
Kenealy, A.J. v3p0473c2s v4p0021c1s v4p0042c2s v4p0064c2s v4p0401c2s v4p0484c1s v4p0498c1m v4p0521c2s v4p0634c2m v5p0067c2m v5p0146c1s v5p0408c1s v5p0624c1s v5p0642c2m v5p0643c1m v5p0643c2s v6p0071c2s v6p0226c2s v6p0227c2s v6p0353c2s v6p0710c1m
Kenealy, A.J., Capt. v5p0129c2m
Kenealy, Arabella v3p0470c2s v6p0630c1s
Kenealy, E. v1p0600c1s
Kenn, M.A. v3p0310c1s
Kenna, E. v1p1400c2s
Kennaday, P. v6p0144c1s v6p0453c1s v6p0660c1s
Kennan, G. v1p0056c1s v1p0077c1s v1p0208c1s v1p0604c1s v1p0701c2s v1p1194c1s v2p0009c1s v3p0223c1s v3p0234c2s v3p0240c2s v3p0369c2s v3p0370c1m v3p0370c2m v3p0391c2m v3p0392c1m v3p0432c1m v3p0435c1s v4p0303c2s v4p0495c2s v4p0496c2s v4p0522c2s v5p0047c2m v5p0092c2s v5p0147c1m v5p0148c1s v5p0239c2s v5p0251c2s v5p0352c1s v5p0445c1s v5p0481c1s v5p0508c2s v5p0528c1s v5p0544c1s v6p0004c1s v6p0110c1s v6p0119c1m v6p0119c2s v6p0316c2s v6p0317c1s v6p0334c2s v6p0335c1s v6p0335c2s v6p0336c1s v6p0336c2s v6p0337c1m v6p0338c2m v6p0354c1m v6p0354c2m v6p0355c1s v6p0378c2s v6p0387c1s v6p0389c1s v6p0416c1s v6p0442c1s v6p0486c2s v6p0491c1s v6p0493c1s v6p0509c1s v6p0534c1s v6p0556c1s v6p0556c2s v6p0557c2s v6p0558c1s v6p0558c2s v6p0560c1s v6p0561c1s v6p0584c1s v6p0613c1s v6p0624c2s v6p0631c1m v6p0631c2s v6p0648c2s v6p0677c2m v6p0696c2s
Kennan, G. and Jones, W.A. v6p0613c1s
Kennard, A.C., Mrs. v3p0351c2s
Kennard, A.S. v5p0454c1s
Kennard, A., Mrs. v3p0123c2s v6p0285c1s
Kennard, C.A. v4p0449c2s
Kennard, E., Mrs. v3p0103c2s v3p0199c1s v3p0389c1s v4p0390c2s
Kennard, J. v1p0430c1s
Kennard, J.W. v6p0101c2s
Kennard, Mary E. v4p0270c1s
Kennard, N. v2p0181c2s
Kennard, N, Mrs. v3p0243c1s
Kennard, N.H. v2p0200c1s v2p0361c2s v2p0478c2s v4p0607c1s
Kennard, N.H., Mrs. v2p0125c1s v2p0158c2s
Kennedy, A. v4p0285c1s
Kennedy, A.B.W. v1p0783c1s v1p0783c2s v2p0135c2s v2p0373c2s v3p0137c1s v3p0137c2s v6p0636c1s
Kennedy, A.G. v6p0111c1s
Kennedy, A.R.S. v5p0058c1s
Kennedy, A.W. v5p0482c1s
Kennedy, B. v4p0308c2s
Kennedy, B.H. v1p0838c1s
Kennedy, C. v6p0608c1s
Kennedy, C.M. v4p0236c1s v5p0514c2s v6p0271c1m
Kennedy, C.R. v1p0196c1s v5p0213c2s
Kennedy, C.W. v2p0208c2s v3p0068c1s v3p0309c2s v3p0375c2s v4p0149c1s
Kennedy, C.W. et al. v3p0156c2s
Kennedy, D.A. v3p0146c1s
Kennedy, E. v1p0876c2s v1p0980c1s v1p1374c1s v3p0154c2s
Kennedy, E., Mrs. v3p0373c1s
Kennedy, F. v5p0546c2s
Kennedy, H.A. v2p0282c2s v3p0107c2s v3p0113c2s v3p0122c1s v3p0124c2s v3p0174c2s v3p0206c2s v3p0260c2s v3p0298c1s v3p0329c2s v3p0384c2s v3p0388c1s v3p0447c2s v4p0040c2s v4p0085c2s v4p0160c2s v4p0173c2s v4p0214c2s v4p0451c2s v4p0517c2s v4p0518c2s v4p0558c1s v5p0083c1s v5p0159c2s v5p0235c2s v5p0486c2s
Kennedy, H.A.A. v5p0059c1s v5p0060c1m v5p0268c2s
Kennedy, H.G. v3p0391c2s
Kennedy, H.M. v1p0417c1s v2p0177c1s v2p0197c2s
Kennedy, Helen P. v4p0226c2s v4p0257c1s
Kennedy, J. v2p0062c1s v2p0130c2s v2p0217c1s v3p0379c1s v4p0056c1s v4p0064c1s v5p0285c2s v5p0286c2s v5p0564c2s v6p0231c2s v6p0313c2s v6p0524c2s v6p0712c1s
Kennedy, J.H. v2p0058c1s v2p0059c1s v2p0061c1s v2p0073c2s v2p0080c1s v2p0089c1m v2p0098c2s v2p0108c2s v2p0110c1s v2p0111c2s v2p0117c1s v2p0136c2s v2p0152c2s v2p0171c1s v2p0183c1s v2p0202c1s v2p0210c1s v2p0229c2s v2p0241c2s v2p0253c1s v2p0270c1s v2p0289c1s v2p0298c1s v2p0300c2s v2p0320c1s v2p0336c1s v2p0353c2s v2p0378c1s v2p0406c1s v2p0416c2s v2p0427c1m v2p0432c1s v2p0443c1s v2p0444c1s v2p0463c2m v2p0468c1s v2p0469c1s v2p0471c1s v2p0472c2s v2p0476c2s v3p0001c2s v3p0121c2s v3p0231c2s v3p0279c2s v3p0280c1s v3p0288c1m v3p0298c2s v3p0307c2s v3p0314c2s v3p0352c2s v3p0422c2s v3p0460c1s v3p0460c2s v4p0191c2s v4p0259c1s v4p0267c2s v4p0324c2s v4p0411c2s v4p0420c2s v4p0554c1s v4p0559c1s v4p0598c2s v5p0059c2s v5p0631c1s v5p0633c1s
Kennedy, J.P. v1p0189c1s v1p0226c1s v1p0291c2s v1p0807c2m v6p0374c2s
Kennedy, J.R. v6p0028c1s
Kennedy, J.R., jr. v6p0251c2s
Kennedy, J.W. v4p0152c1s
Kennedy, Joseph v6p0459c2s
Kennedy, M. v6p0209c1s v6p0263c1s
Kennedy, N.J.D. v4p0052c1s v4p0346c1s v4p0424c2s v5p0113c2s v6p0358c1s v6p0366c2s
Kennedy, P. v1p0369c1s v1p0374c2s v1p0914c2s
Kennedy, Prof. v2p0141c2s v3p0042c2s
Kennedy, R. v3p0222c2s
Kennedy, R.H. v1p1273c2s
Kennedy, S. v3p0066c2s
Kennedy, S.B. v4p0062c2s v4p0091c2s v4p0296c2s v4p0360c1s v4p0560c1s v5p0034c2s v5p0116c1s v5p0130c1s v5p0166c1s v5p0481c2s v6p0046c1s
Kennedy, S.M. v5p0424c2s v6p0469c1s v6p0569c2s
Kennedy, Sara B. v6p0203c2s
Kennedy, W. v2p0022c1s v2p0283c1s v2p0472c2s v4p0547c1s v4p0571c1s
Kennedy, W. and Colyar, A.S. v2p0302c1s
Kennedy, W.R. v5p0472c2s v5p0561c1s
Kennedy, W.S. v1p1008c2s v1p1307c1s v2p0012c2s v2p0029c2s v2p0063c1s v2p0139c1s v2p0140c1s v2p0194c2m v2p0265c2s v2p0346c2s v2p0380c1s v2p0380c2s v2p0383c1s v2p0479c2s v3p0066c2s v3p0068c2s v4p0090c1s v4p0178c2s v4p0391c2s v4p0620c2s v4p0621c1s v5p0103c1s v5p0105c2s v5p0187c1s v5p0275c2s v5p0522c1s v5p0522c2s v5p0523c2s v5p0546c1s v5p0642c1s v6p0089c1s v6p0284c1s v6p0586c2s v6p0697c2s
Kennelly, A.E. v3p0009c2s v3p0134c1s v4p0176c2s v5p0184c1s v5p0184c2s v6p0413c2s
Kennelly, A.E. and Houston, E.J. v4p0175c1s v4p0487c1s
Kennett, J.C. v6p0070c1s
Kennett, R.H. v6p0342c1s
Kenney, C.L. v1p1185c1s
Kenney, G.W. v5p0281c2s
Kenney, J.F. v6p0326c1s
Kenney, L.M. v3p0014c2s
Kenney, M.J. v6p0326c1s
Kenney, M.M. v6p0317c1s v6p0640c1s
Kenney, W. v1p0242c1s
Kenney-Herbert, A. v4p0132c1s v4p0156c1s v4p0266c2s
Kennicott, D. v6p0570c1s v6p0675c2s
Kennington, T.B. v5p0282c1s
Kennion, R.L. v6p0121c1s v6p0291c1s v6p0611c2m v6p0701c2s
Kennion, R.L., Major v6p0036c2s
Kennon, B. et al. v2p0312c1s
Kennon, L.W.V. v5p0050c1s v5p0444c2s
Kenny, B.D. v6p0394c2s
Kenny, C. v1p0496c1s v1p0552c1s v1p0740c2s v4p0051c1s v4p0409c1s v5p0092c1s v6p0099c1s
Kenny, J.T. v5p0418c2s
Kenny, W.J.K. v6p0697c2s
Kenrick, F.P. v2p0081c1s
Kenrick, J. v1p0121c2s v1p0125c2s v1p0204c1s v1p0324c1s
Kenrick, T. v1p0053c1s
Kent, A. v2p0115c1s
Kent, A.E. and Kent, N.A.. v6p0099c1s
Kent, A.T. v1p0616c1s v6p0196c2s
Kent, Armine T. v4p0028c2s v6p0213c1s
Kent, C. v1p0351c2s

v1p0496c1s v1p0619c2s v1p0737c2s
v1p0779c2s v1p0937c1s v1p1022c1s
v1p1287c2s v1p1366c1s v2p0131c1s
Kent, C., Mrs. v2p0322c2s
Kent, C.B.R. v3p0044c2s
v3p0230c2s v3p0238c2s v3p0314c1s
v4p0172c2s v4p0211c1s v4p0394c1s
v4p0417c2s v4p0424c1s v4p0429c1s
v4p0448c1s v4p0452c2s v4p0603c1s
v5p0247c2s v6p0206c2s v6p0271c1s
v6p0308c1s v6p0370c1s v6p0481c1s
v6p0503c1s
Kent, C.B.Roylance v5p0293c1s
v5p0316c2s
Kent, C.F. v4p0055c2s
v4p0056c1s v4p0299c2s v4p0302c2s
v5p0056c2s v5p0308c1s v6p0278c2s
Kent, C.R.R. v4p0210c2s
Kent, C.S. v6p0333c2s
Kent, C.W. v4p0184c1s
v5p0342c1s v5p0455c2s v6p0606c2s
v6p0671c2s
Kent, Cecil S. v6p0246c1s
Kent, E.C. v5p0505c2s
v6p0428c1s v6p0706c2s
Kent, E.N. v1p0563c2s
Kent, H.C. v4p0002c2s
v4p0353c2s v4p0601c1s
Kent, H.R. v5p0390c2s
v5p0642c1s
Kent, H.W. v6p0074c2s
Kent, J. v1p1369c1s
v4p0221c2s v4p0379c1s v4p0527c2s
v5p0072c1s v5p0315c1s
Kent, M.J. v2p0345c2s
Kent, N.A. v6p0467c2s
Kent, N.A. and Kent, A.E.. v6p0099c1s
Kent, P. v1p0097c2s
v2p0032c2s v2p0250c1s v3p0031c2s
v3p0284c2s v3p0431c2s v4p0287c1s
v4p0511c1s v5p0195c1s v5p0347c2s
v5p0510c1s v6p0525c2s
Kent, Philip v5p0469c2s
Kent, R.G. v6p0169c2s
Kent, W. v1p0162c1s
v1p0664c1m v1p1100c2s v1p1261c1s
v2p0090c1s v2p0141c1m v3p0459c1s
v4p0047c2s v4p0061c2s v4p0137c2s
v4p0167c2s v4p0180c2s v4p0252c2s
v4p0292c1s v4p0491c1s v4p0547c1s
v4p0547c2s v6p0016c1s
Kent, W.H. v3p0365c1s
v3p0428c1s v4p0305c1s v4p0354c1s
v4p0424c1s v4p0583c2s v5p0221c1s
v5p0234c2s v5p0289c1s v5p0342c2s
v5p0459c2s v5p0482c1s v5p0485c1s
v5p0493c1s v5p0493c2s v5p0565c1s
v5p0576c2s v6p0030c2s v6p0107c1s
v6p0126c2s v6p0195c2s v6p0286c1s
v6p0310c1s v6p0367c1s v6p0449c1s
v6p0484c1s v6p0549c1s v6p0643c2s
Kent, W.J. v5p0141c2s
Kent, W.P. v6p0655c2s
Kent, W.S. v1p0049c1s
v1p0163c1s v1p0278c2s v1p0327c2s
v1p0366c1s v1p0456c1s v1p0642c1s
v1p0835c2s v1p0891c2s v1p1002c2s
v1p1035c1s v1p1239c1s v2p0205c2s
v3p0016c2s
Kent, W.W. v6p0677c1s
Kentish, I. v1p0602c2s
v1p1158c2s v1p1325c2s
Kenton, E. v6p0178c2s
v6p0434c2s
Kenton, Edna v6p0152c1s
v6p0203c2s v6p0312c1s v6p0388c1s
Kenton, G.E. v5p0474c2s
Kenward, J. v3p0251c1s
v4p0331c2s v5p0338c2s
Kenway, J.L. v4p0469c2s
Kenway, P.N. v4p0252c2s
Kenworthy, J. v5p0069c1s
v5p0404c1s
Kenyon, C.L. v6p0594c1s
Kenyon, E.E. v3p0253c2s
Kenyon, F.C. v4p0041c1s
v4p0209c2s v4p0256c2m v5p0051c2m
v5p0422c2s
Kenyon, F.G. v3p0036c2s
v5p0059c1s v6p0060c2s v6p0130c2s
v6p0274c1s v6p0400c1s
Kenyon, F.G. et al. v3p0195c1s
Kenyon, H. v2p0396c2s
Kenyon, J.B. v4p0309c1s
v4p0492c1m v5p0186c1s v5p0305c1s
v5p0350c1s v5p0553c1s v5p0573c1s
Kenyon, J.G. v4p0353c2s
Kenyon, K. v1p1428c1s
v4p0127c1s
Kenyon, S.B. v4p0249c1s
Kenyon, W.J. v6p0399c2s
v6p0569c2s v6p0574c2s
Keogh, A. v5p0333c2s
v5p0334c2s
Keogh, J.A. v1p0498c1s
v1p0554c1s v1p0994c1s v1p1362c2s
Keogh, J.F. v1p0737c2s
Keogh, J.W. v4p0135c2s
Keon, M.G. v1p0353c1s
Kephart, H. v3p0361c1s
v4p0329c2m v4p0429c2s v5p0070c1s
v5p0089c2s v5p0334c1s v5p0488c2s
v5p0524c2s v5p0599c1s v6p0056c2s
v6p0304c1s
Kephart, Horace v3p0070c1s
Kepley, A.H. v2p0154c1s
Keplinger, L.W. v4p0116c1s
Kepner, W.A. v6p0139c1s
v6p0368c2s
Keppel, D. v6p0484c1s
Keppel, F. v1p0419c2s
v5p0202c2s v5p0376c2s v6p0277c1s
v6p0487c2s
Keppel, Fred v4p0483c1s
Keppel, Susan v4p0523c1s
Kepper, C.A. v4p0129c2s
Ker, D. v1p0138c2s
v1p0139c2s v1p0204c1s v1p0221c2s
v1p0235c1s v1p0268c1s v1p0277c2s
v1p0305c1s v1p0328c2s v1p0454c1s
v1p0517c2s v1p0539c1s v1p0546c1s
v1p0622c2s v1p0691c1s v1p0712c2s
v1p1075c2s v1p1133c2m v1p1135c2m
v1p1136c2s v1p1137c1s v1p1216c1s
v1p1283c2s v1p1292c1s v2p0004c1s
v2p0402c2s v3p0005c2s v3p0029c1s
v3p0069c2s v3p0085c2s v3p0097c2s
v3p0101c2s v3p0179c1s v3p0315c2s
v3p0370c1s v3p0371c2s v3p0391c2s
v3p0409c2s v3p0420c2s v3p0438c1s
v3p0476c2s v4p0005c1s v6p0630c2s
Ker, David v4p0522c2s
Ker, R. v4p0546c2s
Ker, W.P. v4p0609c1s
v5p0280c1s v6p0164c1s v6p0479c1s
Keratry, Count de v1p1332c1s
Keratry, E.de v3p0100c1m
Keravic, Y. v5p0216c2s
v5p0320c2s
Kerby, W.J. v5p0093c2s
v5p0321c2s v5p0536c2s v6p0002c1s
v6p0038c2s v6p0356c1m v6p0357c1m
v6p0425c1s v6p0516c1s v6p0535c1s
v6p0548c1s v6p0600c1m v6p0600c2m
Kercheval, A.W. v1p0038c1s
v1p0216c1s v2p0224c1s
Kercheval, G.T. v3p0265c2s
v3p0312c1m v3p0429c2s v3p0446c1s
v4p0251c2s v4p0282c1s v4p0355c2s
v4p0413c2s v4p0418c1s
Kereven, K.P. v1p0357c1s
v1p0775c1s v1p0942c2s
Kerfoot, F.H. v2p0351c2s
Kerkadec, S.de v1p0334c1s
Kerkadee, Viscountess de . v1p0790c1s
Kerlie, H.M. v3p0468c2s
Kerlin, R.T. v6p0032c1s
v6p0458c1s
Kermode, P.M.C. v2p0072c2s
v4p0362c2s v6p0122c1s v6p0555c1s
Kern, A.A. v6p0020c2s
v6p0595c1s
Kern, H. v2p0059c2s
v4p0467c2s
Kern, O.J. v6p0219c2s
v6p0575c1s
Kern, P.O. v6p0423c2s
Kern, S. v1p0335c1s
Kernahan, C. v2p0140c2s
v2p0200c1s v2p0472c2s v2p0481c1s
v3p0025c1s v3p0362c2s v3p0367c2s
v4p0128c2s v4p0337c1s v4p0358c1s
v4p0385c1s v5p0553c1s
Kernahan, Mary v5p0612c2s
Kernan, F.J. v6p0666c1s
Kernan, M.W. v2p0237c2s
Kernan, T.J. v6p0364c2s
v6p0390c2s
Kernen, C. v1p1117c1s
Kerns, E. v5p0406c1s
Kerr, A. v1p0412c2s
v1p1235c2s v1p1358c2s
Kerr, A.M. v3p0305c2s
v4p0014c1s v5p0342c2s v5p0350c2s
v6p0467c1s
Kerr, C.V. v4p0026c2s
v5p0226c2s
Kerr, D. v6p0267c1s
Kerr, E.E. v6p0364c2s
Kerr, E.T. and Herbertson, A.G.
v6p0516c1s
Kerr, Elizabeth et al. ... v5p0263c1s
Kerr, F. v4p0003c1s
Kerr, F.G. v2p0113c2s
Kerr, J. v1p1191c1s
v3p0378c2s v5p0511c2s v5p0600c2s
Kerr, J.A. v3p0355c2s
Kerr, J.G. v5p0188c1s
Kerr, J.H. v4p0057c1s
v6p0063c1s
Kerr, J.M. v1p0567c1s
v1p0936c2s v2p0239c1s v3p0119c1s
v3p0437c1s
Kerr, J.R. v3p0331c2s
Kerr, M.B. v3p0372c1s
v4p0168c1s
Kerr, M.E.E. v6p0021c2s
Kerr, N. v3p0123c1s
v3p0143c1s
Kerr, Norman v4p0284c1s
Kerr, Prof. v2p0459c1s
Kerr, R. v2p0065c2s
v4p0023c2s v5p0527c2s
Kerr, S.P. v5p0247c2s
v5p0454c2s v6p0327c2s v6p0664c1s
Kerr, W.A.R. v5p0239c1s
v5p0261c2m v5p0379c2s v5p0508c2s
v6p0607c2s
Kerr, W.C. v1p0054c1s
v1p0492c2s v3p0408c2s v4p0551c1s
v5p0482c2s
Kerr, W.J. et al. v6p0309c1s
Kerr, W.R. v5p0208c2s
Kerr, W.S. v5p0396c2s
Kerr, W.W. v6p0244c1s
Kerr-Cross, D., Dr. v4p0409c2s
Kerr-Hillhouse, Florence . v5p0087c2s
v5p0181c1s v5p0505c1s
Kerr-Lawson, J. v6p0637c2s
Kerrich, M. v6p0228c1s
Kerrick, T. v1p1178c1s
v1p1368c2s
Kerrigan, F.H. v4p0324c1s
Kerry, C. v2p0054c1s
v2p0085c2s v2p0111c1s v2p0116c1s
v2p0183c2s v3p0274c2s
Kerschner, J.B. v1p0125c1s
Kerschner, J.E. v1p0123c1s
Kersey, E. v3p0284c1s
v3p0366c1s
Kershaw, F. v2p0157c2s
v2p0364c1s v2p0404c1s v2p0450c1s
Kershaw, J. v2p0131c1s
v2p0309c1s v3p0347c1s
Kershaw, J.B. and Ewell, R.S.
v1p1107c1s
Kershaw, J.B. et al. v1p0518c2s
Kershaw, J.B.C. v5p0042c2s
v5p0138c1s v5p0160c2s v5p0177c2s
v5p0248c1s v5p0435c1s v5p0584c1s
v5p0622c1s v6p0149c1s v6p0199c2s
v6p0203c1s v6p0244c1s v6p0266c2s
v6p0355c2s v6p0514c2s v6p0598c2m
v6p0659c1s
Kershaw, S.W. v2p0443c1s
v4p0066c2s v4p0074c1s v4p0221c2s
v4p0317c2s
Kerslake, T. v2p0014c2m
v2p0289c2s v2p0328c1s v3p0049c2s
v4p0254c1s
Kersley, A.M. v3p0129c2s
v4p0061c2s
Kerswill, W.D. v4p0057c2s
v5p0308c1s
Kespa, H.W. v4p0276c1s
Kessler, D.E. v6p0531c1s
Kessler, J.S. v1p0756c2s
Kester, Paul v5p0598c1s
Kester, V. v5p0464c2s
Kester, Vaughan v5p0089c2s
v5p0375c2s v5p0376c2s
Kesteven, W.H. v2p0119c1s
v2p0442c1s v6p0091c2s
Kestner, F. v6p0322c2s
Kestner, R.F. v6p0708c1s
Ketchum, A. v5p0121c1s
v5p0490c1s v6p0353c1s v6p0580c2s
v6p0603c2s
Ketchum, A.C. v1p0245c1s
v1p0359c2s v1p1177c1s v2p0266c2s
Ketchum, E. v4p0200c2s
Ketchum, R.L. v5p0506c2s
Ketchum, S. v2p0031c2s
v2p0212c2s v2p0311c2s v2p0325c1s
v2p0330c1s v2p0351c1s v2p0385c2m
v2p0400c1s
Ketchum, T.C.L. v4p0086c1s
Ketchum, W.Q. v1p0422c1s
Ketley, J. v1p0512c1s
Kett, C.M. v2p0352c1s
Kettell, T.P. v1p0108c1s
v1p0164c2s v1p0282c2s v1p0284c1s
v1p0284c2s v1p0324c2s v1p0567c2s
v1p0639c1s v1p0835c1s v1p0860c2s
v1p0916c2s v1p0917c2s v1p0938c2s
v1p1221c1s v1p1223c2m v1p1245c1m
Kettle, D.W. v6p0084c2s
Kettle, R. v2p0023c2s
Kettle, R.M. v1p0114c1s
v1p0570c2s v1p0580c2s v1p0737c2s
v2p0064c2s v2p0283c2s v2p0324c2s
v4p0277c1s v4p0543c2s v4p0556c1s
v4p0621c2s
Kettle, T.M. v6p0327c1s
Kettler, J. v3p0467c2s
Kettlewell, S. v2p0241c2s
v3p0235c1s
Key, A. v3p0379c1s
Key, A.C. v5p0308c2s
v6p0006c2s v6p0007c1s v6p0654c2s
Key, A.C., Sir v2p0186c1s
Key, B. v1p0012c2s
Key, B.A. v3p0430c2s
Key, D.M. v6p0466c2s
Key, M. v5p0105c2s
v5p0280c1s v5p0342c1s
Key, Mabel v5p0461c2s
Key, T. v4p0318c2s
Key, W. v4p0009c1s
Key, W.S. v6p0072c1s

Keyes, C.H. v5p0126c1s
Keyes, C.M. v6p0543c1s
Keyes, C.R. v3p0002c2s v3p0060c2s v3p0068c1s v3p0334c2s v3p0374c2s v3p0400c1s v3p0413c1s v4p0196c1s v4p0308c1s v4p0332c2s v5p0229c1s v5p0344c1s v5p0423c1s v5p0580c1s v6p0072c2s v6p0157c1s v6p0185c2s v6p0251c1s v6p0359c1s v6p0545c1s v6p0546c1s v6p0569c2s v6p0657c1s v6p0664c2s
Keyes, Charles R. v6p0185c2s
Keyes, E.L. v3p0121c1s v3p0157c2s v3p0164c2s v3p0167c2s v3p0411c2s v3p0448c2s v4p0083c2s v4p0619c2s
Keyes, E.W. v1p0092c2s
Keyes, H.E. v6p0136c1s v6p0232c1s
Keyes, J.A. v3p0283c1s
Keyes, R.G. v1p0687c2s
Keyes, R.S. v3p0355c1s
Keynes, J.N. v1p0760c2m v5p0528c2s
Keys, C.M. v5p0537c1s v6p0474c1m v6p0528c2s v6p0546c1s v6p0615c1s v6p0696c2s
Keys, D.R. v6p0208c2s v6p0572c2s
Keyser, A. v2p0311c1s v4p0350c2s
Keyser, C.E. v2p0083c1s v2p0450c1s v5p0429c1m
Keyser, C.J. v5p0488c2s v6p0405c2s v6p0462c1s v6p0540c1s v6p0607c1s v6p0670c2s
Keyser, C.J., Prof. v6p0319c1s
Keyser, C.L. v6p0607c1s
Keyser, E.N. v6p0559c1s
Keyser, F. and Holden, E.S. v2p0283c2s
Keyser, F., Mrs. v6p0059c2s
Keyser, Frances v6p0547c1s
Keyser, L.S. v3p0260c1s v4p0060c2s v5p0063c1s v5p0140c2s v5p0351c1s v5p0639c2s v6p0309c2s
Keyser, P.D. v2p0176c1s v2p0338c2s
Keyser, R.S. v3p0062c1s v3p0087c1s v3p0140c1s v3p0184c2s v3p0235c1s v3p0325c1s v4p0144c2s v4p0257c1s
Keyser, S.L. v5p0347c2s
Keyssner, G. v5p0391c1s
Keyworth, T. v3p0150c2s v4p0497c1s
Keyzer, F. v5p0023c1s v5p0095c2s v5p0430c2s
Keyzer, Frances v6p0369c1s
Khan, S.M. v5p0005c1s
Khann, Malcolm v3p0327c2s
Khempke, Dorthea v4p0410c1s
Khnopff, F. v5p0267c2s v5p0337c1s v5p0361c2s v5p0405c2s v6p0103c2s v6p0413c2s
Khnopff, F. et al. v5p0310c1s
Khnopff, Fernand v5p0448c2s
Kiaer, A.T. v5p0340c2s
Kian, Siang v1p1197c2s
Kibbee, W.P. v5p0136c2s v5p0509c2s
Kibler, E. v5p0418c2s
Kiching, E.A. v4p0145c2s
Kidd, A. v5p0139c2s v5p0449c1s v5p0527c1s v6p0183c2s v6p0554c2s
Kidd, B. v2p0038c1s v2p0086c2s v3p0045c2s v3p0130c2s v4p0021c1s v4p0042c1s v4p0204c1s v4p0370c1s v4p0532c1s v5p0591c2s v5p0598c2s v6p0398c1s
Kidd, B. and Galton, F. .. v4p0478c2s
Kidd, B. et al. v6p0310c1s
Kidd, Barrington v6p0257c1s
Kidd, Benj. v6p0657c2s
Kidd, C. v1p0957c2s
Kidd, E.W. v4p0451c2s v6p0688c2s
Kidd, Edwin W. v5p0144c1s
Kidd, G.B. v1p0404c1s v1p0700c1s
Kidd, H.C. v6p0171c1s
Kidd, H.W. v2p0394c2s
Kidd, J. v1p1292c1s v3p0036c2s v3p0137c1s v4p0047c1s v6p0025c1s
Kidd, T.J. v6p0468c1s
Kidd, W. v1p0135c1s v1p0136c1s v2p0066c2s v2p0070c2s v2p0120c2s v5p0610c1s v6p0277c2m
Kidder, B.F. v4p0109c1s v4p0376c1s
Kidder, C.H. v3p0142c2s v4p0403c1s
Kidder, D.P. v1p0233c1s v1p0254c1s v1p0568c2s v1p0831c1s v1p0847c2s v1p1064c1s v1p1435c1s
Kidder, F. v1p0029c2s v1p0067c1s v1p0133c1s v1p0156c1s v1p0637c2s v1p0774c2s v1p0908c2s v1p0926c2s v1p1111c1s v1p1225c1s v1p1274c2s
Kidder, F.A. v5p0431c1s
Kidder, F.A. and Hodge, A.A. v2p0297c2s
Kidder, F.E. v1p0523c1s v1p1427c1s v2p0037c1s v2p0055c2s v2p0153c2s v2p0178c2s v2p0419c1s v4p0023c2s v4p0078c1s v4p0126c1s v4p0577c1s v6p0279c2s
Kidder, J.H. v1p0145c2s v1p0706c1s v1p1188c1s v6p0055c1m v6p0303c2s v6p0544c1s v6p0590c1s
Kidder, W.H. v6p0188c2s
Kiddle, W.W. v1p1192c1s v1p0448c1s
Kidel, B. v6p0240c2s
Kidner, R. v3p0369c2s
Kidney, J.S. v1p0620c1s v1p1098c2s
Kidson, E. v5p0350c2s
Kidwell, E. v4p0180c2s v4p0486c1s v5p0068c2s
Kidwell, E. and Keller, E.R. v3p0167c2s
Kiefer, J.W. v6p0539c2s
Kieffer, F.A. v1p0708c2s
Kieffer, H.M. v2p0310c1s
Kieffer, J.B. v1p0555c1s v2p0179c2s v2p0190c2s v2p0249c1s v4p0013c1s v4p0123c2s
Kieffer, J.B. et al. v6p0376c1s
Kieffer, J.S. v1p0648c2s v1p1270c1s v2p0115c2s v2p0356c1s
Kieffer, M. v1p0003c1s v1p0038c2s v1p0075c1s v1p0081c2s v1p0240c1s v1p0247c2s v1p0487c1s v1p1109c1s v1p1123c2s v1p1141c1s v1p1147c2s v1p1221c2s v1p1302c2s v2p0082c2s v2p0083c1s v3p0244c1s
Kieffer, S. v1p0848c1s
Kieffer, S.B. v1p0440c1s v1p1160c2s
Kiehl, A.H. v1p0680c1s
Kiehle, D.L. v2p0132c1s v4p0171c2s v5p0177c2s v5p0512c2s v6p0447c2s
Kielhorn, F. v3p0075c2s
Kielland, A. v3p0157c2s v4p0308c2s
Kielland, A.L. v5p0425c2s
Kielland, H. v5p0270c1s
Kiely, J.M. v3p0293c1s v4p0046c2s v4p0425c1s
Kiersted, W. v4p0613c2s
Kifton, F.G. v4p0155c1s
Kikkawa, C. v6p0274c2s
Kilbourn, P.K. v1p0666c1s
Kilbourne, F.W. v6p0588c1m v6p0588c2s
Kilbourne, H.S. v5p0375c2s v5p0538c1s
Kilburn, F.D. v6p0658c2s
Kilburn, M.C. v3p0406c1s
Kilby, C.H. v6p0698c1s
Kilby, J.F. v6p0147c2s
Kilby, T.E. v5p0534c2s
Kilby, W.H. v4p0166c2s
Kildare, O. v6p0712c2s
Kildare, Owen v6p0172c2s v6p0339c1s v6p0597c2s
Kilgo, J.C. v6p0193c1s v6p0390c2s v6p0413c1s v6p0605c1s
Kilgo, J.G. v6p0448c1s
Kilgore, Katharine v6p0288c2s
Kilgour, Geo. v4p0310c2s
Kilgour, W.T. v5p0053c1s
Kilham, A.C. v1p1361c2s
Kilham, E. v1p0905c1s v1p0906c1s
Kilham, W.H. v5p0324c2s v6p0076c1s
Kilian, E. v1p0174c2s
Kilian, E.H. v1p0174c2s
Kilian, F. v2p0186c2s v2p0343c1s
Killebrew, J.B. v2p0113c1s v2p0434c2s v6p0276c1s
Killen, Bertha v6p0040c2s
Killen, J.B. v2p0124c2s v2p0170c2s
Killen, W.D. v1p0292c2s v2p0084c2s
Killner, M.L. v3p0375c2s
Killough, F.R. v1p0663c1s
Kilmer, G.L. v3p0103c2s v3p0409c1s v4p0149c2s v4p0633c2s v6p0667c2s
Kilner, W. and Stone, W.H. v2p0138c1s
Kilpatrick, A.R. v1p0772c2s
Kilpatrick, Dr. v1p0154c2s v1p0928c2s
Kilpatrick, T.B. v4p0076c1s v4p0108c2s v5p0306c1s
Kilpatrick, Van Evrie v6p0170c2s
Kilton, F.G. v4p0509c2s v4p0571c1s
Kilvert, B.C. v6p0002c2s
Kim-Hai-Kim, A. v1p0301c2s
Kimball, A.B. v5p0380c2s
Kimball, A.R. v4p0157c2s v4p0431c2s v5p0004c2m v5p0158c1s v5p0253c2s v5p0265c1s v5p0311c1s v5p0409c2s v5p0410c1s v5p0422c2s v5p0469c2s v5p0607c2s v5p0611c1s v5p0643c2m v6p0004c2s v6p0189c1s v6p0346c1s v6p0422c2s v6p0522c2s v6p0670c2s
Kimball, A.S. v1p0491c1m v1p0664c2s v1p1250c2m
Kimball, Alice W. v6p0613c1s
Kimball, B. v4p0440c1s
Kimball, C.C. v2p0291c1s
Kimball, D. v1p0285c1s v1p0448c1s
Kimball, E.A. v3p0191c1s
Kimball, E.F. v4p0078c2s v4p0081c2s
Kimball, F.H. v4p0078c1s v5p0552c1s v6p0197c2s
Kimball, F.M. v6p0197c1s v6p0197c2m
Kimball, G. v3p0231c1s
Kimball, G.A. v5p0072c2s
Kimball, G.M. v6p0434c1s
Kimball, G.S. v4p0117c2s v4p0377c2s
Kimball, G.W. v4p0027c2s
Kimball, H.F. v3p0216c2s v4p0373c2s v6p0326c1s
Kimball, H.I. v5p0547c1s
Kimball, H.McE. v1p0627c1s
Kimball, H.P. v4p0131c1s v5p0316c1s v5p0509c2s
Kimball, H.W. v6p0369c2s
Kimball, J.C. v1p0004c1s v1p0304c1s v1p0685c1s v1p0689c1s v1p0746c1s v1p0783c2s v1p0900c2s v1p1060c1s v1p1066c2s v1p1091c1s v1p1325c2s v1p1389c1s v2p0083c2s v3p0239c2s v3p0454c2s v4p0088c2s v4p0608c1s
Kimball, J.E. v1p1345c2s
Kimball, J.P. v1p0228c2s v1p0509c1s v1p0666c1s v1p0802c1s v1p1199c1s v1p1297c1s v2p0229c2s v2p0386c1s v3p0223c1s v3p0251c2s v3p0392c1s v6p0233c1s
Kimball, J.W. v1p0253c2s
Kimball, K.F. v3p0075c1s v6p0111c1s
Kimball, L.R. v5p0381c1s
Kimball, M.A. v4p0041c2s v5p0294c1s
Kimball, Maris B. v5p0633c1s
Kimball, R.B. v1p0057c1s v1p0093c1s v1p0322c1s v1p0356c2s v1p0406c2s v1p0481c1s v1p0795c1s v1p0800c2s v1p0950c2s v1p0963c2s v1p1102c2s v1p1144c1m v1p1232c2s v1p1314c1s v1p1344c2s v1p1382c1s v1p1387c1s
Kimball, T.R. v5p0200c1s
Kimball, W.H. v1p0686c2s v1p1345c2s v1p1354c1s v2p0037c2s v2p0151c1s v2p0211c1s v2p0428c1s
Kimball, W.P. v6p0092c2s v6p0372c1s
Kimball, W.W. v2p0454c1s v3p0020c1s v3p0396c1s v5p0124c2s v5p0558c2s
Kimber, H. v6p0269c1s
Kimber, H., Sir v6p0481c1s
Kimber, T. v2p0014c1s v2p0393c1s
Kimberly, R.L. v1p0222c2s v1p0228c1s
Kimble, R.G. v5p0034c2s
Kimbrough, G.B. v4p0024c2s v4p0180c2s
Kimm, E.H. v2p0416c1s
Kinahan, G.A. v2p0316c2s v2p0395c1s
Kinahan, G.H. v1p1172c2s v2p0334c1s v2p0394c1s v2p0409c1s v2p0421c1s v2p0473c2s v3p0222c2s v4p0205c1s v4p0289c1s
Kinahan, J.H. et al. v2p0127c2s
Kincaid, J. v3p0459c2s
Kincaid, W. v3p0052c1s v3p0211c1s
Kincaid, W.H. v1p0830c2s
Kinder, F.S. v6p0146c2s
Kinder, P. v2p0116c1s
Kindl, F.H. v5p0551c2s
Kindle, E.M. v6p0456c2m
Kindleberger, C.P. et al.. v5p0360c1s
Kindon, J. v6p0090c2s v6p0592c1s v6p0598c1s v6p0631c2s
Kindrick, A.C. v3p0279c1s
Kindrick, C.W. v5p0387c1s
Kinealy, J.H. v5p0455c1s
King, A. v1p0497c2s v1p0584c2s v1p0782c1s v1p0915c2s v1p0932c2s v1p1086c2s v1p1180c2s v2p0028c2s v2p0201c1s v2p0293c1s v3p0103c1s v3p0188c1s v3p0362c1s v3p0406c2s v4p0133c2s v4p0221c2s v4p0437c2s v6p0586c2m v6p0587c1s v6p0587c2s

King, A.E. v3p0233c1s
v3p0246c1s v4p0063c2s v4p0137c1s
v4p0193c1s v4p0305c1s v4p0527c2s
v4p0605c2s v6p0047c2s
King, A.F. v2p0373c2s
v4p0258c2s v4p0293c2s
King, A.F.A. v1p0354c1s
v2p0119c1s v2p0299c2s
King, A.H. v6p0389c2s
King, A.J. and Watts, B.H.
v0p2236c1s
King, A.J. et al. v2p0036c1s
King, A.M. v1p0588c1s
King, A.T. v1p0466c1s
King, Alice v1p0057c1s
v1p0060c2s v1p0150c1s v1p0213c2s
v1p0223c1s v1p0305c2s v1p0331c1s
v1p0707c2s v1p0863c1s v1p0995c1s
v1p1106c1s v1p1156c1s v1p1183c1s
v1p1195c2m v1p1235c2s v1p1271c2s
v1p1284c1s v1p1423c1s v1p1426c1s
v1p1426c2s v3p0389c2s
King, B. v4p0426c2s
v5p0186c1s v5p0189c1s v5p0281c2s
v5p0300c1s v5p0300c2s v6p0331c2m
v6p0367c1s v6p0553c1s
King, B. and Ashby, J. ... v4p0604c2s
King, Basil v5p0266c1s
v6p0279c2s v6p0362c1s
King, Bolton v6p0331c2s
King, C. v1p0206c1s
v1p0263c1s v1p0282c2s v1p0291c2s
v1p0434c1s v1p0509c1s v1p0524c1s
v1p0524c2s v1p0703c2s v1p0832c1m
v1p0956c2s v1p0987c2s v1p1188c1s
v1p1193c1s v1p1196c1s v1p1351c2s
v1p1385c2s v1p1387c1s v1p1394c1s
v1p1419c1s v2p0198c1s v2p0259c1s
v2p0314c2s v2p0457c2s v2p0480c2s
v3p0020c2s v3p0046c1s v3p0068c1s
v3p0071c1s v3p0076c2s v3p0091c2s
v3p0108c1s v3p0115c2s v3p0124c2s
v3p0165c1s v3p0203c1s v3p0245c2s
v3p0279c1s v3p0279c2s v3p0281c1s
v3p0315c2s v3p0354c1s v3p0372c2s
v3p0406c1s v3p0439c2s v3p0455c1s
v3p0460c2s v3p0466c1s v3p0467c1s
v4p0027c2s v4p0088c2s v4p0093c1s
v4p0102c1s v4p0141c2s v4p0142c2m
v4p0150c1s v4p0165c2s v4p0170c2s
v4p0371c2s v4p0484c1s v4p0498c1s
v4p0515c2s v4p0535c2s v4p0562c2s
v4p0592c1s v4p0611c1s v5p0100c1s
v5p0125c1s v5p0195c1s v5p0479c2s
v5p0591c1s v6p0078c1s v6p0166c2s
v6p0362c1s v6p0377c1s v6p0488c2s
v6p0693c1s
King, C., Capt. v3p0165c1s
King, C.A. v6p0060c1s
King, C.B. v3p0153c1s
King, C.C. v1p0460c2m
v3p0374c2s v4p0502c2s
King, C.H. v6p0351c2s
King, C.J. v3p0374c2s
King, C.R. v2p0195c1s
v2p0243c1s v6p0209c2s v6p0382c1s
v6p0382c2m
King, Carroll v3p0354c1s
King, Charles v5p0093c2s
v5p0150c1s
King, D. v2p0075c1s
v2p0091c1s v3p0367c2s
King, D.B. v2p0108c1s
v2p0142c2s v2p0209c1s v2p0227c1s
v2p0248c2s v2p0330c2s v2p0350c2s
v2p0387c1s
King, D.B. and Strong, H.. v2p0248c1s
King, E. v1p0011c1s
v1p0017c2s v1p0058c1s v1p0080c1s
v1p0089c2s v1p0114c2s v1p0179c2s
v1p0205c1s v1p0226c2s v1p0329c2s
v1p0332c1m v1p0461c2s v1p0512c2s
v1p0615c1s v1p0706c1s v1p0757c2s
v1p0772c2s v1p0854c1m v1p0855c1s
v1p0863c2s v1p0877c1s v1p0927c2s
v1p0943c1s v1p0946c2s v1p0967c2s
v1p0969c2s v1p1115c1s v1p1129c1m
v1p1144c1s v1p1173c2s v1p1223c2m
v1p1225c2s v1p1227c2s v1p1229c2s
v1p1297c1s v1p1330c1s v1p1370c2s
v1p1373c2s v2p0335c2s v3p0089c1s
v3p0163c2s v3p0201c1s v3p0320c1s
v3p0448c2m v4p0029c1s v4p0030c2s
v4p0206c1s v4p0244c1s v4p0304c1s
v4p0524c2s v4p0574c2s v4p0616c1s
v5p0191c2s v6p0386c2s
King, E.A. v4p0363c2s
v4p0428c2s
King, E.A. and Buxton, D.W.
v5p0113c2s
King, E.J. v6p0225c2s
v6p0681c2s
King, E.L. v6p0039c1s
King, E.M. v1p0359c2m
v1p0608c1s v1p0983c1s v2p0124c1s
King, E.M. et al. v2p0477c2s
King, E.M., Mrs. v1p1426c1s
v2p0124c1s v2p0446c2s
King, E.P. v3p0378c1s
v3p0411c1s
King, E.S. v6p0496c2s
King, Eliz.H. v6p0358c2s
King, F. v1p0707c2s
v5p0640c1s
King, F.A. v5p0006c1s
v5p0325c1s v6p0474c2s v6p0582c2s
King, F.B. v5p0644c1s
King, F.G. v2p0160c1s
King, F.H. v2p0344c1s
v6p0602c2s
King, F.L. v3p0125c1s
King, G. v2p0051c1s
v2p0249c2s v3p0036c2s v3p0076c2s
v3p0082c1s v3p0122c1s v3p0126c1s
v3p0217c2s v3p0263c2s v3p0269c1s
v4p0004c2s v4p0019c1s v4p0042c1s
v4p0140c2s v4p0151c2s v4p0158c2s
v4p0190c1s v4p0234c1m v4p0272c1s
v4p0287c2s v4p0335c2s v4p0371c2s
v4p0373c1s v4p0412c2s v4p0467c2s
v4p0551c1s v5p0159c2s v5p0357c1s
v5p0406c1s v6p0234c1s v6p0423c1s
King, G.A. v6p0041c2s
v6p0142c2s v6p0455c1s v6p0630c1s
King, G.S. v2p0419c1s
v2p0447c1s
King, G.W. v3p0192c2s
King, Geo., Sir v5p0073c1s
King, Grace v4p0399c2s
v4p0555c2s v6p0264c1s v6p0467c1s
King, H. v1p0155c2s
v1p0169c2s v1p0172c2s v1p0183c2m
v1p0187c2s v1p0198c2s v1p0285c2s
v1p0286c2s v1p0287c2s v1p0335c1s
v1p0372c2s v1p0436c2s v1p0444c2s
v1p0509c1s v1p0569c1s v1p0622c1s
v1p0638c1s v1p0702c1s v1p0750c2s
v1p0765c1s v1p0795c1s v1p0913c2s
v1p0915c1s v1p0983c2s v1p0990c1s
v1p0991c1s v1p1001c1s v1p1012c1s
v1p1075c1s v1p1344c1s v1p1351c1s
v1p1431c2s v2p0049c1s v2p0059c1m
v2p0220c1s v2p0259c1s v2p0356c1s
v2p0446c1s v2p0481c2s v3p0026c1s
v3p0122c2s v3p0354c1s v3p0460c2s
v4p0255c2s v4p0295c2s v4p0305c2s
v4p0332c2s v4p0399c2s v4p0402c2s
v4p0584c1s v4p0616c1s v5p0236c2s
v5p0253c2s v5p0414c1s v5p0486c2s
v5p0535c2s v6p0113c2s v6p0348c2s
v6p0436c1s v6p0569c1s v6p0592c2s
King, H.B. v1p0193c2s
King, H.C. v4p0049c1s
v4p0520c2s v5p0440c1s v5p0483c1s
v5p0577c1m v6p0055c1s v6p0136c2s
v6p0193c1s v6p0195c1s
King, H.D. v6p0195c1s
King, H.E.H. v2p0032c1s
King, H.F. v3p0112c1s
King, H.M. v1p0097c2s
v1p0130c2s v1p0385c1s v1p1091c2s
v1p1285c2s v2p0297c1s v2p0324c1s
v2p0345c2s v2p0357c2s v2p0428c1s
v4p0078c1s v4p0446c2s v6p0365c2s
King, Hiram v6p0040c2s
v6p0123c1s v6p0214c2s v6p0259c1s
v6p0277c1s
King, Horatio v2p0312c2s
v2p0466c2s
King, I. v6p0512c2s
v6p0513c1s v6p0599c2s v6p0607c1s
King, Irving v6p0623c1s
King, J. v1p0740c2s
v1p0852c1s v1p0915c1m v1p0996c2s
v1p1184c2s v2p0353c2s v3p0057c2s
v4p0152c1s v4p0167c1m v4p0398c2s
v4p0560c1m v4p0610c1s v5p0568c1s
King, J., jr. v3p0138c2s
King, J.A. v5p0266c2s
King, J.B. v4p0446c1s
King, J.G. and Marsh, C. . v1p0098c2s
King, J.H. v6p0213c2s
King, J.L. v5p0339c2s
King, J.M. v3p0083c1s
v4p0143c1s v5p0195c2s v5p0236c2s
King, J.S. v4p0223c1s
King, J.T. v2p0435c2s
v3p0013c1s
King, Jessie M. v5p0637c2s
King, K. v1p0611c1s
King, L.W. v4p0032c2s
v4p0405c1s
King, M. v1p0941c2s
King, M.A. v1p1403c2s
King, M.F. v4p0519c2s
v6p0182c2s
King, P. v2p0140c1s
v4p0138c1s v4p0530c2s v5p0377c2s
v5p0548c1s v6p0163c1s
King, R. v1p0424c2s
v1p0425c1m v1p0725c2s v3p0236c2s
v3p0271c2s v3p0310c2s v4p0411c1s
King, R. and Benson, E. .. v1p0917c2s
King, R.A. v3p0222c2s
v3p0245c2s v3p0322c2s v4p0120c2s
v4p0624c2s
King, R.J. v1p0100c1s
v1p0144c2s v1p0265c1s v1p0333c1s
v1p0348c1s v1p0464c1s v1p0471c1s
v1p0591c1s v1p0708c2s v1p1018c2s
v1p1132c1s
King, R.M., Mrs. v5p0595c1s
King, S. v4p0307c2s
King, S.A. v3p0031c1s
v5p0044c1s
King, S.P. v1p0579c1s
v1p0886c2s
King, S.P., Mrs. v1p0795c1s
King, T. v2p0014c2s
v2p0226c1s
King, T.A. v4p0559c2m
v5p0463c2s
King, T.B. v1p0187c1s
King, T.S. v1p0086c2s
v1p0180c1s v1p0217c2s v1p0244c2s
v1p0289c1s v1p0528c1m v1p0557c2s
v1p0626c1s v1p0686c1s v1p0686c2s
v1p0768c1m v1p0805c2s v1p0877c1s
v1p0923c1s v1p0979c2s v1p1017c1s
v1p1022c2s v1p1042c1s v1p1093c1s
v1p1094c1s v1p1097c1s v1p1147c2m
v1p1387c1s v1p1405c2s v2p0394c1s
v3p0074c1s v3p0233c2s
King, T.W. v1p0501c1s
v1p0813c2s v6p0307c1s v6p0700c2s
King, V.O. v2p0457c2s
v6p0112c1s
King, V.O., Mrs. v1p0455c1s
v1p0645c2s
King, W. v1p0073c1s
v1p1289c2s v2p0274c1s v6p0696c2s
King, W. and Hughes, T.W.H.
v5p0238c2s v5p0285c2s
King, W.A. v5p0099c2s
v5p0107c2s v5p0417c1s
King, W.F. v5p0622c1s
King, W.G. v1p0190c2s
King, W.J.H. v6p0294c1s
v6p0562c2m
King, W.L.M. v4p0469c1s
v5p0584c2s v5p0597c1s v6p0098c1s
King, W.N. v4p0050c2s
v4p0244c1s v4p0601c2m
King, W.N., jr. v3p0101c1s
King, W.R. v4p0180c2s
v4p0349c2s v4p0592c1s v5p0029c2s
v5p0252c2s v5p0602c2s
King, W.S. v5p0305c1s
King, W.Scott v5p0466c1s
v5p0494c2s v6p0205c2s
King, Y. v4p0074c1s
King-Harman, M.J. v3p0180c1s
v3p0211c1s v4p0281c2s v6p0031c2m
v6p0035c1s v6p0534c1s
Kingdon, L.M. v3p0122c1s
Kingdon, S.S. v3p0106c1s
v3p0359c1s
Kingerly, H. v4p0213c2s
v4p0460c2s v4p0563c2s v4p0608c1s
Kingery, H.M. v6p0422c1s
Kinglake, A. v2p0062c1s
Kinglake, A.W. v1p0316c1s
v1p0895c2s
Kinglake, J.A. v1p1425c2s
Kinglake, R.A. v2p0409c2m
Kinglake, W.C. v1p0183c2s
Kingley, B. v3p0259c2s
Kinglsey, C. v1p0014c2s
Kinglsey, F.M. v6p0323c1s
Kinglsey, Mary H. v4p0085c1s
Kingman, B. v1p0927c1s
Kingman, Bradford v4p0621c2s
Kingman, D.C. v5p0290c1s
v5p0622c2s
Kingman, H. v5p0023c2s
Kingman, Henry v6p0093c2s
Kingman, J.A. v5p0041c1m
v6p0044c1s v6p0044c2m
Kingsbury, A.B. v4p0183c2s
Kingsbury, A.G. v5p0010c2s
v5p0011c1s v5p0413c1s v5p0517c2s
v6p0010c2m v6p0476c1s
Kingsbury, C.P. v1p0173c2s
v1p0540c2s v1p0930c2s
Kingsbury, E.M. v6p0249c1s
v6p0262c1s v6p0480c2s v6p0699c2s
Kingsbury, Eliz. v6p0572c1s
Kingsbury, F.J. v1p0092c2s
v1p0397c1s v2p0060c1s v2p0151c1s
v2p0268c1s v2p0335c2s v3p0345c2s
v4p0097c1s v4p0323c1s v4p0434c2s
v4p0534c2s v4p0615c1s v5p0152c1s
v5p0529c2s v5p0623c2s v6p0689c2s
Kingsbury, F.J. et al. ... v3p0345c2s
Kingsbury, F.L. v3p0391c1s
Kingsbury, G.C. v3p0206c1s
Kingsbury, G.E. v6p0498c1s
Kingsbury, J. v1p1288c2s
Kingsbury, J.D. v1p0016c2s
Kingsbury, J.E. v6p0637c1s
Kingsbury, M.H. v6p0020c1s
Kingsbury, M.M. v5p0520c2s
Kingsbury, O.A. v1p0229c1s
v1p0754c1s v1p1270c2s v2p0044c1s
v2p0084c2s v2p0170c1s v2p0375c1s
v2p0463c2s v3p0302c2s
Kingsbury, S.M. v6p0388c2s
Kingsbury-Cooley, Alice .. v5p0214c2s
Kingscote, E. v3p0439c2s
Kingscote, G., Mrs. v3p0053c1s

v3p0211c1s
Kingsford, A. v2p0361c2s
v2p0461c1s
Kingsford, A., Mrs. v1p0817c2s
v1p1123c1s v1p1334c1s v2p0462c2s
Kingsford, C. v1p0161c1s
Kingsford, C.L. v3p0243c2s
v4p0182c2s v4p0361c2s
Kingsford, N. v1p0465c2s
Kingsford, R.E. v5p0019c2s
Kingsford, W. v1p0694c2s
v1p1141c2s v1p1308c2s
Kingsland, Burton, Mrs. .. v6p0124c1s
Kingsland, L.D. v6p0372c1s
Kingsland, W.C. v4p0118c2s
Kingsland, W.G. v3p0056c2s
v3p0057c2s v4p0067c2s v4p0075c2m
v4p0076c1m v4p0076c2m v4p0177c2s
v4p0246c1s v4p0334c2s v4p0383c2s
v4p0492c1s v4p0495c1m v4p0520c1s
v4p0551c2s v5p0078c1s v5p0079c2s
v5p0250c1s v5p0328c2s v5p0525c1s
Kingsley, C. v1p0017c1s
v1p0023c1s v1p0049c1s v1p0135c2s
v1p0159c1s v1p0172c1s v1p0178c2s
v1p0182c1s v1p0214c2s v1p0244c2s
v1p0248c2s v1p0268c1s v1p0348c1s
v1p0368c1s v1p0392c1s v1p0411c1s
v1p0448c1s v1p0458c1s v1p0509c2m
v1p0559c2s v1p0578c2s v1p0584c1s
v1p0588c1s v1p0620c2s v1p0677c1s
v1p0710c2s v1p0715c1s v1p0715c2s
v1p0735c2s v1p0749c2s v1p0766c2s
v1p0785c1s v1p0813c1s v1p0833c2s
v1p0861c2s v1p0889c1s v1p0890c1s
v1p0899c2s v1p0901c2s v1p0926c2s
v1p0966c2s v1p0984c1s v1p1006c1s
v1p1017c1s v1p1032c1s v1p1066c2s
v1p1081c2s v1p1113c2s v1p1119c1s
v1p1127c1s v1p1150c2s v1p1160c2s
v1p1172c1s v1p1189c1s v1p1204c2s
v1p1210c2s v1p1211c2s v1p1234c2s
v1p1271c2s v1p1294c2s v1p1303c2s
v1p1309c1m v1p1323c2s v1p1327c1s
v1p1361c1s v1p1368c2s v1p1390c2s
v1p1391c1s v1p1391c2s v1p1416c1s
v1p1420c2s v1p1421c1s v1p1422c2s
v1p1436c2s v1p1438c2s v2p0038c2s
v2p0119c2s v2p0157c1s v2p0167c1s
v2p0207c1s v2p0235c1s v2p0240c1s
v2p0278c2s v2p0340c2s v2p0371c1s
v2p0389c2s v3p0019c2s v4p0324c1s
Kingsley, D.P. v6p0321c2s
Kingsley, D.P. and Morton, P.
v6p0322c1s
Kingsley, E. v2p0479c1s
v3p0471c1s
Kingsley, F.M. v5p0208c1s
Kingsley, H. v1p0003c1s
v1p0019c1s v1p0079c1s v1p0137c2s
v1p0422c2s v1p0438c2s v1p0499c2s
v1p0540c1s v1p0547c1s v1p0589c1s
v1p0591c1s v1p0675c1s v1p0791c1s
v1p0855c2s v1p0887c2s v1p0890c1s
v1p0952c1s v1p1084c1s v1p1146c2s
v1p1195c2s v1p1197c1s v1p1201c2s
v1p1261c1s v1p1322c1s v1p1335c1s
v1p1370c1s v1p1409c2s
Kingsley, H.C. v1p0034c2s
v1p0627c2s v1p0745c2s v1p1119c1s
v1p1206c2s v1p1230c1s v1p1351c2s
v2p0481c2s
Kingsley, H.C. and Young, M.
v2p0481c2s
Kingsley, H.C. et al. v2p0481c2s
Kingsley, J.L. v1p0143c2m
v1p0222c1s v1p0260c2s v1p0292c1s
v1p0373c2s v1p0404c1s v1p0457c1s
v1p0507c1s v1p0518c1s v1p0525c2s
v1p0554c2s v1p0572c2s v1p0573c1s
v1p0679c2s v1p0727c2m v1p0911c2s
v1p1072c1s v1p1114c2s v1p1254c1s
v1p1262c1s v1p1280c1s v1p1396c1s
v1p1436c1m
Kingsley, J.L. and Everett, E.
v1p0292c1s
Kingsley, J.L. and Silliman, B., Sen.
v1p0827c1s
Kingsley, J.S.
v1p0099c1s v1p0758c1s v1p0858c1s
v1p1188c2m v2p0024c1s v2p0150c2s
v2p0338c1s v2p0483c2s v3p0012c1s
v3p0103c2s v3p0126c2s v3p0191c1s
v3p0213c1s v3p0297c1s v3p0317c1s
v3p0475c2s v4p0016c2s v4p0355c2s
v4p0536c1s v4p0603c1s v5p0136c2s
v5p0204c1s v5p0254c1s v6p0073c1s
v6p0243c1s v6p0281c1s v6p0339c1s
Kingsley, J.S. and Barus, C.
v6p0474c1s
Kingsley, M. v2p0139c2s
v4p0218c2s v4p0225c2s v4p0577c2s
v5p0390c2s
Kingsley, M., Miss v5p0008c1s
Kingsley, M.E. v5p0377c1s
v6p0639c1s v6p0679c2s
Kingsley, M.H. v4p0397c1s
v5p0008c1s v5p0209c1s v5p0340c2s
v5p0433c2s
Kingsley, Mary H. v4p0374c2s
v4p0387c1s v5p0205c2s
Kingsley, Maud E. v5p0159c1s
v5p0491c1s v5p0515c2s v5p0523c1s
v6p0200c2s
Kingsley, P. v1p0484c1s
v1p0846c1s
Kingsley, Prof. v1p0411c2s
Kingsley, R. v2p0148c2s
v2p0397c1s
Kingsley, R.G. v2p0017c1m
v2p0020c2s v2p0059c1s v2p0109c2s
v2p0174c2s v2p0466c1s v3p0053c2s
v3p0135c2s v3p0196c1s v3p0223c2s
v3p0241c1s v3p0242c1s v3p0292c1s
v3p0455c1s v4p0141c2s v4p0244c2s
v4p0247c1s v4p0325c2s v4p0618c1s
v5p0327c1s v5p0496c1s
Kingsley, Rose G. v3p0239c2s
v5p0253c2s
Kingsley, S.C. v6p0116c1s
Kingsley, V.W. v1p0177c2s
v1p0179c2s v1p0186c2s v1p0237c2s
v1p0263c1s v1p0567c2s v1p0585c2s
v1p0680c2s v1p1011c1s v1p1388c1s
v1p1395c2s
Kingsley, W.L. v1p0143c2m
v1p0292c1s v1p0312c1s v1p0417c2s
v1p0779c1s v1p0863c1s v1p0922c1s
v1p0994c2s v1p1129c2s v1p1317c2s
v1p1330c1s v1p1369c2s v1p1378c1s
v3p0235c2s v3p0301c1m v3p0335c2s
v3p0337c2s v3p0349c2m v3p0370c2s
v3p0437c1s v3p0474c1m
Kingsley, W.T. v1p0835c2s
Kingsley, W.W. v1p1189c2s
Kingsmill, E.T. v4p0513c1s
v5p0108c1s v5p0260c1s
Kingsmill, T.W. v2p0079c1s
v3p0126c1s v6p0489c2s v6p0626c1s
Kingstead, J. v6p0162c1s
v6p0362c1s v6p0458c2s v6p0495c2s
Kingston, C.C. v4p0314c2s
Kingston, G. v6p0641c2s
Kingston, G.T. v1p0077c1s
v1p0566c2s v1p0787c2m v1p0829c1s
v1p1256c2s v1p1293c1s v1p1316c2s
Kingston, Gertrude v6p0181c1s
Kingston, W.B. v2p0002c1s
v2p0176c1s v2p0178c1m v2p0303c1s
v2p0378c2s v2p0397c2s v2p0398c2s
Kingston, W.H.G. v1p0304c2s
v1p0321c1s v1p0544c1s v1p0570c1s
v1p1036c2s v1p1037c1m v1p1139c1s
v2p0056c2s v2p0350c1s
Kingstone, A.C. and Boddy, C.A.S.
v4p0206c2s
Kington, J.B. v1p0309c1s
Kingzett, C.T. v3p0170c2s
Kingzett, C.T. and Hake, H.W.
v2p0341c1s
Kinkaid, T.W. v5p0010c1s
Kinkead, A.L. v3p0087c2s
v3p0450c1s
Kinkead, E.B. v4p0411c2s
Kinkead, R.J. v2p0153c1s
Kinkead, T.L. v6p0116c2s
Kinkel, G. v1p0442c2s
v1p0596c2s
Kinley, D. v3p0345c2s
v4p0111c2s v4p0138c2s v4p0144c1s
v4p0582c2s v5p0142c1m v5p0600c2s
Kinley, D. and Andrew, A.P.
v6p0156c2s
Kinley, J. v3p0240c1s
Kinloch, A. v1p0482c2s
v5p0528c1s v6p0076c1s v6p0556c2s
v6p0558c1s v6p0558c2m v6p0559c1s
Kinloch, Alexander v6p0343c2s
Kinloch, F. v6p0261c1s
Kinloch, M.G.J. v4p0168c1s
v6p0104c2s v6p0150c2s v6p0578c2s
Kinlock, M. v2p0078c1s
Kinnaird, Lord v4p0622c2s
Kinnaman, A.J. v6p0425c2s
v6p0486c1s
Kinnaman, N.J. v5p0338c1s
Kinnear, A. v1p0458c1s
v5p0005c2s v5p0422c2s v5p0517c2s
v6p0132c1s v6p0150c2s v6p0481c2s
Kinnear, B.G. v3p0387c2s
Kinnear, B.O. v4p0177c1s
Kinnear, J.B. v1p0398c2s
v1p0696c2s v1p0721c1s v1p0802c2s
v1p0848c2s v1p0850c2s v1p1042c1s
v2p0118c2s v4p0195c1s
Kinnear, W. v4p0094c2s
v4p0331c1m
Kinneir, J.M. v1p1012c1s
Kinnen, E.A. v1p0936c2s
v1p1299c2s v1p1372c2s
Kinney, A. v2p0079c2s
v2p0162c1s v3p0346c2s v4p0423c1s
v6p0092c1m v6p0233c1s v6p0233c2s
v6p0435c2s
Kinney, C. v1p0416c2s
Kinney, E.C. v1p0006c2s
v1p0170c1s
Kinney, H.W. v6p0592c2s
Kinney, J.C. v1p0445c1s
Kinney, M.B. v1p0879c1s
v1p1258c2s
Kinney, R.S. v6p0621c2s
Kinney, T.W. v2p0273c2m
Kinnicutt, F. v4p0202c1s
v4p0307c2s v4p0625c2s
Kinnicutt, L.P. v2p0371c2s
v6p0585c2m v6p0687c2s
Kinnosuke, A. v5p0086c2s
v5p0240c2s v5p0317c1s v5p0370c1s
v5p0479c1s v6p0335c1m v6p0336c1s
v6p0337c1s v6p0337c2s v6p0338c2m
v6p0339c1s v6p0474c2s v6p0561c1m
v6p0565c1m v6p0629c2s v6p0648c2m
Kinnosuke, Adachi v5p0104c2s
v5p0260c1s v6p0119c1s v6p0334c2s
Kinross, A. v5p0521c2s
v6p0014c2s v6p0124c2s v6p0251c2s
v6p0369c2s v6p0581c1s v6p0619c2s
Kinsell, M. v6p0427c2s
v6p0569c1s
Kinsley, C.J. v4p0530c1s
v5p0067c1s
Kinsley, W.W. v1p0167c1m
v1p0312c2s v1p0313c1s v1p0466c2s
v1p0560c1s v1p0613c1m v1p0792c2s
v1p0820c2s v1p0898c2s v1p0964c1s
v1p1152c1s v1p1263c2s v1p1271c1s
v2p0112c2s v3p0341c2m v4p0300c1s
v4p0456c1s
Kinsman, D.O. v6p0312c1s
Kintner, C.J. v2p0137c1s
Kinyoun, J.J. v5p0023c1s
Kioki, Eki v6p0336c2s
Kip, A.L. v5p0057c1s
Kip, L. v1p0076c2s
v1p0198c1s v1p0245c1s v1p0258c1s
v1p0492c1s v1p0608c1s v1p0889c2s
v1p0908c2s v1p0943c1s v1p0952c2s
v1p1030c1s v1p1039c2s v1p1281c1s
v1p1308c2s v1p1323c1s v1p1358c2s
v2p0182c1s v2p0261c1s v2p0436c1s
v3p0069c2s v3p0209c2s v3p0210c1s
v3p0349c2s v3p0419c1s v3p0429c2s
v4p0110c2s v4p0349c2s v4p0426c2s
v4p0551c1s
Kip, Leonard v6p0038c1s
v6p0641c1s
Kip, W.I. v1p0080c1s
v1p0143c1s v1p0187c1s v1p0198c1s
v1p0205c2s v1p0232c1s v1p0599c1s
v1p0917c1s v1p1008c1s v1p1053c1s
v1p1240c2s v1p1362c2s v2p0210c1s
v2p0235c1s
Kipling, J.L. v2p0023c1s
v2p0217c1s v3p0211c1s v4p0158c2s
v4p0279c1s v5p0286c1s
Kipling, R. v3p0025c1s
v3p0095c2s v3p0103c1s v3p0118c2s
v3p0141c1s v3p0153c1s v3p0157c2s
v3p0192c1s v3p0196c2s v3p0210c2s
v3p0211c2s v3p0240c2s v3p0251c1s
v3p0265c2s v3p0312c1s v3p0466c2s
v4p0072c1s v4p0077c1s v4p0089c1s
v4p0108c1s v4p0186c2s v4p0232c1s
v4p0277c1s v4p0307c2s v4p0311c2s
v4p0325c2s v4p0327c2s v4p0365c2s
v4p0390c2s v4p0391c1s v4p0458c2s
v4p0469c2s v4p0536c2m v4p0551c2s
v4p0609c1s v4p0620c1s v5p0001c2s
v5p0052c2s v5p0067c2s v5p0093c2s
v5p0159c2s v5p0204c2s v5p0282c1s
v5p0282c2s v5p0316c1m v5p0373c2s
v5p0425c2s v5p0442c2s v5p0476c2s
v5p0480c1m v5p0521c1s v5p0532c2s
v5p0548c1s v5p0582c1s v5p0629c1s
v5p0633c1s v6p0057c2s v6p0142c2s
v6p0277c1s v6p0314c2s v6p0476c1s
v6p0542c1s v6p0545c2s v6p0643c1s
v6p0701c1s v6p0701c2s
Kipling, R. and Balestier, W.
v3p0297c2s
v4p0395c1s
Kipling, Rudyard v4p0351c1s
v4p0385c2s v4p0521c1s
v5p0523c2s
Kirby, C.V. v6p0074c2s
v6p0130c2s v6p0156c1s
Kirby, G.B. v1p0167c2s
v1p1280c2s
Kirby, M.A. v5p0417c2s
Kirby, T.F. v5p0048c2s
v5p0103c1s v5p0370c1s v5p0632c2s
v6p0110c2s v6p0184c2s v6p0551c2s
Kirby, V.T. v4p0006c1s
Kirby, W. v1p0195c1s
Kirby, W.F. v1p0042c1s
v4p0049c1s v4p0081c1s v4p0384c2s
v4p0573c2s v4p0610c2s v5p0167c1s
v5p0253c2s v5p0331c1s v5p0428c1s
v6p0086c1s
Kirby, W.G. v4p0286c2s
Kirchhammer, A. v1p0543c1s
Kirchhoff, A. v4p0133c2s
Kirchhoff, C. v4p0133c1s
v5p0371c2s v5p0378c1s v6p0248c2s
v6p0616c1s v6p0668c2s
Kirchhoff, C., jr. v2p0102c1s
Kirchner, F. v3p0129c1s
Kirchner, H.W. v4p0499c1s
Kirchwey, G.W. v3p0199c1s

Kirk, A. v1p0141c2m v1p0273c1s v6p0155c2s
Kirk, E.N. v1p1318c2s
Kirk, E.O. v3p0264c1s v4p0029c1s v4p0202c2s v4p0343c1s v4p0409c1s v4p0515c2s v4p0552c1s v4p0602c1s v4p0615c2s v5p0023c1s v5p0262c2s v5p0421c1s v5p0635c2s v6p0069c1s
Kirk, H.C. v3p0134c1s v4p0014c2s v4p0024c1s v4p0180c2s v4p0202c1s v4p0259c1s v4p0286c2s v4p0400c1s
Kirk, H.O. v4p0554c1s
Kirk, H.S. v6p0167c2s v6p0414c1s v6p0711c2s
Kirk, J.F. v1p0201c2s v1p0220c1s v1p0806c2s v1p1142c2s v1p1143c1s v1p1241c1s v1p1298c1s v4p0039c1s v4p0518c1s v4p0603c1s v5p0445c1s v6p0707c2s
Kirk, J.K. v2p0002c2s
Kirk, J.W. v4p0567c1s
Kirk, S. v3p0035c1s v3p0193c1s v3p0323c1s v3p0344c2s v3p0409c2s v3p0418c1s v5p0126c2s
Kirk, Sophia v6p0544c2s
Kirk, T.H. v3p0327c1s v3p0435c2s
Kirk, T.J. v5p0569c2s
Kirk, W. v6p0356c1s
Kirk, W.H. v5p0196c2s v5p0475c1s v6p0679c2s
Kirkaldy, D. v1p0663c2s
Kirkbride, C.N. v3p0019c2s
Kirkbride, F.B. v5p0046c1s v5p0049c2s v6p0175c2m
Kirkbride, W.H. v6p0306c2s v6p0319c2s v6p0599c1s
Kirkcaldie, W.J. v6p0458c1s v6p0632c2s
Kirke, Alice v5p0255c1s
Kirke, E. v2p0089c1s v2p0244c1s v3p0075c1s v3p0299c2s v3p0362c2s v3p0460c2s
Kirke, H. v1p0086c2s v1p0141c1s v1p0708c1s v1p1434c1s v5p0252c1s v6p0120c2s
Kirke, R. v1p1224c1s
Kirkegaard, G. v6p0325c1s
Kirkham, T.N. v1p0501c2s
Kirkland, A.H. v5p0034c2s v6p0276c2s
Kirkland, C.M. v1p0163c2s v1p0534c2s v1p0624c2s v1p0741c1s v1p0916c2s v1p0990c2s v1p1180c1s v1p1386c1s v1p1387c2s v1p1389c1s v1p1392c1s v1p1420c2s
Kirkland, C.M., Mrs. v1p0034c1s v1p0144c1s v1p0560c1s v1p0624c1s v1p0857c1s v1p0876c2s v1p0916c1s v1p0931c2s v1p1242c2s v1p1425c1s
Kirkland, C.M.S. v1p1260c2s
Kirkland, C.M.S., Mrs. ... v1p1179c2s
Kirkland, C.P. v1p1353c2s
Kirkland, C.S. v1p0188c2s
Kirkland, H.S. v5p0613c2s
Kirkland, J. v1p0235c1s v1p0467c2s v1p0599c1s v1p0650c1s v1p0729c2s v1p0750c2s v1p1092c1s v1p1281c2s v1p1317c2s v1p1341c2s v2p0018c1s v2p0021c2s v2p0442c2m v3p0194c1s v3p0296c1s v3p0354c2s v3p0443c1s v3p0448c2s v4p0072c2s v4p0100c1m v4p0101c1s v4p0458c1s v4p0475c1s v4p0558c2s v4p0613c2s
Kirkland, J.H. v4p0123c2s v5p0326c2s v5p0464c1s v6p0635c1s v6p0674c2s
Kirkland, J.T. v1p0753c1s v1p0961c1s v1p1357c2s
Kirkland, J.W.D. v5p0377c2s
Kirkland, James H. v6p0115c1s
Kirkland, W. v1p0212c1s v1p0990c1s v6p0132c1s
Kirkland, W., Mrs. v1p0415c1s
Kirkman, G. v6p0086c2s
Kirkpatrick, A.deL. v5p0425c1s
Kirkpatrick, A.F. v6p0122c2s v6p0347c1s
Kirkpatrick, B. v6p0697c2s
Kirkpatrick, E. v1p0386c1s v6p0020c1s v6p0053c2s v6p0607c1s
Kirkpatrick, E.A. v3p0077c1s v3p0348c2s v3p0419c1s v3p0451c1s v4p0103c1s v4p0103c2s v4p0364c2s v4p0365c1s v5p0107c2s v5p0454c2s v5p0512c2s v5p0542c1s v5p0614c2s v6p0449c2s
Kirkpatrick, E.S. v6p0388c2s
Kirkpatrick, F.A. v5p0384c2s v5p0418c2s v5p0496c2s v5p0597c1s v6p0692c2s
Kirkpatrick, J. v3p0049c1s v5p0039c1s v5p0217c1s
Kirkpatrick, J.A. v1p0829c2s
Kirkpatrick, J.D. v2p0222c2s v2p0308c2s
Kirkpatrick, S.R. et al. . v5p0158c2s
Kirkup, Mary A. v5p0172c1s v5p0299c2s
Kirkup, T. v2p0174c2s v4p0148c1s v4p0533c1s
Kirkus, W. v1p0060c1s v1p0255c1s v1p0314c1s v1p0402c2s v1p0639c1s v1p0686c2s v1p0792c2s v1p0794c1s v1p0869c1s v1p0900c2s v1p1043c1s v1p1083c2s v1p1109c1s v1p1120c1s v2p0376c2s v3p0342c1s v4p0185c2s v4p0450c1s v5p0144c2s v5p0407c1s v5p0463c1s
Kirkus, W.W. v1p1089c2s
Kirkwood, D. v1p0281c2m v1p0580c1s v1p0709c2s v1p0804c1s v1p0827c2m v1p0829c2s v1p0903c2s v1p0904c1s v1p1014c1m v1p1152c2s v1p1218c1m v1p1233c2s v1p1243c2s v1p1268c1s v1p1269c1s v1p1379c1s v2p0025c2m v2p0026c1s v2p0095c1m v2p0095c2s v2p0285c1m v2p0308c2s v2p0343c2s v2p0386c2s v2p0409c1s v3p0003c2s v3p0024c1s v3p0094c1s v4p0033c2m v4p0126c2s v4p0367c1m v4p0381c1s v4p0528c1s
Kirkwood, D. and Walker, S.C. v1p1014c1s
Kirkwood, J.P. v1p1110c2s
Kirkwood, K.E. v4p0528c1s
Kirkwood, T.M. v4p0279c1s
Kirnan, A.V. v1p0476c2s
Kirreh, J.S. v5p0594c2s
Kirsch, A.M. v1p0434c2s
Kirsch, J.S. v6p0567c1s
Kirschbaum, W.G. v6p0405c1s
Kirschmann, A. v4p0125c1s v4p0131c2s v5p0129c1s v6p0167c2s
Kirtland, E.L. v5p0268c2s
Kirtland, J.C. v5p0118c2s
Kirtland, J.C., jr. v6p0135c1s
Kirtland, J.P. v1p0424c1s
Kirwan, A.V. v1p0109c2s v1p0166c2s v1p0384c1s v1p0413c1s v1p0473c1s v1p0477c1s v1p0655c1s v1p0915c1s v1p0967c2s v1p0969c1s v1p1006c1s v1p1314c1s
Kirwan, J.W. v6p0042c1s
Kisbaug, A.H. v6p0026c1s
Kisch, E.H. v3p0317c1s v3p0334c2s
Kiser, S.E. v5p0421c2s
Kishimoto, N. v3p0227c2s v4p0077c2s v4p0297c1s v4p0298c1s v4p0521c1s
Kishimoto, Nobuta v4p0109c2s
Kishinouye, K. v5p0238c1s v5p0250c2s
Kissner, J.G. v6p0308c1s
Kistler, M.S. v5p0319c1s
Kitchel, C.L. v1p0056c2s v1p1270c2s
Kitchel, H.D. v1p0290c1m v1p0291c1s v1p1046c1s v1p1097c2s v1p1400c2s
Kitchen, F.L. v5p0098c2s
Kitchener, H.H. v2p0134c1s v2p0154c1s
Kitchener, Lord et al. ... v6p0312c2s
Kitchin, C. v4p0587c1s
Kitchin, F.H. v5p0292c2m v5p0618c1s v6p0321c2s v6p0385c2s
Kitchin, G.W. v1p0554c1s v5p0532c2s
Kitchin, W.C. v3p0226c2s v3p0227c1s
Kite, W. v1p0451c1s
Kitson, A. v3p0162c2s v3p0167c2s v4p0042c2s v4p0168c1s v4p0223c1s v4p0599c2s v6p0312c1s
Kitson, Arthur v4p0199c1s
Kitson, J. v3p0223c1s
Kitson, J., Sir v3p0409c1s
Kittle, W. v6p0358c2s
Kitto, J. v1p0124c2s v1p0125c2s v1p0179c1s v1p0334c2s v1p0867c1s v1p0875c1s v1p1169c1s v1p1324c1s
Kitto, J.V. v5p0482c1s
Kitton, E.C. v4p0607c2s
Kitton, F.E. v4p0110c2s v4p0143c1s v4p0258c1s v5p0202c2s
Kitton, F.G. v2p0242c1s v3p0117c1m v3p0173c2s v3p0201c2s v3p0252c1s v4p0076c2s v4p0081c2s v4p0155c1s v4p0248c1s v4p0309c1s v4p0325c1m v4p0484c1s v4p0498c1s v4p0569c2s v5p0161c1m v5p0252c1s v5p0482c2s v6p0173c2s v6p0578c2s
Kitton, G.G. v4p0599c1s
Kittredge, C. v5p0376c1s v6p0297c2s
Kittredge, D.W. v6p0583c1s
Kittredge, F.F. v5p0616c2s
Kittredge, G.L. v2p0021c2s v2p0323c1s v2p0404c1s v3p0244c1s v4p0031c2s v4p0042c2s v4p0098c2m v4p0102c2s v4p0183c1s v4p0184c2s v4p0443c1s v4p0518c2s v4p0549c1s v5p0038c2s v5p0086c1s v5p0192c2s v5p0241c1s v5p0242c2s v5p0250c2s v5p0255c1s v5p0523c1s v6p0048c1s v6p0090c2s v6p0495c1s v6p0707c1m
Kittredge, G.L. and Morgan, M.H. v4p0353c2s
Kittredge, H.E. v5p0293c1s v6p0319c1m v6p0581c1s
Kittredge, H.G. v5p0574c2m
Kittredge, M. v6p0295c1s
Kittredge, W.T. v2p0301c2s
Kittrell, T.G. v4p0429c1s
Kitts, E.J. v4p0279c1s v6p0313c2s v6p0314c1s
Kiung, N.Y. v1p1054c2s
Kjelland, A.L. v2p0113c2s v2p0449c2s
Klaczko, J. v4p0071c2s
Klaer, A.N. v4p0504c2s v4p0521c1m
Klapp, E. v4p0177c2s
Klapp, W.A. v3p0437c1s
Klapp, W.H. v5p0127c1s
Klauder, A.L.A. v5p0492c2s
Klausner-Dawoc, L. v5p0631c2s
Klaussmann, A.O. v4p0189c1s v4p0355c2s v5p0054c1s
Klaussmann, O. v5p0526c1s
Klaw, M. v6p0642c1s
Kleberg, R. v5p0593c1s v6p0640c1m
Klebs, A.C. v6p0660c1s
Klebs, Arnold C. v6p0322c1s
Kleene, G.A. v5p0536c1s v6p0408c2s
Kleerkooper, M.M. v6p0538c2s
Kleiber, J. v3p0345c1s
Klein, A. v4p0166c1s v4p0561c2s
Klein, C. v6p0378c1s
Klein, Dr. v3p0024c2s v3p0472c2s v6p0427c2s
Klein, E. v2p0080c2s v2p0387c2s v2p0448c1s v3p0215c2s v3p0376c2s v4p0020c2s v4p0041c1s v4p0107c2s v5p0644c1s v6p0501c2m
Klein, F. v4p0360c2s v6p0238c1s
Klein, F.M. v2p0287c2s
Klein, Felix v6p0236c2s v6p0421c2s
Klein, H. v2p0031c2s v3p0100c2s v6p0439c1s
Klein, H.J. v1p0506c1s
Klein, H.M.J. v5p0060c1s v6p0342c1s v6p0541c2s
Klein, H.Y. v2p0340c1s
Klein, J. v6p0275c2s
Klein, J.F. v1p0580c2s v1p1234c2s
Klein, L. v1p0430c2s v1p1077c1s v1p1077c2s
Klein, L.B. v3p0382c2s
Klein, L.E.B. v3p0274c2s
Klein, L.M. v2p0007c1s v2p0053c1s v2p0081c2s v2p0344c1s
Klein, L.M.B. v4p0190c2s
Klein, M.L. v2p0015c1s v2p0198c2s
Kleine, Lina v5p0630c2s
Kleinert, P. v1p1117c1s
Kleinheksel, J.H. v3p0019c2s
Kleinpeter, H. v6p0204c1s v6p0425c2s
Kleinschmidt, E. v5p0261c1s v5p0265c2s
Kleinschmidt, J.L. v1p0300c1s
Kleist, H.V. v2p0215c1s
Klemm, L.R. v2p0131c2m v2p0204c1s v3p0323c2s v3p0328c1s
Klemm, L.R. and Clark, J.. v3p0196c1s
Klett, F. v1p1442c1s
Klett, J. v2p0445c1s
Kletzsch, A.P. and Gately, S.L. v2p0419c1s
Kliefoth, T. v1p0255c2s
Klinck, J.H. and Williamson, R.B. v5p0279c2s
Kline, B. v6p0200c2s
Kline, Burton v6p0239c1s
Kline, E.W. v5p0592c1s
Kline, L.W. v5p0374c2s v5p0470c2m v6p0116c1s
Kline, L.W. and France, C.J. v5p0426c1s
Klink, J.S. v6p0299c2s v6p0584c2m
Klink, Jane S. v5p0636c1s
Klock, J.E. v4p0151c1s
Kloeber, C.E., jr. v6p0515c2s
Kloos, J.H. v1p1152c2s
Klotz, O.J. v4p0009c1s v4p0321c2s v4p0441c1s v5p0010c2s
Klumpke, D. v5p0044c1s v5p0372c2s
Knap, J.D. v4p0163c1m v5p0064c1s v5p0170c2m
Knapp, A. v4p0501c2s v4p0614c2s v5p0213c2s v5p0251c1s v5p0266c1s v6p0697c1s
Knapp, A. et al. v4p0256c1s
Knapp, A.E. v3p0097c1s
Knapp, A.M. v1p1328c2s

v1p1340c2s v5p0444c2s
Knapp, Adeline v4p0555c1s v5p0088c2s v6p0645c1s
Knapp, C. v4p0221c2s v4p0321c2s v5p0270c2s v6p0680c1s
Knapp, E.A. v5p0501c1s v6p0137c2s
Knapp, F.N. v1p1432c2s
Knapp, Frances v5p0004c2s
Knapp, H. v4p0389c1s
Knapp, H.E. v5p0612c2s
Knapp, H.R. v6p0129c2s
Knapp, J. v1p1022c1s
Knapp, L.M. v3p0427c1s
Knapp, M.A. v4p0471c1s v6p0530c1s v6p0654c1m
Knapp, M.L. v5p0157c1s v5p0359c1s v5p0388c2s v6p0098c2s
Knapp, Margaret L. v6p0499c2s
Knapp, P.C. v3p0216c2s v4p0397c2s
Knapp, S.A. v6p0009c1s v6p0543c1s
Knapp, S.L. v1p0367c2s v1p0483c1s v1p0602c2s
Knapp, W. v4p0044c2s v4p0143c2s v4p0144c1s v4p0144c2s v4p0423c2s
Knapp, W.A. v3p0311c1s
Knapp, W.I. v1p1231c1s v1p1310c1s v2p0052c2s v3p0050c2s v3p0072c2s
Knapp, W.J. v1p1229c2s
Knappen, D.M. v1p0016c2s
Knappen, T.M. v6p0097c2s
Knappen, Theodore M. v6p0097c2s
Knatchbull-Hugessen, E.H.. v1p1063c1s v1p1099c2s v4p0189c1s v4p0420c1m
Knatchbull-Hugessen, Eva . v3p0302c2s
Knatchbull-Hugessen, L. .. v1p0009c1s
Knatchbull-Hugessen, L.K.. v1p0076c2s v1p0371c2s
Knauer, F. v3p0014c2s
Knaufft, E. v4p0100c2s v4p0164c1s v5p0066c2s v5p0069c2s v5p0082c1s v5p0103c1s v5p0160c2s v5p0233c2s v5p0280c1s v5p0406c2s v5p0580c2s v6p0402c1s v6p0442c2s v6p0501c1s v6p0538c2s v6p0695c2s v6p0711c2s
Knaufft, Ernest v6p0116c2s
Kneass, S. v1p0161c1s
Kneass, S.L. v6p0084c1s v6p0319c2s
Kneeland, G.J. v6p0285c1s
Kneeland, S. v1p0063c1s v1p0816c2s v2p0269c2m v2p0308c2s v2p0430c1s v2p0450c1s v3p0266c1s v4p0604c2s
Kneitsch, R. v6p0624c2s
Knerr, E.B. v6p0193c1s
Knevels, J.W. v5p0170c2s
Kniajnine, S. v6p0559c1s
Knickerbocker, C. v1p0228c1s
Knies, K. and Coppock, F.M. v1p0861c1s
Knight, A.A. v2p0461c1s v3p0062c1s v3p0085c1s v3p0243c2s v3p0460c1s
Knight, A.A., Miss v2p0461c2s
Knight, A.A., Mrs. v2p0027c1s
Knight, A.C. v1p0772c1s
Knight, A.F. v6p0664c2s
Knight, A.G. v1p0011c1s v1p0012c2s v1p0021c1s v1p0048c2s v1p0105c2s v1p0202c2s v1p0280c1s v1p0285c2m v1p0297c1s v1p0683c2s v1p0744c1s v1p0771c2s v1p0970c2s v1p0993c1s v1p1052c1s v1p1120c2s
Knight, A.H. v6p0021c2s v6p0686c1s
Knight, A.H. and Knight, C.R. v6p0702c1s
Knight, A.L. v4p0369c2s
Knight, Adeline A. v3p0434c2s
Knight, C. v1p1168c1s v2p0263c2s v2p0302c1s v2p0319c1s v2p0347c2s
Knight, C.R. v6p0021c2m v6p0036c1s v6p0059c1s
Knight, C.R. and Gleeson, M. v6p0368c1s
Knight, C.R. and Knight, A.H. v6p0702c1s
Knight, C.W. v6p0521c1s
Knight, C.W. and Read, T.T. v6p0602c2s
Knight, E. v3p0056c2s v3p0188c2s v4p0577c1s v6p0088c2s v6p0534c2s
Knight, E.H. v1p0651c2s v1p0968c2m v6p0060c2s v6p0065c1s
Knight, F.A. v3p0384c1s
Knight, G. v1p0982c1s v5p0052c1s
Knight, G.H. v4p0196c2s v4p0288c2s v4p0506c1s
Knight, G.K. v6p0574c1s
Knight, G.T. v3p0021c1s v3p0080c2m v3p0166c1s v6p0286c2s
v6p0305c2s v6p0642c1s
Knight, G.W. v4p0123c1s v6p0016c2s
Knight, H.J.C. v5p0503c2s
Knight, H.R. v4p0189c1s
Knight, J. v1p0556c2s v1p0782c2s v1p0824c2s v1p0907c1s v1p1072c1s v1p1202c1s v2p0230c1s v2p0397c2m v2p0443c1s v3p0122c1m v4p0260c2s v5p0054c1s v5p0429c1s v6p0383c2s v6p0587c2s
Knight, J.B. v1p0835c1s v1p1390c2s v2p0347c1s
Knight, J.C. v1p0181c1s
Knight, J.G.D. v5p0049c2s v5p0215c1s
Knight, J.H. v5p0005c2s v6p0442c2s
Knight, J.Hartley v6p0099c2s v6p0692c2s
Knight, J.Huntley v6p0593c2s
Knight, J.T. v4p0581c2s
Knight, J.W. v4p0275c2s v4p0632c2s
Knight, Joseph v6p0329c2s
Knight, L. v6p0084c1s
Knight, L.L. v5p0422c2s v6p0606c2s
Knight, Maria v5p0507c1s
Knight, P. v1p0100c2s
Knight, P.S. v1p0059c1s
Knight, R. v1p1425c2s
Knight, R.P. v1p0210c2s v1p0272c2s v1p1258c2s v1p1278c2s
Knight, W. v1p0294c2s v1p0314c1s v1p0381c2s v1p0426c2s v1p0434c1s v1p0767c1s v1p0827c1s v1p0992c2s v1p1042c1s v1p1042c2s v1p1094c2s v1p1430c1s v3p0105c2s v3p0382c1s v3p0445c1s v4p0140c2s v4p0188c2s v4p0275c2s v4p0381c2s v4p0439c1s v4p0542c1m v5p0166c2s v5p0545c2s v5p0573c1s v6p0088c2s v6p0099c2s v6p0127c1s v6p0396c2s v6p0465c1s v6p0495c2s v6p0505c1s v6p0575c2s v6p0689c1s v6p0707c2m
Knight, W. et al. v3p0146c1s
Knight, W.A. v5p0143c2s
Knight, W.B. v2p0333c2s v2p0422c2s
Knight, W.C. v5p0229c1s v5p0312c2m v5p0642c2s v6p0051c2s
Knight, W.H. v3p0423c2s
Knight, W.J. v6p0571c1s
Knight, W.T. v3p0175c2s
Knight, Wm. v4p0507c2s
Knight-Horsfield, H. v4p0273c2s
Knightley, L.M., Lady v3p0278c1s
Knightley, Lady v3p0150c2s v4p0627c2s
Knighton, W. v1p0112c2s v1p0156c2s v1p0185c2s v1p0201c2s v1p0205c2s v1p0343c1s v1p0396c2s v1p0592c1s v1p0634c2s v1p0749c1s v1p1029c2s v1p1122c1s v1p1239c2s v1p1264c1s v1p1266c1s
Knipe, A.A. v6p0509c2s v6p0623c2s
Knipe, Alden A. v6p0465c1s
Knipe, Emilie B. v6p0431c2s
Knipp, C.T. v5p0185c1s v5p0357c1s
Knobe, B.D. v6p0046c2s v6p0121c2s v6p0643c1s
Knobe, Bertha D. v6p0574c2s
Knoblauch, H.B. v3p0235c2s
Knoblauch, Prof. v1p1427c1s
Knoche, L. v4p0434c1s
Knodel, K. v4p0534c1s v4p0626c1s
Knollys, B.S. v3p0172c2s v3p0252c1s v4p0219c1s v5p0107c2s
Knollys, H. v1p1061c1s v3p0116c2s v3p0247c1s v3p0476c1s v4p0028c1s v4p0107c1s v4p0184c2m v4p0235c2m v4p0466c1s v4p0535c2s v5p0110c1s v5p0181c1s v5p0243c2s v6p0163c2s v6p0340c1s
Knollys, Major v1p0544c2s
Knollys, W.W. v1p0059c2s v1p0155c1s v1p0543c1s v1p1091c2s v1p1218c2s v2p0030c1s v2p0060c1s v2p0142c1s v2p0164c1s v2p0185c2m v2p0186c1s v2p0193c2s v2p0217c2s v2p0221c1s v2p0270c2s v2p0288c2s v2p0293c2s v2p0305c2s v2p0373c1s v2p0429c2s v2p0430c1m v2p0465c2s v3p0022c2m v3p0113c2s v3p0144c2s v3p0160c2s v3p0161c1s v3p0180c1m v3p0187c1s v3p0192c2s v3p0204c2s v3p0283c2s v3p0295c2s v3p0298c2s v3p0341c1s v3p0386c1s v3p0419c1s v3p0454c1s v4p0226c2s v4p0455c2s v5p0091c1s
Knoop, D. and Chapman, S.J. v6p0153c1s
Knopf, S.A. v5p0134c2s v5p0594c1s v6p0660c1m
Knorr, H. v5p0227c1s
v5p0273c2s v5p0278c1s
Knorr, R.H. v6p0211c1s v6p0300c1s
Knortz, K. v1p0768c1s
Knot, H.V. v5p0400c2s
Knott, A.L. v5p0543c1s
Knott, G.H. v4p0049c2m v4p0071c2s v4p0122c1s v4p0157c2s v4p0227c1s v4p0339c1s v4p0340c2s v4p0495c1s v6p0338c1s
Knott, G.H. and Worth, G.C. v5p0609c1s
Knott, J. v6p0046c2s v6p0071c1s v6p0497c2s v6p0586c2s v6p0587c2s
Knott, J.P. v4p0062c2s
Knott, R.W. v2p0346c1s v2p0445c1s
Knower, D. v3p0464c2s
Knowles, A.J. v3p0158c2s
Knowles, E.C. v6p0589c1s
Knowles, E.R. v2p0040c1s v2p0280c2s
Knowles, F.C., Sir v1p0664c1s
Knowles, F.L. v5p0277c2s v6p0122c1s v6p0405c2s v6p0639c1s
Knowles, H. v6p0542c1s
Knowles, Isabel v6p0099c1s
Knowles, J. v3p0134c2s v3p0461c1s v4p0293c2s v4p0541c2s v4p0569c2m v5p0234c2s v5p0289c1s
Knowles, J. and Childers, H.R.E. v5p0243c2s
Knowles, J. and Morris, W. v3p0461c1s
Knowles, J.D. v1p0493c2s v1p0847c1s
Knowles, J.S. v1p0526c2s v1p0887c2s v1p1420c1s
Knowles, L. v3p0201c1s v3p0368c2s v6p0256c2s v6p0399c1s
Knowles, R.B.S. v1p0501c1s v1p0534c2s v2p0038c1s v2p0471c1s v3p0174c2s
Knowles, W.H. v5p0041c2s
Knowles, W.J. v2p0158c2s
Knowling, R.J. v6p0064c1s v6p0389c2s
Knowlson, T.S. v5p0193c1s
Knowlton, E. v1p0881c2s v1p1438c1s
Knowlton, F.H. v4p0013c1s v4p0570c2s v4p0635c2s v6p0067c2s
Knowlton, H.M. v4p0270c1s
Knowlton, H.S. v6p0072c2s v6p0132c2s v6p0152c1s v6p0197c1s v6p0197c2s v6p0198c1s v6p0199c1m v6p0200c1s v6p0235c1s v6p0545c1s v6p0619c1s v6p0621c1s
Knowlton, I.C. v1p0337c2s v1p0613c1s v1p0625c2s v1p0641c1s v1p1043c1s v1p1115c2s v1p1147c2s v1p1340c2s v2p0351c2s v2p0356c2s v2p0371c1s v3p0053c1s v3p0166c1s v3p0198c2s v3p0347c2s
Knowlton, S. v1p1423c2s
Knowlton, S.B. v4p0183c2s
Knox, A. v5p0359c1m
Knox, A.A. v1p0500c2s v1p0604c1s v1p0792c2s v1p0880c2s v2p0401c2s v2p0463c2s
Knox, C.B. v5p0563c1s
Knox, C.E. v1p0850c1s v2p0355c2s
Knox, Dr. v1p1372c1s
Knox, E. v3p0362c2s
Knox, E.F.V. v3p0222c1s v5p0183c2s v5p0295c2s
Knox, G. v4p0137c1s
Knox, G.W. v2p0233c2s v6p0118c1s v6p0121c1s v6p0186c2s v6p0211c2s v6p0312c2s v6p0315c1s v6p0333c2s v6p0536c2s
Knox, G.W. and MacLennan, S.F. v6p0218c1s
Knox, Gen. v2p0221c2s
Knox, Georgia v6p0622c2s
Knox, H.V. v4p0040c1s v5p0200c1s v5p0250c1s
Knox, H.W. v4p0415c2s
Knox, Howard V. v6p0001c2s
Knox, J. v1p0092c1s v1p0092c2s v5p0358c2s
Knox, J.A. v4p0267c1s
Knox, J.A. et al. v3p0236c2s
Knox, J.F. v4p0631c1s
Knox, J.H.M. v6p0417c1s
Knox, J.J. v1p0326c1s v2p0033c2s v3p0032c1s v4p0043c2s v4p0524c2s
Knox, J.W. v1p0231c2s
Knox, Jessie J. v6p0377c1s v6p0551c2s
Knox, K. v6p0022c2s
Knox, L.H. et al. v4p0275c1s
Knox, L.H.B. v6p0113c1s
Knox, M.V.B. v3p0301c2s v4p0586c2s v5p0266c2s
Knox, N.A. v1p0987c2s v1p1033c2s v2p0119c1s v2p0279c1s

v2p0287c1s
Knox, R. v1p0036c2s v1p0312c1s v1p0427c2s v1p1232c2s v2p0226c2s v2p0228c1s
Knox, Robert v6p0107c2s
Knox, T. v1p0235c1s
Knox, T.C. v1p0235c1s
Knox, T.E. v2p0176c1s
Knox, T.F. v1p0534c2s
Knox, T.W. v1p0035c1s v1p0068c1s v1p0279c2s v1p0532c1s v1p0630c2s v1p0699c2s v1p0767c1s v1p0861c2s v1p1135c1s v1p1135c2m v1p1137c1s v1p1194c1s v1p1194c2s v2p0025c1s v2p0197c2s v3p0339c2s v3p0419c1s v4p0038c1s
Knox, T.W., Sir v4p0214c2s
Knox, V. v5p0585c2s
Knox, W. v1p0938c2s
Knox, W.E. v2p0084c2s v2p0085c1s
Knox-Little, W.J. v3p0082c2s v4p0485c1s v4p0507c2s
Knubel, F.H. v5p0059c1s v5p0289c2s v5p0313c1s v5p0482c2s
Knubel, F.H. and Nosgen, D. v4p0053c2s
Knudson, A.A. v4p0537c2s v6p0199c2s
Knupfer, W.R. v5p0132c1s
Knyper, A. v6p0065c1s
Knyvet-Wilson, R. v6p0193c2s
Kobbe, G. v3p0251c1s v3p0312c2s v3p0343c1m v3p0402c2s v3p0427c1s v3p0461c1s v4p0102c1s v4p0157c1s v4p0217c2s v4p0373c1s v4p0633c2s v5p0014c2s v5p0040c1s v5p0075c1s v5p0130c1s v5p0139c2s v5p0151c2s v5p0167c2s v5p0263c2s v5p0337c2s v5p0338c1s v5p0338c2m v5p0366c2s v5p0400c2s v5p0451c2s v5p0454c2s v5p0497c2s v5p0592c1s v5p0616c1m v6p0216c2s v6p0218c1s v6p0280c2s v6p0286c2s v6p0357c2s v6p0620c2s v6p0683c1m
Kobbe, Gustav v4p0390c2s v5p0258c1s v5p0394c2s v6p0379c1s
Kobbel, T.E. v6p0157c1s
Kober, G.M. v5p0277c2s v6p0115c1s v6p0417c1m v6p0687c1s
Kocen, L.D. v5p0373c1s v5p0543c1s
Koch, Dr. v2p0080c2s
Koch, E.W. v6p0613c1s
Koch, F.J. v6p0087c1s v6p0431c2s v6p0597c2s v6p0607c2s
Koch, Felix J. v6p0048c1s
Koch, L. v1p1246c2s
Koch, P. v1p0320c2s v2p0025c2s v2p0267c1s v2p0295c2s v2p0323c1s v2p0387c1s v2p0482c1s
Koch, R. v3p0437c2s v5p0594c1m
Koch, T.W. v6p0102c2s v6p0672c1s
Koch, Theo.W. v6p0102c2s
Koch, W. v6p0083c2s
Kochi, C. v5p0302c2s
Kochi, C. and Comstock, J.H. v6p0321c1s
Kock, H.E. v6p0399c2s
Kockemann, F. v1p0121c2s
Kodis, J. v4p0040c1s
Koe, A.B. v5p0005c1s
Koehler, H.J. v6p0542c2s
Koehler, S.R. v1p0278c2s v1p0596c2s v1p0786c1s v4p0432c1s v4p0454c2s v4p0551c2s v4p0562c2s
Koehler, W. v6p0240c1s
Koenig, E. v6p0590c1s
Koenig, G.A. v5p0381c2s
Koenig, G.A. and Hubbard, L.L. v4p0455c2s
Koeppen, A.L. v1p0008c1s v1p0072c1m v1p0072c2s v1p0075c2s v1p0083c1s v1p0173c2s v1p0329c2m v1p0330c2s v1p0336c2s v1p0361c1s v1p0378c1s v1p0553c1m v1p0553c2m v1p0554c2s v1p0592c1s v1p0926c1s v1p0960c1s v1p0975c2s v1p1011c2s v1p1105c2s v1p1232c1s v1p1279c1s
Koeppen, Prof. v2p0293c2s
Koeppen, W. v1p1293c1s
Koerner, G. v2p0295c2s v4p0100c2s v4p0163c1s v4p0251c1s v4p0379c2s v4p0466c2s v4p0506c2s v4p0553c2s
Koesis, A. v1p0674c2s
Koester, F. v1p0601c1s v6p0198c1s
Koester, Franz v6p0197c2s
Kofoid, C.A. v4p0584c2s v5p0011c1s v5p0204c1s v5p0253c2s v5p0258c2s v5p0277c1s v5p0453c2s v6p0010c2s v6p0227c1s v6p0658c1s v6p0688c2s
Kohfahl, R. v4p0164c2s
Kohl, J.G. v1p0029c2s v1p0151c1s v1p0798c2s v1p1137c2s v1p1388c2s v2p0372c1s
Kohler, H. v3p0417c1s
Kohler, K. v4p0245c2s v4p0341c2s v5p0001c1s
Kohler, Max J. v6p0343c2s
Kohler, P.S. v1p0946c1s v1p1044c1s
Kohlmorgen, O. v6p0143c1s
Kohlrausch, C. v2p0340c2s
Kohlrausch, F. v1p1100c2s
Kohlrausch, F. and Loomis, F.E. v1p1293c1s
Kohn, Annette v6p0342c2s
Kohn, F. v3p0414c1s
Kohut, A. v4p0055c1s v4p0352c1s v4p0637c1s
Kokler, M.J. v6p0239c2s
Kolany, L. v6p0674c1s
Kolbe, F.C. v2p0295c1s v6p0406c2s
Koll, Judith v6p0421c1s
Koller, J.C. v1p0264c2s v1p0686c1s v1p1093c2s v1p1162c2s v2p0383c2s v3p0282c2s v4p0633c1s
Kollmann, J. v4p0468c1s
Kollock, S.K. v1p0120c2s v1p0448c2s v1p0677c2s v1p0683c2s v1p0775c1s v1p0921c1s
Komatz, M. v4p0297c2s v5p0302c1s
Kommen, C. v1p0138c2s
Konig, E. v5p0057c1s v6p0001c2s v6p0045c2s v6p0062c1s v6p0062c2s v6p0065c1s v6p0346c1s v6p0475c2s
Konkie, B.A. v6p0064c2s
Konody, P.G. v5p0048c2s v5p0094c2s v5p0215c2s v5p0241c2s v5p0268c1s v5p0357c1s v5p0609c2s v6p0079c2m v6p0244c2s v6p0589c1s
Konstam, E.M. v6p0313c1s
Koolomzine, A. v1p1137c2s v1p1357c2s
Koons, B.F. v2p0242c2s v2p0435c2s
Koons, E.J. v1p0289c1s
Koopman, H.L. v2p0278c1s v3p0024c1s v3p0070c1s v4p0330c1s v5p0070c2s v5p0252c1s v5p0334c2s v6p0074c2s v6p0373c2s
Koopman, Harry L. v6p0370c2s v6p0542c1s
Kop, A.C.Croiset van der . v4p0021c1s
Kopcke, C. v1p0162c1s
Kopernicki, I. v1p1204c1s
Kopernicki, J. v1p0701c2s
Koplin, A.B. v1p0096c2s v1p0384c2s v1p0853c1s v3p0084c1s
Kopp, H. v1p0436c2s v2p0076c2s
Kopp, M.E. v1p0269c2s v1p0279c2s
Kopsch, H. v5p0034c1s
Kopta, F.P. v4p0065c1s
Koracs, J. v3p0139c2s
Korbay, F. v3p0204c2s v3p0293c1s
Koren, J. v4p0331c1s v4p0334c1s v4p0358c1s v5p0480c1s v6p0106c2s
Koren, W. v6p0059c1s
Korff, S.A. v6p0224c2s
Koristka, C. v1p1029c2s
Korner, S. v3p0387c2s v3p0388c1s v3p0388c2s
Korolenko v6p0352c2s
Korolenko, V. v3p0264c2s v6p0187c1s v6p0362c2s
Korolenko, Y. v5p0295c1s
Korosi, Dr. v4p0471c1s
Korosi, J. v2p0073c1s v4p0062c1s v4p0383c2s v4p0393c2s
Kortrecht, A. v6p0083c2s
Kossmat, F. v5p0024c1s
Kossmat, F. et al. v5p0537c2s
Kossuth, F. v1p0211c2s v6p0303c2m
Kossuth, L. v1p0079c2s v1p0380c1s v1p1133c2s v1p1135c1s
Koster, F. v1p0980c2s
Kostlin, J. v1p0777c1s v4p0213c2s
Koto, B. v2p0005c2s v4p0166c1s
Kottenkamp, F. v1p0412c2s
Kouns, N.C. v2p0369c1s
Kovacs, F. v1p1341c1s
Kovalevsky, M. v4p0146c1s v6p0364c1s
Kowalewsky, P. v4p0356c2s
Koyl, C.H. v1p0279c1s v3p0353c2s v3p0380c1s v3p0384c2s
Kozaki, N. v3p0227c1s
Kozloff, P.K. v6p0646c1s
Kozlowski, W.M. v6p0433c1s v6p0457c1s
Kozmin, P.A. v6p0556c2s
Kraemer, H. v6p0012c2s
Kraepelin, E. v4p0365c1s
Kraft, Max v2p0370c2s
Kral, J.G. v3p0431c1s v3p0435c1s v4p0022c1s
Kral, J.J. v4p0065c1m v4p0078c2s v4p0132c2s v4p0157c1s v4p0165c1s v4p0221c2s v4p0332c1s v4p0388c2m v4p0448c1s v4p0451c1s v4p0530c1s v5p0475c2s
Kramarz, K. v6p0072c2s
Kramer, A.L. v6p0522c2s
Kramer, E.N. and Kramer, S.K. v1p0823c2s
Kramer, F.F. v4p0077c2s v4p0300c1s
Kramer, H. v6p0596c1s
Kramer, J.W. v1p0485c2s
Kramer, M.W. v3p0150c1s
Kramer, S.K. and Kramer, E.N. v1p0823c2s
Krankel, L.K. v6p0405c2s v6p0682c2s
Krans, H.S. v6p0089c1s v6p0189c1s v6p0711c1s
Kransz, Sigmund v6p0043c2s
Kranth, C.P. v1p0966c1s
Kranth, C.P., jr. v1p0076c1s
Krarup, M.C. v5p0041c1s v5p0389c1s v6p0043c2s v6p0044c2m
Krasinski, S. v1p1266c2s v1p1293c2s v1p1339c2s
Krasinski, Z.N. v1p0245c2s
Kratz, H.E. v4p0566c1s v5p0126c2s
Kratzer, H. v2p0161c1s
Kraufft, E. v6p0475c1s
Kraus, C.A. et al. v5p0537c2s
Kraus, E.H. v6p0105c2s v6p0106c1m
Kraus, E.H. and Cook, C.W. v6p0165c2s
Kraus, E.H. and Hunt, W.F. v6p0624c2s
Kraus, F.S. v3p0148c1s v3p0395c2s
Kraus, F.X. v3p0017c2s v3p0467c2s
Kraus, S. v6p0091c1s
Krause, E. v2p0151c1s v2p0157c1s
Krause, G. v5p0252c1s
Krauskopf, M. v2p0375c2s
Krauss, F.S. v3p0287c1s v4p0301c2s
Krauss, S. v4p0159c1s v4p0302c2s v5p0145c2s v5p0362c1s v5p0565c1s v6p0025c1s v6p0345c2m v6p0570c1s
Krausse, A. v5p0109c1s v5p0387c1s
Krausz, S. v6p0153c2s v6p0343c1s v6p0470c1s v6p0510c1m v6p0530c2s v6p0559c1s
Krauth, C.P. v1p0048c1s v1p0096c1m v1p0118c1m v1p0119c1m v1p0125c2s v1p0127c1s v1p0132c2s v1p0206c2s v1p0247c1s v1p0254c1s v1p0254c2s v1p0286c1s v1p0589c1s v1p0601c2s v1p0613c1m v1p0756c2s v1p0769c1s v1p0778c1m v1p0792c1s v1p0794c2s v1p0843c1s v1p1001c1s v1p1085c2s v1p1090c1s v1p1279c2s v1p1286c2s v1p1304c1s v1p1357c1s v1p1418c2s
Krauth, C.P., jr. v1p0095c2s v1p0117c1s v1p0129c1s v1p0447c2s v1p0689c1s v1p0756c2s v1p0769c2s v1p0777c2m v1p0778c1s v1p0808c2s v1p0818c1s v1p1090c1s v1p1302c2s
Krauthoff, E.A. v5p0231c2s
Krauthoff, L.C. v3p0283c2s
Kraybill, L.R. v6p0284c2s
Krebs, H. v2p0111c2s
Krebs, S.L. v5p0223c1s v5p0378c1s v5p0592c1s v6p0611c1s
Krebs, T.L. v5p0224c1s v5p0636c1s
Krebs, W.E. v1p0025c2s v1p0248c2s v1p0688c1s v1p0745c2s v1p1043c1s v1p1050c1s v1p1140c2s v1p1147c2s v3p0444c2s v5p0366c2s v5p0546c2s
Kreeker, A.M. v5p0476c2s
Kreemer, S.I. v6p0709c1s
Krehbiel, H.E. v3p0079c2s v3p0080c1s v3p0293c1s v3p0452c2s v4p0048c1s v4p0165c1s v4p0499c2s v4p0636c2s v5p0052c1s v5p0518c2s v5p0615c2s v6p0124c1s v6p0354c2s v6p0498c2s
Krehbiel, H.E. and Seward, T.F. v3p0432c2s
Kreider, D.A. v4p0316c1s v4p0420c1s v4p0435c1m v5p0146c2s v6p0325c2s
Kreider, D.A. and Breckenridge, J.E. v4p0454c2s v4p0535c2s
Kreider, D.A. and Wright, A.W. v5p0146c2s
Kreider, J.L. v6p0083c2s v6p0305c1s
Kreitner, G. v2p0438c2s
Krejci, J. v4p0065c1s

Kremer, A.H. v1p0646c1m
v1p0948c2s v1p1388c1s
Kremer, A.R. v1p1325c2s
v2p0086c1s v3p0323c2s v4p0190c1s
v4p0336c1s v4p0456c2s v4p0463c1s
v5p0278c1s v6p0450c1s
Kremer, E.N. v6p0251c2s
v6p0535c2s
Kremer, F.W. v1p0206c2s
v1p0561c1s v1p0684c2s v2p0236c1s
Kress, W.S. v3p0131c1s
Kretschmar, H. v5p0042c1m
Kretz, W.C. v5p0549c1s
Kreuzpointner, P. v5p0298c1m
v5p0298c2s v5p0551c2m v5p0552c1s
Kriehn, G. v5p0120c1s
v5p0190c1s v6p0600c1s
Krikorian, J. v2p0404c1s
Krilage, E.H. v4p0227c1s
Krine, J.H.S. v6p0025c1s
Kristeller, Paul v4p0631c1m
Krockow, Countess von v3p0048c2s
v3p0125c1s v3p0127c1s v3p0267c2s
v3p0292c1s v3p0332c2s v4p0091c2s
v5p0556c1s v6p0059c1s
Krockow, L.v. v3p0011c1s
v5p0096c2s
Kroeber, A.L. v5p0024c2s
v5p0105c1s v5p0195c1m v6p0212c1s
v6p0421c1s v6p0424c1s v6p0428c1s
v6p0701c2s
Kroeber, A.L. and Dixon, R.B.
v6p0093c1s v6p0316c2s
Kroeger, A.B. v5p0334c2s
Kroeger, A.B. and Andrews, C.W.
v5p0334c2s
Kroeger, A.E. v1p0222c2s
v1p0390c1s v1p0450c2s v1p0484c2s
v1p0485c1m v1p0485c2s v1p0487c1s
v1p0530c1s v1p0582c2s v1p0585c2s
v1p0702c2m v1p0736c2s v1p0744c2s
v1p0848c2s v1p0884c2s v1p0951c1s
v1p0998c1s v1p0999c2s v1p1000c2s
v1p1105c2s v1p1236c2s v1p1271c2s
v1p1321c1s v1p1328c2s v2p0014c1s
v2p0154c2s
Kroeger, Alice B. v6p0074c2s
v6p0104c1s v6p0374c1s v6p0375c1s
v6p0532c1s v6p0535c1m
Kroeger, E.E. v5p0131c2s
Kroeger, E.R. v6p0287c2s
Kroeger, G.A. v1p1148c1s
Kroeker, K.F. v2p0167c1s
Krohn, W.O. v4p0124c2s
v4p0464c2s v5p0106c1s v5p0449c1s
Kroll, F.X. v2p0233c1s
Kropf, L.L. v5p0261c1s
v5p0564c2s
Kropf, L.L. and Lane-Poole, S.
v5p0381c2s
Kropotkin, P. v2p0168c1s
v3p0370c2s v4p0132c2s v4p0423c1s
v4p0496c2s v4p0522c2s v5p0010c1s
v5p0018c1s v5p0062c1s v5p0090c2s
v5p0130c1s v5p0184c2s v5p0289c2s
v5p0359c2m v5p0372c1s v5p0456c2s
v5p0501c2s v5p0502c1m v5p0513c2m
v5p0581c2s v6p0211c2s v6p0212c2s
v6p0251c1s v6p0371c1s v6p0428c2s
v6p0437c2s v6p0526c2s v6p0534c1s
v6p0556c2s v6p0558c2m v6p0560c1s
v6p0649c1s
Kropotkin, P.A. v6p0444c1s
Kropotkin, P.R. v6p0036c2s
Kropotkin, Prince v2p0156c1s
v2p0173c1s v3p0006c2s v3p0013c1m
v3p0014c2s v3p0120c2s v3p0128c1s
v3p0160c1s v3p0215c1m v3p0266c2s
v3p0376c1s v4p0116c1s v4p0125c1s
v4p0390c2m
Kropotkin, Sophie v5p0636c2s
Krotel, G.F. v1p0769c1s
Krotel, G.F. et al. v2p0106c2s
Krouss, W.C. v4p0523c1s
Krout, J.D. v6p0141c2s
Krout, M.H. v5p0108c2s
v5p0109c1s v5p0110c2s v5p0191c1s
v5p0258c2s v5p0310c2s v5p0408c1s
v5p0408c2s v5p0409c2s v6p0120c2s
v6p0283c2s
Krout, M.K. v5p0578c1s
Krueger, A. v2p0021c1s
Kruekl, F. v5p0328c2s
Kruesi, H. v1p0386c1s
Krug, W.H. v6p0100c2s
Kruger, C. v2p0184c2s
Kruger, G. v5p0556c1s
Kruger, O. v1p0464c1s
Kruill, G. and Pennell, E.R.
v3p0471c1s
Krum, H.J. v4p0388c1s
Krum, J.M. v1p0295c2s
Kuarff, R.C. v3p0473c2s
Kuba, Ludvik v5p0212c1s
v5p0395c1s
Kubel, R. v4p0056c2s
Kucera, M. v6p0131c2s
Kuchler, W. v6p0672c1s
Kuck, Helen S. v6p0332c1s
Kuczynski, R.R. v5p0459c2s
v6p0029c2s v6p0106c2s v6p0405c1s
v6p0694c2s
Kudlich, H.C. v5p0457c1s
Kuehn, Caroline B. v6p0632c1s
Kuelpe, O. v6p0005c2s
v6p0040c2s
Kuenen, A. v1p0318c1s
v1p0529c2s v1p1435c2s v2p0151c1s
Kuenen, J.P. v5p0132c1s
v5p0268c1s
Kuffer, M. v1p0979c2s
Kufferath, M. v5p0133c2s
v5p0157c2s v5p0488c1m
Kugler, Franz v1p0052c2s
Kuhe, E. v4p0226c1s
v4p0465c2s v4p0527c1s v5p0395c1s
v5p0576c1s
Kuhlman, F. v1p0174c2s
Kuhlman, L. v6p0065c2s
v6p0544c2s
Kuhlmann, C. v6p0080c2s
v6p0332c2m
Kuhlmann, F. v1p0665c1s
v1p0955c1s v6p0410c1s v6p0410c2m
Kuhn, Prof. v1p1395c1s
Kuhnast, K. v3p0469c1s
Kuhne, W. v3p0451c1s
Kuhns, L.M. v1p0229c1s
Kuhns, L.O. v4p0147c2s
v5p0275c1s v5p0400c1s v5p0439c2s
v5p0495c2s v5p0562c2s v5p0609c1s
v6p0331c1s v6p0629c2s
Kuhns, O. v5p0152c2s
v5p0646c2s v6p0013c2s v6p0238c2s
v6p0259c2s v6p0657c2s
Kuka, M.N. v6p0046c1s
Kulischer, M. v2p0251c2s
Kuma, Toshi Yasu v6p0521c2s
Kumagusu, Minakato and Dickens, F.V.
v6p0121c2s
Kummel, E.C. v3p0254c1s
Kummell, C.H. v1p1241c1s
Kunkleman, J.A. v1p0235c1s
Kunstlinger, D. v5p0596c1s
Kuntze, D. v1p1014c2s
Kunz, G.F. v2p0005c1s
v2p0016c2s v2p0073c2s v2p0117c2s
v2p0172c2s v2p0285c2m v2p0306c2s
v2p0380c1s v2p0478c2s v3p0116c2m
v3p0156c2s v3p0168c2s v3p0263c2s
v3p0275c2m v3p0276c1m v3p0280c2s
v3p0314c2m v3p0342c1m v4p0016c2s
v4p0101c2s v4p0561c2s v4p0612c2s
v5p0463c2s v5p0502c2s v5p0508c2s
v6p0173c1s v6p0216c2s v6p0249c1s
v6p0332c2m v6p0527c1s v6p0611c1s
Kunz, G.F. and Baskerville, C.
v6p0355c1s v6p0527c2s
Kunz, G.F. and Diller, J.S.
v3p0116c2s
Kunz, G.F. and Huntington, O.W.
v4p0089c1s v4p0154c2s
Kunz, G.F. and Weinschenk, E.
v4p0366c2s v4p0367c1s
Kunz, Geo.F. v6p0129c2s
Kunze, R.E. v2p0102c1s
Kunzman, J.C. v5p0306c1s
Kurino, S. v4p0107c1s
v4p0297c1s
Kurner, F.W. v1p0229c1s
Kurrelmeyer, W. v5p0056c1s
v5p0625c2s
Kurtz, B. v1p0304c1s
v1p0536c2s v1p0668c2s v1p1043c2s
Kurtz, C.M. v4p0510c2s
v5p0132c1s v5p0504c2s v6p0035c2s
v6p0086c2s
Kurtz, J.H. v1p0002c2s
v1p0681c2s v1p0777c2s v1p1200c2s
Kurz, I. v4p0228c2s
Kustermann, O. v6p0071c1s
Kuykendall, J.H. v6p0639c2s
Kuyper, A. v2p0097c2s
v3p0064c1s v3p0343c1s v4p0084c2s
v4p0424c1s
Kuyper, H.S.S. v6p0698c2s
Kyffin, A.E. v5p0344c1s
Kyle, F. v6p0044c1s
Kyle, F. and Patterson, N.
v6p0650c1s
Kyle, H.M. v5p0209c1s
Kyle, J.H. v4p0282c1s
Kyle, J.L. v6p0220c1s
Kyle, J.N. v6p0166c2s
Kyle, J.R.N. v6p0541c1s
Kyle, Joanna N. v5p0642c1s
v6p0483c2s
Kyle, M.G. v6p0562c1s
Kynaston, H. v3p0164c2s
Kynett, A.J. v1p0253c2s
Kyrke, A.V. and Kyrke, H.V.
v5p0609c2s
Kyrke, H.V. and Kyrke, A.V.
v5p0609c2s

L., A.E.H. v6p0408c1s
L., F.A. v5p0517c1s
L., R. v5p0278c2s
L., W.S. v1p0426c1s
Laader, E.T. v4p0511c2s
Labatt, C.B. v4p0131c2s
v4p0226c1s v5p0138c1s v5p0152c1s
v5p0187c2s v5p0467c1s v5p0489c2s
Labilliere, F.P. v2p0142c1s
Labouchere, H. v2p0115c2s
v2p0188c2s v2p0189c2s v2p0330c2s
v3p0114c2s v3p0368c2s v4p0237c1s
Laboulaye, E. v1p0473c2m
v1p0741c2s v1p1351c1s v1p1439c2s
Laboulaye, M. v1p0437c2s
Labrouste, L. v4p0025c1s
Laby, A. v3p0377c1s
Lac, Du v5p0218c1m
Lacaita, J.P. v1p0377c1s
v1p0670c2s
Lacassagne, A. v2p0015c1s
Lacey, H. v4p0126c1s
v4p0345c2s v4p0517c2s
Lacey, J.F. v6p0044c2s
v6p0246c1s
Lacey, T.A. and Catholicus
v4p0112c2s v4p0483c1s
Lacey, W. v1p0698c1s
Lacey, W.J. v3p0088c1s
v3p0166c2s v4p0045c2s v4p0358c2s
v4p0372c2s v4p0591c1s
Lacey-Sites, C.M. v6p0118c2s
Lach-Szyrma, W.S. v2p0016c2s
v2p0103c2s v2p0110c1s v2p0281c1s
v2p0404c2s v4p0205c2m v4p0529c2s
Lachelier, J. v1p0639c2s
Lachlan, R. v1p0718c2s
Lachlan, R.M. v1p0579c1s
Lachman, A. v6p0112c1s
Lack, B.F. v2p0322c1s
Lack, H.R. v1p0480c1s
v1p0845c2s
Lack, W. v5p0524c2s
Lackland, C.E. v2p0233c1s
v2p0283c2s
Lacombe, E.H. v1p0189c1s
v1p0203c1s v1p0316c2s v1p0361c2s
v1p0493c1s v1p0739c2s v1p0892c1s
v1p1070c2s
Lacon v3p0048c1s
v3p0382c2s
Lacon-Watson, E.H. v4p0058c2s
Lacordaire, J.B.H. v1p0937c1s
v1p1275c1s
Lacouperie, A.Terrien de . v3p0078c1s
Lacouperie, T.de v2p0030c2s
v2p0078c2s v2p0080c1m v2p0214c2s
v2p0281c2s v2p0442c2s v3p0058c2s
v3p0079c2s v3p0158c2s v3p0170c1s
v3p0309c1s
Lacroix, Dr. v1p0902c2s
v1p0924c1s
Lacroix, J.P. v1p0255c2s
v1p0266c1s v1p0402c2s v1p0426c2s
v1p0467c2s v1p0481c2s v1p0527c2s
v1p0528c2s v1p0729c1s v1p0935c2s
v1p0993c2s v1p1128c2s v1p1153c2s
v1p1160c1s v1p1200c1s v1p1200c2s
v1p1303c1s v1p1399c1s
Lacroix, Prof. v1p0427c1s
Lacy, B.F. v6p0498c2s
Lacy, B.T. v2p0232c2s
Lacy, G. v5p0068c2s
Lacy, J. v1p1300c1s
Lacy, J.F. v6p0233c1s
Lacy, J.H. v2p0252c2s
Lacy, J.H. et al. v2p0166c2s
Lacy, W.A. v6p0047c1s
Lacy, W.H.De v6p0668c1s
Ladd, B.S. v3p0277c2s
Ladd, C.R. v5p0082c2s
Ladd, C.T. v6p0136c2s
Ladd, E.F. v5p0474c1s
Ladd, E.M. v4p0608c2s
Ladd, G.T. v1p0127c2s
v1p0226c1s v1p0527c2m v1p0901c1s
v1p1174c2s v1p1303c2s v1p1304c1s
v2p0042c1s v2p0045c1s v2p0045c2s
v2p0136c1s v2p0222c2s v2p0266c2s
v2p0273c2s v2p0280c2s v2p0307c2s
v2p0319c2s v2p0371c1s v2p0481c2s
v3p0154c2s v3p0308c1s v3p0348c2s
v3p0444c2s v4p0170c2s v4p0298c1s
v4p0342c2s v4p0365c1s v4p0465c1m
v4p0606c1s v4p0635c1s v5p0286c2s
v5p0302c2s v5p0341c2s v5p0471c1s
v6p0019c2s v6p0025c1s v6p0136c1s
v6p0259c2s v6p0449c1s v6p0495c2m
v6p0518c2s v6p0522c1s v6p0540c2s
v6p0671c2s
Ladd, G.T. and Baldwin, J.M.
v4p0130c1s v4p0190c2s
Ladd, H.O. v1p0001c2s
Ladd, M. v6p0281c2s
Ladd-Franklin, C. v3p0200c2s
Ladegast, R. v5p0406c2s
v6p0251c2s v6p0554c1s v6p0710c2s
Lademan, E.G. v4p0216c2s
v4p0233c2s v4p0445c2s v4p0449c1s
Ladenburg, A. v4p0044c2s
v4p0143c2s
Ladeveze, H.de v6p0340c2s
Ladeveze, Z.de v5p0349c2s
v5p0420c2s
Ladeveze, Zelia de v6p0177c1s
Ladley, A. v1p0464c2s
Ladoff, L. v6p0593c1s
Ladreyt, M.C. v1p0066c2s
Lady, D.B. v2p0236c1s
v3p0240c1s v3p0283c1s v3p0456c2s
v4p0229c2s v4p0461c1s v4p0497c2s
v5p0463c1s v5p0488c1s v6p0419c1s
Lafarge, J. v6p0293c2s
Lafargue, P. v2p0414c1s
v4p0035c1s v5p0536c1s
Lafarque, P. v2p0334c1s
Lafenstre, G. v3p0321c1s
Laffan, B. v3p0412c1s
Laffan, M. v1p0460c2s
Laffan, Miss v1p1396c2s
Laffan, R.S.D. v6p0005c1s
v6p0586c1s
Laffan, R.S.de C. v3p0259c1s
Laffan, W.M. v1p0101c2s
v1p0169c2s v1p0197c2s v1p0340c2s
v1p0505c2s v1p0606c2s v1p1311c1s
v2p0441c1s
Laffan, W.M. and Strahan, E.
v1p1311c1m
Laffineur, J. v1p1110c2s
Laflear, E. v1p0301c1s
Lafler, Henry A. v6p0567c2s
Lafleur, E. v5p0362c2s
Lafleur, P.F. v3p0031c2s
Lafleur, P.T. v3p0162c1s
v3p0351c1s v4p0215c1s v4p0268c2s
v4p0324c2s v5p0041c2s v5p0326c2s
v5p0416c2s v5p0470c2s v5p0528c1s
v6p0127c2s v6p0172c2s v6p0184c1s
v6p0390c1s v6p0504c2s v6p0586c2s
v6p0657c1s
Lafonde, E. v1p0039c1s
Lafonde, M. v1p0526c1s
Lafontaine, H. v5p0486c2s
Lagarde, M.L.Denio de ... v1p1229c2s
Lagarde, P.de v1p0069c2s
v1p0681c1s
Lagardie, H.de v1p0489c2s
Lagden, G.Y. v1p0192c1s
v2p0101c2s
Lagerlof, S. v5p0216c1s
v5p0257c2s v5p0299c2s v5p0425c1s
Lagerlof, Selma v5p0152c1s
v5p0169c2s
Lagerquist, C. v5p0393c2s
Lagrange, Abbe v1p0981c1s
Lagrange, E. v2p0026c1m
v2p0478c1s
Lagrange, F. v3p0076c1s
v3p0146c2s v4p0441c1s
Laguna, F.De v4p0009c2s
v6p0092c2s
Laguna, T.de v5p0122c2s
v6p0211c2m v6p0215c1s
Laharpe, J.H.de v2p0425c2s
Lahee, H.C. v5p0114c1s
v5p0231c1s v5p0343c1s v5p0423c2m
v5p0465c2s v5p0530c2m v6p0438c1s
Lahm, F.P. v6p0048c2s
Lahnier, E.W. v5p0309c2s
Lahnow, C. v6p0599c2s
Laicus v6p0556c1s
Laidlaw, A. v3p0293c1s
v5p0003c1m v5p0167c1s v5p0167c2s
Laidlaw, F.A. v1p1128c1s
v3p0334c2s
Laidlaw, G.E. v5p0270c2s
v5p0463c2s v6p0006c2s
Laidlaw, J. v2p0293c2s
v2p0437c2s v4p0573c1s v5p0497c2s
Laidlaw, P. v5p0632c2s
Laidlaw, R. v1p0930c2s
Laidlaw, W. v3p0058c1s
v5p0118c1s
Laidley, T.T.S. v1p0246c2s
v1p0562c2s
Laine, J.M. v5p0435c1s
Laing, Dr. v1p0557c1s
Laing, G. v6p0348c2s
v6p0363c1s
Laing, G. and Davitt, M. . v2p0227c1s
Laing, G.J. v5p0425c2s
Laing, J. v2p0450c1s
v4p0457c1s v4p0508c2s v6p0032c2s
Laing, J.M. v4p0582c2s
Laing, J.W. v4p0035c2s
v4p0413c2s
Laing, J.W. and Bolton, W.W.
v4p0600c1s v5p0607c2s
Laing, M. v1p0737c2s
Laing, M.E. v4p0103c1s
v5p0293c1s
Laing, R. v1p1120c2m
Laing, S. v1p0159c2s
v1p0356c1s v1p0546c1s v1p0631c1s
v1p1331c2s v2p0179c2s v2p0226c2s
v2p0227c1s v2p0362c1s v2p0363c1s
v2p0380c2s v2p0390c1s v2p0440c1s
v3p0019c2s v3p0052c2s v3p0221c2s
v3p0276c1s v4p0564c2s
Laing, S.H. v5p0561c2s
Laing-Meason v2p0190c1s
Laird, A. v1p0664c1s
Laird, H.P. v1p0793c1s
v1p1136c1s v2p0104c1s v3p0042c1s
v4p0055c1m v4p0172c2s
Laird, J. v4p0391c1s
Laird, S.B. v5p0265c1s
Laird, W.H. v4p0565c1s
Laird, W.P. v4p0024c2s
v4p0438c1s v6p0028c2m
Laisant, M. v5p0107c1s
v5p0366c1s
Laise, A.M. v5p0253c1s
Laist, T.F. v3p0278c1s
v3p0286c2s v3p0289c2s v3p0292c1s
v3p0309c1s v3p0367c2s v3p0448c2s
Laith, A. v4p0527c1s
Lake, B. v4p0134c2s
Lake, C.S. v6p0157c2s
v6p0382c1s
Lake, E. v1p0060c2s
v1p0614c1m
Lake, H. v1p0108c1s
v1p0400c2s v1p0420c1s v1p0837c1s
v1p0882c1s v2p0161c2s v2p0166c2s
v4p0304c1s
Lake, Helen M. v6p0437c2s
Lake, J.J. v1p0376c2s
Lake, K. v6p0061c1s
v6p0063c2m
Lake, K.A. and Harris, W.J.
v6p0271c2s
Lake, Kirsopp v6p0571c2s
Lake, P. v4p0172c2s
v4p0223c1s v4p0498c1s v4p0584c1s
v5p0373c1s
Lake, S. v5p0027c2s
Lake, S. and Baker, R.S. . v5p0027c2s
Lake, T. v5p0461c2s
Lake, W.C. v1p0240c2s
v1p0682c1s v1p0704c1s v1p0861c2s
v1p1124c1s v4p0419c2s v4p0494c2s
Lakes, A. v2p0119c1s
v4p0125c1s v4p0230c2s v4p0402c1s
v4p0631c1s
Laking, G.F. v5p0084c1s
v6p0030c2m v6p0455c2s v6p0684c1s
v6p0700c2s
Lala, R.R. v5p0174c1s
v5p0443c2s v5p0444c1s v5p0444c2m
v5p0445c2s v5p0542c2s
Lala, R.R. et al. v5p0446c1s
Lalanne, M. v2p0329c1s
Lally, Comte de v4p0211c2s
Lalor, J. v1p0390c2s
Lalor, J.J. v1p0218c1s
v1p0346c1s v1p0434c2s v1p0513c1s
v1p0565c1s v1p0745c1s v1p0814c1s
v1p1400c1s v4p0144c1s
Lalor, M.J. v1p0045c1s
v1p0051c2s
Lalor, M.P. v4p0316c2s
Lamaison, L. v4p0148c1s
v4p0591c2s
Lamantia, V. v3p0414c2s
Lamar, C.P. v4p0276c2s
v5p0390c2s v5p0547c1s
Lamar, J.S. v1p0240c2s
v1p0247c1s v1p0806c2s v1p0905c2s
v1p1093c2s v1p1119c2s v1p1121c1s
v1p1211c2s v2p0357c2s
Lamarck, J.B.P.A. v3p0145c2s
Lamarle, M. v1p1321c2s
Lamarque, J.de v1p0979c2s
Lamartine, A. v1p1111c2s
v1p1114c1s
Lamartine, A.de v1p0301c2s
v1p0476c1s v1p1243c1s v1p1361c1s
Lamaster, W.H. v4p0034c1s
v4p0252c2s
Lamb, A. v1p0146c2s
Lamb, A., jr. v1p0387c2s
Lamb, A.M. v2p0250c2s
Lamb, B.W. v6p0677c1s
Lamb, C. v1p0005c1m
v1p0035c1s v1p0098c1s v1p0108c2s
v1p0111c2s v1p0140c2s v1p0228c2s
v1p0231c1s v1p0234c2s v1p0238c2s
v1p0296c1s v1p0304c2s v1p0364c2s
v1p0365c2s v1p0368c1s v1p0374c2s
v1p0497c2s v1p0505c2s v1p0539c1s
v1p0563c2s v1p0601c2s v1p0604c1s
v1p0675c1s v1p0691c1s v1p0711c2s
v1p0739c1s v1p0784c1s v1p0800c1s
v1p0803c2s v1p0887c1s v1p0888c2s
v1p0908c2m v1p0953c2s v1p0982c1s
v1p1010c2s v1p1032c1s v1p1069c2s
v1p1085c1s v1p1109c1s v1p1111c1s
v1p1159c2s v1p1187c1s v1p1195c2s
v1p1226c2s v1p1227c1s v1p1293c2s
v1p1336c1s v1p1361c1s v1p1396c1s
v1p1405c2s v1p1417c2s v1p1430c1s
Lamb, C.R. v5p0388c1s
v5p0391c1s v5p0548c1s v6p0128c2s
Lamb, C.R. and Ferree, B.. v5p0467c2s
Lamb, D. and Merril, T.A.. v1p0846c1s
Lamb, D.S. v5p0384c1s
v5p0391c1s v6p0023c2s
Lamb, E.B. v1p0053c2s

Lamb, F.H. v5p0580c1s v6p0389c2s v6p0647c1s
Lamb, F.J. v5p0307c1s v6p0420c2s
Lamb, F.S. v5p0391c1m v6p0027c2s v6p0128c1s v6p0171c2s v6p0216c2s v6p0258c2s v6p0262c2s v6p0358c2s v6p0431c1s v6p0613c1s v6p0688c2s v6p0700c1s
Lamb, F.S. and Hamlin, A.D.F. v5p0025c2s
Lamb, H. v6p0406c1s
Lamb, H.L. v1p1153c2s
Lamb, H.M. v5p0077c1m
Lamb, J. v5p0013c1s
Lamb, L.A. v3p0303c2s v3p0413c2s v5p0447c2s
Lamb, L.A.F. v5p0448c2s
Lamb, L.M.C. v1p0790c1s
Lamb, Lady v1p1220c2s v2p0085c2s
Lamb, M.J. v1p0172c1s v1p0269c2s v1p0779c2s v1p0908c2s v1p0916c2s v1p0917c1s v1p1019c2s v1p1389c1s v2p0006c2s v2p0031c2s v2p0036c1s v2p0037c2s v2p0049c1s v2p0049c2s v2p0055c2s v2p0056c1s v2p0057c2s v2p0062c1s v2p0062c2s v2p0064c1s v2p0070c1s v2p0082c2s v2p0088c1s v2p0089c2m v2p0090c1s v2p0106c1s v2p0113c1m v2p0118c1s v2p0122c1s v2p0139c1s v2p0139c2s v2p0154c2s v2p0158c1s v2p0167c2s v2p0171c1s v2p0177c1s v2p0178c2s v2p0183c1s v2p0191c1s v2p0195c2s v2p0209c2s v2p0221c2s v2p0234c2s v2p0238c1s v2p0243c1m v2p0246c1s v2p0249c1s v2p0249c2s v2p0258c1s v2p0261c2m v2p0266c2s v2p0270c1m v2p0270c2s v2p0276c2s v2p0278c1m v2p0279c1s v2p0283c2s v2p0288c1s v2p0298c2s v2p0310c1s v2p0313c2m v2p0319c2s v2p0323c1s v2p0332c2s v2p0341c2s v2p0342c1s v2p0382c1s v2p0391c2s v2p0400c1s v2p0412c2s v2p0457c2m v2p0469c2s v2p0474c2m v2p0475c1s v2p0476c1s v2p0482c1s v3p0158c1s
Lamb, M.J., Mrs. v2p0069c2s v2p0313c2s v2p0342c1s v2p0353c1s v2p0373c2s v2p0423c1s v2p0436c2s v2p0441c1s v2p0452c1s v2p0465c1m v2p0481c1s v3p0010c2m v3p0011c1s v3p0013c2s v3p0034c1m v3p0037c1s v3p0056c2s v3p0058c1s v3p0066c1s v3p0069c1s v3p0093c2m v3p0106c2s v3p0125c1s v3p0134c1s v3p0142c1s v3p0197c1s v3p0224c1s v3p0240c1s v3p0244c1s v3p0262c1s v3p0268c1s v3p0271c2s v3p0285c1s v3p0292c1s v3p0304c1m v3p0304c2s v3p0321c1s v3p0329c1s v3p0333c2s v3p0352c2s v3p0379c1s v3p0386c2s v3p0390c1s v3p0402c1s v3p0402c2s v3p0409c2s v3p0453c1s v3p0455c1s v3p0455c2m v3p0456c1m v3p0459c1s v3p0462c2s v4p0119c2s v4p0126c1s v4p0254c2s v4p0310c1s v4p0547c2s v4p0585c1s v4p0609c2s v4p0617c1s v4p0620c1s
Lamb, R. v2p0077c2s v2p0428c2s v3p0255c1s v3p0458c1s
Lamb, W. v4p0200c2s
Lambart, W. v1p0812c2s
Lambdin, A.C. v1p0515c1s v2p0038c2s v2p0144c2s v2p0338c2m v2p0370c1s
Lambec, E. v4p0551c1s
Lamber, J. v1p0479c2s
Lambert, A. v1p0462c2m v2p0078c1s v2p0254c1m v2p0394c1s v4p0574c1s v5p0077c2s v5p0108c1s v6p0548c1s
Lambert, Agnes v2p0375c1s v2p0387c1s v3p0287c2s v3p0376c1s
Lambert, B. v1p0024c1s v1p0218c2s v2p0008c2s v2p0325c1s
Lambert, B. and Mearns, A. v2p0264c1s
Lambert, E. v3p0141c1s v3p0228c2s v5p0449c1s
Lambert, G. v1p0027c1s v1p0950c1s v1p1149c1s v1p1196c1s v2p0041c1s v2p0270c2s v2p0406c1s v3p0155c2s v4p0198c2s v5p0402c2s v5p0505c1s
Lambert, G.T. v6p0271c2s v6p0327c2s
Lambert, H. v4p0117c1s v4p0209c1s v6p0443c2s
Lambert, J., Sir v3p0321c2s
Lambert, J.L. v4p0038c2s
Lambert, L. v4p0423c2s
Lambert, L.V. v5p0055c1s v6p0085c2s
Lambert, Lillian V. v6p0034c2s
Lambert, M. v4p0090c1s
Lambert, W.A. v5p0266c1s v5p0369c1s v6p0040c2s
Lambert, W.H. v6p0378c1s
Lambert-Playfair, R., Sir. v5p0012c1s v5p0080c1s v5p0521c2s v5p0538c2s
Lamberton, N.A. v2p0021c1s
Lambertson, G.M. v2p0219c1s
Lambing, A.A. v3p0058c1s v4p0504c2s
Lamborn, R.C.H. v3p0108c2s
Lamborn, R.H. v1p0855c1s v1p1271c1s v2p0287c1s v3p0277c1s v3p0421c2s v4p0336c1s
Lambre, E. v4p0277c1s
Lambrith, Walker R. v6p0080c1s
Lambros, S. v2p0103c1s v3p0183c2s v6p0273c1s
Lambros, S.P. v2p0027c1m v2p0191c1m v2p0206c2s v3p0025c2m v3p0184c2m v3p0248c2s v3p0377c1s v4p0241c2m v4p0308c1s v5p0036c2s v5p0249c2m v5p0452c1s
Laming, R. v1p0398c2s
Lamington, Lord v2p0006c1s v2p0015c2s v2p0377c2s v3p0068c2s v3p0069c2s v3p0135c1s v3p0432c2s v4p0040c1s v4p0283c1s
Lamm, E. v1p0035c1s
Lamm, E.N. v5p0336c2s
Lamon, E. v2p0012c2s
Lamond, Eliz. v3p0138c2s v3p0406c1s
Lamond, R. v6p0171c2s
Lamont, A. v2p0195c2s v3p0045c2s v3p0057c1s v3p0077c1s v3p0157c2s v3p0198c2s v3p0272c1s v3p0335c2s v3p0425c1s v3p0446c2s v4p0103c2s v4p0227c2s v4p0491c2s v4p0614c2s v5p0083c1s v5p0294c1s v5p0474c2s v5p0596c2s
Lamont, Dr. v1p0787c1s
Lamont, E.M. v1p1167c2s
Lamont, E.N. v1p0770c1s v1p0940c2s
Lamont, H. v5p0040c2s v6p0014c2s v6p0019c2s v6p0038c2s v6p0051c2s v6p0076c1s v6p0081c1s v6p0086c1s v6p0109c1s v6p0131c1s v6p0135c2m v6p0137c1m v6p0137c2s v6p0144c2s v6p0145c2s v6p0156c1s v6p0171c1s v6p0177c1s v6p0178c2s v6p0187c2s v6p0200c2m v6p0207c1m v6p0262c1s v6p0263c2s v6p0285c2s v6p0291c1s v6p0296c1m v6p0305c1s v6p0346c2s v6p0355c1s v6p0364c2s v6p0419c2s v6p0425c1s v6p0443c1s v6p0450c1s v6p0455c2s v6p0456c1s v6p0464c1m v6p0473c2s v6p0476c2s v6p0507c1s v6p0508c1m v6p0511c1m v6p0517c2s v6p0528c2s v6p0534c2s v6p0535c1s v6p0547c2s v6p0550c1s v6p0601c2s v6p0613c1s v6p0617c2s v6p0626c2s v6p0632c1s v6p0635c2s v6p0653c2s v6p0660c1s v6p0677c2s v6p0684c1s v6p0712c1s
Lamont, Hammond v6p0098c2s v6p0116c2s v6p0553c1s
Lamont, R. v2p0424c2s
Lamoroux, W. v1p0482c1s v1p1126c1s
Lamoureaux, A.J. v6p0426c1s v6p0605c2s v6p0606c1s
Lampakes.G. v3p0017c2s
Lampe, J.J. v4p0056c1s
Lampertico, F. and Panzacchi, E. v4p0269c1s v4p0355c1s
Lamphear, O.T. v1p1140c1m v1p1292c2s
Lamplugh, G.W. v2p0179c1s v3p0079c2s v6p0082c2s
Lampman, A. v3p0397c1s v4p0107c1s v4p0247c2s v4p0306c2s v5p0325c2s v5p0571c2s
Lampman, Archibald v4p0436c2s v4p0610c1s
Lampman, C. v6p0665c2s
Lamport, W.J. v1p0739c2s v1p0907c1s v1p0925c1s v1p0975c1s v1p0975c2s v1p1018c1s
Lampson, O.L. v6p0045c2s
Lampton, F.C. v5p0413c1s
Lampton, W.J. v4p0578c1s v4p0618c2s v5p0276c1s v5p0341c1s v5p0519c2s v6p0432c1s v6p0657c2s
Lamson, A. v1p0004c1s v1p0034c2s v1p0047c1s v1p0048c1s v1p0057c1s v1p0058c1s v1p0061c1s v1p0085c2s v1p0116c1s v1p0118c1s v1p0125c2s v1p0127c2s v1p0178c2s v1p0205c2s v1p0222c1s v1p0238c2s v1p0239c2s v1p0242c2s v1p0243c1s v1p0244c2s v1p0254c1m v1p0254c2s v1p0263c2s v1p0313c2s v1p0348c1s v1p0378c2s v1p0414c1s v1p0431c2m v1p0450c1s v1p0603c1s v1p0620c1s v1p0667c1s v1p0681c2s v1p0700c2s v1p0805c2s v1p0809c1s v1p0876c1s v1p0903c1s v1p0946c2s v1p0948c1s v1p0957c2s v1p0985c2s v1p1019c2m v1p1029c2s v1p1066c2s v1p1067c2s v1p1096c2s v1p1190c1s v1p1262c1s v1p1282c2s v1p1286c2s v1p1287c1s v1p1301c2s v1p1304c1s v1p1309c1s v1p1324c1s v1p1325c2s v1p1326c1s v1p1341c1s v1p1357c2s v1p1394c1s v1p1404c2s v1p1430c2s v1p1432c2s
Lamson, C.M. v4p0632c1s v6p0602c1s
Lamson, D.F. v3p0087c2s v3p0194c2s v3p0300c2s v3p0415c2s v3p0420c1s
Lamson, E.R. v5p0508c1s
Lamson, F.L. v6p0012c1s
Lamson, H. v1p0237c2s v1p0846c2s
Lamson, W.O. v2p0129c1s v2p0133c1s
Lamy, T.J. v1p0238c2s v1p0377c2s v1p0554c1s v2p0145c1s
Lanagan, J. v3p0311c1s
Lancaster, A. v5p0334c1m
Lancaster, A.B.M. v2p0265c2s
Lancaster, A.E. v1p0363c1s v1p0468c2s v1p1369c2s v5p0016c2s
Lancaster, E.G. v5p0004c1s
Lancaster, E.R. v1p0212c1s
Lancaster, F.H. v6p0217c1s v6p0599c2s
Lancaster, G. v2p0328c1s
Lancaster, G.B. v6p0079c2s v6p0286c2s v6p0291c2s v6p0311c1m v6p0380c2s v6p0619c2s
Lancaster, H.B. v4p0522c1s
Lancaster, H.C. v6p0208c2s
Lancaster, H.H. v1p0329c2s v1p0485c1s v1p0512c1s v1p0782c1s v1p0907c2s v1p1133c1s v1p1166c2s v1p1170c2s v1p1298c1s
Lancaster, I. v2p0015c2s v2p0047c1m v2p0157c2s v2p0168c2s v3p0045c2s v4p0060c2s
Lancaster, J. v1p0563c1s
Lancaster, M.A. v5p0561c1s
Lancaster, W.P. v1p0450c1s v1p0963c1m
Lancaster-Woodburne, G.B.. v3p0182c2s v4p0215c2s
Lance, W.W. v4p0113c2s v6p0540c2s
Lancefield, R.T. v5p0180c1s
Lancey, E.F.de v1p0023c2s v1p1389c1s v4p0015c2s v4p0125c2s v4p0223c1s
Lancey, Lady De v6p0688c2s
Lanciani, R. v2p0016c1m v2p0147c2s v2p0377c1m v2p0377c2m v2p0442c1s v2p0459c2m v3p0017c1s v3p0070c1s v3p0366c1s v3p0366c2m v4p0122c2s v4p0397c2s v4p0415c2s v4p0424c1s v4p0490c1m v5p0181c1s v5p0495c2m v6p0415c1s v6p0549c1m v6p0549c2m v6p0642c1s
Lanciani, Rodolfo v6p0138c2s
Land, F.De v4p0116c1s v6p0637c1s
Land, J.P.N. v1p0510c1s v1p0760c2s v1p1000c2s v1p1228c1s v1p1236c2s v3p0168c2s
Landa, M.J. v6p0202c2s v6p0308c2s v6p0355c1s
Landeau, J. v1p0785c2s
Landelle, G.de la v1p0728c1s
Landels, W. v1p0565c2s v1p1203c2s v1p1260c2s v2p0105c2s
Lander, B. v6p0508c2s
Lander, E.N. v1p0751c2s
Lander, E.T. v1p0066c1s v1p1423c1s v3p0266c1s v6p0292c1s
Lander, H. v4p0158c1s v5p0260c1s v5p0631c1s
Lander, Louise v5p0073c2s
Lander, M. v1p1426c2s
Lander-Brunton, T. v4p0454c2s
Landerer, M. v1p1332c1s
Landero, C.F.de v3p0185c2s
Landers, J. v2p0098c2s v3p0311c2s
Landers, W.T. v6p0442c2s
Landes, R.W. v1p0527c2s
Landesberger, J. v4p0525c1s
Landesco, A.A. v6p0200c2s v6p0343c2s
Landeveze, Q.de v6p0678c1s
Landfield, J.B. v5p0502c2s
Landfield, J.B., jr. and Purington, C.W. v5p0501c2s v6p0260c2s
Landis, A. v6p0321c2s
Landis, C.K. v1p1372c1s
Landis, E.B. v4p0134c1s v5p0212c2s v5p0319c2m
Landis, H.K. v4p0314c2s v4p0431c2s
Landis, H.R.M. v6p0660c2s
Landis, R.W. v1p0192c1s v1p0626c2s v1p0700c1s v1p1091c1s
Landman, I. v6p0564c2s
Landman, J. v6p0049c2s v6p0629c2s
Landon, C.W. v4p0389c1s v4p0389c2s
Landon, J.S. v6p0498c1s
Landon, L.E. v1p0160c2s v1p0222c2s v1p0491c1s v1p0584c1s

v1p0584c2s v1p0774c1s v1p0837c2s v1p1168c2s
Landon, P. v5p0081c2s v5p0426c1s v6p0019c2s v6p0383c1s v6p0394c2s v6p0473c2s v6p0654c2s v6p0655c1s
Landon, Perceval v6p0645c2s
Landon, W.H. v4p0053c1s
Landor, A.H.S. v4p0522c2s v5p0284c2s v5p0579c2s v6p0018c1s
Landor, A.H.Savage v4p0105c2s v4p0134c1s v4p0297c1s v6p0493c1s
Landor, C. v1p0205c2s v1p0923c1s v1p0968c1s v1p1336c1s
Landor, E.T. v1p0674c1s
Landor, W. v1p1050c1s v1p1326c2s v1p1337c2s
Landor, W.S. v1p0458c2s v1p0625c1s v1p0896c1s v1p0949c2s v1p1226c1s v2p0202c1s
Landreth, B. v4p0316c1s v4p0494c2s v4p0592c1s v5p0329c2s
Landriot, P. v1p0608c1s
Landsberger, H. v4p0079c1s
Landsdell, H. v2p0242c2s v2p0431c1s
Landseer, J. v1p0084c1s v1p0503c2s
Lane, A.C. v2p0174c1s v3p0169c2s v3p0313c1s v4p0165c2s v5p0198c1s v5p0230c1s v6p0202c2s v6p0413c2s v6p0444c1s v6p0690c1s
Lane, A.E. v6p0018c2s v6p0158c1s v6p0208c1s v6p0209c1s v6p0216c2s v6p0466c2s v6p0638c1s v6p0704c2s
Lane, B.W. v6p0402c2s
Lane, C.A. v5p0404c2s
Lane, C.B. v6p0090c1s v6p0318c2s v6p0417c1s
Lane, C.C. v6p0291c2s
Lane, C.D. v4p0526c1s
Lane, C.R. v2p0038c2s v2p0116c1s v2p0180c2s v2p0205c2s v2p0297c1s v2p0359c2s v2p0367c2s v2p0474c1s v3p0026c1s v3p0083c2s v4p0301c2s
Lane, C.S. v3p0446c1s
Lane, D. v2p0172c1s v2p0260c2s v3p0021c1s
Lane, E.E. v4p0587c2s
Lane, E.J. v1p0723c1s
Lane, E.N. and Farrar, I.F. v5p0069c2s v5p0334c2s
Lane, Elinor M. v6p0012c2s
Lane, F.K. v5p0088c1s
Lane, F.T. v5p0505c1s
Lane, G.M. v1p0262c2s v1p0506c1s v1p0727c1s v1p0727c2s v1p1017c1s v1p1177c1s v1p1212c2s v1p1293c2s v1p1357c1s
Lane, G.W. v1p0695c1s
Lane, J. v6p0129c2s
Lane, J., Mrs. v6p0008c1s v6p0352c2s v6p0584c2s v6p0602c2s v6p0631c2s v6p0649c2s
Lane, J.H. v1p0398c2s v1p0399c1s v1p0557c2s v1p0723c1s v1p0825c2s v1p1003c2s v1p1240c1s v1p1269c1s v2p0453c1s v3p0095c2s v3p0154c1s v3p0231c2s v3p0307c1s
Lane, J.H. and Walton, J.B. v1p0518c2s
Lane, J.P. v1p0946c2s v3p0242c1s
Lane, J.W. v6p0279c1s
Lane, John, Mrs. v5p0519c1s
Lane, L.M. and Leuffman, C.B. v4p0094c2s
Lane, L.P. v5p0604c1s
Lane, Laura M. v4p0212c2s
Lane, M.A. v6p0060c1s v6p0185c2s v6p0187c2s v6p0397c1s v6p0397c2s v6p0502c1s v6p0600c2s v6p0602c1s v6p0609c2s v6p0685c1s v6p0702c2s
Lane, M.G. v2p0194c1s
Lane, M.M. v6p0376c1s
Lane, R.A. v4p0438c2s
Lane, R.H. v6p0262c1s
Lane, Stella, Mrs. v6p0290c1s
Lane, T.W. v1p0570c2s v1p1054c1s
Lane, W.A. v6p0659c1s
Lane, W.B. v3p0059c1s v3p0276c2s v4p0216c2s v4p0270c1s v4p0368c1s v4p0592c1s v4p0602c2s
Lane, W.C. v2p0025c2s v2p0152c1s v2p0256c1s v3p0070c1m v4p0092c1s v4p0249c1s v5p0133c1s v5p0479c2s v6p0065c2m v6p0273c2s v6p0282c1s v6p0371c2s v6p0373c1s
Lane, W.C. and Cutter, C.A. v2p0256c1s
Lane, W.C. and Tillinghast, W.H. v5p0633c1m
Lane, Wm.C. v5p0257c1s
Lane-Fox, F. v3p0313c1s
Lane-Poole, S. v2p0343c1s v2p0400c1s v3p0034c1s v3p0082c2s v3p0101c2s v3p0333c1s v4p0082c2s v4p0105c1s v4p0366c2s v4p0503c1s v4p0552c1s v5p0181c1s v5p0305c1s v5p0505c1s v5p0538c1s
Lane-Poole, S. and Kropf, L.L. v5p0381c2s
Lang, A. v1p0066c2s v1p0132c2s v1p0139c1s v1p0168c2s v1p0171c2s v1p0202c1s v1p0394c2s v1p0450c1s v1p0503c1s v1p0553c2s v1p0600c1s v1p0782c2s v1p0879c2s v1p0881c1s v1p0890c2s v1p0891c1s v1p0907c1m v1p0953c2s v1p0992c2s v1p1123c1s v1p1313c1s v1p1371c2s v2p0022c1s v2p0026c2s v2p0036c2s v2p0052c1m v2p0058c1s v2p0107c1m v2p0114c1s v2p0133c2s v2p0152c2s v2p0155c1s v2p0162c2m v2p0169c2s v2p0178c1s v2p0196c2s v2p0208c1s v2p0215c2s v2p0216c2s v2p0229c1s v2p0240c1s v2p0249c1s v2p0260c1s v2p0299c1s v2p0304c2s v2p0305c1s v2p0310c1s v2p0346c1s v2p0369c1s v2p0406c1s v2p0429c1s v2p0483c1s v3p0025c1s v3p0038c1s v3p0047c2s v3p0049c1s v3p0049c2s v3p0057c1s v3p0057c2s v3p0087c2s v3p0092c1s v3p0105c2s v3p0114c2s v3p0117c1s v3p0119c2s v3p0124c1s v3p0152c1s v3p0172c1s v3p0184c2s v3p0187c2s v3p0195c1s v3p0199c2s v3p0228c1s v3p0234c1s v3p0252c2s v3p0260c2s v3p0269c1s v3p0284c2s v3p0289c2s v3p0295c1m v3p0311c2s v3p0332c1s v3p0333c2s v3p0335c1s v3p0355c1s v3p0357c2s v3p0358c2s v3p0360c1s v3p0362c1s v3p0365c2s v3p0366c1s v3p0372c1s v3p0376c1s v3p0387c1s v3p0387c2s v3p0388c1s v3p0388c2s v3p0426c1m v3p0439c1s v3p0441c1s v4p0008c2s v4p0016c1s v4p0030c2s v4p0042c2m v4p0062c2s v4p0084c2s v4p0122c1s v4p0140c2s v4p0156c1s v4p0178c1m v4p0178c2s v4p0179c2s v4p0182c2s v4p0193c2s v4p0198c1s v4p0200c1s v4p0205c1m v4p0211c2s v4p0225c2m v4p0231c2s v4p0262c1m v4p0271c1s v4p0303c1m v4p0306c2s v4p0346c1s v4p0346c2s v4p0355c2s v4p0356c1s v4p0383c1s v4p0408c1s v4p0413c2s v4p0425c1s v4p0434c2s v4p0438c2s v4p0464c1m v4p0469c1s v4p0487c2s v4p0508c2s v4p0518c2s v4p0519c1s v4p0541c1s v4p0549c2s v4p0551c2s v4p0558c1s v4p0571c2s v4p0617c1s v4p0624c2m v5p0016c1s v5p0036c1s v5p0039c1s v5p0039c2s v5p0043c2s v5p0051c1s v5p0071c1s v5p0084c1s v5p0096c1s v5p0099c1m v5p0105c2s v5p0107c1s v5p0134c1s v5p0143c1m v5p0146c2s v5p0149c1s v5p0156c1s v5p0161c1s v5p0166c2m v5p0187c1s v5p0202c1s v5p0205c2s v5p0209c1s v5p0219c2s v5p0225c1s v5p0232c2s v5p0235c2s v5p0236c1s v5p0237c1s v5p0239c1s v5p0241c1s v5p0252c2s v5p0266c2s v5p0290c2s v5p0293c1s v5p0294c1s v5p0298c2s v5p0305c2s v5p0315c1s v5p0340c2s v5p0341c1m v5p0347c2s v5p0352c2m v5p0358c2s v5p0362c2m v5p0364c2s v5p0390c2s v5p0392c1s v5p0392c2s v5p0420c1s v5p0422c1s v5p0475c2s v5p0482c1s v5p0483c2s v5p0515c1s v5p0515c2s v5p0546c1s v5p0573c1s v5p0581c1s v5p0583c2m v6p0013c1s v6p0013c2s v6p0040c2s v6p0048c2m v6p0065c2s v6p0074c1s v6p0074c2s v6p0080c2s v6p0095c1s v6p0099c1s v6p0101c1s v6p0101c2m v6p0158c1s v6p0173c1m v6p0173c2s v6p0182c1s v6p0209c2s v6p0210c2s v6p0219c1s v6p0241c1s v6p0243c2s v6p0259c2s v6p0263c1m v6p0273c2s v6p0283c1m v6p0286c1s v6p0295c1s v6p0295c2s v6p0312c1s v6p0318c1s v6p0353c2s v6p0379c2s v6p0404c1m v6p0440c2s v6p0463c2s v6p0471c1s v6p0490c1s v6p0505c2s v6p0521c1s v6p0547c1s v6p0563c1s v6p0577c2s v6p0578c1s v6p0586c2m v6p0608c2s v6p0623c1s v6p0637c1s v6p0640c2s v6p0650c2s v6p0657c1s v6p0662c1s v6p0662c2s
Lang, A. and Abbey, E.A. . v3p0388c1m v4p0517c1s v4p0518c1s v4p0519c1m
Lang, A. and Atkinson, A.S. v3p0107c2s
Lang, A. and Atkinson, E.G. v5p0364c2s
Lang, A. and Blouet, P. .. v3p0010c2s
Lang, A. and Brown, R., jr. v2p0196c2s
Lang, A. and Cox, G.W. ... v2p0304c2s v3p0013c2s
Lang, A. and Haggard, H.R. v3p0472c2s
Lang, A. and Marett, R.R.. v5p0483c2s
Lang, A. and Taylor, I.M.. v2p0108c2s
Lang, A. and X, a working man v5p0480c1s
Lang, A. et al. v2p0249c1s v3p0106c1s
Lang, A., Mrs. v2p0383c2s v3p0062c2s v3p0361c1s v3p0368c1s
Lang, Andrew v3p0049c2s v3p0056c1s v4p0039c2s v4p0067c2s v4p0097c2s v4p0295c2s v4p0469c1s v5p0012c2s v5p0192c2s v6p0041c2s v6p0353c2s
Lang, Andrew and Mason, A.E.W. v5p0433c2s
Lang, B.J. v4p0388c1s
Lang, C.G. v4p0511c1s v5p0483c1s v6p0478c2s
Lang, H. v1p0701c2s
Lang, H.R. v2p0413c1s v3p0062c2s v3p0242c2s v4p0453c2s
Lang, J. v6p0415c2s
Lang, J.M. v2p0148c1s v2p0197c2s v2p0371c2s v2p0451c2s v3p0174c2s v4p0112c1s v4p0314c2s
Lang, L.B. v4p0221c2s v4p0373c1s v4p0387c1s v4p0603c1s v5p0172c2s v5p0533c1s v5p0557c2s v5p0601c2s v5p0636c1s
Lang, L.L. v5p0149c1s v5p0420c2s v5p0575c2s
Lang, Leonora B. v3p0021c2s
Lang, Ossian v6p0281c1s
Lang, Ossian and Gayley, C.M. v6p0193c2s
Lang, R.H. v1p0080c2s v1p0151c1s v1p0328c1s v1p0328c2s v1p1332c2s v2p0134c2s v3p0108c2s v5p0594c2s v6p0163c1s
Lang, R.H., Sir v6p0163c1s
Lang, R.T. v5p0332c1s v5p0635c1s
Lang, R.von v1p0491c1s
Lang, S.E. v5p0241c2s
Lang, W.H. v5p0013c2s v6p0427c2s
Langbridge, F. v2p0251c2s v2p0395c2s v3p0047c2s v4p0458c1s v5p0153c1s v5p0213c1s v5p0524c1s v6p0259c1s
Langdale, A. v1p0706c2s
Langdell, C.C. v6p0147c2s v6p0411c2s v6p0460c1s
Langdon-Davis, B.N. v5p0434c2s v6p0462c1s
Langdon, D.W. v2p0435c2s
Langdon, D.W., jr. v3p0281c2s
Langdon, F.W. v3p0265c2s
Langdon, H.H. v6p0075c2s
Langdon, M. v4p0581c2s
Langdon, P. v6p0685c2s
Langdon, S. v6p0103c1s
Langdon, Sherman v6p0437c2s
Langdon, W.C. v1p0572c2s v1p0670c2s v1p0673c1s v1p1105c2s v2p0085c1s v2p0085c2s v2p0231c2m v2p0328c2s v2p0377c2s v3p0067c2s v3p0191c1s v3p0238c2s v3p0280c2s v3p0319c1s v3p0360c2s v3p0399c2s v3p0449c1s v5p0434c1s v6p0129c1s v6p0348c2s
Langdon, W.E. v6p0198c2s
Langdon, A.G. v3p0099c2s v3p0106c2s v4p0134c2m v4p0411c1s v5p0145c2s v5p0596c2s v6p0150c2s
Lange, A.F. v6p0128c1s v6p0207c1s v6p0210c1s v6p0389c1s v6p0572c1s v6p0671c1s v6p0672c1s
Lange, A.F.M. v4p0051c2s v4p0554c1s
Lange, C.L. v5p0412c2s
Lange, D.A. v3p0414c1s
Lange, H.O. v6p0373c1s
Lange, J.P. v1p0038c2s v1p0581c1s
Lange, J.P. and Schaff, P. v1p0129c1s
Lange, V.O. v6p0497c1s
Lange, W. v2p0159c1s
Langegg, F.A.J.v. v3p0333c2s
Langegg, F.A.von v3p0435c2s
Langen, G. v3p0236c1s
Langenbeck, K. v5p0462c1s
Langerfeld, E. v2p0101c1s
Langford, J.A. v1p0235c1s v1p1284c1s
Langford, N.P. v1p1437c1m
Langford, S., Mrs. v5p0095c2s
Langhorne, O. v1p0906c1s v5p0165c2s v5p0540c2s v5p0613c1s
Langland, H.M. v5p0065c2s
Langley, A.E. v2p0265c1s
Langley, A.G. v3p0359c2s
Langley, E.M. v3p0015c2s v3p0348c2s
Langley, J.B. v1p0069c2s v1p1328c2s
Langley, J.N. v2p0284c2s
Langley, J.P. v2p0105c2s
Langley, J.W. v1p0225c2s v1p1250c2s v2p0076c1m v4p0532c1s v5p0049c2s v6p0533c2s
Langley, J.W. and McGee, C.K. v2p0384c2s

Langley, M.J. v5p0432c2s
Langley, S.P. v1p0004c2s
v1p0399c2s v1p0428c1m v1p0824c1s
v1p1004c1s v1p1234c1s v1p1267c2s
v1p1268c1m v1p1268c2s v1p1269c1m
v1p1312c1s v1p1321c2s v1p1367c1s
v1p1432c2s v2p0026c1s v2p0027c2s
v2p0126c1s v2p0199c2s v2p0258c2m
v2p0296c2m v2p0343c2s v2p0374c2s
v2p0404c2s v2p0413c2s v2p0425c1m
v2p0425c2m v2p0426c1m v2p0426c2s
v2p0468c1s v3p0064c1s v3p0093c2s
v3p0155c1s v3p0156c2m v3p0192c2s
v3p0275c2s v3p0351c2s v3p0403c2s
v3p0407c1s v3p0414c1s v3p0416c1s
v3p0451c1s v4p0065c2s v4p0202c1s
v4p0540c2s v4p0623c2s v5p0069c1s
v5p0208c1s v5p0211c2s v5p0240c1s
v5p0545c1m v5p0565c2s v5p0633c1s
v6p0230c1s v6p0364c2s v6p0637c1s
v6p0667c2s
Langley, S.P. and Gill, T.
v4p0232c1s
Langley, S.P. and Very, F.W.
v3p0250c2s v3p0287c1s
Langlois, C.V. v3p0137c2s
v3p0159c2s v3p0421c1s v4p0597c1s
v6p0237c1s
Langmuir, J.W. v1p0943c1s
Langridge, I. v6p0591c1s
Langston, C.J. v1p0245c1s
v1p0297c1s v1p0330c2s v1p1175c1s
v2p0331c2s v2p0407c1s v3p0003c1s
v3p0189c1s v4p0218c1s v4p0412c2s
v4p0476c2s v4p0516c1s v5p0140c2s
v5p0217c2s v5p0223c2s v5p0233c1s
Langston, C.L. v2p0162c2m
Langtoft, G. v5p0296c1s
v5p0536c1s
Langton, E. v1p0327c1s
v1p0544c1s
Langton, H.H. v4p0330c1s
v6p0097c1s v6p0371c2s v6p0374c2s
v6p0528c1s
Langton, J. v1p0028c1s
v1p0192c2s v1p0198c1s v1p0926c2s
Langton, J.F. v6p0372c1s
Langton, R. v2p0118c1s
Langtot, G. v5p0034c2s
Langworthy, I.P. v1p0031c1s
v1p0253c1s v1p0289c2m v1p0291c1s
v1p0381c1s v1p1067c1s v1p1141c2s
v1p1366c2s v1p1412c1s
Langzettel, Marion B.B. .. v6p0351c2s
Lanham, W.E. v4p0552c1s
Lanier, C. v4p0320c2s
v5p0388c1s v5p0484c1s
Lanier, C. and Lanier, S.. v1p1040c2s
Lanier, C.D. v4p0021c1s
v4p0037c2s v4p0138c1s v4p0168c2s
v4p0268c1s v4p0347c1m v4p0468c2s
v4p0504c1s v4p0549c1s v4p0587c1s
v4p0620c1s v5p0045c1s v5p0317c1s
v5p0416c2s v5p0518c2s
Lanier, C.S. v4p0178c2s
Lanier, H. v6p0322c1s
Lanier, H.W. v4p0200c2s
v4p0543c1s v5p0095c1s v5p0258c1s
v5p0318c1s v5p0325c1s v5p0400c2s
v5p0420c1s v5p0540c2s v5p0569c1s
v5p0585c2s v6p0311c2s v6p0322c1s
v6p0322c2s v6p0323c1s v6p0464c1s
v6p0489c1s v6p0500c2m v6p0511c2s
v6p0565c2s v6p0670c1s
Lanier, H.Wysham v6p0497c1s
Lanier, R.S. v6p0456c2s
v6p0543c1s
Lanier, S. v1p0558c2s
v1p0576c2s v1p0826c1s v1p0923c2s
v1p0939c2s v1p0946c1s v1p1102c1s
v1p1128c1s v1p1142c2s v1p1148c1s
v1p1224c1s v1p1286c1s v2p0260c1s
v2p0260c2s v2p0297c1s v5p0191c2s
v6p0588c1s
Lanier, S. and Lanier, C.. v1p1040c2s
Lanigan, E. v5p0105c2s
Lanigan, G.T. v2p0032c1s
v2p0066c1s v2p0066c2s v2p0106c2m
v2p0167c2s v2p0174c2s v2p0184c2s
v2p0200c1s v2p0207c2s v2p0228c2s
v2p0241c2s v2p0260c2s v2p0265c1s
v2p0270c1s v2p0318c2s v2p0329c1s
v2p0430c2s v2p0449c1s v2p0472c1s
Lanin, E.B. v3p0020c1s
v3p0153c1s v3p0230c2s v3p0369c2m
v3p0370c1m v3p0370c2s v4p0010c1s
v4p0038c2s v4p0068c2s v4p0107c2s
v4p0256c2s v4p0447c2s v4p0495c2s
v4p0496c1s v4p0496c2m v4p0554c2s
v4p0561c2s v4p0584c2s
Lanin, E.B. and White, A.. v3p0230c2s
Lankester, E. v1p0017c1s
v1p0266c1s v1p0307c1s v1p0313c1s
v1p0465c1s v1p0583c1s v1p0815c1s
v1p0839c1s v1p1155c2s v1p1159c1s
v1p1161c2s v1p1210c1s v2p0263c1s
v2p0390c1s
Lankester, E., Mrs. v1p0967c1s
Lankester, E.R. v1p0040c2s
v1p0042c2s v1p0133c2s v1p0142c2s
v1p0199c2s v1p0297c2s v1p0312c2s
v1p0349c2s v1p0397c2s v1p0587c1s
v1p0618c1s v1p0645c2s v1p0791c2s
v1p0817c2s v1p0835c1s v1p0839c1s
v1p0874c2s v1p0960c1s v1p0975c2s
v1p1002c2s v1p1014c1s v1p1100c2s
v1p1173c1s v1p1295c2s v1p1441c1m
v2p0031c1s v2p0046c1s v2p0069c2s
v2p0080c1m v2p0119c1s v2p0139c2s
v2p0175c1s v2p0213c1s v2p0221c1s
v2p0276c2s v2p0282c2s v2p0317c1s
v2p0332c1s v2p0389c1s v3p0014c1s
v3p0080c1s v3p0111c1m v3p0185c1s
v3p0240c2s v3p0289c1s v4p0017c1s
v4p0191c1s v4p0191c2s v4p0284c1s
v4p0369c2s v4p0490c1s v4p0542c2s
v5p0100c1s v5p0426c1s v5p0646c2m
v6p0193c1s v6p0354c2s v6p0444c1s
v6p0597c2s v6p0691c2s
Lankester, E.R. and Brodrick, G.C.
v5p0426c2s
Lankester, E.R. and Cope, E.D.
v3p0447c1s
Lankester, E.R. and Romanes, G.J.
v3p0111c1s
Lankester, E.R. et al. ... v3p0194c2s
v4p0002c2s v4p0270c2s
Lankester, E.Ray v2p0046c1s
v5p0211c1s v6p0082c2s
Lankester, Mrs. v1p0266c2s
v1p0329c1s
Lankester, R. v2p0158c1s
v3p0284c2s
Lanman, C. v1p0039c1s
v1p0061c1s v1p0082c1s v1p0142c2s
v1p0332c2s v1p0433c1s v1p0455c2s
v1p0456c2m v1p0468c1s v1p0635c2s
v1p0667c2s v1p0732c1s v1p0755c1s
v1p0835c1s v1p0939c2s v1p0958c1s
v1p0959c1s v1p1020c1s v1p1084c1s
v1p1146c1m v1p1260c1s v1p1354c2s
v2p0278c1s v6p0315c2m
Lanman, C.R. v3p0436c1s
v4p0015c1s v4p0620c2m v5p0081c2s
v5p0620c1m v6p0186c1s v6p0333c1s
v6p0474c2s
Lanman, J.H. v1p0014c2s
v1p0094c2s v1p0151c2s v1p0164c2s
v1p0193c1s v1p0235c1s v1p0236c1s
v1p0268c2s v1p0282c2s v1p0283c1m
v1p0284c1s v1p0284c2s v1p0292c1s
v1p0300c1s v1p0307c2s v1p0339c1m
v1p0359c2s v1p0494c2s v1p0522c2s
v1p0543c2s v1p0640c1s v1p0664c2s
v1p0699c2s v1p0789c2s v1p0823c2s
v1p0834c2s v1p0854c1s v1p0902c1s
v1p0928c2s v1p1062c2s v1p1174c1s
v1p1192c2s v1p1214c1s v1p1249c1s
v1p1319c1s v1p1354c1s v1p1403c1s
Lanneau, J.F. v5p0175c1s
v6p0614c2s v6p0625c2s v6p0626c1s
Lanney, J.De v1p0205c2s
Lanphear, O.T. v4p0084c1s
Lanphere, Lydia J. v3p0163c1s
Lansbury, G. v4p0237c2s
v6p0673c2s
Lansdale, E.V. v1p1377c1s
Lansdell, H. v1p1129c1s
v1p1194c2s v2p0025c1s v2p0080c1s
v2p0381c1s v3p0153c1s v3p0208c1s
v3p0369c2s v3p0370c2s v3p0391c2s
v3p0392c1s v3p0438c2s v4p0032c2s
v4p0065c2s v4p0311c2s
Lansen, G. v6p0415c1s
Lansing, D. v6p0171c1s
v6p0407c2s v6p0664c2s
Lansing, David v6p0056c2s
Lansing, G. v1p0397c1s
v2p0135c1s v2p0338c1s
Lansing, G.L. v2p0079c2s
v2p0362c2m v2p0363c1s
Lansing, I. v6p0579c1s
Lansing, I.J. v3p0364c1s
Lansing, J.G. v3p0305c2s
Lansing, K. v5p0152c1s
Lansing, Katharine v5p0211c2s
Lansing, M. v4p0342c2s
Lansing, R. v6p0010c1s
Lanson, G. v5p0221c2s
Lanten, E. v6p0163c2s
Lantheaume, C.A. v6p0288c2s
Lantz, D. v1p0792c2s
v2p0034c2s
Lanyon, O. v3p0038c2s
v3p0237c2s
Lanza, C. v3p0011c1s
v3p0468c1s v4p0109c1s v4p0299c2s
Lanza, C.G. v2p0037c1s
Lanza, G. v1p0328c1s
v2p0435c2s v2p0441c1s v2p0478c2s
v4p0180c2m
Lanzel, A. v2p0361c2s
Lanzendoerfer, G. v2p0062c2s
Lapcho and Mahaffy v4p0544c2s
Lape, T. v1p0206c2s
Lapham, E.C. v2p0477c1s
v5p0637c2s
Lapham, F. v1p0871c2s
Lapham, I.A. v1p0454c2s
v1p0718c1s v1p1256c2s
Lapham, J.A. v6p0460c2s
Lapham, L.E. v6p0230c2s
Lapham, W.B. v1p0171c2s
v1p0991c1s v1p1273c2s
Laplace, C. v6p0039c1s
Laporte, L. v1p0922c2s
Laporte, V. v3p0451c1s
Lapouge, G.V.de v5p0023c1s
v5p0033c2s
Lapoukhyn, V. v1p0002c1s
v1p0706c2s v1p0713c1s
Lapparent, A.de v4p0221c2s
Lapparent, A.de and Faye, H.
v2p0319c1s
Lapsley, C.T. v6p0150c1s
Lapsley, G.T. v5p0190c2s
v5p0298c2s v5p0514c2s v5p0515c1s
v6p0228c2s v6p0360c1s v6p0578c1s
Lapworth, C. v3p0311c2s
v4p0165c2s v4p0433c1s
Lara, D.E.de v2p0167c1s
v2p0199c2s v2p0235c1s v2p0314c2s
v2p0390c1s v2p0404c1s
Larcom, Capt. v1p0653c2s
Larcom, L. v1p0499c1s
v1p0590c2s v1p0775c1s v1p0818c1s
v1p1088c1s v1p1127c2s v1p1204c1s
v1p1277c2s v2p0151c2s v4p0418c1s
Larden, W. v3p0282c1s
Lardner, D. v1p0050c2s
v1p0476c2s v1p1080c2s
Large, J. v5p0043c2s
Larimore, J.W. v1p0228c1s
Larkby, J.R. v5p0118c2m
v5p0125c2s v5p0383c2s v6p0088c1s
v6p0127c1s v6p0154c2s v6p0284c1s
v6p0350c2s v6p0397c1s v6p0471c1s
v6p0514c1s v6p0534c1s
Larkby, J.R. and Dutt, W.A.
v6p0209c2s
Larken, E.P. v5p0465c2s
v5p0517c1s
Larkin, E.L. v2p0026c1s
v2p0028c1s v2p0073c1s v2p0095c2s
v2p0242c2s v2p0299c2s v2p0424c2s
v2p0425c1m v2p0426c2s v2p0459c1s
v5p0389c1s v6p0196c1s v6p0433c1s
v6p0566c2m v6p0567c2s v6p0614c2s
Larkin, E.L. and Kaempffert, W.B.
v6p0187c2s
Larkin, H. v1p0201c2s
v1p0828c2s v1p1014c1s v1p1251c1s
v2p0221c1s
Larking, C. v3p0152c2s
Larkins, C.D. v6p0399c2s
Larkins, E.L. v2p0390c2s
Larkins, W.G. v1p1326c1s
v2p0232c1s v3p0436c1s
Larmer, J.E. v4p0565c1s
Larminie, W. v1p0427c2s
v1p0505c1s v4p0291c2s v4p0367c2s
v4p0406c1s v5p0094c2s v5p0266c2s
v5p0516c1s v5p0525c1s
Larmor, J. v4p0187c2s
v5p0424c2s v6p0198c1s v6p0350c2s
v6p0570c1s
Larmour, R. v5p0205c1s
Larned, C.W. v3p0158c1s
v3p0179c1s v4p0049c1s v4p0370c2s
v5p0626c1s v6p0031c1s v6p0416c2m
v6p0423c2s v6p0485c1s v6p0602c2m
v6p0693c1s
Larned, J.G.E. v1p0808c2s
v1p1225c1m
Larned, J.N. v1p0259c2s
v1p0868c2s v2p0256c1m v2p0256c2m
v2p0339c1s v3p0249c2s v4p0330c1s
v5p0158c1s v5p0189c2s v5p0412c1s
v5p0601c1s
Larned, W.A. v1p0026c2s
v1p0120c2s v1p0191c2s v1p0263c1s
v1p0276c1s v1p0336c2s v1p0342c2s
v1p0477c1s v1p0552c2s v1p0568c1s
v1p0680c1s v1p0743c1s v1p0760c1s
v1p0768c1s v1p0826c2s v1p0905c1s
v1p0921c1s v1p0923c2s v1p0995c2s
v1p1022c1s v1p1134c1s v1p1150c1s
v1p1207c1s v1p1436c1s
Larned, W.C. v2p0326c2s
v3p0279c2s v5p0485c1s v6p0579c2m
Larned, W.J. v5p0387c1s
Larned, W.T. v2p0094c1s
v2p0456c2s v4p0137c2s v4p0252c1s
v4p0282c1s v5p0287c2s v5p0368c1s
v5p0433c2s v6p0435c1s
Larner, E.J. v5p0451c1s
Larner, G.J. v5p0451c1s
Larrabee, W.C. v1p0865c1s
Larrabee, W.H. v2p0077c1s
v2p0128c2s v2p0201c2s v2p0390c2s
v2p0404c1s v2p0426c2s v2p0445c2s
v3p0070c1m v3p0111c1s v3p0252c2s
v3p0383c1s v3p0410c2s v3p0417c2m
v4p0093c1s v4p0119c2s v5p0252c2s
Larremore, W. v2p0266c1s
v2p0448c2s v3p0049c2s v3p0084c1s
v3p0088c1s v3p0260c1s v3p0337c2s
v3p0355c2s v5p0430c1s v6p0005c2s
v6p0016c1s v6p0083c2s v6p0262c2s
v6p0339c1s v6p0379c2s v6p0624c2s

Larremore, Wilbur v6p0176c2s
Larrinaga, Julio v6p0509c2s
Larrison, E.R. v5p0522c1s
Larroumet, G. v5p0275c1s
Larsen, A. v5p0530c1s
Larsen, C. v1p0253c2s
Larsen, C.A. v4p0019c2s
Larsen, T. v6p0305c2s
Larsen, W.F. v5p0178c2s
Larson, L.M. v6p0224c2s
v6p0344c2s v6p0402c1s v6p0428c1s
v6p0441c1s
Larsson, G. v5p0360c2s
v6p0318c1s
Lart, C.E. v5p0401c1m
v6p0484c1s
Lartet, E. v1p0793c1s
Lartet, L. v1p0336c2s
Larus, J.R. v5p0269c2s
Larwood, J. v1p0766c1s
Larymore, C. v6p0153c1s
Larzelere, C.S. v6p0635c1s
Lascaris v6p0272c2s
Lascaris, H. v4p0521c2s
Lascelles, B.P. v6p0696c1s
Lascelles, E.W. v6p0266c2s
Lascelles, G. v2p0114c2s
v4p0194c1s v4p0270c1s v4p0418c2s
v4p0482c1s v4p0542c2s v4p0543c1s
Lascelles, Helen v6p0543c1s
Lascelles-Scott, W.J v4p0192c2s
v4p0309c1s
Lash, Q.A. v4p0049c2s
Lashbroke, H. v1p1266c2s
Lasher, G.W. v2p0222c2s
Lasker, E. v4p0144c2s
v4p0445c1s
Laski, J.De v1p0523c2m
v1p0703c1s
Laslett-Browne, H. v4p0139c1s
Lasley, Mary v6p0561c2s
Lassar, M.O.Baron v6p0582c2s
Lassell, W. v1p0071c1s
Lasselle, S.C. v3p0029c1s
v3p0287c2s
Lassiter, F.R. v5p0029c2s
Lassus, L.A.De v6p0449c1s
Lasswitz, K. v4p0283c1s
v4p0395c1s
Last, J.T. v4p0348c2m
Lasteyrie, F.de v1p0958c2s
v2p0182c1s
Lasteyrie, Mme.de v1p0717c2s
Laszowska, E.de, Mme v2p0427c1s
v2p0445c1s
Latane, J.H. v4p0358c2s
v4p0605c2s v5p0147c2s v6p0098c2s
v6p0138c1s v6p0277c2s v6p0323c2s
Latcha, J.A. v5p0092c1s
v5p0237c2s v5p0476c2s v5p0586c1s
Latchford, H. v4p0268c2s
v4p0336c2s v4p0433c2s v4p0437c1s
Latchmore, F. v3p0365c2s
Latham, A. v1p1349c1s
Latham, B. v1p0619c1s
v1p1181c1s v1p1181c2s v2p0192c2s
v2p0467c2s v3p0457c1m
Latham, C. v4p0558c1s
v4p0617c2s
Latham, C.E. v6p0666c1s
Latham, E.K. v5p0272c1s
v5p0633c1s
Latham, G. v1p1325c1s
Latham, G.E. v4p0034c1s
v4p0472c1s v6p0044c1s
Latham, H. v1p0831c2s
v2p0079c1s
Latham, H.G.D. v5p0123c2s
v6p0457c2s v6p0458c1s v6p0471c2s
v6p0483c1s v6p0603c2s
Latham, H.L. v6p0259c1s
v6p0338c1s v6p0591c1s
Latham, J. v4p0027c2s
Latham, J.B. v4p0046c2s
v4p0404c1s v4p0607c2s
Latham, J.H. v1p0195c1s
v1p1220c2s
Latham, O'N. v5p0322c1s
Latham, O'Neill v5p0187c2s
v5p0349c2s v5p0555c2s v5p0589c2s
Latham, R.G. v1p0013c1s
v1p0018c1s v1p0636c2s v1p0639c2s
v1p0655c1s v1p0875c1s v1p1185c1s
v1p1187c1s
Latham, S. v5p0071c1s
Latham, W. v1p0547c2s
v1p0965c2s v1p1126c2s
Lathbury, Bertha v1p1420c2s
Lathbury, C. v4p0113c1s
v5p0055c2s v5p0561c2s v5p0577c1s
Lathbury, D.C. v1p0072c1s
v1p1348c2s v6p0187c2s v6p0191c1s
v6p0191c2m v6p0299c1s v6p0370c1s
v6p0375c2s
Lathbury, D.C. et al. v6p0191c2s
Lathbury, M.A. v5p0019c1s
v5p0233c2s
Lathbury, M.M. v4p0568c2s
Lathbury, Mrs. v1p0014c2s
Lathbury, T. v1p0781c2s
v1p0987c1s
Lathe, A.M. v3p0075c1s
v3p0146c1s v3p0388c2m v4p0011c2s
v4p0518c2s v4p0519c1s
Lathe, H.W. v2p0106c2s
v2p0201c2s v4p0174c1s
Lathrop, A.J. v2p0465c1s
Lathrop, B. v4p0023c2s
Lathrop, B.H. v3p0433c1s
Lathrop, B.T. v1p0992c1s
Lathrop, C.C. v4p0071c1s
Lathrop, E. v6p0584c1s
Lathrop, G.P. v1p0007c2s
v1p0032c1s v1p0064c1s v1p0151c2m
v1p0274c1s v1p0287c2s v1p0345c1s
v1p0567c1s v1p0575c2m v1p0583c2s
v1p0667c1s v1p0683c1s v1p0717c1s
v1p0734c2s v1p0773c2s v1p0811c2s
v1p0865c1s v1p0931c2m v1p0944c2s
v1p1011c1s v1p1019c2s v1p1109c1s
v1p1111c1s v1p1197c1s v1p1246c1s
v1p1336c1s v1p1388c2s v2p0007c1m
v2p0008c1s v2p0011c1s v2p0029c2s
v2p0110c1s v2p0129c2s v2p0171c1s
v2p0197c1s v2p0198c1s v2p0301c1s
v2p0312c1s v2p0313c1s v2p0314c2s
v2p0317c2s v2p0412c2s v3p0011c2s
v3p0028c2m v3p0048c2s v3p0105c2s
v3p0111c2s v3p0128c1s v3p0172c1s
v3p0191c2s v3p0214c2s v3p0232c2s
v3p0252c2s v3p0265c2s v3p0274c2s
v3p0284c1s v3p0300c2s v3p0303c2s
v3p0308c2s v3p0314c1s v3p0361c1s
v3p0362c1s v3p0364c1s v3p0384c1s
v3p0387c1s v3p0439c2s v3p0443c2s
v3p0451c1s v4p0015c1s v4p0030c1s
v4p0076c2s v4p0079c1s v4p0221c1s
v4p0377c2s v4p0489c1s v4p0570c1s
v4p0606c2s v4p0610c1s v4p0621c2s
v5p0152c1s v5p0259c1s v5p0282c1s
Lathrop, G.P. and Doane, W.C.
v4p0489c1s
Lathrop, G.P. and Sherman, R.
v2p0102c2s
Lathrop, G.P. et al. v3p0099c2s
Lathrop, H. v1p0939c2s
v1p1011c1s v1p1315c1s
Lathrop, H.B. v4p0246c2s
Lathrop, J.C. v6p0518c1s
Lathrop, J.G. v4p0206c2s
Lathrop, J.H. v1p0015c1s
v1p1416c2s v1p1417c1s v5p0377c2s
Lathrop, J.R.T. v5p0268c2s
v6p0536c2s
Lathrop, L. v6p0483c2s
Lathrop, L.A. v4p0622c1s
Lathrop, N. v5p0163c2s
Lathrop, R.H. v2p0355c1s
v4p0251c2m
Lathrop, Rose H. v5p0259c1s
Lathrop, S.P. v1p0829c1s
v1p1375c2s
Lathrop, T.S. v1p0292c2s
v1p0434c1s v1p0440c2s v1p0626c1s
v1p1301c1s v2p0149c2s v2p0437c1s
v3p0206c1s
Lathrop, W.W. v1p0276c2s
v1p1175c1s
Latimer, C.W. v4p0363c2s
v5p0514c1s
Latimer, E.W. v1p1049c2s
v1p1129c1s v1p1174c2s v2p0250c2s
v2p0253c1s v2p0404c1s v3p0071c2s
v3p0072c2s v3p0186c1s v4p0147c2s
v4p0155c1s v5p0418c2s v5p0506c2s
v6p0053c2s
Latimer, E.W., Mrs. v1p0807c2s
v2p0254c2s
Latimer, G.D. v4p0076c1s
v6p0283c2s v6p0504c2s
Latimer, J. v3p0435c2s
Latimer, J.D. v6p0528c2s
Latimer, J.E. v1p0890c2s
v2p0392c1s
Latimer, L. v4p0107c2s
Latimer, L.P. v5p0481c2s
Latimer, M.K. v3p0062c2s
Latimer, R.B., Mrs. v1p1065c2s
Latimer, R.R. v5p0269c2s
Latimer, S.F. v3p0424c1s
Latimore, D. v6p0344c1s
Latrobe, B.H. v1p0145c2s
v1p0146c1s v6p0680c1s v6p0686c2s
v6p0687c1s
Latrobe, J.H.B. v1p0371c1s
v2p0466c2s v2p0469c2s
Latson, W.R.C. v6p0039c1s
v6p0039c2m v6p0204c1s v6p0498c1s
Latta, C.H. v6p0052c1s
v6p0333c2s v6p0388c2s
Latta, Carrie H. v6p0347c2s
Latta, R. v5p0330c1s
v5p0546c1s v6p0673c1s
Latta, T. v1p0056c1s
v1p0927c2s
Latta, T.A. v1p0622c1s
v1p1238c2s
Latter, A.M. v6p0118c2s
v6p0119c1s v6p0186c1s v6p0333c2s
v6p0560c1s
Latter, O.H. v4p0097c2s
v6p0161c1s v6p0320c2s v6p0687c2s
Lattey, C. v5p0499c2s
v6p0064c1s v6p0537c1s
Lattimer, R.B. v6p0193c2s
Lattimer, W. v1p0714c1s
v1p1009c1s
Lattimore, A. v6p0020c1s
Lattimore, S.A. v1p1390c1s
Latto, T.C. v1p0298c2s
Lauck, W.J. v6p0533c2s
Laud, E.F. v6p0511c1s
Laud, M. and Mayo, L.A. .. v5p0541c2s
Laud, P.N. v1p0128c1s
Laud, T.S. v5p0037c2s
Laudels, W. v1p0442c1s
v1p0666c2s
Lauder, T.D. v1p1167c2s
Lauderdale, H. v6p0033c2s
v6p0224c2s
Laudis, H.K. v5p0570c1s
Lauenbruck, Countess von . v1p0516c2s
Lauer, C.N. v6p0152c1s
Lauer, P.E. v4p0111c2s
Lauer, S. v6p0093c1s
v6p0233c1s
Laufer, B. v5p0018c1s
v5p0442c2s v6p0341c2s
Laufroy, A. v2p0193c2s
Laugegg, F.A.Junker von .. v2p0432c1s
Laugel, A. v1p0026c1s
v1p0027c1s v1p0035c1s v1p0045c2s
v1p0090c1s v1p0103c2s v1p0104c1m
v1p0114c1s v1p0128c1s v1p0132c2s
v1p0151c1s v1p0166c2s v1p0175c1s
v1p0186c2s v1p0202c1s v1p0222c1s
v1p0225c2s v1p0243c2s v1p0285c2s
v1p0286c1s v1p0293c2s v1p0294c1s
v1p0334c1m v1p0346c1s v1p0351c2s
v1p0361c2s v1p0371c2m v1p0379c2m
v1p0380c1m v1p0387c2s v1p0395c2s
v1p0402c2s v1p0431c1s v1p0449c2s
v1p0453c1s v1p0474c2s v1p0479c2m
v1p0480c2s v1p0481c2s v1p0497c1s
v1p0498c2s v1p0506c1s v1p0515c1m
v1p0536c2s v1p0561c2m v1p0584c2s
v1p0611c1s v1p0611c2m v1p0612c1m
v1p0615c2s v1p0663c2s v1p0672c2s
v1p0680c1s v1p0683c2s v1p0692c1s
v1p0696c2s v1p0710c1s v1p0720c1s
v1p0744c1s v1p0790c1s v1p0816c2s
v1p0824c1s v1p0831c2s v1p0849c2s
v1p0864c1s v1p0880c2s v1p0886c1s
v1p0894c1s v1p0896c1m v1p0957c2s
v1p0965c2s v1p0967c2s v1p0968c2s
v1p0969c1s v1p0969c2s v1p0970c1m
v1p1023c2s v1p1049c1s v1p1086c2m
v1p1098c1s v1p1098c2m v1p1101c1s
v1p1110c1s v1p1129c2s v1p1143c1m
v1p1194c2s v1p1199c2s v1p1230c1s
v1p1253c1s v1p1281c2s v1p1285c1s
v1p1288c2s v1p1305c2m v1p1317c2s
v1p1323c1s v1p1329c2s v1p1330c1m
v1p1357c1s v1p1366c2s v1p1367c2s
v1p1368c1s v1p1369c2s v1p1371c2s
v1p1378c1s v2p0007c1s v2p0030c2s
v2p0036c2s v2p0037c1s v2p0038c2s
v2p0043c2s v2p0053c2s v2p0057c2s
v2p0060c2s v2p0072c2s v2p0073c2s
v2p0074c1s v2p0097c2s v2p0112c2s
v2p0117c2s v2p0118c1s v2p0125c1s
v2p0125c2m v2p0128c2s v2p0134c1s
v2p0139c1s v2p0141c2s v2p0145c2s
v2p0146c1s v2p0148c1s v2p0154c1s
v2p0154c2m v2p0164c1s v2p0164c2m
v2p0165c1m v2p0165c2m v2p0167c2m
v2p0169c1s v2p0170c2s v2p0175c2s
v2p0192c1m v2p0193c1s v2p0196c1s
v2p0200c1s v2p0210c2m v2p0217c2s
v2p0231c1s v2p0238c2s v2p0239c1s
v2p0266c2s v2p0273c1s v2p0276c2s
v2p0281c1s v2p0282c1s v2p0287c2s
v2p0295c2s v2p0296c1s v2p0320c2s
v2p0329c1s v2p0331c2s v2p0348c2s
v2p0350c1s v2p0370c1m v2p0373c1s
v2p0381c1s v2p0386c2m v2p0395c2s
v2p0415c2s v2p0422c2s v2p0442c2m
v2p0443c2s v2p0453c2s v2p0458c1s
v2p0458c2s v2p0460c2s v2p0462c1s
v2p0463c2s v2p0464c2s v3p0030c2s
v3p0031c2s v3p0034c1s v3p0038c1s
v3p0040c2s v3p0046c2s v3p0049c1s
v3p0050c2s v3p0052c1m v3p0062c1s
v3p0064c1s v3p0074c1s v3p0086c2s
v3p0095c2s v3p0097c2s v3p0111c2m
v3p0116c2s v3p0124c1s v3p0124c2s
v3p0144c1m v3p0155c1s v3p0159c1s
v3p0159c2m v3p0160c1m v3p0161c2m
v3p0162c2s v3p0164c1s v3p0177c1m
v3p0185c2s v3p0186c2s v3p0188c1s
v3p0204c1m v3p0230c1s v3p0239c2s
v3p0247c1s v3p0251c2s v3p0259c1s
v3p0264c2s v3p0267c2m v3p0281c2s
v3p0296c1s v3p0314c2s v3p0320c1m
v3p0320c2s v3p0322c2s v3p0358c2s
v3p0375c2s v3p0380c2s v3p0386c1m
v3p0399c1s v3p0406c1s v3p0418c1s
v3p0419c2m v3p0425c2s v3p0450c1s
v3p0454c2s v3p0461c1s v4p0002c1s
v4p0005c2s v4p0010c1s v4p0017c1s

v4p0045c2s v4p0046c1s v4p0052c1s
v4p0052c2s v4p0058c2s v4p0068c2s
v4p0091c2s v4p0092c2s v4p0096c1s
v4p0097c2s v4p0098c1s v4p0099c2s
v4p0128c1m v4p0130c2s v4p0145c1s
v4p0147c2s v4p0189c1s v4p0196c2s
v4p0211c1m v4p0211c2s v4p0212c1s
v4p0212c2s v4p0213c1s v4p0215c1s
v4p0221c1s v4p0232c1m v4p0254c1s
v4p0268c1s v4p0268c2s v4p0317c1m
v4p0317c2s v4p0321c1s v4p0326c1s
v4p0327c2s v4p0342c2s v4p0355c1s
v4p0361c2s v4p0380c2s v4p0392c2m
v4p0404c1s v4p0413c2s v4p0418c2s
v4p0421c1s v4p0425c1s v4p0425c2s
v4p0426c2s v4p0429c1s v4p0436c1s
v4p0458c1m v4p0480c2m v4p0481c1s
v4p0492c2s v4p0496c2s v4p0498c2s
v4p0499c2s v4p0503c1s v4p0513c2s
v4p0523c2s v4p0562c1s v4p0562c2s
v4p0573c2s v4p0578c1s v4p0578c2s
v4p0584c2s v4p0601c1s v4p0606c1s
v4p0607c1s v5p0013c2s v5p0047c2s
v5p0049c1s v5p0051c1s v5p0069c1s
v5p0072c1s v5p0083c2s v5p0101c1m
v5p0103c1m v5p0115c2s v5p0131c1s
v5p0132c1s v5p0146c1s v5p0156c1s
v5p0157c1s v5p0159c2s v5p0173c2s
v5p0188c1s v5p0215c2s v5p0216c2m
v5p0217c1s v5p0217c2m v5p0219c1s
v5p0220c2s v5p0221c2s v5p0228c1m
v5p0275c1s v5p0310c2m v5p0312c2s
v5p0322c2m v5p0325c2s v5p0337c2s
v5p0348c2m v5p0351c2s v5p0356c2s
v5p0361c2s v5p0368c1s v5p0382c1s
v5p0384c2s v5p0386c2s v5p0392c2s
v5p0397c2m v5p0398c1m v5p0434c2s
v5p0442c1m v5p0475c2s v5p0482c2s
v5p0485c1m v5p0491c1s v5p0492c2s
v5p0495c2s v5p0508c2s v5p0534c2s
v5p0559c1s v5p0565c2s v5p0566c1s
v5p0577c2s v5p0582c1s v5p0583c2s
v5p0612c2s v5p0614c1s v5p0622c2s
v5p0631c2s v6p0011c1s v6p0047c1s
v6p0049c1s v6p0057c1s v6p0059c2s
v6p0073c1s v6p0091c2s v6p0102c1s
v6p0102c2s v6p0108c2s v6p0110c1s
v6p0110c2m v6p0112c1s v6p0121c2m
v6p0134c2s v6p0142c2s v6p0165c2m
v6p0172c1s v6p0183c1s v6p0184c1s
v6p0196c2s v6p0204c1s v6p0222c1s
v6p0228c2s v6p0231c1s v6p0235c1m
v6p0236c2s v6p0261c2s v6p0286c2s
v6p0298c2s v6p0301c2m v6p0354c1s
v6p0354c2s v6p0357c2s v6p0358c2s
v6p0359c1m v6p0363c2m v6p0366c1s
v6p0368c2s v6p0377c2s v6p0390c1s
v6p0395c2s v6p0400c2s v6p0401c1s
v6p0420c1s v6p0426c2m v6p0427c1s
v6p0434c1s v6p0441c2m v6p0442c1m
v6p0449c2s v6p0479c1m v6p0482c1s
v6p0506c1s v6p0508c1s v6p0516c1s
v6p0531c1s v6p0533c2s v6p0536c1s
v6p0549c2m v6p0556c1s v6p0563c1s
v6p0572c1s v6p0584c1s v6p0631c1s
v6p0631c2m v6p0657c1s v6p0668c1s
v6p0678c1s v6p0679c1s v6p0689c1s
v6p0691c1s
Laugel, A. and Bryce, J. . v2p0423c2s
Laugel, A. and Godkin, E.L.
v1p0481c1s
Laugel, A. et al. v1p0380c1s
Laughlin, A.C. v5p0557c1s
Laughlin, C. v6p0330c1s
v6p0644c2s
Laughlin, C.E. v4p0273c1s
v4p0343c1s v5p0030c1s v5p0195c1s
v5p0341c2s v5p0364c1s v5p0489c1s
v6p0083c2s v6p0085c1s v6p0415c1s
v6p0555c1s v6p0639c1s v6p0685c2s
Laughlin, C.F. v6p0504c2s
Laughlin, Clara E. v6p0176c1s
v6p0215c1s
Laughlin, G.H. v2p0456c2s
Laughlin, J.C. and Spahr, C.H.
v4p0524c2s
Laughlin, J.L. v1p0278c1s
v1p1057c1s v2p0099c1s v2p0164c2s
v2p0347c2m v2p0353c1s v2p0367c2s
v2p0403c1s v2p0423c2s v2p0454c2s
v3p0176c1s v3p0343c2s v3p0446c2s
v4p0008c1s v4p0044c1s v4p0100c1s
v4p0167c2s v4p0195c2s v4p0280c1s
v4p0377c2m v4p0378c1m v4p0393c2s
v4p0450c1s v4p0503c1m v4p0525c2s
v5p0125c2s v5p0171c1s v5p0175c2m
v5p0302c2s v5p0354c1s v5p0382c2s
v5p0536c1s v5p0592c2s v5p0600c2s
v5p0601c1s v5p0616c2s v5p0618c1s
v6p0141c1s v6p0162c1s v6p0176c1s
v6p0234c1s v6p0329c2s v6p0357c1m
v6p0425c1m v6p0469c2s v6p0515c2s
v6p0516c1s v6p0524c2s v6p0690c1s
Laughlin, J.L. and Moody, W.G.
v2p0480c1s
Laughlin, J.L. and Tolstoi, Leo
v5p0382c2s
Laughlin, J.L. et al. v2p0403c1m
Laughton, A.N. v4p0261c2s
v4p0429c1s
Laughton, J.K. v1p0080c1s
v1p0269c2s v1p0372c2s v1p0480c1s
v1p0695c1s v1p0902c2s v1p1053c2s
v1p1227c2s v1p1256c2s v1p1289c1s
v1p1309c2s v1p1365c2s v1p1381c2s
v1p1394c2s v1p1433c2s v2p0168c1s
v2p0204c1s v2p0427c1s v2p0475c1s
v3p0228c2s v3p0298c1s v3p0299c2s
v3p0305c2s v3p0396c2s v3p0460c2s
v5p0397c2s v5p0401c1s v6p0268c1s
v6p0268c2s v6p0449c1s v6p0652c2s
Laughton, J.K. and Badham, F.P.
v5p0404c1s
Laughton, J.L. v1p0271c1s
v4p0404c2s
Laughton, L.G. v6p0057c2s
v6p0506c2s
Laughton, L.G.C. v5p0145c1s
v5p0167c1s v5p0172c1s v5p0193c2s
v5p0401c1s v5p0505c1s v5p0585c1s
v6p0177c2s v6p0310c1s v6p0445c1s
v6p0560c1s v6p0591c2s v6p0620c1s
v6p0623c2s
Laughton, W.J. v6p0044c1s
Laun, H.Van v1p0521c1s
v2p0126c1s v2p0387c2s
Laun, Henri Van v4p0164c2s
Laurence, A.H. v5p0244c2s
Laurence, E. v1p0401c1s
v1p0554c1s
Laurence, F. v1p0311c1s
v1p0534c2s
Laurence, P.M. v5p0007c2s
Laurence, S. v1p0279c1s
v1p1008c1s
Laurence, T. v3p0315c1s
Laurens, J.P. v3p0022c1s
Laurenson, A. v1p0948c2s
Laurent, J.C.M. v1p0131c1s
v1p0196c1s v1p0713c2s
Laurentz, C.von v6p0403c1s
Laurie, A.G. v1p0047c1s
v1p0068c2s v1p0243c1s v1p0254c1s
v1p0368c1s v1p0419c2m v1p0668c1s
v1p0708c2s v1p0862c2s v1p1042c1s
v1p1101c2s v1p1121c1s v1p1124c2s
v1p1297c2s v1p1355c2s v2p0236c2s
Laurie, A.P. v2p0136c1s
v3p0412c2s v4p0324c1s v4p0422c1s
v4p0443c1m v6p0278c1s
Laurie, C.F. v6p0437c1s
Laurie, Col. v1p1030c1s
Laurie, H. v4p0283c1s
Laurie, S.S. v1p0391c1s
v1p0392c2s v1p0590c1s v1p0702c1s
v1p0863c1s v3p0128c2s v3p0378c1s
v4p0126c2s v4p0169c1s v4p0169c2s
v4p0171c1m v4p0259c1s v4p0360c2s
v4p0381c2s v4p0480c2s v5p0250c1s
v5p0377c1s
Laurie, S.S. and Hutchison, J.
v2p0455c2s
Laurie, T. v1p0117c1s
v1p0119c2s v1p0733c1s v1p0769c2s
v1p1011c2s v1p1119c2m v1p1415c2s
v1p1437c1s v2p0333c1s v3p0175c1s
Laurie, T.W. v4p0039c1s
Laurie, W.F.B. v1p0632c1s
v1p0731c1s v1p0990c2s v4p0253c2s
Laurie, W.H. v4p0547c1s
Laurier, Wilfrid v6p0096c2s
Laurillard, C.L. v1p0327c2s
Laurvik, J.N. v6p0069c1m
Lauston, A. v5p0186c1s
Laut, A. v6p0180c2s
Laut, A.C. v5p0090c1s
v5p0408c2s v5p0491c2s v6p0010c2s
v6p0054c1s v6p0055c2s v6p0058c2s
v6p0086c2s v6p0091c1s v6p0097c1s
v6p0139c2s v6p0244c2s v6p0285c1s
v6p0301c2s v6p0304c1s v6p0315c1s
v6p0315c2s v6p0354c1s v6p0358c1s
v6p0422c2s v6p0428c1s v6p0433c2s
v6p0460c2s v6p0471c2s v6p0472c1s
v6p0557c2s v6p0559c1s v6p0698c2s
v6p0702c1s
Laut, Agnes C. v6p0051c2s
v6p0097c2s v6p0139c2s v6p0147c2s
v6p0244c2s v6p0264c2s v6p0509c2s
v6p0665c1s v6p0674c1s v6p0693c2m
Lauterbach, E. v4p0450c2s
Lauterbach, E. et al. v4p0384c1s
Lauth, C. v2p0349c2s
v5p0513c1s
Lautreppe, F.Le C.de v4p0201c2s
Lautreppe, L.C.de v4p0013c2s
Lautreppe, L.de v3p0320c1s
v3p0341c1s v3p0358c2s
Lautreppe, LeC.de v3p0151c2s
v4p0355c1s
Lautreppe, LeCocq de v3p0039c1s
v3p0104c1s v3p0111c2s v3p0124c1s
v3p0177c1s v3p0216c2s v3p0331c2s
v3p0459c2s v4p0478c1s v5p0275c1s
Lautz, D. v2p0383c2s
Lautz, F.W. v1p0092c2s
v1p1354c2s
Lautz, W.J. v5p0451c1s
Lauzac, H. v1p0808c1s
Lavedan, H. v5p0220c2s
v5p0432c2s
Laveleye, E. v1p1026c2s
Laveleye, E.D. v2p0251c1s
Laveleye, E.de v1p0010c2s
v1p0079c2s v1p0109c1s v1p0109c2s
v1p0133c2s v1p0431c1s v1p0474c2s
v1p0515c1s v1p0532c2s v1p0546c1m
v1p0672c2s v1p0722c1s v1p0778c2s
v1p0860c1s v1p0860c2s v1p0861c1s
v1p1025c2s v1p1058c1s v1p1119c1s
v1p1120c1s v1p1323c1s v1p1384c1s
v2p0004c1s v2p0038c2m v2p0046c1s
v2p0067c2s v2p0096c2s v2p0098c2s
v2p0115c2s v2p0128c2s v2p0129c2s
v2p0134c1s v2p0165c2s v2p0182c1s
v2p0294c2s v2p0314c2s v2p0337c1s
v2p0351c1s v2p0355c2s v2p0408c1m
v2p0429c1s v2p0444c1s v2p0480c2s
v2p0481c1s v3p0004c1s v3p0038c2s
v3p0094c2s v3p0114c2s v3p0144c1s
v3p0319c1s v3p0322c1s v3p0357c2s
v3p0446c1s v3p0454c1s v4p0294c2s
v4p0534c1s
Laveleye, E.de and Fredericq, P.
v2p0038c2m v3p0038c1m
Laveleye, E.de and Spencer, H.
v2p0414c1s v2p0418c1s
Laveleye, M. v1p1216c1s
Lavell, C.F. v6p0096c2m
v6p0131c2s v6p0147c2s v6p0186c2m
v6p0196c1s v6p0206c1s v6p0206c2s
v6p0237c1s v6p0310c1s v6p0381c2s
v6p0495c1s
Lavell, Cecil F. v6p0273c1s
Lavelle, F. v2p0317c2s
Lavelle, M.J. v3p0365c1s
v4p0488c2s
Lavelye, E. v3p0383c2s
Lavers-Smith, H. v5p0552c1s
v6p0280c2s
Lavery, Urban v6p0548c2s
Laves, K. v5p0194c2s
Laves, Kurt v5p0242c2s
v6p0026c2s v6p0037c2s
Lavilliere, Count de v5p0170c2s
Lavington, S. v1p0528c1s
Lavis, B.M. v6p0611c1s
Lavis, H.J. v2p0460c1s
Lavis, H.J.J. v1p0376c2s
v2p0460c1m
Law, A. v2p0146c2s
v4p0580c2s v5p0041c1s v5p0130c2s
v5p0140c2s v5p0190c1s v5p0191c1s
v5p0526c1s v6p0155c2s v6p0352c1s
v6p0490c2s
Law, Alice v4p0137c2s
v4p0492c1s v4p0619c2s v6p0206c2s
v6p0360c1s
Law, E. v5p0172c2m
Law, E.F. v6p0260c2s
v6p0314c1s
Law, E.F.G. v2p0004c1s
v2p0381c1s v2p0454c2s v3p0327c1s
Law, E.M. v2p0177c2s
v2p0372c2s v3p0090c2s v3p0442c2s
v3p0463c2s
Law, E.M. et al. v5p0541c2s
Law, F.H. v5p0511c1s
Law, Fred.H. v4p0016c1s
Law, G. v4p0531c2s
v5p0150c1s v5p0215c2s v5p0361c1s
v5p0397c2s v5p0474c2s v6p0185c2s
Law, H. v1p1181c1s
v6p0048c1s
Law, H.E. v6p0374c1s
v6p0568c1s
Law, J. v3p0172c1s
v3p0324c1s v4p0315c2s v4p0591c1s
Law, J.G. v2p0039c1s
v2p0103c1s
Law, M.W. v6p0078c2s
v6p0163c2s
Law, O.P. and Gill, W.T. . v6p0042c1s
Law, R.H. v4p0532c2s
v6p0527c1s
Law, S.D. v1p0046c2s
Law, Sidney J. v4p0062c1s
Law, T.G. v1p0806c1s
v3p0038c2s v3p0228c2s v3p0247c1s
v4p0023c1s v4p0054c1s v4p0139c1s
v4p0154c1s v4p0350c2s v4p0358c2s
v4p0540c1s v5p0096c2s v6p0379c1s
Law, V.M. v5p0050c2s
Law, W.H. v6p0436c2s
Lawdeshayne, P. v4p0291c2s
Lawes, J. v2p0395c2s
Lawes, J.B. v3p0386c1s
Lawes, J.B. and Gilbert, J.H.
v1p1404c1s
Lawes, W.G. v2p0311c1s
Lawford, Mr. v1p0161c2s
Lawhead, W.D. v4p0376c2s
Lawhead, L.D. v3p0387c2s
Lawler, A. v2p0349c2s
Lawler, E.J. v3p0116c2s
Lawler, J. v3p0049c2s
v4p0067c1s
Lawler, James v5p0360c1s
Lawler, W. v4p0045c2s
v4p0371c1s v4p0623c1s

Lawler-Wilson, W. v6p0237c2s
v6p0379c2s v6p0386c2s
Lawless, E. v1p0145c1s
v1p0366c1s v2p0047c2s v2p0052c2s
v2p0242c2s v2p0297c2s v3p0264c2s
v3p0311c1s v3p0351c1s v4p0196c1s
v4p0386c2s v4p0492c2s v5p0210c2s
v5p0214c2s v5p0341c1s v5p0414c1s
v6p0145c1s v6p0293c1s v6p0366c1s
v6p0680c1m
Lawless, Emily v5p0266c2s
v6p0432c1s
Lawless, Emily, Hon. v3p0155c1s
v3p0170c2s v3p0219c2s v3p0220c2m
v3p0234c2s
Lawless, M.H. v3p0398c1s
Lawley, A. v5p0005c2s
Lawley, F. v1p1345c1s
v3p0039c1s v3p0296c1s v5p0235c1s
Lawlor, J. v2p0051c2s
Lawney, E.M. v1p0643c2s
Lawrance, S. v5p0282c2s
Lawrence, A. v4p0051c2s
v4p0077c1s v5p0052c1s v5p0053c1s
v5p0067c1s v5p0174c2s v5p0301c2s
v5p0324c2s v5p0360c2s v5p0395c2s
v5p0404c2s v5p0429c1s v5p0479c1s
v5p0632c1s v6p0383c2s v6p0624c2s
Lawrence, A. and Bolton, G.
v5p0340c1s
Lawrence, A.A. v1p0307c1m
Lawrence, A.E. v4p0078c1s
v4p0258c1s v4p0457c1s v5p0529c1s
v5p0538c2s
Lawrence, A.H. v4p0362c1s
v5p0069c1s v5p0137c1s v5p0141c1s
v5p0255c2s v5p0276c2s v5p0530c1m
v5p0560c1s
Lawrence, Arth. v5p0054c2s
Lawrence, B. v1p0796c1s
v1p1440c1s
Lawrence, C. v6p0506c2s
Lawrence, C.A. v4p0373c1s
Lawrence, C.E. v6p0310c2s
Lawrence, C.Napier v6p0267c1s
Lawrence, E. v1p0033c2s
v1p0043c1s v1p0147c1s v1p0206c2s
v1p0258c1s v1p0310c1s v1p0360c1s
v1p0376c2s v1p0388c2s v1p0497c2s
v1p0540c2s v1p0563c2s v1p0612c1s
v1p0618c1s v1p0640c2s v1p0643c1s
v1p0651c2s v1p0654c2s v1p0665c2s
v1p0669c2m v1p0682c2s v1p0683c2s
v1p0691c1s v1p0737c2s v1p0775c1s
v1p0777c1s v1p0857c1s v1p0909c2s
v1p0916c1s v1p0916c2s v1p0938c1s
v1p1124c2s v1p1125c1s v1p1131c2s
v1p1363c2s v1p1382c2s v1p1398c2s
v1p1399c1s v1p1431c2s v3p0140c1s
v3p0257c1s v3p0336c1s v3p0377c2s
v4p0126c1s v4p0280c1s v4p0400c1s
v4p0404c1s v4p0603c1s
Lawrence, E.A. v1p0216c1s
v1p0287c1s v1p0294c2s v1p0313c1s
v1p0575c1s v1p0594c2m v1p0685c1s
v1p0910c1s v1p1303c1s v1p1303c2s
v1p1336c2s v1p1428c1s v2p0064c2s
v2p0151c2s v2p0451c2s v3p0078c2s
v3p0212c1s v3p0212c2m v3p0226c2s
v3p0227c1s v3p0282c2m v3p0283c1s
v6p0581c1s
Lawrence, E.A. and Dodge, M.A.
v3p0096c2s
Lawrence, E.C. v6p0348c1s
Lawrence, E.E. v2p0251c1s
Lawrence, E.W. v6p0511c1s
Lawrence, F. v1p0087c1s
v1p0165c1s v1p0213c2s v1p0324c2s
v1p0422c2s v1p0451c2s v1p0694c1s
v1p0725c2s v1p0728c2s v1p0753c1s
v1p0863c1s v1p1061c1s v1p1211c2s
v1p1226c1s v1p1275c1s v1p1364c1s
v2p0250c1s v6p0489c1s
Lawrence, F.T. v3p0162c2s
v3p0170c2s v3p0296c1s
Lawrence, F.W. v6p0156c1s
Lawrence, G.A. v1p0044c2s
v1p0100c1s v1p0159c1s v1p1150c2s
v1p1277c1s
Lawrence, G.F. v5p0428c2s
Lawrence, G.N. v1p0536c1s
Lawrence, H.N. and Harries, A.
v3p0133c2s
Lawrence, H.T. v5p0318c2s
v6p0156c1s v6p0437c1s
Lawrence, I. v1p0026c1s
Lawrence, Ida E. v6p0564c1s
Lawrence, Isabel v6p0116c1s
Lawrence, J. v6p0483c2s
Lawrence, J.H. v2p0309c2s
v4p0585c2s v5p0380c2s
Lawrence, J.S. v2p0318c2s
Lawrence, M.V. v1p0877c1s
v3p0092c1s
Lawrence, M.W., Mrs. v1p0393c2s
Lawrence, O.L. v5p0360c1s
Lawrence, R.J. v5p0301c1s
Lawrence, R.M. v4p0264c2s
Lawrence, R.R. v5p0472c1s
v6p0244c1s
Lawrence, R.R. and Norton, C.L.
v5p0492c1s
Lawrence, R.R. and Norton, C.S.
v5p0289c1s
Lawrence, S. v3p0289c1s
v3p0354c2s v5p0421c1s
Lawrence, S.B. v6p0215c2s
v6p0495c1s
Lawrence, Sarah B. v6p0485c2s
Lawrence, T.J. v5p0437c2s
Lawrence, W. v3p0092c1s
v3p0347c1s v4p0074c2s v5p0624c1s
v5p0634c2s v6p0282c1s v6p0645c2s
v6p0680c2s v6p0691c2s v6p0702c1s
Lawrence, W.A. v1p0085c2s
Lawrence, W.B. v1p0304c2s
v1p0320c2s v1p0650c2m v1p0801c1s
v1p1348c1s
Lawrence, W.F. v3p0131c1s
Lawrence, W.J. v2p0123c1s
v2p0328c1s v3p0002c2s v3p0071c2s
v3p0148c2s v3p0172c1s v3p0185c2s
v3p0319c1m v3p0334c2s v3p0377c1m
v3p0406c1m v3p0406c2s v3p0456c2s
v4p0088c2s v4p0343c1s v4p0424c1m
v4p0504c2s v4p0541c2s v4p0543c2s
v4p0544c1m v5p0424c1s v5p0429c1s
v5p0523c2s v5p0524c1s v6p0481c2s
v6p0612c2s v6p0641c2s
Lawrence, W.M. v2p0265c2s
v3p0302c1s
Lawrence, W.R. v4p0308c2m
Lawrence, W.T. v5p0104c1s
v5p0442c2s
Lawrence, Walter, Sir v6p0313c2s
Lawrence-Archer v3p0079c1s
Lawrence-Archer, J.H. v3p0034c1s
Lawrence-Archer, J.H., Maj.
v4p0093c2s
Lawrenny, H. v1p0208c2s
v1p0327c1s v1p0346c1s v1p0437c1s
v1p1160c1s v1p1182c1s v1p1284c2s
Lawry, W. v1p1315c2s
Laws, E. v3p0278c2s
v4p0253c2s
Laws, T.C. v4p0018c2s
v4p0168c2s v4p0188c1s v4p0541c2s
Lawson, A.C. v3p0107c1s
v3p0169c2s v3p0353c2s v5p0229c1s
v5p0329c1m
Lawson, A.C. and Leuschner, A.O.
v6p0567c2s
Lawson, A.J. v1p0283c2s
v1p1123c1s
Lawson, E.McG. v4p0002c2s
v4p0094c2s
Lawson, F. v5p0197c2s
Lawson, G. v1p0962c1s
Lawson, G.D. v2p0483c1s
Lawson, G.D. et al. v2p0079c2s
Lawson, H. v1p0301c1s
v1p0541c1s v1p0588c2s v1p0835c1s
v1p0955c2s v1p1003c2s v1p1366c1s
v1p1376c2s v1p1406c2s v3p0146c2s
v5p0042c1s v5p0076c2s v5p0166c1s
v5p0169c2s v5p0344c2s v5p0435c1s
v5p0571c2s v6p0288c2s
Lawson, H.L.W. v4p0006c1s
v5p0093c1s v5p0244c2s v5p0345c1m
Lawson, H.L.W. and Waterhouse, A.
v3p0412c1s
Lawson, H.M. v6p0649c1s
Lawson, J. v3p0178c2s
v3p0295c2s v3p0304c2m v4p0228c2s
v4p0311c1s v4p0313c2s v4p0503c1s
v5p0065c2s v6p0155c2s v6p0440c2s
v6p0647c2s
Lawson, J.A. v1p0963c2m
v4p0263c1s
Lawson, J.D. v1p1204c2s
v2p0148c2s v2p0196c1m v3p0005c2s
Lawson, J.H. v1p0299c2s
Lawson, J.S. v6p0581c2s
Lawson, M.A. v1p0153c1s
Lawson, N.R. v4p0544c1s
Lawson, O.C. v2p0374c2s
Lawson, P.U. v6p0149c1s
Lawson, P.V. v6p0350c2s
v6p0514c1s v6p0701c1m
Lawson, R. v1p0019c2s
v1p0098c1s v3p0098c1m v4p0236c1s
v5p0167c1s v6p0181c1s
Lawson, T.W. v6p0014c1s
v6p0224c1s v6p0242c2m v6p0321c2m
v6p0322c1s v6p0434c2s v6p0613c1s
Lawson, W. v4p0461c2s
v6p0481c2s
Lawson, W., Sir v1p0367c1s
v1p0649c1s v2p0356c1s
Lawson, W.A. v5p0277c1s
v6p0329c1s
Lawson, W.C. v5p0167c1s
Lawson, W.J. v1p0092c1s
v1p0094c1s v1p0912c1s
Lawson, W.R. v2p0108c1s
v3p0019c1m v3p0032c2s v3p0033c1s
v3p0446c1s v4p0006c1s v4p0025c2s
v4p0044c2s v4p0199c1s v4p0279c1s
v4p0307c2s v4p0524c2s v4p0525c2s
v4p0582c1s v5p0046c1s v5p0068c2s
v5p0131c1s v5p0217c2m v5p0231c2s
v5p0270c1s v5p0286c2s v5p0289c1s
v5p0295c1s v5p0303c1s v5p0386c2s
v5p0501c1s v5p0502c1s v5p0529c2s
v6p0049c2s v6p0151c1s v6p0161c2s
v6p0162c1s v6p0267c2s v6p0325c1s
v6p0452c1s v6p0530c1s v6p0655c2s
Lawton, C.E. v6p0263c2s
v6p0290c1s v6p0290c2s v6p0563c2s
Lawton, E.P. v5p0061c1s
v6p0030c2s v6p0136c2s
Lawton, F. v6p0070c1s
Lawton, G.W. v1p0056c2s
v1p0335c1s
Lawton, W.C. v2p0190c2s
v2p0214c1s v2p0451c1s v3p0003c2s
v3p0025c1s v3p0069c1s v3p0114c1s
v3p0144c1m v3p0199c2s v3p0294c1s
v3p0310c1s v3p0448c1s v4p0004c2s
v4p0032c1s v4p0076c1s v4p0092c2s
v4p0169c1s v4p0189c2s v4p0262c1m
v4p0343c2s v4p0430c2s v4p0489c2s
v4p0500c1s v4p0585c1s v4p0597c2s
v4p0626c2s v5p0016c1s v5p0118c2s
v5p0192c1s v5p0249c2m v5p0253c2s
v5p0254c2s v5p0259c1s v5p0264c1s
v5p0269c1s v5p0326c2m v5p0343c2s
v5p0347c1s v5p0405c1s v5p0456c1s
v5p0488c1s v5p0495c2s v5p0612c2s
v6p0002c1s v6p0017c1s v6p0039c1s
v6p0518c2s v6p0570c2s v6p0646c1s
v6p0672c1s
Lawton, W.C. and Ashley, W.J.
v5p0548c2s
Lawton, W.C. and Sturgis, R.
v6p0505c1s
Lawton, W.H. v6p0322c2s
Lawvik, J.N. v6p0069c1s
Lay, B. v6p0304c2s
v6p0694c1s
Lay, H.C. v1p0296c2s
v1p0847c2s v1p0848c1m v1p1103c2s
Lay, J.F. v1p1040c2s
Lay, T.S.De v5p0373c2s
Layard, A. v2p0456c2s
v3p0291c1s
Layard, A.H. v1p0061c1s
v2p0448c2s v3p0098c2s
Layard, Amy v2p0458c2s
v3p0445c2s
Layard, E.L. v2p0047c2s
v3p0384c1s
Layard, F. v3p0295c1s
v3p0405c1s v3p0470c2s
Layard, Florence v3p0060c2s
Layard, G. v2p0069c2s
Layard, G.S. v3p0107c1s
v3p0146c2s v3p0208c2s v3p0246c1m
v3p0426c1s v4p0066c2s v4p0132c1s
v4p0142c1m v4p0151c1s v4p0159c1s
v4p0209c2s v4p0309c1s v4p0343c2s
v4p0371c1s v4p0414c2s v4p0571c2s
v4p0577c2s v5p0033c1s v5p0267c2s
v5p0280c1s v5p0333c2s v5p0502c2s
v6p0089c2s v6p0140c2s v6p0307c2s
v6p0563c1s v6p0586c1s
Layard, Geo.S. v4p0069c2s
v5p0575c1s
Layard, Geo.Somes v5p0574c2s
Layard, J.C. v1p0944c2s
Layard, N.F. v3p0368c1s
Laycock, F.U. v4p0378c1s
Laycock, T. v1p0796c1s
Laye, R. v1p1370c1s
Laying, J. v5p0637c2s
Layman, F.A. v3p0204c1s
Layman, J.M. v2p0425c2s
Layton, W. v4p0127c1s
Layton, W.E. v2p0336c1s
Layton, Walter T. v6p0029c1s
v6p0231c2s
Lazare, B. v5p0168c2s
v6p0343c2s
Lazarus, E. v1p0402c1s
v1p0472c2s v1p0810c1s v1p1278c1s
v2p0037c1s v2p0140c1s v2p0169c1s
v2p0200c1s v2p0236c2m v2p0299c1s
v2p0385c1m v2p0398c1s v3p0061c2s
Lazarus, Emma v2p0368c1s
Lazarus, J. v3p0007c2s
v3p0035c1s v4p0418c1s v5p0645c2s
Lazelle, H.M. v5p0284c1s
v5p0285c1s
Lazenby, A. v5p0611c2s
Lazenby, W.R. v4p0204c1s
v4p0252c1s
Lazzari, R. v5p0609c2s
Lea, F. v2p0214c2s
Lea, G. v5p0622c1s
Lea, H. v6p0701c2s
Lea, H.C. v1p0069c1s
v1p0087c1s v1p0101c2s v1p0148c2s
v1p0247c2s v1p0280c2s v1p0287c1s
v1p0315c2s v1p0436c1s v1p0554c2s
v1p0582c1s v1p0673c1s v1p0697c2s
v1p0861c2s v1p0891c1s v1p0926c1s
v1p0960c1s v1p0992c1m v1p1013c1s
v1p1032c2s v1p1039c2s v1p1085c2s
v1p1109c1s v1p1206c2s v1p1283c1s
v1p1384c2s v2p0049c2s v2p0086c2s

v2p0287c2s v3p0054c1s v3p0096c1s v3p0210c2s v3p0216c2m v3p0217c2s v3p0230c2s v3p0240c1s v3p0329c1s v3p0337c2s v3p0364c1s v3p0424c1s v3p0444c1s v3p0453c1s v4p0109c1s v4p0127c2s v4p0154c2s v4p0156c2s v4p0179c2s v4p0202c2s v4p0213c1s v4p0285c1s v4p0358c2s v4p0433c1s v4p0527c1s v4p0599c1s v4p0602c1s v5p0125c2s v5p0220c1s v5p0264c2s v5p0350c2s v5p0386c2s v5p0459c2s v5p0542c2m v5p0568c2s v5p0583c1s v6p0292c2s v6p0424c1s
Lea, I. v1p0589c2s v1p0929c1s
Lea, J. v1p0376c2s v1p0899c2s
Lea, J.H. v3p0086c2s v3p0245c2s v4p0252c1s v4p0324c2s v4p0433c2s v4p0552c2s v4p0585c2s v5p0049c2s v5p0086c1s v5p0191c1s v6p0049c2s v6p0205c2s v6p0207c2s
Lea, M.C. v1p0224c1m v1p0268c2m v1p0278c2m v1p0518c1s v1p0652c1s v1p0746c2m v1p0747c1s v1p0747c2s v1p0924c1s v1p0955c2m v1p1003c1m v1p1199c1m v3p0008c2s v3p0009c1m v3p0080c1m v3p0208c2s v3p0330c2s v3p0393c1m v3p0393c2m v4p0002c2s v4p0036c2m v4p0125c1s v4p0180c1m v4p0362c2s v4p0376c2s v4p0446c1m v4p0487c1s v4p0519c2s v4p0524c1s v4p0525c2s v4p0526c1s v4p0526c2m v4p0536c1s v5p0237c2s
Lea, M.C. and Johnston, C.C. v4p0632c2s
Leach, A. v4p0276c2s v4p0309c2s v4p0372c2s v4p0408c2s v4p0538c1s v5p0161c1s v5p0186c1s v5p0255c1s v5p0269c1s v5p0323c2s v5p0555c1m v5p0574c2s v5p0611c1s
Leach, A.E. v6p0231c2s
Leach, A.F. v2p0197c2s v2p0208c2s v2p0348c1s v3p0255c1s v3p0337c2s v4p0171c2s v4p0420c1s v4p0499c2s v4p0505c2s v4p0506c1s v4p0623c2s v5p0557c1s v6p0060c1s
Leach, Abby v5p0036c2s
Leach, Anna v5p0024c1s v5p0317c2s
Leach, C. v2p0115c1s v2p0368c2s
Leach, C.J. v6p0030c2s
Leach, E.D. v6p0176c2s
Leach, H. v1p1325c1s v2p0131c1s v6p0090c2s v6p0607c1s v6p0626c2s
Leach, Henry v6p0358c1s v6p0481c2s v6p0657c1s
Leach, J.A. v1p0179c1s v4p0635c2s
Leach, J.G. v4p0165c2s v4p0383c1s v4p0434c1s v4p0474c1s v6p0284c2s
Leach, J.H. v1p1233c2s
Leach, R.B. v4p0107c2s
Leach, S.S. v3p0283c1s
Leach, W. v5p0027c2s
Leacock, R.B. v2p0367c2s
Leacock, S. v5p0270c1s v6p0505c1s
Leadam v6p0320c1s
Leadam, I.S. v2p0180c2s v2p0434c2s v3p0039c1s v4p0066c1s v4p0133c1s v4p0604c2s v5p0270c2s v5p0379c1s v6p0404c1s v6p0677c1s
Leadam, I.S. and Gairdner, J. v6p0287c1s
Leadbeater, C.W. v4p0295c2s
Leader, D.H. v5p0056c2s
Leader, J. v6p0334c1m
Leader, J.D. v2p0091c2s
Leader, J.T. v1p1148c2s
Leadham, J.S. v2p0228c1s
Leadman, A.D.H. v3p0365c2s v6p0172c2s
Leadman, W.M. v6p0698c2s
Leaf, J. v1p0215c1s
Leaf, W. v2p0206c1s v3p0020c1s v3p0073c2s v3p0199c2m
Leaf, W. et al. v2p0229c1s
Leahy, E. v6p0236c1s v6p0326c1s v6p0391c1s v6p0461c1s
Leahy, W.A. v2p0254c1s v3p0139c2m v3p0355c1s v3p0427c1s
Leake, A.H. v5p0360c2s
Leake, D.M. v5p0234c1s
Leake, P., Mrs. v5p0080c1s
Leake, W.M. and Squire, J. v1p1030c1s
Leakin, G.A. v1p0004c1s v1p0594c1s
Leale, C.A. et al. v2p0080c2s
Leaman, C. v3p0042c2m v4p0056c2m
Leaman, W. v1p1164c1s
Leaming, T. v1p0259c1s v3p0219c1s v3p0437c1s v6p0384c1s
Leamington, Lord v2p0337c1s
Lean, F. v1p0065c2s
Leander, Thomas v5p0224c1s
Lear, T. v5p0620c2s
Leared, A. v1p0374c2s v3p0288c2s
Learned, C.A. v6p0525c2s
Learned, D.W. v4p0113c2s
Learned, E. v1p1351c2s
Learned, H.B. v3p0463c1s v4p0268c2s v4p0533c1s v5p0015c2s v5p0267c1s v6p0090c2s v6p0627c1s
Learned, J.C. v1p0108c2s v1p0296c2s v1p1093c1s v3p0067c2s v3p0094c2s v3p0389c2s
Learned, J.E. v2p0081c2s v2p0130c2s v3p0083c2s v3p0157c2s v3p0446c1s v4p0111c2s
Learned, J.G.E. v1p0292c1s
Learned, M.D. v3p0326c1s v4p0438c1s v5p0231c1s v5p0439c2s v6p0192c1s
Learned, R.C. v1p0097c1s v1p1178c1s v1p1414c2s
Learned, W. v3p0025c1s v4p0329c2s
Learned, W.L. v2p0240c1s
Learoyd, H.J. v6p0568c2s
Learoyd, M.W. and Taylor, M.L. v4p0131c2s
Learr, A.F., jr. v5p0135c1s
Leary, J.H.L. v1p1295c1s
Leary, L.G. v6p0106c1s v6p0630c2m
Leary, P. v5p0032c1s v5p0591c1s
Leary, P., jr. v3p0279c1s v3p0448c2s v4p0370c2s v4p0538c2s
Leary, T.H.L. v1p0662c2s v1p0705c1s v1p0953c1s v1p1168c2s v1p1373c1m v2p0042c2s v2p0044c1s v4p0021c1s
Leas, C.A. v1p0258c2s v1p1150c1m
Lease, E.B. v5p0024c1s v5p0278c1s v5p0326c2s
Leask, S.G. v6p0373c1s
Leaske, W.K. v3p0199c2s v3p0328c2s
Leatham, H.B. v5p0242c1s v5p0390c1s v6p0466c2s
Leatham, J. v4p0457c2s v4p0467c1s v4p0508c2s
Leather, F. v5p0319c2s v5p0474c2s v6p0428c1s
Leather, J.W. v6p0602c2s
Leatherdale, G. v5p0390c2s
Leatherdale, G.F. v5p0415c1s
Leathes, S. v1p0242c2s v1p1056c1s v1p1093c1s v1p1338c1s v3p0053c2s v3p0261c2s v3p0425c2s v3p0447c2s
Leathes, S., Mrs. v2p0291c2s
Leathom, G.B. v2p0082c2s v2p0277c1s
Leavens, G.F. v6p0301c1s v6p0567c1s
Leavens, H.W. v3p0311c1s
Leavitt, B. v6p0373c2s
Leavitt, C.P. v1p0008c2s
Leavitt, C.W., jr. v6p0247c2s
Leavitt, E. v3p0300c1s v3p0357c1s
Leavitt, E.W. v4p0323c2s v5p0103c2s v5p0104c2s
Leavitt, E.W., Miss v4p0003c2s
Leavitt, Emily W. v4p0138c1s v4p0546c1s
Leavitt, G.R. v1p0598c2s v1p0944c1s v4p0218c1s
Leavitt, J. v1p0279c2s v1p0283c2s v1p0336c1s v1p0342c2s v1p0426c1s v1p0575c1s v1p0725c1s v1p0833c1s v1p0862c2m v1p1010c1s v1p1023c2s v1p1037c2m v1p1038c1s v1p1038c2s v1p1043c1s v1p1103c2s v1p1174c1s v1p1206c1s v1p1292c2s v1p1350c1s v1p1432c2s
Leavitt, J.B. v2p0439c1s v4p0123c2s v4p0400c1s v5p0116c2s v6p0146c2s v6p0637c1s v6p0666c2s
Leavitt, J.B. et al. v5p0114c2s
Leavitt, J.M. v1p0252c1s v1p1120c1s v2p0336c1s
Leavitt, R.G. v5p0471c1s v5p0496c2s v5p0586c1s
Leavitt, S. v1p0774c1s v2p0444c2s v4p0280c2s
Leavitt, W.H. v5p0430c2s v5p0431c2s
Lebaron, W. v1p0048c2s
Lebermann, F. v4p0182c1s
Lebl, S. v2p0199c2s
Lebon, A. v5p0156c1s v5p0217c2s v6p0237c1s v6p0480c1s
Lebon, Andre v4p0181c1s v4p0211c1s
Lebour, G.A. v1p1371c1s v4p0153c1s
Lebrun, M. v1p0161c1s
Lech, T.W. v5p0209c2s
Leche, K. v6p0640c2s
Lechler, D.K. v1p1095c1s
Lechler, Dr.von v4p0345c2s
Lechler, G. v1p0515c2s v2p0353c1s
Lechmere, Lady v3p0461c2s
Leckie, C.S. v4p0522c1s
Leckie, J.D. v6p0029c2s v6p0478c2s
Leckie-Ewing, R. v6p0168c1s
Lecky, C.S. v5p0293c2s
Lecky, E. v1p0013c1s v3p0338c1s v4p0006c2s v4p0186c2s v4p0242c2s v4p0286c2s v4p0463c2s v4p0505c1s v4p0531c2s v5p0325c1s v5p0381c1s v5p0631c1s v6p0236c1s v6p0323c1s v6p0534c1s v6p0611c2s
Lecky, Eliz. v3p0074c2s
Lecky, G. v5p0437c2s
Lecky, J. v2p0286c1s
Lecky, Mrs. v3p0125c1s v3p0173c2s v3p0289c1s v5p0631c2s
Lecky, W. v4p0003c2s v4p0291c1s v4p0637c1s v5p0493c2s
Lecky, W.E.H. v1p0409c1s v1p0432c1s v1p0655c1s v2p0226c1s v2p0307c1s v3p0068c2s v3p0174c1s v3p0245c1s v3p0406c1s v4p0259c1s v4p0289c2s v4p0302c2s v5p0247c1s v5p0419c1m v5p0610c2s
Lecky, W.E.H. and Gardiner, S.R. v2p0226c1s
Lecky, W.E.H. and Gladstone, W.E. v3p0210c2s
Lecky, W.E.H. et al. v4p0004c1s v4p0133c1s
Lecky, W.S. v1p0151c1s
Leclere, A. v4p0084c2m v5p0089c1s v5p0562c1s
Lecompte, M.B. v1p0282c2s v1p0373c1s
Leconte, J. v2p0127c1s
Leconte, J.L. v1p0108c2s
Lederer, A.M. v6p0173c2s v6p0622c1s v6p0631c2s
Lederle, E.J. v6p0319c1s v6p0453c2s v6p0660c1s
Ledger, A. v2p0073c1s
Ledger, E. v4p0545c1s v5p0194c2s v5p0549c2m v6p0140c2s v6p0187c2s v6p0402c2s v6p0446c1s v6p0613c2s v6p0713c1s
Ledger, G. v3p0009c1s
Ledoux, A.R. v3p0133c1s
Ledoux, M. v1p0621c2s
Leduc and Sacerdote v5p0227c1s
Ledwich, E. v1p0253c1s v1p0367c2s
Ledwith, W.L. v2p0339c2s v5p0463c2s
Ledyard, H. v2p0361c1s v2p0466c2s
Ledyard, L.W. v2p0362c2s
Lee, A. v1p0833c2s v3p0267c1m v5p0274c2s v5p0505c1s v6p0036c2s v6p0093c2s v6p0098c1s v6p0132c1s v6p0268c2s v6p0445c1s v6p0611c2s v6p0662c2s v6p0683c1s
Lee, A. and Pearson, K. .. v5p0475c2s
Lee, A.B. v1p1236c2m
Lee, A.E. v2p0046c1s v2p0060c2s v2p0072c1m v2p0086c2s v2p0108c2s v2p0184c2s v2p0254c2s v2p0349c2s v3p0171c2s v3p0198c2s v3p0310c2s v3p0351c1s v3p0395c2s v4p0411c2s
Lee, A.H. v5p0244c1s
Lee, A.H., Capt. v5p0182c1s
Lee, A.L. v4p0628c1s
Lee, A.W. v5p0164c2s
Lee, Alice L. v5p0021c2s v6p0379c2s
Lee, B. v1p1150c2s v6p0529c1s
Lee, B.P. v3p0264c1s
Lee, C. v1p0726c2s v1p1143c2s v4p0396c2s v6p0434c1s
Lee, C.A. v1p0504c1s
Lee, C.F. v3p0166c1s v3p0206c1s v3p0302c1s v3p0400c2s
Lee, C.F., jr. v1p0776c2s
Lee, C.T. v3p0334c1s
Lee, C.Z. v1p0605c2s
Lee, D. v1p0016c1s
Lee, D.K. v1p0070c2s v1p1174c1s
Lee, E. v1p1081c1s v4p0034c1m v5p0162c2s v5p0599c1s v6p0252c2s v6p0380c1s v6p0461c2s
Lee, E.A. v6p0393c2s
Lee, E.C. v4p0611c2s
Lee, E.G. v1p0813c2s v1p0833c1s
Lee, E.M. v1p1426c1s
Lee, E.M.O'H. v3p0064c2s
Lee, E.P. v4p0129c1s
Lee, Edgar v4p0413c1s
Lee, Elizabeth v4p0633c2s v6p0252c1s
Lee, F. v1p0216c2s v1p0299c1s v1p0518c2s v1p1262c1s

v2p0098c1s v4p0610c1s v4p0615c2s
v5p0146c2s v5p0148c1s
Lee, F. and Stuart, J.E.B.
v1p0704c2s
Lee, F. et al. v1p0518c2s
Lee, F.G. v1p0251c2s
v1p0255c2s v1p0946c2s v3p0164c1s
v4p0478c2s v4p0613c1s v5p0117c2s
v5p0550c2s
Lee, F.R. v5p0401c2s
Lee, F.S. v4p0442c1s
v5p0016c2s v5p0018c2s v5p0449c2s
v6p0409c1m v6p0432c1s v6p0576c2s
Lee, F.W. v3p0172c1s
v5p0336c2s
Lee, Fitz-Hugh v6p0333c2s
Lee, G. v1p1271c1s
Lee, G.A. v2p0019c2m
Lee, G.C. v4p0323c2s
v5p0047c2s v5p0074c2s
Lee, G.H. v3p0091c2s
Lee, G.L. v4p0397c1s
Lee, G.S. v3p0290c2s
v4p0002c2s v4p0089c2s v4p0572c1s
v4p0614c1s v5p0126c1s v5p0145c2m
v5p0206c1s v5p0254c1s v5p0274c2s
v5p0310c2s v5p0341c2s v5p0434c1s
v5p0456c1s v5p0466c2s v5p0502c1s
v5p0555c2s v5p0620c1s v6p0075c1s
v6p0126c1s v6p0126c2s v6p0202c1s
v6p0370c2s v6p0532c1s
Lee, G.W. v4p0591c1s
v6p0278c1s v6p0585c1s
Lee, G.W.C. v1p1107c1s
Lee, H. v1p0038c1s
v1p0307c1s v1p0760c1s v1p0834c1s
v2p0121c1s v2p0157c2s v2p0275c1s
v2p0284c1s v2p0471c1s v3p0311c2s
v4p0309c2s v6p0290c2s
Lee, H.C. v6p0440c1s
Lee, H.T. v1p0999c1s
v1p1183c2s v1p1322c2s
Lee, Henry v4p0515c1s
Lee, I. v6p0454c1s
v6p0571c1s
Lee, J. v1p0652c1s
v2p0261c1s v2p0361c1s v3p0079c1s
v4p0371c1s v4p0452c1s v4p0559c1m
v4p0559c2s v4p0564c2s v4p0580c2m
v5p0199c2s v5p0227c2s v5p0329c2s
v5p0332c2s v5p0391c1s v5p0443c1s
v5p0454c2s v5p0465c1s v5p0574c2s
v5p0598c1s v6p0002c2s v6p0076c2s
v6p0109c2s v6p0405c1s
Lee, J.B. v6p0496c2s
Lee, J.G.C. v5p0029c1s
v5p0029c2s v5p0474c1s v5p0598c2s
v5p0599c1s v6p0667c2s
Lee, J.M. v5p0372c2s
Lee, J.S. v1p0046c1s
v1p0061c2s v1p0120c2m v1p0254c2s
v1p0509c2s v1p0646c1s v1p0724c1s
v1p0724c2s v1p0810c2s v1p0848c1s
v1p0898c2s v1p0961c1s v1p0980c1s
v1p1092c2s v2p0081c2s v2p0181c1s
v2p0223c1s v2p0368c2s v3p0081c1s
v3p0082c2m v3p0229c2s v3p0281c1s
Lee, J.W. v1p0166c2s
v1p1024c2s v3p0178c2s v4p0617c1s
Lee, J.W.M. v1p0914c2s
Lee, Jennette v5p0254c1s
v6p0121c2s v6p0154c2s v6p0166c1s
v6p0299c2s v6p0305c2s v6p0306c1s
v6p0351c2s v6p0380c2s v6p0415c2s
v6p0467c1s v6p0467c2s v6p0491c1s
v6p0503c2m v6p0504c1s v6p0577c1s
v6p0619c1s v6p0644c2m v6p0651c1s
v6p0661c2s v6p0681c2s v6p0700c2s
Lee, L. v1p0383c1s
Lee, M. v3p0228c1s
Lee, M. and Moxom, P.S. .. v3p0119c1s
Lee, M.C. v4p0293c2s
Lee, M.N. v4p0612c1s
v4p0629c2s
Lee, M.V. v3p0287c1s
Lee, Mary C. v5p0628c1s
Lee, Mrs. v1p0024c1s
v1p1429c1s
Lee, O. v6p0264c1s
Lee, P. v5p0365c1s
Lee, P.R. v6p0036c2s
Lee, Prof. v1p0920c1s
Lee, R. v1p1029c1s
v2p0123c1s v2p0338c1s v3p0107c2s
v3p0253c1s v3p0387c2s v3p0465c1s
Lee, R.E. v1p0216c2s
v1p0518c2s v1p0519c1s v1p1344c1s
v1p1346c1s v3p0325c2s
Lee, R.E. et al. v1p1347c1s
Lee, R.W. v4p0183c2s
Lee, S. v1p0238c2s
v1p0356c2s v1p0445c1s v1p0581c2s
v1p0846c2s v4p0059c2s v4p0611c2s
v5p0053c2s v5p0186c1s v5p0207c2s
v5p0383c2s v5p0522c1m v5p0522c2s
v5p0523c1s v6p0074c2s v6p0488c2s
v6p0586c1s v6p0587c1m v6p0587c2s
v6p0588c2s v6p0672c1s
Lee, S. and Stokes, H.P. . v4p0356c1s
Lee, S. et al. v5p0052c1s
Lee, S.A. v1p0121c1s
v1p0810c1s
Lee, S.D. v1p1190c2s
v1p1212c1s v1p1347c2s v1p1369c2s
Lee, S.D. et al. v1p0795c2s
v5p0541c2s
Lee, S.H. v3p0040c2s
v3p0445c1s
Lee, S.L. v1p1185c2s
v2p0144c1m v2p0148c1s v2p0197c2s
v2p0208c1s v2p0271c2s v2p0284c1s
v2p0335c1s v2p0397c1s v3p0074c1s
v3p0104c2s v3p0391c2s v6p0012c1s
Lee, S.L. and Atkinson, E.G.
v2p0024c2s
Lee, S.L. and Sweet, H. .. v2p0144c1s
Lee, S.P. v5p0478c2s
v5p0594c1s
Lee, S.R. v1p1186c2s
Lee, S.T.H. v1p0855c2s
Lee, Sidney v4p0064c1s
v6p0501c2s
Lee, T. v1p0108c2s
Lee, T.I. v5p0037c1s
Lee, V. v1p0009c1s
v1p0051c1s v1p0063c2m v1p0226c1s
v1p0323c2s v1p0446c2s v1p0595c2s
v1p0669c1m v1p0826c2s v1p0883c2s
v1p0884c2s v1p1021c2s v1p1098c1m
v1p1201c1s v1p1338c2s v2p0038c2s
v2p0053c2s v2p0093c2s v2p0123c1s
v2p0195c1s v2p0285c1s v2p0401c1s
v3p0252c2s v3p0358c2s v4p0531c2s
v5p0189c2s v5p0280c1s v6p0555c1s
Lee, V. and Robinson, A.M.F.
v3p0082c1s
Lee, Vernon v4p0274c2s
v4p0326c1s v4p0332c2s v4p0405c2s
v4p0605c1s v6p0438c2s v6p0649c1s
v6p0691c2s v6p0704c1s
Lee, W. v1p0123c2s
v2p0172c2s v3p0051c1s v3p0348c1s
Lee, W.B. v4p0324c2s
Lee, W.M. v6p0488c2s
Lee-Hamilton, E. v4p0059c2s
v4p0482c1s
Lee-Warner, W. v4p0278c2s
v5p0285c1s v5p0286c1s v6p0072c2s
v6p0314c2s
Leebody, Prof. v1p0458c1s
v2p0101c1s
Leech, A.G. v6p0058c2s
v6p0685c1s
Leech, B. v2p0227c1s
Leech, C.A. v6p0499c1s
Leech, D.D. v1p0789c1s
v1p1038c2s
Leech, E.O. v4p0378c2s
v4p0524c2m v4p0525c1m v4p0525c2s
Leech, H.B. v2p0223c2s
v6p0426c1s
Leech, S.H. v4p0564c2s
Leeds, A.R. v1p0224c2s
v1p0225c1s v1p0321c2s v1p0434c1s
v1p0506c2s v1p0509c1m v1p0844c1s
v1p0845c1s v1p1150c2s v1p1234c1s
v1p1391c2s v2p0017c1s v2p0386c1s
v2p0389c1s v5p0206c2s v5p0621c2s
Leeds, B.F. v4p0285c2s
v4p0498c2s
Leeds, C.C. v1p0662c2s
Leeds, Duchess of v6p0571c2s
Leeds, F.G. v4p0613c2s
Leeds, G. v1p0421c2s
v1p0422c1s v1p0998c1s
Leeds, K. v5p0429c1s
Leeds, L.W. v1p0580c2s
v1p1366c1s
Leeds, R.F. v4p0503c1s
Leeds, S.P. v1p0799c1s
Leeds, T.E. v1p0616c2s
Leeds, V.N. v4p0121c1s
Leefe, J.G. v3p0278c2s
Leefe, L.G. v3p0007c1s
Leege, F. v6p0257c2s
v6p0576c2s
Leemans, C.
v1p1122c2s
Leeper, A. and Oppenheim, M.
v5p0347c1s
Leeper, J.A. v5p0238c2s
Leeper, J.L. v5p0310c2m
v6p0340c1s v6p0346c1s v6p0638c1s
Leeper, R.M. v6p0163c2s
Lees, A.B. v5p0309c1s
Lees, B.A. v6p0196c2s
Lees, B.W. v5p0146c1s
v6p0445c2s
Lees, C.H. v6p0082c1s
v6p0082c2s
Lees, E. v4p0153c2s
Lees, F. v1p0478c1s
v1p0605c2s v5p0218c1s v5p0256c1s
v5p0262c1s v5p0304c1s v5p0332c1s
v5p0398c2m v5p0424c1s v5p0431c1s
v5p0431c2s v5p0618c2s v6p0205c1s
v6p0220c2s v6p0483c1s v6p0510c2s
v6p0523c1s v6p0536c1s v6p0579c2s
v6p0620c1s v6p0675c2s v6p0689c2s
Lees, F.S. v1p0934c1s
v1p0934c2s
Lees, Frederic v5p0390c2s
Lees, G.R. v4p0046c2s
v4p0299c2s v5p0305c1s v5p0310c2s
v6p0340c1s
Lees, J.A. v6p0657c2s
Lees, J.C. v1p0590c2s
v1p1137c1s v1p1230c1s v1p1270c1s
v1p1274c2s v3p0363c1s v4p0151c1s
Leese, W. v2p0185c2s
Leeson, G.E. v2p0284c2s
Leet, J.E. v4p0125c1s
Leete, J. v2p0156c1s
v3p0196c2s v3p0266c1s v4p0110c1s
v4p0316c2s v4p0343c1s v4p0520c2s
v5p0589c2s
Lefaivre, P. v3p0114c1s
Lefevre, A. v5p0085c1s
v5p0275c2s v6p0143c2s v6p0209c2s
Lefevre, E. v5p0069c1s
v5p0075c2s v5p0348c1s v5p0359c1s
v5p0451c1s v5p0580c2s v5p0617c1s
v5p0635c1s v6p0043c1s v6p0261c1s
v6p0291c2s v6p0398c1s v6p0410c1s
v6p0431c1s v6p0533c1s v6p0536c1s
v6p0596c1s v6p0647c2s v6p0684c1s
v6p0699c2s
Lefevre, Edwin v6p0276c1s
v6p0617c2s
Lefevre, G. v6p0273c2s
Lefevre, G.J.S. v1p0552c1s
v5p0027c2s
Lefevre, G.J.Shaw v4p0239c1s
Lefevre, G.S. v1p0217c1s
v1p0293c1s v1p0382c2s v1p0392c2s
v1p0423c1s v1p0657c2s v1p0721c1s
v1p1192c1s v2p0005c2s v2p0206c1s
v2p0224c2s v2p0247c2s v2p0264c2m
v2p0291c1s v2p0391c1s v2p0418c2s
v3p0025c2s v3p0097c2s v3p0399c2s
v5p0589c2s v5p0622c2s v6p0047c2s
v6p0445c2s
Lefevre, G.Shaw v2p0189c2s
v3p0161c1s v3p0461c1s
v5p0346c2s
Leffingwell, A. v2p0150c2s
v2p0221c2s v2p0245c1s v2p0340c1s
v2p0355c1s v2p0462c1s v4p0018c2s
v5p0587c1s v6p0680c2m
Leffingwell, A.J. v1p0486c2s
v1p0487c1s v1p1376c2s v1p1410c2s
Leffingwell, W.B. v6p0454c2s
Leffingwell, W.F. v5p0527c1s
Leffmann, H. v5p0004c1s
v5p0161c2s v5p0448c1s v6p0111c2s
v6p0340c1s
Leffmann, Henry v6p0412c1s
Lefroy, A.H.F. v4p0237c1s
v5p0039c1m v5p0468c1s v5p0579c1s
v6p0103c1s v6p0364c1s
Lefroy, B.S. v4p0221c2s
Lefroy, E.C. v5p0369c2s
Lefroy, F.C. v4p0047c1s
Lefroy, F.P. v3p0028c1s
v6p0349c2s
Lefroy, J.H. v1p0077c1s
v1p0164c1s v1p0637c1s v1p1003c2s
v2p0032c1s v2p0040c2s v2p0056c2s
v5p0054c2s
Lefroy, J.H., Sir v2p0173c1s
Lefroy, W. v4p0112c1s
v4p0113c1s v5p0414c2s
Lefroy, W.C. v1p0898c1s
v2p0090c1s v2p0310c2s v2p0350c1s
v2p0482c1s
Leftwich, E. v5p0129c2s
Leftwich, F.S. v5p0043c2s
Leftwich, R.W. v5p0191c2s
v5p0368c1s
Legarda, B. et al. v6p0492c2s
Legare, H.S. v1p0016c1s
v1p0072c1s v1p0113c1s v1p0256c2s
v1p0262c1s v1p0271c1s v1p0343c2s
v1p0551c2s v1p0566c2s v1p0705c2s
v1p1122c1m
Legare, J.De v1p0460c1s
Legare, J.M. v1p0197c2s
v1p0206c1s v1p0748c1s v1p0851c2s
v1p1272c1s
Legend, H.S. v1p1087c2s
Leger, J.N. v6p0284c2s
Legg, J.W. v1p1442c2s
Legg, J.Wickham v3p0254c2s
Legg, W. v1p0736c1s
Legge, A.E.J. v4p0568c1s
Legge, A.O. v2p0423c1s
Legge, E. v1p0277c2s
v1p1138c1s v4p0534c2s v5p0270c1s
Legge, F. v3p0114c2s
v3p0118c2s v3p0138c1s v3p0216c2s
v3p0309c2s v3p0428c1s v3p0466c2s
v4p0117c2s v4p0214c2s v4p0232c2s
v4p0515c2s v4p0625c1s v5p0121c1s
v5p0355c2s v5p0483c1s v6p0011c1s
v6p0013c1s v6p0036c1s v6p0037c2s
v6p0079c2s v6p0092c1s v6p0175c2s
v6p0182c1s v6p0199c1s v6p0203c2s
v6p0204c1s v6p0213c1s v6p0215c1s
v6p0228c2s v6p0293c1s v6p0305c2s
v6p0325c2s v6p0361c1s v6p0375c2s

v6p0376c1s v6p0397c1s v6p0402c2s v6p0410c1s v6p0498c2s v6p0512c1s v6p0613c2s v6p0614c1s v6p0636c1s v6p0638c1s v6p0681c1s v6p0707c2s v6p0709c1s
Legge, H. v4p0590c2s v5p0158c1s v5p0536c1s
Legge, J. v2p0079c2s v2p0080c1m
Legge, J.G. v5p0108c1s
Legge, N.H. v5p0052c2s
Legge, R.F. v6p0416c1s
Legge, W.H. v5p0118c2s v5p0489c1s v5p0612c1s v5p0629c1s v6p0008c2s v6p0013c1s v6p0067c1s v6p0069c1s v6p0081c1s v6p0085c2s v6p0154c2s v6p0167c2s v6p0206c2s v6p0286c1s v6p0469c1s v6p0480c2s v6p0512c1s v6p0513c2s v6p0523c2s v6p0611c2s v6p0699c2s
Leggett, E.H.M. v5p0477c1s
Leggett, M.D. v3p0310c2s v4p0267c2s
Leggett, T.H. v4p0175c2s v5p0160c2s
Leggo, C. v3p0203c2s
Leggo, W. v1p0192c1s v2p0157c2s v2p0186c2m v3p0154c1s
Legh, T.W. v3p0050c2s v3p0059c2s v3p0195c2s v3p0361c2s v5p0239c1s v5p0577c2s
Legler, H.E. v5p0555c2s v6p0374c2s
Legrand, J. v5p0217c1s
Legrange, F. v3p0077c2s v3p0331c2s
Lehlbach, F. v6p0258c2s
Lehman, T.J. v1p1432c1s
Lehman, W.E. v6p0351c1s
Lehmann, C. v6p0278c2s
Lehmann, C.F. v6p0046c1s
Lehmann, J. v3p0377c1s
Lehmann, J.R. v2p0337c1s
Lehmann, R. v6p0689c2s
Lehmann, R.C. v3p0368c1s v4p0410c1s v6p0173c2s v6p0367c1s v6p0663c1s
Lehmann, Rudolf v5p0376c1s
Lehmer, D.N. v6p0435c1s
Leiberg, J.B. v4p0437c2s
Leibnitz, G.W. v1p0859c2s v1p1001c2s v1p1017c1s v1p1237c1s v3p0255c1s
Leibrand, C.H. v5p0199c1s
Leichtlin, Max v4p0586c2s
Leidy, J. v1p1239c1s v1p1368c2s v1p1432c2s
Leifchild, F. v1p0064c1s v1p0959c1s v2p0116c2s v2p0356c2s v2p0397c2s
Leifchild, J.R. v1p0073c2s v1p0267c2s v1p0269c1m v1p0287c2s v1p0460c1s v1p0508c2m v1p0792c2s
Leigh, A. v4p0368c1s
Leigh, A.E. v3p0189c1s
Leigh, C. v4p0303c1s v4p0303c2s v4p0558c2s
Leigh, D. v4p0013c1s
Leigh, E. v1p0089c1s
Leigh, E.E. v5p0564c1s
Leigh, G. v1p1014c1s
Leigh, G.A. v5p0523c2s v5p0567c2s
Leigh, J.G. v5p0259c2s v5p0365c2s v5p0427c1s v5p0506c2m v5p0507c1s v5p0641c1s v5p0641c2s v6p0019c1s v6p0138c1s v6p0203c1s v6p0260c2s v6p0324c1s v6p0324c2s v6p0371c1s v6p0477c1s v6p0532c2s v6p0562c1s
Leigh, J.G. and Holt, A. . v6p0359c2s
Leigh, J.S. v3p0475c1s v4p0536c1s
Leigh, J.W. v4p0232c2s v5p0263c1s
Leigh, K. v3p0362c1s
Leigh, M. v1p0888c2s
Leigh, R. v2p0015c1s v2p0104c1s
Leigh, R.G. v2p0247c2s
Leigh, S. v5p0579c1s
Leighton, A.W. v2p0386c1s
Leighton, C.E. v2p0429c1s
Leighton, D. v4p0561c1s v4p0590c1s
Leighton, E.B. v3p0110c2s
Leighton, F. v1p1115c1s v3p0021c2s v5p0427c2s
Leighton, F. and Wells, H.T. v1p0066c1s v1p0300c2s
Leighton, G.B. v3p0190c2s v4p0471c1s
Leighton, J. v3p0031c1s v3p0049c1s v5p0190c2s v6p0528c2s
Leighton, J.A. v4p0229c1m v6p0317c2s v6p0319c1s v6p0490c1s v6p0582c2s
Leighton, M. v3p0341c1s
Leighton, M.O. v6p0376c1s
Leighton, M.W. v4p0520c1s
v4p0621c2s v5p0254c1s v5p0546c1s
Leighton, R.F. v2p0092c2s v2p0388c2s
Leighton, R.L. v2p0116c1s v5p0245c1s
Leighton, S. v2p0183c1s v2p0315c2s v3p0180c2s v3p0292c1s v3p0306c1s
Leighton, V.L. v4p0549c1s
Leighton, W. v1p0088c2s v1p0526c2s v1p1127c2s v1p1174c1s v6p0305c2s v6p0644c1s v6p0697c1s
Leighton, W. and Shoemaker, W.L. v2p0139c2s
Leighton, W., jr. v1p0526c1s
Leighton, W.R. v4p0305c1s
Leinbach, P.S. v6p0595c2s
Leindeiner-Wildau, H.E.von v6p0473c2s
Leipoldt, C.L. v6p0007c2s v6p0169c1s v6p0228c2s v6p0261c2s v6p0434c2s v6p0533c1s
Leipziger, H.M. v4p0324c2s v5p0329c1s v6p0193c1s
Leiser, J. v6p0155c2s v6p0342c2s v6p0595c1s
Leistikow, B. v4p0122c1s
Leitch, J. v1p0084c2s v1p0166c2s v1p0526c2m v1p1128c2s v1p1204c1s
Leitch, M. v6p0060c1s
Leitch, Marg. and Leitch, Mary v4p0415c1s
Leitch, Mary and Leitch, Marg. v4p0415c1s
Leitch, W. v1p0069c2s v1p0107c1s v1p0194c2s v1p0281c1s v1p0581c1s v1p0866c1s v1p0936c1s v1p1292c1s
Leiter, Joseph v5p0627c2s
Leith, E. v4p0276c1s v4p0318c2s
Leith, G. v5p0007c2s v5p0554c2s
Leith, J.M. v6p0031c1s
Leith-Adams, Mrs. v1p0888c2s v4p0575c2s
Leitner, G.W. v1p1193c2s v2p0237c1s v2p0293c2s v2p0405c1s v3p0129c1s v3p0211c1s v3p0314c1s v4p0001c2s v4p0022c1s v4p0102c2s v4p0107c1m v4p0137c1s v4p0147c2s v4p0170c2s v4p0188c2s v4p0258c1s v4p0270c1m v4p0278c2s v4p0280c1s v4p0307c2s v4p0309c2s v4p0313c1s v4p0320c1s v4p0376c1s v4p0417c1s v4p0587c1s v4p0598c2s v5p0284c1s
Lejeune, L. v1p0605c1s v1p0617c1s v1p0959c1s v1p0968c2s v1p1327c2s
Lelan, L. v1p0729c1s v1p0969c1s
Leland, A. v4p0067c2s v6p0504c1s v6p0582c2s
Leland, C.F. v4p0069c2s v4p0158c1s v4p0570c2s
Leland, C.G. v1p0028c1s v1p0064c1s v1p0067c1s v1p0159c2s v1p0199c1s v1p0223c2s v1p0236c2s v1p0338c2s v1p0380c2s v1p0438c1s v1p0522c1s v1p0558c1s v1p0570c2s v1p0615c1s v1p0635c2s v1p0638c1s v1p0663c1s v1p0674c2s v1p1428c2s v2p0008c1s v2p0101c2s v2p0109c1s v2p0116c2s v2p0194c1s v2p0219c1s v2p0220c2m v2p0226c2s v2p0252c1s v2p0275c2s v2p0293c2s v2p0299c1s v2p0327c2s v2p0332c1s v2p0370c1s v2p0409c1s v2p0420c1s v2p0478c2s v3p0011c1s v3p0048c2s v3p0129c1s v3p0130c1s v3p0172c1s v3p0200c2s v3p0214c2s v3p0289c1s v3p0389c2s v4p0104c2s v4p0277c1s v4p0500c1s v4p0551c2s v4p0552c2s v4p0581c1s v5p0557c2s
Leland, C.P. v3p0352c2s v4p0472c1s
Leland, Charles G. v3p0471c1s
Leland, E.H. v6p0080c2s
Leland, E.R. v1p0004c1s v1p0044c1s v1p0272c2s v1p0842c2s v1p1015c2s v1p1417c1s v2p0034c1s
Leland, F.R. v1p0540c1s
Leland, G. v2p0109c2s
Leland, H.P. v1p0574c2s v1p1055c1s v1p1126c1s
Leland, Mabel v6p0460c2s
Leland, O.S. v1p0476c1s v1p1029c2s
Leland, P.S. v6p0230c2s
Leland, W.G. v6p0069c2s v6p0330c2s
Lelande, A. v6p0495c2s
Leloir, M. and Bergerat, E. v5p0369c1s
Leloutre, G. v2p0351c1s
Lely, J.M. v4p0322c2s v4p0471c2s
Lemaire, C. v6p0144c2s
Lemaitre, J. v3p0038c1s
v4p0110c1s v4p0510c1s v5p0208c1s v5p0386c1s
Lemaitre, Jules v5p0263c1s
Leman v4p0433c2s
Leman, E.M. v4p0044c1s
Lemattre, G. v1p0142c2s
Lembkey, W.I. v6p0236c1s
Lemcke, F. v5p0332c2s v5p0547c2s
Lemieux, R. v6p0096c2s
Lemkes, C.R.L. v4p0547c2s
Lemly, C.S. v6p0598c1s
Lemly, H.R. v1p0050c2s v2p0050c2s v3p0132c1s v3p0400c1s v3p0410c2s v3p0440c1s v3p0460c2s
Lemmon, J.G. v2p0350c2s v3p0093c1s v4p0444c1s v6p0233c2s
Lemmon, L. v4p0458c2s
Lemmy, G.K. v5p0510c2s
Lemoinne, J. and Duff, M.E.G. v1p1330c1s
Lemon, C. v1p0300c1s
Lemon, Ida v4p0323c1s
Lemon, J. v1p1181c2s v1p1366c2s
Lemon, J.S. v4p0615c2s
Lemon, M. v1p0005c1s v1p0076c2s v1p0766c1s v1p1396c2s v1p1405c2s
Lemon, R. v1p0676c2s v1p0691c2s
Lemonnier, C. et al. v6p0237c1s
Lemoran, L. v1p0268c1s
Lemp, H. v4p0175c2s
Lemstrom, S. v2p0028c2s v2p0408c2s
Lena, Hazde and Bassett, R.E. v6p0462c1s
Lenard, P. v4p0164c2s
Lendall, R. v1p0558c1s v1p1144c1s v5p0526c1s
Lendenfeld, R.von v2p0179c1s v3p0170c2s
Lendrum, R.A. v5p0201c2s
Lenfestey, G.H. v5p0161c2s
Leng, J. v3p0199c1s
Leng, J., Sir et al. v4p0290c1s
Lenha, Pont da v4p0481c2s
Lenher, V. and Smith, E.F. v4p0016c1s
Lennard, R.V. v6p0072c1s
Lennard, T.B. v6p0258c2s
Lennard, W. v6p0306c2s v6p0418c1s
Lennes, N.J. v6p0264c2s
Lennig, T. v1p0782c1s
Lennox, H.G., Lord v4p0427c2s
Lennox, W.P. v1p0267c1s v1p0617c1s v1p0707c1m
Lenormand, E. v1p0552c1s v1p1331c1s
Lenormant, F. v1p0050c2s v1p0122c2m v1p0342c1s v1p0402c1s v1p0590c2s v1p0860c2s v1p0968c2s v1p1200c1s v2p0324c1s v2p0458c1s v3p0042c1s
Lenotre, G. v6p0110c2s
Lenox, J.P. v5p0061c2s v5p0227c2s v5p0276c1s v5p0306c1s v5p0330c1s v5p0357c1s v5p0428c2s
Lenox, J.R. v6p0341c2s
Lenox, Margaret v4p0080c2s
Lente, F.D. v2p0159c2s
Lenz, F.G. v4p0145c2s v4p0561c2s v4p0567c1s
Lenz, M. v4p0244c2s
Leo XIII v2p0203c2s v2p0378c1s v3p0053c2s v3p0248c1s v3p0395c1s v4p0054c1s v4p0113c2s v4p0489c1s v5p0017c2s v5p0114c2s v5p0306c2s v5p0493c1s v6p0065c1s v6p0122c1s v6p0386c2s v6p0494c2s v6p0547c1s
Leoinstein, I. v6p0483c2s
Leon, A.E. v3p0391c1s
Leon, D.De v2p0004c2s v2p0040c2s v2p0098c2s
Leon, E.De v1p0001c1s v1p0003c1s v1p0103c2s v1p0294c2s v1p0395c1s v1p0396c1s v1p0571c1s v1p0668c1s v1p0693c1s v1p0738c1m v1p0772c1s v1p0874c2s v1p0895c2s v1p0933c1s v1p0970c1s v1p1142c1s v1p1155c2s v1p1212c2s v1p1224c1m v1p1264c1s v1p1330c2m v1p1332c1m v1p1353c2s v1p1423c2s v2p0230c2s v2p0433c2s v4p0002c1s
Leon, G.De v1p1135c2s
Leon, N. v5p0367c2s
Leon, T.C.De v1p0003c1s v1p0351c1s v1p0488c2s v1p0913c1s v1p0964c1s v1p1264c1s v3p0104c2s v3p0148c1s v5p0160c2s
Leon, X. v5p0447c1s
Leonard, A.B. v3p0154c2s v5p0380c1s
Leonard, A.G. v6p0144c2s
Leonard, A.S. v1p1238c1s
Leonard, C. v4p0589c2s
Leonard, C.H. v5p0269c2s

Leonard, D.L. v2p0298c2m
v3p0288c1m v3p0444c1s v4p0089c2s
v4p0374c2s v4p0376c1s
Leonard, D.M. v1p0458c2s
Leonard, E.B. v1p1009c2s
Leonard, E.M. v5p0615c2s
v6p0141c2s
Leonard, F.E. v5p0449c2s
Leonard, G.H. v5p0217c2s
v5p0428c1s v6p0343c2s
Leonard, G.H., jr. v5p0151c1s
Leonard, G.L. v4p0173c1s
Leonard, H. v6p0325c1s
Leonard, H.F. and Higashi, K.
v6p0344c1s v6p0709c1s
Leonard, H.W. v3p0392c2s
Leonard, J. v1p0666c2s
v1p1076c1s
Leonard, J.W. v5p0126c2s
Leonard, L. v1p0648c2s
v1p0789c2s
Leonard, M. v6p0247c1s
Leonard, M.C. v6p0336c1s
Leonard, M.D. v3p0012c1s
Leonard, M.H. v2p0240c2s
v3p0378c2s v4p0283c1s v5p0198c2s
v5p0362c1s v5p0366c2s v5p0413c2s
v5p0419c2s v5p0491c2m
Leonard, Mabel E. and
Wyer, J.I., jr. v6p0190c1s
Leonard, N.R. v1p0827c1s
Leonard, P. v5p0364c2s
Leonard, P.H. v4p0526c1s
Leonard, Priscilla v4p0564c2s
v4p0619c2s
Leonard, R.M. v4p0158c1s
v5p0615c2s
Leonard, R.W. v6p0441c2s
v6p0688c2s
Leonard, S.W. v3p0278c1s
Leonard, W.A. v5p0249c2s
Leoncavallo, R. v6p0368c1s
Leonhardt, E. v1p0640c1s
Leonowens, A.H. v1p1193c2s
Leonowens, A.H., Mrs. v6p0593c1s
Leonowens, Mrs. v1p0446c2s
Leopardi, G. v3p0116c2s
v6p0388c1s
Leoser, C.McK. v4p0234c1s
v4p0434c1s
Leotsakos, J.P. v4p0241c2s
Leovy, G.J. v5p0042c1s
v5p0642c1s
Lepetit, C.R. v5p0415c1s
Lephron, Mrs. v1p0265c2s
Lepper, A.H. v1p1302c1s
Lepper, C.H. v2p0438c2s
Lepper, G.H. v4p0059c2s
v6p0403c1s
Lepper, G.H. and Ridpath, J.C.
v5p0061c2s
Leppington, B. v2p0012c2s
v4p0351c2s
Leppington, C.H. v3p0427c1s
v4p0097c1s
Leppington, C.H.d'E. v3p0417c1s
v3p0418c1s v4p0314c1s v4p0375c2s
v4p0632c1s v5p0101c2s v5p0102c1s
v5p0459c1s
Lerch, C.H. v3p0107c2s
v3p0135c2s v3p0136c1m v5p0350c1s
Lerch, P. v1p0593c1s
Leroi, P. v4p0028c2s
v4p0486c2s
Leroux, L.P. v1p0613c2s
Leroy, A. v1p0388c1s
Leroy-Beaulieu v3p0370c1s
Leroy-Beaulieu, A. v3p0230c2s
v3p0432c1s v4p0378c2s v6p0668c2s
Leroy-Beaulieu, P. v2p0164c2s
v2p0182c1s v3p0339c2s v4p0014c1s
v4p0059c1s v4p0345c2s v4p0424c2s
v4p0525c2s v4p0596c1s v5p0108c2s
v6p0659c1s
Lerron, D. v4p0277c1s
Lesan, H. v5p0387c1s
Lesart, Hope v6p0022c2s
Lesbald, C. v5p0241c1s
Lescher, H. v2p0045c2s
v2p0329c2s
Lescuyer, M.F. v2p0046c2s
Lesley, A. v3p0461c2s
Lesley, F.P. v1p0507c2s
Lesley, J.P. v1p0197c2s
v1p0268c2s v1p0394c2s v1p0440c1s
v1p0470c1s v1p0506c2s v1p0509c1s
v1p0779c1s v1p0922c2s v1p0934c2s
v1p1257c1s v1p1283c2s v2p0390c2s
v3p0100c2s v3p0209c1s v3p0230c1s
v3p0250c2s
Lesley, J.P., Dr. v2p0337c2s
Lesley, R.W. v5p0099c1s
Lesley, S.I. v1p0421c1s
v1p0623c2s
Leslie, A. v1p0583c2s
v1p1372c2s v5p0409c2s
Leslie, C.D. v5p0054c2s
v5p0255c1s v5p0544c2s
Leslie, E. v1p0043c1s
v1p0429c1s v1p0737c2s
Leslie, F., Mrs. v3p0398c1s
Leslie, G. v5p0296c1s
Leslie, G.D. v2p0024c1s
v4p0493c2s v4p0622c1s v5p0362c1s
v6p0368c2s
Leslie, G.D. and Eaton, F.A.
v4p0084c1s v5p0069c1s v5p0101c1s
v5p0127c2s v5p0135c2s v5p0265c2s
v5p0482c2s v5p0498c2s v5p0533c1s
v5p0619c2s v5p0626c2s v6p0047c2s
v6p0146c1s v6p0212c2s
v6p0364c2s
v6p0553c2s
Leslie, Geraldine v5p0110c1s
Leslie, H. v1p0883c2s
Leslie, J. v1p0056c1s
v1p0613c2m v1p0614c1s v1p1390c1s
Leslie, J., Sir v1p0058c1s
v1p0099c2s v1p0929c1s v1p0929c2s
v1p1024c2s
Leslie, L. v1p0500c2s
v1p0751c2s v1p1041c2s v5p0197c2s
v5p0339c1s v5p0488c1s v6p0442c2s
Leslie, Miss v1p0027c1s
v1p0098c2s v1p0106c1s v1p0143c1s
v1p0265c1s v1p0402c2s v1p0752c1s
v1p0811c2s v1p0878c1s v1p1295c2s
Leslie, R.C. v3p0048c1s
v3p0371c2s v3p0390c2s v4p0327c1s
Leslie, T.E.C. v1p0015c1s
v1p0082c2s v1p0109c2s v1p0380c1s
v1p0406c1s v1p0430c1s v1p0533c1s
v1p0533c2s v1p0647c1s v1p0649c2s
v1p0650c2s v1p0654c2s v1p0656c2m
v1p0657c2m v1p0716c1s v1p0721c1s
v1p0721c2m v1p0728c2s v1p0983c1s
v1p1025c2m v1p1026c1m v1p1026c2s
v1p1027c1s v1p1044c2s v1p1217c1s
v1p1267c1s v1p1285c1s v1p1352c1s
v1p1360c2s v1p1379c2s v1p1402c2s
v2p0223c2s
Lesperance, J. v1p0337c1s
v1p0696c2s v1p0796c2s v1p1220c2s
Lespinasse, H. v6p0072c1s
Lesquereux, L. v1p0268c2m
v1p0470c1s v1p0470c2m v1p0749c1m
v1p1014c2s v1p1015c2s v1p1041c2s
v2p0159c1s v3p0243c1s
Lesseps, F.de v1p0650c2s
v1p0963c1s v1p1264c1s v2p0173c1s
v2p0327c2s
Lessing, B. v6p0066c1s
v6p0083c2s v6p0319c2s v6p0332c1s
v6p0481c2s v6p0517c1s v6p0597c2s
Lessing, Bruno v6p0620c1s
Lester, C. v6p0193c1s
Lester, C.E. v1p0295c1s
v1p0403c2s v1p0425c2s v1p0672c2s
v1p1040c2s v1p1077c1s v1p1248c1s
Lester, C.F. v5p0061c1s
Lester, E. v1p0191c2s
Lester, E.A. v1p1392c1s
Lester, F.E. v4p0335c1s
v4p0575c2s
Lester, G.M.L. v4p0469c1s
v4p0553c2s
Lester, H.F. v1p1308c2s
v2p0171c1s v2p0265c1s v2p0304c2s
v2p0318c1m v2p0443c2s v3p0378c2s
v4p0001c1s v4p0250c1s v4p0447c2s
v4p0567c2s
Lester, J.D. v1p0583c1s
v1p0583c2s
Lester, O.C. v6p0626c1s
Lester, R. v1p0665c1s
Lestocq, W. v4p0003c1s
Lestrade, C.de v3p0032c1s
v3p0370c1s
Lestrich, J.von v6p0322c1s
v6p0364c2s
Lesueur, E.A. v5p0185c1s
Letchworth, W.P. v1p0229c2s
v3p0077c1s v4p0138c1s v4p0185c2m
v5p0159c1s
Lethaby, W.R. v3p0069c2s
v3p0307c1s v5p0240c2s v5p0328c2s
v5p0570c1s v6p0415c2s
Lethbridge, E. v1p0348c1s
Lethbridge, R. v1p0635c1s
v2p0046c1s v2p0186c2s v2p0218c1s
v2p0227c2s v2p0373c1s v2p0401c1s
v4p0049c2s v4p0236c2s v4p0279c1m
v4p0279c2s v4p0280c2m v4p0348c2s
v5p0285c2s v5p0287c1s v6p0312c2s
v6p0313c2m v6p0314c2m v6p0635c1s
Lethbridge, R., Sir v3p0222c2s
Lethbridge, W.C.P. v4p0523c2s
Letheby, Dr. v1p0501c2s
v1p0502c1s v1p1101c1s v3p0157c1m
Letheby, H. v1p1311c1s
Letherbrow, E. v1p0600c1s
Letherbrow, T. v2p0057c2s
v2p0211c1s v3p0204c1s v3p0240c1s
Letheule, P. v6p0479c2s
v6p0688c1s
Lethieullier, S. v1p0150c1s
v1p0750c2s v1p0957c1s v1p1122c1s
v1p1315c1s
Letourneau, C. v4p0334c2s
v4p0610c1s v5p0020c1s v5p0177c2s
Letts, Albina M. v5p0065c2s
Letts, T. v5p0361c1s
v6p0400c1m
Letts, W.M. v6p0478c1s
v6p0562c1s
Leuba, J.H. v4p0397c2s
v4p0480c1s v4p0616c1s v5p0133c2s
v5p0204c1s v5p0281c1s v5p0441c2s
v5p0471c1s v5p0483c2m v6p0167c1s
v6p0309c2s v6p0441c1s
Leuba, J.H. and Hyde, W. . v6p0279c1s
Leuba, James H. v6p0538c1s
Leuffman, C.B. and Lane, L.M.
v4p0094c2s
Leupp, C.M. v1p0733c1s
Leupp, F.E. v1p0105c2s
v4p0282c2s v4p0454c1s v4p0542c2s
v5p0099c2s v5p0113c2s v5p0287c2s
v5p0288c2s v5p0302c1s v5p0343c1s
v5p0410c2s v5p0440c1m v5p0451c2s
v5p0552c2s v5p0610c2s v5p0621c1m
v6p0057c1s v6p0099c1s v6p0144c2s
v6p0165c2s v6p0170c1s v6p0209c2s
v6p0246c2s v6p0315c1s v6p0315c2s
v6p0316c2m v6p0317c1s v6p0433c1s
v6p0539c2s v6p0550c2s v6p0666c1s
v6p0686c2s v6p0687c1s v6p0708c2s
Leupp, Francis E. v6p0317c1s
Leuschner, A.O. v6p0186c1s
v6p0469c1s
Leuschner, A.O. and Lawson, A.C.
v6p0567c2s
Leval, G.de v6p0708c1s
Levallois, J. v3p0163c2s
Levan, F.K. v1p0513c1s
v1p0583c1s v1p0754c2s v1p1090c2s
v2p0269c1s v2p0367c2s v3p0162c1s
v4p0557c1s
Levasseur, E. v2p0140c2s
v2p0418c2s v4p0025c2s v4p0033c2s
v4p0211c2s v4p0452c2s v4p0458c2s
v4p0496c1s v4p0608c1s v4p0632c2s
v5p0602c1s
Levasseur, E. et al. v2p0418c2s
Levay, L.de v6p0202c2s
v6p0303c1s
Leveaux, E.H. v1p1240c2s
v1p1260c2s v3p0412c1s
Levegne, J.M. v5p0139c1s
Levell, W.H. v5p0351c2s
Leveque, C. v2p0037c2s
Lever, C. v1p0065c1s
v1p0157c1s v1p0220c2s v1p0222c1s
v1p0295c2s v1p0335c2s v1p0400c2s
v1p0469c2s v1p0512c2s v1p0572c1s
v1p0608c2s v1p0674c1s v1p0768c2s
v1p0813c1s v1p1099c1s v1p1125c2s
v1p1202c1s v1p1219c1s v1p1299c1s
v1p1403c2s
Lever, C.J. v1p0303c1s
v1p0588c1s v1p0604c2s v1p1201c2s
v1p1315c2s
Lever, D. v4p0248c1s
v4p0544c2s v4p0632c1s v5p0516c2s
Lever, Darcy v4p0010c2s
Lever, W.H. v5p0467c2m
Leverett, C.E. v1p0739c2s
Leverett, F. v3p0335c1s
v4p0186c2s v4p0381c2s
Leverett, F. and Chamberlin, T.C.
v4p0411c2s
Leverett, G.V. v5p0275c1s
Levermore, C. v4p0624c2s
Levermore, C.H. v2p0132c1s
v2p0311c2s v2p0476c1s v3p0068c1s
v3p0097c1s v3p0186c2s v3p0303c1s
v3p0401c2s v4p0259c1s v4p0365c1s
v4p0619c2s v5p0065c1s v5p0197c1m
v5p0277c1s v5p0372c2s v5p0601c2s
Leverrier and Faye v1p1014c1s
Leverrier, M. v1p1014c2s
Leverrier, U.J.J. v1p1014c1s
v1p1014c2s
Leverson, E., Mrs. v5p0282c1s
Leverson, J.J. v4p0006c2s
Leveson-Gowes, G. v4p0088c1s
Levett, N.D. v1p0526c1s
Levett-Yeats, G. v5p0422c2s
Levett-Yeats, G.A. v5p0287c2s
v5p0459c2s
Levetus, A.S. v5p0612c1s
v6p0042c2m v6p0056c1s v6p0107c2s
v6p0155c2m v6p0201c2s v6p0293c2s
v6p0357c2m v6p0409c1s v6p0419c1s
v6p0431c1s v6p0521c1s v6p0630c2s
v6p0651c1s v6p0678c2m v6p0698c1s
Levey, E.J. v3p0304c1s
v5p0407c1s
Levey, G.C. v4p0038c1s
v4p0259c2s v4p0564c1s
Levi, C.M. v1p1002c2s
Levi, E. v1p0787c1s
v5p0086c1s v5p0180c1s v5p0557c2s
Levi, Eugenia v6p0570c2s
Levi, I. v5p0174c2s
Levi, L. v1p0014c1s
v1p0080c2s v1p0087c2s v1p0090c2m
v1p0093c2m v1p0094c2s v1p0095c1s
v1p0268c1s v1p0284c1s v1p0284c2s
v1p0301c1s v1p0307c2s v1p0315c2s

v1p0339c2s v1p0436c1s v1p0545c1s
v1p0545c2s v1p0628c1s v1p0694c2s
v1p0897c2s v1p0963c2m v1p0976c1s
v1p0978c1s v1p1055c1s v1p1135c2s
v1p1163c1s v1p1166c1s v1p1245c2m
v1p1285c1s v2p0033c2s v2p0057c1s
v2p0096c2s v2p0190c1s v2p0231c1s
v2p0231c2s v2p0238c1s v2p0317c1s
v3p0094c1s v3p0113c2s v3p0127c2s
v3p0181c2m v3p0224c2s v3p0274c2s
v3p0292c2s v3p0370c1s v3p0381c1s
v3p0434c1s
Levi, Leone v3p0221c2s
Levi, M. v6p0302c1s
Levias, C. v4p0516c1s
Levick, J.J. v1p0824c1s
v1p1306c2s v2p0090c2s v2p0405c2s
v4p0468c2s
Levick, M.B. v6p0459c2s
Levigne, Capt. v1p0926c2s
Levin, M. v6p0001c1s
Levin, T.W. v1p0346c1s
v1p0702c2s
Levison, J.L. v2p0299c2s
Levison, W.G. v1p0401c1s
v3p0331c1s
Levita, C.B. v5p0294c1s
Levy, A. v1p0429c1s
v1p1435c1s v2p0371c1s v3p0002c2s
v3p0185c2s
Levy, A.A. v2p0238c2s
Levy, Amy v3p0090c1s
v3p0396c1s
Levy, C.H. v4p0054c2s
v4p0250c1s v5p0042c2s v5p0056c1s
v5p0057c2s v5p0176c2s v5p0307c1s
v5p0311c2s v5p0580c2m v6p0061c2s
v6p0169c2m v6p0343c2s
Levy, C.V.S. v1p0796c1s
Levy, E.J. v3p0312c2s
Levy, Florence N. v6p0475c1s
v6p0579c2s
Levy, G.B. v6p0247c1s
Levy, J.C. v4p0525c2s
Levy, J.H. v2p0288c2s
Levy, L.E. v4p0440c2s
v5p0195c1s v6p0211c1s
Levy, L.E. and Sartain, S.
v6p0100c2s
Levy, M. v2p0137c2s
v6p0160c2s
Levy, M.S. v5p0307c2s
Levy, R.G. v5p0231c2m
Levy, S. v6p0343c1s
Levy, S. et al. v6p0343c1s
Levy-Bruhl v4p0489c2s
v4p0533c2s
Levy-Bruhl, L. v4p0212c2s
v5p0050c2s v5p0132c1m v5p0188c1s
v5p0212c2s v5p0356c2s v5p0357c2s
v5p0384c2s v5p0434c2s v5p0447c1m
v5p0498c1s v5p0614c1s
Lewal, Gen. v3p0159c2s
Lewees, F. v1p0592c2s
Lewelling, L.D. v4p0195c1s
Lewes, C.L. v3p0321c1s
Lewes, G.H. v1p0157c1s
v1p0172c2s v1p0287c1m v1p0293c1s
v1p0313c1s v1p0318c1s v1p0333c1s
v1p0350c1s v1p0363c1s v1p0363c2m
v1p0364c1s v1p0364c2s v1p0415c2s
v1p0465c2s v1p0475c1s v1p0485c1s
v1p0510c1s v1p0552c2s v1p0579c1s
v1p0593c2s v1p0595c1s v1p0611c2s
v1p0646c2s v1p0730c1s v1p0738c1s
v1p0745c2s v1p0746c1s v1p0755c1s
v1p0817c1s v1p0857c1s v1p0877c2s
v1p0901c1s v1p0906c2s v1p0921c1m
v1p0932c1s v1p0953c1s v1p1000c1s
v1p1007c2s v1p1016c2s v1p1053c2s
v1p1112c1s v1p1122c1s v1p1124c1s
v1p1161c2s v1p1177c2s v1p1183c1s
v1p1184c2s v1p1233c1s v1p1236c2m
v1p1238c1s v1p1239c1s v1p1253c1s
v1p1280c2s v1p1300c1s v1p1320c2s
v1p1339c1s v2p0310c1s
Lewes, Prof. v3p0167c2s
Lewes, V. v4p0118c2s
Lewes, V.B. v3p0048c2s
v3p0168c1s v3p0341c1s v4p0120c2s
v4p0192c2s v4p0220c2m v4p0271c1s
v4p0542c2s v5p0002c2s v5p0226c1s
v5p0226c2s v6p0225c1s v6p0248c1m
Lewin, P.E. v5p0438c1s
Lewin, R. v1p0626c2s
v2p0395c2s
Lewin, R.D. v2p0099c2s
v2p0239c1m v2p0368c2s v2p0370c1s
Lewin, R.D'C. v2p0313c1s
Lewin, T. v1p0205c1s
v1p0598c2s v1p0682c2s v1p0762c1s
v1p0941c2s v1p0950c1s
Lewin, T. and Airy, G.B. . v1p0184c2s
Lewin, T. and Black, W.H.. v1p1037c1s
Lewin, W. v2p0022c1s
v2p0058c1s v2p0140c1s v2p0140c2s
v2p0183c2s v2p0205c2s v2p0431c2s
v3p0007c2m v3p0037c1s v3p0044c2s
v3p0087c1s v3p0151c2s v3p0191c2s
v3p0259c2s v3p0311c2s v3p0369c1s
v3p0411c2s v3p0429c1s v3p0462c2m
v4p0015c1s v4p0121c1s v4p0144c2s
v4p0248c2s v4p0260c2s v4p0326c1s
v4p0332c2s v4p0421c1s v4p0432c1s
v4p0495c1s v4p0528c2s v4p0620c1s
v4p0620c2s v5p0276c1s v6p0158c2s
Lewin, Walter v2p0439c2s
Lewins, R. v2p0014c2s
v2p0133c1s v2p0213c1s v2p0280c1s
v4p0185c2s v4p0379c1s v4p0575c1s
Lewis, A. v1p0112c1s
v1p0391c1s v1p0667c1s v1p1087c2s
v1p1422c1s v4p0501c2s v4p0505c2s
v4p0634c1s v5p0259c2s v5p0273c1s
v5p0321c1s v5p0507c1s v6p0005c2s
v6p0188c2s v6p0216c2s v6p0573c1s
v6p0665c1s v6p0670c2s v6p0673c2s
v6p0702c2s
Lewis, A.G. v5p0362c2s
v6p0107c1s
Lewis, A.H. v2p0425c2s
v6p0143c1s v6p0184c1s v6p0238c2s
v6p0318c2s v6p0332c2m v6p0339c2s
v6p0346c1s v6p0426c1s v6p0431c1s
v6p0451c1s v6p0465c1s v6p0503c2s
v6p0546c1s v6p0624c2s v6p0645c1s
v6p0690c1s v6p0700c2s
Lewis, A.H. et al. v6p0175c1s
Lewis, A.J. v2p0209c2s
v2p0303c2m v2p0325c1s v2p0327c2s
v2p0329c1s v2p0476c1s v2p0476c2s
Lewis, A.L. v1p0347c2s
v1p0795c1s v2p0141c2s v2p0266c1s
v2p0421c1m v2p0473c2s v4p0134c2s
v4p0192c1s v4p0550c2s v5p0463c2s
v5p0554c1m v5p0554c2s
Lewis, A.S. v4p0561c2s
v5p0308c2s v5p0517c2s v5p0565c1m
v6p0149c1s
Lewis, A.S. et al. v4p0056c2s
Lewis, Agnes S. v4p0300c2s
v4p0561c2s
Lewis, Alfred H. v6p0008c2s
Lewis, Angelo v6p0282c2s
Lewis, Austin v5p0156c1s
v5p0284c1s v5p0599c2s v6p0078c1s
v6p0089c2s v6p0114c2s v6p0352c1s
v6p0366c1s v6p0574c1s v6p0589c2m
Lewis, B.F. v1p0397c2s
v1p1381c1s
Lewis, B.G. v6p0362c2s
Lewis, B.H. v6p0024c1s
Lewis, B.L. v2p0330c1s
Lewis, C.B. v1p0365c2s
v1p0446c1s v5p0127c2s v5p0480c2s
v5p0481c1s v5p0555c1s
Lewis, C.E. v2p0188c1s
Lewis, C.Edgar v5p0413c1s
Lewis, C.L. v6p0625c1s
Lewis, C.M. v6p0207c1s
Lewis, C.S. v5p0464c2s
Lewis, C.T. v1p0600c2s
v1p0647c2s v5p0065c1s v5p0147c1s
v5p0218c2s v5p0439c1s v5p0467c1s
v6p0109c2s v6p0443c2s v6p0487c1m
v6p0659c1s
Lewis, D. v1p0564c2s
v1p0776c2s v1p1005c1s v2p0104c1s
Lewis, D. and Dow, N. v2p0355c2s
v2p0434c1s
Lewis, D. et al. v2p0477c2s
Lewis, D.J. v5p0131c1s
v5p0536c1s
Lewis, D.M. v3p0331c1s
Lewis, D.O. v4p0282c1s
v4p0282c2s v5p0519c2s
Lewis, E. v1p0377c1s
v1p0798c1s v1p1245c1s v1p1324c1s
v3p0400c1s v4p0363c2s v4p0459c1s
Lewis, E., jr. v1p0265c1s
v1p0301c1s v1p0621c2s v1p0647c1s
v1p0759c1s v1p0767c1m v1p1149c2s
v1p1179c1s
Lewis, E.A. v6p0683c2s
Lewis, E.A.M. v4p0158c2s
Lewis, E.B. v1p1409c1s
v4p0496c1s
Lewis, E.D. v5p0021c2s
v6p0689c2s
Lewis, E.H. v4p0140c2s
v4p0183c1s v4p0183c2s v4p0184c2s
v4p0371c2s v4p0415c2s v4p0554c1s
v5p0131c2s v5p0192c1s v5p0523c1s
v6p0207c2s
Lewis, E.I. v6p0218c1s
Lewis, E.M. v5p0162c2s
Lewis, E.P. v4p0536c1s
v6p0040c1s
Lewis, E.P. and Perry, E.S.
v4p0540c2s
Lewis, E.S. v6p0342c2s
Lewis, Eleanor v4p0149c1s
v5p0218c2s v5p0262c1s v5p0348c2s
v5p0368c1s v5p0384c2s v5p0607c1s
Lewis, F. v5p0438c2s
v5p0569c1s v6p0551c2s
Lewis, F.C. v6p0175c1s
v6p0635c1s
Lewis, F.D. v6p0686c1s
Lewis, F.G. v5p0060c1s
Lewis, F.H. v4p0613c1s
v6p0106c2s
Lewis, F.J. v6p0205c2s
Lewis, F.P. v6p0070c2m
Lewis, F.W. v3p0413c2s
v5p0060c1s v5p0274c2s v5p0352c2s
v5p0511c2s v6p0207c1s
Lewis, F.Warburton v6p0259c2s
Lewis, Frances W. v5p0192c1s
Lewis, Fred.H. v4p0619c2s
Lewis, G. v2p0108c1s
v2p0119c2s v2p0178c1s v2p0277c1s
v2p0447c2s
Lewis, G., Sir v1p0149c2s
Lewis, G.A. v1p0447c1s
v1p0779c2s
Lewis, G.C. v1p0428c1m
v1p1063c1s
Lewis, G.C., Sir v1p1431c1s
Lewis, H. v2p0303c2s
Lewis, H.C. v1p1440c2s
v2p0117c2s v2p0174c1s v2p0179c1m
v2p0213c2s v2p0214c1s v2p0297c1s
v2p0335c2s v2p0338c2s v3p0425c2s
Lewis, H.E. v3p0453c1s
v6p0478c2s
Lewis, H.F.M. v5p0319c2s
v6p0347c2s
Lewis, H.H. v5p0343c2s
v5p0397c2s v5p0429c1s v5p0508c1s
v5p0508c2s v5p0516c2s v5p0531c2s
v5p0534c2s v5p0639c1s v5p0644c2s
v6p0016c2s v6p0037c1s v6p0161c1s
v6p0171c1s v6p0443c2s v6p0528c2s
v6p0651c1s
Lewis, H.J. v5p0599c2s
Lewis, H.Leroy v5p0244c2s
Lewis, H.M. v6p0119c2s
Lewis, H.P. v2p0466c1s
v3p0258c2s v4p0273c2s
Lewis, H.R. v5p0337c2s
Lewis, H.S. v6p0627c1s
Lewis, H.W. v1p1427c1s
v4p0103c2s v4p0396c2s
Lewis, Harold v5p0161c2s
Lewis, I.N. v4p0176c2s
Lewis, J. v1p0099c2s
v1p0652c1s v1p0927c2s v1p1188c2s
v5p0092c1s v5p0281c2s v5p0631c1s
v6p0189c2s v6p0203c1s
Lewis, J.A. v1p1051c2s
v2p0053c1m v2p0243c1s v2p0342c1s
Lewis, J.A. and Deane, C.. v2p0342c1s
Lewis, J.C. v1p0428c1s
Lewis, J.D. v1p0252c2s
v1p0264c1s v1p1237c1s
Lewis, J.H. v5p0203c2s
Lewis, J.J. v5p0417c1m
Lewis, J.N. v4p0019c1s
Lewis, J.P. v4p0095c1s
Lewis, J.S. v5p0188c2m
v5p0320c2s v5p0353c2s v5p0544c2s
Lewis, J.T. v1p0118c2s
v1p0248c2s v1p0264c2s
Lewis, L. v6p0499c2s
v6p0528c1s v6p0672c2s v6p0705c1s
Lewis, L., jr. v1p0987c2s
v2p0401c1s
Lewis, L.R. v2p0359c2s
v2p0360c2s v6p0087c2s
Lewis, L.S. v5p0118c1s
v5p0123c1s v5p0174c1s v5p0180c2s
v5p0185c2s v5p0379c1s v5p0632c1s
Lewis, Lawrence v6p0139c2s
v6p0170c2s
Lewis, M. v1p1373c2s
Lewis, M.A. v2p0054c1s
v2p0058c2s v2p0384c2s
Lewis, M.G. v1p0199c2s
Lewis, Mary A. v2p0349c1s
v2p0426c1s
Lewis, Mary S. v6p0672c2s
Lewis, Minna V. v6p0351c2s
Lewis, Mrs. v1p1387c1s
v1p1425c1s
Lewis, N. v5p0010c2s
Lewis, N.P. v5p0490c1s
Lewis, O.F. v6p0135c2s
v6p0136c1s
Lewis, R. v1p0815c1s
Lewis, R.C. v5p0159c2s
Lewis, R.E. v4p0079c2s
v4p0597c2s v5p0110c1s v5p0338c2s
v6p0118c2s v6p0119c2s
Lewis, S. v3p0128c1s
Lewis, S.S. v5p0089c1s
Lewis, S.W. v1p0285c2s
Lewis, T. v1p0008c2s
v1p0069c1s v1p0119c1m v1p0123c2s
v1p0129c1s v1p0133c1s v1p0180c1s
v1p0215c1s v1p0262c1s v1p0263c1s
v1p0312c2s v1p0390c1s v1p0529c1s
v1p0538c1s v1p0554c1s v1p0555c1s
v1p0581c1s v1p0581c2m v1p0613c1s
v1p0613c2s v1p0646c1s v1p0727c1s
v1p0795c1s v1p0825c1s v1p0905c2s
v1p0931c1s v1p0931c2s v1p0945c1s
v1p1017c1m v1p1027c1s v1p1041c2s
v1p1062c1m v1p1083c2s v1p1085c2s
v1p1093c1s v1p1104c1s v1p1147c2s

v1p1162c2s v1p1176c2s v1p1178c1s
v1p1244c2s v1p1328c2s v2p0146c1s
v2p0191c1s v2p0199c1s v2p0344c2s
v6p0144c1s
Lewis, T. et al. v1p0927c1s
Lewis, T.C. v2p0364c1s
v3p0327c2s
Lewis, T.H. v1p0455c2s
v2p0010c2s v2p0019c2m v2p0157c1s
v2p0222c1s v2p0300c1m v3p0018c2s
v3p0052c1s v3p0107c2s v3p0290c1m
v3p0433c2s v3p0435c2s v4p0137c2s
v4p0153c2s v4p0359c1s v4p0385c1m
v4p0456c2m v4p0500c1s v5p0539c2s
Lewis, T.R. v2p0031c1s
v2p0080c2s
Lewis, Tayler v1p0002c2s
v1p0527c2s
Lewis, V.B. v3p0390c2s
v5p0226c2s v6p0216c1s v6p0706c1s
Lewis, W. v1p0141c1s
v1p0533c1s v1p0910c2s v1p1170c2s
v1p1249c1s v1p1416c2s v2p0172c1s
v2p0419c2s v3p0315c2s v4p0594c2s
v5p0343c2s
Lewis, W.A. v6p0566c2s
Lewis, W.B. v4p0139c2s
Lewis, W.D. v3p0420c2s
v4p0387c2s v4p0534c2s v5p0227c1s
v6p0132c1s
Lewis, W.D. et al. v4p0462c2s
Lewis, W.H. v1p0219c1s
v1p0258c2s v1p0643c1s v1p1044c1s
v5p0010c2s v6p0232c1s
Lewis, W.J. v3p0013c2s
Lewis, W.M. v4p0057c2s
v5p0060c1m
Lewis, W.S. v3p0014c2s
v6p0381c1s
Lewis, W.T. v5p0621c2s
Lewis, Will E. v6p0416c1s
Lewisohn, L. v6p0032c1s
v6p0251c2s
Lewkowitsch, J. v6p0465c1s
Lewthwait, E. v5p0091c1s
Lewys, Eleanore F. v6p0196c1s
v6p0568c1s v6p0630c1s v6p0631c2s
Lex v5p0200c1s
Lexis, W. v4p0088c2s
v4p0230c1s v4p0377c2s v5p0553c2s
Ley, M.W. v6p0360c2s
Ley, W. v5p0133c2s
Ley, W.C. v1p0099c2s
v1p0266c2s v2p0259c1s v2p0380c1s
v2p0469c1s v3p0009c1s v3p0034c2s
v3p0458c2s
Leyburn, G.W. v1p0552c1s
v1p0552c2s v2p0191c1s
Leyburn, J. v1p0731c2s
Leyburn, L. v3p0149c2s
Leydekker, R. v6p0256c2s
v6p0297c1s
Leyden, E.M. v4p0636c2s
Leyden, J.A. v5p0290c1s
Leyds, W.J. v5p0588c1s
Leyland, J. v2p0005c1s
v2p0020c1s v2p0023c2s v2p0135c1s
v2p0137c2s v2p0142c1s v2p0229c2s
v2p0263c1s v2p0263c2s v2p0265c1s
v2p0265c2s v2p0322c1s v2p0341c2s
v2p0376c1s v2p0384c2s v2p0411c2s
v2p0448c2s v2p0482c1s v3p0075c1s
v3p0119c2s v3p0121c2s v3p0181c1s
v3p0183c1s v3p0187c2s v3p0197c1s
v3p0255c2s v3p0266c1s v3p0324c2s
v3p0350c1s v3p0376c2s v3p0413c1s
v3p0445c1s v3p0470c2s v3p0474c2s
v4p0052c2s v4p0118c1s v4p0119c1s
v4p0160c1s v4p0294c2s v4p0369c2s
v4p0389c2s v4p0425c2s v4p0503c2s
v4p0504c2s v4p0635c2s v5p0220c2s
v6p0237c2s v6p0269c1s v6p0445c2s
Leyland, Thos. v4p0474c1s
Leyle, E. v2p0228c1s
v3p0350c2s
Leypoldt, Augusta H. v6p0065c2s
Leys, J. v2p0086c1s
v2p0456c1s v3p0168c2s v3p0445c1s
Leys, J.K. v3p0146c1s
v3p0252c1s v3p0258c1s v3p0294c1s
v4p0324c1s v4p0386c1s v5p0596c2s
v5p0631c1s v6p0153c2s
Leys, John v6p0323c1s
Leys, P. v6p0006c2s
v6p0120c2s
Lhamon, W.J. v4p0371c1s
v4p0394c1s v4p0495c1s v4p0549c2s
v4p0573c2s
Liang-Cheng, Chentung v6p0118c1s
Liardet, E.A. v1p1283c2s
Lias, B.de St.P. v3p0430c2s
Lias, J.J. v3p0041c2s
v3p0217c1s v3p0364c2s v4p0112c1s
v5p0117c2s v6p0126c1s
Lias, J.Q. v3p0016c1s
Libbey, W. v5p0315c2s
Libbey, W., jr. v4p0244c2s
Libby, C.F. v4p0318c2s
Libby, D. v1p0575c2s
Libby, E.H. v1p0808c2s
Libby, M. v3p0074c1s
v4p0429c1s
Libby, M.F. v5p0004c1s
v5p0005c1s v5p0522c1m v6p0586c1s
Libby, M.R. v4p0462c1s
Libby, O.G. v5p0600c1s
v6p0067c1s v6p0067c2s v6p0531c1s
Libby, W. v4p0310c2s
Liberty, A.L. v3p0227c1s
v6p0491c1s
Liberty, L. v5p0078c1s
v5p0223c2m v5p0546c2s
Libyarg, L. v2p0100c2s
Lichfield v5p0021c2s
Lichfield, C.R. v6p0300c2s
Lichtenberger, C. v4p0389c1s
v4p0496c1s
Lichtenberger, F. v3p0171c2s
Lichtenstein, J. v6p0374c1s
v6p0375c1s
Lichtenstein, Joy v6p0092c2s
Lichtenstein, R.C. v2p0052c1s
v2p0145c1s v3p0050c1s
Liddeke, F. v6p0290c1s
Liddell, A.G. v2p0226c2s
Liddell, A.G.C. v1p0026c1s
Liddell, E. v4p0498c1s
Liddell, H. v2p0242c2s
v5p0110c1s
Liddell, H.G. v1p0248c2s
v1p0613c1s
Liddell, H.G. and Donne, W.B.
v1p1114c2s
Liddell, M. v5p0103c1m
Liddell, M.H. v5p0148c2s
v5p0191c2s v5p0192c1m v5p0192c2s
v5p0522c2s v5p0524c1m v6p0588c1s
Liddell, S.J.R. v2p0453c2s
Lidgett, E.S. v5p0178c1s
Lidgett, G. v2p0400c2s
Lidgett, J.S. v5p0117c1s
Lidis, B. v6p0305c1s
Lie, J. v1p0558c1s
v2p0258c1s
Lie, Jonas v2p0316c1s
Lieb, H. v4p0199c1s
v4p0384c2s
Lieb, J.W., jr. v6p0204c2s
Lieben, R. v3p0028c2s
Lieber, F. v1p0477c2s
v1p0486c1s v1p0871c2s v1p0895c2s
v1p0900c1s v1p0999c1s v1p1026c1s
v1p1038c2s v1p1073c2s v1p1330c2s
v1p1360c1s v2p0092c2s
Lieber, G.N. v1p0033c2s
v1p0574c2s v1p0805c1s v1p0921c1s
v4p0358c1s v5p0032c1s v5p0199c1s
v5p0375c2s v5p0418c1s
Lieber, G.Norman v5p0312c2s
Lieber, J.T. v1p0899c1s
Lieber, N.B. v5p0562c2s
Lieber, O.M. v1p1225c1s
Lieber, R. v4p0205c2s
v4p0223c2s
Liebermann, F. v4p0353c1s
v4p0536c2s v4p0599c1s v5p0324c2s
v5p0606c2s v5p0631c2s v6p0287c1s
v6p0369c1s
Liebermann, M. v5p0299c2s
Liebetreu, M. v1p1277c2s
Liebhart, H. v2p0357c1s
Liebich, L. v6p0275c2s
Liebig, G.von v5p0010c1s
Liebig, J. v1p0159c1s
v1p0465c2s v1p0526c1s v1p0798c1s
v1p1199c2s v1p1223c1s
Liebig, J.v. v1p0340c1s
Liebig, J.von v1p0085c1s
v1p0085c2s v1p0271c1m v1p0639c2s
Liebknecht, W. v4p0533c2s
v5p0232c1s
Liebling, E. v4p0384c2s
v4p0442c1m v4p0484c2s v4p0506c2s
v5p0114c1s v5p0369c2s v5p0505c1s
Liebreich, O. v1p0924c1s
Liebreich, R. v1p0880c1s
v1p0958c2s v1p0959c2m v1p1333c2m
v1p1375c1s
Lieckfeld, G. v5p0226c2s
v5p0389c1s
Liedeman, C.G. v2p0100c2s
Liefde, I.de v1p0523c1s
Liefde, J.B.De v2p0422c1s
Liefde, J.de v1p0478c2s
v1p0491c2s
Liefde, J.De v1p0597c2s
v1p1175c2s
Liegeard, A. v2p0215c1s
Lies, E. v1p1285c2s
Lies, E.T. v6p0109c1s
v6p0116c1s v6p0129c1s
Lieven, Prince v6p0049c1s
Lievin, L. v1p1305c2s
Liew, C.C.Van v4p0311c1s
v4p0367c1s v4p0505c2s v4p0506c1s
Lifford, Lord v2p0227c2s
v2p0325c1s
Lifford, Lord et al. v1p0657c1s
Liggett, J.T. v2p0123c2s
Light, C.J. v1p1261c1s
Light, G.E. v6p0346c1s
Light, Matilda M. v6p0464c2s
Lightbody, W.M. v6p0006c2s
v6p0161c1s v6p0169c2s v6p0207c2s
v6p0211c2s v6p0240c2m v6p0266c2s
v6p0370c1s v6p0479c1s v6p0519c2s
v6p0520c1s
Lightfoot, G.H. v3p0332c1s
Lightfoot, J.B. v1p0068c1s
v1p0129c2s v1p0431c2s v1p0624c1s
v1p0692c2s v1p0966c1s v1p1029c1s
v1p1271c2s v1p1284c2s v3p0292c1s
Lightfoot, T.B. v2p0163c2s
v2p0214c1s
Lighthall, W.D. v5p0384c2m
v6p0310c1s
Lighthipe, J.A. v5p0184c1s
Lightner, C.A. et al. v6p0489c2s
Lightner, E.W. v2p0466c2s
Lighton, W.R. v5p0061c2s
v5p0212c2s v5p0243c1s v5p0283c1s
v5p0308c2s v5p0327c2s v5p0349c2s
v5p0402c1m v5p0550c1s v6p0019c2s
v6p0220c2s v6p0466c2s v6p0467c1s
v6p0548c2s v6p0586c1s v6p0692c2s
Lighton, W.R. and Duffie, G.C.
v6p0624c1s
Lightone, R. v3p0394c2s
Lightwood, J.M. v4p0454c1s
Lilford, Lord v4p0060c2s
Lilley, A.L. and Dickinson, G.L.
v6p0536c2s v6p0541c1s
Lilley, J.P. v4p0127c2s
v4p0190c1s
Lillie, F.R. v6p0401c1s
Lillie, G.W. v2p0333c2s
v6p0086c2s
Lillie, I.C. v3p0067c2s
Lillie, J. v1p0118c2s
v1p0347c1s v1p0645c2s v3p0090c1s
v3p0284c1s v3p0396c1s v3p0458c1s
v3p0461c1s
Lillie, J. and Collins, M.
v2p0293c2s
Lillie, J., Mrs. v1p0413c2s
v1p0867c1s v1p0882c2s v2p0357c2s
v2p0427c2s
Lillie, J.J. v5p0527c2s
Lillie, L.C. v1p1259c1s
v2p0041c2s v2p0071c1s v2p0114c1s
v2p0117c2s v2p0141c2s v2p0143c1s
v2p0164c1s v2p0220c1s v2p0246c1s
v2p0279c2s v2p0341c1s v3p0007c2s
v3p0021c2s v3p0025c1s v3p0035c2s
v3p0090c2s v3p0170c2s v3p0185c2s
v3p0210c1s v3p0236c1s v3p0252c1s
v3p0255c2s v3p0291c1s v3p0293c2s
v3p0322c1s v3p0459c1s v3p0462c2s
v4p0225c2s v5p0094c2s
Lillie, L.C., Mrs. v3p0046c2s
Lillie, L.W. v1p0820c1s
v1p0874c2s
Lillie, M.E. v5p0585c1s
Lillingston, L.W. v5p0060c2s
v5p0094c2s v5p0115c2s v5p0191c2s
v5p0212c2s v5p0270c2s v5p0327c1s
v5p0346c2s v5p0359c1s v5p0374c2s
v5p0451c1s v5p0451c2s v5p0463c1s
v5p0481c1s v5p0566c1s v5p0584c1s
Lillingston, Leonard W. .. v5p0481c1s
v5p0639c1s v6p0172c2s
Lilly, A.W. v1p0353c2s
v4p0113c1s
Lilly, C., Mrs. v1p0660c1s
Lilly, W.S. v1p0090c1s
v1p0260c1s v1p0397c2s v1p0476c1s
v1p0912c1s v1p1119c2s v2p0081c2s
v2p0082c1s v2p0082c2s v2p0112c2s
v2p0165c2s v2p0167c1s v2p0192c1s
v2p0204c1s v2p0215c1s v2p0227c2s
v2p0230c2s v2p0255c1s v2p0257c2s
v2p0280c1s v2p0288c1s v2p0293c2m
v2p0297c2s v2p0304c2s v2p0369c2s
v2p0376c1s v2p0382c2s v2p0427c1s
v2p0483c1s v3p0021c1s v3p0052c1s
v3p0058c2s v3p0081c2s v3p0138c1s
v3p0143c1s v3p0152c1s v3p0185c1s
v3p0219c2s v3p0221c1s v3p0228c2s
v3p0232c2s v3p0248c2s v3p0250c2s
v3p0268c2s v3p0271c1m v3p0287c2s
v3p0288c1s v3p0302c1s v3p0326c2s
v3p0331c2s v3p0337c2s v3p0346c2s
v3p0348c2s v3p0349c2s v3p0357c2s
v3p0358c2s v3p0361c2s v3p0364c1m
v3p0379c2s v3p0401c1s v3p0404c1m
v3p0406c1s v3p0418c2s v3p0427c1s
v4p0088c2s v4p0108c2s v4p0127c2s
v4p0139c2s v4p0152c1s v4p0233c1s
v4p0247c1s v4p0259c1s v4p0344c2s
v4p0452c2m v4p0458c2s v4p0460c1s
v4p0467c2s v4p0514c1s v4p0533c2m
v4p0611c1s v4p0615c1s v5p0074c1s
v5p0086c1s v5p0115c1s v5p0187c2s
v5p0190c2s v5p0218c1s v5p0245c1s
v5p0246c1s v5p0291c2s v5p0323c2s
v5p0362c2s v5p0434c2s v5p0573c2s
v5p0619c2s v5p0633c2s v6p0020c2s
v6p0086c1m v6p0101c2s v6p0111c1s
v6p0205c1s v6p0255c2s v6p0295c2s
v6p0349c2s v6p0402c1s v6p0455c2s

v6p0508c1s v6p0588c1s v6p0624c1s
Limedorfer, E. v5p0207c2s
v5p0320c1s v5p0553c1s v6p0648c1s
Limerick, P. v5p0484c2s
Linahan, Bart.E. v6p0476c2s
Lincecum, G. v1p0044c1s
v1p1236c1s v1p1282c2s
Lincke, D.A. v4p0033c2s
Lincklaen, L. v1p0507c1s
v1p0960c1s
Lincoln et al. v1p1360c1s
Lincoln, A. v1p0104c2s
Lincoln, A.N. v4p0096c2s
v4p0165c1s v4p0431c2s v5p0072c2s
v5p0365c1s v6p0295c2s
Lincoln, Alice N. v5p0467c1s
Lincoln, B. v1p1391c2s
Lincoln, C.H. v4p0481c2s
v5p0146c2s v5p0217c1s v5p0218c2s
v5p0241c1s v5p0361c2s v5p0439c2s
v5p0498c1s v6p0253c1s v6p0345c2s
v6p0373c2s v6p0669c1s
Lincoln, C.J. v6p0581c2s
Lincoln, C.M. v5p0330c2s
Lincoln, D.F. v1p0744c1s
v1p0903c1s v1p1159c2s v1p1366c2s
v2p0199c1s v4p0199c2s v4p0227c1s
v6p0651c2s
Lincoln, D.F. and Putnam, J.J.
v1p1158c2s
Lincoln, Dean of v5p0235c1s
Lincoln, F.H. v3p0196c2s
v6p0706c1s
Lincoln, G.G. v6p0150c1s
Lincoln, G.W. v2p0075c1s
Lincoln, H. v1p0055c2s
v1p0259c2s v1p0434c2s v1p0640c2s
v1p0667c1s v1p0790c2s v1p0839c2s
v1p0840c2s v1p0846c2s v1p0972c2s
v1p1111c2s v1p1318c2s v1p1341c1s
v1p1363c1s v2p0121c2s v2p0310c2s
v2p0390c1s v3p0174c2s
Lincoln, H.A. v4p0186c1s
v5p0194c1s v5p0396c1s
Lincoln, Helen B. v5p0108c1s
Lincoln, J. v5p0272c2s
v5p0451c1s v6p0467c1s v6p0627c1s
Lincoln, J.C. v6p0024c1s
v6p0123c2s v6p0286c1s v6p0408c1s
v6p0606c2s v6p0633c2s v6p0663c1s
Lincoln, J.L. v1p0045c1s
v1p0531c1s v1p0601c1s v1p0604c1s
v1p0727c1s v1p0891c1s v1p1017c1m
v1p1101c2s v1p1114c2s v1p1221c1s
Lincoln, J.T. v6p0399c2s
Lincoln, Joseph C. v6p0306c2s
v6p0346c1s v6p0595c1s
Lincoln, L.B. v1p0285c1m
Lincoln, L.I. v6p0622c2s
Lincoln, M.D., Mrs. v6p0512c1s
v6p0512c2s
Lincoln, P.M. v6p0013c2s
v6p0198c1s
Lincoln, S. v1p0750c2s
Lincoln, S. et al. v5p0496c2s
Lincoln, V. v1p0014c1s
v1p0424c2s v1p0442c1s v1p0949c2s
v2p0096c2s v2p0146c1s v2p0211c1s
v2p0235c2s v2p0239c1s v3p0084c1s
v3p0209c1s v3p0427c2s
Lincoln, W. v5p0616c2s
v6p0565c2s
Lincoln, W.F. v1p1114c2s
Lindahl, J. v3p0173c2s
Lindau, P. v4p0052c1s
Lindau, R. v1p0336c2s
v1p0999c1s v1p1111c1s v1p1176c1s
v1p1394c2s v2p0261c1s v4p0342c1s
Lindaw, R. v1p0986c2s
Lindberg, C.E. v4p0158c2s
Lindberg, J.C. v6p0464c1s
Linde, C. v4p0477c2s
Linde, C.von v6p0009c2s
Lindeiner-Wildau, H.E.von. v6p0542c2s
Lindemann, F. v3p0331c2s
v6p0040c1s
Linden, A. v5p0254c1s
v5p0266c1s
Linden, M.von v5p0085c2s
Linden, S. v5p0260c1s
Linden, Simeon v6p0020c1s
Lindenau, Col.Von v6p0655c1s
Lindenberg, P. v5p0631c2s
Lindenberger, C.H. v3p0173c1m
v3p0332c1s
Lindenberger, W.E. v2p0092c1s
Lindenkohl, A. v2p0313c1s
v3p0026c1s v3p0203c2s v4p0244c2s
v4p0368c2s v5p0417c2s
Lindenlaub, T. v5p0564c2s
Lindenthal, G. v4p0268c1m
v4p0400c1s v5p0076c1s v5p0188c2s
v5p0563c1s
Linderberg, F. v5p0158c2s
Linderfelt, K.A. v2p0255c2s
v2p0428c1s v3p0248c2s v3p0249c1s
Lindesay, G. v4p0017c2s
v4p0320c2s v4p0406c1s
Lindgren, W. v4p0230c2m
v4p0535c2s v5p0242c1s v5p0382c2s
v5p0424c1s v5p0528c2s
Lindgren, W. and Hillebrand, W.F.
v6p0030c1s
Lindholm, A.T. v2p0115c2s
Lindholm, S.D. v6p0519c1s
Lindholm, S.G. v5p0592c2s
Lindholm, S.V. v5p0584c2s
Lindley, E.H. v4p0365c1s
v5p0473c2s
Lindley, E.H. and Partridge, G.E.
v5p0041c1s
Lindley, E.M. v2p0244c1s
v2p0296c1s v6p0450c2m
Lindley, H. v4p0175c1s
Lindley, J. v1p0492c2s
Lindley, M.J., Mrs. v1p0710c2s
Lindley, N. v4p0323c2s
Lindley, W. v6p0092c1s
Lindley, W.H. v2p0396c1s
Lindo, M.P. v1p0388c1s
Lindsay, A.B. v6p0385c2s
Lindsay, A.D. v6p0035c1s
v6p0428c1s
Lindsay, A.E.T., Mrs. v3p0433c2s
Lindsay, B. v3p0021c2s
v4p0001c1s v4p0137c2s v4p0226c1s
v4p0386c2s v4p0590c1s v5p0320c2s
v5p0507c2s v5p0597c2s v6p0440c2s
Lindsay, C. v3p0044c2s
v4p0073c2s v4p0199c2s
Lindsay, David v4p0358c2s
Lindsay, Dr. v1p1208c2s
Lindsay, F. v4p0570c2s
Lindsay, H. v1p0131c2s
Lindsay, J. v5p0114c2s
v5p0165c1s v5p0279c1s v5p0322c1s
v5p0358c1s v5p0397c1s v5p0480c1s
v5p0482c1s v5p0510c2s v5p0515c1s
v5p0577c1s v6p0032c2s v6p0089c2s
v6p0252c2m v6p0331c1s v6p0368c2s
v6p0412c2s v6p0495c2s v6p0536c2s
v6p0576c1s v6p0577c2s v6p0642c2s
v6p0643c2s
Lindsay, J.A. v2p0319c1s
Lindsay, J.D. v4p0036c2s
v4p0068c2s v4p0192c2s v4p0545c2s
Lindsay, J.S. v2p0352c1s
v6p0596c1s
Lindsay, J.W. v1p0125c1s
v1p0415c2s
Lindsay, Lady v1p1032c1s
v1p1258c1s v2p0184c1s v2p0254c2s
v2p0291c2s v2p0380c1s v2p0444c1s
v3p0069c1s v3p0173c1s v3p0257c2s
v3p0291c2s v3p0329c2s v3p0403c1s
v3p0417c1s v4p0159c2s v4p0190c1s
Lindsay, Lord v1p0077c1s
v1p0742c2s
Lindsay, M. v5p0634c1s
v6p0077c2s
Lindsay, M.B. v5p0334c1s
v6p0075c1s
Lindsay, M.C. v4p0093c1s
v5p0041c2s v5p0197c2s
Lindsay, Mary B. v6p0372c2s
Lindsay, Mayne v5p0529c2s
v6p0043c2s v6p0273c2s
Lindsay, Miss and Ward, Miss
v1p1165c1s
Lindsay, N.A. v1p0605c2s
Lindsay, R. v2p0344c1m
Lindsay, R.L. v2p0050c2s
Lindsay, S.M. v4p0115c2s
v4p0313c1s v4p0560c2s v5p0149c2s
v5p0537c2m v6p0144c2s v6p0355c1s
v6p0509c2s v6p0510c1s
Lindsay, S.M. and Small, A.W.
v5p0537c2s
Lindsay, S.McC. v4p0438c1s
v6p0114c2s v6p0115c1m v6p0510c1s
Lindsay, S.McC. and Worms, R.
v5p0293c2s
Lindsay, S.McC. et al. ... v5p0606c2s
Lindsay, T. v2p0143c1s
v4p0132c2s v4p0269c2s v4p0507c1s
v5p0035c1s v5p0172c2s v5p0417c1s
v5p0453c1s
Lindsay, T.M. v1p0115c1s
v1p0385c1s v1p0582c2s v1p0702c2s
v1p0712c1s v1p0770c2s v1p0954c2s
v1p1165c2s v2p0023c2s v2p0135c2s
v2p0268c2s v2p0345c2s v2p0353c2s
v4p0112c1s v4p0113c2s v4p0510c1s
v4p0530c2m v5p0012c2s v5p0025c1s
v5p0055c2s v5p0117c1s v5p0151c2s
v5p0279c2s v5p0495c2s v5p0499c2s
v6p0063c1s v6p0383c1s v6p0541c2s
Lindsay, W. v5p0315c1s
Lindsay, W.A. v1p0799c1s
v1p0935c2s v1p0985c1m
Lindsay, W.L. v1p0042c2m
v1p0229c2s v1p0622c2s v1p0744c1s
Lindsay, W.M. v2p0153c2s
v3p0334c2s v4p0503c2s v5p0413c1s
v5p0454c1m
Lindsay, W.S. v1p0801c1s
Lindsay of Balcarres, Lady
v2p0472c1s
Lindsell, Alice v6p0229c2s
Lindsey, B.B. v6p0078c1s
v6p0078c2m v6p0128c1s v6p0348c2m
Lindsey, Ben B. v6p0115c1s
v6p0139c1s
Lindsey, C. v1p0192c2m
v1p0457c2s v1p0943c2s v1p1116c2s
v1p1323c2s
Lindsey, F. v6p0324c1s
v6p0398c2s v6p0599c1s
Lindsey, J., jr. v1p1262c1s
Lindsey, J.W., Mrs. v5p0636c2s
Lindsey, J.W. v1p0727c2s
Lindsey, P. v6p0350c2s
Lindsey, T. ...v4p0048c1s v4p0083c2s
Lindsley, Dr. v1p0529c2s
Lindsley, H. v1p0648c2s
v1p1073c1s v1p1420c2s
Lindsley, J.H. v1p1393c2s
Lindsley, P. v1p0636c1s
v1p0794c2s v1p1357c1s
Linebarger, C.E. v4p0124c1s
v4p0154c2s v4p0333c2m v4p0506c2s
v4p0600c2s v4p0606c1s
Linehan, J. v6p0595c2s
Linehan, J.C. v3p0191c2s
v3p0381c1s
Linen, J. v1p0676c1s
Lines, H.H. v3p0062c1s
v3p0098c2s v3p0265c1s v4p0074c1s
v4p0074c2s v4p0081c2s v4p0082c1s
v4p0165c1s v4p0244c2s v4p0248c1s
v4p0336c2s v4p0377c1s v4p0433c2s
Linesman v5p0588c2s
v6p0442c2s v6p0655c1s
Linford, J. v3p0340c1s
Linforth, J.M. v6p0680c1s
Ling, E.E.L. v5p0633c1s
Lingard, J.T. v1p0843c1s
Lingelbach, W.E. v5p0294c2s
Link, S.A. v4p0538c1s
Link, T. v2p0483c1s
Linn, G.W. v4p0271c1s
Linn, J.B. v1p0666c2s
v2p0062c2s v2p0220c1s v3p0356c2s
Linn, J.M. v1p0637c2s
Linn, J.W. v5p0259c2s
v6p0128c2s v6p0257c1s v6p0280c2s
Linn, James W. v6p0114c1s
Linn, W.A. v2p0219c1m
v3p0059c1m v3p0099c2s v4p0083c2s
v4p0116c1s v4p0131c1s v5p0220c1s
v6p0507c2s
Linnett, Amy v4p0630c2s
Linscott, H.F. v6p0572c2s
Linskill, M. v2p0041c1s
v2p0266c2s v2p0472c2s v3p0209c2s
v3p0449c2s
Linskill, Mary v3p0170c1s
Linskill, Miss v2p0194c2s
Linskill, Mrs. v2p0197c2s
Linskill, W.T. v6p0562c2m
v6p0691c2s
Linsley, J.H. v1p0136c1s
v1p0456c2s v1p0573c1s
Linson, C.H. v6p0340c1s
Linson, C.K. v6p0627c1s
v6p0677c2s
Linson, J.T. v6p0330c1s
Linthicum, R. v4p0585c2s
Lintner, G.A. v1p0321c1s
v1p0685c1s v1p0686c1s v1p0852c1s
v1p1103c2s
Lintner, J.A. v1p0108c2s
Linton, E. v4p0635c2s
v6p0019c1s
Linton, E.E. v1p0979c1s
Linton, E.L. v1p0075c1s
v1p0219c1s v1p0263c2s v1p0335c2s
v1p0336c1s v1p0360c1s v1p0461c1s
v1p0492c1s v1p0569c1s v1p0605c2m
v1p0673c1s v1p0722c2m v1p0785c1s
v1p0808c1s v1p0886c2s v1p0907c2s
v1p0937c1s v1p0940c2s v1p0952c1s
v1p1086c2s v1p1179c2s v1p1339c2m
v1p1365c2s v1p1424c2s v1p1432c1s
v1p1438c2s v2p0045c2s v2p0147c2s
v2p0224c2s v2p0238c1s v2p0282c1s
v2p0304c1s v2p0321c2s v2p0332c1s
v2p0416c1s v2p0477c2s v3p0150c2s
v3p0164c1s v3p0166c1s v3p0168c2s
v3p0186c1s v3p0236c1s v3p0267c2s
v3p0268c2s v3p0269c1s v3p0284c1s
v3p0365c2s v3p0384c2s v3p0385c2m
v3p0397c2s v3p0399c2s v3p0432c2s
v3p0468c1m v3p0469c1m v3p0469c2m
v3p0470c1s v4p0105c2s v4p0118c1s
v4p0162c2s v4p0182c1s v4p0265c1s
v4p0340c1s v4p0398c1s v4p0516c1s
v4p0524c1s v4p0530c2s v4p0536c2s
v4p0578c1s v4p0580c1s v4p0629c2s
v4p0630c1s v4p0637c1s
Linton, E.L., Mrs. v4p0159c1s
v4p0182c1m v4p0438c2s
Linton, E.Lynn v2p0332c1s
v2p0401c2s v2p0477c1s v3p0030c1s
v3p0189c1s v3p0203c2s v3p0208c1s
v3p0219c1s v3p0253c2s v4p0215c2s
v4p0356c2s v4p0591c1s
Linton, J.D. v3p0023c1s
v4p0031c1s v4p0613c1s
Linton, L. v3p0219c2s

v4p0138c1s
Linton, L., Mrs. v4p0604c1s
Linton, L., Mrs. et al. .. v3p0151c2s
Linton, L.A. and Peckham, S.F.
v4p0444c2s
Linton, Lynn, Mrs. v3p0399c2s
v4p0270c1s v4p0292c2s v4p0328c1s
v4p0380c1s v4p0531c2s
Linton, R. v5p0632c2s
Linton, W. v1p0286c2s
Linton, W.J. v1p0285c2s
v1p0419c2s v1p1094c2s v1p1427c2m
v2p0041c1m v2p0075c2s v2p0202c1s
v2p0247c1s v2p0281c1s v2p0370c2s
v2p0479c1s v3p0471c1m
Linton, W.S. v4p0513c1s
Lintott, E.S. v1p0551c1s
Linwood, W. v1p0127c1s
Lion, E.J. v2p0064c1s
v2p0357c1s
Lionberger, I.H. v6p0363c2s
v6p0522c2s
Lioy, D. v4p0353c1s
Lipman, J.G. v6p0046c2s
Lipman, M.de v4p0402c2s
Lipman, R.T. v2p0408c1s
Lipman, T.J. v6p0471c1s
Lipmann, R.de v4p0495c2s
Lippert, F.G. v3p0034c2s
v5p0158c2s
Lippincott, B.H. v6p0055c2s
Lippincott, H.C. v6p0322c1s
Lippincott, J.B. v6p0073c2s
v6p0139c2s v6p0688c2s
Lippincott, J.S. v1p0434c2s
v2p0016c1s v2p0159c1s
Lippincott, S.J. v1p0431c2s
v1p0773c1s v1p1258c1s v1p1336c1s
v1p1440c1s v2p0174c2s v3p0030c2s
v3p0306c1s v3p0456c1s
Lippincott, Sara J. v3p0373c2s
v6p0687c1m
Lippincott, T. v1p1427c2s
Lippitt, F.J. v1p0480c1s
v1p0515c2s v1p1032c2s v1p1035c2s
v1p1238c2s v1p1387c2s v2p0193c1s
v2p0370c2s v4p0277c2s v4p0610c1s
v5p0083c1s
Lippmann, E.O.von v3p0388c1s
Lippmann, G. v6p0575c2s
Lippmann, J.M. v3p0209c2s
v4p0034c2s v5p0053c2s v6p0397c2s
Lippmann, Julia M. v4p0321c1s
Lippmann, Julie M. v4p0081c2s
Lipps, T. v6p0005c2s
Lipscomb, A.A. v1p0740c2s
v1p0842c2s v1p1176c2s v1p1422c2s
v2p0235c1s v2p0340c2s v2p0397c2s
v2p0398c2s
Lipscomb, L.A. v1p0684c1s
Lipscomb, W.S. v2p0275c2s
v2p0392c2s
Lipscombe, D. v3p0026c1s
v3p0046c1s v3p0086c1s v3p0356c1s
Lipsett, C. v5p0017c2s
Lipsky, L. v6p0343c1s
Lipton, T. v5p0642c2s
Lipton, T., Sir v6p0710c1m
Liscomb, W.S. v1p0262c2s
v2p0022c2s v2p0088c1s v2p0418c2s
v4p0519c1s v4p0622c1s
Lisle, B.C.de v3p0160c1s
Lisle, E.de v3p0145c1s
Lisle, R.de v1p0804c2s
Lisle, R.M. v2p0299c1s
Lisle, W. v6p0402c2s
Lisle, W.J. v4p0295c2s
Lisle, W.M. v4p0109c1s
v6p0410c2s
Lisman, P.O. v3p0222c2s
Lissauer, Dr. v1p1218c1s
v2p0396c2m
Lisser, H.G.De v5p0626c1s
Lissner, E. v6p0539c2s
Lister, F.S. v5p0502c2s
Lister, J. v1p1068c1s
Lister, J.J. v3p0052c1s
v6p0082c2s
Lister, M. v3p0264c2s
Lister, R. v4p0002c2s
v4p0151c2s
Lister, T.H. v1p0255c1s
v1p0536c1s v1p0653c2s v1p0654c1s
Lister, T.H., Mrs. v1p0871c2s
Liston, W.L. v3p0112c1s
Litchfield, E.H. v5p0050c2s
Litchfield, G. v2p0203c1s
Litchfield, G.A. v3p0217c2s
Litchfield, G.A. and Harper, E.B.
v4p0286c2s
Litchfield, G.D. v2p0011c1s
v2p0243c2s v2p0321c2s v2p0353c2s
v3p0254c1s v3p0384c2s v6p0036c1s
v6p0525c1s
Litchfield, Grace D. v6p0632c1s
Litchfield, I.W. v6p0025c2s
Litchfield, P.H. v5p0371c1s
Litchfield, W.J. v6p0577c1s
Lithgow, R.A.D. v2p0398c1s
Litsey, E.C. v5p0152c2s
v6p0013c1s v6p0272c1s v6p0388c1s
v6p0566c1s
Litta-Visconti-Arese v6p0331c1s
Littehales, G.W. v6p0305c1s
v6p0585c2s
Littel, K.A. v2p0302c2s
Littell, C.W. v1p0675c1s
Littell, E.T. v1p0052c2s
Littell, P. v6p0181c1s
Little, A. v2p0034c2s
v5p0109c1s v5p0111c1s v5p0112c2s
v5p0344c2s v5p0438c2s v5p0501c1s
v5p0643c2m v6p0120c2s
Little, A., Mrs. v6p0486c2s
v6p0593c1s v6p0662c2s v6p0712c2s
Little, A.B. v4p0105c2m
v5p0109c2s v5p0113c1s v5p0579c2s
Little, A.C. v5p0203c1s
v5p0278c2s
Little, A.D. v4p0094c1s
Little, A.G. v3p0046c2s
v3p0120c2s v3p0127c1s v3p0137c2s
v3p0161c2s v3p0172c1s v3p0316c1s
v4p0159c1s v4p0215c2s v5p0219c1s
v6p0238c2s v6p0242c2s v6p0420c1s
Little, A.J. v5p0081c2s
Little, A.J.S.B. v5p0188c2s
v5p0586c1s
Little, A.W. v1p0671c1s
v1p0958c1s v1p1275c1s
Little, A.W., Mrs. v1p0243c1s
Little, Archibald, Mrs. .. v5p0438c2s
v6p0112c1s
Little, C.A. v4p0528c2s
Little, C.F. v2p0139c1s
v3p0068c1s v3p0200c2s v3p0366c1s
v3p0414c2s v4p0124c1s v4p0235c1s
v4p0243c2s v4p0459c2s v4p0460c1s
v4p0536c1s
Little, C.J. v3p0178c1s
v3p0228c1s v3p0240c2s v3p0270c1s
v3p0320c2s v3p0424c2s v4p0456c1s
v4p0479c1s v4p0616c1s v5p0015c1s
v5p0234c2s v5p0306c1s v5p0372c2s
v5p0494c2s v5p0631c1s v6p0245c2s
v6p0288c1s v6p0642c2s
Little, E.D. v5p0456c2s
Little, G.D. v2p0146c2s
Little, G.E. v4p0329c2s
Little, G.T. v2p0255c2m
v4p0330c1s v5p0332c2s v5p0333c1s
v6p0078c1s v6p0374c2s
Little, H.B. v5p0184c2s
v5p0338c2s
Little, J.L. v6p0503c1s
Little, J.P. v1p0461c2m
Little, J.S. v3p0242c1s
v4p0077c2s v4p0298c2s v4p0310c2s
v4p0321c2s v4p0351c1s v4p0434c2s
v4p0514c2s v4p0611c1s v5p0075c1s
v5p0250c1s v5p0555c2s v6p0362c2s
v6p0363c2s
Little, K. v5p0013c2s
v5p0219c1m
Little, L.B. v5p0089c2s
v5p0466c2s v5p0534c1s
Little, R. v3p0148c2s
Little, R.H. v6p0434c2s
Little, S.H. v2p0376c2s
v3p0293c1s
Little, W. v2p0161c2s
v2p0297c1s v3p0174c2s v3p0287c1s
Little, W.C. v3p0390c2s
Little, W.J.K. v4p0112c2s
v4p0157c2s v4p0356c2s
Little, W.J.Knox v4p0356c2s
Little, W.M. v4p0306c1s
Littledale, Dr. and Arnold, T.
v1p1118c1s
Littledale, G.R. v4p0033c1s
Littledale, H. v1p0328c1s
v1p0630c2s v6p0390c2s
Littledale, R.F. v1p0241c2s
v1p0251c1s v1p0255c2s v1p0264c1m
v1p0264c2s v1p0940c1s v1p0964c1s
v1p1028c1s v1p1042c2s v1p1110c1s
v1p1118c1s v1p1179c2s v1p1338c1s
v1p1363c2s v1p1423c1s v2p0008c2s
v2p0081c1s v2p0365c2s v2p0367c2s
v2p0447c1m v3p0339c1s v3p0344c2s
Littledale, St.G.R. v4p0576c1s
Littlefield, C.E. v6p0099c2s
v6p0515c1s v6p0628c1s v6p0659c2s
v6p0667c2s
Littlefield, G.E. v4p0359c2s
Littlefield, G.E. et al. . v6p0667c1s
Littlefield, W. v4p0405c2s
v5p0118c2s v5p0169c1m v5p0300c1s
v5p0645c2s v6p0036c1s v6p0049c1s
v6p0164c2m v6p0184c2s v6p0236c2s
v6p0268c1s v6p0269c1s v6p0303c2s
v6p0440c1s v6p0553c2s v6p0556c2s
v6p0570c2s v6p0713c1s v6p0713c2m
Littlehales, G.W. v4p0411c2s
v4p0511c1m v4p0521c2s v4p0537c2s
v4p0554c2s v5p0401c2s v6p0127c2s
v6p0445c2s v6p0639c2s v6p0646c2s
Littlehales, H. v4p0463c2s
Littlejohn, A.M. v1p0768c2s
Littlejohn, A.N. v1p0240c1s
v1p0274c2s v1p0309c2s v1p0422c1s
v1p0475c1s v1p0568c1s v1p0586c2s
v1p0641c2s v1p1000c2s v1p1094c2s
v2p0087c2s v2p0121c1s v2p0357c1s
Littlejohn, A.W. v1p0846c2s
Littlejohn, H.D. v4p0362c1s
Littlejohn, H.D., Sir v4p0140c1s
v4p0363c1s v4p0440c1s
Littlejohn, J. v3p0334c2s
Littlemore, G. v2p0082c2s
v2p0183c1s
Littleton, J.T. v3p0066c1s
Littleton, L.A. v2p0080c1s
Littleton, M.L. v6p0182c2s
Littlewood, H. v4p0410c1s
Littmann, E. v6p0212c1s
v6p0320c2s v6p0370c2s v6p0516c2s
v6p0616c2s
Littmann, Enno v6p0630c2s
Littre, E. v1p1037c2s
Littrow, C.von v1p1161c2s
Littrow, J.J. v1p0281c2s
Litwin, C.M. v3p0370c2s
Liveing and Dewar v1p1233c2s
v3p0316c2s
Liveing, G.D. v3p0107c1s
v3p0404c1s v4p0420c1s v4p0548c2s
Liveing, G.D. and Dewar, J.
v3p0125c1s v4p0540c2m v5p0037c2s
v5p0614c1s
Livermore, A. v1p0802c1s
Livermore, A.A. v1p0027c2s
v1p0119c2s v1p0564c1s v1p0684c2s
v1p0687c2s v1p0738c2s v1p0777c1s
v1p0792c1s v1p0853c1s v1p0979c2s
v1p0996c2s v1p1005c1s v1p1055c1s
v3p0344c2s v3p0433c2s
Livermore, D.P. v3p0467c2s
Livermore, G. v1p0117c1s
v1p0119c1s v1p0694c1s v1p0743c1s
v1p1363c2s v1p1434c2s
Livermore, L.J. v1p0127c2s
v1p0333c2s v1p0792c2s v1p0794c1s
v1p1321c2s
Livermore, M.A. v2p0478c1s
v3p0048c2s v3p0468c1s v3p0469c1s
v3p0470c1s v4p0270c1s v4p0324c2s
Livermore, M.A. et al. ... v3p0119c1s
Livermore, Mary A. v3p0470c2s
v4p0625c2s
Livermore, T.J. v3p0443c1s
Livermore, T.L. v5p0367c2s
v5p0375c2s v5p0618c1s
Livermore, W.R. v5p0375c1s
v6p0223c2s v6p0509c1s v6p0560c2s
v6p0593c2s
Liverpool, Earl of v1p0094c1s
Liversedge, A.J. v5p0411c2s
Liversidge, A. v6p0576c2s
Liversidge, A., Prof. v5p0038c2s
Livesey, A.W. v5p0006c2s
v5p0133c2s
Livesey, G. v4p0632c2s
v5p0467c2s
Livingston, A. v4p0264c2s
v4p0438c1s
Livingston, C. v5p0053c1s
Livingston, E.B. v3p0254c2s
v4p0150c1s v4p0336c2m
Livingston, F.M. v3p0187c1s
v3p0428c2s v5p0222c2s
Livingston, G. v4p0350c2s
Livingston, Helena v6p0454c1s
Livingston, K. v4p0271c2s
v4p0414c1s
Livingston, L.S. v5p0079c1s
v5p0079c2s v5p0080c2s v5p0122c2s
v5p0187c1s v5p0208c1s v5p0238c2m
v5p0256c2s v5p0259c1s v5p0268c2s
v5p0299c1s v5p0314c1s v5p0317c1m
v5p0317c2s v5p0323c2s v5p0347c1s
v5p0350c1s v5p0444c1s v5p0455c2s
v5p0497c1s v5p0525c1s v5p0553c1s
v5p0573c2s v5p0574c2m v5p0578c1s
v5p0578c2s v5p0629c2s v5p0630c1s
v6p0405c1s v6p0590c2s
v6p0686c2s
Livingston, M. v3p0328c2s
Livingston, S. v4p0062c2s
v4p0276c2s v4p0607c1s
Livingston, W.F. v5p0473c1s
Livingstone, D. v1p0010c1s
v1p0751c2s v2p0299c2s v2p0445c1s
Livingstone, F.B. v4p0285c2s
v4p0588c1s
Livingstone, G. v1p0731c1s
v1p0750c1s
Livingstone, W.F. v4p0336c2s
Livingstone, W.P. v6p0604c2s
v6p0692c2s
Llana, M.G. v2p0412c2s
Llandaff, Viscount v6p0140c1s
v6p0327c2s
Llano, A. v4p0382c1s
v5p0009c1s v5p0196c1s v5p0459c2s
v5p0475c2s
Llewellyn, F. v6p0508c1s
Lloyd, A. v1p0157c2s
v3p0310c1s v6p0040c2s v6p0336c2s
v6p0338c2s v6p0648c2s

Lloyd, A.H. v4p0338c1s v5p0194c1s v5p0198c1s v5p0280c2s v5p0319c1s v5p0447c1s v5p0471c1s v5p0513c2s v5p0537c1s v5p0580c1s v6p0211c2s v6p0273c1s v6p0292c2s v6p0572c2s v6p0600c2s
Lloyd, B.D. v6p0439c2s
Lloyd, C. v5p0049c2s
Lloyd, C.E. v4p0493c1s v5p0082c1s v5p0137c1s v5p0249c1s
Lloyd, C.J. and Carson ... v6p0081c1s
Lloyd, Caro v5p0324c1s
Lloyd, Col. v1p1129c1s
Lloyd, D. v1p0222c1s v6p0304c1s v6p0487c2s
Lloyd, D., Mrs. v1p0904c1s
Lloyd, D.D. v1p0782c1s v2p0349c1s v2p0467c1s
Lloyd, E. v1p0515c1s
Lloyd, E.F. v5p0226c2s
Lloyd, E.M. v4p0092c2s v4p0330c2s v4p0368c1s v4p0392c1s v4p0541c2s v5p0212c2s v5p0331c2s v5p0622c2s v6p0099c1s v6p0265c2s v6p0290c2s
Lloyd, F. v1p0091c1s
Lloyd, F.E. v4p0410c1s v5p0402c1s v6p0015c1s v6p0077c1m v6p0608c2s
Lloyd, F.F. v6p0491c2s
Lloyd, F.J. v3p0141c1s
Lloyd, H. v4p0047c2s v5p0554c2s v6p0460c2s v6p0470c1s
Lloyd, H.D. v1p0862c1s v1p1026c1s v2p0161c1s v2p0183c2s v2p0347c2m v2p0407c1s v3p0138c1s v3p0197c2s v3p0238c2s v4p0179c1s v4p0453c1s v5p0408c2m v6p0041c2s v6p0133c2s v6p0454c2s v6p0528c1s
Lloyd, H.M. v6p0423c2s
Lloyd, H.W. v4p0268c1s v4p0285c2s v4p0623c1s v5p0270c1s
Lloyd, I. v6p0142c2s
Lloyd, J. v4p0125c2s v4p0512c1s v4p0526c2s v4p0586c1s
Lloyd, J.A.T. v5p0250c2s
Lloyd, J.B. v1p0325c1s
Lloyd, J.S. v1p1237c1s v1p1259c1s v1p1335c2s v2p0045c2s v2p0135c1s v2p0139c1s v2p0301c1s v2p0451c1s v3p0046c2s v3p0117c1s v3p0176c2s v3p0411c2s v4p0120c2s
Lloyd, J.S., Mrs. v3p0295c2s v4p0634c1s
Lloyd, J.U. v5p0557c2s v5p0620c1s
Lloyd, L. v4p0453c1s
Lloyd, M. v1p0620c2s
Lloyd, M.A. v1p0153c1s v1p0320c1s v1p0687c2s v1p0824c1s v1p0933c2s v1p1381c1s
Lloyd, M.F. v5p0215c2s
Lloyd, M.G. v1p0170c1s v5p0571c2s v6p0420c2s
Lloyd, N. v6p0004c1s v6p0059c2s v6p0154c2s v6p0232c2s v6p0443c2s v6p0581c1s v6p0599c2s v6p0603c1s v6p0643c2s
Lloyd, Nelson v5p0171c2s v6p0046c1s v6p0176c1s v6p0398c1s
Lloyd, R.J. v4p0017c2s v5p0191c2s v6p0116c1s v6p0361c1s
Lloyd, R.J. et al. v4p0241c2s
Lloyd, R.R. v5p0306c1s
Lloyd, Robert v5p0170c2s
Lloyd, T. v3p0393c2s v4p0043c2s v4p0495c2s v4p0525c1s v5p0285c2s
Lloyd, T. et al. v5p0061c2s
Lloyd, T.G.B. v1p0113c2s v1p0715c2s v1p0910c2s v1p1256c1s
Lloyd, T.W. v6p0617c1s
Lloyd, W. v1p0591c2s v3p0063c2s v3p0261c2s v3p0281c2m v3p0358c1s v3p0384c2s v4p0058c1s v4p0111c2s v4p0112c2s v4p0113c2s v4p0227c2s v4p0286c1s v4p0405c2s v4p0533c2s v4p0534c1s v4p0586c1s v5p0115c2s v5p0376c1s v5p0410c2s v5p0533c1s v6p0061c1s v6p0147c2s
Lloyd, W.A. v1p0049c1m v3p0016c2s
Lloyd, W.H.S. v3p0232c2s
Lloyd, W.W. v1p0066c1s v1p0788c1s v1p0825c1s v1p0964c1s v1p1083c1m v1p1202c2s v1p1372c1s v2p0020c1s v2p0023c1s v2p0025c2s v2p0031c1s v2p0073c2s v2p0119c1s v2p0123c1s v2p0190c2s v2p0249c2s v2p0331c2s v2p0338c1s v2p0397c1s v2p0398c1s v2p0398c2m v2p0399c1s v2p0427c1s v2p0441c2s v2p0442c1m v2p0458c1s v3p0021c1s v3p0025c2s v3p0061c2s v3p0093c2m v3p0141c2s v3p0147c1s v3p0220c1s v3p0267c1s v3p0289c2m v3p0329c1s v3p0332c1s v3p0362c1s v3p0382c2s v3p0387c1s v3p0401c1m v3p0428c1s v4p0262c1m
Lloyd, W.W. and Gairdner, J. v3p0287c2s
Lloyd, W.Watkiss v3p0017c2s v3p0018c2m v3p0332c2s
Lloyd-George, D. v6p0683c2s
Lloyd-Lindsay, R. v1p0543c2s
Lluveras, A.M. v5p0460c2s
Loane, M. v6p0161c1s v6p0304c1s v6p0402c1s v6p0537c1s
Loba, J.F. v4p0017c1s
Lobb, H. v3p0316c2m
Lobb, R.P. v5p0441c1s v5p0539c2s v5p0540c1s
Lobban, J.H. v5p0238c2s v6p0053c2s v6p0071c2s
Lobban, W. v3p0181c1s
Lobdell, H. v1p1435c2s
Lobe, Prof. v1p0820c1s
Lobingier, C.S. v5p0402c1s v6p0174c2s v6p0493c1s v6p0583c1s
Lobingier, H.S. v1p0296c2s v1p0684c1s v2p0434c2s
Lobingier, J.C.S. v6p0494c1s
Lobley, J.L. v4p0166c1s v4p0192c2s v4p0486c2s v4p0543c1s v4p0558c2s v4p0559c1s v4p0582c1s v5p0173c1s v5p0389c2s
Lobley, L.J. v5p0389c2s
Lobnitz, F. v5p0491c2s
Lobstein, T.P. v1p0189c1s
Loch, C.H. v6p0117c1s
Loch, C.S. v3p0273c1s v4p0096c2s v4p0339c2s v4p0412c1s v4p0431c2s v4p0451c2s v4p0452c1m v5p0036c2s v5p0419c1m v5p0459c1s v5p0466c1s v6p0176c1s v6p0484c2s
Lochaber, N. v4p0387c1s v4p0621c2s
Lochaber, Nether v3p0354c2s
Locher, A. v1p0035c2s
Lochman, A.H. v1p1139c2s
Lock, A.G. v3p0176c2s
Lock, C.G.W. v2p0424c2s v3p0207c2s v3p0414c2s v4p0230c2s
Lock, W.G. v2p0214c1s
Locke, Adelaide I. v6p0344c1s
Locke, B.H. v6p0137c2s v6p0518c2s
Locke, C.E. v5p0281c1s v6p0414c1s
Locke, C.G.W. v3p0176c2s
Locke, C.S. v1p0248c2s v1p0685c1s
Locke, D.R. v1p0569c2s v2p0355c2s v3p0249c2s v3p0251c2s
Locke, E. v6p0076c1s v6p0229c2s
Locke, F.B. v5p0476c1s
Locke, G.H. v5p0178c1s v5p0374c1s v5p0517c2s v5p0518c1s v6p0141c1s v6p0454c2s v6p0525c1s v6p0542c2s v6p0574c2s v6p0581c2s
Locke, J. v1p0137c2s v1p0392c2s v1p0401c1s v1p0401c2s v1p0787c2s v1p0788c2s v1p0996c1s v1p1375c2s v6p0072c2m v6p0661c1s
Locke, J. and Jannasch, P. v4p0579c1s
Locke, J.A. v4p0249c1s v4p0463c1s v5p0426c2s
Locke, J.C. v6p0033c2s
Locke, J.G. v1p1374c2s
Locke, James v6p0047c1s
Locke, M.K. v5p0270c1s v5p0389c2s
Locke, S.D. v4p0609c2s
Locke, W. v4p0007c2s
Locke, W.J. v4p0007c1s
Locker, A. v2p0096c2s v2p0131c2s v2p0156c1s v2p0220c2s v2p0363c1s v2p0468c1s
Locker, F. v1p0518c1s v1p1313c1s v1p1358c2s
Locker-Lampson, O. v6p0038c1s
Lockery, Fred, jr. v5p0452c2s
Locket, G.L. v5p0124c1s
Lockett, J. v2p0029c1s v2p0478c2s v3p0119c1m
Lockett, J.L. v6p0688c1s
Lockett, Jeannie v3p0027c2s v3p0238c2s
Lockett, S.H. v2p0017c2s v2p0133c2s v2p0410c2s
Lockett, S.H. and Sedgwick, E.L. v2p0135c1s
Lockhart, A. v1p0951c2s
Lockhart, A.J. v3p0464c2s v6p0213c2s
Lockhart, C. v5p0018c2s v5p0262c2s v5p0283c1s v5p0475c1s v6p0174c2s v6p0257c1s v6p0589c1s v6p0620c1s
Lockhart, C.C. v6p0695c1s
Lockhart, C.G.N. v3p0351c1s
Lockhart, Caroline v6p0075c2s v6p0292c1s v6p0401c2s v6p0571c2s v6p0581c1s v6p0612c2s v6p0694c2s
Lockhart, J.C. v2p0398c1s
Lockhart, J.G. v1p0027c2s v1p0029c2s v1p0160c1s v1p0216c2m v1p0274c1m v1p0274c2s v1p0311c1m v1p0566c2s v1p0602c2s v1p0705c1s v1p0927c1s v1p0929c1s v1p1132c2s v1p1286c1s v1p1326c2s v1p1397c1s v1p1412c2s
Lockhart, J.G. et al. v1p0214c2s
Lockhart, J.H.S. v4p0105c1s v4p0205c1s v4p0353c1s v4p0357c1s
Lockhart, L.B. and Baskerville, C. v6p0527c2s v6p0713c1s
Lockhart, L.M.W. v1p0439c2s
Lockhart, L.W.M. v1p0199c1s v1p0843c2s v1p0921c2s v1p1358c1s v1p1365c2s v1p1385c1s
Lockhart, R.M. v5p0066c1s v5p0080c1s v5p0084c1s v5p0343c2s v5p0362c1s v5p0472c1s
Lockhart, W. v2p0378c2s v3p0302c1s v4p0354c1s
Lockhart, Wm. v3p0078c2s
Lockhart-Ross, H.S. v3p0273c2s v3p0359c2s
Locking, J.F. v3p0051c1m v3p0376c2s
Lockington, W.N. v1p0052c1s v1p0456c1s v1p0456c2s v1p0527c2s v1p1149c1s v2p0004c1s v2p0006c1s v2p0017c1s v2p0020c1s v2p0036c1s v2p0174c1s v2p0214c1s v2p0274c2s v2p0338c2m v2p0345c2s v2p0450c2s v2p0455c2s v3p0034c1s v3p0039c2s v3p0100c2s v3p0193c1s v3p0202c2s v3p0297c1s v3p0368c2s v3p0386c1s v3p0402c2s v3p0412c2s v3p0448c1s v5p0443c1s v6p0022c1s
Lockley, F. v1p0007c2s v1p0397c1s v1p0702c1m v1p0715c1s v1p0914c2s v1p1101c2s
Locksley, L. v3p0027c2s v3p0181c1s
Lockwood, A. v6p0275c1s
Lockwood, Albert v5p0450c1s
Lockwood, B.A. v3p0467c2s v4p0022c2s v4p0101c1s v4p0101c2s v4p0323c2s v4p0432c1s v4p0628c2s
Lockwood, B.A. et al. v4p0629c2s
Lockwood, D.C. v5p0236c1s v6p0599c1s
Lockwood, De Witt C. v6p0275c2s v6p0697c1s
Lockwood, E.H. v3p0367c2s v3p0408c2s
Lockwood, F. v3p0020c2s v4p0343c2s
Lockwood, F.B. v1p0230c1s v1p0495c2s v1p1037c1s v2p0075c1s
Lockwood, F.C. v4p0178c2s v4p0582c1s v6p0283c2s v6p0707c2s
Lockwood, F.W. v5p0451c2s v5p0472c2s
Lockwood, H.C. v1p0457c2s v4p0200c2s
Lockwood, J.A. v3p0039c2s v4p0154c1s v5p0217c2s v5p0437c1s
Lockwood, J.A., Capt. v5p0433c1s
Lockwood, J.B. v1p1040c1s
Lockwood, K.R. v3p0196c2s
Lockwood, L.V. v6p0244c2s
Lockwood, M. v1p0232c1s v5p0154c2s
Lockwood, M.H. and Wheller, E.B. v5p0125c1s
Lockwood, M.S. v4p0189c1s v4p0316c1s
Lockwood, S. v1p0042c1s v1p0108c2s v1p0135c2s v1p0137c1s v1p0216c1s v1p0270c1s v1p0279c2s v1p0311c1m v1p0420c1s v1p0429c1s v1p0463c1s v1p0463c2s v1p0588c2s v1p0645c1s v1p0834c1s v1p0835c2s v1p0877c1s v1p0885c2s v1p0924c1s v1p0948c2s v1p0953c2s v1p0955c2s v1p1112c1s v1p1172c2m v1p1213c1s v1p1213c2s v1p1239c1s v2p0087c2s v2p0279c2s v2p0306c2s v2p0325c2s v2p0361c2s v2p0392c1s v3p0382c1s v3p0383c1s v4p0036c1s v4p0375c2s
Lockwood, S.E.H., Mrs. ... v3p0140c1s
Lockwood, T.D. v4p0174c2s v4p0175c2s
Lockwood, V.H. v4p0430c1s v5p0138c1s
Lockwood, W.L. v6p0279c1s
Lockyer, A.E. v4p0406c2s
Lockyer, J.N. v1p0066c1s v1p0074c1s v1p0224c1s v1p0224c2s v1p0281c2s v1p0375c2s v1p0381c2s v1p0382c1m v1p0401c2m v1p0827c1s v1p0829c2s v1p0866c1s v1p0945c1s v1p1222c1s v1p1233c2m v1p1234c1m v1p1243c2s v1p1267c2m v1p1268c1m v1p1268c2m v1p1269c1s v1p1291c2s v1p1395c1s v2p0127c2m v2p0129c2m v2p0132c1s v2p0220c2s v2p0412c2s v2p0424c2s v2p0426c2s v2p0441c2s v3p0024c2m v3p0127c1s v3p0193c1s v3p0276c1m v3p0281c2s v3p0298c2m v3p0313c1s v3p0379c2s v3p0403c2m v3p0407c1m v3p0407c2m v3p0415c1s v3p0430c2s v4p0033c2s v4p0034c1m v4p0167c1s v4p0172c1s v4p0172c2s v4p0221c1s v4p0253c2m v4p0358c1s

v4p0404c2s v4p0413c2s v4p0417c1s
v4p0468c1s v4p0541c1s v4p0545c2s
v4p0556c2s v4p0557c1s v4p0568c2s
v4p0633c1s v4p0635c1s v5p0174c2s
v5p0402c1s v5p0514c1s v6p0626c1s
Lockyer, J.N. and Hunter, W.W.
v1p0443c1s v1p1269c1s
Lockyér, J.N. and Stewart, B.
v1p1267c2s
Lockyer, J.Norman v2p0425c1s
Lockyer, N. v5p0175c1s
v5p0198c1s v5p0513c2s v5p0545c1m
v5p0549c1m v5p0549c2m v5p0554c2s
v5p0561c1s v6p0079c2s v6p0082c1s
v6p0125c1s v6p0407c2s v6p0444c1s
v6p0507c2s v6p0553c2s v6p0619c1m
v6p0625c2s v6p0681c1s v6p0711c1s
Lockyer, N. and Lockyer, W.J.S.
v5p0478c1s
Lockyer, N., Sir v6p0670c2s
Lockyer, N.J. v4p0337c2s
v5p0343c2s
Lockyer, N.J.S. v6p0187c2s
Lockyer, Norman v5p0174c2s
v6p0127c2s v6p0150c1s v6p0427c1s
Lockyer, Norman, Sir and
Lockyer, W.J.S. v5p0561c1s
Lockyer, S. v1p1257c2s
Lockyer, W.J. v4p0135c2s
v4p0503c2s v4p0602c2s
Lockyer, W.J.S. v4p0242c2s
v4p0307c1s v4p0357c2m v4p0358c1s
v5p0167c1s v5p0338c2s v5p0372c2s
v5p0373c1s v5p0448c1s v5p0513c1s
v5p0549c1s v5p0561c1s v6p0037c2s
v6p0040c1s v6p0042c2s v6p0052c2m
v6p0132c1s v6p0188c1m v6p0314c1s
v6p0330c1s v6p0377c1s v6p0391c2s
v6p0395c1s v6p0403c1s v6p0486c2s
v6p0530c2s v6p0609c1s v6p0613c2s
v6p0625c2m v6p0626c1m v6p0641c1s
v6p0690c2s v6p0711c2s
Lockyer, W.J.S. and Lockyer, N.
v5p0478c1s
Lockyer, W.J.S. and
Lockyer, Norman, Sir .. v5p0561c1s
Lockyer, W.N. v5p0252c2s
Loct, L.C. v5p0156c2s
Locy, W.A. v2p0359c1s
v3p0476c1s v5p0329c2s v5p0357c2s
v5p0563c1s v6p0066c2s v6p0079c2s
Lodeman, A. v5p0391c1s
v6p0574c2s
Lodeman, E.G. v4p0063c1s
Lodge, A. v3p0192c2s
v3p0291c2s v3p0444c2s
Lodge, E. v1p1141c1s
v1p1437c2s
Lodge, E.C. v6p0584c1s
Lodge, G. v5p0121c2s
Lodge, G.E. v2p0047c2s
v2p0428c1s v3p0045c2s
Lodge, Gonzalez v6p0363c1s
Lodge, H.C. v1p0028c1s
v1p0222c2s v1p0237c2s v1p0270c1s
v1p0447c1m v1p0472c1s v1p0497c2s
v1p0567c2s v1p0731c2s v1p0842c1s
v1p0909c2s v1p0964c2s v1p1008c1s
v1p1252c1s v1p1348c2s v1p1412c1s
v2p0105c1s v2p0271c2s v2p0298c2s
v2p0308c1s v2p0329c1s v2p0396c1s
v2p0452c1s v2p0469c1s v3p0001c1s
v3p0010c1s v3p0086c2s v3p0096c2m
v3p0099c2s v3p0132c1s v3p0154c1s
v3p0201c1s v3p0209c1s v3p0261c2s
v3p0323c2s v3p0347c1s v3p0444c1s
v3p0455c2s v4p0016c1m v4p0142c2s
v4p0174c1s v4p0240c1s v4p0256c1s
v4p0260c2s v4p0275c1s v4p0275c2s
v4p0379c2s v4p0481c2s v4p0593c1s
v4p0595c2s v4p0601c2s v5p0017c1s
v5p0086c2s v5p0254c2s v5p0363c2s
v5p0488c1s v5p0543c1s v5p0603c2s
v6p0239c1s v6p0293c1s v6p0293c2s
v6p0308c1s v6p0550c1s v6p0550c2s
v6p0551c1s v6p0558c2s v6p0583c1s
v6p0583c2s
Lodge, H.C. and Adams, H.. v1p1348c2s
Lodge, H.C. and Stewart, W.M.
v4p0515c1s
Lodge, Henry C. v6p0034c2s
Lodge, L.B. v4p0194c1s
Lodge, Mrs. v2p0451c2s
Lodge, O. v2p0036c1s
v2p0138c2s v2p0272c1s v3p0036c1s
v3p0133c2s v3p0134c1s v4p0165c1s
v4p0187c2s v4p0256c2s v4p0487c1s
v5p0382c2s v5p0479c2s v6p0192c1s
v6p0198c2s v6p0199c1m v6p0218c1s
v6p0240c2s v6p0420c1s v6p0490c1s
v6p0527c1s v6p0535c2s v6p0536c2s
v6p0574c2s v6p0575c2m v6p0595c2s
v6p0600c1s v6p0635c1s v6p0665c2s
v6p0707c2s
Lodge, O. et al. v6p0249c2s
Lodge, O., Sir v6p0277c1s
v6p0396c2s v6p0404c1s v6p0406c2s
v6p0595c2s
Lodge, O.J. v1p0400c1s
v1p0401c1s v1p0746c2s v2p0112c1s
v2p0126c1m v2p0137c2s v2p0138c1s
v2p0146c2s v2p0440c1s v3p0133c2s
v3p0134c1s v3p0145c2s v3p0251c1m
v3p0264c1m v3p0331c2s v3p0351c2s
v4p0001c2s v4p0176c1s v4p0177c1s
v4p0222c2s v4p0331c2m v4p0441c2s
v4p0464c1s v5p0366c2s v6p0410c2s
Lodge, O.J. and Clark, J.W.
v2p0126c1s
Lodge, O.J. and Mendenhall, J.C.
v3p0459c1s
Lodge, O.J. and Rudge, W.A.
v3p0133c1s
Lodge, O.J. and Serrell, E.W., jr
v2p0126c1s
Lodge, O.J. et al. v6p0191c1s
Lodge, Oliver v6p0122c2m
Lodge, Oliver, Sir v6p0267c2s
v6p0375c2s v6p0376c1s v6p0418c2s
v6p0627c2s
Lodge, Oliver, Sir et al.. v6p0536c2s
Lodge, R. v3p0159c2m
v4p0211c1s v4p0539c2s v5p0021c2s
v5p0598c1s
Lodge, R.B. v5p0062c2s
v5p0063c2s
Lodge, W.C. v1p0983c1s
Lodian, G. v4p0472c2s
v4p0567c2s
Lodian, L. v5p0606c1s
Lodian, W. v4p0567c1s
Loeb, E. v5p0199c1s
Loeb, J. v5p0034c2s
v5p0180c2s v5p0263c1s v6p0066c2s
v6p0424c1s
Loeb, Jacques v6p0066c2s
Loeb, L. v5p0619c1s
Loeb, M. v4p0222c1s
v5p0226c1s
Loehe, W. v5p0451c2s
Loehr, A.M. v5p0177c1s
v5p0179c2s
Loehr, C.T. v3p0336c1s
Loes, J.M. v4p0049c2s
v5p0638c1s
Loevenhart, A.S. and Kastle, J.H.
v6p0325c2s
Loew, F.A. v6p0651c1s
Loew, H. v1p0644c2s
Loew, O. v1p0867c2s
v1p0955c2s v5p0193c2s
Loew, R. v5p0458c2s
Loew, W.N. v2p0451c2s
Loewe, Herbert v6p0249c2s
Loewe, S. v1p0119c1s
v1p1338c1s
Loewenberg, J. v1p0067c2s
Loewenthal, I. v1p0130c2s
v1p0564c1s v1p0630c1s v1p0631c2s
v1p0633c2s v1p0724c1s v1p0727c1s
v1p1060c2s v1p1303c1s
Loewy, B. et al. v1p1268c2s
Loewy, M. v2p0145c2s
v2p0319c1s v5p0194c2s v5p0408c2s
v5p0431c1s
Loey, W.A. v2p0309c2s
Lofengluh, C. v5p0325c1s
Loffelt, A.C. v4p0361c2s
Lofquest, C.C. v6p0516c2s
Lofthouse, J. v5p0574c2s
Loftie, W.D. v1p0761c2s
Loftie, W.J. v1p0394c2s
v1p0884c1s v1p1101c1s v2p0264c1s
v2p0437c1s v2p0475c2s v3p0058c2s
v3p0135c2s v3p0184c2s v3p0185c1s
v3p0189c1s v3p0235c2s v3p0256c1s
v3p0256c2m v3p0318c1s v3p0361c1s
v3p0372c1s v3p0433c2s v3p0461c1m
v3p0462c2s v3p0465c2s v4p0029c2s
v4p0077c2s v4p0173c1s v4p0179c1s
v4p0244c1s v4p0285c1m v4p0310c1s
v4p0339c1s v4p0339c2m v4p0499c1s
v4p0618c1s v4p0620c1s v6p0194c2s
v6p0385c1s
Loftus, A. v4p0181c1s
Logan, A.M. v3p0237c1s
v4p0248c1s v4p0296c1s v4p0408c2s
v4p0605c2s v5p0021c2s v5p0240c2s
v5p0488c1s v6p0223c2s v6p0281c1s
v6p0284c1s v6p0289c2s v6p0396c2s
v6p0543c1s v6p0640c2s v6p0685c2s
Logan, C. v1p0163c1s
v1p0408c2s
Logan, D. v5p0178c1s
Logan, E.A. v5p0564c2s
Logan, G. v6p0401c1s
Logan, G.W. v1p0528c1s
Logan, H. v6p0171c1s
v6p0512c2s v6p0596c1s
Logan, J. v1p0703c1s
v1p0865c1s v1p1256c1s v2p0222c2s
v5p0593c1s
Logan, J.A. v2p0131c2s
v2p0405c1s v4p0088c2s v4p0288c1s
Logan, J.D. v5p0001c2s
v5p0028c1s v5p0031c1s v5p0101c2s
v5p0159c2s v5p0342c1s v5p0400c2s
v5p0449c1s v5p0468c2s v5p0470c2s
v5p0571c1s v6p0306c2s
Logan, M. v4p0030c1s
v5p0348c2s v5p0417c1s
Logan, M.A. v6p0584c1s
Logan, O. v1p0202c2s
v1p0359c2s v1p0363c1s v1p0363c2s
v1p0606c2s v1p0767c1s v1p0849c1s
v1p0878c2s v1p0930c1s v1p0968c1s
v1p0969c1s v1p1201c2s v1p1241c2s
v1p1242c1s v1p1300c1s v1p1376c2s
v1p1438c1s v2p0086c1s
Logan, R.F. v4p0142c2s
Logan, S.C. v4p0280c1m
Logan, S.J. v4p0195c1s
Logan, S.M. v1p1224c1s
Logan, T. v1p1264c1m
Logan, T.M. v1p0221c1s
v1p0389c1s v1p1223c2s
Logan, W.C. v2p0027c2s
Logan, W.E. and Hunt, T.S.
v1p0751c1s
Logan, W.E., Sir v1p0192c2s
v1p0193c2m v1p0300c1s v1p0508c2s
v1p1070c2m v1p1271c1s
Logan, W.E., Sir and Salter, J.W.
v1p0193c1s
Logan, W.L. v4p0282c2s
v4p0434c2s
Logan, W.S. v4p0022c2s
v4p0368c1s v5p0140c1s v6p0312c1s
v6p0357c1s v6p0460c1s
Logan, W.S. and Butler, W.A.
v4p0022c2s
Logeman, H. v3p0139c2s
Login, T. v1p1389c2s
v3p0223c2s
Logsdael, C. et al. v4p0457c2s
v4p0595c2s
Logsdail, C. v3p0441c2s
v4p0333c1s v4p0575c2s v4p0629c1s
v5p0127c1s
Lohman, W.H.deS. v5p0320c1s
Lohme, G.H. v3p0101c1s
Lohmes, G.H. v3p0025c2s
Loinaz, D. v6p0221c1s
Lointaine, Princess v4p0492c2s
Loiseau, E.F. v1p0268c2s
v1p0493c1m
Loiseaux, Jeanne O. v6p0060c1s
v6p0333c2s
Loisy, A. v6p0237c2s
Loliee, F. v5p0362c2s
Lomas, J. v2p0442c2s
v3p0121c1s
Lomas, J. and Grossmann, K.
v4p0273c1s
Lomas, R. v1p1320c2s
Lomas, S.C. v5p0084c2s
Lomas, S.C., Mrs. v6p0205c2s
Lomax, E.W.P. v5p0344c2s
Lomax, J.A. v3p0173c1s
v3p0244c2s v3p0282c1s
Lomax, J.T. v1p0026c2s
v1p0364c2s v1p0505c1s v1p0774c1s
v1p1073c2s v1p1156c2s v1p1241c2s
Lombard, H.C. v1p0877c1s
Lombard, W.P. v3p0150c1s
v3p0237c1s v3p0292c2s
Lombard, W.P. and Ooge, M.L.D'
v6p0555c2s
Lombroso, C. v3p0013c1s
v3p0105c2s v3p0216c2s v3p0224c1s
v3p0348c1s v4p0017c1s v4p0035c1s
v4p0052c2s v4p0140c1m v4p0191c1s
v4p0373c2s v4p0375c2s v4p0406c1s
v4p0439c1s v4p0441c2s v4p0463c2s
v4p0564c2s v4p0626c1s v5p0018c1s
v5p0061c1s v5p0068c2s v5p0112c1s
v5p0129c2s v5p0198c2s v5p0228c1s
v5p0263c1s v5p0269c2s v5p0291c2s
v5p0300c1s v5p0317c2s v5p0350c2s
v5p0609c1s v6p0019c2s v6p0158c1s
v6p0366c2s v6p0659c1s
Lombroso, P. v5p0107c2s
v5p0436c2s
Lome, Enrique Dupuy de ... v4p0102c1s
Lomel, A.F. v1p1087c2s
Lomet, A.F. v1p0312c2s
Lommel, G.L. ....
v1p1200c1s
Lona, T. ....
v2p0232c1s
Londesborough, Lord v1p1329c2s
London, Bishop of v1p0980c1s
London, H. v3p0385c1s
London, Helen v3p0287c2s
London, J. v3p0032c1s
v5p0131c1s v5p0153c2s v5p0236c2s
v5p0251c1s v5p0302c1s v5p0318c1s
v5p0327c2s v5p0331c2s v5p0340c2s
v5p0359c1s v5p0397c1s v5p0418c1s
v6p0670c2s
London, Jack v5p0131c1s
v5p0165c1s v5p0282c2s v5p0369c2s
v5p0465c2s v5p0514c2s v5p0538c2s
v5p0581c1s v5p0618c1s v5p0628c1s
v5p0629c2s v5p0630c2s v5p0633c2s
v6p0012c2s v6p0056c2s v6p0084c2s
v6p0130c1s v6p0172c2s v6p0223c1s
v6p0260c2s v6p0376c1s v6p0381c2s
v6p0388c1s v6p0405c2s v6p0467c2s
v6p0502c1s v6p0571c2s v6p0580c2s

v6p0586c1s v6p0593c1s v6p0599c1s
v6p0603c2s v6p0626c1s v6p0653c2s
v6p0665c1s v6p0696c2s
London, M. v5p0336c1s
London, W.J. v6p0408c1s
v6p0471c2s
Londonderry, Marchioness of
v1p0072c2s v1p0294c2s v1p0893c1s
v1p1371c1s
Londonderry, Marquis of .. v1p1229c1s
Londonderry, T. v5p0187c2s
Londonderry, T. and Stewart, I.
v6p0462c2s
Lonergan, E.A. v2p0015c1s
Lonergan, T.S. v5p0116c2s
Long, A. v6p0222c1s
Long, A.L. v1p1209c1s
v1p1346c2s v1p1347c1s v1p1347c2s
v2p0100c1s v2p0109c1s v2p0272c1s
v3p0029c2s v3p0125c2s v4p0053c2s
Long, A.L. et al. v1p0518c2s
Long, C. v1p0385c1s
v1p0426c1s
Long, C.C. v5p0180c2s
v5p0539c2s
Long, C.S. v5p0381c1s
Long, C.T. v4p0297c2s
v4p0298c1s
Long, D.P.De v6p0081c1s
Long, E.E. v2p0315c2s
Long, E.V. v5p0281c2s
Long, F. et al. v4p0557c2s
Long, H.C.De v1p0529c1s
Long, H.L. v1p0014c1s
v1p0314c2s
Long, I.H.De v6p0063c1s
Long, J. v1p1332c2s
v3p0369c1s v4p0008c1m v4p0236c2s
v4p0463c1s v5p0594c1s
Long, J.C. v1p0328c1s
v2p0406c1s v2p0432c1s v3p0038c1s
v4p0021c1s v4p0185c2s v4p0283c1s
Long, J.D. v1p0255c1s
v3p0257c2s v3p0404c1s v3p0433c2s
v3p0449c1s v4p0063c1s v5p0354c1s
v5p0602c2s v6p0500c1s v6p0669c1m
Long, J.D. and Mahan, A.T.
v6p0567c1s
Long, J.D. et al. v3p0301c1s
Long, J.F.De v5p0132c1s
v5p0348c1s
Long, J.H. v1p0923c1s
v3p0336c1s v3p0420c2s v4p0057c2s
v4p0217c2s v4p0236c2s v4p0624c2s
v5p0104c1s v6p0011c1s v6p0112c1m
v6p0409c1s
Long, J.L. v3p0343c2s
v5p0163c2s v5p0165c1s v5p0216c1s
v5p0228c1s v5p0354c2s v5p0412c2s
v5p0466c1s v5p0473c1s v5p0534c2s
v6p0375c2s v6p0444c2s v6p0596c1m
v6p0621c2s
Long, J.M. v1p0385c1s
v1p0391c2s v1p0843c1s v1p0843c2m
v1p1062c1m v1p1085c2s v2p0283c2s
v2p0339c2s v3p0271c2s
Long, L.A. v3p0130c2s
v6p0291c2s v6p0407c2s v6p0569c1s
Long, Lily A. v5p0475c1s
Long, M.J.De v1p0646c1s
v2p0214c1s v2p0368c2s v3p0058c1s
v3p0150c2s
Long, M.J.S.De v1p0688c2s
v2p0236c1s
Long, M.V.Le v5p0150c2s
Long, Ossian H. v6p0194c1s
Long, Percy W. v6p0135c1s
Long, R. v6p0071c1s
Long, R.C. v1p0052c1s
v1p0054c1s
Long, R.E.C. v5p0034c1s
v5p0502c2s v5p0527c2s v5p0582c1s
v6p0071c1s v6p0204c2s v6p0457c1s
v6p0556c2s v6p0558c1s v6p0561c1s
v6p0593c1s v6p0634c2s v6p0641c2s
v6p0702c1s
Long, R.H. v2p0179c2s
Long, R.S. v3p0055c1s
v3p0138c1s v3p0322c2s v3p0454c1s
v4p0013c1m v4p0141c2s v4p0370c1s
v4p0436c2s v4p0444c2s v4p0533c1s
v4p0534c1s v4p0622c2s v5p0301c1s
v5p0468c1s
Long, S.B. v1p0199c2s
Long, S.H. v1p0161c1s
v1p0161c2s v1p0759c2s
Long, S.S. v5p0446c1s
Long, W.E. v6p0496c2s
Long, W.H. v4p0337c2s
v6p0021c1s
Long, W.H. and Wheeler, W.M.
v5p0174c2s
Long, W.J. v5p0108c1s
v5p0263c1s v6p0021c1s v6p0021c2s
v6p0022c1m v6p0052c2s v6p0055c1s
v6p0095c2s v6p0226c2s v6p0261c2s
v6p0277c1s v6p0304c1s v6p0309c2s
v6p0350c1s v6p0352c1s v6p0391c1s
v6p0407c1s v6p0444c1s v6p0444c2s
v6p0482c1s v6p0576c1s
Long, W.S. v3p0287c1s
Longan, G.W. v1p0874c1s
v2p0034c2s v2p0042c1s v2p0044c1s
Longan, I.W. v1p0849c2s
Longan, R.E. v6p0625c1s
Longden, A.C. v5p0184c2s
v5p0449c2s v5p0519c1s
Longdon, S. v6p0562c1s
Longdrop, A. v3p0190c2s
Longe, F.D. v1p1319c2s
v4p0553c1s
Longfellow, Alice v5p0347c1s
Longfellow, E.W. v2p0105c2s
Longfellow, H.W. v1p0018c1s
v1p0026c1s v1p0088c1m v1p0099c2s
v1p0110c2s v1p0136c2s v1p0179c1s
v1p0205c1s v1p0215c2s v1p0323c2s
v1p0373c1s v1p0418c1s v1p0488c2m
v1p0497c1s v1p0540c1s v1p0575c2s
v1p0669c1s v1p0706c1s v1p0716c2s
v1p0732c2s v1p0735c1s v1p0761c2s
v1p0763c2s v1p0863c2s v1p0871c2s
v1p0990c1s v1p1021c1s v1p1105c2s
v1p1123c2s v1p1127c2s v1p1155c1s
v1p1231c1s v1p1289c1s v1p1369c2s
v1p1433c1s v2p0039c1s v2p0114c2s
v2p0201c2s v2p0287c1s v6p0404c1s
Longfellow, S. v1p0297c1s
v1p1074c1s v1p1094c1s v1p1096c2s
v1p1300c2s
Longfellow, W.P. and Clark, T.U.
v3p0361c1s
Longfellow, W.P.P. v3p0017c2s
v3p0018c1m v3p0021c2s v3p0109c1s
v3p0447c1s v3p0447c2s v4p0342c2s
v4p0490c1s v4p0490c2s v5p0034c2s
v5p0500c1m v6p0161c2s
Longfield, M. v1p0657c2s
Longford, J.H. v6p0336c1s
v6p0337c2s v6p0354c1m v6p0509c1s
Longhurst, A.E.T. v4p0568c1s
Longhurst, P. v6p0083c2s
Longking, J. v3p0134c2s
Longley, Howard v6p0697c2s
Longley, J. v1p0846c1s
Longley, J.W. v1p1028c1s
v3p0035c2s v3p0065c1s v3p0204c1s
v4p0019c1s v4p0086c1s v4p0217c1s
v4p0265c2s v4p0267c2s v4p0408c1s
v4p0525c2s v4p0533c2s v5p0093c1s
v5p0327c1s v5p0366c1s v5p0415c1s
v5p0468c2s v5p0620c1s v6p0095c2s
v6p0097c2s v6p0428c1s
Longley, T.W. v4p0120c2s
v4p0269c1s
Longman, C.J. v1p0300c2s
v2p0018c2s v4p0070c2s v4p0133c2s
Longman, F.W. v1p0158c2s
Longman, W. v1p0785c2s
v1p1337c2s
Longmuir, P. v5p0215c2m
v6p0235c1s v6p0355c2s v6p0652c1s
v6p0682c2s v6p0708c1s
Longridge, C.C. v2p0317c2s
v2p0337c2s v3p0328c2s
Longridge, J.A. v1p0947c1s
v2p0193c2s v5p0252c2s
Longstaff, G.B. v2p0114c1s
v2p0190c1s v3p0072c1s v3p0180c2m
v3p0339c2s v4p0494c2s
Longstreet, A.B. v1p0442c2s
Longstreet, J. v1p0485c2s
v1p0518c2s v1p0519c1s v1p0795c2s
v1p1180c2s v1p1345c2s v2p0279c1s
v2p0349c1s v2p0372c2s v3p0443c1s
Longstreet, J. et al. ... v2p0166c2s
Longueville, T. v4p0264c1s
Longworth, N. v6p0174c2s
Longworth, Nicholas v6p0146c2s
Lonis, D.A. v3p0306c1s
Lonnegren, A.V. v3p0166c1s
Lonsdale, E. v6p0102c1s
Lonsdale, M. v1p0934c1s
v2p0276c2s v2p0477c1s
Lonsdale, M. et al. v1p0934c1s
Loofs, F. v5p0240c2s
Loogan, G.W. v1p0792c1s
Look, H.M. v2p0031c2s
Loomis, A.W. v1p0232c2s
v1p0233c1s v1p0235c1m v1p0235c2m
v1p0236c1m v1p0236c2m v1p1059c2s
v1p1196c2s
Loomis, C.B. v4p0386c2s
v5p0073c2s v5p0156c1s v5p0313c1s
v5p0347c2s v5p0415c1s v5p0418c2s
v5p0538c2s v5p0628c2s v6p0099c1s
v6p0296c1s v6p0299c2s v6p0397c2s
v6p0440c1s v6p0451c2s v6p0504c1s
Loomis, C.Battell v6p0207c1s
Loomis, E. v1p0070c2s
v1p0074c1s v1p0077c1m v1p0281c1s
v1p0399c1s v1p0565c1s v1p0709c2s
v1p0787c2m v1p0788c1s v1p0788c2s
v1p0827c1m v1p0829c2s v1p0906c2s
v1p0936c1s v1p1014c1s v1p1100c2s
v1p1196c2s v1p1293c1s v1p1316c1s
v1p1359c1s v1p1391c1s v1p1395c1s
v1p1436c1s v2p0035c1s v2p0285c2s
v2p0364c1s v3p0276c1s
Loomis, E. and St.John, S.
v1p0400c1s
Loomis, E.H. v6p0112c1s
Loomis, E.J. and Tood, D.P.
v3p0004c2s
Loomis, E.S. v5p0366c1s
Loomis, F.B. v4p0016c1m
v5p0600c2s v6p0234c2s v6p0272c2s
v6p0305c1s v6p0426c1s v6p0516c1s
v6p0539c2s v6p0666c2s
Loomis, F.B. and Emerson, B.K.
v6p0616c2s
Loomis, F.E. and Kohlrauch, F.
v1p0825c2s
Loomis, F.E. and Kohlrausch, F.
v1p1293c1s
Loomis, F.M. v4p0115c2s
v4p0117c1s v4p0454c2s
Loomis, Francis B. v6p0146c2s
Loomis, G. v5p0347c2s
v5p0571c1s
Loomis, H. v1p0356c2s
v1p1423c2s v3p0396c2s v3p0445c1s
Loomis, H., jr. v1p1103c2s
Loomis, H.B. v5p0218c2s
v5p0229c1s v6p0395c1s
Loomis, J.R. v1p0401c1s
v1p0506c2s
Loomis, L.C. v1p1406c2s
v4p0470c2s
Loomis, M.B. v5p0520c2s
Loomis, S.L. v3p0085c2m
v3p0255c2s v3p0256c1s v4p0113c2s
Loop, D.J.M. v1p0040c1s
v1p0595c2s
Loop, F.E. v1p0334c1s
v1p1213c2s
Loos, C.L. v1p0448c2s
v1p0935c2s v2p0191c1s
Loos, I. v4p0289c1s
Loos, I.A. v6p0141c1s
v6p0352c1s
Loos, I.K. v1p1058c1s
Loos, Isaac v5p0028c1s
Looscan, A.B. v6p0164c1s
v6p0222c1s v6p0569c1s v6p0675c2s
Loose, N.H. v2p0029c2s
Lopez, C.A. v5p0392c1s
v6p0579c2s
Lopez, S. v5p0445c2s
v6p0493c1s
Lopez, Sixto v5p0445c2s
Lorac, L.de v4p0050c1s
Loraine, M.W. v6p0327c2s
Loraine, R. v6p0589c2s
Lorch, E. v5p0025c2s
Lord, A. v4p0447c2s
v5p0215c2s
Lord, A.W. v6p0549c2s
Lord, C. v1p0980c1s
v4p0332c1s
Lord, C.C. v2p0025c2s
v2p0110c1s v2p0207c1m v2p0469c1s
v3p0190c2s v3p0327c1s v3p0385c1s
v3p0466c2s
Lord, C.E. v1p1207c1s
v2p0405c1s
Lord, C.S. v5p0632c1s
Lord, D. v1p0014c1s
Lord, D., jr. v1p0299c2s
v1p0734c2s
Lord, D.N. v1p0107c2s
v1p0119c1s v1p0121c1s v1p0124c2m
v1p0125c1s v1p0131c1s v1p0131c2s
v1p0175c2s v1p0180c1m v1p0254c2s
v1p0274c1s v1p0312c2s v1p0313c1s
v1p0375c1s v1p0375c2s v1p0376c1s
v1p0452c1s v1p0507c1m v1p0508c1s
v1p0514c1s v1p0515c2s v1p0592c2s
v1p0612c1s v1p0688c2s v1p0691c2s
v1p0840c1m v1p0908c1s v1p0923c2s
v1p0964c1s v1p0964c2s v1p0966c1s
v1p0972c1s v1p0980c2s v1p1000c2s
v1p1001c2s v1p1056c1m v1p1056c2s
v1p1062c1s v1p1094c2s v1p1095c1s
v1p1174c2m v1p1200c1s v1p1237c2s
v1p1275c1s v1p1277c2m v1p1278c1s
v1p1432c2s
Lord, E. v1p0243c2s
v1p0253c2s v1p0326c1s v1p0529c1s
v1p0711c2s v1p0816c1s v1p1041c2s
v4p0163c2s v4p0249c2s v4p0361c1s
v4p0432c1s v4p0524c1s v6p0393c1s
Lord, E.C. v1p0236c1s
Lord, E.L. v4p0022c2s
Lord, Eliot v3p0303c1s
Lord, F. v5p0557c2s
Lord, G.D. v5p0038c1s
v5p0291c2s
Lord, G.D. and Heermance, T.W.
v5p0137c2s
Lord, H.B.B., Mrs. v2p0338c2s
Lord, H.C. and Lord, J.L.. v1p0426c2s
Lord, I.E. v5p0333c2s
v5p0335c1s v6p0222c2s
Lord, I.E. and Wyer, J.I., jr.
v5p0176c2m
Lord, Isabel E. v6p0370c2s
v6p0374c2s
Lord, Isabel E. and Wyer, J.I., jr.
v6p0190c1m

Lord, J. v1p0248c1s
v1p0472c1s v1p0893c2s v1p1066c2s
v1p1090c2s v1p1124c2s v6p0571c2s
Lord, J.C. v1p0989c2s
v1p1149c1s
Lord, J.H. v2p0126c2s
Lord, J.K. v1p0256c1s
v1p0472c2s v1p0885c2m v1p1041c2s
v1p1428c1s v2p0015c2s v2p0046c2s
v2p0047c1s v2p0065c2s v2p0070c2s
v2p0091c1s v2p0105c2s v2p0169c2m
v2p0171c1s v2p0177c1s v2p0299c2s
v2p0307c1s v2p0310c1s v2p0325c2s
v2p0347c1s v2p0393c1s v2p0402c2s
v2p0403c2s v2p0465c1s v2p0483c1m
Lord, J.L. and Lord, H.C.. v1p0426c2s
Lord, J.W. v6p0529c1s
Lord, N. v1p0407c1s
v1p0840c1s v1p1106c2s
Lord, R.F. v4p0231c1s
Lord, S. v6p0658c2s
Lord, T. v1p0299c2s
Lord, T.A. v2p0302c2s
Lord, W. v1p1035c2s
Lord, W.B. v1p0983c2s
v5p0067c2s
Lord, W.F. v3p0049c1s
v3p0101c2s v3p0207c1s v3p0219c1s
v3p0228c1s v3p0319c1s v3p0419c2s
v4p0294c2s v4p0462c1s v4p0562c2s
v5p0051c1s v5p0233c1s v5p0240c1s
v5p0352c1s v5p0392c2s v5p0591c1s
v6p0022c2s v6p0041c1s v6p0083c2s
v6p0096c2s v6p0173c1s v6p0262c1s
v6p0352c1s v6p0391c1s v6p0394c2m
v6p0532c1s v6p0564c2s v6p0640c2s
v6p0671c2s
Lord, W.H. v1p0243c2s
v2p0359c1s
Lord, W.W. v1p0180c1s
v1p0542c2s v1p0613c1s v1p0641c2s
v1p0852c2s
v1p1066c2s
v1p1292c1s
Lorec, L.F. v4p0471c1s
v4p0472c1s
Lorence, F. v6p0140c1s
Lorenz, A. v6p0471c1s
Lorenz, E.S. v2p0299c2s
Lorenz, M.O. v6p0529c1s
v6p0690c1s
Loria, A. v3p0118c2s
v3p0127c2s v4p0135c2s v5p0175c2s
v5p0205c1s v5p0532c1s v5p0584c1s
v6p0188c2s v6p0331c2s v6p0359c2s
v6p0445c2s v6p0674c1s
Loria, G. v6p0251c1s
Lorillard, P. v2p0245c1s
Lorimer, C. v6p0463c1s
v6p0653c2s
Lorimer, C.E. v6p0119c1s
Lorimer, G.C. v3p0194c2s
v3p0385c2s v4p0109c1s v5p0592c1s
v6p0526c1s v6p0597c2s
Lorimer, G.H. v6p0060c1s
Lorimer, J. v4p0168c2s
Lorimer, J.C. v4p0127c2s
Lorimer, L. v5p0224c2s
Lorimer, Louise v5p0170c1s
Lorimer, M.F. v5p0496c2s
Lorimer, P. v2p0353c1m
Lorimer, Prof. v1p0242c2s
Lorimer, R. v2p0017c2s
v2p0173c1s v2p0181c1s v2p0378c1s
Lorinda, C. v4p0004c1s
Loring, A.G. and Cutter, W.R.
v5p0451c1s v6p0084c1s v6p0683c2s
Loring, A.H. v4p0236c1s
v6p0266c1m
Loring, C.H. v4p0547c1s
Loring, C.W. v1p0045c2s
Loring, E.G. v1p1196c2s
v2p0073c1s v2p0454c2s
Loring, F.G. v5p0582c1s
Loring, F.W. v1p0329c1s
v1p0626c2s v1p0881c2s v1p1086c2s
v1p1220c2s v1p1335c1s
Loring, G.B. v1p0034c1s
v1p0540c2s v1p1387c1s v3p0149c2s
v3p0322c1s
Loring, J.M. v6p0588c1s
Loring, J.S. v1p0327c1s
v1p0484c1s v1p1232c1s v1p1386c2s
Loring, L.P. v4p0069c1s
v4p0472c1s
Loring, Lucia E. v6p0094c1s
Loring, M.G. v1p0926c1s
Loring, N. v3p0071c1s
Loring, R.P. v2p0268c1s
Loring, S. v1p0155c2s
v1p0848c2s
Loring, W. v1p0841c2s
v4p0156c1s v4p0364c1s v4p0433c1s
Loring, W. et al. v3p0273c2s
Loring, W.W. v2p0135c1s
Lorne, Marquis of v1p0735c2m
v2p0066c1m v2p0196c1s v2p0206c1s
v2p0361c1s v2p0391c1m v3p0004c1s
v3p0004c2s v3p0020c1s v3p0065c1m
v3p0065c2s v3p0136c2s v3p0147c1s
v3p0154c1s v3p0180c2s v3p0265c1s
v3p0316c2s v3p0321c2s v3p0339c2s
v3p0381c2s v3p0463c1s v4p0005c1s
v4p0086c2s v4p0097c2s v4p0213c2s
v4p0219c2s v4p0237c1s v4p0261c2s
v5p0123c2s v5p0201c2s v5p0588c2s
v5p0611c1s
Lorne, Marquis of and Bury, Viscount
v2p0186c2s
Lorne, Marquis of and Butler, B.F.
v4p0049c2s
Lorne, Marquis of and Piril, A.F.
v2p0066c1s
Lorrimer, C. v6p0145c2s
v6p0229c2s v6p0336c1s v6p0338c1s
v6p0423c1s v6p0499c1s
Lorrimer, C.E. v6p0120c2s
v6p0180c1s v6p0244c1s v6p0335c2m
v6p0337c2s v6p0467c2s v6p0485c2s
v6p0509c1s v6p0560c2s v6p0695c1s
Lorsen, K.A. v3p0377c1s
Lort, M. and Vallancey, C.
v1p0644c2s
Lory, C.A. and Duane, W. . v5p0577c2s
Loscher, A.P. v6p0708c2s
Loscombe, A.R. v6p0208c1s
v6p0333c1s v6p0520c2s
Loseby, S.T. v3p0082c1s
Losee, W.F. v6p0695c2s
Loserth, J. v4p0621c1s
Loss, H.V. v5p0371c2s
v5p0551c2s
Loss, H.V.Z. v6p0694c2s
Lossing, B. v6p0203c2s
Lossing, B.J. v1p0018c2s
v1p0021c1s v1p0023c1s v1p0033c1m
v1p0033c2s v1p0034c1s v1p0058c1m
v1p0060c1m v1p0133c2s v1p0149c2s
v1p0151c2s v1p0152c1s v1p0179c1s
v1p0227c2s v1p0326c2s v1p0339c2m
v1p0340c1s v1p0419c2s v1p0571c2s
v1p0572c1s v1p0572c2s v1p0611c1s
v1p0612c2s v1p0636c1s v1p0637c2s
v1p0674c2m v1p0680c2s v1p0694c2s
v1p0695c1s v1p0708c2s v1p0734c1s
v1p0784c1s v1p0801c1s v1p0807c2s
v1p0809c1s v1p0862c1s v1p0864c2s
v1p0867c1s v1p0871c2s v1p0873c1s
v1p0876c2s v1p0894c2s v1p0895c1s
v1p0909c2s v1p0916c1s v1p0988c1s
v1p0989c1s v1p0997c1s v1p1051c1s
v1p1052c1s v1p1053c1s v1p1068c1s
v1p1070c2s v1p1084c2s v1p1125c1s
v1p1141c2s v1p1148c2s v1p1169c2s
v1p1183c1s v1p1188c1s v1p1211c1s
v1p1260c1s v1p1266c2s v1p1290c1s
v1p1307c1s v1p1324c1s v1p1348c2s
v1p1350c1s v1p1351c2s v1p1352c2s
v1p1354c1s v1p1361c1s v1p1368c1s
v1p1384c2m v1p1387c2s v1p1388c1m
v1p1401c2s v1p1405c2s v1p1412c2s
v1p1436c1s v1p1440c1s v1p1440c2s
v2p0306c2s
Lothman, D.W. v6p0594c1s
Lothrop, A.W. v4p0365c2s
Lothrop, J.H. v1p0787c2s
Lothrop, S.K. v1p0068c2s
v1p0239c1s v1p0290c2s v1p0291c1s
v1p0559c1s v1p0705c1s v1p0709c2s
v1p0950c1s v1p0963c1s v1p1256c1s
Lothrop, S.K. and Higginson, T.W.
v5p0257c1s
Lothrop, T.J. v5p0629c1s
Lothrop, T.K. v6p0388c2s
Lothrop, T.S. v1p0496c1s
v1p0723c2s
Loti, P. v3p0227c2s
v3p0359c2s v5p0021c1m
Loti, Pierre v4p0603c2s
v5p0544c2s v6p0678c1s
Lotsy, J.P. v4p0255c1s
Lott, A. v1p0018c2s
Lott, Charles F. v5p0088c1s
Lott, E.S. v6p0002c2s
v6p0321c1s
Lott, F.E. v1p0382c1s
Lott, Judge v1p0452c2s
Lott, T. v1p0154c2s
v1p0764c2s
Lott, W.C. v5p0609c1s
Lotti, P. v2p0013c1s
Lottner, C. v1p0382c2s
Lotz, W. v4p0059c1s
v4p0224c2s
v6p0520c1s
Lotze, H. v1p0529c1s
v1p0623c1s v1p1001c1s v1p1085c2s
Louandre, C. v1p0482c1s
Louch, M. v4p0171c2s
v5p0106c2s
Loud, E.F. v5p0461c2m
Loud, E.S. v4p0073c1s
Loud, Emily S. v6p0275c2s
v6p0606c2s
Loud, G.A. et al. v5p0360c1s
Loud, M.St.Leon, Mrs. ... v1p0019c1s
v1p0683c1s
Loudon, A. v1p1358c2s
Loudon, J. v1p0727c2s
Loudon, J.C. v1p0211c2s
Loudon, J.W., Mrs. v1p0500c1s
Lougee, S.C. v3p0242c2s
Lough, J.E. v4p0331c2s
v4p0435c1s
Lough, T. v5p0296c1s
v6p0327c2s v6p0624c2m
Loughan, W. v2p0074c1s
v2p0088c2s v2p0179c2s
Loughborough, J. v1p0494c2s
v1p0636c1s v1p0740c1s v1p0772c2s
v1p0855c1s v1p0956c1s v1p1400c1m
Loughborough, M.W. v1p1420c2s
Loughead, F.H. v3p0014c2s
v3p0202c2s v3p0209c2s v3p0254c2s
v3p0383c1s v3p0411c1s v3p0411c2s
v4p0071c2s v4p0136c1s v4p0303c2s
v5p0538c2s
Loughead, Flora H. v5p0052c1s
v5p0283c1s v5p0379c1s. v6p0674c2s
Loughlin, Clara E. v6p0043c1s
Loughlin, I. v5p0509c2s
Loughlin, J.F. v1p1115c2s
v3p0033c2s v3p0215c2s v3p0268c2s
v3p0364c2s v3p0377c1s v4p0488c1s
v5p0316c1s v6p0643c2s
Loughlin, J.F. et al. ... v4p0503c2s
Loughman, R.L. v1p0975c2s
Loughman, W. v4p0268c2s
Loughnan, W. v1p0773c1s
v1p0831c2s v2p0165c1s v2p0167c2s
v2p0170c2s v2p0171c1s v2p0201c2s
v2p0234c2s v2p0268c1s v2p0311c1s
v2p0317c2s v2p0460c1s v4p0498c2s
Loughridge, R.H. v1p1218c1s
Louis, A. v3p0462c2s
Louis, A.H. v1p0533c1s
v1p0723c2s v1p0942c1s
Louis, D.A. v3p0176c2s
v3p0330c1s v4p0120c2s v5p0043c1s
v5p0298c2s v5p0325c2s v5p0442c2s
v5p0563c2s
Louis, H. v4p0568c1s
v5p0124c1s v5p0423c1m v6p0328c2s
Louise, Princess v2p0361c1s
Lounsberry, H.A. v4p0173c1s
Lounsbury, E.R. v5p0586c1s
Lounsbury, J.F. v1p0034c2s
Lounsbury, T.K. v1p0879c2s
Lounsbury, T.L. v2p0032c1s
Lounsbury, T.R. v1p0171c2s
v1p0223c1s v1p0416c2s v1p0417c2m
v1p0418c1s v1p0522c2s v1p0606c2s
v1p0723c2s v1p0779c1s v1p0839c1s
v1p1004c1s v1p1184c1s v1p1234c2s
v1p1237c2s v1p1328c2s v1p1378c2s
v1p1401c2s v2p0143c2s v2p0185c1s
v2p0414c1s v3p0075c1m v3p0139c2s
v3p0231c2s v3p0332c1s v3p0395c1m
v3p0425c1s v4p0304c1s v4p0529c1s
v4p0594c2s v5p0079c2s v6p0207c2s
v6p0208c1m v6p0296c1s v6p0319c1s
v6p0361c1s v6p0469c1s v6p0508c2s
v6p0519c1s v6p0707c1s
Loury, H.D. v4p0528c1s
Louther, H. v1p0075c2s
v1p0200c1s v1p0364c2s v1p0501c1s
v1p0571c1s v1p0884c2s v1p1300c2s
v1p1320c1s v2p0191c2s v2p0303c2s
v2p0324c2s v2p0437c1s v2p0449c2s
Louyet, P. v1p0115c2s
Lovart, L. v2p0198c2s
v3p0204c2s
Lovat-Fraser, J.A. v4p0509c1s
v5p0085c1s v6p0084c2s v6p0165c2s
v6p0409c2s v6p0472c2s v6p0501c1s
v6p0578c2s v6p0709c2s
Love, A.C. v2p0352c1s
Love, A.E.H. v4p0492c2s
v6p0406c2s
Love, A.H. v4p0370c1s
v4p0432c1s
Love, D.D. v1p0852c2s
Love, E.F.J. v2p0413c2s
Love, J., Jr. v3p0440c2s
v4p0372c2s
Love, J.L. v3p0309c2s
Love, J.M. v3p0065c2s
v3p0339c2s v4p0497c2s
Love, J.W. v3p0175c1s
v4p0497c1s v4p0534c2s v5p0056c1s
Love, W. v6p0575c2s
Love, W.D. v1p1423c2s
v2p0106c2s
Love, W.De L. v1p0035c2s
v1p0043c2s v1p0296c2s v1p1101c1s
v1p1103c1s v1p1139c1m v1p1140c1s
v1p1206c1s v3p0087c2s v3p0187c2s
v6p0281c2s
Loveday, J. v1p1193c2s
Loveday, R.S. v4p0218c2s
v4p0250c1m v5p0368c1s
Loveday, T. v5p0101c1s
v5p0370c1s
Lovegrove, J. v1p0362c2s
v3p0121c2s
Lovejoy, A. v6p0215c1s
Lovejoy, A.O. v6p0170c1s
v6p0324c1s v6p0349c2m v6p0496c1s
v6p0536c2s v6p0563c2s v6p0647c1s
Lovejoy, B.G. v1p1406c1s

v2p0033c1s v3p0191c2s
Lovejoy, E.M.W. v6p0635c2s
Lovejoy, G.N. v3p0028c2s v3p0071c2s v3p0198c2s v3p0275c1s v4p0041c1s v5p0355c2s v5p0574c1s v5p0620c2s
Lovejoy, O. v6p0114c2s
Lovejoy, O.R. v6p0114c2s v6p0115c1m v6p0356c2s v6p0600c1s
Lovejoy, Owen R. v6p0114c2m v6p0115c1s v6p0202c2s
Lovekin, L.D. v6p0215c2s
Lovelace, Earl v1p1056c1s
Loveland, J.D.E. v6p0474c2s
Loveland, S.C. v1p0849c2s v1p0874c2s
Lovell, A. v4p0274c2s
Lovell, A.T. v3p0458c1s v6p0019c2s v6p0296c1s
Lovell, C. v1p0943c1s v2p0261c1s
Lovell, J. v2p0128c2s
Lovell, J.H. v5p0073c1s v5p0128c2s v5p0211c2s v5p0269c2s v6p0053c1s v6p0229c2m
Lovell, L.N. v5p0551c2s
Lovell, P. v3p0313c2s
Lovell, R.H. v5p0613c1s
Lovell, R.P. v5p0279c2s
Lovely, W.H.C. v5p0039c2s
Loveman, Robert v5p0339c2s v5p0488c1s v5p0581c1s
Lovenjoul, Spoelberich de, Vicomte v6p0049c1s
Lover, S. v1p0099c2s v1p0160c2s v1p0569c2s v1p0662c2s v1p0755c2s v1p0789c1s v1p1020c1s v1p1144c2s
Lovering, Elizabeth C. ... v4p0443c2s
Lovering, F.A. v1p0186c2s
Lovering, J. v1p0071c1m v1p0077c1s v1p0099c2s v1p0149c2s v1p0281c2s v1p0375c1s v1p0400c2m v1p0401c1s v1p0443c2s v1p0580c1s v1p0613c2s v1p0747c2s v1p0783c2s v1p0788c2s v1p0824c1s v1p0828c1s v1p0829c1s v1p0829c2s v1p1005c2m v1p1006c1m v1p1006c2m v1p1050c2s v1p1162c2s v1p1203c2s v1p1219c2s v1p1267c2s v1p1369c1s
Lovering, J.F. v1p1042c2s
Lovering, J.S. v1p1265c2s
Lovett, E. v3p0021c1s v3p0154c1s v4p0202c1s v4p0444c1s v4p0456c2s v5p0035c1s v5p0130c1s v5p0566c1m v6p0425c1s v6p0487c2s
Lovett, Eva v6p0357c2m
Lovett, R. v2p0044c1s v2p0118c1s v2p0184c2s v2p0406c1s v3p0197c2s v3p0236c1s v3p0251c2s v3p0428c1s
Lovett, R.M. v3p0135c1s v3p0259c1s v3p0288c2s v3p0302c1s v3p0309c2s v4p0402c1s v4p0430c2s
Lovett, R.W. v2p0393c2s v2p0395c1s
Lovett, W. v1p0656c2s
Lovett-Cameron, H., Mrs. . v1p0698c1s v3p0259c2s
Lovyed, A.M. and Olney, W. v2p0184c2s
Low, A.A. v1p1227c2s
Low, A.M. v5p0091c1s v5p0162c1s v5p0189c1s v5p0241c1s v5p0245c1s v5p0311c1s v5p0320c2s v5p0354c1s v5p0380c2s v5p0389c2s v5p0464c2s v5p0496c1s v5p0501c1m v5p0598c2s v5p0599c1s v5p0603c2s v5p0604c1s v5p0618c2s v5p0621c1s v6p0015c1s v6p0082c1s v6p0266c1s v6p0334c1s v6p0357c1s v6p0481c1s v6p0558c2s v6p0583c2s v6p0621c2s v6p0622c1s v6p0651c2s v6p0658c2s v6p0669c2s v6p0676c1s v6p0687c2s v6p0699c1s v6p0708c1s
Low, A.P. v3p0283c2s v4p0316c1s v5p0321c2s
Low, A.W. v6p0047c2s
Low, B. v4p0068c1s
Low, C.R. v1p0270c2s v1p0892c2s v2p0334c2s v2p0374c1s
Low, D. v1p0604c2s
Low, E. v4p0586c2s
Low, E.B. v6p0589c2s v6p0688c2s
Low, E.Bruce v5p0622c2s
Low, E.W. v5p0034c2s v5p0482c2s
Low, F.B. v6p0624c1s
Low, F.H. v3p0196c2s v4p0340c2s v5p0042c1s v5p0227c1s v5p0274c1m v5p0484c2s v5p0637c1s v5p0637c2s v6p0182c1s
Low, Florence B. v6p0532c2s
Low, G. v3p0086c1s
Low, G.J. v4p0573c1s v4p0584c1s v5p0164c1s v5p0236c2s v5p0283c1s
Low, H.W. v6p0475c1s
Low, M.A. v5p0042c1s v5p0357c1s
Low, R. v5p0285c2s
Low, S. v3p0073c2s v3p0085c2m v3p0093c1s v3p0260c1m v3p0304c2s v4p0121c1s v4p0152c2s v4p0166c2s v4p0169c2s v4p0213c2s v4p0237c2s v4p0239c2s v4p0257c1s v4p0265c2m v4p0387c1s v4p0432c1s v4p0469c2s v4p0602c1s v5p0028c2s v5p0162c2s v5p0189c1s v5p0189c2s v5p0190c1s v5p0193c2s v5p0245c1s v5p0247c2s v5p0248c2s v5p0382c1s v5p0384c1s v5p0412c1m v5p0437c2m v5p0609c1s v6p0135c2s v6p0267c2s v6p0269c2s v6p0271c2s v6p0298c1s v6p0384c2s v6p0465c1s v6p0542c1s v6p0542c2s v6p0551c1s v6p0613c2s
Low, S. and Shippard, S. . v5p0007c2s
Low, S. et al. v5p0332c1s
Low, S.J. v3p0180c2s v3p0232c1s v3p0257c1s v4p0133c1s v4p0239c2s v4p0289c2s v4p0313c1s v4p0356c1s v4p0480c2s v4p0482c2s
Low, Seth v4p0115c1s v4p0316c1s v4p0597c2s v6p0669c2s
Low, Sidney v5p0246c1s v6p0263c1s v6p0286c2s v6p0354c2s v6p0407c2s v6p0505c2s v6p0514c1s v6p0565c2s
Low, T.H. v6p0543c2s
Low, W.G. v1p0504c2s v2p0085c1s v5p0529c2s
Low, W.H. v3p0406c2s v4p0348c2s v4p0371c1s v4p0381c1s v4p0387c2s v4p0421c2m v5p0014c2s v5p0031c1s v5p0033c1s v5p0428c1s v6p0033c2s v6p0112c2s v6p0442c2s
Low, W.H. and Cox, K. v4p0409c1s
Low, W.H. and Stevenson, R.L. v3p0021c2s
Low, Will H. v4p0100c2s v4p0348c1s v5p0098c2s v6p0034c2s v6p0140c1s v6p0245c2s v6p0246c2s v6p0563c2s
Low, Will H. et al. v6p0345c1s
Lowber, J.W. v4p0450c2s
Lowden, T.S. v5p0106c2s v6p0305c1s v6p0635c1s
Lowe, A.M. v6p0708c1s
Lowe, C. v1p0100c2s v1p0156c2s v1p0389c1s v1p0638c1s v1p0775c1s v1p1219c2s v1p1223c2s v1p1292c2s v1p1340c2m v3p0046c2s v3p0067c2s v3p0171c2s v3p0303c1s v3p0464c2s v4p0121c1s v4p0403c1s v5p0064c2s v5p0240c1s v5p0243c1s v5p0631c2s v6p0236c1s
Lowe, Charles v5p0113c2s
Lowe, E. v4p0038c2s
Lowe, E.J. v1p0077c1m v1p0381c2s v1p0617c2s v1p0827c1m v1p0829c2s v1p0865c2s v1p0900c2s v1p1234c1s v1p1268c1s v1p1293c1s v1p1304c2m
Lowe, E.W. v5p0637c1s
Lowe, F.R.Eaton v2p0475c2s
Lowe, H. v1p1005c1s v6p0474c2s
Lowe, H.F. v4p0436c2s
Lowe, J. v1p1170c2m v1p1191c2s v1p1247c1s v3p0316c2s
Lowe, M. v6p0641c1s
Lowe, M.P. v1p0085c2s v1p0121c1m v1p0217c1m v1p0254c1s v1p0291c1s v1p0357c1s v1p0359c2s v1p0410c2s v1p0435c2s v1p0492c1s v1p0610c2s v1p0632c2s v1p0677c1s v1p0757c1s v1p0775c2s v1p0805c1m v1p0863c2s v1p1068c1s v1p1143c1s v1p1237c2s v1p1243c1s v1p1286c1s v1p1306c1s v1p1340c1s v1p1341c1m v1p1372c1s v1p1422c2m v1p1424c2s v1p1426c1s v2p0284c1s
Lowe, May v5p0106c2s v5p0479c2s v6p0375c1s
Lowe, N.M. v2p0214c1s
Lowe, R. v1p0095c1s v1p0261c2s v1p0338c2s v1p0385c1s v1p0486c2s v1p0544c1s v1p0549c2s v1p0550c1s v1p0626c1s v1p0629c2s v1p0649c1s v1p1025c2s v1p1026c2s v1p1062c2s v1p1086c2s v1p1264c2s v1p1357c1s v1p1376c1s
Lowe, R.W. v3p0148c2s v4p0162c2s v4p0446c2s
Lowe, R.W. and Archer, W.. v3p0388c1s v4p0518c1s
Lowe, Rebecca D. v6p0705c1s
Lowe, T.H. v6p0030c2s
Lowe, V.H. v4p0587c2s
Lowe, W.B. v1p0357c1s
Lowell, A.L. v2p0290c2s v3p0190c2s v3p0222c2s v3p0397c2s v4p0152c1s v4p0284c2s v4p0315c1s v4p0476c2m v5p0434c1s v5p0599c2s v6p0127c1s v6p0137c1s v6p0208c2s
Lowell, C.R. v3p0139c1s v3p0150c2s
Lowell, C.R., Mrs. v3p0017c1s v3p0077c1s v4p0068c1s v4p0096c2s v4p0314c2s v4p0591c1s
Lowell, D.O.S. v6p0019c1s v6p0135c1s v6p0194c2s v6p0195c1s v6p0207c1m v6p0249c1s v6p0407c2s v6p0635c2s
Lowell, E.J. v3p0010c1s v3p0036c1s v3p0071c2s v3p0129c2s v3p0159c2s v3p0161c2s v4p0119c2s
Lowell, F.C. v3p0035c1s v3p0190c1s v3p0196c1s v3p0363c2s v5p0072c1s v5p0072c2s v6p0016c1s v6p0174c2s v6p0293c1s
Lowell, J. v1p0095c1s v1p0247c1s v1p1272c1s
Lowell, J.A. v1p0325c1s v1p0333c2s v1p0675c1s v1p1233c1s
Lowell, J.R. v1p0013c2s v1p0137c2s v1p0159c2s v1p0170c2s v1p0190c2s v1p0201c1s v1p0207c1s v1p0223c1s v1p0287c2s v1p0331c2s v1p0355c1s v1p0368c2s v1p0418c2s v1p0442c2s v1p0458c1s v1p0533c2s v1p0568c2s v1p0600c2s v1p0605c2s v1p0693c2s v1p0738c2s v1p0750c2s v1p0754c2s v1p0768c1s v1p0774c1s v1p0780c2s v1p0782c1s v1p0789c2s v1p0808c1s v1p0825c1s v1p0842c1s v1p0867c2s v1p0871c1s v1p0878c1s v1p0909c2s v1p0910c2s v1p0937c2s v1p0989c2s v1p1032c2s v1p1034c1s v1p1066c2s v1p1067c1s v1p1072c1s v1p1072c2s v1p1087c1s v1p1184c2s v1p1187c1s v1p1234c2s v1p1235c2s v1p1270c2s v1p1275c2s v1p1276c1s v1p1307c1s v1p1321c1s v1p1336c1s v1p1339c1s v1p1344c2s v1p1346c1s v1p1346c2m v1p1347c2s v1p1352c2m v1p1353c2s v1p1416c1s v1p1417c2s v2p0076c1s v2p0092c1s v2p0102c2s v2p0115c1s v2p0146c2s v2p0185c1s v2p0197c1s v2p0205c2s v3p0056c2s v3p0099c2m v3p0137c1s v3p0149c1s v3p0203c1s v3p0242c1s v3p0383c2s v3p0388c1s v3p0438c2s v4p0039c1s v4p0048c2s v4p0096c1s v4p0140c2s v4p0143c1s v4p0183c1s v4p0202c1s v4p0206c2s v4p0207c1s v4p0210c2s v4p0269c1s v4p0274c2s v4p0343c1s v4p0356c1s v4p0360c1s v4p0427c1s v4p0448c1s v4p0503c2s v5p0260c2s v5p0355c1s v5p0524c1s v5p0542c2s v5p0610c1s
Lowell, J.R. et al. v3p0099c2s v3p0190c2s
Lowell, J.S. v4p0022c1m v4p0097c1m v4p0114c2s v4p0591c1s v5p0636c1s
Lowell, J.S., Mrs. v3p0074c1m
Lowell, Josephine S. v4p0553c1s
Lowell, P. v2p0103c1s v2p0366c2s v2p0410c2s v3p0021c2s v3p0226c2m v3p0227c1m v3p0288c1s v3p0308c1s v3p0357c2s v4p0357c2m v4p0358c1m v4p0602c2s v5p0370c2m v5p0609c1s v6p0402c2m v6p0403c1m v6p0677c1m v6p0680c1s
Lowell, Percival v6p0644c2s
Lowell, R. v2p0037c1s v2p0155c1s
Lowell, R.T.S. v1p0585c2s v1p0597c1s v1p0619c2s v1p0776c1s v2p0001c2s v2p0143c2s v2p0173c1s v2p0199c1s v2p0207c1s v2p0277c1s v2p0427c1s v3p0192c2s
Lowenhertz, L.von v1p0768c1s
Lowenstein, Prince v1p0184c1s v1p1036c2s
Lower, H.E. v5p0521c2s
Lowery, W. v6p0533c1s
Lowis, C. v5p0589c2s
Lowles, J. v5p0245c2s
Lown, Jennie v5p0287c2s
Lowndes, A. v3p0083c2s v3p0092c2s v3p0141c2s v3p0150c1s v3p0341c2s v3p0397c2s
Lowndes, B., Mrs. v6p0195c1s
Lowndes, Belloc, Mrs. v6p0002c2s
Lowndes, E.A.S. v5p0500c1s
Lowndes, F.S.A. v5p0310c2s v6p0016c1s v6p0379c1s
Lowndes, J. v4p0019c1s
Lowndes, M.B. v5p0416c2s
Lowndes, M.E. v6p0622c1s
Lowne, B.T. v1p0137c1s
Lowne, B.T. and Hickson, S.J. v2p0150c2s
Lowrey, A. v1p0553c1s
Lowrey, C.E. v2p0008c1s v2p0132c1s v2p0240c2s v2p0339c2s v3p0118c1s v3p0179c2s v3p0246c2s v3p0408c1s v4p0171c2s v4p0330c1s v4p0598c1s
Lowrey, D.M. v4p0287c2s
Lowrey, G.P. v4p0453c1s
Lowrie, C.H. v5p0139c2s
Lowrie, J.C. v1p0628c2s v1p0633c1s v1p0853c2m v2p0219c1s v2p0291c2s v2p0299c2s
Lowrie, R.B. v1p0685c2s
Lowrie, R.W. v1p0264c2s

v1p0870c1s
Lowrie, S.T. v2p0045c1s
v3p0461c1s v4p0057c1s v4p0301c1s
v4p0585c1s v5p0060c1s v5p0561c2s
Lowrie, W. v5p0036c2s
v5p0096c2s v5p0309c2s v6p0263c2s
Lowrie, W.H. v1p0258c2s
v1p0259c2s v1p0406c2s v1p0741c2s
v1p0820c2s v1p1065c2s v1p1228c1s
Lowry, A. v5p0277c1s
Lowry, D. v1p0535c1s
v1p1051c1s v3p0351c2s v4p0084c1s
v4p0251c2s
Lowry, E. v6p0017c1s
v6p0078c1s v6p0231c1s v6p0308c1s
Lowry, E.A. v6p0605c2s
Lowry, E.W. v5p0027c1s
v5p0501c1s v5p0502c1s v6p0256c2s
v6p0567c1s
Lowry, G. v3p0401c2s
Lowry, H.B. v5p0602c1s
Lowry, H.D. v4p0443c1s
v5p0052c2s v5p0098c1s v5p0137c2s
v5p0140c2s v5p0260c1s v5p0350c2s
v6p0103c1s v6p0619c2s
Lowry, H.H. v5p0111c2s
Lowry, J.O'B. v2p0045c1s
Lowry, K.M. v5p0438c2s
Lowry, R. v4p0396c2s
Lowry, S.C. v6p0305c1s
Lowth, G.T. v1p0602c1s
Lowther, H. v1p1242c1s
v2p0202c1s v2p0372c2s v4p0156c1s
Lowther, H.C. v4p0333c2s
v5p0092c1s v5p0142c2s
Lowther, J.W. v4p0005c2s
v4p0181c1s v4p0402c1s
Lowther, T. v6p0221c2s
Lowy, A. v3p0283c2m
Lowy, A. et al. v3p0283c2s
Loy, M. v1p0048c1s
v1p0255c2s v1p0440c1s v1p0447c1s
v1p0846c2s v1p0946c2s v1p1086c1s
v4p0111c2s
Loyson, C. v1p0117c1s
v1p0475c2s v1p0480c1s v1p0957c1s
v1p0970c1s v1p1118c2s
Loyson, E., Mme. v6p0196c1s
Loyson, H. v5p0299c1s
v6p0536c2s
Loyson, H. and Carus, P. . v5p0236c2s
Lozano, C.A. and Erben, H.F.T.
v3p0165c2s
Lozelle, H.M. v5p0618c1s
Lozenraad, C. v5p0231c2s
Lozier, C.S. et al. v2p0477c1s
Lozier, R.T.E. v5p0183c1s
v6p0393c1s
Luard, C.E. v6p0543c2s
Lubach, D. v1p0615c1s
Lubbock, J. v1p0344c1m
v1p0391c2s v1p0545c1s v1p0644c2s
v1p0718c2s v1p0790c2s v1p0865c1s
v1p1014c2s v1p1162c1s v2p0015c2s
v2p0016c1s v2p0029c2s v2p0038c1s
v2p0051c1s v2p0093c2s v2p0120c2s
v2p0162c2s v2p0252c1m v2p0365c2m
v2p0389c2s v2p0390c1s v2p0421c1s
v3p0044c2s v3p0125c2s v3p0245c2s
v3p0249c1s v3p0266c2s v3p0384c1s
v3p0385c1s v4p0165c2s v4p0277c2s
v4p0338c1s v4p0613c2s v5p0045c2s
v5p0173c1s v5p0243c1s v6p0206c2s
Lubbock, J. and Cameron, L.
v2p0410c1s
Lubbock, J. and Carnegie, A.
v4p0525c2s
Lubbock, J. et al. v2p0370c1s
Lubbock, J., Sir v1p0044c1m
v1p0107c1m v1p0385c2s v1p0396c2s
v1p0463c1s v1p0493c1s v1p0593c2s
v1p0644c2s v1p0645c1s v1p0781c1s
v1p0793c1s v1p0860c2s v1p1092c2s
v1p1175c2s v1p1255c2s v1p1256c1s
v2p0186c2m v2p0275c2s v2p0389c2s
v3p0217c1s v3p0333c2s v4p0338c2s
v4p0340c2s v5p0284c2s v5p0297c1s
Lubbock, J., Sir and
Arnold-Forster, H.O. .. v2p0370c1s
Lubbock, J., Sir and Pigorini, L.
v1p1359c1s
Lubbock, J., Sir and Ruskin, J.
v2p0051c1s
Lubbock, J., Sir et al. .. v4p0338c2s
Lubbock, J.W. v2p0296c2s
Lubbock, John v4p0237c1s
Lubbock, M. v2p0093c2s
v5p0453c1s
Lubbock, N. v2p0470c2s
v5p0559c2s v5p0626c1m v6p0692c2s
Lubbock, P. v6p0549c1s
Lubbock, P. and Benson, A.C.
v6p0622c2s
Lubbren, F.M. v1p0269c1s
Lubienski, R.W. v1p0076c2s
v1p0561c2s
Lucas, C. and Bispham, D.. v6p0383c2s
Lucas, C.J. v6p0243c2s
Lucas, C.J.P. v6p0039c1s
Lucas, D.B. v1p0192c1s
Lucas, E. v1p0537c2s
v2p0063c2s v2p0142c1s v2p0376c1s
Lucas, E.V. v4p0448c2s
v5p0075c2s v5p0097c1s v5p0119c1s
v5p0123c2s v5p0138c1s v5p0250c2s
v5p0323c2m v5p0362c1s v5p0379c1s
v5p0469c2s v5p0569c1s v6p0153c2s
v6p0185c1s v6p0359c2s v6p0376c2s
v6p0505c2s v6p0580c2s v6p0638c1s
v6p0649c1s
Lucas, E.V. and Coe, Mrs.. v6p0359c2s
Lucas, F. v4p0298c2s
Lucas, F.A. v2p0138c2s
v3p0026c2s v3p0045c1s v4p0060c2s
v4p0388c1s v4p0528c2s v5p0062c1s
v5p0063c1m v5p0211c2s v5p0216c1s
v5p0270c2s v5p0278c1s v5p0358c1s
v5p0428c1s v6p0041c1s v6p0066c2s
v6p0174c1s v6p0296c2s v6p0405c2s
v6p0580c2s
Lucas, F.C. v6p0674c2s
Lucas, H. v3p0009c2s
v3p0019c1s v3p0125c2s v3p0247c1s
v4p0021c1s v4p0057c1s v4p0336c1m
v5p0030c2s v5p0031c1s v5p0216c1s
v5p0613c2s v6p0381c1s v6p0547c2s
Lucas, H., Mrs. v4p0299c1s
v4p0302c1s
Lucas, H.W. v1p0066c2s
v1p0087c1s v1p0110c1s v1p0265c1s
v1p0427c1s v1p0600c2m v1p0601c1s
v1p0692c2s v1p0891c1s v2p0248c1s
v2p0347c2s v2p0376c1m
Lucas, J. v1p0522c1s
v1p0550c2s v1p1397c2s v3p0022c2s
Lucas, J.R. v1p0775c2s
Lucas, K. v6p0454c2s
v6p0455c1s
Lucas, L. v4p0106c1s
Lucas, L.H. v6p0088c1s
Lucas, M.D.C. v6p0421c1s
Lucas, R. v4p0588c1s
v5p0297c1s v6p0193c1s v6p0201c1s
Lucas, R.N. v6p0157c1s
Lucas, S. v4p0136c1s
v4p0544c1s
Lucas, St.J. v6p0100c1s
v6p0167c1s
Lucas, St.John v6p0242c2s
Lucas, T.J. v1p0062c1s
v2p0306c2s
Luccock, J. v5p0520c2s
v5p0533c1s
Luccock, N. v5p0434c2s
v6p0123c1s
Luce, Grace v5p0434c2s
v5p0627c2s
Luce, J.B. v1p0933c2s
Luce, L.H. and Luce, W.H.. v3p0206c2s
Luce, M. v5p0573c1s
Luce, R. v2p0137c2s
v3p0099c2s v3p0392c2s v3p0431c1s
v3p0433c2s v3p0471c2s v4p0564c2s
v6p0196c2s
Luce, S.B. v1p1068c2s
v1p1091c2s v1p1196c2s v3p0443c2s
v3p0454c1s v4p0395c2s v6p0669c1s
Luce, W.H. and Luce, L.H.. v3p0206c2s
Luce, W.L. v3p0266c1s
v3p0379c1s
Lucier, V.A. v5p0366c1s
Lucipia, L. v6p0479c2s
Lucke, C.E. v6p0248c2m
Luckenbach, W.H. v1p0847c1s
v2p0098c1s v2p0235c2s v2p0236c1s
Luckes, E.C.E. v3p0309c1s
v6p0462c2s
Luckey, G.J. v1p1063c1s
v2p0432c1s v4p0566c1s
Luckey, G.W.A. v4p0125c1s
v5p0106c2s
Luckey, S. v1p0666c2m
v1p0927c1s
Luckock, H.M. v3p0254c2s
v6p0038c2s
Lucy, H.W. v1p0104c1s
v1p0277c2s v1p0355c1s v1p0492c1s
v1p0550c1s v1p0602c1s v1p0607c1s
v1p0705c1s v1p0756c1s v1p0826c1s
v1p0841c1s v1p0973c2m v1p1172c2s
v1p1253c1s v1p1339c2s v1p1405c1s
v2p0051c1s v2p0091c1s v2p0142c1s
v2p0179c2s v2p0197c2s v2p0208c2s
v2p0216c1s v2p0230c2s v2p0233c2s
v2p0243c2s v2p0271c2s v2p0289c1s
v2p0301c1m v2p0331c1s v2p0384c1s
v2p0460c2s v3p0005c2s v3p0036c2s
v3p0039c2s v3p0138c2s v3p0307c1s
v3p0373c1s v4p0022c1s v4p0042c1s
v4p0082c2s v4p0088c1s v4p0227c1s
v4p0236c2s v4p0273c1s v4p0305c2s
v4p0382c2s v4p0386c2s v4p0427c2s
v4p0428c1s v4p0490c2s v4p0491c1s
v5p0100c2s v5p0223c1s v5p0247c1s
v5p0247c2s v5p0433c1s v5p0497c1s
v5p0575c1s v6p0270c1s v6p0299c1m
v6p0481c1s v6p0603c2s v6p0687c1s
Lucy, Henry W. v4p0363c2s
v5p0474c1s v6p0299c1s
Ludeking, C. v4p0141c1s
Ludeking, C. and Starr, J.E.
v4p0016c1s
Luden, E., Mrs. v5p0320c1s
Ludermann, H. v5p0240c1s
Luders, A. v1p0340c2s
Luders, C.H. v3p0008c1s
v3p0013c1s v3p0034c1s v3p0246c2s
v3p0283c2s v3p0335c1s v3p0336c1s
v3p0462c2s
Luders, M.A. v2p0468c1s
Luders, P. v5p0353c1s
Ludlam, R. v1p0621c2s
Ludlow, A.D. v1p0943c2s
v3p0401c1s
Ludlow, F.H. v1p0102c2s
v1p0213c1s v1p0321c1s v1p0542c1s
v1p0650c1s v1p0693c1s v1p0755c2s
v1p0871c2s v1p0915c2s v1p0947c1m
v1p0956c2s v1p1092c1s v1p1286c1s
v1p1309c1s v1p1438c1s
Ludlow, F.W. v2p0026c2s
Ludlow, G.W. v5p0258c1s
Ludlow, H.G. v1p0240c1s
Ludlow, H.H. v2p0423c2s
Ludlow, H.W. v1p0569c1s
v1p0636c2s v2p0129c1s
Ludlow, J. v3p0392c2s
Ludlow, J.M. v1p0016c1s
v1p0048c1s v1p0299c1s v1p0336c1s
v1p0419c1s v1p0477c2s v1p0478c1s
v1p0487c1s v1p0490c2s v1p0502c2s
v1p0503c2s v1p0546c2s v1p0561c1m
v1p0598c1s v1p0611c2s v1p0654c1s
v1p0675c2s v1p0726c1s v1p0808c1s
v1p0875c1s v1p0974c2s v1p0988c2s
v1p1107c2s v1p1114c1s v1p1154c1s
v1p1202c2s v1p1208c1m v1p1261c1s
v1p1288c2s v1p1295c1m v1p1319c2m
v1p1324c2s v1p1342c2s v1p1343c1s
v1p1353c1s v1p1431c1s v2p0124c2s
v3p0013c2s v3p0343c1s v3p0426c2s
v4p0014c2s v4p0067c2s v4p0078c2s
v4p0108c2m v4p0132c2m v4p0179c2s
v4p0215c2s v4p0247c2s v4p0268c1s
v4p0314c1s v4p0391c2m v4p0393c2s
v4p0534c1s v4p0581c1s v5p0136c1m
v5p0237c1s v5p0527c2s v6p0242c2s
Ludlow, J.M. and Snell, W.E.
v5p0136c1s
Ludlow, L.M. v4p0313c2s
Ludlow, T.W. v1p1327c1s
v2p0026c2s v2p0145c2s v2p0339c1s
v2p0436c2s v3p0114c1s
Ludlow, Thomas W. v3p0025c1s
Ludlow, W. v2p0338c2s
v4p0370c1s v5p0410c2s
Ludlum, E. v3p0240c1s
Ludlum, E.M. v2p0015c2s
v3p0030c1s v5p0234c1s
Ludovici, A. v3p0319c1s
v6p0696c1s
Ludwig, G. v4p0009c2s
v4p0393c2s
Ludwig, O. v1p0336c2s
Luedeking, C. and Wheeler, H.A.
v3p0034c1s
Lueder, A.B. v6p0081c1s
Lueders, H.F. v4p0088c1s
Luepp, F.E. v6p0218c1s
Luetscher, G.D. v6p0507c1s
Luffmann, C.B. v5p0233c2s
Luffmann, Laura B. v6p0124c1s
Lufkin, H.L. v4p0175c1s
Lugard, F. v4p0404c2s
Lugard, F.D. v3p0004c1s
v3p0395c1s v4p0005c1s v4p0005c2s
v4p0006c1s v4p0006c2m v4p0068c1s
v4p0404c2s v4p0529c1s v4p0529c2s
v4p0537c2s v4p0582c2s v4p0589c2s
v6p0457c1s
Lugard, F.W. v5p0006c1s
Lugard, Lady v6p0457c1s
Lugrin, C.H. v3p0065c1s
Lugrin, N.B. v6p0131c1s
Lugrin, N.DeB. v6p0462c1s
v6p0500c1s
Luhnow, C.A. v6p0059c1s
Luke, E.M. v4p0630c1s
Luke, P.V. v5p0570c2s
Luke, T.R. v4p0181c1s
Lukens, H.C. v3p0204c2s
Lukens, H.T. v4p0103c2s
v4p0161c2s v4p0320c1s v4p0554c1s
v5p0106c1s v5p0150c1s v5p0157c1s
v5p0511c2s
Lukens, T.P. v6p0593c2s
Lukin and Conder v1p0162c1s
Lukis, F.C. v1p0210c2s
v1p0217c1s v1p0320c1s
Lukis, W. v1p1329c1s
Lukis, W.C. v1p1256c1s
v5p0417c1s
Lull, R.S. v6p0004c1s
v6p0174c1s v6p0174c2s v6p0396c2s
v6p0409c2s v6p0475c2s v6p0616c2s
Lum, D.D. v5p0386c1s
Lum, S.K. v1p1181c2s
v1p1309c1s
Lumby, J.R. v6p0234c1s
Lumholtz, C. v3p0392c1s

v4p0093c1s v4p0563c1m v6p0171c2s
v6p0302c1s v6p0414c1s v6p0414c2s
Lumley, G. v1p1112c2s
v1p1301c1s v6p0042c1s v6p0311c2s
Lumley, J.S. v2p0057c2s
v5p0121c1s
Lumley, W.G. v1p0624c1s
v1p0765c1s v1p1030c2s v1p1115c1s
Lummis, C.F. v3p0302c2s
v3p0325c2s v4p0108c1s v4p0121c1s
v4p0160c1s v4p0205c2s v4p0390c2s
v4p0399c1s v4p0466c2s v4p0469c2s
v5p0053c2s v5p0088c2s v5p0161c1m
v5p0225c2m v5p0253c2s v5p0287c2s
v5p0373c1s v5p0548c2m v5p0574c2s
v6p0002c2m v6p0004c2m v6p0035c2s
v6p0043c2s v6p0049c2s v6p0085c1s
v6p0089c1s v6p0092c1m v6p0092c2m
v6p0093c1m v6p0093c2m v6p0128c2s
v6p0139c2m v6p0153c1s v6p0155c1s
v6p0155c2s v6p0161c2s v6p0162c2s
v6p0177c1s v6p0230c1s v6p0315c1s
v6p0315c2s v6p0316c1m v6p0316c2m
v6p0317c1m v6p0329c1s v6p0369c2s
v6p0370c2s v6p0378c1s v6p0390c1s
v6p0419c1s v6p0421c2s v6p0423c1s
v6p0427c1m v6p0428c1s v6p0443c2s
v6p0444c2s v6p0451c1s v6p0457c1s
v6p0469c1s v6p0471c2s v6p0473c2s
v6p0474c1s v6p0482c2s v6p0483c2m
v6p0511c2s v6p0525c2s v6p0536c1s
v6p0546c2s v6p0552c1s v6p0567c2m
v6p0570c1s v6p0578c1s v6p0603c2s
v6p0607c1s v6p0607c2s v6p0613c1s
v6p0632c1s v6p0654c1s v6p0663c2s
v6p0670c1s v6p0677c1s v6p0686c1s
v6p0696c2s v6p0706c1s v6p0707c1s
Lummis, D. v4p0501c2s
Lummis, E. v4p0193c1s
Lummis, H.B. v6p0638c2s
Lumpkin, J.H. v1p1223c2s
Lumsdaine, Dr. v1p0934c2s
Lumsden, G.E. v4p0567c2s
v5p0035c1s
Lumsden, H.D. v6p0474c1s
Lumsden, H.W. v6p0366c2s
Lumsden, L.I. v2p0477c2s
Luna, Beatriz Bellido de . v6p0203c2s
Lund, G. v3p0038c1s
v3p0078c1s
Lund, J. v6p0458c2s
Lund, L. v1p0427c2s
Lundgren, Fernand v5p0371c1s
Lundie, R.A. v4p0325c1s
Lundstedt, B. v6p0371c1s
v6p0628c2s
Lundt, D. v4p0155c2s
v4p0286c1s
Lunge, G. v5p0104c1s
Lungren, C.M. v1p0876c1s
v1p1040c1s v2p0136c2s v4p0101c1s
Lungren, F.H. v1p0021c1s
Lunn, E. v5p0502c1s
Lunn, G.R. v6p0429c1s
Lunn, H.S. v4p0113c2s
v4p0580c2s v5p0101c1s v5p0311c2s
v5p0561c2s
Lunn, H.S. and Besant, A.. v4p0258c1s
Lunsden, Lt.Col. v3p0264c2s
Lunt, E.C. v3p0072c1s
v4p0246c2s
Lunt, G. v1p0002c2s
v1p0754c2s v1p1298c2s v2p0210c2s
Lunt, H. v2p0046c1s
v2p0047c1s v2p0104c2s v2p0415c2s
Lunt, W. v6p0696c1s
Lunt, W.P. v1p0024c1s
v1p0119c1s v1p0159c2s v1p0172c1s
v1p0310c2s v1p0319c1s v1p0421c1s
v1p0441c1s v1p0452c1s v1p0469c2s
v1p0601c1s v1p0745c1s v1p0809c1s
v1p1022c2s v1p1093c2s v1p1169c1s
Lunyevitza, C.P. v6p0180c1s
Lupan, N. v4p0020c2s
Lupton, J.H. v3p0233c1s
Lupton, J.I. v4p0264c1s
Lupton, N.T. v2p0402c1s
Lupton, S. v2p0090c2s
v3p0345c1s v3p0402c2s v3p0430c2s
Lupton, S. et al. v3p0095c1s
Lupton, S.L. v6p0671c2s
Luqueer, F.L. v5p0512c2s
Luquer, L.M. and Volckening, G.J.
v4p0535c2s
Luquiens, J. v1p0082c2s
v1p1257c1s v1p1440c1s v2p0458c2s
Lury, J.S.De v6p0133c2s
Luscombe, J. v2p0140c2s
v2p0407c2s
Luse, L.A. v2p0091c1s
Lushington, C. v1p1094c1s
v1p1420c2s
Lushington, C.M. v3p0156c2s
Lushington, F. v1p0055c2s
v1p0671c1s
Lushington, G. v5p0168c2m
v5p0169c1m v5p0584c2s v5p0585c1s
Lushington, G., Sir v6p0441c1s
Lushington, H. and Venables, G.S.
v1p0270c1s
Lushington, Lady v1p1394c1s
Lushington, V. v4p0137c1s
v4p0604c1s
Lusk, G. v4p0331c1s
v6p0412c1s
Lusk, H. v1p0919c1s
Lusk, H.H. v4p0016c1s
v4p0042c2s v4p0387c1s v4p0501c1s
v5p0039c1m v5p0265c1s v5p0408c2m
v5p0419c1s v5p0567c2s v5p0638c1s
v6p0041c2m v6p0042c1m v6p0400c1s
v6p0453c1s v6p0622c1s
Lusk, H.H. et al. v5p0445c1s
Lusk, Hugh H. v5p0506c2s
Lusk, L. v5p0171c1s
v6p0278c1s v6p0278c2s v6p0689c2s
Lusk, Lewis v5p0267c2s
v5p0314c2s v6p0180c1s v6p0512c2s
v6p0553c2s v6p0675c2s
Lusk, W.T. v4p0065c1s
Luskod, Count and Vaya, V. v5p0202c2s
Lusted, C. v5p0071c1s
v5p0263c2s v6p0075c1s
Lusted, Charles v5p0064c1s
v5p0071c1s
Lusted, Chas.T. v4p0494c2s
Lustig, A. v5p0453c1s
Luthardt, C.E. v1p0129c1s
v1p0247c1s v1p1120c1s v2p0072c2s
Luthardt, Dr. v1p0979c2s
Luthardt, Prof. v1p0792c2s
Luthell, E.E. v4p0276c1s
Luther, F.N. v2p0234c1s
v3p0347c2s
Luther, M. v1p0769c1s
v5p0584c1s
Luther, M.L. v5p0283c1s
v5p0343c1s v5p0351c2s v5p0414c2s
v5p0421c1s v5p0480c2s v6p0131c1s
v6p0175c1s
Luther, Martin v5p0176c2s
v5p0538c1s
Luthmer v2p0023c2s
Lutkin, P.C. v5p0374c1s
v5p0423c2s
Lutoslawski, W. v4p0275c2s
v4p0283c1s v4p0379c1s
Lutschaunig, A. v3p0230c2s
Luttecke, A.E. v6p0375c2s
Lutton, W. v4p0159c2s
Luttrell, H. v2p0151c2s
v3p0148c1s v3p0260c2s v3p0290c2s
Lutz, E.E. v6p0406c2s
Lutz, Frank E. v6p0037c1s
v6p0402c1s
Lutz, J.J. v5p0474c1s
Lutz, Miss v1p0016c2s
Lutzow v5p0068c2m
Lutzow, C.V. v2p0154c2s
Lutzow, C.von v1p1366c2s
Lutzow, Count v6p0060c1s
Lutzow, F., Count v5p0040c1s
Lux, Herr v2p0268c1s
Lux, J.A. v6p0678c2s
Luxenberg, A. v4p0627c2s
Luxmore, E. v2p0335c1s
Luys, J. v3p0206c2s
v4p0271c2s
Luyster, I.M. v1p0077c2s
v1p0170c1s v1p0512c1s v1p0863c1s
v1p1086c2s v1p1241c2s v1p1298c2s
Luzzatti, L. v6p0666c1s
Lvall, A.C. v1p1081c1s
Lyall, A. v3p0165c1s
v3p0212c1s v3p0212c2s
Lyall, A., Sir v2p0025c1s
Lyall, A.C. v1p0356c1s
v1p0630c1m v1p0634c1m v1p0853c2s
v1p0858c1s v1p1095c2m v1p1417c2s
v3p0101c1s v4p0033c1s v4p0350c1s
v4p0380c2s v4p0394c1s v5p0074c2s
v5p0102c2s v5p0128c1s v5p0287c1s
v5p0521c1s v6p0349c2s v6p0537c1s
Lyall, A.C., Sir v3p0079c2s
v3p0181c1s v3p0347c1s
Lyall, C.J. v2p0039c2s
v2p0243c2s v2p0277c2s v2p0293c2s
v2p0301c2s v2p0305c1s v4p0313c2s
v4p0527c1s v6p0595c2s
Lyall, C.J. and Redhouse, J.W.
v2p0018c1s
Lyall, D. v5p0036c1s
Lyall, Edna v3p0115c2s
Lyall, G.C., Sir v6p0526c1s
Lyall, J.W. v5p0515c1s
Lyall, M. v5p0012c2s
Lyall, W. v1p0006c2s
v1p0191c2s v1p1295c2s
Lybrand, L.M. v5p0089c2s
Lyche, H.T. v3p0281c1s
Lychenheim, J. v4p0084c1s
Lyde, P. v6p0004c2s
v6p0483c1s v6p0645c2s
Lyde, Phoebe v5p0214c2s
v5p0605c2s v6p0001c1s v6p0516c2s
Lydecker, C.E. v2p0288c2s
v6p0417c1s
Lydekker, K. v6p0424c1s
Lydekker, R. v3p0008c2s
v3p0014c2s v3p0015c2s v3p0036c2s
v3p0045c1s v3p0106c1s v3p0119c2s
v3p0121c2s v3p0130c2s v3p0156c2s
v3p0200c2s v3p0254c2s v3p0290c1s
v3p0309c1s v3p0335c1s v3p0341c1s
v3p0359c1s v3p0373c1s v3p0417c2s
v3p0422c2s v3p0433c1s v4p0001c1s
v4p0003c2s v4p0018c2m v4p0021c1s
v4p0027c1s v4p0060c2s v4p0093c1s
v4p0156c1s v4p0177c2s v4p0210c1m
v4p0217c2s v4p0226c2s v4p0237c2s
v4p0258c1s v4p0280c1s v4p0321c1m
v4p0326c1s v4p0348c2s v4p0351c2m
v4p0375c2s v4p0376c2s v4p0379c1s
v4p0409c2s v4p0453c1s v4p0486c2s
v4p0494c2s v4p0503c1s v4p0511c2s
v4p0529c2s v4p0531c1s v4p0543c1s
v4p0543c2s v4p0587c2s v4p0618c2s
v5p0005c1m v5p0020c2m v5p0021c2s
v5p0022c2s v5p0023c1s v5p0027c1s
v5p0039c2s v5p0041c2s v5p0051c1s
v5p0062c2m v5p0064c1s v5p0066c1s
v5p0089c1s v5p0096c2s v5p0098c2s
v5p0140c2s v5p0159c2s v5p0164c2s
v5p0196c1s v5p0207c1s v5p0209c2s
v5p0254c1s v5p0286c1s v5p0287c1s
v5p0288c1s v5p0338c1s v5p0358c1m
v5p0376c2s v5p0381c1s v5p0383c2m
v5p0388c2s v5p0403c1s v5p0414c2s
v5p0448c1s v5p0453c1s v5p0458c1s
v5p0473c2m v5p0514c1s v5p0516c2s
v5p0524c2s v5p0525c1s v5p0545c1s
v5p0547c1s v5p0627c1s v5p0646c1s
v5p0646c2m v6p0005c2s v6p0021c2s
v6p0022c1s v6p0042c2s v6p0054c1s
v6p0094c2s v6p0102c2s v6p0118c1s
v6p0168c1s v6p0200c1s v6p0214c2s
v6p0221c1s v6p0235c2s v6p0244c2s
v6p0262c1s v6p0296c2s v6p0297c1s
v6p0396c2m v6p0472c2s v6p0489c1s
v6p0524c1s v6p0554c1s v6p0580c1s
v6p0580c2s v6p0594c2s v6p0612c1s
v6p0645c2s v6p0646c2s v6p0650c1s
Lydenberg, H.M. v5p0360c2s
Lye, H. v4p0562c2s
Lyell, C. v1p0466c1s
v1p0508c2s v1p0810c1s
Lyell, C., Sir v1p0102c1s
v1p0470c2s v1p0844c2s v1p1376c2s
v1p1377c2s
Lyell, G.A. v5p0307c1s
Lyell, W.D. v6p0393c2s
Lyford, A.C. v3p0045c1s
v3p0156c1s v3p0184c2m
Lyford, W.G. v1p0807c2s
Lykins, W.H.R. v2p0240c2s
Lyle, D.A. v1p0908c1s
v1p1112c1s v1p1428c1s v2p0262c2s
v2p0415c2s
Lyle, E.P. v5p0001c1s
v6p0502c2s v6p0580c1s
Lyle, E.P., jr. v6p0150c1s
v6p0219c2s v6p0333c1s v6p0409c2s
v6p0414c1s v6p0426c2s v6p0477c1s
v6p0510c1s v6p0570c1s v6p0595c1s
v6p0618c2s v6p0636c1s v6p0637c1s
v6p0676c1s
Lyle, E.P., jr. and Whitman, S.F.
v6p0570c2s
Lyle, E.W. v1p0527c2s
Lyle, Eugene P., jr. v6p0101c1s
v6p0047c2s v6p0278c1s
Lyle, L. v1p1113c2s
Lylia, C. et al. v6p0237c1s
Lyman, A. v1p0954c2s
Lyman, A.J. v1p0848c1s
v3p0345c1s v6p0312c1s v6p0484c2s
Lyman, A.T. v6p0153c1s
Lyman, A.W. v3p0456c1s
Lyman, B.S. v1p0070c1s
v1p0508c1s v1p1273c1s v2p0234c1s
v4p0560c2s v5p0131c1s v5p0136c2s
v5p0582c2s v5p0621c2s
Lyman, C. v4p0117c1s
Lyman, C.A. v6p0090c1s
v6p0168c1s
Lyman, C.S. v1p0077c1s
v1p0416c1s v1p0768c2s v1p0827c1s
v1p0941c2s v1p0986c2s v1p1238c1s
v1p1366c2s v1p1393c2s
Lyman, D. v3p0094c1m
Lyman, E. v1p0121c2s
v1p0598c2s
Lyman, E.L. v6p0441c1s
Lyman, F.S. v5p0044c2s
Lyman, G.D. v1p0325c2s
Lyman, H.M. v1p0903c2s
v1p0907c1s v2p0086c1s v2p0222c1s
v2p0283c1s v2p0332c1s v5p0368c2s
Lyman, J. v1p0573c2s
Lyman, J.C. v3p0414c1s
Lyman, J.D. v4p0208c2s
v4p0443c2m
Lyman, J.H. v1p0993c1s
Lyman, O.E. v1p0357c2s
v1p0978c1s v2p0395c2s v2p0433c1s
Lyman, P.W. v5p0202c1s
Lyman, T. v1p0013c2s
v1p0017c2s v1p0302c2s v1p0374c1s
v1p0383c2s v1p0467c1s v1p0692c2s
Lyman, T., jr. v1p1012c1s

Lyman, W.D. v2p0316c2m
v5p0103c2s v5p0621c1s
Lymans, A. v6p0676c2s
Lymburn, J. v3p0308c2s
Lymington, Lord v2p0209c1s
v2p0247c2s v3p0202c1s v3p0248c1s
Lymington, Viscount v3p0102c2s
v3p0137c2s v3p0158c1s v3p0338c2s
v3p0448c2s v4p0582c2s
Lynam, C. v6p0231c1s
Lynch, A. v4p0010c2s
v5p0068c1s v5p0296c1s v5p0311c1s
v6p0221c2s v6p0327c1s v6p0390c2s
v6p0466c2s
Lynch, A.C. v1p0950c1s
v1p1388c2s
Lynch, A.F.B. v6p0489c2s
Lynch, B.J. v3p0224c1s
Lynch, E. v1p0962c2s
Lynch, E.M. v1p0266c1s
v3p0219c2s v3p0221c2s v4p0044c1s
v4p0045c1s v4p0132c2m v4p0600c2s
v5p0043c2s v5p0138c2s v5p0248c2s
v5p0295c2s v5p0297c1s v5p0613c2s
v6p0148c2s v6p0156c2s v6p0424c2s
Lynch, F. v5p0330c2s
Lynch, G. v5p0423c2s
v5p0581c2s v6p0118c1s v6p0119c1s
v6p0696c2s
Lynch, G.D. v5p0019c2s
Lynch, G.F. v4p0334c2s
Lynch, Gertrude v6p0055c2s
v6p0149c2s v6p0710c2s
Lynch, H. v2p0190c2s
v2p0307c2s v3p0254c1s v3p0366c1s
v3p0411c1s v4p0087c1s v4p0167c1s
v4p0241c1s v4p0256c2s v4p0435c1s
v4p0539c1s v5p0048c1s v5p0153c2s
v5p0224c2s v5p0366c2s v5p0469c2m
v5p0543c1m v5p0582c1s v5p0646c1s
v6p0038c2s v6p0078c1s v6p0104c1s
v6p0237c2s v6p0241c2s v6p0302c1s
v6p0304c2s v6p0479c1s v6p0545c2s
v6p0563c1s
Lynch, H. et al. v5p0221c1s
Lynch, H.F.B. v4p0022c1s
v4p0027c1m v4p0344c2s v6p0020c2s
Lynch, Hannah v5p0012c1s
v5p0212c2s v5p0581c2s
Lynch, J. v4p0173c1s
Lynch, J.G. v1p0670c2s
Lynch, K. v6p0569c2s
Lynch, L.R. v6p0388c1s
Lynch, Maj. v1p0519c1s
Lynch, Mrs. v1p1426c1s
Lynch, P. v4p0362c1s
v6p0191c1s
Lynch, P.N. v1p0312c2s
v1p0677c2s v1p0685c1s v1p0850c1s
v1p1363c1s v1p1367c1s v2p0170c1s
Lynd, Grant v5p0542c2s
Lynd, W. v2p0365c2s
v2p0433c1s
Lynde, F. v4p0033c2s
v4p0081c2s v4p0091c2s v4p0098c1s
v4p0244c1s v4p0347c1s v4p0381c1s
v4p0382c1s v4p0411c2s v4p0460c1s
v4p0469c2m v4p0502c1s v4p0515c1s
v4p0553c2s v4p0590c1s v5p0051c2s
v5p0095c2s v5p0105c2s v5p0144c1s
v5p0163c2s v5p0188c1s v5p0318c2s
v5p0433c2s v5p0451c1s v5p0534c1s
v5p0591c2s v5p0597c1s v6p0229c1s
v6p0231c2s v6p0294c1s v6p0301c1s
v6p0449c1s v6p0482c2s v6p0639c1s
v6p0695c1s
Lynde, F.J. v4p0047c1s
Lynde, Francis v5p0248c2s
v6p0221c2s v6p0380c2s v6p0639c2s
Lynde, J.G. v1p0523c1s
Lyndon, E. v1p1383c2s
Lyndon, H. v5p0609c2s
Lyndon, L. v5p0303c2s
Lyndon, Louise v4p0386c1s
Lynn, N.T. v4p0410c1s
Lynn, W.T. v1p0407c1s
v1p1292c1s v2p0064c1s v2p0094c2s
v2p0128c1s v2p0192c1s v2p0285c1s
v2p0285c2s v2p0308c2s v2p0343c2s
v2p0420c1s v3p0002c1s v3p0094c1s
v3p0250c1s v3p0309c2s v3p0359c2s
v3p0376c1s v3p0407c2s v4p0126c2m
v4p0324c1s v4p0465c2s v4p0625c2s
v5p0087c2s v6p0008c1s v6p0187c2s
v6p0626c1m
Lynne, E. v4p0386c1s
Lynton, E.L. v4p0357c1s
Lyon, A.B. v4p0218c1s
Lyon, C. v4p0364c1s
v5p0166c1s v5p0200c2s v5p0282c2s
v5p0359c1s
Lyon, C.H. v1p0262c1s
Lyon, Capt. v1p0635c1s
Lyon, D.Everett v6p0056c2s
Lyon, D.G. v2p0022c2s
v2p0025c2s v2p0030c2s v3p0024c1s
v4p0033c2m v4p0040c2s v4p0055c2s
Lyon, Dorothy W. v5p0114c1s
Lyon, E.C. v5p0335c2s
Lyon, E.N. v5p0365c2s
Lyon, F.P. v6p0130c2s
Lyon, F.E. v6p0158c1s
Lyon, G.E. v2p0438c1s
Lyon, H.L. v6p0013c2s
v6p0020c2s
Lyon, H.N. v4p0018c2s
Lyon, J. v1p1037c1s
Lyon, J.A. v2p0273c2s
Lyon, J.M. v6p0107c2s
Lyon, L. v1p1273c1s
Lyon, LeR.S., Capt. v6p0168c2s
Lyon, P.C. v5p0285c1s
Lyon, W.H. v2p0302c2s
Lyons, A.B. v4p0535c2s
Lyons, C.J. v4p0250c2s
Lyons, D.T. v5p0570c1s
Lyons, H.G. v6p0457c2m
Lyons, J. v1p0288c2s
Lyons, Maude v4p0194c1s
v4p0461c2s
Lyons, R.D. v2p0225c2s
Lyons, T.A. v1p0829c2s
v1p0936c2s v1p0942c2s v3p0094c2s
Lys, F.J. v4p0278c2s
Lys, G.De v1p0803c1s
Lysaght, E. v1p0512c2s
Lysaght, S. v2p0242c2s
Lysaght, S.R. v5p0258c1s
Lysons, D. v1p0542c2s
Lysons, S. v1p0393c1m
v1p0585c1s v1p1071c2s v1p1114c2s
v1p1115c1s v1p1123c1s v1p1296c2s
v1p1317c2s
Lyster, F.E. v3p0335c1s
Lyster, T.W. v2p0028c2s
v2p0181c2s v5p0122c1s v5p0333c1s
Lyte, C.M. v1p0786c2s
Lyte, F.M. v3p0134c2s
v4p0367c2s
Lyte, H.C.M. v3p0143c2s
Lyte, H.M. v6p0178c2s
Lyttelton, A. v3p0143c2s
v4p0231c2s v5p0143c1s v6p0003c1s
v6p0006c2s v6p0007c1s
Lyttelton, A., Mrs. v6p0631c2s
Lyttelton, A.T. v3p0431c1s
v4p0518c1s
Lyttelton, Alfred v6p0592c1s
Lyttelton, C. v1p0160c2s
v1p0464c2s v1p0988c1s v1p1114c2s
v1p1122c1s
Lyttelton, C. and Pegge, S.
v1p1255c2s
Lyttelton, E. v1p1005c2s
v4p0629c2s v5p0107c1s v5p0113c2s
v5p0224c2s v5p0459c2s v6p0193c1s
v6p0574c1s
Lyttelton, E., Mrs. v5p0233c1s
Lyttelton, Edith v5p0264c1s
Lyttelton, K. v3p0161c2s
Lyttelton, Lord v1p1031c1s
Lyttelton, M. v6p0391c1s
Lyttelton, Maud v6p0331c2s
Lyttelton, Maud L. v6p0003c1s
Lyttelton, Maude v5p0352c1m
Lyttelton, N.G. v4p0139c1s
v4p0278c2s v4p0393c1s
Lyttelton, R.H. v4p0139c1m
v4p0233c2s v6p0592c2s
Lyttelton, S., Lady v6p0557c2s
v6p0628c2s
Lyttelton, W.H. v1p0728c1s
Lyttle, B.M. v6p0103c1s
Lyttle, G.B. v6p0164c2s
Lyttleton, A. v4p0266c1s
v4p0453c1s
Lyttleton, C.G. v1p0496c1s
Lyttleton, C.G. and Arnold, A.
v1p0546c2s
Lyttleton, K. v4p0185c1s
Lyttleton, W.H. v1p0250c1s
v1p0900c2s
Lytton, E.B. v1p0308c2s
v1p0429c1s v1p0584c1s v1p0814c1s
v1p1012c1s v1p1391c1s
Lytton, E.B., Lord v1p0534c2s
v1p0574c1s v1p0843c1s v1p0972c1s
v1p1108c1s v1p1404c1s
Lytton, E.B., Sir v1p0169c2s
v1p0172c1s v1p0262c1s v1p0337c2s
v1p0402c2s v1p0417c2s v1p0476c1s
v1p0519c2s v1p0542c1s v1p0548c2s
v1p0712c1s v1p0719c2s v1p1259c2s
v1p1383c1s
Lytton, E.R. v1p0780c2s
v2p0423c2s
Lytton, E.R.B. v1p0439c2s
v1p1059c1s v2p0248c1s v2p0295c2s
Lytton, Earl v2p0123c1s
v2p0416c2s v6p0326c2s
Lytton, Earl of v2p0013c2s
v2p0100c1s v2p0460c2s v6p0108c2s
Lytton, Earl of and Craufurd, H.J.
v6p0522c2s v6p0637c2s
Lytton, Lady v2p0248c2s
Lytton, Lord v1p0144c1s
v3p0361c2s v4p0412c1s
Lytton, Neville v6p0173c2s
Lytton, R. v1p0048c2s
v1p0108c1s v1p0527c2s v1p0583c1s
v1p0741c2s v1p0780c1s v1p1017c1s
v1p1306c1s
Lytton, R., Lord v1p0476c2s
v1p0501c1s
Lytton, R.B. v1p0402c2s
v1p0726c2s v3p0449c2s
Lytton, R.E.B. v1p0334c1s

M. v5p0586c2s
M., A.P. v5p0269c2s
M., B. v3p0181c2s
M., C. v6p0406c2s
M., D.K. v6p0198c2s
M., D.S. v5p0487c1s
M., E. v6p0046c2s
v6p0210c2s
M., E.A. v6p0520c2s
M., E.G.J. v6p0560c1s
M., H.R. v6p0023c1s
v6p0029c1s
M., J. v5p0362c1s
M., K.J. v5p0281c2s
M., W.H. v6p0126c2s
M., W.S. v5p0226c1s
Maack, G.A. v1p0212c2s
Maartens, M. v4p0131c1s
v4p0229c2s v5p0012c2s v5p0040c2s
v5p0161c1s v5p0170c1s v5p0262c2s
v5p0302c1s v5p0309c1s v5p0322c1s
v5p0342c1s v5p0354c2s v5p0368c2s
v5p0560c2s v6p0330c2s v6p0483c1s
v6p0519c1s v6p0676c1s v6p0703c2s
Maartens, Maarten v4p0240c2s
v4p0372c2s v5p0129c2s v5p0337c2s
v5p0388c2s v6p0029c2s v6p0173c1s
Maas, A. v4p0188c1s
v4p0384c1s
Maas, A.G. v5p0436c1s
Maas, A.J. v3p0041c1s
v3p0041c2s v3p0242c1s v3p0429c2s
v4p0054c1s v4p0561c2s v5p0058c1s
v5p0059c1s v5p0059c2s v5p0060c2s
v6p0249c2s v6p0341c1s v6p0341c2s
v6p0404c1s
Maas, E. v5p0610c1s
Maas, O. v4p0355c2m
Maas, P. and Keller, H.F.. v4p0555c2s
v5p0160c2s
Mabee, H. v6p0068c2s
Maber, S. v5p0575c2s
Mabery, C.F. v2p0137c2s
v4p0099c1s v4p0437c2s v4p0507c2s
Mabie, H.W. v2p0210c1s
v2p0260c2s v3p0003c1s v3p0057c1s
v3p0106c1s v3p0151c2s v3p0253c2s
v3p0367c2s v4p0028c1s v4p0037c2s
v4p0067c1s v4p0101c2s v4p0123c2s
v4p0143c1s v4p0198c1s v4p0335c1s
v4p0348c1s v4p0408c1s v4p0548c1s
v4p0569c2s v4p0570c1s v4p0594c2s
v4p0610c2s v5p0013c1s v5p0016c1s
v5p0016c2s v5p0036c2s v5p0070c1s
v5p0082c1s v5p0084c2s v5p0176c1s
v5p0195c1s v5p0196c2s v5p0215c2s
v5p0227c2s v5p0280c1s v5p0280c2s
v5p0309c1s v5p0339c1s v5p0348c1s
v5p0405c1s v5p0426c2s v5p0455c1s
v5p0455c2s v5p0522c1s v5p0523c2s
v5p0533c2s v5p0573c1s v5p0573c2s
v5p0576c2s v5p0607c2s v5p0613c1s
v5p0619c2s v5p0620c1s v5p0625c2s
v5p0638c1s v5p0640c2s v6p0011c2s
v6p0069c2s v6p0079c1s v6p0102c1s
v6p0123c2s v6p0143c1s v6p0178c2s
v6p0202c1m v6p0278c1s v6p0278c2s
v6p0283c2s v6p0291c1s v6p0302c1s
v6p0330c1s v6p0351c2s v6p0354c2s
v6p0361c2s v6p0377c2s v6p0384c1s
v6p0389c2s v6p0452c2s v6p0459c1s
v6p0459c2s v6p0482c2s v6p0578c2s
v6p0598c1m v6p0605c2s v6p0606c2s
v6p0618c1s v6p0644c2s v6p0650c2s
v6p0674c2m v6p0683c1s v6p0685c2s
v6p0697c1s
Mabie, H.W. and Crawford, F.M.
v4p0610c2s
Mabie, H.W. et al. v6p0461c2s
Mabie, L.K. v6p0089c1s
v6p0220c2s v6p0228c2s v6p0325c1s
v6p0533c2s
Mabile, G.A. v1p0636c2s
Mabilleau, L. v6p0635c2s
Mabini, A. v5p0446c1s
Mabon, C.B. v5p0308c1s
Mabry, W.D. v6p0278c2s
Mabson, R.R. v5p0007c1s
Mabury, E.B. v5p0279c2s
Mac, E.A. v2p0367c1s
Mac, W.H. v4p0173c1s
v4p0232c2s v5p0505c2s
McAdam, R.W. v4p0411c2s
v6p0502c1s
Macadam, S. v1p0462c1s
v1p0501c2s
Macadam, T. v1p0939c1s
v6p0618c2s
McAdam, T. v6p0124c1s
v6p0243c2s v6p0246c2s v6p0247c2s
v6p0437c2s v6p0502c2s v6p0656c2s
McAdams, W. v2p0179c1s
v2p0300c1s
McAdie, A. v2p0027c2s
v3p0133c2m v3p0151c1s v4p0177c1s
v4p0332c1m v4p0473c1s v4p0615c2s
v5p0212c1m v5p0219c1s v5p0222c2s
v5p0317c2s v5p0566c1s v5p0579c1s
v6p0473c2s
McAdie, Alex. v5p0038c2s
McAdoo, L.S. v5p0636c2s
McAdoo, W. v6p0054c1s
v3p0208c2s v3p0420c1s v4p0604c1s
v4p0634c1s
McAdoo, Wm. v4p0595c1s
MacAlarney, R. v6p0054c1s
MacAlarney, R.E. v6p0472c1s
McAlexander, N.G. v6p0399c1s
McAlexander, W.G. v5p0468c1s
Macalister, A. v4p0006c2s
v4p0172c2s v4p0352c1s v4p0387c1s
v4p0391c2s v4p0394c2s v4p0458c2s
v4p0573c2s v5p0022c2s v5p0386c1s
v5p0576c1s v5p0578c2s v6p0255c1s
MacAlister, D. v2p0051c1s
v2p0341c1s
MacAlister, D.A. v5p0187c1s
v5p0195c1s
Macalister, J. v2p0447c2s
MacAlister, J. v1p0253c1s
v1p0425c2s v1p0431c2s v1p0959c1s
v1p1327c1s v3p0022c1s v5p0168c2s
MacAlister, J.Y.W. v5p0333c1s
v5p0429c2s
Macalister, R.A.S. v6p0255c1m
Macalister, R.A.S. et al.. v4p0041c2s
v4p0411c1s
Macalister, R.D. v3p0471c2s
Macallam, M.F. v6p0381c2s
McAllister, A.H.T. v5p0590c1s
McAllister, Amelia H. v6p0433c1s
McAllister, F.M. v1p0331c2s
v1p1400c2s
McAllister, W.,jr. v1p0203c1s
Macallum, A.B. v5p0077c2s
v6p0650c1s
McAllum, D. v1p0374c1s
v1p0437c2s
McAlpin, W.L. v5p0010c1s
v5p0171c1s
McAlpine, Charles L. v2p0361c1s
McAlpine, W.J. v1p0018c2s
v1p0329c2s v1p0435c2s v1p0471c1s
v1p1010c1s v2p0006c2m
Macan, H. v4p0512c1s
v5p0134c2s v5p0570c1s
Macan, R.W. v1p0879c2s
v1p0954c2s v4p0026c2s
McAnally, D.R. v3p0092c1s
v3p0459c1s v5p0490c2s
MacAndrew, D.F. v2p0185c2s
MacAndrew, I.F. v2p0221c1s
McAndrew, S. and Gillette, A.D.
v4p0132c1s
McAndrew, W. v5p0569c1s
v6p0193c1s v6p0575c1s v6p0635c1m
v6p0635c2s
McAndrew, W.A. v5p0264c2s
McAndrew, W.S. and Gillette, A.D.
v4p0085c1s
McAneny, G. v4p0116c2s
v5p0134c2s
McAney, C. v5p0120c2s
Macann, F. v3p0052c2s
Macara, C.W. v4p0331c1s
Macarthur, A. v4p0522c1s
McArthur, A. v4p0494c1s
MacArthur, C. v6p0340c2s
Macarthur, D. v4p0073c2s
v4p0268c1s
MacArthur, D. v5p0592c2s
v6p0244c2s
McArthur, E.A. v4p0201c2s
v4p0608c1s v5p0465c1s v5p0615c1s
v5p0615c2s
MacArthur, J. v4p0046c1s
v4p0348c1s v4p0590c2s v5p0013c1s
v5p0392c1s v5p0531c2s v5p0553c1s
McArthur, J. v4p0346c2s
Macarthur, J.S. v2p0103c2s
MacArthur, James v4p0614c1s
McArthur, P. v4p0600c1s
v5p0486c1s v5p0560c2s
MacArthur, R.S. v2p0083c2s
v2p0084c2s v2p0290c2s v2p0332c1s
v3p0081c1s v6p0111c1s
MacArthur, R.S. and Buckley, J.M.
v4p0615c1s
Macarthur, W. v5p0024c2s
v5p0503c2s v5p0526c2s v5p0584c2s
v5p0641c1s v6p0591c2s v6p0652c1s
McArthur, W. v3p0305c1s
McArthur, W.E. v1p0679c2s
Macartney, C.E. v6p0517c1s
Macartney, J. v5p0475c1s
v6p0031c2s
Macartney, J.M. v4p0484c1s
v5p0061c1s v5p0098c2s v5p0101c1s
v5p0195c1s v5p0290c1s
Macartney, M.H.H. v6p0075c2s
v6p0514c1s v6p0578c2s
Macartney, W.E. v3p0222c1s
Macarty, F. v1p0346c1s
Macassey, L. v6p0385c1s
v6p0528c1s
McAtee, W.L. v6p0067c2s
v6p0657c1s
Macau, R.W. v1p0738c1s
Macaulay, A. v3p0234c2s
Macaulay, C.T. v1p1258c1s
Macaulay, G.C. v2p0472c2s
v3p0162c1s v3p0168c2s v3p0173c2s
v3p0319c1s v4p0098c2s v4p0216c1m
v4p0233c2s v6p0644c1s
Macaulay, H. v1p0346c2s
Macaulay, J. v2p0261c1s
v3p0058c2s v3p0103c1s v3p0215c2s
v3p0257c1s v3p0262c2s v3p0292c2s
v3p0369c1s v3p0384c1s v3p0457c2s
v4p0051c1s v4p0077c2s v4p0095c1s
v4p0168c1s v4p0202c1s v4p0226c1s
v4p0347c1s v4p0499c2s v4p0502c1s
v5p0069c2s v6p0133c1m
Macaulay, J.A. v1p0103c2s
Macaulay, J.M. v1p0852c1s
Macaulay, T.B. v1p0006c2s
v1p0051c1s v1p0085c1s v1p0098c2s
v1p0176c1m v1p0176c2s v1p0181c2s
v1p0219c2s v1p0220c1s v1p0247c2s
v1p0265c2s v1p0282c1s v1p0291c2s
v1p0312c1s v1p0319c1s v1p0331c1s
v1p0364c2s v1p0368c2s v1p0412c1s
v1p0415c2s v1p0485c1s v1p0510c2s
v1p0525c1s v1p0534c2m v1p0544c2s
v1p0566c2s v1p0568c2s v1p0573c2m
v1p0593c1s v1p0593c2s v1p0597c1s
v1p0629c1s v1p0690c2s v1p0694c1m
v1p0783c1s v1p0839c1s v1p0841c2s
v1p0849c1s v1p0864c2s v1p0964c2s
v1p1012c1m v1p1021c2m v1p1033c1s
v1p1064c1s v1p1066c2s v1p1226c2s
v1p1230c2s v1p1258c2s v1p1293c1s
v1p1360c1s v1p1360c2m v1p1383c1s
v1p1434c1s v3p0258c1s v3p0459c1s
v4p0483c2s
M'Auley, J.A. v1p1092c1s
McAuley, L.M. v6p0563c2s
McAuliffe, E. v5p0210c2s
v5p0609c1s v5p0610c1s v6p0235c1s
v6p0607c2s
Macauliffe, M. v5p0529c1s
MacBain, A. and Clouston, W.A.
v4p0041c2s
McBeath, S.B. v5p0066c2s
MacBennett, F. v4p0203c1s
v5p0129c2s
Macbeth, H. v4p0145c2s
v4p0584c1s
MacBeth, R.G. v5p0275c1s
McBlain, J.F. v4p0059c2s
Macbrayne, L.E. v5p0558c1s
v6p0309c1s
MacBrayne, L.E. v5p0188c1s
v5p0326c1s v5p0358c2s v5p0521c2s
v6p0389c1s v6p0519c1s v6p0605c2s
v6p0632c1s v6p0661c2s
MacBrayne, L.F. v6p0407c2s
MacBrayne, R.E. v6p0637c1s
McBride, H. v4p0083c2s
v6p0035c2s
McBride, J. v4p0135c1s
McBride, J.H. v6p0594c1s
McBride, J.R. v2p0298c2s
v2p0456c2s
McBride, M.A. v3p0121c1s
v4p0360c1s
McBride, Marion A. v4p0554c1s
McBride, R.E. v6p0389c2s
McBride, R.M. v6p0160c1s
v6p0182c2s
Macbride, T.H. v4p0427c1s
v5p0522c2s v6p0088c1s v6p0250c2s
v6p0437c2s v6p0477c1s
MacBride, T.H. v6p0010c1s
McBride, T.H. v2p0031c1s
v2p0173c2s v2p0181c2s v2p0259c2s
v2p0343c2s v2p0344c1s v2p0458c1s
v3p0165c2m
McBride, W.D. v6p0528c1s
McBroom, J.K. v6p0613c2s
McBryde, J.M., jr. v6p0155c2s
McBryde, M.M. v4p0096c2s
McCabe, D.A. v6p0148c1s
M'Cabe, Dr. v1p0994c1s
M'Cabe, F. v1p0156c2s
McCabe, J. v4p0194c1s
v5p0001c2s v6p0040c2s v6p0277c1s
v6p0305c1s v6p0547c2m
McCabe, J.B. v1p0933c1s
McCabe, J.C. (M') v1p0422c1s
v1p0585c2s v1p1373c2s v2p0279c1s
McCabe, J.D. v2p0098c1m
McCabe, L.D. v4p0457c1s
McCabe, L.R. v3p0108c1s
v3p0203c2s v3p0247c2s v3p0344c2s
v3p0350c1s v5p0151c2m v5p0363c2s
v5p0531c1s v6p0466c2s v6p0505c1s
McCabe, Lida R. v5p0274c2s
v6p0257c1s v6p0314c1s v6p0319c2s
v6p0584c2s
McCabe, T. v6p0631c2s
MacCabe, W.B. v2p0468c1s
McCabe, W.G. (M') v1p0994c2s
v2p0111c2s v2p0347c1s v6p0639c1s
McCaig, D. v4p0277c1s
v4p0571c2s v5p0354c2s
McCain, R. v6p0058c2s
McCaleb, T.H. v1p0007c1s
McCaleb, W.F. (M') v5p0574c2s
v6p0276c2s v6p0414c1s v6p0532c2m

v6p0640c1s
McCaleb, Walter F. v6p0606c2s
McCall, A.G. and Briggs, L.G.
v6p0602c2s
McCall, E. v2p0010c1s
v2p0010c2s v2p0011c2s v2p0100c2s
v2p0102c1s v2p0126c1s v2p0150c2s
v2p0296c2s v2p0306c2s v2p0370c1s
v2p0380c1s v2p0395c2s v2p0404c2s
v2p0408c2s v2p0424c2s v2p0427c1s
v2p0428c2s v2p0439c2s v2p0462c1s
v2p0472c2s
McCall, E., Miss v2p0345c1s
v2p0408c2s
McCall, J.A. v4p0524c2s
McCall, L.M. v6p0564c1s
MacCall, M. v3p0152c1s
McCall, S. v1p0253c2s
McCall, S.W. v1p0893c2s
v1p0237c2s v1p1352c1s v2p0452c2s
v5p0480c2s v5p0621c1s v5p0624c2m
v6p0144c2s v6p0456c1s v6p0540c1s
v6p0583c2s
McCall, S.W. and Shepard, E.M.
v6p0667c1s
McCall, T. v6p0245c1s
v6p0326c2s
McCall, T.B. v6p0192c1s
v6p0328c1s
Maccall, W. v1p0705c1s
v1p0823c2s v4p0007c1s
McCall, W. v1p0670c1s
MacCalla, C.P. v1p0077c2s
McCallie, S.W. v6p0169c1s
McCallum, A.K. v1p0700c2s
McCallum, E.A. v6p0257c1s
McCallum, J.Bruce v6p0382c2s
McCallum, J.I. v6p0048c2s
McCallum, M. v4p0187c2s
McCamant, W. v5p0423c2s
v6p0151c2s v6p0709c1s
McCanachie, W. v6p0701c1s
M'Candlish, J.M. v4p0022c2s
v4p0454c1s
McCann, Anabel P. v6p0622c2s
McCann, F.G. v6p0676c2s
McCann, J. v3p0040c2s
v3p0082c2s v3p0113c2m v3p0287c2s
v4p0151c1s
McCann, R. v5p0068c1s
McCann, W.E. v1p0003c1s
v1p0005c1s v1p0380c2s v1p0469c2s
McCants, E.C. v5p0315c1s
v5p0322c1s v6p0166c2s v6p0226c2s
v6p0235c2s v6p0349c2s v6p0467c1s
v6p0566c2s v6p0620c2s v6p0710c2s
McCants, E.Crayton v6p0026c1s
McCardell, R.L. v6p0456c1s
McCardell, Roy L. v6p0584c2s
McCarter, C. v3p0215c1s
McCarter, H. and Hyde, Douglas
v6p0327c2s
McCarter, J. v1p0280c1s
MacCarthy, B. et al. v3p0411c2s
McCarthy, C. v1p0288c2s
v1p1218c2s v1p1347c1s v2p0098c1s
McCarthy, C.H. v6p0016c2s
MacCarthy, D. v6p0090c1s
McCarthy, D. v6p0333c1s
McCarthy, D.F. (M') v1p0038c2s
v1p0049c1s v1p0186c1m v1p0330c1s
v1p0619c2s v1p0740c2s v1p0814c1s
v1p0817c2s v1p0867c1m v1p1231c2s
v1p1237c1s
McCarthy, D'Alton v4p0353c2s
v4p0505c2s
McCarthy, E. v1p1170c2s
v1p1220c2s v4p0500c2s v5p0011c1s
MacCarthy, E.F.M. v2p0133c1s
v3p0128c2s v5p0178c1s
McCarthy, G. (M') v4p0445c2s
v5p0374c1s v5p0393c1s
MacCarthy, J. v1p0104c1s
v1p0138c2s v1p0353c1s v1p0418c1s
v1p0594c2s v1p0659c2s v1p0661c1s
v1p1118c2s v1p1154c2s v2p0144c1s
v2p0171c1s v2p0225c1s v2p0231c2s
v2p0246c1s v2p0270c2s v2p0292c1s
v2p0297c2s v2p0328c1s v2p0353c2s
v2p0376c1s v3p0238c1s v3p0265c1s
McCarthy, J. (M') v1p0031c2s
v1p0051c1s v1p0056c2s v1p0106c1s
v1p0138c2s v1p0163c1s v1p0190c1s
v1p0219c1s v1p0281c2s v1p0312c1s
v1p0337c2s v1p0347c1m v1p0352c1s
v1p0354c2s v1p0360c2s v1p0361c1s
v1p0369c2s v1p0397c1m v1p0413c2s
v1p0414c1s v1p0417c2s v1p0429c1s
v1p0440c2s v1p0474c2s v1p0480c2s
v1p0492c2s v1p0494c1s v1p0498c2s
v1p0511c2s v1p0524c2s v1p0548c1s
v1p0549c2s v1p0570c2s v1p0599c2s
v1p0608c2s v1p0653c2s v1p0657c2s
v1p0708c2s v1p0716c2s v1p0721c1s
v1p0728c1s v1p0731c2s v1p0737c2s
v1p0740c1s v1p0751c1s v1p0754c2s
v1p0756c1s v1p0758c2s v1p0762c2s
v1p0773c2s v1p0774c2s v1p0780c1s
v1p0786c1s v1p0797c1s v1p0819c2s
v1p0839c1s v1p0851c2s v1p0886c2s
v1p0896c1s v1p0896c2m v1p0912c1s
v1p0931c2s v1p0959c2s v1p1012c2s
v1p1037c2s v1p1045c2s v1p1055c1s
v1p1058c2s v1p1084c2s v1p1093c2s
v1p1100c1s v1p1115c2s v1p1119c2s
v1p1120c2s v1p1133c1s v1p1142c1s
v1p1161c1s v1p1230c2m v1p1242c1s
v1p1243c1s v1p1260c2s v1p1264c2s
v1p1275c2s v1p1305c1s v1p1327c1s
v1p1356c2s v1p1369c2s v1p1370c1s
v1p1411c2s v1p1420c2s v1p1423c2s
v1p1438c1s v2p0124c2s v2p0206c1s
v2p0225c2s v2p0227c2s v2p0272c2s
v2p0408c2s v2p0416c2s v3p0073c2s
v3p0137c2s v3p0138c1s v3p0138c2s
v3p0152c2s v3p0158c2s v3p0221c2s
v3p0223c1m v3p0255c2s v3p0310c1s
v3p0322c1s v3p0391c2s v3p0469c1s
v4p0095c1s v4p0239c1s v4p0239c2s
v4p0240c1m v4p0266c1s v4p0289c1s
v4p0289c2s v4p0290c1s v4p0427c2s
v4p0428c1s v4p0491c1s v4p0530c2s
v5p0040c2s v5p0065c2s v5p0100c2s
v5p0180c1m v5p0130c1s v5p0222c2s
v5p0234c2m v5p0246c1s v5p0247c1m
v5p0247c2s v5p0272c2s v5p0297c2s
v5p0434c1s v5p0467c1s v5p0492c2s
v5p0497c1s v5p0500c2s v5p0505c2s
v5p0587c1s v5p0587c2s v5p0611c1m
v6p0001c1s v6p0047c2s v6p0054c2s
v6p0085c2s v6p0088c2s v6p0095c1s
v6p0194c2m v6p0205c1s v6p0206c2m
v6p0207c1s v6p0269c1s v6p0270c1m
v6p0270c2m v6p0280c1s v6p0326c1s
v6p0326c2s v6p0328c1s v6p0357c2s
v6p0379c2s v6p0383c2m v6p0384c1s
v6p0385c2m v6p0429c1s v6p0481c1m
v6p0534c2s v6p0565c2m
McCarthy, J. and
Blandford, Marquis of . v2p0206c1s
McCarthy, J. and Wilson, D.J.
v1p0599c2s
McCarthy, J. et al. v1p0657c1s
v4p0239c1s
MacCarthy, J.G. v3p0267c1s
McCarthy, J.H. (M') v1p0609c1s
v1p0973c1s v1p1424c2s v2p0134c2s
v2p0206c1s v2p0285c1s v2p0422c2s
v2p0430c1s v3p0049c1s v3p0334c2s
v4p0046c1s v4p0133c1s v4p0160c2s
v4p0161c1s v4p0251c1s v4p0447c1s
v4p0478c1s v4p0512c1s v4p0553c2s
v4p0569c2s v6p0662c1s
McCarthy, J.J. v5p0441c1s
McCarthy, J.M. v3p0199c1s
McCarthy, J.W. v1p1141c2s
McCarthy, John v2p0119c1s
McCarthy, Justin v5p0634c2s
v6p0654c2s
McCarthy, Justin H. v3p0219c2s
v4p0164c1s
McCarthy, M.J.F. v6p0327c1s
MacCartie, J. v5p0396c1s
Maccartney, W.N. v1p0588c2s
McCarty, B. v2p0094c1s
M'Carty, J.H. v3p0475c1s
McCarty, R.J. (M') v2p0095c2s
v2p0244c1s v2p0285c1s v2p0467c1s
McCarty, W.F.M. v5p0501c2s
v5p0502c1s
McCarty, W.P. v1p1328c1s
McCaul, Ethel v5p0416c2s
McCaul, J. v1p0164c1s
v1p0422c2s v1p0727c1s v1p1209c2s
v1p1255c1s v1p1296c2s
MacCauley, C. v1p0217c1s
v6p0336c2s
McCauley, C. v1p1237c2s
M'Cauley, C.A.H. v2p0094c1s
McCauley, D. v1p0391c1s
v1p0614c1s v1p0649c2s
McCauley, J.A. v3p0349c1s
v4p0243c1s
McCauley, L.M. v6p0113c2s
v6p0579c2s
McCauley, Lena M. v6p0033c2s
MacCaulley, E. v6p0292c1s
McCaw, R. v6p0693c2s
McCaw, S.R. v2p0061c1s
McCaw, W.D. v6p0534c2s
McCay, C.F. (M') v1p0306c1s
v1p0306c2m v1p0307c2m v1p0326c1s
v1p0647c2m v1p0873c2s
McCay, L.W. v2p0382c2s
McCharles, A. v3p0290c1s
McChesney, Clara v4p0408c1s
McChesney, D. v6p0700c2s
McChesney, D.G. v5p0579c1s
v6p0074c1s v6p0104c1s v6p0156c1s
v6p0274c1s v6p0383c1s v6p0472c1s
v6p0699c1s
McChesney, Dora G. v6p0265c1s
v6p0301c1s v6p0554c2s v6p0596c2s
McChesney, E. v1p0255c1s
v1p1285c2s v5p0314c2s
McChesney, E.S. v3p0276c2s
McChesney, L.S. v5p0089c2s
v6p0599c1s
McChesney, S. v4p0036c2s
McClain, E. v4p0322c2s
v5p0135c1s v6p0146c1s v6p0283c1s
v6p0347c1s v6p0387c2s
McClain, W.H. v6p0564c1s
McClaire, E. v3p0444c2s
McClanahan, J. v1p0992c2s
M'Claren, J.C. v1p0857c1s
McClatchie, A.J. v4p0060c1s
McClatchie, H.J. v6p0212c2s
M'Claughry, R.W. and Bonfield, J.
v4p0102c1s
McClean, W.A. v4p0084c2s
v4p0318c2s v4p0323c1s v4p0396c1s
v4p0407c1s v4p0471c2s v4p0507c2s
v5p0075c2s v5p0083c2s v5p0164c1s
v5p0326c1s v6p0048c2s v6p0230c2s
v6p0517c2s v6p0609c1s
McClean, Wm.Arch. v5p0529c1s
McCleary, J.T. v6p0633c1s
McCleary, S.F. v1p0392c2s
v1p1264c2s
McCleery, J.C. v6p0162c2s
McClees, S.A. v3p0424c1s
McClellan, G.B. v1p0059c2s
v1p0174c1s v1p0407c2s v1p0922c2s
v1p0960c2s v1p1195c1s v1p1330c1m
v2p0016c2s v2p0135c1s v2p0288c2s
v2p0323c2s v2p0335c1m v5p0599c2s
M'Clellan, G.B. et al. ... v4p0129c1s
McClellan, H.B. v1p1262c1s
McClellan, J.B. v6p0063c1s
McClellan, W. v5p0577c2s
v6p0323c1s
McClelland, A.W. v5p0391c1s
McClelland, G. v1p0454c1s
McClelland, J.L. v6p0134c2s
McClelland, M.G. v3p0284c2s
v3p0384c2s v3p0424c1s v3p0426c2s
v3p0434c2s v4p0580c1s v4p0620c1s
v4p0630c2s v5p0583c2s
McClelland, N.V. v5p0379c1s
v5p0397c1s v5p0416c2s v6p0430c2s
McClelland, Nancy V. v5p0608c1s
McClelland, S. v4p0221c2s
McClenahan, F.M. v6p0305c1s
McClenahan, F.M. and Gooch, F.A.
v6p0121c2s
McClenahan, Howard v5p0624c2s
McClenahan, J. v1p0114c1s
v1p0615c2s v1p1155c1s v1p1331c2s
v1p1350c1s
McClendon, J.F. v6p0664c1s
McClennan, S.F. v6p0357c1s
McClernand, E.J. v5p0290c1s
v6p0433c2s
McClintock, C.W. v4p0330c1s
McClintock, E. v6p0658c1s
McClintock, F.R. v2p0154c1s
v3p0102c1s v3p0107c1s v3p0120c2s
v3p0315c2s
McClintock, J. (M') v1p0060c2s
v1p0123c2s v1p0725c1s v1p0784c1s
v1p0923c2s v1p0941c1s v1p1083c2s
v1p1098c2s v1p1270c1s v1p1304c1s
v1p1306c1s v1p1382c1s v1p1393c1s
v1p1410c2s
McClintock, J.N. v2p0037c1s
v2p0067c1s v2p0074c1s v2p0076c2s
v2p0087c2s v2p0090c2s v2p0097c2s
v2p0163c2s v2p0237c1s v2p0241c2s
v2p0243c1s v2p0278c1s v2p0245c2s
v2p0311c1s v2p0311c2s v2p0321c2s
v2p0375c1s v2p0386c2s v2p0472c2m
v3p0166c2s v3p0258c2s v3p0259c2s
v3p0287c1s
McClintock, L. (M') v1p0209c1s
v1p0464c1s v1p0662c1s v1p1315c1s
v2p0227c2s v2p0232c2s v3p0070c2s
v3p0312c2s v3p0441c1s v5p0630c2s
M'Clintock, Letitia v5p0562c2s
McClintock, S. v6p0106c1s
MacClintock, S.S. v5p0315c1s
McClintock, W. v5p0065c2s
MacClintock, W.D. v6p0428c2s
v6p0653c1s
McClintock, W.D. v3p0087c1s
v3p0140c2s v3p0366c1s v6p0693c1s
McClintock, W.E. v3p0075c2s
v4p0257c1s
McClonnen, S.F. v6p0652c2s
McCloskey, A.G. v6p0025c2m
v6p0068c2s v6p0444c2s
McClounie, J. v6p0463c1s
McClumpha, C.F. v4p0144c2s
M'Clune, J. v1p0967c1s
McClung, H.M. v5p0639c1s
M'Clung, J.C. v2p0244c1s
McClung, N.L. v6p0381c1s
v6p0607c1s
McClure v4p0346c2s
McClure, A.K. v2p0058c1s
v4p0168c2s v4p0332c2m
McClure, A.W. v1p0344c2s
McClure, C.F. v4p0267c1s
McClure, C.F.W. v5p0075c1s
McClure, D.E. (M') v6p0153c2s
v6p0193c1s v6p0219c2s
McClure, E. v4p0003c2s
McClure, J. v6p0406c1s
McClure, J. and Morris, E.
v1p0522c2s

McClure, J.G.K. v6p0483c1s
McClure, M.F. v5p0128c2s
McClure, M.L. v4p0007c2s
McClure, M.L., Mrs. v6p0340c1s
McClure, M.L.H. and Muller, F.M.
v3p0200c2s
McClure, P. v4p0588c2s
McClure, P.F. v3p0109c1s
M'Clure, R. v6p0135c1s
McClure, R.J. v1p0580c2s
v1p1074c1s
McClure, R.L. v6p0350c2s
McClure, S.G. v4p0060c1s
McClure, S.S. v3p0303c2s
v4p0052c2s v4p0341c1s v6p0364c2s
McClure, W.F. v5p0139c2s
v5p0183c2s v5p0552c1s v6p0078c2s
v6p0102c1s v6p0389c2s v6p0400c1s
v6p0694c2s
McClure, W.Frank v6p0097c1s
McClure, W.K. v6p0146c2s
McClurg, A.C. v1p1152c2s
v1p1306c2s v2p0029c2s v2p0030c1s
v2p0040c1s v2p0052c1s v2p0102c2m
v2p0253c2s v2p0453c2s v4p0248c2s
v4p0574c1s
McCoan, J.C. v1p0188c2s
v1p0396c1s v1p0396c2s v1p0657c2m
v1p0857c2s v1p1206c2s v1p1207c2s
v1p1330c1s v1p1331c1m v1p1332c2s
v3p0028c1s
MacColl, D. v2p0024c1s
v2p0083c2m
MacColl, D.C. v6p0244c2s
MacColl, D.S. v3p0340c1s
v4p0066c2s v4p0075c1s v4p0493c1s
v4p0619c2s v5p0031c1s v5p0199c1s
v5p0492c1s v5p0498c2s v6p0028c1s
v6p0032c2s v6p0033c1m v6p0034c1m
v6p0035c2s v6p0108c2m v6p0112c1s
v6p0139c2s v6p0179c1s v6p0215c2s
v6p0219c1s v6p0241c2s v6p0303c2s
v6p0310c2s v6p0325c2s v6p0350c1s
v6p0437c1s v6p0450c2s v6p0473c1s
v6p0474c2s v6p0490c1s v6p0499c1s
v6p0512c2s v6p0514c2s v6p0553c1m
v6p0553c2m v6p0644c1s v6p0675c2m
v6p0676c2s v6p0688c1s v6p0689c1s
v6p0689c2s v6p0695c2m v6p0696c1m
McColl, D.S. v4p0421c2s
v6p0474c2s v6p0475c1m
MacColl, D.S. et al. v6p0108c2s
Maccoll, H. v4p0355c2s
MacColl, H. v3p0291c2s
v5p0480c1s v6p0383c1s v6p0533c1s
v6p0630c1s
McColl, H. v1p0761c1s
v1p1277c2s
Maccoll, M. v1p0010c1s
v1p0114c2s v1p0379c1m v1p0731c2s
v2p0100c1s
MacColl, M. v1p0249c2s
v1p0657c1s v1p1042c2s v1p1109c2m
v1p1116c2s v1p1271c2s v1p1318c2s
v1p1330c2s v1p1331c2s v1p1332c1s
v1p1332c2s v2p0008c1s v2p0084c1s
v2p0244c2s v2p0381c1s v3p0008c1s
v3p0082c2s v3p0119c2s v3p0220c1s
v3p0284c2s v4p0010c1s v4p0027c1s
v4p0047c1s v4p0130c2s v4p0231c2s
v4p0237c2s v4p0261c2s v4p0293c2s
v4p0376c2s v4p0495c2s v4p0515c2s
v4p0582c1s v4p0587c1s v5p0117c1s
v5p0142c2s v5p0173c2s v5p0234c2s
v5p0286c1s v5p0469c1s v5p0489c2m
v6p0003c1s v6p0253c1s v6p0557c1s
v6p0565c2s
Maccoll, M. and Austin, A.
v1p0104c1s
MacColl, M. and Ward, J.H.
v3p0082c2s
MacColl, M. et al. v1p0657c1s
McColl, Malcolm and Round, J.Horace
v5p0116c2s
Mccollester, S.H. v1p0899c2s
v2p0190c2s
McCollester, S.H. v1p0385c1s
v1p1016c1s v2p0041c2s v2p0174c1s
v2p0344c1s
McCollins, P.D. v1p0035c1s
McColloch, R.S. v1p1265c1s
v1p1265c2s
M'Collom, J.T. v1p1302c2s
MacComb, S. v6p0210c2s
v6p0218c1s v6p0341c2s
McComb, S. v3p0427c2s
v5p0306c2s v6p0123c1s v6p0177c2s
McCombie, T. v1p0079c1s
M'Combie, W. v1p0120c2s
McConachie, L.G. v5p0457c1s
v5p0580c1s
McConachie, Wm. v6p0154c1s
McConaughy, D. v1p0723c2s
McConnel, G.M. v1p0558c2s
McConnel, J.C. v3p0101c1s
v3p0107c1s v3p0207c1m v3p0356c1s
McConnell, G.N. v1p1380c1s
McConnell, J.B. v1p0344c2s
M'Connell, J.E. v1p0083c1s
McConnell, J.J. v4p0289c1s
McConnell, J.R. v1p1348c1s
McConnell, M. v1p0422c2s
v1p0609c1m v1p0889c2s
McConnell, M.L. v4p0387c2s
McConnell, R. v5p0090c1s
McConnell, S. v3p0394c1s
McConnell, S.D. v2p0290c2s
v2p0308c2s v3p0008c2s v3p0031c2s
v3p0347c1s v4p0109c2s v4p0463c1s
v5p0116c2m v5p0199c1s v5p0239c1s
v5p0292c2s v5p0378c1s v6p0368c1s
McConnell, W.J. v4p0526c1s
McConnochie, A.I. v5p0216c1s
v5p0610c2s
McCook, Gen. v1p1191c1s
McCook, H.C. v1p0044c2s
v3p0015c1m v3p0130c2s v3p0289c1s
v3p0404c2m v5p0203c2s v6p0022c1s
v6p0024c1m v6p0024c2s v6p0056c2s
v6p0091c1s v6p0127c1s v6p0320c2m
v6p0610c2s v6p0687c2s
McCook, J.J. v4p0531c2s
v4p0581c2m v4p0591c1s v4p0607c2m
v5p0585c2s v6p0653c2s
McCoom, J.C. v1p0386c2s
MacCord, C.W. v3p0142c1s
v4p0362c2s
McCord, D.J. v1p1223c1s
McCord, J. v1p1086c2s
McCord, J.C. v6p0179c1s
McCord, M.N. v5p0564c1s
McCorkle, W.A. v5p0403c2s
McCormac, F.I. v6p0597c1s
v6p0697c1s
MacCormac, H. v1p0367c2s
MacCormac, W. v5p0562c2s
McCormack, T.J. (M') v4p0176c1s
v4p0423c1s v4p0440c2s v4p0487c1s
v5p0080c2s v5p0131c2s v5p0159c1s
v5p0383c1s v5p0390c2s v5p0434c2s
v5p0499c1s v5p0548c1s v6p0169c1s
v6p0549c1s v6p0679c2s
McCormick, Canon v4p0112c1s
MacCormick, E.B. v6p0610c1s
McCormick, E.B. v6p0673c2s
McCormick, F. v5p0139c2s
McCormick, J. (M') v1p0569c2s
v4p0630c2s
McCormick, J.B. v4p0168c2s
McCormick, J.H. v4p0363c2s
McCormick, J.R. v1p1356c2s
McCormick, N. (M')........ v4p0035c1s
v4p0357c1s v4p0543c1s v4p0559c1s
v5p0596c2s
M'Cormick, R.C. v1p0968c2s
McCormick, R.S. v4p0591c2s
McCormick, S.D. v5p0329c1m
v5p0545c2s v5p0600c2s v6p0309c1s
McCormick, W. v3p0308c1s
McCormick, W.B. v4p0015c1s
McCorquodale, D. v2p0162c2s
MacCorrie, J.P. v4p0626c2s
McCorvey, J.C. v4p0457c2s
McCosh, Dr. v1p0568c1s
McCosh, J. (M')........... v1p0014c2s
v1p0208c2m v1p0275c1s v1p0276c1s
v1p0292c2s v1p0313c1s v1p0347c1s
v1p0387c2s v1p0392c2s v1p0427c1s
v1p0432c1s v1p0434c2s v1p0440c2s
v1p0618c1s v1p0625c1s v1p0686c2s
v1p0688c1s v1p0760c2s v1p0840c1s
v1p0843c1s v1p0868c1s v1p0901c1s
v1p1000c1s v1p1000c2s v1p1097c2s
v1p1159c1s v1p1271c2s v1p1328c2s
v2p0040c1s v2p0062c1s v2p0068c2s
v2p0097c2s v2p0101c1s v2p0147c1s
v2p0339c1m v2p0339c2m v2p0354c2m
v2p0366c1s v2p0455c2s v3p0454c2m
McCosh, J. and Eliot, C.W.
v2p0455c2s
McCosh, J. and Osborn, H.F.
v2p0215c1s v2p0289c2s
McCosh, J. and Tyndall, J.
v1p1041c2s
McCosh, J. et al. v3p0091c2s
McCosh, T.O. v5p0319c1s
MacCoun, J. v6p0029c2s
McCowan, H.S. v4p0535c1s
McCowan, J.S. v5p0079c1s
McCoy, A.W. v6p0382c2s
McCoy, C.F. v1p0273c1s
v1p0532c1s
McCoy, Emily M. v6p0500c2s
McCoy, F.R. v6p0607c2s
McCoy, H.N. and Ross, W.H.
v6p0527c1s
McCoy, M.H. v6p0423c2s
McCrackan, Isabel v5p0413c2s
McCrackan, W.D. v3p0009c2s
v3p0417c2s v3p0418c1m v3p0423c2s
v3p0446c1s v3p0465c2s v4p0066c1s
v4p0136c1s v4p0243c2s v4p0259c2s
v4p0284c2m v4p0303c1s v4p0317c1s
v4p0318c1s v4p0476c2m v4p0481c1m
v4p0560c1s v4p0560c2m v4p0593c1s
v5p0114c2m v5p0221c2s v5p0361c1s
v5p0497c1s v5p0500c1s v5p0504c2s
v5p0554c2s v6p0122c2s v6p0189c1s
McCrackan, W.H. v4p0490c2s
McCracken, E. v5p0311c2s
McCracken, Eliz. v6p0019c1s
v6p0073c2s v6p0085c1s v6p0116c2s
v6p0117c1s v6p0132c1s v6p0181c2s
v6p0243c1s v6p0311c2s v6p0398c2s
v6p0401c2m v6p0499c1s v6p0503c2s
v6p0504c1s v6p0586c1s v6p0604c1s
v6p0606c2s v6p0635c1s v6p0638c1s
v6p0703c1s v6p0703c2m v6p0704c1s
v6p0704c2s v6p0705c1m v6p0705c2m
MacCracken, H.M. v5p0254c2s
McCracken, J.C. v6p0093c2s
MacCracken, J.H. v6p0306c2s
McCrackin, Josephine C. .. v5p0061c2s
McCrady, E. v1p0752c1s
v2p0251c1s
McCrady, E., jr. v2p0275c1s
v3p0064c1s v3p0402c1s
McCrady, J.R. v6p0045c2s
M'Crae, G. v5p0324c1s
McCrae, J. v4p0117c1s
v5p0271c2s
v5p0369c2s
v5p0638c2s
McCrae, L. v5p0354c2s
McCraney, G.E. v5p0611c1s
McCrary, F.L. v5p0329c1s
McCrary, G.W. v1p0398c2s
McCrary, G.W. and Hoar, G.F.
v1p1077c2s
McCray, F.T. v3p0439c2s
McCray, F.Y. v3p0411c2s
McCrea, A.E., Mrs. v6p0529c2s
M'Crea, J. v4p0262c2s
McCrea, J. and Pritchard, H.J.
v5p0562c2s
M'Crea, Jas. v4p0305c2s
v4p0362c1s
McCrea, N.G. v5p0144c2s
v6p0363c1s
McCrea, R.C. v5p0478c1s
v6p0151c2s v6p0487c2s v6p0634c1s
McCrea, T. v5p0032c2s
McCready, J.E.B. v6p0096c2s
v6p0098c1s v6p0490c2s
McCreary, E.D. (M')....... v3p0086c1s
v4p0358c2s v4p0481c2s v4p0488c1s
v4p0535c1s v4p0553c2s
McCreary, R.M. v5p0035c2s
McCreath, A.S. v1p0268c1s
McCredie, A.L. v6p0096c2s
M'Crie, C.G. v2p0069c2s
v2p0194c1s v2p0204c2s v2p0297c2s
v2p0378c1s v2p0391c1s v2p0392c1s
v2p0403c2s v2p0475c1s v5p0514c2s
McCrie, G.M. v2p0021c1s
v2p0055c2s v2p0099c2s v2p0158c1s
v3p0119c2s v4p0042c1s v4p0273c2s
v4p0275c2s v4p0328c1s v4p0333c1s
v4p0391c2s v4p0478c2s v4p0554c2s
v4p0555c1s v4p0561c1s
McCrillis, H.O. v6p0487c1s
McCrillis, Herbert O. v6p0279c1s
McCrimmon, N. v6p0578c2m
McCrombie, W. (M') v1p0313c1s
v1p1001c2s v1p1094c2s
McCron, J. v1p0848c1s
McCrory, H.L. v5p0337c1s
McCullagh, F. v6p0337c1s
McCullah, A. v6p0654c1s
MacCullah, A.A. v6p0007c1m
McCulloch, D. v1p0195c1s
v1p1057c2s
McCulloch, E.S. v5p0295c2s
McCulloch, G. v5p0342c1s
McCulloch, Gen. v1p1345c2s
McCulloch, H. (M') v1p0092c2s
v1p0897c2s v1p1349c1m v3p0443c2s
McCulloch, H. et al. v1p1232c2s
McCulloch, H., jr. v3p0031c1s
v3p0036c1s v3p0111c2s v3p0237c1s
v4p0620c2s
M'Culloch, H.M. v1p1232c1s
MacCulloch, Hunter v4p0081c1s
MacCulloch, J. v1p0984c1s
McCulloch, J. v1p0354c1s
v1p0691c2s
Macculloch, J.A. v5p0553c1s
v5p0629c2s
MacCulloch, J.A. v6p0231c1s
v6p0255c2s v6p0262c2s
McCulloch, J.A. v5p0540c1s
McCulloch, J.M. v1p0686c2s
McCulloch, J.R. (M') v1p0095c1s
v1p0211c2s v1p0284c1s v1p0435c2m
v1p0474c1s v1p0494c1s v1p0628c1s
v1p0860c1s v1p1105c2m v1p1285c1m
McCulloch, O.C. v2p0074c2s
v3p0397c2s
McCulloch, R. v5p0551c1s
McCulloch-Williams, M. ... v4p0063c1s
v5p0392c2s v6p0694c2s
McCulloch-Williams, Martha
v6p0711c1s
McCullough, Annie W. v5p0106c2s
McCullough, J. et al. v2p0416c2s
McCumber, P.J. v6p0004c2s
v6p0483c2s
McCune, H. v3p0462c2s
McCune, N.B. v4p0089c2s
Maccunn, F. v3p0072c2s

v3p0274c1s v3p0279c2s v3p0382c1s
v5p0176c2s v5p0316c1s v6p0117c2s
MacCunn, F. v5p0107c2s
v5p0201c2s v5p0348c2s v5p0455c2s
Maccunn, Florence v4p0098c2s
v5p0632c2s v5p0633c1s
MacCunn, Florence v5p0107c2s
v6p0173c2s v6p0677c2s
MacCunn, J. v5p0437c1s
v6p0163c1s
MacCunn, John v5p0138c2s
McCurdy, A.W. v6p0497c2s
McCurdy, C.J. and Field, D.D.
v3p0466c2s
McCurdy, C.J. and Hall, C.S.
v3p0322c1s
Maccurdy, G.G. v6p0209c2s
v6p0514c1s
MacCurdy, G.G. v5p0015c1s
v5p0417c1s v6p0015c1s v6p0018c2s
v6p0023c2m v6p0437c2s v6p0485c1s
McCurdy, G.G. v6p0571c2s
McCurdy, J.F. v1p0066c2s
v1p0124c1s v1p0724c2s v1p1061c2s
v1p1177c1s v2p0025c2s v3p0414c2s
v5p0056c1s v5p0260c2s v5p0307c2s
v6p0061c2s
McCurdy, J.G. v5p0527c1m
v6p0591c2s
McCurdy, R.A. et al. v4p0286c2s
McCurley, W.S. v5p0403c1s
McCurry, J.L. v3p0087c1s
McCutcheon, C.B. v6p0166c1s
McCutcheon, G.B. v4p0019c2s
v5p0566c1s v6p0005c1s v6p0043c1s
v6p0591c1s
McCutcheon, J.T. v5p0360c1s
v6p0103c1s
McD.,W. v6p0522c1s
McDakin, J.G. v1p1212c2s
McDaniel, B.F. v4p0354c1s
McDaniel, E.W. and Steckel, A.
v5p0143c2s
McDaniel, S.W. v1p0105c2s
v1p0387c2s v1p0625c2s v1p0637c1s
McDaniels, J.A. v4p0520c1s
McDaniels, J.H. v1p0603c2s
v3p0122c1s v3p0144c1s v3p0184c2m
v3p0199c2s v3p0295c1s v3p0426c2s
v4p0010c1s v4p0028c1s v4p0241c1s
v4p0241c2s v4p0242c1m v4p0256c1s
v4p0262c1s v4p0263c2s v4p0446c1s
v5p0005c1s v5p0250c1m v6p0170c1s
v6p0174c2s v6p0196c1s v6p0273c2s
v6p0389c1s v6p0459c2s v6p0483c2s
v6p0593c2s v6p0647c2s
McDaniels, J.H. and
Gildersleeve, B.L. v4p0241c1s
McDaniels, J.H. and Nash, F.P.
v4p0021c1m
McDermid, D. v5p0509c2s
McDermot, D. v6p0326c2s
McDermot, G. v3p0220c2s
v3p0221c2s v4p0027c1s v4p0289c2m
v4p0290c1s v4p0290c2s v4p0362c1s
v4p0534c2s v4p0532c1s v4p0535c1s
v4p0552c2s v4p0553c1s v4p0589c2s
v5p0018c2s v5p0019c2s v5p0064c2s
v5p0083c2s v5p0117c2s v5p0145c1m
v5p0151c2s v5p0153c1s v5p0186c1s
v5p0234c2s v5p0245c2s v5p0275c1s
v5p0296c1s v5p0296c2s v5p0297c2s
v5p0362c1s v5p0397c2s v5p0398c1s
v5p0429c2s v5p0458c2m v5p0483c1s
v5p0493c1s v5p0495c2s v5p0497c2s
v5p0500c2s v5p0513c1s v5p0522c2s
v5p0523c1s v5p0528c2s v5p0536c1s
v5p0545c2s v5p0587c1s v5p0600c2s
v6p0171c1s v6p0269c2s v6p0270c1s
MacDermot, T.H. v5p0301c2s
M'Dermott, E. v1p1145c1s
McDermott, E.J. v4p0310c1m
v4p0449c2s v5p0398c2s
McDermott, F. v5p0477c1s
v6p0529c2s
McDermott, H.F. v4p0339c2s
McDermott, P.L. (M') v3p0243c1s
v3p0271c2s v3p0459c2s v4p0070c2s
v4p0226c2s v4p0337c1s v5p0238c2s
McDermott, W. v4p0372c2s
MacDermott, W.R. v6p0320c1s
v6p0624c2s
McDermott, W.R. v6p0478c1s
McDevitt, P.R. v5p0471c2s
v6p0428c2s
Macdonagh, M. v5p0310c2s
v5p0468c1s v5p0485c2s v6p0516c1s
MacDonagh, M. v3p0002c1s
v3p0017c1s v4p0063c1s v4p0265c2m
v4p0266c1s v4p0291c2m v4p0372c2s
v4p0415c2s v4p0469c1s v4p0515c2s
v5p0140c1s v5p0248c2s v5p0272c1s
v5p0272c2m v5p0296c2m v5p0297c1s
v5p0311c1s v5p0417c2s v5p0433c1m
v5p0457c2s v5p0545c2s v5p0605c2s
v5p0610c2s v5p0619c1s v6p0004c2s
v6p0043c1s v6p0180c1s v6p0197c1s
v6p0202c2s v6p0263c1s v6p0277c2s
v6p0299c1m v6p0326c2s v6p0346c2s
v6p0469c1m v6p0481c1m v6p0505c2m
v6p0565c1s v6p0584c1s v6p0608c2s
McDonagh, M. v6p0048c2s
v6p0118c1s
MacDonagh, Michael v5p0467c1s
v6p0299c1s v6p0379c1s v6p0611c1s
McDonagh, Michael v6p0206c1s
Macdonald, A. v1p0876c1s
v2p0252c1s v2p0271c1s v3p0373c1s
v4p0140c2m v4p0188c1m v4p0498c1s
v5p0318c2s v6p0041c2s v6p0042c1s
MacDonald, A. v4p0139c1s
v4p0139c2m v4p0140c1s v4p0162c2s
v5p0278c1m v5p0358c2s v5p0645c2s
McDonald, A. v1p1071c2s
v4p0285c1s v5p0537c1s
Macdonald, A.J. v3p0033c1s
McDonald, A.W. v1p1373c2s
Macdonald, Alexander v6p0018c2s
v6p0643c2s v6p0664c2s
MacDonald, Alexander v6p0386c2s
Macdonald, C. v1p0162c1s
v2p0279c2s
Macdonald, C.B. v5p0239c1s
v5p0239c2s
MacDonald, C.B. v6p0261c1s
Macdonald, C.E. v4p0257c1s
McDonald, D. v5p0157c2s
Macdonald, D.B. v4p0055c2s
v4p0160c2s v4p0514c2s v5p0024c1s
v5p0034c1s v5p0104c2s v5p0385c2s
v5p0425c1s v5p0532c2s v5p0542c1s
v5p0594c2s v6p0001c1s v6p0026c1m
v6p0056c2s v6p0061c2s v6p0063c2s
v6p0089c1s v6p0134c1s v6p0348c1s
v6p0423c2s v6p0428c1m v6p0431c2s
v6p0471c2m v6p0489c2s v6p0674c1s
Macdonald, D.C. v1p0002c1s
v1p0303c2s v1p0696c1s v1p0910c2s
v1p1166c2s v1p1348c2s v1p1403c1s
v4p0278c2s v4p0608c2s v5p0077c2s
MacDonald, D.F. v1p0685c2s
MacDonald, E.P.L. v4p0415c1s
Macdonald, E.R. v6p0247c1s
v6p0510c1s
MacDonald, E.R. v6p0448c2s
McDonald, E.R. v5p0254c2s
Macdonald, F. v1p0987c1s
v2p0059c2s v4p0074c1s
McDonald, F. v4p0162c1s
MacDonald, F.R. v1p0789c1s
Macdonald, G. v1p0024c2s
v1p0574c1s v1p0790c2s v1p1111c1s
v2p0235c1m v2p0351c2m v3p0155c2s
v4p0263c1s v6p0009c2s
MacDonald, G. v1p0021c2s
v1p0245c1s v1p0353c2s v1p0577c1s
v1p0598c2s v1p0735c1s v1p0802c1s
v1p0940c1s v1p1025c1s v1p1035c2s
v1p1185c1s v1p1201c2s v1p1220c1m
v1p1237c2s v1p1252c1s v1p1369c1s
v1p1375c2s v1p1380c2s v1p1410c1s
v1p1433c1s v2p0117c1s v2p0469c2s
v3p0132c1s v6p0680c2s
McDonald, H. v6p0474c2s
McDonald, H.B. v1p0197c1s
Macdonald, H.C. v6p0563c1s
Macdonald, H.S.G. v4p0368c1s
Macdonald, J. v1p0023c2s
v1p0728c1s v2p0057c2s v2p0075c1s
v2p0297c2s v2p0302c1s v2p0392c1s
v2p0410c2s v3p0005c1s v4p0005c2m
v4p0045c1s v4p0559c1s v5p0181c1s
MacDonald, J. v1p1322c1s
v6p0574c2s
McDonald, J. v1p0319c2s
Macdonald, J.A. v5p0090c1s
v6p0133c2s
Macdonald, J.A.M. v4p0591c1s
v5p0247c2m v5p0295c2s
Macdonald, J.A.Murray v3p0131c2s
MacDonald, J.B. v6p0581c1s
McDonald, J.B. v5p0408c1s
Macdonald, J.C. v4p0041c1s
v4p0328c2s v5p0503c2s
MacDonald, J.C. v6p0685c2s
Macdonald, J.D. v1p0374c1s
Macdonald, J.F. v6p0019c2s
v6p0133c2s v6p0169c2s v6p0241c2m
v6p0242c2s v6p0302c2s v6p0365c2s
v6p0387c2m v6p0406c2s v6p0440c2s
v6p0479c1s v6p0479c2s v6p0480c1s
v6p0560c2s
Macdonald, J.H. v1p0921c1s
McDonald, J.H. v5p0229c1s
Macdonald, J.H.A. v2p0328c2s
v4p0236c1s v6p0043c2s
MacDonald, J.H.A. v5p0290c1s
Macdonald, J.K. and Bridle, A.
v5p0083c1s
Macdonald, J.L. v4p0083c2s
Macdonald, J.M. v1p0116c1s
v1p0122c2s v1p0131c1s v1p0440c1s
v1p0520c2s v1p0581c1s v1p1033c1s
v1p1219c1s v1p1235c2s v2p0204c1s
v4p0417c2s
Macdonald, J.R. v5p0481c2s
v6p0356c1s v6p0356c2s
MacDonald, J.R. v4p0202c1s
v5p0121c1s
McDonald, J.R. v3p0464c2s
Macdonald, J.R. and
Hatton-Luck, J.W. v3p0399c1s
MacDonald, J.R. et al. ... v5p0332c1s
Macdonald, J.R.L. v5p0597c1s
MacDonald, J.R.L. v5p0196c2s
MacDonald, J.Ramsay v6p0628c1s
Macdonald, J.Ramsay and
Ramsay, Margaret, E. .. v6p0628c1s
Macdonald, J.W. v3p0086c1s
v3p0243c2s v3p0306c2s v4p0116c2s
MacDonald, J.W. v3p0169c2s
v4p0259c1s v6p0290c1s
Macdonald, Janet v6p0069c2s
MacDonald, Janet v6p0094c1s
v6p0296c1s v6p0410c2s
Macdonald, Lady v3p0065c1s
v3p0431c2s
Macdonald, M. v4p0225c2s
MacDonald, M.B. v6p0415c2s
Macdonald, Menzies v4p0017c1s
MacDonald, N. v4p0483c1s
Macdonald, O. v6p0097c2s
v6p0176c1s v6p0572c2s
McDonald, O. v6p0139c2s
v6p0709c1s
McDonald, R. v4p0148c1s
v4p0459c1s v6p0620c1s
Macdonald, R.C. v3p0469c2s
v4p0070c2s v4p0475c2s
MacDonald, R.C. v3p0230c2s
v3p0379c1s v4p0246c2s
McDonald, R.H. v6p0546c1s
Macdonald, R.H., jr. v6p0131c1s
McDonald, R.H., jr. v6p0356c1s
v6p0456c2s v6p0529c1s v6p0567c2s
McDonald, R.H., jr. and White, S.M.
v6p0632c2s
Macdonald, R.M. v2p0058c1s
v6p0272c1s
MacDonald, S.P. v6p0504c1s
MacDonald, T. v5p0019c2s
McDonald, T.McG. and Calder, W.J.
v6p0565c1s
Macdonald, W. v5p0623c2s
MacDonald, W. v4p0014c2s
v4p0214c2s v4p0233c2s v4p0461c2s
v4p0580c1s v4p0597c2s v5p0015c2m
v5p0092c1s v5p0108c2s v5p0120c1s
v5p0126c1s v5p0127c1m v5p0179c2s
v5p0203c1s v5p0245c1s v5p0266c2m
v5p0281c2m v5p0304c1s v5p0340c2s
v5p0356c2s v5p0370c2s v5p0375c1s
v5p0399c1s v5p0468c1s v5p0544c2s
v5p0568c1s v5p0569c2s v5p0591c1s
v5p0600c1s v5p0613c1s v5p0620c2s
v6p0016c1s v6p0016c2s v6p0018c1s
v6p0039c1s v6p0201c2s v6p0239c1s
v6p0389c1s v6p0408c2s v6p0597c1s
v6p0606c1m
McDonald, W. v6p0136c1s
v6p0145c2s v6p0375c2s
Macdonald, W. et al. v2p0184c2s
MacDonald, Wm. v4p0532c2s
McDonald, Z. v3p0053c1s
McDonald-Valesh, E. v4p0434c2s
Macdonald of Earnscliffe, Baroness
v5p0352c2s
Macdonell, A. v1p0031c2s
v1p0450c2s v4p0320c1s v5p0248c2s
v5p0358c2s
Macdonell, A.A. v2p0386c1s
v4p0633c2s v5p0104c2s
MacDonell, A.A. v4p0492c2s
Macdonell, Annie v4p0296c1s
v5p0079c2s
Macdonell, B.L. v1p0588c2s
v1p0785c2s v4p0205c2s v4p0214c2s
MacDonell, B.L. v6p0525c1s
Macdonell, G.P. v2p0048c2s
v2p0107c2s v2p0142c1s v2p0153c2s
v2p0223c2m v2p0245c1s v2p0273c2s
v2p0407c2s v2p0414c1s v2p0431c2s
v3p0220c1s v3p0441c2s
Macdonell, J. v1p0030c2s
v1p0332c1s v1p0721c1s v1p0806c1s
v1p0971c2s v1p1077c1s v1p1142c2s
v1p1215c2s v1p1264c2s v2p0049c1s
v2p0071c2s v3p0353c1s v4p0071c2s
v4p0335c2s v4p0466c2s v5p0007c1s
v5p0110c2s v5p0180c2s v5p0189c2s
v5p0245c2s v5p0587c1s v5p0589c1s
v5p0604c1s v6p0364c2s v6p0449c2s
v6p0560c2s v6p0606c1s
MacDonell, J. v6p0026c1s
v6p0449c2s
Macdonell, J. et al. v6p0007c1s
Macdonell, J., Sir v6p0277c2s
McDonnel, J.C. v3p0088c2s
McDonnell, E. v1p0241c1s
Macdonnell, J.C. v3p0263c2s
MacDonnell, J.C. v1p0654c1s
Macdonnell, J.deC. v6p0144c1s
Macdonnell, L.C.R. v4p0228c1s
McDonnell, Michael v6p0192c1s
McDonnell, P.E. v6p0009c2s
McDonnell, P.G. v5p0360c1s
Macdonnell, R. v1p1365c1s
MacDonnell, R.W. v1p0432c1s
McDonnell, W. v1p0173c1s
v1p0192c2s v1p1140c1s v2p0382c1s

McDonnell, W.D. v4p0450c1s
McDonnold, B.W. v2p0027c2s
v2p0369c2s v2p0385c2m
Macdonough, A.R. v1p0033c2s
v1p0060c1s v1p0111c2s v1p0168c1m
v1p0259c1m v1p0806c2s v1p0916c2m
v1p0917c2s v1p1139c2s v1p1173c1s
v1p1250c2s v1p1255c1s v1p1282c1s
v1p1409c1s v2p0120c1s v2p0170c1s
v2p0261c2s v2p0389c1s v3p0072c1s
v3p0299c2s
McDonough, A.R. v1p0342c2s
MacDonough, G. v3p0044c1s
v4p0299c1s
McDonough, J.T. v4p0401c1s
Macdougal, D.T. v4p0069c2s
v4p0216c2s v4p0445c2s v5p0073c1s
v5p0338c1s v5p0406c2s v5p0608c2s
v6p0288c1s v6p0503c1s
MacDougal, D.T. v4p0012c1s
v4p0125c1s v4p0273c1s v4p0445c1s
v5p0453c2m v5p0454c1m v6p0015c1s
v6p0066c2s v6p0077c1s v6p0674c2s
v6p0682c1m
Macdougal, Daniel T. v6p0139c2s
McDougal, W.H. v3p0315c2s
v4p0004c1s v4p0502c1s v4p0503c1s
McDougall, A.W. v6p0109c2s
McDougall, D.T. v6p0077c1s
McDougall, E.M.L. (M') ... v4p0578c2s
v4p0632c2s
Macdougall, G. v6p0168c1s
McDougall, H.C. v4p0115c2s
v4p0511c2s v4p0567c2s
McDougall, I. v5p0268c1s
v6p0113c1s v6p0613c2s
McDougall, Isabel v5p0391c1s
v5p0424c2s v6p0471c1s v6p0677c1s
McDougall, J. v3p0461c2s
McDougall, J., Mrs. v3p0467c2s
McDougall, J.A. v1p0956c1s
McDougall, J.L. v6p0096c1s
Macdougall, J.W. v4p0278c2s
v4p0279c2s v4p0280c1s
MacDougall, J.W. v4p0279c2s
v4p0318c2s
MacDougall, P.L. v2p0185c2s
v4p0235c2s
MacDougall, P.L., Sir v2p0185c2s
v2p0429c2s
Macdougall, R. v6p0279c1s
v6p0672c1s
MacDougall, R. v4p0036c2s
v5p0471c1s v6p0060c1s v6p0279c1s
v6p0284c2s v6p0543c1m v6p0583c2s
v6p0647c1s v6p0680c1s
MacDougall, Robert v5p0200c2s
McDougall, W. v5p0338c1s
v5p0470c2s v6p0040c2s v6p0363c1s
v6p0411c1s v6p0490c1s v6p0610c1s
McDougall, W. et al. v6p0522c1s
Macdougall, W.B. v5p0176c1s
McDowall, A. v5p0633c2s
MacDowall, A.B. v3p0136c1s
v3p0253c2s v3p0256c2s v3p0412c2s
v5p0125c2s v5p0561c1m v5p0624c1m
v6p0427c1s
McDowall, A.B. v6p0626c1s
Macdowall, H.C. v3p0227c2s
v4p0121c2s v4p0187c1s v5p0153c1s
v5p0204c1s v5p0373c2s v5p0379c2s
v6p0150c1s v6p0253c2s v6p0283c2s
v6p0302c1s v6p0629c2s
McDowall, H.C. v3p0102c2s
v5p0351c1s
Macdowall, H.G. v6p0237c2s
v6p0624c2s
McDowall, K.A. v6p0273c1m
v6p0287c2s
Macdowall, Prof. v1p0784c1s
McDowell, F.H.B. v2p0290c2s
McDowell, G.S. v4p0551c2s
McDowell, H.B. v2p0080c1s
v4p0106c1s
McDowell, I. v2p0079c1s
M'Dowell, J. v1p1273c2s
McDowell, K. v2p0083c1s
McDowell, M. v4p0118c1s
v5p0510c2s
M'Dowell, M.H. v5p0026c2s
McDowell, W.F. v4p0115c1s
McDowell, W.O. v4p0233c1s
v4p0585c2s v4p0632c2s
McDowell, W.P. v2p0242c1s
Macduff, A.S. v2p0182c2s
v4p0052c1s
Macduff, J.R. v1p0020c1s
v1p0994c1s v1p1299c1s v4p0510c2s
Mace, F.L. v1p0668c2s
v3p0463c1s
Mace, J. v4p0212c2s
Mace, Mrs. v4p0630c2s
Mace, R. v4p0178c2s
v4p0482c2s
Mace, W.H. v4p0584c1s
v5p0413c2s
McElfresh, F. v4p0371c2s
v6p0135c1s
McElhinney, J.J. v1p0248c1s
McElligott, H.R. v4p0495c2s
McElligott, J.N. v1p0338c2s
McElrone, H.P. v1p0790c1s
v2p0072c2s v2p0108c2s v2p0182c2s
v2p0230c2s v2p0269c2s v2p0292c1s
v2p0293c1s v2p0434c1s v3p0296c1s
McElroy, I. v2p0357c1s
McElroy, J. v2p0193c2s
v2p0303c2s v2p0460c1s v3p0206c2s
v5p0395c2s
McElroy, J.G.R. v1p0372c1s
v1p0416c1s v1p0601c1s v1p0724c1s
v1p1194c2s v3p0140c1s v3p0143c2s
McElroy, S. v1p0408c1s
v1p0454c2s v1p0666c2s v1p0708c1s
v1p1065c1m v1p1100c2s v1p1181c2s
v1p1246c2s v4p0613c2s v5p0621c2s
McElroy, W.H. v2p0454c2s
v4p0245c2s
McElroy, W.N. v1p0398c1s
v2p0286c1s v3p0261c1s v3p0369c1s
v4p0345c1s v5p0307c1s
McEnery, S.D. v6p0446c2s
McEnery, S.S. v6p0177c1s
McEntee, J. v1p1362c1s
McEvoy, B. v4p0023c1s
v4p0061c2s v4p0122c2s v4p0273c2s
v4p0385c2s v4p0391c1s v5p0081c1s
v5p0091c2s v5p0337c2s v5p0570c1s
v6p0461c2s
McEvoy, C. v6p0449c2s
McEvoy, J.M. v4p0136c2s
v6p0633c1s
Macewan, A. v4p0082c2s
McEwan, A. v6p0467c2s
MacEwan, E.J. v3p0254c1s
McEwen, A. v1p0395c1s
v4p0602c1s v5p0229c2s v5p0592c2s
v6p0179c2s
Macewen, A.R. v3p0126c2s
v4p0429c2s
MacEwen, A.R. v4p0457c1s
v5p0514c2s
McEwen, B. v5p0313c2s
McEwen, C. v2p0319c2s
McEwen, D. v2p0205c2s
Macewen, M. v1p0997c1s
McEwen, T. (M') v1p1397c1s
v5p0322c1s v5p0596c1s
MacFadden, Bernard v6p0215c2s
McFadden, T. v2p0335c1s
Macfadyen, A. v6p0638c1s
v6p0651c1s v6p0663c2s
MacFadyen, A. v5p0042c2s
Macfadyen, A. and Barnard, J.E.
v5p0042c2s
Macfadyen, A.N. v5p0452c2s
Macfadyen, D. v4p0248c1s
v6p0302c2s v6p0341c1s v6p0541c1s
Macfadyen, Dugald v6p0122c2s
McFadyen, J.F. v5p0055c2s
v5p0080c1s v6p0286c2s v6p0571c1s
McFadyen, T.F. v6p0062c1m
Macfall, H. v5p0141c1s
v6p0001c1s v6p0033c2s v6p0035c1s
v6p0055c1s v6p0130c2s v6p0450c2s
v6p0546c1s v6p0689c1s v6p0704c2s
MacFall, H. v6p0180c1s
v6p0280c2s v6p0411c1s v6p0595c1s
v6p0685c2s v6p0695c2s v6p0697c1s
McFall, H. v6p0352c2s
McFall, Haldane v6p0169c2s
McFarland, A. v1p0357c1s
v2p0097c2s v2p0196c1s v2p0311c1m
v2p0425c2s
McFarland, Albert v6p0499c2s
Macfarland, C.S v5p0533c1s
McFarland, G.F. v6p0500c2s
Macfarland, H. v5p0012c2s
v5p0154c2s v5p0259c1s v5p0496c1s
v5p0544c1m v5p0592c2s
Macfarland, H.B.E. v6p0534c2s
Macfarland, H.B.F. v5p0163c1s
v5p0354c1m v6p0151c2s
MacFarland, H.B.F. v6p0687c1s
McFarland, H.B.F. v6p0122c1s
McFarland, H.H. v1p0167c2m
v1p0558c2s v1p0853c1s v1p1142c1s
v1p1363c1s v1p1424c2s
MacFarland, Harold v4p0364c2s
McFarland, Horace v6p0656c1s
Macfarland, J. v5p0466c1s
McFarland, J.H. v5p0040c2s
v6p0025c2s v6p0128c2s v6p0129c1s
v6p0201c2s v6p0227c2s v6p0230c1s
v6p0243c2s v6p0264c2s v6p0275c1s
v6p0281c1m v6p0307c1s v6p0400c1s
v6p0462c2s v6p0463c1s v6p0656c1m
v6p0656c2s v6p0664c2s v6p0699c2s
McFarland, J.H. and Woodruff, C.R.
v6p0127c2s
McFarland, J.Horace v5p0225c2s
McFarland, J.R. v6p0217c2s
McFarland, J.T. v4p0309c2s
v6p0611c1s
McFarland, R. v6p0347c2s
MacFarland, R.W. v1p0990c1s
McFarland, R.W. v1p0375c2s
v4p0011c2s v4p0083c1s v4p0110c2s
v5p0116c1s v5p0174c2s v6p0125c1s
v6p0188c1s v6p0427c2s
McFarland, T.B. v2p0446c1s
McFarland, W. and Paul, H.M.
v2p0159c1s
Macfarland, W.H. v1p0736c2s
v1p0752c2s v1p0786c1s
McFarland, W.H.
v5p0010c2s
v5p0583c1s
v5p0603c2s
McFarland, W.M. v4p0125c2s
v5p0011c1s v5p0068c2m v5p0195c1s
v5p0602c2s v5p0619c1s v5p0626c2s
v6p0197c2s v6p0204c1s v6p0204c2s
v6p0401c1m v6p0407c1s v6p0409c2s
v6p0413c2s v6p0669c1s v6p0693c2s
M'Farlane, A. v6p0674c2s
Macfarlane, A. v2p0099c2s
v2p0243c2m v4p0285c1s v5p0012c1s
MacFarlane, A.E. v6p0272c1s
McFarlane, A.E. v6p0056c1s
v6p0099c1s v6p0131c1s v6p0138c2s
v6p0175c1s v6p0243c1s v6p0362c1s
v6p0376c1s v6p0494c2s v6p0541c1s
v6p0602c2s v6p0682c1s v6p0697c2s
McFarlane, A.E. and
McFarlane, Margaret ... v6p0623c2s
McFarlane, A.F. v6p0632c1s
Macfarlane, A.R. v2p0155c1s
v6p0572c2s
MacFarlane, A.R. v2p0383c1s
Macfarlane, Alex. v5p0012c1s
Macfarlane, C.S. v5p0473c1s
Macfarlane, C.W. v4p0144c1s
v4p0167c2s v4p0434c1s v4p0481c1s
v6p0176c1s v6p0599c2s
Macfarlane, D.H. v2p0217c2s
McFarlane, D.H. v2p0107c2s
Macfarlane, H. v4p0180c1s
v5p0056c1s v5p0102c1s v5p0115c2s
v5p0124c1s v5p0143c1s v5p0197c1s
v5p0248c1s v5p0312c2s v5p0406c1s
v5p0439c1s v5p0483c1s v6p0075c1s
v6p0157c2s v6p0221c1s v6p0536c1s
v6p0584c1s
Macfarlane, H.B.F. v6p0176c1s
Macfarlane, Harold v6p0232c1s
McFarlane, I. v1p1080c1s
v1p1327c1s v1p1327c2s
Macfarlane, J. v2p0066c2s
v5p0429c1s
MacFarlane, J. v1p0268c1s
McFarlane, J. v1p0229c1s
v1p0770c1s
Macfarlane, J.M. v4p0270c2s
v6p0576c2s
Macfarlane, M. v3p0259c2s
v3p0415c1s
McFarlane, Margaret and
McFarlane, A.E. v6p0623c2s
McFarlane, Miss v1p0065c1s
v1p1051c1s
Macfarlane, T. v1p1210c1s
Macfarlane, W.W. and Clarkson, P.S.
v3p0080c1s
Macfarren, G.A. v1p0569c2s
v1p0877c2s v2p0379c2s
MacFarren, G.A. v1p0819c2s
v1p0883c2s
M'Faul, J.A. v5p0494c1s
Macfayden, Eric v6p0602c2s
McFee, J.R. v2p0355c1s
McFee, K.N. v1p0092c1s
v1p0734c2s
Macfie, M. v1p0929c1s
v1p1148c2s v2p0331c2s v4p0038c2s
v4p0124c2s v4p0368c2s v4p0428c1s
v4p0462c2s v4p0604c1s
Macfie, R.A. v2p0081c1s
McGaffey, E. v4p0146c2s
v4p0395c1s
McGaffey, F. v6p0183c1s
Macgahan, B. v3p0448c2s
McGahie, F.A. v5p0252c2s
McGamble, E.A. and Foster, E.
v6p0644c1s
McGamble, Eleanor A. v6p0040c2s
McGarry, W.R. v3p0066c2s
v4p0158c2s v4p0453c1s v4p0483c1s
v4p0635c2s
McGauley, J.W. (M') v2p0042c2s
v2p0045c1s v2p0232c2s v2p0351c2s
v3p0217c1s
McGarvie, J. v1p0604c1s
v1p0646c2s
McGary, A. v3p0208c2s
McGaskell, C. v4p0617c1s
McGauley, J.W. v1p0026c1s
v1p0399c2s v1p0579c2s v1p0666c1s
v1p0748c1s v1p0877c2s v1p1003c1s
v1p1003c2s v1p1050c2s v1p1055c2s
v1p1161c2s
McGee, A.N. v6p0334c1s
v6p0337c2s v6p0462c2s
McGee, A.N., Mrs. v3p0470c2s
McGee, C.K. and Langley, J.W.
v2p0384c2s
McGee, J.E. v1p0240c1s
v1p0653c2s v1p0660c1s v1p0742c2s
v1p0915c1s
McGee, J.G. v1p0296c1s

v1p0315c2s v1p0448c1s v1p0524c2s
v1p0558c2s v1p0563c1s v1p0594c2s
v1p0625c2s v1p0632c2s v1p0652c2s
v1p0653c2m v1p0656c1s v1p0658c1m
v1p0661c2s v1p0728c2s v1p0730c2s
v1p0742c1s v1p0838c1s v1p0891c1s
v1p0937c1s v1p0979c1s v1p1018c2s
v1p1059c1s v1p1117c2m v1p1118c2s
v1p1119c1s v1p1353c1s
McGee, T.D. v1p0654c1s
McGee, W. v5p0514c1s
McGee, W.C. v3p0205c2s
McGee, W.G. v6p0681c1s
McGee, W.I. v4p0442c2s
MacGee, W.J. v1p1311c2s
McGee, W.J. v1p0265c2s
v1p0523c2s v1p0622c1s v1p0652c1s
v1p0876c1s v1p0876c2s v2p0128c1s
v2p0179c1s v2p0213c2s v2p0281c2s
v3p0016c2s v3p0026c1s v3p0155c2s
v3p0165c1s v3p0169c1s v3p0265c1s
v3p0265c2s v3p0278c1s v3p0315c2s
v3p0318c1s v3p0362c1s v3p0382c2s
v4p0159c2s v4p0165c2s v4p0186c2s
v4p0222c1s v4p0293c2s v4p0368c2s
v4p0443c2s v4p0515c2s v5p0003c1s
v5p0015c1s v5p0034c1s v5p0042c2s
v5p0163c1s v5p0214c1s v5p0224c2s
v5p0228c2s v5p0230c1s v5p0275c2m
v5p0278c2s v5p0358c1s v5p0366c1s
v5p0380c2s v5p0399c1s v5p0399c2s
v5p0429c2s v5p0462c2s v5p0468c1s
v5p0513c2m v5p0578c1s v5p0599c2s
v5p0601c1s v5p0645c1s v6p0015c1s
v6p0023c2s v6p0030c1s v6p0171c2s
v6p0403c2s v6p0474c1s v6p0584c1s
McGee, W.J. and Call, R.E.
v2p0262c2s
McGee, W.J. and Johnson, W.D.
v4p0515c2s
McGee, W.J. and Wright, G.F.
v4p0273c1s
MacGee, W.T. v1p0265c1s
McGeehan, W.O. v5p0359c1s
v5p0427c2s v6p0700c2s
McGeehan, W.O'C. v6p0494c2s
McGehee, M. v3p0163c1s
McGehee, M.H. v1p0306c2s
v1p0307c1s
MacGeorge, A. v2p0253c2s
McGeorge, J. v6p0044c2s
MacGeorge, Madge v5p0294c2s
McGeorge, W., jr. v3p0289c1s
McGhee, Z. v5p0454c2s
v6p0646c2s
McGhee, Zach. v6p0332c2s
McGhie, J. v4p0176c1s
v5p0184c2s v5p0185c1s v5p0377c2s
M'Gibbon, Alex. v5p0235c1s
McGibbon, R.D. v5p0565c2s
v6p0278c2s
McGie, V.C. v4p0412c1s
McGiffert, A.C. v2p0432c1s
v3p0171c1m v3p0171c2s v3p0230c1s
v4p0109c2s v5p0051c2s v5p0118c1s
v5p0442c1s v6p0209c2s v6p0610c2s
McGiffert, J.N. v3p0373c2s
McGiffert, M.C. v5p0193c1s
v6p0220c2s v6p0632c1s v6p0709c1s
McGiffin, C.S. v6p0071c1s
McGiffin, P.N. v4p0635c1s
McGill, A.B. v5p0030c1s
v5p0081c2s v5p0331c1s v5p0497c2s
v5p0499c1s v5p0573c2s v5p0591c1s
v6p0020c2s
McGill, A.T. v1p0336c1s
v1p0808c1s v2p0136c1s
McGill, A.T. and Humphrey, E.P.
v1p1046c1s
McGill, Anna B. v6p0105c2s
v6p0333c1s
McGillicuddy, D. v5p0089c2s
McGillicuddy, O.E. v6p0016c1s
McGillivray, A.J. v6p0344c1s
McGillivray, G. v3p0143c2s
McGillivray, J.D. v6p0010c2s
Macgillivray, W. v1p0135c2s
McGilvary, A.B. v5p0536c2s
McGilvary, E.B. v5p0160c2s
v5p0195c2s v5p0261c1m v5p0344c1s
v5p0344c2s v6p0014c1s v6p0211c2s
v6p0212c1s v6p0286c1s v6p0463c1s
McGinley, A.A. v4p0074c2s
v5p0021c1s v5p0493c2s v5p0514c1s
v5p0536c1m v5p0577c1s
McGinley, J.M. v5p0147c2s
McGinnis, E.L.H. v5p0585c2s
v5p0643c1s
McGinty, W.H. v5p0026c2s
McGlashen, R.B. v4p0555c1s
McGlasson, E.W. v4p0102c2s
v4p0194c2s v4p0373c1s v4p0380c2s
McGloin, F. v3p0230c2s
v4p0342c1s
McGlynn, E. v1p1363c2s
v3p0237c2s v4p0424c1s v5p0509c1s
McGoldrich, D.J. v1p0835c2s
MacGonigle, J.N. v4p0203c1s
v4p0597c1s
MacGonigle, J.N. and Dix, E.A.
v6p0214c1s v6p0229c1s
McGoodwin, H.K. v6p0028c2m
McGovern, J. v6p0003c2s
v6p0239c1s v6p0377c2s v6p0474c2s
v6p0686c2s
McGovern, J.B. v5p0569c2s
v6p0112c2s v6p0327c2s v6p0553c1s
McGovern, J.M. (M') v5p0279c1s
v5p0331c1s v5p0403c1s
McGovney, D.O. v6p0445c2s
MacGowan, A. v4p0071c2s
v4p0092c2s v4p0247c2s v5p0028c1s
v6p0041c1s v6p0121c2s v6p0127c2s
v6p0171c2s v6p0178c2s v6p0295c1s
v6p0378c1s v6p0389c1s v6p0478c1s
v6p0489c1s
McGowan, A. v4p0497c1s
MacGowan, Alice v4p0199c2s
v6p0124c2s v6p0467c1s v6p0551c2s
McGowan, Alice v6p0156c2s
v6p0623c2s
Macgowan, D.B. v6p0416c2s
MacGowan, D.B. v6p0152c1s
v6p0224c2s v6p0506c1s v6p0558c1s
v6p0559c2s v6p0564c2s
Macgowan, D.J. v1p0235c2s
v1p0236c2s v1p0268c1s v1p0637c2s
v1p1018c1s v1p1023c1s v1p1281c2s
v1p1310c1s v2p0128c1s v3p0079c1s
v4p0087c2s
Macgowan, Dr. v1p0232c1s
v1p0678c1s
McGowan, F.X. v4p0364c1s
v5p0134c1s
McGowan, G. v3p0373c2s
v4p0026c1m v4p0253c2s v4p0333c1s
v4p0405c1s
MacGowan, J.E. v2p0434c2s
McGown, A. v1p0192c1s
McGrath, D.J. v3p0359c1s
MacGrath, H. v5p0472c2s
v6p0523c2s v6p0662c2s
McGrath, J. v3p0263c1s
v4p0289c1s
McGrath, P. v6p0636c2s
M'Grath, P.D. v5p0209c1s
MacGrath, P.T. v4p0402c1s
McGrath, P.T. (M') v5p0093c1s
v5p0178c2s v5p0408c2m v5p0409c1m
v5p0504c2s v6p0029c1s v6p0047c2s
v6p0073c1s v6p0091c1s v6p0096c1s
v6p0097c2s v6p0101c1m v6p0171c1s
v6p0187c2s v6p0205c2s v6p0226c2m
v6p0227c2s v6p0289c1s v6p0301c1s
v6p0301c2m v6p0455c1m v6p0455c2m
v6p0459c2s v6p0564c2m v6p0580c2m
v6p0636c2m v6p0694c1m
M'Grath, Wm. v4p0291c1s
McGraw, E.W. v6p0308c2s
v6p0348c1s
McGraw, J.H. v6p0581c1s
McGraw, W.K. v5p0479c1s
McGray, A. v6p0324c1s
McGray, A.N. v6p0460c1m
McGrea, R.C. v6p0634c1s
McGreggor, J. v1p0633c2s
Macgregor, A. v2p0476c1s
Macgregor, B. v5p0207c2s
v5p0348c2s
Macgregor, C.J. v1p0943c1s
Macgregor, D. v1p0437c2s
MacGregor, D.H. v6p0353c2s
McGregor, H. v5p0584c2s
v5p0640c2s
Macgregor, J. v2p0065c2s
v2p0149c2s v2p0422c2s v4p0533c1s
v5p0113c1s
MacGregor, J. v2p0148c2s
v2p0413c1s v3p0317c1s v3p0361c2s
v3p0382c1s
McGregor, J. (M') v1p0951c1s
v2p0201c1s
Macgregor, J., Lt.-Col. .. v6p0133c2s
Macgregor, J.G. v5p0319c1s
MacGregor, J.K. v6p0710c2s
Macgregor, M. v6p0076c1m
MacGregor, M. v2p0158c1s
v2p0352c1s v4p0429c2s
Macgregor, Margaret v6p0001c1s
v6p0057c1s v6p0661c2s
Macgregor, R. v1p0051c2s
v1p0089c1s v1p0315c1s v1p0703c2s
McGregor, R.C. v5p0205c1s
Macgregor, R.R. v1p0111c2s
v1p0155c1s v1p0210c2s v1p0314c2s
v1p0466c1s v1p0499c1m v1p0962c1s
v1p1072c2s v1p1294c2s
Macgregor, W.C. v4p0401c2s
Macgregor, W.D. v6p0267c1s
MacGregor, W.D. v5p0419c1s
McGregor, W.L. v1p1148c2s
Macgregor, W.M. v4p0456c1s
v5p0087c1s v5p0306c1s
MacGregor-Robertson, J. .. v2p0175c2s
McGregor-Robertson, J. ... v2p0360c1s
McGrew, F.F. v6p0628c1s
McGrew, T.F. v6p0512c1s
McGrew, W.K. v5p0485c1s
McGrigor, A.B. v2p0234c2s
McGuffey, Chas.D. v6p0187c1s
McGuire, B.S. v6p0465c1s
McGuire, H. v2p0232c2s
v3p0273c1s
McGuire, J. v6p0086c1s
McGuire, J.D. v2p0001c1s
v3p0332c2s v4p0550c2s
McGuire, W.W. (M') v1p0017c2s
v1p1041c1s
MacGurdy, G.G. v5p0022c2s
McGurdy, J.G. v5p0210c1s
Mach, E. v3p0385c1s
v4p0002c1s v4p0135c2s v4p0169c1s
v4p0177c1s v4p0180c1s v4p0193c1s
v4p0193c2s v4p0248c1s v4p0331c2s
v4p0333c2s v4p0441c1s v4p0441c2s
v4p0475c1s v4p0487c1s v4p0508c1s
v4p0515c1m v4p0561c1s v5p0131c2s
v5p0135c1s v5p0325c1s v5p0364c2s
v5p0397c1s v5p0423c2s v5p0468c1s
v5p0542c1s v6p0251c1s v6p0285c2s
v6p0637c2m v6p0643c1s
Mach, E. and Carus, P. ... v3p0150c2s
v3p0385c1s
Mach, E.Van v6p0224c2s
Mach, E.von v6p0288c2s
Machar, A.M. v1p0173c1m
v1p0314c1s v1p0381c2s v1p0466c2s
v1p0530c1s v1p0708c2s v1p0709c1s
v1p0770c1s v1p0942c1s v1p0981c2s
v1p0996c2s v1p1041c2m v1p1042c1m
v1p1292c2s v1p1356c1s v1p1420c2s
v1p1422c2s v1p1426c2s v2p0382c1s
v3p0142c1s v3p0205c1s v4p0085c1s
v5p0012c2s v5p0425c2s v6p0097c2s
Machar, Agnes M. v2p0270c2s
McHardy, A.A. v6p0035c1s
McHardy, A.B. v3p0180c1s
McHardy, C.M. v5p0246c2s
McHardy, Lieut. v1p1391c2m
MacHarg, W.B. v6p0167c1s
v6p0187c2s
Machell, A.H. v5p0416c2s
Machen, A. v3p0039c2s
Machen, A.W. v1p1305c1s
v6p0634c2s
Machen, E.E. v5p0386c2s
McHenry, G.B. v6p0563c2s
McHenry, K.V. v5p0082c1m
v5p0091c1s
McHenry, M. v5p0156c2s
v5p0206c1s v6p0507c2s
McHenry, May v6p0168c1s
Macheson, C. v2p0005c2s
v2p0208c1s v2p0264c2s v2p0265c1s
v2p0468c1s
Machon, Dr. v5p0087c1s
Machray, R. v1p0610c1s
v2p0449c2s v4p0336c1s v5p0218c1s
v5p0302c2s v6p0096c2s v6p0186c2s
v6p0580c1s
Machugh, K. v6p0455c2s
Macias, J.M. v1p0322c2s
McIlhenny, E.A. v6p0010c2s
v6p0448c2s
McIlhenny, H.A. v6p0694c1s
McIlhiney, P.C. v4p0230c1s
McIlquham, H. (M') v4p0628c1s
v5p0009c2s v5p0035c1s v5p0384c1s
v5p0638c1s v6p0078c2s v6p0402c1s
v6p0703c2s v6p0704c2s v6p0705c1s
MacIlraith, J.R. v2p0289c2s
McIlroy, A. v5p0012c1s
v6p0072c2s v6p0161c2s v6p0564c2s
v6p0621c2s v6p0705c1s
McIlvain, J.W. v3p0036c2s
McIlvaine, A.P. v4p0321c1s
v4p0336c2s v4p0404c1s
McIlvaine, C. v3p0045c2s
v3p0431c1s v4p0190c2s v4p0434c1s
v4p0578c1s v4p0608c2s v5p0051c2s
v6p0135c1s
McIlvaine, Caroline v6p0437c1s
v6p0608c2s
McIlvaine, J.H. (M') v1p0122c1s
v1p0312c2s v1p0385c2s v1p0434c1s
v1p0791c2s v1p0979c2s v1p1030c2s
v1p1102c1s v1p1104c2s v1p1161c2s
v1p1351c2s v2p0371c2s v2p0389c2s
v2p0407c1s v2p0425c2s
Macilwaine, H.C. v5p0150c1s
v5p0304c1s
MacIlwaine, H.C. v5p0039c2s
v5p0040c1s v5p0374c1s
McIlwaine, H.R. v4p0605c2s
MacIlwaine, W. v1p0534c1s
v1p0757c2s v1p1217c2s v1p1242c2s
McIlwaith, Jean N. v6p0701c1s
McIlwraith, I. v4p0179c1s
McIlwraith, J.C. v6p0096c1s
McIlwraith, J.N. v5p0420c2s
v6p0173c1s v6p0299c2s
McIlwraith, J.N. and McLennan, W.
v5p0543c1s
McIlwraith, M. v4p0140c1s
v4p0211c2s v4p0212c1m v4p0294c2s
v4p0559c1s v5p0157c2s
McInnes, A. v1p0784c2s
v1p0995c1s
MacInnes, D. v4p0041c2s
McInnes, J.E. v6p0081c2s

McIntosh, Burr v5p0003c1s
MacIntosh, C.H. v5p0077c1s v5p0238c1s
McIntosh, C.H. v4p0213c2s v4p0347c2s v4p0574c2s
McIntosh, E.H. v4p0082c1s
M'Intosh, I. v5p0222c2s
Macintosh, J., Sir v1p0344c1s
M'Intosh, M.J. v1p1208c1s
Macintosh, M.J. v1p0770c1s
McIntosh, P.D. v6p0089c2s
MacIntosh, S.L. v5p0205c1s v5p0582c1s
MacIntosh, W. v2p0162c1s
McIntosh, W.C. (M') v2p0157c1m v2p0340c1s v3p0153c2s v3p0154c1m v5p0216c1s v6p0226c1s
McIntyre, C.H. et al. v6p0097c2s
McIntyre, D.M. v6p0341c2s v6p0513c1s
McIntyre, H.H. v4p0102c1s v4p0603c1s
Macintyre, J. v4p0481c1s v4p0487c1s
MacIntyre, J. v4p0019c1s
McIntyre, J. v5p0056c1s
McIntyre, J.L. v4p0577c1s v5p0313c2s
McIntyre, J.T. v6p0645c1s
MacIntyre, R. v4p0557c1s v5p0526c1s
McIntyre, R. v4p0548c1s
MacIntyre, Rob. v5p0643c1s
Macirone, C.A. v3p0262c2s v3p0329c1s
Macironi, F. v1p0982c1s
McIver, C.D. v6p0192c2s
Maciver, F.A. v1p0971c2s
MacIvor, A. v4p0004c2s v4p0200c1s v4p0441c1s v5p0044c1s v5p0087c1s
MacIvor, A. v4p0473c1s v4p0502c2s
McJilton, J.N. v1p1050c1s
McJimsey, E.E.E. v3p0351c1s
Mack, A. v2p0034c1s
Mack, C.S. v5p0114c2s
Mack, D. v1p1288c1s
Mack, E. v6p0607c1s
Mack, E.S. v4p0044c2s v6p0158c1s
Mack, F.W. v4p0075c1s
Mackail, J.W. v2p0056c1s v2p0435c1s v3p0149c1s v3p0450c2s v5p0451c1s v5p0576c2s v5p0584c1s v6p0212c2s v6p0273c1s v6p0430c2s v6p0461c1s
MacKain, D. v1p0287c1s v1p1390c1s
Mackall, L.L. v6p0466c2s
McKants, E.C. v6p0005c2s
Mackarness, F. v2p0004c2s v2p0483c2s v3p0005c1s v5p0587c2s v6p0442c2s
Mackarness, J.F. v1p0002c2s v1p0245c1s v1p0402c1s v1p0402c2s v1p0675c1s v1p0695c2s v1p0696c1s v1p0834c1s v1p0874c2s v1p1148c1m v2p0277c2s
Mackay, A. v4p0343c2s v5p0030c1s v5p0253c2s v5p0396c1s v5p0420c2s v5p0486c2s v5p0596c2s
Mackay, A.E. v3p0031c1s
Mackay, A.E.J.G. v5p0075c2s
Mackay, A.H. v5p0570c1s
Mackay, A.J.G. v4p0307c1s v4p0450c2s
Mackay, A.M. v4p0021c1s v4p0074c2s v4p0112c2s v4p0113c2s v4p0405c2s v5p0078c1s v5p0169c2s v6p0179c1s v6p0294c1s v6p0519c1s
Mackay, Agnus M. v2p0270c2s
Mackay, C. v1p0113c2s v1p0145c2s v1p0168c1s v1p0178c2s v1p0193c1s v1p0321c1s v1p0347c2s v1p0489c2s v1p0500c1s v1p0565c2s v1p0574c1s v1p0624c1s v1p0693c1s v1p0693c2s v1p0851c1s v1p0858c1s v1p0923c2s v1p1020c2s v1p1021c1s v1p1241c2s v1p1277c1s v1p1298c2s v1p1305c1s v1p1329c1s v1p1353c2s v2p0069c2s v2p0072c1s v2p0126c2s v2p0253c2s v2p0260c1s v2p0289c1m v2p0306c1s v2p0318c2s v2p0319c2s v2p0330c1s v2p0374c2s v2p0398c2s v2p0409c2s v2p0430c1s v2p0471c2s v3p0139c2s v3p0395c1s v4p0518c2s
McKay, C. v6p0387c1s
McKay, C.F. v1p0647c2s
McKay, C.W. v5p0401c1s
Mackay, D. v6p0155c1s
Mackay, E. v3p0152c1s v4p0043c2s
Mackay, E.J.G. v2p0266c1s
Mackay, F.E. et al. v6p0641c2s
McKay, G. v6p0405c2s
Mackay, G.E. v1p0177c1s v1p0669c1s v1p0801c1s v1p0943c2s
McKay, H. v2p0027c1s
Mackay, H.W. v6p0686c2s
Mackay, H.W.B. v4p0315c2s v4p0564c2s
MacKay, H.W.B. v4p0469c1s
Mackay, I.E. v5p0424c2s v5p0517c1s v5p0532c2s v6p0471c2s
MacKay, I.E. v6p0171c2s
Mackay, J. v1p0721c1s v3p0190c2s v3p0381c2s
McKay, J. v4p0244c2s
McKay, J.F. v4p0588c2s
McKay, J.T. v1p0137c2s v1p0218c2s v1p0199c1s v1p0231c1s v1p0244c2s v1p0257c1s v1p0321c1s v1p0571c1s v1p0698c2s v1p0704c2s v1p0709c2s v1p0725c2s v1p0767c1s v1p0801c1s v1p0864c1s v1p0991c1s v1p0998c1s v1p1011c1s v1p1070c2s v1p1082c2s v1p1113c2s v1p1252c1s v1p1335c1s v2p0087c1s v2p0422c1s v3p0245c2s v3p0363c1s v4p0324c1s v5p0339c2s
Mackay, K. v6p0245c1s
Mackay, L.M. v6p0398c1s
Mackay, M. v1p0365c2s
Mackay, M.N. v1p1421c1s
Mackay, R. v5p0418c1s
Mackay, R.W. v1p1095c2s
McKay, S.A. v3p0288c1s v3p0405c1s
McKay, S.R. v4p0414c2s
Mackay, T. v4p0045c1s v4p0231c2s v4p0265c2s v4p0394c1s v4p0412c1m v4p0450c1s v4p0452c1m v4p0452c2m v4p0521c2s v4p0534c1s v5p0436c2s v6p0508c2s
MacKay, T. v4p0450c2s
McKay, T.C. and Howe, J.C. v5p0184c1s
Mackay, W. v1p0281c1s v1p0354c2s v1p1034c1s v1p1253c1s v1p1275c1s v1p1298c1m v1p1336c1s v4p0307c2s
Mackay, W.R. v4p0527c1s
Mackay, Wm. v4p0289c1s v4p0328c2s v4p0415c2s
Mackay-Smith, Archdeacon . v3p0088c1s v3p0281c1s
McKaye, J. v1p1327c1s
MacKaye, M.E. v2p0349c2s
McKaye, M.E. v2p0037c1s v2p0375c1s
Mackaye, S. v2p0437c1s
McKean, A.G. v2p0356c2s
McKean, H.L. v1p1159c1s
McKean, W.V. v1p1345c2s
McKeay, Anna J. v6p0199c2s
McKechnie, J. v5p0526c1s
McKee, G.W. v6p0286c2s
McKee, J.M. v2p0107c2s v2p0251c1s v2p0309c1s
McKee, O. v4p0263c2s
McKee, Ralph H. v6p0040c1s
McKee, T.H. v2p0455c1s v6p0408c1s
McKee, W.P. v5p0057c1s
McKeen, C. v1p1422c2s
McKeen, J. and Smith, E. . v4p0477c1s
McKeen, S. v1p1208c1s
McKellar, W.H. v5p0048c1s v5p0083c2s v5p0191c2s v5p0573c1s
McKelway, A.I. v5p0340c2s
McKelway, A.J. v5p0414c1s v6p0114c2m v6p0115c1s
McKelway, A.J. et al. v6p0039c2s
M'Kelway, St.C. v4p0115c2m
McKelway, St.Clair v5p0199c2s v6p0346c1s
Mackendrick, A. v6p0428c2s
MacKendrick, A. v6p0288c1s
McKendrick, J. v1p0374c1s
McKendrick, J.G. v1p0278c2s v1p0374c2s v2p0439c2s v3p0047c2s v4p0148c1s v4p0174c2s v4p0176c2s v4p0351c2s v5p0077c1s v5p0447c2m v6p0609c1s v6p0712c1s
McKenna, E.M. v4p0011c2s v4p0570c2s
McKenna, E.M.M. v5p0182c1s v5p0222c1s v6p0339c1s
McKenna, J.A.J. v3p0128c2s v3p0213c2m v3p0364c1s v3p0365c1s v4p0574c2s
McKenna, R. v6p0271c2s
McKenna, Reginald v6p0267c2s
Mackenna, S.J. v1p0773c2s v1p0975c2s v1p1081c1s v1p1164c2s
MacKenna, S.J. v1p0458c2s v1p1317c1s
Mackennal, A. v1p0240c1s v1p0850c1s v2p0030c1s v2p0103c2s v2p0190c1s v2p0291c1s v2p0292c1s v2p0333c1s v3p0096c1s v6p0684c2s
McKenney, Anne P. v6p0038c1s
McKenney, J. v1p0372c2s
McKenney, R.S. v6p0414c1s
Mackenzie, A. v1p0079c1s
McKenzie, A. (M') v1p0190c2s v1p1387c2s v2p0327c1s v3p0383c2s v4p0075c1s v5p0236c1s
Mackenzie, A.B. v3p0168c1s
Mackenzie, A.C. v4p0400c2s v4p0457c1s
McKenzie, A.C. v5p0544c2s v6p0216c1s
Mackenzie, A.M., Sir v6p0294c1s v6p0490c1s
Mackenzie, A.S. v1p0298c2s v1p0339c1s v1p1254c1s v1p1351c2s v6p0040c1s
Mackenzie, A.W. v2p0196c1s
Mackenzie, B.D. v3p0199c1s v3p0318c2s v4p0266c1s v4p0328c2s
Mackenzie, C. v3p0236c2s v5p0157c1s
Mackenzie, D. v3p0004c2s v3p0232c2s v3p0288c2s v6p0429c2s v6p0511c2s
Mackenzie, D.F. v2p0086c1s
Mackenzie, E.K. v5p0348c1s v5p0379c1s v5p0419c2s
McKenzie, F.A. v4p0263c1s v4p0502c2s v4p0548c2s v5p0566c1s v5p0619c1s
Mackenzie, G. v1p0539c2s v1p0609c1s v1p0768c1s v5p0540c1s
McKenzie, G. v4p0150c2s v4p0292c2s v4p0445c1s
Mackenzie, G.A. v1p0195c1s
Mackenzie, G.F. v4p0170c1s
Mackenzie, G.M. and Irby, A.P. v1p0174c2s v1p1180c1s v1p1331c2s
Mackenzie, G.S. v1p1222c2s v4p0005c1s v4p0589c1s v4p0589c2s
Mackenzie, G.T. v4p0374c2s
Mackenzie, H. v6p0670c2s
Mackenzie, H. and Drachmann, H. v5p0169c1s
Mackenzie, H.M. v2p0025c2s
Mackenzie, J. v2p0004c1s v2p0363c1s v3p0004c1s v3p0005c1s v3p0037c1s v4p0471c2s v5p0006c2s v5p0019c2s v5p0051c2s v5p0319c2s
Mackenzie, J. et al. v2p0004c1s
Mackenzie, J.B. v1p0079c2s v6p0180c1s v6p0587c2s v6p0588c2s
Mackenzie, J.C. v4p0122c2s v4p0355c1s v4p0506c2s v4p0512c1s v5p0269c2s v6p0635c2s
Mackenzie, J.C. et al. ... v4p0512c2s
Mackenzie, J.J. v4p0041c1s
Mackenzie, J.S. v3p0348c1s v4p0084c2s v4p0108c1s v4p0164c2s v4p0167c2s v4p0187c2s v4p0188c2m v4p0475c1s v4p0479c2s v4p0484c2s v4p0514c1m v4p0599c2s v5p0179c1s v5p0386c1s v5p0457c2s v5p0468c1s v6p0319c1s v6p0412c2s v6p0533c1s
MacKenzie, J.S. v6p0170c1s
Mackenzie, J.S. et al. ... v4p0475c1s
Mackenzie, J.T. v1p0741c2s
Mackenzie, John v5p0007c1s
Mackenzie, K.R.H. v1p0016c1s
Mackenzie, K.R.H. and Major, R.H. v1p1372c1s
Mackenzie, M. v2p0282c2m v2p0413c1s v2p0462c2m v3p0192c2s v3p0237c2s v3p0396c2s v3p0400c2m v3p0403c2s v3p0416c2s v4p0085c2s v4p0122c2s v4p0143c1s
McKenzie, M. v4p0562c2s
Mackenzie, M., Sir v3p0025c2s v3p0097c2s v3p0098c1s v3p0105c1s v3p0201c2s v3p0215c2s v3p0247c1s v3p0263c1s v3p0424c1s v3p0434c2m v3p0474c1s
Mackenzie, Morell v3p0146c2s
Mackenzie, R. v3p0099c1s v3p0237c1s v4p0571c2s v6p0131c1s v6p0514c2s
MacKenzie, R. v4p0316c2s
Mackenzie, R.D. v5p0043c1s v5p0053c1s v5p0174c2s v5p0287c2s v5p0356c1s
Mackenzie, R.J. v3p0378c1s
Mackenzie, R.S. v1p0409c1s v1p0658c1s v1p0729c1s v1p0795c1s v1p0962c1s v1p0995c1s v1p1144c2s v1p1152c2s v1p1211c2s v1p1408c2s
MacKenzie, R.T. v6p0217c1s
McKenzie, R.T. v4p0528c2s v5p0200c2s v5p0531c2s v6p0080c2s v6p0554c2s
Mackenzie, T.R. v5p0127c2s
Mackenzie, W.A. v5p0039c2s
Mackenzie, W.B. v1p0761c1s
Mackenzie, W.C. v4p0141c1s v5p0204c1s v5p0265c1s v5p0343c1s v5p0345c1s v5p0352c1s v5p0515c1s v5p0517c2s v6p0142c2s v6p0168c1s v6p0382c1s v6p0393c1s v6p0499c1s v6p0577c1s
MacKenzie, W.C. v4p0318c1s
Mackenzie, W.D. v3p0166c2s v3p0398c1s v5p0055c2s v5p0198c1s v6p0024c2s v6p0123c2s v6p0642c2s
Mackenzie, W.G. v5p0207c1s
Mackenzie, W.L. v3p0292c2s v3p0331c2s v6p0410c1s
MacKenzie, W.L. v5p0470c1s

McKenzie, W.P. v4p0111c2s
McKenzie, W.S. v3p0042c1s
v3p0243c2s
McKerlie, H.G. v3p0135c1s
v4p0078c1s
Mackeson, C. v2p0057c1s
v2p0072c2s v2p0126c1s v2p0132c2s
v2p0186c1m v2p0197c2s v2p0209c1s
v2p0262c2s v2p0303c1m v2p0319c1m
v2p0331c1s v2p0358c2s v2p0388c2s
Mackey, A.J. v5p0441c1s
Mackey, D.J. v3p0070c2s
Mackey, E. v1p0849c2s
Mackey, H.B. v2p0166c1s
v3p0161c2s v5p0218c2s v6p0592c2s
Mackey, T.J. v4p0072c1s
v4p0225c1s v4p0594c1s
McKibben, F.P. v5p0554c1s
v5p0627c2s
MacKibbin, S. v3p0086c1s
v3p0197c2s v4p0369c1s
Mackie, C.P. v1p0993c1s
v4p0471c1s
MacKie, C.P. v3p0162c1s
v5p0298c2s
Mackie, J. v4p0420c2s
v5p0013c1s
Mackie, J.B. v6p0393c2s
Mackie, J.M. v1p0372c2s
v1p0477c1s v1p0514c1s v1p0516c1s
v1p0536c2s v1p0606c2s v1p0615c1s
v1p0886c1s v1p1155c2s v1p1228c2s
v1p1251c2s v1p1387c1s v1p1412c1s
Mackie, J.S. v1p0199c1s
v1p0859c2s v1p1334c1s
Mackie, John v4p0206c1s
Mackie, P.B. v5p0490c1s
Mackie, Pauline B. v4p0460c2s
v5p0366c1s
Mackie, S.J. v1p0135c2s
v1p0268c1s v1p0362c2s v1p0401c2s
v1p0428c1s v1p0466c2s v1p0469c1s
v1p0508c2s v1p0562c2s v1p0836c1s
v1p0856c1s v1p0923c2s v1p1018c2s
v1p1019c1s v1p1171c2s v1p1173c1s
v1p1191c1s v1p1227c1s v1p1409c1s
v3p0187c1s v3p0223c2s
M'Kiernan, G.S. v1p0881c2s
McKillop, A. and Guest, A.R.
v5p0314c1s
McKim, Antoinette v6p0483c1s
McKim, C.F. v6p0016c2s
McKim, J.M. v1p1420c1s
McKim, R.H. v1p0519c1s
v1p0686c1s v5p0603c1s
Mackinder v3p0169c1s
Mackinder, H.J. v4p0222c2s
v5p0005c2s v6p0250c1s
v6p0398c1s
Mackinder, H.J. et al. ... v4p0222c1s
McKiney, E.P. v6p0699c2s
McKinley, A. v6p0627c1s
v6p0632c1s
McKinley, A.E. v5p0406c1s
v5p0408c1s v6p0009c2m v6p0680c1s
McKinley, W. et al. v3p0096c2s
McKinley, W., jr. v3p0347c1s
v4p0251c2s
McKinney, D. v1p1047c1s
McKinney, L.F. v5p0139c1s
McKinney, W.A. v1p0200c1s
Mackinnon, Capt. v1p0045c2s
v1p0441c2s v1p1249c2s
McKinnon, Com. v1p0967c1s
McKinnon, D.J. v6p0404c1s
v6p0525c2s
M'Kinnon, J. v2p0305c1s
MacKinnon, J. v5p0180c1s
M'Kinnon, J.B. v2p0004c1m
Mackinnon, W. v4p0062c1s
Mackinslay, J.B. v2p0122c1s
Mackintire, F. v1p0777c1s
v1p1442c2s
Mackintosh, A. v5p0369c1s
v6p0299c1s
Mackintosh, D. v1p0045c2s
Mackintosh, H.R. v5p0037c2s
v5p0059c1s v5p0348c1s v5p0489c2m
v6p0168c2s v6p0259c1s v6p0386c2s
v6p0642c2s v6p0702c1s
MacKintosh, H.R. v6p0544c2s
Mackintosh, H.S. v1p0959c2s
Mackintosh, J. v1p0085c1s
v1p0327c2s v2p0443c1s v6p0420c1s
Mackintosh, J., Sir v1p0142c1s
v1p0190c1s v1p0196c2s v1p0323c1s
v1p0412c2s v1p0479c1s v1p0517c2s
v1p0661c1s v1p0698c2s v1p0783c1s
v1p0842c1s v1p0973c2s v1p1000c1s
v1p1024c1s v1p1036c2s v1p1114c1s
v1p1241c2s v1p1253c2s v1p1261c2s
v1p1265c1s v1p1266c1s v2p0135c2s
Mackintosh, J.B. v3p0223c2s
Mackintosh, J.B. and Hidden, W.E.
v3p0026c2s v3p0338c1m
v3p0414c2s
v3p0475c1s
Mackintosh, M. v2p0178c2s
v2p0275c2s v3p0236c1s v3p0258c1s
v4p0076c2m v4p0431c1s
Mackintosh, May v3p0468c1s
Mackintosh, R. v5p0156c1s
v6p0024c1s
Mackintosh, W. v1p0392c1s
Mackintosh, W.D. v3p0331c2s
v4p0026c2s v5p0012c1s
McKirdy, J.E. et al. v6p0501c1s
McKishine, A.P. v5p0421c2s
v5p0495c2s
McKissick, A.F. v4p0175c1s
v4p0176c2s v4p0195c1s
Macklem, C. v5p0285c1s
Mackleskie, G. v2p0222c2s
Macklin, A. and Macklin, G.E.
v6p0656c2s
Macklin, A. and Macklin, T.E.
v6p0539c1s
Macklin, G.E. and Macklin, A.
v6p0656c2s
Macklin, T.E. and Macklin, A.
v6p0539c1s
McKnight, A.H. (M') v5p0457c1s
v5p0592c1s v5p0623c2s
McKnight, B. v6p0283c1s
McKnight, C. v1p0694c2s
McKnight, C.S. v1p1168c1s
McKnight, D.A. v5p0422c1s
McKnight, G.H. v5p0317c1s
McKnight, G.H. et al. v2p0042c1s
McKnight, L. v1p0645c2s
Macknight, R. v4p0268c1s
M'Knight, W.L. v1p0093c2s
Mackonochie, A.H. v1p0247c2s
v1p0250c1s
M'Kown, C.F. v5p0372c2s
Mackray, R. v2p0366c2s
McKrum, J. v1p0538c2s
Macksey, Charles v5p0437c1s
Mackubin, E. v4p0258c2s
v4p0336c1s v4p0465c2s v4p0491c2s
v5p0159c1s v5p0337c2s v5p0349c2s
Mackubin, N. v2p0105c2s
v4p0571c1s
Mackworth, A. v4p0319c2s
Mackworth, Audley v5p0156c2s
v6p0511c1s
Mackworth, H. v3p0280c2s
McLachlan, A. v1p0148c1s
v1p0888c1s v1p1386c1s
McLachlan, C.M. v1p0623c2s
MacLachlan, J. v4p0236c2s
v4p0261c2s
McLachlan, R. v1p0420c1s
v1p0630c2s v1p1276c2s v2p0252c2s
v2p0483c1s
McLachlan, R.W. (M') v1p1039c2s
v5p0125c1s
Maclagan, Gen. v1p0174c2s
v1p0629c2s v3p0059c1s
Maclagan, R.C. v4p0026c1s
v5p0155c1s v5p0232c2s
Maclagan, T.J. v1p1337c1s
v4p0284c2s v4p0500c1s
Maclagen, R.E. v2p0217c2s
McLain, A.F. v2p0432c2s
McLain, J. v2p0421c2s
Maclan, F. v4p0551c2s
McLanahan, S. v5p0118c2s
v5p0493c1s
McLandburgh, F. v1p0082c1s
v1p0155c2s v1p0890c1s v1p1054c2s
v1p1092c1s
MacLane, J.P. v3p0181c2s
McLane, J.W. (M') v1p0120c1s
v1p0189c2s v1p0240c2s v1p0243c1s
v1p0551c1s v1p1021c2s
McLane, W.W. v3p0145c1s
v3p0209c1s v4p0467c2s v4p0564c2s
v6p0040c2s v6p0523c2s v6p0595c2s
Maclaren, A. v1p0147c2s
v1p0226c2s v1p0564c2s v1p0934c1s
v1p1158c2s v1p1358c1s v1p1422c1s
v5p0248c2s
McLaren, A. v2p0129c1s
v2p0182c2s v2p0183c2s v2p0366c2s
Maclaren, A.C. v6p0157c2s
McLaren, A.C. v1p0238c1s
Maclaren, C. v1p0301c2s
v1p1112c2s
McLaren, C. v4p0073c1s
McLaren, D.C. v1p0342c1s
v1p0507c2s v1p1197c2s
McLaren, D.T. v5p0578c1s
McLaren, E.C. v1p0313c1s
Maclaren, I. v4p0007c1s
v4p0311c1s v4p0360c1s v5p0264c2s
Maclaren, Ian v4p0296c2s
v4p0614c1s v5p0623c1s
McLaren, J. (M') v4p0284c2s
v5p0246c1s v6p0356c2s
McLaren, M.N., jr. v4p0204c2s
MacLaren, M.W. v6p0210c2s
McLaren, N. v3p0254c1s
MacLaren, W. v5p0037c2s
McLaren, W.D. v5p0280c2s
McLaren, W.E. v1p1041c2s
M'Laren, W.S.B. v3p0109c1s
Maclaskie, G. v6p0071c1s
McLauchlan, A. v1p0195c1s
Maclauchlan, H.S. v5p0376c2s
McLaughlin, A. v6p0048c1s
v6p0120c1s v6p0308c1s v6p0308c2m
v6p0309c1m v6p0559c2s v6p0597c1s
McLaughlin, A.C. v3p0012c1s
v3p0188c2s v3p0307c2s v3p0441c2s
v3p0464c1m v4p0359c2s v4p0397c1s
v4p0592c1s v4p0593c2m v4p0618c1s
v5p0267c1s v5p0534c2s v5p0632c1s
v6p0146c1s
McLaughlin, A.J. v6p0308c1s
MacLaughlin, E.T. v4p0334c2s
McLaughlin, E.T. v3p0260c1s
McLaughlin, F. v3p0120c2s
McLaughlin, Frances v6p0508c2s
McLaughlin, J.B. v6p0375c2s
McLaughlin, J.F. v3p0170c1s
v4p0341c1s v5p0566c2s v6p0085c2s
v6p0391c1s
McLaughlin, J.M. v3p0218c2s
McLaughlin, M.J. v1p0870c2s
McLaughlin, T. v3p0274c2s
v3p0459c1s
McLaughlin, W.D. v2p0097c1s
v2p0249c1s v2p0274c1s
McLauglin, M. v6p0308c2s
McLaurin, J.J. v6p0349c1s
v6p0465c1s
McLaurin, J.L. v5p0540c2m
v5p0541c1m
McLaws, L. v1p0518c2s
v5p0396c2s v6p0388c2s
Maclay, E.S. v3p0442c2s
v3p0443c2s v6p0345c2s
Maclay, R.H. v1p0235c2s
Maclay, R.S. v1p0067c2s
v2p0233c2s
Maclay, W.B. v1p1038c2s
McLay, W.S.W. v5p0278c2s
Maclay, W.W. v1p1182c1s
McLean, A. v4p0589c1s
MacLean, A.M. v5p0637c1s
v6p0660c1s v6p0705c2s
Maclean, Annie M. v5p0638c2s
v6p0098c1s v6p0173c1s v6p0628c1s
MacLean, Annie M. v5p0158c2s
v5p0201c1s
McLean, Bruce v6p0550c2s
Maclean, C.D. v2p0250c1s
v2p0367c2s v4p0341c1s
McLean, C.F. v1p1162c1s
v5p0229c2s
McLean, C.F., Mrs. v5p0255c2s
McLean, E. v6p0251c2m
Maclean, F. v6p0510c2s
MacLean, F. v6p0436c2s
McLean, F.H. v5p0384c2s
v5p0572c2s v5p0606c2s v6p0110c1s
v6p0113c2s v6p0623c2s
Maclean, F.W. v1p0880c2s
MacLean, Frank v6p0167c2s
MacLean, G.E. v6p0135c1s
v6p0542c2s
McLean, G.E. v6p0135c1s
Maclean, G.V. v5p0184c1s
MacLean, H. v1p0045c2s
v1p1072c2s v3p0219c2s v3p0381c1s
McLean, H. v1p1166c2s
Maclean, J. v1p0285c1s
v1p1057c1s v2p0236c1s v4p0063c1s
v4p0353c2s v5p0288c1s v5p0384c2s
McLean, J. v4p0063c1s
McLean, J.E. v4p0606c2s
McLean, J.K. v5p0576c2s
Maclean, J.M. v2p0403c1s
v3p0211c1s v3p0211c2s v3p0352c1s
v5p0286c2s v6p0314c2s
Maclean, J.P. v2p0300c1s
MacLean, J.P. v2p0178c1s
v2p0281c1s v3p0193c1s v3p0193c2s
v3p0235c1s
McLean, J.P. v1p0030c2s
v2p0010c2s v2p0027c1s v2p0147c2s
v2p0219c1s v4p0013c1s
Maclean, K.S. v1p1407c1s
v2p0130c2s
Maclean, L. v3p0029c2s
v3p0081c2s v3p0262c2s
McLean, L.May v5p0487c1s
Maclean, M. et al. v4p0177c1s
Maclean, N. v6p0258c2s
v6p0288c2s
McLean, N. v5p0441c1s
MacLean, N.F. v4p0344c2s
Maclean, Norman v6p0174c1s
McLean, S.J. v5p0080c2s
v5p0091c2s v5p0354c1s v5p0476c2s
v5p0477c2s v5p0478c1s v5p0584c1s
v6p0097c1s v6p0528c1s v6p0529c1s
v6p0659c1s
McLean, S.P. v2p0403c2s
MacLean, W. v5p0642c2s
McLean, W. v1p0438c2s
McLean, W.A. v6p0088c1s
Maclean, W.F. v4p0347c1s
Macleane, D. v5p0116c2s
v6p0150c2s
Maclear, J.P. v1p0074c1s
v1p0077c1s v1p0382c1s
Macleay, J. v5p0224c1s
v5p0265c1s

Macleay, W. v1p0911c1s
McLedd, Addison v6p0164c2s
MacLehose, R. v6p0075c1s
Maclehose, Sophia H. v6p0203c1s
McLeish, J.L. v4p0348c2s
McLellan, C.M.S. v3p0015c1s
MacLellan, G.B. v1p0727c2s
McLellan, I. v1p1087c2s
v4p0438c2s
McLellan, J.A. and Burk, F.L.
v4p0026c2s
McLellan, J.F. (M') v1p0436c2s
v1p0551c2s v1p0709c1s v1p0802c2s
v1p1433c1s
Maclellan, J.W. v4p0044c1s
McLellan, R.A. v6p0197c1s
McLellan, S.F. v6p0537c2s
McLenathen, C.H. v6p0451c1s
MacLennan, D. v1p0803c2s
McLennan, E. v3p0088c2s
McLennan, J.F. v1p0160c2s
v1p0728c2s v1p0739c2s v1p0803c1s
v1p1434c1s v3p0146c2s
Maclennan, R.J. v5p0294c1s
M'Lennan, S.F. v4p0153c2s
v4p0179c1s v4p0187c1s
MacLennan, S.F. v5p0261c1s
v5p0480c1s v6p0123c1s v6p0215c2s
v6p0521c2s
McLennan, S.F. and Angell, J.R.
v4p0549c2s
MacLennan, S.F. and Knox, G.W.
v6p0218c1s
McLennan, T. v6p0120c1s
McLennan, W. v3p0273c2s
v4p0004c1s v4p0032c2s v4p0081c2s
v4p0082c1s v4p0243c1s v4p0288c1s
v4p0304c1s v4p0336c1s v4p0351c1s
v4p0355c2s v4p0380c1s v4p0416c2s
v4p0465c2s v5p0140c1s v5p0354c2s
v5p0474c2s v5p0544c2s v6p0001c1s
McLennan, W. and McIlwraith, J.N.
v5p0543c1s
McLennan, W.E. v5p0017c2s
v5p0436c1s v6p0126c1s
Macleod, A. v2p0265c2s
v2p0267c2s v2p0289c2s v2p0473c1s
v3p0193c1s v3p0219c1s v4p0256c2s
MacLeod, A. v2p0044c1s
v2p0078c1s v2p0182c2s v4p0528c2s
McLeod, A. v5p0019c1s
v6p0164c2s v6p0245c1s v6p0679c2s
McLeod, A.A. v4p0120c2s
v4p0474c2s
MacLeod, A.E. v5p0417c1s
Macleod, A.H.M. v4p0320c1s
MacLeod, A.M. v1p1337c2s
McLeod, Addison v5p0073c2s
v6p0415c1s
M'Leod, C. v4p0303c2s
Macleod, C. v6p0155c1s
v6p0451c2s
Macleod, Campbell v6p0002c1s
Macleod, D. v1p0201c2s
v1p0334c2m v1p0590c2s v1p0796c2s
v1p1195c1s v1p1216c2s v1p1234c2s
v2p0076c1s v2p0096c1s v2p0115c2s
v2p0157c1s v2p0169c1s v2p0183c1s
v2p0231c2s v2p0300c2s v2p0334c1s
v2p0347c2s v2p0407c1s v2p0447c1s
v2p0448c1s v3p0097c1s v3p0148c1s
v3p0162c2s v3p0175c1s v3p0196c1s
v3p0225c1s v3p0258c1s v3p0387c1s
v3p0415c2s v3p0448c1s v3p0449c1s
v3p0466c1s v4p0168c1s v4p0309c2s
v4p0311c1s v4p0333c1s v4p0335c2s
v4p0371c1s v4p0413c1s v4p0503c1s
v4p0508c2m v4p0541c2s v4p0545c1s
v5p0239c2s v5p0495c2s v5p0611c1s
v6p0236c1s
McLeod, D. v1p0595c1s
Macleod, Donald v5p0027c2s
v5p0553c2s
MacLeod, Donald v4p0552c1s
McLeod, E.F. v5p0382c2s
McLeod, E.W. v1p0587c2s
Macleod, F. v4p0216c1s
v4p0253c1s v5p0099c1m v5p0163c1s
v5p0224c1s v5p0272c2s v5p0280c2s
v5p0295c1s v5p0579c1s v5p0629c1s
v6p0038c2s v6p0100c2s v6p0328c1s
v6p0407c2s v6p0627c1s v6p0702c2s
v6p0711c1s
MacLeod, F. v6p0245c1s
McLeod, F.F. v5p0430c1s
Macleod, Fiona v5p0625c1s
v6p0391c1s v6p0711c1s
MacLeod, Finoa v6p0580c1s
Macleod, G.H.B. v1p0745c1s
v3p0207c2s
Macleod, G.H.B., Sir v5p0143c2s
Macleod, H. v4p0230c2s
McLeod, H. v2p0426c2s
v4p0009c2s v6p0413c2s
McLeod, H.C. v5p0149c2s
M'Leod, H.D. v1p0094c1s
Macleod, H.D. v1p1027c1s
v2p0388c1s v3p0127c2s
MacLeod, H.D. v4p0059c1s
v4p0230c2s v4p0379c2s v5p0284c1s
v5p0284c2s v5p0285c2s
McLeod, H.D. v4p0526c1s
McLeod, I.M. v2p0449c1s
Macleod, J. v3p0116c2s
v3p0158c2s v3p0268c1s
MacLeod, J. v2p0440c1s
Macleod, J.A. v5p0049c1s
Macleod, J.G. v1p0177c2s
v1p0350c2s v1p0729c1s v1p0959c1s
v1p0995c1s v1p1033c2s v1p1194c1s
v2p0377c2s
MacLeod, J.G. v1p0256c2s
v1p0312c1s v1p0370c2m v1p1227c2s
v1p1332c1s v2p0022c2s v2p0023c1m
v2p0039c1s v2p0040c2s v2p0121c2s
v2p0142c2s v2p0145c1s v2p0145c2s
v2p0215c1s v2p0326c2s v2p0381c1s
McLeod, J.G. v1p0080c1s
v1p0788c2s v1p0807c2s
Macleod, Jessie v3p0306c1s
v4p0350c2s
Macleod, M. v5p0396c2s
McLeod, M. v3p0318c2s
Macleod, N. v1p0072c1s
v1p0076c2s v1p0133c2s v1p0137c2m
v1p0185c1s v1p0185c2s v1p0191c2s
v1p0222c1s v1p0228c2s v1p0229c2s
v1p0244c2s v1p0285c2s v1p0294c1s
v1p0377c1s v1p0377c2m v1p0407c1s
v1p0454c2s v1p0458c2s v1p0527c2s
v1p0528c2s v1p0529c2s v1p0590c2s
v1p0597c1s v1p0633c2s v1p0672c1s
v1p0675c2s v1p0682c1s v1p0685c2s
v1p0689c1s v1p0692c2s v1p0767c1s
v1p0794c2s v1p0852c2s v1p0907c2s
v1p0940c2s v1p0980c2s v1p1054c1s
v1p1134c1s v1p1205c1s v1p1269c2s
v1p1325c1s v1p1384c1m v1p1396c2s
v3p0080c2s v3p0229c1s v3p0392c1s
McLeod, N. (M') v1p0083c1s
v1p0746c2s v4p0458c2s
MacLeod, R. v2p0108c1s
v3p0460c2s
McLeod, R. v1p0199c1s
v3p0106c1s v5p0018c2s v5p0022c1s
v6p0067c1s
McLeod, R.A. v1p0001c1s
v1p0586c2s v1p0672c1s v1p1376c2s
McLeod, T.H. v1p0930c2s
McLeod, W. v1p0866c1s
v1p1406c2s
Macleod, W.J. v4p0433c2s
Maclerie, W. v1p0296c2s
v1p1197c1s v1p1365c1s
McLintock, R. (M') v3p0193c2s
v3p0435c2s v4p0229c2s v4p0253c2s
Maclonagh, M. v6p0327c1s
Macloskie, G. v1p0107c1s
v1p0608c1s v2p0047c2s v2p0458c1s
v3p0289c1s v3p0297c2s v3p0379c2m
v3p0380c2s v4p0020c1s v4p0507c1s
v5p0153c2s v5p0198c2s v6p0210c2s
v6p0397c1s v6p0608c2s v6p0656c1s
v6p0687c2s
Macloskie, George v5p0439c1s
McLoud, J.W. v4p0456c2s
McLoughlin, A.C. v5p0600c1s
McLoughlin, M.J. v1p1024c2s
McLoughlin, T.P. v6p0283c1s
McLoughlin, W.P. v4p0569c1s
McLouth, L.A. v5p0126c2s
McLouth, Lewis v5p0534c2s
Maclure, A. v4p0591c2s
McMackin, A.B. v3p0299c2s
MacMackin, D.J. v6p0368c1s
MacMahan, A.B. v3p0388c1s
v6p0090c2s
McMahan, A.B. v2p0121c1s
v3p0006c1s v3p0057c1s v3p0111c1s
v3p0145c2s v3p0172c2s v4p0011c1s
v4p0022c2s v4p0031c2s v4p0067c1s
v4p0121c1s v4p0137c2s v4p0293c1s
v4p0406c1s v4p0510c1s v4p0628c2s
v5p0014c2s v5p0016c1s v5p0079c2s
v5p0522c2s v5p0548c1s v5p0640c2s
v6p0085c2s v6p0331c1s v6p0590c2s
Macmahan, J.B. v4p0451c1s
MacMahon, A. v6p0367c2s
v6p0663c2s
McMahon, A.H. v5p0005c1s
v6p0582c2m
MacMahon, A.R. v2p0061c2m
v3p0060c2m v3p0070c2s v3p0234c2m
v4p0124c2s v4p0451c2s v4p0522c2m
McMahon, A.R. v5p0503c2s
MacMahon, Anita v6p0072c1s
MacMahon, C.A. v6p0546c2s
McMahon, C.A. v2p0277c1s
MacMahon, E. v4p0245c2s
v4p0309c2s v4p0560c1s v5p0034c2s
v6p0434c1m
McMahon, E. (M') v2p0376c1s
v2p0443c2s v2p0455c1s v3p0444c2s
v6p0292c2s
McMahon, E.J. v2p0063c1s
Macmahon, Ella v6p0303c1s
Macmahon, H. v6p0296c1s
MacMahon, J. v1p0820c2s
McMahon, J. v6p0244c1m
McMahon, J.E. v4p0600c1s
MacMahon, J.H. v1p0594c2s
v1p0882c2s
McMahon, J.H. v2p0332c1s
v4p0488c2s v5p0492c2s v6p0672c1s
MacMahon, J.R. v5p0362c2s
McMahon, L. and Street, I.M.
v3p0141c1s
MacMahon, M. v5p0339c1s
v5p0429c1s v5p0583c2s v6p0606c1s
v6p0674c1s
McMahon, M. v6p0551c2s
McMahon, M.T. v1p0966c2s
v1p0967c1s v1p1347c1s
MacMahon, P.A. v4p0530c2s
v5p0379c1s v5p0564c2s v6p0394c2s
McMahon, P.V. v5p0120c1s
McMahon, R.R. v3p0086c2s
McMahon, Robert C. v6p0179c2s
McMahon, Sarah D. v6p0645c2s
McMahon, T.W. v2p0453c1s
McMahon, W. v6p0321c2s
McMain, E. v6p0451c2m
McManis, J.T. v5p0267c1s
McManus, E. v4p0411c1s
v5p0328c2s
MacManus, J. v5p0275c1s
v5p0630c1s
MacManus, J.E. v3p0385c1s
McManus, J.E. v2p0434c2s
McManus, L. v6p0101c2s
v6p0328c1s
Macmanus, S. v6p0695c1s
v6p0706c1s
MacManus, S. v5p0013c1s
v5p0061c2s v5p0087c1s v5p0099c1s
v5p0195c1s v5p0240c2s v5p0297c1s
v5p0390c2s v5p0435c2s v5p0450c2s
v5p0488c1s v5p0504c2s v5p0550c1s
v5p0557c2s v5p0596c1m v5p0633c2s
v6p0005c1s v6p0046c1s v6p0091c2s
v6p0153c2s v6p0154c2s v6p0159c1s
v6p0218c1s v6p0219c2s v6p0245c1s
v6p0300c2m v6p0327c1m v6p0328c1m
v6p0328c2s v6p0339c1s v6p0362c2s
v6p0386c2s v6p0487c1s v6p0543c2s
v6p0562c1s v6p0616c1s v6p0647c2s
McManus, S. v5p0579c1s
v6p0434c1s v6p0511c2s
McManus, S.B. v6p0545c1s
McManus, S.P. v4p0037c1s
MacManus, Seumas v5p0380c2s
Macmartin, A. v1p1250c2s
M'Master, E. v4p0393c1s
McMaster, G.H. v1p0956c2s
McMaster, J.A. v1p0069c1s
v1p1216c1s v1p1277c1s
McMaster, J.B. v1p0161c2s
v1p0260c1s v1p0329c2s v1p0510c1s
v1p1273c1s v1p1329c2s v2p0353c2s
v2p0371c2s v3p0162c1s v3p0442c1m
v3p0455c2s v4p0044c2s v4p0199c1m
v4p0312c2s v4p0373c1s v4p0449c2s
v4p0457c2m v4p0524c1s v4p0529c1s
v4p0594c1s v4p0617c1s v5p0199c2s
v5p0534c2s v5p0598c2s v5p0620c2m
v5p0624c2m v6p0428c2s v6p0690c2s
McMaster, J.B. and Coudert, F.R.
v4p0015c2s
Macmaster, M. v2p0114c2s
McMasters, S.Y. v1p0259c2s
v1p0594c2s v1p0891c1s v1p0972c2s
v1p1120c2s
McMath, R.E. v1p0854c2s
v2p0299c2s v2p0402c2s
MacMechan, A. v5p0079c2s
v5p0091c2s v5p0095c1s v5p0311c1s
v5p0390c2s v6p0097c2s v6p0169c2s
v6p0461c1m v6p0648c1s
McMichael, C. et al. v4p0214c2s
Macmichael, J.H. v6p0109c1s
v6p0290c2s v6p0383c2s v6p0384c1s
v6p0411c1s v6p0582c1s
MacMichael, J.H. v6p0036c1s
v6p0047c1s v6p0385c1s
v6p0594c1s
McMichael, W.P. v4p0348c1s
McMillan, A.J. v5p0077c1s
McMillan, Alec v6p0313c1s
Macmillan, C. v3p0051c2s
v3p0340c2s v3p0405c1s v4p0060c1s
v4p0069c2s v4p0141c1s
MacMillan, C. v3p0377c2s
v4p0139c1s v4p0171c1s v4p0445c2s
v4p0465c2s v6p0188c1s v6p0420c1s
v6p0650c2s
McMillan, C. v3p0193c2s
v3p0334c1s
McMillan, D.C. v2p0216c2s
v2p0313c2s
MacMillan, D.P. v6p0575c1s
Macmillan, G.A. v1p0677c1s
v3p0025c2s
Macmillan, H. v1p0161c2s
v1p0210c2s v1p0397c2s v1p0590c2s
v1p0613c2s v1p0929c2s v1p0930c1s
v1p0943c1s v1p0967c1s v1p1015c2s
v1p1284c1s v1p1307c2s v1p1323c1s
v2p0009c2s v2p0024c2s v2p0030c1s
v2p0037c2s v2p0066c2s v2p0151c1s
v2p0172c2s v2p0208c1s v2p0246c1s

v2p0247c1s v2p0276c1s v2p0299c2s
v2p0318c2s v2p0321c1s v2p0327c1s
v2p0331c2s v2p0373c2m v2p0383c1s
v2p0429c2s v2p0431c1s v2p0464c2s
v2p0482c1s v3p0035c2s v3p0229c1s
v3p0366c2s v3p0397c2s v4p0054c1s
v4p0191c1s v4p0252c2s v4p0296c2s
v4p0512c2s v5p0001c2s v5p0074c2s
v5p0085c2s v5p0135c1s v5p0151c2s
v5p0283c2s v5p0297c1s v5p0343c2s
v5p0354c2s v5p0416c1s v5p0453c2s
v5p0500c1s v5p0546c1s v5p0556c1s
v5p0569c1s v6p0382c1s v6p0552c2s
MacMillan, H. v4p0262c2s
v5p0145c2s
Macmillan, H.P. v5p0140c1s
v5p0515c1s
Macmillan, Hugh v3p0031c2s
v5p0171c2s v5p0314c2s v5p0433c2s
v5p0473c2s v6p0026c2s v6p0156c1s
v6p0258c2s v6p0462c2s
MacMillan, Hugh v6p0591c1s
McMillan, J. v6p0014c2s
Macmillan, K.D. v5p0057c2s
v6p0061c2s
Macmillan, L. v4p0101c1s
Macmillan, M. v5p0196c1s
McMillan, M. v5p0129c1s
v6p0370c2s
McMillan, Margaret v3p0470c2s
v6p0116c1s v6p0128c1s
Macmillan, Michael v6p0046c2s
McMillan, T. v2p0260c1s
v2p0434c1s v3p0252c2s v4p0401c1s
v4p0488c2s v4p0513c1s v6p0538c1s
v6p0547c1s v6p0547c2s v6p0574c1s
v6p0574c2s
McMillan, W. v1p0591c2s
v4p0427c2s v4p0446c1s
McMillan, W.G. v3p0153c1s
v3p0357c1s
McMillen, W.F. v6p0626c2s
M'Millin, B. et al. v4p0563c2s
MacMorland, P. v1p0728c1s
Macmullen, J. v2p0111c1s
MacMullen, J. v2p0094c1s
v2p0243c1s v4p0241c2s
MacMullen, W. v6p0538c1s
MacMunn, C.A. v2p0083c1s
McMunn, C.A. v2p0080c1s
Macmunn, G.F. v6p0314c2s
MacMunn, G.F. v5p0619c1s
v6p0162c2s v6p0169c1s v6p0265c2s
v6p0403c2s v6p0465c2s v6p0593c1s
McMunn, G.F. v6p0111c2s
v6p0488c2s
MacMurchy, M. v5p0227c1s
v5p0353c2s v5p0453c1s v5p0454c2s
v6p0255c2s
McMurdo, Gen. v3p0212c2s
M'Murdy, R. v1p0158c1s
McMurkie, R.C. v3p0067c2s
McMurray, C.A. v4p0222c1s
McMurray, F.M. v4p0128c1s
v4p0287c2s
McMurrich, J.P. v5p0018c2s
v5p0077c1s
McMurrich, W.B. v1p0640c1s
McMurry, F.M. v6p0199c2s
McMurtie, W. v4p0283c2s
McMurtrie, J. v2p0399c2s
McMurtrie, R.C. v2p0113c2s
McMurtrie, W. v5p0103c2s
v6p0112c1s
McMurtry, L.S. v6p0017c2s
McMurtry, W.J. v3p0392c2s
McMurtry, W.J. and Earle, M.L.
v3p0392c2s
Macnab, B.A. v5p0388c2s
MacNab, F. v4p0485c2s
v6p0348c2s v6p0661c2s
McNab, Frances v4p0170c2s
v4p0451c2s
Macnab, L. v5p0327c1s
McNab, L. v4p0124c1s
Macnab, P. v4p0094c1s
v4p0570c2s
MacNab, P. v4p0625c2s
McNab, P. and Jackson, M.P.
v4p0029c1s
McNab, W.R. (M') v1p0153c1s
v1p1182c1s v1p0321c2s v1p0470c2s
v1p0493c1s v1p0813c1s v1p1014c2s
v1p1015c2s v1p1182c1s v1p1197c1s
McNabb, F.J. v6p0536c2s
McNabb, V. v6p0638c1s
v6p0662c2s
McNabb, V.J. v6p0587c2s
McNabb, Vincent v6p0161c2s
Macnaghten et al. v5p0623c1s
Macnaghten, R.E. v2p0434c1s
v3p0348c2s v3p0423c2s v5p0187c1s
v6p0042c1s v6p0141c1s v6p0216c2s
v6p0240c2s v6p0250c2s v6p0310c2s
v6p0637c2s
MacNaghten, R.E. v6p0522c2s
v6p0637c2s
McNair, F.W. v6p0504c1s
McNair, J.F.A. v6p0468c2s
McNair, T.M. v3p0227c1s
McNally, A. v6p0531c1s
McNally, D.R. v3p0295c2s
McNamara v3p0120c1s
v3p0433c2s
MacNamara, J.F. v4p0387c2s
McNamara, J.J. v6p0507c2s
Macnamara, L. v5p0482c1s
McNamara, M. v1p0083c2s
Macnamara, N.C. v5p0141c2s
v6p0111c2s v6p0375c2s
McNamara, N.C. v5p0075c1s
Macnamara, T.J. v3p0129c1s
v4p0340c1s v4p0480c1s v4p0512c1s
v4p0566c1s v5p0177c2m v5p0346c1s
v5p0511c1s v6p0117c1s v6p0190c1s
v6p0191c1m v6p0191c2m v6p0192c1s
v6p0284c2s v6p0311c1s v6p0326c1s
MacNamara, T.J. v3p0378c1s
v6p0106c2s v6p0581c1s
McNamara, T.J. v4p0169c2s
v4p0170c1s
Macnamara, T.J. et al. ... v6p0191c2s
McNary, S.J. v4p0031c2s
v4p0051c2s
McNaught, W.G. v4p0389c2s
McNaught, W.K. v6p0519c2s
Macnaughton, C. v4p0306c2s
MacNaughton, C. v6p0053c2s
v6p0316c2s
Macnaughton, D.A. v6p0581c2s
McNaughton, J.H. v2p0219c1s
Macnaughton, S. v6p0145c2s
v6p0311c1s
McNeal, A.J. and Mikell, W.E.
v6p0170c1s
MacNeal, J. v5p0095c1s
v5p0140c1s v5p0262c2s
McNeal, M. v5p0151c2s
v5p0561c1s
McNeal, M.I. v4p0381c1s
v5p0013c2s v5p0554c2s
McNeel, J.G. v6p0164c2s
McNeil, A.H. v5p0337c1s
Macneil, H. v1p0209c1s
McNeil, R.J. v4p0616c2s
McNeile, H. v1p0689c2s
v1p1120c1s
McNeill, A. v1p0044c1s
v1p0155c2s v1p1029c1s
MacNeill, D. v3p0060c2s
McNeill, G.E. v3p0239c1s
McNeill, G.E. and Foster, F.K.
v6p0652c1s
M'Neill, G.P. v3p0203c2s
McNeill, H. v1p0117c2s
MacNeill, J.G.S. v5p0162c2s
v5p0296c2m
MacNeill, J.G.Swift v4p0290c1s
McNeill, J.G.Swift v4p0266c1s
McNeill, M. v2p0404c1s
MacNeill, N. v2p0213c1s
v2p0250c1s
McNeill, R. v5p0489c2s
v5p0635c2s v6p0101c2s v6p0241c1s
v6p0243c2m v6p0256c1s v6p0257c2s
v6p0481c1s
McNeill, R. and Traill, H.D.
v5p0278c2s
McNeill, R.J. v4p0333c1s
McNellis, J. v6p0519c2s
Macnicol, D.C. v4p0581c2s
Macnicoll, A.N. v1p0170c1s
v2p0090c2s v4p0167c1s
McNiece, R.G. v1p0872c1s
v3p0288c1m v3p0338c1s v3p0446c1m
MacNish, E. v5p0579c1s
Macnish, N. v1p0950c1s
Macnish, R. v1p0826c2s
Macniver, L. v6p0695c1s
MacNutt, F.A.S. v2p0275c2s
v2p0296c1s
McNutt, G.L. v5p0169c2s
v6p0518c2s
McNutt, Geo.L. v6p0113c2s
Macoane, S.M. v3p0190c2s
Macoane, S.M. and Crocker, U.H.
v3p0315c2s
Macomb, A. v5p0454c1s
Macomber, D.O. v1p1427c1s
Macomber, J.K. v5p0392c1s
Macomber, W. v4p0596c2s
Macomber, W.W. v1p0537c1s
Macon, J. v2p0140c2s
Maconachie, J.K. v5p0610c2s
Maconachie, R. v5p0286c2s
Maconochie, Capt. v1p0297c1s
v1p0925c2s
McOnot, M.E. v5p0409c2s
Macoun, J. and Gibson, J.. v1p0617c2s
McOwan, E. v6p0457c2s
Macphail, A. v5p0061c1s
v5p0302c1s
MacPhail, J.A. v3p0053c2s
v3p0177c2s v4p0035c2s
MacPhail, M. v4p0328c1s
v5p0261c1s
McPhail, R. v2p0324c2s
v2p0441c2s
Macphail, S.R. v2p0470c1s
McPheeters, W.M. v4p0053c1s
v4p0055c1s v6p0344c1s
McPhelim, E.J. v2p0105c2s
v2p0446c1s
Macpherson, A. v1p1251c1s
v2p0202c2s
McPherson, A. v2p0191c1s
Macpherson, C. v6p0577c2s
Macpherson, D. v5p0508c2s
Macpherson, E. v4p0234c1s
v4p0422c2s v4p0560c2s v6p0395c2s
v6p0541c1s
MacPherson, E. v5p0399c2s
McPherson, E. v1p0240c1s
v1p0442c2s v1p0639c1s v2p0198c2s
Macpherson, H. v6p0552c1s
v6p0577c2s v6p0609c2s
Macpherson, H., jr. v6p0670c2s
MacPherson, H.A. v4p0438c2s
MacPherson, H.O. v6p0596c2s
Macpherson, Hector, jr. .. v6p0038c1s
MacPherson, Hector, jr. .. v6p0630c2s
Macpherson, J. v2p0113c2m
v2p0295c2s v5p0236c1s v5p0268c2s
v5p0306c1s v5p0436c1m v5p0511c2s
v5p0627c1s v5p0645c1s
McPherson, J. v4p0483c2s
Macpherson, J.A. v5p0003c2s
McPherson, J.B. v5p0232c2s
McPherson, J.D. v4p0301c1s
McPherson, J.G. v3p0038c2s
v3p0116c2s v3p0124c2s v3p0125c1s
v3p0148c1s v3p0192c1s v4p0072c2s
v4p0120c1s v4p0124c2s v4p0204c2s
v4p0207c1s v4p0251c2s v4p0313c1s
v4p0472c2s v4p0531c1m v4p0557c2s
v5p0023c1s v5p0155c1s v5p0239c1s
v5p0492c1s v6p0178c1s v6p0211c2s
v6p0577c1s
McPherson, J.H.T. v3p0248c1s
Macpherson, J.R. v4p0299c2s
Macpherson, K.L. v6p0098c1s
v6p0179c2s
McPherson, L.G. v4p0096c2s
v4p0134c2s v4p0199c1s v4p0378c2s
v4p0393c2s v4p0585c2s v6p0610c1s
Macpherson, N., jr. v6p0148c2s
MacPherson, T.E. v6p0113c2s
McPherson, W. v5p0077c1s
Macpherson, W.C. v4p0433c1s
McPherson, W.C. v6p0194c2s
McPike, E.F. v6p0065c2m
v6p0082c1s
McPike, H.G. v6p0377c2s
McQuaid, B.J. v1p1063c2s
v2p0357c1s v3p0358c2s v3p0378c2s
McQuaid, L. v5p0374c2s
McQuaid, R.F. v5p0132c1s
Macqueary, H. v4p0188c1s
v4p0450c2s
MacQueary, H. v3p0390c1s
v4p0335c1s v4p0460c2s
Macqueary, T.H. v6p0574c2s
MacQueen, H. v5p0588c2s
M'Queen, J. v1p0011c1s
v1p0544c1s v1p0921c2s v1p1196c1s
Macqueen, P. v6p0494c2s
MacQueen, P. v4p0073c1s
v4p0355c1s v4p0437c2s v4p0509c1s
v5p0005c2s v5p0006c1s v5p0068c2s
v5p0160c2s v5p0266c1s v5p0360c1m
v5p0445c1m v5p0446c1m v5p0460c2s
v5p0501c2s v5p0508c2s v5p0542c1s
v5p0543c1s v5p0544c1s v5p0589c1s
v5p0603c1s v6p0477c1s
McQueen, P. v5p0268c1s
v5p0328c1s v6p0392c2s
MacQueen, P. and Smith, J.H.
v4p0004c1s
MacQueen, Peter v5p0134c1s
McQueen, W. v2p0169c2s
v2p0391c1s
McQuhae, P. v1p0167c2s
McQuillin, E. v2p0340c2s
v3p0355c2s v3p0436c1s v5p0391c2s
v5p0392c1s
Macquoid, G. and Macquoid, K.S.
v4p0406c1s
Macquoid, G.S. v3p0112c1s
v3p0474c2s
Macquoid, K. v4p0521c2s
v5p0047c2s
Macquoid, K.S. v1p0026c2s
v1p0056c2m v1p0082c2s v1p0102c2s
v1p0115c2m v1p0159c1s v1p0166c1s
v1p0189c1s v1p0263c2s v1p0361c1s
v1p0366c1s v1p0444c2s v1p0449c2s
v1p0452c1s v1p0462c1s v1p0483c1s
v1p0680c1s v1p0693c1s v1p0725c1s
v1p0735c2s v1p0774c2s v1p0785c1s
v1p0800c2s v1p0824c1s v1p0840c1s
v1p0875c2s v1p0888c2s v1p0889c1s
v1p0906c2s v1p0921c1s v1p0979c2s
v1p1031c2s v1p1127c1s v1p1143c2s
v1p1144c2s v1p1257c2s v1p1258c1s
v1p1259c1s v1p1261c1s v1p1316c1s
v1p1335c2s v2p0001c1s v2p0051c1m
v2p0076c1s v2p0078c1s v2p0163c2m
v2p0200c2s v2p0216c1s v2p0252c2s
v2p0258c2s v2p0275c2s v2p0278c2s
v2p0283c2s v2p0288c2s v2p0314c2s

v2p0373c1s v2p0374c1s v2p0375c1s
v2p0450c2s v2p0451c1s v2p0470c1s
v2p0472c1s v2p0482c1m v3p0014c2s
v3p0015c2s v3p0109c2s v3p0305c2s
v3p0413c2s v4p0173c2s v4p0295c2s
v5p0441c2s v5p0555c1s v5p0578c1s
v6p0221c1s
Macquoid, K.S. and Macquoid, G.
v4p0406c1s
Macquoid, Mrs. v4p0321c1s
Macquoid, P. v5p0529c2s
v6p0503c1s v6p0595c1s
Macquoid, P.R. v6p0594c2s
Macquoid, T.R. v1p0202c1s
v4p0065c2s v4p0074c1s v4p0569c2s
MacRae, A. v3p0196c1s
McRae, A.L. and Trowbridge, J.
v2p0213c2s
McRae, C. v4p0516c1s
Macrae, C.C. v2p0217c1s
Macrae, D. v6p0202c2s
Macrane, S.M. v5p0437c1s
Macrasty, H.W. v6p0041c1s
Macray, E.L. v6p0510c1s
Macray, W.D. v4p0150c2s
v4p0426c2s v4p0574c1s v5p0021c2s
v6p0053c2s
M'Rea, W.C. v1p1289c2s
McReynolds, S. v6p0451c1s
MacRitchie, D. v4p0008c2s
v4p0369c2s v4p0468c1m v5p0389c1m
v5p0450c2m v5p0452c2s v5p0515c2s
v5p0597c2s v6p0256c2s v6p0656c2s
MacRitchie, W. v5p0346c2s
McRoss, L. v6p0279c2s
Macrosty, H. v6p0263c2s
Macrosty, H.W. v5p0384c1s
v5p0615c2s v6p0240c2s v6p0328c2s
v6p0417c2s v6p0520c1s v6p0659c1s
Macrosty, H.W. and Hobson, S.G.
v5p0552c1s
MacRury, C.W. v5p0287c1s
McShan, J.A. v6p0166c2s
McSherry, G.W. v4p0477c2s
v5p0114c2s
McSherry, J. v1p0775c2s
McSherry, R. v1p0171c2s
v1p0807c2s v1p0832c2m
McSorley, H. v3p0342c1s
McSorley, J. v5p0265c2s
v5p0275c2s v5p0349c1s v5p0350c2s
v5p0400c2m v5p0436c1s v5p0483c2s
v5p0493c1s v6p0108c2s v6p0111c2s
v6p0125c2s v6p0342c1s v6p0348c2s
v6p0409c1s v6p0468c1s v6p0513c2s
v6p0537c2s v6p0547c2m v6p0548c1s
v6p0604c2s v6p0643c1s
McSorley, Joseph v6p0185c1s
McSparran, J. v2p0069c2s
McSweeney, Z.F. v6p0308c2s
McSweeny, E. v1p0127c1s
v2p0219c2s v2p0257c2s v2p0335c2s
v2p0375c1s v2p0482c2s v3p0054c2s
v3p0346c2s v3p0364c2s v3p0399c1s
v3p0467c1s
McSweeny, E.F.X. v1p0434c2s
v2p0295c1m v3p0049c1s
McSweeny, P.F. v2p0388c2s
v3p0364c1s v3p0378c1s v3p0378c2s
v3p0397c2s v4p0557c1s v4p0568c1s
MacSwiney, J. v3p0042c1s
McSwiney, J. (M') v1p0117c1s
v1p0307c2s v1p0314c2s v1p0682c1s
v1p0893c2s v1p1023c2s v1p1092c2s
v1p1121c1s
McTaggart, J.E. v4p0158c2s
v4p0253c1m v4p0577c1s v4p0609c1s
v5p0261c1m v5p0279c1s v5p0499c1s
v5p0536c2s v6p0286c1s v6p0514c1s
v6p0533c1s v6p0554c1s v6p0593c2s
M'Taggart, J.Ellis v6p0057c2s
McTavish, N. v5p0605c2s
McTeague, P. v1p0587c1s
v1p0663c1s v1p0811c2s v1p1231c2s
v1p1393c1s
Mactear and Bald v1p1147c1s
Mactear, J. v1p1040c2s
v3p0069c2s
McTear, J.C. v6p0246c1s
McTear, J.S. v5p0235c2s
v6p0081c1s
McTighe, T.J. v4p0175c2s
Macurdy, Theodosia et al.. v6p0074c2s
McVail, J.C. v6p0673c2s
Macvane, E. v6p0295c2s
Macvane, S.M. v2p0182c1s
v2p0347c2s v2p0464c1s v3p0345c1s
v3p0345c2s v3p0446c2s v3p0452c1s
v4p0088c1s v4p0167c2s v4p0355c2s
v4p0563c1s v5p0215c2s v5p0587c2s
MacVane, S.M. v4p0599c2s
McVane, S.M. v4p0579c2s
Macvane, S.M. and Godkin, E.L.
v4p0602c1s
MacVannel, J.A. v6p0190c1s
McVea, E.W. v6p0680c1s
MacVeagh, F. v1p0443c1s
v4p0115c2s
McVeagh, F. v4p0100c2s
MacVeagh, J. v3p0219c2s
v4p0227c1s
MacVeagh, W. v1p0860c2s
v1p0987c1s v2p0353c1s v3p0114c2s
v5p0603c1s v6p0026c2m v6p0487c2m
v6p0634c1s v6p0676c1s
McVeagh, W. and Davis, H.. v6p0676c1s
McVeigh, W. v5p0434c2s
McVey, A.G. v3p0060c1s
McVey, F.L. v4p0044c2s
v4p0429c1s v4p0453c1s v4p0472c1s
v4p0472c2s v5p0134c2s v5p0136c1s
v5p0321c1s v5p0383c1s v5p0465c2s
v5p0526c2s v5p0559c2s v5p0580c2m
v5p0593c2s v6p0196c2s v6p0318c2s
v6p0411c1s v6p0591c1m v6p0613c1s
v6p0616c1s v6p0684c1s
McVicar, C.W. v3p0076c2s
MacVicar, D.H. v2p0065c2s
v2p0351c2s v2p0376c2s v4p0488c2s
MacVicar, H. and Caven, W.
v5p0464c1s
Macvicar, J.G. v1p1001c2s
MacVicar, M. v4p0171c1s
McVickar, G. v1p0705c2s
McVickar, H.W. v5p0485c2s
McVickar, J. v1p1060c1s
McVickar, W.A. v1p0378c2s
McVicker, A. v1p0430c1s
MacVicker, D.H. v3p0397c2s
McVicker, Dr. v1p0410c2s
McVoy, D. v6p0200c1s
McWhorter, A. v1p0356c2s
v1p0383c1s v1p0470c2s v1p0529c1s
McWhorter, G.C. (M') v1p0118c2s
v1p0123c2s v1p0596c2s v1p1206c2s
v1p1326c1s
Macy, C. v5p0070c1s
Macy, J. v2p0224c2s
v4p0116c2s v4p0181c1s v4p0195c1s
v4p0428c1s v4p0560c2s v5p0158c1s
v5p0241c1s
Macy, J.A. v5p0031c1s
v5p0083c2s v5p0252c1s v5p0294c2s
v5p0328c1s v5p0582c1s v6p0145c1s
v6p0345c2s v6p0456c1s v6p0562c2s
Macy, J.E. v6p0240c2s
Macy, John A. v6p0124c2s
Madan, A.C. v6p0007c2s
Madan, F. v2p0382c2s
v2p0444c2s v3p0042c2s v3p0053c1m
v3p0124c1s v4p0181c2s v4p0459c2s
v5p0426c1s
Madan, F. and Rashdall, H.
v3p0316c1s
Madan, Falconer v4p0058c1s
Madan, H.G. v1p1291c2s
v2p0050c1s v2p0199c1m v2p0320c1m
v2p0347c1s v2p0413c1s v3p0092c2s
v3p0303c2s v3p0344c2s
Madden, A.G. v5p0088c2s
Madden, D.O. v1p0037c2s
Madden, E.A. v4p0011c1s
v5p0415c2s v5p0416c1s
Madden, E.F. v1p0704c1s
v2p0429c1s
Madden, F. v1p0226c2m
v1p0585c1s v1p1129c1s v1p1227c1s
v1p1327c1s
Madden, F., Sir v1p0155c1s
v1p0403c1s v1p0419c1s v1p0585c1s
v1p0928c2s v1p1027c2s v1p1186c2s
v1p1385c1s v1p1385c2s v1p1414c1s
Madden, F.W. v1p0043c1s
Madden, J. v4p0363c1s
v5p0011c2s v5p0151c1s v5p0641c2s
Madden, W.J. v6p0258c1s
v6p0601c1s
Maddison, A.R. v4p0333c1s
Maddison, F. v5p0136c1s
v5p0589c1s v6p0148c2s
Maddock, A.E. v5p0158c1s
v5p0350c2s v5p0366c1s v6p0145c2s
Maddren, A.G. v5p0062c1s
Madeleine, J. v5p0355c1s
Madeley, E. v6p0060c2s
v6p0139c1m v6p0182c2s
Madge, J. v5p0485c2s
Madge, J.H. v2p0448c1s
Madge, T. v1p0346c1s
Madge, W.C. v5p0286c2s
Madison, F. v6p0148c2s
v6p0652c1s
Madison, J. v1p0015c1s
Madison, M. v5p0224c1s
v5p0301c2s
Madison, W.C. v5p0372c2s
Madoc, F. v3p0112c2s
v3p0144c2s v3p0313c1s v3p0432c2s
v4p0198c1s v4p0341c1s v4p0390c2s
v4p0423c1s v4p0476c1s v5p0277c1s
Madras, H. v6p0313c2s
Maedler, J.H. v1p0375c2s
Maedler, J.H. and Beer, W.
v1p0866c1s
Maes, C.P. v2p0099c2s
Maes, J.T. v2p0163c2s
Maeterlinck, M. v4p0011c1s
v4p0287c2s v4p0433c1s v4p0516c1s
v4p0523c2s v5p0051c2s v5p0167c2s
v5p0187c1s v5p0218c1s v5p0313c1s
v5p0316c2s v5p0396c2s v6p0056c1s
v6p0125c1s v6p0167c1s v6p0178c1s
v6p0228c2s v6p0229c2s v6p0230c1m
v6p0233c2s v6p0245c1s v6p0309c1s
v6p0346c2s v6p0348c2s v6p0351c2s
v6p0362c2s v6p0365c2s v6p0388c1s
v6p0408c1s v6p0425c2s v6p0428c2s
v6p0432c1s v6p0471c2s v6p0483c1s
v6p0549c1s v6p0587c2s v6p0595c2s
v6p0624c1s
Maeterlinck, Maurice v6p0685c1s
Maffitt, J.N. v4p0064c1s
Magdala, Napier of v5p0097c2s
v5p0286c2s
Magee, K. v6p0071c2s
Magee, L.J. v5p0141c2s
v5p0200c1s v5p0231c1m
Magee, Louis J. v6p0015c1s
v6p0252c2s
Magee, M.J. v6p0326c2s
Magee, P. v6p0140c1s
Magee, T. v1p1188c1s
v3p0078c2s v4p0209c1s v5p0316c2s
v5p0318c2s v6p0394c2s v6p0677c2s
Magee, W., jr. v4p0416c1s
v5p0447c1s
Magee, W.C. v1p0654c1s
v1p1056c2s v2p0084c2s v2p0318c2s
v3p0040c1s v3p0082c2s v3p0166c2s
v3p0250c1s v3p0313c1s v3p0324c1s
v3p0398c2s v3p0408c1s
Magee, W.J. v5p0076c2s
Magevney, E. v4p0394c2s
v5p0177c2s v5p0178c1s
Magie, B.C., jr. v1p0258c1s
Magie, L.D.W. v5p0184c1s
Magie, W.F. v2p0260c1s
v5p0442c2s v5p0447c1s v6p0204c1s
v6p0603c1s
Magill, D. v2p0159c1s
v2p0282c1s
Magill, E.H. v3p0306c2s
v4p0171c2s v5p0381c1s
Magill, M.T. v2p0175c1s
v2p0404c1s
Magill, S.W. v1p0898c1s
v1p1208c2s
Maginn, W. v1p0183c2s
v1p0419c1s v1p0600c1s v1p0601c1s
v1p1185c2s v1p1187c1s v1p1226c2s
v1p1398c1s
Maginnis, C.D. v5p0026c1s
v6p0126c2s
Maginnis, J.P. v6p0488c1s
Maginnis, J.S. v1p0044c1s
v1p0528c1s
Magister, Artium v6p0193c2s
Magitot, E. v5p0366c1s
Magniac, C. v2p0254c1s
v2p0423c1s v3p0414c1s
Magniac, C.V. v6p0646c1s
Magnus, G.G. v6p0380c2s
Magnus, J. v2p0089c2s
v3p0334c2s v3p0406c1s
Magnus, K. v2p0200c1s
v3p0074c1s v6p0306c2s
Magnus, Kate v6p0532c1s
Magnus, L. v4p0614c1s
v5p0230c1s v5p0230c2s v5p0268c2s
v6p0255c1s v6p0286c1s v6p0343c2s
v6p0347c1s
Magnus, Lady v3p0468c2s
v4p0156c1s v4p0306c1s v4p0408c2s
v5p0201c2s v5p0342c2s v5p0386c1s
Magnus, Laurie v6p0685c2s
Magnus, Mrs. v2p0234c2s
Magnus, P. v1p0690c2s
v2p0275c2s v3p0094c1s v3p0267c1s
v3p0422c2s v4p0147c2s v4p0276c1s
v4p0566c2s v5p0584c1s v6p0343c1s
Magnus, P., Sir v3p0094c1s
v4p0354c1s v5p0584c2s v6p0635c2s
Magnusson, E. v2p0257c1m
v4p0168c1s v5p0585c1s
Magnusson, E. and Morris, W.
v1p1141c2s
Magnusson, P.M.C. v6p0606c1s
v6p0651c1s
Magnusson, S. and Morris, W.
v4p0253c1s
Magonigle, H.V. v5p0325c2s
Magoon, C.E. v6p0670c1s
Magoon, E.L. v1p0282c2s
v1p0553c2s v1p0585c2s v1p0716c1s
v1p0868c1s v1p0884c2s
Magoun, G.A. v1p1081c2s
Magoun, G.F. v1p0017c2s
v1p0052c2m v1p0074c2s v1p0096c1s
v1p0275c1s v1p0275c2s v1p0276c1s
v1p0290c2s v1p0357c2s v1p0359c1s
v1p0385c1s v1p0389c2s v1p0393c2s
v1p0394c1s v1p0427c1s v1p0440c2s
v1p0447c2s v1p0486c1s v1p0650c2s
v1p0652c1m v1p0700c1s v1p0807c2s
v1p0808c1s v1p0847c2s v1p0903c2s
v1p1001c1s v1p1086c2s v1p1099c1s
v1p1267c1s v1p1301c2s v1p1303c1s
v2p0109c2s v2p0117c1s v2p0132c2s
v2p0147c1s v2p0251c1s v2p0279c1s
v2p0307c1s v3p0026c1m v3p0040c2s

v3p0091c1s v3p0107c2s v3p0230c2s
v3p0252c2s v3p0354c1s v4p0381c1s
v4p0431c1m v4p0489
Magoun, G.T. v3p0404c1s
Magoun, H.W. v3p0025c1s
v3p0466c2s v5p0023c2s v5p0265c2s
v6p0413c1s v6p0519c2s
Magrath, E.S. v1p0750c1s
Magrath, V.W. v6p0126c2s
Magrini, E. v6p0416c1s
Magruder, A.B. v1p0309c1s
v1p0750c1s v1p0994c2s
Magruder, J. v1p1438c2s
v3p0025c1s v3p0200c1s v3p0338c1s
v4p0459c1s v5p0155c1s v6p0360c1s
v6p0639c1s
Magruder, J.W. v5p0117c2s
Magruder, Julia v6p0281c1s
v6p0644c2s
Magruder, W.T. v6p0015c1s
v6p0015c2s v6p0408c1s
Magrutor, W. v6p0606c2s
Maguire, A.B. v5p0574c2s
Maguire, C.M. v5p0618c2s
Maguire, E. v5p0193c2s
Maguire, F., jr. v1p0511c2s
Maguire, H.M. v5p0394c2s
Maguire, J.D. v6p0340c2s
v6p0381c2s v6p0679c2m
Maguire, J.M. v6p0035c1s
v6p0253c2s v6p0442c1s
Maguire, M., Dr. v6p0265c2s
v6p0580c1s
Maguire, T.M. v4p0190c1s
v5p0189c2s v5p0244c1s v5p0246c1s
v5p0251c2s v5p0359c2s v5p0375c2s
v5p0556c1s v5p0563c1s v5p0619c2s
v6p0031c2s v6p0083c1s v6p0194c2s
v6p0319c1s v6p0398c2s v6p0399c1s
v6p0490c2s v6p0557c2s v6p0620c2s
v6p0686c1s v6p0691c2s
Maguire, W.H. v3p0191c1s
v3p0201c2s v3p0286c1s v4p0087c2s
v4p0190c1s v4p0422c2s v4p0426c2s
Magurn, A. v6p0594c1s
Magwaza, M. v1p0213c2s
Mahaffy and Lapcho v4p0544c2s
Mahaffy, A. v4p0501c2s
Mahaffy, A.W. v4p0549c2s
Mahaffy, J.P. v1p0051c2s
v1p0553c1s v1p0553c2s v1p0564c2s
v1p0600c1s v1p0702c1s v1p0730c1s
v1p0740c2s v1p0760c2s v1p0889c1s
v1p0941c2s v1p1255c1s v1p1326c1s
v1p1327c1s v2p0003c2s v2p0116c2s
v2p0154c2s v2p0173c1s v2p0190c1s
v2p0190c2s v2p0206c2m v2p0211c2s
v2p0227c1s v2p0232c1s v2p0364c2s
v2p0388c1s v2p0402c2s v2p0410c1s
v2p0441c2s v2p0442c1s v2p0447c2s
v3p0025c2m v3p0065c1s v3p0089c2s
v3p0129c2s v3p0183c2m v3p0184c1m
v3p0208c1s v3p0219c2m v3p0225c1m
v3p0267c1s v3p0271c2s v3p0312c1s
v3p0377c1s v3p0431c2s v4p0023c1s
v4p0130c2s v4p0131c2s v4p0134c1s
v4p0163c1s v4p0169c2s v4p0171c1s
v4p0173c1s v4p0224c2s v4p0235c1s
v4p0287c2s v4p0291c1s v4p0320c2s
v4p0393c2s v4p0404c2s v4p0409c1m
v4p0424c2m v4p0430c2s v4p0465c2s
v4p0549c2s v4p0584c1s v4p0636c2s
v5p0050c1s v5p0178c1s v5p0178c2s
v5p0291c2s v5p0296c2s v5p0297c2s
v5p0533c2s v5p0554c1s v6p0177c1s
Mahaim, E. v4p0050c1s
v4p0322c2s v5p0052c2s v5p0485c2s
v6p0528c2s v6p0621c2s v6p0682c1s
Mahan, A. v1p0241c1s
v1p0989c2s v1p1300c2s
Mahan, A.J. v6p0668c2s
Mahan, A.T. v3p0442c1s
v4p0088c1s v4p0147c2s v4p0192c1s
v4p0250c2s v4p0267c2s v4p0395c2s
v4p0397c2s v4p0499c2s v4p0503c2s
v4p0595c1m v4p0635c1s v5p0034c1s
v5p0068c1s v5p0094c2s v5p0101c1s
v5p0136c2s v5p0310c1s v5p0373c2s
v5p0401c2m v5p0404c1m v5p0411c2s
v5p0437c2s v5p0499c1s v5p0543c1m
v5p0585c1s v5p0588c1m v5p0601c1s
v5p0603c1s v6p0255c1s v6p0267c1s
v6p0293c1s v6p0310c1s v6p0416c2s
v6p0445c1s v6p0445c2s v6p0449c1m
v6p0463c1s v6p0489c2s v6p0561c1m
v6p0567c1s v6p0669c1s v6p0685c1s
Mahan, A.T. and Beresford, C.
v4p0017c2s
Mahan, A.T. and Long, J.D.
v6p0567c1s
Mahan, A.T. and Tilton, W.F.
v5p0543c1s
Mahan, A.T. et al. v4p0180c1s
Mahan, D.H. v1p0478c1s
v1p1401c2s
Mahan, F.A. v4p0438c1s
v5p0032c1s
Mahan, M. v1p0071c2s
v1p0254c1s v1p0328c2s
Mahany, R.B. v4p0378c2s
Maharajah, Gaekwar v5p0196c2s
Mahe, E. v3p0037c1s
v3p0164c1s
Maher, F. v4p0504c2s
Maher, M. v3p0038c2s
v3p0171c1s v3p0208c1s v3p0330c1s
v4p0261c1s v6p0363c1s v6p0396c2s
v6p0575c2s
Mahillon, L. v2p0094c2s
Mahler, P. v6p0228c1s
Mahler, P. and
Thwaite, B.H.
v4p0211c2s
v4p0366c2s
Mahly, J. v1p0281c1s
Mahomed, F.A. and Galton, F.
v2p0100c2s
Mahon, J.L. v3p0183c1s
v4p0239c1s v4p0315c2s
Mahon, J.L. and Hammill, F.
v3p0434c2s
Mahon, K.J. v3p0170c1s
Mahon, Lord v1p0475c2s
v1p0692c1s v1p0795c2s v1p0807c1s
v1p1243c1s v1p1279c2s
Mahon, R.J. v3p0241c1s
v5p0120c1s
Mahon, R.W. v4p0094c1s
Mahon, S. v6p0440c2s
v6p0596c2s
Mahon, Shiela v6p0589c1s
v6p0665c1s
Mahone, W. et al. v3p0031c1s
Mahoney, F. v1p0446c1s
v1p1059c1s
Mahoney, F. et al. v1p0446c1s
Mahoney, F.S. v1p0941c2s
Mahony, Agnes P. v6p0370c1s
Mahony, Lt.-Col. v3p0068c1s
v3p0245c2s v4p0198c2s
Mahony, R.J. v2p0226c2s
Mahood, H.E. v5p0332c2s
Mahood, W., Mrs. v5p0193c1s
Maier, j. v2p0138c1s
Mailliau, E. v4p0196c1s
Maimon, B. v1p0581c2s
v2p0199c2s
Main, A. v1p0082c1s
v1p0293c1s v1p0826c1s v1p0839c1s
v1p1001c1s v1p1054c1s
Main, A. and Hodgson, S.H.
v1p0271c2s
Main, C.T. v4p0613c2s
v5p0360c2s
Main, G.P. v5p0372c2s
Main, J.F. v2p0141c1s
Main, J.H.T. v5p0249c2s
v5p0295c1s v6p0136c1s
Main, P.T. v1p0467c1s
Main, R. v1p0547c2s
v2p0283c2s
Maindron, M. v3p0121c2s
Maine, C.S. v1p0467c2s
v2p0134c2s
v3p0101c2s
Maine, H. v5p0468c2s
Maine, H.C. v2p0404c2s
v4p0097c2s v6p0110c1s
Maine, H.S. v1p0450c1s
v1p0631c1s v1p0707c2s v2p0243c1s
v2p0423c2s
Maine, H.S., Sir v1p0271c1s
v1p1209c1s v2p0115c2s
Mainer, R.H. v5p0392c2s
v6p0662c2s
Mainetty, L.P. v5p0206c2s
Mains, G.P. v3p0276c2s
v4p0016c2s v4p0116c1s v6p0397c1s
Mains, W.C. v5p0158c2s
v6p0533c1s
Mainzer, Dr. v1p0882c1s
Mair, A. v2p0072c2s
v2p0291c1m v2p0450c2s v3p0081c1s
v3p0093c1s v3p0258c2s
Mair, C. v1p0796c2s
Mair, G.R. v5p0183c1s
Mair, R.J.B. v5p0302c2s
v5p0538c1s v6p0256c1m
Mair, R.J.Byford v5p0319c2s
Mair, W. v6p0266c1s
v6p0577c2m
Mairet, Jeanne v6p0239c1s
v6p0367c2s
Maistre, Count de v1p0643c1s
Maistre, G.H.Le v4p0079c2s
Maistre, J.de v1p1141c1s
Maistre, X.de v1p0738c1s
v1p1041c2s
Maitland, A. v5p0469c2s
Maitland, A.C. v2p0062c2s
v2p0101c1m v3p0251c2s v4p0451c2s
Maitland, C. v1p0205c2s
Maitland, Col. v2p0323c1s
v3p0313c2s
Maitland, E. v1p0060c2s
v1p0251c1s v1p0418c2s v1p0421c2s
v1p0790c1s v1p1023c1s v1p1166c1s
v1p1318c2s v5p0536c2s
Maitland, E.A. v5p0379c2s
Maitland, E.F. v5p0531c1s
v5p0578c2s
Maitland, F., Mrs. v3p0209c2s
Maitland, F.M. v3p0034c1s
v3p0228c1s v3p0254c1m
Maitland, F.W. v1p0361c2s
v1p1066c1s v1p1293c2s v2p0251c1s
v2p0408c2s v3p0094c2s v3p0220c1s
v3p0241c2s v3p0246c1s v3p0342c2s
v3p0395c1s v3p0414c2s v4p0068c1s
v4p0087c2s v4p0097c2s v4p0127c2s
v4p0213c1s v4p0254c1s v4p0318c1s
v4p0380c2s v4p0480c1s v4p0513c2m
v4p0584c1s v4p0621c1s v4p0621c2s
v5p0092c2s v5p0138c1s v5p0186c2s
v5p0352c2s v5p0362c2s v5p0558c1s
v5p0606c2s v6p0201c1s v6p0253c2s
Maitland, H. v1p1013c2s
Maitland, J.A. v1p0535c1s
v1p1396c1s
Maitland, J.A.F. v3p0174c2s
v3p0293c1m v4p0194c1s v4p0388c1s
v4p0389c1s v4p0415c1s v4p0574c1s
v5p0422c1s v5p0560c1s v6p0394c1s
v6p0468c1s v6p0648c2s
Maitland, J.A.Fuller v4p0390c1s
Maitland, M. v5p0002c2s
v6p0157c1s
Maitland, M.M. v1p0696c1s
v1p1082c1s v2p0244c2s v2p0383c2s
Maitland, T. v1p1021c2s
v1p1128c2s
Maitland, T.W. v5p0145c2s
Maitland, W. v3p0450c1s
v3p0465c2s v4p0195c1m v4p0462c2s
v6p0006c2s v6p0120c1s
Maitre, H. v6p0542c2s
Majendie, M., Lady v1p1080c1s
v2p0321c2s v4p0142c1s v4p0552c2s
v5p0078c1s v5p0155c1s
v5p0396c1s
Majendie, M.E. v1p0520c1s
Majendie, V.D. v2p0126c2s
v2p0315c1s
Major, B.R. v4p0515c1s
Major, C.I.F. and Goodrich, E.S.
v4p0584c2s
Major, Charles v5p0266c1s
Major, D.R. v6p0464c2s
Major, F.H. v5p0340c1s
v5p0509c2s v6p0095c1s
Major, G.A. v5p0032c2s
Major, J.H. v1p0132c2s
Major, M. v5p0165c2s
Major, R.H. v1p0028c1m
v1p0029c1s v1p0078c2m v1p0184c1s
v1p0280c1s v1p0798c2s v1p1368c1s
v1p1372c1s v2p0028c2s v2p0029c1s
Major, R.H. and Mackenzie, K.R.H.
v1p1372c1s
Major, W. v1p1247c2s
v5p0314c2s
Makaroff, Admiral v5p0278c2s
v5p0644c1s
Makaroff, S. v5p0150c1s
Makee, Walt v6p0090c2s
v6p0319c2s
Makepeace, F.B. v3p0013c1s
Makepeace, J. v1p0629c1s
Makgill, G. v6p0103c1s
v6p0694c1s
Makins, M.A. v3p0470c2s
Makinson, S.P. v6p0065c2s
v6p0418c1s
Makower, S.V. v4p0078c1s
Makuen, G.H. v3p0054c1s
v3p0451c1s
Malagodi, O. v5p0018c1s
Malagrowther, M. v4p0333c2s
Malahide, Lord v2p0265c2s
Malahide, T.de, Lord v2p0192c2s
Malahide, Talbot de, Lord. v4p0133c2s
Malamani, V. v4p0090c2s
v4p0602c1s
Malan, A.H. v3p0255c1s
v4p0337c2m v5p0013c1s v5p0053c1s
v5p0103c1s v5p0171c2s v5p0295c1s
v5p0347c2s v5p0401c2s
Malan, C.H. v1p0543c1s
v1p1087c2s
Malan, S.C. v1p0125c2s
Malato, C. v4p0017c1s
Malberg, M.A. v1p0665c2s
Malcolm, A.G. v1p0438c2s
v1p0578c1s
Malcolm, C. v1p0234c2s
Malcolm, E. v3p0432c2s
Malcolm, E.D. v6p0419c1s
v6p0628c1s
Malcolm, E.H. v1p0446c2s
v1p1300c2s
Malcolm, G. v3p0113c2s
Malcolm, H. v1p1099c1s
Malcolm, I. v5p0050c2s
v5p0301c2s v6p0194c2s v6p0237c1s
v6p0471c1s
Malcolm, Ian v4p0146c1s
Malcolm, J. v4p0274c1s
Malcolm, J.A. v3p0020c1s
Malcolm, J.P. v1p1143c2s
Malcolm, N. v5p0115c2s

v5p0597c1s
Malcolm, W.R. v6p0520c1s
v6p0600c2s
Malcom, H. v1p0097c1s
Malcomb, I. v6p0645c2s
Malden, A.R. v5p0347c1s
Malden, H.E. v2p0007c1s
v2p0142c2s v2p0357c2s v3p0168c2s
v3p0417c1s v4p0350c1s v5p0332c1s
v5p0574c1s v5p0618c1m v6p0059c2s
v6p0073c1s v6p0265c2s v6p0503c2s
v6p0586c2s
Malet, H.P. v1p0101c1s
v1p0147c2s v1p0373c1s v1p0375c1m
v1p0375c2s v1p0443c1s v1p0631c1s
v1p0876c2s v1p0936c2s v1p1172c2s
v3p0049c1s v3p0196c1s v3p0211c2s
v4p0508c2s
Malet, L. v2p0012c2s
v2p0183c1s v3p0102c1s v4p0608c2s
Malet, Lucas v6p0703c1s
Malet, Lucas and Harrison, W., Mrs.
v3p0326c2s
Maletroit, Comte de v6p0238c1s
Malezieux, E. v1p1353c2s
Malezieux, M. v1p0408c1s
Malherbe, C. v5p0390c1s
Maline, J.G. v1p0571c1s
v1p0770c2s
Maling, Miss v1p0499c2s
Mall, F.P. v4p0060c1s
Mallalieu, J.T. v4p0476c2s
Mallalieu, W.F. v1p0163c1s
v3p0153c1s v3p0289c1s v3p0369c2s
v3p0372c2s v4p0190c1s
Mallary, R.D. v4p0113c2s
v5p0118c2s
Mallary, R.DeW. v5p0060c1m
v5p0562c1s v6p0367c2m
Mallery, F. v3p0230c2s
Mallery, G. v1p0059c2s
v1p0179c1s v1p0636c2s v1p0637c2s
v1p0638c1s v1p0722c1s v1p0832c1s
v1p0834c1m v1p1273c1s v1p1342c1s
v2p0220c1s v2p0402c2m v2p0429c1s
v3p0103c1s v3p0185c1s v3p0213c1s
v3p0266c2s v3p0329c2s v3p0373c2s
Malleson, F.A. v2p0479c2s
Malleson, G.B. v2p0006c1s
v2p0029c2s v2p0380c2m v3p0052c1s
v3p0137c2s v3p0159c2s v3p0175c2s
v3p0194c2s v3p0212c2s v3p0213c1s
v3p0369c2s v3p0448c1s
Malleson, H. v6p0549c2s
Malleson, W. v6p0313c1s
Mallet, A. v1p1248c1s
v1p1392c1s
Mallet, C.E. v2p0291c2s
v3p0427c2s
Mallet, C.F. v4p0097c1s
Mallet, E. v1p1376c1s
v2p0009c2s
Mallet, E.J., jr. v2p0094c2s
v2p0169c1s
Mallet, E.T., jr. v1p0542c1s
Mallet, J.W. v1p0502c1s
v1p0827c2s v1p0828c1s v1p1312c2s
v6p0412c2s
Mallet, R. v1p0101c1s
v1p0377c1s v1p0436c2s v1p0664c1s
v1p0665c1s v1p0665c2m v1p1191c2s
v1p1218c2s v1p1261c2s v1p1293c1s
v2p0128c1s
Mallett, J.R. v4p0253c2s
Malley, A.D. v5p0221c1s
v5p0435c2s
Mallins, H. v2p0216c2s
Malloch, D. v6p0348c1s
v6p0393c2s v6p0439c2s v6p0472c1s
Malloch, W.H. v1p1314c2s
Mallock, A. v3p0330c2s
v3p0331c1s v6p0359c2s
Mallock, L.C.R. v6p0236c1s
Mallock, M.M. v1p1208c2s
v3p0236c2s v4p0482c1s v5p0469c1s
Mallock, W.H. v1p0049c1s
v1p0062c1s v1p0071c2m v1p0259c2s
v1p0293c1s v1p0348c2s v1p0359c1s
v1p0423c1s v1p0426c1s v1p0440c1s
v1p0440c2s v1p0570c1s v1p0612c2s
v1p0745c2m v1p0852c1s v1p0869c2s
v1p0908c2m v1p0981c1s v1p0991c1s
v1p1020c1s v1p1037c2s v1p1056c2s
v1p1074c1s v1p1123c1s v1p1177c1s
v2p0099c2s v2p0100c2s v2p0152c1s
v2p0183c1s v2p0188c1s v2p0245c2s
v2p0248c2s v2p0321c1s v2p0348c1s
v2p0362c1m v2p0372c2s v2p0407c2s
v2p0409c1s v2p0468c2s v3p0006c1s
v3p0021c2s v3p0022c1s v3p0052c1s
v3p0086c2s v3p0097c1s v3p0109c1s
v3p0114c2s v3p0127c2m v3p0148c1s
v3p0152c1s v3p0204c1s v3p0239c1s
v3p0239c2s v3p0313c2s v3p0341c1s
v3p0346c1s v3p0346c2s v3p0355c2s
v3p0357c2m v3p0379c2m v3p0434c2s
v3p0440c2s v3p0458c1m v4p0012c2s
v4p0059c1s v4p0108c2s v4p0155c1s
v4p0167c2s v4p0193c1s v4p0195c2s
v4p0233c2s v4p0236c2s v4p0237c1s
v4p0239c1s v4p0248c2s v4p0252c1s
v4p0268c2s v4p0278c1s v4p0314c2m
v4p0340c1s v4p0346c2s v4p0441c2s
v4p0455c2m v4p0462c1s v4p0509c2s
v4p0519c2s v4p0533c2m v4p0534c1s
v4p0535c1s v4p0554c2s v4p0571c2s
v4p0615c1m v5p0114c2s v5p0115c1s
v5p0117c1s v5p0158c1s v5p0245c1s
v5p0330c2s v5p0350c2s v5p0400c1s
v5p0442c2s v5p0483c1s v5p0492c2s
v5p0494c1s v5p0522c2s v5p0545c2s
v5p0557c2s v5p0588c2s v6p0041c1s
v6p0057c2s v6p0100c1s v6p0101c2s
v6p0123c1s v6p0126c1m v6p0234c1s
v6p0270c2s v6p0309c2s v6p0355c2s
v6p0356c2s v6p0382c2m v6p0395c2s
v6p0412c2s v6p0418c2s v6p0440c2s
v6p0490c1s v6p0536c2m v6p0576c2s
v6p0586c2s v6p0633c1s v6p0639c1s
v6p0642c1s v6p0645c1s
Mallock, W.H. et al. v3p0250c2s
v6p0271c1s
Mallon, G.B. v5p0534c1s
v6p0540c2s
Mallory, C. v5p0187c1s
Mallory, F.B. v6p0281c2s
Mallory, G.S. v1p0865c2s
Mallory, H.F. and Davis, J.D.
v4p0302c2s
Mallory, S.R. v5p0601c2s
Malloy, C. v4p0076c1s
v6p0202c1s v6p0202c2m
Malmene, W. v4p0389c2s
Malmesbury, Countess of .. v4p0356c2s
Malmesbury, S. v4p0543c2s
Malmesbury, S., Lady v4p0256c1s
Malmesbury, S.H. v2p0354c1s
v4p0182c2s
Malo, L. v1p0068c2s
Malone, D.R. v1p0117c1s
v1p0507c1s v1p1160c2s
Malone, J. v4p0003c1s
v4p0068c1s v4p0114c1s v4p0517c2s
v4p0520c1s v4p0572c1s v5p0168c2s
v5p0297c2s v5p0523c1s
Malone, John v5p0523c1s
Malone, M.J. v1p0354c2s
v1p0357c2s
Malone, P.B. v5p0446c1s
Malone, P.J. v3p0172c1s
Malone, S. v1p0304c1s
v2p0003c1s v2p0113c1s v2p0224c2s
v2p0332c2s v2p0375c2s v2p0460c2s
v3p0323c2s
Malone, T.A. v1p1004c1s
Malone, T.H. v5p0493c2s
Malone, W. v5p0645c1s
Malortie, Baron de v2p0133c2s
v2p0134c1s v2p0134c2s v5p0065c1s
Maltbie, M.R. v5p0004c2s
v5p0241c1s v5p0338c2s v5p0343c2s
v5p0392c1m v5p0406c2s v5p0443c1s
v5p0622c2s v6p0128c2s v6p0435c1s
v6p0464c2s v6p0522c1s v6p0621c1s
Maltbie, M.R. and Bard, E.F.
v5p0105c1s
Maltbie, W.H. and Coolidge, J.L.
v5p0366c1s
Maltby, A.B. v6p0116c2s
Maltby, A.B. and Root, M.E.
v6p0371c2s
Maltby, T.M. v5p0577c2s
Malthie, M.R. v5p0235c1s
Maltzan, A.von, Baron v6p0072c1s
Man, Alex v4p0209c2s
Man, E.A. v4p0392c1s
Man, E.H. v2p0013c2m
v2p0314c2s v3p0305c1s v4p0393c1s
v4p0455c1s
Man, G. v3p0163c1s
Manager, D. v2p0021c1s
Manatt, J.I. v4p0025c2s
v4p0241c1s v4p0271c1s v4p0505c1s
v5p0004c2s v5p0042c1s v5p0042c2s
v5p0076c2s v5p0249c2s v5p0251c1s
v5p0295c1s v5p0300c2s v5p0322c1s
v5p0436c2s v6p0013c1s v6p0207c2s
v6p0484c2s v6p0647c2s v6p0658c1s
Manavian, G.M. v4p0027c1s
Manby, E. v3p0078c1s
Manby, G.W. v1p0550c2s
Mance, L.S.La v4p0197c1s
v4p0245c1s v4p0420c1s v5p0156c1s
Mance, Laura S.La v4p0291c1s
Manchee, S.H. v1p0226c2s
Manchester, A. v5p0074c2s
Manchester, D.U. v3p0198c1s
Manchester, D.W. v2p0088c2s
v2p0209c2s v2p0413c1s v2p0441c1s
v3p0142c1s v3p0354c2s v3p0460c2s
Manchester, Duke of v1p0128c1s
Manchester, Duke of and Sullivan, E.
v1p0486c2s
Manchester, G.S. v6p0410c1s
Manchester, H.H. and
Manchester, O.L. v5p0446c2s
v5p0518c1s
Manchester, O.L. v5p0325c1s
Manchester, O.L. and
Manchester, H.H. v5p0446c2s
v5p0518c1s
Manchester, T.W. v4p0443c2s
Mancini, E. v4p0331c1s
v5p0571c1s
Mancini, F. v5p0340c1s
v5p0558c2s
Mancini, G.P. v5p0054c1s
Mancini, I. v3p0104c1s
Manclair, C. v5p0428c1s
v5p0464c1s
Mand, C. v5p0347c2s
Mand, W.T. v5p0180c2s
v5p0539c2s
Mandello, J. v4p0144c2s
Mandello, J.G. v6p0615c1s
Mander v1p0949c1s
Manderson, C.F. v5p0349c1s
Manderson, F. and Hazen, C.
v5p0015c1s
Mandes v5p0565c2s
Mandeville, C.E. v6p0141c2s
Mandeville, G.H. v2p0415c1s
Mandeville, H. v1p1044c1s
Mandigo, J.H. v3p0473c2s
v4p0046c2s v4p0543c1m
Mandin, C. v4p0134c1s
Mandy, F. v4p0359c1s
Manecke, F. v6p0520c2s
Mangan, H. v5p0159c1s
Mangano, A. v6p0331c1s
Mangasarian, M.M. v4p0027c1s
v4p0104c1s
Mange, L.S.La v4p0628c1s
Manghas, M.M. v1p0509c1s
Mangin, A. v2p0164c2s
Mangles, J.H. v1p1079c2s
Mangles, R.D. v1p0632c2s
Manhart, F. v3p0141c2s
v4p0476c2s
Manhart, F.P. v4p0062c1s
v4p0169c1s v4p0533c1s v4p0633c1s
v5p0347c2s v5p0535c1s
Maniates, B. v6p0472c1s
v6p0675c2s
Manice, C.F. v6p0261c2s
Manifold, C.C. v6p0118c2s
v6p0119c1s v6p0710c2s
Manifold, Capt. v3p0003c2s
Manigault, G. v1p0486c2s
v1p0861c1s v1p1223c2s v1p1225c2s
v2p0411c1s
Manigault, G.E. v3p0225c2m
Manire, B.F. v2p0042c1s
v2p0083c2s v2p0085c1s v2p0438c2s
v3p0229c2s
Manley, D. v4p0282c2s
Manley, E. v6p0189c2s
v6p0321c1s
Manley, F. v1p0943c1s
Manley, H.B. v5p0110c2s
Manley, J.H. v5p0074c2s
v6p0518c2s
Manley, J.J. v2p0157c2s
v2p0199c1s v2p0224c2s v2p0384c2s
v2p0428c2s v2p0434c1s v2p0440c1s
Manley, Lord de v1p0265c1s
v2p0222c1s
Manley, T.R. v6p0359c2s
Manley, U.R. v2p0047c1s
Manley, W.E. v1p0125c2s
v1p0126c1m v1p0126c2m v1p0426c1s
v1p0503c2s v1p0645c2s v1p1083c2s
v1p1101c1s v1p1178c1s v1p1190c1s
v2p0044c2s v2p0045c1s v2p0371c1s
v3p0043c1s v3p0142c2m v4p0187c2s
v4p0218c1s v4p0254c1s v4p0351c2s
v5p0261c2s
Manly, C. v6p0348c1s
Manly, W.G. v6p0332c1s
v6p0369c1s
Mann, A. v2p0318c1s
v6p0173c1s
Mann, A.H. v5p0347c1s
Mann, A.S. v6p0615c2s
Mann, Abbe v1p0296c1s
v1p1115c1s
Mann, B.P. v1p0271c2s
v1p0742c2s v2p0045c2s v2p0052c1s
v2p0070c2s v2p0256c1s v5p0227c2s
Mann, C.C. v5p0209c1s
Mann, C.H. v6p0061c1s
Mann, C.R. v4p0254c1s
v6p0137c1s v6p0357c1s v6p0468c2s
v6p0498c2s v6p0576c1s
Mann, Dr. v1p0437c2s
v1p0645c1s v1p0897c1m v3p0296c1s
Mann, E.C. v3p0215c2s
v3p0265c2s
Mann, F.C.T. v4p0299c1s
v5p0566c2s
Mann, F.M. v6p0028c1s
v6p0563c2s
Mann, G.H. v1p0326c2s
Mann, G.O. v1p1326c2s
Mann, H. v1p0259c1m
v1p0276c1s v1p0387c1s v1p0390c2s
v1p0414c1s v1p0630c1s v1p1095c2s
v1p1099c2s v1p1235c1s v1p1288c1s
v1p1288c2s v4p0080c1s v4p0301c1s
v4p0523c1s v6p0356c2s

Mann, H., Mrs. v1p0707c2s
v2p0077c2s
Mann, I.J. v1p0211c1s
v2p0072c2s
Mann, J. v1p1043c2s
Mann, J., jr. v4p0331c1s
Mann, J.A. v3p0090c1s
Mann, J.B. v1p1088c1s
v3p0131c2s v3p0434c1s v4p0461c1s
Mann, J.S. v3p0255c2s
v6p0127c1s v6p0213c1s v6p0254c2s
v6p0269c2s v6p0424c2s v6p0530c1s
v6p0607c1s v6p0633c1s
Mann, J.W. v1p0232c2s
v1p0378c1s v1p0595c1s
Mann, K. v6p0552c1s
Mann, L. v1p0255c2s
v1p0983c1s
Mann, L.M. v6p0499c2s
v6p0514c1s
Mann, M. v5p0471c1s
Mann, M.E. v5p0053c1s
v5p0154c1s v5p0425c1s
Mann, M.Y. v4p0505c1s
Mann, Mary E. v4p0163c2s
v4p0624c2s
Mann, N.M. v1p0684c2s
v1p1092c2s v2p0026c1s v2p0287c2s
v2p0371c2s v2p0417c1s v2p0417c2s
v3p0132c1s v3p0441c1s v5p0531c1s
Mann, O. v5p0381c2s
Mann, R. v6p0216c2s
Mann, R.B. v1p0749c1s
Mann, R.J. v1p0748c2s
v1p1441c2s v2p0247c1s v3p0005c1s
v3p0181c1s v3p0240c2s v3p0251c1m
v3p0476c1s
Mann, T. v3p0239c1m
v4p0314c1s v5p0321c2s v6p0041c2s
v6p0455c1s
Mann, T. and Tillett, B. . v4p0314c1s
Mann, T. et al. v4p0428c1s
Mann, T.H. v3p0013c1s
Mann, Tom v4p0182c1s
v4p0315c1s v4p0315c2s v4p0316c1s
Mann, W.H. v6p0366c1s
Mann, W.J. v1p0625c2s
v1p1116c1s v5p0014c2s v6p0025c2s
Mannering, E., Rev. v1p0240c2s
Mannering, M. v5p0081c2s
v5p0096c1s v5p0133c1m v5p0139c2s
v5p0213c2s v5p0214c2s v5p0242c1s
v5p0309c2s v5p0351c1s v5p0384c1s
v5p0454c2s v5p0477c1s v5p0544c1s
v5p0603c2s v6p0141c2s v6p0530c1s
Manners, F. v5p0297c1s
Manners, G. v4p0219c1m
Manners, J. v2p0089c1s
v2p0176c2s v3p0242c1s
Manners, J., Lady v2p0136c1s
v2p0254c2s v3p0271c1s
Manners, Lady v2p0126c2s
v2p0279c2s
Manners, M. v6p0116c2s
Manners, Mary v6p0368c2s
v6p0455c2s v6p0705c1m
Manners, R.R. v4p0388c2s
Manners, V. v6p0487c1s
v6p0677c2s
Manners, Victoria, Lady .. v6p0561c2s
Manning, A. v1p0221c1s
v1p0287c1s v1p0338c2s v1p0608c1s
v1p0855c2s v1p0875c2s v1p1318c1s
v1p1409c1s
Manning, A.M. v1p0574c2m
v1p1324c1s v2p0006c2s v2p0385c1s
Manning, Anne v1p0077c2s
Manning, C.H. v4p0547c2s
Manning, C.R. v4p0065c2s
Manning, C.U. v6p0596c1s
Manning, Cardinal v3p0216c1s
Manning, Cardinal and Burns, J.
v3p0412c2s
Manning, Cardinal and Fawcett, M.G.
v3p0268c2s
Manning, Cardinal and Waugh, B.
v2p0077c2s
Manning, Cardinal et al. . v3p0458c2s
Manning, H.E. v1p0156c2s
v1p0787c1s v1p0935c1s v1p1002c1s
v1p1115c2s v1p1338c2s v1p1363c2s
v1p1410c2s v2p0054c1s v2p0077c2s
v2p0096c2s v2p0107c2s v2p0131c1m
v2p0181c1s v2p0223c2s v2p0302c1s
v2p0331c1s v2p0354c1s v2p0384c2s
v2p0418c1s v2p0466c1s v3p0040c2s
v3p0077c2s v3p0105c1s v3p0136c1s
v3p0244c2s v3p0247c1s v3p0338c2s
v3p0378c1s v3p0379c1s v3p0472c2s
Manning, H.E.C. and Caine, W.S.
v3p0252c2s
Manning, H.E.C. and Farrar, F.W.
v3p0255c1s
Manning, H.F. et al. v4p0108c2s
Manning, J. v1p0079c1s
v1p0143c2s v1p0146c2s v1p0533c2s
v1p0798c2s v1p0818c1s v1p1148c1s
v1p1188c2s v1p1233c1s v2p0354c2s
v4p0560c1s v6p0183c2s
Manning, J.B. v6p0234c1s
Manning, J.F. v1p0519c1s
v1p1280c1s v2p0172c2s
Manning, J.M. v1p0215c2s
v1p0554c1s v1p1050c2s v1p1058c2s
v1p1271c1s
Manning, J.W. v4p0204c1s
v4p0613c1s
Manning, M. v6p0025c1s
v6p0045c1s v6p0101c1s v6p0358c1m
v6p0519c1s v6p0552c1s
Manning, M.L. v4p0029c2s
Manning, P. v6p0473c2s
Manning, R.I. v4p0396c2s
v6p0605c1s
Manning, T.F. v5p0236c2s
Manning, W. v6p0131c1s
v6p0516c1s
Manning, W.C. v1p1063c2s
Manning, W.E. v1p0241c1s
Manning, W.F. v5p0618c1s
Manning, W.H. v5p0605c1s
v6p0033c2s v6p0246c2s v6p0679c1s
Mannix, J.T. v5p0446c1s
Mannix, M.E. v3p0328c1s
Manny, F.A. v5p0265c1s
Manohar, Rajah Murli v3p0210c2s
Manouvrier, L. v5p0452c2s
Manross, N.S. v1p0267c2s
v1p0560c2s v1p0666c1s v1p0844c1s
v1p1012c1s v1p1325c2s
Mans, O. v5p0141c1s
v5p0574c2s
Mansel, H.L. v1p0528c1s
v1p1000c1s v1p1302c1s
Mansell, J.P. v1p0899c1s
Mansergh, H., Mrs. v4p0216c1s
v4p0398c1s v5p0008c2s
Mansergh, J. v3p0457c2s
v5p0366c1s
Mansfield, A.K. v1p0503c2s
v1p0538c2s v1p1064c1s
Mansfield, B. v4p0471c2s
v4p0472c1s
Mansfield, E. v1p0784c1s
Mansfield, E.D. v1p0235c1s
Mansfield, F.A. v2p0433c1s
Mansfield, F.W. v5p0460c1s
Mansfield, G. v1p0222c1s
v1p0537c1s
Mansfield, G.E. v5p0098c1s
Mansfield, G.W. v5p0550c1s
Mansfield, J. v4p0331c1s
v6p0218c1s
Mansfield, R. v2p0380c1s
v4p0002c2s v4p0160c2s v6p0003c1m
v6p0396c2s v6p0631c2s
Mansfield, R.B. v1p0018c2s
v1p1193c1s
Mansfield, Richard, Mrs. . v6p0180c2s
Mansford, C.J. v4p0327c1s
Mansford, F.H. v6p0385c1s
v6p0693c2s
Manson, E. v4p0127c2s
v4p0137c1s v4p0256c1s v4p0270c1s
v4p0323c2s v4p0338c1s v4p0356c1s
v4p0459c2s v5p0155c2s v5p0283c2s
v5p0330c1s v5p0422c2s v5p0487c1s
v5p0575c1s v6p0046c2s v6p0069c2s
v6p0175c1s v6p0273c2s v6p0373c2s
v6p0386c2s v6p0598c2s v6p0701c2s
Manson, G. v1p1276c1s
Manson, G.J. v5p0436c1s
v5p0509c2s
Manson, J. v4p0355c2s
v5p0382c2s v5p0504c1s v6p0566c2s
Manson, J.A. v6p0183c1s
Manson, M. v4p0357c2s
v4p0420c2s v5p0566c1s
Manson, Nathaniel J. v6p0415c1s
Manson, W.L. v5p0131c1s
v5p0624c2s
Manston, A. v3p0100c1s
v3p0440c1s v4p0202c2s v4p0351c1s
v4p0603c1s v5p0138c2s
Manston, A.C. v4p0232c2s
Mant, N. v3p0064c1s
Mant, W.J.N. v3p0359c2s
Mantegazza, P. v5p0198c2s
Mantell, G.A. v1p0470c1s
Mantius, W.E. v4p0404c2s
Manton, W.P. v4p0103c1s
Manus, L. v3p0319c1s
Manzanet, D. v6p0211c1s
Manzi, A. v4p0293c2s
Mapel, J.J. v3p0128c1s
Mapes, E.S. v5p0044c2s
v6p0330c1s v6p0437c1s v6p0656c2s
v6p0690c1s
Mapes, Ella S. v5p0637c2s
Mapes, G.E. v2p0348c1s
v6p0070c1s
Mapes, V. v5p0294c2s
v5p0617c2s
Mapother, E.D. v1p0304c2s
v1p0663c1s v1p1272c2s
Mappin, W.F. v1p0604c1s
v3p0149c2s
Maquarie, A. v5p0328c1m
Mar, A.Del v4p0144c1s
v4p0378c1s v4p0525c2s v5p0094c1s
v6p0092c1s v6p0530c1s v6p0627c2s
Mar, Alex Del v4p0230c1s
v6p0260c2s
Mar, E.Del v6p0240c2s
Mar, F.W. v3p0034c1s
v3p0327c1s v4p0045c2s
Mar, F.W. and Gooch, F.A.. v3p0080c1s
Mar, H. v1p0471c1s
Mar, I. v3p0411c1s
v3p0435c1s v4p0328c1s
Marais, J.I. v5p0482c1s
Marble, A.P. v1p0390c1s
v2p0215c1s v3p0253c2s v3p0296c2s
v4p0183c2s v4p0184c2s v4p0505c1s
Marble, A.R. v5p0013c1s
v5p0062c1s v5p0205c1s v5p0263c2s
v5p0456c1m v5p0500c2s v6p0011c2s
v6p0049c1s v6p0076c2s v6p0078c1s
v6p0085c1s v6p0202c1m v6p0242c2s
v6p0283c2s v6p0296c2s v6p0303c1s
v6p0411c2s v6p0422c2s v6p0461c2s
v6p0471c1s v6p0491c1s v6p0505c2s
v6p0609c1s v6p0644c2s v6p0649c1m
v6p0699c2s
Marble, Annie R. v5p0115c2m
v6p0569c2s v6p0649c1s v6p0686c1s
Marble, C.C. v3p0262c2s
v3p0369c1s v3p0471c2s
Marble, E. v6p0490c2s
Marble, E.K. v6p0299c2s
Marble, Earl v6p0409c2s
Marble, F.L. v6p0469c2s
Marble, J.H. v5p0130c2s
Marble, J.H. et al. v5p0446c1s
Marble, M. v1p1088c1s
Marburg, Edgar v6p0204c1s
Marburg, T. v4p0533c2s
v5p0592c2s
Marbury, E. v3p0468c2s
Marbut, C.F. v6p0422c1s
Marcassey, L.L. v5p0025c2s
Marcel, C. v1p0724c2s
Marcel, G. v1p0078c1s
Marcellus, P.H. v1p1176c2s
Marcet, Dr. v1p0352c1s
Marcet, Prof. v1p0432c2s
Marcet, W. v3p0124c2s
v3p0328c2s
March, Alden v6p0164c2s
March, B.C. v6p0492c1s
March, C. v4p0029c1s
March, C.W. v1p1395c2s
v1p1415c1s
March, D. v1p0229c2s
v1p0239c1s v1p0405c2s v1p0665c2s
v1p0774c2s v1p1071c2s v1p1160c2s
v1p1407c2s
March, E.G. v5p0361c1s
March, F.A. v1p0416c2m
v1p0559c1s v1p0699c2s v1p0948c1s
v1p0989c1s v1p1001c2s v1p1055c2s
v1p1157c2s v1p1184c1s v1p1185c1m
v1p1234c2s v2p0143c2s v2p0339c1s
v3p0022c2m v3p0139c2m v3p0242c2s
v3p0269c2s v3p0387c1s v3p0404c1m
v4p0184c1s v4p0241c2s v4p0519c1s
March, F.A. and Wright, C.
v1p1336c2s
March, H.C. v4p0451c1s
v5p0062c2s v5p0166c1s v5p0210c2s
March, L.G.F. v1p0473c2s
March, T. v2p0216c1s
March-Phillipps, E. v4p0193c1s
v4p0195c2s v4p0403c1s v4p0581c1s
v4p0628c1s v4p0630c1s
March-Phillipps, L. v5p0102c2s
v6p0234c1s v6p0514c2s
Marchal, P. v2p0015c1s
v2p0093c2s v5p0485c2s
Marchant, E.W. v4p0389c1s
Marchant, H. v2p0469c1s
v3p0206c1s
Marchant, H.D.Le v6p0384c2s
Marchant, J.R.V. v6p0415c2s
Marchant, S. v4p0563c1s
v4p0625c2s
Marche, E. v1p1251c1s
Marche, P. v6p0003c1s
v6p0534c2s v6p0592c1s v6p0664c1s
Marchegay, P. and Franks, A.W.
v1p1324c2s
Marchmont, A.W. v5p0283c1s
Marcker, Lieut. v4p0312c1s
Marckwald, W. and Soddy, F.
v6p0527c1s
Marco, De Viti de v4p0295c1s
v5p0300c1s v6p0490c2s
Marcoartu, A.de v1p1291c1s
Marcon, P.B. v1p0326c2s
Marconi, G. v5p0571c1m
v6p0636c2m
Marcosson, I.F. v6p0003c2s
v6p0154c1s v6p0187c1s v6p0203c1s
v6p0228c2s v6p0231c2s v6p0349c1s
v6p0468c1s v6p0474c1s v6p0487c2s
v6p0488c2s v6p0491c2s v6p0524c2s
Marcosson, Isaac F. v6p0102c1s
Marcosson, J.F. v6p0352c1s
Marcosson, O.F. v6p0427c1s
Marcosson, T.E. v6p0159c2s

Marcosson, T.F. v6p0389c1s
Marcou, F.B. v2p0327c1s
Marcou, J. v1p0029c1s
v1p0506c2s v2p0179c1s v4p0429c2s
v5p0312c2s
Marcou, J.B. v2p0173c2s
v2p0224c1s v2p0372c2s v3p0318c1m
Marcou, P.B. v2p0423c1s
Marcou, P.F. v4p0020c2s
v5p0137c2s
Marcow, J. v3p0419c1s
Marcus, H.W. v6p0257c2s
v6p0310c1s
Marcy, O. v1p0804c2s
Marcy, R.B. v1p1011c1s
v1p1132c1s v1p1227c2s v3p0166c2s
v3p0205c1s v3p0460c1s
Marden, H. v2p0161c1s
Marden, O.S. v6p0109c1s
v6p0645c1s
Mardon, E.J. v5p0005c2s
Mare, W.de la v6p0306c2s
Marenholtz-Bulow, B.von .. v1p0491c2s
Marett, R.R. v4p0283c2s
v5p0196c1s v5p0519c1s v6p0513c1s
v6p0609c1s
Marett, R.R. and Lang, A.. v5p0483c2s
Mareu, Honore v6p0222c1s
Marey, A.M. v1p0759c1s
Marey, E.J. v1p0135c2s
v1p0759c1s v2p0329c2s v4p0337c2s
Marey, E.J.H. v3p0045c1s
Marey, Prof. v1p0041c1s
Margesson, H.P. v4p0451c1s
Marget, E. v3p0036c1s
v3p0156c2s v3p0295c2s v3p0400c2s
v3p0467c1s
Marget, Edith v3p0413c1s
Margoliouth, D.S. v5p0055c2s
v5p0356c2s v6p0065c1m v6p0341c1s
v6p0537c1s v6p0714c1s
Margoliouth, D.S. and Harkavy, A.
v5p0503c1s v5p0518c2s
Margoliouth, G. v4p0053c1s
v4p0055c2s v5p0002c1s v5p0057c1m
v5p0174c2s v5p0278c1s v5p0307c2s
v5p0356c2m v6p0112c2s v6p0229c1s
v6p0249c2s v6p0342c1s v6p0349c2s
v6p0566c2s v6p0584c2s v6p0711c2s
Margolis, M.L. v6p0343c1s
Margolis, M.L. and Stevens, G.B.
v6p0347c1s
Margry, P. v2p0250c1s
Marguerittes, Mme.de v1p0327c1s
v1p1073c2s
Mariager, D. v3p0059c1s
v3p0093c1s v3p0258c2s v3p0302c2s
v3p0306c1s v3p0425c2s v3p0452c1s
v3p0476c2s
Mariager, N.D. v2p0216c2s
v2p0240c1s
Mariani, C.F. v5p0032c2s
Mariani, L. v4p0139c1s
v5p0033c2s v5p0240c2s v5p0492c2s
Mariano, R. v4p0424c1s
Marie, G. v2p0262c1s
Marie, J.W. v5p0102c2s
Marie-Davy v1p0829c1s
Marie-Davy, Dr. v2p0329c2s
Mariet, J. v3p0382c2s
Marignac, C. v1p0074c1s
v1p0224c1s
Mariller, C. v1p0959c1s
Marillier v6p0261c2s
Marillier, H.C. v4p0039c2s
v4p0263c2s v5p0089c2s v5p0314c2s
v5p0497c2s v5p0571c1s v5p0578c2s
v5p0607c1s v6p0385c1s v6p0534c1s
Marillier, L. v4p0426c1s
v5p0220c2s v5p0485c1s v5p0497c1s
v5p0641c2s v5p0646c1s
Marin, D. v6p0288c2s
Marindin, G.E. v2p0147c2s
Marini, L. v6p0580c1s
v6p0641c1s
Mario, A. v2p0171c2s
Mario, J.V. v2p0071c1s
Mario, J.W. v1p0027c1s
v1p0207c2s v1p0388c2m v1p0461c1s
v1p0500c2m v1p0669c1s v1p0672c1s
v1p0874c1s v1p1048c2s v1p1365c1m
v2p0080c2s v2p0101c2s v2p0166c2s
v2p0171c1m v2p0231c1m v2p0231c2m
v2p0232c1s v2p0288c1s v2p0383c1s
v2p0449c1s v3p0009c2s v3p0067c2s
v3p0115c1s v3p0167c1s v3p0224c2m
v3p0225c1m v3p0230c1s v3p0263c2s
v3p0295c2s v3p0318c1s v3p0335c2s
v3p0371c2s v3p0465c2s v4p0005c2s
v4p0088c1s v4p0089c1m v4p0094c2s
v4p0209c2s v4p0219c2s v4p0294c1m
v4p0294c2m v4p0295c1m v4p0326c2s
v4p0362c2s v4p0392c2s v4p0422c2s
v4p0443c2s v4p0483c2s v4p0502c1s
v4p0523c1m v4p0584c1s v4p0603c1s
v5p0080c1s v5p0094c1s v5p0097c2s
v5p0098c1s v5p0142c2s v5p0144c1s
v5p0300c1s v5p0300c2s v5p0320c1s
v5p0331c1s v5p0357c2s v5p0367c2s
v5p0392c2s v5p0442c1s v5p0595c2s
v5p0609c2s v5p0612c1s v6p0101c1m
v6p0158c2s v6p0331c1s v6p0331c2m
v6p0408c1s v6p0441c2s v6p0478c1s
v6p0621c2m v6p0676c2s
Mario, J.W. and Griffith, S.S.
v1p0880c1s
Mario, J.W., Mrs. v3p0064c2s
v3p0224c2s v3p0263c2s v3p0302c2s
Mario, J.W.V. v4p0452c1s
Mario, Jessie W. v6p0331c2s
Mario, V. v4p0523c1s
Marion, A. v5p0549c1s
Marion, G.E. v6p0437c1s
Marion, H. v3p0073c2s
v4p0171c1s
Marion, J., Mme. v5p0431c2s
v5p0432c1s
Mariotti, E. v4p0451c2s
v5p0503c1s
Mariotti, L. v1p0199c2s
v1p0295c2s v1p0670c2s v1p0871c1s
Mariotti, Sig. v1p1117c1s
Mariscal, I. v5p0373c1s
Marischal, G.K. v4p0059c1s
v4p0059c2s v4p0377c2s v6p0271c1s
Marischal, W.K. v5p0452c2s
Maritzburg, P. v1p0763c1s
Marius, D. v2p0329c1s
Marjoribanks, E. v2p0158c1s
Mark, E.L. v6p0059c1s
v6p0478c2s
Mark, E.L. and Bristol, C.L.
v6p0059c1s
Mark, H.T. v6p0199c2s
Markby, T. v1p0190c1s
v1p0237c2s v1p1063c1s v1p1357c2s
v1p1421c2s
Marker, G.E. v6p0635c2s
Marker, G.F.H. v1p0996c1s
Markes, J.F. v4p0230c2s
Markham, A.B. v5p0586c2s
Markham, A.H. v1p0055c2m
v1p0056c1s v1p0373c1s v1p0584c2s
v1p0622c1s v1p0931c2s v1p1041c2s
v3p0203c2s v3p0266c1s v4p0025c2s
v4p0406c2s v4p0444c2s v4p0521c2s
v5p0022c1s v5p0108c1s v5p0566c1s
v6p0577c2s
Markham, C. v3p0177c1s
v5p0086c2s
Markham, C., Sir v6p0506c1s
Markham, C.A. v6p0255c2s
Markham, C.E. v6p0113c1s
v6p0465c2s
Markham, C.L. v3p0360c2s
Markham, C.R. v1p0003c1s
v1p0055c1s v1p0055c2s v1p0056c1s
v1p0235c2s v1p0289c2s v1p0439c2s
v1p0455c2s v1p0591c1s v1p0666c2s
v1p0983c2s v1p0992c2s v1p0993c1m
v1p1024c1s v1p1077c1s v1p1225c1s
v2p0020c1s v2p0021c1s v2p0036c1s
v2p0261c1s v2p0471c2s v3p0210c2s
v3p0324c2s v3p0351c1s v3p0360c2s
v4p0012c2s v4p0019c2s v4p0025c1s
v4p0119c1s v4p0222c2m v4p0348c2s
v4p0468c2s v4p0493c2s v4p0543c1s
v4p0602c1s v4p0609c1s v5p0022c1m
v5p0224c2s v5p0228c2s v5p0240c1s
v5p0342c2s v5p0498c2m v5p0621c2s
v6p0023c1m v6p0023c2s v6p0029c1m
v6p0179c1s v6p0200c2s v6p0250c1s
v6p0250c2s v6p0466c2s v6p0490c1m
v6p0553c2m
Markham, C.R., Sir v5p0048c2s
v5p0228c2s v5p0633c1s
Markham, Catherine v6p0074c2s
Markham, Clements R. v6p0055c2s
Markham, E. v5p0359c1s
v5p0539c1s v6p0114c2s v6p0238c2s
v6p0341c2s v6p0356c1s v6p0376c1s
v6p0505c1s
Markham, E. et al. v6p0641c2s
Markham, R.G.L. v6p0044c1s
v6p0615c2s v6p0694c2s
Markham, V.R. v6p0107c2s
v6p0184c2s
v6p0295c1s
Markheim, W. v3p0450c1s
Markino, Y. v6p0656c1s
Markland, J.H. v1p0203c1s
v1p0928c2s v1p1272c2s
Markland, T. v3p0450c1s
Markle, A.L. v5p0636c2s
Markley, A.H. v1p0064c2s
Markley, H.H. v4p0101c2s
Markoe, L.J. v6p0190c1s
v6p0427c1s v6p0522c2s
Markoff, A.V. v4p0027c1s
v5p0111c2s v5p0502c1s
Marks, A. v1p0185c1s
v1p0358c1s v1p0468c1s v1p0773c1s
v4p0605c1m v5p0200c2s v6p0087c2s
v6p0111c2s v6p0385c2s
Marks, A. and Weale, W.H.J.
v6p0216c2s
Marks, A.D. v4p0569c1s
Marks, Alfred v6p0384c2m
Marks, F.W. v3p0120c1s
Marks, G.C. v5p0435c1s
v5p0477c1s
Marks, Isabel v5p0095c2s
v5p0538c2s
Marks, J. v6p0136c2s
v6p0433c1s
Marks, J.A. v5p0625c1s
v6p0648c2s
Marks, Jeannette v6p0307c1s
v6p0430c2s
Marks, Jeannette A. v6p0451c2s
Marks, L.B. v4p0277c1s
Marks, M.A. v4p0325c1s
Marks, M.A.M. v4p0269c1s
v4p0277c1s v4p0517c1s v4p0552c1s
v4p0558c2s v4p0579c1s v4p0587c1s
v4p0588c1s v4p0620c1s v5p0166c2s
v5p0236c1s v5p0349c2s v5p0402c2s
v5p0458c2s v5p0463c1s v5p0558c2s
v5p0579c1s v5p0611c2s v5p0613c2s
Marks, M.A.M.H. v4p0405c2s
Marks, M.B. v5p0282c1s
Marks, M.L. v1p0692c1s
Marks, N. v3p0070c2s
Marks, W.D. v1p0286c2s
v1p0292c2s v1p0312c1s v1p0815c2s
v1p1154c2s v1p1248c1m v1p1248c2s
v2p0110c1s v2p0137c1s v2p0138c1s
v2p0418c2s v2p0419c1m v6p0204c2s
Markwell, M. v5p0633c1s
Markwick, E. v1p0173c1s
v1p1123c1s v2p0198c1s v4p0254c1s
Markwick, E.E. v4p0445c1s
v4p0545c2s v5p0549c2s v5p0645c2s
v6p0614c2s
Marlatt, A.L. v6p0155c2s
Marlatt, C.L. v5p0015c1s
v5p0125c1m v5p0510c1m v6p0101c1s
v6p0568c2s
Marlborough, Duke of v2p0108c2s
v2p0189c2m v2p0216c2s v2p0248c1s
v3p0044c2s v3p0132c2s v3p0182c2s
v3p0201c1s v3p0235c2s v3p0246c1s
v3p0280c1s v3p0321c1s v3p0351c2s
v3p0352c2s v3p0368c1s v4p0029c2s
v4p0182c1s v4p0567c2s
Marlin, J. v5p0216c1s
v5p0373c2s v5p0612c2s
Marlin, J., Mrs. v2p0043c1s
Marlin, Jane v5p0384c2s
Marling, F.H. v5p0395c1s
v6p0437c2s v6p0468c2s
Marlow, A.L. v5p0070c2s
Marlowe, Julia v6p0292c1s
Marmaduke, J.S. v1p1345c1s
Marmande, R.de v6p0560c2s
Marmier, E. v1p0380c2s
Marmol, T.del v6p0607c2s
Marmorek, A. v6p0660c1s
Marnan, B. v5p0135c2s
v5p0327c1s v5p0339c2s v5p0347c2s
v5p0349c2s v5p0433c2s v5p0586c1s
v6p0700c2s
Marneford, Lieut. v1p0001c1s
Marnold v6p0620c2s
Marot, H. v6p0116c2s
v6p0492c1s
Marot, P. v5p0169c1s
Marples, T. v6p0178c1s
Marquand, A. v3p0121c1s
v3p0323c1s v3p0330c1s v3p0344c1s
v3p0362c2s v4p0070c2s v4p0225c1s
v4p0413c1s v4p0485c2m v5p0210c2s
v5p0312c2s v6p0076c1s v6p0163c1s
v6p0458c1m v6p0712c2s
Marquand, H. v3p0021c1s
Marquand, Henry v2p0430c2s
Marquardt, C. v4p0162c2s
Marquis, D.C. v2p0148c1s
v3p0142c2s
Marquis, D.R. v6p0709c2s
Marquis, T.C. v4p0485c2s
Marquis, T.G. v5p0354c2s
v5p0490c2s v6p0070c1s v6p0097c1s
v6p0525c1s v6p0698c1s
Marquis, W.G. v5p0499c2s
Marr, A.E. v6p0134c1s
v6p0289c1s
Marr, C. v3p0274c2s
Marr, J. v2p0093c1s
Marr, J.E. v4p0222c2s
v4p0234c2s v4p0317c1s v4p0385c2s
v4p0422c1s v4p0513c1m v5p0077c2s
v5p0248c1s v5p0323c1s v5p0381c2s
Marr, J.H. v4p0046c2s
v4p0501c2s v5p0270c1s
Marr, R.H. v1p0133c1s
v3p0302c2s
Marrack, Cecil v5p0264c2s
Marras, A. v1p1081c2s
Marriage, C. v6p0090c1s
v6p0604c1s
Marriage, E. v6p0637c1s
Marrin, J.J. v2p0118c2s
Marriner, W.M. v2p0077c1s
Marriner, W.N. v2p0254c2s
v2p0475c1s
Marriott, C. v5p0148c2s
v5p0456c1s v5p0627c1s v6p0260c2s
v6p0347c1s v6p0360c1s v6p0496c1s
v6p0643c2s

Marriott, C.C. v5p0516c2s
Marriott, E.F. v5p0284c2s
Marriott, F.A. v6p0381c1s
v6p0509c2m
Marriott, H.P.F. v3p0449c1s
v4p0012c2s v4p0351c2s v4p0392c1s
v4p0451c2s v4p0528c2s v5p0458c2m
Marriott, H.P.F. and Bristowe, L.W.
v5p0554c2s
Marriott, J.A. v6p0598c1s
Marriott, J.A.R. v5p0241c1s
v5p0276c1s v5p0297c1s v5p0456c1s
v5p0497c1s v5p0605c2s v6p0191c1s
v6p0501c1s v6p0601c1s v6p0672c1s
v6p0708c1s
Marriott, T. v4p0003c1s
Marriott, W. v3p0251c1s
v6p0413c1s v6p0530c2s
Marriott, W.M. v6p0452c2s
Marriott, W.T. v2p0047c2s
v4p0172c2s v4p0173c1s v4p0458c2s
v4p0537c1s
Marriott, W.T., Sir v4p0636c2s
Marriott-Watson, H.B. v5p0155c2s
v5p0427c2s v6p0040c2s
Marris, A.J. v2p0064c1s
Marris, N.M. v5p0213c2s
Marro, A. v5p0385c2s
v5p0471c1m
Marron, W.R. v6p0513c1s
Marryat, A. v4p0350c2s
Marryat, B. v1p0160c1s
Marryat, E. v3p0345c1s
v4p0413c2s v5p0236c2s
Marryat, F. v1p0199c1s
v1p0288c2s v1p0624c1s v1p0996c1s
v1p1032c1s v1p1053c2s v1p1361c1s
v3p0210c1s v4p0356c2s
Marryat, Florence v1p0036c1s
v1p0359c1s
Marryat, R. v2p0385c2s
Marsden, F.E. v5p0081c2s
Marsden, K. v4p0327c1s
Marsden, R.C. v1p0144c1s
Marsden, R.E. v6p0139c1s
Marsden, R.G. v4p0443c2s
v5p0506c1s v6p0016c1s v6p0243c1s
v6p0407c2s v6p0471c1s v6p0591c2s
Marsden, V.F. v6p0555c2s
v6p0558c1s
Marsden, W. v1p1266c2s
Marsden, W. and Bryant, J.
v1p0522c2s
Marsh, A.H. v3p0114c1s
v3p0154c1s v3p0437c2s v5p0128c1s
v6p0338c1s
Marsh, A.R. v2p0109c1s
v3p0128c1s v3p0358c1s v4p0094c2s
v4p0330c2s v4p0334c2s v4p0539c2s
v4p0540c1s
Marsh, B. v5p0253c1s
Marsh, B.C. v6p0116c1m
v6p0625c1s v6p0653c2s
Marsh, B.V. v1p0077c1s
v1p0077c2s v1p0827c1m
Marsh, C. v1p0190c2s
Marsh, C. and King, J.G. . v1p0098c2s
Marsh, C.D. v4p0433c1s
v5p0453c2s
Marsh, C.F. v6p0003c1s
v6p0083c2s v6p0095c1s v6p0235c2s
v6p0415c1s v6p0437c2s v6p0496c1s
v6p0507c2s v6p0583c1s v6p0662c2s
v6p0695c2s v6p0699c1s
Marsh, C.L. v4p0486c2s
Marsh, Dr. v1p0130c2s
Marsh, E.C. v6p0630c1s
Marsh, E.LeB. v4p0333c1s
Marsh, E.M. v3p0376c1s
Marsh, G. v3p0169c2s
v4p0223c1s
Marsh, G.P. v1p0015c2s
v1p0049c2s v1p0118c2s v1p0197c2s
v1p0241c1s v1p0283c2s v1p0351c1s
v1p0379c1s v1p0388c2s v1p0416c1s
v1p0416c2s v1p0428c2s v1p0436c1s
v1p0514c1s v1p0604c1s v1p0622c2s
v1p0669c1s v1p0671c1s v1p0857c2s
v1p0900c2s v1p0901c1s v1p0928c1s
v1p1029c1s v1p1115c2s v1p1123c2s
v1p1131c1s v1p1245c1m v1p1274c2s
v1p1325c1s v1p1331c2s v1p1396c1s
v1p1421c2s v1p1422c2s
Marsh, G.P. and Mycrup, R.
v1p1274c2s
Marsh, H. v6p0120c2s
Marsh, H.A. et al. v4p0629c2s
Marsh, H.C. v5p0212c1s
Marsh, J. v1p0061c1s
v1p0669c1s v1p1021c1s
Marsh, J.B. v1p0285c2s
v1p0639c2s v1p0907c1s v1p0925c1s
v3p0064c2s v3p0084c1s
Marsh, J.P. v2p0037c1s
v3p0098c1s
Marsh, L. v2p0413c1s
Marsh, L.R. v2p0212c2s
Marsh, M.C. v6p0047c1s
v6p0195c1s v6p0226c2s
Marsh, O.C. v1p0137c1m
v1p0352c2m v1p0469c2s v1p0470c1m
v1p0470c2m v1p0503c2s v1p0509c1s
v1p0533c1s v1p0604c2m v1p0699c1m
v1p0718c2s v1p0844c2s v1p0845c1s
v1p0874c2m v1p0876c1m v1p0931c1m
v1p0937c2s v1p0960c1s v1p1062c2s
v1p1099c2m v1p1179c1s v1p1338c1s
v1p1368c2s v2p0119c1m v2p0148c2s
v2p0161c1s v2p0239c2s v2p0358c2s
v3p0022c2s v3p0072c1s v3p0104c2s
v3p0118c1m v3p0159c1s v3p0169c1s
v3p0188c1s v3p0233c2m v3p0275c1s
v3p0281c2s v3p0376c1s v3p0394c2s
v3p0409c2m v3p0436c1s v4p0031c2m
v4p0037c1s v4p0050c2s v4p0064c1s
v4p0085c1s v4p0117c2m v4p0135c2s
v4p0139c1s v4p0156c1m v4p0178c2s
v4p0185c1m v4p0206c2s v4p0256c2s
v4p0264c1s v4p0270c2s v4p0307c1s
v4p0321c1s v4p0332c1s v4p0360c1s
v4p0366c1m v4p0373c1m v4p0417c2s
v4p0444c2m v4p0481c2s v4p0579c2s
v4p0584c1s v4p0614c2s v5p0100c1s
v5p0162c1m v5p0215c2s v5p0264c1s
v5p0312c2s v5p0357c2s v5p0469c1s
v5p0509c2s v5p0558c2s v5p0596c2s
Marsh, O.E. v4p0016c2s
Marsh, R. v3p0060c1s
v3p0263c2s v3p0317c1s v3p0392c2s
v3p0411c2s v3p0413c2s v4p0047c2s
v4p0192c1s v4p0359c1s v4p0462c1s
v4p0588c1s
Marsh, R.B. v4p0478c2s
Marsh, R.V. v1p0281c2s
Marsh, R.W. v1p0034c2s
v1p0843c1s v1p0876c2s v1p1422c2s
Marsh, T.A.P. v4p0236c1s
v4p0278c2s
Marsh, W. v5p0634c2s
Marsh, W.H.H. v1p0096c1s
v1p0097c1s v1p0240c2s v1p1103c2s
v2p0150c1s v3p0175c1s v3p0281c2s
v6p0484c2s
Marsh-Caldwell, A. v1p0739c1s
Marshall, A. v1p0039c1s
v1p0260c1s v1p0419c1m v1p0754c1s
v1p0761c2s v1p0804c2s v1p1026c2s
v1p1057c2s v1p1058c2s v1p1118c2s
v1p1217c1s v1p1361c2s v1p1402c1s
v2p0267c1s v3p0095c1m v3p0343c2s
v3p0345c2m v3p0446c2s v3p0452c1s
v4p0434c1s v4p0481c1s v5p0163c1s
v5p0176c1s v5p0193c1s v5p0202c2s
v6p0140c1s v6p0173c1s v6p0414c1s
v6p0431c2s
Marshall, A. and Bosanquet, B.
v4p0452c1s
Marshall, A. et al. v2p0264c1s
Marshall, A.F. v1p0197c1s
v1p0418c1s v1p0486c1s v1p0797c1s
v1p0954c1s v1p1121c1s v2p0005c1s
v2p0026c2s v2p0083c2s v2p0084c1s
v2p0084c2s v2p0085c1s v2p0085c2s
v2p0087c1s v2p0142c2s v2p0152c1s
v2p0153c2s v2p0178c1s v2p0186c1s
v2p0202c1s v2p0205c2s v2p0238c2s
v2p0325c1s v2p0330c1s v2p0354c2s
v2p0362c1s v2p0368c1s v2p0375c2s
v2p0377c2m v2p0408c2s v2p0426c1s
v2p0456c1s v2p0468c2s v2p0471c1s
v3p0017c1s v3p0041c1s v3p0119c2s
v3p0162c2s v3p0232c2s v3p0247c1s
v3p0257c1s v3p0270c1s v3p0302c1s
v3p0316c1s v3p0319c1m v3p0324c2s
v3p0362c1s v3p0364c2m v3p0369c2s
v3p0374c1s v3p0384c2s v3p0431c1s
v4p0112c1s v4p0112c2s v4p0113c2s
v4p0262c2s v4p0328c2s v4p0353c2s
v4p0405c2s v4p0419c2s v4p0435c2s
v4p0463c1s v4p0488c1s v4p0533c2s
v4p0558c1s v4p0589c2s
Marshall, A.G. v4p0027c2s
Marshall, A.H. v4p0636c1s
Marshall, A.M. v2p0123c2s
v3p0116c1s v4p0183c1s
Marshall, A.T. v2p0387c2s
Marshall, B. v4p0617c1s
v5p0258c1s v5p0411c1s
Marshall, C. v1p0193c1s
v1p0721c1s v1p0872c1s v1p1147c1s
v4p0021c2s v6p0668c1s
Marshall, C.A. v5p0092c2s
Marshall, C.C. v3p0119c2s
Marshall, C.F. v4p0081c1s
v4p0166c1s v4p0217c1s
Marshall, C.K. v1p1223c2s
Marshall, C.T. v3p0431c2s
Marshall, Cloyd v6p0636c1s
Marshall, D. v1p0819c2s
v1p1059c2s v1p1330c2s v5p0490c1s
Marshall, D.T. v4p0411c2s
Marshall, Dexter v6p0274c2s
Marshall, E. v4p0064c1s
v4p0161c1s v4p0317c1s v4p0340c1s
v4p0530c1s v5p0148c1s v5p0425c2s
v6p0185c2s v6p0278c2s v6p0666c2s
v6p0697c2s
Marshall, E. et al. v5p0508c1s
Marshall, E.C. v1p0343c1s
Marshall, E.M.O. v5p0141c1s
v5p0239c2s v5p0363c2s v5p0390c2s
Marshall, E.O. v6p0243c1s
Marshall, Edward and Creelman, James
v5p0049c2s
Marshall, Elizabeth v5p0596c2s
Marshall, Emma S. v4p0458c2s
Marshall, F. v1p0298c1s
v1p0479c1s v1p0481c1s v1p0488c2s
v1p0565c2s v1p0700c1s v1p0934c1s
v1p0970c1s v1p1174c2s v1p1311c2s
v2p0123c1s v2p0329c1s v3p0161c1s
v3p0161c2s v3p0195c2s
Marshall, F.A. v1p0882c2s
v2p0153c2s v2p0416c2s v3p0275c2s
Marshall, F.A. and Fitzgerald, P.
v3p0109c2s v3p0357c1s
Marshall, F.E. v4p0067c1s
Marshall, F.H. v6p0544c2s
Marshall, G.F. v2p0229c2s
v2p0394c2s v3p0088c1s v3p0310c2s
Marshall, G.M. v1p1408c1s
v5p0103c1s
Marshall, G.W. v1p0804c2s
v2p0020c2s v2p0278c1m
Marshall, H. v1p1139c2s
v4p0216c2s v5p0344c2s
Marshall, H.R. v3p0334c2m
v4p0004c2s v4p0023c1s v4p0130c1s
v4p0179c1s v4p0179c2s v4p0421c1s
v4p0447c1m v5p0005c1s v5p0026c1s
v5p0133c2s v5p0156c1s v5p0317c1s
v5p0350c1s v5p0484c1s v5p0484c2s
v5p0590c2s v6p0005c2s v6p0145c2m
v6p0496c1s v6p0515c1s v6p0522c1s
v6p0671c1s v6p0685c2s
Marshall, J. v1p0287c1s
v1p0885c2s v1p1360c2s v6p0559c1s
Marshall, J., Mrs. v1p0988c2s
v4p0388c2s
Marshall, J., Sir v2p0314c2s
v3p0004c2s v3p0283c1s
Marshall, J.B. v1p0623c1s
Marshall, J.F.B. v2p0198c1s
v3p0213c2s
Marshall, J.T. v4p0056c2m
v4p0057c2s v5p0486c1s v5p0496c2s
v6p0312c1s
Marshall, J.W. v1p0727c1s
v6p0406c1s
Marshall, Jeannie A. v4p0368c2s
Marshall, M. v4p0199c1s
Marshall, M.N. v5p0355c1s
v6p0403c1s
Marshall, M.P. v4p0630c2s
Marshall, Mrs. and
O'Connor-Eccles, Miss . v5p0637c1s
Marshall, O.H. v1p0210c1s
v1p0216c1m v1p0939c1s v2p0299c2s
v2p0313c2s
Marshall, P. v3p0217c2m
v4p0261c1s
Marshall, Prof. et al. ... v2p0418c2s
Marshall, S.E. v2p0278c1s
Marshall, T.D. v4p0323c1s
Marshall, T.P. v2p0024c2s
v2p0316c2s v2p0368c1s
Marshall, T.W. v1p1115c1s
v4p0321c1s
Marshall, T.W.M. v1p0392c1s
Marshall, W. v1p0373c2s
v1p0802c2s v3p0045c1s v3p0371c2s
v4p0583c2s v6p0416c2s v6p0710c1s
Marshall, W.B. v4p0451c1s
Marshall, W.H. v1p1217c2s
Marshall, W.K. v4p0130c2s
Marshall, W.M. v1p0999c2s
v1p1021c1s
Marshall, W.P. v2p0342c2s
v3p0352c2s
Marshall, W.R. v3p0466c1s
Marshall, W.W. v1p1319c1s
v4p0323c1m v5p0098c1s
Marshall-Hall v4p0227c1s
Marshall-Hall, A.S. v3p0073c1s
v3p0446c2s
Marshland, Ellis v6p0225c2s
Marsland, G. v1p0092c1s
v1p0093c1s v1p0095c1s v1p0439c1m
v1p0474c2s v1p0627c2s v1p0649c2s
v1p0873c2s v1p0898c2s v1p1027c1s
v1p1078c1s v1p1232c1s v1p1344c1s
v1p1359c2m v1p1360c1m v1p1419c2s
v4p0038c1s
Marson, C.L. v2p0081c2s
v2p0275c2s v2p0407c2s v3p0081c2s
v3p0318c2s v4p0114c1s
Marson, C.L. and Bax, E.B.
v3p0398c1s
Marst, C.F. v6p0627c2s
Marsten, J.F. v6p0059c2s
v6p0261c1s v6p0297c1m v6p0297c2m
v6p0298c1s v6p0344c2s v6p0616c2s
Marsters, J.M. v1p0157c1s
Marsters, V.S. v6p0036c1s
Marston, C.N. v1p0343c1s
Marston, E. v3p0406c2s
v6p0042c2s v6p0465c1s
Marston, J.A. v1p0868c1s
Marston, P.B. v1p0013c2s
v1p0169c1s v1p0346c2s v1p0469c1s

v1p0500c1s v1p0586c1s v1p0851c2s
v1p0952c1s v1p1201c2s v2p0105c1s
v2p0201c1s v2p0301c2s v3p0250c2s
v3p0259c2s v4p0149c1s
Marston, R. v4p0544c1s
Marston, R.B. v4p0181c1s
v4p0206c1s v5p0208c2s v5p0575c1s
v5p0628c1s v6p0226c1s v6p0457c1s
v6p0586c2s
Marston, W. v1p0570c2s
v1p0773c1s v1p1409c1s v2p0293c2s
Marstyn, M. v4p0364c2s
v5p0347c2s
Marteau, H. v5p0113c2s
v5p0427c1s
Martel, C. v6p0252c1s
v6p0371c2s
Martel, E.A. v4p0093c1s
v5p0098c2s
Martel, M.E.A. v5p0098c2s
Martell, G. v4p0017c2s
Marten, C., Mrs. v1p0523c1s
Marten, C.H.K. v6p0293c1s
Martens, F.de v5p0024c2s
v5p0110c1s v6p0301c1s v6p0510c2m
Martensen, H. v1p0095c2s
v1p0289c1s v1p1045c1s v2p0476c2s
v2p0477c1s
Marter, J.G.Van v6p0168c1s
v6p0562c2s
Martillet, G.de v1p0041c2s
Martin, A. v1p0848c1s
v1p1045c1s v3p0443c2s
Martin, A. et al. v6p0342c1s
Martin, A., jr. v1p1303c2s
Martin, A.A. v3p0034c2s
v3p0270c2s v5p0237c1s v6p0242c2s
Martin, A.J. v6p0132c2s
v6p0512c2s v6p0598c2s
Martin, A.P. v2p0182c2s
v3p0177c2s v3p0412c2s v4p0343c2s
v4p0426c2s v4p0520c2s v4p0548c2s
v5p0346c1s
Martin, A.Patchett v4p0216c2s
Martin, A.S. v2p0087c2s
Martin, A.T. v5p0198c2s
v5p0357c2s v5p0360c1s
Martin, A.W.P. v6p0119c2s
Martin, Abbe v1p0473c2s
v1p0479c2s v1p1109c2s v1p1110c1m
v2p0131c2s
Martin, B. v5p0281c1s
v6p0098c1s
Martin, B., jr. v5p0623c2s
Martin, B.E. v1p0350c2s
v1p0473c2s v1p0766c2s v1p1306c2s
v1p1317c1s v2p0076c1s v2p0264c2s
v3p0240c2s v3p0343c1s
Martin, B.E. and Martin, C.M.
v5p0432c1s
Martin, B.N. v1p0348c1s
v1p0393c2s v1p0528c2m v1p0646c1s
v1p0648c2s v1p0740c1s v1p0830c2s
v1p1410c2m v2p0123c2s v2p0408c2s
v2p0437c2s
Martin, C. v5p0057c2s
v5p0114c2s v5p0380c1m
Martin, C., Mrs. v1p0076c2s
v1p0369c1s v1p0703c2s v1p0795c2s
v1p0906c1s v1p0942c2s v1p0982c2s
Martin, C.A. v5p0365c1s
v6p0295c1s
Martin, C.B. v1p0934c1s
v1p1317c2m v1p1440c2s v2p0006c2s
v2p0012c2s v2p0063c1s v2p0075c1s
v2p0197c1s v2p0263c1s v2p0448c2m
Martin, C.B., Mrs. v1p1136c2s
Martin, C.C. v6p0626c2s
Martin, C.D. v5p0258c2s
Martin, C.J. v6p0183c2s
Martin, C.M. v1p0388c1s
Martin, C.M. and Martin, B.E.
v5p0432c1s
Martin, C.S. v3p0349c2s
v4p0310c1s
Martin, C.T. v6p0108c2s
Martin, C.W. v4p0248c2s
Martin, Carew v5p0579c2s
Martin, Charlotte M. v5p0233c2s
Martin, D. v5p0141c2s
Martin, D.B. v6p0013c1s
Martin, D.D. v6p0020c1s
Martin, D.S. v1p0376c2s
v2p0274c2s v3p0146c1s v5p0015c1m
v5p0076c2s v5p0180c2s v5p0229c1s
v5p0234c1s
Martin, E.A. v3p0257c2s
v6p0081c2s v6p0133c2s v6p0255c2s
Martin, E.C. v3p0068c2s
v3p0228c1s v3p0286c1s v3p0458c1s
v4p0004c1s v4p0500c2s v4p0569c2s
Martin, E.G. v1p0076c1s
v1p0522c1s v2p0198c2s v2p0241c1s
v2p0461c1s v3p0070c2s v4p0499c1s
v5p0221c1s v5p0396c2s
Martin, E.H. v5p0581c1s
Martin, E.L. v4p0354c2s
Martin, E.S. v1p1368c1s
v4p0136c2s v4p0210c2s v4p0357c1s
v4p0568c1s v5p0106c2s v5p0107c2s
v5p0257c1s v5p0405c1s v5p0406c2s
v5p0430c1s v5p0434c1s v5p0636c1s
v6p0114c1s v6p0116c2s v6p0153c2s
v6p0175c2s v6p0215c2s v6p0319c1s
v6p0346c1s v6p0376c1s v6p0396c1s
v6p0543c1s v6p0580c1s v6p0580c2s
v6p0701c1s
Martin, F. v1p0291c2s
v1p0431c1s v1p0755c2s v1p1034c2s
v1p1426c2s v2p0021c2s v2p0478c2s
v3p0103c2s
Martin, F.G. v6p0093c1s
Martin, F.W. v6p0695c2s
Martin, Frank G. v6p0376c2s
Martin, G. v1p0500c2s
v5p0635c2s v6p0376c1s
Martin, G.C. v5p0171c2s
Martin, G.E. v3p0108c1s
Martin, G.G. v6p0201c2s
Martin, G.H. v3p0378c2s
v4p0353c2s v4p0359c2m v4p0466c1m
v4p0505c1m v4p0505c2s v4p0506c1m
v5p0179c1s v5p0569c1s v5p0636c2s
v6p0076c2s v6p0089c2s v6p0575c1s
Martin, G.M. v4p0286c1s
v5p0256c1s v5p0278c1s v5p0342c2s
v5p0489c1s v5p0521c2s v6p0259c2s
v6p0299c1s v6p0369c1s v6p0544c1s
Martin, G.W. v6p0349c1s
v6p0382c1s v6p0576c2s
Martin, George v5p0310c2s
Martin, H. v5p0099c1s
v5p0162c1s v5p0314c1s v5p0360c1m
v5p0577c2s v5p0608c2s
Martin, H. et al. v4p0133c2s
Martin, H., Mrs. v1p0016c2s
v1p0105c1s v2p0266c1s
Martin, H.A. v1p1360c1s
v2p0457c1s
Martin, H.F. v1p0944c1s
v1p1035c2s v1p1184c1m v1p1186c1m
v2p0037c1s v2p0239c2s v2p0378c1s
v2p0397c2m v2p0398c1s v3p0195c1s
v3p0387c2s
Martin, H.M. v6p0668c2s
Martin, H.N. v1p0134c2s
v2p0302c2s v2p0341c1s v2p0415c1s
v3p0316c2s
Martin, H.R. v6p0059c2s
v6p0147c2s v6p0175c1s v6p0201c1s
v6p0442c2s
Martin, H.T. v4p0390c1s
v4p0625c2s
Martin, Helen R. v6p0535c2s
Martin, Herbert, Mrs. v6p0356c1s
Martin, J. v1p0519c1s
v1p0918c2s v5p0345c1s v5p0407c1s
v6p0262c1s v6p0652c1s v6p0652c2s
Martin, J., Mrs. v2p0174c2s
v3p0323c2s
Martin, J.A. v2p0240c2s
v6p0050c2s
Martin, J.B. v1p0549c2s
v1p0963c2s v2p0129c2s v2p0136c1s
v2p0186c2s v2p0294c2s v2p0418c2s
Martin, J.C. v3p0286c2s
Martin, J.S. v6p0165c2s
v6p0291c2s v6p0326c1s v6p0436c2s
v6p0631c2s
Martin, J.W. v1p0510c1s
v5p0120c1s v5p0320c2s v5p0391c2s
Martin, K.B. v2p0099c1s
v2p0414c1s
Martin, L. and Tarr, R.S.. v6p0010c2m
Martin, L.J. v2p0076c2s
v2p0170c1s v3p0380c2s v6p0140c2s
v6p0221c1s
Martin, L.P. v2p0390c2s
Martin, M. v2p0457c1s
v5p0140c2s v6p0173c1s v6p0393c2s
Martin, M.B. v1p1426c2s
v2p0351c2s v2p0477c2s v4p0031c1s
Martin, M.E. v1p1380c2s
v3p0346c2s
Martin, McL. v1p0137c1s
Martin, Martha v6p0148c2s
Martin, May v6p0202c1s
Martin, N.R. v6p0133c2s
Martin, N.R. v6p0133c2s
Martin, O.F. v2p0342c2s
v3p0036c2s
Martin, R. v6p0305c1s
Martin, R.B. v1p1075c2s
v6p0270c1s
Martin, R.B. and Hamilton, R.V.
v5p0364c1s
Martin, R.H. v5p0630c2s
Martin, R.M. v1p0545c1s
Martin, R.W. v6p0530c1s
Martin, S. v1p0040c1s
v1p0254c2s v1p0498c2s v1p0637c1s
v1p0640c1s v1p0651c2s v1p0860c1m
v1p0860c2s v1p1205c1s v1p1279c1s
v1p1419c2s v4p0586c1s
Martin, T. v1p0583c1s
v1p0703c2s v1p0705c1s v2p0398c2s
v3p0377c1s v3p0387c1s v4p0408c2s
v5p0611c1s
Martin, T. and Schiller, F.
v3p0118c2s
Martin, T.C. v2p0266c1s
v3p0134c1s v3p0143c2s v3p0148c2s
v4p0176c2m v4p0177c1s v4p0254c1s
v4p0403c2s v4p0570c2m v4p0571c1s
v5p0184c2s v5p0552c2s v6p0091c1s
v6p0151c2s v6p0197c2s v6p0301c2s
v6p0414c2s v6p0458c2s v6p0512c2m
v6p0637c2s
Martin, T.F. v6p0147c2s
Martin, T.M. v5p0463c2s
Martin, W. v6p0019c2s
v6p0083c1s v6p0639c1s v6p0655c2s
Martin, W.A.P. v1p0231c2s
v1p0232c1s v1p0233c2m v1p0236c s
v1p0239c1s v1p0286c2s v1p0426c2s
v2p0223c2s v3p0064c2s v3p0078c2s
v3p0079c2m v3p0096c1s v3p0217c1s
v3p0441c2s v5p0111c1s v5p0112c2s
v5p0113c1s v5p0338c2s v5p0438c2s
v6p0118c1s v6p0119c2s
Martin, W.B. v6p0317c1s
Martin, W.C.L. v1p0137c1s
v1p0456c2s v1p0955c2s v1p1009c2s
v1p1193c2s v1p1213c2s v1p1240c1s
v1p1310c1s
Martin, W.E. v6p0009c2s
Martin, W.J. v4p0406c2s
Martin, W.R. v1p0258c1s
Martin, W.W. v3p0042c1s
v3p0208c2s v4p0041c2s v4p0055c2s
v4p0301c1s v6p0061c2s
Martindale, C.C. v6p0004c2s
v6p0537c2s
Martindale, I.C. v1p0279c1s
Martindale, P. v1p0340c2s
Martineau, E. v5p0536c1s
Martineau, G. v5p0559c2s
v6p0624c2s
Martineau, H. v1p0002c1s
v1p0014c1s v1p0039c1s v1p0059c2m
v1p0066c1s v1p0087c1s v1p0096c1s
v1p0134c1s v1p0183c2s v1p0229c2s
v1p0232c1s v1p0233c2s v1p0280c2s
v1p0305c2s v1p0337c1s v1p0338c2s
v1p0351c2s v1p0359c2s v1p0366c2s
v1p0386c1s v1p0407c1s v1p0413c1s
v1p0442c2s v1p0444c1s v1p0465c1s
v1p0537c2s v1p0539c2s v1p0568c2s
v1p0591c1s v1p0599c1s v1p0599c2s
v1p0618c1s v1p0643c2s v1p0682c1s
v1p0695c2s v1p0718c2s v1p0753c1s
v1p0789c1s v1p0819c2s v1p0823c2s
v1p0876c2s v1p0903c1s v1p0904c2s
v1p0934c1s v1p0934c2s v1p0939c2s
v1p0940c1s v1p0961c2s v1p0993c2s
v1p1025c1m v1p1025c2s v1p1027c2s
v1p1049c2s v1p1068c2s v1p1142c1s
v1p1158c1s v1p1168c1s v1p1168c2m
v1p1175c2s v1p1185c1s v1p1195c1s
v1p1202c1s v1p1203c2s v1p1208c2s
v1p1218c2m v1p1219c2s v1p1245c2m
v1p1251c1s v1p1275c2s v1p1343c1s
v1p1351c1s v1p1394c2s v1p1421c2s
v1p1438c2s v2p0005c2s
Martineau, J. v1p0014c2s
v1p0081c2s v1p0102c2s v1p0129c1s
v1p0129c2s v1p0156c2s v1p0201c2s
v1p0217c1s v1p0247c1s v1p0249c1s
v1p0251c2s v1p0253c1s v1p0274c1s
v1p0287c1s v1p0313c2m v1p0434c2s
v1p0440c1s v1p0527c2s v1p0528c2m
v1p0594c1s v1p0640c2s v1p0810c2m
v1p0839c1s v1p0843c1s v1p0843c2s
v1p0900c2m v1p0912c2s v1p0972c2s
v1p1017c1s v1p1058c1s v1p1097c2s
v1p1102c2s v1p1152c1s v1p1162c2s
v1p1260c1s v1p1293c2s v1p1302c1s
v1p1304c1s v1p1360c2s v1p1378c2s
v2p0084c1s v2p0106c2s v2p0192c1m
v3p0083c1s v3p0136c2s v3p0242c1s
v4p0042c1s v4p0437c1s
Martineau, J. and Fairbairn, A.M.
v4p0042c1s
Martineau, J. et al. v4p0108c2s
Martineau, L.E. v6p0689c2s
Martineau, R. v1p0087c1s
v1p0118c2s v1p0122c2m v1p0125c1s
v1p0312c2s v1p0581c2s v1p0582c1s
v2p0369c1s v4p0055c2s
Martineau, R. and Colenso, J.W.
v1p0313c1s
Martineau, Russell v4p0053c2s
v4p0350c1s v4p0463c2s
Martinengo-Cesaresco, E. . v2p0030c2s
v3p0038c2s v5p0020c2s v5p0115c1s
v5p0116c1s v5p0142c1s v5p0241c1s
v5p0307c1s v5p0326c2s v5p0400c2s
v5p0612c2s v6p0021c2m v6p0022c1s
v6p0040c2s v6p0249c1s v6p0272c1s
v6p0331c2s v6p0333c1s v6p0466c2s
v6p0504c2s v6p0537c1s v6p0549c1s
v6p0581c2s v6p0604c2s v6p0709c2s
Martinez, A.B. v6p0029c1s
Martinez, E. v6p0160c2s
Martinez, J. v5p0148c2s
Martini, F. v4p0295c1s
v4p0597c2s
Martini, T. v1p0751c2s
Martinof, J. v1p0617c2s
Martinoff, I. v5p0499c2s

Martins, C. v1p0134c2s v1p0524c1s v6p0074c1s
Martinson, H. v1p0700c1s
Martius, C.F.P.von v1p0158c2s v1p0196c1s
Martley, H. v5p0025c1s v5p0128c1s v5p0173c2s v5p0404c2s v5p0596c2s v6p0251c2s
Martley, Henry v5p0132c2s
Martley, N. v5p0560c1s
Martling, Harriet v5p0096c2s
Martling, J.A. v1p0600c2s
Marton, C. v1p0712c2s
Marton, W.A.P. v1p0985c2s
Marty, M. v3p0213c2s
Martyn, C. v1p0877c2s v3p0081c1s v3p0083c2s v3p0329c2s
Martyn, C.D. v3p0440c1s
Martyn, C.J. v1p0991c1s
Martyn, E. v3p0220c1m
Martyn, E. and Hannigan, D.F. v3p0469c2s
Martyn, H. v4p0094c2s
Martyn, J.C. v3p0111c2s v3p0411c1s v3p0413c2s
Martyn, M.E. v5p0326c1s
Martyn, Mrs. v1p0693c2s
Martyn, P. v6p0090c1s v6p0629c1s
Martyn, S.S. v2p0041c2s v2p0437c2s
Martyne, R. v6p0691c1s
Martyne, R.A. v6p0645c1s
Martyr, C. v1p0983c2s
Marvel, J. v1p0080c2s v1p0474c1s
Marvel, L.H. v2p0275c2s
Marven, L.C. v1p1194c1s
Marvin, A. v6p0318c1s v6p0581c1s
Marvin, A.P. v1p0005c2s v1p0290c2m v1p1103c2s v1p1206c1s v1p1350c2s v1p1353c1s v1p1395c2s
Marvin, A.S. v5p0088c1s
Marvin, A.T. v6p0493c2s
Marvin, A.W. v6p0510c1s
Marvin, C. v2p0003c2s v2p0036c1s v2p0380c2s v3p0311c1s v4p0365c2s
Marvin, C. and Eastman, W.R. v6p0371c1s
Marvin, C.F. v3p0013c2s v3p0353c2s v5p0317c2s v6p0567c2s
Marvin, C.W. v6p0413c1s
Marvin, Chas. v4p0265c1s v4p0437c2s
Marvin, Cornelia v6p0371c2s
Marvin, E.P. v1p0290c2s v1p0529c2s v1p1237c2s v1p1328c2s
Marvin, Edith D. v6p0432c1s
Marvin, F.O. v4p0180c2m v5p0188c1s
Marvin, F.R. v1p0331c1s v1p0371c1s v1p1221c2s
Marvin, G. v6p0510c1s
Marvin, J.B. v1p1407c1s
Marvin, T.R. v1p0806c1s
Marvin, W. v1p1147c2s v6p0616c1s
Marvin, W.L. v5p0258c1s v5p0370c1s v5p0526c2m v6p0140c2s v6p0141c1s v6p0254c2s v6p0338c2s v6p0411c1s v6p0455c2s v6p0591c1s v6p0616c1s v6p0667c2s
Marvin, W.T. v6p0309c2s v6p0500c2s
Marvin, W.T.R. v5p0085c1s v5p0364c2s v6p0025c2s
Marvyn, J. v6p0709c2s
Marwell, H. v3p0208c2s
Marwick, J.D. v6p0578c1s
Marwick, T.P. v2p0417c1s
Marx, A.B. v1p0108c1s
Marx, C.D. v3p0380c2s v4p0485c1s v6p0204c1s
Marx, C.V. v2p0172c1s
Marx, E. v1p1185c1s v2p0223c2s
Marx, F. v1p1137c2s
Marx, H.F. v6p0074c1s
Marx, K. v3p0067c1s
Marx, K. and Broadhouse, J. v2p0067c1s
Marx, R. v5p0367c2s v5p0368c1s v6p0408c2s
Marx-Aveling, Eleanor v4p0336c1s
Marye, J.L. v4p0225c1s
Marye, L.S. v4p0165c2s
Marzials, F.J. v6p0275c2s
Marzials, F.T. v2p0102c1s v2p0125c1s v2p0193c1s v2p0210c2s v2p0387c2s v3p0240c2s v3p0264c2s v3p0275c1s v3p0368c2s v3p0475c2s v4p0018c1s v4p0124c1s v4p0155c1s v4p0159c2s v4p0197c2s v4p0221c1s v4p0574c1s v6p0228c2s
Mas, A.Del v4p0378c1s
Masao, T. v5p0303c1s
Masaryk, A.G. v6p0072c2s
Mascagni, P. v5p0609c2s
Mascart, E. v2p0093c2s
Mascart, M.E. v1p0647c1s
Mascol, C. v3p0217c1s v3p0229c2s v3p0324c1s v3p0359c2s v3p0374c1s
Masefield, J. v6p0367c2s v6p0580c1s v6p0604c1s v6p0673c1s
Maseres, F. and Mellish, C. v1p0973c1s
Masey, T.A. v1p1290c2s v3p0423c1s
Masham, Lord v4p0214c1s v4p0563c2s
Masham, Lord and Courtney, L. v4p0214c1s
Masham, S.Cunliffe-Lister. v5p0584c1s
Mashek, N. v6p0072c2s
Masiyama, R. v6p0338c1s
Maskell, A. v5p0448c2s v6p0332c1s
Maskell, A.E.C. v1p0199c1s
Maskell, Alfred v6p0033c1s
Maskell, H.P. v3p0135c2s
Maskell, J. v4p0146c1s v4p0146c2s v4p0217c2s v4p0235c1s v4p0339c2s v4p0576c1s v4p0636c2s
Maskell, M. v5p0391c1s
Maskelyne, J.N. v2p0002c1s v2p0030c1s v2p0076c2s v2p0157c1s v2p0239c1s v2p0271c2s v2p0322c2s
Maskelyne, N.S. v1p0008c1s v1p0348c2s v1p0828c1s v1p0828c2m v1p0841c1s v1p0845c1s v1p1195c2s
Maskelyne, N.S. and Ball, V. v3p0116c2s v3p0237c2s
Maslen, A. v4p0491c1s v4p0548c2s
Masoch, S. v1p0738c2s
Mason, A. v4p0323c1s v4p0513c1s v4p0532c2s v6p0419c2s v6p0628c2s
Mason, A.B. v1p0406c1s v1p0713c2s v1p0848c2s v1p1040c1s v4p0097c1s v4p0599c1s v6p0173c1s
Mason, A.E.W. v4p0589c1s v5p0193c2s v5p0425c1s v5p0527c2s v5p0591c2s v6p0235c2s v6p0554c2s v6p0658c1s
Mason, A.E.W. and Lang, Andrew v5p0433c2s
Mason, A.G. v3p0290c2s v3p0373c2m v3p0469c2s v5p0360c1s v5p0520c1s v5p0636c2s
Mason, A.J. v5p0048c1s
Mason, A.L. v5p0392c1s
Mason, A.M. v6p0479c2s
Mason, A.P. v3p0154c2s v3p0271c1s v3p0344c1s v3p0433c2s v3p0452c1s
Mason, A.R. v6p0229c2s
Mason, Amelia G. v5p0638c2s
Mason, B. v1p0883c2s
Mason, C. v1p1082c2s v2p0154c2s v6p0071c2s v6p0399c1s v6p0540c1s
Mason, C.A. v6p0355c1s
Mason, C.A., Mrs. v1p0366c1s v1p0924c1s
Mason, C.J. v3p0036c2s
Mason, C.M. v3p0001c1s v3p0073c2s v3p0077c1s v3p0077c2s v3p0129c2s v3p0405c1s
Mason, C.P. v1p0435c2s
Mason, C.T. v6p0291c1s
Mason, C.W. v1p0776c2s v1p0924c2s v1p1231c2s v1p1396c1s v4p0444c1s v5p0418c2s v5p0643c2s
Mason, D.G. v5p0260c1s v5p0329c1s v6p0059c1s v6p0069c1s v6p0079c1s v6p0121c2s v6p0142c1s v6p0174c1s v6p0176c1s v6p0185c1s v6p0239c1s v6p0239c2s v6p0274c2s v6p0284c1s v6p0404c2s v6p0410c2s v6p0433c2s v6p0437c2s v6p0438c1m v6p0438c2m v6p0439c1s v6p0549c1s v6p0564c2s v6p0575c2m v6p0634c2s
Mason, D.H. v1p0228c1s v1p0640c1s v3p0347c1s
Mason, E. v1p0327c2s v1p0373c1s v1p0459c2s v1p0812c1s v1p0959c2s v1p1131c1s v1p1362c1m v2p0351c1s v2p0382c1s v2p0480c2s v3p0447c1s v6p0142c1s
Mason, E.C. v3p0449c1s v5p0337c2s
Mason, E.E. v1p0599c1s
Mason, E.G. v1p0703c1s v1p0921c1s v1p0973c1s v2p0016c2s v2p0133c1s v2p0214c2m v2p0251c2s v2p0295c2s v2p0383c1s v2p0411c2s v2p0442c1s v3p0074c2s v4p0013c2s v4p0091c1s v4p0099c2s v4p0100c1s v4p0321c1s v4p0406c2s v4p0424c2s v5p0066c1s v6p0437c1s
Mason, E.H. v6p0138c1s
Mason, E.L. v4p0181c1s
Mason, E.V. v6p0298c1s
Mason, Ethel O. v5p0178c2s
Mason, F. v1p0691c1s v1p0702c2m v1p0989c2s v1p1339c2s v3p0369c1s v5p0006c2s
Mason, F.B. v6p0652c2s v6p0682c2s
Mason, F.H. v3p0166c2s v4p0498c2s v4p0552c2s v5p0222c2s v5p0533c2s v6p0011c1s v6p0087c1s v6p0198c1s v6p0244c1s
Mason, G.C. v1p0062c1s v1p0160c2s v1p0203c2s v1p1205c2s v1p1296c1s v2p0229c2s v3p0453c2s v4p0129c1s v4p0635c1s v5p0487c2s
Mason, G.C., jr. v1p0913c2s v2p0020c1s
Mason, G.D. v6p0056c2m
Mason, H.B. v5p0212c2m
Mason, H.D. v3p0189c2s
Mason, H.M. v1p0539c2s v1p1274c1s
Mason, H.T. v6p0131c2s
Mason, J. v1p0464c1s v1p1015c1s v1p1166c1s v2p0302c2m v2p0346c1s v2p0350c1s v2p0418c1s v3p0064c2s v3p0068c2s v3p0091c1s v3p0149c1s v3p0175c2s v3p0198c1m v3p0200c1s v3p0240c2s v3p0287c1s v3p0310c1s v3p0311c1s v3p0326c2s v3p0339c1s v3p0355c2s v3p0383c2s v3p0389c2s v3p0392c2s
Mason, J.D. v4p0414c1s
Mason, J.H. v3p0323c1s
Mason, J.M. v1p1078c2s
Mason, J.T. v5p0525c1s
Mason, J.W. v4p0472c1s v4p0506c1s v4p0525c1s v4p0553c1s
Mason, J.W.T. v6p0012c1s
Mason, J.Y. v1p1374c2s
Mason, L. v1p0019c2s v1p0857c2s v1p0882c2s
Mason, L.B. v1p0243c2s
Mason, L.W. v4p0311c1s
Mason, M. v5p0484c1s
Mason, M.A. v4p0277c1s v5p0423c1s
Mason, M.M. v1p0339c2s
Mason, M.P. v2p0198c1s
Mason, N.T. v4p0022c1s v4p0225c1s v4p0314c2s v4p0315c1s v4p0593c1s
Mason, O.T. v1p0045c2m v1p0324c1s v2p0010c2s v2p0016c1s v2p0018c2s v2p0103c1s v2p0300c1s v2p0370c2s v2p0483c2s v3p0188c1s v3p0205c1s v3p0214c1s v3p0279c2s v3p0467c1s v4p0205c1s v4p0502c1s v5p0049c1m v5p0123c1s v5p0196c1s v5p0196c2s v5p0288c2m v5p0373c1s v5p0589c1s v6p0099c1s v6p0585c2s v6p0700c1s
Mason, R.A. v4p0068c1s
Mason, R.M. v1p0483c1s
Mason, R.O. v1p0041c1s v1p0433c2s v1p1162c1s v1p1360c2s v3p0206c1s v4p0271c2s v5p0209c2s v5p0483c1s
Mason, R.O. and Rabb, R.M. v5p0293c1s
Mason, R.W. v5p0447c2m
Mason, S.B. v6p0323c1s
Mason, S.R. v1p0685c2s v1p1200c2s v1p1270c1s
Mason, S.W. v1p1005c2s
Mason, T. v5p0205c2s v5p0334c2s v5p0347c1s v5p0470c1s
Mason, V.L. v4p0332c2s v4p0592c1s v4p0615c2s
Mason, W. v4p0243c1s v5p0365c1m v6p0564c2s
Mason, W. and Smith, F.M.. v4p0420c2s
Mason, W.A. v4p0161c1s
Mason, W.A.P. v6p0127c2s
Mason, W.E. v5p0004c1s v5p0519c2s
Mason, W.H. v1p0601c1s v1p1157c2s
Mason, W.P. v1p0341c2s v1p0556c2s v1p1399c2s v1p1417c1s v3p0049c1s v3p0456c2s v4p0589c1s v4p0612c2s v5p0104c1s v5p0199c2s v5p0622c1s v6p0688c1s
Mason, Wm. v5p0169c1s
Maspero, G. v2p0134c1s v2p0364c2s v3p0120c1s v3p0131c2s v4p0138c2s
Masqueray, E.L. v6p0563c2s
Mass, A.J. v4p0437c1s
Massaquoi, Momolu v6p0007c2s v6p0675c2s
Massart, Jean v6p0210c2s
Massee, G. v6p0244c1m
Massee, G.E. v1p1428c1s
Masseras, E. v3p0442c1s
Massett, S.C. v1p0294c2s v1p0791c2s
Massey, A.P. v1p0451c1s v1p0742c2s
Massey, G. v1p0019c1s v1p0095c2s v1p0171c1s v1p0500c2s v1p0602c1s v1p0614c2s v1p0719c1s v1p0719c2s v1p0949c2s v1p1008c2s v1p1220c1s v1p1295c2s v3p0295c1s

v3p0433c1s v4p0019c2s
Massey, G.B. v1p0643c2s
Massey, S.F. v5p0127c2s
Massey, W.F. v4p0078c2m
v4p0242c2s v4p0264c2s v4p0414c1s
v4p0415c2s v4p0423c1s
Massey, W.F. and Fletcher, S.W.
v6p0087c1s
Massicks, C.A.B. v4p0565c2s
Massie, E.C. v5p0583c1s
v6p0360c1s
Massie, J. v3p0129c2s
v4p0170c1s v4p0255c2s v5p0024c1s
v5p0178c2s v6p0191c2s
Massie, J.W. v1p0635c1s
Massingberd, W.O. v6p0319c2s
v6p0602c2s
Massingham, H.W. v3p0070c2s
v3p0231c2s v3p0238c2s v4p0227c2m
v4p0238c2s v4p0239c2m v4p0314c1s
v4p0403c1s v4p0428c1s v4p0491c1s
v4p0581c1s v4p0602c2s v5p0141c1m
v5p0176c1s v5p0247c1s v5p0332c2s
v5p0497c1s v5p0581c2s v6p0006c2s
v6p0048c1s v6p0206c1s v6p0238c1s
v6p0270c2m v6p0299c1s v6p0481c1s
v6p0481c2s v6p0512c2s
Massman, S. v2p0482c1s
Masson, D. v1p0002c1s
v1p0169c1s v1p0173c1s v1p0223c1s
v1p0266c2s v1p0276c1s v1p0327c2s
v1p0345c1m v1p0347c2s v1p0368c2s
v1p0384c1s v1p0417c2s v1p0418c1s
v1p0428c1s v1p0497c1s v1p0530c2s
v1p0549c1s v1p0594c1s v1p0602c1s
v1p0704c1s v1p0707c1s v1p0710c2s
v1p0754c1s v1p0755c1s v1p0763c1s
v1p0766c2s v1p0814c2s v1p0819c1s
v1p0840c2s v1p0842c1s v1p0896c1s
v1p0926c2s v1p1023c1s v1p1057c1s
v1p1131c2s v1p1170c1s v1p1176c2s
v1p1177c2s v1p1183c1s v1p1189c2s
v1p1275c1s v1p1306c1s v1p1429c2s
v2p0058c1s v2p0068c2s v4p0226c1s
v4p0304c2s v4p0309c1s v4p0371c2s
Masson, F. v4p0233c1s
v4p0392c2s v4p0421c2s v4p0468c2s
Masson, G. v1p0101c2s
v1p0132c1s v1p0304c2s v1p0346c2s
v1p0489c1s v1p0489c2m v1p0587c2s
v1p0691c1s v1p0791c1s v1p0826c2m
v1p0948c1s v1p0994c2s v1p1070c2s
v1p1121c2s v1p1157c2s v1p1199c2s
v2p0212c1s v2p0375c1s v2p0416c1s
Masson, J. v2p0258c1s
v2p0268c1s v2p0280c2s v2p0341c1s
v2p0450c1s v6p0040c1s v6p0248c2s
Masson, John F., Mrs. v6p0303c2s
Masson, Nancy v6p0333c1s
Masson, O. and Pickering, S.U.
v3p0168c1s
Masson, R. v4p0153c1s
Masson, R.O., Mrs. v1p1011c1s
Masson, R.S. v4p0353c2s
v4p0456c1s
Masson, Rosaline v5p0459c1s
v6p0040c2s v6p0592c2s
Masson, T. v6p0057c2s
v6p0060c1s v6p0541c1s v6p0663c1m
Masson, Tom v6p0078c1s
v6p0124c1s v6p0272c1s v6p0624c2s
v6p0700c1s
Masson-Forestier, A. v5p0311c2s
Massy, P.H.H. v6p0661c2s
Mast, S.O. v6p0005c1s
Masterman, C.F.G. v6p0112c2s
v6p0126c1s v6p0206c1s v6p0206c2s
v6p0208c1s v6p0270c2s v6p0481c1s
v6p0512c1s v6p0592c1s v6p0600c1s
v6p0665c1m
Masterman, E.W. v6p0343c2s
Masterman, E.W.G. v5p0060c2s
v5p0152c1s v5p0212c2s v5p0428c1s
v5p0428c2m v6p0059c2s v6p0163c2s
v6p0166c2m v6p0221c1s v6p0245c2s
v6p0255c1s v6p0340c1s v6p0343c1s
v6p0343c2s v6p0344c1s
Masters, D. v5p0122c2s
Masters, E.L. v3p0029c1s
v3p0473c1s
Masters, F.J. v4p0013c1s
v4p0106c1s v4p0106c2s v4p0415c1s
v6p0086c1s v6p0119c2m v6p0120c1s
v6p0290c2s v6p0468c2s v6p0568c1s
Masters, H. v1p0362c2s
v2p0122c2s
Masters, L. v3p0115c2s
Masters, M.T. v1p0173c1s
v1p0539c1s v1p0732c2s v1p0977c1s
v1p1014c2s v1p1015c2s v1p1175c2s
v1p1177c2s v2p0118c1s v2p0160c1m
v2p0298c2s v3p0405c2s v4p0445c1s
v5p0277c1s
Masters, R. v1p0190c1s
v1p0526c1s v1p1106c1s v1p1254c1s
v1p1382c2s
Masterton, R.K. v4p0232c1s
Mastin, C.H. v2p0282c1s
Maston, O.H. v3p0001c1s
Masure, B.F. v3p0199c1s
Mataja, V. v6p0004c2s
Matchett, C.H. et al. v5p0179c1s
Matchett, W. v6p0173c2s
Mater, A. v6p0236c2s
Mathams, W.J. v5p0244c1s
v5p0490c2s
Mather and Richards v1p1289c2s
Mather, A.I. v4p0231c1s
Mather, E.I. v3p0152c1s
Mather, F. v2p0157c2s
v5p0627c1s
Mather, F.G. v1p0192c1s
v1p0192c2s v1p0194c1s v1p0194c2m
v1p0872c1s v1p0928c2s v1p0951c1s
v1p1367c2s v2p0006c2m v2p0020c1s
v2p0089c2s v2p0171c1s v2p0172c2m
v2p0303c2s v2p0313c2s v2p0373c1s
v2p0384c2s v2p0389c1s v2p0405c1s
v2p0463c2s v3p0066c1s v3p0080c1s
v3p0088c2s v3p0132c2s v3p0144c1s
v3p0304c2s v3p0394c1s v3p0473c2s
v4p0136c1s v4p0461c1s v4p0538c1s
v4p0612c2s
Mather, F.J., jr. v5p0062c1s
v5p0103c1s v5p0147c1s v5p0176c2s
v5p0178c1m v5p0216c2s v5p0271c2s
v5p0300c2s v5p0333c1s v5p0373c1s
v5p0397c2s v5p0435c2s v5p0536c2s
v5p0585c2s v6p0001c1s v6p0001c2s
v6p0004c2s v6p0010c1m v6p0013c1s
v6p0018c2s v6p0021c1s v6p0027c1s
v6p0027c2s v6p0032c2s v6p0033c1s
v6p0034c1m v6p0034c2m v6p0035c1s
v6p0039c1s v6p0040c2s v6p0043c1m
v6p0045c1s v6p0048c1m v6p0055c2s
v6p0056c1s v6p0073c2m v6p0075c1s
v6p0081c2m v6p0089c1s v6p0096c2m
v6p0097c2m v6p0102c1m v6p0106c1s
v6p0107c2s v6p0108c1s v6p0112c2s
v6p0130c2s v6p0131c2s v6p0132c1s
v6p0135c2m v6p0136c1m v6p0137c1m
v6p0137c2s v6p0138c2s v6p0140c1s
v6p0140c2s v6p0142c1s v6p0151c1s
v6p0156c2s v6p0167c2s v6p0168c2s
v6p0169c1s v6p0176c2s v6p0184c1s
v6p0186c1s v6p0189c2s v6p0194c1s
v6p0194c2s v6p0207c2s v6p0211c2s
v6p0213c2s v6p0216c2s v6p0224c1s
v6p0232c2s v6p0236c2s v6p0238c1s
v6p0244c1s v6p0245c2s v6p0248c1s
v6p0256c1s v6p0279c2s v6p0284c1s
v6p0285c1s v6p0286c1s v6p0288c1s
v6p0289c1s v6p0289c2s v6p0292c1s
v6p0294c1s v6p0302c2s v6p0307c2s
v6p0313c1s v6p0333c1s v6p0334c1s
v6p0335c1s v6p0337c1s v6p0344c1s
v6p0344c2s v6p0366c1s v6p0373c2s
v6p0374c2s v6p0378c1s v6p0378c2s
v6p0380c1m v6p0406c2s v6p0408c2s
v6p0429c1s v6p0429c2m v6p0437c1m
v6p0437c2m v6p0442c1s v6p0444c2s
v6p0449c2s v6p0452c1m v6p0452c2m
v6p0453c1m v6p0461c2s v6p0465c1s
v6p0465c2s v6p0468c1s v6p0471c2s
v6p0473c1s v6p0475c1s v6p0476c1s
v6p0476c2s v6p0488c1s v6p0510c2s
v6p0511c1s v6p0511c2s v6p0518c2s
v6p0523c1s v6p0524c2s v6p0531c1s
v6p0532c2s v6p0533c2s v6p0538c2s
v6p0540c1m v6p0541c2s v6p0546c1s
v6p0553c1s v6p0554c1s v6p0560c2m
v6p0561c1m v6p0563c1s v6p0564c1s
v6p0565c2s v6p0569c1s v6p0571c1s
v6p0577c1s v6p0583c2m v6p0584c1s
v6p0588c1s v6p0609c2m v6p0611c2s
v6p0615c1s v6p0621c2s v6p0622c2s
v6p0623c1m v6p0627c1s v6p0635c1s
v6p0646c1s v6p0671c2s v6p0678c1s
v6p0687c1s v6p0690c1s v6p0692c2s
v6p0695c2s v6p0697c2s v6p0713c1s
Mather, F.W. v6p0104c2s
Mather, G.E. v4p0270c1s
Mather, I. v1p0290c1s
Mather, J.C. v1p0694c1s
Mather, M. v1p0738c2s
v2p0064c2s v2p0115c2s v3p0074c2s
v3p0130c2s
Mather, R. v5p0134c1s
v5p0424c1s
Mather, S. v2p0309c2s
v2p0445c1s
Mather, T.W. v2p0160c1s
Mather, W. v4p0313c2s
Mather, W.M. v1p1390c2s
Mather, W.W. v1p0666c1s
v1p0938c2s v1p1271c1s
Mathers, H. v1p0066c2s
v1p1252c1s v1p1314c2s v4p0411c2s
Mathers, H.B. v1p0226c1s
Mathers, H.T. v5p0477c1s
v5p0510c1s
Mathers, W. v6p0387c1s
Mathes, G.P. v3p0079c2s
Mathes, S.J. v5p0594c1s
Matheson, A. v1p0014c1s
v2p0409c2s v2p0478c2s
Matheson, A.H. v2p0174c2s
Matheson, A.P. v6p0041c2s
Matheson, C. v4p0324c1s
Matheson, C.B. v5p0103c2s
Matheson, E. v2p0419c2s
v4p0192c1s v5p0298c1s
Matheson, E.R. v6p0672c2s
Matheson, Ewing v6p0217c2s
Matheson, F.J. v5p0148c1s
Matheson, F.J. and Gossip, G.H.
v5p0543c1s
Matheson, F.P. v4p0629c1s
Matheson, G. v1p0239c2s
v1p0527c2s v1p0625c2s v1p0684c2s
v1p0875c1s v1p1089c2s v2p0122c1s
v2p0129c1s v2p0239c1s v2p0301c2s
v2p0390c1s v3p0001c2s v3p0259c2s
v4p0268c2s v4p0300c2s v4p0431c1s
v5p0060c2s v5p0115c1s v5p0484c2s
v6p0538c2s
Matheson, H.J. v6p0680c2s
Matheson, J. v1p0586c2s
v2p0201c1s v2p0299c2s
Matheson, P.E. v3p0422c1s
v5p0120c1s
Mathew, A. v6p0458c2s
Mathew, F. v4p0034c2s
v4p0064c1s v4p0129c2s v4p0460c2s
v4p0482c2s v4p0519c2s v4p0572c2s
v6p0234c1s
Mathew, J. v4p0093c2s
Mathew, W. v2p0340c1s
v3p0299c2s
Mathew, W.W. v1p1199c1s
Mathews, A. v1p0230c2s
v1p0938c2s v2p0219c2m v2p0276c2s
v2p0320c1m v2p0343c1m v3p0031c2s
v3p0250c1s v3p0454c1m v4p0479c1s
v5p0062c1s v5p0344c1s v5p0518c2s
v6p0085c2s v6p0351c1s
Mathews, A.P. v5p0270c2s
v6p0381c2s v6p0449c1m
Mathews, A.R. v6p0167c1s
Mathews, Amanda v6p0399c2s
v6p0604c1s v6p0703c1s
Mathews, B. v4p0604c2s
Mathews, B.C. v4p0187c2s
v4p0535c1s v5p0101c2s v5p0269c1s
v5p0439c1s
Mathews, B.J. v6p0294c1s
Mathews, C. v1p1190c2s
v2p0118c1s v2p0313c2s
Mathews, C.A. v5p0071c2s
v5p0091c2s v5p0243c2s
Mathews, C.S. v5p0609c1s
Mathews, C.T. v4p0024c1s
v4p0295c2s v4p0296c2s v4p0404c2s
v5p0026c2s v5p0637c2s
Mathews, E.B. v6p0681c1s
Mathews, E.F. v6p0567c2s
Mathews, E.R. and Reed, Clement
v6p0133c2s
Mathews, F.A. v2p0077c1s
v2p0304c1s v2p0325c1s v3p0016c1s
v3p0308c2s v3p0467c2s v4p0002c2s
v4p0448c1s v5p0012c2s v5p0236c1s
v5p0342c2s
Mathews, F.S. v4p0203c2s
v4p0324c2s v5p0041c2s v5p0063c1s
v5p0211c1s v5p0211c2s v6p0220c2s
Mathews, G. v6p0376c2s
Mathews, G.B. v6p0406c1s
Mathews, G.R. v3p0058c2s
Mathews, J. v1p1364c1s
Mathews, J.A. v6p0013c1s
Mathews, J.E. v1p0406c1s
Mathews, J.H. v2p0465c1s
Mathews, J.L. v4p0100c1s
v4p0347c1s v5p0141c1s v5p0393c2s
v5p0394c1s v5p0422c1s v5p0485c1s
v5p0489c1s v6p0575c2s v6p0709c1s
Mathews, Mrs. v1p0005c1s
v1p0312c1s v1p0345c1s v1p0891c2s
v1p1142c2s v1p1309c2s
Mathews, R. v3p0143c1s
v3p0336c2s v4p0188c1s v4p0190c2s
Mathews, R.H. v4p0038c1s
v4p0038c2s v4p0070c2s v4p0308c1s
v4p0624c1s v5p0039c2s v5p0291c1m
v5p0581c1s v5p0639c1s v6p0041c2s
v6p0042c1s v6p0042c2s v6p0121c1s
v6p0644c1s
Mathews, R.T. v2p0044c1s
v2p0082c2s v2p0373c1s
Mathews, S. v4p0057c1s
v4p0301c1s v4p0535c1s v4p0614c2s
v5p0023c1s v5p0055c2s v5p0058c2m
v5p0059c2s v5p0060c1s v5p0116c2s
v5p0118c1s v5p0186c1s v5p0305c2s
v5p0306c2m v5p0371c1s v5p0430c1s
v5p0442c1s v5p0562c1s v6p0063c1s
v6p0135c2s v6p0340c1s v6p0341c1s
v6p0419c1s v6p0475c2s v6p0484c2s
v6p0626c2s v6p0672c1s v6p0692c2s
Mathews, S. and Burton, E.D.
v5p0306c1s
Mathews, Shailer v6p0114c1s
v6p0190c2s v6p0232c1s
Mathews, W. v1p0421c1s
v1p0524c1s v1p0930c2s v1p1257c1s
v1p1429c2s v3p0317c1s v3p0414c2s
v4p0034c2s v4p0151c2s
Mathews, W.A. v3p0084c2s
v3p0168c1s v3p0193c2s

Mathews, W.H. v5p0422c1s
Mathews, W.S.B. v1p0883c1s
v1p0946c1s v4p0049c1s v4p0090c2s
v4p0101c2s v4p0113c2m v4p0219c2s
v4p0248c1s v4p0331c1s v4p0388c2m
v4p0389c1m v4p0389c2s v4p0390c1s
v4p0405c1s v4p0442c1m v4p0491c1s
v4p0506c2s v4p0566c1s v4p0597c2s
v4p0608c2s v5p0004c2m v5p0031c1s
v5p0042c1s v5p0043c2s v5p0052c1s
v5p0073c1m v5p0075c1m v5p0105c2m
v5p0121c2s v5p0152c1s v5p0172c1s
v5p0196c2s v5p0201c1s v5p0223c1s
v5p0224c1s v5p0235c2s v5p0237c1m
v5p0240c2s v5p0251c1s v5p0261c2s
v5p0280c2s v5p0313c2s v5p0352c2s
v5p0365c1m v5p0365c2s v5p0393c1s
v5p0393c2m v5p0394c1m v5p0394c2m
v5p0395c1m v5p0395c2m v5p0403c2s
v5p0408c1s v5p0412c1s v5p0421c2s
v5p0422c1m v5p0423c1s v5p0423c2m
v5p0427c1s v5p0436c1s v5p0450c1m
v5p0450c2s v5p0500c1s v5p0512c2s
v5p0518c2s v5p0525c2s v5p0530c2m
v5p0546c1s v5p0565c1m v5p0567c1s
v5p0578c1s v5p0605c1s v5p0607c2s
v5p0609c2s v5p0646c2s v6p0056c1s
v6p0056c2s v6p0379c1s v6p0439c1s
v6p0439c2m
Mathews, W.S.B. et al. ... v4p0417c1s
Mathewson, A. v5p0159c2s
Mathewson, Albert M. v6p0078c2s
Mathias, E. v3p0068c1s
Mathieson, G. v5p0559c2s
v6p0518c2s
Mathieson, J.E. v2p0291c2s
Mathieson, W.L. v6p0089c1s
v6p0578c2s
Mathieu, E.A. v2p0430c2s
Mathieu, G. and Antoniadi, E.M.
v5p0123c2s
Mathiot, G. v1p0073c1s
v1p0401c2s v1p1347c2s v1p1377c2s
Mathis, J.E. v6p0230c1s
v6p0303c1s v6p0363c2s v6p0552c1s
Mathot, R. v6p0248c2m
Mathot, R.E. v6p0248c1s
Mathot, Rodlophe v6p0044c1s
Mathuisieulx, Vicomte de . v6p0657c1s
Matile, G. v1p0098c1s
Matlack, L.C. v1p0830c2s
v1p0831c1s v1p1149c1s v1p1208c2s
Matlack, R.C. v3p0038c2s
Matlekovits, A. v5p0040c1s
Matlock, L.C. v1p1149c1s
Maton, W.G. v1p1256c1s
Matos, L.J. v4p0063c2s
Matson, C.H. v6p0081c2s
v6p0219c2s v6p0263c2s v6p0309c1s
v6p0349c1m v6p0449c2s v6p0465c1s
v6p0518c2s v6p0574c2s v6p0590c2s
Matson, Esther v6p0036c2s
Matson, H. v1p0440c1s
v1p0711c2s
Matson, K.J. v2p0216c1s
Matson, R.N. v6p0608c1s
Matson, W.A. v2p0194c2s
Matters, C.H. v4p0629c2s
Matteson, S.W. v5p0129c1s
v5p0479c1s
Matteucci, C. v1p0375c1s
Matteucci, R.V. v6p0678c1s
Matthes, F.F. v6p0139c2s
v6p0405c1s
Matthes, G.H. v5p0268c1s
Matthes, J.C. v2p0356c2s
Matthew, F.D. v2p0473c2s
v3p0463c2s v3p0473c1s v4p0054c1s
v4p0621c1s
Matthew, G.F. v3p0001c2s
v3p0319c2m v4p0454c1s v4p0499c1s
Matthew, J. v2p0149c1s
v2p0152c1s v2p0366c2s v3p0016c1s
Matthew, James v5p0048c1s
Matthew, W., jr. v1p0621c2s
Matthew, W.D. v4p0584c1s
v5p0629c2s v6p0125c1s v6p0177c1s
v6p0396c2s
Matthewman, J. v4p0052c1s
Matthews, A. v2p0054c1s
v2p0125c2s v3p0238c2s v4p0011c1s
v4p0592c2s v5p0090c1s v5p0287c2s
v5p0450c2s v5p0632c1s v6p0071c1s
v6p0083c2s v6p0137c2s v6p0145c1s
v6p0179c2s v6p0247c2s v6p0275c2s
v6p0282c2s v6p0302c1s v6p0390c2m
v6p0413c2s v6p0439c1s v6p0475c2s
Matthews, A.F. v2p0078c2s
v4p0047c2s v4p0305c2s v4p0401c1s
v4p0481c1s
Matthews, Albert v4p0419c1s
v5p0318c2s v6p0615c1s
Matthews, B. v2p0139c1s
v2p0146c2s v2p0234c2s v2p0336c1s
v2p0343c2s v2p0346c1s v2p0364c2s
v2p0373c1s v2p0400c1s v2p0401c1s
v2p0464c1s v3p0010c2s v3p0012c1s
v3p0049c2s v3p0055c1s v3p0061c2s
v3p0091c1s v3p0099c2s v3p0100c1s
v3p0105c2s v3p0106c1s v3p0113c2s
v3p0122c2m v3p0149c1s v3p0204c2s
v3p0207c2s v3p0210c1s v3p0228c1s
v3p0246c2s v3p0274c1s v3p0308c1s
v3p0312c1s v3p0334c2s v3p0375c2s
v3p0400c2s v3p0406c1s v3p0411c1s
v3p0435c1s v3p0439c1m v3p0448c2s
v4p0034c2s v4p0049c2s v4p0066c1s
v4p0066c2m v4p0067c2s v4p0073c2s
v4p0079c1s v4p0084c2s v4p0095c1s
v4p0161c2s v4p0184c1s v4p0184c2s
v4p0187c2s v4p0197c2s v4p0198c1s
v4p0216c1s v4p0269c1s v4p0276c2s
v4p0288c1s v4p0311c1s v4p0320c1s
v4p0327c2s v4p0334c2m v4p0364c2s
v4p0370c1s v4p0392c1s v4p0399c1s
v4p0400c2s v4p0426c1s v4p0454c2s
v4p0458c2s v4p0493c2s v4p0529c1s
v4p0538c1s v4p0541c1s v4p0543c1m
v4p0551c2s v4p0571c2s v4p0604c1s
v4p0606c1s v4p0609c2s v5p0016c1s
v5p0025c1s v5p0070c1s v5p0122c2s
v5p0167c2s v5p0191c2m v5p0195c1s
v5p0213c2s v5p0220c2s v5p0266c1s
v5p0282c2s v5p0283c1s v5p0283c2s
v5p0340c2s v5p0341c1s v5p0341c2s
v5p0349c1s v5p0415c2s v5p0421c1s
v5p0487c2s v5p0488c1s v5p0494c2s
v5p0545c2m v5p0640c1m v5p0640c2s
Matthews, B. and Brunner, H.C.
v2p0395c2s
Matthews, B. and Clemens, S.L.
v3p0099c2s
Matthews, B. and Jessop, G.H.
v3p0312c2s
Matthews, B. and Jessopp, G.H.
v3p0075c2s
Matthews, B. and Pollock, W.H.
v2p0130c1s v3p0271c2s
Matthews, B.W. v5p0538c2s
Matthews, Brander v5p0008c2s
v5p0017c2s v5p0167c1s v5p0192c1s
v5p0206c1s v5p0262c2s v5p0422c2s
v5p0575c2s v5p0644c2s v6p0003c2s
v6p0015c2s v6p0018c1s v6p0081c2s
v6p0108c1s v6p0135c1s v6p0140c1m
v6p0158c2s v6p0180c2m v6p0181c1m
v6p0208c1m v6p0209c2m v6p0238c1s
v6p0241c2s v6p0273c1s v6p0301c1s
v6p0306c1s v6p0380c1s v6p0388c1s
v6p0407c1s v6p0437c1s v6p0461c2s
v6p0465c2s v6p0490c1s v6p0501c2m
v6p0503c2s v6p0504c1s v6p0524c2s
v6p0535c1s v6p0545c2s v6p0571c1s
v6p0582c1s v6p0586c2s v6p0587c1s
v6p0592c1s v6p0603c1s v6p0608c1s
v6p0609c2m v6p0612c2m v6p0619c1s
v6p0627c1s v6p0635c2s v6p0641c2m
v6p0642c1s
Matthews, E.B. v6p0499c2s
Matthews, F. v4p0190c1s
v4p0420c2m v5p0268c1s v5p0456c2s
v5p0599c1s v6p0437c1s v6p0453c1s
v6p0454c2s v6p0458c2s v6p0545c1s
v6p0591c1s v6p0623c1s v6p0673c2s
Matthews, H. v5p0590c1s
Matthews, H.C. v5p0408c1s
Matthews, H.W. v5p0426c2s
Matthews, I. v3p0014c1s
Matthews, J. v1p0194c1s
v1p0743c1s v1p0848c2s v1p1099c1m
v1p1342c1s
Matthews, J.B. v1p0005c1m
v1p0076c1s v1p0088c2s v1p0200c1s
v1p0281c1s v1p0347c1s v1p0363c1s
v1p0371c2m v1p0450c1s v1p0468c2s
v1p0488c2s v1p0492c2s v1p0503c2s
v1p0611c2s v1p0713c1s v1p0859c1m
v1p0968c2s v1p0975c1s v1p1017c1s
v1p1105c2s v1p1151c2m v1p1170c2s
v1p1190c2m v1p1220c1s v1p1299c2s
v1p1368c1s v2p0040c2s v2p0120c1s
v2p0122c2s v2p0167c2m v2p0168c1s
v2p0247c1s v2p0262c1s v2p0267c1s
v2p0337c1s v2p0389c1s v2p0400c1s
v2p0459c2s v3p0049c2s v3p0185c2s
v3p0303c1s v4p0059c1s
Matthews, J.B. and Bunner, H.C.
v1p0357c2s
Matthews, J.H. v4p0609c1s
Matthews, J.M. v6p0152c2s
v6p0185c1m v6p0317c1s v6p0707c1s
Matthews, J.N. v3p0336c1s
Matthews, J.R. v2p0094c2s
Matthews, John v3p0174c1s
Matthews, K.V.C. v6p0551c2s
Matthews, M. v1p1406c2s
Matthews, N., jr. v3p0289c1s
Matthews, N., jr. and Thompson, W.G.
v6p0522c2s
Matthews, R.C. v6p0096c1s
Matthews, Robert v1p0812c2s
Matthews, T.R. v1p0656c1s
Matthews, W. v2p0307c2m
v2p0456c2s v3p0266c1s v4p0070c1s
v4p0395c1m v4p0421c1s v5p0100c1s
v5p0196c1s v5p0237c1s v5p0401c1m
v6p0185c2s v6p0316c2s v6p0441c1s
v6p0444c2m
Matthews, W.D. v6p0083c2s
Matthews, W.E. v1p1386c1s
Matthewson, R.C. v1p0375c1s
Matthey, E. v4p0230c1s
Matthiessen, A. v1p1304c2s
Mattison, H. v1p0830c2s
v1p1117c2s v1p1120c2s
Mattison, H.V. v2p0322c2s
Mattison, J.B. v5p0398c2s
Mattocks, C.P. v1p0494c1s
v4p0101c2s v4p0350c1s
Mattos, A.T.de v6p0621c1s
Mattos, K.de v4p0031c2s
v4p0032c1s v4p0203c2s v4p0396c1s
Mattos, W.S.de v3p0398c2s
Mattox, A.H. v5p0431c2s
Matull, K. v6p0699c1s
Matumoto, J.K. v4p0298c1s
v4p0565c2s
Maturin, E. v1p1230c2s
Matz, B.W. v6p0173c2s
Matz, F.P. v4p0550c1s
Matzke, J.E. v5p0164c1s
Mauck, A.V. and Cummings, E.R.
v6p0234c2s
Mauclair, C. v4p0353c1s
v5p0221c1s v5p0492c1s v6p0241c2s
v6p0310c2s v6p0429c1m
Mauclair, Camille v6p0524c1s
Maud, C.E. v6p0027c1s
v6p0241c1s v6p0611c2s
Maud, Constance v6p0111c2s
Maud, Constance E. v6p0221c2s
Maud, Constance Elizabeth. v6p0520c2s
Maud, P. v6p0002c1s
Maud, W.T. v5p0322c2s
v6p0358c2s
Maude, A. v5p0166c2s
v5p0582c1m v6p0179c2s v6p0649c1m
Maude, A. and Wiener, L .. v6p0649c1s
Maude, F.C. v3p0215c1s
v4p0348c1s v4p0348c2s
Maude, F.M. v5p0243c2s
Maude, F.N. v3p0071c1m
v4p0211c1s v4p0284c1s v4p0286c2s
v4p0511c2s v5p0066c2s v5p0089c2s
v5p0098c1m v5p0145c1m v5p0169c2s
v5p0221c2s v5p0243c1s v5p0244c1m
v5p0290c2s v5p0375c2s v5p0588c1s
v5p0618c2s v5p0619c2s v6p0031c2s
v6p0168c2s v6p0205c2s v6p0266c1m
v6p0267c1s v6p0319c1s v6p0620c2s
v6p0654c2m v6p0655c1s v6p0684c2s
v6p0685c1m
Maude, J.E. v2p0132c2s
Maude, L. v6p0649c1s
Maude, R.W. v5p0423c1s
v5p0619c2s
Maude, W.C. v2p0077c2s
v2p0251c1s v2p0297c2s v2p0332c1s
v2p0350c1s v2p0355c1s v2p0368c1s
v3p0060c1s v3p0067c2s v3p0077c1m
v3p0205c1s v3p0244c2s v3p0289c2s
v4p0133c1s v4p0157c2s v4p0226c1s
v4p0332c2s v4p0430c1s v4p0462c1s
v5p0459c1s
Maude, Wm. v6p0080c1s
Maudslay, A.P. v4p0094c2s
v4p0368c1s v5p0367c1s
Maudsley, H. v1p0567c1s
v1p0643c2s v1p0644c1s v1p0810c1s
v1p1006c1s v1p1182c1s v2p0201c2s
v3p0053c1s v3p0072c1s v3p0097c1s
v3p0280c1s
Mauer, Alex A. v6p0215c2s
Maugham, C. v4p0394c1s
Maugham, F.H. v5p0292c1s
Maugham, W.S. v6p0397c2s
Maughan, W.C. v4p0026c1s
Maugras, M.N. v4p0627c1s
Maule, A. v6p0416c1s
Maule, F. v6p0078c2s
Maule, H.P.G. v6p0298c2s
Mauley, De v3p0213c1s
v3p0459c2s
Mauley, Lord De v1p0315c1s
v1p0543c2s v4p0552c1s
Maulsby, D.L. v4p0448c1s
v5p0135c2s v5p0406c1s v5p0630c1s
Maund, E.A. v3p0271c1s
Maund, G.C. v1p0031c1s
Maunder, E.W. v2p0095c2s
v2p0100c1s v2p0277c2s v2p0296c2s
v2p0413c2s v2p0424c2s v3p0019c1m
v3p0024c2s v3p0275c2s v3p0330c2m
v3p0380c1m v3p0403c2s v3p0407c2s
v4p0167c1s v4p0253c2m v4p0306c2s
v4p0357c2m v4p0370c2s v4p0371c1s
v4p0381c1s v4p0396c1s v4p0409c1s
v4p0556c2m v5p0020c1s v5p0028c1s
v5p0035c1m v5p0035c2s v5p0103c1s
v5p0134c1s v5p0174c2m v5p0260c2s
v5p0265c2s v5p0385c1m v5p0402c1s
v5p0448c1s v5p0545c1m v5p0548c2s
v5p0549c1m v5p0560c2s v5p0561c1m
v5p0645c2s v6p0037c2s v6p0038c1s
v6p0092c1s v6p0140c2s v6p0146c1s
v6p0344c1s v6p0395c1m v6p0402c2s
v6p0427c1s v6p0427c2m v6p0614c1m
v6p0625c2s v6p0626c1m
Maunder, E.W. et al. v6p0397c1s
Maunder, M. v4p0541c1s

Maunder, W. v5p0376c1s
Maunder, W.F. v2p0285c1s
Maunder, Walter, Mrs. v6p0552c2s
v6p0625c2s
Maunsell, F.R. v4p0280c2s
v4p0313c2s v5p0320c1s v5p0371c1s
v6p0542c2s
Maunsell, T. v6p0158c1s
v6p0523c2s
Maupassant, G.de v3p0410c2s
v4p0004c1s v4p0021c2s v4p0128c2s
v4p0247c2s v4p0381c1s v6p0280c1s
v6p0319c2s v6p0411c1s v6p0446c1s
v6p0467c1m v6p0499c2s
Maupassant, Guy de v5p0421c1s
Mauran, J.L. v5p0069c2s
v5p0334c1s v5p0471c1s v5p0504c2s
Maurel, M. v3p0064c1s
Maurel, V. v5p0395c1s
v5p0422c1s
Maurenbrecher, M. v5p0321c2s
v5p0641c2s
Maurer, Henry et al. v5p0207c2s
Maurer, M.F. v6p0444c1s
v6p0466c1s
Mauri, Rosita v4p0042c2s
Maurice, A.B. v5p0013c1s
v5p0042c2s v5p0066c1s v5p0096c2s
v5p0153c2s v5p0317c1s v5p0317c2m
v5p0392c2s v5p0407c1s v5p0457c2s
v5p0567c2s v5p0583c2s v6p0042c2s
v6p0165c2s v6p0172c1s v6p0173c2s
v6p0442c2m v6p0620c1s v6p0640c2s
Maurice, A.B. and Cooper, F.T.
v6p0101c2s
Maurice, A.B. and Hapgood, H.
v6p0456c1s
Maurice, Arthur B. v6p0166c1s
Maurice, C.E. v1p0138c2s
v1p0218c2s v1p0484c2s v1p0715c2s
v1p0814c2s v1p0948c1s v4p0272c1s
v4p0432c1s
Maurice, F. v3p0105c1s
v3p0131c1s v3p0182c1s v3p0211c2s
v3p0278c2s v3p0296c2s v3p0298c1s
v3p0459c2s v4p0106c2s v4p0159c1s
v4p0246c2s v4p0541c2s v4p0616c2m
v4p0625c2m v5p0064c1s v5p0219c1s
v5p0252c2s v5p0398c1s v5p0420c2s
v6p0267c2s
Maurice, F., Sir v5p0243c1s
v6p0556c1s
Maurice, F.D. v1p0071c2s
v1p0175c2m v1p0184c2s v1p0284c2s
v1p0339c1s v1p0344c1s v1p0398c2s
v1p0411c1s v1p0593c2s v1p0654c1s
v1p0688c1s v1p0709c1s v1p0722c2s
v1p0777c1s v1p0781c1s v1p0790c1s
v1p0912c2s v1p1001c1s v1p1112c1s
v1p1202c2s v1p1265c1s
Maurice, J. v1p0140c1s
v1p0801c1s
Maurice, J.F. v3p0457c2s
v4p0031c2s v4p0156c2s v4p0370c1s
v5p0032c2s
Maurier, G.Du v1p1087c1m
v3p0328c1m v4p0274c1s v4p0358c1m
v4p0584c1m v5p0314c2m v5p0329c2m
v5p0364c1m v5p0509c1m
Mauris, M. v1p0026c1s
v1p0202c2s v1p0443c1s v1p0666c2s
v1p1180c1s
Maury, C.J. v6p0257c2s
v6p0619c1s
Maury, C.M. v1p1351c2s
Maury, D.F. v1p0134c1s
Maury, D.H. v1p0045c2s
v1p0540c2s v1p0832c1s v1p0856c2m
v1p1287c1s v1p1343c1m v1p1344c1s
v2p0065c1s v3p0400c1s v3p0447c1s
v4p0065c2s v4p0375c2s
Maury, D.H., jr. and Gantt, H.L.
v2p0457c2s
Maury, D.W. v1p0673c2s
Maury, G.B. v5p0176c1s
v5p0325c2s
Maury, M. v1p0280c2s
v1p1118c1s
Maury, M.F. v1p0026c2s
v1p0037c2s v1p0073c1s v1p0073c2s
v1p0099c2s v1p0198c1s v1p0234c1s
v1p0336c2s v1p0340c2s v1p0348c2s
v1p0533c2s v1p0546c1s v1p0562c1m
v1p0718c1s v1p0854c1s v1p0936c1s
v1p0956c1m v1p1171c2s v1p1172c1s
v1p1174c1s v1p1223c1s v1p1227c2s
v1p1243c2s v1p1249c2m v1p1289c2s
v1p1351c2s v1p1414c2s
Maury, N.B. v5p0133c1s
v5p0562c2s
Maury, R. v6p0581c1s
Maury, R.L. v1p1412c1s
v4p0623c1s
Maury, T.B. v1p0055c1s
v1p0056c1m v1p0562c1s v1p0638c2s
v1p0928c1s v1p1196c2s v1p1256c2s
v1p1351c2s v1p1394c2s v1p1395c1m
v2p0443c1s v2p0469c1s
Maury, T.P. v1p1257c1s
Maury, W.A. v4p0371c1s
Maus, O. v5p0052c2s
v6p0696c1s
Mausergh, J. v5p0283c2s
Mautaux, P. v6p0115c2s
Mavall, J. v2p0315c1s
Maver, Alex.A. v6p0615c1s
Maver, W., jr. v4p0567c1s
v5p0182c2s v6p0199c2s v6p0530c1s
v6p0636c1s v6p0636c2s
Maver, William, jr. v6p0636c2m
Maverick, A. v1p0424c1s
v1p1084c2s
Maverick, S. v2p0310c1s
Mavor, J. v3p0092c2s
v3p0412c2s v3p0434c1s v4p0097c1s
v4p0167c2s v4p0182c1s v4p0315c1s
v4p0451c2s v4p0472c1s v4p0500c2s
v4p0591c1s v5p0623c1s v6p0224c1s
Maw, E.H. v4p0404c1s
Maw, G. v3p0014c1s
Maw, T.E. v6p0371c1s
Maw, W.H. v5p0077c1s
Mawby, E.G. v6p0585c2s
Mawer, E.B. v3p0305c2s
Mawer, W. v2p0352c1s
Mawson, H.P. v4p0595c1s
v5p0271c1s
Mawson, T.H. v5p0226c1s
Max, F.L. v1p0642c1s
Max, G. v6p0397c1s
Maxcy, C.L. v4p0519c1s
Maxe, Edwin v6p0430c1s
Maxey, A.E. v6p0154c2s
Maxey, E. v5p0174c1s
v5p0181c2m v5p0212c2s v5p0481c2s
v6p0047c2s v6p0100c2s v6p0186c2m
v6p0270c1s v6p0293c1s v6p0321c2s
v6p0324c1m v6p0334c1s v6p0335c2s
v6p0337c1s v6p0414c2s v6p0423c1s
v6p0476c1s v6p0476c2s v6p0506c2s
v6p0519c1s v6p0533c2s v6p0559c2s
v6p0560c1m v6p0560c2s v6p0561c1s
v6p0570c1s v6p0583c2s v6p0632c2s
v6p0646c1s v6p0655c2s v6p0676c1m
Maxey, Edwin v6p0119c1s
v6p0687c2s
Maxey, S.B. v4p0571c1s
Maxfield, B.L. and Millington, W.H.
v6p0495c1s v6p0680c1s
Maxim, H. v4p0192c2s
v4p0244c2s v5p0200c1m v5p0227c2s
Maxim, H.L. v5p0584c2s
Maxim, H.P. v4p0461c2s
v5p0041c1s
Maxim, H.S. v3p0003c1s
v4p0004c2m v4p0176c1s v4p0204c2m
v5p0200c1s v5p0321c1s v5p0353c2s
v5p0543c2s v6p0007c1s v6p0120c1s
Maxim, Hiram S. v6p0426c2s
Maxim, Hudson v5p0200c1s
v5p0227c1s v5p0367c1s v5p0462c2m
v5p0582c2s v5p0583c1s v6p0650c1s
Maxim, R.H. v4p0204c2s
Maximo, Stella v6p0178c2s
Maxon, H.D. v3p0006c1s
Maxon, W.D. v4p0387c2s
Maxse, F.A. v1p0722c1s
v4p0095c1s v4p0181c1s v4p0189c2s
v4p0211c1s v4p0239c1s v4p0404c2s
v5p0007c1s v5p0008c1s v5p0217c1s
v5p0248c2s v5p0352c1s v5p0476c1s
Maxse, F.A. et al. v4p0239c2s
v4p0476c1s
Maxse, F.I. v4p0133c2s
v4p0236c1m v5p0118c2s v5p0539c2s
v6p0099c2s v6p0401c2s
Maxse, L.J. v4p0601c2s
v5p0168c2s v5p0169c1m v5p0217c2s
v6p0133c2s v6p0271c1s v6p0441c1s
Maxse, L.J. et al. v4p0006c1s
Maxse, Mary v5p0241c1s
Maxson, E.R. v2p0119c1s
Maxson, H.D. v3p0358c1s
Maxson, R.N. v6p0260c1m
Maxwell, A. v6p0235c2s
v6p0246c1s
Maxwell, Anna v3p0200c1s
Maxwell, C. v1p0858c2s
Maxwell, G. v1p0289c2s
v4p0516c1s v4p0529c1s v6p0070c2s
v6p0159c1s v6p0168c1s v6p0200c1s
v6p0429c2s v6p0542c1s v6p0646c2m
v6p0682c2s v6p0697c2s
Maxwell, H. v3p0045c1s
v3p0066c2s v3p0108c1s v3p0283c2s
v3p0471c1s v4p0012c2s v4p0019c1s
v4p0041c1s v4p0061c2s v4p0068c1s
v4p0083c1s v4p0119c2s v4p0136c2s
v4p0142c2s v4p0162c1s v4p0197c2s
v4p0210c2s v4p0215c2s v4p0219c2s
v4p0220c1s v4p0239c2s v4p0287c1s
v4p0343c1s v4p0500c2s v4p0510c1s
v4p0519c2s v4p0549c2s v4p0580c1s
v4p0583c1s v4p0585c1s v4p0607c2s
v5p0014c1s v5p0032c1s v5p0066c1s
v5p0143c1s v5p0242c2s v5p0246c1s
v5p0262c2s v5p0375c2s v5p0397c1s
v5p0414c2s v5p0515c1s v5p0515c2s
v5p0547c1s v5p0594c1s v5p0622c2s
v5p0632c2s v6p0021c2s v6p0157c1s
v6p0230c1s v6p0246c2s v6p0264c2s
v6p0267c2s v6p0270c2m v6p0280c1s
v6p0299c1m v6p0426c2s v6p0444c1s
v6p0482c2s v6p0566c1s v6p0578c1m
v6p0700c1s
Maxwell, H. et al. v4p0240c1s
v6p0271c1s
Maxwell, H., Sir v3p0045c1s
v3p0158c1s v3p0167c1s v3p0412c2s
v4p0114c1s v4p0199c1s v4p0326c2s
v4p0417c2s v4p0447c1s v4p0493c1s
v4p0541c1s v4p0573c2s v4p0585c1s
v5p0021c1s v5p0214c1s v6p0070c2s
v6p0083c1s v6p0233c1s v6p0287c2s
v6p0427c2s v6p0533c2s v6p0550c1s
v6p0706c2s
Maxwell, H.E. v3p0086c2s
v3p0098c1s v3p0186c2s v3p0266c2s
v3p0321c1s v3p0321c2s v5p0610c2s
v6p0404c1s
Maxwell, Herbert v6p0265c1s
Maxwell, Herbert, Sir v6p0246c1s
Maxwell, I.A. v2p0309c1s
Maxwell, J.B. v6p0270c1s
v6p0464c2s
Maxwell, J.C. v1p0278c2s
v1p0352c1s v1p0467c1s v1p0502c1s
v1p0502c2m v1p0584c1s v1p0748c2s
v1p0812c1s v1p0858c2m v1p0899c2s
v1p0966c2s v1p1006c1s v1p1214c1s
v1p1291c2s v1p1304c2s v1p1405c1s
Maxwell, J.Clerk v1p0004c2s
Maxwell, J.K. v2p0359c2s
Maxwell, J.R. v4p0472c1s
Maxwell, L., jr. v6p0051c2m
Maxwell, Laura W. v6p0010c1s
v6p0099c1s
Maxwell, M.C. v5p0402c1s
Maxwell, M.M., Mrs. v6p0578c2s
Maxwell, M.Y. v5p0590c1s
Maxwell, P. v3p0090c1s
v3p0347c2s v4p0172c1s v4p0576c1s
v4p0617c1s v5p0278c2s
Maxwell, Perriton v5p0508c2s
Maxwell, R. v5p0587c2s
Maxwell, S. v2p0105c1s
v3p0016c2s v3p0119c1s v3p0462c2s
v4p0045c2s v4p0337c1m v4p0529c2s
v5p0143c2s v5p0343c2s v5p0600c1s
Maxwell, S.A. v2p0089c2s
v2p0443c1s v2p0469c1s
Maxwell, S.S. v6p0021c1s
v6p0663c2s
Maxwell, T. v4p0408c2s
Maxwell, T.M. v3p0295c2s
Maxwell, W. v1p0833c1s
v6p0652c1s
Maxwell, W.A. v3p0087c2s
Maxwell, W.B. v2p0182c2s
v3p0339c1s
Maxwell, W.H. v1p0153c2s
v1p0292c2s v1p0347c1s v1p0353c1s
v1p0406c2s v1p0483c2s v1p0499c1s
v1p0596c1s v1p0748c1s v1p0773c2s
v1p1071c1s v1p1081c2s v1p1091c1s
v1p1106c1s v1p1239c2s v1p1296c1s
v1p1335c2s v1p1400c2s v3p0129c2s
v3p0421c2s v4p0127c2s v4p0234c1s
v4p0506c1s v5p0471c2s v6p0190c2s
v6p0406c1s v6p0573c1s v6p0635c1m
Maxwell, Wm. v4p0305c2s
v4p0481c1s
Maxwell-Lyte, C. v3p0275c1s
Maxwell-Scott, M.M. v4p0001c1s
v6p0077c2s
Maxwell-Scott, Mrs. v6p0142c1s
May, B. v1p1281c1s
May, D. v5p0155c1s
v5p0455c2s
May, D.W. v6p0377c1s
May, E.S. v3p0160c1s
v3p0457c2s v4p0447c2s v5p0037c2s
v5p0098c1s v5p0270c2s v5p0397c2s
May, E.S., Major v5p0032c1s
May, F. v4p0118c1s
May, H. v2p0033c1s
v2p0420c2s v3p0250c1s v3p0341c1s
May, H.J. v5p0401c2s
May, J. v1p0529c2s
v1p0645c2s v1p0646c1s v1p0810c1s
v1p1200c2s v1p1340c1s v2p0181c1s
May, J.H. v2p0144c1s
v3p0290c1s v4p0327c2s
May, J.P. v3p0047c2s
v3p0186c2s v3p0429c1s
May, Joseph v6p0012c2s
May, Julia H. v5p0004c1s
May, K. v4p0408c2s
May, M.B. v6p0464c2s
May, Major v5p0252c2s
May, P. v5p0367c1s
May, R. v6p0645c2s
May, S. v1p0813c2s
v1p1408c1s v4p0261c1s v5p0339c2s
May, S.J. v1p0285c1s
v1p0374c1s v1p0390c2s v1p0869c2s
v1p0985c2s v1p1438c2s
May, S.P. v2p0393c2s
v3p0044c1s v3p0426c1s
May, Sophie v3p0236c2s

Mayall, J. v2p0380c1s
Mayall, J., jr. v3p0277c2m
Mayberry, E.G. v6p0424c1s
Maybery, C.F. v4p0099c1s
Maycock, W. v3p0383c1s
Mayef, N. v1p0593c1s
v1p0713c2s
Mayer et al. v1p0387c2s
Mayer, A.G. v3p0433c1s
v4p0324c2s v4p0531c1s v5p0261c2s
v6p0047c1s v6p0401c1s v6p0437c2m
v6p0650c2s v6p0670c2s
Mayer, A.M. v1p0004c2m
v1p0074c1s v1p0077c1s v1p0198c1s
v1p0279c1s v1p0398c2s v1p0399c1s
v1p0401c2m v1p0407c2s v1p0463c2m
v1p0466c2s v1p0498c2m v1p0528c2s
v1p0585c2m v1p0640c2s v1p0664c2s
v1p0665c2s v1p0699c1s v1p0787c1s
v1p0787c2s v1p0788c1s v1p0788c2s
v1p0831c2s v1p0858c2s v1p0875c1s
v1p0901c1s v1p1002c2m v1p1006c2s
v1p1222c1s v1p1222c2m v1p1233c2s
v1p1267c2s v1p1268c1s v1p1396c2s
v2p0050c1s v2p0127c1s v2p0414c2s
v3p0107c1s v3p0133c1s v3p0134c2m
v3p0310c2s v3p0328c2s v3p0368c2s
v3p0452c1s v4p0002c2s v4p0124c2s
v4p0125c1s v4p0131c2s v4p0487c1s
v5p0562c2s
Mayer, A.M. and Barnard, C.
v1p0747c2m
Mayer, B. v1p0832c2s
v1p0833c2s v1p1401c2s
Mayer, C. v6p0362c2s
v6p0426c1s
Mayer, F. v1p0089c2s
v5p0431c2s
Mayer, F.B. v1p0807c2s
v1p1196c2s
Mayer, F.H. v5p0022c2s
Mayer, J. v1p0525c1m
v1p0663c2s v1p0892c2s v1p0923c2s
v1p1082c2s v1p1307c1s v2p0315c1s
Mayer, J.H. v5p0082c2s
Mayer, J.M. v6p0114c2s
Mayer, J.R. v1p0210c1s
v1p1218c1s v1p1241c1s
Mayer, L. v1p0036c1s
v1p0039c1s v1p0518c2s v1p1373c2s
v1p1415c2s
Mayer, M.J. v6p0090c2s
v6p0461c1s
Mayer, O.B. v2p0449c2s
Mayer, O.G. v1p1241c1s
Mayer, P.H. v1p0667c1s
Mayer, S.R.T. v1p0168c2s
v1p0181c1s v1p0266c2s v1p0347c2s
v1p0530c1s v1p0566c1s v1p0576c1s
v1p0587c2s v1p0602c1s v1p0616c1m
v1p0708c2s v1p0719c1s v1p0751c1s
v1p0764c2s v1p0804c2s v1p0924c2s
v1p0941c2s v1p1054c1m v1p1201c2s
v1p1211c2s v1p1419c2s
Mayer, S.R.T., Mrs. v1p0445c2s
v1p0998c1s
Mayer, W. v3p0147c2s
Mayer, W., jr. v6p0688c1s
Mayer, W.F. v1p0503c1s
v1p0912c1s v1p1127c2s v1p1365c1s
Mayers, J.M. v4p0559c2s
Mayers, R.C.V. v4p0330c2s
Mayers, W.F. v1p0232c2s
Mayes, W.H. v4p0571c1m
Mayeux, H. v4p0029c1s
Mayhew, A. v1p0018c2s
v4p0042c2s
Mayhew, A.L. v2p0266c2s
v3p0172c1s v3p0186c2s v3p0235c1s
v3p0362c2s v4p0154c1s v4p0430c2s
v4p0531c1s v6p0609c2s
Mayhew, A.L. and Bradley, H.
v3p0388c2s
Mayhew, A.L. and Earle, J.
v3p0215c2s
Mayhew, A.L. and Morris, R.
v3p0175c1s
Mayhew, A.L. et al. v3p0023c1s
v4p0341c2s
Mayhew, A.S. v6p0671c1s
Mayhew, B.F., Mrs. v4p0276c2s
Mayhew, E. v1p0535c1s
v1p0837c1s v1p0871c1s
Mayhew, H. v1p0577c2s
v1p0878c1s
Mayhew, R. v6p0242c2s
v6p0693c2s
Mayhew, W. v6p0710c1s
Mayhew, W.H. v4p0157c2s
v4p0515c2s v5p0058c2s v5p0362c2s
v5p0403c2s v6p0183c1s v6p0283c2s
v6p0309c2s v6p0350c1s v6p0419c1s
v6p0419c2s v6p0483c1s
Mayhew, W.H. and Frost, A.F.
v5p0057c2s
Maynadier, G.H. v3p0166c1s
Maynard, C. v3p0002c2s
v4p0532c2s v4p0572c1s v5p0326c1s
Maynard, C.J. v1p0953c2s
Maynard, C.L. v6p0220c1s
Maynard, Constance L. v6p0462c1s
Maynard, D.H. v6p0338c1s
Maynard, F.M. v5p0041c1s
Maynard, H.W. and Beveridge, W.H.
v6p0665c1s
Maynard, J. v6p0125c1s
v6p0403c2s
Maynard, L. v4p0068c2s
Maynard, L.A. v4p0552c2s
Maynard, M. and Campbell, H.
v3p0120c2s
Maynard, S.T. v6p0247c2s
Maynard, W. v1p0420c2s
v1p0517c2s
Maynard, W.H. v2p0010c2s
Mayne, C.B. v3p0215c2s
v5p0050c1s v5p0286c2s v5p0290c1s
Mayne, F. v4p0392c2s
Mayne, J.D. v3p0211c2s
Mayne, Mary v5p0196c2s
Mayne, R. v3p0290c2s
Mayne, T.E. v4p0351c2s
v4p0507c1s v4p0599c1s
Maynsley, H.G. v3p0418c2s
Mayo, A.D. v1p0006c2m
v1p0106c1s v1p0119c2s v1p0189c2s
v1p0229c1s v1p0243c1s v1p0243c2s
v1p0247c2s v1p0248c2s v1p0255c2s
v1p0259c1s v1p0386c1s v1p0417c2s
v1p0486c1s v1p0576c1s v1p0687c1s
v1p0707c2s v1p0740c2m v1p0805c2s
v1p0848c1s v1p0916c2s v1p0982c2s
v1p1044c1m v1p1097c2s v1p1159c1m
v1p1203c1s v1p1270c1s v1p1295c1s
v1p1302c1s v1p1340c2s v1p1353c1s
v1p1354c1s v1p1355c2s v1p1399c2s
v1p1400c1m v1p1426c1s v2p0131c2s
v2p0310c2s v2p0411c1m v2p0425c2s
v2p0455c2s v3p0299c1s v3p0301c1s
v3p0306c2s v3p0401c2m v3p0402c1m
v3p0467c2s v4p0002c1s v4p0171c1s
v4p0466c1s v4p0506c1s v4p0512c1s
v4p0538c1m v5p0002c1s v5p0017c1s
v5p0178c2s v5p0279c2s v5p0403c1s
Mayo, A.D. et al. v5p0471c2s
Mayo, Dr. v1p0156c1s
Mayo, E. v5p0278c2s
v5p0417c2s v5p0490c2m v5p0574c2s
v6p0018c2s v6p0204c2s v6p0454c1s
v6p0511c1s
Mayo, E.W. v4p0594c1s
v5p0408c1s
Mayo, Earl of v5p0296c1s
v5p0297c1s v6p0105c1s v6p0658c1s
Mayo, Earl of and Synnott, N.
v5p0295c2s
Mayo, F. v5p0036c1s
Mayo, H. v1p0356c2s
v1p1272c1s v1p1361c2s v1p1417c2s
Mayo, I.F. v1p0380c2s
v1p0642c1s v1p0749c1s v1p0936c1s
v1p0938c1s v1p1106c2s v1p1176c2s
v1p1193c2s v1p1426c2s v2p0315c2s
v3p0188c1s v3p0367c2s v3p0440c2s
v3p0451c1s v4p0010c1s v4p0192c1s
v4p0234c1s v4p0234c2s v4p0324c2s
v4p0371c1s v4p0515c2s v4p0620c2s
v5p0047c1s v5p0249c1s v5p0283c2s
v5p0299c1s v5p0312c1s v5p0369c2s
v5p0452c2s v5p0473c1s v5p0554c2s
v5p0596c1s
Mayo, I.F., Mrs. v4p0089c2s
Mayo, I.S. v1p1146c2s
Mayo, Isabella F. v5p0090c1s
v5p0637c1s
Mayo, J. v1p0889c2s
Mayo, J.F. v1p0257c2s
Mayo, L.A. and Laud, M. .. v5p0541c2s
Mayo, Louise A. and Mayo, Mary L.
v4p0612c1s
Mayo, M.L. et al. v5p0529c1s
Mayo, Mary L. and Mayo, Louise A.
v4p0612c1s
Mayo, T. v1p0259c2s
v1p0643c2s v1p0817c1s
Mayo, T.F. v4p0579c1s
v5p0213c2s v5p0266c1s
Mayo, T.H. v5p0074c2s
Mayo, W.J. v6p0408c2s
Mayo, W.S. v1p0153c2s
v1p0284c2s v1p0295c1s v1p1192c1s
Mayo-Smith, R. v4p0094c1s
v4p0212c2s v4p0275c1s v4p0287c1s
v4p0470c1s v4p0524c2s v4p0526c2s
v4p0546c2s v4p0596c2s v4p0608c1s
v5p0382c2s v5p0465c1m
Mayo-Smith, R. and Spahr, C.R.
v4p0524c2s
Mayor, J.B. v1p0251c1s
v1p0496c1s v1p1032c2s v1p1101c1s
v1p1109c2s v1p1421c2s v6p0064c2m
v6p0131c1m v6p0639c2s
Mayor, R. v6p0691c2s
Mayr, G. v2p0418c2s
Mayr, H. v2p0478c2s
Mays, C.V. v1p0564c1s
v1p1158c2s v1p1356c2s
Mays, S.V. v1p0516c1s
Mays, T.J. v3p0213c1s
v4p0072c2s
Mazade, C.de v4p0194c1s
Mazade, F. v5p0431c2s
v6p0028c2m
Mazade, Fernand v4p0156c1s
v4p0425c2s v6p0479c2s
Mazzini, J. v1p0090c1s
v1p0184c2s v1p0285c2s v1p0311c2m
v1p0342c2s v1p0430c2s v1p0471c2s
v1p0477c2s v1p0650c1s v1p0670c1m
v1p0672c1s v1p0673c1m v1p0898c2s
v1p0964c2s v1p1023c2s v1p1098c2s
v1p1131c2s v1p1134c1s v1p1332c2s
v1p1363c2s
Mazzucato, G. v5p0614c1s
Mead, A.D. v5p0549c1s
v6p0209c2s v6p0474c1s
Mead, A.D. et al. v5p0099c2s
Mead, A.R. v6p0655c1s
Mead, C. v1p1304c1s
Mead, C.E. v5p0461c2s
Mead, C.M. v1p0188c2s
v1p0402c1s v1p0426c1s v1p0581c2s
v1p0687c1s v1p1061c1s v2p0042c2s
v2p0269c1s v2p0441c2s v3p0041c2s
v3p0112c1s v3p0351c2s v3p0402c2s
v3p0420c2s v4p0057c1s v4p0228c2s
v4p0431c1s v4p0515c1s v5p0236c2s
v6p0060c1s v6p0158c2s v6p0484c2s
v6p0491c2s v6p0544c2s v6p0642c2s
Mead, C.M., Mrs. v3p0085c1s
v3p0323c2s
Mead, C.S. v6p0463c2s
Mead, C.T., Mrs. v4p0057c1s
Mead, D.W. v4p0613c2s
Mead, E. v4p0199c1s
v4p0434c2s v4p0524c2s v4p0563c1s
v4p0563c2s v5p0027c2s v5p0159c1s
v5p0298c2s v6p0015c1s v6p0329c1s
v6p0329c2m
Mead, E. and Cox, T. v4p0015c2s
Mead, E.C. v2p0029c1s
Mead, E.D. v1p0061c1s
v1p0071c2s v1p0702c1s v1p1111c2m
v1p1243c1s v2p0022c1s v2p0089c1s
v2p0140c1s v2p0283c1s v2p0310c2s
v2p0321c1s v2p0342c1s v2p0382c1s
v2p0471c1s v3p0188c2s v3p0260c1s
v3p0292c1s v3p0329c2s v3p0349c2s
v3p0456c1s v3p0458c1s v4p0621c1s
v5p0176c2s v5p0189c2s v5p0281c2s
v5p0357c1s v5p0455c1s v5p0541c2s
v6p0071c1s v6p0202c1s v6p0389c1s
v6p0485c1s
Mead, E.E. v5p0633c1s
Mead, F. v4p0002c2s
Mead, G.H. v5p0261c1s
v5p0446c2s v5p0535c2s v6p0503c2s
v6p0576c1s v6p0576c2s
Mead, G.R.S. v6p0259c1s
Mead, G.S. v4p0061c1m
v4p0399c1s v4p0503c1s v5p0063c2s
v5p0405c2s
Mead, H. v1p0454c1s
v1p0753c1s v1p1140c1s v6p0225c1s
Mead, H.R. v6p0075c1s
Mead, J.S. v4p0399c1s
Mead, Katherine L. v6p0292c1s
Mead, L. v3p0001c2s
v4p0344c2s v4p0430c1s v4p0580c2s
v4p0627c1s v5p0162c1s v5p0162c2s
v5p0175c1s v5p0294c2s v5p0341c2s
v5p0399c2s v5p0539c1s v5p0640c1s
v6p0337c2s v6p0379c1s v6p0707c1s
Mead, L.A. v5p0391c1s
v6p0026c2s v6p0506c2s
Mead, Leon v6p0620c1s
Mead, M. v3p0137c2s
v3p0418c2s v4p0004c2s v4p0375c2s
Mead, M.E. v6p0208c1s
Mead, N.P. v6p0145c1s
v6p0360c2s
Mead, T.H. v1p0916c2s
Mead, T.L. v6p0229c1s
v6p0469c1s
Mead, W. v1p0844c2s
Mead, W.E. v3p0127c1s
v3p0140c1s v3p0253c2s v4p0067c1s
v4p0273c1m v5p0545c2s v6p0207c2s
Meade, A.P. v5p0401c2s
Meade, C.A. v5p0407c2s
Meade, C.W. v6p0128c2s
Meade, E.F. v6p0308c1s
Meade, E.S. v5p0124c1s
v5p0237c2m v5p0238c2s v5p0383c2s
v5p0399c1s v5p0478c1s v5p0529c2m
v5p0593c1s v5p0604c2s v6p0133c1s
v6p0324c1s v6p0429c1s v6p0519c1s
v6p0627c2s v6p0670c1m
Meade, Emily F. v6p0331c1s
Meade, G.P. v1p0367c1s
Meade, J.R. v4p0489c1s
Meade, L.T. v2p0172c2s
v2p0201c2s v2p0209c2s v2p0243c1s
v2p0349c1s v3p0029c1s v3p0049c1s
v3p0109c1s v3p0117c2s v3p0135c1s
v3p0187c1s v3p0367c2s v3p0466c2s
v4p0020c2s v4p0231c1s v4p0304c2s
v4p0500c1s v4p0590c1s v4p0614c1s
Meade, L.T. and Douglas, R.K.
v4p0483c2s

Meade, L.T. and Eustace, R.
v5p0554c2s
Meade, L.T., Mrs. v6p0619c2s
Meade, R. v4p0417c1s
Meade, R.W. v1p0018c1s
v1p0981c1s v3p0444c2s v5p0355c2s
Meade-King, W.O.E. v5p0622c1s
Meader, C.L. v4p0257c1s
v5p0483c1s v5p0516c1s v6p0378c1s
Meader, E.I. v5p0192c1s
Meader, J.R. v4p0538c1s
Meader, L.H. v5p0139c1s
Meader, W.S. v3p0164c2s
Meadows, A.M. v2p0156c2s
v2p0237c1s v2p0237c2s v2p0304c1s
v2p0304c2s v2p0335c2s v2p0462c1s
v4p0590c1s
Meadows, D. v1p0098c1s
v1p0141c1s
Meadows, K. v1p1012c1s
v1p1284c2s
Meadows, L. v2p0070c2s
v2p0332c2s v2p0459c2s v2p0467c1s
v4p0018c2s v4p0234c2s v4p0550c2s
v5p0038c1s v5p0083c2s v5p0168c1s
v5p0304c2s v5p0466c2s v5p0518c2s
v5p0554c2s v5p0596c1s
Meagher, J.T. v1p0297c1s
v1p0305c1s v1p0574c2m v1p0575c1m
v1p0701c2s v1p0749c2s v1p0993c1s
v1p1071c2s v1p1075c1s
Meagher, T.F. v1p0079c2s
v1p0236c2s v1p0305c1s v1p0863c2s
Meagher, W. v1p0919c2s
Meakin, A.M.B. v5p0378c2s
Meakin, B. v5p0197c2s
v5p0385c2s v5p0387c1m v6p0300c2s
v6p0429c2s v6p0430c1s v6p0600c2s
Meakin, J.E.B. v3p0062c2s
v4p0045c2s v4p0051c2s v4p0302c2s
v4p0381c2s v4p0383c1s
Meakin, N. and Sheringham, H.
v6p0154c2s
Mealey, E.W. v3p0273c2s
Means, C.E. v5p0458c2s
Means, D.M. v1p0208c2s
v1p0235c2s v1p0643c2s v1p0967c1s
v1p1285c2s v2p0245c2s v4p0015c2s
v4p0115c2s v4p0133c1s v4p0608c1s
Means, D.MacG. v1p0057c2m
v1p0434c2s v1p0924c2s v2p0075c1s
v2p0101c2s v2p0105c1s v2p0155c1s
v2p0184c1s v2p0245c1s v2p0273c2s
v2p0333c2s v2p0347c2s v2p0353c2s
v2p0433c1s v2p0460c1s v3p0003c1s
v3p0065c1s v3p0072c1s v3p0089c1s
v3p0091c2s v3p0097c1s v3p0105c1s
v3p0119c1m v3p0149c1s v3p0150c2s
v3p0161c1s v3p0176c1s v3p0185c2s
v3p0206c1s v3p0218c1s v3p0233c2s
v3p0235c2s v3p0241c2s v3p0248c2s
v3p0260c1s v3p0288c1s v3p0289c1s
v3p0301c1s v3p0337c1s v3p0337c2m
v3p0340c1s v3p0344c2s v3p0345c2s
v3p0346c1s v3p0346c2s v3p0347c1s
v3p0347c2s v3p0381c1s v3p0408c2s
v3p0418c1s v3p0420c1s v3p0421c1m
v3p0440c2s v3p0441c2s v3p0452c2s
v4p0022c2s v4p0059c1s v4p0067c2s
v4p0087c1s v4p0115c1s v4p0115c2s
v4p0124c2s v4p0129c1s v4p0140c2s
v4p0150c1s v4p0181c1s v4p0182c1s
v4p0192c2s v4p0193c2s v4p0195c1s
v4p0199c1s v4p0211c2s v4p0214c1s
v4p0214c2s v4p0230c1m v4p0262c2m
v4p0270c2s v4p0280c2s v4p0294c1s
v4p0315c2s v4p0319c1s v4p0325c1m
v4p0331c1s v4p0333c2s v4p0371c2s
v4p0378c1s v4p0394c1s v4p0450c1s
v4p0450c2s v4p0458c1s v4p0462c2m
v4p0474c2s v4p0476c1s v4p0482c2s
v4p0483c2s v4p0524c2s v4p0533c1s
v4p0533c2s v4p0534c1s v4p0534c2s
v4p0535c1s v4p0546c1s v4p0553c1s
v4p0563c2s v4p0608c1s v4p0632c2s
v5p0006c2s v5p0008c2s v5p0025c2s
v5p0045c2s v5p0091c2s v5p0099c2s
v5p0120c2s v5p0121c1m v5p0128c1s
v5p0130c2s v5p0134c2s v5p0135c2s
v5p0159c1s v5p0159c2s v5p0179c1s
v5p0190c2s v5p0199c2s v5p0203c1s
v5p0229c2s v5p0231c2s v5p0238c1m
v5p0241c1s v5p0248c1s v5p0258c2s
v5p0278c2s v5p0281c2s v5p0284c1s
v5p0287c1s v5p0298c2s v5p0321c1s
v5p0327c2s v5p0328c2s v5p0330c1m
v5p0332c2s v5p0351c2s v5p0362c1s
v5p0363c2s v5p0377c2s v5p0383c2m
v5p0391c2s v5p0402c1s v5p0403c2s
v5p0419c1s v5p0435c2s v5p0443c2s
v5p0445c2s v5p0469c1s v5p0476c2m
v5p0487c2s v5p0535c1s v5p0536c1s
v5p0550c1s v5p0556c2s v5p0557c1s
v5p0566c1s v5p0568c1m v5p0568c2m
v5p0584c1s v5p0592c1s v5p0592c2s
v5p0600c1m v5p0602c1s v5p0625c1s
v6p0050c2s v6p0078c1s v6p0086c1s
v6p0129c2s v6p0132c1s v6p0141c1s
v6p0205c2s v6p0206c1s v6p0236c2s
v6p0237c1s v6p0237c2s v6p0364c2m
v6p0378c2s v6p0424c1s v6p0435c2s
v6p0436c2s v6p0448c2s v6p0507c1s
v6p0571c2s v6p0593c2s v6p0618c1s
v6p0622c1s v6p0651c2s v6p0652c1s
Means, D.MacG. et al. v4p0596c1s
Means, J.H. v1p0118c2s
v1p0239c2s v1p0271c1s v1p0599c2s
v1p1109c2s
Means, J.H. and Branner, J.C.
v4p0385c2s v4p0472c1s
Means, J.O. v1p0123c1s
v1p0291c1s v1p0313c1s v1p0724c1s
v1p0949c2s v1p1393c1s v1p1432c2s
Means, J.W. v1p1235c1s
Means, S. v3p0043c2s
Means, T.H. v5p0537c2s
v6p0566c2s
Meany, E.S. v6p0236c1s
Meara, K.O. v1p1144c1s
Meares, W.B. v6p0524c2s
Mearkle, A.L. v5p0326c1s
v5p0362c2s v5p0378c2s v5p0387c1s
v5p0465c2s
Mearkle, Annie L. v5p0635c2s
Mearns, A. v4p0337c2s
Mearns, A. and Lambert, B.
v2p0264c1s
Mearns, E.A. v3p0361c2s
Mearns, J.R. v1p0955c2s
Mearns, P. v1p0096c1s
v1p0130c1s v1p1139c1s v2p0140c2s
v3p0382c1s
Mears, C.A. v6p0565c1s
Mears, D.O. v1p0991c1s
v1p1103c1s
Mears, F.W. v3p0397c2s
Mears, H.D. v1p0987c2s
Mears, J.W. v1p0702c1m
v1p1237c2s v1p1292c2s v2p0437c2s
Mears, M.M. v5p0002c2s
v5p0003c1s v5p0480c1s v5p0597c1s
v5p0609c1s
Mears, Mary M. v5p0154c1s
Measam, T. v1p1320c2s
Mease, J. v1p0301c2s
Meason, M.L. v1p0044c2s
v1p0138c2s v1p0346c2s v1p0368c2s
v1p0397c2s v1p0402c1s v1p0543c2s
v1p0572c1s v1p0596c1s v1p0629c1m
v1p0862c2s v1p0968c1s v1p0970c2s
v1p0971c1s v1p1119c1s v1p1145c2s
v1p1333c2s v1p1408c2s v2p0003c2s
v2p0007c1s v2p0117c1m v2p0126c2s
v2p0166c2s v2p0185c2s v2p0209c2s
v2p0347c1s v2p0404c1s v3p0162c1s
Meath, Countess of v6p0196c1s
Meath, Earl of v3p0010c1s
v3p0014c1s v3p0092c2s v3p0109c1s
v3p0123c1s v3p0137c2s v3p0147c2s
v3p0239c1s v3p0256c1s v3p0321c1s
v3p0324c1s v3p0331c1s v4p0037c2s
v4p0124c2s v4p0266c1m v4p0339c2s
v4p0354c2s v4p0383c1s v4p0414c2s
v4p0427c1s v4p0430c2s v4p0441c1s
v4p0447c1s v4p0592c1s v4p0628c2s
v5p0012c2s v5p0189c2s v5p0398c2s
v6p0266c2s
Meath, Earl of et al. v4p0027c2s
Meath, M.J. v3p0052c2s
v3p0324c1s v5p0387c1m
Meaux, C.de v3p0365c1s
Mebane, G.A. v5p0403c2s
Mechem, F.R. v3p0354c2s
v6p0488c1s
Mechi, J.J. v3p0006c2s
v3p0386c1s
Mechin, E. v2p0007c2s
Mechlin, L. v6p0032c2s
v6p0213c2s v6p0687c1s
Mechlin, Leila v6p0032c2s
v6p0075c2s v6p0350c2s v6p0373c2s
v6p0475c1s v6p0492c1s v6p0706c1s
Mechsler, D. v3p0455c1s
Mecklin, J.M. v6p0273c1s
Mecredy, R.J. v3p0108c1s
v4p0145c1m
Medant, J. v3p0024c1s
Meday, C.H. v1p0839c1s
Medbery, J.K. v1p0038c1s
v1p0956c2s
Medbury, J.K. v1p0693c2s
Medbury, W.K. v1p1080c1s
Medd, J.C. v5p0009c1s
v5p0179c1s v6p0008c2m v6p0192c2s
v6p0449c2s
Medhurst, B. v1p0449c2s
Medhurst, W.H. v1p0236c2s
Medhurst, W.H., Sir v1p0232c2s
v1p0235c1s
Medill, H.C. v6p0555c1s
Medill, J. v1p1290c1s
Medina, C. v6p0477c2s
Medina, L.H. v1p0941c2s
Meding, O. v1p0570c1s
Medini, R. v5p0569c1s
Medley, D.J. v3p0419c2s
Medley, E.P. v6p0068c2s
v6p0229c1s
Medley, G.P. v6p0424c1s
Medley, G.W. v3p0148c1s
v4p0592c2s
Medley, J.G. v1p0408c1s
Medlicott, M. v5p0488c1s
Medlicott, M. and Adler, C.
v5p0393c1s
Medway, H.E. v6p0104c2m
Medway, H.E. and Gooch, F.A.
v6p0552c2s
Medway, J. v1p0130c2s
Medwin, Capt. v1p0090c1s
v1p0370c1s v1p0808c1s v1p1155c2s
Medwin, E. v1p1277c2s
Medwin, T. v1p0008c2m
v1p0009c1s v1p0295c2s v1p0323c1s
v1p0977c1s v1p1308c2s v1p1312c2s
Mee, A. v4p0381c1s
v5p0385c1s v5p0609c2s
Meehan, J. v6p0297c1s
Meehan, T. v1p0449c2s
v1p0462c2s v1p0468c1s v1p0862c1s
v1p1015c2s v1p1176c1s v1p1182c1s
v2p0351c1s v2p0441c1s v2p0463c2s
v4p0438c2s v4p0575c1s
Meehan, T.F. v3p0222c2s
Meehan, W.E. v6p0226c1s
Meek v5p0141c2s
Meek, A. v4p0402c1s
Meek, A.B. v1p1227c2s
Meek, E. v4p0085c2m
v4p0353c2s v4p0447c1s v4p0450c1s
v4p0481c2s
Meek, E.G. v1p0186c2s
v1p0947c1s
Meek, F.B. v1p0301c1s
v1p0469c2m v1p0470c1s v1p0508c2s
v1p0749c1s v1p0903c1s v1p0903c2s
v1p1244c1s
Meek, F.B. and Hayden, F.V.
v1p0508c2m v1p0903c2m
Meek, F.B. and Worthen, A.H.
v1p0317c2s v1p0749c2s v1p1164c2s
Meek, H.J. v1p1156c1s
Meek, S.E. v6p0227c1s
v6p0414c2s v6p0437c2s
Meeker, B.B. v1p0848c2s
v1p0855c1s
Meeker, G.H. v6p0248c1s
Meeker, Harold D. v6p0114c1s
Meeker, J.R. v1p0959c1s
v1p1333c2s
Meeker, L.L. v5p0530c2s
v6p0696c2s
Meeker, N.C. v1p0016c1s
v2p0094c1s
Meeker, R. v3p0071c1s
v6p0591c1m
Meekin, L.R. v6p0243c1s
Meeking, W. v2p0326c2s
Meekins, L.R. v4p0001c2s
v4p0305c1s v4p0325c1s v5p0074c1s
v5p0391c1s v5p0455c2s v5p0593c2s
v6p0054c2s v6p0073c1s
Meelboom, J.A. v6p0552c1s
Meem, J.G. v2p0259c1s
Meen, F. v5p0394c1s
Meerten, H.v. and Haupt, L.M.
v6p0422c1s
Meeson, J.A. v5p0117c2s
Meetkerke, C.E. v1p0444c1s
v1p0531c2s v1p0770c2s v2p0121c2s
v2p0295c1s v2p0322c2s v3p0124c1s
v3p0204c1s v3p0334c2s v4p0039c2s
v4p0047c2s v4p0072c2s v4p0088c1s
v4p0098c1s v4p0159c2s v4p0163c2s
v4p0190c1s v4p0268c2s v4p0316c1s
v4p0324c2s v4p0379c2s v4p0421c2s
v5p0055c1s v5p0169c1s v5p0170c1s
v5p0275c1s v5p0275c2s v5p0282c2s
v5p0331c2s v5p0361c2s v5p0370c2s
v5p0381c1s v5p0421c2s v5p0469c2s
v5p0485c1s v5p0487c1s v5p0494c2s
v5p0504c1s v5p0531c1s v5p0643c2s
v6p0302c1s v6p0395c1s
Meetkerke, C.E. and Hugo, Victor
v4p0193c1s
Meffert, A. v6p0182c2s
Megan, G. v5p0099c2s
v5p0203c2s
Megargee, L.N. v4p0263c2s
v4p0402c2s
Mege, J.B. v1p1005c1s
Meggy, P.R. v4p0037c2s
Meguire, A.S. v5p0634c1s
Mehan, J.D. v5p0530c2m
Mehner, H. v4p0384c2s
Mehr, J.L.Ver v1p0056c2s
v1p0060c1s v1p0465c2s v1p0484c2m
v1p0519c2s v1p0526c2m v1p0535c1s
v1p0627c2s v1p0667c2s v1p0848c1s
v1p1073c2s v1p1127c2s
Meidinger, H. v1p0273c1s
v1p0515c2s v1p0621c2s
Meidinger, M.H. v1p0149c2s
Meidinger, Prof. v2p0111c1s
Meier, E.D. v5p0108c1s
v5p0389c1s v5p0462c2s v6p0204c2s
Meier-Graefe, A.J. v5p0070c2s
Meighan, W.J.C. v4p0135c1s
Meigs, B.C. et al. v1p0204c2s
Meigs, C.D. v1p0874c1s

Meigs, H.V. v3p0102c1s
Meigs, J.F. v6p0030c2s
v6p0469c2s
Meigs, M.C. v2p0055c2s
v2p0127c1s v2p0127c2s v2p0274c2s
v3p0444c1s
Meigs, M.S. v6p0093c1s
Meigs, W.M. v2p0239c1s
v2p0363c1s v3p0178c1s v6p0347c1s
Meikle, J.B. v6p0474c1s
Meikle, W. v3p0376c1s
Meiklejohn, B. v6p0009c2s
v6p0022c1s v6p0048c2s v6p0199c2s
v6p0456c1s
Meily, C. v6p0630c1s
Meinecke, F. v6p0254c2s
Meinertzhagen, R. v6p0031c1s
Meinhardt, A. v5p0259c2s
Meinhold, F. v4p0303c1s
Meinhold, W. v1p1131c1s
Meinong, A. v1p0924c2s
Meirs, H.A. v6p0353c1s
Meisels, I.S. v4p0001c1s
Meissner, F.H. v4p0330c2s
v4p0368c2s
Meissner, S.R.de v3p0189c2s
Meissner, S.Radford de ... v4p0590c1s
Meitzen, A. v3p0408c2s
Melanchthon, P. v1p0777c2s
Melani, A. v3p0018c1m
v3p0018c2s v3p0113c2s v3p0292c2s
v3p0366c2s v4p0024c2s v4p0283c1s
v4p0451c2s v4p0462c1s v5p0026c2s
v5p0156c2s v5p0428c2s v5p0518c2s
v5p0566c2s v6p0033c2s v6p0059c1s
v6p0060c1s v6p0081c1s v6p0157c1s
v6p0168c1s v6p0179c1s v6p0225c2s
v6p0330c2s v6p0331c2m v6p0383c1s
v6p0416c1s v6p0429c1s v6p0515c2s
v6p0545c1s v6p0570c1s v6p0651c1s
v6p0700c2s
Melani, Alfredo v5p0054c2s
v5p0092c1s v5p0300c1s v5p0429c1s
v5p0436c2s v5p0438c2s v5p0479c1s
v5p0594c2s v5p0609c1s v6p0025c2s
v6p0033c1s v6p0057c2s v6p0484c2s
v6p0586c1s v6p0676c2m
Melba, N. v4p0415c1s
Melcher, Elizabeth G. v4p0068c2s
Melcher, R.T. v4p0039c2s
Meldala, R. v4p0186c1s
Melden, C.M. v3p0062c1s
Meldola, E. v4p0440c2s
Meldola, R. v1p0181c1s
v1p0225c2s v1p0374c1s v1p0498c1s
v1p1004c1m v1p1268c2s v2p0020c1s
v2p0090c2s v2p0145c2s v3p0111c1s
v3p0330c2m v4p0036c2s v4p0099c1s
v4p0185c1s v4p0440c2s v5p0012c2s
v5p0104c1s v5p0198c1s v5p0202c2s
v5p0288c2s v5p0377c1s v5p0393c1s
v6p0111c2s v6p0214c1s v6p0285c2s
v6p0317c1s v6p0320c2s v6p0577c1s
v6p0592c2s
Meldrum, C. v1p0327c2s
v1p1244c2s v1p1269c1m v2p0110c2s
v2p0285c1s
Meldrum, D.S. v4p0126c2s
v4p0165c2s v4p0386c1s v4p0493c1s
v4p0580c1s v5p0176c1s v5p0322c2s
v6p0538c2s
Meldrum, J. v1p0077c1s
v4p0376c2s
Melegari, D. v4p0362c2s
Melegari, Dora v5p0635c2s
Melena, E. v1p1439c1s
Melendy, R.L. v5p0506c1s
Meleney, C.E. v2p0388c1s
v3p0422c1s
Melgund, Lord v2p0366c2s
Melgund, Viscount v1p1385c1s
v3p0180c2s v3p0361c2s
Melhuish, W.F. v4p0065c1s
Melinand, C. v4p0064c2s
v4p0322c1s v5p0168c1s v5p0327c1s
Meline, J.C. v1p0692c2s
v1p1033c1s
Meline, J.F. v1p0461c2s
v1p0665c2s v1p0672c1s v1p0795c1s
v1p0886c2s v1p1400c2s
Meline, J.G. v1p0189c2s
v1p0299c2s v1p0411c1s v1p0417c2s
v1p0492c2s v1p0497c2s v1p0571c2s
v1p0665c2s v1p0724c2s v1p0806c2s
v1p0807c1s v1p1095c2s v1p1126c2m
v1p1153c2s v1p1203c1s v1p1227c2s
Meline, M. v1p0461c2s
Meline, M.E. v2p0224c1s
Meline, M.M. v1p0636c2s
v2p0450c2s
Meliss, E. v4p0528c1s
Melius, M. v6p0611c2s
Melius, Marion v6p0156c1s
v6p0438c1s
Mellard, Louis v5p0164c2s
v5p0562c1s
Mellen, C. v3p0316c2s
v3p0368c1s v4p0064c2s v4p0493c1s
v5p0067c2s v5p0498c1s
Mellen, G. v1p0228c2s
v1p0298c2s v1p0886c1s v1p1021c2s
Mellen, G.F. v5p0043c2s
v6p0049c2s v6p0189c2s v6p0339c2s
v6p0692c1s
Mellen, W. v1p1394c1s
Mellen, W.R.G. v1p0472c1s
v1p0813c1s v1p1143c2s v1p1207c2s
Mellick, A.D., jr. v2p0175c2s
v3p0202c2s v3p0301c2m
Mellis, C.J. v4p0621c2s
Mellish, A.E. v5p0203c1s
v5p0465c2s
Mellish, C. and Maseres, F.
v1p0973c1s
Melliss, C.J. v4p0424c1s
Mello, J.M. v1p0209c1s
v1p1113c1m v2p0361c1s
Mellone, M. v1p1268c2s
Mellone, S.H. v4p0188c1s
v4p0464c2s v4p0507c1s v4p0554c2s
v5p0131c2s v5p0364c1s v5p0519c1s
v5p0623c1s v6p0008c1s v6p0212c1s
v6p0302c2s v6p0309c2s v6p0577c2s
Mellone, W.E. v5p0521c1s
Melloni, M. v1p0348c1s
v1p0580c2s v1p1074c1s
Mellor, E. v1p1086c1s
v1p1102c1s v2p0274c1s
Mellor, E.T. v6p0257c2s
Melody, J.W. v6p0402c2m
Melrose, A. v6p0084c2s
Mels, E. v5p0007c1s
v5p0007c2s v5p0285c1s v6p0265c1s
Melson, J.B. v1p0226c1s
Melson, W.N. v1p1151c1s
Melton, F.J. v4p0141c1s
Melton, W.F. v6p0071c2s
v6p0694c2s
Meltza, C.H. v6p0456c2s
Meltzer, C.H. v5p0094c1s
v6p0003c2s v6p0713c2s
Meltzer, S.J. v5p0170c1s
Melvill, Gen. and Douglas, J.
v1p1122c2s
Melville, A. v2p0045c1s
v2p0073c2s v2p0230c2s
Melville, A.G. and Strickland, H.E.
v1p0358c1s
Melville, Capt. v5p0096c2s
Melville, F.H. v5p0316c2s
Melville, G.J.W. v1p0018c1s
v1p0287c1s v1p0352c1s v1p0504c1s
v1p0535c1s v1p0598c1s v1p0605c1s
v1p0651c1s v1p0703c1s v1p0781c1s
v1p0945c1s v1p1083c1s v1p1101c2s
v1p1107c1s v1p1130c1s v1p1152c1s
v1p1257c2s v1p1339c1s v1p1406c2s
v1p1437c1s
Melville, G.J.Whyte v1p0147c2s
Melville, G.W. v2p0020c2s
v4p0047c2s v5p0004c2s v5p0352c2s
v5p0362c1s v5p0401c1m v5p0427c1s
v5p0516c1s v5p0558c2s v5p0602c2s
v5p0619c1s v6p0182c1s v6p0204c2m
v6p0655c2s v6p0669c1m v6p0685c1s
Melville, G.W. et al. v5p0603c1s
v4p0180c1s
v4p0395c2s
Melville, H. v1p0100c2s
v1p0407c1s v1p0668c2s v1p0749c1s
Melville, J. v1p0785c2s
v1p0897c2s v1p1023c1s v1p1358c2s
Melville, J., Mrs. v1p0503c2s
Melville, L. v6p0054c2s
v6p0173c2s v6p0340c1s v6p0369c1s
v6p0391c1m v6p0532c1s v6p0640c2m
v6p0641c1s
Melville, Lewis v6p0216c2s
v6p0235c2s
Melville, R.D. v4p0315c1s
v4p0534c1s v4p0534c2s v5p0024c2s
v5p0187c2s v6p0026c2m v6p0147c1s
v6p0650c2s
Melville, W. v6p0669c2s
Melville, W.H. v3p0107c1s
v3p0117c1s v3p0275c2s v3p0341c2s
v4p0305c1s
Melvin, J. v2p0231c2s
Melzer, S.J. v6p0067c1s
v6p0409c1s
Memes, J.S. v1p0453c2s
v1p0690c1s
Memminger, R.W. v2p0460c1s
Mempes, Dorthy v6p0410c1s
Mempes, M. v4p0003c1s
Menant, J. v2p0110c2s
Menard, J.C. v6p0678c2s
Menard, J.G. v4p0281c2s
v5p0170c1s v5p0219c2s v5p0354c2s
v5p0482c1s
Menard, L. v1p1171c2s
Menard, R. v1p0133c1s
v1p0147c2s v1p0148c1s v1p0153c2m
v1p0160c1s v1p0304c1s v1p0488c1s
v1p0518c1s v1p0581c1s v1p0675c2s
v1p0736c1s v1p1369c1s
Menard, Saint-Yves v3p0088c2s
Menchikoff, M.O. v6p0343c2s
Mendel, L.B. v5p0050c1s
v6p0675c2s
Mendel, M. v5p0492c2s
Mendeleeff, D. v3p0075c2s
Mendelieff, K. v2p0406c2s
Mendels, S. v6p0666c2s
Mendelssohn, P. v1p0938c1s
Mendenhall, C.E. v5p0035c2s
Mendenhall, C.E. and Waidner, C.W.
v5p0224c2s
Mendenhall, Dr. v4p0009c1s
Mendenhall, F.C. v3p0126c1s
Mendenhall, J.C. and Lodge, O.J.
v3p0459c1s
Mendenhall, J.C. and Tittmann, O.H.
v5p0599c2s
Mendenhall, J.W. v2p0339c2s
v2p0369c2s v2p0371c2s v3p0174c1s
v3p0248c1s v3p0442c1s v4p0013c1s
Mendenhall, J.W. et al. .. v3p0073c2s
Mendenhall, L. v4p0039c2s
v5p0440c2s v6p0550c1s
Mendenhall, N.C. v6p0635c2s
Mendenhall, T.C. v1p0541c2m
v1p1337c1s v2p0067c2s v2p0127c2s
v2p0159c1s v2p0341c1s v2p0431c1s
v3p0028c2s v3p0117c1s v3p0126c1m
v3p0380c1s v3p0384c1s v4p0009c1s
v4p0128c1s v4p0175c1s v4p0176c2s
v4p0235c1m v4p0254c1s v4p0341c1s
v4p0362c2s v4p0367c2s v4p0433c2s
v4p0498c2s v4p0508c1s v4p0544c2s
v4p0577c1s v4p0616c1s v5p0054c1m
v5p0372c2s v5p0424c1s v5p0449c2m
v5p0462c2s v5p0492c2s v5p0498c1s
v5p0522c1s v5p0537c1s v6p0413c2s
Mendenhall, T.G. v4p0335c2s
Mendenhall, W.C. v6p0250c2s
v6p0709c1s
Mendes, C. v1p0489c2s
Mendes, F.deS. et al. v3p0216c1s
Mendes, H.P. v3p0230c1s
v4p0610c2s v5p0307c1s v5p0645c2m
Mendes, H.Pereira v6p0277c2s
Mendes, P. v3p0245c1s
Mendivil, J. v1p0047c1s
Mendonca, S.de v4p0072c1m
Mendoza, D. v6p0605c2s
Mendum, G.A. v4p0039c2s
v4p0200c1s
Mendum, S.W. v3p0420c1s
v5p0066c2s
Menefee, E.L. v4p0365c2s
Meneghini, G. v1p0845c1s
Menelas, Constantine v6p0392c1s
Menelaus, W. v1p0663c2s
Mengarini, M.T. v5p0179c1s
Menger, K. v4p0378c1s
Mengert, J.H. v1p0246c2s
Menken, J.S. v5p0101c2s
Menkey, Jill and Gale, Zona
v6p0491c2s
Menmuir, C. v6p0141c1s
v6p0209c1s v6p0431c1s v6p0483c1s
Mennert, A. v3p0049c1s
Menocal, A.G. v1p0332c2s
v4p0087c1s
Menon, C.K. v4p0281c1s
Menpes, M. v4p0030c1s
v4p0187c1s v4p0187c2s v6p0696c1m
Mensbrugghe, G.Van der ... v5p0010c1s
Mensel, E.H. v6p0572c2s
Menteath, P.W.S. v1p0037c2s
Menteth-Beard, Stuart v6p0653c1s
Menzel, W. v1p0514c1s
v1p0827c1s v1p0898c2s v1p0990c1s
Menzies, A. v1p0980c2s
v4p0057c1s v4p0109c1s v4p0109c2s
v4p0374c2s v4p0492c2s v4p0500c1s
v5p0348c1s v5p0503c2s v6p0063c2s
Menzies, A.J.P. v4p0383c2s
v4p0585c2s v5p0342c1s
Menzies, G.K. v4p0269c2s
Menzies, J.J. v3p0215c2s
Menzies, R.S. v3p0221c1s
Menzies, S. v1p0535c1s
Mer, A. v6p0690c2s
Mercadier, E. v1p0885c1s
Mercalli, E. and Ricco, A.
v4p0553c2s
Mercein, D.S. v4p0401c1s
Mercein, T.F.R. v1p0229c1s
v1p0648c2s v1p0677c2s
Merceir, I. v1p0440c2s
Mercer, A. v5p0007c1s
Mercer, C.A. v5p0343c1s
v6p0246c2s
Mercer, Eliz.A. v4p0090c1s
Mercer, H.C. v4p0026c2s
v4p0093c2m v4p0218c2s v4p0281c1s
v4p0298c2s v4p0352c1s v4p0385c1s
v4p0562c2s v4p0636c2s v5p0563c2s
v5p0613c2s
Mercer, H.C. and Hollick, A.
v5p0358c1s
Mercer, L.P. v4p0053c2s
v5p0306c1s v5p0378c1m v5p0563c2s
v5p0597c1s v6p0073c2s
Mercer, T.S. v1p0189c1s
Mercer, W. v2p0040c2s
v2p0365c1s v3p0029c2s v3p0031c2s
v3p0143c2s v3p0191c2m v3p0267c2s

v3p0299c2s v3p0366c2s v3p0392c1s
v4p0084c1s v4p0122c2s v4p0386c1s
v4p0508c1s v4p0584c2s v5p0529c1s
Mercer, W. and Muller, F.Max
v3p0375c2s
Mercer, Wm. v3p0447c1s
Merchant, E.A.J. v1p0666c1s
Merchant, F.I. v5p0313c1s
v6p0583c2s
Mercier, C. v2p0154c1s
v2p0414c1s
Mercier, J. v1p0938c1s
Mercier, J., Mrs. v1p0732c2s
Mercier, M.A. v1p0145c2s
Mercier, Roselle v6p0189c2s
Mercur, J. v4p0370c1s
Meredith, C. v1p0272c2s
Meredith, C., Mrs. v1p1389c1s
Meredith, C.K. v1p0872c2s
Meredith, E. v5p0097c1s
v5p0379c1s v5p0635c1s
Meredith, E. et al. v5p0158c2s
Meredith, E.A. v1p0194c2s
v1p0532c2s v1p1281c1s v2p0249c1s
v2p0354c2s v3p0282c1s v4p0157c2s
v4p0263c1s v5p0410c1s
Meredith, E.R. v4p0629c1s
Meredith, Eliz. v6p0220c2s
Meredith, G. v1p0007c2s
v1p0038c2s v1p0088c1s v1p0105c1s
v1p0108c2s v1p0432c1s v1p0479c1s
v1p0572c1s v1p0577c2s v1p0627c2s
v1p0781c2s v1p0805c1s v1p0940c1s
v1p0996c1s v1p1320c2s v1p1376c1s
v2p0117c2s v2p0440c1s v3p0312c2s
v4p0207c2s v4p0316c1s v4p0368c2s
v5p0083c2s v5p0411c2s v5p0479c2s
v5p0614c2s
Meredith, G.E. v3p0021c1s
v3p0103c2s v3p0114c1m v3p0455c1s
Meredith, G.E., Miss v3p0391c2s
Meredith, Geo. v3p0016c2s
v4p0012c2s
Meredith, Geo.S. v4p0519c2s
Meredith, H.C. v6p0463c2s
Meredith, H.O. v6p0271c2s
v6p0319c1s v6p0520c1s v6p0540c2s
Meredith, I.G. v1p0004c1s
v1p0285c1s v1p0626c2s v1p0966c2s
v1p1324c2s
Meredith, J.C. v5p0488c2s
v6p0496c1s v6p0505c2s
Meredith, K.M.C. v5p0575c1s
Meredith, M. v3p0253c1s
v5p0264c1s
Meredith, Mrs. v1p1397c2s
Meredith, P. v2p0028c1s
Meredith, R. v5p0428c2s
Meredith, S. v1p0587c1s
v1p0868c1s
Meredith, V.C. et al. v4p0102c2s
Meredith, W.H. v3p0055c1s
v5p0625c2s v6p0692c1m
Meren, H. v4p0492c2s
v4p0602c1s v6p0548c2s v6p0676c2s
Merensky, Rev.Dr. v4p0313c1s
Mereu, A. v3p0125c1s
Mereu, H. v3p0017c1s
v3p0021c1s v3p0092c2s v3p0126c1m
v3p0155c2s v3p0187c2s v3p0202c2m
v3p0214c2s v3p0438c1s v3p0448c2s
v4p0071c2s v5p0069c1s v5p0427c1s
v5p0479c1s v5p0485c1s v5p0495c1s
v6p0396c1s v6p0441c2s v6p0508c1m
Mereu, Honore v6p0011c1s
v6p0014c2s
Merewether, J. v1p0145c2s
v1p0587c1s
Mergeland, A.M. v6p0129c2s
Meriam, E. v1p0067c1s
v1p0749c1s v1p1191c2s
Meriam, L.S. v3p0296c1s
Meridith, A.P. v4p0020c1s
Merimee, P. v1p0175c1s
v1p0277c2s v1p0436c1s v1p0761c1s
v1p1229c1s v5p0366c2s
Merington, M. v3p0249c1s
v4p0376c2s v4p0527c1s v4p0528c1s
v5p0064c2s v5p0197c2s v5p0264c1s
v5p0364c1s v5p0379c1s v5p0528c1s
v6p0503c2s v6p0543c1s v6p0620c2s
Merington, M.E. v4p0474c2s
v5p0037c1s v5p0135c1s v5p0249c2s
v5p0640c2s v6p0051c2s
Merington, M.E. et al. ... v5p0218c1s
Merington, Marguerite v4p0058c2s
v4p0390c2s v4p0514c2s v6p0180c2s
v6p0245c2s v6p0648c2s
Merino, S. v4p0293c2s
Merivale, C. v1p0184c2s
v1p0414c2s v1p0727c2s
Merivale, G. v1p0918c2s
Merivale, H. v1p0029c1s
v1p0029c2s v1p0054c1s v1p0387c2s
v1p0531c1s v1p0544c1s v1p0698c2m
v1p0776c2s v1p0804c2s v1p0977c2s
v1p1155c2s v1p1285c1s v1p1338c2s
v1p1378c1s v2p0122c2s v2p0211c2s
v2p0283c1s v2p0445c1s v3p0117c1s
v3p0426c1s v3p0466c2s v5p0522c2s
Merivale, H.C. v1p0336c2s
v1p0716c2s v1p1125c1s v1p1380c1s
v2p0144c2s v2p0267c2s v2p0416c1s
v2p0449c2s
Merivale, H.L. v1p1417c1s
Merivale, H.M. v2p0450c1s
Merivale, Herman v3p0155c2s
Merivale, J.H. v1p0514c1s
v1p0559c1s v1p1246c1s
Merivale, J.H. and Shakespear, Col.
v1p0269c1s
Merivale, M. v1p0026c2s
Meriwether, C. v1p0073c2s
v3p0226c2s v3p0227c2s v4p0297c2s
v4p0359c1s v4p0538c1s v5p0621c1s
Meriwether, L. v3p0119c1s
v3p0144c2s v3p0213c1s v3p0325c1s
v3p0424c2s v3p0472c1s v5p0119c2s
Meriwether, Lee v4p0085c2s
v6p0048c2s v6p0073c2s v6p0563c2s
Meriwether, W.S. v5p0067c1s
v5p0401c2s
Merk, C. v3p0166c2s
v4p0196c1s
Merk, C.H. and Pearson, K.
v4p0345c1s
Merlin, C.L.W. v1p1389c1s
Merlino, S. v4p0073c1s
v4p0085c1s v4p0349c1s
Mero, E.B. v4p0395c2s
v4p0594c2s v4p0595c1s
Merras, W.P. v1p0669c2s
Merrell, W.D. v6p0066c2s
Merriam, A.C. v1p0555c1s
v2p0003c2s v2p0018c2s v2p0183c2s
v2p0458c1s v3p0012c1s v3p0025c2s
v4p0145c2s
Merriam, A.R. v6p0128c2s
v6p0147c2s v6p0213c2s v6p0402c2s
v6p0537c2s v6p0572c2s v6p0673c1s
Merriam, C. v5p0545c1s
Merriam, C.E. v6p0092c1s
v6p0614c2s
Merriam, C.E., jr. v5p0427c2s
v6p0339c2s
Merriam, C.H. v1p0949c1s
v2p0080c1s v2p0393c2m v3p0152c1s
v3p0169c1s v3p0183c2s v4p0018c1s
v4p0060c1s v4p0273c1s v4p0445c2s
v5p0038c1m v5p0053c2s v5p0162c2s
v6p0316c1s v6p0468c2s
Merriam, C.Hart v6p0316c2s
v6p0440c1s
Merriam, C.L. et al. v3p0083c2s
Merriam, E. v1p0055c1s
v1p0943c2s v2p0184c2s
Merriam, E.F. v5p0380c1s
Merriam, Ellis v4p0345c2s
Merriam, F.N. v6p0484c2s
Merriam, G.S. v1p0060c2s
v1p0138c1s v1p0241c1s v1p0441c1s
v2p0053c2s v2p0212c2s v3p0396c2s
Merriam, H.B. v3p0317c2s
Merriam, H.C. v6p0473c1s
Merriam, H.S. v4p0528c1s
Merriam, J.C. v4p0481c2s
v5p0215c1s v5p0309c1s v6p0105c2s
v6p0166c1s v6p0569c1s v6p0657c1s
Merriam, L.P. v3p0279c1s
Merriam, L.S. v4p0432c1s
v4p0532c1s v4p0567c2s v4p0596c2s
Merriam, M. v5p0622c2s
Merriam, W.R. v4p0407c1s
v5p0099c2s v5p0559c2s v6p0106c2m
v6p0659c1s
Merrick and Nystrom v1p1055c2s
Merrick, D.A. v5p0562c1s
v6p0441c2s
Merrick, E.T. v2p0120c1s
v2p0277c1s
Merrick, F.W. v6p0317c2s
Merrick, G.G. v4p0378c2s
Merrick, H. v5p0086c2s
v5p0187c2s
Merrick, J.A. v1p0422c1s
v1p1120c2s
Merrick, J.H. v1p0138c1s
Merrick, J.M. v1p0870c1s
v1p0972c2s v1p1069c2s
Merrick, J.M., jr. v1p0541c1s
Merrick, J.V. v1p0362c1s
v1p0748c2s v1p1247c1s
Merrick, L. v3p0312c2s
v4p0204c1s v4p0614c2s
Merrick, M. v6p0703c1s
Merrick, R.V. v4p0073c1s
Merrifield, C.W. v1p0403c2s
v1p0815c2s v1p0901c2m v1p1250c1s
Merrifield, F. v6p0368c2s
Merrifield, J. v2p0044c1s
v2p0389c1s v3p0341c2s
Merrifield, M.P. v1p0056c1s
v1p0562c1s v2p0007c2m v2p0159c1s
v3p0008c1s
Merrifield, Mrs. v1p0229c1s
v1p0279c1m v1p0346c1s v1p0366c2s
v1p0718c2s v1p0880c2s v1p0959c1s
v1p1150c2s v1p1424c2s
Merrifield, S.B.B. v3p0433c1s
Merrill, A. v6p0702c2s
Merrill, A.H. v5p0393c2s
Merrill, A.P. v2p0212c1s
v2p0245c1s
Merrill, C.C. v5p0623c2s
Merrill, C.D. v2p0109c1s
Merrill, E.B. v4p0144c2s
v4p0295c2s
Merrill, E.H. v3p0329c2s
Merrill, E.T. v4p0321c2s
v6p0332c1s v6p0473c1s v6p0549c2s
v6p0629c2s v6p0630c2s
Merrill, F. v5p0250c2s
Merrill, F.J.H. v3p0036c2s
v3p0203c2s v3p0275c2s v4p0223c1s
v6p0162c2s v6p0257c2s v6p0414c2s
v6p0617c2s
Merrill, G. v1p0473c2s
v1p0479c2s
Merrill, G.A. v4p0103c2s
Merrill, G.B. v1p0350c2s
v1p0574c2s v1p0878c1s v2p0250c2s
Merrill, G.E. v5p0058c2s
v6p0232c1s
Merrill, G.P. v2p0060c1s
v2p0345c1s v3p0026c2s v3p0059c2s
v3p0141c2s v3p0251c1s v3p0276c1s
v3p0313c1s v3p0373c2s v4p0023c1s
v4p0230c1s v4p0367c1s v4p0623c2s
v5p0372c1s v5p0554c2s v6p0257c2s
v6p0412c2s
Merrill, G.P. and Packard, R.L.
v4p0468c1s
Merrill, G.P. and Whitfield, J.E.
v3p0276c1s
Merrill, G.S. v3p0178c2m
Merrill, G.W. v5p0258c2s
v6p0283c1s
Merrill, Geo.B. v5p0258c2s
Merrill, H. v1p0136c2s
Merrill, H.P. v3p0123c2s
Merrill, J. v1p0156c1s
Merrill, J.G. v1p0230c1s
v2p0150c2s v2p0351c2s v2p0426c1s
v3p0340c1s
Merrill, J.W. v4p0634c2s
Merrill, K. v5p0031c2s
v6p0180c2s
Merrill, Katharine v5p0415c1s
Merrill, M. v3p0342c2s
Merrill, M.M. v4p0537c1s
Merrill, M.S. v6p0441c1s
Merrill, N. v1p0284c2s
Merrill, R.W. v2p0366c1s
Merrill, S. v1p0067c2s
v1p0069c1s v1p0069c2s v1p0084c2s
v1p0199c2s v1p0218c1s v1p0684c1s
v1p0975c2s v1p1102c1s v1p1263c2s
v3p0318c1s v4p0295c2s v5p0093c1s
v5p0093c2s v5p0305c1m v5p0401c2s
Merrill, S. and Adams, L.H.
v1p1359c1s
Merrill, S.M. v1p0441c2s
v4p0261c1s v4p0428c2s v4p0457c2s
Merrill, S.P. v3p0463c2m
Merrill, Selah v2p0327c1s
Merrill, T.A. v1p1367c2s
Merrill, T.A. and Lamb, D.
v1p0846c1s
Merrill, T.E. v6p0680c2s
Merrill, W.A. v3p0090c1s
v3p0129c2s v3p0329c2s v5p0350c2s
Merrill, W.E. v1p0161c2m
Merrill, W.H., jr. v6p0225c1s
Merrill, W.P. v6p0024c2s
v6p0341c1s
Merrill, W.S. v4p0401c2s
v5p0014c2s v6p0476c1s v6p0520c2s
v6p0548c1s v6p0614c1s
Merriman, A.C. v2p0145c1s
Merriman, C.C. v1p0524c2s
v1p1112c2s v1p1432c1s
Merriman, D. v1p0426c1s
v1p1292c2s v2p0223c2s v3p0080c2s
Merriman, G. v1p0114c1s
Merriman, G.B. v1p0070c1s
v1p1003c2s
Merriman, G.P. v1p1287c2s
v2p0285c1s
Merriman, H.B. v2p0352c2s
Merriman, H.S. v4p0203c1s
v4p0250c1s v4p0411c1s v4p0425c1s
v4p0460c2s v4p0529c1s v4p0539c1s
v4p0625c1s v5p0282c2s v5p0299c2s
v5p0491c2s v5p0517c1s v6p0052c1s
Merriman, J. v3p0005c1s
v3p0181c1s
Merriman, J.J. v1p0097c2s
v1p0729c2s
Merriman, M. v1p0161c2s
v1p0376c1s v1p0523c1m v1p0760c1s
v1p1241c1m v1p1259c1s v2p0279c2s
v4p0180c2s v5p0293c2s v5p0439c2s
v6p0027c1s v6p0105c1s v6p0204c2s
Merriman, M. and Hazen, H.A.
v4p0381c1s
Merriman, M.L. v6p0222c1s
Merriman, T.M. v6p0699c2s
Merrins, E.M. v6p0024c1s
v6p0170c1s v6p0288c2s v6p0341c1s
v6p0446c1s v6p0501c2s v6p0571c1s

Merris, J.G. v1p0059c2s
Merriton, M. v1p1404c1s
Merritt, A.A. v6p0113c1s
Merritt, A.E. v5p0255c1s
Merritt, A.L. v5p0033c1s v5p0164c2s v5p0225c2m v5p0226c1s v5p0254c1s
Merritt, E. v3p0132c2s v3p0166c2s v4p0331c2s v6p0017c2m v6p0526c2s v6p0527c1s
Merritt, Ernest v5p0492c1s
Merritt, H.F. v4p0336c2s
Merritt, J.S. v5p0371c1s
Merritt, L., Mrs. and Roberts-Austen, Prof. . v4p0387c2m
Merritt, M.F. v1p0863c2s
Merritt, S. v1p0497c1s
Merritt, T. v1p0074c2s v1p0496c1s v1p0830c1s v1p1399c1s
Merritt, W. v3p0213c2s v3p0441c2s v5p0098c1s v5p0160c2s v5p0618c1s v6p0105c2s v6p0366c1s
Merritt, W.H. v1p0195c2s v1p0665c1s v4p0548c1s v5p0238c1m v5p0318c1s
Merritte, E.De v6p0673c2s
Merriwether, C. v4p0096c2s
Merry, A. v5p0212c2s v5p0349c2s v5p0359c1m v5p0565c2s v5p0630c1s
Merry, G.R. v2p0183c2s v4p0164c1s
Merry, W.L. v3p0218c2s v3p0317c1s v3p0374c1s v4p0404c1m v6p0324c1m v6p0456c2m v6p0654c1s
Merryman, J.H. v1p0746c2s
Mershon, W.B. v6p0499c2s
Merson, D. v4p0041c2s
Merton, M. v4p0067c2s v5p0517c2s
Merton, S.D. v6p0496c1s
Merton, S.D. and Carus, P. v6p0496c1s
Mervine, W.M. v6p0258c2s v6p0291c1s
Mervyn, H. v2p0273c1s
Merwin, A.G. v1p0390c1s
Merwin, H.B. v5p0433c1s v5p0455c2s v5p0592c1s
Merwin, H.C. v1p0820c2s v3p0122c2s v3p0153c2s v3p0178c1s v3p0200c2m v3p0201c1m v3p0423c1s v4p0115c2s v4p0162c1s v4p0242c2s v4p0263c2s v4p0264c1m v4p0291c2s v4p0398c2s v4p0412c1s v4p0549c1s v4p0562c2m v5p0053c2s v5p0121c1s v5p0194c1s v5p0376c2s v5p0558c2s v5p0628c2s v5p0629c2s v6p0153c2s v6p0207c2s v6p0219c2s v6p0241c1s v6p0281c1s v6p0297c1s v6p0298c1m v6p0444c1s v6p0450c1s v6p0462c1s v6p0680c2s
Merwin, M.H. v1p0006c2s
Merwin, M.S. v4p0408c1s
Merwin, S. v6p0046c2s v6p0451c1s v6p0564c2s
Merwin, S. and Taylor, N.W. v1p0911c2s
Merwin, Samuel v6p0054c1s
Merwyn, E. v6p0177c2s v6p0421c1s v6p0510c1s v6p0609c1s
Meryon, Commander v4p0413c1s
Merz, J.T. v1p0702c2s
Meshan, J. v4p0190c2s
Mesnil, G.D.Du v5p0001c1s
Messenger, N.O. v5p0094c1s v5p0628c2s v6p0099c1s
Messenger, T. v5p0068c2s
Messer, C. v6p0089c1s
Messer, C.J. v6p0637c2s v6p0651c2s
Messinger, C.S. et al. ... v3p0121c2s
Messinger, G.W. v1p0158c1s v1p0591c2s v1p0825c2s
Messiter, A.H. v3p0084c1s
Messler, A. v1p0979c1s
Messner, H. v1p0047c2s
Mesurier, Mrs.Le v6p0645c1s
Mesurier, T.A.Le v4p0065c1s v4p0266c1s v5p0213c1s
Meta, A. v5p0048c2s
Metcalf, A. v5p0280c2s
Metcalf, F. v6p0216c1s
Metcalf, H. v6p0263c2s
Metcalf, H.B. v2p0067c1s v5p0030c1s
Metcalf, H.H. v2p0046c1s v2p0279c1s v3p0088c1s
Metcalf, I.M. v6p0116c2s
Metcalf, J.C. v1p1007c2s
Metcalf, J.G. v1p0826c2s
Metcalf, J.H. v4p0094c2s v6p0463c2s
Metcalf, J.M.P. v5p0571c2s
Metcalf, M.M. v4p0423c1s v6p0017c2s v6p0197c1s v6p0214c1s v6p0415c2s v6p0440c1s v6p0449c1s
Metcalf, R. v1p0127c2s v1p0566c1s v1p0689c1s
Metcalf, R.C. v1p1085c2s
Metcalf, S.L. v1p0509c2s
Metcalf, T. v1p0729c1s v1p0730c2m
Metcalf, W. v4p0548c1s
Metcalfe, C. and Ruvigny, Marq.de v6p0267c2s
Metcalfe, C. and Ruvigny, Marquis de v5p0542c1m
Metcalfe, C., Sir and Ricarde-Seaver, F.I. .. v3p0004c2s
Metcalfe, F. v6p0127c2s v6p0370c1s v6p0593c2s
Metcalfe, J.S. v3p0267c1s v4p0003c1s v4p0543c2s v4p0572c2s v5p0122c1s v6p0087c2s v6p0242c2s v6p0641c2s
Metcalfe, James A. v6p0443c2s
Metcalfe, R. v4p0206c2s v4p0303c1s v4p0434c1s
Metcalfe, W. v5p0212c1s v5p0277c2s
Metcalfe, W.M. v1p0168c1s v4p0349c2s
Metchnikoff, L. v2p0371c2s v2p0408c2s
Meter, H.H.Van v4p0027c1s v4p0027c2m v4p0106c2s v4p0587c1s
Meteyard, E. v1p0162c2s v1p0213c1s v1p0340c1s v1p0357c2s v1p0551c1s v1p0598c2s v1p0774c1s v1p0855c2s v1p1050c2s v1p1142c2s v1p1238c2s v1p1309c1s v1p1434c1s
Methuen, A.M.S. v5p0521c1s
Methuen, Lord v6p0206c1s
Methven, H. v5p0295c2m v5p0296c2s
Methven, T.H. v1p0982c1s
Mets, J.A. v1p0321c2s
Metters, C. v4p0470c2s
Metzger, E. v2p0127c2s v2p0151c1s
Metzger, F.J. and Wells, H.L. v5p0211c2s
Metzler, E.J. v4p0045c1s
Metzner, H. v3p0439c1s
Meunier, S. v2p0172c1s v2p0258c2s v3p0269c1s v4p0008c2s v4p0152c2s v4p0222c2s
Meurice, P. v5p0275c1s
Meusch, L. v6p0143c1s
Meusiaux, M.de v3p0002c2s v3p0034c2s v3p0063c2s v3p0092c1s v3p0123c2s v3p0186c1m v3p0252c1s v3p0275c1s v3p0277c2s v3p0324c1s v3p0429c2s v3p0436c2s
Mew, C.M. v5p0112c2s v5p0379c1s v6p0083c2s v6p0385c1s v6p0394c1s v6p0401c2s v6p0626c2s
Mew, Charlotte M. v5p0077c2s v5p0538c2s v6p0311c1s v6p0468c1s v6p0696c2s
Mew, E. v3p0439c1s
Mew, J. v1p0018c1s v1p0050c1s v1p0077c2s v1p0145c2s v1p0213c2m v1p0446c2s v1p0619c2m v1p0669c1s v1p0814c1s v1p1071c2s v1p1231c2s v1p1235c2s v1p1312c1s v2p0002c1s v2p0018c1s v2p0062c1s v2p0242c2s v2p0270c2s v3p0193c2m v4p0095c1s v4p0254c1s v4p0347c1s v4p0370c1s v4p0436c1s v4p0467c2s v5p0239c2s v6p0277c1s
Mews, J. v4p0323c2s
Meyer, A. v6p0660c1s
Meyer, A.B. v1p0377c1s v1p0911c1s v1p0998c1s
Meyer, A.G. v6p0625c1s
Meyer, A.J. v1p1395c1s v6p0471c1s
Meyer, A.N. v3p0007c2s v3p0225c2s v3p0468c2s v4p0272c1s v4p0607c2s v5p0415c2s v5p0581c1s v6p0013c1s v6p0135c1s v6p0437c1s v6p0624c2s v6p0663c1s v6p0695c2s v6p0702c2s
Meyer, A.R. v6p0396c1s
Meyer, Alice N. v6p0471c1s
Meyer, Annie N. v6p0361c1s v6p0475c1s v6p0599c1s
Meyer, Annie N. and Ellis, M.B. v5p0232c2s
Meyer, B.H. v5p0292c2s v5p0477c2s v5p0536c2s v5p0565c1s v6p0324c2s v6p0346c2s v6p0438c2s v6p0529c1s v6p0529c2s v6p0530c1s
Meyer, E. v3p0014c2s v6p0011c2s v6p0317c2s
Meyer, E.S. v6p0181c1s v6p0244c1s v6p0252c1s v6p0254c1s v6p0255c1s v6p0283c1s v6p0286c1s v6p0305c2s v6p0624c1s
Meyer, E.T. v5p0194c2s v6p0268c2s
Meyer, Ernest E. v6p0074c1s
Meyer, F.B. v6p0025c1s v6p0122c1s
Meyer, G.von L. v6p0162c1s
Meyer, H. v6p0491c2s v6p0673c1s
Meyer, H.A.W. v1p0128c2s
Meyer, H.H. v6p0344c2s
Meyer, H.R. v5p0427c1s v6p0332c1s v6p0436c1m v6p0528c1m v6p0529c1m
Meyer, I.F. and Colvin, S.S. v6p0117c1s
Meyer, J. v3p0283c1s v4p0611c2s
Meyer, J.A. v6p0261c1s v6p0482c2s v6p0701c2s
Meyer, J.F. v6p0197c1s
Meyer, J.P. v6p0018c2s
Meyer, K. v2p0156c2s v4p0291c2s
Meyer, L. v1p0514c2s
Meyer, L.R. v5p0388c2s
Meyer, M. v5p0369c1s v5p0394c1s v5p0519c2m v6p0040c2s v6p0438c1s v6p0438c2s v6p0439c1s
Meyer, M.A. v6p0475c2s
Meyer, M.W. v4p0503c2s v4p0585c2s
Meyer, O. v2p0327c1s v2p0435c2s v3p0045c2s v3p0118c1s v3p0359c1s
Meyer, Prof. v5p0395c1s
Meyer, R.J. v2p0307c2s
Meyer, R.M. v4p0405c1s v5p0144c2s v5p0230c1s v6p0623c2s
Meyer, W. v4p0381c1s v4p0484c2s v6p0302c2s
Meyerhardt, M.W. v6p0365c2s
Meyers, A. v6p0449c2s
Meyers, C.E. v6p0024c1s
Meyers, C.L. v3p0025c2s
Meyers, F.A. v3p0244c1s
Meyers, F.W. v3p0029c1s
Meyers, F.W.H. v3p0101c2s v3p0348c1s
Meyers, G. v5p0218c2s v5p0407c2s v5p0471c1s
Meyers, G.W. v5p0372c1s v6p0406c1s
Meyers, R.C. v1p0807c1s v1p0938c1s v2p0139c2s
Meyers, R.C.V. v1p0964c1s v4p0199c1s v4p0221c2s v4p0263c1s v4p0618c2s v5p0460c2s
Meyers, W.J. v4p0175c1s
Meyers, W.S. v1p0860c1s
Meyjes, J.W. v5p0371c2s
Meylan, G.L. v6p0282c1s
Meyn, L. v1p0068c2s v3p0024c1s
Meynell, A. v1p0066c2s v1p1130c2s v2p0069c2s v2p0118c1s v2p0279c1s v2p0341c2s v2p0378c2s v2p0479c1s v3p0021c2s v3p0039c2s v3p0193c1s v3p0229c2s v3p0317c2s v3p0460c1s v4p0066c1s v4p0070c1s v4p0079c2s v4p0081c2s v4p0255c2s v4p0257c2s v4p0364c1s v4p0398c1s v4p0416c1s v4p0477c2s v4p0561c1s v5p0554c1s v6p0173c2s v6p0193c2s v6p0303c1s v6p0609c1s v6p0641c1s v6p0705c2s
Meynell, A.C. v4p0030c2s v4p0266c2s
Meynell, Alice v2p0430c1s v3p0034c1s v3p0246c2s v4p0430c2s v4p0492c1s v5p0079c2s v6p0026c2s v6p0665c1s
Meynell, W. v1p0061c1s v1p0624c2s v1p1204c1s v2p0169c2s v2p0207c1s v2p0474c1s v3p0302c1m v4p0011c2m v4p0048c1s v4p0065c1s v4p0207c1s v4p0243c2s v4p0255c2s v4p0260c1s v4p0305c1s v4p0326c1m v4p0327c1s v4p0354c1m v4p0437c2s v4p0459c1s v4p0550c1s v4p0612c2s v4p0614c1s v5p0234c2s v5p0424c1s v6p0003c1s v6p0054c2s v6p0228c1s v6p0258c1s v6p0616c2s
Meynell, W. and Vaughan, H. v4p0354c1s
Meynell, W. et al. v4p0353c2s
Meynell, Wilfrid v5p0127c2s v5p0554c1s
Meynier, E. v5p0331c1s
Meyrick, A.S. v1p1052c2m
Meyrick, G. v3p0296c2s v5p0196c2s v5p0572c1s
Meyrick, J.J. v2p0258c2s
Meyrick, S.R. v1p0059c1m v1p0184c1s v1p0196c1s v1p0216c2s v1p0455c1s v1p0585c1s v1p0770c1s v1p0838c2s v1p1069c2s v1p1182c2s v1p1191c1s v1p1439c2s
Meyrick, T. v1p0067c1s v1p0200c2s v1p0870c2s v1p1262c2s
Meysey-Thompson, H.M. v5p0586c2s
Meza, W.de v4p0082c1s
Mezes, S.E. v4p0129c2s v4p0214c1s v4p0421c1s v4p0447c1s
Mezieres, A. v1p0497c2s
Mezzrocchi, E.C. v1p0209c2s
Miall, A.B. v5p0567c2s
Miall, C.M. v4p0353c2s
Miall, C.S. v2p0084c2s
Miall, L.C. v1p1112c2s

v3p0217c1s v4p0286c1s v4p0613c1s v5p0606c2s v5p0613c2s v5p0629c1s v5p0644c2s
Michael, A.D. v4p0576c2s
Michael, H.A. v4p0089c1s v4p0160c2s v5p0630c1s
Michael, J. v3p0158c1s v3p0211c2s v4p0207c2s
Michael, W.A. v5p0524c1s
Michaelides, C.C. v6p0429c1s v6p0629c1s
Michaelis, A. v2p0338c1s v3p0016c1s v3p0017c2s v3p0267c1s v3p0341c2s v3p0357c1s v3p0375c2s v3p0426c2s v6p0491c1s
Michaelis, Dr. v1p0873c2s
Michaelis, E. v2p0213c2s
Michaelis, J.D. v1p0724c1s
Michaelis, O.E. v2p0138c1s v3p0238c1s v5p0032c1s
Michaelis, P. v4p0500c2s
Michaelis, W. v1p0211c1s
Michaelson, M. v6p0220c2s
Michal, M. v1p0065c1s
Michaud, E. v1p0481c1s v1p0481c2s
Michaud, G. v5p0543c1s v6p0107c1s v6p0526c1s v6p0532c2s v6p0631c2s
Michaux, A. v1p0494c1s
Michel, A. v5p0432c1m
Michel, Andre v4p0426c1s
Michel, H. v4p0337c2s v4p0498c1s
Michel, R.G. v5p0196c2s
Michel, R.L.N. v1p0396c2s
Michel-Levy, M.A. v3p0363c1s
Michelet, C.L. v1p0348c2s
Michelet, J. v1p0301c2s v1p1098c1s v1p1114c1s v1p1241c2s
Micheli, H. v5p0478c1s
Micheli, M.H. v5p0477c2s
Michell, E.B. v2p0152c1m
Michell, L. v6p0542c2s
Michell, N. v1p0262c2m v1p0589c1s v1p1312c2s
Michell, R. v1p0068c1s v1p0449c1s v1p0702c2s v1p0962c2s v1p1137c1s v1p1333c2s v4p0032c2s v4p0423c1s
Michell, T. v1p0315c2s v1p1134c2s
Michels, J. v1p0835c2s
Michels, P.V. v5p0351c1s v5p0624c2s
Michelsen, A. v1p0044c1s v1p0241c1s v1p0515c1s
Michelsen, C. v6p0508c1s
Michelsen, Dr. v1p0305c1s v1p0689c2s v1p0770c2s v1p1123c2s v1p1281c2s v1p1312c2s v1p1377c2s
Michelsen, H. v6p0233c1s v6p0659c1s
Michelson, A. v6p0594c2s
Michelson, A.A. v1p0747c2m v2p0223c2s v2p0367c2s v3p0218c1s v3p0233c1s v3p0250c2s v3p0251c1s v4p0331c2s v4p0362c2s v4p0487c1m v4p0540c2s v5p0195c2s v5p0475c2s v5p0545c1s
Michelson, A.A. and Morley, E.W. v2p0258c2s v3p0143c1s v3p0246c2s v3p0251c1s v3p0399c2s
Michelson, A.A. and Stratton, S.W. v5p0018c1s
Michelson, A.M. v6p0057c1s v6p0474c2s
Michelson, C. v5p0238c1s v5p0323c2s v5p0358c2s v5p0548c1s v5p0612c1s v6p0552c1s v6p0590c1s v6p0653c1s
Michelson, M. v6p0019c2s v6p0106c1s v6p0394c1s v6p0411c2s v6p0474c2s v6p0516c2s
Michener, H.C. v4p0077c2s v4p0433c2s
Michie, A. v1p0327c1s v1p0795c2s v1p0911c1s v4p0006c1s v4p0105c1s v4p0105c2s v4p0133c2s v4p0278c2m v4p0328c1m v5p0110c1m v5p0110c2s v5p0111c1s v5p0111c2s v5p0338c2s v6p0474c1s
Michie, A.S. v4p0045c1s
Michie, C.Y. v2p0156c2s v2p0200c1s
Michie, P.S. v1p1401c2s v4p0617c2s v5p0086c2s v5p0157c1s v5p0375c1s v5p0375c2s
Michie, T.J. v4p0373c1s
Michil, A. v6p0369c2s
Michols, E.L. and Bailey, E.H.S. v2p0405c2s v3p0420c2s
Mickey, D.M. v3p0437c1s
Mickiewiez, A. v1p1136c2s
Micklethwaite, J.T. v1p1402c1s v2p0323c1s v2p0326c2s v4p0114c1s v5p0262c1s v5p0314c2s v5p0626c2s
Mickley, J.J. v1p0728c2s v1p1307c1s
Micklin, J.A. v6p0389c2s
Mickson, E.J. v4p0203c2s
Micou, B. v5p0583c1s
Micou, R.W. v2p0123c2s v4p0057c2s
Middlebrook, C.P. v5p0591c2s
Middleditch, R.T. v1p0871c1s
Middlemass, J. v1p0166c2s v1p0878c1s v1p0994c2s v1p1415c2s v2p0169c1s v2p0451c1s v3p0472c2s
Middlemass, Jean v4p0526c2s
Middlemiss, C.S. v2p0085c2s
Middlemore, J. v6p0271c1s
Middlemore, T. v6p0108c1s
Middleton, A. v1p0351c2s
Middleton, C. v4p0149c1s v4p0521c2s v5p0044c1s v5p0074c2s v5p0083c1s v5p0115c2s v5p0217c2s v5p0247c1s v5p0306c1s v5p0411c2s v5p0499c1s v5p0561c2s v5p0632c2s v5p0645c1s v6p0398c1s v6p0663c1s
Middleton, C.H. v1p0621c1s
Middleton, E.H. v6p0203c2s
Middleton, E.M. v5p0635c1s
Middleton, F. v4p0086c1s v4p0503c1s v5p0631c2s
Middleton, F., Sir v3p0065c2s v4p0284c1s v4p0536c1s
Middleton, G.A. v4p0436c2s
Middleton, G.A.T. v4p0023c2s v4p0212c2s v4p0260c2s v4p0480c2s v5p0026c1m v5p0128c1s v5p0208c1s v5p0271c2s v5p0487c2s v5p0541c1s v6p0220c1s
Middleton, H. v1p0325c1s v1p0537c2s
Middleton, J. v4p0564c2s
Middleton, J.D. v3p0290c1s
Middleton, J.H. v2p0019c2s v2p0023c1s v2p0063c2s v2p0065c1s v2p0072c2s v2p0102c1s v2p0159c2s v2p0177c2s v2p0282c1s v2p0307c2s v2p0326c2s v2p0327c2s v2p0365c1s v2p0383c2s v2p0392c2s v3p0114c1s v3p0424c1s v3p0430c2s v3p0447c2s v5p0087c2s v5p0133c2s v5p0157c1s v5p0495c1m v5p0497c2s v5p0610c1s v6p0454c2s
Middleton, J.S. v6p0524c2s
Middleton, L. v6p0039c1s v6p0479c1s
Middleton, Lady and Gordon-Cumming, C.F. .. v3p0467c1s
Middleton, M.W. v6p0518c1s v6p0633c1s
Middleton, Mathew v4p0316c1s
Middleton, T.H. v6p0552c2s
Middleton, T.J. v4p0538c2s
Middleton, Viscount v1p0590c2s v2p0227c1s
Middleton-Wake, C.H. v2p0479c1s v4p0480c1s
Midgely, J.W. v6p0102c2s v6p0529c1s
Midgley, J.W. v1p1080c1s v4p0472c2s v5p0476c2s v6p0529c1s
Midhat Pasha v1p1332c1s
Midhat, Ali Haydar v6p0186c1s
Midleton, Lord v1p0933c1s
Midworth, H. v5p0332c2s
Miel, C.F.B. v5p0540c1s
Mielatz, C.F.W. v5p0567c2s v6p0633c2s
Miers, A.H. v4p0539c2s
Miers, H.A. v3p0107c1m v4p0142c1m v4p0372c1m v4p0456c2m v4p0468c2s v5p0146c2s v5p0372c1s v5p0566c2s
Miers, H.A. and Andrewes, F.W. v4p0429c2s
Mies, F.P. v6p0704c2s
Mieville, W. v6p0221c2s
Mieville, W.F., Sir v6p0195c2s v6p0221c2s
Mifflin, B.C. v1p0844c1s v1p1199c1s
Mifflin, J., Mrs. v4p0459c2s
Mifflin, J.H. v1p0453c2s
Mifflin, L. v5p0314c1s
Mighels, P.V. v5p0050c1s v5p0596c1s v6p0052c1s v6p0066c1s v6p0121c2s v6p0234c2s v6p0285c1m v6p0380c2s v6p0432c1s v6p0439c1s v6p0440c2s v6p0449c2s v6p0450c1s v6p0464c1s v6p0646c2s v6p0687c2s v6p0695c1s
Migliarini, Prof. v1p0880c1s
Mignet, F.A. v1p0220c2s v1p0806c2s
Mignet, F.A.M. v4p0345c1s
Miguel, Prof. v2p0287c2s
Miguels, P.V. v6p0068c2s
Mijalovics, E.L. v1p1136c1s
Mijatovich, C. v6p0001c1s v6p0661c2s
Mijatovich, C. and Stead, A. v6p0186c2s
Mijatovics, E.L. v1p0963c2s
Mikell, W.E. and McNeal, A.J. v6p0170c1s
Mikhailoff, M. v5p0528c1s
Mikhailovskii, M. v4p0519c1s
Mikkelsen, M.A. v4p0062c1s v4p0116c1s v4p0175c1s
Miklashevsky, A.N. v4p0377c2s
Mikluho-Maclay, N.N. v1p1441c1s
Milborne, H. v5p0517c2s
Milborne, W. v1p1403c1s
Milburn, J.A. v6p0189c2s
Milburn, J.B. v4p0488c1s v5p0241c2s v5p0426c1s v5p0426c2s v5p0604c2s v6p0238c1s v6p0241c2s v6p0400c1s v6p0404c2s
Milburn, N.F. v3p0391c1s v4p0308c1s
Milburn, P. v6p0536c2s
Milburn, W.H. v1p0539c1s v2p0035c2s v2p0270c1s v3p0096c2s
Milecete, H. v6p0220c1s
Miles v6p0556c2s
Miles, C. v4p0465c1s
Miles, E. v5p0511c1s v6p0612c1s
Miles, E.B. v6p0606c2s
Miles, E.H. v5p0475c2s v5p0572c2s
Miles, E.M. v6p0437c2s
Miles, Eustace v6p0080c2s
Miles, G.B. v1p1379c2s
Miles, G.H. v1p0183c1s v1p0244c2s
Miles, G.W. and Schmitt, C.D. v5p0182c2s
Miles, H.A. v1p0095c2s v1p0285c1s v1p0307c1s v1p0420c2s v1p0439c1s v1p0689c2s v1p0700c1s v1p0752c1s v1p1303c2s
Miles, H.H. v1p0906c1s
Miles, J.B. v1p0650c2s v1p0687c2s v1p1101c2s
Miles, J.M. v2p0413c1s
Miles, L.P. v4p0206c2s
Miles, M. v2p0145c1s v2p0153c1s v2p0464c2s v3p0006c1s v3p0006c2m v4p0008c1s v4p0018c1m v4p0255c2s v4p0409c2s
Miles, N.A. v1p0637c2s v3p0223c2s v4p0045c1s v4p0270c1s v4p0597c1s v4p0610c1s v5p0124c2s v5p0173c2s v5p0196c2s v5p0288c2s v5p0375c1s v5p0543c1s
Miles, N.A. et al. v4p0553c2s
Miles, Nelson A. v6p0165c2s
Miles, P. v1p0936c2s v1p1038c1m v1p1038c2s
Miles, R.E. v6p0300c1s
Miles, R.H. v1p0395c1s v1p0960c2s v1p1264c2s
Miles, S.B. v4p0022c1s v5p0250c1s
Miley, J. v1p0069c1s v1p0487c1s v1p0528c1s v1p1304c1s
Miley, J.D., Lt.-Col. v5p0009c2s
Milford, H. v1p0928c1s
Milham, Z. v6p0128c2s
Milhau, Z. v6p0071c1s
Milholland, T.E. v5p0603c1s
Milinowski, A. v5p0206c2s
Milis, C. v6p0069c2s
Mill, H.R. v2p0319c2s v2p0467c1s v3p0089c1s v3p0309c2s v4p0012c1s v4p0019c2s v4p0025c2m v4p0036c1s v4p0073c2s v4p0095c1s v4p0120c1s v4p0222c1m v4p0317c2m v4p0377c1s v4p0410c2s v4p0577c1s v4p0601c2s v5p0019c1s v5p0022c1s v5p0091c1s v5p0162c2s v5p0189c2s v5p0197c1s v5p0207c1s v5p0228c2m v5p0319c2s v5p0323c1s v5p0615c2s v5p0622c1s v6p0023c2m v6p0205c1s v6p0250c1s v6p0250c2s
Mill, H.R. et al. v6p0175c1s
Mill, J. v1p0089c1s v1p0237c2s v1p0429c1s v1p0895c2s
Mill, J.A. v1p1323c2s
Mill, J.S. v1p0029c2s v1p0047c1s v1p0057c2s v1p0077c2s v1p0113c1s v1p0114c1m v1p0193c1s v1p0203c1s v1p0259c2s v1p0274c1m v1p0287c1s v1p0287c2s v1p0326c2s v1p0342c2m v1p0407c2s v1p0412c2s v1p0475c1s v1p0475c2s v1p0477c1s v1p0480c2s v1p0548c2s v1p0552c2m v1p0561c2s v1p0649c1s v1p0655c1s v1p0699c1s v1p0714c1m v1p0721c1s v1p0725c1s v1p0781c2s v1p0839c1s v1p0868c2s v1p0897c2s v1p0925c1m v1p0944c2s v1p0965c2s v1p0974c1s v1p1000c2s v1p1016c2s v1p1026c1s v1p1037c2s v1p1055c2s v1p1062c1s v1p1089c1m v1p1099c1s v1p1100c1s v1p1215c2s v1p1216c2s v1p1295c2s v1p1342c2s v1p1348c2s v1p1357c2s v1p1360c2s v1p1371c1s v1p1371c2s v1p1375c1s v1p1383c1s v1p1386c1s v1p1426c1s
Mill, N. v1p0865c2s
Mill, R.H. v6p0463c2s
Millais, J.G. v4p0030c1s v4p0270c1s v5p0631c1s v6p0455c1s

v6p0455c2s
Millais, J.G. et al. v4p0030c2s
Millar, A. v4p0090c2m
Millar, A.B. v5p0324c2s
Millar, A.C. v4p0169c2s
v5p0177c1s
Millar, A.F. v3p0229c2s
v3p0372c1s
Millar, A.H. v4p0019c1s
v4p0063c1s v4p0265c1s v4p0270c1m
v4p0296c1s v4p0458c1s v4p0509c2m
v4p0510c1s v5p0255c2s v5p0322c2s
v5p0326c2s v5p0515c2s v5p0624c2m
v6p0351c1s v6p0551c1s v6p0577c2s
Millar, C.D. v5p0551c2s
Millar, E.A. v5p0049c2s
Millar, G.M. v6p0193c1s
Millar, J.D. v6p0058c2s
Millar, J.H. v4p0040c1s
v4p0218c2s v4p0335c1s v4p0625c2s
v5p0066c1s
Millar, W.J. v1p0188c2s
v1p1258c2s v1p1261c1s v5p0551c2s
v6p0486c1s
Millard, A. v6p0203c1s
Millard, B. v6p0180c1s
v6p0311c1s v6p0358c1s v6p0367c1s
v6p0376c1s v6p0382c1s v6p0389c2s
v6p0467c2s v6p0674c1s v6p0687c1s
v6p0694c2s v6p0698c1s
Millard, Bailey v6p0608c2s
Millard, C.C. v5p0093c2s
Millard, E.E. v3p0013c2s
Millard, F.B. v3p0103c1s
v4p0273c2s v4p0286c1s v4p0305c1s
v4p0407c2s v5p0560c2s v6p0346c1s
Millard, F.F. v5p0109c1s
Millard, G.B. v5p0047c2s
Millard, J. v6p0217c1s
Millard, O.G. v6p0006c1s
Millard, P. v6p0459c2s
Millard, T.F. v5p0068c1s
v5p0111c2m v5p0589c1s v5p0627c1s
v6p0094c2s v6p0119c1s v6p0317c1s
v6p0335c1s v6p0337c1s v6p0512c2s
v6p0556c1s v6p0561c1s v6p0685c1s
v6p0685c2s
Millard, W.J.N. v2p0020c1s
Millard, W.S. v4p0132c2s
Mille, A.B.De v5p0065c2s
v5p0091c2s v5p0353c2s v5p0491c1s
v6p0290c2s v6p0299c2s
Mille, A.De v6p0142c1s
Mille, J.De v1p0030c2s
v1p0281c1s v1p0358c1s v1p0716c2s
v1p0757c2s v1p0931c1s v1p0943c2s
Millen, F.F. v1p1243c1s
Miller v3p0283c1s
Miller et al. v3p0031c1s
Miller, A. v1p1199c2s
v4p0268c2s v5p0081c1s v6p0210c1s
Miller, A., Sir v6p0327c1s
Miller, A.B. v2p0215c2s
v2p0437c1s
Miller, A.C. v3p0181c2s
v3p0472c2s v4p0199c1s v4p0278c1s
v4p0565c2s v5p0207c1s v5p0365c2s
v5p0568c1s v6p0318c1s v6p0634c1s
Miller, A.C. and Thurston, H.W.
v6p0136c2s
Miller, A.D. v6p0130c1s
v6p0397c2s
Miller, A.E. v6p0007c1m
v6p0327c1s v6p0355c2s v6p0426c1s
Miller, A.E., Sir v6p0099c2s
Miller, A.H. v1p0526c1s
Miller, A.K. et al. v4p0081c1s
v4p0144c1s v4p0564c1s
Miller, A.M. v6p0413c1m
Miller, A.R. v6p0024c2s
Miller, A.S. v1p0374c1s
v1p0757c2s v1p1188c1s
Miller, A.W., Mrs. v6p0574c1s
Miller, Alice D. v6p0203c2s
v6p0333c1s v6p0487c1s v6p0625c1s
v6p0672c2s
Miller, B. v5p0521c2s
Miller, B.A. v5p0628c2s
Miller, B.C. v1p0938c1s
Miller, Barnette v6p0056c1s
Miller, C. v1p1262c2s
v5p0436c1s v5p0481c1s
Miller, C.A. v2p0386c1s
Miller, C.D. v4p0250c2s
Miller, C.G. v5p0593c1s
Miller, C.H. v1p0013c2s
v1p0058c1s v1p0181c2s v1p0182c1s
v1p0187c2s v1p0336c1s v1p0397c2s
v1p0414c2s v1p0504c2s v1p0623c1s
v1p0626c2s v1p0709c2s v1p0726c2s
v1p0947c1s v1p0956c1s v1p1105c1s
v1p1124c2s v1p1182c2m v1p1196c1s
v1p1309c1s v2p0093c1s v4p0149c1s
v4p0416c2s v4p0550c1s v6p0087c1s
Miller, C.L. v6p0447c1s
Miller, C.M. v6p0504c2s
Miller, C.R. v4p0403c1s
v5p0519c2s
Miller, C.W.E. v4p0241c2s
Miller, C.W.E. and
Gildersleeve, B.L. v6p0680c2s
Miller, Capt. v1p0902c1s
Miller, D. v1p0271c2s
v1p1172c1s v2p0192c2s
Miller, D.C. v6p0015c1m
Miller, D.R., Mrs. v4p0082c1s
Miller, D.S. v3p0174c1s
v4p0131c1s v4p0217c2s v4p0418c2s
v4p0585c2s v5p0446c2s
Miller, Dickinson S. v5p0052c2s
v6p0032c1s
Miller, E. v1p0206c2s
v1p0727c1s v1p0956c1s v1p1063c2s
v4p0034c1s v4p0128c2s v4p0190c2s
v4p0381c1s v4p0429c2s v5p0363c1s
v5p0561c1s
Miller, E.C.L. v6p0011c2s
Miller, E.G. v5p0116c2s
Miller, E.H. v4p0207c1s
v4p0551c1s v4p0565c2s v5p0208c2s
v5p0611c2s v6p0020c1s v6p0112c1s
Miller, E.H. et al. v3p0148c1s
Miller, E.J. et al. v2p0417c2s
Miller, E.K. v2p0333c1s
Miller, E.L. v3p0115c2s
v5p0341c1s v6p0272c2s v6p0290c1s
Miller, E.P. v1p0121c2s
v1p0689c2s v1p1270c1s v6p0585c2s
Miller, E.R. v6p0580c1s
Miller, E.S. v3p0071c1s
Miller, E.T. v6p0362c1s
v6p0487c1s
Miller, E.T. and Bolton, T.L.
v6p0210c1s
Miller, E.Y. v5p0270c2s
Miller, E.Z, jr. v3p0355c1s
Miller, Ellen R. v6p0594c2s
Miller, Esther v5p0274c1s
Miller, F. v2p0182c2s
v2p0268c1s v3p0193c1s v3p0256c1s
v4p0032c1s v4p0228c1s v4p0231c2s
v4p0339c2s v4p0379c1s v4p0455c1s
v4p0628c1s v4p0631c1s v5p0070c2s
v5p0102c2s v5p0122c2s v5p0156c1s
v5p0187c2m v5p0208c2m v5p0216c1s
v5p0221c2s v5p0232c2s v5p0301c1s
v5p0314c1s v5p0316c1s v5p0324c2s
v5p0328c2s v5p0346c1s v5p0371c2s
v5p0388c1s v5p0428c1s v5p0485c2s
v5p0490c2s v5p0503c1s v5p0568c2s
v5p0639c1s v5p0639c2s v6p0384c2s
v6p0496c2s v6p0511c2s v6p0624c1s
Miller, F., Mrs. v3p0037c2s
Miller, F.F. v2p0073c2s
v2p0131c1s v2p0407c1s v2p0446c2s
v3p0135c2s v4p0101c2s v4p0102c2s
Miller, F.G. v2p0003c1s
Miller, F.H. v2p0187c1m
v2p0400c2s v2p0451c1s v6p0465c2s
v6p0697c1s
Miller, F.J. v4p0347c2s
v5p0326c2s v6p0130c1s
Miller, F.T. v6p0284c1m
Miller, F.T. and Herisson, J.L.
v6p0278c1s
Miller, Florence H. v6p0081c2s
Miller, Frank J. v6p0331c2s
v6p0680c1s
Miller, Fred v5p0193c2s
v5p0330c1s
Miller, G. v4p0382c2s
v4p0599c1s v4p0627c2s v6p0356c2s
v6p0429c2s
Miller, G.A. v4p0223c1s
v6p0245c2s v6p0275c1s v6p0319c1s
v6p0405c2m v6p0406c2s
Miller, G.B. v1p0262c2s
v1p1088c1s v2p0350c1s
Miller, G.D. v5p0011c1s
v5p0255c2s
Miller, G.M. v1p0470c2s
v6p0048c2s
Miller, G.M. et al. v6p0310c2s
Miller, G.McA. v6p0189c1s
v6p0341c1s v6p0343c2s v6p0431c1s
Miller, G.R. v4p0453c1s
v6p0173c1s v6p0640c2s v6p0669c1s
Miller, G.S. v5p0357c2s
Miller, G.S., jr. v5p0049c2s
Miller, G.W. v6p0228c1s
v6p0368c1s
Miller, Grace v6p0602c1s
Miller, H. v1p0458c1s
v1p0507c1s v1p0874c1s v1p0990c2s
v1p1170c1s v2p0422c2s v3p0439c1s
v4p0257c1s v4p0337c1s v4p0459c1s
Miller, H.A. v6p0526c1s
Miller, H.B. v6p0398c2s
Miller, H.E. v4p0484c1s
v5p0062c2s v5p0136c1s v5p0145c2s
v5p0299c1s v5p0532c2s v5p0544c2s
v5p0567c2s
Miller, H.J. v1p1031c1s
Miller, H.T. v6p0448c2s
Miller, H.W. and Duer, Alice
v5p0340c1s
Miller, J. v1p0252c1s
v1p0325c1s v1p0492c1s v1p0649c1s
v1p0668c1s v1p0714c2s v1p0860c2s
v1p1191c1s v2p0083c1s v3p0064c1s
v3p0290c2s v3p0303c2s v5p0112c2s
v6p0335c2s
Miller, J.A. v5p0441c1s
v5p0584c2s v6p0615c2s v6p0660c1s
Miller, J.B. v2p0119c2s
v2p0315c2s v2p0387c1s v2p0463c1s
Miller, J.C. v1p0121c1s
v1p0126c2s v1p0133c1s v1p0599c2s
v1p0676c2s
Miller, J.D. v4p0086c2s
v4p0261c2s v5p0077c2s v5p0186c2s
v5p0255c1s v5p0333c1s v5p0482c1s
v5p0519c1s v5p0579c1s v5p0592c2s
v6p0109c2s v6p0345c1s v6p0379c2s
v6p0389c1s v6p0550c2s v6p0634c1s
Miller, J.F. v2p0079c2s
v6p0120c1s
Miller, J.J. v5p0212c2s
Miller, J.K. v4p0617c1s
Miller, J.M. v5p0418c2s
v5p0446c1s
Miller, J.O. v1p1432c2s
v5p0317c2s
Miller, J.R. v6p0426c1s
Miller, J.W. v3p0298c1s
v4p0404c1s v4p0610c1s v5p0401c2s
Miller, Joaquin v4p0308c1s
v4p0536c2s v5p0030c1s v5p0129c1s
v5p0318c2s v5p0574c1s v6p0094c1s
v6p0281c2s v6p0353c1s v6p0467c1s
Miller, K. v5p0229c1s
v5p0403c1m v6p0170c2s v6p0446c2m
v6p0447c1s v6p0447c2s v6p0448c1m
v6p0526c1s v6p0658c2s
Miller, K.B. v5p0571c1s
Miller, L. and Ritter, W.E.
v5p0505c1s
Miller, L.B. v4p0432c2s
v6p0311c2s
Miller, L.G.M. v1p0426c1s
Miller, L.H. v6p0565c1s
Miller, L.W. v2p0023c1s
v2p0023c2s v2p0326c2s v2p0338c2m
v2p0371c2s v2p0467c2s v3p0341c1s
v5p0159c2s v6p0128c2s
Miller, M. v4p0380c2s
Miller, M.C. v6p0241c1s
Miller, M.F. v1p0369c2s
v1p1170c1s
Miller, M.L. v4p0155c2s
v4p0626c2s v5p0363c1s
Miller, M.M. v4p0150c1s
v5p0119c2s v5p0171c2s v5p0305c2s
v5p0568c2s v6p0116c2s
Miller, M.M. and Estrem, A.
v4p0627c1s
Miller, M.M. et al. v5p0229c2s
Miller, Marion M. v4p0253c1s
Miller, Mary R. v6p0243c1s
Miller, O.C. v5p0445c2s
Miller, O.D. v1p0069c2s
v1p0084c1s v1p0084c2s v1p0117c1s
v1p0120c2s v1p0127c1s v1p0495c2s
v1p0528c2s v1p0592c2s v1p0691c2s
v1p0923c2s v1p1062c1s v1p1301c2s
v1p1364c1s v1p1412c1s v2p0041c2m
v2p0044c1s v2p0072c1s v2p0113c2s
v2p0119c2s v2p0135c2s v2p0169c2m
v2p0170c2s v2p0181c1s v2p0237c1s
v2p0268c1s v2p0283c1s v2p0315c1s
v2p0352c1s v2p0376c1s v2p0382c2s
v2p0425c2s v2p0434c2s v2p0455c2m
v3p0001c2s v3p0073c2s v3p0082c1s
Miller, O.T. v1p0523c1s
v2p0046c2m v2p0047c1s v2p0071c1m
v2p0261c2s v2p0293c2s v2p0314c2s
v2p0323c2s v2p0374c1s v2p0413c1s
v2p0440c1s v3p0045c1m v3p0045c2m
v3p0047c2s v3p0048c1m v3p0068c1m
v3p0078c1s v3p0087c1s v3p0104c1s
v3p0106c2s v3p0185c2s v3p0233c1s
v3p0236c2m v3p0246c2m v3p0252c2s
v3p0284c1s v3p0314c1m v3p0404c2s
v3p0430c1s v3p0454c2s v3p0471c1m
v4p0060c2m v4p0061c1s v4p0061c2m
v4p0064c2s v4p0210c1s v4p0269c1s
v4p0522c1s v4p0633c2s v5p0096c2s
v5p0554c2s
Miller, P. v1p1249c2s
Miller, P.R. v6p0573c2s
Miller, R. v5p0476c2s
Miller, R.B. v1p0920c1s
Miller, R.T. v6p0209c2s
Miller, R.W. v1p0349c1s
Miller, S. v1p0120c2s
v1p0131c2s v1p0229c1s v1p0240c2s
v1p0244c2s v1p0247c1s v1p0254c2s
v1p0381c1s v1p0393c2s v1p0421c1s
v1p0421c2s v1p0558c2s v1p0610c1s
v1p0756c2s v1p0823c2s v1p0847c2s
v1p0946c2s v1p1047c1m v1p1051c1s
v1p1087c2s v1p1140c1s v1p1292c2m
v1p1301c2s v1p1314c2s v5p0086c2s
v5p0423c2s
v5p0619c1s
Miller, S. and Alexander, A.
v1p0238c2s
v1p1046c1s
Miller, S., jr. v1p1046c1s
Miller, S.A. v4p0026c2s

v5p0004c1s
Miller, S.F. v1p0164c1s v3p0028c2s v3p0219c1s v3p0233c2s
Miller, S.F. et al. v2p0091c1s
Miller, S.H. v2p0154c1s
Miller, S.M. v1p1091c1s v1p1321c1s v4p0071c2m v4p0149c2s v4p0371c2s v4p0372c1s v4p0496c1s v4p0515c1s v4p0614c1s
Miller, S.P.M. v2p0461c2s
Miller, S.P.McD. v2p0254c2s
Miller, T. v1p0229c1s v6p0541c1s
Miller, W. v1p0992c2s v2p0123c1s v2p0292c1s v3p0046c2s v3p0171c2s v3p0212c1s v3p0249c2s v3p0282c2s v3p0337c2s v4p0111c1s v4p0192c1s v4p0241c1s v4p0380c2s v4p0403c2m v4p0419c1s v4p0502c1s v5p0065c1s v5p0071c2s v5p0072c1m v5p0138c2s v5p0142c2s v5p0174c1s v5p0196c2s v5p0224c1s v5p0300c1s v5p0382c1s v5p0384c2s v5p0398c1s v5p0410c1s v5p0433c1s v5p0469c2s v6p0087c1s v6p0090c2s v6p0147c2s v6p0150c1s v6p0157c2s v6p0163c2s v6p0230c1s v6p0246c2s v6p0272c1s v6p0272c2m v6p0314c1s v6p0325c2s v6p0330c2s v6p0332c1s v6p0392c1s v6p0421c2s v6p0426c2s v6p0445c2s v6p0466c2s v6p0469c2s v6p0487c1m v6p0488c1s v6p0549c1s v6p0570c1s v6p0570c2s v6p0597c2s v6p0638c1s v6p0643c1s v6p0678c1s v6p0698c1m v6p0700c1s v6p0709c2s
Miller, W. and Bland, R.P. v4p0596c1s
Miller, W. et al. v4p0384c1s
Miller, W.A. v1p0563c2s v1p1234c1m v6p0400c1s
Miller, W.A. and Huggins, W. v1p1244c1s
Miller, W.C. v1p0408c2s v2p0271c1s v2p0333c2s v3p0062c2s v3p0217c2s v6p0377c1s
Miller, W.D. v1p0407c2s
Miller, W.G. v6p0058c2s v6p0324c1s v6p0364c1s
Miller, W.H. v2p0339c2s v2p0456c1s v6p0524c2s
Miller, W.J. v2p0433c2s
Miller, W.L. v5p0088c1m v5p0259c2s v5p0328c2s v5p0352c2s v5p0465c1s
Miller, W.S. v4p0277c2s
Miller, Walter v5p0425c2s
Miller, Walter L. v5p0327c2s
Miller, Wilhelm v6p0220c1s
Miller, William v5p0507c2s v6p0038c2s v6p0149c2s v6p0239c2s v6p0445c2s
Millerand, M. and Holyoake, G.J. v3p0099c1s
Milles, J. v1p0009c1s v1p0526c2s v1p0605c1s v1p1106c1s v1p1122c1s v1p1173c2s v1p1317c2s v1p1385c2s
Milles, J. and Brooke, J.C. v1p1173c2s v1p1433c1s
Millet, F.D. v1p0471c2s v1p0616c2s v2p0067c1s v2p0083c1s v2p0111c1s v2p0116c1s v2p0169c1s v2p0410c1s v2p0441c1s v2p0460c2s v2p0468c1s v2p0473c2s v2p0482c1s v3p0022c1s v3p0101c2s v3p0147c2s v3p0273c2s v3p0422c2s v4p0101c1m v5p0093c2s v6p0014c2s v6p0549c1s
Millet, J.B. v5p0317c2s v6p0594c1s
Millet, J.B. and Smith, F.H. v3p0066c1s v3p0301c2s v3p0397c1s
Millet, P. v4p0371c1m
Millican, K. v3p0200c1s
Millie, Marie A. v5p0359c2s
Milliet, W. v4p0334c1s
Milligan, A.L. v5p0297c1s v5p0392c2s v5p0630c2s
Milligan, Alice L. v5p0002c2s
Milligan, G. v5p0059c1s v5p0060c1s v5p0305c2m v5p0306c2s v5p0556c1s v6p0064c1s v6p0064c2s v6p0341c2s
Milligan, J. v3p0420c2s
Milligan, Prof. v1p0693c1s
Milligan, R. v1p0117c2s v1p0229c2s
Milligan, W. v1p0128c2m v1p0131c1s v1p0242c1s v1p0378c2s v1p0726c2s v2p0044c2s v2p0473c1s v3p0043c2s v4p0148c2s v4p0527c1s
Milligan, W.J. v1p0857c1s v1p1016c1s
Millikan, R.A. v6p0199c2s v6p0526c2s
Milliken, D. v2p0221c1s
Milliken, D.L. v3p0022c2s
Milliken, J. v1p0357c2s v2p0119c2s
Milliken, J.F. v3p0350c1s
Milliken, O.J. v5p0606c2s
Milliken, W.F. v2p0035c1s v2p0116c1s v2p0204c2s v2p0264c1s v2p0279c1s v2p0471c1s v4p0235c2s v4p0339c2s v4p0499c2s
Millikin, M.A. v6p0222c1s
Millin, G. v3p0344c2s
Millin, G.F. v2p0263c1s v4p0516c1s v5p0332c2s v5p0346c1s v6p0412c2s v6p0690c2s
Millingen, A.V. v1p0182c2s
Millingen, A.Van v2p0060c2s
Millingen, Dr. v1p1266c1s
Millingen, J. and Weston, S. v1p0101c2s v1p0445c1s
Millingen, J.G. v1p1335c2s
Millington, L.A. v1p1236c1s
Millington, L.A., Mrs. ... v1p0449c1s
Millington, P. v5p0084c2s v5p0205c1s v5p0240c2s v5p0266c1s v5p0538c2s v6p0311c1s v6p0312c1s
Millington, Prof. v1p0258c2s
Millington, T. v2p0314c1s
Millington, T.S. v2p0177c2s v2p0250c1s v2p0315c1m v3p0257c2s v3p0400c2s
Millington, W.H. and Maxfield, B.L. v6p0495c1s v6p0680c1s
Million, J.W. v4p0393c2s v4p0472c2s
Mills, H.A. v5p0101c2s v5p0157c1s v5p0159c1m v5p0280c2s v6p0113c1s v6p0113c2s v6p0319c2s
Millis, J. v3p0134c1s
Mills, A. v1p0192c1s v1p0543c2s v1p0544c1s v1p0918c2s v2p0186c2s v2p0209c1s v2p0264c2s v2p0423c2s v4p0144c1s v4p0314c2s v5p0599c1s
Mills, A.H. v1p0244c2s
Mills, A.L. v6p0693c1s
Mills, B.F. v4p0027c1s v5p0358c1s v5p0603c2s
Mills, C. v1p0467c1s v1p1027c1s v1p1265c1s v1p1379c1s v3p0410c1s v4p0283c2s v5p0159c1s v6p0369c1s v6p0525c2s
Mills, C.D.B. v1p0171c2s v1p0381c1s v1p0398c1s v1p0450c2s v1p1000c1s v1p1068c2s v1p1236c2s v1p1441c2s v4p0391c2s
Mills, C.K. v2p0054c2s v4p0284c2s
Mills, C.M. v1p0245c2s v1p0740c2s v1p1182c1s
Mills, C.S. v4p0112c1s
Mills, D. v1p1078c1s v4p0006c1s v4p0182c1s v4p0191c2s v4p0236c2s v4p0379c2s v4p0496c1s v4p0514c1s v5p0020c1s
Mills, D.O. v3p0383c1s
Mills, E.J. v1p0224c2s v1p0269c2s v1p1304c2s
Mills, E.M. v6p0413c1s
Mills, E.T. v5p0287c2s
Mills, Ernest F. v6p0044c1s
Mills, Evan and Caffin, C.H. v6p0570c2s
Mills, F. v2p0148c2s
Mills, F.R. v2p0145c2s
Mills, H. v1p0686c2s v1p1230c1s
Mills, H.E. v5p0085c1s v5p0204c1s
Mills, H.F. v1p1392c1s v2p0078c2s v3p0386c1s
Mills, H.R. v4p0598c1s
Mills, H.V. v3p0050c1s
Mills, Harriet E.D. v6p0311c1s
Mills, J. v1p0122c2s v1p0252c1s v1p0571c1s v1p0682c2s v1p0951c2s v1p1148c1s v5p0009c2s v5p0052c1s v5p0124c1s v5p0321c2s v5p0499c1s v5p0513c1s v5p0570c2s
Mills, J. et al. v5p0611c2s
Mills, J.E. v1p0141c1s v2p0396c2s v4p0112c1s
Mills, J.H. v1p0879c2s
Mills, J.M. v4p0449c2s
Mills, J.R. v1p0533c1s
Mills, J.S. v6p0006c2s v6p0267c1s v6p0269c2s
Mills, J.Warner v6p0139c1s
Mills, L. v5p0055c2s v5p0344c2s v6p0002c2s v6p0045c1m v6p0062c2s v6p0163c1m
Mills, L.H. v3p0474c1s v4p0637c2m v5p0041c2m v5p0227c1m v5p0344c2s v5p0427c1s v5p0441c1s v5p0646c2s v6p0027c1s v6p0045c1m v6p0163c1s v6p0489c2s
Mills, L.H. and Douglas, J. v5p0587c1s
Mills, R.Q. v3p0072c1s v3p0096c2s v3p0162c2s v3p0355c2s v3p0393c2s v3p0420c1s v4p0563c2s
Mills, S. v5p0100c1s
Mills, S.M. v5p0284c2s
Mills, T.A. v1p0248c1s v1p0847c2s v1p1046c2s
Mills, T.L. v5p0625c1s
Mills, T.W. v3p0030c2s v3p0331c2s v3p0348c1s v3p0405c2s
Mills, W. v1p1107c2s v3p0021c1s v3p0117c2s v3p0120c1s v4p0170c2s v4p0255c2s v4p0269c1s v4p0276c2s v5p0021c1s v5p0470c2s v5p0535c1s v6p0071c1s v6p0521c2s
Mills, W.C. v1p0134c1s
Mills, W.H. v2p0022c1s v2p0062c1s v2p0074c1s v2p0207c1s v2p0350c2m v2p0453c1s v4p0259c1s v4p0297c1s
Mills, W.S. v6p0195c1s v6p0351c1s v6p0483c1s
Millspaugh, C., Mrs. v6p0704c1s
Millspaugh, C.F. v4p0069c2s v5p0287c2s v6p0656c1s
Millspaugh, M.L.S. v6p0656c1s
Milman, A. v6p0481c2s
Milman, C. v4p0136c2s v4p0316c2s
Milman, Constance v4p0386c2s
Milman, H. v4p0133c2s
Milman, H.H. v1p0079c2s v1p0085c2s v1p0113c1s v1p0205c2s v1p0219c2s v1p0251c2s v1p0263c2s v1p0264c1s v1p0391c1s v1p0423c2s v1p0481c2s v1p0516c1s v1p0520c2s v1p0580c2s v1p0589c1s v1p0600c2s v1p0603c2s v1p0683c1s v1p0691c2s v1p0754c2s v1p0756c2s v1p0965c1s v1p1016c2s v1p1033c1s v1p1033c2s v1p1061c2s v1p1124c1s v1p1153c2s v1p1178c1s v1p1273c2s v1p1302c2s v1p1306c1s v1p1331c2s
Milman, H.S. v1p1381c1s
Milman, R. v1p0156c2s v1p0381c2s
Milman, W.P. v5p0530c2s
Milne, A. v4p0015c1s
Milne, A.D. v5p0006c1s v5p0412c1s
Milne, B. v5p0497c1s
Milne, D. v1p0281c2s v1p0376c2s
Milne, D., Sir v1p0065c1s
Milne, G.T. v6p0080c1s
Milne, J. v1p0312c1m v2p0127c2m v2p0128c1m v2p0128c2m v2p0233c2s v2p0394c2s v2p0421c1s v2p0463c1s v3p0126c1m v3p0384c1m v4p0036c1s v4p0100c1s v4p0165c2s v4p0166c1m v4p0184c2s v4p0298c1s v4p0433c2s v4p0522c1s v5p0006c2s v5p0071c1s v5p0173c1m v5p0250c2s v5p0346c1s v5p0417c2s v5p0519c1m v6p0185c2m v6p0186c1m v6p0336c2s v6p0582c2m v6p0620c1s v6p0681c1m
Milne, J. and Chree, C. .. v6p0582c2s
Milne, J. and Farr, C.C. . v6p0186c1s
Milne, J.G. v6p0130c2s
Milne, J.R. v4p0603c2s
Milne, Jas. v5p0611c1s
Milne, John v5p0580c1s
Milne, Mabel v5p0085c2s
Milne, R.D. v6p0590c1s
Milne, R.M. v1p1135c1s
Milne, W.J. v4p0566c2s
Milne-Edwards, A. v2p0430c1s
Milne-Rae, Mrs. v2p0296c2s
Milner, A. v2p0444c1s v4p0555c1s
Milner, A.V. v6p0459c1s
Milner, Ange V. v6p0372c2s
Milner, D.C. v4p0461c2s
Milner, F. v5p0366c1s v5p0511c2s v6p0428c2s v6p0569c2s
Milner, Florence v6p0175c1s v6p0177c1s v6p0581c2s v6p0662c2s v6p0712c1s
Milner, G. v2p0101c1s v2p0110c2s v2p0191c2s v2p0241c2s v2p0276c1s
Milner, J. v1p0129c1s v1p0472c2s v1p0526c1s v1p0556c1s v1p0749c2s
Milner, J.G. v1p0863c2s
Milner, J.W. v1p0020c1s
Milner, K. v3p0151c2s
Milner, M.W. v5p0107c1s v5p0321c1s v5p0637c2s
Milner, T. v1p0089c2s v1p0096c2s
Milner, Viscount v6p0006c2s
Milner, W.S. v6p0370c1s
Milnes, A. v4p0599c1s v5p0606c2s
Milnes, A. and Humphreys, N.A. v5p0533c1s
Milnes, J.W. v1p1182c2s
Milnes, R.M. v1p0089c2s v1p0104c1s v1p0395c1s v1p0613c2s v1p1061c1s v1p1135c2s v1p1220c2s v1p1259c2s v1p1358c2s
Milnor, L.D. v5p0643c1s
Milnor, T.W. v4p0120c2s
Milroy, E.A.W. v5p0614c2s
Milroy, J.A. v5p0469c1s

Milroy, T.H. v5p0449c2s
Mils, A. v1p0263c2s
Milsand, J. v1p0481c2s
Milton, G.E. v4p0226c2s
Milton, G.F. v4p0430c1s
v4p0462c2s v4p0538c1s v4p0564c2s
v5p0093c1s v5p0270c2s v5p0320c2s
v5p0540c2s v5p0572c2s
Milton, G.T. v5p0568c1s
Milton, H.A. v4p0520c2s
v6p0526c1s v6p0638c2s
Milton, J. v1p0392c2s
Milton, M. v4p0341c1s
Miltoun, F. v6p0087c2s
v6p0403c2s v6p0544c2s
Miltoun, Francis v6p0520c2m
v6p0563c1s
Milward, M.G. v1p1416c1s
Milward, M.G., Mrs. v1p0308c1s
v1p1436c2s
Milyoukov, P. v3p0370c2m
v4p0497c1m v6p0557c2s
Mims, E. v4p0335c2s
v4p0606c2s v5p0573c2s v5p0607c2s
v6p0312c2s v6p0345c1s v6p0366c1m
v6p0388c2s v6p0450c1m v6p0539c1s
v6p0550c1s v6p0605c1s v6p0617c1s
v6p0671c1s v6p0692c1s
Minakata, K. v4p0106c1s
v4p0199c2s
Minasi, F.J. v1p0339c2s
v3p0113c1s
Minaud, H.M. v4p0090c2s
Minchin, E.A. v4p0369c2s
v5p0547c1s v6p0520c2s v6p0597c2s
Minchin, G.M. v2p0138c2s
v3p0156c1s v3p0380c2s v4p0332c1s
v4p0546c1s v5p0229c2s v5p0513c2s
v6p0091c2s
Minchin, H.C. v4p0228c1s
v5p0309c2s v5p0452c1s v6p0085c1s
v6p0155c2s
Minchin, H.D. v6p0478c2s
Minchin, H.M. v4p0607c2s
Minchin, J.G. v2p0385c2s
v2p0404c2s
Minchin, J.G.C. v4p0164c1s
v4p0224c2s v4p0257c2s v4p0298c2s
v4p0457c1s v4p0544c2s
Minchin, J.I. v2p0007c1s
v2p0250c2s v2p0431c1s v2p0472c1s
v4p0219c1s
Minchin, L.H.J. v5p0394c2s
Mindeleff, C. v5p0096c1s
Mindeleff, Cosmos v4p0579c1s
v5p0472c1s
Mindeleff, D. v3p0432c2s
Mindeleff, V. v3p0349c1s
Miner, A.A. v1p0089c2s
v1p0218c1s v1p0373c2s v1p0613c1s
v1p0687c1s v1p0979c2s v1p1090c1s
v1p1095c2s v1p1096c1s v1p1296c2s
v1p1340c2s v2p0455c2s v2p0456c2s
v4p0160c1s
Miner, A.A. et al. v4p0334c1s
Miner, B.G. v6p0521c1s
Miner, E. v4p0464c1s
Miner, L. v5p0110c1s
v5p0438c2s v6p0121c1s v6p0398c2s
Miner, L.B. v6p0532c2s
Miner, M.L. v6p0348c2s
Miner, T. v1p0292c1s
v1p0816c2s
Mines, F.S. v4p0203c1s
v4p0217c1s
Mines, J.F. v1p0916c2s
v3p0123c1s
Minet, A. v6p0328c2s
Ming, J. v1p0528c1s
v1p0999c2s v1p1001c1s v2p0086c2s
v2p0180c2s v2p0410c2s v3p0379c2s
v3p0403c2s v4p0191c1s
Ming, J.J. v4p0191c2s
v6p0698c2s
Minghi-Tau v5p0097c2s
Minkowsky, G. v5p0609c2s
v6p0468c2s
Minnich, M.R. v4p0257c2m
Minnigedore, C. v1p0554c2s
v1p0555c2s
Minns, G.W. v1p0237c2s
v6p0109c2s
Minor, B. v5p0559c1s
Minor, B.B. v1p0624c1s
v1p0734c2s
Minor, F. v2p0478c2s
v3p0086c1s v3p0467c2s
Minor, J.B., jr. v3p0444c2s
Minor, L. v1p0384c2s
Minor, L.J. v1p0015c1s
Minor, M. v4p0159c2s
Minor, R. v5p0558c1s
Minor, R.C. v6p0364c2s
Minor, R.D. v1p0941c1s
Minor, W.C. v1p0147c2s
Minot, C.S. v1p0134c2s
v1p0213c1s v1p0405c1s v1p0593c1s
v1p0618c1s v1p0836c1s v1p1105c1s
v1p1441c1s v2p0014c2s v2p0113c2s
v2p0162c2m v2p0201c2s v2p0222c1s
v2p0261c2s v2p0284c2s v2p0298c2s
v2p0354c1s v2p0370c2s v2p0379c1s
v2p0439c2s v3p0047c2s v3p0095c1s
v3p0275c1s v3p0278c1s v3p0315c2s
v3p0448c2s v4p0071c2s v4p0255c1s
v4p0369c2s v4p0394c2s v4p0464c1s
v4p0478c1s v5p0099c2s v5p0136c2s
v5p0187c1s v5p0257c1s v5p0319c1s
v5p0321c2s v5p0368c1s v5p0374c1s
v5p0570c2s v6p0145c2s v6p0147c2s
v6p0202c1s v6p0673c2s
Minot, C.S. et al. v6p0018c1s
Minot, H.D. v1p0136c1s
v1p0136c2s
v1p0137c1s
Minot, Mrs. v1p0919c2s
Minot, R.S. v6p0357c1s
v6p0533c1s v6p0684c2s
Minot, W. v1p0499c1s
v1p1285c2s
Minot, W., jr. v1p0053c2s
v1p0062c1s
Minot, W., Mrs. v1p0309c2s
Minra, K. v1p0678c1s
Minto, H.C. v5p0089c1s
Minto, J. v5p0386c2s
v6p0371c1s
Minto, M. v6p0096c2s
Minto, W. v1p0009c2s
v1p0013c1s v1p0308c2s v1p0350c2s
v1p0360c2s v1p0502c2s v1p1019c1s
v1p1141c1s v2p0063c2s v2p0082c2s
v2p0144c1s v2p0144c2s v2p0160c1s
v2p0226c1s v2p0228c1s v2p0269c2s
v2p0270c1s v2p0342c1s v2p0391c2s
v2p0399c2s v3p0140c1s v3p0273c1s
v3p0339c1m v3p0360c1s v3p0472c1s
v4p0509c2m
Minton, F. v4p0113c1s
v4p0615c1s
Minton, H.C. v4p0191c1s
v4p0351c2s v4p0439c2s v4p0475c1s
v4p0532c1s v4p0541c2s v4p0573c1s
v5p0198c1s v5p0236c2s v5p0239c2s
v5p0266c2s v5p0306c1m v5p0306c2s
v5p0319c1m v5p0364c1s v5p0396c2s
v5p0426c1s v5p0447c1m v5p0483c1s
v5p0483c2s v5p0489c2s v5p0576c2m
v5p0577c1s v6p0143c2s v6p0348c2s
Minton, H.C. and Beattie, F.R.
v6p0514c2s
Minton, H.C. and Carus, P.
v6p0103c1s
Minton-Senhouse, R.M. v3p0119c1s
v3p0469c2s
Minturn, E. v1p0523c1s
v1p1357c2s
Minturn, M. v6p0601c2s
Minturn, R.B. v1p0322c2s
v1p0326c1s
Minturn, R.R. v1p0892c2s
Minturn, S.M. v4p0443c2s
Miolati, A. v4p0087c2s
Mir, Miguel v6p0107c1s
Mirbach, Count von v4p0526c1s
Mirecourt, E.de v1p0808c1s
Mirell, G.M. v6p0573c1s
Mirick, C.M. and Flynn, Mr.
v6p0112c1s
Mirrilies, F. v6p0362c1s
Misch, Emil v4p0416c2s
Misch, O.L. v1p0517c1s
v1p0914c2s
Mische, E. v4p0332c2s
Miskovsky, L.F. v5p0493c2s
Misra, U.S. v3p0212c1s
Misra, Uma Sankar v3p0124c1s
v3p0212c1s v4p0279c1m v4p0280c1s
Missimer, H.C. v3p0130c1m
Missy, H.de v5p0049c1s
Mist, H. v4p0238c1s
Mister, J.F. v2p0478c1s
Mitchel, F.A. v3p0436c2s
v4p0617c2s v5p0055c1s v5p0132c2s
Mitchel, J. v2p0226c2s
Mitchel, O.M. v1p0927c2s
v1p0992c1s
Mitchell, A. v1p0218c1s
v1p0353c2s v1p0471c1s v1p0796c2s
v1p1013c2s v1p1048c1s v1p1155c2s
v1p1394c2s v5p0165c2s v5p0272c1s
v6p0300c1s v6p0375c1s
Mitchell, A.A. v2p0268c2s
v6p0364c1s
Mitchell, A.B. v4p0608c2s
Mitchell, A.F. v2p0064c2s
v2p0244c1s v2p0473c2s v4p0312c2s
Mitchell, A.M. v5p0078c2s
v5p0385c1s v5p0414c1s
Mitchell, A.S. v1p0762c2s
Mitchell, Adina v5p0107c2s
Mitchell, Arnold v6p0028c2m
Mitchell, B.W. v5p0156c2s
v5p0547c2s
Mitchell, C.A. v4p0041c1s
v4p0508c2s v4p0531c2s v5p0155c1s
v5p0612c2s
Mitchell, C.B. v5p0590c1s
Mitchell, C.E. v5p0645c1s
Mitchell, C.P. v3p0216c1s
Mitchell, D. v1p1419c2s
Mitchell, D.G. v1p0084c2s
v1p0228c2s v1p0349c2s v1p0357c1s
v1p0445c2s v1p0451c2s v1p0493c1s
v1p0667c1s v1p0717c2s v1p0723c1m
v1p0967c2s v1p0970c2s v1p0996c2s
v1p1132c1s v1p1366c1s v1p1403c1s
v3p0202c1s v3p0369c1s
Mitchell, D.W. v1p0068c2s
Mitchell, E. v1p0533c2s
v1p0927c2s v1p1256c2m v1p1319c2s
v1p1414c1s v2p0338c1s v2p0476c2s
v4p0008c1s v4p0020c2s v4p0038c2s
v4p0084c2s v4p0106c1s v4p0132c1s
v4p0181c2s v4p0225c2s v4p0289c1s
v4p0290c2s v5p0155c1s v5p0167c2s
v5p0292c1s v5p0431c1s v6p0196c2s
v6p0344c2s v6p0412c1s v6p0564c1s
v6p0566c2s
Mitchell, E.C. v1p0242c1s
v1p0742c2s
Mitchell, E.G. v6p0226c1s
Mitchell, E.H. v1p1084c1s
Mitchell, E.K. v5p0024c1s
v5p0114c1m v5p0565c1s v6p0187c1s
v6p0341c2s v6p0471c2s
Mitchell, E.M. v1p1062c1s
v2p0337c1s v3p0334c1s v4p0147c2s
Mitchell, E.M., Mrs. v1p0531c2s
Mitchell, E.P. v1p1279c2s
v4p0146c2s
Mitchell, E.T. v4p0052c1s
Mitchell, Edmund v6p0224c2s
v6p0476c1s
Mitchell, Elmer C. v6p0511c2s
Mitchell, F. v2p0067c1s
Mitchell, F.C. v4p0149c2s
Mitchell, F.J.R. v5p0293c2s
Mitchell, G. v2p0203c2s
Mitchell, G.E. v5p0544c2s
v5p0566c2s v6p0360c1s
Mitchell, G.O. v6p0306c2s
Mitchell, H. v1p0395c2s
v1p0562c1s v1p0916c2s v1p1264c1s
v3p0304c1s
Mitchell, H.B. v6p0670c1s
Mitchell, H.G. v3p0001c2s
v3p0042c1s v3p0042c2s v3p0132c1s
v3p0193c1s v3p0208c2s v3p0322c2s
v3p0430c2s v4p0530c1s v5p0056c2s
v5p0057c1s v5p0058c1s v5p0202c1s
v6p0340c1s
Mitchell, H.K. v6p0261c2s
Mitchell, H.P. v6p0333c2s
Mitchell, I.H. v6p0355c2s
v6p0356c1s v6p0665c1s
Mitchell, J. v1p0238c2s
v1p0624c1s v1p1270c1s v5p0557c1s
v5p0585c1s v6p0621c2s
Mitchell, J.A. v3p0068c1s
v4p0102c1s v4p0386c2s v5p0452c1s
Mitchell, J.B. v2p0114c1s
v2p0367c2s
Mitchell, J.C. v5p0181c1s
Mitchell, J.E. v2p0192c2s
Mitchell, J.H. v4p0416c2s
v4p0515c1s
Mitchell, J.I. v2p0121c1s
Mitchell, J.K. v1p0199c2s
v1p0913c1s v1p1431c1s
Mitchell, J.L. v4p0325c2s
Mitchell, J.M. v1p1440c1s
v2p0299c2s
Mitchell, J.S. v5p0037c1s
Mitchell, J.W. v1p0934c2s
v6p0345c2s v6p0608c1s
Mitchell, John v5p0377c2s
Mitchell, K.M. v4p0220c2s
Mitchell, L.A. v2p0344c2s
Mitchell, L.D. v3p0172c1s
v4p0288c2s v4p0517c1s v4p0554c2s
v4p0575c2s v4p0590c1s v5p0219c1s
v5p0262c2s
Mitchell, L.E. v4p0277c1s
v4p0344c1s v4p0588c2s
Mitchell, L.M. v2p0018c2m
v2p0200c1m v2p0392c2m
Mitchell, L.S. v5p0378c2s
Mitchell, Lt.Col. v2p0114c2s
Mitchell, M. v1p0381c2s
v1p0572c2s v1p0583c2s v1p0699c1s
v1p1152c2s v1p1219c2s v1p1243c2s
v1p1347c2s v1p1422c1s v1p1424c1s
v4p0371c2s
Mitchell, M., Mrs. v2p0097c1s
v2p0218c2s v2p0280c1s
Mitchell, M.A. v5p0636c2s
Mitchell, M.E. v5p0035c1s
v6p0355c1s v6p0552c1s
Mitchell, N. v1p0877c2s
Mitchell, O. v1p0382c1s
Mitchell, P.C. v3p0250c1s
v4p0019c1s v4p0084c1s v4p0178c2s
v4p0190c2s v4p0255c2s v4p0270c2s
v4p0429c2s v4p0463c1s v4p0588c2s
v4p0600c2s v4p0616c2s v5p0075c1s
v5p0368c2s v5p0384c2s v5p0521c2s
v6p0657c2s
Mitchell, P.C. et al. v5p0346c2s
Mitchell, P.G. v6p0526c1s

Mitchell, R. v5p0541c1m
v6p0343c2s
Mitchell, S.A. v5p0174c2s
v6p0188c1s v6p0612c1s
Mitchell, S.C. v6p0447c1s
v6p0605c1s
Mitchell, S.G. v1p0990c1s
Mitchell, S.S. v3p0131c1s
Mitchell, S.W. v1p0081c2s
v1p0204c1s v1p0354c1s v1p0567c1s
v1p0586c1s v1p1023c1s v1p1084c1s
v1p1387c1s v1p1434c2s v1p1437c1s
v2p0216c1s v3p0073c2s v3p0348c1s
v3p0385c2s v4p0096c1s v4p0268c1s
v4p0381c2s v5p0004c2s v5p0040c2s
v5p0129c2s v5p0164c1s v5p0252c1s
v5p0417c1s v5p0420c2s v5p0516c2s
v5p0619c2s v6p0174c2s v6p0289c1s
v6p0451c2s v6p0513c2s v6p0555c1s
v6p0625c1s v6p0686c2s
Mitchell, S.Weir v5p0275c1s
Mitchell, T. v1p0894c2s
Mitchell, T.W. v6p0108c1s
v6p0119c1s v6p0430c2s v6p0528c2s
v6p0618c1s
Mitchell, V.E. v4p0099c2s
v4p0373c2s
Mitchell, Violet E. v4p0070c2s
v4p0398c2s
Mitchell, W. v1p0177c1s
v1p0212c1s v1p0252c2s v1p0281c2s
v1p0282c1s v1p0417c1s v1p0432c2s
v1p0464c1s v1p0614c2s v1p0787c2s
v1p0856c2s v1p0964c2s v1p1164c2s
v1p1353c1s v2p0061c1s v2p0077c2m
v2p0078c1s v2p0220c2s v2p0297c1s
v2p0328c1s v3p0145c2s v3p0199c1s
v3p0381c1m v3p0454c2s v4p0171c1s
v4p0395c2s v4p0588c2s v6p0010c2s
Mitchell, W.C. v4p0458c1s
v5p0040c1s v5p0147c1s v5p0250c2m
v5p0460c1s v5p0568c1s v5p0599c2s
v5p0600c2s v6p0425c1s v6p0682c2s
Mitchell, W.E. v4p0378c2s
Mitchell, W.F. v4p0280c1s
v4p0589c2s v4p0621c1s v6p0334c2s
Mitchell, W.Forbes v4p0233c2s
Mitchell, W.G. v5p0616c2s
v6p0567c2s v6p0568c1s v6p0569c1s
Mitchell, W.H. v1p1177c1s
v2p0194c2s v6p0707c1s
Mitchell, W.M. v4p0471c1s
v6p0041c1s v6p0626c1s
Mitchell, W.S. v1p0073c2s
v2p0160c1s
Mitchell-Innes, N.G. v5p0108c2s
Mitcheson, R. v4p0512c2s
Mitcheson, R.E. v4p0383c2s
Mitchill, S.L. v1p1172c2s
Mitchiner, J.H. v4p0066c1m
v4p0567c2s
Mitchinson, A.W. v3p0118c2s
Mitchinson, J. v1p0509c2s
Mitford, A.B. v1p0469c2s
v1p0570c2s v1p0678c2s v1p0679c1m
v1p0679c2s v2p0265c1s
Mitford, B. v4p0277c2s
Mitford, Bertram v4p0360c1s
Mitford, E.B. v6p0185c1s
v6p0357c2s
Mitford, Evaline B. v6p0536c1s
Mitford, J. v1p0856c1s
Mitford, M.R. v1p0642c2s
v1p1396c2s
Mitford, T. v3p0459c2s
Mitra, S.C. v6p0291c1s
Mitra, S.M. v6p0058c1s
Mitscherlich, E. v1p0224c2s
Mitsukuri, K. v1p0679c1s
v2p0233c2s v5p0303c1s v6p0401c1s
Mitton, G.E. v4p0339c1s
v4p0340c2s v4p0625c2s v5p0084c2s
v5p0420c2s
Mivart, S.G. v2p0166c2s
v2p0376c1s
Mivart, St.G. v1p0014c1s
v1p0036c2s v1p0047c1m v1p0102c1s
v1p0134c2m v1p0216c1s v1p0327c2s
v1p0406c2s v1p0434c1m v1p0467c1s
v1p0491c2s v1p0507c2s v1p0646c2s
v1p0648c1s v1p0701c2s v1p0745c2m
v1p0746c1s v1p0749c2s v1p0758c1s
v1p0899c1m v1p0899c2s v1p1173c1s
v1p1221c2s v1p1229c2s v1p1233c1s
v1p1235c1s v1p1280c1s v1p1368c2s
v2p0015c1s v2p0029c2s v2p0036c2s
v2p0118c2s v2p0129c1s v2p0131c2s
v2p0149c2s v2p0151c2s v2p0176c2s
v2p0187c2s v2p0223c1s v2p0223c2s
v2p0294c2s v2p0323c1m v2p0343c2s
v2p0366c1s v2p0375c1m v2p0390c2s
v3p0038c1s v3p0043c2s v3p0081c1s
v3p0101c2s v3p0111c1s v3p0111c2s
v3p0144c1s v3p0185c2s v3p0194c2s
v3p0233c2s v3p0244c1s v3p0247c1s
v3p0259c1m v3p0284c1s v3p0297c1m
v3p0302c1s v3p0330c1s v3p0364c1s
v3p0365c2s v3p0403c2s v3p0420c2s
v3p0449c2m v3p0459c2s v3p0475c2s
v4p0017c2s v4p0036c1s v4p0042c1s
v4p0048c2s v4p0055c1s v4p0109c1s
v4p0148c1s v4p0190c2s v4p0191c1m
v4p0191c2s v4p0211c2s v4p0218c1s
v4p0229c1s v4p0254c1s v4p0255c1s
v4p0255c2s v4p0270c2s v4p0278c1s
v4p0353c2s v4p0394c2s v4p0419c1s
v4p0420c2s v4p0479c1s v4p0488c2m
v4p0489c2m v4p0507c1m v4p0507c2s
v4p0541c2s v5p0083c2s v5p0117c2s
v5p0277c1s v5p0343c1s v5p0358c1m
v5p0467c1s v5p0470c2s v5p0480c1s
v5p0492c2s v5p0493c2m v5p0494c1s
v5p0581c1s v5p0619c2s v5p0633c2s
Mivart, St.G. and Muller, F.Max
v3p0355c2s
Mivart, St.G. et al. v3p0380c1s
Mixer, M.E. v2p0146c1s
v2p0314c1s
Mixter, C.W. v5p0068c1s
v5p0382c2s v5p0476c1s v5p0509c2s
v6p0100c1s v6p0395c2s
Mixter, W.G. v5p0002c2m
v5p0185c2s v5p0227c1m v6p0002c2s
v6p0100c2s v6p0305c1s
Mladziansky, H.K. v4p0443c2s
Mlodziansky, A.K. v5p0451c2s
Moad, G.L. v2p0353c1s
Mobbs, R. v6p0220c2s
v6p0257c1s v6p0285c2s v6p0629c2s
Moberly, A. v2p0246c1s
v3p0332c2s v4p0321c2s
Moberly, C.E. v3p0387c2s
Moberly, C.H. v2p0050c2s
Moberly, G.W. v1p0250c1s
Moberly, L.G. v5p0093c2s
v5p0157c2s v5p0204c1s v5p0266c1s
v5p0419c1s v5p0433c2s v5p0440c2s
v5p0605c2s v6p0420c2s
Moberly, T.E. v3p0245c2m
Mobius, K. v1p0420c2s
v2p0160c1s
Mobley, D.E. v5p0066c1s
Mobsby, J. v6p0710c2s
Moch, G. v5p0032c1s
v5p0252c1s v5p0252c2m
Mochar, A.M. v2p0384c2s
Mochler, R. v1p0432c1s
Mockler-Ferryman, A.F. ... v4p0146c1s
v4p0404c2s v5p0329c2s v5p0532c2s
v5p0597c1s v6p0224c2s
Modjeska, H. v4p0543c2s
v4p0572c1s v5p0167c2s v5p0457c1s
Modlen, W. v6p0299c1s
Moe, A.K. v6p0226c1s
Moelling, T. v4p0245c1s
Moens, W.J.C. v3p0314c2s
Moeran, E.J. v4p0183c1s
Moeran, L.C. v6p0071c1s
v6p0177c2s v6p0704c1s
Moering, C. v1p1075c1s
Moersch, J. v5p0298c2s
v6p0682c1s
Moffat, A. v4p0551c1s
v4p0569c1s
Moffat, Hilda V. v6p0664c1s
Moffat, J. v1p0174c1s
v5p0305c2s v6p0062c2s v6p0714c1s
Moffat, J.C. v1p0002c2s
v1p0037c1s v1p0122c2s v1p0243c1s
v1p0373c1s v1p0379c1s v1p0391c1s
v1p0396c1s v1p0397c1s v1p0412c1s
v1p0552c2s v1p0554c2s v1p0580c2s
v1p0588c1s v1p0593c2s v1p1027c1s
v1p1090c1s v1p1165c2s v1p1357c2s
v2p0007c1s
Moffat, J.S. v2p0067c1s
v5p0007c1m
Moffat, J.T. v6p0007c1s
Moffat, M. v4p0619c2s
Moffat, Minnie v5p0465c1s
Moffat, R. v1p0011c2s
Moffat, R.B. v6p0447c2s
Moffat, R.S. v2p0220c2s
v4p0074c1s v4p0093c1s v4p0290c1s
Moffat, W.D. v6p0481c2s
Moffatt, A. v5p0040c2s
Moffatt, J. v5p0059c1s
v6p0060c2m v6p0062c2s v6p0064c1s
v6p0340c2s v6p0341c1s v6p0411c2s
v6p0423c1s v6p0523c2s v6p0567c1s
v6p0584c1s
Moffatt, J.C. v3p0098c1s
v3p0359c1s
Moffatt, J.H. v6p0142c2s
Moffatt, L.M. v1p0657c2s
Moffatt, R. v2p0306c2s
Moffatt, R.S. v2p0214c2s
v2p0366c1s v3p0157c1s v3p0321c2s
Moffatt, W. v3p0010c1s
v3p0162c2s v4p0120c1s v4p0173c2s
Moffatt, W.D. v4p0408c1s
Moffet, C. v4p0487c1s
v5p0497c2s
Moffet, C.R. v3p0287c1s
Moffet, J.C. v3p0029c1s
v3p0197c1s v3p0274c1s v4p0105c2s
Moffett, C. v4p0014c1s
v4p0074c2s v4p0090c2s v4p0114c2m
v4p0168c2s v4p0180c1s v4p0198c2s
v4p0234c2s v4p0312c1s v4p0332c2s
v4p0343c2s v4p0364c2s v4p0365c1s
v4p0377c1s v4p0407c1s v4p0432c2s
v4p0451c1s v4p0455c2s v4p0481c1s
v4p0486c2s v4p0559c1s v4p0560c1s
v4p0621c2s v5p0041c1s v5p0161c2s
v5p0173c1s v5p0185c2s v5p0370c1s
v5p0376c2s v5p0398c2s v5p0478c1s
v5p0515c2s v5p0551c1s v5p0571c1s
v5p0580c2s v5p0614c1s v6p0479c2s
v6p0480c1s v6p0483c1s v6p0485c1s
v6p0524c1s v6p0527c2s v6p0627c2s
Moffett, C.R. v3p0076c1s
Moffett, Cleveland v5p0277c1s
Moffett, Cunningham v5p0393c1s
Moffett, Cunninghame v5p0515c2s
Moffett, R. v2p0042c2s
v2p0065c2s v2p0084c2s
Moffett, S.E. v4p0083c2s
v4p0514c2s v5p0015c2s v5p0122c1s
v5p0152c1s v5p0189c1s v5p0303c1s
v5p0481c2s v5p0604c1s v5p0641c2s
v6p0013c1s v6p0041c2s v6p0094c1s
v6p0142c2s v6p0198c1s v6p0260c1s
v6p0308c2s v6p0351c2s v6p0353c1s
v6p0367c2s v6p0463c2s v6p0568c1s
v6p0629c1s v6p0669c1s
Mofras, D.de v1p0188c1s
Moggridge, M.W. v1p0537c1s
v1p0771c1m v1p1021c2s v2p0100c2s
Moggridge, S. v1p0100c1s
v1p0986c2s v1p1145c2s v1p1376c1s
Mohawk, M. v1p0562c1s
Mohn, H. v3p0440c1s
v4p0392c1s
Mohnenti, P. v5p0079c2s
Mohr, C. v4p0577c1m
v4p0583c1s v4p0631c1s
Mohr, F. v1p0225c1s
v1p0487c2s v1p0565c1s
Mohr, M.L.F. v4p0260c1s
Mohun, J.L. v6p0169c1s
v6p0661c1s
Mohun, R.D. v4p0179c1s
v5p0412c1s v5p0645c2s
Moigno, A. v1p0089c1s
v1p0266c1s v1p0401c1s v1p0454c2s
Moigno, Abbe v1p0747c2s
v1p1140c1s
Moigno, F. v1p0640c1s
v1p1024c2s
Moille, T.Y.La v2p0151c1s
Moine, J.M.Le v1p0966c1s
v4p0347c2s v4p0427c1m v4p0469c1m
Moine, Le v1p0716c2s
Moir, D.M. v1p0046c2s
v1p0082c2m v1p0132c2s v1p0204c1s
v1p0205c1s v1p0231c1s v1p0310c1s
v1p0324c1s v1p0332c2s v1p0338c2s
v1p0589c1s v1p0603c2s v1p0720c1s
v1p0735c2s v1p0797c2s v1p0818c2s
v1p0825c1s v1p0926c1s v1p0933c1s
v1p0933c2s v1p1062c2s v1p1072c1s
v1p1098c1s v1p1145c1s v1p1170c1s
v1p1201c2s v1p1213c2s v1p1315c1s
v1p1367c2s v1p1375c2s v1p1416c1s
v1p1433c1s
Moir, E.W. v3p0438c1s
v4p0586c2s
Moir, F.L.M. v3p0004c2s
Moir, G. v1p0693c1s
v1p0864c1s v1p1184c2s v1p1413c2s
Moira, Countess of v1p0613c1s
Moira, G.E. and Jenkins, F.L.
v5p0156c1s
Moise, C. v1p0833c2s
v1p0912c2s v2p0311c2s
Moissan, H. v4p0174c2s
Molden, B. v4p0269c2s
Moldenke, R. v5p0215c2s
v6p0235c1s v6p0328c2m
Moldenke, Richard v6p0235c1s
Mole, R. v1p1027c2s
Moler, G.S. v3p0449c1s
Moleschott, J. v3p0380c2s
Molesworth, G., Sir v3p0044c2s
v3p0413c1s
Molesworth, G.L. v4p0279c1s
v6p0150c1s
Molesworth, G.L., Sir v6p0150c1s
Molesworth, L. v2p0150c1s
v2p0476c2s v3p0411c1s v4p0352c2s
Molesworth, M., Mrs. v2p0451c1s
Molesworth, M.L. v4p0246c1s
v4p0511c2s
Molesworth, Mrs. v2p0277c2s
v3p0120c1s v3p0139c2s v3p0269c1s
v3p0426c2s v4p0412c2s v5p0327c1s
v5p0555c2s
Molesworth, P.B. v6p0403c1s
Molesworth, W. and Conway, H.S.
v1p0368c1s
Molesworth, W., Sir v1p0366c1s
v1p0945c2s
Molesworth, W.N. v1p0548c1s
v1p0550c1s
Molin, P. v5p0555c1s
Molinari, G.de v3p0161c1s
v3p0420c1s v5p0646c1s
Molineux, E.L. v1p0838c2s
v1p1005c2s v5p0489c1s

Molitor, A.P. v1p0533c2s
Molkenboer, N. v5p0397c1s
Moll, G. v1p0401c2s v1p1292c1s
Moller, F.C. v3p0048c1s v3p0274c1s v3p0391c1s v3p0426c2s
Moller, P. v6p0058c2s
Mollet, J.W. v4p0172c2s
Mollett, J.W. v1p0983c2s
Molloy, F. v3p0017c1s v3p0240c2s v4p0453c2s
Molloy, G. v1p0196c1s v1p0399c1s v1p0524c1s v2p0138c2s v3p0133c2s
Molloy, J.F. v1p0090c1s v1p0370c1s v2p0058c2s v2p0089c2s v2p0099c1s v2p0194c1s v2p0216c1s v2p0304c1s v2p0481c1s v3p0088c1s v3p0167c2s v4p0305c1s
Molloy, J.L. v4p0321c1s
Molloy, T.F. v2p0258c2s
Molmenti, P. v4p0602c1s v5p0300c2s
Molmenti, Pompeo v5p0071c2s v5p0609c1s
Moloney, A. v4p0144c1s
Moloney, J.A. v4p0308c2s v4p0544c2s
Molony, F. v5p0476c2s
Molteno, Percy A. v5p0587c2s
Moltke, Count v1p0969c2s
Molyneux, A.J.C. v6p0678c2s
Molyneux, C.C. v5p0309c2s
Molyneux, E. v6p0011c1s
Molyneux, J. v3p0005c1s v3p0116c2m
Molyneux, J.M. v1p0952c2s
Mombert, J.I. v1p0128c1s v1p0468c2s v1p0676c1s v1p0685c1s v1p0732c1s v1p0786c1s v1p1029c1s v1p1059c2s v1p1202c2s v1p1216c1s v2p0175c2s v3p0042c1s
Momerie, A. v3p0236c2s v3p0314c2s v4p0138c2s v4p0478c2s
Mommsen, T. v1p0205c2s v3p0118c1s v4p0156c1s v5p0230c1s v6p0253c1s
Monaghan, J.C. v5p0230c2s v5p0321c1s v5p0598c1s v6p0146c1s v6p0195c1s v6p0237c2s v6p0309c1s v6p0318c1s v6p0322c2s v6p0331c2s v6p0431c1s v6p0479c1s v6p0526c1s
Monahan, M. v6p0048c2s
Monamy, J. v2p0288c2s
Monamy, John v2p0470c2s
Monash, J. v6p0143c1s
Moncel, T.Du v2p0138c2m
Moncheur, Baron v6p0144c1s
Monck, E.C. v4p0620c2m
Monck, M.F.C. v1p1088c1s
Monck, T.K. v5p0597c2s
Monck, W.H. v6p0412c2s
Monck, W.H.S. v1p0049c2s v1p0099c2s v1p0426c2s v1p1000c1s v2p0071c1s v2p0213c2s v2p0241c1s v2p0262c2s v2p0358c2s v3p0094c1m v3p0207c1s v3p0275c2m v3p0407c1m v3p0407c2s v4p0126c2s v4p0367c1s v4p0435c2s v4p0545c2m v4p0556c2s v5p0229c2s v5p0453c2s v5p0549c1s v5p0597c2s v6p0188c1m v6p0614c1s v6p0625c2s v6p0670c2s
Monck, W.H.S. and Halsted, G.B. v5p0229c2s
Monck, W.H.S. and Ranyard, A.C. v3p0407c1s
Monckhouse, W.J. v4p0187c2s
Monckton, H.W. v2p0001c2s
Monckton-Dene, R. v4p0276c2s v4p0460c1s
Monckton-Dene, R.M. v3p0028c1s v3p0440c2s
Moncrief, J.W. v6p0094c1s
Moncrieff, A. v6p0708c1s
Moncrieff, A.H.R. v6p0392c2s
Moncrieff, A.R.H. v3p0433c1s
Moncrieff, C.S. v3p0223c2s v6p0329c1m
Moncrieff, C.Scott v6p0082c1s
Moncrieff, Capt. v1p0065c2s
Moncrieff, G. v1p1028c1s v1p1093c1s
Moncrieff, G.C.S. v1p0633c2s
Moncrieff, G.K.S. v6p0416c2s v6p0523c2s
Moncrieff, G.K.Scott v6p0085c1s v6p0486c2s
Moncrieff, H.W. v1p1375c2s
Moncrieff, J. v1p0017c2s v1p0163c1s v1p0247c2s v1p0270c2s v1p0319c2m v1p0354c2s v1p0384c1s v1p0398c1s v1p0412c1s v1p0420c1s v1p0483c1s v1p0494c1s v1p0504c2s v1p0548c2s v1p0614c1s v1p0654c1s v1p0656c2m v1p0681c1m v1p0712c1s v1p0802c2s v1p0881c1s v1p0973c2s v1p1106c2s v1p1133c1s v1p1164c2s v1p1166c1s v1p1166c2s v1p1167c1m v1p1315c1s
Moncrieff, J., Sir v1p0412c1s
Moncrieff, Joanna S. v6p0484c1s
Moncrieff, Lord v6p0158c1s v6p0677c1s
Moncrieff, S.S. v5p0149c1s
Moncrieff, W.D.S. v1p1212c2s v2p0006c1m v2p0299c2s
Moncrieff, W.T. v1p0404c1s
Mond, F.V.Du v6p0390c2m
Mond, L. v4p0089c1s
Mondell, F.W. v6p0329c1s
Mondesir, Piarron de v1p0022c1s v1p1181c2s
Monete, L. v6p0595c1s
Monette, J.W. v1p0854c2s v1p1062c2s v1p1400c1s
Money, F.B.J. v1p0586c1s
Money, H.D. v5p0147c2s v5p0410c1s v5p0543c1s
Money, H.D. and Scanland, J.M. v5p0199c2s
Money, R.I. and Smith, S.K. v5p0416c2s
Money, W. v4p0187c2s
Money-Coutts, F.B. v5p0012c2s v5p0291c1s v5p0387c2s
Monfort, J.G. v1p1047c1s
Mongan, R. v4p0549c2s
Monin, L.C. v6p0072c1s
Monk, J.H. v1p0386c2s
Monk, Katharine H. v6p0462c2s
Monke, T.K. v5p0585c2s
Monkhouse, C. v1p0153c2s v1p0234c2s v1p0534c2s v1p0953c1s v1p1333c2s v1p1335c1s v2p0023c2m v2p0058c2s v2p0116c2s v2p0195c2s v2p0205c1s v2p0212c1s v2p0351c1s v2p0457c1s v3p0021c2m v3p0022c1m v3p0103c1s v3p0174c1s v3p0185c2s v3p0186c1m v3p0205c1s v3p0242c1s v3p0274c2s v3p0300c1s v3p0322c2s v3p0356c1s v3p0358c2m v3p0363c1s v3p0374c2s v3p0410c1m v3p0411c2s v3p0438c2s v3p0457c1m v3p0471c1s v4p0001c1s v4p0011c2s v4p0030c1s v4p0032c2s v4p0034c2s v4p0042c2s v4p0063c2s v4p0073c2s v4p0079c2s v4p0104c1s v4p0106c1s v4p0149c1s v4p0150c2s v4p0153c2s v4p0157c1s v4p0178c2s v4p0179c2s v4p0276c1s v4p0288c2s v4p0304c2s v4p0325c2m v4p0358c1s v4p0371c1s v4p0381c1s v4p0393c2s v4p0394c1s v4p0417c2s v4p0422c1s v4p0429c1s v4p0454c2s v4p0455c1m v4p0457c1s v4p0480c2s v4p0495c1s v4p0502c1s v4p0549c1s v4p0550c2s v4p0559c1s v4p0577c2s v4p0584c2s v4p0587c1s v4p0589c2s v4p0599c2s v4p0613c1s v4p0614c1s v4p0625c1s v4p0633c2s v5p0223c2s v5p0324c2s v5p0331c1s v5p0423c1s v5p0438c1s v5p0459c2m v5p0461c1s v5p0462c1s v5p0507c2s v5p0563c2s v5p0595c1s v5p0617c2s v5p0623c1s v5p0646c1s
Monkhouse, Cosmo v2p0479c1s
Monkhouse, F. v4p0614c1s
Monkhouse, W.C. v1p1022c2s v1p1368c1s v2p0008c2s v2p0023c1s v2p0024c2s v2p0061c2s v2p0146c2s v2p0170c1s v2p0192c2s v2p0199c2s v2p0230c2s v2p0233c1s v2p0233c2m v2p0251c2s v2p0253c2s v2p0259c2s v2p0271c2s v2p0306c2s v2p0315c2s v2p0323c2s v2p0326c1m v2p0326c2m v2p0347c1s v2p0371c2m v2p0373c2s v2p0378c2m v2p0384c1s v2p0432c2s v2p0449c1s v2p0467c2s v2p0481c1s v4p0226c1s v4p0536c1s v4p0579c1s
Monks, S.P. v1p0758c1s
Monkswell v5p0273c1s
Monkswell, Lord v3p0092c2s v3p0412c1s v5p0482c1s v6p0271c1s v6p0602c2s
Monnett, F.S. v5p0080c2s v5p0586c1s v5p0592c2s
Monod, A. v1p0129c1s v1p0757c2s
Monod, A.F.T. v1p0404c1s
Monod, G. v1p0477c2s v1p0479c2s v1p0834c2s v2p0164c2m v2p0170c2s v3p0160c1m v3p0161c1m v3p0450c1s v4p0212c1s v4p0212c2m v4p0480c2m v4p0562c1s
Monod, J. v2p0136c1s
Monoemy, J. v2p0097c1s
Monot, R.S. v6p0670c1s
Monot, W., jr. v1p1285c2s
Monrey, G. v6p0107c2s
Monro, C.H. v4p0411c1s
Monro, C.J. v1p0760c2s v1p0761c1s v1p0906c2s v1p0980c1s
Monro, D. v5p0610c1s
Monro, D.B. v2p0206c2s v3p0199c2s
Monro, D.C. v5p0428c2s
Monro, F.T. v1p0710c2s v1p0766c2s v1p0974c2s v1p1027c1s v1p1328c2s
Monro, J. v1p0401c1s v3p0336c1s v3p0336c2s
Monro, J.E.C. v3p0131c2s
Monroe, Anne S. v6p0470c1s v6p0531c1s
Monroe, C.H. v4p0378c2s
Monroe, D. v5p0396c1s
Monroe, H. v2p0397c2s v4p0030c2s v5p0008c2s v5p0129c1s v5p0217c1s v5p0463c1s v6p0030c1s v6p0074c2s v6p0108c2s v6p0598c2s v6p0704c2s
Monroe, H.A. v6p0469c1s
Monroe, H.E. v3p0203c2s v3p0216c1s v4p0169c1s v4p0311c1s
Monroe, H.E., Mrs. v3p0089c2s v3p0141c1s v3p0307c1s v3p0377c2s
Monroe, J. v1p1120c2s v4p0054c1s v5p0310c2s
Monroe, J.P. v4p0169c1s v6p0137c2s
Monroe, Kirk v4p0542c2s
Monroe, L. v4p0100c1s v5p0123c2s
Monroe, L.B. v4p0099c2s
Monroe, L.G. v6p0611c1s
Monroe, Lucy v5p0079c2s v5p0226c1s v5p0462c1s
Monroe, P. v4p0461c1s v4p0533c1s v5p0187c2s v5p0293c1s v5p0399c1s v5p0440c1s v5p0467c2s v5p0598c1s
Monroe, R.G. v6p0435c2s v6p0452c2s
Monroe, Robert G. v6p0436c1s v6p0453c1s
Monroe, W.S. v4p0101c1s v4p0126c2m v4p0171c2s v4p0175c1s v4p0249c2s v4p0358c2s v4p0396c1s v5p0106c1m v5p0107c1s v5p0107c2s v5p0108c1s v5p0162c2s v6p0153c2s v6p0252c2s v6p0438c1s v6p0574c2s v6p0649c2s
Monroe, Will S. v6p0116c2s v6p0488c2s
Monselet, C. v2p0370c2s
Monsell, J. v1p0996c1s v1p1199c2s
Monser, J.W. v1p0849c2s v2p0044c2s v2p0235c2s
Monson and Gower v6p0187c2s
Monson, W.J. v6p0212c2s
Mont, P.de v5p0122c1s
Mont, Pol de v5p0165c2s v5p0361c2s v5p0369c1s
Montagnon, L.W. v4p0347c2s
Montagu, G. v1p0658c2s
Montagu, I. v2p0194c1s v2p0465c2s v4p0610c2s
Montagu, Irving v4p0031c2s
Montagu, J.D. v4p0006c1s
Montagu, J.S. v6p0382c1s
Montagu, L.H. v5p0311c2s
Montagu, Lady et al. v4p0452c1s
Montagu, Lily W. v4p0534c1s
Montagu, M.W., Lady v1p0673c1s
Montagu, R., Lord v1p0981c2s
Montagu, S. v3p0055c1s v3p0120c1s v4p0199c1s v4p0279c1s v4p0525c1s
Montague, B. v1p0085c2s
Montague, C. v1p0014c1s v1p0525c1s v1p0709c2s v4p0484c1s
Montague, Capt. v1p0986c1s
Montague, F.C. v3p0060c2s v3p0279c2s v3p0337c1s v3p0417c2s v3p0433c2s v4p0419c2s v4p0533c1s v5p0158c1s v5p0383c2s
Montague, G.H. v6p0613c1m v6p0658c2s v6p0659c1s
Montague, G.P. v4p0403c2s
Montague, J. v5p0145c1s v5p0407c2s
Montague, J.S. and Fowle, T.W. v4p0426c2s
Montague, R. v2p0235c1s v3p0098c2s
Montague, W.E. v1p0154c1s v1p0813c1s v2p0384c1s v4p0028c1s
Montague, W.L. v3p0127c1s v3p0160c1s v3p0261c2s v3p0377c2s
Montague, W.P. v5p0540c1s v6p0302c2s v6p0533c1s v6p0647c1s
Montague, Wm.P. v6p0171c2s
Montaignes, F.des v1p1041c1s v1p1400c2s
Montaigu, Countess de v5p0349c1s
Montalembert, C. v1p0387c2s
Montalembert, C.de v1p1347c2s
Montalembert, C.F.de v1p1124c2s v1p1228c1s v1p1439c1s
Montalembert, Comte de v1p0557c2s v2p0376c2s
Montalivet, Count de v1p0771c2s
Montanari, T. v2p0440c2s
Montbard, G. v4p0393c1s v4p0404c2s v4p0438c2s v5p0205c2s v5p0412c1s v5p0485c2s
Monte, C.B.La v4p0140c2s v4p0217c2s
Monteagle v4p0290c2s
Monteagle, Earl v5p0296c2s

Monteagle, Lord v1p0386c2s v1p0548c2m v1p0604c1s v1p0798c1s v1p1031c2s v1p1317c1s v2p0107c2s v4p0289c1s v4p0290c1s v6p0326c2s
Monteagle, Lord et al. ... v1p0657c1m v4p0291c1s
Monteath, J. v1p0098c2s
Monteath, J.B. v1p0774c1s
Montefiore, A. v3p0010c1s v3p0012c1s v3p0155c2m v3p0156c1m v3p0165c1s v3p0191c1s v3p0303c2s v3p0361c2s v3p0421c2s v4p0012c1s v4p0213c1s v4p0236c2s v4p0295c2s v4p0484c2s v4p0501c2s
Montefiore, C. v2p0230c2s v2p0382c1s
Montefiore, C.C. v6p0343c1s
Montefiore, C.G. v2p0239c1s v4p0053c2s v4p0055c2m v4p0057c1s v4p0150c1s v4p0301c2s v4p0302c1s v4p0306c1s v4p0384c1s v4p0431c1s v4p0438c2s v4p0482c1m v5p0311c1s v5p0311c2m v5p0344c2s v5p0398c2s v5p0417c1s v5p0475c1s v5p0598c1s v6p0123c1s v6p0539c2s
Montefiore, D.B. v6p0222c2s v6p0362c1s
Montefiore, E.L. v2p0312c1s
Montefiore, Francis v5p0346c1s
Montefiore, L. v1p0025c2s
Montefiore, L.A. v1p0516c2s v1p0583c1s
Montefiore, Lady v1p0682c2s
Montefiore-Brice, A. v6p0652c1s
Montegut, E. v3p0266c1s
Montegut, M.E. v1p0559c1s
Monteiro, J.J. v1p0040c2s
Monteiro, M. v3p0229c2s
Monteith, F.P. v1p0768c2s
Monteith, J. v1p0392c1s v1p1096c1s v4p0158c1s v4p0562c2s v4p0633c2s v5p0341c1s v5p0388c2s
Montemerli, M. v1p0669c1s
Montesquieu, C.de v1p0390c1s
Montesquiou, Count De v6p0080c2s
Montet, E. v4p0218c1s v5p0387c1s v5p0423c2s v5p0484c1s v5p0519c2s v6p0430c1m v6p0470c2m v6p0537c2s v6p0583c1s v6p0713c1s
Montgomerie, H.S. v5p0375c2s
Montgomery, A. v2p0303c2s
Montgomery, A.N. v2p0230c1s
Montgomery, B.S. v1p0394c1s
Montgomery, C. v1p0322c2s v1p0956c2s
Montgomery, C.E. v2p0064c2s
Montgomery, C.R. v4p0293c1s
Montgomery, C.S. v4p0572c1s
Montgomery, D.H. v1p0119c1s v1p0613c2s v1p1274c2s v1p1338c1s v2p0121c1s
Montgomery, E. v1p0407c2s v1p0434c1s v1p0746c1m v1p0948c1s v1p1070c1s v2p0071c2s v2p0072c1s v2p0244c1s v2p0412c2s v2p0423c2s v2p0443c2s v3p0147c1s v3p0280c1s v4p0007c1s v4p0039c2s v4p0041c2s v4p0187c2s v4p0191c1s v4p0331c1s v4p0371c2m v4p0379c1m v4p0542c2s v5p0199c2s v5p0534c2s
Montgomery, E. et al. v2p0328c1s
Montgomery, F. v5p0342c1s
Montgomery, Florence v6p0672c2s
Montgomery, G.E. v2p0307c2s v3p0117c1s v3p0168c2s v3p0273c2s v3p0318c2s v3p0334c2s v3p0354c2s v3p0388c2s v4p0194c1s v4p0577c2s v5p0553c1s
Montgomery, G.E. et al. .. v3p0122c1s
Montgomery, G.W. v1p0507c2s v1p1040c2s v1p1355c2s
Montgomery, H. v1p1424c1s v6p0268c1s v6p0397c1s
Montgomery, H.deF. v1p0657c2s v4p0290c2s v4p0318c1s
Montgomery, H.deF. et al.. v4p0291c1s
Montgomery, H.E. v6p0324c2s v6p0356c2s v6p0377c2s v6p0659c1s v6p0659c2s
Montgomery, H.H. v4p0132c1s v4p0364c1s v4p0437c1s
Montgomery, H.J.B. v6p0158c1s v6p0517c2m
Montgomery, H.L. v5p0425c1s
Montgomery, I.T. v5p0403c1s
Montgomery, J. v1p0329c1s v1p1172c2s v1p1385c1s
Montgomery, J.A. v6p0062c2s v6p0501c2s
Montgomery, J.B. v6p0669c1s
Montgomery, J.D. v3p0262c1s
Montgomery, J.E. v1p0777c1s v1p1075c1s
Montgomery, J.H. v3p0317c1s
Montgomery, J.P. v5p0478c2s
Montgomery, Jessie D. v4p0437c1s v6p0592c2s
Montgomery, K.L. v5p0068c2s v5p0203c2s v5p0366c1s v5p0416c2s v5p0608c1s v5p0614c2s v6p0629c1s
Montgomery, L.M. v5p0317c2s v6p0202c2s v6p0304c1s v6p0603c2s
Montgomery, M.C. v3p0149c1s
Montgomery, M.L. v2p0229c1s
Montgomery, M.W. v2p0428c1m
Montgomery, Mrs. v1p0353c2s v1p0528c2s v1p0942c2s
Montgomery, R. v2p0182c1s
Montgomery, R.B.C. v5p0360c1s
Montgomery, S. v5p0316c1s
Montgomery, T.G. v6p0150c1s
Montgomery, T.H. v1p0862c1s v4p0438c1s v5p0426c1s v5p0645c1s v6p0124c2s v6p0713c2s
Montgomery, T.H., jr. v4p0061c1s v4p0255c2s
Montgomery, T.L. v4p0329c1s v4p0597c2s v5p0335c1m
Montgomery, W. v1p0769c2s v3p0149c1s v6p0169c1s
Montgomery, W.A. v6p0368c1s
Montgomery, W.H. v5p0419c1s
Montgomery-M'Govern, J.B.. v5p0311c1s
Monti, L. v1p0163c1s v1p0259c2s v1p0670c1s v1p1194c2m v1p1369c2s v2p0091c1s v2p0281c1s v3p0167c1s
Montillot, L. v3p0217c1s
Montmorency, J.E.G.de v5p0637c2s v6p0022c1s v6p0192c1s
Montresor, C.A. v3p0198c1s
Montresor, F. v4p0194c1s
Montresor, J. v2p0361c1s
Monvel, B.de v4p0303c1s
Monvel, R.Boutet de v6p0117c1s v6p0236c2s v6p0651c2s
Mony, Count de v4p0094c2s
Monypenny, E.L. v6p0674c2s
Mooar, G. v1p0690c1s v1p1362c2s v2p0005c1s v2p0098c2s v2p0291c2s v2p0408c2s v2p0438c1s v3p0024c1s v5p0037c1s
Moodie, A.M. v5p0054c2s
Moodie, E.S. v4p0414c1s
Moodie, Mrs. v1p0193c2s v1p1041c1s v1p1397c2s
Moody, C.A. v6p0229c2s v6p0241c1s v6p0386c2s v6p0451c1s v6p0464c2s v6p0568c2s v6p0674c1s
Moody, F.M. v6p0568c2s
Moody, H.W. v5p0331c2s
Moody, Helen W. v5p0635c2s v5p0637c1s v5p0638c1s
Moody, J. v5p0476c2s v6p0325c2s v6p0425c2s
Moody, J.M. v4p0617c2s
Moody, L. v1p0810c1s v1p1300c2s
Moody, N.L. v2p0273c1s
Moody, S. v4p0338c2s
Moody, S.E. v6p0014c1s
Moody, S.E. and Peters, C.A. v5p0441c2s
Moody, T.B. v6p0460c1s
Moody, W.G. and Laughlin, J.L. v2p0480c1s
Moody, W.H. v5p0461c2s v6p0583c1s
Moody, W.S. v6p0024c2s v6p0090c1s v6p0185c1s v6p0499c1s v6p0541c1s
Moody, W.V. v4p0108c1s v5p0080c2s v5p0239c2s v5p0490c1s v6p0617c2s
Moon, E. v3p0027c2s
Moon, E.M. v5p0054c2s v5p0213c2s v5p0255c1s v5p0260c1s v6p0474c1s
Moon, Elizabeth M. v6p0203c2s v6p0328c1s v6p0426c1s
Moon, H.B. v5p0029c2s
Moon, R.C. v6p0070c2s
Mooney, J. v4p0099c1s v4p0205c1s v5p0092c1s v5p0104c2s v5p0288c1s v5p0398c2s v5p0475c1s v5p0582c2s v5p0630c1s
Mooney, J.A. v2p0038c2s v2p0458c1s v3p0030c1s v3p0037c2s v3p0038c1s v3p0047c2s v3p0058c1s v3p0064c2s v3p0123c1s v3p0161c2s v3p0226c2m v3p0250c2s v3p0339c1m v3p0364c1s v3p0392c1s v4p0126c1s v4p0170c1s v4p0445c1s v4p0488c2s
Mooney, James v4p0099c1s
Mooney, S.F., Mrs. v2p0369c2s
Mooney, V.R. v4p0637c1s
Mooney, W. v3p0251c1s
Mooney, W.D. v5p0126c2s
Moons, J.D. v3p0439c2s
Moor, A.P. v2p0447c2s
Moor, C.R. v1p0493c2s v1p0686c2s v1p1101c2s
Moor, H. v1p1135c2s
Mooran, L.C. v6p0607c2s
Moorby, W.H. and Reynolds, O. v5p0260c1s
Moore, A. v1p1423c2s v5p0051c2s v5p0096c1s v5p0379c1s v6p0250c1s
Moore, A.C. v5p0335c1s v6p0370c2s v6p0375c1s v6p0513c1s v6p0619c2s
Moore, A.E. v2p0032c2s v4p0361c1m
Moore, A.H. v2p0177c2s
Moore, A.J. v4p0521c2s
Moore, A.M. v2p0104c2s v4p0245c2s
Moore, A.W. v3p0265c2m v3p0306c2s v3p0369c2s v3p0370c1s v3p0374c1s v3p0392c2s v3p0399c2s v3p0440c2s v3p0450c1s v4p0205c1s v4p0352c2s v4p0612c2s v4p0616c2s v5p0299c2s v6p0216c1s v6p0302c2s v6p0397c2s v6p0513c1s
Moore, A.W. and Angell, J.R. v4p0036c2s v4p0245c1s
Moore, A.W. and Beddoe, J. v5p0359c1s
Moore, B. v5p0449c2s v6p0511c1s
Moore, B., Mrs. v2p0241c2s v4p0309c1s v4p0507c1s
Moore, B., Mrs. et al. ... v4p0177c1s
Moore, B.G. v4p0366c1s
Moore, Bloomfield, Mrs. .. v4p0309c1m v4p0607c2s
Moore, C. v2p0296c2m v3p0232c2s v4p0407c1s v5p0079c2s v5p0235c1s v5p0391c2s v5p0458c2s v5p0556c2s v6p0687c1m v6p0696c2s
Moore, C.B. v3p0330c2m v3p0331c1s v4p0004c2s v4p0079c2s v4p0385c1s v4p0440c1s v4p0440c2s v4p0520c1s v4p0576c2s v6p0293c2s v6p0673c1s
Moore, C.C. v1p1415c2s
Moore, C.H. v2p0025c2s v2p0073c2s v2p0306c2s v2p0373c1s v2p0408c2s v3p0317c2s v4p0199c2s v4p0233c1s v5p0060c1s v5p0240c2s v5p0455c2s v5p0500c1s v6p0230c2s v6p0279c1s v6p0381c2s
Moore, C.H. et al. v4p0123c1s
Moore, C.J. v4p0309c1s
Moore, C.K. v5p0430c1s
Moore, C.L. v4p0448c2s v5p0005c1s v5p0016c1s v5p0129c2s v5p0144c2m v5p0292c2s v5p0341c1m v5p0341c2m v5p0367c2s v5p0415c1s v5p0455c1s v5p0455c2s v5p0456c1s v6p0017c1s v6p0070c1s v6p0085c2s v6p0106c1s v6p0158c2m v6p0202c1m v6p0303c2s v6p0379c1s v6p0388c2s v6p0582c1s v6p0587c1s v6p0623c1s v6p0627c1s v6p0641c2s
Moore, C.M. v4p0597c2s
Moore, C.R. v6p0149c1s
Moore, C.S. v5p0512c1s v6p0197c1s
Moore, Charles v6p0364c1s
Moore, D. v1p0321c2s v1p1415c2s v2p0475c2s v4p0056c1s v4p0056c2s v4p0084c1s v5p0059c1m v5p0060c2s v6p0058c2s v6p0076c1s
Moore, D.H. v6p0209c2s
Moore, D.McF. v4p0331c2s v6p0673c2s
Moore, Dorothea v5p0275c2s v6p0706c1s
Moore, E. v1p0416c2s v2p0070c1s v2p0111c2m v3p0110c1m v3p0110c2s v4p0147c1s v4p0306c2s v5p0152c2s v6p0533c2s
Moore, E. et al. v3p0110c2s
Moore, E.A. v4p0517c2m v4p0518c1m v4p0519c1s
Moore, E.B. v2p0412c2s
Moore, E.C. v3p0043c2s v3p0229c1s v5p0454c2s v5p0481c2s v5p0506c1s v5p0610c2s v6p0060c2s v6p0191c1m v6p0193c1s
Moore, E.C., jr. v2p0431c1s
Moore, E.G. v3p0419c1s
Moore, E.H. v3p0308c2s v6p0159c2s v6p0406c1m v6p0641c1s
Moore, E.L. v4p0615c2s v5p0336c1s v6p0372c2s
Moore, E.L. and Hunt, C.W. v5p0335c1s
Moore, E.M. v3p0149c1s v5p0342c1s
Moore, E.R. v5p0596c1s
Moore, E.W. v6p0682c1s
Moore, F. v6p0563c1s
Moore, F. and Berth, J.L.C. v6p0392c2s
Moore, F.C. v5p0532c2s
Moore, F.D. v4p0241c2s
Moore, F.F. v1p1111c1s v4p0588c1s v6p0590c1s
Moore, F.G. v5p0429c1s
Moore, F.H. v2p0466c1s
Moore, F.J. v1p0942c2s
Moore, F.M. v6p0136c2s
Moore, F.W. v3p0402c1s v4p0195c1s v4p0538c1s v5p0202c2s v5p0242c1s v6p0233c2s v6p0292c2s v6p0293c1s v6p0387c2s v6p0605c2s
Moore, G. v1p0478c1s

v2p0451c1s v3p0031c2s v3p0122c1m
v3p0273c2s v3p0296c2s v3p0358c2s
v3p0438c1s v4p0029c2s v4p0114c2s
v4p0151c2s v4p0493c1s v4p0493c2s
v4p0637c1m v5p0167c2s v5p0205c2s
v5p0297c2s v5p0396c2s v6p0045c1s
v6p0310c2s v6p0427c1s v6p0450c2s
v6p0483c2s
Moore, G.A. v2p0260c1s
Moore, G.E. v5p0220c1s
v5p0311c2s v5p0402c1s v5p0484c1s
v6p0150c1s v6p0306c2s v6p0393c2s
Moore, G.E. et al. v5p0580c1s
Moore, G.F. v2p0041c2s
v2p0042c2s v2p0169c2s v2p0292c1s
v3p0016c2s v3p0041c1s v3p0041c2s
v3p0042c1m v3p0067c1s v3p0081c1s
v3p0224c1s v3p0228c2s v3p0230c1s
v3p0420c2s v4p0054c2s v4p0056c1s
v5p0188c1s v5p0308c1s v6p0047c1s
v6p0642c2s
Moore, G.F. et al. v5p0055c2s
Moore, G.H. v1p0028c2s
v1p0782c2s v1p0809c1s v1p1205c1s
v1p1207c2m v1p1245c2s v3p0010c1s
v3p0426c2s v3p0455c2s
Moore, G.L. v6p0505c1s
Moore, G.N. v6p0210c2s
Moore, G.T. v6p0077c1s
Moore, G.T. et al. v6p0688c2s
Moore, G.W. v4p0397c1s
Moore, Geo. v4p0003c1s
v4p0128c2s
Moore, H. v1p0384c2s
v1p1288c1s v3p0268c2s v4p0243c2s
v4p0388c1s v4p0527c2s v4p0608c2s
Moore, H.A. v4p0535c1s
Moore, H.C. v4p0080c1s
v6p0091c1s v6p0383c2s v6p0466c2s
Moore, H.D. v1p0980c2s
Moore, H.E. v4p0195c2s
v4p0318c2s v4p0590c2s v5p0009c2s
Moore, H.F. v2p0162c1s
Moore, H.H. v3p0207c2s
v3p0259c1s v3p0427c2s v4p0395c1s
v4p0491c2s v6p0497c1s v6p0609c2s
v6p0680c1s
Moore, H.K. v4p0331c1s
v5p0335c1s v6p0319c2s
Moore, H.L. v4p0576c1s
v4p0608c2s v6p0154c2s
Moore, H.M. v3p0226c2s
Moore, H.S. v3p0047c2s
Moore, I. v6p0223c1s
v6p0223c2s v6p0273c2s
Moore, Isabel v6p0510c2s
Moore, J. v1p0333c2s
v1p1047c1s v1p1160c2s v2p0036c2s
v4p0066c2s v5p0150c1s
Moore, J.B. v1p0006c1s
v1p0023c2s v1p0038c2s v1p0060c1s
v1p0098c2s v1p0100c2s v1p0109c1s
v1p0110c1s v1p0111c1s v1p0115c1s
v1p0154c2s v1p0156c1s v1p0159c2s
v1p0444c1s v1p0909c2s v1p0911c1s
v1p0911c2s v1p0914c2s v1p0950c1s
v1p1249c1s v2p0339c2s v3p0065c1s
v3p0154c1s v3p0442c1s v4p0015c2s
v4p0022c2m v4p0034c2s v4p0104c2s
v4p0142c2s v4p0192c2s v4p0313c1s
v4p0379c2s v4p0394c2s v4p0495c2s
v4p0502c1s v4p0591c2s v5p0010c2s
v5p0024c2s v5p0034c1s v5p0122c1s
v5p0543c2m v5p0598c2s v6p0016c1s
v6p0026c1s v6p0026c2s v6p0141c1s
v6p0174c2s v6p0215c2s v6p0216c1s
v6p0284c1s v6p0381c2s v6p0387c2s
v6p0426c1s v6p0449c2s v6p0570c1s
v6p0580c2s v6p0655c2s v6p0669c2s
Moore, J.Bassett v6p0323c2s
Moore, J.C. v1p0339c1s
Moore, J.E. v5p0184c1s
Moore, J.E.S. v4p0025c1s
v4p0366c2s v4p0463c1s v5p0005c2m
v5p0566c2m v6p0098c2s
Moore, J.G. v1p0295c1s
Moore, J.H. v2p0166c2s
Moore, J.I. v1p0895c2s
Moore, J.M. v6p0617c1s
Moore, J.P. v1p0304c1s
v3p0072c1s v3p0206c1s v6p0336c1s
v6p0421c2s
Moore, J.Q. v1p0450c1s
v1p1199c2s v1p1223c1s v1p1224c1s
Moore, J.R. v5p0591c2s
Moore, J.S. v1p0273c1s
v1p0474c1s
Moore, J.V. v1p0120c2s
v1p1100c1s
Moore, J.W. v1p1289c2s
Moore, Kathleen C. v5p0389c2s
Moore, L. v1p0437c1s
v3p0450c2s
Moore, L.B. v1p1375c2s
Moore, M. v1p0402c2s
v3p0400c1s v4p0219c1s v4p0536c1s
v6p0103c1s
Moore, M.C. v6p0074c2s
v6p0207c1s v6p0263c2s
Moore, M.G. v6p0418c2s
Moore, M.H. v6p0707c2s
Moore, M.I. v4p0502c2s
Moore, M.V. v1p1346c1s
v2p0009c2s v2p0375c1s v3p0395c1s
v3p0395c2s v4p0281c2s v4p0392c1s
Moore, N. v1p0467c1s
v2p0071c1s v3p0186c2s v3p0256c2s
v3p0372c1s v4p0248c1s v4p0476c1s
Moore, N.H. v5p0063c1m
v5p0063c2s v5p0064c1m v5p0400c1s
v5p0400c2s v5p0417c1s v5p0417c2s
v5p0546c1s v6p0052c1s v6p0241c1s
v6p0413c2s v6p0435c1s v6p0475c1m
v6p0656c2s
Moore, N.W. v1p1173c1s
v6p0618c2s
Moore, O.C. v2p0306c1s
Moore, O.H. v6p0193c2s
Moore, P. v2p0268c1s
Moore, R. v1p0860c1s
v1p1182c2s
Moore, R.A. v4p0223c2s
v4p0281c2s v4p0558c1s
Moore, R.W. v4p0303c1s
v5p0230c2s v5p0237c1s
Moore, S. v2p0157c2s
v3p0156c1s
Moore, Susan T. v6p0163c1s
Moore, T. v1p0446c1s
v1p0517c1s v1p0654c1s v1p0660c1s
v1p0952c2s v1p1309c2s
Moore, T.C. v1p1333c2s
Moore, T.J. v1p1149c2s
Moore, T.S. v5p0487c1s
v5p0539c1s v6p0519c2s v6p0546c2s
v6p0641c2m
Moore, T.V. v1p0125c2s
v1p0215c1m v1p0987c1s v1p1001c2s
v1p1073c2s v1p1094c2s v1p1217c2s
v1p1374c1s v5p0221c2s v6p0277c1s
Moore, V.F. v5p0267c1s
Moore, W. v3p0436c2s
v4p0236c1s v5p0289c1s
Moore, W., Sir v4p0108c1s
v4p0280c2s
Moore, W.A. v6p0133c2s
v6p0661c2s
Moore, W.D. v1p0466c1s
Moore, W.E. v2p0136c1s
Moore, W.F. v6p0321c2s
Moore, W.H. v1p0056c1s
v5p0039c1m v5p0457c2s v6p0041c2s
v6p0098c1s v6p0159c2s
Moore, W.J. v3p0212c1s
v3p0268c2s v4p0279c2s
Moore, W.L. v4p0597c1s
v5p0037c2m v5p0554c2s v5p0624c1m
v6p0619c1s v6p0690c1m
Moore, W.O. v2p0119c1s
v2p0266c1s v2p0322c2s
Moore, W.S. v6p0521c1s
Moore, W.T. v1p0027c2s
v1p0097c2s v1p0198c1s v1p0240c2s
v1p0247c2s v1p0252c1s v1p0255c1s
v1p0313c2s v1p0347c2s v1p0353c2s
v1p0713c1s v1p1043c1m v1p1103c2s
v1p1161c1s v1p1430c2s
Moore, W.W. v5p0101c1s
Moore-Ede, W. v3p0166c2s
Moorehead, E. v6p0145c1s
Moorehead, W.K. v3p0158c2s
v4p0017c2s v4p0385c1s v4p0599c1s
v6p0149c1s v6p0432c2s v6p0464c2s
v6p0700c1s
Moorehead, W.K. and Peabody, C.
v6p0015c1s
Moores, George v6p0413c2s
Moorhead, G.O. v5p0589c1s
Moorhead, H.G. v6p0161c2s
Moorhouse, A. v5p0140c2s
Moorhouse, E.H. v6p0449c1s
v6p0525c1s v6p0707c2s
Moorhouse, E.Hallam v6p0561c2s
Moorhouse, H.J. v6p0528c1s
v6p0672c2s
Moorhouse, J. v4p0606c2s
Moorhouse, James v6p0191c2s
Moorley, W.D. v6p0362c2s
Moors, H.J. v6p0567c1s
Moors, J.F. v6p0568c2s
Moors, J.F. and Munroe, Jas.P.
v6p0572c2s
Moors, Jos.B. v6p0121c2s
Moos, F. v5p0045c2s
Moos, J. v4p0389c1s
v4p0389c2s v5p0395c1s
Moot, Adelbert v6p0529c1s
Moque, A.L. v5p0151c1s
v5p0190c1s v5p0366c1s v5p0556c1s
Moque, A.L., Mrs. v4p0145c2s
v4p0182c2s
Mor, J.S. v5p0558c1s
Morais, N. v1p0690c1s
v2p0477c1s
Morais, N. et al. v2p0477c1s
Morais, S. v1p0441c2s
Morales, C.F. v6p0570c1s
Morales, E.A. v6p0138c1s
v6p0476c2s
Morales, G. v5p0164c1s
Moran, E. v2p0401c1s
Moran, E.R. v1p1184c1s
Moran, F.E. v3p0248c1s
Moran, F.J.C. v5p0563c2s
Moran, J.A. v3p0236c1s
Moran, J.W. v6p0035c1s
Moran, P.F. v1p0979c1s
v2p0227c2s
Moran, T. v4p0154c1s
v4p0634c1s v6p0034c1s v6p0353c2s
Moran, T.F. v4p0058c1s
v4p0333c2s v5p0623c2s
Moran, W.H. v6p0581c2s
Morant, L.C. v5p0051c2s
v5p0120c1s v5p0417c1s v5p0557c2s
Morawetz, V. v6p0411c2s
v6p0529c1s v6p0590c2s
Morawitz, C. v6p0661c1s
v6p0661c2s
Moray, A. v2p0321c1s
Morce, A.M. v6p0012c1s
Mordaunt, O. v5p0340c2s
v5p0471c1m
Mordecai, A. v1p0563c1s
v1p0829c1s v1p1293c1s v1p1304c2s
Morden, G.H. v6p0451c2s
Morden, J.H. v1p1125c1m
v1p1125c2s
More, H. v1p0324c1s
v1p0781c2s
More, L.T. v6p0094c2s
More, P. v5p0582c1s
More, P.E. v5p0030c1s
v5p0086c1s v5p0141c1s v5p0157c2s
v5p0193c2s v5p0249c2s v5p0259c1s
v5p0317c2s v5p0367c1s v5p0370c2s
v5p0404c1s v5p0420c1s v5p0508c1s
v5p0578c2s v5p0582c1s v6p0052c2s
v6p0085c2s v6p0180c2s v6p0202c1s
v6p0283c2m v6p0285c1m v6p0292c2s
v6p0326c1s v6p0418c1s v6p0543c1s
v6p0552c1s v6p0563c1s v6p0630c1s
v6p0647c2s v6p0678c1s
More, P.E., jr. v6p0005c1s
More, Paul E. v6p0644c1s
More, Paul Elmer v6p0239c1s
More, Phil v5p0114c1s
v5p0116c2s
More, W.F. v5p0446c1s
v6p0535c2s
Moreau, A. v2p0362c2s
Moreau, T. v6p0626c1s
Morehouse, G.W. v1p0836c1s
Moreing, C.A. v5p0108c1s
v5p0109c1s v5p0110c1s v5p0111c2s
Moreira, M.de v6p0080c2s
v6p0547c2s
Morel, E.C. v6p0582c2s
v6p0660c2s
Morel, E.D. v5p0132c2s
v6p0144c1m v6p0144c2m
Morel, J. v5p0370c1s
Morel, Leon v5p0578c2s
Moreland, R.E. v6p0156c1s
Moreland, S.T. v4p0176c2s
Moreland, W.W. v5p0228c1s
Morell, J.C. v3p0352c1s
Morell, J.R. v2p0055c1s
Morell, T. v1p0301c2s
Morelock, J.F. v6p0348c2s
Morely, G. v1p0675c1s
Moreno, F.P. v5p0027c2s
v5p0435c1m
Moresby, J. v1p0069c1s
v6p0643c2s
Moret, J.C. v2p0212c1s
Moreton, E. v5p0186c1s
Morey v1p0033c2s
Morey, C.A. v1p1002c1s
Morey, S. v1p0280c2s
v1p0579c2s
Morey, W.C. v2p0414c1s
v3p0097c2s v4p0196c1s v4p0490c2s
v4p0546c1s
Morfill, W.R. v2p0009c1s
v2p0400c2s v2p0448c2s v3p0099c1s
v3p0170c1m v3p0172c1s v3p0278c1s
v3p0336c1s v3p0369c2s v3p0370c2s
v4p0187c1s v4p0213c1s v4p0223c2m
v4p0310c1s v4p0369c1s v4p0519c1s
v4p0609c2s v5p0034c2s
Morfit and Alexander v1p0036c2s
Morfit, C. v1p0560c1s
v1p1146c2s v2p0090c1s
Morfit, C. and Alexander, J.H.
v1p0267c2s v1p1265c1s
Morford, E.P. v6p0070c2s
Morford, H. v1p0579c1s
v1p1193c1s v1p1240c2s v1p1419c2s
Morgan, A. v1p1183c2s
v2p0102c2s v2p0112c2s v2p0397c1s
v2p0397c2s v2p0398c2s v2p0409c2s
v3p0002c1m v3p0057c2s v3p0093c2s
v3p0100c1s v3p0109c1s v3p0140c1m
v3p0218c2s v3p0231c2s v3p0352c1m
v3p0352c2s v3p0387c1s v3p0387c2m
v3p0388c1s v3p0388c2s v3p0389c1m
v3p0434c1s v4p0141c2s v4p0175c2s
v4p0288c1s v4p0440c1s v4p0453c1s
v4p0461c2s v4p0471c1s v4p0517c2s

v4p0518c1s v4p0518c2s v5p0293c1s v5p0455c2s v5p0522c2s v5p0523c2s v5p0572c1s
Morgan, A. and Furnivall, F.J. v3p0389c1s
Morgan, A.De v1p0272c2s v1p0595c2s v1p0915c2s v1p1359c2s v2p0021c1m v2p0051c2s v2p0091c2s v2p0114c1s v2p0127c2s v2p0148c1s v2p0160c1s v2p0262c2s v2p0366c2s
Morgan, A.P. v2p0172c2s
Morgan, B. v3p0288c1s v4p0392c2s v4p0488c2s v4p0629c1s
Morgan, B.H. v6p0083c1s
Morgan, Ben.H. v6p0007c1s
Morgan, C.B. v3p0121c2s v3p0157c2s v4p0216c1s v4p0369c2s v5p0363c2s v5p0505c1s v5p0528c2s
Morgan, C.L. v1p1007c1s v2p0015c1m v2p0085c2s v2p0120c1s v2p0120c2s v2p0149c2s v2p0173c2s v2p0174c1s v2p0222c2s v2p0391c1s v3p0014c2s v3p0130c2s v3p0145c2s v3p0297c1s v3p0316c2s v3p0380c1s v3p0397c1s v3p0429c1s v4p0018c2s v4p0039c1s v4p0039c2s v4p0130c1m v4p0163c1s v4p0191c2s v4p0192c1s v4p0255c2m v4p0286c1m v4p0365c1s v4p0379c1s v4p0394c2m v4p0438c1s v4p0464c1s v4p0465c2s v4p0507c2s v4p0566c1s v5p0021c1m v5p0062c1s v5p0098c1s v5p0198c2s v5p0199c2s v5p0292c2s v5p0545c2s v5p0553c2s v5p0613c2s v6p0214c2s v6p0277c1s v6p0293c2s v6p0418c2s v6p0444c1s
Morgan, C.Lloyd v5p0180c2s v5p0468c1s v5p0613c2s v6p0543c2s
Morgan, C.O. v1p0069c2s
Morgan, C.S. v2p0260c2s v3p0345c1s
Morgan, E. v5p0506c2s
Morgan, E.D. v1p0861c2s v4p0065c1s v4p0283c1s v4p0437c2s v4p0496c1s
Morgan, E.D. et al. v1p1353c1s
Morgan, E.K. v6p0364c1s
Morgan, E.S. v3p0224c2s v3p0286c1s v3p0366c1s v3p0366c2s v3p0383c2s v3p0392c1s v4p0294c2s v4p0491c1s v4p0579c2s v4p0587c2m v5p0300c2s
Morgan, E.S., Mrs. v1p0687c2s
Morgan, E.V. v4p0529c2s v5p0506c2s
Morgan, F. v3p0346c1s v3p0392c2s v4p0362c2s v4p0467c2s v4p0548c2s v4p0632c2s
Morgan, F.A. v3p0165c1s
Morgan, F.A.H. v5p0420c2s
Morgan, F.W. v5p0289c2s
Morgan, Forrest v6p0263c2s
Morgan, Frank v5p0232c2s
Morgan, G. v5p0241c2s
Morgan, G.Campbell v6p0126c2s
Morgan, G.O. v1p0721c1s v1p1373c1s v2p0084c1s v3p0083c1s v3p0136c1s v3p0202c1s v3p0321c2s v3p0324c2s v3p0453c1s v4p0010c2s v4p0108c2s v4p0328c2s v4p0340c1s v4p0399c2s v4p0428c1s v4p0446c1s
Morgan, G.O. et al. v3p0199c1s v3p0453c1s
Morgan, G.O., Sir v4p0112c1s
Morgan, G.Osborne v3p0083c1s
Morgan, H.A. and Dupree, J.W. v6p0431c2s
Morgan, H.G. v2p0088c2s v4p0112c2s
Morgan, H.H. v1p0063c1s v1p0064c1s v1p0223c1s v1p0386c1s v1p0391c2s v1p0392c1s v1p0742c2s v1p0752c2s v1p0841c2s v1p0979c2s v1p1021c1s v1p1184c1s v1p1187c2s v1p1232c1s v1p1234c1s v1p1235c2s v1p1244c2s v2p0132c1s v3p0248c2s
Morgan, H.J. v2p0056c2s v2p0066c1s
Morgan, H.R. v6p0653c2s
Morgan, J. v1p0074c1s v1p0075c1s v1p0566c2s v2p0463c2s v6p0231c2m
Morgan, J.B. v5p0052c2s
Morgan, J.D. v5p0344c2s
Morgan, J.De v4p0146c1s v5p0054c1s v5p0137c2s v5p0138c2s v5p0150c1s v5p0181c2s v5p0186c2m v5p0199c1s v5p0321c2s v5p0327c1s v5p0343c1s v5p0345c2s v5p0375c2s v5p0462c1s v5p0554c1s v5p0632c1s v5p0634c2s v6p0348c1s v6p0387c2s v6p0464c1s v6p0506c1s v6p0508c2s v6p0627c2s
Morgan, J.E. v1p1143c2s
Morgan, J.H. and Stewart, Isla v3p0201c2s
Morgan, J.M. v5p0230c1s v5p0332c1s v6p0089c1s
Morgan, J.P. v1p0563c1m
Morgan, J.S. v3p0299c2s
Morgan, J.T. v1p1223c1s v1p1352c2s v1p1353c1s v1p1354c2s v1p1399c2s v2p0286c2s v3p0132c1s v3p0149c2s v3p0190c1s v3p0299c1s v4p0131c2s v4p0403c2s v4p0524c1s v4p0525c1s v5p0258c2s v5p0446c1s v5p0600c2s v5p0603c1s v6p0324c1s
Morgan, J.W. v1p1159c1s v1p1373c1s
Morgan, John De v4p0505c2s
Morgan, L. v3p0155c2s v4p0286c1s
Morgan, L.B. v5p0063c1s
Morgan, L.D. v2p0280c2s v3p0468c1s v4p0414c1s v5p0579c1s
Morgan, L.D., Mrs. v2p0075c2s
Morgan, L.H. v1p0083c2s v1p0303c2s v1p0636c2s v1p0637c1s v1p0637c2m v1p0638c2s v1p0646c2s v1p0876c2s v1p0912c2s v1p0926c2s v1p1365c1s
Morgan, Lloyd v6p0521c2s
Morgan, M. v1p0463c1s
Morgan, M.A.De v5p0471c2s
Morgan, M.De v3p0099c1s
Morgan, M.H. v3p0015c2s v4p0249c1s v4p0302c1s v4p0321c2s v4p0490c2s v4p0528c2s v5p0324c2m v6p0091c1s v6p0691c2s
Morgan, M.H. and Kittredge, G.L. v4p0353c2s
Morgan, M.R. v6p0196c2s
Morgan, O. v1p0184c2s v1p0214c2s v1p0422c2s v1p1108c2s v1p1389c2s
Morgan, P. and Sanborn, A.F. v5p0405c1s
Morgan, P.H. v1p0396c1s v1p1264c1s
Morgan, R. v4p0531c1s
Morgan, S. v6p0149c2s v6p0243c2s v6p0327c2s
Morgan, S.E.De v1p0230c1s v1p1017c2s v1p1431c1s
Morgan, S.O. v1p0658c1s
Morgan, S.O., Lady v1p0308c2s v1p0656c2s v1p1260c2s
Morgan, S.S.De v1p1423c2s
Morgan, T. v2p0009c2s
Morgan, T.F. v2p0315c2s
Morgan, T.H. v3p0103c2s v3p0164c2s v5p0160c1s v5p0180c2s v5p0368c2s v5p0482c2m v5p0641c2s v6p0165c2s v6p0288c1s v6p0320c2s v6p0410c1s v6p0441c2s v6p0535c2s v6p0585c2m v6p0608c2s
Morgan, T.J. v2p0444c2s v3p0128c1s v3p0213c1s v3p0385c1s v3p0396c1s v3p0422c1s v4p0248c2s v5p0256c2s v6p0316c2s
Morgan, Theo.J. v3p0351c1s
Morgan, W.B. v1p0784c2s
Morgan, W.C. v6p0090c1s
Morgan, W.C. and Gooch, F.A. v4p0568c1s
Morgan, W.C. and Tallmon, M.C. v6p0069c1s
Morgan, W.De v4p0345c1s
Morgan, W.J. v1p0596c1s
Morgan-Browne, H. v4p0629c1s v5p0245c1m v6p0224c1s v6p0356c2s v6p0654c2s
Morgan-Browne, H. and Cohen, H. v6p0355c2s
Morgan-Richardson, C. v5p0155c2s
Morgenthal, F. v6p0056c2s
Morhard, E. v6p0241c1s
Morhardt, M. v5p0095c2s
Moriarty, G. v3p0135c2s v3p0284c2s v3p0449c2m
Morice, A.G. v5p0037c2s v5p0161c2s v6p0316c1s
Morier, V.A.L. v3p0309c2s v3p0391c2s v3p0392c1s
Morin v1p1288c2s
Morin, A. v1p0017c1s v1p0111c1s v1p1300c1s v1p1392c1s
Morin, J. v6p0685c2s
Morine, A.B. et al. v3p0301c1s
Morison, A.B. v6p0681c2s
Morison, A.S. v4p0438c2s
Morison, D. v3p0301c1s
Morison, D.B. v4p0190c1s v5p0068c2s
Morison, F. v4p0387c1s
Morison, G. and Chanute, O. v1p0161c1s
Morison, G.S. v1p0362c2s v1p0854c2s v1p0968c2s v1p0997c1s v1p1297c1s v1p1300c1s v2p0055c2s v2p0383c2s v4p0280c1s v4p0403c2s v5p0149c2s v6p0476c2s v6p0477c1s
Morison, G.S. and Abbot, H.L. v6p0477c1s
Morison, J. v2p0292c1s v4p0076c1s
Morison, J.C. v1p0115c1s v1p0202c1s v1p0204c1s v1p0293c1s v1p0475c1s v1p0482c1s v1p0655c1s v1p0771c1s v1p0781c1s v1p0790c1s v1p0849c2s v1p1005c1s v1p1097c2s v1p1109c2s v1p1252c1s v2p0068c2s v2p0070c1s v2p0165c1s v2p0166c1s v2p0200c2s v2p0232c2s v2p0333c1s v2p0462c2s
Morison, J.C. and Cropper, J. v2p0226c1s
Morison, J.H. v1p0127c2s v1p0128c1s v1p0132c1s v1p0158c1s v1p0178c1s v1p0180c1s v1p0202c2s v1p0216c2s v1p0217c1s v1p0227c1s v1p0239c2s v1p0240c2s v1p0273c2s v1p0348c1s v1p0350c1s v1p0386c2s v1p0387c1s v1p0389c1s v1p0405c1s v1p0412c2s v1p0451c2s v1p0495c1s v1p0495c2s v1p0499c2m v1p0557c2s v1p0647c1s v1p0669c2s v1p0687c1m v1p0697c2s v1p0698c1s v1p0714c2s v1p0715c2s v1p0757c1m v1p0770c1s v1p0805c2s v1p0875c2s v1p0876c1s v1p0958c2s v1p0972c2s v1p0982c2s v1p0992c2s v1p1001c2s v1p1008c1s v1p1052c2s v1p1068c1s v1p1094c2s v1p1101c2s v1p1141c1s v1p1171c1s v1p1222c1s v1p1223c2s v1p1234c2s v1p1237c1s v1p1267c1m v1p1286c1s v1p1309c2s v1p1320c2s v1p1340c2m v1p1341c2s v1p1355c1s v1p1381c2m v1p1384c1s v1p1387c1s v1p1395c2s v1p1439c1s v2p0044c2s v3p0450c2s
Morison, L. v5p0525c1s
Morison, M.A. v4p0093c1s
Morison, Margaret v6p0106c1s
Morison, P. v5p0138c2s v6p0251c2s
Morison, R.S. v1p1322c1s
Morison, T. v1p0647c1s v5p0381c2s v6p0314c2m v6p0315c1s
Moritz, R.E. v5p0028c1s v6p0142c2s v6p0542c1s v6p0583c2s
Moritzen, J. v5p0095c1m v5p0128c1s v5p0139c2s v5p0158c2s v5p0207c2s v5p0221c2s v5p0301c2m v5p0314c2s v5p0414c2s v5p0626c1s v6p0225c1s v6p0376c2s v6p0460c2s
Moritzen, Julius v6p0020c1s v6p0122c1s v6p0170c2s v6p0572c1s
Morland, C.E. v3p0084c2s v3p0116c1s v4p0267c2s v4p0539c1s v4p0578c1s
Morland, C.E. and Elmard, A.d' v4p0273c2s
Morland, F.H. v4p0047c2s
Morley, C. v5p0234c2s v5p0259c1s
Morley, D. v3p0461c2s v4p0503c2s
Morley, D.W. v2p0424c2s
Morley, E. v5p0270c1s v5p0640c2s
Morley, E.F. v1p0611c1s
Morley, E.W. v1p0017c1m v1p0452c2s v1p0580c2s v1p0955c1s v2p0424c2s v3p0330c1s v3p0457c1s v4p0009c1s v4p0036c1s v5p0426c2s v5p0514c1s v5p0620c1s
Morley, E.W. and Brush, C.F. v6p0249c1s
Morley, E.W. and Michelson, A.A. v2p0258c2s v3p0143c1s v3p0246c2s v3p0251c1s v3p0399c2s
Morley, F. v3p0417c2s
Morley, F.H. and Gooch, F.A. v5p0237c2s
Morley, G. v3p0006c1s v3p0134c2s v3p0387c2s v4p0177c2s v4p0517c2s v4p0519c1s v5p0078c1s v5p0104c2s v5p0115c2s v5p0139c2s v5p0186c1s v5p0250c2s v5p0259c1s v5p0325c1s v5p0510c2s v5p0524c1s v5p0532c2s v5p0562c2s v5p0620c1s v5p0633c1s
Morley, G.L. v4p0048c1s v4p0308c2s
Morley, H. v1p0114c1s v1p0115c1s v1p0416c1s v1p0959c2s v1p0962c1s v1p1130c1s v1p1437c2s v2p0123c1s
Morley, J. v1p0170c2s v1p0177c2s v1p0181c2s v1p0201c1s v1p0284c2s v1p0287c1s v1p0288c1s v1p0318c1s v1p0323c2s v1p0351c2s v1p0382c2s v1p0390c2s v1p0415c1s v1p0475c2s v1p0477c2m v1p0479c1s v1p0512c1m v1p0546c1s v1p0549c2m v1p0550c1s v1p0571c1s v1p0594c2m v1p0596c2s v1p0607c1s v1p0612c1s v1p0629c1s v1p0631c2s v1p0639c1s v1p0652c2s v1p0654c2s v1p0655c2s v1p0659c1s v1p0661c2s v1p0696c2s v1p0717c1s v1p0720c1s v1p0741c1m v1p0741c2s v1p0757c1s v1p0781c1s v1p0790c1s v1p0839c2m v1p0869c1m v1p0873c1s v1p0889c2s v1p0892c2s v1p1027c1s v1p1037c2s v1p1094c1s v1p1096c1s v1p1098c1s v1p1111c2s v1p1116c2s v1p1129c2m v1p1137c2s v1p1175c2s v1p1183c1s v1p1215c1s v1p1271c2s v1p1320c1s v1p1330c2m v1p1364c1s v1p1377c2s v1p1421c2s v1p1441c2s v2p0115c2s v2p0135c1s

v2p0142c1s v2p0163c2s v2p0174c2s
v2p0227c2s v2p0288c2s v2p0333c1s
v3p0016c1s v3p0160c2s v3p0220c1s
v3p0220c2s v3p0442c2s v4p0128c1s
v4p0152c1s v4p0240c2s v4p0601c2s
v5p0144c2m v5p0252c1s v6p0169c2s
v6p0257c2s v6p0271c2s v6p0281c1s
v6p0293c2s v6p0417c2s v6p0518c2s
v6p0532c1s
Morley, J. and Gladstone, W.E.
v4p0028c1s
Morley, J. and Traill, H.D.
v1p0413c2s
Morley, J.C. v3p0148c1s
v4p0093c2s v4p0336c1s
Morley, M.W. v5p0400c2s
Morley, S.G. v6p0104c1s
v6p0673c2s
Morlot, A. v1p0051c2s
Mornington, S. v6p0359c1s
v6p0623c1s
Morosini, G. v4p0295c1s
Morot, C. v3p0201c1s
Morphy, E.W. v5p0612c2s
Morrah, H. v5p0612c1s
Morras, W.P. v1p0477c2s
v1p0764c2s v1p0841c1s v1p0896c1s
v1p0963c2s v1p1122c1s v1p1308c2s
v1p1342c1s v1p1355c1s v1p1384c1s
v1p1403c2s
Morre, C.F. v6p0630c1s
Morre, J. v1p0907c2s
Morre, V. v6p0409c1s
Morrell, D.M. v5p0048c1s
v5p0051c1s v5p0259c2s v5p0376c2s
v5p0489c1s v5p0567c1s
Morrell, Dora M. v5p0429c2s
Morrell, L.D. v6p0479c2s
Morrell, P.E. v5p0529c1s
Morrell, T. and Barrington, D.
v1p0026c1s
Morrell, W.H. and Rosenberg, A.
v6p0601c1s
Morrill, A.D. v3p0380c1s
Morrill, Bertha F. v5p0106c1s
Morrill, J.S. v2p0366c1s
v3p0065c1s v3p0162c2s v3p0359c1s
v4p0152c2s v4p0524c2s v5p0529c2s
Morrill, S. v3p0248c1s
Morris, A. v1p1148c2s
v2p0393c1s v6p0178c2s
Morris, A.E. v3p0238c1s
Morris, A.F. v6p0655c1s
Morris, A.J. v1p1043c1s
Morris, A.W. v6p0582c1s
Morris, Anna W. v6p0287c2s
Morris, Annie C. v3p0288c2s
Morris, B.R. v1p0137c1s
Morris, B.W. v1p0422c1s
Morris, C. v1p0012c1s
v1p0027c1s v1p0030c2s v1p0051c2s
v1p0493c1s v1p0582c1s v1p0792c2s
v1p0876c2s v1p0947c2s v1p1073c1s
v1p1135c2s v1p1234c1s v2p0015c1s
v2p0072c1s v2p0076c1s v2p0093c1s
v2p0097c1s v2p0129c1s v2p0137c2s
v2p0149c2m v2p0152c1s v2p0161c2s
v2p0185c1s v2p0192c2m v2p0199c1s
v2p0222c1s v2p0257c2s v2p0272c1s
v2p0274c1s v2p0289c2s v2p0294c1s
v2p0323c1m v2p0341c1s v2p0343c2s
v2p0349c2s v2p0357c2s v2p0358c1s
v2p0390c1s v2p0412c2m v2p0414c2s
v3p0002c2s v3p0014c1s v3p0090c2s
v3p0095c1s v3p0265c2s v3p0290c1s
v3p0341c2s v3p0384c1s v3p0424c1s
v3p0462c2s v4p0021c1s v4p0033c1s
v4p0331c1s v4p0345c1s v4p0438c1s
v4p0449c2s v4p0455c2s v4p0470c2s
v4p0471c1s v4p0588c1s v4p0600c2s
v5p0048c1s v5p0071c2s v5p0081c1s
v5p0154c1s v5p0314c1s v5p0379c2s
v5p0387c2s v5p0426c1s v5p0506c2s
v5p0622c2s v6p0040c1s v6p0056c2s
v6p0058c1s v6p0058c2s v6p0069c2s
v6p0182c1s v6p0214c1s v6p0264c2s
v6p0465c2s v6p0471c2s v6p0477c1s
v6p0526c1s v6p0566c2s v6p0590c2s
v6p0593c1s v6p0639c2s
Morris, C.D. v2p0026c2s
v2p0190c2s v2p0335c2s v2p0345c2s
v2p0440c2s v2p0481c1s
Morris, C.M. v1p0781c1s
Morris, C.S. v5p0006c2s
v6p0686c2s
Morris, C.W.G. v6p0378c1s
Morris, Clara v5p0003c2s
v5p0309c2s v5p0548c1s v6p0003c2s
v6p0014c1s v6p0124c1s v6p0163c2s
v6p0185c2s v6p0307c1s v6p0359c1s
v6p0388c1s v6p0465c2s v6p0570c2s
v6p0594c2s v6p0657c2s
Morris, D. v1p0271c2s
v2p0169c1s v2p0344c1s v2p0470c2s
v3p0051c2s v3p0384c1s v4p0162c1s
v4p0197c2s v4p0234c2s v5p0222c2s
v5p0287c1s
Morris, D.K. v5p0298c1s
Morris, E. v1p0161c2s
v1p0374c2s v1p0405c1s v1p0435c2s
v1p0491c1s v1p0604c2s v1p0904c1s
v1p0939c1s v1p1075c1s v1p1171c2s
v1p1210c1s v1p1329c2s v1p1366c2s
v1p1392c1m v1p1414c1s v4p0371c1s
v4p0415c1s
Morris, E. and McClure, J.
v1p0522c2s
Morris, E.B. v5p0542c1s
Morris, E.D. v1p0189c2s
v1p0207c2s v1p0368c1s v1p0613c2s
v1p0731c2s v1p1047c1s v1p1060c1s
v1p1381c1s v2p0027c2s v2p0035c1s
v2p0038c1s v2p0041c2s v2p0146c2s
v2p0282c1s v2p0351c2s v2p0352c2m
v2p0353c1s v3p0097c1s v3p0427c2s
v4p0275c2s v4p0299c2s v4p0618c1s
v5p0236c1s
Morris, E.E. v2p0029c1s
v5p0135c2s v5p0259c1s v5p0281c1s
v5p0309c2s v5p0313c2s v5p0634c2s
Morris, E.H. v3p0120c1s
v3p0271c1s v3p0301c2s v3p0338c2s
v3p0372c1s v3p0386c1s v4p0158c2s
Morris, E.L. v6p0031c2s
Morris, E.P. v3p0243c2s
v3p0385c1s v5p0558c2s
Morris, E.R. v5p0454c1s
Morris, E.W. v6p0468c2s
v6p0660c1s
Morris, Edwin B. v6p0472c2s
Morris, Eliz.C. v6p0422c2s
Morris, F. v3p0083c1s
v4p0146c2s v4p0153c1s v4p0400c2s
v5p0271c1s v5p0503c2s v6p0275c2s
v6p0290c2s v6p0343c2s v6p0457c1s
v6p0636c2s v6p0670c1s
Morris, F.O. v1p0998c1s
v2p0345c2s v2p0393c1s
Morris, Fritz v5p0217c1s
v6p0225c2s v6p0661c1s
Morris, G. v3p0320c2s
v3p0455c2s v5p0441c2s v6p0095c1s
v6p0100c1s v6p0142c2s v6p0351c2s
v6p0380c2s v6p0485c2s v6p0543c1s
v6p0567c2s v6p0700c2s v6p0711c2s
Morris, G.K. v1p0044c2s
v4p0607c1s
Morris, G.L. v5p0026c1s
v5p0027c1s v5p0434c2s
Morris, G.L. and Wood, E.. v6p0102c2s
Morris, G.L. and Wood, Esther
v6p0152c2s
Morris, G.P. v3p0117c2s
v3p0215c1s v4p0479c2s v5p0254c1s
v5p0385c1s v5p0438c1s v5p0546c2s
v6p0015c2s v6p0043c1s v6p0112c2s
v6p0127c1s v6p0144c2s v6p0166c1s
v6p0200c2s v6p0221c1s v6p0257c2s
v6p0282c1s v6p0294c2s v6p0475c2s
Morris, G.P. and Reid, S.. v6p0294c2s
Morris, G.S. v1p0063c2s
v1p0625c2s v1p0702c2s v1p0826c2s
v1p1228c1s v1p1236c2s v1p1311c2s
v1p1324c2s v2p0339c1s v4p0076c2s
v5p0026c2s
Morris, G.V. v6p0222c2s
Morris, Gouverneur v6p0090c1s
v6p0127c1s v6p0404c1s v6p0421c1s
v6p0698c1s
Morris, H. v5p0030c1s
Morris, H.C. v5p0220c2s
Morris, H.L. v6p0221c2s
Morris, H.S. v3p0001c2s
v3p0049c2s v3p0057c2s v3p0059c1s
v3p0081c2s v3p0179c2s v3p0288c1s
v3p0290c2s v3p0409c1s v3p0462c2s
v3p0463c1s v4p0246c2s v4p0618c2s
v5p0011c2s v5p0066c2s v5p0106c2s
v5p0254c2s v5p0262c1s v5p0381c1s
v5p0579c1s v6p0032c2s v6p0273c2s
v6p0367c2s v6p0436c2s v6p0463c1m
v6p0491c2s v6p0598c1s
Morris, H.W. v6p0655c2s
Morris, J. v1p0188c2s
v1p0419c1s v1p0571c2s v1p0793c2s
v1p0960c1s v1p1044c2s v1p1317c2s
v1p1382c2s v1p1437c2s v2p0368c1s
v3p0013c2s v3p0017c2s v3p0036c1s
v3p0037c1s v3p0039c1s v3p0046c1s
v3p0064c2m v3p0067c1m v3p0084c2s
v3p0142c1s v3p0158c2s v3p0174c1s
v3p0194c1s v3p0224c2s v3p0228c2s
v3p0234c1s v3p0270c1m v3p0272c1s
v3p0287c2s v3p0336c1s v3p0356c2s
v3p0362c1s v3p0365c1s v4p0072c2s
v4p0128c2s v4p0146c2s v4p0293c1s
v4p0353c2s v4p0460c1s v4p0489c1s
v5p0087c2s v5p0092c2s v5p0302c2s
Morris, J.A. v6p0231c2s
Morris, J.C. v1p0839c1s
v2p0268c2s
Morris, J.C. and Gooch, F.A.
v5p0030c1s
Morris, J.E. v5p0142c1s
v5p0616c2s v6p0690c2s
Morris, J.G. v1p0076c1s
v1p0145c1s v1p0206c2m v1p0420c1s
v1p0512c2s v1p0519c1s v1p0777c1m
v1p0777c2m v1p0807c2s v1p1306c1s
v2p0269c1m v2p0366c1s v3p0428c2s
v3p0440c1s v4p0383c1s
Morris, J.H. v1p0233c1s
v1p0411c2s v1p0546c2s
Morris, J.J. v3p0304c2s
v3p0373c1s
Morris, J.M. v1p0276c2s
Morris, J.R. v2p0081c1s
Morris, J.W. v1p0469c2s
v1p1436c1s
Morris, L. v2p0030c2s
v2p0132c1s v2p0323c2s v3p0335c2s
v3p0386c1s v3p0394c1s v3p0453c1s
v4p0027c1s v4p0179c2s v5p0055c1s
v5p0486c1s v6p0151c2s
Morris, Lewis v4p0117c2s
v5p0327c1s v5p0420c2s v6p0590c2s
Morris, Lewis, Sir v4p0382c2s
v5p0451c2s
Morris, Lucy Noble v6p0013c1s
Morris, M. v2p0003c2s
v2p0118c1s v2p0122c2s v2p0147c2s
v2p0437c1s v3p0381c2s v4p0002c2s
v4p0034c2s v4p0510c2s v4p0518c1s
v4p0599c1s v5p0134c2s v5p0322c1s
v5p0368c2s v5p0456c1s
Morris, M.C.F. v3p0061c2s
Morris, M.C.O'C. v1p0482c1s
v1p0658c2s v1p0661c1s v1p0768c2s
v1p1125c2s v1p1215c1s
Morris, M.F. v1p0592c1s
Morris, M.O'C. v1p0675c2s
v1p0905c1s v4p0538c2s
Morris, M.P. v1p0910c2s
Morris, Martin v4p0015c2s
Morris, May v4p0178c2s
v6p0404c2s v6p0474c2s
Morris, Mowbray v3p0239c2s
Morris, N. v1p1419c2s
Morris, N.H. v1p0393c1s
v1p0394c1s v1p0914c1s v1p1350c1s
Morris, O. v4p0290c1s
v4p0290c2s
Morris, P.P. v1p0339c1s
Morris, R. v1p0092c2s
v1p0173c2s v1p1349c1m v2p0386c2s
v2p0438c2m v3p0024c1s v3p0318c1m
v4p0422c2s v4p0456c1s v6p0530c1s
v6p0657c2s
Morris, R. and Mayhew, A.L.
v3p0175c1s
Morris, R.G. v1p1205c1s
Morris, R.T. v3p0066c2s
v6p0440c2s
Morris, S. v3p0236c2s
Morris, T. v1p0665c1s
v5p0070c2s
Morris, T.A. v1p0445c2s
Morris, W. v1p0338c1s
v1p0491c2s v1p0529c2s v1p0607c2s
v1p0622c2s v1p0708c1s v1p0942c1s
v1p1336c1s v2p0023c2m v2p0106c1s
v2p0114c2s v2p0116c2s v2p0227c1s
v2p0282c2s v2p0323c2s v2p0370c2s
v2p0379c2s v3p0018c2s v3p0022c1s
v3p0060c1s v3p0174c2s v3p0188c1s
v3p0189c1s v3p0411c1s v4p0274c1s
v4p0533c2s v4p0631c1m v5p0154c2s
v5p0222c1s v5p0232c1s v5p0566c1s
v6p0033c2s v6p0376c1s
Morris, W. and Knowles, J.
v3p0461c1s
Morris, W. and Magnusson, E.
v1p1141c2s
Morris, W. and Magnusson, S.
v4p0253c1s
Morris, W. et al. v3p0399c1s
Morris, W.B. v2p0278c1s
v2p0332c2s v5p0083c2s
Morris, W.F. v5p0446c1s
Morris, W.G. v2p0034c2s
Morris, W.O. v2p0092c1s
v2p0439c1s v3p0007c2s v3p0022c2s
v3p0090c1s v3p0092c1s v3p0105c1s
v3p0139c1s v3p0144c1s v3p0158c2m
v3p0220c2s v3p0221c2m v3p0267c2s
v3p0298c1s v3p0310c1s v4p0004c1s
v4p0026c2s v4p0181c2s v4p0182c1s
v4p0195c2m v4p0613c2s v5p0082c2s
v5p0190c1s v5p0219c2s v5p0362c2s
v6p0086c2s
Morris, W.O'C. v1p0599c2s
v1p0656c1s v1p0657c2s v1p0659c1s
v1p0662c1s v1p0730c2s v1p0802c2s
v1p0917c2s v2p0049c1s v2p0060c1s
v2p0076c2s v2p0166c2s v2p0227c1s
v3p0105c1s v3p0138c1s v3p0160c2s
v3p0161c1s v3p0162c1s v3p0162c2s
v3p0221c2s v3p0268c1s v3p0285c1s
v3p0296c1s v3p0299c2s v3p0348c1s
v3p0384c1s v3p0390c1s v3p0417c1s
v3p0438c1m v3p0459c2s v4p0128c1s
v4p0141c1m v4p0181c2m v4p0193c1s
v4p0289c2s v4p0290c2s v4p0347c1s
v4p0348c1s v4p0356c1s v4p0365c1s
v4p0377c1s v4p0392c2m v4p0604c2s
v5p0136c2s v5p0295c2s v5p0296c1m
v5p0296c2m v5p0297c1s v5p0398c1s
v5p0404c1m v5p0411c2m v5p0438c2s
v5p0505c1s v5p0519c1s v5p0594c2s
v5p0625c1s v6p0258c1s v6p0327c1m

v6p0328c2s
Morris, W.O'Connor v4p0613c2m
Morris, W.P. v1p0459c2s
v1p0914c1s
Morris, W.S. v3p0117c1s
Morris, Wm. v4p0028c2s
Morris-Moore, J. v6p0673c1s
Morrish, G. v3p0040c2s
Morrison, A. v3p0257c1s
v4p0102c2s v4p0325c1s v5p0038c2s
v5p0202c2s v5p0270c1s v5p0309c1s
v5p0346c1s v5p0480c1s v6p0336c1s
Morrison, A.B. v6p0011c1s
v6p0548c2s
Morrison, A.H. v4p0074c1s
v4p0110c2s v4p0138c1s v4p0182c2s
v4p0193c1s v4p0279c1s v4p0280c1s
Morrison, C. v4p0144c1s
Morrison, C.G. v6p0105c2s
Morrison, Caroline W. v6p0525c1s
Morrison, D.M. v6p0665c1s
Morrison, G. v1p0876c2s
Morrison, G.B. v2p0390c1s
v3p0380c1s v6p0290c1s
Morrison, G.J. v1p0233c1s
v1p1366c1s v5p0109c2s v6p0400c1s
Morrison, G.S. v1p0104c2s
Morrison, H. v6p0539c1s
Morrison, J. v1p0468c2s
v1p0596c1s v1p1074c2s v1p1169c1s
v2p0095c1m v2p0095c2s v4p0167c1s
v4p0185c2s v4p0381c1s v4p0445c1s
v4p0523c1s v4p0556c2s v5p0175c1s
v5p0441c2s v5p0509c1m v5p0561c1s
v5p0609c1s v6p0613c2s v6p0625c2s
Morrison, J.C. v1p0475c2s
v1p1280c1s v2p0091c1s v6p0486c1s
Morrison, J.D. v4p0091c2s
Morrison, J.H. v2p0461c2s
v2p0462c1s v3p0069c1s v3p0114c2s
v5p0622c2s
Morrison, L. v6p0148c1s
Morrison, L.A. v2p0021c2s
v3p0465c2s v4p0383c2s
Morrison, M.A. v3p0265c1s
v4p0358c2s v4p0503c2s v5p0065c1s
v5p0411c2s
Morrison, M.G. v1p0336c2s
v2p0250c1s v2p0359c2s v3p0243c1s
Morrison, Mary v6p0296c1s
Morrison, O., Miss v4p0586c1s
Morrison, R. v5p0112c2s
v5p0359c2s
Morrison, R. et al. v3p0343c1s
Morrison, R.H. v4p0278c2s
Morrison, S.C. v6p0616c2s
Morrison, S.G. v6p0662c2s
v6p0670c1s v6p0703c2s
Morrison, T. v1p0945c1s
Morrison, W.D. v4p0139c2m
v4p0307c2s v4p0460c1s v5p0144c1s
v5p0467c1m v6p0158c1s
Morrison, W.M. v6p0144c2m
Morrison, W.R. v3p0347c1s
Morrissette, Kate H. v5p0335c2s
Morrissey, Eliz.L. v6p0115c2s
Morrissey, J.J. v5p0205c2s
v5p0263c1s
Morritt, C. v4p0349c1s
Morrow, E.W. v6p0612c1s
Morrow, F.St.J. v5p0272c2s
v5p0297c1m v6p0361c2s v6p0481c1s
Morrow, F.St.John v6p0392c1s
Morrow, H.W. v5p0062c2s
v5p0563c1s v6p0638c1s v6p0700c2s
Morrow, J. v5p0364c1s
Morrow, J.L. v3p0111c1s
Morrow, P.A. v5p0331c1s
Morrow, W.C. v4p0084c1s
v4p0285c1s v5p0238c2s v5p0257c2s
v5p0263c2s v5p0291c1s v5p0430c2s
v5p0589c2s v6p0130c2s v6p0620c1s
Morrow, W.G. v4p0087c2s
Morse, A. v1p0752c1s
Morse, A.B. v1p1194c1s
Morse, A.D. v2p0232c1m
v3p0011c1s v3p0012c2s v3p0086c1s
v3p0114c2s v3p0188c2s v3p0383c2s
v4p0429c1m v4p0481c2s v5p0003c2s
v5p0158c2s
Morse, A.G. v1p0997c1s
Morse, A.L. v2p0422c2s
Morse, A.P. v1p1343c1s
Morse, A.S. v6p0266c1s
v6p0445c1s
Morse, C. v5p0329c2s
v6p0228c1s v6p0469c1s
Morse, C.A. v5p0497c2s
Morse, C.A.L. v4p0028c1s
v5p0633c2s
Morse, C.F. v1p0818c1s
v1p1107c1s v1p1329c2s
Morse, C.H. v3p0242c1s
v5p0163c2s
Morse, C.M. v3p0356c2s
v3p0472c1s v4p0477c2s
Morse, D. v1p0231c1s
Morse, E. v3p0306c2s
Morse, E.L. v3p0437c1s
v5p0189c1s
Morse, E.L.C. v4p0116c1s
v6p0170c2s v6p0397c2s v6p0512c1s
v6p0572c2s v6p0624c1m
Morse, E.R. v3p0267c2s
Morse, E.S. v1p0041c1s
v1p0156c1m v1p0359c1s v1p0366c1s
v1p0433c2s v1p0578c1s v1p0678c1s
v1p0678c2s v1p0679c1m v1p0681c2s
v1p0751c1s v1p0794c1s v1p0859c1m
v1p1045c2s v1p1173c1s v1p1189c1s
v1p1213c1s v2p0015c2s v2p0233c2s
v2p0274c1s v2p0274c2s v3p0012c1s
v3p0016c1s v3p0146c1s v3p0375c2s
v4p0139c2s v4p0388c1s v4p0394c2s
v4p0465c2s v4p0613c1s v5p0196c2s
v5p0292c1s v5p0319c2s v6p0119c2s
Morse, E.W. v5p0009c2s
Morse, F.H. v1p0437c1s
v1p0650c1s v1p1319c1s v1p1348c1s
Morse, F.L. v1p1189c2s
Morse, F.P. v6p0687c1s
Morse, F.R. v5p0459c1s
v6p0508c1s
Morse, F.W. v2p0340c2m
v4p0439c2s v4p0476c1s
Morse, G.W. v1p1076c1s
Morse, H.B. v6p0118c2s
Morse, J.G. v4p0013c2s
v4p0200c1s
Morse, J.H. v2p0011c1s
v2p0022c1s v2p0058c2s v2p0088c1s
v2p0140c1s v2p0155c1s v2p0191c1s
v2p0197c1s v2p0198c1s v2p0205c2s
v2p0230c1s v2p0233c1s v2p0249c2s
v2p0260c1s v2p0274c1s v2p0345c2s
v2p0346c1s v2p0365c2s v3p0109c2s
v3p0152c1s v3p0463c1s v4p0102c2s
v4p0216c2s v4p0430c2s v4p0551c2s
v5p0011c2s v5p0554c1s v6p0495c1s
Morse, J.T. v1p1349c2s
Morse, J.T., jr. v1p0006c1s
v1p0151c2s v1p0207c2s v1p0326c2s
v1p0350c2s v1p0405c2s v1p0497c2s
v1p0539c1s v1p0605c1s v1p0650c2m
v1p0731c2s v1p0859c1s v1p1330c1s
v1p1382c2s v2p0105c2s v3p0111c2s
v5p0168c2s v5p0646c1s v6p0555c2s
Morse, L.B. v4p0267c2s
v5p0139c1s
Morse, L.W. v2p0105c2s
Morse, M. v6p0069c2s
v6p0325c1s v6p0440c2s v6p0530c2s
Morse, M.A. v1p1358c2s
Morse, M.B. v1p0511c1s
v1p0772c2s v5p0268c2s
Morse, P.A. v1p0772c2s
Morse, R.M. v1p1397c1s
Morse, Ruth v4p0067c2s
Morse, S. v6p0316c1s
v6p0452c2s v6p0546c2s v6p0613c1s
v6p0684c1s
Morse, S.F.B. v1p0184c1s
v1p1290c2s
Morse, S.H. v1p0169c1s
v1p0236c2s v1p0777c1s v1p0852c1s
v1p1009c1s v1p1097c1s v1p1302c2s
v3p0409c1s v4p0478c2s
Morse, T.V. v5p0112c2s
Morse, W.F. v4p0219c2s
v6p0585c1s
Morse, W.H. v2p0253c2s
v3p0466c2s
Morse, W.R. v1p1160c1s
Morseby, J. v1p0535c2s
Morsell, W.F.C. v4p0320c2s
v5p0146c2s
Morselli, H. v2p0424c1s
Morshead, E.D.A. v2p0022c1s
v2p0028c2s v2p0090c1s v2p0181c2m
v2p0206c2m v2p0207c1s v2p0210c2s
v2p0249c1s v2p0298c2s v2p0304c1s
v2p0346c2s v2p0387c2s v2p0428c2s
v2p0435c1s v3p0003c2m v3p0276c2s
v3p0425c1s v4p0263c1s v4p0265c1s
v4p0304c1s v4p0560c1s v6p0155c2s
Morshead, P.A. v1p1095c1s
Morss, C.H. v6p0021c1s
Morss, C.H. and Brooks, Stratton D.
v6p0290c1s
Morss, S.E. v4p0447c2s
Morten, H. v5p0271c2s
v5p0570c1s v6p0462c2s
Mortillet, A.de v5p0385c1s
Mortillet, G.de v1p0793c1s
v5p0642c1s
Mortimer, A.G. and Newton, R.H.
v2p0042c1s
Mortimer, B. and Mortimer, J.R.
v1p0409c1s
Mortimer, F. v1p1367c1s
Mortimer, F.C. v5p0153c2s
v5p0288c2s v5p0317c1s
Mortimer, G. v3p0144c2s
v3p0467c1s v5p0606c1s v6p0201c1s
v6p0531c2s
Mortimer, J. v2p0241c1s
v2p0472c2s v2p0481c2s v4p0391c1s
Mortimer, J.R. v1p0409c1s
v2p0141c2s
Mortimer, J.R. and Garson, J.G.
v4p0046c2s
Mortimer, J.R. and Mortimer, B.
v1p0409c1s
Morton et al. v1p0387c2s
Morton, A. v1p1247c1s
v1p1390c1s v5p0155c1s
Morton, A.B. v5p0263c1s
Morton, A.C. v1p1077c1s
Morton, A.H. v5p0071c1s
v5p0135c1s v5p0196c2s v5p0292c1s
Morton, B. v5p0057c1s
Morton, C.H. v5p0140c1s
v5p0170c2s v5p0323c1s v5p0463c1s
v6p0303c2s v6p0524c2s v6p0679c1s
Morton, Caroline A. v5p0331c2s
Morton, E. v5p0003c1s
v5p0048c1s v5p0416c1s
Morton, E.A. v1p0985c1s
v3p0100c1s v3p0103c1s
Morton, E.H. v1p0665c1s
Morton, E.J.C. v4p0261c2s
Morton, E.P. v5p0192c2s
v5p0500c2s
Morton, E.W. v4p0016c2s
Morton, F. v1p0048c2s
v1p0077c2s v1p0469c1s v1p1244c2s
v1p1342c2s
Morton, F.W. v5p0220c1s
v5p0233c1s v5p0386c1s v5p0417c2s
v5p0466c1s v6p0070c1s v6p0139c1s
v6p0174c1s v6p0295c2s v6p0330c2s
v6p0411c2s v6p0501c1s v6p0598c2s
v6p0678c1s
Morton, G. v2p0092c1s
v4p0332c1s
Morton, G.H.,jr. v2p0093c2s
Morton, G.L. v2p0110c1s
Morton, H. v1p0084c2s
v1p0266c1s v1p0348c2s v1p0399c2s
v1p0400c1s v1p0401c2s v1p0463c2m
v1p0746c2s v1p0747c1s v1p0787c1s
v1p0866c1s v1p0875c2s v1p1019c1s
v1p1234c1s v1p1270c2s v1p1291c2s
v2p0036c2s v2p0138c2m v3p0132c2s
v3p0133c2s v4p0180c2s v4p0219c1s
v4p0435c2s v5p0010c1s v6p0583c1s
Morton, H.E. v6p0364c1s
Morton, Henry v5p0178c2s
Morton, I.W. v5p0130c2s
Morton, J. v6p0217c1s
v6p0311c1s v6p0619c2s
Morton, J.C. v3p0006c1m
v3p0006c2m v3p0279c1s v3p0386c1s
Morton, J.F. v2p0043c1s
Morton, J.M. v2p0114c1s
v2p0150c2s v2p0157c1s v2p0335c2s
v2p0430c1s
Morton, J.S. v4p0195c1s
v4p0462c1s v5p0600c2s
Morton, J.S. et al. v4p0593c1s
Morton, J.W. v2p0238c1s
v2p0453c1s
Morton, M. v2p0388c2s
Morton, M.B. v3p0369c2s
v4p0007c2s v4p0434c1s
Morton, N. v2p0199c2s
Morton, O.P. v1p1048c2s
Morton, O.T. v2p0353c1s
v3p0086c2s v5p0016c2s v5p0028c2s
v5p0457c1s
Morton, P. v6p0445c2s
v6p0515c1s v6p0529c1s v6p0654c1s
Morton, P. and Kingsley, D.P.
v6p0322c1s
Morton, S.G. v1p0311c2s
v1p0396c2s v1p0618c2s v1p0636c1s
v1p0784c2s v1p0947c2s v1p0993c1s
v1p0997c2s
Morton, S.T. v2p0322c1s
Morton, T.C. v3p0433c1s
Morton, T.W. v5p0315c1s
Morton, W. v1p1026c2s
Morton, W.J. v1p0349c1s
Morton, W.K. v3p0106c1s
v4p0044c2s
Morton, W.S. v5p0156c1s
v5p0156c2s
Morwood, V.S. v1p0522c1s
Mory, R.B. v5p0604c2s
v5p0636c2s
Morys, Myra V. v5p0640c2s
Mosby, E.F. v1p0035c2s
v1p0049c1s v1p0245c2s v1p0483c1s
v1p0568c2s v1p0782c1s v2p0023c1s
v2p0051c1s v2p0291c2s v6p0663c1s
Mosby, E.S. v1p1374c1s
Mosby, Harriet E.D. v6p0311c1s
Mosby, J.S. v5p0124c2s
v5p0134c1s v5p0199c2s v5p0446c1s
v6p0517c2s
Mosby, S. v4p0565c1s
Mosby, Speed v5p0138c1s
Mosby, T.S. v6p0146c2s
v6p0154c2s v6p0230c2s v6p0422c2s
Moscheles, C. v1p0936c1s
Moscheles, F. v3p0024c1s
v4p0075c1s v4p0164c1s v5p0367c2s
Moscheles, F. et al. v4p0557c2s
Moscow, M. v5p0458c1s
Moseley, C.B. v5p0416c1s

Moseley, E.A. v6p0528c1s
Moseley, E.L. v5p0194c2s v6p0569c2s
Moseley, E.S. v1p0955c1s
Moseley, G.Van H. v6p0031c1s v6p0400c1s
Moseley, H. v1p0524c1s
Moseley, H.F. v1p0752c1s
Moseley, H.H. v2p0214c2s
Moseley, H.N. v1p0007c1s v1p0214c1s v1p0340c1s v1p0401c2s v1p0621c2s v1p0875c1s v1p1040c1s v1p1263c1s v2p0020c2s v2p0032c1s v2p0069c1s v2p0102c2m v2p0173c1s v2p0201c2s v2p0213c1s v2p0276c2s v2p0334c2m v2p0393c1s v2p0393c2m v2p0396c2s v2p0439c2s v2p0448c1s
Moseley, H.N. et al. v2p0153c2s
Moseley, H.P. and Gooch, F.A. v4p0028c2s
Moseley, L. v1p0314c2s
Moseley, L.H. v5p0054c1s
Mosely, A. v6p0192c2s v6p0240c2s v6p0431c1s v6p0574c2s
Mosely, Alfred v6p0652c1s v6p0708c2s
Mosely, B.L. v2p0058c2s
Mosely, E.L. v6p0412c2s
Mosely, W.S. v1p0912c1s
Mosenthal, H.de v5p0172c2s v5p0412c2s
Moser, C.K. v6p0083c2s
Moser, E.S. v4p0507c1s
Moser, J. v2p0019c1m v2p0027c1s v2p0104c1s v3p0018c1s
Moses, A. v4p0152c1s v4p0233c1s v4p0285c2s v4p0302c2s v5p0363c2s v6p0275c2s
Moses, A.J. v4p0142c1s v5p0180c2s v6p0390c2s v6p0411c1s v6p0424c1s
Moses, B. v1p0430c2s v1p0516c1s v1p0563c2s v1p1254c1s v2p0186c2s v2p0385c1s v3p0086c1s v3p0277c1s v3p0374c2s v3p0398c1s v3p0418c1s v4p0124c1s v4p0144c1s v4p0287c2s v4p0368c1s v4p0501c2s v4p0535c1s v4p0539c2m v5p0036c1s v5p0088c1s v5p0176c1s v5p0302c2s v5p0567c2s v6p0016c2s v6p0026c1s v6p0069c1s v6p0170c1s v6p0170c2s v6p0249c1s v6p0276c2s v6p0370c1s v6p0493c2m v6p0507c1s v6p0561c1s v6p0601c2s v6p0607c2s v6p0608c1s v6p0631c1s
Moses, E.P. v4p0537c2s v4p0632c1s
Moses, F.J. v4p0036c2s v4p0068c2s
Moses, G.H. v4p0370c2s v4p0399c1s
Moses, J. v2p0087c2s v3p0208c1m
Moses, J.Garfield v6p0219c1s
Moses, J.W. v1p0205c1s
Moses, L. v6p0249c1s
Moses, L., jr. v3p0239c2s
Moses, M.J. v6p0074c2s v6p0075c1s v6p0181c2s v6p0461c2s v6p0647c1s
Moses, P.R. v5p0183c1m v5p0185c1s v5p0185c2s v5p0550c2s v6p0024c2m v6p0197c1s v6p0197c2m v6p0198c1s
Moses, R.G. v1p0021c1s v1p0250c1s v3p0074c1s
Moses, T.F. v6p0021c1s v6p0628c2s v6p0670c2s
Mosher, A. v6p0262c2s
Mosher, A.A. v3p0466c1s v4p0578c1s
Mosher, A.M. v3p0372c2s v5p0077c2s v5p0080c1s
Mosher, E.M. v2p0107c2s v4p0505c2s v5p0159c2s
Mosle, G.R. v3p0036c1s
Mosley, J.R. v6p0202c1s
Mosley, P. v2p0090c1s
Mosley, S. v5p0204c2s
Moss, C.E. v6p0486c1s
Moss, C.M. v3p0242c2s v3p0319c1s v4p0242c1s v4p0534c2s
Moss, C.T. v1p0496c2s
Moss, F. v5p0143c2s v5p0406c2s v5p0407c2s v5p0456c2m
Moss, F.J. v4p0354c2s
Moss, Frank v5p0391c2s v6p0506c2s
Moss, J. v4p0390c1m
Moss, J.A. v5p0151c1s
Moss, J.Edwards v5p0065c2s
Moss, J.F. v1p1327c2s
Moss, L. v1p0239c1s v1p0646c1s v1p0686c2s v1p0852c1s v1p1101c2s v1p1355c1s v2p0081c2s v2p0082c2s v2p0389c1s
Moss, M. v6p0124c1s v6p0222c2s v6p0223c1s v6p0243c2s v6p0280c1s v6p0392c2s v6p0401c2s v6p0420c2s v6p0508c1s v6p0543c1s v6p0653c1s
Moss, Mary v6p0052c2s v6p0075c2s v6p0241c2s v6p0347c2m v6p0349c1s v6p0434c1s v6p0461c1s v6p0461c2s v6p0592c1s v6p0618c1s v6p0698c2s
Moss, T.F. v1p0143c1s
Mosser, H. v5p0378c1s
Mosser, H. et al. v3p0300c1s
Mossman, R.C. v4p0050c2s
Mossman, S. v1p0595c1s v1p0947c1s v2p0078c2s v2p0134c1s v2p0233c2s v2p0261c2s v2p0288c2s v2p0411c2s v2p0442c2s
Mosso, A. v4p0071c2s v4p0370c2s v4p0441c1s v4p0442c1s v4p0629c1s
Mostyn, R. v3p0022c2s
Mostyn, S. v1p0339c1s
Moszkowski, A. v5p0395c1s
Moszkowski, M. v4p0189c1s v4p0389c2s v5p0373c2s
Motherwell, J.B. v1p0825c1s
Motherwell, W. v1p0466c1s v1p0711c1s
Motion, J.R. v6p0320c1s
Motley, J.L. v1p0090c1s v1p0354c2s v1p0461c1s v1p0994c1s v1p1066c2s v1p1343c1s
Motora, Y. v6p0449c2s
Motora, Yujiro v6p0575c2s
Motoro, Y. and Hall, G. .. v3p0115c2s
Motoro, Y. and Hall, G.S.. v3p0394c2s
Motschman, L.J. v6p0122c1s
Mott, A.J. v2p0007c1s v2p0027c2s v2p0227c2s v3p0006c2m v3p0111c1s v3p0157c1s v3p0165c1s
Mott, A.J., Miss v4p0096c2s
Mott, F. v6p0055c1s
Mott, E.P. v4p0517c1s
Mott, F.T. v1p0106c1s v1p0434c2s v2p0037c2s v2p0159c2s v4p0125c1s
Mott, G.S. v1p0496c1s v1p0980c2s v2p0015c2s v2p0113c1s v2p0426c1s v5p0620c2s
Mott, H. v1p0209c2s
Mott, J.B. v6p0416c2s
Mott, J.L. and Ewbank, T.. v1p0231c1s
Mott, J.M. v1p0748c2s
Mott, L. v6p0162c1s v6p0166c1s v6p0243c1s v6p0347c2s v6p0357c2s v6p0388c1s v6p0467c1s v6p0467c2s v6p0538c2s v6p0594c2s v6p0653c1s v6p0683c1s v6p0696c2s v6p0698c2s
Mott, L.S. v6p0381c2s
Mott, Lawrence v6p0339c1s
Mott, M.T. v1p0320c2s v2p0206c2s v4p0243c1s
Mott, Mary T. v2p0121c2s
Mott, T.A. v6p0162c1s
Mott, T.B. v5p0258c1s v6p0044c1s v6p0319c1s v6p0398c2s v6p0416c1s v6p0629c2s v6p0681c2s
Mott, T.B., Capt. v5p0360c1s v6p0666c1s
Mott, V. v3p0351c2s
Motte, A.V.La v5p0004c1s v5p0088c2s v5p0208c2s v5p0209c2s
Motte, L. v6p0231c1s
Motte, M.I. v1p0029c1s v1p0994c2s
Motte, M.J. v1p1114c1s v1p1206c1s
Mottern, R.W. v6p0540c2s
Mouat, F.J. v1p0212c1s v1p0230c1s v1p1052c2s v1p1053c1m v2p0208c1s v2p0418c2s v3p0207c2s v3p0344c2m v3p0445c1s v4p0459c2s
Mouchet, Gaston v5p0221c1s
Moudy, R.B. v6p0158c2s
Mougher, A. v3p0258c2s
Mouillard, L.P. v4p0004c2s v4p0228c1s
Mould, W.F. v6p0182c2s
Moulder, P.F. v5p0222c1s v5p0637c2s v5p0641c1s v5p0641c2s v6p0217c2s v6p0428c1s v6p0584c2s v6p0628c1s v6p0679c1s
Moule, C.W. v2p0035c1s
Moule, H. v1p0749c2s v1p0885c1s
Moule, H.C.G. v4p0585c2s
Moule, H.J. v3p0318c2s
Moule, H.M. v1p0004c1s v1p0019c1s v1p0720c2s
Moule, M. v3p0070c2s v4p0157c2s v4p0484c1s v4p0574c1s
Moulins, Amelia Des v6p0182c1s
Moulton, A.F. v6p0125c1s v6p0450c1s
Moulton, F.H. v6p0185c2s v6p0502c1s
Moulton, F.R. v4p0310c1s v4p0540c2s v5p0035c2m v5p0402c1s v5p0441c2s v5p0453c2s v6p0502c1s v6p0647c1s
Moulton, J.E. v1p1381c1s
Moulton, J.F. v3p0186c1s v3p0241c2s v4p0265c2s v4p0266c1s v4p0412c1s
Moulton, J.G. et al. v5p0334c1s
Moulton, J.H. v3p0184c1s v3p0471c2s v4p0057c1s v5p0066c2s v5p0115c1s v5p0433c2s v6p0055c1s v6p0272c2s v6p0273c1s v6p0478c2s
Moulton, L.C. v1p0466c2m v1p0627c2s v1p0747c2s v1p1380c1s v3p0172c1s v3p0177c2s v3p0203c1s v3p0259c2s v3p0269c2m v3p0282c1s v3p0403c1s v3p0420c2s v4p0028c1s v4p0050c2s v4p0240c2s v4p0261c1s v4p0346c1m v4p0383c2s v4p0409c2s v4p0477c2s v4p0577c1s v4p0578c1s v4p0619c1s v5p0348c1s
Moulton, R.G. v3p0087c1s v3p0454c1s v4p0055c1s v4p0058c1s v4p0311c2s v4p0509c2m
Moulton, R.G. et al. v4p0053c1s v4p0597c2s
Moulton, W.F. v5p0131c1s
Moulton, W.J. v6p0155c1s v6p0320c1s v6p0482c2s
Moultrie, G. v1p0459c1s
Moultrie, J. v1p1004c2s
Mount, C.B. v4p0142c1s
Mount, F.J. v3p0015c2s
Mount, M.W. v5p0320c2s v5p0637c1s v5p0639c1s
Mountain, W. v5p0435c2s
Mounteney, C. v5p0610c1s
Mounteney-Jephson, A.J. .. v6p0613c2s
Mountford, W. v1p0343c2s v1p0614c1s v1p0618c1s v1p0850c1s v1p0903c2s v1p1047c2s v1p1101c1s v1p1112c1s v1p1237c1s v1p1338c2s v1p1430c1s
Mountford, W. and Bixby, J.T. v1p0857c1s v1p0858c1s
Mountfort, G. v1p0569c1s
Mountgomery, J. v5p0578c1s
Mountjoy, J.W. v2p0235c2s
Mountmorres, Viscount v6p0005c2s
Mouret, E. v6p0388c1s v6p0552c2s
Mourey, G. v4p0029c2s v5p0011c2s v5p0014c1s v5p0043c1s v5p0094c1s v5p0102c2s v5p0116c1s v5p0122c1s v5p0139c1s v5p0156c2s v5p0171c2s v5p0195c2s v5p0221c2s v5p0277c1s v5p0280c1s v5p0331c1m v5p0332c1s v5p0430c2m v5p0431c1s v5p0432c1m v5p0462c1s v5p0473c1m v5p0473c2s v5p0476c1s v5p0485c1s v5p0490c1s v5p0492c1s v5p0552c1s v5p0575c1s v5p0576c1s v6p0033c2s v6p0545c1s v6p0595c1s
Mousey, G. v5p0326c2s
Moutton, J.H. v5p0430c1s
Mowat, J.G. v5p0091c1s v5p0355c2s
Mowatt, F. v6p0271c2s
Mowbray, J. v5p0330c2s
Mowbray, J.P. v5p0164c2m v5p0203c1s v5p0626c2s v6p0032c1s v6p0101c2s v6p0119c1s v6p0247c2s v6p0301c1s v6p0333c1s v6p0703c1s
Mowell, H.J.S. v4p0422c1s
Mowhawk, M. v1p0854c2s
Mowll, W. and Crundall, W. v5p0166c2s
Mowras, W.P. v1p1134c1s
Mowrey, G. v5p0157c2s
Mowry, A.M. v3p0064c1s v3p0331c2s v3p0433c2s v4p0116c2s v5p0566c1s
Mowry, D. v4p0119c1s v4p0476c2s v4p0596c2s v4p0603c2s v5p0377c1s v5p0443c1s v5p0472c1s v5p0628c2s v5p0636c1s v6p0031c2s v6p0071c2s v6p0125c2s v6p0179c1m v6p0190c1s v6p0194c1s v6p0301c1s v6p0348c1s v6p0377c2s v6p0390c2s v6p0418c1s v6p0423c1s v6p0435c2s v6p0456c1s v6p0535c1s
Mowry, D.E. v6p0367c1s
Mowry, Duane v4p0375c2s
Mowry, J.B. v5p0490c1s
Mowry, W.A. v2p0202c2s v2p0323c1m v2p0380c2s v2p0455c1s v3p0051c1s v3p0249c1s v3p0439c2s v3p0444c2s v4p0171c1s v4p0359c2s v4p0506c1m v5p0120c2s v5p0363c2s v5p0390c1s v5p0439c2s v5p0471c2s
Moxey, E.P. v6p0050c1s
Moxham, A.J. v6p0616c1s
Moxly, J.H.S. v4p0054c1s v4p0263c2s
Moxom, P.S. v2p0002c2s v2p0200c2s v2p0236c1m v3p0081c2s v3p0441c2s v4p0053c2s v4p0075c2s v4p0372c2s v4p0374c2s v4p0432c1s v4p0533c1s v4p0557c2s v5p0056c1s v5p0056c2s v5p0489c1s v5p0561c2s v6p0040c1s v6p0123c1s v6p0176c2s
Moxom, P.S. and Lee, M. .. v3p0119c1s
Moxon, H. v5p0380c1s
Moxon, M.T. v5p0596c1s
Moxon, W. v1p0606c1s

v2p0152c1s
Moy, T. v4p0004c2m
Moyer, F.E. v5p0038c1s
Moyer, R.B. v5p0582c2s
Moyes, D. v5p0165c1s
Moyes, J. v3p0073c2s
v4p0049c1s v4p0058c2s v4p0326c2s
v4p0424c1s v4p0491c1s v4p0611c1s
v5p0117c1s v5p0254c2s v6p0501c2s
Moyes, J. et al. v2p0226c1s
Moyle, E.J. v5p0634c2s
Moyle, H. v5p0089c1s
Moyle, T.N. v4p0422c1s
Moyle, W. v1p0046c2m
Moyna, E.G.J. v6p0006c1s
v6p0303c2s
Moynaham, F.E. v5p0100c2s
Moynahan, F.E. v5p0109c1s
v6p0164c2s
Moyne, S.C.Le and Shipman, C.
v5p0479c2s
Moynihan, H. v5p0459c1s
v6p0280c2s
Moysey, G.E. v5p0119c1s
v5p0458c1s v6p0310c2s
Mozle, E.J. v5p0457c2s
Mozley, F.W. v6p0386c2s
Mozley, J.B. v1p0688c2s
v1p0689c1s v1p0754c2s
Mozley, J.R. v1p0392c2s
v3p0175c2s v3p0295c1s v3p0343c2s
v4p0499c2s v5p0079c1s v6p0576c1s
Mozley, J.R. and Symonds, J.A.
v1p0170c2s
Mozoomdar, P.C. v2p0218c1m
v4p0280c1s v5p0115c1s v5p0284c2s
v5p0286c2m v6p0255c1s
Mozoomdar, Protap Chunder. v4p0071c2s
Muang-Thai v4p0522c2m
Muchall, C. v1p1391c1s
Muchall, M.E. v1p0921c2s
Muckerji, G. v6p0481c2s
Mucky, F.S. v5p0614c1s
Mudd, T. v4p0510c1s
Muddock, J.E. v3p0008c1s
v3p0157c2s v4p0012c1s
Mudford, W. v1p0666c1s
v1p0705c2s
Mudge, B.F. v1p0466c1s
v2p0046c2s v2p0053c1s v2p0149c1m
v2p0173c2s v2p0219c1s v2p0273c2m
Mudge, E.H. v4p0272c2s
v4p0369c1s v5p0242c1s v5p0374c1s
v5p0463c2s
Mudge, G.P. v5p0153c2s
Mudge, Isadore G. v6p0136c2s
Mudge, J. v4p0367c2m
v4p0456c1s v5p0079c2s v5p0080c1s
v5p0315c1s v5p0349c1s v6p0413c1s
v6p0603c1s v6p0707c2s
Mudge, James v4p0260c1s
v6p0202c1s
Mudge, T.H. v1p0130c2s
Mudge, W. v1p0368c1s
v1p0606c2s
Mudge, W.P. v5p0573c1s
Mudie, A. v5p0235c1s
Mudie, M. v2p0201c1s
v3p0216c1s v5p0180c2s
Mueller, A. v1p0793c2s
Mueller, F.M. v4p0473c1s
Mueller, J. v1p0515c2s
Mueller, J.H. v4p0374c1s
Mueller, M. and Douglas, I.A.
v4p0408c1s
Mueller, O.H. v5p0472c2s
Muench, H. v6p0255c1s
Muenscher, J. v1p0119c2s
v1p0123c1s v1p0681c2s
Muenter, H. v1p0690c1s
Mufson, T. v6p0175c2s
Muhlan, Q. v2p0042c2s
Muhleman, M.L. v4p0283c2s
v4p0378c1s v4p0378c2s v4p0595c1s
v5p0237c2s v6p0477c1s
Muhlenberg, F.A. v1p0778c1s
v1p0879c2s
Muir, A. v1p0579c2s
v2p0182c1s v2p0246c1s v4p0354c2s
Muir, A.F. v2p0214c2s
v2p0348c1s v3p0357c1s
Muir, C.H. v5p0290c2s
Muir, F. v3p0116c1s
Muir, H. v4p0567c2s
v5p0037c1s
Muir, J. v1p0152c2s
v1p0187c2s v1p0188c1m v1p0188c2s
v1p0291c2s v1p0524c1s v1p0524c2m
v1p0589c1s v1p0614c2s v1p1178c2s
v1p1188c1m v1p1196c1m v1p1213c2s
v1p1241c1s v1p1329c2s v1p1335c1s
v1p1428c2s v1p1438c1m v2p0038c1s
v3p0236c2s v3p0474c2m v4p0227c1s
v5p0004c1s v5p0011c1s v5p0063c2s
v5p0214c2s v5p0432c2s v5p0481c2s
v5p0626c1s v5p0644c1s v5p0644c2m
v6p0139c2s v6p0257c2s v6p0656c2s
v6p0668c2s v6p0711c2s
Muir, M. v2p0237c1s
Muir, M.M.P. v1p0022c2s
v1p0210c1s v1p0224c1m v1p0225c1m
v1p0401c2s v1p0501c1s v1p0625c1s
v1p0899c2s v1p0996c2s v1p1100c2s
v1p1162c1s v1p1304c2s v2p0027c2s
v2p0076c2m v2p0390c2s v3p0075c2s
v3p0076c1m v4p0099c1m v4p0368c2s
v4p0424c2s
Muir, M.P. v1p1164c1s
Muir, R. v6p0381c1s
Muir, T. v3p0055c2s
Muir, W. v5p0381c2s
Muir, W.K. v1p0395c2s
Muir, Ward v6p0142c2s
v6p0426c2m
Muirhead, A.C. v6p0179c2s
Muirhead, F. v2p0059c2s
v2p0422c2s v2p0449c2s
Muirhead, J.F. v4p0594c2s
v6p0047c1m v6p0276c1s
Muirhead, J.H. v3p0287c2s
v3p0357c2s v4p0128c1s v4p0187c2s
v4p0194c2s v5p0281c2s v5p0319c1s
v5p0426c1s v5p0617c1s v6p0122c1s
v6p0143c2s v6p0191c2s v6p0490c1s
Muirhead, John H. v6p0707c2s
Muirhead, L.A. v5p0316c2s
v5p0520c2s
Muirhead, W. v5p0111c1s
Mukasa, H. v6p0205c1s
Mukhopadhyay, A. v3p0285c2s
Mukhopadhyay, A. et al. .. v3p0096c2s
Mulcaster, R. v1p0391c2s
Mulckow, R. v5p0379c1s
Muldoon, P.J. v1p0948c2s
Mulford, C.E. v6p0051c2s
v6p0103c2s v6p0223c2s
Mulford, E. v1p0812c2s
v2p0455c2s
Mulford, M.J. v5p0579c1s
Mulford, P. v1p0089c2s
v1p0187c1s v1p0188c2s v1p0191c1s
v1p0196c1s v1p0235c2s v1p0298c1s
v1p0323c1s v1p0451c1s v1p0534c1s
v1p0539c2s v1p0597c2s v1p0616c2s
v1p0674c1s v1p0692c1s v1p0757c1s
v1p0845c2m v1p0993c2s v1p1057c1s
v1p1141c2s v1p1222c1s v1p1225c2s
v1p1256c1s v1p1335c1s v1p1371c2s
v1p1403c1s v1p1419c2s v1p1438c1s
v2p0007c1s
Mulford, W.R. v1p0879c2s
Mulhall, M. v2p0007c2s
v2p0134c1s v2p0178c1s v2p0178c2s
v2p0328c2s v2p0378c1s v2p0401c1s
v2p0413c1s v2p0434c2s v2p0448c2s
v3p0240c1s v3p0323c2s v4p0147c1s
v4p0566c2s
Mulhall, M., Mrs. v5p0014c2s
Mulhall, M.G. v1p0640c2s
v2p0087c1s v2p0134c1s v2p0182c1s
v2p0190c1s v2p0206c1s v2p0222c1s
v2p0288c1s v2p0306c2s v2p0353c2s
v2p0424c1s v2p0468c2s v3p0053c2s
v3p0408c2s v4p0059c1s v4p0091c1s
v4p0189c2s v4p0236c1s v4p0294c2s
v4p0352c1s v4p0596c2s v5p0016c2s
v5p0077c1s v5p0099c2s v5p0231c2s
v5p0244c2s v5p0245c1m v5p0248c1m
v5p0600c1s v5p0604c1s
Mulhall, M.G. et al. v2p0264c1s
Mulhall, M.N. v1p0203c1s
Mulhall, Mrs. v2p0373c1s
v3p0374c2s
Mulhall, W.G. v1p0898c2s
Mulhane, L.W. v4p0488c1s
Mulholland, C. v2p0291c2s
v2p0422c1s
Mulholland, R. v1p0461c1s
v1p0523c1s v1p0662c1s v1p0906c1s
v1p0978c1s v1p1040c2s v1p1259c2s
v1p1312c2s v1p1382c1s v1p1409c2s
v2p0041c1s v2p0151c2s v2p0158c1m
v2p0164c1s v2p0177c2s v2p0197c2s
v2p0247c1s v2p0276c1s v2p0276c2s
v2p0280c2s v2p0294c1s v2p0354c2s
v3p0085c2s v3p0100c2s v3p0114c2s
v3p0148c1s v3p0236c1s v3p0252c1s
v3p0317c2s v3p0356c1s v3p0474c1s
Mull, G.F. v2p0297c1s
v2p0358c2s v3p0140c2s v4p0185c2s
Mullaly, F.P. v2p0184c1s
v2p0274c1s
Mullaly, J. v1p0911c1s
Mullany, J.F. v4p0488c2s
v4p0598c1s v6p0104c2s
Mullany, J.J. v6p0547c2s
Mullany, K.F. v5p0307c1s
Mullen, B.H. v5p0334c2s
Mullen, J.M. v3p0443c1s
v6p0566c2s
Mullen, T.A. v1p1335c2s
Mullens, J. v1p0785c1m
Muller, A. v1p0794c2s
v2p0396c1s v6p0146c2s
Muller, A.A. v5p0348c1s
Muller, C. v1p0140c2s
Muller, D. et al. v5p0024c1s
v5p0537c2s
Muller, D.H. v4p0515c1s
v5p0155c2s
Muller, E. v1p0333c2s
v1p0462c2s v1p1181c2s
Muller, F. v1p1041c2s
v1p1073c1s v1p1296c1s
Muller, F.C.G. v1p1250c2s
v2p0419c2s
Muller, F.H. v1p0461c2s
Muller, F.M. v1p0333c2s
v1p0628c2s v2p0061c2s v2p0160c2s
v2p0249c2s v2p0305c1s v3p0015c2s
v3p0056c2s v3p0126c2s v4p0007c1s
v4p0032c2s v4p0063c2s v4p0077c2s
v4p0130c2m v4p0147c2s v4p0200c1s
v4p0228c2s v4p0278c2s v4p0313c2s
v4p0320c1m v4p0320c2m v4p0350c1s
v4p0376c1s v4p0408c1s v4p0436c1s
v4p0478c2m v4p0479c1s v4p0479c2s
v4p0502c2s v4p0503c1s v4p0537c2s
v4p0542c1s v4p0558c1s v4p0575c1m
v4p0601c1m v5p0081c1s v5p0081c2s
v5p0132c2s v5p0231c1s v5p0337c1s
v5p0510c2s v5p0566c2s
Muller, F.M. and Douglas, J.A.
v4p0301c2s
Muller, F.M. and McClure, M.L.H.
v3p0200c2s
Muller, F.M. et al. v3p0146c1s
Muller, F.Max v3p0023c1s
v3p0090c2m v3p0295c1s v3p0306c1s
v3p0311c2s v3p0314c1s v3p0375c1s
v3p0376c1s v3p0420c2s v3p0425c2s
v4p0040c1s v4p0121c2s v4p0541c1s
v4p0637c1s v5p0125c2s v5p0177c2s
v5p0284c2s v5p0316c2s v5p0341c1s
v5p0341c2s v5p0483c2s v5p0499c1s
v5p0640c2s
Muller, F.Max and Mercer, W.
v3p0375c2s
Muller, F.Max and Mivart, St G.
v3p0355c2s
Muller, F.Max et al. v3p0146c1s
Muller, F.P. v1p1383c2s
Muller, F.W. v6p0122c2s
v6p0240c2s
Muller, G. v6p0614c2m
Muller, G.F. v1p1012c2s
v2p0090c1s
Muller, G.M. v4p0587c1s
Muller, Georgina Max v5p0230c1s
Muller, H. v1p0107c1s
v1p0449c2s v1p0462c2m
v2p0417c1s
v4p0422c1s
Muller, H.W. and de la Rive, W.
v2p0137c2s
v1p0400c2s
Muller, J. v1p0003c1s
Muller, J.H. v1p0721c2s
Muller, J.W. v6p0095c1s
v6p0227c2s v6p0301c1s v6p0385c1s
v6p0500c2s v6p0577c1s
Muller, K. v1p0438c2s
Muller, M. v1p0262c2s
v1p0303c2s v1p0333c1s v1p0390c2s
v1p0438c1s v1p0450c1s v1p0514c1s
v1p0584c2s v1p0630c1s v1p0690c1s
v1p0723c2m v1p0724c1s v1p0724c2s
v1p0852c1s v1p0853c2s v1p0858c1s
v1p0891c2s v1p0922c1s v1p1086c1s
v1p1094c2s v1p1095c1s v1p1095c2s
v1p1140c2s v1p1156c1s v1p1157c1m
v1p1234c2s v1p1296c1s v1p1301c1s
v1p1302c2s v2p0045c1s v2p0203c1s
v2p0207c2s v2p0208c1s v2p0217c2s
v2p0218c2s v2p0275c2s v2p0382c2s
v2p0386c2m v2p0409c1s v3p0162c2s
v3p0242c1s v3p0268c2s v4p0018c1s
v4p0077c2s v4p0300c1s v4p0351c2s
v5p0258c1s
Muller, M. and Baker, J.G.
v2p0409c1s
Muller, M. and Gilbert, S.
v4p0479c1s
Muller, M. and Taylor, I.. v2p0319c2s
Muller, Max v1p0037c1s
v1p0071c2s v1p0487c1s v2p0059c2m
v2p0068c2s v2p0074c2s v2p0181c1m
v2p0239c2s v2p0254c1s v2p0274c2s
v2p0305c1s v2p0388c2s v2p0409c1s
v2p0479c2s v3p0015c1s v3p0058c2s
v3p0211c1s v3p0234c1s v3p0242c2m
v3p0245c2s v3p0358c1s v3p0429c1s
v4p0109c1s v4p0193c1s
Muller, Max F. v3p0431c1s
Muller, O.T. v3p0356c1s
Muller, R. v3p0064c2s
Muller, T.M. v1p0604c2s
v4p0388c1s
Muller, W. v1p0922c1s
v1p1201c2s v5p0285c1s
Muller, W.H. v1p1354c2s
Muller, W.M. v4p0076c2s
v6p0073c2s
Mullett, C. v5p0213c1s
v5p0234c1s
Mullett, M. v6p0045c1s
Mullett, M.B. v5p0617c1s
Mullett, Mary B. v5p0040c1s
Mulley, R.E. v1p1416c2s
Mulligan, C.J. v5p0277c1s

Mulligan, J. v1p0262c1s
Mulligan, J.H. v5p0125c1s
Mulligan, J.M. v1p0144c1s
Mullin, E.H. v5p0034c1s
v5p0050c1s v5p0119c2s v5p0123c1s
v5p0171c1s v5p0183c1s v5p0315c1s
v5p0341c1s v5p0344c1s v5p0358c2s
v5p0412c2s v5p0435c1s v5p0553c1s
v5p0622c1s v6p0318c2s
Mullin, R.J. v4p0211c1s
Mullin, R.T. v4p0078c2s
v4p0094c1s v4p0585c1s
Mullinger, J.B. v1p1357c1s
v2p0130c2s v2p0144c2s v2p0169c1s
v2p0367c2s v2p0473c1s v3p0082c1s
v3p0316c2m
Mullinger, J.B. and Freeman, E.A.
v3p0333c1s
Mullins, A. v4p0301c2s
Mullins, E.R. v4p0510c1m
Mullins, J. v1p0744c1s
Mullins, J.D. v1p0742c2s
v1p0743c2s v2p0312c2s v5p0379c2s
Mulloch, D.M. v2p0065c2s
Mulready, W. v1p1262c2s
Mulroy, J. v1p0279c2s
Mulry, T.M. v5p0102c1s
Mulvany, C.P. v1p0014c2s
v1p0369c1s v1p0662c2s v1p0800c1s
Mulvey, T. v4p0408c1s
Mulville, A. v4p0587c1s
Mumford, A.A. v6p0497c2s
Mumford, E.W. v5p0267c1s
v6p0507c2s v6p0580c1s
Mumford, Eben v6p0365c2s
Mumford, G.H. v1p1033c1s
v1p1038c1s v1p1291c1s
Mumford, G.W. v1p1343c2s
Mumford, J.K. v4p0585c1s
v5p0501c1s v6p0386c1s
Mumford, M.E. v6p0233c2s
Mumford, Mrs. v1p1270c1s
Mun, Albert de, Count v6p0236c2s
Munby, A. v1p0204c2s
Munchausen, F.E.von v4p0224c1s
Mundella, A.J. v1p0544c2s
Mundle, T.M. v4p0324c1s
Mundy, A. v4p0280c1s
Mundy, A.J. v3p0265c2s
Munford, J.P. v3p0176c1s
Munford, T.T. v2p0098c1s
Munger, C.A. v1p0039c2s
v1p0044c2s v1p0136c1s v1p0466c1s
v1p0728c1s
Munger, L.M. v2p0206c1s
Munger, R.I. v4p0187c2s
Munger, T.T. v1p0307c2s
v1p0813c2s v2p0149c1s v2p0215c1s
v3p0040c2s v3p0041c1s v3p0128c1s
v3p0208c2s v3p0251c1s v3p0283c1s
v3p0291c2s v3p0380c1s v3p0397c2s
v4p0080c2s v4p0129c1s v4p0260c2s
v4p0388c2s v5p0303c1s v5p0451c1s
v6p0089c1s v6p0126c1s v6p0167c1s
v6p0176c1s v6p0283c2s v6p0284c1s
v6p0397c1s v6p0421c2s v6p0470c1s
v6p0513c2s v6p0696c1s
Munkittrick, R.K. v4p0220c1s
v4p0260c2s v5p0316c2s v6p0103c1s
Munn, C.C. v5p0202c2s
v5p0511c2s
Munn, H.T. v4p0637c1s
Munn, M.J. v6p0152c2s
v6p0389c2s
Munn, W.P. v5p0594c1s
Munnell, J.T. v2p0200c2s
v2p0326c1s
Munnell, T. v1p0107c2s
v1p0239c1s v1p0239c2s v1p0255c2s
v1p0356c2s v1p0440c1s v1p0626c1s
v1p0735c1s v1p1043c1s v1p1047c2s
v1p1237c2s v1p1271c1s v1p1423c2s
v2p0027c2s v2p0043c1s v2p0310c1s
v2p0429c2s
Munro v6p0091c1s
Munro, Alick v5p0479c1s
Munro, Capt. v1p0112c2s
v1p1324c1s
Munro, D.B. v2p0206c1s
Munro, D.C. v5p0095c1s
v5p0192c1s v5p0351c1s v5p0374c1s
v5p0577c2s v6p0673c1s
Munro, G.C. v1p0166c2s
v1p0425c2s v1p0455c2s v1p0560c2s
v1p0567c1s v1p0701c1s v1p0704c2s
v1p0730c1s v1p0735c2s v1p1174c2s
v1p1255c1s v1p1265c2s v1p1335c2s
v1p1361c1s v1p1408c2s v2p0182c2s
Munro, H.A.J. and Kebbel, T.E.
v1p0727c2s
Munro, H.H. v5p0532c1s
Munro, H.I., Mrs. v5p0199c2s
Munro, I. v1p0717c1s
v1p1128c1s v1p1400c1s
Munro, J. v1p0209c2s
v1p0399c1s v1p1052c1s v1p1196c2s
v1p1224c2s v1p1291c1s v2p0037c2s
v2p0136c2s v2p0137c1s v2p0138c1m
v2p0340c2s v2p0432c2s v2p0433c1s
v3p0113c2s v4p0168c2s v4p0176c2m
v4p0309c2s v4p0403c1s v4p0497c1s
Munro, J.A.R. v3p0108c2m
v4p0380c1s v5p0291c2s v5p0396c2s
v5p0458c2s v6p0489c2s v6p0503c1s
Munro, J.A.R. and Anthony, H.M.
v5p0396c2s
Munro, J.A.R. and Hogarth, D.G.
v3p0023c2s
Munro, J.A.R. and Tubbs, H.A.
v4p0145c2s
Munro, J.E.C. v4p0085c2s
Munro, J.K. v6p0161c2s
Munro, J.K. and Collinson, B.W.
v6p0358c1s
Munro, M.F. v5p0106c1s
Munro, N. v4p0517c1s
v4p0522c1s v5p0166c1s v5p0309c1s
v5p0312c2s v5p0317c1m v5p0437c1s
v6p0117c1s
Munro, N.G. v2p0284c1s
v2p0440c1s
Munro, Neil v5p0527c1s
v6p0163c1s
Munro, R. v1p0051c2s
v2p0246c2s v2p0278c1s v3p0204c2s
v3p0315c1s v3p0317c1s v3p0379c1s
v3p0388c1s v3p0410c2s v3p0435c1s
v4p0016c2s v4p0202c1s v4p0457c1s
v4p0536c1s v4p0583c2s v5p0171c1s
v6p0097c2s v6p0278c1s v6p0655c2s
Munro, W. v2p0058c1s
v2p0080c2s v2p0248c2s v2p0369c2s
Munro, W.B. v5p0091c2s
v5p0559c1s v5p0615c1s v6p0323c1s
Munro, W.F. v1p1416c1s
Munro, W.H. v5p0016c2s
Munroe, A.C. v1p1056c1s
Munroe, B. v4p0158c1s
Munroe, C.E. v2p0103c2s
v2p0150c2m v2p0193c2m v2p0239c2s
v3p0076c1s v3p0147c1m v3p0187c1s
v3p0458c1s v4p0611c1s v5p0200c1m
v5p0533c2s v6p0106c2s
Munroe, H. v1p1403c1s
v4p0620c1s
Munroe, J. v4p0567c1m
Munroe, J.E.C. v4p0553c1s
Munroe, J.P. v3p0129c2s
v5p0102c2s v5p0135c1s v5p0178c2s
v5p0517c2s v5p0616c2s v6p0204c1s
v6p0399c2s v6p0405c1s v6p0547c1s
v6p0635c2s
Munroe, Jas.P. and Moors, J.F.
v6p0572c2s
Munroe, K. v3p0384c2s
v4p0011c1s v4p0331c2s v5p0280c2s
Munroe, L. v5p0623c1s
Munroe, N. v1p1288c1s
Munroe, R. v3p0166c1s
Munroe, S. v4p0332c2s
Munscher, J. v1p0685c1s
Munsell, F. v1p0880c2s
Munsell, J. v1p0271c1s
Munsell, L. v6p0665c1s
Munsell, O.S. v1p0687c2s
v1p0797c2s v1p1000c1s v1p1097c2s
Munsen, W.H. v2p0426c2s
Munsey, F. v5p0147c1s
Munsey, F.A. v4p0003c2s
v4p0010c2s v4p0046c1s v4p0107c2s
v4p0153c2s v4p0178c1s v4p0264c1s
v4p0270c1s v4p0305c2s v4p0476c1s
v4p0520c2s v4p0565c2s v4p0620c1s
v5p0311c1s v5p0354c1s v5p0392c1s
v5p0477c1s v5p0485c2s v6p0043c2s
v6p0044c1m v6p0046c2s v6p0131c1s
v6p0346c1s v6p0436c2s v6p0546c1s
v6p0551c1m
Munson, C.L. v4p0120c2s
Munson, C.La R. v4p0438c2s
Munson, E.L. v5p0591c2s
Munson, H.B. v5p0409c1s
Munson, J.W. v6p0431c1s
Munson, L.E. v3p0065c1s
v3p0259c1s v3p0286c1s v5p0091c1s
Munson, L.S. v5p0103c2s
Munson, M.A. v1p0781c2s
v1p1368c2s v1p1389c2s
Munson, W.M. v4p0434c2s
v5p0271c2s
Munson, W.T. v1p0847c2s
Munster, A.M. v1p1309c1s
Munster, A.M., Mrs. v1p1174c1s
v1p1220c2s
Munster, Countess of v3p0376c1s
Munster, M.C.F. v1p0652c2s
Munsterberg, E. v5p0102c1s
v6p0508c1s v6p0508c2s
Munsterberg, H. v4p0033c2s
v4p0036c2s v4p0273c2s v4p0364c2s
v4p0415c2s v4p0465c1s v4p0465c2s
v4p0487c1s v4p0537c2s v4p0549c1s
v4p0561c1s v5p0002c1s v5p0015c1s
v5p0017c1s v5p0031c1s v5p0037c2s
v5p0158c1s v5p0231c1s v5p0257c1s
v5p0397c1m v5p0470c2m v5p0471c1m
v5p0511c1s v5p0512c1s v5p0635c1s
v6p0036c1s v6p0111c1s v6p0211c1s
v6p0309c1s v6p0323c2s v6p0563c2m
Munsterberg, H. et al. ... v6p0102c1s
Munsterberg, Hugo v6p0374c1s
v6p0708c2s
Munthe, A. v3p0067c2s
v3p0117c1s v3p0286c1s
Muntz, A.I. v4p0498c1s
Muntz, E. v2p0054c2s
v2p0299c1m v3p0289c1s v4p0369c1s
v4p0605c1m
Muntz, Eugene v5p0428c1s
v5p0452c1s
Muntz, I. v4p0060c1s
v4p0299c1s v4p0394c2s
Munz, S. v3p0105c2s
v3p0246c2s v4p0242c2s v5p0459c1s
Muralt, C.L.de v6p0199c1s
Murasky, F.J. v4p0636c1s
Murbach, L. v6p0195c1s
v6p0261c2s
Murch, C. v3p0131c1s
Murchison, C. v1p0019c2s
Murchison, R.I. v1p0025c1s
v1p1366c1s
Murchison, R.I., Sir v1p0054c2s
v1p0506c1s v1p0508c1s v1p0509c1s
Murcutt, A.L.A. v6p0336c2s
Murdoch, D. v1p0439c2s
Murdoch, D.L. v5p0473c1s
Murdoch, G.W. v4p0142c2s
v4p0355c1s v4p0375c1s v6p0577c2s
v6p0707c2s
Murdoch, J. v1p0657c1s
v1p0721c2s v1p0964c1s v2p0146c1s
v2p0248c2s v3p0019c2s v3p0142c2m
v3p0336c1s v3p0461c1s v4p0392c1s
v5p0064c1s v5p0074c1s v5p0173c2s
v5p0195c1s
Murdoch, J.E. v3p0387c2s
v3p0388c1s
Murdoch, John v3p0185c1s
v5p0010c2s
Murdoch, W.L. v2p0107c1s
Murdock v1p0215c1s
v1p0217c1s
Murdock, A. v2p0223c2s
Murdock, A.L. v3p0413c2s
Murdock, C.A. v2p0237c1s
v2p0355c2s v3p0057c1s v3p0077c2s
v5p0321c2s v6p0281c2s
Murdock, D.J. v5p0263c2s
Murdock, J. v1p0043c2s
v1p0096c2s v1p0206c2s v1p0289c2s
v1p0359c1s v1p0520c2s v1p0614c2s
v1p0624c1m v1p0677c2s v1p0690c1s
v1p0840c1s v1p1000c1s v1p1302c2s
v1p1321c1s v1p1378c1s
Murdock, J.B. v2p0271c2s
Murdock, J.S. v4p0131c2s
Murdock, W.G.B. v6p0442c2s
Murdock, W.G.Blaikie v6p0404c1s
Mure, W. v1p0601c1s
Muret, M. v5p0402c2s
Murfree, F.D. v3p0391c2s
Murfree, F.N.D. v3p0150c2s
Murfree, M.N. v2p0124c1s
v2p0196c2s v2p0215c2s v2p0356c2s
v2p0468c2s v3p0116c1s v3p0196c2s
v3p0210c1s v4p0258c2s v4p0391c2s
Murfree, W.L. v1p0609c2s
v1p0854c1s v2p0003c1s v2p0104c1s
v4p0592c2s
Murfree, W.L., sr. v2p0363c2s
Murger, H. v1p0522c1s
Murgoci, G.M. v6p0543c2s
Murgue, D. v2p0290c1s
v2p0459c1s
Murie, J. v1p0463c2s
Murison, R. v6p0481c1s
Murison, R.G. v5p0583c2s
v6p0062c1s
Murphy, A. v1p1317c1s
v5p0178c1s
Murphy, A.C. v2p0009c2s
v2p0353c1s v3p0386c1s v6p0631c1s
Murphy, Anna C. v3p0400c1s
Murphy, B. v1p0002c1s
v1p0027c1s v1p0043c1s v1p0049c1s
v1p0052c2m v1p0053c1s v1p0063c2m
v1p0072c2s v1p0080c2s v1p0103c1s
v1p0104c1s v1p0160c1s v1p0209c2s
v1p0223c1s v1p0226c2m v1p0245c1m
v1p0245c2m v1p0286c1s v1p0296c1s
v1p0304c2s v1p0360c2s v1p0378c2s
v1p0386c1s v1p0392c1s v1p0408c2s
v1p0409c2s v1p0412c2s v1p0414c2s
v1p0419c1s v1p0427c2s v1p0431c2s
v1p0479c1s v1p0487c1s v1p0489c2s
v1p0504c2s v1p0515c2s v1p0517c2s
v1p0529c2s v1p0540c1s v1p0555c2s
v1p0587c2s v1p0648c2s v1p0658c1s
v1p0669c2s v1p0673c2s v1p0705c1s
v1p0706c2s v1p0716c1s v1p0725c2s
v1p0727c1m v1p0728c2s v1p0733c2s
v1p0735c2s v1p0738c1s v1p0752c1s
v1p0763c2s v1p0802c2m v1p0817c2s
v1p0825c2s v1p0859c2s v1p0875c1s
v1p0888c2s v1p0890c1s v1p0894c1s
v1p0895c1s v1p0932c2s v1p0951c2s
v1p1029c1s v1p1086c2s v1p1089c2s
v1p1094c1s v1p1098c1s v1p1105c1s
v1p1118c2s v1p1119c2s v1p1125c1s

v1p1126c2s v1p1149c1s v1p1157c2s
v1p1158c1s v1p1197c1s v1p1215c1s
v1p1216c1m v1p1220c1s v1p1274c2s
v1p1278c1s v1p1288c2s v1p1299c1s
v1p1319c2s v1p1337c2s v1p1356c2s
v1p1365c2s v1p1370c2s v1p1387c1s
v1p1414c1m v1p1422c2s v1p1425c2m
v1p1426c2s v1p1439c2s v1p1442c1s
v2p0050c1s v2p0427c1s
Murphy, C. v6p0446c2s
Murphy, C.P. v5p0420c1s
Murphy, D. v1p0346c1s
v1p0937c1s v1p0957c1s v1p1265c1s
v2p0224c2s
Murphy, E. v6p0091c2s
Murphy, E.G. v5p0403c2s
v5p0472c1s v5p0483c2s v6p0448c1s
Murphy, Edgar G. v6p0235c2s
Murphy, F. v5p0572c1s
Murphy, H.C. v1p0594c2s
v1p0707c1s v1p1011c2s
Murphy, I.I. v4p0350c2s
Murphy, J. v1p0258c1s
v1p0698c2s v1p1389c1s v2p0170c1s
v3p0322c1s v3p0379c2s v3p0426c2s
v5p0295c2s v5p0331c1s v5p0491c1s
v6p0262c2s v6p0326c1s v6p0326c2s
v6p0636c2s
Murphy, J.C. v1p1097c2s
v1p1139c1s v1p1328c2s
Murphy, J.D. v6p0468c2s
v6p0496c1s
Murphy, J.G. v1p0581c2s
Murphy, J.H. v3p0120c1s
Murphy, J.J. v1p0056c1s
v1p0441c1s v1p0659c1s v1p0760c2s
v1p0839c1s v2p0005c1s v2p0425c1s
v3p0458c2s
Murphy, J.M. v3p0008c2s
v3p0198c1s v3p0420c2s v3p0439c1s
v4p0060c1s
Murphy, J.N. v1p0657c1s
v1p0891c1s v1p0934c1s v1p1202c2s
Murphy, J.P. v5p0142c1s
Murphy, J.R. v5p0393c1s
Murphy, J.T. v4p0374c2s
v5p0348c1s v5p0493c2s v5p0517c2s
v5p0583c1s v6p0248c1s v6p0253c2s
v6p0556c1s v6p0675c1s
Murphy, J.W. v1p0161c2m
Murphy, Ja. v5p0170c1s
Murphy, M. v1p1125c2s
v2p0227c1s v2p0228c2s
Murphy, N.O. v6p0639c2s
Murphy, N.P. v5p0490c1s
v5p0529c1s v6p0025c1s
Murphy, S.G. v6p0282c1s
Murphy, Starr J. v6p0546c1s
Murphy, T. v3p0154c2s
v3p0159c2s
Murphy, T.J. v3p0001c2s
Murphy, V.R. v3p0120c2s
v3p0333c2s
Murphy, W. v1p0792c1s
Murphy, W.J. v6p0698c2s
Murray, A. v1p0041c2s
v1p0145c2s v1p0188c1s v1p0206c2s
v1p0279c1s v1p0399c1s v1p0456c1s
v1p0534c1s v1p0591c2s v1p0759c2s
v1p0842c2s v1p0855c2s v1p0910c2s
v1p1324c1s v1p1330c1s v2p0384c2s
v3p0217c1s v5p0419c1s
Murray, A.G. v5p0149c1s
Murray, A.M. v3p0028c2s
v3p0171c1s v4p0038c2s v5p0481c1s
Murray, A.S. v1p0328c2s
v1p0555c2s v1p0601c1s v1p0670c2s
v1p0889c1s v1p0941c2s v1p0958c1s
v2p0025c2s v2p0190c1s v2p0249c2s
v2p0281c1s v3p0327c2s v3p0424c1s
v4p0422c1s v4p0600c2s v5p0263c1s
v6p0616c2s
Murray, A.T. v4p0044c2s
v4p0192c1s v6p0002c1s v6p0137c2s
Murray, B. v1p0409c2s
Murray, C. v5p0410c2s
Murray, C., Mrs. v2p0066c1s
Murray, C., Sir v5p0632c2s
Murray, C.A. v2p0181c2s
Murray, C.S. v2p0083c1s
v2p0191c2s v2p0262c1s v2p0467c1s
Murray, C.T. v4p0114c2s
v5p0119c1m
Murray, D. v1p0073c2s
v1p0936c2s v1p1367c1s v2p0313c2s
v6p0091c1s v6p0636c2s
Murray, D.A. v5p0229c2s
Murray, D.C. v1p0175c2s
v1p0316c2s v1p0320c2s v1p0491c2s
v1p0675c2s v1p0696c1s v1p0746c1s
v1p0940c2s v1p1199c1s v2p0028c1s
v2p0047c2s v2p0238c2s v2p0261c2s
v2p0364c1s v2p0389c1s v2p0403c1s
v2p0457c1s v3p0192c1s v3p0231c2s
v3p0311c1s v3p0406c1s v3p0458c1s
v4p0461c2s v5p0048c1s v5p0087c1s
v5p0122c1s v5p0137c1s v5p0144c2s
v5p0161c1s v5p0166c2s v5p0255c2s
v5p0256c2s v5p0274c2s v5p0301c2s
v5p0317c1s v5p0352c2s v5p0357c2s
v5p0370c2s v5p0385c2s v5p0500c2s
v5p0552c2s v5p0619c2s v5p0623c1s
v5p0646c1s v6p0088c2s v6p0298c1s
Murray, D.C. and Atkinson, J.W.
v6p0271c2s
Murray, D.C. and Braddon, E.
v3p0027c2s
Murray, D.C. and Herman, H.
v3p0312c2s v3p0466c1s
Murray, D.C. and Murray, H.
v3p0110c1s
Murray, D.Christie and Herman, H.
v4p0624c2s
Murray, E.C.G. v1p0414c1s
v1p0474c1s v1p0813c2s v1p0893c2s
v1p1280c2s v1p1313c1s v2p0203c2s
Murray, E.H. v2p0456c2s
Murray, E.H. and Taylor, John
v2p0456c2s
Murray, E.W. v3p0116c2s
Murray, G. v1p0896c2s
v1p1438c2s v3p0035c1s v3p0384c1s
v4p0095c1s v4p0355c2s v4p0406c1s
v4p0445c2s v4p0511c2s v5p0399c2s
v5p0516c2s v6p0131c1s v6p0212c2m
Murray, G. and Blackman, V.H.
v5p0125c1s
Murray, G., Sir v1p0987c1s
v1p1398c1s
Murray, G.H. v4p0565c1s
Murray, G.P. v5p0260c1s
Murray, G.R.M. et al. v4p0095c1s
Murray, Geo. v5p0417c2s
Murray, Gilbert v6p0464c1s
v6p0629c1s
Murray, H. v1p0193c2s
v1p0309c1s v1p0494c2s v3p0002c2s
v6p0258c2s v6p0294c1s
Murray, H. and Murray, D.C.
v3p0110c1s
Murray, H.G. v1p0787c1s
v1p1259c1s v2p0089c2s v2p0161c2s
v2p0267c2s v2p0445c2s
Murray, H.J.R. v3p0224c1s
Murray, J. v1p0224c1m
v1p0579c2s v1p1171c2s v1p1240c2s
v2p0220c1s v2p0319c1s v2p0457c1s
v3p0100c2m v3p0291c1s v3p0292c2s
v4p0019c2s v4p0039c1s v4p0230c1s
v4p0402c1s v4p0519c1s v5p0515c1s
v6p0090c2s v6p0388c2s v6p0523c1s
v6p0579c2s v6p0697c2s
Murray, J. and Renard, A.. v2p0393c1s
Murray, J. and Renard, M.A.
v2p0462c2s
Murray, J. et al. v4p0133c1s
v5p0022c1s
Murray, J.A. v1p0475c2s
v4p0413c2s v5p0420c1s
Murray, J.A.H. v3p0098c1s
v4p0153c2s v5p0191c2s v6p0239c2s
v6p0474c1s
Murray, J.A.H. and Platt, J.
v5p0301c2s
Murray, J.A.H. et al. v3p0090c1s
v4p0137c1s v6p0511c1s
Murray, J.C. v1p0074c1s
v1p0365c2s v1p1000c1s v1p1001c2s
v1p1300c2s v2p0272c2s v3p0039c1s
v3p0235c1s v3p0464c1s v4p0085c2s
v4p0138c1s v4p0163c1s v4p0253c1s
v4p0273c2s v4p0283c2s v4p0439c1s
v4p0439c2s v4p0542c1s v5p0498c1s
v6p0402c2s v6p0537c2s
Murray, J.E. v1p1068c2s
Murray, J.F. v1p0764c1m
Murray, J.F. et al. v1p0446c1s
Murray, J.K. v5p0421c2s
Murray, J.N. v1p0388c1s
Murray, J.O. v1p0351c1s
v2p0398c1s v3p0113c2s v4p0620c2s
Murray, J.O.F. v5p0626c2s
Murray, J.P. v6p0025c2s
Murray, John, Sir v5p0417c2m
Murray, John, Sir and Pullar, L.
v6p0578c1s
Murray, K. v5p0043c2s
v5p0169c1s v5p0300c2s v5p0531c1s
v5p0536c1s
Murray, K.B. v3p0094c2s
v3p0209c2s v5p0128c1s
Murray, L. v1p0201c2s
v1p0202c1m v1p0581c1s v1p0653c1s
v1p0698c2s v1p0722c1s v1p0755c2s
v1p0800c1s v1p1186c1s v1p1275c2s
v1p1418c2s
Murray, M.P. v5p0638c2s
Murray, Margaret P. v6p0520c1s
Murray, N. v1p1096c1s
Murray, P.W. v3p0224c2s
Murray, R. v3p0032c1s
v6p0001c2s v6p0313c1s v6p0563c1s
Murray, R.D. v1p0037c1s
v1p0749c2s
Murray, R.F. v3p0167c1s
v4p0135c1s
Murray, R.W. v3p0176c2s
Murray, S. v5p0244c1s
v5p0395c2s v6p0364c1s
Murray, S.J. v4p0038c1s
v4p0401c2s
Murray, S.L. v5p0037c2s
v5p0212c2s v6p0231c1s
Murray, T. v6p0125c1s
Murray, T.A.L. v4p0010c1s
Murray, V.E.H. v1p1082c1s
Murray, W. and Hillier, A.P.
v5p0362c2s
Murray, W., Mrs. v1p0749c1s
Murray, W.B. v4p0427c1s
v4p0519c2s
Murray, W.C. v5p0006c2s
v5p0234c2s
Murray, W.G. v1p0465c2s
Murray, W.H.H. v3p0073c1s
v3p0081c1s v3p0265c1s v3p0303c1s
v3p0441c1s
Murray-Aaron, E. v4p0296c1s
v5p0022c1s v5p0259c2s
Murray-Ayneley, H.G.M. ... v4p0559c1s
Murray-Nairne, C. v1p0758c2s
Murray-Smith, E.T., Mrs. . v6p0258c1s
v6p0476c1s
Murrell, A.E. v6p0107c2s
Mursell, A. v1p0432c2s
Murtfeldt, M.E. v2p0162c2s
Murtha, N.L. v5p0531c2s
Mury, F. v6p0049c2s
Musgrave, A. v1p0198c1s
v1p0839c2s v2p0046c1s v2p0294c2s
Musgrave, A., Sir v1p0486c2s
Musgrave, G.C. v5p0147c2s
Musgrave, G.W. v1p1047c1s
Musgrave, H. v3p0115c2s
v3p0231c1s v3p0254c1s v3p0278c1s
v3p0440c2s v4p0153c2s
Musgrave, W., Sir v1p0413c1s
Mushet, D. v1p0502c2s
v1p0665c1s v3p0223c1s
Mushet, R. v1p0664c1m
Mushet, R.F. v1p1251c1s
Musick, J.R. v1p0586c2s
v4p0250c2s v4p0378c2s v5p0040c1s
v5p0258c2s v5p0582c2s
Musket, R. v1p0272c2s
Muskett, J.J. v1p0012c2s
v1p0144c2s v3p0454c2s
Muss-Arnolt, W. v4p0138c2s
v4p0151c2s v4p0317c1s v4p0380c2s
v5p0058c1s v5p0058c2s v5p0061c1s
v5p0519c2s v6p0484c1s
Musselman, N.H. v5p0374c2s
Musser, J.H. v6p0408c2s
Musser, R.H. v2p0453c1s
Musset, A.de v1p0937c2s
Mussetter, F.S. v3p0405c2s
Mussey, C.F. v2p0355c2s
v2p0415c1s
Mussey, H.R. v6p0321c1s
v6p0451c2s
Musson, W.B. v5p0571c2s
Mustard, W.P. v5p0573c1m
v5p0612c2s v6p0239c2s
Musters, C., Mrs. v3p0246c2s
Musters, G.C. v1p0978c1s
Musters, G.G. v1p0978c1s
Mutch, W.J. v3p0193c1s
v6p0064c2s v6p0582c2s
Mute, C.A. v1p0153c2s
Muthman, W. and Eakle, A.S.
v4p0505c1s
Mutlow, T. v1p0409c1s
Mutsu, Hirokichi v5p0302c1s
v6p0336c2s
Muybridge, E. v2p0015c1s
v3p0014c1s
Muzzey, A.B. v1p0028c2s
v1p0217c1s v1p0275c1s v1p0323c2s
v1p0354c1s v1p0386c1s v1p0443c1s
v1p0527c2s v1p0625c2s v1p0740c2m
v1p0868c1s v1p1159c2m v1p1172c1s
v1p1270c1s v1p1324c1s v1p1407c1s
v1p1430c1s
v4p0249c1s
Muzzey, A.L. v4p0268c2s
v5p0552c2s
Muzzey, A.M. v3p0290c1s
Muzzey, D.S. v5p0094c1s
v5p0256c1s v5p0429c2s v5p0469c1s
v6p0415c2s
Muzzey, L.M v2p0396c2s
Muzzy, C.F. v1p0683c2s
Muzzy, F.E.D. v6p0234c2s
Myakishev, Lieut. v5p0565c2s
Myall, W. v1p0435c2s
v1p1398c2s v1p1406c2s v2p0221c2s
v2p0394c1s
Myatovich, C. v4p0285c1s
Mycrup, R. and Marsh, G.P.
v1p1274c2s
Myers, A.E. v2p0105c2s
v2p0290c2s v2p0445c1s
Myers, A.G. v6p0492c1s
Myers, A.W. v6p0033c2s
Myers, C.S. v4p0528c2s
v5p0279c1s v5p0400c1s v5p0613c2s
v6p0094c2s v6p0680c2s
Myers, D.P. v6p0231c2s
Myers, E. v1p0102c1s
v1p0368c2s v1p0419c1s v1p0781c1s

v1p1152c1s v2p0147c1s v2p0183c1s
v2p0231c1s v2p0346c1s v2p0386c2s
v2p0435c1s v2p0472c1s v3p0225c1s
v3p0271c1s v3p0326c1s v3p0361c2s
v3p0400c2s v4p0086c2s v4p0207c1s
v4p0581c2s v5p0012c1s v6p0492c2s
v6p0678c1s
Myers, E.J. v4p0500c2s
v5p0486c1s v5p0505c2s
Myers, F. v1p1435c1s
Myers, F.A. v4p0443c2s
Myers, F.E. v4p0124c2s
v4p0234c1s v4p0504c1s v4p0537c1s
v4p0594c1s v5p0088c1s v5p0161c2s
Myers, F.J. v5p0095c2s
Myers, F.W.H. v1p0369c2s
v1p0611c1s v1p0680c2s v1p0692c2s
v1p0814c2s v1p0850c2s v1p0913c2s
v1p1098c2s v1p1294c1s v1p1324c2s
v1p1372c2s v1p1424c2s v2p0016c2s
v2p0213c2m v2p0254c1s v2p0307c1s
v2p0337c1s v2p0343c2s v2p0358c1s
v2p0368c2s v2p0378c2s v2p0394c1s
v2p0417c1s v2p0481c1s v3p0006c1s
v3p0020c2s v3p0111c1s v3p0161c2s
v3p0166c1s v3p0188c2s v3p0424c2s
v4p0271c2s v4p0383c2s v4p0449c1s
v4p0464c1s v4p0560c1s v4p0569c2s
v5p0546c2s
Myers, F.W.H. and Gurney, E.
v2p0017c2m v2p0284c1s v2p0284c2s
v2p0338c1s v2p0440c1m v2p0445c1s
Myers, F.W.H. et al. v2p0440c1s
v4p0570c1s
Myers, G. v5p0130c2s
v5p0144c2s v5p0454c1s v5p0566c2s
v6p0151c1s v6p0453c2s
Myers, G.E. v6p0428c2s
Myers, G.L. v4p0038c1s
Myers, G.W. v5p0279c2s
v5p0366c1s v5p0548c2s v5p0549c2s
v6p0012c1s v6p0037c2s v6p0357c1s
v6p0406c1m v6p0406c2s
Myers, H.C. v6p0012c2s
v6p0673c1s
Myers, H.V. v5p0400c1s
Myers, J.H. v4p0384c2s
Myers, J.L. v4p0373c2s
Myers, J.L. and Evans, A.J.
v4p0139c1s
Myers, L.E. v2p0027c1s
Myers, L.S. v4p0453c1s
Myers, M. v6p0583c2s
Myers, M.B. v5p0030c2s
Myers, N.W.H. v1p1189c2s
Myers, P.V.N. v3p0225c1s
Myers, R.C. v1p0466c1s
v1p0609c2s
Myers, R.D. v5p0108c1s
Myers, T.B. v1p0091c1s
v1p0458c2s v1p0815c2s v2p0086c1s
Myers, W. v1p0950c1s
Myers, W.F.H. v2p0174c2s
Myers, W.H. and Gurney, E.
v2p0474c1s
Myers, W.S. v5p0364c2s
Mygatt, O.A. v3p0156c1s
v3p0420c2s
Mykilati, M. v5p0014c2s
Myles, C.E. v5p0174c1s
Myles, J. v1p0372c1s
Myles, M.E. v2p0025c1s
Myles, P. v3p0123c2s
Mylius, E. v1p0166c2s
v1p0237c1s v1p0463c2s v1p0652c1s
Mylne, J. v3p0211c2s
Mylne, R.S. v3p0019c1s
v3p0327c2s v3p0453c1s v4p0110c1s
Myon, R. v6p0392c1s
Myres, J.L. v4p0139c1s
v4p0352c1s v4p0355c1s v5p0136c2s
v5p0272c1s v5p0358c2s v5p0574c2s
v6p0013c2s v6p0641c1s
Myres, J.L. and Paton, W.R.
v4p0308c2s v5p0314c1m
Myrick, A.S. v2p0101c1s
Myrick, H. v5p0559c2s
v6p0308c1s
Myrick, H.W.B. v2p0180c2s
v2p0222c2s
Myrick, L.C.W. v6p0470c1s
Myrick, S. v4p0365c1s
Myrmidon v6p0360c1s
v6p0370c1s
Myrover, J.H. v1p1132c1s

Naake, J.T. v2p0261c1s
Nabersberg, B. v6p0564c2s
Nachtrieb, H.F. v4p0060c1s
v5p0594c1s
Nadaillac, Marquis de v2p0012c1s
v2p0214c2s v2p0352c1s v3p0273c2s
v4p0095c1s v4p0122c1s v4p0252c2s
Nadal, B.H. v1p0029c2s
v1p0169c2s v1p0216c1s v1p0641c1s
v1p0830c1s v1p0847c2s v1p1301c2s
Nadal, E.S. v1p0060c2s
v1p0104c1s v1p0152c2s v1p0169c2s
v1p0171c2s v1p0198c2s v1p0259c1s
v1p0277c1s v1p0354c2s v1p0414c2s
v1p0428c1s v1p0488c1s v1p0572c1s
v1p0765c2s v1p0830c2s v1p0953c2s
v1p1048c1s v1p1223c2s v1p1269c2s
v1p1282c1m v1p1298c1s v1p1337c2s
v1p1406c1s v2p0022c1s v2p0063c1s
v2p0313c1s v2p0452c1s v2p0470c1s
v3p0058c1s v3p0089c1s v3p0146c2s
v3p0476c2s v4p0182c2s v4p0343c2s
v4p0400c2s v4p0504c2s v4p0605c2s
v5p0067c1s v5p0271c1s v5p0574c1s
v6p0329c2s v6p0377c2s
Naden, C.C.W. v2p0037c2s
v2p0328c2s
Nagel, C. v4p0116c1s
v4p0323c2s
Nagel, O. v6p0248c2s
Nageli, C.v. v1p0899c2s
Nagle, A.F. v1p1065c1s
v4p0378c2s v4p0612c2s
Nagle, I.E. v1p1272c1s
Nagle, J.E. v1p0562c1s
v2p0306c1s
Nagler, F.L. v1p0515c2s
v1p0641c1s
Nahmer, H.S. v4p0077c1m
v4p0143c1s
Naidus, M.S. v5p0427c1s
Nair, C.Sankaran v6p0314c1s
Nairn, H. v1p1381c2s
Nairn, J. v5p0187c1s
Nairn, Jas. v5p0492c1s
Nakagawa, A. v5p0292c2s
Nakagawa, T.J. v3p0427c1s
v5p0302c2s
Nakamura, K. v5p0113c1s
v5p0258c2s
Nakamura, K. and Rice, C.E.
v6p0086c1s
Nakamura, Keijiro v4p0439c2s
Nakashima, R. v3p0143c1s
v3p0227c2s v3p0260c1s v3p0330c1s
Nall, E.M. v6p0041c2s
v6p0606c2s
Nall, E.W. v1p0519c2s
Nall, G.H. v5p0325c2s
Nama, T. v6p0338c1s
Name, A.Van v1p0235c2s
v1p0724c2s
Name, R.G.Van v5p0560c1s
v6p0148c2s v6p0159c1s v6p0161c2s
Nampon, A. v1p0519c1s
Nance, J.D. v3p0237c2s
Nance, W.B. v4p0600c1s
Nangis, Marquis de v1p0861c2s
v1p0964c2s v1p1013c1s v1p1369c2s
Nansen, F. v3p0307c1m
v4p0048c2s v4p0187c1s v4p0406c2s
v5p0027c1s v5p0216c1s v5p0397c2s
v5p0456c2s v6p0592c1s
Nanteuil, P.de v4p0590c2s
Naoroji, D. v3p0211c1m
v4p0428c2s
Naoroji, Dadabhai v4p0279c1s
Napier, A.S. v4p0637c2s
Napier, C. v4p0084c2s
Napier, C., Sir v2p0350c2s
Napier, C.O.G. v1p1364c2s
Napier, Capt. v1p1391c2s
Napier, E. v1p0012c2s
v1p0368c1s v1p1278c2s
Napier, E.E. v1p0733c1s
Napier, Eva v6p0619c1s
Napier, G. v5p0076c1s
Napier, J. v4p0205c2s
Napier, J.R. v1p0146c2s
Napier, John, Sir v5p0215c2s
Napier, Lady v6p0578c1s
v6p0706c2s
Napier, Lord v2p0108c1s
Napier, M. v1p0029c1s
v1p0283c1s v1p0558c2s v1p0623c1s
v1p0655c2s v1p1081c2s v1p1253c2s
v1p1388c1s
Napier, R.D. v1p0213c1s
v1p0463c1s
Napier, W., Sir v1p0866c2s
Napier, W.F.P. v1p0558c2s
v1p0987c1s v1p1397c2s
Napoleon III v1p0184c2s
Naquet, A. v1p1273c2s
v3p0052c1s v4p0157c2s
Naquet, A. and Stanton, T.
v4p0174c1s
Nares, G.S. v1p0055c2s
Nares, R. v1p0584c2s
Narey, Hope W. v4p0629c1s
Narrien, J. v1p1121c2s
Nasby, D.S. v6p0095c1s
Nash, A. v1p0277c1s
v1p0283c2s v1p0558c2s v1p0732c1s
v1p0744c2s v1p0801c1m v1p1011c2s
v1p1191c1s v1p1228c2s v3p0027c2s
Nash, A.C. v2p0019c1s
Nash, Anna S. v5p0094c1s
Nash, Augusta v4p0624c2s
Nash, B. v1p0674c1s
Nash, C.E. v3p0048c2s
Nash, C.S. v5p0463c2s
Nash, C.W. v5p0049c1s
v5p0063c1s v5p0063c2s v5p0064c1s
v5p0091c1s v5p0275c2s v6p0068c1s
v6p0499c2s v6p0706c2s
Nash, Clara A. v5p0371c1s
Nash, E. v5p0206c2s
Nash, E.B. v4p0246c2s
v4p0308c2s v4p0523c1s
Nash, E.P. v4p0242c1s
Nash, E.T. v5p0115c2s
Nash, F.B. v5p0587c1s
Nash, F.H. v2p0216c2s
v3p0237c2s
Nash, F.J. v6p0516c2s
Nash, F.P. v1p1150c2s
v4p0137c2s v4p0173c1s v4p0294c2s
v4p0561c1s v5p0300c1s v6p0296c2s
v6p0438c2s
Nash, F.P. and McDaniels, J.H.
v4p0021c1m
Nash, F.W. v5p0444c1s
v6p0192c2s v6p0493c2m v6p0631c1s
Nash, G. v2p0305c1s
v3p0305c1s
Nash, G.V. v6p0469c2s
Nash, H.A. v5p0265c2s
v5p0315c1s v5p0367c2s v5p0378c1s
v5p0419c2s v5p0453c1s v5p0525c1s
v5p0564c2s v5p0595c2s v5p0596c2s
v6p0001c1s v6p0124c2s v6p0287c2s
v6p0330c1s v6p0347c1s v6p0421c1s
v6p0553c1s v6p0608c2s v6p0690c2s
Nash, H.L. v5p0058c2s
Nash, H.S. v4p0020c1s
v5p0400c2s v5p0549c1s v5p0576c1s
v6p0156c2s v6p0296c1s v6p0307c2s
v6p0340c2s v6p0347c1s v6p0383c1s
v6p0536c2s v6p0599c2s
Nash, James L. v6p0072c2s
v6p0419c2s
Nash, L.A. v3p0111c1s
v5p0339c2s
Nash, Louisa O.H. v5p0003c2s
Nash, R.L. v2p0182c1s
v2p0317c1s
Nash, S. v2p0251c1s
Nash, S.P. v2p0096c2s
v2p0357c1s v6p0583c2s
Nash, T. v1p0206c2s
Nash, T.A. v3p0006c2s
Nash, T.R. v1p0756c1s
Nash, V. v4p0179c2s
v4p0314c1s v4p0553c1s v5p0285c1s
v5p0346c2s v5p0419c1s
Nash, W.A. v6p0162c1s
Nash, W.H. v1p1114c2s
Nasmith, J. v5p0353c2s
Nasmyth and Hume v1p0997c2s
Nasmyth, A. v1p0877c2s
Nasmyth, J. v1p0699c1s
v1p1152c2s v2p0296c2s v3p0266c2s
Nason, A.H. v6p0587c1s
Nason, Arthur H. v6p0147c2s
Nason, C.D. v5p0106c1s
v5p0178c2s
Nason, E. v1p0472c1s
v1p0636c2s v1p0909c1s v1p1330c1s
v1p1395c2s v1p1398c1s v1p1413c1s
v2p0361c1s
Nason, E.H. v5p0237c1s
v5p0319c2s v6p0395c2s v6p0500c1s
Nason, Emma H. v4p0259c2s
v4p0620c1s
Nason, F.L. v3p0064c2s
v3p0159c1s v3p0200c1s
Nason, F.S. v5p0339c1s
Nason, H.B. v5p0010c2s
Nassau, R.H. v4p0232c2s
v6p0007c2s v6p0222c1s
Nasse, E. v1p0286c1s
v3p0336c2s
Nast, E. v5p0305c1s
Nast, F. v1p0882c2s
Nast, W. v1p0114c2s
v1p0685c1s v1p0769c1s v1p0830c1s
v1p1155c2s v3p0412c1s
Nathan, G.I. v3p0315c1s
Nathan, G.J. v2p0117c2s
v3p0176c2s v3p0435c1s
Nathan, M. v4p0054c2s
v5p0134c2s
Nathan, Maud v6p0705c2s
Nathan, W. v4p0371c2s
v4p0550c1s
Nathorst, A.G. v3p0342c2s
v4p0445c2s v5p0027c1s v5p0250c2m
Nathusius, M.von v5p0321c1s
Nation, Mrs. v5p0398c2s
Natt, P.D. v1p0064c2m
v2p0403c1s v5p0072c1s
Nattrass, J.C. v4p0179c2s
Naughten, T.E. v5p0296c1s
v5p0297c2s v5p0493c2s v5p0494c1s
v6p0327c2s
Naumburg, Paul S. v6p0168c1s
Nausonty, M.de v2p0443c2s
Navarette, R. v4p0376c1s
Navarro, J.F.de v4p0059c1s
Navarro, J.N. v5p0373c1s
Naville, E. v1p0433c2s
v1p1161c2s v1p1203c2s v1p1300c2s
v2p0135c1s v2p0183c2s v3p0040c2s
v3p0058c1m v3p0131c1s v3p0131c2s
v3p0329c2s v3p0357c2s v4p0173c1s
Naville, E. and Hale, H.P.
v6p0642c1s
Naville, E. et al. v3p0058c1s
Nayler, G. v1p0764c2s
Naylor, C.E. v4p0127c1m
v4p0443c2s v4p0521c1s v5p0088c1s
v5p0417c2s v5p0451c2s v5p0507c1s
v5p0526c2s
Naylor, E.W. v4p0608c2s
Naylor, J. v4p0173c2s
Naylor, J.B. v6p0380c2s
v6p0465c1s v6p0701c2s
Naz, V. v4p0361c2s
Nazarbek, A. v4p0636c2s
Nead, B.M. v1p1054c1s
Nead, D.W. v3p0151c2s
Neal, A.B. v1p0217c2s
v1p0219c1s v1p0272c2s v1p0453c2s
v1p0750c2s v1p1423c1s
Neal, Della R. v6p0621c1s
Neal, J. v1p0064c2s
v1p0113c1s v1p0140c1s v1p0889c2s
v1p0958c1s v1p1009c1s v1p1146c2s
v1p1236c2s v1p1241c1s v1p1258c1s
v1p1411c1s
Neal, J.C. v1p0913c2s
v1p1260c2s
Neal, R.W. v6p0562c2s
Neal, Robert W. v6p0143c2s
Neale, E.V. v1p0173c1s
v1p0761c1s v1p1095c1s v4p0532c2s
Neale, E.V. and Abbot, F.E.
v1p1228c1s
Neale, J.C. v1p0987c2s
Neale, J.M. v1p0620c2s
v5p0240c1s
Neale, P. v2p0244c1s
v2p0463c1s
Neall, J. v1p0449c1s
v1p0505c2s v1p0979c2s v1p1013c1s
v1p1321c2s v1p1416c1s
Nealley, E.B. v1p0863c2s
v1p1437c1s
Nealy, S.H. v5p0356c2s
Neame, L.E. v6p0261c2s
v6p0697c1s
Neander, A. v1p0076c1s
v1p0248c1s v1p0252c2s v1p0427c1s
v1p0432c1s v1p0436c1s v1p0440c2s
v1p0552c1s v1p0976c2s v1p0977c1s
v1p0979c2s v1p1298c2s
Nearing, S. v6p0116c1s
Nearlein, Jane v5p0564c2s
Neate, C. v1p0407c2s
Neaves, C., Lord v1p1232c2s
Neaves, Charles, Lord v1p0724c1s
v1p0793c1s
Neaves, Lord v1p0559c1s
v1p0733c1s v1p0839c2s v1p0860c1s
v1p0929c2s v1p1246c1s
Neber, J.H. v6p0611c2s
Nedhobyty, Anna v6p0072c2s
Needell, J.H., Mrs. v5p0474c2s
v6p0166c2s v6p0389c1s
Needham, E.C. v2p0021c2m
v2p0061c2s v2p0147c2s v2p0216c1s
v2p0232c1s v2p0267c2s v2p0291c1s
v2p0321c2s v2p0326c1s v2p0332c1s
v2p0354c1s v2p0456c1s v3p0137c1s
Needham, H.B. v6p0136c1s
v6p0220c1s v6p0293c1s v6p0551c1m
v6p0583c2s v6p0667c1s
Needham, J.G. v6p0135c1s
v6p0228c2s
Needham, J.G. and Comstock, J.H.
v5p0292c1s
Needham, Violet v5p0362c1s
Needham, W.H. v4p0512c2s
Needles, Edna A. v6p0329c1s
Needles, S.H. v1p0589c2s
v2p0338c2s
Neeley, L. v1p0325c2s
v1p0798c1s v1p0917c1s v1p0918c1s
Neely, F.B. v2p0047c2s
Neely, H.A. v1p0847c2s
v1p0848c1s
Neely, K.J. v1p0878c1s
Neely, T.B. v3p0083c2s
v4p0367c2m v5p0641c2s
Neergaard, N. v2p0480c1s
Neesen, Prof. v4p0012c2s
Neff, E.C. v4p0531c1s
Neff, F.H. v6p0090c1s
v6p0145c1s v6p0449c1s v6p0695c2s

Neff, L.H. v4p0342c1s
Neff, P. v2p0172c1s
Negreponte, M. v4p0133c1s
v4p0363c2s v4p0552c2s v4p0588c2s
Negreponte, Mary v4p0202c2s
v4p0365c2s v4p0426c2s v4p0620c2s
Negri, C. v1p0670c2s
Negris, A. v1p0555c1s
v1p1382c2s
Neher, C.H. v5p0132c1s
Nehrling, H. v4p0203c1m
v5p0265c2s
Neidig, W.J. v6p0109c1s
Neidlinger, W.H. v5p0393c2s
Neiffer, L.M. v4p0563c2s
Neighbor, R.E. v3p0178c2s
v3p0244c1s v4p0269c1s v6p0172c2s
Neihardt, J.C. v6p0598c1s
Neihardt, J.G. v5p0342c2s
v5p0546c2s v5p0591c1s v5p0628c1s
v6p0203c2s v6p0217c2s v6p0362c2s
v6p0386c1s v6p0513c1s
Neil, C.Lang v6p0496c2s
v6p0536c1s
Neil, J. v3p0085c2s
v3p0086c2s v3p0193c1s
Neil, J.W. v1p1362c2s
v4p0150c1s
Neil, M. v1p0422c2s
Neil, S. v4p0481c1s
Neilbardt, J.G. v5p0530c2s
Neill, A.P. v6p0114c2s
Neill, B., Mrs. v3p0393c1s
Neill, C.P. v5p0479c2s
v6p0019c1s v6p0188c2s v6p0547c1s
v6p0634c2s v6p0687c1s
Neill, Charles P. v6p0600c1s
Neill, E.D. v1p0089c2s
v1p0114c2s v1p0160c1s v1p0341c2s
v1p0422c1s v1p0432c2s v1p0695c1s
v1p0807c2s v1p0808c1s v1p0871c2s
v1p0962c1s v1p1018c1m v1p1019c1s
v1p1039c2s v1p1373c1s v1p1374c1m
v1p1374c2m v2p0129c1s v2p0345c1s
v2p0461c2s v2p0475c1s v3p0101c1s
v3p0172c2s v3p0213c1s v3p0226c1s
v3p0270c1s v3p0281c2s v3p0283c2s
v3p0326c2s
v3p0397c1m
Neill, H. v1p0925c2s
v2p0181c1s
Neill, H.H. v2p0253c1s
Neilson, G. v3p0365c2s
v4p0020c2s v4p0304c1s v4p0322c2s
v5p0080c1s v5p0274c2s v5p0316c2s
v5p0515c2s v5p0525c2s v5p0573c2s
v6p0194c2s v6p0301c2s v6p0395c1s
v6p0578c2s v6p0616c2s
Neilson, G. and Bradley, H.
v6p0703c2s
Neilson, G. and Brown, J.T.T.
v5p0047c2s
Neilson, J. v2p0105c1s
Neilson, J.A. et al. v5p0274c2s
Neilson, J.M. v2p0031c2s
Neilson, N. v5p0071c2s
Neilson, R. v6p0615c2s
Neilson, R.M. v6p0673c2s
v6p0700c1s
Neilson, W. v1p0825c1s
Neilson, W.A. v4p0598c2s
v6p0350c1s v6p0386c1s v6p0587c2s
v6p0588c2m
Neiritz, G. v1p0405c2s
Neish, C., Mrs. v5p0021c1s
Neish, R. v5p0347c2s
v5p0381c1s v5p0438c1s v5p0527c1s
Neison, E. v1p0865c2s
v1p0866c1m v1p1291c2s v2p0296c2m
v2p0343c2s
Neison, F.G.P. v1p0079c1s
v1p0315c2s v1p0491c2s v1p0578c2s
v1p0873c1s v1p0873c2m v1p1079c1m
v1p1292c2s v1p1376c1s
Neisser, Emma R. v6p0070c2s
Neisser, G. v4p0635c2s
Nelson, A. v4p0324c2s
v4p0507c2s v6p0353c1s
Nelson, A.H. v5p0019c1s
v5p0105c1s v5p0179c2s v5p0249c1s
v5p0471c2s v6p0573c2s
Nelson, A.J. v3p0229c1s
v4p0431c1s
Nelson, A.S. v5p0171c1s
v5p0523c1s
Nelson, C. v6p0507c2s
Nelson, C.A. v2p0070c2s
v3p0012c1s v3p0249c1s v3p0302c2s
v4p0014c2s v4p0329c2s v4p0435c1s
v6p0373c1s
Nelson, C.Alex. v3p0248c2s
Nelson, C.K. v2p0045c1s
v3p0008c1s v3p0083c2s v3p0362c1s
Nelson, D.E. v4p0364c1s
v4p0418c2s v4p0458c2s
Nelson, E. v6p0029c2s
Nelson, E. et al. v4p0113c2s
Nelson, E.M. v4p0362c2s
Nelson, E.W. v5p0011c1s
v5p0400c1s v6p0414c2s
Nelson, Earl v1p0253c1s
v1p0255c2s v2p0005c2s v2p0185c2s
v3p0080c2s v5p0009c2s v5p0223c1s
v5p0323c2s v6p0305c1s
Nelson, F. v6p0297c1s
v6p0574c2s
Nelson, H. v4p0356c2s
v4p0475c1s v5p0272c2s
Nelson, H.A. v1p0811c1s
v1p1345c1s v2p0116c1s v2p0180c2s
Nelson, H.C. v2p0411c1s
Nelson, H.L. v1p1160c1s
v2p0087c1s v2p0466c2m v2p0467c1s
v3p0202c1s v3p0403c2s v3p0433c2s
v3p0444c1s v4p0050c1s v4p0086c2s
v4p0087c1s v4p0088c2s v4p0196c1s
v4p0457c2s v4p0469c1s v4p0511c2s
v4p0612c2s v4p0623c2s v5p0108c2s
v5p0120c2s v5p0158c1s v5p0199c1s
v5p0440c2s v5p0599c1s v5p0603c2s
v6p0108c1s v6p0108c2s v6p0243c2s
v6p0402c1s v6p0515c1s v6p0551c1s
v6p0583c2s v6p0616c2s v6p0652c2s
v6p0666c2s v6p0687c1s v6p0692c2m
Nelson, H.O. v3p0345c2m
v6p0079c1s
Nelson, I. v5p0049c1s
Nelson, J. v1p0195c1s
v3p0122c2s v3p0386c2s v4p0086c1s
v6p0158c2s v6p0638c1s
Nelson, J. and Sass, E. .. v5p0007c2s
Nelson, J.H. v1p0628c2s
Nelson, J.R. v4p0221c1s
v5p0612c2s v6p0173c2s v6p0625c1s
Nelson, K. v3p0347c1s
v3p0381c1s v5p0600c2s
Nelson, K.G. v5p0030c2s
Nelson, L. v1p0351c2s
Nelson, L.A. v5p0365c1s
Nelson, M.L. v6p0410c1s
Nelson, Maj. v2p0288c2s
Nelson, N.B. v5p0301c1s
Nelson, N.O. v4p0132c1s
v4p0132c2s v4p0314c2s v4p0499c1s
v5p0106c2s v6p0146c2s v6p0295c1s
v6p0518c2s
Nelson, R. v6p0700c2s
Nelson, S.A. v5p0617c1s
v6p0343c2s v6p0464c1s v6p0684c1s
Nelson, W. v1p1387c2s
v2p0011c1s v2p0238c1s v4p0080c1s
v4p0527c1s v6p0451c1s
Nelson, W., Maj. v4p0158c2s
Nelson, W.F. v2p0142c2s
v2p0312c2s v3p0050c1s v4p0172c1s
v4p0245c2s v4p0256c1s v4p0420c1s
Nelson, W.G., Maj. v4p0321c1s
Nelson, W.N. v1p0534c2s
v1p0714c1s v1p1319c2s
Nelson, W.S. v3p0370c1s
Nemenyi, A. v3p0353c1s
Nemos, W. v1p1020c2s
v1p1155c1s v3p0018c1s
Nepean, E., Mrs. v5p0386c2s
Nepean, Maud v5p0085c2s
Nepeau, E. v1p0046c1s
Nerincx, A. v5p0559c2s
v6p0530c1s
Nesbet, A. v1p0053c2s
Nesbet, M.J. v4p0341c1s
Nesbit, A. v1p0526c1s
v1p1125c1s
Nesbit, C.F. et al. v6p0537c1s
Nesbit, E. v2p0001c2s
v2p0246c1s v2p0403c2s v2p0422c1s
v2p0432c2s v2p0449c2s v3p0031c1s
v3p0048c1s v3p0098c2s v3p0116c1s
v3p0127c1s v3p0252c1s v3p0357c1s
v3p0368c2s v3p0372c2s v3p0439c1s
v4p0006c2s v4p0042c2m v4p0293c2s
v4p0333c1s v4p0356c2s v4p0359c2s
v4p0485c1s v4p0536c2s v4p0543c1s
v4p0620c1s v5p0036c1s v5p0052c2s
v5p0096c1s v5p0119c1s v5p0163c2s
v5p0224c1s v5p0239c2s v5p0258c1s
v5p0312c1s v5p0343c1s v5p0347c2s
v5p0379c2s v5p0412c2s v5p0419c2s
v5p0433c2s v5p0490c2s v5p0499c2s
v5p0521c1s v5p0622c2s v5p0628c2s
Nesbit, E. and Jepson, E.. v5p0308c2s
Nesbit, J.T. v1p0425c1s
Nesbit, R.F. v5p0534c1s
Nesbit, W.D. v6p0303c1s
v6p0456c1m v6p0610c2s
Nesbitt, A. v1p0160c2s
v1p0674c1s
Nesbitt, A. and Ganucci, R.
v1p0674c1s
Nesbitt, C. v5p0044c2s
Nesbitt, R.H. v5p0562c2s
Nesfield, D.M., Mrs. and
Danziger, G.A. v4p0302c2s
Nesfield, K.M. v4p0301c2s
v4p0368c1s
Nesmith, G.H. v2p0279c1s
Nesmith, G.T. v6p0554c2s
Nesmith, G.W. v1p1396c1s
v2p0054c2s v2p0060c2s v2p0239c1s
v2p0311c2m v2p0374c1s v2p0386c1s
v2p0424c1s v2p0452c1s v2p0469c1s
v2p0469c2m v3p0459c1s
Nesmith, R.D. v1p0045c1s
Ness, A.W.Van v6p0080c1s
Ness, T.Van v3p0432c1s
v6p0076c2s
Ness, W.W.Van v5p0006c1s
v5p0225c1s
Nest, G.W.Van v2p0215c2s
Nethercott, M. v2p0282c1s
Nettire, N. v5p0628c1s
Nettleship, H. v1p0208c1s
v1p0555c2s v2p0172c2s v2p0207c1m
v2p0315c2s v2p0333c1s v2p0459c2s
v3p0323c2s v4p0039c1s
Nettleship, J.T. v2p0058c2s
v3p0057c1s v3p0367c2s v5p0533c2s
Nettleship, R.L. v1p0176c1s
Nettleship, R.L. and Bryce, J.
v2p0191c2s
Nettleship, W.J. v4p0150c2s
Nettleton, A.B. v4p0594c2s
v5p0354c1s
Nettleton, C.P. v4p0335c1s
Neubauer, A. v2p0043c1s
v2p0076c2s v2p0237c1s v2p0293c1s
v2p0387c2s v2p0394c2s v3p0038c2s
v3p0127c2s v3p0228c1s v3p0231c1s
v3p0264c2s v3p0270c1s v3p0274c2s
v3p0463c1s v3p0473c1s v4p0041c2s
v4p0105c2s v4p0153c1s v4p0295c1s
v4p0302c1m v4p0302c2s v4p0317c1s
v4p0337c2s v4p0480c2s v4p0568c2s
v4p0635c2s v4p0636c2s v4p0637c1s
v5p0304c2s v5p0310c2s
Neubauer, A. and Cheyne, J.K.
v2p0204c1s
Neubauer, A. and Jacobs, J.
v3p0233c1s
Neuman, A.R. v3p0398c2s
Neuman, B.P. v3p0067c2s
v5p0074c1s v6p0345c1s
Neuman, F. v6p0185c1s
Neuman, M. v6p0233c1s
Neuman, P. v5p0164c2s
Neumann, A. v1p0502c1s
Neumann, B.P. v6p0603c2s
Neumann, B.P. and Darlow, T.H.
v3p0096c2s
Neumann, F. v6p0281c2s
Neumann, Felix v6p0517c1s
Neumann, O. v6p0212c1s
Neumann-Spallart, Dr.Von . v2p0444c1s
Neumann-Spallart, F.X.von. v2p0418c2s
v3p0397c2s
Neumayr, G.von v6p0023c1s
Neumayr, M. v3p0088c2s
Neuville, A.de v4p0018c2s
v4p0601c2s
Neve, J.L. v5p0351c1s
v6p0390c1s
Neve, Le v2p0114c2s
v2p0199c2s
Nevers, C.C. v4p0273c2s
Nevers, De v5p0459c2s
Nevers, M.De v5p0609c2s
Nevets, S.D. v1p0784c1s
Nevill, H.L. v5p0626c1s
Nevill, R. v3p0023c2s
v5p0098c1s v6p0039c2s
Nevill, Ralph v5p0032c1s
Neville-Rolfe, E. v5p0458c1s
Neville, C.M. v6p0701c2s
Neville, E. v6p0188c1s
Neville, F.H. v4p0011c1m
v5p0424c2s
Neville, H.F. v1p0657c1s
v1p0814c1s
Neville, H.W. v1p0785c2s
Neville, J.P.C. v5p0285c2s
Neville, L. v1p0749c1s
Neville, N. v1p0331c1s
v1p1361c1s
Neville, P. v5p0618c2s
Neville, R. v5p0157c1s
v6p0240c1s v6p0247c1m v6p0318c1s
v6p0682c1s
Neville, R.C. v1p0100c2s
v1p1122c2s
Nevin, A. v1p0966c1s
Nevin, D.E. v1p0571c1s
v1p0661c2s v1p1083c1s v1p1164c2s
v1p1322c1s v1p1353c1s
Nevin, D.R.B. v3p0409c2s
Nevin, E. v1p0525c1s
Nevin, H.M.O. v3p0307c2s
Nevin, J.J. v5p0626c1s
v6p0131c1s v6p0326c2s
Nevin, J.W. v1p0045c1s
v1p0047c2m v1p0056c2s v1p0071c2m
v1p0074c2s v1p0096c2m v1p0097c1s
v1p0113c2s v1p0121c1s v1p0130c1s
v1p0149c2s v1p0171c1s v1p0207c2s
v1p0218c2s v1p0240c2m v1p0241c1s
v1p0242c1m v1p0243c1s v1p0246c1m
v1p0247c1m v1p0248c1s v1p0248c2s
v1p0250c2s v1p0252c1s v1p0252c2s
v1p0254c2s v1p0255c2m v1p0260c1s
v1p0262c2s v1p0311c1s v1p0313c2m
v1p0328c1s v1p0381c1s v1p0386c1s
v1p0388c2s v1p0398c2s v1p0421c1m

v1p0432c1s v1p0441c1m v1p0484c1s
v1p0487c1s v1p0513c2s v1p0528c2s
v1p0538c2s v1p0583c1m v1p0587c2m
v1p0613c2s v1p0620c2s v1p0684c1m
v1p0684c2s v1p0685c1s v1p0686c2s
v1p0687c1s v1p0687c2s v1p0688c2s
v1p0689c1s v1p0756c1m v1p0756c2s
v1p0769c1m v1p0769c2s v1p0777c1s
v1p0777c2s v1p0794c2s v1p0795c1s
v1p0823c2m v1p0847c1s v1p0850c1s
v1p0868c1s v1p0881c2s v1p0890c1s
v1p0900c2s v1p0940c1s v1p0991c1s
v1p1013c1s v1p1047c1s v1p1053c1m
v1p1056c2s v1p1058c1s v1p1058c2m
v1p1059c1s v1p1062c1s v1p1067c1m
v1p1084c1s v1p1094c2s v1p1101c1s
v1p1102c2s v1p1120c1s v1p1120c2s
v1p1157c1s v1p1175c1s v1p1182c1s
v1p1206c2s v1p1237c2s v1p1271c1s
v1p1303c1s v1p1304c1s v1p1321c2s
v1p1359c1s v1p1375c1s v1p1425c2s
v1p1436c2m v2p0222c2s v2p0235c2s
Nevin, R.B. v1p0988c1s
Nevin, R.J. v2p0065c2s
v2p0231c1s v2p0231c2s v2p0320c2s
v2p0328c1s
Nevin, R.P. v1p0471c1s
v1p0668c1s v1p0849c1s
Nevin, T. v6p0693c2s
Nevin, W.M. v1p0007c1s
v1p0048c2s v1p0088c1s v1p0256c1s
v1p0275c2s v1p0603c2s v1p0727c2s
v1p0845c2s v1p0930c2s v1p0953c1s
v1p1074c1s v1p1279c2s v1p1301c1s
v1p1321c2s v1p1327c1s v2p0008c2s
Nevin, W.W. v1p0322c2s
v3p0002c1s
Nevins, F. v1p0756c2s
v1p1243c2s
Nevins, J. v1p0384c2s
v1p1194c2s
Nevins, J.W. v1p1001c2s
Nevins, W.S. v3p0307c2s
v3p0466c2s v4p0251c2s v4p0625c1s
v6p0146c1s
Nevinson, H.W. v4p0021c1s
v4p0097c1s v4p0229c2s v4p0447c1s
v4p0504c2s v5p0194c1s v5p0269c1s
v6p0007c2s v6p0326c2s v6p0398c2s
v6p0411c2s v6p0415c1s v6p0424c2m
v6p0597c1s v6p0597c2s
Nevitt, C. and Crosby, S.P.
v5p0152c1s
New, C.H. v4p0093c1s
v4p0200c2s v4p0221c2s v4p0547c2s
v5p0019c1s v5p0597c2s
New, F.D. v6p0238c2s
New, H. v1p0689c1s
v1p0841c2s
Newall, F.H. v4p0465c2s
Newall, H.Frank et al. ... v2p0004c2s
Newall, R.S. v2p0073c1s
Newall, W. v1p0763c1s
v1p0764c1s
Newberry, F.E. v4p0099c1s
v4p0491c2s
Newberry, F.H. v6p0391c2s
Newberry, J.S. v1p0231c2s
v1p0267c2m v1p0268c2s v1p0269c2s
v1p0470c1s v1p0470c2s v1p0509c1s
v1p0621c2s v1p0664c2s v1p0718c1m
v1p0749c1s v1p0916c2s v1p0926c2s
v1p1016c1s v1p1163c2s v1p1272c2s
v2p0027c2s v2p0090c1s v2p0179c1s
v2p0182c1s v2p0213c2s v2p0241c1s
v2p0220c2s v2p0316c1s v2p0319c1s
v2p0323c1s v2p0393c1m v2p0440c2m
v3p0045c1s v3p0126c1s v3p0183c2s
v3p0200c1s v3p0213c1s v3p0280c2s
v3p0311c1s v4p0013c1s
Newberry, J.S. and Trowbridge, W.P.
v3p0045c1s
Newberry, P.E. v4p0572c2s
v5p0225c2s
Newberry, S.B. v4p0094c1s
Newbery, F.T. v4p0580c2s
Newbigging, J. v3p0373c2s
Newbigging, T. v3p0167c2s
Newbigin, E.R. v6p0170c1s
Newbigin, M.I. v4p0065c1s
Newbigin, M.J. v4p0018c1s
Newbold, W.R. v4p0019c1s
v4p0039c2m v4p0140c2s v4p0152c2s
v4p0271c2m v4p0274c1s v4p0436c1s
v4p0436c2s v4p0464c1s v4p0464c2s
v4p0465c1m v4p0514c1s v4p0542c1m
v4p0555c2m v4p0573c2s v5p0041c1s
v6p0030c1s
Newbolt, F. v6p0186c1s
Newbolt, Frank v6p0211c1s
Newbolt, H. v5p0001c1s
v5p0068c1s v5p0118c2s v5p0141c2s
v5p0233c2s v5p0244c1s v5p0246c2s
v5p0247c2s v5p0273c1s v5p0295c1s
v5p0332c1s v5p0342c2s v5p0350c2s
v5p0369c1s v5p0371c1s v5p0558c1s
v5p0588c1s v5p0617c2s v6p0208c2s
v6p0265c1s v6p0272c2s v6p0352c2s
v6p0506c1s v6p0510c2s v6p0542c2s
v6p0575c1s v6p0611c2s v6p0616c1s
v6p0652c2s v6p0712c1s
Newbolt, W.C.E. v5p0346c1m
Newbury, J.S. v3p0360c1s
Newbury, S.B. v2p0103c1s
Newcastle, Duchess of v5p0124c1s
Newcomb, C.B. v4p0567c2s
v5p0560c1s
Newcomb, C.L. v4p0613c2s
Newcomb, E. v2p0257c2s
Newcomb, F.W. v5p0448c1s
Newcomb, F.H. v4p0476c1s
Newcomb, G.B. v2p0232c1s
v2p0347c2s v2p0356c1s
Newcomb, H.J. v6p0709c1s
Newcomb, H.O. v1p0201c2s
Newcomb, H.T. v4p0116c2s
v4p0214c2s v4p0470c2m v4p0471c1m
v4p0472c1s v4p0472c2m v5p0121c1s
v5p0476c1m v5p0476c2m v5p0477c1s
v5p0477c2m v5p0598c2s v5p0599c2s
v6p0132c2s v6p0324c2s v6p0355c2s
v6p0454c2s v6p0528c1s v6p0529c2m
v6p0530c1m v6p0615c1s
Newcomb, J.B. v3p0453c1m
Newcomb, J.T. v5p0182c1s
v5p0439c2s v6p0128c1m v6p0128c2s
v6p0203c1s v6p0405c1s v6p0431c1s
v6p0436c1s v6p0452c2s v6p0459c1s
v6p0463c1s v6p0482c1s v6p0516c1s
v6p0615c1s
Newcomb, J.W. v1p1258c1s
Newcomb, L.B. v4p0015c2s
Newcomb, S. v1p0070c1s
v1p0070c2s v1p0071c1m v1p0265c1s
v1p0291c2s v1p0313c2s v1p0325c1s
v1p0356c1s v1p0376c1s v1p0382c1m
v1p0398c1s v1p0434c1s v1p0510c1s
v1p0580c1s v1p0585c2s v1p0647c1s
v1p0647c2s v1p0648c1s v1p0713c1s
v1p0714c2s v1p0827c2s v1p0861c1s
v1p0865c2m v1p0866c1m v1p0900c2s
v1p0901c2s v1p0906c1s v1p0936c1m
v1p0965c2s v1p1025c1s v1p1026c1s
v1p1026c2s v1p1053c2s v1p1162c1s
v1p1198c2s v1p1215c1s v1p1232c2s
v1p1245c1s v1p1261c2s v1p1267c2s
v1p1285c1s v1p1285c2s v1p1292c1s
v1p1319c1s v1p1354c1s v1p1361c2s
v1p1367c1m v1p1379c2s v1p1388c2s
v2p0072c1s v2p0087c2s v2p0089c1s
v2p0089c2s v2p0119c1s v2p0130c1m
v2p0132c1m v2p0177c2s v2p0212c1s
v2p0243c2s v2p0245c2s v2p0258c2s
v2p0299c1s v2p0307c2m v2p0319c1s
v2p0338c2s v2p0341c1s v2p0343c2s
v2p0347c2s v2p0358c1m v2p0389c1s
v2p0390c1s v2p0417c2s v2p0426c2s
v2p0433c2m v2p0455c1s v3p0024c2s
v3p0076c2s v3p0087c1s v3p0158c1s
v3p0276c1s v3p0305c1s v3p0337c1s
v3p0399c1s v4p0034c2s v4p0158c2s
v4p0167c1s v4p0212c2s v4p0360c2s
v4p0361c1m v4p0394c1s v4p0450c1s
v4p0633c2s v5p0004c2s v5p0035c1m
v5p0035c2m v5p0174c2s v5p0218c2s
v5p0261c2s v5p0453c1s v5p0513c1s
v5p0549c1m v6p0038c1s v6p0102c1m
v6p0142c1s v6p0188c2s v6p0203c2s
v6p0230c1s v6p0376c1s v6p0397c1s
v6p0502c1s v6p0563c2s v6p0576c2s
v6p0577c1m v6p0614c2s v6p0629c2s
v6p0670c2m
Newcomb, S. and Dyrenforth, R.G.
v3p0353c2s
Newcomb, S. and Franklin, F.
v2p0347c2s
Newcomb, S. et al. v2p0403c1s
Newcomb, S., jr. v1p0729c1s
Newcomb, Simon v5p0542c1s
v6p0008c1s v6p0030c1s v6p0187c2s
v6p0515c1s
Newcomb, W. and Dutton, C.E.
v3p0126c1s
Newcombe, F.C. v5p0073c1s
v6p0353c1s
Newcombe, J.W., jr. v1p1417c2s
Newcombe, S.P. v1p0820c1s
Newcome, F.N. v1p0453c1s
v1p0897c2s v2p0066c2s
Newcomen, G. v4p0224c1s
v4p0509c2s v4p0528c2s v4p0584c2s
Newcomer, A.G. v4p0448c2s
v5p0488c1s v6p0505c1s
Newdegate, E.N., Sir v5p0243c1s
Newdigate, B.H. v3p0338c2s
Newdigate, Lady v6p0417c1s
Newell, B.E. v5p0496c2s
Newell, C. v4p0449c1s
Newell, C.E. v5p0357c1s
v6p0310c2s v6p0408c2s v6p0544c1s
Newell, C.Ellis v6p0665c1s
Newell, E.J. v5p0066c1s
v5p0400c2s
Newell, F.H. v4p0026c1s
v4p0251c2s v4p0271c1s v4p0409c1s
v5p0027c2s v5p0214c1s v5p0371c1s
v5p0602c1s v6p0329c2s v6p0472c2s
v6p0533c2m v6p0667c2s v6p0692c2s
Newell, J.E. v4p0451c1s
Newell, L.C. v5p0104c1s
Newell, N.E. v3p0092c2s
Newell, P. v5p0164c1s
Newell, S.W. v1p0644c1s
Newell, W. v1p0909c2s
v1p0929c1s v1p1190c1s
Newell, W.S. v6p0128c2s
Newell, W.W. v1p0490c2s
v4p0013c2s v4p0018c1s v4p0041c1s
v4p0102c2s v4p0103c1m v4p0107c1s
v4p0110c2s v4p0114c2s v4p0136c2s
v4p0193c2m v4p0205c1m v4p0205c2m
v4p0219c2s v4p0231c1s v4p0245c1s
v4p0285c1s v4p0290c2s v4p0316c2s
v4p0342c2s v4p0366c1s v4p0392c1s
v4p0395c1s v4p0396c2m v4p0404c2s
v4p0410c1s v4p0416c2s v4p0435c2s
v4p0463c1s v4p0474c1s v4p0497c1s
v4p0536c2s v4p0558c1s v4p0571c1s
v4p0588c1s v4p0607c2m v5p0015c2s
v5p0032c1s v5p0268c2s v6p0218c1s
v6p0230c2s v6p0294c2s v6p0307c1s
v6p0351c1s v6p0407c1s v6p0536c2s
Newell, W.W. and Bergen, F.D.
v4p0103c2s v4p0149c2s
v4p0205c2s
v4p0615c2s
Newell, W.W. and Bergen, F.D., Mrs.
v4p0558c1s
Newfang, O. v6p0156c2s
Newhall, C.S. v5p0524c2s
v6p0233c1s
Newhall, F.C. v2p0453c2s
Newhall, F.H. v1p0842c1s
v1p0847c2s v1p0906c2s v1p0972c2s
v1p1304c1s v1p1410c2s
Newhall, H.M. v2p0401c1s
Newkirk, B.L. v6p0037c1s
Newland, C.B. v6p0321c1s
Newland, D.H. v6p0186c1s
Newlands, F.G. v4p0524c1s
v5p0404c2s v6p0493c1s v6p0494c2s
v6p0530c1s v6p0568c1s
Newlands, Francis G. v6p0570c1s
Newlin, S. v2p0219c2s
Newman, A. v2p0048c2s
Newman, A.E.T. v6p0292c2s
v6p0351c1s
Newman, A.H. v1p0128c2s
v1p0834c1s v2p0045c2s v2p0357c1s
v2p0367c1s v2p0367c2s v2p0437c2s
v2p0464c2s v3p0287c2s v3p0325c1s
v4p0016c2s v4p0622c2s v5p0142c1s
v6p0051c2s
Newman, A.S. v4p0138c2s
Newman, E. v2p0451c1s
v4p0202c1s v5p0054c1s v5p0167c2s
v5p0355c1s v5p0393c2s v5p0394c1s
v5p0593c2s v5p0616c1s v6p0221c1s
v6p0620c2s v6p0702c1s
Newman, Ernest v5p0204c1s
Newman, F.W. v1p0020c1s
v1p0060c2s v1p0072c1s v1p0082c1s
v1p0199c1s v1p0244c1s v1p0250c1s
v1p0259c2s v1p0283c1s v1p0316c1m
v1p0320c2s v1p0404c2s v1p0407c2s
v1p0415c2s v1p0416c2s v1p0417c1s
v1p0420c2s v1p0428c2m v1p0430c2s
v1p0527c2s v1p0538c1s v1p0551c2s
v1p0593c2s v1p0600c2s v1p0607c1s
v1p0630c2s v1p0684c2s v1p0691c1s
v1p0721c1s v1p0751c2s v1p0752c1s
v1p0753c2s v1p0791c2s v1p0802c2s
v1p0857c1s v1p0965c2s v1p0974c2s
v1p1050c1s v1p1055c2s v1p1093c1m
v1p1096c1s v1p1116c1s v1p1121c1s
v1p1121c2s v1p1208c1s v1p1208c2s
v1p1234c2s v1p1269c2s v1p1321c2s
v1p1357c1s v1p1357c2s v1p1364c2s
v1p1384c1s v1p1385c1s v3p0221c1s
v3p0337c1s
Newman, F.W. and Froude, J.A.
v1p0210c1s v1p0948c1s
Newman, F.W. and Grey, M.G.
v1p0427c1s
Newman, H. v4p0081c2s
v4p0258c2s v4p0551c1s
Newman, Hilda v5p0468c1s
Newman, J. v4p0585c1s
Newman, J.A. v5p0076c2s
Newman, J.H. v1p0072c2s
v1p0219c2s v1p0365c1s v1p0518c1s
v1p0671c1s v1p0685c2s v1p1067c2s
v1p1142c1s v1p1158c2s v1p1357c2s
v2p0042c1s v2p0369c2s v4p0254c1s
v5p0493c1s
Newman, J.P. v1p1279c1s
v4p0253c2s
Newman, J.P. et al. v1p0645c2s
Newman, J.T. v5p0304c2s
Newman, L.C. v1p1281c2s
Newman, L.S.M. v6p0327c1s
Newman, Mrs. v1p0726c2s
v1p1315c2s v3p0037c2s v4p0321c2s
v4p0625c1s v5p0563c1s
Newman, N. v3p0359c1s
Newman, O.P. v6p0146c2s
Newman, P., Mrs. v4p0231c2s
Newman, Prof. v1p1034c1s
v1p1045c2s
Newman, R.L. v4p0521c2s

Newman, S.P. v1p1104c2s
Newman, W. v1p0885c1s
Newman, W.W. v1p1153c2s
Newmarch, R. v5p0594c2s
v6p0634c2s v6p0677c1s
Newmarch, Rosa v6p0033c2s
Newmarch, W. v1p0133c1s
v1p0313c2s v1p0410c1s v1p0544c2s
v1p0545c2s v1p1026c1s v1p1026c2s
Newmarch, W. and Giffen, R.
v1p0545c1s
Newmark, N. v1p0296c2s
v3p0465c1s v4p0509c2s v6p0221c1s
Newnes, G., Sir v5p0022c1s
v5p0181c1s v5p0305c1s v5p0514c2s
Newnham, A.J. v5p0118c2s
Newnham, A.T.H. v5p0502c2s
Newport, D. v4p0514c1s
Newport, M. v4p0124c2s
v4p0304c1s
Newsholme, A. v3p0125c1s
v3p0324c2s v4p0523c1s
Newsholme, A. and Stevenson, T.H.C.
v6p0302c1s
Newsom, L.M. v6p0493c2s
Newsome, T.A. v6p0498c2s
Newth, S. v2p0041c2s
v2p0193c2s
Newton, A. v1p0136c1s
v1p0323c1s v1p0723c1s v1p0791c2s
v1p0931c1s v2p0032c1s v2p0463c1s
v3p0045c2s v3p0111c1s v3p0146c1s
v4p0250c2s v5p0137c1s v5p0629c1s
v6p0426c2s v6p0444c2s
Newton, A. and Harting, J.E.
v4p0037c1s
Newton, A.E. v3p0405c1s
Newton, A.F. v4p0568c1s
Newton, Baron v5p0246c1s
Newton, C. v1p0061c1s
v1p0099c1s v1p0167c2s v1p0889c1s
Newton, C.T. v1p0062c1s
v1p0190c2s v1p0552c1s v1p0554c1s
v1p0554c2s v2p0018c2s v2p0279c1s
v3p0025c1s v3p0193c2s v3p0216c2s
Newton, E. v5p0098c2s
v5p0273c1s v5p0351c2s
Newton, E.A. v5p0424c1s
Newton, E.M. v4p0072c2s
Newton, E.T. v5p0358c1s
Newton, Emma M. v4p0273c1s
Newton, F.A. v5p0541c2s
Newton, F.G. v5p0093c1s
v5p0124c1s v5p0320c2s
Newton, F.M. v5p0082c1m
Newton, G.W. v6p0554c1s
Newton, H. v2p0454c2s
Newton, H.A. v1p0077c1s
v1p0282c1s v1p0827c1m v1p0827c2m
v1p0828c2s v1p0873c2s v1p1244c2s
v2p0094c2m v2p0127c2s v2p0285c1s
v2p0285c2s v3p0003c2s v3p0094c1s
v3p0153c2s v3p0258c1m v3p0276c1m
v3p0368c2s v4p0126c2s v4p0306c2s
v4p0367c1m v4p0522c1s v5p0372c1m
Newton, H.C. v4p0149c1s
v4p0304c2s
Newton, I. v1p0102c2s
v1p0902c1m v1p0902c2s v1p1191c2m
Newton, I., Sir v6p0139c2s
v6p0376c2s
Newton, J. v1p0272c2m
v1p0325c2s v1p0678c1s v1p0860c2s
v1p0861c1s v1p1055c2s v1p1396c2m
v1p1427c2s v2p0128c2s v2p0150c2s
v2p0200c2s
Newton, J.K. v2p0088c1s
v2p0132c1s v3p0227c2s
Newton, Lord v6p0299c1s
v6p0392c1s
Newton, M.M.P. v4p0606c1s
Newton, P. v6p0071c2s
Newton, R. v4p0469c1s
Newton, R., jr. v5p0276c2s
v5p0458c1s
Newton, R.H. v2p0097c1m
v2p0101c2m v2p0129c2s v2p0167c1s
v2p0269c1s v2p0376c2s v2p0408c1s
v3p0136c2s v3p0379c2s v4p0137c2s
v5p0078c2s v6p0019c1s v6p0019c2s
v6p0202c1s v6p0536c2s v6p0642c2s
Newton, R.H. and Mortimer, A.G.
v2p0042c1s
Newton, R.H. and Patton, F.L.
v2p0297c1s
Newton, S. v3p0115c1s
v3p0363c1s
Newton, T.M. v4p0543c2s
Newton, T.W. v1p0428c2s
Newton, T.W.L.Baron v5p0243c2s
Newton, V. v4p0128c2s
Newton, W.A. v3p0084c2s
Newton, W.E. v3p0325c1s
Newton, W.W. v1p0101c1s
v1p0909c2s v1p1249c1s v2p0070c1s
v2p0216c2s v3p0206c1s v3p0301c1s
v3p0369c1s
Newton-Robinson, C. v5p0227c2s
Newton-Robinson, J. v4p0248c1s
Newton-Robinson, J.A. v3p0275c1s
v4p0365c2s
Newton-Robinson, Mrs. v4p0080c2s
Newvolt, H. v5p0076c1s
Ney, N. v3p0371c2s
v4p0390c1s
Ney, Napoleon v4p0498c1s
v4p0513c1s
Neymark, A. v3p0160c1s
v3p0161c1s
Ng, Poon Chew v6p0120c1m
Niaudet, A. v1p0399c1m
Nibecker, F.H. v6p0113c1s
v6p0115c2s v6p0349c1s
Nibecker, F.H. and
Kellor, Frances A. v5p0454c2s
Nibecker, F.H. et al. v5p0263c1s
Niblock, W. v1p0096c2s
Nicaise, E. v5p0164c1s
Nicchia, A. v6p0649c1s
Niccol, R. v1p1265c1s
v2p0424c1s
Niccolls, S.J. v2p0300c1s
v3p0084c2s v3p0469c1s
Niccolls, S.J. et al. v4p0477c1s
Nichelson, M. v6p0532c2s
Nichol, J. v1p0674c1s
v1p1214c2s v2p0391c2s v4p0313c1s
Nichol, J.G. v3p0056c2s
Nichol, Prof. v2p0407c1s
Nichol, W.C. v5p0112c2s
Nicholas, A.E. v6p0113c1s
Nicholas, F.C. v5p0127c2s
v6p0476c1s v6p0681c1s
Nicholas, Francis C. v6p0101c1s
Nicholas, H.C. v6p0073c1s
Nicholas, M.A. v4p0299c1s
Nicholas, W. v5p0297c1s
v5p0493c2s
Nicholetts, R.B. v5p0077c2s
v5p0370c1s
Nicholl, A. v1p0214c1s
Nicholl, E.M. v2p0461c2s
v3p0450c2s v4p0185c1s
Nicholl, Edith M. v5p0406c1s
Nicholl, M.W. v6p0371c1s
v6p0445c2s
Nicholl, W. v5p0614c1s
Nicholl, W.R. v6p0191c1s
Nicholls, H.R. v3p0181c1s
Nicholls, J.F. v2p0056c1s
v2p0056c2s
Nicholls, J.H.K. v3p0451c2s
Nicholls, J.J. v1p0604c1s
Nicholls, Joanna R. v5p0009c2s
v5p0027c1s v5p0187c1s
Nicholls, S.C. v5p0333c2s
Nichols, A.H. v6p0076c1s
v6p0541c1s
Nichols, A.W. v6p0535c1s
Nichols, C.F. v3p0200c1s
v4p0194c1s v4p0288c1s v4p0332c1s
v5p0258c2s
Nichols, C.M. v4p0246c2s
v4p0549c2s v4p0557c2s
Nichols, C.S. v5p0625c2s
Nichols, C.W.deL. v6p0220c2s
Nichols, E.H. v5p0198c2s
v6p0098c2s
Nichols, E.L. v1p0400c1s
v1p0945c1s v1p1016c2s v2p0093c2s
v2p0229c1s v2p0272c1s v2p0341c2s
v2p0371c1s v3p0009c2s v3p0090c2s
v3p0092c2s v3p0133c2s v3p0134c1s
v3p0331c1s v4p0277c1s v4p0577c1s
v5p0002c2s v5p0449c2s v6p0015c1s
v6p0230c1s v6p0239c1s v6p0496c2s
v6p0498c1s
Nichols, E.L. and Franklin, W.S.
v3p0132c2s v3p0134c2s v3p0208c1s
v3p0264c1s
Nichols, E.P. and Reid, W.R., jr.
v6p0231c2s
Nichols, F. v5p0495c1s
Nichols, F.D. v5p0464c2s
Nichols, F.E. v6p0114c2s
Nichols, F.H. v5p0018c1s
v5p0148c2s v6p0119c2s v6p0120c2s
v6p0401c1s v6p0660c1s
Nichols, F.M. v1p0303c1s
v1p0317c2s v1p0711c1s v3p0366c2s
Nichols, F.P. v5p0368c1s
Nichols, F.W. v6p0223c1s
Nichols, Francis H. v6p0118c2s
Nichols, G.W. v1p0256c2s
v1p0280c1s v1p0462c1s v1p0595c1s
v1p0854c1s v1p0876c2s v1p1008c2s
v1p1389c1s
Nichols, H. v3p0430c2s
v4p0042c1s v4p0191c2s v4p0196c2s
v4p0273c2s v4p0372c1s v4p0421c1m
v4p0447c1s v4p0464c2m v5p0370c1s
Nichols, H.H. v5p0199c2s
Nichols, H.K. v4p0404c1s
Nichols, H.P. v6p0695c2s
Nichols, J. v1p0835c2s
v1p1294c1s v2p0217c2s
Nichols, J.B. v4p0278c1m
v6p0585c2s
Nichols, J.G. v1p0101c2s
v1p0223c2s v1p0445c2s v1p0586c1s
v1p0596c2m v1p0763c1s v1p0812c1s
v1p1016c1s v1p1051c1s v1p1074c2s
v1p1106c1s v1p1211c2s v1p1219c1s
Nichols, J.G. and Jackson, J.E.
v1p0616c1s v1p0651c2s
Nichols, J.G. and Scharf, G.
v1p0585c1s v1p0596c2s
Nichols, J.H. v1p0264c2s
v1p1399c2s
Nichols, J.H.K. v2p0276c1s
Nichols, L.D. v1p0335c2s
v1p1395c1s
Nichols, M.E. v5p0090c1s
v6p0104c2s v6p0427c1s
Nichols, M.L. v5p0546c1s
v6p0675c1s
Nichols, M.Louise v6p0675c1s
Nichols, May E. v6p0084c2s
Nichols, R.S. v5p0211c1s
v5p0226c1s
Nichols, S.H. v5p0353c2s
v5p0584c2s
Nichols, T. v2p0352c1s
v2p0404c1s v4p0573c1s v5p0386c1s
Nichols, T.E. v1p0104c2s
Nichols, W.A. v1p0072c2s
v1p0596c1s v1p1400c1s
Nichols, W.F. v6p0185c2s
Nichols, W.I. v6p0109c2s
Nichols, W.R. v1p0452c2s
v1p0742c1s v1p1149c2s v2p0076c2s
v2p0155c2s v2p0199c1s
Nichols, W.R. and Allen, C.R.
v2p0396c1s
Nichols, W.R. and Borden, P.D., jr.
v2p0229c2s
Nichols, W.T. v4p0021c2s
v4p0225c1s v4p0391c1s v4p0614c2s
v4p0619c2s v5p0075c1s v5p0283c2s
v5p0557c1s
Nicholson, A. v1p0024c2s
v1p0140c2s v1p0656c2s v4p0041c1s
v4p0517c2s v6p0310c2s v6p0390c1s
Nicholson, A.P. v6p0539c2s
Nicholson, Arthur v5p0524c1s
Nicholson, B. v2p0148c2s
v2p0238c2m v2p0398c2s v2p0421c2s
v3p0075c1s v3p0387c2s v4p0518c2s
v4p0610c1s v5p0054c2s v5p0091c1s
v5p0474c1s
Nicholson, C. v2p0037c2s
v2p0098c2m v2p0377c1s v2p0417c1s
v2p0435c1s v2p0459c2s v3p0271c2s
v3p0321c1s v3p0375c2s v4p0002c1m
v4p0077c1s v4p0404c1s v4p0426c1m
v4p0537c1s
Nicholson, C., Sir v3p0027c1s
Nicholson, C.H. v6p0200c1s
Nicholson, E. v2p0061c2s
v2p0406c2m v2p0445c1s
Nicholson, E.B. v1p0149c1s
v1p0173c1s v1p0764c1s v1p0954c1m
v2p0050c1s v2p0052c1s v2p0070c2s
v2p0153c2s v2p0274c2s
Nicholson, E.J., Mrs. v4p0536c1s
Nicholson, E.P. v4p0245c2s
Nicholson, E.W.B. v4p0222c1s
v4p0295c2s v4p0403c1s v4p0430c2s
v5p0051c2s v6p0588c2s
Nicholson, E.W.B. et al. . v3p0195c1s
v4p0295c2s v4p0442c1s
Nicholson, G. v4p0264c2s
v4p0310c1s v4p0332c1s
Nicholson, G.H. v5p0290c1s
v5p0624c1s v6p0416c1s v6p0543c2m
v6p0544c1s v6p0592c1s
Nicholson, H.A. v1p0194c2s
v1p0506c2s v1p0793c1s v1p0960c1m
v2p0257c2s
Nicholson, H.H. v3p0298c1s
Nicholson, H.L. v1p0111c1s
v1p0968c2s v1p1295c2s
Nicholson, H.O. v6p0301c1s
Nicholson, H.W. v2p0385c1s
Nicholson, I.M.G. v3p0239c2s
Nicholson, J. v1p0581c1s
Nicholson, J.B. v2p0052c1s
Nicholson, J.S. v3p0006c1s
v3p0044c2s v3p0181c2s v3p0285c2m
v3p0343c2s v3p0345c2s v3p0445c2s
v4p0044c2s v4p0280c2s v4p0313c2s
v4p0449c2s v4p0450c1s v4p0524c1s
v4p0525c1s v4p0546c1s v6p0188c2s
v6p0271c1s v6p0520c1s v6p0632c2s
v6p0633c1s
Nicholson, J.S. et al. ... v4p0596c1s
Nicholson, J.T. v3p0407c1s
Nicholson, K.S. v6p0376c2s
Nicholson, L.P. v4p0324c1s
Nicholson, M. v4p0087c2s
v5p0282c2s v6p0195c2s v6p0316c1s
v6p0698c1s
Nicholson, Prof. v2p0347c2s
Nicholson, R.L. v1p0683c2s
Nicholson, S. v4p0199c1s
Nicholson, T. v5p0430c1s
v6p0420c2s
Nickerson, A.C. v3p0116c1s
v3p0287c1s v3p0441c1s
Nickerson, A.H. v4p0225c1s

Nickerson, L. v1p0747c2s
v1p1075c1s v1p1248c1s v1p1259c1s
v1p1390c2s
Nickerson, S.W. v6p0121c1s
Nickerson, Susan D. v5p0525c1s
Nickles, F.J. v1p0825c2s
Nickles, F.J.J. v1p0491c1s
v1p0787c2s v1p0788c1s v1p0788c2s
v1p1049c1s v1p1415c1s
Nickles, J. v1p0401c1s
Nicklin, C.M. v5p0390c1s
Nicklin, J.A. v4p0360c1s
v4p0531c1s v5p0036c1s v5p0222c1s
v5p0250c1s v6p0209c1s v6p0600c1s
Nicol, G. v6p0615c2s
Nicol, H. v1p0916c2s
Nicol, J. v3p0135c2s
v5p0150c2s v5p0448c1m v5p0448c2m
v5p0449c1s
Nicol, J.M. v5p0410c1s
Nicol, T. v5p0058c2s
v5p0595c1s
Nicol, W. v1p0267c2s
Nicolas, N.H. v1p0393c1s
v1p0705c1s v1p0806c1s v1p0937c1s
v1p1106c1s v1p1166c2s v1p1167c2s
v1p1173c2s
Nicolas, N.H. and Planche, J.R.
v1p1051c1s
Nicolas, N.H., Sir v1p0393c1s
v1p0501c1s v1p1385c2s
Nicolay, J.G. v1p1201c2s
v3p0228c1s v3p0252c1s v3p0286c2s
v4p0085c2m v4p0332c2m v4p0379c2s
v4p0503c1s v4p0576c2s v4p0584c1s
Nicolay, J.G. and Hay, J.. v2p0259c1s
v3p0251c2s
Nicolet, T. v5p0411c1s
Nicoll, D.L. v1p1294c2s
Nicoll, De L. v3p0054c1s
Nicoll, E.H. v3p0079c2s
Nicoll, J.A. v4p0614c1s
Nicoll, T. v6p0063c1s
Nicoll, W. and Goldschmidt, V.
v6p0610c2s
Nicoll, W.R. v2p0191c2s
v4p0015c1s v4p0039c1s v4p0334c2s
v4p0365c2s v4p0403c1s v4p0435c1s
v4p0495c1s v4p0497c1s v4p0619c1s
v5p0071c1s v5p0078c1s v5p0114c1s
v5p0169c2s v5p0171c2m v5p0193c1s
v5p0420c1s v5p0463c1s v5p0547c2s
v6p0202c1s v6p0577c2s
Nicolls, E. v5p0052c1s
Nicolls, F.W. v5p0293c2s
Nicolo, A. v1p0893c1s
Nicols, A. v2p0327c2s
v4p0158c1s
Nicols, J. v1p0527c2s
Nicolson, A. v1p1204c1s
v1p1210c2s v2p0261c2s
Nicolson, G. v2p0120c1s
Nicolson, W.M. v2p0044c1s
Nidda, C.K.von v1p0844c2s
Niddrie, W. v5p0308c2s
Niebecker, F.H. v5p0482c1s
Niebuhr, B.G. v1p0921c2s
Niecks, Prof. v6p0438c1s
Niedermasser, A. v1p1118c2s
Niedherhauser, R. v3p0406c1s
Niell, E.D. v1p0028c2s
v1p0433c1s
Nielsen, Alice v5p0227c2s
Nielson, George v5p0215c1s
Nielson, I. v5p0027c1s
Nieman, C.H. v5p0622c2s
Niemeyer, P. v1p0578c2s
Nieritz, G. v2p0430c1s
Nies, J.B. v5p0017c1s
Niesten, L. v3p0024c2s
Nietzsche, F. v4p0608c2s
Nievelt, C.Van v3p0034c2s
Nightingale, A.F. v4p0123c1m
v4p0321c2s v4p0512c2s v4p0566c1s
v5p0126c1m v5p0126c2s v5p0182c2s
v5p0266c2s v5p0326c2s v5p0479c2s
v5p0518c1m v6p0290c1s
Nightingale, F. v1p0606c1s
v1p0632c2s v1p0633c2s v1p0635c1s
v1p0981c2s v1p1093c2s v2p0216c2s
Nightingale, F. and Costa, J.
v2p0040c1s
Nightingale, J.E. v3p0121c1s
v3p0334c1s v4p0612c1s
Nightingale, R.C. v4p0061c2s
v5p0062c2s v5p0372c2s v5p0390c2s
v5p0616c2s
Nightingale, Robt. v5p0064c1s
Nilan, J. v1p0244c1s
v1p1032c2s v2p0133c1s
Niles, C.W. v5p0260c2s
Niles, Grace G. v6p0296c2s
Niles, J.M. v1p0956c1s
v1p1077c2s
Niles, W.H. v1p0524c1s
v1p1361c2s
Niles, W.H. and Wachsmuth, C.
v1p0508c2s
Niles, W.T. v4p0069c1s
Nilson, L.G. v6p0296c2s
Nilsson, Christine v2p0403c2s
Nimmo, J. v2p0105c2s
Nimmo, J., jr. v2p0275c2s
v4p0404c1s v5p0294c1s v5p0294c2s
v5p0410c2s
Nimmo, Joseph, jr. v5p0567c1s
Nims, F.A. v4p0125c1s
Ninde, E.S. v6p0413c1s
Ninde, M.C. v6p0095c2s
v6p0639c1s
Ninde, W.W. v1p0946c1s
Ninet, J. v2p0134c2s
Nino, Antonio de v6p0001c2s
Nipher, F.E. v1p0498c2s
v1p0788c1s v1p0855c1s v1p0881c2m
v1p1375c1s v2p0080c1s v2p0335c1s
v2p0340c2s v3p0143c1s v3p0264c1s
v3p0376c2s v3p0408c2s v5p0175c1s
v5p0402c1s v5p0448c2s v6p0197c1s
v6p0406c2s v6p0407c1s
Nipher, T.E. v2p0272c1s
Nipperdey, H. v3p0151c1s
Nisbet, C. v1p0993c2s
Nisbet, E. v1p0038c2s
v1p0333c2s v1p0792c2s v1p0793c1s
v2p0027c2s v2p0273c2s
Nisbet, H. v3p0114c1s
v3p0289c1s v3p0301c2m v4p0250c1s
v4p0274c2s v4p0551c1s v6p0653c2s
Nisbet, I. v6p0646c2s
Nisbet, J. v3p0158c1s
v4p0209c1s v5p0084c1s v6p0167c1s
v6p0233c1s v6p0687c2s
Nisbet, J.F. v5p0038c1s
v5p0192c1s v5p0409c2s v5p0522c2s
v5p0575c2s
Nisbet, J.M. v5p0188c2s
Nisbet, N. v4p0442c2s
Nissen, H. v1p0388c2s
v4p0245c1s
Nistadt, P. v2p0239c1s
Nitaba, I. v4p0332c1s
Nitchie, J.E. v5p0531c1s
Nithsdale, W. v1p0923c2s
Nitobe, I. v5p0083c2s
Nitobe, M.P.E. v6p0338c1s
Nitsch, A.W. v4p0034c1s
v4p0117c2s
Nitsch, H.A. v1p0878c1s
Nitsche, Dr. v5p0545c2s
Nitti, F.S. v4p0007c2s
v4p0294c2s v4p0295c1m v4p0315c2s
v4p0394c1s v4p0452c1s v4p0553c2s
v5p0018c1s
Nitze, H.B.C. v4p0231c1s
v5p0298c2s v5p0356c1s v5p0382c2s
Nitzsch, C.I. v2p0357c1s
Nitzsch, K.I. v1p0594c2s
v1p1094c1s
Nivedita v6p0314c1s
Niven, G.W. v2p0336c1s
Niven, R. v1p0721c2s
v1p1241c1s v1p1370c1s v2p0171c2s
v3p0057c2s
Niven, W. v5p0420c2s
v6p0247c1s
Nix, P.A. v5p0575c2s
Nixdorf, G.A. v1p0840c1s
Nixdorff, G.A. v1p0296c2s
Nixon, E.R. v6p0603c2s
Nixon, J.K. v1p0178c2s
Nixon, J.O. v6p0107c2s
Nixon, L. v4p0094c1s
v4p0594c2s v5p0526c1m v5p0527c1m
v6p0248c2s
Nixon, M.F. v5p0097c2s
v5p0291c1s v5p0428c2s v5p0506c2s
v5p0580c2s
Nixon, Paul v6p0542c2s
Nixon-Roulet, M.F. v5p0127c2s
v5p0172c1s v5p0367c1s v5p0392c2m
v6p0124c1s v6p0162c2s v6p0184c2s
v6p0249c2s v6p0308c1s v6p0389c2s
v6p0409c2s v6p0545c1s v6p0620c1s
Noa, F.M. v4p0346c1s
v6p0045c1s v6p0045c2s v6p0072c2s
v6p0160c2s v6p0362c2s v6p0569c1s
v6p0570c2s v6p0652c2s v6p0694c2s
Noah, Brother v1p0275c2s
Noah, M.M. v1p0101c1s
Noailles, Duc de v4p0059c1s
Noaillon, E. v6p0222c1s
Noake, J. v1p1429c1s
Noakes, D.W. v5p0642c1s
Nobbs, P.E. v6p0028c2m
Nobel, A. v3p0047c1s
Nobili, R. v3p0001c2s
v4p0426c1s
Nobili-Vitelleschi, F. ... v2p0148c1s
v2p0231c2s v3p0224c2s v4p0295c1s
v4p0382c1s v5p0536c2s
Noble, A. v1p1358c2s
v2p0150c2s v3p0071c2s v5p0042c2s
v5p0570c1s
Noble, Andrew, Sir v5p0188c2s
Noble, C. v6p0445c2s
Noble, C.W. v4p0581c2s
Noble, Capt. v3p0390c2s
Noble, D. v1p1093c1s
Noble, E. v1p0468c2s
v1p0662c2s v1p1085c1s v2p0025c2s
v2p0309c2s v2p0383c2s v3p0069c2s
v3p0077c1s v3p0242c2s v3p0289c1s
v3p0346c1s v3p0369c2s v4p0274c2s
v4p0351c2s v4p0360c2s v4p0483c2s
v5p0198c2s v5p0322c2s v5p0400c2s
v5p0501c2s v5p0535c2s v5p0576c2s
v6p0431c1s v6p0564c2s
Noble, Edmund v6p0425c2s
Noble, F. v4p0040c2s
Noble, F.A. v2p0318c2s
v4p0397c1s v5p0115c1s v6p0684c2s
Noble, F.P. v3p0075c1s
v3p0357c2s v3p0395c1s v4p0005c1m
v4p0100c2s v4p0501c1s
Noble, G. v5p0131c1s
Noble, H.G.S. v3p0094c1s
Noble, J. v5p0256c2s
v5p0532c1s v6p0102c2s
Noble, J.A. v1p0274c2s
v1p0720c2s v1p0788c1s v1p1020c2s
v1p1100c2s v1p1220c2s v2p0026c2s
v2p0057c2m v2p0140c1s v2p0170c1s
v2p0175c1s v2p0181c1s v2p0213c2s
v2p0221c2s v2p0258c1s v2p0273c1s
v2p0278c2s v2p0289c2s v2p0324c1s
v2p0428c2s v2p0448c2s v2p0463c2s
v2p0472c2s v2p0476c2s v3p0027c1m
v3p0094c2s v3p0106c1s v3p0115c2s
v3p0116c1s v3p0140c2s v3p0203c2s
v3p0226c1s v3p0264c2s v3p0335c2s
v4p0026c1s v4p0048c2s v4p0061c2s
v4p0225c1s v4p0232c1s v4p0246c2s
v4p0251c2s v4p0260c2s v4p0269c2s
v4p0347c1s v4p0407c1s v4p0492c1s
v4p0516c2s v4p0548c2s v4p0610c2s
v4p0614c1m v4p0632c1s
Noble, J.D. v4p0074c1s
Noble, J.H. v3p0207c2s
v4p0275c2s v6p0451c2s
Noble, J.W. v5p0256c2s
Noble, L. v3p0128c1s
v4p0262c1s
Noble, L.G. v1p0802c2s
v1p1420c2s v1p1425c2s
Noble, L.L. v1p1316c1s
Noble, M. v1p0220c1m
v1p0272c1s v1p0764c2s v1p0815c2s
v1p1437c2s
Noble, M.W. v3p0299c1s
v4p0630c2s
Noble, Margaret E. v6p0087c2s
Noble, R.E. v4p0453c2s
Noble, T.A. v1p0426c2s
Noble, W. v2p0386c2m
v3p0093c2s v5p0424c1s
Noble, W.B. v2p0081c1s
v2p0290c2s v6p0317c1s
Nobles, G.M. v2p0150c2s
Nockolds, C. v6p0031c1s
v6p0493c1s
Nocquet, P. v6p0005c1s
Nodet, H. v4p0292c1s
Nodet, H. and Saint-Paul, A.
v4p0453c1m
Nodier, C. v1p0142c1s
Noe, H. v6p0524c2s
Noel, A.H. v3p0431c1s
Noel, Annie W. v6p0381c1s
v6p0467c1s
Noel, B.W. v1p0248c1s
v1p0481c2s v1p1103c1s v1p1363c2s
Noel, F. v5p0382c1s
v6p0385c2s
Noel, G. v3p0416c1s
Noel, G.C. v5p0007c2s
v5p0218c1s v5p0248c1s
Noel, G.H. v3p0182c2s
Noel, H. v5p0517c1s
Noel, J. v6p0135c1s
Noel, J.V. v1p0352c2s
v5p0081c2s
Noel, L. v3p0272c1s
Noel, P. v2p0111c1s
Noel, R. v1p0082c1s
v1p0114c1s v1p0172c2s v1p0182c1s
v1p0208c2s v1p0303c2s v1p0304c2s
v1p0436c2s v1p0487c1s v1p0702c1s
v1p0712c2s v1p0810c2s v1p0812c1s
v1p0826c1s v1p0962c1s v1p0989c1s
v1p0993c2s v1p1023c1s v1p1152c1s
v1p1298c2m v1p1407c1s v1p1410c2s
v2p0050c1s v2p0058c2s v2p0183c2s
v2p0184c1s v2p0197c1s v2p0251c1s
v2p0261c2s v2p0283c1s v2p0399c2s
v2p0434c2s v2p0435c1s v3p0057c1s
v3p0204c1s v4p0009c2s v4p0084c2s
v4p0174c1s v4p0405c2s v4p0536c2s
v4p0561c1s v4p0620c2s
Noel, R.R. v1p0305c2s
v1p0831c2s v1p0897c2s v1p1004c2s
v1p1242c1s
Noel, Roden v3p0430c2s
Noguchi, Y. v6p0332c1s
v6p0335c2s v6p0336c1s v6p0336c2s
v6p0337c2s v6p0338c1m v6p0338c2s
v6p0339c1m v6p0354c2s v6p0401c2s
v6p0409c2s v6p0417c2s v6p0648c2s
Noguchi, Yone v6p0285c1s
v6p0552c2s v6p0587c2s v6p0616c1s

Noire, L. v2p0016c2s
v4p0148c1s v4p0320c2s v4p0475c1s
Nokes, W.F. v1p1423c1s
Nolan, D.W. v1p0944c2s
Nolan, E. v1p0781c2s
Nolan, E.J. v1p0736c2s
Nolan, J. v2p0440c2s
Nolan, J. and Darwin, G.H.
v2p0440c2s
Nolan, J.A. v1p0312c1s
v2p0019c2s v2p0411c2s
Nolan, P.L. v3p0222c2s
Nolan, T. v1p1291c2s
v6p0028c2m
Noland, N.B. v1p0026c2s
Nolde, Baroness de v6p0612c1s
Nolen, J. v6p0371c2s
v6p0532c1s v6p0672c1s
Nolen, J. and Olmsted, F.L., jr.
v6p0481c1s
Nolhac, P.de v5p0215c2s
v5p0609c2s
Noll, A. v4p0175c1s
Noll, A.H. v3p0003c1s
v3p0021c2s v3p0029c2s v3p0139c2s
v3p0178c2s v3p0216c2s v3p0226c1s
v3p0244c1s v3p0272c1s v3p0276c2s
v3p0277c1m v3p0322c2s v3p0349c1s
v3p0359c1s v3p0448c1s v4p0036c1s
v4p0043c2s v4p0088c2s v4p0258c2s
v4p0368c2s v4p0451c1s v4p0540c1s
v4p0596c2s v5p0191c1s v5p0373c1s
v5p0380c1s v5p0398c2s v5p0408c1s
v5p0544c2s v5p0573c2s v6p0173c1s
v6p0340c2s v6p0384c1m v6p0414c2s
v6p0593c2m
Noll, Arthur H. v3p0067c2s
Nolle, L. v6p0581c2s
Nollen, H.S. v5p0631c1s
Nollen, J.S. v4p0161c1s
Nolloth, C.F. v6p0342c1s
Nomad v4p0542c2s
Noon, H.S. v6p0595c2s
Noon, J. v1p0441c1s
Noonan, E.A. et al. v3p0085c2s
Nooney, J. v1p0070c1s
v1p0936c1s
Noott, F.H. v1p0543c1s
Noppen, L.C.Van v6p0195c1s
Norbury, E.A. v5p0527c2s
v6p0592c2s
Norcross, F.W. v5p0072c1s
Nordau, M. v4p0037c2s
v4p0151c2s v4p0406c1s v5p0307c2s
v5p0308c1s v5p0618c2s v6p0186c2s
v6p0205c2s v6p0601c1s v6p0623c2s
v6p0713c1s
Nordau, M.S. v6p0380c2s
Nordau, Max v4p0005c1s
v6p0286c1s
Nordell, P.A. v1p0069c1s
v2p0153c1s v2p0351c2s v3p0282c2s
v4p0541c2s
Norden, C.Van v3p0229c1s
v4p0091c2s
Norden, C.von v5p0161c2s
Norden, J.H. v1p0409c1s
Nordenskiold, G. v4p0531c2s
Nordenskjold, A.E. v1p0681c2s
v1p0828c2s v1p1024c1s v1p1274c1s
v2p0028c2s v2p0191c2m v2p0273c2s
v3p0134c2s v3p0142c2s v5p0075c2s
v5p0227c1s
Nordenskjold, E. v5p0210c2s
v6p0072c2m v6p0490c1s
Nordenskjold, O. v5p0435c1s
v6p0023c1m
Nordenskjold, Prof. v1p0827c2s
Nordhausen, R. v5p0482c2s
Nordheimer, I. v1p1072c1s
v1p1281c2s
Nordheimer, J. v1p0581c2s
Nordheimer, Prof. v1p0124c1s
v1p0691c1s
Nordheimer, Prof. and Stuart, Prof.
v1p0581c1s
Nordhoff, C. v1p0010c2s
v1p0012c1s v1p0013c1s v1p0067c2s
v1p0083c2s v1p0185c2s v1p0186c2s
v1p0188c1s v1p0200c1s v1p0226c1s
v1p0280c1s v1p0349c2s v1p0401c2s
v1p0403c1s v1p0443c2s v1p0445c1s
v1p0465c1s v1p0575c1s v1p0647c2s
v1p0748c2s v1p0785c1s v1p0808c2s
v1p0916c2s v1p0937c2s v1p1035c2s
v1p1064c1s v1p1118c2s v1p1142c1s
v1p1171c2s v1p1172c2s v1p1174c1s
v1p1266c1s v1p1272c1s v1p1287c2s
v1p1310c2s v1p1313c2s v1p1416c2s
v1p1417c2s v1p1433c2s
Nordhoff, E.H. v4p0627c1s
v5p0070c2s
Nordhoff, E.S. v4p0253c1s
Nordhoff, W. v1p0570c1s
Norgate, F. v5p0098c2s
Norgate, F. and Goodman, N.
v2p0416c1s
Norgate, G.C.G. v5p0515c2s
Norgate, G.L. v5p0465c2s
Norgate, G.LeG. v4p0028c2s
v5p0089c2s v5p0421c2s
Norgate, G.LeGrys v5p0579c1s
Norgate, K. v3p0069c2s
v3p0310c1s v4p0078c2s v6p0699c1s
Norgate, K. and Archer, J.A.
v4p0250c1s
Norikoff, O. v2p0434c1s
Norlin, G. v6p0152c1s
v6p0590c1s
Norman, A. v6p0636c1s
Norman, A.M. v4p0402c1s
Norman, C. v2p0164c1s
Norman, C.B. v2p0164c1s
v2p0164c2s v3p0211c1s v3p0212c1s
v4p0280c1s v4p0586c2s
Norman, C.H. v6p0477c2s
Norman, F. v5p0206c2s
v5p0398c2s
Norman, F.J. v6p0334c1s
Norman, G. v5p0029c1s
Norman, G.B. v5p0595c1s
Norman, G.W. v1p0479c2s
v1p0721c1m v1p1349c2s
Norman, H. v1p0919c2s
v2p0021c1s v2p0035c2s v2p0139c2s
v2p0140c1s v2p0155c1s v2p0187c1s
v2p0230c1s v2p0238c1m v2p0265c2s
v2p0266c1s v2p0345c1s v4p0042c2s
v4p0172c2s v4p0185c1s v4p0522c2m
v5p0109c1s v5p0109c2s v5p0111c2s
v5p0249c1s v5p0433c1s v5p0501c1s
v5p0502c1s v5p0602c1s v6p0043c2m
v6p0044c1s v6p0044c2s v6p0230c1s
v6p0299c1s v6p0432c2s v6p0560c1s
Norman, H. and Jonson, G.C.Ashton
v6p0385c1s
v6p0618c1s
Norman, H., Sir v1p0631c2s
v2p0251c2s
Norman, H.C. v6p0209c2s
Norman, H.W. v2p0218c1s
Norman, Henry v5p0506c2s
Norman, J.H. v3p0090c2s
v3p0146c2m
v3p0394c1s
Norman, L. v5p0593c1s
Norman, L.E. v6p0005c1s
Norman, L.E.Van v5p0528c2m
v5p0529c1s v5p0620c1s v6p0033c2s
v6p0342c2s v6p0376c1s v6p0453c1s
v6p0476c1s v6p0506c1s v6p0506c2m
v6p0510c2s v6p0550c2s v6p0555c2s
v6p0564c1s v6p0667c1m
Norman, M.M. v5p0143c2s
Norman, N. v4p0134c1s
Norman, P. v3p0256c2m
v3p0392c2s v4p0139c1s v4p0339c1m
v5p0067c1s v5p0428c1s v5p0472c1s
v6p0455c2s
Norman, R.S. v4p0017c2s
Norman, R.W. v1p1423c2s
v2p0300c2s v2p0444c1s
Normandie, J.De v1p0244c1s
v1p0396c2s v1p0796c2s v1p0961c2s
v1p1340c1s v2p0194c1s v4p0177c2s
v4p0493c1s
Normauth, Jacques v5p0419c1s
Norraikow, Countess v4p0404c2s
v4p0496c1s
Norraikow, E. v3p0305c2s
Norregard, J. v6p0247c2s
Norrenberg, C. v5p0333c1s
v6p0254c2s v6p0371c1s
Norris, C.J. v6p0226c1s
v6p0388c1s
Norris, C.M. v4p0342c1s
Norris, C.S. v1p0995c2s
Norris, E.M. v4p0500c1s
v6p0089c2s v6p0164c1s v6p0225c1s
v6p0280c2s v6p0517c1s v6p0674c2s
v6p0700c1s v6p0709c2s
Norris, E.S. v3p0348c2s
Norris, E.T. v3p0110c1s
v3p0114c1s v3p0194c1s v3p0312c2s
Norris, F. v4p0322c1s
v4p0419c1s v5p0130c1s v5p0147c1s
v5p0182c1s v5p0378c2s v5p0416c1s
v5p0578c1s v6p0166c2s v6p0243c2s
v6p0274c2s v6p0387c1s v6p0418c2s
v6p0461c2s v6p0462c1s v6p0482c2s
v6p0591c1s v6p0663c1s v6p0698c1s
Norris, F.E. v3p0132c1s
v3p0309c1s
Norris, F.L. v6p0486c2s
Norris, Frank v4p0582c2s
Norris, G.Perry v6p0085c1s
Norris, G.W. v1p0926c1s
Norris, H. v1p0815c1s
v1p1122c1s v2p0059c1s v6p0438c1s
Norris, H.A. v5p0256c1s
v5p0615c2s
Norris, H.F. v2p0087c2s
Norris, H.H. v6p0198c1s
v6p0661c1s
Norris, H.L. v6p0631c1s
Norris, H.M. v5p0353c2s
v5p0464c1m v5p0527c1s
Norris, H.M., jr. v4p0512c1s
Norris, H.W. v3p0192c1s
Norris, J. v1p0272c1s
v3p0413c1s
Norris, J.A. v3p0258c1s
Norris, J.P. v1p1187c2s
v3p0188c1s v3p0387c2s v3p0448c2s
v4p0246c1s
Norris, K.S. v6p0674c2s
Norris, Lieut. v4p0341c1s
Norris, M. v1p0309c2s
v1p0507c2s v1p1143c1s
Norris, M.H. v6p0707c2s
Norris, Mary H. v4p0467c1s
Norris, O.M. v4p0147c2s
v4p0295c1s
Norris, R.A. v5p0425c1s
Norris, R.V. v6p0133c1s
v6p0294c1s v6p0688c1s
Norris, S.C. v5p0238c1s
v5p0487c2s
Norris, T. v1p0542c2s
v1p0904c2s v1p1146c1m v1p1146c2s
v1p1182c2s v1p1271c2s
Norris, W. v1p0192c2m
v1p0194c1s v1p0195c1m v1p0332c2s
v1p1347c2s
Norris, W.F. v1p0002c2s
v1p0117c1s v1p0940c2s v2p0031c1s
v2p0119c1s v2p0201c2s v2p0274c2s
v2p0304c1s v2p0315c1s v2p0354c1s
v2p0436c2s v3p0009c2s v3p0080c1s
v3p0216c1s v3p0225c2s v3p0264c2s
v3p0267c2s v3p0291c1m v3p0311c1s
v3p0339c1s v3p0350c2s v3p0363c2s
v4p0117c2s v4p0136c2s v4p0153c1s
v4p0160c1s v4p0231c2s v4p0258c2s
v4p0307c2s v4p0361c2s v4p0373c2s
v4p0412c2s v4p0428c2s v4p0528c1s
v4p0568c2s v4p0575c2s v4p0586c1s
v4p0598c2s v5p0206c2s v5p0208c1s
v5p0211c1s v5p0263c2s v5p0630c2s
v6p0223c2s v6p0336c2s v6p0351c2s
v6p0385c2s v6p0434c1s v6p0444c2s
v6p0664c1s
Norris, W.F. v5p0443c2s
v5p0444c1s v6p0448c2m v6p0494c2m
v6p0680c1s
Norris, Z.A. v4p0373c2s
v5p0241c1s v5p0361c1s
Norris-Newman, Capt. v6p0338c2s
Norse, S. v5p0030c2s
North, A. v2p0224c2s
v3p0249c1s
North, A.F. v2p0233c1s
North, C. v3p0368c2s
v3p0417c2s v6p0619c1s
North, Cecil v6p0288c2s
North, Cecil, Capt. v5p0385c2s
North, Christopher v1p1413c1s
v1p1413c2s
North, E. v1p0493c1s
v1p1059c2s
North, E.D. v1p0772c1s
v1p0831c1s v1p0835c2s v1p0836c1s
v1p0989c2s v4p0037c2s v4p0066c2s
v4p0071c1s v4p0164c1s v4p0232c2s
v4p0243c1s v4p0311c2s v4p0317c2s
v4p0411c1s v4p0459c1s v4p0493c1s
v5p0011c2s v5p0070c1s v5p0070c2s
v5p0078c1s v5p0240c2s v5p0280c1s
v5p0314c2s v5p0370c2s v5p0474c1s
v5p0479c1s v5p0525c1s v5p0607c1s
North, E.D. et al. v6p0532c2s
North, E.L. v6p0115c1s
North, E.M. v5p0526c1s
North, E.P. v3p0012c1s
v3p0362c2s v4p0169c1s v4p0186c2s
v5p0194c2s
North, Edward P. v4p0410c2s
North, F. v6p0673c1s
North, F.H. v2p0158c1s
v2p0318c1s v2p0382c2m v2p0431c2s
v2p0480c1s
North, F.M. v4p0116c1s
North, F.P. v1p0913c1s
North, G. v1p0050c1s
North, H. v3p0410c2s
North, H.M. v3p0463c2s
v4p0084c1s v4p0590c1s v4p0620c1s
v5p0085c1s v5p0343c1s v5p0458c2s
v5p0580c2s
North, J.H. v6p0060c2s
North, J.W. v4p0609c1s
v6p0034c1s
North, L. v5p0181c2s
North, L.A. v3p0078c1s
v4p0263c1s v4p0451c2s v5p0614c1s
North, L.S. v1p1418c2s
North, Lord v6p0459c2s
North, O. v5p0264c2s
v5p0312c1s
North, S. v1p0600c2s
v1p0610c1s
North, S.B. v1p1316c1s
North, S.N.D. v1p0917c2s
v1p0948c2s v2p0312c2s v2p0323c2s
v3p0471c2s v4p0022c2s v4p0213c2s
v4p0283c2s v4p0546c2s v4p0631c2s
v5p0190c1s v5p0289c1s v5p0332c1s
v5p0557c1s v6p0399c2s v6p0633c1s
North, S.N.D. and Durfee, W.F.
v3p0011c1s

North, S.N.D. and Wadlin, G.H.
v5p0365c1s
North, T. v2p0039c1s
v2p0259c2s
North, T.M. v3p0268c2s
North, W. v1p0757c1s
v2p0420c1s
Northall, G.F. v5p0359c2s
Northbrook, Lord v1p0633c1s
Northcote, A.F. v1p1110c1s
Northcote, A.S. v4p0015c1s
v4p0092c2s v4p0591c2s v4p0595c1s
Northcote, Dr. v1p1122c1s
Northcote, H.S. v2p0066c1s
v3p0202c1s
Northcote, H.S., Sir v4p0266c1s
Northcote, H.Stafford, Sir
v3p0459c2s
Northcote, J.S. v1p0061c2s
v1p0205c2m v1p0206c1s v1p0808c2s
v1p0994c1s
Northcote, S. v1p0423c1s
Northcote, S.H. v2p0156c1s
v2p0186c2s
Northcott, M. v1p0571c1s
v1p0694c2s v1p0716c2s v1p0726c2s
v1p0930c2s v1p0939c2s v1p1031c2s
v1p1368c2s
Northcott, W.A. v5p0489c1s
Northcroft, G.J.H. v4p0075c2s
v5p0038c2s
Northcroft, Geo.J.H. v3p0056c2s
Northend, C. v1p0285c1s
v1p1398c1s v4p0162c1s v4p0287c1s
Northend, M.H. v6p0035c2s
v6p0320c1s
Northend, Mary H. v6p0565c1m
Northend, W.D. v1p0248c2s
v1p1063c1s v2p0341c2s
Northey, T. v1p1138c1s
Northland, L.G. v6p0212c2s
v6p0628c2s
Northland, Louis G. v6p0644c1s
Northop, J.M. v2p0372c2s
Northrop, B.G. v1p0808c2s
v1p1072c1s v4p0604c2m
Northrop, C. v5p0605c1s
v6p0460c1s
Northrop, C. and Gates, M.E.
v4p0122c2s
Northrop, J.I. v3p0394c2s
Northrop, W.B. v6p0071c2s
Northrop, W.P. v4p0020c2s
Northrup, A.C. v6p0705c1s
Northrup, A.J. v3p0307c1s
Northrup, B. v3p0308c2s
Northrup, E.F. v4p0047c2s
Northrup, G.W. v4p0456c2s
v5p0236c2s
Northrup, H.E. v5p0231c2s
Northrup, M.H. v5p0182c2s
v6p0361c2s
Northrup, W.P. v3p0210c1s
v3p0319c2s
Northumberland, Duke of .. v6p0576c1s
Northup, C.S. v5p0099c1s
v5p0432c2s v6p0161c1s v6p0172c1s
v6p0208c1s v6p0242c2s v6p0597c2s
v6p0617c1s v6p0618c1s v6p0696c1s
Norton, A. v1p0028c2s
v1p0087c1s v1p0130c2s v1p0132c1s
v1p0132c2s v1p0182c1s v1p0217c1s
v1p0221c1s v1p0243c2s v1p0483c2s
v1p0491c2s v1p0495c2s v1p0512c2s
v1p0529c2s v1p0540c1s v1p0584c2s
v1p0620c1s v1p0626c2s v1p0675c1s
v1p0882c2s v1p0962c2s v1p1028c2s
v1p1041c2s v1p1065c2s v1p1094c1s
v1p1175c2s v1p1200c2s v1p1386c1s
Norton, A. and Ticknor, G.
v1p0173c1s
Norton, A.B. v6p0217c1s
Norton, A.H. v4p0570c2s
Norton, A.K., Mrs. v4p0215c2s
Norton, A.O. v6p0191c1s
v6p0362c2s v6p0581c2s
Norton, Arthur O. v6p0362c2s
Norton, B. v3p0352c2s
Norton, C. v4p0109c2s
Norton, C.E. v1p0031c1s
v1p0051c2s v1p0057c2s v1p0082c1s
v1p0140c2s v1p0205c2s v1p0213c2s
v1p0248c2s v1p0258c2s v1p0266c2m
v1p0274c2m v1p0287c1s v1p0291c1s
v1p0321c2s v1p0331c2m v1p0342c2s
v1p0343c1s v1p0350c1s v1p0385c1s
v1p0386c2s v1p0405c2m v1p0406c1s
v1p0411c1s v1p0461c1s v1p0490c2m
v1p0499c2s v1p0573c1m v1p0633c1s
v1p0666c2s v1p0680c2s v1p0685c2s
v1p0693c2s v1p0706c2s v1p0715c2s
v1p0728c2s v1p0750c2s v1p0760c1s
v1p0768c1s v1p0771c1s v1p0795c2s
v1p0797c1s v1p0817c2s v1p0865c1s
v1p0873c1s v1p0877c2s v1p0915c1s
v1p0938c2s v1p0941c1s v1p0942c1s
v1p0960c1s v1p0976c1s v1p0977c1s
v1p0979c1s v1p1011c1s v1p1030c2s
v1p1083c1s v1p1093c1s v1p1141c1s
v1p1171c1m v1p1187c1s v1p1190c1s
v1p1207c2s v1p1210c2s v1p1221c1s
v1p1250c2s v1p1275c2s v1p1295c2s
v1p1310c1s v1p1314c1s v1p1334c2s
v1p1336c2s v1p1344c1m v1p1344c2s
v1p1346c1s v1p1347c1s v1p1355c1s
v1p1363c1s v1p1365c2s v1p1389c2s
v1p1426c1s v2p0069c1s v2p0090c1s
v2p0288c1s v2p0386c1s v3p0010c1s
v3p0056c2s v3p0074c2s v3p0106c2s
v3p0110c1s v3p0110c2m v3p0153c1s
v3p0190c2s v3p0199c1s v3p0320c2s
v4p0117c2s v4p0199c2s v4p0343c2m
v4p0495c1s v5p0025c1s v5p0033c1s
v5p0105c2s v5p0317c1m v5p0475c2s
v6p0038c2s v6p0282c1s v6p0619c1s
Norton, C.E., Mrs. v1p0221c1s
v1p0483c1s v1p0536c1s v1p1128c1s
v1p1131c2s v3p0431c1s
Norton, C.G. v6p0092c2s
Norton, C.H. v5p0067c2s
v6p0274c2s
Norton, C.L. v1p0071c1s
v1p0196c2s v1p0789c2s v1p0886c2s
v2p0012c2s v2p0293c2s v2p0436c2s
v3p0062c1s v3p0064c2s v3p0207c1m
v3p0397c2s v3p0454c1s v4p0083c2s
v4p0125c1s v4p0266c2s v4p0273c1s
v4p0498c1s v4p0634c1s v4p0634c2s
v5p0272c2s v5p0338c1s v5p0643c1s
v6p0604c2s v6p0616c1s
Norton, C.L. and Atkinson, Edward
v6p0087c1s
Norton, C.L. and Lawrence, R.R.
v5p0492c1s
Norton, C.P. v3p0059c1s
Norton, C.S. and Lawrence, R.R.
v5p0289c1s
Norton, C.V. v6p0094c1s
Norton, E. v1p0044c2s
v2p0277c1s v6p0308c1s v6p0308c2s
Norton, E., Mrs. v1p0007c2s
Norton, E.Q. v4p0629c2s
Norton, F.H. v1p0069c2s
v1p0236c1s v1p0368c1s v1p0714c1s
Norton, F.L. v5p0460c1s
Norton, F.W. v5p0014c2s
Norton, G. v2p0032c2s
v2p0063c1s v2p0075c2s v2p0123c2s
v2p0125c1s v2p0155c1s v2p0158c2m
v2p0181c2s v2p0224c1s v2p0260c2s
v2p0283c1s v2p0332c1s v2p0347c2s
v2p0398c1s v2p0399c1s v2p0433c1s
v2p0442c2s v3p0070c2s v4p0025c2s
v4p0355c2s v4p0380c1s v5p0041c2s
Norton, G. and Allen, W.F.
v2p0016c2s
Norton, Grace v6p0426c2s
Norton, H. v1p1377c2s
v3p0235c1s v3p0286c2m
Norton, H.B. v1p0621c2s
Norton, H.E. v2p0355c2s
Norton, J. v3p0286c1s
Norton, J.P. v1p0935c1s
v6p0260c1s v6p0381c2s
Norton, J.S. v2p0421c2s
v3p0086c1s v4p0386c1s
Norton, J.T. v5p0370c2s
v5p0537c2s
Norton, J.T., jr. v5p0298c1s
Norton, J.T., jr. and Gooch, F.A.
v5p0382c1s
Norton, L.A. v2p0322c1s
Norton, Lord v1p0544c1s
v1p0986c1s v2p0084c2s v2p0100c1s
v2p0106c1s v2p0115c2s v2p0130c2s
v2p0131c2s v2p0186c2s v2p0388c1s
v3p0129c1s v3p0356c2s v4p0049c2s
Norton, M. v6p0412c1s
Norton, M.B. v3p0138c2s
v3p0193c2s v3p0406c2s
Norton, M.B., Mrs. v3p0039c1s
Norton, R. v5p0035c1s
v5p0142c2s v5p0369c1s v5p0493c1s
v5p0495c1m v5p0495c2s v6p0163c1s
v6p0549c1s v6p0648c1s
Norton, R.D. v2p0013c2s
Norton, Richard v5p0018c2s
Norton, Roy v6p0696c1s
Norton, Roy E. v6p0348c2s
Norton, S.T. v1p1220c2s
Norton, T.H. v1p0299c2s
v4p0098c2s
Norton, W.A. v1p0104c1s
v1p0189c1s v1p0281c1m v1p0281c2s
v1p0282c1s v1p0295c1s v1p0579c2s
v1p0739c2s v1p0787c2m v1p0858c2m
v1p1006c2m v1p1100c2s v1p1259c1s
v1p1267c2s v1p1268c2s
Norton, W.H. v4p0171c2s
v4p0241c1s v5p0449c1s v5p0513c2s
Norvell, S. v5p0412c2s
Norway, A.H. v3p0294c1s
v4p0078c2s v5p0163c2s v5p0215c1s
v5p0225c1s v5p0443c2s v5p0452c1s
v6p0140c1s
Norway, G. v2p0426c2s
Norwich v4p0124c1s
Norwood, C.J. v3p0089c2s
Norwood, J.C. v5p0315c1s
Nosgen, D. and Knubel, F.H.
v4p0053c2s
Noss, C. v6p0566c2s
Noss, Christopher v6p0335c2s
Noss, J.G. v4p0109c1s
v4p0130c1s v5p0580c2s v6p0285c2s
v6p0534c2s
Nostaw, A.L. v1p1417c2s
Nothnagel, H. v4p0573c2s
Notley, F.E.M. v1p0046c2s
v1p0176c2s v1p0990c1s v1p1252c1s
v1p1261c2s v2p0109c2s v5p0634c2s
Notley, Mrs. v1p0468c2s
v1p0627c1s v1p0851c2s v1p0926c1s
v1p1406c1s
Notman, W.R. v4p0052c1s
v4p0457c1s
Notnor, Hope v3p0272c1s
Nott, C.C. v1p0017c2s
v1p0180c1s v1p0192c1s v1p0222c1s
v1p0228c2s v1p0238c1s v1p0259c1s
v1p0259c2s v1p0275c1s v1p0294c2s
v1p0295c2s v1p0325c2m v1p0356c1s
v1p0487c1s v1p0620c1m v1p0628c1s
v1p0697c2m v1p0698c1s v1p0699c2m
v1p0729c1s v1p0730c2s v1p0862c2s
v1p0880c2s v1p0978c2s v1p1025c2s
v1p1038c2s v1p1048c2m v1p1053c1s
v1p1145c2s v1p1267c1s v1p1323c2s
v1p1378c2s v1p1388c2m v1p1420c2s
v2p0266c2s v2p0353c1s v3p0149c1s
v3p0202c1s v3p0262c1s v3p0379c1s
v3p0443c1s v3p0449c2s v4p0129c1s
v4p0264c1s v4p0306c1s v4p0348c2s
v4p0540c1s v4p0557c2s v4p0562c1s
v4p0592c2s v4p0593c2s
v5p0600c1s
Nott, C.C., jr. v4p0003c2s
v4p0327c2s v6p0176c1s
Nott, F.J. v2p0372c2s
Nott, J. v1p0647c2s
Nott, J.C. v1p0904c2s
v1p1205c1s v1p1436c2s v2p0309c1s
v2p0410c2s
Nott, J.F. v4p0043c1s
v4p0099c2s
Nott, J.W. v2p0473c1s
Nott, R.M. v2p0439c1s
Nott, S. v1p0581c1s
Nott, S., jr. v1p0390c2s
Nottage, G.S. v2p0379c1s
Nottebohm, G. v4p0049c1s
Notter, J.L. v5p0194c1s
Nourse, B.F. v1p0133c2s
v1p0306c2s v1p0325c1s v1p1198c2s
Nourse, D.H. v5p0116c2s
Nourse, E.E. v6p0061c2s
Nourse, H.S. v3p0241c1m
v3p0249c1s v3p0260c2s v3p0343c1s
v4p0329c1s v4p0360c1s v5p0267c1s
v5p0333c2s
Nourse, J.E. v1p0650c2s
v1p0738c1s v1p0920c1s v1p0936c1s
v1p1264c2s
Nourse, M. v1p0283c1s
Nourse, R. v2p0106c1s
v2p0183c1s v2p0234c2s v2p0401c1s
Novicow, J. v5p0133c2s
v5p0189c1s v5p0502c2s v6p0442c2s
Novikoff, O. v3p0370c1s
v3p0370c2s v4p0166c2s v4p0496c2s
v5p0501c1m
Novikoff, O.De v2p0448c2s
Novili-Vitelleschi, F. ... v5p0300c1m
Novy, F.G. v5p0081c1s
Nowell, C.C. v1p1394c1s
Nowell, R. v1p0304c2s
Nowell, W.G. v1p0044c1s
v1p0120c1s v1p0961c2s
Noxon, A.R. v3p0475c2s
Noxon, E.W. v6p0460c2s
Noxon, F.W. v6p0148c2s
v6p0239c1s v6p0249c1s v6p0264c1s
v6p0282c1s v6p0434c2s v6p0476c1s
v6p0570c1s v6p0588c2s v6p0651c2s
v6p0692c1s
Noye, G.R. v6p0661c1s
Noyes, A. v6p0180c2s
v6p0181c2s v6p0185c1s v6p0311c1s
v6p0394c1s
Noyes, A.A. v6p0066c1s
v6p0138c1s v6p0325c2s
Noyes, A.D. v4p0015c2s
v4p0044c2s v4p0143c2s v4p0199c2s
v4p0336c2s v4p0525c1s v4p0550c1s
v4p0593c1s v4p0618c2s v5p0045c2s
v5p0124c1s v5p0149c2s v5p0196c2s
v5p0207c1s v5p0213c1s v5p0237c2s
v5p0551c2s v5p0593c2s v5p0600c2s
v5p0604c1s v5p0627c2m v6p0049c2s
v6p0050c1m v6p0133c1s v6p0151c1s
v6p0188c2s v6p0210c1m v6p0224c1m
v6p0260c1s v6p0260c2s v6p0282c2s
v6p0318c2s v6p0322c2s v6p0324c1s
v6p0400c1s v6p0401c2s v6p0452c1s
v6p0460c1s v6p0478c1s v6p0520c1s
v6p0529c2s v6p0530c2s v6p0658c2s
v6p0665c2s v6p0667c1s v6p0670c1m
v6p0684c1m
Noyes, A.J. v6p0050c1s
Noyes, Alfred v6p0449c1s

Noyes, C. v1p1270c1s
Noyes, C.P. v6p0059c2s
Noyes, D.J. v1p0293c1s
v1p0867c2s
Noyes, D.P. v1p0159c2s
v1p0206c2s v1p0247c1s v1p0290c2s
v1p0528c1s v1p0530c2s v1p0972c2s
v1p1066c2s v1p1400c2s
Noyes, E.C. v6p0130c1s
v6p0142c2s
Noyes, E.F. v2p0165c2s
Noyes, Eliza F. v5p0107c1s
Noyes, F.B. v6p0003c1s
Noyes, F.E. v3p0455c1s
Noyes, G.C. v1p0010c2s
v1p0104c1s v1p0695c2s v2p0061c1s
v2p0103c1s v2p0144c2s v2p0286c2s
v2p0323c1m v2p0338c1s v2p0352c2s
v2p0374c2s v3p0007c1s v3p0029c2s
v3p0186c1s v3p0266c1s v3p0277c1m
v3p0307c2s
Noyes, G.R. v1p0121c2s
v1p0122c1s v1p0123c1s v1p0123c2m
v1p0124c1s v1p0131c1s v1p0132c1m
v1p0179c2s v1p0318c1s v1p0421c1s
v1p0517c1s v1p0529c1s v1p0581c2s
v1p0684c2s v1p0685c2s v1p0761c1s
v1p0813c1s v1p1035c2s v1p1093c2s
v1p1100c2s v1p1141c1s v1p1262c1s
v1p1302c2s v5p0170c1s v6p0559c1s
v6p0559c2s
Noyes, H. v1p0735c2s
Noyes, H.E. v6p0030c1s
v6p0568c1s
Noyes, H.F. v6p0693c2s
Noyes, H.W. v5p0416c1s
Noyes, I.P. v2p0035c1s
v2p0285c2m v2p0366c2s v2p0421c2s
v2p0443c1s v2p0468c2m v2p0469c1m
Noyes, J. v1p1372c1s
Noyes, J.A. v4p0409c1s
v5p0003c2s v5p0048c1s v5p0416c1s
Noyes, J.B. v2p0318c1s
Noyes, J.D. v2p0224c1s
v2p0320c2s
Noyes, J.H. v1p0318c2s
Noyes, J.O. v1p0174c2s
v1p0185c1s v1p0294c1s v1p0304c2s
v1p0307c1s v1p0332c1s v1p0395c2s
v1p0429c2s v1p0522c1m v1p0615c1s
v1p0615c2s v1p0854c1s v1p0858c2s
v1p0917c2s v1p0918c1s v1p1010c2s
v1p1068c2s v1p1224c1s v1p1224c2s
v1p1382c2s v2p0299c2s
Noyes, N. v1p0590c1s
Noyes, N.D. v5p0122c1s
v6p0051c1s v6p0616c1s v6p0654c2s
Noyes, S.B. v1p0628c2s
v2p0070c2s
Noyes, T. v1p0846c2m
v1p0925c2s v1p1429c1s
Noyes, T.H. v1p1308c1s
Noyes, W. v3p0082c1s
v3p0105c2s v3p0206c2s v3p0216c2s
v3p0319c2s v4p0312c1s v6p0078c2s
v6p0115c1s
Noyes, W.A. v4p0099c1s
v6p0112c1m
Noyes, W.B. v4p0158c1s
Noyes, W.S.G. v4p0616c1s
Nuckols, Emma D. v5p0224c1s
Nuel, Fr. et al. v6p0173c1s
Nugent, J. v1p0642c1s
Nugent, Lord v1p0185c1s
v1p0315c1s v1p0787c1s
Nugent, R. v1p0411c1s
Nugent, W.T. v4p0027c2s
Nugent-Bankes, G. v5p0208c1s
Nugisch, E. v1p0084c1s
Numsen, W.H. v2p0014c1m
v2p0095c2s
Numsen, W.H. and Swift, L.
v2p0014c1s
Nundy, A. v5p0196c2s
v6p0313c1s
Nundy, Alfred v5p0286c1s
Nunez, E. v5p0148c1s
Nunn, E.A. v2p0305c2s
Nunn, P.N. v6p0198c1s
Nunn, T.H. v4p0340c1s
Nunn, T.W. v4p0206c1s
Nunneley, T. v2p0322c1s
Nunns, T. v5p0212c1s
v5p0263c1s
Nursey, P.E. v2p0008c2s
Nursey, P.F. v1p0526c1s
v1p1204c2s v2p0057c2s v3p0174c2s
v4p0324c1s
Nusbaum, S. v4p0260c2s
Nussbaum, Dr.von v3p0163c1s
Nusse, E. v3p0077c2s
Nussey, H.G. v6p0408c2s
v6p0708c1s
Nute, M.C., Mrs. v1p0050c2s
Nutt, A. v2p0024c1s
v2p0133c1s v4p0085c1s v4p0094c1m
v4p0177c2s v4p0261c1s v4p0336c1s
v4p0346c2s v4p0397c2s v4p0512c1s
v5p0201c2s v5p0212c1m v6p0034c2s
v6p0479c1s v6p0481c2s v6p0594c1s
Nutt, A. and Besant, W. .. v5p0070c1s
Nutt, A. and Jacobs, J. .. v4p0155c2s
v4p0361c1s
Nutt, A. et al. v3p0315c1s
v4p0114c2s
v5p0170c2s
Nutt, G. v3p0144c2s
v3p0349c2s
Nutt, G. et al. v2p0416c1s
Nutt, H.G. v6p0450c2s
Nutt, Harry G. v6p0295c2s
Nutt, J.J. v6p0109c2s
Nutt, N. v4p0140c2s
v4p0433c1s
Nutt, R. v1p1041c2s
Nutt, T. v6p0070c1s
Nuttall, G. v6p0409c1s
Nuttall, G.C. v4p0048c1s
v4p0162c1s v4p0633c2s v5p0024c1s
v5p0025c1s v5p0043c2s v5p0085c2s
v5p0103c2s v5p0123c2s v5p0135c1s
v5p0166c2s v5p0173c1s v5p0360c1s
v5p0374c1s v5p0400c2s v5p0447c2s
v5p0518c2s v5p0521c2s v5p0534c2s
v5p0569c1s v5p0581c2s v5p0590c1s
v5p0642c2s v6p0049c1s v6p0230c1s
v6p0502c2m v6p0503c1s
Nuttall, G.C. and Farman, A.E.
v4p0430c2s
Nuttall, G.Clarke v5p0066c2s
Nuttall, G.H.F. v5p0067c1s
v5p0430c1s
Nuttall, T.K. v4p0169c1s
v4p0350c1s v5p0637c2s
Nuttall, Z. v2p0435c1s
v5p0562c2s
Nuttall, Zelia v4p0368c1s
v5p0100c2s v6p0092c1s v6p0407c2s
v6p0414c1s
Nutter, C.S. v4p0008c2s
v4p0300c1s
Nutter, F.H. v5p0504c1s
Nutter, G.R. v6p0047c2s
Nutting, A. v4p0409c2s
Nutting, C.C. v3p0002c1s
v3p0332c2s v4p0255c2s v4p0271c1s
v4p0637c2s v5p0021c1s v5p0447c2m
v5p0455c1s v5p0516c2s v6p0365c1s
v6p0630c2s v6p0650c2s
Nutting, H.C. v5p0326c2s
v6p0143c2s
Nutting, J.D. v6p0429c1s
Nutting, J.H. v1p0416c1s
Nutting, M.A. v6p0660c1s
Nutting, M.E. v3p0176c1s
Nyana, R. v5p0393c1s
Nyblom, Helena v5p0019c1s
v5p0419c2s
Nydia v6p0094c1s
Nye, A.B. v2p0354c1s
v6p0479c1s
Nye, A.C. v4p0218c1s
v4p0384c1s v4p0631c2s v5p0223c2m
Nye, A.G. v5p0113c2s
Nye, Bill v6p0463c1s
Nye, E.W. v3p0029c1s
v4p0449c2s
Nye, E.W. et al. v3p0236c2s
Nye, G. v1p1287c2m
Nye, G.H.F. v5p0117c1s
Nye, H.R. v1p0495c2s
v1p0496c1s v1p0536c2s v2p0044c2s
Nye, W. v2p0343c1s
Nyevelt, S.I.de Zuylen de. v3p0028c1s
v4p0039c1s v4p0194c1s v4p0260c1s
v4p0260c2s v4p0554c1s
v6p0678c2s
Nyhuus, H. v6p0372c1s
Nyhuus, Haakon and Hammer, S.C.
v6p0679c1s
Nylan, J.N. v1p0362c1s
v1p0458c2s
Nylander, P.E. v5p0258c1s
Nymanover, E. v2p0289c1s
Nyren, M. v5p0563c2s
Nyren, M. and Watson, Isa. v6p0622c1s
Nys, E. v4p0156c2s
Nystrom and Merrick v1p1055c2s
Nystrom, J.W. v1p0057c2s
v1p0145c2s v1p0146c1m v1p0200c1s
v1p0366c1s v1p0374c2s v1p0442c1s
v1p0491c1s v1p0541c2s v1p0831c2s
v1p1006c1s v1p1055c2m v1p1191c2m
v1p1222c1s v1p1249c2s v1p1315c2s
v1p1430c2s v2p0039c1m v2p0078c2m
v2p0419c2s
Nyttelton, N.G. v3p0187c1s

O., E.B. v6p0095c2s
Oak, H.L. v1p0030c2s
Oakeley, Canon v4p0420c1s
Oakeley, F. v1p0390c1s
v1p1120c2s
Oakeley, F.C. v1p0253c1s
Oakeley, H.D. v5p0020c1s
v6p0427c1s v6p0704c1s
Oakely, Thornton v6p0132c2s
Oakes, R.A. v1p0886c2s
v3p0401c1s
Oakes, W.W. v5p0612c2s
Oakeshott, B.N. v5p0030c1s
v5p0522c2s
Oakeshott, G. v5p0637c1s
Oakey, A.F. v1p0004c2s
v1p0052c1s v1p0054c2s v1p0253c1s
v1p0339c2s v1p0405c1s v1p1008c1s
v2p0022c2s v2p0100c2s v2p0114c1s
v2p0114c2s v3p0374c1s
Oakey, M.R. v1p0367c1s
v1p0616c2s v1p1011c1s
Oakey, S.W. v1p0034c1s
Oakley, A.F. v2p0435c2s
Oakley, C.S. v4p0163c1s
v4p0628c1s
Oakley, F. v1p1318c2s
Oakley, H. v5p0219c2s
v5p0467c2s v6p0518c2s
Oakley, H.C. v5p0349c2s
Oakley, I.G. v5p0454c2s
Oakley, J. v1p0391c2s
Oakley, J.G. v2p0377c1s
Oakley, J.M. v3p0248c1s
Oakley, John v5p0228c1s
Oakley, T. v6p0422c1s
v6p0425c2s v6p0383c2s
Oakley, Thornton v6p0453c2s
Oakley-Williams, P.H. v5p0346c2s
Oakman, W.G. v5p0540c2s
Oaksmith, A. v1p0325c2s
v1p1226c1s v1p1348c1s
Oates, A. v3p0077c1s
v5p0171c2s
Oates, A.G. v2p0038c2m
v2p0373c1s
Oates, J.W. v6p0030c1s
v6p0315c2s v6p0604c1s v6p0687c2s
Oates, W.C. v1p0518c2s
v4p0262c1s v4p0538c1s
Obach, E.F.A. v5p0253c1m
Obenchain, W.A. v3p0225c2s
Ober, C.K. v3p0123c1s
Ober, F.A. v1p0939c2s
v1p1172c2s v3p0002c1s v3p0060c1s
v3p0093c2m v3p0318c2s v3p0403c1s
v4p0126c1s v5p0433c2s v5p0460c1s
v5p0507c1s v6p0403c2s
Ober, S.E. v6p0287c2s
Oberholser, H.C. v4p0540c1s
Oberholtzer, E.P. v3p0245c1s
v3p0356c1s v4p0387c2s v4p0492c2s
v5p0162c1s v5p0567c1s v6p0147c2s
v6p0181c1s v6p0239c1s v6p0332c2s
v6p0430c2m v6p0505c2s v6p0668c1s
Oberholtzer, S.L. v4p0504c1m
Oberly, H.H. v2p0096c2s
Obersteiner, H. v5p0404c2s
Obersteiner, Heinrich v5p0194c2s
O'Brien, A. v1p0770c2s
v1p0942c2s v1p1255c2s v2p0197c2s
v2p0295c1s
O'Brien, Alice v6p0123c2s
O'Brien, C. v1p0657c2s
O'Brien, C. et al. v1p0657c1s
O'Brien, C.G. v1p0655c2s
v2p0313c1s
O'Brien, C.M. v5p0414c2s
O'Brien, D. v1p1408c2s
v2p0113c2s v3p0208c1s
O'Brien, E.W. v2p0227c2s
O'Brien, E.Y. v6p0687c1s
O'Brien, F.J. v1p0081c1s
v1p0349c1s v1p0384c1s v1p0567c1s
v1p0570c2s v1p0779c2s v1p0818c2s
v1p0855c2s v1p0878c2s v1p1182c1s
v1p1187c2s v1p1201c2s v1p1294c1s
v1p1427c1s
O'Brien, F.M. v3p0069c1s
v3p0470c2s
O'Brien, G. v2p0154c2s
v2p0290c1s
O'Brien, H. v1p0115c1s
O'Brien, J.E. v3p0423c1s
O'Brien, L.R. v1p0064c1s
O'Brien, Lt.Col. v4p0370c2s
O'Brien, M. v1p0657c2s
v1p0658c2s v2p0428c2s v2p0431c2s
v2p0458c1s v3p0161c2s v3p0186c2s
v3p0220c1s v3p0220c2s v3p0221c1s
v3p0221c2m v4p0289c2s v4p0290c1m
v4p0560c2s v5p0295c2s v5p0296c2s
v6p0326c1m v6p0326c2m v6p0327c1s
v6p0484c1s v6p0629c2s
O'Brien, M.D. v5p0068c1s
v5p0234c2s v6p0114c1s v6p0258c1s
v6p0270c2s v6p0492c2s v6p0654c1m
O'Brien, R.B. v2p0225c1s
v2p0228c1m v2p0228c2s v2p0405c2s
v3p0220c2s v5p0149c1s v5p0509c1s
v6p0184c1s
O'Brien, R.L. v6p0144c2s
v6p0209c1s v6p0488c1s v6p0583c2s
v6p0696c2s
O'Brien, T.F. v5p0374c2s
O'Brien, V.L. v5p0129c1s
O'Brien, W. v1p0195c2s
v1p1022c1s v1p1234c2s v3p0158c2s
v4p0289c1m v4p0290c1s v4p0339c2s
v4p0428c1s v5p0085c1s v5p0296c2s
O'Brien, W. et al. v4p0291c1s
O'Brien, W.S. v6p0110c1s
O'Byrne, J.P. v4p0381c2s
O'Byrne, M.A. v4p0094c1s
v5p0129c1s
O'Byrne, M.C. v4p0007c1s
v4p0186c2s v4p0187c2s v4p0391c2s
v4p0478c1s v4p0479c1s
O'Byrne, M.C. and Keane, J.J.
v2p0375c2s
O'Byrne, R. v3p0143c2s
Ocagne, M.D' v3p0017c2s
O'Callaghan, D. v6p0069c2s
v6p0168c2s
O'Callaghan, E. v2p0113c1s
v2p0459c1s v2p0464c2s v3p0019c1s
v3p0055c2s v3p0243c2s v3p0266c1s
v3p0296c1s v3p0338c1s v3p0372c1s
v3p0372c2s v3p0374c2s v3p0430c1s
v3p0449c2s
O'Callaghan, E., Capt. v3p0172c2s
O'Callaghan, E.B. v1p0677c1s
v1p0680c2s v1p0683c2s v1p0842c2s
v1p1143c1s v1p1212c1s v1p1374c1s
O'Callaghan, E.J. v3p0215c2s
O'Callaghan, P. v4p0398c1s
O'Callaghan, P.T. v2p0218c1s
O'Callaghan, R.E. v4p0534c1s
Ochiltree, J.C. v5p0268c1s
Ochino, B. v1p0700c1s
Ochs, G.W. v4p0116c1s
v6p0346c1s
Ochsenius, K. v2p0463c1s
Ockershausen, G.P. v1p0418c1s
O'Connell, C.H. v4p0237c2s
O'Connell, D. v1p0875c1s
v1p0908c2s v1p0976c1s v5p0417c2s
O'Connell, J. v1p0404c2s
v1p1157c2s v1p1359c2s v5p0353c1s
v6p0393c1s
O'Connell, J.J. v4p0224c1s
v4p0553c1s v5p0028c2s v5p0108c1s
v5p0196c2s v5p0216c2s v5p0622c2s
O'Connell, L. v6p0631c1s
O'Connell, M.D. v2p0082c2s
O'Connell, M.J., Mrs. v2p0399c1s
O'Connor, B.F. v2p0167c2s
O'Connor, C.J. v5p0495c2s
v5p0590c2s
O'Connor, C.M. v5p0599c1s
O'Connor, D.M. v3p0152c1s
v4p0584c1s v6p0143c1s v6p0181c1s
O'Connor, H. v3p0461c2s
v5p0197c2s
O'Connor, J. v1p0252c2s
v1p0405c1s v1p1058c1s v1p1118c1s
v1p1175c2s v2p0067c1s v2p0244c2s
v2p0349c1s v2p0407c2s
O'Connor, J.E. v6p0313c2s
O'Connor, J.F.X. v2p0022c2s
O'Connor, J.J. v6p0226c2s
O'Connor, J.T. v3p0206c1s
O'Connor, L.S. v1p0073c1s
O'Connor, M. v1p1115c2s
v1p1324c2s v5p0196c2s v5p0218c2s
v5p0494c1s v6p0202c2s v6p0416c2s
O'Connor, M.J. v1p0253c1s
O'Connor, R.F. v2p0004c1s
v2p0073c2s v2p0105c1s v2p0125c2s
v2p0272c2s v2p0460c1s v4p0536c1s
v6p0032c2s v6p0052c2s v6p0195c2s
v6p0256c2s v6p0334c1s v6p0336c2s
v6p0398c2s v6p0709c2s
O'Connor, T.P. v1p0080c1s
v1p0657c2s v1p0861c1s v2p0142c1s
v2p0224c2s v2p0226c1s v2p0227c2s
v3p0174c1s v3p0220c2s v3p0221c2m
v3p0222c1s v3p0232c2s v4p0261c2s
v4p0265c2s v4p0289c2s v4p0290c1s
v5p0272c1s v5p0272c2s v6p0047c2s
v6p0326c2s v6p0357c2s v6p0542c1s
v6p0565c2s v6p0614c2s v6p0644c1s
O'Connor, T.P. and Hill, F.H.
v4p0289c2s
O'Connor, T.P., Mrs. v6p0592c1s
O'Connor, V.C.S. v5p0089c2s
v5p0298c2s v5p0573c1s
O'Connor, W.A. v2p0003c2s
O'Connor, W.D. v1p0088c1s
v1p0202c2s v1p0711c1s v1p0746c2s
v1p0770c1s v1p1313c1s v1p1403c2s
v3p0053c2s
O'Conor, C.P. v2p0337c1s
O'Conor, J.V. v1p0032c1s
v1p0201c1s v1p0230c1s v1p0256c1s
v1p0372c1s v1p0412c2s v1p0417c2s
v1p0451c1s v1p0575c2s v1p0578c1s
v1p0619c2s v1p0752c2m v1p0754c2s
v1p0838c2s v1p0892c2s v1p0932c1s
v1p0990c2s v1p1022c2s v1p1024c2s
v1p1057c2s v1p1094c2s v1p1104c2s
v1p1158c1s v1p1161c2s v1p1266c2s
v1p1275c2s v1p1286c1s v1p1307c1s
v1p1321c1s v2p0053c2s v4p0467c1s
O'Conor, J.V. et al. v1p0356c1s
O'Conor, W.A. v2p0022c2s
v2p0163c2s v2p0247c1s v2p0297c2s
v2p0369c1s v2p0399c2s
O'Conor-Eccles, C. v5p0612c1s
O'Conor-Eccles, Miss and
Marshall, Mrs. v5p0637c1s
Odell, W. v2p0070c2s
v2p0194c2s v2p0402c2s v2p0456c1s
Odell, W., jr. v1p0743c2s
Odell, W.H. v4p0065c2s
Odell, W.P. v4p0228c2s
Odenbaugh, Katherine v6p0093c1s
Odescalchi, B. v5p0300c2s
Odgen, R. v5p0147c1s
v6p0632c1s
Odger, G. v1p0317c1s
v1p0721c2s v1p1431c2s
Odgers, J. v5p0483c2s
Odgers, J.E. v1p1129c2s
v2p0044c1s v2p0234c2s
Odgers, J.F. v4p0482c1s
Odgers, W.B. v1p0219c2s
v1p0397c2s v2p0049c1s v2p0201c2s
v6p0364c2s
Odhner, C.T. v1p0915c1s
v5p0224c2s
Odiorne, J.C. v1p0152c1s
Odling, Dr. v1p0225c1s
Odling, Prof. v3p0457c1s
Odling, W. v1p0224c1s
v1p0224c2s v1p0348c2s v1p1002c1s
v2p0138c2s v2p0389c2s v3p0054c1s
Odlum, E. v5p0318c1s
v5p0594c1s
Odlum, St.G. v4p0473c2s
O'Donahue, D.J. v3p0116c1s
O'Donavan, P.D. v1p0887c1s
O'Donnell, C.R. v1p0587c2s
v1p1134c1s
O'Donnell, F.H. v1p0516c1s
v1p0653c2s v1p0963c2s v1p1136c1s
v2p0154c2s
O'Donnell, J.D. v5p0210c1s
O'Donnell, J.F. v3p0201c1s
v3p0317c1s v4p0264c1s v4p0350c1s
v5p0270c2s
O'Donnell, K. v1p1163c2s
O'Donnell, T. v5p0224c1s
O'Donnell, T.F. v1p0452c2s
v1p0659c1s v1p0982c1s v1p1309c2s
O'Donoghue, D.J. v6p0398c2s
O'Donoghue, J. v1p0039c1s
v2p0195c1s v2p0228c2s v2p0268c1s
v2p0361c2s v2p0380c1s v2p0446c1s
O'Donoghue, J.G. v6p0652c2s
O'Donoghue, M.F. v6p0129c1s
O'Donoghue, M.F. and
Withee, L.J.Young v6p0241c1s
O'Donoghue, P., Mrs. v2p0208c1s
O'Donoghue, T.G. v2p0069c1s
O'Donovan, E. v2p0296c1s
v3p0438c1s
O'Donovan, J. v6p0116c1s
v6p0189c2s
O'Donovan, L. v6p0562c1s
O'Donovan, W. v2p0313c1s
v2p0329c2s
O'Donovan, W.R. v1p1139c2s
v1p1186c2s
O'Donovan, W.R. and Parsons, S.
v6p0361c1s
O'Driscoll, F. v4p0088c1m
v4p0106c1s
O'Dwyer, E. v5p0297c1s
O'Dwyer, E.Thomas v6p0672c1s
O'Dwyer, K. v6p0648c2s
O'Dwyer, M.F. v5p0034c1s
v5p0284c1s
O'Dwyer, W.M. v4p0368c2s
Oehlenschlager, A. v1p0521c1s
v1p0565c2s v2p0012c2s v2p0195c2s
v2p0382c2s
Oehler, G.F. v1p0120c1s
Oehler, Prof. v1p0891c2s
Oelrichs, H. v4p0560c1s
Oersted, H.C. v1p1391c2m
Oertel, H. v4p0298c2s
v5p0325c1s
Oertel, J.R. v1p0129c2s
Oesterley, W.O.E. v6p0063c2m
v6p0425c2s
Oettli v4p0054c2s
O'Fallon, J.M. v2p0180c1s
v4p0072c1s v4p0292c1s v4p0301c2s
v4p0455c1s v4p0526c2s v5p0462c1s
v5p0530c1s v6p0161c1s v6p0429c1s
O'Farrell, P.A. v3p0185c2s
v3p0189c1s v3p0195c2s v3p0263c1s
v4p0075c2s
Ofella v3p0200c2s
O'Ferrall, M. v1p1148c2s
Offen, C.R.W. v5p0107c2s
Offenbach, J. v2p0465c1s
Officer, M. v1p0599c2s
v1p0853c2s v1p0980c2s v1p1205c2s

Offord, J. v2p0030c2s
v4p0066c1s v4p0173c1s v6p0036c2s
v6p0037c1s v6p0046c1m v6p0060c1s
v6p0103c1s v6p0195c2s v6p0271c1s
v6p0416c1s v6p0458c1s v6p0478c2m
v6p0491c2s v6p0548c2s v6p0626c1s
O'Flanagan, J.R. v1p0880c2s
v2p0067c2s v2p0415c2s v3p0223c1s
Ogan, Mena K. v4p0009c1s
O'Gara, P.J. v6p0098c2s
Ogden, A. v4p0063c1s
Ogden, C.E. v5p0349c2s
Ogden, D.B. v1p0643c2s
v6p0056c1s
Ogden, D.L. v1p0097c1s
v1p0276c2s v1p0285c2s v1p0612c2s
v1p0908c2s v1p1120c2s
Ogden, E.L. v4p0375c1s
Ogden, G.W. v6p0056c1s
v6p0230c1s v6p0231c2s v6p0396c1s
v6p0422c1m v6p0484c2s v6p0615c2s
v6p0698c1s
Ogden, H.G. v3p0089c2s
v3p0169c1m v4p0121c1s
Ogden, H.G. and Baker, M.. v3p0417c1s
Ogden, H.G. et al. v4p0222c1s
Ogden, H.N. v4p0466c2s
Ogden, H.W. v1p1391c2m
Ogden, J. v2p0145c2s
v3p0186c1s v4p0128c1s v4p0320c1s
v5p0467c2s v5p0512c2s v5p0558c1s
v6p0459c1s v6p0521c2s
Ogden, J.De P. v1p0710c2s
Ogden, R. v2p0013c1s
v2p0286c2m v2p0287c1m v2p0369c2s
v2p0437c2s v2p0480c1s v3p0013c1s
v3p0019c1m v3p0053c2m v3p0054c2s
v3p0072c1s v3p0078c1s v3p0084c2m
v3p0104c1s v3p0110c2s v3p0135c1s
v3p0145c1s v3p0160c1s v3p0161c1s
v3p0186c1s v3p0252c2s v3p0272c1s
v3p0277c1m v3p0282c2s v3p0298c2s
v3p0308c2s v3p0309c1s v3p0318c2s
v3p0399c2s v3p0402c1s v3p0403c1m
v3p0420c1s v3p0471c2s v3p0472c2s
v3p0476c1s v4p0006c1s v4p0035c2s
v4p0038c1s v4p0042c1s v4p0045c1s
v4p0049c2s v4p0053c1m v4p0054c2s
v4p0072c1m v4p0091c2s v4p0104c2s
v4p0105c1s v4p0106c1s v4p0107c2s
v4p0111c2s v4p0113c2m v4p0119c1s
v4p0123c2s v4p0129c1m v4p0141c1s
v4p0142c1m v4p0142c2s v4p0152c2s
v4p0157c2s v4p0190c2s v4p0216c1s
v4p0233c2s v4p0240c2s v4p0248c2s
v4p0250c2m v4p0251c1m v4p0252c1s
v4p0255c2s v4p0266c2s v4p0277c2m
v4p0287c2s v4p0288c1s v4p0305c2s
v4p0312c2s v4p0315c1s v4p0323c2s
v4p0334c2s v4p0335c1s v4p0374c2m
v4p0380c1s v4p0387c2m v4p0408c2m
v4p0412c1s v4p0423c2s v4p0449c1s
v4p0452c1s v4p0466c2s v4p0467c1s
v4p0474c2s v4p0488c1s v4p0489c1s
v4p0501c1s v4p0506c2m v4p0514c2s
v4p0533c2m v4p0553c1s v4p0562c1s
v4p0565c2s v4p0568c2s v4p0573c1s
v4p0575c2s v4p0580c2s v4p0586c2s
v4p0591c1s v4p0593c1s v4p0593c2s
v4p0595c1m v4p0595c2s v4p0598c2s
v4p0599c1s v4p0601c2m v4p0606c2s
v4p0609c1s v4p0616c1s v4p0632c2s
v5p0006c2s v5p0039c1s v5p0050c2s
v5p0069c2s v5p0072c1m v5p0079c2s
v5p0092c2s v5p0100c1s v5p0100c2s
v5p0109c1s v5p0109c2s v5p0110c1s
v5p0110c2s v5p0111c2m v5p0112c1s
v5p0128c2m v5p0133c1s v5p0136c2s
v5p0137c1s v5p0141c2s v5p0145c1s
v5p0146c2s v5p0147c1m v5p0147c2m
v5p0148c1m v5p0149c2s v5p0151c2s
v5p0157c2s v5p0158c1s v5p0159c1s
v5p0168c1s v5p0168c2m v5p0169c1s
v5p0172c1s v5p0180c1s v5p0181c1s
v5p0189c1s v5p0190c2s v5p0206c1s
v5p0209c2s v5p0213c2s v5p0221c2s
v5p0234c2s v5p0244c2s v5p0247c2s
v5p0256c2s v5p0258c1s v5p0258c2m
v5p0281c2s v5p0292c2s v5p0294c1m
v5p0294c2s v5p0300c1s v5p0308c2s
v5p0317c2s v5p0326c2s v5p0331c2s
v5p0341c1s v5p0354c1m v5p0381c1s
v5p0386c2s v5p0407c1s v5p0418c1s
v5p0420c2s v5p0422c2s v5p0429c1m
v5p0435c2s v5p0437c2m v5p0443c2m
v5p0444c1m v5p0444c2m v5p0445c1m
v5p0445c2m v5p0454c1s v5p0460c1s
v5p0460c2m v5p0464c2s v5p0468c2m
v5p0486c1s v5p0487c2s v5p0494c1s
v5p0496c1s v5p0497c1s v5p0501c2s
v5p0505c2s v5p0506c2s v5p0508c1s
v5p0508c2s v5p0510c2s v5p0513c1s
v5p0514c2s v5p0518c1s v5p0519c2m
v5p0520c1s v5p0526c2s v5p0537c2s
v5p0542c1s v5p0542c2m v5p0543c2s
v5p0557c1s v5p0562c2s v5p0566c1s
v5p0567c1m v5p0567c2s v5p0580c2s
v5p0584c1s v5p0586c1s v5p0586c2s
v5p0587c1s v5p0587c2s v5p0588c1s
v5p0589c2m v5p0595c2s v5p0604c1s
v5p0609c1s v5p0618c1s v5p0618c2s
v6p0003c2s v6p0004c1s v6p0019c2m
v6p0024c1s v6p0026c2s v6p0048c1s
v6p0060c1s v6p0061c1s v6p0075c1s
v6p0081c1s v6p0085c2m v6p0087c2s
v6p0089c2s v6p0099c1s v6p0106c1s
v6p0107c2m v6p0108c1m v6p0113c1s
v6p0119c1s v6p0119c2s v6p0129c1s
v6p0129c2s v6p0131c1s v6p0138c1s
v6p0141c1s v6p0144c2m v6p0150c1s
v6p0151c1s v6p0151c2s v6p0156c2s
v6p0158c1s v6p0160c2m v6p0170c1m
v6p0174c2m v6p0175c1s v6p0189c1s
v6p0189c2s v6p0195c1m v6p0202c1s
v6p0210c1m v6p0215c2m v6p0216c1s
v6p0230c2s v6p0232c1s v6p0253c1s
v6p0256c2s v6p0258c1m v6p0262c2s
v6p0263c2s v6p0269c2s v6p0274c2s
v6p0279c2s v6p0284c1s v6p0293c1s
v6p0294c1s v6p0303c1s v6p0305c2s
v6p0306c2s v6p0310c1m v6p0312c1s
v6p0312c2s v6p0316c1s v6p0321c1s
v6p0322c1s v6p0323c1s v6p0324c2s
v6p0330c1s v6p0331c1s v6p0334c1s
v6p0335c2s v6p0340c1m v6p0346c2s
v6p0347c1s v6p0347c2s v6p0364c2s
v6p0366c2s v6p0368c1s v6p0370c1m
v6p0388c2s v6p0390c1s v6p0390c2m
v6p0391c1m v6p0396c2s v6p0416c1s
v6p0426c1s v6p0429c2s v6p0434c2s
v6p0436c1m v6p0436c2s v6p0443c1s
v6p0447c1m v6p0447c2s v6p0451c1s
v6p0455c2m v6p0460c1s v6p0468c2s
v6p0476c2m v6p0477c1s v6p0480c2s
v6p0481c1s v6p0485c1s v6p0493c1m
v6p0493c2s v6p0494c1s v6p0494c2s
v6p0495c1s v6p0504c1s v6p0507c1m
v6p0514c2m v6p0515c1m v6p0515c2s
v6p0519c2s v6p0522c2m v6p0528c2s
v6p0529c1s v6p0534c2s v6p0535c1m
v6p0535c2s v6p0539c2m v6p0540c1m
v6p0540c2s v6p0542c1s v6p0550c1m
v6p0550c2m v6p0551c1m v6p0556c1s
v6p0556c2s v6p0557c2s v6p0558c1s
v6p0565c2s v6p0570c1m v6p0575c2s
v6p0577c1s v6p0581c2s v6p0582c2s
v6p0583c1m v6p0583c2m v6p0591c2s
v6p0597c1s v6p0601c2m v6p0605c1s
v6p0606c1s v6p0607c2s v6p0608c1m
v6p0608c2s v6p0609c2s v6p0616c2s
v6p0621c1m v6p0621c2m v6p0623c2s
v6p0624c1s v6p0631c1s v6p0632c1s
v6p0633c1m v6p0634c1s v6p0649c1s
v6p0651c2s v6p0652c1s v6p0655c2s
v6p0659c1s v6p0661c1s v6p0665c2s
v6p0666c1s v6p0666c2m v6p0667c1s
v6p0669c1s v6p0676c1m v6p0684c1s
v6p0699c1s
Ogden, R. et al. v5p0157c2s
Ogden, R.C. v6p0192c2s
v6p0605c1s
Ogden, R.M. v5p0486c2s
v6p0249c2s
Ogden, Rollo v6p0013c1s
v6p0325c2s
Ogg, F.A. v5p0228c2s
v5p0293c2s v6p0014c2s v6p0016c1s
v6p0018c1s v6p0029c2s v6p0036c2s
v6p0042c1s v6p0084c2s v6p0097c2s
v6p0119c2s v6p0134c2s v6p0170c1s
v6p0170c2s v6p0186c2s v6p0187c1s
v6p0205c1s v6p0205c2s v6p0206c1s
v6p0209c1s v6p0213c1m v6p0213c2s
v6p0215c2s v6p0237c2m v6p0253c2s
v6p0265c1s v6p0267c1m v6p0292c2s
v6p0308c1s v6p0308c2m v6p0309c1s
v6p0313c1s v6p0315c2s v6p0318c2s
v6p0331c2s v6p0332c1s v6p0416c2s
v6p0422c1s v6p0456c1s v6p0478c2s
v6p0508c2s v6p0528c2s v6p0535c1s
v6p0555c2s v6p0556c1s v6p0557c1s
v6p0558c2s v6p0559c1s v6p0559c2s
v6p0560c2s v6p0571c2s v6p0593c1s
v6p0600c1s v6p0601c1s v6p0606c1s
v6p0650c2s v6p0668c2s v6p0684c2s
Ogg, F.W. v6p0242c1s
Ogilby, J.P. v1p0918c2s
Ogilby, Prof. v1p0679c2s
Ogilvie, A. v5p0165c2s
v5p0443c2s
Ogilvie, A.M. v4p0454c1s
Ogilvie, G. v5p0130c2s
Ogilvie, G.F. v5p0274c1s
Ogilvie, M.M. v4p0040c1s
v5p0355c1s
Ogilvie, W. v4p0347c2s
v4p0636c2s v5p0645c1s
Ogilvie, W.H. v6p0042c1s
Ogilvy, A. v1p0035c2s
v1p0143c2s v1p0257c2s v1p0537c2s
v1p0571c1s v1p0574c2s v1p1242c1s
v1p1260c2s v1p1300c1s v1p1317c2s
Ogilvy, A.J. v3p0265c1s
Ogilvy, M. v4p0147c1s
Ogle, J. v3p0121c1s
Ogle, J.J. v5p0097c1s
v5p0336c1s v5p0336c2s v5p0337c1s
v6p0374c2s
Ogle, O. v2p0429c2s
Ogle, W. v1p0462c2s
v1p1015c1s v1p1147c2s v2p0282c1s
v2p0424c1s v3p0139c1s v3p0269c1s
v4p0339c1s
Oglesby, Robert v5p0011c1s
v5p0318c1s
Oglesby, T.K. v3p0170c2s
v3p0442c1s
Ogleston, M. v2p0248c2s
O'Gorman, M. v6p0044c2s
O'Gorman, T. v4p0170c1s
v4p0289c1s v4p0303c1s v6p0016c1s
v6p0104c2s
O'Grady, M. v5p0032c1s
v5p0048c1s v5p0353c2s
O'Grady, S. v1p0660c1s
v1p0950c1s v2p0068c2s v3p0220c2s
v3p0438c2s v4p0290c1s v5p0188c1s
v5p0266c2s v5p0280c1s v5p0296c2m
O'Grady, S.H. v3p0194c1s
O'Grady, W.L.D. v1p1191c2s
v1p1435c1s
O'Hagan, A. v5p0036c2s
v5p0062c1s v5p0068c2s v5p0070c1s
v5p0115c2s v5p0141c2s v5p0158c2s
v5p0283c2s v5p0379c1s v5p0407c2m
v5p0500c2s v5p0637c1s v6p0001c1s
v6p0055c2s
O'Hagan, Anne v5p0489c1s
v6p0019c2s v6p0121c2s v6p0124c2m
v6p0155c1s v6p0180c1s v6p0213c2s
v6p0216c2s v6p0220c2s v6p0222c1s
v6p0242c2s v6p0247c2s v6p0272c1s
v6p0288c2s v6p0344c1s v6p0358c1s
v6p0394c1s v6p0400c2s v6p0407c2s
v6p0421c1s v6p0496c1s v6p0497c2s
v6p0525c2s v6p0534c1s v6p0545c1s
v6p0608c2s v6p0610c2s v6p0623c1s
v6p0678c1s v6p0680c1s v6p0683c1s
v6p0688c2s v6p0703c1s v6p0712c1s
O'Hagan, J. v1p0806c2s
v1p0870c2s v1p1245c2s v1p1295c2s
v3p0111c2m
O'Hagan, T. v4p0087c1s
v4p0299c2s v4p0335c2s v4p0474c2s
v4p0630c2s v5p0090c2s v5p0493c2s
v6p0083c1s v6p0182c2s v6p0539c1s
v6p0707c2s
O'Hallaran, B. v1p0956c2s
O'Halloran, G. v6p0420c2s
O'Halloran, G.B. v4p0072c1s
v4p0360c1s v4p0517c1s v6p0310c2s
v6p0405c2s
O'Halloran, R. v5p0444c1s
O'Halloran, Rose v6p0417c1s
v6p0614c1s v6p0626c1s
O'Hanlan, W.M. v1p1140c1s
O'Hanlon, Alice v2p0451c1s
O'Hanly, T.L.P. v4p0574c2s
O'Hara, E. v1p0139c2s
v1p0588c1s v1p0803c2s v1p0940c2s
v1p1376c1s v1p1404c2s v1p1406c2s
O'Hara, E.V. v6p0165c2s
v6p0536c2s v6p0596c2s
O'Hara, J.B. v6p0031c2s
v6p0199c1s
O'Hara, J.C. v6p0323c1s
O'Hara, R. v2p0227c1s
O'Hara Family v1p0662c2s
O'Hare, A.E. v5p0409c1s
O'Hare, F. v1p1115c1s
O'Hare, Kate, R. v6p0176c2s
O'Hea, Capt. v1p1107c2s
v2p0012c2s v2p0193c2s v2p0288c2s
O'Higgins, H.J. v5p0467c2s
v5p0572c1s v6p0025c1s v6p0080c1s
v6p0100c2s v6p0215c2s v6p0311c1s
v6p0311c2s v6p0362c1s v6p0375c2s
v6p0452c2s v6p0465c2s v6p0490c1s
v6p0517c2s v6p0525c1s v6p0615c1s
v6p0632c1s v6p0656c2s v6p0663c1s
O'Higgins, Harvey J. v6p0296c1s
O'Higgins, J.S. v5p0544c1s
Ohl, J.K. v4p0036c1s
Ohl, T. v3p0073c1s
v3p0117c1s v3p0186c2s v3p0327c1s
v3p0363c2s v3p0367c1s v3p0392c1s
Ohlmietz, C.C. v6p0107c2s
Ohlson, J.L. v1p1401c1s
Oille, L. v1p0967c1s
Oishi, K. v4p0106c2s
Oishi, Kuma v3p0226c2s
Okada, T. v4p0565c1s
Okakura, K. v6p0337c2s
Okakura, Kakuzo v6p0338c2s
v6p0634c2m
Okamura, T. v4p0297c1s
O'Kane, M.M. v5p0615c1s
v6p0145c2s
O'Keefe, C.M. v2p0009c1s
v2p0091c2s v2p0228c2m v2p0305c1s
v2p0398c1s v3p0048c2s v3p0142c2s
O'Keefe, H.E. v6p0289c1s
v6p0327c2s
O'Keefe, P.J. v4p0100c1s
v5p0028c2s v5p0330c2s
O'Keeffe, C.M. v2p0078c1m
v2p0175c2s v2p0197c2s v3p0221c1s
v3p0222c2s v3p0323c2s
O'Keeffe, H.E. v5p0409c1s
v5p0435c2s

O'Keene, F. v2p0386c1s v4p0490c2s
Oker, C.W. v4p0458c1s
Oker, J. v4p0378c2s
Okey, I. v4p0159c1s
Okey, T. v6p0676c2s
Okie, J. v3p0007c1s
Okuma v6p0336c1s
Okuma, Count v6p0337c1s v6p0354c1s v6p0560c1s
Okuma, S. v6p0335c2s
Okuma, S., Count v5p0302c1s v5p0302c2s
O'Laughlin, J.C. v6p0015c2s v6p0151c2s v6p0237c1s v6p0246c1s v6p0288c1s v6p0369c2s v6p0560c1s v6p0580c2s v6p0668c2s v6p0669c1s v6p0676c1m
Olcott, E.E. v3p0176c2s
Olcott, F.J. v5p0334c2s v5p0452c2s v6p0371c1s
Olcott, Frances J. v6p0116c2s v6p0375c1s
Olcott, G.N. v5p0291c2s v5p0492c2s v6p0134c2s
Olcott, H.S. v3p0428c1m v5p0577c1s v6p0579c1s
Olcott, J.B. v3p0362c2s
Olcott, W.T. v5p0276c2s
Old, R.O. v3p0155c1s v3p0363c1s
Old, W.W. v2p0200c2s
Old Harrovian, An v6p0157c2s
Oldbuck, J. v4p0288c2s
Oldcastle, A. v4p0296c1s
Oldcastle, J. v1p1130c2s v2p0008c1s v4p0016c2s v4p0063c2s v4p0081c1s v4p0157c2s v4p0251c2s v4p0308c2s v4p0371c1s v4p0421c2s v4p0442c2s v4p0528c2s v4p0565c2s v4p0603c2s
Oldcastle, John v3p0410c1s v4p0226c1s
Olden, J. v5p0013c2s v5p0179c1s v5p0293c1s
Oldenberg, H. v4p0188c2s v4p0391c2s v4p0480c1m v4p0502c2s v4p0601c1m
Oldfield, E. v1p1115c1s v5p0254c1s
Oldfield, J. v4p0049c1s v5p0608c2s v5p0613c2m v6p0151c2s v6p0314c1s v6p0408c1s v6p0462c2s v6p0501c2s
Oldfield, S.H. v5p0235c1s
Oldforde, T. v6p0109c1s v6p0155c2s
Oldham, A. v5p0117c2s
Oldham, Alice v3p0398c2s
Oldham, B.D. v2p0209c1s
Oldham, C.F. v2p0203c1s v4p0623c2m
Oldham, E.A. v3p0116c2s v3p0126c2s v4p0013c2s v4p0125c2s
Oldham, H.G.V. v5p0551c1s
Oldham, H.Y. v4p0013c1s v4p0353c1s
Oldham, J.R. v4p0547c2s v5p0323c1s v5p0362c1s v5p0526c1s v5p0526c2s v5p0551c2s v6p0054c1s v6p0616c1s
Oldham, R.D. v3p0089c2s v4p0272c2s v4p0279c2s v4p0373c1s v4p0437c2s v5p0173c1m v6p0186c1s
Oldham, W.F. v3p0394c1s v5p0285c2s v5p0380c1s v5p0484c1s
Oldham, W.S. v2p0098c1s v2p0453c2s
Olding, W.H. v2p0029c2s v2p0051c2s v2p0065c1s v2p0260c2s v2p0314c2s v2p0395c1s v4p0334c2s v5p0417c1s
Oldknow, R.C. v3p0298c1s v4p0237c2s
Oldnall, H.C. v5p0588c1s
Oldrieve, W.T. v2p0060c1s
Oldright, C.D. v4p0633c2s
Oldrini, A. v4p0170c1s v4p0294c1s v4p0294c2m v4p0295c1s
Olds, F.A. v5p0116c1s v5p0135c2s v5p0422c2s
Oldschool, O. v1p0937c2s
Oldys, H. v5p0064c1s v6p0067c1s v6p0068c1m
Oldys, H.W. v6p0438c1s
O'Leary, C. v1p0816c2s v2p0149c1s
O'Leary, C.M. v1p0259c2s v1p0317c1s v1p0356c2s v1p0613c2s v1p0810c2s v1p0826c1s v1p0843c2s v1p1007c1s v1p1161c1s v2p0003c2s v2p0008c2s v2p0283c1s v4p0190c1s v4p0439c1s
O'Leary, Dr. v1p0907c1s
O'Leary, J. v1p0653c1m
O'Leary, M.M. v4p0163c1s
O'Leary, T.L. v1p1214c1s
Olerich, H. v4p0430c1s v6p0044c1s
Oleron, P. v4p0632c1s
Oleson, W.B. v4p0250c2s
Olin, J.M. v1p0278c1s v1p0757c2s
Olin, S. v1p0852c1s v1p1097c2s v1p1438c2s
Olin, S.H. v4p0400c1s v4p0466c1s
Olina, D. v5p0197c1s v5p0300c1s
Oliphant, C.H. v5p0372c2s v6p0513c2s
Oliphant, D. v1p0117c1s v1p0574c2s
Oliphant, F.R. v3p0194c1s v4p0164c1s
Oliphant, J. v3p0109c2s v4p0219c1s v5p0178c2s v5p0521c2m v6p0402c1s v6p0428c1s
Oliphant, J.T.K. v2p0021c1s
Oliphant, L. v1p0011c2s v1p0234c1s v1p0678c2s v1p0864c1s v1p0922c2s v1p1007c2m v1p1331c2s v2p0059c2s v2p0064c1s v2p0066c1s v2p0069c1m v2p0072c1s v2p0073c1s v2p0107c2s v2p0124c2s v2p0128c2s v2p0146c2s v2p0170c1s v2p0190c1s v2p0231c2m v2p0236c2s v2p0299c2s v2p0380c2s v2p0415c2s v2p0466c2m v3p0166c1s v3p0289c2s
Oliphant, M. v1p0027c1s v1p0044c1s v1p0071c1s v1p0072c1s v1p0114c1s v1p0171c1s v1p0200c2s v1p0201c2s v1p0202c2s v1p0246c1m v1p0265c1s v1p0324c1s v1p0335c2s v1p0376c1s v1p0380c2s v1p0383c1s v1p0412c1s v1p0492c1s v1p0577c1s v1p0596c1s v1p0614c1s v1p0627c1s v1p0642c2m v1p0666c2s v1p0667c2s v1p0693c1s v1p0703c2s v1p0786c1s v1p0799c2s v1p0851c2s v1p0863c1s v1p0925c1s v1p1032c1s v1p1071c2s v1p1087c2s v1p1106c2s v1p1127c2s v1p1149c1s v1p1153c2s v1p1175c1s v1p1182c2s v1p1191c1s v1p1219c2s v1p1257c1s v1p1258c1m v1p1308c1s v1p1335c2m v1p1370c1s v1p1383c1s v1p1418c2s v1p1423c2s v1p1439c1s v2p0046c1s v2p0068c1m v2p0104c2s v2p0200c1s v2p0208c2s v2p0246c1m v2p0271c1s v2p0323c2s v2p0349c1s v2p0448c1s v2p0458c2s v2p0476c2s
Oliphant, M. and Carducci. v2p0210c2s
Oliphant, M.O. v5p0528c2s
Oliphant, M.O.W. v2p0120c1s v2p0460c2s v3p0103c2s v3p0128c1s v3p0152c1s v3p0239c2s v3p0267c2s v3p0311c2s v4p0003c2s v4p0019c1m v4p0119c2s v4p0151c1s v4p0226c2s v4p0293c1s v4p0356c1s v4p0412c1s v4p0412c2s v4p0502c1s v4p0560c1s v4p0606c1s v4p0621c1s v5p0610c2s
Oliphant, M.O.W. and Aldrich, T.B. v3p0383c2s
Oliphant, Mrs. v1p0043c2s v2p0261c1s v2p0361c1s v3p0237c1s v3p0241c2s v3p0263c1s v3p0269c1s v4p0356c2s v4p0552c1m v4p0621c2s v5p0174c1s v5p0610c2s
Oliphant, P.L. v6p0042c1s
Oliphant, P.L., Capt. v6p0319c2s
Oliphant, W.J. v2p0021c2s
Oliveira, B. v2p0475c2s
Oliver, A. v1p0748c2s v1p1309c1s v1p1391c2s
Oliver, A.J. v6p0643c2s
Oliver, Andrew v6p0709c1s
Oliver, B.L. v1p0882c1s v1p1061c1s
Oliver, C. v6p0001c1s v6p0019c1s v6p0058c1s v6p0066c1s v6p0141c1s v6p0196c1s v6p0212c1s v6p0221c2s v6p0242c2s v6p0394c1s v6p0400c2s v6p0405c2s v6p0426c1s v6p0480c1s v6p0484c1s v6p0559c2s v6p0663c1s
Oliver, C.A. v2p0309c1s v3p0285c2s
Oliver, D. v1p1015c1s v1p1324c2s
Oliver, E.E. v3p0212c1s
Oliver, F.E. v4p0402c2s
Oliver, F.O. v6p0082c2s v6p0582c1s
Oliver, F.W. v4p0204c2s v6p0077c2s
Oliver, G. v6p0648c1s
Oliver, G.J. v1p0378c2s v1p0680c1s
Oliver, G.T. v5p0289c1s v5p0593c1s
Oliver, G.W. v4p0162c1s v4p0197c1s v4p0235c1s v4p0613c1s
Oliver, H.K. v1p0861c2s v1p1158c2s v2p0139c2s
Oliver, J.A.B. v1p0752c2s v1p0828c1s
Oliver, J.A.W. v1p0621c2s v2p0095c2s v2p0285c2s v3p0126c1m
Oliver, J.E. v1p0257c2s v4p0214c1s
Oliver, J.E. and Hervey, F.L. v3p0012c2s
Oliver, J.H. v1p0259c2s v1p1244c2s
Oliver, J.N. v6p0035c2s v6p0182c1s v6p0564c1s
Oliver, J.R. v4p0280c1s v6p0049c1s
Oliver, J.W. v3p0286c2s v3p0458c2s v4p0080c1s
Oliver, Jean N. v6p0148c2s
Oliver, L. v2p0287c2s
Oliver, M.I.G. v6p0033c1s v6p0057c1s v6p0184c2s v6p0228c2s v6p0251c2s v6p0564c1s v6p0628c2s
Oliver, M.N. v4p0301c1s
Oliver, Maude I.G. v6p0113c1s v6p0114c1s v6p0252c2s v6p0337c2s v6p0564c1s v6p0602c1s
Oliver, O. v6p0163c1s v6p0286c2s
Oliver, Owen v6p0081c1s v6p0398c1s
Oliver, P. v1p0809c1s v1p1066c2s v1p1067c1s v4p0348c1s v4p0348c2s v6p0340c2s
Oliver, Pasfield v4p0274c2s
Oliver, S.P. v1p0065c2s v1p0166c1s v1p0359c1s v1p0558c2s v1p0611c2s v1p0682c1s v1p0817c2s v1p1151c2s v1p1256c1m v2p0024c1s v2p0057c1s v2p0074c1s v2p0121c1s v2p0323c1m v2p0423c2s v2p0443c2s v3p0109c1s v4p0006c2s v4p0088c1s v4p0151c2s v4p0308c1s v4p0348c1s v4p0348c2s v4p0350c2s v4p0410c2s v4p0537c2s v5p0348c2s v5p0354c2s
Oliver, T. v4p0632c2s v6p0009c1s v6p0091c2s
Oliver, W. v1p0829c1s v3p0369c2s
Oliver, W.F. v5p0615c1s
Olivier, L. v2p0027c2s v2p0175c2s v3p0075c2s
Olivier, S. v2p0407c2s v2p0408c1s v3p0398c1s v3p0398c2s v4p0553c1s v5p0388c2s v5p0461c1s v5p0484c2s v6p0307c2s v6p0447c1m v6p0448c1s v6p0649c1s v6p0696c2s
Olivier, Sydney v6p0203c1s
Olivieri, A. v2p0111c2s v2p0276c1s
Ollason, J. v3p0066c2s
Ollie, W.F. v6p0596c1s
Ollier, C. v1p0418c2s v1p0574c1s v1p0922c1s
Ollier, E. v4p0421c2s v4p0623c1s
Ollivant, A. v4p0280c2s v5p0596c1s v6p0164c1s v6p0407c2s
Ollivier, E. v3p0238c2s v4p0211c1s v5p0014c2s v5p0216c2s v5p0542c1s
Ollivier, Emile v4p0342c2s
Olmstead, A.F. v1p0941c1s
Olmstead, C.H. v2p0075c1s
Olmstead, J.M. v6p0051c1s
Olmstead, J.W. v1p1203c2s
Olmstead, L.G. v1p0021c1s v1p0328c1s
Olmstead, Millicent v5p0505c1s
Olmstead, V.H. and Fessenden, S.D. v4p0179c2s
Olmsted, A.F. v1p1405c2s
Olmsted, D. v1p0077c1m v1p0106c1s v1p0225c2s v1p0240c1s v1p0267c2s v1p0292c1s v1p0335c1s v1p0349c2s v1p0373c2s v1p0431c2s v1p0457c1s v1p0533c2s v1p0565c1m v1p0808c1s v1p0827c2m v1p0829c1s v1p0829c2s v1p0835c2s v1p0900c1s v1p0906c2s v1p0927c2s v1p0929c2s v1p0936c2s v1p0961c1s v1p1088c1s v1p1159c2s v1p1161c2s v1p1268c2s v1p1288c1s v1p1316c1s v1p1321c2s v1p1323c1s v1p1328c1s v1p1407c1s v1p1432c1m v1p1440c2m
Olmsted, D. and Clarke, W.A. v1p0827c1s v1p0827c2s
Olmsted, F.L. v1p0227c2s v1p0723c1s v1p0972c1s v2p0330c1s v2p0446c1s v3p0421c1s v3p0431c2s v4p0101c2s v4p0427c2s v5p0256c2s v6p0128c1s v6p0481c1s
Olmsted, F.L., jr. v5p0004c2s v5p0324c2s v6p0360c2s
Olmsted, F.L., jr. and Nolen, J. v6p0481c1s
Olmsted, G.K. v5p0148c2s
Olmsted, J.C. v3p0017c1s v5p0433c1s
Olmsted, W.C. v4p0087c1s
Olney, C.M. v6p0712c2s
Olney, Caroline M. v6p0090c1s v6p0711c2s
Olney, E.W. v1p0075c2s v1p0590c1s v1p0773c2s v1p0851c2s v1p0942c2s v1p1202c1s v1p1309c1s v1p1315c1s
Olney, R. v5p0199c2s

v5p0363c2m v5p0601c1s v5p0602c1s v6p0528c2s v6p0529c1s v6p0669c2s
Olney, W. v2p0306c1s v2p0400c2s v3p0223c2s v4p0144c2s
Olney, W. and Lovyed, A.M. v2p0184c2s
Olphert, R.F. v3p0220c1s
Olsaver, F.T. v4p0512c2s
Olsen, J. v6p0325c2s
Olshausen, H. v1p0126c2s v1p0127c1s
Olson, J.E. v3p0142c1s v3p0307c1s v3p0307c2s v4p0407c2s v5p0361c2s
Olssen, W.W. v1p0353c1s v1p1060c1s v2p0043c1m v2p0432c1s v3p0231c2s
Olssen, W.W. and Spalding, J.F. v3p0347c1s
Olsson-Seffer, P. v6p0470c1s
Oltmans, A. v5p0379c2s
Olyphant, V.M. v4p0058c1s v4p0507c1s
O'Malley, A. v5p0493c2s
O'Malley, C.J. v4p0179c2s v4p0559c1s
O'Malley, C.L. v6p0195c1s
O'Malley, J. v1p1125c1s
Oman, C. v2p0282c1s v3p0017c2s v3p0025c1s v3p0090c2s v4p0121c2s v5p0375c1s v5p0588c1s v5p0622c2s v6p0209c1s v6p0688c2s
Oman, C.W.C. v2p0091c2s v3p0325c1s v6p0162c1s v6p0506c2s
Oman, J. v5p0058c1s
O'Meara, B.E. v5p0398c1s
O'Meara, E. v1p0375c1s
O'Meara, J. v2p0079c2s v2p0342c2s v2p0385c1s v3p0063c1s v3p0066c1s v3p0458c2s v6p0040c2s v6p0283c1m v6p0604c1s v6p0640c1s v6p0678c1s v6p0683c2s
O'Meara, J.B. v1p0662c1s v1p0887c1s v1p1175c1s
O'Meara, J.O. v3p0063c1s
O'Meara, K. v1p0018c1s v1p0056c2s v1p0084c1s v1p0111c2s v1p0341c1s v1p0372c2s v1p0414c1s v1p0464c2m v1p0475c1s v1p0476c1s v1p0482c1s v1p0539c1s v1p0683c2s v1p0703c2s v1p0726c1s v1p0728c2s v1p0735c1s v1p0771c2s v1p0825c1s v1p0841c1s v1p0859c1s v1p0862c2m v1p0933c2s v1p0970c1s v1p0970c2s v1p0983c2s v1p1012c2s v1p1085c2s v1p1111c2s v1p1112c1s v1p1241c2s v1p1275c1s v1p1292c1s v1p1329c1s v1p1368c1s v2p0084c2s v2p0168c1s v2p0232c1s v2p0294c1s v2p0337c2s v2p0384c1s v2p0404c1s v3p0296c1s
Omega v6p0335c2s
Ommen, A.E. v6p0158c1s
Omond, G.W.T. v4p0453c1s v5p0553c1s
Omond, R.T. v2p0406c2s
Omond, T.S. v1p0881c2s v1p1368c1s v5p0468c2s
O'Monroy, Richard v5p0504c1s
O'Morris, M.C. v1p0024c2s
Omwake, G.L. v6p0066c2s
Onahan, M.J. v4p0484c2s v4p0603c2s
Onahan, W.J. v1p0624c2s v1p0661c2s v1p1117c2s v1p1399c2s v2p0132c1s v2p0375c2s
Oncken, A. v4p0450c1s v4p0560c2s v5p0175c2s v5p0533c1s v5p0564c2s
Oncken, H. v6p0293c1s
Ondaatje, M.P.J. v3p0273c2s
Onderdonck, J.L. v1p0027c1s v1p1017c1s v1p1045c1s
Onderdonk, H. v1p1069c2s
Onderdonk, J.L. v1p0028c1s v1p0794c1s v1p0872c1s v4p0076c1s v4p0151c2s v4p0321c1s v4p0335c1s v4p0447c2m v4p0536c2s
O'Neal, E. v6p0539c2s
O'Neale, D.H. v2p0363c1s
O'Neale, J.B. v1p0206c2s
O'Neil, Charles v6p0030c2s
O'Neil, H. v1p1008c2s
O'Neil, H.C. v6p0378c1s
O'Neil, J. v6p0467c2s
O'Neil, J.H. et al. v4p0434c1s
O'Neil, M. v3p0388c1s
O'Neill, A.B. v4p0284c1s
O'Neill, A.W. v6p0113c2s
O'Neill, E. v6p0491c1s
O'Neill, F.R. v5p0627c1s v6p0387c1s
O'Neill, G. v6p0046c2s v6p0182c2s
O'Neill, H. v1p1437c1s
O'Neill, Hugh v6p0055c1s
O'Neill, Hugh and Steele, J.M. v6p0349c2s
O'Neill, J. v2p0140c2s v3p0006c2s v3p0155c1s v3p0244c1s v4p0077c2s
O'Neill, J.D. v6p0561c2s
O'Neill, J.J. v4p0277c2s v4p0450c1s
O'Neill, J.R. v1p1222c1s
O'Neill, John v4p0106c2s v4p0552c2s
O'Neill, M. v3p0050c2s v4p0147c2s v4p0289c2s v4p0536c1s v5p0090c2s v5p0309c1s
O'Neill, Rose C. v6p0358c1s
O'Neill, T.W. v1p1268c1s
O'Neill, Miss v1p0106c1s
Onimus, M. v1p0907c1s
Onions, O. v6p0218c1s
Ono, Y. v3p0227c1s
Onslow, B. v2p0013c1s
Onslow, Countess of v5p0296c1s
Onslow, Earl of v3p0120c1s v4p0060c2s v6p0382c1s
Onslow, Lady v6p0327c2s
Onslow, P. v1p1087c2s
Ooge, B.L.D' v3p0087c1s v3p0243c2s v4p0321c2s v5p0374c1s v6p0363c1s
Ooge, M.L.D' v2p0130c1s v2p0339c1s v3p0184c2s v3p0199c2s v4p0035c1s v5p0249c2s v5p0269c1s v6p0024c2s v6p0169c2s v6p0323c2s
Ooge, M.L.D' and Lombard, W.P. v6p0555c2s
Ookhtomsky, Prince and Holmstrem, V. v5p0247c1s
Oort, H. v2p0430c2s
Oosterzee, J.J.van v1p0151c1s v1p0154c1s v1p0688c2s v1p0689c1s v1p0809c2s v2p0205c1s
Opdycke, L.E. v2p0003c2s v6p0573c2s
Opdyke, G. v1p0325c2s
Opdyke, G.H. v5p0138c1s
Oper, T. v1p0143c1s v1p1123c1s
Opie, A. v1p0109c2s
Opie, J.N. v3p0053c2s
Opp, J.F. v4p0147c1s
Opp, Julia F. v4p0084c1s
Oppe, A.P. v6p0169c2s
Oppenheim, A. v1p0089c1s v1p0224c1s v1p0501c2s v1p0514c1s v1p0619c1m v1p0788c2s v1p0955c1m v1p1390c1s
Oppenheim, A.T. v5p0194c1s
Oppenheim, E.P. v4p0543c1s
Oppenheim, L. v5p0181c2s v5p0398c2s v5p0546c1s v5p0611c2s v6p0547c1s
Oppenheim, M. v2p0170c1s v2p0215c2s v2p0445c2s v3p0182c1s v4p0182c1s v4p0238c1m
Oppenheim, M. and Leeper, A. v5p0347c1s
Oppenheim, M. and Wingfellde, A. v5p0633c1s
Oppenheim, N. v3p0170c1s v3p0272c1s v4p0139c2s v4p0345c2s v4p0363c1s
Oppenheim, Phillips v5p0576c1s
Oppenheimer, M.S. v5p0187c2s
Opper, E.A. v5p0539c2s
Oppert, G. v1p0167c1s
Oppizi, P. v1p0759c2s
Oppler-Legbaud, Else v6p0182c1s
Oppolzer, E.R.von v4p0556c2s
Oppolzer, E.von v4p0557c1s
Oral, T.O. v3p0215c2s
Orange, H.W. v3p0039c1s
Oratesi, M. v1p1084c1s
Orb, S.A. v4p0111c2s
Orban, A. v3p0435c1s
Orchardson, J. v5p0563c1s
Orcutt, C. v1p0169c2s
Orcutt, C.R. v6p0091c1s
Orcutt, H. v5p0126c1s v5p0162c2s
Orcutt, H.F.L. v5p0353c1m
Orcutt, H.M. v6p0308c1s
Orcutt, W.D. v4p0035c2s v4p0249c1m
Ord, C. v1p0177c1s v1p0203c2s v1p0320c2s v1p0393c2s v1p0558c1s v1p0585c1s v1p0767c1s v1p1053c2s
Ord, L.R. v4p0078c1s
Ord, W.E. v5p0011c1s
Ord, W.M. v2p0180c1s
Orde, E.L. v5p0223c1s
Orde-Ward, F.W. v6p0685c1s
Ordega, L. v4p0038c2s v4p0065c1s
Ordinaire, E. v1p0870c1s
Ordinaire, M. v4p0348c2s
Ordish, T.F. v2p0061c1s v2p0068c2s v2p0073c2s v2p0108c1s v2p0171c2s v2p0264c2m v2p0265c1s v3p0123c1s v3p0148c1s v4p0517c2s v4p0518c2s v5p0346c1s v6p0693c2s
Ordonez, E. and Braschi, V.M. v6p0414c1s
Ordway, A. v2p0288c2s
Ordway, C.E. v6p0081c1s v6p0126c2s v6p0470c1s v6p0517c1s
Ordway, J.K. v3p0455c2s
Ordway, J.M. v1p1391c1s v2p0419c1s v3p0192c2s
O'Reilly, B. v2p0067c1m v2p0084c1s v2p0231c1s v2p0375c2s v2p0412c2s v3p0039c2s v3p0159c2m v3p0160c1m v3p0222c1s v3p0222c2s v3p0244c1s v3p0319c1s v3p0366c1s v3p0441c1s v4p0127c2s v4p0424c1m v4p0490c2s
O'Reilly, B.B. v6p0243c1s
O'Reilly, B.J. v1p0697c1s
O'Reilly, Boyle v6p0695c2s
O'Reilly, E.J. v1p0252c2s v1p0288c2s v1p0388c1s v1p0389c1s v1p0802c1s v1p1032c2s v1p1033c1m v2p0084c2s
O'Reilly, F.J. v4p0546c1s v5p0440c1s
O'Reilly, G.R. v4p0121c1s v4p0515c2s v5p0534c1s
O'Reilly, I.M. v4p0303c1s
O'Reilly, J. v5p0441c1s
O'Reilly, J.B. v1p0781c1s v2p0224c2s v2p0226c2m v2p0227c1s v2p0228c1s v3p0220c1s v3p0220c2s v3p0322c1s
O'Reilly, J.P. v2p0128c1s v3p0226c1s v6p0545c1s
O'Reilly, J.R. v1p0726c2s
O'Reilly, M.B. v4p0373c2s v4p0505c2s
O'Reilly, M.F. v1p0399c2s v1p0539c2s
O'Reilly, P. v1p0654c2s
O'Reilly, P.J. v3p0309c1s
O'Rell, M. v2p0143c1s v4p0015c1s v4p0070c1s v4p0118c2s v4p0275c2s v4p0625c1s v5p0103c2s v5p0304c2s v5p0485c1s
O'Rell, M. et al. v4p0630c1s
O'Rell, Max v3p0231c1s v4p0236c2s
Orelli, A.D' v2p0148c2s
Orelli, C.von v2p0044c2s
Organ, T.A. v3p0379c1s v5p0130c2s v5p0570c1s
O'Rielly, H. v1p0772c2s v1p1051c2s v1p1290c1s
O'Riordan, M. v2p0351c2s v4p0451c2s v4p0488c1s v5p0133c2s v5p0367c1s
Orischinsky, C. v1p1137c1s
Orleans, Henri d' v4p0283c1s v5p0579c2s
Orleans, Henry of, Prince. v4p0636c2s
Orleans, L.P.d' v1p0519c1s
Orleans, L.P.d' and Sheibert, I. v1p0518c2s
Orm, M. v2p0279c2s
Ormathwaite, F. v5p0398c1s v5p0442c1s v5p0523c2s
Orme, B. v1p0343c2s
Orme, E. v2p0477c1s v5p0143c2s v5p0274c1s v5p0637c1s
Ormerod, E.A. v2p0222c1m v2p0474c2s v4p0286c1s
Ormerod, E.L. v1p1389c1s
Ormerod, G. v1p1122c2s
Ormiston, T.S. v1p0917c1s
Ormond, A.J. v2p0005c1s
Ormond, A.T. v1p0014c2s v3p0204c1s v4p0214c1s v4p0439c1s v5p0370c1s v5p0402c2s v5p0535c1s v6p0345c1s v6p0495c2s v6p0609c2s
Ormond, A.T. and Hamilton, S.M. v4p0346c2s
Ormond, J.R. v6p0287c1s v6p0606c2s v6p0713c2s
Ormonde, Marquis of v4p0407c1s
Ormrod, J. v1p0754c2s v1p0820c1s v1p1159c1s
Ormsby, G.F. v6p0310c2s v6p0669c1s
Ormsby, J. v2p0457c2s
Ormsby, M.F. et al. v4p0629c2s
Ormsby, W.E. v4p0579c2s
Ormsby-Johnson, F.C. v5p0290c1s v5p0362c1s v5p0517c1s v6p0488c1s
Ormsby-Johnson, T.C. v5p0362c1s
Orne, A.S. v1p1398c1s
Orne, J. v4p0050c1s
Orne, V. v6p0679c1s
Ornsby, R. v1p0256c1s v1p0263c2s v1p0619c2s v1p0948c1s
Ornum, W.H.Van v4p0199c2s v5p0321c1s v5p0537c2s
Orobio, I. v2p0235c2s v2p0284c2s
Oronhyatekha v1p0858c1s
O'Rourke, L. v6p0126c2s
Orpen, A.E. v3p0294c2s
Orpen, G.E. v4p0291c1s
Orpen, G.H. v3p0017c1s v3p0068c2s v4p0289c1s v6p0431c2s
Orpen, Goddard H. v6p0327c1s
Orpen, J.M. v4p0360c2s v5p0245c1s

Orpen, Mrs. v5p0108c1s v5p0273c2s

Orpet, E.O. v4p0012c2s v4p0083c1m v4p0093c1s v4p0145c2s v4p0197c1s v4p0203c1s v4p0203c2m v4p0220c1s v4p0228c2s v4p0242c2s v4p0291c1s v4p0332c1m v4p0332c2s v4p0388c1s v4p0393c1m v4p0416c1m v4p0416c2m v4p0446c1s v4p0449c1s v4p0458c2m v4p0468c1s v4p0491c2s v4p0552c2s v4p0586c2s v4p0605c1m v5p0082c2s v5p0261c2s v5p0393c1s v6p0469c2s

Orr, A. v1p0170c2m v1p0482c1s v1p1311c2s v1p1424c1s v3p0057c2s v5p0065c2s

Orr, A.C. v5p0510c2s

Orr, C.A. v4p0359c1s v4p0409c2s

Orr, F. v3p0123c1s

Orr, H. v1p0161c1s v1p1051c2s v1p1311c1m

Orr, I. v1p0819c1s v1p1356c1s

Orr, J. v2p0224c2s v2p0444c2s v3p0082c1s v3p0224c1s v3p0279c1s v3p0281c2s v4p0054c2s v4p0056c2s v4p0193c2s v4p0274c2s v4p0300c2s v4p0308c2s v4p0484c2m v5p0024c1s v5p0347c2s v5p0489c2s v6p0152c1s v6p0218c1s v6p0351c2s

Orr, J. and Borland, W. .. v6p0514c2s

Orr, J. et al. v5p0464c1m

Orr, J.D. v1p1223c2s

Orr, L. v6p0391c1s v6p0402c1s v6p0705c1s

Orr, Leyndon v6p0173c2s

Orr, M.A. v5p0363c1s

Orr, S. v6p0600c2s

Orr, S., Mrs. v1p0170c2s v1p0610c2s v4p0076c2s

Orr, Solon v6p0557c2s

Orr, T.E. v6p0512c1s v6p0709c2s

Orr, W. v6p0437c2s v6p0498c1s

Orr, W., jr. v4p0329c2s

Orrery, Countess of and Cork, Countess of v5p0140c1s v5p0196c2s

Orrick, J.L. v5p0615c2s

Orrick, L.S. v6p0447c1s

Orrick, Lucy S. v6p0607c1s

Orrick, W.P. v2p0047c2s

Orridge, B.B. v1p0762c1s

Orrock, J. v4p0130c2s v4p0137c2m v4p0154c2s v4p0270c1s v4p0386c2s

Orrock, Ja. v5p0048c1s v5p0140c2s v5p0160c2s

Orsey, A.J.D.D' v1p1085c2s

Orsi, Count v1p0285c2s v3p0226c2s

Orsi, J. v1p0896c1m

Orsi, P. v5p0396c2s v5p0608c1s

Orsman, W.J. and Russell, W.J. v3p0089c2s

Ort, S.A. v1p0778c1s v1p0847c1s v1p1101c2s v1p1163c2s v1p1301c1s v3p0436c1s v4p0113c2s v4p0528c2s v5p0240c2s v5p0400c1s v6p0390c1s

Orth, S.P. v6p0131c2s v6p0274c1s v6p0367c1m v6p0436c2s v6p0464c2s v6p0573c1s

Ortmann, A.E. v4p0119c2s v4p0515c2s v4p0637c2s v5p0022c1s v5p0062c2s v5p0141c2s v5p0295c1s v5p0340c1s v5p0355c2s v5p0426c2s v5p0574c1s v6p0214c1m v6p0214c2s v6p0330c2s v6p0413c2s v6p0440c1s v6p0483c1s

Orton, E. v1p0938c2s v1p0984c1s v2p0090c2s v2p0171c2s v2p0337c2s v3p0167c2s v3p0297c1s v4p0469c1s v5p0015c1s

Orton, G.W. v5p0037c1s v5p0091c1s v5p0213c1s v5p0262c1s

Orton, J. v1p0026c2s v1p0037c2m v1p0076c2s v1p0137c1s v1p0305c2s v1p0314c1s v1p0508c2s v1p1072c2s v1p1142c2s v1p1363c1s

Orton, J.F. v4p0377c2s

Orton, J.R. v1p1248c1s v1p1325c1s

Orton, W., jr. v1p0117c1s

Ortt, F.L. v5p0579c2s

Orvis, E.E. v2p0236c1s

O'Ryan, J. v1p1312c2s v2p0175c1s

O'Ryan, J.F. v6p0417c1s

O'Ryan, J.M. v1p0887c2s v3p0308c1s

O'Ryan, J.P. v6p0054c1s

Osbon, A.M. v1p0179c2s v1p0691c2s v1p0770c2s v1p1056c1s v1p1101c1s

Osborn, A.F. v2p0103c2s

Osborn, A.S. v6p0216c1s

Osborn, C. v4p0115c2s v4p0350c1s v5p0340c2s v5p0476c2s v5p0585c1s v5p0592c1s

Osborn, C.S. v6p0012c1s

Osborn, D. v4p0082c1s

Osborn, E.B. v4p0035c2s v4p0217c2s v5p0091c2s v5p0131c2s v5p0223c2s v5p0287c1s v5p0516c1s v6p0096c1s v6p0098c1s v6p0216c1s v6p0232c1s

Osborn, F.W. v4p0104c1s v4p0171c2s v5p0209c2s v5p0479c2s v5p0569c1s v5p0640c2s

Osborn, H. v6p0021c1s

Osborn, H.D. v2p0135c1s

Osborn, H.E. v6p0083c2s v6p0193c2s

Osborn, H.F. v2p0283c1s v2p0322c2s v3p0002c1s v3p0104c2s v3p0194c2m v3p0216c1s v3p0275c1s v3p0422c2s v4p0060c1m v4p0148c1s v4p0191c1s v4p0191c2s v4p0255c1s v4p0255c2s v4p0270c2s v4p0351c2m v4p0419c1s v4p0456c2s v4p0463c1s v4p0567c1s v4p0600c2s v4p0603c1s v5p0002c2s v5p0020c1s v5p0136c2m v5p0138c2s v5p0162c1s v5p0204c1s v5p0215c1s v5p0234c1s v5p0343c1s v5p0357c2m v5p0388c1m v5p0519c1s v5p0546c1s v5p0591c1s v5p0610c1s v6p0019c2s v6p0143c1s v6p0174c2s v6p0234c2m v6p0235c1s v6p0295c2s v6p0297c1m v6p0306c2s v6p0378c1s v6p0396c2s v6p0454c1m v6p0475c2s v6p0514c1s v6p0526c2s v6p0539c2m v6p0577c1s v6p0598c2s v6p0657c2s v6p0677c2s v6p0697c2s v6p0706c2s v6p0713c1s

Osborn, H.F. and McCosh, J. v2p0215c1s v2p0289c2s

Osborn, H.F. and Poulton, E.B. v5p0519c1s

Osborn, H.F. et al. v5p0514c1s

Osborn, H.L. v1p1241c1s v2p0289c2s v3p0044c2s v3p0331c2s v4p0018c1s v4p0223c2m v4p0255c2s v4p0369c2s v5p0041c2s v5p0458c1s v5p0517c1s v5p0607c2s v5p0646c2s v6p0220c1s

Osborn, H.L. and Hargitt, C.W. v4p0435c1s

Osborn, H.P. v2p0032c1s

Osborn, H.S. v1p0050c1s v1p0948c1s v1p1333c1s

Osborn, J.L. v5p0039c2s

Osborn, M. v6p0595c2s

Osborn, M.C. v1p0852c2s

Osborn, Max v6p0172c1s

Osborn, P.L. v5p0447c1s

Osborn, R. v1p0631c1s v1p0858c1s

Osborn, R.D. v1p0009c2s v1p0010c1m v1p0191c1s v1p0316c2s v1p0342c1s v1p0476c1s v1p0539c1s v1p0591c1s v1p0629c2s v1p0631c1m v1p0632c1s v1p0632c2s v1p0857c2s v1p0952c2s v1p1294c2s v1p1441c2s v2p0008c1s v2p0060c1s v2p0061c2s v2p0068c1s v2p0122c2s v2p0126c1s v2p0182c2s v2p0183c1m v2p0186c1s v2p0217c1m v2p0218c1m v2p0218c2m v2p0239c2s v2p0251c2m v2p0270c2s v2p0284c1s v2p0291c1s v2p0293c2s v2p0295c1s v2p0305c2m v2p0404c2s v2p0410c2s v2p0434c2s v2p0442c2s v3p0003c2s v3p0023c2s v3p0040c1s v3p0059c2s v3p0060c2s v3p0211c1s v3p0212c2s v3p0245c1s v3p0401c1s v3p0435c2s v3p0451c1s

Osborn, S. v1p0007c1s v1p0056c1s v1p0484c1m v1p0679c2s

Osborn, T.N. v2p0411c2s

Osborn, T.W. v1p0332c2s v1p0650c2s

Osborn, W.E. v5p0459c2s

Osborne, A. v5p0631c2s

Osborne, A.F. v2p0223c1s

Osborne, C. v1p0574c1s

Osborne, C.A. v6p0298c1s

Osborne, C.C. v5p0318c1m v5p0424c1s v6p0278c1s v6p0302c2s v6p0486c1s

Osborne, C.F. v4p0023c2s

Osborne, C.P. v2p0384c2s

Osborne, D. v3p0159c2s v3p0341c2s v3p0349c1s v3p0416c2s v4p0413c1s v5p0312c1s v5p0389c2s v5p0564c1s v5p0633c2s v6p0053c2s v6p0512c1s

Osborne, E. v3p0470c2s

Osborne, E.A. v4p0156c2s

Osborne, F.H. v4p0142c1s

Osborne, H.L. v4p0427c2s

Osborne, J.A. v5p0443c2s

Osborne, J.B. v4p0050c1s v4p0107c1s v5p0480c2m v6p0146c2s v6p0283c2s v6p0509c2s v6p0533c2m v6p0632c2s v6p0655c1s

Osborne, J.D. v1p0215c2s v1p0479c2s v1p0498c2s v1p0677c1s v1p0834c2s v1p0968c1s v1p0969c1s v1p0969c2s v1p0970c1s v1p1170c2s v1p1367c2s v2p0329c1s v3p0320c2s

Osborne, J.H. v1p0472c1s v1p0903c1s v1p1038c2s v1p1153c2s

Osborne, Lloyd v5p0541c2s

Osborne, M.L. v5p0048c1s v5p0066c2s v5p0133c1s v5p0301c1s v5p0344c2s v5p0380c2s v5p0385c1s v5p0624c2s v5p0626c2s v5p0627c1s

Osborne, R.S. v4p0064c2s v4p0086c2s v4p0151c1s v4p0270c1s v4p0395c2s v4p0401c1s v6p0613c1s

Osborne, T.B. v1p1349c2s v2p0102c1s v2p0315c1s

Osborne, T.M. v1p0603c1s v1p0674c1s v4p0206c2s v5p0230c1s

Osborne, W.H. v5p0424c1s v6p0010c1s v6p0012c2s v6p0024c2s v6p0087c2s v6p0173c2s v6p0274c1s v6p0385c2s v6p0572c1s v6p0589c1s

Osborne, W.L. v4p0077c1s

Osbourne, B. v2p0198c1s

Osbourne, F.M. v1p1152c1s

Osbourne, L. v4p0267c1s v4p0549c1s v5p0221c2s v5p0506c2s v6p0234c2s v6p0244c1m v6p0258c2s v6p0380c2s v6p0572c2s v6p0645c1s v6p0698c2s

Osbourne, L. and Stevenson, R.L. v3p0473c1s v4p0166c2s v4p0633c2s

Osbourne, Lloyd v5p0051c1s v5p0171c2s v5p0262c2s v5p0474c2s v5p0553c1s v6p0465c2m

Osburn, R.C. v6p0180c1s v6p0225c1s v6p0396c2s

Osburn, W. v1p0436c2s

Oscar, A. v5p0067c2s v5p0371c1s

Oscar Fredrik, King v3p0074c2s v4p0097c2m v6p0187c2s

Oscar II, King v2p0074c1s v2p0316c2s v3p0383c1s v6p0038c1m

Oseroff, I. v5p0501c2s

Osgood, F. v4p0069c1s v4p0606c2s v5p0253c2s v6p0001c1s v6p0500c1s v6p0608c1s

Osgood, H. v1p0097c1s v2p0045c1s v2p0096c1s v2p0230c2s v2p0235c1s v2p0236c2m v3p0041c2s v3p0229c1s v3p0319c2s v3p0359c2s v4p0055c1s v4p0057c2m v4p0058c1m v4p0179c1s v4p0349c1s v5p0047c1s v5p0299c1s v5p0307c1s v5p0386c1s v6p0540c2s

Osgood, H.L. v2p0374c2s v2p0408c1s v3p0012c2s v3p0137c2s v3p0349c2s v4p0134c2s v4p0463c2s v5p0077c1s v5p0128c1s v5p0133c2s v5p0468c2s v5p0541c1m v5p0601c1s v5p0601c2s v6p0016c1s v6p0450c1s v6p0701c1s

Osgood, I. v6p0564c2s

Osgood, J. v3p0003c1s

Osgood, J.B.F. v1p0447c2s

Osgood, K,P. v1p0108c2s v1p0469c1s v1p0587c1s v1p0626c2s v1p0726c2s v1p0888c2s v1p1114c1s v1p1293c2s v1p1339c1s v1p1387c1s v2p0154c1s v3p0232c2s

Osgood, R.C. v6p0571c2s

Osgood, S. v1p0027c1s v1p0069c1s v1p0120c1s v1p0127c2s v1p0175c2s v1p0189c1s v1p0211c1s v1p0229c1s v1p0239c1s v1p0241c2s v1p0243c2s v1p0246c2s v1p0254c1m v1p0261c2s v1p0288c2s v1p0296c1s v1p0331c2s v1p0348c1m v1p0372c2s v1p0373c2s v1p0378c2s v1p0389c2s v1p0390c1s v1p0393c2s v1p0426c2m v1p0471c2s v1p0492c2s v1p0512c2s v1p0559c2s v1p0598c2s v1p0610c1s v1p0613c1s v1p0647c1s v1p0682c1s v1p0686c2s v1p0692c1s v1p0697c1s v1p0697c2s v1p0714c2s v1p0755c1s v1p0773c2s v1p0777c1s v1p0842c1s v1p0867c2s v1p0875c2s v1p0906c2s v1p0910c1s v1p0910c2s v1p0916c1s v1p0980c1s v1p1043c1s v1p1062c1s v1p1064c2s v1p1067c2s v1p1096c1s v1p1111c2s v1p1120c2s v1p1128c1s v1p1128c2s v1p1129c2s v1p1152c1s v1p1157c1s v1p1158c2s v1p1172c2s v1p1182c1s v1p1215c2s v1p1217c1s v1p1222c1s v1p1236c2s v1p1274c2s v1p1286c2s v1p1296c1s v1p1321c1s v1p1340c2s v1p1381c2s v1p1384c1s v1p1398c2s v1p1400c1s v1p1404c1s v1p1422c1s v2p0379c1s

Osgood, W.H. v6p0129c2s

O'Shaughnessy, R. v1p0391c1s v2p0379c2s

O'Shea, J.A. v1p0311c2s v1p0316c2s v1p0448c1s v1p0574c2s v1p0626c1s v1p0627c1s v1p0738c2s v1p0810c1s v1p1231c1s v1p1335c2s v2p0040c1s v2p0068c1s v2p0150c1s v2p0150c2s v2p0208c1s v2p0261c1s

v2p0367c2s v2p0395c2s v2p0413c1s
v2p0427c2s v2p0447c2s v3p0443c1s
O'Shea, J.J. v4p0002c1s
v4p0027c1s v4p0037c2s v4p0102c1s
v4p0125c2s v4p0168c1s v4p0186c2s
v4p0213c1s v4p0266c1s v4p0289c1s
v4p0289c2s v4p0290c1s v4p0303c1s
v4p0315c1s v4p0365c1s v4p0385c1s
v4p0400c1s v4p0409c1s v4p0452c2s
v4p0605c1s v5p0065c1s v5p0084c1s
v5p0144c1s v5p0152c2s v5p0177c1s
v5p0234c2s v5p0285c1s v5p0295c2s
v5p0296c1s v5p0297c1s v5p0297c2s
v5p0315c1s v5p0323c2s v5p0373c2s
v5p0416c2s v5p0420c1s v5p0433c2s
v5p0458c2s v6p0002c1s v6p0094c1s
v6p0103c1s v6p0200c2s v6p0212c2s
v6p0228c1s v6p0326c1s v6p0504c2s
v6p0520c2s v6p0571c2s v6p0572c1s
v6p0605c2s
O'Shea, J.O. v1p0994c2s
O'Shea, John J. v5p0296c1s
O'Shea, K.F.M. v5p0030c2s
O'Shea, M.N. v6p0707c2s
O'Shea, M.V. v4p0103c1s
v4p0161c1s v4p0406c1s v4p0441c2s
v4p0464c2s v4p0506c1s v4p0566c1s
v5p0101c2s v5p0106c2m v5p0107c1s
v5p0107c2s v5p0167c2s v5p0168c1s
v5p0325c1s v5p0370c1m v5p0416c1s
v5p0517c2s v5p0569c2m v5p0633c2s
v6p0136c1s v6p0190c2s v6p0193c1s
v6p0211c2s v6p0290c2s v6p0498c1s
v6p0540c1s v6p0625c1s
O'Shea, T.J. v6p0191c1s
O'Shea, W.W. v5p0177c1s
Oshio, T. v6p0434c2s
Oshio, Tokutaro v6p0338c2s
Oskison, J. v6p0097c1s
v6p0144c2m v6p0170c1s v6p0196c2s
v6p0315c2s v6p0316c2s v6p0346c2s
v6p0435c1s v6p0447c2s v6p0491c2s
v6p0535c1s v6p0592c1s v6p0651c1s
v6p0692c2s
Oskison, J.M. v5p0062c1s
v5p0421c2s v5p0628c1s v6p0329c1s
v6p0524c2s
Osler, W. v3p0273c1s
v3p0450c2s
Osman, Bey v3p0469c2s
Osmond, I.T. v1p0810c2s
v6p0280c2s
Oss, S.F.Van v4p0038c2s
v4p0130c1s v4p0475c1s v4p0550c1s
v5p0131c1s
Ostberg, P. v2p0070c1s
Osterberg, M. v4p0174c2s
Osterhout, W.J.V. v6p0288c2s
v6p0502c1s
Ostertag, B. v5p0271c1s
v5p0303c2s v6p0123c2s v6p0124c1s
Ostien, L.A. v6p0290c1s
Ostrogorski, M. v3p0470c1s
v4p0239c1s v5p0413c1s
Ostrom, J.N. v5p0225c1s
Ostwald, W. v4p0099c1s
v4p0176c2s v4p0360c2m v6p0066c2s
v6p0104c1s v6p0200c1s v6p0204c1s
v6p0280c1s v6p0576c1s
O'Sullivan, D. v5p0087c2s
O'Sullivan, D.A. v2p0065c2s
v2p0361c1s v2p0375c1s v2p0375c2s
v2p0445c2s v3p0062c1s v3p0065c1s
v3p0137c2s v3p0350c2s v3p0358c1s
v3p0444c1s
O'Sullivan, D.E. v2p0012c2s
v2p0320c1s
O'Sullivan, D.R. v4p0576c2s
O'Sullivan, D.T. v4p0034c1s
O'Sullivan, M.P. v5p0496c2s
Oswald, E. v2p0243c2s
v2p0248c2s v2p0321c1s
Oswald, E.J. v1p0622c2s
Oswald, F. v6p0098c2s
Oswald, F.L. v1p0030c2s
v1p0056c2s v1p0209c1s v1p0212c2s
v1p0274c2s v1p0351c2s v1p0358c2s
v1p0374c1s v1p0450c1s v1p0465c1s
v1p0467c2m v1p0560c1s v1p0564c1s
v1p0649c1s v1p0675c2m v1p0832c2s
v1p0833c2s v1p0845c1s v1p0863c2s
v1p0935c1s v1p1005c1s v1p1179c1s
v1p1196c1m v1p1209c2s v1p1220c2s
v1p1310c2s v1p1326c2s v1p1439c2s
v1p1440c2s v2p0007c1s v2p0014c2s
v2p0024c2s v2p0025c2s v2p0053c2s
v2p0071c1s v2p0089c1s v2p0100c2s
v2p0108c2s v2p0126c2s v2p0127c2s
v2p0154c2s v2p0198c2s v2p0205c2s
v2p0209c1s v2p0212c1s v2p0213c1s
v2p0222c2s v2p0265c1s v2p0266c1s
v2p0295c1s v2p0332c2s v2p0337c1m
v2p0340c2s v2p0341c1s v2p0345c1s
v2p0360c2s v2p0369c2s v2p0374c2s
v2p0410c2s v2p0424c2s v2p0427c1m
v2p0430c2s v2p0434c1s v2p0436c1s
v2p0445c1s v3p0039c2s v3p0059c1s
v3p0086c2m v3p0088c2s v3p0155c2s
v3p0192c1s v3p0229c1s v3p0257c2s
v3p0263c2s v3p0276c1m v3p0280c1s
v3p0285c2s v3p0357c1s v3p0410c2s
v3p0414c2s v3p0456c2s v4p0007c1s
v4p0020c2s v4p0035c1s v4p0035c2s
v4p0039c2s v4p0065c1s v4p0085c1s
v4p0121c2s v4p0130c1s v4p0161c2s
v4p0188c1s v4p0200c1m v4p0207c2s
v4p0216c2s v4p0252c1s v4p0260c2s
v4p0270c2s v4p0286c2s v4p0313c1s
v4p0345c1s v4p0404c1s v4p0410c2s
v4p0429c2m v4p0459c2s v4p0461c1s
v4p0476c2m v4p0480c2s v4p0497c2s
v4p0502c2s v4p0513c1s v4p0516c2s
v4p0538c1s v4p0538c2s v4p0550c2s
v4p0575c2s v4p0581c1s v4p0627c1s
v4p0636c1s v5p0021c2s v5p0034c2s
v5p0064c1s v5p0064c2s v5p0081c1s
v5p0147c2m v5p0148c1s v5p0161c1s
v5p0205c2s v5p0222c2s v5p0229c2s
v5p0252c2s v5p0291c2s v5p0316c2s
v5p0318c1s v5p0332c2s v5p0351c2s
v5p0357c2s v5p0383c1s v5p0442c1s
v5p0508c1s v5p0534c2s v5p0544c1s
v5p0618c1s v5p0626c1m v6p0138c2s
v6p0154c1s v6p0542c1s
Oswald, F.L. and Conway, M.D.
v4p0588c2s
Oswald, F.L. and Roberts, E.H.
v5p0018c2s
Oswald, F.S. v1p0349c2s
v5p0092c2s
Oswald, J. v1p0096c2s
v1p0778c1s v1p0847c1s v1p1056c2s
Oswald, R. v6p0129c2s
Otani, K. v6p0296c1s
v6p0338c2s
Otey, J.H. v1p1315c1s
Otheman, E. v1p0454c1s
Otheman, E.B. v1p0481c2s
v1p0612c1s v2p0079c1s
Otis, A. v1p0197c2s
v1p1112c1s
Otis, A.L. v1p0887c2s
Otis, E.A. v4p0148c1s
Otis, E.O. v6p0660c1s
Otis, E.S. v5p0489c1s
Otis, F.D. v1p0962c2s
Otis, F.N. v1p0963c1s
v1p1326c2s v3p0359c2s
Otis, G. v1p0143c2s
v1p0727c1s v1p0833c1s
Otis, H.G. v1p1270c1s
Otis, H.N. v1p0472c1s
v1p0950c2s v1p1299c2s
Otis, J.F. v1p0023c2s
v1p0177c2s v1p0178c2s v1p0322c1s
Otis, N.A. v1p0156c1s
Otis, W.S.C. v1p0130c1s
Ott and Jackson v1p0533c1s
Ott, A. v1p0224c2s
v1p0533c1s v1p0624c2s v1p0664c1s
v1p0873c2s v1p1192c2s v1p1250c2s
Ottarson, F.J. v1p0915c2s
Otte, E.C. v1p0983c2s
Ottendorfer, O. v3p0208c2s
v3p0398c2s v4p0152c1s
Ottley, E.B. v6p0538c1s
Ottley, H. v1p0067c2s
v1p0171c2s v1p0353c1s v1p0992c1s
Ottley, R.L. v4p0188c1s
v6p0125c1s v6p0211c2s
Ottley, R.R. v4p0580c1s
Ottley, W.G. v1p1434c1s
Otto, Count of Mosloy v4p0126c1s
Ottolengui, R. v4p0033c2s
v4p0380c2s v4p0392c1s v4p0527c2s
Otts, J.M. v2p0148c1s
Otway, A. v3p0164c1s
Otzbacker, O.E. v6p0370c1s
Oudemans, J.A.C. v2p0064c1s
v2p0234c1s
Oudin, Maurice A. v6p0141c1s
Oughter-Lonie, A.C. v1p0043c1s
Ouida v1p1082c1s
v2p0155c1s v2p0390c1s v6p0685c2s
v6p0687c2s
Oukhtomsky, E., Prince ... v6p0645c2s
Oulahan, R.V. v6p0274c2s
v6p0687c1s
Ould, R. v1p1346c1s
v2p0453c1s
Oulet, B. v4p0333c1s
Ousley, C. v5p0224c2s
Ousley, C.N. v3p0099c1s
Ouspensky, G. v6p0142c2s
Oustalet, E. v1p0001c1s
v1p1009c2s
Outerbridge, A. v1p0812c1s
Outerbridge, A.E. v1p0532c1s
v1p0825c2m v1p0849c1s v1p1198c1m
v1p1233c2s v2p0280c2s v4p0173c2s
v4p0314c1s v4p0347c2m v5p0125c1s
v5p0289c2s v5p0353c2s v5p0408c2s
v5p0554c1s v6p0400c1s v6p0412c1s
Outerbridge, A.E., jr. ... v1p0532c2s
v2p0413c2s v3p0069c2s v3p0223c1m
v4p0138c1m v4p0180c1s v4p0362c2s
v4p0607c2s v5p0011c1s v5p0078c2s
v5p0237c2m v5p0289c2s v5p0353c2s
v5p0529c2s v6p0328c2m v6p0399c2s
v6p0400c1s v6p0407c1s v6p0652c1s
v6p0682c2s
Outerbridge, A.H. v1p0314c2s
Outisky, Prince v2p0048c1s
Outram, L. v4p0107c1s
Outran, J. v6p0036c2s
v6p0232c2s v6p0546c2s
Ouvry, F. v1p0256c1s
v1p0409c1s
Ovenden, C.T. v6p0644c2s
Overall, W.H. v2p0057c2s
Overbeck, Baron von v4p0078c1s
Overbury, F. v5p0185c2s
Overmyer, D. v5p0158c2s
Overstreet, H.A. v6p0136c1s
v6p0473c1s v6p0659c2s
Overton, E.E. v4p0419c2s
Overton, F. v6p0044c1s
v6p0156c1s
Overton, J.H. v2p0033c1s
v2p0145c1s v2p0401c1s v2p0470c1s
v3p0038c2s v3p0193c1s v3p0252c1m
v6p0692c1s
Overy, H. v5p0356c2s
Oviatt, A.P. v5p0496c2s
Oviatt, E. v5p0643c2s
v6p0325c1s
Oviatt, F.C. v6p0321c2m
v6p0322c1s
Ovington, C.O. v5p0198c1s
v5p0618c1s
Ovington, M.W. v6p0446c2s
v6p0447c2s v6p0456c2s
Ovington, Mary W. v6p0448c1s
Owen, A.K. v4p0138c2s
v4p0420c2s
Owen, Alan v4p0600c2s
v6p0265c1s v6p0463c1s
Owen, B.F. v5p0275c1s
v5p0343c2s v5p0386c2s
Owen, C. v1p0522c1s
v1p0627c1s v1p0774c1s v1p0943c1s
v1p1335c2s v3p0426c2s v5p0610c2s
Owen, C. et al. v3p0202c2s
v3p0269c1s
Owen, C.E. v6p0395c2s
Owen, C.H. v2p0031c1s
v2p0397c1s v3p0087c2s v3p0180c1s
v3p0375c1s v3p0417c1s v5p0423c1s
v5p0587c2s v6p0035c1s
Owen, D. v2p0313c2s
v4p0633c2s
Owen, D.D. v1p0612c2s
Owen, E. v5p0118c1s
v5p0335c2s v5p0625c1s v6p0003c2s
Owen, E.B. v6p0281c2s
Owen, E.S.D. and Bunce, Louise M.
v6p0171c2s
Owen, East v4p0172c1s
Owen, Ernest Dale v6p0176c2s
Owen, F.C. v1p0922c1s
v1p1136c1s v5p0180c1s
Owen, F.Cunliffe v5p0077c2s
v6p0516c2s
Owen, F.D. v1p1342c2s
v5p0267c1s v5p0330c2s
Owen, F.M. v2p0241c1s
Owen, G. v6p0100c2s
Owen, G.S. v5p0109c2s
Owen, H. v1p0184c2s
v4p0323c2s
Owen, J. v1p0231c1s
v1p0346c2s v1p0559c2s v1p0625c2s
v1p0810c2s v1p1000c2s v1p1001c1s
v1p1412c1m v3p0019c1s v3p0081c1s
v3p0261c1s v3p0262c2s v3p0266c1s
v3p0302c1s v3p0358c1s v3p0358c2s
v3p0416c1s v4p0074c1s v4p0158c1s
v4p0302c1s v4p0611c1s
Owen, J. and Charles, R.H.
v4p0056c1s v4p0185c1s
Owen, J.A. v1p1082c1s
v2p0004c2s v2p0006c1s v2p0078c1s
v2p0327c2s v3p0146c2s v3p0197c1s
v3p0219c1s v4p0124c1s v4p0285c1s
v4p0528c1s
Owen, J.B. v1p0941c1s
v1p1281c1s v2p0029c1s
Owen, J.E. v5p0139c2s
Owen, J.F. v5p0007c1s
v5p0128c2s v5p0244c2s
Owen, J.H. v1p0288c1s
Owen, J.J. v1p0048c1s
v1p0124c1s v1p0343c2s v1p0846c2s
v1p0847c1s
Owen, J.M. v6p0209c1s
Owen, J.P. v4p0120c2s
v4p0138c1s
Owen, J.P. et al. v4p0527c1s
Owen, L. v5p0191c2s
v5p0562c1s
Owen, L.A. v6p0397c1s
Owen, M. v1p1277c1s
Owen, M.A. v3p0419c2s
v4p0413c1s
Owen, M.L. v1p0153c1s
Owen, R. v1p0040c2s
v1p0042c1s v1p0143c1s v1p0396c2s
v1p0470c1s v1p0497c2s v1p0509c2s
v1p0641c2s v1p0730c1s v1p0745c1s
v1p0767c2s v1p0788c2s v1p0791c2s

v1p0818c1s v1p0841c2s v1p0995c2s v1p1213c1s v1p1232c2s v2p0133c2s v2p0274c2s v5p0355c1s
Owen, R. et al. v1p1376c2s
Owen, R., Sir v3p0225c2s
Owen, R.D. v1p0116c2s v1p0297c1s v1p0306c2s v1p0399c1s v1p0400c2s v1p0439c1s v1p0595c2m v1p0953c1s v1p1208c1s v1p1216c1s v1p1297c1s v1p1400c2s v1p1412c1s
Owen, S.J. v1p0629c2s v2p0125c2s v3p0048c2s v3p0212c2s v3p0240c2s v4p0250c1s
Owen, T.M. v2p0209c1s
Owen, W. v1p1398c1s
Owen, W.B. v6p0078c2s v6p0239c2s v6p0290c2s
Owen, W.H. v4p0182c2s
Owen, W.M. v3p0114c1s v3p0185c1s
Owen, W.O. v3p0044c1s v3p0474c2s v5p0242c1s v5p0389c2s v5p0449c1s
Owen-Smith, C.E. v4p0265c1s
Owens, J.E. v5p0006c2s
Owens, J.G. v3p0476c2s v4p0205c1s
Owens, M.J. v4p0080c2s
Owens, R.B. v5p0184c2s
Owens, R.C. v6p0570c1s
Owens, W. v1p0464c2s v1p0905c1s
Owens, W.G. v4p0367c1s
Ower, E.M. v3p0391c2s
Oxe, O. v6p0307c1s
Oxeley, J.M. v6p0380c2s
Oxenden, L. v5p0331c2s
Oxenden, M. v5p0494c1s
Oxenden, Maud v6p0155c1s
Oxenford, J. v1p0080c2s v1p0115c1s v1p0160c1s v1p0175c1m v1p0186c1s v1p0205c1s v1p0446c2s v1p0502c2s v1p0701c2m v1p0739c1s v1p0801c2s v1p0863c1s v1p0925c1s v1p1044c2s v1p1072c1s v1p1081c2s v1p1107c1s v1p1148c1s v1p1202c1s v1p1230c2m v1p1231c1s v1p1318c2s v1p1371c1s v1p1417c2s v2p0410c1s
Oxenford, J. and Calderon. v1p0019c1s
Oxenham, E.J. v6p0694c1s
Oxenham, H.N. v1p0426c1s v1p1355c1s v1p1376c2s v2p0042c2s v2p0166c2s v3p0264c2s
Oxenham, J. v5p0053c2s v5p0064c2s v5p0067c1s v5p0096c2s v5p0266c1s v5p0313c1s v5p0425c1s v6p0031c1s v6p0052c1s v6p0073c1s v6p0134c1s v6p0248c2s v6p0255c2s v6p0311c2s v6p0366c2s v6p0467c1s v6p0467c2s v6p0518c2s v6p0570c2s v6p0603c2s v6p0626c2s v6p0644c2s v6p0648c2s
Oxenham, John v5p0115c2s v6p0100c1s
Oxland, C. v1p0056c2s
Oxley, J.M. v2p0157c2s v2p0270c2s v2p0400c2s v3p0015c2s v3p0065c2s v3p0142c2s v3p0154c1s v3p0203c2m v3p0205c1s v3p0261c1s v3p0290c2s v3p0327c1s v3p0371c1s v3p0372c2s v4p0086c2s v4p0168c2s v4p0519c2s v5p0045c1s v5p0090c2s v5p0115c2s v5p0252c1s v5p0338c1s v5p0384c2s v5p0424c2s v6p0181c1s v6p0456c2s v6p0461c2s v6p0546c2s v6p0596c1s v6p0662c2s
Oxley, J.McD. v2p0382c2s
Oxley, J.Macdonald v6p0096c2s
Oxley, T. v1p0563c2s
Oxley, W. v2p0135c2s
Oxley, W.MacD. v3p0213c2s
Oyen, H. v6p0362c1s v6p0398c1s
Oyly, C.J.D' v1p0793c2s
Oyly, W.H.D' v6p0022c2s
Ozaki, Y. v5p0303c1s
Ozaki, Y.T. v6p0336c1s
Ozaki, Yei Theodora v6p0024c2s v6p0350c2s
Ozanne, C.H. v3p0062c2s v3p0092c1s
Ozanne, J.W. v1p1129c1s v1p1322c1s

P., A.W. v3p0326c2s
P., E.B. v5p0377c1s
P., E.R. v3p0100c1s
P., J.E. v5p0208c1s
P., W.N. v6p0301c2s
P., W.R. v5p0274c1s
Pace, E.A. v4p0465c1m
v5p0613c1s v6p0049c1s v6p0190c1s
v6p0193c2s v6p0241c1s v6p0309c2m
v6p0382c1s v6p0419c2s v6p0495c2s
v6p0496c1s v6p0521c1s v6p0521c2s
v6p0537c1s v6p0548c1s v6p0571c1s
v6p0642c2s v6p0643c2m v6p0690c1s
v6p0708c2s
Pacha, Hobart ....
v2p0443c2s
Pack-Beresford ....
v5p0032c1s
Packard, A.S. v1p0132c2s
v1p0154c2s v1p0276c1s v1p0600c1s
v1p0724c2s v1p0898c2s v1p0899c2s
v1p1213c1s v1p1325c2s v1p1412c2s
v2p0120c2s v2p0146c1s v2p0173c2s
v2p0222c1s v2p0222c2s v2p0245c2s
v2p0324c1s v2p0349c2s v2p0444c1s
v2p0459c2s v2p0483c2s v3p0055c2s
v3p0071c1s v3p0120c1s v3p0145c1s
v3p0145c2s v4p0156c2s v4p0223c1s
v4p0327c1s v4p0484c2s v4p0519c2s
v4p0554c2s v4p0607c1s v5p0008c2s
v5p0198c1s v5p0292c1s v5p0323c1m
v5p0582c1s v5p0646c2s v6p0111c2s
v6p0214c2s v6p0359c1s
Packard, A.S., jr. v1p0042c1s
v1p0073c1s v1p0107c1m v1p0181c1s
v1p0209c1m v1p0279c1s v1p0311c1m
v1p0321c2s v1p0327c2s v1p0362c2s
v1p0366c1s v1p0367c1s v1p0394c1s
v1p0435c1s v1p0463c2m v1p0523c2s
v1p0524c1m v1p0551c1s v1p0644c2m
v1p0645c1m v1p0645c2m v1p0715c2s
v1p0758c1s v1p0759c2m v1p0792c1m
v1p0855c2s v1p0859c1s v1p0875c1m
v1p0929c2s v1p0930c1s v1p0956c1s
v1p0967c1s v1p1059c1s v1p1074c1m
v1p1147c1s v1p1164c2s v1p1197c2s
v1p1342c2s v1p1432c2m v1p1441c1s
v2p0179c1s v2p0259c1s v2p0308c1s
Packard, A.S., jr. and Cope, E.D.
v1p0920c2s
Packard, E.N. v3p0281c1s
Packard, F.A. v1p0285c1s
v1p0388c2s v1p1093c1s v1p1096c2s
v1p1160c1s
Packard, G.F. v1p0154c2s
Packard, G.T. v1p0789c2m
v2p0096c2s
Packard, H. v6p0351c2s
v6p0428c1s
Packard, Harry A. v6p0400c1s
Packard, J. v1p0050c1s
v1p0246c2s v1p0689c1s v1p0693c2s
v1p1120c1s
Packard, J., jr. v2p0437c2s
Packard, J.C. et al. v6p0406c1s
Packard, J.H. v1p0934c1s
Packard, L.R. v1p0262c2s
v1p0552c1m v1p0553c1s v1p0553c2m
v1p0555c1s v1p0600c1s v1p0889c1s
v1p0990c1s v1p1234c2s v2p0206c2s
v2p0321c2s
Packard, R.L. v4p0133c1m
v4p0403c1s v4p0600c2s v5p0446c1s
Packard, R.L. and Merrill, G.P.
v4p0468c1s
Packard, R.S. v5p0614c1s
Packard, S.S. v3p0061c1m
v3p0310c2s
Packard, W. v4p0089c1s
v4p0200c1s v4p0497c2s v4p0620c1s
v5p0010c2s v5p0027c1s v5p0061c2s
v5p0096c2s v5p0124c1s v5p0125c1s
v5p0267c1s v5p0317c1s v5p0338c2s
v5p0447c2s v5p0450c2s v5p0463c1s
v5p0517c2s v5p0518c2s v5p0526c2s
v5p0580c1s v5p0617c1s v6p0229c1s
v6p0463c2s v6p0570c1m v6p0616c2s
v6p0636c1s v6p0687c1s
Packard, W.A. v1p0700c2s
v6p0009c1s
Packard, Winthrop v6p0137c1s
Padan, R.S. v5p0465c1s
v5p0607c1s v5p0615c1s v6p0400c2s
Paddock, B.H. v1p1044c1s
Paddock, Cornelia v2p0298c1s
Paddock, M.H. v4p0222c2s
v4p0257c1s v5p0552c2s v6p0498c1s
Paddock, W. v5p0438c1s
Paddock, Z. v1p0027c2s
v1p0097c1s v1p0240c1s v1p0558c2s
v1p0830c1s v1p0831c1s v1p1057c1s
v1p1106c2s v1p1292c2s v1p1434c2s
Paden, M.S. v5p0214c2s
Pagan, Isabelle M. v6p0173c2s
Page, A. v1p0648c1s
v3p0255c2s
Page, A.G. v5p0630c2s
Page, Arthur W. v6p0153c1s
Page, C.E. v2p0092c1s
v4p0589c1s v5p0042c2s
Page, C.G. v1p0400c1s
v1p0401c1m v1p0401c2m v1p0462c2s
v1p0498c1m v1p0498c2m v1p0787c2s
v1p0788c1s
Page, C.H. v4p0577c2s
v5p0273c2s v5p0317c2s
Page, D. v2p0387c2s
Page, D.P. v1p0390c2s
v1p0391c2s
Page, E.D. v2p0197c1s
v2p0481c2m v6p0089c2s
Page, G.H. v3p0016c2s
v3p0284c1s v3p0396c1s v4p0030c2s
v4p0140c2s v4p0276c1s v4p0308c2s
v4p0310c1s v4p0598c2s v5p0555c2s
Page, H.A. v1p0063c2s
v1p0137c2s v1p0157c2s v1p0163c2s
v1p0176c1s v1p0179c1s v1p0229c1s
v1p0271c2s v1p0438c1s v1p0521c1s
v1p0557c2s v1p0605c2s v1p0708c2s
v1p0752c2s v1p0758c2s v1p0765c1s
v1p0866c2s v1p0869c2s v1p1022c2s
v1p1030c2s v1p1035c1s v1p1141c2s
v1p1142c1s v1p1162c2s v1p1165c2s
v1p1170c1s v1p1174c1s v1p1177c1s
v1p1188c2m v1p1202c2s v1p1416c1s
Page, H.E. v2p0008c1s
v2p0222c2s v2p0422c1s v3p0306c1s
Page, J. v2p0293c1s
v3p0402c1s v5p0073c2s v6p0477c1s
v6p0681c1s
Page, J.L.W. v1p0667c1s
v3p0110c2s v3p0400c1s v4p0122c1s
v4p0154c2s
Page, James v6p0463c2s
Page, L.R. v1p0468c2s
Page, O.O. v4p0444c2s
Page, R. v3p0152c1s
v4p0429c2s
Page, R.A. v1p0904c1s
Page, R.L. v1p0871c1s
v2p0298c1s
Page, S.F. v1p0163c1s
v1p0607c1m v3p0180c2s
Page, Sarah C. v6p0059c2s
v6p0680c1s
Page, T. v1p0161c2s
v3p0139c1s
Page, T.N. v1p1438c1s
v2p0278c1s v2p0282c2s v2p0321c1s
v2p0348c1s v2p0409c1s v2p0450c2s
v3p0135c2s v3p0170c1s v3p0306c1s
v3p0334c1s v3p0369c1s v3p0401c2m
v4p0079c2s v4p0235c2s v4p0267c1s
v4p0335c2s v4p0373c2s v4p0390c2s
v4p0397c1s v4p0412c2s v4p0605c2s
v5p0075c2s v5p0480c2s v5p0481c1s
v5p0545c1s v5p0613c1m v6p0084c1s
v6p0391c1s v6p0421c1s v6p0446c2s
v6p0447c1s v6p0447c2s v6p0465c2s
v6p0590c2s v6p0671c2s
Page, T.N. and Smith, W.B.
v6p0448c2s
Page, T.W. v5p0351c2s
v6p0081c2s v6p0293c1s v6p0364c2s
v6p0666c2s
Page, W. v1p0793c2s
v1p0825c2s v1p1186c1s v2p0411c1s
v3p0084c1s v5p0414c1s v6p0475c1s
Page, W.G. v3p0283c2s
v4p0477c2s v5p0539c2s
Page, W.H. v1p1223c2s
v1p1224c1s v2p0123c2s v2p0309c1s
v3p0401c2s v4p0346c1s v5p0040c2s
v5p0081c2s v6p0393c1m v6p0458c1s
v6p0460c1s v6p0523c1s v6p0605c2s
v6p0686c2s
Page, W.Y. v4p0193c2s
v4p0242c2s
Page, Walter H. v6p0137c2s
v6p0550c1s
Page-Roberts, R. v6p0052c1s
Page-Roberts, W. v3p0247c1s
v4p0382c1s
Pagelsen, E.N. v5p0451c1s
Paget, A.L. v5p0068c1s
v5p0504c1s
Paget, E. v4p0141c1s
Paget, F.A. v1p0146c2s
v1p0214c1s v1p0664c1s v3p0048c2s
Paget, F.V. v2p0210c2s
v2p0246c2s
Paget, H.C., Mrs. v5p0112c1s
v5p0499c2s
Paget, J. v1p0181c2s
v2p0198c2m v2p0366c2m v3p0188c2s
v3p0323c1s v6p0050c1s
Paget, J., Sir v1p0036c1s
v1p0426c1s v1p0816c2s
Paget, J., Sir and Bernays, J.
v1p0019c2s
Paget, J., Sir et al. v1p1376c2s
Paget, J.C. v1p0059c2s
v1p0316c1s v1p0379c2m v1p0429c1s
v1p0545c2s v1p0547c2s v1p0642c2s
v1p0650c2s v1p0706c2s v1p0817c2s
v1p0902c1m v1p1133c2s v1p1331c2s
v1p1362c2s v5p0026c2s v5p0127c2s
v5p0165c1s v5p0345c1s v5p0440c2s
Paget, J.G. v4p0317c2s
Paget, J.N. v6p0051c1s
Paget, J.R. v4p0044c1s
Paget, Lady v3p0066c2s
Paget, Lucy Gordon v6p0704c1s
Paget, M.C. v6p0594c1s
Paget, R.A. v6p0543c2s
Paget, S. v6p0058c2s
v6p0497c2s v6p0680c2s
Paget, Stephen v6p0363c1s
Paget, V. v1p1334c1s
v2p0122c2s v2p0214c2s v2p0303c1s
v2p0317c2s v2p0326c2s v2p0336c1s
v2p0346c2m v2p0350c1s v2p0365c1s
v2p0385c1s v2p0401c1s v2p0416c1s
v2p0450c2s v2p0462c2s v3p0006c1s
v3p0012c2m v3p0016c1s v3p0155c2s
v3p0214c2s v3p0246c1s v3p0300c1s
v3p0314c2s v3p0355c1s v3p0394c1s
v3p0419c2s v3p0451c1s v3p0472c2s
v3p0473c1s v4p0029c1s v4p0048c2s
v4p0131c1s v4p0179c1s v4p0188c2s
v4p0215c2s v4p0220c1s v4p0266c2s
v4p0293c2s v4p0334c2s v4p0349c1s
v4p0474c1s v4p0499c2s v4p0510c2s
v4p0542c1s v4p0582c2s v4p0587c2s
v4p0632c1s v4p0633c2s v4p0637c1s
v5p0018c2s v5p0030c2s v5p0031c1s
v5p0052c2s v5p0301c2s v5p0595c2s
v6p0033c1s v6p0171c1s v6p0360c2s
v6p0596c1s v6p0662c1s v6p0673c1s
Paget, V. and Anstruther-Thomson, C.
v5p0051c1s
Paget, Violet v6p0101c2s
v6p0380c1s
Paget, W. v2p0334c1s
v3p0271c2s v4p0601c1s v6p0005c2s
v6p0083c1s v6p0536c1s v6p0678c1s
Paget, W., Lady v6p0678c2s
Paget, W.C. v6p0542c2s
Pagliari, R. v4p0492c2s
Paige, E.R. v2p0028c2s
Paige, J.W., Mrs. v2p0469c2s
Paige, L.R. v1p0837c1s
v1p1101c2s v1p1416c1s v2p0057c2s
v2p0472c1s v2p0473c1s
Paige, S. v6p0010c2s
v6p0632c1s
Paige, W.H. v6p0161c1m
Pain, A. v5p0021c2s
v5p0435c1s
Pain, A.C. v1p1255c2s
Pain, B. v4p0127c2s
v4p0145c2s v4p0194c1s v4p0259c1s
v4p0311c1s v4p0430c2s v4p0453c2s
v4p0589c2s v5p0033c1s v5p0103c2s
v5p0491c1s
Pain, Barry v4p0113c2s
v4p0341c2s v6p0388c2s
Pain, J. v4p0050c1s
Pain, W. v4p0278c1s
v5p0361c1s
Paine, A.B. v4p0487c2s
v4p0566c2s v4p0577c2s v5p0075c2s
v5p0094c2s v5p0134c1s v5p0201c2s
v5p0419c1s v5p0420c2s v5p0486c1s
v5p0578c1s v5p0644c1s v6p0040c2s
v6p0081c1s v6p0124c2s v6p0143c2s
v6p0179c1s v6p0185c2s v6p0198c1s
v6p0227c2s v6p0228c2s v6p0298c2s
v6p0398c1s v6p0434c1s v6p0500c2s
v6p0657c2s v6p0670c1s
Paine, A.B. and Stuart, R.McE.
v4p0343c1s
Paine, A.B. et al. v6p0055c1s
Paine, A.W. v1p0532c1m
v2p0403c1s v3p0132c1s v3p0451c2s
Paine, Albert B. v6p0485c1s
Paine, B. v1p1101c2s
v4p0494c2s
Paine, C. v5p0429c1s
Paine, C.M. v6p0458c1s
Paine, David v6p0153c2s
Paine, E. v1p1009c2s
Paine, E.E. v6p0550c2s
Paine, F.B. v4p0079c1s
Paine, F.H. v5p0360c1s
Paine, G.E. v6p0477c2s
v6p0617c1s
Paine, G.H. v4p0471c2s
v5p0188c1s v5p0476c1s v5p0477c1m
Paine, H.G. v4p0079c1s
v4p0557c2s v5p0048c2s v5p0340c1s
Paine, J. v1p0487c2s
v1p0957c2s
Paine, J.A. v1p1263c2s
v3p0041c1s v3p0042c1s v3p0064c1s
v3p0239c2s v3p0328c2s
Paine, J.K. v1p0884c1s
v1p1380c1s v4p0415c1s
Paine, L.L. v1p0244c1s
v2p0324c1s v4p0035c1s v4p0037c1s
v4p0584c1m
Paine, R.D. v4p0493c1s
v6p0050c1s v6p0054c1s v6p0086c2s
v6p0105c2s v6p0137c1m v6p0149c2s
v6p0150c2s v6p0164c1s v6p0175c2s
v6p0223c2s v6p0224c1s v6p0231c2s
v6p0232c1s v6p0256c2s v6p0260c2m
v6p0279c1s v6p0332c2s v6p0359c1s
v6p0362c1s v6p0382c2s v6p0384c1s

v6p0386c2s v6p0389c2s v6p0405c2s
v6p0426c2s v6p0449c2s v6p0450c1s
v6p0451c2s v6p0453c2s v6p0459c2s
v6p0474c1s v6p0492c1s v6p0513c2s
v6p0553c1m v6p0627c1s v6p0661c2s
v6p0678c2s v6p0690c1s
Paine, R.T. v4p0022c2s
v4p0096c2s v4p0097c1m v4p0178c2s
v4p0431c2s v6p0076c2s v6p0484c2s
v6p0579c2s v6p0638c1s
Paine, R.T., jr. v2p0074c2s
v2p0205c2s
Paine, Ralph D. v6p0100c1s
v6p0378c1s v6p0384c1s v6p0611c2s
Paine, S.W. v4p0147c1s
Paine, T. v1p0538c1s
v1p0997c1s
Paine, V.B. v2p0358c2s
Paine, W. v6p0654c1s
Paine, W.S. v2p0403c1s
v3p0376c2s
Painter, A.F. v3p0021c1s
Painter, C.C. v3p0214c1s
Painter, F.V.N. v1p1118c1s
v2p0269c1s v3p0242c2s v3p0243c1s
Pais, E. v6p0508c1s
v6p0596c1s
Pal, B.C. v5p0055c1s
Palache, C. v4p0141c1s
v4p0232c1s v4p0564c1s v4p0583c1s
v5p0194c1s v5p0226c1s v5p0228c2s
v5p0462c2s v5p0571c2s v6p0323c2s
Palache, C. and Wood, H.O.
v6p0417c2s
Paladilhe, Dr. v1p0646c2s
Palaeologae-Nicephorae-Comnenae,
Princess v5p0554c2s
Palamedes v6p0679c1s
Palandier, Lieut. v1p0928c1s
Paleologue, J. v6p0684c1s
Paleologue, M. v6p0549c2s
Paley, F. v1p1097c2s
v1p1357c1s
Paley, F.A. v1p0420c2s
v1p0554c1s v1p0555c2s v1p0600c1s
v1p1218c1s v1p1222c1s v1p1309c1s
v1p1327c1s v1p1327c2s v2p0071c2s
v2p0182c1s v2p0185c1s v2p0471c2s
Paley, W.B. v4p0050c2s
v4p0073c2s v5p0345c2s v5p0461c1s
v5p0490c2s v5p0494c2s v5p0571c1s
v6p0098c1s v6p0482c2s
Palfrey, C. v1p0023c1s
v1p0060c2s v1p0247c2s v1p0293c2s
v1p0535c2s v1p0687c1s v1p0850c2s
v1p0945c1s v1p0982c2s v1p1042c1s
v1p1087c1s v1p1101c2s v1p1393c2s
v2p0081c1s
Palfrey, E.A. v1p0519c1s
Palfrey, F.W. v1p0037c2s
v1p0080c2s v1p0191c1s v1p0216c2s
v1p0303c1s v1p0327c1s v1p0489c2s
v1p0540c2m v1p0597c2s v1p0675c1s
v1p0695c1s v1p0734c1m v1p0907c2s
v1p1032c2s v1p1190c1s v1p1190c2m
v1p1280c1s v1p1342c2s v1p1344c1s
v1p1355c1s
Palfrey, J.C. v1p0445c1s
v1p0459c1s v1p0856c2s v1p1065c1s
v2p0049c2s
Palfrey, J.G. v1p0005c2s
v1p0029c1s v1p0031c1s v1p0032c1s
v1p0032c2s v1p0033c1s v1p0112c2s
v1p0124c2s v1p0154c1s v1p0162c2s
v1p0202c2s v1p0212c2s v1p0285c1s
v1p0291c2s v1p0300c2s v1p0348c1s
v1p0351c1s v1p0382c2s v1p0412c1s
v1p0445c1s v1p0447c1s v1p0466c2s
v1p0504c1s v1p0537c2s v1p0546c1s
v1p0548c2s v1p0572c2m v1p0578c2s
v1p0581c2s v1p0591c1s v1p0596c2s
v1p0598c1s v1p0784c1s v1p0808c2s
v1p0809c1s v1p0847c2s v1p0909c1s
v1p0910c1s v1p0910c2m v1p0933c1s
v1p0961c2s v1p0990c2s v1p1009c1s
v1p1082c1s v1p1091c2s v1p1099c2s
v1p1112c1s v1p1169c2s v1p1175c2s
v1p1231c2s v1p1340c1s v1p1341c1s
v1p1436c1s v2p0293c2s v2p0452c2s
v2p0453c1s
Palfrey, J.G. and Felton, C.C.
v1p1011c1s
Palfrey, J.G. and Hillard, G.S.
v1p0285c1s
Palfrey, J.G. and Sparks, J.
v1p0126c2s
Palfrey, S. v1p0424c1s
v1p1181c2s v1p1219c2s v1p1437c1s
Palfrey, S.H. v1p0703c1s
v1p1422c2s v3p0054c1s v3p0291c1s
v5p0089c1s
Palgrave, E.T. v1p0418c2s
v1p0620c2s
Palgrave, F. v1p0184c2s
Palgrave, F., Sir v1p0040c2s
v1p0309c1s v1p0481c1s v1p0577c1s
v1p0593c2s
Palgrave, F.T. v1p0053c1s
v1p0053c2s v1p0062c2s
v1p0064c1s
v1p0105c2s v1p0159c2s v1p0266c2s
v1p0340c1s v1p0365c1s v1p0425c2s
v1p0431c2s v1p0482c2s v1p0588c2s
v1p0593c1s v1p0616c2s v1p0773c1s
v1p0896c2s v1p0958c2s v1p1022c2s
v1p1049c1s v1p1071c2s v1p1085c1s
v1p1092c1m v1p1109c2s v1p1122c1s
v1p1259c2s v1p1284c2s v1p1370c1s
v1p1373c1s v1p1393c1s v1p1421c1s
v2p0024c1s v2p0333c2s v2p0346c2m
v3p0021c1s v3p0034c1s v3p0075c1m
v3p0140c2s v3p0188c1s v3p0316c1s
v3p0335c2s v3p0400c2s v4p0305c2s
v4p0493c2s
Palgrave, F.T. and Forman, H.B.
v2p0241c1s
Palgrave, F.T. and Herford, C.H.
v3p0075c1s
Palgrave, M.E. v3p0202c2s
v3p0343c1s
Palgrave, Mary E. v3p0151c1s
Palgrave, R. v1p0177c2s
Palgrave, R.F.D. v1p1258c2s
v3p0096c2s v3p0106c1m v4p0265c2s
v4p0266c1s v5p0145c1m
Palgrave, R.H. v1p1034c2s
v6p0260c1s
Palgrave, R.H.I. v1p0091c1s
v1p0093c2s v1p0094c1s v1p0094c2s
v1p0212c1s v1p0326c1s v1p0607c2s
v1p1285c2s v2p0033c2s v2p0129c2m
v3p0255c1s v3p0421c1s v4p0283c2s
v4p0288c2s v6p0008c2m v6p0050c2s
v6p0206c1s v6p0235c2s v6p0266c1s
v6p0266c2s v6p0267c1s v6p0282c2s
Palgrave, R.H.Inglis v6p0050c1s
Palgrave, W.G. v1p0002c1s
v1p0022c2s v1p0036c2s v1p0073c2s
v1p0163c1s v1p0197c2s v1p0208c1s
v1p0232c2s v1p0238c2s v1p0377c2s
v1p0397c1s v1p0523c1s v1p0561c1s
v1p0710c1s v1p0790c2s v1p0829c2s
v1p0844c2s v1p0857c2s v1p0858c1s
v1p0941c2s v1p0998c1s v1p1194c1s
v1p1266c2s v1p1279c1s v1p1323c2s
v1p1333c1s v1p1333c2s v1p1401c1m
v2p0243c2s v2p0340c2s
Pall, A.C. v4p0441c2s
Pallen, C.B. v2p0005c1s
v2p0011c2s v2p0180c2s v2p0214c1s
v2p0351c1s v2p0387c2s v2p0435c1s
v2p0436c2s v3p0095c1s v3p0110c1s
v4p0466c1s v4p0479c1s v4p0489c1s
Pallicia, G.M. v6p0508c2s
Palliser, B., Mrs. v1p0086c1s
v1p1039c1s v1p1192c2s v4p0316c1s
Palliser, F.B. v1p1373c1s
Palliser, F.W. v4p0240c2s
Palm, A.J. v4p0117c1s
v4p0134c2s v4p0460c1s v4p0610c1s
Palma, R. v1p0850c1s
Palma, T.E. v6p0160c2s
Palmer, A. et al. v3p0195c1s
Palmer, A.B. v2p0161c2s
v2p0206c2s
Palmer, A.D. v4p0128c1s
Palmer, A.D., jr. v5p0184c2s
Palmer, A.De F., jr. v4p0253c2s
v5p0370c2s
Palmer, A.E. v3p0303c2s
v3p0361c2s
Palmer, A.F. v3p0129c2s
v3p0468c2s v4p0102c1s v4p0170c1m
v4p0566c1s v5p0255c2s
Palmer, A.H. v2p0327c2s
v3p0200c1s v3p0206c2s v3p0409c2s
v3p0467c1s
Palmer, A.M. v4p0447c1s
v4p0592c1s v5p0474c1s
Palmer, A.M. et al. v2p0123c1s
Palmer, A.N. v3p0460c1s
Palmer, A.S. v5p0104c2s
v6p0649c2s
Palmer, A.Smythe v6p0714c1s
Palmer, A.V. v3p0036c1s
v3p0180c1s v3p0423c1s v5p0244c1s
Palmer, B. v6p0259c1s
v6p0340c2s
Palmer, B.M. v2p0405c1s
v2p0411c2s
Palmer, C. v1p1178c2s
v3p0019c2s
Palmer, C.B. v4p0444c2s
Palmer, C.F. v6p0049c1s
Palmer, C.F.R. v1p0490c2s
v2p0048c2s v2p0077c1s v3p0046c2s
v3p0095c2s v3p0106c2s v4p0062c2s
Palmer, C.H. v3p0269c1s
v4p0009c1s v4p0197c2s v4p0380c1s
Palmer, C.M. v6p0125c1s
Palmer, C.S. v4p0115c1s
v4p0123c1s v4p0391c1s v5p0513c2s
Palmer, C.T. v4p0135c1s
Palmer, C.T.H. v2p0334c1s
v6p0129c1s
Palmer, C.von v1p0778c2s
Palmer, E. v1p0637c1m
v1p0876c1s v1p1016c1s v2p0286c2s
v6p0066c1s
Palmer, E.D. v5p0202c1s
Palmer, E.H. v1p0050c2s
v1p0345c2s v1p0346c1s v1p0396c2s
v1p0454c2s v1p0565c1s v1p1059c2s
v1p1183c1s v4p0085c1s
Palmer, E.H., Prof. v4p0173c2s
Palmer, E.V. v6p0042c2s
Palmer, F. v3p0013c1s
v3p0116c1s v3p0137c1s v4p0463c1s
v5p0318c1s v5p0318c2m v5p0389c1s
v5p0400c2s v5p0438c2s v5p0446c1s
v5p0644c2s v6p0230c2s v6p0446c1s
v6p0520c1s v6p0669c1s v6p0693c1s
v6p0695c1s
Palmer, F.B. v1p0208c2s
v5p0155c2s
Palmer, F.H. v4p0002c1s
v4p0250c2s v4p0589c1s v5p0138c1s
v5p0268c2s
Palmer, F.L. v6p0012c2s
Palmer, F.M. v5p0464c2s
v6p0030c1s v6p0093c1s
Palmer, F.P. v1p0244c2s
v1p0756c1s v6p0161c1s
Palmer, F.R. v3p0164c2s
Palmer, F.S. v2p0202c1s
v3p0232c1s v5p0052c1s
Palmer, F.W. v6p0428c2s
Palmer, Frederick v5p0050c1s
v5p0249c1s v5p0300c2s v6p0086c1s
Palmer, G. v2p0374c2s
v2p0406c2s v5p0299c1s
Palmer, G.G. v6p0390c1s
Palmer, G.H. v2p0136c1m
v2p0241c1s v3p0195c2s v3p0200c1s
v3p0401c1s v4p0381c2s v4p0597c2s
v5p0081c2s v6p0211c2s v6p0288c1s
v6p0476c1s v6p0583c1s v6p0589c2s
v6p0676c2s
Palmer, H. v3p0035c1m
Palmer, H.D. v2p0256c2s
Palmer, H.J. v2p0058c1s
v2p0110c1s v2p0399c2s v5p0004c2s
Palmer, H.K. v6p0117c2s
Palmer, H.P. v1p0596c1s
v3p0151c1s v4p0513c2s v4p0619c2s
Palmer, H.R. v1p0103c2s
v4p0064c2s v4p0256c1s v4p0399c1s
v4p0483c1s v5p0079c1s v5p0335c1s
v5p0487c2s v5p0554c2s v6p0226c2s
Palmer, H.S. v2p0233c2s
Palmer, H.W. v6p0357c2s
Palmer, J.A. v1p0151c2s
Palmer, J.A., jr. v1p0235c1s
v1p0378c2s v1p0882c1s v1p1313c2s
Palmer, J.F. v2p0072c2s
v2p0141c2s v2p0337c1s v2p0387c1s
v2p0423c1s v5p0588c2s v6p0523c2s
v6p0611c1s
Palmer, J.M. v6p0138c1s
v6p0224c1s v6p0320c1s v6p0396c2s
v6p0403c2s v6p0478c2s v6p0528c1s
v6p0609c1s
Palmer, J.McA. v6p0151c2s
v6p0301c1s v6p0482c1s
Palmer, J.S. v2p0143c1s
Palmer, J.W. v1p0076c2s
v1p0082c2s v1p0089c2m v1p0133c2s
v1p0156c2s v1p0178c1s v1p0190c2s
v1p0233c2s v1p0367c2s v1p0521c1s
v1p0591c2m v1p0630c1s v1p0638c1s
v1p0640c2m v1p0852c1s v1p0939c2s
v1p0995c2s v1p1188c1s v1p1425c1s
v4p0080c2s v4p0099c1s v4p0359c1m
v4p0501c2s v5p0230c1s
Palmer, L. v1p0864c1s
v3p0325c2s
Palmer, L.E. v6p0454c1s
v6p0638c2s
Palmer, L.M. v1p0142c2s
v1p0735c2s v1p0908c1s v6p0203c1s
Palmer, M.M. v6p0137c2s
Palmer, M.T. v2p0414c2s
v3p0383c2s
Palmer, P., Mrs. v4p0102c2s
v4p0628c2s
Palmer, R. v1p0171c2s
v1p0240c2s v1p0290c1s v1p0392c2s
v1p0558c2s v1p0598c1s v1p0774c2s
v1p0856c2s v1p0857c1s v1p0868c1s
v1p0868c2s v1p0910c1s v1p1067c1s
v1p1198c1s v1p1227c2s v1p1314c1s
v1p1419c2s v4p0186c1s
Palmer, R.S. v5p0643c1s
Palmer, Ray v1p0239c2s
Palmer, S.M. v2p0337c2s
v5p0182c1s
Palmer, T. v5p0611c2s
Palmer, T.A. v5p0525c1s
Palmer, T.C. v3p0255c2s
v3p0404c1s
Palmer, T.H. v1p1158c2s
Palmer, T.R. v1p0002c2s
Palmer, T.S. v5p0002c1s
v5p0166c1s
Palmer, W. v1p0649c2s
v2p0325c1s
Palmer, W., Mrs. v4p0316c2s
Palmer, W.H., Mrs. v1p0492c1s
v1p0571c1s v1p0725c1s v1p1420c1s
Palmer, W.J. v5p0146c2s

Palmer, W.K. v5p0294c2s
Palmer, W.L. v4p0354c1s v6p0089c1s
Palmer, W.M. v5p0333c1s
Palmer, W.S. v1p0783c2s v6p0008c1s v6p0540c2s
Palmer, W.T. v5p0204c2s v5p0209c1s v5p0232c2s v5p0323c1s v5p0380c2s v5p0507c2s v6p0221c2m v6p0359c1s v6p0467c1s v6p0590c1s v6p0644c2s v6p0700c1s
Paltsits, V.H. v5p0073c1s v6p0232c2s
Paludan-Muller, F. v1p0016c1s
Pammel, L.H. v4p0217c2s v6p0055c1s
Pammel, L.M. v4p0129c2s
Panckridge, W. v2p0085c1s
Pancoast, H.S. v3p0005c2s v3p0010c1s v3p0057c2s v3p0279c2s v3p0404c1s v4p0076c1s v4p0183c2s v4p0411c2s v5p0107c2s v5p0342c1m v5p0479c2s v6p0085c1s v6p0166c1s
Pang, S. v6p0120c1s
Pangalo, George v5p0087c2s v5p0105c2s
Pangborn, F.W. v4p0634c2s
Pangborn, G.W. v6p0264c2s
Pangborn, Georgia W. v6p0147c1s v6p0175c2s v6p0179c2s v6p0185c1s v6p0235c2s
Pangloss, A. v5p0404c1s
Pangman, C.C. v5p0607c1s
Panin, I. v1p0020c2s
Panizzi, A. v1p0060c1s v1p0479c2s v1p0483c1s v1p0488c1s v1p0669c2s v1p0683c2s v1p0906c1s v1p1025c1s v1p1038c2s v1p1137c2s
Pannekoek, A. v5p0376c1m
Pansch, A. v1p0557c1s
Pantaleoni, M. v5p0557c2s v5p0564c2s
Pantin, M. v3p0036c2s
Pantin, W.E.P. v3p0150c2s
Panting, J.H. v6p0566c1s
Pantini, R. v5p0033c1s v5p0299c2s v6p0247c2s
Pantoleon, A. v1p1002c2s
Panton, J.E. v2p0031c1s v2p0104c2s v2p0122c1s v2p0142c1s v2p0171c2s v2p0224c1s v2p0268c1s v2p0279c2s v2p0316c1s v2p0359c2s v2p0380c1s v2p0393c2s v2p0456c2s v2p0473c2s v3p0070c1s v3p0315c1s v3p0405c2s
Panzacchi, E. v4p0293c2s v4p0602c2s
Panzacchi, E. and Lampertico, F. v4p0269c1s v4p0355c1s
Paoli, G.C. v2p0316c2s
Papa, F.D. v5p0300c1s v5p0300c2s
Papendick, E. v1p0013c2s
Papillon, E.C. v3p0425c1s
Papillon, F. v1p0338c1s v1p0400c2s v1p0437c1s v1p0449c1s v1p0579c2s v1p0587c1s v1p0746c2s v1p0812c1s v1p0930c2s v1p0938c1s v1p0977c1m
Papillon, T.L. v4p0604c2s
Papin, T. v5p0339c2s
Papini, G. v6p0495c2s
Papworth, J.W. v3p0202c2s v4p0161c2s
Paquin, P. v4p0131c1s
Paracelsus, A. v1p0627c1m
Paranelli, F. v6p0012c1s
Paratt and Kelly v6p0413c1s
Parcell, G.A. v5p0627c2s
Pardee, A. et al. v5p0557c1s
Pardee, G.C. v6p0194c1s v6p0672c2s
Pardee, H.E.G. v1p0866c1s
Pardee, J.N. v6p0076c2s
Pardee-Clark, J. v4p0245c1s
Pardee-Clark, Jean v6p0332c1s
Pardepp, R. v4p0099c1s v4p0527c1s v4p0552c1s v5p0434c2s
Pardoe, J. v1p0111c2s v1p0474c1s v1p0577c2s v1p1242c2s v1p1284c1s v1p1333c1s v1p1335c2s
Pardoe, L. v1p0406c2s v1p0615c2s
Pardoe, Miss v1p0037c1s v1p1437c1s
Pare, W. v1p0286c1s v1p0423c1s
Parel, G. and Colonies, Les v6p0564c2s
Parent, M.B. v6p0110c2s v6p0241c2s
Pares, B. v4p0275c2s v4p0578c1s v6p0431c1s v6p0556c2m v6p0558c1s
Pares, Bernard v5p0439c1s
Paret, J.P. v3p0052c1s v3p0424c2m v5p0037c1s v5p0049c1s v5p0074c1s v5p0129c1s v5p0267c2s v5p0328c1s v5p0572c2m v5p0573c1m v6p0638c2m
Paret, T.D. v3p0136c1s v4p0179c1m v4p0539c1s v6p0202c2s
Pareto, V. v4p0294c2m v4p0295c1s v5p0175c2s
Parham, E. v4p0396c2s v6p0084c1s
Parieu, E.de v1p0779c1s v1p1285c1s
Paris, Count de v1p0518c2s
Paris, Gaston v4p0147c2s
Paris, J.de v2p0394c1s
Paris, Philippe, Comte de. v4p0309c1s
Parish, A. v1p1284c2s
Parish, Amy M. v6p0255c2s
Parish, S.B. v4p0217c1s
Parish, W.F., jr. v6p0418c1s
Park, A.L. v6p0568c2s
Park, C.E. v1p0692c2s v1p0975c1s v1p1141c1m
Park, C.F. v6p0389c1s
Park, C.S. v1p0517c2s
Park, C.W. v2p0054c2s v2p0382c2s v3p0282c2s
Park, E.A. v1p0020c2s v1p0057c2s v1p0074c2m v1p0103c1s v1p0110c1s v1p0122c1s v1p0124c1s v1p0261c1s v1p0276c2s v1p0393c2m v1p0529c1s v1p0847c2s v1p0910c1s v1p0972c1s v1p0998c2s v1p1043c2m v1p1044c1m v1p1064c2s v1p1065c1s v1p1066c2s v1p1104c2s v1p1120c2s v1p1179c1m v1p1200c1s v1p1287c1m v1p1301c2s v1p1302c1m v1p1303c2m v1p1304c1s v1p1326c1s v1p1405c1s v2p0027c2s v3p0178c1s
Park, F. and Ireland, E.N. v3p0152c1s
Park, J. v6p0407c2s
Park, J.C. v1p0699c2s v1p0705c2s
Park, L.J. v1p0584c2s v1p1289c1s
Park, L.M. v1p0037c2s
Park, M. v5p0495c1s
Park, M.H. v2p0081c1s v2p0099c2s
Park, O.K. v6p0086c1s
Park, P. v1p1171c1s
Park, R. v1p0630c2s v1p0817c2s v1p1096c1s v2p0137c1s
Park, R.E. v1p1180c2s v1p1346c2s v1p1414c1s v5p0231c1s v6p0144c2s
Park, Robert E. v6p0368c2s
Park, W.E. v1p1176c2s
Park, W.H. v4p0020c2s v6p0175c2s
Parke, E. v1p0181c2s
Parke, F. v1p0152c2s v1p0159c2s v1p0182c2m v1p0183c1s v1p0230c1s v1p0256c2s v1p0260c1s v1p0318c1s v1p0334c2s v1p0343c2s v1p0344c2s v1p0363c1s v1p0384c1s v1p0420c2s v1p0426c1s v1p0452c2s v1p0504c2s v1p0511c1s v1p0557c2s v1p0587c2s v1p0588c1s v1p0677c2s v1p0704c1s v1p0753c2s v1p0757c1s v1p0773c2s v1p0781c1s v1p0791c2s v1p0872c1s v1p0979c1s v1p1177c2s v1p1202c1s v1p1211c1s v1p1233c1s v1p1278c1s v1p1283c2s v1p1414c2s v1p1427c2s v2p0232c1s v2p0304c1s
Parke, J. v4p0558c2s
Parke, J.S. v5p0375c2s
Parke, P.G. v2p0001c1s v2p0191c1s
Parke, T.H. v4p0005c2s v4p0232c2s v4p0604c1s
Parke, W. v3p0294c2s v4p0090c2s
Parker, A. v1p0583c1s v3p0079c2s v5p0166c2s v6p0198c2s v6p0500c1s
Parker, A.B. v6p0002c1s v6p0179c1s v6p0363c2m v6p0365c1s
Parker, A.H. v1p0053c2s
Parker, A.K. v4p0218c2s v4p0299c2s v4p0396c1s v5p0562c1s
Parker, A.P. v4p0337c2s
Parker, Adella M. v6p0621c1s v6p0693c1s
Parker, B. v6p0028c1s
Parker, B.S. v4p0600c1s
Parker, C. v4p0071c2s
Parker, C.G. v6p0053c2s
Parker, C.H. v4p0105c1s
Parker, C.M. v5p0361c2s
Parker, C.P. v2p0325c2s v4p0242c1s v5p0404c2s
Parker, C.S. v1p0262c1s v5p0220c1s
Parker, Clara M. v4p0344c1s
Parker, D.F. v1p0457c2s
Parker, D.G. v6p0571c1s
Parker, E. v5p0512c1s v5p0512c2s v5p0530c2s
Parker, E.C. v6p0220c1s
Parker, E.D. v5p0216c2s
Parker, E.G. v1p0237c2s v1p0256c1s v1p0263c1s v1p0605c2s
Parker, E.H. v4p0105c1s v4p0106c2s v4p0120c1s v4p0133c2s v4p0328c1s v4p0415c1s v4p0417c2s v4p0495c2s v4p0500c2s v4p0510c1s v4p0587c1s v5p0014c1s v5p0021c1s v5p0084c1m v5p0097c1s v5p0108c2m v5p0109c1m v5p0109c2s v5p0110c1m v5p0110c2m v5p0111c1s v5p0111c2s v5p0112c1m v5p0112c2s v5p0113c1m v5p0132c2m v5p0289c1s v5p0313c1s v5p0314c2s v5p0319c2s v5p0359c2m v5p0379c2s v5p0501c2s v5p0502c1s v5p0527c2m v5p0560c1s v5p0566c2s v5p0580c2s v5p0595c1s v6p0035c1s v6p0086c1s v6p0118c1m v6p0118c2m v6p0119c2s v6p0120c2m v6p0213c1s v6p0334c2s v6p0337c1s v6p0507c2s v6p0548c2s v6p0555c2s v6p0560c1s v6p0566c2s v6p0611c1s v6p0632c1m v6p0645c2s v6p0646c1s v6p0661c2m v6p0710c2s
Parker, E.M. v6p0215c2s
Parker, E.M.W. v1p1148c2s
Parker, E.P. v2p0037c2s v2p0112c2s v6p0381c1s
Parker, E.S. v3p0374c1s
Parker, E.W. v5p0124c1s v5p0298c1s v5p0327c1s v5p0590c2s v6p0133c1m
Parker, Edmund M. v6p0614c2s
Parker, Edward H. v5p0472c2s
Parker, F. v1p0125c1s v1p0246c2m v1p0831c1s v1p1056c2m v1p1178c1s v1p1277c2s
Parker, F. and Hincks, E.. v1p0246c2s
Parker, F.A. v1p0033c2s v1p0102c2s
Parker, F.J. v1p0175c2s v1p0972c2s v2p0064c1s v2p0084c1s v2p0342c1s v2p0359c2s v3p0126c2s v3p0204c1s v3p0361c2s
Parker, F.W. v4p0222c2m v4p0234c1s v4p0353c2s v4p0512c1s v5p0475c1s v6p0113c2s v6p0392c2s v6p0436c1s
Parker, F.W. et al. v3p0422c1s
Parker, Francis W. v6p0112c2s v6p0435c2s v6p0607c1s
Parker, G. v3p0022c1s v3p0054c2s v3p0065c2s v3p0069c2s v3p0267c2s v3p0467c2s v4p0034c2s v4p0035c1s v4p0046c1s v4p0155c1s v4p0199c2s v4p0215c2s v4p0216c1s v4p0226c1s v4p0229c2s v4p0240c2s v4p0254c1s v4p0266c2m v4p0317c1s v4p0335c2s v4p0350c2s v4p0397c2s v4p0409c2s v4p0412c2s v4p0443c2s v4p0458c1s v4p0476c1s v4p0504c2m v4p0512c1s v4p0527c2s v4p0542c2s v4p0562c2s v4p0573c2m v4p0575c2s v4p0582c2s v4p0583c2s v4p0598c1s v4p0607c2s v4p0620c1s v5p0036c1s v5p0039c1s v5p0200c2s v5p0205c2s v5p0206c2s v5p0211c1s v5p0252c2s v5p0282c1s v5p0338c1s v5p0358c2s v5p0366c2s v5p0373c2s v5p0421c1s v5p0465c1s v5p0489c1s v5p0589c2s v5p0594c1s v5p0628c2s v6p0095c2s v6p0327c1s v6p0690c2s
Parker, G. et al. v6p0271c1s
Parker, G., Sir v6p0047c2s v6p0096c2s v6p0481c1s v6p0533c2s v6p0695c2s
Parker, G.A. v6p0480c2s
Parker, G.F. v4p0058c2s v4p0061c2s v4p0115c1s v4p0119c1s v4p0275c1s v4p0457c2s v4p0524c2s v4p0594c2s v5p0050c2s v5p0134c1s v5p0339c2s v6p0326c2s v6p0497c1s v6p0563c2s v6p0564c1s v6p0618c2s
Parker, G.H. v5p0583c1s v6p0195c2s v6p0227c1s v6p0713c2s
Parker, G.M. v6p0121c2s
Parker, G.W. v2p0209c2s v2p0271c1m
Parker, Gilbert v4p0065c2s v4p0236c2s v4p0628c2s v5p0050c1s v6p0210c2s v6p0613c1s v6p0687c2s
Parker, Gilbert and Sewall, M.W. v5p0637c2s
Parker, H. v3p0248c1s v4p0079c1s v4p0104c2s v4p0257c2s v4p0304c1s v4p0316c1s v4p0328c1s v4p0427c1s v4p0457c2s v4p0498c1s v4p0607c2s v6p0108c1s
Parker, H.A. v4p0267c1s v5p0309c1s
Parker, H.C. v4p0628c1s
Parker, H.H. v6p0028c1s
Parker, H.M. v1p0809c1s v1p1067c1s
Parker, H.N. and Whipple, G.C. v5p0357c2s
Parker, H.T. v3p0140c2s v3p0141c1s v3p0203c2s v3p0388c2s v3p0417c2s v6p0504c1s v6p0641c2s
Parker, H.W. v1p0061c2s v1p0949c1s v1p1041c1s v1p1081c1s v1p1378c2s v2p0161c1s v2p0443c1s v3p0445c2m v4p0357c2s

Parker, I. v1p0297c2s v1p1341c1s
Parker, J. v1p0564c1s v1p0601c2s v1p0648c1s v1p0650c2s v1p0729c2s v1p0802c1s v1p0808c1m v1p0907c2s v1p1342c2s v1p1346c2m v1p1396c1s v2p0045c1s v2p0096c2s v2p0119c1s v3p0037c1m v3p0104c1s v3p0118c2s v3p0149c1s v3p0174c1s v3p0189c2s v3p0362c2s v4p0339c2s v5p0011c2s v5p0041c2s v5p0132c1s v5p0374c2s v5p0375c1s v5p0395c2s v5p0443c2s v5p0614c2m v5p0642c2s v6p0061c1s v6p0105c2s v6p0223c2s v6p0417c1s v6p0513c2m
Parker, J.A. v1p0264c2s v1p0702c1s v1p1069c1s
Parker, J.D. v2p0020c2s v2p0024c1s v2p0031c1s v2p0050c2s v2p0061c2s v2p0174c1s v2p0301c2s v2p0339c1s v2p0373c2s v2p0411c2s v2p0443c1m v6p0463c2s
Parker, J.G. v6p0074c1s
Parker, J.H. v1p0053c1s v1p0053c2m v1p0253c2s v1p0335c1s v1p1125c1s v2p0094c1s v2p0183c2s v2p0259c2s v2p0376c2s v2p0377c1m v2p0377c2s v3p0372c1s v5p0027c2s v5p0252c2s v5p0253c1s v5p0353c1s v5p0375c2s v5p0445c1s v5p0445c2s v5p0543c2s v5p0599c1m v5p0599c2s v6p0495c1s v6p0666c1s
Parker, J.H. and Ashpitel, A. v1p0237c2s
Parker, J.M. v2p0261c1s v3p0192c1s v3p0195c2s v3p0203c1s v3p0207c1s v3p0228c1s v3p0279c2s v3p0324c1s v3p0422c2s v4p0086c1s v4p0219c2s v4p0299c2s v4p0344c1s v5p0165c2s v5p0348c2s v5p0361c2s v5p0467c2s v5p0481c1s v5p0545c2s v6p0115c2s v6p0566c1s v6p0573c2s
Parker, J.R. v6p0251c2s v6p0391c1s
Parker, J.S. v2p0126c1s v2p0258c1s
Parker, J.W. v4p0254c2s
Parker, Jane M. v3p0151c2s v4p0160c1s v4p0432c1s v5p0468c1s v6p0110c1s
Parker, K. v5p0070c2s
Parker, Katherine H. v4p0031c1s v4p0600c1s
Parker, L.F. v2p0184c2s
Parker, L.N. v6p0474c2s
Parker, L.S. v6p0479c1s
Parker, M. v2p0229c1s
Parker, M.D. v1p0013c1s
Parker, N.L. v4p0161c1s v4p0446c2s
Parker, O. v6p0423c1s
Parker, P. v1p0828c1s
Parker, P.L. v6p0647c2s
Parker, Prof. v1p1334c1s v1p1368c1s
Parker, R.A. v4p0292c1s v4p0344c2s
Parker, R.G. v1p0287c1s v1p0416c1s
Parker, R.W. v3p0077c1s v6p0010c1s
Parker, S.J. v3p0203c2s
Parker, Sarah v6p0705c2s
Parker, T. v1p0054c2s v1p0107c2s v1p0259c2s v1p0323c1s v1p0347c1s v1p0527c1s v1p0688c2s v1p0715c2s v1p0809c1s v1p0836c2s v1p0870c2s v1p1016c2s v1p1047c2s v1p1260c1s v1p1434c1s
Parker, T., Rev. v4p0293c1s
Parker, T.C. v4p0262c2s
Parker, T.J. v1p0134c2s v1p1441c1s v2p0317c1s v2p0340c2s v3p0044c2s v4p0270c2s
Parker, T.Jeffrey v2p0327c2s
Parker, U.S. v6p0132c2s
Parker, W. v1p0487c1s v2p0050c2s v2p0103c2s
Parker, W.B. v5p0052c2s v5p0317c1s
Parker, W.G. v4p0163c2s
Parker, W.H. v1p0021c2s v6p0528c2s
Parker, W.K. v1p0394c1s v1p0872c2s v1p1204c1s v1p1213c1s v2p0015c1s v2p0108c1s v2p0149c2s v3p0045c1s
Parker, W.N. v3p0347c2s
Parker, W.S. v6p0260c1s
Parker, W.T. v3p0288c2s v4p0131c1s v5p0288c2s v5p0368c2s v5p0403c1s v6p0316c1s
Parker, Z. v1p1392c1m
Parker-Scammon, E. v4p0617c2s
Parker-Smith, J. et al. .. v4p0239c2s
Parkes, A. v1p0972c2s
Parkes, B.R. v1p0001c1s v1p0021c2s v1p0103c1s v1p0154c2s v1p0465c1s v1p0537c1s v1p0735c2s v1p0749c2s v1p0815c1s v1p1104c2s v1p1177c2s v1p1317c1s v1p1317c2s v1p1396c1s
Parkes, D. v2p0274c1s
Parkes, G. v6p0712c1s
Parkes, H. v2p0029c1m v3p0027c1s v4p0038c2s v4p0399c2m
Parkes, J. v1p1248c1s
Parkes, K. v4p0520c1s v4p0524c1s v5p0187c1s v5p0413c1s
Parkes, S. v1p0383c1s v1p1146c2s v1p1312c2s
Parkes, W. v1p0748c2s
Parkes-Belloc, B. v3p0035c2s
Parkhurst, C. v1p0182c2s v1p0840c2s v1p1257c1s
Parkhurst, C. et al. v3p0207c2s
Parkhurst, C.D. v5p0032c2s v5p0538c1s
Parkhurst, C.H. v2p0082c1s v2p0249c1s v2p0356c1s v2p0456c1s v2p0479c2s v3p0197c1s v3p0347c2s v3p0378c2s v4p0012c1s v4p0115c1s v4p0401c1s v5p0019c2s v6p0043c1s v6p0600c2s
Parkhurst, E.T.Y. v6p0134c2s v6p0706c1s
Parkhurst, H.L. v5p0548c1s
Parkhurst, H.M. v1p0282c1s v1p1004c1s v1p1244c2s v2p0014c1s v2p0118c2s v2p0323c2s v2p0340c2m v3p0219c1s v4p0545c2s
Parkhurst, J.A. v4p0373c1s v4p0545c2m v5p0119c1s v5p0548c2s v5p0549c2s v6p0497c1s v6p0614c1s
Parkhurst, J.L. v1p0407c1s
Parkhurst, R.M. v1p1426c2s
Parkin, C.W. v1p0351c2s
Parkin, G.R. v3p0013c2s v3p0027c2s v3p0028c1s v3p0181c2s v3p0445c2s v4p0172c2s v4p0251c1s v5p0573c1s v5p0610c2s
Parkin, W. v1p0133c1s v1p1392c1s
Parkinson, C. v2p0124c1s v3p0045c1s v3p0092c1s v3p0135c2s v3p0165c1s v3p0285c2s v3p0373c1s v3p0386c1m v3p0418c1s v3p0423c2s v4p0003c2s v4p0136c1s v4p0318c1s v4p0560c2s v4p0632c1s v4p0634c1s v5p0063c1s v5p0283c2s v5p0351c1s v5p0383c2s v5p0484c2s v5p0504c1s v5p0509c1s v5p0525c1s
Parkinson, D.C. v4p0185c1s v5p0474c2s
Parkinson, F.B. and Brander-Dunbar, Lieut.. v5p0538c2s
Parkinson, G.H. v2p0186c2s
Parkinson, J.B. v1p0683c2s
Parkinson, J.C. v1p0608c1s v1p0765c1s v1p0820c1s v1p1030c2s v1p1031c2s v1p1091c1s v1p1431c1s
Parkinson, M. v6p0011c1s
Parkinson, R. v1p0972c1s v1p1084c2s v2p0108c2s v2p0330c1s
Parkinson, R.H. v1p0585c1s v1p1042c2s
Parkinson, T.B. v1p0140c2s v1p0525c1s v1p0602c1s v1p0807c1s v1p0814c2s v1p0836c2s v1p0991c1s v1p1033c2s v1p1039c2s v1p1337c1s
Parkinson, W.D. v4p0165c2s v5p0178c1s v5p0468c1s v6p0126c1s v6p0572c2s
Parkman, C.M. v1p0255c2s
Parkman, F. v1p0030c2s v1p0085c2s v1p0097c2s v1p0103c1s v1p0110c1s v1p0115c1s v1p0141c1s v1p0169c2s v1p0180c1s v1p0193c1s v1p0198c2s v1p0219c1s v1p0242c2s v1p0298c2s v1p0306c1s v1p0317c2s v1p0392c2s v1p0461c2s v1p0462c1s v1p0470c2s v1p0487c2m v1p0542c1s v1p0557c2s v1p0566c2s v1p0573c1s v1p0637c2s v1p0638c1s v1p0641c1s v1p0698c1s v1p0705c1s v1p0709c1s v1p0726c1s v1p0765c1s v1p0864c2s v1p0870c2s v1p0947c2s v1p0956c2s v1p0961c2s v1p1002c1s v1p1024c2s v1p1043c2s v1p1046c1s v1p1052c2s v1p1062c2s v1p1070c2s v1p1096c1s v1p1155c1s v1p1195c2s v1p1225c2s v1p1261c2s v1p1265c1s v1p1378c1s v1p1385c2s v1p1386c1m v1p1393c1s v1p1406c2s v1p1409c1s v1p1412c1s v1p1418c1m v1p1420c1s v1p1429c1s v2p0001c2m v2p0130c1s v2p0162c1s v2p0174c2s v2p0317c2s v2p0476c2s v3p0098c1s v3p0244c1s v3p0259c1s v3p0285c1s v3p0363c1s v3p0455c2s v4p0002c1s
Parkman, J. v1p0482c1s v1p0618c1s v1p0889c2s v1p1341c1s
Parkman, S., Mrs. v1p0387c1s
Parkman, T. v1p0636c2s
Parks, E.H. v6p0025c2s
Parks, F. v2p0470c1s
Parks, F.W. v4p0501c2m v5p0271c2s
Parks, I.W. v5p0402c2s v5p0631c1s
Parks, J.L. v5p0194c1s
Parks, L. v2p0054c1s v4p0074c2s v6p0695c1s
Parks, L., jr. v1p0500c2s
Parks, LaF.I. v5p0569c1s
Parks, Leighton v6p0668c1s
Parks, N.G. v2p0246c2s v2p0476c1s
Parks, S.C. v5p0281c1s v6p0167c2s v6p0492c2s v6p0494c2s v6p0608c1s
Parks, W.A. v6p0479c1s
Parks, W.H. v3p0100c1s
Parkyn, E.A. v5p0422c2s
Parley, W.B. v5p0134c1s
Parlin, C.C. v6p0039c1s
Parloa, M. et al. v3p0202c2s
Parlss, S.C. v6p0551c1s
Parmara, E. v1p0834c1s
Parmeighe, E. v1p0833c2s
Parmele, M. v3p0126c2s v3p0285c2s v3p0357c1s v3p0399c2s
Parmele, Mary v4p0603c2s
Parmele, Mary, Mrs. v4p0180c1s
Parmelee, E. v1p1231c2s
Parmelee, J.H. v6p0672c1s
Parmelee, J.W. v2p0130c1s v2p0312c1s v2p0372c1s
Parmelee, M.P. v5p0304c1s
Parmelee, T.N. v1p1353c1s
Parmer, E. v1p0083c2s v1p0403c2s v1p0813c2s v1p0832c2s v1p0833c2m v1p0844c1s v1p1071c2s v1p1158c1s v2p0011c1s
Parmerter, A.L. v5p0375c1s
Parminter, A.V. v4p0167c1s
Parmiter, S.C. v4p0394c1s
Parnell, A. v2p0128c1s v2p0139c1s v2p0141c1s v2p0259c1m v2p0379c2s v2p0440c2s v3p0068c1m v3p0113c2s v3p0278c2s v3p0295c2s v3p0403c1s v3p0417c2s v5p0354c2s
Parnell, C.S. v1p0657c2s v2p0227c2s v3p0221c2s
Parnell, W.R. v3p0213c1s v3p0304c2s
Parodi, L. v1p1266c2s
Parpped, R. v4p0138c2s
Parr, A.W. v5p0224c2s
Parr, C.F. v3p0101c2s
Parr, F.C.W. v2p0234c1s
Parr, H. v1p0067c1s v1p0168c1s v1p0574c1s v1p0799c2s
Parr, H.H. v1p0701c1s
Parr, J. v4p0166c2s
Parr, L. v1p0005c2s v1p0361c1s v1p0439c2s v1p0903c1s v1p1047c2s v2p0267c1s v2p0316c1s v2p0374c1s v3p0149c1s v3p0158c1s v3p0328c1s v3p0369c1s v3p0373c1s v4p0251c2s v4p0345c2s v5p0076c2s v5p0374c1s v5p0531c2s
Parr, Lilla v5p0394c1s
Parr, Louisa v3p0260c2s v5p0454c2s
Parr, M.A. v6p0675c1s
Parr, Mrs. v1p0459c2s
Parr, Olive K. v6p0675c1s
Parr, W.A. v5p0224c2s v6p0026c2s v6p0229c1s
Parrish, C.S. v5p0150c1s v5p0636c2s v5p0638c1s
Parrish, E. v1p0995c2s
Parrish, G.S. v4p0539c1s
Parrish, J. v2p0065c1s
Parrish, S.L. v5p0198c1s v5p0199c1s
Parritt, M. v4p0233c1s
Parrot, M. v1p1293c1s
Parrott, A.G. v5p0141c2s
Parrott, J. and Dougherty, F.C. v6p0667c2s
Parrott, J., jr. v2p0464c1s
Parrott, J.M. v6p0407c1s
Parrott, T.M. v5p0239c1s v6p0016c2s v6p0032c1s v6p0130c2s v6p0189c2s v6p0222c2s v6p0289c2s v6p0345c1s v6p0495c1s v6p0578c1s v6p0712c2s
Parry, C.C. v1p0586c2s v1p1113c2s v1p1360c1s v1p1435c1s v2p0053c1s v3p0354c1s
Parry, C.H. and Brougham, H. v1p0959c1s
Parry, D.M. v6p0100c1s
Parry, E.A. v2p0324c1s v2p0367c2s v3p0314c2s v4p0575c1s v5p0458c2s v5p0641c1s v6p0154c2m v6p0296c2s
Parry, E.B. v4p0304c1s
Parry, E.G. v3p0008c1s v3p0167c1s
Parry, E.Gambier v4p0542c2s
Parry, F. v4p0005c1s
Parry, H. v1p0583c1s
Parry, J. v1p0663c1s v4p0291c2m v4p0292c1s v4p0390c1s v4p0540c2s v5p0423c1s
Parry, J.S. v1p0229c2s v1p1360c2s

Parry, J.W. v4p0280c2s
v5p0286c2s v5p0331c1s v5p0426c1s
Parry, W.E. v1p0805c2s
Parsey, L. v4p0635c2s
Parshall, H.F. v4p0175c2s
v4p0176c1s v4p0548c1s v6p0198c1s
Parsloe, J. v1p1078c1s
v2p0362c2s
Parson, W.E. v1p0244c1s
v1p0435c1s v1p0901c1s v1p1300c2s
v1p1435c1s v3p0271c1s v4p0456c1s
v5p0503c2s v5p0546c2s
Parsons, A. v4p0217c1s
v4p0297c1m v4p0298c1m
Parsons, A.R. v1p1380c1s
Parsons, Anna F. et al. .. v4p0557c2s
Parsons, B. v2p0251c2s
Parsons, C. v1p0863c2s
v3p0393c2s
Parsons, C.A. v5p0389c1s
v5p0551c2s v5p0594c2m v6p0325c1s
Parsons, C.G. and Dakyns, H.G., jr.
v6p0661c1s
Parsons, C.L. v3p0006c1s
v6p0059c2s
Parsons, C.L. and Waters, C.E.
v6p0015c2m
Parsons, C.W. v1p0155c2s
v2p0039c1s v2p0242c2s v2p0365c1s
v3p0464c1s v4p0464c1s
Parsons, E. v1p1200c1s
v3p0075c1s v3p0424c2s v3p0425c1s
v4p0101c1s v4p0262c1s v4p0570c1s
v4p0570c2m v5p0093c2s v5p0105c1s
v5p0244c2s v5p0484c2s v5p0522c2s
v5p0573c1s v5p0573c2s v5p0597c1s
v6p0113c1s v6p0128c2s v6p0138c2s
v6p0276c2s v6p0671c2s
Parsons, E.C. v6p0257c1m
v6p0493c2s v6p0573c2s v6p0638c1s
Parsons, E.S. v3p0341c2s
v3p0398c2s v6p0134c2s v6p0418c1s
Parsons, Elsie C. v6p0189c2s
v6p0492c2s v6p0585c2s v6p0705c1s
Parsons, F. v4p0174c2s
v4p0257c2s v4p0380c1s v4p0390c2s
v4p0525c1m v5p0024c2s v5p0158c1s
v5p0281c2s v5p0412c1m v5p0457c1s
v5p0457c2s v5p0543c1s v5p0556c2s
v5p0570c2s v5p0593c2s v6p0148c1s
v6p0148c2s v6p0258c1s v6p0308c2s
v6p0318c1s v6p0435c2s v6p0436c1m
v6p0460c1s v6p0488c1s v6p0522c2s
v6p0530c1s v6p0551c1s v6p0621c2s
v6p0636c1s v6p0659c2s
Parsons, F. et al. v4p0567c1s
v6p0621c2s v6p0667c1s
Parsons, F.G. v4p0391c1s
v6p0117c2m
Parsons, F.H. v4p0355c1s
Parsons, F.M. v5p0196c2s
v5p0259c1s v5p0331c2s v5p0404c2s
v5p0480c2s v5p0629c2s v6p0054c2s
v6p0255c2s v6p0471c1s v6p0547c1s
Parsons, F.M.W. v5p0639c2s
Parsons, F.Mary Wilson ... v4p0365c2s
v4p0611c1s
Parsons, F.T. v5p0547c2s
Parsons, F.W. v6p0164c2s
v6p0236c2s v6p0238c1s v6p0593c2s
Parsons, Florence M. v5p0042c1s
v6p0115c2s v6p0368c2s v6p0375c2s
v6p0598c1s
Parsons, Frank v6p0528c1m
v6p0529c1s v6p0573c2s
Parsons, G.F. v1p0145c2s
v1p0696c2s v2p0032c2s v2p0245c1s
v2p0260c1s v2p0384c2s v3p0125c1s
v3p0271c1s v3p0373c2s
Parsons, G.L. v6p0661c1s
Parsons, H.B. v2p0410c1s
Parsons, H.C. v5p0250c2s
Parsons, H.F. v2p0119c2s
Parsons, H.G. v5p0039c1s
v5p0597c1s v6p0268c1s v6p0598c1s
v6p0693c2s
Parsons, H.deB. v4p0200c1s
v5p0082c2s v5p0207c2m
Parsons, I. v1p0868c1s
Parsons, I.D. v6p0197c2s
Parsons, J. v6p0217c1s
Parsons, J.C. v1p0529c1s
v1p0753c2s v1p0843c1s v1p1095c1m
v2p0369c2s v2p0414c1s v2p0414c2s
v4p0229c1s
Parsons, J.E. v6p0151c1s
Parsons, J.H. v4p0002c1s
v4p0199c2s v4p0245c2s v4p0436c1s
v5p0441c1s
Parsons, J.L. v2p0029c1s
v4p0017c2s
Parsons, J.R. v1p0684c1s
Parsons, J.R., jr. v4p0184c1s
v6p0290c1s v6p0574c1m
Parsons, J.R., jr. and Ellis, A.C.
v6p0290c1s
Parsons, K.L. v3p0297c1s
Parsons, L. v3p0322c2s
Parsons, L.H. v1p1256c2s
v3p0229c2s
Parsons, M.C. v4p0463c2s
Parsons, M.H. v1p0007c1s
v1p0875c1s
Parsons, M.H., Mrs. v1p0403c1s
v1p0773c1s v1p1408c2s
Parsons, N. v6p0488c2s
Parsons, P.M. v2p0275c1s
Parsons, R. v1p0202c1s
v3p0001c1s v3p0058c2s v3p0071c2s
v3p0087c2s v3p0110c1s v3p0424c1s
v4p0168c1s v4p0213c1s v4p0244c2s
v4p0358c1s v4p0451c1s v4p0483c1s
v5p0220c1s v5p0322c1s v5p0323c2s
v5p0348c2s v5p0456c2s v5p0502c2s
v6p0141c2s v6p0222c2s v6p0308c1s
v6p0459c1s
Parsons, R.C. v1p1065c1s
v2p0031c1s
Parsons, Reuben v5p0493c1s
Parsons, Richard v4p0431c1s
Parsons, S. v1p0903c2s
Parsons, S. and O'Donovan, W.R.
v6p0361c1s
Parsons, S., jr. v1p0731c1m
v1p1015c2s v1p1324c1s v3p0338c1s
v4p0116c2s v4p0445c2s v5p0431c1s
v5p0432c2s v6p0592c2s
Parsons, S.B. v1p0605c2s
v1p0723c1s
Parsons, S.F., Mrs. v4p0612c1s
Parsons, S.W., jr. v4p0319c2s
Parsons, T. v1p0383c1s
v1p0417c2s v1p0592c1s v1p0632c2s
v1p0705c2s v1p0867c1s v1p0904c2s
v1p1122c1s v1p1163c1s v1p1233c1s
v1p1241c1s
Parsons, T.W. v1p0331c2s
v1p0737c2s v1p0834c2s v2p0111c2m
v2p0259c1s v3p0209c2s v3p0295c1s
v3p0400c2s
Parsons, U. v1p0087c2s
v1p0156c2s v1p0424c1m v1p0492c2m
v1p0591c1s v1p0718c1s v1p0816c2s
v1p0934c2s v1p0989c1s v1p1070c1s
v1p1105c2s
Parsons, W. v3p0164c2s
Parsons, W.B. v4p0115c2s
v5p0108c1s v5p0108c2s v5p0109c1m
v5p0109c2s v5p0110c2s v5p0407c2s
v5p0477c2s v6p0476c2s v6p0710c2s
Parsons, W.B., jr. v3p0137c1s
Parsons, W.E. v6p0530c1s
Parsons, W.F. v4p0632c1s
Parsons, W.G. v6p0192c2s
Parsons, W.L. v1p0043c2s
Partington, A.T. v1p0452c2s
Partington, C.F. v1p0419c2m
v1p0425c2s v1p1427c2s
Partington, F.E. v4p0405c2s
v4p0624c1s
Parton, E. v3p0300c2s
v5p0434c1s
Parton, G. v6p0427c1s
Parton, J. v1p0107c2s
v1p0112c2s v1p0133c2s v1p0179c2s
v1p0186c2s v1p0200c2s v1p0227c2s
v1p0230c2s v1p0256c2s v1p0259c1s
v1p0259c2s v1p0263c1s v1p0291c2m
v1p0300c2s v1p0366c2s v1p0409c1s
v1p0504c1s v1p0522c2s v1p0535c2s
v1p0640c2s v1p0680c2m v1p0681c1m
v1p0691c1s v1p0692c1s v1p0894c1s
v1p0910c2s v1p0914c1s v1p0915c1s
v1p0916c2s v1p1007c2s v1p1012c2s
v1p1082c2s v1p1117c2s v1p1144c1s
v1p1182c1s v1p1199c1s v1p1199c2s
v1p1212c2s v1p1271c1s v1p1374c1s
v1p1378c1m v1p1388c1s v1p1395c2s
v1p1415c2s v2p0086c2s v2p0210c2s
v2p0312c2s v3p0050c1s v3p0086c1s
v3p0100c1s v3p0232c2s v3p0282c1s
v3p0292c1s v3p0343c1s v3p0356c2s
v3p0409c2s v3p0443c2s
Parton, J., Mrs. v1p0752c2s
Parton, W.F. v5p0168c2s
Partridge v5p0112c1s
Partridge, C. v6p0307c1s
Partridge, C.H. v6p0482c1s
Partridge, E.A. v3p0026c1s
v3p0062c1s v3p0319c2s v3p0328c2s
v5p0545c1s v6p0251c1s
Partridge, E.A. and Whitaker, H.C.
v4p0218c2s
Partridge, E.A. and Bradbury, R.H.
v6p0526c2s
Partridge, Ella S. v5p0291c1s
v5p0442c1s
Partridge, F.A. v5p0347c1s
v5p0534c1s
Partridge, G.E. v5p0011c2s
v5p0067c2s v5p0075c2s v5p0487c1s
Partridge, G.E. and Lindley, E.H.
v5p0041c1s
Partridge, G.T. v6p0628c1s
Partridge, J.A. v3p0181c1s
v3p0219c2s v3p0370c1s
Partridge, J.H. v1p0494c2s
v1p0614c2s
Partridge, M. v5p0107c2s
Partridge, M.E. v4p0088c1s
Partridge, N.A. v6p0113c2s
Partridge, S.M. v1p0977c2s
v1p1283c2s
Partridge, T.H. v1p0136c2s
Partridge, T.J. v6p0020c1s
v6p0282c2s v6p0298c1s v6p0500c2s
v6p0617c1s v6p0623c2s
Partridge, W. v1p0586c2s
v1p0639c1s
Partridge, W.O. v2p0123c1s
v4p0030c1s v4p0030c2s v4p0042c2s
v4p0487c2s v4p0510c1s v4p0510c2m
v5p0026c2s v5p0031c2s
v5p0516c1m
v6p0033c1s
v6p0443c2s
v6p0579c2m
v6p0601c2s
v6p0708c2s
Partridge, W.S. v6p0543c1s
Partridge, W.T. v4p0064c1s
v5p0496c1s v6p0374c2s
Parville, H.de v1p0211c2s
v2p0093c2s v5p0101c1s
Parvin, T.S. v1p0652c1s
v5p0220c1s
Pascalis, F. v1p0463c1s
Paschen, F. and Runge, C.. v4p0220c2s
Pasco, S. v6p0324c2s
Pascoe, C. v1p0960c1s
Pascoe, C.E. v1p0399c2s
v1p0428c1s v1p0761c2s v1p0763c1s
v1p0765c1s v1p1052c1s v2p0123c1s
v2p0271c2s v2p0283c2s v2p0333c1s
v2p0359c1m v2p0373c2s v2p0383c2s
v3p0031c2s v3p0058c2s v3p0086c2s
v3p0121c2s v3p0164c2s v3p0235c2s
v3p0315c1s
v3p0449c1s
v3p0465c2m
Pask, A.P. v2p0361c1s
Pask, A.T. v1p1259c2s
v1p1278c1s v4p0187c1s v4p0406c1s
Paske, Deputy Surgeon-Gen.
v4p0280c1s
Paske, E. v1p0173c2s
v2p0381c1s
Paske, E.H. v2p0104c1s
v3p0003c2s v3p0327c2s v3p0369c2s
Paslew, J. v3p0306c1s
Pasley, C.M.S. v4p0065c2s
v4p0433c1s
Pasley, C.W. v1p0362c1s
v1p0437c1s v3p0459c2s
Pasmore, A. v5p0311c2s
Paspati, A.G. v1p0328c2s
Pasquier, Baron v1p0327c2s
Pass, H.L. and Arendzen, J.
v5p0332c1s
Passarge, Dr. v4p0003c2s
Passarini, F. and Gale, R.
v1p1235c1s
Passavant, M. v1p0408c1s
Passepont, J. v4p0077c2s
Passepont, L. v4p0274c2s
v4p0504c2s
Passmore, J.C. v1p0155c1s
v1p1429c2s
Passy, F. v1p1027c1s
v4p0432c1s v5p0437c2s v6p0026c1s
v6p0458c2s
Passy, J. v5p0440c2s
Passy, M. v1p1055c2s
Passy, P. v6p0238c1s
Past, R.H. v5p0622c2s
Pasteur, L. v2p0175c2s
v2p0213c1m v3p0351c2s
Pasteur, L. and Huxley, T.H.
v3p0205c2s
Pastnor, P. v1p0367c2s
v4p0151c1s v5p0213c1s v5p0393c1s
Paston, G. v4p0316c2s
v5p0093c1s v5p0143c2s v5p0204c2s
v5p0242c1s v5p0340c1s v5p0345c1s
v5p0349c2s v5p0357c1s v5p0461c1s
v5p0579c2s v5p0632c1s v6p0026c2s
Pasture, H. de la, Mrs. .. v6p0385c2s
Pasture, Henry de la, Mrs.
v6p0490c2s
Patay, J. v6p0059c2s
Patch, C.A. v2p0114c1s
v2p0415c2s v3p0312c1s
Patch, C.A. and Dodge, T.A.
v3p0443c1s
Patch, G.B. v1p1262c2s
Patch, K.W. v4p0374c1s
v5p0390c2s v6p0071c2s v6p0247c1s
v6p0516c2s v6p0695c1s
Patch, Kate v6p0663c1s
Patch, Kate W. v5p0301c1s
Patchell, W.H. v4p0547c1s
Pate, J.T. v2p0024c2s
Pater, W. v2p0058c2s
v2p0116c1s v2p0398c1s v2p0421c2s
v2p0468c1s v3p0022c1s v3p0058c1s
v3p0124c1s v3p0144c1s v3p0147c2s
v3p0160c2s v3p0168c1s v3p0196c2s
v3p0243c2s v3p0275c1s v3p0387c2s
v3p0413c2s v4p0016c1s v4p0021c1s
v4p0035c2s v4p0178c2s v4p0241c1s

v4p0316c2s v4p0429c1s v4p0446c1s
v4p0446c2s v4p0473c2s v4p0603c2s
Pater, W.H. v1p0008c1s
v1p0098c1s v1p0153c2s v1p0342c2s
v1p0353c1s v1p0614c2s v1p0719c2s
v1p0834c2s v1p1008c1s v1p1123c2s
v1p1171c1s v1p1171c2s v1p1185c2s
v1p1372c1s v1p1429c2s
Paterson, A. v3p0040c1s
v3p0056c1s v3p0294c1s v3p0312c2s
v4p0086c2s v4p0368c1s v5p0097c1s
v5p0197c2s v5p0548c2s
Paterson, A.B. v6p0613c1s
Paterson, A.D. v1p0717c2s
Paterson, A.H. v2p0351c1s
v2p0366c2s v2p0395c2s v3p0363c1s
Paterson, A.N. v3p0261c2s
Paterson, B. v5p0171c1s
Paterson, Burd S. et al. . v6p0501c1s
Paterson, C.G. v6p0577c1s
v6p0702c2s
Paterson, D. v5p0124c1s
Paterson, H.S. v2p0450c2s
Paterson, J. v1p0810c2s
v1p1365c1s v2p0068c2s
Paterson, J.L. v6p0332c2s
Paterson, J.S. v1p0905c1s
v2p0372c1s
Paterson, M.C. v1p0195c2s
Paterson, O. v5p0548c1s
Paterson, R. v1p0064c2s
v1p1293c1s
Paterson, S. v1p0302c1s
v5p0424c1m v5p0608c2s
Paterson, W.G.S. v2p0463c1s
Paterson, W.P. v4p0096c1s
v5p0301c2s v5p0489c2s
Paterson, W.R. v5p0306c1s
Patey, J. v4p0296c2s
v5p0206c1s v5p0253c1s v5p0590c1s
Patmore, C. v1p0165c1m
v1p0818c1s v1p1370c2s v1p1426c1s
v2p0035c1s v3p0118c2s v3p0142c1s
v3p0237c2s v3p0313c1s v4p0109c1s
v4p0248c2s v4p0368c2m v4p0437c1s
v4p0574c2s v4p0599c2s
Patmore, F.G. v1p0577c1s
Patmore, G.A. v1p1181c2s
Patmore, K.A. v5p0202c1s
v6p0169c1s
Patmore, P.G. v1p0141c2s
Paton, A. v2p0013c2s
v2p0016c1s
Paton, C.M. v2p0178c2s
Paton, D. v4p0118c2s
v4p0137c1s v4p0190c1s v4p0353c1s
v4p0562c1s v4p0614c1s v5p0033c2s
v5p0145c2s v5p0163c1s v5p0353c2s
Paton, E.B. v6p0061c2s
Paton, F.N. v3p0015c1s
v3p0120c2s v3p0222c1s
Paton, G. v4p0557c1s
Paton, J.B. v1p0441c2s
v1p0515c2s v1p0810c2s v2p0298c1s
Paton, J.G. v4p0132c1s
v4p0334c1s
Paton, J.L. v6p0575c1s
Paton, J.N. v1p1338c2s
Paton, L.A. v4p0028c1s
v4p0063c2s
Paton, L.B. v3p0030c2s
v3p0041c2s v4p0055c1s v4p0056c1m
v4p0066c1s v4p0312c2s v5p0057c1m
v5p0058c2s v5p0116c1s v5p0308c1s
v5p0311c2s v5p0468c2s v6p0095c2s
v6p0165c2s v6p0167c1s v6p0285c2s
v6p0339c2s v6p0340c1m v6p0475c2s
v6p0484c1s v6p0519c2m
Paton, L.P. v4p0430c2s
Paton, R. v1p0837c1s
v1p0886c2s
Paton, R.S.G. v2p0406c1s
Paton, S. v6p0435c1s
Paton, T.B. v6p0345c1s
Paton, T.L. v4p0073c2s
Paton, W. v1p0136c1s
v1p0188c1s v1p0441c2s
Paton, W.A. v3p0093c2s
Paton, W.B. v3p0370c1s
v3p0383c2s v4p0179c1s
Paton, W.R. v3p0068c1s
v3p0447c2s v4p0159c1s v5p0004c2s
v5p0212c1s v5p0212c2s v5p0314c1s
v5p0331c1s
Paton, W.R. and Myres, J.L.
v4p0308c2s v5p0314c1m
Paton, W.R. and Tarbell, F.B.
v3p0026c2s
Patrici, M.L. v5p0394c1s
Patrick, D. v1p1329c1s
Patrick, G.T.W. v3p0194c1s
v3p0325c1s v3p0342c2s v3p0385c1s
v4p0364c2s v4p0409c1s v4p0626c1s
v5p0157c1s v5p0179c1s v5p0467c2s
v5p0479c2s v6p0232c1s
Patrick, G.T.W. and Gilbert, J.A.
v4p0529c2s
Patrick, J. v5p0094c2s
v6p0105c2s
Patrick, M.M. v4p0587c1s
v5p0638c1s v6p0394c1s v6p0610c2s
v6p0676c2s
Patrick, Mary Ellis v6p0704c2s
Patrick, Mary M. v5p0637c1s
v6p0661c2s
Patrick, P. v6p0698c1s
Patridge, J.M. v1p0854c1s
Patritsch, L. v6p0271c1s
Pattee, C.H. v3p0334c2s
v4p0068c2s v4p0160c2s
Pattee, C.R. v6p0092c2s
v6p0263c2s
Pattee, F.A. v6p0711c2s
Pattee, F.L. v4p0015c1s
v5p0136c1s v5p0187c1s v5p0221c2s
v5p0347c1s v5p0455c2s v5p0523c1s
Pattee, F.L. et al. v5p0016c1s
Pattee, Fred L. v6p0386c1s
Pattee, J.C. v1p0081c2s
Pattee, W.S. v3p0444c2s
Patten, A.B. v5p0484c2s
Patten, A.N. v5p0047c1s
Patten, A.W. v6p0122c1s
Patten, Anna B. v5p0379c2s
Patten, F.B. v2p0033c1s
v2p0103c2s v5p0194c2s
Patten, F.C. v6p0373c2s
Patten, F.J. v4p0175c1s
v4p0455c2s v4p0552c2s v4p0570c2s
v4p0571c1s
Patten, F.L. v3p0198c1s
Patten, Frank C. v6p0366c1s
Patten, G.E. v1p0018c1s
v1p0165c2s v1p1338c2s
Patten, J.W.D. v1p1147c2s
Patten, S.F. v4p0532c1s
Patten, S.N. v3p0019c2s
v3p0067c1s v3p0092c1s v3p0107c1s
v3p0127c2s v3p0178c1s v3p0241c2s
v3p0265c1s v3p0272c2s v3p0336c2s
v3p0343c2s v3p0346c1s v3p0360c2s
v3p0421c1s v3p0452c1s v3p0458c1s
v4p0135c2m v4p0165c1s v4p0323c2s
v4p0382c1s v4p0450c1m v4p0453c1s
v4p0464c2s v4p0483c2s v4p0507c2s
v4p0534c2m v4p0599c1s v5p0425c2s
v6p0193c2s v6p0292c2s v6p0672c2s
Patten, W. v4p0417c1s
v5p0080c1s v5p0129c1s v5p0277c1s
v5p0314c2s v6p0656c2m
Patterson, A.H. and Arnold, C.H.
v4p0175c1s
Patterson, A.J. v1p0014c2s
v1p0318c2s v1p0615c2m v1p1036c2s
v1p1355c1s v2p0018c1s v2p0029c2s
v2p0108c2s v2p0131c2s v2p0379c1s
v2p0455c2s v3p0204c2s v4p0492c2s
Patterson, A.M. v1p0917c2s
v6p0016c1m
Patterson, Ada v6p0045c2s
Patterson, Annie W. v6p0575c2s
Patterson, B. v4p0571c2s
Patterson, C. v6p0293c2s
Patterson, C.B. v5p0102c1s
v5p0115c1s v5p0377c1s v5p0469c1s
v6p0467c1s
Patterson, C.B. et al. ... v5p0114c2s
Patterson, C.R. v6p0029c1s
Patterson, C.S. v1p1089c1s
v2p0096c2s v2p0098c2s v2p0120c2s
v2p0201c2s v2p0240c1s v2p0286c2s
v2p0363c2s v2p0373c1s v2p0397c2s
v3p0081c1s v3p0314c1s v3p0444c2s
Patterson, D.L., jr. v6p0339c2s
v6p0655c2s
Patterson, D.N. v3p0201c1s
Patterson, D.W. v1p1273c1s
v1p1434c2s
Patterson, E.H. v5p0397c2s
Patterson, G. v2p0425c2s
v3p0340c1s v5p0408c2s
Patterson, G.L. v6p0070c1s
v6p0444c2s
Patterson, G.S. v4p0139c1s
Patterson, G.W. v2p0170c2s
Patterson, George v4p0402c1m
Patterson, J. v1p0423c1s
v1p1267c2s v4p0137c1s v5p0018c1s
v5p0158c2s
Patterson, J. et al. v4p0596c1s
Patterson, J.C. v1p1218c1s
v5p0368c1s
Patterson, J.E. v5p0503c2s
Patterson, J.H. v4p0438c2s
v5p0201c1m v5p0565c2s
Patterson, J.L. v1p0047c2s
v1p0558c1s v1p0994c1s v1p1033c1s
v2p0337c2s
Patterson, J.O. v1p0161c2s
Patterson, J.S. v1p0027c2s
v1p0043c1s v1p0467c2s v1p0493c1s
v1p0745c2s v1p0792c2s v1p0826c1s
v1p0900c1s v1p1093c1s v1p1093c2s
v1p1095c1s v1p1160c2s v1p1235c1s
v1p1255c2s v1p1308c1s v1p1345c1s
v1p1421c1s v1p1422c1s v2p0067c1s
v2p0463c2s
Patterson, J.W. v1p0389c2s
v1p0390c2s v2p0342c1s v3p0379c1s
v5p0083c2s
Patterson, John v4p0413c2s
v5p0196c2s v5p0509c1s
Patterson, Joseph M. v6p0144c1s
Patterson, M.M. v1p1391c1s
Patterson, M.S. v5p0391c1s
Patterson, M.W. v5p0028c1s
Patterson, N. v5p0091c1m
v5p0091c2m v5p0180c1s v5p0229c2m
v5p0378c2s v5p0473c2s v5p0498c2s
v5p0587c1s v5p0587c2s v5p0588c2s
v6p0010c1s v6p0096c1s v6p0096c2s
v6p0097c1s v6p0098c1m v6p0121c2s
v6p0170c2s v6p0194c2s v6p0215c2s
v6p0244c1s v6p0264c1s v6p0280c1s
v6p0317c1s v6p0335c2s v6p0363c2s
v6p0384c1s v6p0390c1s v6p0511c1s
v6p0650c1s v6p0654c2s
Patterson, N. and Kyle, F.
v6p0650c1s
Patterson, R. v1p0241c2s
v1p0486c1s v1p0509c2s v1p0638c1s
v1p0792c2s v1p1002c2s v1p1158c2s
v1p1239c1s v1p1244c2s v5p0445c2s
v5p0565c2s
Patterson, R.E. v1p0850c1s
Patterson, R.H. v1p0078c2s
v1p0093c1s v1p0186c2s v1p0198c1s
v1p0325c1s v1p0325c2s v1p0327c2s
v1p0335c2s v1p0378c1s v1p0407c1s
v1p0421c1s v1p0532c1s v1p0532c2s
v1p0533c2s v1p0649c2s v1p0747c1s
v1p0762c1s v1p0861c1m v1p1004c1s
v1p1174c1s v1p1199c1s v1p1218c1s
v1p1267c2s v1p1319c1s v1p1432c2s
v2p0029c1s v2p0337c1s
Patterson, R.H. and Williamson, S.
v1p1319c1s
Patterson, R.M. v1p0132c1s
v1p0484c2s v1p0846c2s v1p1045c2s
v2p0352c2s v5p0464c1s
Patterson, R.W. v1p1046c1s
v1p1047c1s v2p0394c1s
Patterson, T.C. v5p0271c1s
Patterson, T.G. v4p0273c1s
Patterson, T.H. v6p0419c1s
Patterson, T.J. v1p1395c2s
Patterson, T.L. v4p0064c1s
Patterson, T.M. v2p0094c1s
Patterson, W. v3p0454c1s
Patterson, W.C. v1p1035c2s
Patterson, W.H. v3p0255c1s
v4p0141c2s
Patterson, W.R. v5p0159c1s
v6p0196c2s v6p0638c2s
Patteson, C. v4p0152c2s
Patteson, S.L. v5p0442c1s
Patteson, S.S.P. v4p0605c2s
v5p0301c1s v5p0329c1s v5p0347c2s
v5p0465c2s
Patti, Adelina v6p0595c2s
Pattinson, H.L. v6p0249c1s
Pattinson, J. v1p0796c1s
Pattison, A.S.P. v5p0411c1s
Pattison, E.F.S. v1p0053c2s
v1p0203c1s v1p0309c2s v1p0482c1s
v1p0490c1s v1p0537c1s v1p0962c1s
v1p1010c2s v1p1040c1s v2p0329c2s
v2p0379c1s v4p0322c1s v4p0455c2s
Pattison, E.W. v1p1319c2s
v1p1321c2s
Pattison, F.A. v5p0183c1s
Pattison, J.W. v5p0105c1s
v5p0156c1s v5p0208c1s v5p0377c1m
v5p0428c1s v6p0030c2s v6p0033c2s
v6p0049c1s v6p0070c1s v6p0403c1s
v6p0410c2s v6p0420c1s v6p0436c2s
v6p0556c1s v6p0661c2s
Pattison, M. v1p0148c1s
v1p0318c1s v1p0359c1s v1p0419c1s
v1p0434c1s v1p0841c2s v1p0954c2s
v1p1000c1s v1p1037c2m v1p1054c2s
v1p1086c1s v1p1305c2s v2p0283c2s
v2p0325c1s
Pattison, M., Mrs. v1p1098c1s
Pattison, M.B. v4p0002c2s
Pattison, M.M. v1p0074c1s
v1p0401c2s v1p0858c2s
Pattison, P., Mrs. v4p0273c2s
Pattison, R.E. v1p0528c1s
v1p0850c2s
Pattison, S.R. v2p0057c1s
v2p0072c2s v2p0245c1s v2p0273c2s
v2p0274c2s v3p0100c2s
Pattison, T.H. v1p0033c2s
v1p0909c1s v1p0941c1s v2p0022c2s
v3p0472c1s
Pattison-Muir, M.M. and Dewar, J.
v4p0221c1s
Pattisson, P.B., Mrs. v3p0216c1s
v3p0284c1s v3p0294c1s v3p0386c2s
v4p0034c2s
Patton, A.B. v3p0347c2s
Patton, A.S. v1p0365c2s
v1p0689c1s v1p1096c2s
Patton, C.S. v6p0214c2s
v6p0519c2s
Patton, F.J. v6p0484c2s
Patton, F.L. v1p0568c1s
v1p0595c2s v1p0912c2s v1p1000c1s
v1p1101c2s v1p1165c2s v2p0043c1s

v2p0147c1m v2p0180c2s v2p0285c1s
v2p0290c2s v2p0324c2s v2p0332c1s
v2p0339c2s v2p0352c2s v2p0414c2s
v2p0437c1m v2p0437c2s v3p0013c1s
v3p0342c1s v3p0342c2s v4p0346c2s
Patton, F.L. and Newton, R.H.
v2p0297c1s
Patton, G.A. v2p0148c2s
Patton, G.S. v4p0188c2s
v5p0196c1s v5p0386c1s v5p0576c1s
Patton, J. v6p0373c1s
Patton, J.H. v1p1438c1s
v2p0083c2s v2p0461c2s v3p0290c1s
v3p0355c2s v3p0426c2s v3p0443c2s
v4p0473c1s
Patton, J.M. v1p0815c1s
v1p1397c1s
Patton, N.S. v3p0248c2s
v4p0132c2s v5p0336c1s
Patton, R.B. v1p0725c1s
v1p0743c1s
Patton, S.N. v6p0704c2s
Patton, W. v1p0253c1s
v1p0258c1s v1p0946c2s
Patton, W.M. v5p0067c1s
v5p0381c2s v5p0571c2s v6p0195c2s
v6p0343c1s v6p0583c1m v6p0630c2s
Patton, W.W. v1p0035c2s
v1p0043c2s v1p0096c2s v1p0240c2s
v1p0290c1s v1p0290c2m v1p0323c1s
v1p0336c1s v1p0392c1s v1p0397c2s
v1p0731c2s v1p0853c1s v1p0986c1s
v1p1101c1s v1p1103c2s v1p1203c2s
v2p0045c1s v2p0086c2s v2p0099c1s
v2p0148c1s v2p0404c1s v2p0415c1s
v2p0478c1s v3p0010c2s v3p0283c1s
Pattullo, G.R., jr. v5p0253c2s
Paul, A.B. v4p0544c2s
v4p0604c1s
Paul, A.L. v4p0406c2s
Paul, B.H. v1p0367c1s
v1p0747c1s v1p0995c2s v1p1181c1s
v2p0213c2s v3p0163c1s v3p0165c1s
v3p0250c2s
Paul, C.F. v5p0504c1s
v6p0674c2s
Paul, C.K. v1p0045c2s
v1p0047c2s v1p0118c2s v1p0175c2s
v1p0185c2s v1p0241c1s v1p0253c2s
v1p0423c2s v1p0511c2s v1p0542c1s
v1p0571c1s v1p0666c2s v1p0682c2s
v1p0685c2s v1p0704c1s v1p0744c2s
v1p0819c1s v1p0980c1s v1p0980c2s
v1p1098c2s v1p1203c2s v1p1412c1s
v1p1419c2s v2p0001c2s v2p0005c2s
v2p0051c2s v2p0131c1s v2p0151c2s
v2p0264c1s v2p0269c2s v2p0275c2s
v2p0311c2s v2p0331c2s v3p0095c2s
v3p0302c1s v4p0077c1s v4p0189c1s
v4p0214c1s v4p0373c1s v4p0468c1s
v4p0545c1s v4p0548c2s v5p0016c1s
v5p0099c1s v5p0197c2s
Paul, C.Kegan v2p0358c1s
v4p0214c2s
Paul, D. v1p0082c2s
v1p0200c1s v1p0670c2m v1p0672c2m
v1p0737c2s v1p0993c1s v1p1013c1s
v1p1126c1s v2p0313c1s
Paul, E.G. v3p0315c1s
Paul, F. v3p0204c1s
v3p0452c2s
Paul, G.F. v6p0413c2s
v6p0423c1m v6p0509c1s v6p0677c1s
Paul, G.H. et al. v6p0225c1s
Paul, H. v2p0248c1s
v3p0237c1s v3p0460c2m v4p0118c1s
v4p0217c1s v4p0448c1s v4p0549c1s
v4p0569c2s v5p0118c2s v5p0142c1s
v5p0233c1s v5p0247c2m v5p0254c2s
v5p0272c1s v5p0320c1s v5p0331c2s
v5p0406c1s v5p0476c1s v5p0519c1s
v5p0564c1s v6p0068c2s v6p0125c2s
v6p0173c2s v6p0191c2s v6p0200c2s
v6p0269c2m v6p0270c1s v6p0270c2m
v6p0273c1s v6p0273c2s v6p0280c1s
v6p0303c2s v6p0334c1s v6p0485c2s
v6p0534c2s v6p0622c2s
Paul, H. and Gosse, E. ... v4p0569c1s
Paul, H. and Hedley, J.C.. v5p0289c1s
Paul, H. et al. v6p0191c2s
Paul, H.M. v2p0128c1m
v2p0136c2s v2p0244c1s v2p0345c1s
v2p0386c2s
Paul, H.M. and McFarland, W.
v2p0159c1s
Paul, H.M. et al. v2p0285c1s
Paul, H.W. v4p0028c1s
v6p0411c2s v6p0469c2s
Paul, Herbert v6p0127c1s
v6p0152c1s v6p0268c1s v6p0270c1s
v6p0359c1s
Paul, J.B. v4p0168c1s
v4p0254c2s v4p0341c1s v4p0549c2s
v5p0467c2s
Paul, J.Balfour v6p0194c2s
Paul, M. v6p0032c2s
Paul, M.E. v5p0303c1s
Paul, Mrs. v1p0500c1s
Paul, N. v5p0416c2s
Paul, R.W. v5p0262c2s
Paul, S.C. v2p0148c2s
v2p0263c1s
Paul, T. v3p0201c2s
v3p0307c2s
Paul, W. v1p0477c1s
v3p0142c1s v3p0165c1s
Paulding, J. v1p0038c1s
Paulding, J.K. v1p0445c1s
v1p0782c2s v1p1375c2s v3p0009c2s
v3p0036c1s v3p0061c2s v3p0464c2s
v4p0051c2s v4p0096c2s v4p0257c2s
v4p0319c2s v5p0407c2s v5p0471c2s
v5p0582c1s v6p0185c1s v6p0456c1m
Paulding, P.R. v4p0274c2s
v4p0421c2s v5p0488c2s
Paulding, W.I. v1p0650c1s
v1p0915c2s v1p0938c1s v1p1323c1s
v1p1415c2s
Paulding, W.J. v1p0804c2s
Paulet, H., Lady v4p0483c1s
Paulham, F. v4p0389c2s
v4p0464c2s
Paulhan, Fr. v5p0447c1s
Pauli, G.R. v1p0515c2s
v1p1060c2s
Pauli, W.B. v1p0377c1s
v1p0796c1s
Paullan, L. v4p0049c2s
v4p0425c1s
Pauline, G. v1p0567c1s
Paull, H.M. v5p0399c1s
v5p0538c1s v6p0442c2s v6p0586c2s
Paull, J.W. v6p0541c1s
v6p0555c1s
Paullin, C.O. v6p0606c2s
v6p0669c1m
Paullin, W.T., jr. v6p0467c2s
Paulsen, A. v2p0028c2s
v3p0027c1s
Paulsen, F. v4p0597c2s
v5p0179c2s v5p0198c2s v5p0326c2s
v6p0253c1s v6p0679c1s
Paumier, M. v1p1161c1s
Pauncefort, M. v6p0686c2s
Paux, R. v6p0222c2s
Pavey, F.D. v5p0119c2s
v5p0147c1s v5p0407c2s v5p0445c1s
v5p0457c2s
Pavey, G.M. v3p0012c1s
v3p0062c1s v3p0097c2s
Pavey, H.A. v2p0014c1s
Pavie, T.H. v1p0790c2s
Pavin, I. v3p0274c1s
Pavlovsky, I. v4p0020c2s
Pavoux, E. v1p0197c2m
Pavy, F.W. v3p0297c2s
Pavy, L.M. v2p0333c2s
Pawling, H.C. v1p1196c1s
Pawling, J. v5p0356c1s
Pawson, J. v1p0926c2s
Paxson, F.L. v5p0218c2s
v6p0139c1m v6p0284c2s v6p0339c2s
v6p0414c1m
Paxson, S.A. v6p0160c1s
Paxton, G. v4p0032c2s
v4p0049c1s v4p0060c1s v4p0333c1s
Paxton, M.W. v2p0104c2s
Paxton, W.M. v3p0281c1s
v4p0473c2s
Payen, A. v1p1427c1s
Payen, C.E. v5p0438c2s
Payen, M. v1p1265c2s
Payer, J.V. v4p0406c2s
Payle, ... v4p0134c2s
Payler, F. v6p0154c2m
v6p0176c2s v6p0201c2s v6p0278c2s
v6p0347c1s v6p0363c1s v6p0364c1s
Payn, H. v5p0604c2s
Payn, J. v1p0007c1s
v1p0007c2s v1p0021c1s v1p0051c1s
v1p0071c1s v1p0076c2s v1p0088c1s
v1p0102c1s v1p0116c1s v1p0142c2s
v1p0181c2s v1p0199c1s v1p0202c1s
v1p0209c2s v1p0216c2s v1p0218c2s
v1p0229c2s v1p0267c1s v1p0289c1m
v1p0296c2s v1p0318c1s v1p0372c2s
v1p0378c2s v1p0442c1s v1p0443c1s
v1p0445c2s v1p0451c1s v1p0453c2s
v1p0455c2s v1p0471c1s v1p0491c2s
v1p0535c2s v1p0541c1s v1p0561c2s
v1p0563c2s v1p0567c2s v1p0586c1s
v1p0601c2s v1p0627c1s v1p0628c1s
v1p0639c1s v1p0752c2s v1p0755c1s
v1p0769c1s v1p0770c2s v1p0773c2s
v1p0803c1s v1p0803c2s v1p0813c2s
v1p0814c1s v1p0816c1s v1p0837c2s
v1p0850c2s v1p0856c2s v1p0860c2s
v1p0881c1s v1p0930c2s v1p0933c2s
v1p0938c1s v1p0942c2s v1p0944c1s
v1p0952c2s v1p0979c1s v1p0988c1s
v1p0989c2s v1p1040c2s v1p1054c2s
v1p1088c2s v1p1187c2s v1p1195c2s
v1p1200c1s v1p1214c2s v1p1258c1s
v1p1259c1s v1p1273c2s v1p1281c1s
v1p1284c1s v1p1289c2s v1p1318c1s
v1p1321c2s v1p1339c1s v1p1358c2s
v1p1368c2s v1p1369c2s v1p1371c2s
v1p1383c1s v1p1403c2s v1p1420c1s
v2p0090c1s v2p0145c2s v2p0155c1s
v2p0166c2s v2p0185c1s v2p0234c1s
v2p0268c1s v2p0307c1s v2p0423c2s
v2p0430c1s v2p0438c2s v2p0449c2s
v3p0029c1s v3p0061c1s v3p0112c2s
v3p0127c1s v4p0041c1s v4p0156c2s
v4p0254c2s v4p0331c1s v4p0432c1m
v4p0590c1s v5p0135c1s v5p0176c2s
v5p0418c2s
Payn, Neville v5p0170c2s
Payne, A. v1p0031c2s
v1p0054c2s v1p1267c1s v2p0097c2s
v2p0378c1s
Payne, A. and Sheffield, W.F.
v2p0372c1s
Payne, A.E. v4p0634c2s
Payne, A.M. v3p0469c1s
v6p0278c1s
Payne, B. v6p0399c2s
Payne, B.H. v1p0854c2s
v1p0913c1m
Payne, B.R. v6p0211c2s
v6p0399c2s
Payne, C.H. v1p0391c2s
v3p0121c1s
Payne, E.B. v3p0315c2s
v4p0012c2s v5p0088c2s v5p0276c2s
v5p0339c1s v5p0362c1s v5p0399c1s
Payne, E.J. v1p0973c1s
v2p0309c1s v4p0427c1s
Payne, G. v1p0601c2s
v4p0350c1s v4p0388c1s v6p0538c2s
Payne, Geo.A. v4p0312c2s
Payne, H. v1p1281c1s
v4p0033c2s v4p0089c2s v4p0274c2s
Payne, H.C. v5p0400c2s
v6p0018c1s v6p0570c2s v6p0579c2s
Payne, H.R. v2p0175c2s
Payne, Harriet E. v5p0126c2s
Payne, J. v1p0088c1s
v1p0668c2s v1p1163c1s v1p1257c2s
Payne, J.B. v1p0062c2s
Payne, J.F. v1p0592c2s
v4p0255c1s
Payne, J.F. et al. v3p0445c1s
Payne, J.H. v1p0556c1s
Payne, J.L. v2p0065c2s
v3p0448c2s v4p0070c2s v4p0085c2s
v4p0262c1s v4p0418c1s v4p0636c1s
Payne, J.O. v3p0350c2s
Payne, L.W., jr. v5p0013c1s
v5p0574c2s v6p0256c1s v6p0361c2s
Payne, Laura A. v6p0441c1s
Payne, M.S., Mrs. v4p0612c1s
Payne, M.W. v6p0486c1s
Payne, R.M.Horne v6p0325c1s
Payne, S. v2p0433c1s
Payne, S.E. v5p0370c1s
v5p0567c1s
Payne, W. v1p0245c2s
v1p0284c2s v1p0596c2s v4p0527c1s
v5p0100c1s v5p0159c2s v5p0207c2s
v5p0283c1s v5p0323c2s v5p0390c1s
v5p0466c1s v5p0627c2s v6p0113c1m
v6p0377c1s v6p0427c2s v6p0534c1s
v6p0566c1s
Payne, W.A. v4p0100c2s
Payne, W.H. v2p0315c2s
v2p0432c1s v3p0130c1s v3p0196c1s
v5p0131c1s v5p0569c2s
Payne, W.M. v2p0022c1s
v2p0048c1s v2p0155c1s v2p0210c2s
v2p0241c1s v2p0318c2s v2p0339c2s
v2p0346c2s v2p0388c2s v2p0390c2s
v2p0394c2s v2p0399c2s v2p0428c1s
v2p0428c2s v2p0443c1s v2p0446c2s
v3p0110c1m v3p0336c1s v3p0390c1s
v3p0425c1s v4p0037c2s v4p0047c2s
v4p0100c1s v4p0184c1s v4p0184c2s
v4p0218c1s v4p0257c1s v4p0272c1m
v4p0376c1s v4p0402c2s v4p0448c2m
v4p0465c1s v4p0495c1s v4p0504c2s
v4p0608c2s v4p0620c2s v5p0016c1m
v5p0030c1m v5p0075c1s v5p0152c2m
v5p0194c1s v5p0205c2s v5p0206c1m
v5p0250c1s v5p0267c2s v5p0278c1m
v5p0340c2s v5p0341c2s v5p0350c1s
v5p0385c1s v5p0412c1s v5p0418c1s
v5p0456c1s v5p0494c2s v5p0512c2s
v5p0615c2s v6p0018c1s v6p0032c1s
v6p0059c2s v6p0069c1s v6p0079c2s
v6p0113c1s v6p0200c2s v6p0284c2s
v6p0305c2m v6p0388c2s v6p0506c1s
v6p0610c1s v6p0629c2s v6p0631c1s
v6p0644c1s v6p0689c2s
Payne, W.M. and Hawthorne, J.
v6p0088c2s
Payne, W.W. v2p0026c1s
v2p0068c1s v2p0086c1s v2p0095c1s
v2p0095c2m v2p0257c2s v2p0278c1s
v2p0322c1s v2p0386c2s v2p0417c1s
v2p0417c2s v2p0424c2s v2p0426c2s
v2p0433c2s v2p0441c2s v3p0024c2s
v3p0333c2s v3p0407c1s v3p0415c1s
v3p0415c2s v4p0034c1s v4p0034c2s
v4p0126c2s v4p0253c2s v4p0306c2s
v4p0357c2s v4p0381c1s v4p0447c1s
v4p0545c1s v4p0556c2s v4p0567c2s
v5p0035c2m v5p0080c1s v5p0130c1s
v5p0167c1s v5p0172c2s v5p0194c2s
v5p0350c1s v5p0370c2s v5p0372c1s
v5p0372c2m v5p0402c1s v5p0549c1s

v5p0549c2s v5p0560c2s v5p0602c2m
v5p0641c2s v5p0644c1m v6p0018c2s
v6p0037c2m v6p0140c2m v6p0187c2s
v6p0188c1s v6p0274c1s v6p0344c1s
v6p0347c2s v6p0348c1s v6p0363c1s
v6p0402c2s v6p0406c1s v6p0454c2s
v6p0496c2s v6p0509c1s v6p0571c1s
v6p0596c2s v6p0614c1s v6p0614c2m
v6p0625c2m v6p0637c1s v6p0637c2m
v6p0668c2s v6p0711c2s
Payne, W.W. and Todd, D.P.
v3p0415c1s
Payne, W.W. et al. v2p0285c1s
v5p0174c2s
Payne, Will v6p0049c2s
v6p0689c2s v6p0692c1s
Payne, Wm. v4p0507c1s
Payne, Wm.W. v6p0037c2s
v6p0188c1s
Paynter, A. v1p0517c2s
v1p0597c2s v1p0672c1s
Payson, E. v1p0423c1s
v1p0625c2s v1p0729c2s v1p1041c2s
Payson, E.P. v2p0431c2s
v5p0328c1s v5p0364c1s
Payson, E.R. v3p0196c1s
Payson, G.S. v3p0378c2s
Payson, W.F. v5p0321c2s
v5p0456c2s
Payton, H.T. v6p0227c1s
Payton, J.K. v6p0628c2s
Payton, T.K. v6p0115c2s
v6p0277c1s v6p0670c2s
Peabody, A.P. v1p0014c1s
v1p0027c2s v1p0031c2s v1p0032c2s
v1p0045c1s v1p0063c1s v1p0073c1s
v1p0075c1s v1p0097c2s v1p0100c2s
v1p0106c1s v1p0117c2s v1p0119c2s
v1p0120c2m v1p0121c2s v1p0124c2s
v1p0127c1s v1p0127c2m v1p0128c1s
v1p0129c1s v1p0129c2s v1p0132c2s
v1p0152c2s v1p0158c1s v1p0165c2s
v1p0187c1s v1p0194c2m v1p0198c2s
v1p0215c1s v1p0216c1s v1p0224c2s
v1p0234c2s v1p0235c1s v1p0239c1s
v1p0242c2s v1p0244c1s v1p0248c2s
v1p0252c2s v1p0254c2s v1p0285c1s
v1p0291c1s v1p0293c1s v1p0312c1s
v1p0348c1s v1p0349c2s v1p0376c1s
v1p0378c1s v1p0413c2s v1p0425c1s
v1p0429c2s v1p0431c2s v1p0433c2s
v1p0441c1s v1p0451c1s v1p0454c2s
v1p0470c2s v1p0472c1s v1p0514c2m
v1p0566c1s v1p0566c2s v1p0571c2s
v1p0572c2s v1p0574c2s v1p0575c2m
v1p0582c1s v1p0592c2s v1p0617c1s
v1p0637c1s v1p0646c1s v1p0684c1s
v1p0685c2s v1p0688c2s v1p0691c1s
v1p0697c2s v1p0714c2s v1p0727c1s
v1p0731c1s v1p0754c2s v1p0768c1s
v1p0769c1s v1p0775c1m v1p0782c2s
v1p0784c1s v1p0786c1s v1p0792c1s
v1p0797c1s v1p0805c2s v1p0816c2s
v1p0824c2s v1p0848c1s v1p0852c1s
v1p0869c1m v1p0869c2s v1p0890c2s
v1p0900c2s v1p0902c2s v1p0905c1s
v1p0909c2s v1p0921c1s v1p0929c1s
v1p0933c1s v1p0961c2s v1p0963c1s
v1p0972c2m v1p0975c2s v1p0982c2s
v1p0990c2m v1p0992c2s v1p0997c1s
v1p0997c2s v1p1000c2s v1p1006c1s
v1p1011c2s v1p1018c2s v1p1025c2s
v1p1037c2s v1p1043c1s v1p1053c2s
v1p1058c1s v1p1063c1s v1p1083c2s
v1p1092c2s v1p1093c1s v1p1093c2s
v1p1099c2s v1p1102c1s v1p1121c2m
v1p1124c1s v1p1139c1s v1p1148c2s
v1p1159c1s v1p1159c2s v1p1161c1m
v1p1161c2s v1p1203c2s v1p1206c1m
v1p1207c1s v1p1217c1s v1p1232c2s
v1p1238c1s v1p1240c2s v1p1254c2s
v1p1286c2s v1p1333c2s v1p1346c2s
v1p1348c1s v1p1373c1s v1p1381c2s
v1p1384c1s v1p1386c1s v1p1386c2s
v1p1387c2s v1p1398c2s v1p1406c2s
v1p1407c1s v1p1426c1s v1p1429c2s
v2p0010c2s v2p0132c1s v2p0139c1s
v2p0191c1s v2p0234c1s v2p0333c1s
v2p0339c1s v2p0345c2s v2p0351c2s
v2p0419c2s v2p0425c2s v3p0012c1s
v3p0049c2s v3p0108c1s v3p0143c1s
v3p0318c1s v3p0321c1s v3p0334c1s
v3p0361c2s v3p0395c2s v3p0413c2s
v3p0441c1s v4p0057c1m v4p0597c2s
v4p0615c1s v5p0640c2s
Peabody, A.P. et al. v2p0233c1s
v2p0328c1s
Peabody, C. v6p0446c2s
Peabody, C. and Moorhead, W.K.
v6p0015c1s
Peabody, C.A. v1p0772c2s
Peabody, C.H. v3p0064c1s
v4p0467c1s v4p0547c2s v6p0445c1s
Peabody, D. v1p0032c1s
v1p0426c2s v1p0436c2s
Peabody, E. v1p0032c2s
v1p0035c2s v1p0048c2m v1p0174c2s
v1p0178c2s v1p0218c1s v1p0242c2s
v1p0357c2s v1p0404c1s v1p0495c2s
v1p0542c1m v1p0545c1s v1p0603c1s
v1p0619c2s v1p0620c1s v1p0629c1s
v1p0641c2s v1p0671c2s v1p0684c2s
v1p0690c1s v1p0949c2s v1p0955c1s
v1p0977c2s v1p0981c2s v1p0982c2s
v1p1065c1m v1p1094c1s v1p1175c2s
v1p1204c2s v1p1208c1s v4p0505c2s
Peabody, E. and Eliot, C.W.
v5p0511c1s
Peabody, E.P. v1p0112c1s
v1p0122c1s v1p0167c2s v1p0217c1s
v1p0312c2s v1p0341c1s v1p0491c2s
v1p0527c2s v1p0575c2m v1p0707c2s
v1p0813c1s v1p1401c2s v1p1426c2s
v1p1433c1s v2p0208c1s v2p0243c1s
v2p0274c2s
Peabody, F.D. v5p0230c1s
Peabody, F.G. v1p0243c1s
v1p0395c1m v1p0395c2m v1p1043c1s
v1p1062c1s v1p1093c2s v1p1095c1s
v1p1303c2s v2p0181c1s v2p0255c1s
v2p0358c2s v3p0099c1s v3p0215c1s
v3p0398c1s v3p0399c1s v3p0444c2s
v4p0097c1s v4p0124c2s v4p0162c1s
v4p0249c2s v4p0387c1s v4p0452c1s
v4p0455c2s v4p0456c2s v4p0581c2s
v4p0591c2s v5p0102c1s v5p0127c1s
v5p0340c2s v5p0488c1s v5p0536c1s
v6p0002c1s v6p0341c1s
Peabody, F.P. v4p0500c2s
Peabody, G.F. v5p0525c1s
Peabody, H.P. v1p0388c1s
Peabody, J.D. v5p0316c2s
v5p0567c2s
Peabody, J.P. v4p0147c2s
v5p0188c1s v5p0255c2s v5p0278c1s
v5p0419c1s v5p0452c2s v5p0474c2s
Peabody, Josephine P. v6p0221c1s
v6p0505c2s
Peabody, L.G. v5p0092c2s
Peabody, O.W.B. v1p0022c2s
v1p0031c1m v1p0091c1s v1p0135c1s
v1p0165c1s v1p0178c2s v1p0278c1s
v1p0298c2s v1p0311c1s v1p0362c2s
v1p0418c1s v1p0418c2s v1p0537c1s
v1p0555c2s v1p0622c2s v1p0680c1s
v1p0768c1s v1p0872c2s v1p1022c2s
v1p1051c2s v1p1068c1s v1p1151c1s
v1p1168c1s v1p1211c1s v1p1231c2m
v1p1266c1s v1p1272c1s v1p1318c1s
v1p1429c1s
Peabody, R.S. v1p0053c1s
v2p0019c2s v3p0018c1m v4p0023c2s
v4p0114c1s v4p0182c2s v4p0249c1s
v4p0602c2s v5p0025c1s
Peabody, S.H. v1p0055c1s
v1p0925c2s v2p0009c2s v2p0079c2s
v2p0128c1m v2p0233c2s v2p0234c1s
v3p0079c1s v3p0111c1s v3p0136c2s
v3p0142c1s v3p0276c1s v3p0406c2s
v3p0451c2s v3p0458c2s v4p0041c2s
v5p0027c1s v5p0109c1s v5p0533c2s
Peabody, S.P. v1p0243c2s
Peabody, W.B.O. v1p0006c2s
v1p0066c2s v1p0120c2m v1p0124c1s
v1p0157c1s v1p0159c2s v1p0168c2s
v1p0182c2s v1p0183c1s v1p0216c2s
v1p0243c2s v1p0288c1s v1p0310c2s
v1p0383c1m v1p0420c1s v1p0468c1s
v1p0483c2s v1p0505c1s v1p0507c2s
v1p0515c2s v1p0574c2s v1p0577c2s
v1p0582c1s v1p0594c1s v1p0595c2s
v1p0609c2s v1p0610c2s v1p0636c1s
v1p0645c1s v1p0683c2s v1p0690c1s
v1p0694c1s v1p0697c2s v1p0723c1s
v1p0738c1s v1p0758c2s v1p0777c2s
v1p0806c2s v1p0808c2s v1p0811c1m
v1p0819c2s v1p0841c1s v1p0870c2s
v1p0874c2s v1p0876c2s v1p0893c2s
v1p0899c2s v1p0931c2m v1p0933c1s
v1p0938c2s v1p0949c1s v1p0997c1s
v1p1021c1s v1p1050c1m v1p1088c2s
v1p1089c2s v1p1168c1s v1p1169c2s
v1p1197c1s v1p1240c1s v1p1262c1s
v1p1286c1s v1p1324c1s v1p1328c1s
v1p1371c2s v1p1384c2s v1p1385c1s
v1p1412c2s
Peabody, W.O.B. v1p0098c1s
v1p0181c2s v1p1101c2s v1p1115c1s
Peabody, W.R. v6p0174c2s
Peabody, W.Rodman v6p0128c2s
Peace, W. v3p0448c2s
Peach, B.N. v2p0006c1s
Peach, B.N. and Horne, J.. v2p0174c1s
Peach, R.W. v5p0437c2s
Peache, J.C. v5p0551c1s
Peachey, G.C. v5p0081c1s
Peacock, A.W. v6p0530c1s
Peacock, B. v4p0621c1s
Peacock, C.K. v4p0500c1s
Peacock, E. v1p0256c1s
v1p0739c2s v1p1240c1s v1p1416c2s
v2p0061c1s v2p0085c2s v2p0105c1s
v2p0108c1s v2p0124c1s v2p0161c1s
v2p0181c2s v2p0192c1s v2p0235c1s
v2p0246c2s v2p0259c2m v2p0287c2s
v2p0294c2s v2p0315c2s v2p0324c1s
v2p0360c2s v2p0364c1s v2p0367c2s
v2p0405c2s v2p0482c1s v3p0050c2s
v3p0054c1s v3p0056c1s v3p0083c2s
v3p0198c1s v3p0201c2s v3p0237c1s
v3p0246c2s v3p0264c1s v4p0114c1s
v4p0137c1s v4p0165c2s v4p0218c2s
v4p0252c1s v4p0254c2s v4p0463c1s
v5p0073c2s v5p0294c2s v5p0339c2s
v5p0360c2s v5p0382c1s v5p0478c1s
v5p0515c2s v5p0556c1s v6p0071c1s
Peacock, E. et al. v2p0416c1s
Peacock, E.R. v5p0446c2s
Peacock, F. v4p0050c2s
v4p0079c2s v4p0141c2s v4p0149c2s
v4p0484c2s v4p0552c2s v4p0558c2s
v5p0025c1s v5p0174c1s v5p0275c2s
v5p0388c1s v5p0402c1s v5p0427c1s
v5p0507c1s v5p0561c1s v5p0592c1s
Peacock, Florence v4p0027c2s
Peacock, G. v1p0831c1s
v1p1397c1s
Peacock, G.J. v3p0016c2s
Peacock, J.S. v1p0772c2s
Peacock, M. v4p0333c1s
v5p0043c2s
Peacock, Mabel v4p0050c2s
v4p0110c1s v4p0140c1s v4p0150c1s
v4p0205c2s v5p0270c1s v5p0270c2s
v5p0339c2s
Peacock, N. v5p0156c2s
v5p0344c1s v5p0502c2s
Peacock, R. v1p0568c2s
Peacock, R.A. v1p1246c2m
Peacock, T.L. v1p0217c2s
v1p0342c2s v1p0555c1s v1p0560c1s
v1p0603c2s v1p0908c2s v1p1189c2m
v3p0465c2s
Peacock, V.T. v5p0069c1s
v5p0084c2s v5p0150c1s v5p0510c2s
v6p0380c2s
Peacock, W.F. v1p0350c2s
Peak, H. v6p0153c2s
Peake, A.S. v4p0099c2s
v6p0040c1s v6p0341c1s
Peake, E.E. v5p0093c2s
v5p0263c2s v5p0265c2s v5p0269c2s
v5p0272c2s v5p0389c2s v5p0411c2s
v5p0425c2s v5p0442c2s v5p0458c1s
v5p0494c2s v6p0007c2s v6p0046c1s
v6p0140c2s v6p0229c1s v6p0285c1s
v6p0709c1s
Peake, F. v4p0557c2s
v6p0626c2s
Peake, H. v6p0663c1s
Peake, R.B. v1p0038c2s
v1p0574c1s v1p0692c2s v1p1033c1s
v1p1038c1s v1p1314c2s v1p1322c1s
Peal, S.E. v1p0233c2s
v2p0025c1s v2p0179c1s v2p0289c2s
v2p0296c2s v2p0342c1s v2p0344c2s
v3p0045c2s v3p0155c2s v4p0357c2m
v4p0383c1s
Peale, A.C. v1p0551c1s
v1p1147c1s v1p1304c2s v2p0177c2m
v2p0245c2s
Peale, A.C. et al. v2p0467c1s
Peale, F. v1p0087c2s
v1p0635c2s
Peale, R. v1p0983c2s
v1p1388c1s
Peale, T.R. v1p0437c1s
Pearce, E.H. v3p0082c1s
v4p0110c2s v4p0125c2s
Pearce, E.K. v4p0001c1s
v4p0509c2s
Pearce, F.B. v5p0005c2s
Pearce, H. v1p0009c1s
v1p0286c2s v1p0506c2s v1p0524c1s
v1p0922c1s v1p0983c1s v1p1381c2m
v1p1416c1s
Pearce, H.G. v4p0007c2s
Pearce, H.J. v6p0040c2s
v6p0307c2s
Pearce, R. v3p0176c1s
Pearce, S. v1p1266c1s
Pearce, S.A. v1p0571c1s
v1p0883c2s v1p0884c1s v1p1007c2s
v2p0302c2s
Pearce, S.H. and Penfield, S.L.
v4p0451c1s
Peard, F.M. v1p0786c2s
v2p0318c1s v2p0402c1s v3p0324c1s
v4p0062c2s v5p0094c1s v5p0165c2s
v6p0164c2s v6p0292c1s
Peard, Frances M. v4p0089c1s
v4p0287c2s v6p0248c1s v6p0485c2s
Peard, G. v1p0592c2s
v1p1336c2s
Peard, W. v3p0373c1s
Peareson, P.E. v6p0684c1s
Pearis, C.F. v5p0146c1s
Pearl, R. v6p0077c2s
v6p0151c2s v6p0387c1s
Pearle, Mary v4p0469c1s
Pearmain, A.V. v5p0512c1s
Pearman, M.T. v4p0104c2s
Pearman, W.D. v1p0256c1s
v1p0262c1s
Pearne, T.H. v1p0487c1s
v2p0362c2s v3p0299c1s v4p0367c2m
v4p0478c2s v4p0588c1s
Pearre, S.E. v1p0450c2s
v1p0980c2s
Pears, E. v1p1332c2s

v4p0539c2s
Pears, S.A. and Jewitt, L.
v1p1311c1s
Pearsall, R. v1p0567c1s
Pearsall, R.L. v1p0370c1s
v1p0709c2s
Pearse, A.L. v4p0230c1s
Pearse, A.S. v6p0148c2s
v6p0173c1s v6p0660c2s
Pearse, C.G. et al. v5p0512c1s
Pearse, H. v5p0089c2s
v5p0166c1s v5p0285c2s v5p0313c1s
v5p0332c1s v5p0529c1s v5p0562c2s
v5p0586c2s v6p0399c2s
Pearse, H.H.S. v4p0097c2s
v6p0132c1s
Pearse, H.W. v5p0313c1s
v5p0614c2s
Pearse, J. v4p0079c2s
v4p0150c1s
Pearse, J.B. v1p0666c1s
v1p0844c2s v1p1075c1m v1p1250c2s
v1p1251c2s
Pearse, M.G. v2p0205c1s
v2p0206c1s v3p0101c1s v3p0319c2s
v6p0543c2s
Pearse, Mark G. v6p0663c2s
Pearse, R.L. v5p0563c1s
Pearse, T.F. v1p0265c1s
Pearson, A. v2p0403c2s
Pearson, A.C. v3p0076c1s
v5p0018c1s
Pearson, A.N. v2p0035c1m
Pearson, A.W. v4p0233c2s
v4p0234c2m
Pearson, C. v4p0235c2s
v4p0284c1s v4p0617c2s
Pearson, C.A. v6p0240c2s
Pearson, C.B. v1p0619c2s
v1p0620c2s v2p0085c2s v2p0243c2s
Pearson, C.H. v1p0078c2s
v1p0974c2s v1p1351c1s v1p1370c1s
v2p0029c1s v4p0351c2s v4p0394c1s
v4p0436c2s
Pearson, C.W. v6p0060c2s
Pearson, F.S. v5p0182c2s
Pearson, G.F. v2p0162c1s
v2p0162c2m v3p0158c1s
Pearson, H.C. v4p0021c2s
v4p0095c2s v4p0118c1s v4p0317c2s
v5p0516c1s
Pearson, H.G. v4p0446c2s
Pearson, H.H.W. v5p0453c2s
Pearson, Helen C. v6p0703c2s
Pearson, J. v2p0037c2s
v2p0440c2s v3p0085c1s v3p0373c2s
Pearson, John v4p0367c2s
Pearson, K. v2p0116c1s
v2p0129c2s v2p0135c2s v2p0268c1s
v2p0269c1s v2p0301c2s v2p0383c2s
v2p0414c2s v2p0451c2s v2p0455c2s
v2p0473c2s v2p0479c1s v3p0125c2s
v3p0157c2s v3p0169c2m v3p0257c2s
v3p0339c1s v4p0103c2s v4p0186c1s
v4p0340c2s v4p0366c2s v4p0375c2s
v4p0380c1s v4p0394c2s v4p0450c2s
v4p0507c2s v4p0514c1s v4p0533c1s
v4p0597c2s v4p0625c2s v5p0263c1s
v5p0366c1s v6p0067c1s v6p0319c2s
Pearson, K. and Beeton, Mary
v5p0347c1s
Pearson, K. and Hutchinson, J.
v2p0042c1s
Pearson, K. and Lee, A. .. v5p0475c2s
Pearson, K. and Merk, C.H.
v4p0345c1s
Pearson, K. and Watts, C.A.
v5p0008c2s
Pearson, K. et al. v3p0257c2s
Pearson, Karl v5p0485c2s
v6p0067c1s
Pearson, N. v2p0027c1s
v2p0111c1s v2p0123c1s v2p0169c2s
v2p0251c1s v2p0264c2s v2p0325c2s
v2p0362c1s v2p0391c1s v2p0391c2s
v2p0410c2s v2p0424c1s v3p0014c1s
v3p0209c1s v4p0394c2s v4p0456c1s
v6p0214c1s v6p0352c2s v6p0391c2s
v6p0428c2s
Pearson, N. and Thornely, T.
v1p0989c2s
Pearson, P.H. v5p0053c1s
Pearson, P.M. v6p0390c2s
Pearson, R.A. v5p0015c1s
v5p0376c1s
Pearson, R.M. v6p0111c1s
Pearson, S. v1p0291c1s
v2p0098c2s v2p0099c1s v2p0342c1s
v2p0352c1s v2p0359c1s v2p0392c2s
v3p0166c1s v3p0276c2s
Pearson, T. v1p0639c1s
Pearson, T.R. v5p0003c2s
v5p0562c2s v6p0597c1s
Pearsons, G.W. v2p0240c2s
Pearsons, J.C. and Hutchins, C.C.
v6p0009c2s
Peart, S.E. v3p0388c2s
v4p0517c1s
Peart-Robinson, W. v4p0236c1s
Peary, F.P. v6p0271c2s
Peary, R.E. v3p0305c1m
v4p0242c2s v4p0403c2s v5p0027c1s
v5p0250c2s v5p0414c1s v6p0029c1m
v6p0123c2s v6p0250c1s v6p0486c1s
v6p0561c2s v6p0597c1s
Peary, R.E. and Bridgman, H.L.
v5p0438c1s
Peary, Robert E. v6p0016c2s
Pease, A.E. v4p0005c2s
v5p0538c2s
Pease, A.G. v1p0129c1s
v1p0598c2s
Pease, Alfred E. v6p0654c2s
Pease, C. v1p0262c2s
v1p1043c2s v1p1065c1s
Pease, E.R. v2p0115c2s
v3p0238c2s v5p0273c1s v6p0508c2s
Pease, F.C. v4p0372c2s
Pease, F.S. v1p0617c1m
v1p0984c1m
Pease, G.C. v4p0407c2s
Pease, G.W. v5p0561c2s
v6p0626c2m
Pease, H.M. v5p0176c1m
v6p0189c1s
Pease, Marion F. v4p0629c2s
Pease, T.C. v2p0059c1s
v5p0059c1s
Pease, V.S. v4p0328c1s
Peaslee, C.L. v4p0138c1s
Peaslee, E.R. v1p0019c2s
Peaslee, J.B. v2p0297c1s
v2p0358c2s
Peaslee, R.J. v6p0176c2s
v6p0584c1s
Peat, H. v2p0416c2s
Peat, J.B. v4p0044c1s
v4p0199c1s v4p0458c1s
Peatfield, J.J. v1p0271c1s
v1p0560c1s v4p0043c2s v4p0084c1s
v4p0161c2s v4p0374c1s v4p0543c1s
v6p0070c1s v6p0092c2s v6p0246c2s
v6p0404c2s v6p0439c2s v6p0444c2s
v6p0508c1s v6p0606c2s
Peattie, E.W. v3p0105c1s
v3p0118c1s v3p0277c2s v3p0375c1s
v4p0088c2s v4p0303c1s v5p0008c2s
v5p0105c1s v5p0195c1s v5p0349c2s
v5p0358c2s v6p0394c1s v6p0434c1s
v6p0501c2s v6p0612c2s v6p0644c2s
Peattie, Eliz W. v6p0249c1s
Peavey, Amy Z. v5p0393c2s
Pebody, C. v1p0178c2s
v1p0200c1s v1p0370c1s v1p0383c2s
v1p0441c2s v1p0596c2s v1p0681c1s
v1p0719c2s v1p0781c2s v1p1033c1s
v1p1168c2s v1p1211c2s
Pecant, F. v3p0335c2s
Pecco and Prinetti v2p0406c2s
Pechell, M. v4p0153c1s
v4p0373c1s v4p0436c1s
Pechenard, P.L. v5p0493c1s
Pechey, W.A. v1p0303c1s
Peck, A.C. v3p0342c1s
Peck, A.L. v2p0180c2s
v4p0329c1s v5p0335c1s v5p0479c2s
Peck, A.M. v4p0397c2s
v4p0463c1s
Peck, A.S. v4p0241c1s
v4p0361c2s v4p0429c2s v5p0389c1s
v6p0020c1s
Peck, C.H. v2p0088c1s
v3p0061c1s v3p0446c2s v5p0343c1s
Peck, D. v1p0247c1s
v1p0248c1s v1p0293c1s
Peck, E. v3p0244c2s
v5p0327c2s v5p0336c1s v6p0144c2s
Peck, E.B. v5p0024c2s
v5p0414c1s
Peck, E.F. v6p0308c1s
v6p0344c1s v6p0403c1s v6p0510c2s
Peck, E.J. v5p0323c1s
Peck, F. v1p0426c1s
v2p0371c1s v3p0257c1s
Peck, F.W. v5p0431c2s
Peck, G. v1p0130c2s
v1p0171c1s v1p0238c2s v1p0430c2s
v1p0432c1s v1p0470c2s v1p0782c1s
v1p0872c1s v1p0980c2s v1p0990c1s
v1p1085c1s v1p1089c2s v1p1120c2s
v1p1165c2s v1p1434c2s
Peck, G.A. v4p0558c1s
Peck, G.B. v6p0032c2s
Peck, G.M. v6p0106c2s
Peck, G.R. v5p0600c1s
v6p0323c1s
Peck, G.W. v1p0050c1s
v1p0081c1s v1p0167c1s v1p0231c1s
v1p0237c2s v1p0258c1s v1p0443c2s
v1p0520c1s v1p0569c2s v1p0596c1s
v1p0616c2s v1p0719c2s v1p0768c1s
v1p0818c2s v1p1136c1s v1p1185c1s
v1p1383c2s v1p1416c2s
Peck, H.J. v1p0340c2s
v1p0772c2s v6p0699c2s
Peck, H.T. v3p0005c2s
v3p0312c2s v4p0146c2s v4p0163c1s
v4p0202c1s v4p0229c2s v4p0305c1s
v4p0381c2s v4p0405c2s v4p0415c2s
v4p0449c1s v4p0536c2s v5p0028c1s
v5p0040c2s v5p0044c2s v5p0051c1s
v5p0058c2s v5p0064c2s v5p0096c1s
v5p0123c1s v5p0144c2s v5p0153c2s
v5p0154c1s v5p0167c1s v5p0169c2m
v5p0171c2s v5p0191c2s v5p0235c1s
v5p0242c1s v5p0270c2s v5p0274c2s
v5p0290c2s v5p0317c1s v5p0341c1s
v5p0341c2s v5p0342c2s v5p0354c1s
v5p0357c2s v5p0369c2s v5p0383c1s
v5p0385c2s v5p0397c1s v5p0409c2s
v5p0411c1s v5p0440c2s v5p0465c1s
v5p0466c1s v5p0486c2s v5p0514c1s
v5p0545c2s v5p0581c1s v5p0583c2s
v5p0587c1s v5p0591c1s v5p0597c2s
v5p0620c1m v5p0635c2m v5p0636c2s
v5p0638c1s v6p0011c1s v6p0055c2s
v6p0075c1s v6p0101c2s v6p0154c2s
v6p0220c2m v6p0278c2s v6p0287c1s
v6p0289c1s v6p0290c2s v6p0352c1s
v6p0473c1s v6p0491c1s v6p0503c2s
v6p0515c1s v6p0587c1s v6p0625c1s
v6p0657c2s v6p0670c1s v6p0671c1s
v6p0689c1s v6p0713c1s
Peck, H.T. and Walker, J.B.
v5p0178c2s
Peck, H.W. v6p0032c1s
Peck, Harvey W. v6p0202c1s
Peck, J. v1p0533c2s
Peck, J.M. v1p0097c1s
v1p0097c2m v1p0136c2s v1p0149c2m
v1p0192c1s v1p0624c1s v1p0772c1s
v1p0852c2s v1p0854c2s v1p0855c1s
v1p1048c2s v1p1399c2s
Peck, J.O. et al. v2p0106c2s
v4p0482c2s
Peck, J.S. v6p0653c2s
Peck, J.T. v1p0597c1s
v1p0830c1s v1p0831c1s v1p0989c2s
v1p1004c2s v1p1104c2m v1p1307c1s
v2p0286c1s
Peck, L.H. v5p0504c1s
Peck, L.W. v1p0033c1s
v1p0144c2s v1p0169c2s v1p0437c1s
v1p0854c2s v1p1292c2s v1p1435c1s
v2p0150c2s
Peck, M. v4p0148c2s
Peck, M.A. v4p0233c2s
v4p0453c2s
Peck, M.B. v5p0294c1s
Peck, S.M. v5p0167c1s
v5p0274c1s v5p0429c2s v5p0591c2s
Peck, T. v2p0481c2s
v3p0243c2s v6p0595c1s
Peck, T.B. v6p0130c1s
v6p0546c1s
Peck, W.F. v3p0179c1s
v3p0401c2s
Peck, W.F.G. v1p0221c1s
Peck, W.T. v3p0243c2s
Peckham, A.W. v5p0193c2s
Peckham, G. v2p0198c2s
v2p0221c1s
Peckham, G.W. v4p0329c1s
Peckham, Grace v3p0300c1s
v3p0331c2s
Peckham, H.E. v5p0065c2s
Peckham, S.F. v1p0840c1s
v1p0848c2s v1p0995c2m v2p0048c1s
v2p0242c2s v4p0033c1m v4p0062c2m
v4p0444c2s v5p0034c2m v5p0065c2s
v5p0099c1s v5p0430c1s v5p0442c2m
v5p0486c2s v6p0484c2s v6p0486c1s
v6p0545c1s v6p0578c1s v6p0620c2s
Peckham, S.F. and Hall, C.W.
v1p0751c1s
Peckham, S.F. and Linton, L.A.
v4p0444c2s
Peckham, S.P. v6p0363c1s
Peckham, W.C. v5p0010c1s
v5p0645c2s
Peckham, W.G. v6p0365c1s
Peclet, E. v1p0579c2s
Pedder, D.C. v5p0203c1s
v6p0060c1s v6p0126c1s v6p0178c2s
v6p0192c1s v6p0206c1s v6p0360c1s
v6p0378c2s v6p0404c1s v6p0481c2s
v6p0499c2s v6p0664c2s v6p0679c1m
Pedder, H.C. v1p1086c1s
v2p0052c2s v2p0190c2s v2p0211c1s
v2p0265c2s v2p0397c2s v2p0477c1s
v2p0479c2s
Pedder, W.G. v1p0631c1s
v2p0218c2s v3p0186c2s v3p0211c2s
v3p0212c2m v3p0242c1s v3p0424c1s
v3p0450c1s
Peddie, J.W. v4p0324c1s
Peddie, R.A. v6p0312c1m
Peddie, W. v2p0299c2s
Pedler, A. v4p0281c1s
Pedley, H. v1p1302c1s
Pedrick, J.G. v5p0515c2s
Peebles, H.P. v3p0446c1s
Peebles, J.K. v4p0299c1s
Peebles, J.M. v6p0455c1s
Peebles, P. v1p0112c2s
Peek, C.E. and Ranyard, A.C.
v3p0407c2s
Peek, F. v1p0015c2s
v1p0387c2s v1p0441c1s v1p0649c1s
v1p0700c1s v1p0949c2s v1p0981c2s

v1p1065c2s v1p1097c2s v2p0152c1s v2p0252c1s v2p0349c1s v2p0355c1s v2p0384c2s v3p0050c1s v3p0233c2s v3p0371c1s v3p0472c2s v4p0068c1s v4p0113c1s v4p0497c2s v5p0117c2s v5p0177c2s
Peek, F. and Hall, E.T. .. v4p0115c2s
Peek, G.M. v6p0524c1s
Peek, H. v4p0397c2s v5p0547c1s
Peeke, M.B. v4p0410c1m v4p0463c2s v4p0542c1s v4p0622c1s
Peel, C. v6p0266c1s
Peel, E.L. v2p0030c1s v2p0447c1s v2p0459c2s
Peel, E.Lennox v2p0078c1s
Peel, G. v4p0034c2s v4p0378c1s v4p0433c1s v4p0525c1s v4p0526c1s v5p0421c1s v5p0589c1s v6p0095c2s v6p0108c1s
Peel, Geo. v6p0162c2s v6p0169c1s
Peel, R., Sir v1p0326c1s
Peel, S. v4p0418c1s v5p0148c2s v5p0424c1s v6p0195c2s v6p0329c1s
Peel, W.L. v3p0121c1s
Peel, W.Laidlaw v4p0571c1s
Peele, F. v2p0389c2s
Peer, F.S. v5p0097c2m
Peer, P.S. v4p0317c2s v4p0634c2s
Peerce, J.B. v2p0197c2s
Peers, C.R. v5p0495c2s
Peery, J.C. v6p0575c1s
Peery, R.B. v5p0307c1s v5p0319c2s v6p0159c2m
Peet, E.W. v4p0336c2s
Peet, H.L. v1p0337c1s
Peet, H.P. v1p0337c1m
Peet, J.S. v2p0100c1s
Peet, L.R. v3p0195c1s
Peet, S. v3p0350c1s
Peet, S.D. v2p0010c1s v2p0010c2s v2p0012c1s v2p0014c2s v2p0016c2s v2p0018c2m v2p0020c1s v2p0045c1s v2p0115c1s v2p0211c1s v2p0219c2m v2p0220c1m v2p0274c1s v2p0300c1m v2p0320c1s v2p0352c1s v2p0395c1s v2p0429c1m v2p0434c2s v2p0443c2s v2p0461c1m v3p0014c1s v3p0018c1s v3p0085c2s v3p0088c1s v3p0106c2s v3p0130c2s v3p0155c2s v3p0202c2s v3p0277c2s v3p0289c2m v3p0290c1m v3p0342c2m v3p0385c2s v3p0410c2m v3p0416c1m v3p0450c1s v4p0020c1s v4p0034c1s v4p0043c2s v4p0083c1s v4p0119c2s v4p0126c1s v4p0138c2s v4p0157c1s v4p0229c2s v4p0256c1s v4p0258c2s v4p0273c2s v4p0282c1s v4p0311c2s v4p0351c2s v4p0355c1s v4p0360c1s v4p0385c1m v4p0391c2m v4p0456c2s v4p0466c2m v4p0473c1s v4p0479c1s v4p0497c2s v4p0515c2s v4p0529c1s v4p0587c2s v4p0624c1s v5p0014c2s v5p0026c2m v5p0041c2s v5p0069c1s v5p0076c2s v5p0092c1s v5p0098c2s v5p0123c1m v5p0129c1s v5p0172c1m v5p0299c1s v5p0367c1s v5p0463c2m v5p0472c1m v5p0490c1s v5p0520c2s v5p0554c1m v5p0582c1s v5p0583c2s v6p0013c2s v6p0014c2s v6p0015c1s v6p0018c1s v6p0023c2s v6p0027c2s v6p0033c1s v6p0033c2s v6p0069c2s v6p0107c1s v6p0128c1m v6p0146c1s v6p0149c1m v6p0169c2s v6p0295c2s v6p0309c2s v6p0316c2m v6p0317c1s v6p0432c2m v6p0490c1s v6p0512c1s v6p0540c2s v6p0581c2s v6p0638c1m v6p0656c1s v6p0679c1s
Peet, W. v1p0312c1s
Peet, W.B. v4p0149c2s
Peffer, W.A. v3p0149c2s v4p0453c1s v5p0281c1s v5p0313c2s v5p0382c2s v5p0440c1s v5p0445c2s v5p0468c1s v5p0519c2m v5p0593c1m
Pegge, S. v1p0020c1s v1p0021c1s v1p0084c2s v1p0109c1s v1p0159c2s v1p0165c2s v1p0175c1s v1p0210c2s v1p0218c2s v1p0227c1s v1p0270c2s v1p0272c1m v1p0272c2s v1p0296c2s v1p0311c2s v1p0320c2s v1p0335c2s v1p0345c2s v1p0368c1m v1p0384c1s v1p0393c1s v1p0464c2s v1p0521c2s v1p0557c2s v1p0604c1m v1p0605c1s v1p0616c2s v1p0660c1s v1p0691c2m v1p0693c1s v1p0710c1s v1p0732c1s v1p0750c2s v1p0848c2s v1p0924c1s v1p1013c2s v1p1113c2s v1p1115c1s v1p1122c1s v1p1131c2s v1p1140c1s v1p1149c2s v1p1154c2m v1p1173c2m v1p1178c2s v1p1179c1s v1p1255c2s v1p1299c1s v1p1329c1s v1p1359c1s v1p1372c1m v2p0174c2s
Pegge, S. and Brander, G.. v1p0135c1s
Pegge, S. and Lyttelton, C. v1p1255c2s
Pegler, A.J. v5p0643c1s
Pegram, G.B. v5p0475c2s
Pelle, J.H.F. v6p0078c2s v6p0473c1s
Peill, J. v3p0263c1s
Peipers, C. v1p1251c1s
Peirce, A.W. v4p0514c1m
Peirce, A.W. and Gooch, F.A. v4p0514c1m
Peirce, B. v1p0154c2s v1p0281c2s v1p0375c1m v1p0725c1s v1p0827c1s v1p0902c2s v1p1161c1s
Peirce, B.K. v1p0700c2s
Peirce, B.O. v4p0349c2s v4p0353c1s v4p0446c1s v5p0356c1s v5p0440c2s
Peirce, B.O. and Willson, R.W. v3p0036c1s v4p0355c1s
Peirce, B.O. and Wilson, R.W. v4p0529c1s
Peirce, C. v1p1085c1s
Peirce, C.L. v4p0176c1s v5p0251c1s
Peirce, C.S. v1p0114c1s v1p0224c2s v1p0278c2s v1p0417c1s v1p0439c1s v1p0623c1s v1p0627c2s v1p0648c2s v1p0760c2m v1p0843c2s v1p0986c2m v1p1000c2s v1p1014c1s v1p1162c1s v1p1234c1s v1p1275c1s v2p0312c1s v2p0335c1s v3p0255c1s v3p0255c2s v3p0348c2s v3p0428c1s v4p0009c2s v4p0034c1s v4p0128c1m v4p0148c1s v4p0183c2s v4p0217c2s v4p0223c1s v4p0270c2s v4p0326c1s v4p0338c1s v4p0343c1s v4p0349c2s v4p0352c1m v4p0363c1s v4p0372c1s v4p0396c1m v4p0398c2s v4p0465c1s v4p0468c1s v4p0478c1s v4p0509c2s v4p0542c1s v4p0573c1s v5p0054c1s v5p0264c1s v5p0344c2s v5p0377c1s v5p0454c2s v5p0470c2s v5p0483c1s v5p0513c2s v5p0559c2s v6p0030c1s v6p0038c1s v6p0085c1s v6p0112c1s v6p0142c2s v6p0171c1s v6p0185c1s v6p0286c1s v6p0349c2s v6p0383c1s v6p0413c2s v6p0442c2m v6p0496c1s v6p0513c1m v6p0527c1s v6p0602c1s v6p0610c1s v6p0610c2s v6p0689c1s
Peirce, C.S. and Sturgis, R. v1p0246c1s
Peirce, E.L. v1p0698c1s v1p1369c1s
Peirce, E.W. v1p0099c1s v1p0335c1s v1p0957c2s v1p1009c1s v1p1129c2s v1p1259c1s v1p1395c1s
Peirce, G.H. v1p0016c2s v2p0068c1s v2p0077c2s v2p0275c2s v2p0283c2s v2p0365c2s v3p0286c1s v4p0206c2s v4p0243c1s
Peirce, G.Howard v5p0055c1s
Peirce, G.J. v5p0073c1s v5p0486c1s v6p0288c1s v6p0503c1s
Peirce, H.H.D. v5p0162c1s v6p0557c2s
Peirce, J. v1p0268c2s
Peirce, J.B. v2p0171c1s
Peirce, J.M. v1p0791c1s v4p0010c2s v5p0016c2s
Peirce, J.O. v6p0018c1s
Peirce, Mary F. v4p0631c2s
Peirce, W.S. v1p0258c1s
Peirce, Z.F. v1p1388c2s
Peirse, B.M. v3p0044c2s
Peirson, A.L. v1p1005c1s
Peirson, L.J. v1p1280c2s
Peixotto, E.C. v4p0501c2s v5p0011c1s v5p0094c1s v5p0113c2s v5p0137c1s v5p0214c2s v5p0291c1s v5p0343c2s v5p0431c2s v5p0432c1s v5p0583c2s v6p0131c2s v6p0163c2s v6p0210c1s v6p0241c2s v6p0281c1s v6p0396c2s v6p0401c1s v6p0531c2s v6p0545c1s v6p0660c2s
Peixotto, M. v6p0569c2s
Peixotto, M.H. v6p0131c2s v6p0257c2s
Peixotto, Mary A. v5p0560c1s
Peixotto, Mary H. v6p0431c2s v6p0662c2s v6p0676c2s
Peixotto, S.S. v6p0139c2s
Peladan, J. v6p0481c2s
Peladan, Sar v6p0027c1s
Pelet, P. v6p0634c2s
Pelet-Narbonne, Lieut.-Gen.Von v6p0105c2s
Pelford, W.H. v6p0282c2s
Pelham, A.F. v2p0377c2s
Pelham, H.F. v1p1018c1s v4p0028c2s v6p0548c1s v6p0548c2s
Pelham-Clinton, C.S. v3p0047c1s v3p0124c1s v3p0127c1s v3p0159c2s v3p0406c1s v3p0459c2s v3p0471c2s v4p0356c1s v5p0253c1s v5p0457c1s v5p0611c2s
Pell, Albert v2p0431c2s
Pell, E.L. v5p0351c2s
Pell, H. v4p0342c2s
Pellatt, A. v1p1039c1s
Pellatt, F. v1p0525c2s v1p0664c1s
Pelletan, C. v3p0052c1s v3p0159c2s v3p0171c2s
Pelletier, J. v1p1364c2s
Pelletier, M.C. v4p0068c2s v4p0482c2s
Pelletier, Mabel C. v4p0013c1s v4p0305c1s
Pelletreau, W.S. v3p0119c2s v3p0235c2s v3p0329c2s
Pellew, C.E. v5p0011c2s
Pellew, C.E. and Chandler, C.F. v6p0195c2s
Pellew, E.F. v2p0346c1s
Pellew, F.H. v3p0195c1s v5p0199c1s
Pellew, G. v3p0011c2s v3p0015c2s v3p0151c2s v3p0355c1s v3p0469c2s v4p0575c2s
Pelly, Col. v1p0629c1s
Pelly, F.W. v4p0194c2s v5p0495c1s v6p0514c1s
Pelly, L. v4p0089c2s
Peloubet, F.N. v4p0557c2s
Pelt, D.Van v1p0419c2s v1p1093c1s v2p0235c1s v3p0043c1s v3p0332c2s v4p0164c2s v4p0246c2s v4p0317c2s v4p0380c2s v4p0401c1s v4p0603c1s
Pelt, J.R.Van v6p0293c2m
Pelton, J.C. v3p0063c1s
Pelton, J.L. v4p0550c2s
Peltz, P. v1p1090c2s
Peltzer, R. v1p0939c1s
Pelz, P.J. v4p0129c2s
Pember, A. v1p0550c2s v1p1109c2s v2p0085c1s v3p0052c2m v3p0077c1s v3p0378c2s
Pember, E.H. v6p0274c2s
Pember, G.H. v3p0405c1s
Pember, P.Y. v1p0851c2s v2p0462c1s
Pember, P.Y., Mrs. v6p0516c2s
Pemberton, C.F. v2p0167c2s
Pemberton, C.H. v4p0104c1s v5p0403c2s v5p0473c1s
Pemberton, E.L. v2p0189c2s v2p0247c2s v3p0431c1s
Pemberton, H. v1p0749c2s v3p0009c2s
Pemberton, H., jr. v2p0009c1s v2p0154c1s v2p0340c1s v2p0424c2s v4p0440c1s
Pemberton, H.L.C. v2p0271c1s v2p0338c2s
Pemberton, J. v5p0359c2s
Pemberton, J.C. v2p0460c1s
Pemberton, Jeannette v6p0398c2s
Pemberton, M. v4p0045c2s v4p0090c2s v4p0295c2s v4p0301c2s v4p0414c2s v4p0425c1s v4p0562c2s v4p0572c1s v5p0225c2s v5p0282c1s v5p0467c1s v5p0635c2s v6p0165c2s v6p0261c1s
Pemberton, Max v5p0252c1s
Pemberton, T.E. v3p0401c1s v4p0003c1s v4p0424c1s v4p0518c2s v4p0572c2s v6p0108c1s v6p0173c1s v6p0330c1s
Pemberton, T,E. v6p0020c1s
Pemberton-Grund, J. v4p0163c2s v5p0170c2s
Pembrey, M.S. v4p0018c2s
Pembroke v4p0266c1s
Pembroke, Beatrix, Countess of v5p0632c1s
Pembroke, Earl v3p0163c1s v3p0202c1s
Pembroke, Earl of v1p0145c1s v1p0452c1s v1p0714c1s v2p0209c1s v2p0255c1m v2p0407c2s
Penard, E. v4p0483c1s
Pence, C.R. v3p0442c1s
Penck, A. v4p0633c1s v5p0449c1s v6p0131c2m v6p0400c1s
Pendered, M.L. v3p0196c2s v5p0053c1s v5p0240c1s v5p0274c1s v5p0424c1s v5p0530c1s v5p0577c2s v6p0003c2s v6p0327c2s
Pendered, Mary L. v4p0310c2s v4p0374c1s v5p0547c1s v5p0563c1s
Penderel-Brodhurst, J. ... v3p0050c2s v3p0382c1s v3p0462c2s v4p0182c2s v4p0250c1s v4p0345c2s v4p0493c1s v4p0493c2m v4p0571c2s v4p0587c1s v5p0352c2s
Pendexter, H. v6p0466c1s v6p0469c1s v6p0651c1s v6p0695c1s
Pendexter, Hugh v6p0029c1s v6p0176c1s v6p0287c2s v6p0679c2s
Pendlebury, W.H. v5p0076c2s
Pendleton, A.M. v1p0742c2s
Pendleton, E.P. v6p0319c1s
Pendleton, H.B. v6p0446c2s
Pendleton, J. v4p0099c2s v4p0168c2s v4p0372c1s v4p0402c2s v5p0124c1s v5p0409c2m v5p0410c1s v5p0477c1s v5p0504c2s v5p0561c2s v5p0594c2s v6p0050c1s v6p0079c1s v6p0549c1s v6p0551c2s v6p0703c1s
Pendleton, J.M. v2p0099c2s
Pendleton, J.S. v1p0112c1s
Pendleton, John v4p0402c2s

v4p0471c1s v5p0176c2s v5p0232c1s v5p0414c2s
Pendleton, L. v2p0048c2s v4p0134c2s v4p0396c2s
Pendleton, W.E. v6p0049c1s v6p0684c1s
Pendleton, W.K. v1p0074c2s v1p0095c2s v1p0240c1s v1p0359c1s v1p0626c1s v1p1222c1s v2p0083c2s v2p0389c1s
Pendleton, W.N. v1p0288c2s v1p0367c1s v1p0518c2s v1p0660c2s v1p0734c1s
Pendred, H.W. v1p1079c2s v1p1141c2s
Pendred, V. v1p0759c1s
Penfield, E. v5p0124c1s v6p0123c2s v6p0294c2m v6p0607c2s
Penfield, F.C. v4p0172c2m v5p0001c1m v5p0087c2s v5p0181c1s v5p0356c1s v5p0411c2s v5p0412c1s v5p0497c1s v6p0008c1s v6p0152c2s v6p0334c2s v6p0395c2s v6p0426c1s v6p0457c2s v6p0476c2s v6p0477c2s v6p0485c2s v6p0624c1s
Penfield, F.E. v4p0173c2s
Penfield, S.L. v1p0047c1s v1p0230c2s v2p0013c1s v2p0108c2s v2p0160c1s v2p0171c2s v2p0290c1s v2p0294c2s v2p0438c2s v2p0457c2s v3p0015c1s v3p0027c1s v3p0039c2m v3p0072c2s v3p0097c1s v3p0329c1s v3p0350c1s v3p0403c1s v4p0026c1s v4p0082c2m v4p0087c1s v4p0132c1s v4p0255c1s v4p0353c1s v4p0372c1s v4p0432c1s v4p0434c2s v4p0613c1s v5p0241c2s v5p0255c1s v5p0377c1s v5p0552c2s v5p0560c1s v5p0595c1s v6p0160c1m v6p0510c2s v6p0617c1s
Penfield, S.L. and Dana, E.S. v2p0285c2s v3p0336c1s
Penfield, S.L. and Foote, H.W. v5p0065c2s v5p0123c1s v5p0280c1s v5p0492c1s v5p0583c2s
Penfield, S.L. and Forbes, E.H. v4p0380c2s
Penfield, S.L. and Ford, W.E. v5p0087c2m v6p0617c2s
Penfield, S.L. and Genth, F.A. v3p0242c2s
Penfield, S.L. and Harper, D.N. v2p0041c1s v2p0201c1s v2p0364c2s
Penfield, S.L. and Hidden, W.E. v3p0188c2s
Penfield, S.L. and Hillebrand, W.F. v6p0014c1s
Penfield, S.L. and Iddings, J.P. v3p0150c2s
Penfield, S.L. and Jamieson, G.S. v6p0663c1s
Penfield, S.L. and Pearce, S.H. v4p0451c1s
Penfield, S.L. and Pratt, J.H. v4p0546c2s v4p0572c1s v4p0617c2s
Penfield, S.L. and Sperry, E.S. v3p0203c2s
Penfield, S.L. and Sperry, F.L. v2p0171c2s v3p0150c2s
Penfield, S.L. and Warren, C.H. v5p0225c2s v5p0432c2s v5p0645c2s
Penfield, S.L. and Wells, H.L. v2p0175c1s v4p0255c1s v6p0610c2s
Penfield, S.N. v5p0521c1s
Penfield, W.L. v1p0779c1s v2p0452c1s v3p0246c1s v5p0452c1s v5p0550c1s v6p0265c1s v6p0500c2s v6p0676c1s
Pengelly, A. v2p0162c2s
Pengelly, W. v1p0209c1s v1p0347c2s v1p0556c2s v1p0706c1s v2p0016c2s v2p0072c1s v2p0158c2s v2p0186c1s v2p0270c2s v2p0273c2s v2p0352c1s v2p0364c1s
Penguin v2p0392c2s v5p0492c1s
Penhallow, D.P. v1p0016c2s v2p0234c1s v2p0282c2s v2p0344c1m v2p0434c2s v2p0467c1s v4p0197c1s v4p0449c1s v5p0371c1s v5p0428c1s v5p0639c2s v6p0070c2s v6p0104c1s v6p0145c1m v6p0412c1s v6p0565c2s
Penhallow, J.D.P. v4p0186c1s
Penhallow, P.W. v1p0986c2s
Penman, F. v5p0302c1s v5p0379c2s
Penman, H.C. v6p0618c2s
Penn, A. v2p0051c1s v2p0051c2s v2p0052c1s v2p0068c1s v6p0209c2s v6p0391c1s
Penn, A.G. v1p0007c1s v1p0073c1s v1p0155c2s v1p0225c1s v1p1202c2s
Penn, Arthur v5p0040c2s v6p0148c1s
Penn, H. v5p0165c2s v5p0271c2s
Penn, H.C. v3p0340c2s
Penn, J.A. v5p0017c2s v5p0290c1s
Penn, M.E. v1p0627c1s v1p0921c2s v1p0941c1s v2p0123c1s v2p0216c1s v2p0321c2s v2p0326c1s v2p0434c2s v3p0216c1s v3p0286c1s v4p0552c1s
Penn, M.E.S. v4p0213c2s v4p0285c1s v4p0391c2s v4p0590c2s v4p0605c1s v5p0518c1s
Penn, Mary E. v3p0209c2s
Penn, R. v4p0196c1s v4p0413c1s v4p0571c2s
Penn, W. v2p0335c2s
Penna, F. v1p1201c1s
Pennant, D.F. v6p0323c1s
Pennant, J. v1p0335c2s
Penne, A. v5p0125c1s
Pennefather, F.W. v2p0313c2s
Pennefather, J.P. v1p0314c1s v1p0579c1s
Pennell, A.F. v3p0316c2s
Pennell, E. v3p0470c1s
Pennell, E.B. v4p0312c1s
Pennell, E.R. v2p0049c2s v2p0060c2s v2p0096c1s v2p0151c2s v2p0231c1s v2p0253c2s v2p0264c2s v2p0377c2m v2p0436c2s v2p0457c2s v2p0458c1s v2p0476c1s v3p0021c1s v3p0028c2s v3p0039c2s v3p0058c1s v3p0069c1s v3p0070c2s v3p0094c1s v3p0106c1s v3p0124c2s v3p0130c2s v3p0150c2s v3p0161c2s v3p0172c2s v3p0186c1s v3p0193c1s v3p0195c1s v3p0207c1m v3p0242c1s v3p0256c2s v3p0257c2s v3p0261c2s v3p0290c2s v3p0303c1s v3p0315c2s v3p0317c2s v3p0321c1m v3p0347c2m v3p0367c2s v3p0368c1s v3p0399c1s v3p0426c2s v3p0437c2s v3p0448c1s v3p0449c2s v3p0452c2s v3p0457c2s v3p0467c2s v4p0010c2s v4p0029c2s v4p0031c1m v4p0032c1s v4p0069c1s v4p0089c2s v4p0098c2s v4p0101c1s v4p0163c2s v4p0227c2s v4p0245c1s v4p0269c2s v4p0304c2s v4p0309c2s v4p0335c2s v4p0340c2s v4p0371c1s v4p0383c1s v4p0389c1s v4p0421c2s v4p0425c2s v4p0426c1m v4p0442c2s v4p0486c1s v4p0493c2s v4p0539c2m v4p0571c2s v4p0580c1s v4p0601c2m v4p0616c2s v4p0619c2s v5p0013c2s v5p0030c2s v5p0031c1s v5p0067c2s v5p0135c2s v5p0170c2s v5p0172c1s v5p0172c2s v5p0190c1s v5p0217c1s v5p0235c1s v5p0250c1s v5p0280c1s v5p0300c1s v5p0310c1m v5p0330c1s v5p0342c1s v5p0344c2s v5p0345c2m v5p0346c1s v5p0346c2s v5p0349c1s v5p0365c1s v5p0387c2s v5p0430c2s v5p0450c2s v5p0484c2m v5p0497c1s v5p0505c2s v5p0575c2s v5p0595c1s v5p0609c1s v5p0628c2s v6p0013c2s v6p0035c2s v6p0104c2s v6p0108c2s v6p0205c1s
Pennell, E.R. and Kruill, G. v3p0471c1s
Pennell, E.R. and Pennell, J. v3p0009c1s v3p0108c1s v3p0449c2s v4p0371c1s v4p0442c2s v5p0151c1s v5p0342c1s
Pennell, E.R. and Sturgis, R. v5p0156c2s
Pennell, Eliz.R. v6p0147c2s v6p0148c1m v6p0209c1s v6p0228c2s v6p0241c2s v6p0251c2s v6p0255c1s v6p0258c2s v6p0276c1s v6p0300c2s v6p0303c2s v6p0306c2s v6p0311c1s v6p0324c1s v6p0331c2s v6p0367c2m v6p0383c1s v6p0383c2s v6p0384c1s v6p0384c2s v6p0385c2s v6p0401c2s v6p0415c1m v6p0464c2s v6p0474c2s v6p0480c1m v6p0517c1s v6p0538c2s v6p0553c1s v6p0553c2m v6p0563c1m v6p0564c2s v6p0579c1s v6p0662c1s v6p0689c1s v6p0695c2s v6p0696c1m v6p0703c2s
Pennell, H.C. v1p0209c2s v1p0814c1s v1p1092c1s
Pennell, J. v3p0059c2s v3p0060c1s v3p0208c2s v3p0347c2s v4p0196c1s v4p0274c1s v4p0274c2s v4p0463c1s v4p0483c2s v4p0631c1s v5p0018c2s v5p0051c1s v5p0061c1m v5p0150c2m v5p0151c1s v5p0151c2s v5p0314c2s v5p0342c1s v5p0409c1s v5p0448c2s v5p0542c1s v5p0542c2s v5p0616c2s v6p0013c2s v6p0065c2s v6p0432c1s v6p0432c2s v6p0695c2s
Pennell, J. and Pennell, E.R. v3p0009c1s v3p0108c1s v3p0449c2s v4p0371c1s v4p0442c2s v5p0151c1s v5p0342c1s
Pennell, Joseph v4p0414c1s v6p0676c2s
Penney, E. v4p0477c2s
Penniman, J.H. v4p0466c1s v6p0046c1s
Penniman, T.D. and Rowland, H.A. v5p0184c2s
Penning, W.H. v1p0333c2s v1p0408c1s v1p0507c2s v1p0844c1s v1p0899c2s v1p1160c2s v3p0176c2m
Pennington, A.R. v2p0166c2s
Pennington, F. v5p0084c2s
Pennington, Ed. v5p0301c2s
Pennington, H. v6p0676c2s v6p0695c2s
Pennington, J.B. v4p0500c2s v6p0313c1s v6p0313c2s v6p0566c2s
Pennington, J.F. v2p0115c1s
Pennington, R. v1p0314c1s v1p1329c1s
Pennington, R.L.A. v5p0049c2s v5p0244c1s v5p0290c1s
Pennock, B.W. v5p0334c1s v5p0335c1s
Pennoyer, S. v3p0322c2s v4p0277c2m v4p0355c1s v4p0595c2s v5p0592c2s
Penny, B. v4p0500c1s
Penny, C.B. v6p0537c1s
Penny, F., Mrs. v3p0428c2s
Penny, Frank, Mrs. v4p0494c2s
Penny, R. v4p0127c2s v4p0460c1m
Penny, S.M. v5p0265c1s
Pennypacker, F.R. v6p0509c2s
Pennypacker, I.R. v5p0231c1s v5p0352c1s
Pennypacker, Percy V., Mrs. v6p0706c1s
Pennypacker, S.W. v1p0073c2s v1p0515c1s v1p1106c2m v3p0326c1s v3p0329c1s v3p0402c2s v5p0263c1s v5p0440c1s v5p0639c2s v6p0619c1s v6p0686c2s
Penrhyn, J.E. v1p0438c2s
Penrodil, M. v2p0350c1s
Penrose, B. v6p0120c1s v6p0309c1s
Penrose, B. and Allinson, E.P. v2p0338c2s v3p0086c1s v3p0186c1s v3p0329c1s v3p0359c1s
Penrose, C.B. v2p0172c1s
Penrose, C.B. and Trowbridge, J. v2p0439c2s
Penrose, C.W. v3p0446c1s
Penrose, E. v4p0600c1s
Penrose, F.C. v2p0426c1s v3p0183c2s v4p0035c1s v4p0253c1s v4p0417c1s v4p0568c2s v5p0250c1s v5p0346c1s
Penrose, H.H., Mrs. v4p0082c1s v4p0247c2s v5p0055c1s
Penrose, M. v5p0486c1s v5p0487c1s
Penrose, R.A.F. v1p0816c1s
Penrose, R.A.F., jr. and Hill, R.T. v3p0104c2s
Penrose-Fitzgerald, C.C. v3p0268c1s
Pense, E.J.B. v5p0064c2s
Penstone, W. v1p1212c1s
Pentecost, G.F. v3p0349c1s v4p0108c2s v4p0278c2s v4p0374c1s v4p0562c1s v5p0385c1s v6p0492c2s v6p0631c1s
Pentecost, G.F., jr. v5p0324c2s v6p0247c1s v6p0247c2m v6p0361c1m
Pentecost, H.O. v3p0067c2s v3p0215c1s
Pentecost, H.O. et al. v3p0086c1s
Penthorne, F. v1p0728c1s
Pentin, H. v6p0080c1s v6p0088c1s v6p0424c2s
Pentland-Smith, J. v4p0155c2s v4p0245c2s
Penton, E. v6p0489c2s
Penton, E. and Ronaldshay, Earl v6p0058c1s
Pentrill, F., Mrs. v2p0148c2s v4p0070c1s
Pentz, A.D. v4p0207c1s v4p0288c2s
Penwyn, M.J. v1p1010c1s
Penzance, Lord v2p0167c1m v3p0347c1s
Peple, E. v6p0649c2s
Peple, E.H. v6p0177c2s v6p0396c2s
Peplow, F.J. v6p0370c1s
Peppei, L.L. v6p0248c1s
Pepper, C.M. v5p0146c2s v5p0147c1s v5p0460c1s v6p0107c1s v6p0477c2m v6p0606c1m
Pepper, D., jr. v5p0183c2s
Pepper, G.D.B. v1p0095c2s v1p0097c1s v1p0210c1s v1p0286c1s v1p0385c1s v1p0769c1s v2p0180c2s v2p0205c2s v2p0371c1s v3p0379c2s v3p0427c2s v5p0196c1s
Pepper, G.H. v6p0444c2s v6p0523c1s
Pepper, G.W. v6p0495c1s
Pepper, J.H. v1p0793c1s v1p0955c1s
Pepper, L.L. v5p0300c1s v6p0095c2s v6p0100c1s
Pepper, M.S. v5p0002c1s v5p0090c2s v5p0094c1s v5p0384c2s v5p0438c1s v5p0474c1s v6p0332c1s

Pepper, W. v3p0162c1s
Pepper, W.A. v3p0149c2s
Pepperell, G.W. v4p0089c2s
v4p0378c1s v4p0520c2s
Peppler, C.W. v6p0647c2s
Pepys, W. v1p0574c2s
v1p0872c2s v1p0964c1s
Pepys, W.C. v1p0178c1s
Perceval, C.P.S. v2p0251c2s
Perceval, C.S. v1p0078c1s
v1p0197c1s v1p1114c2s v2p0393c2s
v5p0246c2s v5p0328c1s
Perceval, K.J. v2p0433c1s
Perceval, W.B. v4p0237c1s
Perceval-Clark, P. v3p0209c2s
Percival, C.B. v6p0604c1s
Percival, F. v1p0017c2s
Percival, G. v1p0312c2s
v1p0968c1s v5p0244c2s
Percival, H. v6p0400c1s
Percival, H.R. v2p0066c2s
v2p0153c1s v5p0115c1s v5p0348c1s
Percival, J. v4p0263c1s
v5p0117c2s
Percival, J. et al. v4p0557c2s
Percival, J.G. v1p0901c2s
v1p1209c1s v1p1396c2s
Percival, John v6p0194c1s
Percival, O. v6p0337c2s
v6p0565c1s
Percival, Olive v6p0120c1s
Percy, C.E. v1p1057c1s
Percy, C.M. v4p0553c1s
v6p0676c2s
Percy, Dr. v1p0340c2s
Percy, E. v6p0205c1s
Percy, Earl v2p0188c1s
v2p0472c1s v4p0318c1s
Percy, G.W. v3p0095c2s
v3p0223c1s v5p0382c1s
Percy, J. v1p1250c2s
v5p0032c2s v5p0098c1s
Percy, J.H. v3p0239c2s
Percy, R.T. v1p1199c1s
Perdicario, G.A. v1p0301c2s
Perdicaris, I. v1p0972c1s
v1p1130c1s v3p0288c1s v5p0387c1s
v6p0429c2s v6p0430c1m v6p0632c1s
Perdicaris, Ion v3p0288c1s
v4p0017c2s v4p0383c1m
Perdicaris, Prof. v1p0950c2s
Pereira, H.W. v3p0230c1s
v4p0067c1s
Pereira, Mrs. v3p0046c2s
v3p0459c2s
Pereira, S.M. v3p0460c1s
Pereira, S.M.S. v2p0105c1s
v3p0101c1s v3p0102c2s v4p0003c2s
v4p0313c1s v4p0375c2s v4p0523c1s
Pereira, Sarah M.S. v3p0026c2s
Pereles, J.M. v5p0533c1s
Pereyra, G. v1p0145c2s
Perez, A.G. v5p0147c1m
v5p0148c1m
Perez, R. v6p0138c1s
v6p0476c2s
Perhault, E. v1p0331c1s
v1p1274c2s
Peries, G. v4p0087c2s
v4p0603c2s
Perigord, Louis de, Count and
Gronkowski, Camille ... v6p0424c2s
v6p0479c2s
Perine, F.L. v3p0273c2s
Perini, N. v5p0152c2s
Perisse, I. v6p0044c2s
Perisse, J.S. v1p1251c1s
Perisse, L. v6p0044c2s
Peritz, I.J. v5p0635c1s
Periwinkle, Pauline v6p0016c2s
Perkin, F.M. v5p0099c1s
v5p0103c2s v5p0184c1s v5p0185c2s
v5p0288c2m v6p0192c1s v6p0192c2s
v6p0199c2s v6p0624c1s v6p0632c1s
Perkin, W.H. v1p0022c2s
v1p0279c2s v1p0640c1s v2p0076c2s
Perkins, A.C. v5p0154c2s
v6p0653c2s
Perkins, A.D., Mrs. v1p0105c1s
Perkins, A.T. v1p0371c1s
Perkins, A.W. v6p0073c2s
Perkins, C.A. v2p0314c2s
v3p0414c2s
Perkins, C.C. v1p0063c2s
v1p0064c1m v1p0148c2s v2p0239c2s
Perkins, C.E. v3p0281c1s
v3p0349c1s v3p0349c2s
Perkins, D.H. v5p0026c1s
Perkins, Dwight H. v6p0113c2s
Perkins, E.S. v4p0393c1s
Perkins, F.B. v1p0228c2s
v1p0286c2s v1p0292c1s v1p0297c1s
v1p0347c2s v1p0357c2s v1p0361c2s
v1p0450c2s v1p0457c2s v1p0474c1s
v1p0625c1s v1p0628c2s v1p0652c1s
v1p0730c1s v1p0731c2s v1p0742c2s
v1p0754c1s v1p0797c2s v1p0888c2s
v1p0911c2s v1p0932c1s v1p0990c2s
v1p0991c1s v1p1028c1s v1p1092c2s
v1p1171c1s v1p1178c2s v1p1203c2s
v1p1237c2s v1p1264c2s v1p1289c2s
v1p1311c1s v1p1319c2s v1p1334c2s
v1p1336c2s v1p1404c2s v1p1428c1s
v2p0109c2s v2p0256c1s v2p0256c2s
v2p0317c2s v2p0385c1s v3p0064c1s
v3p0270c2s v5p0601c2s
Perkins, F.B. and Schwartz, J.
v2p0256c1s
Perkins, F.C. v5p0184c2s
v6p0197c1s v6p0197c2s v6p0356c1s
v6p0580c2s v6p0685c2s
Perkins, F.E. v6p0002c2s
v6p0678c1s
Perkins, Frances B. v5p0425c2s
Perkins, G. v1p0237c2s
v1p0861c2s
Perkins, G.A. v1p0044c1s
v1p0644c2s
Perkins, G.C. v4p0083c1s
v4p0297c1s v5p0010c2s v6p0583c1s
Perkins, G.H. v1p0216c1s
v1p0505c2s v1p0624c2s v1p0637c2s
v1p0977c1s v1p1015c1s v1p1241c1s
v1p1367c1s v2p0340c2s v2p0421c1s
v4p0084c1s v4p0444c1s
Perkins, G.H. and Bentley, W.A.
v5p0534c2s
Perkins, G.R. v1p0649c2s
v1p0850c2s
Perkins, G.W. v1p0404c2s
v1p0676c1s
Perkins, Geo.C. v6p0120c1s
Perkins, H.A. v6p0245c2s
v6p0395c1s
Perkins, H.G. v5p0039c1s
Perkins, H.N. v1p0990c2s
Perkins, H.P. v6p0121c1s
Perkins, J. v1p0907c1s
v1p0980c2s v1p1248c1s v1p1391c2s
v1p1414c1s
Perkins, J., jr. v1p1062c2s
v1p1226c1s
Perkins, J.B. v1p0317c2s
v1p0349c1s v1p0480c2s v1p0974c2s
v3p0076c2s v3p0095c2s v3p0168c1s
v3p0248c2s v3p0258c1s v3p0298c2s
v4p0484c1s v5p0217c1s v5p0488c2s
Perkins, J.G. v3p0005c2s
Perkins, J.H. v1p0012c2s
v1p0028c2s v1p0033c1s v1p0078c2s
v1p0485c2s v1p0490c1s v1p0557c2s
v1p0559c1s v1p0584c2s v1p0635c2s
v1p0683c2s v1p0706c1s v1p0729c1s
v1p0771c1s v1p0775c1s v1p0854c2s
v1p0857c1s v1p0929c1s v1p0938c2s
v1p0939c1s v1p1274c2s v1p1341c1s
v1p1400c1s
Perkins, J.H.T. v6p0108c2s
v6p0150c2s v6p0206c2s v6p0578c1s
Perkins, J.W. v5p0386c2s
Perkins, L. v1p1247c2m
Perkins, L.F. v5p0637c1s
v6p0435c1s
Perkins, Lucy F. v6p0301c2s
Perkins, N.C. v1p0348c2s
v1p0417c1s v1p0712c2s v1p0989c1s
v1p1065c2s v1p1131c2s v3p0327c1s
Perkins, N.S.G. v6p0413c1s
Perkins, O. v1p1104c1s
v1p1200c1s
Perkins, R. v4p0058c1s
Perkins, R.A. v3p0094c1s
v3p0441c2s
Perkins, S.B. v4p0449c1s
Perkins, S.H. v1p0547c1s
v1p0836c2s
Perkins, T. v1p1389c2s
v4p0556c2s
Perkins, W.R. v4p0131c1s
Perkins, W.S. v1p0966c2s
v2p0299c2s v2p0328c2s
Perkins, W.T. v6p0010c1s
Perks, J.H., Mrs. v5p0418c1s
Perles, F. v6p0280c2s
Perles, Felix, Dr. v6p0489c1s
Perley, C.W. v6p0130c2s
Pernet, G. v6p0175c2s
v6p0225c1s v6p0368c2s v6p0376c2s
Pernin, Father v5p0101c2s
v5p0505c2s
Pernter, J.M. v3p0400c2s
v4p0036c1s
Perosi, L. v6p0438c2s
Perot, A. v4p0252c2s
Perott, J.De v4p0395c2s
Perowne, J.J.S. v1p0125c1s
v1p0127c1s v1p0264c1s v1p1041c2s
v2p0043c1s v2p0181c1s v2p0273c2s
v2p0337c2s v3p0041c2s v4p0437c1s
Perrault, E. v1p0579c2s
Perret, F.A. v6p0678c1s
Perret, Paul v4p0353c1s
Perrey, A. v1p0377c1s
Perreyve, H. v2p0082c2s
v2p0157c1s
Perrien, A. v1p0872c2s
Perrier, E. v1p0042c2s
v1p1441c1s
Perriet, E. v1p0040c2s
Perrill, W.H. v3p0303c1s
Perrin, A. v4p0093c1s
v4p0276c2s v4p0321c2s
Perrin, B. v2p0268c1s
v2p0338c1s v3p0199c2s v5p0027c2s
v5p0121c1s v5p0126c2s v5p0266c2s
v5p0443c2s v5p0643c2s v6p0272c2s
v6p0643c1s
Perrin, H.E. v5p0435c2s
Perrin, J.B. v1p0792c1s
Perrin, J.H. v4p0309c2s
Perrin, J.W. v5p0175c1s
v5p0221c2s v5p0452c2s v5p0535c1s
v5p0600c2s v6p0190c2m
Perrin, L. v1p0257c2s
v1p1207c2s
Perrin, P.A. v1p0775c2s
Perrin, R.S. v4p0584c1s
Perrin, W.H. v1p1045c2s
v3p0213c1s v3p0298c1s v3p0338c2s
Perrine, A.C. v4p0174c2s
Perrine, C.D. v5p0129c2m
v5p0130c1s v5p0372c1s v6p0188c1s
v6p0502c1s v6p0613c2s v6p0625c1s
Perrine, C.D. and Brashear, J.A.
v5p0314c2s
Perrine, C.D. and Campbell, W.W.
v6p0571c1s
Perrine, F.A.C. v4p0175c1s
v4p0176c2s v4p0244c2s v4p0598c1s
v4p0632c2s v6p0688c1s
Perrine, W. v5p0439c2s
Perris, G.H. v5p0502c1s
v5p0582c1s v6p0354c2s
Perrodil, M.de v1p0618c2s
Perrot, E.G. v6p0143c1s
Perrot, G. v5p0031c1s
Perrotin, M. v4p0357c2s
Perrott, G. v4p0241c1s
Perrucchetti v5p0013c2s
Perry, A. v1p1380c2s
v2p0008c2s v2p0128c2s v2p0165c1s
v3p0232c1s
Perry, A.F. v1p1012c2s
Perry, A.F., Mrs. v1p1039c2s
Perry, A.L. v1p1283c2s
v2p0245c1s v3p0086c1s v3p0347c1s
v3p0391c1s v4p0462c2s
Perry, A.T. v6p0061c1s
v6p0135c2s
Perry, B. v3p0055c1s
v3p0081c1s v3p0403c1s v3p0434c2s
v4p0127c1s v4p0251c2s v4p0278c1s
v4p0348c2s v5p0208c2s v5p0266c1s
v5p0283c2s v6p0039c2m v6p0137c1s
v6p0227c2s v6p0235c2s v6p0283c2s
v6p0317c1s v6p0379c2s v6p0462c1s
v6p0592c1s v6p0710c2s
Perry, Bliss v3p0061c2s
v3p0109c1s v3p0330c1s v5p0127c1s
v5p0437c2s v5p0629c1s v6p0039c2s
Perry, C. v1p0609c1s
v2p0268c2s
Perry, C.B. v3p0299c1s
Perry, C.C. v5p0178c1s
v5p0231c1s
Perry, C.E. v6p0071c1s
Perry, C.H.H. v4p0467c2s
Perry, C.R. v5p0070c1s
v6p0074c2s
Perry, Com. v1p1250c1s
Perry, E. v1p0631c2s
Perry, E., Sir v1p0287c1s
Perry, E.A. v1p0216c2s
v1p1292c2s v2p0333c1s v2p0434c1s
v2p0480c1s v3p0105c2s v3p0332c2s
v3p0344c2s v3p0414c2s
Perry, E.B. v4p0031c2s
v4p0360c1s v4p0388c2s v4p0389c1s
v4p0442c1s v5p0031c2s v5p0325c2s
v5p0394c1s v5p0450c1s
Perry, E.D. v4p0224c1s
v6p0089c2s v6p0177c1s v6p0671c1s
Perry, E.S. and Lewis, E.P.
v4p0540c2s
Perry, E.W. v4p0087c2s
v4p0262c2s v4p0268c2s
Perry, G.B. v1p0391c2s
v3p0095c1s v3p0349c1s v3p0439c2s
Perry, G.C. v3p0083c1s
v3p0195c2s
Perry, G.G. v1p0087c2s
v1p0251c1s v1p0433c1s v1p0611c1s
v1p0729c1s v1p0859c2s v3p0137c2s
v3p0285c1m v3p0426c1s v4p0049c1s
Perry, G.H. v6p0014c1s
Perry, G.W. v5p0579c2s
Perry, H.A. v2p0134c1s
v2p0134c2s v2p0141c2m v2p0298c2s
v3p0092c2s v3p0108c2s v3p0161c1s
v3p0172c2s v3p0273c1s v3p0285c1s
v3p0288c1s v4p0172c2s
Perry, H.A. et al. v3p0146c1s
Perry, H.F. v5p0102c1s
v5p0118c1s v5p0561c2s v6p0109c2s
Perry, H.H. v4p0021c2s
v4p0593c2s
Perry, H.J. v4p0126c1s
v4p0249c1s
Perry, H.T. v3p0410c1s
v4p0390c1s

Perry, H.W. v5p0490c2s
Perry, Harold A. v2p0164c1s
Perry, J. v1p0082c2s
v1p0236c2s v1p0399c2s v1p0771c1s
v1p1432c2s v3p0133c1s v3p0331c2s
v5p0184c1s v5p0184c2s v5p0185c1s
v5p0188c2s v5p0366c1m v5p0549c1s
v5p0572c1s v6p0132c2s v6p0204c2m
v6p0209c1s v6p0213c2s v6p0406c1m
v6p0406c2m v6p0444c1s v6p0473c1s
v6p0575c2s
Perry, J. and Ayrton, W.E.
v2p0281c2s v3p0383c2s
Perry, J. et al. v4p0165c2s
Perry, J.B. v1p0507c2s
v1p0508c1s v1p0509c2s v1p1367c2s
v3p0119c2s v4p0603c1s v5p0263c2s
v5p0491c1s v5p0524c2s v5p0630c1s
v5p0636c2s
Perry, J.H. v1p0316c1m
v1p0615c1s v1p0712c2s v1p0830c1s
v1p1398c2s
Perry, J.R. v3p0061c1s
v5p0145c1s v5p0396c1s v6p0076c1s
v6p0388c1s v6p0471c2s
Perry, J.T. v2p0025c1s
v2p0082c2s v2p0199c2s v2p0221c1s
v2p0472c2s v3p0310c1s v4p0024c1s
v5p0089c2s v6p0569c1s
Perry, Katharine v6p0623c2s
Perry, L. v6p0022c1s
v6p0225c1s v6p0275c1s v6p0616c1s
v6p0636c1s v6p0673c2s
Perry, L.C. v3p0334c2s
v6p0448c1s
Perry, L.J. v4p0332c2s
v5p0029c1s v5p0339c1s v6p0377c2s
Perry, M. v6p0619c2s
Perry, M.C. v2p0237c1s
v5p0352c1s v5p0560c1s
Perry, Margaret v6p0335c2s
Perry, N. v1p0359c1s
v1p0465c2s v1p0492c1s v1p0716c2s
v1p0951c2s v1p1123c1s v1p1127c2s
v1p1407c1s v2p0053c1s v2p0108c2s
v3p0473c1s
Perry, N.W. v4p0020c1s
v4p0101c1s v4p0132c1s v4p0174c2m
v4p0175c1s v4p0175c2s v4p0176c2s
v4p0177c1s v4p0220c2m v4p0349c2s
v4p0570c2s v5p0183c1s v5p0183c2s
v5p0482c2s
Perry, Norah v3p0439c2s
Perry, Prof. v3p0205c2s
Perry, Prof. and Ayrton, Prof.
v1p0788c2s
Perry, R.B. v5p0303c2s
v5p0313c2s v5p0525c2s v6p0145c2s
v6p0240c2s v6p0505c1s v6p0512c2s
v6p0537c2s v6p0538c1s v6p0554c1s
Perry, R.H. v6p0021c2s
v6p0033c1s v6p0039c2s
Perry, S. v1p0382c1s
v1p1367c1m
Perry, S.J. v1p0706c2s
v1p0788c1s v1p0788c2m v2p0072c1s
v2p0129c2m v2p0340c1s v2p0425c1s
Perry, T.D. v6p0626c2s
Perry, T.Doane v6p0180c1s
Perry, T.H. v1p0787c2s
v1p1014c1s
Perry, T.S. v1p0035c1s
v1p0076c1s v1p0089c2s v1p0105c1s
v1p0183c1s v1p0225c2s v1p0241c2s
v1p0266c2s v1p0277c1s v1p0361c2s
v1p0369c2s v1p0417c2s v1p0489c1s
v1p0511c2s v1p0542c1s v1p0611c1s
v1p0750c1s v1p0789c2s v1p0876c2s
v1p0885c2s v1p0931c2s v1p1102c1s
v1p1157c2s v1p1169c1s v1p1309c2s
v1p1317c2m v1p1378c1s v1p1398c1s
v1p1440c2s v2p0068c2s v2p0099c2s
v2p0101c2s v2p0144c2s v2p0210c1s
v2p0215c1s v2p0250c2s v2p0317c2s
v2p0389c1s v3p0134c2s v3p0232c1s
v3p0370c2s v4p0215c1s v6p0227c2s
Perry, W.C. v1p0190c1s
v1p0388c1s v1p0518c1s v1p0954c1s
v1p0990c1s v1p1357c1s v2p0269c2s
v2p0308c2s v2p0404c1s
Perry, W.F. v1p1410c1s
Perry, W.G.J. v3p0095c1s
Perry, W.O.H. v2p0389c2s
Perry, W.S. v1p0148c1s
v1p0808c2s v1p0935c2s v1p1060c1s
v1p1173c2s v1p1406c1s v2p0123c2s
v3p0083c2s v3p0141c2m v3p0216c1s
v3p0347c1s v3p0462c1s v4p0612c1s
v5p0210c1s v5p0609c2s v6p0034c2s
v6p0035c2s
Perseus v6p0213c1s
v6p0236c1s v6p0429c2s v6p0558c2s
Pershing, H.T. v4p0320c1s
Pershing, J.K. v4p0139c2s
Person, H.L. v6p0089c2s
Person, Harlow S. v6p0089c2s
Persons, W.F. v6p0508c1s
v6p0532c1s
Perton, C. v4p0285c2s
Pertz, D.F.M. v4p0409c2s
Perugini, Kate Dickens ... v6p0173c2s
Pestalozzi, J.H. v1p0390c1s
v1p0647c1s v1p0737c2s
Petch, A.T. v6p0304c2s
Peter, A. v6p0183c1s
v6p0272c1s v6p0373c1s
Peter, F.L. v3p0212c1s
Peter, K. v4p0253c2s
Peterborough, Bishop of .. v3p0258c2s
Petermann, A. v1p0055c1m
v1p0055c2s v1p0056c1m v1p0484c1s
v1p1024c1s
Peters, A. v1p0853c2s
v1p0990c1m v1p1046c1s
Peters, A.H. v3p0006c1s
v3p0028c2s v3p0069c2s v3p0128c2s
v3p0143c1s v3p0149c2s v3p0246c2s
v3p0441c1s v4p0049c1s v4p0088c2s
v4p0127c2s v4p0178c2s v4p0314c1s
v4p0353c1s v4p0541c1s
Peters, A.W. v5p0290c2s
Peters, B. v1p0285c1s
v1p0750c2s v1p1355c2m
Peters, C. v3p0406c2s
v4p0006c1s v5p0354c2s
Peters, C.A. v5p0136c2s
v5p0370c2s v5p0426c1s
Peters, C.A. and Gooch, F.A.
v5p0254c2s v5p0426c1s v5p0571c2s
Peters, C.A. and Moody, S.E.
v5p0441c2s
Peters, C.H.F. v1p0351c2s
v1p0749c1s
Peters, Carl, Dr. v5p0422c1s
Peters, E. v2p0097c1s
Peters, E.B. v5p0442c1s
Peters, E.S. v2p0248c2s
Peters, E.T. v3p0158c2s
Peters, G.N.H. v1p0684c1s
v1p0706c2s
Peters, J. v6p0078c2s
Peters, J.A. v1p0532c2s
v2p0098c1s v2p0343c1s
Peters, J.C. v1p0238c1s
Peters, J.C. et al. v2p0080c2s
Peters, J.H. v6p0291c1s
Peters, J.P. v2p0284c2s
v3p0115c2s v3p0226c1s v3p0392c1s
v3p0475c1s v3p0475c2s v4p0054c2m
v4p0055c2s v4p0130c2s v4p0405c1m
v4p0567c2s v4p0586c2s v5p0025c1s
v5p0035c1s v5p0042c1m v5p0060c2s
v5p0134c1s v5p0268c1s v5p0388c1s
v5p0434c2s v5p0479c2s v6p0046c1m
v6p0062c1s v6p0196c1s v6p0458c1m
v6p0475c2m v6p0583c1s v6p0630c2s
v6p0692c1s
Peters, J.W.S. v6p0349c2s
Peters, James W.S. v6p0295c1s
Peters, John P. v3p0232c1s
v4p0118c1s
Peters, M.C. v4p0565c1m
Peters, M.S. v2p0202c2s
Peters, M.S., Mrs. v2p0111c1s
Peters, S.J. v1p0913c1s
Peters, S.S. v5p0342c2s
Peters, T.McC. v1p0853c1s
v1p0916c1s
Peterselia, L.M. v1p0463c2s
v1p1236c1s
Petersen, C. v1p0344c1s
v1p0344c2s v1p1155c1s v1p1371c1s
v2p0048c1m v2p0054c2s v2p0204c2s
v2p0250c2s v2p0278c1s v2p0317c1s
v2p0388c2s
Petersen, E. v6p0020c1s
Petersen, E.O. v5p0424c2s
Petersen, H.S. v6p0305c1s
Petersen, Henrik G. v6p0320c1s
Petersen, M. v1p1051c1s
Petersen, M.H. v4p0152c2s
Petersen, V. v2p0116c1m
v3p0110c1m
Petersen, W. v6p0670c2s
Peterson, A.F. v3p0320c1s
Peterson, C.H. v6p0296c1s
Peterson, C.J. v1p0497c1s
v1p0935c1s
Peterson, C.W. v5p0627c2s
Peterson, E.L. v2p0294c2s
Peterson, E.O. v5p0227c1s
v5p0385c1s
Peterson, F. v2p0445c1s
v3p0319c2s v4p0273c2s v4p0276c2s
v6p0046c1s v6p0470c1s
Peterson, H.A. v6p0130c2s
Peterson, H.C. v6p0170c2s
Peterson, J.B. v5p0098c1s
v5p0313c2s v5p0564c2s
Peterson, K.D. v3p0293c2s
v3p0332c2s
Peterson, M.H. v5p0304c1s
Peterson, O.M. v6p0007c2s
Peterson, P. v2p0217c1s
v2p0386c1s v3p0040c2s v3p0375c1s
Peterson, T. v4p0027c1s
Peterson, W. v3p0445c1s
v5p0570c1s v6p0127c1s
Peterson, W.A. v5p0264c1s
Petheram, W.C. v5p0265c2s
v5p0616c1s
Petherbridge, M. v5p0337c1s
Petherick, E.A. v2p0028c2s
v4p0246c1s v6p0555c1s v6p0627c2s
Petherick, Mrs. v1p0010c1s
Pethick, W.N. v5p0438c2s
Pethick-Lawrence, F.W. ... v6p0634c1m
Petit, J. v4p0355c1s
Petofi, A. v1p1258c1s
Petot, M. v1p0749c2s
v1p0873c2s
Petre, C. v1p0115c1s
Petre, F.L. v5p0287c1s
Petre, F.Loraine v6p0313c2s
Petre, M. v1p1060c2s
v2p0069c1s v2p0210c2s v3p0136c1s
Petre, M.D. v5p0332c2s
v5p0349c2s v5p0466c2s v6p0388c1s
v6p0457c1s v6p0490c2s
Petre, M.D. and Streeter, A.
v5p0637c2s
Petrey, H.J.H. v3p0436c2s
Petrie, Alice H. v6p0701c2s
Petrie, C.G. and Giltner, L.G.
v6p0694c2s
Petrie, F. v4p0029c1s
v4p0117c2s v5p0399c2s
Petrie, Flinders v4p0185c2s
Petrie, G. v4p0037c1s
v4p0111c2s v5p0602c1s v6p0010c1s
Petrie, M. v5p0610c1s
Petrie, W.F. v3p0150c2s
v3p0318c1s v4p0334c2s v4p0421c1s
Petrie, W.F. and Torr, C.. v4p0004c2s
Petrie, W.M.F. v1p0831c2s
v2p0134c1s v2p0281c2s v2p0345c1s
v2p0360c2s v2p0385c1s v3p0070c1s
v3p0130c2s v3p0131c1m v3p0173c2s
v3p0191c2s v3p0351c2s v4p0172c1m
v4p0172c2s v4p0241c1s v4p0352c1s
v4p0365c2s v4p0391c1s v4p0438c1s
v5p0002c1s v5p0180c2s v5p0181c1m
v5p0181c2s v5p0463c2s v6p0001c2s
v6p0002c1s v6p0195c2s v6p0196c1m
v6p0595c2s
Petrie, W.M.F. et al. v2p0127c1s
v2p0156c2s v3p0351c2s v4p0172c1s
Petrie, W.M.Flinders v6p0330c2s
Petrina, M. v1p1289c2s
Petritsch, L. v6p0042c2s
Petroff, I. v2p0006c2m
Petrunkevitch, A. v6p0482c1s
v6p0556c2m
Pettas, I.M. v5p0329c2s
Pettee, G.D. v6p0049c1s
Pettee, J.E. v6p0371c2s
Pettee, J.I. v6p0372c1s
Pettee, W.H. v2p0136c1s
Pettegrew, J.A. v6p0656c2s
Pettengill, A.G. v5p0383c1s
Pettengill, L. v6p0178c2s
Pettengill, S.B. v3p0346c1s
Pettenkofer, M. v2p0409c1s
Pettenkoffer, M.von v1p0017c1m
v1p0266c1s v1p0559c2s v1p0608c1s
v1p0744c2s v1p1015c1s v2p0080c2s
Petter, J.M. v6p0274c1s
Pettersen, K. v2p0020c2s
v2p0158c1s v2p0179c1s
Petterson, Elias v2p0419c2s
Pettersson, O. v5p0037c1s
v5p0209c1s v6p0463c2s
Pettibone, Hawley v6p0248c2s
Pettigrew, J.B. v1p0460c1s
Pettigrew, J.J. v1p1206c1s
Pettigrew, T.J. v1p0644c2s
v1p0803c2s v1p0880c1s
Pettigrove, F.G. v4p0139c2s
Pettingal, J. v1p0497c1s
Pettingal, J. and Adee, S.
v1p0026c1s
Pettingall, J. v1p1068c1s
Pettingell, J.H. v1p0046c2s
Pettis, C.R. v6p0657c2s
Pettit, H. v4p0288c2s
Pettit, J.S. v4p0284c1s
v5p0023c2s v5p0375c1s v5p0573c2s
v6p0666c1s
Pettit, M. v5p0003c1s
v6p0664c2s
Pettit, W. v1p0300c1s
Pettit, W.V. v5p0460c1s
Pettitt, T. v6p0638c2s
Petts, R.G. v6p0044c2s
Pettus, C.P. v6p0687c2s
Pettus, I.M. v5p0637c2s
Petty, W. v1p0640c1m
Pettypiece, H.J. v6p0529c2s
Peucker, C. v4p0126c1s
Peucker, K. v4p0147c2s
v6p0048c1s
Peverel, R.de v1p0542c1s
v1p1255c1s
Peyster, F.De v1p0463c1s
Peyster, J.W.De v1p0176c2s
v1p0192c2s v1p0708c1m v1p0789c1s
v1p0862c1s v1p0917c2s v1p0948c2m
v1p1344c2s v1p1369c2s v2p0211c2s
v2p0468c2s v3p0188c2s v3p0456c1s
v4p0505c1s v4p0636c1s

Peyton, C.S. v1p0518c2s
Peyton, E. v5p0503c1s v6p0699c1s
Peyton, J.E.H. v3p0126c1s
Peyton, J.L. v1p0624c2s v2p0338c1s
Peyton, W.W. v3p0043c1s v4p0057c1s v4p0277c2s v5p0022c2s v5p0146c1s v5p0305c2s v5p0483c1s v5p0486c1s
Peytoulbard, B. v1p0977c1s
Pezet, F.A. v4p0436c2s
Pfaehler, G.J. v6p0549c2s
Pfahler, W.H. v6p0355c1s v6p0468c1s v6p0652c1s
Pfanstiehl, A.A. v2p0215c2s v2p0236c1s v2p0257c2s v2p0290c2s v2p0292c1s v2p0368c2s v2p0371c1s v3p0006c1s v3p0135c1s v3p0175c2s v3p0229c2s v4p0058c1s v4p0111c2s v4p0622c2s
Pfeiderer, O. v4p0382c1s v4p0432c1s v6p0341c2s
Pfeifer, C. v1p0161c2s
Pfeiffer and Dingler v1p1247c1s
Pfeiffer, C. v1p0747c2s
Pfeiffer, E. v1p0786c1s v1p1010c2s v1p1426c1s v2p0321c2s v2p0372c1s v2p0478c1s
Pfeil, G.V. v5p0369c1s
Pfeil, J.Count v4p0006c2s
Pfeil, S. v5p0460c2s
Pfirshing, Mrs. v5p0355c2s
Pfleiderer, O. v3p0261c1s v4p0109c1s v4p0224c1s v4p0479c1s v4p0573c1s v5p0198c1s v5p0306c1s v5p0386c1s v6p0537c1s
Pflugk-Harttung, J.von ... v6p0182c2s v6p0328c1s
Pfordte, O.F. v4p0372c2s v4p0526c2s
Pfoundes, C. v2p0233c1s v2p0233c2m v3p0021c2s v4p0077c2s v4p0297c1s v4p0298c1s v5p0110c1s v5p0112c2s v5p0302c1m
Pfoundes, C.J.W. v6p0470c2s
Pfungst, A. v5p0305c1s
Pharo, H.A. v6p0197c2s
Phayre, A., Sir v3p0060c2s
Phayre, A.P. v2p0061c2s
Phees, R. v4p0300c2s
Phelan, D.S. v2p0167c1s
Phelan, J. v2p0434c2s
Phelan, J.D. v2p0136c1s v2p0223c2s v2p0255c1s v3p0472c2s v4p0501c2m v5p0088c1s v5p0112c2s v6p0568c2m
Phelan, J.D. et al. v6p0567c2s
Phelan, J.H. v3p0347c1s
Phelan, R.V. v6p0162c1s
Phelps, A. v1p0239c1s v1p0296c2m v1p0529c1s v1p0620c1s v1p1044c1s v1p1091c1s v1p1091c2s v5p0036c1s v5p0355c2s v5p0406c1s v5p0474c1s v5p0480c2s v6p0262c1s
Phelps, A.L. v1p0153c1s v1p0411c2s v1p1421c2s v6p0444c2s
Phelps, A.L., Mrs. v1p0029c2s v1p0453c2s v1p0790c1s v1p0904c1s v1p1153c1s v1p1214c2s
Phelps, A.McA. v2p0116c2s
Phelps, A.R. v4p0330c1s v6p0258c2s v6p0372c1s
Phelps, Arthur S. v6p0153c2s
Phelps, C.G. v6p0161c1s
Phelps, C.H. v2p0398c2s
Phelps, C.S. v5p0405c1s
Phelps, D. v1p0885c2s
Phelps, E. v1p0023c1s v1p0027c2s v1p0227c2s v1p0236c1s v1p0259c2s v1p0336c1s v1p0357c2s v1p0418c2s v1p0573c2s v1p0717c1s v1p0874c2s v1p0886c2s v1p0917c1s v1p0931c1s v1p0951c1s v1p1189c1s v1p1221c2s v1p1223c1s v1p1343c1s v1p1349c2s v1p1358c2s v1p1387c1s v2p0474c2s
Phelps, E.H. v6p0003c2s
Phelps, E.J. v3p0005c2s v3p0037c2s v3p0119c1s v3p0215c1s v3p0441c2s v4p0022c2s v4p0116c2s v4p0457c2s v4p0597c1s
Phelps, E.S. v1p0038c1s v1p0335c2s v1p0438c2s v1p0491c1s v1p0528c1s v1p0531c2s v1p0627c1s v1p0677c1s v1p0706c1s v1p0851c2s v1p0924c1s v1p0930c2s v1p0951c2s v1p0995c2s v1p1142c2s v1p1295c2s v1p1299c2s v1p1378c2s v1p1419c2s v1p1420c1s v1p1440c1s v2p0120c2s v2p0175c1s v2p0215c2s v2p0271c2s v2p0358c1m v2p0371c1s v3p0014c2s v3p0081c1s v3p0113c1s v3p0159c1s v3p0225c2s v3p0393c1s v4p0218c1s v4p0252c2s v4p0261c1s v4p0341c1s v4p0410c1s v4p0478c1s v4p0527c2s v4p0551c2s v4p0558c2s v4p0588c1s v4p0614c1s v4p0620c2s v4p0621c1s v5p0266c1s v5p0349c2s v5p0410c2s v5p0416c2s v6p0043c1s v6p0109c1s
Phelps, E.S. et al. v2p0477c2s v3p0119c1s v3p0216c1s
Phelps, Eliz.S. v6p0155c1s v6p0166c2s v6p0345c2s v6p0562c1s v6p0665c1s
Phelps, Eliz.Stuart v4p0230c1s
Phelps, F.B. v4p0133c1s
Phelps, G.T. v6p0683c1s
Phelps, I.K. v4p0089c1s v5p0129c2s v6p0222c1s v6p0458c2m
Phelps, I.K. and Gooch, F.A. v4p0028c2s v4p0089c1s
Phelps, J.B.T. v4p0576c2s
Phelps, J.M. v1p1068c2s
Phelps, J.W. v1p1074c2s v1p1309c1s v1p1367c2s
Phelps, K.E. v5p0182c1s
Phelps, L., Mrs. v1p0292c1s v1p0531c1s v1p1020c1s v1p1197c1s
Phelps, L.L. v5p0134c1s
Phelps, L.R. v4p0096c1s v4p0412c1s v4p0548c2s v4p0608c1s v4p0632c2s v5p0392c1s v5p0459c1m v6p0206c2s v6p0271c1s
Phelps, M.A. and Gooch, F.A. v6p0032c2s
Phelps, M.H. v6p0313c1s
Phelps, M.S. v1p0045c2s v1p0297c2s v1p0305c1s v1p1235c1s v2p0437c1s
Phelps, Mary v6p0085c1s
Phelps, Minnie B. v6p0301c1s
Phelps, P.F. v1p1033c2s v1p1116c1s
Phelps, R.S. v5p0048c2s
Phelps, S. v2p0201c2s v6p0274c2s
Phelps, S. and Vye, B. ... v5p0229c2s
Phelps, S.D. v1p0751c1s v1p1153c1s v2p0235c2s v2p0236c1s v2p0351c2s
Phelps, T.G. v6p0430c2s
Phelps, T.S. v4p0512c1s
Phelps, W.F. v1p0925c2s v3p0124c1s
Phelps, W.J. v5p0282c1s v6p0511c1s
Phelps, W.L. v3p0057c1s v3p0247c2s v3p0249c2s v3p0312c1s v3p0345c2s v3p0379c1s v4p0091c1s v4p0351c1s v4p0622c2s v5p0066c1s v5p0488c1s v6p0231c2s v6p0394c1s v6p0461c2s v6p0556c1s v6p0587c2s v6p0697c2s
Phelps, W.W. v2p0049c1s v4p0130c2s v4p0596c2s v4p0611c2s v4p0628c2s
Phelps-Stokes, J.G. v6p0512c1s
Phelps-Stokes, Rose H. ... v6p0704c1s
Philbrick, E. v1p1366c1s
Philbrick, E.A. v2p0035c2s
Philbrick, E.H. v2p0399c2s
Philbrick, E.S. v1p0362c2m v1p1181c2m
Philbrick, E.S. and Bowditch, E.W. v2p0122c2s
Philbrick, G.D. v2p0432c1s
Philbrick, J.D. v1p0898c1s v1p1072c1s v1p1158c1s v1p1190c2s v2p0325c1s v3p0034c1s
Philbrick, J.E. v1p0385c2s
Philbrick, P.H. v1p1328c1s v2p0037c1s v2p0475c1s
Philip, A.J. v6p0657c1s
Philip, J.W. v5p0508c2s
Philip, J.W. et al. v5p0603c1s
Philip, L. v2p0436c1s v3p0460c1s
Philip, R. v1p0206c2s
Philippovich, E. v5p0557c1s
Philippovich, E.von v3p0136c1s v3p0171c2s v6p0042c2s
Philipps, E. v5p0118c2s
Philippsohn, L. v2p0016c2s v2p0236c2s v2p0239c1m v2p0294c1s v2p0356c2s v2p0368c2s v2p0430c2m
Philips, B. v2p0120c2s
Philips, C. v3p0275c2s
Philips, F.C. v4p0636c1s
Philips, J.F. v6p0363c2s
Philips, M. v3p0247c1s v3p0325c2s v4p0168c2s v4p0471c1s
Philips, N. v6p0603c2s
Philips, T.E.R. v6p0347c2s
Philips, W.H. v5p0146c2s
Philips, W.L. v6p0573c2s
Philipson, D. v4p0306c1s v5p0307c2s v6p0347c1s v6p0525c2s
Philleo, C.W. v1p0017c2s v1p1018c2s v1p1242c2s v1p1335c1s
Phillimore, C.M. v1p0020c1s v1p0363c2s v1p1051c2s v1p1284c1s v2p0443c2s v3p0120c2s v3p0155c2s v6p0036c1s
Phillimore, E.L. v4p0059c2s
Phillimore, G. v6p0006c1s
Phillimore, J.S. v5p0411c2s v6p0368c1s
Phillimore, L., Mrs. v5p0345c2s
Phillimore, M. v5p0009c1m
Phillimore, Miss v1p0798c2s v1p0995c1s
Phillimore, W.G.F. v6p0402c1s v6p0611c2s
Phillimore, W.P. v2p0397c1s
Phillimore, W.P.W. v2p0085c1s v2p0171c1s v3p0356c1s v4p0220c1s v5p0415c1s
Phillip, D.G. v6p0512c2s
Phillip, M.L. v5p0250c1s
Phillipi, F.A. and Frank, F.H.R. v1p1302c2s
Phillipps, E.M. v4p0305c2s v4p0316c2s v4p0337c2s v4p0516c1s v5p0492c2s v6p0059c1s v6p0619c1s v6p0648c1s
Phillipps, H. v1p0933c2s
Phillipps, T., Sir v1p0176c2s v1p0200c1s v1p0261c1s v1p0799c2s v1p0803c2s v1p1009c2s v1p1328c1s
Phillipps-Wolley, C. v2p0014c1s v3p0002c1s v3p0044c1s v3p0071c1s v4p0500c1s v5p0077c1s v5p0090c2s v5p0100c1s v5p0238c1s v5p0405c1s v6p0045c1s
Phillippson, A. v4p0241c1s
Phillips, A. v1p0634c2s v3p0168c2s
Phillips, A., Mrs. v1p0942c2s v1p1259c1s v1p1311c1s v2p0139c1s v2p0150c1s v3p0035c2s v3p0190c1s v3p0312c1s v4p0048c2s
Phillips, A.C. et al. v3p0394c2s
Phillips, A.H. v4p0544c2s v5p0589c1s
Phillips, B. v1p0371c2s v1p0886c2s v1p0942c1s v1p0948c2s v1p1261c2s v1p1372c2s v1p1388c1s v2p0109c1s v2p0157c2s v2p0159c2s v3p0154c2s v3p0410c2s v3p0455c1s
Phillips, C. v2p0379c2s v3p0046c1s v3p0068c1s v3p0073c1s v3p0121c1s v3p0186c2s v3p0194c1s v3p0224c2s v3p0287c2s v3p0320c1m v3p0320c2s v3p0368c1m v3p0402c2s v3p0406c1s v3p0413c1s v3p0440c1s v3p0447c1s v3p0448c2s v4p0028c2s v4p0029c1m v4p0029c2m v4p0030c1m v4p0047c1s v4p0047c2s v4p0048c1s v4p0065c1s v4p0066c1s v4p0146c2s v4p0159c2s v4p0226c2s v4p0231c2s v4p0233c2s v4p0259c2s v4p0265c2s v4p0304c2s v4p0326c1s v4p0328c1s v4p0344c1s v4p0363c1s v4p0364c1s v4p0369c1s v4p0382c2m v4p0387c1s v4p0398c1s v4p0399c1s v4p0426c1m v4p0436c2s v4p0442c2s v4p0468c1s v4p0473c2m v4p0486c2s v4p0493c1m v4p0493c2m v4p0497c1s v4p0500c2s v4p0510c1s v4p0510c2m v4p0577c2s v4p0601c2s v4p0609c1s v4p0614c1s v5p0224c1s v5p0267c2s v5p0347c2s v5p0376c1s v5p0432c1s v5p0476c1s v5p0487c1s v5p0499c2s v5p0505c1s v5p0580c2s v6p0033c2s v6p0034c2s v6p0085c2s v6p0245c1s v6p0378c2s v6p0648c1m v6p0675c2s v6p0681c2s
Phillips, C. and Wedmore, F. v4p0029c1s
Phillips, C.C. v5p0588c1s
Phillips, C.J. v5p0381c2s
Phillips, C.L. v1p0196c2s
Phillips, Claude v3p0022c1s v3p0244c1s v5p0172c2s v5p0427c2s v5p0497c1s v5p0509c1s v5p0609c2s v5p0617c1m v6p0179c2s v6p0473c2s v6p0510c2s v6p0531c2s v6p0684c1m
Phillips, D. v2p0229c1s
Phillips, D.B. v2p0284c1s
Phillips, D.C. v6p0616c2s
Phillips, D.E. v5p0182c2s v5p0416c1m v5p0569c2s
Phillips, D.G. v6p0125c1s v6p0237c2s v6p0259c2s v6p0261c1s v6p0291c2s v6p0297c1s v6p0345c1s v6p0504c2s v6p0546c1s v6p0550c2s v6p0552c2s v6p0583c2s v6p0641c1s v6p0645c2s v6p0690c1s v6p0695c1s
Phillips, D.W. v1p0376c1s v1p0470c2s v1p0571c2s v1p0849c2s v2p0017c1s
Phillips, David G. v6p0601c1s
Phillips, E. v1p1077c2s v5p0297c2m v5p0311c1s
Phillips, F. v6p0062c1s v6p0087c2s v6p0410c1s
Phillips, F.C. v2p0284c2s v3p0167c2s
Phillips, F.S. v6p0158c2s
Phillips, Forbes v6p0019c2s
Phillips, G. v1p0965c2s v1p1023c1s
Phillips, G.Claude v6p0650c1s
Phillips, G.L. v1p0460c2s v1p0655c2s v6p0343c2s
Phillips, G.S. v1p0201c1s v1p0345c1s v1p0682c1s v1p0815c1s v1p1191c1s
Phillips, H., jr. v1p1272c1s

v3p0242c2m v3p0322c2s v4p0458c2s
Phillips, H.A. v2p0218c2s
v2p0260c1s v3p0471c2s v4p0078c2s
Phillips, H.A.D. v4p0224c1s
v5p0384c2s v5p0468c1s
Phillips, H.B. v6p0057c1s
Phillips, H.L. v5p0403c1s
Phillips, H.W. v5p0101c1s
v5p0232c2s v5p0366c2s v5p0481c1s
v5p0597c2s v6p0066c1s v6p0090c1s
v6p0162c2s v6p0310c2s v6p0353c2s
v6p0380c2s v6p0471c1s v6p0501c2s
v6p0534c2s v6p0650c2s
Phillips, J. v1p0826c1s
v1p1175c2s v1p1181c2s v1p1237c1s
v3p0106c2s v4p0141c2s v4p0229c2s
v5p0143c1s
Phillips, J., Sir v1p1392c1s
Phillips, J.A. v1p0022c2s
v1p0187c1s v1p0666c1s v1p0825c2s
v2p0008c1m v2p0182c1s v3p0176c1s
v3p0280c2s
Phillips, J.B. v6p0146c1s
v6p0188c2s v6p0203c1s v6p0348c1m
v6p0529c1s v6p0530c1s v6p0614c2s
v6p0624c1s v6p0659c2s
Phillips, J.H. v4p0278c1s
Phillips, J.L.T. v1p0072c2s
v1p0171c2s
Phillips, J.M. and Hornaday, W.T.
v6p0433c1s
Phillips, J.N. v5p0136c1s
v5p0191c2s
Phillips, J.R. v1p0304c1s
v1p0460c2s v1p0764c2s v1p1288c2s
Phillips, J.S. v2p0237c1s
Phillips, J.S.R. v5p0166c2s
Phillips, Jos. v5p0639c1s
Phillips, L. v5p0007c1m
v5p0561c2s v6p0008c2s v6p0659c1s
Phillips, L. et al. v6p0271c1s
Phillips, L.A. v4p0398c2s
v4p0464c1s
Phillips, L.C. v5p0207c1s
Phillips, L.M. v6p0087c1s
Phillips, M.L. v5p0620c2s
Phillips, M.W. v1p0307c1s
Phillips, O.P. v6p0230c1s
Phillips, P. v4p0426c1s
Phillips, P.C. v6p0554c2s
Phillips, P.L. v5p0361c1s
Phillips, R. v3p0251c1s
v6p0131c1s v6p0394c2s v6p0679c2s
v6p0685c2s
Phillips, R.A. v6p0095c2m
v6p0704c1s
Phillips, R.C. v3p0096c1s
Phillips, R.E. v5p0122c2s
v5p0136c1s v5p0187c2s v5p0230c1s
v5p0641c1s
Phillips, Rena A. v6p0702c2s
Phillips, S. v1p0186c1s
v5p0008c2s v5p0086c1s v5p0120c1s
v5p0140c2s v5p0188c1s v5p0251c1s
v5p0352c1s v5p0405c1s v5p0581c1s
Phillips, S.C. v1p0779c1s
v6p0478c2s
Phillips, S.E. v2p0413c2s
Phillips, S.M. v1p0832c2s
Phillips, T. v1p0196c2s
Phillips, T.B. v6p0300c2s
Phillips, T.B. et al. v6p0225c1s
Phillips, T.L. v5p0365c2s
Phillips, U.B. v6p0152c2m
v6p0153c1s v6p0502c2m v6p0527c2s
v6p0597c1s v6p0605c1s v6p0605c2s
Phillips, W. v1p0082c2s
v1p0113c1s v1p0139c2s v1p0172c1s
v1p0181c2s v1p0195c2s v1p0265c2s
v1p0298c2s v1p0300c2s v1p0310c2s
v1p0322c1m v1p0324c2s v1p0383c1s
v1p0498c1m v1p0501c1s v1p0530c1s
v1p0533c2s v1p0556c2s v1p0562c1s
v1p0613c1s v1p0689c2s v1p0705c2s
v1p0730c2s v1p0760c2s v1p0780c1s
v1p0780c2m v1p0783c2s v1p0944c2s
v1p0991c1s v1p1105c1s v1p1223c2s
v1p1227c2s v1p1230c2s v1p1303c2s
v1p1352c2s v1p1425c1s
Phillips, W. et al. v1p0198c2s
Phillips, W.A. v1p0169c1s
v1p1178c2s v2p0433c1s v3p0234c1s
v4p0347c1s v4p0476c2s v4p0609c2s
v5p0288c1s v5p0352c2s
Phillips, W.A. et al. v2p0403c1s
Phillips, W.B. v6p0447c2s
Phillips, W.F. v5p0053c1s
Phillips, W.H. v1p0356c2s
v5p0536c2s
Phillips, W.S. v6p0566c1s
Phillips, Willard v1p0345c1s
Phillpotts, A.H.C. v5p0032c2s
v6p0297c1s
Phillpotts, E. v2p0001c1s
v2p0112c1s v2p0209c2s v3p0095c1s
v3p0142c1s v3p0157c1s v3p0187c2s
v3p0383c1s v3p0467c1s v4p0033c2s
v4p0090c2s v4p0134c1s v4p0188c2s
v4p0215c2s v4p0269c1s v4p0276c2s
v4p0414c1s v4p0442c2s v4p0462c2s
v4p0494c1s v4p0494c2s v4p0528c2s
v4p0531c1s v4p0540c2s v5p0211c1s
v5p0387c2s v5p0416c1s v5p0469c2s
v5p0481c1s v5p0506c2s v5p0634c1s
v6p0004c2s v6p0298c1s v6p0304c2s
v6p0346c1s v6p0380c1m v6p0499c1s
v6p0534c2s v6p0581c2s v6p0644c2s
v6p0695c2s
Phillpotts, Eden v5p0079c1s
v5p0145c2s v5p0242c1s v5p0487c1s
v5p0507c1s v6p0185c2s v6p0324c2s
Phillpotts, W. v1p0214c1s
v1p0666c2s
Philp, E. v1p1201c1s
Philp, R.K. v1p0436c1s
Philpot, W.B. v1p0409c1s
Philpott, H.B. v5p0346c2s
v5p0347c1s v5p0371c2s v5p0450c1s
v6p0056c2s v6p0104c2m v6p0384c2s
v6p0385c1s v6p0626c2s v6p0693c2s
v6p0708c1s
Philpott, H.J. v3p0031c1s
v3p0223c2s v3p0346c2s
v3p0398c1s v3p0403c2s
v3p0442c1s
v4p0011c2s
Philps, A.D. v3p0289c1s
v3p0427c1s
Philps, A.M. v3p0069c1s
Phin, J. v1p0211c1s
v1p0621c2s v1p0749c1s
Phinney, Emma D. and
Hallam, Florence M. ... v4p0161c2s
Phinney, J.I. and Gooch, F.A.
v4p0494c1s
Phinney, S.M. v6p0262c2s
Phipard, C.B. v6p0492c1s
Phippen, G.D. v1p1015c2s
Phipps, D.W. v1p0702c1s
Phipps, Dr. v1p1435c1s
Phipps, E. v1p0103c1s
v1p0837c2s
Phipps, J.H. v1p0581c1s
v1p1221c1s
Phipps, R.W. v1p1057c2s
Phipps, S.A. v3p0077c1s
Phipson, C.B. v4p0458c1s
v6p0314c2s
Phipson, S.L. v6p0214c1m
Phipson, T.L. v1p0004c2s
v1p0036c1s v1p0040c2s v1p0400c2s
v1p0532c2s v1p0924c2s v1p1002c2s
v1p1015c2s v1p1171c2s v1p1410c2s
v4p0420c1s v4p0575c1s v5p0363c2s
v5p0411c1s v5p0417c2s v5p0529c1s
v6p0259c1s
Phipson, T.S. v2p0254c2s
v2p0287c2s
Phister, N.P. v5p0290c1s
Phoebus, G.A. v1p1399c1s
v2p0286c1s v3p0090c2s
Phoebus, V.C. v1p0856c1s
v1p0935c2s
Phoebus, V.C., Mrs. v2p0004c2s
Piatt, A.S. v3p0113c1s
Piatt, D. v1p0104c2s
v1p0358c1s v1p0595c2s v1p1227c2s
v2p0075c2s v2p0417c1s
Piatt, Don v3p0088c1s
Piatt, H.S. v4p0597c2s
Piatt, J.J. v1p1250c2s
v1p1412c2s v6p0038c1s
Piatt, S.M.B. v1p0105c1s
v1p0938c1s v2p0364c2s
Piazzi-Smyth, C. et al. .. v2p0090c1m
Pica, V. v6p0053c1s
v6p0403c2s v6p0582c1s
Picard, G.H. v5p0355c1s
Picard, P.K. v2p0236c2s
Piccard, J. v3p0457c1s
Picciotto, J. v1p0199c2s
v1p0469c2s v1p0473c2s v1p0511c2s
v1p0534c2s v1p0673c2s v1p0934c1s
v1p0951c2s v1p1126c1s v1p1299c2s
v1p1326c2s
Pichler, A. v1p1324c2s
Pick, B. v1p0122c2s
v1p0126c2s v1p0691c1s v1p1171c1s
v1p1281c2s v2p0199c2m v2p0401c2s
v3p0002c2s v3p0142c2s v3p0193c1s
v3p0232c1s v3p0329c2s v3p0428c1s
v4p0302c2s v4p0542c1s v5p0056c2s
v5p0308c1s v6p0062c2s
Pickard, C.E. v4p0115c1s
Pickard, E. v6p0405c2s
Pickard, J. v3p0142c1s
v4p0165c1s v4p0186c2s v4p0242c1s
v5p0032c1s v5p0424c1s
Pickard, J.L. v1p1063c2s
v2p0107c2s v2p0202c2s v3p0296c2s
v3p0378c1s v3p0466c1s v4p0121c2s
v4p0512c2s v5p0144c1s v5p0177c1s
v5p0605c1s
Pickard, S.T. v5p0597c2s
Pickard-Cambridge, A.W. .. v6p0130c1s
v6p0341c1s v6p0554c2s
Picken, A. v1p0265c1s
Pickering, C.J. v3p0001c2s
v3p0029c1s v3p0048c2s v3p0153c1s
v3p0296c1s v3p0312c1s v3p0327c2s
v3p0368c2s
Pickering, E.C. v1p0326c2s
v1p0352c1s v1p0382c1m v1p0541c1s
v1p0747c2s v1p0865c2s v1p0903c2m
v1p1005c2s v1p1024c2s v1p1233c2s
v1p1267c2s v1p1292c1s v2p0300c2s
v2p0319c1s v2p0340c1s v2p0340c2m
v2p0413c2m v2p0417c2s v3p0399c2s
v3p0403c2s v3p0407c2s v4p0037c2s
v4p0540c2s v4p0545c1s v4p0545c2s
v4p0577c1s v5p0028c1s v5p0188c1s
v5p0194c2m v5p0257c1s v5p0277c2s
v5p0293c2s v5p0372c1m v5p0447c2s
v5p0503c2s v5p0509c1m v5p0548c2s
v5p0549c2m v5p0571c2s v6p0012c1s
v6p0037c1s v6p0037c2m v6p0210c2s
v6p0377c1s v6p0427c2s v6p0614c1s
v6p0614c2m v6p0637c1s
Pickering, J. v1p0236c2s
v1p0261c2s v1p0270c2s v1p0372c2s
v1p0385c2s v1p0392c1s v1p0396c1s
v1p0449c1s v1p0555c1s v1p0572c2s
v1p0636c2s v1p0637c2s v1p0679c2s
v1p0724c2s v1p0727c2s
Pickering, J.E.L. v2p0136c2s
Pickering, O. v1p0870c2s
Pickering, S. v3p0400c2s
v4p0453c2s v4p0601c1s v5p0190c1s
v5p0200c2s v5p0295c1s v6p0053c1s
v6p0291c2s v6p0332c2s v6p0347c2s
v6p0351c1s
Pickering, S.U. v3p0075c2s
v3p0400c1s
Pickering, S.U. and Masson, O.
v3p0168c1s
Pickering, W.A. v1p0235c1s
v1p0790c2s v4p0350c2s v4p0351c1s
Pickering, W.F. v2p0343c2s
Pickering, W.H. v2p0208c1s
v2p0413c2s v2p0424c2s v2p0425c1s
v3p0127c1m v3p0269c2s v4p0037c2s
v4p0133c2s v4p0249c2s v4p0306c2m
v4p0307c1m v4p0357c2m v4p0358c1m
v4p0381c1s v4p0406c1s v4p0568c1s
v5p0174c2s v5p0227c2s v5p0372c1s
v5p0372c2m v5p0385c1m v6p0140c2s
v6p0187c2s v6p0397c1s v6p0403c1m
v6p0413c1m v6p0427c1m v6p0427c2s
v6p0463c2s v6p0571c1s v6p0637c2s
Pickering, W.H. and Huggins, W.
v2p0425c1s
Pickering, W.H. et al. ... v5p0174c2s
Pickernell, F.A. v2p0137c1s
Pickersgill, W. v1p0397c1s
v1p0521c1s
Pickett, A.J. v1p0017c2s
Pickett, J.C. v1p0038c1s
Pickett, L.C. v4p0276c2s
v5p0420c1s
Pickett, Mrs.General v6p0377c2s
Pickett, T.J. v1p0288c2s
Pickford, A.M. v6p0258c2s
Pickford, J. v4p0141c2s
v4p0435c1s
Pickles, J.D. v4p0053c2s
Pickrel, A.R. v6p0424c1s
Pickstone, C.H. v5p0131c2s
Pickthall, M. v6p0407c1s
v6p0467c1s
Pickthall, M.L. v6p0057c2s
Pickthall, M.L.C. v6p0431c2s
Picquart, G. v6p0041c1s
v6p0688c2s
Pictet, F.J. v1p0352c1s
v1p1070c2s
Pictet, R. v1p0619c1m
v1p0955c1m v2p0028c1s v2p0294c1s
v2p0325c2m v3p0424c1s
Picton, J.A. v1p0054c1s
v1p0385c2s v1p0386c2m v1p0392c1s
v1p0537c1s v1p0586c2s v1p0687c1s
v1p1042c1s v1p1063c1s v1p1159c1m
v1p1176c2s v1p1318c1s v1p1366c1s
v2p0061c1s v2p0094c1s v2p0108c1s
v2p0153c2s v2p0201c1s v2p0310c1s
v3p0409c1s v3p0431c1s v3p0446c1s
v4p0405c2s v4p0599c1s
Picton, J.A. et al. v4p0557c2s
Piderit, T. v3p0290c2s
Pidgeon, D. v1p0226c1s
v1p1309c2s v2p0352c1s v2p0393c1s
v3p0006c1s v3p0133c2s v3p0238c2s
v3p0452c1s
Pidgeon, H. v1p0561c1s
v1p1193c2s
Pidgin, C.F. v3p0408c2s
Pidoux, M. v4p0349c1s
Pienar, P. v5p0589c1s
v5p0627c1s
Piens, C. v6p0712c2s
Pieper, F. v4p0053c2s
Pier, A.S. v4p0256c1s
v6p0141c2s v6p0163c1s v6p0525c2s
v6p0629c1s v6p0638c2s v6p0657c2s
v6p0672c2s v6p0707c2s
Pier, F. v6p0421c1s
Pier, F.S. v6p0236c1s
Pier, Florida v6p0512c2s
Pierantoni, A. v6p0390c2s
Pierce, A.H. v5p0279c2s

v5p0280c1s v5p0422c2s v6p0521c2s
Pierce, A.H. and Angell, J.R. v4p0036c2s
Pierce, B. v2p0407c1s
Pierce, B.K. v1p0317c1s v1p0337c1s v1p0707c2s v1p0783c2s v1p1089c1s v2p0256c2s v3p0052c2s
Pierce, C.C. v5p0445c2s
Pierce, C.H. v1p0946c2s
Pierce, C.S. v1p0110c1s v4p0026c1s v4p0140c2s v4p0153c2s v4p0240c2s v6p0001c1s v6p0245c2s v6p0483c1s v6p0554c1s v6p0576c1s
Pierce, D.T. v5p0464c2s v6p0014c2s v6p0078c2s v6p0561c2s
Pierce, Daniel J. v6p0018c2s
Pierce, Daniel T. v6p0301c2s v6p0308c2s
Pierce, E. v3p0123c2s v4p0004c2s
Pierce, E.C. v3p0345c2s
Pierce, E.L. v1p0487c1m v1p0870c2s v1p1148c1s v1p1267c1s v4p0520c2s
Pierce, E.T. v4p0566c2s
Pierce, E.T. et al. v5p0413c2s
Pierce, E.W. v1p1361c1s
Pierce, F.C. v2p0178c1s v6p0596c2s
Pierce, F.H. v2p0203c1s
Pierce, G. v1p0228c1s
Pierce, G.A. v1p0717c2s v2p0234c1s v5p0539c1s v6p0048c1s
Pierce, G.H. v1p0855c2s
Pierce, G.J. v4p0069c2s
Pierce, G.W. v1p0194c2s v2p0297c1s v5p0476c1s
Pierce, Grace A. v6p0225c1s
Pierce, H.A. v3p0393c1s v3p0461c2s v6p0283c1s
Pierce, H.H.D. v6p0555c2s
Pierce, H.W. v6p0366c2s
Pierce, J. v1p0240c1s v1p0834c2s v4p0598c1s
Pierce, J., jr. v1p0024c1s v3p0313c2s v4p0238c1s
Pierce, J.D. v1p0291c1s
Pierce, J.O. v1p0805c1s v1p0838c1s v2p0115c2s v2p0184c1s v2p0223c1s v2p0251c1m v2p0290c1s v2p0299c1s v2p0398c1s v3p0010c2s v3p0011c2s v3p0097c2m v3p0218c2m v3p0235c2s v3p0244c2s v3p0292c1s v3p0310c2s v3p0424c2s v3p0442c1m v3p0450c1s v3p0455c1s v4p0181c1s v4p0560c2s v4p0592c2s v4p0623c1s v5p0074c2s v5p0130c1s v5p0189c2s v5p0494c2s v5p0600c1s v6p0205c2s v6p0339c2s v6p0426c1s v6p0700c1s
Pierce, M.E. v6p0405c1s
Pierce, M.T. v6p0093c1s
Pierce, Mary v6p0335c1s
Pierce, N. v1p1091c1s
Pierce, N.B. v6p0485c2s
Pierce, O.W. v4p0076c1s
Pierce, P.B. v5p0386c2s
Pierce, P.E. v6p0494c2s
Pierce, S.O. v2p0223c1s
Pierce, V.M. and Emery, Clay v6p0299c2s
Pierce, Z.F. v1p0608c1s
Piercy, E.B. v5p0495c1s
Piercy, J.W. v5p0122c1s v6p0263c1s v6p0466c1s
Pierides, G.D. v5p0510c1s
Pieron et al. v6p0521c1s
Pieron, H. and Vaschide, N. v5p0168c1s
Pierpont, J. v6p0091c2s v6p0210c1s
Pierpont, James v5p0223c1s
Pierra, F.G. v5p0147c2s
Pierre, A. v4p0047c1s
Pierrelee, S.De v6p0544c2s
Pierrepont, E. v3p0036c2s v3p0393c1s
Pierrepont, E. et al. v3p0360c2s
Pierson, A. v2p0352c1s
Pierson, A.J. v1p0432c2s
Pierson, A.T. v3p0084c1s
Pierson, Arthur T. v6p0005c2s
Pierson, C.W. v3p0178c2s v3p0179c1s v4p0131c2s
Pierson, D.L. v6p0019c1s v6p0313c2s
Pierson, H. v1p1189c1s v3p0058c1s v3p0177c1s v3p0186c2s v3p0373c1s v4p0293c1s
Pierson, H.C. v5p0213c1s v5p0489c1s
Pierson, H.W. v1p0196c1s v2p0198c2s
Pierson, Helen W. v5p0499c2s
Pierson, J. v3p0258c2s
Pierson, N.E. v6p0621c2s
Pierson, N.G. v4p0230c1s v4p0458c1s v5p0172c1s v6p0300c1s
Pierson, W.H. v1p0576c2s v2p0158c1s v2p0451c2s v3p0345c1s
Piesse, S. v1p0225c1s
Pieters, A.J. v5p0581c2s
Pietersen, J.F.G. v4p0285c1s
Pietrement, C.A. v2p0121c2s
Pietrie, A.J. v6p0084c1s
Pietsch, T.W. v6p0264c1s v6p0518c1s
Pietschmann, R. v6p0185c1s
Piffard, H. v3p0419c2s
Pigeon, A. v4p0091c1s
Pigeon, C.D. v1p0001c2s v1p0440c1s v1p0700c1s v1p0911c2s v1p1201c1s v1p1302c1s v1p1302c2s v1p1303c2s
Piggot, J. v1p0055c2s v1p0103c2s v1p0110c2s v1p0157c2s v1p0257c2s v1p0806c2s v1p1180c2s
Piggot, J., jr. v1p0546c2s v1p0593c2s
Piggot, M.M. v4p0276c2s
Piggott, A.S. v1p0014c2s v1p0036c1s v1p0771c1s
Piggott, F.T. v3p0227c1s v4p0296c2m v4p0297c2s v4p0298c2s
Piggott, H.J. v5p0459c1s
Piggott, M.T. v5p0259c1s
Pignatorre, G. v6p0038c2s v6p0549c1s
Pigon, A.C. v6p0263c2s v6p0411c2s
Pigorini, L. and Lubbock, J., Sir v1p1359c1s
Pigot, J.H. v5p0170c1s
Pigott, A.S. v1p0237c2s v1p0450c1s
Pigott, F.T. v2p0466c1s
Pigott, G.W.R. v1p0583c2s
Pigott, R. v1p0735c1s v2p0227c1m v2p0227c2s v2p0228c2s
Pigott, T.D. v3p0036c2s v3p0045c2s v3p0046c1s v3p0149c2s v3p0390c2s v4p0260c1s v4p0519c2s v5p0504c2s v6p0067c1s v6p0183c1s
Pigott, W. v4p0481c2s v5p0168c1s v5p0496c2s
Pigou, A. v6p0425c2s
Pigou, A.C. v6p0085c1s v6p0108c1s v6p0184c1s v6p0188c2s v6p0240c1s v6p0271c1m v6p0469c1s v6p0507c1s v6p0596c1s v6p0634c1s v6p0673c1s
Pike, A. v1p0047c1s v1p0058c1s v1p0620c1s
Pike, C. v3p0196c2s v3p0272c1s
Pike, C.W. v3p0002c1s v4p0174c2s
Pike, G.H. v2p0041c2s v2p0047c1s v2p0264c2s v2p0362c1s v2p0396c2s v2p0438c2s v3p0005c2s v3p0008c2s v3p0358c1s v3p0369c2s v3p0428c2s v3p0464c2s v4p0064c1s v4p0149c2s v4p0312c1s v4p0338c2s v4p0347c1s v4p0414c2s v5p0211c2s v6p0517c2s
Pike, G.R. v3p0349c1s
Pike, H.L. v6p0382c2s
Pike, J. v1p0441c1s
Pike, L.O. v1p0352c1s v1p1073c2s v1p1296c2s v1p1421c1s v4p0095c2s v5p0643c2s
Pike, L.W. v5p0587c2s
Pike, M.C. v1p0159c1s
Pike, N. v2p0312c2s v4p0560c2s
Pike, R. v1p0689c1s v1p1040c2s
Pike, R.S. v6p0623c1s
Pike, W.A. v2p0422c2s v4p0547c2s
Pikler, J. v3p0331c2s
Pilbrow, J. v1p1121c1s
Pilchau, G.Pilar Von v4p0502c2s
Pilcher, J.E. v3p0152c1s v3p0315c2s v4p0535c2s v5p0162c2s v5p0208c1s v5p0449c2s v5p0626c2s
Pilcher, L.W. v1p0173c1s v1p0725c1s
Pilcher, T.D. v5p0032c1s
Pile, W.H. v1p1233c1s
Pilgrim, C.W. v3p0216c2s v3p0414c2s v4p0221c2s v4p0285c2s v4p0555c2s
Piling v2p0438c2s
Pitkington, H.L. v5p0098c1s
Pilkington, R. v1p0525c2s
Pillai, G.P. v5p0006c2s v5p0286c2s
Pillai, P.P. v5p0355c1s
Pillet, A. v6p0232c2s
Pillet, E. v2p0337c1s
Pillsbury, A. v2p0056c2s v3p0269c2s
Pillsbury, A.E. v5p0329c2s v6p0302c2s v6p0390c2s
Pillsbury, A.J. v4p0596c1s v5p0088c1s v5p0159c2s
Pillsbury, H.N. v4p0099c1s
Pillsbury, J.E. v4p0244c2s
Pillsbury, J.H. v4p0125c1m
Pillsbury, P. v2p0163c2s
v2p0374c2s
Pillsbury, R. v6p0603c2s
Pillsbury, R.L. v6p0390c1s
Pillsbury, W.B. v4p0528c2s v5p0024c1s v5p0292c2s v5p0389c2s v5p0486c2s v6p0105c1s v6p0215c1s v6p0220c2s
Pilon, M.R. v1p0028c1s
Pilsbry, H.A. v4p0531c1s v5p0382c1s v5p0534c1s v6p0229c1s
Pilsbury, C.A. v1p1406c2s v2p0194c2s v2p0411c1s v2p0412c1s
Pilsbury, P. v2p0171c2s
Pim, B. v1p1294c1s v2p0158c1s v2p0451c1s v3p0305c1s v3p0318c2s
Pinard, E. v4p0212c1s
Pinch, P. v3p0298c2s
Pinches, T.G. v3p0029c2m v3p0104c1s v3p0275c1s v4p0040c2m v4p0173c2s
Pinchot, G. v3p0158c1s v4p0208c1s v4p0208c2m v5p0408c1s v5p0589c2s v6p0233c1s v6p0329c2s
Pinchot, Gifford v4p0207c2s v5p0214c1s v6p0233c1s
Pinchot, J.W. v6p0233c2s
Pinckney, C.C. v5p0088c1s v5p0567c1s
Pinckney, F.S. v3p0473c2s
Pinckney, G.M. v6p0092c1s
Pinckney, H.L. v1p1237c1s
Pinckney, P. v5p0029c1s
Pinckney, T. v1p0503c1s
Pincoffs, A.L. v1p0730c1s v2p0205c1s v4p0260c1s
Pincott, F. v2p0217c1s v3p0019c2s v3p0023c1s v3p0130c1s v3p0131c2s v3p0199c1s v3p0211c1s v3p0211c2s v3p0212c1m v3p0268c2s v4p0026c2s
Pincus, J.W. v6p0706c2s
Pinder, N. v4p0214c2s
Pine, B. v1p0144c2s v1p0963c1s v1p1441c2s
Pine, J.B. v6p0187c2s v6p0281c1s v6p0427c2m v6p0649c2s
Pinero, A.W. v3p0139c2s v6p0617c2s
Pingey, D.H. v3p0150c2s
Pingree, H.P. v4p0444c1s
Pingree, H.S. v4p0115c2s v4p0154c1s v4p0452c1s v5p0119c2s v5p0207c1s v5p0556c2s
Pingrey, D.H. v4p0087c1s v5p0600c1s
Pink, L.A. v6p0453c1s
Pink, L.R. v6p0566c1s
Pink, Louis B. v6p0091c1s
Pink, R. v1p0664c1s
Pink, W.D. v1p0100c1s v1p0154c1s
Pinkerton, B.J. v1p0687c1s
Pinkerton, L.L. v1p0239c2s
Pinkerton, P. v3p0024c1s v3p0322c2s
Pinkerton, P.E. v1p1127c1s v1p1419c1s v4p0033c1s v4p0429c2s v4p0600c1s
Pinkerton, R.A. v4p0209c2s v5p0018c1s
Pinkerton, W. v1p0069c2s
Pinkerton, W.A. v4p0471c2s
Pinkham, G.R. v5p0413c2s
Pinkham, J.W. v1p1391c2s v2p0396c1s
Pinkney, E.C. v5p0260c1s
Pinkus, N. v6p0034c2s v6p0255c1s v6p0322c2s
Pinnington, E. v5p0073c2s v5p0079c1s v5p0100c2s v5p0326c2s v5p0354c2s v5p0384c2s v5p0505c2s v5p0515c1s v6p0095c1s v6p0239c2s v6p0484c1s v6p0578c1s
Pinnington, Edward v5p0171c1s v5p0207c2s
Pinon, R. v5p0112c2s
Pinsent, R.J. v3p0301c1s
Pinzger, L. v2p0078c2s
Pio, L. v2p0403c2s v2p0480c1s
Pipe, W. v4p0479c1s
Piper, C.V. v6p0264c2s v6p0432c2s
Piper, Dr. v1p1323c2s
Piper, E.B. v6p0509c2s
Piper, F. v1p0865c1s
Piper, H.L. v4p0331c1s
Piper, P. v6p0164c1s
Piper, P.F. v5p0126c2s
Pipson, T.L. v4p0047c1s
Pireau, M. v4p0590c1s
Piril, A.F. and Lorne, Marquis of v2p0066c1s
Pirkey, O. v3p0416c1s
Pirkis, C.L. v1p0674c1s v2p0112c2s v3p0025c1s v3p0111c2s v3p0356c1s
Pirsson et al. v4p0020c2s
Pirsson, L.V. v3p0062c2s

v3p0174c2s v3p0287c2s v3p0360c2s v4p0128c1s v4p0148c1s v4p0155c2s v4p0179c2s v4p0439c2m v4p0607c1s v5p0004c2s v5p0138c2s v5p0279c2s v6p0426c2s v6p0487c2s
Pirsson, L.V. and Robinson, H.H. v5p0377c2s
Pirsson, L.V. and Washington, H.S. v6p0057c2m v6p0450c2s
Pirsson, L.V. and Weed, W.H. v4p0048c2s v4p0274c1m v4p0375c1s v5p0527c1s
Pirsson, L.V. and Wells, H.L. v4p0324c1s
Pirtle, J.B. . . . v1p1369c2s
Pirtsch, H. . . . v2p0345c2s
Pise, C.C. . . . v1p1372c1s
Pitcairn-Knowles, A. . . . v6p0648c2s
Pitcher, F.B. . . . v3p0403c2s
Pitcher, J. . . . v4p0228c2s
Pitcher, J.R. . . . v3p0001c2s
Pite, B. . . . v5p0333c1s v6p0028c2m
Pitkin, L. . . . v3p0170c2s
Pitkin, T. . . . v1p0353c1s v1p1350c1s
Pitkin, T.C. . . . v1p0229c1s v1p0240c1s v1p0292c1s v1p0422c1s v1p0422c2s v1p0756c2s v1p1436c1s
Pitkin, W.B. . . . v6p0353c2s v6p0495c2s v6p0583c2s
Pitman, A.J. . . . v4p0030c2s
Pitman, C.B. . . . v2p0075c2s v2p0294c2s
Pitman, E.R. . . . v2p0085c1s v2p0461c1s
Pitman, F.I. . . . v3p0048c1s
Pitman, H.A. . . . v5p0557c1s
Pitman, I. . . . v4p0522c1s
Pitman, J.C.R. . . . v2p0476c2s
Pitman, J.H. . . . v4p0538c2s
Pitman, M.J. . . . v2p0384c2s
Pitman, R.C. . . . v1p0170c1s v1p0752c1s v1p0775c1s v1p1292c1s v2p0240c1s v3p0049c2s v3p0373c2s v3p0378c2s
Pitman, W. . . . v3p0113c2s
Pitre, G. . . . v1p0803c2s v1p1195c1s v4p0491c1s
Pitt, B.J. . . . v3p0057c1s
Pitt, J. . . . v1p1430c2s
Pitt, W. . . . v4p0132c1s
Pitt-Lewis, G. . . . v4p0190c2s v4p0261c2s v5p0143c2s v5p0392c2s
Pitt-Rivers . . . v5p0212c2s
Pitt-Rivers, F. . . . v3p0015c1s v3p0286c2s
Pitt-Rivers, Lt.-Gen. . . . v4p0589c1s
Pittenger, W. . . . v3p0255c1s
Pittman, E.F. . . . v1p0584c2s
Pitts, G.L. . . . v6p0331c1s
Pitts, Mabel P. . . . v6p0366c2s v6p0461c1s
Pitzer, A.W. . . . v1p0255c1s v1p1285c2s v2p0394c1s
Pitzer, R.G. . . . v6p0619c2s
Pius X. . . . v6p0241c2s v6p0274c1s v6p0308c1s v6p0438c2m v6p0509c1s v6p0513c2s v6p0547c1s v6p0547c2s
Pixley, F.M. . . . v6p0092c1m
Pixley, M. . . . v6p0121c1s
Placci, C. . . . v2p0125c2s
Place, Francis La . . . v6p0124c2s
Place, Helen . . . v5p0393c1s v5p0395c1s
Place, Helen M. . . . v5p0394c2m
Placzek, B. . . . v2p0017c1s v2p0047c1s
Plain, H. . . . v3p0046c2s
Plamer, E. . . . v1p0637c2s
Plamer, G.H. . . . v3p0132c2s
Planat, P. . . . v3p0018c1s v3p0018c2s v4p0024c1s v4p0024c2s
Planch, J.G. . . . v1p1089c1s
Planche, J.R. . . . v1p1242c1s v2p0021c2s v2p0078c1s
Planche, J.R. and Nicolas, N.H. v1p1051c1s
Planchut, E. . . . v1p0998c1s v1p1129c2s v3p0395c1s v3p0438c1s
Planck, A. . . . v1p0775c2s
Planck, C. . . . v6p0395c1s
Planck, D.A. . . . v2p0211c2s
Planck, J.C.Ver . . . v1p0593c1m v3p0428c1s
Planck, Prof. . . . v1p0554c2s
Planck, W.E.Ver . . . v4p0114c2s v4p0266c2m v4p0268c1m
Plank, E.N. . . . v4p0069c2m v4p0399c1s v4p0514c1s v4p0571c1m
Plank, G.J. . . . v1p0126c1s
Plant, A.W. . . . v4p0241c1s
Plant, H.B. . . . v4p0471c2s
Plant, J.C. . . . v3p0396c1s
Plante, G. . . . v1p1104c2s
Plantz, S. . . . v6p0418c2s
Plantz, Samuel . . . v4p0218c1s
Plarr, M.J. . . . v4p0452c2s v5p0499c1s
Plarr, V. . . . v3p0447c1s v5p0498c2s
Plassmann, P. . . . v4p0010c2s
Plat, E.A.Du . . . v5p0240c1m
Platano, G. . . . v4p0189c1s
Plateau, F. . . . v1p0644c2s
Platfield, J.J. . . . v6p0113c1s v6p0261c1s
Platner, J.W. . . . v6p0024c2s v6p0281c2s v6p0710c2s
Platner, S.B. . . . v3p0023c1s v3p0172c1s v3p0295c1s v3p0335c1s v3p0419c1s v4p0092c2s v4p0225c1s v4p0447c2s v5p0119c1m v5p0458c1s v6p0549c2s
Platt, C.A. . . . v4p0220c1s
Platt, C.C. . . . v3p0431c2s
Platt, C.M. . . . v2p0313c2s v3p0233c2s v4p0233c2s v4p0323c1s v4p0539c1s v4p0546c1s
Platt, Dr. . . . v1p1031c2s
Platt, F. . . . v5p0089c1s v5p0473c1s
Platt, Frederic . . . v6p0094c1s
Platt, H.E. . . . v5p0012c1s
Platt, H.E.P. . . . v1p1171c1s v1p1216c1s
Platt, I.H. . . . v4p0520c1s v4p0620c2s v6p0587c1s v6p0697c1s
Platt, J. . . . v4p0106c2s v4p0415c1s v5p0272c1s v5p0383c2s v5p0402c2s v5p0582c2s v5p0622c2s
Platt, J. and Murray, J.A.H. v5p0301c2s
Platt, J.C. . . . v4p0105c1s
Platt, J.I. . . . v1p0259c1s
Platt, J.T. . . . v1p0438c2s v2p0372c2s
Platt, James . . . v4p0245c1s
Platt, L.B. . . . v3p0029c2s v3p0038c1s v3p0275c2s v3p0394c2s v3p0420c2s
Platt, O.H. . . . v4p0281c2s v5p0146c2s v5p0147c2s v5p0148c1s v6p0160c1s
Platt, T.C. . . . v4p0596c1s v5p0603c2s
Platt, T.C. et al. . . . v4p0384c1s
Platt, W. . . . v5p0382c1s
Platt, W.B. . . . v3p0086c1m
Platt, W.H. . . . v2p0375c2s
Platts, W.C. . . . v4p0004c2s v4p0568c2s v4p0579c1s v5p0339c2s v5p0443c1s
Platz, E. . . . v5p0095c2s
Plautz, S. . . . v6p0534c2s
Playfair and Bensen . . . v1p0502c1s v1p0502c2s
Playfair and Bunsen . . . v1p0495c1s
Playfair, A. . . . v4p0371c2s
Playfair, G.J. . . . v1p1331c1s
Playfair, J. . . . v1p0014c1s v1p0075c2s v1p0429c1s v1p0506c2s v1p0510c1m v1p0706c1s v1p0725c1m v1p0824c1s v1p0986c2s v1p1053c2s v1p1325c2s
Playfair, J. and Smith, Syd. v1p0954c1s
Playfair, J.E. . . . v4p0244c1s
Playfair, L. . . . v1p0380c1s v1p0465c2s v1p0630c1s v1p0747c1s v1p0762c2s v1p0978c2s v1p1288c2m v1p1356c2s v1p1400c1s v2p0337c2s v2p0356c2s v2p0390c1s v3p0176c1s v3p0346c2s v3p0379c2s v3p0380c1s v3p0393c1s v4p0340c2s v4p0612c2s v5p0069c2s
Playfair, L., Sir . . . v2p0113c2s v2p0457c1s v3p0017c1s v3p0422c2s v3p0444c1s v4p0565c1s
Playfair, Lyon . . . v2p0454c1s
Playfair, R.C. . . . v5p0004c1m
Playfair, R.L. . . . v3p0273c1s
Playfair, R.L., Sir . . . v2p0336c1s
Playter, G.F. . . . v1p1398c2s
Pleasanton, A. and Howard, O.O. v2p0074c1s
Pleasants, H.R. . . . v1p1224c1s v1p1373c2s
Pleasants, J.H. . . . v1p0183c2s
Pleasants, L.L. . . . v1p0569c2s v4p0276c2s
Pledge, J.H. . . . v5p0479c1s
Pledge, J.L.de. . . . v4p0409c2s
Plehn, C.C. . . . v3p0347c2s v4p0083c2s v5p0088c1s v5p0088c2s v5p0207c1s v5p0293c2s v5p0445c2s v5p0568c1m v6p0141c1s v6p0188c2s v6p0211c2s v6p0238c2m v6p0493c1s v6p0494c2m v6p0608c1s v6p0634c1s v6p0651c2s v6p0682c2s
Plehn, C.C. et al. . . . v6p0318c1s
Plehve, M.de . . . v6p0224c2s
Pleydell, E.F. . . . v1p1165c2s
Pleyte, C.M. and Ray, S. . v3p0440c1s
Plimpton, E.L. . . . v1p0307c1s
Plimpton, F.B. . . . v1p0246c1s
Plimsoll, S. . . . v1p0269c1s v2p0157c2s v2p0330c2s v3p0391c1s v3p0437c1s
Plimsoll, S. and Scrutton, T. v3p0218c1s
Plitt, Dr. . . . v1p0255c2s v1p0848c1s
Plitt, G.L. . . . v1p0076c1s
Plomer, H.R. . . . v4p0011c2m v4p0067c1s v4p0258c2s v4p0341c1s v4p0459c1s v4p0461c1s v4p0474c1s v4p0580c1s v5p0173c1s v5p0336c2s v5p0453c1s v5p0466c2m v5p0528c2s v5p0607c1s v5p0630c1s v6p0075c1m v6p0105c1s v6p0284c2s v6p0385c1s v6p0411c1s v6p0473c2s v6p0515c2s v6p0517c1m v6p0523c1s v6p0588c2s v6p0693c2s
Plongeon, A.D.Le . . . v2p0482c2s v3p0475c1s v4p0454c2s
Plongeon, A.D.Le, Mme. . . . v4p0024c2s
Plongeon, A.D.Le, Mrs. . . . v3p0272c1s v3p0475c1s v4p0362c1s
Plongeon, A.Le . . . v1p0376c2m v1p1439c2s v3p0404c1s
Plongeon, Alice D.Le . . . v4p0636c2s
Ploss, E.B. . . . v6p0053c1s
Plowden, T.C. . . . v2p0018c1s v2p0449c1s
Plowman, A.B. . . . v6p0502c1s v6p0502c2s v6p0551c2s
Plowman, H. . . . v3p0268c1s
Plowman, T.F. . . . v5p0244c2s
Plowright, C.B. . . . v5p0634c2s v6p0019c1s
Plues, M. . . . v1p0494c2s v1p0698c2s
Plumacher, O. . . . v1p0993c2s
Plumandon, J.R. . . . v5p0478c1s
Plumasier, A. . . . v1p0341c2s
Plumassier, A. . . . v1p0461c2s
Plumb, A.H. . . . v3p0303c1s v4p0573c1s
Plumb, C.S. . . . v3p0006c2s v4p0195c1s v4p0207c2s v4p0208c1s v4p0354c2m v4p0436c1s v4p0454c2s v4p0605c1s
Plumb, D. . . . v1p1264c2s
Plumb, D.H. . . . v3p0073c2s v3p0383c2s
Plumbe, G.E. . . . v1p1263c1s
Plumbe, R. . . . v1p0211c1s v1p1110c2s
Plumer, J. . . . v2p0119c2s
Plumer, W. . . . v1p0911c1s
Plumer, W.S. . . . v1p0370c1s v1p0596c1s v1p1120c2s v1p1275c1s v1p1277c2s
Plumley, G.S. . . . v3p0455c2s
Plumly, B.R. . . . v1p0001c2s
Plummer, A. . . . v3p0043c1s v4p0057c1s v4p0158c1s v4p0300c1s v4p0436c2s v5p0059c2s
Plummer, E.C. . . . v4p0047c1s v4p0356c1s v4p0460c1s v5p0526c2s
Plummer, E.H. . . . v5p0029c2s
Plummer, F.G. . . . v4p0498c2s
Plummer, J. . . . v1p0113c1s v1p0261c1m v1p0299c2s v1p0315c1s v1p0472c2s v1p0501c1s v1p0503c2s v1p0714c1s v1p0762c1s v1p0762c2s v1p0782c2s v1p0844c1s v1p0972c1s v1p1043c1s v1p1132c2s v1p1246c1s v1p1260c1s v1p1321c2s v1p1379c2s v1p1423c1s v2p0023c2s v2p0024c2s v2p0029c1m v2p0067c1s v2p0077c2s v2p0126c1s v2p0126c2s v2p0312c2s v2p0340c1s v2p0396c2s v2p0432c2s v2p0444c2s v2p0465c2s v2p0479c2s v2p0480c1m
Plummer, J.J. . . . v1p0828c2s v1p0904c1s
Plummer, J.T. . . . v1p0067c1m
Plummer, John . . . v6p0706c2s
Plummer, M.R. . . . v6p0417c1s
Plummer, M.W. . . . v3p0249c2m v4p0329c2s v4p0330c1s v5p0332c2s v5p0333c1s v5p0335c1m v5p0463c1s v6p0017c1s v6p0370c1s
Plummer, M.W. et al. . . . v6p0375c1s
Plummer, T. . . . v3p0136c1s
Plummer, W.E. . . . v3p0127c1s v4p0126c2s v4p0258c1s v4p0460c1s v4p0550c2s v5p0093c1s v5p0100c1s v5p0265c2s v5p0338c1s v5p0549c2s v5p0641c2s v6p0055c1s v6p0094c1s v6p0221c1s v6p0280c2s v6p0287c1s v6p0348c1s v6p0361c1s v6p0554c1s v6p0595c1s
Plummer, W.S. and Woods, L. v1p0239c2s
Plumptre, C. . . . v1p0904c1s v1p0999c2s
Plumptre, C.E. . . . v2p0457c2s v3p0030c1s v3p0053c1s v3p0058c1s v6p0403c2s
Plumptre, E.H. . . . v1p0046c2s v1p0076c1s v1p0085c2s v1p0251c1m v1p0293c1s v1p0331c2s v1p0385c1s v1p0406c2s v1p0440c1s v1p0668c1s v1p0700c1s v1p0879c2s v1p0953c2s

v1p0980c1s v1p0980c2s v1p1056c2s
v1p1095c1s v1p1139c1s v1p1269c2s
v1p1281c2s v2p0084c1s v2p0111c2m
v3p0231c1s v3p0389c1s v3p0398c1s
v3p0459c2s
Plumptre, E.H. and Godet, F.
v2p0478c1s
Plumstead, E. v5p0456c2s
Plunket, F.L. v5p0564c1s
Plunkett, A.H. v1p1148c1s
Plunkett, G.N. v3p0314c1s
Plunkett, G.T. v6p0034c2s
Plunkett, H. v4p0290c2s
v5p0295c2m v5p0296c2s v6p0326c2s
Plunkett, H.C. v3p0099c2s
Plunkett, H.M. v5p0194c1s
Plunkett, H.M., Mrs. v1p0606c2s
v2p0378c1s v3p0258c1s v4p0041c1s
v4p0311c1s v4p0354c1s v4p0363c2s
v4p0380c1s v4p0444c2s v4p0599c1s
v5p0554c1s v6p0134c1s
Plunkett, L. v6p0007c2s
Plush, S.M. v1p1002c2s
v1p1291c1m v1p1291c2s
Plutarch v1p0386c1s
v1p0691c2s
Pluvinel, De la B. v4p0167c1s
Plympton, G.W. v2p0382c2m
Pobedonostseff, C. v5p0501c1s
Pobedonostseff, C.P. v6p0043c2s
v6p0170c1s
Pochet, L. v1p1249c1s
Pockels, A. v4p0411c2s
Pocock, N. v2p0041c2s
v2p0042c1m v2p0044c1s v2p0084c2s
v3p0040c2s v3p0042c2s v3p0083c1s
v3p0150c2s v3p0264c2s v4p0182c1s
v4p0260c1s v5p0076c2s v5p0262c1s
Pocock, R. v5p0091c2s
v5p0220c1s v5p0299c1s v5p0318c2s
v5p0412c2s v5p0629c2s v6p0055c2s
v6p0243c2s
Pocock, R.I. v3p0404c2s
v4p0508c1m v4p0508c2m v4p0541c2m
v4p0615c2s v5p0022c2s v5p0280c2s
v5p0538c2s v5p0546c1m v6p0610c2s
Pocock, R.L. v6p0524c1s
Pocock, Wm.W. v3p0002c1s
Pococke, R. v1p0656c1s
Podgorski, C.M. v4p0459c1s
Podmore, F. v4p0063c2s
v4p0437c2s v4p0464c1m v6p0148c2s
v6p0472c2s v6p0611c1s
Poe, C.H. v6p0391c1s
v6p0459c2s v6p0554c2s v6p0574c2s
v6p0624c1s v6p0665c2s
Poe, Clarence H. v6p0152c2s
Poe, Clarence H. and Burkett, C.W.
v6p0152c2s
Poe, D.A. v3p0066c1s
Poe, E.A. v1p0024c2s
v1p0113c2s v1p0147c1s v1p0217c1s
v1p0363c1s v1p0421c1s v1p0441c2s
v1p0570c1s v1p0577c2s v1p0740c1s
v1p0751c2s v1p0770c1s v1p0798c1s
v1p0800c1m v1p0818c2s v1p0832c1s
v1p0880c1s v1p0917c1s v1p1280c2s
v1p1308c1s v1p1361c1s v1p1368c1s
v1p1375c2s v3p0038c2s v4p0206c2s
v6p0699c2s
Poe, F. v1p0188c2s
v1p0574c2s v1p0956c1s
Poe, W.B. v6p0446c2s
Poech, F. v2p0090c1s
Poel, W. v3p0388c2s
v4p0002c2s v4p0178c1s v4p0572c1s
v6p0616c1s
Poels, H.A. v6p0292c2s
v6p0321c1m
Poesche, E. v4p0326c1s
Poey, A. v1p0266c1s
v1p0747c2s v1p0748c2s
Poey, Prof. v1p0266c2s
Poggendorff, J.C. v1p0400c1s
Pogson, F.L. v6p0065c1s
v6p0623c2s
Pogue, B.C. v3p0307c2s
Pogue, M.P. v6p0046c1s
Pohl, M. v1p0563c1s
Pohli, E. v3p0332c1s
Pohlman v2p0175c2s
Pohlman, A.V. v6p0370c1s
Poincare, H. v5p0229c1s
v6p0406c1s v6p0406c2s v6p0417c1s
v6p0498c2s
Poincare, M.H. v6p0576c2s
Poindexter, A.M. v1p0847c2s
Poindexter, J.W. v2p0205c1s
v2p0385c2m
Poindexter, P. v3p0056c2s
Poingdestre, E. v2p0422c2s
Poinier, P. v1p0579c2s
Poinier, P.P. v1p1362c2s
Poinsett, J.R. v1p0437c1s
v1p0832c2s v1p0834c1s v1p1224c1s
v1p1352c1s
Pointer, E.F. v2p0140c2s
Poirel, M. v1p0022c1s
Poison, M. v1p1293c1s
Poisson, A. and Hallopeau, L.A.
v4p0482c2s
Poisson, J. v1p1362c2s
v3p0318c2s
Pokagon, S. v4p0282c2s
v4p0443c1s v5p0155c1s v5p0288c1m
v5p0462c1s
Poland, A.E. v3p0422c1s
Poland, H. v6p0099c1s
Poland, H.B. and Edgcumbe, R
v6p0157c1s
Poland, H.B. et al. v4p0139c2s
Poland, W. v3p0331c2s
v3p0379c2s v4p0295c1s v4p0439c2s
v5p0126c1s v5p0177c1s v6p0191c1s
v6p0199c2s v6p0575c1s
Poland, W.C. v4p0285c2s
Pole, Prof. v1p0381c2s
Pole, W. v1p0008c1s
v1p0089c1s v1p0200c1s v1p0211c2s
v1p0278c2m v1p0329c2s v1p0348c2s
v1p0404c1s v1p0723c1s v1p0882c2s
v1p0885c1s v1p0885c2s v1p1003c2s
v1p1144c2s v1p1160c1s v1p1248c1m
v1p1375c1s v1p1405c2m v2p0003c1m
v2p0467c2s v3p0290c2s v3p0293c1s
Polenburg, A. v1p0308c2s
Polignac, C.de v4p0589c2s
Politis, N.G. v4p0217c2s
Polk, C.J. v1p0934c2s
Polk, L.L. v3p0149c2s
Polk, R.T. v3p0230c1s
Polk, W.M. v1p1191c1m
v2p0077c1s
Polk, W.N. v1p0228c1s
v2p0077c1m
Polko, E. v1p0020c1s
v1p0197c2s v1p0472c2s v1p0589c1s
v1p0703c2s v1p0789c1s v1p1188c1s
v5p0078c1s v5p0580c2s
Pollak, G. v1p0168c1s
v1p0651c2s v1p0995c1s v1p1301c1s
v3p0031c1s v3p0171c1s v4p0121c2s
v5p0230c2s v6p0048c1s v6p0251c2s
v6p0254c1s v6p0478c1s v6p0574c2s
v6p0621c1s
Pollard, A. v3p0350c2s
v4p0357c1s v5p0400c1s
Pollard, A.F. v5p0538c2s
Pollard, A.W. v3p0178c1s
v3p0266c1s v3p0421c2s v3p0468c2s
v3p0470c1s v4p0067c1m v4p0067c2m
v4p0098c1s v4p0098c2s v4p0110c2s
v4p0256c1s v4p0274c2s v4p0284c2s
v4p0631c1m v5p0061c1s v5p0070c1s
v5p0071c1s v5p0162c2s v5p0280c1s
v5p0454c2s v6p0018c2s v6p0065c1s
v6p0073c2s v6p0074c2s v6p0083c1s
v6p0105c2s v6p0110c2s v6p0139c1s
v6p0293c1s v6p0518c1m v6p0542c2s
v6p0588c1s v6p0648c1s
Pollard, Alfred W. v4p0577c2s
Pollard, Annie A. v6p0373c2s
Pollard, Aylmer v5p0498c1s
Pollard, C.L. v4p0157c1s
v5p0413c1s
Pollard, C.S. v5p0073c1s
Pollard, E.A. v1p0046c2s
v1p0048c2s v1p0110c1s v1p0288c2s
v1p0585c2s v1p0675c1s v1p0698c2s
v1p0904c2s v1p0905c1s v1p1027c2s
v1p1124c1s v1p1224c1s v1p1374c1s
v1p1374c2s v1p1394c1s
Pollard, E.B. v4p0299c2s
v5p0057c1s v5p0468c2m v6p0342c1s
Pollard, F. v2p0048c2s
Pollard, J.P. v4p0131c2s
Pollard, P. v4p0031c2s
v5p0042c2s v5p0151c1s v5p0152c1s
v5p0433c2s
Pollard, W. v1p0983c1s
Polle, F. v2p0284c1s
Pollen, C.B. v2p0423c1s
Pollen, G. v6p0526c1s
Pollen, G.C.H. v5p0229c1s
Pollen, J.H. v1p0054c2s
v1p0061c1s v1p0105c2s v1p0369c1s
v1p1227c1s v1p1297c2s v2p0070c1s
v2p0077c2s v2p0169c2s v2p0180c2s
v2p0182c2s v2p0403c1s v3p0069c2s
v3p0165c2s v3p0167c1m v3p0174c2s
v3p0187c1s v3p0374c2s v3p0471c1s
v4p0030c1s v4p0049c1s v4p0091c1s
v4p0093c2s v4p0095c1s v4p0150c2s
v4p0218c1s v4p0366c2s v4p0549c1s
v4p0561c2s v5p0090c1s v5p0305c1s
v5p0364c2m v5p0434c1s v5p0441c1s
v5p0607c1s v5p0639c2s v6p0095c2s
v6p0200c2m v6p0256c1s v6p0326c2s
v6p0328c1s v6p0333c1s v6p0381c1s
v6p0403c2s v6p0404c1s v6p0548c1m
Pollens, L. v3p0450c1s
v4p0482c2s
Pollington, Lord v1p0992c1s
Pollock, A. v6p0265c1s
v6p0266c1s v6p0266c2s
Pollock, A.W. v5p0527c1s
Pollock, A.W.A. v4p0284c1s
v5p0050c1s v6p0083c1s v6p0265c1s
v6p0265c2m v6p0266c1m v6p0271c2s
v6p0416c2s v6p0560c1s
Pollock, Alsager v6p0007c1s
Pollock, C.F. v3p0035c2s
v3p0047c2s v3p0049c1s v3p0088c2s
v3p0117c2s v3p0123c1s v3p0147c2s
v3p0261c1s v3p0292c2s v3p0300c1s
Pollock, E. v1p0043c2s
v1p0216c2s v1p0441c2s v1p0878c1s
v1p0887c2s v1p0943c2s v1p1023c1s
v1p1428c1s
Pollock, F. v1p0046c2s
v1p0265c1s v1p0305c1s v1p0426c2m
v1p0433c2s v1p0570c1s v1p0723c2s
v1p0729c1s v1p0868c2s v1p0935c1s
v1p1236c2m v1p1255c1s v2p0009c1s
v2p0066c1s v2p0085c1s v2p0112c1s
v2p0248c1s v2p0297c2s v2p0348c1m
v2p0414c2s v2p0429c1s v3p0100c1s
v3p0241c2s v3p0244c2s v3p0264c2s
v3p0404c2s v4p0237c1s v4p0259c2s
v4p0289c2s v4p0322c2s v4p0480c2s
v4p0528c1s v4p0542c1s v4p0548c2s
v5p0012c1s v5p0150c2s v6p0310c1s
v6p0363c2s v6p0364c2s v6p0403c2s
v6p0426c1s v6p0616c2m
Pollock, F. and Pollock, W.H.
v1p0363c2s
Pollock, F., Sir v1p1212c2s
v2p0046c1s v3p0279c2s v4p0042c1s
v4p0158c2s v4p0311c2s v4p0322c2s
v4p0323c1m v4p0419c2s v5p0053c2s
v6p0411c2s
Pollock, F., Sir et al. .. v3p0146c1s
Pollock, F.L. v4p0519c1s
v5p0348c2s
Pollock, F.T. v5p0185c2s
Pollock, G.C. and Pollock, W.H.
v6p0284c1s
Pollock, J. v1p0032c1s
v1p0062c1s v1p0199c2s v1p0281c1s
v1p0363c1m v1p0364c1s v1p0450c2s
v1p0488c2m v1p0513c1s v1p1079c2s
v6p0003c1s v6p0280c1s
Pollock, J.B. v6p0507c2s
Pollock, J.F. v4p0371c1s
v5p0307c2s
Pollock, Lady v1p0005c1s
v1p0115c2s v1p0309c1s v1p0318c2m
v1p0364c2s v1p0462c2s v1p0610c1s
v1p0841c1s v1p0931c2s v1p0997c2s
v1p1036c1s v1p1241c2s v1p1257c2s
v1p1372c1s v2p0028c1s v2p0210c2s
v2p0276c2s v2p0367c1s v2p0397c2s
v2p0421c2s
Pollock, M.I. v6p0096c2s
Pollock, Margaret I. v6p0358c2m
Pollock, W. v1p1092c2s
v3p0435c2s v3p0436c1s
Pollock, W.F. v1p1212c2s
Pollock, W.H. v1p0363c1s
v1p0371c1s v1p0408c2s v1p0583c1s
v1p0726c1s v1p0749c1s v1p0819c1s
v1p0886c1s v1p1106c2s v1p1339c2s
v2p0122c2s v2p0123c2s v2p0147c2s
v2p0153c2s v2p0171c2s v2p0181c2s
v2p0399c1s v2p0410c1s v2p0416c1s
v2p0447c1s v3p0168c1s v3p0175c2s
v3p0185c1s v3p0223c2s v4p0037c2s
v4p0092c1s v4p0124c1s v4p0258c2s
v4p0273c2s v4p0350c1s v4p0358c1s
v4p0518c2s v4p0560c2s v4p0572c2s
v5p0052c2s v5p0150c1s v5p0167c2s
v5p0232c2s v5p0398c1s v5p0442c2s
v5p0472c2s v5p0522c2s v5p0576c1s
v5p0597c2s v6p0221c1s v6p0401c1s
v6p0442c1s v6p0534c1s v6p0630c1m
Pollock, W.H. and Besant, Walter
v4p0097c2s
Pollock, W.H. and Matthews, B.
v2p0130c1s v3p0271c2s
Pollock, W.H. and Pollock, F.
v1p0363c2s
Pollock, W.H. and Pollock, G.C.
v6p0284c1s
Pollock, W.H. et al. v4p0239c2s
Pollok, F.T. v5p0005c2s
Pollough-Pogue, M. v5p0555c1s
Polsue, R. v6p0399c2s
Polton, E.S. v6p0427c1s
Pomar, Duke de v1p1175c1s
Pomeroy, D. et al. v6p0169c2s
Pomeroy, E. v4p0476c2s
v4p0615c1s v5p0049c2s v5p0134c1s
v5p0330c1s v5p0383c1s v5p0399c2s
v5p0482c1s v6p0165c2s v6p0170c1s
v6p0174c2s v6p0193c1s v6p0242c2s
v6p0430c2s v6p0450c1s v6p0481c2s
v6p0507c1s v6p0533c1s v6p0535c1s
v6p0535c2s v6p0539c2s v6p0667c1s
v6p0669c2s
Pomeroy, E. and Brown, A.A.
v5p0162c1s
Pomeroy, E.N. v6p0171c1s
Pomeroy, Eltweed v4p0325c2s
v6p0175c1m v6p0319c2s v6p0387c1s
v6p0449c1s
Pomeroy, F.W. v4p0446c1s
Pomeroy, H.S. v3p0339c2s
Pomeroy, J.A. v1p0699c2s
v2p0370c2s
Pomeroy, J.N. v1p1108c1s

Pomeroy, J.N. v1p0018c1s
v1p0025c2s v1p0035c1s v1p0039c2s
v1p0231c2s v1p0247c2s v1p0257c2s
v1p0259c1s v1p0283c1s v1p0288c1s
v1p0292c2s v1p0317c2m v1p0338c2s
v1p0424c1s v1p0431c1s v1p0447c1s
v1p0457c2m v1p0467c1s v1p0477c2s
v1p0478c1s v1p0504c2m v1p0538c2s
v1p0551c2s v1p0638c1s v1p0650c2m
v1p0713c2s v1p0772c2s v1p0803c1s
v1p0902c1s v1p0908c1s v1p0987c2s
v1p1028c2s v1p1048c2s v1p1075c2s
v1p1079c2s v1p1086c2s v1p1121c2s
v1p1122c1s v1p1124c2s v1p1246c1s
v1p1272c1m v1p1323c2m v1p1350c1s
v1p1353c2s v1p1375c1s v1p1426c1s
Pomeroy, J.N. and Godkin, E.L.
v1p0322c2s v1p1375c1s
Pomeroy, J.N. et al. v1p0927c1s
Pomeroy, W.M. v1p0505c2s
Pompeius v6p0181c2s
Poncelet, J.V. v1p1103c1s
Ponci, Fomoaley v6p0307c1s
Poncins, E.de v5p0370c1s
Pond, A.B. v5p0031c1s
Pond, E. v1p0002c1s
v1p0035c2s v1p0047c1s v1p0048c1s
v1p0058c1s v1p0071c2s v1p0074c1s
v1p0076c1s v1p0090c2m v1p0118c1s
v1p0119c1s v1p0119c2s v1p0120c2s
v1p0121c2m v1p0122c2s v1p0123c1s
v1p0130c2s v1p0131c1s v1p0210c1m
v1p0217c1s v1p0241c2s v1p0246c2s
v1p0252c2s v1p0254c1s v1p0289c2s
v1p0296c1s v1p0314c1s v1p0323c1s
v1p0340c1s v1p0361c1s v1p0420c2s
v1p0423c2s v1p0432c2s v1p0433c2s
v1p0452c1s v1p0493c2s v1p0507c1s
v1p0527c2s v1p0528c2m v1p0529c2s
v1p0573c1s v1p0580c2s v1p0595c2s
v1p0603c1s v1p0640c2s v1p0646c1s
v1p0649c2s v1p0653c2s v1p0689c1s
v1p0691c1s v1p0696c1s v1p0698c1s
v1p0700c1s v1p0794c1s v1p0811c1m
v1p0826c1s v1p0849c2s v1p0852c1s
v1p0852c2s v1p0853c2s v1p0857c1s
v1p0868c1s v1p0909c2s v1p0979c1s
v1p0989c2s v1p1004c2s v1p1009c1s
v1p1009c2s v1p1017c1s v1p1035c1s
v1p1056c1s v1p1100c1s v1p1134c2s
v1p1140c2s v1p1154c1s v1p1207c1s
v1p1217c2s v1p1219c2s v1p1233c1m
v1p1296c2s v1p1301c2s v1p1303c2s
v1p1306c1s v1p1378c1s v1p1406c2s
v1p1410c2m v1p1433c2s
Pond, G.E. v1p0430c2s
v1p0594c1s v1p0636c2s v1p0710c1s
v1p1137c2s v1p1351c2s v4p0370c1s
Pond, I.K. v6p0028c1s
v6p0035c2s
Pond, J.B. v4p0345c2m
v5p0625c2s
Pond, R. v6p0227c1s
Pond, W.F. v6p0298c1s
Pond, W.P. v6p0059c2s
v6p0297c1m
Ponsard, E. v1p0971c1s
Ponsonby, A. v5p0074c2s
v5p0339c1s v6p0690c1s
Ponsonby, M.E. v4p0415c2s
v5p0638c1s v6p0482c1s
Ponsonby, Mary E. v5p0186c1s
v5p0507c2s
Ponte, Prof.Da v1p1331c2s
Pontifex, D.D. v5p0061c2s
Pontiff, L. v1p1274c2s
Ponting, C.E. et al. v3p0465c2s
Ponting, H.C. v6p0337c1s
Ponting, H.G. v6p0036c1s
Pontius, J.W. v1p1321c2s
Pontius, W.H. v4p0389c1s
Pontmartin, A.de v4p0351c1s
Pontoffidan, E. v6p0139c1s
Ponton, B. et al. v6p0090c2s
Ponton, M. v2p0002c1s
v2p0093c2s v2p0294c1s v2p0413c2m
Pool, F.J. v6p0141c2s
Pool, M.L. v1p0209c1s
v1p0362c1s v1p0466c2s v1p0571c1s
v1p0607c2s v1p0785c2s v1p0851c2s
v1p0996c1s v1p1314c2s v2p0090c1s
v2p0175c1s v3p0079c2s v3p0149c1s
v3p0165c2s v3p0194c1s v3p0216c2s
v5p0370c2s
Poole, C.P. v6p0185c1s
Poole, E. v1p0026c1s
v6p0058c2s v6p0105c1s v6p0113c2s
v6p0146c2s v6p0171c1s v6p0181c2s
v6p0242c1s v6p0296c1s v6p0343c1s
v6p0454c1s v6p0465c2s v6p0558c1m
v6p0559c2m v6p0621c1m v6p0628c1s
v6p0663c1s v6p0679c1s
Poole, E. and Hurd, W. ... v6p0621c1s
Poole, E. and Walling, W.E.
v6p0558c2s
Poole, Ernest v6p0179c2s
v6p0308c2s v6p0453c2s v6p0456c1s
v6p0535c1s
Poole, F. v5p0110c2s
v5p0113c1s
Poole, H. v2p0471c1m
Poole, H.J. v2p0035c1s
v2p0426c1s
Poole, H.M. v4p0389c1s
v4p0464c1s v4p0517c1s
Poole, H.W. v1p0429c1s
v1p0883c2s v1p0884c1s v1p0884c2s
v1p0885c1s v1p0885c2s v1p0947c2s
v1p1050c2s
Poole, J. v1p0505c2s
v1p0627c1s v1p0692c2s v1p0756c1s
v1p1002c1s v1p1121c1s v1p1132c1s
v1p1300c1s v2p0052c2s
Poole, J.P. v5p0332c2s
v5p0443c2s
Poole, R. v5p0186c1s
v6p0459c2s v6p0552c2s
Poole, R.B. v2p0255c1s
v2p0482c2s v3p0049c2s v3p0070c1s
v3p0151c2s v4p0354c2s
Poole, R.B. and Johnston, D.V.R.
v4p0066c2s
Poole, R.L. v2p0017c1s
v2p0473c2s v3p0149c1s v3p0463c2s
v4p0181c2s v4p0424c1s v4p0621c2s
v5p0020c1s v6p0003c1s v6p0277c1s
Poole, R.S. v1p0049c2s
v1p0050c1s v1p0117c1s v1p0118c1s
v1p0118c2s v1p0216c1s v1p0272c2s
v1p0328c2m v1p0394c2m v1p0395c1s
v1p0581c1s v1p0590c1s v1p0889c1s
v1p0935c1s v1p0979c2s v1p0992c1s
v1p1282c1s v2p0018c1s v2p0091c2s
v2p0102c1s v2p0133c1s v2p0135c1s
v2p0343c1s v3p0029c2s v3p0041c2s
v3p0265c2s v3p0470c2s v4p0621c2s
Poole, R.S. and Cotton, J.S.
v4p0171c2s
Poole, R.S. and Smith, W.R.
v3p0041c2s
Poole, S.L. v1p0703c2s
v1p1275c1s v1p1431c1s v2p0017c2s
v2p0018c1s v2p0022c1s v2p0022c2m
v2p0030c2s v2p0063c2m v2p0068c1s
v2p0091c2m v2p0102c1s v2p0133c2s
v2p0135c1s v2p0233c1s v2p0238c2s
v2p0428c1s v4p0403c1s v5p0492c1s
v6p0026c1s
Poole, S.Lane v2p0324c2s
Poole, T.C. v4p0585c2s
Poole, W.F. v1p0031c1s
v1p0152c1s v1p0290c2s v1p0327c1m
v1p0451c1s v1p0584c2s v1p0628c2m
v1p0742c2m v1p0743c2m v1p0744c1s
v1p0768c1s v1p0770c1s v1p0774c1s
v1p0811c1s v1p0927c1s v1p0939c1s
v1p0946c2m v1p1033c2s v1p1143c1s
v1p1350c2s v1p1418c1m v1p1438c1s
v2p0002c2s v2p0009c2s v2p0010c1s
v2p0010c2s v2p0011c1m v2p0027c1s
v2p0052c1s v2p0077c1s v2p0092c1s
v2p0202c1s v2p0212c2s v2p0216c2m
v2p0257c1m v2p0259c1s v2p0279c2s
v2p0345c2s v2p0360c2m v2p0383c1s
v2p0454c1m v3p0010c1m v3p0049c2s
v3p0117c2s v3p0197c1s v3p0249c1s
v3p0270c2s v3p0301c1s v3p0304c2s
v3p0447c1s v3p0460c1s v3p0460c2s
v4p0126c1s v4p0254c2s v4p0330c1s
v4p0359c2s
Poole, W.F. and Fletcher, W.I.
v2p0216c2s v2p0336c1s
Poole, W.F. et al. v2p0255c2s
Pooler, C.K. v6p0505c2s
Pooley, J.H. v2p0427c2s
Poor, A.B. v4p0335c2s
v5p0072c1s v5p0596c1s
Poor, C.L. v4p0126c2s
Poor, C.Lane v6p0140c2s
Poor, D. et al. v1p0204c2s
Poor, H.V. v1p0095c1s
v1p0735c1s v1p0956c1s v1p1344c1s
Poor, H.V. and Bland, R.P.
v1p0273c1s
Poor, J.A. v1p0789c2s
v1p1033c2s
Poor, J.M. v6p0712c1s
Poore, B.P. v1p0291c2s
v1p1267c1s v1p1388c2s v2p0466c2s
v3p0022c2s v3p0096c2s v3p0383c2s
Poore, D.S. v2p0006c1s
Poore, G.V. v1p0619c1s
v1p0972c2s v3p0088c2s v3p0255c2s
Poore, H.P. v5p0067c1s
Poore, L.C. v5p0337c2s
Poore, Lady v5p0128c1s
Poore, Vivian v5p0508c1s
Poortugael, Den B. v5p0587c1s
Poortugael, J.C.C.den Beer
v5p0006c2s
Pope, A. v1p0361c1s
v2p0071c1s
Pope, A.A. v4p0485c2m
v5p0490c2s
Pope, A.M. v1p0193c1s
v2p0016c2s v2p0071c2s v2p0180c1s
v2p0254c1s v2p0271c2s v2p0320c2s
v2p0354c1s v2p0444c1s
Pope, A.R. v1p0741c2s
v1p1055c1s
Pope, A.W. v6p0450c1s
Pope, C.H. v3p0121c1s
v3p0335c1s
Pope, E.A. v2p0477c1s
Pope, E.H. v6p0672c1s
Pope, Elfrieda H. v6p0518c2s
Pope, F.H. v3p0302c2s
Pope, F.L. v1p1290c2s
v3p0133c1s v3p0339c1s v3p0422c2s
v3p0446c2s v4p0175c1s v4p0176c2s
v4p0403c2s
Pope, G.U. v5p0566c1s
Pope, H. v5p0171c2s
v5p0323c2s v6p0061c2s v6p0062c1s
v6p0176c2s v6p0383c1s v6p0404c1s
v6p0435c1s v6p0562c2s
Pope, Hugh v6p0065c1s
Pope, J. v1p1223c1s
v2p0060c2s v3p0086c2s v3p0443c1s
v4p0082c1s
Pope, J.J. v3p0375c1s
Pope, J.O'F. v1p0639c2s
Pope, J.W. v3p0115c2s
v3p0278c2s v4p0282c1s v5p0375c1s
v5p0446c1s v6p0031c2s v6p0171c2s
Pope, M.G. v5p0590c2s
Pope, M.M. v4p0149c1s
v4p0306c1s v4p0485c1s v4p0566c2s
v5p0134c1s v5p0262c2s v5p0478c2s
v5p0606c1s
Pope, R.M. v5p0306c1s
v5p0306c2s
Pope, R.W. v3p0133c1s
v3p0134c1s v5p0570c2s
Pope, W.J. v5p0205c1s
v5p0590c2s v6p0222c1s v6p0617c1s
Popenoe, F.O. v3p0232c2s
Popham, J. v1p0503c1s
v1p1030c1s v1p1187c2s
Popham, J.S. v6p0159c2s
Popoff, Adm. v1p0665c2s
Popoff, L. v3p0317c2s
v4p0030c2s
Popoff, M.N. v6p0087c1s
Popoff, P.J. v2p0011c2s
v2p0380c2s
Popplewell, W.C. v6p0385c1s
Poradowzka, Marguerite ... v5p0530c1s
Porch, F.M. v4p0171c2s
v5p0435c1s
Porcher, C.G. v6p0053c1s
Porcher, F.A. v2p0411c2s
Porcher, F.P. v2p0412c1s
v3p0095c2s
Pordage, Arthur v6p0225c2s
Pore, C. v5p0172c2s
Porges, N. and Bacher, W.. v5p0228c1s
Poriel, M. v1p0618c2s
Porphyrius, F. v1p0853c2s
Porrett, R. v1p0115c2s
v1p1256c1s
Porritt, A.G. v5p0415c1s
v6p0267c2s v6p0367c1s
Porritt, E. v4p0115c1m
v4p0136c1s v4p0169c2m v4p0170c1s
v4p0181c2s v4p0182c1s v4p0182c2s
v4p0195c1s v4p0197c2s v4p0239c2m
v4p0277c2s v4p0314c1s v4p0323c2s
v4p0333c2s v4p0353c1s v4p0398c2s
v4p0400c1s v4p0427c2s v4p0428c2s
v4p0429c1s v4p0452c1m v4p0534c1s
v4p0538c1s v4p0543c2s v4p0569c1s
v4p0590c2s v4p0628c2s v4p0632c2s
v5p0068c1s v5p0072c1s v5p0090c1s
v5p0091c1s v5p0182c1s v5p0189c2s
v5p0190c1s v5p0246c1m v5p0247c1m
v5p0247c2s v5p0254c2s v5p0272c1s
v5p0272c2s v5p0330c1s v5p0340c1s
v5p0410c1s v5p0433c1s v5p0438c2s
v5p0442c2s v5p0468c1s v5p0471c2s
v5p0481c2s v5p0485c2s v5p0598c2s
v6p0068c2s v6p0157c1s v6p0206c2m
v6p0269c1s v6p0281c2s v6p0317c2s
v6p0327c1s v6p0367c1s v6p0511c1s
v6p0632c2s
Porritt, E. and Shaw, A. . v4p0174c2s
Porritt, M. v5p0177c1s
v5p0177c2s
Porro, F. v2p0095c1s
Porteous, J. et al. v6p0342c1s
Porteous, W.W. and Christy, M.
v5p0075c2m
Porter, A. v1p0851c2s
v1p0889c1s v1p0923c2s v2p0026c2s
v2p0146c1s v2p0290c2s
v3p0224c1s
v6p0488c2s
Porter, A.E. v1p0068c2s
Porter, A.E., Mrs. v1p0743c1s
Porter, A.H. v4p0403c2s
Porter, A.S. v3p0430c1s
Porter, A.W. v6p0404c2s
Porter, B.F. v1p0029c1s
v1p0030c2s v1p0095c1s v1p0282c2s
v1p0283c2s v1p0339c1m v1p0734c2s
v1p0772c2s v1p0794c2s v1p1018c1s
v1p1104c2s v1p1256c1s v1p1319c1s
Porter, C. v1p0659c1s
v3p0057c2m v3p0266c2s v3p0387c2s
v3p0425c1s v3p0468c1s v4p0015c1s

v4p0076c1s v4p0076c2s v4p0133c1s
v4p0335c1s v4p0518c1s v4p0626c2s
v5p0016c1s v5p0072c1s v5p0079c2s
v5p0278c1s v5p0317c2s v5p0446c2s
v5p0636c1s v6p0467c2s
Porter, C. and Clarke, H.A.
v5p0079c2s v5p0080c1s v5p0153c2s
v5p0203c2s v5p0278c1s v5p0468c1s
v5p0522c1m v5p0523c1m v5p0523c2s
v5p0539c2s v5p0630c2s v6p0202c2s
v6p0587c2s
Porter, C.H. v6p0519c2s
Porter, C.J.A. v2p0222c1s
Porter, C.T. v1p1248c1s
v4p0541c1s v4p0547c1s
Porter, C.W. v3p0468c2s
v5p0234c1s
Porter, Charlotte v6p0388c1s
Porter, Charlotte and
Clarke, Helen A. v4p0519c1s
v6p0588c2m
Porter, D. v3p0367c1s
v4p0129c2s
Porter, D.D. v1p1148c2s
v1p1316c2s v1p1353c2s v2p0312c1s
v3p0007c2s v3p0298c1s v3p0339c2s
v3p0443c2s
Porter, D.G. v1p0095c2m
v1p0255c1s v1p0262c1s v1p1422c1s
v1p1422c2s v1p1426c1s v4p0183c1s
v5p0324c1s
Porter, D.L. v4p0214c1s
Porter, E. v1p0566c2s
v1p1042c1s v1p1042c2s v1p1044c1s
v1p1103c1s
Porter, E.E. v6p0124c2s
Porter, E.G. v4p0027c1s
v4p0416c2s v5p0072c1s v5p0086c2s
v5p0128c1s v5p0133c1s
Porter, E.H. v6p0145c1s
v6p0169c1s v6p0218c2s v6p0258c2s
v6p0286c2s v6p0351c1s v6p0450c1s
v6p0625c1s v6p0641c1s v6p0665c1s
Porter, E.L. v1p0906c2s
Porter, E.S. v1p0342c2s
v1p1090c2s
Porter, E.W. v6p0054c2s
Porter, Eleanor H. v6p0020c2s
v6p0103c2m v6p0163c2s v6p0311c1s
v6p0396c1s v6p0463c1s v6p0467c1s
v6p0524c2s
Porter, F.C. v3p0328c1s
v3p0329c2s v3p0404c2s v4p0021c1s
v4p0054c1s v4p0055c2s v4p0275c1s
v5p0468c2s v5p0576c2s v6p0226c1s
v6p0341c1s
Porter, F.G. v5p0033c2s
v6p0001c1s
Porter, F.H. v6p0056c1s
Porter, F.J. v2p0273c2s
v2p0293c2s v2p0372c2s
Porter, F.J. and Hill, D.H.
v2p0170c1s
Porter, G. v1p0387c1s
v1p0426c1s v2p0032c2m
Porter, G.M. v1p0468c2s
Porter, G.R. v1p0164c1s
v1p0283c2s v1p0307c1s v1p0315c1s
v1p0480c1s v1p0845c2m v1p0970c2s
v1p1153c2s v1p1265c2s
Porter, G.S. v5p0051c1s
v5p0316c2s v5p0615c1s v6p0022c1s
v6p0068c1s v6p0068c2s v6p0403c1s
v6p0444c1s v6p0461c1s v6p0515c2s
Porter, H. v2p0184c2m
v2p0259c1s v3p0102c2s v3p0179c1s
v3p0279c1s v3p0353c1m v4p0033c1s
v4p0234c2s v5p0242c1s v5p0242c2s
v6p0366c1s
Porter, H. et al. v3p0138c1s
v4p0234c2s
Porter, H.D. v3p0078c2s
v5p0524c1s v6p0064c1s
Porter, H.DeB. v4p0577c2s
Porter, H.F.J. v4p0180c1s
v4p0548c1s v5p0204c1s v5p0298c1s
v5p0353c2s v5p0615c2s v6p0190c1s
v6p0203c1s v6p0225c1s v6p0318c1s
v6p0518c2s v6p0616c1s v6p0624c2s
Porter, H.J. v1p0758c1s
v1p0982c1s
Porter, H.J.F. v6p0290c2s
Porter, H.T. v5p0217c2s
v5p0252c1s
Porter, Helen v6p0138c2s
Porter, Horace v4p0481c2s
v6p0345c2s
Porter, I.M. v1p0704c2s
Porter, J. v1p0095c2s
v1p0254c1s v1p0336c1s v1p0729c1s
v1p0830c2s v1p1025c2s v1p1147c2s
Porter, J.A. v1p0014c2s
v2p0079c1s v2p0092c2s v2p0466c2s
v2p0481c2s v3p0076c1s v3p0091c2s
v3p0097c1s v3p0167c2s v4p0220c1s
Porter, J.C. v1p0423c1s
Porter, J.D. v2p0076c1s
v6p0251c2s
Porter, J.G. v2p0095c1s
v2p0181c1s v2p0308c1s v2p0417c2s
v3p0283c2s v3p0328c1s v5p0549c2s
v6p0411c2s
Porter, J.H. v2p0219c2s
v4p0205c1s v4p0281c1s v4p0385c2s
v4p0576c2m v5p0340c1s v5p0579c2s
Porter, J.L. v1p0101c1m
v1p0119c1s v1p0127c2s v1p0329c2s
v1p0420c2s v1p0587c2s v1p0673c2s
v1p0688c2s v1p0705c1s v1p0849c2s
v1p0980c1s v2p0041c2s
Porter, J.N. v1p0061c2s
v1p0364c2s v1p1312c1s v1p1424c1s
v2p0085c2s v2p0255c1s v2p0459c1s
v4p0024c2s v4p0086c2s v4p0466c2s
v4p0548c1s
Porter, J.P. v6p0608c1s
v6p0610c2s
Porter, J.R. v2p0198c1s
Porter, J.S. v1p1035c2s
Porter, J.W. v3p0376c1s
v4p0221c2s v4p0435c1s v4p0574c2s
v4p0618c2s v5p0398c2s v5p0629c1s
Porter, Jane M. v6p0631c2s
Porter, Judge v1p0317c1s
Porter, L.H. v2p0204c1s
v3p0450c2s
Porter, L.S. v4p0185c1s
v5p0349c2s v5p0478c1s v5p0596c2s
Porter, M. v1p0517c1s
Porter, M.E. v1p1422c1s
Porter, M.S. v4p0009c2s
v4p0432c1s v5p0434c1s v6p0435c1s
Porter, Maria S. v4p0260c2s
v4p0550c1s
Porter, Mary B. v6p0508c2s
Porter, N. v1p0032c1s
v1p0060c2s v1p0071c2s v1p0074c2s
v1p0085c2s v1p0107c2s v1p0130c2s
v1p0172c2s v1p0180c1m v1p0238c2s
v1p0242c2s v1p0256c1s v1p0265c1s
v1p0274c1s v1p0275c1s v1p0286c1s
v1p0291c1m v1p0318c2s v1p0346c1s
v1p0359c2s v1p0382c2s v1p0390c1s
v1p0393c2m v1p0394c1s v1p0405c2s
v1p0410c1s v1p0411c1s v1p0416c1s
v1p0416c2s v1p0417c2s v1p0421c2s
v1p0422c2s v1p0426c2s v1p0444c2s
v1p0467c1s v1p0518c1m v1p0565c1s
v1p0572c1s v1p0603c1s v1p0614c2s
v1p0618c1s v1p0641c2s v1p0686c2s
v1p0702c1s v1p0729c2s v1p0743c1s
v1p0752c1s v1p0769c1s v1p0782c2s
v1p0826c2s v1p0839c1s v1p0840c1s
v1p0843c1s v1p0843c2s v1p0972c2m
v1p0978c1s v1p0990c2s v1p1000c2s
v1p1001c1s v1p1001c2s v1p1009c2s
v1p1025c1s v1p1062c2s v1p1066c2s
v1p1085c1s v1p1094c2s v1p1103c1m
v1p1103c2s v1p1105c1s v1p1157c2s
v1p1198c1s v1p1211c2m v1p1217c2s
v1p1227c1s v1p1261c2s v1p1271c1s
v1p1287c1s v1p1321c1s v1p1336c2s
v1p1341c1s v1p1396c1s v1p1429c2s
v1p1430c1s v2p0071c1s v2p0081c2s
v2p0088c1s v2p0092c2s v2p0151c2s
v2p0212c2s v2p0282c2s v2p0290c2s
v2p0388c1s v2p0389c1s v2p0436c1s
v3p0010c2s v3p0111c1s v3p0143c1s
v3p0185c1s v3p0255c1s v3p0396c2s
v3p0454c2s v4p0107c1s
Porter, N. et al. v2p0481c2s
Porter, N., jr. v1p0239c2s
v1p0285c1s v1p0826c2s v1p1160c1s
Porter, O.H. v6p0603c1s
Porter, P.A. v4p0403c2s
Porter, P.B. v1p1195c2s
Porter, R.K. v1p0270c1s
Porter, R.P. v1p0029c2s
v1p0339c1s v1p0538c1s v1p0880c2m
v1p1038c2s v1p1100c1s v1p1153c2s
v1p1245c1s v1p1261c1s v1p1319c1s
v1p1348c2s v1p1354c1m v1p1400c2s
v2p0073c1s v2p0262c1s v2p0452c1s
v2p0470c2s v3p0072c1m v3p0113c1s
v4p0115c1s v4p0297c1s v4p0476c1s
v4p0592c1s v5p0099c2s v5p0147c1s
v5p0303c2s v5p0567c1s v5p0584c1s
v6p0198c1s v6p0384c1s v6p0436c2s
v6p0638c2s
Porter, R.P., Mrs. v4p0246c2s
Porter, R.S. v6p0051c2s
v6p0165c2s v6p0494c2s
Porter, R.W. v5p0250c2s
v5p0275c1s
Porter, S. v1p0723c2s
v1p0724c1s v1p1234c2s v1p1378c2s
v5p0066c1s v6p0467c2s
Porter, S.O'B. v5p0555c1s
Porter, Sophie E. v5p0027c2s
Porter, T.C. v1p0108c2s
v1p0686c1s v1p0701c2s v1p0739c2s
v1p0768c1s v1p0794c2s v1p0949c2s
v1p1053c1s v4p0349c2s v4p0437c1s
v4p0444c1s v5p0161c2s
Porter, T.G. v1p1070c2s
Porter, T.K. v2p0159c2s
Porter, T.P. v5p0591c1s
Porter, W. v2p0320c2s
v4p0013c1s
Porter, W.A. v1p0549c1s
v1p1035c2s
Porter, W.H. v6p0166c1s
v6p0591c1s v6p0645c1s
Porter, W.S. v1p0292c1s
Porter, W.T. v4p0020c1s
v4p0103c2s v4p0104c1s v5p0449c2m
v5p0450c1m v6p0127c2s v6p0199c2s
Porterfield, C. v3p0350c2s
Portlock, J.E. v1p0297c1s
v1p0946c1s
Portman, M.V. v4p0440c2s
Portman, S. v1p1155c2s
v1p1408c2s
Portor, Laura S. v6p0565c2s
Portsmouth, Earl of v5p0499c1s
Portugal, Adele v4p0392c2s
Posada, J.de la C. v4p0124c1s
Poseck, Helena v6p0120c2s
Posnett, H.M. v5p0039c1s
v5p0079c1s v5p0131c1s v5p0452c1s
v6p0267c1s v6p0328c1s v6p0559c2s
Posse, M. v3p0187c1s
Post, A. v6p0043c2s
v6p0044c1s v6p0360c1s
Post, A.A. v4p0607c1s
Post, A.C. v6p0294c2s
Post, A.H. v3p0143c2s
v4p0307c1s v5p0312c2s
Post, C.A. v4p0490c2s
Post, C.C. v4p0554c2s
Post, C.J. v6p0316c2s
v6p0366c1s v6p0438c2s v6p0606c1s
Post, C.W. v5p0461c2s
Post, D.H. v1p0223c2s
Post, E. v4p0451c1s
v5p0311c2s v6p0135c2s
Post, F. v1p0458c2s
Post, G.B. v4p0024c1s
v6p0452c1s
Post, G.E. v1p0960c2s
Post, H.D. v3p0353c2s
Post, H.S. v1p1441c2s
Post, J.W. v2p0405c2s
Post, L.F. v4p0318c2s
Post, L.F. and Croffut, W.A.
v2p0245c2s
Post, L.F. et al. v5p0567c2s
Post, M.D. v5p0328c1s
Post, T. v1p0343c1s
Post, T.M. v1p0290c1s
v1p0291c1s v1p0342c2s v1p0625c2s
v1p0626c1s v1p0855c1s v1p0860c2s
v1p1117c2s v1p1206c1s v2p0148c2s
v2p0171c2s v2p0369c2s
Posta, Angla de Oleveira Cesar de
v6p0122c1s
Postans, M., Mrs. v1p0875c1s
Postans, Mrs. v1p0119c1s
v1p0122c1s v1p0270c2s v1p0592c1s
v1p0706c2s v1p0871c1s v1p0975c2s
v1p1077c1s v1p1087c1s v1p1178c1s
Postans, R. v1p0561c2s
v1p0587c2s v1p0895c2s v1p1049c1s
Postgate, I.J. v3p0029c2s
v4p0343c2s v5p0582c2s
Postgate, Isa J. v4p0201c1s
v4p0349c1s v4p0618c1s v5p0633c1s
Postgate, J.P. v2p0071c2s
v2p0146c2s v2p0325c1s v3p0468c2s
v4p0409c2s v5p0325c1s v5p0367c2s
v6p0130c1s
Postlethwaite, H.L. v4p0032c1s
v4p0157c1s v4p0421c2s
Postlethwaite, H.W. v6p0567c2s
Postlethwaite, R.H. v6p0260c1s
Postlethwaites, H. v5p0033c1s
Poston, C.D. v4p0020c2s
v4p0026c2s
Potamian, Brother v5p0233c2s
Poteat, W.L. v4p0507c2s
v5p0198c1s v5p0350c2s v6p0575c2s
Potocka, A. v6p0368c2s
Pott, A. v3p0250c1s
Pottecher, M. v5p0575c2s
Potter v5p0152c2s
Potter, A. v1p0275c1s
v1p0529c1s v1p1161c1s
Potter, A.C. v5p0333c2s
Potter, A.de v3p0305c2s
v5p0210c1s
Potter, A.M. v4p0461c2s
Potter, B. v3p0256c1s
v3p0417c1m v3p0419c1s v3p0472c1s
Potter, E.L. v5p0572c2s
Potter, E.N. v1p0883c1s
v2p0302c2s v3p0084c2s
Potter, E.T. v1p0225c2s
v3p0085c2s v3p0359c1m v4p0569c1s
v5p0273c1s v5p0609c1s
Potter, F.H. v5p0017c1s
Potter, F.S. v4p0480c1s
v5p0387c2s v6p0219c2s
Potter, G. v1p0198c1s
v1p0249c1s v1p0486c2s v1p0713c2s
v1p1261c1m v1p1261c2s v1p1319c2m
v2p0140c2s
Potter, G. and Arch, J. .. v1p0715c1s
Potter, G. and Arde, J. .. v1p0483c1s
Potter, G. and Howell, G.. v1p0379c1s
Potter, G.A. v1p0235c1s

v1p0325c2s v1p1027c1s v1p1385c1s
Potter, H. v5p0167c2s
v6p0104c2s
Potter, H.C. v1p0450c2s
v2p0075c1s v2p0290c2s v2p0357c1s
v3p0083c2s v3p0088c1s v3p0202c1s
v3p0284c1s v3p0377c2s v3p0433c2s
v3p0458c2s v4p0092c1s v4p0102c1m
v4p0110c1s v4p0162c1s v5p0102c1s
v5p0113c2s v5p0199c2s v5p0258c2s
v5p0285c2s v5p0302c2s v5p0321c1s
v5p0388c2s v5p0445c1s v5p0536c1s
Potter, H.C. and Abbott, L.
v5p0506c1s
Potter, H.C. et al. v2p0106c2s
v3p0119c1s
Potter, H.N. v6p0612c1s
Potter, H.P. v1p1013c2s
Potter, I.B. v3p0362c2m
v4p0058c2s v4p0485c2s
Potter, J. v1p0391c2s
v1p0943c2s v5p0610c1s
Potter, J.R. v3p0169c1s
Potter, M. v6p0463c2s
Potter, M.A. v5p0305c2s
Potter, M.H. v6p0394c1s
Potter, M.K. v5p0572c1s
v6p0311c2s
Potter, P. v6p0181c2s
Potter, P.M. v1p0104c1s
v2p0112c2s v2p0210c2s v2p0378c2s
v2p0417c1s
Potter, Prof. v1p1246c2s
Potter, R.M. v1p0018c1s
v1p0810c1s v1p1149c1s v1p1297c1s
v1p1297c2s v2p0436c1m v5p0236c2s
v5p0367c1s v5p0377c1s v5p0502c2s
v5p0618c1s v6p0349c2s v6p0640c1s
Potter, T. v2p0097c2s
v6p0143c1s
Potter, Thomas v5p0207c2s
Potter, W.A. v1p0052c1s
Potter, W.D. v1p0256c2s
v1p0360c2s
Potter, W.J. v1p0241c1s
v1p0626c1s v1p0684c2s v1p0686c1s
v1p0688c1s v1p1045c1s v1p1059c1s
v1p1320c1s v1p1336c1s v4p0382c1s
Potter, Z.H. v1p1122c1s
Pottinger, H. v3p0113c2s
v3p0193c2s v3p0306c2s v3p0307c2s
Pottinger, H., Sir v1p0708c1s
v3p0135c1s v3p0307c2s v3p0436c2s
v4p0178c1s
Pottle, E. v6p0020c2s
v6p0055c2s v6p0056c2s v6p0073c1s
v6p0103c1s v6p0106c1s v6p0220c2s
v6p0235c1s v6p0330c1s v6p0432c1s
v6p0539c2s v6p0634c2s v6p0647c2s
v6p0663c1s v6p0701c1s
Pottow, A. v5p0239c2s
v6p0205c2s v6p0261c1s v6p0261c2s
Potts, A.F. v5p0391c2s
Potts, C. v1p0579c2s
v1p0718c1s v1p1248c2s
Potts, C.S. v6p0147c2s
v6p0224c1s v6p0640c2s
Potts, E. v5p0304c2s
Potts, H.E.F. v4p0065c2s
Potts, J.D. v1p0283c1s
v1p1077c1s v1p1079c1s v1p1321c2s
Potts, J.H. v2p0085c2s
v2p0359c1s v2p0404c1s v2p0470c1s
v4p0367c2s v5p0194c1s v6p0126c2s
Potts, L.M. v5p0185c1s
Potts, Olive M. v6p0496c2s
Potts, R.H. v4p0034c2s
Potts, T.H. v1p0394c1s
v1p0703c2s
Potts, W. v1p1069c2s
v3p0046c1s v5p0203c1s v5p0620c1s
v6p0469c1s v6p0539c1s
Potts, W.J. v2p0012c1s
v2p0338c2s v3p0124c2s
Potts, W.J. and Allen, J.L.
v2p0033c1s
Potwin, Eliz.B. v5p0369c1s
Potwin, F.S. v4p0056c1s
Potwin, L.S. v1p0074c2m
v1p0121c1s v1p0126c1s v1p0554c2m
v1p0689c1s v1p1187c2s v1p1235c1s
v1p1302c2s v1p1410c2m v2p0432c1s
v3p0043c1s v3p0229c2s v4p0186c1s
v6p0240c2s
Potwin, L.S. and Thacher, T.A.
v1p0727c2s
Potwin, T.S. v1p0336c1s
v1p0397c2s v1p0903c1s v2p0245c1s
v3p0114c2s v3p0145c1s v3p0148c2s
v4p0055c1s v4p0218c1s v4p0357c2s
v4p0534c1s
Poucher, J. v2p0286c1s
v3p0042c1s v4p0054c1s v4p0252c2m
v4p0430c2s v6p0575c2s
Pouchet, A. v1p0420c1s
Pouchet, G. v1p0388c1s
v1p0645c1s v1p0907c1s v4p0209c2s
Pougin, A. v5p0043c1s
v5p0071c2s v5p0235c2s v5p0389c2s
v5p0422c1s v5p0489c1s v5p0502c2s
Poulson, N. v4p0200c1s
Poulsson, Emilie v5p0115c2s
Poulton, E.B. v2p0070c2s
v3p0082c1s v3p0447c1s v4p0124c2s
v5p0020c2s v5p0022c1s v5p0085c2s
v5p0128c2s v5p0153c2s v5p0198c2s
v5p0253c2s v5p0465c2s v6p0107c1s
v6p0674c2s v6p0697c1s
Poulton, E.B. and Osborn, H.F.
v5p0519c1s
Poulton, E.B. et al. v3p0111c1s
Pound, E. v6p0088c1s
v6p0363c1s
Pound, R. v4p0158c1s
v4p0224c2s v4p0316c1s v4p0330c2s
v4p0405c2s v6p0348c1s v6p0348c2s
v6p0363c2s
Pound, R. and Clements, F.E.
v5p0323c1s
Poundstone, J. v3p0112c1s
Pourcel, A. v2p0275c1s
Pourcel, M. v1p1250c2s
Pourtales, L.F. v1p0301c1s
Pourtales, L.F.de v1p0462c1s
Pouting, C.E. v3p0402c2s
Poutzen, E. v2p0396c2s
Pouvillion, E. v4p0348c2s
Powderly, P.Y. v6p0309c1s
Powderly, T.V. v2p0119c1s
v2p0244c2s v2p0245c1s v2p0422c2s
v3p0132c1s v3p0208c2m v3p0237c2s
v3p0393c2s v4p0262c1s v4p0314c2s
v4p0472c1s v4p0569c2s v4p0596c2s
Powderly, V. v3p0131c2s
Powel, T. v2p0156c1s
Powell, A. v5p0349c2s
Powell, A.C. v4p0279c2s
Powell, A.M. v2p0434c1s
v6p0497c1s
Powell, A.M. et al. v4p0007c1s
Powell, A.W. v1p1141c2s
v1p1173c1s
Powell, Alice v4p0588c1s
Powell, B. v1p0117c2s
v1p0729c1s v1p0915c2s v1p1303c1s
v6p0024c2s v6p0320c2s
Powell, B. and Sears, J.M., jr.
v6p0464c1s
Powell, B.B. v4p0004c2s
v4p0042c2s
Powell, B.Baden v4p0009c1s
v5p0004c2s
Powell, B.E. v6p0146c2s
Powell, B.H.B. v2p0217c2s
v3p0212c1s
Powell, Benj. v6p0149c2s
Powell, C.A. v4p0169c1s
v4p0171c2s v5p0001c2s v5p0056c2s
v5p0388c1s
Powell, C.H. v5p0050c2s
v5p0598c1s
Powell, Caroline A. v5p0107c2s
v5p0152c1s
Powell, E. v6p0011c2s
v6p0182c1s
Powell, E.A. v6p0368c2s
v6p0382c1s v6p0411c2s
Powell, E.B. v3p0356c2s
v4p0599c2s v6p0673c1s
Powell, E.C. v6p0690c2s
Powell, E.E. v6p0537c2s
Powell, E.P. v3p0188c2s
v3p0228c1s v3p0318c2s v3p0359c1s
v4p0018c2s v4p0022c2s v4p0123c2s
v4p0130c1s v4p0162c2s v4p0168c2s
v4p0169c2s v4p0171c2s v4p0191c1s
v4p0195c2s v4p0213c1s v4p0213c2s
v4p0234c2m v4p0246c2s v4p0286c1s
v4p0299c1m v4p0320c1s v4p0320c2s
v4p0325c2s v4p0345c2s v4p0358c2s
v4p0369c1s v4p0421c1s v4p0431c1s
v4p0446c2s v4p0460c2s v4p0462c1s
v4p0481c2s v4p0484c2s v4p0485c2s
v4p0490c2s v4p0505c2s v4p0507c2s
v4p0535c1s v4p0552c2s v4p0555c1s
v4p0597c2s v4p0610c1s v5p0003c2m
v5p0123c2s v5p0126c2s v5p0139c2s
v5p0176c2s v5p0203c1s v5p0255c1s
v5p0304c1s v5p0361c1s v5p0405c1s
v5p0452c1s v5p0562c2s v5p0599c2s
v6p0025c2s v6p0043c2m v6p0045c1s
v6p0059c1m v6p0112c1s v6p0128c2s
v6p0149c2s v6p0154c1m v6p0170c1s
v6p0214c2s v6p0220c1s v6p0229c1s
v6p0246c2s v6p0264c2s v6p0386c1s
v6p0407c2s v6p0416c1s v6p0454c2s
v6p0465c2s v6p0469c1s v6p0472c1s
v6p0511c2s v6p0513c1s v6p0534c1s
v6p0597c1s v6p0611c2s v6p0701c1s
Powell, E.R. v6p0128c2s
v6p0153c2s
Powell, Edgar v6p0486c1s
Powell, F.M. v5p0204c2s
Powell, F.T. v5p0130c1s
Powell, F.Y. v2p0214c1s
v2p0305c1s v2p0325c1s v2p0460c2s
v2p0474c2s v3p0090c2s v3p0097c2s
v3p0197c1s v4p0391c2s v4p0498c1s
v4p0571c1s v5p0012c1s v5p0424c2s
v6p0208c2s v6p0247c2s v6p0367c2s
v6p0652c2s
Powell, F.Y. et al. v3p0088c1s
v3p0449c2s
Powell, F.York v2p0040c1s
Powell, G.B. v1p0031c1s
v1p1057c2s v1p1265c2s v1p1370c1s
v2p0004c2s v2p0356c2s v3p0174c1s
v3p0265c1s
Powell, G.Baden v3p0027c1s
Powell, G.H. v3p0368c2s
v4p0203c2s v4p0217c1s v4p0295c2s
v4p0444c2s v5p0145c1s v5p0252c2s
v5p0394c2s v5p0439c1s v5p0567c2s
v6p0017c1s v6p0074c2s v6p0112c1s
v6p0256c2s v6p0663c1s
Powell, G.M. v2p0018c1s
v2p0244c2s v2p0423c1s
Powell, George H. v3p0250c2s
v4p0220c2s
Powell, H. v6p0258c1s
v6p0258c2s
Powell, H.A. v6p0523c2s
Powell, H.J. v1p0525c2s
v3p0174c2s v4p0384c1s v4p0499c2s
v5p0570c1s
Powell, H.Y. v2p0165c1s
v2p0309c1s v2p0465c2s
Powell, J.L. v4p0048c2s
v4p0554c2s v5p0188c2s v5p0542c2s
v5p0629c1s v5p0641c2s
Powell, J.W. v1p0027c1s
v1p0279c2m v1p0509c1s v1p0871c1s
v1p0890c2s v1p0949c2s v1p1001c1s
v1p1334c1s v2p0017c2s v2p0127c1s
v2p0128c1s v2p0149c2s v2p0219c2s
v2p0221c2s v2p0277c2s v2p0300c1s
v2p0332c2s v2p0390c2s v2p0455c1s
v3p0010c2s v3p0015c1m v3p0017c2s
v3p0019c1m v3p0030c2s v3p0093c1s
v3p0095c2s v3p0098c2s v3p0145c2s
v3p0169c1s v3p0204c1s v3p0213c2s
v3p0223c2s v3p0250c1s v3p0293c1s
v3p0342c2s v3p0380c2s v3p0385c1s
v3p0458c2s v4p0094c2s v4p0121c1s
v4p0125c1s v4p0146c2s v4p0202c2s
v4p0205c1s v4p0258c2s v4p0269c1s
v4p0272c2s v4p0282c1s v4p0282c2s
v4p0384c2s v4p0537c2s v4p0593c2s
v5p0005c1s v5p0097c1s v5p0116c2s
v5p0122c1s v5p0212c1s v5p0288c2s
v5p0293c1s v5p0322c1s v5p0440c2s
v5p0446c2s v5p0447c1s v5p0483c2s
v5p0509c2s v5p0537c1s v5p0539c2s
v5p0632c1s v6p0688c2s
Powell, J.W. and Boas, F.. v3p0143c2s
Powell, J.W. and Rhodes, C.D.
v6p0666c2s
Powell, L.P. v4p0014c1s
v4p0443c1s v5p0339c2s v5p0605c1s
v5p0620c2s v6p0295c1s
Powell, L.W. v1p0928c2s
v1p1063c2s
Powell, M. v1p0188c1s
Powell, M.B. v4p0579c1s
Powell, M.G. v4p0398c2s
Powell, N. v5p0138c2s
v5p0398c1s v6p0054c2s v6p0683c1s
Powell, R. v1p1212c1s
Powell, R.F. v6p0673c2s
Powell, S.W. v2p0159c1s
v2p0162c2s
Powell, T. v1p1042c1s
Powell, T.E. v4p0059c2s
v4p0596c1s
Powell, T.E. et al. v4p0525c1s
Powell, W. v3p0300c2s
v6p0075c1s
Powell, W.B. v4p0222c2s
v5p0512c2s
Powell, W.H. v3p0020c1s
v3p0103c2s v3p0213c1s v3p0213c2s
v3p0359c2s v3p0430c2s v3p0441c2s
v4p0284c1s
Power, A. v2p0372c1s
v3p0429c1s
Power, A., Sir v1p0017c2s
v1p0955c2s v1p1434c1s
Power, C. v2p0030c2s
v2p0339c1s
Power, F.D. v2p0085c1s
Power, H. v1p0352c1s
v1p0767c2s v1p0793c2s v1p0944c1m
Power, J.O'C. v1p0599c2s
v1p0656c1s v1p0661c2s v2p0186c2s
v3p0219c2s v4p0624c2s v5p0083c2s
Power, J.W. v4p0601c2s
Power, John O'c. v4p0615c1s
Power, L.G. v2p0225c2s
v4p0428c1s v4p0605c1s v6p0097c1s
Power, Lady v1p0858c2s
v1p1126c2s
Power, M.A. v1p1377c2s
v3p0043c1s
Power, P.B. v1p1159c2s
Power, R. v2p0153c1s
Power, R.M. v5p0439c1s
Power, S. v2p0206c1s
v2p0325c2s v6p0486c1s
Power, T.R. v3p0219c2s
Power, W.B. v5p0472c1s

Power, W.P. v2p0085c2s
Power, Walter S. v6p0487c2s
Powers, A.H., jr. v4p0243c1s
Powers, C.J. v4p0112c2s
Powers, E. v3p0353c2s
Powers, E.M. v5p0177c1s
Powers, E.P. v4p0524c2s
Powers, F.P. v1p0623c1s
v1p0795c1s v2p0220c2s v3p0028c1m
v3p0086c2s v3p0185c1s v3p0208c2s
v3p0241c2s v3p0340c2s v3p0347c1s
v3p0353c1s v3p0358c2s v3p0416c2s
v3p0421c1s v3p0441c2s v3p0460c2s
v4p0187c2s v4p0195c1s v4p0197c2s
v4p0374c2s v5p0228c1s v5p0237c2s
v5p0241c1s v5p0329c1s v5p0542c2s
v5p0584c1s v5p0592c2s v5p0599c2s
v5p0618c1s
Powers, G.F. v5p0031c1s
v6p0472c1s
Powers, G.W. v1p0714c2s
v1p1288c2s
Powers, H. v1p0856c2s
v4p0135c1s
Powers, H.G. v3p0020c1s
Powers, H.H. v4p0535c1s
v5p0199c1s v5p0199c2s v5p0232c1s
v5p0543c1s v5p0623c2s v6p0033c1s
v6p0229c1s
Powers, H.N. v1p0171c2m
v1p0172c1s v1p0228c1s v1p0245c2s
v1p0419c1s v1p0567c2s v1p1021c2s
v2p0011c2s v2p0012c2s v2p0022c1s
v2p0059c1m v2p0140c1s v2p0195c1s
v2p0248c2s v2p0280c2s v2p0332c2s
v2p0377c2s v2p0431c2s v2p0439c2s
v3p0011c2m v3p0020c2s v3p0317c2s
Powers, Henry v4p0452c1s
Powers, J.O. v6p0004c2s
Powers, J.T. v1p0505c1s
Powers, L.B. v6p0421c2s
Powers, L.G. v4p0230c1s
v5p0289c2s v5p0535c2s v5p0568c1s
Powers, Laura B. v6p0092c2s
v6p0568c1s
Powers, Le G. v5p0009c2s
Powers, M.A. v2p0078c1s
Powers, S. v1p0058c1s
v1p0080c1s v1p0187c1s v1p0187c2m
v1p0188c1m v1p0188c2m v1p0234c2s
v1p0236c1s v1p0366c2s v1p0379c2s
v1p0517c1s v1p0518c1s v1p0637c1m
v1p0793c1s v1p0814c2s v1p0854c1s
v1p0956c1s v1p1011c1s v1p1012c1s
v1p1060c1s v1p1060c2s v1p1061c1s
v1p1297c2s v1p1352c1s v2p0089c2s
v3p0063c2s
Powers, S.L. v1p0843c1s
v1p0900c2s v4p0466c2s
Powers, Stanley v6p0113c2s
Powers, W.R. v1p0096c1s
v1p0096c2s v1p0663c1s
Powerscourt v3p0221c1s
Powerscourt, Lord v4p0289c1s
Powerscourt, Visc. v2p0225c1s
Powicke, F.J. v5p0454c1s
v5p0470c2s
Powicke, F.M. v6p0020c2s
v6p0459c1s v6p0546c2s
Powicke, J.F. v4p0437c1s
Powles, L.D. v4p0554c2s
Powlett, N. v2p0127c1s
v2p0336c1s
Pownal, C.A.W. v6p0556c1s
Pownall, G.H. v4p0237c1s
v5p0045c1s
Pownall, J. v1p1114c2s
Pownall, T. v1p0053c1s
v1p0156c2s v1p0165c2s v1p0320c2s
v1p0487c2s v1p0653c1s v1p0958c2s
v1p0987c1s v1p1121c1s v1p1122c1s
v1p1122c2s v1p1123c1s v1p1192c1m
v1p1234c1s v1p1329c1s v1p1363c1m
v1p1400c2s
Powys, N. v5p0494c2s
Powys, R. v6p0618c1s
Poyen-Bellisle, R.de v4p0580c1s
v6p0242c1s
Poynder, G. v1p0251c2s
v1p1033c2s
Poynder, J.D. v4p0280c1s
Poynter, E.F. v2p0216c1s
v2p0221c2s
Poynter, E.J. v1p0105c2s
v1p0365c1s v1p0834c2s v4p0605c1s
v4p0619c1s
Poynter, H.M. v4p0365c2s
v5p0417c1s v5p0541c2s
Poynting, J. v6p0376c2s
Poynting, J.H. v2p0353c2s
v2p0471c2s v3p0192c1s v4p0165c2s
v5p0242c2s v6p0376c1s v6p0498c1s
v6p0526c2m
Poynting, T.E. v1p0810c2s
Poyntz, A. v1p0266c2s
v1p0297c2s v1p0711c1s v1p0886c2s
Poyntz, L. v1p0087c2s
v1p0175c2s v1p0782c1s v1p1345c1s
Poznanski, S. v5p0053c1s
v5p0307c1s v5p0503c1s v6p0347c1s
v6p0561c2s
Pozzoni, C. v1p0670c2s
v1p0671c1s v1p1025c2s v1p1369c2s
Praed, B.C. v4p0160c1s
Praed, C. v6p0387c1s
Praed, C., Mrs. v2p0483c1s
v3p0467c2s v3p0469c2s
Praeger, F. v3p0293c2s
Praeger, R.L. v5p0211c1s
v5p0296c1s v5p0454c1s v6p0072c1s
v6p0083c1s v6p0229c2s v6p0267c2s
Praeger, W.E. v5p0534c1s
Praelatus v6p0548c1s
Praetorius, C. v6p0603c1s
Praetorius, C.J. v5p0149c1s
v5p0361c1m v5p0408c1s v5p0452c1s
v5p0639c1s v6p0226c2s v6p0450c2m
Prag, F. v3p0050c1s
Prag, J. v5p0428c2s
Praga, A. v5p0377c2s
Prang, L. v1p0246c1s
Prasil, F. v5p0594c2s
Prater, H. v1p0874c2s
Prather, H.B. v5p0167c2s
v5p0222c2s
Prather, W.L. et al. v5p0327c1s
Pratt, A. v1p1015c2s
v5p0039c2s v6p0315c2s
Pratt, A.E. v5p0014c1s
Pratt, C.A. v4p0515c2s
v4p0625c1s v5p0086c2s v5p0240c2s
v5p0274c2s v5p0301c2m v5p0370c2m
v5p0432c2s v5p0540c1s v5p0620c1s
Pratt, C.E. v1p0132c2s
v3p0044c1m v3p0339c1s
Pratt, C.L. v5p0360c2s
v6p0573c1s
Pratt, C.S. v3p0309c2s
v4p0154c2s v4p0432c1s v6p0323c2s
v6p0418c1s
Pratt, D. v1p0307c1s
Pratt, D.M. v6p0084c1s
v6p0341c1s
Pratt, E. v1p0099c2s
v1p0846c1s v5p0189c1s v5p0284c1m
Pratt, E.A. v6p0529c1s
v6p0534c1s v6p0708c2s
Pratt, E.A. and Barbour, J.F.
v5p0215c1s
Pratt, F. v2p0259c1s
Pratt, F.H. v6p0366c1s
Pratt, F.L. v3p0312c2s
Pratt, G. v1p0941c1s
Pratt, G.C. v2p0362c2s
Pratt, H. et al. v4p0557c2s
Pratt, H.C. v6p0564c1s
Pratt, H.G. v4p0416c2s
v4p0491c2s
Pratt, I. v2p0243c1s
Pratt, J. v1p0128c2s
v1p0129c1s v1p0451c1s v1p1056c2m
v2p0257c2s v2p0467c1s v5p0012c2s
v6p0168c1s
Pratt, J.A. v5p0333c1s
v6p0066c1s
Pratt, J.B. v6p0400c2s
Pratt, J.H. v1p0375c1s
v3p0063c2s v3p0318c2s v4p0082c2s
v4p0292c1s v5p0014c1s v5p0022c2s
v5p0054c2s v5p0116c1s v5p0138c2m
v5p0150c2s v5p0193c2s v5p0414c1s
v5p0440c2s v5p0508c2s
Pratt, J.H. and Foote, H.W.
v5p0625c1s
Pratt, J.H. and Hidden, W.E.
v5p0487c2m v5p0645c2s
Pratt, J.H. and Penfield, S.L.
v4p0546c2s v4p0572c1s v4p0617c2s
Pratt, J.H., jr. v3p0134c2s
Pratt, J.W. v4p0512c1s
Pratt, L.W. v6p0630c2s
Pratt, M. v1p0712c1s
v5p0378c1s
Pratt, M.C. v4p0412c2s
Pratt, M.E. v5p0379c2s
Pratt, M.L. v3p0398c1s
v4p0104c1s v4p0441c1s
Pratt, P.E. v4p0300c2s
Pratt, R.H. v4p0282c1s
v4p0282c2s v5p0288c1s
Pratt, S. v3p0272c2s
v5p0567c1s
Pratt, S.C. v6p0379c1s
Pratt, S.G. v4p0414c2s
Pratt, S.S. v6p0224c1s
v6p0321c1s v6p0452c2s v6p0550c2s
v6p0670c1s
Pratt, Sereno S. v6p0051c1s
Pratt, W.M. v6p0213c1s
Pratt, W.S. v1p0885c1s
v1p0947c2s v2p0105c2s v4p0388c2s
v4p0389c1s v5p0057c2s v5p0277c2s
v5p0342c2s v5p0395c1s v6p0121c2s
v6p0126c2s v6p0172c2s v6p0381c1s
v6p0513c2s v6p0611c1s
Pratten, B.P. v1p0125c1s
Pratten, H. v1p0136c2s
Pratz, C.de v4p0170c1s
v4p0425c2s v6p0081c2s v6p0161c2s
Pratz, Claire de v5p0506c1s
Pravieux, G.J. v5p0221c1m
Pravieux, J. v6p0242c1m
Pray, Florence v6p0117c2s
v6p0246c1s
Pray, I.C. v1p0150c1s
v1p1283c1s v1p1374c2s
Pray, J.C. v1p1057c2s
Pray, J.S. v5p0299c2s
Pray, M.L. v1p1301c1s
Pray, S. v1p1112c2s
Pray, T. v3p0201c1s
Pray, T., jr. v3p0102c1s
v3p0408c2s v4p0547c2s v4p0600c1s
Pre, L.J.Du v1p0853c2s
v2p0410c1m
Preble, E.L. v6p0142c1s
Preble, Ethel L. v6p0301c1s
Preble, G.H. v1p0059c1s
v1p0449c2s v1p0459c1s v1p0556c1s
v1p1044c2m v1p1192c1s v1p1349c2s
v1p1437c2s v2p0436c2s v4p0521c1s
v4p0547c2s
Preble, H. v5p0326c1s
Preece, F.J.C. v2p0162c2s
Preece, W. v6p0196c1s
Preece, W., Sir v6p0634c1s
Preece, W.H. v1p0077c1s
v1p0376c1m v1p0399c2m v1p0401c1s
v1p0501c2s v1p0749c1m v1p0835c1s
v1p1076c1s v1p1222c2s v1p1291c1s
v2p0136c2m v2p0137c1m v2p0138c1s
v2p0433c1s v2p0433c2s v3p0132c2m
v3p0133c2m v3p0134c1s v3p0251c1s
v3p0330c1s v3p0401c2s v3p0423c1m
v4p0175c2s v4p0176c1s v4p0567c2s
v5p0184c2s v5p0188c1s v5p0529c1s
v5p0571c1s v6p0082c1s v6p0457c2s
v6p0576c1s
Preece, Wm.H. v6p0601c2s
Preisinger, H. v4p0229c2s
Prel, C.Du v1p0903c2m
Prelooker, J. v4p0588c1s
Prence, Katharine v6p0130c2s
Prendegast, W.A. v6p0051c1s
Prendergast, F.E. v1p0833c2s
v2p0363c1s
Prendergast, H.N.D. v4p0079c2s
v4p0211c1s v4p0278c2s v4p0283c1s
v4p0522c2s
Prendergast, J.P. v2p0111c2s
v2p0284c1s
Prendergast, T. v1p0672c2s
Prendergast, T.F. v2p0066c1s
v2p0316c2s
Prendeville, Mary v5p0071c1s
Prentice, C. v5p0200c2s
v6p0216c2s
Prentice, E.P. v5p0152c1s
v5p0312c2s v6p0324c2m
Prentice, E.Parmalee v6p0151c1s
Prentice, G. v1p0358c1s
v1p0398c1s v1p0405c1s v1p0972c2s
v1p1047c2s v1p1098c2s
Prentice, J.M. v4p0390c1s
Prentice, M.L. and Warren, I.
v5p0334c1s
Prentice, S.D. v4p0220c2s
v4p0411c2s
Prentice, T.M. v4p0070c2s
Prentice, W.K. v6p0174c2s
Prentice, W.P. v4p0401c1s
v4p0459c2s
Prentice, W.R. v6p0182c2s
Prentiss, A.N. v1p0645c1s
v4p0203c1s
Prentiss, C.W. v5p0021c2s
v6p0174c1s
Prentiss, D.W. v2p0015c1s
v2p0284c2s v3p0187c2s
Prentiss, E. v1p0485c1s
Prentiss, E.L. v6p0162c2m
Prentiss, F.F. v4p0180c2s
v4p0296c2s
Prentiss, G.D. v1p1182c2s
Prentiss, G.L. v1p1204c1s
v1p1352c2s v1p1353c2s v2p0221c1s
Prentiss, H.M. v3p0307c1s
Prentiss, M.A. v2p0251c1s
Prentiss, Mabel E. v6p0075c1s
v6p0371c2s v6p0372c2s
Prentiss, N.A. v2p0201c2s
Prentiss, R.W. v3p0134c1s
Presbrey, O.F. v4p0144c2s
Presby, F.H. v6p0546c1s
Presbyter Anglicanus v1p0122c2s
Prescott, A. v2p0091c1s
Prescott, A.B. v1p0493c1s
v1p0745c2s v2p0258c1s v2p0432c1s
v4p0098c2s
Prescott, A.B. and Demmon, I.M.
v6p0491c1s
Prescott, B.F. v1p0911c2s
v3p0339c2s v4p0453c2s
Prescott, C. v4p0243c2s
v4p0468c2s
Prescott, D. v3p0148c1s
v3p0339c1s v3p0411c1s v3p0463c1s
v4p0015c1s v4p0091c2s v4p0376c1s
v4p0578c2s v5p0016c1s
Prescott, E. v1p1002c2s

Prescott, E.B. v3p0159c1s
v3p0403c1s
Prescott, E.L. v5p0019c1s
v5p0162c2s
Prescott, F.C. v6p0380c1s
Prescott, G.B. v1p0077c1s
v1p0384c1s v1p0542c1s v1p1240c2s
v1p1290c2m v1p1291c2m
Prescott, G.B., jr. v3p0132c2s
v3p0133c1s
Prescott, H.E. v1p0107c1s
v1p0361c2s v1p0446c1s v1p0626c2s
v1p0711c1s v1p0837c1s v1p1029c2s
Prescott, H.W. v6p0273c1s
Prescott, Harriet E. v1p0026c2s
Prescott, J.E. v1p0807c1s
v1p1293c2s
Prescott, K.E. v1p0452c1s
Prescott, K.T. v3p0308c2s
Prescott, M.N. v1p0203c1s
Prescott, S.C. v6p0047c1s
v6p0417c1s v6p0527c2s
Prescott, S.C. and Underwood, W.S.
v5p0552c2s
Prescott, W. v1p1397c1s
Prescott, W.B. v6p0356c1s
Prescott, W.H. v1p0057c1s
v1p0142c1s v1p0145c2s v1p0169c1s
v1p0182c2s v1p0213c2s v1p0360c1s
v1p0417c2m v1p0425c1s v1p0539c2s
v1p0556c2s v1p0593c1s v1p0667c2s
v1p0668c2s v1p0669c2s v1p0672c2s
v1p0706c1s v1p0738c1s v1p0833c1s
v1p0859c1s v1p1032c1s v1p1168c1s
v1p1170c2s v1p1231c1s v1p1320c1s
v1p1350c1s v1p1434c1s
Preskin, H. v5p0237c2s
v5p0421c2s
Pressense, E. v1p0431c1s
Pressense, E.de v1p0117c2m
v1p0479c2m v1p0480c1m v1p0481c2s
v1p0489c1s v1p0518c1s v1p0683c1s
v1p0683c2s v1p0684c1s v1p0684c2s
v1p0688c1s v1p0862c1s v1p0869c2s
v1p0895c1s v1p1117c1s v1p1140c1s
v1p1199c2s v1p1305c1s v2p0092c1s
v2p0164c1s v2p0164c2s v2p0165c2m
v2p0297c2s v2p0329c2s v2p0461c1s
v2p0463c2s v3p0072c2s v3p0161c2s
v3p0343c1s
Pressense, F. v5p0142c2s
Pressense, F.de v2p0167c2m
v4p0027c1s v4p0181c1m v4p0211c1s
v5p0170c1s v5p0173c2s v5p0189c1s
v5p0189c2s v5p0216c2m v5p0243c1s
v5p0501c2s v5p0611c1s v6p0205c2s
v6p0237c1s
Pressey, E.P. v5p0365c1s
v5p0562c1s
Pressinger, W.P. v4p0008c2m
v5p0455c1s
Pressley, J.G. v2p0424c2s
v3p0459c1s
Pressy, E.P. v6p0296c1s
Prest, C. v1p0243c2s
Prestage, E. v4p0011c2s
v4p0091c2s v4p0453c2s
Prestel, M.A.F. v1p1394c2s
Preston, A.J. v6p0544c1s
Preston, C.E. v6p0002c1s
Preston, E. v6p0074c1s
v6p0133c2s
Preston, E.D. v3p0125c2s
v3p0191c2s v3p0263c2s v3p0325c2s
v3p0328c1s v3p0407c1s v4p0250c2m
v5p0134c1s v5p0136c2s v5p0228c1s
v5p0258c2s v5p0599c2s
Preston, G.H. v6p0160c1s
v6p0311c2s
Preston, G.J. v2p0201c1s
Preston, G.R. v6p0667c2s
Preston, H.L. v4p0367c1m
v5p0279c2s v5p0372c1m
Preston, H.W. v1p0065c1s
v1p0075c2s v1p0197c1s v1p0418c2s
v1p0680c1s v1p0790c1s v1p0855c2s
v1p0956c1s v1p1059c2s v1p1327c1s
v2p0012c2s v2p0017c1s v2p0022c1s
v2p0221c1s v2p0231c1s v2p0232c1s
v2p0293c1s v2p0317c2s v2p0321c1s
v2p0325c1s v2p0326c1s v2p0341c1s
v2p0345c1s v2p0364c2s v2p0382c1s
v2p0464c2s v3p0024c1s v3p0085c1m
v3p0158c2s v3p0165c1s v3p0251c2s
v3p0261c2s v3p0317c1s v3p0347c2s
v3p0371c1s v3p0386c1s v3p0392c1s
v3p0447c2s v4p0004c1s v4p0189c2s
v4p0248c1s v5p0079c2s v5p0420c1m
Preston, H.W. and Dodge, L.
v3p0010c1s v3p0023c2s v3p0027c1s
v3p0048c2s v3p0228c2s v3p0233c1s
v3p0261c1s v3p0324c1s v3p0366c2s
v3p0371c1s v3p0385c1s v3p0418c2s
v4p0118c2s v4p0124c2s v4p0437c1s
v4p0449c2s v4p0484c1s v4p0490c1s
v4p0561c1s
Preston, Harriet W. v6p0301c1s
v6p0411c1s v6p0474c2s v6p0685c2s
Preston, Harriet Waters .. v6p0086c1s
v6p0333c1s
Preston, J.H. v1p0235c1s
Preston, J.L.T. v1p0485c2s
Preston, J.T.L. v1p0010c2s
v1p0073c1s v1p0782c2s v1p0905c2s
v1p0996c1s v2p0058c1s v3p0422c1s
Preston, J.W. v1p0201c1s
v1p1228c2s
Preston, K.D. v5p0206c2s
Preston, M. v2p0009c2s
Preston, M.J. v1p0024c2s
v1p0370c2s v1p0576c2s v1p0722c2s
v1p0856c1s v1p0930c2s v1p1112c1s
v1p1363c1s v1p1419c2s v1p1428c1s
v2p0101c1s v2p0151c1s v2p0198c2s
v2p0232c2s v2p0329c1s v3p0026c2s
v3p0125c1s v3p0245c2m v3p0262c1s
v3p0269c2s v3p0294c2s
Preston, N.K. v6p0374c2s
Preston, R.E. v4p0230c1s
Preston, R.J. v4p0134c2s
Preston, S. v6p0157c2s
v6p0523c2s v6p0535c2s v6p0625c1s
Preston, S.H. v3p0440c1s
v5p0250c1s v5p0425c1s v6p0249c1s
Preston, S.J. v3p0298c2s
Preston, S.O. v4p0096c2s
v4p0591c1s
Preston, S.T. v1p0074c1s
v1p0426c1s v1p0434c1s v1p0502c2s
v1p0580c2s v1p0747c2m v1p0787c1s
v1p1074c1s v1p1222c2s v1p1356c1s
v1p1378c2s v2p0146c2s v2p0307c1s
v2p0412c2s v2p0455c2s v3p0430c2s
v4p0439c1s v4p0507c2s v5p0545c2s
Preston, Sydney v6p0150c1s
Preston, T. v5p0475c2s
v5p0545c1s
Preston, T.B. v3p0012c1s
v3p0066c2s v3p0081c1s v3p0247c1s
v3p0340c2s v3p0408c1m v3p0443c2s
v4p0027c2s v4p0404c1s v4p0425c1s
v4p0425c2s v4p0450c2s v4p0533c2s
v5p0135c2s v5p0218c1s v5p0232c1s
v5p0409c2m v5p0430c2m v5p0440c2s
Preston, T.F. v1p0289c1s
Preston, T.S. v1p0023c2s
v1p0422c1m v1p1109c2m v1p1337c1s
v2p0375c1s v3p0347c1s v3p0358c1s
v3p0364c1s v3p0365c1s v3p0398c1s
Preston, T.W. v1p1340c1s
Preston, W.C. v2p0049c2s
v2p0202c1s v2p0207c1s v2p0288c1s
v2p0328c1s v3p0047c1s v3p0067c2s
v3p0077c2s v3p0136c1s v3p0234c1s
v3p0240c1s v3p0256c1s v3p0373c2s
v3p0395c1s v3p0395c2s v3p0466c2s
v4p0047c2s v4p0130c2s v4p0165c1s
v4p0271c2s v4p0360c2s v4p0363c1s
v4p0392c1s v4p0467c1s v4p0468c1s
v4p0501c1s v4p0586c1s v5p0346c2s
v5p0574c2s
Preston, W.T.R. v6p0098c1s
Preston, Wm.C. v3p0402c2s
v4p0320c2s v4p0386c2s v4p0530c2s
Preston-Thomas, H. v3p0193c2s
v3p0446c1s v4p0260c1s v4p0385c2s
Prestwich, G.A. v3p0315c2s
Prestwich, J. v1p0268c2s
v1p0506c2s v1p0509c2s v1p1299c1s
v2p0434c1s v2p0463c1s v3p0169c1s
v4p0202c1s v4p0223c1s v4p0351c2s
Prestwich, Mrs. v2p0127c1s
v2p0151c1s
Prestwick, L. v2p0224c1s
Pretlow, M.D. v6p0201c2s
Pretlow, M.D. et al. v6p0635c1s
Prettyman, V. v6p0038c2s
v6p0290c1s
Pretyman, G.T. v4p0307c2s
Pretyman, J.R. v1p0250c1s
Prevey, C.E. v5p0102c1s
Prevost, A.L. v6p0583c2s
Prevost, Agnes L. v6p0223c2s
Prevost, Dr. v2p0055c1s
Prevost, E.W. v2p0155c2m
v2p0315c1s v2p0344c1s
Prevost, F. v3p0019c1s
v3p0198c1s v3p0206c1s v4p0178c1s
v4p0225c1s v4p0606c2s
Prevost, Francis v5p0438c1s
Prevost, L.M. v1p0161c1s
Prevost, M. v5p0052c1s
v5p0464c1s v5p0537c2s
Prevost-Paradol, L.A. v1p0785c1s
Prewitt, F.W. v1p0637c2s
Preyer, D.C. v5p0406c2s
v6p0084c2s
Preyer, W. v1p0041c1s
v1p1061c2s v2p0104c2s v2p0394c2s
v3p0102c1s v3p0208c2s v3p0215c2s
v3p0250c2s v3p0332c1s v4p0247c1s
v4p0331c1s v4p0507c1s
Price, A. v3p0294c2s
v3p0334c2s v4p0293c1s
Price, B. v1p0079c2s
v1p0091c1s v1p0091c2m v1p0092c1s
v1p0093c2s v1p0207c2s v1p0248c2s
v1p0262c2s v1p0272c2s v1p0313c2s
v1p0325c1m v1p0326c1m v1p0453c1s
v1p0486c2s v1p0549c1s v1p0615c1s
v1p0649c2s v1p0761c1s v1p0860c2s
v1p0861c1m v1p0942c2s v1p0953c2s
v1p0963c2m v1p1026c1s v1p1086c2m
v1p1099c1s v1p1116c1s v1p1319c2s
v2p0046c1s v2p0110c1s v2p0132c2s
v2p0167c1s v2p0209c1s v2p0217c2s
v2p0294c2s v3p0202c1s
Price, C.A. v4p0080c1s
v4p0081c2s v4p0137c2s v4p0231c2s
v4p0263c1s v4p0383c2s v4p0399c2s
v4p0482c1s v4p0498c2s v4p0520c1s
v4p0527c2s
Price, C.W. v6p0289c1s
Price, Daisy v6p0516c2s
Price, E.A. v4p0309c1s
Price, E.C. v2p0007c2s
v2p0161c2s v2p0175c1s v3p0014c2s
v3p0039c2s v3p0356c1s v4p0052c1s
v4p0052c2s v4p0212c2s v4p0373c2s
v4p0536c2s v5p0074c1s v5p0261c2s
Price, E.C.H. v4p0071c1s
v4p0240c2s v4p0619c2s v4p0630c2s
Price, E.D. v3p0132c1s
v3p0327c2m v3p0349c1s v3p0382c2s
v3p0446c1s v3p0448c2s
Price, F.E. v6p0275c2s
Price, F.G.H. v1p1072c2s
v2p0273c2s v5p0180c2s
Price, F.G.H. and Price, J.E.
v2p0377c1s v2p0393c2s
Price, F.G.H. et al. v3p0384c1s
Price, F.G.Hilton v2p0133c1s
Price, F.M. v5p0427c1s
Price, F.T. v1p0600c1s
v1p1366c2s
Price, G.B. v3p0272c2s
Price, G.E. v6p0569c1s
Price, G.F. v5p0388c1s
Price, H. v1p0252c1s
v1p0483c1s v3p0213c1s v4p0500c2s
Price, H.B. v1p0772c2s
Price, H.M. v5p0605c2s
Price, I.M. v3p0041c1s
v4p0056c1s v4p0065c2s v4p0302c1s
v5p0055c2s v5p0056c1m v5p0058c1s
v5p0199c1s v5p0308c1s v5p0412c2s
v5p0432c1s v5p0444c2s v5p0613c1s
v6p0030c2s v6p0036c1s v6p0064c2s
v6p0216c1s v6p0279c1s v6p0470c1s
Price, I.N. v6p0255c1s
Price, J. v1p1122c1s
Price, J.C. v3p0298c2s
Price, J.E. v1p0993c1s
v1p1173c2s v2p0037c1s v2p0448c1s
v3p0142c1s v3p0256c1s v3p0415c2s
Price, J.E. and Price, F.G.H.
v2p0377c1s v2p0393c2s
Price, J.M. v4p0331c2s
v5p0530c1s v6p0033c1s v6p0434c2s
v6p0559c1s v6p0561c1s
Price, J.R. v1p0386c2s
Price, L.C. v6p0136c2s
Price, L.G. v6p0136c1s
v6p0137c2s v6p0439c1s
Price, L.L. v3p0215c1m
v3p0280c1s v3p0359c1s v4p0008c1m
v4p0059c2m v4p0167c2m v4p0199c1s
v4p0279c1s v4p0314c1s v4p0377c2s
v4p0419c2s v4p0450c1m v4p0461c1s
v4p0530c1s v4p0535c1s v4p0565c1s
v5p0028c1s v5p0121c1s v5p0175c2m
v5p0289c1m v5p0300c2s v5p0320c2s
v5p0344c2s v5p0345c2s v5p0563c1s
v5p0616c2s v6p0026c1s v6p0082c2s
v6p0142c1m v6p0188c2m v6p0206c2s
v6p0240c1s v6p0262c1s v6p0269c2s
v6p0271c1m v6p0271c2m v6p0318c1m
v6p0472c2s v6p0506c2m v6p0512c1s
v6p0632c2s v6p0633c1s
Price, L.L.F.R. v3p0452c2s
Price, L.V. v4p0381c2s
Price, M. v1p0854c1s
Price, M.L. v6p0660c2s
Price, M.M. v3p0283c1s
v3p0301c2s
Price, Mary A. v3p0130c1s
Price, Miss v6p0525c1s
Price, Mrs. v1p1108c1s
Price, O.J. v6p0403c2s
Price, O.W. v6p0233c1s
v6p0233c2m
Price, R. v5p0597c1s
Price, R.D.G. v1p1086c2s
v2p0378c1s v2p0444c1s
Price, R.H. v5p0438c1s
Price, S. v1p0855c1s
v1p0934c2s
Price, S.F. v4p0197c1s
Price, Sadie F. v5p0315c1s
Price, T. v1p1122c2s
Price, T.R. v1p0385c1s
v1p0390c2s v2p0461c1s v3p0298c2s
v4p0320c1s v4p0334c2s v5p0278c2s
Price, W. v3p0164c1s
v3p0372c2s v5p0081c1s
Price, W.H. v3p0238c1s
v6p0047c2s v6p0153c1s v6p0241c1s
v6p0312c1s v6p0651c2s
Price, W.J. v6p0282c2s
v6p0336c2s v6p0492c1s

Price, W.L. v6p0027c2s v6p0028c1s
Price, W.L.T. v1p0515c2s
Price, W.S. v1p0820c2s v1p1207c1s v1p1208c2s
Price, W.W. v4p0153c2s v5p0464c2s v5p0538c1s v6p0393c2s v6p0550c2s
Price, Wm.T. v6p0143c1s
Price-Edwards, E. v3p0392c2s v6p0594c1s v6p0604c2s
Price-Williams, R. v3p0089c2s
Prichard, C.E. v1p0063c2s
Prichard, F.P. v4p0387c2s
Prichard, H. v5p0254c1s v5p0377c1s v5p0422c2s v6p0080c2s v6p0201c1s
Prichard, H. and Prichard, K. v5p0197c2s v5p0211c2s v5p0274c1s v5p0412c2s
Prichard, H.A. v6p0533c1s
Prichard, J.C. v1p0427c2s
Prichard, J.V. v3p0210c1s
Prichard, K. and Prichard, H. v5p0197c2s v5p0211c2s v5p0274c1s v5p0412c2s
Prichard, K. and Prichard, H. v5p0260c1s
Prichard, S.J. v1p0246c1s
Prichard, W.T. v1p0832c2s
Prichett, H.S. v6p0102c1s v6p0691c1s
Prichett, R.T. v2p0205c1m
Prick, P.L. v6p0537c1s
Prideaux, J. v1p0143c1s
Prideaux, S.T. v3p0426c2s v4p0066c1m v4p0066c2m v4p0164c2s v5p0070c2m v5p0437c1s v6p0484c1s
Prideaux, T.S. v1p0202c2s v1p0948c1s v1p1004c2s v1p1005c1m v1p1076c1s v1p1292c1s v2p0054c2s
Prideaux, W.F. v6p0080c1s v6p0164c1s
Prideaux, W.F. and Blunt, R. v5p0103c2s
Prideaux, W.F. and Ramsey, J.H. v5p0065c2s
Prideaux, W.F. and Roberts, W. v5p0591c1s
Pridmore, J.E.O. v6p0641c2s
Priebsch, R. v6p0481c2s
Priest, C.M. v4p0623c1s v5p0390c1s
Priest, G.M. v6p0187c2s
Priestley, Dr. et al. v3p0146c1s
Priestley, E. v3p0264c2s v3p0356c1s v4p0266c2m v5p0210c1s v5p0416c2s v5p0435c1s v5p0486c1s v6p0241c2s v6p0364c2s v6p0474c2s v6p0483c1s
Priestley, E., Lady v5p0042c2s
Priestley, E., Mrs. v3p0170c2s v3p0205c2s v3p0323c1m v3p0393c1s
Priestley, J. v1p0002c2m v1p0047c2s v1p0057c1m v1p0075c1s v1p0096c1s v1p0122c1s v1p0124c2s v1p0128c1s v1p0129c2s v1p0130c2s v1p0440c2s v1p0531c2s v1p0645c2s v1p0646c1m v1p0684c1s v1p0685c1s v1p0685c2s v1p0686c2s v1p0687c1s v1p0688c1s v1p0692c1s v1p0697c2s v1p0812c2s v1p0825c1s v1p0875c1s v1p0962c1s v1p0980c2m v1p0998c2s v1p1016c2s v1p1017c1m v1p1094c1s v1p1101c1s v1p1139c2s v1p1286c2s
Priestley, Lady v4p0502c2s
Priestman, M.T. v6p0148c2s
Priestman, Mabel T. v6p0298c2s v6p0509c2s
Prigg, H. v2p0274c2s
Prillerman, B. v6p0686c2s
Prime, E.D.G. v2p0449c1s
Prime, F., jr. v1p0141c1s v1p0470c1s v1p0509c1s
Prime, R.E. v5p0138c1s
Prime, S.I. v1p0301c1s v1p1276c2s v2p0109c2s
Prime, W.C. v1p0041c2s v1p0119c2s v1p0148c2s v1p0272c1m v1p0294c1s v1p0377c2s v1p0395c2s v1p0497c2s v1p0553c1s v1p0682c1s v1p0815c1s v1p0817c1s v1p0960c2s v1p0980c2s v1p1039c1s v1p1051c2s v1p1200c2s v1p1300c2s v1p1389c2s v2p0059c1s v2p0104c2s
Prime-Stevenson, E.I. v5p0219c1s v6p0303c2s v6p0354c2s v6p0453c1s v6p0472c2s v6p0482c2s v6p0506c1s v6p0552c2s
Primensnyder, J.B. v3p0394c1s
Primer, S. v2p0315c2s v3p0074c2s
Primerano, D. v5p0526c2s
Primrose, W. v4p0328c1s
Prince, A.T. v6p0678c2s v6p0712c2s
Prince, B.F. v3p0083c1s v3p0415c2s
Prince, C.A. v6p0469c1s
Prince, E.E. v3p0154c1s v3p0268c1s v4p0201c1s
Prince, H.C. v5p0024c1s v5p0210c1s v6p0550c1s
Prince, H.L. v3p0443c2s
Prince, J. v4p0520c2s
Prince, J.D. v3p0008c2s v4p0056c1s v5p0057c2s v5p0058c1s v5p0287c2s v5p0378c2s v6p0001c1s v6p0062c2s v6p0107c2s v6p0149c1s v6p0301c2s v6p0458c1m
Prince, J.D. and Speck, F.G. v6p0423c2s v6p0488c2s
Prince, J.T. v2p0297c1s v2p0388c2s v3p0377c2s v3p0378c1s v4p0170c2s v4p0245c1s v4p0255c1s v4p0315c1s v5p0056c1s v5p0106c2s v5p0186c1s v5p0511c1s v5p0512c1s v6p0168c2s v6p0190c2s v6p0307c2s v6p0626c2s v6p0628c2s
Prince, L.B. v2p0357c1s v3p0084c1s v4p0059c2s v4p0399c1s v5p0508c1s
Prince, L.C. v5p0281c2s v6p0340c2s
Prince, M. v6p0418c2m
Prince, M.S. v2p0207c2s
Prince, Morton v6p0521c1s
Prince, W.C. v1p0213c2s
Prince, Wm.L. v5p0393c2s
Prindiville, K. v5p0493c2s
Prindiville, K.G. v6p0113c1s
Prindle, E.J. v5p0253c1s v5p0435c1s v5p0624c1s v6p0483c2s
Prindle, F.C. v1p1010c1m
Prindle, H.B. v3p0133c1s
Prinetti and Pecco v2p0406c2s
Pring, J.H. v4p0246c1s v4p0247c1s v4p0453c2s
Pringle, A. v2p0038c1s v3p0200c1s v4p0018c2s v4p0188c1s v5p0448c2s
Pringle, C.D. v1p0306c2s v1p1071c1s
Pringle, C.G. v4p0208c2s v4p0265c1s v4p0368c2s v4p0583c1s v5p0373c1s
Pringle, E.W. v1p0790c2s
Pringle, G. v5p0251c2s v5p0528c2s
Pringle, G.O.S. v5p0376c1s
Pringle, J.C. v6p0356c1s
Pringle, J.W. v4p0604c1s
Pringle, R. v3p0396c1s
Pringle-Pattison, A.S. ... v6p0351c1s v6p0383c1s v6p0403c2s v6p0593c2s v6p0610c1s
Prinsep, D.G. v5p0032c2s
Prinsep, H.T. v1p0020c1s
Prinsep, V. v3p0451c1s v4p0328c1s
Prinsep, V.C. v4p0122c2s v6p0033c2s
Prinsep, Val. v4p0492c1s
Prior, E.J. v6p0012c2s v6p0158c1m v6p0298c1s v6p0308c2s v6p0320c1s v6p0408c2s v6p0517c2s
Prior, E.S. v5p0225c2m v6p0028c1s
Prior, H.M. v1p1175c1s
Prior, J. v1p0758c1s
Prior, M. v4p0130c2s v4p0582c1s
Prior, W.R. v5p0530c1s
Prisse, S. v1p1002c2s
Pritchard, C. v1p0070c2s v1p0073c2s v1p0381c2s v1p0382c1s v1p0827c2s v1p0989c1s v1p1234c1s v1p1243c2m v1p1432c2s
Pritchard, E. and Tait, L. v2p0395c2s
Pritchard, H. v5p0268c2s
Pritchard, H.B. v1p0089c1s v1p0141c2s v1p0401c1s v1p1003c1m v1p1003c2s v1p1218c2s v1p1384c1s v1p1385c1s v2p0200c2s v2p0465c2s v4p0440c2s
Pritchard, H.J. and McCrea, J. v5p0562c2s
Pritchard, Prof. v2p0389c1s
Pritchard, S.J. v1p0877c2s v1p0942c1s v1p1257c1s
Pritchard, W.T. v1p0202c2s v1p0452c1s v1p0833c1s
Pritchard, W.T.E. v1p1406c2s
Pritchett, A.H. v6p0610c2s
Pritchett, C.W. v2p0459c1s
Pritchett, H.H. v6p0099c2s
Pritchett, H.S. v2p0137c1s v2p0277c2s v2p0390c2s v2p0433c2s v3p0444c1s v4p0167c1s v5p0514c2s v5p0603c2s v6p0082c1s v6p0189c2s v6p0198c1s v6p0254c1s v6p0317c2s v6p0428c1s v6p0450c1s v6p0575c2s v6p0636c1s v6p0659c2s v6p0671c1m
Pritchett, J.A. v2p0456c2s
Pritchett, R.S. v5p0343c2s
Pritchett, R.T. v1p0597c1s v1p0597c2s v1p0929c2s v1p1230c1s v3p0050c2s
Priuli-Bon, L. v6p0675c2s
Priuli-Bon, Lilian v5p0413c1s
Prjevalsky, N. v3p0023c2s
Probert, C.K. v2p0104c1s
Probert, I. v2p0137c1s v3p0132c2s
Probert, W.G. v4p0189c1s
Probst, J.B. v6p0709c1s
Probyn, J.W. v1p0670c1s v1p0670c2s v1p1096c2s v1p1194c2s
Probyn, L.C. v4p0280c1s v4p0378c1s v5p0285c1s v5p0285c2s
Probyn, M. v2p0003c1s v2p0438c1s v3p0281c2s
Probyn, May v3p0440c1s
Procter, A. v1p1094c1s
Procter, A.A. v1p0534c1s v1p1315c1s v1p1327c2s
Procter, B.W. v1p0496c2s v1p0746c1s v1p1338c1s v2p0365c2s
Procter, H.R. v1p0077c1s v5p0328c2s
Procter, J. v3p0019c1s
Procter, J.J. v1p0763c2s
Procter, J.R. v4p0127c1s v4p0403c2s v4p0454c1s v5p0081c1s v5p0242c1s v5p0258c1s v5p0358c1s v5p0410c2s v5p0602c1s
Procter, L.J. v1p0757c2s
Procter, R. v5p0056c1s
Procter, Z. v5p0008c2s
Proctor, B.F. v1p0436c2s
Proctor, B.S. v1p0747c2s
Proctor, E.D. v1p0815c1s v1p0874c2s v1p1136c1s v1p1137c1s v1p1144c2s v2p0276c2s v3p0285c1s
Proctor, Edna D. v6p0229c2s
Proctor, G.H. v1p0527c1s v1p1172c2s
Proctor, H. v6p0060c1s v6p0120c2s v6p0285c2m v6p0709c1s
Proctor, L.B. v4p0080c1s
Proctor, M. v3p0148c1m v3p0213c1s v4p0092c1s v4p0490c1s v5p0035c2s v5p0549c1s
Proctor, Mary v4p0034c1s v4p0389c1s v6p0188c1s
Proctor, R. v4p0002c1s v4p0537c1s v5p0284c1s v6p0032c2s v6p0517c1s v6p0664c1s
Proctor, R.A. v1p0004c1s v1p0055c2m v1p0069c2m v1p0070c1s v1p0070c2m v1p0071c1m v1p0077c2s v1p0116c2s v1p0144c1s v1p0168c1s v1p0185c2s v1p0226c2s v1p0281c1m v1p0281c2m v1p0282c1m v1p0294c2s v1p0365c2s v1p0375c2s v1p0376c2s v1p0377c1m v1p0381c2s v1p0382c1m v1p0407c1s v1p0415c2s v1p0423c1s v1p0428c1s v1p0443c1s v1p0452c1s v1p0465c2s v1p0499c1s v1p0526c2s v1p0536c2s v1p0562c1s v1p0581c1s v1p0605c1s v1p0641c2s v1p0699c1m v1p0748c1s v1p0757c1s v1p0776c2s v1p0787c1s v1p0788c2s v1p0804c1m v1p0824c1s v1p0827c1m v1p0827c2m v1p0829c2s v1p0865c2s v1p0866c1m v1p0902c2s v1p0903c2m v1p0913c2s v1p1002c2s v1p1014c1m v1p1068c1m v1p1068c2s v1p1080c2s v1p1100c2s v1p1129c2s v1p1139c2s v1p1152c2m v1p1172c2s v1p1173c1m v1p1202c1m v1p1219c2s v1p1233c2m v1p1243c2m v1p1244c1m v1p1244c2m v1p1256c2s v1p1267c2m v1p1268c1m v1p1268c2m v1p1269c1m v1p1269c2s v1p1273c1s v1p1275c1s v1p1291c1s v1p1291c2m v1p1316c2s v1p1321c2s v1p1356c1m v1p1359c1s v1p1366c2m v1p1367c1m v1p1394c2s v1p1396c2s v1p1414c2s v1p1416c1s v1p1432c2s v2p0001c2s v2p0002c1s v2p0008c2s v2p0011c2m v2p0012c2s v2p0014c1s v2p0015c1s v2p0016c1s v2p0021c1s v2p0021c2s v2p0025c2s v2p0026c1m v2p0029c2s v2p0032c1s v2p0039c2s v2p0041c1m v2p0043c1s v2p0054c1s v2p0054c2s v2p0056c1s v2p0056c2s v2p0062c2s v2p0063c2s v2p0067c2s v2p0072c1s v2p0073c1s v2p0088c1s v2p0089c2m v2p0090c1s v2p0091c2m v2p0093c1s v2p0094c2m v2p0095c1m v2p0095c2m v2p0096c1m v2p0097c2s v2p0100c1s v2p0103c2s v2p0104c1m v2p0106c2s v2p0108c1s v2p0112c1m v2p0118c1s v2p0123c2m v2p0126c2m v2p0127c1m v2p0127c2m v2p0128c1m v2p0128c2s v2p0129c2m v2p0144c1s v2p0146c1s v2p0147c2s v2p0148c2s v2p0152c1s v2p0155c2m v2p0158c2s v2p0160c1s v2p0161c1s v2p0170c1s v2p0170c2m v2p0174c1m v2p0175c1s v2p0177c1s v2p0177c2s v2p0194c1s v2p0199c2m v2p0201c2s v2p0202c1s v2p0207c2m v2p0214c1s v2p0215c1s v2p0221c1s v2p0230c2s v2p0234c1s v2p0239c2m v2p0242c2s v2p0249c1s v2p0252c2m v2p0257c2s v2p0258c1s v2p0266c2s v2p0268c1m v2p0274c2s v2p0275c2s v2p0276c1s v2p0277c1s v2p0277c2m

v2p0278c1m v2p028-c1s v2p0280c1m
v2p0281c2s v2p0283c2s v2p0284c1s
v2p0285c1m v2p0285c2m v2p0291c2m
v2p0296c2m v2p0302c2s v2p0303c2s
v2p0307c1s v2p0308c1s v2p0312c1s
v2p0313c1s v2p0314c1s v2p0314c2s
v2p0328c2m v2p0335c1s v2p0340c1m
v2p0340c2s v2p0343c2m v2p0344c1s
v2p0347c1m v2p0349c2s v2p0351c2s
v2p0359c2s v2p0360c1m v2p0360c2m
v2p0364c1s v2p0365c2s v2p0371c1s
v2p0382c2s v2p0386c2m v2p0388c1s
v2p0389c1s v2p0389c2m v2p0390c1s
v2p0393c1m v2p0393c2s v2p0395c1s
v2p0404c1s v2p0404c2s v2p0412c2s
v2p0414c1m v2p0417c1m v2p0417c2m
v2p0418c1m v2p0418c2m v2p0420c2s
v2p0424c2m v2p0425c1m v2p0425c2m
v2p0426c2m v2p0427c1m v2p0429c1s
v2p0440c1m v2p0450c1s v2p0454c1m
v2p0456c1s v2p0459c1m v2p0459c2s
v2p0460c1s v2p0463c2s v2p0471c1s
v2p0472c1m v2p0480c1m v2p0480c2s
v3p0010c1s v3p0011c2s v3p0012c1s
v3p0013c2s v3p0030c1s v3p0035c1m
v3p0040c2s v3p0062c2m v3p0073c1s
v3p0077c1s v3p0081c1s v3p0085c1m
v3p0092c2s v3p0093c2s v3p0094c1m
v3p0104c2s v3p0105c1s v3p0120c1s
v3p0126c1s v3p0130c1s v3p0137c1s
v3p0140c1s v3p0155c2s v3p0157c2s
v3p0166c2s v3p0172c1m v3p0204c1s
v3p0232c1s v3p0250c1m v3p0250c2s
v3p0257c2s v3p0265c2s v3p0269c1s
v3p0271c2s v3p0274c1s v3p0275c2m
v3p0279c1s v3p0280c1m v3p0286c2s
v3p0290c2s v3p0310c2s v3p0328c1s
v3p0333c2m v3p0337c2s v3p0341c1s
v3p0343c2s v3p0344c2s v3p0358c1s
v3p0371c2s v3p0379c2s v3p0380c1m
v3p0383c1m v3p0387c1s v3p0387c2s
v3p0388c1s v3p0407c1m v3p0407c2m
v3p0416c1s v3p0423c1s v3p0423c2s
v3p0439c2s v3p0444c2m v3p0445c2s
v3p0462c1m v3p0467c1s v4p0127c1s
v4p0331c1s v4p0517c2s v4p0541c1s
v4p0557c1s
Proctor, R.A. and Ballou, W.H.
v2p0193c1s
Proctor, R.A. and Edwards, A.B.
v2p0360c1s
Proctor, R.H. et al. v3p0216c1s
Proctor, W.C. v1p1369c1s
v2p0028c2s v2p0109c1s v2p0327c2s
v2p0334c1s v2p0373c1s v2p0384c2s
v3p0225c1s v4p0461c1s
Prodt, G.H. v6p0588c2s
Proffatt, J. v1p0740c2s
v1p1411c1s
Prokop, I.A. v1p0145c1s
v1p0154c1s v1p0181c2s v1p0398c1s
v1p0467c2s v1p0770c2s v1p0810c1s
Prokop, Ita A. v1p0016c2s
Proost, L. v1p1030c1s
Propert, J.L. v4p0372c2s
v5p0377c2s
Prorok, N.E. v5p0040c1s
Prosper, K. v1p0536c2s
v1p1209c2s
Prospero, G. v3p0323c1s
Prosser, C.S. v4p0154c2s
v5p0418c2s
Prosser, F.R.W. v2p0244c1s
v2p0255c1s
Prosser, Mrs. v2p0107c2s
v2p0151c1s v2p0279c2s v2p0429c2s
Prosser, R.B. and Romanes, C.H.
v2p0475c1s
Prosser, T. v1p0145c2s
v1p1246c1s v1p1246c2s v1p1247c1m
Prosser, W.F. v3p0464c2s
v4p0592c2s
Prosser, Wm.F. v5p0601c2s
Prothero, A. v4p0196c2s
Prothero, E. and Prothero, R.
v3p0347c2s
Prothero, E. and Prothero, R.E.
v3p0099c2s
Prothero, G.W. v2p0191c1s
v2p0409c2s v2p0468c1s v3p0137c2s
v3p0138c1s v3p0321c2s v3p0434c2s
v4p0002c2s v4p0170c2s v4p0214c1s
v4p0259c1s v4p0265c2s v4p0328c1s
v4p0428c1s v4p0521c2s v4p0597c2s
v5p0433c1s v6p0206c1s v6p0292c2s
v6p0458c1s
Prothero, M. v6p0313c2s
Prothero, R. and Prothero, E.
v3p0347c2s
Prothero, R.E. v2p0166c1s
v2p0205c2s v2p0334c1s v2p0473c1s
v3p0006c1s v3p0033c2s v3p0052c2s
v3p0083c1s v3p0140c2s v3p0160c1s
v3p0162c2s v3p0185c1s v3p0223c1s
v3p0241c2s v3p0382c2s v3p0431c1s
v3p0460c1s v4p0164c1s v4p0225c2s
v4p0618c1s v5p0086c1s v5p0218c1s
v6p0155c2s v6p0157c1s v6p0684c2s
Prothero, R.E. and Burns, J.
v4p0338c2s
Prothero, R.E. and Prothero, E.
v3p0099c2s
Prothero, Rowland E. v6p0090c2s
Protheroe, E. v5p0092c1s
v5p0177c2s v6p0397c1s
Proudfit, A. v1p0278c1s
Proudfit, J. v1p0363c1s
v1p0496c2s v1p0554c2s v1p0879c1s
Proudfit, J.W. v1p0047c2s
v1p0583c1s
Proudfit, S.V. v2p0293c1s
Proudfoot, W. v4p0498c1s
Proudhon, P.J. v1p0382c2s
Proust, A. v4p0362c2s
v4p0443c1s v5p0359c2s v6p0363c1s
Prout, E., Prof. v5p0114c1s
Prout, F.S. v2p0043c1s
Prout, H.A. v1p0055c1s
v1p0854c2s v1p0855c1s
Prout, H.G. v2p0183c1s
v3p0136c2s v3p0353c2s v4p0470c2s
v4p0471c1s v4p0471c2m v4p0472c1s
v4p0472c2m v5p0007c1s v5p0008c1s
v5p0093c1s v5p0139c2s v5p0210c2s
v5p0476c2s v5p0477c1s v5p0478c1m
Prout, J.S. v3p0243c1s
Prouty, C.A. v5p0294c2m
v5p0476c2s v5p0477c2s v6p0460c1s
v6p0528c2m v6p0530c1s v6p0530c2s
v6p0550c1s
Provand, A.D. v4p0179c2m
v5p0124c1s v5p0641c1s
Provine, J.C. v2p0353c1s
Provis, W.A. v1p0195c2s
Provost, A. v5p0470c2s
v5p0530c2s
Provost, A.L. v4p0512c1s
v5p0369c2s v5p0425c2s v6p0332c2s
v6p0643c1s v6p0674c1s
Provost, Agnes L. v5p0260c2s
Prower, M. v5p0125c2s
v5p0351c2s v5p0612c1s v6p0641c2s
Prower, Maude v5p0141c1s
Prowett, C.G. v1p0049c1s
v1p0698c1s v1p0775c2s v1p0998c2s
Prowse, C.M. v6p0418c1s
Prowse, D.W. v5p0209c1s
v6p0226c2s v6p0275c1s v6p0455c1s
v6p0455c2m
Prowse, P.O. v3p0466c1s
Prowse, R.O. v4p0195c2s
Prowse, W.J. v1p0907c1s
v1p1051c1s v1p1112c2s v1p1212c2s
Pruckner, M.C.P. v1p1338c1s
Prudden, H.T.M. v5p0472c1s
Prudden, T.M. v3p0030c1s
v3p0098c1s v3p0207c1s v4p0119c2s
v4p0252c1s v4p0272c2s v4p0363c2s
v4p0400c2s v4p0586c1s v5p0049c1s
v5p0092c2s v6p0175c2s v6p0569c1s
Prudden, T.M. et al. v3p0278c1s
Prudhomme, R.F.A.S. v5p0078c1s
v5p0139c1s v5p0532c2s
Prudhomme, R.G.A.S. v5p0085c2s
v5p0419c1s v5p0442c1s v5p0486c1s
v5p0563c1s v5p0581c1s
Prudnik, H.Von v2p0127c2s
Prugh, J.H. v5p0469c1s
Pruner-Bey v1p0565c2s
Prunier, O. v5p0469c1s
Prusoe, J. v1p0342c1s
v1p1244c1s
Prusol, J. v1p0070c1s
v1p0375c1s v1p0746c2s v1p1356c1s
Prussing, E.E. v6p0113c1s
Prutz, H. v5p0146c1s
Pryce, D.H. v6p0570c2s
Pryce, G. v1p0163c2s
v6p0508c2s
Pryce, J. v4p0380c2s
v5p0615c2s
Pryce, L. v2p0196c2s
Pryce, T.D. and Armitage, E.S.
v6p0103c2s
Pryde, D. v4p0436c2s
Pryde, T. v3p0161c2s
v3p0193c2s
Pryer, W.B. v2p0052c2s
Pryor, J.H. v5p0572c2s
Pryor, J.W. v5p0407c1s
Pryor, P. v6p0703c1s
Pryor, R.A. v3p0097c2s
v3p0299c1s
Pryor, R.A. et al. v2p0353c1s
Pryor, R.A., Mrs. v3p0012c1s
v3p0399c2s v4p0136c1s v4p0385c1s
Pryor, S.A. v4p0511c2s
Puaux, R. v6p0225c1s
Puckler Muskau, Prince ... v1p0308c2s
v1p0895c1s
Puddefoot, W.G. v4p0275c1s
Pudor, H. v6p0279c2s
v6p0317c2s v6p0342c2s
Pudor, Heinrich v6p0182c1s
Pue, E.Spence de v6p0022c2s
v6p0256c1s
Puente, F.G. v6p0160c2s
Puffer, A.F. v1p0180c2s
Puffer, E.D. v5p0005c1s
v5p0144c1s v5p0441c2s
Puffer, Ethel D. v6p0055c2s
Puffer, J.A. v6p0246c2s
Puffer, J.Adams v6p0078c2s
Pugh, E. v4p0284c1s
v4p0352c2s v4p0358c2s v4p0384c2s
v5p0031c2s v5p0140c2s v5p0555c2s
Pugh, E.W. v4p0019c2s
Pugh, L.P. v2p0217c2s
Pugh, M.M. v6p0178c2s
Puibaraud, L. v4p0627c2s
Pulbrook, A. v6p0240c2s
Pulitz, M.de v2p0176c2s
Pulitzer, J. v5p0600c1s
v6p0346c2s
Pullan, R.P. v5p0032c1s
Pullar, A. v3p0267c1s
Pullar, L. and Murray, John, Sir
v6p0578c1s
Pullein, Catherine v5p0224c2s
Pullen, C. v5p0318c2s
Pullen, C.B. v2p0075c2s
v2p0312c2s
Pullen, E. v4p0068c1s
v4p0114c2s v4p0626c2s
Pullen, R.P. v2p0383c2s
Pulling, F.S. v4p0266c1s
Pullman, G.H. v4p0046c2s
Pullman, G.M. v4p0553c1s
Pullman, J. v1p0830c1s
v2p0286c1s
Pullman, J.M. v4p0097c1s
Pullman, J.M. et al. v2p0085c1s
Pullman, J.W. v6p0016c1s
v6p0086c2s
Pulman, O.S., jr. v6p0673c1s
Pulman, O.S., jr. and Gooch, F.A.
v5p0382c1s
Pulsford, E. v3p0347c1s
Pulsford, S. v3p0027c2s
Pultz, J.L. v6p0132c2s
Pulvertaft, T.J. v6p0320c1s
Pumpelly, R. v1p0232c2s
v1p0233c2m v1p0235c1s v1p0236c1s
v1p0298c1s v1p0300c1s v1p0508c2s
v1p0509c1s v1p0678c2s v1p0679c1s
v1p0912c2s v1p1112c2s v1p1333c2s
v1p1437c1s v2p0097c1s v2p0409c1s
v4p0373c1s
Pumpelly, R. and Brooks, T.B.
v1p0300c1s v1p1271c1s
Pumpelly, R. and Hise, C.R.Van.
v4p0270c1s
Punchard, E.G. v2p0402c2s
Punchard, G. v1p1434c2s
Punnett, J.T. v1p0394c1s
v2p0147c1s
Punshon, E.R. v5p0093c2s
Punshon, W.M. v1p0176c1s
v1p0402c1s v1p0781c1s v1p1409c1s
Pupin, M.I. v4p0012c1s
v4p0175c1s v4p0175c2s v4p0176c1m
v4p0177c1m v4p0467c1s v4p0487c1m
v4p0599c1s v5p0183c2s v5p0571c1s
Purcell, E. v2p0009c1s
v2p0023c2s v2p0059c1s v2p0116c1s
v2p0125c1s v2p0155c2s v2p0165c1s
v2p0204c1s v2p0309c2s v2p0321c1s
v2p0333c1s v2p0370c1s v4p0011c1s
v4p0168c1s v4p0211c2s v4p0299c1s
v4p0405c2s v4p0549c2m v4p0614c1s
Purcell, E.S. v4p0059c2s
v4p0354c1m v4p0490c1s v4p0586c2s
v4p0601c1s
Purcell, William et al. .. v2p0353c1s
Purchas, J.R.P. v6p0588c1s
Purchas, W.R. v3p0454c1s
Purdie, T. v3p0113c2s
v3p0208c2s
Purdon, J.E. v4p0542c1s
Purdon, K.F. v5p0125c2s
v5p0209c2s
Purdy, B. v6p0296c2s
v6p0297c1m v6p0297c2s v6p0416c2s
v6p0616c2s
Purdy, B. and T., E.R. ... v6p0182c2s
Purdy, C. v4p0069c2s
v4p0209c1s v5p0103c2s v5p0339c1m
v5p0355c1s v5p0416c2s v5p0597c1s
v6p0053c1s v6p0053c2s
Purdy, C.T. v6p0027c1s
Purdy, C.W. v5p0277c2s
Purdy, Carl v4p0069c2s
v4p0083c2s v4p0136c2s v4p0332c1s
Purdy, F. v1p0550c2s
v1p0981c2s v1p1031c2s v1p1285c2s
v1p1379c1m
Purdy, L. v5p0018c2s
v5p0083c1s v5p0157c2s v5p0568c2s
Purdy, L.E. v4p0111c1s
v6p0594c1s
Purdy, Lillian E. v6p0091c2s
Purdy, T. v4p0137c2s
v5p0609c1s
Purdy, T.C. v4p0217c2s
Purey-Cust, A.P. v4p0635c2s
v5p0137c2s
Purey-Cust, H.E. v4p0399c1s
Purington, C.W. v5p0528c1s
v6p0013c2s v6p0303c2s
Purington, C.W. and

Landfield, J.B., jr. .. v5p0501c2s v6p0260c2s
Purinton, D.B. v5p0550c1s
Purnell, J. v3p0228c2s
Purnell, T. v1p0551c1s v2p0311c2s
Puron, J.G. v4p0540c1s
Purple, S.S. v1p0538c2s
Purrington, W.A. v2p0360c2s v3p0273c1s v5p0114c2m v6p0506c2s
Purroy, H.D. v2p0157c1s
Pursee, J. v6p0278c2s
Purser, A.M. v5p0396c1s
Pursey, G.G. v1p1292c2s
Purves, A. v6p0162c1s v6p0355c1s v6p0405c1s v6p0435c2s
Purves, D. v6p0060c1s v6p0123c1s v6p0341c1s
Purves, G.T. v2p0044c2s v3p0081c1s v3p0317c1s v3p0328c1s v4p0056c2s v4p0057c1s v4p0286c1s v4p0300c1s v4p0431c1m v5p0024c1s v5p0059c1s v5p0307c1s
Purves, J. v1p0072c1s v1p0152c2s v1p0925c1s v1p0952c2s v1p1019c2m v1p1337c1s v2p0101c2s v2p0108c2s v2p0127c1s v2p0158c2s v2p0266c2m v2p0294c1s v2p0332c1s v2p0345c2s v2p0391c1m v2p0439c2s v3p0373c1s
Purves, J.A. v5p0226c2s v5p0338c2s
Purves, James v2p0464c2s v4p0177c2s
Purves, M. v6p0471c2s
Purves, W.L. v6p0168c2m
Purvis, F.P. v5p0210c2s v5p0526c2s
Purvis, M. v4p0149c1s
Puseley, D. v3p0048c1s
Pusey, E.B. v1p0125c1s v1p1301c2s v2p0043c2s
Pusey, J. v2p0469c1s
Pushkin, A.S. v1p1281c1s
Pushkin, Alex v5p0170c2s
Put, A.Van de v6p0292c1s
Putlitz, G.zu v1p0468c2s v1p1232c1s
Putman, C.E. and Thomas, C. v2p0112c2s
Putman, C.E. et al. v2p0112c2s
Putnam, A.B. v1p1079c2s
Putnam, A.P. v1p0089c2s v1p0617c2s v1p0620c1s v1p0980c2s v1p1411c2s v1p1422c1s v2p0168c1s v2p0333c1s
Putnam, B.A. v6p0569c1s
Putnam, B.H. v6p0348c2s
Putnam, B.L. v4p0204c1s v4p0445c2s v4p0593c2s v5p0196c1s v6p0573c2s
Putnam, Bessie L. v5p0204c1s v5p0211c2s v5p0339c1s v6p0221c1s
Putnam, C.M. v1p0968c1s
Putnam, C.P. v1p0934c1s
Putnam, D. v1p0175c2s v1p1068c1s
Putnam, E. v1p0718c2s v2p0110c2s v2p0111c1s v2p0130c1s v2p0384c1m
Putnam, E.C. v5p0107c1s v6p0405c1s
Putnam, E.L. v2p0473c1s
Putnam, F. v5p0003c2s v5p0105c1s v5p0256c2s v5p0362c1s v6p0160c2s v6p0219c2s v6p0285c1s v6p0287c1s v6p0353c2m v6p0357c1s v6p0456c1s v6p0539c2s v6p0601c1s v6p0612c1s
Putnam, F.A. v5p0171c2s
Putnam, F.W. v1p0051c2s v1p0209c1s v1p0301c1s v1p0456c1m v1p0639c1s v1p0706c1s v1p0792c1s v1p0876c2s v1p1039c1s v1p1045c1s v1p1203c1s v1p1255c2s v2p0300c1m v2p0320c1s v2p0333c2s v2p0399c2s v2p0434c2s v3p0010c2s v3p0289c2s v3p0290c1s v3p0342c2s v4p0014c1s v4p0385c1s v5p0022c2s v6p0524c2s
Putnam, F.W. and Wheeler, B.I. v6p0092c2s
Putnam, G. v1p0146c2s v1p0186c2s v1p0201c1s v1p0240c2s v1p0274c2s v1p0402c2s v1p0429c1s v1p0823c2s v1p1069c2s v1p1340c2s v2p0122c1s
Putnam, G., jr. v1p0916c1s
Putnam, G.B. v3p0035c2s v3p0045c2s v3p0187c1s
Putnam, G.H. v1p0572c2s v1p1439c2s v3p0099c2s v3p0100c1m v3p0349c1s v4p0133c1m v4p0466c2s v6p0149c1s
Putnam, G.H. and Eggleston, E. v3p0099c2s
Putnam, G.I. v4p0091c2s v4p0194c1s v4p0277c1s v4p0317c1s v4p0574c1s
Putnam, G.P. v1p0175c1s v1p0667c2s v1p0761c2s v1p0765c1s v1p1063c2s
Putnam, G.R. v4p0433c2s v5p0010c2s v5p0027c1s
Putnam, G.W. v1p0350c1s
Putnam, Geo.L. v4p0207c1s
Putnam, H. ... v2p0091c1s v2p0150c1s v2p0400c2s v2p0431c1s v3p0043c2s v3p0249c1s v3p0281c2s v3p0394c1s v4p0329c1s v5p0133c1m v5p0333c2s v5p0334c2s v5p0335c1s v5p0335c2s v5p0336c1s v5p0337c1s v6p0104c1s v6p0140c1s v6p0149c1s v6p0373c1s v6p0373c2m v6p0540c1s v6p0668c1s
Putnam, H.C. v5p0606c2s
Putnam, H.H. v6p0322c1s
Putnam, H.W. v5p0257c1s
Putnam, Herbert v6p0372c1s v6p0373c2s
Putnam, I. v4p0355c2s
Putnam, J.B. v1p0678c2s v1p0680c2s v1p1150c1s
Putnam, J.J. v1p0564c1s
Putnam, J.J. and Lincoln, D.F. v1p1158c2s
Putnam, J.N. v1p0393c2s
Putnam, J.P. v1p0455c1s v1p0831c2s v3p0016c1s v3p0018c2s v3p0457c2s v5p0640c2s v6p0504c1s
Putnam, J.P. and Brown, J. v3p0435c1s
Putnam, J.W. v1p0740c2s
Putnam, M.C. v1p0480c2s v1p0625c1s
Putnam, M.L. v1p0472c2s v1p0512c2s v1p0615c2s
Putnam, M.L., Mrs. v1p0024c2s v1p0616c1s v1p0727c2s v1p0921c1s
Putnam, N.B. v1p0377c1s
Putnam, R. v1p0285c1s v6p0022c2s v6p0678c1s
Putnam, S.R., Mrs. v1p0709c2s v1p1025c1s
Putnam, T.H. v1p1437c2s
Putnam-Jacobi, M. v2p0354c1s
Putney, Edith M. v6p0136c1s
Putney, H.M. v2p0056c1s
Putron, J.P.De v5p0410c2s v5p0626c1s
Putzker, A. v1p0019c2s v2p0182c1s v3p0247c2s
Puxley, H.L. v6p0090c1s v6p0417c1s
Puy, C.M.Du v1p0663c2m v1p0664c2m v1p0947c1s
Puy, Herbert Du v6p0425c2m
Puy, W.H.De v1p0831c1s v4p0014c2s
Pyburn, G. v2p0433c2s
Pychowska, L.D. v1p0029c1s v1p0882c1s v1p0882c2s v2p0111c2s v3p0101c1s v3p0110c2s
Pycraft, W. v5p0085c1s
Pycraft, W.P. v4p0023c1s v4p0196c1s v6p0009c2s v6p0067c2s v6p0068c1s v6p0068c2s v6p0174c2s v6p0412c2s v6p0504c2s
Pycroft, J. v2p0107c1s
Pycroft, Miss v5p0165c2s
Pye, Walter v4p0265c1s
Pye-Smith, P.H. v1p0036c2m v1p0040c2s v1p0792c1s v1p0793c1s v1p1007c2s v1p1441c1s v5p0368c1s
Pyke, M.J. v3p0160c1s
Pyke, R. v6p0388c2s v6p0402c2m v6p0410c1s v6p0705c2s v6p0706c1s
Pyle, A. v4p0254c1s
Pyle, H. v1p0101c1s v1p0519c1s v1p0726c2s v1p0807c2s v1p1308c1s v1p1373c2s v1p1412c2s v2p0281c1s v2p0335c1s v2p0360c2s v3p0058c1s v3p0073c2m v3p0124c2s v3p0226c1s v3p0333c1s v3p0409c2s v4p0050c2s v4p0081c2s v4p0121c1s v4p0268c1s v4p0277c1s v4p0376c1s v4p0482c1s v4p0489c2s v4p0528c2s v4p0535c2s v4p0578c1s v5p0019c1s v5p0270c1s v5p0472c2s v6p0224c1s v6p0604c2s
Pyle, Howard v5p0337c2s
Pyle, I.A. v5p0167c1s v5p0223c2s v5p0387c2s v5p0458c2s v5p0539c1s v5p0548c1s v6p0101c1s v6p0129c2s v6p0329c2s v6p0437c2s v6p0442c2s v6p0579c1m v6p0639c2s
Pyle, J.G. v1p1234c2s v2p0299c2s v2p0370c2s
Pyle, J.S. v4p0140c1s
Pyle, Katherine v4p0375c2s
Pyle, M.C. v2p0124c1s v2p0184c2s
Pyle, W. v5p0070c2s
Pynchon, E. v5p0267c1s
Pyne, E. v2p0066c2s v3p0334c1s v3p0350c1s v3p0417c1s v4p0468c2s
Pyne, J. v1p0054c1s v1p0090c1s v1p0105c2s v1p0156c2s v1p0173c2s v1p0242c1s v1p0282c1s v1p0289c1m v1p0305c1s v1p0363c1s v1p0378c2s v1p0479c2s v1p0497c1s v1p0553c2s v1p0647c1s v1p0857c1s v1p0937c1s v1p0945c1s v1p1002c1s v1p1078c1s v1p1171c2s v1p1209c1s v1p1441c2s
Pyne, J.B. v1p0063c2s v1p1008c2s
Pyne, M. v1p0513c1s v1p1105c1s v1p1424c1s
Pyre, J.F.A. v5p0160c2s

Q., J. v1p1283c1s
Qilliamson, C.N. v4p0503c1s
Quackenbos, J.D. v5p0278c1m
v5p0591c2s v6p0654c1s
Quad, M. v5p0274c1s
Quaife, Miss v5p0416c2s
Quail, A. v5p0487c2s
Quail, J. v4p0201c1s
v6p0511c2s v6p0620c1s
Quail, Jesse v6p0267c2s
Quaintance, A.L. v6p0037c1s
Quaintance, H.W. v4p0416c2s
v4p0529c1s v6p0008c2s
Quaintance, W.H. v4p0615c1s
Qualtrough, E.F. v3p0298c1s
Quamoclit, A. v1p0350c1s
Quantz, J.O. v4p0125c1s
v5p0025c1s v5p0158c2s
Quaritch, B. v2p0360c2s
v4p0066c1s v5p0140c2s
Quarles, J. v6p0162c2s
Quarles, J.A. v4p0377c2s
v4p0594c2s v5p0632c1s
Quarles, J.V., jr. v6p0439c2s
Quarry, A. v4p0312c1s
v4p0448c1s v4p0550c2s v4p0622c1s
v4p0625c2s v5p0048c2s v5p0052c1s
v5p0114c1s v5p0270c1s
Quarry, J. v1p0663c1m
Quartermass, W.W. v4p0593c1s
Quasimodo v3p0275c1s
Quatermass, W.W. v4p0466c1s
Quatrefages, A.de v1p0613c1s
v1p0792c2s v1p0793c2m v1p0795c1m
v1p1002c2s v1p1073c1m v1p1197c2m
v3p0010c2s
Quay, M.P. v5p0013c1s
Quay, M.S. et al. v4p0595c2s
Quayle, W.A. v4p0149c1s
v5p0228c1s v5p0275c1s v5p0523c1s
v6p0380c1s v6p0513c2m v6p0683c2s
v6p0703c2s
Quekett, M. v5p0027c2s
v5p0095c2s v5p0159c2s
Quellhorst, G.A. v6p0258c2s
Queneau, A.L. v6p0458c2s
Quennell, C.H.B. v5p0139c1s
Quenstedt, dr. v2p0205c2s
Quentin, C. v5p0186c2s
v5p0492c1m v5p0632c2s v6p0546c2s
Quesada, G.de v6p0160c1s
Quesnel, L. v2p0011c2s
Quest, A. v3p0190c2s
Quest, I.C. v6p0536c1s
Quetelet, M.A. v1p0647c2s
Quetil, C.J. v1p1076c2s
v2p0447c2s
Queux, W.L. v3p0234c1s
Queux, W.Le v5p0042c1s
v5p0079c1s v5p0280c1s v5p0300c1s
v5p0418c1s v5p0465c2s v5p0528c2s
v5p0608c2s v6p0024c1s v6p0132c1s
v6p0398c1s
Quibell, J.E. v4p0173c1s
v4p0330c2s
Quick, E.A. v6p0241c1s
Quick, E.R. and Butler, A.W.
v2p0024c2s
Quick, H. v6p0171c2s
v6p0220c1s v6p0463c2s
Quick, H.P. v6p0198c1s
Quick, J. v1p0210c1s
v1p0457c2s v1p1010c1s v1p1035c1s
v2p0079c2s v2p0351c1s v2p0418c2s
v3p0456c2s v5p0123c2s v5p0476c1s
Quick, J.W. v6p0655c2s
Quick, R. v5p0051c2s
v5p0053c1s v5p0053c2s v5p0566c1s
v5p0622c2s v5p0639c1s v6p0057c2s
v6p0101c1s v6p0302c1s v6p0460c2s
v6p0500c2s v6p0611c1s v6p0648c2s
v6p0654c1s
Quick, R.H. v1p0392c1s
v1p0675c2s v1p0724c2s v2p0094c2s
v3p0358c2s v3p0413c2s
Quicke, F.C. and Gibbons, A.St.H.
v5p0362c2s
Quiddam, R. v1p0112c1s
v1p0244c2s v1p0317c1s v1p0463c1s
v1p0649c1s v1p0700c1s v1p0753c2s
v1p1109c2s v1p1202c1s v1p1366c1s
v1p1376c1s
Quigg, L.E. v3p0348c2s
Quigley, F. v6p0295c1s
Quigley, J. v6p0083c1m
v6p0179c2s
Quigley, Jane v6p0681c2s
Quigley, M.G. v6p0619c2s
Quigley, May G. v6p0619c1s
Quigley, Sarah R. v6p0272c1s
Quigley, T. v1p0388c1s
v1p0657c1s v1p0659c1s
Quille, D.De v3p0011c2s
v3p0260c2s v3p0386c1s v3p0392c1s
v3p0410c2s
Quille, Dan De v2p0439c2s
v3p0125c2s v3p0131c1s v4p0523c2s
v6p0685c2s
Quiller-Couch, A.T. v4p0046c2s
v4p0164c1s v5p0076c1s v5p0079c1s
v5p0222c1s v5p0322c2m v5p0328c2s
v5p0383c2s v5p0415c2m v5p0426c2s
v5p0435c2s v5p0447c1s v5p0525c1m
v5p0526c1s v5p0566c1s v5p0626c2s
v6p0234c1s v6p0595c2s v6p0596c1s
v6p0678c1s v6p0693c1s
Quiller-Couch, L. v5p0050c1s
v5p0605c2s
Quiller-Couch, M. v5p0036c1s
v5p0373c2s v5p0546c2s
Quilliam, W. v6p0562c2s
Quillin, E.M. v3p0073c2s
Quillin, F.U. v6p0448c1s
Quilter, H. v1p0063c2s
v1p0649c1s v1p1098c2s v1p1391c1s
v2p0023c2m v2p0059c1s v2p0378c2s
v2p0379c2m v3p0021c2s v3p0092c1s
v3p0122c1s v4p0029c1s v4p0124c1s
v4p0136c2s v4p0141c1s v4p0199c2s
v4p0273c2s v4p0335c1s v4p0371c1s
v4p0426c1s v4p0493c1s v4p0493c2s
v4p0545c1m v4p0582c2s v4p0627c2m
v5p0080c1s v6p0108c2s v6p0696c1s
Quilter, Harry v2p0468c1s
v4p0030c2m v4p0199c2s v4p0234c2s
v4p0341c1s v6p0499c1s
Quilter, W.C. v3p0037c2s
Quimby, A.W. v4p0204c2s
v5p0118c2s v5p0273c1s v5p0545c1s
v5p0571c2s v6p0112c2s v6p0634c2s
Quimby, E.E. v1p0110c1s
v1p0978c1s v1p0978c2s v1p1291c2s
Quimby, G.A. v3p0351c1s
Quimby, G.W. v1p0495c2s
Quimby, Harriet v6p0244c2s
Quin, C.W. v1p1162c1s
v2p0136c2s
Quin, E.W. v3p0013c2s
v3p0299c2s v4p0582c2s
Quin, J.J. v2p0245c2s
Quin, M.J. v1p0037c1s
v1p0765c2s v1p0971c1s v1p1332c1s
Quinan, W.R. v5p0006c2s
v5p0645c1s
Quinby, A.W. v6p0532c1s
Quinby, J.W. v3p0007c1s
v3p0342c1s v3p0448c1s
Quincey, A.De v1p0734c1s
Quincey, T.De v1p0082c2s
v1p0184c2m v1p0186c2m v1p0201c1s
v1p0213c2s v1p0219c2s v1p0231c1s
v1p0241c2s v1p0256c1s v1p0274c1m
v1p0274c2s v1p0289c1s v1p0296c1m
v1p0335c1s v1p0369c1s v1p0370c1s
v1p0402c1s v1p0410c1s v1p0410c2s
v1p0413c1s v1p0416c1s v1p0416c2s
v1p0417c1s v1p0425c1s v1p0442c1s
v1p0487c2m v1p0489c2s v1p0521c2s
v1p0530c1s v1p0533c2s v1p0541c1s
v1p0552c2s v1p0553c1s v1p0555c1s
v1p0556c1s v1p0568c1s v1p0577c1s
v1p0588c1s v1p0600c1s v1p0656c1s
v1p0692c1s v1p0702c1s v1p0702c2m
v1p0704c1s v1p0711c2s v1p0718c2s
v1p0719c2s v1p0722c2s v1p0724c2s
v1p0738c2s v1p0739c1s v1p0754c1s
v1p0760c1s v1p0761c2s v1p0775c1s
v1p0784c1s v1p0786c1s v1p0791c2s
v1p0797c1s v1p0881c1s v1p0944c2m
v1p0949c2s v1p0953c2s v1p0956c2s
v1p1017c1s v1p1032c1s v1p1047c2s
v1p1058c1s v1p1072c1s v1p1107c1s
v1p1124c1m v1p1128c1s v1p1175c1m
v1p1189c1s v1p1189c2s v1p1210c2s
v1p1227c1s v1p1231c2s v1p1236c1s
v1p1254c1s v1p1263c1s v1p1270c2s
v1p1271c2s v1p1279c1s v1p1292c2s
v1p1320c1s v1p1322c2s v1p1393c1s
v1p1402c2s v1p1413c1m v1p1429c2s
v1p1430c1m v2p0221c1s
Quincke, G. v6p0257c2s
v6p0301c1s
Quincy, E. v1p0005c2s
v1p0006c1s v1p0034c2s v1p0077c2s
v1p0098c1s v1p0183c2s v1p0318c2s
v1p0329c2s v1p0355c1s v1p0372c2s
v1p0457c1s v1p0529c2s v1p0570c1s
v1p0680c2s v1p0706c1s v1p0859c2s
v1p0905c2s v1p0962c1s v1p0972c2s
v1p1037c1s v1p1049c2s v1p1087c1s
v1p1130c2s v1p1207c1s v1p1211c2s
v1p1240c1s v1p1261c2s v1p1285c1s
v1p1305c1s v1p1306c2m v1p1388c2m
v1p1398c1s v1p1407c2s
Quincy, E., jr. v2p0120c1s
Quincy, E.S. v1p1072c1s
v2p0361c1s v6p0569c2s
Quincy, J. v1p0283c1s
v1p1080c2s v3p0254c2s v4p0135c1s
v4p0466c1s v5p0049c2s v5p0072c2s
v5p0108c2s v5p0112c1s v5p0119c1s
v5p0454c2s v5p0501c1s v6p0160c2s
Quincy, J. and Chandler, W.E.
v4p0596c1s
Quincy, J. et al. v4p0174c1s
Quincy, J.P. v1p0104c2s
v1p0116c1s v1p0219c1s v1p0254c2s
v1p0255c1s v1p0276c1s v1p0287c1s
v1p0335c2s v1p0445c2s v1p0651c1s
v1p0681c1s v1p0743c2s v1p0811c2s
v1p0819c1s v1p0941c1s v1p1054c2s
v1p1072c1s v1p1085c1s v1p1099c1s
v1p1285c1s v1p1285c2m v1p1315c1s
v2p0334c1s v2p0397c2s v3p0103c2s
v3p0282c1s v3p0440c2s
Quincy, M.P. v5p0505c2s
Quincy, S.M. v1p0183c1s
Quinlan, M.F. v6p0019c2s
v6p0086c2s v6p0172c1s v6p0180c1m
v6p0231c1s v6p0311c1m v6p0311c2s
v6p0377c2s v6p0381c2s v6p0383c2s
v6p0469c1s v6p0601c1s v6p0620c1s
Quinn, A.H. v5p0259c1s
Quinn, C.H. v6p0210c1s
v6p0518c2s
Quinn, D. v4p0169c2s
v4p0241c1s v5p0036c2s v5p0185c2s
v5p0196c2s v5p0223c2s v5p0368c2s
v5p0493c1s v6p0030c2s v6p0038c2m
v6p0157c1s v6p0272c2s v6p0292c1s
v6p0466c2s v6p0603c1s
Quinn, D. and Shahan, T.J.
v6p0272c2s
Quinn, P.E. v4p0111c1s
v4p0618c2s
Quinn, P.T. v1p0015c2s
Quinn, T.C. v4p0229c2s
v4p0417c2s v4p0554c1s
Quint, A.H. v1p0178c2s
v1p0252c2s v1p0253c1s v1p0289c2m
v1p0290c1s v1p0290c2s v1p0344c2m
v1p0362c1s v1p0381c1m v1p0711c1s
v1p0809c1s v1p0811c1s v1p0846c2m
v1p0892c2s v1p0910c1s v1p0926c1s
v1p0977c2s v1p1033c2s v1p1103c1s
v1p1107c1s v1p1154c1s v1p1302c1m
v1p1336c1s v2p0122c1s v2p0125c2s
v2p0195c1s v4p0621c1s
Quint, W.D. v6p0230c2s
Quintard, C.T. v3p0075c2s
Quintero, L.C. v3p0259c1s
v3p0437c2s
Quinton, A.R. v6p0694c1s
v6p0709c2s
Quinton, W. v5p0318c2s
Quirinus v6p0553c2s
Quirk, E.P. v3p0388c1s
Quirk, L.W. v6p0291c2s
Quisenberry, A.C. v4p0612c1s
Quisenberry, E.B. v5p0209c1s

R., C. ... v6p0041c2s
R., C.H. ... v6p0549c2s
R., J.de ... v5p0123c1s
R., T.K. ... v6p0412c1s
R., W. ... v6p0696c2s
Rabb, K.H. ... v4p0531c2s v6p0421c1s v6p0451c1s v6p0503c1s
Rabb, R.M. and Mason, R.O. v5p0293c1s
Rabbeno, U. ... v3p0224c2s v4p0294c1s v4p0341c2s
Rabino, J. ... v2p0135c1s v3p0414c1s v5p0441c1s
Rabinovitch, I.E. ... v6p0251c1s
Raborg, S.A. ... v1p0605c2s v1p0916c1s v1p0916c2s v1p0917c1s v1p1052c1s
Rabot, C. ... v6p0006c1s v6p0257c2s v6p0562c2s
Race, H. ... v3p0162c1s
Racey, N.W. ... v1p0490c2s v1p0888c1s
Rackermann, F. ... v6p0151c2s
Rackett, T. ... v1p0409c1s v1p1203c1s
Radau, H. ... v6p0057c1s v6p016c1s v6p0156c2s v6p0278c2s v6p0583c1s
Radau, R. ... v1p0375c2s v1p1410c2s v2p0027c1s v2p0089c2s v2p0459c1s
Radcliffe, A.G. ... v3p0135c2s
Radcliffe, C.B. ... v1p0019c2s v1p0365c2s v1p0401c2s v1p0434c1s v1p0794c1s v1p0794c2s v2p0161c1s
Radcliffe, F.R.Y. ... v3p0413c1s v4p0239c1s v4p0461c1s v4p0579c2s
Radcliffe, Francis ... v2p0463c2s
Radcliffe, G.L. ... v5p0264c2s
Radcliffe-Cooke, C.W. ... v3p0202c1s v4p0174c1s
Radclyffe, D.E. ... v6p0531c1s
Radclyffe, R. ... v4p0571c2s
Raddin, C.S. ... v5p0105c1s
Radford, A. ... v5p0361c2s
Radford, B.J. ... v2p0042c1s v2p0149c1s v2p0350c1s
Radford, Dollie ... v5p0456c1s
Radford, E. ... v2p0041c1s v2p0479c1s v4p0326c1s v4p0497c1s v5p0033c2s v5p0139c1s v5p0230c1s v5p0385c1s v5p0420c2s v5p0455c1s v5p0608c2s v6p0050c1m v6p0332c2s v6p0350c2s v6p0365c2s v6p0481c2s v6p0503c1s
Radford, Ernest ... v5p0342c2s v5p0608c2s v6p0079c1s v6p0156c1s v6p0302c1s v6p0606c2s
Radford, G. ... v2p0120c2s v2p0393c1s v2p0449c1s v2p0482c1s v3p0389c2s v4p0244c1s v6p0629c1s
Radford, Geo. ... v5p0342c2s
Radford, J.A. ... v4p0031c1s v4p0100c2s
Radford, M.L. ... v4p0332c1s
Radford, R.S. ... v6p0307c1s v6p0362c2s
Radice, A.E. ... v6p0209c1s
Radiguet, M. ... v1p0749c2s
Radnor, Earl of ... v1p1067c2s
Radwell, C. ... v2p0133c1s
Radziszewski, B. ... v2p0340c1s
Radziwill, C. ... v5p0487c2s
Radziwill, Princess ... v6p0049c1s
Rae, A. ... v6p0440c2s
Rae, Betty ... v5p0641c2s
Rae, C.J. ... v2p0389c1s
Rae, F.B., jr. ... v5p0332c1s
Rae, F.J. ... v4p0506c2s
Rae, G. ... v3p0032c2m
Rae, J. ... v1p0055c2s v1p0425c1s v1p0551c2s v1p0622c1s v1p1095c1s v1p1136c2s v1p1216c1m v2p0048c1s v2p0101c2s v2p0106c2s v2p0108c1s v2p0160c1s v2p0169c1s v2p0202c2s v2p0213c2m v2p0315c2s v2p0389c1s v2p0391c2s v2p0407c1s v2p0407c2s v2p0461c1s v3p0040c1s v3p0127c2s v3p0131c2s v3p0175c2s v3p0213c2s v3p0217c2s v3p0238c2s v3p0399c1m v4p0173c2m v4p0283c2s v4p0412c1s v4p0434c1s v4p0581c1s v4p0590c2s v5p0322c2s v5p0457c1s v6p0591c2s
Rae, J. and Wharton, H.T.. v2p0372c2s
Rae, John ... v2p0179c2s v3p0387c1s
Rae, L.M. ... v6p0462c2s
Rae, T. ... v4p0049c1s
Rae, W.F. ... v1p0017c2s v1p0140c2s v1p0156c1s v1p0300c2s v1p0482c2s v1p0511c2s v1p0583c2s v1p0621c2s v1p0808c1s v1p0909c2s v1p0958c2s v1p1190c1s v1p1242c2s v1p1280c1m v1p1362c2s v1p1410c1s v1p1411c2s v1p1416c2s v2p0139c1s v2p0241c1s v2p0265c1s v2p0297c1s v2p0367c1s v2p0474c2s v3p0048c2s v3p0064c2s v3p0103c1s v3p0103c2s v3p0161c2m v3p0233c1m v3p0262c1s v3p0286c1s v3p0292c2s vp0311c2s v3p0362c1s v3p0382c1s v3p0421c2s v3p0453c2s v4p0137c1s v4p0173c1s v4p0225c2s v4p0306c2m v4p0403c1s v4p0601c1s v5p0233c1s v5p0312c2m v5p0525c1s v5p0525c2m v6p0183c2s v6p0347c2s
Rae-Brown, Colin ... v4p0153c1s
Raeb, B. et al. ... v4p0215c2s
Raeburn, D.L. and Brooks, A.H. v6p0393c2s
Raeburn, H. ... v6p0595c2s
Raffaelli, J.F. ... v4p0276c1s v5p0153c2m v6p0475c1m
Raffalovich, A. ... v3p0105c2s v3p0399c1s v5p0340c2s v6p0556c2s
Raffalovich, A. et al. ... v6p0167c1s
Raffensperger, E.B. ... v1p0760c1s v1p1183c1s
Raffensperger, Mrs. ... v1p0872c1s
Rafferty, F.W. ... v6p0083c1s
Rafferty, W.C. ... v5p0207c2s
Raffles, T. ... v1p0646c1s
Raffles, W.H. ... v3p0156c2s v3p0256c1s
Rafinesque, C.S. ... v1p0030c2s v1p0456c2s v1p0706c1s v1p0939c1s
Rafter, E. ... v6p0247c2s
Rafter, G.W. ... v1p1366c1s v2p0459c1s v3p0141c2s v3p0349c2s v3p0352c2s v3p0457c1s v4p0516c2s v4p0613c2s
Ragan, H.H. ... v4p0155c1m v4p0181c2s v4p0611c2s v5p0268c1s v5p0431c2s v5p0564c2s
Ragg, A.E. ... v5p0090c2s v5p0369c2s v5p0582c1s
Raglan, Lord ... v4p0236c1s v6p0416c2s
Ragoonath, R. ... v3p0196c2s
Ragozin, Z. ... v1p0922c1s v2p0236c2s
Ragozin, Z.A. ... v5p0473c1s
Raguet, C. ... v1p0373c1s
Rahda-Ananda ... v6p0377c1s
Rahlfs, A. et al. ... v4p0056c2s
Rahn, S.S. ... v3p0041c1s
Raikes, H.C. ... v1p0607c1s v1p0936c1s v1p0973c2s v2p0136c1s v2p0186c1s v2p0189c1s v2p0331c1s v2p0478c1s
Raikes, H.St.J. ... v5p0235c1s
Raikes, Henry Cecil ... v2p0322c2s
Raikes, T. ... v1p0132c2s
Raimond, C.E. ... v4p0050c2s v4p0244c2s v4p0373c2s v5p0053c1s v5p0579c1s
Raimondy, A. ... v1p0637c2s
Raine, A.J. ... v5p0405c1s
Raine, F. ... v3p0002c1s
Raine, J. et al. ... v3p0074c2s
Raine, W.M. ... v5p0008c2s v5p0380c2s v5p0412c2s v5p0591c2s v5p0633c1s v6p0024c2s v6p0127c2s v6p0243c2s v6p0311c2s v6p0348c2s v6p0377c1s v6p0378c1s v6p0467c2s v6p0470c1s v6p0472c1s v6p0516c1s v6p0654c1s v6p0705c1s
Raine, W.McL. ... v5p0036c1s v5p0485c1s v5p0548c2s v6p0161c2s
Raines, C.W. ... v6p0640c1s v6p0640c2s
Rainey, P. ... v1p0368c2s
Rains, G.J. ... v1p1316c2s
Rains, G.W. ... v1p0401c1s
Rainsford, W.H. ... v6p0311c2s v6p0346c1s v6p0633c2s v6p0663c1s v6p0689c1s
Rainsford, W.S. ... v3p0338c2s v3p0391c2s v4p0334c1s v6p0419c2s
Rainy, H. and Stiles, H.J. v5p0531c2s
Rainy, R. ... v2p0073c2s v2p0284c1s v2p0290c2s v2p0391c1s v2p0437c2s v2p0471c1s v4p0277c2s v4p0478c2s
Rait, R.S. ... v5p0117c1s v5p0130c2s v5p0220c1s v5p0244c2s v5p0369c1s v5p0515c1m v6p0047c2s v6p0126c1s v6p0205c1s v6p0245c2s v6p0353c2s v6p0512c1s v6p0577c2s v6p0627c2s
Ral, J. ... v4p0314c1s
Ralegh, Walter, Sir ... v6p0203c1s
Raleigh, A. ... v1p0241c1s v1p0688c2s v1p1040c1s v1p1055c1s v3p0077c2s v3p0229c1s
Raleigh, E. ... v3p0060c1s
Raleigh, E.A. ... v4p0259c1s
Raleigh, S. ... v1p0647c1s
Raleigh, T. ... v2p0189c2m v2p0226c1s v3p0350c1s v4p0261c2s v4p0345c1s v4p0427c2s v4p0450c2s v4p0508c2m v5p0159c1s v5p0369c1s
Raleigh, W. ... v1p0288c1s v4p0184c2s v4p0248c1s v5p0068c1s v6p0043c1s
Raleigh, W.A. ... v4p0582c1s
Raleigh, W., Sir ... v6p0541c1s
Ralli, P. ... v5p0443c2s v5p0444c2s
Ralli, Pantia ... v5p0195c1s
Ralling, G. ... v5p0093c1m v5p0487c2s v6p0542c1s
Ralling, George ... v5p0093c1s
Ralph and Gorton ... v3p0046c2s
Ralph, J. ... v3p0024c1s v3p0046c1s v3p0052c1s v3p0074c2s v3p0079c2s v3p0109c2s v3p0287c1s v4p0009c1s v4p0011c2s v4p0047c2s v4p0068c2s v4p0073c2s v4p0074c2s v4p0097c2s v4p0099c2s v4p0100c1s v4p0100c2s v4p0105c1m v4p0105c2m v4p0125c1s v4p0128c1s v4p0133c2s v4p0146c1s v4p0153c1s v4p0164c2s v4p0174c1s v4p0203c1s v4p0223c1s v4p0268c1s v4p0333c1s v4p0335c2s v4p0343c1m v4p0373c1s v4p0375c1m v4p0380c1s v4p0384c2s v4p0387c2s v4p0399c2s v4p0402c2s v4p0406c2s v4p0407c1s v4p0412c2s v4p0434c2s v4p0437c1s v4p0444c1s v4p0447c2s v4p0491c1s v4p0499c1m v4p0538c1m v4p0538c2s v4p0551c2s v4p0558c1s v4p0612c1s v4p0612c2s v4p0619c1s v4p0634c1s v5p0008c1s v5p0019c1s v5p0019c2s v5p0053c2s v5p0060c1s v5p0173c2s v5p0191c1s v5p0249c1s v5p0345c2s v5p0425c1s v5p0439c1s v5p0453c1s v5p0466c1s v5p0501c1s v5p0502c1s v5p0587c1s v5p0588c2s v5p0628c1s v6p0025c1s
Ralph, Julian ... v4p0390c2s v4p0497c2s v5p0228c1s v6p0013c1s v6p0017c1s v6p0118c1s v6p0145c1s v6p0161c2s v6p0223c1s v6p0285c1s v6p0433c2s v6p0565c2s v6p0647c2s v6p0653c2s v6p0654c2s v6p0677c1m
Ralph, T. ... v4p0569c1s
Ralph, W.S. ... v2p0087c1s
Ralston, G. ... v1p0741c1s v3p0248c1s
Ralston, J.H. et al. ... v5p0567c2s
Ralston, W.R.S. ... v1p0105c2s v1p0244c2s v1p0257c1s v1p0440c1s v1p0522c1s v1p0558c1s v1p0589c1s v1p0618c1s v1p0712c2s v1p0713c1s v1p0730c2s v1p0890c2s v1p0926c1s v1p0970c2s v1p0982c1s v1p1017c1s v1p1024c1s v1p1030c2s v1p1041c1m v1p1133c2s v1p1134c2s v1p1136c1s v1p1136c2m v1p1137c2s v1p1138c2s v1p1194c2s v1p1282c2s v1p1315c1s v1p1333c2s v2p0039c2s v2p0065c2s v2p0153c2s v2p0289c1s v2p0359c2s v2p0360c1s v2p0438c2s v2p0448c2s v4p0205c2s
Ralston, W.S. ... v1p1138c1s
Ram, F. ... v2p0037c2s
Ram, G.S. ... v6p0643c1s
Ramage, B.J. ... v2p0184c1s v2p0262c1s v2p0277c1s v2p0411c2s v5p0006c1s v5p0064c2s v5p0091c2s v5p0103c1s v5p0109c1s v5p0112c1s v5p0182c2s v5p0187c1s v5p0273c2s v5p0352c2s v5p0363c2s v5p0392c1s v5p0459c1s v5p0476c2s v5p0501c2s v5p0532c1s v5p0540c2s v5p0561c2s v5p0568c1s v5p0572c2s v6p0344c2s v6p0366c2s v6p0474c1s v6p0506c2s
Ramage, B.J. and Dubose, W.P. v6p0279c1s
Ramage, C.T. ... v1p0054c1s v1p0174c2s v1p0673c2s v1p1124c2s
Ramage, T.C. ... v1p1029c2s
Ramakers, L. ... v6p0199c1s v6p0375c2s
Ramal, W. ... v4p0384c2s v4p0604c2s v5p0385c1s
Ramaley, F. ... v6p0077c1s v6p0087c1s v6p0135c1s v6p0502c2s
Ramann, L. ... v2p0030c2s v2p0195c2s
Rambaud, A. ... v5p0501c1s v6p0559c1s
Rambaut, A.A. ... v6p0350c2s
Rambaut, T.D. ... v3p0361c1s
Rambler, The ... v5p0548c2s
Rambo, W.P. ... v3p0247c2s
Rambold, T.F. ... v2p0457c1s
Ramchundra ... v1p0813c2s
Rame, L.de L. ... v1p0588c1s
Rame, L.de la ... v3p0390c1s
Rameau, E. ... v1p1117c2s
Rameau, J. ... v3p0071c2s
Rameau, Jean ... v5p0142c2s v5p0203c2s v5p0236c1s v5p0459c2s v6p0220c2s
Ramee, D. ... v1p1240c2s
Ramee, J.de la ... v1p0358c1s v1p0732c2s
Ramee, J.L.de la ... v1p0157c2s
Ramee, L.de la ... v1p0105c1s v1p0106c1s v1p0135c2s v1p0143c1s v1p0202c1s v1p0222c1s v1p0301c1s v1p0334c1s v1p0446c2s v1p0453c2s v1p0460c1m v1p0541c1s v1p0563c2s v1p0598c1s v1p0609c1s v1p0623c1s

v1p0726c1s v1p0755c2s v1p0802c1s
v1p0952c1s v1p1011c2s v1p1059c2s
v1p1199c1s v1p1260c1s v1p1282c1s
v1p1324c2s v1p1432c2s v2p0026c2s
v2p0168c2s v2p0216c1s v2p0231c1s
v2p0231c2s v2p0287c1s v2p0365c2s
v2p0370c2s v2p0462c2s v2p0478c1s
v3p0045c1s v3p0119c2s v3p0130c1s
v3p0155c2s v3p0167c1s v3p0452c1s
v4p0018c1s v4p0060c1s v4p0067c1s
v4p0099c1s v4p0130c1s v4p0139c2m
v4p0140c2s v4p0142c1s v4p0172c1s
v4p0194c1s v4p0212c2s v4p0255c1s
v4p0293c1s v4p0294c1m v4p0325c1s
v4p0350c2s v4p0408c2s v4p0441c2s
v4p0472c1s v4p0492c1s v4p0494c1m
v4p0534c2s v4p0579c1s v4p0589c2s
v4p0603c2s v4p0606c2s v4p0626c1s
v5p0021c2s v5p0098c1s v5p0100c2s
v5p0141c2s v5p0153c1s v5p0164c2s
v5p0168c2s v5p0300c1s v5p0300c2m
v5p0341c1s v5p0342c2s
Ramien, G. ... v1p1000c1s
Ramiere, F. ... v1p0482c1s v1p1214c1s
Ramiere, H. ... v1p1118c1s v1p1118c2s
Ramieu, G. ... v1p0386c1s
Ramm, C.A. ... v3p0404c1s v4p0223c1s
Rammelkamp, C.H. ... v6p0144c2s v6p0196c2s v6p0237c1s v6p0666c2s v6p0696c1s
Ramp, H.M. et al. ... v5p0321c1s
Rampini, C. ... v3p0164c1s v3p0431c2s v3p0465c1s
Rampini, Sheriff ... v2p0400c1m v2p0400c2s
Ramsay, A. ... v1p0618c2s v1p0848c2s v2p0029c2s v4p0482c1s
Ramsay, A.C. ... v1p0295c2s v1p0523c2m v1p0713c1m v1p0940c1s v1p1019c1s v1p1263c2s
Ramsay, A.M. ... v6p0330c1s
Ramsay, Alex. ... v5p0364c1s
Ramsay, C.C. ... v4p0123c2s v5p0126c1s v5p0178c2s v5p0182c2s v5p0413c2s v6p0443c1s
Ramsay, C.C. et al. ... v5p0265c1s
Ramsay, C.G. ... v4p0406c1s
Ramsay, C.H. ... v6p0272c2s
Ramsay, G. ... v1p0285c2s v1p1031c1s v1p1144c1s v1p1204c1s
Ramsay, G.G. ... v1p0389c1s v2p0066c1s v2p0132c2s v2p0202c2s v3p0129c2s v3p0422c1s v4p0582c1s v6p0549c1s
Ramsay, H.C. ... v1p1105c1s
Ramsay, J. ... v2p0230c1s v3p0451c2s v4p0143c1s
Ramsay, J.H. ... v2p0075c2s v2p0200c2m v2p0305c1s v2p0372c1s v2p0473c1s v3p0130c1s v3p0203c2s v4p0046c1s v5p0114c1s v6p0125c1s
Ramsay, J.H. et al. ... v3p0318c1s
Ramsay, J.H., Sir ... v2p0200c2s
Ramsay, J.S. ... v6p0686c1m
Ramsay, L. ... v3p0131c2s v4p0382c1s
Ramsay, Lady ... v4p0007c1s
Ramsay, Margaret, E. and Macdonald, J.Ramsay ... v6p0628c1s
Ramsay, R. ... v4p0124c1s v4p0156c2s v5p0101c1s v5p0160c2s v5p0390c2s v5p0517c1s v5p0564c1s
Ramsay, R.A. ... v1p1137c1s
Ramsay, W. ... v2p0405c2s v4p0026c1s v4p0597c1s v5p0037c1s v5p0113c2s v5p0226c2s v5p0227c1s v5p0320c1s v5p0371c2s v5p0479c1s v5p0605c1s v6p0056c1s v6p0112c1s v6p0199c2m v6p0200c1m v6p0286c2s
Ramsay, W. and Rayleigh, Lord v4p0026c1s
Ramsay, W. et al. ... v4p0253c2s
Ramsay, W., Sir ... v6p0168c2s v6p0527c1m
Ramsay, W.M. ... v1p0766c2s v2p0025c1m v2p0073c1s v3p0001c1s v3p0003c1s v3p0016c1s v3p0021c2s v3p0022c2s v3p0023c2s v3p0108c1s v3p0217c1s v3p0331c1m v3p0333c1s v3p0385c1s v3p0394c2s v3p0396c2s v4p0027c2m v4p0156c1s v4p0256c2s v4p0403c1s v4p0441c1s v4p0489c2s v4p0508c2s v5p0058c2s v5p0059c1s v5p0059c2m v5p0060c1s v5p0173c2s v5p0194c1s v5p0270c2m v5p0434c2s v5p0436c1m v5p0436c2s v6p0036c2m v6p0063c2s v6p0064c2s v6p0073c2s v6p0123c2s v6p0127c1s v6p0128c1s v6p0171c1s v6p0209c2s v6p0294c2s v6p0306c2s v6p0320c1s v6p0343c2s v6p0390c2m v6p0404c1s v6p0461c1m v6p0466c1s v6p0484c1s v6p0484c2s v6p0486c1s v6p0489c2s v6p0497c2s v6p0585c1s v6p0630c1s v6p0633c2m v6p0659c2s
Ramsay, W.W. ... v4p0287c1s
Ramsay, William ... v5p0404c1s
Ramsdell, F.W. ... v5p0442c1s
Ramsdell, L.R. ... v5p0206c1s
Ramsdell, T.J. ... v4p0311c1s v5p0293c2s
Ramsden, F.W. ... v5p0508c2m
Ramsden, G. ... v5p0168c1s
Ramsden, G., Lady ... v6p0601c2s
Ramsden, H. ... v5p0510c1s v6p0224c2s
Ramsden, R. ... v1p0721c2s
Ramseeve, S.D. ... v1p1343c2s
Ramsey, A.C. ... v1p0280c2s v1p0928c2s v1p1221c2s
Ramsey, A.R. ... v5p0635c2s
Ramsey, G.G. ... v1p0024c2s v1p0727c2s
Ramsey, H.A. ... v1p1247c2s
Ramsey, J.G.M. ... v1p0576c2s v1p0708c1s v1p0815c2s v1p0927c2s
Ramsey, J.H. and Prideaux, W.F. v5p0065c2s
Ramsey, J.H. et al. ... v5p0012c1s
Ramsey, L. ... v3p0099c1s v3p0358c1s
Ramsey, Miss ... v1p0245c2s v1p1266c2s
Ramsey, R.W. ... v4p0118c2m v4p0141c2s v5p0144c2s v6p0298c2s
Ramsey, W. ... v5p0230c1s
Ramsey, W.C. ... v4p0550c1s
Rance, C.De ... v1p0267c2s
Rance, C.E.De ... v1p0049c1s v1p0056c1s v1p0508c2s v1p0757c1s v1p0897c1s v1p1227c1s v1p1391c2s v1p1441c2s
Rance, C.E.De et al. ... v2p0127c2s
Ranciman, J. ... v3p0187c2s v3p0307c1s
Ranciman, J.F. ... v6p0604c2s
Ranck, G.W. ... v2p0179c1s v4p0310c1s
Ranck, H.H. ... v6p0061c1s v6p0365c1s v6p0545c2s
Ranck, S.H. ... v4p0133c2s v4p0329c1s v5p0070c2s v5p0126c2s v5p0335c2m v5p0337c1s v5p0472c2s v6p0049c1s v6p0264c1s v6p0374c1s v6p0374c2s v6p0472c2s
Ranck, S.H. and Steiner, B.C. v4p0329c1s v4p0330c1s
Rand, B. ... v1p0734c2s v1p0789c2s v3p0088c1s
Rand, B.H. ... v1p0224c2s v1p0564c2s
Rand, E.J., jr. ... v1p0738c2s
Rand, E.K. ... v6p0472c2s v6p0617c2s
Rand, E.L., jr. ... v1p1219c2s
Rand, E.S., jr. ... v1p0580c2s
Rand, H.W. ... v5p0067c1s
Rand, H.W. and Ulrich, J.L. v6p0596c1s
Rand, J. ... v4p0166c1s
Rand, S.B. ... v5p0094c1s v5p0116c1s v6p0486c1s
Rand, S.T. ... v3p0277c2s
Rand, T.D. ... v1p0834c1s v1p0845c1s
Rand, T.H. ... v4p0081c2s v4p0192c2s v4p0537c1s v4p0551c1s v4p0623c1s v5p0067c1s v5p0516c2s
Randal, F.H. ... v5p0424c2s v5p0546c2s v6p0072c1s v6p0638c1s
Randall, Alice S. ... v5p0397c1s
Randall, C.D. ... v4p0103c1m
Randall, C.P. ... v2p0464c2s
Randall, D.L. ... v6p0222c1s
Randall, D.R. ... v2p0279c1s v2p0359c2s
Randall, D.T. ... v6p0133c1s
Randall, E.A. ... v5p0505c1s
Randall, E.C. ... v5p0033c1s
Randall, F.E. ... v3p0090c2s
Randall, G. ... v4p0036c2s v4p0477c2s
Randall, H.J. ... v6p0058c2s v6p0149c1s v6p0364c2s v6p0375c1s
Randall, J. ... v1p0491c2s v1p1180c2s v1p1193c2s v1p1433c2s v3p0422c1s
Randall, Marion ... v6p0095c1s v6p0359c1s
Randall, S.S. ... v1p0225c2s v1p0391c2s
Randall, S.W. ... v5p0605c1s
Randall, T.G. ... v4p0004c1s v4p0256c1s v4p0346c2s v5p0325c2s v5p0623c2s
Randall, T.H. ... v4p0019c1s v4p0024c1s
Randall, T.M. ... v4p0201c2s
Randall, W.H. ... v6p0630c2s
Randall, W.S. ... v3p0400c1s
Randall-Maciver, D. ... v6p0542c2s
Randell, M.A. ... v6p0683c2s
Randle, E.B. ... v5p0462c2s
Randolph, A.D.F. ... v3p0103c1s
Randolph, B.R. ... v2p0110c1s
Randolph, B.S. ... v2p0018c2s
Randolph, C. ... v1p0227c2m
Randolph, C.F. ... v3p0360c1s v4p0179c1s v5p0593c1s v6p0460c1s
Randolph, C.H. ... v2p0117c2s v2p0198c2s
Randolph, D.F. ... v5p0062c2s v5p0099c2s
Randolph, E., jr. ... v1p0339c2s v2p0301c2s v2p0376c1s v2p0430c1s
Randolph, E.H.L. ... v5p0126c2s
Randolph, F.F. ... v1p0783c1s
Randolph, F.M. ... v6p0044c1s
Randolph, H.F. ... v3p0328c1s v3p0417c2s v4p0572c2s
Randolph, J. ... v1p1142c1s
Randolph, L.S. ... v4p0180c2s v4p0566c2s v5p0188c2s v6p0132c2s
Randolph, N.A. ... v2p0067c2s v2p0161c1s v2p0438c2s
Randolph, R. ... v1p0218c1s v1p1263c1s v2p0127c1s v2p0127c2s v2p0174c1s v2p0194c1s v2p0318c2s v2p0342c1s v2p0412c2s v2p0414c2s
Randolph, R.C., Mrs. ... v1p1375c1s
Randolph, S.N. ... v3p0236c1s
Randolph, Thomas ... v6p0505c1s
Rands, W.B. ... v1p0575c2s v1p0883c2s
Ranfurly, Earl of ... v6p0455c1s
Ranger, H.W. ... v4p0407c1s
Ranger, W.E. ... v6p0444c2s
Ranjitsinhji, Prince ... v5p0142c2s
Ranke, F.von ... v6p0531c2s
Ranken, I. ... v5p0303c1s v5p0303c2s
Ranken, J. ... v5p0173c2s v5p0580c2s
Ranken, J.Elliot ... v6p0711c2s
Ranken, T.Elliot ... v6p0535c1s
Ranken, W.B. ... v1p0267c1s
Ranken, W.L. ... v1p1227c2s
Rankin, A. ... v3p0372c1s v4p0164c2s
Rankin, C.W. ... v1p0168c1s v6p0583c1s v6p0689c2s
Rankin, D. ... v6p0220c1s
Rankin, D.C. and Roberts, W.H. v5p0464c1s
Rankin, D.J. ... v3p0004c2s v3p0264c2s v4p0636c2s v5p0319c2s
Rankin, D.N. ... v4p0613c1s
Rankin, E.A. ... v3p0232c2s
Rankin, F. ... v5p0503c2s
Rankin, F.H. ... v1p0134c1s
Rankin, G. ... v6p0449c2s
Rankin, H.W. ... v1p0751c2s v5p0108c2s v6p0591c1s
Rankin, J. ... v3p0136c1s
Rankin, J.C. ... v1p0058c2s v1p0096c2s v1p0538c2s v1p0847c1s
Rankin, J.E. ... v1p0441c1s v1p0568c2s v1p1152c1s v1p1311c1s v1p1364c1s v1p1376c2s v3p0055c2s v3p0216c1s v3p0299c1s v3p0427c2s v4p0006c2s v4p0160c1s v4p0328c2s v4p0396c2s v5p0015c1s v5p0056c1m v6p0179c2s
Rankin, J.F. ... v6p0480c2s
Rankin, J.H. ... v2p0391c1s
Rankin, N.S. ... v5p0301c2s
Rankin, R. ... v6p0002c2s
Rankin, R.G. ... v1p1080c2s
Rankin, T.E. ... v6p0592c1s
Rankin, W. ... v4p0422c1s
Rankine, A. ... v3p0019c2s v3p0200c2s v3p0296c1s
Rankine, J.C. ... v1p0096c2m
Rankine, W.J.M. ... v1p0017c1m v1p0397c2s v1p0580c1s v1p0751c2s v1p1191c2s v1p1246c1s v1p1246c2s v1p1247c1s v1p1248c2s v1p1362c2s v1p1390c2s
Ranking, B.M. ... v1p0374c1s v1p0520c2s v2p0152c1s v3p0150c1s v4p0447c2s v4p0509c1s
Ranking, E.M. ... v3p0270c1s
Ranlett, Alice ... v6p0609c2s
Ranlett, S.A. ... v4p0192c1s v4p0375c1s
Ranlett, S.Alice ... v4p0159c2s
Rann, Wm. ... v6p0350c2s
Ranney, A.L. ... v2p0054c2m
Rannie, D.W. ... v4p0141c2s v4p0237c2s v6p0201c2s v6p0262c2s
Ransford, E. ... v1p0046c2s
Ransford, H. ... v1p1131c1s
Ransmeier, J.C. ... v6p0423c2m
Ransom, A. ... v2p0446c1s v3p0336c2s v5p0214c1s v6p0141c2s v6p0679c1s
Ransom, E. ... v1p0208c1s
Ransom, J.B. ... v6p0660c1s
Ransom, J.H. ... v6p0111c2s
Ransom, R.S. ... v4p0623c1s
Ransom, S.H. ... v4p0116c1s
Ransome, A. ... v3p0471c1s v6p0294c1s v6p0500c2s v6p0504c2s v6p0597c2s
Ransome, C. ... v3p0075c1s v3p0180c2s v3p0433c2s
Ransome, E.L. ... v4p0128c1s

Ransome, F. v1p0065c2s
v1p1255c1m
Ransome, F.L. v5p0327c1s
v5p0404c1s v6p0486c2s v6p0567c2s
Ransome, F.L. and Hillebrand, W.F.
v5p0095c1s
Ransome, J. v1p0357c1s
v1p1199c1s
Ransome, S. v5p0303c1s
v6p0335c2s
Rantoul, R. v1p0388c2s
v1p0389c2s
Rantoul, R., jr. v1p0285c1m
v1p0315c2s v1p0384c2s
Rantoul, R.S. v4p0432c1s
v5p0159c1s v5p0332c1s v5p0474c2s
v6p0282c1s v6p0565c1s
Ranyard, A.C. v2p0094c2s
v2p0095c1s v2p0095c2s v2p0096c1s
v2p0115c2s v2p0129c2s v2p0244c1s
v2p0296c2s v2p0360c1s v2p0406c2s
v2p0426c2s v3p0026c1s v3p0092c1s
v3p0108c2s v3p0127c1s v3p0146c1s
v3p0190c2s v3p0248c2s v3p0251c1m
v3p0279c1m v3p0286c2m v3p0298c1s
v3p0298c2m v3p0309c2s v3p0334c2s
v3p0405c2s v3p0407c1s v3p0407c2s
v3p0415c1s v3p0415c2m v3p0423c2m
v3p0432c2s v4p0126c2s v4p0381c1s
v4p0516c2s
Ranyard, A.C. and Monck, W.H.S.
v3p0407c1s
Ranyard, A.C. and Peek, C.E.
v3p0407c2s
Ranyard, A.C. et al. v2p0426c2s
v3p0252c1s
Ranyard, C.A. v2p0096c1s
Ranzabe, A. v1p1282c2s
Rao, D.S.R.C. v6p0708c2s
Rapalje, S. v2p0476c2s
v3p0214c2s v3p0322c2s
Rapallo, E.S. v6p0426c1s
Raper, C.L. v6p0153c1s
Raper, G. v5p0164c2s
v6p0177c2s
Raper, G.A. v5p0431c2s
v6p0241c1s
Raphael, Hadji v4p0173c1s
Raphall, M.J. v1p0384c2s
Rapoport, S. v5p0501c1s
Rappoport, A.S. v6p0556c1s
v6p0556c2s v6p0557c2s v6p0558c1s
Rapsher, W.M. v3p0437c1s
Rapson, E.J. v4p0143c1s
Raqueni, Signor v5p0144c1s
Rasay, C.E.S. v3p0013c1s
Rasch, F.C. v5p0244c2s
v5p0545c2s
Rasch, Maj. et al. v5p0244c2s
Rashdall, H. v2p0062c2s
v2p0147c1s v2p0457c1s v3p0270c1s
v3p0316c1s v3p0445c1m v3p0451c1s
v4p0092c1s v4p0113c1s v4p0283c1s
v4p0307c2s v4p0482c2s v4p0533c1s
v4p0546c1s v5p0097c2s v5p0117c2s
v5p0214c2s v5p0289c1s v5p0455c1s
v5p0484c1s v5p0535c2s v6p0157c1s
v6p0278c1s v6p0333c2s v6p0375c2s
v6p0383c2s v6p0504c1s v6p0507c1s
v6p0533c1s v6p0638c1s v6p0671c1s
Rashdall, H. and Holland, T.E.
v3p0316c2s
Rashdall, H. and Madan, F.
v3p0316c1s
Rashidi, Ar v4p0173c1s
Rashleigh, P. v1p0409c1s
v1p1227c1s
Rasmussen, R.T. v6p0638c2s
Rassam, C.A. v1p0581c2s
Rassam, H. v5p0580c1s
Rassam, Hormuzd v4p0027c1s
v4p0033c2s v4p0040c2s
Rat, J.N. v5p0094c2s
Rateau, A. v6p0661c1s
Rath, E.J. v6p0247c1s
v6p0276c1s
Rath, O.vom v4p0390c1s
Rathbone, A.M. v6p0401c1s
Rathbone, C.K. v4p0101c2s
v4p0409c1s v4p0429c2s
Rathbone, E.P. v6p0007c1m
Rathbone, F. v2p0469c2s
Rathbone, F.L. v5p0070c2s
v6p0223c1s v6p0372c1s
Rathbone, H.B. v6p0178c1m
v6p0246c1s
Rathbone, H.M. v1p0455c2s
v1p0703c1s
Rathbone, J.A. v5p0334c1s
v6p0372c1s
Rathbone, P.H. v1p1431c1s
Rathbone, St.G. v3p0214c1s
v3p0233c2s
Rathbone, W. v1p0973c1s
v2p0184c1s v2p0225c1s v2p0423c2s
v4p0239c2s
Rathbun, E.P. and Bigelow, R.P.
v6p0381c1s
Rathbun, M.J. et al. v5p0295c1s
v6p0010c2s
Rathbun, R. v1p0026c2s
v1p0158c2m v1p0301c1s v1p0381c2s
v1p0572c2s v1p0582c2s v2p0393c1m
v2p0415c2s
Rathbun, S.B. v2p0018c2s
Rathburn, R. v3p0405c1s
Rathenau, E. v5p0183c1s
v5p0487c1s
Rather, E.Z. v6p0172c2s
v6p0639c2s
Rather, E.Z. and Austin, S.F.
v6p0640c1s
Rathmore, D.R.P., Baron .. v6p0326c1s
Rathom, J.R. v6p0439c2s
Ratnagar, N.J. v2p0051c1s
Ratoin, E. v4p0424c2s
Rattigan, W. v6p0315c1s
Rattigan, W.H. v5p0042c1m
v5p0081c1s v5p0285c1s v5p0312c2s
v5p0381c2m v5p0482c1s
Rattray, A. v3p0212c1s
Rattray, W.J. v1p0192c2s
v1p0194c2s
Ratzel, F. v5p0457c2s
Ratzenhofer, G. v6p0602c1s
Rau, C. v1p0352c1s
v1p0638c2s v1p1255c2m v1p1256c1s
v2p0118c2s v2p0219c2s v2p0246c2s
Rau, O.M. v4p0175c2s
Rau, R.V. v4p0010c1s
Rauch, F.A. v1p0063c2s
v1p0384c2s v1p0440c1s v1p0530c2s
v1p0614c2s v1p1049c2s v1p1086c1s
v6p0187c2s
Rauch, J.H. v2p0077c1s
Rauch, J.H. et al. v2p0080c2s
Rauline, H. v4p0380c2s
Raulston, J.J. v4p0386c2s
Raum, G.B. v2p0087c1s
v3p0326c1s
Raumer, K.v. v1p1102c1s
Raumer, K.von v1p0057c2s
v1p0085c1s v1p0101c1s v1p0262c1m
v1p0281c1s v1p0387c2s v1p0388c1s
v1p0388c2m v1p0390c1m v1p0392c2s
v1p0424c1s v1p0483c2s v1p0506c1s
v1p0510c1s v1p0518c1s v1p0518c2s
v1p0567c2s v1p0587c1s v1p0590c1s
v1p0595c1s v1p0683c1s v1p0727c2s
v1p0758c2s v1p0777c2s v1p0818c1s
v1p0863c1s v1p0903c1s v1p0907c2s
v1p0993c2s v1p0997c2s v1p1083c2s
v1p1085c2m v1p1096c2s v1p1157c2s
v1p1159c1s v1p1163c1s v1p1262c2s
v1p1288c1s v1p1329c1s v1p1357c1m
v1p1419c1s v1p1422c1s
Raumer, R.von v1p0513c2s
v1p1005c1s
Raunsley, H.D. v2p0161c1s
Raupert, J.G. v6p0259c1s
v6p0664c1s
Rauschenbusch, W. v4p0532c2s
v5p0118c1s v5p0305c2s v5p0486c2s
v6p0177c1s v6p0213c2s v6p0434c2s
Rausford, H.K. v6p0124c1s
Rauwenhoff, L.W.E. v1p0479c2s
v1p0683c2s
Ravaisson, F. v1p0365c1s
Rave, H. v4p0163c1s
v4p0210c2s v4p0390c2s v4p0470c1s
v4p0556c1s v5p0475c1s
Raven, C. v5p0023c2s
v6p0024c1s v6p0569c1s
Raven, Canon v6p0461c1s
Raven, J.H. v1p1288c2s
v2p0094c2s v2p0334c1s v3p0129c2s
v3p0325c1s
Raven, J.J. v3p0461c1s
v5p0432c2s
Ravenal, H.W. v1p0266c2s
v1p0541c1m v1p0983c1s v1p1015c2s
Ravene, G. v2p0095c1s
v3p0244c2s v4p0244c1s v5p0327c2s
Ravene, Gustave v5p0453c1s
Ravenel, H.W. v1p0617c2s
Ravenhill, A. v6p0498c1s
Ravenhill, A. and Scharlieb, M.
v6p0498c1s
Ravenshaw, H.W. v6p0419c1s
Ravenshear, A.F. v5p0574c1s
Ravenstein, E.G. v1p0012c1s
v1p0035c1s v1p0055c1s v1p0210c2s
v1p0452c1s v1p0468c2s v1p1136c2s
v1p1332c2s v1p1370c2s v2p0288c1s
v3p0278c1s v4p0005c2s v4p0041c2m
v4p0051c2s v4p0128c2s v4p0305c2s
v4p0487c2s v4p0574c2s v5p0001c1s
v5p0008c1s v5p0137c1s v5p0412c1s
v5p0452c1s v5p0611c2s v6p0183c1s
v6p0543c2s v6p0571c2s v6p0701c2s
Ravenstein, E.J. v3p0092c2s
Raverly, H.G. v4p0005c1s
Raverty, H.G. v6p0046c2s
v6p0112c2s
Ravisi, Baron Textor de .. v4p0522c2s
Ravoux, A. v1p0652c1s
Rawdon, H. v4p0614c2s
v5p0347c2s
Rawle, J. v1p0306c1s
v1p0306c2s
Rawle, W.B. v2p0338c2s
v4p0433c2s v5p0439c2m
Rawle, W.H. v2p0063c2s
Rawlence, Guy v6p0140c1s
Rawling, C.G. v6p0645c2s
Rawlings, B.B. v2p0208c1m
v2p0443c1s v5p0164c1s
Rawlings, G.B. v4p0411c1s
v4p0494c2s
Rawlings, R. v5p0377c1s
Rawlings, R.B. v1p0606c1s
Rawlins, B.F. v4p0367c2s
v5p0376c1s v5p0507c1s
Rawlins, W.D. v1p0190c2s
v1p0415c2s v1p1274c1s
Rawlins, W.D. and Hughes, T
v1p0031c1s
v1p0303c1s
v1p0573c1s
Rawlinson, C.G. v2p0449c1s
Rawlinson, E. v1p0351c1s
Rawlinson, G. v1p0011c2s
v1p0256c2s v1p0328c2s v1p0377c2s
v1p0379c1s v1p0856c1s v1p1073c1s
v1p1124c1s v2p0025c2s v2p0087c1s
v2p0133c2s v2p0147c2s v2p0179c2m
v2p0273c2s v2p0339c2s v2p0434c2s
Rawlinson, H. v1p0324c1s
v2p0380c2s
Rawlinson, H., Sir v2p0025c1s
Rawlinson, H.C., Sir v1p0010c1m
Rawlinson, H.E. v1p0010c1s
Rawlinson, R. v1p0362c2s
v1p1150c1s v1p1150c2s v1p1391c2s
v2p0223c1s v3p0121c2s v3p0202c2s
v3p0386c2m
Rawlinson, W.G. v1p1333c2s
v2p0449c1s v3p0438c2s
Rawn, G.B. v5p0121c1s
Rawnsley, Canon v5p0087c1s
Rawnsley, H.D. v3p0045c2s
v3p0054c2s v3p0236c1s v3p0315c1s
v3p0335c2s v3p0350c1s v3p0396c2s
v3p0407c1s v3p0425c1s v3p0473c1s
v4p0252c1s v4p0328c1s v4p0398c1s
v4p0429c2s v4p0563c1s v5p0180c2s
v5p0219c1s v5p0327c1s v5p0417c1s
v5p0424c1s v5p0452c2s v5p0500c1s
v6p0196c1s
Raworth, J.S. v5p0551c1s
Rawson, A.L. v1p0644c2s
v1p0856c1s v1p1008c2s v1p1271c1s
Rawson, C. v5p0288c2s
Rawson, E.K. v2p0381c2s
v2p0407c2s v2p0408c1s v4p0096c1s
v4p0195c2s
Rawson, H. v1p0733c2s
Rawson, M.C. v6p0099c2s
Rawson, M.S. v5p0316c1s
v6p0358c2s v6p0440c1s v6p0613c1s
Rawson, Maud S. v6p0106c2s
Rawson, R.W. v1p0317c1s
v1p0317c2s v1p0386c1s v1p0798c1s
v1p1049c2s v1p1076c2s v2p0093c1s
v2p0418c2s
Rawson, R.W. and Hamilton, G.
v4p0410c2s
Rawson, S. v5p0503c1s
Rawson, S., Mrs. v6p0612c1s
Rawson, S.G. v5p0570c1s
Rawstorne, Canon v3p0319c2s
Ray, A.C. v6p0166c1s
Ray, Anna C. v6p0166c1s
Ray, C. v6p0294c2s
v6p0321c1s v6p0336c2s v6p0346c1s
v6p0369c2s v6p0384c1s v6p0405c1s
v6p0513c2s v6p0562c2s v6p0566c2s
v6p0599c2s v6p0612c1s v6p0626c2s
v6p0650c2s v6p0679c2s v6p0689c2s
Ray, D.G. v3p0296c1s
Ray, E.A. v6p0497c2s
Ray, I. v1p0157c1s
v1p0259c2s v1p0421c1s v1p0510c2s
v1p0643c2m v1p0644c1s v1p1004c2s
Ray, I.T. v6p0350c2s
Ray, J. v1p0644c1s
Ray, J.M. v2p0067c2s
Ray, L. v1p0153c1s
v1p0292c1m v1p0637c1s v1p1179c1s
Ray, L.D. v3p0377c2s
Ray, M.F. v3p0035c2s
Ray, M.J. v2p0317c2s
Ray, M.L. v6p0328c1s
Ray, Rex v5p0626c2s
Ray, S. and Pleyte, C.M. . v3p0440c1s
Ray, S.H. v3p0301c2s
v3p0304c2s v4p0399c1s
Ray, T. v4p0021c1s
Ray, W.H. v3p0108c1s
v3p0162c1s v3p0296c1s v3p0345c2s
v3p0370c1s
Rayburn, C.C. v6p0691c2s
Rayet, G. v1p0672c1s
v1p0936c1s
Rayleigh v2p0112c1s
v3p0107c1s v3p0456c2s
Rayleigh, Baron v2p0136c2s
Rayleigh, Baron and Vincent, E.
v3p0256c2s
Rayleigh, E. v5p0472c2s

Rayleigh, G. v3p0205c2s
Rayleigh, J.W. et al. v2p0151c1s
Rayleigh, J.W.S. v3p0401c2s
Rayleigh, Lady v2p0136c1s
Rayleigh, Lord v1p0004c2s v1p0381c2s v1p0400c2s v1p0407c2s v1p0579c2s v1p0747c2s v1p0947c2s v1p1004c1s v1p1222c2s v2p0047c1s v2p0093c2s v2p0220c2s v2p0340c2s v3p0149c1s v3p0252c2s v3p0330c2s v3p0457c1s v4p0026c1m v4p0220c2s v4p0271c1s v4p0420c1s v4p0545c2s v4p0589c1s v5p0421c2s v5p0457c1s v5p0538c2s v5p0571c1s v5p0586c1s v6p0604c2s v6p0647c1s
Rayleigh, Lord and Ramsay, W. v4p0026c1s
Rayleigh, Lord et al. v4p0026c1s
Raylton, M. v5p0197c2s v5p0199c1s
Raymond, A.V.V. v5p0173c2s
Raymond, B.P. v5p0196c1s v6p0692c1s
Raymond, C. v1p0308c2s
Raymond, C.A. v1p1205c1s
Raymond, C.W. v1p0018c1s v1p0804c1s v1p0898c1s v1p1291c2s
Raymond, D. v1p0095c1s v1p0730c2s v1p1283c2s
Raymond, E.M. v1p0221c2s
Raymond, F. v6p0033c1s
Raymond, F.E.H. v3p0034c2s
Raymond, G. v1p0368c1s v1p1053c2s
Raymond, G.L. v5p0176c2s v5p0179c2s
Raymond, G.M. v1p0148c1s v1p0249c1s v1p0940c1s v1p1008c2s
Raymond, H. v1p0480c1s v5p0048c1s
Raymond, H.J. v1p0186c2s
Raymond, H.W. v1p1084c2s v2p0109c1s v3p0391c1s v3p0413c2s v5p0217c1s v5p0231c1s v5p0411c1s v5p0602c2s
Raymond, I.H. v6p0490c2s
Raymond, J.H. v1p0240c2s v1p0432c1s v1p0568c1s v1p1075c2s v1p1363c1s v5p0127c1s
Raymond, J.L. v4p0164c2s
Raymond, M. v1p0359c2s v1p0688c2s v1p0692c1s v1p0726c1s v1p1030c1s
Raymond, M.D. v3p0396c2s v3p0420c2s v3p0455c2s
Raymond, Miss v1p0479c2s
Raymond, Mrs. v1p0230c2s v1p1053c1s
Raymond, P. v4p0369c2s
Raymond, P.E. v6p0019c1s v6p0079c1s v6p0111c1s
Raymond, R. v6p0282c2s
Raymond, R.H. v1p1280c2s
Raymond, R.L. v6p0659c2s
Raymond, R.W. v1p0542c1s v1p0622c1s v1p0664c2s v1p0897c2s v1p1163c2s v2p0119c2s v2p0205c1s v4p0372c2s v5p0264c1s v5p0378c1s v6p0176c1s
Raymond, Robert L. v6p0151c1s
Raymond, S. v3p0136c1s
Raymond, T.H. v1p0978c2s
Raymond, W. v4p0097c1s v4p0276c2s v5p0089c1s v5p0189c2m v5p0190c2s v5p0412c2s v5p0518c2s v5p0538c2s v5p0596c1s v6p0384c1s v6p0551c2s
Raymond, W.G. v2p0275c2s
Raymond, W.R. v6p0681c1s
Raymond, Walter v6p0002c2s
Raymond-Barker, E. v2p0016c1s v3p0419c2s v5p0307c2s
Rayne, M.L., Mrs. v1p0003c2s v1p1212c2s
Rayner, I. v3p0443c2s v6p0529c1s
Rayner, M.C. v2p0160c1s
Raynolds, E.V. v4p0450c1s v4p0476c2m
Raynor, E.C. v2p0234c1s v2p0253c2s
Raynor, L. v4p0201c2s
Rea, J. v1p0408c2s v1p0553c1s v2p0143c1s
Rea, L. v6p0589c1m
Rea, Lilian v6p0513c2s
Rea, R. v1p0391c2s v1p1090c1s v6p0047c2s v6p0270c2s
Rea, S.J. v2p0264c2s
Rea, W.F. v1p1025c1s
Reach, A.B. v1p0039c2s v1p0114c1s v1p0560c1s v1p0722c1s v1p0945c1s v1p0988c2s v1p1078c2s v1p1105c1s v1p1105c2s v1p1300c1s v1p1322c2s v1p1338c2s
Reach, E. v6p0683c1s
Read, C. v1p0342c2s v1p0761c1m v1p0993c2s v1p1000c2m v1p1001c1s v1p1088c2s v2p0154c1s v2p0241c1s v2p0283c2s v2p0285c1s v2p0340c2s v2p0358c2s v3p0255c2s
Read, C.C. v1p0321c1s
Read, C.F. v6p0057c1s v6p0532c1s
Read, C.H. v4p0263c2s v4p0417c2s v4p0550c2s v5p0198c2s v5p0373c1s v6p0258c2s v6p0682c1s v6p0699c1s
Read, C.H. and Dalton, O.M. v5p0053c2s
Read, C.Hercules v6p0260c2s
Read, C.S. v2p0434c2s
Read, C.W. v1p1343c2s
Read, D.B. v1p0098c1s v1p0699c2s v1p0700c2s v1p0945c2s v2p0007c1s v2p0139c2s v2p0324c1s v2p0351c1s v2p0443c1s v3p0007c2s v3p0135c2s v3p0315c1s v3p0341c2s v3p0432c2s v4p0268c1s
Read, D.H. v6p0408c2s
Read, E. v1p0227c1s v1p0610c1m v1p0611c1s v1p0952c1s v3p0112c2s
Read, E.A. v1p1196c1s v5p0282c2s
Read, F.C. v4p0500c2s
Read, F.W. v4p0557c1s
Read, G.W. v5p0029c1s
Read, H. v1p0978c1s v4p0608c1s
Read, J.M. v2p0097c2s v2p0178c1s v2p0313c2s v2p0365c2s v3p0403c2s v3p0455c2s v4p0551c2s v4p0611c2s
Read, J.M., jr. v1p0997c1s v1p0997c2s
Read, M.C. v2p0171c1s v2p0274c2s v2p0374c2s
Read, N. v4p0474c1s
Read, O. v4p0374c1s
Read, R.H. v2p0228c2s
Read, S.C. v1p0321c2s
Read, S.P. v4p0105c2s v4p0156c2s v4p0221c1s v5p0110c1s v5p0111c2s v5p0112c2s
Read, Sewall v4p0233c2s
Read, T.B. v1p0154c2s v1p0579c1s v1p0886c2s v1p1086c1s
Read, T.T. and Knight, C.W. v6p0602c2s
Read, W. v1p0035c2s
Read, W.B. v1p0957c2s
Read, W.G. v1p0106c1s v1p0408c2s v1p0807c2s
Read, W.H.A. v2p0030c2s v2p0311c2s
Read, Wm.E. v4p0282c2s
Reade, A. v2p0247c1s v3p0221c1s v5p0415c1s v5p0604c2s
Reade, A.A. v2p0052c2s v2p0056c1s v3p0002c1s v3p0054c2s v4p0071c2s v4p0506c1s
Reade, C. v1p0022c2s v1p0062c1s v1p0063c1s v1p0064c1s v1p0064c2s v1p0144c2s v1p0190c2s v1p0230c2s v1p0266c2s v1p0535c1s v1p0535c2s v1p0558c2s v1p0586c2s v1p0609c1s v1p0643c2s v1p0674c1s v1p0710c2s v1p0865c1s v1p0953c2s v1p1067c2s v1p1084c2s v1p1145c1s v1p1193c2s v1p1199c2s v1p1204c1s v1p1280c1s v1p1296c1s v1p1358c1s v1p1368c2s v1p1372c2s v1p1420c1s v2p0052c2s v2p0173c1s v2p0336c1s v2p0341c2s v2p0365c2s v2p0380c1s v2p0438c1s v3p0006c1s v3p0043c2s v3p0232c1s v3p0333c1s v3p0354c2s v4p0577c2s v4p0608c1s v5p0360c2s
Reade, C. and Boucicault, D. v1p0471c1s
Reade, C., Mrs. v1p0336c2s v1p0586c1s v1p1262c2s v1p1275c2s
Reade, C.W. v1p0267c1s
Reade, Compton v5p0189c2s v6p0532c1s
Reade, E.M. v1p1429c1s
Reade, H. v6p0006c1s v6p0006c2m v6p0007c1m v6p0091c2m v6p0200c2s v6p0239c1s v6p0254c1s v6p0333c2s v6p0352c1s v6p0542c2s v6p0587c1s v6p0605c2s v6p0677c1s
Reade, J. v1p0023c2s v1p0120c2s v1p0193c1s v1p0193c2s v1p0220c1m v1p0582c1s v1p0624c2s v1p0892c1s v1p0895c2s v1p1429c1s v2p0082c2s v3p0351c2s v5p0412c1s v6p0310c1s
Reade, J.B. v1p0836c1s
Reade, P. v3p0236c2s v6p0101c1s
Reade, R.H. v4p0578c2s
Reade, R.N.R. v6p0685c1s
Reade, T.M. v1p0362c2s v1p0607c2s v2p0116c1s v3p0150c1s v3p0363c1s v3p0374c2m v4p0131c2s v4p0133c1s v4p0385c2s v4p0502c2s
Reade, W. v1p0491c2s
Reade, W.W. v1p0011c2s v1p0013c2s v1p0329c1s v1p0536c2m v1p0583c2s v1p0718c1s v1p0761c2s v1p1164c1s v1p1241c2s v1p1275c2s
Reading, C. v1p0183c2s
Ready, A. v3p0076c2s
Ready, A.W. v4p0466c1s v5p0121c2s
Reagan, J.H. v6p0112c1s v6p0300c2s
Realf, J. v3p0223c2s
Realf, J., jr. v3p0080c1s v3p0174c1s v3p0394c2s v4p0146c1s v4p0157c2s v4p0432c2s v4p0486c1s v6p0278c1s v6p0301c1m v6p0388c2s v6p0470c1s
Ream, S. v5p0580c2s
Reamer, C.W. v5p0309c1s v5p0641c2s
Reamer, L. v6p0468c1s v6p0683c1s
Reaney, G.S. v2p0264c1s v2p0288c2s v2p0407c2s v2p0477c1s v3p0256c1m v3p0353c1s v3p0358c1s
Reaney, G.S., Mrs. v2p0182c2s v2p0196c1s v2p0444c2s v3p0254c1s v3p0257c1s
Reaney, I. v1p0415c2m v1p0523c1s v1p1422c2s v2p0143c2s v2p0178c2s v2p0263c1s v2p0477c2s
Rearden, M. v2p0469c1s
Rearden, T.A. v1p0959c2s
Rearden, T.H. v1p0389c2s v1p1419c2s v2p0435c1s v6p0176c1s v6p0275c1s v6p0491c1s v6p0541c1s
Reardon, J.M. v6p0449c2s v6p0637c2s
Reasoner, E. v6p0579c1s
Reasoner, E.N. v6p0243c2s
Reasoner, Elsie v5p0420c1m
Reavell, J.A. v5p0622c1s
Reay, Lord v3p0128c2s
Rebec, G. v5p0642c1s v6p0033c2s v6p0090c2s
Rebec, George v5p0344c1s
Rebeur-Paschwitz, E.V. ... v3p0126c1s v4p0166c1s
Rebigger, H.A. v6p0429c2s
Reboux, M. v1p0026c2s
Reckenzaun, A. v2p0136c2s v2p0137c1s v3p0133c1s v3p0244c1s
Reclam, Prof. v2p0031c2s
Reclus, E. v1p0153c2s v1p0448c1s v1p0535c1s v1p0772c1s v1p0784c2s v1p0802c2s v1p0911c1s v1p1230c1s v1p1264c2s v1p1441c2s v2p0013c1s v2p0013c2s v3p0027c1s v3p0185c1s v4p0105c2s v4p0114c2s v4p0166c1s v4p0461c1s v4p0496c1s v4p0596c2s v5p0034c1s v5p0112c1s v5p0236c1s v5p0468c1s v6p0400c1s v6p0610c2s
Record, G.L. v5p0392c1s
Record, L.L. v1p1101c1s
Rector, E.L. v4p0143c2s v4p0378c1s v4p0580c2s
Rector, L.E. v4p0512c2s v5p0165c2s
Rector, S. v6p0503c2s
Redan, H. v5p0451c2s
Redbranche, A.F. v5p0379c2s
Redcliffe, I.Y. v1p0222c1s
Redcliffe, Stratford de, Lord v1p0553c1s v1p0650c2s v1p1332c1m
Redcliffe, Stratford de, Visc. v1p0196c2s
Reddale, F. v5p0096c2s v5p0224c2s v6p0223c2s v6p0286c1s v6p0399c1s v6p0471c2s v6p0653c2s
Reddall, F. v5p0214c2s
Reddall, H.F. v2p0264c2s
Reddaway, W.F. v6p0240c1s
Redden, L.C. v1p0107c2s
Reddick, J.E. v4p0021c2s
Reddie, C. v3p0129c2s
Reddie, J. v1p1206c1s
Redding, B.B. v1p1255c2s v6p0094c1s v6p0308c2s v6p0463c2s
Redding, C. v1p0062c2s v1p0080c2s v1p0106c2s v1p0146c2s v1p0168c1s v1p0191c2m v1p0198c2s v1p0307c1s v1p0344c1s v1p0353c1s v1p0365c2s v1p0378c1s v1p0448c2m v1p0542c1s v1p0549c1m v1p0549c2s v1p0550c2s v1p0573c2s v1p0611c1s v1p0628c2s v1p0634c1s v1p0667c1s v1p0670c1s v1p0764c1s v1p0851c1s v1p0858c2s v1p0871c1s v1p0964c2s v1p0995c1s v1p1023c2s v1p1027c2s v1p1032c1s v1p1060c2s v1p1084c2s v1p1133c2s v1p1134c1s v1p1174c2s v1p1184c2s v1p1188c2s v1p1238c2s v1p1281c1s v1p1294c1s v1p1333c2s v1p1341c2s v1p1342c2s v1p1344c1s v1p1352c2s v1p1415c1m v1p1415c2s v1p1435c1s
Redding, G.H. v4p0035c1s
Redding, J.D. v3p0154c1s
Reddington, A. v1p0484c1s
Reddington, J. v6p0179c2s
Reddy, E. v1p0876c2s
Reddy, T.F. v3p0120c2s
Rede, A. v5p0204c1s

Rede, L. v1p1088c2s
Redenbaugh, W.A. v4p0355c2s
Redepenning, Dr. v1p0521c1s
Rederus, S. v5p0172c1s
Redesdale, Earl of v1p1118c2s
Redfarn, W.B. v2p0400c2s
v2p0474c1s
Redfern, D. v6p0507c2s
Redfield, A.A. v3p0039c1s
Redfield, C. v1p1247c1s
Redfield, C.L. v4p0288c1s
v4p0430c1s v5p0019c2s v5p0462c2s
v6p0355c1s v6p0516c1s
Redfield, I.F. v1p1067c1s
v1p1215c2s
Redfield, J.F. v1p0935c1s
Redfield, J.W. v1p0843c2s
Redfield, W.B. v1p0984c1s
Redfield, W.C. v1p0327c2s
v1p0367c1s v1p0470c1s v1p0497c1s
v1p0562c1s v1p0617c2m v1p0622c1s
v1p0829c2s v1p0956c1s v1p1247c1s
v1p1256c2m v1p1257c1s v1p1316c1s
v1p1316c2m v1p1401c1s v1p1405c2m
Redford, G. v3p0022c1s
Redford, R.A. v1p0645c2s
v5p0204c1s
Redford, W.K.R. v4p0351c1s
Redgrave and Cole, H. v1p0064c1s
Redgrave, A. v1p0767c1s
v3p0128c2s v3p0426c1s
Redgrave, E. v3p0286c1s
v3p0372c2s
Redgrave, G. v3p0395c1s
Redgrave, G.R. v2p0238c2s
v2p0354c2m v3p0022c1s v3p0050c1s
v3p0053c2s v3p0373c2s v3p0426c1s
v4p0072c1s v4p0220c1s v4p0586c1s
v5p0191c1s v6p0043c1s v6p0174c1s
v6p0478c2s
Redgrave, G.T. v5p0570c1s
Redgrave, R. v1p0063c1s
Redgrave, R.G. v2p0314c2s
Redgrave, S. v1p1130c1s
Redgrove, G.R. v2p0411c2s
Redhead, C.H. v1p0006c1s
Redhouse, J.W. and Lyall, C.J.
v2p0018c1s
Redington, A. v1p0705c1s
Redlich, Josef v6p0303c1s
Redman, J.B. v2p0440c2s
v3p0426c2m
Redman, J.C. v4p0072c1s
Redman, R.A. v1p0013c2s
Redmayne, R.A.S. v6p0133c1s
Redmond, J.E. v4p0262c1s
v4p0289c2m v4p0290c1m v4p0290c2s
v5p0295c2m v5p0296c1s v5p0296c2m
v5p0297c1s v5p0297c2s
Redmond, J.E. et al. v4p0265c2s
v4p0289c2s
Redmond, Wm.A. v3p0475c1s
Redon, G. v4p0021c2s
v4p0221c1s v4p0572c1s
Redpath, Alice E. v6p0632c1s
Redpath, H.A. v4p0054c1s
v4p0624c2s v5p0509c1s v6p0063c1s
v6p0259c2s v6p0584c1m
Redpath, J. v1p1032c1s
v2p0224c2s v2p0227c1s
Redshawe, L.S. v1p1200c1s
Redstone, V.B. v6p0686c1s
Redway, J.W. v3p0186c2s
v4p0125c2s v4p0171c2s v4p0190c1s
v4p0222c2m v4p0441c2m v4p0445c1s
v5p0175c1s v5p0584c2s v6p0622c2s
Redwitz, O.v. v1p1099c2s
Redwood, A.C. v1p0155c1s
v1p0297c2s v1p0469c1s v1p0693c2s
v1p0995c1s v1p1374c1s v2p0232c2s
v2p0275c1s
Redwood, B. v3p0328c2s
Redwood, B.R. v6p0432c1s
Reece, B. v3p0244c2s
v3p0352c1s v3p0353c1s v3p0378c1s
v4p0471c1s
Reece, G. v6p0492c2s
Reece, R. v1p0579c1s
v2p0416c2m
Reed, A. v2p0481c2s
v6p0158c1s
Reed, A.L. v2p0362c2s
Reed, A.Z. v5p0122c1s
Reed, Anna M. v6p0380c2s
Reed, C. v1p0388c2s
v2p0141c2s
Reed, C.A. v4p0022c1s
v4p0070c2s
Reed, C.A.L. v5p0016c2s
v6p0017c1s
Reed, C.J. v4p0026c1s
v4p0089c1s v4p0177c1s v5p0185c2s
v5p0577c2s v6p0506c1s
Reed, C.J. et al. v4p0177c1s
Reed, C.O. v5p0450c1s
Reed, Clement and Mathews, E.R.
v6p0133c2s
Reed, E. v2p0187c1s
v4p0041c1s v4p0517c2s
Reed, E.A. v4p0622c2s
v6p0155c2s
Reed, E.B. v6p0013c1s
v6p0422c2s
Reed, E.C. v6p0681c1s
Reed, E.H. v5p0473c2s
Reed, E.J. v1p0547c1s
v1p0551c1s v1p0901c2s v2p0187c1s
v2p0283c2s v2p0401c1m v2p0419c2s
v2p0465c2s v3p0182c1s v3p0390c2s
Reed, E.J., Sir v3p0161c1s
v3p0298c1s v5p0264c1s
Reed, E.T. v5p0275c2s
Reed, F. et al. v5p0388c2s
Reed, F.H. v6p0131c1s
v6p0213c2s
Reed, F.W. v6p0465c1s
Reed, F.W.H. v6p0191c2s
v6p0482c2s
Reed, G.E. v3p0362c2s
Reed, H. v1p0274c2s
v1p0294c2s v1p0575c2s v1p0762c2s
v1p1088c2s v1p1238c1s v1p1348c1s
Reed, H.A. v4p0092c2s
v5p0032c2s v5p0573c2s v6p0564c2s
Reed, H.E. v6p0692c2s
Reed, H.L. v4p0026c2s
v4p0034c2s v4p0226c2s v4p0322c1s
v4p0374c1s v4p0470c1s v5p0079c2s
Reed, H.S. v5p0194c2s
v6p0479c1s
Reed, H.T. v6p0413c2s
Reed, H.V., Mrs. v1p0595c2s
Reed, H.W. v5p0510c2s
Reed, J. v1p1275c1s
v3p0417c2s v4p0096c2s v4p0109c2s
v4p0112c1s v4p0113c1s v4p0233c1s
v4p0331c1s v4p0463c1s v4p0476c2s
v4p0489c1s v4p0559c2s v5p0009c1s
v5p0020c2s v5p0056c1s v5p0078c2s
v5p0118c1s v5p0154c1s v5p0189c1s
v5p0378c2s v5p0405c1m v5p0561c2m
v5p0563c2m v5p0631c1s v6p0060c1s
v6p0125c2s v6p0126c2s v6p0192c2s
v6p0202c1s v6p0259c1s v6p0342c1s
v6p0402c1s v6p0450c1s v6p0541c1s
v6p0541c2s v6p0626c2s v6p0708c2s
Reed, J.A. v1p0750c1s
Reed, J.C. v1p1226c1s
v6p0291c1s
Reed, J.H. v6p0237c1s
Reed, J.J. v1p0065c1s
v1p0210c2s v1p0239c2s v1p0370c1s
v1p0832c2s v1p0882c2s v1p0975c2s
v5p0623c1s v6p0117c2s
Reed, J.M. v3p0134c2s
Reed, J.O. v3p0422c1s
Reed, J.P. v3p0213c1s
v3p0280c2s
Reed, J.P. and Walsh, W.S.
v4p0543c2s
Reed, James v5p0640c1s
v6p0523c2s
Reed, K. v6p0645c1s
Reed, L.B. v6p0370c1s
v6p0377c2s
Reed, L.L. v5p0610c2s
Reed, M. v4p0028c1s
v5p0283c1s v5p0480c1s v5p0527c2s
v5p0629c2s v6p0026c2s v6p0055c2s
v6p0089c2s v6p0206c2s v6p0338c2s
v6p0402c2s v6p0442c2s v6p0482c2s
v6p0488c2s v6p0595c1s v6p0617c1s
v6p0630c1s v6p0654c1s v6p0704c1s
v6p0705c2s
Reed, M.G. v4p0027c2s
Reed, Marcus v6p0295c1s
Reed, Myron v5p0411c2s
Reed, Myrtle v5p0319c1s
Reed, R.R. v6p0618c1s
Reed, S. v4p0578c2s
Reed, S., Mrs. v3p0469c1s
Reed, S.A. v4p0200c1m
Reed, T. v4p0540c2m
Reed, T. and Young, C.A. . v4p0037c2s
Reed, T.A. and Eames, R.L.
v2p0401c1s
Reed, T.B. v3p0007c1s
v3p0047c1s v3p0088c1s v3p0114c2s
v3p0132c1s v3p0202c1m v3p0440c1s
v4p0129c1s v4p0213c2s v4p0350c1s
v4p0563c1s v4p0595c1s v4p0595c2m
v4p0596c1m v5p0204c1s v5p0272c2s
v5p0410c1s v5p0433c2s v5p0525c2s
v5p0597c1s v5p0600c1s v6p0633c1s
Reed, T.B. and Carlisle, J.G.
v3p0202c2s
Reed, T.B. and Wilson, W.L.
v4p0595c2s
Reed, V. v3p0288c1s
v3p0344c1s v4p0342c2s v4p0434c2s
Reed, V. and Cooke, Grace MacG.
v6p0464c1s
Reed, V.L. v4p0342c1s
Reed, V.Z. v4p0017c2s
v4p0342c1m v6p0171c1s v6p0317c1s
v6p0480c1s v6p0562c2s
Reed, W., Sir v6p0069c2s
Reed, W.A. v6p0446c1s
Reed, W.B. v1p0231c2s
v1p0234c2s v1p0385c1s v1p0522c2s
v1p0833c1s v1p0833c2s v1p1012c2s
v1p1088c2s v1p1298c1s
Reed, W.D. v1p0359c2s
Reed, W.H. v1p1088c2s
Reed, W.O. v5p0447c2s
Reede, F. v3p0158c1s
Reeder, C. v1p0146c1s
Reeder, J.L. v4p0336c1s
Reeder, R.P. v5p0328c1s
Reeder, R.R. v5p0480c1s
v6p0116c1s v6p0116c2s v6p0152c2m
v6p0153c2s
Reedy, W.M. v6p0568c1s
Reeks, M.E. v6p0121c1s
Rees, A.F. v5p0560c1s
Rees, A.W. v5p0020c2s
v5p0282c2s v6p0067c1s v6p0465c2s
v6p0504c2s v6p0706c2s
Rees, Alfred W. v6p0305c2s
v6p0428c1s
Rees, F.A. v6p0122c1s
Rees, H.K. v6p0555c1s
Rees, J.D. v3p0007c2s
v3p0079c1s v3p0100c2s v3p0268c2s
v3p0327c1m v3p0430c1s v4p0040c1s
v4p0150c1s v4p0189c2s v4p0199c2s
v4p0217c2s v4p0280c2s v4p0391c1s
v4p0496c1m v5p0111c2s v5p0185c2s
v5p0265c2s v5p0285c1m v5p0286c2s
v5p0355c1s v6p0186c1s v6p0313c1s
v6p0313c2s v6p0314c1s v6p0315c1s
v6p0394c1s v6p0634c2s
Rees, J.E.R. v2p0194c1s
Rees, J.K. v2p0441c2s
v4p0034c1s v4p0034c2s v4p0321c2s
v4p0497c1s v5p0326c2s v5p0372c2s
v5p0453c2s v5p0514c1s v6p0037c2s
v6p0038c1s
Rees, J.R. v2p0051c1s
v2p0052c1s v2p0114c2s v3p0285c1s
Rees, Janet E.R. v3p0467c2s
Rees, L.D. v4p0333c2s
Rees, L.E. v1p0592c2s
Rees, Malcolm v5p0627c2s
Rees, T. v6p0527c2s
Rees, T.H. v5p0188c2s
Rees, W.L. v3p0374c1s
Reese, A.M. v5p0013c1s
v6p0160c1s v6p0243c1s
Reese, C.L. v4p0439c2s
Reese, D.M. v1p0794c1s
Reese, D.M. and Sunterland, L.
v1p1301c2s
Reese, E.P. v4p0389c2s
Reese, F.D. v6p0183c1s
Reese, G.C. v5p0224c2s
Reese, G.P. v1p1106c2s
Reese, H.M. v5p0645c2s
Reese, J. v1p0664c1s
v1p1250c2s
Reese, L.W. v5p0272c2s
v5p0566c2s v6p0150c1s v6p0363c2s
Reese, Lizette W. v6p0287c1s
Reese, W.B., jr. v2p0239c2s
v2p0465c1s
Reeser, T.F. v4p0497c2s
Reeve, A.B. v6p0232c1s
v6p0660c2s
Reeve, C.G.J. v3p0122c2m
v3p0173c2s v3p0201c2s v4p0221c2s
v4p0516c1s v5p0038c1s
Reeve, C.H. v4p0139c2s
v4p0169c1s v4p0337c1s v4p0450c2s
v4p0481c2s v4p0537c2s v4p0553c2s
Reeve, Dr. v1p0588c1s
Reeve, E.P. v3p0172c1s
Reeve, H., Mrs. v2p0101c1s
v3p0098c2s
Reeve, H.M. v5p0351c2s
v6p0047c2s v6p0472c1s
Reeve, J.K. v3p0006c1s
v3p0006c2m v3p0099c1s v3p0149c2s
v3p0187c2s v3p0326c2s v4p0049c1s
v4p0051c1s v4p0083c2s v4p0120c2s
v4p0142c2s v4p0162c1s v4p0250c1s
v4p0410c2s v4p0517c1s v6p0648c1s
Reeve, S.A. v6p0660c2s
Reeve, Sidney A. v6p0248c2s
Reeve, T.R. v5p0631c2s
Reeve, W. v6p0077c2s
Reeve, W.P. v5p0381c2s
Reeve, Wybert v6p0138c1s
Reeves, D.M. v1p0684c2s
Reeves, E. v4p0314c2s
v4p0339c2s v4p0401c2m v4p0630c1s
Reeves, E.A. v6p0314c2s
v6p0627c2s v6p0674c2s
Reeves, E.B. v4p0542c2s
Reeves, H. v1p0034c2s
Reeves, J. v4p0336c1s
Reeves, J.B. v4p0476c1s
v5p0481c2s
Reeves, J.C. v3p0149c2s
Reeves, J.S. v4p0128c2s
v6p0144c2s v6p0364c1s
Reeves, M.S. v6p0455c1s
Reeves, R.M. v4p0614c2s
Reeves, R.N. v5p0445c2s
v5p0559c2s v5p0623c2s v6p0377c2s
v6p0583c1s

Reeves, S. v5p0530c2s
Reeves, S.W. v6p0470c1s
Reeves, W.P. v4p0085c2s
v4p0150c1s v4p0233c2s v4p0315c2s
v4p0401c2s v5p0014c2s v5p0038c2s
v5p0039c1m v5p0615c2s v6p0026c1s
v6p0138c2s v6p0266c2s v6p0322c2s
v6p0355c2s v6p0455c1s v6p0673c1s
Regal, F. v4p0078c1s
Regal, F.E. v4p0081c2s
v4p0285c1s v4p0390c1s
Regal, Mary L. v5p0394c1s
Regan, J. v5p0127c1s
v5p0375c1s v6p0399c1s v6p0631c1m
Regel, E. v1p0975c2s
Regg, J.M. v2p0021c1s
Regidor, A. v5p0444c1s
Regin, E.S. v3p0120c1s
Regnard, A. v1p0223c1s
Regnault, F. v4p0191c2s
v4p0206c2s
Regnault, H.V. v1p1016c1s
Regnault, M.V. v1p0502c1s
v1p0581c1s v1p1248c1s v1p1362c2s
Regnier, C. v5p0217c1s
Rehder, A. v6p0709c2s
Rehmann, A. v6p0298c2s
Rehmke, J. v5p0133c2s
v5p0199c2s
Rehn, J.A.G. v6p0522c1s
Reibenack, M. v4p0472c2s
Reich, E. v4p0269c2s
v4p0302c2s v4p0601c2s v5p0040c1s
v5p0645c2s v6p0018c1s v6p0042c2s
v6p0065c1s v6p0213c1m v6p0254c1s
v6p0292c1s v6p0292c2s v6p0303c2s
v6p0363c1s v6p0424c2s v6p0597c1s
Reich, E., Dr. v6p0667c1s
Reich, Emil v6p0303c2s
Reichard, P. v3p0299c1s
Reichardt, A. v3p0284c2s
Reichardt, A., Mrs. v3p0469c2s
Reichardt, Mrs. v4p0303c1s
Reichel, C.F. v1p1302c1s
Reichel, C.P. v1p0653c2s
v1p0732c1s
Reichel, H.R. v6p0670c2s
Reichenan, Von v5p0162c2s
Reichenbach, A. v3p0413c2s
v4p0455c2s v4p0566c1s v5p0099c2s
Reichenbach, M.von v4p0090c2s
Reichenbach, O. v2p0020c1s
v2p0149c1s v2p0173c2s v2p0258c2s
v2p0309c2s v2p0409c1s
Reichensperger, A. v1p1117c1s
Reichhelm, E.P. v5p0468c1s
Reichman, C. v4p0284c1s
v5p0375c2s
Reichmann, C. v5p0290c2s
v5p0587c2s
Reichmann, Carl v4p0567c1s
Reid, A. v2p0312c2s
v3p0303c1s v3p0303c2s v4p0214c1s
v5p0004c2s v5p0528c1m
Reid, A. et al. v3p0221c2s
Reid, A.D.D. and Reid, G.Archdall
v6p0288c1s
Reid, A.P. v1p0194c1s
v1p0566c1s v1p0939c2s
Reid, Anna M. v6p0260c2s
Reid, B. v6p0054c1s
v6p0545c1s
Reid, C. v2p0345c1s
v3p0126c1s v4p0272c2s v4p0289c1s
v4p0316c2s v4p0317c2s v4p0442c2s
v4p0490c2s v4p0520c1s v4p0636c2s
v6p0306c2s
Reid, C. and Fisher, F.C.. v1p1257c2s
Reid, C.S. v6p0312c1s
Reid, Christian v4p0098c1s
Reid, D. v6p0697c2s
Reid, D.B. v1p0052c2s
v1p1070c1s v1p1366c1s
Reid, D.M. v4p0041c2s
Reid, D.N. v4p0049c2s
v4p0253c1s v4p0278c1s v4p0279c2s
v5p0285c1s v5p0286c2s v6p0047c1s
v6p0468c2s
Reid, Donald N. v5p0119c1s
Reid, E. v5p0189c1s
Reid, E.W. v4p0002c1s
Reid, F. v6p0180c1s
Reid, G. v4p0105c1s
v4p0106c1m v5p0108c2s v5p0110c1s
v5p0111c1s v5p0111c2m v5p0112c1s
v5p0347c2s v5p0438c2s v6p0119c1s
v6p0369c2s
Reid, G.A. v4p0191c1s
v4p0286c1s v4p0476c2s v5p0101c2s
v5p0392c1s v5p0486c2s v6p0602c1s
v6p0673c2s
Reid, G.Archdall v6p0288c1s
v6p0675c1s
Reid, G.Archdall and Reid, A.D.D.
v6p0288c1s
Reid, G.H. v3p0027c1s
Reid, G.J. v6p0060c2m
v6p0185c2s
Reid, G.W. v1p0133c2s
v2p0125c1s
Reid, H. v1p0599c2s
v2p0072c2s
Reid, H.A. v2p0046c1s
v2p0274c2m v2p0352c1s v6p0387c1s
v6p0482c1s
Reid, H.F. v3p0049c1s
v4p0387c1s v5p0498c1s v6p0257c2s
Reid, H.G. v1p1167c1s
v3p0381c1s
Reid, H.J. v3p0120c2s
v3p0372c2s
Reid, H.M.B. v5p0623c1s
Reid, Harriet v6p0230c2s
Reid, Henry v2p0404c2s
Reid, J. v1p1391c1s
v4p0149c2s v4p0154c2s v4p0390c2s
v4p0562c2s v4p0568c2s v5p0239c2s
v5p0503c2s v5p0572c2s v6p0235c2s
Reid, J. and Clarke, F.N.. v4p0045c2s
Reid, J.A. v5p0233c1s
v5p0270c2s v5p0411c1s
Reid, J.B. v6p0029c1s
v6p0592c2s
Reid, J.E. v6p0171c2s
Reid, J.L. v4p0002c2s
Reid, J.M. v1p0231c2s
Reid, J.W. v3p0158c2s
v3p0220c2s
Reid, John v4p0221c2s
Reid, M. v1p0168c1s
v1p0459c1s v1p0679c2s v1p0937c1s
v1p1279c2s v1p1385c1s v1p1409c2s
v3p0021c1s v4p0048c2s v4p0258c2s
Reid, M.C. v2p0421c1s
v3p0039c1s
Reid, M.J. v4p0448c1s
v4p0630c2s v5p0042c2s
Reid, Mary J. v4p0548c1s
v5p0220c2s v5p0480c1s
Reid, O. v4p0276c2s
Reid, P.C. v5p0340c1s
Reid, P.Y. v1p0979c2s
v1p1200c1s
Reid, R. v2p0248c1m
v6p0026c1s
Reid, R.R. v6p0206c2s
Reid, R.T. v2p0133c2s
v2p0423c2s v3p0440c1s v4p0261c2s
Reid, R.W. v4p0369c1s
Reid, S. v1p0192c1s
v3p0107c1s v4p0303c1s v5p0407c2s
v6p0657c2s v6p0710c1s
Reid, S. and Morris, G.P.. v6p0294c2s
Reid, S.J. v2p0097c2s
v2p0139c2s v2p0386c1s v5p0066c1s
v6p0071c1s v6p0552c1s v6p0555c2s
Reid, T. v3p0385c1s
v5p0183c2s v6p0688c1m
Reid, T.H. v6p0119c2s
v6p0186c2s
Reid, T.H. et al. v5p0445c1s
Reid, T.W. v1p0166c2s
v1p0345c1s v1p0696c2s v1p1063c1s
v1p1129c1s v2p0163c1m v4p0227c2s
v4p0238c2s v4p0266c1s
Reid, Thorburn v6p0204c1s
v6p0204c2s
Reid, W. v1p0696c2s
v1p0817c2s v1p1028c2s v1p1157c2s
v4p0074c1s v4p0172c2s v4p0239c2s
v4p0401c2s v4p0495c2s v5p0146c2s
v5p0234c2s v5p0310c2s v5p0354c1s
v5p0409c2s v5p0443c2s v5p0502c1s
v5p0505c1s v6p0667c1s v6p0669c2s
Reid, W. and Rogers, J.G.. v5p0594c2s
Reid, W., Sir v5p0247c2s
v5p0602c1s
Reid, W.C.J. v5p0034c1s
v5p0111c1s v6p0118c1s v6p0646c1m
Reid, W.F. v4p0270c2s
v6p0056c1s v6p0197c1s v6p0563c2s
Reid, W.J. v5p0012c1s
v5p0151c1m v5p0355c1s v5p0528c1s
v5p0579c1s v5p0579c2s v5p0643c2s
v6p0645c2s
Reid, W.M. v6p0575c2s
Reid, W.R., jr. and Nichols, E.P.
v6p0231c2s
Reid, W.T., jr. v6p0039c1s
Reid, Whitelaw v6p0492c2s
v6p0703c2s
Reid-Matheson, E. v6p0709c2s
Reifsnider, C.K. v4p0052c2s
Reigart, J.F. v3p0422c1s
v6p0549c2s
Reigart, S.W. v4p0360c1s
Reighard, J. v6p0227c1s
Reighard, K.F. v5p0069c2s
v5p0092c2s v5p0170c2s v5p0504c2s
Reignolds-Winslow, Catherine M.
v4p0474c2s
Reihl, C.W. v6p0049c2s
v6p0050c2s
Reik, H.O. v5p0200c2s
Reilly, B.J. v4p0469c1s
Reilly, B.O. v2p0356c1s
Reilly, C. v1p0523c1s
Reilly, F.W. v2p0482c1s
Reilly, H.J. v5p0032c2s
v5p0049c2s v5p0290c2s
Reilly, I.W. v6p0122c2s
Reilly, L.W. v2p0124c2s
v5p0322c2s v5p0479c1s
Reilly, M. v5p0393c1s
Reilly, R.J. v3p0367c2s
Reilly, T.B. v5p0373c2m
v6p0106c1s v6p0236c1s v6p0539c1s
v6p0623c1s
Reily, W.M. v1p0024c1s
v1p0065c2s v1p0106c1s v1p0303c1s
v1p0380c2s v1p0443c1s v1p1042c2s
v1p1157c1s v2p0069c1s v2p0139c2s
v3p0043c2s v3p0057c1s v3p0120c1s
Reimensnyder, J.M. v2p0426c1s
Reimensnyder, J.R. v3p0422c1s
Reimer, W.E.De v5p0009c1s
Reimers, J. v5p0140c1s
v5p0397c1s v6p0617c2s
Reimers, Johannes v5p0253c1s
Rein, J. v4p0013c2s
Rein, W. v4p0171c2s
v4p0255c1s v4p0432c2s v4p0437c1s
v5p0148c2s v5p0176c2s v5p0511c1s
Reinach, J. v1p0482c2s
v1p1171c1s v2p0134c2s v2p0141c2s
v2p0164c2s v2p0165c2s v2p0170c2s
v2p0226c1s v2p0312c2s v3p0160c1s
v3p0161c1s v3p0163c2s v3p0164c1m
v4p0215c1m v4p0239c1s v5p0169c1s
v5p0221c1m v5p0224c2s v6p0558c2s
Reinach, P.S. v6p0136c1s
Reinach, S. v2p0004c1s
v2p0018c2s v2p0024c1s v2p0069c2s
v2p0222c1s v2p0435c2s v2p0448c1s
v2p0449c1s v3p0069c2s v3p0160c1s
v3p0294c2s v3p0334c1s v3p0377c2s
v3p0425c2s v4p0322c2s v4p0428c2s
v4p0576c1s v5p0609c1s
Reinecke, C. v5p0513c1s
Reinecke, E.W. v1p0121c2s
v1p0589c1s v1p1160c2s
Reinhard, G.L. v6p0364c2s
Reinhard, J. v5p0204c1s
v5p0275c1s v5p0358c2s v5p0370c1s
v5p0427c1s v5p0544c2s v6p0360c2s
Reinhardt, L. v6p0059c2s
Reinhart, A. v5p0510c1s
Reinhart, G.S. v4p0361c2s
Reinhart, J.A. v2p0132c1s
v2p0432c1s v3p0422c1s v5p0179c2s
Reinhart, L. v6p0142c1s
Reinherz, H. v6p0472c1s
Reinholt, O.H. v6p0493c1s
Reinick, W.R. v5p0604c1s
v6p0522c1s
Reinicke, Karl v5p0340c2s
Reinisch, L. v5p0180c2s
Reinkens, Prof. v1p0640c2s
v1p1363c1s
Reinold, A.W. v2p0341c1s
v3p0410c1s v4p0127c2s v4p0199c1s
Reinold, A.W. and Rucker, A.W.
v2p0155c2s
Reinsch, P.S. v5p0108c1s
v5p0109c2s v5p0111c2s v5p0173c2s
v5p0289c2s v5p0412c1s v5p0445c1s
v5p0457c2s v5p0626c1s v6p0036c1s
v6p0138c2s v6p0144c2s v6p0167c2s
v6p0224c2s v6p0287c1s v6p0334c1s
v6p0414c2s v6p0426c1s v6p0447c1s
v6p0493c1s v6p0510c2s v6p0539c2s
Reinsch, Paul S. v6p0411c1s
Reinstein, J.B. v5p0088c2s
Reinwald, C. v6p0419c1s
Reisch, T. v6p0513c1s
Reiss, G.T. v6p0393c1s
Reiss, W. and Stuebel, A.. v1p0382c2s
Reiter, I.H. v1p1090c2s
Reith, J., jr. v6p0706c2s
Reitz, F.W. v6p0006c2m
Reizenstein, M. v4p0043c1s
v4p0609c2s v5p0044c2s
Rejane, Mme. v6p0181c1s
Relton, F. v4p0122c2s
v4p0283c1s
Rembaugh, A.C. v1p1073c2s
v1p1288c2s
Remensnyder, J.B. v3p0261c1s
v4p0345c1s v4p0443c1s
Remick, J.W. v6p0127c1s
Remick, M.C. v4p0283c2s
v5p0031c1s
Remick, O.P. v4p0480c1s
Remington, F. v3p0076c2s
v3p0201c1s v3p0213c2s v3p0351c1s
v3p0382c1s v4p0048c1s v4p0087c2s
v4p0137c1s v4p0146c1s v4p0267c1s
v4p0368c2s v4p0468c2s v4p0473c2s
v4p0486c2s v4p0492c2s v4p0523c2s
v4p0552c1s v5p0029c1s v5p0061c2s
v5p0098c2s v5p0201c1s v5p0214c2s
v5p0269c2s v5p0274c1m v5p0310c2s
v5p0365c2s v5p0398c2s v5p0527c2s
v5p0531c2s v5p0539c2s v5p0544c1s
v5p0546c2s v5p0555c1s v5p0561c1m
v5p0577c2s v5p0591c2s v6p0171c2s
v6p0689c2s v6p0693c2s
Remington, Frederic v5p0606c2s
Remington, H. v5p0046c2s
Remington, J. v6p0689c2s

Remington, J.R. v1p0031c2s
Remington, M.E. v6p0363c1s
Remington, S. v1p1096c2s
v1p1441c2s
Remley, H. and Jameson, C.D.
v3p0071c2s
Remnitz, V.Y. v5p0342c2s
v5p0592c1s v6p0584c2s v6p0620c1s
Remnitz, V.Y. and Brown, A.G.
v5p0463c1s
Remnitz, Virginia Y. v6p0287c2s
Remondino, P.C. v6p0092c1s
v6p0093c1s v6p0442c1s
Remsen, D.S. v3p0264c2s
v4p0428c2s
Remsen, I. v1p0200c1s
v1p0224c2s v1p0225c2s v1p0817c1s
v1p0947c2s v1p1258c1s v2p0076c1s
v2p0237c2s v2p0272c1s v2p0338c1s
v3p0075c2s v3p0444c2s v4p0099c1s
v4p0360c2s v5p0010c1s v5p0104c1s
v6p0575c2s v6p0576c2s
Remsen, I. and Gilman, D.C.
v6p0344c2s
Remsen, Ira v4p0026c1s
Remusat, C.de v1p1398c2m
Remusat, P.de v1p0828c2s
Remy, C.F. v5p0192c1s
Renan, E. v1p0046c2s
v1p0123c1s v1p0123c2s v1p0128c2s
v1p0387c2s v1p0690c1s v1p0691c1s
v1p1236c2s v2p0210c2s v4p0054c2s
v5p0513c2s
Renard, A. v3p0451c2s
Renard, A. and Murray, J.. v2p0393c1s
Renard, M.A. and Murray, J.
v2p0462c2s
Renaud, E. v1p0320c2s
v1p0627c1s
Renaud, G. v5p0451c1s
Renault, B. v5p0374c1s
Rendall, F. v4p0122c2s
v5p0307c2s v5p0436c1s
Rendall, V. v4p0224c1s
Rendel, J.M. v1p0162c1s
Rendel, S. v2p0084c1s
v2p0464c2s
Render, W.H. v6p0134c2s
Rendle, A.B. v4p0092c1s
v4p0197c2s v4#324c2s v4p0422c2s
v4p0513c1s v6p0077c1s
Rendle, R. v1p0036c1s
Rendle, W. v1p0330c2s
v1p1029c1s v2p0276c2s v3p0372c2s
v3p0418c2s v4p0045c1s v4p0339c2m
Rendu, E. v1p0387c2s
v1p0388c2s
Renee, A. v1p0864c2s
Renick, E.I. v3p0086c2s
v3p0095c1s v3p0103c1s v3p0443c2s
v4p0117c1s v4p0597c1s v5p0024c2s
v5p0464c2s
v5p0468c2s
Rennell, Maj. v1p0184c2s
Rennell, Major v1p0084c2s
v1p0184c2s v1p0410c2s v1p0980c2s
Rennert, H.A. v6p0386c2s
Rennie, G. v1p0051c1s
v1p0463c1s v1p0491c1s v1p0618c2s
v1p0956c2s
Rennie, G.B. v1p0357c1s
v1p1249c1s
Rennie, J. v1p0141c2m
v2p0170c2s
Renninger, Eliz.D. v6p0374c1s
Reno, C. v3p0098c1s
v3p0306c2s v4p0022c1s v4p0405c2s
v4p0563c2s v4p0607c2s v5p0155c2s
Reno, G. v4p0259c2s
v5p0147c2s v5p0148c2s v5p0225c2s
v5p0628c1s
Renouf, E. v5p0002c2s
Renouf, P.L.P. v4p0092c1s
Renshaw, C.S. v1p0404c2s
v1p0675c2s v1p0676c1s
Renshaw, J.A. v1p0561c1s
Rensselaer, G.van v2p0185c1s
v2p0391c2s
Rensselaer, H.Van v3p0286c1s
v3p0384c1s
Rensselaer, J.K.Van, Mrs.. v4p0311c2s
v5p0407c2s v6p0089c1s v6p0424c2s
Rensselaer, J.T.Van v6p0601c1s
Rensselaer, J.Van v1p0140c2s
v1p0749c1s v1p0936c2s
Rensselaer, M.G.v. v1p0445c1s
Rensselaer, M.G.van v2p0298c1s
v2p0449c1s
Rensselaer, M.G.Van v1p0062c1s
v1p0115c1s v1p0140c2s v1p0341c1s
v1p0450c2s v1p0915c2s v1p1262c1s
v2p0008c1s v2p0019c2m v2p0022c2m
v2p0023c1m v2p0023c2m v2p0031c2s
v2p0032c2s v2p0036c2s v2p0040c2s
v2p0077c2s v2p0085c1s v2p0114c2s
v2p0116c2s v2p0126c1s v2p0133c2s
v2p0139c2s v2p0143c1s v2p0145c1s
v2p0146c2m v2p0169c1m v2p0178c1s
v2p0195c1s v2p0206c2s v2p0272c2s
v2p0289c1s v2p0301c2s v2p0313c1s
v2p0318c1s v2p0326c1s v2p0326c2m
v2p0337c2s v2p0341c2m v2p0351c1s
v2p0365c1s v2p0373c2s v2p0378c2s
v2p0408c2s v2p0430c2s v2p0449c1s
v2p0464c1s v2p0478c2s v2p0479c1s
v2p0481c1s v3p0017c2s v3p0067c1s
v3p0070c2s v3p0101c1s v3p0113c2s
v3p0124c2s v3p0135c2s v3p0174c2s
v3p0242c1s v3p0252c1s v3p0320c1s
v3p0328c1s v3p0372c1s v3p0373c1s
v3p0455c2s v3p0459c2s v3p0474c2s
v4p0011c1s v4p0018c1s v4p0023c2s
v4p0069c1s 'v4p0075c1s v4p0100c2s
v4p0114c1m v4p0121c1s v4p0134c1s
v4p0136c2s v4p0198c2s v4p0203c2m
v4p0208c2s v4p0262c1s v4p0297c2s
v4p0319c1s v4p0339c2s v4p0345c1s
v4p0348c2s v4p0380c2s v4p0400c2m
v4p0413c1s v4p0416c1s v4p0427c2s
v4p0435c1s v4p0463c1s v4p0480c1s
v4p0485c2s v4p0549c1s v4p0628c2s
v4p0637c2s v5p0406c2s v5p0408c1s
v5p0471c2s
Rensselaer, M.Van v1p0242c1s
v4p0361c2s v6p0498c1s v6p0573c1s
Rensselaer, M.Van et al. . v6p0532c2s
Rensselaer, S.Van, Mrs. .. v2p0332c1s
v3p0018c1s v3p0250c1s v3p0252c1s
v3p0408c2s v3p0465c1s v4p0358c2s
v4p0414c1s v5p0018c2s v5p0041c2s
v5p0087c1s v5p0209c2s v5p0268c1s
v5p0331c1s v5p0406c2s v5p0407c1s
v5p0407c2s v5p0410c1s v5p0456c2s
v5p0509c1s v5p0559c1s
Rensselaer, Schuyler Van, Mrs.
v5p0405c1s
Rensselaer, Van v6p0231c1s
Rent, G. v4p0003c2s
Renton, A.W. v4p0117c2s
v4p0236c1s v4p0284c2s v4p0311c2s
v4p0377c2s v4p0428c1s v4p0430c1s
v4p0486c1s v4p0617c2s v4p0635c1s
v5p0289c2s v5p0291c2m v5p0499c1s
Renton, D. v4p0236c2s
v5p0245c2s
Renton, J. v5p0482c1s
Rentoul, Robert R. v6p0168c2s
Renwick, J. v1p0375c2s
v1p0494c1s v1p1109c1s v1p1249c2s
v1p1306c2s
Renwick, W.H. v6p0132c2s
Renwick, W.R. v6p0240c1s
Renyon, J.B. v5p0387c2s
Renzy, J.De v5p0271c2s
Repass, S.A. v1p0440c2s
v2p0352c1s v2p0403c2s
Repington, C.A., Court ... v6p0560c1s
Replogle, M.A. v5p0622c1s
Repplier, A. v1p1257c1s
v2p0078c1s v2p0152c1m v2p0164c2s
v2p0198c1s v2p0199c2s v2p0211c2s
v2p0213c1s v2p0215c2s v2p0238c2s
v2p0254c2s v2p0332c2s v2p0380c1s
v2p0421c2s v2p0444c2s v2p0463c2s
v3p0022c1s v3p0027c1s v3p0049c2s
v3p0071c1s v3p0077c2s v3p0081c2s
v3p0099c1s v3p0105c2s v3p0127c2m
v3p0151c2s v3p0152c1m v3p0204c2s
v3p0207c2s v3p0225c2s v3p0253c1s
v3p0259c2s v3p0283c2s v3p0308c1s
v3p0328c1s v3p0334c2s v3p0376c2s
v3p0385c1s v3p0414c2s v3p0426c1s
v3p0450c1s v3p0454c1s v4p0033c2s
v4p0067c2s v4p0083c1s v4p0092c1m
v4p0185c1s v4p0197c2s v4p0216c1s
v4p0225c2s v4p0244c1s v4p0269c1s
v4p0276c2s v4p0324c2s v4p0326c1s
v4p0388c1s v4p0408c2s v4p0413c1s
v4p0415c1s v4p0425c1s v4p0448c2s
v4p0624c2s v4p0625c2s v4p0632c1s
v5p0038c2s v5p0065c2s v5p0074c1s
v5p0161c1s v5p0169c2s v5p0233c2s
v5p0456c1s v5p0635c1s
Repplier, Agnes v2p0427c1s
v4p0336c1s v4p0408c1s v4p0570c2s
v5p0204c2s v5p0369c1s v6p0011c1s
v6p0012c2s v6p0056c2s v6p0074c2s
v6p0083c2s v6p0115c2s v6p0144c1s
v6p0147c1s v6p0157c2s v6p0223c1s
v6p0249c1s v6p0284c2s v6p0301c1s
v6p0309c2s v6p0311c2s v6p0388c1s
v6p0400c2s v6p0402c2s v6p0541c2s
v6p0609c1s v6p0650c2s v6p0655c2s
v6p0664c2s v6p0673c2s
Repplier, Emma v6p0239c1s
v6p0345c2s
Repton, J.A. v1p0174c1s
v1p0334c1s v1p0424c2s v1p0464c2s
v1p0577c2m v1p1060c1s
Republican, A. and
Breckenridge, W.C.P. .. v3p0443c2s
Resor, J.H., Mrs. v6p0078c1s
Respighi, L. v1p0077c1s
v1p0382c1s v1p1268c2s
Resser, G.B. v3p0033c2s
Restelle, H. v6p0685c1s
Restelle, W. v6p0684c2s
Reston, J.T.L. v1p0485c2s
Retallack, F. v1p0828c2s
Rett, C.W. v2p0316c1s
Rettock, C.M. v5p0073c1s
v5p0140c2s v5p0477c1s v5p0494c2s
Reubelt, J.A. v1p0003c1s
v1p0047c2s v1p0058c2s v1p0117c2s
v1p0243c2s v1p0255c2s v1p0424c2s
v1p0427c2s v1p0432c1s v1p0515c2s
v1p0684c2s v1p0686c1s v1p0761c1s
v1p0775c2s v1p1098c2s v1p1101c2s
v1p1157c1s v1p1221c2s v1p1260c1s
v1p1398c2s
Reubelt, J.F. v1p0686c1s
Reuben, L. v1p0060c2s
v1p0384c2s v1p1308c1s
Reuchlin, H. v1p0683c2s
Reufs, S. v1p0119c1s
Reunert, T. v5p0007c2s
Reusch, H. v3p0276c1s
Reusch, Prof. v1p0497c2s
Reuss, E. v1p0131c1s
Reuss, E.W.E. v1p0124c1s
Reutenik, H.J. v1p0117c1s
v1p0583c1s
Reuter, F. v1p0593c1s
v1p0609c1s v1p1176c1s
Reuter, Gabriele v5p0282c2s
Reuter, J.N. v5p0207c2s
Reuterdahl, A. v6p0198c2s
Reuterdahl, H. v6p0668c2s
Reuthe, G. v4p0332c1s
Reutnick, H.J. v1p1178c2s
Reutter, F. v4p0170c1s
Reveillaud, E. v2p0165c2s
Revell, W.F. v4p0365c2s
Reverchon, J. v4p0571c1s
v4p0583c2s
Revere, C. v6p0203c2s
Revere, C.T. v6p0664c2s
Revett, A. v4p0412c1s
Reville, A. v1p0018c1s
v1p0301c1s v1p0434c2s v1p0481c2s
v1p0597c1s v1p0684c1m v1p0810c2s
v1p0985c2s v1p0994c1s v1p1097c1s
v1p1159c2s v2p0106c2s v4p0111c2s
v4p0300c1s v4p0301c1s v4p0373c2s
v5p0168c2s
Reville, J. v4p0478c2s
v4p0479c1s v5p0431c1s v6p0236c2s
Reville, R. v1p0898c1s
Revillout, E. v2p0343c1s
v3p0131c2s
Revorg, E.A. v1p1111c1s
v1p1148c1s
Rew, C.A. v1p0808c2s
Rew, C.H. v1p0054c1s
Rew, P.H. v3p0006c1s
Rew, R.H. v4p0370c2s
v5p0212c2s v6p0163c2s v6p0408c1s
v6p0417c1s v6p0590c1s
Rex, A.P. v6p0189c1s
Rexford, A. v3p0087c1s
v3p0168c2s v3p0207c2s v3p0291c2s
Rexford, E.E. v1p0819c1s
v4p0414c1s v5p0023c2s v5p0041c1s
v5p0082c2s v5p0213c2s v5p0225c2s
v5p0612c1s v6p0154c1m v6p0247c1m
v6p0247c2m v6p0310c2s v6p0503c1s
v6p0679c1s
Rexford, Eben E. v6p0246c2s
v6p0476c1s v6p0502c2s v6p0503c1s
Reyall, W.S. v5p0232c2s
Reybaud, C. v1p0496c1s
Reyd, P. v4p0437c1s
v5p0442c1m
Reyd, Penley v4p0418c2s
v5p0379c2s v5p0547c1s
Reyer, E. v2p0284c2s
v2p0441c2s v4p0038c2s v4p0052c1s
v4p0165c2s v6p0375c1s
Reyes, R. v6p0138c1s
v6p0377c1s
Reymann, O.C. v5p0452c2s
Reymond, E.Du.B. v2p0112c1s
Reymond, E.Du-Bois v1p0259c2s
Reynal, C. v6p0464c1s
Reynal, Carlotta v5p0507c2s
v5p0527c1s v6p0380c1s v6p0441c2s
Reynaud, A. v6p0177c2s
v6p0496c1s v6p0548c1s
Reynaud, G. v4p0443c1s
Reynegom, F.W.Van v1p1370c2s
Reynier, E. v1p0399c2s
v2p0036c2s
Reynold, M. v5p0562c1s
Reynolds, A. v3p0396c2s
Reynolds, A.M. v5p0045c2s
v5p0326c1s v5p0377c1s
Reynolds, C. v5p0011c1s
v5p0084c2s v5p0214c1s v5p0620c1s
Reynolds, Cuyler v5p0485c1s
Reynolds, D.S. v2p0071c1s
Reynolds, E. v1p0438c1s
v1p1005c1s v1p1007c1s
Reynolds, E.A. v3p0093c1s
Reynolds, E.C. v2p0359c2s
v4p0569c1s
Reynolds, E.F. v6p0028c1s
v6p0032c2s v6p0090c2s
Reynolds, E.V. v2p0100c1s
v3p0337c1s v4p0224c2s
Reynolds, E.W. v1p0085c2s

v1p0218c1s v1p0241c1s v1p0244c1s
v1p0248c2s v1p0254c1s v1p0587c2s
v1p0847c1s v1p1044c1s v1p1302c2s
v1p1344c2s v1p1355c2s v1p1387c1s
Reynolds, Elizabeth v5p0053c1s
Reynolds, F.W. v3p0092c2s
Reynolds, G. v1p0003c2s
v1p0150c2s v1p0152c1s v1p0167c2s
v1p0189c1s v1p0217c1s v1p0287c2s
v1p0482c2s v1p0492c2s v1p0547c1s
v1p0638c1s v1p0676c1s v1p0833c2s
v1p0972c1s v1p1005c1s v1p1038c1s
v1p1042c2s v1p1094c1s v1p1301c1s
v1p1301c2s v1p1310c1s v1p1355c1s
v2p0219c1s v3p0127c1s
Reynolds, G.G. v1p0254c2s
v4p0629c1s
Reynolds, H. v1p0863c1s
v5p0589c2s
Reynolds, H.L. v3p0283c1s
Reynolds, H.L., jr. v3p0277c1s
Reynolds, H.M. v4p0570c1s
Reynolds, H.R. v3p0281c1s
v4p0020c1s v4p0109c2s
Reynolds, H.R. and Conder, E.R.
v1p1118c1s
Reynolds, H.R., jr. v2p0373c2s
Reynolds, H.W. v2p0334c2s
Reynolds, Isabel M. v6p0349c1s
Reynolds, J. v1p0261c1s
v2p0083c2s v2p0103c2s
Reynolds, J.B. v2p0481c2s
v4p0451c2s v4p0535c1s v5p0350c1s
Reynolds, J.C. v1p0322c2s
v2p0191c1s v2p0413c2s v2p0455c2s
Reynolds, J.E. v1p0225c1s
v4p0217c1s
Reynolds, J.E. and Haughton, S.
v1p1390c1s
Reynolds, J.H. v1p0557c1s
v1p0705c1s v1p0862c2s
Reynolds, J.H. et al. v5p0570c1s
Reynolds, J.L. v1p1204c2s
Reynolds, J.N. v1p0856c2s
Reynolds, J.P. v1p0154c2s
v1p0771c1s
Reynolds, J.W. v3p0145c2s
v3p0209c1s v3p0275c2s v3p0281c2s
v3p0416c1s
Reynolds, L. v2p0411c1s
Reynolds, M.J. v6p0155c1s
v6p0209c2s v6p0483c2s
Reynolds, M.T. v4p0009c2s
v4p0024c1s v4p0266c2s v5p0495c2s
Reynolds, M.W. v1p0638c2s
v2p0240c2s
Reynolds, Minnie J. v6p0069c2s
Reynolds, O. v1p1074c2s
v1p0017c1s v1p0111c1s v1p0408c1s
v1p0463c1s v1p0491c1s v1p0565c1s
v1p0812c1s v1p1079c1s v1p1080c2s
v1p1081c1s v1p1082c2s v1p1181c2s
v1p1246c2s v1p1252c2s v1p1378c2s
v1p1416c2s v2p0118c2m v2p0141c1s
v2p0163c1m v2p0268c1s v2p0364c1s
v2p0419c1s v2p0438c1m v2p0463c2s
v2p0467c1m v3p0137c1s v3p0272c2s
Reynolds, O. and Moorby, W.H.
v5p0260c1s
Reynolds, R.D. v2p0043c2s
Reynolds, T. v5p0052c1s
Reynolds, T.C. v1p0777c1m
v1p1205c1s
Reynolds, T.T. v3p0383c1s
Reynolds, W. v1p1085c2s
v2p0251c1s v3p0345c1s v6p0049c1s
v6p0073c1s
Reynolds, W.G. v1p0827c2s
Reynolds, W.G. and Gooch, F.A.
v4p0514c1s
Reynolds, W.J. v4p0142c1s
v6p0219c2s
Reynolds, W.M. v1p0010c2s
v1p0121c1s v1p0124c2s v1p0132c1s
v1p0229c2m v1p0238c2s v1p0239c2s
v1p0247c1s v1p0254c1m v1p0361c1s
v1p0394c2s v1p0432c2s v1p0513c1s
v1p0620c1m v1p0620c2m v1p0777c1s
v1p0777c2m v1p0778c1m v1p0778c2m
v1p0806c1s v1p0847c1s v1p0976c1s
v1p0981c1s v1p1155c1s v1p1274c2s
v1p1279c2s v1p1342c2s
Reynolds-Ball, E. v6p0313c1s
v6p0499c2s v6p0580c1s
v6p0639c2s
Reynolds-Ball, E.A. v5p0111c1s
v5p0525c1s v6p0098c1s
Reynolds-Stephens, W. v5p0137c1s
v6p0579c2s
Rhea, F.M. v1p0972c2s
Rhea, H. v6p0011c2s
Rhead, F. v5p0462c1s
Rhead, L. v6p0056c1s
v6p0227c2s v6p0565c2s v6p0658c1m
Rhead, L.J. v4p0454c2s
Rhees, J. v1p1212c1s
Rhees, R. v5p0059c1s
v5p0398c2s v6p0060c2s v6p0644c2s
Rhees, R. and Butler, H.M.
v6p0136c1s
Rhees, W.J. v5p0044c1s
Rhett, C. v2p0196c2s
v2p0293c1s v2p0299c1s
Rhett, E.B. v1p1343c2s
Rhett, R.B. v1p0538c2s
v2p0098c1s
Rhett, R.B., Sen. v1p1353c1s
Rhiel, H. v5p0215c2s
Rhind, A.H. v1p0010c1s
Rhine, A.B. v6p0262c1s
Rhine, A.H. v1p0267c1s
v1p0752c2s v1p1158c2s v2p0068c1s
v2p0396c1s v3p0230c2s v3p0470c2s
Rhineheart, J.B. v4p0417c1s
Rhoades, H.E. v6p0333c2s
Rhoades, J. v5p0418c1s
v6p0150c2s
Rhoades, J.H. and Bland, R.P.
v4p0524c1s
Rhoades, L.A. v6p0069c1s
v6p0259c2s v6p0699c1s
Rhoades, W.C. v6p0062c1s
v6p0200c2s v6p0344c1s v6p0589c2s
Rhoads, E. v6p0120c1s
Rhoads, J.E. v3p0213c2s
Rhoads, S.N. v2p0387c2s
v2p0449c1s v3p0045c2m v4p0271c1s
v4p0351c2s v4p0486c2m v5p0646c2s
v6p0415c1s
Rhoda, F. v2p0253c1s
Rhodes, A. v1p0002c2s
v1p0031c2s v1p0049c2s v1p0089c2s
v1p0106c2s v1p0113c2s v1p0138c2s
v1p0200c2s v1p0235c1s v1p0282c1s
v1p0291c2s v1p0320c1s v1p0359c1s
v1p0397c1s v1p0412c2s v1p0450c1s
v1p0465c2s v1p0471c2s v1p0479c2m
v1p0481c1m v1p0487c2s v1p0488c1s
v1p0489c2m v1p0490c1s v1p0490c2s
v1p0503c2s v1p0522c2s v1p0565c1s
v1p0597c2s v1p0677c1s v1p0682c2s
v1p0709c2s v1p0717c2s v1p0751c2s
v1p0803c1s v1p0804c1s v1p0958c1s
v1p0967c2m v1p0969c2s v1p0970c2s
v1p1103c1s v1p1151c2s v1p1263c2s
v1p1265c2s v1p1292c2s v1p1299c2s
v1p1348c2s v1p1369c1s v1p1415c1s
v1p1423c1s v5p0460c1s
Rhodes, C.A. v5p0243c1s
Rhodes, C.D. v4p0352c2s
v4p0475c1s v5p0271c1s v5p0467c1s
v5p0599c1s v6p0105c1s v6p0666c1s
Rhodes, C.D. and Powell, J.W.
v6p0666c2s
Rhodes, E. v1p1084c2s
v4p0025c2s v4p0470c2s v5p0051c1s
v5p0279c1s v5p0337c2s v6p0394c1s
Rhodes, E.H. v2p0116c2s
v2p0441c2s
Rhodes, E.M. v5p0633c1s
v6p0291c2s
Rhodes, Elsie v4p0418c1s
Rhodes, Eugene M. v6p0604c1s
Rhodes, F.S. v5p0269c2s
Rhodes, G.M. v3p0464c1s
Rhodes, G.W. v6p0599c1s
Rhodes, H.G. v6p0310c2s
v6p0385c1s
Rhodes, Harrison v6p0378c1s
Rhodes, J.A. v5p0538c2s
Rhodes, J.F. v2p0089c1s
v2p0099c1m v2p0154c1s v2p0203c2s
v2p0454c1s v4p0346c2s v4p0433c2s
v5p0145c1s v5p0232c2s v5p0266c2s
v5p0525c2s v6p0139c2s v6p0247c2s
v6p0515c1s
Rhodes, L.R. v6p0388c2s
Rhodes, M. v2p0258c1s
v3p0278c1s v4p0169c1s
Rhodes, O.B. v3p0091c2s
Rhodes, T. v4p0554c2s
Rhodes, W.E. v4p0318c1s
v5p0299c1s
Rhodes, W.H. v1p0534c1s
v1p0608c2s v1p0959c2s
Rhone, Rosamond D. v6p0133c1s
Rhoscomyl, O. v4p0148c2s
Rhymer-Jones, T.M. v2p0478c2s
Rhyn, G.A.F.Van v1p0322c1s
v1p0776c1s v1p1201c1s
Rhys, E. v2p0092c1s
v3p0097c2s v3p0243c1s v4p0094c1s
v4p0340c2s v4p0635c1s v5p0354c2s
v5p0397c1s v5p0629c1s v6p0263c2s
v6p0307c2s v6p0345c2s v6p0610c1s
v6p0629c1s v6p0683c2s
Rhys, E. and Abbey, E.A. . v6p0587c2m
Rhys, G. v6p0110c1s
Rhys, J. v2p0024c1s
v2p0036c1s v2p0142c1s v2p0160c2s
v2p0320c1s v3p0055c1m v3p0071c2m
v3p0076c1s v3p0166c1s v3p0351c2s
v3p0365c2s v3p0381c2s v4p0091c2s
v4p0205c1s v4p0352c2s v4p0411c1m
v4p0434c2s v4p0609c1s v6p0397c2s
Rhys, J. and Hager, H. ... v2p0249c1s
Rhys, J. and Higgins, T.W.E.
v4p0200c2s
Rhys, John v3p0148c1s
Rhys, Rhys ap v3p0094c2s
Rhys-Davids, C.A.F. v5p0285c1s
Rhys-Davids, T.W. v2p0404c1s
v6p0086c1m v6p0122c2s
Rhysaght, S. v2p0225c1s
Riale, F.N. v3p0357c2s
v4p0102c2s v4p0478c2s v5p0484c1s
Rialle, M.G.De v4p0435c2s
Riano, E.Gayangos de v5p0350c1s
Riano, J.F. v2p0413c1m
v3p0403c1m v4p0540c1m
Ribaux, Adolphe v5p0355c1s
Ribbentrop, B. v2p0162c2s
Ribblesdale, C.Lady v6p0258c1s
Ribblesdale, Lord v2p0337c2s
v3p0098c2s v3p0172c2s v3p0220c2s
v3p0322c1s v4p0077c2s v4p0266c1s
Ribchester, J. v4p0225c1s
Ribot, T. v1p1000c2s
v4p0036c2m v4p0130c1s v4p0168c1s
v4p0179c2s v4p0246c1s v4p0364c2s
v4p0421c1s v4p0436c1m v4p0436c2m
v4p0447c1s v4p0622c1s v5p0021c1s
v5p0107c1s v5p0280c1s v5p0545c1m
v5p0545c2m
Ricalton, J. v3p0015c2s
v3p0019c1s v3p0144c2s v3p0307c2s
v3p0409c2s v3p0435c2s
Ricarde-Seaver, F.I. v4p0006c1s
v4p0065c1s v4p0154c2s v4p0582c1s
Ricarde-Seaver, F.I. and
Metcalfe, C., Sir v3p0004c2s
Ricardo, D. v4p0143c2s
Ricardo, F. v2p0460c1s
Ricardo, H. v4p0150c2s
v5p0139c2s v6p0646c2s
Ricardo, Halsey v5p0120c1s
v5p0165c2s
Ricci, G.S. v4p0092c1s
Riccio, V. v4p0140c2s
Ricco, A. v2p0095c1s
v2p0417c1s v2p0426c2s v2p0463c1s
v6p0497c1s
Ricco, A. and Mercalli, E.
v4p0553c2s
Rice, A.F. v4p0620c2s
Rice, A.H. v6p0400c1s
v6p0441c2s v6p0569c2s v6p0604c2s
v6p0698c1s
Rice, A.H. et al. v6p0074c2s
Rice, A.T. v1p0212c2s
v1p0758c2s v1p0958c1s v2p0032c2s
v2p0089c1s v2p0115c1s v2p0184c2s
v2p0259c1s v3p0101c2s v3p0162c2s
v3p0179c2s v3p0260c1s v3p0296c1s
v3p0441c2s
Rice, A.T. et al. v3p0420c2s
Rice, B. v1p0124c2s
Rice, B.E. v6p0466c1s
Rice, Beatrice E. v6p0069c1s
Rice, C. v4p0247c2s
v6p0370c1s
Rice, C.B. v1p0529c1s
v4p0129c1s v4p0219c1s
Rice, C.E. and Nakamura, K.
v6p0086c1s
Rice, C.H. v4p0558c2s
Rice, C.I. v5p0394c1s
v5p0394c2s
Rice, E.D. v1p0870c2s
Rice, E.G. v3p0474c1s
v5p0541c1m
Rice, E.J. v3p0294c2s
v4p0259c1s
Rice, E.W. v3p0318c1s
Rice, F., jr. v6p0187c1s
v6p0450c1s v6p0660c2s
Rice, F.P. v6p0052c2s
v6p0294c1s
Rice, F.S. v5p0368c1s
Rice, G.E. v1p1382c2s
v1p1418c1s
Rice, H. v1p0748c2s
v2p0013c2s v2p0031c2s v2p0062c1s
v2p0069c2s v2p0088c2s v2p0334c1s
v2p0359c2s v2p0365c1s v2p0471c1m
v3p0061c1s v3p0063c2s
Rice, H.C.P. v2p0039c2s
Rice, H.G. v1p0474c1s
v1p0490c1s v1p0797c2s v1p1086c2s
v1p1263c2s v1p1283c2s v1p1323c1s
v1p1396c2s
Rice, H.J. v1p0035c2s
Rice, Herbert L. v6p0037c1s
v6p0174c1s
Rice, I.L. v2p0255c1s
v2p0407c2s v2p0452c1s v3p0054c1s
v3p0353c1s v4p0131c1s v4p0135c1s
v4p0471c1s v4p0525c1s v4p0602c1s
Rice, I.L. and White, A.D.
v4p0596c1s
Rice, I.L. et al. v4p0601c2s
Rice, I.M. v5p0446c1s
Rice, Isaac L., Mrs. v6p0458c2s
Rice, J. and Besant, W. .. v1p0181c2s
v1p0199c1s v1p0674c1s v1p0861c2s
v1p0888c1s v1p0952c2s v1p1085c2s
v1p1174c1s v1p1264c1s v1p1306c1s
v1p1418c1s v2p0008c1s v2p0067c2s
v4p0511c2s
Rice, J.E. v6p0512c1s

v6p0637c1s v6p0661c2s
Rice, J.H. v1p0244c1s
v1p0848c1s v1p1046c2s v1p1262c1s
Rice, J.L. v2p0247c2s
v2p0311c2s v2p0318c1s v2p0363c1s
v2p0459c2s
Rice, J.M. v3p0377c2s
v4p0043c1s v4p0078c1s v4p0114c1s
v4p0169c2s v4p0281c2s v4p0400c2s
v4p0441c2s v4p0466c1m v4p0466c2m
v4p0499c1s v4p0505c2m v4p0554c1s
v4p0566c1s v4p0571c1s v4p0582c2s
v5p0177c1s v5p0222c2s v5p0399c1s
v5p0399c2s v5p0545c2s v5p0569c2m
v6p0030c1m v6p0193c1s v6p0194c1s
v6p0194c2m v6p0361c1s v6p0367c1s
v6p0443c1s v6p0635c2s
Rice, M.E. et al. v5p0537c2s
Rice, R. v6p0697c1s
Rice, R.R. and Foshay, P.M.
v3p0173c2s
Rice, S. v1p1027c1s
Rice, T.S. v6p0618c1s
Rice, W. v3p0249c1s
v5p0020c1s v5p0108c2s v5p0110c2s
v5p0164c1s v5p0374c1s v5p0408c2s
v5p0428c2s v5p0445c2s v5p0508c2s
v6p0029c1s v6p0294c2s v6p0307c1s
v6p0354c2s v6p0366c1s v6p0494c1s
v6p0550c2s v6p0557c1s v6p0572c2s
v6p0674c1s
Rice, W.A. v6p0704c2s
Rice, W.de Groot v5p0405c2s
v5p0484c1s
Rice, W.E. v6p0612c1s
Rice, W.G. v4p0116c2s
v4p0144c2s
Rice, W.H. v1p1191c1s
Rice, W.N. v1p0333c2s
v1p1399c1s v2p0153c1s v2p0179c1s
v3p0380c2m v4p0301c1s v4p0508c1s
v5p0023c2s v5p0514c2s v6p0692c1s
Rice, W.P. v2p0246c2s
Rice, W.S. v6p0090c1s
v6p0503c1s v6p0506c1s v6p0548c2s
v6p0627c2s
Rice, Wallace v6p0113c2s
Rice, Wm.S. v6p0260c1s
Rice, Wolff v6p0580c2s
Rich, A.B. v1p0019c2s
v1p0118c1s v1p0581c2s v1p1292c1s
v1p1399c2s
Rich, A.C. v6p0255c2s
Rich, A.H. v4p0425c1s
v4p0566c1s
Rich, A.J. v3p0173c1s
Rich, Alice H. v5p0396c1s
Rich, B.A. v5p0034c2s
Rich, C. v1p0748c2s
Rich, C.A. v3p0403c1s
v4p0025c1s v4p0040c1s v5p0026c2s
v5p0382c2s v5p0501c2s
Rich, E. v2p0301c2s
Rich, E.J. v6p0032c1s
v6p0114c1s
Rich, G. v3p0102c1s
v4p0234c1s
Rich, G.A. v4p0068c1s
v4p0200c2m v4p0214c2s v4p0324c1s
v4p0585c2s
Rich, H. v1p0733c1s
v1p0963c2s v1p1204c1s v1p1310c1s
v1p1363c1s v2p0015c2s
Rich, H., Sir v1p1036c2s
Rich, M.N. v6p0509c2s
Rich, R. v2p0461c2s
Rich, S.W. v3p0009c2s
v3p0386c1s
Rich, T.H. v3p0113c1s
Richard, E. v6p0684c2s
Richard, H. v1p1306c2s
v2p0084c2s v2p0315c2s
Richard, J.A. v2p0097c1s
Richard, J.H. v6p0125c2s
Richard, J.W. v1p0117c2s
v1p0230c1s v1p0390c1s v1p0846c2s
v1p1162c2s v1p1214c1s v2p0044c1s
v2p0235c1s v2p0351c2s v2p0357c1s
v3p0229c2s v3p0254c2s v3p0258c2m
v3p0261c1m v3p0342c1s v3p0349c1s
v3p0476c2s v4p0021c1s v4p0128c2s
v4p0345c1m v4p0345c2m v4p0497c2s
v5p0038c1s v5p0182c2s v5p0351c1s
v5p0369c1s v5p0469c1s v6p0094c1s
v6p0176c1s v6p0176c2s v6p0193c2s
v6p0240c2s v6p0348c2s v6p0514c1s
v6p0520c2s
Richard, L.S. v4p0134c2s
Richard, T. v6p0118c1s
v6p0118c2s
Richards and Mather v1p1289c2s
Richards, A.B. v1p0583c2s
Richards, A.E. v2p0024c2s
v2p0036c1s v2p0422c1s
Richards, Ap v3p0119c1s
Richards, B. v6p0405c2s
Richards, B.G. v6p0713c1s
Richards, Burton v6p0084c2s
Richards, C.A.L. v3p0093c2s
v3p0130c2s v3p0387c1s v3p0409c1s
v3p0454c2s v4p0022c2s v4p0052c1s
v4p0081c1s v4p0111c1s v4p0116c1s
v4p0186c1s v4p0213c1s v4p0218c1s
v4p0468c1s v4p0545c1s v5p0078c2s
v5p0311c1s v5p0633c2s
Richards, C.B. v1p0017c1s
v1p0829c2s v1p1255c2s
Richards, C.H. v6p0213c2s
v6p0386c2s
Richards, C.R. v5p0137c2s
Richards, C.W. v6p0368c1s
Richards, E. v3p0003c1s
v3p0040c1s v3p0061c2s v3p0157c1m
v3p0311c2m
Richards, E.A. v6p0647c2s
Richards, E.H. v4p0132c1s
v4p0398c2s
Richards, E.H. and Jordan, E.O.
v3p0306c1s
Richards, E.J. v2p0119c2s
Richards, E.L. v2p0027c1s
v2p0092c2s v2p0150c1s v2p0161c1s
v2p0174c1s v3p0025c2s v3p0474c1s
v4p0170c2s v4p0206c2s v4p0223c1s
v4p0609c1s
Richards, E.S. v4p0441c1s
Richards, Ellen H. v5p0423c2s
Richards, F. v4p0008c2s
v4p0288c2s v5p0409c1s v5p0609c1s
Richards, F.B. v6p0646c1s
Richards, F.H. v5p0320c2s
v5p0353c2s
Richards, F.T. v2p0017c1s
v2p0049c1s v2p0147c1s v2p0190c1s
v2p0377c1s v2p0429c2m v3p0334c1s
v3p0339c2s v3p0366c2s v3p0475c2s
v4p0109c1s
Richards, G. v1p0328c1s
v1p0815c1s v4p0148c2s v4p0618c2s
Richards, G.C. v4p0035c1s
v4p0478c1s v4p0600c2m
Richards, G.D. v6p0346c2s
v6p0499c1s
Richards, G.M. v6p0357c2s
v6p0684c1s
Richards, G.N. v1p0348c2s
v1p1034c2s
Richards, G.R. v1p1034c1s
v6p0399c2s
Richards, G.S.S. v1p0987c2s
v1p1218c2s v1p1374c2s
Richards, G.W. v5p0060c2s
v5p0201c2s v5p0463c2s v5p0468c2s
v5p0562c1s v6p0538c1s v6p0554c2s
Richards, G.W. et al. v6p0376c1s
Richards, H. v1p0249c1s
v1p1356c2s v2p0021c1s v2p0190c2s
v2p0347c2s v5p0257c1s v6p0383c2s
Richards, H.C. v1p0543c2s
v1p1022c1s v2p0256c1s v6p0179c1s
v6p0379c1s
Richards, H.E. v4p0060c2s
v6p0403c1s v6p0472c1s
Richards, H.L. v2p0451c2s
Richards, H.L., jr. v3p0035c2s
v3p0303c2s
Richards, H.M. v3p0158c1s
v6p0077c2s
Richards, H.M.M. v4p0214c2s
v4p0616c2s
Richards, H.S. v1p0728c1s
v6p0151c1s v6p0518c2s
Richards, J. v1p0310c1s
v1p0365c1s v1p0402c1s v1p0408c1s
v1p0503c1s v1p0536c2s v1p0688c2s
v1p0815c1s v1p0840c2s v1p0884c2s
v1p0978c2s v1p1427c2s v4p0012c2s
v4p0600c1s v4p0613c2m v5p0161c1s
v5p0289c2s v5p0328c2s v5p0353c2s
v5p0510c1m v5p0621c2s v5p0639c2s
Richards, J.B. v2p0179c2s
v2p0180c1m
Richards, J.K. v5p0600c1s
v6p0019c2s
Richards, J.W. v2p0428c1s
v3p0009c2s v3p0156c1s v4p0012c2m
v4p0177c1m v4p0230c1s v4p0366c2s
v4p0524c1s v5p0014c1m v5p0089c1s
v5p0103c2s v5p0150c2s v5p0185c2s
v5p0226c2s v5p0238c1m v5p0371c2s
v5p0377c2s v5p0381c2s v6p0199c2m
v6p0390c1s v6p0688c1s
Richards, J.W. and Thomson, J.A.
v5p0014c1s
Richards, J.W. and Trowbridge, J.
v5p0185c2s
Richards, L. v2p0372c1s
Richards, L.F. v5p0169c2s
Richards, L.N. v6p0386c1s
Richards, L.P. v6p0069c1s
v6p0367c2s v6p0392c1s
Richards, Laura E. v6p0608c1s
Richards, M.H. v2p0438c2s
v3p0088c1s v3p0238c2s v3p0265c2s
v3p0316c1s v3p0424c1s v4p0109c1s
v4p0229c1s v4p0273c2s v4p0314c2s
v4p0534c2s v5p0133c2s
Richards, M.T. v3p0214c1s
Richards, O.W. and Johnson, R.A.
v5p0426c1s
Richards, R. v6p0072c1s
Richards, R.C. v3p0241c2s
Richards, R.H. v2p0229c1m
v3p0375c1s v4p0366c2s
Richards, R.W. v6p0107c2s
Richards, S. v2p0415c1s
Richards, S.C. v4p0300c1s
Richards, St.J. v6p0636c2s
Richards, St.John v6p0211c1s
Richards, T.A. v1p0006c2m
v1p0198c1s v1p0207c2s v1p0292c2s
v1p0511c1s v1p0611c1s v1p0667c1s
v1p0698c2s v1p0913c1s v1p0916c1m
v1p1106c1s v1p1151c2s v1p1223c2s
v1p1273c1s v1p1412c1s
Richards, T.C. v6p0418c1s
Richards, T.H. v1p0930c1s
Richards, T.W. v5p0104c1s
v5p0537c2s v6p0307c2s v6p0491c2s
Richards, T.W. and Trowbridge, J.
v5p0027c2s v5p0227c1s
Richards, W. v4p0577c1s
v5p0278c1s v5p0316c1s v5p0396c2s
v5p0606c2s v6p0587c1s
Richards, W. and Trowbridge, J.
v5p0227c1s
Richards, W.C. v1p0239c1s
v1p0309c1s v1p1234c1s v2p0356c2s
v3p0262c2s v3p0294c1s
Richards, W.J.B. v3p0103c1s
v6p0192c1s
Richards, W.R. v6p0128c2s
Richards, Z. v1p0353c2s
v1p1288c1s v2p0354c1s v4p0354c2s
v4p0607c1s
Richardson, A. v3p0371c2s
v4p0403c2s
Richardson, A.C. v2p0087c2s
Richardson, A.D. v1p0235c1s
v1p0845c2s v1p0855c1s v1p1389c2s
Richardson, A.J. v6p0193c2s
v6p0445c1s
Richardson, A.S. v1p0236c1s
v1p0511c2s v1p0801c2s v1p1183c2s
v2p0119c1s v3p0120c2s
Richardson, A.T. v6p0711c1s
Richardson, B.B. v6p0361c2s
Richardson, B.W. v1p0019c2m
v1p0043c1s v1p0076c1s v1p0157c1s
v1p0177c1s v1p0229c2s v1p0237c1s
v1p0237c2s v1p0273c2s v1p0295c1s
v1p0338c1m v1p0354c1s v1p0356c1s
v1p0366c2s v1p0426c1m v1p0432c1s
v1p0445c2s v1p0491c2s v1p0542c1s
v1p0554c2s v1p0567c1s v1p0573c2s
v1p0577c2s v1p0578c1m v1p0578c2s
v1p0707c2s v1p0732c2s v1p0746c1s
v1p0881c2s v1p0892c1s v1p0896c2s
v1p0955c2s v1p0977c1s v1p1087c2s
v1p1150c2m v1p1209c2s v1p1254c1s
v1p1269c2s v1p1289c1s v1p1376c1s
v1p1393c1s v1p1415c1s v1p1415c2s
v1p1421c1s v2p0013c1s v2p0015c1s
v2p0100c2s v2p0110c2s v2p0196c1s
v2p0198c2s v2p0199c1s v2p0203c2s
v2p0258c1s v2p0361c2s v2p0386c1s
v2p0446c1s v2p0446c2s v2p0477c1s
v3p0007c2s v3p0129c1s v3p0157c1s
v3p0172c2s v3p0192c1m v3p0218c1s
v3p0250c2s v3p0265c1s v3p0272c2s
v3p0280c1s v3p0297c2s v3p0350c1s
v3p0375c1m v3p0426c2s v3p0433c2s
v3p0434c1s v3p0472c1s v4p0016c2s
v4p0035c2s v4p0036c1s v4p0145c2s
v4p0502c2s v4p0529c1s
Richardson, B.W., Sir v4p0331c1s
v4p0409c2s v4p0502c2s v4p0568c1s
Richardson, C. v1p1110c2s
v4p0387c1s v4p0429c1s v6p0491c1s
v6p0576c1s
Richardson, C.F. v1p0190c2s
v1p0817c2s v2p0011c2s v2p0092c2s
v2p0254c2s v2p0305c1s v2p0317c2s
v2p0474c2s v3p0012c1s v3p0313c1s
v4p0015c1s v4p0017c2s v4p0066c2s
v4p0130c2s v4p0595c1s v6p0504c2s
Richardson, C.J. v1p0995c2s
Richardson, C.Morgan v5p0324c1s
Richardson, C.W.G. v5p0388c1s
Richardson, D. v6p0287c2s
Richardson, D.S. v2p0056c1s
v2p0158c2s v2p0360c1s v2p0442c1s
v3p0072c2s v3p0124c1s v3p0339c1s
v6p0414c1s v6p0414c2s
Richardson, Dorothy v5p0272c2s
v6p0705c2s
Richardson, E.A. v5p0634c2s
Richardson, E.A. et al. .. v5p0388c2s
Richardson, E.C. v2p0141c1s
v2p0255c2s v2p0256c1m v2p0256c2s
v2p0257c1s v2p0437c2s v3p0028c2s
v3p0248c2s v3p0249c1s v3p0250c1s
v4p0118c2s v4p0330c1s v5p0070c1s
v5p0071c1s v5p0114c2s v5p0122c1s
v5p0333c2s v5p0334c2s v5p0636c1s
v6p0065c2s v6p0075c1s v6p0213c2s
v6p0370c2s v6p0371c1s v6p0373c2s
v6p0375c1s
Richardson, E.H. v6p0178c1s
Richardson, E.S.L. v1p1106c2s

Richardson, Ernest C. v6p0373c2s
Richardson, F. v1p1408c2s
v5p0114c2s v5p0416c1s v6p0055c1s
v6p0161c2s v6p0505c2s v6p0565c1s
Richardson, F.D. v2p0432c1s
Richardson, F.T. v1p1440c2s
Richardson, G. v5p0228c1s
v6p0485c1s v6p0591c1s v6p0625c1s
Richardson, G. and Slosson, E.E.
v6p0476c2m v6p0477c1m v6p0477c2s
v6p0630c2s
Richardson, G.A. v5p0290c2s
Richardson, G.L. v5p0539c1s
Richardson, G.H. v6p0131c2s
Richardson, H. v6p0075c2s
Richardson, H.D. v4p0218c2s
v6p0029c2s
Richardson, H.H. v2p0012c2s
v2p0316c1s v4p0069c1s v6p0027c1s
Richardson, H.J. v1p0687c2s
Richardson, H.M. v5p0516c1s
Richardson, H.S. v1p0805c1s
Richardson, H.W. v1p0092c2s
v1p0342c2s v2p0032c2s v2p0064c2s
v2p0091c2s v2p0180c1s v3p0276c2s
Richardson, Helen E. v6p0089c2s
Richardson, Hugh v6p0082c2s
Richardson, J. v1p0424c1s
v1p0437c1s v1p0455c1s v1p0906c2s
v1p0915c2s v1p0917c1s v1p0919c2s
v1p0945c1s v1p0955c2s v1p0978c2s
v1p1015c1s v1p1061c2s v1p1234c1s
v1p1432c2s v2p0446c1s v4p0317c1s
v6p0032c2s
Richardson, J., jr. v1p0581c1s
Richardson, J., Sir v1p0484c1s
Richardson, J.B. v5p0032c1s
v5p0124c2s v5p0252c2s
Richardson, J.D. v2p0069c2s
v5p0460c2s
Richardson, J.E. v1p0584c1s
Richardson, J.H. v3p0071c1s
v3p0381c2s v3p0413c1s v4p0287c1s
v6p0202c2s v6p0430c1s v6p0474c1s
Richardson, J.L. v3p0016c1s
v3p0084c1s v3p0177c2s
Richardson, J.M. v1p0099c2s
v1p0161c1s v1p0429c1s v1p0583c2s
v1p1076c1s v1p1325c2s v3p0146c1s
v3p0422c1s v4p0262c2s v4p0566c2s
Richardson, J.M. and Welch, L.B.
v2p0352c1s
Richardson, J.W. v6p0216c1s
v6p0322c1s
Richardson, L. v3p0437c1s
v4p0517c2s
Richardson, L.J. v6p0671c2s
Richardson, L.P. v1p0139c2s
Richardson, L.S. v1p0842c1s
Richardson, M. v1p0201c2m
v1p0319c2s v2p0074c2s v4p0198c2s
v4p0266c2s v4p0386c2s v4p0489c2s
Richardson, M., Mrs. v4p0032c2s
v4p0574c2s
Richardson, M.C. v6p0646c1s
Richardson, M.E. v6p0427c1s
Richardson, M.L. v1p1190c1s
Richardson, M.M. v3p0209c2s
Richardson, Margaret F. .. v6p0224c2s
Richardson, Mary K. v6p0409c2s
Richardson, N.S. v1p0031c1s
v1p0031c2s v1p0048c1m v1p0052c2s
v1p0097c1s v1p0110c1s v1p0217c2s
v1p0241c2s v1p0250c2m v1p0254c2s
v1p0255c2s v1p0275c2s v1p0313c2s
v1p0378c2s v1p0379c1s v1p0422c1m
v1p0422c2m v1p0432c1s v1p0487c1s
v1p0573c1s v1p0575c1s v1p0673c2s
v1p0679c2s v1p0683c1s v1p0704c2s
v1p0756c2s v1p0769c2s v1p0852c2s
v1p0853c1s v1p0870c1s v1p0881c1s
v1p0910c1s v1p0916c1m v1p0950c2s
v1p0964c1s v1p0994c1s v1p1000c2s
v1p1033c1s v1p1033c2s v1p1046c1s
v1p1066c2m v1p1067c1s v1p1089c2s
v1p1091c1s v1p1120c2s v1p1134c1s
v1p1141c1s v1p1150c1s v1p1173c2s
v1p1209c1s v1p1224c2s v1p1229c2s
v1p1318c2s v1p1331c1s v1p1399c1s
v1p1433c2s v2p0010c2s
Richardson, N.S. v1p0289c1s
Richardson, Norval v6p0332c2s
Richardson, P. v1p0487c1s
v1p1082c1s v1p1244c2s
Richardson, R. v1p0096c1s
v1p0190c1s v1p0741c2s v5p0181c2s
v5p0493c2s v6p0578c2s
Richardson, R.B. v1p0037c2s
v1p0046c2s v1p0588c1s v2p0181c2s
v2p0450c2s v3p0039c2s v3p0262c1s
v3p0334c1s v4p0026c1s v4p0083c1s
v4p0186c2s v4p0338c1s v4p0366c1s
v4p0413c2s v4p0446c1s v4p0577c1s
v4p0579c2s v5p0004c2s v5p0137c1m
v5p0137c2s v5p0181c1s v5p0185c2s
v5p0194c2s v5p0206c2s v5p0214c2s
v5p0248c2s v5p0249c1s v5p0452c1m
v5p0516c1s v5p0528c1s v5p0573c1s
v6p0038c2s v6p0149c2m v6p0157c1s
v6p0174c2s v6p0209c2m v6p0272c2s
v6p0395c1s v6p0412c1s v6p0420c1s
v6p0500c2s v6p0570c2s v6p0598c2s
v6p0643c1m
Richardson, R.B. and Heermance, T.W.
v5p0194c2s
Richardson, R.B. et al. .. v4p0186c2m
Richardson, R.L. v5p0477c2s
Richardson, R.M. v1p0086c1s
Richardson, Rufus B. v5p0027c2s
v6p0130c1s v6p0157c1s
Richardson, S.D. v2p0233c1s
Richardson, S.F. v5p0037c1s
Richardson, T. v1p0047c1s
v3p0402c1s
Richardson, W. v6p0534c1s
Richardson, W.A. v3p0190c1m
v4p0143c2s v4p0249c1s v4p0558c2s
v5p0257c1s
Richardson, W.C. v3p0084c1s
Richardson, W.G. v4p0594c2s
Richardson, W.H. v5p0017c2s
v5p0123c2s v5p0607c1s
Richardson, W.J. v6p0593c2s
Richardson, W.L. v6p0079c1s
Richardson, W.P. v5p0374c2s
v5p0530c2s
Richardson, W.W. and Wissler, C.
v5p0389c1s
Richart, M.B.J. v4p0209c2s
Richberg, D. v6p0273c2s
v6p0631c2s
Riche, E.Le v4p0008c1s
Richel, C. v1p0621c2s
Richelieu, A.de v1p1145c2s
Richepin, J. v4p0110c2s
Richert, E. v6p0401c1s
Richet, C. v1p0237c1s
v1p0343c2s v1p0573c2s v1p0944c2s
v2p0015c1s v2p0153c2s v2p0462c2s
v3p0150c1s v3p0274c2s v3p0348c1s
v3p0407c2s v4p0394c1s v5p0435c1s
Richet, Chas. v5p0404c2s
Richey, A.G. v1p0919c2s
v1p1280c1s
Richey, T. v1p0240c2s
v1p0273c2s v2p0082c1s v2p0096c2s
v2p0277c2s v2p0290c2s v2p0439c1s
v2p0473c1s
Richings, E.A. v4p0134c1s
v4p0251c1s v4p0257c2s v4p0317c2s
v4p0376c1s v5p0009c1s v5p0010c2s
v5p0039c2s v5p0067c1s v5p0098c2s
v5p0116c1s v5p0350c2s v5p0356c2s
v5p0541c2s v5p0567c2s v6p0261c1s
v6p0319c2s v6p0329c1s v6p0336c1s
v6p0431c1s v6p0648c2s
Richman, I.B. v3p0086c1s
v3p0244c2s v4p0063c1s v4p0388c1s
Richman, J. v5p0468c1s
v5p0562c1s v6p0114c1s
Richman, Julia v5p0471c2s
v6p0312c1s
Richmond, A. v2p0013c2s
v2p0036c2s v2p0440c2s v3p0036c1s
v6p0240c2s v6p0271c1s
Richmond, A.B. v3p0105c1s
v3p0166c1s v3p0218c1s
Richmond, C.A. v4p0107c2s
v4p0129c1s
Richmond, C.L.V. v5p0470c1s
v5p0546c2s
Richmond, C.Q. v5p0003c2s
Richmond, C.W. v2p0280c1s
Richmond, D. v1p1309c2s
Richmond, E.M. v4p0536c2s
Richmond, E.T.C. v5p0253c2s
Richmond, F.H. v6p0509c2s
Richmond, G. v2p0214c1s
v4p0176c2s v4p0220c2s v5p0226c2s
v5p0482c2s
Richmond, G.S. v6p0029c2s
v6p0351c1s v6p0525c2s v6p0627c1s
Richmond, Grace S. v6p0066c1s
v6p0466c2s
Richmond, H.A. v5p0051c1s
Richmond, J.C. v1p0751c1s
Richmond, J.F. v1p0330c2s
v1p1090c2s v1p1108c2s v1p1353c1s
v1p1427c1s v2p0159c2s v4p0415c2s
Richmond, Kate v3p0193c2s
Richmond, M.E. v4p0096c2s
v4p0599c1m v5p0102c1s v5p0102c2s
v6p0321c1s
Richmond, M.W. v6p0365c1s
Richmond, Mary E. v5p0102c1m
v6p0535c1s
Richmond, W. v4p0167c1s
v5p0623c1s v6p0532c2s
Richmond, W.B. v4p0325c2s
v4p0499c2m v5p0025c1s v5p0345c1s
v5p0346c1s v6p0689c1s
Richter, C. v5p0231c1s
v5p0405c2s
Richter, E. v3p0088c2s
v4p0534c1s
Richter, E.J. v2p0147c2s
v2p0266c1s
Richter, G.E. v4p0553c1s
Richter, J.E. v2p0071c2s
Richter, J.P. v1p0776c2s
v1p1241c2s v1p1274c1s v1p1366c1s
v2p0061c2s v2p0348c2s v2p0461c1s
v3p0317c2s v3p0354c2s v4p0079c2s
v4p0393c2s v4p0399c1s v4p0421c2s
v4p0422c1s v4p0605c1s v4p0605c2s
v5p0077c2s v6p0088c2s
Richter, L.M. v6p0242c1s
v6p0689c1s v6p0695c2s
Richter, Louise M. v5p0537c2s
Richter, M.O. v3p0373c1s
Richthofen, Baron von v1p0591c1s
Richthofen, F.V. v4p0033c1s
Richthofen, F.von v1p0232c2s
v1p0233c1s v1p0233c2s v1p1035c1s
v4p0133c2s v6p0250c2s
Richthofen, F.von, Baron . v1p0508c2s
Rickaby, J. v1p0117c2s
v1p0247c1s v1p0287c1s v1p0313c1s
v1p0434c1s v1p0529c2s v1p0557c2s
v1p0760c2s v1p0793c1s v1p0839c2s
v1p0850c1m v1p0870c2s v1p1017c1m
v1p1037c2s v1p1083c2s v1p1093c2s
v1p1095c2s v1p1200c2s v1p1203c2s
v1p1301c1s v1p1302c2s v1p1303c2s
v1p1304c2s v1p1305c2s v1p1336c2s
v2p0084c2s v2p0184c1s v2p0269c2s
v2p0390c1s v2p0427c1s v2p0456c2s
v3p0057c1s v3p0070c1s v3p0082c2s
v3p0087c2m v3p0184c2s v3p0287c2s
v3p0329c2s v3p0339c1s v3p0379c2s
v4p0051c2s v4p0300c2s v5p0037c2s
v5p0097c2s v5p0132c1s v5p0279c1s
v5p0279c2s v5p0386c1s v5p0402c1s
v5p0473c1s v5p0489c2s v5p0509c2s
v5p0576c2s v5p0595c2s v5p0641c1s
v6p0032c1s v6p0040c2s v6p0045c1s
v6p0088c1s v6p0212c1s v6p0473c1s
v6p0602c1s
Rickard, J.A. v6p0419c1s
Rickard, J.L. v5p0630c1s
Rickard, T.A. v4p0140c2s
v4p0230c1m v4p0230c2s v4p0231c1m
v4p0502c1s v5p0131c2s v5p0377c2s
v6p0576c1s
Rickards, E.C. v3p0034c1s
Rickards, G.R. v1p0198c1s
Ricker, David S. v6p0574c1s
v6p0635c1s
Ricker, E.W. v3p0312c2s
Ricker, G.W. v1p1107c1s
Ricker, N.C. v2p0078c2s
v2p0178c2m v2p0318c1m
Rickert, E. v5p0077c2s
v6p0129c2s v6p0222c1s v6p0286c1s
v6p0353c2s v6p0511c2s
Rickert, Edith v6p0052c1s
v6p0091c1s v6p0264c1s v6p0483c1s
Rickett, A. v4p0141c1s
Rickett, J.C. v5p0247c1s
Ricketts, C. v5p0330c1s
v6p0034c1s
Ricketts, E.B. v4p0271c1s
Ricketts, Maj. v4p0325c1s
Ricketts, P.C. v2p0070c1s
v2p0229c1s
Rickey, A.G. and Campbell, G., Sir
v1p0657c2s
Rickey, Nellie v6p0459c2s
Rickleby, J. v1p0839c2s
Rickman, J. v1p1256c1s
Rickman, T. v1p0052c2s
Rickman, T.M. et al. v3p0059c2s
Rickmers, W.R. v5p0069c1s
Rickoff, A.J. v1p1348c2s
Rickoff, B.M. v4p0627c1s
Rickoff, R.D. v2p0275c2s
Ricord, F.W. v4p0401c2s
v4p0426c2s v4p0486c2s
Ricour, T. v1p0747c1s
Riddall, W. v4p0113c1s
Riddel, Dr. v1p1055c1s
Riddel, S.H. v1p0033c2s
v1p0909c1s v1p1261c2s
Riddell, A. v1p0957c1s
Riddell, D.L. v1p0273c1m
v1p0849c1s
Riddell, J.H. v1p1072c2s
v2p0293c1s v2p0395c1s v2p0440c1s
v5p0452c2s
Riddell, J.H., Mrs. v1p0002c2s
v1p0078c1s v1p0627c1s v1p0716c2s
v1p0746c1s v1p0889c2s v1p1177c2s
v2p0266c2s v3p0351c1s
Riddell, J.L. v1p0835c2s
v1p0938c2m
Riddell, L.C. v1p1180c2s
Riddell, R. v1p0469c1m
v1p0498c1s v1p0651c2s v1p1165c1s
v1p1299c1s
Riddell, W.B. v6p0326c2s
Riddell, W.P. v1p0597c2s
v1p1140c1s v1p1265c2s
Ridder, P.J.de v4p0623c2s
Ridding, Laura E. v5p0178c1s
Riddle, A.G. v2p0038c1s
v2p0320c1s v2p0331c2s v2p0335c1s
v2p0463c2s v3p0037c1s v3p0310c2s
Riddle, D.H. v1p0229c1s
v1p0243c2s v1p0840c1s v1p0889c2s
v1p0996c1s v1p1009c2s v1p1047c2s

v1p1101c1s v1p1417c1s
Riddle, G. v3p0427c1s
Riddle, J.L. v1p0854c2s
Riddle, J.W. v4p0219c1s
Riddle, M.B. v1p1259c2s
v4p0057c1s
Riddle, N.T. v3p0254c1s
Riddle, W. v3p0157c1s
Riddleberger, H.H. v2p0461c2s
Rideal, Dr. v6p0688c1s
Rideal, S. v4p0012c2s
v4p0199c1s v5p0212c2s v5p0521c1s
v5p0521c2s
Rideing, W.H. v1p0007c2s
v1p0065c2s v1p0179c1s v1p0223c2s
v1p0279c1s v1p0279c2s v1p0303c2s
v1p0320c2s v1p0381c2s v1p0414c2s
v1p0424c1s v1p0437c1s v1p0455c1s
v1p0538c2s v1p0606c1s v1p0607c1s
v1p0625c2s v1p0757c1s v1p0795c1s
v1p0849c1s v1p0908c1s v1p0911c2s
v1p0912c2s v1p0914c2s v1p0915c2s
v1p0916c1s v1p0916c2m v1p0917c1m
v1p0917c2s v1p0956c2s v1p1017c1s
v1p1083c1s v1p1142c1s v1p1147c1s
v1p1159c2s v1p1166c2s v1p1199c1s
v1p1227c1s v1p1245c2s v1p1319c2s
v1p1334c1s v1p1367c2s v1p1391c2s
v1p1406c2s v1p1426c2s v2p0033c1s
v2p0053c1s v2p0066c2s v2p0195c2s
v2p0251c2s v2p0263c2m v2p0282c1s
v2p0361c1s v2p0399c2s v2p0436c1m
v2p0471c1s v2p0481c2s v2p0482c1s
v3p0007c2s v3p0023c1s v3p0026c1m
v3p0136c1s v3p0191c2s v3p0198c2s
v3p0258c1s v3p0260c1s v3p0289c2s
v3p0329c1s v3p0360c2s v3p0390c2s
v3p0409c1s v3p0453c1s v3p0455c1s
v3p0463c1m v3p0465c2s v4p0120c2s
v4p0159c2s v4p0227c2s v4p0338c2s
v4p0547c2s v5p0345c2s v5p0573c1s
v6p0258c1s
Ridenour, W.E. v5p0012c2s
v5p0550c2s v6p0104c1s
Rideout, H. v6p0554c2s
Rideout, H.M. v6p0071c2s
v6p0100c1s v6p0185c2s v6p0280c1s
v6p0347c1s v6p0474c1s v6p0698c1s
Rideout, W.L. v5p0208c2s
Rider, A.H. v1p0724c1s
Rider, G.T. v2p0238c2s
v4p0088c1s
Rider, R.P. v3p0292c2s
v4p0388c2s
Rider, S.S. v3p0360c2s
Ridewood, W.G. v4p0201c1s
v4p0263c2s v4p0383c1s
Ridgaway, H.B. v1p0075c1s
v2p0403c2s
Ridge, F. v6p0175c1s
Ridge, W.P. v3p0256c2s
v4p0012c1s v4p0128c2s v4p0153c2s
v4p0375c2s v5p0153c2s v5p0188c1s
v5p0345c1s v5p0358c2s v5p0468c2s
v5p0486c1s v5p0635c2s
Ridge, W.Pett v4p0093c1s
v4p0284c1s v4p0457c2s v4p0554c2s
v5p0219c2s v5p0390c1s v5p0405c1s
Ridgely, B.H. v5p0017c2s
v5p0186c1s v5p0350c2s v5p0359c1s
v6p0020c1s v6p0382c1s v6p0397c2s
v6p0421c1s
Ridgely, Ben.H. v4p0126c2s
Ridgely, G.W. v1p0422c1s
Ridgely, W.B. v6p0051c1s
Ridgeway, W. v3p0199c2s
v3p0200c1s v3p0200c2m v3p0241c2s
v3p0419c1s v4p0235c2s v4p0242c1s
v4p0391c1s v5p0457c1s
Ridgeway, W. and Taylor, I.
v4p0143c2s
Ridgeway, W. et al. v4p0262c1s
Ridgeway, W., Sir v3p0003c2s
v6p0370c1s
Ridgway, A.R. v1p0232c2s
v1p0329c1s
Ridgway, E.J. v5p0126c2s
Ridgway, H.B. v2p0087c2s
Ridgway, R. v1p0135c1s
v1p0135c2s v1p0136c1s v1p0136c2m
v1p0137c1m v1p0953c2s v1p1379c1s
v4p0208c2s v4p0581c2s
Ridgway, T. v6p0035c1s
Ridgway, T.S. v1p0939c2s
Ridgway, W. v2p0480c2s
Ridley, H.N. v3p0151c1s
v4p0060c1s v4p0351c2s v4p0513c1s
Ridley, J.J. v1p1064c2s
Ridley, M.W. v6p0152c2s
Ridley, W. v1p0079c1m
Ridley, W.D. v5p0398c2s
Ridlon, G.T. v5p0418c2s
Ridout, C.G. v4p0049c1s
v4p0262c2s
Ridout, R.H. v1p0300c1s
v1p1177c2s
Ridpath, J.C. v3p0060c1s
v3p0076c2s v3p0115c1s v3p0143c2s
v3p0257c2s v3p0344c1s v3p0351c2s
v3p0436c1s v4p0186c2s v4p0219c2s
v4p0304c2s v4p0332c2s v4p0435c2s
v4p0593c1s v5p0019c1s v5p0019c2s
v5p0053c1s v5p0080c2s v5p0133c1m
v5p0149c2s v5p0158c1s v5p0198c2s
v5p0251c1m v5p0266c2s v5p0281c2s
v5p0332c2s v5p0358c1s v5p0383c1s
v5p0399c1s v5p0458c2s v5p0499c1s
v5p0604c1s v5p0604c2s v5p0617c1s
v5p0618c2s
Ridpath, J.C. and Julian, G.W.
v5p0600c2s
Ridpath, J.C. and Lepper, G.H.
v5p0061c2s
Ridpath, J.C. et al. v5p0115c2s
v5p0610c1s
Riebestein, R. von v3p0300c1s
Riedel, L. v5p0157c2s
Rieffer, J.B. v4p0474c2s
Riehl, F.C. v4p0536c2s
Riehl, W.H. v1p0517c1s
v1p1336c1s v2p0120c1s v2p0303c2s
v2p0366c1s
Riehm, E. v1p0226c1s
v2p0268c2m
Riemann, B. v1p0510c1s
Ries, E.E. v4p0175c2s
v4p0180c2s
Riess, E. v4p0447c2s
v5p0562c2s
Rietschel, G. v4p0633c1s
Rieu, W.N.Du v2p0070c2m
Rigakushi, Shogoro Tsuboi. v4p0578c2s
Rigby, E.A. v3p0194c2s
Rigby, J.A. v6p0627c1s
Rigby, Miss v1p0229c1s
v1p0513c2s v1p0717c1s v1p0959c1s
v1p1254c1s v1p1322c2s
Rigby, T. v6p0306c2s
v6p0438c2s
Rigg, A. v1p0083c1s
v1p0568c2s v1p0618c2s v1p0815c2s
v1p1316c1s v3p0209c2s v3p0272c2s
v3p0344c1s v3p0432c2s v5p0609c1s
Rigg, E. v3p0088c2s
v3p0456c2m
Rigg, J. v1p1398c2s
Rigg, J.H. v1p0085c1s
v1p0085c2s v1p0117c1s v1p0250c1s
v1p0386c2s v1p0387c1s v1p0571c1s
v1p0813c1s v2p0432c2s v5p0519c1s
Rigg, J.M. v3p0206c2s
v6p0343c2s
Rigg, Mrs. v2p0039c2s
Rigge, W.F. v3p0274c2s
v4p0167c1s v4p0410c1s v6p0187c2s
v6p0471c1s
Riggen, S.B. v4p0318c2s
v4p0564c2s
Riggs, A.L. v1p0329c1s
v1p0637c2s v3p0213c2s
Riggs, A.S. v6p0224c1m
v6p0494c1s
Riggs, Arthur S. v6p0180c1s
Riggs, C.F. v1p0350c1s
Riggs, E. v1p0124c1s
v1p0175c1s v2p0025c1s v2p0100c1s
v2p0449c1s v3p0040c2s v6p0361c1s
Riggs, E.G. v6p0147c1s
v6p0507c1s
Riggs, E.G. et al. v4p0609c1s
Riggs, E.S. v5p0018c1s
v5p0162c1s v6p0079c1s v6p0174c1s
v6p0235c1s
Riggs, J.F. v3p0197c2s
v6p0374c1s
Riggs, J.M. v2p0280c2s
Riggs, J.S. v4p0218c2s
v4p0299c2s v4p0305c1s v4p0422c2s
v4p0501c1s v5p0311c2s v6p0342c1s
Riggs, R.B. v3p0275c2s
v3p0433c1s v4p0083c1s v4p0110c2s
v4p0292c1s v4p0349c2s v4p0353c1s
Riggs, S.L. v2p0111c1s
Riggs, S.P. v1p0637c2s
Riggs, S.R. v2p0111c1s
v2p0403c2s
Riggs, W.F. v6p0286c2s
Riggs, W.P. v6p0427c2s
Right, F.L. v4p0354c2s
Righton, E. v3p0056c2s
Rightor, H. v6p0655c2s
Rightsell, L.T. v5p0104c2s
Riis, J. v6p0580c1s
Riis, J.A. v3p0361c2s
v3p0424c1s v4p0104c1s v4p0104c2m
v4p0302c2s v4p0387c1s v4p0400c2m
v4p0406c2s v4p0418c2s v4p0447c1s
v4p0449c2s v4p0452c1s v4p0491c1s
v4p0568c2s v4p0574c1s v4p0618c2s
v4p0632c1s v5p0096c2s v5p0115c2s
v5p0128c2s v5p0207c2s v5p0225c1s
v5p0255c1s v5p0308c2s v5p0315c2s
v5p0326c1s v5p0342c2s v5p0407c2m
v5p0408c1s v5p0434c2s v5p0478c2s
v5p0481c2s v5p0496c1m v5p0533c1s
v5p0555c1s v5p0566c1s v5p0572c2m
v5p0610c2s v6p0078c2s v6p0116c1s
v6p0116c2s v6p0170c2s v6p0181c2s
v6p0240c1s v6p0308c1s v6p0448c2s
v6p0453c2s v6p0515c1s v6p0550c2s
v6p0599c1s
Riis, J.A. et al. v6p0225c1s
Riker, A.B. v5p0044c1s
v5p0216c1s
Riland-Bedford, W.K. v4p0351c1s
Riley, A. v3p0438c2s
v4p0480c1s v4p0506c2s v5p0177c2s
Riley, A. and Diggle, J.R.
v4p0169c2s
Riley, C.V. v1p0107c2s
v1p0108c2s v1p0181c1m v1p0541c1m
v1p0759c2s v1p0855c2m v1p0875c1s
v1p1005c1s v1p1012c1s v1p1039c1s
v1p1175c2s v2p0038c1s v2p0085c2s
v2p0139c1s v2p0155c2m v2p0262c2s
v2p0305c2s v2p0340c2s v2p0402c2s
v3p0141c2s v3p0145c1s v3p0200c2s
v3p0447c1s v4p0286c1s v4p0636c2s
Riley, E.S. v5p0364c2s
v6p0415c2s
Riley, E.S., jr. v1p0028c1s
v1p0034c1s v1p0807c2s v1p1044c2s
v1p1326c1s v1p1384c2s v1p1418c1s
Riley, F. v6p0480c1s
Riley, F.L. v4p0398c2s
v4p0515c1s v6p0425c1s
Riley, H.H. v1p1063c2s
Riley, I. v1p0124c2s
Riley, I.W. v5p0060c1s
v5p0312c1s
Riley, J. v1p1059c1s
v1p1250c2s v5p0526c1s
Riley, J.H. v1p0637c1s
Riley, J.W. v3p0254c1s
v3p0385c1s v4p0110c1s v4p0154c2s
v4p0196c2s v4p0261c2s v4p0572c2s
v4p0598c2s v5p0270c1s v5p0312c2s
v5p0419c2s v5p0425c1s v5p0499c1s
v5p0520c2s v5p0628c1s v6p0169c1s
v6p0448c2s v6p0694c1s v6p0710c2s
Riley, J.W. et al. v5p0115c2s
Riley, J.Woodbridge v6p0451c2s
Riley, L.W. v6p0490c1s
Riley, M.B. v6p0444c2s
Riley, M.L. v6p0491c2s
Riley, P.M. v2p0385c2s
Riley, R.S. v6p0215c2s
Riley, T.J. v6p0575c1s
Riley, W.A. v6p0070c2s
Riley, W.H. v2p0454c1s
Rimbault, E.F. v2p0011c2s
v2p0196c1s v2p0198c2s v2p0211c1s
v2p0213c1s v2p0227c1s v2p0296c1s
v2p0302c2s v2p0303c1m v2p0318c1s
v2p0341c1s v2p0391c2s v2p0470c1s
Rimbault, E.F. and Hopkins, E.J.
v1p0947c2s
Rimington, E.C. v2p0137c2s
v2p0141c1s
Rimmel, E. v3p0156c1s
v3p0326c2s
Rimmer, A. v1p0152c2s
v1p0193c1s v1p0194c2s v1p0308c2s
v1p0320c1s v1p0428c1s v1p0456c2s
v1p0572c1s v1p1255c2s v1p1409c2s
v2p0066c1s v2p0076c1s v2p0077c1s
Rinck, Dr. v1p0433c2s
Rindell, A. v6p0367c2s
Rinder, E.W. v5p0077c2s
Rinder, F. v5p0031c2s
v5p0070c2s v5p0081c1s v5p0345c2m
v5p0349c1s v5p0476c1s v5p0479c1s
v5p0498c2m v5p0499c1s v5p0500c1s
v5p0524c1s v5p0541c2s v6p0034c1s
v6p0069c1s v6p0215c2s v6p0384c1m
v6p0450c2m v6p0475c1s v6p0553c1m
v6p0589c1m v6p0673c2s v6p0677c1s
Rinder, F.K. v5p0413c2s
v6p0079c2s v6p0232c2s
Rinder, Frank v4p0083c1s
v4p0253c1s v4p0559c1s v5p0617c1s
v6p0278c1s v6p0323c2s v6p0383c2s
Rinehart, M.R. v6p0083c2s
v6p0292c1s v6p0465c2s
Ring, J. v1p0424c1s
Ringeling, D.D. v3p0322c2s
Ringgold, J.T. v3p0415c2s
Ringler-Thomson, E.C. v6p0653c2s
Ringling, A.T. v5p0119c1s
Ringueberg, E.N.S. v2p0120c2s
Ringwalt, J.L. v1p0419c2s
Ringwalt, May C. v5p0496c1s
v6p0407c1s v6p0431c2s v6p0648c1s
Ringwalt, R.C. v5p0155c2m
v6p0608c2s
Ringwault, J.E. v1p0997c2s
Rink, H. and Boas, F. v4p0187c1s
Rio, Juan de v6p0093c1s
v6p0260c1s v6p0332c2s v6p0399c1s
v6p0421c1s v6p0421c2s
Riordan, J.J. v2p0070c1s
Riordan, M.J. v3p0297c2s
Riordan, R. v1p1290c2s
v2p0019c1s v2p0062c1s v2p0323c2s
v2p0342c1s v2p0349c2s v3p0298c1s
v3p0321c1s v3p0450c1s v4p0196c2s
v4p0318c1s v5p0223c1s v5p0257c2s
v5p0367c1s v5p0473c1s v5p0500c1s
v5p0533c1s v6p0067c1s v6p0247c1s
v6p0452c1s

Rios, A.Morales de los ... v6p0544c2s
Rios, E.M. v6p0430c1s
Ripley, A.C. v6p0381c1s
Ripley, A.L. v2p0027c1s
v4p0045c1s v4p0143c2s v4p0546c1m
v4p0592c2s v5p0149c2s v6p0051c1s
Ripley, E.B. v3p0173c1s
Ripley, F.H. v5p0394c1s
Ripley, G. v1p0090c1s
v1p0370c1s v1p0392c1s v1p0464c2s
v1p0481c2m v1p0513c2s v1p0587c1s
v1p0597c2s v1p0784c1s v1p0805c2s
v1p0907c2s v1p0993c2s v1p1058c2s
v1p1096c2s v1p1157c1s v1p1176c2s
v1p1360c2s
Ripley, H.J. v1p0096c2s
v1p0555c1s v1p1104c2s
Ripley, L.W. v6p0371c1s
Ripley, M.A. v3p0139c2s
Ripley, R.S. v1p1345c1s
Ripley, W. v6p0658c2s
Ripley, W.C. v5p0475c2s
Ripley, W.Z. v4p0002c1s
v4p0123c2s v4p0189c2s v4p0222c1s
v4p0252c1s v4p0606c2s v5p0043c2s
v5p0049c1s v5p0100c1s v5p0131c1s
v5p0138c1s v5p0148c2s v5p0289c1s
v5p0308c1s v5p0361c1s v5p0459c2s
v5p0475c2s v5p0502c1s v5p0532c1s
v6p0142c1s v6p0318c1s v6p0357c1s
v6p0528c2m v6p0529c1s v6p0530c2s
v6p0551c1s v6p0651c2s v6p0654c1s
v6p0670c1s
Ripon, Lord v1p0820c1s
Ripon, Marquis of v1p0299c1s
v1p0650c2s
Ripon, W.B. v2p0111c2s
Rippel, J.A. v6p0611c2s
v6p0707c1s
Ripper, W. v5p0551c1s
v5p0570c1s
Rippingille, E.V. v1p0066c1s
v1p0576c1s v1p0949c2s v1p0950c2s
v1p1105c1s v1p1125c2s
Rippl, W. v2p0370c2s
Rippon-Seymour, H. v6p0498c1s
Riseley, H.M. v6p0122c2s
v6p0452c1s
Rishell, C.W. v3p0362c1s
v4p0057c1s v4p0429c2s v4p0502c1s
v5p0059c1s v5p0383c2s v6p0063c2s
v6p0341c1s v6p0692c1s
Rising, W.B. and Conte, J.Le
v2p0284c2s
Risk, T.F. v1p0639c1s
v1p1214c2s
Risley, H.H. v2p0039c2s
v2p0277c1s v3p0143c2s v3p0212c1s
v3p0212c2s v3p0268c2m v3p0392c2s
v4p0224c2s v4p0278c2s
Risley, H.M. v6p0452c2s
Risley, R.V. v5p0023c2s
v5p0341c1s v5p0485c1s
Risley, S.D. v4p0606c1s
Risom, F. v4p0267c1s
Risser, E.S. v5p0012c1s
Risteen, F.H. v4p0381c2s
v5p0050c2s v5p0094c2s v5p0156c2s
v5p0209c1s v5p0385c2m v5p0505c2s
v6p0055c2s v6p0428c1s
Ristori, A. v5p0489c2s
Ristori, Adelaide v5p0575c2s
Ristori, E. v2p0356c1s
v5p0014c1s
Rita v4p0575c1s
Ritchey, G.W. v6p0427c2s
v6p0446c1s v6p0613c2s
Ritchie, A. v1p0476c1s
v1p0680c2s v1p1241c2s v3p0421c2s
v3p0426c1s v4p0052c2s v4p0308c2s
Ritchie, A.C. v1p0278c1s
v1p1153c2s
Ritchie, A.I. v5p0308c2s
v6p0069c2s v6p0289c2s
Ritchie, A.I., Mrs. v1p0309c2s
v1p1088c1s v1p1406c1s
Ritchie, A.P.F. v5p0023c2s
Ritchie, A.S. v1p0041c1s
v1p1313c1s v2p0076c1s
Ritchie, A.T. v2p0435c1s
v3p0195c1s v3p0369c1s v4p0075c2s
v4p0341c2s
Ritchie, A.T., Mrs. v5p0066c1s
Ritchie, Anne T. v5p0574c2s
Ritchie, C. v5p0396c1s
Ritchie, D.G. v2p0344c2s
v3p0058c2s v3p0138c1s v3p0185c1s
v3p0281c2s v3p0297c1s v3p0314c1s
v3p0316c2s v3p0337c1s v3p0397c2s
v3p0402c2s v4p0167c1s v4p0186c1m
v4p0191c2s v4p0212c1s v4p0214c1s
v4p0225c2s v4p0338c1s v4p0366c2s
v4p0384c2s v4p0439c1s v4p0462c1s
v4p0465c1s v4p0475c1s v4p0482c1s
v4p0496c1s v4p0532c1m v4p0541c2m
v4p0546c1s v4p0604c1s v5p0344c2s
v5p0354c2s v5p0383c2s v5p0400c1s
v5p0446c2s v5p0471c1s v5p0618c1s
v6p0495c2s
Ritchie, D.M. v4p0442c2s
Ritchie, E. v4p0154c1s
v4p0188c2s v4p0382c1s v4p0479c1s
v5p0386c1s v5p0400c1s v5p0483c1s
v5p0593c2s v5p0636c1s v6p0210c2s
v6p0259c2s v6p0610c2s
Ritchie, E. and Gulliver, J.H.
v4p0154c1s
Ritchie, Ellen S.H. v4p0626c1s
Ritchie, F. v5p0341c2s
v5p0393c1s v5p0487c2s v6p0609c1s
Ritchie, F.J. v3p0088c2s
Ritchie, I.K. v5p0137c1s
v5p0342c2s v5p0421c2s
Ritchie, J. v1p1313c2s
v2p0214c1s
Ritchie, J., jr. v3p0269c1s
v4p0257c2s v5p0015c1s
Ritchie, J.F. v1p0020c2s
v1p0109c2s v1p0398c2s v2p0070c2s
v2p0074c2s v2p0120c2s v2p0178c2s
v2p0183c2s v2p0220c2s v2p0263c1s
Ritchie, L. v1p0348c2s
v1p0631c2s v1p0632c1s v1p0816c1s
v1p0837c1s v1p0898c2s v1p0921c2s
v1p1069c2s v1p1134c2s v1p1287c2s
v1p1288c2s v1p1394c2s
Ritchie, Mrs. v2p0431c2s
v3p0056c1s v3p0121c1s v3p0204c2s
v4p0309c2s v4p0571c1s
Ritchie, R. v2p0182c2s
v2p0266c1s
Ritchie, R., Mrs. v2p0301c1s
v4p0134c2s v5p0259c2s v5p0262c1s
v5p0503c2s v6p0248c2s
Ritenom, J.S. v3p0423c1s
Rites, F.M. v4p0547c1s
v4p0547c2s
Ritschl, A. v1p0989c2s
Rittenhouse, J.B. v6p0209c1s
Ritter, C. v1p0336c2s
v1p0961c1s v5p0010c1s
Ritter, F.R. v1p1421c1s
Ritter, F.W. v1p1438c1s
Ritter, H. v5p0499c2s
Ritter, I.H. v4p0260c1s
Ritter, J.H. v6p0344c2s
Ritter, J.P. v3p0377c1s
v4p0064c1s v4p0096c2s v4p0401c1s
v4p0584c2s
Ritter, L. v1p1039c2s
Ritter, W. v5p0251c1s
Ritter, W.E. v6p0010c2s
v6p0066c2s v6p0209c1s v6p0288c2s
v6p0401c1s v6p0474c1s v6p0577c1s
v6p0671c1s v6p0713c2s
Ritter, W.E. and Miller, L.
v5p0505c1s
Ritter, W.L. v2p0279c1s
v2p0453c1s
Ritter, W.L. et al. v6p0102c1s
Rive, A.de la v1p0077c1s
v1p0443c2s v1p0787c2s
Rive, M.de la v1p0565c1m
Rive, W.de la and Muller, H.W.
v1p0400c2s v2p0137c2s
River, J. v6p0586c1s
Rivers, F. v4p0295c2s
Rivers, J. v6p0033c2s
v6p0175c1s v6p0242c2s v6p0418c2s
Rivers, P. v2p0052c2s
v2p0076c2s v2p0111c1s v4p0412c2s
Rivers, P., Gen. v2p0128c2s
Rivers, W.C. v6p0556c1s
Rivers, W.H.R. v4p0528c1s
v5p0129c1s v6p0648c2s
Rives, A. v3p0002c1s
v3p0150c1s v3p0195c1s v3p0216c1s
v3p0264c1s v3p0309c1s v3p0351c1s
v3p0410c2s v3p0451c1s v3p0466c2s
v4p0035c1s v4p0170c2s v5p0370c2s
Rives, Amelie v3p0455c1s
v5p0555c1s v6p0229c1s v6p0423c1s
Rives, G.L. v5p0162c1s
v5p0294c1s v5p0407c1s v5p0542c1s
v5p0544c2s
Rives, J.P. v5p0218c1s
Rives, R.W. v6p0132c2s
Rives, W.C. v1p0474c1s
v1p0479c1m
Rivet, M.B. v5p0004c2s
Rivett-Carnac, J.H. v5p0488c2s
Rivett-Carnac, S. v3p0020c1s
v3p0211c1s
Rivier, A. v4p0303c1s
v4p0623c2s
Rivier, M.A. v2p0223c2s
Rivington, C.J. v3p0100c1s
Rivington, C.R. v6p0615c1s
Rivington, J.A. v2p0326c2s
Rivington, L. v3p0083c1s
v3p0083c2s v3p0365c2s v4p0185c2s
v4p0424c1s v4p0489c2s v5p0612c2s
Rivington, R. v4p0298c2s
Rivington, S. v4p0185c2s
Rivoalen, E. v4p0025c1s
v4p0159c2s v4p0480c2s
Rix, E.A. v5p0010c1s
v6p0009c1s
Rix, H. v2p0055c1s
v2p0379c1s v3p0315c2s v4p0163c1s
v4p0250c1s v4p0268c1s v4p0413c1s
v4p0494c1s
Rix, W.J. v4p0158c1s
Rix, W.P. v4p0455c1s
v5p0235c2s v6p0107c1s
Rizer, P. v1p1101c2s
v1p1271c2s
Roach, A.M. v6p0024c2s
v6p0210c1s v6p0291c2s v6p0319c2s
v6p0369c1s v6p0450c1s v6p0544c1s
v6p0610c2s v6p0672c2s v6p0674c2s
v6p0707c2s
Roach, Abby M. v6p0249c2s
v6p0376c2s v6p0434c1s
Roach, J. v1p0034c1s
v1p0839c1s v2p0012c1s v2p0431c1s
Roach, J. et al. v2p0356c2s
Roach, J.A.J. v2p0109c2s
Roach, J.J.A. v2p0332c1s
Roach, John et al. v2p0431c1s
Roach, L.J. v5p0380c2s
Roach, N., Mrs. v5p0573c2s
Roach, O.C. v6p0594c1s
Road, L.B. v1p0213c2s
Roads, S., jr. v3p0267c2s
Roalf, J., jr. v6p0289c2s
Roane v1p1099c2s
Roane, A. v1p0416c1m
v1p1073c1s v2p0453c2s
Roane, A.J. v1p1208c2s
Robarts, C.H. v1p0743c2m
v1p1357c2s
Robarts, L.W. v3p0360c2s
v3p0439c1s
Robarts, W.H. v5p0398c1s
Robb, C. v1p0194c1m
v1p0508c2s v1p0995c2s v1p1324c1s
Robb, D.W. v6p0615c2s
Robb, J. v1p1248c1s
Robb, J.H. v2p0314c1s
Robb, Juliet E. v6p0034c2s
Robb, R. v4p0176c1s
Robb, T.D. v3p0122c1s
v3p0308c1s
Robb, W.L. v5p0492c1s
Robberds, J. v1p1286c1s
v2p0439c1s
Robbie, E. v1p1200c1s
Robbins, A. v1p0505c1s
v1p0693c2s v1p0780c1s
Robbins, A.F. v4p0048c1s
Robbins, A.J. v4p0227c2s
Robbins, Alfred F. v5p0545c2s
Robbins, C. v1p0074c1s
v1p0163c1s v1p0492c2s v1p1042c1s
v1p1386c1m
Robbins, E. v6p0434c1s
Robbins, E.D.C. v2p0044c2s
Robbins, E.W. v1p0575c2s
v1p0989c2s
Robbins, E.Y. v2p0199c2s
Robbins, G.S. v4p0564c2s
Robbins, H. v6p0087c1s
v6p0114c2s v6p0202c1s v6p0217c2s
v6p0355c2s v6p0491c2s v6p0577c1s
Robbins, H.E. v3p0404c2s
Robbins, H.H. v4p0050c1s
v5p0017c1s v5p0175c2s v5p0176c2s
v5p0409c2s v5p0468c1s
Robbins, Hayes v6p0522c2s
Robbins, J.E. v4p0097c1s
v6p0232c2s v6p0330c2s
Robbins, J.J. v1p0608c2s
v1p0681c2s v1p1339c2s
Robbins, L.O. v4p0390c2s
Robbins, M.C. v4p0028c2m
v4p0043c1s v4p0094c1m v4p0100c1m
v4p0129c2s v4p0136c2s v4p0203c2m
v4p0204c1m v4p0208c1s v4p0219c2m
v4p0220c1s v4p0319c2m v4p0380c2s
v4p0422c1s v4p0427c2s v4p0444c1m
v4p0463c2s v4p0465c2s v4p0468c1s
v5p0433c1m v5p0504c1s v5p0612c1s
Robbins, M.E. v4p0330c2s
v6p0375c1s
Robbins, Mrs. v2p0016c1s
Robbins, R. v1p0254c1s
v1p0310c2s v1p0338c2s v1p0420c1s
v1p0443c1s v1p0505c1s v1p0534c2s
v1p0581c1s v1p0610c1s v1p0620c1s
v1p0676c2s v1p0798c1s v1p0842c2s
v1p0855c2s v1p0868c2s v1p0932c2m
v1p1006c1s v1p1067c1s v1p1087c2s
v1p1096c1s v1p1216c2s v1p1237c2s
v1p1348c2s v1p1351c1s v1p1393c2s
v1p1404c2s v1p1419c1s v2p0148c2s
Robbins, R.C. v4p0414c1s
Robbins, R.D.C. v1p0087c1s
v1p0117c1s v1p0122c2s v1p0130c2s
v1p0131c1s v1p0396c1s v1p0496c1s
v1p0668c2s v1p0811c1s v1p1180c1s
v1p1418c1s v1p1442c2s
Robbins, S.S., Mrs. v1p0504c2s
v2p0420c1s
Robbins, T., jr. v4p0050c2s
Robbins, W.A. v6p0655c2s
Robbins, W.L. v3p0143c1s
Robeck, G.de v1p0452c1s
v4p0761c1s
Robeck, G.H. v1p0886c1s

Roberson, E.L. v6p0475c2s
Roberson, F.R. v5p0443c2s v5p0587c1s
Roberson, P. v4p0378c2s
Roberston, W. v3p0149c2s
Robert, C. v5p0494c2s
Robert, P.G. v1p0259c2s
Roberts, A. v1p0127c1s v1p0199c2s v1p1090c1s v2p0012c1s v2p0391c2s v3p0098c2s v4p0077c1s v4p0131c2s v4p0378c1s
Roberts, A.C. v4p0196c1s
Roberts, A.L. v3p0405c1s v3p0434c1s
Roberts, A.W. v2p0431c1s v5p0549c1s v5p0549c2s v6p0037c2s v6p0613c2s v6p0614c1m v6p0625c2s v6p0670c2s
Roberts, Alex.W. v6p0614c2s v6p0627c1s
Roberts, B.S. v1p0854c2s
Roberts, C. v1p0438c2s v2p0151c1s v2p0178c2s v3p0271c1s v4p0268c2s v4p0370c1s v4p0475c2s v5p0005c2s v5p0017c1s v5p0028c2s v5p0087c2s v5p0099c1s v5p0370c1s v5p0436c2s v6p0015c2s v6p0018c2s v6p0108c1s v6p0174c2s v6p0194c2s v6p0356c2s v6p0381c2s v6p0383c2s v6p0384c2s v6p0457c2s v6p0565c2s v6p0645c2s
Roberts, C.D. v5p0627c1s
Roberts, C.F. v4p0288c2m
Roberts, C.G.D. v1p0819c1s v2p0405c2s v2p0421c1s v3p0066c1s v3p0067c2s v3p0077c1s v3p0191c2s v3p0323c1s v3p0324c2s v3p0371c2s v3p0431c2s v4p0034c2s v4p0086c2s v4p0152c2s v4p0157c2s v4p0186c1s v4p0261c1s v4p0344c1s v4p0489c2s v4p0550c2s v4p0625c1s v5p0054c2s v5p0078c2s v5p0081c1s v5p0201c1s v5p0227c1s v5p0251c2s v5p0260c1s v5p0269c1s v5p0273c2s v5p0329c2s v5p0356c2s v5p0374c1s v5p0385c2s v5p0388c2s v5p0411c2s v5p0413c2s v5p0456c1s v5p0475c1s v5p0478c2s v5p0631c1s v6p0012c2s v6p0021c1s v6p0038c1s v6p0231c2s v6p0240c1s v6p0265c1s v6p0283c2s v6p0380c2s v6p0391c1s v6p0424c1s v6p0478c1s v6p0509c1s v6p0515c2s v6p0517c2s v6p0525c2s v6p0534c1s v6p0548c2s v6p0566c1s v6p0579c1s v6p0584c2s v6p0620c1s v6p0658c1s v6p0702c2s
Roberts, C.H. v3p0376c1s v5p0176c2s
Roberts, C.P. v5p0117c2s
Roberts, C.R. v3p0351c2s
Roberts, C.S. v5p0017c2s v5p0567c1s
Roberts, Chalmers v6p0267c2s
Roberts, Charles G.D. v6p0311c1s
Roberts, Charlotte F. v4p0107c1s v4p0405c1m
Roberts, D. v4p0160c1s
Roberts, D.E. v5p0621c1s
Roberts, E. v1p0582c2s v1p0629c2s v1p0948c2s v1p1191c1s v2p0157c2s v2p0193c1s v2p0297c1s v2p0342c1s v2p0359c1s v2p0374c2s v2p0386c1s v2p0406c2s v2p0456c2m v3p0061c2s v3p0115c1s v3p0193c2s v3p0363c2s v3p0374c2s v3p0375c1m v3p0473c2s v3p0474c2s v4p0501c2s v5p0063c1s v6p0035c1s v6p0439c2s
Roberts, E.A. v6p0131c1s v6p0568c2s
Roberts, E.D. v5p0425c1s
Roberts, E.G. v3p0112c2s
Roberts, E.H. v3p0420c1s v3p0432c1s v6p0162c1s v6p0472c1s
Roberts, E.H. and Oswald, F.L. v5p0018c2s
Roberts, E.P. v4p0180c2s
Roberts, E.S. v2p0190c2s v3p0217c1s
Roberts, E.W. v5p0377c1s v6p0432c1s
Roberts, Eric J. v6p0503c2s
Roberts, F.C. v2p0127c1s
Roberts, F.H.H. v6p0129c1s
Roberts, F.L. v1p0799c2s
Roberts, F.S. v2p0185c2m v6p0265c1s
Roberts, F.S., Sir v5p0243c2s
Roberts, G. v1p0090c2s v1p0862c1s v4p0392c1s v5p0156c2s v5p0592c1s
Roberts, G.E. v1p0279c2s v1p0900c1s v1p1045c1s v4p0195c1s v5p0047c1s v5p0080c2s v5p0207c1s v5p0237c2m v5p0241c1s v5p0592c1s v5p0593c2s v6p0260c2s v6p0515c2s v6p0589c2s
Roberts, G.L. v6p0673c1s
Roberts, G.N. v2p0448c1s
Roberts, H. v6p0168c2s v6p0346c2s
Roberts, H.D. v5p0336c1s v6p0370c2s
Roberts, H.F. v6p0216c1s
Roberts, H.H. v5p0638c1s
Roberts, H.P. v3p0448c2s
Roberts, I. v4p0396c1s v5p0402c1m v5p0549c1s v5p0549c2m v6p0140c2m
Roberts, I.B. v5p0262c2s v5p0338c1s v6p0167c2s v6p0215c2s v6p0223c2s v6p0282c2s v6p0536c1s
Roberts, I.J. v4p0310c2s
Roberts, I.R. v6p0515c2s
Roberts, Ina B. v6p0232c1s v6p0285c2s v6p0533c1s
Roberts, J. v5p0402c1s v6p0241c1s v6p0568c1s
Roberts, J.A. v5p0291c1s v5p0568c2s
Roberts, J.B. v2p0130c2s v2p0132c1s v2p0358c1s v3p0136c2s
Roberts, J.F. v2p0252c1s
Roberts, J.G. v1p0639c2s v1p1303c1s v2p0390c1s v5p0631c1s
Roberts, J.H. v5p0236c1s
Roberts, J.P. v6p0021c2s
Roberts, J.S. v6p0201c1s v6p0449c1s
Roberts, Kate L. v6p0375c1s v6p0455c1s
Roberts, L. v3p0088c2s
Roberts, L.A. v1p1037c1s v1p1227c2s v1p1243c1s v1p1256c2m v3p0362c2s
Roberts, L.H. v1p1123c2s
Roberts, L.M. v4p0080c1s v5p0276c1s v6p0390c1s
Roberts, Lord v6p0105c2s
Roberts, M. v1p1257c2s v3p0005c2s v3p0027c2m v3p0050c2m v3p0061c1s v3p0062c1s v3p0255c2s v3p0257c1s v3p0409c1s v3p0409c2s v3p0426c2s v3p0453c1s v3p0464c1s v4p0022c2s v4p0168c2s v4p0198c2s v4p0231c1s v4p0340c1s v4p0352c2s v4p0588c2s v5p0005c1s v5p0008c1s v5p0164c1s v5p0206c1s v5p0359c1s v5p0362c1s v5p0434c2s v5p0437c1s v5p0585c1s v5p0621c1s v6p0001c1s v6p0593c2s
Roberts, M.R. v5p0143c1s
Roberts, Miss v1p0396c2s
Roberts, Morley v3p0325c2s v5p0451c2s
Roberts, O. v6p0256c2s
Roberts, O.H. v2p0194c2s
Roberts, O.M. v6p0639c2s v6p0640c1s v6p0640c2s v6p0671c2s
Roberts, P. v1p0665c1s v1p1034c1s v1p1241c1s v6p0114c2s v6p0132c2s v6p0257c1s v6p0418c2s v6p0566c1s v6p0597c1s v6p0621c1s v6p0621c2m v6p0665c2s
Roberts, P.E. v6p0240c2s v6p0651c2s
Roberts, R. v1p0109c1s v1p1176c2s v3p0042c2s
Roberts, R.D. v2p0290c1s
Roberts, R.H. v1p1041c2s
Roberts, S.H. v3p0157c2s
Roberts, S.W. v1p0311c2s v1p0939c1s v1p1035c2s v1p1075c1s
Roberts, T. v5p0419c1s v5p0425c1s v5p0534c2s v5p0633c1s v5p0645c1s v6p0027c1s v6p0142c1s v6p0187c1s v6p0234c1s v6p0278c1s v6p0285c2s v6p0299c1s v6p0333c1s v6p0377c1s v6p0592c1s v6p0603c2s v6p0664c1s
Roberts, T.S. v1p0311c2s
Roberts, V.H. v6p0175c2s
Roberts, W. v2p0145c1s v2p0335c2s v2p0384c2s v3p0095c2s v3p0146c2s v3p0168c2s v3p0186c1s v3p0290c2s v4p0021c1s v4p0066c2s v4p0067c2m v4p0068c1s v4p0079c1s v4p0118c1s v4p0122c2s v4p0185c2s v4p0200c1s v4p0216c2s v4p0222c1s v4p0225c2s v4p0227c1s v4p0243c2s v4p0259c2s v4p0270c2s v4p0317c2s v4p0329c1s v4p0337c1s v4p0340c2s v4p0346c1s v4p0354c2s v4p0355c1s v4p0406c1s v4p0411c1s v4p0429c2s v4p0442c2m v4p0455c1s v4p0490c2s v4p0544c2s v4p0623c2s v5p0031c2m v5p0070c2s v5p0071c1s v5p0148c2s v5p0151c2s v5p0152c1s v5p0160c1m v5p0174c1s v5p0233c1s v5p0242c1s v5p0257c2s v5p0290c2s v5p0310c1s v5p0332c2s v5p0356c1s v5p0368c1s v5p0373c2s v5p0438c2s v5p0450c2s v5p0466c2s v5p0479c1s v5p0495c2s v5p0513c1s v5p0553c1s v5p0607c1s v5p0610c1s v5p0615c1s v5p0623c1s v6p0034c2s v6p0075c1s v6p0101c2s v6p0245c2s v6p0282c2s v6p0346c1s v6p0382c2s v6p0429c1s v6p0475c1s v6p0480c1s v6p0499c1s v6p0521c1s v6p0550c1s v6p0586c2s v6p0618c1s v6p0713c1s
Roberts, W. and Claretie, J. v5p0432c1s
Roberts, W. and Prideaux, W.F. v5p0591c1s
Roberts, W. and Rome, W. . v5p0151c2s
Roberts, W.C. v1p0023c2s v1p0224c1s v1p0751c2s v1p0826c1s v1p1242c2s v3p0090c1s v3p0091c2s v3p0128c2s v6p0097c1s v6p0363c2s
Roberts, W.D. v6p0653c2s
Roberts, W.H. v1p0444c2s v1p1031c1s v3p0083c2s v3p0342c2s v4p0132c2s v4p0477c1s v4p0573c1s v5p0406c1s v5p0464c1m v5p0482c1s
Roberts, W.H. and Rankin, D.C. v5p0464c1s
Roberts, W.J. v6p0100c1s
Roberts, W.M. v1p0158c2s v1p0939c1s
Roberts, W.P. v1p0314c1s v3p0020c1s v3p0270c1s v4p0131c1s v4p0345c2s v5p0366c2s
Roberts, W.R. v5p0087c1s
Roberts, W.Rhys v5p0028c1s
Roberts, W.T. v6p0436c2s
Roberts, W.V. v6p0069c1s v6p0270c1s v6p0299c2s
Roberts-Austen, Prof. and Merritt, L., Mrs. v4p0387c2m
Roberts-Austen, W.C. v2p0284c2s v3p0009c1s v3p0024c1s v3p0326c2s v3p0409c1s v4p0011c1s v4p0174c2s v4p0366c2m v4p0369c1s v5p0013c1s
Roberts-Austen, W.C. and Rose, T.K. v5p0013c1s
Robertson, A. v3p0225c1s v3p0365c1s v3p0448c1s v4p0229c1s v4p0294c2s v5p0059c2s v5p0580c2s v5p0608c2s v6p0288c1s v6p0676c2s
Robertson, A.C. v6p0653c1s
Robertson, A.E. v6p0577c2s
Robertson, A.F. v5p0065c2s v5p0349c1s v5p0374c1s v5p0406c1s v5p0421c2s
Robertson, A.H. v6p0646c2s
Robertson, A.J. v5p0305c2s
Robertson, A.K. v3p0057c1s
Robertson, A.W. v5p0001c2s v5p0332c2s v5p0334c1s v5p0336c2s
Robertson, Alex. v5p0500c1s
Robertson, B. v5p0142c1s
Robertson, C. v1p0711c2s v4p0202c2s v6p0188c1s
Robertson, C.D. v6p0214c1s v6p0512c2s
Robertson, C.F. v1p1411c2s v2p0062c1m v2p0470c2m
Robertson, C.G. v4p0630c1s v5p0166c2s v5p0392c1s v6p0247c2s
Robertson, C.H. v1p0181c1s v1p0426c1s v1p0883c1s
Robertson, D. v3p0112c1s v3p0122c1s v3p0281c2s v3p0295c1s v3p0404c1s v6p0513c1s
Robertson, D.C. and Strunk, W., jr. v3p0424c2s
Robertson, D.J. v3p0258c2s v4p0309c2s v4p0318c2s v5p0423c1s v5p0424c1s v6p0469c1s v6p0470c2s
Robertson, E. v2p0130c2s v2p0174c2s v2p0264c1s v2p0348c1s v2p0428c2s v4p0417c1s v5p0006c2s v5p0085c1s v5p0116c2s v5p0120c2s v5p0247c2s v5p0433c1s v5p0558c2m v6p0206c1s v6p0268c1s v6p0378c2s v6p0445c1s v6p0616c1m
Robertson, E. and Hurd, A.S. v5p0368c2s
Robertson, E.H. v4p0348c2s v6p0419c1m
Robertson, E.O. v5p0229c2s
Robertson, E.S. v1p0657c1s v1p0698c1s v1p1034c2s v1p1099c1s v1p1210c1s v2p0131c1s v4p0011c2s v4p0266c1s v5p0590c2s v6p0327c2s v6p0391c2s
Robertson, Ed.H. v5p0338c2s
Robertson, Edmund v6p0100c2s
Robertson, F.F. v1p0703c1s v4p0305c1s v4p0380c1s
Robertson, Frances F. v6p0420c2s
Robertson, G. v1p0287c2s v1p1245c2s v6p0312c1s
Robertson, G.A. v2p0279c1s v3p0270c2s
Robertson, G.C. v1p0082c1m v1p0085c2s v1p0114c1s v1p0156c2s v1p0157c1s v1p0213c1s v1p0614c1s v1p0624c1s v1p0625c1s v1p0649c1s v1p0760c1s v1p0760c2m v1p0819c1s v1p0839c2s v1p0843c2s v1p1000c1s v1p1000c2m v1p1062c1m v1p1098c2s v1p1177c1s v1p1228c1s v1p1328c2s v2p0054c2s v2p0059c2s v2p0339c1s v2p0358c1s v3p0198c1s v3p0292c2s v4p0041c1s
Robertson, G.C. et al. ... v1p0839c2s
Robertson, G.D. v3p0462c2s
Robertson, G.H. v4p0174c2s
Robertson, G.S. v4p0307c2s v4p0413c1s v5p0228c2s v5p0313c1s

Robertson, G.S., Sir v5p0163c1s
v5p0313c1s
Robertson, H. v3p0203c1s
v4p0137c1s v4p0483c2s v4p0519c2s
v5p0160c1s v5p0169c2s v5p0627c1s
Robertson, H.R. v1p1299c1s
v2p0057c1s v3p0254c1s
Robertson, H.W. v2p0152c1s
Robertson, I.W. v5p0570c1s
Robertson, J. v1p0244c2s
v1p0379c1s v1p0559c2s v1p0711c1s
v1p0891c1s v1p0944c2s v1p0992c1s
v1p1165c1s v1p1224c2s v1p1281c2s
v3p0026c2s v3p0272c2s v3p0289c1s
v4p0042c1s v5p0057c2s v6p0343c1s
Robertson, J.A. v6p0493c1s
Robertson, J.B. v1p0133c2s
v1p0232c1s v1p0630c2s v1p0631c1s
v3p0044c2s v3p0176c2s v3p0393c1s
v4p0059c1s v4p0144c1s v4p0144c2s
v4p0206c2s v4p0279c1s v6p0313c1s
Robertson, J.B. et al. ... v1p0518c2s
Robertson, J.C. v1p0106c2s
Robertson, J.D. v3p0475c2s
v4p0138c2s
Robertson, J.F. v1p0857c1s
v2p0233c1s v2p0460c2s v4p0029c2s
v4p0074c2s v4p0439c1s v4p0583c2s
Robertson, J.G. v4p0215c2s
v4p0387c1s v4p0408c1s v4p0413c2s
v4p0435c1s v4p0550c2s v6p0079c2s
Robertson, J.L. v1p0930c1s
v2p0364c2s v2p0448c1s v5p0351c1s
Robertson, J.M. v4p0375c2s
v5p0220c1s v5p0227c2s v5p0324c2s
v5p0415c2s v5p0422c2s v5p0618c2s
v6p0192c1s v6p0196c1s v6p0260c2s
v6p0342c1s v6p0447c2s v6p0531c2s
Robertson, J.R. v6p0371c1s
Robertson, J.S. v4p0175c1s
v4p0344c2s
Robertson, J.W. v5p0360c2s
v6p0087c1s
Robertson, James C., Mrs.. v3p0013c2s
Robertson, M. v4p0511c1s
v5p0154c2s v5p0159c1s v5p0202c1s
v5p0421c1s v5p0465c2s v5p0506c1s
v5p0628c1s v6p0147c2s v6p0395c1s
v6p0422c2s v6p0623c1m
Robertson, M.A. v6p0364c2s
Robertson, M.J.M. v2p0267c1s
Robertson, Madge v2p0241c2s
Robertson, Morgan v6p0043c1s
Robertson, P. v6p0329c2s
v6p0486c2s
Robertson, R.S. v1p0876c2s
v1p1111c2s v2p0280c2s v3p0130c1s
v3p0179c1s v3p0313c2s v3p0463c2s
v4p0407c1s v4p0508c2s
Robertson, S. v3p0088c1s
v3p0244c1s v3p0453c2s v3p0474c2s
Robertson, S.C. v3p0166c2s
v5p0098c2s
Robertson, S.J. v4p0037c1s
v4p0261c2s
Robertson, T. v2p0244c1s
Robertson, T.W. v2p0324c2s
Robertson, W. v1p0629c2s
v1p1019c1s v2p0345c2s v4p0037c2s
v4p0105c1s v4p0221c1s v5p0111c1s
Robertson, W.A. v5p0150c1s
v6p0528c2s
Robertson, W.B. v4p0121c2s
v4p0350c1s v5p0021c1s v6p0088c1s
v6p0332c1s v6p0384c2s v6p0464c1s
v6p0542c2s v6p0636c2s v6p0698c1s
Robertson, W.C. v3p0009c1s
Robertson, W.F. v5p0291c2s
Robertson, W.J. v3p0457c2s
v6p0643c2s
Robertson, W.R. v3p0006c2m
v3p0210c2s v3p0212c2s
Robertson, W.S. v3p0277c2s
Robertson, W.S.S. v3p0453c2s
Robertson, W.W. v3p0434c1s
v4p0207c2s
Robertson-Scott, J.W. v4p0061c2s
v4p0138c2s
Robeson, S.S. v4p0267c2s
Robhouse, C. v6p0271c2s
Robie, C.E. v4p0315c2s
Robie, E. v1p0119c1s
v1p1325c2s
Robie, L.P. v3p0201c1s
Robie, S. v4p0544c2s
Robie, V.H. v5p0128c1s
v5p0405c1s v5p0406c2s v5p0540c2s
Robin, Abbe C.C. v3p0455c2s
Robin, Felix v4p0173c1s
Robin, G.T. v6p0278c1s
Robin, M. v1p0267c2s
v1p1210c1s
Robinet, M.G. v1p0211c2s
Robins, A.E. v3p0428c1s
Robins, C.E. v1p0296c1s
v2p0374c2s
Robins, Dr. v1p0685c1s
Robins, E. v1p0851c1s
v2p0060c1s v2p0124c2s v2p0146c2s
v2p0148c2s v2p0152c2s v2p0203c1s
v2p0218c2s v2p0220c2s v2p0262c2s
v2p0271c2m v2p0336c2s v2p0338c2s
v2p0369c1s v5p0017c2s v5p0054c2s
v5p0280c2s v6p0010c1s v6p0239c1s
v6p0419c1s v6p0425c2s
Robins, E.C. v1p1150c2m
v2p0100c1s v3p0023c1s v3p0153c1s
v3p0378c2s v3p0422c1s
Robins, E.P. v5p0311c2s
Robins, Elizabeth v4p0013c1s
v5p0413c1s v6p0358c2s
Robins, H.M. v5p0322c1s
Robins, J. v1p0195c2s
Robins, M.H. v5p0388c2s
Robins, R.B. v1p1403c2s
Robins, R.P. v3p0102c1s
v3p0206c2s v3p0254c1s v3p0461c1s
Robins, S.N. v4p0243c1s
v5p0322c1s
Robins, Sally N. v5p0613c1s
Robins, W.M. v3p0225c2s
Robinson, A.C. v4p0134c1s
v6p0004c1s v6p0330c1s v6p0346c1s
v6p0387c1s v6p0457c2s v6p0492c1s
v6p0516c2s
Robinson, A.G. v5p0007c1s
v5p0147c1m v5p0148c1m v5p0213c1s
v5p0444c1s v5p0445c1s v5p0445c2m
v6p0160c1s v6p0160c2m v6p0509c2s
Robinson, A.G. et al. v6p0342c1s
Robinson, A.M.F. v1p0365c1s
v1p1158c1s v2p0177c1s v2p0182c2s
v2p0200c2s v2p0233c1s v2p0273c1s
v2p0305c2s v2p0318c1s v2p0365c2s
v3p0161c1s v3p0273c1s v3p0278c2s
v3p0320c2s v3p0429c2s v3p0451c1s
v3p0472c2s v4p0049c2s v4p0078c2s
v4p0097c2s v4p0120c1s v4p0136c2s
v4p0151c2s v4p0155c1s v4p0212c1s
v4p0213c1s v4p0233c1s v4p0277c1s
v4p0302c2s v4p0327c1s v4p0343c1s
v4p0421c2s v4p0458c2s v4p0463c1s
v4p0492c2s v4p0587c2s v4p0601c1s
v6p0631c1s
Robinson, A.M.F. and Lee, V.
v3p0082c1s
Robinson, A.M.F., Miss ... v3p0135c1s
Robinson, A.Mary F. v3p0074c1s
Robinson, A.W. v4p0161c2s
v4p0522c1s v5p0237c2s v5p0238c1s
v6p0182c1s v6p0215c1m v6p0476c2s
v6p0477c1s v6p0592c2s
Robinson, Albert G. v6p0160c1s
Robinson, B.L. v5p0073c1s
v6p0077c1s
Robinson, B.W. v6p0341c1s
Robinson, C. v1p0218c1s
v1p0314c1s v1p0796c2s v1p0980c1s
v1p1207c1s v1p1340c2s v4p0015c2s
v4p0030c2s v4p0039c2s v4p0213c2s
v4p0240c2s v4p0250c2s v4p0318c1s
v4p0377c1s v4p0397c2s v4p0411c1m
v4p0445c1s v4p0487c2m v4p0498c2s
v4p0600c1s v5p0031c2s v5p0378c1s
v6p0299c2s
Robinson, C., Sir v4p0030c2s
Robinson, C.B. v1p1049c2s
Robinson, C.C. v3p0066c2s
Robinson, C.D. v1p0644c2s
v1p0776c2s v3p0021c2s v4p0083c2s
v4p0585c2s v4p0636c1s v6p0534c2s
Robinson, C.H. v1p0187c1s
v1p1119c1s v2p0368c2s v4p0232c2s
v4p0247c2s v4p0250c1s v5p0532c1s
Robinson, C.J. v1p0494c2s
v1p0879c2s v1p1145c2s v1p1239c2s
v2p0008c1s v2p0057c2s v2p0090c2s
v2p0092c1s v2p0115c2s v2p0164c1s
v2p0195c2s v2p0197c1s v2p0249c2s
v2p0300c2s v2p0422c2s v2p0449c2s
v2p0475c1s v2p0479c2s v4p0246c1s
v4p0255c2s
Robinson, C.K. v1p1178c2s
Robinson, C.M. v4p0549c2s
v5p0120c1s v5p0176c1s v5p0431c1s
v5p0467c1s v5p0606c2s v6p0004c2m
v6p0034c1s v6p0057c1s v6p0128c1s
v6p0128c2s v6p0435c2m v6p0621c1s
Robinson, C.M. and Ellwanger, W.D.
v4p0202c1s
Robinson, C.N. v4p0395c2s
v5p0543c1s v6p0597c2s v6p0629c2s
Robinson, C.S. v1p0049c2s
v1p0118c2s v1p0909c1s v1p1040c2s
v1p1270c2s v1p1421c1s v2p0337c2s
v3p0064c1s
Robinson, C.W. v1p0007c1s
v6p0183c2s v6p0265c1s v6p0464c2s
Robinson, Chas.A. v4p0168c2s
Robinson, D. v4p0148c1s
v4p0203c1s v6p0596c1s
Robinson, D.M. v6p0149c2s
v6p0169c1s v6p0320c2m v6p0465c1s
v6p0595c2s
Robinson, D.W. v6p0660c1s
Robinson, E. v1p0050c1s
v1p0117c1s v1p0126c1s v1p0127c1s
v1p0132c1m v1p0198c1s v1p0336c2m
v1p0368c2s v1p0430c2s v1p0518c1s
v1p0598c1s v1p0638c1s v1p0668c2s
v1p0682c2m v1p0689c1s v1p0695c2s
v1p0754c1s v1p0803c2s v1p0907c1m
v1p0925c2s v1p0960c2s v1p0961c1m
v1p0961c2s v1p0985c2s v1p1096c2s
v1p1174c2s v1p1207c2s v1p1301c2s
v2p0404c1s v3p0324c2s v3p0325c2s
v3p0354c2s v3p0448c1s v4p0026c1s
v4p0095c1s v4p0241c1s v4p0453c2s
v4p0510c2s v5p0063c2s v5p0127c2s
v5p0200c2s v5p0362c1s v5p0434c1s
v5p0573c2s v5p0609c1s v6p0067c2s
v6p0120c2s v6p0325c2s v6p0420c2s
v6p0423c1s v6p0606c2s v6p0674c2s
Robinson, E.A. v4p0303c1s
v5p0308c2s
Robinson, E.C. v3p0143c1s
Robinson, E.F. v4p0272c2s
Robinson, E.G. v1p1109c2s
v1p1303c1s v2p0131c1s
Robinson, E.G. et al. v2p0017c1s
Robinson, E.K. v2p0062c2s
v2p0171c1s v2p0200c1s v2p0274c2s
v2p0442c1s v4p0004c2s v4p0278c2s
v4p0311c2s v4p0395c1s v4p0419c1s
v5p0214c2s v5p0226c1s v5p0285c2s
v5p0479c2s v6p0145c2s v6p0161c1s
v6p0247c2s v6p0397c1s
Robinson, E.Kay v5p0563c2s
v6p0090c1s v6p0246c2s v6p0247c1s
v6p0525c2s v6p0691c1s
Robinson, E.L. v6p0141c2s
Robinson, E.P. v3p0376c1s
Robinson, E.S. v2p0348c2s
Robinson, E.S.K. v6p0272c1s
Robinson, E.V. v4p0196c1s
v4p0546c1s v5p0294c1s v5p0602c1s
v5p0618c1s v6p0272c1s
Robinson, E.V.D. v5p0142c2s
Robinson, E.Van D. v5p0016c2s
v5p0264c2s v5p0266c2m v5p0267c1s
v5p0558c1s
Robinson, E.Van Dyke v5p0410c2s
Robinson, E.W. v1p0867c2s
Robinson, Edgar E. and
Gruhl, Edwin F. v6p0529c1s
Robinson, Ednah v4p0353c1s
v5p0586c1s
Robinson, Eugene v4p0579c2s
Robinson, F. v2p0366c2s
Robinson, F.B. v5p0498c2s
Robinson, F.C. and Hutchins, C.C.
v4p0141c2s
Robinson, F.K. v6p0472c2s
Robinson, F.M. v2p0372c2s
v2p0442c1s v3p0324c2s v3p0470c2s
v4p0031c1s v4p0076c2s v4p0090c2s
v4p0099c2s v4p0125c2s v4p0213c1s
v4p0245c1s v4p0260c1m v4p0316c2s
v4p0326c2s v4p0362c1s v4p0422c2s
v4p0435c1s v4p0473c1s v4p0536c1s
v4p0579c2s v4p0600c1m v4p0600c2s
Robinson, F.Mabel v6p0110c1s
Robinson, F.N. v6p0106c2s
v6p0328c1s
Robinson, F.P. v6p0599c2s
Robinson, F.R. v4p0157c1s
v6p0052c1s
Robinson, F.S. v4p0356c1s
v4p0446c1s v4p0526c2s v5p0029c1s
v5p0073c2m v5p0078c2m v5p0081c1s
v5p0092c1s v5p0123c2m v5p0156c2s
v5p0223c2m v5p0291c1s v5p0322c1s
v5p0459c2m v5p0566c2s v5p0632c2s
Robinson, F.T. v3p0339c1s
v4p0187c1s v4p0407c1s
Robinson, F.T. and Downes, W.H.
v4p0032c1s v4p0064c2s
Robinson, F.W. v1p0066c2s
v1p0183c1s v1p0202c1s v1p0230c1s
v1p0245c2s v1p0378c1s v1p0749c2s
v1p0805c1s v1p0851c1s v1p1083c1s
v1p1123c1s v1p1253c1s v1p1438c2s
v2p0045c2s v2p0058c1s v2p0118c1s
v2p0216c1s v2p0355c1s v4p0063c2s
v4p0588c1s
Robinson, G. v1p0200c1s
v1p0210c1s v1p0215c2m v1p0334c1s
v3p0004c2s v3p0126c1s v6p0121c1s
v6p0249c2s v6p0257c1s
Robinson, G.H. v4p0186c2s
Robinson, G.L. v4p0155c2s
v5p0052c1s v5p0057c1m v5p0058c1s
v5p0199c1s v5p0260c2s v5p0264c2s
v5p0305c1s v5p0313c1s v5p0428c2s
v5p0442c1s v6p0029c2s v6p0061c1s
v6p0062c2s
Robinson, G.P. v6p0418c1s
v6p0671c2s
Robinson, G.T. v1p0495c1s
v2p0114c2s v2p0169c2s v2p0209c1s
v2p0465c1s v3p0334c1s v3p0413c1s
v4p0093c2s
Robinson, G.W. v6p0649c1s
Robinson, Geo.H. v4p0243c1s
Robinson, H. v1p0188c1m
v1p0537c2s v1p1040c2s v1p1148c2s
v1p1181c1s v2p0074c1s v3p0417c1s
v4p0174c2s
Robinson, H.C. v1p0060c1s
v1p0808c2s v2p0355c2s v3p0104c1s

Robinson, H.G. v1p0219c1s
v1p0386c1s v1p0392c1s v1p0417c2s
Robinson, H.H. v2p0151c1s
v2p0267c2s v2p0374c1s v3p0260c1s
v5p0417c2s
Robinson, H.H. and Pirsson, L.V.
v5p0377c2s
Robinson, H.H., Mrs. v3p0056c2s
Robinson, H.M. v1p0140c1s
v1p0164c1m v1p0174c1s v1p0359c1s
v1p0611c1m v1p0638c1s v1p0817c1s
v1p1379c1s
Robinson, H.P. v3p0172c2s
v3p0176c2s v3p0331c1s v4p0102c2s
v4p0321c2s v4p0324c2s v4p0405c2s
v4p0471c1s v4p0472c2s v4p0553c1s
v5p0321c1s v5p0354c1s v5p0448c2s
v5p0477c1s v5p0478c1s v6p0171c1s
v6p0398c1s
Robinson, H.P. et al. v4p0553c2s
Robinson, H.S. v5p0469c1s
Robinson, H.W. v6p0490c1s
v6p0711c1s
Robinson, Harry P. v6p0256c1s
Robinson, Isabel v6p0338c1s
Robinson, J. v1p0434c1s
v1p0860c1s v1p1311c2s v1p1359c2s
v2p0162c1s v3p0005c1s v3p0119c1s
v3p0138c2s v3p0181c1s v3p0296c2s
v4p0516c1s v4p0540c1s v5p0250c2s
v5p0459c1s
Robinson, J., Sir v5p0007c2s
Robinson, J.A. v2p0267c1s
v4p0437c1s v5p0060c1s v5p0458c1s
v6p0341c2s v6p0693c2s
Robinson, J.A.A. v3p0113c2s
v4p0468c2s v4p0484c1s
Robinson, J.A.L. v1p0446c2s
Robinson, J.B. v2p0019c1s
v3p0018c2s v3p0070c2s v3p0238c2s
v4p0023c1s v4p0023c2m v4p0025c1s
v4p0088c1s v4p0266c2m v5p0007c2s
v5p0025c2s v5p0407c2s v5p0511c2s
v5p0608c1s
Robinson, J.B. and Henry, E.
v3p0059c2s
Robinson, J.C. v1p0063c2s
v1p0958c2s v1p1008c2s v1p1227c1s
v2p0024c1s v2p0032c2s v2p0374c2s
v2p0392c2s v2p0456c2s v2p0467c2s
v3p0022c1s v3p0189c1s v3p0332c1s
v4p0029c1s v4p0031c1s v4p0442c2s
v4p0480c1s v4p0483c1s v4p0517c1s
v5p0031c2s v5p0556c2s v6p0198c1s
Robinson, J.F. v2p0038c1s
Robinson, J.H. v1p0813c2s
v1p0833c1s v3p0170c2s v3p0442c1s
v4p0450c2s v4p0463c2s v4p0569c1s
v5p0217c1s v5p0220c2s v5p0266c1s
v5p0266c2s v5p0374c2s v5p0489c1s
v5p0493c1s v6p0094c2s v6p0196c2s
v6p0236c2s v6p0238c1s v6p0238c2s
v6p0390c1s v6p0535c2s
Robinson, J.K. v5p0185c1s
v5p0551c1s v5p0619c2s
Robinson, J.L. v6p0447c2s
Robinson, J.M. v6p0647c1s
Robinson, J.N. v4p0032c1s
v4p0138c1s
Robinson, J.R. v4p0318c1s
v5p0364c1s v6p0173c2s
Robinson, Janetta Newton . v4p0549c2s
Robinson, K.E. v4p0342c1s
Robinson, L. v1p0149c1s
v3p0111c1s v3p0145c2s v3p0215c2s
v3p0231c2s v4p0019c1s v4p0092c1s
v4p0092c2s v4p0102c2s v4p0103c1s
v4p0103c2s v4p0142c1s v4p0158c1s
v4p0158c2m v4p0159c1s v4p0161c2s
v4p0192c2m v4p0193c1m v4p0206c1s
v4p0258c2s v4p0263c2s v4p0271c1s
v4p0328c1s v4p0379c1s v4p0443c1s
v4p0560c1s v4p0581c1s v5p0137c2s
v5p0198c1s v5p0200c2s v5p0236c1s
v5p0239c1s v5p0414c2s v6p0224c2s
v6p0425c2s
Robinson, L.B. v5p0092c2s
v5p0295c1s
Robinson, L.G. v1p0503c2s
v1p1244c2s v2p0023c1m v2p0040c2s
v2p0125c1s v2p0275c1s v2p0421c1s
v3p0197c2s v6p0303c2s v6p0375c2s
v6p0413c2s
Robinson, L.J. v3p0468c1s
Robinson, L.L. v3p0423c2s
Robinson, L.V. v6p0076c2m
v6p0098c2s v6p0284c1s v6p0660c2s
Robinson, M. v2p0378c2s
v3p0321c1s v4p0473c2s v5p0139c1s
v5p0172c1s v5p0548c2s v5p0584c2s
v6p0240c1s
Robinson, M. and Walhouse, M.J.
v4p0410c1s
Robinson, M.C. v6p0523c2s
Robinson, M.E. v6p0130c1s
v6p0295c1s v6p0470c2s
Robinson, M.F. v4p0456c1s
v6p0444c2s
Robinson, M.H. v5p0593c1s
v6p0634c1s
Robinson, M.H. et al. v6p0318c1s
Robinson, M.S. v1p1088c2s
v4p0078c2s v4p0147c2s v4p0157c2s
Robinson, Mabel F. v3p0239c2s
Robinson, Margaret F. v6p0056c1s
Robinson, Marion v4p0552c1s
Robinson, Mary C. v6p0635c1s
Robinson, Mrs. v1p0514c1s
v1p1022c1s v1p1022c2m v1p1209c1s
v1p1231c2s v1p1296c2s
Robinson, N. v1p0089c2s
v1p0141c1s v1p0150c1s v1p0275c1s
v1p0369c1s v1p0593c1s v1p0600c1s
v1p0710c1s v1p0739c2s v1p0755c2s
v1p0790c1s v1p0833c2s v1p0835c1s
v1p0841c1s v1p0852c1s v1p0878c2s
v1p0886c2s v1p0887c2s v1p0996c2s
v1p1123c1s v1p1315c1s v2p0063c2s
v4p0020c2s v5p0143c2s v5p0381c1s
v5p0505c1s v5p0514c2s
Robinson, N.H. v5p0383c2s
Robinson, O.D. v4p0512c1s
v5p0264c2s
Robinson, O.H. v1p0742c2m
v1p1112c2s
Robinson, P. v1p0348c1s
v2p0016c1s v2p0017c1s v2p0025c1s
v2p0037c1m v2p0046c2s v2p0047c1m
v2p0050c1s v2p0070c2s v2p0108c1s
v2p0108c2s v2p0109c2s v2p0121c1s
v2p0122c1s v2p0126c2m v2p0133c2s
v2p0168c2s v2p0207c2s v2p0216c1s
v2p0242c1s v2p0259c2s v2p0299c2s
v2p0324c1s v2p0346c1s v2p0354c1s
v2p0370c2s v2p0395c1s v2p0400c2m
v2p0449c2s v2p0456c2s v3p0260c2s
v4p0021c2s v4p0051c1s v4p0204c1s
v4p0247c1s v4p0308c1s v4p0321c1s
v4p0340c2s v4p0353c2s v4p0409c2s
v4p0416c1s v4p0448c2s v4p0490c2s
v4p0518c2s v4p0540c1s v4p0543c1s
v4p0558c1s v4p0624c1s v5p0063c1s
v5p0164c2s v5p0202c2s v5p0225c2s
v5p0301c2m v5p0362c2s v5p0496c1s
Robinson, P.A. v5p0321c2s
v5p0383c2s v6p0357c1s
Robinson, Paschal v6p0239c1s
Robinson, Phil. v2p0406c2s
v2p0441c1s v3p0155c1s v3p0179c1s
v3p0226c2s v3p0404c2s
v5p0063c1m
v5p0416c1s
Robinson, R.E. v1p0107c1s
v1p0444c1s v1p0448c1s v1p0472c2s
v2p0158c1m v2p0399c1s v3p0178c2s
v3p0267c2s v4p0021c2s v4p0064c1s
v4p0354c2s v4p0398c2s v4p0607c2s
v5p0331c2s v5p0425c1s v5p0473c2s
v5p0533c2s v6p0400c2s v6p0523c2s
Robinson, R.E. and Smith, L.P.
v5p0474c1s
Robinson, R.E.L. v6p0030c1m
v6p0389c1s v6p0712c2s
Robinson, R.G. v4p0531c1s
v5p0211c1m v5p0643c2s
Robinson, R.S. v1p0543c2s
v2p0187c1s v3p0298c1s
Robinson, R.S., Sir v1p0641c2s
v1p0665c2s
Robinson, R.T. v1p0290c1s
v1p1393c1s
Robinson, S. v1p0846c1s
v1p1064c2s v1p1203c1s v1p1207c2s
v2p0353c1s v2p0425c2s v4p0519c2s
Robinson, S.W. v1p0104c1s
v1p0162c1m v1p0400c2s v1p0502c2s
v1p0503c2s v1p0523c1s v1p0739c2s
v1p0937c2s v1p1012c1s v1p1110c1m
v1p1222c2s v1p1236c2s v1p1248c1s
v1p1273c1s v1p1289c1s v1p1390c2s
v2p0056c1s v2p0094c2s v2p0172c1s
v2p0363c1s v2p0363c2s v2p0419c1s
v2p0457c2s
Robinson, T. v1p0104c2s
v1p0465c1s v1p1042c1s v2p0082c1s
v2p0366c1s v2p0373c1s v4p0376c1s
v4p0377c2s v6p0049c1s
Robinson, T., Mrs. v1p0219c2s
v1p0489c2s v1p1137c1s v1p1207c2s
Robinson, T.A.L.V.I. v1p0555c1s
Robinson, T.C. v4p0067c2s
Robinson, T.H. v1p0060c2s
v1p1217c2s v6p0436c2s
Robinson, T.L. v3p0299c1s
Robinson, T.R. v1p0903c2s
v1p1291c2s v4p0196c1s v4p0606c1s
Robinson, T.W. v6p0328c2s
Robinson, Tracy v6p0476c1s
v6p0476c2s
Robinson, V.J. v3p0069c1s
Robinson, W. v1p0013c1s
v1p0334c1s v1p0406c1s v2p0023c1s
v2p0264c2s v3p0228c2s v3p0282c2s
v3p0328c2s v4p0319c1s v4p0416c1s
v4p0416c2s v4p0437c2s v6p0247c1s
Robinson, W.A. v4p0413c1s
Robinson, W.C. v1p0026c1s
v1p0201c1s v1p0220c1s v1p0220c2s
v1p0444c2s v1p0447c2s v1p0483c2s
v1p0523c2s v1p0540c2s v1p0818c2s
v1p0907c2m v1p0994c2s v1p0998c1s
v1p1314c1s v1p1411c2s v2p0120c1s
v3p0387c2s v4p0050c1s v4p0295c1s
v4p0367c2s v4p0488c1s v4p0488c2s
v5p0327c1s v6p0366c2s v6p0414c1s
Robinson, W.F. v4p0634c2s
v5p0643c1s
Robinson, W.G. v5p0430c2s
v6p0417c2s
Robinson, W.H. v4p0152c1s
v4p0239c1s v4p0328c2s
Robinson, W.J. v2p0064c2s
Robinson, Wilfrid C. v6p0182c2s
Robinson, Wm. v4p0416c2s
Robiquet, P. v4p0212c2s
Robison, J. v1p1246c1s
Robjohns, S. v1p0194c1s
v1p0380c1s v1p0679c2s v1p1071c2s
v1p1421c1s v2p0023c1s v2p0023c2s
v2p0059c2s v2p0066c1s v2p0122c2s
v2p0192c2s v2p0289c1s v2p0327c2s
v2p0341c2s v2p0357c2s v2p0361c1s
v2p0379c1m v2p0379c2s
Roblin, R.P. v6p0097c2s
Robson, A. v5p0342c2s
Robson, I.S. v6p0081c1s
v6p0408c2s
Robson, J. v2p0292c1m
v5p0115c1s
Robson, J.S. v5p0255c1s
v6p0217c1s
Robson, M.H. v1p0463c2s
Robson, N. v1p0195c2s
Robson, S. v5p0003c1s
Roby, E.W. v6p0507c2s
Roby, H.J. v2p0111c1s
v3p0365c2s v3p0388c1s
Roby, H.J. et al. v2p0250c1s
Rochard, J. v4p0107c2s
v4p0162c1s v4p0189c2s v4p0578c1s
Rochas, A.de v2p0156c2s
v3p0007c2s v3p0176c1s v3p0380c2s
Rochas, A.de and Espitallier, G.
v3p0018c2s
Rochat, F. v5p0021c2s
Roche, C. v3p0234c2s
v5p0268c1s
Roche, E.De La v2p0318c1s
Roche, J. v5p0094c2s
v5p0155c2s v5p0217c2s
Roche, J.A. v2p0391c2s
v3p0124c2s
Roche, J.H.La v5p0238c1s
v5p0532c2s
Roche, J.J. v1p0103c2s
v3p0314c1m v4p0131c1s v5p0473c1s
Roche, J.P. v5p0239c1s
v5p0642c2s
Roche, K. v1p0398c1s
v1p0627c1s v1p0748c1s v2p0196c1s
Roche, M.de la v6p0603c2s
v6p0643c1s
Rochefort, H. v1p0478c2s
v2p0165c2s v3p0052c1s v5p0146c2s
Rochelle, J.H. v2p0098c1s
Rochelle, R.de v1p1322c2s
Rochester, A.T. v1p1237c2s
Rochussen, T.A. v1p1077c2s
Rock, J. v5p0286c1s
Rock, M. v3p0198c1s
v6p0023c1s
Rockefeller, J.D. et al. . v5p0593c1s
Rockenbach, S.D. v6p0095c2s
Rockewell, C.H. v4p0089c1s
Rockham, R.B. v4p0334c1s
Rockhill, W.W. v3p0078c2m
v3p0285c2s v3p0428c2m v3p0474c1s
v4p0078c1s v4p0378c2s v4p0576c1s
v4p0634c1s v5p0083c2s v5p0109c2s
v5p0112c1s v5p0134c2s v5p0320c1s
Rockstro, W.S. v2p0270c1s
v2p0475c2s
Rockstroh, E. v6p0275c2s
Rockwell, A.D. v2p0400c1s
v5p0011c2s
Rockwell, A.E.P. v6p0175c2s
v6p0599c2s
Rockwell, A.F. v2p0171c1s
Rockwell, A.G. v6p0222c2s
Rockwell, Anna G. v6p0374c1s
v6p0561c2s
Rockwell, C. v2p0094c1s
Rockwell, C.H. v1p1264c1s
v1p1264c2s v2p0129c2s v4p0130c2s
v4p0395c2s v4p0511c1s v4p0511c2s
v4p0592c2s v4p0594c2s
Rockwell, E.A. v1p0452c2s
Rockwell, E.F. v1p0226c1s
v1p0927c2m v1p0965c2s v1p1082c2s
v1p1306c2s
Rockwell, J.H. v5p0416c1s
v6p0634c2s
Rockwood, C.G. v1p0875c2s
Rockwood, C.G., jr. v1p0377c1m
v1p0679c2s v2p0128c1m
Rockwood, F.E. v4p0321c2s
Rockwood, G.I. and Green, S.M.
v4p0547c2s
Rockwood, J.G. v6p0160c2s
Rockwood, Laura C. v6p0299c2s

Rod, E. v4p0215c1s v4p0460c1s v5p0144c1s v5p0210c1s v5p0238c2s v5p0576c1s v5p0581c2s v5p0604c2s v5p0615c2s v6p0241c2s v6p0289c1s v6p0334c2s v6p0713c2s
Rod, Edouard v5p0646c1s
Rodd, A.E. v3p0074c2s
Rodd, E.A. v3p0172c2s
Rodd, R. v2p0006c2s v2p0346c1s v2p0404c2s v3p0031c1s v3p0081c2s v3p0183c2s v3p0405c2s v3p0428c1s v3p0446c2s v4p0030c2s v4p0190c1s v4p0350c1s v4p0377c1s v4p0421c2s v4p0483c2s v4p0609c2s
Rodd, Rennell v4p0434c1s v4p0607c2s
Rodeffer, J.D. v6p0136c1s v6p0373c2s
Roden, C.B. v6p0522c1s
Rodenbach, Georges v4p0551c2s
Rodenberg, J. v4p0351c1s v4p0494c1s
Rodenbough, T.F. v1p0864c2s v4p0400c2s v4p0594c1s v5p0376c1s
Roderick, Stella V. v6p0540c1s
Rodes, R.E. v1p0216c2s v1p0518c2s
Rodet, M. v1p0902c2s
Rodet, M.D.L. v1p0283c1s v1p0480c1s v1p0798c1s v1p1282c2s v1p1283c1s
Rodey, B.S. v6p0030c1s v6p0451c1s
Rodger, A.M. v4p0436c2s
Rodger, J.W. v4p0099c1m v4p0333c2s v4p0536c1m
Rodgers, F. v6p0668c2s
Rodgers, J. v1p0824c1s v1p1280c1s v1p1310c1s v1p1359c1s
Rodgers, J. and Schoenborn, A. v1p0327c2s
Rodgers, J.B. v5p0444c2s v5p0445c2s
Rodgers, M.A. v6p0660c1s
Rodgers, R. v5p0121c2s
Rodgers, S.A. v2p0161c2s
Rodgers, W.C. v5p0363c1s
Rodgers, W.R. v6p0476c1s
Rodin, A. v6p0237c1s v6p0262c2s
Rodman, E. v1p0888c1s
Rodman, G.H. v6p0198c2s
Rodman, S., jr. v2p0094c1s
Rodman, T. v6p0686c2s
Rodman, T.P. v1p0385c1s v1p0820c1s
Rodman, W. v6p0531c1s v6p0593c2m v6p0711c2s
Rodman, W.A. v4p0612c2s
Rodman, W.W. v3p0338c1s v6p0508c1s
Rodney, G.B. v5p0271c1s v5p0416c1s v6p0182c1s
Rodrigues, J.C. v1p0158c1s v1p0191c1s v1p0963c1s v3p0053c2s
Rodriguez, J.I. v2p0457c2s v3p0359c1s v3p0403c1s v3p0453c2s v4p0215c2s v5p0147c1s v5p0544c2s
Rodway, A.J. v3p0142c1s
Rodway, J. v4p0087c2s v4p0209c1s v4p0213c2s v4p0244c1m v4p0395c1s v4p0416c2s v4p0472c2s v4p0538c2s v5p0158c1s v6p0082c2s v6p0276c1s
Rodwell and Fergus v1p1159c1s
Rodwell, G.F. v1p0017c1s v1p0072c2s v1p0224c2s v1p0225c1s v1p0428c1m v1p0497c2m v1p0579c2s v1p0582c1m v1p0622c2s v1p0652c1s v1p0669c1s v1p0751c2s v1p0933c1s v1p1006c2m v1p1161c2s v1p1163c2s v1p1228c1s v1p1304c2s v1p1368c2s v1p1369c1s v1p1377c1s v2p0020c2s v2p0127c1s v2p0325c2m v2p0460c1s v2p0462c2s
Rodwell, J.M. v1p0003c1s v1p0123c2s v1p0427c2m v1p0620c1s v1p0620c2s
Roe, A.C. v2p0198c1s v2p0317c2s
Roe, A.H. v5p0575c1s
Roe, A.S. v5p0044c2s v5p0072c2s v5p0640c1s v6p0405c1s v6p0693c1s
Roe, A.S. and Hoar, G.F. . v6p0325c1s v6p0707c1s
Roe, C. v5p0189c1s v5p0284c2s v5p0472c2s
Roe, C.A. v5p0117c1s v5p0189c2s v6p0007c1s v6p0314c2s v6p0315c1s
Roe, E.D., jr. v4p0542c1s v4p0622c1s
Roe, E.P. v1p0115c2s v1p0493c1s v1p1210c1s v1p1260c2s v2p0110c1s v2p0177c2s v2p0243c2s v2p0248c2s v2p0307c2s v2p0365c1s v2p0422c2s v3p0151c2s v3p0237c1s v3p0282c1s v3p0350c2s v3p0363c2s
Roe, F.A. v3p0277c2s v3p0326c1s v4p0085c2s v4p0482c2s
Roe, G.M. v2p0409c2s
Roe, H.G., Mrs. v3p0058c1s v3p0301c1s
Roe, J. v3p0369c2s
Roe, Mary W. v5p0541c2s
Roe, R.S. v6p0390c2s
Roe, V.E. v6p0090c2s v6p0619c2s
Roe, W.C. v5p0381c2s
Roe, W.J. v5p0155c2s v5p0620c1s v6p0470c2s v6p0688c2s v6p0693c1s
Roe, W.M. v2p0180c2s
Roebling, J.A. v1p0161c1m v1p0162c1s v1p0919c2s v4p0275c1s v4p0457c2s
Roebling, W.A. v1p0161c1s v5p0620c1s
Roebling, W.A., Mrs. v6p0686c1s
Roebuck, J.A. v1p0193c2s v1p0880c2s
Roechling, H.A. v5p0521c2s
Roeder, A. v4p0014c1s v4p0116c2s v6p0002c2s v6p0060c2s v6p0061c1s v6p0129c1m v6p0481c2s v6p0533c1s
Roeder, Adolph v4p0116c1s
Roelker, C.R. v1p0463c1s v1p0663c1s v1p1250c1s
Roemer, F. v1p1297c1s
Roepper, W.T. v1p0844c2s
Roepstorff, F.A.de v1p0037c1s v1p0921c1s
Roesler, F.E. v1p0030c2s
Roess, E. v6p0020c1s
Roewade, A.J. v6p0659c1s
Roffe, W. v3p0104c2s
Roge, C.F.B. v6p0075c2s
Roger, C. v2p0295c1s
Roger, W.M. v5p0597c2s
Roger-Miles, L. v6p0524c1s
Rogers and Boye v1p0750c1s
Rogers, A. v3p0166c2s v3p0211c2s v4p0244c1s v4p0279c2s v4p0527c1s v6p0162c2s v6p0312c2s v6p0313c1m v6p0313c2s v6p0314c2s
Rogers, A.A. v4p0016c1s v5p0045c2s v5p0130c2s v5p0222c2s v5p0564c1s v6p0603c2s
Rogers, A.C. v4p0470c2s
Rogers, A.D. v1p1114c1s
Rogers, A.E. v2p0457c1s v6p0324c1s
Rogers, A.F. v5p0546c1s v6p0160c1s
Rogers, A.F. and Winslow, C.-E.A. v6p0066c2s
Rogers, A.G. v2p0205c1s
Rogers, A.K. v5p0001c2s v5p0194c1s v5p0199c2s v5p0261c1s v5p0404c1s v5p0519c1s v5p0578c2s v6p0001c2s v6p0004c2s v6p0057c2s v6p0309c2s v6p0425c2s v6p0531c2s v6p0533c1m v6p0596c2s
Rogers, Alma A. v6p0702c2s v6p0706c1s
Rogers, Anna A. v5p0202c2s v5p0396c1s v6p0381c1s
Rogers, B. v4p0221c2s
Rogers, B.F. v3p0209c1s
Rogers, C. v1p1296c1s v2p0007c2s v2p0016c1s v2p0030c2s v2p0032c2s v2p0106c1s v2p0112c2s v2p0180c1s v2p0194c2s v2p0204c1s v2p0232c2s v2p0253c2s v2p0345c1s v2p0374c2s v2p0391c1m v2p0392c1m v2p0476c1s
Rogers, C.C. v3p0318c2s v4p0543c1s
Rogers, C.G. v4p0142c1s v4p0162c2s v4p0259c2s v4p0260c1s v4p0267c1s v4p0412c2s v4p0448c2s v4p0619c1s v5p0095c1s v5p0309c1s v5p0531c1s
Rogers, C.R. v4p0087c2s v5p0392c1s
Rogers, D. v3p0213c2s
Rogers, E. v5p0560c2s
Rogers, E. and Rogers, E.T. v1p0396c1s
Rogers, E.B. v4p0298c2s
Rogers, E.M. v1p0627c2s
Rogers, E.P. v1p0689c1s v4p0089c2s
Rogers, E.R. v6p0634c2s
Rogers, E.T. v1p0329c2s v1p0345c2s v2p0091c2s v2p0135c1s
Rogers, E.T. and Rogers, E. v1p0396c1s
Rogers, E.T. and Rogers, M.E. v1p0185c1s v1p0395c2s v1p1264c1s
Rogers, E.V. v5p0637c1s v6p0705c2s
Rogers, E.W. v6p0292c2s v6p0584c2s
Rogers, E.W., Mrs. v5p0120c1s
Rogers, Elmer E. v6p0657c1s
Rogers, F. v1p0269c2s v1p0453c1s v1p0605c1s v1p0788c1s v1p0788c2s v3p0268c1s v6p0652c2s
Rogers, F.J. v4p0349c2s
Rogers, G. v2p0183c2s v6p0270c2s
Rogers, G.A. v1p0304c2s v1p0383c2s v4p0631c1s
Rogers, G.M. v4p0011c1s
Rogers, H. v1p0040c1s v1p0047c2s v1p0073c1s v1p0100c2s v1p0165c2s v1p0169c1s v1p0180c2s v1p0273c2s v1p0315c1s v1p0315c2s v1p0317c1s v1p0345c2s v1p0391c1s v1p0416c2s v1p0417c1s v1p0423c2m v1p0436c1s v1p0440c1s v1p0494c1s v1p0513c1s v1p0517c2s v1p0520c2s v1p0566c2s v1p0618c1s v1p0736c2s v1p0743c1s v1p0755c1s v1p0758c2s v1p0777c1s v1p0794c2s v1p0806c1s v1p0868c1s v1p0908c2s v1p0954c1m v1p0976c2s v1p0991c1s v1p1016c2s v1p1049c1s v1p1053c1s v1p1057c1s v1p1060c1s v1p1064c2s v1p1067c2s v1p1079c1s v1p1086c1s v1p1088c2s v1p1098c2s v1p1103c2s v1p1104c2s v1p1108c1s v1p1121c1s v1p1164c1s v1p1203c1s v1p1203c2m v1p1217c2s v1p1261c1s v1p1318c2s v1p1338c1s v2p0162c1s v5p0061c2s v6p0079c1s
Rogers, H.B. v2p0049c1s
Rogers, H.D. v1p0267c2m v1p0268c1m v1p0268c2s v1p0508c1s v1p0919c2m v1p0995c2s v1p1005c2s
Rogers, H.D. and Rogers, W.B. v1p1406c2s
Rogers, H.J. v5p0431c1s v6p0318c1s
Rogers, H.W. v1p0752c1s v2p0096c2s v2p0100c1s v2p0260c1s v3p0147c1s v3p0444c2s v4p0157c1s v5p0122c1s v5p0162c1s v5p0294c1s v5p0327c2s v5p0494c1s v5p0543c2s v5p0574c1s v6p0324c1s v6p0366c2s
Rogers, H.W. et al. v3p0091c2s
Rogers, Howard J. v6p0194c1s
Rogers, I.G. v4p0405c2s
Rogers, Ida C. v6p0283c1s
Rogers, J. v6p0639c1s
Rogers, J., jr. v6p0553c1s
Rogers, J.C. v6p0191c2s
Rogers, J.D. v5p0027c2s v6p0577c1s v6p0653c1s
Rogers, J.E. v4p0047c2s v6p0074c2s v6p0156c1s v6p0349c1s v6p0567c2s v6p0656c1s
Rogers, J.E.T. v1p0015c2s v1p0139c1s v1p0198c1s v1p0264c1s v1p0386c1s v1p0412c2s v1p0545c2s v1p0607c1m v1p0627c2s v1p0713c2s v1p0714c1s v1p0954c2m v1p0963c2s v1p0973c1s v1p0978c2s v1p0998c2s v1p1049c2m v1p1099c1s v1p1285c2s v1p1358c1s v1p1379c1s v2p0130c1s v2p0143c1s v2p0143c2s v2p0145c1s v2p0208c2m v2p0367c1s v2p0405c2s v2p0408c1s v2p0461c1s v3p0015c2s v3p0141c1s v3p0398c1m v3p0449c1s
Rogers, J.E.Thorold v4p0073c1s
Rogers, J.G. v1p0146c1s v1p0177c1s v1p0249c2s v1p0250c1s v1p0250c2s v1p0550c1s v1p0741c1s v1p0847c1s v1p0925c1s v1p1025c2s v1p1341c1s v2p0058c1s v2p0083c2s v2p0084c1s v2p0084c2m v2p0085c2m v2p0089c2s v2p0098c2m v2p0099c1m v2p0113c1s v2p0113c2s v2p0179c2m v2p0188c2s v2p0189c1s v2p0190c1s v2p0210c1s v2p0225c2s v2p0226c1s v2p0235c2s v2p0279c1s v2p0296c1m v2p0298c1s v2p0315c2s v2p0330c1s v2p0332c1s v2p0351c2m v2p0364c2s v2p0384c2s v2p0416c1s v2p0426c1m v2p0447c2s v2p0469c2s v2p0475c2s v3p0096c1s v3p0096c2s v3p0182c2s v3p0248c1s v3p0405c2m v3p0447c2s v4p0011c1s v4p0169c2s v4p0227c2s v4p0239c1s v4p0240c2m v4p0328c2s v4p0589c2s v5p0117c1m v5p0163c1s v5p0197c2s v5p0234c2s v5p0247c1s v5p0247c2s v5p0332c1m v5p0332c2s v5p0410c2s v5p0425c1s v5p0489c2s v5p0490c1s v5p0587c2s v6p0066c2s v6p0191c2m v6p0269c2s v6p0459c1s
Rogers, J.G. and Dicey, E. v4p0239c2s
Rogers, J.G. and Reid, W.. v5p0594c2s
Rogers, J.G. et al. v4p0027c2s v5p0332c1s v6p0191c2s
Rogers, J.Guinness v5p0588c1s
Rogers, J.H. v6p0092c1s
Rogers, J.I. v5p0443c1s
Rogers, J.K. v3p0327c1s v3p0459c1s
Rogers, J.M. v4p0365c1s v5p0200c1s v5p0208c2s v5p0634c1s v6p0049c1s v6p0147c1m v6p0284c1s v6p0293c1s v6p0382c2s v6p0488c1s v6p0491c2s v6p0503c2s v6p0515c1s v6p0524c2s v6p0578c2s v6p0589c2s v6p0644c1s v6p0663c2s v6p0689c1s
Rogers, J.R. v5p0220c1s

Rogers, J.S. v5p0492c2s
Rogers, J.T. v1p0984c1s
v5p0226c2s
Rogers, J.Z. v3p0255c1s
v3p0262c2s v3p0418c1s
v4p0582c2s
Rogers, James D. v6p0320c2s
Rogers, Julia E. v6p0395c1s
v6p0590c2s
Rogers, L.B. v2p0197c2s
Rogers, L.L. v6p0462c2s
Rogers, M.A.H. and Sidgwick, A.
v4p0627c2s
Rogers, M.E. v1p0064c2s
v1p0289c1s v1p0960c2s v1p1278c2s
v1p1427c2s
Rogers, M.E. and Rogers, E.T.
v1p0185c1s v1p0395c2s v1p1264c1s
Rogers, R. v3p0035c1s
Rogers, R.A.P. v6p0647c1s
Rogers, R.B. v6p0277c2s
Rogers, R.C. v1p1403c2s
Rogers, R.E. and Rogers, W.B.
v1p0844c2s
Rogers, R.S. v4p0612c1s
Rogers, R.V. v3p0070c1s
v4p0060c2s v4p0185c1s v4p0281c1s
v4p0542c1s v4p0572c1s v4p0579c1s
v5p0112c2s v5p0160c1s v5p0220c2s
v5p0225c2s v5p0308c2s v5p0363c1s
v5p0381c2s v5p0416c2s v6p0166c2s
v6p0402c1s v6p0499c2s v6p0545c2s
v6p0702c2s
Rogers, R.W. v3p0024c1s
v4p0033c2s v4p0172c2s
Rogers, S. v4p0036c2s
v4p0287c1s v5p0196c1s v5p0328c1s
Rogers, S.S. v4p0117c1s
v4p0144c2s
Rogers, T. v3p0316c1m
Rogers, T.H. v1p0742c1s
v5p0093c2s v5p0478c1s v5p0597c2s
Rogers, Thorold v3p0321c1s
Rogers, W.A. v1p1132c1s
v2p0026c1s v2p0283c2s v2p0382c2s
v2p0392c1s v2p0417c2m v3p0097c2s
v5p0132c1s
Rogers, W.B. v1p0665c1s
v1p1101c2s v1p1108c2s v1p1222c2s
v1p1375c1s
Rogers, W.B. and Rogers, H.D.
v1p1406c2s
Rogers, W.B. and Rogers, R.E.
v1p0844c2s
Rogers, W.C. v2p0083c2s
v2p0250c2s v2p0369c2s v4p0567c1s
Rogers, W.F. v4p0430c1s
Rogers, W.G. v1p0311c2s
Rogers, W.H.H. v1p0363c1s
v5p0140c1s
Rogers, W.R.C. v1p0282c2s
v1p0318c2s v1p0397c2s v1p0428c2s
v1p0646c1s v1p0825c1s
Rogers, W.S. v6p0131c2s
v6p0485c1s
Rogerson, J.B. v1p0796c1s
Roget, I.L. v3p0054c2s
Roget, J.L. v1p0061c2s
v1p0365c1s v1p0900c2s
Rogge, A. v1p1179c1s
Rohe, G.H. v2p0199c1s
v3p0279c1s v4p0613c2s
Rohn, A. v1p0874c1s
Rohn, S.S. et al. v5p0348c1s
Rohne, H. v5p0290c1s
Rohrbach, C.A.P. v5p0028c2s
Rohree, A.L. v6p0235c1s
Roka, F.C. v1p0394c2s
Rokewoode, J.G. v1p0100c1s
v1p0933c2s v1p0951c1s
Roland, E. v1p0450c1s
v1p0738c1s
Roland, H. v4p0522c1s
v5p0353c1m v5p0516c1s v5p0527c1m
v5p0621c2s
Rolfe, C. v2p0183c2s
v2p0215c1s
Rolfe, E.S. v5p0064c1s
Rolfe, F.W. v6p0292c1s
v6p0508c2s
Rolfe, G.B. v4p0092c1s
v4p0252c2s v4p0254c1s
Rolfe, H.W. v4p0037c2s
Rolfe, J.C. v3p0015c1s
v3p0428c2s v4p0321c2s v5p0326c2s
v5p0634c2s v6p0130c1s v6p0363c1s
v6p0580c1s
Rolfe, J.C. et al. v3p0334c1s
Rolfe, R.A. v4p0416c1s
v4p0416c2s
Rolfe, W.J. v2p0031c1s
v2p0391c2m v2p0397c1m v2p0397c2s
v2p0435c1s v3p0057c2m v3p0382c1s
v3p0387c2s v3p0388c1s v3p0388c2s
v4p0076c1s v4p0263c1s v4p0448c2s
v4p0517c2s v4p0518c1m v4p0518c2m
v4p0519c1m v4p0570c1m v5p0197c1s
v5p0522c1s v5p0522c2m v5p0523c1m
v5p0523c2m v5p0524c1s v5p0556c1s
v5p0573c1s v6p0588c2s v6p0639c1s
v6p0650c2s
Rolfs, P.H. v4p0444c1s
v6p0500c1s v6p0650c2s
Rolin, A. v3p0108c1s
Rolin-Taequemyns, G. v1p0744c2s
Rolker, A.W. v6p0022c1m
v6p0048c2s v6p0069c2s v6p0176c1s
v6p0200c1s v6p0512c1s v6p0598c2s
v6p0655c1s v6p0698c1s
Roller, F.A. v5p0424c2s
Roller, G.C. v5p0216c1s
v6p0616c2s
Rolleston, C. v3p0288c1s
v4p0284c1s v4p0383c1s v4p0410c2s
v4p0604c2s v6p0057c1s v6p0058c1s
v6p0109c2s v6p0246c1s v6p0309c1s
v6p0498c1s v6p0598c2m v6p0600c1s
Rolleston, D. v4p0634c2s
Rolleston, G. v1p0041c1s
v1p0261c2s v1p0411c1s v1p0435c2s
v1p1258c1s
Rolleston, M. v6p0014c1s
Rolleston, T.W. v3p0057c2s
v3p0105c2s v3p0111c2s v3p0221c2s
v4p0327c2s v4p0504c2s v6p0540c2s
Rollins, A.W. v2p0003c1s
v2p0205c2s v2p0211c2s v2p0232c2s
v2p0240c2s v2p0246c2s v2p0298c2s
v2p0364c2s v2p0456c2s v2p0477c2s
v3p0037c1s v3p0103c2s v3p0151c2s
v3p0208c1s v3p0267c1s v3p0355c2s
v3p0424c1m v3p0435c1s v3p0474c2s
v4p0045c2s v4p0149c2s v4p0161c1s
v4p0192c2s v5p0317c1s
Rollins, Alice W. v4p0123c1s
Rollins, F.W. v5p0405c1s
v5p0406c1s v6p0463c2s
Rollins, G.S. v5p0486c2s
v6p0024c2s
Rollins, G.W. v3p0011c1s
Rollins, J.R. v1p1084c2s
v1p1114c2s v2p0332c2s
Rollins, R. v1p0013c2s
Rollins, W. v5p0642c2s
v6p0264c2s
Rollins, W. and Towbridge, J.
v6p0527c1s
Rollins, W.E. v6p0164c1s
Rollit, A. v5p0130c2s
Rollit, A.K. v2p0258c1s
Rolls, J.E.W. v1p1435c2s
Rolph, J.F. v2p0153c2s
v3p0201c2s
Rolph, J.F. and Waddington, S.
v2p0429c1s
Rolph, John F. v4p0339c2s
Rolston, W.E. v6p0581c1s
v6p0625c2s
Romain, C.E. v3p0233c1s
v3p0397c1s
Roman, A. v2p0037c1s
v5p0425c2s
Roman, A.B. v1p0352c1s
Roman, S.R. v5p0049c1s
Romanes, C.H. and Prosser, R.B.
v2p0475c1s
Romanes, F.E. v6p0366c2s
Romanes, Francis E. v6p0220c2s
Romanes, G.J. v1p0042c1s
v1p0044c2s v1p0117c2s v1p0292c2s
v1p0433c2s v1p0434c2s v1p0435c1s
v1p0450c1s v1p0620c2m v1p0624c2s
v1p0646c2s v1p0648c2s v1p0817c2s
v1p0819c1s v1p0843c1s v1p0843c2s
v1p0907c1m v1p1007c1s v1p1042c2s
v1p1087c1s v1p1308c1s v1p1311c2s
v1p1432c2s v2p0015c1m v2p0016c1m
v2p0038c1s v2p0078c1s v2p0099c2s
v2p0112c1s v2p0148c2s v2p0149c1s
v2p0149c2m v2p0211c1s v2p0212c2s
v2p0222c2m v2p0273c2s v2p0283c1s
v2p0289c2m v2p0295c1s v2p0307c1m
v2p0307c2m v2p0389c1s v2p0394c2s
v2p0424c1s v2p0439c2s v2p0459c2s
v2p0480c1s v3p0014c1m v3p0019c2s
v3p0078c1s v3p0111c1m v3p0120c1s
v3p0145c2s v3p0194c2m v3p0205c2s
v3p0242c1s v3p0250c2s v3p0265c2s
v3p0274c1s v3p0280c1s v3p0297c1s
v3p0314c1s v3p0384c2m v3p0386c2s
v3p0403c2m v3p0407c2s v3p0429c1s
v3p0468c1m v3p0470c2s v4p0148c1s
v4p0166c1s v4p0275c2s v4p0320c1s
v4p0341c1s v4p0369c2s v4p0394c2s
v4p0423c2s v4p0464c1s v4p0514c1m
v4p0562c1s v4p0575c1s v4p0616c2s
v5p0198c2s
Romanes, G.J. and Allman, G.J.
v1p0681c2s
Romanes, G.J. and Conder, E.R.
v2p0437c2s
Romanes, G.J. and Goodwin, H.
v2p0280c1s
Romanes, G.J. and Hartog, M.
v4p0514c1s
Romanes, G.J. and Lankester, E.R.
v3p0111c1s
Romanes, G.J. et al. v3p0166c2s
v3p0318c2s v4p0423c2s
Romanes, J.H. v6p0658c2s
Romanis, J.M. v1p1291c2s
Romanoff, H.C. v3p0369c2s
Romanus v6p0341c1s
Romayne, M. v1p1005c2s
v2p0211c2s
Romayne, R. v1p0299c2s
Rombauer, R.S. v6p0363c2s
Rombouts, J.E. v2p0158c2s
Rome, L.S. v5p0226c2s
Rome, W. and Roberts, W. . v5p0151c2s
Romeiser, T.H. v6p0446c1s
Romer, I. v1p0891c1s
Romer, I.F. v1p1112c2s
v1p1266c2s
Romer, J.F. v1p0904c1s
Romer, J.I. v3p0016c1s
v6p0297c2s
Romer, Mrs. v1p0007c1s
v1p0477c1s v1p0574c1s v1p0774c2s
v1p0994c2s v1p1107c2s v1p1145c1s
v1p1258c1s
Romero, C. v4p0368c2s
Romero, M. v2p0287c1s
v3p0318c2s v4p0140c1s v4p0160c2s
v4p0220c2s v4p0368c1s v4p0368c2m
v4p0526c1s v4p0567c1s v5p0024c2s
v5p0373c1m v5p0543c1m
Romero, M. and Felsenthal, E.T.
v4p0140c1s
Romeyn, H. v4p0484c1s
v4p0484c2s v4p0592c1s v5p0337c1s
v6p0297c2s
Romieux, J. v6p0236c2s
Romig, Lida v6p0349c1s
Romilly, F. v1p0486c2s
v1p1285c1s
Romilly, H.H. v3p0301c2s
v3p0401c1s
Romilly, S., Sir v1p0113c1s
v1p0271c1s
Romney, A.B. v5p0577c2s
Romney, A.D. v5p0454c2s
Ronald, E.B. v6p0695c1s
Ronaldshay, Earl v6p0057c2s
v6p0489c2s
Ronaldshay, Earl and Penton, E.
v6p0058c1s
Ronaldshay, Lord v6p0047c2s
Ronaldson, C.E. v1p0367c1s
Ronan, A.S. v5p0091c2s
Ronayne, J. v5p0206c2s
Ronayne, M. v1p0746c1s
v3p0241c1s
Rondani, A. v4p0029c2s
v4p0294c1s
Rondinella, L.F. v4p0221c1s
Rondot, N. v4p0631c1s
Rondthaler, J.A. v4p0427c2s
v4p0633c1s
Roney, C.H. v1p0268c1s
v1p1003c1s v2p0238c2s v2p0359c2s
Roney, T.C. v5p0078c2s
Roney, W.R. v4p0160c1s
v5p0554c1s
Ronne, A.B. v4p0370c1s
v5p0543c2s
Ronse, W.H.D. v5p0041c2s
v5p0321c2s
Rontgen, W.C. v1p1291c2s
v4p0487c1m
Rood, A.E. v4p0306c2s
Rood, H. v1p0651c1s
v4p0372c1s
Rood, H.E. v5p0127c2s
v5p0585c2s v6p0133c1s v6p0425c1s
Rood, J.B. v5p0226c1s
Rood, O.N. v1p0017c1s
v1p0278c1s v1p0278c2s v1p0352c1s
v1p0399c1m v1p0399c2s v1p0437c2s
v1p0747c1m v1p0748c2s v1p0777c1m
v1p0835c2s v1p0836c1s v1p0945c1s
v1p0959c1s v1p0986c2s v1p0989c1s
v1p1003c2s v1p1004c1m v1p1222c2s
v1p1233c2m v1p1234c1s v1p1252c2m
v1p1291c2s v1p1360c2s v1p1369c1s
v2p0093c2s v2p0340c1s v4p0125c1m
v4p0441c1s v4p0487c1m v5p0128c2s
v5p0129c1s v5p0184c2s v5p0449c1m
v6p0199c1s
Roof, K.M. v6p0052c1s
v6p0187c1s v6p0245c1s v6p0329c1s
v6p0395c2s v6p0458c2s v6p0482c2s
v6p0662c2s
Roof, Katharine M. v6p0350c2s
v6p0468c2s
Roof, T.H. v1p1362c1s
Roofs, N. v4p0297c1s
Rook, C. v4p0091c2s
v5p0361c2s v5p0548c1s v6p0017c1s
v6p0212c1s
Rooke, H. v1p0163c1s
v1p0345c2s v1p0368c1m v1p1012c1s
v1p1115c1m v1p1122c2m v1p1123c1s
Rooker, A. v1p1089c2s
Rooker, F.Z. v4p0294c2s
v6p0478c1s
Rooney, J.J. v5p0169c2s
v5p0187c1s v5p0623c1s
Rooney, L.J.F. v5p0496c1s
Roop, C.Y. v6p0546c1s
Rooper, G. v6p0099c2s

v6p0127c2s v6p0196c2s v6p0205c2s
Rooper, W.O. v2p0140c2s
Roorbach, Eloise J. v6p0711c2s
Roorbach, Eloise T. v6p0420c2s
Roork, R.N. v6p0459c1s
Roos, J.D.C.De v1p0751c1s
Roos, W. v4p0604c2s
Roosa, D.B.S. v4p0193c1s
Roosa, D.B.St.J. v1p0437c2s
v4p0107c2s v5p0368c1s
Roosa, D.B.St.J. et al. .. v4p0206c2s
Roosa, H. v6p0213c2s
Roose, P. v3p0263c1s
Roose, P.W. v3p0068c2s
v3p0122c2s v3p0231c2s v3p0240c2s
v4p0075c1s v4p0093c1s v4p0104c1s
v4p0151c2s v4p0218c1s v4p0364c2s
v4p0424c1s v4p0501c1s v4p0620c1s
v5p0008c2s v5p0099c1s v5p0155c1m
v5p0155c2s v5p0168c1s v5p0223c2s
v5p0224c1s v5p0251c1s v5p0260c2m
v5p0281c1m v5p0369c2s v5p0370c2s
v5p0379c2s v5p0394c2s v5p0466c1s
v5p0527c1s v5p0578c1s v6p0465c2s
v6p0534c1s
Roose, Pauline W. v4p0149c2s
v4p0615c2s v5p0456c1s
Roose, R. v2p0199c1s
v2p0263c2m v3p0118c2m v3p0150c1s
v3p0215c2s v3p0247c1s v3p0250c1s
v3p0257c2s v3p0457c2s v4p0006c1s
v4p0009c2s v4p0108c1s v4p0119c2s
v4p0156c2s v4p0363c1s
Roosevelt, J.A. v6p0301c1s
Roosevelt, J.W. v4p0058c2s
v4p0157c1s v4p0264c2s v4p0341c1s
v4p0474c1s
Roosevelt, M. v6p0515c2s
v6p0600c1s
Roosevelt, R.B. v1p0311c1s
Roosevelt, T. v2p0037c1s
v2p0087c1s v2p0253c1s v2p0313c1s
v3p0010c2s v3p0086c2m v3p0099c2s
v3p0165c1s v3p0203c2s v3p0209c1s
v3p0214c1s v3p0225c2s v3p0354c1m
v3p0368c1s v3p0390c1s v3p0444c1s
v3p0460c1s v4p0014c2s v4p0016c1s
v4p0017c2s v4p0033c1s v4p0117c1m
v4p0123c2s v4p0124c2s v4p0137c1s
v4p0178c1s v4p0219c1s v4p0259c2s
v4p0366c1s v4p0401c1m v4p0450c2s
v4p0476c1s v4p0498c2s v4p0516c2s
v4p0532c1s v4p0540c1s v4p0596c1s
v4p0603c2s v4p0614c1s v4p0614c2s
v5p0021c1s v5p0029c2s v5p0101c2s
v5p0120c2s v5p0121c1s v5p0144c2s
v5p0204c2s v5p0214c1s v5p0224c2s
v5p0276c2s v5p0375c1s v5p0399c2s
v5p0407c2m v5p0413c1s v5p0456c2s
v5p0457c1s v5p0457c2s v5p0481c2s
v5p0482c1s v5p0498c1s v5p0535c1s
v5p0565c2s v5p0599c2s v5p0602c2s
v5p0639c1s v5p0640c2s v6p0055c1s
v6p0087c1s v6p0128c1s v6p0151c1s
v6p0398c1s v6p0453c1s v6p0533c2s
v6p0539c2s v6p0551c2s v6p0599c2s
v6p0600c1s v6p0631c1s v6p0659c1s
Roosevelt, T. and Stickney, J.L.
v5p0160c1s
Roosevelt, T. et al. v2p0089c1s
v5p0603c1s
Roosevelt, Theodore v4p0114c2s
v4p0400c2s v5p0139c1s v6p0232c2s
v6p0281c2s v6p0674c1s v6p0687c1s
v6p0702c1s v6p0706c1s
Root, A.S. v6p0065c2s
Root, D. v5p0211c1s
Root, E. v5p0539c1s
v6p0477c2s v6p0540c1s
Root, E.A. v4p0592c1s
Root, E.T. v5p0064c2s
v6p0126c2s
Root, F.D. v6p0458c1m
Root, F.S. v5p0167c1s
v5p0620c1s
Root, F.W. v4p0389c2m
v4p0586c1s v4p0606c2s v4p0607c1s
v5p0530c2s v5p0614c1s
Root, G.F. v4p0333c1s
v4p0430c2s
Root, J.A. v1p0285c1s
v1p0292c1s
Root, J.C. v5p0115c2s
Root, J.P. v2p0473c2s
Root, J.W. v3p0202c1s
v4p0428c1s v5p0077c1s v5p0526c2s
v6p0271c1s v6p0326c2s
Root, M.E. and Maltby, A.B.
v6p0371c2s
Root, N.W.T. v1p0911c2s
Root, O. et al. v3p0091c2s
Root, T.H. v4p0301c1s
Root, W. v3p0188c2s
v5p0148c1s
Roote, C.B. v6p0290c1s
Roots, L.S. and Jones, J.K.
v3p0087c2s
Roper, C. v4p0219c1s
v4p0625c1s
Roper, D.C. v6p0153c1s
Roper, E. v6p0491c2s
Roper, R.C. v6p0377c2s
Roper, S.C.D. v4p0086c2s
v4p0619c1s v5p0091c1s v5p0628c1s
Roper, T.W. v5p0457c2s
Ropes, A.E. v6p0240c1s
Ropes, A.R. v2p0203c2s
v2p0367c2s v3p0010c1s v3p0162c2s
v3p0386c1s v3p0403c1s v5p0090c2s
v5p0355c1s v5p0634c2s
Ropes, A.R. and Austin, L.F.
v4p0619c2s
Ropes, C.H.J. v5p0306c2s
Ropes, C.J.H. v1p0242c1s
v1p0663c1s v2p0042c2s v2p0044c1s
v2p0088c2s v4p0301c1s v6p0641c1m
Ropes, E.H. v1p1308c1s
v3p0326c1s
Ropes, I.C. v1p0573c1s
Ropes, J. v1p0326c1s
Ropes, J.C. v1p0894c2s
v1p0895c2s v1p1392c2s v2p0036c2s
v2p0060c2s v2p0453c2s v3p0062c1s
v3p0296c1s v3p0383c2s v3p0390c2s
v3p0442c2s v3p0443c1s v3p0457c2s
v4p0601c2s
Ropes, J.H. v4p0026c2s
v4p0057c1s v4p0248c1s v4p0616c2s
v5p0009c1s v6p0063c1s v6p0544c1s
Ropes, J.H. and Torrey, C.C.
v5p0306c2s
Ropes, J.S. v1p0024c2s
v1p0092c2s v1p0093c1s v1p0093c2s
v1p0325c1s v1p0325c2s v1p0326c1m
v1p0556c1s v1p0620c2s v1p0963c1s
v1p0990c2s v1p1264c2s v1p1344c1s
v1p1349c1s v1p1351c2s
Ropes, J.S. et al. v1p1232c2s
Ropes, W.L. v1p0290c2s
v2p0148c2s
Roquette, O. v1p1323c2s
Rordan, Torkild S. v6p0063c2s
Rorer, Jona.T. v6p0037c2s
Ros, Dowager Lady De v3p0459c2s
Rosa, C. v3p0312c2s
Rosa, E.B. v4p0175c1s
v5p0275c2s v6p0443c1s v6p0613c1m
Rosa, J.C. v6p0157c2s
Rosamund, B. v5p0465c2s
Rosanoff, M.A. v6p0169c1s
v6p0527c1s v6p0555c2s
Rosaro, N. v1p0609c1s
Rosavo, A. v1p1193c2s
Rosavo, N. v3p0273c1s
Roscher, W. v1p1309c1s
Roscoe, E. v1p0198c2s
v1p0300c2s v1p0315c1s v1p0350c1s
v1p0773c1s v1p0780c1s v1p0811c2s
v1p1040c1s v1p1184c2s v1p1185c1s
v1p1186c1s v1p1189c1s v1p1425c1s
v1p1426c1s v2p0246c2s
Roscoe, E.S. v1p0245c1s
v1p0437c2s v1p0648c1s v1p0697c2s
v1p0721c2s v1p0770c1s v1p0908c2s
v1p1160c1s v4p0147c1s v4p0193c2s
v4p0202c1s v4p0323c1s v4p0579c2s
Roscoe, E.S. and Clergue, H.
v5p0323c1s
Roscoe, G. v5p0157c2s
v5p0437c1s
Roscoe, Gertrude v6p0163c1s
Roscoe, H. v3p0009c2s
v3p0422c1s
Roscoe, H.E. v1p0074c1s
v1p0176c1s v1p0225c2s v1p0639c1m
v1p0744c2s v1p1100c2s v1p1163c2s
v1p1234c1m v1p1266c2s v2p0076c2m
v2p0090c2s v3p0026c1s v3p0055c1s
v3p0075c2s v4p0098c2s v4p0170c1s
v4p0353c1s v4p0506c2s v5p0083c1s
v5p0584c1s
Roscoe, R. v6p0120c1s
Roscoe, T. v1p0200c1s
v1p0304c2s v1p0309c1s v1p0711c1s
v1p1040c1s v1p1318c1s
Rose, A. v4p0241c2s
Rose, A.C. v1p0131c1s
Rose, A.G., Mrs. v4p0308c2s
Rose, A.J. v6p0117c1s
Rose, A.M. v5p0373c2s
Rose, A.P. v4p0461c2s
Rose, D.A. v4p0133c1s
Rose, D.M. v6p0404c1s
Rose, E. v1p0440c1s
v1p0568c2s v1p0808c1s v1p1183c2m
v1p1379c2s v2p0094c2s v4p0312c1s
v4p0518c1s
Rose, E.B. v6p0072c1s
Rose, F.H. v6p0393c1s
Rose, F.J. v5p0526c2s
Rose, G.B. v4p0026c2s
v5p0011c2s v5p0021c2s v5p0031c2s
v5p0237c1s v5p0385c1s v5p0427c2s
v5p0485c1s v6p0022c2s v6p0036c2s
v6p0072c1s v6p0394c2s v6p0427c1s
v6p0539c1s v6p0593c2s
Rose, G.W. v5p0248c2s
Rose, H. v1p0115c2m
v1p0786c2s v1p0967c1s v3p0449c1s
v3p0472c2s
Rose, H.A. v6p0672c2s
Rose, H.C. v1p0437c2s
Rose, H.J. v1p0047c1s
v1p0604c1s v1p1229c2s v1p1230c1s
v1p1440c1s
Rose, I.N. v4p0007c1s
Rose, J. v1p0452c2s
v1p0701c1s v1p1154c1s
Rose, J.A. v1p1410c1s
Rose, J.C. v2p0072c2s
v2p0392c2s v2p0451c2s v2p0455c1s
v3p0072c1m v3p0270c2s v3p0299c1s
v3p0301c2s v3p0339c2s v3p0442c1s
v4p0008c1s v4p0009c1s v4p0238c2s
v4p0262c1s v4p0265c2s v4p0350c1s
v4p0494c2s v5p0099c2s v5p0403c1m
v5p0540c2s v6p0049c1s v6p0108c1s
v6p0270c1s v6p0447c2s v6p0454c2s
Rose, J.H. v4p0087c2s
v4p0392c2s v5p0017c2s v5p0239c2s
v5p0241c2s v5p0350c1s v5p0409c2s
v6p0041c1s v6p0099c1s v6p0146c2s
v6p0157c1s v6p0231c2s v6p0236c1s
v6p0269c1s v6p0339c2s v6p0416c1s
v6p0436c2s v6p0442c1m v6p0443c2s
v6p0688c2s
Rose, J.Holland v6p0099c1s
v6p0653c1s
Rose, J.N. v4p0135c2s
v4p0289c1s v4p0409c2s
Rose, J.W. v4p0613c1s
Rose, M. v4p0308c1s
v4p0348c1s
Rose, Mary H. v5p0327c2s
v5p0361c2s
Rose, N.J. v4p0186c1s
v4p0306c2s v4p0423c1s
Rose, N.M. v5p0134c1s
Rose, P.La v5p0086c1s
v6p0594c1s
Rose, R.Geo. v6p0689c1s
Rose, T.K. v4p0011c1s
v4p0133c1s v4p0230c1s v4p0637c1s
v5p0237c2s v5p0318c2s v5p0371c2s
Rose, T.K. and Roberts-Austen, W.C.
v5p0013c1s
Rose, U.M. v1p1408c1s
v2p0442c1s v4p0553c2s v5p0051c2s
v5p0125c2s v5p0312c2s v5p0327c2s
v6p0134c1s
Rose, W.J. v1p1326c2s
Rose, W.K. v1p0782c2s
v1p1177c2s v1p1192c1s v2p0404c2s
v4p0038c1s v5p0618c1s
Rose, W.W. v6p0349c2s
Rose-Soley, A.J. v4p0038c2s
v4p0127c2s v4p0310c2s v4p0320c1s
v4p0398c1s
Rose-Soley, A.R. v5p0607c1s
v6p0477c2s
Rose-Soley, J.F. v4p0501c1s
v5p0234c1s v5p0531c1s v5p0570c2s
v5p0595c2s v6p0683c1s
Rosebault, C.J. et al. ... v4p0609c1s
Rosebery, Earl of v5p0144c2s
v5p0245c1s v5p0550c1s
Rosebery, Lord v5p0398c1s
v5p0452c2s v5p0552c2s
Roseboro', V. v3p0077c1s
v3p0078c1s v3p0089c1s v3p0157c2s
v3p0224c1s v3p0228c2s v3p0243c1s
v3p0249c1s v3p0295c2s v3p0304c1m
v3p0357c1s v3p0368c2s v4p0051c2s
v4p0226c2s v4p0254c2s v4p0504c2s
v4p0604c2m v5p0425c1s v6p0027c1s
v6p0695c2s v6p0712c1s
Roseboro', V. and Bronson, H.
v5p0282c2s
Roseboro', Viola v4p0228c1s
Rosebrugh, A.M. v1p0437c2s
Rosecrans, L. v1p0006c2s
v1p0386c1s v1p0540c2m v1p1396c2s
Rosecrans, W.S. v1p1076c1s
v2p0103c1s v2p0184c2s v3p0075c1s
Rosegger, P. v5p0163c1s
v5p0214c1s v5p0517c1s v5p0536c2s
Rosegger, P.K. v4p0578c2s
Rosell, C.R. and Speyers, C.L.
v5p0486c1s
Rosen, L. v5p0398c1s
v6p0442c1s
Rosenau, N.S. v4p0100c2s
v5p0101c2s
Rosenbach, H.P. v2p0297c1s
v3p0335c1s
Rosenbaum, S. v6p0343c2s
Rosenbaum, W.A. v5p0184c2s
Rosenberg, A. v1p0691c1s
v1p0960c2s v1p0961c1s v6p0344c1s
Rosenberg, A. and Morrell, W.H.
v6p0601c1s
Rosenberg, C.C. and Balliet, H.S.
v6p0198c1s
Rosenberg, C.G. v1p0966c1s
v1p1041c1s v1p1151c1s
Rosenberg, E. v1p1234c1s
Rosenberg, Ida L. v6p0372c2s
Rosenberger, J.C. v4p0558c2s
Rosenblatt, H. v1p1148c2s
Rosenblatt, L.G. v4p0286c1s

Rosenblatt, W.M. v1p0690c1s
v1p0691c2s
Rosenburg, C.G. v1p0054c2s
Rosenfeld, G.H. v4p0151c1s
Rosenfeld, J. v6p0608c2s
Rosenfeld, S. v3p0334c2s
Rosengarten, J.G. v1p0049c1s
v1p0169c1s v1p0259c1m v1p0408c2s
v1p0514c1s v1p0986c1s v1p0988c1s
v1p1030c2s v1p1050c2s v1p1384c2s
v1p1419c2s v2p0070c1s v2p0087c1s
v2p0107c2s v2p0151c2s v2p0167c1s
v2p0175c2s v2p0209c1s v2p0232c1s
v2p0257c2s v2p0261c1s v2p0288c2m
v2p0312c1s v2p0329c2s v2p0345c1s
v2p0347c2s v2p0364c2s v2p0365c2s
v2p0452c2s v2p0453c2s v2p0466c1s
v2p0470c2s v2p0477c2s v2p0482c2s
v3p0124c2s v3p0302c2s v4p0486c1s
v4p0548c2s v5p0194c2s v5p0264c1s
v5p0439c2s v6p0017c2s v6p0239c1s
v6p0252c1s v6p0509c1s v6p0650c2s
v6p0667c2s
Rosengarten, J.J. v1p1350c1s
v1p1365c2s
Rosenhain, W. v6p0132c2s
Rosenkranz, K. v1p0530c2m
v1p0531c1s v1p0531c2s v1p0582c2m
v1p0594c2s v1p0702c1s v1p0761c1s
v1p0843c1s v1p0984c1s
Rosenkranz, P.H. v1p0642c2s
Rosenkranz, R. v1p0392c1s
Rosenraad, C. v5p0383c1s
Rosenthal, H. v6p0289c1s
v6p0420c2s v6p0559c2s
Rosenthal, Herman v6p0010c2s
Rosenthal, I. v4p0018c1s
Rosenthal, L. v2p0197c1s
v2p0379c1s
Rosevelt, H. v1p0188c2s
v1p0444c2s v1p0448c1s v1p0584c2s
v1p0848c2s v1p0875c2s v1p0877c2s
v1p0942c2s v1p1144c2s v1p1440c1s
Rosewater, Frank v4p0059c2s
Rosewater, V. v4p0175c1s
v4p0336c2s v6p0197c2s v6p0541c1s
v6p0634c2s
Rosin, D. v4p0221c1s
v4p0252c2s
Rosland, W.P. v1p0325c1s
Roslyn, G. v1p0407c1s
v1p0471c1s v1p0800c2s v1p1186c1s
v1p1186c2s v1p1193c2s v1p1220c1s
v1p1240c1s v2p0055c2s v2p0130c1s
Rosmead, Lord v6p0417c1s
Rosny, J.H. v3p0305c2s
v3p0398c2s v4p0528c1s v5p0359c1s
v5p0572c1s v6p0261c2s
Rospide, R. v4p0490c2s
Ross, A. v2p0477c2s
v3p0209c1s v5p0086c1s
Ross, A.F. v6p0517c2s
Ross, A.H. v1p0289c2s
v1p0290c1m v1p0290c2s v1p0291c1s
v1p0769c2m v1p0846c2s v1p1118c1s
v1p1140c2s v1p1423c2s v2p0098c2m
v2p0154c1s v3p0010c2s v3p0096c1s
v3p0096c2s v4p0111c2s v4p0129c1m
Ross, A.H.D. v4p0086c1s
v4p0375c1s
Ross, C. v2p0267c1s
v4p0125c1s v4p0128c2s v4p0192c2s
v4p0543c2s v5p0001c1s v5p0129c2m
v5p0322c1s v5p0362c1s v5p0432c2s
v5p0589c2s v5p0595c1s v6p0560c2s
Ross, C.H. v5p0127c2s
v5p0368c2s v5p0452c1s v5p0580c2s
v5p0623c1s
Ross, C.S. v4p0034c2s
v4p0145c2s v4p0429c2s
Ross, Clinton v5p0517c1s
Ross, D.M. v2p0251c1s
v4p0614c1s v5p0169c2s
Ross, D.W. v6p0035c2s
v6p0171c2s v6p0636c1s
Ross, E. v2p0114c2s
Ross, E.A. v3p0306c1s
v4p0143c2s v4p0283c2s v4p0322c2s
v4p0337c1s v4p0432c1m v4p0460c2s
v4p0466c1s v4p0527c2s v4p0531c2s
v4p0534c2s v4p0555c2s v4p0565c1m
v4p0565c2s v4p0599c2s v5p0019c2s
v5p0034c2s v5p0175c2s v5p0176c2s
v5p0195c2s v5p0381c1s v5p0475c2s
v5p0535c1m v5p0536c1s v6p0506c2s
v6p0595c2m v6p0599c2m v6p0600c1s
v6p0602c1m v6p0665c2s
Ross, E.D. v5p0042c1s
v5p0441c2s
Ross, E.G. v4p0026c1s
v4p0304c1m v4p0450c1s v4p0594c2s
Ross, F.E. v6p0287c1s
Ross, G.R.T. v6p0175c2s
Ross, G.W. v4p0476c2s
v4p0566c1s v5p0213c1s v5p0245c2s
v5p0365c2s v6p0098c1s v6p0459c2s
Ross, H.H. v6p0330c1s
v6p0400c2s
Ross, H.R. v3p0076c2s
Ross, H.V. v6p0318c2s
v6p0574c2s
Ross, J. v1p0178c1s
v1p0939c2s v1p1220c1s v1p1334c2m
v2p0021c2s v2p0036c1s v2p0159c1s
v2p0190c2s v2p0380c2s v2p0430c2s
v2p0449c2s v3p0110c2s v3p0167c1s
v3p0193c1s v3p0220c2s v3p0222c1s
v3p0290c2s v3p0383c2s v3p0393c1s
v4p0037c2s v4p0318c2s v4p0368c2s
v5p0079c1s v5p0109c1s v5p0110c1s
v6p0475c2s
Ross, J., Mrs. v2p0170c1s
v3p0451c2s
Ross, J.A. v4p0549c1s
Ross, J.B. v4p0406c2s
Ross, J.C. v4p0196c1s
Ross, J.C., Sir v1p0073c2s
Ross, J.D. v4p0211c1s
v4p0496c1s
Ross, J.E. v6p0472c1s
v6p0531c1s
Ross, J.H. v2p0029c1s
v4p0271c2s v4p0359c2s v4p0374c2s
v5p0380c1s v5p0580c1s v5p0644c2s
v6p0351c2s v6p0452c1s
Ross, J.W. v6p0259c1s
Ross, James H. v6p0122c1s
Ross, Janet v3p0116c2s
v4p0065c1s v6p0239c1s
Ross, Janet, Mrs. v3p0061c2s
Ross, L. v4p0511c1s
v5p0136c1s
Ross, L.S. v5p0121c1s
Ross, M. v3p0210c1s
v3p0222c1s v3p0304c2s v3p0406c1s
v4p0086c2s v4p0518c2s v5p0032c2s
v6p0232c1s
Ross, M. and Somerville, E.Ae.
v5p0297c2s
Ross, M. and Somerville, E.O.
v6p0145c1s v6p0164c1s
Ross, M.A. v2p0301c1s
Ross, M.R.S. v1p0270c2s
Ross, O.C.D. v1p0420c1s
v1p0994c2s v4p0204c2s
Ross, P. v2p0293c2s
v3p0148c2s v4p0595c2s
Ross, P.D. v3p0439c2s
Ross, R. v5p0096c1s
v5p0357c1m v5p0388c2m v6p0396c1s
v6p0431c2m v6p0603c1s
Ross, R.T. v5p0205c1s
Ross, Robert v6p0055c1s
Ross, T. v1p0108c1s
v1p0819c2s
Ross, W. v1p0206c2s
v2p0392c1s
Ross, W.A. v2p0049c2s
v2p0191c2s
Ross, W.G. v2p0371c1s
v2p0454c2s v3p0106c1s v3p0106c2s
v3p0127c2s v3p0138c1s v3p0296c1s
v6p0621c1s
Ross, W.H. and McCoy, H.N.
v6p0527c1s
Ross, W.L. v6p0130c2s
Ross, W.P. v1p0226c1s
Ross, W.S. v4p0379c1s
Ross-Johnson, C. v6p0516c2s
Rosse, I.C. v5p0404c2s
Rosselli, Amelia v6p0295c2s
Rosser, F. v5p0174c2s
Rosser, R.H. v5p0285c2s
v5p0375c1s
Rosset, C.W. v2p0273c1s
Rossetti, C.G. v1p0181c2s
v1p0245c1s v1p0402c1s v1p0812c2s
v1p1129c1s v2p0111c2s v2p0476c1s
v4p0167c1s v4p0614c2s
Rossetti, D.G. v1p0266c2s
v1p0565c2s v1p0569c1s v1p1220c2s
v1p1372c2s
Rossetti, L.M. v4p0075c1s
Rossetti, W.M. v1p0040c2s
v1p0064c2m v1p0165c1s v1p0169c1s
v1p0611c1s v1p0762c2s v1p0786c1s
v1p0840c2s v1p1020c2s v1p1130c1m
v1p1132c2s v1p1169c2s v1p1171c1s
v1p1189c2m v1p1232c1s v1p1344c1s
v1p1414c2s v2p0378c2s v2p0399c2s
v2p0446c1s v4p0076c2s v4p0324c1s
v4p0457c1s v4p0492c1s v4p0509c2s
v5p0497c1s v5p0497c2s
Rossi, A. v5p0160c1s
v5p0261c2s v5p0579c2s v6p0330c2s
v6p0331c2s
Rossi, A.J. v6p0328c2s
v6p0648c1s
Rossi, J.B.de v1p1363c1s
Rossi, L. v5p0033c2s
Rossignol, J.E.Le v4p0018c2m
v5p0175c2s v5p0638c1s v6p0529c2s
Rossiter, A.M.S. v4p0416c1s
Rossiter, C. v2p0023c2s
Rossiter, E. v1p0228c2s
v2p0077c2s v2p0078c1s
Rossiter, N.L. v1p1197c2s
Rossiter, W. v2p0425c2s
v3p0025c1s v3p0472c1s
Rossiter, W.S. v6p0106c2s
v6p0153c2s v6p0489c1s v6p0517c1m
v6p0522c2s v6p0555c1s v6p0667c2s
Rosslyn, Earl v3p0440c1s
Rossman, V.D. v4p0609c2s
v5p0130c2s
Rost, E.C. v5p0251c2s
v6p0470c2s v6p0648c1s
Rost, R. v2p0061c2s
v2p0194c1s
Rost, R. and Chandler, H.W.
v3p0048c1s
Rostand, E. v5p0010c1s
v5p0311c1s
Roswell, E.P. v1p1316c1s
Roswell, F.W. v1p0001c1s
v1p0258c2s v1p0441c2s v1p0838c2s
v2p0133c2s
Roszel, S.A. v1p1017c2s
Rotberg, Baroness v5p0092c1s
v5p0312c1s
Rotch, A. v1p0176c2s
v4p0023c2s
Rotch, A.L. v2p0364c1s
v4p0367c1s v5p0077c1s v5p0317c2m
v6p0040c1s v6p0239c2s v6p0353c1s
v6p0377c1s v6p0412c2m
v6p0700c1s
Rotch, A.L. and
Brot, L.Teisserenc de . v6p0040c1s
v6p0412c2s
Rotch, L.A. v6p0005c1s
Rotch, W.J. v6p0118c1s
Roth, C.L. v5p0052c2s
Roth, H.L. v2p0006c1s
v2p0018c1s v2p0334c1s v3p0050c2s
v3p0373c2s v4p0068c1s v4p0137c1s
v4p0493c2s v5p0039c2s v5p0053c2s
v5p0411c1s v5p0567c2s
Roth, H.Ling v5p0053c2s
Roth, J. v1p1146c2s
v1p1390c2s
Roth, J.D. v5p0135c2s
Roth, S. v5p0014c1s
Roth, W.E. v3p0427c1s
Rothe, C.E. v1p0533c2s
Rothe, Prof. v4p0057c2s
Rothe, R. v1p1102c2s
v2p0027c2s v3p0365c1s
Rothenstein, W. v4p0233c2s
v5p0524c1s
Rothenstein, W. and Way, T.R.
v5p0342c1s
Rothera, G.B. v4p0218c2s
Rotherham, F. v4p0521c1s
Rothermel, J.G. v4p0352c1s
Rothery, G.C. v2p0419c2s
v2p0428c2s v3p0372c1s v4p0135c2s
Rothery, H.J. v3p0217c2s
Rothery, S.E. v5p0565c2s
Rothery, S.E., Mrs. v5p0507c1s
Rothpletz, A. v3p0126c2s
Rothrock, A.M. v6p0091c2s
v6p0660c2s
Rothrock, J.F. v4p0209c1s
Rothrock, J.T. v1p0907c1s
v1p0927c1s v1p1015c1s v1p1375c2s
Rothschild v5p0284c2s
Rothschild, A.de v4p0059c1s
Rothschild, C.de v1p1423c2s
Rothschild, F. v2p0023c1s
v3p0054c2s v3p0160c2s v3p0259c1s
v4p0211c2s
Rothschild, F., Baron v3p0088c1s
v3p0138c1s
Rothschild, W. v5p0049c1s
v5p0063c2s
Rothwell, A. v1p0082c2s
v4p0449c1s
Rothwell, C.C. v3p0079c1s
v3p0440c1s
Rothwell, J.S. v3p0085c1s
v3p0436c2m v4p0486c1s v4p0584c2m
Rothwell, R. v1p1218c1s
Rottenburg, Baron de v1p0906c2s
v1p1244c1s v1p1269c1s
Rotter, A.T. v4p0198c1s
Rottermund, Count v1p1271c1s
Rottier, M. v1p1311c2s
Rottmann, A. v5p0156c2s
Rouble, C.T.W. v4p0097c2s
Roucher, C. v1p1297c2s
Roudebush, V. v5p0291c1s
Rouge, M. v6p0648c1s
Rougemont, F.de v1p0506c1s
v1p1073c1s
Rouillion, L. v5p0560c1s
Roulhac, T.R. v4p0406c2s
Round, J.A. and Russell, G.W.E.
v5p0365c1s
Round, J.H. v2p0036c2s
v2p0051c1s v2p0054c2s v2p0121c1s
v2p0167c1s v2p0193c2s v2p0208c2s
v2p0248c1s v2p0259c2s v2p0302c1s
v2p0315c2s v2p0392c1s v2p0409c2s
v2p0444c1s v3p0069c2s v3p0076c1s
v3p0085c1s v3p0110c1s v3p0120c2m
v3p0138c2m v3p0194c1s v3p0216c1s
v3p0237c2s v3p0241c2s v3p0247c2s
v3p0256c1s v3p0361c2s v3p0362c2s
v3p0372c2s v3p0450c2s v3p0464c1s

v4p0049c2s v4p0097c2s v4p0099c2s v4p0118c1s v4p0136c2s v4p0177c2s v4p0178c1s v4p0181c2m v4p0250c1s v4p0312c2s v4p0318c1s v4p0355c1s v4p0404c2s v4p0419c2s v4p0420c1s v4p0453c2s v4p0462c2s v4p0467c1s v4p0521c2s v4p0548c2s v5p0116c2s v5p0117c1s v5p0117c2s v5p0123c1s v5p0125c2s v5p0137c2s v5p0144c2s v5p0165c1s v5p0186c2m v5p0207c1s v5p0257c2m v5p0262c1s v5p0265c1s v5p0266c1s v5p0299c1s v5p0345c2s v5p0414c1s v5p0469c1s v5p0504c1s v5p0504c2s v5p0573c2s v5p0631c2s v6p0054c2s v6p0108c1s v6p0134c2s v6p0160c1s v6p0167c2s v6p0194c2s v6p0248c1s v6p0344c2s v6p0389c1s v6p0486c2s v6p0561c2s

Round, J.H. and Gairdner, J. v2p0015c2s

Round, J.H. and Stevenson, W.H. v3p0069c2s v5p0631c2s

Round, J.H. and Yeatman, P. v2p0107c1s

Round, J.Horace and McColl, Malcolm v5p0116c2s

Round, O.S. v1p0049c1s v1p0135c1s v1p0137c1m v1p0171c2s v1p0839c1s v1p1324c1s

Round, W.F. v5p0504c1s

Round, W.M.F. v1p0135c1s v2p0107c2s v3p0208c2m v4p0139c2s v4p0251c2s v4p0255c1s v5p0467c1s

Roundell v3p0082c2s

Roundell, C.S. v1p0014c2s v6p0258c1s

Roundell, J. v6p0496c1s

Roundell, J.E. v4p0087c2s v4p0234c2s v4p0491c1s v4p0579c1s

Rounds, C. v1p0114c2s

Rounds, I. v2p0432c1s

Rounds, N. v1p0097c2s v1p0124c2s v1p1232c1s v1p1411c1s

Rounds, O.A. v1p0434c1s v2p0149c1s v2p0152c1s v2p0161c2s v2p0280c1s

Rounds, R.S. v3p0012c2s

Roundy, A.M. v5p0316c2s v5p0594c1s

Roundy, H. v1p0235c2s

Rountree, E.K. v4p0585c2s

Rouquie, G. v5p0309c1s

Rous-Marten, C. v5p0343c2s v5p0344c1m v5p0431c1s v5p0477c2s v5p0478c1s v6p0382c1s v6p0382c2m

Rouse, F.P.P. v5p0089c2s

Rouse, W.H.D. v4p0205c1s v4p0295c1m v4p0327c1s v4p0362c1s v4p0480c1s v5p0178c1s v5p0391c1s v5p0505c1s v5p0547c1s v6p0272c2s v6p0572c2s v6p0650c2s v6p0673c1s

Rouse, W.J. v3p0252c1s

Rousiers, P.de v4p0532c2s v5p0281c1s

Rousse, P.W. v1p0998c1s

Rousseau, E. v1p0108c1s

Rousseau, M. v3p0329c2s

Rousselet, C.F. v6p0552c2s

Rousselot, C.F. v6p0508c1s

Roussillon, L.E. v6p0242c1s v6p0391c2s

Routh, E. v6p0632c1s

Routh, E.M.G., Miss v6p0213c1s

Routh, J.E. v6p0304c2s

Routh, J.E., jr. v6p0248c1s v6p0647c2s

Routh, W. v4p0219c1s v4p0558c1s

Routledge, F. v3p0434c1s

Routledge, J. v1p0630c2s v1p0633c2s

Routledge, R.W. v3p0180c2s

Routzahn, E.G. v6p0016c2s v6p0129c1s v6p0347c2s v6p0436c2s v6p0656c1s

Rouvet, M. v4p0605c2s

Rouvier, F. v2p0132c2s v2p0166c1s

Roux, H.Le v3p0105c1s v3p0320c1s v4p0074c2s v4p0139c2m v4p0473c1s v4p0480c2s v4p0503c1s v5p0419c2s v6p0002c1s

Roux, L.C. v5p0068c2s

Roux, P. v6p0393c1s

Rouyer, J. v2p0113c2s

Rovinsky, A. et al. v6p0343c2s

Rovnianek, P.V. v6p0597c2s

Row, C.A. v1p0128c1s v1p0241c2s v1p0251c1s v1p1056c2s v1p1326c1s v1p1356c2s v2p0297c1s v2p0356c2s

Row, C.B.Le v3p0355c1s

Row, P. v1p0980c2s

Row, R.R. v3p0196c2s v3p0212c2s

Row-Fogo, J. v5p0392c1s v5p0568c1s

Row-Fogo, J.A. v5p0515c1s

Rowan, A.S. v5p0147c2s v6p0256c1s

Rowan, Dr. v1p0777c1s

Rowan, F. v1p1131c1s

Rowan, F.J. v1p1247c2m v6p0248c1s v6p0615c2s

Rowan, M. v3p0453c1s

Rowan, T. v1p0664c2s v1p1250c2s

Rowan-Robinson, H. v6p0168c2s

Rowbotham, J. v2p0199c1s

Rowbotham, J.F. v1p0884c1s v2p0303c1s v3p0109c2s v3p0144c1s v3p0293c1m v3p0293c2m v3p0299c2s v3p0328c2s v3p0379c1s v3p0436c2s v3p0452c2s v4p0020c2s v4p0033c2s v4p0231c1s v4p0233c1s v4p0357c1s v4p0373c1s v4p0415c1m v4p0415c2s v4p0564c1s v4p0585c1s v4p0609c2s v5p0225c1m v5p0276c1s v5p0331c1s v6p0057c2s v6p0182c2s v6p0230c1s v6p0588c1s v6p0658c2s

Rowcroft, C. v1p1309c2s

Rowe, A.D. v1p0592c1s v1p0632c2s v1p0852c2s

Rowe, A.W. v4p0210c1s

Rowe, C.J. v3p0027c2s

Rowe, E.C. v6p0162c1s

Rowe, E.G. v6p0251c2s

Rowe, Eliz. G. v6p0380c2s

Rowe, H.K. v5p0187c2s

Rowe, J.B. v1p0385c2s v1p1119c2s

Rowe, J.F. v1p0191c1s v1p0240c1s v1p0244c1s v1p0442c2s v1p0687c2s v1p0964c1s v1p1091c1s v1p1353c2s

Rowe, J.G. v4p0510c2s

Rowe, J.P. v6p0521c1s

Rowe, L.S. v3p0244c2s v3p0336c2s v4p0115c1s v4p0316c1s v4p0340c1s v4p0597c1s v4p0604c1s v5p0119c2m v5p0120c1s v5p0457c2s v5p0460c2m v5p0536c2s v5p0543c2s v5p0556c2s v5p0602c1s v5p0641c1s v6p0160c2s v6p0173c1s v6p0414c1s v6p0435c2s v6p0436c1m v6p0477c2s v6p0493c2s v6p0510c1s v6p0621c1s v6p0692c2s

Rowe, N. v1p0419c1s v1p1048c2s v1p1137c1s

Rowe, O.M.E. v2p0318c1s v4p0192c2s

Rowe, O.O'F. v6p0255c2s

Rowe, P.T. v5p0645c1s

Rowe, R. v1p0140c1s v1p0332c2s v1p0463c1s v1p0677c1s v1p0682c1s v1p0762c2s v1p0763c2s v1p0765c2s v1p0766c1s v1p0767c1s v1p1142c1s v1p1142c2s v2p0300c2s

Rowe, R. and Strahan, A. . v1p0764c2s

Rowe, R.P.P. v4p0493c1s

Rowe, S. v2p0344c2s

Rowe, S.H. v5p0106c1s v5p0106c2s v5p0107c1s v5p0304c2s v6p0293c2s

Rowe, W.H. v5p0271c1m v5p0475c2s v5p0630c1s

Rowe, W.R. v4p0404c2s

Rowell, E.P. v6p0286c1s

Rowell, F. v5p0430c2s

Rowell, G.A. v1p0077c1m v1p0432c2s v1p1080c2s

Rowell, G.R. v1p0957c2s

Rowell, J.B. v4p0257c2s

Rowell, J.C. v3p0261c2s v4p0329c1s v4p0508c1s v6p0136c2s

Rowell, M.W. v5p0271c1s

Rowett, E. v2p0061c2s v3p0060c2s

Rowland, A. v2p0089c2s v3p0213c1s v3p0288c1s v6p0124c1s

Rowland, A.J. v2p0434c2s v2p0480c2s v5p0183c1s

Rowland, A.O. v3p0033c2s

Rowland, F.A.A. v5p0281c2s

Rowland, F.F. v6p0543c2s

Rowland, H.A. v1p0398c2s v1p0400c1s v1p0787c2s v1p0788c1s v1p1100c2s v1p1369c1s v2p0245c2s v2p0322c2s v2p0390c1m v3p0036c1s v3p0458c1s v4p0176c2s v5p0184c2s v5p0449c2s v5p0513c2s

Rowland, H.A. and Barker, G.F. v1p0399c2s

Rowland, H.A. and Bell, L. v3p0263c2s

Rowland, H.A. and Penniman, T.D. v5p0184c2s

Rowland, H.A. et al. v3p0134c1s v4p0487c1s

Rowland, H.C. v5p0219c1s v6p0049c1s v6p0071c2s v6p0121c2s v6p0179c2s v6p0231c1s v6p0242c2s v6p0249c2s v6p0282c2s v6p0312c1s v6p0329c1s v6p0389c2s v6p0464c2s v6p0476c2s v6p0477c1s v6p0493c2s v6p0494c2s v6p0540c2s v6p0551c2s v6p0589c2s v6p0637c2s v6p0710c1s

Rowland, Henry C. v6p0472c1s

Rowland, J. v1p0120c2s v1p1064c2s

Rowland, J.F., jr. v6p0464c2s

Rowland, K.M. v1p0510c2s v2p0058c2s v2p0231c2s v2p0461c2s v3p0270c2s v4p0070c1s v5p0443c1s v5p0533c2s v5p0554c1s

Rowland, K,M. v3p0124c1s

Rowland, Kate M. v3p0290c1s v4p0091c1s

Rowland, L.G. v5p0182c2s

Rowland, O. v6p0604c2s

Rowland, P.F. v5p0039c1s v6p0041c2s v6p0042c1m v6p0042c2s v6p0520c1s

Rowlands, E.B. v3p0166c2s v5p0144c1s v6p0154c2s

Rowlands, H.O. v3p0142c2s

Rowlands, L.B. v3p0350c1s

Rowlands, W. v3p0021c2s v3p0467c1s

Rowlands, Walter v3p0021c2s

Rowlatt, S.A.T. v4p0323c1s

Rowlee, M. v4p0513c1s

Rowlee, W.W. v5p0424c2s v5p0563c1s

Rowlett, W.T. v3p0237c2s

Rowley, F.R. v5p0161c1s

Rowley, H.M. v3p0269c2s

Rowley, H.T. v6p0304c2s

Rowley, J. v1p0085c2s v1p0410c2s v1p0595c1s v1p1262c2s v3p0060c2s

Rowley, S. v1p1375c1s

Rowley, T. v5p0198c2s

Rowney, T. v1p0036c2s v1p0746c1s v1p0835c2s v1p0836c1s v1p1234c1s

Rowntree, B.Seebohm v6p0219c2s

Rowsell, E.P. v1p0143c2s v1p0644c2s v1p0715c1s v1p0729c1s v1p0733c2s v1p0932c2s v1p0995c1s v1p1043c2s v1p1116c1s v1p1244c2s v1p1269c2s v1p1270c2s v1p1328c2s v1p1431c1s

Rowsell, F.W. v1p0112c1m v1p0198c2s v1p0366c2s v1p0381c1s v1p0394c2s v1p0545c2s v1p0546c2s v1p0607c1s v1p0791c1s v1p1149c2s v1p1201c1s v1p1244c1s

Rowsell, M.C. v3p0142c1s v3p0328c2s v5p0363c2s

Rowton, F. v1p0198c2m

Roy, A.L. v2p0217c1s

Roy, B.N. v5p0331c2s

Roy, Bun Le v2p0435c2s

Roy, C. et al. v3p0080c1s

Roy, C.O. v3p0038c2s

Roy, C.S. v2p0415c1s v4p0385c2s

Roy, C.S. and Adami, J.G.. v3p0453c1s

Roy, Coomar, Raj v3p0077c1s

Roy, J. v1p0874c2s

Roy, J.A.Le v5p0010c1s v5p0027c2s v5p0444c1s v5p0444c2m v6p0315c2s v6p0337c1s v6p0429c2s v6p0492c2m v6p0493c1m v6p0493c2m v6p0494c1m v6p0494c2m v6p0631c1m v6p0632c1s

Roy, J.C. v1p0521c1s

Roy, J.E. v1p0275c2s v1p0496c1s v1p0599c2m v1p0624c2s v1p0649c2s v1p1053c2s v3p0299c1s

Roy, K. v4p0445c1s

Roy, M.J. v2p0011c2s

Roy, P.C. v4p0278c2s

Roy, T.B. v1p0073c1s

Roy-Lewis, H.Le v6p0265c1s

Royall, E. v1p0114c2s

Royce, A.A. v1p0347c1s

Royce, A.L. v3p0124c1s v3p0172c1s v4p0392c2s v4p0636c2s

Royce, C.C. v2p0399c1m

Royce, C.M. v6p0536c1s

Royce, G.M. v2p0178c1s v2p0192c2s v2p0380c2s v4p0467c1s v6p0519c1s v6p0599c2s

Royce, J. v1p0702c2s v1p0843c2s v1p1021c1s v1p1085c2s v2p0064c2s v2p0147c1s v2p0278c2s v2p0283c2s v2p0289c2s v2p0432c1s v2p0437c1s v2p0439c2s v3p0006c1s v3p0027c1s v3p0027c2s v3p0028c1s v3p0063c1s v3p0130c1s v3p0143c1s v3p0145c2s v3p0163c1m v3p0188c1s v3p0193c1s v3p0253c1s v3p0274c1s v3p0319c2s v3p0348c1s v3p0348c2s v3p0379c1s v3p0423c1s v3p0424c2s v3p0445c2s v4p0076c1s v4p0076c2s v4p0079c1s v4p0188c2s v4p0191c1s v4p0232c1s v4p0249c1s v4p0274c2m v4p0365c1s v4p0366c2s v4p0382c1s v4p0394c2s v4p0395c1s v4p0439c2m v4p0514c1m v4p0633c1s v5p0197c2s v5p0209c2s v5p0261c1s v5p0329c1s v5p0427c1s v5p0470c2s v6p0093c2s v6p0200c2s v6p0211c1s v6p0306c2s v6p0319c1s v6p0349c2s v6p0444c1s v6p0513c1s v6p0526c1s v6p0536c2s v6p0590c1s v6p0610c1s

Royce, Josiah v6p0185c2s

Royer, C. v3p0014c1s

v4p0229c1s
Roylance-Kent, C.B. v4p0017c1s
v4p0211c1s v4p0212c1s v4p0266c1s
v4p0295c1s v4p0297c1s v4p0428c1s
v4p0429c1s v4p0476c1s v4p0496c2s
v5p0040c1s v5p0452c2s v5p0492c1s
Royle, E.J. v6p0397c2s
Royle, E.M. v5p0608c1s
v6p0612c1s
Royle, E.T. v5p0279c1s
Royle, J.F. v1p0306c2m
v1p0621c2s v1p0886c1s
Royle, J.R. v2p0110c2s
v2p0217c1s v2p0218c1s v2p0219c1s
v2p0322c1s v2p0329c2s v4p0366c2s
Roys, Sarah L. v4p0042c2s
Roysdon, A.W. v2p0286c2s
Royston, Alice G. v4p0253c2s
Royston-Pigott v1p0339c2s
Royston-Pigott, G.W. v1p0196c2s
Ruadh, G. v6p0080c1s
Ruben, P. v5p0056c2s
v5p0057c1s
Rubens, H. and Trowbridge, A.
v5p0290c2s
Rubens, H.S. v5p0147c2s
Rubenstein, J.S. v4p0323c2s
Rubin, M. v5p0064c2s
Rubinow, I.M. v6p0321c1m
v6p0321c2s v6p0343c2s v6p0512c1s
v6p0584c2s v6p0651c2s
Rubinow, J.M. v6p0178c2s
v6p0514c2s
Rubinsohn, T. v1p0121c1s
v1p0121c2s v1p0701c1s v1p0998c2s
Rubovito, E. v6p0342c2s
Ruby, S.V. v4p0183c2s
Rucker, A. v5p0319c2s
Rucker, A.W. v1p1214c1m
v2p0155c2s v3p0133c2s v3p0277c2s
v3p0440c2s v4p0156c1s v4p0254c1s
v4p0316c1s v5p0077c1s v5p0356c1s
Rucker, A.W. and Harkness, W.
v3p0264c1s
Rucker, A.W. and Reinold, A.W.
v2p0155c2s
Rucker, A.W. and Thorpe, T.E.
v1p1173c1s
Rucker, A.W., Sir v6p0385c2s
Rucker, Prof. v2p0406c1s
v5p0605c1s
Ruckert, F. v1p0116c1s
v1p0443c1s v1p0949c2s
Ruckman, J.W. v6p0168c2s
Ruckman, J.W. and Stuart, E.R.
v6p0168c2s
Ruckstuhl, F.W. v4p0376c1s
v6p0579c1s v6p0579c2s
Rudd, E.H. v5p0478c2s
v6p0478c1s
Rudd, F.A. v1p0600c2s
v1p0837c2s v1p1054c1s v1p1128c1s
v2p0117c1m
Rudd, J.C. v2p0117c1s
Rudd, J.P. v3p0207c1s
v3p0458c1s v4p0046c2s v4p0145c2s
v4p0228c2s v4p0267c2s v4p0276c2s
v4p0336c1s v4p0419c1s v4p0421c1s
v4p0477c2s v5p0163c1s v5p0299c2s
Rudd, M.B. v4p0099c2s
Ruddiman, W.H. v1p0835c1s
Ruddock, J.C. v6p0664c1s
Rudelbach, Prof. v1p0038c2s
Rudge, E. v1p0433c2s
v1p1428c2s
Rudge, W.A. and Lodge, O.J.
v3p0133c1s
Ruding, R. v1p0324c1s
v1p1069c2s
Rudler, F.W. v1p0014c1s
v1p0348c2s v1p0675c2s v2p0262c2s
v2p0455c1s v3p0396c2s v4p0473c2s
Rudolf, C.C. v4p0233c2s
Rudolf, R.D. v6p0434c1s
Rudolf, R.W. v6p0471c2s
Rudolph, A.J. v4p0092c1s
v5p0227c2s v5p0333c1s
Rudy, C. v1p1135c1s
v1p1136c1s v2p0369c1s v6p0525c1s
v6p0579c2s v6p0607c2s
Rudy, F. v6p0525c1s
Rue, A.S.B. v5p0042c2s
Rue, Abbe de la v1p0039c2m
v1p0103c2s
Rue, De la v1p1379c1s
Rue, E.D., jr. v6p0463c2s
Rue, W. et al. v1p1268c2s
Ruedemann, R. v4p0156c2s
v5p0242c2s
Ruediger, W.C. v6p0459c1s
Rueling, J.F. v1p0680c2s
Ruetenik, H.J. v3p0109c1s
Ruff, J.D. v5p0359c1s
Ruff, M.D. v1p0875c2s
Ruffer, A. v3p0030c1s
v3p0273c1s v3p0351c2s v4p0363c2s
Ruffer, M.A. v4p0156c1s
v4p0234c2s
Ruffer, M.A. and Horsley, V.
v4p0606c2s
Ruffin, E. v1p0741c1s
v1p1204c2s v1p1207c1s v2p0405c1s
Ruffin, F.G. v2p0098c1s
Ruffini, G. v1p0200c2s
v1p1149c1s
Ruffini, J. v1p0699c1s
v1p1071c2s v1p1372c1s
Ruffner, D. v1p1147c1s
Ruffner, H. v1p1374c2s
Ruffner, W.H. v1p1073c1s
Ruge, C. v5p0433c1s
Ruge, Clara v6p0035c2s
v6p0107c1s v6p0275c1s v6p0649c2s
Ruge, S. v4p0125c2s
Ruggles, D. v1p0300c1s
v1p0811c2s v1p1310c1s
Ruggles, E.R. v3p0074c2s
Ruggles, G.D. v4p0592c1s
Ruggles, J. v1p1240c1s
Ruggles, L.B. v6p0239c1s
Ruggles, M.B. and Doherty, E.P.
v3p0050c1s
Ruggles, S.B. v1p0177c1s
Ruggles, S.P. v1p1289c1s
Ruggles, T. v1p0209c1s
v1p0561c1s
Ruhl, A. v5p0037c1s
v5p0160c1s v5p0572c2s v6p0071c2s
v6p0159c2s v6p0215c2s v6p0231c2s
v6p0261c1s v6p0410c1s v6p0454c1s
v6p0472c1s v6p0496c2s v6p0525c2s
v6p0526c1s v6p0554c2s v6p0642c1s
Ruhl, A.B. v5p0456c1s
Ruhl, Arthur v6p0080c1s
v6p0366c2s
Ruhne v2p0055c2s
Rukhmabai v3p0268c2s
Ruland, C. v1p0159c2s
v1p0471c2s v1p0959c1s
Rule, M. v2p0016c1s
v5p0021c2s v6p0011c2m
Rule, M. et al. v3p0041c1s
Rule, Martin v6p0274c1s
Rulison, H.F. v5p0565c1s
Rumbold, H. v6p0059c1s
v6p0119c2s v6p0174c2s v6p0238c2s
v6p0554c2s v6p0557c2s v6p0678c2s
Rumler, E. v3p0349c1s
v4p0388c1s v4p0580c1s
Rumsey, C.A. v6p0094c2s
Rumsey, O. v4p0407c1s
Runcie, J.E. v5p0146c2s
Runciman, J. v2p0204c1s
v2p0332c1s v3p0061c1s v3p0123c1s
v3p0128c2s v3p0154c2s v3p0201c1s
v3p0255c2s v3p0333c2s v3p0423c2s
v4p0161c1s v4p0598c2s
Runciman, J.F. v4p0048c1s
v4p0049c1s v4p0389c2m v4p0442c1s
v4p0467c2s v5p0042c1s v5p0048c2s
v5p0050c1s v5p0050c2s v5p0052c1s
v5p0065c2s v5p0086c1s v5p0095c2s
v5p0113c2s v5p0116c1s v5p0131c2m
v5p0154c2s v5p0165c1s v5p0166c2s
v5p0233c2s v5p0236c1s v5p0253c2m
v5p0276c1s v5p0323c1s v5p0325c2s
v5p0337c1s v5p0345c1s v5p0365c2s
v5p0393c1m v5p0393c2m v5p0394c1m
v5p0394c2m v5p0395c1s v5p0395c2m
v5p0409c1s v5p0422c1m v5p0423c1m
v5p0423c2s v5p0427c1m v5p0441c1s
v5p0450c1m v5p0465c2s v5p0472c1s
v5p0497c2s v5p0505c1s v5p0530c2s
v5p0539c1s v5p0548c2s v5p0565c1s
v5p0609c2m v5p0611c2s v5p0615c2m
v5p0616c1m v5p0645c1s v6p0031c2s
v6p0046c1m v6p0049c2s v6p0053c2s
v6p0056c2m v6p0059c1m v6p0069c1m
v6p0083c2s v6p0084c2s v6p0088c2s
v6p0104c2s v6p0121c2s v6p0142c2s
v6p0155c1s v6p0158c2s v6p0194c2s
v6p0200c1s v6p0259c2s v6p0262c2m
v6p0275c1s v6p0278c2s v6p0283c1s
v6p0284c1s v6p0303c1s v6p0328c1s
v6p0344c1s v6p0346c2s v6p0384c2s
v6p0399c1m v6p0432c2s v6p0434c1m
v6p0437c2m v6p0438c1m v6p0438c2m
v6p0439c1m v6p0439c2m v6p0457c1s
v6p0457c2s v6p0464c2s v6p0468c1m
v6p0468c2m v6p0469c1s v6p0470c1m
v6p0499c1m v6p0500c2s v6p0501c2s
v6p0516c1s v6p0523c2s v6p0525c1s
v6p0540c2s v6p0551c2s v6p0572c1s
v6p0595c2s v6p0620c1s v6p0620c2m
v6p0624c2s v6p0626c2s v6p0677c1m
v6p0683c1m
Runciman, T. v4p0340c1s
v4p0440c1s
Rundal, F.H. v2p0423c2s
v3p0414c1s v3p0456c2s
Rundall, F.M. v3p0211c1s
Rundell, J.B. v1p1234c2s
Rundell, M.A. v6p0319c1s
Runeberg, J.L. v2p0106c1s
Rung, W. v5p0183c2s
Runge, C. v4p0204c2s
v4p0321c2s v4p0540c2s
Runge, C. and Paschen, F.. v4p0220c2s
Runge, E.C. v6p0109c2s
Runiberg, J.L. v2p0156c1s
Runk, E.J. v3p0300c2s
Runke, R. and Watson, J.C.
v5p0526c2s
Runkle, B. v5p0261c2s
Runkle, Bertha v6p0285c2s
Runkle, E.W. v6p0487c2s
Runkle, L.G. v2p0477c2s
Runnels, M.T. v1p1432c1s
Runnion, J.B. v1p0024c1s
v1p0227c1s v1p0227c2s v1p0680c2s
v1p0875c1s v1p0881c1s v1p0905c2s
v1p0971c2s v1p1242c1m v2p0168c1s
v2p0210c1s v2p0229c2s v2p0230c1s
v3p0228c1s v4p0501c1s
Runtz-Rees, J.E. v3p0452c2s
Runyon, L.L. v5p0178c2s
Rupp, A. v6p0252c2s
Rupp, A.J. v4p0126c1s
Rupp, J.C.F. v3p0192c2s
v3p0261c1s v3p0473c2s v4p0113c1s
v4p0581c1s
Rupp, W. v1p0117c2s
v1p0242c1s v1p0248c1s v1p0257c2s
v1p0684c2s v1p0792c2s v1p0988c2s
v1p1091c1s v1p1160c2s v1p1175c1s
v2p0027c2s v2p0081c2s v2p0136c1s
v2p0355c2s v2p0403c2s v2p0407c1s
v2p0437c2s v3p0026c1m v3p0082c1s
v3p0105c2s v3p0145c1m v3p0359c2s
v3p0428c1s v4p0053c2s v4p0174c1s
v4p0286c1s v4p0300c2s v4p0477c1s
v4p0505c1s v4p0527c2s v4p0573c1s
v4p0633c1s v5p0013c2s v5p0037c2m
v5p0055c1s v5p0055c2s v5p0060c2s
v5p0116c1s v5p0196c1s v5p0199c1s
v5p0236c2s v5p0261c1s v5p0289c2s
v5p0294c2s v5p0306c1s v5p0306c2s
v5p0385c2s v5p0436c1m v5p0464c1s
v5p0469c1s v5p0482c1s v5p0486c2s
v5p0493c1s v5p0506c2s v5p0530c1s
v5p0538c1s v5p0572c1s v5p0576c2s
v5p0593c1s v5p0597c2s v5p0611c1s
v6p0123c2s
Ruppell, Dr. v1p0318c2s
v1p0592c2s
Ruppenthal, J.C. v6p0196c2s
Ruppert, J., jr. v5p0399c2s
Ruprecht, J.T. v5p0416c1s
Ruricola v2p0005c2s
Rusby, H.H. v6p0698c1m
Ruschenberger, C.W. v3p0007c1s
Ruschenberger, W.N.S. v1p0902c1s
Ruschenberger, W.S.W. v1p0993c1s
v1p1100c2s
Ruscoconi, A.J. v6p0012c1s
Rusden, H.K. v3p0384c2s
Rush, B. v1p0868c1s
v1p1066c1s v4p0406c2s v5p0348c2s
Rush, C.J. v3p0147c2s
Rush, R. v1p0548c1s
Rush, W. v1p0643c2s
Rushforth, G.McN. v3p0186c2s
Rushmore, D.B. v5p0182c2s
v6p0013c2s v6p0552c2s
Rushton, W. v1p1162c1s
Rusk, C.E. v4p0003c2s
Rusk, E.L.H. v4p0363c2s
Rusk, J.M. v3p0006c2s
v4p0008c1s
Ruskin, J. v1p0181c2s
v1p0450c2s v1p0599c1s v1p0639c2s
v1p0648c2s v1p0769c1s v1p0850c1s
v1p0881c2s v1p0908c1s v1p1026c1s
v1p1027c1s v1p1045c2s v1p1168c2s
v1p1366c1s v1p1386c1s v2p0012c2s
v2p0159c1s v2p0383c1s v2p0421c2s
v4p0031c1s
Ruskin, J. and Fraser, J.. v1p1359c2s
Ruskin, J. and Lubbock, J., Sir
v2p0051c1s
Rusling, J.F. v1p0767c2s
v1p1342c2s
v1p1436c1s
Russ, C. v1p0003c1s
Russ, H.M. v5p0639c1s
Russ, K. v3p0045c2s
Russ, S.B. v1p0043c2s
Russ, W.A. v2p0053c1m
Russel, G.F. v5p0092c2s
Russel, I.C. v4p0498c2s
Russel, J.S. et al. v1p1247c1s
Russel, R. v4p0216c2s
Russel, W.E. v4p0199c1s
Russell and Williamson ... v1p0502c2s
Russell, A. v1p0003c1s
v3p0103c1s v3p0233c2s v4p0148c1s
v4p0230c2s v4p0626c2s v5p0363c2s
v6p0217c1s
Russell, A.D. v5p0568c1s
Russell, A.H. v2p0433c1s
v5p0029c1s v5p0066c2s v6p0276c2s
Russell, B. v3p0065c1s
v4p0019c1s v4p0087c1s v5p0339c2s
v5p0366c1s v5p0414c1s v5p0416c1s
v5p0423c1s v5p0580c1s v6p0142c1s
v6p0170c2s v6p0251c1s v6p0271c1s
v6p0319c1s v6p0367c1s v6p0659c2s
Russell, B., Mrs. v6p0255c2s
v6p0432c1s
Russell, B.A.W. v4p0223c1s

Russell, B.B. v4p0395c1s
v6p0555c2s
Russell, B.F.W. v6p0388c2s
Russell, Bertrand v6p0292c1s
Russell, C. v1p0298c1s
v1p0798c2s v1p1141c2s v1p1239c2s
v1p1353c2s v4p0162c2s v4p0324c1s
v4p0397c2s v4p0511c1s v4p0572c1s
v5p0642c2s v6p0119c1s
Russell, C.E. v5p0103c1s
v5p0317c1s v5p0346c1s v5p0412c1s
v5p0431c1s v6p0014c2s v6p0041c2m
v6p0056c1s v6p0103c2s v6p0253c1s
v6p0263c1s v6p0313c1m v6p0335c1s
v6p0356c1s v6p0383c2s v6p0436c1s
v6p0455c1s v6p0530c1m v6p0629c2s
v6p0644c1s v6p0658c2s
Russell, C.E.B. and Campagnac, E.T.
v5p0224c2s v5p0359c2s v5p0585c1s
Russell, C.J.W. v1p0457c2s
Russell, C.P. v1p0619c1s
v1p0790c2s
Russell, C.W. v1p0216c2s
v1p0692c1s v1p1111c2s v1p1226c1s
v2p0154c2s v2p0253c1s v3p0246c2s
v3p0473c2s
Russell, D.J. v5p0312c1s
Russell, E. v1p1062c1s
v1p1101c1s v2p0274c2s v6p0154c2s
v6p0291c1s v6p0313c1s v6p0314c1s
v6p0314c2s v6p0315c1s v6p0342c2s
Russell, E., Sir v5p0299c1s
v5p0575c2s
Russell, E.A. v6p0216c2s
Russell, E.E. v4p0563c2s
Russell, E.E.B. and Campagnac, E.T.
v5p0394c1s
Russell, E.H. v3p0309c2s
v4p0104c2s v6p0192c2s v6p0293c1s
v6p0532c2s v6p0644c1s
Russell, E.J. v4p0293c1s
Russell, E.K. v2p0398c2s
Russell, E.R. v1p0035c2s
v1p0318c2s v1p0754c1s v1p0755c1s
v1p0974c1s v1p1185c1s v1p1186c2s
v2p0186c2s v2p0230c1m v4p0240c1s
Russell, Earl and Thwaite, B.H.
v4p0176c2s
Russell, Edmund v6p0022c1s
Russell, F. v3p0289c2s
v3p0315c2s v5p0328c1s v5p0358c1m
v5p0359c1s v5p0520c1s v5p0538c2s
v5p0583c1s v6p0500c1s
Russell, F. and Strong, J.
v3p0084c2s
Russell, F. et al. v5p0244c2s
Russell, F.A. v6p0154c1s
v6p0417c2s
Russell, F.A.R. v1p0098c1s
v3p0192c1s
Russell, F.C. v4p0130c1s
v4p0338c1s v4p0542c1s v5p0344c1s
Russell, F.E. v3p0122c2s
v4p0162c1m v4p0314c2s
Russell, F.E. and Gay, S.M.
v4p0564c2s
Russell, F.E. et al. v4p0564c2s
Russell, F.J. v6p0127c2s
Russell, F.S. v2p0185c2s
v2p0207c2s v5p0244c1s v5p0618c2s
v6p0266c1s v6p0266c2s
Russell, Fox v4p0405c2s
Russell, Frank v4p0390c1s
v5p0014c2s v6p0023c2m
Russell, G.B. v1p0254c1s
v1p0441c1s v1p0476c2s v1p0513c1s
v1p0514c2s v1p0564c2s v1p0949c2s
v1p1028c1s v1p1050c1s
Russell, G.R. v1p0283c1s
v1p0823c2s
Russell, G.W.E. v2p0084c2s
v2p0189c2s v2p0330c2s v2p0472c1s
v3p0182c2s v3p0248c1s v3p0369c1m
v3p0419c1s v3p0451c1s v4p0113c1s
v4p0177c2s v4p0328c2s v4p0476c2s
v5p0117c2m v5p0186c2s v5p0235c1s
v5p0323c2s v5p0365c1s v5p0489c2s
v6p0270c1s v6p0280c1s v6p0369c2s
Russell, G.W.E. and Round, J.A.
v5p0365c1s
Russell, G.W.E. et al. ... v4p0240c1s
Russell, Geo.W.E. v4p0028c1s
Russell, H. v3p0036c2s
v4p0078c1s v4p0119c2s v4p0548c1s
v5p0064c1s v5p0278c2s v5p0283c2s
v6p0268c2s
Russell, H.B. v4p0564c1s
v4p0593c1s
Russell, H.C. v2p0139c1s
v4p0034c1s v4p0366c2s v4p0399c2s
v4p0440c1s
Russell, H.E. v1p1343c2s
v1p1345c2s v1p1352c2s v1p1353c2s
Russell, H.H. v4p0410c1s
v4p0500c2m
Russell, H.L. v4p0041c1s
v6p0111c2s
Russell, H.M. v2p0004c2s
v2p0146c2s v2p0321c1s v2p0478c2s
Russell, H.N. v5p0549c1s
v6p0613c2s
Russell, H.P. v6p0126c1s
v6p0544c2s
Russell, H.R. v3p0266c2s
Russell, Herbert v5p0344c1s
Russell, I. v1p1163c1s
Russell, I.C. v1p0136c2s
v1p0280c1s v1p0466c1s v1p0718c1s
v1p0912c1m v1p0918c2s v1p0919c1s
v1p1325c1s v1p1380c1s v2p0008c1s
v2p0345c1s v3p0035c2s v3p0300c2s
v3p0372c1s v4p0114c2s v4p0227c1s
v4p0361c1s v4p0498c2m v4p0607c1s
v5p0234c1s v5p0278c2s v5p0410c2s
v5p0449c1s v5p0478c2s v6p0077c2s
v6p0105c2s v6p0250c1s v6p0403c2s
v6p0487c1s v6p0540c1s v6p0647c1s
v6p0681c1m v6p0692c2s
Russell, I.C. and Schwatka, F.
v3p0372c1s
Russell, I.F. v5p0293c2s
v5p0327c2s v5p0397c1s
Russell, J. v1p0389c1s
v1p0405c2s v2p0321c1s v3p0070c2s
v3p0332c1s v5p0179c2s v5p0608c2s
Russell, J., Lord v1p0558c1s
v1p1012c2s
Russell, J.A. v3p0116c1s
Russell, J.B. v1p0374c2s
v1p1269c2s v1p1375c2s
Russell, J.C. v1p0459c2s
v2p0179c1s v2p0246c2s
Russell, J.E. v3p0330c1s
v4p0064c2s v4p0183c2s v4p0223c2s
v4p0241c1s v4p0321c2s v4p0360c2s
v4p0373c1s v4p0514c1s v5p0192c1s
v5p0194c1s v5p0228c2s v5p0266c2s
v5p0514c1s v5p0518c1s v5p0569c1s
v5p0569c2s v5p0576c1s v6p0135c1s
v6p0189c2s v6p0513c1s v6p0573c1s
Russell, J.E. et al. v4p0512c2s
Russell, J.F. v5p0608c2s
Russell, J.J. v1p0145c2s
Russell, J.L. v1p0449c1s
v1p0494c2s v1p0882c1s v1p0899c2s
v1p1039c1s v1p1173c1s
Russell, J.R. v1p1055c1s
Russell, J.S. v1p0199c1s
v1p0436c2s v1p0443c2s v1p1078c2m
v1p1079c2s v1p1248c2s v1p1288c2s
v1p1289c1m v1p1368c1s v1p1393c2s
v2p0193c2s
Russell, J.Scott v1p0459c2s
Russell, J.W. v1p1289c1s
v4p0086c1m v4p0393c1s v4p0563c2s
v5p0039c1s v5p0327c1s
Russell, James E. v4p0597c1s
Russell, John v4p0050c2s
v6p0134c1s
Russell, John, Lord v1p1055c1s
Russell, L. v6p0302c1s
Russell, L.S. v4p0608c2s
Russell, Lord v4p0022c2s
v4p0122c1s v4p0287c2s
Russell, M. v1p0172c2s
v1p0218c2s v1p0334c2s v1p0347c1s
v1p0362c1s v1p0540c2s v1p0614c2s
v1p0661c2s v1p0662c1s v1p0667c2s
v1p0697c1s v1p0743c1s v1p0863c2s
v1p0941c2s v1p0949c2s v1p0950c2s
v1p0979c1s v1p1054c1s v1p1411c2s
v1p1424c2s v2p0270c1s
Russell, P. v2p0161c1s
v2p0217c1s v2p0319c1s v2p0389c2s
v2p0393c2m
Russell, R. v1p0314c2s
v1p0562c1s v1p1256c2s v3p0192c1s
v4p0154c2s v4p0284c2s v6p0230c2s
v6p0442c2s v6p0690c2s
Russell, R.H. v4p0228c1s
v4p0598c2s v5p0223c1s
Russell, S. v1p0901c2s
v1p1080c2s v1p1192c1s v1p1249c2s
Russell, S.L. v2p0152c1s
Russell, T. v1p1304c2s
v3p0090c2m v3p0458c2s v4p0340c2s
v4p0504c1s v6p0428c1s v6p0647c1s
Russell, T.A. v6p0044c1s
Russell, T.B. v4p0014c2s
v6p0279c1s v6p0319c1s v6p0613c2s
Russell, T.J. v1p0301c2s
Russell, T.O. v2p0072c2s
v2p0228c2s v6p0245c1s
Russell, T.O'N. v2p0065c2s
v2p0086c1s v3p0220c1s
Russell, T.W. v3p0219c2s
v3p0220c1s v3p0220c2s v3p0221c1m
v3p0221c2m v3p0222c2s v3p0252c2s
v3p0423c2s v4p0170c1s v4p0190c2s
v4p0237c2s v4p0289c1m v4p0289c2s
v4p0290c1m v4p0290c2s v5p0190c1s
v5p0247c2s v5p0272c1s v5p0295c2s
v5p0296c1s v5p0297c1s v5p0383c1s
v5p0598c1s v6p0326c2s v6p0327c1s
v6p0327c2s
Russell, T.W. et al. v4p0239c2s
v4p0265c2s
Russell, Theresa v6p0027c1s
v6p0292c1s v6p0311c2s
Russell, Tom v5p0223c1s
Russell, V.F. v1p0574c1s
v1p0941c2s
Russell, W. v1p0007c1s
v1p0021c2s v1p0315c2s v1p0385c2s
v1p0389c2s v1p0391c1s v1p0641c1s
v1p0783c1s v1p0867c2s v1p1085c2s
v1p1086c2s v1p1088c2s v1p1288c1s
v1p1422c1s v5p0146c2s v5p0507c1s
Russell, W.C. v1p0464c2s
v1p0534c2s v1p0608c2s v1p0715c2s
v1p0774c1s v1p0803c2s v1p1336c1s
v2p0232c1s v2p0393c1s v2p0393c2s
v2p0401c1s v2p0422c1s v3p0055c2s
v3p0118c1s v3p0121c2s v3p0165c1s
v3p0228c2m v3p0241c1s v3p0268c1s
v3p0268c2s v3p0294c2m v3p0382c2s
v3p0383c1s v3p0400c2s v3p0411c2s
v3p0428c2s v4p0074c1s v4p0088c2s
v4p0146c2s v4p0438c1s v4p0498c1s
v4p0552c1s v4p0575c2s v4p0586c1s
v5p0115c2s v5p0404c1s v5p0415c2s
v5p0526c1m v5p0526c2s v5p0619c1s
Russell, W.Clark v3p0297c2s
Russell, W.E. v3p0270c2s
v4p0152c1s v4p0152c2s v4p0188c1s
v4p0299c1s v4p0596c1s
Russell, W.E. et al. v4p0517c2s
Russell, W.H. v1p0007c2s
v1p0073c1s v1p0165c1s v1p0505c1s
v1p0742c1s v2p0007c1s v2p0134c2s
v2p0230c2m v2p0385c2s v3p0105c1s
v3p0222c1s v4p0140c1s v4p0280c1s
v4p0344c1s v4p0428c2s v4p0512c1s
v5p0601c2s v6p0087c1s v6p0411c1s
Russell, W.H.L. v1p0434c2s
v1p0747c2s
Russell, W.J. v1p0224c2s
v1p1234c1s v2p0080c1s v3p0156c2s
v4p0370c1s v4p0443c1s v5p0448c2s
v6p0184c2s v6p0497c1s
Russell, W.J. and Orsman, W.J.
v3p0089c2s
Russell, W.L. v5p0134c2s
Russell, W.R. v1p0455c2s
Russell, W.W. v6p0477c1s
Russell of Killowen, Lord. v5p0293c2s
Russling, J.F. v1p0211c2s
Rust, H. v1p0252c2s
v1p0514c2s v1p1089c1s
Rust, H.N. v2p0300c1s
v6p0032c1s v6p0107c1s v6p0223c2s
v6p0412c2s v6p0463c2s v6p0491c1s
v6p0500c1s v6p0522c1s v6p0546c2s
v6p0566c2s v6p0598c2s v6p0618c2s
Rust, J.B. v3p0041c1s
v3p0145c2s v3p0401c1s v4p0259c1s
v4p0341c2s v5p0548c2s
Rust, J.W. v2p0099c2s
Rust, R.S. v1p0256c1s
v1p1006c2s
Rust, R.S., Mrs. v3p0467c2s
Rustafjaell, R.de v6p0163c1s
Rustafjaell, R.de and Smith, Cecil
v6p0163c1s
Rustem, A. v5p0034c1s
Rutan, Eliz.Y. v5p0308c2s
Rutherford, E. v6p0526c2m
v6p0527c1s
Rutherford, E. and Boltwood, B.B.
v6p0527c1s
Rutherford, E.M. v5p0172c2s
v5p0299c2s v5p0406c2s v5p0481c1s
v6p0177c2s v6p0466c1s v6p0688c2s
Rutherford, L.M. v6p0057c2s
Rutherford, M.A. v6p0291c2s
Rutherford, R. v6p0113c1s
Rutherford, R.C. v2p0319c2s
Rutherford, W. v1p0756c2s
v4p0231c2s v6p0171c1s v6p0440c2s
Rutherford, W.G. v6p0449c1s
Rutherford, W.L. v6p0013c2s
Rutherfurd, C.L. v2p0074c2s
Rutherfurd, H. et al. v4p0557c2s
Rutherfurd, L.M. v1p0039c1s
v1p0070c1s v1p0070c2s v1p1003c2s
v1p1233c2s
Ruthrauff, C.C. v1p0169c2s
Ruthrauff, J.M. v5p0126c1s
Ruthven, J.F. v5p0401c2s
Ruthven, W. v4p0037c1s
Rutland, Duchess of v4p0050c2s
v4p0287c1s
Rutland, Duchess of et al.
v4p0452c1s
Rutledge, J. v1p0730c1s
Rutley, F. v1p0835c2s
Rutson, A. v1p1332c1s
Rutter, C. v6p0227c1s
v6p0566c1m v6p0658c1s
Rutter, F.R. v5p0541c1m
v5p0584c1s v6p0624c1s
Rutter, H.C. v5p0194c1s
Rutter, J.A. v6p0432c2s
Rutter, J.P. v1p0801c1s
Rutton, W.L. v5p0250c2m
v5p0262c1s
Rutz, G.A. v4p0294c1s
Ruvigny, Marquis de and Metcalfe, C.
v5p0542c1m v6p0267c2s
Ruvigny, Marquis of v5p0330c1s

Ruxton, G.F. v1p0832c1s
Ryan, A.W. v3p0149c1s
Ryan, C. v1p1027c2s v1p1090c1s v5p0421c2s
Ryan, D. v1p0291c2s
Ryan, D.J. v1p0870c2s v1p1141c1s v3p0089c1s
Ryan, E. v6p0570c2s
Ryan, E. and Dredd, F. ... v6p0346c2s
Ryan, Edward v5p0544c2s
Ryan, F. v1p0700c2s v1p0818c2s
Ryan, F.J. v6p0618c1s
Ryan, F.M. v1p0468c2s
Ryan, G.H. v3p0217c2s
Ryan, Grace F. v5p0315c1s
Ryan, H.J. and Bedel, F. . v4p0384c2s
Ryan, J. v1p0658c2s
Ryan, J.A. v5p0408c2s v5p0557c2s v6p0416c2s v6p0609c1s v6p0651c2s v6p0664c2s v6p0682c1m v6p0682c2m
Ryan, J.J. v1p0058c2s v1p0535c1s v1p1135c1s
Ryan, J.P. v1p0657c1s v3p0364c2s
Ryan, J.T. v4p0038c2s v4p0155c1s
Ryan, M.E. v3p0209c2s
Ryan, M.J. v6p0135c1s
Ryan, R.M. v4p0028c1s v4p0138c2s v4p0151c2s v4p0299c2s
Ryan, R.P. v5p0073c2s v5p0101c2s
Ryan, T.F. v6p0605c2s
Ryan, W.P. v6p0384c2s
Rybakoff, S.I. v6p0559c1s
Ryckman, J.W. v6p0322c2s v6p0418c1s v6p0425c2s
Rycroft, E.H. v6p0626c2s
Rycroft, Maj. v6p0196c1s
Ryde, H.T. v1p1143c2s
Ryder, A.H. v1p0283c2s v1p1162c2s
Ryder, A.R. v1p0283c1s
Ryder, C.E. v2p0365c1s
Ryder, C.H.D. v6p0119c2s v6p0645c2s
Ryder, C.J. v4p0015c1s v4p0283c2s v4p0608c2s v5p0389c2s
Ryder, Dr. v1p0251c1s v1p1237c2s
Ryder, E.A. v1p1319c1s
Ryder, F.W. v2p0119c1s v4p0505c2s
Ryder, H.I.D. v1p0450c2s v1p1109c2s v2p0413c2s v3p0055c1s v3p0110c2s v3p0136c1s v3p0166c1s v3p0281c2s v3p0302c1s v4p0053c2s v4p0057c2s v5p0117c2s v5p0348c1s v5p0618c1s
Ryder, I. v1p0019c2s
Ryder, J.A. v1p0058c2s v1p0352c1s v1p0812c1s v1p0889c1s v1p1239c1s v2p0139c2s v2p0157c1s v2p0262c1s v2p0287c2s v2p0325c2m v2p0426c1s v2p0443c1s v3p0451c2s v4p0284c2s v4p0417c1s
Ryder, J.F. v4p0622c1s v5p0079c1s
Ryder, Spencer v4p0605c2s
Ryder, T. v1p1148c1s
Ryder, W.H. v1p0069c1s v1p0395c1s v1p0468c2s v1p0612c1s v1p0689c2s v1p0726c2s v1p0960c2s v1p1065c2s v1p1147c2m v3p0043c1s v3p0303c1s v4p0300c2s v5p0059c2s
Rydzewski, A. v5p0087c2s
Rye, A. v1p0063c1s v1p0856c2s v1p0958c1s
Rye, E.C. v1p0108c2s v1p0645c1s v1p0645c2s v1p1143c2s
Rye, F. v1p0173c1s v1p0949c1s v1p1035c1s v1p1421c1s v1p1425c1s v2p0456c1s
Rye, F., Mrs. v1p0221c2s v1p1085c1s v1p1132c2s
Rye, J.B. v5p0398c1s
Rye, W. v2p0075c2s v2p0108c2s v2p0317c1s v3p0048c2s
Rye, W. et al. v2p0416c1m
Rye, W.B. v3p0226c1s v6p0080c2s
Ryecroft, H. v6p0043c1s
Ryerson, G.S. v5p0481c1s
Rylance, J.H. v2p0222c2s v2p0438c1s v4p0118c2s
Rylance, J.H. et al. v2p0085c1s
Ryland, F. v3p0288c2s v4p0338c1s
Rylands, J.P. v4p0361c1m v5p0067c1s
Ryle, H.E. v4p0054c2s
Ryle, J.C. v1p0103c1s
Rylett, H. v3p0295c2s
Ryley, G.B. v2p0084c2s v3p0082c2s
Ryley, H.B. v4p0466c1s
Ryley, J.H. v4p0072c1s v4p0291c2s v4p0303c1s v4p0576c1s
Ryley, J.Horton v4p0201c2s
Ryley, M.B. and Uzanne, O. v6p0547c1s
Rymaelje-Suwarof, M. v4p0496c1s
Ryman, W.P. v6p0390c1s
Rymer, I. v6p0158c2s
Ryn, B.van v6p0411c2s
Ryn, Jan Van v6p0275c2s
Rynd, Evelyne E. v6p0552c1s
Rysden, O. v5p0534c1s v6p0455c1s v6p0651c1s
Rysier, J.A. v1p0792c1s

S., A.M. v6p0303c1s
S., E.A. v5p0449c2s
S., E.M. v5p0598c1s
S., F. v6p0440c2s
S., F.R.G. v5p0373c1s
S., G. v5p0220c1s
S., G.W. v1p0536c2s
S., H. v6p0644c2s
S., H.T. v6p0215c2s
S., J.B. v4p0627c2s
S., M. v6p0014c1s
v6p0054c1s
S., M.C. v5p0441c1s
Saabye, O.A.F. v4p0423c2s
Saadeh, K. v6p0436c2s
Saalschutz, J.L. v1p0691c1s
v1p0874c1s
Saarpless, I. v2p0285c1s
v2p0404c1s
Sabatier, A. v4p0331c1s
v5p0114c1s v5p0483c1s
Sabatier, P. v6p0237c1s
v6p0238c1s v6p0238c2s
Sabatini, R. v6p0593c2s
Sabin, A.H. v6p0474c2s
v6p0675c1s
Sabin, E.L. v5p0043c1s
v5p0103c2s v5p0114c1s v5p0131c2s
v5p0154c2s v5p0348c1s v5p0521c1s
v6p0078c2s v6p0177c2s v6p0260c1s
v6p0301c1s v6p0310c2s v6p0381c1s
v6p0388c2s v6p0394c2s v6p0405c2s
v6p0415c2s v6p0517c2s v6p0590c1s
v6p0681c2s v6p0701c1s v6p0711c2s
Sabin, Edward L. v6p0472c1s
Sabin, H. v4p0506c1s
v4p0506c2s v5p0198c2s v5p0265c2s
v5p0386c1s v5p0512c1m v5p0558c1s
v5p0572c1s v6p0428c2s v6p0622c2s
Sabin, J. v1p0149c2s
v1p1417c1s
Sabin, L. v1p1091c2s
Sabin, W.W. v1p1097c2s
Sabine, E. v1p0788c2s
Sabine, G.H. v6p0203c1s
v6p0292c2s v6p0302c2s
Sabine, G.H. and Bentley, I.M.
v6p0649c2s.
Sabine, L. v1p0006c1s
v1p0031c1m v1p0032c2s v1p0086c2s
v1p0095c1s v1p0164c2s v1p0189c2s
v1p0194c1m v1p0204c1s v1p0283c1s
v1p0457c2m v1p0468c1s v1p0543c2s
v1p0637c1s v1p0775c1s v1p0789c2s
v1p0848c1s v1p0867c2s v1p0910c1s
v1p0988c1s v1p1018c2s v1p1044c2s
v1p1386c2s
Sabine, R. v1p0017c1s
v1p1019c1s
Sabine, W.C. v5p0002c2s
Sabine, W.C. and Trowbridge, J.
v3p0408c2s
Sacc, Dr. v1p0307c1s
Saccardo, P. v6p0676c2s
Saccardo, P.A. v4p0446c1s
Sacchi, F. v4p0114c1s
Sacerdote and Leduc v5p0227c1s
Sacher-Masoch, L.von v4p0377c2s
Sacheverel-Coke, A. v4p0150c2s
Sachs, E. v2p0159c2s
Sachs, E.O. v4p0200c1s
v4p0572c2s v5p0025c2s v5p0254c2s
v5p0548c1s v5p0570c1s v6p0225c1s
Sachs, E.T. v2p0061c2s
Sachs, J. v4p0087c1s
v4p0128c1s v4p0175c2s v4p0176c1s
v4p0177c2s v4p0200c1s v4p0512c1s
v5p0095c2s v6p0198c1s
Sachs, J. and Sharpless, I.
v5p0179c1s
Sachs, Julius v6p0136c1s
v6p0423c2s
Sachs, W.von v3p0449c2s
v4p0389c2s v4p0604c1s
Sachse, J.F. v3p0141c2s
v3p0329c1s v4p0214c2m v4p0217c2s
v4p0440c2s v5p0451c1s v6p0239c1s
Sachtleben, W.L. and
Allen, T.G., jr. v4p0032c2s
v4p0058c2s
Sack, K.H. v1p0442c1s
Sacken, C.R.Osten v5p0258c2s
Sackett, G. v6p0371c1s
Sackville, M. v5p0298c2s
Sackville, Margaret v6p0004c2s
Sadler, A. v1p0330c2s
Sadler, H. v3p0407c1s
v3p0407c2s
Sadler, H.C. v5p0551c2s
v6p0204c2s
Sadler, H.E. v2p0402c2s
Sadler, M.E. v5p0518c1s
v6p0190c2s v6p0191c1s v6p0191c2s
v6p0192c1s v6p0202c1s v6p0573c1m
Sadler, M.E. and Stuart, L.E.
v4p0597c2s
Sadlier, A.F. v4p0147c2s
Sadlier, A.T. v2p0066c1s
v2p0237c2s v2p0361c1s v2p0383c1s
v3p0262c2s v4p0561c2s v6p0219c1s
Sadlier, J. v3p0065c2s
Sadlier, J., Mrs. v1p0661c2s
Sadtler, B. v1p0423c2s
v1p0777c1s v1p1237c2s
Sadtler, S.P. v1p0810c2s
v2p0090c2s v3p0076c1s v3p0328c2s
v4p0033c1m v4p0062c2s v4p0094c1s
v4p0098c2s v6p0225c2s
Sadtler, S.S. v6p0011c2s
v6p0390c1s v6p0615c2s
Saemann, L. v1p0506c2s
v1p1218c1s
Saffell, W.T.R. v1p0221c2s
v1p0359c1s
Saffi, A. v1p0500c2s
v1p0670c1s v1p0671c2s v1p0834c1s
Safford, F. v5p0586c2s
Safford, G.B. v1p0336c1s
Safford, H.G. v2p0044c2s
Safford, I.A. v1p0551c1s
v4p0364c2s
Safford, J.M. v1p0995c2s
v1p1294c2m
Safford, J.M. and Schuchert, C.
v5p0089c1s v5p0424c1s
Safford, L.H. v4p0360c2s
Safford, M.J. v2p0382c2s
v6p0488c2s
Safford, M.Y. v1p1369c1s
Safford, O.F. v1p0119c2s
v2p0032c2s v2p0101c1s v2p0140c1s
Safford, S.H. v1p0883c2s
Safford, T.H. v1p0227c2s
v1p0382c1s v1p1154c2s v3p0019c2s
v3p0024c2s v3p0092c1s v3p0275c1s
v3p0330c2s v5p0035c2s v5p0441c2s
v5p0602c2s
Safford, W.E. v6p0108c1s
v6p0275c2m
Sage, A. v1p0568c2s
Sage, A.C. v4p0110c1s
v4p0454c2s v4p0616c1s v5p0416c2s
v5p0529c1s
Sage, B.J. v1p1348c1s
v1p1354c1s v2p0113c1s
Sage, D. v1p1146c2s
v2p0243c2s v3p0379c1s v5p0474c1s
v5p0505c2s
Sage, J.H. v5p0016c2s
v6p0017c2s
Sage, Lillian B. v5p0229c1s
Sage, M.W. v5p0037c1s
Sage, R. v1p1078c2s
v5p0593c1s
Sage, Russell, Mrs. v6p0705c1s
Sage, W. v5p0252c1s
Sage, W.H. v6p0183c1s
Sagebeer, J.E. v5p0480c1s
Saglio, A. v6p0066c1s
v6p0083c1s
Saglio, Andre v6p0177c1s
Saglio, Maurice v4p0020c2s
Sague, J.E. v2p0086c2s
Sahler, Emma F. v6p0310c2s
Sahler, L.H.von v5p0243c1s
Sahlin, Axel v6p0248c1s
v6p0328c2s v6p0356c2s
Saillens, R. v2p0210c2s
Saillier, E. v5p0204c2s
Sainsbury, W.N. v1p0533c2s
v2p0010c1s v2p0010c2s v2p0210c2s
v2p0330c1s v3p0300c2s
St.Albans, Duke of v2p0208c2s
v4p0296c1s
St.Andre, A.de and Thomas, G.G.
v5p0369c2s
v5p0465c1s
St.Arnaud, P. v1p0889c2s
St.Aubyn, J. v5p0504c2s
St.Chelt, R. v1p0446c1s
v1p1041c2s
St.Clair, D.F. v5p0540c2s
St.Clair, G. v3p0025c1s
v4p0252c2s v5p0023c2s v5p0027c2s
v5p0087c2s v5p0096c2s v5p0181c1m
v5p0194c2s v5p0301c1s v5p0517c2s
v6p0633c2s
St.Clair-Tisdall, W. v5p0299c1s
St.Clement, J. v1p0837c1s
St.Cyres, S.H.N. v6p0296c1s
v6p0347c1m
St.Cyres, Viscount v6p0109c1s
v6p0221c2s v6p0347c1s
v6p0395c2m v6p0598c1m
v6p0660c2s
St.Denys, C.M. v2p0267c1s
St.Edme, E. v1p0399c2s
Saint-Etienne, R. v3p0160c2s
St.Foix, De v1p0413c2s
Saint-Gaudens, A. v6p0579c1s
St.Gaudens, H. v6p0052c2s
v6p0055c2s v6p0085c2s v6p0110c2s
Saint-Gaudens, H. v6p0150c1s
v6p0161c2s v6p0172c2s v6p0202c2s
v6p0228c1s v6p0239c2s v6p0287c1s
v6p0342c2s v6p0366c1s v6p0393c2s
v6p0419c1s v6p0433c2s v6p0470c2s
v6p0481c2s v6p0559c2s v6p0570c2s
v6p0632c2s v6p0641c1s
St.Gaudens, Homer v6p0070c1s
Saint-Gaudens, Homer v6p0014c2s
v6p0048c2s
v6p0155c2s
Saint-Genix, E. v5p0382c2s
St.George v5p0245c2s
St.George, F.K.E. v5p0176c1s
St.Georges, H.De v1p0307c2s
St.Hilaire, R. v1p0738c1s
St.John, B. v1p0396c1s
v1p0799c2s v1p0861c2s v6p0479c2s
St.John, C. v6p0272c1s
v6p0300c2s
St.John, C.E. v4p0177c1s
v4p0591c2s v5p0486c2s
St.John, C.M. v4p0184c1s
St.John, H. v1p0049c1s
v1p0167c2s v1p0336c1s v1p0484c1s
v1p0722c1m v1p0761c1s v1p0778c2s
v1p0790c2s
v1p1137c1s
v1p1147c1s
St.John, H.C. v1p0016c2s
St.John, H.R. v1p0367c1s
v1p0932c1s
St.John, I.M. v1p1343c2s
St.John, J.A. v1p0167c2m
v1p0330c1s v1p0396c2s v1p0544c2s
v1p0553c2s v1p0673c1s v1p0782c1s
v1p1304c2s
v1p1335c2s
St.John, J.P. v4p0333c2s
St.John, N.M. v5p0146c1s
St.John, O. v2p0069c2s
St.John, P. v1p1280c2s
St.John, P.B. v1p0477c1s
v1p0850c2s v1p0960c1s v1p1233c1s
St.John, R.D. v3p0322c1s
v4p0632c2s
St.John, R.F.St.A. v1p0050c2s
v1p0591c1s
St.John, R.F.St.Andrew ... v4p0053c1s
St.John, R.P. v5p0179c1s
St.John, S. and Loomis, E.
v1p0400c1s
St.John, W.P. v3p0393c1s
v4p0278c1s
v4p0524c2s
St.Johnston, A. v2p0029c1s
v2p0066c2m v4p0029c2s v4p0061c2m
v4p0125c1s v4p0228c1s v4p0414c2s
v4p0455c1s v4p0526c2s
v4p0604c1s
Saint Just, I. v5p0547c2s
St.Lawrence, B. v6p0539c1s
St.Leger, A. v6p0448c2s
Saint Leger, E. v4p0316c2s
v4p0414c2s
St.Leger, W. v4p0343c1s
St.Matthew, J.H. v1p0702c1s
v1p1342c1s
St.Maur, E. v1p1228c2s
St.Maur, H. v1p0571c1s
v4p0245c1s
Saint-Maur, H. v4p0293c1s
Saint-Maur, Kate V. v6p0114c1s
St.Michael-Podmore v6p0706c2s
St.Paul v6p0192c1s
Saint-Paul, A. v4p0024c1s
v4p0024c2s v4p0480c2s v4p0580c1s
Saint-Paul, A. and Nodet, H.
v4p0453c1m
St.Pierre, T. v2p0117c1s
v6p0435c2s
St.Pol, Baron de v4p0393c1s
Saint-Pollias, B.De v6p0479c2s
Saint-Saens v5p0395c1s
Saint-Saens, C. v4p0052c1s
v4p0331c1s v4p0389c1s v4p0494c1s
v5p0241c1s v5p0422c1s v5p0546c2s
v5p0616c1s v6p0438c1s
St.Simon, Mrs. v1p1066c1s
St.Victor, M.Niepce de ... v1p0463c2s
v1p1002c2s
v1p1004c1m
Ste.Beuve v1p0864c1s
Ste.Beuve, C.A. v1p1180c2s
Sainte-Beuve, C.A. v1p0113c2s
v1p0127c2s v1p0425c2s v1p0512c2s
v1p0799c2s v1p0814c2s
Sainte-Foi, C. v1p1352c1s
Ste.Toe, C. v2p0477c1s
Sainter, J.D. v2p0094c2s
v2p0421c1s
Saintine, X.B. v1p0238c1s
Saintsbury, G. v1p0103c1s
v1p0115c1s v1p0216c1s v1p0225c2s
v1p0359c1s v1p0371c1s v1p0418c1s
v1p0450c1s v1p0459c2s v1p0490c1s
v1p0503c1s v1p0503c2s v1p0612c1s
v1p0739c2s v1p0881c1s v1p1098c2s
v1p1110c1s v1p1143c1s v1p1149c2s
v1p1377c2s v1p1378c1s v2p0001c2s
v2p0052c2s v2p0075c1s v2p0144c1s
v2p0154c2s v2p0195c1s v2p0210c2s
v2p0262c1s v2p0334c1s v2p0361c2m
v2p0395c1s v2p0406c1s v2p0428c1s
v2p0475c1s v3p0089c2s v3p0103c2s
v3p0111c2s v3p0115c1s v3p0140c1s
v3p0152c1s v3p0163c2s v3p0188c2s
v3p0198c1s v3p0200c1s v3p0204c2s

v3p0228c1s v3p0287c1s v3p0308c1s
v3p0341c2s v3p0359c1s v3p0375c2s
v3p0400c2s v3p0454c2s v4p0030c2s
v4p0043c1s v4p0045c2s v4p0048c1s
v4p0059c2s v4p0063c1s v4p0082c2s
v4p0121c1s v4p0163c2s v4p0258c2s
v4p0263c1s v4p0269c1s v4p0319c1s
v4p0346c1s v4p0349c2s v4p0361c2s
v4p0383c2s v4p0405c2s v4p0481c2s
v4p0495c1s v4p0509c2s v5p0415c2s
v5p0487c1s v5p0605c2s v6p0208c2s
Saintsbury, G. and Craik, H.
v5p0515c2s
Saintsbury, G.E.B. v5p0585c1s
Saintsbury, Geo. v3p0192c1s
v3p0396c2s v4p0168c1s v4p0408c1s
v4p0539c1s
Saisset, E. v1p0085c2s
v1p0287c2s v1p0904c1s v1p1060c1s
Sakai, V.K. v5p0394c2s
Sakney, N. v3p0370c1s
Sakolski, A.M. v6p0652c2s
Sakuma, H. v6p0334c2s
v6p0435c2s
Sakurai, J. v2p0169c1s
Sala, E. v1p0889c1s
Sala, G. v1p1079c1s
Sala, G.A. v1p0010c1s
v1p0022c1s v1p0071c1s v1p0084c1s
v1p0108c2s v1p0114c2s v1p0150c1s
v1p0151c1s v1p0153c2s v1p0159c1s
v1p0168c1s v1p0199c1m v1p0203c1s
v1p0218c2s v1p0245c2s v1p0270c1s
v1p0277c2s v1p0298c1m v1p0299c2s
v1p0318c1s v1p0321c1m v1p0324c1s
v1p0350c2s v1p0352c2m v1p0357c1s
v1p0360c1s v1p0362c1s v1p0369c1s
v1p0414c2s v1p0439c2s v1p0442c1s
v1p0451c2s v1p0483c2s v1p0505c1s
v1p0519c2m v1p0521c2s v1p0525c2m
v1p0539c2s v1p0550c2s v1p0559c1s
v1p0567c2s v1p0569c2s v1p0574c2s
v1p0583c2s v1p0596c1s v1p0606c2s
v1p0607c1s v1p0609c1s v1p0641c1s
v1p0696c2s v1p0739c1s v1p0757c1s
v1p0762c1s v1p0763c1s v1p0763c2s
v1p0764c1s v1p0764c2m v1p0765c2s
v1p0766c1s v1p0786c1s v1p0795c2s
v1p0797c1s v1p0804c2s v1p0812c2s
v1p0837c2s v1p0851c1s v1p0864c2s
v1p0878c1s v1p0879c1s v1p0880c1s
v1p0885c1s v1p0916c1m v1p0917c1s
v1p0951c2s v1p0961c2s v1p0964c1m
v1p0966c2s v1p0970c1s v1p0970c2s
v1p0971c2s v1p0978c2s v1p0989c2s
v1p1019c1s v1p1021c1s v1p1025c1s
v1p1030c1s v1p1060c1s v1p1072c2s
v1p1087c2s v1p1098c2s v1p1112c2m
v1p1125c1s v1p1144c2m v1p1177c2s
v1p1179c2s v1p1180c2s v1p1193c1s
v1p1193c2s v1p1197c1s v1p1227c1s
v1p1232c1s v1p1242c1s v1p1258c1s
v1p1259c1s v1p1260c2s v1p1298c2s
v1p1326c1s v1p1331c2s v1p1350c2s
v1p1365c2m v1p1366c1s v1p1366c2s
v1p1389c1s v1p1400c2s v1p1411c1s
v1p1421c2s v1p1438c2s v2p0325c2s
v2p0383c2s v3p0124c2s v3p0267c2s
v4p0340c1s
Saladin, H. v3p0018c2s
Salaman, C. v5p0450c1s
v6p0498c2s
Salaman, M.C. v5p0376c1s
Salamon, A.G. v3p0037c2s
v3p0474c1s
Salano, E.J. v6p0645c2s
Salatini, R. v6p0291c2s
Salazar, L. v6p0331c1s
Salazar, Lorenzo v5p0304c2s
Salazaro, F.Z. v3p0173c2s
Sale, A.E. v3p0210c1s
Sale, M.T. v1p0630c1s
v1p1256c1s
Saleeby, C. v6p0264c2s
Saleeby, C.W. v6p0004c2s
v6p0011c1m v6p0014c1s v6p0037c1s
v6p0040c1m v6p0048c1s v6p0067c1s
v6p0098c2s v6p0106c1s v6p0140c2s
v6p0145c2s v6p0152c1m v6p0167c1s
v6p0172c2s v6p0175c1s v6p0175c2m
v6p0193c1s v6p0203c1s v6p0209c2s
v6p0211c1s v6p0212c2s v6p0223c1s
v6p0258c1s v6p0273c1s v6p0284c2s
v6p0285c1s v6p0287c2s v6p0288c2m
v6p0294c1s v6p0296c2s v6p0305c1s
v6p0307c2s v6p0309c2s v6p0319c1s
v6p0334c2s v6p0337c2s v6p0375c2s
v6p0376c1m v6p0376c2s v6p0379c1s
v6p0382c1s v6p0397c1s v6p0402c1s
v6p0402c2s v6p0407c1s v6p0410c1s
v6p0418c2s v6p0446c1m v6p0469c1s
v6p0479c1s v6p0497c2s v6p0502c1s
v6p0526c1s v6p0572c1m v6p0533c1s
v6p0537c2m v6p0544c1s v6p0576c1s
v6p0577c1s v6p0583c2s v6p0595c2s
v6p0602c1s v6p0603c2s v6p0609c2s
v6p0610c1m v6p0624c2s v6p0625c2s
v6p0629c1s v6p0630c1s v6p0644c2s
v6p0660c1s v6p0680c1s v6p0698c2s
v6p0708c2s
Saleilles, R. v4p0211c2s
Salerno, G.R. v5p0291c1s
Sales, H.H. v3p0380c2s
Salford, Bp.of v3p0246c2s
v4p0171c1s v4p0182c2s v4p0506c1s
Salis, E.de v5p0155c1s
Salis-Schwabe, G. v6p0638c1s
Salisbury, A. v2p0308c2s
v4p0102c2s
Salisbury, E.E. v1p0353c1s
v1p0360c1s v1p0608c1s v1p0692c2s
v1p0834c2s v1p0858c1s v2p0192c2s
v3p0185c1s
Salisbury, E.E., Mrs. v2p0474c2s
Salisbury, E.G. v4p0481c2s
Salisbury, Lord v4p0236c2s
v4p0266c1s
Salisbury, Marquis of v2p0126c1s
v2p0330c2s
v4p0073c2s
Salisbury, Ph. v5p0005c2s
v5p0028c2s v5p0205c2s v5p0220c2s
Salisbury, R.D. v3p0313c2s
v3p0425c2s v4p0025c1s v4p0272c2m
v4p0351c2s v4p0396c1s v5p0228c2s
v5p0413c2s v5p0590c1s v5p0614c1m
Salisbury, R.D. and Chamberlin, T.C.
v3p0334c2s
Salisbury, Rollin D. v6p0186c1s
Salle, G.De v6p0586c1s
Sallet, F.von v1p0751c1s
Sallwurk, E.von v4p0171c2s
Salm-Salm, Princess v1p0833c2s
Salmeron, D.L. v6p0607c2s
Salmon, A. v4p0604c2s
Salmon, A.L. v3p0077c1s
v4p0074c1s v4p0098c1s v4p0159c2s
v4p0161c2s v4p0216c1s v4p0350c1s
v4p0476c1s v4p0482c1s v5p0212c1s
v5p0645c1s v6p0020c1s v6p0034c2s
v6p0135c1s v6p0230c2s v6p0580c2s
v6p0639c1s v6p0647c2s
Salmon, C.L. v2p0004c2s
Salmon, C.S. v2p0004c2s
Salmon, D. v5p0015c2s
v5p0178c2s
Salmon, D.E. v2p0175c1s
v2p0175c2s v2p0428c2s
Salmon, E. v3p0036c2s
v3p0116c1s v3p0120c2s v3p0122c1s
v3p0180c2s v3p0295c1s v3p0355c1s
v3p0358c1s v3p0385c2s v3p0472c1s
v4p0038c1s v4p0124c2s v4p0213c2s
v4p0256c2s v4p0315c1s v4p0533c2s
v5p0189c2s v5p0215c2s v5p0229c2s
v5p0244c2s v5p0245c2s v6p0089c2s
v6p0108c1s v6p0240c1s
Salmon, E.G. v2p0205c1s
v2p0365c2m v4p0522c1s v4p0557c2s
Salmon, G. v1p0097c1s
v1p0496c1s v1p1237c1s v2p0017c2s
v2p0045c1s v2p0054c1s v2p0072c1s
v2p0224c2s v2p0348c1s v2p0359c2s
v5p0297c1s
Salmon, L.M. v2p0131c2s
v3p0090c1s v3p0091c2s v3p0197c1s
v3p0197c2s v4p0122c2m v4p0127c1s
v4p0159c1m v4p0171c1s v4p0258c2s
v4p0266c2s v4p0626c2s v5p0127c1s
v5p0179c1s v5p0266c2s v5p0348c2s
v5p0569c2s v6p0152c2s v6p0292c2s
v6p0293c1s v6p0584c2s
Salmon, Lucy M. v6p0190c1s
v6p0192c1s
Salmond, C.A. v1p1033c1s
v1p1117c1s v2p0204c2s v2p0403c2s
v4p0229c1s v5p0380c1s
Salmond, J.L. v5p0249c2s
Salmond, J.M. v5p0120c1s
Salmond, J.W. v4p0131c2s
v4p0190c2s v4p0323c1s v5p0327c2s
v5p0463c2s v6p0128c1s
Salmond, L.M. v5p0165c2s
Salmond, S.D.F. v2p0044c1s
v2p0044c2s v2p0333c1s v3p0357c2s
v4p0042c1s v4p0533c2s v5p0055c2m
v5p0058c2s v5p0084c2s v5p0085c1s
v5p0118c1s v5p0236c1s v5p0281c1s
v5p0515c1s v6p0063c1s v6p0125c1s
v6p0403c2s
Salmond, W. v1p0690c1s
Salmone, H.A. v3p0035c1s
v4p0022c1s v4p0587c1m
Salmone, H.A. et al. v4p0027c2s
Salom, P.G. v2p0050c2s
v2p0419c2m v3p0133c1s v4p0047c2s
v4p0090c2s v4p0174c2s v4p0175c1s
v4p0550c2m
Salomon, C.S. v6p0570c1s
Salomon, Felix v6p0501c1s
Salomon, M. v5p0528c1s
v6p0384c2s
Salomon, W. v4p0131c2s
v4p0144c1s
Salomons, D. v3p0132c2s
v4p0415c2s
Salomons, D., Sir v5p0389c1s
Salt, H. v1p0111c2s
v1p0289c2s v1p0395c1m v1p0396c2s
Salt, H. et al. v3p0399c1s
Salt, H.A. v3p0253c2s
Salt, H.S. v2p0087c2s
v2p0147c2s v2p0161c1s v2p0289c1s
v2p0346c1s v2p0399c2m v2p0408c1s
v2p0439c2m v3p0061c1s v3p0128c2s
v3p0175c2s v3p0204c1s v3p0228c1s
v3p0289c2s v3p0390c1s v3p0410c1s
v3p0429c1s v4p0142c1s v4p0155c2s
v4p0169c1s v4p0229c2s v4p0364c1s
v4p0543c1s v4p0569c2s v4p0574c2s
v5p0578c2s v6p0150c2s v6p0339c1s
v6p0611c1s v6p0611c2s
Salt, H.S. and Dowden, E.. v3p0390c1s
Salt, H.S. et al. v5p0021c1s
Salt, W.H. v5p0156c2s
Salter, D.M. v2p0076c2s
Salter, E. v3p0081c2s
Salter, E.A. v1p0197c1s
Salter, E.G. v6p0238c2s
Salter, G.A. v1p0418c1s
Salter, H. v6p0473c2s
Salter, J.W. and Logan, W.E., Sir
v1p0193c1s
Salter, M. v2p0234c2m
v2p0392c2s
Salter, Miss v1p0069c1s
Salter, N.M. v4p0479c1s
Salter, W. v1p1010c1s
v2p0140c1s
Salter, W.M. v1p0447c1s
v1p1094c2s v2p0214c2s v3p0073c1s
v3p0136c1s v3p0143c1s v3p0280c1s
v3p0302c1s v3p0330c1s v3p0441c1s
v4p0017c1s v4p0109c1s v4p0177c2s
v4p0188c1m v4p0194c1s v4p0196c2s
v4p0273c1s v4p0273c2s v4p0307c2m
v4p0314c2s v4p0372c1s v4p0382c1s
v4p0463c2s v4p0476c2s v4p0514c2m
v4p0610c2s v4p0628c2s v5p0337c2s
v6p0019c2s v6p0108c2s v6p0202c2s
v6p0492c2s v6p0702c2s
Saltus, E. v3p0151c2s
v3p0178c2s v3p0287c2s v3p0328c1s
v3p0435c1s v4p0503c1s v5p0051c1s
v5p0265c1s v5p0467c1s v6p0054c2s
v6p0069c1s v6p0352c1s v6p0452c1s
v6p0452c2s v6p0490c2s v6p0516c2s
v6p0517c1s v6p0556c2s
Saltus, Edgar v5p0067c1s
v5p0140c1s v5p0202c2s v5p0238c2s
v5p0579c1s
Saltus, J.Sanford v6p0339c1s
Salvado, R. v1p0078c1s
Salvador, Althea v4p0178c2s
Salvador, Althea, Baroness
v3p0320c2s
Salvage, W.B. v6p0156c1s
Salvesen, E.T. v5p0127c1s
v6p0154c2s
Salvetat and Ebelmen v1p1035c1s
Salviati, G. v3p0174c2s
Salvini, T. v2p0397c1s
v2p0398c1m v3p0002c2s v4p0501c1s
Salwey, C.M. v4p0297c1m
v4p0564c1s v5p0303c1s v5p0303c2m
v5p0319c2s v6p0335c2m v6p0338c2s
Salwey, C.M., Mrs. v4p0298c1s
Salzmann, L.F. v6p0627c2s
Sambon, L.W. v5p0591c2s
Samborn, K. v1p0826c1s
Sambourne, L. v4p0091c1s
Sampey, J.R. v3p0041c2s
v5p0506c2s
Sample, J.A. v6p0162c1s
Sample, R.F. v5p0463c2s
Sampsell, L.D. v5p0642c2s
v5p0643c1s
Sampson, A. v6p0644c2s
Sampson, D. v3p0340c2s
v4p0039c2s v5p0296c1s v5p0300c1s
v5p0300c2s v5p0479c1s v5p0489c1s
v6p0105c1s v6p0334c1s v6p0387c2s
v6p0390c2s v6p0478c1s v6p0501c1s
Sampson, Donat v5p0429c2s
v6p0242c1s
Sampson, F. v6p0469c1s
Sampson, F.A. v2p0399c2m
Sampson, L. v2p0366c1s
Sampson, M.G. v5p0197c2s
v6p0347c2s
Sampson, M.W. v3p0382c1s
v4p0183c1s v4p0184c1s v5p0012c1s
v5p0297c2s v6p0500c1s v6p0713c2s
Sampson, R.A. v6p0013c1s
v6p0625c2s
Sampson, T.R. v2p0026c2s
Sampson, W. v1p0652c1s
v1p1315c2s
Sampson, W.T. v1p1233c2s
v2p0025c2m v2p0095c2s v4p0395c2s
v5p0160c2s v5p0543c1s
Sampson, W.T. and Frisby, E.
v2p0095c2s
Sampson, W.T. v2p0095c1s
Sams, G.F. v4p0490c1s
Sams, S. v6p0338c1s
v6p0338c2s v6p0447c1s v6p0591c1s
Samson, B.M. v2p0276c2s
Samson, G.W. v1p0053c1s
v1p0129c2s v1p0185c1s v1p0234c1s

v1p0246c2s v1p0333c2s v1p0395c1s
v1p0435c1s v1p0536c2s v1p0565c1s
v1p0625c1s v1p0686c1s v1p0857c2s
v1p0872c1s v1p0994c1s v1p1332c2s
v2p0369c2s
Samson, J. v1p1113c2s
Samuel, B. v2p0255c2s
v2p0338c2s v5p0453c1s v5p0461c1s
Samuel, G.E. v4p0133c1s
Samuel, H. v6p0119c1s
v6p0133c2s v6p0308c2s v6p0342c2s
v6p0664c1s v6p0679c1s
Samuel, H.B. v6p0054c2s
v6p0286c1s
Samuel, Herbert v6p0144c1s
Samuel, J. v1p1248c1s
Samuel, M., Sir v5p0223c1s
Samuel, S.M. v2p0315c1s
v4p0302c2s
Samuels, A.W. v6p0326c1s
Samuels, E. v5p0107c2s
Samuels, E.A. v1p0181c1s
v1p0645c1s v5p0529c2s
Samuels, M. v2p0283c1s
Samuels, S. v3p0294c1s
Samuelson, B. v1p1288c2m
v2p0229c1s v4p0566c2s
Samuelson, H. v1p0387c2s
Samuelson, J. v1p0013c1s
v1p0070c2s v1p0099c1s v1p0108c2s
v1p0110c2s v1p0299c1s v1p0745c2s
v1p1007c1s v1p1378c2s v2p0038c1s
v2p0258c2s v2p0261c2s v2p0281c2s
v2p0415c2s v3p0202c1s v3p0239c1s
Samuelson, M. v2p0419c1s
San Carlos, L.de v4p0211c2s
v4p0212c1s v4p0215c1s v4p0629c1s
San Carlos, P.de v6p0607c2s
San Giuliano, A.di v4p0476c1s
San Juan v3p0425c2s
Sanborn, A.F. v4p0035c1s
v4p0049c2s v4p0071c1s v4p0336c2s
v4p0369c2s v4p0425c2m v4p0426c1s
v4p0426c2s v4p0474c2s v4p0569c1s
v4p0632c1m v5p0074c1s v5p0078c1s
v5p0217c2s v5p0221c1s v5p0280c2s
v5p0405c1s v5p0431c1s v5p0564c2s
v6p0003c2s v6p0238c1s v6p0238c2m
v6p0422c2s v6p0451c2s v6p0459c1s
v6p0491c1s v6p0631c2s v6p0682c2s
v6p0683c1s
Sanborn, A.F. and Morgan, P.
v5p0405c1s
Sanborn, A.L. v3p0091c2s
v6p0085c2s
Sanborn, Alvan F. v6p0242c1s
v6p0242c2s v6p0417c2s v6p0427c1s
Sanborn, B.F. v6p0143c1s
Sanborn, D.H. v1p1149c1s
Sanborn, E.D. v1p0261c1s
v1p0262c1s v1p0313c2s v1p0594c2s
v1p0723c2s v1p0840c1s v1p0932c1s
v1p1158c2s v1p1203c1s v1p1217c1s
v1p1356c2s v1p1424c1s v2p0108c1s
v2p0144c1s v2p0173c1s v2p0311c1m
v2p0311c2s v2p0332c2s v2p0436c1s
v2p0469c2s v3p0295c2s
Sanborn, E.H. v3p0335c2s
Sanborn, E.R. v1p1065c2s
Sanborn, E.W. v4p0467c1s
Sanborn, F.B. v1p0169c1m
v1p0219c1m v1p0337c1m v1p0405c2s
v1p0696c2s v1p0809c1s v1p0910c1m
v1p0914c1s v1p0981c2s v1p0997c2s
v1p1031c2s v1p1052c1s v1p1052c2m
v1p1090c2s v1p1180c2s v1p1214c1s
v1p1215c1m v2p0111c2s v2p0133c1s
v2p0139c2s v2p0140c2m v2p0341c2s
v2p0359c2s v2p0405c1s v2p0407c1m
v2p0407c2s v2p0439c2s v3p0067c1s
v3p0095c1s v3p0136c1s v3p0260c1s
v3p0261c1s v3p0301c2s v4p0096c1s
v4p0104c1s v4p0108c1s v4p0144c2s
v4p0178c2s v4p0179c1m v4p0532c1s
v4p0532c2s v4p0533c1s v4p0575c1m
v5p0019c1s v5p0046c1s v5p0086c1s
v5p0101c1s v5p0259c1s v5p0291c2m
v5p0324c1s v5p0351c1s v5p0406c1s
v5p0466c2s v5p0522c1s v5p0534c2s
v5p0535c1s v5p0535c2s v5p0539c2s
v5p0560c1s v5p0578c2s v5p0612c1s
v5p0626c1s v6p0011c2s v6p0084c2s
v6p0108c2m v6p0109c2s v6p0133c2s
v6p0143c1s v6p0201c2s v6p0202c1m
v6p0369c2s v6p0471c1s v6p0480c2s
v6p0544c2s v6p0563c1s v6p0598c1s
v6p0600c1s v6p0644c1s
Sanborn, F.B. and Boteler, A.R.
v2p0058c1s
Sanborn, F.B. et al. v2p0139c2s
Sanborn, F.P. v3p0059c1s
Sanborn, J.B. v5p0269c1s
v5p0308c1s v6p0151c1s
Sanborn, J.L. v1p0188c1s
Sanborn, K. v2p0076c1s
v2p0172c2s
Sanborn, K.A. v1p0871c1s
Sanborn, Kate v3p0219c1s
v6p0262c2s v6p0303c1s v6p0696c1s
Sanborn, May F. v6p0541c1s
Sanborn, N. v1p1149c1s
Sanborn, Prof. v1p1396c1s
Sanborn, V.C. v2p0385c1s
v4p0312c1s v5p0506c2s v6p0077c1s
v6p0167c1s
Sanchez, A.M. v6p0493c1s
v6p0648c2s
Sanchez, J.F. v6p0570c1s
Sanchez, N.V.De v6p0671c2s
Sand, G. v1p0802c1m
v1p0862c2s v1p1359c1s
Sand, George v1p0197c1s
v1p0520c1s v1p0755c2s v1p1114c2s
v1p1281c2s v2p0125c1s v4p0163c1s
Sand, L. v1p0492c1s
v1p0571c2s v1p0892c1s v1p1070c2s
v1p1072c1s v1p1088c1s v1p1112c1s
v1p1113c2s
Sandars, H. v6p0547c1s
v6p0607c2s
Sandars, M.F. v6p0049c1s
v6p0165c2m
Sandars, Mary F. v6p0049c1m
Sandars, R. v2p0120c2s
Sandars, V. v2p0404c1s
v4p0434c2s
Sandars, W.C. v1p1260c2s
v1p1328c1s
Sanday, W. v1p0126c2s
v1p0128c1s v1p0691c1s v1p0799c2s
v1p0862c2s v3p0043c1s v3p0043c2s
v3p0081c1s v3p0141c1s v3p0184c1s
v3p0191c1s v3p0251c1m v4p0053c2s
v4p0054c1s v4p0057c1s v4p0057c2s
v4p0109c1s v4p0111c1s v4p0270c2s
v5p0037c2s v5p0271c2s v6p0061c1s
v6p0342c1s
Sanday, W. and Hort, F.J.A.
v3p0385c1s
Sanday, W.H. v4p0532c1s
Sandberg, C.P. v1p1075c1m
Sandberg, G. v3p0058c2s
v3p0175c1s v3p0248c1s v3p0428c2m
v4p0279c2s v5p0374c2s
Sandeman, G. v4p0096c1s
Sandeman, W. v6p0185c2s
Sandernan, J.W. v1p1311c2s
Sanders, A.J. v3p0071c2s
Sanders, C.F. v5p0040c2s
v5p0115c1s v5p0378c1s v6p0150c1s
v6p0513c2s
Sanders, C.S. v6p0443c2s
Sanders, C.W. v6p0131c1s
Sanders, D.W. v2p0207c1s
Sanders, F.K. v5p0058c2s
v6p0538c1m
Sanders, F.W. v4p0287c2s
v4p0293c2s
Sanders, H.A. v6p0521c1s
v6p0675c1s
Sanders, H.F. v6p0256c1s
Sanders, H.M. v4p0256c1s
v4p0448c1s v4p0503c2s v5p0079c2s
v5p0094c1s v5p0165c2s v5p0213c2s
v5p0274c2s v5p0329c1s v5p0341c2s
v5p0425c1s v5p0433c2s v5p0456c1s
v5p0466c2s v6p0182c2s
Sanders, H.N. v5p0310c1s
Sanders, Helen F. v6p0090c1s
v6p0362c1s v6p0467c2s v6p0485c1s
v6p0568c2s v6p0670c1s
Sanders, L. v6p0331c1s
v6p0661c2s v6p0695c2s
Sanders, L.C. v3p0363c1s
Sanders, M.A. v3p0249c1m
v4p0337c1s
Sanders, M.F. v6p0387c2s
Sanders, M.T. v4p0144c1s
Sanders, Mrs. v6p0417c1s
Sanders, T.C. v1p0259c2s
Sanders, V., Lady v5p0390c2s
Sanders, W. v1p0757c1s
Sanderson, A. v5p0466c2s
Sanderson, B. v1p1366c2s
v2p0344c1s
Sanderson, C. v1p1251c1m
v3p0223c1s v3p0409c1s
Sanderson, C.P. v6p0014c2s
Sanderson, E.D. v6p0153c1s
v6p0320c2s
Sanderson, F.R. v6p0026c1s
v6p0027c1s v6p0451c2s
Sanderson, J. v1p0415c2s
v1p0701c1s v1p1255c2s v1p1322c1s
v1p1441c2s v2p0284c2s v4p0492c2s
Sanderson, J.B. v1p0086c1s
v1p1007c1s v2p0080c2s v4p0070c2s
v4p0344c2s v4p0442c1s
Sanderson, J.B. and Hilton, H.
v6p0286c2s
Sanderson, J.F. v1p0216c1s
Sanderson, J.G. v5p0282c1s
v5p0369c1s v5p0441c2s v5p0467c2s
v6p0066c1s
Sanderson, J.P. v1p0769c1s
Sanderson, J.S.B. v3p0331c2s
Sanderson, L.J. v4p0186c2s
Sanderson, Lydia E. v6p0705c2s
Sanderson, Miss v1p0110c1s
v1p0942c1s v1p1339c1s
Sandford, A.B. v5p0276c1s
Sandford, C.W. v2p0084c2s
Sandford, D.K. v1p0057c2m
v1p0072c1s v1p0554c2s v1p0601c1s
v1p0601c2s
Sandford, D.K., Sir v1p0009c1s
v1p0019c2s v1p0068c1s v1p0506c1s
v1p0551c2s v1p0554c1m v1p0780c1s
v1p1010c2s v1p1284c2s
Sandford, E.A. v1p0026c2s
Sandford, Lord v3p0128c2s
Sandford, Mrs. v1p1422c2s
v4p0627c2s
Sandham, A.F. v2p0324c1s
Sandham, H. v1p0215c2s
v5p0259c2s
Sandier, Alex. v6p0388c1s
Sandison, G.H. v3p0034c2s
v4p0017c1s v4p0615c1s v5p0145c2s
Sandison, J. v4p0109c1s
v4p0454c1s v5p0081c1s v5p0114c2s
v5p0577c1s
Sandow, E. v4p0441c1s
Sandoz, M. v5p0045c2s
v5p0564c2s
Sandraz, Esther v3p0186c1s
Sandrock, M.L. v3p0279c2s
Sands, A.H. v1p1421c2s
Sands, H. v5p0474c1s
v6p0082c2m v6p0183c2s v6p0663c1s
Sands, J. v4p0499c1s
Sands, J.D. v4p0608c1s
Sands, R.C. v1p0569c2s
Sands, Susan v5p0403c1s
v5p0620c1s
Sands, W.F. v6p0354c1s
Sands, W.H. v5p0587c1s
Sandwick, R.L. v6p0426c2s
v6p0569c1s v6p0575c1s
Sandwith, H. v1p0027c1s
v1p0058c2s v1p0109c2m v1p0151c1s
v1p0285c2s v1p0553c1s v1p0578c2s
v1p0766c2s v1p0830c2s v1p0935c2s
v1p0951c1s v1p1180c1m
Sandwith, T.B. v1p0328c2s
v1p0759c2s v1p1039c1s
Sandy, W. v2p0044c2s
Sandys, E. v3p0304c2s
v5p0251c1s v5p0623c2m v5p0639c2s
v6p0053c2m v6p0067c2m v6p0068c1s
v6p0071c2s v6p0095c2s v6p0177c2m
v6p0183c1s v6p0227c1s v6p0227c2m
v6p0228c1s v6p0235c2s v6p0246c1m
v6p0275c1s v6p0280c2m v6p0399c1s
v6p0403c1s v6p0439c2s v6p0499c1s
v6p0524c1s v6p0524c2s v6p0545c2s
v6p0599c1s v6p0611c2s v6p0658c1m
v6p0661c2s v6p0698c1s v6p0700c1s
v6p0701c2s v6p0706c2s
Sandys, E.W. v3p0066c2s
v3p0203c1s v3p0293c2s v3p0405c2s
v3p0426c2s v3p0438c2s v3p0471c1m
v4p0048c2s v4p0061c1s v4p0064c2s
v4p0086c2s v4p0131c2s v4p0151c1s
v4p0200c2s v4p0201c1m v4p0210c2s
v4p0219c1s v4p0221c1s v4p0244c2s
v4p0248c1s v4p0270c1m v4p0348c2s
v4p0376c1s v4p0390c1m v4p0468c2m
v4p0470c2s v4p0521c2s v4p0528c1s
v4p0531c2s v4p0543c1s v4p0560c1s
v4p0582c2s v4p0585c1s v4p0587c1m
v4p0624c1s v5p0038c1s v5p0049c1m
v5p0063c1s v5p0089c2s v5p0092c2s
v5p0115c2s v5p0164c2m v5p0170c2s
v5p0197c2s v5p0208c2s v5p0209c1s
v5p0216c1s v5p0230c1s v5p0240c1s
v5p0276c2s v5p0385c2s v5p0395c2m
v5p0425c1s v5p0455c1s v5p0473c2s
v5p0475c1s v5p0490c1s v5p0505c2s
v5p0527c1m v5p0568c2s v5p0581c2s
v5p0589c1s v5p0591c2s v5p0592c1s
Sandys, E.W. and Currie, D.
v3p0186c1s
Sandys, Ed.W. v4p0431c2s
Sandys, F.W. v5p0547c2s
Sandys, G. v1p0300c1s
Sandys, J.E. v4p0189c1s
Sandys, J.E. and Edwards, A.B.
v3p0401c1s
Sandys, J.E. et al. v3p0019c2s
Sandys, W. v1p0972c2s
Sanford, D.S. v5p0265c1s
v6p0056c1s v6p0193c2s v6p0307c2s
Sanford, E.C. v2p0056c1s
v3p0082c1s v3p0327c2s v3p0348c2s
v3p0439c2s v4p0110c2s v4p0464c2m
v4p0465c1s v4p0539c1s v5p0116c1m
v6p0227c1s v6p0276c1s v6p0410c2s
v6p0521c2m v6p0522c1s
Sanford, E.C. and Triplett, N.
v5p0488c1s
Sanford, E.J. v5p0149c2s
Sanford, E.P. v6p0566c1s
Sanford, F. v4p0473c1s
Sanford, H.E. v1p0199c2s
Sanford, H.S. v2p0394c1s
Sanford, J. v6p0620c1s
Sanford, L.E., Mrs. v2p0195c1s
Sanford, L.J. v1p0536c2s
Sanford, Laura v6p0071c1s

Sanford, M. v1p0051c2s v1p0313c1s
Sanford, M.B. v4p0153c2s
Sanford, M.E. v2p0348c2s
Sanford, M.R. v5p0494c1s
Sanford, M.W. v6p0245c2s
Sanford, Mary B. v6p0167c1s
Sanford, O.M. v2p0431c2s
Sanford, P. v5p0049c1s
Sang, E. v1p0783c1m v1p0986c2s v1p1077c1s
Sanger, C.F. v3p0119c1s v3p0416c1s
Sanger, C.P. v4p0021c2s v4p0167c2s v5p0550c2s v5p0568c1m v6p0518c2s
Sanger, C.P. and Sweet, C. v6p0151c1s
Sanger, C.R. v6p0291c1s
Sanger, E.B. v2p0029c1m v2p0273c2s
Sanger, J.P. v5p0032c2m v5p0276c2s
Sanger, W.C. v5p0029c2s
Sangree, A. v5p0006c1s
Sangree, Allen v5p0587c1s v5p0627c1s v6p0053c1s
Sangster, C. v1p0457c2s v1p0666c2s
Sangster, M. v1p0423c2s v4p0040c1s
Sangster, M.E. v4p0284c1s v4p0627c1s v5p0419c2s
Sanguinetti, E.P. v3p0017c1s
Sanial, L. v3p0304c2s
Sanial, L. et al. v5p0179c1s
Sankey, H.R. v6p0615c2s
Sankey, R., Sir v6p0326c1s
Sankey, W.H.V. v1p1329c2s
Sannomiya, A.Y. v4p0521c1s v5p0303c1s
Sansom, A.E. v2p0175c2s
Sansone, F. v2p0127c2s v2p0173c1s
Sansone, J. v3p0104c2s
Santa Cruz, J.M. v3p0078c1s
Santayana, G. v2p0414c2s v3p0207c2s v3p0462c2s v4p0035c2s v4p0249c2s v4p0438c2s v4p0488c2s v4p0517c1s v4p0635c1s v5p0038c1s v5p0250c1s v6p0491c1s v6p0503c2s v6p0663c1s
Santee, J.W. v1p0097c1s v1p0243c2m v1p0252c1s v1p0254c2s v1p0402c2s v1p0425c2s v1p0442c2s v1p0585c1s v1p0758c2s v1p1057c2s v1p1089c2s v1p1103c2s v1p1174c2s v1p1175c2s v1p1270c1s v4p0113c2s v4p0186c1s v4p0345c2s v4p0475c1s
Santini, C.F. v6p0331c2s
Santini, F. v6p0331c2s
Santley, H. v1p0802c1s v1p1420c2s
Santos-Dumont, A. v6p0005c1s v6p0009c2m v6p0048c2s
Santvoord, C.Van v1p0784c2s v1p0897c1s v2p0259c1s v2p0279c1s
Saphir, A. v1p0684c2s
Saplin, W.H. v4p0217c1s
Saporta, A.de v2p0028c2s v2p0393c2s
Saporta, Count de v1p1015c2s
Saporta, G.De v2p0274c1s v2p0352c1s
Saporta, Marquis de v3p0158c1s
Sapp, R. v1p0831c1s
Sarafoff, B. v6p0392c1s
Sarasin, E. v4p0122c2s
Sarbiewski, C. v1p0461c1s
Sarcey, F. v1p0281c1s v1p0970c1s v3p0320c1s v4p0121c2s v4p0126c1s v4p0429c2s v5p0241c2s
Sarcey, T. v1p0488c2s
Sardeson, F.W. v5p0337c1s v5p0344c1s v6p0536c2s v6p0575c2s
Sardon, V. v1p0139c2s
Sardou, V. v1p1072c1s
Sarel, C.W. v4p0009c1s
Sargant, C.H. v3p0186c1s v3p0241c2s
Sargant, G.H. v3p0377c2s
Sargant, W.L. v1p0385c2s v1p0628c1m v1p1376c1s
Sargeant, A. v1p0469c2s
Sargeant, A.M. v1p0792c2s v1p0979c1s
Sargeant, H.B. v6p0107c1s v6p0138c1s
Sargeant, J. v1p0821c1s
Sargeant, L. v4p0621c1s
Sargeaunt, J. v5p0309c2s
Sargent, A. v1p0006c1s v1p0203c2s v1p0920c2s
Sargent, A.A. v2p0013c1s v2p0079c2s v2p0176c2s v2p0229c2s
Sargent, A.J. v6p0013c2s
Sargent, A.L. v4p0330c1s v5p0334c2s
Sargent, A.L. et al. v5p0106c2s
Sargent, B.G. v4p0295c2s
Sargent, C.C., jr. v5p0129c1s v5p0434c1s
Sargent, C.S. v1p0467c2s v1p0468c1m v1p0908c1s v2p0002c2s v2p0162c1m v2p0162c2m v2p0268c1s v2p0310c2s v2p0325c2s v2p0342c1s v2p0446c1s v4p0003c2m v4p0007c2m v4p0008c1m v4p0008c2m v4p0022c2s v4p0023c2s v4p0024c2s v4p0030c1s v4p0032c2m v4p0039c2m v4p0059c1m v4p0060c1s v4p0068c2m v4p0069c1s v4p0069c2m v4p0070c1s v4p0070c2s v4p0078c1s v4p0083c2s v4p0093c2s v4p0094c2m v4p0097c2s v4p0100c1s v4p0101c2m v4p0102c2s v4p0116c1s v4p0129c2s v4p0132c1s v4p0134c1s v4p0136c2m v4p0145c2s v4p0146c1s v4p0160c1s v4p0160c2s v4p0166c1s v4p0176c1s v4p0178c1s v4p0180c2s v4p0186c1s v4p0192c1s v4p0192c2s v4p0194c2s v4p0195c1s v4p0197c2s v4p0202c2m v4p0203c1s v4p0203c2m v4p0204c1m v4p0207c2m v4p0208c1m v4p0208c2m v4p0209c1m v4p0219c2m v4p0220c1m v4p0248c1s v4p0264c2m v4p0265c1m v4p0285c2m v4p0319c1m v4p0319c2m v4p0321c1s v4p0322c1s v4p0344c2m v4p0349c2s v4p0353c1s v4p0354c2s v4p0358c1s v4p0376c2s v4p0380c2s v4p0385c2s v4p0387c1s v4p0394c2s v4p0395c1s v4p0399c1s v4p0400c2m v4p0410c1m v4p0422c2s v4p0423c1s v4p0426c2s v4p0427c1m v4p0427c2m v4p0431c1s v4p0432c2s v4p0435c1s v4p0444c1m v4p0445c1m v4p0445c2m v4p0446c1s v4p0447c1s v4p0447c2m v4p0463c2s v4p0465c2s v4p0468c1s v4p0481c2s v4p0483c2s v4p0502c1m v4p0503c2s v4p0504c2s v4p0505c2s v4p0510c1s v4p0513c1s v4p0513c2s v4p0522c1m v4p0524c1s v4p0535c2s v4p0542c1m v4p0543c1s v4p0543c2s v4p0546c2m v4p0552c2s v4p0556c1s v4p0566c2s v4p0577c1s v4p0583c1m v4p0583c2m v4p0592c2s v4p0600c1s v4p0604c2s v4p0605c1s v4p0609c2s v4p0611c2s v4p0613c1s v4p0614c2s v4p0616c1s v4p0623c2s v4p0635c2m v4p0636c2m v5p0001c1s v5p0004c1s v5p0004c2s v5p0009c1m v5p0010c2s v5p0038c1s v5p0072c2s v5p0133c1s v5p0211c1s v5p0214c1m v5p0214c2s v5p0225c2s v5p0251c1s v5p0256c1s v5p0324c2m v5p0393c1s v5p0407c2s v5p0432c2s v5p0433c1m v5p0440c1s v5p0453c2s v5p0454c1m v5p0454c2s v5p0455c1s v5p0474c1s v5p0481c2s v5p0486c1s v5p0511c2s v5p0553c2s v5p0589c2s v5p0590c1m v5p0630c2s v5p0634c2s
Sargent, C.S. and Eliot, C. v5p0590c1s
Sargent, C.S. et al. v5p0214c1s
Sargent, D. v1p1152c1s
Sargent, D.A. v2p0027c1s v2p0340c2m v3p0025c2m v3p0190c2s v3p0192c2s v3p0265c2s v3p0470c1s v4p0441c1s v5p0148c2s v5p0199c1s v5p0257c1s v5p0347c1s
Sargent, E. v1p0424c1s v1p0887c2s v1p1037c2s v1p1259c2s
Sargent, E.B. v6p0215c1s
Sargent, E.W. v5p0457c1s
Sargent, Ellen C. v6p0432c2s
Sargent, F.L. v3p0367c1s
Sargent, F.LeR. v4p0045c2s
Sargent, F.P. v4p0552c2s v6p0308c2s v6p0309c1s
Sargent, G.E. v2p0476c2s
Sargent, G.H. v5p0239c2s
Sargent, H. v2p0307c2s v2p0428c2s v3p0339c1s
Sargent, H.B. v1p1059c1s v6p0005c1s
Sargent, H.G. v4p0244c1s v5p0012c2s v5p0067c1s
Sargent, H.H. v5p0556c1s v6p0365c1s
Sargent, I. v6p0005c2s v6p0028c1s v6p0033c1s v6p0033c2s v6p0034c1s v6p0053c1s v6p0074c1s v6p0076c2s v6p0102c2s v6p0131c2s v6p0139c1s v6p0154c1s v6p0155c2s v6p0167c2m v6p0171c2s v6p0194c2s v6p0220c2s v6p0226c1s v6p0239c2s v6p0241c1s v6p0256c2m v6p0262c2s v6p0279c2s v6p0299c2s v6p0320c2s v6p0354c2s v6p0359c1s v6p0384c1s v6p0430c2m v6p0435c1s v6p0472c2s v6p0511c2s v6p0512c1m v6p0536c1s v6p0538c2s v6p0555c1s v6p0595c1s v6p0640c2s v6p0647c1s
Sargent, I. and Schopfer, J., v6p0595c1s
Sargent, J.E. v2p0031c2s v2p0088c2s v2p0311c2s v2p0361c2s v2p0441c1s
Sargent, J.S. v5p0385c2s
Sargent, J.T. v1p0972c2s v1p1092c2s
Sargent, J.Y. v2p0287c1s
Sargent, L.M. v1p0140c1s v1p0809c2s
Sargent, L.R. v5p0444c1m v5p0444c2s
Sargent, Lucy v6p0315c2s
Sargent, M.E. v4p0066c2s v5p0106c2s v5p0335c2s v6p0709c1s
Sargent, Maud E. v6p0327c1s
Sargent, R.M. v1p1013c2s
Sargent, W. v1p0034c1s v1p0038c1m v1p0105c1s v1p0149c1s v1p0149c2s v1p0228c2s v1p0233c1s v1p0234c1s v1p0257c1s v1p0281c1s v1p0350c1s v1p0371c2s v1p0412c1s v1p0475c2s v1p0680c1s v1p0744c1s v1p0753c1s v1p0771c2s v1p0998c1s v1p1133c2s v1p1138c2s v1p1212c2s v1p1213c2s v1p1331c1s v2p0381c1s v2p0448c2s v5p0511c2s v6p0573c2s
Sargent, W.H. v6p0056c1s v6p0358c2s
Sargent, W.M. v2p0238c2s
Sarmiento, D.F. v1p1159c2s
Saroni, H.S. v1p0883c2s v1p0884c2s v5p0116c1s
Sarrazin, G. v3p0163c2s v4p0075c2s v4p0620c1s
Sars, G.D. v1p0055c1s
Sars, G.O. v1p0082c1s
Sars, J.E. v4p0407c1s
Sarson, G. v1p0201c2s v2p0174c2s v2p0355c2s
Sartain v2p0141c1s
Sartain, J. v1p0419c2s v2p0326c2s v3p0335c1s
Sartain, S. and Levy, L.E. v6p0100c2s
Sartain, W. v4p0030c1s v4p0538c1s
Sartiaux, A. v1p0399c2s
Sartoris, A., Mrs. v1p1396c2s
Sartorius, Dr. v1p0769c2s
Sartorius, E.W.C. v1p0814c2s
Sarver, J.M. v6p0039c1s
Sarwey, C. v1p0929c2s
Sasaki, C. v2p0402c2s
Sasmal, B.N. v6p0312c2s
Sasnett, W.J. v1p1352c1s
Sass, E. and Nelson, J. v5p0007c2s
Sass, G.H. v1p0190c2s v1p0266c2s v1p0443c2s
Sass, M. v1p0785c2s
Sassenach, A. v6p0162c1s
Sasseville, E.de v5p0411c1s v5p0525c1s
Sassoon, D. v1p0617c1s
Sassoon, D.S. v6p0521c1s
Sassoon, E. v5p0284c2s v5p0568c1s v6p0312c2s
Sassoon, E. et al. v5p0529c2s
Sassoon, E.A. v2p0403c1s v5p0570c2s
Satchell, W. v6p0649c1s
Sato, S. v2p0248c1s v2p0267c1s v2p0436c1s v2p0454c1s
Sato, Shosuke v2p0006c2s v2p0159c2s v2p0233c2s v3p0226c2s
Satolli, F. v4p0488c2s
Satolli, F.A. v4p0331c1s
Satow, E. v4p0320c2s v4p0522c2m
Satterlee, C.B. v5p0049c2s
Satterlee, H.Y. v2p0140c2s v3p0415c2s v6p0016c1s
Satterthwait, L. v3p0071c1s v3p0239c1s v3p0337c2s v3p0343c1s v4p0116c1s v4p0135c2s v4p0278c1s v4p0330c2s v4p0450c2s v4p0595c2s v6p0530c2m
Satterthwait, Linton v4p0603c2s v6p0447c2s
Satterthwait, Louise v6p0201c2s
Satterthwaite, F. v2p0341c2s v3p0014c1s v3p0166c2s v3p0397c1s
Satthianadhan, S. v6p0314c1s
Sauber, H.H. v5p0592c1s
Saudier, A. v6p0028c1s
Sauerbeck, A. v2p0352c1s v2p0353c2s v4p0458c1m v5p0465c1s v5p0465c2m v6p0312c2s v6p0516c1m
Saulsbury, W. v5p0157c2s
Saunder, S.A. v1p0733c2s v5p0561c1s
Saunders, C. v4p0449c1s
Saunders, C.F. v6p0545c1s
Saunders, E.M. v2p0130c2s
Saunders, F. v1p0667c1s v1p0812c1s v1p0847c2s v1p1280c1s v1p1314c2s v3p0054c1s v3p0090c1s v4p0033c2s v4p0412c1s
Saunders, F.H. and Hall, G.Stanley v5p0452c2s
Saunders, F.K. v3p0024c1s
Saunders, G. v1p0053c1s v1p1402c1s
Saunders, G.F. v5p0324c1s
Saunders, G.H. v6p0513c2s v6p0517c1s
Saunders, H. v4p0513c1s

Saunders, H.M. v4p0423c1s
Saunders, J. v1p0238c1s
v1p0406c2s v1p0472c1s v1p0477c1s
v1p0499c2s v1p0501c1s v1p0592c2s
v1p0609c2s v1p0680c1s v1p0706c2s
v1p1020c2s v1p1112c1s v1p1190c2s
v1p1264c2s v1p1305c1s
Saunders, J.L. v5p0260c2s
Saunders, K. v1p0799c2s
v2p0310c1s
Saunders, L.S.B. v5p0518c1s
v5p0638c2s
Saunders, Miss v1p0645c2s
Saunders, P.H. v6p0605c1s
Saunders, T. v1p0702c2s
v2p0004c1s v2p0110c2s v3p0031c2s
v3p0316c2s
Saunders, T.B. v3p0111c1s
v3p0150c2m v3p0247c2s v3p0355c2s
v4p0234c1s v4p0475c1s v5p0411c1s
v5p0619c2s v6p0177c2s v6p0288c1s
Saunders, T.W. v1p0633c1s
Saunders, W. v1p0194c1s
v1p0645c2s v1p1015c2s v6p0694c2s
Saunders, W.F. v5p0182c2s
v5p0504c2s v6p0564c2s
Saunders, W.H. v2p0134c2s
Saunders, W.H.B. v6p0697c2s
Saunders, W.L. v3p0119c1s
v3p0350c2s v4p0008c2m v4p0468c2s
v5p0010c1s v5p0567c1s v6p0009c1m
v6p0393c1s
Saunderson, H.S. v4p0133c2s
Saussaye, P.D.Chautepie de la
v4p0019c1s v4p0391c2s
Saussure, C.de v6p0150c2s
v6p0251c1s
Saussure, R.de v4p0436c2s
v4p0573c2s v6p0230c1s v6p0251c1s
Sauter, G. v5p0294c1s
Sauvage, E. v1p0051c2s
v1p0456c1s v1p0810c1s
Sauvage, G.M. v6p0496c1s
Sauvage, H.E. v2p0483c1s
Sauvel, F.B. v4p0484c1s
Sauveur, A. v5p0274c2s
v5p0371c2s v6p0412c1s
Sauville, F.L. v6p0114c2s
v6p0492c1s
Savage, A.D. v5p0132c1s
v5p0390c1s
Savage, C.C. v2p0364c1s
Savage, D.L. v5p0063c2m
Savage, E.A. v5p0446c2s
v6p0072c1s v6p0488c2s
Savage, G.C. v6p0217c1s
Savage, G.H. v3p0200c1s
v3p0216c2s
Savage, G.W. v1p0578c1s
v1p0647c1s v1p1195c1s
Savage, Gertrude v4p0624c2s
Savage, H. v5p0226c2s
Savage, H.W. v5p0422c1s
Savage, J. v1p0239c1s
v1p0616c1s v1p0909c2s v1p0997c1s
v1p1019c2s v1p1180c2s
Savage, J.B. v3p0272c2s
Savage, J.F. v4p0503c2s
Savage, J.W. v3p0054c2s
v3p0235c2s v3p0279c2s v3p0312c1s
Savage, M. v1p0657c1s
v1p1093c1s v2p0351c2s
Savage, M.J. v1p0242c1s
v1p0427c1m v1p0434c1s v1p0796c1s
v1p1300c2s v2p0147c1s v2p0215c1s
v2p0238c2s v2p0369c1s v2p0369c2s
v2p0388c2s v2p0389c2s v2p0414c1s
v3p0177c1m v3p0268c2s v3p0296c2s
v3p0314c2s v3p0354c2s v3p0378c2m
v3p0405c1s v3p0428c1s v4p0104c1s
v4p0232c1s v4p0261c1s v4p0341c1s
v4p0343c2m v4p0372c1s v4p0464c1m
v4p0479c2s v4p0532c2s v4p0620c2s
v5p0424c1s
Savage, M.J. and Hale, E.E.
v3p0385c2s
Savage, M.J. and Hawthorne, J.
v3p0405c1s
Savage, M.J. et al. v2p0139c2s
v3p0083c2s v4p0517c2s
v5p0115c2s
Savage, M.W. v1p0436c1s
v1p1174c2s v1p1308c2s
Savage, P.H. v5p0041c1s
v5p0222c2s v5p0282c1s v5p0404c2s
Savage, R.C. v4p0450c2s
Savage, R.H. v4p0204c2s
v4p0374c1s
Savage, W.H. v4p0179c1s
v4p0229c1s v4p0341c1s v4p0570c1s
v4p0614c1s v4p0621c1s
Savage, W.M. v1p1420c1s
Savage, W.T. v1p0050c1s
v1p0290c1s v1p0396c2s v1p0503c2s
Savary, A.W. v4p0168c2s
v6p0002c1s v6p0022c2s v6p0461c1s
Savary, A.W. and Smith, G.
v5p0511c2s
Savery, A.W. v2p0382c1s
v3p0376c1s
Savidge, E.C. v5p0149c1s
Savignoni, L. v5p0142c2s
Savigny, F.C. v1p0147c1s
v1p1357c1s
Savigny, F.C.von v1p0518c1s
Savile, A. v2p0161c2s
Savile, A.R. v4p0058c2s
v4p0145c2s
Savile, B.W. v1p0109c1s
v1p0397c1s v1p0668c2s v1p1161c2s
v1p1330c2s v1p1336c2s
Savile, C.S. v1p0007c2s
v1p0084c2s v1p0992c1s v1p1192c2s
v1p1310c2s
Savile, F. v5p0425c1s
v6p0140c1s v6p0209c2s v6p0434c2s
Savile, G.W.W. v5p0290c2s
Savile, Lord v5p0325c2s
v5p0499c2s
Savile-Clarke, C. v4p0231c1s
Saville, E.S. v5p0386c2s
Saville, Elizabeth J. v5p0038c1s
Saville, Frank v6p0311c2s
Saville, H.F. v1p0981c1s
Saville, M. v1p1433c1s
Saville, M.H. v4p0256c2s
v5p0373c1s v6p0111c1s
Saville, S.E. v5p0063c1s
v5p0301c2s v5p0349c1s v5p0428c2s
v5p0537c2s v5p0539c2s v5p0624c1s
v6p0644c1s v6p0705c1s
Saville-Kent, W. v4p0336c2s
v5p0573c2s
Savine, A. v6p0149c1s
v6p0360c2s v6p0639c1s
Savine, Alex. v6p0073c1s
Savinien, Francois P. v6p0103c2s
v6p0138c1s
Sawaki, Y. v6p0334c2s
Saward, B.C. v4p0012c1s
Saward, F.E. v5p0124c1m
v6p0133c1s
Sawer, J.C. v3p0326c2s
Sawin, T.P. v5p0079c2s
Sawin, W.G. v5p0093c1s
Sawtell, A. v6p0312c2s
Sawtell, R.W. v5p0066c1s
Sawtelle, H.A. v1p0038c2s
v1p0236c1s v1p0236c2s v1p0688c2s
v1p0966c2s v2p0289c1s v2p0374c1s
Sawter, George v5p0082c2s
Sawvel, F.B. v4p0289c2s
v4p0341c1s v4p0519c1s v4p0606c2s
v5p0013c2s v5p0016c1s v5p0031c1s
v5p0330c1s v5p0342c1s v5p0450c2s
v5p0497c2s v6p0015c1s v6p0033c1s
v6p0034c1s
Sawyer, A.L. et al. v2p0313c1s
Sawyer, A.W. v1p1043c1s
Sawyer, C.A. v3p0072c1s
v3p0277c1s v3p0327c2s
Sawyer, C.F. v3p0025c2s
Sawyer, C.M. v1p0814c2s
v1p0888c2s v3p0322c1s
Sawyer, C.P. v6p0296c2s
v6p0638c2s
Sawyer, D. v2p0467c1s
Sawyer, Dr. v5p0532c1s
Sawyer, E. v2p0039c2s
v3p0279c1s
Sawyer, E.A. v5p0013c1s
v5p0616c2s v5p0617c2s v6p0235c2s
v6p0606c2s
Sawyer, E.F. v1p0827c2s
v2p0285c1s v2p0319c1s v2p0417c2m
Sawyer, E.M. and Burgess, J.A.
v6p0246c1s v6p0496c2s
Sawyer, E.O., jr. v6p0031c1s
v6p0668c2s
Sawyer, F.A. v1p0273c1s
v1p1149c1s v3p0393c1s
Sawyer, F.E. v2p0155c1s
v4p0084c1s v4p0127c2s
Sawyer, F.W. v1p1425c2s
Sawyer, G.C. v3p0184c2s
v3p0243c2s v3p0315c2s
Sawyer, H.A. v4p0041c2s
v4p0173c2s
Sawyer, H.D. v5p0401c1s
Sawyer, J.E.C. v3p0046c1s
v5p0152c2s
Sawyer, L. v1p1222c1s
Sawyer, L.M. v6p0619c2s
v6p0692c1s
Sawyer, L.R. v6p0510c1s
Sawyer, Lucy M. v6p0381c2s
Sawyer, P. v6p0049c2s
Sawyer, R.M. v1p0013c2s
v1p1437c2s
Sawyer, R.T. v2p0237c2s
v2p0455c2s
Sawyer, T.G. v2p0455c2s
Sawyer, T.J. v1p0038c2s
v1p0097c1s v1p0129c2s v1p0238c2s
v1p0357c2s v1p0426c1m v1p0777c2s
v1p0796c1s v1p0850c2s v1p0948c2s
v1p0979c1s v1p1038c1s v1p1059c1s
v1p1063c2s v1p1066c1s v1p1099c1s
v1p1101c2s v1p1200c1s v1p1211c1s
v1p1218c1s v1p1219c2s v1p1301c2s
v1p1306c1s v1p1355c2m v2p0146c2s
v2p0169c2s v2p0205c2s v2p0403c2s
v3p0098c2s v3p0444c2s
Sawyer, W. v1p0349c1s
v1p0350c2s v1p0353c2s v1p0462c1s
v1p0523c1s v1p0751c1s v1p0764c2s
v1p0891c2s v1p0933c1s v1p0978c2s
Sawyer, W.C. v1p0675c2s
v5p0599c2s
Sawyer, W.C., Mrs. v4p0636c1s
Sawyer, W.E. v1p0399c1s
Sawyer, W.L. v4p0398c2s
v5p0288c2s v5p0316c1s
Saxby, A. v6p0443c2s
v6p0456c1s
Saxby, F.W. v5p0448c1s
Saxby, J.E. v2p0474c1s
Saxby, J.M.E. v2p0160c2s
v3p0332c1s v6p0591c1s
Saxby, Jessie M.E. v5p0100c2s
Saxe, A. v1p0292c2s
v1p0868c1s v3p0215c2s
Saxe, J.A. v4p0359c2s
Saxe, J.G. v1p0371c1s
v1p0805c1s
Saxe, L. v3p0239c2s
Saxelby, F.M. v6p0406c1s
Saxon, C. v6p0658c2s
Saxon, E.L. v3p0470c1s
Saxon, J.W. v1p1305c2s
Saxon, W.E. v4p0273c2s
Saxton, C.T. v4p0481c2s
Saxton, C.T. et al. v3p0031c1s
Saxton, H.A. v2p0291c2s
Saxton, M.L. v3p0063c2s
Say and Seale, Lord v1p0138c1s
v1p0756c2s
Say, J.B. v1p1025c2s
Say, L. v2p0062c2s
v2p0134c1s v2p0418c1s v2p0423c2s
Sayah v1p1194c2s
Sayce, A. v1p0903c2s
Sayce, A.H. v1p0068c1s
v1p0069c1s v1p0070c1s v1p0101c2s
v1p0122c2s v1p0125c1s v1p0214c2m
v1p0342c1s v1p0435c2s v1p0551c2s
v1p0559c1s v1p0595c1s v1p0636c2s
v1p0723c2m v1p0724c1m v1p0879c2s
v1p0923c1s v1p0960c1s v1p0999c1m
v1p1002c1s v1p1008c1s v1p1015c2s
v1p1072c2s v1p1140c2s v1p1196c2s
v1p1210c2s v1p1278c2s v1p1357c1s
v1p1434c1s v2p0009c1m v2p0012c2s
v2p0016c2s v2p0021c1s v2p0024c1s
v2p0024c2m v2p0025c2s v2p0045c1s
v2p0065c2s v2p0133c2m v2p0134c1s
v2p0134c2m v2p0135c1m v2p0181c1s
v2p0190c2s v2p0204c1s v2p0206c1s
v2p0206c2m v2p0230c2s v2p0231c2s
v2p0234c2s v2p0238c2s v2p0240c1s
v2p0249c1s v2p0254c2s v2p0282c2s
v2p0304c2s v2p0323c2s v2p0339c2s
v2p0448c1s v2p0483c1s v3p0003c1s
v3p0010c1s v3p0012c2s v3p0016c2m
v3p0023c1m v3p0072c2s v3p0108c2s
v3p0126c2s v3p0130c2m v3p0131c1m
v3p0232c2s v3p0242c2s v3p0261c2s
v3p0273c1s v3p0283c2s v3p0314c1s
v3p0318c1m v3p0384c2m v3p0392c2s
v3p0397c2s v3p0411c1s v3p0436c2s
v3p0447c1s v4p0004c1s v4p0032c2s
v4p0040c2s v4p0046c2s v4p0055c1m
v4p0056c1s v4p0057c2m v4p0058c1s
v4p0189c1m v4p0259c1m v4p0302c1s
v4p0302c2s v4p0405c1s v4p0515c2s
v4p0527c1s v4p0527c2s v4p0620c2s
v5p0042c1s v5p0087c2s v5p0131c1s
v5p0269c2s v5p0358c1s v6p0001c2s
v6p0046c1m v6p0095c2m v6p0156c2s
v6p0273c2s v6p0293c1m v6p0305c1s
Sayce, A.H. and Hogarth, D.G.
v4p0172c1s
Sayce, A.H. et al. v3p0023c1s
v3p0197c2s v3p0289c1s v3p0420c1s
Sayen, H.L. v5p0492c1s
Sayen, H.L. and Willyoung, E.G.
v5p0125c1s v5p0492c1s
Sayers, J.D. v5p0592c2s
Sayle, C. v5p0608c1s
Sayler, H.L. v6p0211c1s
v6p0386c1s
Sayles, I. v3p0125c2s
Sayles, M.B. v6p0300c1s
v6p0300c2s v6p0462c2s v6p0585c1s
v6p0638c1s v6p0638c2s
Sayous, A.E. v6p0102c2s
v6p0132c2s v6p0659c1s
Sayres, H.M. v4p0145c1s
v5p0283c1s
Scacchi, A. v1p0614c2s
Scadding, H. v1p0001c2s
v1p0069c2s v1p0082c1s v1p0190c1s
v1p0193c2m v1p0194c2s v1p0195c1m
v1p0216c1s v1p0272c1s v1p0390c2s
v1p0424c2s v1p0718c1s v1p0741c2s
v1p0824c2s v1p0831c1s v1p0882c1s
v1p0892c1s v1p1061c2m v1p1316c2m
v4p0086c1s v4p0260c1s v4p0317c2s
v4p0579c2s
Scadding, S.W. v3p0313c2s

v3p0344c1s
Scaife, W.B. v2p0176c2s
v2p0266c2s v2p0279c1s v2p0299c2s
v2p0335c1s v2p0357c2s v2p0370c1s
v4p0116c2s v4p0221c2s v4p0325c1s
v4p0627c1s v5p0218c2s v5p0320c2m
v5p0321c1s v5p0564c2s
Scaife, W.L. v5p0452c2s
Scaife, W.L. et al. v6p0501c1s
Scales, J. v1p1111c1s
v2p0060c2s v2p0112c1s
Scammell, A. v6p0230c1s
Scammell, E.T. v6p0042c1s
Scammon, C.M. v1p0018c1s
v1p0020c1s v1p0069c2s v1p0187c1s
v1p0271c1s v1p0443c2s v1p0776c2s
v1p0951c1s v1p0956c1s v1p1011c1s
v1p1064c1s v1p1134c2s v1p1172c2m
v1p1173c2s v1p1174c1s v1p1403c1m
v3p0382c2s
Scammon, E.P. v1p0832c1s
v2p0286c2s v4p0203c1s v4p0350c1s
v4p0538c1s
Scammon, Gen. v1p0004c2s
v1p0164c1s
Scammon, J.G. v1p0457c2s
Scammon, L.E. v4p0467c2s
Scandlin, W.G. v1p1147c1s
Scanlan, J.M. v6p0139c2s
Scanlan, M. v1p1239c1s
v2p0478c2s
Scanlan, W.M. v5p0207c2s
Scanland, A.L. v1p1040c2s
Scanland, J.M. v4p0305c1s
v4p0374c1s v4p0388c1s v5p0112c2s
v5p0379c2s v5p0380c1s v5p0387c1s
v5p0542c2s v6p0092c2s v6p0121c1s
v6p0149c2s v6p0331c1s v6p0362c1s
v6p0377c1s v6p0567c2s v6p0568c1m
Scanland, J.M. and Money, H.D.
v5p0199c2s
Scanlon, T. v4p0240c1s
v4p0283c2s v4p0291c2s v4p0412c1s
v4p0533c1s v5p0229c2s v5p0293c1s
v5p0321c1s v5p0419c1s v5p0593c1s
v6p0175c1s v6p0595c2s v6p0610c1s
v6p0634c1s
Scannell, F.B. v3p0010c2s
v3p0373c1s
Scannell, T.B. v3p0137c2s
v3p0333c1s v3p0419c2s v4p0010c1s
v4p0052c1s v4p0452c2m v5p0495c1s
Scarboro, A. v5p0088c2s
Scarborough, W.S. v3p0013c1s
v3p0017c1s v3p0132c1s v3p0243c2s
v3p0298c2s v3p0299c1m v3p0450c2s
v4p0005c2s v4p0446c2s v4p0575c2s
v5p0196c2s v5p0402c2s v5p0403c1m
v5p0403c2s v5p0620c1s v6p0446c2s
Scarff, C.A., Mrs. v5p0419c2s
Scarlett, B.F. v3p0102c1s
v3p0193c2s
Scarritt, W. v6p0414c1s
Scarritt, W.E. v6p0044c1s
Scarritt, W.R. v3p0427c2s
Scarritt, Winthrop E. v6p0043c2s
Scartazzini, J.A. v3p0110c1s
Scarth, H. v6p0410c2s
Scarth, H.M. v1p0191c1s
v1p0265c1s v1p1082c1s v2p0247c2s
Schaack, H.C.Van v1p0261c2s
v1p0707c2m v1p1362c1s v2p0214c2s
v2p0298c2s
Schaafhausen, H. v1p0613c2s
v1p0794c2s v1p1204c1s
Schaarschmidt, J. et al. . v2p0357c2s
Schachner, A. v4p0368c1s
Schackelford, Ethel v6p0705c1s
Schadd, J.E. v1p0116c2s
Schade, L. v1p0625c2s
v1p1313c2s
Schaeberle, J.M. v2p0367c2s
v3p0055c2s v4p0167c1s v4p0440c2s
v5p0430c1s v5p0548c2s v5p0571c2s
v6p0301c1s v6p0446c1s
Schaeberle, J.M. and Colton, A.L.
v5p0371c2s
Schaefer v1p0620c2s
Schaefer, F. v6p0024c2s
v6p0163c1s v6p0404c1s
Schaeffer, C.E. v6p0536c2s
v6p0642c2s
Schaeffer, C.F. v1p0071c2s
v1p0074c2s v1p0097c1s v1p0123c1s
v1p0125c2s v1p0126c2s v1p0127c1s
v1p0128c2s v1p0254c1s v1p0254c2s
v1p0339c1s v1p0398c2s v1p0459c1s
v1p0601c2s v1p0645c2s v1p0777c2m
v1p1154c2s
v1p1277c2s
Schaeffer, C.W. v1p0505c2s
v1p0777c2s
Schaeffer, E.S. v6p0465c2s
Schaeffer, K.L. v6p0121c1s
v6p0627c1s
Schaeffer, M.F. v6p0351c2s
Schaeffer, N.C. v1p0072c2s
v1p0515c2s v1p0683c1s v1p1120c1s
v1p1122c1s v1p1159c2s v3p0342c1s
v5p0159c2s v5p0442c1m v5p0569c2s
v6p0341c1s
Schaeffer, W. v4p0537c1s
Schaeffer, W.C. v4p0111c2s
v5p0182c1s v5p0306c1s v5p0590c2s
v6p0215c1s v6p0537c1m
Schaeffer, W.G. v5p0188c1s
Schafer, D. v5p0064c2s
Schafer, E.A. v1p1007c1s
v3p0072c1s v4p0186c2s
Schafer, J. v6p0469c2s
Schafer, Joseph v6p0460c2s
Schaff, D.S. v1p0336c1s
v1p0460c1s v4p0457c1s v5p0429c2s
v6p0016c1s v6p0170c1s v6p0343c2s
v6p0415c2s v6p0424c2s
Schaff, P. v1p0027c2s
v1p0032c1s v1p0045c1m v1p0048c1s
v1p0067c1s v1p0071c2m v1p0076c2s
v1p0096c1s v1p0111c2s v1p0112c1s
v1p0117c1s v1p0118c1s v1p0126c2s
v1p0127c1s v1p0129c1s v1p0130c1s
v1p0189c1s v1p0210c1s v1p0240c1s
v1p0243c1s v1p0243c2s v1p0244c1s
v1p0247c2s v1p0248c1s v1p0248c2s
v1p0252c2m v1p0254c1m v1p0293c2m
v1p0307c2s v1p0314c1s v1p0331c2s
v1p0351c2s v1p0360c1s v1p0412c2s
v1p0416c1s v1p0432c1m v1p0442c2s
v1p0513c1s v1p0514c2s v1p0515c2s
v1p0527c1s v1p0570c2s v1p0582c1s
v1p0583c1m v1p0587c2s v1p0620c1s
v1p0620c2s v1p0642c2s v1p0684c2m
v1p0687c1s v1p0687c2s v1p0688c1m
v1p0692c2s v1p0712c2s v1p0727c2s
v1p0737c2s v1p0756c2m v1p0769c2s
v1p0806c2s v1p0812c1s v1p0849c2s
v1p0860c1s v1p0861c2s v1p0862c1s
v1p0903c1m v1p0920c1s v1p0938c1s
v1p0960c2s v1p0964c2s v1p0980c1s
v1p0980c2s v1p0985c2s v1p0988c2s
v1p0994c1s v1p1031c1s v1p1092c2s
v1p1120c2s v1p1121c2s v1p1139c1s
v1p1140c2s v1p1154c1s v1p1178c1s
v1p1206c2m v1p1241c1s v1p1245c1s
v1p1252c1s v1p1277c2s v1p1278c1s
v1p1296c2s v1p1325c2s v1p1341c1s
v1p1357c2s v1p1402c2s v1p1442c2s
v2p0042c1s v2p0044c1s v2p0064c2s
v2p0082c2s v2p0146c1s v2p0236c1s
v2p0237c2s v2p0268c1s v2p0282c2s
v2p0295c2s v2p0333c1s v2p0337c2s
v2p0354c1s v2p0418c1s v2p0438c1s
v2p0458c1s v3p0012c2s v3p0060c1s
v3p0070c1s v3p0082c2m v3p0084c1s
v3p0261c1s v3p0356c2m v3p0358c2s
v3p0422c1s v3p0446c2s v3p0461c1s
v3p0476c2s v4p0019c2s v4p0073c1s
v4p0084c1m v4p0084c2s v4p0142c1s
v4p0153c1s v4p0171c2s v4p0513c1s
v4p0516c1s v4p0573c1s
Schaff, P. and Witt, J.De. v3p0461c1s
Schaff, P. and Lange, J.P.
v1p0129c1s
Schaff, Philip v2p0369c2s
v4p0225c1s
Schaffer, H.M. v2p0237c2s
Schaffle, A.von v5p0040c1s
v5p0231c1s v5p0243c1s
Schafft, A. v2p0352c1s
Schafhaentl, C. v1p1251c1s
Schaick, E.Van v3p0055c2s
v3p0151c1s v4p0196c2s
Schal, E. v1p0966c2s
Schalk, E. v4p0378c2s
Schallenberger, M. v5p0128c2s
Schallenberger, M.E. v4p0104c1s
Schaller, F. v1p0311c2s
v1p0477c2s v1p0516c1s v1p0521c1s
v1p0530c2s v1p0738c2s v1p0777c1s
v1p1156c2s v1p1221c2s v1p1223c2s
v1p1306c1s v1p1356c2s v1p1386c2s
v1p1392c1s v1p1402c2s
Schaller, W.T. v6p0184c1s
v6p0368c2s v6p0593c2s v6p0650c2s
Schaller, W.T. and Graton, L.C.
v6p0523c2s
Schaller, W.T. and Hillebrand, W.F.
v6p0365c1s
Schamberg, J.F. v5p0331c1s
Schanck, J.S. v1p0159c1s
Scharf, G. v1p0065c1s
v1p0310c1s v1p0526c2s v1p0569c1s
v1p0726c1s v1p0837c2s v1p0997c2s
v1p1036c1m v1p1106c1s v1p1171c2s
v1p1282c2s v1p1413c2s v1p1414c2s
v4p0235c1m v4p0346c1s v4p0495c1s
v5p0094c1s v5p0186c1s v5p0364c2s
Scharf, G. and Nichols, J.G.
v1p0585c1s v1p0596c2s
Scharf, J.T. v4p0488c1s
v5p0112c2s
Scharf, R.F. v5p0204c1s
Scharlieb, M. and Ravenhill, A.
v6p0498c1s
Scharlieb, Mary v4p0626c1s
Schaubach, E. v1p0128c2s
Schauffler, A.F. v2p0152c1s
v3p0283c1s v4p0309c2s v4p0481c2s
Schauffler, R.H. v6p0146c1s
v6p0201c1s v6p0285c2s v6p0397c2s
v6p0439c2m v6p0468c1s v6p0559c1s
Schauffler, W.C. v1p1415c2s
Schaumberg, A. v4p0595c1s
Schaumburg, A. v4p0629c2s
Schaw, H.S. v4p0433c2s
Schayer, J. v1p0859c1s
v1p1266c2s v1p1306c1s v1p1310c2s
v2p0148c2s v3p0264c2s v3p0283c2s
v4p0074c2s v5p0092c1s
Schechter, S. v4p0084c2s
v4p0102c2s v4p0252c2s v4p0303c1s
v4p0306c1s v4p0391c2s v4p0482c1s
v4p0523c2s v4p0536c1s v4p0573c1m
v5p0174c1m v5p0174c2s v5p0228c1m
v5p0268c1s v5p0307c2s v5p0475c1s
v6p0061c2s v6p0249c2s v6p0561c2s
Schechter, S. and Adler, E.N.
v5p0174c1s
Scheckter, S. v2p0430c2s
Schefer, C. v4p0170c1s
v4p0211c1m v4p0212c2m v4p0423c2s
v4p0496c2s v4p0553c1s v4p0598c1s
Schefer, L. v1p0066c1s
v1p0178c2s
Scheffauer, H. v6p0032c1s
v6p0528c1s v6p0568c2s v6p0678c1s
Scheffer, J.G.D. v1p0820c1s
v1p0987c2s
Scheffler, F.A. v4p0176c2s
v6p0615c2s
Scheffler, H. v1p1247c2s
Scheffler, J. v1p0226c1s
Scheffler, L.Von v3p0176c1s
Scheffler, T.F. v4p0547c1s
Schei, P. and Sverdrup, O.
v6p0236c1s
Scheibert, F. v2p0400c1s
Scheibert, J. v3p0095c2s
v3p0111c2s
Scheibler, F. v5p0580c1s
Schell, E.A. v4p0186c1s
v5p0024c1s v6p0025c1s v6p0684c1s
Schell, E.R.De v5p0068c2s
v6p0215c2s
Schell, F.H. v6p0024c1s
Schell, H.S. v1p1375c2s
Schellen, H. v1p0827c1s
v1p0903c2s
Schellenberg, F.Z. v1p0320c1s
Schelling, F.E. v3p0140c1s
v3p0384c2s v4p0184c1s v5p0522c1s
v6p0181c1s v6p0456c1s v6p0641c2s
Schelling, F.W.J. v1p0454c1s
v1p0623c1s v1p0817c1s
Schelling, F.W.J.von v1p0243c1s
v1p0899c2s v1p1001c2m v1p1002c1s
v1p1006c1s v1p1160c2s v1p1357c1s
v1p1358c1s
Scheltema, J.F. v6p0079c2s
v6p0184c2s v6p0339c1m
Schem, A.J. v1p0584c2s
v1p0975c2s v1p1058c2s
Schenck, A.D. v3p0441c2s
v4p0592c1s v5p0252c2s
Schenck, A.O. v5p0032c1s
Schenck, C.A. v5p0214c2s
Schenck, E.H., Mrs. v3p0247c2s
Schenck, Margaret v6p0691c1s
Schenck, N.H. v1p1433c1s
Schenck, R.C. v3p0205c1s
Schenck, S.L. v6p0585c2s
Schenk, A.D. v5p0222c2s
Schenk, Caspar v4p0551c1s
Schenk, G.W. v1p0427c2s
Scheppegrell, W. v5p0172c2s
v5p0579c1s v6p0681c1s
Scherb, E.V. v1p0331c2s
v1p0347c1s v1p0825c1s
Scherer, A.B. v4p0431c1s
Scherer, E. v1p0477c2s
v1p1116c2s v1p1271c2s
Scherer, J.A.B. v4p0538c1s
v5p0560c2s v5p0580c2s v6p0136c2s
v6p0160c1s
Scherer, J.F. v4p0345c1s
Scherer, J.W. v1p0530c1s
Scherer, L.C. v5p0399c2s
Schermerhorn, E.W. v5p0063c1s
v6p0246c2s
Schermerhorn, I.Y. v4p0485c1s
Schermerhorn, L.Y. v3p0240c1s
v6p0285c1s
Scherpf, G.A. v1p0665c1s
Scherren, H. v4p0637c2s
Schetty, J.A. v6p0289c2s
Schey, W.F. v5p0039c1s
Schiaparelli, G. v4p0357c2s
v5p0363c1s
Schiaparelli, G.V. v3p0274c2s
Schick, J.M. v4p0633c1s
v5p0280c2s
Schidrowitz, S. v5p0040c1m
Schiedt, R.C. v3p0026c1s
v3p0128c2s v3p0297c1s v3p0308c1s
v4p0149c2s v4p0212c1s v4p0213c1s
v5p0198c1m v5p0253c2s v5p0263c1s
v5p0337c2s v5p0514c1s v6p0107c2s
v6p0531c2s v6p0609c2s
Schiele, F.M. v6p0064c1s
Schierbrand, W.von v3p0305c2s

v3p0327c1s v3p0327c2m v4p0422c1s
v4p0436c1s v4p0629c1s v6p0192c1s
v6p0252c1s v6p0252c2s v6p0253c2m
v6p0254c1m v6p0254c2s v6p0255c1m
v6p0258c1s v6p0278c2s v6p0334c2s
v6p0351c1s v6p0389c2s v6p0489c1s
v6p0506c2s v6p0521c1s v6p0555c2s
v6p0556c2s v6p0558c1s v6p0560c1s
v6p0600c2s v6p0632c2s v6p0696c2s
v6p0699c1m
Schierbrand, Wolf von v5p0213c1s
v5p0348c2s v6p0005c1s v6p0428c2s
Schiff, A.G. v4p0526c1s
Schiff, J.H. v3p0393c2s
v6p0162c1s v6p0333c2s
Schiller, C.J. v1p1293c2s
Schiller, F. v1p0362c1s
v1p1375c2s v3p0195c1s v4p0229c2s
v4p0609c2s
Schiller, F. and Martin, T.
v3p0118c2s
Schiller, F.C.S. v4p0191c2s
v4p0223c1s v4p0342c2m v4p0379c1s
v4p0404c2s v4p0475c1s v4p0537c2s
v4p0577c1s v5p0028c1s v5p0052c2s
v5p0153c2s v5p0281c1s v5p0426c2s
v5p0441c2s v5p0604c2s v6p0014c1s
v6p0025c1s v6p0137c1s v6p0182c1s
v6p0203c1s v6p0218c2s v6p0245c1s
v6p0383c1s v6p0412c2s v6p0457c1s
v6p0473c1s v6p0490c1s v6p0503c1s
v6p0513c1m v6p0521c1s v6p0536c2s
v6p0565c2s v6p0610c1s v6p0659c2s
v6p0673c1s
Schiller, F.von v3p0201c2s
Schiller-Szinessy, S.M. .. v3p0190c2s
Schilling, Dr. and Bunte, H.
v2p0172c1s
Schilling, G. v4p0261c1s
Schilling, H.K. v4p0376c1s
v6p0691c1s
Schillings, C.B. v6p0006c1s
Schindler, A.H. v2p0190c2s
Schindler, J.F. v2p0180c2s
Schindler, R. v3p0264c1s
Schindler, S. v3p0046c1s
v3p0119c1s v3p0171c2s v3p0197c2s
v3p0208c2s v3p0218c1s v3p0278c1s
v4p0022c1s v4p0176c2s v4p0284c1s
v4p0285c1s v4p0286c2s v4p0394c1s
v4p0417c2s v4p0466c1s v4p0472c1s
Schindler, S. and Garland, H.
v4p0464c2s
Schindler, Solomon v6p0116c1s
Schinz, A. v5p0054c2s
v5p0335c1s v5p0341c2s v5p0381c1s
v6p0002c1s v6p0130c2s v6p0181c1s
v6p0211c1m v6p0222c1s v6p0239c2s
v6p0242c1s v6p0302c1s v6p0361c1m
v6p0379c2s v6p0380c1s v6p0468c1s
v6p0678c1s
Schinz, Albert v6p0237c1s
v6p0421c1s
Schinz, C. v1p0495c1s
v1p0502c1s
Schlagintweit, A. and
Schlagintweit, H. v1p0025c2s
Schlagintweit, H. and
Schlagintweit, A. v1p0025c2s
Schlagintweit, H.de and
Schlagintweit, R.de ... v1p0068c1s
v1p0631c2s
Schlagintweit, R.de and
Schlagintweit, H.de ... v1p0068c1s
v1p0631c2s
Schlegel, H. v1p1179c1s
Schlegel, J.F.W. v1p0331c1s
Schleiermacher, F. v1p0528c2s
Schleisner, P.A. v1p0622c2s
v1p1376c1s
Schlesinger, A.R. v4p0388c1s
Schlesinger, F. v5p0532c1s
Schlesinger, K. v5p0140c2s
Schlesinger, Kathleen v5p0422c1s
Schlesinger, L. v1p0322c1s
Schlesinger, M. v1p0138c1s
Schlesinger, W.M. v2p0137c2s
Schley, B.G. v3p0128c1s
Schlich, W. v3p0158c1s
v5p0285c2s v5p0580c1s v6p0646c2s
Schlicher, J.J. v6p0317c2s
v6p0363c1m v6p0525c2s
Schlicht, P.J. v3p0343c1s
v5p0129c2s
Schlichter, H. v4p0281c2s
v4p0637c1s v5p0487c2s
Schlichter, H.G. v4p0440c2s
Schlichting, J. v1p1110c2s
Schliemann, H. v1p0601c1s
v1p1327c1s v2p0276c1s v2p0447c2s
v3p0313c2s
Schliemann, Henry v2p0441c2s
Schloss, D.F. v3p0098c1s
v3p0099c1s v3p0199c1s v3p0230c1s
v3p0238c2s v3p0345c2s v3p0398c1s
v3p0417c1m v3p0470c2s v3p0472c1s
v4p0132c2s v4p0283c2s v4p0314c1m
v4p0339c2s v4p0442c2s v4p0553c1s
v4p0559c2m v4p0608c1s v6p0318c1s
v6p0518c2s
Schlosser, F. v2p0017c1s
v2p0304c2s v2p0344c2s
Schlumberger v5p0086c1s
Schlutter, O.B. v5p0099c1s
v5p0297c2s
Schmahl, J.E. v4p0630c2s
Schmalz, F. v4p0527c1s
Schmalz, H. v4p0029c1s
v4p0052c2s v4p0299c2s
Schmeckebier, L.F. v5p0230c1s
v5p0319c1s
Schmid, F. v5p0350c1s
Schmid, H. v1p0687c2s
Schmidt, A.M. v4p0109c2s
Schmidt, A.S. v6p0001c2s
v6p0083c1s v6p0310c2s v6p0413c1s
Schmidt, Alex.R. v6p0129c2s
Schmidt, Anna S. v6p0461c1s
Schmidt, C.F. v2p0294c2s
v2p0370c2s
Schmidt, E. v4p0229c2s
v5p0572c1s v6p0245c1s
Schmidt, F. v2p0288c1s
Schmidt, F.G.G. v6p0305c2s
Schmidt, F.S. v1p0072c2s
v1p0775c2s
Schmidt, G. v1p0833c2s
v1p1155c1s
Schmidt, G.A. v1p0324c1s
Schmidt, H. v4p0059c1s
Schmidt, H. et al. v4p0525c1s
Schmidt, H.I. v1p0130c1s
v1p0130c2s v1p0255c2s v1p0685c1s
v1p0689c2s v1p0769c2s v1p0777c2s
v1p0778c1s v1p1254c1m v2p0309c2s
Schmidt, J.G. v6p0390c1s
Schmidt, K. v1p0386c1s
v1p1062c1s
Schmidt, N. v4p0046c1s
v4p0341c2s v4p0384c1s v5p0058c1s
v5p0403c2s v5p0484c1s v5p0538c2s
v5p0577c1s v6p0166c2s
Schmidt, O. v1p1215c2s
v2p0432c2s
Schmidt, S. v5p0535c1s
Schmidt, W. v1p1303c1s
Schmidt-Wartenberg, H. ... v4p0076c2s
Schmiedel, P.W. v6p0064c1s
v6p0484c2s
Schmitt, C.D. and Miles, G.W.
v5p0182c2s
Schmitt, E.J.P. v6p0400c2s
v6p0563c1s
Schmitt, F. v6p0366c2s
Schmitz, E.E. v6p0568c1s
Schmitz, L. v1p0884c2s
v1p1160c1s
Schmoll, A. v1p0471c1s
v1p0491c1s
Schmoller, G. v4p0450c1s
Schmucker, B.M. v3p0474c2s
Schmucker, S.D. v6p0126c1s
Schmucker, S.M. v1p0677c2s
Schmucker, S.S. v1p0096c2s
v1p0240c2s v1p0248c1s v1p0344c2s
v1p0684c2s v1p0769c2s v1p0778c1m
v1p0778c2s v1p1067c2s v1p1158c1s
v1p1303c2s v1p1304c1s
Schnaase, C. v2p0037c2s
Schnadhorst, F. v2p0071c2s
Schneder, D.B. v5p0081c2m
v5p0132c2s v5p0303c1s
Schneider, A. v6p0046c2s
v6p0430c1m
Schneider, A.V. v6p0005c1s
Schneider, A.von v6p0038c2s
Schneider, C.C. v6p0622c1s
Schneider, D.B. v5p0230c2s
Schneider, E.A. v3p0399c2s
Schneider, E.A. and Clarke, F.W.
v4p0368c2s
Schneider, Emil v4p0451c1s
Schneider, F.A. v4p0490c1s
Schneider, F.A. and Clarke, F.W.
v3p0392c2s
Schneider, G.H. v4p0384c2s
Schneider, H. v5p0616c1s
Schneider, H.G. v4p0556c1s
v5p0168c1s
Schneider, P.F. v5p0302c1s
v6p0174c1s v6p0472c2s
Schneiderman, Rose v6p0099c2s
Schnitzler, A. v6p0358c1s
v6p0381c1s
Schobert, E. v5p0560c2s
Schobinger, J.J. v4p0098c2s
Schock, G. v6p0068c2s
v6p0124c1s v6p0358c1s v6p0483c2s
v6p0697c2s
Schock, Georg v6p0500c1s
Schock, J.L. v1p1278c1s
Schodde, G.H. v1p0123c1s
v1p0131c1s v1p0668c1s v1p0850c2s
v2p0042c1s v2p0043c2s v2p0105c2s
v2p0147c2m v2p0230c1s v2p0235c1s
v2p0236c2s v2p0239c1s v2p0284c2s
v2p0299c2s v3p0001c2s v3p0016c1s
v3p0041c1s v3p0042c2s v3p0143c2s
v3p0230c1s v3p0230c2s v3p0232c2s
v3p0445c1s v4p0058c1s v4p0185c1s
v4p0306c1s v5p0060c2s v5p0179c2s
v5p0306c2s v6p0547c2s
Schoeberlein, L. v1p0685c1s
v1p1101c2s v1p1433c1m
Schoefer, H. v2p0273c1s
Schoeffler, H. v2p0364c1s
Schoek, G. v6p0165c2s
Schoen, E. v6p0246c2s
v6p0679c2s
Schoenborn, A. and Rodgers, J.
v1p0327c2s
Schoenfeld, H. v4p0315c2s
Schoenhof, J. v3p0422c2s
v5p0009c2s v5p0131c1s v5p0199c1s
v5p0200c1s v5p0218c2s v5p0230c2s
v5p0289c2s v5p0298c1s v5p0400c1s
v5p0412c1s v5p0567c1m v5p0570c2s
v5p0615c1s v6p0317c2s v6p0633c1s
v6p0707c2s
Schoepf, J.D. v1p0988c1s
Schoff, H.K. v6p0116c2s
Schoff, W.H. v4p0128c1s
v5p0443c1s v6p0606c1s
Schoffer, J. v6p0108c2s
Schofield, A. v3p0215c2s
v3p0311c1s v4p0271c1s v4p0529c2s
Schofield, A.T. v3p0025c2s
v3p0053c1s v3p0122c2s v3p0125c1s
v3p0125c2s v3p0147c2s v3p0170c2s
v3p0192c1m v3p0198c1s v3p0205c2s
v3p0206c2s v3p0300c1s
Schofield, J.M. v5p0309c1s
v5p0373c1s v5p0604c2s v5p0618c2s
Schofield, V.M. v5p0217c1s
Schofield, W.H. v5p0278c2s
Scholefield, E.O.S. v6p0371c1s
Scholefield, G.H. v6p0041c1s
Scholermann, W. v5p0031c1s
Scholes, F.E.S. v5p0248c2s
Scholey, H. v5p0183c1s
v5p0205c1s
Scholl, Baron von v1p0544c2s
Scholl, G. v1p1042c2s
v2p0039c2s
Scholten, J.H. v1p1095c2s
v1p1260c1m
Scholz, R.F. v6p0542c2s
Schomberg, G.A. v2p0276c2s
Schomburgk, R. v1p0561c1s
Schomburgk, R.H., Sir v1p0098c1m
v1p0294c2s
Schomp, H.A. v2p0109c1s
Schon; H.Von v6p0512c2s
Schon, V. v5p0130c1s
Schonberg, S.K. v4p0313c1s
Schone, A. v2p0050c1s
Schonfeld, H. v4p0522c2s
Schonix, R.Le v3p0159c2s
v3p0349c2s v4p0233c2s v4p0523c2s
Schonix, Roach v3p0342c1s
Schonix, Roach Le v3p0053c1s
v3p0120c2s
Schonland, S. v2p0344c1s
Schonthan, P.von v4p0042c1s
Schoolcraft, H.R. v1p0029c2s
v1p0236c2s v1p0268c1s v1p0300c1s
v1p0636c1m v1p0636c2s v1p0718c1s
v1p0858c1s v1p1271c1s v1p1321c1s
Schoolcraft, J.R. v1p0767c1s
Schooley, J.S. v1p0939c2s
Schooling, J.H. v4p0145c1s
v4p0225c1s v5p0094c2s v5p0143c1s
v5p0169c1s v5p0173c1s v5p0245c2s
v5p0246c1s v5p0272c2s v5p0297c1s
v5p0347c1m v5p0348c2m v5p0362c2s
v5p0363c1s v5p0401c2m v5p0419c1s
v5p0459c2s v5p0472c2s v5p0517c1s
v6p0083c1s v6p0098c2s v6p0132c2s
v6p0138c2s v6p0182c1s v6p0205c2m
v6p0224c1m v6p0239c2s v6p0255c1s
v6p0266c2s v6p0269c1s v6p0299c1s
v6p0463c2s v6p0484c2s v6p0509c1s
v6p0586c2s v6p0621c2s v6p0708c1s
Schooling, J.Holt v5p0190c2s
Schooling, W. v3p0148c1s
v3p0268c2s v3p0330c2s v3p0407c2s
v4p0125c1s v4p0283c1s v4p0447c1s
v4p0511c1s v6p0261c1s v6p0322c1s
Schoonhoven, J.J. v6p0304c2s
Schoonmaker, Edwin D. v6p0017c1s
Schoonmaker, L.M. v1p0919c2s
Schoonover, F.E. v6p0080c2s
v6p0189c1s
Schopenhauer, A. v1p0384c2s
v1p0648c1s v1p0760c1s v1p0999c2s
v1p1410c2s
Schopfer, J. v5p0026c1s
v5p0026c2s v5p0156c1s v5p0430c2s
v5p0477c1m v5p0607c1s v5p0639c2s
v6p0024c2s v6p0033c1s v6p0033c2s
v6p0106c2s v6p0107c1s v6p0128c1s
v6p0128c2s v6p0241c2s v6p0273c2s
v6p0342c2s v6p0479c2s v6p0480c2s
v6p0595c1m
Schopfer, J. and Anet, C.. v6p0546c2s
Schopfer, J. and Sargent, I.
v6p0595c1s
Schopfer, Jean v6p0547c1s
Schott v1p0236c2s
Schott, C.A. v1p0787c2s

v1p0788c1s v2p0257c2s v2p0319c1s
v2p0393c1s v5p0172c2s v5p0173c1s
Schott, G. v5p0607c1s
Schott, H. v6p0349c2s
Schottky, E. v3p0089c1s
Schouler, J. v1p0833c1s
v1p1343c2s v2p0146c2s v2p0246c1s
v2p0295c2s v2p0371c2s v2p0394c2s
v2p0418c2s v2p0474c1s v3p0069c2s
v3p0197c1m v3p0225c2s v3p0426c1s
v4p0116c2s v4p0250c2s v4p0258c2m
v4p0284c2s v4p0427c1s v4p0451c1m
v4p0457c2s v4p0571c1s v4p0623c1s
v5p0123c1s v5p0519c2s v5p0600c1s
v5p0614c2s v6p0332c2s v6p0345c1m
v6p0426c1s v6p0669c2s v6p0674c1s
Schouler, J. et al. v4p0595c2s
Schoultz-Adlewsky, E.de .. v5p0539c1s
Schoute, P.H. v4p0637c2s
Schovelin, T.A. v2p0111c2s
v2p0213c2s
Schrader, B. v5p0253c2s
Schrader, C.L. v6p0498c1s
Schrader, E. v6p0037c1s
v6p0122c1s v6p0410c2s
Schrader, F.C. v5p0413c1s
Schramm, R. v2p0239c2s
Schrauf, A. and Dana, E.S.
v1p0844c2s
Schreck, E.J.E. v5p0260c2s
v5p0405c1s v6p0479c1s
Schreiber, A. v2p0424c2s
Schreiber, E. v2p0108c2s
v2p0154c2s v2p0180c2s v2p0389c1s
v2p0473c1s v3p0106c2s v3p0107c1s
v3p0144c1s v3p0231c1s v3p0331c1s
v3p0334c1s v3p0368c1s v4p0349c1s
v4p0405c1s v6p0013c2s v6p0030c2s
v6p0099c2s
Schreiber, Ellis v6p0085c2s
v6p0235c2s
Schreiber, J. v6p0038c1s
Schreiner, O. v3p0416c1s
v4p0006c1s v4p0611c2s v5p0635c2s
Schreiner, Olive v3p0122c2s
v3p0467c2s v5p0068c1s
Schreiner, S.C.C. v5p0547c2s
Schreiner, S.C.Cronwright. v6p0026c1s
Schreiner, T.W. v5p0531c2s
Schrenk, H.von v6p0025c2s
Schrenk, Hermann von v6p0069c1s
Schribner, G.H. v2p0258c1s
v4p0071c2s
Schrodde, G.H. v1p0101c1s
Schroder, C. v4p0077c2s
v4p0108c2s
Schrodter, E. v5p0320c1s
Schroeder, A.T. and Curtis, T.W.
v5p0490c2s
Schroeder, D. v1p1147c2s
Schroeder, E. v4p0523c2s
v4p0561c1s v5p0434c2s
Schroeder, F. v1p1250c2s
v6p0336c2s
Schroeder, F.C. v6p0010c1s
Schroeder, J. v3p0046c1s
v3p0244c1s v3p0465c2s v4p0452c2m
v4p0489c1s
Schroeder, S. v1p0065c1s
v1p1141c2s v6p0275c2s
Schroeder, T. v6p0176c2s
v6p0370c1s v6p0402c2s v6p0507c2s
Schroeder, W. v6p0258c2s
Schubarth, Prof. v1p0526c1s
Schubert, Dr.von v1p0342c1s
Schubert, H. v3p0085c2s
v4p0114c2s v4p0210c1s v4p0349c2s
v4p0360c2s v4p0379c1s v4p0409c1s
v4p0487c1s
Schuchert, C. v5p0215c1s
v5p0596c2s v6p0056c1s v6p0100c2s
v6p0251c1s v6p0657c1s
Schuchert, C. and Buckman, S.S.
v6p0663c2s
Schuchert, C. and Clark, J.M.
v5p0229c1s
Schuchert, C. and Diller, J.S.
v4p0154c2s
Schuchert, C. and Safford, J.M.
v5p0089c1s v5p0424c1s
Schuckburgh, E.S. v4p0135c2s
Schucking, L. v1p0361c2s
v1p1202c1s
Schuerman, W.H. v6p0304c2s
Schuler, H.A. v3p0140c1s
v4p0632c1s
Schulte, F.v. v1p0176c2s
Schulte, F.von v1p0515c2s
v1p0517c2s v1p1117c1s
Schulte, L.E. v6p0544c2s
Schulten, Jessie L. v6p0344c1s
Schultz, C. v5p0501c2s
Schultz, E. v6p0253c2s
v6p0603c1s
Schultz, H. v1p1369c1s
v4p0478c2s v5p0503c2s
Schultz, J. v4p0268c1s
Schultz, J.W. v5p0236c1s
v5p0491c2s v5p0524c2s
Schultz, L.V. v2p0061c1s
Schultz, R.W. v4p0502c1s
Schultz, R.W. and Gardner, E.A.
v4p0186c2s
Schultze, E.A. v5p0453c2s
Schultze, F. v1p0323c1s
Schultze-Naumburg, P. v5p0156c2m
v5p0511c1s v5p0558c1s
Schultze-Naumburg, Paul .. v5p0368c2s
Schulz, E.H. v6p0168c2s
Schulze, A. v5p0585c1s
Schulze, P. v4p0571c1s
Schumacher, J. v1p0071c1s
v1p1199c1s
Schumacher, P. v1p0541c2s
v1p0956c2s v1p1149c1m
Schumann, C.H. v4p0072c2s
Schumann, F. v4p0224c2s
v4p0552c1s v5p0633c2s
Schumm, G. v4p0404c1s
Schumpeter, J. v6p0041c1s
Schunck, E. v3p0075c2s
Schupphaus, R.C. v5p0252c2s
Schur, W. and Holden, E.S.
v2p0283c2s
Schure, E. v3p0074c2s
v3p0098c1s
Schure, S.E. v5p0616c1s
Schurer, E. v3p0043c1s
Schurman, G.W. v6p0301c2s
Schurman, J.G. v3p0065c1s
v3p0091c2s v4p0007c1s v4p0007c2s
v4p0042c1s v4p0051c1s v4p0096c2s
v4p0144c2s v4p0188c2s v4p0307c2s
v4p0308c1s v4p0382c1s v4p0439c2s
v4p0465c1s v4p0478c2s v4p0566c2s
v5p0144c1s v5p0199c2s v5p0445c1m
v5p0447c1s v5p0520c1s v5p0597c2s
v5p0605c1s v6p0136c1s v6p0493c2s
Schurman, J.G. and Huling, R.G.
v4p0512c1s
v5p0160c2s
Schurman, J.G. et al. v4p0206c2s
v4p0512c2s
Schurman, J.S. v4p0134c2s
Schurz, C. v1p0637c2s
v1p1348c2s v2p0103c2s v2p0131c2s
v2p0135c2s v2p0167c2s v2p0177c1m
v2p0250c1s v2p0271c1s v2p0331c2s
v2p0334c1s v2p0356c2s v2p0410c2s
v3p0251c2s v4p0019c1s v4p0115c1s
v4p0117c1m v4p0353c2s v4p0542c2s
v4p0592c1s v5p0019c2s v5p0123c1s
v5p0602c1s v5p0624c2s v6p0162c2s
v6p0310c1s v6p0447c1s v6p0526c1s
v6p0594c1s
Schurz, C. and Eddy, T.A.. v4p0192c2s
Schurz, Carl v6p0253c2s
Schuster, A. v1p0224c1s
v1p0400c2s v1p0401c1s v1p0591c2s
v1p0959c2s v1p1074c1s v1p1194c1s
v1p1233c2s v1p1268c1m v2p0138c1m
v2p0258c2s v2p0272c1s v2p0280c1s
v3p0133c2s v4p0176c1s v4p0376c2s
v5p0173c1s v5p0426c2s v5p0449c2s
v5p0545c1s v6p0324c1s v6p0432c1s
v6p0526c2s v6p0576c1s v6p0626c1s
v6p0678c2s
Schuster, E. v1p0690c2s
v4p0224c1s v4p0430c1s v5p0205c2s
v5p0468c1s
Schuster, E.J. v6p0322c2s
Schuster, F. v6p0205c2s
Schutt, W.E. v6p0542c2s
Schutz, E. v5p0414c2s
Schutz-Wilson, H. v1p0352c2s
v1p0435c2s v1p0475c2s v1p0856c2s
Schutze, M. v6p0444c1s
Schutzenberger, P. v1p1239c1s
Schuyler, A. v1p0811c1s
v1p1044c1s
Schuyler, E. v1p0009c1s
v1p0016c1s v1p0067c2s v1p0114c2s
v1p0137c2s v1p0299c2s v1p0352c2s
v1p0378c2s v1p0379c1s v1p0417c2m
v1p0428c2s v1p0568c2s v1p0701c2s
v1p0730c2s v1p0874c2m v1p0880c2s
v1p0994c1s v1p0997c2s v1p0999c1s
v1p1134c1s v1p1134c2m v1p1135c1m
v1p1135c2s v1p1136c1m v1p1136c2m
v1p1137c2s v1p1138c1m v1p1330c2s
v1p1333c2s v1p1357c2s v2p0025c1s
v2p0060c2s v2p0103c1s v2p0151c2s
v2p0379c1m v2p0385c2s v3p0011c1s
v3p0048c2s v3p0049c1s v3p0056c2s
v3p0059c2s v3p0066c2s v3p0070c1s
v3p0100c2s v3p0110c1m v3p0115c2s
v3p0124c1s v3p0191c2s v3p0207c2s
v3p0224c1s v3p0269c1s v3p0279c2s
v3p0362c1s v3p0370c2s v3p0385c2m
v3p0390c1s v3p0396c2s v3p0406c1s
v3p0432c1s v3p0435c1s
Schuyler, H. v3p0155c1s
Schuyler, J. v3p0254c2s
Schuyler, L.R. v6p0515c2s
Schuyler, M. v1p0018c2s
v2p0020c1s v2p0023c2s v2p0313c1s
v2p0313c2s v2p0322c1s v2p0392c2s
v2p0446c2s v3p0018c2m v3p0076c2s
v3p0281c1s v3p0372c2s v4p0024c1m
v4p0024c2s v4p0025c1m v4p0100c2s
v4p0102c1s v4p0173c1s v4p0269c2s
v4p0285c1s v4p0309c1s v4p0311c2s
v4p0490c1s v4p0593c2s v5p0026c2m
v5p0076c1m v5p0082c2s v5p0087c1s
v5p0133c1s v5p0146c2s v5p0226c1s
v5p0255c2s v5p0258c2s v5p0272c1s
v5p0443c2s v5p0553c1s v5p0583c2s
v6p0027c2s v6p0076c1s v6p0081c2s
v6p0087c1s v6p0126c2s v6p0128c2s
v6p0208c2s v6p0300c1s v6p0333c1s
v6p0452c2m v6p0453c1s v6p0454c1s
v6p0563c2s v6p0564c2s v6p0596c2s
v6p0693c1s
Schuyler, M., jr. and Gray, L.H.
v5p0264c1s
Schuyler, M.R. v3p0473c2s
Schuyler, Montgomery v4p0486c1s
v5p0409c1s v6p0030c2s v6p0452c2s
v6p0696c2s
Schuyler, W. v4p0108c1s
v4p0518c2s v4p0628c1s v5p0026c2s
v5p0620c1s v6p0207c1s v6p0252c2s
v6p0495c2s v6p0564c1s
Schuyler, W.H. v2p0001c2s
Schwab, C.M. v5p0095c1s
v5p0593c1s
Schwab, F.A. v1p0970c1s
v2p0459c2s v4p0016c2s v6p0221c2s
Schwab, G. v1p0082c2s
v1p0284c2s v1p0513c1s v1p1265c2s
v1p1283c2m v1p1428c2s
Schwab, G.H. v4p0275c1s
v5p0313c1s v6p0349c1s
Schwab, J.C. v3p0398c2s
v4p0128c2m v4p0364c1s v5p0132c1s
v5p0465c1s v5p0643c2m
Schwab, J.S. v3p0304c2s
v3p0421c1s
Schwab, L.H. v5p0489c2s
Schwab, M. v3p0013c1s
v3p0105c2s v4p0017c1s v4p0338c1s
v5p0316c2s
Schwabe, M.J.S. v2p0400c1s
Schwalbach, A. v6p0044c2s
Schwan, T. v6p0249c2s
Schwarm, S. v2p0370c1s
v3p0230c1s v3p0261c1s v3p0330c1s
v3p0423c2s v4p0045c1s v4p0480c1s
v6p0040c1s
Schwarts, W.P. v4p0497c2s
Schwartz, A. v1p0311c2s
v1p0351c2s v1p0481c2s v1p0490c1s
v1p0517c1s v1p0531c1s v1p0597c2s
v1p1118c2s v1p1241c1s v1p1418c2s
v5p0307c2s
Schwartz, A.J. v1p0581c2s
Schwartz, D.G. v1p1351c2s
Schwartz, G.F. v4p0631c2s
Schwartz, J. v1p0206c1s
v1p0628c2s v1p0742c1s v1p0742c2m
v1p0743c1s v2p0051c2s v2p0070c2s
v2p0213c2s v2p0216c2s v2p0256c1m
v2p0256c2s v2p0313c1s v3p0043c2s
v3p0082c1s v3p0146c2m v3p0328c2s
Schwartz, J. and Perkins, F.B.
v2p0256c1s
Schwartz, J.M.W.van der P.
v5p0347c2s
Schwartz, J.W. v4p0300c2s
v4p0394c2s
Schwartz, M.S. v1p0561c1s
Schwartz, T. v4p0010c1s
v4p0062c1s v4p0152c2s v4p0327c1s
v4p0342c2s
Schwartzkopff, P. v5p0306c2s
Schwarz, E.H.L. v6p0099c2s
Schwarz, E.H.L. and Gardiner, J.S.
v6p0149c2s
Schwarz, G.F. v6p0305c1s
Schwarz, H. v2p0050c2s
Schwarz, T. v5p0065c1s
Schwatka, F. v2p0020c2m
v2p0146c1s v2p0146c2m v2p0214c1m
v2p0303c2s v2p0406c2s v2p0482c2m
v3p0015c2s v3p0019c1s v3p0027c1s
v3p0135c1s v3p0142c2s v3p0147c1s
v3p0185c2s v3p0207c1s v3p0336c1s
v3p0383c1s v3p0394c2s v3p0415c2s
v3p0453c2s v3p0461c1s v4p0119c2s
v5p0027c1s
Schwatka, F. and Russell, I.C.
v3p0372c1s
Schwatka, F., Mrs. v5p0312c1s
v5p0645c1s
Schwedes, G.A. v5p0463c2s
Schwedoff, Prof. v2p0194c2s
Schweinfurth, G. v1p0010c2s
v1p0779c1s v2p0134c1s v2p0159c1s
Schweinfurth, J.A. v4p0040c1s
Schweinitz, E.A.de v4p0367c1s
v5p0374c1s
Schweinitz, E.De v2p0483c1s
Schweitzer, G. v1p1173c1s
Schweitzer, H. v6p0133c1s
Schweizer-Lerchenfeld, A.von
v4p0027c1s
Schwickerath, R. v6p0340c2s
v6p0537c1s
Schwiedland, E. v6p0628c1s
Schwill, F. v6p0504c2s

Schwimmer, Rosika v6p0303c1s
Schwob, M. v4p0059c2s
Schwob, Marcel v4p0549c1s
Scidmore, E.R. v3p0227c2s
v3p0422c1s v4p0009c1m v4p0207c2s
v4p0227c1s v4p0298c1s v4p0375c2s
v4p0562c1s v5p0071c2m v5p0109c1s
v5p0304c1s v5p0387c1s v5p0438c2s
v5p0579c2s v5p0643c2m
v6p0010c1s
Scidmore, Eliza R. v5p0438c2s
v5p0553c2s v5p0645c1s
Scisco, L.D. v4p0400c1s
v4p0401c1s v4p0410c2s v5p0408c1s
v6p0138c1s
Sciurus, B.B. v5p0569c1s
Sclater, B.L. v4p0409c2s
Sclater, P.L. v1p0042c1s
v1p0098c2s v1p0110c2s v1p0136c2m
v1p0204c2s v1p0800c2s v1p0879c1s
v1p0899c1s v1p1105c1s v1p1392c1s
v1p1440c2m v2p0161c2s v2p0271c1s
v2p0273c2s v2p0311c1s v3p0008c1s
v3p0218c2s v3p0296c1s v3p0360c1s
v4p0019c2s v4p0050c1s v4p0310c2s
v4p0348c1s v5p0005c2s v5p0163c1s
v6p0021c2s v6p0276c1s v6p0305c2s
Sclater, W.L. v4p0189c1s
v4p0351c2s v5p0357c2s
Scobey, J.E. v3p0083c1s
v3p0215c2s
Scoble, T.C. v5p0091c2s
v5p0558c2s
Scoffern, Dr. v1p1229c2s
Scoffern, H.E. v1p1288c2s
Scoffern, J. v1p0108c1s
v1p0196c1s v1p0203c2s v1p0209c1s
v1p0268c1s v1p0288c1s v1p0304c2m
v1p0376c2s v1p0432c1s v1p0443c2s
v1p0454c1s v1p0562c2s v1p0563c1m
v1p0565c2s v1p0619c1s v1p0643c2s
v1p0748c2s v1p0798c2s v1p0810c1s
v1p0919c1s v1p0923c2s v1p0937c2s
v1p0957c2s v1p0959c1s v1p1005c1s
v1p1023c2s v1p1145c2s v1p1174c2s
v1p1177c2s v1p1204c1s v1p1213c2s
v1p1232c2s v1p1237c1s v1p1265c1m
v1p1265c2s v1p1289c1s v1p1291c1s
v1p1316c2s v1p1361c2s v1p1375c1s
v1p1376c1s v1p1417c2s
Scoles, I. v2p0057c1s
v2p0299c1s
Scoles, J.J. v1p1068c1s
Scollard, C. v3p0126c2s
v3p0135c1s v4p0119c1s v5p0135c1s
v5p0154c1s v5p0279c1s v5p0282c2s
v5p0318c2s v5p0425c2s v5p0434c2s
v5p0532c2s v5p0538c2s v5p0564c2s
v5p0583c2s v5p0609c2s v5p0639c2s
v6p0048c2s v6p0052c2s v6p0525c1s
v6p0567c1s
Scollard, Clinton v4p0119c2s
v5p0633c2s
Scomp, H.A. v3p0170c2s
v3p0299c1s v4p0059c1s v5p0249c2s
v5p0571c2s v6p0063c1s
Scomp, H.A. et al. v6p0408c2s
Scoones, W.B. v1p0258c2s
v1p0630c1s v2p0086c2s v2p0144c1s
v3p0146c1s v4p0236c1s
Scoones, W.Baptiste v5p0555c2s
Scoresby, Dr. v1p1393c1s
Scoresby, W. v1p0286c2s
v1p0927c2s v1p1213c2s v1p1291c2s
v1p1393c1s
Scotford, F.E. v6p0645c1s
Scott, A. v1p0354c1s
v1p1191c2s v3p0121c2s v4p0036c2s
v4p0509c1s v5p0268c2s v5p0332c2s
v5p0406c1s v6p0360c2s v6p0372c1s
v6p0460c2s v6p0555c1s
Scott, A.C. v6p0497c2s
Scott, A.R. et al. v4p0095c1s
Scott, Addie E. v5p0326c1s
Scott, Alex. v4p0127c2s
Scott, Ann v5p0357c1s
Scott, Austin v2p0311c2s
Scott, B. v1p1010c1s
v2p0264c1s v2p0468c2s v3p0294c1s
v3p0458c2s
Scott, Benj. v3p0300c1s
Scott, C. v1p0536c2s
v1p0950c1s v2p0013c1s v2p0014c1s
v2p0082c2s v2p0123c1s v2p0288c1s
v2p0299c1s v2p0324c2s v2p0344c2s
v2p0354c1s v2p0397c2s v2p0416c1s
v2p0416c2s v3p0047c1s v3p0087c2s
v3p0122c1m v3p0206c2s v3p0256c2s
v3p0286c1s v3p0294c1s v4p0023c1s
v4p0028c1s v4p0097c1s v4p0141c1s
v4p0161c1s v4p0200c2s v4p0261c2s
v4p0285c1s v4p0297c1s v4p0446c2s
v4p0504c2s v4p0508c2s v4p0516c2s
v4p0588c1s v5p0167c1s v5p0167c2s
v5p0191c2s v5p0251c1s v5p0299c1s
Scott, C.A. v4p0085c1s
v4p0109c1s v4p0149c2s v4p0213c1s
v5p0130c2s v5p0219c1s v5p0236c1s
v5p0331c2s v5p0348c1s v5p0366c1m
v5p0369c2s v5p0378c1s v5p0436c1s
v5p0482c1s v6p0342c1s v6p0399c2s
v6p0576c2s
Scott, C.F. v5p0013c2s
v5p0182c2s v5p0183c1s v5p0223c1s
v5p0226c2s v6p0013c2s v6p0197c2s
v6p0198c1s
Scott, C.N. v2p0077c1s
Scott, C.P.G. v5p0191c2s
v6p0315c1s
Scott, C.W. v1p0333c1s
v1p0944c1s v2p0257c1s
Scott, Canon v4p0475c2s
v4p0555c1s
Scott, Colin A. v4p0411c2s
Scott, D. v1p0527c1s
v1p1232c1s
Scott, D.C. v3p0123c2s
v3p0210c1s v3p0471c2s v4p0085c2s
v4p0277c1s v4p0584c2s v5p0091c2s
v5p0329c2s v5p0596c1s v5p0607c1s
v6p0317c1s v6p0613c2s v6p0620c1s
v6p0700c2s
Scott, D.H. v3p0295c1s
v4p0089c1s v4p0459c1s v6p0502c2s
Scott, D.M. v2p0478c2s
Scott, D.S. v2p0071c1s
v6p0004c2s
Scott, Dr. v1p0284c1s
Scott, E. v4p0048c2s
v5p0161c2s v5p0240c2s v5p0500c1s
Scott, E., Sir v1p0254c1s
Scott, E.A. v2p0363c1s
v5p0533c1s v6p0465c2s
Scott, E.G. v1p0005c2s
v1p1181c1s v3p0065c1s v3p0065c2s
v4p0324c2s v4p0346c2s v6p0706c2s
Scott, E.J.L. v3p0147c2s
v5p0239c1s
Scott, E.K. v5p0312c1s
Scott, E.N. v6p0089c1s
v6p0107c1s
Scott, E.S. v6p0403c2s
Scott, F. v1p0643c2s
Scott, F.G. v4p0537c2s
v5p0083c2s
Scott, F.J. v4p0059c1s
v4p0059c2s
Scott, F.J. et al. v2p0034c1s
Scott, F.N. v3p0253c2s
v4p0121c2s v4p0184c1s v5p0126c1s
v5p0192c1m v5p0192c2s v5p0523c1s
v6p0164c2s
Scott, G. v6p0105c1s
v6p0314c1s v6p0629c1s
Scott, G., Sir v6p0310c2s
v6p0599c2s
Scott, G.A. v4p0371c1s
v4p0497c1s
Scott, G.E. v6p0149c2s
Scott, G.F. v5p0039c2s
v5p0282c2s v5p0362c1s v5p0404c2s
v5p0503c1s
Scott, G.G. v1p1101c1s
Scott, G.R. v5p0440c1s
Scott, G.R. et al. v5p0610c1s
Scott, G.R.W. v1p0323c1s
v4p0480c2s v4p0572c2s v6p0480c2s
Scott, G.W. v6p0180c1s
v6p0362c2s v6p0476c1s
Scott, Gilbert v6p0288c2s
Scott, H. v5p0151c2s
v6p0200c1s
Scott, H.A. v5p0251c2s
v5p0475c1s v6p0468c1s
Scott, H.B. v6p0152c2s
Scott, H.K. v5p0152c1s
v5p0384c2s
Scott, H.L. v1p0341c1s
v1p0838c1s v1p1342c1s
Scott, H.M. v2p0070c2s
v2p0132c2s v2p0176c2s v2p0357c2s
v3p0083c2s v3p0427c2m v4p0013c1s
v4p0108c1s v4p0109c2s v4p0301c2s
v4p0366c1s v5p0116c2s v5p0174c1s
v5p0399c2s v5p0577c1s v6p0162c2m
v6p0344c1s v6p0536c2s v6p0642c2s
Scott, H.R. v1p0011c2s
v1p0421c2s
Scott, H.S. v5p0391c1s
v6p0607c1s
Scott, H.W. v6p0036c2s
Scott, H.Y.D. v1p0211c1s
v1p0362c2s v1p0749c2s v1p0873c2s
v1p1181c1m v3p0386c1s
Scott, I. v1p0134c1s
v1p0140c1s v1p0147c2s v1p0167c2s
v1p0169c1s v1p0443c2s v1p0512c2s
v1p0588c2s v1p0681c2s v1p0781c2s
v1p0831c2s v1p1219c2s v1p1425c2s
Scott, I.M. v2p0245c1s
v3p0125c2s v3p0205c2s v3p0223c1s
v3p0237c2s v3p0416c2s v4p0059c1s
v4p0247c2m v4p0395c2s v5p0088c2s
v5p0443c2s
Scott, I.M. et al. v4p0521c1s
Scott, I.W. v1p1400c1s
Scott, Ida v3p0113c2s
v3p0304c2s
Scott, J. v1p0116c1s
v1p0218c1s v1p1183c1s v2p0239c1s
v2p0339c2s v4p0543c2s v5p0180c2s
v5p0284c2s v5p0292c1s
Scott, J., Sir v5p0181c1s
Scott, J.A. v6p0680c2m
Scott, J.B. v6p0293c1s
v6p0324c1s v6p0364c1s
Scott, J.C. v2p0115c1s
v2p0250c1s v2p0261c2s v2p0339c2s
v2p0447c2s v3p0124c1s v3p0153c2s
v3p0155c1s v3p0176c2s v3p0210c1s
v3p0290c2s v3p0376c2s v3p0429c2s
v3p0431c1s
Scott, J.E. v1p0632c2m
v1p1192c1s v2p0203c1s v5p0320c1s
v6p0421c2s
Scott, J.G. v2p0078c2s
v3p0060c2s v3p0389c1s v4p0079c2s
v4p0607c2s v6p0589c1s
Scott, J.G., Sir v6p0114c1s
Scott, J.H. v5p0127c2s
Scott, J.L. v1p0898c1s
v4p0231c2s v4p0546c1s
Scott, J.McD. v1p1043c1s
Scott, J.W. v1p0265c1s
v1p0265c2s v1p0539c2s v1p0650c1m
v1p0718c2s v1p0939c1s v1p1041c1s
v1p1041c2s v1p1075c2s v1p1078c1s
v1p1080c1s v1p1314c2s v1p1318c1s
v1p1319c1m v1p1400c2s
Scott, L. v2p0102c2s
v2p0342c2s v2p0430c2s v4p0030c1s
v4p0202c2s v5p0023c2s v5p0097c1s
v5p0099c1s v5p0101c1s v5p0232c2s
v5p0234c1s v5p0402c1s v5p0609c1s
v6p0043c2s v6p0296c1s v6p0297c1s
v6p0340c1s v6p0442c2s v6p0464c2s
v6p0517c2s v6p0526c1s v6p0530c2s
v6p0621c2s v6p0648c1s
Scott, L. and Seely, A.C.. v6p0627c1s
Scott, L.F. v4p0604c2s
v5p0127c2s
Scott, Leader v5p0210c2s
v6p0054c2s
Scott, Leroy v6p0219c2s
v6p0321c2s v6p0528c1s v6p0665c1s
v6p0708c1s
Scott, M. v1p0321c1s
v1p0415c1s v1p1315c1s v5p0465c1s
v6p0681c1s
Scott, M., Mrs. v2p0315c1s
v2p0391c1s v4p0341c2s
Scott, M.A. v5p0123c2s
v6p0211c1s v6p0331c1s v6p0704c2s
Scott, M.B. v1p1112c1s
v1p1168c1s v5p0153c1s
Scott, M.H.B. v5p0026c1s
v5p0156c1s v5p0207c2s v5p0559c1m
Scott, M.M. v1p0537c2s
v3p0076c2s v6p0283c1s
Scott, M.M.M. v2p0286c2s
v3p0373c1s
Scott, M.M.Maxwell v6p0001c1s
v6p0221c2s v6p0344c1s v6p0629c1s
Scott, M.M.Maxwell, Mrs. . v6p0333c1s
v6p0420c2s
Scott, M.O. v5p0081c1s
v5p0090c1s v5p0288c2s v6p0400c2s
v6p0561c2s
Scott, Mary A. v4p0098c1s
v5p0589c2m v6p0367c1s v6p0426c2s
Scott, N.B. v6p0324c2s
Scott, N.H. v6p0693c1s
Scott, O. v5p0229c1s
Scott, O.S. v5p0074c1s
Scott, P.T. et al. v3p0301c1s
Scott, R. v1p0008c2m
v1p0263c2s v1p0621c1s v1p1157c2s
v1p1284c1s v1p1301c1s v6p0198c1s
Scott, R.A.E. v4p0237c2s
Scott, R.E. v4p0169c1s
Scott, R.E.A. v3p0181c2s
Scott, R.F. v6p0023c1s
Scott, R.F. et al. v6p0023c1s
Scott, R.H. v1p0077c1s
v1p0829c1s v1p0829c2s v1p1256c2s
v1p1394c2m v2p0006c1s v2p0146c1s
v2p0285c2s v2p0426c2s v2p0469c1s
v3p0088c2s v3p0236c1s v3p0256c1s
v3p0430c1s v3p0458c2m v4p0119c2s
v4p0236c1s v4p0615c2m
Scott, R.H. and Curtis, R.H.
v2p0196c2s
Scott, R.N. v5p0364c1s
Scott, R.P. v5p0178c1s
Scott, R.W. v1p0258c1s
Scott, S.H. v6p0384c2s
v6p0575c1s
Scott, S.P. v1p0022c1s
v1p0301c2s v1p0539c2s v1p0866c2s
v1p1195c2s v2p0013c2s v2p0069c2s
v2p0386c1s v2p0395c2s v2p0442c2s
v2p0448c1s
Scott, T. v1p0848c1s
v5p0071c1s
Scott, T.A. v1p1261c1s
Scott, T.F. v1p0255c2s
Scott, T.J. v1p0156c2s
v1p0857c2s v6p0315c1s
Scott, T.S. v5p0318c1s
Scott, W. v1p0130c1s

v1p0539c1s v1p0691c1s v1p0776c2s
v1p1235c2s v1p1303c1s v3p0031c1s
v3p0459c2s v4p0145c1s v4p0189c1s
v4p0197c1m v4p0327c2s v4p0491c2s
v4p0494c1s v4p0509c2s v4p0513c2s
v4p0602c2s v5p0264c2s v5p0452c2s
v5p0569c1s v6p0419c2s v6p0684c2s
Scott, W., Sir v1p0026c1s
v1p0077c2s v1p0162c1s v1p0176c1s
v1p0178c2s v1p0182c1s v1p0186c1s
v1p0222c2s v1p0223c1m v1p0246c1s
v1p0298c1s v1p0317c2m v1p0323c1s
v1p0335c1s v1p0383c1s v1p0418c1s
v1p0418c2s v1p0492c1s v1p0522c1s
v1p0530c1s v1p0586c2s v1p0595c2s
v1p0599c1s v1p0704c2s v1p0705c1s
v1p0722c1s v1p0723c1s v1p0739c1s
v1p0812c2s v1p0838c1s v1p0859c1s
v1p0871c2s v1p0894c1s v1p0949c1s
v1p0950c1s v1p0989c1m v1p1016c1s
v1p1109c1s v1p1165c1s v1p1165c2s
v1p1166c1s v1p1166c2m v1p1170c1s
v1p1189c1s v1p1226c2s v1p1228c1s
v1p1235c2s v1p1264c2s v1p1307c2s
v1p1392c2s v3p0001c1s
Scott, W., Sir and Grey, C.E., Sir
v1p0191c2s
Scott, W., Sir and Jeffrey, F.
v1p0851c1s
Scott, W.A. v1p0284c1s
v1p0392c2s v5p0229c2s v5p0474c1s
v6p0089c2s v6p0193c1s v6p0671c1m
Scott, W.B. v1p0045c1s
v1p0140c2s v1p0419c2s v1p0567c1s
v1p0834c1s v1p0836c2s v1p0949c1s
v1p1027c2s v1p1054c1s v1p1165c2s
v1p1202c2s v1p1214c1s v2p0054c2s
v2p0119c1s v2p0193c2s v2p0207c2s
v2p0343c1s v3p0134c2s v3p0436c1s
v4p0422c1m v4p0600c2s v5p0357c2s
v5p0358c1s v6p0189c1s v6p0282c2s
Scott, W.D. v6p0004c2s
Scott, W.E.D. v5p0044c2s
v5p0062c2s v6p0067c2m v6p0068c1m
v6p0071c2s v6p0178c1s v6p0224c1s
v6p0662c1s
Scott, W.F. v4p0058c1s
Scott, W.J. v5p0117c1s
Scott, W.K. v1p0556c2s
Scott, W.L. v2p0106c2s
v2p0240c1s v3p0003c1m
Scott, W.M. v1p0415c2s
v1p1056c1s v6p0197c1s
Scott, W.R. v4p0584c1s
v5p0025c1s v6p0553c2s v6p0577c2s
v6p0578c2s
Scott, W.S. v3p0157c1s
Scott, W.T. v6p0379c2s
Scott, W.W. v4p0148c2s
v4p0295c2s v4p0324c2s v4p0361c2s
v6p0696c1s
Scott, Winifred v6p0042c1s
Scott-James, R.A. v6p0392c1s
Scott-Moncrief, Mrs. v5p0223c2s
v5p0273c1s
Scott-Moncrieff, C. v4p0404c2s
Scott-Moncrieff, C.C. v2p0134c2s
v2p0229c2s
Scott-Moncrieff, J.M. v3p0325c1s
v4p0432c1s
Scott-Moncrieff, S. v6p0226c1s
Scott-Moncrieff, W.D. v1p0016c2s
Scott-Moncrieff, W.G. v4p0119c1s
v4p0140c1s
Scott-Montagu, J. v6p0044c1m
Scott-Uda, M. v4p0294c1s
v4p0332c1s v5p0397c2s
Scotter, R. v4p0354c1s
Scouler, J. v1p0636c2s
Scovel, J.M. v3p0252c1m
v4p0121c1s v4p0333c1s v4p0516c2s
v5p0290c2s v5p0339c1s v5p0339c2m
v5p0552c2s v6p0031c2s v6p0345c1s
v6p0377c2m v6p0617c1s v6p0697c1s
Scovel, S.F. v1p1043c2s
v3p0091c2s v3p0214c2s v3p0273c1s
Scovel, S.F. et al. v3p0073c2s
Scovell, J.T. v4p0417c2s
Scoville, A.B. v5p0251c1s
v5p0288c1s
Scoville, S. v5p0612c1s
Scoville, S., jr. v4p0035c2s
v4p0036c1m v4p0254c1s v4p0470c1s
Scoville, W.S. and Gooch, F.A.
v4p0514c1s
Scranton, B.S. v1p0693c1s
Screven, W.E. v1p0470c2s
Scribe, E. v5p0232c2s
v6p0255c2s v6p0513c2s v6p0571c1s
Scribe, M. v1p1049c2s
Scribner, C.W. v5p0294c2s
Scribner, F.L. v4p0008c2s
Scribner, W. v1p0357c2s
v1p0438c1s
Scripps, J.E. v5p0253c1s
Scripture, E.W. v3p0019c2s
v3p0348c2s v4p0087c1s v4p0103c1s
v4p0125c1s v4p0169c1s v4p0193c1s
v4p0363c1s v4p0365c1s v4p0372c1s
v4p0464c2m v4p0505c2s v5p0100c1s
v5p0128c2s v5p0177c1s v5p0184c2s
v5p0325c2s v5p0470c2s v5p0471c1s
v5p0488c1s v5p0552c2s v5p0614c2s
v6p0609c1s v6p0681c1s v6p0699c1s
Scriven, G.P. v3p0441c2s
v5p0410c2s
Scriven, J. v6p0256c1s
Scroggs, Josephine V. v6p0458c2m
Scroggs, W.O. v6p0456c2s
Scroggs, W.Oscar v6p0683c2s
Scrope, G.P. v1p0312c1s
v1p1377c1s
Scruggs, W.L. v2p0086c2s
v2p0424c1s v3p0086c1s v3p0087c2s
v3p0194c2s v3p0277c1s v3p0286c1s
v3p0359c1s v3p0402c1s v3p0403c1s
v4p0287c2s v4p0529c1s v4p0601c2s
v6p0016c1s v6p0128c1m v6p0426c1s
v6p0624c1s
Scrutator v6p0089c2s
v6p0095c1s v6p0144c1s v6p0699c1s
Scrutton, T. v2p0257c2s
v2p0393c1s
Scrutton, T. and Plimsoll, S.
v3p0218c1s
Scrutton, T.E. v4p0127c1s
Scudamore, Amy L. v4p0400c2s
Scudamore, F. v3p0186c2s
v4p0173c1s v4p0247c1s
Scudamore, F.I. v4p0212c1s
Scudder, D. v6p0120c2s
Scudder, D.C. v1p0592c1s
v1p0628c2s
Scudder, Dr. v1p0393c1s
Scudder, H.E. v1p0004c1s
v1p0037c2m v1p0038c1s v1p0140c2m
v1p0152c1s v1p0175c2s v1p0262c1s
v1p0324c1s v1p0436c1s v1p0459c1s
v1p0572c2s v1p0583c2s v1p0607c1s
v1p0748c1s v1p0795c1s v1p0878c2s
v1p1072c1s v1p1097c1s v1p1132c2s
v1p1143c2s v1p1157c2s v1p1288c2s
v1p1416c2s v2p0013c2s v2p0077c2m
v2p0102c1s v2p0102c2s v2p0143c2s
v2p0301c2s v2p0321c2s v2p0422c1s
v2p0458c1s v3p0011c2s v3p0082c2s
v3p0130c1s v3p0253c2s v3p0258c1s
v3p0309c1s v3p0355c1s v4p0171c1s
v4p0183c1s v4p0260c2s v4p0330c1s
v4p0458c2s v4p0474c2s v4p0505c2s
v5p0414c2s
Scudder, H.E. et al. v2p0058c2s
Scudder, J.L. v3p0383c2s
Scudder, J.W. v5p0119c1s
Scudder, M.L. v1p0846c2s
v4p0443c1s
Scudder, M.L., jr. v2p0170c1s
v2p0408c1s
Scudder, M.T. v5p0265c1s
Scudder, N.D. v2p0215c1s
Scudder, S.H. v1p0181c1m
v1p0206c2s v1p0270c2s v1p0420c1s
v1p0470c1s v1p0541c1s v1p0644c2s
v1p0645c1s v1p0858c2s v1p0924c2s
v2p0304c2s v2p0307c1s v2p0338c1s
v3p0249c1s v3p0475c2s v4p0083c2s
v4p0089c1s v4p0139c1s v4p0406c2s
v4p0609c1s
Scudder, S.K. and Scudder, V.D.
v3p0155c2s
Scudder, V.D. v2p0149c1s
v3p0020c2s v3p0284c1s v3p0293c2s
v3p0335c2s v3p0398c2s v3p0468c1s
v3p0473c1s v4p0520c1s v4p0598c1s
v4p0626c2s v5p0127c1s v5p0191c2s
v5p0535c2s v5p0641c1s
Scudder, V.D. and Scudder, S.K.
v3p0155c2s
Scudder, Vida D. v3p0386c2s
v6p0125c1s v6p0137c1s v6p0169c2m
v6p0170c1s v6p0190c2s v6p0238c2s
v6p0328c1s v6p0601c2s
Scudo, P. v1p0360c2s
Scull, G.D. v2p0032c1s
v2p0055c2s v2p0105c2s v2p0139c1s
v2p0279c2s v2p0310c1s v2p0310c2m
v2p0337c2m v2p0364c2s v2p0408c2s
v2p0470c1s v2p0475c2s
Scull, G.H. v5p0516c2s
v5p0538c1s v5p0634c1s
Scull, W.D. v1p0905c2s
v4p0164c1s
Scully, C.D. v6p0501c1s
Scully, Nora and Scully, W.C.
v5p0394c1s
Scully, W.C. v5p0085c2s
v5p0331c1s
Scully, W.C. and Scully, Nora
v5p0394c1s
Scupham, J.R. v1p1012c1s
Scurry, W.R. v3p0361c2s
Sea, E.S. v4p0186c1s
Seaber, L. v6p0492c1s
Seabright, L. v6p0301c1s
Seabrook, E.B. v1p0346c1s
v1p0449c1s v1p1172c2s v1p1224c1s
v1p1225c2s v2p0099c2s
Seabrooke, W. v5p0519c2s
Seabury, E.P. v4p0021c2s
Seabury, S. v6p0319c2s
Seabury, W.J. v1p1173c2s
v2p0357c1s v2p0393c2s
Seadman, A.D.H. v3p0116c1s
Seafield, F. v2p0068c1s
v2p0110c2s v2p0239c1s
Seager, H.R. v4p0167c2s
v4p0450c1s v5p0015c2s v6p0016c1s
v6p0039c2s v6p0356c1s v6p0385c1s
v6p0519c2s
Seager, R.B. v6p0589c1s
v6p0633c2s
Seagrave, F.E. v6p0571c1s
Seagrave, F.H. v5p0258c2s
Seal, G.D. v5p0623c2s
Seal, H. v4p0143c1s
v4p0450c2s v4p0546c2s v5p0125c1s
v5p0146c1s v5p0288c2s v5p0440c1s
v5p0446c2s v5p0542c1s v5p0550c2s
v5p0580c1s v6p0038c1s v6p0660c2s
Seal, M. v6p0197c1s
Seaman, E.C. v1p0963c1s
v1p1044c2s
Seaman, L.L. v2p0313c2s
v5p0479c1m v5p0599c1s v5p0599c2s
v6p0099c2s v6p0334c2m v6p0560c2s
Seaman, O. v5p0474c1s
v5p0475c1s v5p0511c2s v6p0396c1s
Seaman, R.F. v1p1238c2s
Seaman, S.A. v2p0286c1s
v2p0420c2s
Seaman, W.H. v3p0278c1s
v6p0413c2s
Seamon, W.H. v3p0475c2s
Search, P.W. v4p0466c1s
v4p0466c2s v4p0566c2s v5p0264c2s
v6p0217c1s
Search, T.C. v4p0593c2s
v5p0619c2s
Searchfield, E. v4p0390c2s
Seares, F.H. v6p0012c2s
v6p0506c1s
Seargill, W.P. v1p0323c1s
Searing, A.E.P. v3p0023c1s
v4p0335c2s v4p0353c1s v4p0369c2s
v4p0422c1s v5p0092c1s v5p0191c2s
v5p0198c1s v5p0202c1s v5p0420c2s
v5p0578c2s
Searing, L. and Hoffmann, S.V.
v3p0125c2s
Searle, A. v1p0199c2s
v1p0804c1s v4p0010c2s v4p0548c2s
Searle, G. v1p0387c2s
Searle, G.F.C. v6p0199c2s
Searle, G.G. v1p0089c1s
v1p0858c2s
Searle, G.M. v1p0850c1s
v1p1119c1s v1p1163c1s v2p0095c1m
v2p0095c2s v2p0141c1s v2p0255c1s
v2p0357c2s v2p0369c2s v2p0389c1s
v2p0480c2s v3p0119c1s v3p0407c1s
v4p0034c2s v4p0190c2s v4p0440c1s
v4p0445c1s v4p0482c1s v4p0497c2s
v5p0141c2s v5p0174c2s v5p0381c1s
v5p0613c2s v6p0092c1s v6p0171c2s
v6p0172c1s v6p0218c2s v6p0406c1s
v6p0537c1s v6p0609c2s v6p0625c2s
Searle, G.W. v1p0433c1s
v1p1282c1s
Searle, J. v1p0559c2s
v1p0876c2s v1p1189c2s v1p1201c2s
v1p1424c2s
Searle, J.P. v4p0095c2s
Searle, R. v1p0871c1s
Searle, T.J. v4p0287c1s
Searle, W.S. v3p0007c2s
v3p0037c2s v3p0192c1s v3p0410c1s
Searles, O. v3p0412c2s
Searles, S. v6p0379c1s
Sears, A. v1p1076c2s
v3p0342c2s
Sears, A.F. v1p1078c1s
v3p0408c1s v4p0136c1s v4p0436c2m
v4p0552c2s
Sears, A.F., jr. v5p0219c2s
Sears, A.W. v4p0626c1s
v5p0628c1s
Sears, B. v1p0009c1s
v1p0254c2s v1p0389c2s v1p0595c1s
v1p0777c1s v1p0777c2s v1p0778c1s
v1p0903c1s v1p0948c1s v1p1090c2s
v1p1121c2s v1p1354c2s v1p1421c2s
Sears, C.H. v5p0472c2s
v5p0488c1s v6p0543c1s
Sears, D. v1p0788c1s
Sears, E.A. v1p1048c1s
Sears, E.G. v1p0528c2s
Sears, E.H. v1p0012c1s
v1p0086c1s v1p0128c1s v1p0128c2s
v1p0129c1s v1p0148c1s v1p0239c1s
v1p0239c2s v1p0240c2s v1p0243c1s
v1p0252c1s v1p0255c1s v1p0279c2s
v1p0361c1s v1p0527c1s v1p0529c1s
v1p0579c1s v1p0646c1s v1p0687c1s
v1p0688c1s v1p0692c2s v1p0847c2s
v1p0849c2s v1p0900c1m v1p1085c1s
v1p1269c2s v1p1340c1s v1p1340c2m
v1p1341c1s v1p1346c2s v1p1429c1s
v3p0302c1s v6p0135c1s
Sears, E.H. and Folsom, N.S.
v1p0687c1s

Sears, E.H. and Wellington, A.M.
v1p1325c2s
Sears, E.I. v1p0021c1s
v1p0027c2s v1p0042c2s v1p0050c1s
v1p0057c1m v1p0057c2s v1p0068c2s
v1p0081c1s v1p0107c2s v1p0112c2s
v1p0155c2s v1p0158c1s v1p0168c1s
v1p0184c2s v1p0191c1s v1p0210c2s
v1p0225c1s v1p0236c1s v1p0259c1s
v1p0259c2s v1p0261c2s v1p0275c1s
v1p0275c2s v1p0276c1s v1p0276c2s
v1p0280c1m v1p0282c2s v1p0292c2s
v1p0298c2s v1p0299c2s v1p0317c1s
v1p0318c1s v1p0318c2s v1p0331c1s
v1p0331c2s v1p0335c1s v1p0353c1s
v1p0357c2s v1p0363c2s v1p0367c2s
v1p0385c1s v1p0386c1s v1p0390c2s
v1p0393c1m v1p0394c2s v1p0420c2s
v1p0423c2s v1p0429c2s v1p0431c2s
v1p0488c2s v1p0490c1s v1p0497c2s
v1p0531c2s v1p0540c2m v1p0554c1m
v1p0555c2s v1p0556c1m v1p0583c1s
v1p0591c2s v1p0600c1s v1p0604c2s
v1p0628c1s v1p0633c1s v1p0641c1s
v1p0643c1s v1p0647c1s v1p0648c1m
v1p0655c1m v1p0658c2s v1p0669c2s
v1p0683c2s v1p0689c2s v1p0693c2s
v1p0706c1s v1p0710c1s v1p0725c1s
v1p0736c2s v1p0754c1s v1p0776c1s
v1p0777c1s v1p0783c1s v1p0796c1s
v1p0816c1s v1p0832c1s v1p0835c1s
v1p0850c2s v1p0859c1s v1p0883c2s
v1p0915c2m v1p0916c1s v1p0916c2m
v1p0917c1s v1p0923c1s v1p0937c1s
v1p0944c1s v1p0945c2s v1p0950c1s
v1p0967c1s v1p0992c1s v1p0995c1s
v1p0995c2s v1p0999c1s v1p1002c1s
v1p1004c2s v1p1010c2s v1p1038c2s
v1p1048c1m v1p1063c2s v1p1064c1m
v1p1068c2s v1p1069c1m v1p1158c1s
v1p1181c2s v1p1217c2s v1p1221c1m
v1p1236c2s v1p1266c2s v1p1284c1s
v1p1334c2s v1p1353c1m v1p1356c2m
v1p1363c1s v1p1365c2s v1p1372c2s
v1p1384c2s v1p1408c2s v1p1422c1s
v1p1422c2s v1p1429c1s
Sears, F.C. v4p0208c1s
v5p0632c2s v6p0054c2s
Sears, G.E. v4p0053c1s
Sears, G.W. v1p0951c2s
Sears, H. v4p0163c1s
v4p0270c1s v5p0037c1s v5p0231c2s
v5p0385c2s v5p0482c2s v6p0710c1s
Sears, J.H. v5p0541c1m
Sears, J.M., jr. v6p0366c1s
Sears, J.M., jr. and Powell, B.
v6p0464c1s
Sears, J.V. v1p0222c1s
v4p0066c1s v4p0066c2s v4p0274c1s
v5p0044c1s
Sears, L. v3p0055c2s
v3p0267c1s v3p0387c1s v5p0269c1s
v6p0110c2s v6p0379c1s
Sears, P.H. v1p1092c2s
Sears, R.S. v1p0913c2s
Sears, S.E. v6p0060c2s
Sears, W.I. v1p0600c2s
Seart, J.V. v1p0608c1s
Seashore, C.E. v5p0107c2s
v5p0624c1s
Seashore, C.E. and Williams, M.C.
v5p0279c2s
Seat, E.F. v4p0102c2s
v4p0110c1s v4p0558c1s v5p0236c1s
Seaton, A.E. v3p0409c1s
Seaton, F. v6p0392c2s
Seaton, R.C. v1p1189c1s
v2p0068c2s v2p0081c2s v2p0140c1s
v3p0418c2s v5p0350c1s v5p0458c1s
v6p0388c2s
Seaton, W.J. v2p0162c2s
Seaver, E.P. v3p0266c2s
v4p0585c1s v5p0264c2s v6p0196c2s
v6p0575c1s
Seaver, J.W. v5p0581c2s
Seaver, W.A. v1p0373c2s
v1p0498c2s v1p0520c2s
Seavey, F.C. v4p0111c1s
v4p0203c2s v4p0491c1s v5p0380c2s
v6p0656c2s
Seaward, S. v1p1249c2s
Seawell, M.E. v3p0188c1s
v3p0237c2s v3p0288c1s v3p0468c2s
v4p0215c1s v4p0304c2s v4p0590c1s
v4p0627c2s v5p0267c1s v5p0310c1s
v5p0430c2s
Seawell, Molly E. v5p0592c1s
Seay, S. v2p0421c1s
v3p0223c1s
Sebastian, C.H. v5p0398c2s
Sebenius, J.L. v4p0548c1s
Sebillot, P. v6p0619c1s
Sebree, U. v6p0567c1s
Sebree, W. v4p0548c1s
Secchi, A. v1p0381c2s
v1p0827c2s v1p0866c1s v1p1267c2s
Seccombe, T. v5p0216c2s
v5p0533c2s v6p0505c2s
Seccombe, T. and Brandin, L.
v6p0288c1s
Secomb, D.F. v2p0012c2s
Secor, W.B. v5p0479c2s
Secretan, C. v2p0429c1s
Secretan, W.C. v6p0091c1s
Sedding, E. v1p0245c1s
v1p0736c1s v4p0561c1s
Sedding, J.D. v2p0020c1s
v3p0018c1s
Sedding, J.R. v2p0018c2s
Seddon, H.C. v1p1150c2s
Seddon, J.A. v6p0113c1s
Seddon, J.P. v1p1386c2s
v2p0019c2s v2p0020c1s v2p0078c2m
v2p0437c1s v4p0228c1s
Seddon, R.J. v6p0454c2s
Seddon, W.L. v2p0432c2s
Sedgewick, M.K. v4p0409c2s
Sedgwick, A. v1p0313c1s
v1p0960c1s v6p0397c2s
Sedgwick, A.D. v5p0340c1s
v5p0486c1s v6p0234c1s v6p0394c1s
v6p0540c1s v6p0624c2s
Sedgwick, A.G. v1p0017c2s
v1p0018c1s v1p0029c1s v1p0095c1s
v1p0097c2s v1p0100c2s v1p0101c1s
v1p0104c1m v1p0115c1m v1p0144c1s
v1p0152c1s v1p0152c2s v1p0160c1s
v1p0176c1s v1p0180c2s v1p0188c1s
v1p0194c2s v1p0201c1s v1p0208c2s
v1p0213c1s v1p0229c1s v1p0258c2s
v1p0259c1s v1p0284c2s v1p0286c1s
v1p0291c1s v1p0295c1s v1p0300c2m
v1p0313c2s v1p0317c1s v1p0322c2m
v1p0326c2s v1p0333c1s v1p0334c1s
v1p0341c1s v1p0380c1s v1p0428c1s
v1p0437c2m v1p0442c2s v1p0451c2s
v1p0499c1s v1p0511c2s v1p0525c1s
v1p0540c1m v1p0591c1s v1p0614c2s
v1p0638c1s v1p0647c1s v1p0650c2s
v1p0659c2s v1p0680c2s v1p0696c1s
v1p0699c2s v1p0715c1s v1p0719c1s
v1p0736c1m v1p0739c2s v1p0744c2s
v1p0745c2s v1p0758c1s v1p0797c1s
v1p0808c2s v1p0862c2s v1p0865c1s
v1p0909c2s v1p0914c1s v1p0916c1s
v1p0916c2s v1p0956c1s v1p0967c1s
v1p0983c1s v1p0997c1s v1p1048c1s
v1p1048c2m v1p1053c1s v1p1055c1s
v1p1063c1s v1p1077c2s v1p1099c2s
v1p1100c1s v1p1104c2s v1p1132c2s
v1p1148c1s v1p1175c1s v1p1176c2s
v1p1183c2s v1p1186c2s v1p1216c2m
v1p1217c1s v1p1245c1s v1p1266c2s
v1p1272c1s v1p1284c2s v1p1289c2s
v1p1292c2s v1p1298c2s v1p1326c2s
v1p1334c2s v1p1344c1s v1p1348c1s
v1p1350c1s v1p1352c1s v1p1352c2s
v1p1354c1s v1p1371c2s v2p0002c2s
v2p0005c1s v2p0005c2s v2p0034c1s
v2p0049c1m v2p0059c1s v2p0068c2s
v2p0069c1s v2p0083c1s v2p0090c1s
v2p0091c1s v2p0092c2m v2p0098c2s
v2p0099c1s v2p0100c2m v2p0101c1s
v2p0102c2m v2p0111c1s v2p0118c1s
v2p0118c2s v2p0119c1s v2p0120c1s
v2p0120c2s v2p0124c1s v2p0132c1s
v2p0150c2s v2p0170c1s v2p0172c2s
v2p0195c1s v2p0215c1s v2p0222c1m
v2p0223c2s v2p0224c1s v2p0227c2s
v2p0230c1s v2p0240c1m v2p0251c2s
v2p0253c1m v2p0260c1s v2p0262c1s
v2p0269c2s v2p0289c1s v2p0298c1s
v2p0310c1s v2p0312c2s v2p0324c1s
v2p0332c1s v2p0333c1s v2p0348c1s
v2p0353c1s v2p0353c2s v2p0355c1s
v2p0356c1s v2p0362c2s v2p0363c1s
v2p0365c2s v2p0370c2s v2p0372c1s
v2p0384c2s v2p0413c1m v2p0414c1s
v2p0415c2s v2p0416c2s v2p0418c1m
v2p0420c2s v2p0424c2s v2p0427c1s
v2p0435c2s v2p0439c2s v2p0452c1m
v2p0465c2s v2p0466c2s v2p0474c1m
v2p0477c2s v2p0478c1s v3p0240c1s
v3p0268c2s v3p0313c1s v4p0050c2s
v4p0102c2s v4p0142c2s v4p0152c1s
v4p0323c2s v4p0520c2s v5p0014c2s
v5p0024c2s v5p0046c2s v5p0053c1s
v5p0066c1s v5p0067c1m v5p0090c2s
v5p0094c1s v5p0109c2s v5p0120c2s
v5p0122c1s v5p0123c1s v5p0145c2s
v5p0189c2s v5p0190c2s v5p0191c1s
v5p0213c2s v5p0220c1s v5p0254c2s
v5p0291c1m v5p0312c2s v5p0315c1s
v5p0324c1s v5p0328c1s v5p0362c1s
v5p0374c2s v5p0384c1s v5p0410c1s
v5p0418c1s v5p0443c2s v5p0476c2m
v5p0478c1s v5p0550c1s v5p0578c2s
v5p0583c2s v5p0592c2s v5p0618c2s
v6p0098c2s v6p0101c2s v6p0159c2s
v6p0186c2s v6p0214c1s v6p0278c2s
v6p0293c1s v6p0529c2s v6p0651c2s
v6p0656c2s v6p0667c2s v6p0673c1s
Sedgwick, A.G. and Godkin, E.L.
v1p0504c2s v2p0414c1s
v2p0420c2s
Sedgwick, A.G. and White, H.
v2p0049c1s
Sedgwick, Adam v5p0607c2s
Sedgwick, Anne D. v5p0379c1s
Sedgwick, C.B. v4p0137c2s
v4p0324c2s
Sedgwick, C.M. v1p0334c2s
v1p0335c2s v1p0612c2s v1p0662c1s
v1p1097c1s v1p1142c2s v1p1155c2s
v1p1207c2s v1p1386c1s v1p1406c2s
Sedgwick, E. v5p0497c2s
Sedgwick, E.L. and Locket, S.H.
v2p0135c1s
Sedgwick, E.M. v4p0575c1s
Sedgwick, Gen. v1p0485c2s
Sedgwick, H. v4p0153c2s
v4p0307c2s
Sedgwick, H.D. v1p0729c1s
v1p0847c2s v4p0051c2s v5p0221c1s
v6p0016c1s v6p0018c1s v6p0380c1s
v6p0423c1s v6p0491c1s v6p0647c2s
v6p0694c1s
Sedgwick, H.D., jr. v4p0094c2s
v4p0380c1s v5p0021c2s v5p0080c2s
v5p0192c1s v5p0300c1s v5p0352c1s
v5p0400c1s v5p0493c1s v5p0521c2s
v5p0575c1s v5p0604c1s v6p0014c2s
v6p0022c2s v6p0368c1s v6p0382c1s
v6p0426c2s v6p0440c1s v6p0501c1s
v6p0578c2s v6p0649c1s v6p0711c2s
Sedgwick, H.S. v6p0702c1s
Sedgwick, M.K. v5p0638c1s
Sedgwick, N.C. v6p0086c1s
Sedgwick, O.G. v5p0078c2s
Sedgwick, S.N. v6p0548c2s
Sedgwick, T. v1p0113c2s
v1p0163c2s v1p0730c2s v1p1439c1s
Sedgwick, W.T. v2p0429c1s
v2p0458c1s v4p0502c2s v4p0507c1s
v5p0042c2s v6p0522c2s v6p0569c2s
v6p0576c2s
Sedgwick, W.T. and Hough, T.
v6p0498c2s
Sedgwick-Hough v6p0498c2s
Sedille, P. v2p0019c2s
v3p0018c2m
Sedley, H. v1p0028c2s
v1p0697c1s v1p0851c2s v1p0914c1s
v3p0076c1s
Sedley, H.W. v1p0952c1s
See, H. v3p0409c1s
See, T.J.J. v3p0407c2s
v4p0034c2s v4p0070c2s v4p0178c1s
v4p0344c1s v4p0357c2s v4p0410c2s
v4p0433c1s v4p0439c2s v4p0528c1m
v4p0545c1s v4p0545c2m v5p0010c2s
v5p0035c1s v5p0035c2m v5p0037c2s
v5p0227c1s v5p0312c2s v5p0328c1m
v5p0385c1s v5p0453c2s v5p0509c1s
v5p0538c1s v5p0549c1m v5p0560c2s
v5p0561c1s v5p0571c2s v5p0579c2s
v5p0604c2s v6p0037c2s v6p0038c1s
v6p0185c2m v6p0361c1s v6p0446c1s
v6p0540c1s v6p0596c2s v6p0626c1s
v6p0671c2s v6p0681c1s
See, W. v1p0177c1s
Seebach, J.F. v5p0177c1s
v5p0263c1s v5p0369c1s v5p0631c1s
v6p0125c2s
Seebach, M.R. v6p0705c1s
Seeberg, R. v5p0351c1s
Seeberger, C.D. v6p0210c2s
Seebohm, F. v1p0139c1m
v1p0359c2s v1p0385c1s v1p0387c1s
v1p0410c1s v1p0626c1s v1p0658c1s
v1p0721c1m v1p0850c1s v1p0870c2s
v1p0953c2s v1p1090c2s v1p1215c2s
v2p0163c1m v2p0291c1s v2p0370c1s
v3p0048c2s v3p0325c1s v4p0604c2s
Seebohm, F. et al. v1p0657c1s
Seebohm, H. v2p0419c2s
v3p0036c1s v3p0046c1s v4p0406c2s
v4p0522c2s
Seebohm, H.E. v6p0247c1s
Seebohm, H.E. et al. v6p0007c1s
Seed, T.A. v6p0203c1s
Seeds, R.M. v6p0393c1s
Seeger, F. v1p0725c2s
v2p0086c2s
Seeger, M.K. v6p0490c1s
Seeger, Mary K. v5p0644c1s
Seeger, W.T. v6p0291c1s
Seegmiller, W. v5p0369c1s
Seeler, E.V. v5p0572c2s
v5p0601c1s v6p0148c2s v6p0608c2s
Seeley, E.L. v3p0080c1s
Seeley, F.P. v6p0033c2s
Seeley, H.G. v1p0352c2s
Seeley, J. v6p0265c1s
Seeley, J.E.B. v6p0006c2s
Seeley, J.H. v1p0040c1s
Seeley, J.R. v1p0165c2s
v1p0417c1s v1p0431c2s v1p0546c2s
v1p0594c1s v1p0595c1s v1p0842c2s
v1p0893c1s v1p0894c1s v1p1028c1m
v1p1028c2s v1p1060c2s v1p1121c2s
v1p1124c2s v1p1357c1s v1p1431c1s
v2p0053c2s v2p0075c1s v2p0131c2s
v2p0142c1s v2p0181c1s v2p0203c2s
v2p0204c1s v2p0223c1s v3p0132c1s
v3p0137c2s v3p0138c1s v3p0138c2s
v3p0143c1s v3p0185c1s v3p0253c1s
v3p0337c2s v3p0445c1s v4p0182c1s
v5p0617c2s
Seeley, L. v5p0484c2s

Seeley, R.H. v1p0871c2s
v1p1147c1s
Seeliger, H. v4p0037c2m
v5p0035c2s v5p0242c2s
Seeliger, H. and Holden, E.S.
v2p0417c1s
Seeliger, Prof. v4p0545c1s
Seely, A.C. and Scott, L.. v6p0627c1s
Seely, A.C., Dr. v6p0423c2s
Seely, C.A. v1p0825c2s
Seely, G.B. v2p0214c1s
v3p0295c2s
Seely, H. v3p0439c1s
Seely, H.B. v4p0200c1s
v6p0225c2s
Seely, H.M. v2p0422c2s
Seely, J. v6p0265c2s
Seelye, E.E. v4p0072c2s
Seelye, H.C. v4p0530c2s
Seelye, J. v1p0594c2s
Seelye, J.H. v1p0035c2s
v1p0589c2s v1p1000c2s v1p1055c1s
v1p1065c2s v1p1139c1s v1p1158c1s
v2p0126c2s v2p0132c2m v2p0348c1s
v3p0337c1s v3p0346c1s
Seelye, J.H. et al. v3p0091c2m
Seelye, L.C. v1p0210c2s
v1p0448c2s v1p0655c1s v5p0127c1s
Seelye, L.Clark v6p0137c2s
v6p0704c1s
Seeman, B. v1p0078c1s
v1p0993c1s v1p1149c2s
Seeman, E. and Dames, M.L.
v6p0045c2s
Seemuller, A.M.C., Mrs. .. v1p0905c2s
Seerley, F.N. v6p0585c2s
Seerley, H.H. v4p0360c2s
v5p0413c2s v6p0575c1s
Sefi, M. v1p1170c2s
Segar, M.G. v5p0348c2s
Segg, J.W. v3p0403c1s
Seghers, C.J. v2p0399c1s
Segsworth, A.E. v4p0539c1s
Seguin, E. v1p0623c2s
v1p0641c1s
Seguin, E.C. et al. v2p0221c2s
Seguin, L. v1p0285c2s
Seguin, L.G. v3p0274c2s
v3p0286c2s v3p0306c1s
Segur, Comte de v6p0242c1s
v6p0368c2s
Segur, S.D. v3p0312c2s
Sehon, J.L. v5p0512c2s
Seibold, L. v5p0144c2s
v5p0496c1s
Seidel, H. v5p0589c2s
Seidel, M. v1p0035c1s
v1p0924c1s
Seidenadel, C.W. v5p0249c2s
Seidensticker, O. v1p0531c2s
v1p0978c1s v1p0987c2s v1p1002c2s
v1p1207c2m v2p0145c1s v3p0140c1s
v3p0195c1s v3p0291c2s v4p0182c2s
v4p0223c2s
Seidl, A. v4p0388c2s
v4p0608c2s
Seidl, A. et al. v4p0405c2s
Seigfried, A. and Seigfried, J.
v6p0708c1s
Seigfried, C.A. v3p0131c1s
v3p0184c1s
Seigfried, J. and Seigfried, A.
v6p0708c1s
Seigneur, M.du v3p0369c1m
Seignobos, C. v5p0218c1s
Seiler, C. v1p1376c2s
Seiler, G.F. v1p0341c2s
Seilhamer, G.O. v1p0676c1s
v5p0148c2s
Seip, E.C. v5p0634c1s
Seiple, W.C. v6p0493c2s
Seiple, W.G. v6p0062c1s
Seiss, C.F. v2p0294c1s
v2p0461c1s
Seiss, J.A. v1p0119c2s
v1p0248c1s v1p0255c1s v1p0420c2s
v1p0529c1s v1p0690c1s v1p0756c2s
v1p0777c2s v1p0840c2s v1p0964c2s
v1p1056c2s v1p1139c1s v1p1302c2s
v4p0336c1s
Seitz, D.C. v4p0075c2s
Seitz, Don C. v1p0169c2s
Sekiya, S. v2p0128c2s
Seklemian, A.G. v5p0630c1s
Sekon, G.A. v4p0074c1s
v5p0477c1s
Selbie, J.A. v5p0056c2s
Selbie, W.B. v3p0229c2s
Selbon, L. v1p0886c2s
v1p0887c1s
Selborne, Countess of v6p0705c2s
Selborne, Earl of v3p0083c1s
v3p0086c2s v3p0182c2m
Selborne, Lord and Gale, F.
v3p0465c1s
Selby, A.D. v5p0073c1s
v6p0675c2s
Selby, A.P. v1p0551c1s
Selby, H.M. v5p0468c1s
Selby, P. v5p0339c2s
Selby, T.G. v3p0191c1s
v5p0347c2s
Selby, W.D. v2p0075c2s
v3p0075c1m v3p0356c1s
Selby-Bigge, D. v4p0176c2s
Selby-Bigge, L.A. v4p0122c2s
v4p0420c1s
Selden, C. v4p0389c2s
v4p0630c1s
Selden, C.A. v6p0188c2s
Selden, C.B. v4p0556c1s
Selden, C.P. v4p0357c1s
v4p0384c2s
Selden, G.C. v5p0425c2s
v6p0651c2s v6p0670c1s
Seler, E. v6p0015c1s
Self, E. v2p0086c2s
v2p0215c1m
Self, E.D. v3p0009c2s
Selfridge, A.J. v3p0287c1s
v3p0412c2s
Selfridge, Susan W. v5p0065c1s
v5p0235c1s
Selfridge, T.O., jr. v4p0143c1s
v4p0366c1s
Seliger, W. v4p0208c1s
Seligman, A.L. v6p0438c1s
Seligman, E.R. v6p0431c1s
Seligman, E.R.A. v2p0325c1s
v2p0347c2s v2p0408c1m v3p0049c2s
v3p0101c2s v3p0152c2s v3p0186c2s
v3p0218c2s v3p0421c1m v4p0199c1s
v4p0277c2s v4p0278c1s v4p0482c2s
v4p0565c1m v4p0565c2s v5p0175c1s
v5p0175c2s v5p0207c1s v5p0241c1s
v5p0567c2s v5p0568c2m v5p0607c1s
v6p0188c2m v6p0189c1s v6p0224c1s
v6p0238c2s v6p0292c2s v6p0386c1s
v6p0407c2s v6p0531c1s v6p0532c1s
v6p0550c1s v6p0575c2s
Seligman, E.R.A. and Taussig, T.W.
v6p0189c1s
Seligmann, C.G. v6p0450c2s
Seligsberg, A.L. v5p0186c2s
Seligsohn, M. v6p0285c2s
Selincourt, B.de v6p0037c1m
Selincourt, Basil de v6p0088c2s
v6p0411c1s
Selkirk, J.B. v2p0394c1s
v3p0206c1s v3p0258c1s
Sell, E. v4p0293c2s
Sell, H.T. v6p0341c1s
Sellack, C.S. v1p1004c1s
Sellar, A.C. v1p0267c1s
v1p0380c1s v1p0389c1s v1p0443c1s
v1p0543c1s v1p0607c1s v1p0631c1s
v1p0954c2s v1p1049c1s v1p1299c1s
v1p1356c2s v1p1357c2s v2p0253c1s
Sellar, A.G. v1p0005c2s
Sellar, E.C. v3p0077c2s
v3p0452c2s
Sellar, W.Y. v1p0184c2s
Sellards, E.H. v6p0134c1m
v6p0222c1s v6p0234c2s v6p0320c2s
v6p0489c1m v6p0598c2s
Sellars, E. v5p0459c1s
v6p0385c2s v6p0465c1s
Selle-Brandenberg, Dr. ... v4p0440c2s
Selleck, L. v6p0379c2s
Selleck, W.G. v4p0088c1s
v4p0313c2s v4p0459c2s
Sellers, C. v1p0467c1s
v1p0726c2s v1p0831c2m v1p0875c2s
v1p0997c1s v1p1003c1s v2p0148c2s
v2p0262c1s v2p0281c2m v3p0272c2s
v3p0305c1m v4p0180c1s v4p0363c1s
v4p0383c2s v4p0435c2s v5p0353c1s
v5p0367c2s v5p0372c2s
Sellers, C., jr. v2p0281c2s
Sellers, E. v3p0166c1s
v3p0267c2s v3p0344c1s v4p0104c1s
v4p0185c2s v4p0241c2s v4p0313c1s
v4p0326c1s v4p0330c2s v4p0412c1s
v4p0431c2s v4p0434c2s v4p0452c1s
v4p0456c1s v4p0482c1s v4p0528c2s
v4p0604c1s v5p0023c1s v5p0107c1s
v5p0229c2s v5p0419c1s v5p0436c2s
v5p0437c1s v5p0442c1s v5p0482c1s
v5p0575c2s v5p0612c1s v6p0055c2s
v6p0347c2s v6p0354c2s v6p0415c1s
v6p0508c2s v6p0534c2s v6p0541c1s
v6p0557c2s v6p0637c2s v6p0707c2s
Sellers, E.J. v3p0227c2s
Sellers, Edith v4p0031c1s
v4p0146c1s v4p0243c1s v4p0244c2s
v4p0308c2s v4p0452c1s v4p0481c1s
v4p0484c1s v4p0495c2s v5p0207c2s
v5p0640c2s v6p0381c2s v6p0508c1s
v6p0508c2s
Sellers, G. v2p0432c2s
Sellers, G.E. v1p0638c2s
v1p1039c1s
Sellers, H.W. v4p0514c2s
v6p0339c2s v6p0485c2s
Sellers, J.F. v6p0112c1s
Sellers, M. v4p0635c2s
v5p0644c2s
Sellers, M.P. v6p0450c1s
Sellers, W. v1p1110c2s
Sellier, C. v6p0034c2s
Selmes, M.Russell v6p0429c1s
Selmes, P.M.F. v4p0625c2s
Selon, M. v5p0005c2s
Selons, F. v3p0191c1s
v3p0232c2s v3p0463c2s
Selous, E. v6p0045c1m
v6p0067c1m v6p0067c2s v6p0068c1s
v6p0069c2m v6p0196c1s v6p0276c2m
v6p0332c1s v6p0473c2m v6p0491c1s
v6p0504c1s v6p0590c1s v6p0596c2s
v6p0611c1s v6p0614c1m v6p0628c1m
v6p0639c1m v6p0639c2s v6p0645c1m
Selous, Edmund v5p0475c1s
Selous, F. v5p0425c1s
Selous, F.C. v3p0270c2s
v4p0360c2s v4p0636c2s v5p0385c2s
Selwyn, A.R.C. v3p0314c1s
v4p0560c2s
Selwyn, E.C. v5p0436c1m
v6p0519c2s
Selwyn, G. v2p0472c2s
v5p0451c1s v5p0485c1s
Selwyn, J.H. v1p0493c2s
v2p0212c2s
Semibreve v3p0281c2s
Semly, H. v2p0219c2s
Semper, B.M. v6p0641c2s
Semper, H. v3p0018c1s
Sempers, C.T. v2p0175c1s
v2p0457c1s v3p0397c1s v3p0454c2s
v3p0463c1s
Semple, E.C. v5p0315c1s
v5p0535c2s
Semple, Ellen C. v6p0563c1s
Semple, P.B. v2p0249c2s
v2p0435c1s v3p0209c2s v3p0235c2s
Semsch, O.F. v4p0554c1s
v5p0557c2s v6p0024c2s
Sen, A.P. v6p0313c2s
Sen, Chuan v5p0438c2s
Sendall, R. v5p0538c2s
Sendall, W.J. v2p0064c2s
Senger, L.C. v5p0036c1s
v5p0585c2s
Senger, Louis C. v5p0634c1s
Senhouse, H. v5p0398c1s
v5p0585c1s
Senior, A.W. v1p1169c1s
v1p1169c2s
Senior, H. v5p0467c1s
Senior, N.W. v1p0257c2s
v1p0288c1s v1p0316c1s v1p0396c1s
v1p0398c1s v1p0486c2s v1p0517c1s
v1p0650c2s v1p0653c1s v1p0656c2s
v1p0659c1s v1p0707c2s v1p0896c1s
v1p0896c2s v1p0947c2s v1p0954c1s
v1p1031c2s v1p1245c1s v1p1305c2s
v1p1356c2s v3p0182c2s
Senior, W. v1p0021c2s
v1p0079c2s v1p0588c2s v1p0709c1s
v1p1071c1m v1p1071c2s v1p1108c1s
v1p1137c2s v1p1284c1s v1p1322c2s
v1p1436c2s v2p0436c2s v4p0338c2s
Senior, W.S. v4p0623c2s
Senior, William v3p0103c1s
Senner, J.H. v4p0224c2s
v4p0275c1m v5p0280c2s
Sennett, A.R. v5p0271c1s
v6p0247c1s
Sennett, G.B. v2p0046c2s
Sennett, R. v2p0276c2s
Sensier, A. v1p0841c1s
Senter, J.H. v1p0560c2s
Senter, O.S. v1p0198c1s
v1p0909c2s v1p0913c2s v1p1240c2s
v1p1406c2s
Seppings-Wright, H.C. v5p0618c2s
Serae, G. v5p0623c1s
Serao, M. v6p0619c2s
Serao, Matilde v5p0203c2s
v5p0531c1s
Serch, C.H. v6p0032c1s
Serge, G. v2p0016c1s
Sergeant, A. v3p0300c1s
Sergeant, H.B. v6p0507c1s
Sergeant, L. v3p0076c1s
v4p0621c1s
Sergel, C.H. v3p0028c2s
Sergi, G. v4p0352c1s
v5p0033c2s v5p0197c1s v5p0228c1s
v5p0263c1s v5p0326c2s v6p0409c1s
v6p0549c2s
Serle, L. v3p0252c1s
v3p0257c1s
Serle, T. v1p0695c2s
Serle, T.J. v1p0364c2s
Serrancino, N. v6p0441c2s
Serrano, M.J. v1p0346c2s
v5p0090c1s v5p0586c1s v6p0462c2s
Serrell, E.W. v1p0075c1s
v6p0230c1s
Serrell, E.W., jr and Lodge, O.J.
v2p0126c1s
Serrell, G. v4p0113c1s
v4p0157c2s v4p0356c2s v4p0541c2s
v5p0094c2s v5p0227c1s v5p0325c1s
v5p0377c1s v5p0460c1s v5p0528c2s
Serrell, L.W. v4p0175c2s
v5p0183c2s
Serres, M.de v1p0042c2s

v1p0117c2s v1p0795c1s v1p1160c2s
Serrin, M. v1p0399c2s
Servaes, F. v5p0054c1s
Service, J. v1p0296c2s
v1p0334c2s v1p0495c2s v1p1069c1s
v1p1109c1s
Service, J. and Fontanes, E.
v1p1243c1s
Servier, M. v1p0501c2s
Servier, O'N. v6p0297c2s
Serviss, G.P. v2p0014c1s
v2p0028c2s v2p0272c1s v2p0426c2m
v3p0024c2m v3p0269c2s v3p0274c2s
v3p0286c2m v3p0287c1s v3p0298c2s
v3p0333c2s v3p0407c1s v3p0407c2s
v3p0415c1m v3p0415c2s v4p0034c2m
v4p0063c2s v4p0361c1s v4p0441c1s
v4p0445c1s v4p0545c2s v4p0567c2s
v4p0597c1s v5p0453c1s v5p0453c2s
v6p0009c1s v6p0088c1m v6p0347c2s
v6p0375c2s v6p0497c1s v6p0502c2s
v6p0503c1s v6p0614c2s
Serviss, Garrett P. v6p0037c2s
Sessions, Carlotta L. v5p0451c1s
Sessions, F.C. v2p0006c2s
v2p0022c2s v2p0320c1s v3p0007c1m
v3p0060c1s v3p0100c2s v3p0161c2s
v3p0168c2s v3p0173c2s v3p0178c2s
v3p0191c2s v3p0263c2s v3p0265c1s
v3p0276c2s v3p0320c1s v3p0366c1s
v3p0386c1s v3p0392c1s v3p0419c2s
v3p0438c1s v3p0474c2s v4p0010c2s
v4p0082c1s
Sessions, H. v1p0741c1s
Sessions, H.C. v1p0891c2s
Sessions, R.H. v5p0164c1s
v5p0479c2s
Setchell, W.A. v6p0010c1s
v6p0376c1s v6p0638c1s
Seter, M.P. v5p0349c1s
Seth, A. v1p0450c2s
v1p0582c2s v1p1000c1s v2p0241c1s
v3p0193c1s v3p0234c2s v3p0287c1s
v4p0002c1s v4p0042c1s v4p0186c1m
v4p0253c1s v4p0308c1s v4p0337c1s
v4p0352c1s v4p0394c2s v4p0414c2s
v4p0464c2s v4p0465c1s v4p0475c1s
v5p0411c1s
Seth, Andrew v4p0168c2s
Seth, H. v2p0280c1s
Seth, J. v3p0287c2s
v3p0330c1s v4p0039c2s v4p0042c1s
v4p0179c2s v4p0192c1s v4p0447c1s
v4p0467c2s v4p0478c2s v4p0572c2s
v5p0196c1m v5p0233c1s v5p0319c1s
v5p0528c2s v5p0576c1m v6p0211c2s
v6p0378c2s
Seth, T. v4p0007c2s
Sethbridge, R. v3p0210c2s
Seton, C. v1p1175c1s
Seton, E. v6p0510c1s
v6p0653c1s
Seton, E.T. v5p0329c2s
v5p0585c1s v6p0021c1s v6p0023c2s
v6p0027c1s v6p0068c1s v6p0070c2s
v6p0086c2s v6p0101c1s v6p0168c1m
v6p0217c1s v6p0225c1s v6p0231c2s
v6p0244c2s v6p0261c2s v6p0382c2s
v6p0428c1s v6p0653c1s v6p0656c1s
v6p0684c2s v6p0706c2s
Seton, G. v2p0278c2s
Seton, Grace G. v6p0225c1s
Seton, J. v1p0941c1s
Seton, J.L. v1p0059c2s
v1p0543c1s
Seton, M. v1p0261c1s
v1p0460c2s v1p0603c1s v1p0603c2s
v1p0773c2s v1p1028c1s v1p1184c2s
v1p1187c2s v1p1195c2s v1p1372c2s
v2p0203c2s v5p0049c1s v5p0297c1s
v5p0504c1s
Seton, Mgr. v1p0200c1s
v1p1117c1s
Seton, R. v1p0111c2s
v1p0219c1s v1p0238c2s v1p0278c1s
v1p0283c1s v1p0586c1s v1p0586c2s
v1p0690c2m v1p0800c1s v1p0882c1s
v1p1032c2s v1p1119c1s v2p0270c1s
v3p0060c1s v3p0070c1s v3p0080c1s
v4p0108c1m v4p0490c1s v4p0561c1s
Seton, R., Mgr. v1p0670c2s
Seton, S.R. v4p0488c1s
Seton, W. v1p0292c2s
v1p0320c1s v1p0464c1s v1p0520c1s
v1p0583c2s v1p0781c1s v1p1030c1s
v1p1073c2s v1p1187c2s v1p1396c2s
v1p1433c1s v2p0034c2s v2p0069c2s
v2p0083c1s v2p0147c2s v2p0153c2s
v2p0342c1s v2p0349c1s v2p0409c1s
v2p0444c2s v2p0473c1s v2p0476c2s
v3p0014c1m v3p0015c1s v3p0104c2s
v3p0206c1s v3p0242c2s v3p0297c2s
v3p0300c1s v3p0357c1s v3p0382c2s
v3p0410c2s v4p0015c1s v4p0038c1s
v4p0081c1s v4p0096c1s v4p0161c2s
v4p0191c2s v4p0223c1s v4p0246c1s
v4p0317c2s v4p0351c2s v4p0449c1s
v4p0531c2s v4p0622c1s v5p0051c2s
v5p0062c2s v5p0194c1s v5p0198c1s
v5p0263c1s v5p0288c2s v5p0291c2s
v5p0400c2s v5p0441c2s v5p0513c1s
v5p0519c1s v5p0532c2s v5p0579c2s
v5p0636c2s v6p0041c2s v6p0165c2s
v6p0205c1s v6p0206c1m v6p0238c1s
v6p0245c1s v6p0450c2s v6p0531c2s
v6p0547c2s v6p0548c1s v6p0579c2s
Seton-Karr, H. v3p0454c1s
v5p0189c2s v6p0304c1s v6p0428c1s
v6p0460c2s v6p0709c2s
Seton-Karr, H.W. v3p0007c1s
v4p0333c2s v4p0536c1s v5p0210c2s
v5p0276c2s
Seton-Karr, W.S. v2p0370c1s
v3p0006c2s v3p0210c2s v3p0211c1s
v3p0212c1s v3p0461c2s v4p0194c2s
v4p0278c2s
Seton-Thompson, E. v5p0050c2s
v5p0251c1s v5p0309c1s v5p0313c2s
v5p0320c1s
Setoun, G. v5p0277c1s
Settlemier, C.R. v6p0644c1s
Settlemyer, W.H. v1p0128c1s
Sevander, J.I. v1p0857c2s
Sevasly, M. v3p0020c1s
Seve, E. v4p0020c2s
Severance, A.D. v6p0122c2s
Severance, H.O. v6p0104c1s
Severance, M.H. v5p0265c1s
Severance, M.S. v1p0046c2s
v1p1239c2s v1p1307c2s v6p0589c1s
Severance, M.S. and Wise, K.
v1p1315c1s
Severing, P. v6p0071c2s
v6p0112c2s v6p0432c1s v6p0636c2s
Severinghaus, J.D. v1p0513c2s
v1p0516c1s v1p0778c1s v4p0345c1s
v5p0047c1s v6p0642c2s
Severn, J. v1p0704c1s
Severn, W. v1p1204c1s
v1p1391c1s
Severson, T.B. v5p0565c2s
Severy, M.L. v5p0282c1s
Seville, S.H. v3p0034c1s
Sewall, A.A. v4p0343c1s
v4p0348c2s
Sewall, A.C. v2p0041c2s
v2p0414c1s
Sewall, B. v3p0284c2s
Sewall, E.D. v1p1036c1s
Sewall, E.Q. v1p0224c2s
v1p0390c1s v1p0435c2s v1p0805c2s
Sewall, F. v2p0180c2s
v2p0181c1s v2p0222c2s v3p0068c1s
v3p0150c2s v4p0013c1s v4p0243c2s
v4p0331c1s v4p0465c2s v4p0516c2s
v4p0559c2m v4p0561c1s v4p0573c1s
v5p0051c1s v5p0313c2s v5p0447c1s
v5p0483c1s v5p0563c2s v5p0621c1s
v6p0033c1s v6p0075c2s v6p0240c2s
v6p0306c2s v6p0420c1s v6p0495c2s
v6p0521c2s v6p0523c1s v6p0538c1s
v6p0602c1s v6p0628c2s v6p0642c2s
v6p0653c2s
Sewall, Frank v4p0380c2s
v5p0042c1s
Sewall, H. v3p0044c2s
Sewall, J., jr. v1p0570c1s
Sewall, J.B. v1p0224c2s
v1p0874c1s v1p1092c2s v3p0325c1s
v3p0433c2s
Sewall, J.S. v1p0003c1s
v1p0170c2s v1p0232c2s v1p0253c2s
v1p0323c2s v1p0595c1s v1p0651c1s
v1p0793c1s v1p0847c2s v1p0892c1s
v1p1064c2s v2p0198c1s v2p0265c2s
v3p0227c1s v3p0342c1s v3p0439c2s
v4p0301c2s v5p0452c1s v6p0489c1s
Sewall, M.W. v2p0205c2s
v5p0125c1s
Sewall, M.W. and Parker, Gilbert
v5p0637c2s
Sewall, M.W. et al. v4p0120c1s
v4p0162c1s
Sewall, R.K. v2p0219c2s
v2p0385c1s v5p0339c2s
Sewall, S. v1p0221c1s
v1p0837c1s v1p0846c2s v1p1181c1s
v1p1392c2s v4p0182c1s
Sewall, S.C. v1p0961c2s
Sewall, S.E. v1p0158c2s
v1p0384c2s v1p0637c2s v1p1208c2s
Sewall, S.L. v1p0700c1s
Sewall, S.S. v1p1303c2s
Sewall, W.G. v1p0298c1s
v1p0675c2s v1p0929c1s
Seward, A. v4p0013c1s
Seward, A.C. v4p0013c1s
v4p0051c1s v4p0120c2s v4p0191c1s
v4p0422c1m v4p0503c1s v4p0541c2s
v5p0210c2m v5p0236c1s v5p0623c2s
v6p0234c2s v6p0582c2s
Seward, G.F. v2p0012c1s
v2p0079c2s v4p0105c1s v4p0296c2s
v5p0445c1s
Seward, G.H. v6p0217c2s
Seward, J.L. v3p0190c2s
Seward, O.R. v3p0372c2s
v4p0322c1s
Seward, S.S. v4p0112c1s
v4p0229c1s v4p0456c2s v6p0536c2s
Seward, T.F. v4p0075c1s
v6p0261c1s v6p0347c1s
Seward, T.F. and Krehbiel, H.E.
v3p0432c2s
Seward, T.F. et al. v4p0324c1s
Seward, T.W. v2p0474c2s
Seward, W.F. v6p0066c2s
Seward, W.H. v1p0740c2s
v3p0301c1s
Sewel, J. v1p0146c1s
Sewell, E. v4p0280c2s
Sewell, E.H.D. v6p0157c2s
v6p0231c2s v6p0232c1s
Sewell, E.M. v1p0336c1m
v1p0701c1s v3p0173c2s
Sewell, H.D. v1p0332c2s
Sewell, J.A. v4p0157c1s
v4p0356c2s
Sewell, J.S. v5p0076c1s
v6p0028c2m v6p0031c1s v6p0049c1s
v6p0337c1s
Sewell, J.W. v5p0191c2s
Sewell, J.W.S. v6p0527c2s
Sewell, M.A. v1p0387c1s
Sewell, R. v1p0094c1s
v4p0278c1s v4p0627c1s v5p0284c2s
Sewell, R.V.V. v4p0032c1s
v4p0042c2s
Sewell, S.C. v1p0225c2s
Sewell, S.E. v1p0512c1s
Sewell, W. v1p0020c2s
v1p0053c1s v1p0207c1s v1p0250c1s
v1p0652c2s v1p0653c1s v1p0653c2s
v1p0656c2s v1p0954c1s v1p0954c2s
v1p1117c1s
Sexis, W. v2p0294c2s
Sexton, A.H. v4p0220c2s
v5p0066c2s v6p0248c1s
Sexton, A.Humboldt v6p0151c2s
Sexton, C. v6p0417c2s
Sexton, E.M. v4p0220c1s
v6p0568c2s v6p0697c1s
Sexton, Ella M. v6p0463c1s
v6p0703c1s
Sexton, F.B. v6p0286c2s
Sexton, F.M. v2p0216c2s
Sexton, P.T. v4p0593c1s
Sexton, S. v2p0028c2s
v3p0125c2s v3p0383c1s
Seybold, S.V. v6p0672c1s
Seyburn, S.Y. v5p0599c1s
Seyd, E. v1p0091c2s
v1p0272c2s v1p1198c2s v3p0094c1s
v3p0393c1s v3p0458c2s
Seyffarth, G. v1p0230c2s
v1p1121c2s v2p0133c2s
Seyley v4p0535c2s
Seymour, A. v1p0366c1s
Seymour, A.B. v3p0179c2s
Seymour, A.H. v4p0404c2s
Seymour, B.N. v1p1047c1s
Seymour, C. v3p0202c2s
v3p0375c2s v3p0387c2s v3p0388c2s
Seymour, E. v1p1327c2s
Seymour, E.G. v3p0105c2s
Seymour, E.G. and Seymour, I.
v5p0105c2s
Seymour, E.H. v4p0423c2s
Seymour, E.R. v1p0298c1s
v1p0779c2s v1p0934c1s v1p1439c2s
Seymour, G.F. v2p0071c1s
v2p0294c2s v2p0376c2s v4p0471c1s
Seymour, H. v1p0315c1s
v1p0918c1s v5p0396c2s v5p0425c2s
v5p0474c2s
Seymour, H. and Boutwell, G.S.
v2p0454c2s
Seymour, H., jr. v1p1078c1s
Seymour, H.D. v1p0974c1s
Seymour, H.J. v2p0059c1s
v2p0073c2s v2p0180c1s v2p0270c2m
v2p0440c2s
Seymour, H.R. v6p0498c1s
Seymour, H.W. v4p0524c2s
v6p0216c1s
Seymour, I. v5p0479c1s
v5p0482c2s
Seymour, I. and Seymour, E.G.
v5p0105c2s
Seymour, J.F. v3p0141c2s
Seymour, J.H. v2p0101c1s
v2p0123c2s v2p0180c1s v2p0184c1s
v2p0191c2s v2p0234c2s v2p0270c1s
v2p0283c1s v2p0343c1s v2p0373c1s
v2p0431c2s v2p0457c2s v2p0470c1s
v2p0476c2s
Seymour, J.S. v6p0002c2s
Seymour, L.S. v6p0236c2s
Seymour, Lucy M. v5p0267c1s
Seymour, M.A. v2p0008c1s
Seymour, M.C. v4p0049c2s
v6p0409c2s
Seymour, M.H. v1p0118c2s
v1p0659c2s v1p1120c1s
Seymour, N.P. v1p0555c1s
Seymour, R.L. v4p0017c1s
v4p0058c2s v4p0263c2s
Seymour, T.D. v2p0388c1s
v3p0005c2s v3p0012c1s v3p0025c1s
v3p0115c1s v3p0184c1m v3p0184c2s

v3p0199c2s v3p0305c1s v3p0326c2s
v3p0348c2s v3p0377c1s v3p0399c2s
v3p0400c1s v3p0427c2s v4p0241c2s
v4p0242c1s v4p0446c2s v4p0620c2s
v5p0025c1s v5p0126c2s v5p0235c1s
v5p0249c1s v6p0027c1m v6p0030c1s
v6p0037c1s v6p0038c2s v6p0295c2m
v6p0302c2s v6p0657c2s
Seymour, W. v2p0012c1s
Seymour, W.D. v2p0405c2s
Seymour, W.F. v3p0350c1s
Seyton, S. v1p0579c1s
Shackelford, C. v4p0397c2s
Shackford, C.C. v1p0061c2s
v1p0310c1s v1p0342c2s v1p0431c2s
v1p0744c2s v1p0746c1s v1p1095c1s
v1p1117c1s v1p1183c2s v1p1185c1s
v1p1214c2s v1p1277c2s v1p1378c2s
v1p1423c2s v3p0003c2s v3p0019c2s
v3p0197c1s v3p0418c2s v3p0451c2s
Shackford, J.W. v2p0027c1s
v2p0160c1s v2p0214c1s v2p0258c1s
v2p0393c1s
Shackford, M.H. v6p0215c1s
v6p0250c1s v6p0380c1m v6p0444c2s
v6p0697c2s
Shackford, Martha H. v6p0207c2s
Shackford, S. v3p0251c2s
Shackleford, A. v1p0357c1s
v1p0564c2s
Shackleford, C. v6p0058c2s
Shackleford, Ethel v6p0464c1s
Shackleton, R. v4p0075c2s
v4p0209c2s v4p0311c2s v4p0618c1s
v5p0083c2s v5p0274c1s v5p0379c1s
v6p0100c2s v6p0232c2s v6p0375c2s
v6p0382c1s v6p0577c1s v6p0587c2s
v6p0627c1s v6p0668c1s
Shackleton, R., jr. v2p0217c2s
v4p0075c1s v4p0137c2s v4p0218c2s
v4p0322c1s
Shackleton, Robert v6p0036c1s
Shackleton, W. v5p0022c1s
v5p0466c2s v6p0187c2m
Shadwell, A. v3p0120c1s
v3p0351c2s v4p0058c1s v4p0162c2s
v4p0287c1s v4p0338c2s v4p0426c1s
v4p0465c2m v4p0568c1s v5p0090c1s
v5p0091c1s v5p0150c2s v5p0170c1s
v5p0310c2s v5p0346c2s v5p0368c2s
v5p0422c2s v5p0464c2s v5p0596c2s
Shadwell, J.L. v1p1379c2s
Shadwell, L.L. v4p0585c2s
Shaen, W., Mrs. v1p0608c1s
Shafer, S.A. v6p0078c2s
v6p0177c1s v6p0362c2s v6p0664c2s
Shafer, Sara A. v6p0007c2s
Shaffer, A.W. v3p0132c1s
Shaffer, E.L. v3p0357c2s
Shaffer, N.M. v6p0386c2m
Shaffner, R. v4p0273c1m
v4p0282c1s
Shaffner, T.P. v1p1289c2s
Shafroth, J.F. v5p0133c1s
v6p0492c2s
Shafter, Helen v5p0269c1s
Shafter, W.R. v5p0508c1s
Shafto, H. v6p0216c1s
Shahan, T.J. v4p0094c1s
v4p0111c2s v4p0242c2s v4p0492c2s
v5p0151c2s v5p0313c1s v5p0461c1s
v5p0493c2s v5p0494c1s v5p0495c2s
v6p0006c1s v6p0085c2s v6p0104c2m
v6p0123c1s v6p0126c2s v6p0139c2s
v6p0160c1s v6p0252c2s v6p0277c2s
v6p0291c2s v6p0327c2s v6p0350c1s
v6p0456c2s v6p0478c1s v6p0484c2m
v6p0516c1s v6p0537c1s v6p0539c1s
v6p0548c1m v6p0558c2s v6p0582c1s
v6p0635c1s v6p0668c1s
Shahan, T.J. and Quinn, D.
v6p0272c2s
Shairp, J.C. v1p0014c2s
v1p0082c1s v1p0088c2s v1p0171c1m
v1p0178c2s v1p0318c1s v1p0441c1s
v1p0590c2s v1p0606c2s v1p0720c1s
v1p0783c2s v1p0784c2s v1p0799c2s
v1p0842c1s v1p0852c2s v1p0877c1s
v1p0877c2s v1p0950c1m v1p0959c1s
v1p1021c1s v1p1022c1s v1p1022c2m
v1p1169c1s v1p1170c1s v1p1170c2s
v1p1189c2s v1p1373c1s v1p1410c1s
v1p1430c1s v1p1430c2m v2p0003c2s
v2p0144c2m v2p0168c2m v2p0194c1s
v2p0203c1s v2p0346c1s v2p0360c1s
v2p0378c2s v2p0458c1s v2p0461c2s
v2p0479c2s
Shairp, T. v1p0240c2s
v1p0725c1s v1p1016c1s v2p0384c1s
v5p0486c1s
Shakespear, Col. and Merivale, J.H.
v1p0269c1s
Shakespear, J. v4p0345c1s
Shakespeare, E.O. v4p0468c2s
Shakespeare, W. v4p0293c2s
Shakspear, H. v2p0218c2s
Shakspeare, C. v1p1243c1s
v1p1280c1s
Shakspeare, L. v5p0338c1s
Shaku, S. v6p0684c2s
Shalders, E.W. v2p0085c2s
Shaler, N.S. v1p0279c2s
v1p0323c2s v1p0365c2s v1p0376c2m
v1p0377c1m v1p0487c1s v1p0507c2s
v1p0508c2s v1p0509c1s v1p0646c2s
v1p0792c1s v1p0805c1s v1p0809c1s
v1p0865c2s v1p0877c1s v1p0896c2s
v1p0900c1s v1p0926c2s v1p0927c2s
v1p0933c2s v1p1028c2s v1p1044c2s
v1p1084c1s v1p1174c1s v1p1198c2s
v1p1209c1s v1p1353c2s v1p1354c2s
v1p1394c2s v1p1403c1s v2p0027c1s
v2p0110c2s v2p0159c1s v2p0211c1s
v2p0212c1s v2p0299c2s v2p0309c1s
v2p0332c1s v2p0361c2s v2p0390c2s
v2p0426c2s v2p0427c2s v3p0014c1s
v3p0025c2s v3p0026c1s v3p0071c1s
v3p0073c1s v3p0091c2s v3p0098c1s
v3p0126c1s v3p0128c2s v3p0129c2s
v3p0146c1s v3p0150c1s v3p0156c2s
v3p0158c1s v3p0167c2m v3p0169c1s
v3p0173c2m v3p0177c2s v3p0200c1s
v3p0245c2s v3p0265c1s v3p0290c2s
v3p0297c2s v3p0298c2s v3p0299c1m
v3p0330c1s v3p0362c1s v3p0362c2s
v3p0380c2s v3p0383c1s v3p0384c1s
v3p0399c2s v3p0401c2s v3p0402c1s
v3p0417c1s v3p0433c1s v3p0445c1m
v3p0446c1s v3p0451c2s v3p0457c1s
v3p0458c1s v4p0048c1s v4p0048c2s
v4p0060c2s v4p0158c1s v4p0166c1s
v4p0168c2s v4p0169c1s v4p0180c1s
v4p0185c1s v4p0186c2s v4p0222c2m
v4p0223c1s v4p0263c2s v4p0273c1s
v4p0275c1s v4p0288c2s v4p0397c1s
v4p0405c1s v4p0460c2s v4p0485c1s
v4p0507c2s v4p0508c2s v4p0510c2s
v4p0511c1s v4p0566c2s v4p0593c2m
v4p0597c2s v4p0610c1s v5p0017c1s
v5p0024c1s v5p0041c1s v5p0237c2s
v5p0277c1s v5p0324c2s v5p0397c2s
v5p0403c2m v5p0517c2s v5p0561c1s
v5p0607c1s v6p0021c1s v6p0185c2s
v6p0216c1s v6p0218c1s v6p0272c1s
v6p0323c1s v6p0393c1s v6p0412c1s
v6p0490c1s v6p0502c2s v6p0674c1s
v6p0681c1s v6p0685c1s
Shaler, N.S. et al. v3p0091c2s
v5p0182c2s
Shallock, M. v1p1125c1s
Shamel, A.D. v6p0149c2s
Shami, A. v5p0170c1s
Shami, Abdullah v4p0162c2s
Shanahan, E.T. v6p0214c2m
v6p0259c1m v6p0368c1s v6p0397c1s
v6p0520c1s v6p0533c1s v6p0698c2s
Shand, A.F. v3p0097c1s
v3p0402c2s v3p0429c2s v4p0036c2m
v4p0096c1s v4p0622c1s v5p0204c2s
v5p0382c2s v5p0631c1s
Shand, A.H. v3p0097c1s
Shand, A.I. v1p0013c2s
v1p1433c2s v2p0228c1s v2p0317c2s
v2p0347c1s v3p0046c1s v3p0049c2s
v3p0208c1s v3p0392c1s v3p0430c2s
v4p0076c2s v5p0014c1s v5p0080c1s
v5p0095c2s v5p0164c1s v5p0251c2s
v5p0443c1s v6p0020c2s v6p0068c1s
v6p0068c2s v6p0108c1s v6p0132c1s
v6p0169c1s v6p0182c2s v6p0189c1s
v6p0206c2s v6p0207c2s v6p0208c2s
v6p0248c2s v6p0261c1s v6p0261c2s
v6p0275c1s v6p0379c2s v6p0383c2m
v6p0384c2m v6p0501c2s v6p0545c1m
v6p0578c2s v6p0647c2s v6p0653c2s
v6p0689c1s v6p0700c2s
Shand, Alex.I. v6p0078c1s
v6p0247c2s
Shand, J.L. v3p0072c2s
Shand, W. v1p1222c1s
Shane, C. v5p0494c1s
Shane, ara.I. v6p0301c1s
Shanet, V. v4p0081c2s
Shanhan, T.J. v5p0067c2s
Shankland, E.C. v6p0235c1s
Shanks, C.G. v1p1045c2s
Shanks, W.F.G. v1p0069c1s
v1p0167c2s v1p0171c1s v1p0222c2s
v1p0236c1s v1p0304c2s v1p0457c1s
v1p0540c2s v1p0768c2s v1p0955c2s
v1p1129c2s v1p1190c1s v1p1190c2s
v1p1433c2s v1p1435c1s
v4p0153c2s
Shanley, J.J. v6p0615c1s
Shanly, C.D. v1p0195c1s
v1p0358c2m v1p0458c1s v1p0513c1s
v1p0565c2s v1p0700c2s v1p0769c2s
v1p0916c2s v1p1193c2s
Shann, G. v6p0086c1s
Shannon, O.P. v4p0410c2s
Shannon, R.W. v5p0020c1s
v5p0316c2s v5p0475c1s v6p0095c2s
Shannon, T. v1p1363c2s
Shannon, W.F. v5p0093c2s
v5p0202c2s v5p0214c1s v6p0212c1s
Shansfield, W.N. v5p0310c2s
Sharkey, S. et al. v1p0934c1s
Sharkey, S.J. v3p0288c2s
Sharp, A. v5p0150c2s
Sharp, B. v4p0025c2s
v4p0304c1s
Sharp, B. and Hughes, W.E.
v4p0025c1s
Sharp, C.H. v6p0168c1s
Sharp, D.L. v4p0300c1s
v5p0060c2m v5p0085c2s v5p0253c2s
v5p0305c2s v5p0310c2s v5p0463c1s
v6p0067c2s v6p0180c1s v6p0403c1s
v6p0444c2s v6p0472c1s v6p0612c1s
v6p0701c1s
Sharp, Dallas L. v6p0121c1s
Sharp, E. v5p0276c1s
v5p0283c1s v5p0342c2s v6p0273c2s
Sharp, Evelyn v4p0390c2s
v4p0413c2s v6p0344c1s
Sharp, F.C. v4p0188c1s
v4p0307c2s v4p0410c1s v4p0475c1s
v5p0319c1s v5p0386c1s
Sharp, Frank C. v5p0386c1s
Sharp, G. v1p0092c2s
Sharp, H. v5p0285c1s
v5p0462c2s v5p0490c1m
Sharp, I.S. v1p0735c1s
Sharp, J. v2p0039c2s
Sharp, J.H. v5p0287c2s
Sharp, K.L. v4p0014c2s
v4p0027c2s v4p0329c1m v4p0624c2s
v5p0336c2s
Sharp, Luke v4p0153c2s
v4p0558c1s
Sharp, Luke and Burgin, G.B.
v4p0249c1s
Sharp, N. v4p0081c1s
Sharp, R.F. v3p0206c2s
v3p0406c1s v4p0444c1s v4p0561c1s
Sharp, S. v1p1122c2s
Sharp, Stella E. v5p0470c2s
Sharp, T. v5p0158c2s
Sharp, W. v2p0022c2s
v2p0036c2s v2p0076c1s v2p0126c1s
v2p0195c1s v2p0329c2s v2p0378c2m
v2p0441c2s v2p0458c2s v3p0011c2s
v3p0028c1s v3p0103c2s v3p0203c2s
v3p0245c2s v3p0247c2s v3p0267c2s
v3p0269c2s v3p0367c2s v3p0368c1s
v3p0400c2s v3p0429c1s v3p0432c1s
v3p0471c1s v4p0005c2m v4p0015c1s
v4p0031c1s v4p0050c1s v4p0090c1s
v4p0136c1s v4p0146c2s v4p0202c1s
v4p0216c1s v4p0220c1s v4p0248c1s
v4p0294c1s v4p0322c2s v4p0343c1s
v4p0349c1s v4p0358c1s v4p0383c2s
v4p0426c1s v4p0430c1s v4p0458c2s
v4p0485c2s v4p0492c1m v4p0509c2s
v4p0516c1s v4p0550c1s v4p0561c1s
v4p0577c2s v4p0605c1s v4p0613c1s
v5p0021c2s v5p0032c1s v5p0038c2s
v5p0085c1s v5p0100c2s v5p0171c2s
v5p0310c1m v5p0370c2s v5p0424c1s
v5p0473c1s v5p0495c1s v5p0532c2s
v5p0564c1s v5p0566c2s v6p0246c2s
v6p0350c1s v6p0394c2s v6p0578c2s
v6p0585c1s v6p0593c1m v6p0617c2s
v6p0642c1s
Sharp, William v2p0385c1s
v2p0391c2s v3p0448c1s v3p0448c2s
v4p0426c1s v4p0493c2s v4p0586c2s
v4p0628c2s
Sharpe, A. v3p0017c1s
v4p0005c1m v4p0344c1s v4p0390c2s
v5p0185c2s v6p0399c1s
Sharpe, A.B. v6p0156c2s
v6p0217c1s v6p0531c2s v6p0646c1s
Sharpe, A.C. v3p0020c1s
v3p0279c1m v4p0370c2s v4p0610c1s
v5p0375c2s v5p0401c2s v5p0512c2s
v6p0175c1s v6p0234c1s v6p0629c2s
v6p0664c1s
Sharpe, B.F. v5p0540c1s
Sharpe, E. v1p1422c2s
Sharpe, F. and Haigh, D.H.
v1p0272c1s
Sharpe, F.S. v5p0557c2s
Sharpe, G. v1p0103c2s
Sharpe, H.B. v6p0241c1s
v6p0249c2s v6p0322c2m
Sharpe, H.G. v4p0610c1s
v5p0028c2s v5p0501c1s
Sharpe, J. v3p0166c2s
v3p0414c1s v6p0561c2s v6p0579c1s
v6p0591c1s
Sharpe, L. v1p1318c1s
Sharpe, N.W. v6p0421c2s
Sharpe, R.B. v1p0911c1s
v1p0998c1s v2p0046c2s v3p0030c2s
v3p0314c2s v3p0407c2s v4p0060c1s
v4p0060c2s v4p0061c1s v4p0417c2s
Sharpe, R.R. v3p0013c2s
v3p0256c1s
Sharpe, S. v1p0119c1s
v1p0684c2s v2p0434c1s
Sharpey, W. v1p0157c1s
Sharples, S.P. v1p0498c1m
v1p0562c1s v2p0478c2s
Sharpless, I. v2p0026c1s
v2p0095c1s v2p0095c2s v2p0340c1s
v2p0441c2s v2p0459c1s v4p0171c1s
Sharpless, I. and Sachs, J.
v5p0179c1s
Sharpless, J.T. v1p1198c1s

Sharr, F.J. v1p0446c1s
Sharswood, G. v1p0407c2s
v1p0823c1s
Shastin, Vamadeva v2p0218c1s
Shastri v4p0107c2s
Shastri, V. v5p0287c1s
Shastri, Vamadeo v4p0042c1s
v4p0071c2s
Shattock, M. v1p1271c2s
Shattuck, G.B. v5p0257c1s
v6p0015c1s v6p0047c1s
Shattuck, H.R. v3p0029c1s
v3p0247c2s v3p0359c1s v3p0473c1s
Shattuck, L. v1p0152c1m
v1p0504c1s v1p0848c2s v1p1091c2s
v1p1416c1s
Shattuck, S.D. v3p0034c2s
Shaw, A. v2p0099c1s
v2p0119c2s v2p0130c1s v2p0184c1m
v2p0214c2s v2p0223c2s v2p0245c1m
v2p0262c1m v2p0290c2s v2p0347c1s
v2p0347c2s v2p0407c1s v2p0407c2s
v2p0452c2s v3p0009c2s v3p0012c1s
v3p0038c1s v3p0059c2s v3p0085c2s
v3p0097c2s v3p0099c1s v3p0127c2s
v3p0144c2s v3p0156c1s v3p0160c1s
v3p0174c1s v3p0184c2s v3p0204c2s
v3p0256c2s v3p0257c1s v3p0281c1s
v3p0292c1s v3p0320c2s v3p0326c2s
v3p0337c1s v3p0376c2s v3p0385c2s
v3p0398c1s v3p0408c1m v3p0420c1s
v3p0438c1s v4p0011c1s v4p0052c1s
v4p0068c1s v4p0075c1s v4p0077c2s
v4p0115c1m v4p0116c2s v4p0120c1s
v4p0129c1s v4p0224c1s v4p0246c1s
v4p0246c2s v4p0261c2s v4p0294c1s
v4p0337c2s v4p0338c2s v4p0387c2s
v4p0400c1m v4p0413c2s v4p0441c1s
v4p0499c1s v4p0502c2s v4p0509c1s
v4p0538c2s v4p0544c2s v4p0579c2s
v4p0587c2s v4p0591c1s v4p0599c1s
v5p0139c1s v5p0147c1s v5p0163c1s
v5p0197c2s v5p0227c1s v5p0234c2s
v5p0255c1s v5p0407c1s v5p0420c1s
v5p0430c2s v5p0464c2s v5p0496c1s
v5p0507c1s v5p0511c2s v5p0602c1s
v5p0603c1s v5p0603c2m v5p0620c1s
v5p0644c2s v6p0188c2s v6p0219c2s
v6p0279c1s v6p0291c1s v6p0500c2s
v6p0515c1s v6p0659c2s
Shaw, A. and Porritt, E. . v4p0174c2s
Shaw, A.A. v6p0124c2s
Shaw, A.C. v4p0151c1s
v4p0381c2s v4p0557c1s v5p0225c1s
Shaw, A.G. v5p0430c1s
Shaw, A.H. v5p0637c1s
Shaw, A.M. v6p0045c2s
v6p0464c1s v6p0467c2s v6p0540c2s
Shaw, A.N. v3p0102c1s
Shaw, A.W. v4p0431c1s
Shaw, Adele M. v5p0180c2s
v6p0116c2s v6p0213c2s v6p0231c2s
v6p0316c1s v6p0349c2s v6p0370c1s
v6p0410c2s v6p0457c2s v6p0574c2m
v6p0575c1s v6p0627c2s v6p0635c1s
v6p0658c1s v6p0673c2s
Shaw, Albert v4p0006c1s
v4p0289c1s v5p0082c1s v6p0346c1s
v6p0651c2s
Shaw, Anna v4p0630c1s
Shaw, Annette J. v4p0384c2s
Shaw, B. v1p0465c2s
v1p0762c1s v1p1109c2m v4p0193c1s
Shaw, C.A. v2p0027c2s
v2p0285c2s
Shaw, C.B. v5p0601c2s
Shaw, C.G. v2p0391c2s
v3p0255c1s v5p0115c1s v5p0607c1s
v6p0123c2s v6p0211c2s v6p0340c2s
v6p0341c1s v6p0342c2s v6p0428c2s
v6p0536c2s v6p0537c2s
Shaw, C.L. v3p0191c2s
v5p0164c1s v5p0317c2s v5p0433c2s
v5p0590c2s v5p0645c1s v6p0262c1s
v6p0377c1s v6p0650c1s
Shaw, Capt. v1p0455c1s
Shaw, E. v2p0383c1s
v5p0452c1s
Shaw, E.H. v5p0427c2s
Shaw, E.M. v1p0159c1s
v1p0454c2s v1p0455c2s v3p0153c1m
v3p0217c2s v3p0427c1m v4p0101c2s
v4p0399c1s
Shaw, E.R. v2p0265c1s
v2p0283c1s v3p0169c2s v4p0566c2s
Shaw, Edith M. v5p0640c2s
Shaw, Esther E. v6p0622c2s
Shaw, F.A. v1p0772c1s
Shaw, F.G. v4p0360c2s
Shaw, F.J. v6p0444c1s
v6p0705c2s
Shaw, F.L. v2p0145c2s
v2p0378c1s v3p0004c2s v3p0172c2s
v3p0180c2s v3p0264c2s v3p0274c2s
v3p0419c2s v3p0424c2s v3p0475c1s
Shaw, G.A. v2p0271c1s
Shaw, G.B. v2p0067c1s
v2p0278c2s v2p0456c1s v3p0337c2s
v3p0399c1s v3p0413c1s v3p0446c2s
v3p0452c2s v4p0161c1s v4p0251c2s
v4p0272c1s v4p0272c2s v4p0351c1s
v4p0358c1s v4p0371c2s v4p0383c2s
v4p0442c1s v4p0446c2s v4p0517c2s
v4p0519c1s v4p0533c2s v5p0003c1m
v5p0048c1m v5p0052c2s v5p0055c2s
v5p0079c1s v5p0083c2s v5p0112c2s
v5p0129c2m v5p0136c2s v5p0142c1s
v5p0152c1s v5p0154c2s v5p0171c1s
v5p0210c2s v5p0246c2s v5p0261c2s
v5p0278c1m v5p0278c2s v5p0299c1s
v5p0310c1s v5p0319c1s v5p0324c2s
v5p0327c1s v5p0345c2m v5p0388c1s
v5p0396c1s v5p0418c1m v5p0429c2s
v5p0432c2m v5p0451c2m v5p0485c2s
v5p0491c1m v5p0522c1s v5p0523c1s
v5p0523c2s v5p0536c1s v5p0547c2s
v5p0552c2s v5p0574c1m v5p0575c2m
v5p0585c2s v5p0623c1s v6p0673c2s
Shaw, G.B. and Goldie, G.. v2p0070c1s
Shaw, G.B. et al. v3p0399c1s
Shaw, G.F. v6p0057c2s
Shaw, G.L. v6p0652c1s
Shaw, G.M. v1p0384c1s
v1p1222c2s v1p1291c2s
Shaw, G.W. v1p0867c2s
v1p1284c1s v6p0056c2s v6p0215c2s
Shaw, H. v3p0327c1s
v3p0363c2s v3p0422c1s v6p0033c2s
Shaw, H.S.H. v1p0876c1s
v2p0223c1s v2p0270c2s v3p0062c2s
v3p0262c2s
Shaw, J. v1p0563c1s
v2p0372c2s v4p0577c1s v5p0515c1s
Shaw, J.C. v4p0104c1s
v4p0364c2s
Shaw, J.D. v2p0086c2s
v4p0199c2s
Shaw, J.G. v3p0112c2s
Shaw, L. v1p0855c1s
v1p1206c2s
Shaw, L.M. v5p0149c1s
v6p0162c1s
Shaw, Leslie M. v6p0202c1s
Shaw, Louise M. v6p0648c1s
Shaw, N. v6p0234c1s
v6p0284c2s
Shaw, P.E. v6p0197c2s
Shaw, R.B. v1p0702c2s
Shaw, R.D. v6p0680c1s
Shaw, R.Dykes v6p0607c2s
Shaw, R.G. v1p0918c1s
Shaw, T. v5p0090c1s
v5p0587c2s v6p0352c1s v6p0378c2s
Shaw, T.B. v1p0035c1s
v1p1067c2s v1p1296c1s
Shaw, V. v5p0108c1s
Shaw, Val. v6p0534c2s
Shaw, W.A. v3p0343c1s
v4p0477c2s v6p0267c2s v6p0425c1s
Shaw, W.B. v3p0379c1s
v3p0408c1s v3p0442c2s v4p0090c2s
v4p0151c1s v4p0167c1s v4p0167c2s
v4p0169c1s v4p0210c2s v4p0505c2s
v4p0531c2m v5p0175c1s v5p0266c2s
v5p0335c2s v5p0534c2s v6p0048c2s
v6p0077c2s v6p0129c1m v6p0550c2s
v6p0552c1s v6p0574c2s v6p0701c1s
Shaw, W.H. v4p0152c1s
Shaw, W.J. v1p0583c2s
v5p0092c2s
Shaw, W.J. and Baldwin, J.M.
v4p0364c2s
Shaw, W.M. v6p0413c1s
Shaw, W.N. v2p0160c1s
v5p0254c1s v5p0345c2s v6p0040c1m
v6p0048c2s v6p0082c1s v6p0581c1s
Shaw-Lefevre, G. v2p0370c1s
v3p0255c2s v3p0257c1s v3p0267c2s
v4p0355c1s
Shaw-Lefevre, G.J. v1p1246c1s
Shaw-Lefevre, J.G. et al.. v3p0221c2s
Shaw-Sparrow, W. v4p0422c1s
v4p0544c1s v5p0402c1s
v6p0598c2s v6p0676c2s v6p0690c2s
Shawham, J.M. et al. v6p0123c2s
Shawmut, W.G. v1p0987c2s
Shawn, E. v6p0344c2s
Shayler, J. v6p0460c2s
Shaylor, J. v4p0067c2s
v4p0291c1s v5p0069c2s v5p0070c1m
v5p0323c1s v5p0440c1s v6p0075c1s
v6p0124c1s v6p0539c2s
Shea, C.C. v5p0506c1s
Shea, C.E. v3p0431c1s
Shea, D.W. v3p0134c2s
Shea, J. v1p0071c2s
Shea, J.A. v1p0421c1s
Shea, J.G. v1p0003c2s
v1p0028c2s v1p0029c1s v1p0100c2s
v1p0119c1s v1p0119c2s v1p0143c2s
v1p0195c1s v1p0209c2s v1p0216c1m
v1p0227c1s v1p0330c2s v1p0448c2s
v1p0492c2s v1p0500c1s v1p0637c1s
v1p0643c1s v1p0658c1s v1p0676c2s
v1p0683c2m v1p0692c1s v1p0726c1s
v1p0784c1s v1p0802c1s v1p0805c1s
v1p0806c1s v1p0852c2s v1p0906c2s
v1p0915c2s v1p0918c1s v1p0936c1s
v1p0957c1s v1p1115c2s v1p1116c1s
v1p1117c1m v1p1117c2m v1p1119c2s
v1p1120c2s v1p1142c2s v1p1155c1s
v1p1184c2s v1p1242c2s v1p1374c1s
v1p1433c1s v2p0010c2s v2p0011c1s
v2p0032c2s v2p0037c1s v2p0071c2s
v2p0094c2s v2p0166c1s v2p0245c1s
v2p0279c1s v2p0286c1s v2p0357c1m
v2p0360c1s v2p0375c1s v2p0375c2m
v2p0376c1m v2p0383c1s v2p0425c2s
v2p0452c2s v3p0010c1s v3p0041c1s
v3p0047c1s v3p0051c1s v3p0093c2s
v3p0129c2s v3p0225c1s v3p0226c2s
v3p0228c2s v3p0235c1s v3p0329c1s
v3p0349c2s v3p0364c1s
v3p0364c2m
Sheaf, E.T. v6p0450c2s
v6p0508c1s
Sheafer, F.B. v5p0452c2s
v5p0552c2s v6p0145c1s
Sheafer, H.C. v1p0965c2s
v1p0988c1s v6p0005c1s
Sheafer, P.W. v1p0267c2s
Sheafer Bros. v1p0269c1s
v1p1182c2s
Sheahan, J.W. v1p0147c2s
v1p0352c2s v1p0446c1s v1p0744c2s
Sheak, W.H. v6p0210c2s
Shean, A.W.C. v3p0153c1s
v3p0427c1s
Shean, C.M. v5p0156c1s
v6p0033c2s v6p0436c2s
Shear, C.L. v6p0077c2s
Sheard, C. v5p0372c2s
v6p0111c2s v6p0498c1s
Sheard, V. v5p0116c1s
v5p0339c1s v5p0356c2s v5p0371c2s
v5p0437c2s v5p0486c1s v6p0057c1s
v6p0084c1s v6p0234c1s v6p0287c2s
v6p0300c2s v6p0467c1s v6p0467c2s
v6p0551c2s v6p0625c1s
Sheardown, A.F. v4p0607c1s
Shearer, G.L. v4p0016c1s
Shearer, H. v5p0082c1s
Shearer, W.J. v5p0265c1s
v5p0471c2s v5p0512c2s v6p0263c1s
v6p0575c1s
Shearman, A. v1p1035c1s
Shearman, M. v3p0157c2s
Shearman, M.A. v1p0037c2s
Shearman, T.G. v1p0097c2s
v1p0107c2s v1p0258c2s v1p0294c2s
v1p0693c2s v1p0729c2s v1p0734c2s
v1p0916c1s v1p0976c2s v1p1057c2s
v1p1087c1m v1p1226c1s v1p1234c1s
v1p1245c1s v1p1252c1s v1p1265c1s
v1p1285c2s v1p1355c1s v1p1426c1s
v3p0044c1s v3p0163c1s v3p0170c1s
v3p0347c1s v3p0420c1s v3p0421c1m
v3p0458c1s v4p0192c1s v4p0378c1s
v5p0147c2s v5p0486c1s v5p0567c2s
v5p0568c1s
Shearman, T.G. et al. v4p0462c2s
Shears, G.F. v6p0409c1s
Shearwood, J.A. v5p0143c1s
Sheavyn, P. v6p0709c1s
Shebbeare, C.J. v4p0030c1s
v5p0117c2s v6p0225c1s v6p0370c1s
Sheble, F. and Smith, W.C.
v3p0456c2s
Shedd, E.C. v5p0552c1s
v5p0590c1s
Shedd, G.T. v2p0181c1s
Shedd, H.F. v4p0430c1m
Shedd, J.C. v6p0052c2s
Shedd, J.G. v6p0113c1s
Shedd, J.H. v2p0230c2s
Shedd, W.A. v4p0056c1s
v5p0380c1s v6p0630c2s
Shedd, W.B. v1p1379c1s
Shedd, W.G.T. v1p0011c1s
v1p0074c1s v1p0125c2s v1p0276c1s
v1p0290c2s v1p0419c1s v1p0593c1s
v1p0601c2s v1p0723c2s v1p0850c1s
v1p0858c2s v1p1043c2s v1p1044c1s
v1p1179c1m v1p1263c1m v2p0146c2s
v2p0169c2s v2p0285c1s v2p0340c2s
v3p0054c2s v3p0229c1s v3p0271c2s
v3p0345c1s
Shedlock, J.S. v2p0031c2m
v2p0040c2s v2p0047c2s v2p0093c1s
v2p0180c2s v2p0195c2m v2p0252c2s
v2p0260c1s v2p0300c2s v2p0303c1s
v2p0314c1s v2p0362c1s v2p0388c2s
v2p0416c1s v2p0464c1m v3p0039c2s
v3p0100c2s v3p0107c1s v3p0189c2s
v3p0246c1m v3p0293c2s v3p0414c2s
v4p0040c2s v4p0049c2s v4p0061c2s
v4p0213c1s v4p0228c2s v4p0233c1s
v4p0248c2s v4p0254c1s v4p0325c1s
v4p0337c2s v4p0388c2s v4p0389c2s
v4p0467c2s v4p0494c1s v4p0506c2s
v4p0586c1s v4p0602c2s v5p0575c2s
Shee, G. v1p0662c2s
v2p0228c2s
Shee, G.F. v6p0031c2s
v6p0268c2s v6p0498c2s
Shee, W.A. v2p0326c1s
Sheedy, M.M. v3p0238c2s
v3p0364c1m v3p0378c1s v4p0488c2s
v5p0366c1s
Sheedy, Morgan M. v6p0326c2s

Sheehan, J. v1p0445c2s v1p0468c1s v1p0520c1s v1p0541c1s v1p0695c2s v1p0710c2s v1p0773c1s v1p0775c2s v1p0814c1m v1p0957c1s v1p1072c2s v1p1101c2s v1p1102c1s v1p1230c1s v1p1287c1s v1p1288c2s v1p1327c1s v1p1334c1s
Sheehan, J.F., jr. v4p0502c1s
Sheehan, P. v3p0223c1s
Sheehan, P.A. v3p0026c2s v4p0213c1s
Sheehan, P.P. v6p0456c1s
Sheehan, T. v1p0407c1s
Sheehan, W.F. v6p0480c2s
Sheehy-Skeffington, F. ... v6p0166c1s
Sheeleigh, M. v1p0778c1s v1p1270c1s v2p0361c1s
Sheepshanks, J. v4p0077c2s
Sheets, B.F. et al. v4p0459c2s
Sheeve, S.H. v1p1259c1s
Sheffauer, H. v6p0485c1s
Sheffey, H.W. v2p0096c2s v3p0347c1s
Sheffey-Peters, M. v4p0198c1s
Sheffield, D.C. v2p0081c2s
Sheffield, D.Z. v2p0098c2s v2p0369c1s v3p0058c2s v5p0109c1s v5p0110c2s v5p0113c1s
Sheffield, E.L. v3p0444c2s
Sheffield, E.N. v2p0257c2s v2p0477c1s v3p0345c2s
Sheffield, H. v4p0107c2s
Sheffield, J.R. v5p0207c2s
Sheffield, M.W. v4p0201c1s
Sheffield, W.F. and Payne, A. v2p0372c1s
Sheffield, W.M. v4p0162c2s v5p0318c2s
Sheffield, W.P. v3p0154c1s v3p0327c1s v4p0232c2s
Shehan, J.W. v1p0227c1s v1p0228c1s
Sheibert, I. and Orleans, L.P.d' v1p0518c2s
Sheil, R.L. v1p0458c2s
Sheilds, E.D. v6p0011c2s v6p0101c2s v6p0280c2s v6p0450c2s v6p0665c1s
Sheilds, E.Douglas v6p0179c2s v6p0295c1s v6p0545c2s v6p0662c1s
Sheirber, E. v3p0264c2s
Sheirr, R.J. v1p0877c2s v1p1171c2s v1p1306c2s v1p1386c2s
Shelby, J.T. v5p0315c1s
Sheldahl, Della R. v5p0469c2s
Sheldon, A. v2p0133c2s
Sheldon, A.E. v6p0225c2s
Sheldon, A.Z. v3p0266c2s
Sheldon, C. v5p0578c2s
Sheldon, C. and Barrows, A.C. v5p0455c2s
Sheldon, C.M. v3p0281c1s v3p0399c2s v5p0016c2s v5p0409c2s v5p0575c2s v6p0122c2s v6p0139c1s v6p0349c2s v6p0514c2s v6p0518c2s v6p0675c2s v6p0708c2s
Sheldon, C.M. and Bliss, W.D.P. v6p0125c1s
Sheldon, C.M. et al v3p0083c2s
Sheldon, C.P. v1p0603c1s
Sheldon, Caroline v6p0307c2s v6p0385c2s v6p0486c1s
Sheldon, D.N. v1p0598c2s
Sheldon, E.A. v1p0935c2s
Sheldon, E.S. v5p0152c2s
Sheldon, F. v1p0098c1s v1p0103c2s v1p0292c1s v1p0311c1s v1p0350c2s v1p0471c2s v1p0572c2s v1p0681c1m v1p0850c2s v1p0957c2m v1p1092c1s v1p1417c1s v1p1420c2s v2p0035c1s v2p0320c2s
Sheldon, F.E. v2p0040c1s v2p0079c2s v3p0063c2s v3p0068c1s v3p0109c1s v4p0501c2s
Sheldon, G. v3p0113c2s v4p0151c1s v4p0529c1s v5p0157c1s v5p0288c1s v5p0365c2s v5p0595c1s v6p0057c1s v6p0072c2s v6p0168c1s
Sheldon, G. and Upham, W.P. v4p0328c1s
Sheldon, G.W. v1p0213c2s v1p0328c2s v1p0916c2s v1p1385c2s v2p0089c2s v2p0326c1s v2p0400c2m v3p0082c2s v4p0285c1s v4p0365c2s
Sheldon, H.C. v1p0074c2s v3p0339c1s v4p0326c2s v5p0511c1s v6p0065c1s v6p0413c1s
Sheldon, H.D. v4p0282c2s v5p0107c1s v6p0193c1s
Sheldon, H.G. v5p0334c1s
Sheldon, J. v1p0680c2s v2p0351c2s v2p0366c2s v3p0066c1s v3p0318c2s v3p0393c1s
Sheldon, L.A. v3p0063c1s v3p0165c1s v4p0328c1s v4p0342c2s v4p0472c1s v6p0070c1s v6p0144c2s v6p0248c1s v6p0329c2s v6p0594c2s
Sheldon, L.H. v1p0818c1s
Sheldon, L.V. and Austen, E.J. v4p0342c1s
Sheldon, L.W. v5p0430c1s
Sheldon, M.B. v4p0334c2s
Sheldon, N.L. v5p0414c2s v6p0168c1s v6p0482c1s
Sheldon, S. v3p0133c2s v3p0134c1m v3p0380c2s
Sheldon, S. and Trowbridge, J. v3p0214c2s v3p0305c1s
Sheldon, W.D. v3p0091c2s v3p0128c2s v4p0118c1s v4p0123c1s v6p0211c2m v6p0391c1s v6p0572c2m
Sheldon, W.H. v5p0470c1s v6p0412c2s v6p0446c1s v6p0670c1s
Sheldon, W.L. v3p0302c1s v3p0355c1s v4p0187c2s v4p0224c1s v4p0241c1s v4p0314c2m v4p0462c1s v4p0518c1s v4p0537c1s v4p0542c1s v4p0562c1s v4p0578c2s v5p0523c2s v6p0145c2s
Sheldrake, S. v5p0397c1s
Sheldrake, T. v1p0181c2s
Shelfer, L.H. v6p0648c1s
Shelford, W. v2p0065c2s
Shellabarger, S. v1p0282c2s
Shelle, K.La v6p0459c1s
Shelle, Kirke La v5p0576c1s
Shelley, C. v4p0215c2s v4p0277c2s v4p0588c1s v5p0149c1s v5p0262c2s v5p0326c1s
Shelley, F. v4p0357c1s
Shelley, H.C. v4p0089c2s v4p0162c2s v4p0166c2s v4p0231c2s v4p0270c1s v4p0331c1s v4p0336c2s v5p0270c1m v5p0295c1s v5p0413c1s v5p0439c2s v5p0440c1s v5p0505c1s v5p0519c1s v5p0528c2s v5p0546c1s v5p0554c1m v5p0616c2s v5p0629c1s v5p0642c1s v5p0646c1s v6p0201c1s v6p0261c1s v6p0264c2s v6p0541c2s v6p0593c2s
Shelley, Lady v2p0399c2s
Shelley, M.W. v1p0583c1s
Shelley, M.W., Mrs. v1p1321c2s
Shelley, P.B. v1p1383c2s
Shelling, F.E. v3p0276c2s v5p0485c1s
Shelly, J. v2p0256c2s
Shelton, A. v1p1331c1s
Shelton, C.M. v6p0223c1s v6p0541c2s
Shelton, F.H. v5p0226c2s v6p0307c2s
Shelton, F.W. v1p0066c2s v1p0084c2s v1p0152c2s v1p0350c2s v1p0602c1m v1p0719c2s v1p0720c1s v1p0972c1s v1p1180c2s v1p1211c2s
Shelton, J.DeF. v4p0268c2s v4p0396c2s
Shelton, J.W. v1p0719c1s
Shelton, Jane De F. v4p0405c1s
Shelton, K. v2p0110c2s v4p0234c2s
Shelton, Keziah v6p0001c2s
Shelton, R.B. v6p0627c1s
Shelton, Rosa T. v5p0531c1s
Shelton, S. v4p0193c1s
Shelton, W.H. v3p0189c2s v3p0443c1s v4p0162c2s v4p0352c2s v4p0590c1s v4p0616c1s v5p0071c1s v5p0130c1s v5p0359c1s v5p0635c2s v6p0452c1s v6p0565c2s v6p0598c1s
Shenck, W.A. v5p0294c2s
Sheneman, S. v1p1349c1s
Shenstone, J.C. v6p0288c1s
Shenstone, W.A. v5p0613c2s v6p0040c1m v6p0100c2s v6p0112c1m v6p0185c2s v6p0211c2s v6p0222c1s v6p0375c2s v6p0376c1s v6p0376c2s v6p0406c2m v6p0424c1s v6p0432c1s v6p0526c2m v6p0527c1s v6p0603c1s v6p0691c1s
Shenton, F.K.J. v1p0756c1s v1p1414c1s
Shepard, B.F. v1p0989c2s
Shepard, C.U. v1p0225c2s v1p0304c2s v1p0508c2s v1p0509c1s v1p0666c2s v1p0809c1s v1p0827c1s v1p0827c2s v1p0828c1m v1p0828c2m v1p0845c1m v1p0989c2s v1p1002c2s v1p1240c2s v1p1251c2s v2p0285c2s v2p0294c2s v2p0295c1s
Shepard, C.U., jr. v1p1002c2s
Shepard, C.U., Sen. v1p0828c1m v1p0845c1s
Shepard, E. v3p0298c2s
Shepard, E.A. v4p0163c1s
Shepard, E.M. v2p0086c2s v4p0074c2s v4p0115c1s v4p0576c2s v5p0301c1s v5p0407c1s v5p0445c1s v5p0603c2s v6p0151c1s v6p0170c1s v6p0289c1s v6p0365c1s v6p0453c2s
Shepard, E.M. and McCall, S.W. v6p0667c1s
Shepard, E.S. v5p0448c1s
Shepard, F.J. v4p0078c1s v6p0088c2s v6p0345c1s
Shepard, F.N. v6p0407c2s
Shepard, G. v1p0177c2s v1p0256c1s v1p0261c2s v1p0343c2s v1p0404c1s v1p0472c1s v1p0558c2s v1p0566c2s v1p0847c1s v1p0946c1s v1p1043c1s v1p1043c2s v1p1223c1s
Shepard, G.H. v5p0050c1s v5p0184c2s v5p0619c1s
Shepard, H.M. v4p0307c1s
Shepard, H.N. v4p0115c1s v6p0107c1s v6p0170c1s v6p0172c1s
Shepard, I. v5p0413c2s
Shepard, I.S. v6p0173c2s
Shepard, J. v3p0320c1s v3p0323c1s v4p0129c2s v4p0550c2s v5p0357c2s v5p0462c1s v5p0629c2s v6p0070c1s v6p0345c1s v6p0389c2s
Shepard, J.F. v6p0470c1s
Shepard, J.H. and Griffis, H.L. v3p0075c2s
Shepard, J.S. v6p0205c2s v6p0291c1s v6p0460c2s v6p0484c1s
Shepard, M.D. v5p0405c1s
Shepard, R.H. v2p0247c1s
Shepard, S.E. v1p0040c2s v1p0048c1s v1p0096c1s v1p0096c2s v1p0138c1s v1p0255c1m v1p0296c2s v1p0432c2s v1p0440c1s v1p0507c1s v1p0536c2s v1p1093c2s v1p1139c1s v1p1175c2s
Shepard, T. v1p1105c1s
Shepard, W.K. v5p0538c2s
Shepardson, F.W. v4p0015c1s v4p0260c1s v4p0584c1s v5p0015c2s v5p0242c2s v5p0301c1s v5p0367c2s v5p0511c1s v5p0599c1s v5p0600c1s v5p0601c2m v6p0345c2s v6p0515c1s
Shepardson, Francis W. ... v6p0160c2s
Shepardson, G.D. v5p0476c1s
Shephard, A.K. v1p0833c1s
Shephard, C.U. v1p0327c2s
Shephard, H.H. v6p0291c1s v6p0313c1s
Shephard, J. v4p0002c2s
Shephard, J.S. v6p0460c1s
Shepheard, W.P.B. v4p0555c1s
Shepherd, A.Hill v3p0389c2s
Shepherd, A.K. v1p1148c1s
Shepherd, C.M. v5p0470c1s
Shepherd, C.O. v6p0293c2s
Shepherd, E.S. and Day, A.L. v6p0418c2s
Shepherd, F.J. v2p0015c2s v2p0211c1s v2p0360c2s
Shepherd, H.E. v1p1288c1s v2p0040c1s v2p0091c2s v2p0148c2s v3p0140c2m v3p0355c1s v5p0192c2s v5p0342c1s v5p0540c2s v5p0573c1s v6p0081c2s
Shepherd, H.L. v6p0497c1s
Shepherd, J.A. v6p0588c2s
Shepherd, Lettie E. v5p0565c2s
Shepherd, N.G. v1p0166c1s
Shepherd, R.H. v1p0201c1s v1p0719c2s v2p0058c2s v2p0068c2s v2p0151c2s v2p0246c2s v2p0264c2s v2p0265c2s v2p0380c2s v2p0435c1s v3p0117c1s v3p0385c1s v3p0417c2s
Shepherd, T.B. v6p0107c1s v6p0478c2s v6p0551c2s
Shepherd, W.R. v5p0457c1m v6p0387c2m v6p0698c2m
Shepley, G.F. v1p1107c1s
Sheppard, E. v1p0230c1s
Sheppard, E.T. v6p0146c1s
Sheppard, F.H. v1p0837c1s
Sheppard, H.J. v1p1329c1s
Sheppard, J. v6p0143c1s
Sheppard, J.G. v1p0217c2s v1p0450c1s
Sheppard, J.H. v1p0048c2m v1p0165c1s v1p0363c1s v1p0371c1s v1p0557c1s v1p0602c2s v1p0740c1m v1p0910c2s v1p1152c1s v1p1363c2s v1p1410c1s v1p1416c1s
Sheppard, M. v1p1107c2s
Sheppard, N. v1p0354c2s v1p0524c2s v1p0546c1s v1p0714c1s v1p0971c1s v1p1341c2s v1p1379c1s
Sheppard, R.S. v1p1178c1s
Sheppard, S.T. v6p0416c2s
Sheppard, T. v5p0358c2s v6p0020c2s v6p0084c2s v6p0302c1m v6p0548c2s v6p0629c2s
Sheppard, W.F. v5p0550c2s
Sheppard, W.L. v5p0396c1s
Shepperd, E. v3p0466c2s
Shepstone, H. v6p0117c2s
Shepstone, H.J. v5p0108c1s v5p0150c2s v6p0180c1s v6p0653c2s
Sheran, W. v6p0020c2s
Sheran, W.H. v5p0393c1s v5p0409c1s v5p0522c2s
Sherard, R. v5p0169c1s
Sherard, R.H. v2p0070c1s v3p0009c2s v3p0315c2s v4p0032c1s v4p0042c2s v4p0076c2s v4p0080c2s v4p0082c2s v4p0099c1s v4p0141c1s v4p0148c1s v4p0164c1s v4p0201c1s v4p0232c1s v4p0251c1s v4p0271c2s v4p0301c2s v4p0577c2m v4p0603c1s v4p0618c1s v4p0637c1s v5p0021c2s v5p0034c1s v5p0137c2s v5p0219c2s

v5p0261c1s v5p0607c1s
Sherard, R.N. v4p0360c1s
Sherard, R.R. v4p0327c1s
Sheraton, J.P. v4p0468c1s
v5p0174c1s v5p0429c2s v5p0495c2s
Sherborn, C.D. v4p0394c2s
v4p0419c1s
Sherborn, C.D. and Woodward, A.S.
v4p0584c1s
Sherbourn, C.S. v3p0157c2s
Sherbrooke, Lord v1p0658c1s
v1p0936c1m v1p0973c2m v2p0295c1s
v2p0330c1s
Sherbrooke, Visc. v2p0331c1s
Sherburne, E.R. v6p0590c2m
Sherck, C.R. v5p0464c1s
Sherer, E. v1p1054c2s
v2p0070c2s
Sherer, J.W. v1p0790c1s
v2p0032c2m v2p0253c2s v2p0458c1s
v2p0464c1s v3p0031c2s v3p0214c1s
v3p0333c1s v3p0396c1s v3p0447c1s
v3p0465c2s v4p0229c2s v4p0285c1s
v4p0306c1s v4p0341c2s v4p0345c2s
v4p0346c1s v4p0366c1s v4p0381c1s
v4p0494c2s v4p0500c2s v4p0509c2s
v4p0574c2s v4p0620c2s v5p0068c1s
v5p0203c2s v5p0342c2s v5p0390c1s
v5p0520c2s v5p0563c1s v6p0177c1s
v6p0699c2s
Sheridan, A. v3p0384c2s
Sheridan, H. v2p0447c2s
Sheridan, M. v4p0153c1s
Sheridan, N. v6p0535c2s
Sheridan, P.H. v2p0453c1s
v3p0161c1s v3p0179c1s v3p0443c1s
Sheridan, S. v2p0163c2s
v2p0201c2s v2p0216c1s v2p0237c2s
Sheridan, S.N., jr. v2p0216c1s
v3p0115c1s v3p0210c1s v3p0238c1s
v3p0286c2s
Sheridan, Sol.N. v5p0359c1s
Sheriff, A.M.E. v6p0694c1s
Sheringham, H. and Meakin, N.
v6p0154c2s
Sheringham, H.T. v5p0211c2s
v6p0084c1s v6p0658c1s
Sherington, R.O. v6p0642c1s
v6p0650c2s
Sherlock, C.R. v5p0403c2s
v6p0209c1s
Sherlock, F. v4p0243c1s
Sherman, A.S. v4p0104c1s
Sherman, A.W. v4p0496c2s
Sherman, B.R. v2p0356c1s
Sherman, C. v2p0288c1s
Sherman, C.K. v5p0499c1s
Sherman, C.P. v3p0291c1s
Sherman, D. v1p0847c1s
v1p1190c2s v2p0219c2s v2p0229c2s
v2p0400c1s v3p0339c2s
Sherman, E.B. v4p0352c1s
v4p0371c1s v5p0013c1s v5p0070c1s
v5p0164c1s v5p0276c1s v5p0362c1s
v5p0415c1s v5p0443c1s v5p0506c1s
v5p0532c1s v6p0538c2s
Sherman, F. v4p0485c2s
v5p0640c1s v6p0663c2s
Sherman, F.D. v3p0008c1s
v3p0305c2s v3p0312c1s v3p0366c1s
v4p0079c1s v4p0482c1s v4p0522c1s
v6p0407c2s
Sherman, H. v1p0947c1s
v1p1350c1s
Sherman, Hoyt v5p0242c2s
Sherman, J. v1p0023c2s
v1p1232c2s v3p0305c1s v4p0593c1s
Sherman, J. et al. v1p1232c2s
Sherman, J.Dickinson, Mrs.
v6p0706c1s
Sherman, J.L. v2p0357c2s
Sherman, John et al. v4p0526c1s
Sherman, L.A. v1p0999c1s
v2p0386c1s v4p0076c1s v4p0184c1m
v4p0269c1s v4p0335c1s v4p0508c1s
v5p0016c1m v5p0144c2s v6p0234c1s
v6p0583c2s
Sherman, L.A. et al. v4p0335c2s
Sherman, L.D. v6p0099c1s
v6p0145c1s v6p0599c1s
Sherman, M. v6p0114c1s
v6p0638c2s
Sherman, Minnie E. v3p0390c2s
Sherman, O.T. v1p0055c1s
v1p0159c2s v2p0095c2s v2p0335c1s
v2p0413c2s v2p0438c2s v3p0407c1s
v3p0416c1s v3p0475c2m v4p0556c2s
Sherman, P.E. v6p0308c2s
Sherman, R. v4p0116c1s
v4p0544c2s v6p0611c1s
Sherman, R. and Lathrop, G.P.
v2p0102c2s
Sherman, R.E. v2p0292c1s
Sherman, S.A. v5p0392c1s
Sherman, S.O. v3p0050c2s
Sherman, S.O. and Hutchins, W.F.
v6p0365c1s
Sherman, Stephen O. and
Hutchins, Weston F. ... v6p0405c1s
Sherman, T. v5p0283c1s
Sherman, T.E. v2p0280c2s
Sherman, T.I. v4p0201c1s
Sherman, T.T. v6p0590c2s
Sherman, W.T. v1p0784c2s
v1p1148c2s v2p0184c2s v3p0047c1s
v3p0063c2s v3p0178c2s v3p0179c1s
v3p0298c2s v3p0390c2s v3p0443c1s
v3p0449c2s v5p0219c1s v5p0375c1s
v5p0375c2s v5p0525c2s v6p0264c1s
Sherman, W.T. et al. v3p0360c2s
Sherrington, C.S. v4p0327c2s
v5p0187c1s v6p0082c1s v6p0409c1s
v6p0449c2s v6p0535c1s v6p0575c2s
Sherrington, M. v6p0011c2s
v6p0012c1s v6p0014c2s v6p0040c2s
v6p0200c2s v6p0286c2s v6p0401c1s
v6p0466c1s v6p0604c1s v6p0698c2s
Shervinton, C.R.St.Leger . v5p0354c2s
Shervinton, M.C.I. v6p0466c2s
v6p0679c1s
Sherwell, A. v4p0159c2s
v5p0265c1s v5p0378c2s v6p0637c2s
Sherwin, T. v1p0442c1s
v1p0627c2s v1p0811c1s v1p0986c1s
Sherwood, A. v1p0732c2s
v3p0072c2s v3p0410c1s
Sherwood, E. v4p0584c1s
v6p0484c1s
Sherwood, Eleanor P. v4p0389c1s
Sherwood, G.W. v4p0403c2s
Sherwood, I. v1p0304c2s
Sherwood, J. v3p0173c1s
Sherwood, J.D. v1p0202c1s
v1p0230c1s v1p0336c2s v1p0350c2s
v1p0709c2s v1p0922c1s v1p1010c1s
v1p1100c1s v1p1105c1s v1p1254c2s
v1p1295c1s
Sherwood, J.M. v1p0145c1s
v1p0846c2m v1p1046c2s v1p1089c2s
v1p1171c1s v1p1198c1s v1p1240c1s
v1p1347c2s v2p0260c2s v2p0405c2s
Sherwood, K.B. v3p0289c2s
v3p0327c2s
Sherwood, L. v1p0343c1s
v1p0650c1s v1p1206c2s v1p1347c1s
Sherwood, M. v5p0052c2s
v5p0326c1s v6p0131c2s
Sherwood, M.E.W. v1p0511c1s
v1p1329c1s v2p0223c2s v3p0011c2s
v3p0012c2s v3p0107c1s v3p0141c2s
v3p0385c2s v3p0444c1s v4p0003c1s
v4p0048c2s v4p0593c2s v4p0612c1s
v5p0407c1s v5p0565c2s
Sherwood, M.E.W., Mrs. ... v1p0744c2s
v1p1426c2s
Sherwood, Margaret v5p0608c1s
v6p0140c2s v6p0164c2s v6p0516c2m
v6p0525c1s v6p0585c1s v6p0680c2s
Sherwood, R.H. v1p0789c2s
v1p1119c1s
Sherwood, S. v4p0138c2s
v4p0199c1s v4p0378c1s v4p0472c2s
v4p0593c1s v5p0045c2s v5p0175c2m
v5p0176c1s v5p0593c1s
Sherwood, V. v1p0910c1s
v1p1223c2s v1p1420c2s
Sherwood, V., Mrs. v1p0034c2s
Sherwood, W.A. v4p0030c1s
v4p0082c2s v4p0199c2s v4p0455c2s
Sherzer, W.H. v4p0555c2s
v5p0374c1s v6p0257c2s
Shetfield, H.E.M. v3p0228c1s
v3p0413c2s
Shettle, G.T. v4p0127c1s
Shevitch, S.E. v1p1138c1s
Shew, W. v1p1003c2s
Shewin, H. v2p0079c2s
v2p0288c1s
Shibley, F.W. v5p0628c1s
v6p0352c2s v6p0574c1s
Shibley, G.H. v5p0281c2s
v5p0465c1s v5p0605c1s v6p0395c2m
v6p0470c1s v6p0535c1s v6p0539c2s
Shibley, S.H. et al. v6p0169c2s
Shibusawa, Baron v6p0335c1s
Shiedt, R.C. v5p0514c1s
Shiel, M.P. v5p0411c2s
Shield, A. v4p0181c2s
v4p0296c1s v4p0554c1s v5p0102c2m
v5p0122c2s v5p0348c2s v5p0361c2s
v5p0496c2s v6p0333c1s v6p0705c1s
Shields, C.W. v1p0003c1s
v1p0047c2s v1p0342c1s v1p1001c2s
v1p1037c2s v2p0085c1s v2p0390c2s
v3p0083c2s v3p0084c2s v3p0120c1s
v3p0206c2s v3p0215c2s v4p0053c1s
v4p0516c1s v5p0010c1s v5p0313c2s
v5p0571c2s v5p0573c2s v6p0706c2s
Shields, F.D. v6p0541c2s
v6p0683c2s
Shields, G.O. v2p0016c1s
v2p0295c2s v3p0036c2s v3p0059c1s
v3p0135c1s v3p0255c1s v3p0437c1s
Shields, J. v5p0449c2s
Shields, R. v6p0071c2s
Shields, S.A. v1p0570c2s
Shields, S.J. v4p0042c2s
v4p0520c1s
Shields, T.E. v6p0548c1s
Shilleto, A.R. v2p0395c2s
Shillington, V. v6p0510c2s
Shimer, H. v1p0645c1s
Shimer, H.W. v6p0079c1s
v6p0639c1s
Shimer, P.W. and Drown, T.M.
v1p0665c1s
Shimizu, S. and Honda, K.. v5p0557c2s
Shindler, E.B. v6p0567c1s
Shindler, R. v1p0500c1s
v3p0008c2s v3p0048c2s v3p0076c1s
v3p0087c2s v3p0117c2s v3p0153c2s
v3p0189c2s v3p0200c1s v3p0282c1s
v3p0290c2s v3p0291c1s v3p0417c2s
v4p0435c2s v4p0519c1s v4p0560c1s
Shindley, R. v3p0203c1s
Shinn, C.H. v1p0931c2s
v2p0064c1s v2p0064c2m v2p0193c2s
v2p0211c1s v2p0248c1s v2p0262c2s
v2p0288c1s v2p0290c1s v2p0325c1s
v2p0372c1s v2p0399c1s v2p0413c1s
v3p0022c2s v3p0031c2s v3p0062c2s
v3p0063c1m v3p0063c2m v3p0226c1s
v3p0237c1s v3p0248c2s v3p0258c2s
v3p0277c1s v3p0286c1s v3p0318c2s
v3p0374c2s v3p0389c2s v3p0400c2s
v3p0402c2s v3p0421c2s v3p0435c1s
v3p0473c1s v4p0007c2s v4p0021c2s
v4p0050c2s v4p0083c2m v4p0084c1s
v4p0106c1s v4p0192c2s v4p0203c1s
v4p0208c1s v4p0208c2m v4p0209c1m
v4p0216c2m v4p0217c1s v4p0234c2s
v4p0264c2m v4p0265c1s v4p0292c2s
v4p0298c2s v4p0326c1s v4p0337c2s
v4p0398c1s v4p0415c2s v4p0445c2s
v4p0471c2s v4p0473c2s v4p0476c1s
v4p0501c2s v4p0523c2s v4p0524c1s
v4p0544c2s v4p0583c1s v4p0599c2s
v4p0634c2s v4p0636c1s v5p0088c1m
v5p0151c1s v5p0173c2s v5p0214c2s
v5p0390c2s v5p0426c2s v5p0439c1s
v5p0458c1s v5p0507c1s v5p0580c2s
v6p0032c1s v6p0088c1s v6p0093c1m
v6p0101c2s v6p0243c2s v6p0421c1s
v6p0523c2s v6p0681c2s
Shinn, E. v1p0064c2s
v1p0213c2s v1p0996c2m v1p0997c1s
v1p1147c2s v2p0023c2s v2p0284c1s
Shinn, G.W. v2p0081c2s
v2p0106c2s v3p0218c1s v3p0347c1s
v3p0414c2s v3p0416c1s v5p0261c2s
v5p0271c2s v6p0003c2m
Shinn, J. v2p0158c2s
Shinn, M.W. v2p0232c2s
v2p0247c2s v2p0423c1s v2p0424c2s
v2p0439c1s v2p0477c2s v2p0482c2s
v3p0063c1s v3p0076c1s v3p0077c1s
v3p0246c2s v3p0374c2s v3p0469c2s
v4p0040c2s v4p0084c1s v4p0123c2s
v4p0330c1s v4p0330c2s v4p0419c1s
v6p0200c2s
Shinn, M.W. and Whitney, C.A.
v3p0137c1s
Shinn, Milicent W. v5p0425c2s
Shinoda, M. v5p0302c1s
Shipe, Maud M. and Ellis, A.C.
v6p0220c2s
Shipley, A.E. v2p0113c2s
v4p0425c1s v5p0430c1s v6p0320c2s
v6p0485c2s
Shipley, A.S. v6p0228c2s
Shipley, F.W. v6p0363c1s
v6p0561c2s
Shipley, G.T. v1p0361c1s
v1p1149c1s v1p1219c1s
Shipley, J.B. v3p0307c2s
v4p0073c2s v4p0406c2s
Shipley, M. v6p0002c1s
v6p0100c1m v6p0295c2s v6p0308c2s
Shipley, Maynard v6p0100c1s
Shipley, O. v1p0247c2s
v1p0249c2s v1p0250c1s v1p0251c1s
v1p0288c2s v1p1067c2s v2p0124c2s
v2p0225c1s v2p0375c1s v3p0123c2s
v3p0220c1s v4p0271c2m v4p0353c2s
v4p0490c1s v4p0490c2s
Shipley, W.P. and Warder, R.B.
v1p0787c1s
Shipman v6p0101c2s
Shipman, C. v5p0016c1s
v5p0066c1s v5p0078c1s v5p0104c2s
v5p0151c2s v5p0192c1s v5p0488c1s
v5p0558c1s v5p0569c2s v6p0130c1s
v6p0223c1s v6p0284c1s v6p0495c2s
v6p0618c1s
Shipman, C. and Moyne, S.C.Le
v5p0479c2s
Shipman, C.W. v4p0344c1s
Shipman, Carolyn v5p0575c1s
Shipman, E.C. v4p0080c2s
v5p0140c1s v5p0390c1s
Shipman, F.R. v4p0478c2s
Shipman, H. v6p0695c1s
Shipman, L.E. v4p0549c1s
v5p0478c2s
Shipman, P.R. v1p0417c1s
v1p0804c2s v1p0920c2s v2p0280c2s
v2p0341c1s v2p0462c1s v3p0205c2s
v3p0271c1s v4p0007c1s v4p0007c2s
v4p0108c2s v4p0180c1s v4p0361c1s
v4p0379c1s v6p0145c2s v6p0577c1s

Shipman, R.P. v1p0261c2s
Shipman, W.D. v2p0087c2s v3p0026c1s v3p0329c2s
Shipp, M.B. v6p0218c1s v6p0287c2s v6p0594c1s
Shipp, T.R. v6p0218c1s
Shippard, S. v5p0588c1s
Shippard, S. and Low, S. . v5p0007c2s
Shippard, S., Sir v5p0006c1s
Shippen, E. v2p0308c1s v3p0026c2s v3p0074c2s v3p0120c1s v3p0178c2s v3p0183c2s v3p0317c1s v3p0385c2s v3p0390c2s v4p0166c2s v4p0360c1s v4p0443c1s
Shippen, Edward v5p0029c2s
Shippen, J. v3p0314c1s v3p0346c1s
Shippen, R.L. v5p0548c2s
Shippen, R.L., Mrs. v5p0304c1s
Shippen, R.R. v2p0419c2s
Shipton, G. v3p0434c2s
Shipton, H. v3p0151c1s v3p0208c1s v3p0243c1s v5p0583c2s
Shipton, Helen v4p0012c1s v5p0400c2s
Shipton, J.A. v6p0031c2s v6p0105c2s v6p0560c2s
Shiras, G. v6p0496c2s
Shirk, A.H. v6p0242c2s
Shirlaw, W. v4p0282c1s v5p0394c1s
Shirlaw, W., jr. v5p0139c1s v5p0215c2s
Shirley, E.P. v1p0494c1s v1p0863c1s v1p0928c1m v2p0052c1s
Shirley, G. v1p0013c2s
Shirley, J. v5p0201c1s v6p0269c2s
Shirley, J.M. v2p0252c2s v2p0311c2s v2p0449c1s
Shirley, L.C. v4p0470c1s v5p0301c2s
Shirley, M. v6p0258c1s
Shirley, W.M. v6p0408c1s
Shiro, Shiba v2p0103c1s v6p0458c2s
Shirreff, E. v1p0523c1s v1p0707c2s v1p1421c2s v1p1422c1s
Shirres, A.H. v5p0596c1s v6p0638c1s
Shishkoff, N. v5p0189c1s
Shock, G. v6p0678c1s
Shock, W.H. v1p1191c2s v1p1261c1s v4p0105c1s v4p0106c1s v4p0137c1s
Shodde, G.H. v1p0691c1s v4p0021c1s v4p0302c2s
Shoemaker, H.B. v4p0288c1s
Shoemaker, T.H. v4p0224c1m
Shoemaker, W.L. and Leighton, W. v2p0139c2s
Shoemaker, W.R. v4p0010c1s v4p0511c2s v6p0286c1s v6p0504c2s v6p0554c1s
Shoest, L. v1p0493c2s
Shogren, E.W. v3p0252c1s
Shokalsky, J. v5p0027c1s
Sholes, C.H. v2p0293c2s
Sholl, A.M. v6p0298c2s v6p0466c1s
Sholl, A.McC. v4p0148c2s v4p0574c2s v4p0614c1s v6p0299c2s v6p0694c2s
Sholl, Anna M. v6p0235c1s
Sholl, Anna McC. v4p0556c1s v4p0627c2s v6p0140c1s v6p0479c1s
Shomaker, J. v6p0429c2s
Shonts, T.P. v6p0477c1s
Shonts, Theodore P. v6p0476c2s
Shoolbred, J.N. v2p0138c1s v3p0132c2s v3p0134c1s v4p0176c2s v6p0199c1s
Shopfer, J. v5p0432c1s
Shore, A. v2p0395c2s v3p0308c1s v3p0390c1s
Shore, F.T. v6p0478c2s
Shore, Florence T. v6p0104c2s
Shore, H.A. v2p0401c2s v6p0234c1s
Shore, H.N. v2p0079c2s v3p0078c2m v3p0079c1s v3p0190c2s v3p0227c2s v5p0109c2s v6p0127c2s v6p0133c2s v6p0184c1s v6p0279c2s v6p0315c2s v6p0441c2s v6p0445c1m v6p0580c1s v6p0691c2s
Shore, J.W. v6p0021c1s
Shore, T.T. v4p0113c1s v4p0128c2s v4p0632c1s
Shore, T.T. and Carter, T.T. v4p0112c1s
Shore, T.W. v2p0255c2s v3p0223c2s v4p0247c1s v4p0307c2s v4p0485c2s v5p0128c1s v6p0416c1s
Shore, W.T. v6p0073c2s v6p0099c2s v6p0385c2s v6p0473c1s v6p0683c2s
Shorey, D.L. v4p0212c1s v4p0317c1s v4p0586c2s
Shorey, M.A. v1p0227c2s
Shorey, P. v2p0017c1s v2p0191c1s v2p0206c2s v2p0442c1s v2p0451c1s v3p0019c2s v3p0184c1s v3p0295c1s v3p0334c1s v3p0334c2s v3p0429c2s v3p0471c2s v4p0051c1s v4p0191c1s v4p0241c2s v4p0242c1s v4p0262c1s v4p0307c2s v4p0334c2s v4p0371c2s v4p0413c1s v4p0425c2s v4p0439c1s v4p0446c1s v4p0446c2m v5p0028c1s v5p0162c2s v5p0249c2m v5p0269c1s v5p0436c2s v5p0454c1s v5p0517c2s v5p0519c2s v5p0606c1s v6p0017c1s v6p0130c2s v6p0273c2s v6p0330c1s v6p0389c1s v6p0503c1s
Shorey, Paul v6p0022c1s v6p0029c2s
Shorley, P. v4p0569c2s
Short, C. v1p0261c2s v1p0262c2s v2p0044c1m v5p0369c1s v5p0564c2s
Short, J.T. v1p0028c1s v1p0320c1s v1p1141c2s
Short, S.H. v5p0183c2s
Shorter, C. v5p0282c2s v6p0262c2s
Shorter, C.K. v4p0074c1s v4p0221c1s v5p0012c2s v5p0069c2s v5p0078c1s v5p0192c2s v5p0235c1s v5p0280c1s v5p0311c1s v5p0365c2s
Shorter, D.S. v5p0043c2s v5p0172c2s v5p0205c1s v5p0466c2s
Shorter, Dora S. v5p0479c1s
Shorthouse, E. v4p0218c1s
Shorthouse, J.H. v2p0017c1s v2p0035c2s v2p0211c2s v2p0261c1s v2p0277c1s v2p0280c2s v2p0341c2s v3p0421c2s v4p0557c1s v6p0402c1s
Shorthouse, J.H. and Clapperton, J.H. v2p0005c1s
Shorthouse, L. v1p1192c2s
Shortis, W. v5p0478c1s
Shortland, H.V. v2p0442c2s
Shortrede, J. v4p0314c1s v4p0318c1s
Shortt, A. v3p0038c2s v3p0067c1s v5p0091c1s v5p0096c1s v5p0376c2s v5p0410c1s v5p0536c2s v6p0097c2s v6p0310c1s v6p0598c1s v6p0632c2s v6p0652c2s
Shortt, J. v1p0712c2s
Shott, J.A. v4p0507c2s
Shotton, S. v6p0360c1s
Shoup, E.G. v6p0568c2s
Shoup, F. v1p1224c1s
Shoup, F.A. v5p0118c1s v5p0236c2s v5p0369c2s v5p0555c2s
Shoup, P. v5p0489c2s
Shoup, Paul v5p0146c1s
Shoup, S.W. v6p0279c2s
Shoup, W.J. v3p0209c2s v3p0412c1s
Shovelin, T.A. v2p0428c2s v2p0476c1s
Show, A. v6p0045c1s
Showerman, G. v6p0127c1s v6p0136c1s v6p0518c1s
Showerman, Grant v6p0190c2s
Showers, S. v5p0624c2s
Shrady, C.F. v4p0107c2s
Shrady, G.F. v3p0067c2s v4p0441c2s v4p0558c2s v5p0163c1s v5p0368c1s
Shrady, J. v2p0255c1s
Shreve, F. v6p0233c2s v6p0320c2s
Shreve, J.P. v3p0290c1s
Shreve, S.H. v1p1127c1s v1p1259c1s v1p1328c1s
Shreve, T.H. v1p0309c1s v1p0442c2s v1p0445c2s v1p0648c1s v1p1216c2s v1p1281c1s
Shrewsbury, Countess of .. v2p0178c2s
Shrewsbury, W.J. v1p1206c2s
Shrimpton, R.J. v6p0097c1s
Shriver, E.J. v3p0032c2s v3p0108c1s v3p0223c1s v3p0241c2s v4p0564c2s v4p0596c1s v4p0601c2s
Shroder, W.J. v6p0051c1s
Shrotter, A.von v1p0810c1s v1p1003c1s
Shrubsall, F. v5p0141c2s v5p0532c1s
Shrubsole, G.W. v4p0099c2s
Shrubsole, O.A. v2p0326c2s v4p0202c1s v4p0601c2s
Shrubsole, W.H. v3p0117c1s v3p0278c1m
Shubert, G. v6p0506c2s
Shuck, H., Mrs. v1p0191c1s
Shuck, L.H. v1p0241c1s v1p0259c2s v3p0365c2s
Shuckburg, E.S. v3p0017c1s
Shuckburgh, E.S. v2p0291c1s
Shuddick, R. v5p0136c2s v5p0315c2s
Shuey, E.L. v5p0154c2s v5p0644c2s
Shuey, L.H. v2p0113c1s v2p0476c1s v3p0428c2s v4p0083c1s
Shufeldt, G.A. v1p0718c2s
Shufeldt, M.A. v3p0263c1s
Shufeldt, R.W. v1p0135c2s v2p0046c2s v2p0073c2s v2p0141c1s v2p0168c2s v2p0169c2s v2p0212c1s v2p0348c1s v2p0390c2s v2p0404c1s v2p0483c2s v3p0060c2s v3p0195c1s v3p0213c2s v3p0247c1s v3p0265c2m v3p0297c2m v3p0330c2s v3p0475c2s v4p0047c2s v4p0052c2s v4p0061c2s v4p0079c2s v4p0216c1s v4p0282c1m v4p0341c1s v4p0404c2s v4p0417c2m v4p0422c1s v4p0565c2s v4p0619c2s v5p0051c2s v5p0062c2s v5p0064c1s v5p0111c1s v5p0208c2m v5p0448c1m v5p0448c2s v5p0507c2s v5p0516c1s v5p0521c2s v5p0544c2s v5p0621c2s v6p0067c2m v6p0068c1s v6p0256c1s v6p0349c1s v6p0352c1s v6p0497c1s v6p0524c1s v6p0695c2s
Shugio, H. v4p0298c1s
Shuldham, E.B. v1p0583c1s v1p1130c1s v5p0128c2s v5p0261c1s
Shull, G.H. v6p0675c1s
Shuller, M.D. v3p0229c2s
Shultz, J.S. v6p0182c2m
Shumacher, G. v6p0712c2s
Shuman, A. v1p0227c2m v1p0228c1s v1p0315c1s v1p1052c1s
Shuman, E.L. v5p0409c2s
Shumard, B.F. v1p1297c2s
Shumway, H.L. v6p0144c2s v6p0159c2s v6p0322c2s v6p0440c2s v6p0494c1s v6p0660c1s
Shurtleff, A.A. v5p0226c1s v6p0247c2s
Shurtleff, N.B. v1p0152c1s v1p0203c2s v1p0739c2s v1p0804c2s v1p0814c1s
Shurtliff, Benj. v5p0524c2s
Shute, A.A. v5p0385c2s
Shute, C.E. v4p0065c2s v4p0393c1s v4p0578c2s v5p0088c2s
Shute, H.A. v6p0448c2s v6p0504c2m
Shute, K.H. v3p0095c1s v6p0207c1s
Shute, K.H. et al. v5p0511c1s
Shute, Katherine H. v6p0380c1s
Shute, S.M. v1p0040c1s v1p0625c2s v1p1336c2s
Shutter, M.D. v2p0042c1s v3p0061c1s v3p0208c2s v4p0328c2s v4p0597c1s
Shuttleworth, H.C. v4p0051c1s v4p0164c2s
Shuttleworth, H.C. and Hall, N. v4p0572c1s
Shuttleworth, J.K., Sir .. v1p0387c1s
Shuttleworth, R.J. v1p1213c2s
Shutts, G.C. v4p0223c1s
Sibbald, A.F. v3p0156c2s v6p0107c2s
Sibbald, A.T. v2p0054c2s v2p0150c2s v2p0160c2s v2p0289c2s v2p0309c2s v2p0449c1s v2p0462c1s v3p0003c1s v3p0020c1s v3p0048c1s v3p0078c2s v3p0126c2s v3p0144c2s v3p0193c2s v3p0224c1s v3p0418c1s v4p0002c2m v4p0124c2s v4p0141c2s v4p0217c1s v4p0219c1s v4p0224c2s v4p0407c2s v4p0504c1s v4p0582c2s v4p0594c2s v4p0617c2s v5p0074c2s v6p0058c1s v6p0119c1s v6p0223c2s v6p0335c1s v6p0394c2s v6p0487c1s
Sibbald, W.A. v6p0032c1s v6p0200c2m
Sibert, W.L. v6p0390c1s v6p0485c1s
Sibert, W.T. v6p0204c1s
Sibley, G.C. v1p0799c1s v4p0462c2s v4p0633c1s
Sibley, H.L. v4p0328c2s v4p0367c2s v4p0450c2s
Sibley, H.L. et al. v4p0157c1s
Sibley, J.L. v1p0380c2s v1p1040c2s
Sibley, J.Langdon v1p0103c1s
Sibley, L.L. v5p0338c2s v6p0467c1s
Sibley, N.M. v6p0404c1s
Sibley, N.W. v5p0067c1s v5p0083c2s v5p0138c1s v5p0312c2s v5p0331c2s v5p0470c1s v5p0492c1s v5p0588c2s v6p0214c1s v6p0328c2s
Sibley, W.K. v3p0246c1m
Sibley, W.N. v5p0312c1s
Sibree, J. v4p0091c1s v4p0348c1s
Sibree, J., jr. v1p0785c1s v2p0271c1s v2p0272c2s v3p0263c1s v4p0205c1s v4p0348c1s v4p0350c2s
Sicard, C. v1p0953c2s
Sicard, W.F. v4p0530c2s v4p0583c2s
Siccama, H.T.H. v6p0235c1s
Sichel, E. v3p0040c1s v3p0173c2s v5p0268c1s v5p0475c1s v5p0636c1s v6p0009c1m v6p0675c1s
Sichel, Edith v4p0589c1s v5p0215c1s v5p0644c1s
Sichel, H.D. v5p0273c2s

Sichel, W. v3p0426c1s
v4p0048c1s v4p0571c1s v5p0050c2s
v5p0086c1s v5p0161c1s v5p0494c1s
v5p0583c1s v6p0054c2s v6p0206c1s
v6p0223c1s v6p0252c2s
Sichel, W.S. v1p0104c1s
v2p0181c2s v2p0200c1s
Sichel, Walter v6p0260c1s
Sicher, D.F. v6p0524c1s
Sickels, Frank E. v5p0122c2s
Sickert, O. v5p0294c1s
v6p0450c2s v6p0696c1s
Sickert, W. v4p0335c2s
v4p0619c2s
Sickles, D.E. v5p0528c1s
Sickley, J.C. v2p0351c1s
v3p0355c1s
Siclen, G.W.Van v3p0447c1s
v5p0587c2s
Siclen, G.W.Van and Ireland, A.
v5p0587c1s
Siddons, J.H. v1p0992c1s
v1p1227c2s v1p1300c2s v2p0122c2s
Sidebotham, H. v3p0286c1s
Sidebotham, J. v1p1003c2s
v1p1004c1m
Sidebotham, W. v5p0235c1s
v5p0255c2s v6p0693c2s
Sidebotham, Wm. v6p0090c2s
v6p0385c2s
Sidgreaves, W. v2p0153c2s
v4p0037c2s v4p0540c2s v4p0556c2s
v4p0557c1s v6p0613c2s
Sidgreaves, W. and Townsend, J.S.
v4p0556c2s
Sidgreaves, W. and Turner, H.
v4p0556c2s
Sidgwick, A. v1p0341c1s
v1p0711c2s v1p0760c2m v2p0114c2s
v2p0152c1s v2p0356c2s v4p0131c1s
v4p0338c1m v4p0447c1s v6p0045c2s
v6p0302c2s v6p0440c2s
Sidgwick, A. and Rogers, M.A.H.
v4p0627c2s
Sidgwick, A. et al. v4p0475c1s
Sidgwick, A., Mrs. v6p0253c2s
v6p0299c2s v6p0512c1s v6p0664c1s
Sidgwick, A.G. v1p0904c1s
Sidgwick, E.M. v4p0003c1s
Sidgwick, F. v6p0701c2s
Sidgwick, H. v1p0060c2s
v1p0110c1s v1p0113c1s v1p0382c2s
v1p0420c2s v1p0426c2m v1p0427c1m
v1p0435c1s v1p0447c2s v1p0582c2s
v1p0702c2s v1p0715c1s v1p0861c1s
v1p1000c1s v1p1017c2s v1p1062c1s
v1p1082c2s v1p1108c1s v1p1314c1s
v1p1379c2s v2p0046c1s v2p0116c2s
v2p0129c2s v2p0147c1m v2p0191c2s
v2p0203c2s v2p0241c1s v2p0339c1m
v2p0407c2s v2p0418c2s v2p0440c1s
v3p0143c1m v3p0188c2s v3p0207c2s
v3p0234c2s v3p0244c2s v3p0245c2s
v3p0398c2s v3p0399c2s v3p0412c2s
v4p0127c1s v4p0187c2s v4p0345c2s
v4p0450c2s v4p0479c2s v4p0533c2s
v4p0535c1m v4p0573c2s v4p0577c1s
v5p0196c1s v5p0250c1s v5p0537c1s
v5p0593c2s
Sidgwick, H. and Barratt, A.
v1p0394c1s
Sidgwick, H. and Caird, E.
v1p0623c1s
Sidgwick, I. v3p0242c1s
Sidgwick, J. v3p0144c1s
Sidgwick, M. v6p0488c1s
Sidgwick, M.C. v5p0462c2s
Sidgwick, R. v6p0417c2s
Sidis, B. v4p0365c1s
v4p0375c2s v6p0278c2s
Sidney, A. v2p0267c2s
Sidney, E. ....
v1p0494c2s
v1p0967c1s
Sidney, M. v4p0575c1s
Sidney, P. v6p0036c2s
v6p0110c1m v6p0222c2s v6p0333c1s
v6p0369c2s v6p0481c2s v6p0508c2s
v6p0546c1s v6p0548c1s v6p0622c2s
v6p0646c1s
Sidney, Philip v6p0551c2s
Sidney, S. v3p0344c2s
Sidney, W.C. v4p0498c1s
Siebel, G. v6p0649c2s
Sieber, J.L. v6p0523c2s
Sieber, L.L. v6p0213c2s
Siebert, Albert v5p0482c2s
Siebert, G. v6p0204c2s
Siebert, W.H. v4p0529c2s
v4p0590c2s v6p0664c2s
Siedhof, C. v1p0555c1s
Siegbold, K.P. v4p0380c2s
Siegfried, A. v3p0465c2s
v5p0536c2s v6p0585c1s
Siegfried, A.H. v1p0197c1s
v1p0854c2s
Siegfried, C.A. v3p0131c1s
v3p0362c1s v3p0436c2s v4p0363c1s
Sieghart, R. v5p0040c1s
Sieghold, K.P. v6p0259c1s
Sieghold, Kate P. v4p0179c2s
Siegmund, G.F. v1p0239c1s
Siemens, A. v1p0399c2s
v4p0082c1s v5p0435c1s v6p0483c2s
Siemens, A. and Hopkinson, E.
v3p0134c1s
Siemens, C.W. v1p0399c1m
v1p0399c2m v1p0400c2m v1p0436c2m
v1p0493c1m v1p0493c2m v1p0495c1m
v1p0501c1m v1p0501c2m v1p0580c2m
v1p0663c2m v1p0665c1m v1p0815c1m
v1p0815c2m v1p1068c2m v1p1160c2m
v1p1212c2m v1p1246c2m v1p1249c1m
v1p1290c2m v1p1291c1m v1p1293c1m
v2p0056c2m v2p0126c2m v2p0136c2m
v2p0137c2s v2p0389c1s v2p0389c2s
v2p0425c1m v3p0422c2s
Siemens, C.W. and Archibald, E.D.
v2p0425c1s
Siemens, F. v2p0094c2s
v2p0180c1m v2p0434c1s v4p0220c2s
Siemens, G.W. v1p0408c1s
Siemens, W. v2p0394c2s
v3p0380c2s
Sienkiewicz, H. v5p0033c1s
v5p0187c1s v5p0312c1s v5p0331c2s
v5p0337c2s v5p0423c2s
Sienkiewicz-Litwos, H. ... v2p0333c1s
Sieveking, A.F. v4p0309c1s
v4p0607c1s
Sieveking, G. v6p0088c2s
Sieveking, I.G. v6p0080c2s
v6p0133c2s v6p0272c2s v6p0290c2s
v6p0422c2s v6p0474c2s v6p0612c1s
v6p0627c2s v6p0692c1s
Sieveking, J.G. v5p0261c1s
v6p0108c2s v6p0179c1m v6p0207c2s
v6p0531c1s
Siewers, C. v2p0317c1s
v2p0428c1s v4p0407c2s v4p0578c2s
Siewers, C.G. v1p0645c1s
v1p0858c2s
Sifton, C. v4p0353c2s
v6p0097c1s
Sigel, F. v1p1341c2s
v1p1354c1s v5p0502c1s
Sigerfoos, C.P. v5p0277c2s
Sigerson, G. v4p0291c2s
Sighele, S. v6p0310c1s
Sigma v5p0518c2s
Sigmund, F.L. v6p0191c1s
Sigmund, G.F. v1p1300c1s
Sigmund, W.S. v4p0341c2s
Sigourney, L.H. v1p0188c1s
v1p0424c2s v1p0577c2s v1p0605c2s
v1p0693c2s v1p0717c1s v1p0875c2s
v1p1281c1s v1p1284c2s v1p1288c1s
v1p1422c1s v2p0212c2s
Sigourney, L.H., Mrs. v1p0105c2s
v1p0175c2s v1p0889c1s v1p1270c2s
v1p1280c2s
Sigrid, E. v4p0229c2s
v4p0616c1s
Sigsbee, C.D. v5p0087c1s
v5p0356c2s
Sihler, E.G. v1p1309c2s
v6p0137c2s v6p0643c1s
Sikes, E.W. v5p0414c1s
v6p0598c2s
Sikes, G.C. v4p0021c2s
v5p0218c2s v6p0113c1s v6p0113c2m
v6p0131c2s v6p0238c2s v6p0345c1s
v6p0435c2s
Sikes, W. v1p0183c1s
v1p0245c1s v1p0271c2s v1p0439c1s
v1p0526c2s v1p0606c2s v1p0737c1s
v1p0753c1s v1p0967c2s v1p0970c1s
v1p1031c2s v1p1280c1s v1p1294c1s
v1p1359c2s v1p1381c1m v1p1398c1s
v1p1408c2s v2p0464c2m
Sikes, W.W. v1p0169c2s
Silberman, T.J. v1p1051c2s
Silberrad, U.L. v4p0489c2s
v5p0466c1s v6p0180c1s v6p0295c2s
v6p0300c2s v6p0400c2s v6p0517c1s
v6p0638c1s v6p0700c2s v6p0701c2s
Silburn, P.A. v6p0168c2s
v6p0268c1s v6p0309c2m v6p0579c1s
Silcock, C. v4p0528c1s
Silikovitsch, G. v3p0131c2s
Sill, Alice H. v6p0397c2s
Sill, E. v1p0947c1s
Sill, E.M. v6p0117c1s
Sill, E.R. v1p0889c2s
v1p1186c1s v2p0023c2s v2p0092c2s
v2p0132c2s v2p0140c1s v2p0459c2s
v3p0112c1s v6p0202c1s v6p0386c1s
v6p0671c2s v6p0690c1s
Sill, J. v1p0625c2s
v2p0367c1s v3p0356c1s
Sill, L.M. v5p0211c2s
v6p0359c1s
Sillard, P.A. v5p0073c1s
v5p0144c2s v6p0099c1s v6p0213c2s
v6p0395c1s v6p0395c2s v6p0427c2s
v6p0590c1s v6p0684c2s
Sillard, R.M. v5p0048c2s
v5p0161c1s v5p0342c1s v5p0440c2s
v5p0575c2s v5p0576c1s v6p0326c1s
v6p0327c2s v6p0427c2s
Silliman, B. v1p0058c1s
v1p0261c1s v1p0267c2s v1p0268c1s
v1p0268c2m v1p0269c2s v1p0279c2s
v1p0292c1s v1p0326c2s v1p0444c1s
v1p0469c2s v1p0501c2s v1p0502c1s
v1p0508c1m v1p0509c2s v1p0532c2m
v1p0533c2s v1p0534c1s v1p0541c1s
v1p0619c1s v1p0621c1s v1p0732c1s
v1p0788c1s v1p0810c1s v1p0828c1s
v1p0845c1m v1p0845c2s v1p0892c2s
v1p0911c2s v1p0930c1s v1p0995c2s
v1p1070c2s v1p1071c2m v1p1183c1s
v1p1198c2s v1p1235c2s v1p1292c1s
v1p1322c1s v1p1334c1s v1p1360c1s
v1p1390c1s v1p1393c2s v2p0229c1s
Silliman, B. and Wurtz, H.
v1p0459c1s v1p0501c2s v1p1293c1s
Silliman, B., jr. v1p0237c1s
v1p0329c1s v1p0428c1s v1p0493c2s
v1p0792c1s v1p0844c1s v1p0908c2s
v1p1377c2s
Silliman, B., jr. and Whitney, J.D.
v1p0300c1s
Silliman, B., jr. and Whitney, J.S.
v1p0163c2s
Silliman, B., Sen. and
Kingsley, J.L. v1p0827c1s
Silliman, J.M. v1p0664c1s
Silliman, R.D. v5p0453c1s
Sillingston, Leonard W. .. v6p0709c1s
Silsbee, F.H. v1p0307c1s
Silsbee, J. v1p1202c1s
Silsbee, W. v1p0001c2s
v1p0440c1s v1p0714c2s v1p1176c2s
v1p1201c1s v1p1214c2s v1p1267c1s
Silsby, M.E. v6p0067c2s
Silsby, M.R. v5p0016c2s
v5p0063c1s
Siltman, A.H. v5p0049c2s
Siltwell, W. v4p0360c1s
Silver, A.P. v5p0225c1s
v5p0227c2s v6p0101c1s v6p0376c2s
v6p0455c1s
Silver, C.F. v6p0411c1s
Silver, E.C. v6p0537c2s
Silver, Ednah C. v5p0260c2s
v6p0394c1s
Silver, Ednah D. v4p0302c1s
v6p0628c2s
Silver, G. v6p0685c2s
v6p0703c2s
Silver, H. v1p0095c1s
v1p0315c1s v4p0325c1m
Silver, J.A. v4p0359c1s
Silver, J.S. v1p0187c2s
v1p0188c2s v1p0235c1s v1p1415c1s
Silversmith, J. v5p0328c1s
Silvester, K. v5p0053c1s
v5p0283c2s v5p0486c1s
Silvester, Katharine v5p0565c2s
Silvester, T.H. v1p1272c2s
Silvestre, J.de S. v4p0081c1s
Sim, A.C.G. v4p0409c1s
Sim, A.G. v4p0504c1s
Sim, C.A. v4p0171c1s
Simas, E.M. v5p0049c2s
Simboli, R. v6p0022c2s
v6p0130c2s v6p0331c1s v6p0368c1s
v6p0547c1s v6p0549c2s
Simcox, E. v1p0202c2s
v1p0337c2s v1p0511c2s v1p0640c1s
v1p0839c2s v1p0979c2s v1p1423c1s
v2p0023c2s v2p0101c2m v2p0130c1s
v2p0132c2s v2p0147c1m v2p0250c2s
v2p0299c1s v2p0358c1s v2p0414c2s
v2p0444c1s v3p0099c1s v4p0564c1s
v5p0039c2s
Simcox, E.J. v2p0131c2s
Simcox, Edith v3p0468c1s
Simcox, G.A. v1p0026c1s
v1p0053c2s v1p0061c1m v1p0061c2s
v1p0062c1s v1p0063c2s v1p0173c1s
v1p0351c2s v1p0438c2s v1p0453c2s
v1p0454c1s v1p0487c1s v1p0503c2s
v1p0511c2s v1p0681c2s v1p0692c1s
v1p0708c2s v1p0778c2s v1p0805c1s
v1p0813c2s v1p0869c1s v1p0880c1s
v1p0949c2s v1p0993c1s v1p1054c1s
v1p1280c1s v1p1307c1s v1p1409c1s
v1p1417c1s v1p1427c1s v1p1435c2s
v2p0002c2s v2p0147c1s v2p0148c2s
v2p0167c1s v2p0192c1s v2p0241c2s
v2p0245c2s v2p0280c2s v2p0300c2s
v2p0322c1s v2p0339c1s v2p0339c2s
v2p0360c1s v2p0368c2s v2p0428c2s
v2p0437c1s v3p0020c2s v3p0367c1s
v3p0419c1s v3p0454c2s v4p0056c2s
v4p0079c1s v4p0111c1s v4p0271c2s
v4p0309c1s v4p0354c1s v4p0468c1m
v5p0010c1s
Simcox, W.H. v2p0007c2s
v2p0045c1s v2p0057c1s v2p0201c2s
v2p0368c2s v3p0143c1s
Sime, D. v2p0061c1s
v2p0062c1s v2p0105c2s
Sime, J. v2p0108c1s
v2p0268c1s v2p0298c1s v3p0061c1s
v5p0141c2s
Sime, W. v2p0170c1s
v3p0139c1s

Sime, Wm. v4p0137c2s
Simeon, C. v1p0061c1s v1p0899c2s
Simey, E. v5p0175c1s v6p0390c1s
Simkhovitch, M.K. v6p0453c2s v6p0507c1s v6p0585c1s
Simkhovitch, Mary K. v6p0279c2s
Simkhovitch, V.G. v5p0502c2s v6p0556c1s v6p0558c1m v6p0559c1m v6p0613c1s v6p0639c2s
Simkins, A.C. v6p0171c1s
Simmel, G. v4p0381c2s v4p0535c1m v5p0535c1s v5p0607c1s v6p0144c1s v6p0220c1s v6p0252c1s v6p0537c2s v6p0581c2s v6p0602c1s
Simmonds, C. v6p0090c1s v6p0310c1s v6p0319c2s v6p0515c1s v6p0554c1s
Simmonds, P.L. v1p0063c1s v1p0167c1s v1p0380c2s v1p0532c1s v1p0562c1s v1p0914c2s v1p0949c1s v1p0965c2s v1p1100c2s v1p1154c2s v1p1198c1s v1p1427c1s v2p0390c1s v3p0009c2s v3p0040c2s v3p0100c1s v3p0126c2s v3p0130c2s v3p0156c1s v3p0181c1s v3p0186c2s v3p0272c2s v3p0309c1s v3p0315c1s v3p0319c2s v3p0324c2s v3p0359c1s v3p0359c2s v3p0373c2s v3p0392c2s v3p0393c1s v3p0397c1s v3p0407c2s v3p0408c2s v3p0422c1s v3p0430c2s v3p0456c2s v3p0465c2s v3p0471c2s
Simmons, A.M. v6p0601c1s v6p0601c2s
Simmons, A.T. v5p0265c1s v5p0359c2s v5p0458c1s v5p0514c1s v6p0335c1s v6p0704c1s
Simmons, B. v1p0188c2s v1p0997c2s v1p1053c1s v1p1219c2s v1p1273c2s v1p1375c2s
Simmons, C. v6p0193c1s v6p0573c1s
Simmons, C.L. v2p0270c2s
Simmons, D.B. v1p0678c1s v1p0679c1s
Simmons, Eleanor B. v5p0014c2s
Simmons, F.M. v6p0448c1s
Simmons, G. v3p0238c2s v3p0374c1s v6p0191c1s v6p0192c1s
Simmons, G.A. v1p0006c1s
Simmons, G.F. v1p0128c1s v1p0254c2s v1p0404c1s v1p0535c2s v1p0689c1s v1p0726c2s v1p0903c1m v1p0958c1s v1p1321c2s v1p1372c1s
Simmons, H.E. v3p0449c1s
Simmons, H.M. v5p0618c2s
Simmons, J.E. v4p0081c1s
Simmons, J.F. v1p1040c2s v1p1093c2s v2p0368c2s v6p0310c1s
Simmons, J.L.A. v2p0185c2m v4p0084c2s v4p0189c1s v4p0212c1s v4p0235c2s v4p0236c1s
Simmons, J.W. v1p0031c2s v1p0182c1s
Simmons, L. v6p0094c1s
Simmons, L., Sir v5p0501c1s
Simmons, L.M. v4p0007c1s v4p0072c2s v4p0306c1s
Simmons, L.M. and Harris, E. v4p0171c1s
Simmons, M.B. v4p0424c2s
Simmons, N.B. v4p0047c2s
Simmons, O.L. v4p0541c2s
Simmons, R. v4p0165c2s v4p0412c1s
Simmons, T.F. v1p1109c2s
Simmons, W. v1p0725c2s
Simmons, W.E. v1p0501c2s v6p0710c1s
Simmons, W.E., jr. v1p0049c1s v1p0104c2s
Simmons, W.H. v1p0949c2s
Simmons, W.I. v4p0632c2s
Simms, A.E. v5p0060c1s
Simms, A.E.N. v6p0535c2s
Simms, C.S. v6p0412c2s
Simms, G.E., jr. v2p0457c1s
Simms, J. v3p0053c1s v5p0075c1s
Simms, M.E. v4p0105c2s v4p0388c2s
Simms, S.C. v6p0570c2s v6p0648c2s
Simms, W. v1p0924c2s
Simms, W.G. v1p0049c1s v1p0058c1s v1p0105c1s v1p0221c1s v1p0222c1s v1p0300c2s v1p0397c2s v1p0609c2s v1p0624c1s v1p0638c1s v1p0638c2s v1p0703c1s v1p0751c2s v1p0825c2s v1p0926c1s v1p0942c1s v1p0977c1s v1p0983c1s v1p1010c2s v1p1070c2s
Simon, A. v6p0343c1s
Simon, A.M. v6p0367c2s
Simon, D.W. v1p0074c2s v1p0263c2s v1p0625c1s v1p0685c1s v1p0879c1s v2p0041c2s v2p0120c2s v2p0476c2s v3p0121c1s v3p0199c1s v3p0436c1s v4p0479c2s v4p0572c2s v4p0573c1s v5p0202c1s
Simon, H. v3p0229c2s
Simon, J. v1p0198c2s v1p0817c1s v2p0131c2s v2p0165c2m v3p0161c2s v3p0164c1s v4p0156c2s v4p0173c1s v4p0211c1s v4p0535c1s
Simon, J.A. v5p0061c1s
Simon, J.S. v5p0235c2s v6p0413c1s
Simon, Jules v3p0469c1s v4p0600c2s v5p0125c2s
Simon, L. v6p0400c1s
Simon, O.J. v4p0306c1m v4p0480c1s v5p0307c2s v5p0484c1s v5p0484c2s
Simon, O.J. et al. v5p0311c2s
Simon, R. v3p0241c1s
Simon, T. and Black, C. .. v3p0468c1s
Simon, T.C. v1p0114c1s v1p0356c1s v1p0582c2s v1p0794c2s v1p0826c2s v1p1375c1s
Simon, W. v3p0003c1s
Simonds, A.B. v6p0608c1s
Simonds, F.H. v6p0301c2s v6p0340c1s
Simonds, F.W. v1p0665c2s v5p0574c1m v6p0640c2s
Simonds, G. v2p0057c2s v2p0156c1s v2p0281c2s v3p0056c1s v4p0074c2m
Simonds, G.F. v3p0363c2s v4p0042c2s
Simonds, George v2p0418c2s
Simonds, J.A. v4p0120c1s
Simonds, J.W. v1p0388c2s
Simonds, O.C. v6p0106c2m v6p0656c1s
Simonds, P.L. v1p0462c2s
Simonds, S.D. v1p0527c2s
Simonds, W.E. v3p0193c2s v3p0206c2s v3p0207c1s v4p0430c1s v4p0432c1s v5p0053c2s v5p0523c1s v6p0104c2s v6p0113c2s v6p0361c2s v6p0389c1s v6p0480c2s v6p0515c1s v6p0588c2s v6p0697c1s
Simonin, L. v1p1268c1s
Simons, A.M. v5p0462c2s v6p0033c1s v6p0057c2s v6p0188c2s
Simons, E.D. v2p0045c1s
Simons, G.J. v1p1293c1s
Simons, L. v4p0272c1s
Simons, S.E. v5p0062c1s v5p0535c1s
Simons, Sadie E. and Angell, J.R. v5p0193c1s
Simons, Sarah E. v5p0534c2s v6p0599c2s
Simonson, G.A. v1p0435c2s v6p0275c2s
Simonson, G.M. v4p0026c2s
Simonton, T.D. v6p0213c1s
Simony, O. et al. v5p0024c1s v5p0537c2s
Simpkinson, J.N. v1p1388c2s
Simpson, A. v6p0153c1s
Simpson, A.H. v1p0995c1s
Simpson, A.N. v5p0501c1s
Simpson, B. v5p0185c2s
Simpson, C.T. v4p0355c2s v4p0377c1s v4p0591c2m
Simpson, C.W., Mrs. v6p0194c2s
Simpson, E. v1p0065c2s v1p0902c1s v2p0308c1s v2p0454c1m
Simpson, E.B. v3p0120c1s v3p0464c1s v4p0107c2s v4p0158c2s v4p0527c1s v5p0552c2s
Simpson, E.E. v5p0171c2s v5p0394c1s v5p0395c2s v5p0502c1s v5p0593c2s v5p0616c1s
Simpson, E.G. v2p0344c2s v2p0472c1s v3p0437c1s
Simpson, E.O. v1p0285c1s
Simpson, Eve B. v3p0120c1s v5p0164c2s v5p0515c2s v5p0553c1s
Simpson, F.M. v6p0027c2s
Simpson, G. v1p1150c1s
Simpson, G., Sir v1p0697c1s
Simpson, G.W. v1p0082c1s
Simpson, H. v6p0074c2s v6p0589c2s
Simpson, H.B. v4p0130c2s v4p0139c2s v5p0439c1s
Simpson, H.C.C.D. v3p0022c2s v5p0032c2s
Simpson, H.F.Morland v6p0055c1s
Simpson, H.G. v5p0394c1s
Simpson, H.M. v6p0101c2s
Simpson, Henry v6p0616c2s
Simpson, J. v1p0385c1s v1p0390c2s v1p0391c2s v1p0392c1s v1p0641c1s v2p0075c1s v2p0376c2s v2p0417c1s
Simpson, J.A.H. v6p0165c2s
Simpson, J.F. v5p0585c1s
Simpson, J.G. v6p0655c1s
Simpson, J.H. v3p0389c2s
Simpson, J.P. v2p0087c2s v2p0152c2s v2p0267c2s v2p0343c2s v2p0362c1s v2p0392c2s v2p0416c1m v2p0416c2s v2p0437c1m v2p0445c1s v2p0469c1s v3p0178c2s v4p0250c1s
Simpson, J.Y. v5p0098c1s v5p0309c1s v5p0382c1s v5p0467c1s v5p0528c1s v5p0529c2s v5p0577c1s v6p0165c2s v6p0182c2s
Simpson, Jane A.H. v4p0270c2s v4p0557c1s
Simpson, L.D. v1p1048c2s
Simpson, M.C.M. v1p1179c2s v4p0221c2s v4p0515c1s v4p0527c1m v5p0203c2s
Simpson, M.C.M., Mrs. v2p0294c1s
Simpson, M.H. v1p0797c2s
Simpson, P. v6p0405c1s
Simpson, P.A. v2p0006c1s
Simpson, P.C. v5p0301c1s
Simpson, Prof. v2p0346c2s v2p0467c2s
Simpson, R.L. v4p0533c1s
Simpson, S. v6p0195c1s v6p0353c2s
Simpson, S.L. v1p0169c2s v1p0446c1s v1p0770c1s
Simpson, T.A. v5p0623c2s
Simpson, V.A. v5p0274c1s v5p0634c2s v5p0640c1s v6p0481c2s
Simpson, Violet A. v6p0073c2s v6p0572c2s v6p0584c2s
Simpson, W. v1p0003c1s v1p0058c1s v1p0236c1s v1p0342c1s v1p0889c1s v1p1009c2s v1p1051c1s v1p1157c2s v1p1390c2s v2p0003c2s v2p0109c2s v2p0239c1s v3p0003c2m v3p0019c1s v3p0254c1s v3p0294c2s v3p0314c2s v4p0024c2s v4p0140c1s v4p0276c1s v4p0386c2s v4p0417c1s v4p0512c1m v5p0157c2s v5p0208c1s v5p0291c1s v5p0517c2s
Simpson, W.A. v5p0032c2s v5p0588c1s
Simpson, W.G. v4p0263c2s
Simpson, W.H. v6p0431c1s
Simpson, W.L. v4p0443c1s v5p0622c2s
Simpson, W.S. v1p1144c2s v2p0383c2s v4p0217c2s
Simpson-Moore, Jennie v5p0638c2s
Sims, C.N. v3p0132c2s
Sims, C.N. et al. v3p0129c2s
Sims, G.C. and Aldrich, W.S. v5p0401c2s v5p0615c1s
Sims, G.C. et al. v4p0180c1s v4p0395c2s
Sims, G.R. v2p0422c2s v2p0440c2s v3p0079c1s
Sims, H.A. v1p0052c1s
Sims, J.M. v1p0784c2s v2p0269c2s
Sims, J.M. et al. v1p0500c1s
Sims, S.C. v6p0694c2s
Sims, W.R. v3p0164c1s v3p0403c1s
Simson, A. v1p1011c1s v1p1439c1m v2p0305c2s
Simson, J. v2p0251c1s v2p0406c2s
Sinclair and Babson v3p0159c1s
Sinclair, A. v5p0477c1s
Sinclair, A.H. v3p0412c1s
Sinclair, A.T. v6p0256c2s
Sinclair, Angus v5p0344c1s
Sinclair, Archdeacon v4p0112c1s
Sinclair, C.M. v4p0090c1s v4p0498c2s
Sinclair, G.A. v5p0150c2s v6p0407c2s v6p0489c1s v6p0595c2s v6p0603c1s v6p0638c2s v6p0701c2s
Sinclair, G.T. v1p1036c2s v1p1345c1s v5p0211c1s
Sinclair, I.A. v6p0606c2s
Sinclair, J. v3p0179c2s
Sinclair, M. v4p0305c2s v5p0263c2s v6p0017c2s v6p0427c1s v6p0541c1s v6p0545c2s v6p0650c1s
Sinclair, M.L. v4p0441c2s v4p0618c1m
Sinclair, Magnus v6p0486c1s
Sinclair, May v4p0273c1s v6p0114c1s
Sinclair, N. v5p0206c2s
Sinclair, P. v3p0436c2s
Sinclair, R.A. v3p0381c2s
Sinclair, S.B. v4p0086c1s
Sinclair, T. v3p0270c1s v4p0589c2s
Sinclair, U. v6p0142c1s v6p0161c2s v6p0295c1s v6p0361c2m v6p0376c1s v6p0401c2s v6p0541c2s v6p0601c2s
Sinclair, Upton v6p0408c1s
Sinclair, W. v3p0362c2s v4p0112c2s v4p0275c2s v4p0458c2s v4p0506c1s v5p0235c2s v5p0362c1s v6p0385c1s v6p0393c2s v6p0475c2s v6p0555c1m
Sinclair, W. et al. v4p0170c1s
Sinclair, W.J. v6p0440c2s v6p0511c2s
Sinclair, W.M. v1p0856c2s v4p0193c1s v4p0331c2s v4p0515c2s

v5p0140c2s v6p0173c1s v6p0272c1s
Sinding, P.C. v1p0684c2s
Sinding, T.C. v1p1311c2s
Sing, O.P. v4p0497c1s
Singelbach, W.E. v6p0411c1m
Singer, C. v6p0218c2s
Singer, E. v6p0642c1s
Singer, E.A. v5p0311c2s
v5p0519c2s v6p0408c1s
Singer, E.A., jr. v5p0519c2s
v6p0121c2s
Singer, H.W. v5p0068c1s
v5p0250c1s v5p0318c1s v5p0342c1s
v5p0578c1s v6p0182c1s v6p0274c1s
v6p0365c2s v6p0380c1s v6p0517c1s
v6p0617c1s
Singer, Hans W. v6p0226c1s
Singer, I. v6p0343c1s
v6p0556c1s v6p0702c1s
Singer, J.W. v2p0237c1s
Singer, S. v3p0371c1s
v3p0418c2s
Singer, W. v4p0077c2s
Singer, W.H. v3p0394c1s
Singh, O.P. v4p0279c1s
v4p0279c2s
Singh, S.A. v6p0314c1s
Single Trigger v5p0547c1s
Singleton, A. v5p0228c1s
Singleton, A.H. v6p0327c2s
v6p0691c1s
Singleton, E. v3p0024c2s
v3p0058c1s v3p0228c2s v3p0468c1s
v4p0435c1s v4p0540c2s v5p0195c1s
v5p0356c2s
v5p0394c1s
Singleton, Esther v4p0156c2s
v4p0625c1s v5p0390c1s v5p0421c2s
v5p0422c1m
Singleton, L. v1p0921c2s
v1p0951c2s
Singleton, M., Mrs. v4p0537c1s
Singleton, M.M. v4p0381c1s
Singleton, R. v3p0046c2s
v3p0081c2s v3p0179c2s v3p0273c2s
v3p0280c1s v3p0307c2s v3p0426c2s
v3p0453c1s
Singleton, V. v2p0304c1s
v2p0321c2s
Singmaster, E. v6p0287c2s
v6p0417c2s
Singmaster, Elsie v6p0066c1s
v6p0311c1s v6p0368c2s v6p0420c1s
v6p0673c2s
Singmaster, J.A. v1p0432c2s
v3p0258c1s v3p0283c1s v3p0419c2s
v4p0374c2s v5p0060c2s v5p0132c1s
v6p0642c2s
Sinjohn, J. v5p0318c2s
Sinker, R. v6p0123c2s
Sinks, J.L. v6p0221c1s
v6p0561c1s
Sinnett, A.P. v2p0217c1s
v4p0063c2s v4p0077c2m v4p0395c1s
v5p0523c2s v6p0463c2s
Sinnett, A.P. and Stead, W.T.
v3p0047c1s
Sinnett, C.N. v6p0187c1s
Sinnett, J.F. v1p0682c1s
Sinnett, P., Mrs. v1p0294c1s
v1p0344c2s v1p0583c2s v1p0755c1s
v1p1425c2s
Sinnickson, Lina v6p0543c2s
Sinnott, J.E. v2p0210c1s
v2p0234c2s
Sionara v1p1350c1s
v1p1351c1s
Siordet, H.L. v5p0124c1s
Sioussat, G.L. v6p0184c1s
v6p0404c2s
Sioussat, St.G.L. v6p0206c2s
v6p0667c2m v6p0668c2s
Sirks, J.L. v4p0235c1s
Sirr, H. v2p0114c2s
v2p0478c2s
Sirr, H.S. v1p0213c2s
v1p0231c1s
Sise, R.W. v5p0263c2s
Sisley, R. v4p0284c1s
Sismondi, J.C.L. v1p0897c1s
Sismondi, J.C.L.de v1p1207c1s
Sisson, E.G. v6p0526c1s
Sisson, E.O. v6p0046c2s
v6p0130c1s v6p0190c2s v6p0192c2s
v6p0194c1s v6p0538c1s
Sisson, F.T. v4p0375c2s
Sisson, H.T. v4p0256c2s
Sisson, S. v6p0525c1s
v6p0678c2s
Sites, C.M.L. v6p0398c2s
Sitterly, C.F. v5p0426c1s
v6p0341c1s
Sitwell, F. v3p0037c1s
Sitwell, G.R. v2p0107c1s
Six, J. v3p0177c2s
v3p0424c1s v3p0475c2s v4p0040c1s
Sizeranne, R.de la v4p0440c1s
v5p0094c2s v5p0101c1s v5p0448c1s
v5p0448c2s v5p0464c1s
v5p0500c2s
v5p0558c2s
Sizeranne, R.de la et al.. v5p0310c1s
Skae, W. v1p0127c1s
Skaife, W. v5p0147c1s
v5p0559c2s
Skan, S.A. v5p0368c2s
Skarstedt, C.W. v4p0439c2s
v4p0504c2s
Skeat, E.G. v3p0388c2s
v4p0193c2s
Skeat, W. v6p0396c1s
v6p0611c1s
Skeat, W.W. v1p0040c1s
v2p0014c2s v2p0145c2m v2p0160c2s
v3p0075c1s v3p0102c2s v3p0139c2m
v3p0194c2s v3p0198c1s v3p0243c2s
v3p0288c2s v3p0362c2s v3p0366c1s
v3p0368c1s v3p0388c1s v3p0431c2s
v4p0079c2s v4p0098c1s v4p0098c2s
v4p0156c2s v4p0341c2s v4p0362c1s
v5p0103c1s v5p0141c2s v5p0193c1s
v5p0359c2s v5p0580c2s v6p0013c1s
v6p0111c1s v6p0201c2s v6p0229c2s
v6p0609c2m
Skeat, W.W. and Birdwood, G.
v5p0488c1s
Skeat, W.W. and Humphreys, Jennett
v4p0098c1s
Skeat, W.W. et al. v3p0118c2s
v3p0369c1s v4p0098c1s v4p0111c1s
v5p0170c2s
v5p0198c2s
Skeats, H.S. v1p1096c2s
Skeel, E.E.F. v6p0119c2s
Skeel, Emily E.F. v6p0234c1s
Skeel, M.C. v6p0203c2s
Skeel, M.H. v4p0558c1s
Skeel, T. v1p1065c2s
v1p1247c2s v1p1248c1s
Skeel, T. and Hunt, G.P. . v1p1249c1s
Skeen, W. v1p0984c2s
Skelding, E. v4p0120c1s
v4p0261c1s v4p0344c1s v4p0635c2m
Skelford, W. v2p0210c1s
Skeltie, J. v1p0371c2s
Skelton, H.J. v5p0298c2s
Skelton, J. v1p0060c1s
v1p0082c1s v1p0132c2s v1p0149c1s
v1p0166c2s v1p0169c1s v1p0170c1s
v1p0172c1s v1p0230c1s v1p0318c1s
v1p0355c1s v1p0368c2s v1p0512c1s
v1p0595c1s v1p0643c1s v1p0709c1s
v1p0734c1s v1p0781c2s v1p0873c1s
v1p0892c2s v1p0935c1s v1p0946c1s
v1p0949c1s v1p0958c1s v1p0981c1s
v1p1060c1s v1p1111c2s v1p1128c2s
v1p1132c2m v1p1165c2s v1p1166c1s
v1p1167c2s v1p1170c1s v1p1210c2s
v1p1236c1s v1p1314c2s v1p1328c2s
v1p1411c2s v2p0391c2s v2p0393c2s
v3p0039c2s v3p0270c1m v4p0216c2s
v4p0444c2s v4p0492c1s v4p0509c2s
Skelton, John v3p0381c2s
Skelton, L.J. v6p0332c1s
Skelton, O.D. v6p0514c2s
v6p0706c2s
Skelton, P. v1p0182c2s
v1p0699c1s
Skelton, R.A. v5p0560c1s
Skelton, T.A. v1p0748c2s
Skene, F.M.F. v1p0478c1s
v1p0557c2s v1p0725c2s v1p1030c2s
v1p1053c1s v1p1090c2s v1p1092c2s
v1p1308c2s v3p0348c1s v4p0088c2s
v4p0093c2s v4p0210c1s v4p0241c2s
v4p0482c2s v4p0581c2s v4p0634c1s
v5p0349c1s v5p0478c2s v5p0515c2s
v5p0518c1s v5p0585c2s
Skene, H. v1p0018c2s
Skene, J.H. v1p0018c2s
v1p0431c2s v1p0553c2s v1p0672c2s
v1p1333c1s v2p0107c2s v2p0422c2s
Skerne, S. v1p1077c1s
Skerrett, R.G. v4p0256c2s
Skertchly, S.B.J. v1p0265c1s
v3p0153c2s
Sketchley, A. v1p0878c2m
Sketchley, J. v2p0075c2s
Sketchley, R.E.D. v5p0441c2s
v6p0070c1s v6p0073c2s v6p0086c1s
v6p0150c2s v6p0282c2s v6p0357c2s
v6p0446c1s v6p0689c2s
Skidmore, Eliza R. v6p0200c1s
Skidmore, H. v1p0038c2s
Skidmore, S.T. v3p0445c1m
Skiff, F.J.V. v4p0101c2s
Skillman, W.J. v3p0343c2s
Skilton, C.S. v4p0448c1s
v5p0040c2s
Skilton, J.A. v3p0006c1s
Skinn, C.H. v6p0074c2s
Skinner, A.B. v5p0541c2s
v6p0455c2s
Skinner, A.G. v5p0367c1s
Skinner, A.N. v1p0281c2s
v1p1244c1s v5p0602c2s v6p0280c2s
Skinner, A.W. v6p0250c2s
v6p0293c1s
Skinner, C.A. v1p0775c1s
v1p1398c2s
Skinner, C.E. v3p0139c2s
Skinner, C.M. v2p0298c2s
v3p0185c1s v4p0079c1s v4p0151c1s
v4p0346c2s v5p0021c1s v5p0119c1s
v5p0160c1s v5p0206c1s v5p0211c2s
v5p0417c2s v5p0532c1s v5p0533c1s
v5p0562c2s v5p0607c2s v6p0197c1s
v6p0255c2s v6p0301c2s v6p0455c2s
v6p0475c2s v6p0645c1s v6p0697c1s
Skinner, C.R. v4p0116c1s
v4p0466c1s v6p0428c1s
Skinner, D. v1p1224c1s
Skinner, F.C. v6p0483c2s
Skinner, F.W. v5p0076c1m
v6p0079c2s v6p0187c1s v6p0454c1s
Skinner, G.A. v6p0103c1s
Skinner, G.W. v1p1355c2s
Skinner, H. v4p0610c2s
Skinner, H.D. v5p0429c1s
v6p0018c1s
Skinner, H.M. v5p0566c1s
v6p0608c1s
Skinner, J. v5p0506c2s
v6p0701c2s
Skinner, J.J. v1p0859c1s
v1p1240c2s
Skinner, J.O. v1p0125c2s
v1p0130c2s v1p0675c2s v1p0681c2s
v1p0685c2s v1p0686c1s v1p0687c2s
v1p0697c2s v1p0760c2s v1p1093c2s
v1p1142c2s v1p1346c2s v1p1355c1s
Skinner, M.M. v4p0055c1s
v4p0252c1s
Skinner, O.A. v1p0239c2s
v1p0357c2s v1p0380c2s v1p0528c1s
v1p0925c1s v1p1000c2s v1p1147c2s
Skinner, R.P. v4p0072c2s
v6p0410c2s v6p0422c2s
Skinner, R.R. v6p0410c2s
Skinner, Robert P. v6p0002c1s
Skinner, T.A. v1p1063c2s
v1p1103c2s
Skinner, T.H. v1p0075c1s
v1p0243c2s v1p0252c2s v1p0687c2s
v1p0820c1s v1p0850c2s v1p0966c1s
v1p1043c2m v1p1044c1m v1p1099c1s
v1p1139c2s v1p1149c1s v1p1210c1s
v1p1237c2s v2p0100c2s v2p0235c1s
v2p0352c1s v3p0175c1s
Skinner, T.H., jr. v1p0120c1s
v1p1085c2s v1p1302c2s v1p1326c1s
Skipton, H.G. v4p0093c2s
Skipwith, G.H. v4p0056c1m
v5p0084c1s v5p0176c1s v5p0260c2s
v5p0574c1s v6p0036c1s v6p0259c2s
v6p0330c2s
Skipworth, G.H. v5p0308c1s
Skirving, R. v6p0654c2s
Skirving, R.S. v1p0465c2s
Skitaletz, J.B. v6p0347c1s
Sklodowska-Curie, Mad. ... v6p0526c2s
Skordalsvold, J.J. v3p0039c1s
Skottowe, B. v3p0446c1s
Skottowe, B.C. v4p0095c1s
v5p0611c1s
Skottsberg, C. v6p0023c2s
v6p0675c2s
Skovgaard-Pedersen, Mrs. . v6p0440c1s
Skrine, F.A. v6p0312c2s
Skrine, F.H. v5p0043c1s
v5p0192c1s v5p0286c2s v6p0058c1s
v6p0305c1s
Skrine, J.H. v5p0511c1s
v6p0072c1s v6p0490c1s
Skrine, M.J.H. v5p0222c1s
v5p0273c2s v5p0386c2s v6p0644c2s
Skrine, Mary J.H. v5p0438c1s
Skull, G.D. v2p0194c2s
Skurray, F. v6p0041c2s
Slaby, A. v5p0571c1s
Slack, A.F. v4p0225c1s
Slack, C. v5p0406c1s
Slack, C.W. v3p0444c2s
Slack, H.J. v1p0699c1s
v1p0745c1s v1p0745c2s v1p0805c1s
v1p0812c1s v1p0835c1s v1p0836c1m
v1p0865c2s v1p0992c2s v1p1029c1s
v1p1030c1m v1p1128c2s v1p1172c1s
v1p1239c1s v1p1364c1s v1p1366c2s
v1p1372c1s v2p0093c2s v2p0119c1s
v2p0150c2s v2p0215c1s v2p0258c1s
v2p0278c2s v2p0287c2m v3p0216c1s
v3p0278c1m v3p0465c1s
Slack, H.S. v1p0278c2s
v1p0835c2s
Slack, J. v1p1239c1s
Slade, A. v5p0489c2s
Slade, C.B. v6p0023c2s
v6p0389c1s v6p0590c1s
Slade, D.D. v1p0166c2s
v1p0343c2s v3p0056c1s v3p0080c1s
v3p0271c1s v4p0187c2s v4p0220c1s
v4p0242c2s v4p0342c2s v4p0387c2s
v4p0427c1s
Slade, E. v6p0601c2s
Slade, F.J. v1p1246c2m
v1p1248c1s
Slade, R.J. v4p0029c1s
v4p0032c1s v4p0447c1s v4p0493c2m
v4p0546c2s v4p0608c2s

Slade, R.J. and Jackson, M.P. v4p0029c1s
Slade, R.J. and Sparrow, W.S. v4p0052c2s
Slade, W. v4p0131c1s
Slade, W.A. v5p0268c1s v5p0396c2s v5p0443c2s
Sladen, D. v4p0098c2s v4p0400c1s v5p0404c1s v5p0590c2s
Sladen, Douglas v5p0411c1s
Slafter, E.F. v1p1045c1s v2p0250c2s v3p0010c1s v4p0050c1s
Slagg, J. v1p0284c2s v2p0217c2m v2p0218c1s v2p0218c2s
Slaney, R.A. v3p0322c2s
Slate, F. v3p0245c2s v6p0204c1s v6p0498c1s v6p0498c2s v6p0581c2s
Slater, A., jr. v2p0200c1s
Slater, E. v5p0177c2s
Slater, Edith and Freshfield, F.H. v5p0275c2s
Slater, F.W. v5p0645c1s
Slater, G. v5p0034c2s v5p0273c1s v5p0420c1s v6p0300c1s
Slater, H. et al. v4p0474c1s
Slater, H.D. v5p0528c2s
Slater, J. v2p0020c1s v2p0097c2s v2p0378c1s v2p0399c2s v3p0059c2s v6p0680c1s
Slater, J.B. v6p0692c2s
Slater, J.H. v2p0135c2s v3p0050c1s v4p0067c1s v5p0071c1m v5p0129c1s v5p0345c2s v5p0374c1s v5p0580c1s v6p0073c2m v6p0200c2s v6p0401c2s
Slater, J.R. v5p0200c2s v5p0304c2s v6p0113c1s v6p0329c1s v6p0592c1s
Slater, J.W. v1p1161c2s v1p1162c1s v2p0001c2s v2p0014c2s v2p0158c2s v2p0159c2s v2p0212c2s v2p0215c1s v2p0222c1s v2p0222c2m v2p0319c2s v2p0340c2s v2p0346c2s v2p0390c1s v2p0396c1m v2p0402c2s v2p0444c2s v2p0467c2s v3p0014c1s
Slater, P.F. v5p0235c1s v5p0640c1s
Slater, T. v2p0140c1s v3p0230c1s v5p0019c2s v5p0120c2s
Slater, T.E. v2p0217c1s v3p0428c1s
Slater, W. v3p0349c1s
Slater, W.B. v2p0355c1s
Slater, W.F. v4p0341c2s
Slatterthwaite, L. v6p0600c1s
Slattery, C.L. v3p0052c1s v3p0058c1s v3p0329c2s v4p0506c2s
Slattery, J. v4p0397c1s
Slattery, J.R. v2p0034c2s v2p0308c2s v2p0309c1m v2p0471c2s v3p0282c2s v3p0299c2s v3p0395c1s v4p0322c2s v4p0396c2s v4p0397c1s v5p0402c2s v5p0403c1s v6p0236c2s v6p0516c1s
Slaught, H.E. v4p0223c1s v5p0012c1m v6p0406c1s
Slaughter, C.W. v5p0039c2s
Slaughter, J.W. v5p0024c1s v5p0038c1s v6p0410c2s v6p0427c1s v6p0437c2s
Slaughter, W.B. v1p1432c1s
Slauser, J.A. v6p0355c2s
Slauson, A.B. v6p0373c2s
Slayden, E.M. v4p0368c1s
Slaymaher, G.B. v6p0216c1s
Sledd, A. v5p0279c2s v6p0446c2s
Sleeman, C. v2p0193c2s v2p0196c1s v2p0290c1s v4p0554c2s
Sleeman, P.R. v2p0347c1s
Sleeper, H.D. v5p0640c1s
Sleeper, J.K.C. v3p0389c2s
Sleeper, J.S. v1p0246c2s
Sleeper, Kathrine v5p0318c1s
Sleet, J.C. v6p0257c1s v6p0462c2s
Sleigh, J. v1p0345c2s v1p0782c1s
Slessor, A.K. v5p0008c1s v5p0008c2s v5p0159c1s v5p0243c1s v5p0580c2s v5p0604c2s v6p0449c2s
Slicer, A.E.H. v4p0467c2s
Slicer, T.R. v2p0368c2s v2p0369c2s v3p0084c1s v4p0042c1s v4p0053c1s v4p0206c1s v4p0229c1s v5p0118c1s v5p0392c1s v5p0467c2s v6p0212c1s v6p0259c2s
Slifer, H.J. v5p0298c2s
Slingerland, E. v1p0753c2s
Slingerland, M.V. v4p0445c2s
Slingo, W. v2p0136c2s v2p0137c1m v2p0137c2m v2p0138c1s v2p0138c2m v2p0171c2s v2p0258c2m v2p0272c1s v2p0340c1s v2p0348c2s v2p0390c1s v2p0433c1m v2p0433c2s v3p0133c2s v5p0570c1s
Slipher, V.M. v6p0348c1s
Sloan, C.W. v5p0054c1s v5p0198c2s v6p0273c2s
Sloan, J.M. v2p0292c1s v6p0577c2s
Sloan, M.M. v5p0298c1s v6p0328c2s v6p0616c1s
Sloan, R.I. v4p0552c2s
Sloan, W.H. v2p0059c2s v2p0111c1s v2p0275c2s
Sloane, J.R.W. v2p0042c1s v2p0045c1s
Sloane, R.R. v3p0440c2s
Sloane, T.O. et al. v2p0150c2s
Sloane, T.O'C. v1p0267c2s v2p0426c1s
Sloane, W.M. v1p1063c1s v2p0132c2s v2p0370c1s v3p0031c2s v3p0081c1s v3p0326c1s v3p0344c1s v3p0431c2s v4p0258c2s v4p0392c2s v5p0064c2m v5p0065c1m v5p0128c1s v5p0134c2s v5p0266c2s v5p0373c2s v5p0398c1m v5p0460c1s v5p0620c1s v6p0195c2s v6p0237c2s v6p0388c1s v6p0388c2s v6p0651c1s v6p0671c2s
Sloat, L.W. v1p0188c2s
Slocombe, S. v6p0211c1s
Slocum, C.E. v1p1209c2s v6p0317c1s
Slocum, Grace L. v6p0390c2s
Slocum, H.W. v1p1345c2s v3p0390c2s v4p0434c1s
Slocum, J. v5p0503c2s v5p0547c1s v5p0614c2s v6p0086c1s v6p0172c1s v6p0284c1s v6p0682c1s
Slocum, M.G. v6p0139c1s
Slocum, S.E. v6p0408c1s
Slocum, V. v6p0500c1s
Slocum, V.J. v6p0226c2s
Slocum, W.F. v4p0097c1s v5p0576c2s v6p0139c2s v6p0708c2s
Slocum, W.F., jr. v4p0466c1s
Slocum, W.H. v3p0424c2s
Slocum, W.N. v1p0018c1s
Slomen, A. et al. v6p0214c1s
Slonaker, J.R. v4p0606c1s
Sloss, F.A. v6p0080c2s
Slosson, A.T. v2p0053c2s v2p0209c2s v3p0027c1s v3p0061c2s v3p0112c1s v3p0154c2s v3p0403c2s v4p0093c2s v4p0164c1s v5p0074c1s v5p0586c1s v6p0175c2s
Slosson, Annie T. v6p0509c2s
Slosson, E.E. v4p0367c2s v5p0446c1s v6p0134c1s v6p0186c2s v6p0295c1s v6p0305c2s v6p0411c2s v6p0520c2s v6p0563c2s
Slosson, E.E. and Richardson, G. v6p0476c2m v6p0477c1m v6p0477c2s v6p0630c2s
Slosson, Edwin E. v6p0176c2s
Slosson, M.H. v1p0434c2s v1p0652c1s
Slosson, W.B. v6p0245c2s
Sloughton, J. v2p0278c2s
Sloyd, F.J. v5p0009c1s
Slupp, Margaret B. v6p0090c1s
Slutzski, A. v4p0303c1s
Slyck, F.G.N.Van v5p0192c1s
Slye, R. v5p0368c1s
Slyke, J.G.Van v3p0436c1s v6p0480c2m
Slyke, L.L.Van et al. v3p0236c1s
Smade, W. v6p0172c1s
Smail, J. v5p0496c1s
Smales, H. v1p0476c2m
Small, A. v4p0449c1s
Small, A.D. v3p0378c1s
Small, A.M. v4p0531c2s
Small, A.S. v6p0235c1s
Small, A.W. v2p0452c1s v3p0011c2s v3p0090c2s v3p0442c1s v3p0442c2s v4p0080c2s v4p0100c1s v4p0135c1s v4p0167c2s v4p0531c2s v4p0534c1s v4p0534c2m v4p0535c1s v4p0596c2s v5p0116c2s v5p0132c1s v5p0136c1s v5p0534c2s v5p0535c1m v5p0535c2s v5p0537c2m v5p0567c1s v6p0002c1s v6p0137c2s v6p0572c1s v6p0602c1m v6p0685c2s
Small, A.W. and Abbott, W.J. v5p0002c1s
Small, A.W. and Bawden, H.H. v6p0602c1s
Small, A.W. and Lindsay, S.M. v5p0537c2s
Small, C.H. v5p0079c1s
Small, E.S. v6p0172c1s v6p0501c2s
Small, H. v3p0450c1s
Small, H.C. v6p0259c1s
Small, H.M. v5p0100c1s
Small, M.H. v4p0104c2s v4p0555c2s v5p0536c2s
Small, W.H. v5p0028c1s v5p0512c1s v6p0257c1s v6p0263c2s
Small, W.S. v5p0479c1m
Small, Walter H. v6p0263c2s
Smalley, E. v1p0406c2s v1p0820c1s v1p1406c2s
Smalley, E.M. v1p0366c1s v1p0495c2s v1p0939c2s v1p1084c1s v1p1209c2s
Smalley, E.V. v2p0056c2s v2p0075c1s v2p0091c1s v2p0159c2s v2p0171c1s v2p0175c2s v2p0238c2s v2p0240c2s v2p0290c2s v2p0312c1s v2p0316c2m v2p0320c2s v2p0335c2s v2p0338c2s v2p0359c1s v2p0400c1s v2p0454c2s v2p0472c2s v3p0283c2s v3p0414c1s v4p0026c1m v4p0194c2s v4p0195c1s v4p0317c2s v4p0347c2s v4p0353c2s v4p0456c1s v4p0614c1s v5p0085c1s v5p0309c1s v5p0429c1s v5p0435c1s
Smalley, G.W. v2p0051c1s v2p0052c1s v2p0429c2s v3p0029c1s v3p0304c1s v4p0062c2s v4p0266c1s v4p0270c2s v4p0305c1s v4p0343c2s v4p0592c2s v5p0139c2s v5p0180c1s v5p0190c2s v5p0235c1s v5p0311c1s v6p0043c1s v6p0047c2s v6p0208c2s v6p0209c1s v6p0379c2s v6p0570c2s v6p0695c2s
Smalley, H.A. v2p0454c2s
Smalley, H.S. v6p0529c1s
Smalley, J. v1p0195c1s
Smalley, J.C. v1p0135c1s v1p0245c2s v1p0494c2s v1p1426c2s
Smalley, J.G. v1p0215c2s
Smalley, J.M. v1p0848c2s
Smalley, M.A. v1p0735c2s v1p1116c2s
Smalley, M.G. v1p0215c2s v1p0910c1s v1p1409c2s v1p1439c1s
Smalley, Mrs. v1p0952c1s v1p1108c1s v1p1350c2s v1p1425c2s
Smalley, P.G. v6p0609c2s
Smalley, Phoebe G. v6p0695c2s
Smalls, R. v3p0132c1s
Smallwood, C. v1p0829c2m v1p0936c1s
Smallwood, Martin v5p0387c2s
Smallwood, W.M. v6p0168c1s v6p0590c2s
Smart, C. v5p0029c1m v5p0368c1s
Smart, C.S. v4p0466c1s
Smart, G.T. v6p0109c2s
Smart, H. v1p0887c2s v1p0952c2s v1p1072c2s v1p1270c2s v1p1403c2s v2p0448c2s v3p0154c2s v3p0156c2s
Smart, H.C. v5p0112c2s
Smart, H.T. v4p0601c1s
Smart, R.A. v5p0344c1s
Smart, R.D., jr. v6p0448c1s
Smart, W. v3p0215c1s v3p0218c1s v3p0337c1s v3p0472c1s v4p0157c1s v4p0227c2m v4p0283c2s v4p0378c1s v4p0615c1s v5p0391c2s v6p0300c1s v6p0659c1s
Smeaton, O. v4p0038c1s v4p0071c1s v4p0090c1s v4p0159c1s v4p0166c2s v4p0190c1s v4p0232c2s v4p0296c1s v4p0309c2s v4p0420c2s v4p0548c2s v5p0039c2s v5p0128c1s v5p0140c1s v5p0160c1s v5p0251c1s v5p0301c2s v5p0309c1s v5p0386c2s v5p0515c2s v5p0545c2s v5p0567c2s
Smeaton, Oliphant v5p0565c2s
Smeaton, T.H. v6p0042c2s
Smedberg, O. v1p1228c2s
Smedes, A.K. v1p0854c1s
Smedley, A.Constance v6p0673c1s
Smedley, Constance v6p0525c1s v6p0663c1s
Smedley, F.E. v1p0483c2s v1p0572c1s v1p0804c1s
Smedley, Ida v6p0520c1s
Smedley, M.B. v1p0588c1s v1p0981c1s v1p1422c2s
Smedley, Miss v1p1431c1s
Smedley, W.L. v6p0074c2s v6p0203c2s
Smedt, E.J.De v2p0072c2m
Smee, A. v1p0826c1s v3p0386c2s
Smee, E.M. v1p0184c1s
Smellie, E.S. v5p0488c1s
Smeltzer, J.P. v1p0649c2s
Smet, I.J.De v1p0947c1s
Smet, P.J.De v1p0280c1s v1p0637c1s v1p0638c2s
Smiles, Dr. v1p0090c1s v1p0742c2s
Smiles, R. v1p0810c1s v2p0186c1s v2p0264c1s
Smiles, S. v1p0035c2s v1p0117c1s v1p0190c2s v1p0197c2s v1p0439c1s v1p0611c1s v1p0612c2s v1p0661c1s v1p0712c1s v1p0734c2s v1p0921c1m v1p0984c1s v1p0988c2s v1p1051c2s v1p1083c1s v1p1252c2s v1p1307c1s v1p1363c2s v1p1428c1s v1p1430c2s v2p0197c1s v2p0201c1s v2p0431c2s v3p0028c2s
Smiley, C. v4p0060c2s v4p0061c1s v4p0061c2s
Smiley, C.W. v3p0009c2s
Smiley, E. v1p0777c1s v1p0870c1s v1p1157c1s v1p1355c2s

v3p0230c1s
Smiley, W.H. v4p0512c1s
Smillie, J.D. v4p0187c1s
Smirke, S. v1p0051c1s
v1p0808c2s v1p1011c2s v1p1084c1m
v1p1178c1s v1p1278c2s v1p1301c2s
v1p1402c2m v1p1407c1s
Smirnov v1p0624c2s
Smit, D. v6p0294c2s
v6p0371c1s
Smit, M.J.A.R. v1p0606c2s
Smith, A. v1p0082c1s
v1p0088c2s v1p0100c2s v1p0137c2s
v1p0140c2s v1p0153c2s v1p0163c1s
v1p0216c1s v1p0292c2s v1p0345c1s
v1p0394c1s v1p0439c1s v1p0469c2s
v1p0519c2s v1p0578c1s v1p0582c1s
v1p0753c2s v1p0764c1s v1p0799c2s
v1p0878c1s v1p0923c2s v1p0971c1s
v1p1004c2s v1p1054c1s v1p1165c1s
v1p1201c2s v1p1313c2s v1p1357c1s
v1p1416c1s v1p1441c1s v2p0271c1s
v3p0043c2s v3p0051c2s v3p0146c1s
v3p0258c1s v3p0370c2s v4p0107c2s
v4p0213c1s v4p0496c1s v5p0360c2s
v5p0370c2s v5p0453c2s v5p0514c1s
v5p0550c1s v6p0095c2s v6p0113c2s
v6p0189c2s v6p0223c1s v6p0445c2s
v6p0470c2s v6p0486c1s
Smith, A., Mrs. v1p0034c2s
v1p0774c1s v1p0859c2s v1p1240c1s
v1p1322c2s v2p0113c2s
Smith, A.Beverly v6p0356c1s
Smith, A.C. v5p0200c2s
v5p0437c2s v5p0519c2s v5p0568c2s
v5p0595c1s v6p0171c1s v6p0362c2s
v6p0398c1s v6p0694c1s v6p0710c1s
Smith, A.D. v1p0333c1s
v1p0687c2s v4p0536c1s v4p0594c1s
v5p0005c2s v5p0315c2s
Smith, A.H. v3p0023c2s
v3p0025c1s v3p0137c1s v3p0195c1s
v3p0331c2s v3p0341c2s v4p0423c2s
v4p0428c2m v5p0109c1m v5p0109c2m
v5p0110c2s v5p0111c1m v5p0111c2s
v5p0112c1m v5p0112c2s v5p0113c1s
v5p0254c2s v5p0438c2m v6p0118c1m
v6p0119c1m v6p0239c1s v6p0421c2s
Smith, A.L. v4p0020c2s
v4p0324c2s v4p0511c2s v5p0267c1s
v6p0526c1s v6p0704c1s
Smith, A.M., Mrs. v5p0330c2s
v5p0488c2s v6p0150c2s v6p0693c2s
Smith, A.P. and Cameron, M.
v5p0024c1s
Smith, A.R. v4p0070c1s
v4p0462c2s v4p0521c1s v5p0200c1s
v5p0526c1m v5p0526c2m
Smith, A.T. v2p0006c1s
v2p0131c1s v2p0315c2s v2p0388c1s
v3p0086c1s v3p0421c2s v4p0076c2s
v4p0419c2s v4p0512c1s v5p0177c1s
v5p0178c1s v5p0179c2s v5p0319c2s
v5p0431c1m v5p0475c2s v5p0636c2s
v6p0001c2s v6p0168c2s v6p0190c2s
v6p0192c1s v6p0192c2s v6p0193c2s
v6p0213c2s v6p0224c2s v6p0238c1s
v6p0495c2s v6p0498c1s v6p0521c1s
v6p0563c2s v6p0573c2s v6p0600c2s
v6p0628c2s v6p0705c2s
Smith, A.W. v3p0021c1s
v4p0479c1s v4p0488c1s v6p0054c1s
Smith, A.W.P. v4p0148c2s
v4p0629c2s
Smith, A.W.P., Miss v3p0058c1s
Smith, Alex. v1p0357c1s
v1p0365c2s v1p0782c2s v1p1204c1s
v1p1307c1s v6p0037c2s
Smith, Alice P. v6p0703c1s
Smith, Anna T. v6p0667c1s
Smith, Ashbel v1p1296c2s
Smith, B. v1p0048c1s
v1p0129c2s v1p0248c2s v1p0682c2s
v1p1312c1s v1p1355c2s v2p0060c2s
v3p0088c1s
Smith, B., Mrs. v4p0384c2s
Smith, B.A. v1p0435c2s
v5p0527c2s v6p0389c1s
Smith, B.B. v1p0096c2s
v1p0240c2s v1p0251c2s
Smith, B.E. v4p0541c1s
v5p0153c2s v5p0390c2s v5p0427c1s
v5p0475c2s v5p0545c2s v6p0609c2s
Smith, B.F. v3p0083c1s
Smith, B.G. v1p0282c2s
v1p1394c1s
Smith, B.H. v6p0022c1s
v6p0053c2s v6p0116c1s v6p0126c2s
v6p0278c2s v6p0284c2s v6p0411c2s
v6p0453c2s v6p0504c1s v6p0524c1s
v6p0635c2s v6p0638c2s
Smith, B.W. v2p0466c1s
Smith, Barrett v6p0120c2s
Smith, Bertha M. v6p0469c1s
Smith, Bessie S. v6p0532c2s
Smith, Blanche v6p0073c1s
Smith, C. v1p0323c1s
v1p0535c1s v1p0666c1s v1p0978c2s
v2p0087c1s v2p0224c1s v3p0305c2s
v3p0317c2s v3p0323c1s v3p0371c2s
v3p0426c1s v3p0447c1s v3p0447c2s
v4p0023c1s v4p0124c2s v4p0148c1s
v4p0205c2s v4p0322c1s v4p0326c1s
v4p0393c1s v4p0435c2s v4p0451c1s
v5p0154c2s v5p0212c2s v5p0234c1s
v5p0355c2s v5p0429c2s v6p0164c1s
Smith, C.A. v1p0759c1s
v1p1248c2s v5p0079c2s v5p0540c2s
v5p0573c1s v6p0380c1s v6p0429c1s
v6p0461c2s
Smith, C.Alphonso v6p0296c1s
Smith, C.B. v6p0456c1s
Smith, C.C. v1p0006c1s
v1p0026c2s v1p0032c1s v1p0038c1s
v1p0060c1s v1p0099c1s v1p0110c1s
v1p0152c1s v1p0169c2s v1p0170c2s
v1p0177c2s v1p0179c2s v1p0194c1s
v1p0196c2s v1p0303c2s v1p0321c1s
v1p0355c1s v1p0412c1m v1p0483c2s
v1p0490c2s v1p0497c2s v1p0529c2s
v1p0544c2s v1p0567c1s v1p0572c2s
v1p0593c1s v1p0694c2s v1p0698c2s
v1p0768c1m v1p0781c2s v1p0782c1s
v1p0786c1s v1p0805c2s v1p0808c2s
v1p0811c2s v1p0830c2s v1p0832c2s
v1p0837c2s v1p0861c2s v1p0909c2m
v1p0914c1s v1p0920c1s v1p0987c2s
v1p1047c2s v1p1111c2s v1p1121c2s
v1p1176c2s v1p1182c2s v1p1195c2s
v1p1211c2s v1p1219c2s v1p1224c2s
v1p1280c1s v1p1314c1s v1p1348c1s
v1p1350c2s v1p1386c2s v1p1395c2s
v1p1405c2s v1p1413c1s v1p1416c2m
v1p1425c2s v4p0398c1s v5p0324c2s
v6p0447c2s
Smith, C.D. v5p0339c2s
Smith, C.E. v1p0664c2s
v2p0034c2s v2p0480c1s v4p0010c1s
v4p0467c1s v4p0496c1s v5p0603c2m
v5p0624c2s v6p0515c2s v6p0555c2m
v6p0557c1s v6p0701c2s
Smith, C.E., Sir v1p1165c2s
Smith, C.E.S. v1p0279c1s
Smith, C.F. v2p0411c1s
v2p0412c1s v4p0123c1s v4p0628c1s
v5p0029c2s v5p0153c1s v5p0446c2s
v6p0003c2s v6p0495c1s v6p0701c1s
Smith, C.Fox v6p0707c1s
Smith, C.G. v1p1011c1s
v2p0034c2s v2p0045c1s v3p0311c2s
Smith, C.G. and Gooch, F.A.
v3p0080c1s
Smith, C.H. v1p0027c1s
v2p0174c1s v4p0397c1s v4p0600c2s
v6p0675c1s
Smith, C.H. and Townsend, J.P.
v4p0504c1s v4p0524c2s
Smith, C.J. v6p0321c2s
Smith, C.L. v2p0165c1s
v2p0461c2s v3p0160c2s v5p0126c1s
Smith, C.M. v2p0425c1s
v3p0134c1s v5p0449c1s
Smith, C.McD. v4p0346c2s
Smith, C.McK. v5p0085c1s
Smith, C.P. v3p0276c2s
v3p0416c1s
Smith, C.Piazzi v2p0364c1s
Smith, C.R. v1p0040c1s
v1p0373c1s v1p0409c1s v1p0732c1s
v1p1115c1s v1p1122c2m v1p1154c2m
v1p1296c2s v2p0376c2s v2p0377c1s
v3p0076c2m v3p0365c2s
Smith, C.R.G. v5p0232c2s
Smith, C.S. v1p0051c1s
v1p0558c1s v1p1414c1s v2p0163c1m
v3p0012c1s v3p0061c1s v3p0207c2s
v3p0415c2s v3p0449c2s v4p0005c1s
v4p0457c2s v6p0641c2s
Smith, C.S. and Thurber, F.B.
v5p0468c2s
Smith, C.S. and Weber, J.B.
v4p0275c1s
Smith, C.S. et al. v4p0081c1s
v4p0564c1s
Smith, C.S., Prof. v3p0444c2s
Smith, C.T.R. v3p0008c1s
Smith, C.V. v5p0394c1s
v6p0439c1s
Smith, C.W. v3p0409c1s
v6p0371c1m v6p0581c1s
Smith, C.W. et al. v4p0157c1s
Smith, Campbell v5p0514c2s
Smith, Cecil v4p0248c1s
v5p0320c2s v5p0369c1s v6p0675c1s
Smith, Cecil and Rustafjaell, R.de
v6p0163c1s
Smith, Charlotte F. v6p0429c1s
Smith, Constance v5p0137c1s
v5p0412c2s v5p0499c2s v6p0122c2s
Smith, D. v1p0260c1s
v1p0578c1s v1p1056c1s v1p1270c1s
v5p0058c2s v5p0098c2s v5p0350c2s
v6p0341c1s v6p0342c1s
Smith, D.A.W. v2p0292c1s
Smith, D.C. v3p0337c1s
Smith, D.E. v4p0026c2m
v4p0516c2s v5p0028c1m v5p0178c2s
v5p0366c1s v5p0413c2s v5p0637c1s
v6p0406c1s v6p0406c2s
Smith, D.T. v2p0393c1s
v6p0162c2s
Smith, D.W. v5p0322c2s
Smith, DeCost v4p0154c1s
v4p0292c2s v4p0414c2m v4p0625c1m
Smith, E. v1p0219c1s
v1p0400c2s v1p0465c2s v1p1015c1s
v1p1052c2s v2p0161c2s v2p0418c1s
v3p0007c2s v3p0117c2s v3p0157c1s
v3p0421c2s v3p0448c1s v4p0459c2s
v4p0484c2s v5p0293c1s v5p0343c1s
v6p0386c1s
Smith, E. and McKeen, J. . v4p0477c1s
Smith, E.A. v1p0026c2s
v1p0461c2s v1p0799c1s v2p0229c2s
v2p0435c2s v4p0009c1s v4p0230c2s
v4p0389c1s v4p0454c1s v4p0571c1s
v4p0590c2s v5p0088c2s v5p0155c2s
v5p0465c1s v5p0467c1s v5p0529c1s
v5p0529c2s v5p0585c1s v5p0592c1s
v5p0596c2s v5p0610c2s v6p0168c1s
v6p0276c1s v6p0380c2s v6p0422c2s
v6p0518c1s
Smith, E.A. and Aldrich, T.H.
v6p0264c1m
Smith, E.B. v1p0154c2s
v1p0239c2s v1p0376c2s v1p0811c1s
v1p0890c2s v1p1139c1s v1p1340c2m
v5p0047c2s v5p0105c1m v5p0391c2s
v5p0469c1s v5p0474c1s v6p0169c2s
v6p0307c1s v6p0436c1s v6p0621c1s
Smith, E.C. v2p0229c2s
v6p0092c1s
Smith, E.D. v1p0242c1s
v1p1099c2s
Smith, E.E. v6p0635c2s
Smith, E.F. v1p0664c1m
v3p0316c2s v3p0329c1s v3p0414c2s
v4p0020c2s v4p0041c1m v4p0142c2s
v4p0233c2s v4p0317c1s v4p0325c2s
v4p0445c2s v4p0560c2s v5p0042c2s
v5p0104c1m v5p0182c2s v5p0223c1s
v5p0277c1s v5p0330c1s v5p0337c1s
v5p0453c2m v5p0461c2s v5p0537c1s
v6p0199c2s v6p0503c1s
Smith, E.F. and Desi, E.D.
v4p0586c2s
Smith, E.F. and Frankel, L.K.
v3p0134c1s
Smith, E.F. and Lenher, V.
v4p0016c1s
Smith, E.F. and Swingle, D.B.
v6p0046c2s
Smith, E.F. et al. v4p0613c2s
Smith, E.G. v1p0232c2s
v1p0303c1s v1p0359c2s v1p0626c1s
v1p1042c1s v1p1096c1s v1p1197c1s
v1p1326c1s v1p1340c2s v1p1383c2s
v1p1406c2s
Smith, E.H. v1p0727c2s
Smith, E.H., Prof. v5p0483c2s
Smith, E.J. v4p0185c1s
v4p0242c1s v5p0584c1m v5p0585c1s
v5p0615c2s v6p0652c2s
Smith, E.L. v1p0784c2s
Smith, E.M. v2p0115c1s
v4p0086c2s v5p0019c1s v5p0301c2s
v6p0097c2s v6p0439c2s
Smith, E.O. v1p0523c1s
v1p0789c2s v1p0798c2s v1p0856c2s
v1p0876c1s v1p1308c2s v1p1372c1s
v1p1419c2s v1p1436c2s v2p0080c1s
v4p0061c2s v4p0115c1s
Smith, E.O., Mrs. v1p0930c2s
v5p0088c1s
Smith, E.P. v1p0486c2s
v1p1027c1s v1p1057c2s v3p0174c1s
Smith, E.R. v5p0025c2m
v6p0028c2m v6p0140c1s v6p0370c2s
v6p0579c2s v6p0624c1s
Smith, E.T.M. v5p0626c2m
Smith, E.V. v1p0837c2s
Smith, E.V., Mrs. v1p1019c2s
v1p1084c2s
Smith, E.W. v5p0447c2s
Smith, Edwin B. v6p0170c2s
Smith, Eli v1p1333c2s
Smith, Elizabeth L. v5p0095c1s
Smith, Ellen A. v5p0283c1s
v6p0461c1s
Smith, Ellen D. v5p0012c1s
Smith, Ellen G. v6p0113c1s
Smith, Eugene v2p0418c1s
v6p0157c2s v6p0583c2s
Smith, F. v1p0333c2s
v1p0637c2s v4p0110c2s v4p0264c1s
v5p0158c1m v5p0289c2s v5p0368c2s
v5p0437c1s v5p0457c2s v5p0535c2s
v5p0550c1s v5p0568c1s v5p0600c2s
Smith, F.A. v4p0194c1s
v6p0084c2s
Smith, F.B. v6p0482c2s
Smith, F.C. v5p0154c1s
v5p0219c2s v5p0222c2s
Smith, F.Clifford v5p0475c2s
Smith, F.E. v5p0097c1s
Smith, F.E.G. v3p0270c1s
Smith, F.G. v5p0542c1s
Smith, F.H. v1p0022c1s
v1p0161c2s v1p1162c2s v1p1171c2s
v1p1268c2s v3p0059c2s v3p0067c2s

v3p0092c2s v3p0112c1s v3p0142c2m
v3p0224c2s v3p0277c1s v3p0349c1s
v3p0394c2s v3p0440c2s v4p0001c1s
v4p0002c1s v4p0040c1s v4p0102c1m
v4p0129c2s v4p0130c2s v4p0158c1s
v4p0222c1s v4p0232c1s v4p0303c2s
v4p0304c2s v4p0312c2s v4p0317c1s
v4p0478c1s v4p0578c2s v4p0602c1s
v5p0166c1s v5p0215c1s v5p0359c1s
v5p0398c2s v5p0431c2s v6p0008c1s
v6p0142c1s v6p0216c2s v6p0234c2s
v6p0346c2s v6p0434c2s v6p0457c2s
v6p0458c2s v6p0518c1s
v6p0646c2s
v6p0675c2s
Smith, F.H. and Millet, J.B.
v3p0066c1s v3p0301c2s v3p0397c1s
Smith, F.H., jr. v6p0088c1s
Smith, F.Hargraves v5p0172c2s
Smith, F.Hopkinson v5p0087c2s
Smith, F.J. v3p0125c2s
v3p0401c2s v6p0508c1s
Smith, F.L. v1p0533c2s
Smith, F.M. v4p0147c1s
v4p0442c1s v5p0282c1s v5p0339c2s
v5p0578c2s v6p0422c2s v6p0617c2s
Smith, F.M. and Bartlett, Boyd
v6p0095c1s
Smith, F.M. and Mason, W.. v4p0420c2s
Smith, F.N. v4p0123c2s
Smith, F.O.J. v1p0093c1s
v1p0295c2s v1p0304c1s v1p0325c2s
v1p1038c1s v1p1054c2s v1p1078c1s
v1p1264c2s v1p1289c2s
Smith, F.P. v3p0222c1s
v3p0361c1s
Smith, F.W. v6p0191c1s
v6p0574c2s v6p0581c2m
Smith, FitzHenry, jr. v6p0580c2s
Smith, Frances v5p0376c2s
Smith, Franklin v6p0167c1s
v6p0614c2s
Smith, G. v1p0011c2s
v1p0043c1s v1p0058c2s v1p0068c1s
v1p0077c2s v1p0172c1s v1p0192c2s
v1p0193c1s v1p0195c2s v1p0201c1s
v1p0209c2s v1p0251c1s v1p0303c1s
v1p0310c2s v1p0368c1s v1p0370c2s
v1p0372c2s v1p0384c1s v1p0408c1s
v1p0428c1s v1p0439c1s v1p0439c2s
v1p0526c1s v1p0546c1s v1p0595c1s
v1p0600c2s v1p0625c2s v1p0632c2s
v1p0666c2m v1p0689c2s v1p0704c1s
v1p0731c1s v1p0741c1s v1p0768c1s
v1p0779c1s v1p0779c2s v1p0800c2s
v1p0842c2s v1p0926c1s v1p0943c1s
v1p0954c1s v1p0979c2s v1p1066c2m
v1p1088c2s v1p1106c1s v1p1109c2s
v1p1133c2s v1p1181c2s v1p1230c2s
v1p1294c2s v1p1330c1s v1p1332c2m
v1p1357c2s v1p1358c1s v1p1405c1s
v2p0061c1s v2p0142c1s v2p0143c1s
v2p0147c1s v2p0171c2s v2p0186c1s
v2p0251c2s v2p0270c2s v2p0292c1s
v2p0293c1s v2p0325c1s v3p0036c1m
v3p0066c1s v3p0138c1s v3p0155c1s
v3p0160c2s v3p0167c2s v3p0179c1s
v3p0230c2s v3p0234c2s v3p0266c1s
v3p0287c2s v3p0296c2s v3p0300c1s
v3p0345c2s v3p0346c1s v3p0437c2s
v3p0467c2s v3p0470c1s v4p0009c2s
v4p0018c1s v4p0028c2s v4p0052c2s
v4p0070c1s v4p0072c2s v4p0079c2s
v4p0122c2s v4p0137c2s v4p0181c2m
v4p0212c2s v4p0216c1s v4p0216c2s
v4p0219c1s v4p0237c2s v4p0239c2s
v4p0250c1s v4p0253c1s v4p0266c1s
v4p0331c1s v4p0338c1s v4p0353c1s
v4p0353c2m v4p0365c2s v4p0374c1s
Smith, G. v4p0414c1s
v4p0419c2s v4p0420c1s v4p0434c2s
v4p0444c2s v4p0473c2s v4p0523c1s
v4p0545c1s v4p0595c1s v4p0595c2m
v4p0596c1s v4p0596c2s v5p0054c1s
v5p0086c2s v5p0092c1s v5p0145c1s
v5p0190c1s v5p0234c2s v5p0247c2s
v5p0269c1s v5p0284c2s v5p0296c2s
v5p0299c2s v5p0341c1s v5p0434c1s
v5p0452c2s v5p0522c2s v5p0543c2s
v5p0600c1s v6p0003c1s v6p0025c1s
v6p0054c2s v6p0097c2s v6p0101c2s
v6p0191c1s v6p0208c2s v6p0310c1s
v6p0666c2s
Smith, G. and Savary, A.W.
v5p0511c2s
Smith, G. et al. v2p0143c2s
v4p0596c1s
Smith, G., Dr. v5p0285c2s
Smith, G.A. v2p0245c2s
v2p0408c1s v4p0010c2s v4p0049c1s
v4p0054c2s v4p0055c1s v4p0055c2s
v4p0285c2s v4p0396c1s v5p0169c2s
v5p0260c2s v5p0385c1s v6p0061c2s
v6p0165c2s v6p0217c1s v6p0340c1m
v6p0343c1s v6p0443c2s v6p0583c2s
v6p0596c1s v6p0713c1s
Smith, G.B. v1p0086c2s
v1p0125c2s v1p0169c1s v1p0170c1s
v1p0172c2s v1p0349c2s v1p0413c1s
v1p0451c2s v1p0511c2s v1p0530c1s
v1p0540c2s v1p0541c2s v1p0842c1s
v1p1019c2s v1p1192c2s v1p1212c2s
v1p1275c1s v1p1294c2s v1p1386c2s
v2p0009c2s v2p0028c2s v2p0196c2s
v2p0246c2s v2p0267c2s v2p0430c2s
v3p0058c2s v3p0076c2s v3p0164c2s
v4p0288c2s v4p0427c2s v5p0148c2s
v5p0398c1s v5p0469c2s v5p0632c1s
v6p0521c2s
Smith, G.Barnett v4p0048c2s
v4p0492c1s v6p0134c2s
Smith, G.C. v2p0110c2s
v2p0443c1s v4p0509c2s
Smith, G.C.M. v5p0042c2s
v6p0627c2s v6p0688c2s
Smith, G.C.Moore v6p0441c2s
Smith, G.E. v5p0005c2s
Smith, G.F. v4p0145c2s
v5p0139c1s
Smith, G.G. v3p0040c1s
v3p0058c2s v3p0262c2s v3p0425c1s
v3p0467c1s v6p0348c2s
Smith, G.H. v1p0113c1s
v1p0729c2s v1p0736c1s v2p0481c2s
v3p0046c2s v3p0233c2s v3p0244c2s
v3p0246c1s v4p0307c1s v4p0378c1s
v4p0420c2s v4p0592c2s v5p0061c2s
v5p0460c1s v6p0348c1m v6p0364c1s
v6p0469c1s v6p0533c1s v6p0544c1s
Smith, G.J. v4p0184c1s
v5p0027c2s v6p0697c1s
Smith, G.L. v3p0212c1s
v6p0159c2s v6p0173c2s v6p0231c1m
v6p0514c2m
Smith, G.Le Blanc v5p0212c2s
v5p0413c1s v6p0514c2s v6p0616c2s
Smith, G.M. v5p0137c2s
v5p0327c2s v5p0533c1s
Smith, G.M., Sir v5p0078c1s
v5p0276c1s v5p0574c2s
Smith, G.N. v1p0377c1s
v1p1399c2s
Smith, G.P. v3p0351c2s
v3p0400c2s
Smith, G.T. v2p0059c2s
v2p0233c2s
Smith, G.V. v1p0074c2s
v1p0124c2s v1p0130c1s v1p0243c2s
v1p0314c1s v1p0751c1s v1p0983c1s
v1p1174c2s v2p0041c2s v2p0085c1s
v2p0451c2s v4p0255c2s
Smith, G.Vance v1p0127c1s
Smith, G.W. v2p0037c1m
v2p0395c2s v2p0453c2s
Smith, G.W.V. v1p1211c2s
Smith, Garnet v3p0168c1m
v4p0202c1s v5p0520c1s v6p0242c1s
Smith, Geo., Dr. v4p0473c2s
v5p0343c1s v5p0607c2s
Smith, Geo.A. v5p0058c1s
Smith, Geo.B. v1p1264c1s
Smith, Geo.M. v5p0533c2s
Smith, George v1p1197c1s
v2p0194c1s v5p0380c1s
Smith, Gertrude v3p0427c1s
v4p0442c2s v4p0492c2s
Smith, Goldwin v1p0014c1s
v1p0017c2s v1p0021c1s v1p0034c2s
v1p0157c2s v1p0164c1s v1p0168c2s
v1p0170c2s v1p0192c1s v1p0194c1s
v1p0194c2s v1p0195c1s v1p0270c1s
v1p0410c1s v1p0419c1s v1p0441c2s
v1p0476c2s v1p0487c1s v1p0538c1s
v1p0545c1s v1p0546c2s v1p0657c1s
v1p0690c2s v1p0715c1m v1p0750c1m
v1p0793c1s v1p0807c1s v1p0808c1s
v1p0856c1s v1p0868c1m v1p0869c2s
v1p0943c2m v1p0954c1s v1p0976c2s
v1p0987c2s v1p0993c2s v1p1089c2s
v1p1095c1s v1p1124c1m v1p1215c2s
v1p1230c2s v1p1254c2s v1p1261c1s
v1p1283c1s v1p1295c2s v1p1306c1s
v1p1331c1s v1p1344c1s v1p1352c2s
v1p1355c1s v1p1357c2s v1p1399c1s
v1p1425c2s v1p1426c1s v1p1437c2s
v2p0015c2s v2p0066c1s v2p0090c2m
v2p0115c2s v2p0130c1s v2p0136c1s
v2p0149c2s v2p0189c2m v2p0206c1s
v2p0208c2s v2p0224c2m v2p0225c1s
v2p0225c2m v2p0236c2s v2p0239c1s
v2p0297c2s v2p0306c1s v2p0334c2s
v2p0466c2s v2p0482c1s v3p0012c1s
v3p0062c2s v3p0065c1m v3p0083c1s
v3p0181c1s v3p0225c2s v3p0269c2s
v3p0310c1s v3p0325c1s v3p0333c1m
v3p0347c1s v3p0388c2s v3p0405c1s
v3p0408c1s v3p0420c1s v3p0441c2s
v3p0459c1s v4p0054c2s v4p0133c1s
v4p0163c2s v4p0180c2s v4p0210c1s
v4p0223c1s v4p0275c2s v4p0322c1s
v4p0344c2s v4p0356c1s v4p0382c2s
v4p0514c2s v4p0520c2s v4p0546c2s
v4p0628c1s v5p0272c2s v5p0281c1s
v5p0281c2m v5p0484c1s v5p0497c1s
v5p0604c2s v5p0618c1s v5p0625c1s
v6p0029c1s v6p0088c2s v6p0095c2s
v6p0096c2s v6p0143c2s v6p0159c1m
v6p0183c2s v6p0193c2s v6p0200c1s
v6p0243c2s v6p0257c2m v6p0258c1s
v6p0293c1s v6p0299c2s v6p0309c1s
v6p0313c1s v6p0327c2s v6p0343c2s
v6p0442c1s v6p0473c2s v6p0482c1s
v6p0484c1s v6p0536c1s v6p0538c1s
v6p0542c2s v6p0578c2s v6p0601c1s
v6p0667c1s v6p0667c2s
Smith, H. v1p0140c1s
v1p0306c2s v1p0773c1s v1p0854c2s
v1p0885c2s v1p1075c2s v2p0117c1s
v2p0125c2s v2p0196c2s v3p0064c1s
v3p0123c2s v3p0291c2s v3p0306c2s
v3p0346c2s v3p0418c2s v4p0207c1s
v4p0230c2s v4p0282c2s v4p0538c1s
v5p0486c2s v6p0278c1s v6p0285c2s
v6p0377c1s
Smith, H., Mrs. v1p0007c1s
Smith, H., Rev. v3p0229c1s
v4p0010c1s
Smith, H., Sir v5p0486c2s
v6p0385c1s
Smith, H.A. v2p0426c2s
v5p0110c1s v5p0643c2s
Smith, H.A. and Allen, G.. v4p0094c1s
Smith, H.Arthur v4p0128c1s
v4p0388c2s v4p0389c1s
Smith, H.Atterbury v6p0154c1s
Smith, H.B. v1p0027c2s
v1p0254c1s v1p0254c2s v1p0432c1s
v1p0514c1s v1p0568c1s v1p0625c1s
v1p0684c2s v1p0688c1s v1p0839c2s
v1p0903c1s v1p1001c1s v1p1046c2s
v1p1047c1s v1p1088c1s v1p1111c2s
v1p1363c2s v2p0017c1m v2p0143c2s
v2p0207c1s v2p0422c2s v5p0319c2s
v5p0322c2s v6p0132c1s
Smith, H.B.L. v6p0652c1s
Smith, H.B.Lees v6p0665c1s
Smith, H.C. v6p0509c2s
Smith, H.D. v1p0770c1s
v3p0097c2s v3p0180c1s v3p0190c1s
v3p0196c2s v3p0294c1s v3p0360c1s
v3p0441c1s v4p0131c1s v4p0319c1s
v4p0558c2s v5p0487c1s
Smith, H.D., jr. v6p0572c1s
Smith, H.DeF. v5p0126c2s
v5p0249c2s
Smith, H.E. v3p0081c2s
v3p0122c2s v3p0183c2s v3p0195c1s
v3p0232c2s v3p0243c1s v4p0014c2s
v4p0186c1s v4p0402c2s v5p0407c1s
v6p0246c2s v6p0535c2s
Smith, H.F.H. v3p0401c1s
Smith, H.G. v1p0339c1s
v2p0380c1s v4p0580c1s v6p0003c2s
v6p0183c1s v6p0210c1s v6p0316c1s
v6p0707c1s
Smith, H.G. et al. v6p0537c1s
Smith, H.H. v1p0026c1s
v1p0271c1s v1p0423c2s v1p0966c1s
v1p1108c2s v2p0009c2s v2p0055c1s
v3p0115c1s v3p0372c2s v4p0420c2s
v4p0444c2s v4p0540c1s v5p0272c2s
v6p0501c2s v6p0692c2s
Smith, H.H. and
Fitzmaurice, E., Lord . v2p0247c2s
Smith, H.H. and Trepplin, E.C.
v4p0146c1s
Smith, H.I. v4p0187c1s
v4p0369c1s v5p0077c1m v5p0427c1s
v5p0503c2s v6p0023c2s v6p0460c1s
v6p0465c1s v6p0500c2s v6p0590c1s
v6p0710c2s
Smith, H.J. v3p0340c2m
v5p0066c1s v6p0012c2s v6p0391c2s
v6p0415c1s
Smith, H.J.S. v2p0281c1s
Smith, H.K. v4p0344c1s
Smith, H.L. v1p0835c2s
v1p1068c1s v2p0433c2s v4p0314c2s
v4p0340c1s v4p0340c2s v4p0566c2s
v6p0102c2s
Smith, H.Lavers v6p0629c1s
Smith, H.M. v4p0200c2s
v5p0011c1s v5p0208c2s v5p0509c1s
v6p0182c2s v6p0226c2s v6p0244c2s
v6p0335c1s v6p0396c2s v6p0401c1s
v6p0677c2s
Smith, H.N. v1p1336c1s
Smith, H.P. v1p0692c1s
v2p0043c1s v2p0052c1s v2p0279c2s
v2p0470c1s v3p0041c2s v3p0042c1s
v4p0055c1s v6p0040c1s v6p0061c2s
Smith, H.Preserved v6p0288c2s
Smith, H.S.S. v2p0275c1s
v2p0459c1s
Smith, H.W. v5p0269c1s
Smith, Harlan F. v6p0701c1s
Smith, Harlan I. v6p0139c2s
Smith, Harry v5p0021c2s
Smith, Helen E. v5p0380c2s
Smith, Horace v1p1193c1s
Smith, Hugh M. v6p0226c2s
Smith, I. v5p0223c1s
v5p0475c1s
Smith, I.G. v1p0262c2s
v3p0409c2s v5p0590c2s
Smith, I.T. v1p0630c2s
v3p0051c1s
Smith, I.W. v3p0087c1s
Smith, Isabel v5p0421c2s

v1p1271c1s v2p0043c1s v3p0100c1m
Smith, R.R. v3p0306c2s
v5p0632c2s
Smith, R.S. v2p0357c2s
Smith, R.T. v6p0567c1s
Smith, R.W. v2p0213c2s
Smith, Robinson v6p0512c1s
Smith, Roger v4p0078c1s
Smith, S. v1p0295c1s
v1p0336c1s v1p0774c2s v1p1007c1s
v1p1013c2s v1p1070c1s v1p1198c2s
v1p1373c1s v2p0077c2s v2p0078c1s
v2p0116c2s v2p0218c2s v2p0220c2s
v2p0247c2s v2p0256c1s v2p0407c1s
v3p0105c2s v3p0128c2s v3p0129c1s
v3p0377c2s v4p0502c2s v5p0332c2s
v5p0368c1s v5p0482c1s v5p0503c1s
v5p0512c2s v5p0590c1s v6p0175c2s
v6p0320c1s v6p0430c2s
Smith, S., Mrs. v1p0943c2s
Smith, S.A. v6p0089c1s
Smith, S.B. v1p0207c1s
v1p0286c1s v1p0859c2s v1p1096c1s
v6p0461c2s v6p0705c2s
Smith, S.D., jr. v6p0441c2s
v6p0442c1s
Smith, S.F. v1p0038c2s
v1p0060c2s v1p0097c1s v1p0097c2s
v1p0123c1s v1p0132c1s v1p0180c2s
v1p0234c2s v1p0242c2s v1p0244c2s
v1p0264c2s v1p0276c1s v1p0310c1s
v1p0319c1s v1p0320c1s v1p0372c2s
v1p0398c1s v1p0432c2s v1p0470c2s
v1p0641c1s v1p0698c2s v1p0726c1s
v1p0732c2s v1p0782c1s v1p0824c1s
v1p0832c2s v1p0841c1s v1p0923c1s
v1p0923c2s v1p0982c2s v1p1140c2s
v1p1167c2s v1p1396c1s v2p0081c1s
v2p0214c2s v3p0013c2s v3p0083c1s
v3p0135c1s v3p0175c1s v3p0215c2s
v3p0229c2s v3p0254c1s v3p0261c2s
v3p0311c2s v3p0355c2s v3p0356c2s
v3p0362c1s v4p0039c1s v4p0040c1s
v4p0131c2s v4p0227c2s v4p0249c2s
v4p0269c2s v4p0285c1s v4p0353c2s
v4p0359c2s v4p0437c1s v6p0057c2s
v6p0151c1s v6p0156c2s v6p0160c1s
v6p0191c2s v6p0274c1s v6p0287c1s
v6p0321c1s v6p0340c2s v6p0518c1s
v6p0547c2m v6p0675c2s v6p0683c2s
v6p0690c2s
Smith, S.F. et al. v3p0190c2s
Smith, S.G. v3p0389c1s
v4p0139c2s v4p0285c1m v4p0449c2s
v5p0143c2s v5p0154c1s v5p0378c2s
Smith, S.H. v1p0367c1s
Smith, S.I. v1p0042c1s
v1p0321c2s v1p0470c1s v1p0758c1s
Smith, S.K. and Money, R.I.
v5p0416c2s
Smith, S.P. v1p1043c2s
v2p0369c1m v3p0378c1s
Smith, S.R. v1p0247c1s
v1p0688c2s v1p0993c1s v1p1055c1s
v1p1404c1s v6p0239c2s
Smith, S.S. v1p0287c1s
v4p0141c1s
Smith, S.T. v1p0942c2s
v1p1220c1s v1p1277c2s v2p0216c1s
Smith, S.W. v6p0039c2s
Smith, Saml. v1p1198c2s
Smith, Samuel Harrison, Mrs.
v6p0687c1m
Smith, Seba v1p0033c1s
v1p0909c2s v1p1374c2s
Smith, Seba, Mrs. v1p0503c2s
v1p0620c2s v1p1189c1s
Smith, Sigma v4p0274c2s
v4p0510c1s
Smith, Southworth v1p0036c2s
Smith, Syd. v1p0027c1s
v1p0027c2s v1p0030c1s v1p0036c2s
v1p0067c1s v1p0113c1s v1p0138c1s
v1p0153c2m v1p0155c1s v1p0214c1s
v1p0231c1s v1p0262c1s v1p0264c2s
v1p0265c2s v1p0307c2s v1p0315c2s
v1p0324c2s v1p0344c1s v1p0387c2s
v1p0390c1s v1p0391c2s v1p0395c2s
v1p0421c1s v1p0442c1s v1p0452c1s
v1p0472c1m v1p0475c2s v1p0499c1s
v1p0539c2s v1p0552c1s v1p0568c2s
v1p0602c2s v1p0622c1s v1p0632c2s
v1p0643c2s v1p0647c1s v1p0653c1m
v1p0661c2s v1p0676c2s v1p0720c2s
v1p0723c2s v1p0725c1s v1p0727c1s
v1p0740c1s v1p0786c1s v1p0789c1s
v1p0795c2s v1p0830c1m v1p0870c1s
v1p0896c2s v1p0904c1s v1p0913c2s
v1p0960c2s v1p0961c1s v1p0974c2s
v1p0975c1s v1p0994c2s v1p1005c1s
v1p1031c1s v1p1031c2s v1p1052c1s
v1p1053c1m v1p1054c2s v1p1062c2s
v1p1066c1s v1p1069c2s v1p1096c2s
v1p1098c2s v1p1112c2s v1p1116c2m
v1p1196c1s v1p1225c1s v1p1240c2s
v1p1241c2s v1p1314c2s v1p1323c1s
v1p1331c1s v1p1369c2s v1p1418c2s
v1p1422c1s
Smith, Syd. and Playfair, J.
v1p0954c1s
Smith, T. v1p0447c1s
v1p0639c1s v1p0784c2s v1p1052c1s
v1p1211c1s v3p0030c1s v6p0175c2s
v6p0408c2s v6p0415c2s v6p0425c1s
Smith, T., Mrs. v2p0449c2s
Smith, T.B. v2p0076c2s
v2p0083c1s v2p0307c1s v2p0390c2m
v2p0451c1s
Smith, T.C. v3p0235c1s
v3p0360c2s v5p0183c1s v5p0462c2s
v5p0600c2s v6p0110c1s v6p0293c1s
v6p0645c1s v6p0668c1s
Smith, T.G. v5p0253c1s
Smith, T.G., jr. v4p0165c1s
v4p0547c1s
Smith, T.K. v5p0467c1s
Smith, T.L. v6p0005c2s
v6p0116c2s v6p0166c1s v6p0521c2s
v6p0526c1s
Smith, T.L. and Hall, G.S.
v6p0137c1s v6p0323c1s v6p0376c2s
Smith, T.O. v5p0132c2s
Smith, T.P. v2p0356c1s
v3p0281c1s v4p0601c2s
Smith, T.R. v1p0052c1s
v1p0174c1s v1p0647c2s v2p0019c1s
v2p0378c1s v2p0464c2s v3p0017c2m
v3p0018c2s v3p0035c2s v3p0069c1s
v3p0378c2s v4p0023c1s
Smith, T.R. and White, W.H.
v3p0125c1s
Smith, T.Roger v3p0054c1s
Smith, T.T.V. v1p0928c2s
v1p1404c1s
Smith, Theodate L. v4p0364c2s
v6p0115c2s v6p0463c2s
Smith, Theodate L. and Hall, G.S.
v6p0053c1s v6p0592c2s
Smith, V. v1p1263c2s
v3p0170c2s v3p0436c1s
Smith, V.A. v3p0309c1s
Smith, V.G. v1p0910c2s
Smith, V.T. v3p0077c1s
Smith, Victor v6p0394c2s
Smith, W. v1p0168c1s
v1p0207c2s v1p0557c2s v1p0639c2s
v1p0711c1s v1p0790c2s v1p0849c2s
v1p0921c2s v1p1246c2s v1p1375c2m
v2p0229c2s v2p0275c1s v2p0305c1s
v2p0369c2s v2p0455c2s v4p0057c1s
v4p0094c2s v4p0171c1s v4p0312c2s
v4p0554c2s v4p0606c1s v5p0056c1s
v5p0293c1s v6p0159c2s v6p0185c2s
v6p0607c1s v6p0647c1s
Smith, W.A. v1p0374c2s
v4p0098c1s v4p0127c1s v4p0200c2m
v4p0253c1s v4p0445c2s v4p0447c2s
v4p0582c2s
Smith, W.B. v3p0308c2s
v5p0059c2m v5p0256c1s v6p0041c1s
v6p0064c1m v6p0445c2s v6p0484c2m
v6p0640c2s
Smith, W.B. and Page, T.N.
v6p0448c2s
Smith, W.C. v1p0023c1s
v1p0372c1s v1p0424c2s v1p0784c2m
v1p0873c1s v1p1167c1s v1p1387c2s
v1p1434c2s v2p0058c1s v2p0181c1s
v2p0212c1s v2p0290c2s v3p0362c2s
v3p0381c1s v4p0153c2s v4p0157c1s
v4p0209c2s v4p0508c2s v4p0585c2s
v5p0515c1s v6p0142c1s v6p0164c2s
v6p0347c1s v6p0364c1s v6p0532c1s
v6p0659c2s
Smith, W.C. and Sheble, F.
v3p0456c2s
Smith, W.E. v1p0081c2s
Smith, W.F. v1p0228c1s
v1p0256c2s v1p1011c2s v1p1152c2s
v2p0121c2s v2p0400c2s v2p0453c1s
v2p0454c2s v3p0036c1s v3p0349c1s
Smith, W.G. v1p0882c1s
v1p0960c1s v1p1039c1m v2p0037c1s
v2p0274c1s v2p0326c2m v2p0421c1s
v3p0318c1s v4p0033c2s v4p0364c2m
v4p0422c1s v4p0490c1s v5p0627c2s
v6p0498c2s v6p0711c2s
Smith, W.G. and Waterhouse, J.
v6p0592c2s
Smith, W.G.P. v4p0152c1s
v5p0158c1s v6p0129c2s
Smith, W.H. v1p0335c1s
v1p0349c2s v1p0500c1s v1p0946c2s
v1p1143c1s v1p1183c2s v2p0002c2s
v2p0011c1s v2p0059c1s v2p0155c2s
v2p0187c1s v2p0271c2s v2p0295c2s
v2p0354c2s v2p0364c2s v2p0383c1s
v2p0469c2s v3p0087c2s v3p0288c2s
v3p0343c2s v3p0380c1s v3p0424c2s
v4p0299c1s v4p0312c2s v4p0411c2s
v4p0544c2s v4p0556c1s v4p0565c1s
v4p0595c2s v5p0098c1s v5p0178c2s
v5p0182c2s v5p0399c2s v6p0095c2s
v6p0447c1s
Smith, W.H., Mrs. v5p0314c1s
Smith, W.J. v1p0545c1s
v4p0589c2s v6p0684c1s
Smith, W.J. and Hyde, G.W.
v3p0071c2s
Smith, W.O. v5p0252c2s
Smith, W.R. v1p0039c1s
v1p0117c1s v1p0121c2s v1p0125c2s
v1p0334c2s v1p1212c1s v2p0042c2s
v2p0272c1s v2p0327c1s v3p0041c2s
v3p0107c1s v3p0230c1s v3p0286c2s
v3p0384c2s v4p0253c1s v5p0632c1s
v6p0129c2s v6p0606c1s v6p0640c1s
Smith, W.R. and Conder, C.R.
v3p0041c1s
Smith, W.R. and Poole, R.S.
v3p0041c2s
Smith, W.Robertson v2p0327c2s
v3p0230c1s
Smith, W.Roy v6p0159c1s
Smith, W.S. v1p0486c1s
v3p0203c1s v5p0205c1s v6p0204c1s
v6p0616c1s
Smith, W.S.T. v6p0093c2s
Smith, W.Sooy v1p1019c1s
Smith, W.T. v3p0029c2s
v5p0174c1s
Smith, W.Taylor v4p0054c2s
Smith, W.W. v1p0734c1s
v3p0382c1s v4p0510c1m v5p0515c2s
Smith, Wilberforce v4p0567c1s
Smith, Wilder v1p0246c2s
Smith, Z.B. v2p0472c2s
Smith, Z.D. v3p0341c1s
Smith-Gordon, L. v3p0310c1s
Smith-Rossie, Charlotte .. v6p0115c2s
v6p0479c2s
Smithells, A. v4p0201c2s
v5p0103c2s v6p0031c1s v6p0673c2s
Smithmeyer, J.L. v1p0291c2s
v3p0159c1s v4p0330c2s
Smock, J.C. v1p0666c1m
Smoot, T.A. v6p0459c2s
Smucker, I. v1p0693c2s
v1p0928c2s v1p0938c2s v1p1400c1s
v1p1413c1s v2p0061c2s v2p0220c1s
v2p0299c2s v2p0300c1s v2p0316c2m
v2p0320c1m v2p0435c2s v3p0066c2s
v3p0086c2s v3p0214c2s v3p0235c2m
v3p0307c2m v3p0310c2m v3p0360c1s
v3p0424c2s v3p0455c2s v4p0576c2s
Smucker, Isaac v3p0377c1s
Smylie, R. v5p0390c1s
Smyser, B.B. v1p1356c2s
Smyser, W.E. v4p0520c1s
v5p0057c2s
Smyth, A.H. v3p0387c2s
v5p0223c2s v5p0259c1m v6p0239c1s
v6p0239c2s v6p0333c1s
Smyth, C. v6p0066c1s
v6p0138c1s v6p0453c2s
Smyth, C. and Davis, H. .. v6p0222c2s
Smyth, C.H. v4p0011c2s
Smyth, C.H., jr. v4p0011c2s
v4p0218c2m v4p0291c2s v4p0435c1s
v4p0499c1s v6p0174c1s v6p0524c2s
Smyth, C.P. v1p0502c1s
v1p1068c1s v1p1134c2s v1p1292c1s
v1p1305c1s v1p1311c2s v2p0110c2s
v2p0127c1s v2p0360c1s v2p0413c2m
v2p0434c2m v2p0468c2m v3p0407c1s
Smyth, C.Piazzi v2p0095c2s
Smyth, D.D. v6p0690c1s
Smyth, E. and Burrage, H.S.
v2p0034c2s
Smyth, E.C. v1p0148c1s
v1p0373c2s v1p0432c1s v1p0567c1s
v1p1063c2s v1p1275c1s v1p1382c1s
v2p0013c2s v2p0034c2s v2p0355c2s
v2p0432c1m v3p0120c1s v3p0130c2s
v3p0229c1s v3p0345c1s v3p0346c2s
v3p0472c2s v4p0417c2s v5p0180c1s
Smyth, F. v4p0139c2s
Smyth, F.O.J. v1p0322c1s
Smyth, G.B. v5p0108c2s
v5p0109c1s
Smyth, G.H. v1p0029c2s
v1p1164c2s v2p0391c1s
Smyth, H. v1p0436c1s
Smyth, H.L. v3p0409c2s
v4p0369c1s
Smyth, H.P. v2p0153c1s
Smyth, H.W. v2p0135c2s
v2p0206c2s v3p0117c2s v4p0522c2s
v5p0527c2s v6p0396c1s
Smyth, H.Weir v3p0184c1s
Smyth, J.H. v6p0185c1s
Smyth, J.J. v1p0244c1s
v1p0618c1s
Smyth, J.K. v4p0036c2s
v4p0053c1m v4p0053c2m v4p0108c1s
v4p0109c1s v4p0191c1s v4p0229c1s
v4p0300c2s v4p0301c1s v4p0314c2s
v4p0417c1s v4p0430c2s v5p0024c2s
v5p0125c1s v5p0197c2s v5p0240c1s
v5p0519c1s v5p0544c1m v5p0563c2s
v5p0618c2s v6p0419c2s
Smyth, L.T. v6p0389c2s
Smyth, N. v1p0651c1s
v2p0067c1s v2p0122c1s v2p0245c1s
v2p0365c1s v2p0407c1s v2p0425c2s
v2p0437c1s v3p0010c2s v3p0240c2s
v3p0344c1s v4p0054c2s v4p0219c1s
v4p0342c1s v6p0506c2s
Smyth, N. et al. v2p0106c2s
v2p0438c1s

v5p0494c2s v6p0213c2s v6p0584c2s
Smith, Isabel, Mrs. v5p0433c2s
v5p0485c1s v6p0177c1s v6p0420c2s
v6p0673c2s
Smith, J. v1p0159c1s
v1p0275c2s v1p1020c2s v1p1165c2s
v1p1249c1m v1p1250c1s v1p1386c1s
v2p0082c1s v2p0147c1s v2p0291c2s
v2p0318c2s v2p0343c2s v2p0382c1m
v5p0109c1s v5p0110c2s v5p0380c1s
v5p0498c2s v6p0136c2s v6p0507c2m
Smith, J. et al. v6p0429c1s
Smith, J.A. v1p0045c2s
v1p0331c2s v1p0973c1s v1p1058c2s
v1p1096c1s v1p1303c1s v3p0058c2s
v3p0126c2s v3p0253c2s v3p0342c2m
v3p0475c1s v4p0377c2s v4p0554c1s
v5p0250c1s
Smith, J.B. v1p1267c1s
v2p0016c1s v3p0289c2s v4p0064c1s
v4p0093c1s v4p0202c1s v4p0235c1s
v4p0242c2s v4p0256c2s v4p0362c1s
v4p0409c2s v4p0432c1s v4p0450c2s
v4p0631c2s v5p0231c2s v5p0292c1s
v6p0022c2s v6p0431c2m
Smith, J.Bainbridge v6p0038c2s
Smith, J.C. v1p0248c2s
v1p0752c2s v1p0803c1s v2p0294c2s
v6p0711c1s v6p0713c1s
Smith, J.D. v1p0407c1s
v1p0579c1s
Smith, J.E. v1p0117c2s
v1p1160c2s v1p1391c2s v3p0109c1s
v5p0101c2s v5p0215c2s
Smith, J.F. v1p0441c2s
v1p0483c2s v1p0517c2s v1p0530c1s
v1p0587c1s v1p0738c2s v1p1042c2s
v1p1157c1s v1p1236c2s v2p0043c2s
v2p0176c2s v2p0356c2s v6p0429c1s
Smith, J.F. et al. v6p0429c1s
Smith, J.Few v1p0119c2s
v1p0528c2s v1p0687c2s v1p1043c1s
v1p1043c2s v1p1065c1s v1p1104c2s
Smith, J.G. v4p0090c2s
v5p0318c1s v6p0194c1s v6p0472c1s
Smith, J.G. and Godley, A.D.
v5p0426c1s
Smith, J.Gordon v6p0334c2s
v6p0580c2s v6p0632c1s
Smith, J.H. v2p0388c2s
v4p0034c1s v4p0079c1s v4p0138c2s
v6p0018c1m v6p0031c2s v6p0404c2s
v6p0616c1s
Smith, J.H. and MacQueen, P.
v4p0004c1s
Smith, J.J. v1p0987c2s
v5p0518c1s
Smith, J.L. v1p0022c2s
v1p0061c1s v1p0065c1s v1p0146c1s
v1p0304c2s v1p0405c2s v1p0507c2s
v1p0580c2s v1p0664c1m v1p0827c2m
v1p0828c1m v1p0828c2m v1p0835c2s
v1p0844c1m v1p0986c2s v1p1162c1s
v1p1162c2s v1p1304c2s v2p0229c1s
v2p0340c1s v6p0565c1s
Smith, J.L. and Brush, G.J.
v1p0844c1s
Smith, J.L. and Hall, G.S.
Smith, J.L.C. v2p0199c1s
Smith, J.Lawrence v1p0405c2s
Smith, J.Lawrence v1p0405c2s
Smith, J.M. v1p0647c2s
v4p0328c2s v4p0546c1s
Smith, J.M.C. v1p0989c1s
Smith, J.M.P. v5p0154c2s
v6p0215c1s v6p0317c2s
Smith, J.M.P. and Kelso, J.A.
v6p0598c1s
Smith, J.M.P., and Wildeboode
v5p0056c2s
Smith, J.McCune v1p0265c2s
v1p0767c2s
Smith, J.McL. v1p0452c2s
v2p0156c1s
Smith, J.N. v4p0401c2s
v4p0529c2s v4p0588c1s
Smith, J.O.,Mrs. et al. .. v2p0265c2s
Smith, J.Obed v6p0097c1s
Smith, J.P. v1p0130c2s
v1p0338c1s v2p0074c1s v2p0232c2s
v2p0291c1s v3p0151c1m v3p0165c2m
v3p0222c1s v3p0290c1s v3p0292c2s
v3p0331c1s v3p0333c2m v3p0384c1s
v4p0235c1s v4p0491c1s v5p0043c1s
v5p0272c1s v6p0138c2s v6p0474c1s
Smith, J.P.G. et al. v2p0422c2s
Smith, J.Pye v1p0124c2m
v1p0646c1s
Smith, J.R. v3p0042c2s
v3p0043c2s v4p0057c1s v4p0151c1s
v4p0202c1s v5p0059c1s v5p0174c2s
v5p0194c1s v5p0249c1s v5p0300c2s
v5p0307c1s v5p0396c2s v5p0398c1s
v5p0443c2s v5p0541c1m v5p0553c1s
v5p0618c1s v6p0040c2s v6p0117c2s
v6p0119c1s v6p0141c1s v6p0157c1s
v6p0233c1s v6p0236c2s v6p0241c1s
v6p0431c2s v6p0442c1s v6p0520c2s
v6p0681c2s
Smith, J.Ritchie v5p0060c1s
Smith, J.Russell v6p0029c1s
v6p0241c1s v6p0463c2s v6p0503c1s
Smith, J.S. v1p0161c1s
v2p0240c1s v3p0370c1s v3p0370c2s
v4p0197c2s v4p0480c2s v4p0569c1s
v5p0395c2s
Smith, J.T. v1p0038c2s
v1p0087c1s v1p0096c2s v1p0201c2s
v1p0688c2s v1p0737c1s v1p1101c1s
v1p1420c1s v2p0034c2s v2p0035c2s
v2p0077c2s v2p0135c2s v2p0409c1s
v2p0462c2s v3p0052c2s v3p0065c2s
v3p0170c1s v3p0238c1s v3p0241c1s
v3p0252c2s v3p0452c2s v4p0043c1s
v4p0354c1s v4p0503c2s v6p0181c1s
v6p0255c2s v6p0380c1s v6p0508c2s
v6p0547c1s v6p0596c1s v6p0658c2s
Smith, J.V.C. v1p0273c1s
v1p0456c2s v1p1044c2s
Smith, J.W. v1p1043c2s
v4p0137c1s v4p0229c1s v4p0533c1s
v5p0044c1s v5p0067c2s v5p0082c2s
v5p0261c1s v5p0524c2s v5p0582c2s
v5p0630c2s v6p0022c1s v6p0452c1s
Smith, James v1p0128c1m
Smith, Jessie G. v6p0522c1s
Smith, Joe v6p0428c1s
Smith, John v5p0307c2s
Smith, Josiah R. v6p0538c2s
Smith, Judson v4p0374c2s
Smith, K. v6p0389c2s
Smith, K.F. v4p0156c1s
v5p0185c2s v5p0396c1s v6p0276c2s
v6p0403c1s
Smith, K.L. v5p0053c2s
v5p0335c1s v5p0335c2s v6p0033c1s
v6p0035c2s v6p0279c2s v6p0370c2s
v6p0420c1s v6p0443c2s v6p0528c2s
v6p0572c1s
Smith, K.V. v1p0573c1s
Smith, Kate D. v6p0202c2s
Smith, Kate E. v6p0222c1s
Smith, Kate L. v6p0617c2s
Smith, Katherine L. v5p0098c2s
v5p0409c2s v6p0131c2s v6p0564c2s
Smith, L. v3p0427c1s
v6p0104c1s v6p0398c1s v6p0573c1s
Smith, L.A. v3p0205c1s
v3p0368c1s v3p0400c2s v4p0249c2s
v4p0297c2s v4p0536c2m v4p0602c1s
v4p0612c2s v5p0376c1s
Smith, L.E. v1p0075c1s
v1p0118c2s v1p0180c1s v1p0381c1s
v1p0412c1s v1p0909c2s v1p1147c2s
v1p1230c1s v2p0044c2s v3p0281c2s
v5p0439c1s v6p0023c1s v6p0174c2s
v6p0548c2s
Smith, L.E., Mrs. v4p0089c2s
Smith, L.E.M. v4p0588c1s
Smith, L.G. v6p0132c1s
v6p0599c2s
Smith, L.H. v4p0565c2s
Smith, L.Horton v4p0225c1s
v5p0232c2s
Smith, L.K. v5p0126c1s
Smith, L.M. v4p0474c1s
Smith, L.P. v1p0184c2s
v1p0359c2s v1p0742c1s v1p0894c2s
v1p0997c2s v1p1013c2s v1p1182c1s
v1p1257c2s v2p0045c2s v2p0255c2s
v2p0256c1s v5p0629c1s v6p0624c2s
Smith, L.P. and Robinson, R.E.
v5p0474c1s
Smith, L.R. v3p0447c2s
Smith, L.S. v6p0187c1s
Smith, L.T. v1p0977c2s
v2p0118c1s v2p0127c1s v2p0143c2m
v2p0256c2s v2p0275c2s v3p0450c1s
v5p0317c1s v6p0395c2s
Smith, L.T. and Ward, Humphry, Mrs.
v5p0317c1s
Smith, L.W. v4p0121c2s
v4p0161c2s v5p0079c2s v5p0282c1s
v5p0323c1s v6p0085c1s v6p0588c2s
v6p0638c2s v6p0664c2s
Smith, Laura A. v3p0454c2s
v4p0344c2s v5p0276c2s v5p0539c1s
Smith, Laura G. v6p0305c1s
Smith, Lena R. v6p0124c2s
Smith, Lewis W. v6p0161c2s
Smith, Lt.Comdr. v6p0031c1s
Smith, Lucy T. v4p0213c1s
Smith, Lucy Toulmin v4p0071c1s
Smith, M. v1p0240c2s
v2p0048c1s v2p0150c1s v2p0175c2s
v2p0176c2s v2p0307c1s v3p0090c1s
v3p0171c2m v3p0244c2s v3p0348c1s
v4p0062c1s v4p0077c1s v4p0100c1m
v4p0212c1s v4p0224c1s v4p0224c2s
v4p0228c2s v4p0303c1s v4p0377c1s
v4p0623c2s v5p0064c2s v5p0065c1m
v5p0080c2s v5p0193c1s v5p0236c1s
v5p0308c2s v5p0374c1s v5p0457c1s
v5p0632c2s v6p0010c1s v6p0363c2s
v6p0424c2s v6p0518c1s
Smith, M. and Dunning, W.A.
v5p0457c1s
Smith, M. and Stimson, F.J.
v3p0090c1s v3p0244c2s
Smith, M., Mrs. v5p0352c1s
Smith, M.B. v4p0469c1s
Smith, M.C. v2p0249c1s
v2p0477c2s v3p0464c1s v4p0032c2s
v4p0436c2s v5p0096c1s v5p0220c1s
v5p0300c1s v6p0087c2s
Smith, M.E. v2p0002c1s
v2p0009c2s v2p0184c2s
Smith, M.E.C. v4p0347c1s
Smith, M.H. v1p0180c1s
v1p0750c1s v1p0755c2s v1p1396c2s
v5p0294c2m v5p0476c2s
Smith, M.J. v6p0288c2s
Smith, M.K. v4p0021c2s
v4p0566c1s
Smith, M.P. v4p0624c2s
v5p0003c1s v5p0305c2m v5p0531c1s
Smith, M.R. v4p0628c1s
v4p0628c2s v5p0165c2m v5p0636c2s
v6p0536c2s
Smith, M.R.D. v1p0146c2s
Smith, M.S. v3p0039c1s
v3p0456c1s v6p0470c2s
Smith, Margaret Bayard ... v6p0687c1s
Smith, Margaret K. v2p0132c1s
v6p0361c1s
Smith, Mary Campbell v4p0092c1s
v4p0604c2s
Smith, Mary R. v4p0011c2s
v4p0626c2s v5p0407c2s v5p0636c2s
v6p0283c2s
Smith, Minna C. v3p0019c2s
v5p0263c1s v6p0276c2s
Smith, Minnie R. v5p0555c1s
Smith, Munroe v4p0224c1s
v4p0450c2s v4p0560c2s v5p0064c2s
v5p0065c1m v5p0236c1s v6p0139c2s
v6p0237c1s v6p0366c2s
Smith, N. v2p0293c2s
v2p0303c2s v5p0387c2s v6p0156c2s
v6p0216c1s v6p0302c2s
Smith, N.A. v4p0311c1s
v5p0106c1s v5p0108c1s v5p0280c2s
v5p0316c1s v6p0608c1s
Smith, N.B. v6p0338c2s
Smith, N.C. v4p0122c1s
Smith, N.F. et al. v2p0166c2s
Smith, N.H. v4p0354c1s
v5p0424c2s
Smith, N.L. v4p0001c1s
v4p0509c2s
Smith, N.W. v4p0477c2s
Smith, Nora A. v6p0409c2s
v6p0500c1s
Smith, Nowell v5p0144c2s
v6p0078c2s
Smith, O. v2p0281c2s
v3p0209c1s v3p0352c1s v3p0379c2s
v4p0180c1s v4p0347c1m v4p0347c2s
v4p0413c1s v4p0470c2s v5p0308c2s
v5p0353c1s v5p0371c2s v6p0649c2m
Smith, O.B. v6p0068c1s
Smith, O.H.P. v5p0198c1s
Smith, O.M. v5p0599c1s
Smith, Oberlin and Janvier, H.A.
v6p0134c2s
Smith, P.C. v4p0396c2s
Smith, P.H. v2p0001c2s
Smith, P.V. v2p0188c2s
v2p0272c1s v2p0478c1s v4p0052c2s
v6p0125c2s
Smith, P.W.B. v3p0169c2s
Smith, Piazzi v2p0296c2s
Smith, Q.D., Mrs. et al. . v4p0215c2s
Smith, R. v1p0171c1s
v1p0522c1s v1p0700c1s v1p0842c2s
v1p1261c2s v3p0017c2s v3p0212c1s
v4p0151c1s
Smith, R.A. v1p0035c1s
v1p0517c1s v1p0844c1s v1p1143c2s
v1p1366c2s v2p0284c2s v2p0290c1m
v3p0118c2s v3p0380c1s v3p0396c1s
Smith, R.B. v1p0379c1s
v2p0226c1s v3p0004c2s v3p0284c2s
v3p0391c1s v5p0117c1s v6p0067c1s
v6p0395c1s v6p0472c2s v6p0531c2s
Smith, R.C. v5p0582c2s
v5p0583c1m v6p0669c1s v6p0685c2s
Smith, R.D. v5p0146c1s
v5p0627c2s v6p0079c1s v6p0081c2s
v6p0617c1s
Smith, R.D. and Steiner, B.C.
v6p0088c1s
Smith, R.D.O. v4p0036c1s
v5p0462c2s
Smith, R.E. v5p0277c2s
v5p0627c2s
Smith, R.F. v6p0091c2s
Smith, R.H. v1p0466c2s
v2p0044c1s v3p0309c2s v6p0170c1s
v6p0318c1s
Smith, R.H. and Gildersleeve, B.L.
v4p0128c1s
Smith, R.L. v5p0403c2s
Smith, R.M. v2p0220c2s
v2p0245c1m v2p0245c2s v2p0347c2s
v2p0349c2s v3p0072c1m v3p0127c2s
v3p0136c2s v3p0208c2s v3p0408c1s
v3p0452c2s v4p0050c1s v4p0596c2s
v5p0099c2s
Smith, R.P. v1p0095c2s

Smyth, P. v1p1234c1s
v2p0441c2s
Smyth, P.G. v4p0349c2s
v5p0105c1s v5p0296c1s
Smyth, P.J. v1p0661c1s
Smyth, Piazzi v2p0095c1s
Smyth, R. v5p0409c2s
Smyth, R.B. v1p1370c1s
v2p0027c2s
Smyth, R.D. v5p0054c1s
v5p0084c2s v5p0121c1s v5p0171c2s
v5p0216c1s v5p0255c1s v5p0329c1s
v5p0391c1s v5p0414c2s v5p0433c2s
v5p0497c2s v6p0053c1s v6p0070c2s
v6p0107c2s v6p0111c1s v6p0129c2s
v6p0243c1s v6p0291c1s v6p0293c2m
v6p0346c1s v6p0546c1s v6p0589c2s
Smyth, R.D. and Steiner, B.C.
v6p0091c2s v6p0264c2s
v6p0590c2s
v6p0709c1s
v6p0345c1s
Smyth, R.S. v6p0369c1s
v6p0002c2s
Smyth, T. v1p0398c1s
v1p0447c2s v1p0792c1s v1p1175c1s
v3p0334c1s
Smyth, T.C. v3p0413c2s
Smyth, W. v6p0502c2s
Smyth, W.H. v1p0265c2s
v1p0273c2s v1p0403c1s v1p0538c2s
v1p0575c1s v1p1122c2s v4p0288c2s
v5p0294c2m v5p0353c1s v5p0582c2s
Smyth, W.W. v1p0267c2s
v1p0666c1s
Smythe, A.H. v2p0281c2s
Smythe, C. v5p0122c1s
v5p0367c1s v5p0589c1s
Smythe, C.W.E. v5p0404c2s
Smythe, F. v1p1359c1s
Smythe, G.S. v1p0627c1s
v1p1105c1s
Smythe, Lillian C. v6p0002c2s
Smythe, N.E. v6p0092c1s
Smythe, R. v6p0635c2s
Smythe, W.D. v5p0582c2s
Smythe, W.E. v4p0026c1m
v4p0083c2s v4p0292c2m v4p0596c2s
v4p0599c1s v5p0299c1s v5p0606c1s
v5p0621c2s v5p0625c2s v6p0139c2s
v6p0327c1s v6p0329c1m v6p0329c2m
v6p0350c1s v6p0472c2s v6p0473c2s
v6p0567c1s v6p0658c2s
Smythe, W.G. v5p0255c2s
Smythe, W.H. v1p0102c1s
Smythe, W.M. v1p0130c1s
Smythies, F.K. v3p0019c1s
Smythies, W.G. v2p0022c2s
v3p0045c2s v3p0112c1s v3p0148c1s
v4p0521c2s
Smythies, W.Gordon v5p0233c1s
Snagge, T.W. v1p0271c2s
v5p0139c2s
Snaith, J.C. v5p0322c1s
Snead, L.W. v5p0272c2s
Snead, T.L. v2p0121c2s
Sneath, R.G. v3p0109c1s
v3p0312c1s v3p0465c2s
Snedden, D.S. v6p0290c1s
Snedeker, F.W. v3p0202c2s
v4p0460c2s v4p0572c2s
Sneed, H.P. v6p0448c1s
Snell, A.S. v6p0298c1s
Snell, B.J. v4p0263c1s
v4p0626c1s v4p0633c1s v5p0019c1s
Snell, B.J. et al. v4p0557c2s
Snell, E.L. v4p0016c2s
v4p0384c1s v4p0599c2s
Snell, E.Lisle v6p0263c2s
Snell, E.S. v1p0564c2s
v1p0747c2s v1p1081c1s v1p1293c1s
Snell, F.J. v4p0147c2s
v5p0021c1s v5p0121c1s v6p0303c1s
v6p0541c2s v6p0685c1s
Snell, H.I. v6p0285c2s
Snell, H.M. v2p0180c2s
v2p0389c2s v2p0395c1s v2p0433c1s
Snell, H.S. v2p0208c1s
Snell, M.M. v3p0058c2s
v3p0229c1s v3p0265c2s v3p0322c1s
v3p0364c2s v4p0077c2s v4p0229c1s
v4p0258c1m v4p0478c2m v4p0487c2s
v4p0507c2s v4p0573c2s v5p0342c2s
v5p0409c2s v5p0483c1s v5p0493c2s
v5p0578c1s v6p0249c2s
v6p0381c1s v6p0456c1s
Snell, T. v1p0504c1s
v1p0809c1s
Snell, W.D.P. v5p0535c2s
Snell, W.E. v4p0132c2m
v4p0461c1s v5p0004c1s v5p0292c2s
Snell, W.E. and Ludlow, J.M.
v5p0136c1s
Snelling, G.T. v2p0100c1s
Snelling, S. v5p0534c1s
Snelling, W.J. v1p0139c2s
v1p0172c1s v1p0636c1s v1p1404c1s
Snelus, G.J. v1p0455c1s
v1p0665c1s v1p1091c1s
Snevets, S.D. v1p0136c1s
Sneyd, H. v1p0712c2s
v1p1332c2s
Sneyd, W. v2p0211c1s
Snider, D.J. v1p1183c1s
v1p1183c2m v1p1184c1m v1p1184c2s
v1p1185c1m v1p1185c2m v1p1186c1m
v1p1186c2m v1p1187c1m v2p0206c2s
v3p0199c2s
Snider, G.E. v6p0530c2s
Snively, D. v1p1042c1s
Snively, J.H. v1p0110c2s
v1p0405c1s v1p0990c1s v1p1044c2s
v1p1218c1s
Snively, W.A. v1p1120c1s
Snoad, W. v4p0629c2s
Snoddy, J.S. v5p0191c2s
v5p0232c2s v5p0325c2s v5p0558c2s
Snoddy, Ja.S. v5p0191c1s
Snodgrass, A.E. v5p0004c1s
Snodgrass, J.E. v1p0086c2s
v1p1072c2s
Snoilsky, C. v2p0146c1s
Snook, F.W.G. v5p0311c1s
Snook, H.C. v6p0019c1s
Snow, A. v4p0338c1s
Snow, B.M. v6p0071c1s
v6p0077c1s
Snow, B.W. v5p0009c1s
v5p0627c2s
Snow, C.H. v3p0439c1s
Snow, C.L. v1p1423c1s
Snow, D.E. v1p0107c2s
v1p0170c1s v1p0626c2s v1p1311c2s
v4p0210c1s
Snow, F. v3p0154c1s
v4p0081c2s v4p0104c2s v4p0250c2s
Snow, F.E. v2p0355c2s
v6p0273c2s
Snow, F.H. v1p0108c2s
v2p0145c1s v2p0240c2s v3p0353c2s
v6p0490c2s
Snow, F.L. ....
v5p0080c1s v4p0636c2s
Snow, Florence L. v5p0497c1s
Snow, G.D'O. v1p0946c2s
v1p1303c1s
Snow, H. v1p0660c2s
v1p1029c1s v3p0066c2m v3p0271c2s
Snow, J. v1p1014c2s
v1p1111c1s
Snow, L.F. v6p0302c2s
Snow, Lorenzo v6p0429c1s
Snow, M.B. v1p0921c2s
Snow, M.E.O. v5p0054c2s
v6p0173c2s
Snow, M.S. v1p0219c2s
v1p0994c1s v1p1134c2s v1p1137c1s
v1p1377c2s v4p0092c2s v5p0092c2m
v5p0632c2s v6p0136c1s v6p0200c2s
v6p0290c2s
Snow, O.T. v4p0474c2s
Snow, T. v5p0328c1s
v6p0154c2s
Snow, T.B. v4p0246c1s
v5p0233c2s
Snow, T.C. v4p0112c2s
v5p0433c1s
Snow, T.R. v3p0211c1m
Snow, W.B. v3p0147c2s
v4p0252c2s v4p0602c2s v5p0167c2s
v5p0260c2s v6p0071c2m v6p0619c1s
Snow, W.B. and Fontaine, C.
v6p0241c1s
Snow, W.P. v1p0018c1s
v1p0078c1s v1p0425c1s v1p0936c2s
Snow, Walter B. v6p0180c1s
Snowden, A.L. v6p0048c1s
v6p0584c2s
Snowden, C.L. v5p0105c1s
Snowden, Col. v4p0593c2s
Snowden, J.K. v6p0150c1s
Snowden, J.R. v1p0341c2s
v2p0110c1s
Snowden, K. v6p0078c1s
v6p0204c1s v6p0465c2s v6p0516c2s
v6p0626c2s
Snowden, P. v6p0356c2s
v6p0652c1s
Snowden, Philip v6p0355c2s
v6p0356c2s
Snowdon, F.S. v5p0127c2s
Snowdon, J.S. v2p0155c2s
Snowdon, J.W. v2p0039c1m
Snure, J. v5p0295c2s
Snyder, C. v4p0081c1s
v4p0119c1s v4p0197c1s v4p0231c1s
v4p0474c2s v4p0612c2s v5p0092c1s
v6p0079c2s v6p0112c1s v6p0199c1s
v6p0318c2s v6p0375c2s v6p0376c1s
v6p0382c2s v6p0408c1s v6p0465c1s
v6p0498c2s v6p0575c2s v6p0636c1s
v6p0712c1s
Snyder, C.B.J. v5p0407c2s
Snyder, C.J. v6p0309c2s
Snyder, F.E. v4p0037c2s
Snyder, G.D. v6p0443c1s
v6p0681c2s
Snyder, G.W. v2p0203c2s
Snyder, H. v6p0602c2s
Snyder, H.M. v6p0605c1s
Snyder, H.N. v6p0136c2s
v6p0170c2s v6p0555c1s v6p0713c1s
Snyder, H.P. v5p0125c2s
Snyder, J. v3p0165c2s
v3p0299c1s v3p0346c1s v4p0499c1s
Snyder, J.F. v2p0300c1s
v2p0421c1s
Snyder, M.B. v2p0137c2s
v4p0034c1s v4p0598c1s v5p0256c2s
v6p0614c2s
Snyder, P. v3p0244c2s
Snyder, P.W. v4p0560c2s
Snyder, W. v4p0412c1s
Snyder, W.S. v5p0343c2s
Soames, C. v1p0990c1s
Soames, J.M. v4p0271c2s
v4p0580c2s
Soane, G. v1p0098c1s
Soanes, F. v1p1280c1s
Soar, C.D. v6p0422c2s
Soares, G.De M. v1p0606c2s
Soares, G.M. v1p1129c1s
Soares, T.G. v4p0056c1s
v4p0252c2s v5p0057c2s v5p0308c1s
v5p0572c1s v6p0065c1s v6p0341c1s
Soares, Victor E. v6p0114c1s
Sobko, N. v4p0435c2s
v4p0602c2s
Sobolev v3p0369c2s
Sobolewski, E. v1p0819c2s
v1p0883c1s v1p0884c1s v1p1160c1s
Sobral, J.G. v5p0410c2s
Socyer, J.N. v1p1393c2s
Soddy, F. v6p0526c2s
v6p0527c1m
Soddy, F. and Marckwald, W.
v6p0527c1s
Soddy, F. et al. v6p0040c1s
Soden-Smith, R.H. v4p0031c1s
v4p0455c1s
Soderholm, J.W. v2p0046c1s
Sodian, L. v5p0476c2s
Sohm, R. v5p0231c2s
Sohn, J. v4p0506c2s
v5p0019c2s v5p0299c2s v5p0361c1s
v6p0438c1s
Sohncke, L. v2p0108c2s
v2p0440c2s v4p0120c2s
Soignie, D. v1p1075c1s
Soigvolk, P. v1p0230c1s
v1p1156c1s
Soissons, Count de v5p0220c2s
v5p0221c1s v5p0230c2s v5p0492c1s
v6p0461c2s v6p0500c2s v6p0544c1s
Soissons, S.C.de v5p0017c1s
v5p0068c1s v5p0101c1s v5p0253c1s
v5p0348c1s v5p0355c2s v5p0498c1s
v5p0509c2s v5p0510c2s v5p0609c2s
v5p0635c1s v6p0072c1s v6p0242c1s
v6p0252c1m v6p0252c2s v6p0262c1s
v6p0394c1s v6p0559c2s v6p0593c2s
Soissons, S.C.de, Count .. v5p0240c2s
v5p0441c2s
Sokal, E. v4p0483c2s
Solano, E.J. v6p0036c2s
v6p0265c1s v6p0266c2s v6p0571c2s
Solano, E.T. v6p0312c2s
Solaville, M.de v2p0265c1s
Solberg, A. v4p0042c1s
Solberg, F. v4p0067c2s
Solberg, T. v2p0075c2s
v2p0102c2m v2p0251c2s v2p0387c1s
v3p0022c1s v3p0049c2s v3p0100c1m
v3p0141c1s v3p0206c2s v3p0249c2s
v4p0133c1s v4p0133c2m v5p0070c1s
v5p0136c2s v5p0137c1m v6p0149c1m
v6p0162c2s
Soldan, F.L. v2p0312c1s
v4p0257c1s v5p0569c2s v6p0199c2s
Soldan, F.L. and Brown, J.S.
v6p0136c1s
Soldan, L. v1p0391c2s
v1p1089c1s
Soldan, L.F. v1p0323c1s
v1p0331c1s v1p0331c2s v1p0390c1s
v1p0729c1s
Soleman, W. v2p0022c1s
v2p0133c1s v2p0432c1s
Solenberger, E.D. v6p0109c1s
v6p0219c1s
Soley, A.R.R. v5p0507c1s
Soley, J.F.Rose v5p0506c2s
Soley, J.R. v2p0330c1s
v3p0095c2s v3p0159c2s v3p0263c1s
v3p0298c1s v3p0443c2s v3p0454c1s
Solis-Cohen, S. v3p0245c1s
v6p0216c1s
Solis-Cohen, S. and Weed, E.D.
v5p0281c2s
Sollas, W.J. v4p0018c2s
v4p0351c2s v4p0444c2s v5p0077c1s
v5p0137c1s v5p0223c1s v5p0229c1s
Sollas, W.T. v4p0152c1s
v4p0222c2s
Solly, E. v1p0339c2s
v1p1147c1s v2p0016c1s v2p0031c1s
v2p0130c2s v2p0135c2s v2p0166c1s
v2p0185c1s v2p0204c1s v2p0254c2s
v2p0270c2s v2p0312c1s v2p0473c1s
v3p0267c1s v3p0433c2s v4p0259c2s

v4p0560c1m
Solly, H. v1p1289c1s v2p0142c1s v2p0432c2s v3p0105c2s v3p0450c1s
Solly, H.S. v1p1026c1s v1p1160c1s v1p1377c2s v2p0254c1s v2p0349c1s
Solly, J.R. v4p0161c1s
Solms-Laubach, H. v4p0623c1s
Solomon, B. v5p0459c1s v6p0276c1s v6p0384c1s
Solomon, E. v3p0077c2s
Solomon, M. v6p0248c2s v6p0546c2s v6p0636c2m v6p0663c2s
Solomon, Maurice v6p0636c1s
Solomon, S.J. v5p0311c2s v6p0377c1s
Solomons, L.M. v4p0125c1s v5p0041c1s v5p0188c1s v5p0430c1s v5p0520c1s v5p0624c1s
Solomons, L.M. and Stein, G. v4p0039c2s
Solomons, S. v4p0626c2s
Solomons, S.S. v5p0008c2s
Solomons, T.S. v4p0523c2s v5p0570c2s v5p0644c2s
Solon, L. v5p0100c1s v5p0435c1s
Solovieff, V. v4p0109c2s
Solter, M. v2p0048c1s v2p0168c2s
Sombart, W. v6p0254c1s
Somerby, H.G. v1p0731c1s v1p1380c2s
Somers, A.N. v4p0087c2s v4p0436c1s v4p0531c2s v5p0387c1s
Somers, F.M. v3p0158c1s v6p0567c2s
Somers, H.O. v4p0475c2s
Somers, R. v1p1223c2s
Somers, R., jr. v1p0559c2s
Somers, R.O. v2p0324c1s
Somers, W.A. v5p0120c1s
Somerset, A. v3p0397c1s v3p0404c2s
Somerset, Duchess of v5p0640c2s
Somerset, Duke of v3p0275c1s v3p0285c2s
Somerset, H., Lady v4p0150c1s v4p0622c1s v5p0570c2s v5p0616c2s v5p0631c1m v6p0384c2s
Somerset, H.S. v4p0601c2s v5p0217c1s v6p0352c2s
Somerset, Henry, Lady v4p0104c2s v5p0572c1s v6p0206c2s v6p0619c2s
Somerset, I. v4p0629c2s
Somerset, I. et al. v4p0629c1s
Somerset, S. v6p0380c2s v6p0605c2s
Somervell, A. v6p0437c2s
Somerville, B.T. v4p0399c1m v4p0405c1s v5p0538c2s
Somerville, D. v5p0037c2s v5p0115c2s v5p0313c1s v5p0515c1s
Somerville, E.A. v3p0305c2s
Somerville, E.A.E. and Ross, M. v5p0297c2s
Somerville, E.E. v3p0439c2s
Somerville, E.O. v4p0031c1s
Somerville, E.O. and Ross, M. v6p0145c1s v6p0164c1s
Somerville, E.O'E. v6p0009c2s
Somerville, H.M. v6p0391c1s
Somerville, J.E. v2p0438c2s
Somerville, R.S. v6p0377c1s
Somerville, T. v1p0361c2s v1p1064c1s
Somerville, T.H. v5p0380c2s
Somerville, W.A. v5p0343c2s v5p0486c2s v6p0565c2s
Somerville, Wm. v5p0009c1s
Somes, J.J. v6p0258c2m
Sommel, E. v1p0461c2s
Sommer, H.O. v3p0234c1s v4p0325c1s
Sommerville, C.W. v5p0256c1s
Sommerville, M. v6p0249c1s
Sommerville, W.A. v5p0498c2s
Sondley, F.A. v3p0354c2s
Sondresen, S. v5p0278c1s
Songey, W.F. v2p0156c1s
Sonneck, O.G. v5p0393c1s v5p0393c2s
Sonnenburg, A.Falkner von. v5p0360c1s v5p0444c2s
Sonnenschein, A. v4p0169c1s v4p0192c1m v6p0413c2s
Sonnenschein, E.A. v2p0109c2s v2p0278c1s v4p0234c1s v5p0605c1s v6p0362c2s
Sonnichsen, A. v5p0612c1s
Sooysmith, C. v2p0432c2s v5p0082c2s
Sooysmith, Chas. v3p0163c1s
Soper, F.L. v3p0241c1m
Soper, G.A. v6p0305c1s v6p0568c2s
Soper, G.W. v3p0270c2s
Sopwith, T. v1p0211c2s v1p0572c2s v3p0417c1s
Sorabji, C. v4p0002c2s v4p0428c2s v4p0598c2s v5p0052c1s v5p0287c1s v5p0287c2s v5p0479c1s v6p0117c1s v6p0314c2s v6p0315c1s v6p0346c2s
Sorabji, Cornelia v3p0268c2s v5p0042c1s v6p0207c2s v6p0434c2s v6p0518c1s
Sorby, H.C. v1p0070c1s v1p0237c2s v1p0279c2s v1p0464c1s v1p0467c1s v1p0494c2s v1p0565c2s v1p0750c1m v1p0828c2s v1p0835c2m v1p0844c2s v1p0899c2s v1p1113c1s v1p1204c2s v2p0030c1s v2p0047c2s v2p0093c2s v2p0160c2s v2p0229c1s v2p0413c2s v5p0361c2s
Sorby, T.C. v5p0026c1s v6p0028c1s
Sorensen, C.W. v6p0008c2s
Sorley, W.R. v1p0692c1s v1p1236c2s v2p0147c1s v3p0281c1s v3p0287c2s v4p0255c1s v5p0009c1s v5p0288c2s v5p0400c1s v5p0528c2s v6p0059c2s v6p0188c2s v6p0212c1s v6p0261c2s v6p0306c2s
Sorrel, L. v5p0442c2s
Sorrel, Lucian v5p0271c2s
Sorsbie, R.F. v5p0157c1s v5p0206c2s v6p0685c2s
Sosinsky, T.S. v1p0905c2s
Sosnosky, T.von v5p0243c2s
Sostegno, Alfiera de, Marchese v3p0224c2s
Sotheran, A.H. v5p0500c2s
Sotheran, C. v1p0487c2s v1p0504c1s v1p0536c1s v2p0399c2s
Sotheran, C.S. v4p0351c1s
Sothern, Una v6p0234c1s
Sothern, W. v5p0638c1s
Sotten, G.O. v5p0025c1s
Sotter, M. v2p0160c2s
Souef, D.Le v5p0039c1s
Soule, A.L. v1p0644c1s
Soule, A.M. v6p0284c2s
Soule, C.C. v2p0256c1s v3p0249c2m v3p0300c2s v4p0069c1s v5p0223c1s v6p0084c1s v6p0374c2m
Soule, C.C. et al. v3p0245c1s
Soule, C.G. v5p0097c1s
Soule, Caroline G. v5p0400c2m
Soule, F. v1p0406c2s v1p0755c2s v1p0978c2s v6p0545c1s
Soule, J.B.L. v1p0492c1s v1p0889c2s v1p1010c1s
Soule, S. v3p0020c2s
Soule, T.J. v1p1116c2s
Soulie, F. v1p0720c1s
Soulsby, B.H. v6p0014c2s
Soulsby, L.H.M. v2p0105c1s v2p0114c2s v2p0243c2s v2p0328c2s
Soumet, A. v5p0397c1s
Souper, C.E., Col. v6p0652c2s
Souriaou, P. v3p0289c2s
Souriau, M.P. v4p0125c1s v4p0510c1s
Souriau, P. v4p0124c2s
Sousa, J.P. v5p0423c1s v6p0438c2s
Souter, A. v6p0014c2s v6p0063c1s
South, A. v5p0293c2s v5p0485c1s
South, M. v1p0983c1s
Southall, J.C. v1p0792c1s v1p0794c1m
Southard, L. v6p0247c1s v6p0573c2s
Souther, H. v6p0044c2s
Souther, Hal v4p0619c2s
Souther, T.E. v4p0292c2s
Souther, W.H. v6p0377c2s
Southerland, W.H.H. v6p0668c1s
Southern, H. v1p0178c2s v1p0200c1s v1p0217c2s v1p0312c1s v1p0334c1s v1p0341c1s v1p0368c2s v1p0375c1s v1p0423c2s v1p0433c1s v1p0580c2s v1p0586c1s v1p0601c1s v1p0681c2s v1p0690c2s v1p0727c1s v1p0777c2s v1p0926c2s v1p0952c2s v1p1013c2s v1p1074c1s v1p1081c2s v1p1082c2s v1p1203c1s v1p1359c1s v1p1363c2s v1p1419c2s
Southern, H. and Butler, E.H. v1p0950c1s v1p0950c2s
Southerner, A v3p0401c2s
Southesk v2p0480c2s
Southesk, Earl of v1p0627c1s v2p0320c1s v3p0310c2s v4p0616c1s
Southesk, Lord v1p1152c1s v5p0023c2s
Southey, M. v5p0473c2s
Southey, Mrs. v1p1438c2s
Southey, R. v1p0002c1s v1p0021c1s v1p0022c2s v1p0026c2s v1p0028c2s v1p0047c1s v1p0081c1s v1p0097c2s v1p0103c2s v1p0106c1s v1p0110c1s v1p0126c2s v1p0131c2s v1p0151c1s v1p0158c2s v1p0165c2s v1p0176c2s v1p0178c1m v1p0178c2s v1p0191c1s v1p0207c1s v1p0211c1s v1p0247c1s v1p0249c1s v1p0253c1s v1p0261c1s v1p0261c2m v1p0276c2s v1p0300c2s v1p0319c1s v1p0332c1s v1p0334c2m v1p0347c2s v1p0353c2s v1p0355c1s v1p0355c2m v1p0372c2s v1p0373c2s v1p0374c1s v1p0377c2s v1p0381c1m v1p0385c1s v1p0385c2s v1p0390c1s v1p0395c1s v1p0396c2s v1p0406c1s v1p0412c1s v1p0414c1m v1p0414c2s v1p0415c2s v1p0418c2s v1p0432c2s v1p0433c1s v1p0444c2s v1p0476c1s v1p0539c1s v1p0544c2s v1p0548c1m v1p0568c2s v1p0576c2s v1p0577c2m v1p0598c1s v1p0610c1s v1p0617c1s v1p0622c2s v1p0629c2s v1p0640c1s v1p0641c2s v1p0643c1s v1p0650c1s v1p0653c1s v1p0654c1s v1p0733c2s v1p0740c1s v1p0752c1s v1p0754c1s v1p0775c1s v1p0798c1s v1p0801c2s v1p0813c2s v1p0820c1s v1p0851c1s v1p0852c2m v1p0853c2s v1p0859c2s v1p0864c1s v1p0864c2s v1p0866c2s v1p0869c2s v1p0872c2s v1p0898c2s v1p0904c2s v1p0905c2s v1p0906c1s v1p0909c2s v1p0921c1s v1p0927c1s v1p0935c2s v1p0962c2s v1p0968c1s v1p0973c2m v1p0981c2m v1p1004c2s v1p1025c1s v1p1025c2s v1p1029c1s v1p1030c2m v1p1031c1s v1p1034c1s v1p1037c1m v1p1089c2s v1p1097c1s v1p1104c1s v1p1111c2s v1p1115c1s v1p1115c2s v1p1116c2s v1p1117c1s v1p1119c1s v1p1134c2s v1p1137c1s v1p1154c2s v1p1195c2s v1p1227c1s v1p1228c1m v1p1231c1s v1p1231c2s v1p1266c2s v1p1304c2s v1p1313c1s v1p1315c2m v1p1356c1s v1p1361c1s v1p1363c2s v1p1364c1s v1p1378c1s v1p1380c2m v1p1397c2s v1p1398c1s v1p1401c1s v1p1438c2s
Southgate, H. v1p0378c1s v1p0378c2m v1p0485c2s v1p0853c1s v1p0920c2s v1p1109c1s v1p1131c1s
Southgate, W.S. v1p0205c2s
Southward, J. v4p0589c1s
Southwark, H. v5p0491c2s
Southwell, T. v3p0383c1s v4p0019c2s v4p0172c1s v4p0443c1s v5p0627c1s v6p0611c1s
Southwick, A.P. v1p0371c1s
Southwick, E.B., Dr. v4p0587c2s
Southwick, G.N. v4p0592c2s
Southwick, G.N. et al. ... v4p0129c1s
Southwick, W. v6p0184c1s
Southworth, A.S. v1p0279c1s
Southworth, Mae E. v6p0032c1s
Southworth, R.J. v1p0835c2s
Soutif, E. v4p0326c2s v4p0601c1s
Souttar, R. v4p0447c1s
Souvestre, E. v1p0019c1s v1p0036c1s v1p0075c2s v1p0216c1s v1p0559c1s v1p0921c2s v1p0983c2s v1p1323c1s
Sowerby, A. v5p0109c2s
Sowerby, W. v3p0176c2s v5p0287c1s
Sowers, E. v4p0555c1s
Soyeda, J. v4p0297c1s v4p0297c2s v5p0046c2s v5p0238c1s v5p0238c2s v5p0302c2m v6p0335c1s
Soyeda, Jinchi v4p0450c1s
Soyen, Shaku v4p0405c1s v6p0560c1s
Sozinskey, T.S. v1p0017c1s v1p0143c2s v1p0450c2s v1p0541c2s v1p0810c2s
Spadoni, Adriana v6p0172c2s v6p0325c1s v6p0362c2s
Spagnoletti, C.E. v5p0477c2s
Spahn, J. v1p1273c2s v3p0067c2s
Spahr, C.B. v2p0245c1s v2p0431c2s v3p0346c1s v3p0398c2s v3p0414c1m v3p0421c1m v4p0059c1s v4p0462c1s v4p0472c1s v4p0476c2s v4p0525c2s v4p0526c2s v5p0028c1s v5p0080c2m v5p0106c1s v5p0124c1s v5p0201c1s v5p0202c2s v5p0298c1s v5p0387c1s v5p0403c1m v5p0410c2s v5p0540c2s v5p0584c2s v6p0621c2s
Spahr, C.B. and Hazard, R. v4p0059c1s
Spahr, C.H. and Laughlin, J.C. v4p0524c2s
Spahr, C.R. and Mayo-Smith, R. v4p0524c2s
Spaid, A.R.M. v4p0434c1s v6p0072c1s v6p0381c2s
Spalding, A.F. v6p0066c1s
Spalding, A.G. v3p0035c1s
Spalding, A.T. v6p0512c1s
Spalding, B.F. v4p0090c2s
Spalding, D.A. v1p0271c2s v1p0305c1s v1p0646c2s v1p0740c1s v1p0745c2s v1p0843c1s v1p0843c2m v1p1053c2s v1p1062c1m v1p1177c2s v6p0321c1s
Spalding, E.S. v5p0488c1s

Spalding, G.B. v3p0342c1s v3p0346c2s
Spalding, G.L. v1p1096c2s
Spalding, H. v3p0272c1s
Spalding, H.G. v1p0487c1s v1p1345c2s
Spalding, J. v1p0599c2s v1p0656c1s
Spalding, J.F. v1p0138c1s v1p0361c2s v1p0421c2s v1p1096c1s v4p0487c2s
Spalding, J.F. and Olssen, W.W. v3p0347c1s
Spalding, J.H. et al. v6p0214c1s
Spalding, J.L. v1p0323c1s v1p0384c2s v1p0492c2s v1p0655c1s v1p0660c1s v1p0696c2s v1p0774c2s v1p0839c2s v1p0893c2s v1p1060c1s v1p1115c2s v1p1116c1s v1p1117c1m v1p1117c2m v1p1176c2s v1p1407c2s v2p0349c2s v2p0371c2s v3p0175c1s v3p0358c1s v3p0378c2s v3p0397c2s v3p0398c1s v3p0442c1s v4p0015c1s v4p0125c2s v4p0466c1s v4p0488c1s v4p0488c2s v4p0636c1s v6p0194c1s v6p0671c1s
Spalding, J.L. and Stanton, E.C. v2p0477c1s
Spalding, J.R. v1p1422c1s
Spalding, J.W. v1p1117c2s
Spalding, K.J. v5p0542c2s
Spalding, M.J. v1p0202c1s v1p0254c1s v1p0832c2s v1p0856c1s
Spalding, N.De v6p0056c2s
Spalding, S. v1p0869c1s
Spalding, S.J. v1p0425c1s
Spalding, T.A. v1p1186c2s v4p0428c1s
Spalding, T.L. v1p0390c2s
Spalding, V.M. v2p0287c2s v3p0333c2s v5p0214c1s v6p0188c1s v6p0233c1s v6p0329c1s v6p0657c2s
Spalding, W. v1p0105c2s v1p0780c2s v1p1186c2s
Spalding, W.A. v2p0284c1s v6p0305c2s
Spalding, W.F. v4p0139c2s v4p0162c2s v4p0459c2s v4p0515c1s v6p0213c2s
Spangenberg, L. v1p0826c1s v1p1259c1s
Spangler, E.W. v4p0117c2s
Spangler, H.T. v4p0123c1s
Spangler, H.W. v2p0098c1s v4p0220c2s v5p0125c2s v6p0179c2s
Spangler, I.M. v5p0543c1s
Spanhoofd, E. v3p0330c1s
Spanhorfd, E. v3p0170c2s
Spare, J. v1p0746c1s
Spargo, J. v6p0102c2s v6p0117c1s v6p0128c2s v6p0182c1s v6p0262c1s v6p0595c2s v6p0664c2s
Sparhawk, F.C. v2p0219c2s v2p0371c2s v3p0012c2s v3p0100c1s v3p0135c1s v3p0217c1s v3p0412c2s v3p0454c1s v4p0183c2s v4p0281c2s v4p0293c2s v4p0376c2s v4p0620c2s v6p0316c2s
Sparhawk, F.E. v2p0424c1s v2p0478c1s
Sparkes, J. v3p0240c2s v3p0341c1m v4p0325c2s
Sparkman, D. v3p0343c1s
Sparkman, J.R. v1p0404c2s
Sparkman, P.S. v6p0389c2s
Sparks, E.E. v4p0116c2s v5p0014c2s v5p0015c2m v5p0016c2s v5p0095c2s v5p0162c1s v5p0266c1s v5p0279c2s v5p0349c1s v5p0506c1s v5p0600c2s v5p0620c2s v6p0113c1m v6p0240c1s v6p0248c2s v6p0329c1s v6p0377c2s v6p0422c1s v6p0667c1m v6p0668c1s
Sparks, E.S. v5p0199c2s
Sparks, F.E. v4p0359c1s
Sparks, F.M. v6p0571c1s
Sparks, G.D. v5p0057c1s v5p0057c2s v5p0058c1s v6p0062c1s v6p0431c1s
Sparks, G.R. v5p0461c2s
Sparks, J. v1p0005c1s v1p0005c2s v1p0015c1s v1p0023c1s v1p0027c2s v1p0028c2s v1p0030c1s v1p0031c2s v1p0060c1s v1p0064c1s v1p0067c1s v1p0073c2s v1p0085c2s v1p0089c2s v1p0103c2s v1p0157c1s v1p0169c2s v1p0171c2s v1p0174c1s v1p0175c2s v1p0180c2s v1p0195c1s v1p0277c2s v1p0278c1s v1p0280c2s v1p0311c2s v1p0322c2s v1p0376c1s v1p0388c2s v1p0406c1s v1p0433c1s v1p0497c1m v1p0512c2s v1p0532c1s v1p0574c2s v1p0585c2s v1p0598c1s v1p0635c2s v1p0637c2s v1p0642c1s v1p0650c1s v1p0669c1s v1p0725c2s v1p0726c1s v1p0730c2s v1p0733c2m v1p0767c1s v1p0772c2s v1p0802c1s v1p0833c2s v1p0899c1s v1p0918c1m v1p0927c2s v1p0931c1s v1p0931c2s v1p0938c2s v1p0939c1s v1p0949c1s v1p0997c1s v1p0999c2s v1p1034c1s v1p1036c2s v1p1063c1s v1p1064c1m v1p1078c2s v1p1105c2s v1p1107c2s v1p1108c1s v1p1149c2s v1p1158c2s v1p1159c1m v1p1181c2s v1p1224c2s v1p1226c1s v1p1231c1s v1p1294c1s v1p1348c1s v1p1348c2s v1p1350c2s v1p1393c2s
Sparks, J. and Felton, C.C. v1p0636c2s
Sparks, J. and Palfrey, J.G. v1p0126c2s
Sparlin, E.M. v6p0574c2s
Sparling, H.H. v3p0140c2s v4p0332c1s
Sparling, S.E. v5p0139c2s v5p0550c1s v6p0017c2s v6p0114c1s
Sparrow, T. v3p0312c1s v3p0404c2s v4p0277c1s v4p0337c2s
Sparrow, W. v5p0628c1s v6p0489c2s
Sparrow, W.S. v4p0050c2s v4p0244c1s v4p0254c1s v4p0260c2s v4p0310c2s v4p0600c2s v5p0030c2s v5p0156c1s v5p0158c2m v5p0171c1s v5p0203c1s v5p0215c1s v5p0226c1s v5p0237c1s v5p0254c1s v5p0265c2s v5p0275c2s v5p0298c1s v5p0315c2s v5p0373c1s v5p0619c2s v5p0632c1s v6p0054c2s v6p0202c1s v6p0257c1s v6p0367c1s v6p0546c2s
Sparrow, W.S. and Slade, R.J. v4p0052c2s
Sparrow, Walter S. v5p0371c2s v5p0429c2s
Sparroy, W. v5p0441c1m
Sparry, C. v1p0994c1s
Sparvel-Bayly, J.A. v2p0055c1s v2p0296c1s v3p0038c1s v3p0044c1s v3p0083c2m v3p0110c2m v3p0142c2s v3p0158c2s v3p0167c1s v3p0185c1s v3p0186c2s v3p0187c2s v3p0417c1m v4p0310c1s v4p0437c2s
Spaulding, C.S. v3p0246c2s
Spaulding, D.A. v1p0135c2s v1p0646c2m
Spaulding, E.G. v1p0556c2s v1p1349c1s v2p0110c1s v6p0066c2s v6p0214c2s
Spaulding, E.S. v5p0633c2s
Spaulding, H.C. v3p0134c1s v4p0175c2s v4p0541c1s
Spaulding, H.G. v1p0125c2s v1p0126c2s v1p0511c2s v1p0601c1s v1p0646c1s v1p0682c1s v1p0684c1s v1p1125c2s v1p1341c2s v1p1423c2s v4p0075c1s
Spaulding, J. v1p0107c1s
Spaulding, J.L. v4p0102c1s
Spaulding, Leila C. v6p0320c2s
Spaulding, S.J. v1p0099c1s
Spaulding, V.M. v3p0051c2s v3p0179c2s v3p0380c2s
Spaulding, W. v1p0117c1s v1p0468c2s v1p0867c2s v1p1087c1s
Spaulding, W.F. v4p0434c2s
Speakman, E. v6p0298c1s
Speakman, Eliz. v6p0571c1s
Speakman, T.S. v1p1312c2s
Spear, E.P. v6p0045c2s
Spear, Emily P. v5p0085c1s
Spear, F. v5p0202c2s
Spear, J. v1p0831c1s
Spear, P.B. v1p0581c1s v1p1114c2s
Spear, S.T. v1p0119c2s v1p0179c2s v1p0259c2s v1p0735c1s v1p0741c2s v1p0792c2s v1p0849c2s v1p1101c1s v1p1158c1s v1p1353c2s
Spear, W.A. v1p0234c2s
Speare, A. v3p0238c1s
Speare, C.F. v6p0149c1s v6p0236c2s v6p0616c2s
Speare, L.B. v4p0466c1s v4p0487c2s
Speare, S.L.B. v3p0356c2s
Spearman, C. v6p0151c2s v6p0323c1s
Spearman, E.R. v3p0015c2s v3p0105c2m v3p0207c2s v3p0283c2s v3p0320c2s v3p0467c1s v3p0470c2s v4p0020c1s v4p0140c1s v4p0273c2s v4p0402c1s v4p0425c1m v4p0431c2s v4p0459c2s v4p0460c1s v4p0552c2s v4p0628c2s v5p0313c1s v6p0604c1s
Spearman, F. v6p0529c2s
Spearman, F.H. v3p0115c2s v3p0460c1s v5p0065c2s v5p0081c1s v5p0132c1s v5p0202c2s v5p0274c1s v5p0356c2s v5p0376c2s v5p0418c1s v5p0435c2s v5p0490c1s v5p0500c1s v5p0508c1s v5p0527c1s v5p0557c1s v6p0143c2s v6p0153c1s v6p0382c2s v6p0457c2m v6p0468c2s v6p0527c2s v6p0571c1s v6p0585c2s v6p0665c2s v6p0693c2s v6p0697c1s
Spearman, M.C. v6p0037c1s
Spears, J.D. v5p0643c1s
Spears, J.R. v3p0003c1s v3p0153c1s v3p0199c1s v3p0297c2s v3p0305c1s v3p0306c1s v3p0311c1s v3p0339c2s v3p0371c2s v3p0374c2s v3p0411c1s v3p0443c2s v4p0166c2s v4p0376c2s v4p0399c2s v4p0430c1s v4p0531c1s v4p0634c2s v5p0004c1m v5p0081c1s v5p0100c1s v5p0132c2s v5p0134c1s v5p0209c2s v5p0396c1s v5p0409c1s v5p0417c2s v5p0452c1s v5p0532c1s v5p0555c1s v5p0555c2s v5p0583c1s v5p0625c2s v5p0642c1s v5p0642c2m v6p0031c2s v6p0054c1s v6p0086c1s v6p0145c1s v6p0166c2s v6p0167c1s v6p0180c2s v6p0209c1s v6p0358c2s v6p0376c2s v6p0429c1s v6p0536c1s v6p0562c2s v6p0580c1s v6p0591c2s v6p0668c2s v6p0690c1m v6p0694c1s v6p0710c1m v6p0710c2s
Spears, R.B. v1p0525c2s
Spears, R.S. v5p0202c1s v5p0406c2s v6p0160c1s
Specht, G.J. v1p1316c1s
Specht, R. v6p0552c1s
Speck, F.G. v6p0424c1m v6p0488c2s
Speck, F.G. and Prince, J.D. v6p0423c2s v6p0488c2s
Spedding, J. v1p0085c1s v1p0085c2s v1p0165c1s v1p0219c2s v1p0392c2s v1p0402c2s v1p0905c2s v1p0952c2s v1p1085c1s v1p1185c2s v1p1208c2s v1p1234c2s v1p1333c2s
Speed, J. v3p0251c2s
Speed, J. and Holt, J. ... v3p0416c2s
Speed, J.G. v3p0362c2m v4p0004c1s v4p0058c1m v4p0098c1s v4p0119c1s v4p0175c2s v4p0194c2s v4p0231c2s v4p0264c1s v4p0264c2s v4p0309c1s v4p0346c1s v4p0393c2s v4p0402c2s v4p0454c2s v4p0460c1s v4p0485c1m v4p0491c2s v4p0566c1s v4p0572c2s v4p0588c2s v5p0041c1m v5p0270c2s v5p0315c2s v5p0418c2s v5p0576c1s v5p0619c1s v6p0263c2s v6p0297c1s v6p0545c1s v6p0647c2s
Speed, J.J. v1p0807c2s v1p1100c1s
Speed, T. v2p0037c1s v2p0166c2s
Speedy, C.M. v3p0082c1s v3p0419c2s
Speedy, T. v4p0151c1s
Speedy, T.C.S. v5p0416c1s v5p0539c2s v6p0462c1s
Speer, L. v3p0324c2s
Speer, R.E. v6p0354c1s
Speer, W. v1p0028c1s v1p0187c1s v1p0232c1s v1p0235c1s v1p0302c1s v1p1047c2s
Speight, I.W. v5p0518c1s
Speight, R. v4p0472c2s
Speight, T. v1p0168c2s v1p0321c2s
Speight, T.W. v1p0889c2s v2p0026c2s v2p0070c1s v2p0161c2s v2p0191c2s v2p0322c1s v2p0449c2s v3p0049c1s v3p0112c2s v3p0189c1s v3p0291c1s v3p0294c1s v3p0311c2s v3p0400c1s v3p0431c2s v3p0460c2s v3p0464c1s v4p0079c1s v4p0136c2s v4p0243c1s v4p0352c2s v4p0399c2s v5p0055c1s v5p0104c2s v5p0188c1s v5p0323c2s v5p0492c2s v6p0179c2s v6p0220c2s
Speir, F., jr. v3p0097c1s
Speirs, E.B. v3p0374c1s
Speirs, F.W. v4p0108c2s v4p0590c2s v5p0556c2s
Speirs, F.W. et al. v5p0606c2s
Speke, J.H. v1p0010c2s v2p0460c2s
Spellier, L.H. v1p1312c1s v2p0136c1m v2p0441c2s
Spence, A.M. v4p0234c1s v4p0272c1s
Spence, C.H. v4p0013c2s v4p0481c1s v4p0630c1s
Spence, D.M. v4p0092c1s v4p0190c2s
Spence, E.F. v2p0003c1s v2p0405c2s v4p0126c1s v5p0144c2s v5p0255c2s v6p0180c2s
Spence, F. v4p0485c1s
Spence, G. v1p1293c2s
Spence, G.S.G. v1p1091c2s
Spence, H.B. v4p0287c1s v4p0547c2s
Spence, H.D.M. v3p0122c2s v3p0148c2s v3p0178c1s v3p0191c1s v3p0306c2s v3p0367c2s v3p0425c2s v4p0228c2s v4p0418c1s v4p0523c2s v4p0571c1s
Spence, J.D. v5p0090c1s
Spence, M. v4p0548c2s
Spence, M. and Donald, H.. v4p0119c2s
Spence, P. v1p0074c1s v1p0406c2s v2p0214c1s v2p0335c2s v3p0385c1s
Spence, T.R. v4p0609c1s v5p0159c2s
Spence, T.W.L. v4p0431c1s

Spence, W. v5p0198c1m
Spence, W.H. v5p0152c1s
v5p0174c1s
Spencer, A. v6p0035c2s
v6p0466c1s
Spencer, A.Brownell v6p0165c2s
v6p0673c2s
Spencer, A.C. v5p0160c1s
Spencer, A.C. and Arnold, R.
v6p0567c2s
Spencer, A.C. and Vaughn, T.W.
v6p0160c2s
Spencer, A.G. v1p1424c2s
v3p0355c2s v4p0102c2s v4p0104c2s
v4p0428c1s v5p0302c1s v6p0046c2s
Spencer, A.W. v6p0618c1s
Spencer, B. and Gillen, F.J.
v5p0193c2s
v5p0583c1s
Spencer, C.H. v6p0324c2s
Spencer, Capt. v1p1332c2s
Spencer, Countess v1p0219c1s
Spencer, D.E. v3p0178c1s
v3p0466c1s
Spencer, Dorcas J. v6p0703c2s
Spencer, E. v1p0033c2s
v1p0048c2s v1p0060c1s v1p0261c1s
v1p0306c2s v1p0308c1s v1p0455c2s
v1p0487c1s v1p0491c2s v1p0519c2s
v1p0526c1s v1p0542c2s v1p0560c1s
v1p0578c2s v1p0583c1s v1p0598c2s
v1p0610c1s v1p0616c2s v1p0621c1s
v1p0693c2s v1p0716c2s v1p0775c1s
v1p0817c1s v1p0873c1s v1p0898c1s
v1p0959c1s v1p0962c1m v1p1020c2s
v1p1028c1s v1p1034c1s v1p1078c1s
v1p1176c2s v1p1266c1s v1p1280c2s
v1p1326c1s v1p1345c2s v1p1346c1s
v1p1353c1s v1p1354c1s v1p1357c2s
v1p1369c2s v1p1420c1s v3p0069c1s
v3p0224c1m v3p0296c1s v3p0388c1s
v4p0309c2s v5p0271c1s v6p0009c1s
v6p0111c1s v6p0171c1s v6p0564c1s
v6p0579c1m v6p0579c2s
Spencer, E.B.T. v6p0429c1s
Spencer, E.C. and Berle, A.A.
v3p0208c2s
Spencer, E.E. v5p0030c2s
Spencer, E.F. v6p0386c2s
Spencer, E.H. v5p0137c1s
Spencer, Ema v5p0448c2s
Spencer, F.A. v5p0055c1s
v5p0465c2s
Spencer, F.B. v4p0299c1s
Spencer, F.H. v5p0107c1s
Spencer, F.M. v6p0039c2s
Spencer, G.L. v3p0003c1s
Spencer, H. v1p0006c2s
v1p0071c1s v1p0093c1s v1p0213c1s
v1p0237c1s v1p0265c1s v1p0293c1s
v1p0385c1s v1p0392c1s v1p0392c2s
v1p0406c2s v1p0427c1s v1p0434c2m
v1p0442c2s v1p0445c1s v1p0450c1s
v1p0537c2s v1p0538c1s v1p0556c1s
v1p0623c2s v1p0728c1s v1p0736c1s
v1p0739c2s v1p0793c1m v1p0794c2s
v1p0797c1s v1p0803c1s v1p0805c2s
v1p0868c2s v1p0903c2s v1p0974c1s
v1p1004c2m v1p1005c1s v1p1007c2s
v1p1027c2s v1p1038c2s v1p1055c1s
v1p1062c1m v1p1080c1s v1p1099c2s
v1p1162c1s v1p1177c2s v1p1182c1s
v1p1216c2s v1p1217c1s v1p1217c2m
v1p1235c2s v1p1239c1s v1p1244c2s
v1p1263c1s v1p1271c2s v1p1313c1s
v1p1319c1s v1p1420c2s v1p1432c2s
v2p0005c1s v2p0011c2s v2p0012c2s
v2p0149c2m v2p0184c1s v2p0188c1s
v2p0220c2s v2p0253c1s v2p0315c2s
v2p0331c1s v2p0348c1s v2p0349c1s
v2p0366c2s v2p0369c1s v2p0405c1s
v2p0405c2s v2p0407c2s v2p0429c2s
v2p0443c2s v2p0448c1s v3p0053c1s
v3p0145c2s v3p0233c2s v3p0234c2s
v3p0293c2m v3p0297c1s v3p0398c2s
v3p0402c2s v3p0408c1s v4p0020c2s
v4p0023c2s v4p0025c1s v4p0029c1s
v4p0042c1s v4p0060c1s v4p0097c1s
v4p0125c1s v4p0146c2s v4p0191c1s
v4p0191c2s v4p0255c2m v4p0367c2s
v4p0375c2s v4p0421c1s v4p0441c2s
v4p0460c2s v4p0464c2s v4p0510c1s
v4p0510c2s v4p0514c1s v4p0534c2s
v4p0566c1s v4p0588c2m v4p0602c2s
v4p0616c2s v5p0009c1s v5p0099c1s
v5p0198c2m v5p0400c1s v5p0535c1s
v5p0536c1s v5p0545c2s v5p0558c2s
v5p0619c2s v6p0353c2s
Spencer, H. and Laveleye, E.de
v2p0414c1s v2p0418c1s
Spencer, H. and Tylor, E.B.
v1p0036c2s
Spencer, H. et al. v1p0839c1s
v3p0194c2s v3p0241c2s
Spencer, H.B. v1p0268c1s
v1p0438c1s v1p1415c1m
Spencer, H.D.M. v3p0074c2s
v3p0335c1s
Spencer, H.L. v4p0499c1s
Spencer, Herbert v3p0337c1s
Spencer, Herman v6p0596c2s
Spencer, I.L. v1p0641c2s
Spencer, I.S. v1p0071c2s
Spencer, J. v4p0373c2s
Spencer, J.A. v1p0031c2s
v1p0704c2s v1p0857c1s v1p1121c2s
v1p1142c2s v1p1185c1s v2p0191c1s
v3p0260c1s
Spencer, J.H. v3p0433c2s
v6p0619c1s
Spencer, J.J. v5p0616c2s
Spencer, J.P. v2p0385c2s
Spencer, J.W. v2p0299c2s
v2p0322c1s v2p0435c2s v3p0008c2s
v3p0173c2s v3p0205c1s v3p0223c2s
v3p0240c1s v3p0312c2s v3p0374c2s
v4p0186c2s v4p0317c2s v4p0345c1s
v4p0403c1m v5p0099c2s v5p0410c1s
v5p0626c1s v6p0301c2s v6p0321c1s
v6p0460c1s v6p0573c2s v6p0623c1s
v6p0687c2s
Spencer, L.J. v5p0161c1s
v5p0374c2s
Spencer, Lady v1p0762c2s
Spencer, M. v3p0152c2s
v3p0154c1s
Spencer, N.S. v5p0556c2s
Spencer, O.M. v1p0209c2s
v1p0245c1s v1p0280c2s v1p0452c1s
v1p0461c1m v1p0505c1s v1p0505c2s
v1p0673c2s v1p0799c2s v1p1029c1s
v1p1197c2s v1p1365c1s v4p0424c2s
Spencer, R. v1p0207c1s
v3p0101c1s
Spencer, R.C. v5p0642c1s
v6p0220c1s
Spencer, R.C., jr. v5p0203c1s
v6p0225c2s
Spencer, S. v6p0529c1s
Spencer, T. v4p0174c2s
v4p0175c1s
Spencer, T.D. v1p0338c1s
Spencer, W.B. v2p0197c2s
v2p0295c2s v3p0324c2s v4p0469c1s
Spencer, W.B. et al. v3p0126c2s
Spencer, W.E. v3p0177c2s
Spencers, A.W. v5p0616c1s
Spences, E. v5p0180c1s
Spender, A.E. v5p0111c1s
v5p0140c2s v5p0412c2s v5p0419c1s
v5p0546c1s
Spender, A.F. v5p0096c2s
v5p0428c2s
Spender, A.S. v5p0278c1s
Spender, C. v6p0633c2s
Spender, C.M. v6p0699c2s
Spender, E. v1p1214c1s
v1p1292c2s v5p0534c1s
Spender, H. v4p0265c2s
v4p0352c2s v5p0018c2s v5p0390c1s
v5p0468c2s v5p0479c1s v5p0573c2s
v6p0013c2s v6p0059c2s v6p0108c1s
v6p0116c2s v6p0195c2s v6p0220c1s
v6p0433c1s v6p0457c2s v6p0462c1s
v6p0522c2s v6p0639c1s v6p0686c1s
v6p0686c2s
Spender, Harold v5p0013c2m
v6p0144c1s
Spender, I.K., Mrs. v4p0316c2s
Spender, J.A. v5p0247c2m
v6p0047c2s v6p0048c1s v6p0191c1s
v6p0240c1s v6p0253c1s v6p0265c1s
v6p0269c2s v6p0270c1m v6p0270c2m
v6p0300c2s v6p0370c1s
Spender, J.K. v1p1307c2s
Spender, J.K., Mrs. v1p0530c1s
Spender, R. v6p0433c2s
Spender, W.B. v5p0131c1s
Spener, P. v4p0045c1s
Spens, J. v6p0552c1s
Spenser, E. v1p0209c2s
Spenser, H. v5p0165c1s
Spenser, H.J. v5p0036c2s
Spenser, J.G. v4p0074c1s
Spensley, J.C. v6p0385c2s
Speranza, C.L. v3p0224c1m
Speranza, G.C. v5p0143c2s
v5p0355c2s v5p0368c2s v6p0116c1s
v6p0202c2m v6p0213c1s v6p0286c1s
v6p0308c1s v6p0308c2s v6p0309c1s
v6p0331c1m v6p0331c2s v6p0355c2s
v6p0466c1s v6p0487c1s
Sperbeck, H.C. v6p0125c1s
Spero, A.K. v5p0390c2s
Sperra, W.E. v5p0549c1s
Sperry, A. v4p0137c2s
Sperry, E. v6p0104c2s
v6p0542c1s
Sperry, E.S. and Penfield, S.L.
v3p0203c2s
Sperry, F.L. and Penfield, S.L.
v2p0171c2s v3p0150c2s
Speyers, C.L. v5p0069c1s
v6p0100c2s v6p0285c2s v6p0378c2s
Speyers, C.L. and Rosell, C.R.
v5p0486c1s
Spice, R. v1p1222c2m
v1p1329c2s
Spicer, H. v1p0716c2s
v1p1071c1s v1p1325c1s
Spicer, S.D. v3p0439c2s
Spieker, E.H. v2p0172c2s
Spielhagen, F. v4p0051c2m
v4p0160c2s
Spielmann, I. v6p0563c2s
Spielmann, I. and Jacobs, J.
v3p0230c1s
Spielmann, M.H. v3p0349c2s
v3p0368c1s v4p0010c1s v4p0011c2s
v4p0012c2s v4p0029c1s v4p0029c2s
v4p0030c1m v4p0030c2s v4p0032c1m
v4p0051c1s v4p0065c1s v4p0070c1s
v4p0084c1s v4p0092c1s v4p0109c2s
v4p0133c1s v4p0151c1s v4p0151c2s
v4p0257c2s v4p0260c1s v4p0267c2s
v4p0309c1s v4p0309c2s v4p0310c1s
v4p0325c2s v4p0335c2s v4p0339c1m
v4p0362c1s v4p0362c2s v4p0371c1s
v4p0381c2s v4p0393c2s v4p0426c1s
v4p0442c2s v4p0454c2s v4p0457c2s
v4p0467c2m v4p0472c2s v4p0490c2s
v4p0493c1m v4p0493c2m v4p0495c1m
v4p0501c1s v4p0518c1s v4p0518c2s
v4p0538c2m v4p0544c1s v4p0554c1s
v4p0564c1s v4p0569c1s v4p0600c1m
v4p0604c1s v4p0614c2s v4p0631c1s
v5p0001c1s v5p0030c2s v5p0031c2s
v5p0061c2s v5p0073c2s v5p0102c2s
v5p0103c1s v5p0104c2s v5p0159c2s
v5p0219c2s v5p0220c2s v5p0223c2s
v5p0233c2s v5p0255c2m v5p0256c2s
v5p0263c1s v5p0270c1s v5p0310c1s
v5p0342c1s v5p0370c1s v5p0371c1s
v5p0386c2s v5p0396c2s v5p0399c1s
v5p0432c1m v5p0441c2s v5p0462c2m
v5p0487c1s v5p0491c1s v5p0498c2m
v5p0500c1m v5p0500c2s v5p0516c1s
v5p0541c2s v5p0575c1s v5p0610c2s
v5p0617c1m v5p0623c1m v5p0631c2s
v6p0058c1s v6p0079c2s v6p0139c3s
v6p0224c2s v6p0233c2s v6p0256c1s
v6p0274c1s v6p0339c2s v6p0350c1s
v6p0409c2s v6p0512c2s v6p0553c1s
v6p0678c1s v6p0689c2s v6p0695c2s
Spielmann, M.H. and Armstrong, W.
v4p0029c1s
Spielmann, M.H. and Frith, W.P.
v4p0004c1s
Spielmann, M.H. and Wedmore, F.
v4p0029c1s
Spielmann, Mabel v6p0465c2s
Spiers, E.B. v3p0074c2s
Spiers, F.E. v6p0473c1s
Spiers, F.W. v5p0443c1m
Spiers, G.R.P. v4p0023c2s
Spiers, J. v1p0111c1s
Spiers, J.B. v6p0189c1s
Spiers, R.P. v1p0597c1s
v2p0019c1s v3p0036c1s v4p0024c1s
v5p0026c2s v5p0503c1s
Spiers, R.Phene v3p0300c1s
Spies, A. v4p0220c2s
v4p0292c1s v4p0443c1s v4p0547c2s
Spies, P. v4p0614c2s
Spiess, E. v1p0406c1s
v1p0513c1s
Spillane, D. v4p0373c1s
v4p0389c2s v4p0417c1s v4p0442c1s
Spiller, G. v5p0038c1s
v5p0498c1s v6p0203c1s v6p0323c1s
v6p0531c2s v6p0681c2s
Spiller, J. v2p0009c1s
v2p0154c1s v3p0331c1s
Spillman, W.J. v6p0159c2s
v6p0410c1m v6p0413c2s v6p0432c2s
v6p0629c2s v6p0639c2s v6p0694c2s
Spilsbury, A.G. v5p0387c1s
v5p0583c2s
Spilsbury, E.G. v5p0439c1s
Spindler, F.N. v5p0583c2s
Spingarn, J.E. v5p0439c2s
v6p0103c2s v6p0390c2s v6p0539c1s
Spink, W. v2p0397c1s
Spinner, Alice v4p0225c2s
Spinner, R. v4p0045c2s
v4p0194c2s
Spinney, G.F. v6p0355c2s
Spitta, P. v4p0049c2s
Spitta, W. v1p0188c2s
v1p0378c1s
Spitz, M. v6p0052c2s
Spitzer, L.S. v6p0073c1s
Spitzka, E.A. v6p0079c1s
v6p0079c2m v6p0234c1s v6p0337c2s
v6p0357c1s v6p0512c2s
Spitzka, E.C. v3p0007c2s
v3p0205c2s v3p0383c1s
Spivak, C.D. v5p0415c2s
Splaine, J.F. v2p0022c1s
v2p0131c1s v2p0131c2s v2p0132c1s
v2p0214c1s v2p0446c2s
Splegelberg, A.F. v6p0444c2s
Spode, A. v4p0458c1s
Spoer, H.H. v6p0019c1s
v6p0061c2s v6p0221c2s v6p0691c1s
Spoer, H.H. and Barton, G.A.
v6p0633c2s
Spofford, A.R. v1p0149c1s
v1p0300c2s v1p0611c2s v1p0743c2s
v1p1388c2s v2p0099c1s v2p0336c2s

v4p0129c1m v4p0330c1s v4p0331c1s v4p0596c2s v5p0133c1s v5p0288c2s v5p0305c1s v5p0621c1s v6p0372c2s
Spofford, H.E. v1p0155c2s v1p1407c1s
Spofford, H.P. v1p0071c1s v1p0139c1s v1p0327c1s v1p0332c2s v1p0362c1s v1p0402c2s v1p0455c2s v1p0462c1s v1p0466c1s v1p0495c1m v1p0586c1s v1p0642c1s v1p0649c2s v1p0755c2s v1p0771c1s v1p0785c2s v1p0833c2s v1p0840c2s v1p0851c2s v1p0909c1s v1p0947c1s v1p1010c2s v1p1017c2s v1p1084c2m v1p1108c1s v1p1128c1s v1p1129c1s v1p1148c1s v1p1190c1s v1p1225c1s v1p1259c1s v1p1260c1s v1p1280c2s v1p1361c1s v1p1388c2s v1p1437c1s v2p0026c2s v2p0041c1s v2p0062c2s v2p0284c2s v2p0300c1s v2p0301c1s v2p0440c1s v2p0444c2s v2p0445c1s v2p0473c1m v3p0007c2s v3p0077c2s v3p0236c2s v3p0283c2s v3p0291c2s v3p0322c2s v3p0343c2s v3p0440c2m v4p0124c1s v4p0229c2s v4p0276c2s v4p0277c1s v4p0312c2s v4p0555c1s v4p0571c2s v4p0580c1s v4p0612c2s v5p0055c1s v5p0096c1s v5p0251c2s v5p0312c1s
Spofford, H.P. et al. v4p0629c1s v4p0630c1s
Spofford, Harriet P. v6p0307c1s v6p0465c2s v6p0562c1s v6p0619c2s v6p0679c1s
Spofford, Harriet Prescott v6p0020c1s v6p0124c2s v6p0220c2s v6p0292c1s
Spofford, J. v1p1239c1s
Spofford, P. v1p0495c1s
Spofford, W.P. v5p0106c1s
Spofforth, T.R. v4p0139c1s
Spooner, A.C. v1p0339c1s v1p1145c2s v1p1257c1s
Spooner, D.B.S. v5p0081c2s
Spooner, Florence v5p0093c2m
Spooner, J.C. v5p0544c1s
Spooner, L. v1p0453c2s v1p0532c1s v1p1049c2s v1p1361c2s v2p0034c1s v2p0411c1s
Spooner, T. v1p1239c2s
Spooner, W.A. v3p0189c1s v5p0426c1s v5p0459c1m v6p0699c1s
Spooner, W.J. v1p0324c2s v1p0809c1s v1p0946c1s v1p0998c2s
Spooner, W.S. v1p1034c2s
Spooner, W.T. v1p0624c1s
Spoonts, M.A. v5p0294c1s
Spotswood, W. v6p0608c1s
Spottiswoode, G.A. v3p0046c1s v4p0506c2s
Spottiswoode, W. v1p0321c2s v1p0399c1s v1p0747c2s v1p0810c2s v1p0885c1s v1p1024c2s v1p1130c2s v2p0272c1s v2p0390c2s v2p0405c2s
Spottsberg, C. v6p0606c2s
Spragge, E.M. v4p0073c2m
Sprague, A.P. v1p0013c2s v1p0435c1s v1p0453c1s v1p0839c2s v1p1021c1s v1p1222c1s
Sprague, C.E. v3p0451c2s v5p0388c1s v6p0171c1s
Sprague, C.J. v1p0333c2s v1p0462c2s v1p0463c1s v1p0711c2s
Sprague, Carleton v5p0200c1s
Sprague, D. v5p0056c2s
Sprague, D.G. v1p1400c1s
Sprague, Eliz.C. v6p0408c1s
Sprague, F.J. v3p0133c1m v3p0134c1s v4p0175c2m v4p0484c1s v5p0183c2s v5p0184c1s v5p0346c1s v6p0198c1m
Sprague, F.W. v4p0232c2s v5p0240c1m v5p0424c2s v6p0262c1m
Sprague, H.B. v2p0460c1s v3p0253c2s v3p0342c2s v3p0388c1s v4p0299c1s v4p0362c1s
Sprague, J.A. v1p0797c1s
Sprague, J.T. v1p0399c1m v1p0501c1s v2p0137c1s v2p0138c1s
Sprague, L.S. v6p0645c1s
Sprague, L.T. v5p0063c1s v5p0063c2m v5p0210c2s v5p0400c2s v5p0634c2s v5p0639c2m v6p0021c2s v6p0068c1s v6p0236c1s v6p0246c1s v6p0332c2s v6p0345c2s v6p0366c1s v6p0401c1s v6p0429c1s v6p0429c2s v6p0444c1s v6p0524c1s v6p0580c2s v6p0690c1s
Sprague, O.M.W. v5p0125c2s v6p0050c2s v6p0425c1m
Sprague, P.W. v2p0145c2s v2p0207c1s
Sprague, W. v1p0769c2s
Sprague, W.B. v1p0242c2s v1p0252c2s v1p0373c2m v1p0535c2s v1p0566c2s v1p0585c2m v1p0676c2s v1p0808c1s v1p0846c2s v1p0847c1s v1p0881c2s v1p1201c2s v1p1270c2s v1p1338c2s v1p1436c1m
Spratling, E.J. v5p0210c2s
Spratling, W.P. v6p0209c2m
Spratt, D.E.W. v4p0511c1s v5p0109c2s v5p0524c2s
Spratt, L.W. v1p1206c1s v2p0405c1s
Spratt, T.A.B. v5p0162c1s v5p0166c1s
Sprecher, S. v1p0243c1s v1p1090c1m v2p0073c1s v2p0082c1s v2p0240c1s
Spreckels, J.D. v4p0250c2s
Sprengel, H. v1p1360c2s
Sprigg, S. v6p0398c1s
Sprigge, S.S. v4p0039c1s
Spriggs, S.S. v4p0449c1s
Sprinchorn, C.K. v2p0312c2s
Spring, A. v6p0226c1s v6p0426c1s v6p0476c1s
Spring, A.L. v4p0359c2s v4p0370c2s
Spring, E.T. v4p0047c1s
Spring, G. v1p1149c1m v6p0231c2s
Spring, L.W. v1p0345c1s v1p1223c1s v2p0058c1m v2p0126c1s v3p0234c1s v4p0184c2s v4p0334c2s v4p0372c2s v4p0517c2s v4p0518c1s v4p0622c2s v5p0324c2s v5p0361c2s v5p0377c1s v5p0380c2s v5p0523c1s
Spring, M.W. v2p0467c1s
Spring, R. v1p1308c2s
Spring, W. v1p0110c1s v3p0341c1s
Springer, A. v4p0369c2s v6p0175c2s
Springer, F. v1p0288c2s v1p0778c1s v1p0778c2s v1p1121c1s v1p1156c1s v2p0061c2s
Springer, F. and Wachsmuth, C. v1p0317c2s
Springer, J.F. v6p0576c2s
Springer, M.E. v4p0142c2s
Springer, W.M. v1p1290c1s v3p0085c2s v3p0416c2s v4p0251c1s v4p0563c1s
Springer, W.M. et al. v4p0230c2s v4p0525c1s v4p0593c1s v4p0595c2s
Springer, W.S. v2p0356c2s v2p0431c2s
Springfield, L. v4p0156c2s v4p0207c1s v4p0271c1s v4p0361c1s v4p0376c2s v6p0648c2s
Springmuhl, F. v1p0516c2s
Sprogle, J.L. v5p0485c2s
Sprott, R.J. v6p0361c2s
Sproule, J. v1p0660c2s v1p1265c1s
Sproull, J.W. v4p0349c1s
Sproull, W.O. v3p0129c2s
Spry, I.H. v1p0585c1s
Spurgeon, C.H. v1p0308c1s v1p1055c2s
Spurgeon, J.W. v5p0114c1s
Spurgin, W.F. v5p0029c1s
Spurr, E. v5p0318c1s
Spurr, H.A. v4p0258c2s v5p0210c1s v5p0263c2m v5p0598c1s v6p0036c1s
Spurr, J.E. v4p0529c1s v5p0474c1s v5p0510c1s v6p0649c2s
Squarey, T.F. v2p0261c2s
Squier, E.G. v1p0022c1s v1p0030c2m v1p0037c2s v1p0187c1s v1p0212c2m v1p0300c1s v1p0377c1s v1p0533c2s v1p0636c2s v1p0799c1s v1p0876c1s v1p0920c1s v1p0992c2s v1p1073c1s v1p1149c1s v1p1377c2s v3p0072c1s v3p0218c2s
Squier, G.O. v4p0349c2s v5p0086c2s v5p0252c2s v5p0426c2s
Squier, G.O. and Crehore, A.C. v5p0565c1s
Squier, H.G. v6p0599c1s
Squier, M.P. v1p0237c2s v1p0527c2s v1p1043c2s
Squire, B. v5p0450c1s
Squire, C.R. v5p0487c2s v6p0220c2s
Squire, G.H. v6p0272c1s
Squire, J. and Leake, W.M. v1p1030c1s
Squire, W. v2p0416c1s
Squire, W.B. v3p0061c2s v4p0058c2s v4p0389c1s v4p0583c2s
Squire, W.S. v2p0303c2s
Squires, G. v5p0543c2s v5p0618c2s
Squires, L.H. v3p0113c2s
Squires, V.P. v5p0377c1s
Squirrell, H.S. v6p0154c1s
Srygley, F.D. v2p0261c1s
Staaff, K. and Braekstad, H.L. v6p0460c2s
Staats, J. v4p0013c1s
Staats, W.C.M. v1p1233c1s
Stab, S. v3p0129c2s
Stabler, H.S. and Washington, E.B. v4p0612c1s
Stabler, Marguerite v5p0505c1s
Stables, G. v1p0237c1s v1p1439c1s v2p0070c2s v2p0120c2m v2p0228c2s v2p0424c2s v3p0014c2s v3p0047c2m v3p0068c1s v3p0070c1s v3p0120c1s v3p0126c2s v4p0406c1s
Stables, J.C. v3p0035c2s
Stace, A.J. v3p0308c1s
Stack, C.M. v6p0156c2s v6p0218c1s
Stack, H.J. v3p0319c2s
Stack, J.H. v1p0350c2s v1p0448c2s v1p0661c1s v1p0932c1s
Stackhouse, P. v1p0573c2s
Stackhouse, V.E. v6p0383c2s
Stackpole, C.A. v1p0313c2s
Stackpole, E.S. v5p0054c2s
Stackpole, J.L. v1p0729c2s v1p1267c1s
Stackpole, S.H. v1p0557c2s v2p0181c1s
Stacpoole, H.de V. v4p0348c2s
Stacpoole, W.H. v2p0152c2s v2p0300c2s v2p0433c2s v3p0131c2s v3p0234c2s v3p0243c1s v3p0267c1s v3p0291c1s v3p0292c1s v3p0299c2s v3p0300c2s v3p0308c2s v3p0382c1s v3p0411c2s v3p0445c2s
Stacy, F.N. v6p0328c2s v6p0591c2s
Stadden, C.M. v5p0410c2m
Stadelman, P.C. v5p0091c1s
Stadling, J. v4p0496c1m v4p0578c2s v5p0325c2s v5p0524c1s v5p0528c1s
Stadling, Jonas v5p0027c1s
Staehelin, E. v1p0769c2s
Staehlin, L. v4p0053c1s
Stael, A.De v4p0181c2s
Stael, M.de v1p0420c1s v1p0448c1s
Stael, Mad.de v1p0754c1s
Stafford, B.T. v6p0122c2s v6p0259c1s v6p0602c1s
Stafford, H.M. v5p0581c1s
Stafford, J. v4p0159c2s v4p0178c2s v4p0603c2s v5p0377c2s v5p0397c2s v5p0440c2s v5p0503c1s v5p0632c2s v6p0459c1s v6p0473c2s
Stafford, John v5p0238c2s v6p0583c2s
Stafford, W.C. v1p0440c1s
Stafford, W.P. v3p0329c2s v4p0046c2s v5p0456c2s v6p0631c1s
Stager, L.A. v3p0198c2s v3p0378c1s
Stagg, E. v1p0111c1s v1p0843c2s v1p1085c1s v1p1359c1s
Stahl, A.W. v1p1040c2s v1p1416c2s v4p0410c2s
Stahl, J.M. v4p0350c1s v4p0524c2s v4p0596c1s v5p0137c2s
Stahley, G.D. v3p0084c1s v3p0216c2s v6p0066c2s
Stahley, G.D. et al. v5p0348c1s
Stahlschmidt, J.C.L. v2p0039c1m
Stahr, J.S. v1p0435c1s v1p0738c1s v1p0988c1s v2p0127c1s v2p0368c1s v2p0390c1s v3p0204c1s v4p0171c1s v4p0191c2s v4p0478c1s v5p0399c2s v5p0482c1s
Stainforth, J.W. v2p0469c1m
Stairly, C. v3p0023c1s
Stairs, W.G. v3p0004c1s v3p0005c1s
Stakely, C.A. v3p0155c2s v3p0298c2s
Stakley, C.A. v3p0395c2s
Staley, A.E. v2p0254c1s
Staley, E. v6p0294c2s v6p0361c2s v6p0502c2s v6p0688c2s
Staley, G.L. v1p0025c2s v1p0240c2s v1p0769c2s v1p1043c2s v1p1050c1s
Staley, Kathryn v4p0440c1s
Stalker, A.W. v6p0688c1s
Stalker, J. v3p0428c1s v4p0056c1s v4p0109c2s v4p0113c1s v4p0224c1s v4p0301c2s v4p0303c2s v5p0306c1s v5p0307c1s v5p0385c1s v6p0122c1s
Stalker, James, Rev. v6p0341c1s
Stalker, T. v3p0026c1s v6p0566c1s
Stall, S. v2p0269c1s v4p0345c1s
Stallard, J.H. v1p0981c2m v3p0125c1s v3p0192c1s v3p0452c1s v5p0443c1s v5p0507c1s
Stallings, L.F. v6p0571c1s
Stallo, J.B. v1p1006c1s v1p1162c2s v2p0341c1s v2p0390c1s
Stallybrass, H.M. v2p0099c1s
Stamford, P. v4p0423c2s
Stammer, M. v1p1265c2s
Stamp, A.E. v5p0261c1s v6p0401c2s
Stampenbourg, Baron de ... v5p0011c2s v5p0278c1s v6p0277c1s
Standage, H.C. v2p0093c2s v4p0411c2s

Standart, E.C. v2p0078c1s
Standiland, C.J. v2p0258c1s
Standing, G.M. v4p0086c1s
Standing, H. v2p0437c1s
Standing, P.C. v3p0320c2s
v4p0043c2s v5p0010c2s v5p0072c1s
v5p0078c1m v5p0142c2s v5p0224c1s
v5p0262c1s v5p0369c1s v5p0439c1s
v5p0500c1s v5p0527c2m v5p0539c2s
v5p0548c1s v5p0557c1s v6p0293c2s
v6p0448c2s
Standing, Percy C. v6p0070c1s
Standish, G.F. v1p0801c2s
Standish, P.C. v3p0060c1s
Standish, W.H. v4p0230c2s
Standish, W.W. v4p0525c2s
v4p0526c1s
Standring, G. v3p0446c1s
Stanesby, A.J. v3p0350c2s
Stanford, C. and Taio-ko . v5p0111c2s
Stanford, C.V. v2p0424c1s
v3p0162c1s v3p0322c1s v3p0452c2s
v4p0389c2s v5p0401c1s
Stanford, C.V., Sir. v6p0079c1s
Stanford, E.C.C. v3p0383c1s
Stanford, H. v5p0390c1s
Stanford, J.V. v6p0615c1s
Stanford, P. v5p0592c1s
Stanford, V. v4p0602c2s
Stanford, V.F.B. v3p0263c1s
Stang, W. v2p0281c1s
Stange, C. v6p0514c1s
Stange, D. v4p0059c1s
Stanhope, E. v1p1079c1s
v2p0165c2s v2p0254c1s
Stanhope, Earl v1p0050c1s
v1p0184c2s v1p0219c2s v1p0238c2s
v1p1000c1s v1p1230c2s
Stanhope, G. v5p0102c2s
v5p0349c2s
Staniels, C.E. v2p0129c1s
Staniforth, E. v3p0044c1s
v3p0430c2s v4p0602c2s
Stanlaws, P. v5p0051c1s
v5p0051c2s
Stanley, A. v5p0588c2s
Stanley, A.P. v1p0003c1s
v1p0027c2s v1p0047c2s v1p0053c1s
v1p0060c2s v1p0071c2s v1p0095c2s
v1p0103c1s v1p0176c1s v1p0177c1s
v1p0230c1m v1p0239c2s v1p0241c2s
v1p0248c1s v1p0250c1s v1p0251c2s
v1p0255c2s v1p0286c1s v1p0313c2s
v1p0339c1s v1p0351c2s v1p0390c2s
v1p0509c2s v1p0536c2s v1p0594c1s
v1p0594c2s v1p0602c2s v1p0651c2s
v1p0685c2s v1p0752c1s v1p0769c1s
v1p0775c2s v1p0812c2s v1p0841c1s
v1p0928c2s v1p0940c1s v1p0960c2s
v1p0964c2s v1p0977c2s v1p0997c2s
v1p1095c1s v1p1096c2s v1p1109c2s
v1p1118c2s v1p1131c2s v1p1161c1s
v1p1171c2s v1p1219c1s v1p1220c1s
v1p1263c2s v1p1303c1s v1p1310c1s
v1p1321c2s v1p1322c2s v1p1338c1s
v1p1338c2s v1p1350c1s v1p1355c1s
v1p1402c1s v1p1402c2s v1p1417c1s
v2p0071c1s v2p0113c2s v2p0374c1s
v6p0325c1s v6p0646c1s
Stanley, C.A. v5p0248c2s
v6p0024c1s v6p0418c2s
Stanley, C.H. v3p0234c1m
v5p0084c2s
Stanley, C.H., Mrs. v3p0277c2s
v3p0434c2s
Stanley, D. v5p0331c1s
Stanley, D.M. v1p0016c2s
Stanley, E.L. v1p0359c2s
v1p0387c1s v1p0511c1s v1p0558c1s
v1p0640c1s v1p0650c2s v1p0813c1s
v2p0131c1s v2p0264c2s v3p0128c2s
v3p0129c1s v3p0378c1s v4p0169c2m
v4p0170c1s v4p0339c2m v5p0177c2s
v5p0178c1s v6p0191c1s v6p0384c1s
Stanley, E.L. and Gregory, R.
v3p0129c1s
Stanley, E.Lyulph v5p0177c2s
Stanley, G.E. v4p0625c2s
Stanley, H.A. v5p0414c1s
v5p0621c1s
Stanley, H.H. v5p0078c2s
v5p0107c1s
Stanley, H.M. v1p0013c1s
v2p0088c1s v2p0116c2s v2p0154c1s
v2p0233c1s v2p0390c2s v3p0004c2s
v3p0021c2s v3p0022c1s v3p0136c2s
v3p0150c2s v3p0194c2s v3p0214c2s
v3p0269c1s v3p0332c2m v4p0006c2s
v4p0036c2s v4p0128c2s v4p0130c1s
v4p0177c2s v4p0204c2s v4p0351c2s
v4p0464c2s v4p0529c1s v4p0575c1s
v4p0589c2s v4p0602c1s v5p0005c2s
v5p0006c1s v5p0034c1s v5p0039c2s
v5p0176c2s v5p0179c1s v5p0187c2s
v5p0190c2s v5p0239c2s v5p0279c1s
v5p0325c1s v5p0381c2s v5p0402c2s
v5p0523c2s v5p0542c1s v5p0580c1s
v5p0589c2s v5p0597c1s v6p0006c1s
v6p0089c1m v6p0639c1s v6p0678c2s
Stanley, H.S. v2p0149c1s
Stanley, Henry M. v5p0020c1s
Stanley, Hiram M. v3p0384c1s
v4p0012c1s v4p0169c1m v4p0196c1s
v4p0312c2s v4p0328c2s v4p0357c1s
v4p0357c2s v4p0475c1s v4p0513c2s
v5p0044c2s v5p0067c1s v5p0079c2s
v5p0102c2s v5p0168c1s v5p0169c2s
v5p0327c1s v5p0386c1s v5p0454c2s
v5p0471c1s v5p0484c1m v5p0577c2s
v5p0579c2s v5p0583c1s
Stanley, J. v2p0240c1s
v4p0091c2s v5p0565c2s
Stanley, Lady v1p1421c2s
Stanley, Lord v5p0467c1s
Stanley, M. v1p0462c2s
v1p0766c2s v3p0385c2s v5p0641c1s
Stanley, Maude, Hon. v3p0089c1s
v3p0472c1s
Stanley, Miss v1p0463c1s
Stanley, Prof. v5p0605c2s
Stanley, S.S. v2p0421c2s
v4p0050c2s
Stanley, T. v5p0275c2s
Stanley, W.F. v3p0408c2s
Stanley-Brown, J. v4p0050c1s
v5p0527c1s
Stanley of Alderley v4p0072c1s
v6p0191c1s
Stanley of Alderley, Lord. v2p0005c2s
v2p0057c1s v2p0247c2s v2p0431c1s
v3p0083c1s v4p0318c2s v4p0609c1s
v5p0265c2s
Stanmore, Lord v5p0234c2s
Stanmore, Lord et al. v4p0290c1s
Stannard, A. v2p0183c1s
Stannard, H.E.V. v4p0355c2s
Stannard, H.E.V., Mrs. ... v4p0609c1s
Stannard, W.G. v6p0388c2s
Stannus, H. v4p0199c2s
v4p0204c2s v4p0550c2s v5p0214c2s
v5p0495c1s
Stansbury, Alta L. v6p0374c2s
Stansbury, C.F. v3p0314c1s
v6p0333c2s v6p0473c2s
Stansbury, E.A. v1p0116c2s
Stansbury, M.A.P. v3p0401c1s
v4p0095c2s v4p0579c1s
Stansfeld, J. v1p0295c1s
v1p0816c2s v2p0189c1s
Stansfield, A. v2p0318c1s
v2p0482c1s
Stansfield, H. v1p0091c1s
Stansfield, H. and Edser, E.
v5p0338c1s
Stansfield, W.L. v4p0305c1s
Stantford, F.A.Van v4p0348c2s
v4p0388c2s
Stanton, A.G. v4p0565c2s
v6p0634c2s
Stanton, E. v5p0159c1s
Stanton, E.C. v1p1420c2s
v2p0425c2s v3p0119c1s v3p0322c1s
v3p0345c2s v3p0473c2s v4p0054c1s
v4p0229c1s v4p0555c1s v5p0017c1s
v5p0163c2s
Stanton, E.C. and Grant, C.R.
v5p0484c2s
Stanton, E.C. and Spalding, J.L.
v2p0477c1s
Stanton, E.C., Mrs. v3p0113c1s
Stanton, E.C. et al. v2p0477c2s
Stanton, E.E. v4p0295c2s
Stanton, E.F. v1p0797c2s
Stanton, E.P. v5p0554c2s
v6p0274c2s
Stanton, Eliz.C. v3p0074c2s
Stanton, Elizabeth Cady .. v4p0622c1s
Stanton, F.B. v1p0487c1s
Stanton, F.M. v6p0259c2s
Stanton, F.P. v1p0741c2s
v1p1048c2s v1p1343c1s v1p1343c2s
v1p1344c2s v1p1347c2m v1p1353c2s
v1p1414c1s
Stanton, G. v4p0226c1s
Stanton, G.B. v4p0158c1s
v4p0575c2s
Stanton, Gertrude v5p0557c2s
Stanton, H. v1p0574c1s
v1p0703c1s v1p1255c1s v1p1378c2s
v1p1407c2s
Stanton, H.A., Mrs. v4p0550c2s
Stanton, H.B. v1p0917c2s
Stanton, H.C.W. v2p0046c2s
v2p0346c1s
Stanton, H.M.E. v5p0101c2s
Stanton, H.P. v5p0642c1s
Stanton, H.T. v4p0621c2s
Stanton, J. v4p0564c2s
Stanton, J.A. v4p0501c2s
Stanton, J.H. v4p0444c1s
Stanton, R.B. v3p0093c1s
v4p0125c1s
Stanton, R.L. v1p0481c1s
v2p0352c2s
Stanton, R.L. and Vincent, M.R.
v2p0152c1s
Stanton, R.M. v3p0302c1s
Stanton, S.A. et al. v4p0180c1s
Stanton, S.B. v5p0024c1s
Stanton, S.W. v4p0268c1s
v4p0547c1s v4p0548c1m
Stanton, T. v3p0179c1s
v3p0242c2s v3p0251c2s v3p0351c1s
v4p0046c2s v4p0056c2s v4p0071c1s
v4p0073c1s v4p0091c2s v4p0095c2s
v4p0101c1m v4p0121c1s v4p0134c2s
v4p0137c1s v4p0155c2s v4p0160c1s
v4p0192c1s v4p0211c1m v4p0212c2m
v4p0215c1s v4p0216c2s v4p0229c2s
v4p0277c2s v4p0305c1s v4p0320c2s
v4p0367c1s v4p0392c2s v4p0425c2s
v4p0426c2s v4p0485c2s v4p0505c1m
v4p0577c2s v4p0592c2s v4p0593c2s
v4p0630c1s v5p0002c1s v5p0054c2s
v5p0066c1s v5p0069c1s v5p0080c1s
v5p0101c2s v5p0124c1s v5p0153c2s
v5p0162c1s v5p0166c2s v5p0169c1s
v5p0227c1s v5p0252c1s v5p0341c1s
v5p0373c2s v5p0430c2s v5p0431c1s
v5p0431c2s v5p0432c1m v5p0484c1s
v5p0535c2s v5p0604c2s v5p0641c1s
v6p0069c1s v6p0073c1s v6p0284c2s
v6p0358c2s v6p0713c2s
Stanton, T. and Naquet, A.
v4p0174c1s
Stanton, T.W. v4p0048c1s
v6p0251c1s
Stanton, T.W. and Vaughan, T.W.
v4p0139c1s
Stanton, Theodore v3p0161c2s
v6p0243c2s v6p0460c2s
Stanton, V.H. v1p0685c2s
v1p1025c2s v2p0084c2s v4p0108c2s
v4p0109c1s v4p0532c1s
Stanton, W.A. v3p0081c1s
v3p0081c2s
Stanton, W.S. v6p0110c2s
Stanus, H. v3p0156c2s
Stanwood, C. v6p0564c1s
Stanwood, E. v1p0444c2s
v1p0556c2s v1p0715c1s v1p0848c2s
v1p1049c2s v1p1075c2s v1p1098c1s
v1p1239c2s v1p1261c1s v2p0065c2s
v2p0215c2s v2p0277c1s v2p0348c2s
v2p0452c1s v2p0454c1s v4p0136c1s
v5p0614c2s v6p0170c1s v6p0426c1s
Stanwood, J.B. v4p0145c1s
v5p0550c2s v5p0551c1m
Stanwood, J.R. v2p0312c1s
v2p0470c1s
Stapf, O. v3p0272c1s
v4p0262c2s v5p0315c1s
Stapfer, P. v4p0095c2s
v4p0517c1s
Stapff, F.M. v1p1329c2s
Staples, C.A. v3p0087c1s
v3p0189c1s v3p0197c2s v3p0247c2s
Staples, C.J. v6p0613c2s
Staples, F.P. v4p0475c2s
Staples, J. v1p1191c2s
Staples, R. v2p0227c1s
v2p0442c1s
Staples, R., jr. v2p0227c2s
Staples, S. v5p0228c1s
Staples, S.F. v5p0163c2s
Staples, W.R. v1p1105c2s
Stapleton, A. v3p0106c2m
v3p0308c1s v6p0208c1s
Stapleton, A.G. v1p0196c2s
v1p0490c2s v1p0558c1s v1p0987c2s
Stapleton, F. v2p0095c1s
Stapleton, Gregory, Mrs. . v6p0326c1s
Stapleton, H. v5p0051c1s
Stapleton, P. v3p0067c2s
v3p0068c1s v3p0315c1s v3p0337c2s
v3p0466c1s v4p0581c2s v4p0585c1s
v4p0626c2s
Stapleton, S. v6p0346c2s
v6p0602c1s
Stapleton, T. v1p0006c2s
v1p0393c1s v1p0926c1s v1p1385c2s
v1p1411c2s
Stapley, A. v2p0389c1s
Stapley, A.M. v3p0075c2s
Stapley, M. v1p0079c1s
Stapp, E.B. v5p0311c2s
v5p0555c1s
Star, M.A. v3p0133c2s
Starbird, R.S. v6p0032c1s
Starbuck, A. v1p0892c2s
Starbuck, C.C. v1p0675c2m
v1p0686c1s v2p0073c2s v2p0217c2s
v2p0218c1s v2p0236c1s v2p0292c1m
v2p0320c2s v2p0336c2s v2p0376c2s
v2p0432c1s v2p0449c1s v3p0005c1m
v3p0020c2s v3p0042c2m v3p0055c1s
v3p0081c2s v3p0096c1s v3p0119c2m
v3p0139c1s v3p0141c2s v3p0144c2s
v3p0162c1s v3p0166c1s v3p0191c2s
v3p0205c1s v3p0227c1s v3p0228c2s
v3p0263c1s v3p0282c2m v3p0285c1s
v3p0294c2s v3p0301c1s v3p0323c1s
v3p0338c1s v3p0342c1s v3p0365c1s
v3p0367c2s v3p0383c2s v3p0422c1s
v3p0438c2s v3p0455c1s v4p0045c1s
v4p0057c1s v4p0226c1s v4p0255c2s
v4p0277c2s v4p0299c2s v4p0321c1s
v4p0344c1s v4p0357c1s v4p0374c2m
v4p0375c1s v4p0463c1s v4p0487c2s
v4p0488c1s v5p0071c2s v5p0224c1s

v5p0308c1s v5p0380c1s v5p0464c1s
v5p0469c1s v5p0510c1s v6p0021c1s
Starbuck, E.D. v5p0135c1s
v5p0484c1s v6p0536c2s v6p0537c1m
v6p0538c1s
Starbuck, M.E. v5p0299c2s
v6p0441c2s
Starbuck, W.G. v1p0197c2s
v1p0559c2s
Starcke, C.N. v3p0236c2s
v3p0338c1s v4p0129c2s v4p0357c1s
Starey, A.B. v3p0424c2s
Starey, J.H. v3p0072c2s
Stark, A.B. v1p0416c2s
v1p0417c1s
Stark, B. v6p0009c1s
v6p0345c2s v6p0353c2s
Stark, E.D. v3p0393c1s
Stark, F.G. v2p0238c2s
Stark, J. v1p1146c1s
v1p1167c2s v1p1376c1s v6p0325c2s
Stark, J.A. v2p0060c1s
Stark, J.H. v2p0040c2s
v3p0039c2s
Stark, W.E. v1p1370c1s
Starke, G.von v2p0048c1s
Starkey, D.P. v1p0693c2s
Starks, E.C. v6p0226c1s
Starks, W.J. v1p0322c2s
Starkweather, G.P. v5p0141c2s
v5p0482c2s v5p0550c2m v5p0577c2s
Starkweather, W.G. v4p0128c1s
v4p0292c2s v5p0141c1s
Starley, J.K. v4p0058c2s
v5p0150c2s
Starley, W.K. v5p0150c2s
Starling, E. v4p0418c1s
v4p0513c1s
Starling, E.H. v5p0604c2s
v6p0581c2s
Starling, W. v3p0283c1s
v4p0328c1s v4p0375c1s v5p0112c1s
Starnes, H.N. v2p0069c1s
v2p0104c1m v2p0372c1s
Starnes, V. v4p0277c1s
Starr, E.A. v2p0310c2s
v3p0003c2s v3p0015c1s v3p0229c2s
v4p0399c2s v4p0408c1s v5p0306c1s
Starr, E.S. v2p0341c2m
v3p0121c2s
Starr, F. v3p0122c2s
v4p0005c2s v4p0008c2s v4p0013c2s
v4p0014c2s v4p0020c1m v4p0036c1s
v4p0041c2s v4p0100c2s v4p0101c1s
v4p0102c2s v4p0134c1s v4p0148c1s
v4p0152c2s v4p0187c1s v4p0196c2s
v4p0201c2s v4p0205c2m v4p0219c1s
v4p0235c1s v4p0255c1s v4p0282c2s
v4p0309c2s v4p0354c1s v4p0362c1s
v4p0365c1s v4p0369c1s v4p0388c1s
v4p0433c2s v4p0468c1s v4p0522c2s
v4p0550c2s v4p0558c1s v4p0636c1s
v4p0636c2s v5p0033c2s v5p0053c2s
v5p0105c1s v5p0143c2s v5p0154c1s
v5p0198c2s v5p0236c2s v5p0269c2s
v5p0286c1s v5p0359c1s v5p0359c2s
v5p0367c1s v5p0368c2s v5p0373c1m
v5p0373c2s v5p0401c1s v5p0403c1s
v5p0429c2s v5p0454c2s v5p0475c2s
v5p0504c2s v6p0042c2s v6p0144c1s
v6p0364c1s v6p0414c2m v6p0485c1s
v6p0494c2s v6p0600c1s v6p0633c2s
v6p0714c1s
Starr, F. and Carus, P. .. v5p0373c2s
Starr, F.F. v1p0255c2s
v4p0357c1s
Starr, Florence v6p0404c1s
Starr, Frederick v4p0368c2s
v6p0524c1s
Starr, I.B. v5p0389c1s
v5p0639c2s
Starr, J.E. and Ludeking, C.
v4p0016c1s
Starr, L. v2p0273c1s
Starr, L.B. v4p0105c2s
v4p0297c1s v4p0298c2s v5p0028c1s
v5p0152c1s v5p0181c2s v5p0395c1s
v5p0409c1s v5p0569c1m
Starr, Laura B. v4p0414c2s
v5p0159c1s
Starr, Laura C. v6p0139c2s
Starr, Laura E. v5p0624c2s
Starr, M. v2p0088c2s
v4p0323c2s
Starr, M.A. v2p0283c1s
v2p0413c2s v3p0331c1s v4p0388c1s
v4p0465c2s v4p0574c1s
Starr, M.L. v4p0616c2s
Starr, R.H. v5p0114c2s
Starr, R.H.E. v4p0110c1s
v5p0267c2s v5p0350c2s v5p0434c2s
v5p0564c2m v5p0611c1s
Starr, S. v1p0943c1s
Starr, T. v3p0128c1s
Starr-Martin, E. v5p0635c2s
Starrett, H.E. v3p0202c2s
v3p0468c1s v4p0250c1s v4p0457c1s
v4p0466c1s
Starrett, H.E., Mrs. v3p0422c1s
Starrett, Helen E. v4p0334c2s
v5p0178c2s
Starrett, T. v6p0580c2s
v6p0687c1s
Start, E.A. v2p0439c1s
v3p0039c1s v3p0261c2s v3p0301c2s
v3p0302c2m v3p0372c1s v4p0028c1s
v4p0228c2s v4p0247c1s v4p0434c1s
v5p0174c1s v5p0197c1s v5p0400c1s
v5p0641c2s v6p0080c1s v6p0410c2s
v6p0456c2s
Start, J.E. v4p0477c2s
Stassoff, V. v4p0030c2s
Statham, E. v5p0505c2s
Statham, E.P. v2p0216c1s
v5p0041c2s
Statham, F.R. v1p0012c2s
v1p0329c2s v1p1203c2s v4p0138c1s
v4p0360c2s v4p0610c2s v5p0123c2s
v5p0320c1s v5p0356c1s v5p0586c2s
Statham, F.Reginald v5p0320c1s
Statham, H. v4p0493c1s
Statham, H.H. v1p0053c2s
v1p0054c1s v1p0108c1s v1p0140c2s
v1p0559c2s v1p0884c2s v1p0885c1s
v1p1130c1m v2p0019c2s v2p0264c2s
v2p0300c2s v2p0323c2s v2p0358c2s
v3p0017c2s v3p0018c2s v3p0246c1m
v3p0255c2s v4p0023c2s v4p0040c2s
v4p0181c1s v4p0339c1s v4p0365c1s
v5p0054c2s v5p0082c2s v5p0084c1s
v5p0188c2s v5p0253c2m v5p0330c1s
v5p0344c2s v5p0427c2s v5p0430c2s
v5p0431c2s v5p0432c1m v5p0498c2m
v5p0500c2s v5p0505c2s v5p0556c2s
v5p0623c1s v6p0081c1s v6p0499c1s
v6p0566c1s v6p0640c2s
Statham, H.S. v5p0394c2s
Statham, S.H. v4p0243c2s
Statham, S.P.H. v4p0357c1s
Statham, W.M. v2p0204c2s
v2p0212c1s v2p0301c2s v2p0365c1s
v2p0379c2s v4p0422c2s
Staudt, C.K. v6p0348c2s
Staufen, K.v. v4p0287c1s
Staufen, K.von v4p0106c2s
Stauffer, D.McN. v1p0051c1s
v3p0241c1s v5p0409c1s v6p0456c1s
Stauffer, F.H. v1p0135c2s
Stauffer, J.H. v6p0538c2s
Stauffer, N.P. v6p0039c1s
v6p0137c1s v6p0553c1s
Staunton, S.A. v4p0047c2s
v5p0543c2s
Staunton, W. v1p0238c1s
v2p0085c1s
Stauss, R. v5p0193c2s
Stav, M.A. v1p0529c2s
Staveley, Canon v6p0327c2s
Staveley, R. v5p0385c2s
v5p0622c2s v6p0696c2s
Stavenhagen, B. v4p0269c2s
Stawell, F.M. v6p0030c1s
v6p0286c2s v6p0411c1s
Stawell, F.Melian v6p0575c1s
Staymaker, G.B. v6p0012c2s
Stayton, W.H. v4p0395c2s
Stead, A. v6p0019c2s
v6p0042c1s v6p0087c1s v6p0089c1s
v6p0110c1s v6p0186c2m v6p0334c1m
v6p0334c2s v6p0336c1s v6p0336c2s
v6p0337c1s v6p0354c1m v6p0354c2s
v6p0398c2s v6p0478c1s v6p0509c1s
v6p0556c1s v6p0560c1m v6p0560c2m
v6p0561c1m v6p0584c2s
Stead, A. and Mijatovich, C.
v6p0186c2s
Stead, Alfred v6p0283c1s
v6p0337c1s
Stead, F.H. v4p0100c1s
v4p0101c1s v4p0479c1s v6p0078c1s
v6p0384c1s v6p0665c1s
Stead, H. v6p0041c1s
v6p0163c2s v6p0414c2s
Stead, Henry v6p0042c1s
Stead, J.L. v4p0412c1s
Stead, R.J.C. v6p0182c1s
Stead, S. v1p0047c2s
v1p0255c2s
Stead, W.F. v6p0057c1s
Stead, W.J. v5p0293c2s
Stead, W.T. v1p0271c1s
v2p0353c2s v3p0007c2s v3p0030c2s
v3p0046c2s v3p0050c1s v3p0051c2s
v3p0084c2s v3p0159c2s v3p0204c1s
v3p0084c2s v3p0159c2s v3p0204c1s
v3p0260c1s v3p0276c2s v3p0319c1s
v3p0372c2s v3p0460c1s v3p0464c1s
v4p0001c2s v4p0010c1m v4p0033c1s
v4p0042c1s v4p0046c1s v4p0064c1s
v4p0067c2s v4p0086c1s v4p0100c1s
v4p0116c2s v4p0227c1m v4p0233c1s
v4p0238c2m v4p0240c2s v4p0247c2s
v4p0261c2s v4p0303c1s v4p0320c1s
v4p0320c2s v4p0340c1s v4p0347c2s
v4p0353c2s v4p0369c1s v4p0404c1s
v4p0443c1s v4p0457c2s v4p0483c1s
v4p0491c1s v4p0496c1s v4p0500c1s
v4p0514c2s v4p0536c1s v4p0543c2s
v4p0553c1s v4p0569c1m v4p0586c1s
v4p0604c1s v4p0622c1s v5p0011c2s
v5p0025c1s v5p0065c1s v5p0093c1s
v5p0100c2s v5p0138c1s v5p0145c1s
v5p0168c2s v5p0180c1s v5p0190c2s
v5p0234c2s v5p0245c1s v5p0245c2s
v5p0247c1s v5p0248c1s v5p0277c2s
v5p0389c2s v5p0390c2s v5p0406c1s
v5p0410c2m v5p0430c2s v5p0437c2m
v5p0487c2m v5p0500c2s v5p0501c1s
v5p0502c2s v5p0610c2s v5p0611c2s
v5p0631c2s v6p0007c1s v6p0095c1m
v6p0129c2s v6p0130c2s v6p0191c1s
v6p0191c2m v6p0194c2s v6p0210c2s
v6p0224c2s v6p0226c2s v6p0258c1s
v6p0268c1s v6p0269c1s v6p0269c2s
v6p0274c2s v6p0277c2m v6p0296c2s
v6p0299c2s v6p0368c1s v6p0368c2s
v6p0410c2s v6p0457c1s v6p0459c1s
v6p0471c2s v6p0501c1s v6p0510c2s
v6p0541c2s v6p0542c1s v6p0556c2s
v6p0558c2m v6p0612c2s v6p0649c1m
v6p0689c1s v6p0709c2s
Stead, W.T. and Sinnett, A.P.
v3p0047c1s
Stead, W.T. et al. v4p0111c2s
Steadman, A. v4p0077c1s
Stearns, A.S. v1p0295c2s
Stearns, C. v1p1068c1s
Stearns, C.A. v4p0523c2s
Stearns, C.C. v6p0293c1s
Stearns, C.M. v6p0085c2s
v6p0255c1s v6p0279c2s v6p0291c1s
v6p0651c1s
Stearns, E. v1p0240c1s
Stearns, E.J. v1p1375c1s
v2p0320c2s v2p0415c1s
Stearns, E.S. v4p0398c1s
v5p0171c2s v5p0209c2s v5p0347c1s
v5p0385c2m v5p0553c2s v6p0228c1s
v6p0684c1s
Stearns, F.P. v1p0760c2s
v3p0087c1s v3p0136c1s v3p0355c1s
v5p0237c1s
Stearns, G. v1p1092c2s
v1p1093c1s
Stearns, G.F. v4p0054c1s
Stearns, Geo. v4p0235c1s
Stearns, H.P. v1p0643c2s
v1p1007c2s
Stearns, J. v1p0843c2s
Stearns, J.F. v1p1047c1m
Stearns, J.M. v1p1055c2s
v1p1394c1s
Stearns, J.W. v1p0046c2s
v1p0601c1s v1p0842c1s v6p0052c1s
Stearns, L.E. v4p0329c1s
v4p0330c1s v4p0474c2s v4p0624c2s
v5p0334c1s v5p0334c2s v5p0336c2s
v6p0370c2s v6p0373c1s v6p0655c2m
Stearns, L.F. v2p0027c2s
v2p0247c1s v2p0438c1s v2p0451c2s
v3p0064c1s v3p0096c1s v3p0460c1s
Stearns, Lutie E. v6p0256c2s
v6p0374c2s v6p0375c1m
Stearns, O. v1p0121c2s
v1p0293c1s v1p1083c2s
Stearns, O.O. v1p0097c2s
Stearns, O.S. v1p0125c1s
v1p0241c2s v1p0273c2s v2p0042c2s
v2p0393c2s
Stearns, R. v6p0440c2s
Stearns, R.E.C. v1p0279c2s
v1p0462c1s v1p0637c2s v1p0859c1s
v1p0860c1s v1p0889c1s v1p0984c1s
v1p1015c2s v1p1176c1s v1p1189c1m
v2p0001c1s v2p0399c2s v2p0435c1s
v3p0479c1s v3p0017c1s v3p0293c2s
v6p0212c2s v6p0620c2s
Stearns, Richard v5p0167c2s
Stearns, W.A. v1p0393c2s
v1p0495c2s v1p0689c1s v1p0846c1s
v1p1250c1s v1p1286c2s v1p1338c2s
v1p1340c1s
Stearns, W.N. v6p0272c2s
v6p0641c1s v6p0672c1s
Stebbing, T.R.R. v1p0435c1s
v1p1291c1s v4p0016c2s v4p0018c2s
v4p0142c1s v4p0270c1s v4p0337c1s
v4p0344c2s v4p0466c2s v4p0637c2s
v5p0146c1m v5p0424c2s v6p0111c2s
v6p0458c2s
Stebbing, W. v1p0397c2s
Stebbins, D. v1p1250c2s
Stebbins, G.B. v4p0159c2s
v4p0464c1s v5p0257c2s v5p0533c2m
Stebbins, H. v2p0054c2s
Stebbins, H.W. v6p0318c1s
Stebbins, J. and Faith, E.A.
v6p0068c1s
Stebbins, Joel v6p0067c2s
Stebbins, M.C. v3p0428c1s
Stebbins, N.L. v3p0267c2s
Stebbins, O.B. v4p0068c2s
v4p0069c1s v4p0341c1s
Stebbins, R. v1p1428c1s
v4p0136c2s
Stebbins, R.P. v1p0038c1s
v1p0069c1s v1p0084c2s v1p0118c1s
v1p0122c2s v1p0125c1s v1p0126c2s
v1p0303c1s v1p0333c2s v1p0394c2s
v1p0434c2s v1p0507c1s v1p0508c1s

v1p0686c1s v1p0690c2s v1p0757c1s
v1p0847c1s v1p1051c1s v1p1063c1s
v1p1235c1s v1p1262c1s v1p1340c1s
v1p1388c2s v1p1415c2s v2p0043c1s
v2p0199c2s v2p0211c1s v3p0385c2s
Stebbins, W. v1p1359c1s
Stechhan, H.O. v6p0316c1s
v6p0435c1s
Steck, D. v1p0847c1s
Steckel, A. v5p0241c1s
Steckel, A. and McDaniel, E.W.
v5p0143c2s
Stecker, C.C. v3p0329c2m
v3p0338c2s v3p0422c2s
Stedman, A. v3p0274c1s
Stedman, C.M. v3p0355c2s
Stedman, E.C. v1p0008c1s
v1p0032c2s v1p0060c1s v1p0116c2s
v1p0150c1s v1p0165c2s v1p0170c1m
v1p0171c2s v1p0301c2s v1p0311c2s
v1p0354c1s v1p0360c2s v1p0418c2s
v1p0419c1s v1p0446c2s v1p0492c2s
v1p0569c2s v1p0579c1s v1p0602c1s
v1p0620c2s v1p0703c2s v1p0722c2s
v1p0918c1s v1p0939c2s v1p1019c1s
v1p1020c1s v1p1021c1s v1p1021c2s
v1p1054c1s v1p1202c1s v1p1204c1s
v1p1275c2s v1p1286c1s v1p1294c2m
v1p1301c1s v1p1386c2s v1p1407c1s
v2p0003c1s v2p0049c1s v2p0139c2s
v2p0173c1s v2p0241c1s v2p0249c2s
v2p0255c1s v2p0265c2s v2p0267c2s
v2p0321c1s v2p0346c1s v2p0473c1s
v3p0055c2s v3p0140c2s v3p0189c2s
v3p0263c1s v3p0436c1s v4p0196c1s
v4p0216c2s v4p0310c1s v4p0448c2s
v4p0511c1s v4p0518c1s v4p0520c1s
v5p0274c2s v5p0509c1s v6p0454c1s
v6p0618c1m v6p0697c2s
Stedman, E.C. et al. v2p0205c1s
v4p0517c2s
Stedman, H.R. v5p0291c2s
Stedman, J.M. v4p0352c1s
Stedman, W.P. and Wilson, J.H.
v3p0111c2s
Steed, J.G. v6p0297c2s
Steede, M. v4p0120c1s
Steege, K.R. v6p0491c1s
Steel, C.D. v6p0423c2s
Steel, F.A. v3p0193c1s
v4p0034c2s v4p0062c2s v4p0197c1s
v4p0228c2s v4p0311c2s v4p0374c1s
v4p0414c1s v4p0419c1s v4p0473c1s
v4p0477c1s v5p0271c2s v5p0282c2s
v5p0287c1s v5p0342c2s v5p0412c1s
v5p0440c2s v5p0562c2s v6p0021c2s
v6p0114c1m v6p0117c1s v6p0147c2s
v6p0165c2s v6p0169c1m v6p0182c1s
v6p0189c1s v6p0229c2s v6p0246c2s
v6p0247c1s v6p0294c1s v6p0314c1s
v6p0314c2s v6p0315c1s v6p0365c2s
v6p0388c1s v6p0462c2s v6p0478c2s
v6p0573c1s v6p0575c1s v6p0702c2s
v6p0703c2s v6p0705c1m
Steel, Flora A. v5p0043c1s
v6p0257c1s v6p0314c2s v6p0402c1s
v6p0525c1s
Steel, J.H. v1p0844c2s
Steel, J.L. v6p0053c1s
Steel, J.W. v4p0164c1s
Steel, M.D. v3p0205c1s
Steel, Mrs. v4p0276c2s
Steel, R. v2p0311c2s
v2p0352c2s
Steel, W. v6p0003c1s
Steel, W.A. v4p0430c2s
Steel, W.B. v3p0415c2s
Steelcroft, F. v5p0042c1s
v5p0135c1s v5p0135c2s v5p0200c1s
v5p0225c1s v5p0245c2s
Steele, A.B. v4p0369c2s
v5p0201c2s
Steele, A.C., Mrs. v1p1214c1s
Steele, A.G. v6p0085c2s
Steele, A.H. v5p0505c1s
Steele, B.W. v4p0257c2s
Steele, D. v1p0008c2s
v1p0343c2s v1p1064c1s v2p0437c2s
v3p0184c1s v6p0123c1s
Steele, D. et al. v3p0242c2s
Steele, D.M. v6p0419c2s
v6p0638c2s
Steele, Dr. v1p1064c1s
v3p0273c1s
Steele, E. v1p0560c1s
v6p0222c2s
Steele, E.S. v3p0292c2s
Steele, F.A. v5p0490c2s
Steele, F.E. v4p0044c1s
v4p0044c2m v4p0086c2s v4p0127c2s
v4p0199c1s v5p0046c2s v6p0050c1s
v6p0050c2s v6p0051c1m v6p0051c2s
Steele, F.E.M. v2p0362c1s
v2p0407c2s v3p0122c2s v3p0178c1s
v3p0337c1s v3p0414c1s
Steele, F.M. v6p0132c1s
Steele, Francesca M. v5p0462c1s
Steele, G.M. v1p0020c2s
v1p0059c1s v1p0078c1s v1p0242c2s
v1p0276c2s v1p0760c2s v1p0826c2s
v1p0831c1s v1p0928c1s v1p0989c2s
v1p1215c1s v2p0291c1s v3p0026c1s
v3p0215c1s v4p0002c1s v4p0169c1s
v4p0192c1s v4p0615c1s v4p0622c1s
Steele, H.M. v4p0271c2s
v4p0366c2s v4p0440c1s v4p0561c1s
v5p0500c1s
Steele, H.T. v2p0147c1s
Steele, J. v1p0846c2s
v1p1138c2s
Steele, J.C. v1p0563c2s
v1p0873c2s v4p0008c1s
Steele, J.D. v1p1076c1s
v3p0156c1s
Steele, J.L. v5p0361c1s
v6p0133c2s v6p0649c2s
Steele, J.M. and O'Neill, Hugh
v6p0349c2s
Steele, J.S. v4p0610c2s
Steele, J.S. et al. v5p0158c2s
Steele, L.E. v5p0552c2s
Steele, M.D. v2p0039c2s
v2p0483c1s v3p0144c2s v3p0170c2s
v3p0178c1s v4p0494c1s
Steele, M.F. v5p0162c2s
v5p0538c1s v5p0599c1s v5p0644c2s
Steele, M.P. v3p0310c2s
Steele, Mary D. v5p0533c1s
Steele, Matthew F. v6p0666c1s
Steele, R. v4p0009c2s
v4p0213c1s v4p0383c1s v5p0094c1s
v5p0454c2s v6p0074c2m v6p0504c1s
Steele, R.B. v4p0561c2m
v4p0605c2s v5p0005c1s v5p0052c2s
v5p0118c2s v5p0201c2s v5p0206c2s
v5p0520c2m v6p0001c2s v6p0105c1s
v6p0255c1s v6p0381c2m v6p0389c2s
v6p0472c2s
Steele, R.M. v5p0283c1s
Steele, R.W. v2p0089c1s
v2p0180c1s
Steele, T. v1p0718c2s
Steele, W.F. v4p0300c1s
v4p0561c2s v5p0001c2s
Steen, A.S. v2p0086c1s
Steen, S.P. v5p0282c1s
Steenberg, A.S. v6p0170c2s
v6p0370c2s v6p0372c1s
Steenstra, P.H. v3p0042c1s
v4p0384c1s
Steep, T.W. v5p0147c2s
v5p0148c1s
Steer, P.W. v4p0121c2s
Steer, W.H.H. v3p0413c2s
Steere, J.B. v3p0014c1s
v3p0141c2s v3p0280c1s v3p0318c1s
v3p0329c2m v4p0372c1s
Steet, G.C. v3p0157c1s
Steevens, G.W. v4p0042c1s
v4p0210c1s v4p0272c1s v4p0575c2s
v4p0596c1s v5p0150c1s v5p0168c2s
v5p0169c1s v5p0231c2s v5p0322c2s
v5p0384c1s v5p0466c2s v5p0577c2s
Steevers, Lt.Col. v1p0291c2s
Steeves, G.W. v4p0252c1s
v4p0502c2s
Stefan v3p0207c1s
Stefani, C.de v4p0042c1s
Stefansson, J. v3p0207c2s
v4p0166c1s v4p0517c2s
Stefansson, V. v6p0301c1m
Steffee, J.G. v6p0347c1s
v6p0631c1s
Steffen, G.F. v4p0608c1s
Steffen, H. v5p0137c1s
Steffens, J.B. v4p0627c2s
Steffens, J.B. et al. v4p0627c2s
Steffens, J.L. v4p0560c1s
v5p0082c2s v5p0085c1s v5p0152c1s
v5p0318c1s v5p0409c1s v5p0419c2s
v5p0496c1m
Steffens, L. v6p0017c1s
v6p0083c2s v6p0113c2s v6p0134c2s
v6p0217c2s v6p0285c1s v6p0307c1s
v6p0346c2s v6p0358c2s v6p0378c1s
v6p0419c2s v6p0422c2s v6p0451c1s
v6p0452c2s v6p0464c2s v6p0492c1s
v6p0501c1s v6p0506c2s v6p0542c1s
v6p0544c1s v6p0550c2s v6p0564c1s
v6p0618c2s
Steffens, L. and Wetmore, C.H.
v6p0564c1s
Steffens, Lincoln v6p0127c2s
v6p0131c1s
Steffens, N.M. v4p0084c2s
v4p0153c1s v4p0374c2s v4p0457c1s
v4p0476c1s v5p0089c1s v5p0196c1s
v5p0564c2s
Steffens, N.M. et al. v4p0477c1s
Steger, E. v4p0375c2s
Steggall, J.E.A. v2p0413c2s
Steggall, R. v1p0458c1s
v1p1440c1s v2p0299c2s v2p0380c1s
v2p0438c2s v3p0103c2s v3p0203c1s
v3p0332c2s
Stegman, H.M. v5p0147c2s
Steichen, L. v6p0590c2s
Steiger, A. v5p0594c2s
Steiger, G. v6p0594c2s
Steiger, G. and Clarke, F.W.
v5p0017c2m v5p0438c1s v6p0594c2s
Stein, A. v1p0854c1m
v1p0856c2s v1p1110c1s v2p0003c2s
v2p0293c1s v2p0299c2m
Stein, C. v4p0093c1s
v4p0196c2s v4p0201c1s v4p0202c2s
v4p0511c2s v4p0517c1s v5p0066c1s
v5p0225c1s v5p0582c2s
Stein, E. v5p0302c1s
Stein, G. and Solomons, L.M.
v4p0039c2s
Stein, M. v1p0944c1s
Stein, M.A. v5p0594c2s
v6p0661c1s
Stein, R. v4p0009c1s
v4p0027c1s v4p0059c2s v4p0449c1s
v5p0274c2s v6p0013c2s v6p0496c1m
Stein, Sigmund v6p0056c2s
Stein, W. v1p0459c1s
Steinback, E. v6p0659c1s
Steinberg, G. v6p0058c2s
Steindorf, G. v6p0195c2s
Steiner, B.C. v3p0270c2s
v4p0072c1s v4p0129c2s v4p0246c2s
v4p0329c1s v4p0529c1s v4p0603c1s
v4p0637c1s v5p0042c2s v5p0176c1s
v5p0260c2s v5p0328c1s v5p0335c2s
v5p0351c2s v5p0364c2m v5p0510c2s
v5p0521c2s v5p0600c1s v6p0054c2s
v6p0058c2s v6p0080c1s v6p0165c2s
v6p0218c2s v6p0251c2s v6p0289c2s
v6p0346c1s v6p0352c2s v6p0372c1s
v6p0379c1s v6p0392c2s v6p0394c1s
v6p0399c1s v6p0404c2m v6p0471c2s
v6p0598c2s v6p0610c2s v6p0684c2s
v6p0710c2s v6p0711c2s
Steiner, B.C. and Ranck, S.H.
v4p0329c1s v4p0330c1s
Steiner, B.C. and Smith, R.D.
v6p0088c1s
Steiner, B.C. and Smyth, R.D.
v6p0091c2s v6p0264c2s v6p0345c1s
v6p0590c2s v6p0709c1s
Steiner, B.M. v5p0309c2s
Steiner, E.A. v5p0258c1s
v5p0265c1s v5p0355c2s v5p0384c2s
v5p0532c2s v5p0535c1s v5p0559c1s
v5p0582c1m v6p0072c2s v6p0252c1s
v6p0303c1s v6p0308c1s v6p0344c1s
v6p0354c2s v6p0506c1m v6p0557c2s
v6p0597c2s v6p0649c1m
Steiner, E.J. v6p0649c1s
Steiner, L.H. v1p0041c1s
v1p0045c1s v1p0186c2s v1p0240c2s
v1p0262c1s v1p0275c1s v1p0354c1s
v1p0356c2s v1p0454c2s v1p0528c2s
v1p0594c1s v1p0620c2s v1p0725c1s
v1p0756c2s v1p0806c1s v1p0850c1s
v1p0966c2s v1p1007c1s v1p1058c1s
v1p1150c2s v1p1160c2s v1p1162c1s
v1p1237c1s v1p1245c1s v1p1342c1s
v1p1342c2s v1p1347c1s v3p0162c1s
v3p0249c1s v3p0249c2s
Steiner, P.C. v6p0222c2s
Steiner, R. v5p0133c1s
Steinman, G. v3p0402c1s
Steinman, G.S. v1p0171c1s
v1p0220c1s
Steinmetz, A. v1p1290c2s
Steinmetz, C.P. v6p0199c1s
Steinmetz, J.A. v5p0014c1m
Steinmitz, A. v1p0766c2s
v1p1391c2s
Steinmitz, J.W. v1p0243c2s
Steinschneider, M. v5p0024c2m
v5p0307c2s v6p0343c1s
Steinthal, S.A. v1p0387c1s
v2p0090c2s
Steinway, W. v4p0253c2s
Stejneger, L. v2p0088c1s
v3p0383c1s v5p0021c2s v5p0063c1s
v5p0197c2s v5p0414c2s v5p0534c1s
v6p0019c1s v6p0168c1s v6p0214c2s
v6p0576c1s v6p0648c1s
Stejneger, Le v6p0066c2s
Stella, A. v6p0660c1s
Stellman, L.J. v6p0171c2s
Stelzle, C. v5p0074c2s
v5p0641c1s v6p0356c2s v6p0620c2s
Stelzner, A. v2p0318c2s
Stem, F.D. v1p0613c1s
Stemons, J.S. v6p0647c2s
Stempel, G.H. v5p0103c1s
v6p0161c1s v6p0207c2s
Stenhouse, E. v5p0167c1s
v5p0369c2s v5p0517c1s
Stenhouse, I. v2p0130c1s
Stenhouse, J. v1p1338c1s
Stenning, R. v1p0857c1s
v1p0872c2s v1p1329c2s v2p0233c2s
v3p0438c1s
Stenson, M. v3p0072c2s
v3p0236c1s
Step, E. v4p0137c2s
v4p0347c2s v4p0583c1s v4p0601c1s
v5p0141c1m v5p0292c1s v5p0417c2s
v6p0444c2s v6p0503c1s
Step, Ed. v5p0132c2s
Stephen, A. v3p0119c1s
v4p0411c2s

Stephen, C. v3p0212c1s v3p0212c2s
Stephen, C.E. v1p0855c2s v1p1086c2s v1p1179c2s
Stephen, F. v1p1319c2s
Stephen, H. v2p0327c2s v4p0190c2s
Stephen, H., Sir v4p0140c1s
Stephen, H.L. v4p0282c2s v4p0484c2s v4p0557c1s v5p0224c2s v5p0269c2s v5p0528c2s v5p0616c2s
Stephen, Herbert v4p0021c2s
Stephen, J. v1p0073c1s v1p0775c1s v1p0777c1s v1p1035c2s v1p1409c1s v4p0200c1s v5p0409c1s
Stephen, J., Sir v1p0103c1s v1p0111c2s v1p0260c2s v1p0432c2s v1p0483c1s v1p0495c2s v1p0542c1s v1p0557c2s v1p1006c1s v1p1085c1s v1p1286c2s v1p1406c2s
Stephen, J.B.C. v4p0091c1s
Stephen, J.F. v1p0184c2s v1p0198c2s v1p0251c1s v1p0271c1s v1p0309c1s v1p0317c2s v1p0547c2s v1p0904c1s v1p0974c2s v1p0986c1s v1p1097c1s v1p1338c1s v2p0049c1s v2p0054c1s v2p0107c2m v2p0248c1s v2p0355c1s v2p0456c1s v3p0043c2s v3p0364c1s v3p0365c2s v3p0429c2s
Stephen, J.F., Sir v1p0317c2s v1p0729c2s v1p0944c1s v3p0166c2s v3p0313c1s
Stephen, J.W.W. v6p0597c2s
Stephen, L. v1p0014c1s v1p0025c1s v1p0025c2s v1p0060c1s v1p0072c2s v1p0090c1s v1p0110c1s v1p0133c1s v1p0156c2s v1p0166c1s v1p0166c2s v1p0169c2s v1p0201c1s v1p0201c2s v1p0227c1s v1p0248c2s v1p0249c2s v1p0311c1m v1p0318c2s v1p0345c1s v1p0355c1s v1p0361c2s v1p0365c2s v1p0379c2s v1p0384c1s v1p0394c1s v1p0417c2s v1p0427c1s v1p0438c1s v1p0451c2s v1p0493c2s v1p0494c1s v1p0511c2s v1p0529c2s v1p0549c2s v1p0575c2s v1p0577c1s v1p0594c2s v1p0612c1s v1p0694c2s v1p0708c2s v1p0722c2s v1p0729c1s v1p0781c1s v1p0796c1s v1p0809c2s v1p0813c1s v1p0839c1s v1p0869c1s v1p0912c2s v1p1027c2s v1p1032c1m v1p1094c1s v1p1109c1s v1p1129c2s v1p1132c2s v1p1168c1s v1p1182c2s v1p1189c1s v1p1203c2s v1p1236c2s v1p1253c1s v1p1358c1m v1p1382c2s v1p1385c1s v1p1430c1s v2p0005c2s v2p0072c2s v3p0038c1s v3p0095c2s v3p0140c2s v3p0233c1s v3p0302c1s v3p0333c1s v3p0397c2s v3p0437c2s v4p0028c1s v4p0059c2m v4p0067c1s v4p0081c1s v4p0081c2s v4p0085c1s v4p0090c1s v4p0121c1s v4p0122c1s v4p0168c2s v4p0188c1s v4p0257c2s v4p0260c2s v4p0421c1s v4p0554c1s v4p0636c1s v5p0043c1s v5p0079c2s v5p0165c2s v5p0187c1s v5p0222c2s v5p0233c1s v5p0262c2s v5p0277c1s v5p0309c2s v5p0311c1s v5p0341c2s v5p0397c2s v5p0434c2s v5p0437c1s v5p0457c2s v5p0494c2s v5p0500c1s v5p0515c2s v5p0522c1s v5p0522c2s v5p0528c2s v5p0533c1m v5p0541c2s v5p0591c1s v5p0617c1s v5p0640c2s v6p0036c1s v6p0085c1s v6p0259c2s v6p0269c2s v6p0327c2s v6p0586c2s v6p0609c1s v6p0617c1s v6p0657c2s v6p0712c1s
Stephen, L., Sir v1p0530c1s v1p0946c2s
Stephen, Leslie v2p0389c2s v4p0039c1s v4p0345c2s v6p0616c2s
Stephen, T. v3p0161c2s
Stephen, V. v6p0211c1s v6p0439c1s
Stephen, W. v5p0515c1s
Stephens, A.C. v4p0050c1s v4p0248c1s v4p0308c1s v5p0002c2s v5p0454c1s
Stephens, A.F. v5p0348c2s
Stephens, A.G. v6p0163c2s
Stephens, A.H. v1p0698c2s v1p1048c1s v1p1344c2s v1p1352c2s v2p0252c2s
Stephens, A.M. v4p0381c2s
Stephens, A.M. and Fewkes, J.W. v4p0587c2m
Stephens, A.S., Mrs. v1p1425c1s
Stephens, Anna C. v5p0393c2s v5p0475c1s
Stephens, C.H. v2p0240c1s
Stephens, D.S. v1p0383c2s
Stephens, F. v3p0118c1s
Stephens, F.G. v1p0032c2s v1p0305c2s v1p0321c1s v1p0602c1s v1p0616c2s v1p0705c2s v1p0723c1s v1p0751c1s v1p0880c1s v1p0954c2s v1p0962c1s v1p1171c1s v2p0057c1s v2p0076c2s v2p0080c1s v2p0113c1s v2p0195c2s v2p0204c2m v2p0212c1s v2p0238c1s v2p0248c2s v2p0378c2s v2p0400c2s v2p0466c1s v3p0021c1s v3p0036c2s v3p0061c1s v3p0103c2s v3p0205c1s v3p0232c1s v3p0291c2s v3p0318c2s v3p0320c2s v3p0331c1s v3p0332c1s v3p0353c2s v3p0362c2s v3p0368c1s v3p0401c1s v3p0424c2s v3p0458c1s v4p0075c1s v4p0142c1s v4p0286c1s v4p0312c2s v4p0333c1s v4p0446c1s v4p0453c2s v4p0476c1s v4p0485c1s v4p0486c1s v4p0492c1m v4p0494c1s v4p0498c1s v4p0504c1s v4p0510c2s v4p0575c1s v4p0631c2s v5p0474c2s
Stephens, F.J. v3p0368c2s
Stephens, G. v1p0040c1s v1p0708c1s v1p0817c1s v1p1002c1s v1p1155c1s v2p0116c1s v2p0316c1s v2p0320c2s v2p0333c2s v2p0459c2s v3p0073c2s v3p0383c1s v3p0450c1s v3p0474c2s v5p0437c1s v5p0609c2s
Stephens, G.F. v4p0215c2s
Stephens, H. v1p0714c1s
Stephens, H.B. v1p1300c1s
Stephens, H.G. v6p0310c2s v6p0500c2s
Stephens, H.J. v1p0020c1s
Stephens, H.M. v2p0061c1s v2p0164c2s v2p0165c1s v2p0241c2s v2p0252c2s v2p0266c2s v2p0278c1s v2p0288c1s v3p0160c2s v3p0189c2s v3p0197c1s v3p0249c2s v3p0290c1s v3p0419c2s v3p0437c2s v4p0051c1s v4p0151c1s v4p0211c2m v4p0212c1s v4p0237c1s v4p0237c2s v4p0284c2s v4p0322c2s v4p0347c1s v4p0373c1s v4p0392c2s v4p0562c2s v4p0613c2s v5p0043c1s v5p0083c2s v5p0173c2s v5p0217c2s v5p0233c1s v5p0266c2m v5p0414c2s v5p0438c2s v5p0505c2s v6p0227c2s v6p0292c1s v6p0292c2s v6p0352c2s v6p0365c1s v6p0459c2s v6p0542c2m v6p0662c1s v6p0672c1s
Stephens, H.P. v4p0386c1s
Stephens, J. v2p0188c1s v2p0217c2s v2p0226c2s
Stephens, J.B. v1p1138c2s v1p1375c1s
Stephens, J.E.R. v4p0307c1s v4p0323c1s v4p0511c2s v5p0293c2s v5p0312c2s v5p0328c2s v5p0520c1s v5p0611c2s v6p0099c1s v6p0154c2s v6p0547c1s
Stephens, J.L. v1p1135c1s
Stephens, J.R. v2p0363c1s
Stephens, J.W. v6p0431c2s
Stephens, J.W.W. v6p0711c1s
Stephens, K. v3p0468c2s v4p0630c1s v5p0071c1s v5p0635c2s
Stephens, Kate v4p0213c1s v5p0218c2s
Stephens, R. v4p0335c2s v5p0169c2s v5p0440c2s
Stephens, R.N. v3p0046c2s v4p0035c1s v4p0452c2s v4p0584c2s
Stephens, W.P. v4p0087c2s v4p0634c2m v5p0582c2s v5p0643c1m v6p0363c2s v6p0710c1m
Stephens, W.R.W. v1p0274c2s
Stephenson, A. v3p0366c2s
Stephenson, D. v1p0757c1s
Stephenson, F. v4p0050c2s
Stephenson, H.T. v6p0355c1s
Stephenson, J. v1p0793c1s
Stephenson, J.J. v1p0795c1s
Stephenson, Mill v3p0072c2s
Stephenson, N. v4p0203c1s v5p0576c1s v6p0222c2s v6p0535c2s
Stephenson, N.W. v3p0425c1s
Stephenson, P.H. v2p0021c2s
Stephenson, R. v1p0161c2s v1p1075c1s v1p1075c2s v1p1078c2s v1p1290c2s
Stephenson, R.A.M. v3p0163c1s
Stephenson, T. and Voysey, C. v1p1042c1s
Stephenson, T.B. v3p0460c1s v4p0013c2s v4p0072c2s v4p0281c2s v4p0303c2s
Stephenson, T.G. v4p0190c1s
Stephenson, W.T. v4p0570c2s v5p0181c2s
Stepler, J.H. v6p0123c1s
Stepniak v2p0154c1s v2p0315c1s v2p0380c2m v2p0381c2m v3p0281c2s v3p0305c2s v3p0369c2s v3p0391c2s v4p0220c1s v4p0496c1s
Stepniak, S. v2p0007c2s v3p0370c2m v4p0010c1s v4p0165c1s v4p0404c2s v4p0495c2s v4p0496c1s
Steptoe, E. v4p0636c1s
Sterki, V. v5p0290c2s v5p0553c2s v6p0665c2m
Sterling, A. v5p0322c1m v5p0402c1s v5p0614c1s v6p0162c2s v6p0357c2s
Sterling, F.C. v5p0008c1s
Sterling, J. v1p0112c2s v1p0202c1s v1p0246c1s v1p0321c2s v1p0619c2s v1p0736c1s v1p0863c1s v1p0943c2s v1p0950c2s v1p0960c1s v1p1182c1s v1p1199c2s v1p1266c1s v1p1308c1s v1p1397c2s
Sterling, S.A. v6p0358c2s
Sterling, S.A. and Dapprich, E. v6p0552c1s
Stern, A. v5p0181c1s
Stern, A.von v4p0189c2s
Stern, C.E. v2p0272c1s
Stern, L. v4p0209c2s v4p0432c2m
Stern, Louis v4p0631c1s
Stern, S.A. v1p0019c1s v2p0303c2s
Stern, S.M. v3p0242c2s
Sternberg, C. v4p0388c2s v4p0506c2s
Sternberg, C.H. v2p0159c1s v2p0239c1s v2p0240c2s v2p0315c1s
Sternberg, Dr. v2p0177c1s
Sternberg, G.H. v6p0200c1s
Sternberg, G.M. v2p0096c1s v2p0119c2s v2p0273c1s v2p0385c2s v4p0041c1s v4p0156c2s v4p0252c1s v4p0284c1s v4p0429c2s v5p0258c1s v5p0290c2s v5p0357c1m v5p0368c2s v5p0374c1s v5p0388c1s v5p0388c2s v5p0453c1s v5p0644c1s v6p0024c1s v6p0319c1s v6p0324c2s v6p0515c2s v6p0687c1s
Sternberg, G.M. et al. ... v6p0102c1s
Sternberg, L. v1p0507c1s v1p0769c1s v1p1103c1s v1p1328c2s v1p1433c1s
Sternberg, S.von v6p0252c1s v6p0606c1s
Sternbergh, P.L. v3p0232c1s
Sternburg, Hermann Speck von v6p0193c1s
Sternburg, S.Von v6p0672c1s
Sterndale, R.A. v3p0338c1s v4p0017c2s v4p0023c2s v4p0279c1s v4p0451c1s v5p0261c2m
Sterne, C. v1p1044c2s v1p1302c1s v3p0407c2s v4p0191c1s v4p0284c1s v4p0351c2s v4p0425c1s v4p0537c2s v4p0546c1s v5p0136c2s v5p0224c2s v5p0291c1s v5p0315c1s v5p0596c2s
Sterne, S. v1p0258c1s v1p0736c1s v1p0848c2s v1p1078c1s v1p1282c1s v2p0253c1m v3p0064c2s v3p0183c2s v3p0352c1s v3p0353c1s v3p0440c2s v4p0471c1s v4p0471c2s v5p0282c2s v5p0407c2s v5p0437c2s v5p0561c1s
Sterne, W. v1p0245c1s v1p0739c1s v1p0746c2s v1p0887c1s v1p0988c1s
Sterns, E.E. v1p0135c1s v1p0917c1s
Sterns, E.J. v2p0045c1s
Sterns, W.P. v5p0149c2s v5p0599c2s v5p0600c2m
Sterrett, D.B. v6p0091c2s v6p0650c2s
Sterrett, F.R. v5p0351c1s v6p0610c2s
Sterrett, J.E. v6p0002c2s
Sterrett, J.M. v1p0440c2s v1p1161c1s v2p0003c2s v2p0017c1s v2p0081c2s v2p0200c1m v2p0339c1s v2p0368c2m v3p0081c1s v3p0143c1s v4p0039c1s v4p0138c2s v4p0167c1s v4p0167c2s v4p0253c1s
Sterrett, J.R.S. v3p0021c2s v3p0023c2m v3p0108c2s v4p0189c1s v4p0199c2s v5p0034c1m v5p0036c2s v5p0093c1s v5p0249c1s v5p0267c1s v5p0315c2s v5p0434c1s v5p0449c1s v5p0494c2s v5p0581c2s v5p0582c2s v5p0591c1s v6p0100c2s
Sterrett, R.J. v5p0628c1s
Sterry, J.A. v3p0257c1s
Sterry, W. v5p0252c1s
Stetham, W.M. v3p0077c1s
Stetson, A. v4p0174c2s
Stetson, C. v1p0029c1s v1p0078c2s v1p0094c1s v1p0187c2s v1p0360c1s v1p0685c1s v1p1292c2s v1p1429c1s v1p1432c2s v6p0710c2s
Stetson, C.P. v3p0466c1s v4p0635c2s v5p0051c2s v5p0195c2s v5p0605c2s v5p0635c1s v5p0637c2s v5p0640c2s
Stetson, C.W. v6p0218c1s
Stetson, F.L. v3p0085c2s v4p0403c2s
Stetson, G.R. v2p0107c1s v2p0279c2s v2p0358c2s v3p0105c1m v3p0299c1m v4p0085c2s v4p0111c2s v4p0140c2s v4p0632c2s v5p0204c1s v5p0369c2s v5p0475c2s
Stetson, J.D. v1p0758c2s v1p1141c2s
Stetson, R.H. v4p0274c2s v5p0450c1s v6p0542c2s
Stetson, W.K. v2p0070c2s v2p0216c2s v3p0070c1s v6p0074c1s
Steuart, A.F. v6p0313c2s v6p0387c2s v6p0419c1s v6p0424c2s

v6p0445c2s v6p0474c2s v6p0482c2s
v6p0493c2s v6p0570c2s v6p0578c2m
v6p0632c1s v6p0691c2s
Steuart, A.Francis v6p0680c1s
Steuart, J.A. v4p0289c1s
v5p0040c2s v5p0071c1s v5p0273c2s
Steuart, R.H.J. v6p0359c2s
v6p0394c2s v6p0549c1s
Steuben, J. v4p0115c2s
Steudel, Dr. v1p0047c2s
v1p0646c1s
Stevart, A. v1p1078c1s
Steven, G. v5p0056c1s
Steven, H.F. v6p0154c1s
Steveni, W.B. v4p0033c1s
v4p0177c2s v4p0181c1s
Stevens, A. v1p0034c2s
v1p0076c1s v1p0090c1s v1p0112c1s
v1p0181c2s v1p0205c2s v1p0217c1s
v1p0285c1s v1p0298c1s v1p0372c2s
v1p0421c2s v1p0561c2s v1p0667c2s
v1p0718c1s v1p0719c1s v1p0781c1s
v1p0830c1m v1p0830c2s v1p0831c1m
v1p0836c2s v1p0941c2s v1p0967c2s
v1p1065c1s v1p1117c2s v1p1200c1m
v1p1207c1s v1p1208c1s v1p1219c2s
v1p1241c2s v1p1293c2s v1p1363c2s
v1p1377c2s v1p1383c1s v1p1398c2s
v1p1418c2s v2p0040c2s v2p0309c1s
v2p0349c2s v3p0211c2s
Stevens, A. and Gervex, H.
v3p0306c1s v3p0320c1s
Stevens, A.A. v6p0161c1s
Stevens, A.C. v3p0113c1s
v3p0461c2s v4p0199c1s v4p0423c2s
v4p0541c1s v4p0619c1s v5p0292c2s
Stevens, A.DeG. v2p0234c1s
v2p0246c1s v2p0321c1s v4p0118c2s
Stevens, A.J. v5p0124c1s
Stevens, A.M. v5p0518c2s
v5p0618c2s v5p0620c1s v6p0055c2s
v6p0549c2s v6p0648c2s
Stevens, A.P. et al. v4p0103c1s
Stevens, Alice J. v5p0250c2s
Stevens, B.F. v4p0069c1m
v4p0285c1s
Stevens, C.A. v1p1160c2s
v1p1439c1s
Stevens, C.C. v5p0087c2s
Stevens, C.F. v6p0207c1s
Stevens, C.L.M. v5p0436c2s
Stevens, C.L.McC. v5p0596c2s
Stevens, C.W. v5p0072c2s
Stevens, D.W. v4p0296c2s
v5p0110c2s v5p0302c2s
Stevens, D.W. et al. v4p0133c2s
Stevens, E.A. v4p0197c2s
Stevens, E.M. v2p0448c2s
v3p0412c2s
Stevens, E.O. v4p0618c1m
v5p0538c1s
Stevens, E.R. v5p0002c2s
v6p0701c1s
Stevens, F.B. v2p0156c2s
v4p0510c1s
Stevens, F.E. v2p0094c1s
v2p0116c1s v2p0311c2s v2p0312c1s
v6p0378c1s
Stevens, F.G. v2p0259c2m
v4p0635c2s v6p0108c1s
Stevens, F.H. v6p0366c2s
Stevens, F.L. v3p0171c1s
v6p0502c2s
Stevens, G.B. v1p0440c2s
v2p0027c2s v2p0042c2s v2p0214c2s
v2p0251c1s v2p0351c2s v2p0410c2s
v2p0437c1m v3p0324c1s v3p0329c2s
v3p0357c2s v3p0389c2s v3p0413c1s
v3p0427c1s v3p0427c2s v4p0057c1s
v4p0301c2s v4p0303c2m v4p0431c1s
v4p0573c1s v5p0483c2s v5p0576c2s
v6p0040c1s v6p0089c1m v6p0123c1s
v6p0210c2s v6p0259c2s v6p0342c2s
v6p0348c2s v6p0419c2s v6p0544c2m
v6p0561c2m v6p0595c2m
Stevens, G.B. and Margolis, M.L.
v6p0347c1s
Stevens, G.L. v3p0426c2s
Stevens, G.P. v6p0210c1m
Stevens, G.T. v5p0461c1s
v6p0296c2s
Stevens, H. v1p0028c1s
v1p0132c2s v1p0206c1s v1p0613c2s
v1p0743c1s v1p1003c1s v1p1280c1s
v2p0057c1s v2p0451c2s v4p0054c1s
Stevens, H.C. v1p1366c1s
v6p0040c2s v6p0221c2s v6p0647c1s
Stevens, H.D. v3p0074c1s
Stevens, H.M. v5p0361c2s
Stevens, H.W. v3p0329c2s
Stevens, Harriet F. v2p0360c2s
Stevens, J. v1p1012c1m
Stevens, J.A. v1p0025c2s
v1p0033c1m v1p0033c2s v1p0060c1s
v1p0084c2s v1p0190c2s v1p0227c1s
v1p0276c2s v1p0348c1s v1p0503c1s
v1p0571c1s v1p0717c2s v1p0728c2s
v1p0733c2s v1p0757c2s v1p0800c1s
v1p0823c2s v1p0917c1m v1p0917c2m
v1p0918c1s v1p0989c1s v1p1242c2s
v1p1253c2s v1p1282c2s v1p1383c2s
v1p1388c1m v1p1395c2s v1p1406c1s
v1p1437c2s v2p0091c1s v2p0313c1s
v3p0304c2s v3p0420c2s v4p0015c2s
v4p0610c1s
Stevens, J.E. v5p0359c2s
v5p0443c2s
Stevens, J.G. v1p0424c1s
Stevens, J.H. v3p0281c1s
Stevens, J.L. v1p0640c2s
Stevens, J.L. et al. v4p0251c1s
Stevens, J.S. v5p0184c2s
v5p0439c1s v5p0562c2s v6p0498c2s
v6p0621c2s
Stevens, John v5p0378c2s
Stevens, Kate v6p0115c2s
v6p0189c2s
Stevens, L.M.N. v6p0099c2s
Stevens, L.T. v2p0441c2s
Stevens, Montague v5p0222c2s
Stevens, O.C. v4p0489c2s
Stevens, O.L. v6p0044c1s
Stevens, R. v4p0603c1s
v6p0025c1s v6p0089c2s v6p0318c2s
v6p0391c2s v6p0712c1s
Stevens, R.P. v1p0268c2s
v1p0469c2s v1p0523c2s v1p0524c2s
v1p0624c1s v1p0938c2s v1p1373c2s
v2p0179c1s
Stevens, S. v6p0529c1s
Stevens, S.M. v4p0136c2s
v4p0149c1s v4p0213c2s v4p0277c1s
Stevens, S.W. v3p0300c2s
v6p0088c1s
Stevens, T. v3p0005c2s
v3p0044c1s v3p0275c1s v4p0058c2s
v4p0189c2s v4p0634c2s
Stevens, T.H. v3p0047c2s
v3p0274c1s v3p0400c2s
Stevens, T.W. v6p0139c2s
v6p0369c1s
Stevens, W. v2p0280c2s
Stevens, W.A. v1p0420c2s
v1p0601c1s v1p0724c1s v1p1045c1s
v2p0150c1s v2p0173c1s v3p0003c1s
v3p0043c2s v3p0166c1s v3p0265c2s
v4p0301c1s v5p0520c2s
Stevens, W.B. v1p0512c2s
v2p0357c1s v2p0470c1s v3p0201c1s
v5p0224c2s v6p0387c2s v6p0563c2s
v6p0593c1s
Stevens, W.B. et al. v6p0563c2s
Stevens, W.E. v2p0453c2s
Stevens, W.J. v4p0472c1s
v5p0476c2s v5p0477c1s v6p0435c1s
Stevens, W.L. v3p0278c1s
v3p0356c2s v3p0451c1s v4p0192c1s
v5p0180c1s v5p0319c2s v6p0413c2m
v6p0498c2s v6p0550c1s v6p0648c1s
Stevens, W.L.C. v1p1252c2s
Stevens, W.LeC. v2p0003c1s
v2p0137c1s v2p0322c2s v2p0323c1s
v2p0337c1s v2p0409c2s v2p0420c1m
v2p0477c2s v3p0237c2s v3p0245c2s
v3p0385c1m v3p0401c2m v4p0244c2s
v4p0252c2s v4p0346c1s v4p0367c2s
v4p0415c2m v5p0367c1s v6p0137c2s
v6p0296c1s
Stevens, W.LeC. et al. ... v5p0129c1s
Stevens, W.Le Conte v5p0252c2s
Stevens, W.W. v6p0027c2s
Stevenson, A. v1p1252c2s
v4p0104c1s v4p0541c1s
Stevenson, A.E. v5p0603c2s
Stevenson, A.L. v5p0139c2s
Stevenson, A.M. v5p0440c1s
Stevenson, B.C. v5p0304c2s
Stevenson, B.E. v5p0476c1s
v6p0070c1s v6p0664c1s
Stevenson, C.A. v2p0394c2s
v4p0326c2s
Stevenson, C.H. v6p0667c2s
Stevenson, C.L. v1p1343c2s
v1p1347c2s
Stevenson, C.W. v2p0388c1s
v6p0662c2s
Stevenson, Cornelius, Mrs.
v4p0115c1s
Stevenson, D. v1p0174c2s
v1p0570c2s v1p0718c1s v1p0748c1m
v1p1110c1s v1p1311c2s v2p0242c1s
v2p0278c1s
Stevenson, D.A. v2p0024c2s
Stevenson, D.M. v3p0050c1s
v4p0315c1s
Stevenson, Daniel v4p0367c2s
Stevenson, E. v6p0442c2s
v6p0607c1s
Stevenson, E.I. v2p0012c2s
v2p0301c1s v2p0355c2s v3p0183c2s
v4p0091c2s v4p0123c2s v4p0233c1s
v4p0269c2s v5p0050c2s v5p0322c2s
Stevenson, E.L. v6p0683c2s
Stevenson, F. v5p0006c2s
Stevenson, F.A. v3p0048c1m
v3p0474c1s
Stevenson, F.S. v2p0005c2s
v3p0094c2s v4p0027c1s v4p0027c2s
v4p0239c1s v4p0636c1s
Stevenson, F.S. and Coore, G.B.M.
v4p0027c2s
Stevenson, F.V. v4p0590c1s
Stevenson, F.V.DeG. v1p0235c2s
v3p0188c1s v5p0021c1s
Stevenson, F.V.G. v2p0466c1s
Stevenson, F.Van deG. v4p0405c1s
Stevenson, Geo. v6p0664c2s
Stevenson, H. v1p0940c1s
Stevenson, H., Mrs. v1p0170c1s
v1p1006c1s v1p1215c1s
Stevenson, I.P. v5p0077c2s
v5p0219c2s v5p0395c2s v5p0413c2s
v5p0583c2s v5p0609c2s v5p0624c1s
Stevenson, J. v1p0043c1s
v1p0373c2s v1p0806c2s v1p1231c2s
v1p1334c2s v2p0015c2m v2p0200c2m
v2p0201c1s v2p0262c2s v2p0337c1s
v2p0367c2s v2p0473c1s v2p0473c2s
v2p0476c2m v4p0138c1s v4p0178c1s
v4p0610c2s
Stevenson, J.E. v2p0300c1s
Stevenson, J.F. v1p0869c1s
v1p1210c2s
Stevenson, J.G. v4p0283c2s
Stevenson, J.H. v4p0474c1s
v6p0561c2s v6p0578c2s
Stevenson, J.J. v1p0053c1s
v1p0053c2s v1p0279c1m v1p0497c2s
v1p0607c2s v1p0988c1s v1p1113c2s
v3p0016c1s v3p0251c2s v3p0450c2s
v4p0092c2s v4p0094c2s v5p0122c1s
v5p0229c1s v6p0038c2s v6p0136c1s
v6p0137c1s v6p0168c2s v6p0323c1s
v6p0368c2s v6p0672c1s
Stevenson, J.M. v2p0478c1s
Stevenson, J.S. v4p0445c1s
Stevenson, L. v2p0317c2
Stevenson, M.C. v6p0714c1s
Stevenson, M.H. v4p0490c2s
Stevenson, O.J. v6p0068c2s
v6p0272c1s v6p0311c1s
Stevenson, P. v1p1167c1s
Stevenson, P.E. v5p0087c2s
v5p0287c1s
Stevenson, R. v4p0509c2s
Stevenson, R.A. v5p0458c2s
v5p0506c1s v5p0598c1s v6p0614c1s
Stevenson, R.A.M. v3p0087c2s
v3p0101c1s v3p0185c2s v3p0375c2s
v3p0384c1s v4p0028c2s v4p0029c1s
v4p0029c2s v4p0030c1s v4p0032c1s
v4p0134c2s v4p0149c1s v4p0159c1s
v4p0168c1s v4p0243c1s v4p0245c2s
v4p0309c2s v4p0319c1s v4p0341c2s
v4p0399c1s v4p0453c2s v4p0493c1s
v4p0493c2s v4p0528c2s v4p0559c1s
v5p0031c1s v5p0310c1s v5p0319c1s
v5p0344c2s v5p0362c1s v5p0376c1s
v5p0435c1s v5p0484c2s v5p0555c2s
v5p0578c2s v6p0527c2s
Stevenson, R.L. v1p0383c2s
v1p0651c2s v1p0712c1s v1p0739c1s
v1p0752c2s v1p0781c1s v1p0869c2s
v1p1155c2s v1p1257c2s v1p1307c1s
v2p0120c2s v2p0155c1s v2p0234c2s
v2p0261c1s v2p0321c1s v2p0343c2s
v2p0354c1s v2p0377c1s v2p0403c1s
v2p0423c2s v2p0430c1s v2p0445c2s
v2p0451c2s v3p0028c2s v3p0037c2s
v3p0049c2s v3p0082c1s v3p0109c2s
v3p0112c1s v3p0122c2s v3p0128c1s
v3p0129c2s v3p0152c1s v3p0168c2m
v3p0202c2s v3p0242c2s v3p0266c2s
v3p0271c1s v3p0323c1s v3p0349c1s
v3p0398c2s v3p0410c1s v4p0079c1s
v4p0137c1s v4p0206c1s v4p0207c1s
v4p0232c1s v4p0274c2s v4p0293c2s
v4p0318c2s v4p0360c2s v4p0407c1s
v4p0501c1s v4p0528c2s v4p0536c2s
v4p0549c1s v4p0554c2m v4p0578c1s
v4p0580c1s v4p0581c2s v4p0599c1s
v4p0606c1s v4p0623c2s v4p0631c2s
v5p0083c1s v5p0203c2s v5p0504c1s
Stevenson, R.L. and Henley, W.E.
v4p0346c2s
Stevenson, R.L. and Low, W.H.
v3p0021c2s
Stevenson, R.L. and Osbourne, L.
v3p0473c1s v4p0166c2s v4p0633c2s
Stevenson, R.L., Mrs. v3p0282c1s
Stevenson, R.S. v1p0864c1s
v5p0269c2s
Stevenson, R.T. v4p0118c2s
v4p0358c1s v4p0431c1s v4p0474c1s
v5p0268c2s v6p0016c1s
Stevenson, S.H. v1p0134c2s
Stevenson, S.T. v5p0638c1s
Stevenson, S.Y. v3p0130c2s
v3p0194c1s v4p0313c1s v5p0069c2s
v5p0367c1m v5p0373c1m v5p0373c2s
v6p0045c2s v6p0323c1s v6p0414c1s
v6p0442c1s v6p0456c2s
Stevenson, Sara Y. v4p0066c1s
Stevenson, T. v1p0265c2s
v1p0266c1s v1p0271c2s v1p0748c2m
v1p0829c1s v1p1256c2s v1p1393c1s
v1p1393c2s v2p0065c2s v2p0440c2s
v2p0475c1s
Stevenson, T.H.C. and Newsholme, A.
v6p0302c1s

Stevenson, V.E. v1p1059c1s
Stevenson, W. v4p0530c1s
Stevenson, W.B. v6p0063c1s
Stevenson, W.F. v1p0039c1s
v1p0148c2s v1p0150c1s v1p0233c1s
v1p0238c1s v1p0262c2s v1p0336c1s
v1p0348c1s v1p0394c1s v1p0441c2s
v1p0448c2s v1p0617c2s v1p0619c2s
v1p0620c2s v1p0632c2s v1p0678c2s
v1p0701c1s v1p0853c1s v1p0905c2s
v1p1090c1s v1p1111c2s v1p1142c1s
v1p1360c2s v1p1440c1m v2p0045c1s
v2p0292c1s v2p0327c2s v5p0049c2s
Stevenson, W.G. v2p0258c1s
v2p0462c1s v3p0168c2s v3p0216c2s
Stevenson, W.H. v2p0014c2s
v3p0031c2s v3p0120c2m v3p0132c1s
v3p0139c2s v3p0188c1s v3p0204c2s
v3p0363c2s v3p0372c1s v4p0226c1s
,v4p0499c1s v5p0012c1s v5p0083c2s
v5p0159c2s v5p0176c1s v5p0625c2s
v6p0005c2s v6p0276c1s v6p0480c2s
Stevenson, W.H. and Cook, A.S.
v3p0088c1s
Stevenson, W.H. and Davidson, J.B.
v2p0014c2s
Stevenson, W.H. and Round, J.H.
v3p0069c2s v5p0631c2s
Stevenson, W.H. et al. ... v3p0316c1s
Stevenson, W.M. v5p0012c2s
v5p0206c1s v5p0334c2s
Stevenson-Hamilton, J. ... v6p0246c1s
v6p0654c1s
Stevinus v5p0244c1s
Steward, H.J. v3p0252c2s
Steward, J.E. and Brook, M.
v2p0172c1s
Steward, T.G. v4p0396c2m
v6p0284c1s
Steward, T.T. v4p0075c1s
Steward, W.A. v5p0570c1s
Stewardson, J. v4p0024c1s
Stewardson, L.C. v4p0118c2s
Stewardson, T. v4p0358c1s
v4p0617c1s
Stewart, A. v1p0668c1s
v1p1283c1s v2p0081c2s v2p0268c1s
v4p0192c2s v5p0080c1s v5p0236c1s
v5p0484c1m
Stewart, A.D. v4p0368c1s
Stewart, A.F. v6p0578c2s
Stewart, A.G. v6p0068c2s
Stewart, A.K. v4p0047c1s
Stewart, A.M. v6p0186c2s
Stewart, A.T. v5p0184c1s
v5p0184c2s
Stewart, A.W. v4p0082c2s
v4p0143c2s v4p0168c1m v4p0348c1s
v4p0530c2s v4p0558c2s v5p0176c1s
v5p0366c2s v5p0378c1s v5p0392c1s
v5p0514c2s v5p0525c1s
Stewart, B. v1p0099c2s
v1p0169c1s v1p0376c1s v1p0407c2m
v1p0496c2s v1p0580c1s v1p0580c2s
v1p0747c1s v1p0788c1m v1p0788c2m
v1p0818c2s v1p0829c1m v1p0829c2m
v1p1006c2m v1p1061c2s v1p1081c1s
v1p1234c1m v1p1257c1s v1p1268c2s
v1p1269c1m v1p1395c1s v2p0141c1s
v2p0258c1s v2p0272c1s v2p0315c1s
v2p0362c1s v2p0425c1s v2p0436c2s
v2p0455c2s v3p0036c1s
Stewart, B. and Lockyer, J.N.
v1p1267c2s
Stewart, B. et al. v1p1268c2s
Stewart, C. v1p0707c1s
v2p0405c1s v4p0010c2s v4p0352c2s
v4p0419c1s v6p0480c2s
Stewart, C.D. v6p0138c2s
v6p0539c1s v6p0690c1s
Stewart, C.E. v3p0328c2s
Stewart, C.P. v1p1035c1s
Stewart, C.R.S. v6p0214c2s
Stewart, C.S. v1p1355c1s
Stewart, Cora v6p0585c1s
Stewart, D. v2p0015c1s
v2p0120c1s v2p0277c2s v5p0340c1s
v6p0005c2s
Stewart, D.A. v6p0239c1s
v6p0546c1s
Stewart, D.H. v4p0506c2s
Stewart, David v6p0224c2s
Stewart, E. v4p0085c1s
v4p0207c2s v5p0144c2s v6p0142c1s
v6p0646c2s v6p0656c2s
Stewart, E.F. v1p0256c1s
Stewart, E.S. v5p0637c2s
Stewart, F. v5p0281c2s
v5p0526c2s
Stewart, F.C. and Harding, H.A.
v6p0090c2s
Stewart, F.L. v4p0134c1s
v4p0555c1s
Stewart, Florence v6p0278c1s
Stewart, G. v1p1154c2s
v3p0065c2s v3p0135c2s v3p0198c2s
v3p0259c2s v3p0463c1s v4p0085c2m
v4p0086c2s v4p0100c2s v4p0114c2s
v4p0346c1s v4p0569c1s v4p0575c1s
v5p0052c1s v5p0091c2s v5p0432c2s
v5p0474c1m v6p0097c1s v6p0363c2s
v6p0427c1s v6p0553c1s v6p0604c1s
Stewart, G. and Brown, F.C.
v5p0090c1s
Stewart, G., jr. v1p0320c1s
v3p0154c1s
Stewart, G.A. v2p0120c1s
v2p0277c1s v4p0634c1s v4p0634c2m
Stewart, G.C. v1p1265c2s
Stewart, G.N. v5p0449c2s
Stewart, G.N. and Guthrie, C.C.
v6p0456c1s
Stewart, G.W. v2p0220c1s
v5p0348c1s v5p0430c1s v6p0064c1s
v6p0199c1s v6p0507c2s
Stewart, Geo. v4p0216c2s
Stewart, H. v4p0531c1s
v4p0619c1s
Stewart, I. v3p0309c1s
Stewart, I. and Holland, S.
v6p0462c2s
Stewart, I. and Londonderry, T.
v6p0462c2s
Stewart, Isla and Morgan, J.H.
v3p0201c2s
Stewart, J. v1p0947c2s
v5p0464c1s v5p0587c2s
Stewart, J.A. v1p1062c1s
v1p1228c1s v2p0191c1s v2p0209c2s
v2p0288c2s v2p0339c2s v2p0392c1s
v5p0049c2s v5p0072c2s v5p0564c1s
v5p0569c1s v5p0574c2m v5p0638c2s
v6p0141c1s v6p0306c2s v6p0491c2s
v6p0503c2s
Stewart, J.D. v6p0371c2s
v6p0635c2s
Stewart, J.J. v3p0133c2s
v3p0137c1s v4p0008c2s v4p0124c2s
v4p0220c2s v4p0440c2s v4p0487c1s
v4p0541c1s v6p0441c1s
Stewart, J.L. v1p0245c2s
v1p0277c1s v1p0739c2s v1p1241c2s
v3p0461c2s v5p0193c1s v5p0601c2s
v6p0519c2s
Stewart, J.S. v5p0235c2s
Stewart, Jane A. v5p0049c2s
v6p0137c2s
Stewart, K.J. v1p0007c2s
v1p1343c1s
Stewart, L.C. v5p0210c2s
Stewart, M. v6p0549c2s
Stewart, M.B. v6p0031c1s
v6p0245c1s
Stewart, McLeod v5p0091c1s
v5p0424c2s
Stewart, O.W. v6p0519c1s
Stewart, P.M. v6p0225c2m
Stewart, R. v1p0564c2s
v4p0139c1s v4p0254c2s v4p0317c1s
v4p0450c2s v5p0064c2s v5p0123c2s
v5p0407c1s
Stewart, S. v6p0044c1s
v6p0404c1s
Stewart, S.B. v3p0321c1s
Stewart, S.S. v5p0436c1s
Stewart, S.T. v5p0606c2s
Stewart, T. v2p0364c1s
v2p0467c2s
Stewart, T.G. v4p0363c2s
v4p0599c1s
Stewart, T.M. v1p0293c1s
Stewart, W.J. v1p0164c1s
v4p0307c1s
Stewart, W.M. v3p0107c2s
v3p0393c1s v3p0460c2s v4p0230c2m
v4p0525c2s v4p0526c1s v5p0093c2s
v5p0603c2s
Stewart, W.M. and Lodge, H.C.
v4p0515c1s
Stewart, W.M. et al. v4p0230c2s
v4p0525c1s
Stewart, W.R. v5p0431c1s
v5p0495c1s v6p0010c2s v6p0051c2s
v6p0075c2s v6p0095c2s v6p0096c2s
v6p0131c1s v6p0133c1s v6p0152c2s
v6p0160c2s v6p0258c2s v6p0286c1s
v6p0318c2m v6p0363c2s v6p0369c2s
v6p0407c1s v6p0594c2s v6p0620c2s
v6p0647c2s v6p0664c2s v6p0674c2s
v6p0690c2s
Stewart, Y. v4p0210c2s
v5p0216c1s v5p0225c1s v5p0233c1s
v5p0590c2s v5p0646c1s
Stibbard, L.H. v5p0222c1s
Stibitz, G. v5p0468c2s
Stibitz, G.W. v5p0304c2s
Stichter, Minnie v5p0629c1s
Stickley, G. v6p0033c1s
v6p0091c1s v6p0093c1s v6p0139c2s
v6p0393c1s v6p0470c2s v6p0564c1s
Stickney, A. v1p0018c2s
v1p0259c1s v2p0240c1s v4p0429c1s
Stickney, A.B. v6p0529c1s
Stickney, C. v3p0163c2s
v3p0170c2s
Stickney, F.D. v3p0346c1s
v4p0537c1s
Stickney, F.H. v2p0262c1s
Stickney, H.C. v4p0577c1s
Stickney, J. v6p0554c2s
Stickney, J.A. v2p0311c1s
Stickney, J.L. v5p0360c1s
Stickney, J.L. and Roosevelt, T.
v5p0160c1s
Stickney, Jos. T. v4p0603c1s
Stickney, L. v6p0385c1s
Stickney, L.D. v2p0159c2s
Stickney, M.E. v3p0085c2s
v4p0026c2s v4p0153c2s v4p0305c1s
v4p0412c2s v4p0420c2s v5p0377c2s
v5p0548c2s
Stickney, M.E.S. v3p0363c1s
Stickney, T. v6p0563c1s
Stiedra, W. v4p0102c2s
Stieglitz, A. v5p0448c2s
v6p0497c1s
Stieren, E. v1p1147c1s
Stieringer, L. v5p0200c1s
Stiff, W.P.W. v1p0110c2s
Stiffe, A.W. v1p0221c2s
v1p0604c1s v1p0949c1s v4p0436c1s
v4p0528c1s v5p0441c2m
Stifler, J.M. v2p0043c1s
v2p0044c1s v4p0109c2s v4p0306c1s
v5p0116c2s
Stifler, W.H. v2p0289c2s
Stigan, K.E. v4p0515c2s
Stigand, I.A. v6p0491c1s
v6p0598c1s
Stigand, W. v1p0066c1s
v1p0103c1s v1p0182c1s v1p0220c2s
v1p0482c2s v1p0483c1s v1p0529c2s
v1p0771c2s v1p0880c1s v1p0971c1s
v1p1137c2s v1p1230c2s v1p1281c2s
Stigant, W. v1p0668c2s
v1p0928c1s
Stiles, C.W. v1p0868c2s
v5p0378c2s
Stiles, G. v2p0341c2s
Stiles, H.H. v5p0192c1s
Stiles, H.J. and Rainy, H.
v5p0531c2s
Stiles, H.R. v5p0488c2s
Stiles, P.G. v6p0597c1s
Stiles, R. v1p0734c1s
v3p0252c1s v3p0450c2s
Stiles, R.A. v1p0296c2s
Stiles, W.A. v2p0373c2s
v4p0416c1s
Stiles, W.C. v1p0684c1s
v1p1016c2s v1p1200c1s v1p1355c2m
v2p0455c2m v3p0175c1s v3p0454c2s
Stiles, W.H. v1p0881c1s
Still, A.T. v6p0471c1s
Stille, C.J. v1p0572c2s
v1p0997c1s v1p1422c2s v2p0335c2s
v2p0360c2s v2p0478c1s v3p0036c2s
v3p0055c2s v3p0113c1s v3p0325c2s
v3p0336c1s v4p0013c2s v4p0149c2s
v4p0317c1s
Stille, G.J. v3p0011c1s
Stille, K.B. v6p0350c1s
Stille, W.A. v4p0402c2s
v4p0464c2s v6p0650c2s
Stille, Werner A. v6p0249c2s
Stilling, M. v2p0175c1s
Stillman and Freedlander . v6p0152c2s
Stillman, B.H. v3p0225c1m
v3p0225c2s
Stillman, C.A. v2p0167c1s
Stillman, G.A. v1p0746c1s
Stillman, J.D.B. v1p0187c2m
v1p0376c2s v1p0492c1s v1p0532c2s
v1p0920c1s v1p0956c2s v1p1149c1s
Stillman, J.M. v1p0715c2s
v2p0302c2s v6p0672c1s
Stillman, J.W. v5p0093c2s
v5p0098c2s v5p0291c1s v5p0418c1s
v5p0574c1m
Stillman, M.S. v1p0199c1s
v1p0922c1s v1p1197c1s v1p1366c2s
v2p0483c1s v3p0050c2s v3p0368c1s
v4p0033c2s v4p0213c1s v4p0241c1s
v4p0295c1s v4p0444c1s v4p0613c1s
v6p0088c2s v6p0152c1s v6p0229c1m
v6p0274c1s v6p0325c2s v6p0332c1s
v6p0383c2s v6p0514c2s v6p0582c2s
Stillman, W. v3p0331c1s
Stillman, W.G. v2p0170c1s
v2p0258c2s
Stillman, W.J. v1p0009c1s
v1p0061c2s v1p0079c2s v1p0169c1s
v1p0213c2s v1p0295c1m v1p0314c2m
v1p0341c2s v1p0353c1s v1p0379c2s
v1p0465c2s v1p0467c2s v1p0551c2s
v1p0552c1s v1p0553c1s v1p0553c2s
v1p0562c2s v1p0669c2s v1p0864c2s
v1p0958c1s v1p0958c2s v1p0959c2s
v1p0968c2m v1p1019c2s v1p1050c2s
v1p1098c1s v1p1108c1s v1p1128c2s
v1p1132c2s v1p1148c2s v1p1155c2s
v1p1171c2s v1p1327c1s v1p1331c1s
v1p1333c2s v1p1366c2s v2p0002c2s
v2p0018c2s v2p0022c2s v2p0023c1m
v2p0024c1s v2p0025c2s v2p0026c2s
v2p0073c1s v2p0104c2s v2p0121c2s
v2p0143c1s v2p0156c1s v2p0190c1s
v2p0192c2s v2p0206c2s v2p0214c2s
v2p0248c2s v2p0263c1s v2p0264c1s
v2p0278c1s v2p0282c2s v2p0299c1s

v2p0304c1m v2p0306c2s v2p0326c1s
v2p0326c2s v2p0329c1s v2p0350c1s
v2p0366c1s v2p0379c2s v2p0383c1m
v2p0419c1s v2p0441c2s v2p0450c2s
v2p0458c1s v2p0458c2s v2p0459c2s
v2p0461c1s v2p0467c2s v2p0468c1s
v3p0003c1s v3p0007c2s v3p0008c1s
v3p0009c1s v3p0017c2s v3p0019c1s
v3p0021c2s v3p0035c1s v3p0038c2s
v3p0051c2s v3p0062c1s v3p0082c1s
v3p0085c1s v3p0086c2s v3p0090c2m
v3p0104c2s v3p0114c1s v3p0155c2s
v3p0161c2m v3p0166c1s v3p0168c2s
v3p0172c1m v3p0178c2s v3p0184c1s
v3p0208c2s v3p0221c1s v3p0222c1s
v3p0224c1s v3p0224c2s v3p0225c1m
v3p0232c2s v3p0252c2s v3p0258c2s
v3p0259c2s v3p0263c2s v3p0314c2s
v3p0328c1s v3p0328c2s v3p0354c2s
v3p0366c2s v3p0369c1s v3p0377c2s
v3p0384c2s v3p0392c1m v3p0392c2s
v3p0404c2s v3p0439c1s v3p0448c2s
v3p0450c1s v4p0003c2s v4p0030c2s
v4p0090c2s v4p0135c1s v4p0140c2s
v4p0156c2s v4p0166c2s v4p0226c1s
v4p0294c1s v4p0294c2s v4p0295c1s
v4p0313c1s v4p0342c2s v4p0343c2s
v4p0344c2s v4p0428c2s v4p0439c1s
v4p0466c1s v4p0490c2s v4p0494c2s
v4p0495c1m v4p0503c2s v4p0523c1s
v4p0530c1s v4p0577c2m v4p0602c2s
v4p0603c1s v5p0021c1s v5p0028c2s
v5p0030c2s v5p0051c1s v5p0061c2s
v5p0067c2s v5p0080c2s v5p0189c2s
v5p0191c1s v5p0197c1s v5p0248c2s
v5p0249c1m v5p0300c2m v5p0305c1s
v5p0396c2s v5p0415c1s v5p0417c2s
v5p0490c1s v5p0492c2s v5p0497c2s
v5p0500c1m v5p0581c2s v5p0609c1s
v6p0612c1s
Stillman, W.J. and Cole, T.
v3p0013c2s v3p0147c2s v3p0173c1s
v3p0258c2s v3p0266c2s v3p0270c1s
v3p0270c2s v3p0274c1s v3p0313c2s
v3p0317c2s
Stillman, W.O. v2p0343c1s
v3p0035c1s
Stillman, W.S. v2p0259c1s
Stillwell, L.B. v4p0403c1s
v6p0198c1s
Stillwell, S.M. v1p0325c2s
v1p1351c2s
Stilson, W.B. v1p0639c1s
Stilt, E.F.R. v4p0076c1s
Stilwell, S.S. v5p0225c2s
Stimers, A.C. v1p0580c2s
v1p1246c2m v1p1248c1s v1p1250c1s
Stimpson, F.E. v1p0444c1s
v1p0501c2s
Stimpson, H.B. v5p0405c2s
Stimpson, M.S. v6p0094c2s
v6p0099c2s v6p0220c1s v6p0353c2s
v6p0546c1s v6p0622c1s v6p0644c1s
Stimpson, Mary S. v6p0450c1s
Stimpson, W. v1p0835c1s
v1p1189c1s
Stimpson, W.A. v6p0586c1s
Stimson, A.L. v1p0284c2s
v4p0483c2s
Stimson, A.S. v1p0437c1s
Stimson, F.J. v2p0216c1s
v2p0301c1s v2p0324c2s v2p0332c1s
v2p0430c1s v2p0449c2s v3p0007c1s
v3p0114c2s v3p0119c2s v3p0153c2s
v3p0190c2s v3p0359c2s v3p0369c1s
v4p0089c1s v4p0152c1s v4p0284c2s
v4p0315c1s v4p0323c1s v4p0444c2s
v4p0546c1s v4p0596c2s v5p0024c2s
v5p0158c1s v5p0321c2m v5p0525c2s
v5p0529c2s v5p0602c1s v5p0616c1s
v5p0623c2s v6p0311c1s v6p0342c2s
v6p0423c1s
Stimson, F.J. and Smith, M.
v3p0090c1s v3p0244c2s
Stimson, F.S. v5p0634c2s
Stimson, H.A. v1p0291c1s
v2p0074c2s v2p0114c1s v2p0147c1s
v5p0055c2s v5p0056c2s v5p0127c1s
v5p0130c2s v5p0378c1s v5p0492c2s
v5p0493c1s v6p0054c2s v6p0089c2s
v6p0110c2s v6p0137c2s v6p0147c1s
v6p0194c1s v6p0417c2s v6p0419c2s
v6p0447c1s
Stimson, H.B. v4p0599c2s
Stimson, J.W. v5p0030c2s
v6p0033c1s v6p0034c1s v6p0055c2s
v6p0062c2s v6p0338c2s v6p0350c1s
v6p0533c1s v6p0590c1s v6p0600c1s
Stimson, L.A. v1p0086c1s
v4p0429c2s
Stinchcomb, J.K. v6p0449c2s
Stinde, J. v2p0161c1s
v2p0360c1s v3p0416c1s
Stine, W.M. v5p0527c2s
v6p0367c2s
Stiness, J.H. v5p0487c2s
Stingley, L.L. v5p0207c2s
Stinner, T.H. v6p0405c1s
Stirling, A.H. v2p0324c1s
v2p0438c2s v5p0123c2s
Stirling, A.W. v3p0350c2s
Stirling, E.C. v4p0083c1s
Stirling, I.R. v5p0472c2s
Stirling, J. v1p0513c2s
v1p1154c2s v2p0179c1s
Stirling, J.D.M. v1p0664c2s
Stirling, J.H. v1p0114c1s
v1p0173c1s v1p0208c2s v1p0568c1s
v1p0614c1s v1p0702c1m v1p0702c2m
v1p0730c1s v1p1000c1s v1p1160c1s
v1p1263c1s v1p1278c1s v2p0071c2s
v2p0240c2m
Stirling, M.C. v1p0723c1s
Stirling, W. v4p0344c2s
v6p0080c2s
Stisted, G.M. v3p0061c1s
Stitt, E.F.R. v4p0569c2s
Stobart, M. v4p0581c1s
Stobart, M.A. v5p0073c1s
v5p0207c1s v5p0278c1s v6p0122c2s
v6p0352c2s v6p0654c1s
Stobart, W.L. v4p0240c1s
v4p0283c2s v4p0432c1s v4p0491c1s
v5p0332c2s
Stobart, W.L. and Academicus
v5p0497c1s
Stobie, W. v2p0209c2s
v3p0039c1s
Stock, E. v3p0282c2s
v3p0457c2s
Stock, E.E. v6p0013c2s
v6p0099c2s v6p0433c1s v6p0629c2s
Stock, St.G. v1p0114c1s
v5p0315c2s v5p0553c2s v6p0319c1s
Stock, St.George v6p0214c1s
Stockalper, E. v1p0017c1s
Stockbauer, Dr. v1p0984c1s
Stockbridge, G.H. v3p0134c1s
v4p0176c2s v4p0177c1s v5p0185c1s
Stockbridge, H. v1p0089c2s
v4p0209c2s v6p0444c1s
Stockbridge, J.C. v1p0033c1s
v1p0033c2s v1p0034c1s v1p0038c1s
v1p0169c1s v1p0797c1s v1p1101c2s
v1p1438c1s v2p0012c1s v2p0197c1s
v2p0208c2s v2p0461c2s
Stocker, C.D. v2p0271c1s
Stocker, C.H.D. v2p0301c1s
v2p0315c1s
Stockfleth, G. v4p0217c1s
Stocking, F.M. v3p0202c2s
v3p0203c1m v3p0424c2s v4p0125c2s
v4p0568c1s v5p0237c2s v6p0638c2m
Stocklager, Guy N. v6p0010c2s
Stockley, W.F. v3p0066c1s
v3p0260c2s v3p0385c2s v4p0085c2s
v4p0609c2s
Stockley, W.F.P. v5p0393c2s
v5p0492c2s v5p0494c1s v6p0088c2s
v6p0096c1s v6p0098c1s v6p0520c1s
v6p0547c2s v6p0548c1s v6p0549c2s
Stocks, A. v4p0078c1s
Stocks, G.A. v2p0380c1s
Stockton, C.H. v3p0019c1s
v3p0093c2s v3p0383c1s v4p0009c1s
v4p0106c2s v4p0212c1s v4p0395c2s
v4p0511c2s v4p0595c1m v5p0094c1s
v5p0146c2s v5p0167c1m v5p0310c1s
v5p0595c2s v5p0618c1s
Stockton, C.R. v3p0443c2s
Stockton, C.S. v3p0443c2s
Stockton, Chas.S. v4p0573c2s
Stockton, F. v1p0952c1s
Stockton, F.R. v1p0192c1s
v1p0439c2s v1p0523c1s v1p0789c1s
v1p0878c2s v1p0886c2s v1p0897c1s
v1p0908c2s v1p0951c1s v1p1009c1s
v1p1010c1s v1p1029c2m v1p1131c1s
v1p1252c1s v1p1299c2s v2p0052c2s
v2p0070c1s v2p0090c1s v2p0119c1s
v2p0148c1s v2p0153c1s v2p0203c2s
v2p0211c2s v2p0216c1s v2p0246c1s
v2p0303c2s v2p0324c2s v2p0329c1s
v2p0348c2s v2p0369c2s v2p0371c1s
v2p0380c1s v2p0382c1s v2p0413c2s
v2p0421c2s v2p0422c1s v2p0430c1s
v2p0444c2s v3p0082c1s v3p0124c2s
v3p0202c2s v3p0204c2s v3p0275c1s
v3p0286c2s v3p0406c1s v3p0457c1s
v4p0032c2s v4p0088c2s v4p0118c2s
v4p0349c1s v4p0386c1s v4p0391c1s
v4p0439c2s v4p0546c2s v4p0612c2s
v5p0061c1s v5p0066c1m v5p0083c1s
v5p0085c1s v5p0133c2s v5p0138c2s
v5p0241c1s v5p0248c2s v5p0309c1s
v5p0322c1s v5p0415c2s v5p0458c1s
v5p0494c2s v5p0531c2s v5p0534c2s
v5p0613c2s
Stockton, Frank R. v5p0610c2s
Stockton, J.D. v1p0327c1s
v1p1359c1s
Stockton, L. v1p0336c2s
v1p0601c2s v1p0912c1s v1p1277c2s
v2p0201c1s v3p0016c2s v3p0116c1s
v4p0366c1s v4p0408c2s v6p0539c2s
Stockton, Louise v4p0120c1s
Stockton, M. v1p0940c1s
Stockton, M.E. v1p0776c1s
Stockton, R. v4p0146c2s
v4p0321c1s
Stockton, T.H. v1p0935c2s
Stockton-Hough, J. v1p1376c1s
Stockwell, A. v4p0151c2s
Stockwell, G. v5p0334c2s
v6p0489c1s
Stockwell, G.A. v1p0143c2s
v1p0200c1s v2p0037c2s v2p0067c2s
v2p0219c1s v2p0472c2s v3p0292c2s
v3p0437c1s v4p0064c2s v4p0105c1s
v4p0260c1s v4p0598c2s v5p0352c2s
v5p0634c2s
Stockwell, H.G. v6p0025c2s
Stockwell, J.L. v1p0375c2s
Stockwell, J.N. v1p0865c2m
v1p0866c1s v5p0174c2s
Stockwell, Lillian v6p0272c1s
Stockwell, T.A. v4p0151c1s
Stocquart, E. v3p0268c2s
v3p0269c1s v4p0157c2s v5p0363c1s
v5p0646c1s
Stocqueler, J.H. v1p0943c1s
Stodart, R. v5p0575c2s
Stoddard, A. v3p0367c1s
Stoddard, A.M. v6p0231c1s
Stoddard, C.A.
v1p0237c2s
Stoddard, C.W. v1p0143c1s
v1p0188c1s v1p0188c2s v1p0196c2s
v1p0215c2s v1p0217c2s v1p0288c2s
v1p0297c2s v1p0566c1s v1p0579c1s
v1p0607c2m v1p0626c2s v1p0627c2s
v1p0680c1s v1p0701c1s v1p0738c1s
v1p0774c1s v1p0811c2s v1p0888c1s
v1p0888c2s v1p0901c2s v1p0922c1s
v1p0942c2m v1p0983c2s v1p1154c1s
v1p1227c1s v1p1259c2m v1p1280c1s
v1p1326c2s v1p1360c2s v1p1418c2s
v1p1438c1s v2p0123c1s v2p0198c1s
v2p0252c1s v2p0387c2s v2p0447c1s
v3p0191c2s v4p0248c2s v4p0371c1s
v5p0323c1s v5p0396c1s v6p0014c1s
v6p0093c1s v6p0129c2s v6p0186c1s
v6p0223c1s v6p0311c2s v6p0350c1s
v6p0352c2s v6p0361c2s v6p0366c1s
v6p0410c2s v6p0420c2s v6p0434c2m
v6p0470c2s v6p0607c1s v6p0617c2s
Stoddard, C.Warren v6p0278c2s
v6p0417c2s
Stoddard, D.T. v1p0829c2s
Stoddard, E. v1p0004c1s
v1p1372c2s v3p0337c2s v3p0381c2s
v3p0429c1s v3p0461c2s v4p0355c1s
Stoddard, E.D.B. v2p0267c2s
Stoddard, E.P. v1p0749c2s
v1p0965c1s
Stoddard, F.H. v2p0174c2s
v2p0260c2s v2p0317c2s v2p0477c2s
v3p0020c2s v3p0238c2s v3p0431c2s
v4p0334c2s v6p0473c1s
Stoddard, H.H. v3p0360c1s
Stoddard, H.L. v6p0491c2s
v6p0514c1s
Stoddard, J.C. v6p0242c1s
Stoddard, J.L. v1p0427c1s
v1p0685c2s
Stoddard, J.M. v6p0184c2s
Stoddard, J.T. v2p0097c1s
v2p0320c2s v3p0095c1s v3p0330c2s
v3p0401c2s v3p0458c1s v4p0026c1m
v4p0458c2s
Stoddard, L. v4p0281c2s
Stoddard, O.N. v1p1316c1m
Stoddard, R.H. v1p0037c1s
v1p0081c1s v1p0099c1s v1p0112c2s
v1p0139c1s v1p0170c1s v1p0171c2s
v1p0172c2s v1p0244c2s v1p0286c2s
v1p0330c1s v1p0332c2s v1p0345c1s
v1p0351c2s v1p0462c1s v1p0503c1s
v1p0556c2s v1p0575c2s v1p0605c2s
v1p0704c1m v1p0708c1s v1p0719c1s
v1p0733c2s v1p0750c2s v1p0767c2s
v1p0770c2s v1p0781c1s v1p0799c2s
v1p0801c1s v1p0803c2s v1p0864c2s
v1p0866c2s v1p0873c1s v1p1019c2s
v1p1068c1s v1p1084c2s v1p1106c1s
v1p1107c1s v1p1123c1s v1p1142c1s
v1p1147c2s v1p1160c1s v1p1220c2s
v1p1244c2s v1p1266c1s v1p1286c1s
v1p1294c2m v1p1295c2s v1p1298c1s
v1p1361c2s v1p1393c2s v1p1404c2s
v1p1406c2s v1p1407c2m v1p1433c2s
v2p0036c2s v2p0059c1s v2p0061c2s
v2p0198c1s v2p0239c1s v2p0277c1s
v2p0288c1s v2p0318c2s v2p0335c2s
v2p0346c2s v2p0351c2s v2p0431c2s
v2p0472c2s v3p0020c2s v3p0029c1s
v3p0048c2s v3p0057c1s v3p0058c1s
v3p0061c2s v3p0188c1s v3p0191c2s
v3p0259c2m v3p0269c1s v3p0274c1s
v3p0335c1s v3p0354c2s v3p0421c2s
v3p0464c2s v4p0160c2s v4p0341c1s
v4p0343c2s v4p0449c1s v4p0574c1s
v5p0339c1s v5p0340c1s v5p0509c1s
v5p0630c1s v6p0283c2s v6p0466c1s
v6p0505c1s v6p0645c1s
Stoddard, R.H. et al. v1p0534c1s
Stoddard, R.H., Mrs. v1p0274c2s
v1p0888c2s
Stoddard, S. v6p0293c2s
Stoddard, T.H. v6p0136c2s

Stoddard, W.O. v1p0915c2s
v1p0916c2s v1p0982c1s v1p1088c1s
v1p1264c1s v2p0015c2s v2p0033c2s
v2p0193c2s v2p0259c1s v2p0317c1s
Stoddard, W.O. et al. v4p0550c2s
Stoddart, A. v3p0268c1s
v4p0028c1s v4p0622c1s v6p0084c2s
v6p0133c2s v6p0154c2s v6p0163c1s
v6p0164c2s v6p0165c2s v6p0187c1s
v6p0236c1s v6p0300c2s v6p0310c2s
v6p0377c1s v6p0472c1s v6p0525c1s
v6p0546c1s v6p0571c1s v6p0616c2s
v6p0631c2s v6p0647c2s v6p0701c2s
Stoddart, A.M. v4p0477c2s
v5p0066c1s
Stoddart, Alfred v6p0274c2s
v6p0300c2s
Stoddart, B.B. v6p0300c2s
Stoddart, J.M. v3p0216c1s
v3p0367c2s
Stoddart, J.T. v4p0349c1s
v4p0536c1s
Stoddart, W.W. v1p0579c1s
Stodder, C. v1p0836c1s
Stodola, A. v5p0551c1s
Stoeckel, G.J. v1p1379c2s
v3p0293c1m
Stoeckhardt, J.A. v1p1427c1s
Stoessl, O. v5p0418c2s
v5p0611c2s
Stoever, M.L. v1p0027c1s
v1p0076c2s v1p0239c1s v1p0276c1m
v1p0385c1s v1p0483c2s v1p0519c1m
v1p0571c2s v1p0599c1s v1p0687c2s
v1p0696c1s v1p0750c1s v1p0777c2s
v1p0778c1m v1p0778c2s v1p0847c1s
v1p0852c1s v1p0935c2s v1p0980c1s
v1p0988c1s v1p1072c2s v1p1097c1s
v1p1176c1s v1p1176c2s v1p1237c1s
v1p1355c1s
Stoever, S.E. v6p0532c2s
Stoffel, L.M. v1p0664c2s
Stofford, F. v6p0530c2s
Stoker, A. v1p0321c2s
Stoker, B. v4p0161c1s
Stoker, B. et al. v3p0406c1s
Stoker, Bram v4p0476c1s
v5p0574c1s
Stoker, G.A. v5p0360c2s
Stoker, H.M. v3p0079c1s
Stoker, M. v3p0390c1s
Stoker, T. v5p0472c2s
Stokes, A. v2p0067c2s
v3p0252c2s
Stokes, A.C. v1p0840c2s
v2p0221c1m v2p0414c2s v3p0044c1s
v3p0108c1s v3p0108c2s v4p0019c2s
v4p0286c1s
Stokes, A.P., jr. v6p0419c2s
Stokes, F.W. v4p0025c2m
v5p0027c1s v6p0023c1m v6p0041c1s
Stokes, G.C. v2p0367c1s
Stokes, G.G. v1p0038c2s
v1p1074c2m v1p1268c2s v2p0228c1s
v3p0359c2s v3p0379c2s v4p0331c2s
Stokes, G.G. and Webb, S.. v5p0338c2s
Stokes, G.G., Sir v4p0187c2s
Stokes, G.J. v4p0228c2s
v4p0424c1s v5p0280c1s
Stokes, G.T. v1p0644c2m
v2p0002c1s v2p0050c2s v2p0112c1s
v2p0153c2s v2p0206c1s v3p0019c1s
v3p0127c1s v3p0237c2s
Stokes, H. v2p0060c1s
v5p0224c1s
Stokes, H.M. v4p0026c1s
Stokes, H.N. v4p0253c2s
v5p0037c2s v5p0104c1s v5p0473c2s
v6p0015c1s
Stokes, H.N. et al. v5p0062c2s
Stokes, H.P. v4p0517c1s
Stokes, H.P. and Lee, S. . v4p0356c1s
Stokes, H.P. and Yeatman, J.P.
v4p0517c1s v4p0517c2s
Stokes, J., Sir v3p0110c2s
Stokes, J.G.P. v5p0521c1s
v6p0574c2s
Stokes, J.S. v5p0404c1s
Stokes, M. v2p0022c1s
v2p0103c2s v2p0108c2s v2p0117c1s
v2p0194c1s v2p0259c1s v2p0391c2s
v5p0295c2s
Stokes, Miss v1p0159c1s
v1p0660c2s
Stokes, S. v5p0448c1s
Stokes, W. v2p0041c2s
v2p0224c2s v2p0228c2s v2p0229c1s
v2p0375c1s v2p0457c1s v3p0247c2s
v3p0310c2s v4p0049c1s v4p0065c1s
v4p0156c1m v4p0168c2s v4p0195c2s
v4p0456c1s v4p0578c1s v4p0589c2s
Stokes, W. et al. v3p0311c2s
v4p0403c1s
Stokes, W.A. v1p0807c2s
Stokes, Whitley v6p0216c2s
Stokoe, T.H. v6p0061c1s
Stolle, E. v3p0414c1s
Stolle, F. v1p0309c2s
Stoller, J.H. v3p0194c2s
v3p0359c1s v6p0047c1s
Stonaker, C.L. v6p0479c1s
Stone, A. v1p0174c2s
v5p0276c1s
Stone, A.B. v4p0322c1s
v5p0640c2s
Stone, A.H. v6p0184c2s
v6p0331c1s v6p0434c2s v6p0448c1s
v6p0502c2s
Stone, A.H. and Bois, W.E.B.Du
v6p0447c2s
Stone, A.J. v5p0011c1s
v5p0027c1s v5p0094c2s v5p0164c2s
v5p0385c2s v6p0010c2s v6p0028c2s
v6p0029c1s v6p0460c2s v6p0590c1s
Stone, A.L. v1p0252c2m
Stone, A.P. v4p0385c2s
Stone, Alfred v5p0580c1s
Stone, B.F. v5p0418c2s
Stone, B.N. v6p0419c2s
v6p0513c2s
Stone, C.H. v6p0422c1m
Stone, C.J. v1p0543c1s
v1p1091c2s v2p0272c1s
Stone, C.P. v1p0833c2s
v2p0315c1s v2p0391c2s v2p0410c1m
v2p0453c2s v2p0466c2m v5p0181c1s
Stone, C.R. v6p0138c1s
Stone, C.W. v4p0121c2s
Stone, D.M. v4p0546c1s
Stone, E. v4p0550c1s
v5p0251c1s
Stone, E.A. v5p0035c1s
v5p0549c1s
Stone, E.B. v4p0181c1s
v4p0365c1s v4p0626c1s v4p0628c2m
v5p0362c2s v5p0435c1s
Stone, E.J. v1p0903c2s
Stone, Ellen M. v6p0081c2m
Stone, F. v1p0585c1s
v2p0063c2s v2p0135c1s
Stone, F.D. v1p0997c2s
v2p0310c2s v2p0335c1m v3p0313c2s
v4p0565c2s
Stone, F.G. v2p0071c1s
v5p0091c1s v5p0091c2s v6p0654c1s
Stone, F.M. v2p0150c2s
Stone, F.Z. v6p0147c2s
Stone, G.E. v4p0552c2s
Stone, G.H. v2p0124c1s
v2p0475c1s v3p0024c1s v3p0173c2m
v3p0174c1s v3p0317c1s v3p0425c2s
v5p0234c1s v5p0242c1m
Stone, G.W. v2p0347c1s
Stone, H. v1p0212c1s
v3p0200c1s v3p0424c2s v3p0429c1s
v6p0706c1m
Stone, H.L. v6p0528c1s
v6p0529c2s
Stone, H.N. v1p0713c1s
v1p1343c1s
Stone, H.S. v6p0569c1s
Stone, J.F. v1p0888c2s
Stone, J.H. v1p1371c1s
v2p0460c2s v5p0591c2s v6p0002c2s
v6p0145c1s v6p0293c2s
Stone, J.M. v2p0232c2s
v2p0273c1s v2p0364c2s v2p0372c1s
v3p0083c2s v3p0194c1s v3p0270c1m
v3p0288c2s v3p0329c2s v3p0364c2s
v3p0425c1s v4p0035c1s v4p0177c2s
v4p0186c1m v4p0407c1s v4p0480c2s
v4p0494c2s v4p0504c1s v4p0538c1s
v5p0049c1s v5p0360c2s v5p0364c2s
v5p0452c1s v5p0482c1s v5p0485c1s
v5p0499c1s v5p0556c1s v5p0622c2s
v6p0022c2s v6p0200c2s v6p0259c2s
v6p0340c2s v6p0390c1s v6p0535c1m
v6p0535c2s v6p0701c2s
Stone, J.S. v1p0411c1s
v1p0761c1s v1p0977c2s v1p0989c1s
v1p1139c1s v3p0251c1s v3p0302c1s
v3p0349c2s v3p0358c1s
Stone, J.W. v5p0070c1s
Stone, Jane D. v6p0305c2s
Stone, L. v1p0049c1s
v1p0228c1s v2p0478c1s
Stone, L. et al. v3p0470c1s
Stone, L.B. v1p1265c2s
Stone, L.H. v2p0161c2s
v2p0477c2s v4p0030c1s
Stone, L.H., Mrs. v1p0069c2s
Stone, M. v1p0646c1s
Stone, M.E. v4p0099c2s
v6p0037c1m v6p0559c1s
Stone, M.O. v6p0480c2s
Stone, Melville E. v4p0100c1s
Stone, N.I. v5p0009c2s
v5p0093c2s v6p0252c1s v6p0253c2s
v6p0255c1s v6p0323c2s v6p0558c1s
v6p0633c1s
Stone, O. v1p0911c1s
v2p0423c1s v3p0400c1s
Stone, P.C.R. v4p0067c2s
Stone, R. v5p0460c1m
Stone, R., Gen. v4p0485c2s
Stone, Roy v5p0460c2s
v6p0510c1s
Stone, S. v6p0143c2s
v6p0298c2s
Stone, S. and Akerman, J.Y.
v1p0211c1s
Stone, S.F. v6p0651c1s
Stone, S.H. v6p0318c1s
Stone, S.J. v1p0452c1s
v2p0287c1s v2p0409c2s v2p0435c1s
Stone, T.D.P. v1p0404c1s
Stone, T.T. v1p0032c1s
v1p0048c2s v1p0218c1s v1p1321c2s
v1p1360c2s
Stone, W. v1p1163c1s
v2p0421c1s v3p0092c2s v4p0061c1s
v6p0440c1s v6p0539c2s v6p0608c2s
Stone, W.A. v6p0026c1s
v6p0632c2s
Stone, W.H. v1p0399c1m
v1p0464c1s v1p0885c2s v1p1074c2s
v1p1163c2s v2p0136c2s v2p0137c2s
v2p0138c1s v2p0138c2s v2p0302c2s
v2p0462c2s v4p0399c1s v4p0443c2s
v5p0406c1s
Stone, W.H. and Kilner, W.
v2p0138c1s
Stone, W.J. v5p0158c2s
v5p0603c2s
Stone, W.L. v1p0004c2m
v1p0051c2s v1p0152c1s v1p0157c2m
v1p0172c1m v1p0176c2m v1p0265c2m
v1p0782c2m v1p0792c1s v1p0871c1s
v1p0876c2s v1p0914c1m v1p1051c2s
v1p1127c2m v1p1151c2s v1p1160c1s
v1p1233c1s v1p1393c2s v2p0114c1s
v2p0278c1s v2p0386c1s v3p0305c1s
v4p0050c2s v4p0134c1s v4p0444c1s
Stone, W.W. v2p0079c2s
Stone, Witmer v5p0472c1s
Stonecheek, Robert v6p0535c1s
Stones, W. v3p0304c2s
Stonestreet, C.H. v2p0083c2s
Stonestreet, G.D. v3p0116c2s
Stoneven, L.S. v1p1111c1s
Stoney, B.B. v1p1010c2s
Stoney, G.J. v1p0827c2s
v1p1074c2s v2p0286c1s v4p0326c2s
v6p0548c1s
Stoney, G.J. and Argyll .. v2p0439c2s
Stoney, G.J. and Downing, A.M.W.
v5p0372c2s
Stooke, E.H. v5p0201c2s
Stookey, L.B. and Gooch, F.A.
v6p0674c1s
Stoops, J.D. v5p0519c1s
v6p0317c2s v6p0582c2s
Stop, E. v3p0382c2s
Stopes, C. v3p0154c2s
Stopes, C.C. v3p0204c2s
v3p0388c2s v4p0025c2s v4p0073c1s
v4p0303c2s v4p0344c2s v4p0517c2s
v4p0518c2s v5p0069c2s v5p0070c1s
v5p0257c2s v5p0276c1m v5p0301c1s
v5p0450c2s v5p0470c1s v5p0522c1s
v5p0524c1s v6p0389c2s v6p0404c1s
Stopes, C.C., Mrs. v4p0269c2s
Stopes, Charlotte C. v4p0517c2s
v5p0346c2s v6p0110c2s v6p0287c1m
v6p0333c2s v6p0404c1s v6p0586c1s
v6p0588c1m v6p0606c2s
Stopes, H. v3p0265c1s
v4p0310c1s v5p0358c2s
Stopford, J.G. v4p0079c2s
Stopford, J.G.B. v5p0007c2s
v5p0190c1s v5p0244c2s
Stordy, R.J. v6p0712c2s
Storer, A.C. v5p0295c1s
v5p0564c1s v6p0164c2s v6p0289c2s
v6p0401c2s
Storer, B. et al. v4p0596c1s
Storer, D.H. v1p0456c2s
v1p0588c2s
Storer, F.H. v1p0061c1s
v1p0923c2s v1p1221c1s v2p0155c2s
Storer, F.H. and Eliot, C.W.
v1p0061c1s
Storer, H.R. v1p1034c1s
Storer, J.J. v1p0258c2s
v1p1150c1s v1p1181c1s
Storey, A.B. v1p0031c2s
Storey, A.T. v5p0048c2s
v5p0533c1s
Storey, C.W. v1p0259c1s
Storey, F.D. v2p0300c2s
v2p0301c1s v2p0314c2s v2p0424c1s
Storey, G.A. v5p0087c2s
v5p0448c2s v6p0553c2s
Storey, H.V. v6p0102c2s
v6p0271c1s
Storey, M. v1p0031c1s
v1p0705c1s v1p1282c1s v1p1353c1s
v4p0115c1s v5p0138c1s v5p0257c1s
v6p0667c1s
Storey, M. et al. v5p0592c1s
Storey, Max v6p0441c1s
Storey, Moorfield v3p0337c2s
Storey, R.H. v1p0856c2s
Stork, C.A. v1p0014c1s
v1p0074c1s v1p0112c1s v1p0168c1s
v1p0180c2s v1p0229c1s v1p0241c2s
v1p0242c1s v1p0286c1s v1p0289c1s
v1p0386c1s v1p0434c1s v1p0434c2s
v1p0454c1s v1p0626c1s v1p0686c2s
v1p0700c1s v1p0769c1s v1p0839c2s

v1p0848c1s v1p0977c2s v1p1042c2s
v1p1044c1s v1p1132c2s v1p1302c1s
v2p0058c1s v2p0266c1s v2p0384c2s
Stork, T. v1p0849c2s
Stork, T.B. v1p0116c2s
v4p0054c1s v4p0480c1s v4p0615c1s
v5p0545c2s v6p0170c1s v6p0698c2s
Storm, O.J. v4p0443c1s
Storm, T. v1p0627c2s
v1p1267c1s v1p1273c2s
Storms, A.B. v6p0064c2s
Storms, J.B. v6p0161c1s
Storojenko, N. v2p0381c2m
Storr, F. v2p0442c2s
Storr-Best, L. v4p0271c2s
Storrey, J.B.S. v3p0053c2s
Storrow, E. v2p0293c2s
Storrow, J.J. v1p0978c2s
Storrow, T.W. v1p0380c2s
v1p0489c1s v1p0950c1s v1p1311c2s
Storrs, A. v1p0109c2s
Storrs, A.B. v1p0017c2s
v1p1419c1s
Storrs, A.P. v1p0982c1s
v1p1110c2s
Storrs, E.A. v1p0343c1s
Storrs, H.M. v1p0247c1s
v1p0291c1s
Storrs, J.B. v1p1006c2s
Storrs, L.C. v6p0109c1s
v6p0312c2s v6p0415c2s v6p0535c2s
Storrs, R.S. v1p0241c1s
v3p0086c2s v3p0094c1s v3p0197c1s
v3p0444c1s v4p0054c1s v5p0469c1s
Storrs, R.S., jr. v1p0686c1s
v1p1043c1s v1p1263c2s
Storrs, W.M. v1p0444c1s
Story, A.J. v4p0190c1s
Story, A.T. v1p1388c2s
v2p0335c1s v3p0157c1s v3p0191c1s
v3p0205c1s v3p0309c1m v4p0063c2m
v4p0217c2s v4p0333c1m v4p0384c2s
v4p0423c1s v4p0430c2s v4p0551c2s
v4p0598c1s v5p0263c2s v5p0551c2s
Story, D. v1p0773c1s
v5p0083c1s v5p0181c2s v5p0248c1s
v5p0604c2s v6p0007c2s v6p0033c1s
v6p0035c2s v6p0076c1s v6p0211c1s
v6p0261c1s v6p0286c2s v6p0289c1s
v6p0356c1s v6p0368c1s v6p0369c1s
v6p0440c1s v6p0469c2s v6p0472c1s
v6p0523c1s v6p0555c2s v6p0571c2s
v6p0577c2m v6p0702c2s
Story, Douglas v6p0561c1s
Story, Elinor H. v6p0114c2s
Story, G.A. v4p0599c2s
Story, G.D. v1p0837c1s
Story, J. v1p0216c2s
v1p0537c2s v1p0729c1s v1p0735c1s
v1p0801c1s v1p0804c2s
Story, J.A. v5p0483c2s
Story, J.C. v6p0283c2s
Story, Judge v1p0648c1s
Story, M. v4p0325c2s
Story, R. v1p0666c2s
Story, R.H. v1p0335c2s
v1p1002c1s v1p1056c2s v4p0110c1s
v5p0440c2s
Story, W.E. v6p0406c2s
Story, W.O. v3p0301c2s
Story, W.W. v1p0061c1s
v1p0082c1s v1p0204c2s v1p0226c1s
v1p0228c2s v1p0264c1s v1p0286c2s
v1p0295c2s v1p0346c2s v1p0407c1s
v1p0520c1s v1p0522c1s v1p0523c1s
v1p0523c2s v1p0627c1s v1p0627c2s
v1p0669c1s v1p0727c2s v1p0856c2s
v1p0872c1s v1p0923c1s v1p0947c2s
v1p0957c1s v1p0996c2s v1p1050c2m
v1p1122c1s v1p1125c1s v1p1125c2s
v1p1126c1s v1p1267c1s v1p1277c2s
v1p1282c2s v1p1372c1s v1p1389c1s
v2p0035c2s v2p0224c1s v2p0287c1s
v3p0021c1s v3p0098c2s v3p0260c1s
v3p0277c2s v3p0366c2s v4p0010c1s
v4p0068c1s v4p0412c2s
Stoss, W. v4p0166c1s
v4p0235c1s
Stosz, W. v3p0027c1s
Stotesbury, H. v5p0089c1s
Stothart, C. v1p0103c2s
v1p0105c1s v1p0147c1s v1p0881c1s
Stothart, J. v1p1082c2s
Stothart, M.C. v1p0061c2s
Stotherd, E.A. v5p0098c2s
Stotherd, E.A.W. v4p0278c2s
v4p0524c1s
Stotherd, R.H. v3p0020c2s
Stothert, J. v1p0886c1s
Stothert, J.A. v1p1161c2s
Stott, D. v4p0067c1s
Stott, G. v1p0349c2s
v1p0559c1s v1p0648c1s v1p1280c2s
v1p1420c1s
Stott, R.G. v6p0279c2s
Stott, W.T. v2p0147c1s
Stottlemyer, W.B. v5p0437c2s
Stottler, V.E. v5p0131c1s
Stoudt, J.B. v6p0488c1s
Stough, J.H. v5p0121c2s
v6p0190c1s
Stoughton, C.W. v2p0121c1s
Stoughton, E.W. v1p0234c2s
v1p0283c1s v1p0284c1s v1p0647c1s
v1p0648c1m v1p0818c1s v1p0944c2s
v1p1227c1s v1p1330c2s v1p1352c2s
v1p1365c2s
Stoughton, E.W. and Black, J.S.
v1p1048c1s
Stoughton, J. v1p0039c2s
v1p0040c1s v1p0117c2s v1p1123c2s
v2p0007c2s v2p0048c2s v2p0051c2s
v2p0075c2s v2p0082c1s v2p0085c2s
v2p0159c1s v2p0209c2s v2p0282c1s
v2p0295c1s v2p0391c1s v2p0397c1s
v2p0430c1m v2p0471c1s v3p0014c2s
Stout, A.B. v1p0283c1s
v2p0007c1s v2p0020c1s
Stout, C.B. v1p0421c2s
Stout, C.E.E. v2p0163c2s
Stout, E.A. v6p0458c2s
Stout, G.F. v3p0016c2s
v3p0038c1s v3p0194c2m v3p0355c2s
v3p0366c1s v3p0429c1s v4p0607c1s
v5p0101c1s v5p0470c2s v6p0490c1s
Stout, R. v2p0314c1s
v3p0181c1s v4p0401c2s v5p0038c2s
v5p0408c2s v6p0518c1s
Stout, R., Sir v4p0401c2m
v5p0038c2s
Stout, Robert, Sir v5p0408c1s
Stout, W.O. v5p0225c1s
Stovall, D.H. v6p0201c1s
v6p0261c1s v6p0368c1s v6p0649c2s
Stovel, C. v1p0244c1s
Stovell, G. v5p0375c2s
Stover, C.B. v3p0186c2s
v5p0454c2s v6p0546c1s
Stover, M.L. v1p0879c2s
Stow, D. v1p0497c2s
v1p0945c1s
Stow, E. v6p0431c1s
Stowe, C.E. v1p0107c2s
v1p0119c2s v1p0122c1s v1p0124c1s
v1p0128c1m v1p0238c2s v1p0262c1s
v1p0276c1s v1p0392c1s v1p0582c2s
v1p0685c2s v1p0690c1s v1p0695c1s
v1p0700c2s v1p0777c2s v1p0909c2s
v1p0925c2m v1p1009c2s v1p1041c2s
v1p1043c2s v1p1047c1s v1p1096c1s
v1p1214c1s v1p1258c2s v1p1282c1s
v1p1288c1s v1p1302c1s v1p1321c1s
v1p1354c1s v5p0253c2s
Stowe, E. v1p0405c1s
v2p0075c1s v2p0201c1s
Stowe, H.B. v1p0014c1s
v1p0183c2s v1p0199c1s v1p0231c1s
v1p0264c2s v1p0277c2s v1p0359c2s
v1p0402c2s v1p0462c1s v1p0519c1s
v1p0738c2s v1p0750c1s v1p0846c1s
v1p0851c2s v1p0856c2s v1p0877c1s
v1p0905c1s v1p0940c1s v1p0940c2s
v1p0952c1s v1p0975c2s v1p1011c1s
v1p1218c1s v1p1262c2s v1p1273c2s
v1p1287c2s v1p1408c2s v2p0397c2s
Stowe, H.B., Mrs. v1p0195c2s
v1p0801c2s
Stowe, J.A. v5p0143c1s
Stowe, L.B. v6p0437c1s
Stowe, W.T. v1p1407c2s
Stowell, A.D. v1p0254c1s
v1p1217c1s
Stowell, F.W.O. v2p0177c1s
Stowell, H. v1p0014c1s
v1p0120c2s v1p0121c2s v1p0122c1s
v1p0402c2s v1p0641c1s v1p0687c2s
v1p0714c2s v1p0979c1s v1p1103c1s
v1p1176c2s v1p1237c2s
Stowell, Lord v1p0171c1s
Stowell, M.L. v6p0139c1s
v6p0338c1s
Stowell, T.B. v3p0297c1s
v3p0377c2s v5p0062c1s
Stowell, W. v6p0103c2s
Stoyell, M. v2p0209c2s
Strach, M. v4p0633c2s
Strachan, A. v1p1219c2s
Strachan, G.B. v3p0324c2s
Strachan, G.R. v2p0396c1s
Strachan, R. v2p0119c2s
Strachan, W. v5p0324c1s
v5p0328c2s v6p0100c1s v6p0360c2s
v6p0431c1s v6p0609c1s
Strachan-Davidson, J.L. .. v3p0366c2s
v5p0494c1s
Strachan-Porgan, E. v3p0321c1s
Strachey, A. v5p0273c1s
Strachey, A. et al. v1p0839c2s
Strachey, Amy v4p0146c1s
v4p0167c2s
Strachey, C. v5p0361c1s
Strachey, E. v1p0384c2s
v1p1218c1s v4p0033c2s v4p0084c2s
v4p0312c1s v5p0083c1s v5p0366c2s
Strachey, E. and Hamilton, J.
v1p0657c2s
Strachey, E. et al. v2p0021c1s
Strachey, E., Sir v2p0165c1s
v3p0102c2s v4p0110c1s v4p0181c2s
v4p0343c1s v4p0356c2s v4p0436c1s
v4p0450c2s v4p0518c1s v4p0551c2s
v4p0562c2s
Strachey, G. v2p0166c2s
v3p0144c1s v4p0089c2s v4p0090c1s
Strachey, G.L. v6p0070c1s
v6p0085c1s v6p0368c2s v6p0587c1s
v6p0681c2s v6p0684c2s
Strachey, H. v5p0001c1s
v5p0101c1s
Strachey, J. and Strachey, R.
v6p0083c2s v6p0162c2s
Strachey, J.S. v6p0505c2s
Strachey, J.St.L. v4p0237c1s
v4p0291c1s v4p0495c2s v4p0565c1s
v6p0240c2m v6p0293c1s v6p0541c1s
Strachey, J.St.Loe v4p0247c2s
v4p0586c2s v5p0018c1s
Strachey, L. v5p0018c1s
v5p0497c2s v6p0206c2s v6p0252c2s
v6p0281c1s v6p0523c1s v6p0589c2s
v6p0681c2s v6p0685c2s v6p0713c1s
Strachey, Lionel v5p0243c2s
Strachey, M. v6p0587c2s
Strachey, R. v1p0434c2s
v1p0506c1m v1p0631c1s v1p1005c2s
v2p0283c2s v3p0126c1s v5p0579c2s
Strachey, R. and Strachey, J.
v6p0083c2s v6p0162c2s
Strachey, R. et al. v2p0128c1s
Strachey, S.L. v2p0172c1s
Strachey, St.L. v4p0265c2s
v4p0491c1s v4p0589c2s
Strachey, St.L., Mrs. v4p0590c2s
Strachey, St.Loe v3p0222c2s
v4p0240c2s v4p0256c1s v4p0266c1s
v4p0289c2s v4p0290c2s v4p0314c2s
v4p0476c1s
Stradley, W.P. v3p0354c1s
Stradling, A. v1p0465c2s
v2p0406c2s v2p0442c1s v3p0305c1s
v3p0397c1s v4p0415c1s v4p0481c2s
v4p0515c2s v4p0531c1m v4p0605c2s
Stradling, A., Dr. v4p0515c2s
Stradling, G.F. v4p0288c2s
v5p0621c2s
Stradling, J.M. v6p0387c1s
Strahan, A. v1p0710c2s
v1p0754c1s v1p0754c2s v1p0784c2s
v2p0006c1s v2p0143c2s v4p0440c1s
v6p0082c1s
Strahan, A. and Rowe, R. . v1p0764c2s
Strahan, C.M. v3p0170c2s
v3p0383c1s
Strahan, E. v1p0162c2s
v1p0517c1s v1p1282c1s v1p1296c1s
Strahan, E. and Laffan, W.M.
v1p1311c1m
Strahan, S.A.K. v3p0268c2s
v4p0140c1s
Strahorn, R.E. v4p0407c1s
v4p0486c2s v5p0614c1s
Straight, H.H. v2p0220c2m
Straight, M.W. v5p0070c1s
v6p0075c1s
Straight, W. v6p0121c1s
v6p0354c1s
Strait, H. v1p0008c1s
Strang, J. v1p0550c1s
v1p1167c1s v1p1391c2s v5p0343c2s
v5p0345c2s
Strange, A. v1p0167c1s
v1p0829c2s v1p1161c2s v1p1164c1s
v1p1367c1s
Strange, C. v1p0456c2s
v1p0608c2s
Strange, D. v4p0462c2s
v4p0580c2s
Strange, E.F. v4p0084c1s
v4p0245c1s v4p0297c1s v4p0343c1s
v4p0388c1s v4p0455c1s v4p0634c1s
v5p0033c2s v5p0098c2s v5p0154c2s
v5p0170c1s v5p0255c1s v5p0298c2s
v5p0310c2s v5p0331c2m v5p0342c1s
v5p0385c1s v5p0440c1s v5p0496c1m
v5p0552c1s v5p0629c1s v6p0338c1s
v6p0360c1s v6p0446c1s v6p0592c1s
v6p0612c2s
Strange, G.le v4p0178c1s
Strange, Guy le v4p0296c1m
Strange, J. v1p1114c2s
v1p1115c1s v1p1122c1s v1p1122c2s
v1p1380c2s
Strange, J.B. v6p0416c1s
Strange, K. v4p0552c2s
v4p0562c1s v4p0619c1s
v5p0496c2s
Strange, Mark v6p0458c1s
Strange, T.B. v3p0066c1s
v3p0181c1s v5p0033c1s v5p0090c2s
v5p0410c1s v6p0221c1s v6p0297c1m
v6p0309c2s
Strange, W. v1p0102c1s
v1p1275c2s
Strangford, Lady v1p1129c1s
Strangs, A. v1p0415c1s
Strappini, W. v2p0053c1s
Strappini, W.D. v1p0312c2s
v1p1066c1s v2p0053c1s v2p0122c2s
v2p0159c2s v2p0183c1s v2p0234c1s
v2p0344c1s v2p0382c2s v3p0114c2s

v3p0267c2s v3p0423c1s v4p0244c1s
v4p0573c2s
Strasburger, E. v4p0243c2s
Strassburger, N.S. v1p0641c1s
Strassmaier, J.N. v1p0069c1s
Stratford, S.P. v1p0919c1s
Stratham, H.H. v1p0569c2s
Strathcona, Lord v6p0267c1s
Stratiotes v6p0265c2s
Straton, Col. v1p0177c1s
Straton, J. v1p0213c1s
v1p1004c2m
Straton, J.R. v5p0403c1s
Straton, N.D.J. v6p0192c1s
Stratten, T. v1p0599c2s
Stratton, A.W. v5p0033c2s
v5p0286c1s
Stratton, C.C. v6p0671c1s
Stratton, F. v4p0539c1s
Stratton, F.N. v6p0166c2s
v6p0380c2s v6p0686c1s v6p0695c1s
v6p0703c1s
Stratton, F.S. v4p0094c2s
v5p0327c2s
Stratton, G. v4p0606c1s
Stratton, G.M. v4p0326c1s
v4p0338c1s v4p0464c2s v5p0106c1s
v5p0576c1s v5p0583c2s v5p0606c1s
v5p0613c1m v5p0613c2s v6p0630c1s
Stratton, H.W. v5p0395c2s
v6p0157c2s v6p0437c2s
Stratton, J.Y. v1p0647c2s
v2p0168c2s
Stratton, M.C. v5p0493c2s
Stratton, Margaret v6p0264c1s
Stratton, S.W. v6p0613c1s
Stratton, S.W. and Michelson, A.A.
v5p0018c1s
Stratton, W. v1p1139c2s
Straub, J. v2p0389c2s
Straubenmueller, G. v6p0308c2s
Straus, N. v4p0096c2s
v4p0370c2s v4p0400c1s
Straus, O.S. v3p0358c1s
v4p0131c1s v4p0258c1s v4p0380c1s
v5p0120c1s v6p0146c1s v6p0318c1m
v6p0443c1m v6p0559c1s v6p0666c1s
Straus, O.S. et al. v4p0601c2s
Straus-Frank, V. v6p0239c1s
Strauss, D.F. et al. v4p0379c1s
Strauss, D.T. v1p0517c2s
Strauss, I.L. v5p0600c1s
Strauss, J. v3p0176c1s
v4p0229c2s v4p0365c1s v4p0542c1s
v6p0291c1s v6p0713c1s
Strauss, L.F. v6p0601c1s
Strauss, P. v6p0237c2s
Strauss, V.von v1p0231c1s
Strayler, A. v1p0626c2s
Streaker, G.H. v5p0150c2s
v5p0151c1s
Streatfield, G.S. v6p0065c1s
v6p0123c1s v6p0259c1s
Streatfield, R.A. v5p0062c1s
v5p0446c2s v6p0090c1s
Streator, M.L. v2p0235c2s
Strecey, R. v3p0169c1s
Streckenberg, J.W.H. v1p0690c1s
Streddler, E. v3p0354c2s
Street, A.B. v1p0034c1s
v1p0176c2s v1p0273c1s v1p0442c1s
v1p1151c2s
Street, A.E. v3p0112c2s
v3p0448c2s v3p0454c1s v3p0461c1s
v4p0171c1s
Street, A.L. v5p0310c2s
Street, C.S. v6p0705c1s
Street, F. v6p0377c1s
Street, G.E. v1p0054c2m
v1p1365c2s v2p0019c2s v5p0261c1s
Street, G.S. v4p0097c2s
v4p0276c1s v4p0340c1s v4p0572c1s
v5p0078c2s v5p0086c1m v5p0163c1s
v5p0216c1s v5p0219c1s v5p0239c2s
v5p0263c2s v5p0308c1s v5p0339c1s
v5p0519c2s v5p0524c2s v5p0525c2s
v5p0548c2s v5p0590c2s v5p0591c1s
v5p0617c2s v5p0645c1s v6p0046c2s
v6p0081c2m v6p0103c2s v6p0129c2s
v6p0157c1s v6p0172c2s v6p0185c2s
v6p0255c2s v6p0396c2s v6p0401c2s
v6p0496c1s v6p0520c2s v6p0522c1s
v6p0525c1s v6p0601c2s v6p0644c2s
v6p0662c2s v6p0678c2s v6p0709c1s
v6p0712c1s
Street, H. v2p0033c1s
Street, H.A. v3p0412c1s
Street, I.M. v3p0057c1s
v3p0134c2s v3p0387c2s v5p0192c1s
Street, I.M. and McMahon, L.
v3p0141c1s
Street, J.A. v5p0290c2s
Street, J.R. v5p0281c1s
v5p0325c1s v5p0386c1s
Street, Julian v6p0102c1s
v6p0440c1s
Street, L. v4p0324c2s
v4p0555c1s v4p0578c2s v4p0589c2s
v5p0491c1s
Street, O. v1p0122c1s
Street, W. v3p0214c2s
Street, W.C. v2p0163c2s
Street, W.D.C. v4p0118c2s
Streeter, A. v4p0338c2s
v4p0591c1s v5p0030c2s v5p0031c1s
v5p0310c1s v5p0387c2s v5p0450c2s
v5p0484c2s
Streeter, A. and Petre, M.D.
v5p0637c2s
Streeter, E.W. v4p0432c1s
Streeter, G.S. v3p0368c2m
v3p0464c1s
Streeter, L.C. v6p0143c1s
Streeter, R. v1p0867c2s
Streeter, S.F. v1p0056c2s
v1p0325c2s v1p1127c2s v1p1273c1s
Streeter, W.B. v6p0170c2s
Streets, T.H. v1p0188c2s
v1p0443c2s
Streissguth, W. v1p0333c2s
v1p0810c2s
Strela, K.N. v2p0216c1s
Strengell, G. v6p0608c1s
Streton, Col. v1p0394c2s
Strettell, A. v2p0094c1s
v2p0359c1s
Stretton, H. v2p0069c1s
v2p0112c2s v2p0214c2s v2p0383c2s
v2p0438c2s v3p0002c1s v4p0246c1s
Stretton, J. v1p0564c1s
v1p0680c1s v1p0939c2s v1p1092c2s
Stribling, T.S. v6p0606c2s
Stricker, S. v1p0816c2s
Strickland, A. v1p0510c1s
v1p0583c2s v1p0593c2s v1p1143c2s
Strickland, C.P. v1p1335c2s
Strickland, F.L. v6p0490c1s
Strickland, H.E. v1p1440c2s
Strickland, H.E. and Melville, A.G.
v1p0358c1s
Strickland, J. v1p1362c2s
Strickland, M. v2p0478c1s
v3p0468c1s
Strickland, M.W. v6p0201c2s
Strickland, T.A.G. v5p0449c1s
v5p0538c2s
Strickland, W. v1p1075c1s
Strickland, W.P. v1p0830c1s
v1p0852c1s
Stride, W.K. v4p0027c1s
v4p0166c2s v4p0420c1s v5p0199c1s
v5p0426c1s v5p0429c2s v5p0516c2s
v6p0163c1s
Strieby, M.E. v4p0282c2s
v4p0508c2s
Strigil v6p0559c1s
v6p0627c1s
Strindberg, A. v4p0343c1s
v4p0439c2s v6p0622c1s
Stringer, A. v5p0074c1s
v5p0262c2s v5p0637c1s v6p0362c1s
v6p0430c2s v6p0526c1s v6p0645c1s
Stringer, A.J. v4p0318c1s
v5p0187c1s v5p0421c1s v5p0539c2s
v5p0605c2s v5p0635c2s v6p0058c1s
Stringfellow, C.S. v1p0288c2s
Stringfellow, H. v3p0218c2s
Stringfellow, J. v1p0723c1s
Stringfield, T. v1p0684c1s
Stringham, I. v2p0348c1s
v6p0037c1s
Strobel, A. v3p0093c2s
v3p0164c1s
Strobel, E.H. v6p0292c2s
Strobel, W. v1p0063c1s
Strobel, W.D. v1p1023c1s
Strobell, A. v3p0320c1s
Strobridge, H.L. v3p0035c2s
v4p0087c2s
Strobridge, I.M. v5p0248c2s
v6p0280c1s v6p0568c1s
Strobridge, J.M. v6p0311c2s
v6p0501c2s v6p0612c2s
Strobridge, W.H. v1p0503c2s
Strode, W.S. v3p0045c1s
v3p0316c1s v4p0591c2s
Stroever, C. v5p0607c1s
Strohm, A.J. v6p0656c2s
Strombeck, H.von v3p0012c2m
v4p0016c1s v4p0073c1s
Stromeyer, C.E. v2p0199c1s
v2p0419c2s
Stromeyer, C.E. and Backhouse, T.W.
v3p0093c1s
Stromstadt, D.M. v6p0010c1s
Stronach, G. v4p0495c1s
v6p0046c2s v6p0586c2s
Strong, A.B. v5p0576c2s
Strong, A.H. v1p0999c2s
v2p0064c2s v2p0291c1s v2p0474c1m
v3p0119c1s v3p0175c1s v3p0207c2s
v3p0427c2s v4p0300c2s v6p0642c2s
Strong, Arthur v6p0070c2s
Strong, C.A. v3p0348c1s
v4p0130c1s v4p0371c2s v4p0421c1m
v4p0465c1s v4p0577c1s v6p0047c2s
v6p0195c2s v6p0306c2s
Strong, C.L. v4p0373c2s
Strong, C.S. v4p0295c1s
v4p0523c1s v5p0076c2s v6p0393c2s
Strong, C.Sorel v5p0612c2s
Strong, Clare v4p0485c2s
Strong, Clare S. v5p0197c1s
Strong, D.M. v5p0081c2s
Strong, E. v1p0127c1s
v1p0146c1s v1p0226c2s v1p0445c1s
v1p1043c2s v4p0039c2s
Strong, E.A. v5p0449c2s
Strong, E.E. v2p0069c2s
v5p0095c2s
Strong, Eliz.H. v5p0063c2s
Strong, Eugenie v6p0224c2s
Strong, F. v1p0552c1s
v5p0145c1s v5p0405c1s
Strong, F.L. v5p0444c2s
Strong, F.S. v5p0032c1s
Strong, G.A. v3p0343c2s
v4p0073c1s
Strong, G.A., Mrs. v6p0034c1s
Strong, G.D. v1p0237c2s
Strong, G.S. v2p0154c1s
Strong, H. v2p0184c2s
v4p0038c1s
Strong, H. and King, D.B.. v2p0248c1s
Strong, H.A. v2p0314c1s
v4p0092c1s v4p0432c2s v5p0387c2s
v6p0292c1s
Strong, H.M. v5p0051c1s
v5p0054c2s
Strong, H.W. v5p0086c2s
v5p0426c2s v6p0600c2s v6p0660c2s
Strong, H.W.R. v4p0423c1s
Strong, I. v5p0553c1m
Strong, I.O. v5p0553c1s
v6p0567c1s v6p0617c2s
Strong, Isobel v4p0549c1s
v5p0081c1s v5p0342c2s
Strong, J. v1p0097c1s
v1p0122c2s v1p0132c1s v1p0246c2m
v1p0395c2s v1p0416c1s v1p0495c2s
v1p0554c2s v1p0564c1s v1p0581c2s
v1p0686c1s v1p1088c1s v2p0042c2s
v2p0043c1s v3p0042c1s v3p0083c2s
v3p0086c1s v3p0193c1s v3p0427c2s
v4p0113c2s v4p0271c2s v4p0561c2s
v5p0118c2s v5p0119c2s v6p0419c2s
v6p0600c2s v6p0668c1s
Strong, J. and Dodge, W.E.
v3p0378c1s
Strong, J. and Russell, F.
v3p0084c2s
Strong, J. et al. v3p0242c2s
v4p0108c2s
Strong, J.L. v1p0187c1s
v1p0306c1s v1p0306c2s
Strong, J.W. v2p0307c2s
Strong, L.J. v6p0672c2s
Strong, P.B. v4p0362c1s
Strong, R.M. v4p0195c2s
v4p0209c2s v5p0527c2s
Strong, S.A. v4p0040c1s
v4p0256c2s v5p0160c1s v5p0348c2s
v6p0282c2s
Strong, T. v1p0423c1s
v1p0739c2s
Strong, W. v1p0736c1s
v1p1215c1s v1p1272c1s v1p1354c2s
v3p0416c2s v6p0637c2s
Strong, W.J. v5p0066c1s
Strong, W.L. v5p0119c2s
Strong, W.T. v4p0356c1s
v4p0539c2s v5p0197c1s v5p0261c1s
Strother, D.H. v1p0023c1s
v1p0084c1s v1p0089c2s v1p0155c2s
v1p0177c1s v1p0288c2s v1p0422c2s
v1p0487c1s v1p0805c1s v1p0809c1s
v1p0892c2s v1p0908c2s v1p0927c2s
v1p0986c1s v1p1126c1s v1p1346c1s
v1p1374c1s v1p1374c2m v1p1392c2s
v1p1406c2s
Strother, F. v6p0053c2s
v6p0325c1s v6p0409c1s v6p0456c2s
v6p0568c1s v6p0607c1s
Strother, French v6p0242c2s
v6p0393c2s
Strother, H.D. v1p1224c2s
Strother, H.E. v1p0354c2s
Strothers, D.H. v3p0377c2s
Stroud, W. v1p1418c2s
Stroudley, W. v2p0262c1s
Strouhal, V. and Barus, C.
v2p0101c2s v2p0419c2m v3p0409c1s
Stroumbo, D.S. v1p0400c1s
Stround, W. v5p0478c2s
Strouse, I.R. v3p0452c1s
Strout, J.W. v6p0216c2s
v6p0255c2s v6p0574c1s
Struder, B. v1p0155c1s
Strugis, R. v1p0246c1s
v5p0026c2s
Strugis, R.C. v5p0583c2s
Strugis, Russell v5p0322c2s
Strunk, W., jr. v5p0432c1s
Strunk, W., jr. and Robertson, D.C.
v3p0424c2s
Strunsky, S. v6p0250c1s
v6p0292c2s v6p0557c2s
Struthers, J. v2p0282c2s
v6p0412c1s
Struthers, P. v5p0006c1s

Strutt, E.C. v5p0300c1s
Strutt, J.W. v1p0278c2s
 v1p0399c1s
Strutt, R.J. v6p0526c2s
 v6p0527c1s
Struve, G.F. v1p0191c1s
Struve, O. v2p0417c2s
Stryker, G.L. v6p0133c2s
Stryker, H.B. v1p0153c2s
Stryker, W.S. v1p1171c1s
 v2p0354c2s v2p0427c2s v6p0516c2s
 v6p0656c2s
Stuart, A. v3p0204c2s
 v3p0462c1s v4p0088c2m v4p0394c2s
 v4p0614c1s v6p0622c2s
Stuart, A.F. v6p0532c1s
Stuart, A.H.H. et al. v2p0411c1s
 v2p0461c2s
Stuart, A.J.C. v5p0268c1s
Stuart, A.R. v5p0066c1s
Stuart, C. v2p0298c2s
 v4p0609c1s
Stuart, C.A. v4p0086c1s
Stuart, C.B. v1p0269c2s
 v1p0361c2s
Stuart, C.D. v1p1440c1s
 v6p0038c1s v6p0592c1s
Stuart, C.J. v6p0636c1s
Stuart, C.M. v4p0507c1s
 v5p0205c1s v5p0385c1s v5p0401c2s
 v6p0458c1s
Stuart, D.R. v6p0320c1s
Stuart, Dr. v2p0014c2s
Stuart, E. v1p1180c2s
 v2p0276c1s v2p0295c2s v2p0430c2s
 v3p0061c2s v3p0236c1s v3p0261c2s
 v3p0294c1s v3p0305c2s v3p0457c2s
 v4p0004c1s v4p0047c2s v4p0081c2s
 v4p0097c2s v4p0276c2s v4p0324c2s
 v4p0357c2s v4p0447c2s v4p0629c2s
 v5p0322c1s v6p0101c1s v6p0169c2s
 v6p0275c1s
Stuart, E.L. v6p0084c2s
Stuart, E.R. v6p0035c1s
 v6p0416c2s
Stuart, E.R. and Ruckman, J.W.
 v6p0168c2s
Stuart, Eleanor v5p0556c1s
 v6p0201c2s v6p0375c2s v6p0664c2s
Stuart, F. v5p0481c1s
Stuart, Frances v5p0544c2s
Stuart, G. v3p0196c1s
Stuart, G.A. v5p0264c2s
Stuart, G.B. v1p0514c2s
 v1p0572c1s v2p0104c2s v2p0451c1s
 v3p0052c2s v3p0088c2s v3p0187c2s
 v3p0284c2s v3p0407c2s v4p0065c2s
 v4p0164c1s v4p0393c1s v4p0405c1s
 v4p0554c1s v4p0572c1s v5p0036c1s
 v5p0038c2s v5p0078c2s v5p0387c2s
 v5p0464c2m v5p0483c1s v5p0634c1s
 v6p0319c1s v6p0515c2m
Stuart, G.P. v4p0536c2s
Stuart, H. v2p0262c2s
 v5p0143c1s v5p0213c1s v5p0261c1s
 v6p0658c1s
Stuart, H.M. v1p1056c2s
Stuart, H.W. v4p0230c2s
 v4p0599c2m
Stuart, J. v1p0352c1s
 v1p0788c1s v1p0899c2s v1p1163c2s
 v1p1262c1m v1p1336c2s v1p1388c1s
 v1p1431c2s v3p0336c1s v3p0404c2s
 v3p0445c1s v4p0340c2s v5p0108c2s
 v5p0284c1s v6p0520c2s
Stuart, J., Mrs. v4p0499c1s
Stuart, J.B. v4p0350c2s
Stuart, J.E.B. v1p0216c2s
 v1p0518c2s v1p1345c1s v1p1346c1s
 v2p0098c1s
Stuart, J.E.B. and Lee, F.
 v1p0704c2s
Stuart, J.M. v1p0669c1s
 v1p0670c2s v1p1117c1s v1p1369c2s
 v5p0170c1s
Stuart, L. v4p0080c1s
Stuart, L.E. and Sadler, M.E.
 v4p0597c2s
Stuart, M. v1p0038c2s
 v1p0059c1s v1p0074c1s v1p0096c2s
 v1p0117c2s v1p0119c2s v1p0120c2s
 v1p0121c2s v1p0122c2m v1p0124c1s
 v1p0126c1s v1p0126c2s v1p0127c2s
 v1p0128c2s v1p0129c1s v1p0130c1s
 v1p0262c1m v1p0373c2s v1p0378c1s
 v1p0393c1s v1p0496c1s v1p0507c1s
 v1p0521c2s v1p0554c1s v1p0555c1m
 v1p0581c2m v1p0713c2s v1p0769c2m
 v1p0933c2s v1p1056c1s v1p1200c2s
 v1p1406c2s
Stuart, M.P. v6p0694c1s
Stuart, M.S. v1p1056c2s
Stuart, N. v2p0227c2s
 v3p0258c2s v3p0350c1s v4p0505c2s
 v5p0081c2s v5p0570c2s
Stuart, O.K. v5p0620c2s
 v6p0295c2s
Stuart, P.C. v4p0052c1s
 v4p0058c2s v4p0145c1s v4p0620c1s
 v5p0026c2s v5p0129c1s v5p0407c2s
 v5p0572c2s v5p0621c1s
Stuart, Prof. and Nordheimer, Prof.
 v1p0581c1s
Stuart, R. v1p0079c2s
Stuart, R.M. v3p0176c2s
 v3p0241c1s v4p0070c2s v4p0110c2s
 v4p0369c2s v4p0529c2s v4p0537c1m
 v5p0040c2s v5p0415c1s v5p0597c2m
 v5p0638c2s v6p0250c1s v6p0420c2s
 v6p0491c1s v6p0690c1s
Stuart, R.McE. v3p0064c2s
 v3p0068c2s v3p0082c1s v3p0440c2s
 v3p0463c2s v4p0077c2s v4p0157c1s
 v4p0299c2s v4p0616c1s v4p0626c2s
 v5p0023c2s v5p0450c2s v5p0494c2s
 v5p0517c2s v6p0416c1s
Stuart, R.McE. and Paine, A.B.
 v4p0343c1s
Stuart, R.McEnery v4p0598c1s
Stuart, S.E. v5p0029c2s
 v5p0032c1s
Stuart, T.M. v4p0109c1s
 v4p0188c2s
Stuart, T.McK. v5p0281c1s
 v6p0214c1s v6p0340c2s
Stuart, V. v2p0133c2s
Stuart, W. v1p0261c2s
 v1p1382c2s
Stuart, W.L. v1p0185c2s
Stuart, W.M. v5p0550c2s
Stuart-Baker, H. v6p0696c2s
Stuart-Glennie, J.S. v1p0101c1s
 v1p0173c1s v2p0397c1s v3p0387c1s
 v4p0019c1s v4p0032c2s v4p0240c1s
 v5p0002c2s v5p0249c2s v5p0266c2s
 v5p0293c1s v6p0292c2s v6p0346c1s
Stuart-Langford, E. v5p0564c1s
 v5p0566c1s v5p0575c2s
Stuart-Langford, Eliz. ... v5p0379c2s
Stuart-Wortley, C. v4p0365c2s
Stuart-Wortley, E., Mrs. . v6p0061c2s
Stuart-Wortley, Edward, Mrs.
 v6p0205c1s v6p0236c1s
Stuart-Wortley, J., Mrs. . v3p0256c1s
Stubblefield, D.R. v6p0429c1s
Stubbs, C. v2p0024c1s
 v2p0040c2s
Stubbs, C.W. v2p0290c1s
 v2p0355c2s v5p0014c2s v5p0041c2s
 v5p0117c1s v6p0059c2s v6p0126c1s
 v6p0525c1s v6p0587c1s v6p0624c1s
Stubenrauch, A.V. v6p0092c2s
Stuck, H. v5p0397c2s
Stuckenberg, A. v2p0336c2s
Stuckenberg, H.C. v3p0361c1s
Stuckenberg, J.H.W. v1p0076c1s
 v1p0106c1s v1p0240c1s v1p0587c1s
 v1p0778c2s v1p0903c1s v2p0176c2s
 v2p0177c1m v2p0389c1s v2p0437c2s
 v2p0439c1m v3p0039c1s v3p0171c1s
 v3p0171c2m v3p0225c1s v3p0354c1s
 v3p0428c2s v3p0468c2s v5p0489c2s
Stuckenberg, J.H.W., Mrs.. v2p0375c2s
Studd, A.H. v4p0540c1s
Studer, A.G. v2p0404c2s
Studley, P. v5p0269c2s
 v5p0531c1s
Studnitz, A.P. v2p0115c2s
Stuebel, A. and Reiss, W.. v1p0382c2s
Stukeley, W. v1p1402c1s
Stull, A.F. v6p0026c2s
Stump, A. v2p0085c2s
 v3p0070c1s v3p0239c1s v3p0261c1s
 v4p0053c1s v4p0337c1s v5p0292c2s
 v6p0123c2s v6p0390c1s v6p0483c1s
Stumpf, C. v4p0254c1s
 v4p0465c1s
Sturdee, J. v6p0420c1s
Sturdee, R.J. v5p0228c1s
 v6p0231c2s v6p0685c1s
Sturdy, E.W. v1p0057c1s
 v1p0804c1s v2p0244c1s v2p0463c1s
Sturge, J.M. v6p0597c1s
Sturge, L.J. v6p0425c1s
Sturgeon, E. v5p0260c1s
Sturgeon, J. v2p0006c1s
 v2p0396c1s
Sturgeon, W. v1p0077c1s
 v1p0498c2s
Sturges, J. v3p0093c2s
 v3p0287c1s v3p0462c2s
Sturges, M.U. v1p1358c2s
Sturges, O. et al. v1p0934c1s
Sturgis, D. v4p0064c1s
 v4p0311c1s
Sturgis, D.N.B. v6p0056c1s
 v6p0081c1s v6p0540c1s
Sturgis, Dinah v5p0499c2s
Sturgis, F.R. v2p0282c1s
Sturgis, H.O. v5p0420c1s
Sturgis, J. v1p0048c2s
 v1p0834c1s v2p0189c2s v2p0266c1s
 v2p0271c1s v2p0304c1s v2p0377c1s
 v3p0077c1s v3p0219c2s v3p0337c2s
 v3p0429c2s
Sturgis, J.R. v1p1187c2s
Sturgis, N. v1p0808c1s
 v1p0884c1s v1p0884c2s
Sturgis, R. v1p0053c2s
 v1p0882c1s
 v1p0064c1m v1p0203c1s v1p0212c2s
 v1p0213c1s v1p0321c1s v1p0328c2s
 v1p0361c1s v1p0370c2s v1p0425c2s
 v1p0460c2s v1p0490c2s v1p0537c1s
 v1p0542c1s v1p0677c2s v1p0678c2s
 v1p0703c2s v1p0734c1s v1p0751c1s
 v1p0824c2s v1p0834c2s v1p0865c1s
 v1p0958c2s v1p0959c1s v1p0966c1s
 v1p0968c2m v1p0997c1s v1p1039c2s
 v1p1045c2s v1p1048c1s v1p1098c1s
 v1p1101c1s v1p1132c2m v1p1276c1s
 v1p1298c1s v1p1361c2s v1p1372c2s
 v1p1414c2s v1p1427c2s v2p0026c2s
 v2p0070c1s v2p0231c1s v2p0377c2s
 v2p0392c2m v2p0430c2s v2p0458c2m
 v3p0121c1s v3p0177c2s v3p0183c2s
 v3p0202c1s v3p0382c2m v4p0023c2s
 v4p0024c2s v4p0227c2s v4p0326c1s
 v4p0381c1s v4p0421c2s v4p0467c2s
 v4p0510c2s v5p0025c1m v5p0025c2s
 v5p0026c1s v5p0026c2s v5p0031c2s
 v5p0121c2s v5p0123c1s v5p0133c1s
 v5p0156c1m v5p0160c2s v5p0161c2s
 v5p0207c1s v5p0207c2s v5p0254c2s
 v5p0272c1s v5p0276c1s v5p0303c2s
 v5p0387c2m v5p0392c2s v5p0431c1s
 v5p0453c2s v5p0464c1s v5p0499c2s
 v5p0521c1s v5p0554c1s v5p0556c1s
 v5p0632c2s v6p0027c2s v6p0028c1m
 v6p0028c2m v6p0033c1s v6p0034c1m
 v6p0035c2s v6p0045c1s v6p0113c1s
 v6p0113c2s v6p0128c2s v6p0138c1s
 v6p0139c1m v6p0179c1s v6p0288c1s
 v6p0402c1s v6p0595c1s
Sturgis, R. and Cox, K. .. v5p0447c2s
Sturgis, R. and Crowninshield, F.
 v5p0324c2s
Sturgis, R. and Fowler, F.
 v6p0570c2s
Sturgis, R. and Lawton, W.C.
 v6p0505c1s
Sturgis, R. and Peirce, C.S.
 v1p0246c1s
Sturgis, R. and Pennell, E.R.
 v5p0156c2s
Sturgis, R., jr. v1p0054c1s
 v1p0054c2s v1p0062c1s v1p1133c1s
 v3p0051c2s v3p0475c1m
Sturgis, R.C. v4p0555c1s
 v5p0025c2s v5p0073c1s v5p0225c2s
 v5p0226c1s v5p0496c1s v6p0052c1s
 v6p0148c2s v6p0187c2s
Sturgis, Russell v3p0051c1s
 v4p0211c2s v5p0025c2s v5p0030c2s
 v5p0031c2s v5p0048c2s v5p0097c1s
 v5p0373c2s v6p0033c1s v6p0033c2s
 v6p0076c2m v6p0080c2s v6p0084c1s
 v6p0085c1s v6p0104c2s v6p0156c1s
 v6p0167c2m v6p0171c2s v6p0179c1s
 v6p0195c1s v6p0217c1s v6p0217c2s
 v6p0224c2s v6p0225c2m v6p0298c1s
 v6p0323c2s v6p0338c2s v6p0358c2s
 v6p0420c1s v6p0433c1s v6p0452c1s
 v6p0453c2m v6p0454c1m v6p0474c2s
 v6p0475c1s v6p0479c2s v6p0497c1s
 v6p0510c1s v6p0511c2s v6p0517c1s
 v6p0555c1s v6p0564c2s v6p0572c2s
 v6p0604c1s v6p0651c1s v6p0685c2s
 v6p0686c1s v6p0700c2s v6p0706c2s
Sturgis, T. v1p1254c2m
Sturgis, W. v1p0494c2s
 v1p0929c1s
Sturley, J.M. v2p0251c1s
Sturt, B.M. v5p0558c1s
Sturt, H. v4p0129c2s
 v5p0172c1s v5p0249c2s v5p0519c1s
 v5p0531c2s v5p0560c2s v6p0123c1s
Sturtevant, E.D. v4p0021c2s
 v6p0487c1s
Sturtevant, E.L. v1p0207c2s
 v2p0053c1s v2p0072c1s v2p0103c1s
 v2p0111c1s v2p0146c1s v2p0212c2s
 v2p0254c2s v2p0272c2s v2p0394c1s
 v3p0447c2s
Sturtevant, J. v1p0627c2s
Sturtevant, J.M. v1p0060c2s
 v1p0087c2s v1p0117c2s v1p0203c2s
 v1p0247c2s v1p0275c2m v1p0276c1s
 v1p0279c2s v1p0323c1s v1p0393c1s
 v1p0708c2s v1p0714c1s v1p0848c1s
 v1p0872c1s v1p0905c1s v1p0928c2s
 v1p1026c2s v1p1058c2s v1p1092c2s
 v1p1175c2s v1p1264c2s v1p1286c1s
 v1p1345c1s v1p1354c1s v1p1357c2s
 v2p0248c1s
Stutfield, G.H. v3p0166c2s
 v3p0351c2s v5p0475c2s
Stutfield, H.E.M. v3p0073c1s
 v3p0401c1m v4p0035c1s v4p0042c1s
 v4p0093c2s v4p0095c2m v4p0135c1s
 v4p0288c2s v4p0335c1s v4p0579c1s
 v5p0131c1s v5p0207c1s v5p0265c1s
 v5p0270c1s v5p0387c1s v5p0491c2s
 v5p0635c2s v6p0596c2s
Stutz, E. v6p0014c1s
 v6p0643c1s
Stutz, M.S. v1p0759c2s
Stutzer, A. v1p0148c2s
 v1p1299c2s
Stuxberg, A. v2p0393c1s

Styles, C.W. v6p0713c2s
Styles, G. v5p0185c1s
v6p0349c1s
Suares, A. v5p0434c2s
Suckert, J.J. and Willson, T.L.
v4p0002c2s v4p0089c1s
Sudduth, H.T. v6p0467c1s
Sudduth, M.A. v4p0083c2s
v4p0217c1s
Sudeley, Lady v3p0188c2s
Sudermann, H. v5p0308c2s
v5p0386c2s v5p0578c2s v6p0325c2s
v6p0451c2s v6p0563c1s
Sudley, G. v5p0351c1s
Sudworth, G.B. v4p0208c2s
v4p0444c1s
Suess, E. v1p0025c2s
v4p0410c2s v6p0298c2s
Sueur, E.A.Le v4p0291c2s
v4p0403c2m
Sueur, W.D.Le v1p0115c1s
v1p0201c2s v1p0318c1s v1p0427c1s
v1p0435c1s v1p0623c1s v1p0648c2s
v1p0810c2s v1p0869c1s v1p0869c2m
v1p0976c2s v1p1041c2m v1p1055c1s
v1p1164c1s v1p1235c1s v2p0149c1m
v2p0149c2s v2p0215c2s v2p0280c1s
v2p0293c2s v2p0341c1s v2p0348c1s
v2p0350c1s v2p0414c1s v3p0104c1m
v3p0145c2s v3p0313c2s v3p0379c2s
v4p0171c1s v4p0532c1s v4p0610c1s
Sueur, W.Le v1p0060c2s
v1p0741c2s
Suffern, J.W. v4p0527c2s
Suffield, R.R. v1p0859c2s
v2p0370c1s v2p0376c2s v5p0316c2s
Suffling, E.R. v5p0180c2s
v5p0235c2s v5p0347c1s v5p0413c2s
v5p0548c1s v6p0707c1s
Suffolk, Earl of v4p0195c1s
v4p0210c2s
Suffolk, Earl of and
Berkshire, Earl of v5p0216c1s
Sugg, W. v2p0172c1m
v3p0167c2s
Sugiyama, S. v4p0297c2s
v4p0318c2s v4p0565c1s
Suha, E. v1p0795c2s
v1p0909c1s
Suhrawardy, A.M. v6p0330c1s
Sui, Sin Fah v5p0113c1s
v6p0120c1s
Sulley, J. v3p0348c2s
Sulley, J.P. v3p0080c1s
Sulley, R. v1p0093c2s
v1p0198c1s v1p0324c2s v1p0325c1s
v1p0486c2s v1p0713c1s v1p0860c1s
v1p0860c2m v1p0861c1s v1p1026c2s
v1p1027c1s v1p1057c1s v1p1394c1s
Sullivan, A. v1p0615c1s
v2p0228c2s v2p0451c2s v3p0221c1s
v3p0322c1s v4p0010c2s v4p0344c2s
v5p0267c1s
Sullivan, A.M. v1p0656c1s
v2p0225c1s
Sullivan, Capt. v1p0441c2s
Sullivan, E. v6p0074c1s
v6p0275c2s
Sullivan, E. and Manchester, Duke of
v1p0486c2s
Sullivan, I.T. v4p0386c1s
Sullivan, J. v5p0363c2s
v5p0417c2s v5p0631c2s v6p0403c1s
Sullivan, J.E. v5p0082c1s
v6p0466c2m
Sullivan, J.F. v4p0095c2s
v4p0126c2s v4p0158c1s v4p0578c1s
v4p0598c2s
Sullivan, J.L. v1p0357c1s
v1p0650c1s v1p0801c1s v1p1079c2m
v1p1225c2s v1p1247c1s v1p1249c1s
Sullivan, J.M. v5p0075c2m
v5p0634c1s v6p0041c1s v6p0235c1s
v6p0350c2s v6p0463c1s v6p0484c1m
v6p0648c2s
Sullivan, J.W. v3p0356c1s
Sullivan, K.F.M. v4p0397c2s
v4p0554c2s v5p0075c2s v5p0280c2s
v5p0356c2s
Sullivan, K.L. v6p0426c2s
Sullivan, L.H. v4p0024c2s
v4p0025c1s v5p0026c2s v6p0028c1s
v6p0028c2s
Sullivan, M. v1p0104c1s
v1p0340c1s v1p1261c2s v5p0409c2s
v6p0030c1s v6p0149c1s v6p0200c2s
v6p0614c2s
Sullivan, M.C. v6p0337c2s
v6p0594c1s
Sullivan, M.F. v1p0095c2s
v1p0201c1s v1p0347c1s v1p0511c2s
v1p0537c2s v1p0657c2m v1p0658c1s
v1p0660c2s v1p0721c2s v1p1021c2s
v1p1022c2s v1p1116c1s v1p1335c1s
v1p1423c2s v2p0077c1s v2p0117c1s
v2p0123c1s v2p0131c1s v2p0206c1s
v2p0225c2s v2p0227c2s v2p0303c2s
v2p0312c1s v2p0364c2s v3p0277c1s
v5p0341c1s v5p0493c2s v6p0462c2s
Sullivan, M.F., Mrs. v1p0032c1s
Sullivan, Mark v6p0093c2s
v6p0508c1s
Sullivan, P.O. v1p0570c2s
v1p1279c2s
Sullivan, T.R. v3p0013c1s
v3p0088c1s v3p0100c2s v3p0258c2s
v3p0263c2s v3p0315c2s v3p0363c1s
v3p0413c2s v3p0429c2s v3p0431c2s
v4p0028c2s v4p0069c1s v4p0295c2s
v4p0352c2s v4p0438c1s v4p0571c2s
v4p0572c1s v4p0578c1s v4p0590c1s
v4p0590c2s v4p0619c2s v5p0133c2s
v5p0274c2s v5p0343c2s v5p0355c1s
v5p0524c2s v6p0012c1s v6p0255c2s
v6p0279c1s v6p0376c2s v6p0547c1s
v6p0662c1s
Sullivan, W. v1p0384c2s
v1p0495c2s v1p0932c2s
Sullivan, W.C. v6p0011c2s
v6p0223c1s v6p0323c1s v6p0402c2s
v6p0436c2s
Sullivan, W.H. v4p0374c1s
Sullivan, W.L. v5p0115c1s
v5p0379c2s v5p0380c1s v6p0123c1s
v6p0321c1s v6p0335c2s v6p0359c2s
v6p0396c2s v6p0421c2s
Sullivan, W.R. v4p0375c2s
v4p0479c1s v4p0489c1s v4p0532c2s
v4p0601c1s
Sully, D.J. v6p0152c2s
Sully, J. v1p0009c1m
v1p0041c1s v1p0042c2s v1p0061c2s
v1p0218c1s v1p0259c2s v1p0278c2s
v1p0279c1s v1p0366c1s v1p0436c2s
v1p0452c2s v1p0468c2s v1p0612c2s
v1p0640c2s v1p0647c1s v1p0651c1s
v1p0760c1s v1p0760c2s v1p0819c1s
v1p0884c1s v1p0885c1m v1p0885c2s
v1p0924c2s v1p0943c2s v1p0957c2s
v1p0984c1s v1p1001c2s v1p1017c2s
v1p1062c1s v1p1067c2s v1p1164c1s
v1p1196c2s v1p1222c1s v1p1222c2s
v1p1234c2s v1p1375c1m v2p0003c2s
v2p0009c1s v2p0015c1s v2p0097c1s
v2p0149c1s v2p0173c1m v2p0201c1s
v2p0221c2s v2p0238c2s v2p0259c2s
v2p0266c2s v2p0283c2s v2p0297c1s
v2p0350c1s v2p0352c1s v2p0439c2s
v2p0442c2s v2p0459c2s v3p0095c1s
v3p0120c1s v3p0122c2s v3p0123c2s
v3p0124c1s v3p0129c2s v3p0151c2s
v3p0164c2s v3p0274c2s v3p0333c1s
v3p0348c2s v3p0355c2s v3p0432c1s
v3p0449c1s v4p0103c1m v4p0128c1s
v4p0161c1s v4p0161c2s v4p0196c1s
v4p0274c2s v4p0465c1m v4p0475c1s
v5p0105c2s v5p0106c1s v5p0165c1s
v5p0275c2s v5p0327c1m v5p0446c2s
v6p0114c1s v6p0279c1s v6p0593c2s
v6p0616c2s v6p0646c1s
Sully, J. and Allen, Grant
v1p0009c1s
Sully, James v3p0168c2s
v3p0336c2s
Sully, T. v1p1062c1s
v6p0115c2s
Sully-Prudhomme v3p0175c1s
v3p0209c1s
Sulman, T. v4p0121c2s
v4p0246c1s v4p0250c1s v4p0587c1s
Sulman, Thos. v4p0393c2s
v5p0031c2s v5p0566c2s
Sulte, B. v5p0305c1s
v6p0241c2s v6p0272c1s
Sulzberger, C.I. v6p0309c1s
Sulzberger, C.L. v6p0343c1s
Sulzberger, M. v1p0690c2s
v1p0925c1s
Sumichrast, De v6p0097c2s
Sumichrast, F.C. v3p0473c2m
v3p0474c1s
Sumichrast, F.C.de v4p0249c1s
v4p0361c2s v4p0518c2s v5p0172c1s
v5p0256c2s v5p0275c1s v6p0249c1s
v6p0302c1s
Summer, W.G. v3p0360c2s
Summer, W.G. and Hadley, A.T.
v2p0100c2s
Summers, E.B. v6p0461c1s
Summers, W. v1p0486c2s
v3p0182c2s v3p0231c2s v3p0240c2s
v3p0288c1s v4p0227c2s
Summers, Wm. v3p0162c1s
Sumner, A. v4p0074c2s
Sumner, C. v1p0029c2s
v1p0312c2s v1p0560c1s v1p0623c2s
v1p0886c1s v1p1052c1s v1p1052c2s
v1p1219c1s v1p1257c1s v1p1348c2s
v1p1350c1s
Sumner, C.P. v2p0220c1s
v2p0314c2s
Sumner, Canon v2p0084c1s
Sumner, E.V. v3p0446c1s
Sumner, F.B. v6p0226c2s
v6p0608c2s v6p0706c2m
Sumner, G. v1p0552c2s
v3p0405c1s
Sumner, G.H. v1p1109c2s
Sumner, H. v3p0386c2s
v5p0030c2s v6p0319c2s
Sumner, Heywood v5p0639c2s
v6p0586c1s
Sumner, J.R.E. v5p0572c2s
v6p0349c1s v6p0531c1s v6p0638c1s
Sumner, J.S. v1p1117c2s
Sumner, Mary O. v6p0129c2s
Sumner, W.G. v1p0034c1s
v1p0114c1s v1p0133c2s v1p0232c1s
v1p0235c2s v1p0275c2s v1p0325c1s
v1p0398c2s v1p0421c2s v1p0540c1s
v1p0709c1s v1p0860c2s v1p1025c2s
v1p1027c1s v1p1031c1s v1p1048c1s
v1p1057c2s v1p1085c2s v1p1161c1s
v1p1198c2s v1p1215c2s v1p1217c1s
v1p1349c1s v1p1352c1s v1p1358c1s
v2p0092c2s v2p0245c2s v2p0347c2s
v2p0348c1s v2p0357c1s v2p0407c2s
v2p0408c2s v2p0430c2s v2p0463c2s
v3p0086c2s v3p0115c1s v3p0213c1s
v3p0215c1s v3p0248c1s v3p0279c1s
v3p0399c1s v3p0408c1s v4p0045c1s
v4p0162c2s v4p0230c1s v4p0380c1s
v4p0534c2s v4p0597c1s v5p0125c1s
v5p0281c2s v5p0525c2s v5p0544c1s
Sumner, W.G. and Walker, F.A.
v1p0133c2s
Sumner, W.G. et al. v2p0403c1s
Sumner, W.H. v1p0175c2s
v1p0402c2s v1p0569c1s v1p0612c2s
v1p0717c2s v1p1267c1m v1p1388c2s
Sumulong, J. v6p0494c2s
Sun, Yat Sen v5p0111c1s
Sundberg, J.C. v3p0354c1s
Sunderland, B. v2p0382c1s
Sunderland, E.M. v6p0484c1s
Sunderland, J.T. v1p1044c2s
v1p1341c1s v5p0285c1s v5p0286c1m
v5p0317c1s
Sunderland, L. v1p1045c1s
v1p1141c1s
Sundermann, H. v3p0305c1s
Sunterland, L. and Reese, D.M.
v1p1301c2s
Super, C.H. v1p0384c2s
Super, C.W. v1p0021c1m
v1p1377c2s v3p0402c2s v4p0011c2s
v4p0109c1s v4p0123c2s v4p0321c2s
v4p0532c2s v4p0597c1s v4p0597c2s
v5p0033c2s v5p0121c1s v5p0195c2s
v5p0196c1m v5p0248c2s v5p0263c1s
v5p0267c1m v5p0358c1s v5p0399c2s
v6p0193c2s v6p0211c2s v6p0361c2s
v6p0380c1s v6p0495c2s v6p0498c1s
v6p0521c2s v6p0566c1s v6p0607c2s
v6p0637c2s v6p0678c1s
Super, H.W. v1p1090c2s
Super, O.B. v3p0014c1s
v3p0023c1s v5p0614c1s
Super, R.C. v5p0542c2s
v6p0018c1s
Suplee, H.H. v4p0138c1s
v4p0288c2s v4p0403c2s v4p0504c1s
v4p0613c2s v5p0002c2s v5p0025c1s
v5p0431c2s v6p0204c2s v6p0413c2s
Surette, T.W. v6p0056c2s
v6p0279c1s v6p0284c1s v6p0433c2s
v6p0439c1s v6p0575c1s v6p0575c2s
v6p0683c1s
Surface, G.T. v6p0680c1s
Suring, R. v6p0040c1s
Surr, Mrs. v1p0700c2s
Surrage, E.J.R. v4p0391c2s
v5p0613c2s
Surrette, T.W. v5p0640c1s
Surtees, F.R. v2p0053c2s
Surtees, W.E. v1p0322c2s
v1p1353c2s
Surveyer, E.F. v5p0474c1s
Sutcliff, R. v1p1397c2s
Sutcliffe, C. v4p0244c1s
v4p0587c1s v5p0424c1s v5p0510c1s
Sutcliffe, H. v5p0036c1s
v5p0351c2s v6p0362c1s v6p0467c1s
Sutcliffe, J.D. v6p0285c1s
Sutcliffe, S. v6p0246c1s
Suter, G.A. v5p0260c2s
Suter, H.M. v6p0232c2s
v6p0233c1s v6p0233c2s
Sutherland, A. v1p0122c1s
v1p0395c1s v2p0403c2s v4p0046c1s
v4p0431c1s v5p0179c1s v5p0486c1s
v5p0572c1s v5p0619c2s v5p0635c1s
v6p0469c1s
Sutherland, A.T. v6p0107c2s
Sutherland, Allan v6p0128c2s
Sutherland, D. v4p0492c1s
v5p0342c1s
Sutherland, D.M. v5p0638c2s
Sutherland, Duchess of ... v5p0321c1s
Sutherland, E. v5p0224c1s
Sutherland, E.L. v6p0219c1s
Sutherland, G. v3p0373c2s
v3p0393c2s
Sutherland, H. v4p0268c1m
v6p0247c2s v6p0418c1s v6p0431c2s
v6p0596c2s v6p0615c1s
Sutherland, J. v1p0539c2s
v5p0514c1s
Sutherland, J.C. v6p0204c2s
Sutherland, J.R. v4p0382c1s

Sutherland, M. v4p0224c2s
v6p0702c2s
Sutherland, P.M. v3p0296c1s
Sutherland, W. v2p0446c1s
v6p0470c1s
Sutherland, W.A. v6p0144c2s
Sutlive, W.G. v5p0509c2s
v5p0642c2s
Sutphen, H.R. v5p0041c1s
v5p0226c2s
Sutphen, J.M. v2p0474c1s
Sutphen, J.Q. v6p0363c1s
Sutphen, M.C. v1p0792c2s
v5p0469c2s
Sutphen, V.T. v5p0573c2s
Sutphen, Van T. v6p0059c2s
v6p0090c2s v6p0112c2s v6p0166c2s
v6p0234c1s v6p0261c1m v6p0299c1s
v6p0323c2s v6p0396c1s v6p0415c2s
v6p0511c2s v6p0608c2s
Sutphen, W.G.V.T. v5p0566c2s
Sutphen, W.T.van Tassel .. v5p0239c1s
Sutro, A. v6p0080c1s
v6p0388c1s
Sutro, T. v1p1273c2s
v6p0114c2s
Sutter, J. v2p0472c1s
v2p0473c1s v2p0480c2s
Suttner, B.von v5p0437c1s
v5p0437c2s
Sutton, C.H. v6p0413c2s
Sutton, C.T. v6p0377c2s
Sutton, C.W. v2p0054c1s
v2p0256c2s v2p0275c1m v2p0366c1s
Sutton, E. v6p0287c1s
Sutton, E.V. v4p0149c2s
v4p0171c2s v4p0309c2s
Sutton, Elizabeth v5p0315c2s
Sutton, F. v3p0338c1s
Sutton, G. v1p1309c1s
Sutton, H. v1p1020c1s
v3p0077c1s v3p0083c2s v4p0103c1s
v4p0103c2s
Sutton, J.R. v2p0296c2s
v2p0417c2s v3p0279c1s v3p0407c2s
v4p0369c1s v4p0460c2s
Sutton, J.R. and Eliot, J.
v6p0531c1s
Sutton, S.W. v1p0241c2s
v2p0081c2s v3p0444c2s
Sutton, W. v1p0646c2s
v1p0900c2s v1p1336c2s v2p0118c1s
v2p0367c1s v2p0423c1m v3p0036c2s
v3p0178c2s v3p0198c1s v3p0250c2s
Sutton, W.A. v1p1085c1s
v1p1086c1s v3p0466c1s v5p0565c1s
Sutton, W.P. v5p0460c2s
Sutton, W.S. v5p0157c1s
v5p0574c2s v6p0581c2s
Suydam, A. v1p0031c1s
v1p0275c1s v1p1054c1s
Suydam, J.H. v3p0456c1s
Suyematsu, Baron v6p0186c2s
v6p0280c1s v6p0285c1s v6p0334c1m
v6p0335c1s v6p0335c2s v6p0336c1s
v6p0336c2s v6p0440c1s v6p0555c2s
v6p0560c1s v6p0560c2s
Suyematsu, K. v6p0335c1s
v6p0416c1s
Suzuki, S. v6p0336c1s
Suzuki, T. v5p0003c2s
v5p0081c2s v6p0086c2s
Suzuki, T. and Carus, P. . v5p0325c2s
v5p0566c2s
Suzuki, Teitaro v5p0132c2s
Suzzatti, S. v6p0009c1s
Svendsen, C.C. v5p0055c1s
v5p0305c1s
Svenson, J. v5p0631c1s
Sverdrup, O. and Schei, P.
v6p0236c1s
Swaffam, J. v6p0515c2s
Swain, C.F. v6p0286c2s
Swain, D.L. v1p0638c1s
Swain, G.F. v1p0051c1s
v1p0104c1s v1p1255c2s v2p0127c2s
v2p0458c2s v3p0457c1s v5p0570c1s
Swain, G.R. v6p0617c1s
Swain, H.H. v5p0468c2s
v5p0477c2m
Swain, J. v3p0039c1s
v3p0135c2s v3p0332c2s v3p0453c1s
v5p0284c1s v6p0180c1s v6p0369c2s
v6p0386c2s v6p0406c2s v6p0442c2s
v6p0577c1s
Swain, L. v1p0290c1s
v1p0688c2s v1p1172c1s
Swaine, S.A. v2p0125c2s
Swainson, C.A. v1p0284c2s
Swainson, E.G. v3p0386c1s
Swainson, F. v5p0232c2s
Swainson, G. v4p0369c2s
Swainson, J. v2p0047c2s
v2p0233c1s v2p0269c1s
Swallow, C.W. v4p0060c1s
Swallow, G.C. v1p0508c2s
v2p0106c2s v2p0148c2s v2p0149c2s
Swallow, R.W. v6p0118c2s
Swallow, S.C. v6p0519c1m
Swallow, W.H. v2p0098c1s
v2p0166c2s v2p0177c2s
v2p0438c2s
Swalm, P., Mrs. v1p0540c1s
Swan, A.M. v6p0618c2s
Swan, A.S. v3p0102c2s
v3p0264c2s v4p0342c1s v5p0481c1s
v5p0628c1s
Swan, Annie S. v3p0463c1s
Swan, C. v3p0277c2s
v3p0307c2s
Swan, J.C. v3p0121c1s
Swan, J.G. v1p0035c1s
Swan, J.N. v6p0135c2s
Swan, J.W. v2p0137c1m
v4p0177c1s v5p0185c2s
Swan, K.R. v6p0704c2s
Swan, M. v5p0598c1s
Swan, R.M.W. v4p0359c1s
Swan, R.T. v4p0159c2s
v4p0284c2s v4p0424c2s v5p0094c2s
Swan, S.H. v5p0072c2s
Swan, W. v2p0463c1s
Swan, W.D. v1p0285c1s
v5p0257c1s
Swander, J.I. v1p0242c1s
v1p0314c2s v1p0685c1s v1p0966c1s
v1p1317c2s v2p0195c1s v5p0116c1s
v5p0266c2s v5p0576c2s v5p0577c1s
Swank, J.M. v4p0292c1s
v6p0530c2s
Swank, J.W. v6p0487c2s
Swann, E.H. v1p0286c2s
Swann, J. v2p0248c1s
Swann, J.S. v1p1113c1s
Swann, M.F. v1p0116c2s
Swann, N.E.E. v5p0120c1s
Swanton, J.R. v5p0113c2s
v5p0126c1s v5p0563c2m v6p0129c2s
v6p0218c2s v6p0277c2m v6p0317c1s
v6p0650c2s
Swanwick, A. v1p0434c1s
Swanwick, F. v1p0698c1s
Swart, Rose C. v2p0322c2s
Swartwout, C.E. v4p0281c1s
Swartz, H.B. v3p0471c2s
Swartz, J. v1p0069c1s
v1p0980c1s v1p1237c1s
Swartz, L.K. v2p0432c2s
Swarzfeld, F. v6p0343c2s
Swasey, A.C. v1p0735c1s
Swasey, G.R. v3p0051c1s
Swayne, E. v4p0069c1s
v4p0099c1s v4p0100c1s v4p0364c1s
v4p0602c2s v5p0052c1m v5p0075c1m
v5p0233c1s v5p0276c1m v5p0325c2s
v5p0368c2s v5p0393c2s v5p0423c2s
v5p0450c1s v5p0450c2s v5p0560c1s
v5p0616c1s v6p0016c1s v6p0438c2s
v6p0439c1s v6p0443c1s v6p0468c2s
v6p0474c1s
Swayne, Egbert v5p0081c2s
v5p0422c1s v5p0530c2s v5p0539c1s
Swayne, G.C. v1p0016c1s
v1p0025c2m v1p0048c2s v1p0139c2s
v1p0361c1s v1p0487c2s v1p0519c2s
v1p0525c1s v1p0642c1s v1p0666c1s
v1p0681c2s v1p0682c1s v1p0750c2s
v1p0770c1s v1p0789c1m v1p0874c2s
v1p0937c2s v1p1177c1s v1p1219c1s
v1p1337c1s v1p1358c2s v1p1396c2s
v1p1397c1s v1p1409c2s v1p1440c1s
v2p0226c2s v3p0418c1s
Swayne, M. v1p1389c2s
v1p1419c1s
Swayne, W. v1p1389c1s
Swayze, F.J. v6p0518c1s
Sweat, M.J., Mrs. v1p0167c1s
v1p0932c2s
Sweat, M.J.M. v1p0780c2s
Sweeney, C.P. v5p0147c1s
v5p0151c1s
Sweeney, G.M. v1p1322c2s
Sweeney, H.M. v4p0179c1s
v4p0275c1s v4p0296c1s v4p0400c2s
v4p0612c2s
Sweeney, J.S. v1p0095c2s
v1p0096c1s
Sweeney, Z.T. v5p0249c2s
v5p0382c1s
Sweeny, E.M. v2p0482c2s
Sweet, A.C. v5p0459c1s
Sweet, C. v4p0007c1s
v4p0108c1s v4p0278c1s v4p0454c1s
v4p0513c2s v4p0585c2s v5p0441c1s
v5p0468c2s v6p0489c1s
Sweet, C. and Sanger, C.P.
v6p0151c1s
Sweet, E.M. v6p0471c1s
Sweet, Emelie T. v2p0377c1s
Sweet, F.H. v4p0267c1s
v4p0342c1s v4p0554c1s v5p0062c2s
v5p0085c2s v5p0089c1s v5p0339c1s
v5p0361c2s v5p0397c1s v5p0438c1s
v6p0067c1s v6p0081c1s v6p0227c1s
v6p0504c1s v6p0610c2s
Sweet, Frank A. v6p0275c1s
Sweet, Frank H. v6p0165c2s
v6p0291c2s v6p0663c1s
Sweet, H. v1p0723c2s
v2p0143c2s v2p0145c2s v2p0339c2s
Sweet, H. and Lee, S.L. .. v2p0144c1s
Sweet, J.B. v2p0168c2s
v3p0345c1s
Sweet, J.D. v2p0474c2m
Sweet, J.E. v1p1316c1s
v3p0262c2s v4p0153c1s v4p0347c1s
v4p0444c2s v4p0547c1m v5p0367c2s
v6p0615c2m
Sweet, M. v4p0602c2s
Sweet, O.J. v5p0560c1s
Sweeting, R.D.R. v2p0354c2s
Sweetman, G. v5p0297c2s
Sweetman, W. v5p0337c2s
v5p0422c2s v6p0326c2s v6p0327c1s
Sweetser, A.L. v5p0125c1s
Sweetser, E.C. v2p0455c2s
v3p0026c1s v3p0229c1s
Sweetser, S. v1p0001c1s
v1p0115c1s v1p0120c1s v1p1328c2s
Swem, E.G. v5p0061c1s
Swenson, B.V. v6p0312c1s
Swenson, R.B. v6p0381c2s
Swensson, C.A. v4p0345c1s
Sweny, H.W. v4p0032c1m
v4p0291c1s v4p0456c1s v4p0610c2s
Swete, H.B. v6p0063c2s
v6p0342c1s v6p0519c2s
Swets, A. v5p0172c1s
Swett, E.T.J. v2p0445c1s
Swett, E.T.V. v3p0367c1s
Swett, E.T.Y. v3p0246c1s
Swett, J. v1p0105c2s
v1p0887c2s v1p0941c1s v4p0386c2s
v5p0512c1s
Swett, L. v3p0442c2s
Swett, O.J. v6p0429c2s
Swett, S. v1p0175c2s
v1p1275c1s v2p0048c2s v2p0151c1s
v2p0321c2s v2p0443c1s v2p0482c1s
v3p0226c1s v5p0211c1s
Swett, S.H. v2p0031c1s
v2p0230c2s v2p0291c2s v2p0442c2s
Swift, A. v6p0550c1s
Swift, A.M. v2p0209c1s
Swift, B. v5p0549c2s
v6p0222c2s
Swift, Baroness v2p0373c1s
Swift, C. v1p0197c1s
Swift, C.J. v4p0250c2s
v4p0277c2s
Swift, E. v5p0351c2s
v6p0488c1s
Swift, E.J. v4p0036c2s
v5p0144c1s v5p0200c2s v5p0330c2s
v5p0427c2s v6p0190c1s v6p0195c1s
v6p0317c2s v6p0365c2s v6p0410c1s
v6p0572c2s
Swift, F.E. v3p0017c1s
v3p0130c1s
Swift, H. v6p0666c1s
Swift, Ivan v6p0213c1s
Swift, J.A. v5p0570c2s
Swift, J.L. v1p0027c1s
v1p0424c1s
Swift, J.M. v5p0179c2s
Swift, L. v1p1014c1m
v2p0095c1s v2p0095c2s v2p0096c1s
v2p0285c1s v2p0308c2m v2p0343c2s
v2p0466c1s v3p0162c1s v3p0275c2s
v3p0318c2s v4p0069c1s v4p0126c2s
v4p0354c2s v4p0361c1s v4p0396c1s
v5p0035c1s v5p0072c2s v5p0213c2s
v5p0335c1m v5p0335c2s v5p0360c2s
v5p0372c1s v5p0402c1s v5p0564c1s
v6p0279c1s v6p0301c1s
Swift, L. and Nimsen, W.H.
v2p0014c1s
Swift, L.B. v4p0117c1s
Swift, Lewis v5p0035c2s
v5p0129c2s
Swift, M.I. v2p0331c2s
v3p0085c2s v3p0129c2s v3p0215c1s
v3p0331c1s v3p0345c1s v3p0398c1s
v3p0398c2s v3p0422c1s v3p0437c2s
v3p0445c2s v4p0113c1s v4p0188c2s
v4p0221c2s v4p0477c1m v4p0597c2s
Swift, M.J. v3p0192c1s
v3p0445c1s
Swift, M.L. v4p0314c1s
v5p0013c2s
Swift, P.H. v5p0120c1s
v5p0347c1s v5p0542c1s v6p0189c1s
Swift, S. v6p0018c2s
v6p0341c2s
Swift, S.T. v5p0066c2s
v5p0118c1s
Swift, T. v4p0003c2s
v4p0165c2s v5p0004c2s v5p0480c2s
Swift, W.H. v1p0103c2s
Swiggett, C.L. v6p0549c1s
Swiggett, G.L. v5p0220c2s
v5p0325c1s v5p0455c2m v5p0612c2s
v6p0361c2s
Swimmerton, E. v3p0309c1s
v3p0455c1s
Swinburne, A. v1p0264c1s
Swinburne, A.C. v1p0060c2s
v1p0062c2s v1p0082c2s v1p0228c2s
v1p0287c1s v1p0336c2s v1p0368c2s
v1p0407c2s v1p0418c2s v1p0419c1s

v1p0461c1s v1p0467c2s v1p0484c2s
v1p0503c2s v1p0567c2s v1p0611c2m
v1p0612c1s v1p0649c1s v1p0726c2s
v1p0770c2s v1p0873c1m v1p0886c1s
v1p0920c2s v1p0959c2s v1p0982c2s
v1p1054c1s v1p1114c2s v1p1128c2s
v1p1142c1s v1p1184c1s v1p1187c1s
v1p1189c2s v1p1199c2s v1p1201c2s
v1p1219c2s v1p1246c1s v1p1270c2s
v1p1294c2s v1p1375c2s v1p1389c2s
v1p1398c1s v1p1436c2s v2p0032c1s
v2p0049c1s v2p0057c2s v2p0063c1s
v2p0070c1s v2p0144c2m v2p0182c2s
v2p0210c2m v2p0224c1s v2p0246c2s
v2p0278c2s v2p0288c1s v2p0365c2s
v2p0457c1s v2p0469c2s v2p0476c2s
v2p0479c2s v3p0020c1s v3p0022c1s
v3p0031c1m v3p0057c2s v3p0058c1s
v3p0061c1s v3p0092c1s v3p0111c2s
v3p0114c1s v3p0138c2s v3p0204c1m
v3p0217c1s v3p0226c1s v3p0232c1m
v3p0267c2s v3p0269c2s v3p0271c1s
v3p0312c1s v3p0318c2s v3p0369c1s
v3p0371c2s v3p0382c1s v3p0387c2s
v3p0391c1s v3p0417c2s v3p0425c1s
v3p0433c1s v3p0439c2s v3p0448c2s
v3p0462c1s v3p0462c2s v3p0463c1s
v4p0021c1s v4p0021c2s v4p0037c1s
v4p0074c1s v4p0080c1s v4p0090c2m
v4p0150c1s v4p0177c1s v4p0196c1s
v4p0240c2s v4p0256c2s v4p0257c1s
v4p0268c1s v4p0268c2m v4p0295c2s
v4p0296c2s v4p0305c2s v4p0306c2m
v4p0324c2s v4p0337c1s v4p0355c1s
v4p0362c1s v4p0383c2s v4p0408c2s
v4p0410c2s v4p0422c1s v4p0492c1s
v4p0509c2m v4p0515c2s v4p0570c1s
v4p0577c2s v4p0581c2s v4p0591c2s
v5p0036c1s v5p0048c1s v5p0101c1s
v5p0154c2s v5p0169c1s v5p0248c2s
v5p0259c1s v5p0322c2s v5p0468c1s
v5p0596c1s v5p0624c2s v6p0163c1s
v6p0184c1s v6p0587c2m
Swinburne, A.C. and Abbey, E.A.
v6p0588c1s
Swinburne, A.C. and Collins, Churton
v2p0361c1s
Swinburne, H.L. v3p0182c1s
v4p0521c1s v4p0610c2s v6p0269c1s
Swinburne, J. v4p0177c1s
v5p0183c1s v5p0183c2s v6p0198c2s
v6p0221c2s
Swinburne, Jas. v5p0584c1s
Swinburne, L. v2p0232c2s
v3p0116c2s
Swinburne, L.J. v1p1358c2s
v2p0022c1s v2p0140c1s v2p0378c2s
v3p0132c1s v3p0335c2s
Swindells, W. v4p0456c2s
Swindlehurst, A. v5p0143c2s
v5p0329c2s
Swindlehurst, F. v6p0156c2s
v6p0210c2s
Swineford, H.B. v5p0635c1s
Swiney, F. v5p0064c2s
v6p0125c1s v6p0191c2s v6p0396c1s
v6p0703c1s v6p0703c2m v6p0707c1s
Swiney, F.L. v6p0259c1s
Swiney, J.M. v1p1266c2s
Swing, A.T. v4p0258c2s
v5p0165c1s v5p0207c2s
Swing, D. v1p0044c2s
v1p0228c1s v1p0414c1s v1p0724c1s
v1p1224c1s v1p1373c1s v2p0017c1s
v2p0083c2s v2p0351c2s v3p0037c1s
v3p0081c2s v3p0153c1s v3p0446c1s
v4p0111c2s v4p0382c1s v4p0557c1s
Swing, D. et al. v4p0214c2s
Swing, David v4p0100c1s
Swingle, D.B. and Smith, E.F.
v6p0046c2s
Swinnerton, S.N. v6p0235c2s
Swinny, S.H. v2p0104c2s
v2p0238c2s v2p0418c2s v3p0259c1s
v3p0433c2s v3p0447c2s v5p0646c1s
Swinstead, J.H. v5p0527c2s
Swinton, A.A.C. v2p0136c2s
v2p0340c1s v4p0487c1m v4p0541c1s
v5p0184c1s v5p0289c1s v5p0314c1s
Swinton, A.A.Campbell v3p0132c2s
Swinton, A.H. v2p0128c1s
v2p0425c1m v2p0426c2m v2p0463c1s
Swinton, G.S.C. v6p0110c2s
v6p0383c2s v6p0385c1m
Swinton, J. v5p0152c1s
v5p0406c2s
Swinton, W. v1p0417c1s
v1p0518c2s v1p0594c2s v1p0706c1s
v1p0932c1s v1p1344c2s
Swirles, R.S. v4p0163c1s
Swisshelm, J.G. v1p0032c1s
Swithin, S. v4p0557c1s
Switzler, W.F. v5p0387c1s
Swofford, R.P. et al. v6p0537c1s
Swynnerton, C. v2p0429c1m
v3p0418c1s
Sy, A.P. v6p0458c2s
Sybel, H.v. v1p0516c1s
Sybel, H.von v1p0475c2s
v1p1024c1s v1p1357c1s
Sydenham, A.H. v4p0131c2s
v4p0252c1s v4p0301c2s v4p0342c1s
v4p0409c1s v4p0535c2s v4p0551c1s
v4p0592c1s v4p0614c2s
Sydenham, Col. v1p1121c1s
Sydenham, J. v1p0100c2s
Sydney, A. v2p0246c2s
Sydney, S. v2p0272c2s
Sydney, W. v3p0013c1s
v3p0156c2s v4p0255c2s
Sydney, W.C. v3p0255c2s
v4p0093c2s v4p0102c2s v4p0164c2s
v4p0217c2s v4p0250c1s v4p0260c2s
v4p0317c1s v4p0339c2s v4p0482c1s
v4p0499c2s v4p0588c1s v5p0137c2s
v5p0255c1s v5p0346c1s v5p0451c2s
v5p0562c2s v5p0563c1s v6p0627c2s
Syester, A.K. v1p0213c1s
v1p0741c2s
Sykes, A.C. v6p0359c1s
v6p0685c2s
Sykes, A.G.P. v4p0626c2s
Sykes, A.L. v6p0300c2s
v6p0344c2s
Sykes, D.E., Mrs. v1p1362c1s
Sykes, E.A. v6p0489c2s
Sykes, E.C. v5p0212c1s
Sykes, E.T. v2p0054c2s
v2p0077c1s v2p0453c1s
Sykes, F.H. v6p0207c1s
Sykes, J. v5p0272c2s
v5p0428c2s v5p0433c1s v5p0452c2s
v5p0457c2s v5p0570c2s v5p0590c1s
v6p0055c1s v6p0089c2s v6p0184c1s
v6p0463c2s
Sykes, J., Lady and
Grey-Egerton, H., Lady. v4p0594c2s
Sykes, J.F.J. v5p0273c1s
Sykes, J.H. v1p0514c2s
Sykes, L.C. v5p0441c1s
Sykes, M. v6p0406c2s
v6p0480c2s
Sykes, M.L. v6p0540c1s
Sykes, M'Cready v6p0004c1s
v6p0235c2s v6p0305c1s
Sykes, Mr. v1p1079c2s
Sykes, P.M. v5p0053c1s
v5p0315c1s v5p0441c1s v6p0481c2s
v6p0489c2m
Sykes, R. v5p0093c1s
Sykes, T.P. v3p0128c2s
v3p0147c2s
Sykes, W.H. v1p0059c2s
v1p0094c1s v1p0112c2s v1p0184c1s
v1p0234c1s v1p0473c2s v1p0480c1s
v1p0482c2s v1p0483c2s v1p0542c2s
v1p0547c2s v1p0629c1s v1p0630c1s
v1p0630c2s v1p0631c1s v1p0633c2s
v1p0634c1s v1p0680c1s v1p0902c2s
v1p0920c1s v1p1049c2s v1p1265c2s
v1p1376c1s
Sykes, W.J. v1p0322c1s
v1p0322c2s v1p1223c2s v2p0309c1s
v2p0370c2s
Syle, E.W. v1p0236c1s
v1p0985c2s v2p0052c2s v2p0292c1s
Sylva, C. v3p0409c2s
v5p0106c1s v5p0555c1s
Sylva, Carmen v3p0305c2s
v3p0324c2s v3p0367c2s v4p0262c1s
v4p0548c2s v4p0625c1s v5p0230c2s
v5p0636c1s v6p0405c2s v6p0608c1s
v6p0645c1s v6p0685c1s v6p0703c1s
Sylvan, Urbanus v5p0469c2s
v6p0089c1s v6p0520c2s
Sylvester, C. v1p0608c1s
v1p1366c1s v1p1386c1s
Sylvester, H.H. v5p0280c1s
Sylvester, H.M. v4p0489c2s
Sylvester, J.J. v1p0224c2s
v1p0811c1s v1p0815c2s v1p1013c2s
v2p0118c2s v2p0145c2s v2p0174c1s
v2p0221c1s v2p0366c1s v3p0019c2s
v3p0058c2s v3p0119c1s v3p0188c2s
v3p0308c2s
Sylvester, K. v6p0155c2s
v6p0219c1s
Sylvester, Katharine v5p0605c2s
Sylvester, P. v3p0166c1s
v3p0185c2s v3p0252c2s v3p0403c1s
v3p0439c1s
Sylvester, Prof. v1p1284c1s
v1p1340c1s
Sylvester, R.H. v4p0275c2s
Sylvester, W. v5p0131c1s
v5p0271c2s v6p0407c2s
Sylvestre, M. v6p0394c1s
Sym, J.D. v5p0641c1s
Sym, R. v6p0479c2s
Syme, D. v1p1026c2s
Symes, J.E. v4p0173c2s
v4p0283c1s v4p0534c1s
Symington, A.J. v1p1333c2s
Symington, A.M. v1p0061c1s
v1p0172c2s v1p0196c1s v1p0349c2s
v1p0374c1s v1p0535c2s v1p0537c1s
v2p0024c2s v2p0196c2s v2p0292c1s
v2p0359c2s v2p0364c2s v2p0387c1s
v2p0388c2s v2p0403c2s v2p0471c2s
v3p0323c2s v3p0410c1s v3p0411c2s
Symington, J. v4p0358c2s
Symington, Maggie v4p0547c1s
Symmes, E. v5p0038c2s
Symmes, F. v6p0609c1s
Symmes, F.J. v2p0197c1s
Symmes, H.S. v6p0176c1s
v6p0489c2s
Symon, J.D. v4p0046c1s
v4p0066c1s v4p0181c1s v4p0195c2s
v4p0216c2s v4p0417c1s v4p0493c2s
v4p0550c2s v5p0050c1s v5p0092c2s
v5p0195c1s v5p0450c1s v5p0510c2s
v5p0554c2s v5p0642c1s
Symon, J.H. v5p0039c2s
Symonds, A.J. v5p0282c1s
Symonds, J. v3p0207c2s
Symonds, J.A. v1p0046c1s
v1p0145c2s v1p0202c2s v1p0266c2s
v1p0335c1m v1p0398c1s v1p0418c1s
v1p0461c1s v1p0589c1s v1p0669c1s
v1p0673c1s v1p0776c1s v1p0817c1s
v1p0834c2s v1p0842c1s v1p1028c2s
v1p1149c1s v1p1221c1s v1p1334c2s
v1p1430c1s v2p0058c2s v2p0120c1s
v2p0158c2s v2p0182c2s v2p0238c2s
v2p0252c2s v2p0296c1s v2p0378c2m
v2p0393c1s v2p0409c2s v2p0423c1s
v2p0428c2s v2p0456c2s v2p0458c2s
v2p0475c2s v2p0483c2s v3p0021c1s
v3p0025c2s v3p0068c1s v3p0071c2s
v3p0110c1s v3p0114c1s v3p0122c1s
v3p0143c2s v3p0178c1s v3p0207c2s
v3p0259c2s v3p0284c1s v3p0306c1s
v3p0317c1s v3p0317c2s v3p0335c2s
v3p0355c1s v3p0390c1s v3p0400c2s
v3p0418c1s v3p0427c2s v3p0429c2s
v3p0463c1s v3p0475c2s v4p0143c1s
v4p0294c1s v4p0295c1s v4p0299c2s
v4p0325c1s v4p0480c2m v4p0491c1s
v4p0570c1s v4p0601c2s
Symonds, J.A. and Mozley, J.R.
v1p0170c2s
Symonds, J.C. v1p1159c2s
Symonds, Margaret v5p0441c2s
Symonds, S. v1p0583c2s
v1p1087c2s v1p1218c1s
Symonds, T., Sir v4p0238c1s
Symonds, T.A. v2p0402c1s
Symonds, T.E. v3p0382c1s
v3p0409c1s
Symonds, W.L. v1p0719c2s
v1p0754c1s v1p1123c2s v1p1211c2s
Symonds, W.S. v1p0082c2s
v1p0376c2s v1p0377c1s v1p0524c1s
v1p0524c2s v1p1377c1s v1p1377c2s
Symons, A. v2p0293c1s
v3p0033c2s v3p0037c1s v3p0057c1s
v3p0205c1s v3p0274c2s v3p0287c1s
v3p0367c2s v3p0448c2s v3p0450c1s
v4p0085c1s v4p0163c2s v4p0232c1s
v4p0254c1s v4p0271c1s v4p0272c1s
v4p0298c2s v4p0335c1s v4p0361c2s
v4p0383c2s v4p0430c1s v4p0520c1s
v4p0540c1s v4p0602c2s v4p0603c1m
v5p0028c1s v5p0031c1s v5p0043c2s
v5p0044c2s v5p0051c1s v5p0069c1s
v5p0076c1s v5p0080c2s v5p0090c1s
v5p0127c2s v5p0137c1s v5p0141c1s
v5p0153c2s v5p0154c2s v5p0163c2s
v5p0165c2s v5p0166c2s v5p0171c2s
v5p0277c1s v5p0290c2s v5p0314c1s
v5p0355c2s v5p0357c2m v5p0362c1s
v5p0370c2s v5p0388c1s v5p0397c2s
v5p0404c2s v5p0427c2s v5p0430c2s
v5p0435c2s v5p0463c1s v5p0521c1m
v5p0552c2s v5p0567c2s v5p0570c2s
v5p0573c2s v5p0577c2s v5p0609c1s
v5p0609c2s v5p0612c2s v5p0623c1s
v5p0625c1s v5p0631c2s v5p0637c2s
v5p0644c1s v6p0022c2s v6p0056c2s
v6p0057c2s v6p0059c1s v6p0070c1m
v6p0071c2s v6p0091c1s v6p0095c1s
v6p0103c1s v6p0129c2s v6p0131c1s
v6p0135c1s v6p0146c1m v6p0150c1m
v6p0150c2m v6p0156c1s v6p0181c1s
v6p0275c1s v6p0280c1s v6p0283c2s
v6p0288c1m v6p0294c1s v6p0305c2s
v6p0359c1s v6p0360c2s v6p0365c2s
v6p0391c2s v6p0407c1s v6p0409c2s
v6p0427c2s v6p0428c2s v6p0434c1s
v6p0439c1s v6p0449c2s v6p0450c2s
v6p0456c1s v6p0473c2s v6p0475c1s
v6p0480c1s v6p0483c2s v6p0490c2s
v6p0500c2s v6p0532c1s v6p0546c2s
v6p0547c1s v6p0559c2s v6p0578c2s
v6p0602c2s v6p0620c2s v6p0649c1s
v6p0676c2m v6p0677c2s v6p0683c1s
v6p0700c1s v6p0707c2s
Symons, A. and Abbey, E.A.
v6p0588c1s
Symons, A. et al. v4p0324c2s
v4p0582c2s
Symons, Arthur v5p0012c2s
v5p0021c2s v5p0081c1s v5p0083c1s
v5p0100c2s v5p0137c2s v5p0322c2s
v5p0331c1s v5p0342c1s v5p0384c2s
v5p0466c2s v5p0489c1s v5p0503c1s
v5p0530c1s v5p0607c1s v6p0248c1s
v6p0483c2s v6p0538c2s v6p0550c1s
v6p0607c1s

Symons, G.J. v1p1081c1s
v3p0056c1s v3p0187c2s v4p0216c2s
v4p0473c1s v4p0615c2s
Symons, J. v1p0001c1s
v3p0234c1s
Symons, J.C. v1p0066c1s
v1p0798c1s v1p1194c2s v1p1276c1s
v1p1276c2s v1p1379c2s
Symons, T.W. v5p0092c1s
v5p0599c1s
Symons, T.W., Col. v6p0098c1s
Symons, W.C. v4p0292c1s
v4p0402c1s
Sympson, E.M. v3p0126c2s
v3p0151c1s
Sympson, G.W. v6p0157c2s
Syms, P. v5p0385c2s
Syms, R.H. v4p0437c2s
Synge, G.M. v4p0636c1s
v5p0277c1s
Synge, Gen. v1p1150c2s
Synge, H., Mrs. v5p0069c1s
v5p0390c1s
Synge, J.M. v6p0543c2s
Synge, J.M. and Hyde, D. . v6p0328c1s
Synge, W.W.F. v1p0979c2s
Synnott, H.L. v1p0218c2s
v1p0981c1s
Synnott, M.J. v3p0150c1s
Synnott, N. v5p0248c1s
Synnott, N. and Mayo, Earl of
v5p0295c2s
Synnott, N.J. v2p0255c1s
Synon, Mary K. v6p0255c2s
Sypesteyn, J.C.A.van v1p1378c1s
Sypherd, H.M. v6p0049c2s
Syrett, N. v3p0426c2s
v4p0062c1s v5p0105c2s v6p0116c1s
v6p0141c2s v6p0175c2s v6p0220c1s
v6p0306c2s v6p0541c1s
Syrett, Netta v4p0193c2s
Syveton, G. v6p0237c2s
Szabad, Col. v1p0740c2s
Szabo, Col. v1p0330c2s
v1p1274c2s
Szabo, Prof. v1p0376c2s
Szyrma, W.S.L. v2p0335c2s

T., A.E. v6p0361c1s
T., E.R. and Purdy, B. ... v6p0182c2s
T., R.H. v5p0590c1s
T., S.B. v5p0096c1s
Taaffe, T.G. v4p0614c2s
Tabb, J.B. v1p1375c2s
v2p0033c1s v4p0444c2s v5p0174c2s
v5p0366c2s v5p0367c2s v5p0380c2s
v5p0537c2s v6p0121c2s v6p0179c2s
v6p0280c1s
Taber, R.B. v6p0413c1s
Taber, R.G. v4p0025c1s
v4p0253c1s v4p0316c1m
v5p0617c2s
Taber, S.R. v6p0390c2s
Taber, W.M. v2p0120c2s
v3p0429c2s
Tabley, Lord de v4p0417c2s
Tabor, F.H. v5p0037c1s
Tabor, H. v4p0376c2s
Tabor, I.G. v6p0098c1s
v6p0154c2s v6p0386c2s v6p0502c1s
v6p0579c1s
Tabor, M.C. v3p0077c2s
v3p0355c1s
Tacchella, A. v1p0535c1s
Tadd, J.L. v5p0031c2s
v6p0034c1s
Tadema, L.A. v3p0429c2s
v4p0343c1s v4p0590c2s
Tadema, L.Alma v4p0523c2s
v6p0394c2s
Tafel, L. and Tafel, R.L.. v1p0539c2s
v1p0999c1s
Tafel, L.H. v4p0054c1s
v5p0056c1s
Tafel, R.L. v1p0724c1s
v1p1037c1s v1p1274c2s
Tafel, R.L. and Tafel, L.. v1p0539c2s
v1p0999c1s
Taff, J.A. v5p0034c2s
Taffinder, Adelia H. v5p0041c2s
Taffinder, Will G. v6p0175c2s
Taft, C.P. et al. v4p0129c1s
Taft, L. v4p0510c1s
v5p0053c2s v5p0078c1s v5p0241c2s
v5p0279c2s v5p0430c2s v5p0447c2s
v5p0467c2s v5p0629c1s
Taft, M.A. v4p0046c1s
Taft, M.L. v4p0106c2s
v4p0433c1s v6p0711c1s
Taft, O., jr. v5p0323c2s
Taft, O.B. v4p0315c2s
v6p0107c1s
Taft, R. v5p0043c2s
Taft, R.S. v4p0603c1s
v5p0048c1s
Taft, R.W. v6p0075c2s
v6p0552c1s
Taft, W.H. v4p0594c2s
v6p0477c2s v6p0492c2s v6p0493c1s
v6p0493c2m v6p0494c1m v6p0494c2s
Taggart, L.L. v5p0262c1s
Taggart, M.A. v2p0063c1s
v2p0291c1s v4p0163c2s v4p0260c1s
v4p0354c2s v4p0497c2s v6p0387c1s
Tahi, A. v5p0326c1s
Tailer, T.S. v4p0120c1s
Taillandier, St.R. v1p1262c1s
v2p0297c2s
Taillandier, St.Rene v1p0961c2s
Taine, H. v1p0475c1m
v1p0475c2s v1p0479c2s v1p0723c2s
v1p1419c2s v2p0221c1s v3p0140c2s
v3p0296c1s
Taine, H.A. v1p0802c1s
v1p1423c1s v2p0407c2s v3p0296c1s
Tainsh, E.C. v1p0315c1s
Tainter, H.D. v2p0310c2s
Tainton, C.F. v5p0006c2s
Taintor, C.M. v1p0157c2s
v1p1280c1s
Taio-ko and Stanford, C. . v5p0111c2s
Tait, A.C. v1p0682c2s
v1p1095c1s v1p1338c2m v2p0300c2s
v2p0302c1s
Tait, A.G. v5p0494c2s
Tait, C.G. v2p0291c1s
Tait, E.C. v4p0091c2s
v4p0165c1s v4p0310c2s v4p0543c2s
Tait, G. v1p1309c1s
Tait, H.R. v2p0321c1s
Tait, H.T. v5p0377c1s
Tait, J. v3p0175c2s
v4p0224c2s v4p0611c1s v5p0165c1m
v5p0180c1m v6p0054c1s v6p0289c2s
Tait, J.H. v4p0585c2s
Tait, J.R. v1p0880c2s
v1p1084c2s v2p0032c2s v2p0353c2s
v3p0411c1s v4p0396c1s
Tait, J.S. v3p0032c1s
v3p0067c2s v4p0045c1s v4p0471c1s
v4p0525c1s
Tait, L. v1p0312c1s
v2p0113c2s v2p0462c2s
Tait, L. and Pritchard, E.
v2p0395c2s
Tait, N. v4p0220c2s
Tait, P.G. v1p0070c1s
v1p0276c1s v1p0374c2s v1p0401c1s
v1p0434c2s v1p0466c2m v1p0813c2s
v1p0899c2m v1p1006c2m v1p1102c2s
v1p1255c1s v1p1440c2s v2p0093c1s
v2p0138c1s v2p0260c1s v2p0438c2s
v3p0177c1s v3p0237c1s v3p0410c1s
v3p0456c2s v4p0231c2s
Tait, P.G. and Gibbs, J.W.
v3p0350c2s
Tait, P.S. v2p0138c2s
Takahashi, K.T. v4p0297c1s
Takahashi, K.T. and Gronlund, L.
v5p0537c1s
Takahira, K. v5p0302c2s
v6p0561c1s
Takahira, Kogoro v6p0665c2s
Takaki, M. v6p0338c2s
v6p0478c2s
Takakusu, J. v6p0335c1s
Takano, F. v4p0297c2s
v4p0314c2s v5p0302c2s v5p0303c2s
Takegoshi, J. v6p0565c1s
Takona, F. v4p0298c1s
v4p0316c1s
Talandier, A. v1p0479c2s
v1p0480c2s v1p0481c1s
Talbot, A.A. v6p0304c1s
Talbot, A.L. v5p0524c2s
Talbot, C.A.P. v3p0154c2s
Talbot, Canon v3p0052c2s
v3p0077c2s v3p0124c2s
Talbot, E. v2p0132c2s
v2p0221c1s v3p0051c1s v6p0421c2m
v6p0502c1s v6p0693c1s
Talbot, E., Mrs. and Harris, W.T.
v3p0398c1s
Talbot, E.B. v4p0464c2s
v6p0222c2s
Talbot, E.B. and Darlington, L.
v5p0038c1s
Talbot, E.F. v2p0360c1s
Talbot, E.S. v1p1025c2s
v3p0187c1s v4p0232c2s v4p0533c1s
v6p0122c1s
Talbot, Ellen B. v5p0205c2s
Talbot, F. v1p0177c1s
v1p0442c2s v1p0593c1s v1p0599c1s
v1p0608c2m v1p0624c1s v1p0674c1s
v1p0789c1s v1p0796c1s v1p0887c1s
v1p0889c1s v1p1078c2s v1p1131c1s
v1p1183c1s v1p1187c1s v1p1299c1s
v1p1309c1s v1p1436c2s v3p0210c1s
Talbot, F.A. v5p0181c2s
v5p0298c2s v6p0637c1s
Talbot, G. v6p0538c1s
v6p0595c1s
Talbot, G., Sir v1p0691c2s
Talbot, G.F. v1p0350c2s
v1p1232c1s v4p0629c1s
Talbot, H.F. v1p1003c1s
v1p1003c2s
Talbot, H.P. v6p0182c2s
Talbot, J.E. v4p0174c2s
v4p0176c2s v4p0547c1s
Talbot, J.J. v1p0012c2s
v1p0213c1s v1p0327c1s v1p0523c1s
v1p0639c2s
Talbot, M. v1p0109c2s
v1p0597c1s v4p0502c2s v4p0534c2s
v4p0598c1s v5p0637c1s v6p0286c2s
v6p0612c1s
Talbot, M.J. v5p0501c2s
Talbot, Marion v6p0300c1s
Talbot, R. v2p0001c2s
v4p0433c1s
Talbot, R.T. v3p0195c2s
v4p0053c1s
Talbot, S. v1p0426c2s
v1p0681c2s v1p0685c1s v1p0793c1s
v1p0810c1s v1p1001c1s v2p0474c1s
Talbot, T.H. v2p0253c1s
Talbot, T.T. v2p0328c2s
Talbot, W.H.F. v1p0419c2s
Talbot, W.T. v6p0078c2s
v6p0625c1s
Talcott, A.M. v3p0225c2s
Talcott, E.C. v6p0479c1s
Talcott, M.C. v5p0405c1s
Talcott, M.K. v1p1427c2s
v2p0481c1s v5p0069c1m v5p0629c1s
v6p0072c2s v6p0187c1s v6p0677c2s
Talcott, Mary K. v3p0135c1s
Talfourd, T.N. v1p0169c2s
v1p0256c1s v1p0344c2s v1p0363c1s
v1p0398c1s v1p0561c1s v1p1139c2s
v1p1258c2s v1p1320c2s v1p1382c1s
v2p0444c2s
Tallack, W. v2p0183c2s
v3p0092c2s v3p0198c2s
Tallberg, A. v6p0628c2s
Tallberg, Axel v6p0628c2s
v6p0640c2s
Tallentyre, S.G. v5p0104c2s
v5p0106c2s v5p0116c2s v5p0130c2s
v5p0170c2s v5p0191c1m v5p0194c1s
v5p0221c2s v5p0228c1s v5p0257c2s
v5p0331c2s v5p0384c1s v5p0398c1s
v5p0402c1s v5p0477c1s v5p0480c1s
v5p0505c2s v5p0521c1s v5p0547c2s
v5p0617c1s v5p0640c2s v6p0011c2s
v6p0055c2s v6p0143c2s v6p0173c2s
v6p0175c2s v6p0206c2s v6p0222c1s
v6p0274c2s v6p0399c1s v6p0401c1s
v6p0661c1s v6p0681c2m
Talley, S.A. v1p0776c2s
Talleyrand, M.de v1p1092c1s
Tallichet, E. v6p0429c2s
Tallman, H.B. v5p0164c2s
Tallmon, M.C. and Morgan, W.C.
v6p0069c1s
Talmadge, D.H. v5p0213c2s
v5p0219c2s v5p0265c2m v6p0146c1s
v6p0183c2s v6p0243c2s v6p0346c2s
Talmadge, J.F.N. v1p0233c1s
Talmage, J.E. v3p0183c2s
v4p0514c1s
Talmage, T.D. v1p1392c1s
Talmage, T.DeW. v1p0290c1s
v1p0595c2s
Talman, J. v1p0799c1s
v3p0405c2s v5p0086c1s v5p0329c1s
Talman, W.H. v4p0569c1s
Talmeyer, M. v5p0461c2s
Talmeyr, M. and Brodhurst, J.P.
v4p0206c1s
Tamm, H. v1p0796c1s
Tams, J.F. v6p0710c1s
Tamura, S.T. v6p0336c2s
v6p0338c2s
Tanaka, Tatsu v6p0591c1s
Tandy, F.D. v5p0284c1s
v5p0557c2s v6p0130c2s
Taney, E.S. v4p0562c2s
Tangye, R. v4p0049c2s
v5p0145c1s v5p0319c1s v5p0474c1s
v6p0131c1s v6p0150c2s v6p0465c2s
Tannehill, W. v1p0866c2s
Tannenbaum, S. v6p0587c1s
Tanner, A. and Anderson, K.
v4p0515c1s
Tanner, Amy E. v6p0115c2s
v6p0137c2s
Tanner, Dr. v2p0419c1s
Tanner, E.P. v5p0015c1s
Tanner, H. v6p0329c1s
Tanner, H.C.B. v3p0196c2s
Tanner, J.R. v3p0175c2s
v3p0273c2s v3p0369c1s v3p0386c2s
v4p0181c2s v4p0182c1s v4p0434c2s
v4p0513c2s v5p0246c1s v5p0636c2s
Tanner, M.E. v5p0336c1s
Tanqueray, B., Mrs. v5p0374c2s
Tanqueray, K. v6p0008c2s
Tansley, A.G. v4p0446c1s
v4p0548c2s
Tansley, A.J. v3p0412c1s
Tantivy, T. v2p0188c2s
v2p0189c1s v2p0190c1s v2p0192c2s
v2p0306c2s v2p0331c2s v2p0448c1s
Tanzer, A. v1p0733c2s
v2p0089c1s v2p0447c1s v3p0012c1s
v3p0089c2s v3p0109c1s v3p0148c2s
v3p0160c1s v3p0339c1s v3p0339c2s
v3p0428c2s v3p0449c2s v4p0088c2s
v4p0127c1s v4p0224c2s v4p0393c2s
v4p0490c2s v6p0018c2s v6p0575c2s
Tapley, E. v4p0504c1s
Tapley, W. v4p0222c2s
Tapley, W.H. v5p0183c1s
v5p0185c1s
Taplin, G. v1p0079c1m
Taplin, W.H. v4p0033c1s
v4p0047c1s v4p0078c2s v4p0119c1s
v4p0130c1m v4p0197c1m v4p0203c2s
v4p0204c2m v4p0264c2s v4p0444c2s
v4p0445c2s v4p0491c2m
Tapp, E. v1p0733c2s
Tappan, B. v1p0048c2s
v1p1282c2s
Tappan, B., jr. v1p0061c1s
v1p0850c2s
Tappan, Dr. v1p0021c2s
Tappan, E.T. v2p0455c2s
Tappan, G.A. v6p0501c1s
Tappan, H. v1p0255c2s
v1p1282c2s
Tappan, H.P. v1p0076c2s
v1p0120c1s v1p0180c1s v1p0276c1s
v1p0387c2s v1p0946c1s v1p1043c1s
v1p1115c2s v1p1120c1m
Tappan, L. v1p1052c1s
v1p1052c2s
Tapper, T. v4p0389c1s
v4p0390c1s
Tapper, T.W. v3p0355c1s
Tar, K. v6p0356c2s
Tar, K.R. v6p0557c2s
Taramelli, A. v5p0089c1s
v5p0373c2s v5p0442c2s v6p0262c1s
Taran, A. v1p1135c1s
Tarbell, A. v6p0595c1s
Tarbell, A.W. v4p0231c2s
v4p0328c1s v4p0482c2s v5p0048c1s
v5p0078c2s v5p0127c1s v5p0176c2s
v5p0211c1s v5p0234c1s
Tarbell, Arthur W. v6p0708c1s
Tarbell, F.B. v3p0274c2s
v4p0035c1s v4p0241c1s v5p0151c1s
v5p0171c2s v5p0396c2s v6p0273c1s
Tarbell, F.B. and Bates, W.N.
v4p0568c2s

Tarbell, F.B. and Buck, C.D. v3p0015c1s

Tarbell, F.B. and Paton, W.R. v3p0026c2s

Tarbell, F.B. and Waldstein, C. v3p0406c2s

Tarbell, H.S. v2p0091c1s v4p0506c1s

Tarbell, H.S. et al. v4p0566c1s

Tarbell, I.M. v3p0341c1s v3p0363c2s v3p0406c1s v3p0468c1s v3p0469c1s v4p0004c1s v4p0063c2s v4p0127c2s v4p0140c1s v4p0332c2s v4p0392c2s v4p0393c1m v4p0410c1s v4p0425c2s v4p0426c1s v4p0429c2s v4p0487c2s v4p0500c2s v4p0605c1s v5p0152c1s v5p0156c1s v5p0206c2s v5p0339c2s v5p0447c2s v5p0601c2s v6p0089c1s v6p0483c1s

Tarbell, Ida M. v4p0210c2s v5p0430c2s v6p0392c2s v6p0546c1s v6p0613c1m v6p0632c2s

Tarbell, J. v3p0355c2s v6p0068c1s

Tarbell, J.H. v6p0448c1s

Tarbox, I.N. v1p0006c1s v1p0024c1s v1p0060c1s v1p0069c1s v1p0172c2s v1p0175c2s v1p0179c2s v1p0275c1s v1p0275c2s v1p0276c1s v1p0280c1m v1p0292c1s v1p0373c1s v1p0373c2s v1p0393c2s v1p0394c1s v1p0398c1s v1p0405c1s v1p0691c2s v1p0809c1s v1p0909c2s v1p0910c1s v1p0972c2s v1p1010c1s v1p1018c2s v1p1021c2s v1p1061c2s v1p1157c2s v1p1257c1s v1p1265c1s v1p1299c1s v1p1323c1s v1p1341c1s v1p1353c2s v1p1372c2s v1p1396c1s v1p1416c2s v2p0007c1s v2p0008c2s v2p0031c1s v2p0091c1s v2p0099c2s v2p0116c1s v2p0133c1s v2p0191c2s v2p0197c1s v2p0333c2s v2p0374c1s v2p0401c1s v2p0423c1s v2p0439c1s v2p0481c2s v3p0038c1s v3p0247c1s v3p0420c1s

Tarde, G. v4p0139c2s v4p0375c2s v5p0144c1s v6p0324c2s v6p0521c2s

Target, F. v1p1390c1s

Tarick, B. v1p0872c2s

Tarkington, B. v5p0104c2s v5p0228c1s v5p0384c1s v6p0043c1s v6p0218c1s

Tarkington, Booth v6p0012c2s v6p0055c1s v6p0055c2s v6p0076c1s v6p0145c1s v6p0286c1s v6p0386c2s v6p0434c2s v6p0446c1s v6p0519c1s v6p0663c1s v6p0675c1s v6p0692c2s

Tarkington, Edwin v6p0434c1s

Tarkington, Louisa F. v6p0376c2s

Tarleton, F.A. v1p1357c1s

Tarleton, G. v2p0355c1s

Tarn, W.W. v5p0436c1s v6p0273c2s v6p0286c2s

Tarpey, J.T.K. v4p0588c2s v5p0396c1s v5p0585c1s

Tarpey, W.B. v3p0431c1s

Tarpey, W.K. v4p0473c1s v5p0167c2s v5p0310c1s v5p0524c2s

Tarpey, W.Kingsley v5p0451c2s

Tarr, R.S. v2p0091c1s v2p0106c1s v2p0128c1s v2p0157c2s v2p0212c2s v2p0303c2s v2p0328c2s v2p0441c1s v2p0483c2s v3p0121c2s v3p0142c1s v3p0179c1s v3p0186c2s v3p0244c1s v3p0425c2s v4p0123c1s v4p0134c2s v4p0222c2s v4p0227c1s v4p0381c2s v4p0435c2s v4p0441c1s v5p0154c1s v5p0229c1m v5p0278c2s v5p0449c1s v5p0506c1s v6p0010c2s v6p0186c1s v6p0250c2s v6p0454c2s v6p0689c1s

Tarr, R.S. and Aitken, J.. v4p0317c1s

Tarr, R.S. and Martin, L.. v6p0010c2m

Tarr, S.R. v4p0075c2s v4p0085c2s v4p0086c2s v5p0168c1s v5p0186c1s v5p0420c2s v6p0323c1s

Tarrant, M.E. v6p0388c1s v6p0504c1s

Tarrant, W.G. v5p0097c1s

Tartt, W.M. v1p0317c2s

Tarver, E.J. v1p0066c1s v3p0018c2s

Tarver, J.C. v5p0079c1s v5p0140c2s v5p0425c1s v5p0471c2s v5p0512c2s v6p0549c1s v6p0573c2s

Tarver, M. v1p0014c2s v1p0093c2s v1p0106c1s v1p0258c1s v1p0259c2s v1p0265c1s v1p0304c1s v1p0315c1s v1p0322c1s v1p0373c1s v1p0384c2s v1p0406c1s v1p0435c2s v1p0459c2s v1p0509c1s v1p0533c1s v1p0562c1s v1p0584c2s v1p0595c1s v1p0649c2s v1p0650c1s v1p0651c2s v1p0652c1s v1p0665c1s v1p0666c1s v1p0711c2s v1p0773c1s v1p0783c2s v1p0824c2s v1p0854c2s v1p0855c1m v1p0875c1s v1p0956c2s v1p0990c2s v1p1014c2s v1p1015c1s v1p1015c2s v1p1025c2s v1p1049c1s v1p1057c2s v1p1062c2s v1p1075c1s v1p1089c1s v1p1110c2m v1p1113c2s v1p1144c1s v1p1201c2s v1p1208c1s v1p1400c1s

Tasistro, L.F. v1p1025c2s

Tasker, A. v5p0364c2s v6p0328c2s v6p0404c1s

Tasker, F.E. v4p0313c2s

Tasker, J.C. v6p0123c1s

Tasker, S.P.M. v6p0615c2s

Tassin, A. v4p0588c1s

Tassin, A.G. v2p0094c2s v3p0015c2s v3p0064c2s v3p0082c1s v3p0186c1s v3p0191c1s v3p0203c1s v3p0214c1s v3p0258c1s v3p0270c1s v3p0300c2s v3p0306c1s v3p0351c1s v3p0431c2s v3p0455c1s

Tate and Fairbairn v1p0526c1s

Tate, A.C. v3p0389c1s

Tate, F.B. v1p1232c1s

Tate, H.R. v6p0006c1s

Tate, J.S. v1p1382c1s

Tate, J.W. v4p0445c1s

Tate, R. v2p0169c1s v4p0038c2s

Tate, S. v1p1249c2s

Tate, T. and Fairbairn, W. v1p1247c1s

Tate, W.J. v1p0056c2s v1p0608c2s v1p1020c2s

Tateno, G. v4p0101c2s

Tatham, E.H. v3p0305c1s

Tatham, E.H.R. v4p0186c1s v6p0491c1s

Tatham, F.S. v5p0007c1s v6p0205c1s v6p0442c2s

Tatham, W. v4p0324c1s v5p0238c1s

Tatham, W.P. v1p0374c2s v2p0126c2m v3p0276c1s

Tatistcheff, S. v6p0456c2s

Tatlock, J. v2p0417c1s

Tatlock, J., jr. v2p0028c2s v2p0284c1s v2p0404c2s

Tatlock, W. and Coxe, A.C. v1p0255c2s

Tatnall, R. and Crew, H. . v4p0540c2s

Tatsuo, H. v6p0648c2s

Tatsuo, Hirala v6p0355c1s

Tattersall, H. v4p0082c2s v4p0153c1s v4p0383c2s

Tattersall, W. v2p0459c1s v4p0318c1s v4p0462c2s

Tattle, C.W. v1p0216c1s

Tau, Sein Ko v5p0111c1m v5p0111c2s v5p0112c1s

Taube, G.von v3p0215c1s

Taubeneck, H.E. v5p0623c2s

Tauber-Harper, B.V. v4p0513c1s

Taubman-Goldie, G. v4p0237c2s

Taulane, J.H. v4p0324c1s

Taumey, J.W. v4p0082c1m

Taunton, E. v6p0236c2s v6p0318c2s v6p0643c2s

Taunton, E.L. v5p0122c2s v5p0174c2s v6p0248c2s v6p0433c2s v6p0501c2s v6p0515c2s

Taunton, E.L. and Galton, A. v6p0547c2s

Taunton, Ethelred v6p0248c2s

Taunton, Ethelred L. v6p0003c1s

Taurnier, W. v4p0532c1s

Tauska, C. v1p1024c1s

Taussig, F. v4p0525c2s

Taussig, F.W. v1p0690c2s v2p0092c2s v2p0223c1s v2p0353c2s v2p0364c1s v2p0413c2s v2p0424c1s v3p0157c2s v3p0218c1m v3p0336c2s v3p0337c1s v3p0347c1s v3p0353c1s v3p0393c1s v3p0393c2s v3p0412c2s v3p0420c1m v3p0452c1s v4p0014c1s v4p0036c1s v4p0179c2s v4p0199c1s v4p0231c1s v4p0262c1s v4p0458c1m v4p0460c2s v4p0462c2s v4p0469c2s v4p0472c1s v4p0475c2s v4p0525c1s v4p0525c2m v4p0563c2m v4p0608c2s v4p0631c2s v5p0149c2s v5p0171c1s v5p0257c1s v5p0298c1s v5p0383c1s v5p0517c2s v5p0567c1m v5p0568c2s v5p0600c1s v5p0604c1s v6p0240c1s v6p0519c2s v6p0522c2s v6p0572c2s v6p0624c1s v6p0682c1s v6p0690c1s v6p0707c1s

Taussig, F.W. and James, E.J. v2p0418c1s

Taussig, T.W. and Seligman, E.R.A. v6p0189c1s

Taussig, W. v6p0563c2s v6p0564c1s

Tavaststjerna, K. v5p0634c1s

Tavener, L. v5p0500c1s

Tavenor-Perry, J. v6p0231c1s

Tavera, T.H.P.de et al. .. v6p0492c2s

Tavernier, E. v6p0236c2m v6p0288c1s v6p0424c1s

Taw, Sein Ko v4p0105c1s v5p0112c1s

Tawney, C.H. v4p0473c1s v5p0508c1s

Tawney, G. v4p0539c1s

Tawney, G.A. v5p0292c2s v5p0565c2s v6p0147c2s v6p0533c1s

Tawney, G.A. and Hodge, C.W. v5p0166c1s

Tawse, G. v1p1150c1s v2p0468c1s v3p0234c2s v3p0235c2s v3p0252c1s

Tayler, B.W.K. v1p0195c1s

Tayler, C.B. v2p0123c2s

Tayler, F. v6p0158c1s

Tayler, G. v1p0312c2s

Tayler, J.J. v1p0109c1s v1p0126c1s v1p0240c1s v1p0597c1s v1p0880c2s v1p1322c1s

Tayler, J.L. v5p0176c2s v6p0214c2s

Tayler, J.W. v6p0590c2s

Tayler, N.M. v6p0240c1s

Tayler, W. v1p0547c1s v3p0367c1s v3p0435c2s

Tayler, W.B. v1p0464c1s

Tayler, W.C. v6p0686c2s

Tayleur, E. v6p0447c1s

Taylor et al. v1p0831c2s

Taylor, A. v1p0537c1s v1p0765c1s v2p0074c2s v2p0256c2s v4p0113c1s v4p0440c2s v4p0597c1s

Taylor, A.A.E. v1p0392c1s v2p0352c2m

Taylor, A.B. v2p0295c1s v2p0469c2s v5p0305c2s v5p0378c2s

Taylor, A.C. v5p0614c2s v6p0549c2s

Taylor, A.D. v6p0665c1s

Taylor, A.E. v4p0275c2s v4p0446c2s v4p0514c2s v4p0542c1s v5p0371c2s v5p0454c1s v5p0619c2s v6p0412c2s v6p0418c2m v6p0434c2s v6p0444c1s v6p0503c2m v6p0521c2s v6p0537c1s v6p0659c2m

Taylor, A.H. v6p0453c2s

Taylor, A.H.E. v5p0520c2s

Taylor, A.J. v6p0041c2s

Taylor, A.K. v4p0592c1s

Taylor, A.R. v4p0576c1s v6p0012c1s

Taylor, Alicia C. v5p0119c1s

Taylor, Annie R. v4p0576c1s

Taylor, Austin v5p0490c1s

Taylor, B. v1p0041c1s v1p0041c1s v1p0048c2s v1p0049c2s v1p0076c1m v1p0087c2s v1p0102c1s v1p0105c2s v1p0146c2s v1p0170c2s v1p0192c1s v1p0199c1s v1p0204c1s v1p0289c1s v1p0335c2s v1p0356c1s v1p0427c2s v1p0429c2s v1p0436c2s v1p0451c2s v1p0491c1s v1p0516c2s v1p0517c2s v1p0521c2s v1p0567c1s v1p0571c2s v1p0573c2s v1p0574c1s v1p0581c1m v1p0613c2s v1p0614c1s v1p0621c1m v1p0626c2s v1p0663c1s v1p0668c1s v1p0680c2s v1p0693c2s v1p0696c1s v1p0707c1s v1p0716c1s v1p0727c1s v1p0770c1s v1p0785c2s v1p0807c2s v1p0814c1s v1p0893c2s v1p0931c1s v1p0933c1s v1p0963c1s v1p0964c1s v1p0983c1s v1p1030c1s v1p1045c2s v1p1069c2s v1p1131c2s v1p1134c2s v1p1145c1s v1p1188c2s v1p1228c2s v1p1229c2m v1p1259c1s v1p1270c2s v1p1273c2s v1p1276c1m v1p1277c1s v1p1294c2s v1p1298c1s v1p1335c1s v1p1335c2m v1p1397c1m v1p1407c2s v1p1408c1s v3p0112c1s v3p0280c2s v4p0143c2s v4p0147c2s v4p0227c2s v4p0337c1s v4p0565c1s v5p0111c2s v5p0122c1s v5p0124c1m v5p0130c1s v5p0186c2s v5p0235c1m v5p0245c1m v5p0289c2s v5p0321c1s v5p0427c1s v5p0516c2s v5p0526c1m v5p0539c1s v5p0556c1s v5p0556c2s v5p0584c2m v5p0602c1s v6p0083c1s v6p0108c1s v6p0152c2s v6p0284c1s v6p0300c1m v6p0355c2s v6p0357c1s v6p0445c2s v6p0533c2s v6p0591c1s v6p0591c2s v6p0624c1s v6p0634c1s v6p0652c2s v6p0655c2m v6p0681c2s

Taylor, B. and Wilson, H.W. v5p0600c1s

Taylor, B. et al. v1p0534c1s v6p0271c1s

Taylor, B.B. v1p1076c2s v1p1080c1s v1p1354c1s

Taylor, B.F. v1p0098c2s v1p0167c2s v1p0199c1s v1p0212c1s v1p0228c1s v1p0356c1s v1p0626c2s v1p0745c2s v1p0807c1s v1p0887c1s v1p0888c2s v1p0941c1m v1p1061c2s v1p1236c2s v1p1362c2s v2p0185c1s

Taylor, B.G. v5p0196c2s

Taylor, B.M. v5p0596c2s

Taylor, B.N. v4p0413c2s v4p0619c1s

Taylor, B.S. v1p0442c1s

Taylor, Benj. v4p0295c2s v4p0539c1s v5p0130c1s v5p0526c2s v5p0613c2s v6p0275c2s v6p0324c1s v6p0476c2s

Taylor, Bessie v4p0085c1s v6p0476c2s

Taylor, C. v1p0459c2s v1p0463c2s v1p0638c2s v1p0645c1m

v1p0759c2s v1p0855c2s v1p0875c1s
v1p1198c1s v1p1236c1s v1p1404c1s
v4p0121c2s v5p0053c1s v5p0174c1s
v5p0325c1s v6p0058c1s
Taylor, C., Sir v1p0458c1s
v1p0929c2s
Taylor, C.B. v3p0323c1s
v5p0327c2s v6p0022c1s v6p0175c1s
v6p0187c1s v6p0414c1s v6p0440c1s
v6p0677c1s v6p0706c2s
Taylor, C.Bryson v6p0019c2s
v6p0519c1s
Taylor, C.C. v5p0249c1s
Taylor, C.E. v6p0164c1s
Taylor, C.E., jr. v4p0412c2s
Taylor, C.F. v1p0558c2s
v1p0843c1s v3p0176c1s v4p0119c2s
v4p0284c2s
Taylor, C.H. v3p0309c2s
v5p0252c1s v5p0311c1s
Taylor, C.S. v3p0127c1s
Taylor, C.W. v4p0197c1s
Taylor, D.M. v3p0270c2s
v3p0278c2m v5p0399c1s
Taylor, Dr. v1p0670c1s
Taylor, E. v1p0110c1s
v1p0151c2s v1p0589c2s v1p0712c2s
v1p0726c1s v1p0859c2s v4p0347c2s
v5p0313c2s v5p0414c2m v6p0001c2s
v6p0163c2s v6p0457c2s
Taylor, E.B. v2p0280c2s
v4p0559c1s
Taylor, E.C. v1p1198c2s
v1p1199c2s
Taylor, E.E. v5p0213c1s
v5p0518c2s v6p0235c2s v6p0487c2s
Taylor, E.F. v1p0767c2s
v1p1365c1s
Taylor, E.G. v4p0063c2s
v4p0513c1s v6p0196c2s
Taylor, E.H. v5p0222c1s
Taylor, E.M. v3p0263c1s
Taylor, E.R. v4p0466c2s
Taylor, Elizabeth v5p0181c2s
v5p0203c1s v5p0565c2s
Taylor, F. v1p0089c1s
v1p0193c1s v3p0352c2m v4p0348c1s
Taylor, F.B. v4p0347c2s
v4p0403c1s v5p0366c2s
Taylor, F.H. v1p0574c2s
v1p0718c2s v1p1297c2s v2p0066c1s
v6p0005c1s v6p0173c1s v6p0414c2s
v6p0476c2s
Taylor, F.M. v3p0244c1s
v4p0143c2s v5p0149c2s v5p0382c2m
Taylor, F.R. v6p0497c1s
Taylor, F.W. v2p0084c1s
v4p0442c2s v4p0608c1s v5p0203c1s
v6p0143c2s v6p0671c1s
Taylor, Father v4p0565c2s
Taylor, G. v1p0156c1s
v1p1403c1s v1p1433c1s v3p0341c2s
v5p0118c1s v6p0113c2s v6p0114c2s
v6p0118c2s v6p0125c1s v6p0128c2m
v6p0153c2s v6p0318c2s v6p0585c1m
Taylor, G.B. v1p0327c2s
v1p0769c2s v1p1216c2s
Taylor, G.H. v4p0531c2s
Taylor, G.L. v1p0454c1s
v1p1430c2s v3p0004c1s v3p0004c2s
v3p0169c2s
Taylor, G.R. v6p0113c2s
v6p0348c2s v6p0585c1s v6p0658c1s
Taylor, Geo.E. v6p0443c2s
Taylor, Graham v6p0115c1s
Taylor, H. v1p0317c2s
v1p0339c2s v1p0347c1s v1p0451c2s
v1p0472c2s v1p0631c2s v1p0870c2s
v1p0932c2s v1p1430c1s v1p1430c2s
v3p0202c1s v4p0214c1s v4p0236c1s
v4p0265c2s v4p0266c1s v4p0350c1s
v4p0428c1s v5p0147c2s v5p0218c1s
v5p0292c2s v5p0542c2s v5p0544c1s
v5p0601c2s v6p0026c1m v6p0138c2s
v6p0146c1s v6p0263c1s v6p0347c2s
v6p0364c1m v6p0449c2m v6p0477c2m
v6p0608c1s
Taylor, H. et al. v6p0401c2s
v6p0685c1s
Taylor, H., Sir v1p0202c1s
v1p0417c1s v1p1426c1s
Taylor, H.A. v3p0424c2s
Taylor, H.C. v3p0089c1s
v3p0218c2s v3p0304c1s v3p0305c1s
v3p0317c1s v3p0457c2s v4p0101c2s
v4p0610c2s v5p0134c1s v5p0383c2s
v5p0508c2s v5p0542c2s v5p0602c2s
v6p0539c1s v6p0624c1s
Taylor, H.C.C. v5p0239c1s
Taylor, H.D. v2p0129c2s
Taylor, H.G. v1p0386c2s
v1p0388c1s v1p0727c1s
Taylor, H.L. v4p0103c1s
v4p0192c1s v5p0431c1m v5p0517c2s
v6p0572c2s
Taylor, H.O. v1p0031c1s
v2p0103c2s v5p0144c2s v6p0286c2s
v6p0565c2s
Taylor, H.Osborn v6p0302c2s
Taylor, H.S. v2p0269c1s
v2p0367c1s
Taylor, Hannis v6p0026c1s
v6p0077c2s v6p0558c2s
Taylor, Henry, Sir v2p0310c1s
Taylor, I. v1p0122c2s
v1p0148c1s v1p0149c1s v1p0303c2s
v1p0308c1s v1p0428c2s v1p0470c2s
v1p0471c1s v1p0473c1s v1p0722c2s
v1p0960c2s v1p1384c1s v1p1404c1s
v2p0018c1s v2p0121c1s v2p0190c2s
v2p0204c1s v2p0249c1s v2p0305c1s
v3p0008c1s v3p0023c1m v3p0037c1s
v3p0120c2s v3p0172c1s v3p0176c2s
v3p0199c2s v3p0200c2s v3p0205c2s
v3p0225c1s v3p0230c1s v3p0261c2s
v3p0266c2s v3p0282c2m v3p0327c1s
v3p0382c2s v3p0450c1s v4p0011c2s
v4p0490c2s v4p0523c1m v6p0101c2s
v6p0378c1s
Taylor, I. and Abercromby, J.
v3p0153c1s
Taylor, I. and Freeman, E.A.
v3p0392c1s
Taylor, I. and Muller, M.. v2p0319c2s
Taylor, I. and Ridgeway, W.
v4p0143c2s
Taylor, I. et al. v2p0249c1s
v3p0107c2s v3p0427c1s
Taylor, I.A. v2p0221c2s
v3p0029c1s v4p0165c1s v4p0186c1s
v4p0229c2s v4p0277c2s v4p0305c2s
v4p0522c1s v5p0138c2s v5p0153c1s
v5p0160c1s v5p0209c2m v5p0222c1s
v5p0296c1s v5p0349c1s v5p0414c2s
v5p0427c2s
Taylor, I.M. and Lang, A.. v2p0108c2s
Taylor, I.N. v4p0479c1s
Taylor, Ida v5p0462c2s
Taylor, Isaac v3p0224c1s
Taylor, Isaac and Evans, A.J.
v2p0058c1s
Taylor, J. v1p0329c2s
v1p0709c2s v1p0837c1s v2p0056c1s
v2p0256c1s v3p0055c1s v3p0236c1s
v3p0248c2s v4p0480c2s v5p0488c2s
v5p0489c1s v5p0516c1s v6p0033c1s
v6p0035c1s v6p0062c2s v6p0171c2s
v6p0258c1s
Taylor, J. et al. v1p0627c2s
v3p0369c1s
Taylor, J., jr. v3p0102c1s
Taylor, J.B. v1p0420c2s
v5p0126c2s
Taylor, J.C. v6p0312c2s
Taylor, J.E. v1p0308c2s
v1p0462c2s v1p0510c1s v1p0514c1s
v1p0645c1s v1p0845c1s v1p0908c2s
v1p1009c2s v2p0289c2s v3p0008c1m
v3p0291c2s v4p0555c1s
Taylor, J.F. v5p0064c2s
v5p0085c2s v5p0091c2s v5p0297c2m
v5p0342c1s v5p0423c1s v5p0446c2s
v5p0488c2s v5p0531c1s
Taylor, J.G. v4p0532c1s
Taylor, J.H. v1p1225c2s
Taylor, J.J. v1p0047c1s
v2p0233c2s
Taylor, J.L. v1p0016c2s
v1p0030c2s v1p0998c2s v6p0211c2s
v6p0317c2m v6p0520c1s
Taylor, J.M. v1p0206c2s
v2p0352c1s v4p0123c1s v4p0361c1s
v4p0441c1s v4p0512c1s v5p0608c1s
v6p0055c2s v6p0078c2s v6p0465c1s
v6p0597c1s v6p0704c1s
Taylor, J.P. v2p0025c2s
v2p0406c1s v3p0130c2s v3p0418c2s
v4p0053c1s
Taylor, J.R. v5p0025c1s
v5p0067c2s v5p0350c2s v5p0479c1s
v6p0389c2s v6p0444c2s v6p0500c2s
v6p0711c1s
Taylor, J.R.M. v6p0224c1s
Taylor, J.S. v5p0293c1s
Taylor, J.S., Mrs. v1p1419c1s
Taylor, J.T. v1p1003c1s
v1p1004c1s v1p1427c2s v4p0597c2s
Taylor, J.W. v6p0068c2s
Taylor, J.Y. v4p0605c1s
Taylor, J.Z. v1p0810c1s
Taylor, James v4p0570c2m
Taylor, John and Murray, E.H.
v2p0456c2s
Taylor, L.E. v6p0528c2s
Taylor, L.P. v3p0095c1s
Taylor, M. v1p0904c2s
v1p1420c2s v1p1423c1s
Taylor, M.A. v4p0163c1s
v5p0154c1s v5p0238c1s v6p0035c1s
Taylor, M.C. v1p0641c2s
v1p0689c1s
Taylor, M.D. v4p0224c2s
v4p0388c2s
Taylor, M.F. v1p0032c1s
v1p0356c2s v1p0639c1s v1p0802c1s
Taylor, M.I. v5p0281c1s
Taylor, M.L. and Learoyd, M.W.
v4p0131c2s
Taylor, M.S. v4p0135c1s
Taylor, Mary I. v6p0700c1s
Taylor, Miss v1p0581c1s
v1p0609c1s v1p0609c2s v1p0674c1s
v1p0716c1s v1p0773c2s v1p0878c2s
v1p0921c2s v1p1408c1s v1p1409c1s
v1p1411c1s
Taylor, N.M. v5p0190c1s
v5p0269c1s
Taylor, N.T. v4p0002c1s
Taylor, N.W. v1p0099c1s
v1p0626c2s v1p1091c2s v1p1102c1s
v1p1200c2s v1p1240c1s v1p1287c1m
v1p1336c2m v2p0259c1s
Taylor, N.W. and Merwin, S.
v1p0911c2s
Taylor, O.A. v1p0038c1s
v1p0076c1s v1p0885c1s
Taylor, O.F. v5p0134c1s
Taylor, O.S. v1p0074c2s
v1p0688c1s v1p0708c2s
Taylor, P. v2p0457c1s
Taylor, P.K. v6p0352c1s
Taylor, P.M. v2p0279c1s
Taylor, P.T. v1p1289c2s
Taylor, Prof. v2p0008c1s
Taylor, R. v1p0261c2s
v1p1245c2s v1p1343c2m v1p1347c1s
Taylor, R.C. v1p0030c2s
v1p0268c2s v1p0269c1s
Taylor, R.J. v6p0493c1s
Taylor, R.S. v2p0299c2m
v4p0457c2s v5p0149c2s v5p0332c1s
v6p0422c1s
Taylor, R.S. and Dyes, Gustave
v5p0380c2s
Taylor, R.W. v5p0038c1s
Taylor, S. v1p0004c2m
v1p0081c2s v1p0198c2s v1p0286c2s
v1p0299c1s v1p0497c2m v1p0733c2s
v1p0876c1s v1p1006c1s v1p1222c2s
v2p0006c1s v3p0345c2s
Taylor, S.H. v1p0555c1s
v1p0739c1s
Taylor, S.J. v3p0128c1s
v4p0113c1s v4p0429c2s
Taylor, S.M. v4p0206c1s
v4p0279c1s
Taylor, T. v1p0082c1s
v1p0099c2s v1p0370c2s v1p0958c2s
v1p1130c1s v1p1241c2s v1p1299c2s
v2p0059c2s v2p0062c2s v2p0209c1s
v2p0338c1s v2p0473c2s
Taylor, T.W. v4p0307c1s
Taylor, T.W., jr. v5p0327c2s
v5p0486c1s
Taylor, Tom v1p0186c1s
v1p0595c2s v1p0738c1s v1p0769c1s
v1p0786c2s v1p1013c2s v1p1256c1s
v1p1434c2s v1p1436c2s
Taylor, W. v1p0849c2s
v2p0354c2s v4p0015c1s v4p0016c1s
v4p0168c2s v4p0182c2s v4p0399c2s
v4p0400c1s v4p0400c2s v4p0562c2s
v4p0571c2s v6p0678c1s
Taylor, W., jr. v3p0303c1s
Taylor, W.A. v6p0025c2s
Taylor, W.B. v1p0426c1s
v1p1222c2s v2p0127c1s
Taylor, W.C. v1p0014c2s
v1p0019c1s v1p0088c1s v1p0143c1s
v1p0165c2s v1p0199c2s v1p0218c2s
v1p0227c1s v1p0258c1s v1p0315c1s
v1p0372c1s v1p0438c2s v1p0439c1s
v1p0525c1s v1p0570c2s v1p0614c1s
v1p0652c2s v1p0700c2m v1p0757c1s
v1p0801c2s v1p0836c2s v1p0859c2s
v1p0897c1s v1p0904c1s v1p0906c1s
v1p0952c2s v1p1066c1s v1p1142c2s
v1p1151c2s v1p1182c1s v1p1197c1s
v1p1231c2s v1p1327c1s v1p1426c1s
v2p0296c2s v2p0340c1s
Taylor, W.D. v6p0530c1s
Taylor, W.E. v1p0343c2s
v3p0169c2s v4p0531c1s
Taylor, W.F. v2p0072c1s
v2p0235c2s
Taylor, W.G.L. v4p0450c1s
v4p0599c2s v5p0175c1s v5p0607c1m
v6p0141c1s v6p0156c2s v6p0158c2s
v6p0254c1s v6p0458c1s v6p0516c1s
v6p0519c2s v6p0520c1s v6p0651c2s
v6p0659c2s
Taylor, W.G.Langworthy ... v6p0224c1s
Taylor, W.H. v1p0519c1s
v5p0214c1s
Taylor, W.H. et al. v1p0518c2s
Taylor, W.I. v1p0355c1s
Taylor, W.J. v1p0560c1s
v1p0793c2s v1p0828c1s v1p1096c2s
v1p1440c1s
Taylor, W.J.R. v2p0286c1s
v3p0283c1s
Taylor, W.L. v4p0316c2s
v5p0334c2s
Taylor, W.L. et al. v5p0106c2s
Taylor, W.M. v1p0784c1s
v1p1042c1s v1p1044c1s v2p0440c1s
v3p0135c2s v3p0255c2s v3p0281c1s
Taylor, W.V. v4p0114c2s
v4p0320c2s v4p0570c1s v5p0118c2s
Taylor, W.W. v3p0011c1s

v3p0114c1s v3p0465c1s v4p0459c1s
Taylor, Z.B. v3p0331c2s
Taylor, Zula M. v6p0315c2s
Taylor-Cameron, J.S. v4p0489c2s
Tchaykovsky, N.W. v6p0558c2s
Tchekhof, A. v6p0164c2s
v6p0311c1s
Tcheng-Ki-Tong v4p0106c1s
Tcheng-Ki-Tong, Gen. v3p0223c2s
v3p0393c1s
Tchernoff, D.K. v1p1251c2s
Tchertkoff, V. v5p0437c2s
Tchihatchef, P.de v3p0328c2s
Teachenor, R.B. v3p0413c2s
Teague, J.J. v3p0235c1s
v4p0504c1s
Teague, M.A. v6p0572c2s
Teague, Merrill A. v6p0086c1s
Teal, A. v2p0290c1s
v3p0200c2s v3p0268c1s
Teal, A.H. v1p0886c2s
Teal, B. v4p0075c2s
Teale, L. v6p0378c1s
Teale, T.P. v2p0157c1m
v3p0125c1s v4p0164c2m
Teall, F.A. v4p0483c1s
Teall, F.H. v4p0518c1s
Teall, G. v5p0235c2s
Teall, G.C. v5p0030c1s
v5p0204c1s v5p0279c2s v5p0303c2s
v5p0377c2s v5p0378c2s v6p0338c1s
v6p0695c2m
Teall, J.J.H. v2p0337c2s
v4p0486c2s v4p0511c1s
Teall, O.S. v3p0085c2s
Tearle, C. v6p0244c2s
v6p0531c1s
Teasdale, G.T. v6p0236c1s
Teasdale, T.C. v1p0097c1s
Teasdale-Buckell, G. v6p0275c1s
Tebaldini, G. v4p0233c1s
v5p0438c1s
Tebb, W. v3p0446c2s
Tebbets, T. v1p0230c2s
v1p0688c1s v1p1103c2s v2p0236c1s
Tebbs, H.V. v1p0272c1s
Tebbutt, E. v6p0127c2s
v6p0548c2s
Tebbutt, S. v5p0327c1s
Tedder, H.R. v2p0035c1s
v2p0045c1s v2p0045c2s v2p0047c2s
v2p0057c1s v2p0117c2s v2p0255c2s
v2p0256c1s v2p0256c2s v2p0257c1m
v2p0399c1s v5p0192c1s v5p0217c2s
Teebay, C. v1p0483c1s
Teele, R.P. v5p0299c1s
v6p0329c1s v6p0329c2m v6p0620c2s
Teeling, B. v4p0570c2s
v6p0302c1s v6p0552c1s
Teeling, Bartle v6p0486c2s
Teeling, C.G. v2p0134c1s
Teeling, T.L. v3p0475c1s
Teeling, T.L.L. v1p0611c2s
v2p0077c1s v3p0240c1s v3p0246c1s
v3p0350c1s v4p0255c2s v4p0350c2s
v4p0536c2s v5p0170c2s v5p0227c2s
v5p0371c1s v5p0494c1s v5p0510c1s
v5p0589c1s v6p0275c2s v6p0627c1s
Teeple, C.L. v6p0054c1s
Teeple, L. v5p0036c1s
Teeple, Lou R. v5p0338c1s
v6p0608c1s
Teetling, B. v6p0328c1s
Teetor, H.D. v2p0086c1m
v2p0161c2s v2p0238c2s v2p0259c2s
v2p0268c1s v2p0270c1m v2p0293c1s
v3p0047c1s v3p0061c2s v3p0072c2s
v3p0085c1m v3p0088c1s v3p0089c1s
v3p0093c1s v3p0104c2s v3p0111c2s
v3p0113c1s v3p0115c1s v3p0130c1s
v3p0132c1s v3p0144c2s v3p0188c1s
v3p0188c2s v3p0193c2s v3p0198c1s
v3p0207c2s v3p0213c2s v3p0225c2s
v3p0245c1s v3p0245c2s v3p0266c1s
v3p0266c2s v3p0268c1s v3p0272c1s
v3p0275c2s v3p0280c1s v3p0280c2s
v3p0290c1s v3p0324c2s v3p0332c2s
v3p0350c2s v3p0352c2s v3p0354c2s
v3p0363c1s v3p0363c2s v3p0367c1s
v3p0368c1s v3p0393c2s v3p0410c1s
v3p0410c2s v3p0411c2s v3p0422c2s
v3p0436c2s v3p0455c1s v3p0461c2s
v3p0465c2s v3p0467c1s v3p0471c1s
v4p0028c1s v4p0043c2s v4p0075c1s
v4p0080c1s v4p0084c1s
Tefft, J.A. v1p0273c1s
Tefft, L.B. v1p0729c2s
v1p0977c2s
Tegetmeier, W.B. v1p0083c1s
v1p0322c2m v1p0986c2s v1p1040c1s
v2p0261c2s v4p0121c1s v4p0387c1s
v4p0443c1s v5p0216c1s v6p0178c1s
v6p0545c1s
Tegetmeier, W.B. et al. .. v4p0030c2s
Teggart, F.J. v4p0345c2s
v5p0012c1s v5p0088c1s v5p0332c2s
v5p0333c1m v5p0333c2m v5p0335c1s
v5p0336c2m v6p0092c2s v6p0104c1s
v6p0636c1s
Tegima, S. v2p0131c2s
Tegner, E. v2p0427c2s
Tegner, Esaias v2p0409c2s
Teichmueller, H. v4p0044c2s
v4p0167c1s v4p0233c2s v5p0269c1s
v5p0311c2s v5p0312c2s v5p0593c2s
Teichmueller, H.Teich v4p0322c2s
Teignmouth-Shore, T. v5p0640c1s
Teisen, A. v4p0195c1s
Telang, P.R. v4p0278c2s
v4p0356c2s v4p0374c2s
Telbin, W. v3p0207c2s
v4p0504c2s v4p0544c1m v5p0429c1s
Telfer, J.B. v3p0020c1s
Telfer-Smollett v5p0244c1s
v5p0244c2s v5p0375c2s
Telfer-Smollett, Col. v6p0083c1s
v6p0417c1s
Telford, E.P. v5p0134c1s
v5p0412c1s v5p0594c2s v5p0595c1s
v6p0081c2s
Telford, Emma P. v6p0415c1s
Telford, J. v2p0078c1s
v3p0060c1s v3p0302c1s v3p0460c1s
v4p0081c2s v4p0271c2s v4p0495c1s
v4p0580c1s v5p0144c2s v5p0500c2s
v5p0644c2s
Telford, John v4p0618c1s
Telford, T. v5p0625c2s
v6p0525c1s
Teller, C. v2p0017c1s
v6p0004c1s
Teller, Charlotte v5p0510c2s
Teller, H.M. v4p0617c1s
Teller, Nora v4p0052c1s
Tellet, R. v4p0156c2s
Tellkampf, J.L. v1p0073c2s
v1p0092c1s v1p0284c2s v1p0324c2s
v1p0515c1s v1p0515c2s v1p0860c1s
v1p1250c1s v1p1323c2s
Tellkampf, T.A. v1p0318c2s
v1p0415c2s
Tempany, T.W. v2p0055c1s
v2p0143c1s v2p0251c1s v2p0277c2s
v3p0089c1s
Temperley, H.W.V. v6p0266c2s
v6p0345c2s
Tempest, Adolphus V. v6p0612c2s
Tempest, M. v4p0568c2s
Tempest, W. v1p0238c1s
Templar, C.
v1p0756c1s
v1p1106c1s
Temple, A.G. v4p0125c2s
v4p0244c1s v4p0338c2s v5p0544c1s
v5p0595c1s v6p0248c2s
Temple, Bp. v2p0258c1s
Temple, C. v1p1041c2s
Temple, F. v2p0149c1s
v2p0368c1s
Temple, G.T. v1p0114c1s
v2p0007c1s v2p0009c2s v2p0020c2s
v2p0102c2s v2p0234c1s v2p0316c1s
v2p0420c2s v2p0447c1s v3p0185c1s
Temple, J.H. v1p0741c2s
v1p0760c2s v1p0851c1s v3p0002c2s
v3p0172c2s
Temple, J.W. v4p0489c2s
Temple, Lieut. v1p1401c2s
Temple, M. v5p0335c2s
Temple, R. v2p0079c1s
v2p0134c2s v2p0190c1s v2p0217c1s
v2p0218c2s v2p0407c1s v2p0410c1s
v3p0211c1s v3p0214c2s v3p0266c1m
v4p0132c1s v4p0279c2s v4p0280c2s
v4p0604c1s v5p0019c2s v5p0034c1s
v6p0127c1s
Temple, R., Sir v2p0162c2s
v2p0186c2s v2p0218c2s v2p0272c2s
v3p0023c2s v3p0158c1s v3p0182c1s
v3p0200c1s v3p0212c2s v3p0434c1s
v4p0522c2s v4p0525c1s v4p0566c1s
Temple, R., Sir and Wade, T.Sir
v2p0079c1s
Temple, R.C. v2p0166c2s
v2p0181c1s v3p0060c2s v3p0213c1s
v3p0234c2s v3p0469c1s v4p0205c1s
v4p0278c1s v4p0353c1s v5p0018c2m
v5p0149c1m v5p0212c1s v5p0411c1s
v5p0472c2s
Temple, T. v3p0086c1s
v3p0184c2s v3p0266c2s
Temple-Barre, R.
v4p0337c2s
Templer, J. v6p0340c1s
v6p0396c2s
Templer, J.C.
v1p1413c2s
Templeton, A.
v2p0082c2s
v2p0236c1s
Templeton, H.
v5p0153c1s
v6p0051c2s
v6p0147c2s
v6p0300c2s
Templeton, Herminie
v6p0036c1s
v6p0351c1s
Templeton, J.
v2p0039c1s
Templeton, J.M.
v4p0051c1s
v4p0413c2s
Templin, L.J. v2p0007c1s
v2p0169c2s v2p0252c1s v2p0273c2s
v2p0307c2s v2p0344c1m v2p0350c2s
v2p0394c1s
v2p0458c1m
v2p0480c1s
Tener, G.C. v3p0052c1s
Tenger, M. v4p0049c1s
Tenison-Woods, J.E. v2p0090c1s
Teniswood, C.G.H. v2p0067c2s
v3p0120c2s v3p0368c2s
Teniswood, G.F. v1p0459c2m
Tennal, R. v6p0467c1s
Tennant, D. v2p0264c2s
Tennant, H.J. v5p0585c1s
v6p0355c1s v6p0708c1s
Tennant, J.F. v2p0089c2s
Tennant, J.R. v6p0674c1s
Tennant, M. v5p0639c1s
Tennant, P. v6p0117c2s
Tennent, J.E. v1p0213c2s
v1p0618c2s v1p1010c1s
Tennent, J.E., Sir v1p1415c1s
Tenney, A.A. v6p0383c1s
Tenney, A.H. v6p0058c2s
v6p0116c1s
Tenney, E. v1p1103c1s
Tenney, E.P. v1p0243c1s
v1p0496c1s v1p1084c1m v1p1302c2s
Tenney, H.C. v3p0209c2s
Tenney, H.M. v5p0236c2s
Tenney, J.B. v5p0358c1s
Tenney, J.M. v5p0575c1s
Tenney, S. v1p0456c2s
v1p0877c1s v1p1016c1s v1p1155c2s
v1p1173c1s
Tenney, S.E., Mrs. et al.. v4p0215c2s
Tenney, W.A. v5p0151c2s
v5p0414c1s v6p0367c2s v6p0377c1s
v6p0660c2s
Tenney, W.J. v2p0452c1s
Tennyson, A. v1p0004c1s
v1p0022c2s v1p0335c2s v1p0346c2s
v1p0539c2s v1p0612c1s v1p0726c2s
v1p0776c1m v1p0831c1s v1p0863c2s
v1p0942c1s v1p1102c2s v1p1313c1s
v1p1369c2s v1p1397c2s v2p0074c2s
v2p0116c2s v2p0166c2s v2p0167c1s
v2p0182c2s v2p0262c1s v2p0458c1s
v2p0461c2s v4p0117c2s v4p0158c2s
v4p0409c2s
Tennyson, F. v1p0573c1s
v1p1219c2s
Tennyson, H. v1p0171c1s
v3p0141c1s v3p0454c2s
Tennyson, L. v1p0363c1s
v1p0992c1s v1p0996c1s
Tennyson, Lady v4p0409c2s
Tennyson, Lord v3p0068c2s
v3p0106c2s
Tennyson, M.H. v2p0457c2s
v3p0131c2s
Tennyson-D'Eyncourt, E.H.. v5p0551c2s
Tepper, J.G.O. v5p0385c1s
Terhune, A.P. v5p0051c1s
v5p0338c2s v6p0398c1s v6p0412c1s
v6p0480c2s
v6p0580c2s
Terhune, E.B. v4p0505c2s
v5p0081c1s
Terhune, H.R. v3p0331c1s
Terhune, J. v3p0424c1s
Terhune, M.V. v1p0107c2s
v1p0139c2s v1p0617c2s v1p0878c1s
v1p0996c2s v1p1180c2s v1p1270c2s
v1p1280c1s v2p0055c1s v3p0056c1s
v4p0382c2s v4p0447c2s v5p0078c1s
Terhune, M.V., Mrs. v3p0469c2s
Terhune, Mrs. v1p0849c1s
Terman, L.M. v6p0249c2s
v6p0514c1s
Ternant, A.de v4p0182c2s
v4p0215c1s v4p0341c2s v4p0376c2s
v5p0038c1s v5p0140c1s v5p0398c1s
Terne, B. v3p0090c2s
v3p0343c1s v4p0066c1s v4p0219c2m
v5p0017c2s v6p0111c2s
Teros, A.P. v5p0211c2s
Terrasson, E.de v5p0134c2s
Terrel, A.K., Mrs. v5p0458c2s
Terrell, A.P. v3p0467c1s
Terrell, A.W. v5p0001c1s
Terrell, G. v6p0024c2s
Terrell, J.W. v4p0152c2s
Terrell, M.C. v6p0390c2s
v6p0605c2s
Terriss, Ellaline v6p0612c2s
Terry, A. v5p0586c1s
Terry, B. v5p0145c1s
v5p0190c1s v6p0020c2s
Terry, B.S. v4p0214c2s
v4p0303c1s
Terry, C.S. v5p0102c2s
v5p0504c1s v6p0189c1s v6p0258c2s
v6p0263c2s
Terry, C.Sanford v6p0425c2s
Terry, E. v2p0060c2s

v3p0406c1s
Terry, Ellen v6p0274c1s
Terry, F. v5p0288c2s
Terry, F.C.B. et al. v4p0371c2s
Terry, G.C. v6p0523c1s
Terry, H.T. v1p0208c2s
v1p0848c2s v2p0244c2s v2p0464c1s
v6p0650c1s
Terry, L.M. v5p0125c1s
v5p0160c2s v5p0434c2s v6p0414c2s
Terry, L.M., Mrs. v5p0298c2s
Terry, M.S. v1p0047c1s
v1p0087c2s v1p0438c2s v1p0668c1s
v1p0681c2s v1p1417c2s v2p0043c1s
v3p0042c1s v3p0192c2s v3p0237c2s
v3p0385c2s v4p0056c1s v4p0057c2s
v4p0058c1s v4p0158c2s v4p0275c2s
v5p0057c1s v5p0058c1s v5p0060c1s
v5p0305c2s v5p0352c2s v6p0024c2s
v6p0121c2s v6p0124c2s v6p0235c1s
v6p0262c1s v6p0543c2s
Terry, R. v1p0208c2s
v1p0468c1s v1p0520c1s v1p1028c2s
Terry, S.H. v5p0551c2s
Terry, T. v6p0338c2s
Terry, T.P. v3p0462c1s
v4p0145c1s v4p0178c2s v4p0368c1s
v4p0578c2s v5p0109c2s v5p0150c2s
v5p0151c1m v5p0258c2s v5p0302c2s
v5p0303c1s v5p0373c2s v5p0560c1s
v6p0337c2s v6p0339c1m v6p0354c2s
v6p0709c1s
Tertzky, R.K. v1p0615c2m
Terzian, P. v4p0027c1s
v5p0028c2s
Teschemacher, J.E. v1p0268c1s
v1p0470c2s
Teskey, A.M. v6p0391c2s
Tesla, N. v4p0288c2s
v4p0331c2m v5p0184c1s v5p0184c2s
v5p0275c2s v5p0560c2s
Tessan, J.F.L'Espigarie de
v6p0110c2s
Test, Z. v1p0857c2s
Tetedoux, C. v4p0607c1s
v4p0608c2s
Teters, E.C. v6p0690c1s
Teters, L.C. v6p0421c1s
Teters, Luellen C. v6p0040c2s
Tetley, J.G. v6p0367c2s
Tetlow, E.H. v4p0416c2s
Totlow, J. v1p1422c1s
v3p0242c2s v3p0287c1s v4p0026c2s
v4p0122c2s v4p0183c1s v4p0320c2s
v4p0627c2s v5p0182c2s v5p0264c2s
v5p0265c1s v6p0208c2s
v6p0514c2s
Tetlow, J. and Kellogg, M.
v4p0122c2s
Tetlow, J. et al. v5p0182c2s
Tetmajer, L. v2p0229c1s
Tetzel, J.M. v1p1270c1s
Teubner, C. v2p0220c1s
Tewkesbury, E.G. v5p0113c1s
Texima, S. v2p0233c2s
Texte, J. v5p0221c1s
Thacher, B.B. v1p0419c1s
v1p1018c2s v1p1207c2s v1p1255c1s
Thacher, E.S. v6p0059c2s
Thacher, G.A. v6p0175c1s
Thacher, H.F. v6p0502c1s
Thacher, J. v1p0038c1s
v3p0244c2s
Thacher, J.B. v5p0120c1s
Thacher, M. v1p0020c1s
Thacher, M.B. v4p0452c1s
Thacher, S.D. v2p0054c1s
Thacher, S.O. v2p0152c2s
Thacher, T. v5p0327c2s
Thacher, T.A. v1p0184c2s
v1p0588c2s v1p0709c1s v1p0727c2s
v1p1279c2s v1p1321c2s
Thacher, T.A. and Potwin, L.S.
v1p0727c2s
Thackara, E.S. v3p0122c2s
v3p0127c2s
Thacker, J.K. v1p0875c2s
Thackeray, A.E. v1p0984c1s
Thackeray, A.I. v1p0105c2s
v1p0257c1s v1p0328c1s v1p0492c1s
v1p0493c2s v1p0674c1m v1p0723c1s
v1p0756c1m v1p0765c2s v1p0851c1s
v1p0940c2s v1p0952c1s v1p1109c1s
v1p1141c1s v1p1177c2s v1p1209c2s
v1p1218c1s v1p1257c2s v1p1313c1s
v1p1314c2s v1p1371c1s v1p1423c1s
Thackeray, E.A. v3p0468c1s
Thackeray, F.S.J. v2p0030c2s
Thackeray, F.St.J. v3p0347c2s
v4p0147c1s v4p0186c1s v4p0571c2s
v6p0231c1s
Thackeray, F.T.St. v4p0569c2s
Thackeray, H.St.J. v6p0029c2s
Thackeray, W.M. v1p0007c2s
v1p0141c1s v1p0143c1s v1p0166c2s
v1p0229c1m v1p0245c1s v1p0343c2s
v1p0350c2s v1p0454c1s v1p0458c2s
v1p0510c1m v1p0510c2s v1p0511c1m
v1p0536c2s v1p0551c1s v1p0624c2s
v1p0682c1s v1p0753c1s v1p0774c1s
v1p0776c1s v1p0780c2s v1p0814c1s
v1p0819c2s v1p0878c2s v1p0895c2s
v1p0909c1s v1p0932c1s v1p0958c2s
v1p1008c1s v1p1008c2s v1p1129c2m
v1p1148c1s v1p1182c2s v1p1362c2s
v1p1375c1s v1p1377c2s v1p1412c1s
v1p1437c1m
Thackray, E.A. v3p0242c1s
v3p0400c2s
Thalberg, S. v1p1007c2s
Thaler, K. v1p0338c1s
v1p0601c2s
Thallon, Ida C. v6p0163c2s
Thane, G.D. v1p0536c2s
v2p0305c1s
Thanet, O. v1p0286c1s
v1p0888c1s v1p0981c1s v1p1317c2s
v1p1320c2s v1p1431c2s v2p0047c2s
v2p0090c1s v3p0188c1s v3p0463c1s
v4p0082c1s v4p0151c1s v4p0258c1s
v4p0272c1s v4p0374c1s v5p0066c2s
v5p0094c1s v5p0307c1s v5p0396c1s
v5p0555c2s
Thanet, Octave v4p0403c1s
v4p0404c2s v5p0133c2s v5p0168c2s
v5p0309c1s v5p0382c1s v5p0417c1s
v5p0635c2s v6p0016c2s v6p0084c2s
v6p0544c1s v6p0678c1s
Thanque, H.H.La v4p0031c1s
Thatcher, B.B. v1p0050c2s
v1p0067c2s v1p0073c2s v1p0084c2s
v1p0152c2s v1p0157c2s v1p0185c1m
v1p0278c1m v1p0287c2s v1p0636c1s
v1p0722c1s v1p0815c1s v1p0921c2s
v1p0950c1s v1p1378c1s
Thatcher, M.P. v1p0303c2s
v1p0712c1s
Thatcher, N. v1p1419c2s
Thatcher, O.J. v4p0306c1s
v5p0197c1s v5p0266c2s
Thaw, A.B. v4p0401c1s
v5p0269c1s v6p0052c1s
Thaxter, C. v1p0108c2s
v1p0466c1s v1p0560c2s v1p0579c1s
v1p0668c1s v1p0725c2s v1p0933c1s
v1p1230c2s v1p1328c2s v1p1380c1s
v1p1389c2s v1p1433c2s
Thayer, A.S. v6p0364c1s
v6p0511c1s
Thayer, A.W. v1p0108c1s
v2p0150c1s v2p0230c2s v3p0230c1s
v5p0052c1s
Thayer, Alice v6p0229c2s
Thayer, C. v6p0664c2s
Thayer, C.T. v1p0038c1s
v1p0100c2s
Thayer, Catherine v6p0005c2s
Thayer, E.M. v1p0919c2s
Thayer, E.R. v3p0194c1s
v6p0264c2s
Thayer, G.A. v3p0080c2s
v5p0352c1s v5p0428c2s v5p0601c2s
v6p0163c1s v6p0598c1s
Thayer, G.F. v1p0309c1s
v1p0506c2s v1p0796c2s v1p0867c2s
v1p1053c2s v1p1085c2s v1p1158c2s
v1p1159c2s v1p1234c2s v1p1235c1s
v1p1288c1s v1p1429c2s v1p1434c1s
Thayer, H.O. v5p0441c1s
Thayer, H.W. v6p0517c1s
Thayer, J., Mrs. v1p0420c1s
v1p0471c2s
Thayer, J.B. v1p0427c1s
v1p0600c2m v2p0110c1s v2p0133c1s
v2p0140c1s v2p0186c1s v2p0253c1s
v3p0097c2s v3p0135c2s v3p0213c1s
v3p0213c2s v3p0233c1s v3p0245c1s
v3p0466c2s v4p0548c2s v5p0363c2s
v6p0491c2s v6p0671c2s
Thayer, J.H. v1p0130c2s
v3p0042c2s v3p0471c2s v4p0056c2s
v5p0017c1s v5p0306c1s v5p0348c1s
Thayer, J.M. v4p0234c2s
v5p0003c2s v5p0548c2s
Thayer, Jessie M. v5p0612c1s
Thayer, L.R. v1p1380c1s
Thayer, Mabel v4p0516c2s
Thayer, R. v5p0044c1s
Thayer, S.H. v3p0020c2s
v3p0396c1s v4p0569c1s v5p0203c2s
v6p0701c1s
Thayer, S.R. v4p0096c2s
Thayer, S.S. v4p0225c2s
Thayer, S.W. v1p1029c2s
Thayer, T.B. v1p0070c1s
v1p0089c2s v1p0127c2s v1p0180c1s
v1p0293c1s v1p0343c2s v1p0347c1s
v1p0433c2s v1p0481c2s v1p0495c2m
v1p0560c1s v1p0593c2s v1p0625c2s
v1p0711c1s v1p0721c2s v1p0821c1s
v1p0849c2s v1p0857c2s v1p0874c1s
v1p0891c1s v1p0977c2s v1p1028c2s
v1p1058c2s v1p1088c1s v1p1097c1s
v1p1207c1s v1p1215c1s v1p1238c2s
v1p1337c1s v1p1338c2s v1p1369c2s
Thayer, W.G. v5p0472c2s
Thayer, W.K. v5p0299c2s
Thayer, W.M. v2p0082c1s
v3p0049c2s v3p0128c2s v4p0183c2s
v4p0474c2s v4p0505c1s v4p0514c1s
Thayer, W.R. v2p0050c2s
v2p0063c1s v2p0072c1m v2p0198c1m
v2p0200c1s v2p0231c2s v2p0270c1s
v2p0401c2s v2p0409c1s v2p0472c2s
v3p0028c1s v3p0057c1s v3p0058c1s
v3p0110c1m v3p0114c1s v3p0144c1s
v3p0262c2s v3p0387c1s v3p0392c1s
v3p0424c2s v3p0430c2s v3p0454c2s
v4p0077c1m v4p0090c1s v4p0109c1s
v4p0147c1m v4p0147c2s v4p0152c1s
v4p0197c2s v4p0198c1s v4p0249c1s
v4p0249c2s v4p0294c1s v4p0320c2s
v4p0347c1s v4p0419c2s v4p0452c2s
v4p0475c1s v4p0481c2s v4p0523c1s
v4p0551c2s v4p0602c1s v4p0605c1s
v4p0632c1s v5p0064c2s v5p0098c2s
v5p0144c2s v5p0209c2s v5p0256c2m
v5p0300c1s v5p0347c1s v5p0608c2s
v6p0066c2s v6p0112c2s v6p0164c1s
v6p0202c1s v6p0230c2s v6p0282c1m
v6p0292c2m v6p0294c1s v6p0331c1s
v6p0403c2s v6p0408c1m v6p0441c2m
v6p0565c2s v6p0571c2s v6p0572c1s
v6p0588c2m v6p0676c2m v6p0684c2s
Thayer, W.S. v1p1407c2s
v3p0225c1s v6p0409c1s
Thayer, W.S. and Howland, W.
v1p0774c2s
Thayer, W.W. v5p0644c1s
Thearle, L.N. v5p0551c2s
Thearle, T. v5p0282c1s
Thebaud, A. v1p0637c1s
v1p1119c1s
Thebaud, A.J. v1p0247c2s
v1p0387c2s v1p0431c1s v1p0487c2s
v1p0617c2s v1p1109c2s v1p1115c2m
v1p1116c1s v1p1118c2s v1p1216c1m
v2p0092c2s v2p0168c1s v2p0241c2s
v2p0480c2s
Theed, M.F. v5p0484c2s
Thelberg, E.B. v5p0271c2s
v5p0334c1s
Thelwall, A.S. v1p0240c2s
Thelwall, S. v3p0315c1s
Theobald, F.V. v4p0061c2s
Theobold, J. v1p0953c2s
Theophilus, D. et al. v4p0379c1s
Thesca, H. v1p1065c1s
Thesiger, E.P. v3p0084c2s
v3p0416c1s v4p0388c2s
Theuriet, A. v1p0022c2s
v1p0262c2s v4p0166c2s v4p0202c1s
v5p0210c1s v5p0355c2s
Theuriet, Andre v4p0583c2s
Theuriet, M.A. v1p1339c2s
Theuriot, M. v1p0849c2s
Thevenin, M. v1p0472c2s
v1p0475c1s v1p0516c2s v1p0824c2s
v1p1122c1s
Thicke, F.E. v3p0202c2s
v3p0448c1s
Thicknesse, L. v5p0137c1s
Thiergen, O. v4p0015c1s
v5p0192c1m v5p0230c1s v5p0232c1s
v5p0293c2s v5p0381c1s v6p0192c1s
v6p0215c1s v6p0252c1m v6p0252c2s
v6p0363c1s v6p0581c2s
Thierry, C.de v4p0016c1s
v5p0112c2s v5p0124c2s v5p0128c1m
v5p0187c2s v5p0244c2s v5p0245c1m
v5p0247c1s v5p0281c1s v5p0328c2s
v5p0356c1s v5p0588c1s v5p0602c1s
v5p0611c1s v6p0024c1s v6p0138c2m
v6p0205c1s v6p0267c1s
Thiers, L.A. v1p1392c2s
Thiersch, H.G.J. v1p1058c1s
Thijon, A. v1p0516c2s
Thilby, F. v4p0439c2s
Thilly, F. v4p0439c1s
v4p0622c1s v5p0133c2s v5p0293c1s
v5p0343c2s v5p0386c1s v5p0605c1s
v6p0277c1s v6p0317c2s v6p0325c1s
v6p0457c1s v6p0495c2s v6p0496c1s
v6p0521c2m v6p0604c2s
Thilly, F. et al. v6p0002c1s
Thilly, Frank v6p0563c2s
Thimme, Edw. v4p0315c2s
Thin, G. v4p0327c1s
Thinker, S.H. v5p0395c2s
Thirkield, W.P. v6p0016c2s
Thirlmere, R. v4p0079c1s
v4p0309c1s v4p0396c2s
Thirlwall, F.J. v4p0066c2s
Thirsk, R. v6p0465c1s
Thiry, J.H. v3p0376c1s
Thiselton, A.E. v5p0270c2s
Thiselton-Dyer, W.T. v3p0051c2s
v4p0087c1s v4p0340c2s v4p0543c2s
v4p0600c2s v5p0137c2s v5p0277c1s
v6p0008c2s
Thiselton-Dyer, W.T. et al.
v6p0576c1s
Thistleton, A.C. v3p0273c1s
v3p0427c2s
Thiusch, H.G.J. v1p0769c1s
Thoburn, J.M. v1p0853c2s
v3p0264c2s v3p0283c1s v4p0367c2s
v4p0374c2s v4p0573c2s v5p0118c1s
v5p0380c1s v6p0321c1s
Thoburn, J.M. et al. v4p0374c2s

Thoits, A.T. v6p0264c1s
Tholuck, A. v1p0262c2s
v1p0580c2s v1p0673c1s v1p0681c1s
v1p0769c1s v1p0769c2s v1p1178c1s
v1p1301c2s v1p1356c2s
Tholuck, Dr. v1p0646c1s
Tholuck, F. v1p0515c1s
Tholuck, F.A. v1p0126c1s
v1p0126c2s v1p0129c1s v1p0517c1s
Tholuck, F.A.G. v1p0121c2s
v1p0127c1s v1p0189c1s v1p0645c2s
v1p1044c1s v1p1083c2s v1p1271c2s
Thom, J.H. v1p0409c2s
v1p0414c1s v1p0720c1s v1p1041c2s
v1p1096c2s v1p1404c1s
Thom, W.T. v5p0613c1s
Thoma, F.de v6p0567c1s
Thoma, Frank de v6p0451c1s
Thomas, A. v1p0466c2s
v1p0484c2s v1p0609c2s v1p1201c2s
v1p1301c1s v4p0336c1s v5p0591c1s
Thomas, A.C. v1p0043c2s
v1p0697c2s v1p1147c2s v1p1200c2s
v1p1279c1s v4p0139c1s v4p0250c1s
v5p0397c1s
Thomas, A.E. v6p0298c2s
v6p0706c2s
Thomas, A.G. v2p0468c2s
Thomas, A.P. v2p0399c1s
Thomas, B. v1p0014c1s
v1p0081c2s v1p0314c2s v1p0584c1s
v1p1059c1s v1p1372c2s v2p0139c1s
v2p0261c1s v2p0464c1s v3p0039c2s
v6p0112c2s
Thomas, B.D. v4p0467c1s
Thomas, Bertha v3p0097c1s
Thomas, C. v1p0769c2s
v1p0793c1s v1p0814c1s v1p0900c1s
v1p1091c1s v1p1326c2s v2p0010c1m
v2p0076c1s v2p0076c2s v2p0185c1s
v2p0281c1s v2p0286c2s v2p0299c2m
v2p0300c1m v2p0339c1s v2p0361c2s
v2p0388c2s v2p0465c2s v3p0068c2s
v3p0076c1s v3p0105c2s v3p0125c1s
v3p0129c2m v3p0170c2m v3p0175c2s
v3p0176c1m v3p0180c2s v3p0208c1s
v3p0232c2s v3p0247c2s v3p0277c2s
v3p0290c1m v3p0417c2s v4p0013c2s
v4p0094c2s v4p0154c1s v4p0223c2s
v4p0224c2s v4p0229c1s v4p0229c2m
v4p0250c1s v4p0282c2m v4p0343c1s
v4p0362c1m v4p0406c2s v4p0422c2s
v4p0448c1s v4p0481c2s v4p0482c2s
v4p0610c1s v5p0099c2s v5p0157c2s
v5p0288c2s v5p0358c1s v5p0366c1s
v5p0367c1s v5p0455c2s v5p0525c2s
v5p0617c2s v5p0630c1s v6p0262c2s
v6p0305c2s v6p0349c2s v6p0414c1s
v6p0460c2s v6p0554c1s v6p0554c2s
v6p0609c2s
Thomas, C. and Carney, W.J.
v6p0031c1s v6p0352c2s
Thomas, C. and Hewitt, J.N.B.
v6p0275c2s v6p0709c2s
Thomas, C. and Putman, C.E.
v2p0112c2s
Thomas, C.E. v6p0075c2s
v6p0393c2s v6p0440c2s v6p0465c2s
v6p0598c1s v6p0617c1s
Thomas, C.H. v3p0164c2s
Thomas, C.S. v4p0059c1s
v4p0379c2s v4p0462c2s v4p0525c1s
v4p0526c1m
Thomas, C.W. v6p0667c1s
Thomas, D.A. v4p0173c2s
v5p0124c1s v6p0129c1s v6p0132c2s
Thomas, D.V. v6p0345c1s
v6p0605c1s
Thomas, D.Y. v6p0016c2s
v6p0213c1s v6p0215c2s v6p0668c2s
Thomas, E. v1p0835c1s
v1p0835c2s v1p1148c2s v1p1240c1s
v4p0412c1s v4p0578c1s v5p0422c2s
v6p0171c1s v6p0221c1s v6p0339c1s
v6p0532c2s v6p0672c2s v6p0696c2s
Thomas, E., Mrs. v5p0394c1m
v5p0394c2s
Thomas, E.A. v1p0871c2m
v2p0240c1s v2p0318c2s v2p0474c1s
v2p0478c2s v3p0233c2s v5p0394c1s
Thomas, E.C. v2p0045c2s
v2p0057c1m v2p0062c1m v2p0070c2s
v2p0088c1s v2p0133c1s v2p0216c2s
v2p0256c1m v2p0256c2m v2p0257c1m
v2p0336c1s v4p0253c1s v5p0084c2s
Thomas, E.E. v2p0121c1s
Thomas, E.M. v2p0026c2s
v2p0030c1s v2p0048c2s v2p0062c1s
v2p0121c2s v2p0139c2s v2p0146c1s
v2p0185c1s v2p0294c2s v2p0307c2s
v2p0364c1s v2p0371c1s v2p0404c2s
v2p0475c1s v3p0113c2s v3p0156c1s
v3p0312c1s v3p0382c2s v3p0435c2s
v4p0018c2s v4p0021c2s v4p0060c1s
v4p0214c1s v4p0227c2s v4p0243c2s
v4p0277c1s v4p0345c2s v4p0375c2s
v4p0411c1s v4p0494c2s v4p0550c1s
v4p0556c1s v4p0577c1s v4p0585c2s
v4p0607c1s v4p0607c2s v5p0003c2s
v5p0063c1s v5p0079c2s v5p0093c2s
v5p0115c2s v5p0211c1s v5p0283c1s
v5p0564c1s v5p0609c2s v5p0622c1s
v6p0089c1s v6p0345c2s v6p0485c1s
v6p0495c1s v6p0505c2s
Thomas, E.M. and Goodrich, S.F.
v3p0207c1s
Thomas, Edith M. v2p0406c2s
v2p0415c2s v4p0630c2s v6p0124c1s
v6p0165c2s
Thomas, Edward v5p0416c1s
v5p0596c2s v6p0045c1s v6p0205c2s
Thomas, F.E. v4p0145c1s
v4p0364c1s v4p0426c2s v6p0439c1s
Thomas, F.F. v1p0844c2s
Thomas, F.G. v5p0332c1s
Thomas, F.I. v4p0219c2m
v5p0324c2s
Thomas, F.M. v3p0121c1s
Thomas, F.R. v1p0539c2s
v1p0859c1s v1p0993c2s v1p1424c1s
v1p1426c1s
Thomas, F.S. v4p0151c2s
v6p0177c1s
Thomas, F.W.L. v1p0210c2s
v1p0948c2s
Thomas, G. v3p0213c2s
v4p0561c1s
Thomas, G.E. v4p0210c1s
Thomas, G.G. v5p0051c2s
v5p0394c1s v6p0045c1s v6p0071c1s
Thomas, G.G. and
St.Andre, A.de
v5p0369c2s
v5p0465c1s
Thomas, G.J. v6p0136c2s
Thomas, H. v4p0139c2s
v4p0316c1s v4p0455c1s v4p0523c2s
v4p0608c1s v5p0196c1s v5p0320c2s
v5p0535c1s
Thomas, H.A. v2p0045c1s
v2p0081c2s
Thomas, H.E. v3p0459c2s
v6p0333c2s v6p0456c1s v6p0660c1s
v6p0662c1s
Thomas, H.G. v3p0328c2s
Thomas, H.O. v4p0567c1m
v5p0626c1s
Thomas, H.P. v2p0428c2s
Thomas, H.S. v3p0071c1s
v3p0340c2s v6p0525c2s
Thomas, H.T. v6p0333c1s
Thomas, H.W. v2p0355c2s
v5p0067c1s v5p0592c2s v6p0347c1s
v6p0600c1s
Thomas, Harlan v6p0087c2s
Thomas, I. v3p0039c1s
v3p0129c2s v4p0512c2s v6p0247c2s
v6p0450c1s
Thomas, J. v1p0772c1s
v2p0324c1s v3p0236c2s v5p0305c1s
Thomas, J.B. v1p0468c2s
v2p0247c1s v6p0493c2s v6p0559c1s
Thomas, J.B. et al. v2p0106c2s
Thomas, J.F. v4p0115c2s
Thomas, J.H. v3p0321c1s
Thomas, J.L. v5p0641c1s
Thomas, J.O. v3p0050c2s
v3p0294c1s
Thomas, J.P. v6p0048c2m
Thomas, J.R. v3p0018c2s
Thomas, J.W. v4p0327c2s
Thomas, Jennie L. v5p0530c2s
Thomas, Julian P. v6p0048c2s
Thomas, K.E. v6p0022c2s
v6p0397c2s v6p0515c1s
Thomas, Katherine E. v6p0124c1s
v6p0676c2s
Thomas, L. v1p0065c2s
v4p0047c1s v4p0147c1s v4p0329c1s
Thomas, L.A. and Hanna, C.A.
v4p0433c2s
Thomas, L.B. v4p0323c2s
Thomas, M. v1p0081c1s
v2p0195c2s
Thomas, M.A. v1p0319c2s
Thomas, M.C. v5p0636c2s
Thomas, M.Carey v6p0135c1s
Thomas, M.T. v2p0071c2s
Thomas, M.W.B. v1p1395c1s
Thomas, Moy v1p1309c2s
Thomas, N.W. v1p0939c1s
v3p0386c2s v5p0020c2s v5p0271c1s
v5p0583c1s v5p0624c1s v6p0036c1s
v6p0402c1s v6p0572c1s
Thomas, O. v1p1043c1s
v2p0443c2s v3p0124c2s v4p0033c2s
v5p0396c2s
Thomas, P. v5p0081c1s
Thomas, P.H. v6p0197c1s
Thomas, R. v4p0146c1s
v4p0331c1s v5p0283c2s v5p0578c1s
v6p0489c2s v6p0529c2s
Thomas, R.B. v2p0211c1s
v2p0280c1s
Thomas, R.W. v5p0487c1s
Thomas, Rose F. v5p0395c1s
v5p0638c2s
Thomas, Rowland v6p0038c2s
Thomas, S. v3p0215c1s
Thomas, S.H. v1p0300c1s
Thomas, T. v1p0883c2s
Thomas, T., Mrs. v4p0099c2s
Thomas, T.B. v6p0537c2s
Thomas, T.E. v2p0151c1s
Thomas, T.H. v4p0141c2s
v6p0683c2s
Thomas, T.P. v4p0043c1s
v4p0115c1s
Thomas, T.S. v5p0352c1s
Thomas, Theodore, Mrs. ... v6p0113c2s
Thomas, W.B. v5p0036c2s
v5p0225c1s v5p0261c2s v5p0512c1s
v6p0040c1s v6p0041c1s v6p0067c2s
v6p0068c1s v6p0096c1s v6p0168c2s
v6p0472c1s v6p0542c2s v6p0573c1s
v6p0611c2s
Thomas, W.C. v2p0131c1s
v2p0151c1s v2p0280c1s v2p0395c1s
Thomas, W.H. v3p0299c1s
v5p0402c2s v5p0632c2s v6p0258c2s
v6p0317c2s v6p0431c1s v6p0613c1s
Thomas, W.H.G. v6p0125c2s
Thomas, W.I. v4p0205c2s
v5p0123c2s v5p0225c1s v5p0381c2s
v5p0521c2m v5p0535c1s v6p0079c1s
v6p0526c1s v6p0600c1s v6p0702c2s
Thomas, W.J. v3p0453c1s
Thomas, W.L. v4p0234c2s
Thomas, W.L. et al. v4p0557c2s
Thomas, W.M. v2p0182c2s
v4p0395c1s v6p0226c1s
Thomas, W.W., jr. v3p0081c2s
v3p0109c1s v3p0177c2s v3p0417c2s
v3p0466c1s
Thomasius, G. v1p0119c1m
v1p0700c1s v1p1058c1m v1p1089c1s
Thomason, F. v4p0347c1s
Thomason, F.T. v4p0487c1s
Thomasson, F. v5p0324c1m
v5p0457c2s v5p0618c1s v6p0211c2s
v6p0300c2s v6p0370c1s v6p0519c1s
Thome, J.M. v4p0133c2s
Thomoff, S. v4p0424c1s
Thompson v6p0216c1s
Thompson, A. v1p0716c1s
v2p0299c1s v2p0309c2s v3p0464c1s
v4p0142c1s v6p0392c2s
Thompson, A.B. v4p0258c2s
v5p0266c2s
Thompson, A.C. v1p0120c1s
v1p0851c1s v6p0419c2s v6p0501c2s
v6p0519c1s v6p0525c2s v6p0579c1s
v6p0634c1s
Thompson, A.E. v3p0371c1s
v5p0049c1s v6p0523c1s
Thompson, A.G. v5p0267c2s
Thompson, A.H. v2p0057c1s
v4p0193c1s v5p0242c2s v5p0554c1s
v5p0572c2s v6p0131c2s v6p0411c2s
v6p0514c1s v6p0636c1s
Thompson, A.I. v5p0512c1s
Thompson, A.L. v1p0290c2s
Thompson, A.S. v5p0530c2s
Thompson, A.T. v1p1313c2s
Thompson, A.W. v6p0592c1s
v6p0682c2s
Thompson, B. v1p0595c2s
v5p0315c2s v5p0506c2s
Thompson, B.F. v6p0011c2s
Thompson, B.J. v5p0013c2s
Thompson, C. v1p0175c2s
v6p0595c1s
Thompson, C.G. v1p0426c1s
Thompson, C.H. v1p0486c2s
v1p0829c1s v1p1086c2s
Thompson, C.L. v2p0307c1s
Thompson, C.M. v3p0117c2s
v5p0122c1s v5p0631c1s v6p0084c2s
v6p0342c2s v6p0586c1s
Thompson, C.O. v1p0365c1s
v2p0202c2s v2p0275c2s
Thompson, C.S. v5p0392c2s
Thompson, C.T. v4p0126c1s
Thompson, C.W. v1p0366c1s
v4p0635c2s
Thompson, D. v3p0473c1s
Thompson, D.C. v2p0481c1s
v6p0578c2m v6p0689c2s
Thompson, D.D. v2p0162c1s
v2p0465c2s v3p0378c1s v5p0339c1s
v6p0637c2s
Thompson, D.G. v1p0110c1s
v1p0570c1s v1p0641c1s v1p0651c1s
v1p0711c1s v1p0839c2s v1p0989c1s
v1p1000c2s v1p1267c1s v3p0242c1s
v3p0358c1s v3p0429c1s v4p0382c1s
Thompson, D'Arcy W. v1p0498c2s
Thompson, E. v1p0694c2s
v1p0810c2s v1p1229c2s v1p1314c2s
v1p1330c2s v2p0067c2s v3p0474c2s
v5p0029c2s v5p0183c1s
Thompson, E.C. v4p0118c1s
v5p0394c1s
Thompson, E.E. v3p0243c1s
v4p0061c2s v4p0311c1s
Thompson, E.H. v2p0027c1s
v6p0286c2s
Thompson, E.M. v2p0083c1s
v2p0203c2s v2p0296c1s v4p0057c2s
v4p0084c1s v4p0243c2s v4p0274c1m

v5p0156c2s v5p0279c2s v5p0333c2s
v6p0003c2s v6p0083c1s v6p0335c1s
v6p0370c2s
Thompson, E.M., Sir v4p0073c2s
Thompson, E.P. v1p0795c1s
v1p0940c1s v1p1204c1s v1p1256c1s
v3p0159c1s v3p0351c1s v4p0207c1s
v4p0289c1s v4p0355c1s v4p0382c2s
v4p0430c1m v4p0522c2s v5p0054c2s
v5p0324c2s v5p0418c1s v6p0604c1s
Thompson, E.S. v5p0216c1s
v5p0329c2s v5p0530c1s v5p0581c1m
Thompson, E.Seton v5p0646c1s
Thompson, E.W. v1p0022c2s
v1p0542c1s v1p0884c2s v1p1408c2s
v4p0136c1s v4p0412c2s
Thompson, Edith v3p0085c1s
Thompson, Ellinor F.B. ... v6p0087c1s
Thompson, Elroy S. v6p0083c2s
Thompson, F. v3p0222c2s
v3p0388c1s v5p0079c2s v5p0084c1s
v5p0094c2s v5p0100c1s v5p0125c2s
v5p0141c2s v5p0299c2s v5p0352c1s
v5p0359c2s v5p0370c2s v5p0376c2s
v5p0410c1s v5p0412c1s v5p0573c1m
v6p0172c1s v6p0261c1m v6p0286c2s
v6p0629c1s
Thompson, F.D. v3p0438c2s
Thompson, F.L. v4p0346c1s
v5p0455c2s
Thompson, F.M. v5p0017c1s
v5p0520c2s v6p0702c1s v6p0704c2s
Thompson, Flora M. v6p0312c1s
Thompson, G. v1p1081c1s
Thompson, G.A. v6p0029c1s
v6p0282c1s v6p0499c2s
Thompson, G.C.K. v4p0251c1s
Thompson, G.G. v4p0275c2s
Thompson, G.W. v4p0593c2s
Thompson, Grace A. v6p0360c1s
v6p0463c2s v6p0614c2s
Thompson, Grace Agnes v6p0037c1s
v6p0674c2s
Thompson, H. v1p0160c2s
v1p0314c1s v1p0442c1s v5p0376c1s
v5p0608c2m v6p0001c1s v6p0259c2s
v6p0318c2s
Thompson, H., Sir v1p0465c1s
v2p0118c2s v3p0104c1s
Thompson, H.A. v6p0404c1s
Thompson, H.B. and Angell, J.R.
v5p0133c2s
Thompson, H.C. v5p0091c2s
v5p0456c2s
Thompson, H.G. v6p0346c1s
Thompson, H.H.S. v2p0233c2s
v3p0227c1s v3p0227c2s v3p0356c1s
Thompson, H.L. v5p0426c1s
Thompson, H.M. v1p0259c2s
v1p0421c2m v1p0744c2s v1p0897c1s
v1p1091c1s v1p1098c2s v1p1103c1s
v1p1117c2s v1p1306c1s v1p1347c1s
v3p0200c2s v4p0587c2s v5p0243c2s
Thompson, H.N.S. v2p0234c1s
Thompson, H.S. v1p1410c2m
v3p0281c2s v3p0333c1s v6p0281c2s
Thompson, H.Yates v6p0400c1s
Thompson, Herbert M. v6p0428c1s
Thompson, J. v1p0023c2s
v1p0409c1s v1p1106c1s v1p1110c2s
v1p1188c1s v3p0284c2s v4p0043c2s
v6p0263c1s
Thompson, J.A. v5p0198c2s
v5p0482c2s v6p0103c1s v6p0376c1s
Thompson, J.B. v1p0503c2s
v1p0918c1s v2p0373c1s v4p0597c2s
v5p0603c2s v6p0183c1s
Thompson, J.C. v1p0213c2s
v3p0226c1s
Thompson, J.D. v6p0601c2s
Thompson, J.E. v3p0315c2s
v3p0406c2s v5p0090c1s v5p0093c2s
Thompson, J.G. v5p0178c1s
v5p0413c2s
Thompson, J.H. v1p0154c2s
Thompson, J.J. v4p0174c2s
v4p0451c1s v5p0138c1s
Thompson, J.L. v1p0524c1s
Thompson, J.M. v6p0267c2s
v6p0600c2s
Thompson, J.O. v4p0173c2s
Thompson, J.P. v1p0011c1s
v1p0027c2s v1p0058c2s v1p0061c2s
v1p0128c1s v1p0240c2s v1p0242c2s
v1p0243c2s v1p0244c2s v1p0246c2s
v1p0249c1s v1p0252c2s v1p0289c2s
v1p0290c2s v1p0291c1s v1p0306c1s
v1p0314c1s v1p0336c2s v1p0343c1s
v1p0350c1s v1p0372c2s v1p0393c2s
v1p0394c2s v1p0395c2s v1p0397c1m
v1p0421c1s v1p0430c1s v1p0432c2s
v1p0435c1s v1p0436c2s v1p0496c2s
v1p0497c1s v1p0502c2s v1p0519c1s
v1p0538c1m v1p0612c2s v1p0634c2s
v1p0652c2s v1p0656c2s v1p0682c2m
v1p0684c2s v1p0714c2s v1p0775c2s
v1p0792c2s v1p0794c1s v1p0810c2s
v1p0852c2s v1p0853c1s v1p0853c2s
v1p0893c2s v1p0897c1s v1p0916c1s
v1p0925c1s v1p0960c2s v1p0961c1s
v1p0997c2s v1p1032c2s v1p1082c2s
v1p1083c2s v1p1095c2s v1p1096c2s
v1p1101c1s v1p1108c2s v1p1117c1s
v1p1118c1s v1p1119c1s v1p1127c1s
v1p1161c2s v1p1163c1s v1p1190c2s
v1p1214c1s v1p1238c1s v1p1255c2s
v1p1264c1s v1p1287c1s v1p1340c1s
v1p1341c1m v1p1344c1s v1p1347c2s
v1p1363c1m v1p1384c1s v5p0561c2s
v6p0629c1m
Thompson, J.R. v1p0089c1s
v1p0347c2s v1p0413c1s v1p0424c2s
v1p0430c2s v1p0973c1s v1p0979c2s
v1p1019c2s v1p1374c2s v1p1437c2s
Thompson, J.W. v1p0002c2s
v1p0005c1s v1p0277c1m v1p0460c1s
v1p0528c2s v1p0624c1s v1p0648c2s
v1p0667c2s v1p0687c2s v1p0695c2s
v1p0867c2s v1p0869c1s v1p0874c1s
v1p0875c1s v1p0924c1s v1p0982c2s
v1p1088c1s v1p1325c2s v1p1340c1m
v4p0229c1s v4p0303c2s v4p0609c1m
v5p0167c1s v5p0435c1s v6p0253c2s
v6p0441c2s v6p0679c2s
Thompson, Joseph v2p0314c2s
Thompson, Juliet W. v6p0488c1s
Thompson, Kate V. and Ford, Julia E
v6p0711c1s
Thompson, Kathleen v6p0045c1s
Thompson, L. v1p1278c2s
v2p0282c1s v2p0304c1s
Thompson, L. et al. v2p0184c2s
Thompson, L., Mrs. v3p0251c1s
Thompson, L.B. v4p0332c1s
v5p0089c2s v5p0525c1s
Thompson, L.Beatrice v5p0156c1s
v5p0340c1s
Thompson, L.G. v2p0483c1s
Thompson, Lady v6p0392c1s
Thompson, Launt, Mrs. v4p0153c1s
Thompson, M. v1p0039c2s
v1p0051c2m v1p0135c1s v1p0135c2m
v1p0262c2s v1p0444c1s v1p0461c2s
v1p0539c2s v1p0542c2s v2p0025c1s
v2p0033c1s v2p0047c1s v2p0150c2s
v2p0155c1s v2p0204c2s v2p0243c1s
v2p0293c2s v2p0366c1s v2p0404c1s
v2p0448c1s v3p0017c2s v3p0033c2s
v3p0038c2s v3p0044c1s v3p0046c1s
v3p0106c2s v3p0124c2s v3p0151c2s
v3p0253c1s v3p0318c1s v3p0351c2s
v3p0361c1s v3p0365c2s v3p0405c1s
v3p0424c2s v3p0443c1s v3p0453c2s
v3p0475c1s v4p0035c2s v4p0039c1s
v4p0042c1s v4p0148c1s v4p0215c2s
v4p0242c1s v4p0248c1s v4p0251c1s
v4p0267c2s v4p0335c1m v4p0375c2s
v4p0408c1s v4p0411c2s v4p0448c2s
v4p0481c2s v4p0484c1s v4p0494c1s
v4p0503c1s v4p0530c2s v4p0560c1s
v4p0578c2s v5p0025c1m v5p0063c1s
v5p0074c1s v5p0132c2s v5p0157c1s
v5p0160c2s v5p0225c2s v5p0259c2s
v5p0304c2s v5p0313c2s v5p0351c2s
v5p0489c1s v5p0491c2s v5p0496c2s
v5p0540c2s v5p0561c2s
Thompson, M.L. v1p0338c1s
v1p0607c2s v2p0032c1s v2p0120c1s
v2p0231c1s v2p0362c1s v4p0564c2s
Thompson, M.P. v1p0045c1s
v1p0056c2s v1p0057c1s v1p0058c1s
v1p0068c2s v1p0082c2s v1p0090c1s
v1p0101c1s v1p0101c2s v1p0103c2s
v1p0112c1s v1p0118c1s v1p0138c2s
v1p0150c1s v1p0159c1s v1p0168c1s
v1p0171c2s v1p0189c2s v1p0209c2s
v1p0221c2s v1p0222c1s v1p0277c1s
v1p0330c1s v1p0477c2s v1p0505c2s
v1p0537c2s v1p0598c1s v1p0668c1s
v1p0673c2s v1p0680c1s v1p0719c1s
v1p0722c1s v1p0728c2s v1p0738c1s
v1p0762c1s v1p0773c1m v1p0779c2s
v1p0785c1s v1p0788c2s v1p0797c2s
v1p0865c1s v1p0931c1m v1p0948c2s
v1p0968c1s v1p0979c2s v1p0995c1s
v1p1011c2s v1p1068c2m v1p1112c2s
v1p1122c2s v1p1142c1s v1p1144c1m
v1p1144c2s v1p1150c2s v1p1152c2s
v1p1154c1s v1p1180c2s v1p1196c1s
v1p1221c2s v1p1284c1s v1p1312c2s
v1p1314c2s v1p1334c1s v2p0005c1s
v2p0030c1m v2p0045c2s v2p0074c1s
v2p0075c2s v2p0082c2s v2p0083c1s
v2p0239c2s v2p0254c1s v2p0288c1s
v2p0299c1s v2p0347c1s v2p0395c1s
v2p0440c1s v2p0458c1s v2p0459c2s
v3p0121c2s v3p0301c2s v3p0364c2s
v4p0327c1s v5p0162c2s
Thompson, Maurice v4p0303c2s
v4p0397c2s v5p0030c1s v5p0639c2s
v6p0379c1s
Thompson, N.A. v6p0191c1s
v6p0193c1s
Thompson, N.F. v2p0356c1s
v4p0088c1s v4p0313c2s
Thompson, N.H. v2p0087c1s
v2p0319c2s v4p0593c1s
Thompson, O.R.H. v6p0222c2s
Thompson, P. v1p0138c1s
v1p0694c2s v4p0208c2s
Thompson, P.W. v4p0482c2s
Thompson, R., Sir v5p0613c2s
Thompson, R.A. v6p0092c1s
v6p0093c2s v6p0219c2s v6p0490c2s
v6p0570c1s
Thompson, R.E. v1p0023c2s
v1p0118c2s v1p0144c2s v1p0170c2s
v1p0200c1s v1p0201c1s v1p0243c1s
v1p0286c1m v1p0333c1s v1p0390c2s
v1p0391c1s v1p0410c2s v1p0435c2s
v1p0473c1s v1p0487c2s v1p0570c2s
v1p0637c1s v1p0661c1s v1p0705c1s
v1p0728c2s v1p0890c1m v1p0906c1s
v1p0926c1s v1p0988c1m v1p0999c2s
v1p1025c2m v1p1026c2s v1p1048c1s
v1p1057c2s v1p1063c1s v1p1066c2s
v1p1073c2s v1p1134c2s v1p1137c1s
v1p1198c2s v1p1215c1s v1p1215c2s
v1p1216c1s v1p1238c1s v1p1296c2s
v1p1308c1s v1p1336c2s v1p1338c1s
v1p1439c2m v2p0009c2s v2p0011c2s
v2p0012c2s v2p0041c1s v2p0066c1s
v2p0078c1s v2p0092c2s v2p0102c2s
v2p0131c2s v2p0133c2s v2p0134c1s
v2p0136c1s v2p0148c1s v2p0171c1m
v2p0191c1s v2p0215c1s v2p0224c2s
v2p0225c1s v2p0227c1s v2p0227c2s
v2p0228c1s v2p0233c2s v2p0269c1m
v2p0270c2s v2p0272c2s v2p0282c1s
v2p0290c2s v2p0298c2m v2p0312c2s
v2p0316c2s v2p0321c2s v2p0331c1s
v2p0335c1m v2p0347c2s v2p0356c2m
v2p0358c2s v2p0360c1s v2p0371c1m
v2p0381c2s v2p0408c1s v2p0414c1s
v2p0418c1s v2p0431c1s v2p0444c1s
v2p0451c2s v2p0460c2s v2p0472c1s
v3p0064c2s v3p0067c2s v3p0088c2s
v3p0206c1s v3p0280c1s v3p0346c2s
v3p0347c1s v3p0398c1s v3p0404c2s
v3p0405c1s v3p0421c2s v6p0107c2s
Thompson, R.F.M. v5p0271c1s
Thompson, R.J. v6p0170c2s
v6p0382c1s v6p0550c2s v6p0707c1s
Thompson, R.S. and Ferriss, J.H.
v5p0082c1s
Thompson, R.W. v2p0004c1s
v2p0079c1s v5p0373c2s v5p0506c2s
Thompson, Robert J. v6p0365c2s
Thompson, S. v1p0195c1s
v2p0367c2s v2p0441c1s v3p0028c1m
v3p0136c2s v4p0038c1s v4p0064c2s
v4p0294c2s v4p0382c2s v4p0403c1s
v4p0416c2s v4p0501c2s v4p0579c1s
v4p0589c2s v4p0603c1s v5p0448c2s
v6p0155c2s v6p0278c2s v6p0622c1s
Thompson, S.A. v4p0086c1s
v4p0163c2s v4p0407c1s v6p0688c2s
Thompson, S.D. v1p0484c2s
v1p0601c2s v2p0161c2s v2p0194c1s
v3p0069c1s v3p0147c1s v3p0233c2s
v3p0245c1s v4p0131c2s v4p0134c2m
v4p0135c1m v4p0138c2s v4p0196c1s
v4p0471c2s v4p0592c2s v5p0074c2s
v5p0119c2s v5p0140c1s v5p0152c1s
v5p0169c1s v5p0219c2s v5p0301c1s
v5p0324c1s v5p0327c2s v5p0328c1s
v5p0328c2s v5p0402c2s v5p0520c2s
v5p0562c2s v5p0600c2s v6p0293c1s
v6p0377c2s v6p0550c1s v6p0628c2s
Thompson, S.E. v5p0451c1s
v6p0143c1s v6p0143c2s v6p0499c2s
Thompson, S.H. v1p0313c1s
Thompson, S.H., jr. v5p0239c1s
Thompson, S.P. v1p0049c1s
v1p0246c1s v1p0399c1s v1p0401c1m
v1p0640c1s v1p0788c2s v1p0875c2s
v1p0968c2s v1p1291c2s v1p1375c1s
v2p0017c2s v2p0126c2s v2p0137c1m
v2p0138c2m v2p0223c1s v2p0322c2s
v2p0341c1s v2p0347c1s v2p0410c2s
v2p0463c1s v3p0016c2s v3p0125c2s
v3p0129c1s v3p0132c2s v3p0134c1m
v3p0153c1s v3p0250c2s v3p0293c2s
v3p0422c2s v4p0174c2s v4p0176c2s
v4p0309c2s v4p0326c2s v4p0340c2s
v4p0403c2s v4p0440c1s v4p0440c2s
v5p0184c1s v5p0319c2s v5p0570c1s
v5p0571c1m v6p0150c1s v6p0197c2s
v6p0256c1s v6p0469c1s v6p0636c2s
Thompson, S.P. et al. v5p0346c2s
Thompson, S.T. v4p0475c1s
Thompson, Stephen v3p0255c1s
Thompson, T. v3p0357c2s
v4p0304c1s
Thompson, T.B. v6p0475c2s
Thompson, T.L. v5p0075c2s
Thompson, T.P. v1p0002c2s
v1p0029c2s v1p0049c2s v1p0090c2s
v1p0091c1s v1p0109c1m v1p0109c2s
v1p0113c1m v1p0113c2s v1p0162c2s
v1p0183c1s v1p0215c1s v1p0264c1s
v1p0274c2s v1p0279c2s v1p0283c2s
v1p0284c1s v1p0302c2m v1p0341c1s
v1p0373c1s v1p0378c1s v1p0382c2s
v1p0391c2s v1p0419c2m v1p0423c1s
v1p0429c1s v1p0430c2s v1p0435c2s
v1p0439c1s v1p0460c2s v1p0469c1s
v1p0474c1s v1p0476c2s v1p0484c2s
v1p0486c1s v1p0486c2s v1p0489c1s
v1p0500c1s v1p0510c1s v1p0544c2s

v1p0546c1s v1p0626c2s v1p0630c1s
v1p0632c1s v1p0635c1s v1p0652c2m
v1p0662c1s v1p0690c2s v1p0692c1s
v1p0707c1s v1p0711c2s v1p0736c1s
v1p0755c1s v1p0765c2s v1p0771c1s
v1p0783c2s v1p0839c1s v1p0871c1s
v1p0882c1s v1p0883c1m v1p0884c1m
v1p0884c2s v1p0885c1m v1p0895c1s
v1p0961c2s v1p0973c2m v1p0992c1s
v1p0993c1s v1p0997c2s v1p1007c2s
v1p1026c1m v1p1027c1s v1p1032c1s
v1p1056c1s v1p1081c1s v1p1096c1s
v1p1116c2s v1p1130c2s v1p1145c1s
v1p1174c1s v1p1197c2s v1p1208c1s
v1p1208c2s v1p1264c2s v1p1284c2s
v1p1285c1s v1p1313c1s v1p1328c2s
v1p1360c2s v1p1371c2s v1p1372c2m
v2p0208c2s
Thompson, V. v5p0202c1s
v5p0278c1s v5p0282c2s v5p0430c2s
v5p0485c2s v5p0536c2s v5p0547c2s
v5p0613c2s v5p0634c2s v6p0012c1s
v6p0017c2s v6p0058c2s v6p0081c1s
v6p0091c1m v6p0148c2s v6p0218c2m
v6p0242c1s v6p0255c1s v6p0261c2s
v6p0297c1s v6p0297c2m v6p0327c2s
v6p0354c2s v6p0387c2s v6p0430c1s
v6p0458c2s v6p0463c2s v6p0480c1m
v6p0596c1s v6p0597c2s v6p0712c2s
Thompson, Vance v5p0003c2s
v5p0014c2s v5p0461c1s v5p0496c1s
v6p0172c1s v6p0480c2s v6p0552c2s
v6p0557c2s v6p0651c1s
Thompson, W. v1p0360c2s
v1p0833c1s v2p0027c2s v3p0050c2s
v3p0092c2s v4p0146c2s v4p0309c2s
Thompson, W., Sir v1p0788c1s
Thompson, W.A. v1p0024c1s
v1p0609c1s v1p1202c1s v1p1264c1s
v1p1313c2s
Thompson, W.D. v5p0437c2s
Thompson, W.G. v2p0282c1s
Thompson, W.G. and Matthews, N., jr.
v6p0522c2s
Thompson, W.H. v1p1007c2s
v4p0013c1s v5p0065c2s v5p0069c1s
v5p0103c1s v6p0059c2s v6p0219c2s
v6p0495c1s v6p0568c1s v6p0613c1s
Thompson, W.H., Mrs. v6p0297c2s
Thompson, W.M. v4p0028c2s
v4p0201c1s v4p0322c2s v4p0325c1s
v5p0276c1s v6p0588c2s v6p0617c1s
v6p0710c1s v6p0710c2s
Thompson, W.O. v5p0333c1s
v6p0135c2s
Thompson, W.R. v2p0148c2s
Thompson, W.S. v2p0055c2s
v2p0056c1s
Thompson, W.V.B. v5p0530c1s
v1p1290c2s
Thompson, Z. v1p0470c1s
v1p0829c1s
Thoms, W.J. v1p0149c2s
v1p0176c2s v1p0266c2s v1p0363c1s
v1p0415c2s v1p0513c1s v1p0840c2s
v1p0994c2s v1p1187c1s v1p1368c1s
v1p1406c1s v2p0074c2s v2p0183c2s
v4p0098c2s v4p0157c1s
Thomsen, C. v6p0584c1s
Thomsen, J. v2p0438c1s
Thomson and Houston v1p0426c1s
v1p0835c1s
Thomson, A. v1p0040c2s
v1p0042c2s v2p0013c2s v2p0166c2s
v2p0231c2s v4p0307c1s v4p0323c1s
v5p0022c2s v5p0128c2s v6p0085c1s
v6p0588c1s
Thomson, A.E. v4p0527c1s
v5p0037c2s v6p0295c1s
Thomson, A.F. v6p0461c1s
Thomson, A.J. v2p0084c2s
Thomson, A.R. v5p0158c1s
v5p0316c2s
Thomson, A.S. v1p0295c1s
v1p0919c1m
Thomson, A.T. v1p1006c1s
Thomson, A.T., Mrs. v1p0221c2s
v1p0557c1s v1p0567c2s v1p0569c1s
v1p0597c1s v1p0705c1s v1p0727c1s
v1p0863c1s v1p1063c2s
Thomson, B. v3p0066c2s
v4p0062c1s v4p0135c2s v4p0198c2s
v4p0201c1s v5p0322c1s v5p0397c1s
v5p0631c1s v5p0642c1s
Thomson, B.H. v4p0017c1s
v4p0198c2s
Thomson, Basil v4p0240c2s
Thomson, C. v1p0982c1s
v1p0997c1s v1p1008c1s v2p0156c2m
v5p0180c2s v5p0206c2s v5p0242c1s
v5p0380c1s v5p0488c1s
Thomson, C.A. v3p0469c2s
Thomson, C.E. v4p0012c1s
Thomson, C.W. v1p0214c2m
v1p0340c1s v1p0441c2s v1p1030c1s
v1p1171c2s v1p1411c1s
Thomson, C.W., Sir v1p0044c2s
Thomson, D.C. v1p0116c2s
v1p0959c2s v2p0041c1s v2p0283c1s
v4p0045c2s v4p0134c2s v4p0148c1s
v4p0155c1s v4p0293c2s v4p0371c1s
v4p0492c2s v5p0031c2s v5p0095c1s
v5p0235c1s v6p0060c1s v6p0443c1m
v6p0527c2s v6p0696c1s
Thomson, E. v1p0400c1s
v1p0626c1s v1p0628c2s v1p0767c2s
v1p1206c1s v1p1234c1s v2p0126c2s
v2p0250c1s v3p0132c2s v3p0133c1s
v3p0208c2s v4p0176c1s v4p0176c2m
v4p0349c2s v5p0010c1s v5p0184c1s
v5p0199c2s v6p0199c1s v6p0681c1s
Thomson, E. and Houston, E.J.
v1p0374c1s v1p0398c2s v1p0399c2m
v1p0400c1s v1p0401c1s v2p0137c2s
Thomson, E.A. v2p0045c1s
v2p0333c1s
Thomson, E.C.R. v5p0287c1s
v5p0501c2s
Thomson, E.P. v5p0259c2s
v5p0524c2s v5p0638c1s
Thomson, E.W. v4p0085c2s
v5p0630c1s v6p0076c1s v6p0514c1s
v6p0628c1s
Thomson, Edgar B. v6p0113c2s
Thomson, Elihu v6p0011c1s
v6p0198c2m
Thomson, Estelle v6p0093c2s
Thomson, F. v5p0504c2s
Thomson, F.D. v5p0182c2s
Thomson, G. v1p0495c1s
v5p0326c1s v5p0531c2s
Thomson, G.M. v2p0313c2s
v3p0304c2s
Thomson, H. v5p0271c1s
Thomson, H.C. v4p0086c1s
v5p0006c2s v5p0102c2s v5p0110c2s
v5p0111c1s v5p0352c2s v5p0438c2s
v5p0586c2s v6p0096c2s v6p0120c2s
v6p0349c1s v6p0455c2s v6p0654c1s
v6p0675c1s
Thomson, H.S. v1p1004c2s
Thomson, J. v1p0010c2s
v1p0011c1s v1p0100c2s v1p0120c2s
v1p0150c1s v1p0170c2s v1p0342c1s
v1p0503c1s v1p0648c1s v1p0812c1m
v1p0815c2s v1p1240c1s v1p1266c2s
v1p1282c1s v1p1390c2m v2p0281c2s
v2p0294c1s v2p0379c1s v2p0405c2s
v2p0462c2s v2p0472c1s v3p0004c1m
v3p0004c2s v3p0203c1s v3p0270c2m
v3p0401c1s v3p0473c1s v4p0005c1s
v4p0589c2s v5p0335c1s v5p0335c2s
v5p0515c2s v6p0065c2s
Thomson, J. et al. v6p0017c1s
Thomson, J.A. v4p0178c2s
v4p0179c2s v5p0205c1s v5p0291c1s
Thomson, J.A. and Geddes, P.
v4p0429c2s
Thomson, J.A. and Richards, J.W.
v5p0014c1s
Thomson, J.A.S. v3p0356c1s
Thomson, J.B. v1p1111c2s
Thomson, J.C. v3p0416c2s
v4p0135c1s v4p0150c1s v6p0639c1s
Thomson, J.E.H. v4p0056c1s
Thomson, J.H. v6p0197c2s
Thomson, J.J. v1p0787c2s
v4p0220c2s v4p0487c1m v5p0037c2s
v5p0492c1s v6p0056c1s v6p0197c1s
v6p0527c1s
Thomson, J.M. v1p0744c2s
v1p1288c2s v2p0341c2s v3p0350c1s
v4p0366c2s v6p0139c2s
Thomson, J.P. v4p0399c1s
Thomson, J.R. v2p0082c2m
v2p0175c1s v2p0337c1s v2p0368c2s
v2p0457c1s v2p0473c1s v3p0145c2s
Thomson, J.S. v5p0248c2s
v5p0473c1s v5p0481c2s v5p0520c1s
v6p0066c1s v6p0259c2s v6p0296c1s
v6p0300c2s v6p0328c1s v6p0427c2s
v6p0610c2s
Thomson, M. v1p0533c2s
v1p0534c1s v2p0047c1s v2p0366c2s
Thomson, M.P. v3p0428c2s
Thomson, Mrs. v1p1407c1s
Thomson, R. v1p0090c1s
Thomson, R.D. v1p0073c2s
v1p0237c2s
Thomson, R.T. v5p0641c1s
Thomson, S. v1p1396c2s
Thomson, S.D. v2p0221c2s
v6p0151c1s
Thomson, St.C. v3p0206c1s
Thomson, T. v1p0225c1s
v1p0333c1s v1p0501c2s v1p0591c2s
v1p0823c1s
Thomson, T.K. v3p0066c1s
v3p0386c1s v4p0073c1s
Thomson, W. v1p0017c1s
v1p0073c1s v1p0134c2s v1p0214c2s
v1p0286c2m v1p0317c2s v1p0340c1s
v1p0375c2s v1p0401c1s v1p0407c2m
v1p0449c1s v1p0498c1s v1p0526c1s
v1p0751c2s v1p0787c1s v1p0788c2s
v1p0829c1s v1p1172c1s v1p1172c2s
v1p1268c1s v1p1290c2s v1p1293c1s
v2p0067c1s v2p0093c2s v2p0097c1s
v2p0141c1s v2p0243c1s v2p0245c2s
v2p0258c2m v2p0294c1s v2p0340c2s
v2p0363c2s v2p0395c1s v2p0402c1s
v3p0007c1s v3p0132c2s v3p0134c1s
v3p0134c2s v3p0159c1s v3p0214c2s
v3p0261c1s v3p0297c1s v3p0415c1m
v4p0052c2s v4p0091c1s v4p0201c1s
v4p0311c2s v4p0418c1s v5p0030c1s
v5p0075c2s v5p0425c2s v5p0494c2s
v5p0526c1s v6p0032c2s
Thomson, W., Sir v1p0044c2s
v1p0074c1s v1p0375c2s v1p0400c1s
v1p0407c2s v1p0506c2s v1p0748c2s
v1p0936c2m v1p1109c1s v2p0137c2s
v2p0141c1s v2p0395c1s v3p0132c2s
v3p0251c1s
Thomson, W.H. v1p0049c2s
v1p0368c2s v1p0802c1s v4p0022c1s
v4p0166c2s v6p0337c2s v6p0568c1s
Thomson, W.J. v4p0166c2s
Thomson, W.M. v1p0109c1s
v1p0529c1s v1p0695c2s v1p0961c1s
v1p0966c1s v1p1237c2s v1p1269c2s
v1p1337c1s
Thomson, W.P. v2p0459c1s
Thomson, W.T. v4p0173c2s
v4p0318c2s v4p0372c2s
Thon, O. v5p0537c1s
Thorburn, J.M. v6p0421c2s
Thorburn, S.S. v4p0278c1s
v6p0313c2m v6p0315c1s
Thorden, K.M. v1p1358c2m
Thoreau, H.D. v1p0048c2s
v1p0049c1s v1p0082c1s v1p0193c1s
v1p0197c2s v1p0198c1s v1p0223c1s
v1p0287c2s v1p0600c2s v1p0698c2s
v1p0789c2s v1p0814c1s v1p1010c2s
v1p1382c1s v1p1397c2s v1p1416c2s
v2p0476c1s v6p0376c1s
Thorel, R. v6p0033c2s
Thoresby, F. v6p0665c1s
v6p0705c1s
Thormanby v5p0404c1s
v6p0056c1s v6p0351c2s v6p0543c1s
Thormanby, Lord v2p0207c2s
Thorn, C. v5p0327c2s
Thorn, C.R. and Dillingham, M.W.
v4p0397c1s
Thorn, J.C. v2p0097c2s
Thornbury, F.J. v4p0613c2s
v5p0621c2m
Thornbury, G.W. v1p0223c1s
v1p0323c1s v1p0497c1s v1p0596c1s
v1p0626c2s v1p0766c1s v1p0952c2s
v1p0969c1s v1p1132c1s v1p1219c1s
v1p1220c1s
Thornbury, J. v1p1017c2s
v1p1371c1s
Thornbury, W. v1p0007c2s
v1p0066c1s v1p0072c2m v1p0172c2s
v1p0208c2s v1p0222c1s v1p0267c1s
v1p0305c2s v1p0321c1s v1p0336c1s
v1p0446c1s v1p0454c2s v1p0536c1s
v1p0705c2s v1p0761c2s v1p0763c2s
v1p0764c2m v1p0765c2m v1p0766c1s
v1p0824c2s v1p0852c1s v1p0887c2s
v1p0923c1s v1p0927c2s v1p0971c1s
v1p0989c2s v1p1105c1s v1p1108c2s
v1p1140c1s v1p1143c2s v1p1144c2m
v1p1190c2s v1p1202c1s v1p1228c1s
v1p1230c1s v1p1231c1s v1p1275c1s
v1p1300c1s v1p1409c2s v1p1410c1s
Thornbury, W.G. v1p0088c1s
Thorndike, A.H. v4p0019c1s
Thorndike, E. v5p0020c2s
v5p0021c1m v5p0105c2s v5p0208c2s
v5p0370c1m v5p0471c1s v5p0514c1s
Thorndike, E. and Woodworth, R.S.
v5p0356c1s
Thorndike, E.L. v5p0293c1s
v5p0383c2s v5p0400c2s v5p0470c2s
v6p0004c2s v6p0021c2s v6p0135c2s
v6p0136c2m v6p0137c1s v6p0193c1s
v6p0193c2m v6p0219c2s v6p0290c2s
v6p0402c1s v6p0521c2m v6p0572c2s
v6p0704c1s
Thorndike, E.L. and Woodworth, R.S.
v5p0370c1s
Thorndike, Edward v5p0204c1s
Thorndike, J.L. v6p0233c2s
Thorne, C. v5p0312c2s
Thorne, C.E. v4p0618c2s
Thorne, F. v3p0165c2s
Thorne, G. v6p0695c1s
Thorne, J. v2p0019c2m
v2p0023c2s v2p0162c1s v2p0306c2m
v2p0341c2s v2p0362c2s v2p0379c2s
v2p0392c2s
Thorne, J.F. v5p0421c2s
v6p0009c2s
Thorne, L.T. v2p0136c2s
v2p0350c1s v2p0406c1s v2p0432c2s
Thorne, N.C. v6p0052c1s
Thorne, O. v1p0148c1s
v1p1408c2s v5p0095c2s
Thorne, P. v1p1040c1s
v1p1419c2s
Thorne, R. v5p0521c2s
v5p0635c1s
Thorne, R.T. v2p0221c1s
Thorne, T. v2p0208c1s
Thorne, W.B. v5p0488c1s

v6p0148c1s
Thorne, W.H. v1p0089c2s
v1p0891c2s v1p1412c2s
Thornely, J.L. v2p0465c1s
Thornely, Laura B. v5p0390c2s
Thornely, T. v4p0450c2s
Thornely, T. and Pearson, N.
v1p0989c2s
Thorngate, Ella v6p0155c1s
Thornley, G.W. v5p0160c2s
v5p0499c2s
Thornley, J.C. v4p0338c2s
v5p0345c1s v5p0419c1s
Thornton, A. v5p0120c1s
Thornton, C.W. v5p0504c1s
Thornton, E. v1p1328c1s
v2p0455c1s
Thornton, E.L.H. v6p0196c2s
Thornton, G. v1p0141c2s
Thornton, J.S. v4p0500c2s
Thornton, J.W. v1p0151c2s
v1p0306c1s v1p0327c2s v1p0402c2s
v1p0521c2s v1p0535c2s v1p0536c1m
v1p0536c2s v1p0909c1s v1p0985c2s
v1p1033c2s v1p1148c1s v1p1187c2s
v1p1418c1s
Thornton, L.M. v6p0463c1s
Thornton, M.E. v6p0462c2s
Thornton, M.G. v4p0010c1s
Thornton, P.M. v3p0190c1s
Thornton, R. v2p0144c2s
Thornton, Robinson v6p0553c1s
Thornton, T.H. v3p0038c2s
v3p0223c2s v3p0417c1s
Thornton, W.B. v6p0025c2s
v6p0040c2s v6p0219c2s v6p0243c2s
v6p0347c2m v6p0428c1s v6p0462c1s
v6p0464c1s v6p0684c1s v6p0701c1s
Thornton, W.J. v1p0834c1s
Thornton, W.L. v1p1336c2s
Thornton, W.M. v1p1076c1s
v1p1382c1s v4p0543c1s
Thornton, W.T. v1p0111c1s
v1p0198c2s v1p0313c2s v1p0388c1s
v1p0594c1s v1p0618c2s v1p0628c2s
v1p0630c2s v1p0657c2s v1p0666c2s
v1p0714c1s v1p0715c1s v1p0907c2s
v1p0908c1s v1p0976c1s v1p0983c2s
v1p1027c1m v1p1108c1s v1p1272c1s
v1p1288c2s v1p1320c1m v1p1360c2s
v1p1361c2s v1p1379c2s v1p1394c1s
v3p0223c2m
Thornton, W.W. v2p0240c1s
v4p0281c2s v6p0281c1s v6p0286c2s
v6p0681c2s
Thornwell, J.H. v2p0405c1s
Thornycroft, J.I. v5p0551c2s
Thornycroft, J.S. v2p0443c2s
Thoroddsen, T. v2p0214c1m
Thoroddsen, Th. v5p0278c2s
Thorold, A. v3p0040c1s
v4p0098c1s v4p0169c2s v6p0236c1s
Thorold, A.C.E. v4p0575c1s
Thorold, A.C.E., Rev. v5p0416c2s
Thorold, A.W. v1p0874c2s
v1p0919c2s v1p1139c1s v1p1144c2s
v1p1228c2s v1p1327c1s v2p0100c2s
v2p0255c1s v2p0474c1s v3p0077c1s
v3p0175c2s v3p0466c1s v4p0108c2s
v4p0301c1m v4p0343c1s
Thorold, Algar v6p0127c1s
v6p0231c1s v6p0394c1s
Thorold, E.H. v5p0202c1s
Thorold, W. v4p0614c2s
Thorold, W.J. v5p0003c1m
v6p0195c1s
Thorp, E. v2p0461c1s
Thorp, J. v2p0035c2s
Thorp, J.G. v5p0467c1s
Thorp, J.G., jr. v3p0123c1s
Thorp, N.J. v5p0026c2s
Thorp, T. v2p0099c1s
v6p0174c1s
Thorp, W. v3p0362c1s
v5p0091c1s v5p0317c1s v5p0626c1s
v6p0336c2s v6p0477c1s v6p0558c2s
v6p0561c2s v6p0570c1m
Thorp, W.H. v2p0019c2s
Thorpe, C.E. v3p0423c1s
Thorpe, E. v1p1362c2s
Thorpe, F.N. v2p0204c1m
v3p0075c1s v3p0086c1m v3p0097c2s
v3p0101c1s v3p0108c1s v3p0197c1s
v3p0251c2s v3p0266c2s v3p0267c1m
v3p0356c1s v3p0367c1s v3p0408c1s
v3p0442c1s v3p0450c1s v4p0152c1m
v4p0434c1s v4p0636c2s v5p0120c2s
v5p0128c2s v5p0134c1s v5p0218c2s
v5p0219c1s v5p0304c1s v5p0440c1s
v5p0464c2s v5p0550c1s v6p0667c1s
Thorpe, F.T. v3p0143c1s
v3p0456c1s
Thorpe, H.W. v1p0115c1s
v1p0154c2s v1p0262c2s v1p0952c2s
Thorpe, J. v1p0362c1s
v2p0083c1s
Thorpe, J.E. v3p0330c1s
v6p0253c2s v6p0463c2s
Thorpe, K. v1p0836c2s
Thorpe, L. v1p0939c2s
Thorpe, Mrs. v3p0356c1s
Thorpe, Prof. v3p0092c1s
Thorpe, S.P. and Wakeman, R.P.
v6p0644c2s
Thorpe, T.B. v1p0006c2s
v1p0023c2s v1p0104c2s v1p0106c2s
v1p0144c1s v1p0261c1s v1p0306c1s
v1p0340c2s v1p0358c2s v1p0370c1s
v1p0465c2s v1p0472c2s v1p0604c2s
v1p0605c1s v1p0751c1s v1p0772c2s
v1p0854c2s v1p0916c1s v1p1045c2m
v1p1083c1s v1p1084c1s v1p1243c2s
v1p1265c1s v1p1313c2s v1p1354c2s
v1p1396c2s v1p1400c2s v1p1403c1s
v1p1404c1s v1p1427c2s
Thorpe, T.E. v1p0016c2s
v1p0224c1s v1p0225c1s v1p1070c1s
v2p0076c1s v2p0090c2s v2p0126c1s
v2p0279c2s v2p0390c2s v2p0406c1s
v2p0476c2s v3p0029c2s v3p0244c1m
v3p0271c2s v3p0274c1s v3p0285c1s
v3p0343c2s v3p0372c2s v3p0456c2s
v4p0099c1s v4p0167c1s v4p0313c1s
v4p0322c2s v4p0420c1s v4p0504c2m
v4p0507c1s v5p0092c1s v5p0104c1s
v5p0462c1s v5p0623c1s v6p0059c2s
v6p0545c2s v6p0699c2s
Thorpe, T.E. and Rucker, A.W.
v1p1173c1s
Thorpe, W. v4p0572c1s
v6p0186c2s
Thorpe, W.G. v3p0060c1s
v3p0074c1s v3p0219c1s
Thoulet, J. v5p0417c2s
Thoulet, M.J. v2p0290c1s
Thovez, E. v6p0167c2s
Thow, G. v4p0376c1s
v5p0452c1s
Thoyts, E.E. v4p0424c2s
Thrall, A. v6p0697c1s
Thrall, J.B. v2p0290c2s
v2p0428c1s
Thrall, S.C. v1p0138c1s
Thrall, W.G. v3p0385c2s
v3p0431c1s
Thrasher, B.B. v6p0233c1s
Thrasher, J.S. v1p0322c1s
Thrasher, M.B. v4p0158c1s
v4p0324c2s v5p0010c2s v5p0074c1s
v5p0085c2s v5p0092c1s v5p0139c1s
v5p0139c2s v5p0205c1s v5p0361c1s
v5p0384c2s v5p0473c1s v5p0505c2s
v5p0578c1s v5p0595c2m v5p0609c2s
v5p0620c1s v5p0620c2s v6p0554c2s
Threlfall, J.R. v3p0434c2s
Threlfall, R. v5p0184c1s
Threlfall, T.R. v4p0314c2s
v4p0581c1s v5p0520c1s v6p0553c2s
Thresh, J.C. v4p0612c2s
Thresher, C.P. v6p0488c2s
Thresher, E. v2p0116c1s
Thring, G.H. v5p0136c2s
v5p0137c1m
Thring, G.Herbert v6p0149c1s
Thring, H., Sir v2p0215c2s
Thring, Henry, Baron v5p0136c2s
Thring, Lord v3p0199c1s
v3p0219c2s v3p0255c1s v5p0588c2s
v6p0267c1s
Thring, Lord et al. v4p0314c1s
v4p0318c1s
Thrum, T.G. v4p0250c2s
Thrupp, G.A. v3p0022c1s
v3p0089c1s
Thrupp, G.H. v4p0090c2s
Thruston, E.H. v5p0597c1s
Thruston, Prof. v6p0043c2s
Thudicum, J.L.W. v1p0711c2s
v1p0744c2s v3p0250c1s v3p0272c2s
v3p0333c2s v3p0465c2s
Thum, P. v4p0204c1s
Thurber, C.C. v6p0462c2s
Thurber, C.H. v3p0171c2s
v4p0022c1s v4p0393c2s v4p0505c2s
v4p0512c1s v5p0030c1m v5p0048c1m
v5p0106c1s v5p0106c2s v5p0126c1s
v5p0177c1s v5p0177c2s v5p0178c2s
v5p0179c2s v5p0182c2m v5p0191c2s
v5p0204c2s v5p0231c2s v5p0264c2s
v5p0360c1s v5p0466c1s v5p0471c1s
v5p0479c2s v5p0512c1s v6p0399c1s
Thurber, C.H. and Chase, W.J.
v4p0123c1s
Thurber, C.H. and Yoe, F.E.De
v5p0264c2s
Thurber, F.B. v1p0235c1s
v1p1075c2s v1p1246c1s v2p0245c1s
v2p0247c2s v2p0363c2s v3p0099c1s
v4p0457c2s v5p0129c2s v5p0135c1s
v5p0407c1s v5p0593c1s v6p0435c2s
Thurber, F.B. and Abad, L.V.de
v6p0161c1s
Thurber, F.B. and Smith, C.S.
v5p0468c2s
Thurber, S. v3p0087c1s
v3p0095c1m v3p0139c1s v3p0140c1s
v3p0140c2s v3p0141c1s v3p0196c1s
v3p0242c2s v3p0262c1s v3p0383c2s
v4p0183c1m v4p0184c1m v4p0184c2s
v4p0335c2s v4p0415c2s v4p0478c1s
v5p0131c2s v5p0192c1m v5p0264c2s
v5p0342c1s v6p0207c2s v6p0532c2s
Thurber, S. et al. v5p0182c2s
Thurber, T.B. v5p0289c2s
Thurburn, A. v5p0461c1s
Thurlow, M.C. v6p0532c1s
v6p0706c1s
Thurlow, S.L. v5p0544c1s
Thurman, A.G. and Frye, W.P.
v3p0347c1s
Thurman, J. v1p0100c1s
v1p0613c1s
Thurman, W.D. v6p0262c1s
Thurn, E.F.Im v2p0015c2s
v2p0193c1s v2p0421c1m v2p0470c2s
v4p0440c1s v5p0225c1s
Thurnam, J. v1p0100c2s
v1p0643c2s
Thursfield, J.R. v1p0550c1s
v6p0168c2s
Thursfield, R. v1p1011c2s
Thurston, A.A.W. v5p0528c1s
Thurston, A.S. v3p0430c1s
v4p0486c1s
Thurston, C.R. v4p0096c1s
v4p0402c2s v5p0054c1s
Thurston, D. v1p0752c2s
v1p0923c1s
Thurston, E. v3p0214c1s
v3p0277c2s v3p0306c1s v3p0324c2s
v5p0022c2s
Thurston, E.A. v4p0344c1s
Thurston, E.L. v6p0141c2s
v6p0406c1s
Thurston, E.P. v1p0458c2s
Thurston, E.P. et al. v4p0408c2s
Thurston, Emma A. v4p0585c2s
v4p0634c1s
Thurston, G.P. v2p0077c1s
v2p0219c2s v3p0290c1s v4p0385c1s
Thurston, H. v1p0417c1s
v1p0804c1s v2p0376c1s v2p0398c1s
v3p0001c1m v3p0048c2s v3p0270c1s
v4p0032c2s v4p0088c1s v4p0141c2s
v4p0223c1s v4p0244c1s v4p0326c2s
v4p0422c2s v4p0539c1s v4p0601c2s
v5p0012c1s v5p0019c1m v5p0023c1s
v5p0117c1s v5p0145c2s v5p0160c1m
v5p0200c2s v5p0289c1s v5p0305c1m
v5p0331c1s v5p0364c2m v5p0365c1m
v5p0369c1s v5p0442c1s v5p0459c1s
v5p0496c2s v5p0503c2s v5p0561c2s
v5p0643c2s v6p0012c1s v6p0020c2m
v6p0022c2s v6p0024c1s v6p0046c2s
v6p0058c1s v6p0131c1s v6p0143c1s
v6p0150c2s v6p0187c1s v6p0189c2s
v6p0201c2s v6p0228c1s v6p0267c2s
v6p0274c1s v6p0287c1s v6p0307c2s
v6p0328c1s v6p0335c1s v6p0335c2m
v6p0336c2m v6p0365c1s v6p0413c2s
v6p0478c1s v6p0484c1s v6p0499c2s
v6p0531c1s v6p0551c2m v6p0554c2s
v6p0586c2s v6p0609c1s v6p0648c2s
v6p0675c1s
Thurston, H.W. v3p0228c1s
v3p0234c1s v3p0442c2s v4p0167c2s
v5p0120c1s v5p0120c2s v6p0113c1s
v6p0348c2s
Thurston, H.W. and Miller, A.C.
v6p0136c2s
Thurston, Herbert v5p0493c1s
v6p0003c1s
Thurston, J.M. v5p0413c1s
v5p0625c2s v6p0144c2s v6p0563c2s
Thurston, J.R. v5p0146c1s
v6p0214c2s
Thurston, K.C. v6p0302c2s
v6p0344c2s v6p0441c1s v6p0645c2s
Thurston, L.A. v4p0310c2s
v4p0420c2s v5p0165c1s
Thurston, L.A. and Curtis, G.T.
v4p0250c2s
Thurston, M.N. v5p0140c1s
v5p0518v1s v5p0552c1s v6p0201c2s
v6p0467c1s v6p0690c1s
Thurston, Mabel N. v6p0160c1s
Thurston, R.B. v1p0112c1s
v1p0290c1s v1p0687c1s v1p1064c2s
v1p1104c1s v1p1244c2s
Thurston, R.F. v6p0576c2s
Thurston, R.H. v1p0017c1s
v1p0102c2s v1p0146c1m v1p0167c1s
v1p0295c1s v1p0300c1s v1p0408c1s
v1p0491c1s v1p0493c2s v1p0495c1s
v1p0580c1s v1p0664c2s v1p0665c1m
v1p0715c1s v1p0759c2s v1p0783c1s
v1p0810c1m v1p0815c2s v1p0825c2s
v1p0956c2s v1p1011c1s v1p1100c2m
v1p1111c1s v1p1141c2s v1p1246c2m
v1p1247c2m v1p1248c2m v1p1250c1s
v1p1253c2s v1p1259c1s v1p1261c1s
v1p1296c2s v1p1311c2s v1p1317c1s
v1p1319c1s v1p1427c1m v2p0003c1s
v2p0006c1s v2p0050c2m v2p0124c1m
v2p0126c2s v2p0131c2s v2p0141c1s
v2p0150c1s v2p0150c2s v2p0168c2s
v2p0195c1s v2p0229c1s v2p0268c1m
v2p0281c2m v2p0319c2m v2p0320c2s
v2p0356c1s v2p0390c1m v2p0418c2m
v2p0419c1m v2p0419c2s v2p0448c2m

v2p0467c2s v3p0003c1m v3p0020c1s
v3p0038c1s v3p0059c1s v3p0137c1m
v3p0164c2s v3p0305c1s v3p0352c2s
v3p0379c2s v3p0408c2m v3p0422c1s
v3p0473c2s v4p0018c1m v4p0052c2s
v4p0090c2s v4p0180c2s v4p0204c2s
v4p0215c2s v4p0288c2s v4p0292c1s
v4p0362c2s v4p0430c1s v4p0507c1s
v4p0547c1m v4p0547c2m v4p0558c2s
v4p0563c1s v4p0567c1s v4p0573c2s
v4p0596c2s v4p0623c2s v5p0023c1s
v5p0028c1s v5p0085c1s v5p0172c1s
v5p0175c2s v5p0176c2s v5p0185c1s
v5p0188c2s v5p0226c2s v5p0256c2s
v5p0265c2s v5p0287c2s v5p0299c1s
v5p0367c2s v5p0435c1s v5p0467c2s
v5p0471c2s v5p0526c2s v5p0533c2s
v5p0550c2s v5p0551c1m v5p0552c1s
v5p0558c2s v5p0560c2s v5p0570c1s
v5p0577c2s v5p0602c2s v5p0614c2s
v6p0008c1s v6p0136c2s v6p0137c2s
v6p0150c1s v6p0194c1s v6p0204c1m
v6p0204c2s v6p0244c1s v6p0285c2s
v6p0318c1s v6p0332c1s v6p0356c2s
v6p0362c2s v6p0409c2s v6p0431c1s
v6p0445c1s v6p0457c1s v6p0518c2s
v6p0526c2s v6p0577c1s v6p0643c1s
v6p0669c1s v6p0674c2s
Thurtell, E. v4p0007c1s
v4p0244c2s v4p0478c2s v4p0491c2s
v4p0513c2s
Thurwanger, C. v4p0134c2s
v5p0095c2s
Thwaite, B.H. v4p0176c2s
v4p0181c1s v4p0204c2s v4p0601c2s
v5p0068c2s v5p0069c1s v5p0184c1s
v5p0189c1s v5p0231c1s v6p0432c1s
Thwaite, B.H. and Mahler, P.
v4p0211c2s v4p0366c2s
Thwaite, B.H. and Russell, Earl
v4p0176c2s
Thwaites, C. v2p0406c2s
Thwaites, R.G. v2p0028c1s
v2p0048c2s v2p0123c2s v3p0122c2s
v3p0466c1m v4p0014c2s v4p0045c2s
v4p0071c1s v4p0156c2s v4p0182c2s
v4p0624c2s v5p0337c1s v5p0353c2s
v6p0022c2s v6p0049c2s v6p0220c1s
v6p0369c2s v6p0374c1s v6p0387c2s
v6p0422c1m
Thwaites, R.G. and Fletcher, W.I.
v5p0337c1s
Thwing, C. v4p0123c1s
Thwing, C.B. v3p0331c1s
v4p0349c2s
Thwing, C.F. v1p0110c1s
v1p0134c1s v1p0236c2s v1p0275c2s
v1p0276c1s v1p0276c2m v1p0577c1s
v1p0624c1s v1p0679c2s v1p0847c1s
v1p0982c2s v1p1001c2s v1p1160c1s
v1p1162c2s v1p1422c2s v2p0066c2s
v2p0092c2s v2p0098c2s v2p0131c2s
v2p0152c2s v2p0219c1s v2p0297c1s
v2p0300c2s v2p0306c2s v2p0355c1s
v2p0406c1s v2p0455c2s v2p0456c1s
v3p0002c2s v3p0091c1s v3p0105c2s
v3p0199c1s v4p0015c1s v4p0075c1s
v4p0109c1s v4p0122c2s v4p0123c1m
v4p0123c2m v4p0169c2s v4p0170c1s
v4p0177c2s v4p0249c1s v4p0305c1s
v4p0323c1s v4p0411c1s v4p0441c2s
v4p0627c2m v4p0635c1s v5p0056c1s
v5p0078c2s v5p0126c1m v5p0126c2m
v5p0127c1m v5p0127c2s v5p0157c1s
v5p0180c1s v5p0187c1s v5p0213c1s
v5p0264c2s v5p0327c2s v5p0368c1s
v5p0474c2s v5p0512c1s v5p0558c1s
v5p0568c1s v5p0636c2s v6p0038c2s
v6p0135c2m v6p0137c1m v6p0137c2m
v6p0190c2m v6p0191c1s v6p0219c1s
v6p0232c1s v6p0249c2s v6p0321c1s
v6p0385c2s v6p0473c1s v6p0518c2s
v6p0564c2s v6p0672c2s
Thwing, C.F. and Warfield, B.B.
v4p0573c1s
Thwing, C.T. v2p0088c2s
Thwing, E.P. v1p1036c1s
v3p0126c2s
Thygeson, N.M. v5p0204c2s
v5p0238c1s
Thynne, R. v1p0101c1s
Thys, Capt. v3p0096c1s
Thysius, A. v1p0769c1s
Tibbets, A.G. v6p0366c2s
Tibbetts, C.B. v6p0181c2s
Tibbetts, H.C. v6p0030c1s
Tibbey, T.G. v5p0267c1s
Tibbits, A.O. v5p0239c2s
Tibbles, S. v3p0213c1s
Tibbles, T.H. v3p0213c2s
Tibbot, N.W. v6p0519c2s
v6p0619c2s
Tice, J.H. v1p0384c2s
Tichener, E.B. v4p0364c2s
v4p0371c2s
Tichener, E.B. and Bentley, I.M.
v6p0055c1s
Tichenor, C.O. v5p0600c1s
Tichomoroff, L. v2p0381c1s
Tickell, G. v3p0270c2s
Tickle, W.W. v3p0054c2s
v3p0319c2s
Ticknor, C. v1p1004c2s
v4p0041c2s v4p0195c2s v4p0272c1s
v4p0413c1s v5p0230c1s v5p0434c2s
v5p0552c1s v5p0596c1s v6p0024c1s
v6p0111c2s v6p0173c2s v6p0489c1s
Ticknor, Caroline v4p0551c2s
Ticknor, G. v1p0036c1s
v1p0102c1s v1p0285c1s v1p0559c1s
v1p0670c2s v1p0717c1s v1p0866c2s
v1p1158c2s v1p1228c1s v1p1231c1s
v1p1254c1s v1p1297c2s v1p1396c1s
Ticknor, G. and Norton, A.
v1p0173c1s
Ticknor, H.M. v6p0077c1s
v6p0283c2s
Tidball, J.C. v5p0033c1s
v5p0601c2s
Tidball, W.L. v1p0270c2s
Tiddeman, L.E. v4p0305c1s
v4p0380c1s v4p0484c1s v5p0085c2s
v5p0251c2s v6p0083c2s v6p0426c2s
Tiddeman, R.H. v1p0794c2s
Tidmarsh, H.E. v2p0085c1s
v4p0022c2s v4p0042c1s v4p0105c1s
Tidy, C.M. v2p0107c1s
v2p0396c1m v3p0313c1s v3p0386c1s
Tidy, Dr. v1p1390c2s
Tieck, L. v1p1009c1s
Tiedeman, C.G. v2p0347c1s
v4p0277c2s v5p0529c2s v5p0610c2s
v6p0263c1s
Tiedman, P.G. v2p0248c1s
Tiempo, M. v5p0263c2s
v5p0629c2s
Tiernan, F.C. v4p0318c2s
v4p0368c1s
Tiernan, M.S. v3p0439c1s
Tierney, A. v5p0645c1s
Tierney, J. v1p0007c2s
Tierney, R.H. v6p0256c2s
v6p0276c1s
Tiffany, C.C. v1p0242c1s
v1p0427c1s v1p0514c2s v1p0879c1s
v1p1083c2s v1p1121c1s v3p0036c2s
v3p0461c1s v4p0353c2s
Tiffany, E.B. v5p0366c1s
v6p0022c1s v6p0153c2s v6p0466c2s
v6p0579c1s
Tiffany, F. v1p0323c2s
v1p0335c2s v1p0516c2s v1p0579c1s
v1p0738c1s v1p1040c2s v1p1059c1s
v1p1185c2s v1p1344c1s v2p0462c1s
v3p0435c1s v4p0478c2s v5p0387c2s
v5p0432c2s v6p0395c2s v6p0706c2s
Tiffany, J.B. v5p0450c1s
Tiffany, L.C. v4p0228c1s
Tiffany, Mary A. v6p0289c1s
Tiffany, N.M. v3p0061c1s
v3p0103c2s v3p0386c2s v3p0394c1s
v3p0395c1s
Tiffany, O. v1p0106c2s
v1p0232c1s v1p0337c1s v1p0485c1s
v1p0497c2s v1p0570c2s v1p0591c2s
v1p0723c1s v1p0759c2s v1p0975c2s
v1p1252c2s v1p1287c2s v1p1365c2s
v4p0402c2s
Tiffany, W.L. v1p0445c2s
v1p1420c2s
Tigerschiold, H. v4p0559c2m
v5p0564c1s
Tigert, J.J. v2p0027c2s
v3p0461c2s v5p0366c1s v6p0175c1s
Tighe, W. v1p0707c1s
Tight, W.G. v4p0227c1s
v6p0451c1s
Tilbury, Dr. v2p0048c1s
v2p0054c2s v2p0122c2s v2p0387c2s
v2p0388c1s v2p0403c2s v2p0404c2s
Tilden, D. v2p0113c2s
v4p0029c2s
Tilden, Douglas v5p0462c2s
Tilden, F. v6p0605c1s
v6p0606c1s
Tilden, Freeman v6p0379c1s
Tilden, H.C. v6p0595c1s
v6p0612c2s
Tilden, H.P. v6p0258c1s
Tilden, Kate T. v5p0266c1s
Tilden, M. v1p0841c2s
Tilden, W.A. v3p0076c1s
v5p0260c1s
Tilden, W.P. v1p0685c2s
v1p0977c2s v1p1011c2s
Tilden-Brown, C.M. v4p0336c1s
Tildesley, J.C. v1p0663c1s
v1p0758c2s
Tileston, W.M. v1p0358c2m
v1p0698c1s v1p0983c2s v1p1287c2s
Tilghman, R.A. v1p0339c2s
v1p1390c1s
Tillbury, Dr. v2p0155c1m
v2p0204c2s v2p0209c2m v2p0242c2s
v2p0260c1s v2p0389c1s
Tille, A. v4p0110c1s
v4p0110c2s
Tille, V. v4p0065c1m
v5p0068c2m v6p0072c2m
Tillett, B. v3p0412c2s
v4p0238c1s v5p0602c1s
Tillett, B. and Mann, T. . v4p0314c1s
Tillett, W.F. v3p0401c2s
v3p0402c1s
Tilley, A. v1p1023c1s
v2p0087c2s v2p0155c1s v2p0175c1s
v2p0210c1s v2p0233c1s v2p0246c1s
v2p0346c1s v2p0448c2s v3p0026c2s
v3p0163c2s v3p0284c2s v3p0286c1s
v3p0335c1s v3p0338c1s v4p0254c2s
v4p0380c1s v5p0218c2s v5p0275c2s
Tilley, B.F. v5p0506c2m
Tilley, L.L. v5p0230c2s
Tillinghast, C.B. v4p0329c2s
Tillinghast, J.A. v6p0447c2s
v6p0526c1s
Tillinghast, W.H. v3p0307c1s
v4p0013c1s v4p0013c2s v4p0058c1s
v4p0259c1s v5p0336c2s v6p0372c2s
Tillinghast, W.H. and Lane, W.C.
v5p0633c1m
Tillman, B.R. v4p0331c1m
v4p0596c1s v5p0603c2s
Tillman, B.R. and Dargan, W.F.
v4p0331c1s
Tillman, S.D. v1p0074c1s
Tillman, S.E. v4p0253c2s
v4p0324c1s v4p0362c1s v4p0529c1s
v4p0537c1s v4p0555c2s v4p0601c2s
v4p0635c2s v5p0002c2s v5p0377c1s
v6p0603c1s v6p0693c1s
Tillman, S.E., Lieut.Col.. v3p0133c2s
Tillmanns, H. v4p0331c1s
Tillotson, W.D., Mrs. v5p0081c2s
v6p0339c1s
Tilly, A. v4p0229c2s
Tilly, H.L. v4p0028c2s
Tilman, S.E. v4p0487c1s
v6p0693c1s
Tilney, F.C. v6p0496c2s
Tilney, H.C. v5p0415c2s
Tilt, E.J. v2p0446c1s
Tilton, A.C. v6p0692c2s
Tilton, J.H. v4p0525c1s
Tilton, T. v1p0875c2s
Tilton, W.E. v5p0087c2s
Tilton, W.F. v4p0079c1s
v4p0178c1s v4p0539c2m v5p0167c1s
v5p0186c1s
Tilton, W.F. and Mahan, A.T.
v5p0543c1s
Tilyard, Aelfrida C.W. ... v6p0229c1s
Timbs, J. v1p0090c1s
v1p0197c1s v1p0965c2s v2p0036c2s
v2p0051c2m v2p0075c2s v2p0076c1s
v2p0230c2s v2p0247c1s v2p0263c1s
v2p0264c1s v2p0279c1s v2p0326c1s
v2p0359c2s v2p0383c2s v2p0438c2s
v2p0460c2s
Timins, D.T. v5p0285c2s
Timiriazeff, C. v2p0080c1m
Timlow, H.R. v1p1051c1s
Timmins, S. and Jeaffreson, J.C.
v2p0063c1s
Timmins, W.E. v1p0053c2s
Timmis, I.A. v2p0363c2s
Timms, J. v2p0435c2s
Timpson, L. v3p0338c1s
Timrod, H. v1p1240c1s
v1p1336c1s v5p0456c1s v6p0505c2s
v6p0604c1s
Timsol, R. v3p0107c1s
v5p0400c1s
Tincker, M.A. v1p0154c1s
v1p0335c2s v1p0541c1s v1p0569c1s
v1p0607c2m v1p0693c1s v1p0715c2s
v1p0746c1s v1p0755c2s v1p0888c1s
v1p0952c1s v1p1131c2s v1p1202c2m
v1p1266c2s v1p1309c1s v1p1338c2s
v1p1367c1s v1p1412c1s v1p1415c2s
v2p0028c1s v2p0169c1s v2p0237c1s
v2p0262c2s v2p0327c2s v3p0439c1s
v5p0197c2s
Tincombe-Fernandez, W.C. . v6p0546c2s
Tincombe-Fernandez, W.G. . v6p0338c1s
Tindal, A., Mrs. v1p0196c1s
v1p0568c2s v1p1237c1s v1p1359c1s
Tindal-Robertson, P. v6p0481c2s
Tindall, S. v6p0230c2s
Tindell, W.H. v6p0422c2s
Tingey, J.G. v5p0615c2s
Tingle, J.B. v6p0011c2s
v6p0021c1s v6p0091c2s v6p0317c1s
v6p0473c2s
Tingley, C.E. v4p0471c2s
Tinling, J.F.B. v2p0168c1s
Tinsley, H.G. v5p0475c1s
v6p0055c1s v6p0094c2s
Tinsley, L. v2p0026c2s
v2p0105c1s v2p0216c1s v2p0259c2s
v2p0265c1s v2p0480c2s v3p0110c2s
Tinsley, W. v5p0580c2s
Tinson, H. v3p0009c2s
v3p0436c2s
Tipping, E. v2p0227c1s
Tipping, H.A. v2p0151c2s
v2p0202c1s v2p0354c1s v2p0451c2s
Tipping, J.W. v1p0115c1s
v1p0337c2s v1p0963c2s v1p1134c1s
Tipple, E.S. v6p0141c2s

v6p0291c1s
Tipple, S.A. v3p0177c1s
Tippy, W.M. v5p0565c1s
Tipton, T.L.M. v4p0234c1s
Tipton, W.M. v6p0533c1s
Tirand, Max v6p0049c1s
v6p0174c1s
Tirard, N. v2p0155c1s
v2p0208c1s
Tirebuck, W. v2p0062c1s
v2p0275c1s v2p0378c2s v4p0030c2s
v4p0033c1s
Tirebuck, W.E. v4p0386c1s
Tirrell, A.M. v4p0546c2s
Tischendorf, C. v1p0126c1m
v1p0126c2s v1p0127c2s v1p1312c2s
Tischendorf, C.von v2p0044c1s
Tisdale, L.B. v4p0335c2s
Tisdale, S.T. v1p0101c2s
Tisdale, W.H. v4p0217c1s
Tisdale, W.M. v4p0217c1s
v4p0316c2s v4p0326c1m v4p0413c1s
v4p0415c2m v5p0088c1s v5p0113c1s
v5p0120c1s v5p0422c2s v6p0534c2s
Tisdall, W.S.C. v6p0489c2s
Tisdel, W.P. v4p0168c1m
Tisdell, W.St.C. v6p0156c2s
Tisistro, L.F. v1p0218c2s
Tison, A. v6p0335c2s
Tissandier, A. v4p0078c2s
Tissandier, G. v1p0019c2s
v1p0373c1s v1p0502c2s v1p1304c2s
v2p0119c2s v2p0258c2s v2p0340c1s
v2p0409c1s
Tissandier, Gaston v4p0004c2s
Tisserand, F.F. v3p0333c2s
Tissot, E. v4p0272c2s
Tissot, J.J. v5p0055c1s
v5p0305c1s
Tiswolde, C.O. v4p0360c2s
Titchener, E.B. v3p0348c1s
v4p0020c1s v4p0036c2s v4p0067c1s
v4p0092c1s v4p0161c2s v4p0386c2s
v4p0430c1s v4p0464c2m v4p0465c1m
v4p0465c2s v4p0474c1m v4p0478c1s
v4p0606c2s v5p0204c2s v5p0470c1s
v5p0470c2s v5p0471c1m v5p0548c2s
v6p0521c2m
Titchener, E.B. et al. ... v5p0129c1s
Titcomb, M. v1p0135c1s
v1p0179c2s v1p0197c1s
Titcomb, Mary L. v6p0277c1s
Tite, W. v1p0226c2s
v1p0765c1s v1p0873c2s v1p0971c2s
v1p1115c1s v1p1122c1s v1p1122c2s
v1p1123c1s v1p1260c2s
Titelbach, Vl. v5p0207c2s
Titherington, R.H. v4p0009c1s
v4p0010c2s v4p0023c1s v4p0045c2s
v4p0049c1s v4p0104c2s v4p0163c2s
v4p0183c1s v4p0189c1s v4p0198c2s
v4p0201c2s v4p0210c2s v4p0211c2s
v4p0212c1s v4p0301c1s v4p0341c1s
v4p0356c1s v4p0392c2s v4p0400c1m
v4p0401c1s v4p0408c1s v4p0419c2s
v4p0421c2s v4p0449c1s v4p0463c1s
v4p0467c1s v4p0477c1s v4p0584c1s
v4p0595c1s v4p0600c1s v4p0620c1s
v5p0354c1s v5p0397c2s v5p0426c2s
v5p0460c1s v5p0542c2s v5p0543c1s
v6p0121c2s v6p0162c2s v6p0243c2s
v6p0247c2s v6p0255c1s v6p0262c2s
v6p0289c1s v6p0294c1s v6p0377c2s
v6p0385c1s v6p0393c1s v6p0393c2s
v6p0426c1s v6p0452c1s v6p0510c2s
v6p0556c2s v6p0558c2s v6p0602c2s
v6p0674c1s
Titley, A. v5p0590c1s
Tittle, E.F. v5p0379c1s
Tittman, E.D. v6p0528c2s
Tittmann, C.H. v1p1109c1s
Tittmann, J.A.H. v1p0126c1s
v1p0687c1s
Tittmann, O.H. v3p0428c1s
v6p0250c1m v6p0666c2m
Tittmann, O.H. and Mendenhall, J.C.
v5p0599c2s
Tittmann, Prof. v1p0554c2s
Titus, A. v2p0074c2s
v2p0455c2s v2p0469c2s v2p0476c1s
v3p0159c1s v3p0366c2s v3p0397c2s
v3p0404c2s v4p0580c1s v5p0094c2s
v5p0425c1s
Titus, A., jr. v1p1355c2s
v2p0382c1s
Titus, Cap'n v6p0643c1s
Titus, E.K. v6p0389c2s
v6p0433c1s v6p0506c1s
Titus, E.Kirk v6p0371c1s
Titus, G.M. v6p0373c1s
Titus, H. v1p0198c2s
Titus, J. v1p0459c2s
Titus, L.B. v4p0079c1s
Titus, Ruth v6p0025c1s
Titus, T.T. v1p0667c2s
v1p1188c2s
Titzel, J.M. v1p0120c1s
v1p0685c1s v1p0686c1s v1p0688c2m
v1p0794c1s v1p1048c1s v1p1244c2s
v2p0081c2s v2p0359c1s v3p0021c1s
v3p0037c1s v3p0145c1s v3p0175c2s
v3p0218c1s v3p0281c1s v4p0149c2s
Tizard, T.H. v3p0426c2s
v4p0271c1s
Tobey, A. v1p0641c1s
Tobey, E.S. v3p0459c1s
Tobey, R.B. v4p0068c2s
v4p0265c1s
Tobias, D.E. v5p0403c2s
Tobie, W.N. v6p0537c1s
Tobin, J.A. v1p0664c2s
Tobin, T.W. v1p0281c2s
v1p0986c2m v1p1375c1s v2p0150c2s
v3p0116c2s
Tobin, W. v5p0376c1s
Toboso, D.de v4p0539c2s
Tochman, G. v1p1023c2s
v1p1209c1s v2p0347c1s
Tocke, A.W. v4p0095c1s
Tocque, P. v1p0910c2s
v1p1173c2s
Tocqueville, A.de v5p0602c2s
Tocs, J.M. v1p0458c1s
Tod, I.M. v2p0101c2s
Tod, I.M.S. v2p0178c2s
v2p0246c1s v2p0380c1s v2p0478c2s
Tod, M.N. v6p0189c1s
v6p0412c1s
Tod, M.N. and Bosanquet, R.C.
v6p0272c1s
Tod-Mercer, C. and Tod-Mercer, L.
v5p0299c2s
Tod-Mercer, L. and Tod-Mercer, C.
v5p0299c2s
Todd, A. v1p0193c2s
v5p0032c1s
Todd, A.J. v3p0303c1s
v6p0398c1s
Todd, C. v4p0367c1s
Todd, C.A. v1p0338c2s
v1p0374c1s v1p1144c1s
Todd, C.B. v1p0099c1s
v1p0292c1s v1p0378c1s v1p0559c1s
v1p0863c2s v1p0911c1s v1p0912c1s
v2p0012c1s v2p0049c2s v2p0060c1s
v2p0090c1s v2p0116c2s v2p0129c1s
v2p0159c2s v2p0242c2s v2p0256c2s
v2p0283c1s v2p0320c2s v2p0327c1s
v2p0355c1s v2p0386c2s v2p0430c2s
v2p0471c2s v3p0007c2s v3p0277c2s
v3p0301c1s v3p0409c1s v4p0039c1s
v4p0046c1s v4p0131c1s v4p0202c1s
v4p0270c1s v4p0309c2s v4p0326c1s
v4p0380c2s v4p0444c1s v4p0612c1s
v4p0618c2s v5p0051c1s v5p0230c1s
v5p0240c2s v5p0407c1s v5p0461c2s
v5p0521c1s v6p0534c2s
Todd, C.C. v4p0595c1s
Todd, D. v6p0018c2s
v6p0637c1s
Todd, D. and Baker, R.H. . v6p0188c1m
Todd, D.P. v1p0382c1s
v1p1014c1s v1p1268c1m v2p0011c2s
v2p0012c2s v2p0027c2s v2p0195c2s
v2p0245c2s v2p0257c2s v2p0319c1s
v2p0343c2s v2p0394c1s v2p0417c2s
v2p0425c2s v2p0426c2m v2p0433c2s
v2p0455c1s v3p0005c1s v3p0024c2s
v3p0067c1s v3p0127c1m v3p0372c1s
v4p0358c1s v4p0410c1s v4p0556c1s
v5p0035c2s v5p0174c2s v5p0175c1s
v5p0644c1s
Todd, D.P. and Loomis, E.J.
v3p0004c2s
Todd, D.P. and Payne, W.W.
v3p0415c1s
Todd, D.P. and Todd, M.L.. v4p0217c1s
Todd, David v6p0188c1s
Todd, E. v2p0053c2s
Todd, E.E. v4p0442c1s
Todd, E.S. v1p0235c1s
v3p0424c1s
Todd, F.W. v5p0270c1s
Todd, G. v4p0484c1s
Todd, G.E. v3p0205c1s
v3p0369c1s
Todd, H.A. v6p0241c2s
Todd, H.M. v4p0097c1s
v4p0460c1s
Todd, H.S. v6p0035c2s
Todd, J. v1p0119c1s
v1p0711c1s v2p0149c1s v2p0368c2s
v4p0347c2s
Todd, J.A. v1p0990c1s
v1p1237c2s v3p0112c1s
Todd, J.C. v6p0060c1s
Todd, J.E. v1p0462c2s
v1p1041c2s v1p1154c1s v1p1311c1s
v1p1416c1s v2p0127c2s v2p0462c2s
v3p0067c1s v3p0092c2s v5p0378c2s
Todd, J.H. v6p0095c2s
Todd, M.L. v3p0127c1s
v3p0165c1s v3p0466c2s v4p0123c2s
v4p0125c1s v4p0155c2s v4p0167c1s
v4p0443c1s v5p0035c1s v5p0045c1s
v5p0174c2m v5p0257c1s v5p0302c2s
v5p0351c2s v5p0417c1s v5p0430c2s
v5p0444c1m v5p0444c2s v5p0527c2s
v5p0530c1s v5p0559c1s v5p0580c2s
v6p0563c2s
Todd, M.L. and Todd, D.P.. v4p0217c1s
Todd, Mabel L. v5p0010c1s
v6p0188c1s
Todd, Mabel Loomis v6p0012c1s
v6p0132c1s v6p0187c2s v6p0657c1s
Todd, W.C. v1p0072c2s
v2p0117c2s v3p0008c2s v3p0091c2s
v3p0116c2s v4p0144c2s v4p0432c1m
v4p0616c1s v5p0388c1s
Todd, W.G. v1p0138c2s
v1p0198c1s v1p0384c2s v1p0653c2s
v1p0803c1s v1p1090c2s v4p0135c2s
Todhunter, I. v1p0276c1s
v1p1262c2s v2p0144c1s
Todhunter, J. v3p0311c2s
v3p0465c1s v3p0474c1s v4p0178c1s
v5p0161c2s v5p0399c1s v5p0530c2s
v6p0070c1s v6p0181c1s v6p0434c1s
v6p0612c2s
Todhunter, M. v4p0042c1s
v4p0053c2s v4p0062c1s v4p0070c1s
v4p0184c2s v4p0201c2s v4p0227c2s
v4p0246c2s v4p0407c2s v4p0506c2s
v4p0513c2s v4p0528c1s v4p0586c2s
v5p0211c1s v5p0367c2s v5p0510c2s
v5p0552c1s v5p0590c2s
Todleben, F.E., Gen. v1p0316c1s
Todt, M. v3p0171c2s
v3p0352c1s
Toft, P. v1p0464c1s
v1p0596c2s v1p0776c2s v1p1188c2s
v1p1439c2s v4p0132c1s
Toit, D.F.Du v5p0487c2s
Toker, E.J. v4p0619c1s
v5p0090c1s
Toker, E.T. v4p0209c1s
Toland, M.H. v1p0220c2s
Toldridge, Eliz.B. v6p0344c2s
Tolefree, R. jr. v1p1376c2s
Tolerton, J. v6p0102c2s
Tolfrey, F. v1p0194c2s
Toll, E.von, Baron v5p0508c1s
Toll, Ed.von v6p0029c1s
Tolland, N. v1p0846c1s
Tollemache, Beatrix L. ... v4p0138c1s
Tollemache, L. v1p0308c2s
v1p0407c2s v1p0767c2s v1p0838c2s
v1p1295c2s
Tollemache, L.A. v1p0077c2s
v1p0084c1s v1p0559c2s v1p0584c1s
v1p0593c2s v1p0752c2s v4p0419c1s
v4p0578c2s v5p0322c2s
Tolles, C.W. v1p0059c2s
v1p1136c1s
Tolman, A.H. v2p0289c2s
v2p0423c1s v3p0140c1s v4p0183c2s
v4p0184c1s v4p0507c1s v4p0518c2s
v5p0207c2s v6p0208c1s
Tolman, E. v5p0636c2s
v6p0462c1s
Tolman, Edgar B. v6p0113c2s
Tolman, F.L. v6p0065c2m
v6p0602c1s
Tolman, G.R. v6p0131c2s
Tolman, H.C. v5p0269c1s
Tolman, H.L. v2p0143c2s
v4p0209c1s
Tolman, H.S. v3p0175c1s
Tolman, L.D. v6p0497c1s
Tolman, W.H. v4p0115c2s
v4p0132c1s v4p0215c2s v4p0266c2s
v4p0533c1s v4p0554c1s v4p0567c1s
v4p0569c1s v5p0049c2s v5p0086c2s
v5p0136c1s v5p0157c2s v5p0201c1s
v5p0273c1s v5p0321c1s v5p0406c2s
v5p0431c2s v5p0512c2s v5p0535c2s
v5p0544c1s v5p0641c1s v6p0002c2s
v6p0052c1s v6p0246c2s v6p0252c1s
v6p0354c2s v6p0401c2s v6p0437c2s
v6p0535c2s v6p0566c1m v6p0600c1s
Tolstoi, Count and Ballou, A.
v3p0306c2s
Tolstoi, L. v2p0471c2s
v3p0082c2s v3p0146c2s v3p0332c2s
v3p0360c1s v3p0383c2s v3p0396c2s
v3p0431c2s v3p0465c2s v3p0472c1s
v4p0109c2m v4p0206c1s v4p0356c2s
v4p0382c1s v4p0478c1s v4p0496c2s
v5p0030c2m v5p0041c2s v5p0115c1s
v5p0116c2s v5p0199c1s v5p0229c2s
v5p0437c2s v5p0502c1s v5p0514c1s
v5p0616c1s v5p0617c2s v6p0120c2s
v6p0123c1s v6p0176c1s v6p0203c2m
v6p0248c1s v6p0286c2s v6p0376c1s
v6p0471c1s v6p0513c1s v6p0536c2s
v6p0557c1m v6p0557c2s v6p0586c1s
v6p0685c1s
Tolstoi, L., Count v3p0155c1s
v5p0501c2s
Tolstoi, L.N. v4p0361c2s
Tolstoi, Leo v4p0109c1s
v5p0403c2s v5p0502c1s v6p0272c1s
Tolstoi, Leo and Laughlin, J.L.
v5p0382c2s
Tombo, R. v6p0137c2s
v6p0672c1s
Tombo, R., jr. v6p0136c1s
v6p0169c1s v6p0190c2s v6p0622c2s
Tomes, R. v1p0032c2s
v1p0106c1s v1p0350c1s v1p0425c2s

v1p0535c2s v1p0570c1s v1p0678c2s
v1p0790c2s v1p0916c1s v1p1408c2s
Tomilson, G.W. v2p0320c1s
Tomkins, G. v2p0223c1s
Tomkins, H.G. v2p0204c1s
v2p0327c1s v3p0012c2s v3p0390c1s
v3p0438c1s
Tomkins, I.G. v5p0523c2m
Tomkins, J.N. v1p0900c1s
Tomlins, W.L. v2p0403c2s
v2p0462c2s v4p0390c1m v5p0394c1s
v5p0530c2s
Tomlinson, C. v1p0749c1s
v1p0810c1s v1p0958c2s v1p1003c1s
v1p1162c1s v1p1210c1s v1p1271c2s
v1p1282c2s v2p0111c2s v2p0260c1s
v2p0325c2m v3p0110c1s v3p0133c2s
v3p0187c2s v3p0319c2s v4p0332c1s
v5p0215c2s
Tomlinson, C. and Griffith, A.F.
v3p0251c1s
Tomlinson, C.W. v3p0282c1s
Tomlinson, D. v1p1310c1s
Tomlinson, E.T. v2p0001c2s
v2p0088c1s v3p0001c2s v5p0479c2s
v6p0346c1s v6p0419c2s v6p0642c2s
Tomlinson, H. v2p0135c2s
v2p0163c1m v2p0272c1s v2p0413c1s
v3p0272c1s
Tomlinson, H.A. v6p0110c1s
Tomlinson, H.W. v6p0170c2s
Tomlinson, J. v1p0130c1s
v1p0507c2s v1p0759c1s v1p1001c1s
v1p1082c1s v2p0154c1s v3p0198c2s
v3p0258c2s v4p0045c1s v4p0053c2s
v4p0112c1s v4p0497c2s v4p0502c1s
v5p0114c2s v5p0135c1s v5p0306c2s
v5p0507c2s
Tomlinson, N. v2p0422c2s
Tomlinson, T. v4p0174c2s
Tomlinson, W. v2p0172c1s
Tommasi-Crudeli, C. v1p0388c2s
Tomn, L. v5p0481c2s
Tompkins, A. v4p0432c2s
v4p0534c2s v5p0262c2s
Tompkins, C.E. v4p0631c2s
Tompkins, D.A. v4p0136c1s
v4p0406c2s v4p0485c1s v6p0153c1m
v6p0708c1s
Tompkins, D.M. v6p0259c1s
Tompkins, E. v1p0353c1s
Tompkins, E.A. v3p0456c1m
Tompkins, E.K. v4p0519c2s
v5p0065c1s v5p0275c1s v6p0291c2s
v6p0671c1s
Tompkins, E.K. et al. v5p0048c2s
Tompkins, E.S.de G. v3p0152c1s
v3p0327c2s
Tompkins, E.W. v6p0580c1s
Tompkins, G. v5p0271c1s
v5p0489c1s v6p0603c2s
Tompkins, H., Dr. v2p0457c1s
Tompkins, H.B. v3p0171c1s
Tompkins, H.C. v5p0053c2s
Tompkins, H.W. v5p0476c1s
v5p0589c2s v6p0013c1s v6p0019c1s
v6p0359c1s v6p0485c1s v6p0617c1s
Tompkins, I.G. v4p0321c1s
v4p0333c1s v4p0404c2s v4p0519c1s
v5p0523c1s
Tompkins, J.A. v3p0375c1s
Tompkins, J.E. v6p0504c1s
Tompkins, J.W. v4p0266c2s
v4p0414c1s v5p0085c2s v5p0116c1s
v5p0361c2s v5p0421c1s v5p0480c1s
v6p0078c2s v6p0093c1s v6p0232c1s
v6p0235c1s v6p0262c2s v6p0310c2s
v6p0342c2s v6p0347c1s v6p0408c1s
v6p0433c2s v6p0532c1s v6p0603c1s
v6p0690c2s v6p0703c1s
Tompkins, Juliet W. v6p0124c1s
v6p0358c1s v6p0387c2s v6p0432c1m
v6p0434c1s v6p0458c1s v6p0700c1s
Tompkins, L.A. v3p0201c1s
Tompkins, O.D. v5p0396c2s
Tompkins, W.E. v1p0349c2s
Tomson, A. v5p0050c1s
v5p0096c2s v5p0195c1s v5p0498c2s
v6p0107c1s v6p0622c2s
Tomson, Arthur v5p0166c1s
v5p0376c2s v5p0439c2s
Tomson, G.R. v3p0025c1s
v3p0141c2s v3p0195c2s v3p0332c1s
v3p0458c1s v3p0460c1s v4p0218c2s
v4p0225c2s v4p0270c1s v4p0320c1s
v4p0559c1s v4p0574c2s v4p0614c1s
Tondini, F. v1p1134c2s
Tondorf, F.A. v6p0037c2s
Toner, J.M. v3p0219c1s
v3p0455c2s v3p0456c1s v4p0611c2m
v4p0612c1s
Toney, S.B. v2p0359c1s
Tonge, F. v4p0629c2s
Tonge, T. v4p0153c1s
v4p0231c1s v5p0028c1s v5p0129c1m
v5p0144c1s v5p0238c1s v5p0594c1s
Tonjoroff, S.I. v5p0002c1s
v5p0197c1s v5p0501c2s v5p0535c1s
Tonks, J.W. v4p0301c2s
Tonks, O.S. v6p0024c1s
v6p0134c2s
Tonks, Oliver S. v6p0497c2s
Tonks, T.W. v1p0052c1s
Tonnies, F. v5p0446c2s
v6p0254c2s v6p0600c2s
Tonnochy v5p0029c2s
Tonsor, J. v4p0396c2s
Toof, J.T. v2p0085c1m
Tooke, C.W. v5p0391c2s
Tooke, M.A. v1p0149c1s
v1p0149c2s
Tooke, W. v1p1283c2s
Tooker, L.F. v5p0259c2s
v5p0326c1s v5p0580c2s v6p0171c1s
v6p0311c1s v6p0311c2s v6p0350c2s
v6p0664c2s
Tooker, W.W. v4p0098c2s
v4p0423c1s v4p0559c1s v5p0012c1s
v5p0371c1s v5p0459c2s v5p0563c2s
v6p0012c2s v6p0512c2m v6p0680c1m
Toole, J.L. v2p0470c1s
v4p0269c1s
Tooley, G.W. v4p0306c1s
Tooley, H. v1p1316c1s
Tooley, S. v6p0194c2s
Tooley, S.A. v6p0124c1s
v6p0194c2s v6p0569c2s
Toombs, R. v1p1206c1s
Toombs, R.Y. v3p0340c2s
v4p0306c1s v4p0594c1s
Toomey, M.V. v5p0493c2s
Topham, A.F. v6p0027c1s
v6p0051c1s
Topham, F.W.W., Mrs. v4p0436c2s
Topham, J. v1p0393c1m
v1p0393c2s v1p0424c2s v1p0585c1s
Topin, M. v1p0665c2s
v2p0030c1s
Topinard, P. v2p0016c2s
v3p0265c2s v4p0193c2s v4p0352c1s
v4p0507c1s v5p0077c2s v5p0358c1s
v5p0513c1s v5p0535c2s v6p0238c1s
Topley, S. v1p0415c1s
Topley, W. v1p0198c1s
v1p0972c1s v1p1149c2s v1p1391c2s
v2p0122c1s v2p0231c1s v3p0167c2s
v3p0328c2s v4p0269c2s v4p0502c2s
Topley, W.G. v3p0457c2s
Topliff, G.F. v6p0649c2s
Toppan, R.N. v1p0272c2s
Topsham, F.W.W., Mrs. v4p0590c2s
Torbert, J.B. v5p0005c2s
Torbett, J.E. v1p0895c2s
v1p1143c2s
Torbett, J.R. v6p0400c1s
Torneoko, K. v6p0338c2s
Tornow, Max L. v5p0444c1s
Torr, C. v3p0201c2s
v3p0357c1s v4p0573c2s
Torr, C. and Petrie, W.F.. v4p0004c2s
Torr, C. et al. v4p0091c2s
Torr, H.J. v6p0356c1s
Torrance, T. v3p0294c2s
v3p0437c1s
Torre, L. v4p0202c1s
v5p0089c2s v5p0160c1s
Torrence, R. v6p0404c2s
v6p0677c2s
Torrens, A.E. v4p0345c2s
Torrens, R. v1p0721c1s
v1p1303c2s
Torrens, T.McC. v1p1210c1s
Torrens, W.M. v1p0398c2s
v1p0406c1s v1p0758c2s v1p0763c1s
v1p1092c1s v3p0395c1s v3p0457c1s
Torrens, W.T.M. v1p0543c1s
v1p0606c1s v1p0733c1s
Torrey, B. v2p0046c2m
v2p0047c1m v2p0047c2s v2p0472c2s
v2p0479c1s v3p0100c2s v3p0113c1s
v3p0125c1s v3p0156c1s v3p0162c1s
v3p0204c2m v3p0290c1s v3p0290c2s
v3p0301c1s v3p0308c2s v3p0363c1s
v3p0391c2s v3p0450c2s v4p0061c1m
v4p0061c2s v4p0102c2s v4p0149c1s
v4p0203c1m v4p0257c2s v4p0341c2s
v4p0374c1s v4p0498c2s v4p0499c1s
v4p0575c1s v5p0012c2s v5p0016c1s
v5p0041c1s v5p0063c1s v5p0095c1s
v5p0209c2s v5p0219c1m v5p0283c1s
v5p0385c2s v5p0400c1s v5p0475c1s
v5p0578c2s v5p0609c2s v6p0067c1m
v6p0068c1s v6p0229c1s v6p0236c1s
v6p0284c2s v6p0350c1s v6p0617c1s
v6p0707c2s
Torrey, Bates v3p0439c2s
Torrey, Bradford v6p0644c1s
Torrey, C.A. v5p0335c1s
Torrey, C.C. v4p0056c1s
v5p0058c2s v5p0176c2s v5p0316c1s
v6p0360c2s v6p0370c2s v6p0391c2s
v6p0496c1s v6p0710c2s
Torrey, C.C. and Ropes, J.H.
v5p0306c2s
Torrey, C.W. v1p0458c2s
v1p1423c2s
Torrey, D.C. v3p0105c1s
Torrey, E. v1p1181c2s
Torrey, Eliz. v5p0303c1s
Torrey, G.F. v1p1360c1s
Torrey, H.A.P. v2p0253c1s
v3p0348c1s
Torrey, H.B. v6p0105c1s
v6p0174c1s
Torrey, H.W. v1p0060c2s
v1p0078c2s v1p0106c1s v1p0111c1s
v1p0317c2s v1p0447c1s v1p0617c2s
v1p0650c2s v1p0738c2s v1p0907c2s
v1p0923c2s v1p1124c1s
Torrey, J. v1p0645c2s
v4p0180c2s v4p0347c1s
Torrey, J., jr. v4p0099c1s
Torrey, J., jr. and Barbour, E.H.
v3p0312c2s
Torrey, J.L. v5p0046c2s
Torricelli, G. v2p0229c2s
Torricelli, J.B. v1p0207c2s
v1p0500c2s v1p0522c1s v1p0668c2s
v1p1032c2s v1p1033c1s v1p1058c1m
v1p1120c1s v1p1363c1s
Torrington, J.A. v4p0003c2s
v5p0018c2s
Tosti, G. v5p0016c1s
v5p0018c1s v5p0560c1s v5p0567c1s
v6p0330c2s v6p0331c2m
Tosti, Gustavo v6p0202c2s
Totten, C.A.L. v2p0360c1s
v5p0556c1s
Totten, C.A.S. v1p1040c2s
Totten, H.S. v1p0445c1s
Totten, J.G. v1p0621c2s
v1p0749c2s v1p0873c2s
Totten, S. v1p0096c2s
v1p0222c1s
Tottenham, H.R. v3p0444c2s
Tottie, J.W. v1p0627c2s
Totyl, J. v3p0011c1s
v3p0012c1s v3p0218c2m
Touche, T.D.La v4p0486c1s
v5p0173c1s
Touche, T.D.La and Hansen, A.M.
v4p0317c1s
Tougenieff, I. v1p1050c1s
Toulouse et al. v6p0521c1s
Toumey, J.W. v4p0583c1s
v5p0086c2s v5p0214c1s v6p0502c1s
Tourette, G.de la v3p0014c1s
Tourgee, A.W. v1p0001c1s
v1p0259c1s v2p0029c2s v2p0064c1s
v2p0232c2s v2p0286c2s v3p0101c1s
v3p0296c2s v3p0315c2s v3p0401c2s
v3p0402c1s v3p0414c1s v3p0466c2s
v4p0143c2s v4p0351c1s v4p0453c1s
v4p0585c2s v4p0594c1s v5p0437c1s
v5p0600c2s v6p0146c1s
Tourgenieff, I. v1p0044c2s
v1p0069c1s v1p0162c2s v1p0352c1s
v1p0358c1s v1p0403c2s v1p0445c2s
v1p0446c1s v1p0609c1s v1p0623c1s
v1p0708c1s v1p0757c2s v1p0862c2s
v1p0876c1s v1p0924c2s v1p1240c1s
v1p1308c2s v1p1309c1s v1p1375c2s
v1p1389c2s v1p1437c1s v2p0156c2s
v2p0284c2s v2p0394c2s v2p0415c2s
v2p0422c1s v3p0116c1s v3p0400c2s
v3p0462c2s v4p0079c1s v4p0094c2s
v4p0159c1s v4p0196c1s v4p0246c2s
v4p0518c1s v5p0164c2s
Tourgenieff, Ivan v5p0419c1s
Tourgenieff, N. v1p1137c1m
Tourneur, N. v5p0412c1s
Tourney, J.W. v4p0119c2s
Tousey, S. v1p1245c1s
Toussaint, B. v1p1335c1s
Tout, J.F. v3p0030c2s
Tout, T.F. v3p0329c1s
v4p0181c2s v6p0076c1s v6p0142c1s
v6p0194c2s v6p0223c2s v6p0378c1s
v6p0424c2s
Touzel, T.P. v2p0232c1s
Tovel, A. v3p0297c2s
Tovell, A. v1p0692c1s
v2p0174c1s
Tovey, D.C. v4p0574c2s
Tovey, D.F. v6p0344c1s
Tovey, Dr. v1p1115c1s
Tovey, O. v5p0488c2s
Tower, C. v6p0112c1s
v6p0303c2s v6p0559c1s
Tower, C.V. v6p0582c2s
Tower, E.B. v6p0294c1s
Tower, Ellen M. v4p0069c1s
Tower, Grace M. v6p0093c2s
Tower, S. v1p1288c1s
Tower, W.B. v6p0408c1s
Tower, W.L. v5p0277c2s
Tower, W.S. v6p0250c2s
v6p0493c1s v6p0544c2s
Tower, Walter S. v6p0127c2s
Tower, Z.B. v1p0622c1s
Towers, C.M.D. v4p0371c1s
v4p0618c1s
Towle, C. v6p0172c1s
Towle, C., Mrs. v6p0172c1s
v6p0228c1s
Towle, E.A. v5p0140c2s
v5p0340c2s
Towle, Eleanor A. v5p0160c1s
Towle, G.M. v1p0015c2s
v1p0056c2m v1p0067c1s v1p0076c2s

v1p0082c1s v1p0163c1m v1p0165c1s
v1p0165c2s v1p0166c1s v1p0201c2s
v1p0209c2s v1p0265c2s v1p0267c1s
v1p0274c2s v1p0295c2s v1p0332c1s
v1p0355c1s v1p0397c2s v1p0412c2m
v1p0413c2s v1p0473c1s v1p0477c2s
v1p0479c1s v1p0480c1s v1p0480c2s
v1p0498c2s v1p0514c2s v1p0520c2s
v1p0524c2s v1p0534c2m v1p0547c2s
v1p0550c1s v1p0550c2s v1p0559c2s
v1p0572c2s v1p0583c1s v1p0607c1s
v1p0616c1s v1p0633c2s v1p0670c2s
v1p0708c2s v1p0727c2s v1p0729c2s
v1p0740c1s v1p0757c2s v1p0779c1s
v1p0780c2s v1p0802c2s v1p0814c2s
v1p0889c1s v1p0892c1s v1p0892c2s
v1p0895c2s v1p0913c1s v1p0941c2s
v1p0948c2s v1p0960c1s v1p0962c1s
v1p0968c2s v1p0969c1s v1p0969c2s
v1p0970c1s v1p0975c2s v1p1084c2s
v1p1129c1s v1p1146c2s v1p1151c2s
v1p1305c1s v1p1314c1s v1p1329c1s
v1p1342c1s v1p1348c2s v1p1354c1s
v1p1406c2s v1p1436c1m v2p0454c2s
v3p0085c2s v3p0233c2s
Towle, H.E. v1p1023c2s
Towle, L. v5p0396c2s
Towle, M.R. v6p0554c1s
Towle, S. v4p0431c2s
Towle, W.W. v5p0194c2s
Town, C.M., Mrs. v1p1325c1s
Town, K.T. v1p0855c2s
Townbridge, E. v1p0100c2m
v1p0177c2s v1p0324c2s v1p0534c2s
v1p0609c2s v1p0624c1s v1p0628c2s
v1p0631c1s v1p0692c2s v1p0795c1s
v1p0879c1s v1p0888c1s v1p0908c2s
v1p0941c1s v1p1371c2s v1p1376c2s
v1p1380c1s v1p1403c2s
Towndrow, G.E. v6p0586c1s
Towndrow, R.F. v6p0098c2s
Towne, A.N. v3p0163c1s
v3p0191c1s v3p0235c2s v3p0263c1s
v3p0333c1s v3p0389c2s v3p0396c2s
v3p0439c1s v3p0466c2s v4p0027c1s
v4p0368c1s v4p0404c1s v4p0549c1s
Towne, A.W. v3p0464c1s
Towne, C.A. v5p0019c1s
v5p0053c1s v5p0431c2s v5p0482c1s
v5p0603c2s v5p0604c1s
Towne, C.M. v5p0089c2s
Towne, E.C. v1p0027c2s
v1p0050c1s v1p0107c2s v1p0241c2s
v1p0242c1s v1p0380c2s v1p0496c2s
v1p0712c1s v1p0848c1s v1p1095c2s
v2p0009c2s v2p0010c2s v2p0189c2s
v3p0007c2s v3p0135c1s
Towne, F.E. v6p0228c2s
Towne, H.A. et al. v1p1247c2s
Towne, H.R. v1p0111c1s
v2p0106c1m v4p0461c1s
Towne, W.B. v1p1318c1s
Towner, A. v1p0406c2s
Towner, Harriet C. v5p0030c1s
v5p0638c2m
Townes, J.C. v6p0640c1m
Townley, D.O'C. v1p0066c1s
v1p1280c2s
Townley, H.C. v1p0641c1s
Townley, J. v1p1116c1s
v2p0015c1s v2p0025c2s v2p0272c2s
v2p0318c2s v2p0430c1s v2p0430c2s
v2p0482c2s
Townley, M.M. v5p0423c2s
Townley, S., Lady v6p0476c2s
Townley, S.D. v6p0647c1s
Townley, Susan v6p0582c2s
Townsend, A. v3p0234c1s
Townsend, A.B. v6p0496c2s
Townsend, B.L. and Ballard, M.L.
v3p0424c2s
Townsend, C. v1p0339c1s
v6p0351c2s
Townsend, C.C. v5p0285c1s
v6p0016c2s
Townsend, C.E. v1p0401c1s
v1p0865c2s v1p1268c1s v5p0351c2s
Townsend, C.F. v4p0010c2s
v4p0482c1s v5p0211c2s v5p0213c2s
v5p0412c2s
Townsend, C.H. v2p0385c2s
v4p0384c1s v5p0031c2s v5p0517c1s
v6p0485c2s v6p0580c1s
Townsend, C.H. and Fassett, E.C.B.
v6p0338c1s
Townsend, C.H.T. v4p0417c1s
Townsend, D. v1p0825c2s
v1p1003c2s
Townsend, D.M. v5p0029c2s
Townsend, E.J. v3p0426c1s
v6p0406c1s
Townsend, E.W. v5p0156c1s
v6p0043c1s v6p0164c1s v6p0166c2s
v6p0350c1s v6p0539c2s v6p0552c2s
v6p0567c2s
Townsend, F. v1p0162c2s
Townsend, F.S. v4p0198c1s
v5p0178c1s
Townsend, G. v6p0180c1s
Townsend, G.A. v1p0032c2s
v1p0472c2s v1p0807c2s v1p1388c2s
v2p0052c2s v2p0183c2s v3p0303c1s
v4p0126c1s v4p0152c1s v4p0252c1s
v4p0475c2s
Townsend, G.E. v6p0711c2s
Townsend, G.F. v1p1414c2s
Townsend, H. v3p0128c1s
v4p0024c2m v4p0043c2s v4p0274c1s
v4p0421c1s v4p0484c1s v4p0526c2s
v4p0572c1s v5p0010c2s v5p0030c2s
v5p0139c1s v5p0268c1s v5p0343c1s
v5p0428c1s v5p0553c1s
Townsend, H.A. v5p0443c2s
Townsend, H.C. v4p0177c1s
Townsend, H.S. v5p0258c2m
v6p0429c2s v6p0493c1s
Townsend, J.B. v4p0058c2s
Townsend, J.D., Mrs. v4p0103c2s
Townsend, J.P. v1p1153c1s
v3p0376c1s v5p0509c2s
Townsend, J.P. and Smith, C.H.
v4p0504c1s v4p0524c2s
Townsend, J.S. v6p0325c2s
Townsend, J.S. and Sidgreaves, W.
v4p0556c2s
Townsend, L.T. v1p1252c1s
v3p0042c2s v3p0091c1s v3p0120c1s
v3p0190c1s v3p0364c1s v3p0378c1s
v4p0056c2s v4p0489c1s
Townsend, L.T. and Dunn, J.B.
v3p0426c1s
Townsend, M. v1p0630c2s
v3p0213c1s v3p0283c1s v5p0034c1s
v5p0197c1s v5p0420c1s
Townsend, M.E. v6p0501c1s
Townsend, M.T. v4p0228c2s
v5p0209c2s v5p0591c2s v5p0592c1s
v5p0644c1s
Townsend, N. v1p0801c1s
Townsend, P. v2p0040c1s
Townsend, R.D. v6p0523c1s
Townsend, T.F. v3p0310c2s
Townsend, T.S. v4p0359c2s
Townsend, V.F. v1p0013c2s
v1p0609c2s v1p0680c1s v1p0799c2s
v1p0921c2s v1p0939c2s v1p0941c1s
v1p1175c1s
Townsend, W. v1p0060c2s
v1p0667c1s v1p0775c2s v1p1189c1s
v1p1226c1s v1p1253c1s v4p0120c1s
v4p0518c2s v4p0519c1s
Townsend, W.G.Paulson v6p0129c2s
Townsend, W.K. v4p0307c1s
Townsend, W.K., Mrs. v5p0003c1s
Townshend, C. v1p0490c2s
Townshend, C.C. v1p0053c1s
Townshend, C.H. v1p1052c2s
v2p0031c1s v2p0039c1s v3p0090c1s
v4p0041c1s v4p0125c2s v4p0362c1s
v4p0393c1s v4p0620c1s v5p0264c1s
v5p0479c2s v5p0643c2s
Townshend, D. v6p0193c2s
v6p0599c1s v6p0700c2s
Townshend, E.C. v4p0637c1m
Townshend, N.S. v3p0310c2s
Townshend, R.B. v3p0002c1s
v4p0346c1s v4p0390c2s v5p0061c2s
v5p0391c1s v5p0489c1s v5p0495c1s
v6p0086c2s v6p0087c2m v6p0411c2s
v6p0599c1s v6p0643c2s
Townshend, T.B. v5p0357c1s
Townsley, C.P. v1p0174c2s
Towry, M.H. v2p0256c2s
v2p0414c2s v3p0297c1s
Towse, J.R. v2p0229c2s
v2p0230c1s v2p0293c2s v3p0138c2s
v3p0139c1s v3p0172c2s v3p0220c1s
v3p0260c2s v3p0453c2s v4p0068c1s
v4p0164c2s v4p0182c2s v5p0003c2s
v5p0152c1s v5p0274c1s v5p0360c2s
v5p0415c1s v5p0539c2s v5p0575c2m
v6p0180c2s v6p0184c2s v6p0256c1s
v6p0329c2s v6p0391c2s v6p0495c1s
v6p0504c1s v6p0586c1s v6p0586c2s
v6p0641c2m
Towse, J.Rankin v5p0054c2s
v5p0209c2s v5p0451c2s v6p0500c1s
Towse, R. v6p0544c2s
Towson, M.R. v6p0703c2s
Toy, C.H. v1p0096c2s
v1p0121c2s v1p0394c2s v1p0438c2s
v1p0879c2s v1p1177c1s v1p1329c1s
v2p0018c1m v2p0043c1m v2p0043c2s
v2p0135c1s v2p0143c2s v2p0270c1s
v2p0339c1s v2p0394c2m v2p0399c1s
v3p0016c2s v3p0041c1s v3p0041c2s
v3p0042c1m v3p0043c2s v3p0143c1m
v3p0145c1s v3p0330c1s v3p0357c2s
v4p0053c1s v4p0056c1s v4p0077c2s
v4p0145c2s v4p0302c2m v4p0313c2m
v4p0479c1s v5p0195c1s v5p0299c1s
v5p0316c2s v5p0385c1s v5p0483c2s
v5p0503c1s v6p0125c1s v6p0302c2s
v6p0423c2s v6p0538c1s v6p0641c1s
v6p0672c1s
Toy, C.H. and Gilman, N.P. v5p0197c2s
Toy, E.P. v2p0138c2s
Toynbee, C.M. v5p0459c1s
Toynbee, H. v3p0391c1s
v4p0609c2s v5p0386c2s
Toynbee, H.V. v4p0097c1s
v4p0314c1s v4p0591c1s v5p0222c1s
v6p0665c1s
Toynbee, Helen v5p0617c2m
Toynbee, P. v3p0075c1s
v3p0110c1s v3p0110c2s v3p0163c2s
v3p0267c1s v3p0377c1s v3p0409c2s
v3p0446c2s v4p0147c1m v4p0147c2m
v4p0157c1s v4p0622c2s v5p0067c2s
v5p0074c2s v5p0430c1s v6p0164c2s
Toynbee, P. et al. v3p0135c2s
v3p0191c1s v4p0562c1s
v5p0152c2s
Toynbee, W. v4p0276c2s
v4p0515c2s v4p0599c2s v4p0619c1s
v5p0452c2s v5p0476c1s
Tozer, A. v3p0315c1s
Tozer, B. v4p0158c1s
v6p0236c1s v6p0461c2s v6p0582c2s
v6p0611c1s
Tozer, Basil v6p0081c1s
v6p0346c2s v6p0369c1s v6p0515c2s
v6p0548c1s
Tozer, H.F. v2p0111c2s
v2p0160c2s v2p0190c2s v2p0191c1s
v2p0254c1s v2p0332c2s v2p0372c1s
v2p0374c2s v3p0025c2s v3p0062c1m
v3p0082c2s v3p0100c2s v3p0109c1s
v3p0184c2s v3p0225c1s v3p0325c2s
v3p0335c1s v3p0360c1s v3p0375c2s
v5p0436c2s
Tozer, H.J. v5p0287c1s
v6p0314c1s
Tozer, W.H. v6p0708c1s
Tozier, J. v6p0298c1s
Tozier, Josephine v5p0430c2s
v5p0431c1s v5p0431c2s v6p0041c1s
Tracey, C. et al. v4p0596c1s
Tracey, T. v4p0215c1s
v4p0346c2s
Tracy, A.T. v1p0845c2s
v1p1237c2s
Tracy, B.F. v3p0443c2s
v4p0049c2s
Tracy, C. v1p1256c2s
Tracy, C.M. v1p0946c1s
v1p1015c2s
Tracy, E.C. v1p0330c1s
Tracy, F. v4p0320c2s
v5p0470c1s v6p0610c1s
Tracy, F.B. v4p0453c1s
v4p0533c2s v5p0066c2s v5p0202c2s
v5p0358c2s v6p0096c1s v6p0382c2s
v6p0482c1s v6p0550c2s v5p0669c2s
Tracy, F.P. v1p0189c2s
v1p0910c1s v1p1355c2s
Tracy, H. v1p0195c2s
Tracy, H.A. v2p0115c1s
Tracy, I. v1p0289c2m
Tracy, J. v1p0096c2s
v1p0277c1s v1p0356c2s v1p1108c1s
v1p1150c1s
Tracy, J.J. v6p0610c1s
Tracy, J.M. v1p0063c2s
v1p0106c1s
Tracy, J.T. v6p0405c1s
Tracy, J.V. v3p0302c1s
v3p0324c1s v3p0345c2s v3p0365c1s
v3p0373c2s v4p0137c2s v4p0300c2s
v4p0621c1s v5p0486c1s
Tracy, Joseph V. v5p0324c2s
Tracy, L. v4p0451c2s
Tracy, Louis v6p0157c2s
Tracy, M. v4p0090c2s
v4p0267c2s v4p0325c1s v4p0580c2s
v5p0439c1s
Tracy, Marguerite v6p0283c2s
Tracy, R.S. v1p0258c2s
v1p0367c2s v1p0957c2s v1p1436c2s
v5p0119c2s v6p0386c1m
Tracy, S. v1p0096c1s
v1p0254c2s
Tracy, V. v6p0516c2s
Tracy, W. v1p0636c2s
Tracy, W.W. v4p0033c1s
v4p0579c1s v6p0369c1s v6p0582c1s
Trader, G.D. v6p0071c1s
Trafton, A. v1p0013c2s
v1p0167c1s v1p0402c1s v1p0484c2s
v1p0593c1s v1p0703c1s v1p0889c1s
v1p0896c2s
Trafton, G.H. v6p0077c1s
Traherne, J.M. v1p1258c2s
Trahey, J.J. v6p0209c1s
Trail, J.W.H. v5p0122c1s
Traill, A. v1p0657c2s
v3p0221c1s v4p0290c1s v5p0296c2s
v5p0590c2s v6p0327c1s
Traill, C. v4p0281c2s
Traill, C., Mrs. v1p0195c1s
Traill, C.P. v1p0209c2s
Traill, H.D. v1p0044c2s
v1p0308c2s v1p0335c2s v1p0342c2s
v1p0391c1s v1p0540c1s v1p0977c1s
v1p1027c1s v1p1027c2s v2p0015c1s
v2p0022c1s v2p0036c1s v2p0039c2s
v2p0059c1s v2p0082c1s v2p0092c1s
v2p0100c1s v2p0102c2s v2p0185c1s
v2p0187c2s v2p0188c1s v2p0189c2s
v2p0204c1s v2p0208c2s v2p0211c2s

v2p0247c2s v2p0261c1s v2p0267c2s
v2p0312c2s v2p0317c2s v2p0331c1s
v2p0337c1s v2p0357c1s v2p0358c2s
v2p0372c1s v2p0401c2s v2p0409c2s
v2p0411c2s v2p0470c2s v2p0473c2s
v2p0474c1s v3p0020c2s v3p0057c1s
v3p0102c2s v3p0122c1s v3p0152c1s
v3p0204c2s v3p0228c1s v3p0260c2s
v3p0321c2s v3p0339c1m v3p0345c2s
v3p0366c1s v3p0384c2s v3p0386c2s
v3p0390c1s v4p0019c1s v4p0027c2s
v4p0081c2s v4p0148c2s v4p0160c2s
v4p0172c2s v4p0173c1s v4p0227c2s
v4p0240c2s v4p0247c2s v4p0260c1s
v4p0266c1s v4p0269c1m v4p0289c2s
v4p0293c1s v4p0352c1s v4p0428c1s
v4p0432c2s v4p0448c2m v4p0449c1s
v4p0466c2s v4p0500c1s v4p0540c1s
v4p0544c2s v4p0569c2m v4p0574c2s
v4p0583c1s v4p0585c2s v4p0588c2s
v4p0611c1s v4p0614c1s v5p0192c2s
v5p0248c2s v5p0480c1s
Traill, H.D. and McNeill, R.
v5p0278c2s
Traill, H.D. and Morley, J.
v1p0413c2s
Traill, J. v5p0264c1s
v5p0306c2s
Traill, Mrs. v1p0160c2s
v1p0193c1m v1p0194c2s v1p0236c2s
v1p1324c1s
Traill, T.S. v1p0102c2s
Train, A. v6p0104c2s
v6p0210c2s v6p0216c2m v6p0239c2s
v6p0263c1s v6p0332c2s v6p0340c1s
v6p0391c2s v6p0523c2s v6p0701c1s
Train, Arthur v6p0311c1s
Train, E.P. v4p0039c2s
v4p0356c1s v4p0532c1s
Trammel, W.D. v1p1223c2s
Trammell, W.D. v2p0115c1s
Transeau, E.N. v6p0232c2s
v6p0365c2s
Transom, L.H. v4p0378c2s
Trant, W. v1p1320c1s
v2p0383c2s v3p0066c1s v4p0282c1s
v5p0081c2s v5p0091c2s v5p0430c2s
v5p0434c1s
Tranthim-Fryer, J.R. v5p0570c1s
Traphagan, F.W. v6p0711c2s
Trapier, P. v1p1179c1s
Trapman, A. v5p0624c2s
Traquair, E.M. v3p0328c1s
Traquair, R.H. v1p0470c1s
Trarieux, L. v5p0169c1s
Trasenster, L. v1p1391c1s
Trask, Blanche v6p0569c2s
Trask, J. v6p0490c2s
Trask, J.B. v1p0187c2s
v1p0376c2s v1p1196c1s
Trask, J.N. v1p0637c2s
Trask, K. v4p0052c2s
v4p0116c1s v4p0277c1s v4p0384c2s
v5p0003c2s v6p0311c2s
Trask, Katrina v4p0042c2s
v4p0246c1s v5p0134c1s v6p0176c2s
v6p0340c2s v6p0376c2s
Trask, W.B. v1p0034c2s
v1p0135c1s v1p0348c1s v1p0363c1s
v1p0376c2s v1p0460c1s v1p0556c2s
v1p0711c1s v1p0737c1s v1p1009c1s
v1p1130c1s v1p1174c1s v1p1264c2s
v1p1267c1s v1p1315c1s v1p1385c2s
v1p1386c1s v1p1401c1s v2p0051c1s
v2p0121c2s v2p0341c2s v2p0470c1s
v3p0203c1s v3p0235c2s v3p0296c1s
v3p0460c2s v4p0117c2s v4p0321c1s
v5p0166c1s v5p0589c1m
Trask, W.B. and Clapp, E.. v1p0260c2s
Trask, W.B. and Fairbanks, M.B.
v6p0655c1s
Tratman, E.E.R. v5p0072c2s
Traub, P.E. v6p0416c2s
v6p0566c2s v6p0666c1s
Traubel, H. v6p0697c2s
Traubel, H.L. v3p0262c2s
v3p0462c2m v3p0463c1s v4p0343c2s
v4p0620c2m
Traughber, E. v4p0625c2s
Traut, W. v1p0635c1s
Trautmann, M.E. v5p0508c1s
Trautvetter, A. v2p0315c1s
Trautwine, J.C. v1p0049c2s
v1p0051c1s v1p0075c1s v1p0161c2s
v1p0162c1s v1p0326c2s v1p0332c1s
v1p0405c1s v1p0435c2s v1p0467c1m
v1p0640c2s v1p0875c2s v1p1010c1s
v1p1074c2s v1p1075c1m v1p1077c2s
v1p1078c2s v1p1223c2s v1p1369c1s
v1p1427c1s v4p0471c1s
Trautwine, J.C., jr. v6p0204c1s
Trautwine, W. v1p0160c2s
Traver, A. v1p0346c2s
v1p0353c2s v1p0496c1s v1p0724c1s
v1p0745c1s v1p1222c1s v1p1305c2s
v2p0366c1s v2p0368c2s v3p0022c2s
Traver, M. v1p1223c1s
Traver, S. v1p1221c2s
Travers, F. v1p0244c2s
v3p0412c1s
Travers, G. v4p0626c2s
Travers, G.W. v3p0087c2s
v3p0135c2s v3p0165c2s v3p0192c1s
v3p0237c1s v3p0238c1s v3p0262c1s
v3p0266c2s v3p0360c1s v3p0393c1s
v3p0454c2s v4p0010c2s
Travers, J. v1p0455c2s
v1p0744c1s
Travis, H. v1p1410c2s
Travis, I.D. v5p0294c1s
Travis, W.J. v5p0239c1s
v6p0261c1s
Travis, W.J. and Ford, S.. v6p0261c2s
Travous, C.N. v6p0432c1s
Traylor, M.C. v5p0194c2s
Traylor, Mary C. v5p0194c1s
Trayner, J. v4p0287c1s
Traynor, W.J.H. v4p0015c2m
v4p0489c1s
Trayser, R.E. v2p0423c1s
Treacy v5p0270c2s
Treacy, M.J. v5p0503c2s
Treacy, W.P. v2p0102c1s
v2p0294c1s
Treadwell, A.L. v3p0279c1s
Treadwell, D. v1p0783c2s
v1p1289c1s v1p1366c2s
Treadwell, D. and Gray, A.
v1p1233c1s v1p1303c2s
Treadwell, J.H. v1p1039c1s
v2p0333c2s
Treanor, T.S. v4p0149c2s
v4p0331c2s v4p0332c1s
Treat, B.F. v2p0222c2s
Treat, C.G. v6p0464c2s
Treat, C.R. v3p0112c1s
Treat, F.S. v6p0325c2s
Treat, M. v1p0044c2m
v1p0135c2s v1p0136c1m v1p0181c1s
v1p0206c2s v1p0462c1s v1p1014c2s
v1p1236c1s v1p1270c2s v2p0016c1s
v2p0342c2s v3p0155c1s v3p0217c1m
v4p0021c2s v4p0060c2s v4p0217c1s
v4p0443c2m v4p0446c1s v5p0033c2s
v5p0211c1s v5p0222c2s v5p0624c2s
Treat, M., Mrs. v1p0836c1s
v1p1282c2s
Treat, Mary v1p0044c1s
v2p0047c1s v4p0061c2s v4p0209c1s
v4p0235c1s v4p0445c2s
Treat, S.B. v1p0561c2s
v1p0742c1s
Treat, W.B.F. v3p0376c1s
Treat, W.F.B. v3p0258c2s
Treat, W.P. v6p0059c2s
Treat, W.T.B. v3p0359c2s
Trebutien, M. v1p0560c2s
Trede, T. v5p0493c1s
Tredgold, T. v1p1311c1m
v1p1311c2m v1p1427c2s
Tredick, G.B. v5p0024c1s
Tredway, W.T. v4p0546c2s
Tredwell, J.H. v1p1196c1s
Tree, H.B. v3p0406c1s
v5p0167c2s v5p0523c2s v6p0587c1s
Tree, H.B. and Jones, H.A.
v3p0002c2s v3p0406c1s
Tree, H.Beerbohm v4p0518c1s
Tree, L. v4p0077c1s
v6p0559c1s
Treffry, F. v6p0265c2s
v6p0266c2s v6p0268c1s v6p0484c1s
Tregarthen, H.P. v3p0132c1s
v3p0324c1s
Tregarthen, J.C. v6p0471c2s
Tregear, E. v3p0136c1s
v3p0155c2s v3p0267c1s v3p0308c2s
v3p0338c1s v3p0430c1s v4p0354c2s
v5p0408c2s v5p0419c1s v6p0026c1s
v6p0454c2s v6p0455c1s v6p0528c2s
Tregellas, W.H. v2p0030c1s
v2p0103c2s v2p0310c2s v3p0101c1s
v4p0032c1s v4p0134c2s
Tregelles, S.P. v1p0117c2s
v1p0126c2s v1p0128c1s v1p0128c2s
v1p0160c1s
Tregent, M. v1p1102c2s
v1p1308c2s
Tregent, M.E. v1p0574c2s
Tregent, Mrs. v1p0776c1s
Treherne, E. v1p0158c2s
Treherne, E.R. v5p0418c2s
Trehonnais, F.R.de la v3p0006c2s
Trelawney, D. v4p0522c1s
Trelease, W. v1p0449c2m
v1p0758c1s v2p0038c1s v2p0325c1s
v4p0069c2s v5p0073c1s v5p0073c2s
v5p0101c1s v5p0563c1s v6p0422c2s
v6p0480c2s v6p0563c2m
Trelease, W. et al. v6p0018c1s
Tremain, H.E. v5p0218c2s
v5p0383c2s
Tremain, R.A. v5p0591c2s
Tremayne, H. v6p0008c2s
Trembly, C. v5p0041c2s
Tremenheere, H.S. v1p0648c1m
v1p1309c1s
Tremlett, F.S. v2p0121c1s
v4p0158c2s v4p0365c1s
Tremper, F.E. v2p0401c1s
Trench, F. v1p0572c1s
v1p0588c1s v4p0224c1s
Trench, F.C. v3p0180c1m
v3p0278c2s v3p0303c1s v3p0370c2s
Trench, F.H. v3p0029c2s
v3p0168c2s
Trench, H. v5p0370c2s
Trench, J.T. v2p0226c2s
Trench, M. v1p0934c1s
v2p0404c1s
Trench, M.E. v6p0038c2s
Trench, Maria v2p0178c2s
Trench, R.C. v1p0563c2s
v1p0655c1s v1p1306c1s
Trenchard, P. v6p0204c1s
v6p0564c1s
Trendelenburg, Prof. v1p0582c2s
Trendell, A.J.R. v3p0180c2s
v3p0300c1s
Trendly, F. v3p0005c2s
Trenholm, W.L. v1p1223c2s
v1p1224c1m v3p0287c1s
Trenholme, N.M. v5p0382c2s
v6p0569c1s
Trenor, J.D. v6p0309c1s
Trent, A.G. v1p1221c2s
Trent, P. v4p0425c1s
v5p0018c2s v5p0349c2s v6p0025c2s
Trent, W.P. v3p0173c1s
v3p0444c2s v3p0469c1s v4p0043c1s
v4p0118c2s v4p0248c1s v4p0335c2s
v4p0438c2s v4p0468c2s v4p0491c1s
v4p0584c2s v5p0015c2s v5p0016c1s
v5p0016c2m v5p0017c1s v5p0044c2m
v5p0086c1s v5p0138c2s v5p0141c2s
v5p0144c1s v5p0176c1s v5p0185c2m
v5p0192c2s v4p0219c1s v5p0249c2s
v5p0256c1s v5p0256c2s v5p0270c2s
v5p0341c2m v5p0352c1s v5p0366c2m
v5p0376c2s v5p0409c2s v5p0434c1s
v5p0446c2s v5p0458c1s v5p0480c2s
v5p0522c2s v5p0533c1s v5p0540c2m
v5p0553c1s v5p0573c1s v5p0596c2s
v5p0601c2s v5p0617c2s v5p0620c2s
v5p0634c2s v6p0002c1s v6p0011c2s
v6p0032c1s v6p0085c1s v6p0168c2s
v6p0202c1s v6p0208c2s v6p0239c1s
v6p0272c1s v6p0345c1s v6p0379c2s
v6p0380c1s v6p0515c2s v6p0678c1s
Trent, W.P. and Adams, H.B.
v3p0183c2s
Trent, W.P. et al. v5p0281c1s
Trentowski, E. v2p0091c1s
Trepplin, E.C. and Smith, H.H.
v4p0146c1s
Tresca, H. v1p0462c1m
v1p1218c2m v2p0280c1s
Tresca, M. v1p0167c2s
v1p0783c2s v1p1370c2s
Tresca, Prof. v1p0579c2s
Trescot, W.H. v1p0322c2s
v1p0906c1s v1p1224c1s v1p1349c2s
Tress, Lucy Van v5p0610c1s
Tressilian, F.B. v1p1345c1s
Trettien, A.W. v5p0142c1s
v5p0617c1s v6p0361c1s
Trettien, A.W.T. v6p0116c2s
Treuenpreuss, Dr. v1p0059c2s
v1p0076c1s
Treussart, Gen. v1p0749c2m
v1p0873c2s v1p1322c1s
Trevarthen, J. v5p0270c1s
Trevathan, C.E. v4p0145c1s
v4p0534c2s v6p0296c2s v6p0297c1s
v6p0297c2s v6p0464c1s v6p0570c2s
Trevelvan, C. v6p0360c1s
Trevelyan, C. v1p0219c1s
v6p0299c1s v6p0520c1s
Trevelyan, C., Sir v1p0543c1s
v1p1309c1s
Trevelyan, C.E. v1p0543c2s
Trevelyan, C.E., Sir v1p0656c2s
Trevelyan, C.P. v6p0299c1s
Trevelyan, E.J. v5p0286c1s
Trevelyan, F. v3p0203c1s
v3p0351c2s v3p0405c1s v3p0426c2s
v4p0470c1s v4p0555c1s v4p0586c2s
v4p0588c2s v6p0297c1m
Trevelyan, Francis v5p0458c2s
Trevelyan, G. v6p0207c1s
Trevelyan, G.A. v1p0632c1s
Trevelyan, G.M. v5p0094c2s
v5p0190c1s v5p0464c2s v6p0008c1s
v6p0099c1s v6p0144c1s v6p0292c2s
v6p0400c2s v6p0411c2m v6p0515c2s
Trevelyan, G.O. v1p0144c1s
v1p0335c1s v1p0551c2s v1p0848c2s
v1p1345c1s
Trevelyan, Janet v6p0260c1s
Trevelyan, Lady v6p0704c2s
v6p0705c1s
Trevelyan, R. v6p0427c2s
Trevena, R. v3p0013c2s
Trever, G.H. v5p0325c2s
v6p0537c1s v6p0610c1s
Treves, F. v5p0541c1m
Trevett, R. v1p0204c1s
Trevithick, F. v1p1324c2s
Trevor, C.S.I., Col. v5p0285c1s
Trevor, C.W. v5p0243c1s

Trevor, E. v1p0261c1s
Trevor, G. v2p0373c1s
Trevor, G.H. v5p0168c1s
v5p0277c2s v5p0287c1s v5p0312c1s
v5p0397c2s v6p0186c1s v6p0314c1s
Trevor, H.R. v6p0441c2s
Trevor, J. v4p0315c1s
v4p0478c1s
Trevor, K. v1p1086c2s
Trevor, L.G. v3p0449c1s
Trevor, P. v5p0029c1s
v6p0157c2s
Trevor, P.C.W. v5p0029c1s
v5p0142c2s v5p0317c1s
Trevor, T.G. v6p0654c2s
Trevor-Battye, A. v4p0312c2s
v4p0620c1s v5p0634c2s
Tribe, A. and Gladstone, J.H.
v2p0137c2s
Tribe, W.H. v5p0520c2s
Tribus, L.L. v4p0544c2s
Tricker, W. v4p0022c1m
v4p0234c2s v4p0323c2s v4p0445c2s
v4p0446c1s v4p0613c1m v5p0404c1s
Trickett, A.W. v6p0165c2s
Trickett, N. v4p0278c1s
Trickett, W. v6p0221c1s
v6p0673c1s
Trieber, J. v6p0151c1s
Trier, F. v2p0421c1s
Trigge, A.St.L. v6p0162c1s
Triggs, O.L. v4p0124c1s
v4p0335c1s v4p0383c2s v4p0508c1s
v4p0620c1s v5p0005c1s v5p0016c2s
v5p0030c1s v5p0030c2s v5p0144c1s
v5p0541c2s v5p0629c2s v6p0035c2s
v6p0059c2s v6p0092c1s v6p0156c1s
v6p0186c2s v6p0194c1s v6p0317c2s
v6p0318c2s v6p0380c1s v6p0504c1s
v6p0649c1s v6p0708c2s
Triggs, O.L. et al. v4p0335c2s
Trilton, J.H. v4p0059c1s
Trimble, H. v3p0419c2s
v4p0060c1s v4p0411c2s v4p0562c2m
v5p0486c1s
Trimble, H.H. v4p0144c1s
Trimen, H. v1p1015c2s
Trimen, R. v2p0062c2s
v4p0001c1s v5p0377c1s
Tripe, J.W. v2p0285c2s
Tripier, N. v1p0098c1s
v1p1153c1s
Tripler, C.E. v5p0010c1s
Triplett, G.V. v5p0209c1s
Triplett, N. v5p0133c1s
v5p0426c2s v5p0440c2s v6p0116c1s
v6p0486c1s v6p0521c2s
Triplett, N. and Sanford, E.C.
v5p0488c1s
Triplett, R. v1p0147c1s
Tripp, C. v4p0578c1s
v5p0230c2s
Tripp, C.H. v6p0378c2s
Tripp, D.K. v1p0187c2s
Tripp, F.E. v1p1359c1s
Tripp, G.H. v6p0371c2s
Tripp, Margaret E.B. v6p0604c1s
Tripp, W.B. v2p0364c1s
Trippe, T.M. v1p0136c1s
v1p0136c2s v1p0137c1s v1p0139c2s
Trippel, E.J. v3p0475c1s
Trippel, H.F. v6p0314c2s
Tripplin, J. v3p0088c2s
v3p0456c2s
Triqueti, H.de v1p0165c1s
v1p1171c1m v1p1171c2s v1p1227c1s
Triscott, Y. v6p0482c1s
Trist, J. v5p0247c2s
v5p0419c1s
Trist, N. v5p0259c2s
Trist, N.B. v3p0462c1s
Tristram, F.J. v2p0298c2s
Tristram, H.B. v1p0668c1s
v1p1073c1s v1p1441c1s v4p0297c2s
v6p0232c1s
Tristram, O. v5p0518c1s
Tristram, W.O. v2p0037c2s
v3p0062c1s v3p0076c1s v3p0089c1s
v3p0170c1s v3p0199c1s v3p0392c1s
v4p0016c2s
Trobridge, C. v6p0164c1s
Trobridge, G. v5p0532c2s
v6p0139c1s v6p0141c1s v6p0202c1s
v6p0375c2s v6p0428c2s v6p0443c2s
v6p0462c1s v6p0483c2s v6p0555c1s
Troelstra, P.J. v6p0294c2s
Trohne, H.W. v6p0524c1s
Troili, M. v6p0092c2s
Troili, Margaret v6p0646c2s
Troilius, M. v1p1251c1s
Trollope, A. v1p0034c1s
v1p0044c1s v1p0071c1s v1p0111c2s
v1p0256c1m v1p0258c2s v1p0263c1s
v1p0309c1s v1p0350c1s v1p0357c2s
v1p0371c1s v1p0384c1s v1p0432c1s
v1p0451c2s v1p0471c2s v1p0472c2s
v1p0505c2s v1p0534c1s v1p0572c1s
v1p0575c2s v1p0577c1s v1p0617c1s
v1p0622c1s v1p0653c2s v1p0667c2s
v1p0692c1s v1p0696c1s v1p0701c1s
v1p0716c1s v1p0726c1s v1p0737c2s
v1p0740c1s v1p0750c2s v1p0766c1s
v1p0767c2s v1p0770c2s v1p0790c2s
v1p0807c1s v1p0851c1s v1p0898c1s
v1p0923c1s v1p0932c2s v1p0933c1s
v1p0949c1s v1p0963c2s v1p1002c1s
v1p1063c1s v1p1081c2s v1p1201c2s
v1p1210c1s v1p1240c1s v1p1261c2s
v1p1269c2s v1p1286c2s v1p1298c1m
v1p1333c1s v1p1335c2s v1p1369c1s
v1p1393c2s v1p1408c1s v1p1408c2s
v1p1421c1s v1p1428c1s v2p0242c2s
v2p0301c1s v2p0415c2s v2p0449c2s
Trollope, C. v5p0025c1s
v5p0064c1s v5p0164c2s v5p0560c1s
v5p0562c2s
Trollope, E. v1p0007c1s
v1p0152c2s v1p0750c2s
Trollope, F. v1p0863c1s
Trollope, F., Mrs. v1p0017c2s
v1p0099c1s v1p0181c1s v1p0745c2s
v1p1111c2s v1p1129c2s v1p1154c1s
v1p1408c2s
Trollope, F.E. v1p0021c1s
v1p0111c1s v1p0221c2s v1p0278c1s
v1p0523c2s v1p0669c1s v1p0669c2s
v1p0952c1s v1p1284c1s v1p1367c2s
Trollope, H.C. v5p0263c1m
Trollope, H.M. v1p0363c2s
v1p0858c2s v1p1242c1s v2p0036c1s
v2p0103c1s v2p0250c1s v2p0361c2s
v3p0085c1s v3p0239c2s v3p0284c2m
v3p0453c2s v4p0376c2s v4p0564c1s
Trollope, J.A. v1p0893c1s
Trollope, Mrs. v1p0979c2s
Trollope, T.A. v1p0023c2s
v1p0057c1s v1p0066c1s v1p0083c2s
v1p0086c1s v1p0113c2s v1p0115c1s
v1p0127c2s v1p0144c2s v1p0217c2s
v1p0297c1s v1p0331c2s v1p0442c2s
v1p0461c1s v1p0461c2s v1p0497c1s
v1p0560c1s v1p0617c1s v1p0671c2m
v1p0672c2s v1p0691c2s v1p0722c2s
v1p0737c1s v1p0750c2s v1p0751c2s
v1p0834c1s v1p0834c2s v1p0866c2s
v1p0959c2s v1p1040c2s v1p1118c2s
v1p1123c1s v1p1125c1m v1p1126c1s
v1p1126c2s v1p1195c1m v1p1276c1s
v1p1284c1s v1p1312c2s v1p1334c1m
v1p1404c1s v1p1427c2s v2p0065c1s
v2p0065c2s v2p0066c2s v2p0071c2s
v2p0328c2s v3p0206c1s v3p0463c1s
v4p0094c1m v4p0244c1s v4p0350c2s
Trollope, T.A., Mrs. v1p0043c1s
v1p1141c1s
Trollope, T.E. v1p0995c1s
Tromholt, S. v2p0028c2m
v2p0272c1s v2p0426c2s v2p0433c1s
Tronton, F.T. v3p0250c2s
Trood, T. v2p0462c1s
Troop, J. v4p0152c2s
v4p0197c2s v4p0323c2s
Troost, L. v1p1223c1s
v2p0412c1s
Troplong, R.T. v1p1122c1s
Troshine, Y. v5p0028c2s
Trostler, J. v4p0052c1s
Troth, H. v6p0246c2s
Troth, S. v4p0458c1s
Trott, L.L. v6p0415c2s
Trotter, A.M. v3p0005c2s
v3p0195c2s v3p0315c1s v4p0035c1s
v4p0134c1s v4p0299c1s v4p0359c2s
v4p0412c2s v5p0163c2s
Trotter, A.P. v6p0129c2s
Trotter, Ada M. v3p0366c2s
Trotter, C. v2p0025c1s
v2p0273c1s v2p0310c1s v2p0311c1s
v2p0348c2s v2p0385c1s v2p0401c2s
v2p0448c1s v3p0027c2s v3p0049c1s
v3p0152c2m v3p0164c2s v3p0244c1s
v3p0317c1s v3p0338c1s v3p0432c1s
v4p0040c2s v4p0422c2s
Trotter, J.K. v5p0411c1s
v6p0031c2s
Trotter, L.J. v1p0629c2s
v1p0632c1s v1p1179c2s v1p1324c2s
Trotter, L.K. v3p0323c2s
Trotter, P.D. v3p0015c2s
Trotter, S. v2p0138c2s
v2p0273c2s v3p0123c2s v3p0362c2s
v4p0061c1s v5p0084c2s v5p0097c1s
v5p0413c2s v5p0540c2s
Trotter, W.F. v5p0199c1s
v6p0022c1s
Troubridge, E.C.T. v5p0591c2s
Trouessart, E. v4p0376c2s
Trouessart, E.L. v3p0201c1s
v4p0263c2s
Troup, E.D. v5p0457c2s
Troup, F.B. v4p0353c1s
v5p0002c2s
Troup, G.E. v3p0048c2s
Troup, J. v6p0086c2s
Troup, J.R. v3p0035c1s
v3p0406c2s
Trousdale, J.A. v2p0434c2s
Trout, J.M. v6p0063c2s
Trout, W.H. v4p0504c1s
v5p0510c1s
Troutbeck, G.E. v6p0344c1s
Troutman, H.C. v6p0580c2s
Trouton, F.T. v3p0134c2s
v3p0428c1s
Trouve, G. v1p0399c1s
v4p0204c2s
Trouvelot, E.L. v2p0386c2s
v3p0375c2s
Trouvelot, L. v1p0645c2s
v1p0824c1s v1p0866c1s v1p1152c2s
v1p1197c2s v1p1268c2s v1p1269c1s
Trow, G. v6p0588c2s
Trowbridge, A. v5p0125c1s
Trowbridge, A. and Rubens, H.
v5p0290c2s
Trowbridge, A.B. v5p0025c2s
Trowbridge, A.W. v4p0296c1s
Trowbridge, C.C. v4p0271c1s
v5p0010c1s v6p0067c2s v6p0221c1s
v6p0498c2s v6p0700c1s
Trowbridge, C.W. v2p0229c1s
Trowbridge, D. v1p0069c2m
v1p0070c2s v1p0071c1s v1p0212c2m
v1p0281c2s v1p0375c1s v1p0375c2s
v1p0376c1s v1p0382c1s v1p0429c1s
v1p0506c2s v1p0523c1s v1p0524c1s
v1p0588c2s v1p0592c2s v1p0804c1s
v1p0866c1s v1p0876c2s v1p0903c2m
v1p0904c1s v1p1014c2s v1p1045c1s
v1p1062c2s v1p1110c1s v1p1152c2s
v1p1161c1s v1p1222c2s v1p1243c2s
v1p1244c1s v1p1261c2s v1p1267c2m
v1p1366c2s v1p1406c1s
Trowbridge, E.T. v6p0449c1s
Trowbridge, G. v5p0152c1s
v5p0380c1s v6p0628c2s
Trowbridge, H.S. v2p0010c2s
Trowbridge, J. v1p0220c2s
v1p0308c1s v1p0399c1s v1p0399c2s
v1p0400c1s v1p0400c2s v1p0401c1s
v1p0454c2s v1p0498c2s v1p0502c1m
v1p0748c2s v1p0751c2m v1p0788c1s
v1p1006c2s v1p1081c1s v1p1162c1s
v2p0137c2s v2p0138c1s v2p0138c2m
v2p0258c2s v2p0314c1s v2p0402c2s
v2p0440c2s v3p0092c1s v3p0133c1s
v3p0133c2m v3p0156c2s v3p0330c2s
v3p0351c2s v4p0037c2s v4p0175c2s
v4p0176c2s v4p0177c1s v4p0324c2s
v4p0332c1s v4p0403c1s v4p0430c1s
v4p0438c1s v4p0487c1m v4p0556c2s
v4p0567c2s v5p0014c1s v5p0037c1s
v5p0095c2s v5p0182c2s v5p0184c1m
v5p0185c1m v5p0185c2s v5p0195c2s
v5p0277c2s v5p0338c2s v5p0492c1m
v5p0513c2m v5p0545c1s v5p0554c2s
v5p0571c1m v5p0642c2s v6p0193c2s
v6p0199c1s v6p0199c2s v6p0239c1s
v6p0248c2s v6p0319c1s v6p0395c1s
v6p0576c1m v6p0609c1s v6p0637c1m
v6p0685c1s
Trowbridge, J. and Adams, E.P.
v5p0356c1s
Trowbridge, J. and Bauer, L.A.
v5p0356c1s
Trowbridge, J. and Burbank, J.E.
v5p0447c2s v5p0492c1s
Trowbridge, J. and Duane, W.
v4p0175c2s
Trowbridge, J. and Hayes, H.V.
v2p0170c2s v2p0340c1s
Trowbridge, J. and Hutchins, C.C.
v3p0415c1m
Trowbridge, J. and McRae, A.L.
v2p0213c2s
Trowbridge, J. and Penrose, C.B.
v2p0439c2s
Trowbridge, J. and Richards, J.W.
v5p0185c2s
Trowbridge, J. and Richards, T.W.
v5p0027c2s v5p0227c1s
Trowbridge, J. and Richards, W.
v5p0227c1s
Trowbridge, J. and Rollins, W.
v6p0527c1s
Trowbridge, J. and Sabine, W.C.
v3p0408c2s
Trowbridge, J. and Sheldon, S.
v3p0214c2s v3p0305c1s
Trowbridge, J.M. v2p0288c2s
Trowbridge, J.P. v1p0986c1s
Trowbridge, J.R. v6p0507c1s
Trowbridge, J.T. v1p0076c2s
v1p0080c2s v1p0088c1s v1p0148c1s
v1p0181c2s v1p0222c1s v1p0258c1s
v1p0308c2s v1p0361c1s v1p0371c1s
v1p0405c2s v1p0485c1s v1p0492c2s
v1p0518c2s v1p0651c2s v1p0675c2s
v1p0726c2s v1p0785c1s v1p0795c1s
v1p0820c1s v1p0852c1s v1p0886c2s
v1p0940c2m v1p0942c2s v1p0987c2s
v1p0996c1s v1p1073c2s v1p1123c1s
v1p1190c2s v1p1240c2s v1p1271c1s
v1p1315c1s v1p1403c2s v2p0068c1s
v2p0473c2s v3p0011c1s v3p0258c2s
v4p0590c2s v5p0633c1s v6p0020c1s
v6p0076c2s v6p0278c2s v6p0697c1s
Trowbridge, John v5p0492c1s
Trowbridge, S.B.P. v3p0219c1s
Trowbridge, S.H. v2p0041c2s

v2p0173c2s v2p0293c1s v2p0307c1s
v2p0307c2s v2p0351c2s v2p0390c1s
v2p0447c2s
Trowbridge, T.C. v1p0058c2s
v1p1332c1m v2p0293c2s v2p0324c2s
v2p0448c2s
Trowbridge, W.P. v1p0073c1s
v1p0340c1m v1p0340c2s v1p1222c2s
v1p1223c1s v1p1347c2s v1p1392c1s
v2p0281c2s v2p0385c2s v2p0419c1s
Trowbridge, W.P. and Bell, A.N.
v2p0199c2s
Trowbridge, W.P. and Newberry, J.S.
v3p0045c1s
Trowbridge, W.R.H. v6p0403c2s
v6p0480c1s
Trower, H.S. v4p0398c1s
Trowsdale, T.B. v2p0318c2s
v2p0366c1s v4p0570c2s
Troy, D.S. v1p1206c1s
v3p0458c1s v4p0384c2s
Troyon, F. v1p0223c2s
Troyte, C.A.W. v2p0039c1s
v2p0383c2s
Truax, C. v5p0134c1s
Truax, C.H. v1p1204c2s
Trubetzkoi, Michael, Prince
v6p0556c2s
Trudeau, E.L. v6p0660c1s
Trudell, I. v5p0410c1s
Trudinger, O. v5p0469c1s
True, A. v6p0635c2s
True, A.C. v5p0009c1m
v5p0009c2m v5p0199c2s v5p0202c2s
v5p0583c2s v5p0598c2s v6p0008c2m
v6p0554c2s
True, A.C., Dr. v5p0034c2s
True, B.O. v3p0083c1s
v4p0056c2s
True, C.K. v1p0273c1s
v1p0639c2s v1p0672c2s v1p0868c2s
v1p1058c2s v1p1301c1s v1p1398c2s
True, F.W. v2p0015c1s
v2p0057c1s v2p0121c1s v2p0406c2s
v4p0467c1s v5p0100c1s
True, J.P. v3p0311c2s
v6p0349c1s
True, K.M., Mrs. v5p0334c2s
True, M.B.C. v1p0842c1s
v1p1234c2m v1p1272c2s v3p0355c1s
v3p0379c1s v4p0116c1s v4p0462c2s
v4p0474c2s
True, R.H. v5p0366c1s
v6p0580c2s v6p0634c2s
Trueb, M.M. v3p0051c2s
Trueba, A. v1p0202c1s
Trueba, A.de v6p0153c2s
Trueblood, B.F. v4p0022c2s
v4p0110c1s v4p0288c1s v5p0381c2s
v5p0437c2s v6p0026c1s v6p0277c2s
Trueblood, Lyra D. v6p0078c1s
v6p0300c1s
Trueblood, M.E. v5p0273c1s
Truesdell, C.G. v4p0452c1s
Truitt, W. v4p0448c2s
v4p0519c1s
Truman, B.C. v4p0410c1s
Truman, Ben C. v5p0464c2s
v5p0525c2s v5p0548c1s v5p0601c2s
v6p0155c1s v6p0482c2s
Truman, E.B. v1p0437c2s
Truman, J. v1p0308c2s
v3p0003c1s v3p0294c1s v5p0065c2s
v6p0069c2s
Trumble, A. v4p0029c1s
v4p0138c1s v4p0155c2s v4p0194c1s
v4p0309c2s v4p0319c1s v4p0384c1s
v4p0410c2s v4p0549c2s
Trumbull, A.E. v2p0259c1s
v3p0113c1s v3p0164c2s v3p0363c1s
v3p0393c2s v5p0024c2s v5p0591c1s
Trumbull, Annie v4p0032c2s
Trumbull, Annie E. v3p0440c2s
Trumbull, H.C. v4p0304c1s
v6p0644c1s
Trumbull, J. v1p1248c1s
v3p0389c1s v3p0462c2s v4p0104c2s
v4p0407c2s v6p0372c1s
Trumbull, J.H. v1p0374c1s
v1p0636c2s v1p0638c2s v1p0737c2s
v1p0796c2s v1p0947c1s v1p1219c2s
v1p1254c1s v1p1328c1s v2p0113c2s
Trumbull, J.H. and Gray, A.
v1p0065c1s
Trumbull, John v3p0078c1s
Trumbull, Jonathan v6p0460c2s
Trumbull, L. v4p0456c2s
v4p0592c2s
Trumbull, L. et al. v1p1048c2s
Trumbull, M.M. v2p0021c1s
v2p0451c2s v3p0274c1s v3p0326c1s
v4p0071c2s v4p0080c1s v4p0121c1s
v4p0131c2s v4p0132c1s v4p0150c1s
v4p0159c2s v4p0171c1s v4p0188c1s
v4p0220c2s v4p0223c1s v4p0263c1s
v4p0313c1s v4p0318c2s v4p0325c1s
v4p0360c1s v4p0377c2s v4p0378c1s
v4p0399c2s v4p0424c2s v4p0425c1s
v4p0455c1s v4p0475c2m v4p0479c1s
v4p0501c1s v4p0514c2s v4p0535c2s
v4p0558c1m v4p0599c2s v4p0607c2s
Trumbull, M.R. v6p0469c2s
Trumbull, R.L. v3p0078c1s
Trumbull, W. v1p1437c1s
Truran, W. v1p1075c1s
v1p1079c2s
Truscott, W. v3p0413c2s
Trusdell, C.G. v3p0444c1s
Truslow, A. v5p0454c2s
v5p0593c2s
Truslow, S.W. v6p0673c2s
Trux, J.J. v1p0905c2s
Truxal, A.E. v4p0477c1m
v4p0592c2s v5p0059c2s v5p0115c1s
v5p0117c2s v5p0268c2s v5p0292c2s
v5p0520c2s v5p0577c1s v6p0172c2s
v6p0536c2s v6p0642c2s
Trybom, F. v3p0417c2s
Tryde, O. v5p0416c2s
v5p0550c2s
Tryon, F. v1p0017c2s
Tryon, G., Sir et al. v3p0218c1s
Tryon, G.C. v6p0141c1s
Tryon, J.R. v5p0401c1s
Tsakni, N. v3p0328c1s
v3p0370c1s
Tsanoff, S.V. v5p0406c2s
v5p0454c2s
Tschudi, J.J.von v1p0993c1m
Tseng v3p0079c1m
Tsybikoff, G.G. v6p0369c2s
Tubbs, F.H. v4p0527c2s
Tubbs, H.A. and Munro, J.A.R.
v4p0145c2s
Tuck, E. v1p0471c2s
v2p0163c2s
Tuck, Edward v5p0061c2s
Tuck, F. v1p0123c1s
Tuck, T. v4p0059c2s
Tuck, W.J. v1p0263c1s
Tucker, B. v1p0447c1s
v1p0537c2s v1p0538c1s v1p0730c1s
v1p1027c2s v2p0119c2s
Tucker, B.R. et al. v5p0179c1s
Tucker, D. v1p0648c2s
v1p0791c2s v1p0794c2s
Tucker, F. v5p0102c1s
v5p0483c1s v6p0298c1s v6p0381c1s
Tucker, F.E.S. v6p0054c1s
Tucker, G. v1p0031c2s
v1p0093c1s v1p0187c2s v1p0212c1s
v1p0232c1s v1p0324c2s v1p0326c1s
v1p0384c2s v1p0389c2s v1p0406c1s
v1p0532c2s v1p0533c2s v1p0639c2s
v1p0640c1s v1p0791c2s v1p1001c2s
v1p1027c2s v1p1034c1s v1p1034c2m
v1p1044c2s v1p1054c2s v1p1099c2s
v1p1207c2s v1p1353c1s v1p1382c1s
v1p1394c1s v2p0474c2s
Tucker, G.F. v3p0475c1s
v4p0002c2s v4p0398c1s v4p0468c2s
v6p0539c2s
Tucker, G.M. v2p0012c2s
v2p0144c1s v2p0250c2s v2p0323c2s
v2p0479c2s
Tucker, G.T. v2p0020c2s
Tucker, G.W. v1p0373c1s
v1p1285c1s
Tucker, H.A. v6p0447c2s
Tucker, H.F. v4p0604c1s
Tucker, H.R. v6p0290c1m
Tucker, H.S. v1p1348c2s
Tucker, H.St.G. v6p0367c1s
Tucker, J.C. v4p0634c1s
Tucker, J.P. v5p0639c2s
Tucker, J.R. v1p1353c2s
v2p0361c2s v2p0411c1s v3p0150c2s
v3p0421c1s v3p0450c2s v4p0022c2s
Tucker, J.R., jr. v5p0599c2s
Tucker, J.T. v1p0074c2s
v1p0123c1s v1p0496c1s v1p0641c1s
v1p0689c1s v1p0820c1s v1p0882c2s
v1p0912c2s v1p0989c2s v1p1033c2s
v1p1044c1s v1p1086c1s v1p1095c1s
v1p1121c1s v1p1200c1s v1p1271c1s
v1p1286c2s
Tucker, M. v1p0320c1s
v1p0690c1s v1p1064c2s v1p1065c1s
v1p1145c1s
Tucker, M., Mrs. v3p0191c1s
Tucker, M.A. v5p0267c1s
v5p0295c1s v5p0569c2s v6p0255c2s
v6p0574c1s
Tucker, M.A.R., Miss v4p0148c2s
v4p0498c2s
Tucker, P. v4p0232c1s
Tucker, P.A. v4p0266c2s
Tucker, R. v1p0075c2s
v1p0222c1s v1p0503c1s v2p0089c1s
v3p0386c1s
Tucker, R.H. v6p0263c2s
v6p0539c2s
Tucker, R.H., jr. v2p0095c2s
Tucker, S. v3p0168c1s
Tucker, T. v1p1034c2s
Tucker, T.G. v4p0364c1s
Tucker, T.G. et al. v4p0256c1s
Tucker, T.W. v1p0823c2s
Tucker, W. v1p1095c2s
v2p0107c2s v2p0147c1s v2p0153c1s
v2p0251c1s v2p0280c1s v2p0339c2s
v2p0356c1s v2p0357c1s v2p0369c1s
v2p0389c2s v2p0404c1s v2p0457c1s
v3p0053c1s v3p0104c1s v3p0157c2s
v3p0216c2s v3p0271c2s v3p0277c2s
v3p0297c2s v3p0347c2s v3p0404c2s
v3p0464c1s v5p0239c1s v5p0239c2s
Tucker, W.C. v6p0585c2s
Tucker, W.G. v4p0613c1s
Tucker, W.J. v2p0148c1s
v2p0359c1s v2p0437c2s v2p0480c1s
v3p0105c1m v3p0283c1s v3p0324c1m
v3p0346c1s v3p0349c1s v3p0397c2s
v3p0399c2s v3p0458c1s v4p0269c1s
v4p0300c1s v5p0127c1s v5p0264c2s
v5p0378c1s v6p0135c1s v6p0135c2s
v6p0137c2m v6p0523c2s
Tucker, W.T. v5p0574c1s
Tuckerman, B. v2p0246c1s
v2p0269c2s v2p0447c1s v2p0448c2s
Tuckerman, C.K. v1p0072c2s
v1p0162c2s v1p0298c2s v1p0302c1s
v1p0553c1s v1p0799c1s v2p0093c2s
v2p0446c1s v3p0031c2s v3p0051c1s
v3p0052c1s v3p0078c2s v3p0088c1s
v3p0179c1s v3p0184c1s v3p0231c2s
v3p0252c1s v3p0304c1s v3p0377c1s
v3p0386c2s v3p0395c2m v3p0436c1s
v3p0438c2s v3p0439c1s v3p0456c2s
v4p0341c1s v4p0594c1s
Tuckerman, F. v3p0099c1s
v3p0189c2s v5p0136c1s
Tuckerman, H.S. v1p1275c1s
Tuckerman, H.T. v1p0006c2s
v1p0017c2m v1p0029c2s v1p0031c2s
v1p0060c2s v1p0068c2s v1p0073c2s
v1p0076c1s v1p0083c2m v1p0090c1s
v1p0100c2s v1p0106c2s v1p0109c1s
v1p0133c1s v1p0133c2s v1p0135c1s
v1p0169c2s v1p0173c1s v1p0177c1s
v1p0177c2s v1p0178c2s v1p0191c2s
v1p0217c1s v1p0222c1s v1p0227c1s
v1p0229c1s v1p0247c1s v1p0258c1s
v1p0265c2s v1p0274c1s v1p0298c2s
v1p0305c2s v1p0310c2s v1p0331c2s
v1p0332c1s v1p0335c2s v1p0341c1s
v1p0345c1s v1p0352c1s v1p0353c1s
v1p0355c1s v1p0357c2s v1p0385c1s
v1p0404c1s v1p0447c1s v1p0451c1s
v1p0461c1s v1p0462c2s v1p0468c1s
v1p0469c2s v1p0483c2s v1p0488c1s
v1p0500c2s v1p0530c1s v1p0533c2s
v1p0534c2s v1p0567c1s v1p0567c2s
v1p0575c2m v1p0577c1m v1p0577c2s
v1p0584c1s v1p0591c1s v1p0596c2s
v1p0610c1s v1p0613c2s v1p0614c2s
v1p0616c1s v1p0617c1s v1p0626c2s
v1p0640c2s v1p0642c2s v1p0667c2s
v1p0669c2m v1p0671c1s v1p0671c2m
v1p0680c1s v1p0681c1s v1p0704c1s
v1p0712c1s v1p0717c2s v1p0719c2m
v1p0723c2s v1p0733c1s v1p0737c2s
v1p0738c1s v1p0739c1s v1p0753c2s
v1p0787c1s v1p0797c1s v1p0798c2s
v1p0855c2s v1p0863c1s v1p0913c1m
v1p0916c1s v1p0917c2s v1p0950c2s
v1p0967c2s v1p0969c2m v1p0971c2s
v1p0985c2s v1p0995c1s v1p1032c1s
v1p1084c2s v1p1105c2s v1p1127c2m
v1p1128c1s v1p1132c1s v1p1149c1s
v1p1151c2s v1p1180c2s v1p1189c1s
v1p1194c2s v1p1209c1s v1p1211c2s
v1p1221c2s v1p1226c1s v1p1251c2m
v1p1253c1m v1p1260c2s v1p1298c1s
v1p1307c1s v1p1322c1m v1p1322c2s
v1p1326c2s v1p1373c1s v1p1374c1s
v1p1382c1s v1p1387c2s v1p1390c2s
v1p1414c2s v1p1420c2s v1p1429c2s
v1p1438c1s v2p0074c1s
Tuckerman, J. v1p0625c2s
v1p0630c1s v1p0847c1s v1p0852c1s
v1p1082c1s
Tuckerman, J.H. v5p0308c2s
v5p0512c2s v6p0178c1s v6p0230c2s
v6p0297c2m v6p0380c2s v6p0452c1s
v6p0480c2s v6p0490c2s v6p0531c2s
Tuckett, C. v2p0208c1s
Tuckett, H.G. v1p0647c2s
Tuckey, C.L. v3p0148c2s
v3p0206c1m v3p0250c1s v4p0271c2m
Tuckey, J. v1p0141c1s
Tuckwell, G.M. v5p0201c1s
v5p0320c2s v6p0705c1s
Tuckwell, Gertrude v5p0130c2s
v6p0682c2s
Tuckwell, Gertrude M. v6p0704c2s
Tuckwell, W. v1p0153c1s
v1p1014c2s v1p1163c1m v1p1163c2s
v1p1409c2s v4p0182c2s v4p0212c2s
v6p0507c2s
Tudor, F. v1p1366c1s
Tudor, Frederic v5p0609c1s
Tudor, H. v1p0987c2s
Tudor, Heinrich v6p0462c2s
Tudor, W. v1p0027c2s
v1p0030c1s v1p0257c1s v1p0291c1s
v1p0294c2s v1p0414c2s v1p0454c1s
v1p0476c2s v1p0559c1s v1p0596c1s
v1p0610c1s v1p0615c1s v1p0616c2s
v1p0622c2s v1p0772c2s v1p0809c2s

v1p0855c1s v1p0969c1s v1p0971c1s v1p0987c1s v1p1168c2s v1p1169c1s v1p1225c1s v1p1341c2m v1p1354c2s v1p1389c1s v1p1410c1s v2p0009c2s
Tuel, J.E. v1p1224c1s
Tuell, H.E. v5p0277c1s
Tuer, A.W. v3p0392c2s
Tufferd, F. v2p0140c2s v2p0247c2s
Tufnell, E.C. v1p0387c1s
Tufts, F.L. v5p0540c1s v6p0497c2s v6p0604c2s
Tufts, G.E. v5p0304c2s v5p0463c1s
Tufts, J.H. v4p0212c2s v4p0273c2s v5p0194c1s v6p0005c2s v6p0348c2s
Tufts, L.T. and Booth, E.C. v5p0594c1s
Tufts, W.W. v4p0043c1s
Tugman, F.W. v5p0244c1m v5p0245c1s v5p0457c1s v5p0477c2s v6p0270c1s v6p0340c2s v6p0675c1s
Tugman, J.B. v6p0144c1s
Tuke, D.H. v1p0565c2s v1p0643c1s v1p0643c2s v1p0644c1s v1p0775c2s v1p0952c2s v1p1262c2s
Tuke, D.Hack v4p0624c2s
Tuke, H.S. v5p0202c1s
Tuke, J.B. v3p0216c2s v4p0162c2s v6p0320c1s
Tuke, J.H. v1p0658c2s v1p0983c2s v2p0140c2s v2p0225c1s v3p0136c2s v3p0222c2s
Tuke, J.H. et al. v1p0657c1s
Tukeman, H. v5p0315c2s
Tuker, M.A.R. v6p0104c1s v6p0104c2s v6p0478c1s v6p0549c2s v6p0595c2s
Tulle, J.K. v6p0616c2s
Tullidge, E.H. v1p0872c1s v1p1360c1s
Tullidge, E.M. v1p0872c1m v1p1438c1s
Tulloch v5p0618c1s
Tulloch, A.B. v5p0244c1s v6p0606c1s
Tulloch, A.M. v1p0873c1s v1p1401c1s
Tulloch, A.M., Sir v1p1218c2s
Tulloch, Alex.B. v4p0428c1s
Tulloch, J. v1p0021c1s v1p0027c1s v1p0205c2s v1p0230c2s v1p0239c2s v1p0240c1s v1p0242c1s v1p0249c1s v1p0255c2s v1p0355c1s v1p0359c1m v1p0360c1s v1p0414c1s v1p0423c2s v1p0484c2s v1p0528c1s v1p0566c1s v1p0663c1s v1p0683c1s v1p0775c1s v1p0849c2s v1p0870c2s v1p1017c1s v1p1058c1s v1p1083c2s v1p1089c2s v1p1093c2s v1p1165c2s v1p1167c1s v1p1211c1s v1p1211c2s v1p1243c1m v1p1253c1s v1p1254c1s v1p1286c2s v1p1302c2s v1p1405c1s v1p1409c1s v1p1411c2s v2p0084c1s v2p0092c1s v2p0268c1s v2p0391c1s v2p0417c1s v3p0044c1s v3p0189c2s v3p0203c1s v3p0254c1s v3p0306c2s
Tulloch, J. et al. v2p0438c1s
Tulloch, W.W. v1p0535c1s v1p0797c1s v1p0814c2s v1p1125c2s v1p1240c2s v2p0364c2s v3p0284c2s
Tullock, T.L. v2p0013c2s v2p0252c1m v2p0308c1s v2p0350c1m v2p0448c1s
Tullock, W.W. v1p0604c1s
Tully, J.C. v2p0084c2s v2p0266c2s
Tully, R.W. v6p0388c1s v6p0388c2s
Tunell, G.G. v5p0241c2s v5p0440c1s v5p0461c2m v6p0529c2s v6p0530c1s
Tunis, J. v3p0102c2s v3p0121c1s v3p0131c1s v3p0175c1m v3p0282c2s v3p0297c1s v3p0384c1s v3p0441c1s v4p0069c1s v4p0192c1s v4p0338c2s v4p0532c2s v4p0546c1s v4p0569c1s
Tunison, J.S. v2p0282c1s v5p0071c1s v5p0341c1s
Tunner, Prof. v1p0141c1s
Tunnicliffe, F.W. v5p0077c1s v5p0361c1s v5p0368c1s v5p0427c1s v5p0594c1s v6p0098c2s
Tunzelmann, G.W.de v3p0087c2s v3p0331c2s v3p0351c2s v5p0571c1m
Tuomey, Honoria R.P. v6p0088c1s
Tuomey, J.W. v5p0451c2s
Tuomey, M. v1p0462c1s
Tupes, H. v6p0449c2s v6p0543c2s
Tupman, G.L. v1p0827c1s
Tupp, A.C. v4p0524c1s v4p0524c2s
Tupper, C. v3p0065c1s v3p0065c2s v4p0237c1s v4p0564c1s
Tupper, C., Sir v4p0236c1s
Tupper, C.H. v4p0353c2s v4p0511c2s v5p0090c2s
Tupper, C.L. v3p0211c2s v5p0356c2s
Tupper, Charles, Sir v3p0181c1s
Tupper, E. v4p0547c2s
Tupper, E.S. v3p0048c1s v3p0282c1s v3p0440c2s v4p0469c1s v5p0254c2s
Tupper, F., jr. v4p0311c2s v4p0497c1s v5p0488c1s v5p0610c1s v6p0208c1s
Tupper, F.A. v3p0438c1s v4p0022c2s
Tupper, J.L. v1p0059c1s v1p1306c2s v1p1428c2s
Tupper, J.W. v6p0355c1s v6p0426c2s
Tupper, K.B. v2p0203c2s
Tupper, L. v6p0313c1s
Tupper, M.F. v1p0368c1s v1p1107c2s v1p1220c2s v1p1436c1s v2p0416c1s
Tuque, L. Dutilh de la v4p0210c2s
Tur, M.P. v6p0535c2s
Turbyne, A. v4p0256c1s
Turgan, L. v5p0236c1s
Turique, B.de v3p0121c1s
Turk, J.C. v5p0076c1s v5p0237c2s
Turlay, W.W. et al. v5p0163c2s
Turley, L.A. and Aldrich, J.M. v5p0210c1s
Turley, R.T. v5p0276c1s v6p0398c2m
Turley, W. v1p0072c2s
Turmann, Max v6p0236c2s v6p0238c1s
Turnbull, Edward v5p0070c1s
Turnbull, F.L. v2p0058c2s v2p0150c2s v2p0346c1s
Turnbull, G.B. v4p0125c1s
Turnbull, L. v1p0839c2s v1p0854c2s v1p1094c1s v1p1223c2s v1p1289c2s v1p1290c1m v1p1290c2m v1p1291c1s
Turnbull, L., Mrs. v5p0609c1s v5p0623c1s
Turnbull, L.S. v5p0138c2s
Turnbull, M.M. v5p0606c2s v6p0052c1s v6p0280c1s v6p0692c1s
Turnbull, M.P. v5p0276c2s
Turnbull, Montagu, Mrs. v5p0259c2s v5p0287c1s
Turnbull, R. v1p0096c2s v1p0169c2s v1p0213c2s v1p0243c2s v1p0274c1s v1p0613c1s v1p0689c1s v1p0863c1s v1p1001c2s v1p1073c2s v1p1234c2s v1p1236c2s
Turnbull, S.E. v4p0069c1s
Turnbull, W.R. v1p0564c2s v1p0832c2s v1p0833c2s v2p0139c2s v2p0341c1s v2p0473c1s
Turner, A. v3p0436c1s v4p0285c1s v4p0591c1s v5p0349c2s v6p0360c2s v6p0577c1s
Turner, A.E. v4p0290c2s v4p0350c1s v4p0605c2s v5p0231c1m v5p0382c1s v5p0610c2s v6p0253c2s v6p0266c1s
Turner, A.J. v2p0156c1s
Turner, A.T. v5p0456c1s
Turner, C. v3p0015c2s v3p0025c2s v3p0064c1s v3p0104c2s v3p0108c1s v3p0113c2s v3p0180c1s v3p0302c2s v3p0322c2s v3p0329c1s v4p0182c1s v4p0310c2s v4p0407c1s v4p0508c2s v4p0528c1s v4p0612c2s v5p0053c1s v5p0089c1s v5p0239c1m v5p0239c2m v5p0268c1s v5p0374c2s v5p0400c2s v5p0407c1s v5p0508c1s v5p0628c1s
Turner, C.E. v1p0531c2s v1p0698c1s v1p0702c2m v1p0761c2s v1p0906c1s v1p1067c2s v1p1138c1s v2p0448c2s
Turner, C.F. v1p0927c1s
Turner, C.H. v3p0328c1s v4p0060c2s v4p0429c1s
Turner, C.Q. v5p0202c1s v6p0178c2s v6p0246c1s v6p0415c1s v6p0507c2s v6p0525c2s v6p0530c2s v6p0543c2s
Turner, C.T. v1p0331c1s
Turner, C.W. v5p0012c1s v5p0329c1s v5p0435c1s v6p0669c2s
Turner, C.Y. v5p0082c1s v6p0086c2s
Turner, Colonel v5p0388c1s
Turner, D. v3p0112c2s
Turner, D.L. v6p0282c1s
Turner, Dawson v5p0389c1s v6p0432c2s
Turner, E. v1p0351c2s v1p0455c1s v1p0585c1s v1p0646c1s v1p0806c1s v1p1042c2s v1p1129c1s v1p1355c2s v2p0350c2s v4p0343c1s v4p0447c1s v5p0152c1s
Turner, E.B. v5p0061c1s
Turner, E.C. v1p0713c1s
Turner, E.F. v4p0267c2s
Turner, E.S. v1p0577c2s v1p1005c1s
Turner, Ethel v6p0402c2s
Turner, F. v4p0090c2s v5p0334c2s
Turner, F.H. v6p0409c2s
Turner, F.J. v3p0162c1m v3p0214c1s v3p0263c1s v3p0460c1s v4p0013c2s v4p0086c2s v4p0617c1m v4p0618c1s v5p0227c2s v5p0304c1s v5p0349c1m v5p0414c1s v5p0601c2s v5p0625c2m v6p0016c1s v6p0185c2s v6p0192c2s v6p0282c2s v6p0387c2s v6p0422c1m v6p0605c1s v6p0670c1s v6p0692c2m
Turner, F.M. v4p0064c2s v4p0501c1m v4p0501c2s
Turner, F.S. v5p0319c1s v6p0107c1s v6p0540c2s
Turner, F.T. v4p0328c1s
Turner, G. v1p0035c2s v1p0036c2s v1p0221c2s v1p0278c2s v1p0534c1s v1p0675c2s v1p0914c1s v1p1185c2s v2p0031c1s v2p0075c2s v2p0090c1s v2p0101c1s v2p0118c1s v2p0144c1s v2p0255c1s v2p0260c2s v2p0340c2s v2p0387c2s v2p0397c2s v2p0416c1s v2p0416c2m v2p0437c1s v2p0482c1s v3p0153c2s v3p0257c1s v3p0280c2s v3p0345c2s v3p0346c1s v3p0388c1s v3p0406c1s v3p0419c1s
Turner, G.F. v6p0662c2s
Turner, G.J. v6p0287c1s v6p0348c2s v6p0378c1s v6p0590c2s v6p0693c2s
Turner, G.K. v5p0120c1s v5p0442c2s v5p0474c2s v5p0572c1s v5p0629c2s v6p0003c1s v6p0245c2s v6p0501c2s
Turner, G.L. v3p0385c1s
Turner, G.W. v4p0089c2s
Turner, Gilbert v6p0164c1s
Turner, Grace B. v6p0241c1s
Turner, Grace Baldwin v6p0281c2s
Turner, H. v1p1063c2s v2p0044c1s v2p0107c1s v2p0304c1s v2p0379c2s v2p0382c1s v2p0416c2s v4p0636c2s
Turner, H. and Sidgreaves, W. v4p0556c2s
Turner, H.E. v3p0103c2s
Turner, H.H. v3p0140c2s v5p0175c1s v5p0499c1s v6p0037c2m v6p0141c2s v6p0186c1s v6p0210c2s v6p0397c1s v6p0455c1s v6p0496c2s v6p0497c1s
Turner, H.S. v4p0141c1s v4p0295c2s
Turner, H.W. v4p0227c1s v4p0231c1s v4p0284c2s v4p0322c1s v5p0088c2s v6p0418c2s
Turner, H.W. et al. v5p0496c2s
Turner, J. v4p0588c2s
Turner, J.A. v1p0192c1s v1p0675c1s v1p0999c1s v1p1177c1s
Turner, J.B. v1p0093c2s
Turner, J.D. v6p0181c2s v6p0287c2s
Turner, J.G. v1p1329c2s
Turner, J.R. v4p0622c1s
Turner, J.T. v5p0077c1s
Turner, L. v3p0137c1s
Turner, M.M. v1p0441c2s v1p1147c2s
Turner, Marg. v6p0179c2s
Turner, May v5p0325c2s
Turner, R. v2p0169c2m v2p0458c1s v6p0174c1s v6p0522c2s
Turner, R.W. v4p0035c2s
Turner, Reginald v6p0208c2s
Turner, S. v1p1105c2s v2p0322c1s v5p0013c2s v5p0366c2s
Turner, S.E. v2p0254c2s v4p0275c1s
Turner, S.H. v1p0031c1s v1p0124c2s v1p0130c1s v5p0581c2s v1p0617c1s v1p1412c2s v6p0436c2m v6p0508c2s
Turner, T. v2p0229c1s v5p0139c2s
Turner, T.A. v1p0172c1s
Turner, W. v2p0163c1s v3p0071c2s v3p0194c2s v5p0196c2s v5p0358c2s v6p0210c2s v6p0251c2s
Turner, W., Sir v5p0077c1s v5p0358c1s
Turner, W.D. v3p0241c2s v3p0433c1s v5p0324c1s
Turner, W.L. v1p1063c1s
Turner, W.M. v1p0457c1s v1p0533c2s v1p0857c1s v1p0947c1s
Turner, W.S. v1p1150c1s v1p1377c1s
Turner, W.Y. v1p0876c1s
Turney, E. v1p0096c1m
Turney, P. v3p0095c2s
Turnock, F.H. v5p0488c2s v6p0010c1s
Turnor, E. v1p0163c2s v1p0219c2s v1p0297c1s v1p0608c1s v1p1115c1s

Turnour, E. v6p0212c2s
Turnour, Viscount v6p0134c2s
v6p0299c1s
Turpie, D. v5p0294c1s
Turpin, B.S. v4p0048c1s
v4p0270c1s
Turpin, E. v4p0288c2s
Turquand, P.J. v2p0088c1s
v2p0318c2s
Turquet, A. v6p0054c2s
Turrell, E. v1p0425c2s
Turrell, G. v4p0278c1s
v4p0317c2s v4p0564c2s
Turrell, G.G. v4p0292c1s
v4p0317c2s
Turrell, G.G. and Hadley, A.T.
v4p0167c2s
Turrettini, T. v4p0613c2s
Turtle, R. and Jarvis, A.W.
v6p0083c1s
Turtle, T. v5p0157c1s
Turtle, T. and Haupt, L.M.
v3p0371c1s
Turton, J.J. v1p0189c2s
Tuska, S. v1p0625c2s
Tustin, J.P. v1p0286c1m
v2p0017c2s
Tuthill, C.L. v1p1374c2s
Tuthill, F. v1p0059c2s
Tuthill, L.W.C. v6p0046c1s
Tuthill, M. v1p1308c1s
v2p0037c2s v2p0366c1s v2p0456c2s
Tuthill, W.H. v1p1334c2s
Tuttiet, M.G. v4p0197c2s
v5p0637c2s v6p0461c2s
Tuttle, A.E. v6p0208c1s
Tuttle, A.H. v1p0859c2s
v4p0043c1s v4p0122c2s v4p0302c1s
v5p0463c1s v5p0463c2s v5p0577c2s
v6p0285c2s v6p0545c2s
Tuttle, C.A. v3p0458c2s
v5p0175c2s v5p0623c2s v6p0100c1m
v6p0708c1s
Tuttle, C.H. v1p0448c2s
v5p0479c1s
Tuttle, C.W. v1p0006c1s
v1p0668c1s v1p0707c1s v1p0739c2s
v1p1030c2s v1p1334c2s
Tuttle, E. v5p0621c1s
Tuttle, F.G. v5p0096c1s
Tuttle, G.W. v6p0453c2s
Tuttle, H. v1p0114c2s
v1p0151c1s v1p0259c1s v1p0441c2m
v1p0515c2s v1p0516c1s v1p0517c1m
v1p0559c1s v1p0863c1s v1p0900c2s
v1p1060c2s v1p1061c1s v1p1065c2s
v1p1134c1s v1p1238c1s v1p1398c1s
v2p0048c1m v2p0117c2s v2p0129c1s
v2p0152c1s v2p0176c2s v2p0204c2s
v2p0210c2s v2p0331c2s v2p0348c1s
v2p0407c2s v2p0459c2s v3p0070c2s
v3p0162c2s v3p0204c1s v3p0338c1s
v3p0339c1s v3p0358c1s v3p0405c1s
v3p0464c1s v5p0349c1s v5p0470c1s
Tuttle, H.B. v4p0500c2s
Tuttle, H.P. v5p0129c2m
v5p0615c1s
Tuttle, J.E. v1p0034c1s
v1p1387c2s v5p0101c1s v6p0404c2s
Tuttle, J.F. v1p0107c2s
v1p0275c1s v1p0538c2s v1p0873c1s
v1p0912c1s v1p0938c2s v1p1011c1s
v1p1047c2s v1p1387c2m v1p1399c2s
v1p1400c1s v1p1400c2s v1p1418c1s
v2p0353c1s
Tuttle, J.M. v1p0848c2s
Tuttle, J.T. v1p0832c1s
Tuttle, L. v5p0568c1s
v6p0529c1s
Tuttle, L.T. v6p0696c2s
Tuttle, Lauren T. v6p0438c1s
Tuttle, M.C. v5p0210c2s
Tuttle, M.M. v3p0464c1s
Tuttle, S.L. v1p0786c1s
Tuttle, S.W. v1p1148c1s
Tuttle, T. v1p0535c1s
v1p0912c1s
Tuttle, T.R. v6p0364c2s
Tuttle, W.R. v5p0177c1s
Tuttle-Schuthof v5p0129c2s
Tutton, A.E. v3p0029c2s
v3p0080c1s v3p0107c1s v3p0156c1m
v3p0167c2s v3p0174c2s v3p0205c2s
v3p0305c1s v4p0051c2s v4p0142c1s
v4p0204c1s v4p0271c1m v4p0359c2s
v4p0366c2s v4p0405c1s v4p0418c1s
v4p0440c1s v4p0555c2s v5p0299c2s
Tutton, C.H. v1p1259c1s
Tutweiler, J. v2p0477c2s
Tutwiler, J.R. v6p0396c2s
Tutwiler, Julia R. v6p0466c1s
v6p0606c2s
Tuxton, I. v1p1210c1s
v1p1417c1s
Twain, Mark v3p0260c2s
v4p0014c1s v4p0118c2s v4p0365c1s
v5p0155c2s v5p0254c1s v6p0094c1s
v6p0177c2s v6p0179c2s v6p0214c1s
v6p0297c2s v6p0301c1s v6p0330c2s
v6p0344c1s v6p0347c2s v6p0661c2s
Tweddell, R.H. v4p0271c1s
Tweed, B.F. v1p0152c1s
v1p0218c1s v1p0390c1s v1p0890c2s
v1p0925c1s v1p1085c2s v2p0304c2s
v3p0077c1s
Tweedale, V. v6p0212c1s
Tweedale, V.C. v4p0066c2s
Tweedale, Violet v6p0626c1s
Tweedie, A., Mrs. v3p0307c2s
v4p0081c1s v5p0570c2s
Tweedie, Alec., Mrs. v4p0062c2s
v4p0333c1s
Tweedie, E.B., Mrs. v3p0323c1s
Tweedie, Ethel B. v4p0272c1s
v4p0392c1s
Tweedie, Maj.-Gen. v6p0169c1s
v6p0531c2s
Tweedie, W. v5p0077c2s
v6p0314c1s
Tweedie, W., Maj.-Gen. ... v6p0590c1s
Tweedy, A.B. v3p0279c1s
v3p0289c2s v3p0468c2s v4p0245c1s
v4p0629c2s
Twells, J.H. v4p0275c1s
Twells, J.H., jr. v6p0201c2s
Twells, T.H. v6p0012c1s
Twelvetrees, W.N. v5p0078c2s
v5p0260c2s v5p0621c2s v6p0529c2s
Twemlow, G. v2p0147c2s
Twemlow, J.A. v5p0180c1s
v5p0630c1s
Twesten, A.D.C. v1p1094c1s
v1p1325c2s
Twesten, Prof. v1p0120c1s
Twichell, J.H. v1p0719c2s
v1p1103c1s v2p0422c1s v2p0466c1s
v3p0235c1s v4p0118c2s v6p0115c2s
v6p0565c2s v6p0686c1s
Twigg, J.H. v5p0284c1s
Twigg, R.H. v1p1219c1s
Twigge, R. v4p0009c2s
v4p0037c1s v4p0516c1s v5p0520c2s
Twigge, R.W. v5p0011c1s
Twiggs, H.D.D. v4p0608c2s
Twing, C.F. v2p0418c1s
Twing, M.A.E. v3p0082c2s
v3p0112c1s v3p0467c1s v3p0469c1s
Twining, A. v1p0278c1s
Twining, A.C. v1p0077c1m
v1p0077c2s v1p0361c2s v1p0376c2s
v1p0404c2s v1p0827c2m v1p0828c1s
v1p0903c2s v1p0907c1s v1p1208c1s
v1p1401c2s
Twining, E.H. v1p0727c2s
Twining, G. v3p0469c2s
Twining, K. v1p0254c2s
v1p0314c1s v1p0756c2s v1p1063c1s
v1p1432c2s
Twining, L. v2p0208c1s
v2p0480c1s v3p0036c2s v3p0339c1s
v3p0470c2s v4p0096c2s v4p0465c2s
v4p0627c1s v5p0459c1s v6p0236c2s
Twining, Louisa v3p0086c2s
v3p0338c2s v3p0468c1s
Twining, T. v1p1289c1s
Twisden, J.F. v1p0815c1s
Twiss, H. v1p0811c2s
Twiss, J.J. v1p1422c1s
Twiss, J.W. v1p0529c1s
v1p1410c2s
Twiss, T. v2p0223c2s
v2p0286c2s v2p0305c2s v2p0315c2s
Twist, A.C. v4p0083c2s
Twombley, W. v6p0287c1s
Twombley, W.McK. v5p0211c1s
Twombly, A.S. v1p0047c1s
v1p0687c2s v1p0690c1s v1p1044c1s
v1p1144c1s v1p1289c2s v2p0155c1s
v6p0578c1s
Twombly, M. v3p0469c1s
v5p0450c2s v6p0223c1s
Twombly, Mary v5p0031c2s
Twomey, D.H.R. v6p0086c2s
Twomey, M. v1p0300c1s
Twose, G.M.R. v4p0570c2s
v5p0226c1s v5p0387c2s v6p0244c2s
Twycross, M. v5p0213c2s
Twycross, N. v5p0122c2s
Tyack, L. v5p0067c1s
Tybout, E.M. v5p0294c2s
v6p0019c1s v6p0036c2s v6p0070c1s
v6p0084c1s v6p0221c1s v6p0298c2s
v6p0431c1s v6p0464c1s v6p0515c2s
v6p0535c2s v6p0541c1s v6p0648c2s
v6p0672c2s v6p0677c2s v6p0681c1s
Tybout, Ella M. v6p0273c2s
v6p0301c1s v6p0413c1s v6p0424c1s
v6p0661c2s
Tybout, H.R. v5p0344c2s
Tylden, H.J. v4p0430c2s
Tylee, E.S. v6p0134c2s
Tyler, A. v5p0036c2s
Tyler, A.M. v6p0543c2s
Tyler, A.S. v6p0370c2s
Tyler, A.W. v1p0688c1s
v1p0773c2s v3p0351c1s
Tyler, Alice S. v6p0374c1s
v6p0374c2m
Tyler, B. v1p0097c1s
v1p1287c1m
Tyler, B.B. v3p0084c1s
Tyler, B.P. v6p0078c2s
Tyler, C.D. v4p0392c2s
Tyler, C.M. v1p0869c2s
v5p0483c2s
Tyler, C.W. v4p0232c1s
v6p0354c2s
Tyler, Capt. v1p1079c2s
v2p0364c1s v3p0352c2s
Tyler, E. v1p0619c1s
v2p0144c2s
Tyler, E.R. v1p0131c2m
v1p0198c2s v1p0247c1s v1p0248c1s
v1p0254c2s v1p0279c2s v1p0290c2m
v1p0535c2s v1p0538c1s v1p0613c1s
v1p0708c2s v1p0779c1m v1p0903c1s
v1p0905c1s v1p0990c1s v1p1096c1s
v1p1117c2s v1p1206c1s v1p1391c1s
Tyler, E.S. v3p0259c2s
Tyler, G.R. v4p0339c1s
Tyler, H.M. v4p0535c2s
Tyler, H.W. v1p0535c1s
v1p1078c2s v1p1079c1s v3p0352c2s
v3p0422c2s v5p0616c2s v6p0406c1s
v6p0636c1s v6p0671c2s v6p0714c2s
Tyler, J. v1p0823c2s
v1p1348c2s v1p1411c2s v2p0412c1s
v5p0458c1s v6p0573c2s
Tyler, J.B. v1p0435c2s
Tyler, J.G., Miss v4p0621c1s
Tyler, J.G., Mrs. v1p1208c1s
Tyler, J.M. v5p0198c1s
v5p0280c1s v5p0343c1s v6p0191c1s
v6p0193c1s v6p0256c2s v6p0290c1s
Tyler, J.Z. v2p0098c2s
v2p0235c2s
Tyler, L.G. v2p0323c1s
v2p0436c1s v2p0450c1s v6p0292c2s
Tyler, M. v1p1363c1s
Tyler, M.C. v1p0271c1s
v1p0733c2s v1p0761c2s v1p0835c1m
v1p1311c1s v2p0255c2s v4p0150c2s
v4p0254c2s v4p0344c1s v4p0625c1s
Tyler, M.F. v2p0433c2s
v3p0432c1s v5p0641c1s
Tyler, N.C. v1p0163c1s
Tyler, R. v1p0111c1s
v1p0665c2s
Tyler, R.U. v5p0606c1s
Tyler, R.W. v6p0554c2s
Tyler, S. v1p0009c1s
v1p0085c1s v1p0179c2s v1p0527c2s
v1p0568c1m v1p0613c2s v1p0737c1s
v1p0761c1s v1p0900c2s v1p1000c1s
v1p1007c2s v1p1028c1s v1p1062c1s
v1p1102c2s v1p1221c2s v1p1355c2s
Tyler, T. v1p0681c1s
v1p1237c1s v2p0030c2s v2p0043c2m
v2p0204c1s v2p0234c2s v2p0265c1s
v2p0322c1s v2p0334c2s v2p0428c1s
v3p0042c1s v3p0154c2s v3p0197c2m
v3p0234c1s v3p0348c1s v3p0371c2s
v4p0021c1s v4p0023c1s v4p0201c2s
v4p0259c1s v5p0174c1s v5p0574c1s
Tyler, T. and Furnivall, F.J.
v3p0154c2s
Tyler, T. and Wright, W. . v2p0204c1s
Tyler, T. et al. v4p0259c1s
Tyler, Thos. v4p0374c1s
v4p0560c1s
Tyler, W.S. v1p0009c1m
v1p0020c2s v1p0057c2s v1p0072c1m
v1p0118c1s v1p0248c2s v1p0258c2s
v1p0294c1s v1p0329c2s v1p0504c2s
v1p0529c1s v1p0577c2s v1p0601c1s
v1p0682c1s v1p0688c2m v1p1000c1s
v1p1016c2s v1p1018c2m v1p1124c2s
v1p1140c1s v1p1217c2m v1p1221c1s
v1p1250c1s v1p1337c1s v1p1422c2s
v2p0044c1s
Tyler, W.S. et al. v1p0496c1s
Tylor, A. v1p0035c1s
v1p0613c1s v1p0933c2s v1p1172c2s
v2p0441c2s v5p0492c2s
Tylor, D. v5p0336c2s
Tylor, E. v2p0010c1s
Tylor, E.B. v1p0012c1s
v1p0045c2s v1p0078c1s v1p0083c2s
v1p0085c1s v1p0260c1s v1p0427c2s
v1p0499c1s v1p0718c2s v1p0724c1s
v1p0747c2s v1p0794c2m v1p0879c2s
v1p0885c2s v1p0891c1s v1p0935c1s
v1p0946c2s v1p0979c1s v1p0992c2s
v1p1003c1s v1p1018c1s v1p1045c2s
v1p1050c2s v1p1071c2s v1p1072c2s
v1p1073c1s v1p1073c2s v1p1094c2s
v1p1153c1s v1p1204c2s v1p1217c1s
v1p1217c2m v1p1314c1s v1p1409c2s
v1p1432c1s v2p0010c1s v2p0016c2m
v2p0061c2s v2p0110c1s v2p0142c1s
v2p0193c1s v2p0345c1s v2p0347c2s
v2p0348c2s v2p0471c2s v3p0012c2s
v3p0115c2s v3p0267c1s v3p0268c1s
v3p0268c2s v4p0047c2s v4p0205c2s
v4p0270c2s v4p0361c1s v4p0467c2s
v4p0479c1s v4p0550c2s v4p0564c1s
v5p0583c1m
Tylor, E.B. and Spencer, H.
v1p0036c2s
Tylor, G.S. v2p0364c2s

Tylor, J.J. v1p0829c2s
Tymms, T.V. v3p0005c2s
v3p0106c2s v3p0209c1s v3p0255c1s
v3p0289c1s v4p0402c1m
Tynan, A.E. v5p0555c1s
Tynan, K. v2p0199c1s
v2p0216c1s v3p0048c1s v3p0064c1s
v3p0309c2s v3p0316c1s v3p0322c1s
v3p0474c2s v4p0096c1s v4p0163c1s
v4p0291c2s v4p0353c2s v4p0360c2s
v4p0387c2s v4p0418c2s v4p0442c2s
v4p0443c2s v4p0495c1s v5p0070c1s
v5p0146c1s v5p0387c2s v5p0548c1s
v5p0628c2s v6p0114c1s v6p0504c2s
v6p0589c1s
Tynan, Katharine v4p0219c2s
v6p0058c1s v6p0147c1s v6p0287c2s
v6p0347c2s v6p0358c1s v6p0387c1s
v6p0409c2s v6p0416c1s v6p0464c1s
Tynan, R. v2p0374c1s
Tyndale, T.H. v1p0304c1s
Tyndall, Fanny v1p0025c2s
Tyndall, J. v1p0004c2s
v1p0024c2m v1p0025c1m v1p0073c2m
v1p0202c2s v1p0278c2s v1p0279c1s
v1p0348c2s v1p0354c1m v1p0373c1m
v1p0382c1s v1p0399c1m v1p0399c2s
v1p0401c1s v1p0433c2s v1p0435c1m
v1p0443c2m v1p0449c1m v1p0455c1s
v1p0459c1s v1p0464c1m v1p0466c2m
v1p0467c1s v1p0502c2s v1p0504c2s
v1p0512c2m v1p0524c1s v1p0526c2s
v1p0531c2s v1p0577c1s v1p0579c2s
v1p0580c1m v1p0622c2s v1p0696c1s
v1p0746c2s v1p0747c1s v1p0747c2s
v1p0788c2s v1p0792c2s v1p0805c2s
v1p0810c1m v1p0810c2m v1p0812c1s
v1p0814c1s v1p0849c2s v1p0919c2s
v1p1036c2s v1p1074c1s v1p1098c2s
v1p1139c1s v1p1161c1m v1p1164c1s
v1p1198c1s v1p1204c1s v1p1222c1s
v1p1222c2m v1p1239c1m v1p1356c1s
v1p1372c2s v1p1407c2s v2p0027c2m
v2p0100c2s v2p0175c2m v2p0199c1s
v2p0304c1s v2p0332c1s v2p0362c1m
v2p0364c1s v2p0389c2s v2p0410c2s
v2p0439c2s v2p0448c1s v2p0467c1s
v3p0009c1s v3p0068c2s v3p0158c1s
v3p0251c1m v3p0331c1s v4p0181c1s
v4p0429c2s
Tyndall, J. and McCosh, J.
v1p1041c2s
Tyne, J. v1p0428c2s
Tyner, C.E. v2p0022c1s
Tyner, M. v4p0193c2s
v4p0291c1s
Tyner, P. v4p0465c2s
v4p0528c1s v4p0535c1s v5p0116c2s
v5p0600c2s v6p0412c2s
Tyner, Paul v4p0574c1s
Tyng, C. v1p0574c2s
Tyng, C.D. v6p0012c2s
Tyng, C.M. v2p0289c1s
Tyng, E.M. v2p0275c2s
Tyng, J.A. v5p0239c2s
Tyng, S.H., jr. v1p0647c2s
Tyng, T.S. v3p0227c1m
Tyrrell, F.H. v3p0438c1s
v4p0045c2s v4p0139c1s v4p0278c2s
v4p0495c2s v4p0586c2s v5p0217c1m
v5p0220c2s v5p0503c1s v6p0236c2s
Tyrrell, G. v2p0215c2s
v3p0098c1s v3p0237c2s v4p0042c1s
v4p0199c1s v4p0535c1s v4p0637c2s
v5p0023c2m v5p0031c1s v5p0097c2s
v5p0118c1s v5p0122c2s v5p0165c1s
v5p0174c1s v5p0198c1s v5p0323c2s
v5p0397c1s v5p0435c2s v5p0479c1s
v5p0483c2s v5p0486c2s v5p0488c2s
v5p0493c2s v5p0511c1s v5p0576c2s
v5p0584c1s v5p0590c2s v5p0633c2s
v5p0635c2s v6p0122c2s v6p0172c1s
v6p0262c2s v6p0296c2s v6p0342c1s
v6p0376c1s v6p0386c2s v6p0440c2s
v6p0536c2s
Tyrrell, H. v2p0247c1s
v3p0036c2s v5p0329c1m v6p0180c2s
v6p0228c1s
Tyrrell, H.G. v5p0076c1m
Tyrrell, Henry v6p0181c2s
Tyrrell, J.B. v3p0104c2s
v4p0086c1m v4p0268c1s v5p0090c2s
Tyrrell, J.W. v4p0086c1s
v4p0187c1s
Tyrrell, Lieut.-Gen. v5p0216c2s
Tyrrell, R.L. v6p0552c1s
Tyrrell, R.Y. v2p0410c1s
v3p0057c1s v3p0087c1s v3p0454c2s
v4p0189c2s v4p0248c1s v4p0269c1s
v4p0321c2s v4p0344c2s v5p0170c1s
v5p0275c2s v5p0324c2s v6p0029c2s
v6p0046c1s v6p0127c1s v6p0130c1s
v6p0130c2s v6p0272c2m v6p0303c1s
v6p0339c1s v6p0361c1s v6p0427c2s
v6p0500c1s v6p0504c2s v6p0604c1s
v6p0707c2s
Tyrrell-Gill, F. v5p0635c2s
Tyrwhitt, R.S. v1p1204c1s
Tyrwhitt, R.St.J. v1p0061c1s
v1p0061c2s v1p0062c1s v1p0062c2s
v1p0064c1m v1p0064c2s v1p0066c1s
v1p0106c1s v1p0301c1s v1p0323c1s
v1p0340c2s v1p0361c1s v1p0438c1s
v1p0555c2s v1p0640c1s v1p0840c1s
v1p0935c1s v1p0964c1s v1p0996c2s
v4p0098c1s v4p0138c1s v4p0161c1s
v4p0528c2s
Tyrwhitt, St.J. v1p0434c1s
Tyrwhitt, T. v1p0165c1s
Tyson, A.H. v2p0468c1s
Tyson, J.A. v4p0578c1s
v6p0409c2s v6p0528c2s
Tyson, J.R. v1p0997c1s
Tyson, M. v1p0798c1s
Tyson, R. v1p0144c1s
v1p0197c1s v6p0196c2s v6p0335c1s
v6p0539c2m
Tyson, Robert v6p0519c2s
Tytler, C.C.F. v1p0825c1s
v2p0318c2s
Tytler, S. v1p0204c2s
v1p0504c1s v1p0522c2s v1p0716c1s
v1p0891c1s v1p1131c1s v1p1203c1s
v1p1403c2s v2p0037c2s v3p0046c2s
v3p0118c1s v3p0449c1s v6p0626c2s
Tytus, G.S.H. v6p0457c2s
v6p0643c2s v6p0662c1s
Tytus, R.de P. v6p0457c2s
Tyver, T. v6p0011c1s
Tzschirner, H.T. v1p0241c1s

Uchimura, J.K. v2p0233c2s
Udal, J.S. v2p0318c2s
Udden, J.A. v4p0164c2s
v5p0614c1s v6p0432c2s
Udell, C. v5p0154c1s
Udney, S. v2p0342c1s
v3p0069c1s
Udny, S. v6p0164c2s
Uebelacker, C.F. v5p0183c2s
Uehling, E.A. v6p0070c1s
Ufer, C. v3p0325c1s
v4p0255c1s v4p0432c2s v5p0230c2s
v6p0536c1s
Ufford, H.P. v5p0129c1s
Ufford, W.S. v5p0107c1s
v6p0049c1s
Uhland, J.L. v1p0228c2s
v1p0307c2s
Uhland, L. v1p0848c2s
Uhland, W.H. v1p1370c2s
Uhle, J.B. v3p0132c1s
v4p0401c1s
Uhle, M. v6p0490c1s
v6p0606c1s
Uhlenhuth, Paul v6p0024c2s
Uhler, G. et al. v4p0180c1s
v4p0395c2s
Uhler, P.R. v1p1389c1s
v3p0031c2s v4p0221c1s
Uhlhorn, C. v6p0520c2s
Uhlhorn, G. v6p0548c1s
Uhlig, G. v5p0447c1s
Uhlrich, E. v5p0635c1s
v6p0076c1s
Ukhtomksi, H. v6p0118c2s
Ular, A. v6p0251c2s
v6p0557c2s v6p0558c2s v6p0645c2s
v6p0646c1m
Ule, M. v1p1308c1s
Ule, O. v1p0347c1s
v1p0465c1s
Ulery, W.F. v4p0287c2s
Ulke, T. v5p0028c2s
v5p0136c2s v5p0377c2s v5p0411c1s
Ullathorne, W.B. v3p0465c1s
Ullman, K. v1p1090c1s
Ullmann, C. v1p0242c1s
v1p0685c2s
Ulrich, E. v6p0069c2s
Ulrich, H.L. v6p0639c1s
Ulrich, J.L. and Rand, H.W.
v6p0596c1s
Ulrich, Mabel S. v6p0629c1s
Ulrici, H. v2p0410c2s
v2p0415c1m
Umbreit, F.W.C. v1p0536c2s
v1p1056c2s
Umpherston, F.A. v6p0652c1s
v6p0708c1s
Umsted, L.D. v1p0767c1s
Unamuno, M.De v6p0192c2s
Unden, J.A. v4p0551c1s
Underdown, E.M. v3p0434c1s
Underhill, C.B. v6p0467c2s
Underhill, C.M. v6p0075c1s
Underhill, E. v6p0404c1s
Underhill, E.B. v1p0097c1s
Underhill, F.T. v6p0297c2s
Underhill, G.E. v3p0183c2s
v6p0105c1s
Underhill, G.F. v3p0022c1s
v4p0404c2s v5p0216c1s
Underhill, J. v3p0339c1s
v4p0052c1s
Underhill, M.H. v1p0752c2s
Underhill, R. v5p0630c1s
Underhill, Z.D. v4p0285c1s
v4p0445c1s
Underwood, B.F. v1p0338c2s
v3p0442c2s v4p0371c2s v4p0478c1s
v4p0542c1s v4p0633c2s
Underwood, E.B. v3p0350c1s
v3p0371c2s v6p0567c1s
Underwood, E.L. v6p0484c1s
Underwood, F.H. v1p0175c1s
v1p0394c2s v1p0405c1s v1p0598c1s
v1p0709c1s v1p0774c2s v1p0908c2s
v1p1044c2s v1p1067c1s v1p1091c1s
v1p1314c2s v1p1417c2s v3p0135c2s
v3p0191c2s v3p0198c2s v3p0258c1s
v3p0259c2m v3p0260c1s v3p0300c2s
v3p0321c1s v3p0429c1s v3p0463c1s
Underwood, F.K. v3p0455c1s
Underwood, G.H. v3p0294c1s
v3p0296c1s
Underwood, H. v3p0359c1s
Underwood, H.S. v3p0456c2s
v5p0410c1s
Underwood, Helen v5p0424c2s
Underwood, J. v1p0642c2s
v6p0467c2s
Underwood, Julia G. v6p0111c1s
Underwood, L. v6p0143c1s
Underwood, L.M. v2p0451c1s
v3p0017c1s v4p0384c2s v5p0315c2s
v6p0160c1s v6p0222c1m
Underwood, M.G. v6p0244c1s
Underwood, M.G.L. v4p0584c2s
v4p0589c2s
Underwood, M.L. v4p0015c1s
Underwood, O.W. v5p0403c2s
v5p0436c1s
Underwood, S.A. v3p0348c1s
v3p0470c2s v4p0626c2s v5p0287c2s
v5p0342c1s v5p0420c1s
Underwood, S.A. et al. ... v2p0477c1s
Underwood, S.J. v5p0038c1s
Underwood, W.L. v5p0388c2s
v6p0431c2m v6p0688c1s
Underwood, W.S. and Prescott, S.C.
v5p0552c2s
Undy, S. v2p0183c2s
Unger, F.W. v6p0685c2s
Unger, Frederic William .. v6p0047c1s
Union, W.C. v4p0271c1s
Unite, P. v5p0154c1s
v5p0635c1s
Univiera, Y.de v2p0211c2s
Unsworth, T. v3p0165c2s
Unwin, A.H. v6p0096c2s
Unwin, G. v5p0585c1s
Unwin, M.L.H. v5p0454c1s
Unwin, R. v3p0399c1s
v6p0651c1s
Unwin, W.C. v1p0145c2s
v1p0162c1s v2p0467c2s v4p0146c2s
v4p0175c1s v4p0180c1s v4p0252c2s
v4p0547c1s v4p0547c2s v4p0613c2s
v6p0615c2s
Updegraff, M. v3p0435c1s
v6p0614c1s v6p0647c1s
Updike, W. v1p1399c2s
Upham, A.A. v5p0511c2s
Upham, A.E. v6p0535c2s
Upham, C.W. v1p0005c2s
v1p0121c1s v1p0194c2s v1p0317c2s
v1p0447c2s v1p0476c1s v1p0512c2s
v1p0523c1s v1p0604c1s v1p0709c1s
v1p0719c1s v1p0789c2s v1p0811c1s
v1p0898c1s v1p0902c2s v1p0911c2s
v1p0931c1s v1p0987c1s v1p0993c1s
v1p1047c2m v1p1050c2s v1p1088c2s
v1p1089c2s v1p1145c2s v1p1350c2s
v1p1362c2s v1p1373c1s v1p1400c1s
v1p1418c1s
Upham, Caroline E. v3p0466c2s
Upham, F.K. v1p1358c2s
v2p0201c2s v3p0234c1s
Upham, F.N. v4p0194c1s
Upham, J.B. v1p0174c1s
v1p0883c2s v1p1222c2s
Upham, J.C. v1p0119c2s
Upham, M.B. v2p0031c1s
Upham, N. v4p0403c2s
Upham, T.C. v1p0119c2s
v1p0437c2s v1p0867c2s v1p0911c2s
v1p1043c2s v1p1262c1s
Upham, W. v1p0270c2s
v1p0292c2s v1p0824c2s v1p0927c1s
v2p0290c2s v3p0115c1s v3p0290c2s
v3p0350c2s v3p0389c2s v3p0430c1s
v4p0045c1s v4p0165c2s v4p0210c1s
v4p0222c2m v4p0226c2s v4p0227c1s
v4p0272c2m v4p0273c1s v4p0469c1s
v4p0499c1s v4p0520c2s v5p0015c1s
v5p0288c1s v6p0244c2s v6p0251c1s
v6p0397c1m v6p0419c2s v6p0422c1s
v6p0432c2s v6p0531c1s v6p0618c2s
v6p0647c1s
Upham, W.P. and Sheldon, G.
v4p0328c1s
Upham, Warren v6p0359c1s
v6p0456c2s
Upshur, A.P. v1p0538c2s
v1p0680c2s v1p1207c1s v1p1373c1s
Upshur, T.T. v4p0605c2s
Upsom, A.J. v2p0351c2s
Upson, A.J. v1p0892c1s
v4p0309c2s
Upson, D. v4p0098c1s
Upson, W.H. v4p0284c2s
v4p0553c2s
Upton, C.B. v1p0026c2s
v1p0071c2s v1p0434c1s v1p0839c2s
v1p0964c1s v1p1041c1s v1p1094c1s
v1p1095c2s v1p1164c1s v2p0241c1s
v2p0414c2m v2p0466c1s v2p0474c1s
v4p0242c1s
Upton, C.R. v1p0592c2s
Upton, E. v1p0839c1s
v1p1060c2s
Upton, F.E. v2p0136c1s
Upton, F.H. v1p0339c1s
Upton, F.R. v1p0384c1s
v1p0399c2s
Upton, G.B. v1p1192c2s
v4p0101c2s
Upton, G.E. v5p0479c2s
Upton, G.M. v2p0304c1s
Upton, G.P. v1p0168c2s
v1p0227c1s v1p0227c2m v1p0256c2s
v1p0515c1s v1p0885c1s v2p0140c1s
v2p0303c2s v2p0443c1s v2p0464c1s
v3p0293c1m v3p0293c2s v3p0300c2s
v4p0100c1s v4p0401c2s v5p0105c1s
v6p0437c2s v6p0624c2s
Upton, Geo.P. v6p0390c2s
Upton, H.T. v3p0237c2s
v5p0261c2s
Upton, J.H. v1p0286c2s
Upton, J.K. v4p0540c1s
v5p0545c1s
Upton, M.F. v4p0398c1s
v5p0027c2s v5p0222c2s
Upton, M.G. v1p0333c1s
v1p0377c1s v1p0415c2s v1p0914c1s
v1p1148c2s v1p1276c1s v1p1289c2s
v1p1386c1s v6p0251c2s
Upton, M.R. v3p0027c1s
v3p0200c2s
Upton, R.D. v1p0106c2s
v1p0604c2s
Upton, S. and Goodell, D.H.
v3p0423c2s
Upton, S.C. v3p0311c2s
v4p0189c1s v4p0470c1s
Upton, Sara C. v3p0372c2s
Upton, W. v2p0129c2s
v2p0179c1s v2p0364c1s v2p0426c2s
v3p0239c2s v3p0309c2m v3p0415c1s
v4p0130c2s
Upton, W.H. v2p0456c2s
Upton, W.S. v1p0339c1s
v1p0356c2s v1p0772c2s
Upward, A. v4p0263c2s
v4p0336c1s v4p0442c2s v5p0452c1s
Upward, Allen v5p0077c2s
v5p0099c1s v5p0346c1s
Urann, C.A. v5p0638c2s
Urban, G. v6p0544c1s
Urban, S. v4p0395c1s
v4p0459c1s v5p0186c2s v5p0218c1s
v5p0393c2s v6p0179c1s v6p0319c2s
v6p0418c1s v6p0532c1s v6p0586c1s
v6p0599c2s
Urban, Sylvanus v5p0451c1s
v6p0071c2s v6p0103c1s
Urban, W.M. v4p0372c1s
v5p0280c1s v5p0369c2s v5p0559c1s
v6p0025c2s v6p0171c1s v6p0317c2s
Urdahl, T.K. v5p0204c2s
Urdahl, T.K. and Ely, R.T.
v5p0536c2m
Ure, A. v1p0068c2s
v1p0141c2s v1p0237c1s v1p0562c2s
v1p0635c2s v1p0810c1s v1p0982c1s
v1p1236c2s v5p0223c1s v6p0036c1s
v6p0652c2s
Ure, P. v6p0663c2s
U'Ren, W.S. v6p0319c2s
v6p0470c1s
Urgindi, J. v1p0828c2s
Uricoechea, E. v1p0224c1s
Urmston, E. v2p0324c2s
Urmy, C. v5p0455c2s
v6p0182c1s
Urner, C.H. v5p0173c1s
v5p0633c1s
Urner, Mabel H. v6p0132c1s
Urquhart, A. v1p1122c1s
Urquhart, D. v3p0438c2s
Urquhart, F. v3p0234c2s
v4p0244c2s
Urquhart, F.F. v5p0146c1s
Urquhart, G. v4p0116c1s
v4p0459c1s
Urquhart, J. v2p0139c2s
v2p0234c2s v5p0055c2s
Urquhart, J.W. v3p0386c2s
Urusov v6p0557c2s
Urwick, W. v2p0026c2s
Usborne, Com. v1p0557c1s
v1p0901c2s
Usher, A.P. v6p0150c1s
v6p0241c2s
Usher, E.B. v5p0633c2s
v6p0701c1s
Usher, E.C.S. v2p0132c2s
Usher, J.N. v4p0066c1s
Usher, L.W. v5p0423c1s
Usher, R. v1p0392c1s
v1p0819c1s v1p0820c1s v1p1176c2s
v1p1222c2s v1p1264c2s
Usher, R.G. v6p0333c1s
Ussher, Beverley, Mrs. ... v6p0575c1s
Ussher, R. v2p0277c1s
v2p0324c1s v2p0353c2m
Ussher, T. v1p0894c2s
v4p0392c2s
Utley, A.J. v4p0059c1s
v5p0142c1s
Utley, G.B. v6p0448c1s
Utley, G.P. v6p0332c2s
Utley, H.M. v2p0256c2s
v3p0116c1s v3p0248c2s v3p0303c1s
v4p0329c2s v5p0066c2s v5p0336c2s
v6p0373c1s
Utley, T.F. v4p0022c2s
v4p0104c2s v4p0425c1s
Utter, D. v2p0058c1s
v5p0487c1s
Utter, D.N. v1p0235c1s
v2p0058c1s
Uwins, D. v1p0238c1s
v1p0643c2s v1p0644c1s v1p1004c2s
v1p1210c1s
Uyeno, T.M. v4p0107c1s
Uzanne, O. v4p0066c2s
v4p0067c2s v4p0268c1s v4p0439c2s
v4p0627c1s v5p0070c2s v5p0157c1s

v5p0242c2s v5p0301c2s v5p0315c1s
v5p0411c1s v6p0086c2s v6p0219c1s
v6p0237c2s v6p0242c1s v6p0277c2s
v6p0298c2s v6p0324c2s v6p0363c1s
v6p0365c2s v6p0483c1s v6p0703c1m
Uzanne, O. and Ryley, M.B.
v6p0547c1s
Uzanne, Octave v4p0058c1s

V., H.A. v5p0578c2s
Vaart, H.M.Van der v6p0115c1s
Vacaresco, H. v6p0011c2s
v6p0352c1s v6p0426c2s
Vacaresco, Helene v5p0498c1s
v6p0302c1s v6p0400c2s v6p0486c2s
v6p0552c2s
Vacchide, N. v6p0637c1s
Vachell, Guy C. v6p0166c1s
Vachell, H.A. v4p0095c2s
v4p0110c2s v4p0276c1s v4p0469c2s
v4p0483c2s v5p0209c1s v5p0209c2s
v5p0236c1s v5p0304c1s v5p0359c1s
v5p0419c2s v5p0473c2s v5p0629c2s
v6p0011c2s v6p0093c2s v6p0168c1s
v6p0217c1s v6p0287c2s v6p0289c1s
v6p0303c1s v6p0527c2s v6p0657c2s
Vachell, M.C. v2p0089c1s
Vacher, F. v3p0007c1s
Vackell, H.A. v5p0075c2s
Vaihinger, T.G. v1p0123c2s
Vail, A.M. v4p0416c1s
Vail, Anna M. v4p0069c2s
v4p0217c2s
Vail, C.D. v3p0340c2s
Vail, Dr. v1p1088c1s
Vail, H.M. v4p0202c2s
Vail, J.H. v4p0175c2s
Vail, R.P.H. v6p0301c2s
Vail, S. v3p0422c2s
v5p0388c1s v5p0411c2s
Vail, S.M. v1p0124c1m
v1p0131c2s v1p0587c2s v1p0601c2s
v1p0820c1s
Vail, T.H. v1p0994c1s
v1p1237c1s v2p0047c2s v2p0309c1s
Vail, W.S. v2p0022c1s
v2p0140c1s
Vailati, G. v6p0503c2s
v6p0513c1s
Vaile, C.M. v5p0051c1s
v5p0440c2s
Vaile, E.O. v1p0058c1s
v1p0720c2s v1p1085c1s v1p1183c2s
v4p0144c2s v6p0609c2s
Vaile, H.S. v4p0321c2s
Vaile, J.F. v4p0453c1s
Vaill, J. v1p0085c1s
v1p1301c2s
Vaill, J.H. v4p0129c2s
Vaill, S.M. v1p0186c1s
Vaillant, L. v2p0157c1s
Vaissaire, M. v1p1260c2s
Vaissiere, M. v1p0971c1s
Val, C.Du v2p0324c1s
v2p0471c2s
Valance, A. v5p0087c2s
v6p0244c2s
Valbert, G. v3p0050c1s
v3p0191c1m v4p0011c2s v4p0089c2s
v5p0065c1s v5p0128c1s v5p0132c2s
v5p0217c1s v5p0219c2s v5p0495c1s
v5p0519c1s v5p0537c1s v5p0637c1s
Valbert, M.G. v4p0480c1s
Valdes, A.P. v4p0417c2s
v5p0355c1s v6p0523c2s
Valdes, E. v4p0559c1s
v5p0063c2s v5p0573c1s
Valenciennes, A. and Fremy, E.
v1p0394c1s v1p0881c2s
Valentine, B.B. v2p0266c2s
Valentine, C.R. v4p0236c2s
v5p0367c2s
Valentine, E.A.U. v4p0253c1s
v5p0623c1s v5p0629c2s
Valentine, E.E. v3p0029c1s
Valentine, E.S. v5p0587c1s
v6p0472c1s
Valentine, E.V. v1p0464c1s
v6p0366c1s
Valentine, F.C. v2p0456c2s
v3p0386c2s
Valentine, J. v1p0002c1s
v1p0883c2s
Valentine, J.J. v4p0059c2s
v4p0378c1s v4p0461c1s
Valentine, M. v1p0068c2s
v1p0229c1s v1p0238c2s v1p0274c1s
v1p0275c1s v1p0285c2s v1p0292c2s
v1p0293c1s v1p0432c1s v1p0440c1s
v1p0442c2s v1p0445c2s v1p0452c2s
v1p0528c1s v1p0613c1s v1p0711c1s
v1p0746c1s v1p0777c2s v1p0778c2s
v1p0794c1s v1p0796c1s v1p0820c2s
v1p0847c2s v1p0882c2s v1p0980c2s
v1p1051c1s v1p1054c2s v1p1088c2s
v1p1089c1s v1p1089c2s v1p1093c1s
v1p1103c1s v1p1139c2s v1p1232c2s
v1p1263c2s v1p1270c1m v1p1328c2s
v1p1422c1s v1p1423c1s v2p0044c1s
v2p0269c1s v2p0295c2s v2p0356c2s
v2p0367c1s v2p0417c1s v2p0438c1s
v2p0482c2s v3p0229c2m v3p0261c1s
v3p0281c1s v3p0442c2s v4p0057c1s
v4p0109c1s v4p0341c2s v4p0345c1s
v5p0056c2s v5p0289c2m v6p0123c1s
v6p0259c2s v6p0312c1s
Valentine, M.H. v5p0196c1s
v5p0198c1s
Valentine, R.G. v5p0275c1s
v6p0642c1s
Valentine, S.G. v4p0168c2s
Valentine, W. et al. v5p0062c2s
Valentini, P. v1p1439c2s
Valentini, P.J.J. v4p0040c1s
Valentini, Ph.J.J. v5p0591c1s
Valery, P. v4p0163c1s
v4p0265c2s v5p0232c1s
Valesh, E.M. v4p0568c2s
Valette, H.F. v3p0157c2s
Valgsmigli, A. v6p0110c1s
Valhasky, M. v4p0083c2s
Valhasky, Marie v4p0253c1s
Valise, E. v5p0115c2s
v5p0532c2s
Valkenburg, D.Van v1p0686c2s
Valkenburg, E.Van v4p0389c2s
Valkenburgh, Agnes Van ... v6p0104c1s
Vallance, A. v3p0022c1s
v3p0084c1s v3p0296c2s v3p0447c2s
v4p0031c1s v4p0266c2s v4p0301c2s
v4p0312c2s v5p0031c2s v5p0051c1s
v5p0115c2s v5p0141c1s v5p0156c2m
v5p0315c2s v5p0354c2s v5p0371c2s
v5p0402c1s v5p0405c2s v5p0428c1s
v5p0450c1s v5p0450c2s v5p0530c1s
v5p0566c2s v5p0617c1m v5p0632c2s
v6p0034c1s v6p0035c2s v6p0050c1m
v6p0163c1s v6p0244c2s v6p0365c2s
v6p0445c2s v6p0558c1s v6p0637c2s
v6p0682c1s v6p0684c1s
Vallance, A. and Eastlake, C.L.
v6p0167c2s
Vallance, Aymer v5p0272c2s
v6p0034c2s
Vallance, Z. v6p0704c1s
Vallancey, C. v1p0662c1s
Vallancey, C. and Lort, M.
v1p0644c2s
Vallandigham, E.N. v3p0163c1s
v3p0259c1s v3p0304c1s v6p0164c1s
v6p0679c1s v6p0680c1s
Vallas, A. v1p0423c1s
v2p0252c1s
Vallejo, G. v3p0062c2s
Vallence, A. v6p0074c1s
Vallentine, B.B. v2p0112c1s
Vallette, M.F. v4p0519c2s
Vallings, H. v2p0324c2s
v5p0492c2s v5p0552c2s v6p0102c2s
v6p0165c2s v6p0201c2s v6p0306c2s
v6p0307c1s v6p0552c2s
Valpy, R. v1p0316c2s
v1p0544c1s v1p0845c2s v1p1135c1s
v1p1283c2s
Valvedre, A.de v1p0370c1s
v1p1420c1s v2p0304c2s
Vambery, A. v1p0067c2s
v1p0146c2s v1p0345c2m v1p0379c1s
v1p0706c2s v1p0707c1s v1p0712c2s
v1p0713c2s v1p0992c1m v1p1205c2s
v1p1313c2s v2p0003c2s v2p0025c1s
v2p0211c2m v2p0218c2s v2p0342c2s
v2p0381c2s v2p0448c2s v2p0457c2s
v3p0001c1s v3p0003c2s v3p0023c2s
v3p0028c1s v3p0138c2s v3p0187c2s
v3p0194c2s v3p0204c2m v3p0264c1s
v3p0351c1s v3p0369c2s v3p0370c1m
v3p0387c1s v3p0435c1s v4p0032c2s
v4p0181c1s v4p0182c1s v4p0189c2s
v4p0423c1s v4p0436c1s v4p0495c2m
v4p0497c1s v4p0522c2s v5p0500c2s
v5p0528c1s v6p0005c2s v6p0026c1s
v6p0206c2s v6p0303c2s v6p0330c1s
v6p0334c1s v6p0478c1m v6p0633c2m
v6p0661c2s
Vambery, A. and Baker, S.W., Sir
v2p0129c1s v2p0380c2s
Vambery, H. v2p0242c2s
v2p0303c2s v5p0034c1s
Van, Lila v6p0117c1s
Van, W.B.Le v1p0146c1s
v1p0402c1s v1p0881c1s v1p1065c2s
v1p1076c2s v1p1247c2m v1p1248c1s
v2p0362c2s v2p0363c1s v2p0418c2s
v2p0419c1s v2p0445c1s v3p0048c2s
v3p0137c1s
Vance, A.C. v4p0624c1s
Vance, A.T. v5p0603c1s
Vance, H.A. v6p0617c1s
Vance, I.J. v4p0205c2s
Vance, J.B. v1p0927c1s
Vance, J.G. v1p1293c2s
Vance, L.J. v2p0338c2s
v3p0156c2s v3p0267c1s v3p0273c1s
v4p0042c2s v4p0045c1m v4p0087c2s
v4p0095c2s v4p0123c2s v4p0128c2s
v4p0146c2s v4p0148c1s v4p0157c1s
v4p0160c1s v4p0166c2s v4p0204c2s
v4p0205c1s v4p0205c2m v4p0206c1s
v4p0225c2s v4p0234c2m v4p0344c2s
v4p0349c1s v4p0395c2s v4p0432c1s
v4p0444c1s v4p0558c1s v4p0561c2s
v4p0587c2s v4p0600c1s v5p0617c1s
v6p0099c2s v6p0416c1s v6p0610c2s
Vance, L.T. v4p0483c1s
Vance, R.L. v3p0156c2m
Vance, W.R. v6p0322c2s
Vance, Z.B. v5p0288c1s
Vance, Z.B. et al. v2p0353c1s
Vandam, A.D. v1p0138c1s
v1p0145c1s v1p0220c2s v1p0337c2s
v1p0364c1s v1p0465c2s v1p0520c2s
v1p0772c2s v1p0773c2s v1p1377c2s
v4p0037c1s v4p0126c1s v4p0158c1s
v4p0164c1s v4p0198c2s v4p0212c1m
v4p0212c2s v4p0233c1s v4p0348c1s
v4p0375c2s v4p0425c2m v4p0480c2m
v4p0526c2m v4p0546c1s v5p0065c1s
v5p0092c2s v5p0169c1s v5p0217c1m
v5p0218c1m v5p0220c2s v5p0229c2s
v5p0234c1s v5p0307c2s v5p0424c1s
v5p0431c2m v5p0456c1s v5p0488c2s
v5p0547c2s
Vandegrift, M. v1p0320c1s
v1p0785c2s v2p0154c2s v2p0345c1s
v5p0474c2s v5p0581c1s
Vandegrift, Margaret v3p0236c2s
Vandeleur, C.F.S. v5p0597c1s
Vandeleur, S. v5p0416c2s
Vandenberg, A.H. v6p0052c1s
Vandenberg, Arthur H. v6p0075c1s
Vandenburgh, O. v1p0917c1s
Vanderberg, A.H. v6p0592c2s
Vanderbilt, A.T. v4p0629c1s
Vanderbilt, C. v6p0199c1s
Vanderbilt, W.K. v6p0306c2s
Vanderburck, E. v1p0952c1s
Vandercook, J. v6p0195c1s
v6p0678c2s
Vanderem, F. v4p0273c1s
Vanderheyden, Helen v6p0619c1s
Vanderhoof, Herbert v6p0097c1s
Vanderlip, F.A. v5p0444c1s
v5p0543c2s v5p0600c1s v5p0601c1s
v5p0619c1s v6p0213c1m v6p0224c1s
v6p0322c1s v6p0560c1s v6p0601c1s
v6p0651c2s v6p0670c1s
Vanderlip, F.A. and Bolce, H.
v5p0314c1s
Vanderpoel, I. v1p0918c1s
Vanderpoel, J.H. v5p0167c2m
Vanderpoel, S.O. v2p0360c2s
Vanderpoole, L. v2p0266c2s
v3p0028c2s v3p0029c1s v3p0123c2s
v3p0308c2s v3p0356c1s v5p0218c1s
Vandersloot, J.S. v1p0323c1s
Vandervelde, E. v6p0057c1s
v6p0600c2s v6p0601c1m
Vandervell, H. v5p0211c1s
Vandervort, J.W. v5p0626c2s
Vandervort, L. v5p0633c1s
v6p0039c1s v6p0043c2s v6p0135c2s
v6p0154c1s v6p0233c2s v6p0443c2s
v6p0688c1s
Vanderweyde, P.H. v1p0467c1s
Vandewalker, N.C. v5p0316c1s
v5p0370c1s
Vandewalker, Nina C. v5p0023c1s
Vandiver, W.D. v6p0230c2s
v6p0323c1s
Vandyke, H., jr. v1p0959c1s
Vandyke, John v1p0682c1s
Vandyne, M.E. v2p0305c2s
v3p0067c2s
Vane, D. v3p0031c1s
v3p0139c2s v3p0240c1s v3p0258c2s
v3p0291c1s v3p0291c2s v3p0410c2s
v3p0475c1s v4p0295c2s v5p0378c1s
Vane, F. v6p0604c2s
Vane, Geraldine v5p0613c1s
Vane, H. v1p0006c2s
Vanham, A.D. v5p0047c2s
Vaniatsky, V. v6p0394c1s
v6p0653c1s
Vaniatsky, V., Prince v6p0650c2s
Vaniatsky, Vladimir, Prince
v6p0165c2s v6p0220c2s v6p0712c2s
Vann, I.G. v6p0366c2s
Vann, L. v5p0383c1s
Vannah, K. v2p0193c1s
Vansant, N. v1p0687c2s
Vansittart, E.C. v4p0313c2s
v5p0012c2s v5p0028c1s v5p0083c2s
v5p0141c1s v5p0166c2s v5p0300c1s
v5p0497c1s v5p0583c2s v6p0302c2s
v6p0330c2m v6p0341c2s v6p0402c2s
v6p0461c1s v6p0483c2s v6p0548c1s
v6p0548c2s v6p0552c2s v6p0568c2m
v6p0619c2s v6p0621c1s v6p0676c2s
Vantvoord, C. v1p0749c2s
Vara, W.B.Le v4p0472c2s
Vardd, A. v1p0098c2s
v1p0367c2s
Vardon, H. v5p0239c1m
Vare, D.B. v5p0365c2s
v6p0311c2s v6p0416c1s v6p0474c1s
Varese v5p0501c1s
Varian, I.J. v1p0721c1s
Varian, W.A. v4p0560c1s
Varien, A. v1p0328c1s
v1p0421c2s v1p0994c1s
Varigny, C.de v3p0027c1s
v3p0040c1s v3p0174c1s v3p0329c2s
v3p0409c1s v4p0625c2s
Varigny, H.de v1p0213c1s
v2p0077c1s v2p0177c2s v3p0333c2s
v4p0212c1s
Varley, C. v1p0663c2s
v1p1250c2s v6p0429c2s

Varley, F.J. v6p0022c1s
Varley, S.A. v1p1290c2s
v3p0423c1s
Varley, W.B. v5p0421c2s
Varney, G.J. v1p0502c1s
v1p0749c1s v2p0001c2s v2p0012c1s
v2p0310c1s v2p0317c2s v4p0009c1s
v4p0175c1s v4p0175c2s v4p0350c1s
v4p0567c2s v5p0029c2s v5p0044c1s
v5p0072c2m v5p0184c2s v5p0041c1s
v5p0288c2s v5p0309c2s v5p0317c2s
v5p0365c1s v5p0406c1s v5p0440c1s
v5p0529c1s v5p0597c2s v6p0228c1s
Varney, G.L. v5p0037c1s
Varney, G.T.
v5p0502c1s
Varney, T. v5p0002c2s
Varnhagen, F.A.De v1p1368c2s
Varnum, J.B. v1p0253c1s
v1p0284c1s v1p1354c1s v1p1388c2s
Varnum, J.M. v3p0447c1s
Varnum, V.B. v1p1077c2s
Varra, O. v1p0382c2s
Vars, N.V. v2p0458c1s
Vas, S. v5p0286c2s
Vaschalde, A. v6p0525c2s
Vaschide et al. v6p0521c1s
Vaschide, N. and Binet, A.
v5p0293c1s
Vaschide, N. and Binet-Valmer, G.
v6p0170c1s
Vaschide, N. and Pieron, H.
v5p0168c1s
Vase, G.L. v1p0161c2s
Vaselot, J.J. Marquet de . v6p0388c1s
Vasquez, E. v4p0142c2s
Vassall, H. v3p0157c2s
Vassall, O.R. v3p0198c1s
Vassault, F.I. v3p0026c2s
v3p0031c2s v3p0050c2s v3p0063c1s
v3p0149c2s v3p0163c1s v3p0296c2s
v3p0412c2s v3p0443c1s v4p0344c2s
v4p0430c2s v4p0525c2s v6p0687c2s
Vassault, F.J. v2p0319c2s
Vassault, L.S. v5p0054c2s
Vater, T.G. v2p0221c2s
Vatralsky, S.K. v4p0544c2s
v6p0259c1s v6p0659c2s
Vattemare, M.H. v1p1363c2s
Vauclain, S.M. v6p0047c2s
v6p0100c2s v6p0190c2s
Vaughan, A.O. v6p0257c1s
v6p0423c1s v6p0579c1s
Vaughan, B. v1p0160c2s
v1p0775c2s v2p0413c1s
Vaughan, C.B. v6p0467c2s
Vaughan, C.J. v1p0239c2s
v1p0256c1s v1p0382c2s v1p0441c1s
v1p0584c2s v1p0599c2s v1p0618c1s
v1p0687c1s v1p1430c2s
Vaughan, C.R. v1p0850c1s
Vaughan, C.W. v6p0358c1s
Vaughan, Capt. v6p0257c1s
Vaughan, Cardinal v4p0170c2s
v4p0480c1s
Vaughan, D.J. v1p1170c1s
Vaughan, D.W. v1p1245c2s
Vaughan, E.T. v1p0021c1s
v1p0594c1s v1p0685c2m v1p0686c2s
v1p0704c1s v1p0912c2s v1p1005c2s
v1p1109c2s
Vaughan, F.W. v1p0161c1s
Vaughan, H. v2p0375c1s
v3p0319c1s v4p0437c1s v5p0178c1s
v6p0598c2s
Vaughan, H. and Meynell, W.
v4p0354c1s
Vaughan, H.B. v4p0436c1s
Vaughan, H.H. v6p0349c1s
Vaughan, H.M. v5p0019c2s
v5p0429c2s v6p0074c2s v6p0169c2s
v6p0330c1s v6p0445c1s v6p0622c2s
Vaughan, Herbert v4p0112c2s
Vaughan, I.C. v4p0554c2s
v5p0065c2s
Vaughan, J. v3p0384c1s
v4p0098c2s v4p0513c2s v4p0604c2s
v5p0189c2s v5p0195c1s v5p0221c2s
v5p0222c2s v5p0245c2m v5p0262c2m
v5p0523c2s v5p0541c2s v5p0580c2s
v5p0587c2s v5p0612c1s v5p0617c1s
v5p0629c1s v6p0242c2s v6p0279c1s
v6p0503c1s v6p0598c2s v6p0684c2s
v6p0686c1s v6p0691c1s
Vaughan, J.L. v1p0629c1s
Vaughan, J.S. v2p0106c2s
v2p0125c2s v2p0149c1s v2p0223c2s
v2p0272c1s v2p0321c1s v2p0407c1s
v2p0455c2s v3p0097c1s v3p0125c2s
v3p0145c2s v3p0148c1m v3p0414c1s
v4p0316c1s v4p0572c2s v4p0584c1s
Vaughan, K. v4p0054c1s
v4p0368c1s v4p0589c2s
Vaughan, M.M. v4p0269c1s
Vaughan, R. v1p0247c2s
v1p0319c2s v1p0355c1s v1p0470c2s
v1p0514c1s v1p0566c2s v1p0654c2s
v1p0739c1s v1p0758c2s v1p0779c1s
v1p0847c2s v1p0954c1s v1p1010c1s
v1p1050c1s v1p1060c2s v1p1133c1s
v1p1203c1m v1p1302c2s
Vaughan, T.W. v4p0376c2s
v5p0129c2s v6p0214c1s v6p0620c2s
v6p0682c1s
Vaughan, T.W. and Stanton, T.W.
v4p0139c1s
Vaughan, V. v1p0056c2s
v1p0335c2s v1p0522c2s v1p0560c2s
v1p1112c2s v4p0369c1s
Vaughan, V.C. v5p0212c2s
v5p0453c1m v5p0456c2s v5p0544c1s
v6p0047c1s v6p0272c2s
Vaughan, V.U. v4p0156c2s
Vaughan, W. v4p0364c2s
Vaughan, W.W. v5p0038c2s
Vaughn, D. v1p1014c1s
v1p1432c1s v1p1432c2s
Vaughn, J. v6p0637c1s
Vaughn, T.W. and Spencer, A.C.
v6p0160c2s
Vaun, L. v5p0476c2s
Vauthier, M. v4p0050c1s
Vautier, J.D. v2p0177c2s
Vaux, C. v1p0046c2s
v1p0607c2s
Vaux, C. et al. v2p0184c2s
Vaux, C.B. v3p0066c2m
v3p0332c1s v3p0367c2s v3p0394c2s
v4p0528c2s v4p0599c1s
Vaux, C.C. v4p0087c2s
Vaux, D. v4p0023c2s
v4p0319c2s
Vaux, F. v1p0267c2s
Vaux, G. v3p0063c2s
v3p0190c1s v3p0268c1s v3p0275c1s
Vaux, G.Le v1p0890c2s
Vaux, G.V.Le v1p1071c2s
Vaux, J.E. v4p0113c1s
Vaux, P. v5p0067c1s
v5p0125c1s v6p0275c1s v6p0397c2s
v6p0445c1m
Vaux, W.S.W. v1p0798c2s
v1p0919c1s
Vawser, R. v1p0362c2s
Vaya, Vay de, and Luskod, Count
v6p0202c2s
Vazaha v3p0263c1s
v4p0348c1m v4p0348c2s
Vazarbek, A. v4p0027c2s
Veatch, A.C. v6p0347c2s
v6p0348c1s v6p0432c2s
Veazey, D. v5p0120c2s
Veazey, W.G. et al. v4p0434c1s
Veazie, G.A., jr. v4p0466c2s
Veblen, J.B. v4p0608c1s
Veblen, O. v6p0251c1m
Veblen, T. v4p0627c2s
v5p0175c1s v5p0175c2m v5p0320c2s
v5p0330c2s v5p0426c1s v5p0636c2s
v6p0404c1s v6p0515c2s v6p0576c1s
v6p0601c2s
Veblen, T.B. v2p0240c2s
v3p0398c2s v4p0088c1s v4p0137c2s
v4p0206c1s v4p0533c2m v4p0618c2m
v5p0028c1s
Veblen, T.V. v4p0419c1s
Veblen, Thorstein v6p0156c2s
Vecchia, G.D. v5p0012c2s
v5p0144c1s
Vecchia, G.della v5p0429c2m
v5p0489c2s
Vecchia, G.Dalla v5p0093c1s
v5p0300c1m v5p0300c2m v5p0361c2s
Vecchia, Giovanni D. v5p0330c2s
Vechten, J.Van v1p0381c1s
v1p0852c1s
Vedal, P. v4p0132c2s
Vedant, M.D. v4p0100c2s
Vedder, D. v1p0948c2s
Vedder, H. v4p0386c1m
Vedder, H.C. v1p0127c2s
v2p0034c2m v2p0235c2s v2p0236c1s
v2p0255c1s v2p0437c2s v3p0013c1s
v3p0064c2m v3p0084c2s v4p0045c2s
v4p0254c2s v4p0543c2s v4p0553c2s
v5p0047c2s v5p0459c1s v5p0616c2s
v6p0125c2s
Vedel, Emile v5p0134c1s
Vedel, P. v4p0165c2s
v4p0272c2s v4p0314c2s v4p0315c1s
Veditz, C.W.A. v5p0537c1s
v5p0537c2s v6p0018c1s
Veeder, M.A. v3p0027c1s
v6p0041c1s
Veeder, V.V. v5p0312c1s
Veeder, Van V. v6p0079c1s
v6p0208c1s v6p0223c2s v6p0264c2s
v6p0370c1s v6p0668c1s
Veel, W. v1p0220c1s
Veen, C.V. v2p0235c2s
Veen, M.van der v5p0269c1s
Veer, L. v1p0480c2s
Veer, L.van der v6p0287c1s
v3p0343c1s
Veer, L.Van der v6p0034c2s
v6p0054c2s v6p0124c2s v6p0169c2s
v6p0174c1s v6p0304c2s v6p0361c1s
v6p0385c1s v6p0435c1s
v6p0700c1s
Veer, L.Vander v6p0287c1s
Vegrier, Gen.de v6p0654c2s
Vegus, H.L. v6p0414c1s
Vehling, E.A. v6p0328c2s
Veiller, B. v6p0311c2s
Veiller, L. v5p0407c2s
v5p0538c1s v5p0572c2m v6p0300c1s
v6p0638c2s
Veit, A. v4p0127c2s
v4p0359c1s v4p0390c1s v4p0442c1s
v5p0472c1s
Veitch, F.P. v6p0222c1s
Veitch, J. v1p0524c2s
v1p0614c1s v1p1000c2s v2p0195c2s
v3p0031c1s v3p0307c2s v3p0381c2s
v4p0508c2s v4p0635c1m
Veitch, S.F.F. v3p0179c1s
Velain, C. v1p1377c1s
v2p0128c1s v2p0230c1s
Velde, M.S.Van de v3p0286c1s
v4p0163c2s v6p0281c2s
Velde, M.van de, Mme v3p0320c1s
Veley, M. v1p0466c2s
v1p0841c1s v2p0171c1s
Velez, M. v1p0911c1s
Vellacott, C.H. v4p0529c1s
v5p0520c2s v6p0343c1s
Velloso, Llas v6p0080c1s
Velschow, F.A. v3p0090c2s
v3p0156c2s
Venable, C.S. v1p1347c1s
v2p0474c1s
Venable, E. v6p0532c2s
v6p0588c1s
Venable, E.P. v3p0275c2s
v5p0103c2s
Venable, F.P. v4p0435c1m
v5p0037c2s v5p0185c2s
Venable, F.P. and Gore, J.W.
v2p0438c2s
Venable, W.H. v2p0086c1s
v2p0320c1s v2p0361c2s v6p0696c2s
Venable, W.H. et al. v5p0229c2s
Venable, W.M. v6p0451c2s
Venables, Canon v4p0491c1s
Venables, E. v1p0757c1s
v1p1004c1s v2p0259c2s v2p0375c1s
v3p0417c1s v4p0037c1s v4p0062c1s
v4p0178c2s v4p0195c2s v4p0214c1s
v4p0333c1s v4p0407c2s v4p0500c1s
v4p0574c1s
Venables, G. v1p1271c2s
v2p0277c1s v2p0322c1s v4p0500c1s
Venables, G.S. v1p0558c1s
v1p0929c1s v2p0063c1s v2p0068c2s
v2p0069c1s
Venables, G.S. and Lushington, H.
v1p0270c1s
Venables, P. v2p0069c2s
Venables, W.H. v3p0327c1s
Venegas, E. v6p0645c1s
Venn, H.W. v6p0042c1s
Venn, J. v1p0216c1s
v1p0621c1s v1p0760c1m v1p0760c2m
v1p0761c1m v1p1228c1s v1p1311c2s
v2p0262c2m v3p0262c2s v3p0451c1s
v4p0040c1s v4p0372c1s
Venn, J. and Galton, F. .. v3p0015c2s
Venn, J. et al. v3p0142c1s
Venner, A. v1p0148c1s
v1p0489c1s v1p0574c2s v1p0893c2s
Venner, G.U. v4p0113c2s
Venning, K. v3p0002c1s
v3p0039c2s v3p0122c1s v3p0163c2s
v3p0406c1s
Venning, R. v3p0015c2s
Venning, W.M. v2p0310c2s
Venton, F. v1p0742c2s
Ventura, L.D. v5p0115c2s
v6p0331c1s v6p0676c2s
Venturi, A. v3p0471c1s
Venturi, E.A. v1p0717c1s
v1p0814c2s v1p1097c1s
Ventzke v1p1265c1s
Venuti, Ceresa v5p0095c2s
Venyukof, M. v1p1137c1s
Vera, A. v1p0582c2s
v1p0623c1m v1p0760c1s v1p1234c2s
Veragua, Duke of v4p0125c2s
Verbeck, W. v6p0246c2s
Verbeek, R.D.M. v2p0244c1s
v2p0462c2s
Vercellone, C. v1p0076c2s
Verdery, M.J. v3p0401c2s
v4p0083c1s
Verdon, R. v1p0468c2s
Verdun, M.P. v2p0157c1s
Vere, A.De v1p0008c2s
v1p0044c2s v1p0253c2s v1p0429c2m
v1p0518c1s v1p0708c1s v1p0709c2s
v1p0754c1s v1p0755c1s
v1p0939c2s
v1p1023c2s
v1p1430c1s
v1p1430c2s
v2p0007c2s
v2p0148c1s
v2p0161c2s
v2p0166c1s
v2p0195c2s
v2p0328c1s

v2p0370c1s v2p0450c2s v2p0479c2s
v3p0057c2s v3p0246c1s v3p0339c1s
v3p0372c2s v3p0436c1s v4p0114c1s
v4p0154c1s v4p0345c2s v4p0354c1s
v4p0402c1s
Vere, A.T.De v1p1189c2s
Vere, E. v4p0110c1s
Vere, G.E.De v3p0221c2s
Vere, M.A.de v1p0774c1s
Vere, M.De v1p0467c2s
Vere, M.S.de v1p0159c2s
Vere, M.S.De v1p0271c1s
v2p0148c1s v2p0305c2s v2p0427c2s
Vere, M.Schele de v1p0110c2s
v1p0136c1s v1p0205c1s v1p0301c1s
v1p0366c2s v1p0376c2s v1p0420c2s
v1p0456c2s v1p0459c2s v1p0460c1s
v1p0472c2s v1p0506c1s v1p0514c1s
v1p0640c2s v1p0645c1s v1p0645c2s
v1p0748c1s v1p0748c2s v1p0777c1s
v1p0810c1s v1p0823c2s v1p0844c1s
v1p0866c1m v1p0870c1s v1p0875c2s
v1p0884c1s v1p0892c1m v1p0936c1s
v1p0936c2s v1p0955c2s v1p0965c2s
v1p0983c2s v1p1014c2s v1p1015c2s
v1p1146c2s v1p1172c2s v1p1354c1s
v1p1374c2s v1p1440c2m
Vere, S.De v1p0935c2s
Vere, S.De, Sir v2p0318c2s
Vere, S.E.De v2p0207c1m
v3p0200c2s v4p0263c1m
Vere, W.C.De v1p0706c2s
v1p0795c2s
Vereker, C.G. v6p0168c2s
Verestchagin, V. v3p0370c2s
v5p0368c2s
Verestchagin, V.V. v3p0394c2s
Verhaegen, P. v6p0057c1s
v6p0165c2s
Verhaeren, E. v4p0235c1s
v4p0355c1s v4p0364c1s v4p0491c1s
v5p0052c2m v5p0221c2s v5p0548c2s
Verhaeren, Emile v5p0373c1s
Verhoeff, F.H. v5p0521c2s
Vericour, De v1p0065c1s
Vericour, L.R.De v1p1107c2s
v1p1292c1s v2p0050c2s v2p0204c1s
v2p0232c2s v2p0450c1s
Vericour, Prof.de v1p0256c2s
v1p0441c2s
Verlaine, P. v4p0182c1s
v4p0470c1s v4p0517c1s
Verlaine, Paul v4p0019c1s
Verlenden, W.L., Mrs. ... v5p0017c1s
Vermilye, A.G. v2p0313c2s
v2p0350c1s v4p0326c1s v4p0343c2s
v4p0400c1s
Vermilye, R.G. v1p0529c1s
Vermorcken, E.M. v4p0202c1s
Verne, E. v3p0279c2s
Verne, J. v1p0007c2s
v1p0492c1s v1p0834c2s v1p0865c2s
v1p0889c2s v2p0038c2s v2p0079c2s
v3p0474c1s
Verne, N. v4p0572c2s
Verneau, R. v1p0937c1s
Vernede, R.E. v5p0565c2s
v6p0089c2s v6p0150c2s v6p0167c2s
v6p0318c2s v6p0379c1s v6p0421c1s
v6p0457c2s
Verner, S.P. v5p0005c2s
v5p0473c2s v6p0005c2s v6p0007c2s
v6p0144c1s v6p0524c1m v6p0711c1s
Verner, W. v3p0022c2s
v3p0045c2s v3p0089c2s v3p0368c2s
v3p0402c2s v4p0236c2s v5p0242c2s
v5p0368c2s v5p0412c2s v5p0439c1s
v5p0602c1s v6p0044c2s v6p0249c1s
v6p0256c1s v6p0265c2s v6p0401c1s
v6p0432c2s v6p0592c1s v6p0694c2s
Vernet, E.R. v1p0717c1s
Verneuil, M.P. v6p0036c1s
v6p0202c1s v6p0470c2s
Verney, E. v5p0174c2s
v5p0179c1s v5p0289c2s v5p0376c1s
v5p0500c1s v6p0017c2s v6p0117c1s
v6p0195c2s v6p0508c2s
Verney, E., Sir v5p0009c1m
v5p0009c2s v5p0361c1s v6p0154c1s
Verney, E.H. v1p1400c2s
Verney, E.P. v2p0012c2s
Verney, Edmund v6p0192c1s
v6p0293c2s
Verney, Edmund, Sir v5p0143c2s
Verney, F. v4p0522c1s
v6p0126c1s v6p0142c2s v6p0384c2s
Verney, F.P. v2p0010c1s
v2p0208c1s v2p0209c2s v3p0161c1s
Verney, F.P., Lady v1p0062c2s
v1p0364c1s v1p1277c1s
Verney, F.W. v2p0217c1s
v3p0434c1s
Verney, H. v1p0164c1s
v1p0195c1s
Verney, H., Sir v4p0182c1s
Verney, Lady v1p0107c1s
v1p0135c1s v1p0175c2s v1p0278c2s
v1p0415c1s v1p0429c2s v1p0431c2s
v1p0553c1s v1p0597c2s v1p0862c1s
v1p0950c2s v1p0968c2s v1p1214c1s
v1p1277c2s v1p1381c1s v2p0008c2s
v2p0030c1s v2p0061c2s v2p0165c1s
v2p0231c2s v2p0247c2s v2p0248c1s
v2p0334c1m v3p0209c2s v3p0325c1s
v3p0369c2s v3p0370c1s
Verney, M.M. v4p0079c2s
v4p0153c1s v4p0181c1s v5p0254c2s
v5p0392c2s v6p0429c2s
Verney, R.F. v6p0327c1s
Vernham, R.E. v5p0065c1s
Vernois, J.von Verdy du .. v4p0377c1s
Vernon, C.W. v4p0189c1s
Vernon, H.C. v5p0084c2s
Vernon, H.M. v5p0198c2s
v5p0607c2s
Vernon, I.R. v1p0340c1s
v1p0359c1s
Vernon, J. v4p0469c2s
Vernon, J.J. v6p0409c2s
Vernon, J.R. v1p0505c2s
v3p0174c2s v3p0200c2s v4p0371c2s
Vernon, K.D. v5p0368c1s
Vernon, L. v5p0539c1s
Vernon, L.T. v6p0613c1s
Vernon, Lord v3p0289c1s
v4p0146c1s v4p0318c1m
Vernon, M. v3p0176c2s
Vernon, M.V. v4p0179c2s
Vernon, P. v4p0570c2s
v5p0043c1s v5p0325c2s
Vernon, S.M. v5p0372c2s
v6p0576c2s
Vernon, W. v6p0538c2s
Vernon-Harcourt, L.F. ... v3p0066c1s
v4p0180c2s v5p0291c1s
Verny, E. v5p0333c2s
Verplanck, F.A. v6p0319c1s
Verplanck, G.C. v1p0099c1s
v1p0169c1s
Verrall, A.W. v3p0434c2s
v4p0021c1s v4p0081c1s v4p0189c2s
v4p0343c1s v4p0358c1s v4p0461c2s
v4p0503c2s v4p0577c2s v5p0022c2s
Verres, J. v2p0269c1s
v2p0358c1s v6p0424c2s
Verrill, A.E. v1p0042c1s
v1p0136c2s v1p0213c1s v1p0301c1m
v1p0301c2s v1p0321c2m v1p0327c2s
v1p0366c1s v1p0381c2s v1p0456c2s
v1p0469c2s v1p0800c2m v1p0859c1s
v1p0927c1s v1p0937c2s v1p1172c2s
v1p1173c1s v1p1189c1s v2p0193c2s
v2p0276c2s v2p0329c1s v2p0393c1s
v2p0410c2s v4p0167c1s v4p0376c2s
v4p0415c1s v5p0003c1s v5p0054c2s
v5p0087c1s v5p0129c1s v5p0208c2s
v5p0211c1s v5p0412c2s v5p0516c2s
Verrill, A.E. and Bush, K.J.
v5p0329c1s
Verrill, A.H. v4p0135c2s
v5p0395c2s
Verschoyle, J. v2p0226c2s
v2p0242c2s v2p0399c2s v3p0017c1s
v3p0298c1s v3p0390c1s v4p0042c1s
v4p0296c1s v4p0483c1s v6p0126c1s
v6p0133c2s
Verschoyle, J. et al. v4p0582c2s
Verschoyle, J.H. v6p0225c1s
Vert, E.J. v5p0574c2s
Vert, O.W.Le v1p0170c1s
Vertue, G. v1p0393c1s
Verwey, A.J. v1p1376c1s
Verworn, M. v4p0441c2s
v5p0099c1s
Very, E.W. v1p1230c1s
Very, F.W. v1p0835c2s
v5p0107c1s v5p0513c2s v6p0152c1s
v6p0245c2s v6p0458c2s
v6p0613c2s
Very, F.W. and Langley, S.P.
v3p0250c2s v3p0287c1s
Very, J. v1p0241c1s
v1p1021c2s
Vesci, Lord De et al. v1p0657c1s
Vesci, Viscount de v3p0221c2s
Vesci, Viscount de (J.R.W.V.)
v5p0246c1s
Vesselovsky, A. v1p0721c2s
Vest, G.G. v3p0114c2s
v4p0563c2s v5p0061c2s v5p0443c2s
Vest, G.G. and Dolph, J.N.
v4p0129c1s
Vester, A.L. v5p0320c2s
Veteran v3p0397c1s
Veth, Jan v6p0330c2s
Vethake, H. v1p0103c1s
v1p0430c2s v1p1027c2s
Vetter, T. v2p0096c2s
v2p0381c1s
Viajero, L. v5p0171c2s
v5p0381c1s v5p0499c1s v5p0563c2s
v5p0590c2s v6p0661c2s
Viallate, A. v6p0335c1s
Viardot, L. v1p0041c2s
Viaud, J. v4p0335c1s
v5p0153c2s
Vibart, E. v5p0286c1s
Vibert, J.G. v4p0235c1s
v4p0374c2s v4p0404c2s v4p0430c2s
Vicars, E. v4p0448c2s
Vicars, E.R. v4p0344c1s
Vicars, F. v6p0506c1s
Vicars, G.R. v4p0088c2s
v4p0371c1s v4p0434c1s v4p0449c2s
v4p0459c2s v4p0460c1m v4p0515c1s
v4p0633c1s v5p0122c2s v5p0143c1s
v5p0467c1s
Vicars, G.Rayleigh v4p0140c1s
Viccars, S.J. v4p0325c2s
v4p0393c2s
Vicholkovska, A. v6p0490c1s
Vick, E.C. v6p0256c1s
Vickars-Gaskell, G. v2p0387c2s
v3p0194c1s
Vickers, E.H. v6p0186c2s
v6p0335c1s v6p0335c2s v6p0336c1s
v6p0336c2s v6p0337c1s
Vickers, J. v1p1331c2s
Vickers, L. v1p0173c2s
Vickers, R.H. v1p0176c2s
Vickers, S. v2p0242c2s
Vickers, T. v1p0529c2s
v1p0777c1s v4p0257c1s
Vickers, T.E. v1p1251c1s
Vickery, J.H. v5p0158c1s
v5p0293c2s v5p0437c2m
Vickroy, T.R. v1p1002c1s
Victim, A. v6p0190c2s
Victor, F.F. v1p0004c1s
v1p0280c1m v1p0397c2s v1p0637c2s
v1p0779c2s v1p0832c1s v1p0851c2s
v1p0878c1s v1p0908c1s v1p0929c1s
v1p0940c1s v1p0947c1m v1p1123c1s
v1p1148c1s v1p1399c2s v1p1403c2s
v2p0300c2s v2p0323c1s v4p0083c2s
v4p0132c2s v4p0420c2s v4p0629c2s
Victor, F.F., Mrs. v1p0609c1s
v1p0942c1s v6p0469c2s
Victor, Frances F. v6p0049c2s
v6p0092c2s
Victor, H. v3p0109c2s
v3p0468c2s
Victor, O.J. v5p0461c2s
Victor, W. v4p0320c2s
Victorin, A. v4p0138c1s
Vidal, R.S. v1p0713c2s
v1p0946c1s v1p1325c1s
Vidari, Ercole v5p0300c1s
Vidocq, M. v1p1280c2s
Vieille and Berthelot v2p0150c2s
Vieira, J.A. v2p0254c2s
Viele, E.L. v1p0917c1s
v2p0313c2s v2p0349c2s v5p0089c2s
Viele, F.L. v1p0750c2s
Viele, H.K. v6p0043c1s
v6p0091c2s v6p0101c1s v6p0102c2s
v6p0166c2s v6p0408c2s v6p0425c1s
v6p0463c2s
Viereck, G.S. v6p0698c2s
Viereck, L. v5p0232c1s
Vigfusson, G. v2p0214c1s
v2p0319c2s v3p0265c2s v3p0307c1s
Vigfusson, G. and Gaidoz, H.
v2p0319c2s
Viggars, F. v4p0306c2s
Vigil v6p0326c1s
Vignaud, H. v6p0140c1s
Vignoles, O.J. v3p0169c1s
v4p0148c1s v4p0549c2s
Vigny, De v1p0728c2s
Vigor, H.D. and Yule, G.U.
v6p0585c2s
Vijaya-Raghavan, T. v3p0196c2s
v3p0212c1s v3p0268c2s
Viktorov, R.S. v4p0315c2s
Vilain, J. v1p0041c2s
Vilaro, J. v5p0252c2s
Vilas, W.F. v3p0039c1s
v3p0466c1s v4p0525c2s
Vilas, Wm.F. et al. v4p0524c2s
Vilet, M. v1p0561c2s
Viljoen, H.D. v5p0588c2s
Vilks, S. v2p0462c2s
Villa, G. v6p0293c1s
v6p0521c1s
Villa-Maior, Visc.de v1p1415c2s
Villamil, M.P. v3p0230c1s
v3p0364c2s v3p0403c1s v4p0013c2s
v4p0302c2m
Villard, H. v1p0059c2s
v1p0093c1s v1p0138c2s v1p0423c2s
v1p0988c2s v1p1215c1s v1p1349c2m
v6p0069c1s v6p0377c2s
Villard, H. and Farnam, H.W.
v4p0563c1s
Villard, O.G. v4p0172c1s
v4p0364c1s v5p0011c2s v5p0044c1s
v5p0092c2s v5p0129c2s v5p0148c1s
v5p0231c1s v5p0363c2s v5p0403c1s
v5p0444c1s v5p0445c1s v5p0513c1s
v5p0550c1s v5p0599c1m v5p0599c2s
v5p0626c2s v6p0030c2s v6p0031c1s
v6p0031c2m v6p0039c1s v6p0047c2s
v6p0054c1s v6p0058c2m v6p0066c1s
v6p0069c1s v6p0084c2s v6p0089c2s
v6p0095c1s v6p0099c2s v6p0117c2s
v6p0118c2s v6p0119c1s v6p0119c2s
v6p0120c1s v6p0129c1s v6p0132c2s
v6p0133c1s v6p0145c1s v6p0146c2s
v6p0147c1s v6p0195c2s v6p0196c2s

v6p0197c1s v6p0224c1s v6p0224c2s
v6p0231c2s v6p0232c1m v6p0234c2s
v6p0251c2s v6p0252c1s v6p0252c2s
v6p0253c2m v6p0254c1m v6p0277c2s
v6p0282c1s v6p0299c1s v6p0301c2s
v6p0310c1s v6p0336c2s v6p0346c2s
v6p0354c2s v6p0357c1s v6p0367c1s
v6p0378c2s v6p0391c1s v6p0391c2s
v6p0398c1s v6p0416c1s v6p0417c1s
v6p0429c2s v6p0431c1s v6p0447c1m
v6p0447c2m v6p0448c1m v6p0453c1s
v6p0454c1s v6p0464c1s v6p0484c1s
v6p0485c1s v6p0487c2s v6p0488c1s
v6p0492c1s v6p0493c1s v6p0493c2s
v6p0494c1m v6p0503c1s v6p0505c2s
v6p0519c1m v6p0543c2s v6p0551c1m
v6p0555c2s v6p0556c1s v6p0557c2m
v6p0560c1s v6p0561c1s v6p0567c1s
v6p0583c2s v6p0591c1s v6p0601c1s
v6p0605c1m v6p0606c1s v6p0623c1s
v6p0625c1s v6p0632c1s v6p0637c2s
v6p0650c1m v6p0666c1m v6p0666c2s
v6p0668c2m v6p0669c1m v6p0671c2s
v6p0681c1s v6p0685c1s v6p0694c2s
v6p0704c1s v6p0710c1m
Villard, O.G. and Williams, H.S.
v6p0679c2s
Villari, G. v4p0607c1s
Villari, L. v1p0098c2s
v1p0669c1s v1p0737c2s v1p1054c2s
v1p1153c2s v2p0039c2s v2p0143c2s
v2p0160c2s v2p0184c1s v2p0230c2s
v2p0231c2s v2p0318c1s v2p0376c2s
v2p0377c2s v2p0385c2s v2p0429c1s
v3p0024c1s v3p0067c2s v3p0102c2s
v3p0290c2s v3p0366c2s v3p0373c1s
v3p0374c2s v3p0446c2s v4p0045c2s
v4p0102c2s v4p0213c1s v4p0490c2m
v4p0576c2s v5p0293c2s v5p0300c2s
v5p0634c2s v6p0042c2s v6p0105c1s
v6p0299c2s v6p0331c2s v6p0392c1s
v6p0392c2s v6p0558c1s v6p0559c1s
v6p0560c1s
Villari, L. and Creighton, M.
v2p0203c1s
Villari, Linda v2p0401c2s
v6p0557c2s
Villari, Mad. v1p0147c1s
v1p1424c2s
Villari, P. v2p0231c2s
v4p0294c2s v5p0187c2s v5p0300c2s
Villaro, J. v5p0514c2s
Villars, P. v3p0138c1s
v3p0254c2s v3p0256c1s v3p0316c1s
v4p0426c1s v6p0385c1s
Villemain, M. v1p0836c2s
Villemarque, H. v1p0210c2s
Villiers, A. v5p0251c1s
Villiers, Brougham v6p0355c2s
Villiers, F. v3p0454c1s
v4p0002c1s v4p0100c2s v4p0397c1s
v4p0453c1s v5p0011c2s v5p0181c1s
v5p0520c2s v5p0539c2s v5p0540c1m
v5p0594c2m v5p0595c1s
Villiers, H.M. v1p0532c1s
v1p0764c1s v1p1384c2s
Villiers, J.H.de v2p0038c1s
Villiers, M.de v4p0006c2s
v5p0006c2s v5p0416c1s
Villiers, P. v2p0302c1s
v2p0458c2s
Villiers de L'Isle Adam .. v4p0016c2s
v4p0343c1s v4p0371c2s
v4p0579c2s
v5p0487c1s
Vilmorin, M.L.de v4p0416c2s
v5p0451c2s v5p0452c1s
Vimbert, P.S. v5p0497c2s
Vince, C. v1p0128c1s
v1p0683c2s
Vince, H.S. v1p0086c2s
v1p0245c2s v4p0032c2s
Vincent, B. v5p0271c1s
Vincent, C. v2p0190c2s
v2p0336c2s v4p0525c2s v6p0148c1s
Vincent, C.E.H. v2p0355c1s
v3p0336c1s v4p0275c1s v4p0563c1s
Vincent, C.E.H. and Gray, A.
v3p0274c2s
Vincent, C.E.Howard v4p0236c1s
Vincent, C.W. v1p0665c1s
v1p1239c1s v3p0132c2s v3p0405c1s
Vincent, D'A.G. v3p0182c1s
v3p0390c2s v3p0432c2s v4p0238c1s
Vincent, E. v3p0453c1s
v4p0341c1s
Vincent, E. and Rayleigh, Baron
v3p0256c2s
Vincent, E.H. v2p0185c2s
Vincent, F. v3p0325c1s
v4p0065c2s v4p0348c2s
Vincent, F., jr. v1p0068c1s
v1p0111c2s
Vincent, Frank v4p0041c2s
v4p0501c1m
Vincent, G.C. v6p0542c2s
Vincent, G.E. v3p0473c2s
v4p0501c1s v4p0534c2s v4p0535c1s
v4p0539c2s v5p0103c1s v5p0231c2s
v5p0315c1s v6p0111c1s v6p0137c1s
v6p0189c2s v6p0195c1s v6p0278c2s
v6p0288c2s v6p0346c2s v6p0357c1s
v6p0373c2s v6p0428c2s v6p0600c1s
v6p0602c1m v6p0610c1s v6p0625c1s
v6p0671c2s v6p0673c1s
Vincent, H. v3p0180c1s
v4p0020c1s v4p0140c1s v4p0236c2s
v4p0276c1s v5p0588c1s v5p0614c2s
v6p0207c1s v6p0266c1s v6p0556c1s
Vincent, H.P. v2p0110c1s
Vincent, J. v1p1102c1s
Vincent, J.B. v6p0158c2s
Vincent, J.E. v6p0641c1s
v6p0682c1s v6p0692c1s
Vincent, J.H. v1p1270c1s
v2p0131c1s v3p0075c1m v3p0129c1s
v3p0130c1s v3p0225c2s v4p0072c2s
v4p0294c2s v4p0300c2s v4p0367c2s
v4p0372c2s v4p0406c1s v4p0415c2s
v4p0435c2s v5p0121c2s v5p0242c1s
v5p0376c1s v5p0419c2s v5p0577c1s
v6p0111c1s v6p0280c2s v6p0626c2s
v6p0671c1s
Vincent, J.H. et al. v4p0503c2s
v5p0060c2s
Vincent, J.M. v3p0097c2s
v3p0418c1s v3p0449c2s v4p0050c1s
v4p0377c1s v4p0560c1s v4p0626c1s
v6p0249c2s v6p0436c1s v6p0461c2s
v6p0629c2m
Vincent, J.W. v5p0602c2s
Vincent, L.H. v4p0058c1s
v4p0309c1s v5p0196c2s v5p0227c1s
v5p0491c1s v5p0524c2s v6p0684c2s
Vincent, M.R. v1p0127c1s
v1p1084c1s v2p0291c1s v2p0405c2s
v3p0110c1s v4p0053c2s v4p0054c1s
v4p0056c2s v5p0060c1s
Vincent, M.R. and Stanton, R.L.
v2p0152c1s
Vincent, Mme. v4p0213c1s
Vincent, S.H. v6p0677c2s
Vincotte, M. v1p0267c1s
Vindex v5p0173c2s
Vindex Justitiae v5p0007c1s
Vine, C.H. v6p0179c2s
Vine, S. v4p0339c1s
Vine, S., Sir v4p0276c1s
Vines, B. v1p0788c1s
Vines, J.H. v6p0573c1s
v6p0578c2s
Vines, S.H. v1p0237c2m
v1p0891c1s v2p0323c1s v3p0194c2s
v5p0371c2s v5p0454c1s v6p0685c2s
Vingut, G.De, Mrs. v1p1354c2s
Vining, P. v3p0237c1s
Vinkbooms, C.Van v1p0026c1s
v1p0523c2s
Vinne, T.L.De v1p0563c2s
v1p0798c2s v1p1427c2s v2p0101c2s
v3p0072c1s v3p0334c1s v3p0431c1s
v4p0459c2s v4p0589c1s v5p0253c1s
v5p0387c2s v5p0429c2s v5p0466c2m
Vinne, T.L.De and Whittaker, J.V.
v1p0743c1s
Vinogradoff, P. v2p0456c1s
v4p0071c1s v4p0204c2s v4p0318c1s
v4p0354c1s v5p0009c2s v6p0303c2s
v6p0395c1s v6p0395c2s v6p0527c2s
v6p0556c1s v6p0556c2s v6p0558c1s
v6p0625c1s
Vinson, J. v2p0217c2s
Vinton, A.D. v2p0054c1s
v2p0154c2s v3p0141c2s v3p0253c2s
v3p0287c2s v3p0387c1s v3p0412c2s
Vinton, A.H. v1p0679c2s
v1p1395c2s
Vinton, F. v1p0121c2s
v1p0148c2s v1p0641c1s v1p0677c2s
v1p0744c1s v1p0771c2s v1p0979c1s
v1p1033c1s v1p1051c1s v1p1411c2s
v2p0025c2s v2p0255c2s v2p0417c1s
v2p0447c2s v2p0457c1s
Vinton, J. v1p0975c2s
Vinton, J.A. v1p0006c1s
v1p0297c2s v1p0564c1s v1p0750c2s
v1p0946c2s
Vinton, S.F. v1p0929c1s
Vintras, L. v5p0486c2s
v5p0523c2s
Violette, M. v1p0200c1s
v1p1427c1s
Violle, J. v1p0580c1s
Viollet-le-Duc v3p0185c2s
v3p0202c2s v4p0023c2s
Viollet-le-Duc, M. v1p0564c1s
Viollier, J. v1p1276c2s
Virchow, R. v1p0979c1s
v1p1162c1s v2p0001c2s v3p0292c2s
v3p0378c2s v4p0020c1s v4p0430c2s
v5p0445c1s v6p0409c1s v6p0576c2s
Virstow, H. v5p0348c1s
Virtue, G.O. v4p0120c2s
v4p0230c2s v4p0372c1s v5p0557c1s
v6p0148c2s
Virtue, J. v1p0540c2s
Virtue, Mgr. v1p0952c2s
v1p1092c2s
Vis, C.W.De v3p0283c2s
Vischer, Hans v6p0457c1s
Vischer, W.L. v3p0460c1s
Visetti, A. v6p0262c2s
Visher, J. v2p0043c1s
v4p0100c1s v4p0136c2s v4p0438c2s
v4p0574c2s
Visilini, M.P. v1p0706c1s
v1p1119c1s
Visscher, W.L. v3p0070c2s
v3p0103c2s v3p0168c1s v3p0197c2s
v3p0344c2s v3p0372c1s v3p0376c2s
v3p0379c1s v3p0396c1s v3p0397c1s
v3p0419c1s v3p0439c2s v4p0011c2s
v4p0017c2s v4p0032c2s v4p0085c1s
Visser, De v4p0354c2s
Vitelleschi, F.N. v2p0231c1s
v2p0231c2s
Vitet, L. v1p0481c2s
Vitringa, C. v1p0178c2s
Vitry, P. v6p0579c2s
Vittum, E.M. v3p0431c2s
Vitu, A. v1p1308c2s
v2p0164c2s
Vivanti, A. v6p0101c1s
Vivaria, K. v5p0637c2s
Vivian, C.A. v5p0644c2s
Vivian, E. v6p0090c1s
v6p0275c2s v6p0584c1s
Vivian, H. v4p0132c2m
v4p0501c1m v4p0516c1s v5p0002c1s
v5p0381c2s v5p0390c2s v5p0594c1s
v6p0048c1s v6p0127c1s v6p0295c1s
v6p0300c1s v6p0356c2s v6p0392c1s
v6p0584c2s v6p0660c2s
Vivian, H. and Williams, A.
v4p0314c1s v5p0136c1s
Vivian, H.H. v4p0132c2s
Vivian, Herbert v4p0296c1s
v4p0498c2s v5p0077c2s v6p0086c1s
v6p0107c2s v6p0248c2s
Vivian, T.J. v1p0235c1s
v1p1016c2s
Vivian, W. v3p0340c1s
v6p0570c1s
Vizetelly, E. v1p0143c1s
v4p0027c2s v4p0267c1s v5p0142c2s
Vizetelly, E.A. v1p0969c2s
v3p0319c1s v4p0637c1s
Vizetelly, E.H. v1p0021c2s
v1p0022c1m v1p0049c2s
Vizetelly, F.H. v5p0068c1s
Vizetelly, H. v1p0467c2s
Vlachos, N.P. v6p0519c2s
v6p0604c1s
Vleck, F.Van v4p0385c1s
Vleet, T.S.Van v4p0395c1s
Voast, J.Van, Mrs. v4p0565c2m
Vocke, W. and Carus, P. .. v5p0231c1s
Voe, A.De v5p0570c2s
Voe, T.F.De v1p0167c2s
v1p0916c1s v1p1254c2s v1p1341c1s
v6p0618c1s
Voelcker, A. v1p0839c1s
v2p0288c2s v3p0396c2s v3p0414c1s
Voelcker, J.A. v4p0278c1s
Voeux, G.W.Des v4p0038c1s
v4p0415c1s
Voeux, W.Des v5p0173c2s
v6p0654c1s
Voeux, Wm.Des v5p0408c2s
Vogdes, I. v1p1345c2s
Vogdez, A.W. v1p0207c2s
Vogel, A. v1p0224c1s
v1p0744c2s v1p1014c2s v2p0093c2s
v2p0159c2s
Vogel, E. v2p0027c2s
Vogel, F.W. v1p0107c1s
Vogel, H. v1p0237c1s
v1p0282c1s v1p1003c2s v1p1004c1s
Vogel, H.C. v4p0037c2m
v4p0346c1s v4p0540c2s v4p0545c2s
Vogel, J. v1p0079c1s
v1p0163c2s v1p0545c1s v1p0626c1s
v1p0918c2m v1p0956c1s v4p0236c2s
v4p0237c1s v4p0286c2s v5p0039c1s
v5p0611c1s
Vogel, J., Sir v1p0544c1s
v1p0919c1s v1p1290c1s v2p0311c1s
v3p0181c1s v4p0038c1s v4p0401c2s
v4p0550c1s
Vogel, Julius v4p0303c2s
Vogeles, A.W. v1p0027c1s
Vogelstein, H. v4p0052c2s
v4p0519c2s
Voges, E. v3p0015c1s
Vogler, W.H. v3p0287c2s
Vogt, C. v1p0045c2s
v1p0794c2s v1p1032c2s v1p1213c2s
v3p0061c2s v3p0252c1s v4p0612c2s
Vogt, J.G. v4p0361c1s
Vogue, E.M.de v3p0071c1s
v3p0133c2s v3p0273c2s v3p0320c1s
v3p0370c2s v4p0212c1s v4p0317c2s
v4p0397c2s v5p0217c2s v5p0330c2m
v5p0430c2s v6p0677c2s
Voight, Dr. v1p1092c2s
Voigt, A.G. v4p0036c2s
v4p0328c2s v4p0462c1s v5p0625c2s
Voigt, C.A. v4p0121c1s
v4p0211c1s v4p0224c1s v4p0455c2s
v4p0484c2s

Voigt, J. v1p0557c2s
Voigt, J.C. v5p0398c2s v5p0586c2s
Voisines, A.G.Des v5p0349c1s
Voisins, D'Aubuisson v1p1390c2s
Voit, C. v1p0465c1s v1p0465c2s
Voit, Prof. v1p0288c1s v1p0352c1s v1p0465c2s
Vola, R.E. v2p0387c1s
Volck, A.J. v1p0874c2s
Volckening, G.J. and Luquer, L.M. v4p0535c2s
Volk, D. v5p0051c1s
Volk, L.W. v2p0259c1s
Volkhovsky, F. v3p0370c1s v3p0391c2s v4p0496c1s v4p0522c2s v5p0501c2s v6p0556c1s v6p0557c2s
Volkmar, W.J. v5p0217c1m
Volkonski, Princess v5p0421c1s
Vollers, K. v5p0181c2s v5p0278c1s
Vollert, W. v6p0698c2s
Vollmar, G.von v6p0599c2s
Vollmer, P. v4p0054c2s v6p0215c2s
Volpicelli, P. v1p0399c1s v1p1074c2s v1p1404c2s
Volta, R.Dalla v4p0294c1s
Voltaire, R.M.A. v1p1372c2s
Volz, R. v1p1347c2s
Voorhees, D.W. v3p0393c1s
Voorhees, E.B. v6p0008c1s v6p0496c1s
Voorhees, T. v3p0163c1s v4p0470c2s v4p0553c1s
Voorsanger, J. v4p0301c1s
Vore, E. v6p0074c2s
Vore, E.A. v5p0078c1s v5p0264c2s
Vore, Elizabeth v5p0620c1s v6p0124c1s
Vorse, A.W. v5p0022c1s v5p0179c2s v5p0357c1s v5p0454c2s v5p0470c1s v6p0486c1s
Vorse, Albert W. v6p0029c1s
Vorse, M.H. v6p0045c2s
Vorse, Mary H. v6p0080c2s v6p0103c2s v6p0244c2s v6p0285c1s v6p0310c2s v6p0400c2s v6p0420c1s v6p0549c1s
Vorse, Mary Heaton v6p0179c1s
Vorst, B.McG.van v5p0488c2s
Vorst, B.Van v5p0054c2s v5p0318c2s v5p0608c1s v6p0024c1s v6p0704c2s v6p0705c2m
Vorst, B.Van and Vorst, M.Van. v6p0704c2s
Vorst, J.Van, Mrs. v6p0085c2s v6p0479c2s v6p0703c1s
Vorst, M.L.van v5p0640c1s
Vorst, M.L.Van v5p0153c2s v5p0227c1s v5p0357c2s v5p0385c1s v5p0559c1s
Vorst, M.Van v5p0191c1s v5p0435c2s v5p0473c1s v5p0576c1s v5p0578c2s v6p0020c1s v6p0178c2s v6p0301c2s v6p0308c1s v6p0358c1s
Vorst, M.Van and Vorst, B.Van. v6p0704c2s
Vorst, Marie Van v5p0169c2s v5p0492c1s v5p0552c1s v6p0014c1s v6p0087c2m v6p0168c2s v6p0405c2s v6p0420c1s v6p0422c2s v6p0426c1s v6p0516c2s v6p0590c1s v6p0645c2s v6p0683c1s v6p0695c1s v6p0700c2s
Vortriede, Helen A. and Heywood, Alice v6p0598c1s
Vos, G. v4p0109c2s v4p0366c1s v4p0573c1s v5p0058c1m v5p0058c2s v5p0307c2s v5p0436c2s v5p0576c2s v6p0259c1s v6p0342c1s
Vosburg, J.H. v1p0113c2s v1p0179c1s v1p1072c1s v1p1129c2s v1p1327c1s
Vosburgh, J.H. v1p1080c1s
Vosburgh, W.S. v5p0271c1s v5p0304c2s v6p0297c1s
Vose, G.L. v1p0524c1m v1p0541c1s v1p1347c2s v2p0141c1s v2p0359c1s v2p0364c1s
Vose, J.E. v2p0042c2s v2p0426c1s v3p0086c1s
Vose, J.G. v1p0853c2s v2p0235c1s v3p0011c1s
Vose, J.T. v4p0079c1s
Vose, R.H. v5p0591c2s
Voss, R. v5p0042c2s
Vossion, L. v4p0079c2s v4p0393c1s
Vostock, D. v6p0354c1s
Vostock, Dalni v6p0333c2s
Vostrovsky, C. v4p0274c2s v5p0479c2s v5p0562c2s v6p0092c1s
Vostrovsky, Clara v5p0451c2s v5p0511c1s
Votaw, C.W. v3p0080c2s v3p0148c2s v4p0057c2s v4p0218c2s v5p0024c1s v5p0057c1s v5p0059c2s v5p0571c2m v6p0063c1s v6p0340c1s v6p0341c1s v6p0341c2s v6p0473c2s v6p0488c1s v6p0537c2s v6p0538c1s
Votaw, C.W. and Bradley, C.F. v5p0058c2s
Voth, H.R. v5p0363c1s
Vouzay, M. v5p0074c2s
Voxall, J.H. and Ainslie, W.L. v5p0077c2s
Voynich, W. v6p0074c2s
Voysey, C. v6p0537c2s
Voysey, C. and Clifford, W. v3p0356c2s v3p0428c1s
Voysey, C. and Stephenson, T. v1p1042c1s
Voysey, C.F.A. v5p0026c1m v5p0273c1s
Vozoff, Ivan v5p0569c1s
Vredenburg, E. v3p0279c2s
Vreeland, H.H. v5p0391c2s v6p0356c1s v6p0488c1s
Vregille, P.De v6p0626c1s
Vries, H.De v2p0344c1s v6p0088c1m v6p0214c2s v6p0608c2m
Vries, Hugo de v6p0674c2s
Vries, J.C.E.de v5p0172c1s
Vring, C. v5p0479c2s
Vroom, G.D.W. v6p0088c2s
Vroom, J. v5p0205c1s
Vrooman, A.L. v5p0520c2s
Vrooman, C. v5p0158c1s
Vrooman, C.S. v6p0479c1s v6p0584c2s
Vrooman, Carl S. v6p0332c1s v6p0629c2s
Vrooman, C. v4p0150c1s
Vrooman, F. v6p0373c2s
Vrooman, F.B. v4p0053c2s v4p0102c2s v4p0252c1s v4p0311c1s v4p0451c2s v4p0546c1s
Vrooman, Frank v6p0664c2s v6p0665c2s
Vrooman, G. v4p0159c1s v4p0354c1s
Vrooman, H. v5p0136c1s v5p0260c2s v5p0546c2s v6p0148c2m
Vrooman, H.C. v4p0096c2s v4p0139c2s v4p0322c2s
Vrooman, H.C. and Will, T.E. v4p0610c1s
Vrooman, J.S. v6p0595c1s v6p0617c2s
Vrooman, W. v4p0111c2s v4p0476c2s
Vrooman, W. et al. v4p0427c2s
Vross, F.A. v2p0002c2s
Vulpius, W. v5p0574c2s v5p0624c2s
Vye, B. v4p0034c2s v4p0052c2s v4p0306c2s v4p0537c2s
Vye, B. and Phelps, S. ... v5p0229c2s
Vyle, S. v5p0527c2s
Vynne, E.S. v3p0173c1s
Vynne, N. v3p0047c2s v3p0168c2s v3p0200c1s v3p0315c2s v4p0241c1s v4p0361c2s v4p0555c2s v4p0589c2s
Vyse, G.W. v3p0003c2s
Vyvian, C. v4p0140c2s v4p0405c2s

W., A.R. v5p0570c1s
W., F.G. v4p0604c2s
W., T.P. v5p0056c2s
    v5p0638c1s
Waage, C.M. v3p0110c1s
    v3p0228c2s v3p0323c2s v6p0041c2s
    v6p0305c2s v6p0644c2s
Waagen, G.F. v1p0062c2s
    v1p1083c1s v1p1139c1s
Wabeman, G. v1p0781c1s
Wace, A.J.B. v6p0286c2s
    v6p0487c1s v6p0661c1s
Wace, H. v1p0057c1s
    v1p0071c2s v1p0110c1s v1p0427c1s
    v1p0777c1s v1p0859c2s v1p1090c1s
    v1p1100c1s v2p0044c1s v2p0044c2s
    v2p0414c1s v5p0117c1s
Wace, H. et al. v3p0005c2s
Wachs, O. v3p0160c2s
    v4p0173c1s v5p0410c2s
Wachsmuth, C. v1p0317c2s
Wachsmuth, C. and Niles, W.H.
    v1p0508c2s
Wachsmuth, C. and Springer, F.
    v1p0317c2s
Wack, A.W. v4p0493c1s
Wack, H.W. v4p0527c1s
    v5p0464c2s
Waddell, A.M. v2p0013c2s
    v4p0503c2s
Waddell, J. v6p0624c1s
    v6p0665c2s
Waddell, J.A.L. v1p1080c2s
    v2p0056c1s
Waddell, J.D. v2p0040c1s
Waddell, L.A. v4p0317c2m
    v4p0576c2s v5p0197c2s v6p0369c2s
Waddell, P.H. v1p0013c1s
Waddilove, R.D. v1p0464c2s
    v1p1109c1s v1p1171c1s
Waddington, C. v1p0789c2s
Waddington, H. v1p0333c1s
Waddington, J. v3p0233c1s
Waddington, M.K. v6p0011c2s
    v6p0205c2s
Waddington, Mary K. v6p0123c2s
    v6p0331c1s v6p0459c1s v6p0674c1s
Waddington, P. v4p0480c2s
Waddington, R. v4p0169c2s
    v4p0506c2s
Waddington, S. v1p0266c2s
    v1p0423c2s v1p0950c1s v1p1220c2s
    v1p1417c2s v2p0479c2s v3p0400c1s
    v5p0358c1s
Waddington, S. and Rolph, J.F.
    v2p0429c1s
Waddington, W.H. v3p0161c1s
    v3p0255c1s
Waddle, A.H. v5p0580c1s
Waddle, C.C. v3p0009c2s
    v3p0423c2s
Waddle, E. v3p0025c2s
    v3p0037c1s
Waddle, W., jr v3p0310c2s
Waddy, C. v6p0046c1s
    v1p0159c2s v1p0244c2s v1p0270c2s
    v1p0455c1m v1p0562c2m v1p0563c1s
    v1p0565c2s v1p0769c1s v1p1213c2s
    v1p1239c2m
Waddy, R. v1p0309c2s
Waddy, S.D. v1p1201c1s
Wade, B.E. v6p0618c2s
Wade, D.S. v1p1296c1s
Wade, E.I. v4p0092c1s
Wade, Elizabeth F. v6p0235c2s
Wade, F.C. v3p0353c1s
    v6p0353c1s v6p0596c1s
Wade, G.A. v5p0125c2s
    v5p0227c2s v5p0230c1s v5p0243c2s
    v5p0296c1s v5p0345c1s v5p0409c2s
    v5p0584c1s v6p0522c2s v6p0693c2s
Wade, Geo.A. v6p0305c1s
Wade, H. v6p0044c2s
Wade, H.D. v6p0682c1s
Wade, H.T. v4p0419c1s
    v6p0139c2s
Wade, J.A. v1p0332c1s
    v1p0349c2s v1p0800c2s
Wade, J.H. v6p0208c1s
Wade, J.M. v5p0379c1s
Wade, J.P. v6p0544c1s
Wade, J.R. v5p0124c2s
Wade, M.S. v5p0318c1s
    v6p0082c2s v6p0589c2s
Wade, S. v4p0154c1s
Wade, T., Sir v3p0078c2s
Wade, T., Sir and Temple, R., Sir
    v2p0079c2s
Wade, T.F. v4p0106c1s
Wade, W. v4p0528c2s
Wade, W.C. v2p0073c2s
Wade, W.F. v5p0234c1s
Wade, W.P. v2p0317c1s
Wadhams, A.V. v3p0443c2s
    v4p0595c1s
Wadleigh, B. v2p0452c2s
Wadleigh, F.E. v4p0469c2s
    v1p0609c1s v1p0627c1s v1p0906c1s
    v1p1389c1s v2p0185c1s v3p0178c1s
    v3p0283c2s

Wadleigh, G. v2p0311c1s
    v2p0405c1s
Wadlin, G.H. and North, S.N.D.
    v5p0365c1s
Wadlin, H.G. v3p0270c2s
    v4p0314c2s v4p0559c2s v5p0360c2s
    v6p0223c1s v6p0374c1s
Wadsworth, D. v1p0052c1s
Wadsworth, F.L.O. v4p0034c1s
    v4p0092c2s v4p0114c2s v4p0159c2s
    v4p0186c1s v4p0283c1s v4p0540c2m
    v4p0552c1s v5p0260c1s v5p0350c2s
    v5p0448c1m v5p0571c2m v6p0478c2s
Wadsworth, H.A. v1p1356c1s
Wadsworth, H.R. v5p0385c2s
Wadsworth, J. v1p0847c2s
Wadsworth, M.E. v2p0127c1s
    v2p0174c2s v2p0290c1s v2p0311c1s
    v2p0319c2s v2p0374c2s v2p0383c2s
    v3p0402c2s
Wadsworth, O.A. v1p0076c2s
    v1p0805c2s v1p0951c2s
Wadsworth, R. v6p0132c2s
Wadsworth, R.C.W. v6p0651c1s
Wadsworth, W.R. v5p0421c2s
Wady, C.S. v4p0161c2s
    v5p0516c1s v5p0642c1s
Waern, C. v4p0417c2s
    v4p0029c2s v4p0276c1s v4p0317c1s
    v4p0385c1s v5p0473c1s v6p0362c1s
Waern, Cecilia v5p0427c2s
    v6p0442c1s
Waffle, A.E. v2p0027c2s
    v3p0191c2s v3p0238c2s
Wagenen, T.F.Van v3p0393c2s
    v5p0027c1s v6p0678c2s
Wagenen, W.Van v1p0249c1s
Wagener, J.A. v2p0215c1s
Wager, C.H.A. v6p0572c2s
    v6p0587c1m v6p0588c2s
Wager, H. and Herbert, A.. v4p0008c2s
Wager, Harold v6p0082c1s
    v6p0106c1s
Wager, J. v1p0104c2s
    v1p1156c2s v1p1377c2s v1p1421c1s
Wager, M.A.E. v1p0703c2s
Wager, N. and Herbert, A.. v3p0007c1s
Waggaman, M.T. v1p0735c2s
    v5p0493c2s v6p0216c2s
Waggener, W.J. v3p0034c2s
Waggoner, C. v4p0544c2s
Waghorn, A.E. v5p0287c1s
Wagle, N.B. v6p0314c1s
Wagmire, J.A. v5p0298c2s
Wagner, A. v6p0253c2s
    v6p0521c1s
Wagner, A.L. v5p0033c1s
    v5p0090c1s v5p0294c2s v5p0602c2m
    v5p0618c2s v6p0399c1s v6p0666c1s
Wagner, Ad. v3p0337c1s
Wagner, C. v5p0431c2m
    v6p0124c2s v6p0242c1s v6p0306c2s
    v6p0466c1s v6p0550c2s v6p0595c1s
Wagner, C.E. v4p0123c2s
    v4p0273c1s v6p0143c1s v6p0659c2s
Wagner, Edith v4p0177c2s
    v6p0245c1s
Wagner, F.R. v6p0341c1s
Wagner, G. v6p0507c2s
Wagner, H.A. v5p0184c2s
Wagner, J. v3p0349c1s
    v4p0345c1s v5p0055c2s
Wagner, J.C. v3p0062c1s
Wagner, J.H. v5p0408c2s
Wagner, J.R. v4p0217c1s
    v2p0440c2s
Wagner, L. v4p0079c2s
    v4p0079c2s v4p0447c1s v5p0576c1s
Wagner, M.A.E. v1p0021c1s
    v1p1362c2s
Wagner, R. v1p0157c1s
    v1p0563c1s v1p0793c1s v1p1380c1s
    v5p0052c1s
Wagner, S. v2p0083c2s
Wagner, S., jr v1p0845c2s
Wagner, S.G. v1p1042c2s
Wagoner, L. v1p0787c2s
    v1p1311c2s
Wagstaff, E.W. v4p0071c2s
Wagstaff, F. v1p0229c2s
Wagstaff, H.McG. v6p0459c2s
Wagstaffe, W.W. v1p1209c2s
    v4p0473c1s v5p0624c2s
Wagtail, W. v1p1280c2s
Wahis, Baron v6p0144c2s
Wahl, G.M. v3p0046c1s
    v3p0171c1s v3p0187c1s
Wahl, R. v1p0121c2s
    v1p0425c1s v1p1115c2s
Wahl, W.H. v1p0210c1s
    v1p0269c1s v1p0322c1s v1p0376c1s
    v1p0455c1s v1p0467c1s v1p0642c1m
    v1p0995c2s v2p0138c2s v2p0221c1s
    v3p0334c1s
Wahl, W.H. and Greene, W.H.
    v4p0353c1s v4p0366c2s
Wahly, W.H. v5p0496c2s
Waidner, C.W. and Mendenhall, C.E.
    v5p0224c2s
Wailly, A. v3p0049c1s
Wain, L. v5p0389c2s

Wainwright, A. v2p0313c1s
Wainwright, A.G. v6p0342c2s
Wainwright, A.S. v6p0065c2s
    v6p0068c2s
Wainwright, C.E. v3p0453c1s
Wainwright, J.A. v2p0277c2s
Wainwright, J.M. v1p0337c1s
    v4p0435c1s
Wainwright, R. v3p0074c2s
    v3p0089c2s v3p0297c2s v3p0390c2s
    v3p0441c2s v5p0508c2s v5p0619c1s
    v6p0668c2s
Wainwright, S.S. v5p0246c2s
    v6p0247c1s v6p0639c2s
Wait, B.W. v5p0429c2s
Wait, D.G. v1p0118c2s
Wait, F.E. v3p0294c1s
Wait, H.L. v3p0473c2s
    v4p0195c2s v5p0066c2s v5p0601c2s
Wait, J.C. v4p0089c1s
Wait, J.J. v2p0440c1s
    v5p0220c2s v5p0477c2s
Wait, M. v5p0447c2s
Wait, S.P. v3p0041c2s
    v3p0042c2s v3p0429c1s v4p0218c1s
Wait, W.B. v6p0070c2s
Wait, W.H., Mrs. v4p0049c1s
Waite, A. v5p0309c1s
Waite, A.E. v2p0267c2s
    v3p0367c1s v4p0435c1s
Waite, C.B. v1p1360c1s
Waite, D. v5p0401c2s
Waite, D.H. v4p0526c2s
Waite, D.H. and Crounse, L.
    v4p0630c1s
Waite, E.F. v4p0434c1s
Waite, E.G. v1p0722c1s
    v1p0956c1s v3p0063c2s v3p0425c2s
Waite, E.R. v4p0368c2s
Waite, F.C. v5p0054c2s
Waite, G.B. v4p0416c1s
Waite, H.E. v1p1380c1s
    v2p0058c1s v2p0310c2s v2p0464c1s
Waite, H.R. v2p0131c2s
    v2p0298c2s v2p0424c1s v2p0435c2s
    v2p0454c2s v4p0014c2s v4p0116c1s
    v4p0116c2m v4p0286c2s v5p0015c2s
Waite, J.K. v2p0256c1s
Waite, J.T. v1p1380c1s
Waite, N.E. v5p0512c2s
Waite, V. v5p0065c2s
    v5p0386c2s
Waites, A. v6p0586c2s
Waitt, A.M. v6p0304c2s
Wake, C.H.M. v2p0057c1s
    v2p0105c1s
Wake, C.S. v1p0005c2s
    v1p0792c1s v1p0794c2m v1p1092c2s
    v1p1179c2s v2p0272c2s v2p0309c2s
    v2p0328c2s v2p0348c2s v3p0146c2s
    v3p0157c1s v4p0433c1s v4p0003c1s
    v4p0229c1s v4p0382c1s v4p0389c2s
    v4p0396c2s v4p0441c1s v4p0575c2s
    v5p0297c1s v5p0325c1s v5p0395c2s
    v5p0400c1s v5p0417c2s v6p0017c2s
    v6p0036c2s v6p0055c1s v6p0316c1s
    v6p0316c2s v6p0349c2s v6p0396c2s
    v6p0407c2s v6p0441c1s v6p0444c2s
    v6p0457c2s v6p0507c2s
Wake, C.Stanliland v6p0317c1s
Wake, S. v6p0014c2s
Wakecook, E. v5p0364c1s
    v6p0032c2s
Wakefield, A.M. v3p0069c1s
    v3p0293c1s v3p0347c2s v3p0369c1s
    v4p0143c1s v5p0125c1s v5p0252c1m
    v5p0367c1s v6p0593c1s
Wakefield, E. v2p0186c1s
    v2p0313c2s v3p0031c1s v3p0165c1s
    v3p0177c1s v3p0200c1s v3p0347c2s
    v4p0262c2s v4p0267c2s v4p0308c1s
    v4p0397c2s v4p0401c2s
Wakefield, G.W. v4p0307c2s
    v4p0330c2s
Wakefield, H.R. v6p0265c2s
Wakefield, W.H.T. v4p0481c1s
Wakefield, W.W. v3p0256c1s
Wakeley, A. v4p0400c1s
Wakely, A.R. v5p0180c1s
Wakeman, A.V. v4p0628c1s
Wakeman, A.VanH. v5p0105c2s
Wakeman, Emma F. v6p0374c1s
Wakeman, G. v1p0007c2s
    v1p0024c2s v1p0296c1s v1p0417c1s
    v1p0826c1m v1p1105c2s v1p1220c1m
    v1p1222c1s v1p1315c2s v1p1367c1s
    v1p1429c1s v1p1429c2m
Wakeman, H.O. v3p0083c1s
Wakeman, R.P. and Thorpe, S.P.
    v6p0644c2s
Wakeman, T.B. v3p0083c2s
    v3p0135c2s v4p0255c1s v4p0275c2s
    v4p0396c2s v4p0451c1s v4p0537c2s
    v4p0541c2s v4p0616c1s v4p0633c1s
    v6p0309c2s
Wakeman, T.B. and Anderson, G.
    v2p0351c2s
Wakeman, W.H. v4p0065c1s
    v4p0371c2s v4p0547c1s v4p0547c2s

v5p0551c1s
Walaeus, A. v1p0095c2s
Walbey, C. v1p0187c2s
v1p0382c2s
Walbridge, H. v1p1077c2s
Walby, C. v1p0451c1s
Walch, Jas.J. v6p0107c1s
Walcot, W. v1p1082c1s
Walcott, C.B. v3p0064c1s
Walcott, C.D. v2p0065c1s
v2p0358c2s v2p0446c2s v3p0017c2s
v3p0064c1s v3p0136c2s v3p0311c2s
v3p0350c2s v3p0419c1m v4p0021c2s
v4p0084c2m v4p0394c1s v4p0593c2s
v5p0074c2s v5p0214c1s v5p0340c1s
v5p0602c2s v6p0190c2s v6p0329c2s
Walcott, C.D. and Branner, J.C.
v6p0667c2s
Walcott, E.A. v2p0114c1s
v3p0291c1s v5p0240c2s v5p0454c2s
v5p0543c1s v5p0597c2s
Walcott, H.P. v6p0709c2s
Walcott, J. v1p0625c2s
v1p0770c1s
Walcott, M.E.C. v1p0228c1s
v1p0244c2s v1p0254c1s v1p0371c1s
v1p0452c2s v1p0543c2s v1p1096c2s
v1p1142c2s v1p1428c2s v2p0291c1s
Walcott, S. v1p0941c1s
Wald, L.D. v4p0606c1s
v6p0408c2s v6p0462c2s v6p0573c2s
v6p0575c1s
Wald, S.T. v6p0113c1s
Waldau, O. v3p0163c2s
Waldeck, R.W. v6p0245c2s
Walden, J.M. v3p0019c1s
Walden, J.T. v1p1382c1s
Walden, O. v4p0490c1s
Walden, P.T. v4p0074c1s
Walden, P.T. and Wells, H.L.
v4p0082c2m
Walden, T. v1p0826c1s
v1p0930c2s v1p1099c1s v1p1255c2s
v1p1370c1s v1p1402c2s v2p0471c1s
Waldenberg, L. v1p0218c1s
Waldner, H. v1p0073c2s
Waldo, A. v1p1361c2m
v5p0607c1s
Waldo, C.A. v6p0015c2s
v6p0039c2s v6p0204c2s v6p0406c2s
Waldo, C.A. et al. v6p0039c1s
Waldo, F. v3p0088c2s
v3p0276c1m v3p0276c2s v3p0449c1s
v3p0465c2s v4p0367c1s v4p0623c2m
v5p0024c1s v5p0067c1s v6p0094c2s
v6p0281c2s v6p0413c1s v6p0560c1s
v6p0663c2s
Waldo, F.J. and Walsh, D.. v4p0362c2s
Waldo, F.K. v6p0227c2s
v6p0444c2s
Waldo, F.L. v6p0477c1m
v6p0518c2s
Waldo, J.F. and Walsh, D.. v4p0162c1s
Waldo, L. v1p0835c1s
v1p1305c1s v1p1312c1s v2p0200c2s
v2p0441c2s v2p0467c1s v3p0456c2s
v5p0061c1s
Waldo, W. v1p0113c1s
Waldon, A. v2p0166c1s
v2p0326c2s
Waldorf, L. v6p0018c1s
Waldron, A.C. v2p0330c1s
v3p0349c1s v5p0257c2s
Waldron, D.W. v4p0451c2s
Waldron, G. v4p0086c2s
Waldron, G.B. v4p0615c1s
v5p0015c1s v5p0020c1s v5p0130c2s
v5p0212c2s v5p0360c2s v5p0407c1s
v5p0477c2s v5p0480c2s v5p0526c1s
v5p0599c2s v5p0618c1s v5p0632c2s
v6p0005c1s v6p0253c2s v6p0426c1s
v6p0527c2s v6p0606c1s
Waldron, H.D. v4p0091c1s
Waldron, J.A. v6p0003c1s
v6p0641c2s
Waldstein, C. v1p0517c1s
v1p0922c1s v2p0145c1s v2p0190c2s
v2p0328c1s v2p0331c2m v2p0464c2s
v3p0019c2s v3p0114c1s v3p0222c2m
v3p0261c2s v3p0267c1s v3p0274c2s
v3p0322c1s v3p0322c2s v3p0334c1s
v3p0350c1s v3p0369c1s v3p0448c1s
v4p0026c1s v4p0026c2s v4p0241c1s
v4p0306c2s v4p0361c1s v4p0365c2s
v4p0380c2s v4p0428c2s v4p0451c1s
v5p0019c2s v5p0027c2m v5p0193c1s
v5p0249c1s v5p0261c2s v5p0262c2s
v5p0434c1s v5p0458c2s v5p0500c1s
v5p0516c1s v6p0083c2s v6p0288c1s
v6p0599c2s v6p0671c1s
Waldstein, C. and Daniel, A.M.
v6p0163c2s
Waldstein, C. and Tarbell, F.B.
v3p0406c2s
Waldstein, C. et al. v4p0186c2s
Walenn, W.H. v1p0400c1s
v3p0132c2s v3p0331c1s
Wales, A.D. v6p0264c1s
Wales, H.A., Mrs. v5p0388c2s
Wales, L.E. v2p0088c2s
Wales, M.E. v4p0358c1s
Wales, P. v5p0538c1m
Wales, W.G. v5p0241c2s
Walesby, T. v2p0039c1s
Waley, J. v1p1261c1s
Walford, C. v1p0149c1s
v1p0206c1m v1p0338c2s v1p0443c1s
v1p0647c1s v1p0742c1s v1p0743c2s
v1p1349c2s v2p0008c2s v2p0051c1s
v2p0051c2s v2p0052c1s v2p0055c2s
v2p0066c1s v2p0151c2s v2p0156c2s
v2p0161c1s v2p0191c2s v2p0196c1s
v2p0243c1s v2p0281c1s v2p0299c1s
v2p0336c1s v2p0354c2s v2p0373c2s
v2p0411c2s v2p0471c1s v3p0147c1s
v3p0153c1s v4p0244c1s
Walford, E. v1p0023c1s
v1p0081c2s v1p0105c1s v1p0157c1s
v1p0178c2m v1p0226c1s v1p0237c1s
v1p0257c1s v1p0264c2s v1p0266c2s
v1p0280c2s v1p0361c1s v1p0383c1s
v1p0521c1s v1p0525c1s v1p0526c1s
v1p0565c1s v1p0569c1s v1p0624c1s
v1p0765c2s v1p0803c1s v1p0855c2s
v1p0871c1s v1p0874c2s v1p0906c2s
v1p0909c1s v1p0941c2s v1p1142c2s
v1p1143c1s v1p1144c2s v1p1193c1s
v1p1242c2s v1p1317c2s v1p1383c1s
v1p1419c2s v2p0006c2s v2p0036c1s
v2p0087c2s v2p0196c1s v2p0284c1s
v2p0378c2s v2p0444c1s v3p0098c2s
v3p0104c2s v3p0124c2s v3p0146c1s
v3p0303c2s v3p0372c2s v4p0032c2s
v4p0033c2s v4p0073c1s v4p0082c1s
v4p0163c2s v4p0242c2s v4p0332c1s
v4p0340c2s v4p0366c1s v4p0401c2s
v5p0137c2s
Walford, G. v4p0558c2s
Walford, Henry v2p0123c2s
Walford, J. v1p0428c2s
Walford, L.B. v1p0107c2s
v1p0349c2s v1p0716c1s v1p0892c1s
v1p0981c1s v2p0050c1s v2p0126c1s
v2p0275c2s v2p0384c2s v3p0056c1s
v3p0069c1s v3p0226c1s v3p0282c1s
v4p0119c1s v4p0166c2s v4p0335c2s
v4p0336c1s v4p0360c2s v4p0391c1s
v4p0414c1s v4p0414c2m v4p0469c2s
v5p0071c2s v5p0225c1s v5p0321c2s
v5p0421c1s v6p0641c1s
Walford, N.L. v5p0290c1s
Walford, T. v1p0192c1s
v1p1114c2s v1p1115c1s
Walford, W. v1p0118c1s
v1p0129c2s v1p0130c2s v1p0495c2m
v1p0500c1s v1p0646c1s
Walford, W.S. v1p0059c1s
v1p0340c1s v1p0761c2s v1p0941c1s
v1p1114c2s
Walger, J.P. v6p0005c1s
Walhouse, M.J. v1p0347c2s
v1p0501c1s v1p0555c2s v1p0632c1s
v1p0732c2s v1p0865c1s v1p1391c1s
v2p0061c1s v2p0211c1s v2p0356c2s
v4p0225c2s v5p0212c1s
Walhouse, M.J. and Robinson, M.
v4p0410c1s
Walk, D. v1p0035c2s
v1p0640c2s
Walker, A. v1p0019c2s
v1p0091c2s v1p0147c2s v1p0187c1s
v1p0188c1s v1p0203c2s v1p0242c2s
v1p0277c1s v1p0325c1m v1p0326c1m
v1p0453c1s v1p0478c1s v1p0532c2s
v1p0533c1s v1p0708c1s v1p0713c2s
v1p0714c1s v1p0782c2s v1p0798c1s
v1p0861c1s v1p1025c2s v1p1041c2s
v1p1099c1s v1p1211c1s v1p1285c1s
v1p1319c1s v1p1342c1s v1p1348c2s
v1p1349c1s v1p1351c2s v1p1355c2s
v1p1361c2s v1p1379c1s v4p0225c1s
v4p0600c2s
Walker, A. and Breen, J.W.
v1p1342c1s
Walker, A.F. v3p0095c1s
v3p0218c2s v4p0288c1s v4p0315c1s
v5p0294c1s v5p0592c2s v6p0266c1s
Walker, A.H. v5p0312c2s
Walker, A.L. v1p0627c1s
v2p0301c2s
Walker, A.S. v6p0014c1s
v6p0330c1s v6p0695c2s
Walker, A.T. v5p0118c2s
Walker, B. v5p0008c1s
v6p0303c1s v6p0423c2s
Walker, B.E. v4p0044c1s
Walker, C. v1p0629c1s
v1p0846c2s v1p0857c1s v1p1414c2s
v2p0027c2s v2p0149c2s v2p0351c2s
v3p0148c1s v3p0297c2s v4p0174c1s
v4p0207c2s v4p0334c1s v4p0359c2s
v5p0236c2s v6p0595c2s
Walker, C.A. v1p1286c1s
Walker, C.C. v3p0007c1s
v3p0035c2s
Walker, C.F. v5p0295c1s
v5p0537c2s
Walker, C.F. and Gillespie, D.H.M.
v5p0295c1s
Walker, C.F. and Gooch, F.A.
v5p0295c1s
Walker, C.H. v2p0100c1s
v2p0462c1s v4p0069c1s v4p0505c2s
v5p0389c1s v5p0420c1m v5p0471c1s
v6p0028c1s v6p0033c2s v6p0154c1s
v6p0171c2s v6p0563c2s
Walker, C.H. and Brunt, H.van.
v2p0208c2s
Walker, C.Howard v2p0337c1s
Walker, C.L. v1p0346c2s
Walker, C.S. v2p0140c1s
v2p0142c2s v2p0236c1s v2p0245c2s
v3p0149c2s v4p0013c1s v4p0195c1s
v5p0149c2s v5p0365c1s v5p0533c2s
Walker, C.V. v1p0102c2s
v1p1078c2s
Walker, D. v1p0055c1s
v1p0055c2s v1p0077c1s v1p0077c2s
v1p0557c1s v5p0059c2s
Walker, D.A. v4p0513c1s
v5p0059c1s v5p0307c1s v5p0465c2s
v6p0519c2s
Walker, D.B. v5p0117c1s
Walker, Dean A. v5p0057c2s
v6p0061c2s
Walker, Dr. v1p0646c2s
v1p0687c1m v1p0689c2s v1p1109c1s
v1p1242c1s v1p1284c1s
Walker, E. v6p0145c2s
v6p0168c2s v6p0228c2s v6p0332c2s
v6p0369c2s v6p0396c1s v6p0415c2s
v6p0620c2s v6p0656c2s v6p0664c1s
v6p0694c2s
Walker, E.A. v1p0229c1s
v1p0248c1s v1p0265c2s v1p0300c2s
v1p0443c2s v1p0513c2s v1p0515c1s
v1p0878c2s v1p1147c2s
Walker, E.A., Mrs. v1p1416c2s
Walker, E.D. v3p0301c1s
v3p0363c2s v3p0463c2s v4p0573c2s
Walker, E.E. v2p0439c2s
Walker, E.H. v5p0541c1m
Walker, E.O. v4p0105c1s
v4p0278c2s v4p0279c2s v4p0473c1s
v4p0527c1s v4p0567c1s v5p0023c2s
v5p0608c2s v6p0313c1s
Walker, E.S. v2p0239c2s
v2p0318c1s
Walker, F. v1p0706c1s
v1p0871c1s v5p0129c1s v5p0530c2s
v6p0133c1s v6p0151c2s v6p0252c2s
v6p0289c2s v6p0425c2s v6p0616c2s
v6p0624c2s v6p0651c2s
Walker, F.A. v1p0212c1s
v1p0342c2s v1p0350c1s v1p0360c1s
v1p0636c1s v1p0637c2m v1p0860c1s
v1p0996c2s v1p1025c2s v1p1034c1s
v1p1198c2m v1p1262c2s v1p1285c2s
v1p1351c1s v1p1351c2s v1p1379c2s
v1p1384c2s v1p1421c2s v2p0005c2s
v2p0072c2s v2p0220c2s v2p0227c1s
v2p0275c2s v2p0407c1s v2p0452c2s
v2p0455c1s v3p0010c1s v3p0019c2s
v3p0038c2s v3p0072c1m v3p0114c2s
v3p0127c2s v3p0131c2s v3p0157c2s
v3p0208c2s v3p0237c1s v3p0238c1s
v3p0297c1s v3p0299c1m v3p0337c1s
v3p0345c2s v3p0346c2s v3p0358c2s
v3p0398c1s v3p0399c1s v3p0421c1s
v3p0422c2s v3p0441c2s v3p0452c2s
v3p0453c1s v3p0458c1s v3p0472c1s
v3p0472c2s v4p0015c1s v4p0035c2s
v4p0059c2s v4p0144c2s v4p0171c1s
v4p0265c1s v4p0275c1s v4p0275c2s
v4p0287c2s v4p0378c2m v4p0397c2s
v4p0524c2s v4p0525c1s v4p0566c2s
v4p0596c2s v4p0604c1s v4p0618c1s
v4p0627c2s v5p0462c2s v6p0039c1s
Walker, F.A. and Allan, W.
v3p0246c1m
Walker, F.A. and Sumner, W.G.
v1p0133c2s
Walker, F.A. and Walker, Q.J.
v3p0345c2s
Walker, F.A. et al. v2p0403c1s
v3p0215c1s
Walker, F.J. v6p0508c1s
Walker, F.T. v5p0197c2s
Walker, Francis v6p0056c1s
Walker, G. v1p0086c2m
v1p0091c1m v1p0092c1s v1p0092c2m
v1p0093c1s v1p0094c1m v1p0095c1s
v1p0109c2s v1p0133c2s v1p0185c1s
v1p0212c1s v1p0325c1s v1p0325c2s
v1p0326c1s v1p0463c1s v1p0486c2m
v1p0532c2s v1p0540c2s v1p0545c2s
v1p0556c2s v1p0672c1s v1p0715c1s
v1p0801c2s v1p0965c2s v1p0992c1s
v1p1198c2m v1p1283c2s v1p1349c1s
v1p1351c1s v1p1394c2s
Walker, G.B. v2p0290c1s
v3p0089c2s v5p0358c2s
Walker, G.F. v1p0285c1s
v1p0323c2s v1p0391c2s
Walker, G.H. v3p0096c2s
v4p0129c1s
Walker, G.J. v1p0075c1s
Walker, G.L. v1p0846c1s
v1p1381c2s v2p0133c1s v2p0194c2s
Walker, G.M. v5p0111c1s

v6p0118c1s v6p0118c2s v6p0528c2s
Walker, G.T. v1p0946c2s
v5p0071c2s
Walker, Guy M. v6p0119c2s
Walker, H. v1p0523c2s
v2p0015c2s v2p0047c1s v2p0053c2s
v2p0057c1s v2p0155c1s v2p0222c2s
v2p0287c2s v2p0352c1s v4p0028c1s
v4p0124c1s v4p0270c2s v5p0329c1s
v5p0632c2s v6p0075c2s
Walker, H.DeR. v5p0038c2s
v6p0097c1s v6p0172c2s
Walker, H.K. v6p0467c2s
Walker, Hugh v6p0698c2s
Walker, J. v1p0069c1s
v1p0107c2s v1p0111c1s v1p0112c1s
v1p0112c2s v1p0122c1s v1p0127c2s
v1p0133c1s v1p0176c1s v1p0190c2s
v1p0240c1s v1p0243c1s v1p0254c2s
v1p0271c1s v1p0359c1s v1p0384c2s
v1p0440c2s v1p0452c2s v1p0459c1s
v1p0513c1s v1p0567c2s v1p0572c2s
v1p0578c1s v1p0597c2s v1p0614c1s
v1p0791c2s v1p0794c1s v1p0803c1s
v1p0805c2s v1p0846c2s v1p0857c1s
v1p0859c2s v1p0868c1s v1p0869c1s
v1p0869c2s v1p0901c1s v1p0903c1s
v1p0942c2s v1p0961c2m v1p0971c2s
v1p0982c2s v1p0990c1s v1p1000c2s
v1p1001c2s v1p1008c1s v1p1050c2s
v1p1083c2s v1p1088c2s v1p1094c2s
v1p1103c1s v1p1103c2s v1p1115c1s
v1p1127c1s v1p1200c2m v1p1211c2s
v1p1214c2s v1p1262c1s v1p1299c1s
v1p1301c2s v1p1303c2s v1p1328c2s
v1p1329c1s v1p1340c1m v1p1341c2s
v1p1404c2s v1p1406c1s v1p1406c2s
v1p1407c1s v1p1429c1s v4p0098c2s
v4p0536c1s v5p0104c1s v5p0504c1s
v5p0580c1s
Walker, J.A. v1p1414c1s
Walker, J.B. v1p0529c1s
v1p0796c2s v1p0911c1s v1p1306c2s
v2p0054c1s v2p0097c2s v2p0374c2s
v3p0006c2s v3p0008c1s v3p0036c1s
v3p0085c2s v3p0301c1s v3p0363c2s
v4p0004c2s v4p0022c2s v4p0102c1s
v4p0102c2s v4p0118c1s v4p0121c1s
v4p0262c2s v4p0264c1s v4p0472c1s
v4p0473c2s v5p0108c2s v5p0119c2s
v5p0126c2s v5p0135c1s v5p0149c1s
v5p0152c1s v5p0228c1s v5p0229c2s
v5p0248c1s v5p0294c2s v5p0367c2s
v5p0381c2s v5p0388c2s v5p0407c2s
v5p0485c2s v5p0496c1s v5p0544c2s
v5p0552c1s v5p0556c1s v5p0619c2s
v6p0005c1s v6p0044c2s v6p0151c1s
v6p0154c2s v6p0193c1s v6p0193c2s
v6p0209c1s v6p0231c1s v6p0363c2s
v6p0378c2s v6p0429c1s v6p0452c2s
v6p0479c1s v6p0493c1s v6p0507c1s
v6p0511c1s v6p0542c1s v6p0556c2s
v6p0563c2s v6p0565c2s v6p0623c2s
v6p0624c1s v6p0634c1s v6p0669c2s
v6p0670c1s v6p0693c1s
Walker, J.B. and Ansell, F.G.
v6p0685c1s
Walker, J.B. and Peck, H.T.
v5p0178c2s
Walker, J.B., jr. v5p0284c1s
v5p0462c1s
Walker, J.B.R., Mrs. v1p1257c2s
Walker, J.C. v6p0281c2s
Walker, J.E. v4p0163c1s
v6p0507c2s v6p0657c1m
Walker, J.F. v5p0190c1s
v5p0262c2s v5p0297c1s v5p0505c2s
Walker, J.G. v1p1018c1s
v2p0196c2s v2p0399c1s
Walker, J.G. et al. v4p0180c1s
Walker, J.H. v1p0186c2s
v4p0044c2s v4p0115c2s v5p0600c2s
v6p0666c2s
Walker, J.L. v4p0427c1s
Walker, J.M. v1p1350c1s
Walker, J.R. v6p0596c1s
Walker, J.S. v3p0133c1s
Walker, J.T. v2p0128c2s
v2p0217c2s v2p0218c2s v4p0304c1s
v4p0576c1s
Walker, J.W. v1p0772c2s
Walker, J.W.G. v6p0107c1s
Walker, John B. v6p0629c2s
Walker, Joseph H. v4p0314c2s
Walker, K.C. v1p1126c1s
Walker, K.K.C. v1p0672c1s
v1p1317c1s
Walker, L. v3p0466c2s
v4p0179c2s
Walker, L., jr. v5p0241c2s
Walker, L.B. v5p0029c2s
v5p0527c1s v6p0031c2s v6p0591c2s
Walker, L.M.R. v4p0079c2s
v4p0218c2s v4p0430c1s v4p0539c2s
Walker, M. v1p1332c2s
Walker, M.M. v2p0320c2s
Walker, M.P. v1p1306c2s
Walker, Mrs. v1p0102c1s
v1p0168c2s v1p0214c2s v1p1333c1s
Walker, N. v2p0084c1s
Walker, N.L. v2p0391c1s
v4p0508c2s v4p0509c1s v5p0464c1s
v6p0598c1s
Walker, N.L. and Campbell, D.
v5p0464c1s
Walker, N.L. and Fergusson, A.W.
v5p0464c1s
Walker, N.L. et al. v5p0464c1m
Walker, N.M. v2p0205c1s
v2p0267c1m
Walker, N.McF. v2p0305c1s
Walker, N.S. v4p0457c1s
Walker, P. v1p0197c1s
Walker, Q.J. and Walker, F.A.
v3p0345c2s
Walker, R. v1p0273c1s
v2p0041c1s v2p0151c2s v2p0180c1s
v2p0200c2s v2p0246c2s v2p0254c2m
v2p0434c2s v3p0089c1m v3p0189c2s
v3p0335c1s v4p0032c1s v4p0050c1s
v4p0070c1s v4p0129c2s v4p0227c2s
v4p0263c1s v4p0312c1s v4p0362c1s
v4p0381c2s v4p0437c2s v4p0477c2s
v4p0631c1s v5p0013c2s v6p0052c1s
Walker, R.B.N. v3p0166c1s
Walker, R.J. v1p0058c1s
v1p0195c2s v1p0335c1s v1p0532c1s
v1p0601c1s v1p0639c2s v1p0854c1s
v1p0933c2s v1p1025c2s v1p1174c2s
v1p1205c1s v1p1344c1s v1p1349c1m
v1p1350c2s v1p1354c2s
Walker, R.K. v2p0282c1s
v2p0335c1s
Walker, Robert v3p0232c1s
Walker, S. v1p0696c2s
Walker, S.A. v5p0026c1s
v5p0484c2s v5p0537c1s
Walker, S.B. v6p0708c1s
Walker, S.C. v1p0024c1s
v1p0269c2s v1p0381c2s v1p0835c1s
v1p1291c1s v1p1397c1s v6p0208c1s
Walker, S.C. and Kirkwood, D.
v1p1014c1s
Walker, S.D. v2p0071c2s
Walker, S.F. v2p0409c2s
v5p0183c1s v5p0183c2s v5p0185c1s
v6p0591c2m
Walker, S.G. v4p0077c1s
Walker, S.R. v1p0322c1s
Walker, Sophia A. v6p0027c2s
Walker, T. v1p0044c1s
v1p0122c2s v1p0198c2s v1p0271c1s
v1p0284c1s v1p0391c1s v1p0391c2s
v1p0582c2s v1p0695c1s v1p0730c2s
v1p0811c1s v1p0815c2s v1p1028c2s
v1p1359c2s v1p1418c1s v2p0251c1s
v2p0297c2s v2p0368c2s v2p0408c1s
Walker, T.B. v2p0446c2s
Walker, T.J. v4p0064c2s
Walker, T.L. v4p0404c1s
v4p0435c1s v4p0541c2s v5p0279c2s
v5p0373c2s v5p0582c2s v5p0590c2s
Walker, V.M. v6p0045c2s
Walker, W. v1p1365c2s
v3p0172c1s v4p0246c1s v4p0268c2s
v4p0359c2m v4p0406c2s v4p0467c2s
v4p0469c2s v4p0580c1s v4p0584c1s
v4p0622c2s v5p0048c2s v5p0139c2s
v6p0108c2s v6p0144c2s v6p0617c2s
Walker, W.A. v5p0366c1s
Walker, W.D. v5p0210c2s
Walker, W.E. v4p0561c1s
Walker, W.H. v6p0112c1s
v6p0234c1s v6p0341c2s v6p0405c1s
Walker, W.J. and Jeune, Mrs.
v3p0468c1s
Walker, W.L. v6p0159c2s
Walker, W.R. v1p1098c2s
v1p1275c1s
Walker, W.S. v1p0227c2s
v1p0437c1s
Walker, Williston v6p0144c2s
v6p0708c2s
Walkes, W.R. v3p0194c1s
v4p0307c1s v4p0473c1s
Walkley, A. v2p0154c2s
v3p0441c1s v4p0213c2s v4p0462c1s
Walkley, A.B. v4p0161c1s
v4p0465c2s v4p0486c1s v4p0569c2s
v4p0600c2s
Wall, A. v1p0361c2s
v1p0796c2s v1p0864c1s v1p1123c2s
v1p1136c2s v3p0435c1s
Wall, A.G. v5p0592c2s
Wall, A.H. v1p1317c1s
v1p1405c1s v2p0002c2s v2p0006c1s
v2p0031c2s v2p0052c1s v2p0065c2s
v2p0094c1s v2p0150c2s v2p0187c1s
v2p0307c2s v2p0448c1s v2p0460c2s
v2p0468c1s v3p0387c2s v4p0042c2s
v4p0309c2s v4p0392c2s v4p0562c2s
v4p0609c1s
Wall, A.R. v3p0110c1s
v4p0147c1s v4p0518c1s v4p0519c1s
Wall, C.H. v2p0265c1s
v2p0275c2s
Wall, C.W. v1p0590c1s
Wall, E. v6p0475c2s
Wall, E.J. v6p0609c1s
Wall, G.E. v4p0399c2s
Wall, J.C. v4p0443c2s
v6p0362c2s v6p0459c1s
Wall, J.W. v1p0114c2s
v1p0205c2m v1p0223c1s v1p0364c1s
v1p0807c1s v1p0973c1s v1p1260c2m
v1p1264c1s v1p1383c1s
Wall, L.H. v4p0209c1s
v4p0263c1s v4p0338c1s v4p0612c2s
v5p0002c1s v5p0260c1s v5p0283c1s
v6p0358c1s v6p0568c1s
Wall, M. Mack v5p0013c1s
Wall, N.G. v3p0133c2s
Wall, W.A. v5p0472c2s
Wallace, A. v3p0392c2s
Wallace, A. and Darwin, C.
v5p0545c1s v5p0608c1s
Wallace, A.F. v6p0203c1s
Wallace, A.R. v1p0013c1s
v1p0041c2s v1p0042c1m v1p0044c1m
v1p0045c2s v1p0107c1s v1p0134c1s
v1p0136c2s v1p0137c2s v1p0250c1s
v1p0278c2s v1p0279c1s v1p0333c2s
v1p0420c1s v1p0423c1s v1p0435c1s
v1p0486c2s v1p0505c1s v1p0507c1s
v1p0523c2s v1p0524c2s v1p0614c2s
v1p0644c2s v1p0645c1s v1p0657c2s
v1p0700c1s v1p0721c1s v1p0745c1s
v1p0745c2s v1p0792c1s v1p0792c2s
v1p0793c1m v1p0882c1s v1p0899c2s
v1p0900c1m v1p0911c1m v1p0920c1s
v1p1005c2s v1p1014c2s v1p1073c1s
v1p1086c2m v1p1162c1s v1p1176c1s
v1p1176c2s v1p1232c2s v1p1233c1s
v1p1237c1s v1p1238c1m v1p1238c2s
v1p1440c2s v2p0106c2s v2p0112c1s
v2p0149c2s v2p0214c1s v2p0247c2s
v2p0248c1s v2p0288c1s v2p0295c1s
v2p0325c1s v2p0348c2s v2p0377c1s
v2p0465c2s v3p0010c1s v3p0010c2s
v3p0014c1m v3p0016c2s v3p0145c1s
v3p0146c1s v3p0156c1s v3p0190c2s
v3p0240c2s v3p0265c1s v3p0292c2s
v3p0328c2s v3p0384c1s v3p0384c2m
v3p0417c1s v4p0001c1s v4p0060c2s
v4p0148c1s v4p0165c2m v4p0191c2m
v4p0203c2s v4p0222c1s v4p0228c2s
v4p0254c2s v4p0255c1s v4p0266c1s
v4p0272c2s v4p0321c1s v4p0410c2s
v4p0441c1s v4p0464c2s v4p0497c2s
v4p0513c2s v4p0532c1s v4p0532c2s
v4p0541c1s v4p0543c1s v4p0599c2s
v4p0637c2s v5p0162c2s v5p0429c2s
v6p0068c1s v6p0397c1m v6p0443c2s
v6p0505c1s v6p0544c1s
Wallace, A.R. and Blackman, W.F.
v5p0591c2s
Wallace, A.R. and Carpenter, G.H.
v4p0422c1s
Wallace, A.R. and Howorth, H.H.
v4p0317c1s
Wallace, A.R. et al
v3p0241c1s
v4p0517c2s
Wallace, B.J. v1p0010c1s
v1p0010c2s v1p0018c2s v1p0032c1s
v1p0049c2s v1p0061c1s v1p0074c2s
v1p0166c2s v1p0203c2s v1p0255c1s
v1p0291c1s v1p0416c2s v1p0521c1s
v1p0554c2s v1p0581c2s v1p0620c1s
v1p0644c2s v1p0682c2s v1p0691c1s
v1p0718c2s v1p0727c1s v1p0732c1s
v1p0754c1s v1p0853c1m v1p0907c2s
v1p0961c2s v1p0982c2s v1p0988c1s
v1p0999c2s v1p1002c1s v1p1022c2s
v1p1046c1m v1p1046c2s v1p1047c1s
v1p1047c2m v1p1093c1s v1p1263c1s
v1p1322c2s v1p1342c2s v1p1347c1s
v1p1438c2s
Wallace, C. v1p0497c1s
Wallace, C.E. v5p0107c1s
Wallace, C.M. v1p0460c2s
Wallace, C.W. v2p0012c2s
v2p0209c2s v2p0332c2s v3p0354c1s
v6p0588c1s
Wallace, D. v6p0357c2s
Wallace, D.D. v5p0541c1m
v6p0604c2s
Wallace, D.M. v1p0922c1s
v1p1136c2s v1p1137c1s v1p1137c2s
v1p1175c1s v1p1371c2s v3p0023c2s
v3p0315c2s
Wallace, D.W. v6p0606c1s
Wallace, E. v2p0191c1s
v3p0330c2m v3p0331c1m v4p0104c2s
v4p0193c1s v4p0413c1s v4p0440c2s
v6p0172c2s
Wallace, E.G. v6p0218c1s
Wallace, E.S. v5p0308c1s
Wallace, E.W. v5p0051c2s
v6p0101c2s
Wallace, F. v6p0613c1s
Wallace, F.H. v5p0307c2s
v6p0484c2s
Wallace, G. v6p0561c1s
v6p0686c1s
Wallace, G.H. v6p0131c2s
Wallace, G.M. v3p0346c2s
Wallace, H. v2p0446c2s
v3p0012c2s v3p0266c1s v6p0099c1s
Wallace, H.E., jr. v6p0321c1s

Wallace, I.R. v6p0030c2s
Wallace, J. v1p0579c2s
v5p0139c1s v5p0284c2s v5p0287c1s
v5p0570c1s v6p0314c1s
Wallace, J.F. v4p0471c1s
v4p0484c1s v6p0476c2s v6p0477c1m
Wallace, J.S. v1p0799c2s
Wallace, J.W. v1p0156c1s
v1p0744c1s v1p0997c1s v1p1051c2s
Wallace, L. v1p0174c1s
v1p0833c2s v2p0121c2s v2p0235c1s
v3p0094c2s v5p0034c2s v5p0273c2s
v5p0640c1s
Wallace, L., jr. v5p0118c1s
Wallace, L.A. and Boileau, F.F.R.
v5p0416c2s
Wallace, L.J. v4p0606c2s
Wallace, Lew v6p0591c1s
Wallace, Lew, Mrs. v4p0551c1s
Wallace, M.A. v2p0049c1s
Wallace, O. v6p0709c2s
Wallace, P.M. v2p0397c1s
Wallace, R. v1p0741c1s
v3p0006c1s v3p0006c2s v3p0210c2s
v4p0152c2s v4p0172c1s v4p0238c2s
v4p0261c2s v4p0266c1s v4p0290c1s
v4p0313c2s v4p0609c1s v5p0006c1s
v5p0281c2s v5p0284c1s v5p0287c1s
Wallace, R.H. v4p0370c2s
v4p0601c2s v4p0618c2s v5p0009c1s
v5p0009c2s v5p0027c2s v5p0097c2s
v5p0276c1s v5p0393c1s v5p0414c2s
v6p0572c1s
Wallace, S.E. v1p1063c2s
Wallace, S.W. v5p0181c1s
v5p0412c1s
Wallace, W. v1p0141c2s
v1p0179c1s v1p0501c2s v1p0502c1s
v1p0529c2s v1p0873c2s v1p1167c2s
v1p1225c2s v2p0008c1s v2p0031c1s
v2p0048c1s v2p0068c1s v2p0068c2m
v2p0069c1m v2p0146c1s v2p0147c1s
v2p0191c2m v2p0204c2s v2p0209c1s
v2p0240c2m v2p0314c2s v2p0406c1s
v2p0408c2s v3p0152c1s v3p0167c2s
v3p0199c1m v3p0234c2s v3p0262c2s
v3p0297c1s v3p0381c1s v4p0042c1s
v4p0080c1m v4p0082c2s v4p0141c1s
v4p0218c2s v4p0270c2s v4p0293c1s
v4p0377c1s v4p0404c1s v4p0448c2s
v4p0484c2s v4p0535c2s v5p0029c1s
v5p0048c1s v5p0392c1s v5p0514c2s
v5p0515c1s v5p0605c1s v6p0294c1s
v6p0579c1s
Wallace, W. et al. v4p0141c1s
Wallace, W.A. v2p0065c2s
v2p0121c1s v3p0064c2s
Wallace, W.B. v4p0246c1s
v4p0322c1s v5p0036c2s v5p0041c2s
v5p0054c1s v5p0073c2s v5p0086c2s
v5p0097c2s v5p0127c2s v5p0210c1s
v5p0331c1s v5p0381c1s v5p0436c2s
v5p0455c1s v5p0458c1s v5p0465c1s
v5p0595c2s v5p0597c2s v5p0612c2s
v6p0007c1s v6p0010c1s v6p0101c1s
v6p0163c1s v6p0259c2s v6p0287c1s
v6p0320c1s v6p0449c1s v6p0489c2s
v6p0496c1s v6p0647c2s
Wallace, W.F.S. v5p0497c2s
v5p0616c1s
Wallace, W.T. v1p0097c1s
Wallace, W.W. v5p0525c2s
Wallace, William v4p0289c2s
v5p0239c1s v5p0552c2s v5p0603c1s
Wallace-Dunlop, M.A. v4p0072c1s
v4p0301c2s
Wallace-Goodbody, F.G. ... v3p0097c1s
v3p0224c2s
Wallach, H. v3p0186c1s
Wallach, I.R. v6p0299c2s
Wallack, L. v3p0453c2s
Wallah, J. v6p0105c2s
Wallas, A. v5p0332c1s
Wallas, G. v3p0346c1s
v3p0399c1s v3p0446c2s v4p0164c1s
v4p0238c2s v5p0535c2s
Wallas, G., Mrs. v6p0397c2s
Wallaschek, R. v4p0188c2s
v4p0388c1s v4p0388c2m v5p0395c2s
Wallaschek, R. and Cattell, J.M.
v3p0293c2s
Wallaston, A.N. v2p0203c2s
Wallbridge, A. v1p0885c1s
Wallbridge, T.C. v1p0876c2s
Wallenstein, J.D. v1p0193c1s
v1p0453c2s v1p0513c1s v1p0515c2s
v1p0701c2s v1p1060c1s v1p1197c2s
Waller, A.D. v3p0134c2s
v4p0219c1s v4p0397c2s
Waller, C.H. v3p0041c2s
v3p0146c2m v3p0346c2m v3p0394c1s
Waller, E. v2p0003c1s
Waller, F. v3p0036c1s
Waller, H. v1p1205c2s
v3p0395c1s v4p0354c2s v4p0589c2s
Waller, H.D. v3p0341c2s
Waller, J.F. v1p0049c1s
v1p0082c1s v1p0087c2s v1p0143c1s
v1p0179c2s v1p0245c1m v1p0378c2s
v1p0432c2s v1p0490c1s v1p0493c1s
v1p0837c1m v1p0890c1s v1p0908c2m
v1p0921c2s v1p0994c2s v1p1019c1s
v1p1123c2s v1p1144c2s v1p1145c1s
v1p1167c1s v1p1167c2s v1p1213c1s
v1p1308c2s v1p1334c2s v1p1396c1s
v1p1416c1s
Waller, J.G. v1p1092c2s
v2p0091c1s v2p0365c1s v4p0152c2s
v5p0124c2s v5p0374c2s v5p0393c1s
v5p0617c1s v6p0282c2s
Waller, J.J. v4p0426c2s
v5p0142c1s v5p0164c2s v5p0431c1s
v5p0432c1s
Waller, J.O., Mrs. v3p0077c2s
Waller, S.E. v3p0155c1s
v4p0031c1s v4p0442c2s
Waller, W.F. v2p0153c2s
v2p0345c1s v2p0386c2s
Waller, W.G. v1p0305c1s
v2p0299c1s
Walley, S.H. v1p0770c2s
v1p1049c2s
Walley, S.H., jr. v1p1101c1s
Wallhofen, Von v5p0098c1s
Wallian, S.S. v6p0134c2s
Wallich, G. v1p1074c2s
Wallich, G.C. v1p0041c1s
v1p0346c1s v1p0349c2s v1p0465c2s
v1p0936c2s v1p1037c1s v2p0027c1s
v2p0433c1s
Wallich, Maj. v1p0435c1s
Wallie, A. v6p0525c2s
v6p0533c1s
Wallihan, A.G. v4p0440c1s
v4p0486c2s v6p0496c2s
Walliker, J.F. v4p0065c1s
v5p0362c1s
Walling, E.B. v3p0009c1s
v3p0271c1s v4p0146c2s
Walling, H.F. v1p0541c2s
v1p1273c1s v2p0427c2m
Walling, R.A.J. v5p0023c1s
v5p0213c2s
Walling, R.J. v5p0510c1s
Walling, W.E. v6p0016c2s
v6p0087c1s v6p0117c2s v6p0139c1s
v6p0158c2s v6p0217c2s v6p0355c2s
v6p0357c1s v6p0468c1s v6p0506c1s
v6p0558c1s v6p0559c1s v6p0559c2s
v6p0600c2s v6p0652c1m v6p0652c2s
Walling, W.E. and Poole, E.
v6p0558c2s
Wallington, Miss v1p1421c1s
Wallis, A. v1p0221c2s
v1p0436c2s
Wallis, A.B.R. v5p0161c1s
Wallis, A.F. v6p0301c1s
v6p0580c1s
Wallis, Alfred v3p0256c1s
Wallis, C.J. v1p0227c1s
v1p0474c1s v1p0479c2s v1p0480c1s
v1p0480c2s v1p0696c2s v2p0329c2s
v3p0034c2s v3p0267c2s v4p0243c1s
Wallis, D. v4p0389c2s
Wallis, E.A. v6p0195c2s
Wallis, E.W. v2p0406c1s
Wallis, G. v1p0064c1s
v1p0082c1s v1p0405c1s v2p0403c1s
v3p0115c2s v3p0135c2s v4p0029c1s
v4p0074c2s v4p0292c1s v4p0292c2s
v4p0587c2s
Wallis, H. v2p0034c2s
v2p0070c1s v2p0163c2s v2p0275c2s
v2p0287c1s v2p0326c1s v2p0365c1m
v2p0461c1s v2p0467c2s v3p0025c1s
v3p0051c2s v3p0062c2s v3p0131c1s
v3p0174c2s v3p0259c1s v3p0261c1s
v3p0261c2s v4p0074c2s v4p0163c2s
v5p0100c1s v5p0462c1s
Wallis, H.W. v6p0472c2s
Wallis, Henry v2p0306c2s
v3p0072c1s v3p0131c2s v3p0261c2s
v6p0091c1s
Wallis, J.P. v5p0145c1s
v5p0217c2s v6p0266c2s
Wallis, L. v6p0599c2s
Wallis, R. v1p1057c1s
Wallis, S.T. v1p0090c1s
v1p0270c2s v1p0327c1s v1p0335c1s
v1p0699c2s v1p0734c1s v1p0807c2s
v1p0808c1s v1p0982c1s v1p1181c2s
v1p1344c2s
Wallis, T.H. v3p0248c2s
Wallis, W. v3p0024c1s
v3p0392c1s v3p0418c2s v4p0422c2s
Wallop, G. v6p0459c1s
Walmesley, O. v2p0005c2s
Walmsley, E. v3p0111c1m
Walpole, F. v1p0378c1s
v1p0681c2s v1p0733c1s v1p0837c1s
Walpole, F.G. v2p0475c2s
Walpole, Maud v4p0131c1s
Walpole, S. v1p0172c2s
v1p0417c2s v1p1146c2s v3p0154c1s
v3p0225c2s v3p0325c1s v4p0357c1s
v4p0444c2s v4p0458c2s v5p0186c2s
v5p0419c1s
Walras, L. v4p0458c1s
Walree, E.C.W.van v1p0176c2s
Walrod, H. v3p0183c2s
Walrond, T. v1p0127c1s
Walsh, A. v6p0284c2s
Walsh, C. v5p0385c2s
Walsh, C.E. v5p0299c1s
Walsh, C.M. v4p0059c2s
v5p0383c1s v6p0239c1s v6p0349c2s
Walsh, D. and Waldo, F.J.. v4p0362c2s
Walsh, D. and Waldo, J.F.. v4p0162c1s
Walsh, E. v6p0411c2s
Walsh, G.E. v2p0341c2s
v3p0149c1s v3p0311c2s v4p0121c1s
v4p0176c1s v4p0275c1s v4p0288c1s
v4p0501c1s v4p0556c1s v4p0559c2s
v4p0576c2s v5p0009c2m v5p0044c1s
v5p0051c2s v5p0086c2s v5p0103c2s
v5p0164c2s v5p0184c1s v5p0185c1s
v5p0214c1s v5p0225c1s v5p0225c2s
v5p0226c1s v5p0226c2s v5p0238c1m
v5p0271c2m v5p0278c2s v5p0289c1s
v5p0294c2s v5p0317c2s v5p0323c1s
v5p0388c1s v5p0401c1s v5p0418c2s
v5p0467c1s v5p0490c1s v5p0526c1s
v5p0526c2s v5p0551c2s v5p0589c1s
v5p0619c1m v5p0627c2s v5p0642c1s
v6p0002c2s v6p0005c1s v6p0029c1s
v6p0044c2s v6p0090c1s v6p0198c2s
v6p0225c2s v6p0233c2s v6p0325c1s
v6p0425c2s v6p0477c2s v6p0491c1s
v6p0495c1s v6p0513c1s v6p0528c1s
v6p0670c1s v6p0690c1s v6p0706c2s
Walsh, G.F. v6p0527c1s
Walsh, H.A. v5p0049c2s
v5p0092c2s
Walsh, H.C. v2p0104c2s
v3p0039c2m v3p0329c1s v4p0247c1s
v4p0266c2s v4p0469c2s v5p0384c2s
v5p0414c1s v5p0496c2s
Walsh, J. v2p0375c2s
v6p0376c1s
Walsh, J.D. v2p0411c1s
v3p0276c2s v4p0221c2s v4p0367c2s
v5p0363c2s
Walsh, J.J. v5p0054c2s
v5p0062c2s v5p0337c2s v5p0374c1s
v5p0417c1s v5p0431c2s v5p0453c1s
v5p0471c1s v5p0513c1s v5p0520c2s
v5p0612c2s v6p0073c1s v6p0164c2s
v6p0329c2s v6p0487c1s v6p0501c1s
v6p0536c2s v6p0673c2s v6p0679c2s
v6p0683c1s
Walsh, J.T. v2p0017c2s
v2p0180c2s
Walsh, J.W. v6p0322c1s
Walsh, Jas.J. v6p0165c2s
Walsh, L.S. v6p0405c1s
v6p0537c2s
Walsh, M. v1p0030c1s
v1p0432c2s v1p0558c1s v1p1250c2s
Walsh, M.A. v2p0424c2s
v3p0145c1s
Walsh, M.D. v5p0038c2s
v5p0485c1s v6p0072c2s v6p0106c1s
v6p0233c2s v6p0274c1s v6p0704c2s
Walsh, R. v1p0967c1s
Walsh, R.F. v3p0102c2s
v3p0154c2s v3p0195c1s v4p0200c2s
v4p0347c2s v4p0420c1s v4p0554c2s
Walsh, R.M. v1p0075c1s
v1p0305c1s v1p0421c1s v1p0739c1s
v1p0962c1s v1p1108c2s v1p1148c2s
v2p0249c2s
Walsh, R.T. v3p0222c2s
Walsh, T. v5p0003c2s
v5p0158c2s
Walsh, T.F. v5p0298c2s
v6p0329c2s
Walsh, V.H. v6p0237c1s
Walsh, W. v1p0247c2s
v1p0656c1s v1p0660c2s v1p0814c1s
v1p0911c2s v4p0080c1s v4p0300c2s
v4p0476c2s v4p0478c1s v4p0513c1s
v4p0570c1s v5p0074c1s v5p0168c1s
v5p0518c2s
Walsh, W.F. v6p0136c1s
Walsh, W.J. v3p0221c2m
v4p0289c1s v4p0489c1s v4p0495c1s
Walsh, W.S. v3p0002c1s
v3p0049c2s v3p0135c1s v3p0152c1s
v3p0189c1s v3p0197c1s v3p0198c1s
v3p0204c2s v3p0250c1s v3p0253c2s
v3p0332c2s v3p0346c2s v3p0350c1s
v3p0363c2s v3p0376c2s v3p0410c1s
v4p0035c2s v4p0263c1s v4p0277c2s
v4p0512c1s v4p0627c2s v5p0021c1s
Walsh, W.S. and Reed, J.P.
v4p0543c2s
Walshe, W.G. v6p0119c2m
Walshe, W.H. v2p0341c1s
Walsingham, J.DeG. v3p0167c1s
Walsingham, Lord v3p0429c2s
Walsingham, M. v1p0597c1s
Walstein, C. v1p0406c2s
Walt, F. v4p0541c2s
Walter, Carrie S. v2p0327c2s
Walter, Catherine v4p0507c2s
Walter, D.A. v5p0644c2s
Walter, D.Alleyne v3p0106c2s
Walter, F.G. v5p0345c1s
Walter, G.E. v6p0495c1s
Walter, G.W. v6p0470c1s

Walter, H. v6p0236c2s
Walter, H.D. v6p0038c2s
Walter, H.E. v5p0062c1s
v6p0067c1s
Walter, H.W. v1p1205c1s
Walter, L. v1p0627c2s
Walter, L.E. v5p0165c2s
Walter, L.H. v5p0075c1s
Walter, P.G. v5p0007c1s
Walter, T.U. v1p0052c2s
v1p0522c2m
Walter, W.E. v6p0404c2s
v6p0683c1s
Walter, W.J. v1p0418c2s
v1p0448c2s v1p0460c2s v1p0462c2s
v1p0538c2s v1p0546c2s v1p1020c2s
v1p1227c2s v1p1231c2s v1p1329c1s
Walterhofer, O. v2p0415c2s
Walters, A. v4p0097c2s
v4p0293c2s v4p0455c2s v4p0605c2s
v5p0528c1s v5p0539c1s
Walters, Alan v4p0351c1s
Walters, C.A. v6p0085c1s
Walters, C.F. v4p0518c1s
Walters, Carrie S. v6p0066c1s
Walters, E.C. v2p0107c1s
Walters, F. v2p0397c2s
v2p0398c2s
Walters, F.G. v2p0355c1s
v3p0002c2s v3p0064c2s v3p0147c2s
v3p0268c1s v3p0294c2s v3p0339c1s
v5p0019c1s v5p0077c2s v5p0169c2s
v5p0292c1s v5p0364c1s v5p0398c1s
v5p0510c1s v5p0527c1s v5p0594c1s
v5p0617c1s
Walters, G. v5p0100c2s
Walters, H.B. v4p0411c1s
v4p0454c1m v4p0584c1s v4p0600c2s
v5p0608c1s
Walters, H.M. v1p0505c1s
v1p1241c2s
Walters, J.C. v6p0281c1s
Walters, J.W. v4p0250c1s
Walthall, W.T. v1p0335c1s
v2p0453c1s
Waltham, R.C. v1p0948c1s
v1p1360c2s
Walther, C.F.W. v1p1178c2s
Walther, J., Dr. v4p0153c2s
Walther, W. v1p0504c2s
Walton, C. v3p0388c2s
Walton, C.S. v5p0400c1s
v5p0630c2s v6p0323c2s
Walton, E.C., Mrs. v1p0413c2s
Walton, E.M. v1p0751c2s
Walton, F. v3p0187c1s
v3p0368c2s
Walton, F. and Flynt, J. . v5p0061c2s
v5p0215c2s v5p0282c2s v5p0486c2s
Walton, F.P. v4p0245c2s
v4p0269c2s v4p0377c2s v4p0490c1s
v5p0327c1s v5p0637c2s v6p0237c2s
v6p0252c1s v6p0364c1s
Walton, G.E. v2p0159c2s
Walton, Genevieve M. v6p0374c2s
Walton, H. v5p0637c2s
Walton, H.E. v5p0515c2s
Walton, J. v1p0216c2s
v1p0611c1s v1p0802c2s v1p1256c1s
v5p0109c2s v6p0118c2s v6p0207c2s
Walton, J.B. and Lane, J.H.
v1p0518c2s
Walton, J.C. v1p0848c1s
v1p1042c1s
Walton, J.E. v1p1237c2s
Walton, J.G. v6p0081c1s
Walton, J.L. v5p0281c2s
v6p0125c2s
Walton, J.P. v4p0544c1s
Walton, J.S. v5p0413c1s
Walton, J.W. v4p0462c1s
Walton, Jos. v4p0280c2s
Walton, L.B. v6p0441c1s
Walton, P. v6p0456c1s
Walton, T. v1p1205c2s
Walton, T.H. v1p0269c1s
Walton, W. v1p1154c1s
v5p0051c1s v6p0032c2m v6p0070c1s
v6p0117c1s v6p0262c2s v6p0436c2m
v6p0452c2s v6p0453c2s v6p0462c1s
v6p0510c2s v6p0537c2s v6p0579c2s
v6p0709c2s
Walton, Wm. v4p0091c2s
Waltz, E.C. v5p0396c2s
v5p0463c1s v5p0630c2s v6p0182c2s
v6p0301c1s v6p0353c2s v6p0482c2s
v6p0534c2s v6p0653c2s v6p0680c1s
v6p0697c1s
Waltz, Eliz.C. v6p0358c1s
Waltz, Eliz.Cherry v6p0304c1s
Waltzing, J.P. v4p0244c1s
Walworth, C.A. v1p0351c2s
v2p0222c2s v2p0356c1s v2p0446c2s
v4p0221c2s v4p0607c2s
Walworth, C.L. v5p0494c1s
Walworth, E.H. v1p0173c2s
v1p0176c2s v1p1151c2s
Walworth, F. v6p0298c1s
v6p0471c2s v6p0699c2s
Walworth, H. v4p0226c1s
v4p0503c1s
Walworth, J.H. v2p0306c2s
v4p0243c2s v4p0358c2s v5p0055c1s
v5p0250c1s
Walworth, Jeannette H. ... v5p0358c1s
Walworth, M.T. v1p0570c2s
Walworth, R.H. v1p0156c1s
v1p0341c2s v1p0808c1s
Walz, F.J. v6p0690c2s
Walz, I. v2p0307c2s
Walz, N.E. v5p0302c1s
Wambaugh, E. v5p0018c1s
v5p0241c1s v6p0361c1s v6p0652c2s
Wambaugh, E. et al.
v6p0361c1s
Wanamaker, J. v4p0504c1s
Wanamaker, J. et al. v4p0596c1s
Wandby, W.S. v6p0356c1s
Wandell, C. v6p0373c1s
Wandell, S.H. v4p0157c2s
Wandesford-Butler, J. v4p0027c1s
Wandle, J.T. v4p0216c1s
v4p0543c1s
Wannamake, W.H. v6p0252c1s
Wansbrough, W.D. v5p0068c2m
v5p0235c1s v5p0343c2s v5p0550c2s
v5p0551c1m
Wantage, Lord v3p0149c1s
v3p0180c2s
Wanton, E. v1p0217c2s
Warburton, C. v3p0404c2s
Warburton, E. v1p0209c1s
v1p1132c1s
Warburton, W.J. v4p0087c2s
Ward and Howell v3p0276c1s
Ward, A. v1p1275c2s
v5p0181c1s
Ward, A.B. v4p0101c2s
v4p0159c1s
Ward, A.H. v1p0035c2s
v1p0325c2s v1p0910c1s v1p1106c1s
v1p1193c2s v1p1272c2s v1p1385c2s
Ward, A.M. v3p0014c2s
Ward, A.S. v6p0368c2s
Ward, A.W. v1p0145c1s
v1p0342c1s v1p1357c1s v2p0065c1s
v2p0332c2s v2p0346c2s v2p0409c2s
v2p0473c1s v3p0162c2s v3p0323c2s
v3p0377c1s v3p0400c2s v3p0445c1s
v4p0181c2s v4p0210c2s v4p0226c1s
v4p0365c2s v5p0349c1s v6p0009c1s
v6p0057c2s v6p0333c1s
Ward, Artemus v5p0079c1s
Ward, B.E. v6p0034c2s
v6p0085c2s
Ward, B.M. v5p0199c1s
Ward, B.P. v1p1173c1s
v2p0002c2s
Ward, C.A. v1p0421c1s
v2p0139c2s v2p0198c2s v2p0210c1s
v3p0034c2m v3p0059c2s v3p0107c1s
v3p0120c1s v3p0231c2s v3p0308c1s
v3p0314c1s v4p0067c2s v4p0304c1s
v4p0329c1s v4p0463c2s v4p0474c2s
v4p0530c1s
Ward, C.A. et al. v5p0084c1s
Ward, C.C. v1p0200c2s
v1p0867c1s v1p1035c1s v2p0037c1s
Ward, C.E. v6p0535c2s
Ward, C.H. v3p0019c2s
Ward, C.J. v3p0039c1s
v3p0060c1s v3p0069c1s v3p0082c2s
v3p0129c2s v3p0427c2s
Ward, C.O. v3p0270c1s
v5p0585c1s
Ward, C.T. v3p0302c1s
Ward, C.W. v4p0090c1s
Ward, Dr. v3p0356c2s
Ward, E.A. v6p0684c1s
Ward, E.C. v1p0902c2s
Ward, E.D. v5p0088c1s
v5p0591c2s
Ward, E.M. v4p0421c2m
v4p0443c2s
Ward, E.M., Mrs. v1p1385c2s
Ward, E.P. v5p0165c2s
Ward, E.S.Phelps v4p0449c1s
v5p0204c2s v5p0634c1s
Ward, Effie M. v5p0107c1s
Ward, Elizabeth A. v6p0093c1s
Ward, F.L. v2p0118c1s
Ward, F.W. v5p0354c2s
Ward, F.W.Orde v6p0342c1s
Ward, G.A. v1p0989c1s
Ward, G.C. v1p1199c1s
Ward, G.E. v6p0313c1s
Ward, G.W. v5p0104c2s
Ward, H. v2p0168c2s
v3p0081c2s v3p0096c1s v3p0225c2s
v4p0006c2s v4p0015c1s v4p0041c2m
v4p0128c2s v4p0323c2s v4p0392c1m
v4p0427c1s v4p0449c2s v4p0480c1s
v4p0480c2s v5p0200c1s
Ward, H., Mrs. v2p0037c2s
v2p0115c2s v4p0323c2s v4p0527c2s
v4p0551c1s v5p0182c1s v6p0358c2s
v6p0402c2s v6p0403c2s
Ward, H., Mrs. and Harnack, A.
v4p0021c1s
Ward, H.A. v1p0881c2s
v4p0367c1m v5p0372c1s v5p0609c2s
v6p0066c1s v6p0412c2m v6p0448c2s
Ward, H.B. v4p0095c1s
v5p0016c2s v5p0062c1s v6p0175c2s
v6p0415c2s v6p0576c2s
Ward, H.B. and Barbour, E.H.
v6p0432c2s
Ward, H.C. v3p0036c1s
v3p0309c1s
Ward, H.C.E. v4p0053c1s
v4p0279c1s v5p0055c1s
Ward, H.D. v3p0312c2s
v3p0462c2s v4p0091c2s v4p0240c2s
v4p0245c2s v4p0374c1s v4p0489c2s
v4p0514c2s v4p0523c2s v5p0143c2s
v5p0263c2s v6p0177c1s v6p0239c1s
v6p0434c1s v6p0488c1s v6p0536c1s
v6p0543c2s v6p0569c2s v6p0632c1s
Ward, H.D.A. v1p1350c2s
Ward, H.E. v4p0543c1s
v4p0556c1s v4p0558c2m
Ward, H.F. v5p0170c2s
v5p0317c1s
Ward, H.G. v2p0342c1s
Ward, H.L. v3p0383c1s
v4p0060c2s v5p0005c1s v5p0372c1s
v6p0053c2s v6p0289c1s
Ward, H.M. v2p0080c1s
v2p0350c2s v2p0378c1m v2p0418c1s
v3p0035c1s v3p0037c1s v3p0257c1s
v3p0347c2s v3p0430c2s v4p0041c1s
v4p0405c1m v5p0073c1s v5p0458c1s
v5p0485c2s
Ward, H.Marshall v6p0244c1s
Ward, H.O. v4p0333c2s
Ward, H.O., Mrs. v4p0507c2s
Ward, H.S. v4p0487c1s
v5p0184c2s v5p0316c1s v5p0347c1s
v5p0447c2s v5p0448c1m v5p0448c2m
v5p0462c1s v6p0497c1s
Ward, Herbert v4p0025c2s
Ward, Herbert D. v6p0012c2s
Ward, Hon. Mrs. v1p0824c1s
Ward, Humphry, Mrs. v3p0043c2s
v6p0222c1s v6p0283c2s
Ward, Humphry, Mrs. and Smith, L.T.
v5p0317c1s
Ward, I.W. v4p0460c2s
Ward, J. v1p0002c1s
v1p0104c1s v1p0295c2s v1p0447c1s
v1p0480c1s v1p0561c2s v1p0771c2s
v1p0843c1s v2p0131c2s v2p0289c2s
v2p0318c2s v2p0358c2s v2p0419c2s
v3p0034c2s v3p0053c1s v3p0085c1s
v3p0143c2s v3p0280c1s v3p0330c1s
v3p0348c1s v3p0425c2s v3p0437c1s
v4p0033c2s v4p0465c1m v4p0475c1s
v4p0632c1s v5p0048c2s v5p0049c1s
v5p0098c2s v5p0119c1s v5p0181c1s
v5p0210c1s v5p0412c1s v5p0459c2s
v5p0546c1m v6p0012c2s v6p0034c2s
v6p0196c1s v6p0349c2s v6p0351c1s
v6p0408c2s v6p0457c2m v6p0495c2s
v6p0521c2s v6p0577c1s v6p0623c2s
Ward, J. and James, W. ... v3p0147c1s
Ward, J. et al. v4p0475c1s
Ward, J.B. v6p0126c2s
Ward, J.C. v1p0621c2s
v1p0718c2s v1p1283c2s v2p0102c2s
Ward, J.H. v1p0061c1s
v1p0169c1s v1p0256c1s v1p0261c2s
v1p0287c2s v1p0330c1s v1p0421c2s
v1p0557c1s v1p0691c2s v1p0694c2s
v1p0722c2s v1p0775c1s v1p0839c1s
v1p0839c2s v1p0855c2s v1p0867c2s
v1p0910c1s v1p0932c2s v1p0964c1s
v1p0973c1s v1p0989c2s v1p1047c2s
v1p1111c2s v1p1139c2s v1p1295c2s
v1p1412c1s v2p0085c2s v2p0265c2s
v2p0280c2s v2p0378c2s v2p0425c2s
v2p0469c1s v3p0046c1s v3p0102c2s
v3p0136c1s v3p0274c2s v3p0462c1s
v4p0068c2s v4p0074c2m v4p0209c1s
v4p0265c2s v4p0427c1s v4p0429c1s
v4p0551c2s v4p0612c2s
Ward, J.H. and MacColl, M.
v3p0082c2s
Ward, J.J. v5p0292c1s
v6p0077c2s v6p0104c1s v6p0259c1s
v6p0320c2s v6p0420c1s v6p0428c1s
v6p0502c1s v6p0502c2m v6p0583c2s
v6p0592c2s v6p0603c1s v6p0615c1s
Ward, J.M. v2p0035c2s
v3p0035c1m v6p0315c1s
Ward, J.S. v4p0594c1s
Ward, J.W. v1p0527c2s
v1p0551c1s v1p1065c1s v3p0345c1s
v3p0433c2s v6p0666c1s
Ward, John v3p0189c2s
v3p0353c2s v3p0365c2s v3p0430c1s
Ward, L. v6p0305c1s
v6p0351c1s
Ward, L.A. v1p1041c2s
Ward, L.E. v1p0356c1s
Ward, L.F. v1p0224c1s
v1p0351c1s v1p0434c1s v1p0702c1s
v1p0794c1s v1p1015c1s v1p1015c2s
v1p1028c1s v1p1214c2s v2p0149c1s
v2p0178c2s v2p0229c2s v2p0252c1s
v2p0258c1s v2p0289c2s v2p0293c1s

v2p0326c2s v2p0343c2s v2p0344c1s
v2p0347c2s v2p0423c2s v3p0107c2s
v3p0127c2s v3p0151c1s v3p0168c2s
v3p0178c1s v3p0194c2s v3p0209c1s
v3p0333c2s v3p0340c2s v3p0397c2s
v3p0444c2s v3p0458c2s v3p0467c2s
v3p0469c2s v4p0020c1s v4p0060c1s
v4p0069c2s v4p0135c2s v4p0180c1s
v4p0253c1s v4p0255c2s v4p0275c2s
v4p0366c1s v4p0379c1s v4p0430c1s
v4p0447c2s v4p0464c2s v4p0503c1s
v4p0532c1m v4p0532c2s v4p0534c2m
v4p0535c1m v4p0541c2s v4p0546c1s
v4p0616c2s v4p0623c1s v4p0628c1s
v5p0215c1s v5p0240c2s v5p0342c1s
v5p0461c2s v5p0483c1s v5p0535c1s
v5p0535c2s v5p0537c1s v5p0553c2s
v5p0571c2s v6p0142c2s v6p0162c2s
v6p0234c2s v6p0458c2s v6p0475c2s
v6p0522c1s v6p0585c2s v6p0599c2s
v6p0600c2s v6p0602c1m v6p0610c1m
Ward, L.F. and Brooks, W.K.
v5p0447c1s
Ward, L.H. v3p0378c2s
Ward, L.L. v6p0371c2s
Ward, L.M. v3p0325c2s
Ward, L.T. v1p0304c2s
v1p0434c2s
Ward, Lester F. v4p0210c1s
Ward, Lillian D. v6p0705c2s
Ward, M. v1p0021c1s
v1p0491c1s v3p0051c2m v5p0154c1s
v6p0345c2s v6p0457c1s
Ward, M., Mrs. v1p0699c1s
Ward, M.A. v1p1131c2s
v2p0413c1s v3p0440c1s v4p0169c1s
v5p0117c2s
Ward, M.A., Mrs. v3p0042c2s
v3p0302c1s v4p0408c2s
Ward, M.C. v1p0816c2s
Ward, M.E. v5p0163c1s
Ward, Marshall H. v6p0244c1s
Ward, May A. v6p0706c1s
Ward, Miss and Lindsay, Miss
v1p1165c1s
Ward, Mrs. v1p0144c1s
v1p0191c1s v1p0381c2s v1p0614c2s
v1p0898c2s v1p1036c2s v1p1292c1m
Ward, N. v1p0792c1s
Ward, N.M. v4p0409c2s
Ward, O.A. v5p0538c2s
Ward, R. v2p0127c1s
v2p0174c1s v2p0199c1s v2p0390c2s
v5p0568c1s v6p0685c1s
Ward, R.D. v5p0190c2s
v6p0005c2s v6p0014c1s v6p0023c1s
v6p0040c1m v6p0052c2s v6p0071c1s
v6p0092c1s v6p0117c2s v6p0132c1s
v6p0162c2m v6p0182c2s v6p0284c2s
v6p0304c1s v6p0308c2s v6p0313c1s
v6p0353c1m v6p0413c1m v6p0433c2m
v6p0486c2s v6p0530c2m v6p0614c2s
v6p0645c2s v6p0690c1s v6p0690c2m
Ward, R.DeC. v4p0275c1s
v5p0424c1s v6p0131c2m v6p0308c1m
v6p0309c1m v6p0605c1s v6p0606c1s
v6p0638c1s v6p0666c2s
Ward, R.H. v1p0835c2m
v1p0836c1m
Ward, S. v2p0265c2s
Ward, S., jr. v1p0767c1s
Ward, S.F. v1p1015c1s
Ward, S.H. v3p0201c2s
v3p0469c1s v3p0469c2s v3p0470c2s
v4p0031c1s v5p0455c2s
Ward, Susan H. v6p0618c1s
Ward, Susan Hayes v6p0574c2s
Ward, T. v1p0058c2s
v1p0723c1s v1p0997c1s v1p0997c2s
v1p1104c2s v2p0148c2s v2p0176c1s
v2p0201c2s v4p0500c2s v6p0364c2s
Ward, T.H. v1p0291c2s
Ward, V. v1p1412c1s
Ward, W. v2p0005c1s
v2p0038c2m v2p0081c2s v2p0197c1s
v2p0368c2s v2p0414c1s v3p0081c2s
v3p0148c2s v3p0205c1s v3p0302c1m
v3p0302c2s v3p0340c1s v3p0357c2s
v3p0364c2s v3p0377c2s v4p0059c2s
v4p0270c2s v4p0488c1s v4p0569c1s
v4p0570c1s v4p0601c1s v5p0040c2s
v5p0170c2s v5p0332c2s v5p0381c1s
v5p0409c1m v5p0429c2s v5p0494c1s
v5p0503c1s v6p0043c1s v6p0048c1s
v6p0236c2s v6p0368c1s v6p0507c1s
v6p0536c2s v6p0548c1s
Ward, W.C. v2p0399c2s
v3p0361c1s v4p0135c1s
Ward, W.E. v2p0041c1s
v2p0157c1s
Ward, W.G. v1p0213c2s
v1p0426c2s v1p0595c2s v1p0904c1s
v1p1095c1s v1p1235c1s v1p1300c2s
v1p1410c2m v2p0437c1s
Ward, W.H. v1p0069c1m
v1p0069c2s v1p0695c2s v1p0856c1s
v1p0890c2s v1p0999c1s v1p1179c1s
v2p0043c2s v2p0181c1s v2p0204c1s
v2p0249c2s v2p0284c2s v3p0029c2m
v3p0204c1s v3p0314c1s v3p0373c2s
v3p0416c1s v3p0467c1s v4p0259c1s
v4p0300c1s v4p0422c2s v4p0548c2s
v5p0267c1s v5p0267c2s v5p0270c2s
v5p0279c1s v5p0290c2s v5p0416c1s
v5p0460c1s v5p0460c2s v5p0520c2s
v5p0555c1s v5p0560c2s v6p0123c1s
v6p0126c2s v6p0195c1s v6p0221c2s
v6p0279c1s v6p0485c1s v6p0663c1s
Ward, W.H. and Boscawen, W.St.C.
v5p0517c1s
Ward, W.H. and
Frothingham, A.L., jr.. v3p0197c2s
Ward, W.H. et al. v2p0085c1s
v4p0168c2s
Ward, W.Hayes v6p0126c2s
Ward, W.J. v6p0067c2s
Ward, W.S. v1p0049c1s
v1p0915c2s v1p1149c2s
Ward, Wilfred v6p0108c1s
Ward, Wilfrid v5p0484c2s
Warde, A. v6p0462c2s
Warde, J. v6p0195c2s
Warden, F. v3p0429c1s
v3p0466c2s
Warden, Florence v4p0119c2s
Warden, H.F. v2p0156c2s
v2p0437c1s
Warden, W.L. v6p0044c2s
v6p0479c1s
Warder, G.A. v4p0142c1s
Warder, G.W. v6p0625c2s
Warder, R.B. v4p0099c1s
v4p0500c2s
Warder, R.B. and Shipley, W.P.
v1p0787c1s
Wardlaw, R. v1p0123c2s
Wardle, E.J. v6p0005c2s
Wardle, G. v3p0074c2s
Wardle, G.Y. v5p0146c1s
Wardle, H.N. v5p0518c2s
v6p0433c1s v6p0499c2s
Wardle, T. v3p0393c1m
v4p0524c1s
Wardlow, S.A. v5p0067c1s
Wardman, E. v3p0291c1s
v4p0124c1s v6p0301c2s v6p0452c2s
Wardman, G. v2p0006c2s
v2p0169c1s
v2p0383c2s
v3p0374c2s
Wardwell, M.E. v5p0219c2s
Wardwell, Mary E. v5p0631c1s
Ware, D.E. v1p0897c1s
v4p0259c2s
Ware, E.F. v3p0454c2s
v5p0374c2s
Ware, E.T. et al. v6p0039c2s
Ware, F.M. v5p0271c1m
v6p0182c1s v6p0297c2m v6p0297c2m
v6p0298c1m v6p0612c1s v6p0675c2s
Ware, H. v1p0120c1s
v1p0132c2s v1p0238c2m v1p0240c1s
v1p0310c2s v1p0504c2s v1p0599c1s
v1p0649c1s v1p0817c1s v1p0884c2s
v1p0975c1s v1p0989c2s v1p0997c2s
v1p1086c1s v1p1301c2s v1p1325c2s
v1p1340c2m v1p1433c2s
Ware, H., jr. v1p0023c2s
v1p0050c1s v1p0075c1s v1p0239c2s
v1p0472c1s v1p0504c2s v1p0535c2s
v1p0557c2s v1p0574c2s v1p0591c1s
v1p0619c2s v1p0649c1s v1p0699c1s
v1p0841c2s v1p0845c2s v1p0850c2s
v1p0877c1s v1p0890c2s v1p0983c1s
v1p1226c2s v1p1252c2s v1p1270c1s
v1p1286c1s v1p1292c2s v1p1333c2s
v1p1393c2s v1p1438c2s
Ware, H., Mrs. v1p0841c1s
v1p1334c2s v1p1392c1s v1p1439c2s
Ware, J. v1p0036c2s
v1p0041c1s v1p0042c2s v1p0078c1s
v1p0225c1s v1p0649c1s v1p0752c1s
v1p0810c1s v1p0816c2s v1p0900c1s
v1p1093c1s v1p1160c2s v1p1210c1s
v1p1375c2s
Ware, J., Mrs. v1p0040c1s
v1p0840c2s
Ware, J.E. v1p1014c2s
Ware, J.F.W. v1p0116c1s
v1p0357c2s v1p0433c1s v1p0599c1m
v1p0599c2m v1p0701c2s v1p0837c1s
v1p0855c1s v1p0904c1s v1p0910c2s
v1p1269c2s v1p1270c1s v1p1299c1s
v1p1344c2s v1p1426c2m
Ware, J.R. v1p0361c1s
v1p0834c1s v1p1112c2s v1p1127c2s
Ware, L.G. v1p0027c2s
v1p0061c2m v1p0065c1s v1p0331c2s
v1p0834c1s v1p0834c2s v1p0841c1s
v1p0958c1s v1p1276c2s
Ware, L.S. v1p0051c1s
v1p1218c2s v1p1325c1s
Ware, L.S. and Grimshaw, R.
v2p0424c1s
Ware, R.C. v1p0450c2s
v1p0702c1s
Ware, R.D. v6p0101c1s
Ware, S. v1p0053c1s
v1p1364c1s
Ware, W. v1p0085c2s
v1p0404c2s v1p0464c2s v1p0557c2s
v1p0697c2s v1p0768c1s v1p0817c1s
v1p1067c2s
Ware, W.K. v6p0028c2m
Ware, W.R. v1p0064c1s
v1p0848c2s v5p0025c2m v5p0026c1s
v5p0026c2m v5p0441c2s
Ware, W.R. and Allen, E.H.
v2p0240c2s
Warfield, B.B. v1p0686c1s
v1p1296c2s v2p0017c1s v2p0042c2s
v2p0044c1m v2p0045c1m v2p0432c1m
v3p0043c1m v3p0111c1s v3p0135c1s
v3p0215c2s v3p0233c2s v3p0342c2s
v3p0422c1s v3p0427c2s v4p0037c1s
v4p0045c1s v4p0053c1s v4p0053c2m
v4p0054c2s v4p0058c1s v4p0109c2s
v4p0191c2s v4p0213c1s v4p0286c1s
v4p0433c1s v4p0468c1s v4p0573c1m
v5p0038c1s v5p0043c2s v5p0055c2m
v5p0056c1s v5p0056c2s v5p0058c2s
v5p0089c1s v5p0195c1s v5p0271c2s
v5p0290c1s v5p0306c1s v5p0422c2s
v5p0438c2s v5p0463c2s v5p0464c1s
v5p0483c2s v5p0489c2s v5p0562c1s
v5p0627c1m v5p0640c2s v6p0040c2s
v6p0060c1s v6p0060c2m v6p0063c1s
v6p0125c2s v6p0177c2s v6p0235c2s
v6p0394c2s v6p0535c1s v6p0693c2s
Warfield, B.B. and Hodge, A.A.
v1p0645c2s
Warfield, B.B. and Thwing, C.F.
v4p0573c1s
Warfield, C. v6p0133c1s
Warfield, E.D. v2p0047c2s
v2p0055c1s v2p0065c2s v2p0197c1s
v2p0243c1s v2p0452c1s v3p0057c1s
v3p0064c2s v3p0235c2s v3p0236c1s
v3p0263c1s v4p0062c1s v4p0123c1m
v4p0259c1m v4p0454c2s v4p0593c1s
v4p0598c1s v5p0126c1s v5p0145c1s
v5p0190c2s v5p0191c2s v5p0232c2s
v5p0294c1s v5p0368c2s v5p0369c1s
v5p0391c1s v5p0451c2s v5p0541c2s
v5p0604c2s v5p0613c1s v5p0627c1s
Warfield, E.D. et al. v4p0206c2s
v5p0558c1s
Warfield, G. v6p0652c2s
Warfield, G.A. v6p0712c1s
Warfield, J.D. v4p0348c2s
Warfield, K. v5p0228c1s
v5p0563c1s
Warfield, R. v4p0386c2s
Warfield, R.B. v3p0184c2s
Warfield, R.B. et al. v3p0141c2s
Waring, C. v2p0055c1s
v2p0101c2s v2p0220c2s v2p0362c2s
v2p0363c1s v2p0444c2s
Waring, C.B. v1p0312c2s
v2p0089c2s
Waring, C.H. v1p0520c1s
Waring, Chas. v2p0424c1s
Waring, E. v3p0435c1s
Waring, G. v1p1369c2s
Waring, G.A. v6p0524c2s
Waring, G.E. v1p0472c2s
v1p0913c1s v1p0997c1s v1p1343c1s
v2p0122c2m v2p0283c1s v2p0396c2s
v4p0114c2s v4p0612c2s v5p0061c1s
v5p0165c1s v5p0258c1s v5p0436c2s
v5p0556c1s
Waring, G.E. et al. v5p0407c2s
Waring, G.E., jr. v1p0015c1s
v1p0025c2s v1p0181c1s v1p0299c1m
v1p0362c2m v1p0444c1s v1p0444c2m
v1p0560c2s v1p0578c2m v1p0597c2m
v1p0604c2m v1p0682c1s v1p0839c1s
v1p0874c2s v1p0897c1s v1p0917c1s
v1p0926c1s v1p0950c2s v1p0996c2m
v1p0997c1m v1p1105c1s v1p1131c1s
v1p1150c1s v1p1152c1s v1p1157c2s
v1p1181c1s v1p1181c2m v1p1337c2s
v1p1371c2s v1p1380c2s v1p1389c1s
v1p1396c1s v2p0063c1s v2p0114c1s
v2p0122c2m v2p0207c2s v2p0209c1s
v2p0283c1s v2p0345c2s v2p0396c1m
v3p0121c2s v3p0264c2s v4p0429c1s
v4p0516c2m v5p0061c1s v5p0169c2s
v5p0225c2s v5p0407c1s v5p0457c2s
v5p0556c1m v5p0597c1s v5p0626c2s
Waring, G.L. v6p0570c1s
Waring, George E., jr. ... v2p0396c2s
Waring, H. v4p0272c1s
Waring, H.W. v4p0503c1s
Waring, J.B. v1p0175c1s
Waring, J.G. v4p0319c2s
Waring, J.H.N. v6p0447c2s
Warington, G. v1p1218c1s
Warington, R. v1p0923c2s
v1p1061c1s v2p0315c1s v3p0399c2s
v5p0598c2s
Warker, E.Van de v1p0036c2s
v1p0315c2s v1p0643c1s v1p0643c2s
v1p0981c2s v1p0990c2s v1p1182c1s
v1p1292c1s v1p1337c1s v1p1419c2s
v1p1425c2m
Warland, C. v2p0419c2s
Warlow, P., Col. and Hobart, Pasha
v2p0129c1s v2p0448c2s
Warman, C. v4p0047c2s

v4p0092c1s v4p0140c2s v4p0147c2s
v4p0150c1s v4p0204c2s v4p0292c2s
v4p0337c2m v4p0470c2s v4p0471c1s
v4p0471c2m v4p0548c1s v4p0575c2s
v5p0103c2s v5p0139c2s v5p0206c2s
v5p0275c1s v5p0301c1s v5p0314c1s
v5p0318c1s v5p0343c2s v5p0422c2s
v5p0434c2s v5p0477c1s v5p0478c1s
v5p0586c1s v5p0610c2s
Warman, Cy v6p0038c2s
v6p0097c1m v6p0098c1s v6p0177c1s
v6p0177c2s v6p0430c2s v6p0467c1s
v6p0474c1s v6p0489c2s v6p0530c2s
v6p0550c1s v6p0571c1s v6p0604c1s
v6p0631c2s v6p0674c2s v6p0691c1s
v6p0698c2s v6p0708c1s
Warman, E.B. and Cox, H.C.
v4p0274c2s
Warman, P.G. v6p0576c1s
Warming, L. v6p0460c1s
Warmont, C. v1p0372c2s
Warnack, H.C. v6p0386c1s
Warne, C. v1p0046c2s
v1p0621c1s v1p1122c2s v1p1368c2s
Warne, F.J. v4p0116c2s
v5p0557c1s v6p0132c2m v6p0133c1s
v6p0418c2s v6p0422c2s v6p0652c1s
Warne, F.L. v5p0291c2s
Warneck, G. v2p0376c1s
Warneford, Lieut. v1p1434c1s
Warner, A. v6p0149c2s
v6p0166c2s v6p0287c2s v6p0339c1s
v6p0394c1s v6p0627c2s v6p0652c2s
Warner, A.G. v2p0407c1s
v3p0032c2s v3p0074c1s v3p0092c2s
v3p0099c1s v3p0101c2s v3p0216c2s
v3p0341c1s v3p0441c1s v4p0096c2s
v4p0139c2s v4p0206c1s v4p0315c1s
v4p0450c2s v4p0455c1s v4p0460c1s
Warner, A.H. v6p0090c1s
Warner, A.J. v1p0326c2s
v1p1232c2m v4p0059c1s v4p0059c2s
v4p0524c1s v4p0526c1s v5p0149c2s
Warner, Anne v6p0013c2s
v6p0019c2s v6p0303c1s v6p0402c2s
v6p0420c2s v6p0434c1s v6p0582c1s
Warner, B. v6p0451c2s
Warner, B.E. v3p0328c1s
Warner, C. v4p0213c2s
v4p0349c1s
Warner, C.D. v1p0006c2s
v1p0029c1s v1p0084c2s v1p0189c2s
v1p0205c1s v1p0253c1s v1p0294c1s
v1p0323c1s v1p0349c2s v1p0395c1s
v1p0413c1s v1p0492c2s v1p0667c1s
v1p0682c1s v1p0909c1s v1p0910c1s
v1p0922c2s v1p0951c2s v1p0960c2s
v1p1147c1s v1p1183c1s v1p1186c1s
v1p1221c1s v1p1240c1s v1p1329c1s
v1p1351c1s v1p1402c1s v2p0011c2s
v2p0060c2s v2p0082c2s v2p0139c2s
v2p0155c1s v2p0183c2s v2p0220c2s
v2p0230c1s v2p0295c2s v2p0298c2s
v2p0312c1s v2p0321c2s v2p0355c1m
v2p0411c1m v2p0412c2m v2p0437c1s
v2p0464c1s v3p0001c2s v3p0063c1s
v3p0063c2m v3p0065c1s v3p0076c2s
v3p0085c1s v3p0089c2s v3p0093c2s
v3p0105c1m v3p0107c1s v3p0173c1s
v3p0214c2s v3p0225c2s v3p0234c2s
v3p0235c2s v3p0253c1s v3p0254c1m
v3p0259c1s v3p0274c1s v3p0277c1m
v3p0281c2s v3p0287c2s v3p0302c2s
v3p0303c1s v3p0307c2s v3p0308c1s
v3p0323c2s v3p0355c1s v3p0372c2s
v3p0389c2s v3p0394c1s v3p0402c1s
v3p0405c2s v3p0421c2s v3p0446c1s
v3p0466c1s v4p0178c1s v4p0231c1s
v4p0293c1s v4p0293c2s v4p0362c2s
v4p0363c2s v4p0405c2s v4p0514c2s
v4p0551c2s v4p0592c2s v5p0003c1s
v5p0016c1s v5p0040c2s v5p0143c2s
v5p0164c2s v5p0179c2s v5p0255c2s
v5p0256c2s v5p0341c1s v5p0341c2s
v5p0403c1s v6p0526c1s
Warner, C.D. et al. v2p0477c2s
Warner, C.E. v2p0054c1s
v2p0436c2s
Warner, Clarence D. v4p0008c1s
v4p0176c2m
Warner, E.E.K. v6p0193c1s
Warner, E.N. v6p0129c1s
Warner, E.P. v1p1131c2s
Warner, F. v1p1270c2s
v2p0309c2s v3p0077c1s v4p0103c2s
v4p0104c1s v4p0365c1s v4p0505c2s
v6p0594c2s
Warner, G. v5p0336c1s
Warner, G.F. v3p0066c1s
v3p0429c1s v4p0296c1s v4p0509c1s
v6p0333c1m
Warner, G.T. v3p0186c2s
Warner, H. v1p0442c1s
v4p0592c1s v6p0625c1s
Warner, H.D. v2p0067c2s
v2p0130c1s v2p0212c1s v2p0411c1s
v2p0463c1s
Warner, H.E. v1p0420c2s
v1p0627c2s v3p0155c1s v5p0418c1s
Warner, H.H. v2p0096c1s
v2p0466c1s
Warner, H.J. v1p0021c1s
v1p0063c1s v1p0071c2s v1p0076c1s
v1p0083c2s v1p0108c1s v1p0233c1s
v1p0256c1s v1p0264c1s v1p0314c2m
v1p0322c1s v1p0329c2s v1p0552c1m
v1p0669c2s v1p0673c2s v1p0722c2s
v1p1107c2s v1p1121c2s v1p1124c1s
v1p1125c2s v1p1126c1s v1p1157c2s
v1p1160c2s v1p1305c2s v1p1337c2s
Warner, H.L. v2p0050c1s
Warner, H.L. and Hughes, T.
v3p0368c2s
Warner, Horace v5p0617c1s
Warner, J. v1p0187c1s
v1p0377c1s
Warner, J.B. v4p0470c1s
v5p0328c2s
Warner, J.D. v3p0393c2s
v4p0434c1s v4p0524c2s v5p0004c2m
v5p0076c1s v5p0406c2s v5p0407c1s
v5p0526c2m v5p0568c2s v6p0128c2s
v6p0435c2s v6p0454c1s
Warner, J.DeW. v4p0563c2s
v5p0391c1s v5p0391c2s v5p0556c2s
Warner, J.H. v1p0436c2s
v1p0583c2s v1p1121c2s v1p1170c2s
v1p1246c2s
Warner, J.L. v1p1244c2s
Warner, J.W. v6p0507c1s
Warner, L. v6p0346c2s
v6p0349c2s v6p0351c1s v6p0588c2s
Warner, L.C. v4p0088c1s
v6p0283c1s v6p0455c1s
Warner, M. v6p0077c1s
Warner, M.L. v5p0191c1s
Warner, O.L. et al. v2p0184c2s
Warner, R.L. v4p0585c1s
v5p0276c2s
Warner, R.S. v6p0203c1s
Warner, S.M. v1p0696c1s
Warner, W.D. v5p0091c2s
v5p0402c2s
Warner, W.L., Mrs. v5p0284c2s
Warner, W.R. v4p0568c1s
v6p0509c1s
Warnerke, L. v1p1004c1s
Warr, Constance de la, Countess
v6p0441c2s
Warr, Countess de la v6p0239c1s
Warr, Earl De la v1p0012c1s
v1p1329c2s
v2p0131c1s
Warr, G.C. v2p0377c1s
Warrand, H. v6p0227c1s
Warrand, H.M. v6p0168c1s
v6p0440c1s
Warre, E. v3p0351c2s
v3p0440c1s
Warren, A. v2p0377c1s
v4p0027c2s v4p0195c2s v4p0274c1s
v4p0430c2s v5p0093c2s v5p0188c2s
v5p0567c1s v5p0608c1s v6p0411c1s
v6p0429c2s
Warren, Arthur v6p0660c2s
Warren, Arthur and Williams, J.L.
v4p0031c2s v4p0110c2s
Warren, B.E. v6p0442c2s
Warren, B.W. v6p0621c1s
Warren, C. v1p0742c2s
v2p0004c2s v2p0434c2s v3p0005c1s
v3p0120c1s v3p0169c1s v3p0257c1s
v3p0279c1s v3p0336c1s v5p0014c1s
v5p0127c2s v5p0136c2s v5p0154c1s
v5p0168c1s v5p0235c2s v5p0241c1s
v5p0243c2s v5p0274c1s v5p0360c2s
v5p0588c1s v6p0007c1s v6p0100c1s
v6p0643c2s
Warren, C., Gen. v5p0160c2s
Warren, C., Sir v3p0004c2s
v5p0587c2s v6p0542c1s
Warren, C.E. v2p0030c2s
v2p0046c1s v2p0048c1s v2p0061c1s
v2p0089c1m v2p0171c2s v2p0196c1s
v2p0203c1s v2p0208c1s v2p0232c1s
v2p0250c2s v2p0261c2s v2p0280c1s
v2p0324c1s v2p0328c1s v2p0336c2s
v2p0343c1s v2p0414c1s v2p0414c2s
v3p0268c1s
Warren, C.F.S. v3p0106c1s
v3p0117c2s v3p0148c2s v4p0048c2s
v4p0244c2s v4p0467c2s v4p0541c1s
Warren, C.H. v1p0100c1s
v5p0377c2s
Warren, C.H. and Penfield, S.L.
v5p0225c2s v5p0432c2s v5p0645c2s
Warren, Cecilia v5p0331c2s
Warren, Charles v6p0300c2s
Warren, Charles, Gen. v5p0093c1s
Warren, Cornelia v6p0106c1s
v6p0357c2s
Warren, E. v1p0228c2s
v1p0426c2s v1p0730c1s v2p0283c2s
v2p0479c2s
Warren, E.A. v5p0364c2s
Warren, E.C. v6p0432c2s
Warren, E.P. v5p0454c1s
v5p0627c1s v6p0473c2s
Warren, E.R. v3p0363c1s
v3p0397c1s
Warren, F. v2p0298c2s
v3p0097c1s
Warren, F.E. v2p0054c1s
v2p0228c2s v2p0373c1s v5p0489c2s
v6p0178c2s
Warren, F.E. and Westwood, I.O.
v3p0144c2s
Warren, F.E. et al. v3p0323c2s
Warren, F.M. v3p0101c1s
v3p0171c1s v3p0320c2s v4p0214c2s
v4p0294c2s v5p0002c1s v5p0115c2s
v5p0275c1s v5p0384c1s v5p0432c1s
v5p0478c2s v5p0492c2s v5p0591c2s
Warren, F.M. et al. v5p0221c1s
Warren, F.P. v5p0327c1s
Warren, Francis E. v6p0021c1s
Warren, G.K. v1p0162c2s
v1p0848c2s v1p0854c2s
Warren, G.W. v1p0074c1s
v1p0452c1s v1p0829c2s v1p0993c2s
v1p1068c1s v1p1395c1m
Warren, H. v6p0147c2s
Warren, H.C. v4p0492c2s
v4p0529c2s v5p0016c2s v5p0106c1s
v5p0139c2s v5p0370c1s v5p0427c2s
v5p0470c2s v5p0486c2s
Warren, H.C. and Farrand, L.
v4p0464c2s
Warren, H.L. v4p0125c1s
v5p0025c2s v5p0073c1s v6p0027c2s
v6p0028c1m
Warren, H.L. and Cram, R.A.
v5p0026c2s
Warren, H.L. and Fox, J.A.
v4p0023c2s
Warren, H.L. et al. v3p0456c1s
Warren, H.P. v2p0311c1s
v5p0025c2s
Warren, H.Valette v6p0334c2s
Warren, H.W. v1p0119c1s
v1p0141c2s v1p0538c1s v1p1099c2m
v1p1341c1s v3p0107c2s v3p0474c1s
v4p0186c2s v4p0511c2s v5p0059c2s
v5p0218c1s v5p0590c1s v6p0014c2s
v6p0216c2s v6p0292c2s v6p0315c1s
v6p0418c2s
Warren, I. and Prentice, M.L.
v5p0334c1s
Warren, I.P. v2p0042c2s
v2p0222c2s
Warren, Irene v6p0375c1s
Warren, J.A. v5p0472c1s
v5p0547c1s
Warren, J.C. v1p0810c1s
v1p1005c1s v1p1194c1s v1p1386c2s
Warren, J.E. v1p0026c2s
v1p0966c1s v1p1230c2s v4p0300c2s
Warren, J.G. v1p0598c2s
Warren, J.L. v1p0057c2s
v1p1294c2s
Warren, J.P. v1p0990c1s
v6p0589c2s
Warren, J.P. et al. v5p0445c1s
Warren, J.T. v5p0595c1s
Warren, K.M. v4p0079c1s
v4p0265c1s v4p0618c1s
Warren, Kate M. v4p0320c1s
Warren, L. v1p1275c2s
v1p1312c1s
Warren, L.E. v4p0149c2s
Warren, M. v2p0040c1s
v2p0212c2s v2p0250c1s v2p0339c1s
v3p0085c1s v5p0028c2s v5p0326c2s
v5p0401c1s v5p0600c2s v6p0271c2s
v6p0651c2s
Warren, M.S. v5p0040c1s
v5p0158c2s v5p0186c1s v5p0382c1s
v5p0410c2s v5p0610c2s v5p0611c1s
v5p0631c1s
Warren, Mary S. v6p0453c1s
Warren, O.H. v3p0276c2s
Warren, S. v1p0155c2s
v1p0185c2s v1p0257c2s v1p0349c2s
v1p0351c1s v1p0464c2s v1p0681c2s
v1p0801c2s v1p0886c1s v1p0887c1s
v1p0956c1s v1p0985c1s v1p1012c1s
v1p1178c2s v1p1211c1s v1p1234c2s
v1p1244c1s v1p1245c2m v1p1258c2s
v1p1293c2s v1p1413c2m v1p1432c2s
Warren, S.E. v1p0258c2s
v1p0365c1s v1p0408c1s v1p1163c2s
v2p0123c2s v2p0220c2s v3p0378c2s
v4p0381c2s v5p0512c2s v6p0507c2s
Warren, S.M. v4p0559c2s
v5p0358c1s v5p0484c1s v6p0340c2s
v6p0628c2s
Warren, T.H. v4p0605c2s
v5p0242c2s v5p0456c1s v6p0032c1s
v6p0130c1s v6p0164c1s v6p0604c1s
v6p0639c1s
Warren, T.P.B. v3p0368c2s
Warren, T.R. v1p1193c1s
v1p1435c2s v2p0411c2s
Warren, T.T.P.B. v3p0280c2s
Warren, W. v1p0260c1s
v1p0608c1s v1p1410c2s v2p0342c1s
v5p0162c1s
Warren, W.F. v1p0059c1s
v1p0074c2s v1p0128c1s v1p0305c1s
v1p0847c2m v1p1099c2s v1p1302c1s

v2p0106c2s v2p0384c2s v3p0265c2s
v3p0395c2s v4p0032c2s v4p0367c2m
v4p0629c1s v5p0057c1s v5p0319c2s
v6p0210c1s v6p0354c1s v6p0425c2s
Warren, W.I. v1p0110c1s
Warren, W.L. v1p1245c1s
Warrender, H.V. v5p0567c2s
Warriner, E.C. v5p0015c2s
v5p0374c1s
Warring, C.B. v1p0305c1s
v1p0455c2s v1p0509c2s v1p1015c1s
v2p0173c2s v3p0044c1s v3p0103c2s
v4p0135c2s v4p0271c1s v4p0357c2s
v6p0420c2s
Warrington, F.M. v6p0470c1s
Warrington, J. v3p0205c2s
Warrington, J.N. v2p0356c1s
Warrington, R. v1p1287c2s
Warschauer, J. v5p0436c1m
Wartegg, E.v.H. v6p0347c2s
Warth, H. v4p0468c2s
Wartmann, L.F. v1p0281c1s
Warvelle, G.W. v2p0206c2m
v3p0342c1s
Warwick, C. v4p0610c1s
Warwick, Countess of v5p0061c2s
v5p0177c2s v5p0570c1s v5p0620c1s
v6p0116c2s v6p0497c2s v6p0566c2s
Warwick, Frances E., Countess of
v6p0009c1s
Warwick, H.S. and Applin, A.
v5p0608c2s
Wash, R. v3p0398c1s
v3p0399c1s
Wash, R.F. v6p0226c2s
Washburn, A.H. v4p0131c1s
v5p0134c2s v6p0633c1s
Washburn, C. v6p0604c1s
Washburn, C.A. v1p0282c2s
v1p0361c2s v1p0600c1s v1p1048c1s
v1p1278c1s v6p0238c2s v6p0606c1s
Washburn, C.G. v6p0635c2s
Washburn, C.H. v1p0668c2s
v1p0719c2s v1p1101c1s
Washburn, E. v1p0290c1s
v1p0436c2s v1p0485c2s v1p0650c2s
v1p0689c1s v1p0697c2s v1p0715c2s
v1p0736c2s v1p0867c1s v1p1159c2s
v1p1206c1s v1p1244c1s v5p0112c1s
v6p0531c2s
Washburn, E.A. v1p0132c1s
v1p0242c1s v1p1101c2s v1p1161c1s
v1p1215c1s v1p1301c1s v1p1302c1s
Washburn, E.A. et al. v1p0645c2s
Washburn, E.B. v1p0339c1m
v1p0732c1s
Washburn, E.H. v1p0842c1s
Washburn, F.L. v4p0414c2s
v5p0426c2m v5p0581c1s v6p0320c2s
v6p0473c2s
Washburn, F.T. v1p0043c2s
v1p0119c2s v1p0239c2s v1p0286c1s
v1p0358c1s v1p0645c2s v1p1085c1s
v1p1118c2s v1p1158c1s
Washburn, G. v1p0151c1s
v1p0508c2s v1p0546c1s v1p1330c2s
v4p0376c1s v5p0501c1s v5p0532c1s
v5p0595c1s v6p0450c2s v6p0545c2s
Washburn, G.F. et al. v6p0667c1s
Washburn, J. v1p0719c1s
v1p0722c2s
Washburn, L.M. v4p0009c1s
Washburn, M. v4p0462c1s
v4p0465c1s v5p0344c1s v5p0480c2s
Washburn, M.F. v5p0008c2s
v5p0129c1s v6p0184c2s v6p0410c2s
v6p0521c1s v6p0709c2s
Washburn, Margaret F. v6p0433c2s
Washburn, O.M. v6p0109c1s
v6p0149c2s v6p0210c1s
Washburn, O.R. v6p0122c2s
Washburn, S. v5p0477c1s
Washburn, W.D. v6p0633c1s
Washburn, W.D., jr. v5p0378c2s
Washburn, W.P. v1p0730c2s
Washburn, W.T. v1p1326c2s
Washburne, E.A. v1p0672c2s
v1p1384c1s
Washburne, E.B. v1p0957c2s
v2p0259c1s v2p0438c2s v3p0094c2s
v3p0320c2s
Washburne, F.D. v1p0924c1s
Washburne, I. v1p0086c2s
v1p0260c1s
Washburne, I., jr. v1p0392c1m
v1p1265c1m v1p1345c1s
Washburne, M.F. v4p0100c1s
v6p0302c1s v6p0356c2s v6p0705c1s
Washburne, W.D. v4p0218c2s
v4p0415c2s
Washer, B.A. v5p0522c1s
Washer, B.F. v4p0276c1s
Washington, A. v2p0457c2s
Washington, B.C. v5p0079c1s
v5p0132c1s v5p0620c2m v6p0648c2s
Washington, B.C., jr. v5p0184c2s
Washington, B.T. v4p0283c2s
v4p0396c2m v4p0397c1s v4p0587c2m
v5p0105c2s v5p0384c2s v5p0402c2s
v5p0403c1m v5p0403c2m v6p0144c1s
v6p0219c2s
Washington, B.T. et al. .. v5p0524c2s
Washington, B.T., Mrs. ... v6p0447c1s
Washington, Booker T. v6p0006c1s
v6p0039c2s v6p0318c2s v6p0340c2s
v6p0399c2m v6p0446c2m v6p0447c2m
v6p0448c1m v6p0448c2m v6p0595c1s
v6p0662c1m
Washington, Booker T. et al.
v6p0447c1s
Washington, Capt. v1p0901c2s
Washington, E. v6p0099c2s
Washington, E.B. v2p0466c2s
v4p0611c2s
Washington, E.B. and Stabler, H.S.
v4p0612c1s
Washington, G. v4p0071c1s
v6p0686c2s
Washington, H.A. v1p1373c2s
v2p0361c2s
Washington, H.L. v5p0196c2s
Washington, H.S. v3p0334c1s
v4p0040c1s v4p0046c2s v4p0446c1s
v4p0580c2s v5p0235c2s v5p0279c2s
v5p0361c1s v5p0372c1s v5p0491c2s
v5p0580c2s v5p0614c1s v6p0593c1s
v6p0630c1s
Washington, H.S. and Hidden, W.E.
v3p0280c2s
Washington, H.S. and
Hillebrand, W.F. v3p0099c2s
Washington, H.S. and Pirsson, L.V.
v6p0057c2m v6p0450c2s
Washington, L.Q. v5p0132c1s
Washington, M.V., Mrs. ... v3p0179c1s
Washington, T.A. v4p0560c2s
v4p0612c1s
Waska, F.E. v5p0623c1s
Wasmuth, H.A. v3p0015c1m
v3p0089c2s
Wason, R.A. v6p0045c2s
Wason, Robert A. v6p0161c2s
Wassa, Pasco, Pasha and Colquhoun, P.
v4p0433c1s
Wassell, W. v5p0004c1s
Wassell, W.H. v4p0523c2s
v4p0527c2s
Wassermann, L. v2p0372c1s
v2p0449c2s v2p0483c1s v3p0067c2s
v3p0107c1s v3p0233c1s v3p0312c1s
v3p0394c1s v4p0088c2s v4p0358c2s
Wasson, D.A. v1p0003c1s
v1p0085c1s v1p0100c1s v1p0109c1s
v1p0109c2s v1p0173c1s v1p0208c2s
v1p0247c2s v1p0297c2s v1p0361c2s
v1p0420c2s v1p0515c2s v1p0531c2s
v1p0594c1s v1p0600c2s v1p0686c2s
v1p0715c2s v1p0745c2s v1p0900c1m
v1p0901c1s v1p0972c2m v1p0998c2s
v1p1021c2s v1p1022c1s v1p1040c2s
v1p1045c1s v1p1074c1m v1p1092c2s
v1p1095c2s v1p1108c1s v1p1141c1s
v1p1214c1s v1p1260c1s v1p1384c1s
v1p1431c2s v2p0196c1s v2p0473c1s
Wasson, G.S. v5p0641c2s
v6p0076c1s v6p0405c2s v6p0472c2s
v6p0552c2s v6p0561c1s v6p0580c1s
v6p0635c2s v6p0657c1s v6p0663c1s
v6p0697c2s v6p0701c2s
Wasson, J.B. v3p0084c2s
Wasson, L. v5p0420c2s
Watanabe, R. v4p0415c2s
v4p0474c1s
Watanabe, R. and Hill, A.R.
v4p0388c1s v4p0515c1s
Watanabe, Seitei v6p0337c2s
Watanna, O. v5p0596c1s
v6p0388c1s v6p0388c2s
Watanna, Onoto v5p0317c2s
v6p0338c1s
Watch, A.F. v4p0016c2s
Watchorn, R. v4p0193c2s
Watchorn, R. et al. v6p0309c1s
Water, G.R.Van De v3p0084c2s
v3p0415c2s
Waterbury, E.B. v6p0648c2s
Waterbury, I.C. v6p0318c2s
v6p0506c1s v6p0511c2s
Waterbury, J.B. v1p0846c1s
v5p0014c2s v5p0266c1s
Waterbury, J.I. v6p0636c2s
Waterbury, J.W. v1p0402c1s
Waterbury, Jennie B. v5p0494c2s
Waterbury, L. and Iliff, E.
v4p0577c1s
Waterbury, Mrs. v1p0851c2s
Waterbury, S.J. v1p0466c1s
Waterer, C. v4p0071c1s
v4p0122c2s v4p0171c1s v4p0584c1s
v5p0587c1s
Waterfield, O.C. v2p0423c2s
Waterfield, W. v2p0024c1s
Waterford, Marquis of v3p0221c1s
Waterhouse, A. v2p0020c1s
v3p0361c1s
Waterhouse, A. and Lawson, H.L.W.
v3p0412c1s
Waterhouse, Buck v5p0209c1s
Waterhouse, C.W. v2p0335c2s
Waterhouse, F.A. v4p0123c1s
Waterhouse, J. and Smith, W.G.
v6p0592c2s
Waterhouse, P. v5p0026c2s
v5p0218c1s v6p0028c2m v6p0474c2s
v6p0641c2s
Waterhouse, S. v2p0293c1s
v2p0383c2m
Waterloo, S. v4p0099c2s
v5p0066c2s v5p0135c2s v6p0612c1s
v6p0702c2s
Waterlow, D.S. v5p0273c1s
Waterlow, E.A. v6p0360c2s
Waterlow, S. v6p0333c1s
Waterlow, S.P. v6p0267c1s
Waterman, A.N. v6p0634c1s
Waterman, F.A. v5p0072c2s
Waterman, G. v1p0070c1s
Waterman, J. v4p0074c2s
Waterman, R., jr. v4p0101c1s
v4p0171c2m
Waterman, T. v1p1392c2s
Waterman, T.T. v3p0272c1s
v6p0352c1s
Waters, A. v4p0007c1s
v4p0101c2s v4p0182c1s v4p0346c2s
v4p0379c1s v4p0436c2s v4p0565c2s
v5p0106c2s
Waters, A. et al. v5p0613c2s
Waters, A.C. and Hayward, T.E.
v5p0459c2s
Waters, A.T. v6p0649c2s
Waters, B. v6p0177c2m
v6p0178c1s
Waters, C. v4p0546c2s
Waters, C.A. v3p0172c2s
Waters, C.E. v5p0460c2s
v6p0016c1s v6p0222c1s
Waters, C.E. and Parsons, C.L.
v6p0015c2m
Waters, E. v6p0249c2s
v6p0332c2s v6p0676c2s
Waters, E.C. v2p0020c1s
v2p0040c1m v2p0076c2s v2p0392c1s
v2p0398c1s v2p0401c1s v2p0409c2s
Waters, F. v5p0622c1s
v6p0505c2s
Waters, H. v1p0141c1s
Waters, H.F. v2p0133c1s
v2p0172c2s v2p0197c1m v3p0138c1s
v3p0168c2s v3p0363c2s v3p0455c1m
v3p0464c2s v4p0221c2s v4p0514c2s
v5p0189c2s v5p0227c2s v5p0267c2s
v5p0360c1s
Waters, J. v1p0104c2s
Waters, M. v4p0321c1s
Waters, Miriam Van v6p0140c2s
Waters, N.R. v1p0148c2s
Waters, T. v5p0277c2s
v5p0298c2s v5p0378c1s v5p0496c2s
v6p0053c1s v6p0056c2s v6p0094c1s
v6p0149c1s v6p0230c2s v6p0433c2s
v6p0444c1s v6p0453c1s v6p0466c1s
v6p0527c1s
Waters, Theo. v6p0056c2s
Waters, W.E. v4p0035c2m
v5p0229c2s v5p0538c1s
Waters, W.G. v2p0104c2s
v3p0068c1s v4p0079c1s
Waters, W.G. and Harcourt, A.F.P.
v6p0679c1s
Waters, W.R. v1p0239c1s
Waterston, A.M. v1p0077c2s
Waterston, C. v5p0252c1s
v5p0314c1s
Waterston, G. v1p0291c2s
v1p0541c2s
Waterston, J.J. v1p0401c1s
Waterston, R.C. v1p0062c1s
v1p0064c2s v1p0274c1s v1p0390c1s
v1p0644c1s v1p0700c2s v1p0738c1s
v1p0867c2s v1p0877c1s v1p1052c2s
v1p1089c1s v1p1257c1s v1p1309c2s
v1p1408c2s v1p1438c2s
Waterston, R.C., Mrs. v1p1424c1s
Waterton, E. v1p0625c1s
v1p1033c1s v1p1108c1s v2p0241c2s
Waterworth, W. v1p0994c1s
v1p1058c1s v1p1116c2s
Watherston, E.J. v1p1197c2s
v1p1423c1s v2p0172c2m
Watkin, E. v4p0002c1s
Watkin, E., Sir v4p0472c2s
Watkin, E.W., Sir v3p0139c1s
Watkin, W.T. v2p0056c2s
v2p0376c2m v2p0423c1s v2p0458c2s
v3p0365c2m v3p0382c2s
Watkin, W.T. et al. v3p0076c1s
v3p0365c2s
Watkins, A. v4p0160c1s
v5p0080c2m v5p0158c1s v5p0199c2s
v5p0434c1s v5p0471c2s v5p0475c2s
v5p0536c1s v5p0628c2s v6p0497c2s
v6p0516c1s
Watkins, B.U. v1p0313c2s
v1p1203c1s v1p1425c2s v2p0044c1s
v2p0080c2s v2p0106c2s v2p0148c2s
v2p0201c2s
Watkins, F. v6p0007c1s
Watkins, G.P. v5p0469c1s
v6p0690c1s

Watkins, H.T. v6p0421c1s
Watkins, J. v1p0403c2m
v1p0643c1s v1p0893c2s
Watkins, J.A. v4p0107c2m
Watkins, J.E. v5p0188c1s
v6p0144c2s v6p0146c2s
Watkins, J.E., jr. v6p0597c1s
Watkins, J.F. v1p0068c2s
v1p0627c2s v1p1148c2s
Watkins, J.R. v5p0047c2s
v5p0506c1s
Watkins, J.T. v1p0368c1s
v1p0380c1s
Watkins, L.R. v6p0142c1s
Watkins, M.G. v1p0039c2m
v1p0042c2s v1p0088c1s v1p0136c2s
v1p0137c1s v1p0155c2s v1p0198c1s
v1p0333c1s v1p0459c1s v1p0500c1s
v1p0540c1s v1p0708c2s v1p0887c1s
v1p0898c2s v1p0951c1s v1p1146c2s
v1p1172c2s v1p1179c2s v1p1239c2s
v1p1244c2s v1p1310c2s v1p1327c1s
v1p1327c2s v1p1383c2s v1p1406c1s
v2p0014c1s v2p0014c2m v2p0030c1s
v2p0046c1s v2p0046c2m v2p0047c1s
v2p0047c2s v2p0059c2s v2p0062c1s
v2p0104c1s v2p0114c2m v2p0120c2s
v2p0158c1m v2p0160c1s v2p0160c2m
v2p0241c2s v2p0255c2s v2p0262c1s
v2p0288c1s v2p0401c2s v2p0427c2s
v3p0102c2s v3p0149c2s v3p0154c1s
v3p0254c1s v3p0305c2s v3p0315c1s
v3p0354c2s v3p0362c1s v3p0381c2s
v3p0461c1s v3p0471c1s v4p0060c2s
v4p0084c2s v4p0253c1s v4p0371c2s
v4p0412c2s v4p0432c2s v4p0485c1s
v4p0528c1s v4p0583c1s v4p0624c1s
v5p0021c1s v5p0222c2s v5p0347c1s
v5p0433c2s v5p0490c1s v5p0525c2s
v6p0584c1s
Watkins, O.D. v6p0125c2s
Watkins, P.M. v4p0090c2s
v4p0517c1s
Watkins, S.C. v6p0067c2s
v6p0068c2s v6p0288c2s
Watkins, S.G. v6p0620c2s
Watkins, S.R. v2p0207c1s
v2p0434c2s
Watkins, S.R. and Jackman, J.S.
v2p0299c2s
Watkins, W.K. v3p0420c2s
v3p0457c2s v4p0433c1s v4p0623c1s
v5p0140c2s v5p0256c2s v5p0408c1s
v5p0524c2s v6p0289c1s v6p0463c2s
Watkinson, W.L. v5p0372c2m
v5p0463c1s v5p0463c2s
Watney, D. v3p0213c1s
Watrin, P.F. v2p0267c1s
Watrous, A.E. v3p0302c2s
v3p0359c1s v4p0402c2s
Watrous, E.F. v5p0397c1s
v6p0620c1s
Watrous, G.D. v2p0193c1s
v2p0231c1s
Watrous, G.J. v2p0231c2s
Watrous, J.A. v5p0631c2s
v6p0119c1s
Watson and Galton v1p0442c2s
Watson, A. v1p0406c2s
v1p0527c2s v2p0157c1s v2p0163c2s
v2p0207c2s v4p0065c2s v4p0201c1s
v4p0571c2s v4p0589c1s v5p0480c1s
v5p0566c2s v6p0244c1s v6p0660c2s
Watson, A.B. v5p0396c1s
Watson, A.E.T. v1p0022c2s
v1p0535c2s v1p1214c1s v1p1221c1s
v2p0120c2s v2p0420c1s v4p0141c1s
Watson, A.M. v6p0225c1s
v6p0384c1s
Watson, A.R. v4p0364c2s
v4p0565c2s v4p0629c2s v5p0199c2s
Watson, A.T., Sir v5p0329c2s
Watson, C. v3p0303c1s
Watson, C.H. v3p0281c1s
v5p0091c2s
Watson, C.K. v1p0261c1s
v1p0710c2s v1p1433c1s
Watson, C.W. v1p0208c1s
v1p1185c2s v4p0117c1s
Watson, D. v1p0566c1s
v4p0017c1s
Watson, E. v6p0656c1s
Watson, E.H.L. v4p0187c1s
v4p0231c2s v4p0398c2s v4p0469c2s
v4p0540c1s v5p0008c2s v6p0463c1s
v6p0519c1s v6p0711c2s
Watson, E.H.Lacon v4p0185c1s
v4p0430c1s
Watson, E.P. v5p0194c2s
v5p0344c1s v6p0072c2s v6p0127c2s
v6p0328c2s v6p0355c1s v6p0392c2s
v6p0393c1s v6p0408c1s v6p0615c2m
v6p0708c2s
Watson, E.R. v6p0449c2s
Watson, E.W. v5p0349c1s
Watson, Egbert P. v6p0217c2m
v6p0615c2s
Watson, Ellen v6p0288c1s
Watson, Elsie v5p0119c2s
v5p0414c2s
Watson, Emma L. v4p0409c2s
Watson, Eugene S. v6p0120c2s
v6p0476c2s
Watson, F. v4p0009c2s
v4p0021c2s v4p0066c1s v4p0126c2s
v4p0169c2s v4p0170c1s v4p0246c1s
v4p0255c1s v4p0322c1s v4p0344c1s
v4p0492c1s v4p0633c1s v5p0087c2s
v5p0138c1s v5p0178c1s v5p0179c2s
v5p0180c1s v5p0242c2s v5p0270c1m
v5p0413c1s v5p0437c2s v5p0639c2s
v5p0642c1s v6p0149c2s v6p0192c1s
v6p0193c1s v6p0201c1s v6p0205c2s
v6p0215c1s v6p0399c2s v6p0459c1s
v6p0478c1s v6p0491c1s v6p0573c2s
v6p0618c1s v6p0635c1s
v6p0689c2s
Watson, Foster v5p0003c1s
v5p0028c1s v5p0569c1s
Watson, G. v1p0603c1s
Watson, G.C. v5p0170c2s
Watson, G.E. v1p0467c1s
v1p0529c1s v1p1136c2s v2p0099c2s
v2p0283c1s
Watson, G.R. v4p0001c1s
Watson, G.W. v2p0009c2s
Watson, H.B.M. v4p0254c1s
v4p0306c1s v4p0311c2s v4p0317c1s
v4p0411c1s v4p0468c2s v4p0497c1s
v5p0322c2s v5p0347c2s v5p0425c2s
v5p0466c1s v5p0531c2s v5p0589c2s
v6p0010c1s v6p0018c2s v6p0223c1s
v6p0286c2s v6p0304c1s v6p0342c2s
v6p0512c1s v6p0611c2s v6p0617c2s
v6p0672c2s
v6p0702c2m
Watson, H.B.Marriott v6p0420c2s
v6p0662c1s
Watson, H.L. v5p0460c2s
Watson, H.S. v6p0650c2s
Watson, H.W. v3p0133c2s
v3p0264c1s
Watson, Ida L. v6p0614c2s
Watson, Isa. v6p0173c1s
Watson, Isa and Nyren, M.. v6p0622c1s
Watson, J. v1p0270c1s
v1p0333c2m v1p0368c1s v1p0407c1s
v1p0408c2s v1p0435c1s v1p0469c1s
v1p0614c1s v1p0702c2m v1p0711c2s
v1p0760c2s v1p0869c1s v1p1122c2m
v1p1235c1m v1p1336c2s v1p1432c1s
v2p0120c2s v2p0240c2s v3p0045c1s
v3p0045c2s v3p0123c2s v3p0129c2s
v3p0145c2s v3p0166c2s v3p0263c1s
v3p0373c1s v3p0402c2s v3p0436c2s
v4p0002c1s v4p0104c2s v4p0113c1s
v4p0151c1s v4p0153c1s v4p0162c2s
v4p0193c2s v4p0206c2s v4p0253c1s
v4p0262c1s v4p0267c1s v4p0308c2s
v4p0325c2m v4p0331c1s v4p0366c2s
v4p0374c1s v4p0439c1s v4p0463c2s
v4p0464c2s v4p0477c1s v4p0480c1s
v4p0584c1s v4p0600c1s v4p0601c2s
v4p0633c1s v5p0016c2s v5p0028c1s
v5p0043c1s v5p0108c1s v5p0131c1s
v5p0169c2s v5p0190c2s v5p0241c2s
v5p0297c2s v5p0304c1s v5p0306c1s
v5p0306c2s v5p0463c2s v5p0486c1s
v5p0486c2m v5p0518c2s v5p0571c1s
v5p0602c1s v6p0030c1m v6p0055c1s
v6p0087c2s v6p0134c1s v6p0177c2s
v6p0178c1s v6p0236c1s v6p0330c1s
v6p0393c2s v6p0403c2s v6p0533c2s
v6p0577c2s v6p0639c2s v6p0702c1s
v6p0703c2s
Watson, J. et al. v4p0540c1s
Watson, J.C. v1p0282c1s
v1p1014c1m v1p1289c1s v1p1379c1s
v1p1389c2s v5p0445c1s
Watson, J.C. and Runke, R.
v5p0526c2s
Watson, J.F. v3p0073c2s
v3p0102c1s v3p0151c2s v3p0178c2s
v3p0360c1s
Watson, J.M. v4p0618c2s
Watson, J.Maclaren v4p0233c2s
v4p0429c2s
Watson, J.S. v1p0047c2s
v6p0009c2s
Watson, J.W. v1p0329c1s
v1p0348c2s v1p0501c2s v1p0503c2s
v1p0607c2s v1p0751c2s v1p0810c1s
v1p0851c2s v1p0917c2s v1p0983c2s
v1p1192c1s v3p0087c2s v3p0109c1s
Watson, John v4p0157c2s
v5p0196c1s
Watson, K. v4p0411c1s
v4p0412c2s v4p0598c2s v4p0619c1s
v5p0261c2s
Watson, L.H. v2p0005c1s
Watson, Lily v4p0492c1s
Watson, M. v1p0078c1m
v1p0079c1s v3p0335c1s v3p0406c1s
v4p0451c1s v4p0484c1s v4p0549c1s
v5p0144c1s v5p0410c1s v5p0617c2s
v6p0679c1s
Watson, M.A. v3p0360c1s
Watson, M.P. v6p0451c1s
Watson, Margaret v5p0410c1s
v5p0570c2s v6p0264c2s v6p0466c1s
Watson, P. v6p0574c1s
Watson, P.B. v1p0028c1s
Watson, R. v1p1301c2s
Watson, R.A. v1p0046c2s
v1p0666c1s v2p0022c1s v2p0251c1s
v2p0307c2s
Watson, R.D. v6p0689c1s
Watson, R.S. v2p0479c2s
v3p0212c1s v3p0239c1m v3p0369c2s
v4p0227c2s v4p0557c2s
Watson, S. v1p0031c2s
v1p0560c1s v1p1033c2s
Watson, S.E. v5p0088c1s
Watson, S.J. v1p0195c1m
Watson, T. v1p1210c1s
Watson, T., Sir v1p0619c1s
v1p1376c1s v1p1442c2s
Watson, T.E. v4p0397c1s
v6p0488c2s
Watson, T.E. et al. v4p0595c2s
Watson, T.L. v6p0673c1s
Watson, T.M. v3p0122c1s
v3p0306c1s
Watson, T.S. v6p0664c1s
Watson, W. v1p0195c2s
v1p0368c1s v1p0783c2s v1p1110c1s
v1p1258c2s v2p0257c2s v2p0394c2s
v2p0429c2s v3p0048c1s v3p0054c2s
v3p0105c2s v3p0152c1s v3p0235c1m
v3p0253c1s v3p0261c2s v3p0335c2m
v3p0363c1s v3p0418c2s v3p0458c1s
v3p0472c1s v4p0021c2s v4p0032c2s
v4p0043c1s v4p0065c2s v4p0069c2m
v4p0078c2s v4p0087c1s v4p0111c1s
v4p0159c1s v4p0197c1s v4p0200c2s
v4p0203c2s v4p0204c2s v4p0243c2s
v4p0248c1s v4p0252c2s v4p0264c2s
v4p0310c1s v4p0310c2s v4p0317c2s
v4p0410c2s v4p0416c1m v4p0416c2m
v4p0423c1s v4p0433c1s v4p0446c1m
v4p0458c2s v4p0486c2s v4p0520c1s
v4p0523c1s v4p0537c1s v4p0545c1s
v4p0554c2s v4p0569c2s v4p0579c1m
v4p0581c2s v4p0586c2s v4p0613c1s
v5p0323c2s v5p0348c1s v5p0404c1s
v5p0446c2m v5p0523c2s v5p0539c1s
v5p0605c2s v6p0345c1s v6p0380c1s
Watson, W.C. v1p0033c2s
v1p0060c1s
Watson, W.L. v5p0272c1s
Watson, W.P. v6p0335c1s
Watson, W.R. v6p0299c2s
v6p0351c2s
Watson, W.S. v4p0053c1s
v4p0055c1m
Watson, W.S., jr. v4p0055c1s
Watson, William v6p0525c2s
Watt, A. v5p0292c2s
Watt, F. v1p0486c2s
v1p1131c2s v3p0029c2s v3p0187c2s
v3p0256c2s v4p0299c1s v4p0339c1s
v4p0357c1s v4p0406c2s v4p0443c2s
v4p0470c1s v4p0549c1s v4p0588c2s
v4p0619c2s v4p0635c1s v5p0071c2s
v5p0323c2s v5p0345c2s v5p0596c2s
v6p0117c2s v6p0287c1s
Watt, Francis v4p0509c1s
v5p0075c2s
Watt, Fs. v5p0346c1s
Watt, G. v1p0844c2s
v1p0845c1m v3p0211c1s v3p0266c1s
Watt, J.C. v1p0634c1s
v4p0140c1s v6p0184c2s v6p0658c2s
Watt, J.H. v5p0304c1s
Watt, L.M. v6p0194c2s
Watt, M.R. v4p0395c2s
Watt, W. v2p0253c1s
Watt, W.A. v6p0323c2s
v6p0400c2s
Watte, O.Le v1p0683c1s
Watters, A. v4p0281c2s
Watters, T. v4p0134c1s
Watterson, H. v1p1224c1s
v2p0411c1s v2p0454c2s v3p0115c1s
v3p0299c1s v3p0383c1s v3p0383c2s
v3p0420c1s v4p0128c2s v4p0396c2s
v4p0626c1s v5p0603c1s v6p0213c1s
v6p0346c2s
Watteville, A. v3p0395c2s
Watteville, A.de v3p0206c1s
Watton, F.P. v4p0357c1s
Watts, A. v2p0090c2s
v3p0089c1s
Watts, A.A. v1p0942c2s
Watts, A.M.H. v1p0518c1s
v2p0427c2s
Watts, A.M.H. and Jewitt, L.
v1p1397c2s
Watts, B.H. and King, A.J.
v0p2236c1s
Watts, C. v2p0266c1s
Watts, C.A. and Pearson, K.
v5p0008c2s
Watts, D.G. v3p0403c2s
v4p0172c1s v4p0620c1s
Watts, G.F. v1p0063c2s
v1p0064c2s v2p0124c1s v4p0028c2s
v4p0030c2m v5p0452c1s v6p0474c2s
Watts, G.F. and Alford, M.
v1p0904c2s

Watts, G.F., Mrs. ... v5p0388c1s
Watts, H.E. ... v1p1401c1s
Watts, H.M. ... v3p0279c2s v5p0111c1s v5p0624c1s v6p0276c1s v6p0298c2s
Watts, I. ... v6p0248c1s
Watts, J. ... v1p1261c1s
Watts, J.K. ... v2p0075c1s v2p0110c1s
Watts, N.W. ... v4p0222c2s
Watts, P. ... v1p1191c2s
Watts, R. ... v1p0074c2s v2p0005c1s v2p0104c1s v2p0136c1s v2p0212c2s v2p0251c1s v2p0269c1s v2p0307c1s v3p0083c2s v3p0145c1s v3p0198c2s v3p0217c1m v3p0217c2s v3p0261c2s v3p0379c2s v4p0301c1s v4p0456c2s
Watts, R. et al. ... v2p0438c1s
Watts, S.H. ... v4p0090c2s
Watts, S.J. ... v4p0206c2s
Watts, T. ... v2p0077c2s v2p0378c2m v3p0011c2s v3p0020c1s v3p0243c2s v3p0259c2s v3p0269c2s v3p0424c2s v3p0425c1s v4p0153c2s v4p0163c2s v4p0245c2s v4p0327c2s v4p0404c1s v4p0492c1m v4p0569c1s v4p0569c2m v4p0570c1s v4p0570c2s v4p0616c1s v4p0620c1s
Watts, W.A. ... v2p0390c2s
Watts, W.H. ... v1p1024c2s v1p1179c2s v6p0600c2s
Watts, W.L. ... v1p0622c2s v1p1363c2s v1p1377c1s v3p0207c2s v3p0451c2s v5p0442c2s
Watts, W.M. ... v1p0199c2s v2p0413c2s
Watts, W.W. ... v2p0207c2s v4p0133c2s v5p0448c1s v6p0110c1s
Watts-Dunton, T. ... v4p0063c2s v4p0383c1s v4p0570c2s v5p0253c1s v5p0350c2s v5p0491c1s v6p0275c1s v6p0281c1s v6p0545c2s v6p0587c1s
Watts-Dunton, T. and Abbey, E.A. v6p0587c2s
Watts-Jones, Mrs. ... v3p0344c2s
Wauchope, A. ... v4p0154c2s
Waud, A.R. and Keeler, R.. v1p0102c2s v1p0148c1s v1p0227c2s v1p0580c2s v1p0792c1s v1p0819c2s v1p0854c1s v1p0897c1s v1p0913c1m v1p1144c1s v1p1223c2s v1p1369c2s
Waugh, A. ... v3p0288c2s v4p0039c1s v4p0232c2s v4p0335c1s v4p0424c2s v4p0569c2s v6p0138c1s v6p0257c1s v6p0489c1s
Waugh, A.S. ... v1p0454c1s
Waugh, B. ... v2p0078c1s v2p0235c1s v2p0480c2s v3p0001c2s v3p0008c2s v3p0029c2s v3p0040c2s v3p0077c2s v3p0107c1s v3p0156c1s v3p0168c1s v3p0168c2s v3p0175c1s v3p0217c2s v3p0229c2s v3p0236c2s v3p0244c2s v3p0263c2s v3p0289c1s v3p0319c1s v3p0326c2s v3p0359c2s v3p0361c2s v3p0404c2s v3p0415c2s v4p0061c2s v4p0103c2s v4p0104c1s v4p0456c1s v6p0490c2s
Waugh, B. and Manning, Cardinal v2p0077c2s
Waugh, B. et al. ... v4p0353c2s
Waugh, E. ... v3p0147c2s
Waugh, F.A. ... v4p0209c1s v4p0217c1s v4p0577c1s v4p0579c1s v5p0624c2s v6p0025c1s v6p0185c1s v6p0504c1s
Waugh, F.F. ... v4p0088c1s
Waugh, F.G. ... v4p0263c1s
Waugh, J.J. ... v6p0364c2s
Waugh, J.W. ... v1p0632c1s
Waugh, W.T. ... v6p0466c1s
Wauters, A.J. ... v4p0614c2s v5p0623c1s
Wavell, A.H. ... v1p1330c1s
Wavertree, O.M. ... v1p1267c1s v2p0469c2s v3p0440c1s
Waxweiler, E. ... v4p0608c1s
Way, A. ... v1p0274c2s v1p0962c1s v1p1106c1s v1p1178c2s v1p1279c2s v6p0094c1s
Way, A.F. and Havens, F.S. v5p0277c2s v5p0298c1s
Way, A.S. ... v4p0518c1s
Way, T.R. ... v5p0342c1s v5p0628c2s v6p0384c1s v6p0695c2s
Way, T.R. and Rothenstein, W. v5p0342c1s
Way, W.I. ... v3p0253c2s v4p0066c2m v4p0198c2s v4p0269c2s v4p0561c1s v5p0171c2s v5p0209c2s
Waybrook, R. ... v5p0424c2s
Wayland, F. ... v1p0157c1s v1p0384c2s v1p0390c2s v1p0436c2s v1p0496c1s v1p0607c1s v1p1052c2s v1p1103c2s v2p0067c2s v2p0329c1s v2p0407c1s v3p0210c2s v4p0103c1s
Wayland, F., jr. ... v1p0261c2s v1p0607c1s v1p0905c2s
Wayland, H.A. ... v4p0097c1s
Wayland, H.L. ... v1p0095c2s v1p0157c2s v1p0392c2s v1p0649c2s v1p1289c2s v2p0331c2s v2p0414c1s v2p0438c2s v3p0057c2s v3p0137c1s v3p0289c1s v3p0340c2s v4p0022c1s v4p0045c1s v4p0076c2s v4p0397c1s v4p0546c1s v4p0546c2s
Wayland, J. ... v1p0378c2s
Waylen, J. ... v3p0106c2s v3p0122c1s
Waymire, J.A. ... v4p0481c2s
Wayne, C.S. ... v1p0526c1s v1p0593c1s v1p1155c2s v1p1410c2s
Wayne, E.S. ... v4p0254c2s
Wayne, F. ... v5p0115c2s v5p0140c1s v5p0263c2s v5p0299c1s v5p0399c2s v5p0533c2s
Wayne, M.W. ... v1p0038c1s
Wayte, A. ... v5p0282c2s v5p0379c2s
Wead, C.K. ... v2p0341c1s v3p0314c1s v3p0401c2s v5p0003c1s v5p0369c1s v5p0394c2m v5p0423c2s v6p0439c1s v6p0439c2s v6p0495c2s v6p0564c2s
Weage, E.D. ... v4p0374c2s
Weale, W.H.J. ... v2p0178c2s v2p0344c2s v3p0038c2s v3p0049c2s v3p0050c1s v3p0344c1s v4p0223c2s v5p0031c2s v5p0200c2m
Weale, W.H.J. and Marks, A. v6p0216c2s
Weare, J. ... v5p0545c1s
Weatherbee, M. ... v2p0148c1s
Weatherbee, R.S. et al. .. v2p0091c1s
Weatherby, A.H. ... v4p0070c2s v4p0091c1m
Weatherby, F.E. ... v1p0693c1s v1p0800c1s
Weathergage ... v5p0585c1s
Weatherly, F.E. ... v1p0583c1s v1p0725c2s v1p0985c2m v1p1385c2s v5p0340c2s
Weatherly, J.T. ... v5p0601c2s
Weatherly, L.A. ... v4p0437c2s
Weatherly, P. ... v5p0045c1s
Weatherly, U.G. ... v4p0463c2s
Weathers, J. ... v4p0416c1s
Weaver, C.C. ... v5p0064c2s
Weaver, E.A. ... v5p0015c2s
Weaver, E.A., Mrs. ... v4p0096c2s
Weaver, E.M. ... v3p0020c1s v3p0278c2s v3p0304c1s v3p0400c1s v4p0031c2s v5p0032c2s v5p0124c2s v5p0157c1s v6p0031c2s
Weaver, E.P. ... v5p0002c1s v5p0316c2s v5p0443c1s v5p0556c1s v6p0002c1s v6p0022c2s v6p0461c1s
Weaver, Emily P. ... v6p0301c1m
Weaver, F.L. ... v3p0339c1s
Weaver, F.W. ... v4p0332c1s
Weaver, G.C. ... v6p0459c2s
Weaver, G.S. ... v1p0688c2s v3p0083c1s v3p0229c2s
Weaver, J.B. ... v4p0284c1s v4p0524c2s
Weaver, J.H. ... v5p0268c2s
Weaver, Louise ... v6p0449c1s
Weaver, O. ... v6p0366c2s
Weaver, P. ... v4p0206c2s
Weaver, P., jr. ... v4p0084c1m v4p0110c1s v4p0325c1s v4p0443c1s
Weaver, P.L. ... v6p0360c2s
Weaver, P.L., jr. ... v4p0036c1s v4p0200c2s
Weaver, Phil., jr. ... v4p0501c2s
Weaver, R. ... v1p1181c2s v1p1391c1s
Weaver, W.D. ... v2p0137c1s
Webb, A. ... v2p0038c2s v2p0074c1s v2p0189c2s v2p0225c1s v2p0225c2m v2p0226c1m v2p0226c2m v2p0227c1m v2p0227c2m v2p0228c1s v2p0231c2s v2p0331c1s v2p0367c2s v2p0450c2s v3p0048c2s v3p0053c1s v3p0055c2s v3p0157c1s v3p0158c2s v3p0165c1s v3p0190c1s v3p0219c2s v3p0220c2s v3p0221c1m v3p0222c1m v3p0222c2s v3p0322c1m v3p0389c2s v3p0391c1s v3p0394c2s v3p0430c2s v4p0071c1s v4p0074c1s v4p0189c2s v4p0227c2s v4p0258c1s v4p0261c2s v4p0265c2s v4p0289c2s v4p0290c2s v4p0291c1s v4p0339c2s v4p0354c2s v4p0360c2s v4p0460c1s v4p0564c1s v4p0609c1s v5p0073c2s v5p0171c1s v5p0295c2m v5p0296c2m v5p0433c2m v5p0580c1s v5p0587c1s v6p0027c2s v6p0181c1s v6p0279c2s v6p0295c1s v6p0313c1s v6p0326c1m v6p0326c2s v6p0385c1s v6p0665c2s
Webb, A. and Bryce, J. ... v5p0611c1s
Webb, A. and Dicey, A.V. . v5p0433c1s
Webb, A.J. ... v4p0378c2s
Webb, A.S. ... v5p0375c2s
Webb, A.Z. ... v2p0410c1s
Webb, B. ... v4p0314c1s
Webb, B. and Webb, S. ... v4p0022c1s v4p0581c1m v4p0608c1s v6p0080c1s v6p0208c2s v6p0480c1s
Webb, B.J. ... v1p0397c2s v1p0706c1s v1p1200c1s
Webb, B.R. ... v5p0591c1s
Webb, C. ... v6p0178c2s
Webb, C.H. ... v1p0229c1s v4p0092c1s v5p0008c2s
Webb, E.A. ... v6p0041c1s
Webb, E.B. ... v1p0074c2s v1p0440c2s v1p0664c1s
Webb, F.C. ... v1p0400c1s
Webb, G. ... v2p0078c2s
Webb, H.H. and Yeatman, P. v5p0238c1s v5p0634c2s
Webb, H.L. ... v3p0062c1s v3p0133c1s v3p0423c1s v4p0176c1s v4p0176c2s v4p0567c2m v5p0086c2s v6p0637c1m
Webb, J. ... v1p0135c2s v1p0396c1s v1p0411c2s v1p0608c1s v1p1106c1s v1p1293c1s
Webb, J.A. ... v5p0055c1s v5p0638c1s
Webb, J.B. ... v2p0438c1s v3p0230c1s v3p0354c2s
Webb, J.S. ... v5p0318c2s
Webb, J.W. ... v3p0314c2s v4p0312c2s v5p0163c1s
Webb, Judge ... v6p0588c2s
Webb, M. ... v5p0232c2m
Webb, M. and Frampton, G.. v5p0516c1s
Webb, N. ... v5p0359c1s
Webb, P.G.L. ... v6p0689c1s
Webb, R. ... v1p0235c1s v5p0205c1s v5p0480c1s v6p0701c2s
Webb, R.D. ... v1p0295c1s v1p1364c1s
Webb, R.J. ... v5p0228c1s
Webb, S. ... v3p0118c2s v3p0214c2s v3p0218c1m v3p0238c2s v3p0239c1s v3p0338c2s v3p0339c1s v3p0398c2s v3p0452c2s v3p0470c2s v4p0238c2s v4p0338c2s v5p0130c2s v5p0334c2s v5p0497c1s v6p0269c1s v6p0384c1s v6p0385c2s v6p0526c1s v6p0652c2s v6p0659c2s
Webb, S. and Stokes, G.G.. v5p0338c2s
Webb, S. and Webb, B. ... v4p0022c1s v4p0152c1s v4p0581c1m v4p0608c1s v6p0080c1s v6p0208c2s v6p0480c1s
Webb, Sidney ... v6p0670c2s
Webb, Stephen ... v5p0293c1s
Webb, T. ... v1p0865c2s
Webb, T.E. ... v1p0826c2s
Webb, T.W. ... v1p0070c2s v1p0374c2s v1p0588c2s v1p0699c1m v1p0804c1m v1p0865c2m v1p0903c2s v1p1014c1s v1p1152c2m v1p1243c2m v1p1244c1s v1p1366c2s v2p0014c1s v2p0030c1s v2p0039c1s v2p0095c1s v2p0128c1s v2p0277c2m v2p0278c1s v2p0296c2s v2p0426c2s
Webb, W.A. ... v6p0605c2s
Webb, W.B. ... v6p0694c2s
Webb, W.E. ... v1p1400c2s
Webb, W.L. ... v4p0110c2s v6p0143c1s
Webb, W.M. ... v4p0637c2s v5p0062c1s v5p0277c1s v5p0462c1s v5p0641c2s v6p0227c1s v6p0444c2s v6p0498c1s
Webb, W.N. ... v6p0576c2s
Webb, Wilfred M. ... v5p0406c1s
Webb, Winifred ... v5p0571c2s v6p0017c1s
Webb-Peploe, H.W. ... v4p0381c1s
Webbe, E. ... v1p1156c2s
Webber, A. ... v5p0616c1s
Webber, B. ... v1p0004c1s v1p0572c1s v1p0668c2s v1p0907c2s v1p1221c1s v2p0004c2s v2p0010c1s v4p0260c2s v4p0325c2s v6p0471c1s
Webber, Byron ... v1p0022c2s
Webber, C.E. ... v3p0132c2s v3p0423c1s
Webber, C.W. ... v1p0042c2s v1p0133c1s v1p0575c2s v1p1069c1s v1p1327c2s
Webber, Col. ... v3p0423c1s
Webber, F.W. ... v3p0363c1s v4p0548c2s
Webber, H.J. ... v4p0196c1s v4p0445c2s v6p0077c1s v6p0469c1s v6p0579c2s
Webber, J.E. ... v6p0180c2s v6p0181c1s v6p0329c2s
Webber, S. ... v1p0066c1s v1p0374c2s v1p1366c1m v1p1386c2s v1p1392c1s v3p0168c1s v3p0457c1s v3p0457c2s v4p0586c2s v4p0613c2m v5p0372c2s v5p0621c2s
Webber, S.S. ... v6p0701c1s
Webber, T.W. ... v3p0158c1s
Webber, W. ... v6p0417c1s
Webber, W.H.Y. ... v5p0064c2s v6p0384c2s
Webber, W.O. ... v4p0065c1s v4p0233c2s v5p0010c1s v5p0068c2s v5p0551c1m v5p0622c1s v6p0017c2s v6p0523c1s
Weber, A.D. ... v6p0318c1s

Weber, A.F. v5p0009c1s
v5p0176c1s v5p0321c1s v5p0559c1s
v5p0584c2s v5p0585c2s v6p0128c1s
v6p0203c1s v6p0317c2s
Weber, A.S. v4p0108c2s
v4p0171c2s v4p0300c2s v4p0465c1s
v5p0236c2s v5p0306c2s v5p0489c2s
v5p0577c1s v5p0623c1s v6p0123c1s
v6p0513c2s v6p0537c2s
Weber, Adna F. v5p0119c2s
Weber, C. v1p0264c2s
Weber, C. and Goddard, J.. v1p0246c1s
Weber, E. v6p0311c2s
Weber, F. v3p0273c2s
v3p0404c1s
Weber, G.A. v5p0572c2s
Weber, H.A. v6p0463c2s
Weber, J.B. v4p0139c2s
v4p0431c1s
Weber, J.B. and Smith, C.S.
v4p0275c1s
Weber, P.E. v5p0143c2s
Weber, W. v5p0024c1s
v5p0306c2s v5p0444c1s v5p0576c1s
v6p0334c1s v6p0626c2s
Weber, Wm. v5p0231c1s
Weber-Ebenhof, A.von v6p0689c1s
Webling, A.F. v6p0373c2s
Webling, Peggy v5p0017c1s
Webster, A. v1p0137c1s
v1p0169c1s v1p1222c1s v5p0349c2s
Webster, A. et al. v4p0557c2s
Webster, A., jr. v1p0103c1s
v1p0402c1s v1p0851c2s v1p1052c1s
Webster, A.D. v2p0162c1s
v2p0322c2s
Webster, A.F. v1p0439c1s
v1p1151c1s
Webster, A.G. v4p0441c1s
v5p0020c1s v5p0182c2s v5p0184c2s
v6p0088c1s
Webster, B. v3p0310c1s
Webster, C.E. v6p0146c2s
Webster, C.L. v3p0173c2s
v3p0219c1m v4p0119c1s v5p0240c1s
Webster, D. v1p0175c2s
v1p0339c1s v1p0437c2s v1p0730c2s
v1p1362c1s v5p0125c1s
Webster, D.H. v6p0402c1s
Webster, Evelyn v5p0041c1s
v5p0164c2s
Webster, F. v3p0153c1s
Webster, F.M. v4p0285c2s
v5p0066c2s v6p0320c2s v6p0321c1s
v6p0713c2s
Webster, G. v1p0678c1s
v2p0375c1s
Webster, G.S. v6p0169c1s
Webster, G.T. v1p1329c1s
Webster, G.W. v4p0445c2s
Webster, H. v4p0600c1s
v5p0108c2m v5p0226c2s v5p0302c1s
v5p0319c2s v5p0506c2s v5p0619c1s
Webster, H.A. v3p0317c1s
Webster, H.J. v6p0574c1s
Webster, H.K. v6p0102c1s
v6p0153c1m v6p0167c1s v6p0348c2s
v6p0356c1s v6p0436c1s v6p0617c1s
v6p0621c1s
Webster, J. v1p0160c2s
v1p1115c1s v1p1123c1s v6p0434c1s
Webster, J.C. v1p1433c1s
v5p0634c2s
Webster, J.G. v6p0531c1s
Webster, J.J. v1p0663c2s
v2p0178c2s
Webster, J.L. v6p0707c1s
Webster, J.W. v1p0108c1s
v1p0224c2s v1p0507c2s v1p0509c2s
v1p0785c2s
Webster, Jean v6p0255c1s
v6p0420c2s v6p0478c2s
Webster, L. v3p0325c2s
Webster, M.P. v6p0624c1s
Webster, N. v1p0389c2m
v1p0428c2s v1p0458c2s v1p0469c1s
v1p0998c2m v1p1159c1s
Webster, N.B. v1p0354c2s
Webster, P. v3p0086c1s
v3p0297c1s v5p0116c2s
Webster, R.E. v4p0100c2s
Webster, R.E. and Boscawen, A.G.
v4p0112c2s
Webster, R.E. and
Griffith-Boscawen, A. . v4p0609c1s
Webster, R.G. v3p0256c2s
v3p0414c1s
Webster, S. v2p0109c2s
v3p0034c2s v3p0038c1s v3p0393c2s
v4p0049c2s v4p0142c2s v4p0156c2s
v4p0278c1s v4p0288c1s v4p0594c1s
v5p0603c1s v6p0494c1s
Webster, T. v1p0830c2s
v3p0219c1s v3p0292c2s v3p0323c1s
v3p0422c1s v3p0423c1s
Webster, V.B. v6p0471c2s
Webster, W. v1p0101c2m
v1p0131c1s v1p0482c2s v1p0491c2s
v1p1214c2s v2p0036c1m v2p0201c1s
v2p0241c2s v2p0296c1s v2p0356c1s
v2p0413c1s v3p0035c2s v3p0048c2s
v3p0071c2s v3p0072c2s v3p0199c2s
v4p0013c2s v4p0047c1s v4p0167c1s
v4p0233c2s v4p0283c1s v4p0341c2s
v4p0344c1s v4p0391c2s v4p0468c1s
v4p0539c1s v4p0570c2s v4p0626c1s
v5p0180c1s
Webster, W. et al. v4p0215c1s
Webster, W.C. v5p0134c1s
v5p0179c2s
Webster, W.F. v5p0249c2s
Webster, W.G. v3p0087c1s
Webster, W.R. v5p0551c2s
Webster, Wentworth v2p0412c2s
Wedd, N. v6p0257c1s
Wedd, W. v1p1316c1s
Weddell, A.J. v1p0436c1s
v1p0620c1s
Weddell, J.W. v2p0082c1s
v2p0345c2s
Wedderburn, D. v1p0236c2s
v1p0344c1s v1p0919c1s v1p1335c2s
Wedderburn, D., Sir v1p0078c1s
v1p0339c1s v1p0622c1s v1p0633c1s
v1p0678c2s v1p0679c2s v1p0680c1s
v1p0775c1s v1p0798c2s v1p0872c1s
v1p1029c1s v1p1073c1s v2p0004c1s
v2p0208c2s
Wedderburn, S.A. v4p0551c2s
Wedderburn, W. v4p0107c1s
v4p0278c1s v5p0284c1s v6p0314c2s
Wedderburn, W., Sir v4p0065c2s
v4p0280c2s
Wedding, Dr. v2p0229c1s
Wedding, H. v1p0664c1s
Weddle, I. v3p0023c1s
v3p0049c1s v3p0123c1s v3p0263c1s
v3p0275c1s v3p0406c2s
Weddle, Isabella v4p0066c1s
Wedekind, A.C. v1p0112c1s
Wedel, E.von v4p0626c2s
Wedel, L.von v6p0205c1s
Wedgwood, H. v1p0058c1s
v1p0760c2s v1p0811c1s v3p0068c1s
Wedgwood, J. v1p0202c1s
v1p0418c1s v1p0492c2s v1p0729c1s
v1p1018c2s v1p1168c2s v1p1243c1s
v1p1372c2s v1p1426c1s v2p0003c2s
v2p0280c2s v2p0397c1s v2p0397c2s
v3p0043c1s v3p0064c1s v3p0144c1s
v3p0223c1s v3p0311c2s v3p0386c2s
v3p0388c2s v3p0431c2s v3p0467c1s
v4p0053c1s v4p0054c1s v4p0054c2s
v4p0122c1s v4p0242c1s v4p0301c2s
v4p0405c1s v4p0518c1s v4p0548c2s
v4p0569c2s v4p0610c2s v5p0196c1s
v5p0277c1s v5p0500c1s v5p0513c2s
v6p0403c2s v6p0407c1s
Wedgwood, J.C. v6p0360c2s
Wedgwood, J.W. v2p0155c1s
Wedgwood, Julia v3p0337c2s
v5p0196c1s
Wedgwood, W. v2p0154c2s
Wedmore, F. v1p0064c1s
v1p0066c1s v1p0140c2s v1p0310c2s
v1p0321c1s v1p0383c2s v1p0425c2s
v1p0459c1s v1p0471c2s v1p0675c2s
v1p0695c1s v1p0726c1s v1p0824c2m
v1p0866c2s v1p0900c1s v1p0959c2s
v1p1104c2s v1p1251c2s v1p1277c1s
v1p1439c2s v1p1440c2s v2p0010c1s
v2p0013c2m v2p0023c1m v2p0058c1s
v2p0059c1s v2p0074c2s v2p0088c1s
v2p0101c1s v2p0109c1s v2p0117c2s
v2p0123c1s v2p0146c2m v2p0154c1s
v2p0155c2s v2p0192c2m v2p0194c1s
v2p0215c1s v2p0215c2s v2p0230c1m
v2p0233c1s v2p0266c1s v2p0276c2s
v2p0298c1s v2p0301c2s v2p0326c1s
v2p0326c2s v2p0329c2s v2p0338c1s
v2p0360c1s v2p0400c1s v2p0435c1s
v2p0436c2s v2p0437c1s v2p0449c1s
v2p0454c1s v2p0467c2s v2p0468c1s
v2p0472c1s v2p0479c2s v3p0075c2s
v3p0102c1s v3p0142c2s v3p0172c2s
v3p0206c2s v3p0232c1s v3p0252c1s
v3p0269c2s v3p0300c1s v3p0362c2s
v3p0388c1s v3p0391c1s v3p0411c2s
v4p0030c1s v4p0093c2s v4p0136c1s
v4p0164c1m v4p0187c1m v4p0229c2s
v4p0232c1s v4p0243c1s v4p0245c1s
v4p0246c2s v4p0251c2s v4p0254c1m
v4p0258c1s v4p0259c2s v4p0269c2s
v4p0319c2s v4p0325c2s v4p0333c1s
v4p0335c2s v4p0355c2s v4p0389c2s
v4p0406c2s v4p0417c1s v4p0442c2s
v4p0448c1s v4p0454c2s v4p0458c1s
v4p0480c1m v4p0493c1s v4p0518c1s
v4p0564c1s v4p0569c2s v4p0614c1s
v4p0616c1s v5p0031c1s v5p0084c1s
v5p0089c2s v5p0101c2s v5p0134c1s
v5p0168c1s v5p0173c1s v5p0193c1s
v5p0193c2s v5p0195c1s v5p0195c2s
v5p0207c2s v5p0301c2s v5p0371c1s
v5p0405c2s v5p0427c2s v5p0428c1s
v5p0435c1m v5p0454c2s v5p0456c1s
v5p0461c1m v5p0466c1s v5p0484c2s
v5p0499c1m v5p0527c1s v5p0555c1s
v5p0575c2s v5p0595c1s v5p0608c2s
v6p0077c2s v6p0138c1s v6p0146c1s
v6p0168c2s v6p0180c2s v6p0219c1s
v6p0226c1s v6p0398c2s v6p0415c1s
v6p0475c1s v6p0539c1s v6p0592c1s
v6p0678c2s
Wedmore, F. and Phillips, C.
v4p0029c1s
Wedmore, F. and Spielmann, M.H.
v4p0029c1s
Wedmore, Frederick v2p0326c1s
Wedmore, M. v5p0610c1s
Wedmore, P. v6p0696c1s
Wedmore, T.F. v1p0060c1s
v1p0170c2s v1p0428c2s v1p0459c1s
v1p0642c1m v1p0751c2s v1p0962c1s
v1p1130c1s v1p1152c1s v1p1324c2s
Weed, C.M. v3p0044c2s
v3p0404c2s v4p0007c2s v4p0022c2s
v4p0050c2s v4p0216c1s v4p0257c1s
v4p0541c2m v4p0613c1s v4p0637c2s
v5p0128c2s v5p0238c2s v5p0292c1m
v5p0400c2s v5p0448c2s v6p0104c2s
v6p0229c2m v6p0338c1s
Weed, E.D. v5p0444c1s
v5p0445c1s
Weed, E.D. and Solis-Cohen, S.
v5p0281c2s
Weed, H.L. v4p0611c1s
Weed, H.R. v1p0239c1s
Weed, J. v1p1148c2s
Weed, Maria v5p0162c2s
v5p0282c1s
Weed, S.M. v4p0245c1s
Weed, T. v1p0556c1s
v1p0698c2s v1p0717c2s v1p0750c1s
v1p1242c2s v1p1344c1s
Weed, T.M. v6p0581c2s
Weed, W.H. v3p0168c1s
v3p0176c2s v3p0201c2s v3p0392c2s
v3p0474c2s
Weed, W.H. and Pirsson, L.V.
v4p0048c2s v4p0274c1m v4p0375c1s
v5p0527c1s
Weeden, C.F. v6p0419c1s
Weeden, W.B. v1p0032c2s
v1p0715c1s v1p0793c1s v1p0809c1s
v1p0988c2s v1p1040c1s v2p0011c2s
v2p0097c1s v2p0220c1s v2p0310c2s
v4p0182c2s v4p0398c2s v4p0534c1s
v4p0605c2s v5p0405c1s v5p0472c2s
Weeden, W.B. and Brown, W.
v1p1040c1s
Weedon, A.L.P. v6p0602c1s
v6p0664c2s
Week, Maria v5p0172c1s
Weekes, A.R. v6p0285c1s
Weekes, C. v5p0355c2s
Weekes, G.N. v5p0443c1s
Weekes, R.K. v6p0653c2s
Weeks, A.D. v6p0208c1s
Weeks, C. v4p0564c2s
Weeks, C.F. v5p0239c2s
v5p0505c2s
Weeks, C.J. v2p0450c1s
v4p0031c1m v4p0340c2s v4p0565c2s
Weeks, C.L. v1p1201c2s
v1p1439c1s
Weeks, C.S. v2p0318c1s
v2p0402c1s
Weeks, E.H. v4p0435c2s
Weeks, E.L. v3p0212c2s
v4p0030c1s v4p0089c1s v4p0258c1s
v4p0278c2s v4p0280c1s v4p0293c2s
v4p0317c1s v4p0384c1s v4p0385c2s
v4p0418c2s v4p0435c2s v4p0467c2s
v4p0473c1s v5p0154c1s v5p0385c2s
v5p0607c2s
Weeks, F.B. v4p0508c1s
v5p0229c1s v6p0323c2s
Weeks, F.C. v6p0509c2s
Weeks, G.F. v3p0093c1s
v3p0313c2s
Weeks, H.C. v3p0470c2m
Weeks, H.C. and Howard, L.O.
v6p0431c2s
Weeks, J.D. v1p0639c2s
v2p0419c2s v3p0167c2m v3p0174c2s
v4p0217c1s v4p0262c1s v4p0553c1s
Weeks, J.W. v2p0247c2s
v6p0456c2s
Weeks, L.H. v1p0083c2s
v4p0003c1s v4p0040c1s v4p0065c2s
v4p0091c1s v4p0258c1s v4p0554c1s
v4p0560c2s v4p0578c1s v4p0597c1s
Weeks, N.A. v5p0295c1s
Weeks, R. v6p0155c1s
Weeks, R.K. v1p0873c1s
Weeks, R.L. v3p0337c2s
Weeks, R.W. v6p0312c1s
v6p0321c2s
Weeks, S.B. v3p0124c1s
v3p0362c2s v3p0395c1s v3p0438c2s
v4p0023c1s v4p0162c2s v4p0397c1s
v4p0406c2m v4p0605c2s v4p0634c1s
Weems, J.B. v6p0193c2s
Weese, Dall de v5p0524c2s
Weese, T.A. v3p0330c2s
Weese, T.A.De v4p0090c2s
v5p0311c1s v5p0511c1s v6p0114c1s
v6p0456c2s v6p0712c1s
Wegg-Prosser, F.R. v2p0327c1s

v2p0437c1s v2p0440c2s v3p0145c1s
v4p0151c2s v4p0545c2s v5p0224c2s
v6p0397c1s
Wehle, T. v1p0647c2m
Wehrling, H. v4p0423c1s
Weibel, G.F. v6p0396c2s
Weidemeyer, J.W. v1p1219c2s
Weidenmann, J. v1p0211c2s
Weidman, S. v6p0301c2s
Weidner, R.F. v3p0041c1s
Weigal, J.W. v5p0318c2s
Weigall, C.E.C. v4p0447c2s
v5p0085c2s v5p0203c1s v5p0252c2s
v5p0379c1s v5p0474c2s v5p0528c1s
v5p0614c1s
Weightman, H. v2p0121c2s
v2p0144c1s v2p0187c1s v2p0277c1s
v2p0334c2s
Weightman, R. v5p0603c1s
v6p0141c1s v6p0421c2s
Weightman, R.C. v6p0395c1s
Weightman, Richard v6p0099c1s
Weightman, W.H. v4p0128c1s
Weightman, W.J. v6p0458c1s
Weigle, E.D. v2p0085c2s
v2p0290c2s v3p0149c1s v4p0185c2s
v4p0372c2s
Weik, J.W. v5p0339c1s
v6p0377c2s v6p0637c1s
Weil, G. v1p0120c1s
v4p0313c1s
Weil, I.H. v1p0085c2s
Weil, L. v3p0133c1s
Weil, M. v6p0497c1s
Weil, O. v6p0437c2s
Weiler, L. v2p0136c1s
Weiller, L. v4p0440c2s
Weiller, Lazare v5p0163c1s
Weinek, L. v5p0385c1s
Weinel, H. v6p0683c1s
Weiner, A. v6p0343c1s
Weingartner, F. v5p0565c1s
Weinland, D.F. v1p0042c2s
v1p0577c1s v1p1441c1s
Weinschenk, E. and Kunz, G.F.
v4p0366c2s v4p0367c1s
Weinstock, H. v4p0107c1s
v4p0533c1s v6p0178c2s v6p0463c2s
Weintraub, E. v6p0411c1s
Weippiert, G.W. v3p0303c1s
v4p0044c1s v4p0289c1s v4p0315c2s
Weir, D.B. v6p0469c1s
Weir, D.H. v1p0856c1s
v6p0062c1s
Weir, F. v3p0157c2s
Weir, F.R. v6p0380c2s
v6p0397c2s v6p0504c2s
Weir, H. v3p0159c1s
v6p0512c1s
Weir, J. v4p0018c2s
v4p0232c2s v4p0494c2s v5p0021c2s
v5p0337c1s
Weir, J., jr. v4p0018c2s
v4p0124c2s v4p0262c2s v4p0271c2s
v4p0394c2s v4p0468c1s v4p0475c2s
v4p0515c1s v4p0629c2s v5p0020c1s
v5p0020c2s
Weir, J.F. v1p0061c2s
v1p0062c1s v1p0063c2s v1p0064c1s
v1p0616c2s v1p0907c2s v1p1160c2s
v1p1171c2s v2p0018c2s v2p0023c2s
v2p0326c1m v2p0480c2s v3p0043c1s
v3p0189c1s
Weir, J.J. v2p0149c2s
v2p0213c2s
Weir, R.S. v1p0704c1s
v6p0353c2s
Weir, S. v4p0109c2s
v6p0240c1s v6p0342c1s
Weir, T.H. v6p0354c1s
v6p0429c2m
Weir, W.A. v5p0241c1s
Weisbach, A. v1p0157c1s
Weiser, C.Z. v1p0009c1s
v1p0262c2s v1p0385c2s v1p0391c1s
v1p0435c2s v1p0441c1s v1p0640c2s
v1p0793c2s v1p1090c2s v1p1102c1s
v1p1160c2s v1p1161c2s v1p1176c2s
v1p1271c2s v1p1274c2s v1p1301c2s
v2p0027c2s v2p0081c2s v2p0113c2s
v2p0136c1s v2p0146c1s v2p0239c1s
v2p0370c2m v2p0450c2s v3p0175c2s
v3p0347c2s v3p0371c1s v3p0458c1s
Weiser, R. v1p0076c1s
v1p0519c1s v1p0685c1s v1p0777c2s
v1p0778c2s v1p0806c1s v1p0872c1s
v1p1044c2s v1p1088c1s v1p1235c2s
Weismann, A. v3p0194c2s
v3p0293c2s v3p0336c1s v4p0154c1s
v4p0255c2s v4p0331c1s v4p0513c2m
Weismann, A. and Ischikawa, C.
v3p0209c2s
Weiss, B. v1p0184c2s
v1p0686c2s v2p0235c1s v4p0232c2s
v5p0059c2s v6p0262c2s
Weiss, C. v1p1230c1s
Weiss, E. v1p0394c2s
v1p0944c2s v1p1088c1m v1p1264c1s
Weiss, J. v1p0334c2s
v1p0440c2s v1p0486c1s v1p0517c2s
v1p0564c1s v1p0576c2s v1p0577c1s
v1p0597c2s v1p0685c2s v1p0688c2s
v1p0754c1s v1p0802c1s v1p0820c2s
v1p0876c2s v1p0948c1s v1p1022c2s
v1p1043c1s v1p1095c1m v1p1103c2s
v1p1148c2s v1p1161c1s v1p1187c1s
v1p1241c2s v1p1295c1s v1p1307c1s
v1p1317c2s v1p1352c1s v1p1384c1s
v1p1387c1s v1p1420c2s v1p1426c1s
v3p0098c1s
Weiss, J.H. v4p0562c2s
Weiss, L.I.H. v4p0637c2s
Weiss, N. v3p0358c1s
Weiss, S. v3p0005c2s
Weiss, S.A. v1p0316c1s
v1p0574c1s v1p0994c2s v5p0081c2s
Weiss, S.A.T. v1p1019c2s
Weiss, Susan A., Mrs. v6p0505c1s
Weisse, H.V. v5p0107c2s
v5p0479c2s v6p0537c1s v6p0573c1s
Weisse, S. v2p0364c2s
v3p0207c2s v3p0385c2s v3p0410c2s
Weissman, A. v1p0463c2s
Weissmann, A. v1p0136c1s
Weitenkampf, F. v3p0028c2s
v3p0348c1s v4p0546c2s v5p0161c1s
v5p0193c2s v5p0303c2s v5p0429c1s
v5p0466c2s v6p0101c2m v6p0121c2s
v6p0195c2s v6p0219c1s v6p0302c1m
v6p0328c1s v6p0335c2s v6p0354c2s
v6p0370c2m v6p0373c2s v6p0453c2s
v6p0474c2s v6p0510c2s v6p0517c1m
v6p0543c2s
Weitenkampf, Frank v6p0370c2s
v6p0599c2s
Weitzel, G. v2p0112c1s
v5p0219c1s
Weitzel, S.W. v3p0073c2s
v3p0079c1s v3p0201c2s v3p0374c1s
Welby, F.A. v4p0606c2s
Welby, Lady v3p0274c2s
v4p0537c2s
Welby, Lord v6p0167c1s
v6p0224c1s v6p0269c2s v6p0543c1s
Welby, R.E. v5p0345c1s
Welby, V. v4p0515c1s
v5p0446c2s
Welby, V., Lady v4p0362c2s
v5p0499c1s
Welby-Gregory, W.E. v4p0096c2s
Welch, A. v1p1075c1s
v2p0141c2s
Welch, A.C. v5p0308c1s
Welch, A.K. v6p0604c1s
Welch, C. v1p0206c1s
v5p0252c1s v5p0336c2s v5p0343c1s
v6p0117c1s v6p0276c1s
Welch, D. v3p0093c2s
v5p0100c1s v6p0173c2s v6p0595c1s
Welch, F.H. v5p0618c1s
Welch, H. v5p0276c1s
v6p0540c2s v6p0692c1s
Welch, J. v2p0320c1s
v3p0146c1s v3p0148c2s v3p0460c2s
Welch, J.C. v2p0445c1s
v3p0218c2s v3p0435c1s
Welch, J.C. and Camden, J.N.
v2p0320c2s v2p0417c1s
Welch, J.M. v2p0060c1s
v3p0218c2s v3p0304c2s
Welch, L.B. and Richardson, J.M.
v2p0352c1s
Welch, M.C. v1p0797c2s
v1p0977c2s v1p1064c2s
Welch, M.H. v4p0402c2s
v4p0629c1s
Welch, R. v3p0149c2m
v3p0341c1s v3p0460c1s
Welch, R.B. v1p0239c2s
v1p0441c1s v1p0554c1m v1p0857c1s
v1p1203c1s v1p1302c2s v2p0021c1s
v2p0152c1s v2p0161c2s v2p0372c1s
v3p0026c1m v3p0083c2s v3p0218c1s
v3p0421c2s
Welch, R.G. v1p1365c1s
Welch, R.W. v2p0276c1s
Welch, W.H. v3p0215c2s
v3p0273c1s v4p0502c2s v5p0062c1s
v5p0368c1s v5p0435c2s v5p0643c2s
v6p0066c2s v6p0309c2s v6p0408c2s
v6p0409c1s
Welch, W.H. et al. v6p0540c1s
Welcker, H. v1p0331c2s
Weld, A. v1p0042c1s
v1p0045c2s v1p0382c1s v1p0434c2m
v1p0460c1s v1p0683c2s v1p0792c2s
v1p0793c1s v1p0860c1s v1p0936c1s
v1p1299c1s v1p1336c2s v4p0388c1s
v4p0416c1s v5p0292c2s
Weld, A.C.G. v5p0395c1s
v5p0422c1s
Weld, A.G. v5p0573c1s
Weld, A.G., jr. v4p0570c1s
Weld, A.H. v1p0262c1s
v3p0417c1s
Weld, A.T. v1p0757c2s
Weld, Arthur v5p0394c2s
Weld, C. v1p1068c2s
v1p1272c1s v1p1360c1s
Weld, C.R. v1p0376c2m
v1p0690c2s v1p0968c2s v1p0999c2s
v1p1377c1m
Weld, C.S.F. v1p0473c1s
v1p0833c1s
Weld, F.E. v3p0005c2s
v3p0054c1s
Weld, H.H. v1p0639c1s
v1p1396c2s v1p1425c1s
Weld, I. v1p0919c2s
v1p1113c1s
Weld, L.G. v4p0087c2s
v5p0372c2s v6p0015c1s v6p0015c2m
v6p0037c2s
Weld, Le R.D. v5p0022c1s
Weld, S.F. v3p0218c2s
v3p0318c2m
Weldon, F.R. v5p0153c2s
Weldon, G. v2p0268c2s
Weldon, J.C. v1p0963c2s
Weldon, J.E.C. v6p0159c1s
Weldon, Mrs. v1p1201c1s
Weldon, W. v1p0749c2s
v1p0752c1s v2p0408c2s
Weldon, W.F.R. v4p0600c2m
v5p0319c2s
Welford, B.R. v1p0976c1s
Welford, E. v1p1414c1s
Welford, R. v2p0310c1s
Welker, P.A. v4p0175c2s
Well, T.E. v5p0127c1s
Wellby, M.S. v5p0002c1m
v5p0004c1s v5p0579c2s
Wellcome, H.S. v1p0256c2s
Wellcome, M.D. v3p0121c1s
Welldon, J.E.C. v3p0129c1s
v3p0130c1s v3p0184c1s v3p0253c2s
v3p0378c2s v4p0241c2s v4p0466c1s
v4p0474c2s v4p0566c1s v6p0038c2s
v6p0126c1s v6p0130c1s v6p0131c1s
v6p0513c2s v6p0575c1s
Weller, C.F. v5p0222c1s
v6p0039c2s v6p0109c2s
Weller, C.H. v6p0002c2s
Weller, C.W. et al. v6p0674c2s
Weller, E.F. v5p0525c2s
Weller, H.W. v5p0072c2s
Weller, J. v5p0114c2s
Weller, J.H. v1p0706c1s
Weller, S. v1p1372c1m
v1p1415c1m v1p1415c2s v4p0543c1s
Weller, S.H. v6p0111c1s
Welles, C.S. v1p0922c2s
Welles, E.L. v2p0094c1s
v2p0453c2s
Welles, G. v1p0404c2s
v1p0444c2s v1p0537c1s v1p0693c2s
v1p0750c1m v1p0750c2s v1p0808c1s
v1p0913c1s v1p1007c2s v1p1207c1s
v1p1267c1s v1p1353c2s
Welles, M.E. v2p0173c1s
Welles, N.J. v4p0037c1s
v5p0420c2s
Welles, W. v1p0522c2s
v1p0992c1s
Wellesley, Marquis v4p0497c2s
Wellhausen, J. v4p0302c1s
Welling, J.C. v1p0404c2s
v1p0651c1s v1p0753c1s v1p0815c2s
v1p1022c2s v1p1027c2s v1p1222c2s
v1p1230c2s v1p1267c1s v2p0029c2s
v2p0132c2s v2p0370c2s v2p0467c1s
v3p0012c1s v3p0046c1s v3p0086c1s
v3p0117c2s v3p0204c2s v3p0228c1s
v3p0236c1s v3p0263c1s v3p0272c2s
v3p0354c1s v3p0403c1s v3p0442c2m
v3p0443c1s v4p0163c1s v4p0254c2s
v4p0267c1s v4p0359c2m v4p0430c1s
v4p0529c2s v4p0594c1s v4p0594c2s
v4p0614c2s
Welling, J.C. et al. v6p0408c2s
Wellington, A. v4p0092c1s
Wellington, A.M. v1p1089c1s
v1p1176c2s v1p1340c1s
Wellington, A.M. and Sears, E.H.
v1p1325c2s
Wellington, Arthur, Duke of
v5p0429c1s
Wellington, G. v6p0417c2s
Wellington, S. v6p0201c1s
Wellington, T.S. v2p0062c2s
Wellman, F.L. v1p0097c2s
Wellman, H.C. v5p0334c1s
v6p0017c1s v6p0117c1s v6p0371c2s
Wellman, H.C. et al. v6p0371c1s
Wellman, J.W. v1p0085c2s
v1p0742c2s v3p0130c2s v4p0460c1s
Wellman, Mabel T. v4p0245c1s
Wellman, W. v5p0019c1s
v5p0027c1m v5p0041c1s v5p0044c1s
v5p0120c1s v5p0313c2s v5p0319c2s
v5p0354c1s v5p0384c1s v5p0414c1s
v5p0544c1s v5p0625c1m v6p0284c1s
v6p0326c1s v6p0358c2s v6p0477c2s
v6p0485c1s v6p0510c2s v6p0518c2s
v6p0551c1s v6p0592c1s v6p0611c1s
v6p0621c2s v6p0689c1s v6p0714c2s
Wellman, Walter v6p0009c2s
v6p0321c2s
Wells, A.E.
v2p0141c2s

v2p0168c2s v2p0461c1s
Wells, A.J. v6p0092c1s v6p0093c1s v6p0093c2m
Wells, A.M. v1p0277c1s
Wells, A.R. v5p0114c1s
Wells, B.W. v3p0134c2s v3p0323c2s v3p0463c2s v5p0074c2s v5p0083c1s v5p0099c1s v5p0103c1s v5p0153c2s v5p0171c1s v5p0192c2s v5p0195c1s v5p0206c1s v5p0217c1s v5p0220c2m v5p0221c2s v5p0230c2s v5p0237c1s v5p0298c2s v5p0321c2s v5p0330c2s v5p0362c1s v5p0370c2s v5p0377c2s v5p0412c1s v5p0414c1s v5p0475c2s v5p0485c1s v5p0496c1s v5p0516c1s v5p0539c2s v5p0540c2s v5p0544c2s v5p0559c1s v5p0576c2s v5p0606c1s v5p0614c1s v5p0637c2s v5p0646c1s v6p0014c1s
Wells, C. v1p0377c2s v1p0724c2s v4p0606c2s v5p0232c2s v5p0369c2s v6p0168c2s v6p0303c1s
Wells, C.B. v6p0564c1s
Wells, C.C. v6p0458c2s
Wells, C.L. v4p0112c1s v5p0189c2s
Wells, C.W. v6p0610c2s
Wells, Carolyn v5p0153c2s v5p0313c1s v5p0390c1s v5p0413c1s v5p0425c2s v6p0043c1s v6p0390c1s v6p0440c2s
Wells, D.A. v1p0109c1s v1p0540c1s v1p0628c1s v1p0640c1s v1p0649c2s v1p0677c2s v1p0796c1s v1p0897c2s v1p0902c2s v1p1055c2s v1p1164c1s v1p1242c2s v1p1260c1s v1p1265c1s v1p1285c1s v1p1285c2m v1p1297c1s v1p1342c2m v1p1349c1s v1p1349c2m v1p1351c2m v1p1394c1m v2p0260c1s v2p0286c2s v2p0356c2s v2p0430c2m v2p0431c1s v2p0431c2s v3p0044c2s v3p0071c2s v3p0127c2m v3p0173c2s v3p0178c1s v3p0342c1s v3p0343c2s v3p0347c1s v3p0434c1m v3p0442c1s v4p0070c2s v4p0167c1s v4p0235c2s v4p0278c1m v4p0283c2s v4p0415c2s v4p0462c2s v4p0524c2s v4p0563c1s v4p0563c2s v4p0565c1s v4p0591c2s v5p0317c2s v5p0568c1s v5p0568c2s v5p0604c1s
Wells, D.A. et al. v1p1232c2s v2p0356c2s v2p0431c1s
Wells, D.C. v3p0101c1s v3p0129c2s v3p0238c2s v3p0336c2s v3p0371c1s v3p0464c2s v4p0234c1s v5p0241c1s v5p0330c2s v6p0479c1s
Wells, D.D. v4p0205c1s
Wells, Dr. v1p1133c2s
Wells, E.C. v6p0679c1s
Wells, E.L. v2p0242c2s
Wells, E.P. v4p0348c1s
Wells, E.T. v4p0102c2s
Wells, F.J. v4p0047c1s v4p0210c2s v4p0564c1s v5p0049c2s
Wells, F.M. v6p0230c1s
Wells, G. v1p1181c2s
Wells, G.E. v6p0153c2s
Wells, H.C. v6p0231c1s v6p0596c2s
Wells, H.G. v3p0444c2s v3p0475c2s v4p0021c2s v4p0132c1s v4p0191c1s v4p0192c1s v4p0369c2s v4p0381c1s v4p0432c2s v4p0446c2s v4p0507c2m v4p0551c1s v4p0554c1s v4p0555c2s v4p0577c1s v4p0590c1s v5p0023c1s v5p0061c1s v5p0141c1s v5p0146c2s v5p0149c1s v5p0151c1s v5p0208c1s v5p0234c1s v5p0236c2s v5p0308c2s v5p0356c1s v5p0359c1s v5p0386c1s v5p0390c1s v5p0412c2s v5p0554c2s v5p0595c2s v5p0597c2s v5p0606c2s v5p0618c2s v5p0623c2s v6p0075c1s v6p0179c1s v6p0245c1s v6p0257c1s v6p0311c1s v6p0389c1s v6p0399c1s v6p0423c2s v6p0600c2m v6p0601c1s v6p0602c1m v6p0673c1s
Wells, H.G. et al. v5p0346c2s
Wells, H.L. v2p0342c2s v3p0046c2s v3p0163c1s v3p0195c1s v3p0244c1s v3p0337c2s v3p0349c2s v3p0371c2s v4p0082c2m v4p0288c2s v4p0324c1m v4p0385c2s v4p0435c2s v4p0436c1s v5p0496c2s v5p0508c1s v6p0681c2s
Wells, H.L. and Boltwood, B.B. v4p0082c2s
Wells, H.L. and Campbell, G.F. v4p0082c2s
Wells, H.L. and Dupee, L.C. v4p0082c2s
Wells, H.L. and Foote, H.W. v4p0082c2s v4p0637c1s v5p0087c1s v5p0499c2s v5p0645c2s
Wells, H.L. and Hurlburt, E.B. v4p0016c1s
Wells, H.L. and Johnston, W.R. v4p0016c2s
Wells, H.L. and Metzger, F.J. v5p0211c2s
Wells, H.L. and Penfield, S.L. v2p0175c1s v4p0255c1s v6p0610c2s
Wells, H.L. and Pirsson, L.V. v4p0324c1s
Wells, H.L. and Walden, P.T. v4p0082c2m
Wells, H.L. and Wheeler, H.L. v4p0010c2s v4p0082c2s v4p0494c1s v4p0524c1s
Wells, H.L. and Willis, J.M. v5p0087c1m
Wells, H.P. v2p0114c2s v2p0157c1s v2p0158c1s v2p0384c1s v2p0393c1s v3p0037c1s v3p0068c1s v3p0287c1s
Wells, H.T. and Leighton, F. v1p0066c1s v1p0300c2s
Wells, I.B. v4p0346c1s
Wells, J. v2p0073c2s v2p0392c1s v4p0046c2s v4p0102c2s v4p0226c1s v4p0316c2s v4p0363c1s v4p0422c2m v4p0438c2s v4p0597c2s v4p0632c2s v5p0181c1m v5p0181c2s v5p0283c2s v5p0284c2s v5p0286c1m v5p0312c1s v5p0320c1s v5p0379c1s v5p0406c2s v5p0421c2s v5p0632c2s v6p0131c1s
Wells, J.A. v5p0020c1s
Wells, J.C. v2p0316c2s
Wells, J.E. v1p0195c1s v1p0297c1s v1p0625c2s v1p0793c1s v1p1041c2s v1p1042c2s
Wells, J.G. v1p1002c1s
Wells, J.G.C. v4p0145c1s
Wells, J.M. v6p0369c2s
Wells, J.S.C. v2p0229c1s
Wells, J.T. v1p1052c2s v1p1053c1s
Wells, J.W. v3p0053c2s
Wells, K.G. v1p0034c1s v1p0219c1s v1p0230c1s v1p0386c1s v1p1085c1s v1p1420c1s v1p1424c1s v2p0158c1s v2p0336c2s v2p0420c2s v3p0128c2s v4p0019c2s v4p0068c2s v4p0104c2s v4p0158c2s v4p0386c2s v4p0409c2s v4p0501c2s v4p0549c2s v4p0556c1s v5p0204c2s v5p0362c2s v5p0485c1s v5p0617c2s v5p0620c1s v5p0636c2s
Wells, K.G., Mrs. v1p0707c2s v5p0163c2s
Wells, Kate G. v2p0408c1s v6p0301c1s v6p0702c2s
Wells, Kate Gannett v6p0705c1s
Wells, M.L. v4p0399c2s
Wells, N.A. v1p0786c1s v5p0279c2s v5p0392c2s
Wells, N.J. v5p0001c1s
Wells, N.W. v2p0037c2s v2p0068c2s v2p0247c1s v3p0152c2s
Wells, R. v6p0563c2s
Wells, R.G. v2p0003c1s
Wells, R.W. v1p1041c2s
Wells, S. v4p0107c2s
Wells, S.C. v1p1111c1s v2p0211c1s v2p0257c2s v3p0091c1s v3p0265c2s v4p0054c1s
Wells, S.H. v5p0569c2s
Wells, T.S. v3p0104c1s
Wells, W. v1p0011c2s v1p0048c2s v1p0114c2m v1p0223c2s v1p0478c1s v1p0481c2s v1p0513c1s v1p0515c2m v1p0516c1s v1p0516c2s v1p0517c1s v1p0522c2s v1p0637c1s v1p0683c1s v1p0740c1s v1p0789c2s v1p0823c1s v1p0880c1s v1p0961c1s v1p1129c1m v1p1143c1s v1p1163c1s v1p1199c2s v1p1261c1s v1p1270c2s v1p1307c2s v1p1312c2s v1p1340c1s
Wells, W.A. v4p0412c2s
Wells, W.G. .. v3p0064c2s v4p0383c2s
Wells, W.H. v1p0227c2s v1p0228c1s v1p0416c1s v2p0143c2m
Wells, W.L. v1p1218c1s v4p0082c2s v4p0454c2s
Wells, W.V. v1p0271c1s v1p0534c1s v1p0833c1m v1p0834c1s v1p0908c2s v1p0910c2s v1p0947c1s v1p1033c2s v1p1071c2s
Wells, W.Y. v1p0166c1s
Wells-Barnett, I.B. v5p0351c2s
Welman, C.C. v3p0286c1s
Welsford, J.W. v6p0053c2s v6p0133c2s
Welsh, A.H. v2p0011c2s v2p0343c1s
Welsh, C. v2p0265c1s v5p0106c2m v5p0107c2s v5p0190c1s v5p0479c2s v5p0641c1s v6p0115c2s v6p0218c1s v6p0328c1s
Welsh, D. v1p0254c2s v1p1404c1s
Welsh, H. v3p0213c2m v3p0214c1s v3p0326c1s v4p0027c2s v4p0115c1s v4p0117c1m v4p0135c2s v4p0281c1s v4p0282c1m v4p0282c2s v4p0314c1s v4p0387c2s v5p0445c1s
Welsh, Herbert v3p0213c2s
Welsh, J. v2p0167c1s v3p0438c2s
Welsh, J.J. v6p0471c1s
Welsh, L.S. v5p0643c2s
Welsh, M.C. v1p0874c2s
Welsh, O. v5p0146c2s
Welsh, R.E. v4p0067c1s v5p0056c1s v5p0402c1s
Welsh, R.F. v3p0045c2s
Welsh, R.G. v6p0339c2s
Welsh, Silvia M. v6p0367c2s
Welsh, W. v1p0255c2s v1p0916c1s
Welton, J. v5p0262c2s
Welton, R. v4p0192c2s v5p0393c2s v5p0395c1s
Welton, T. v1p1014c1s
Welton, T.A. v1p0338c2s v1p0481c1s v1p0873c2s v1p0936c1s v1p1354c1s v4p0546c2s v6p0383c2s v6p0509c1s v6p0673c1s
Welton, Thos. v4p0286c2s
Wemley, W. v4p0104c1s v4p0449c2s v4p0516c2s
Wemyss, M.E. v3p0177c2s v3p0232c1s v4p0537c1s
Wemyss, T. v1p0595c1s v1p1053c1s
Wendel, F.C.H. v3p0130c2s v4p0172c1s v5p0283c2s
Wendell, B. v2p0123c2s v3p0190c2m v3p0243c1s v3p0367c1s v4p0071c1s v4p0100c2s v4p0149c2s v4p0184c1m v4p0184c2s v4p0467c2s v5p0121c1s v5p0122c2s v5p0478c2s v6p0192c2s v6p0617c2s
Wendell, E.J. v3p0025c2s v3p0089c1s v4p0476c2s
Wendell, O.C. v2p0095c1m v2p0096c1s v2p0285c1s
Wendell, O.C. and Chandler, S.C. v2p0095c1s
Wendell, W.L. v5p0091c2s v5p0564c2s v6p0409c2s
Wendlandt, W. v6p0666c2s
Wendt, H.H. v4p0056c2s
Wendte, C. v6p0673c2s
Wendte, C.W. v1p0235c1s v2p0083c2s v2p0284c2s v5p0176c2s
Wenham, Canon v2p0366c1s
Wenham, F.H. v1p0463c2s v1p0935c2s v1p1240c2s
Wenham, J.C. v2p0244c1s
Wenham, J.L. v3p0253c2s
Wenley, R.M. v3p0328c1s v3p0358c1s v3p0399c2s v4p0202c1s v4p0259c1s v4p0439c1s v4p0474c1s v4p0478c2s v5p0087c2m v5p0193c1s v5p0233c1s v5p0279c1s v5p0311c2s v5p0381c2s v5p0447c1s v5p0455c1s v5p0455c2s v5p0483c2m v5p0484c1s v5p0513c1s v5p0604c2s v5p0607c1s v6p0161c2s v6p0503c2s v6p0554c1s
Wenley, R.M. et al. v6p0002c1s
Wenlock, Prof. v1p1003c1s
Wenner, G.U. v1p0229c1s v1p0255c2s v1p0289c1s v1p1433c1s v3p0112c1s v3p0254c2s v4p0045c1s v4p0057c1s v4p0311c1s v4p0352c2s v4p0477c2s v4p0630c1s v4p0633c1s v5p0033c2s v5p0083c2s v5p0378c1s v5p0577c1s v6p0060c2s v6p0245c1s v6p0419c2s v6p0483c1s
Went, G.H. v5p0242c2s
Went, G.M. v5p0203c2s
Wentworth v1p0149c2s
Wentworth, B.H. v6p0568c2s
Wentworth, Dr. v1p0873c1s
Wentworth, E. v1p0011c2s v1p0234c2s v1p0882c2s v2p0042c1s v2p0078c2s
Wentworth, E.L. v1p0512c1s
Wentworth, F. v1p0721c1s
Wentworth, F.H. v6p0659c2s
Wentworth, I.H. v6p0315c2s
Wentworth, J. v1p1398c2s v2p0469c2s v2p0470c1m v3p0188c1s v3p0460c1s
Wentworth, M. v1p0750c1s
Wentworth, Pres. v1p0959c1s
Wentz, G. v1p0080c2s
Wentz, V.L. v5p0079c2s v6p0404c1s
Wenzel, H. v3p0201c2s
Wenzel, H. and Bendall, C. v3p0428c2s
Wenzel, H.W. v3p0318c1s
Wergeland, A.M. v5p0193c1s v5p0532c1s v6p0237c1s v6p0238c2s v6p0274c2s v6p0434c2s v6p0707c2s
Wergeland, H. v2p0060c2s
Wergeland, M. v4p0024c1s v4p0147c1s v4p0272c1s v6p0597c1s
Wermuth, O. v1p0233c2s v1p1052c1s
Werncke, B. v1p1410c2s
Werner, A. v2p0021c1s v2p0048c2s v2p0053c1s v2p0054c1s v2p0453c2s v2p0469c2s v3p0004c2s v3p0050c2s v3p0054c1s v3p0234c2s v3p0263c1s v3p0332c2s v4p0204c2s v4p0521c2s v5p0020c1s v5p0047c1s v5p0129c1s v5p0140c2s v5p0344c1s

v5p0379c1s v5p0452c2s v5p0527c1s
v5p0546c1s v5p0563c1s v5p0566c2s
v5p0646c2s v6p0489c1s v6p0702c1s
Werner, A. and Colenso, H.E.
v4p0393c1s
Werner, A.E. v6p0583c2s
Werner, C.H. v4p0403c2s
v4p0566c2s v4p0634c2s
Werner, E. v3p0404c1s
Werner, E.A. v2p0178c2s
v3p0173c1s v4p0023c1s
Werner, E.T.C. v4p0105c2s
v4p0327c1s v4p0558c1s
Werner, J.C. v4p0040c1s
v4p0599c1s
Werner, J.R. v3p0409c1s
v5p0313c2s
Werner, W. v2p0324c1s
Werner-Spanhoofd, A. v6p0252c1s
Werren, J.E. v4p0320c1s
v5p0056c1s v5p0563c2s v6p0628c2s
Werry, I. v1p0005c1s
Werschler, A. v5p0391c1s
v5p0516c1s
Wertenbaker, W. v1p1356c2s
Wertheimer, J. v3p0200c1s
v3p0269c1s v6p0191c2s v6p0635c2s
Wertropp, H.M. v2p0232c2s
Wesche, W. v5p0211c2s
Wesley, E.B. v6p0454c2s
Wesley, H.W. v5p0560c2s
Wesley, P. v4p0235c1s
v5p0157c2s v5p0196c2s
Wesley, W.H. v3p0100c2s
v3p0342c2s v3p0451c2s v4p0473c2s
Wessely, C. v3p0353c1s
Wesslau, O.E. and Hake, A.E.
v3p0420c1s
Wesson, E. v2p0314c1s
West, A. v4p0114c1s
v4p0460c1s v5p0150c1s v5p0190c2s
v5p0340c2s v5p0345c1s v5p0605c2s
v5p0611c2s v5p0628c2s v6p0258c1s
v6p0341c2s v6p0383c1s v6p0407c2s
v6p0641c2s
West, A. and Gell, P.L. .. v5p0471c2s
West, A., Sir v6p0462c1s
v6p0640c2s
West, A.F. v2p0088c1s
v2p0092c2s v3p0334c2s v4p0321c2s
v4p0459c1s v5p0038c1s v5p0121c2s
v5p0178c2s v5p0518c1s v6p0130c1s
v6p0136c1s v6p0192c2s v6p0217c2s
v6p0363c1m
West, Algernon v6p0152c1s
West, Andrew F. v6p0662c2s
West, C.E. v1p0377c1s
West, C.S. v6p0031c2s
West, E.D. v1p0170c2s
West, E.H. v6p0166c2s
v6p0640c1s
West, E.P. v2p0211c1s
v2p0240c2m v2p0293c1s v2p0300c1m
v2p0354c1s v2p0409c1s
West, E.W. v3p0474c1s
v4p0428c2s
West, E.W. and Harlez, C.de.
v3p0029c1s
West, F. v5p0375c2s
West, F.S. v6p0038c1s
West, G. v1p1264c1s
West, G.A. v6p0440c1s
West, G.H. v1p1163c2s
West, G.M. v3p0147c2s
v4p0243c2s v4p0287c1s
West, H. v3p0002c1s
West, H.H. v5p0551c2s
West, H.L. v4p0588c2s
v5p0133c1m v5p0163c1s v5p0354c1m
v5p0414c1s v5p0425c2s v5p0464c2m
v5p0519c2m v5p0543c2s v5p0603c2s
v6p0666c2s
West, H.W. v5p0600c1s
West, J. v5p0164c2s
West, J.B. et al. v3p0245c1s
West, J.C. v6p0182c1s
West, Jean L. v6p0243c1s
West, K. v4p0217c2s
v4p0309c1m v4p0433c2s v4p0520c1m
v4p0601c2s v5p0314c2s v5p0344c1s
v5p0512c2s v6p0302c1s v6p0399c2s
West, Kenyon v4p0309c1s
v4p0457c1s v5p0223c1s v6p0055c2s
v6p0180c2s
West, L.H. v3p0102c2s
v4p0287c2s v5p0071c2s
West, Lady v3p0294c2s
West, M. v4p0102c2s
v4p0233c1s v4p0268c2s v4p0565c1s
v5p0075c1s v5p0207c1s v5p0283c2s
v5p0291c1m v5p0316c1s v5p0403c2s
v5p0407c1s v5p0464c2s v5p0500c2s
v5p0568c1s v5p0568c2m v5p0600c1s
v5p0638c1s v6p0045c2s v6p0051c2s
v6p0109c2s v6p0274c1s v6p0367c1s
v6p0410c1s v6p0424c1s v6p0584c1s
v6p0585c1s v6p0612c2s v6p0687c1s
West, M., Mrs. v5p0376c1s
West, M.A. v3p0120c2s
West, M.G. v5p0506c1s
West, Mr. et al. v6p0634c2s
West, Mrs. v1p0206c1s
West, N. v1p0336c1s
v2p0415c1s v3p0042c1s
West, R. v4p0150c1s
v5p0286c1s
West, R.A. v1p0158c1s
v1p0176c1s v1p0261c2s v1p0357c1s
v1p0846c1s
West, R.H. v4p0545c2s
West, R.W. v2p0341c2s
West, T. v1p0349c2m
v1p0982c2s v1p1016c1s v1p1115c1s
v1p1296c2s v1p1427c1s v4p0301c1s
v4p0371c2s
West, T.H. v2p0255c2s
v4p0329c1s
West, W.H.G. v1p1065c1s
v1p1248c1s v1p1248c2m
West, W.K. v6p0166c1s
v6p0325c2s v6p0541c2s v6p0553c2s
v6p0706c1s
West, W.M. v4p0194c2s
v5p0601c2s
Westall, A.St.L. v6p0220c2s
v6p0448c2s
Westall, A.St.Leger v6p0125c2s
Westall, W. v1p1199c1s
v2p0060c1s v2p0179c1s v2p0200c2s
v2p0401c2s v3p0152c1s v3p0191c1s
v3p0308c2s v5p0458c1s v5p0546c1s
Westall, Wm. v3p0194c1s
v6p0220c2s v6p0282c2s
Westbrook, H., Mrs. v1p1422c1s
Westbrook, R.B. v4p0284c1s
Westcott, A. v6p0693c1s
Westcott, B.F. v1p0008c2s
v1p0240c1s v1p0241c2s v1p0242c1s
v1p0243c1s v1p0249c2s v1p0287c1s
v1p0353c1s v1p0688c1s v1p0948c1s
v1p1001c2s v1p1017c1s v1p1037c2m
v2p0081c2s v2p0148c1s
Westcott, B.J. v4p0132c2s
Westcott, C. v6p0290c2s
Westcott, C.M. v6p0177c2s
Westcott, Canon v1p0207c1s
v3p0081c1s
Westcott, E.N. v5p0571c2s
Westcott, J.F.X. v5p0305c1s
Westcott, M. v1p0358c2s
Westdahl, F. v6p0665c2s
Westenholz, M. v5p0396c1s
Westenholz, Mary v6p0629c2s
Westenholz, R.A. v6p0170c2s
Wester, A.I. v1p0943c1s
Westerby, G.W. v1p0327c2s
Westergaard, H. v1p0873c2s
v4p0131c1s v5p0158c2s v5p0188c1s
v5p0343c2s v5p0388c1s
Westermarck, E. v4p0357c1s
v5p0024c1s v5p0207c1s v5p0386c1s
v5p0486c2s v6p0416c1s v6p0430c1s
Western, E.J. v6p0637c2s
Western, J. v1p0015c2s
v1p0044c2s v1p0267c2s v1p0663c1s
v1p1057c1s v1p1057c2s v1p1285c1s
Western, Lord v1p0161c2s
Western, W. v4p0365c2s
Western, W.H. v4p0119c2s
Westervelt, E. v1p0212c2s
Westervelt, J.P. v1p0133c1s
v1p0688c1s v1p0688c2s v1p0962c1s
v1p1098c2s v1p1260c1s v1p1304c1s
Westfield, Emily H. v6p0385c1s
Westgarth, W. v1p0078c1s
v2p0186c2s
Westgate, A.L. v6p0387c2s
Westhall, W. v4p0493c1s
Westinghouse, G., jr. v3p0132c2m
Westlake, J. v1p0701c1s
v2p0092c1s v2p0133c2s v2p0370c1s
v3p0218c2s v3p0258c2s v3p0297c1s
v4p0022c2s v5p0008c1s v5p0113c2s
v5p0133c2s v5p0207c1s v5p0568c2s
v6p0048c1s v6p0272c2s v6p0323c2s
Westlake, J. et al. v2p0370c1s
Westlake, N.H.J. v2p0417c1s
v4p0228c1s v5p0036c2s
Westland, A.B. v4p0319c2s
v4p0416c1s v4p0470c1s v4p0601c1s
v5p0113c1s
Westley, G.H. v4p0021c2s
v4p0120c1s v4p0267c2s v4p0306c1s
v4p0352c2s v4p0469c2s v4p0502c1s
v4p0587c2s v4p0601c2s v5p0006c1s
v5p0119c1s v5p0135c2s v5p0143c2s
v5p0148c2s v5p0155c2s v5p0156c1s
v5p0163c2s v5p0204c2s v5p0253c2s
v5p0328c2s v5p0392c2s v5p0423c1s
v5p0506c2s v5p0520c1s v5p0527c2s
v5p0546c1s v5p0560c2s v5p0606c2s
v6p0162c1s v6p0486c2s v6p0650c2s
Westmacott, P. v1p0618c2s
Westmacott, Prof. v3p0408c2s
Westman, G.M. v6p0248c2s
Westminster, Archbishop of et al.
v6p0191c2s
Westminster, Duke of and
Barnett, S.A. v5p0311c2s
Weston, A.J. v4p0383c1s
Weston, C. v1p1355c2s
Weston, C.H. v1p0639c1s
Weston, E.M. v6p0476c1s
Weston, G.F. v6p0066c1s
Weston, G.M. v1p0133c2s
v1p0282c2s v1p0283c1s v1p0313c2s
v1p0339c1s v1p0396c1s v1p0532c1m
v1p0630c2s v1p0634c2s v1p0714c1s
v1p0722c1s v1p0860c1s v1p1054c2s
v1p1198c1s v1p1198c2m v1p1199c1s
v1p1201c2s v1p1319c1s v1p1349c1s
v1p1351c2s v2p0033c2s v2p0170c1s
v2p0223c2s v2p0244c2s v2p0294c2s
v2p0328c2s v2p0353c2s v2p0452c1m
Weston, H.G. v2p0044c2s
v5p0306c2s
Weston, J. v1p0323c2s
v5p0222c1s v6p0669c2s
Weston, J.L. v6p0488c2s
Weston, N.A. v5p0137c2s
Weston, S. v1p0066c2s
v1p0167c1s v1p0272c1s v1p0323c1s
v1p0531c2s v1p0584c1s v1p0775c2s
v1p0924c1s v1p0938c1s v1p1002c1s
v1p1123c1s
Weston, S. and Howes, S.B.
v1p0272c1s v1p0554c1s
Weston, S. and Millingen, J.
v1p0101c2s v1p0445c1s
Weston, S.B. v4p0331c1s
Weston, T., jr. v2p0321c1s
v3p0461c1s
Weston, W. v2p0385c2s
v4p0296c2s v6p0333c2s
Weston, W.S. v2p0094c2s
Westrope, R. v4p0213c2s
Westropp, H.M. v1p0658c2s
v1p0938c1s v2p0377c2s v2p0473c2s
v3p0361c2s
Westrum, A.S.Van v4p0254c2s
v5p0004c1s v5p0044c2s v5p0087c1s
v5p0147c1s v5p0153c2s v5p0168c1s
v5p0197c1s v5p0264c1s v5p0275c1s
v5p0276c2s v5p0413c2s v5p0609c2s
v6p0074c1s v6p0119c1s v6p0301c1s
v6p0367c2s v6p0404c2s v6p0459c2s
v6p0598c1s v6p0698c1s
Westrum, A.Schade Van v4p0039c2s
v5p0083c1s v5p0221c1s
Westrup, E. v6p0487c1s
Westrup, M. v5p0315c1s
v6p0620c2s
Westrup, Margaret v5p0349c2s
v6p0066c1m v6p0216c2s v6p0632c1s
Westwood, F.B. v6p0571c2s
Westwood, I.O. and Warren, F.E.
v3p0144c2s
Westwood, J.O. v2p0062c2s
v3p0280c2s
Westwood, J.O. and Cook, A.S.
v3p0279c2s
Westwood, T. v1p0282c1s
v1p0599c1s v2p0389c1s
Wet, C.R.De v6p0655c1s
Wetherald, A.E. v1p0520c1s
Wetherald, E. v1p0424c1s
v4p0376c1s
Wetherbee, G.D. v5p0119c1s
Wetherbee, J. v1p1238c2s
Wetherbee, M. v2p0264c2s
Wetherby, A.G. v2p0294c1s
Wethered, C. v3p0450c2s
Wethered, F.T. v4p0012c1s
v4p0560c1s
Wethered, J. v1p1246c2s
Wetherell, E. v5p0120c2s
Wetherell, J.E. v4p0509c1s
Wetherell, Jane J. v3p0353c1s
Wetherell, L. v5p0159c1s
Wetherell, W. v4p0073c2s
v4p0144c2s v6p0017c2s v6p0083c1s
Wetherill, C.M. v1p0036c1s
v1p0065c1s v1p0159c1s v1p0502c1s
v1p0525c2s v1p0939c1s v1p1266c2s
v1p1362c2s
Wetherill, C.M. and Dalson, A.T.
v1p0271c1s
Wetherill, J.K. v2p0063c1s
v2p0317c1s v3p0117c1s v3p0263c1s
v3p0392c2s
Wetmore, A.D. v4p0043c1s
Wetmore, C.A. v1p0818c1s
v6p0700c2s
Wetmore, C.H. v5p0274c2s
Wetmore, C.H. and Steffens, L.
v6p0564c1s
Wetmore, C.W. v6p0025c2s
Wetmore, H.H. v6p0233c2s
Wetmore, P.M. v1p0915c2s
Wetmore, S. v3p0082c2s
v3p0083c2s v3p0271c1s
Wetmore, S.A. v5p0072c2s
Wetmore, W.S. v1p0090c2s
Wette, W.M.L.De v1p0123c2s
Wetter, A.A. v6p0629c2s
Wetzel, A. v6p0622c2s
Wetzel, W.A. v4p0213c1s
v6p0290c1s v6p0290c2s
Wetzler, J. v3p0133c1s
v4p0175c1s

Wex, G.R.von v2p0373c2s
Wey, A. v4p0502c1s
v6p0095c1s v6p0569c1s
Wey, Auguste v6p0092c2s
v6p0181c2s v6p0315c2s v6p0332c2s
v6p0386c2s
Weyde, H.Van der v4p0440c2s
Weyde, Van der v2p0433c1s
Weyer, E.M. v4p0164c1s
Weyers, J.L. v1p1077c2s
Weygandt, C. v6p0058c2s
v6p0328c1s v6p0514c2s v6p0582c2s
v6p0589c1s v6p0689c1s v6p0711c1s
Weyl, W.E. v4p0564c2s
v5p0320c2s v5p0477c2s v6p0355c2s
v6p0418c2m v6p0422c2s v6p0621c2s
Weyl, W.E. et al. v4p0275c1s
Weyler, R. v4p0461c1s
Weyler, S. v4p0431c1s
Weyman, C.S. v1p0059c2s
v1p1039c1s v1p1344c2s
Weyman, S. v5p0096c2s
Weyman, S.J. v2p0030c2s
v2p0421c2s v3p0049c1s v3p0106c1s
v3p0149c1s v3p0157c2s v3p0159c1s
v3p0160c1s v3p0170c2s v3p0202c2s
v3p0246c2s v3p0411c1s v3p0414c2s
v3p0446c2s v4p0004c1s v4p0010c2s
v4p0092c1s v4p0119c2s v4p0173c1s
v4p0195c2s v4p0216c1s v4p0220c1s
v4p0222c1s v4p0233c2s v4p0276c2s
v4p0322c1s v4p0336c1s v4p0342c1s
v4p0352c2s v4p0364c1s v4p0383c1s
v4p0414c2s v4p0468c1s v4p0569c1s
v4p0586c2s v4p0588c2s v5p0139c2s
v5p0455c1s v5p0527c2s v5p0539c2s
v6p0001c1s v6p0121c1s
Weymouth, R.F. v3p0015c2s
v3p0025c1s v3p0040c2s v3p0043c1s
v3p0184c1s
Weymouth, S.J. v2p0412c2s
Weymouth, W.J. v5p0162c1s
v6p0464c1s
Weyrauch, J. v1p1261c1s
v2p0118c2s
Weyrauch, J.J. v1p0663c2s
Weysse, A.W. v6p0021c2s
v6p0489c1s
Weysse, A.W. and Burgess, W.S.
v6p0540c2s
Whale, G. v3p0098c2s
v4p0304c1s v5p0334c2s
Whaley, W.B.S. v6p0197c2s
Whall, W.B. v2p0283c2s
Whalley, J.W. v5p0327c2s
Whalley, P.C. v4p0236c1s
Whannel, G.B. v1p0660c1s
Wharton, A.H. v1p1403c2m
v3p0011c2s v3p0055c2s v3p0057c1s
v3p0117c2s v3p0151c2s v3p0161c2s
v3p0247c2s v3p0255c1s v3p0259c2s
v3p0415c1s v3p0456c1s v3p0466c1s
v3p0469c2s v4p0124c2s v4p0221c2s
v4p0611c2m v4p0629c2s v5p0301c1s
v5p0443c1s v5p0500c1s v5p0621c1s
v6p0085c2s
Wharton, A.H. and Hawthorne, J.
v3p0463c2s
Wharton, Anne H. v6p0359c1s
v6p0491c2s v6p0664c1s
Wharton, E. v4p0571c2s
v4p0599c2s v5p0013c2s v5p0339c2s
v5p0389c1s v5p0389c2s v5p0480c2s
v5p0485c1s v6p0032c1s v6p0174c1s
v6p0247c2s v6p0299c1s v6p0362c1s
v6p0369c1s v6p0383c1s v6p0421c1s
v6p0432c2s v6p0525c2s v6p0532c2s
v6p0533c2s v6p0677c2s v6p0679c1m
Wharton, E.R. v2p0191c1s
v4p0241c2s
Wharton, Edith v3p0291c2s
v4p0217c2s v4p0318c1s v4p0587c2s
v5p0019c1s v5p0136c2s v5p0170c1s
v5p0299c2s v5p0393c1s v5p0439c1s
v5p0583c2s v6p0171c1s v6p0200c2s
v6p0216c1s v6p0237c2s v6p0288c2s
v6p0299c2s v6p0311c2s v6p0331c1s
v6p0331c2s v6p0358c2s v6p0394c1s
v6p0416c1s v6p0481c2s v6p0487c2s
v6p0511c2s v6p0548c2s v6p0550c1s
v6p0569c1s v6p0645c1s v6p0676c1s
Wharton, F. v1p0034c2s
v1p0047c2s v1p0081c2s v1p0091c2s
v1p0202c2s v1p0205c1s v1p0231c1s
v1p0234c2s v1p0255c1s v1p0283c2s
v1p0284c1m v1p0317c1s v1p0336c1s
v1p0378c1s v1p0406c1s v1p0431c2s
v1p0474c1s v1p0540c1s v1p0554c1s
v1p0697c2s v1p0699c1s v1p0854c1s
v1p0855c1s v1p0897c2s v1p0904c1s
v1p0944c2s v1p1036c2s v1p1067c2s
v1p1075c2s v1p1102c1s v1p1118c2s
v1p1121c1s v1p1134c2s v1p1202c2s
v1p1228c2s v1p1238c1s v1p1283c1s
v1p1354c1s v1p1418c2s v2p0252c2s
Wharton, F.W. v5p0098c2s
v5p0379c2s v5p0381c1s v5p0390c1s
v5p0412c2s v5p0421c1s v5p0425c1s
v5p0555c1s v5p0589c2s v6p0168c1s
v6p0171c2s v6p0511c1s v6p0541c1s
v6p0600c1s v6p0607c1s v6p0686c2s
v6p0698c1s v6p0709c2s
Wharton, G.M. v1p0300c2s
Wharton, G.W. v6p0116c1s
v6p0290c1s v6p0573c2s
Wharton, H.M. v6p0131c1s
Wharton, H.T. v2p0035c1s
v2p0201c1s
Wharton, H.T. and Rae, J.. v2p0372c2s
Wharton, J. v1p0082c1s
v1p0102c1s v1p0216c1s v1p0639c2s
v1p0650c1s v1p0920c2s v1p1057c1s
v1p1235c1s v1p1243c2s v1p1283c1s
Wharton, J.H. v2p0471c2s
Wharton, J.M. v1p0384c1s
v2p0291c1s
Wharton, R. v1p0603c1s
Wharton, T. v2p0246c1s
v2p0420c1s v4p0064c2s v4p0139c1s
v4p0321c1s v5p0425c2s v5p0474c1s
Wharton, W. v6p0250c1s
Wharton, W.F. v4p0131c1s
Wharton, W.J.L. v2p0179c1s
v3p0100c2s v3p0356c1s v4p0410c2m
v5p0137c1s v6p0082c1s v6p0250c2s
v6p0567c1s
Wharton, W.J.L. et al. ... v3p0100c1s
Whately, E. v2p0168c2s
v2p0246c2s
Whately, E.J. v2p0080c2s
v2p0118c1s v2p0243c1s v3p0370c2s
Whately, M.L. v2p0063c2s
v2p0134c1s v2p0134c2s v2p0252c1s
v2p0421c2s
Whately, R. v1p0077c2s
v1p0260c1s v1p0293c2s v1p0465c1s
v1p0892c1s v1p0932c1s v1p1026c2s
v1p1043c2s
Whates, H. v4p0244c1s
v5p0100c2s v5p0247c2s v5p0325c2s
v5p0609c1s
Whatham, A.E. v5p0261c1s
v5p0308c2s v6p0046c1s
Wheat, L. v3p0461c2s
Wheat, Q.A. v6p0188c1s
Wheatcroft, F.G. v1p0479c2s
v1p0481c1s v1p0481c2s v1p1117c1s
Wheatcroft, H.J. v2p0165c2s
Wheater, W. v3p0295c2s
v3p0363c1s v4p0003c1s v4p0107c1s
v4p0361c1s v4p0467c2s
Wheatley, B.R. v1p0149c1s
v1p0628c2s v1p0742c1s v1p0742c2s
v1p1313c1s v2p0051c2s v2p0052c1s
v2p0257c1s
Wheatley, C.M. v1p0073c1s
v1p0469c2s
Wheatley, G.W. v1p1379c2s
Wheatley, H.B. v1p0206c1s
v1p0628c2m v2p0002c2s v2p0015c2s
v2p0039c1s v2p0045c2s v2p0052c1m
v2p0062c2s v2p0076c1s v2p0091c1s
v2p0093c1m v2p0117c2s v2p0160c2s
v2p0208c2m v2p0264c1s v2p0271c2s
v2p0327c2s v2p0335c2s v2p0352c1s
v2p0378c1s v2p0398c1s v2p0398c2s
v2p0418c2s v2p0428c2s v2p0433c1s
v3p0049c2m v3p0101c1s v3p0326c2s
v4p0154c1s v4p0434c2m v4p0552c2s
v4p0617c1s v5p0070c2s v5p0077c2s
Wheatley, H.B. et al. v2p0458c1s
Wheatley, J. v1p1191c2s
Wheatley, J.H. v1p0735c2s
Wheatley, L.A. v2p0104c1s
v2p0130c2s v2p0241c2s v2p0253c2s
v2p0344c2s v4p0309c2s
Wheatley, R. v2p0004c1s
v2p0110c1s v2p0151c2s v2p0271c1s
v2p0286c1s v2p0313c2s v2p0420c2s
v2p0450c1s v3p0032c2s v3p0079c2s
v3p0199c1s v3p0253c2s v3p0265c2m
v3p0301c1s v3p0303c2s v3p0304c1m
v3p0336c2s v3p0346c2s v3p0355c1s
v3p0375c1s v3p0410c1s v3p0428c2s
v3p0474c2s v4p0127c1s v4p0302c2s
v4p0334c1s v4p0438c2s v4p0449c2s
v5p0407c1s
Wheatley, T.A. v5p0641c1s
Wheatley, W.W. v6p0454c1s
Wheaton, A. v1p0476c1s
Wheaton, E.F. v6p0567c2s
Wheaton, H. v1p0040c1s
v1p0295c2s v1p0344c1s v1p0395c1s
v1p0535c2s v1p0680c1s v1p0730c1s
v1p0730c2m v1p0801c1s v1p0978c2s
v1p1011c1s v1p1155c1s
Wheaton, J.W. v5p0103c2s
v5p0151c2s
Wheaton, R. v1p0019c1s
v1p0301c1s v1p0331c1s v1p0331c2s
v1p0476c2s v1p0481c2s v1p0926c1s
v1p1058c2s v1p1061c1s v1p1195c1m
v1p1305c1s
Wheatstone, C. v1p0747c2s
v1p1290c2s v1p1375c1s
Whedon, D.A. v1p0126c1s
v1p0203c2s v1p0535c2s v1p0831c1m
v2p0355c2s
Whedon, D.D. v1p0058c2s
v1p0059c1s v1p0441c2s v1p0458c1s
v1p0731c2s v1p0830c1m v1p0830c2s
v1p0831c1s v1p0840c1s v1p0840c2s
v1p0867c2s v1p0980c1s v1p1053c2s
v1p1287c1s v1p1347c1s v1p1399c1s
v2p0044c2m v2p0351c2s v2p0432c1s
Whedon, M.A. v4p0169c1s
Wheelan, F.H. v6p0550c2s
Wheeler, A.A. v1p0058c2s
v1p0103c2s v1p0757c2s v1p1137c2s
v1p1379c2m v2p0398c1s v2p0464c1s
v6p0275c1s v6p0558c1s v6p0629c1s
Wheeler, A.C. v1p0704c2s
v1p1227c2s v3p0051c2s v3p0387c2s
v4p0003c1s v4p0427c1s v4p0515c1s
v5p0232c2s v5p0557c2s
Wheeler, A.D. v1p0036c2s
v1p0353c1s
Wheeler, A.L. v6p0309c2s
Wheeler, A.M. v5p0378c2m
Wheeler, A.S. v1p1122c1s
v2p0245c1s v6p0004c2s
Wheeler, B.F. v5p0483c2s
Wheeler, B.I. v4p0241c2m
v4p0428c2s v5p0011c2s v5p0012c1s
v5p0042c1s v5p0129c1s v5p0161c1s
v5p0173c2s v5p0248c2s v5p0249c1m
v5p0325c1m v5p0367c1s v5p0419c2s
v5p0473c2s v5p0521c1s v5p0597c1s
v5p0639c1s v5p0645c2s v6p0093c2m
v6p0140c2s v6p0161c1s v6p0190c1s
v6p0192c2s v6p0195c1s v6p0242c2s
v6p0312c2s v6p0376c1s v6p0381c1s
v6p0495c2s v6p0568c1m v6p0609c2m
v6p0643c1s v6p0671c2s
Wheeler, B.I. and Hale, W.G.
v2p0430c1s
Wheeler, B.I. and Putnam, F.W.
v6p0092c2s
Wheeler, B.L. v4p0184c2s
Wheeler, B.S. v5p0437c1s
Wheeler, Blanche E. v6p0157c2s
Wheeler, C. v3p0044c1s
v3p0174c1s v4p0101c1s v4p0198c2s
v4p0263c2s v5p0225c2s v5p0269c1s
v6p0024c1s v6p0230c1s v6p0462c2s
v6p0690c2s
Wheeler, C.B. v6p0140c2s
v6p0158c2s v6p0176c2s v6p0256c1s
v6p0575c2s
Wheeler, C.G. v1p0056c2s
Wheeler, C.P. v6p0355c1s
Wheeler, C.S. v1p0577c1s
v1p0591c1s v1p0775c1s
Wheeler, Candace v4p0150c2s
v5p0636c1s
Wheeler, Chris. v3p0044c1s
Wheeler, D.H. v1p0227c2s
v1p0286c1s v1p0353c1s v1p0723c2s
v1p0724c1s v1p0860c1s v1p0904c1s
v1p1028c2s v1p1048c1s v1p1062c2s
v1p1216c2s v1p1282c1s v1p1285c2s
v1p1335c1s v1p1352c2s v2p0081c1s
v2p0398c2s v2p0438c1s v3p0056c2s
v4p0108c2s v4p0152c1s v4p0183c1s
v4p0230c1s v4p0283c2s v4p0382c1s
v4p0448c2s v4p0518c1s v4p0520c1s
v4p0532c1s v4p0533c1s v4p0554c2s
v4p0558c2s v4p0615c1s v5p0613c1s
Wheeler, E. v5p0085c2s
Wheeler, E.B. and Lockwood, M.H.
v5p0125c1s
Wheeler, E.C. v6p0600c1s
Wheeler, E.F. v1p0611c2s
v1p0728c1s v2p0057c2s v2p0198c1s
v2p0284c1s v2p0317c1s v3p0028c2s
v3p0105c2s v3p0411c1s v3p0468c2s
v4p0242c1s v4p0365c2s v4p0628c2m
v5p0554c1s v5p0637c2s
Wheeler, E.F. et al. v3p0468c2s
Wheeler, E.G.L. v2p0251c2s
Wheeler, E.G.L., Mrs.
v2p0312c1s
v2p0319c2s
Wheeler, E.J. v5p0468c1s
v5p0527c2s
Wheeler, E.P. v2p0081c2s
v5p0120c1s v5p0120c2s v5p0256c2s
v5p0535c1s v6p0026c2s v6p0218c2s
v6p0347c1s v6p0356c1s
Wheeler, Ethel v5p0355c2s
Wheeler, F. v6p0396c1s
Wheeler, F.B. v2p0295c1s
Wheeler, F.L. v5p0419c1s
Wheeler, F.M. v4p0467c1s
v5p0472c2s v5p0619c1s
Wheeler, F.P. v5p0267c1s
Wheeler, Frances E. v6p0183c1s
Wheeler, G.C. v6p0507c2s
Wheeler, G.M. v1p0506c1s
v5p0375c2s v5p0547c2s
Wheeler, G.S. v6p0276c2s
Wheeler, H. v1p1292c2s
v2p0221c2s
Wheeler, H.A. v2p0252c1s
v2p0290c1s v3p0151c1s
Wheeler, H.A. and Luedeking, C.
v3p0034c1s
Wheeler, H.F.B. v6p0189c1s
v6p0647c2s
Wheeler, H.L. v4p0020c1s

v4p0028c2s v4p0288c2s v4p0568c1s
Wheeler, H.L. and Wells, H.L.
v4p0010c2s v4p0082c2s v4p0494c1s
v4p0524c1s
Wheeler, H.M.K. v2p0324c2s
Wheeler, H.N. v5p0348c2s
Wheeler, J. v1p0057c2s
v4p0594c1s v5p0154c1s v6p0225c2s
Wheeler, J. and Grosvenor, C.H.
v4p0602c1s
Wheeler, J. et al. v5p0541c2s
Wheeler, J.C. v5p0095c1s
v5p0266c1s
Wheeler, J.E. v3p0453c2s
Wheeler, J.R. v3p0026c2s
v3p0237c2s v4p0026c1s v4p0035c1s
v5p0025c1s v6p0038c2s v6p0287c2s
Wheeler, J.T. v1p0112c2s
v3p0196c2s v3p0212c1s v3p0212c2s
v3p0333c1s v3p0420c2s v4p0193c2s
v4p0258c1s
Wheeler, L.P. and Bumstead, H.A.
v6p0526c2m
Wheeler, M.S. v3p0394c1s
Wheeler, N.M. v2p0048c1s
v2p0130c2s v2p0132c1s v2p0204c1m
v2p0315c1s v2p0381c2s
Wheeler, O.C. v2p0064c1s
Wheeler, O.E. v1p0698c2s
Wheeler, R.A. v3p0440c1s
v6p0613c2s
Wheeler, S. v3p0003c2s
v3p0211c1s v3p0211c2s v4p0279c1s
v4p0444c1s v5p0150c1s v5p0186c1s
v5p0324c1s
Wheeler, S.S. v5p0183c1s
Wheeler, T. v4p0354c2s
Wheeler, T.H. v2p0035c2s
Wheeler, W.A. v1p0031c1s
v1p0875c2s v1p1184c2s
Wheeler, W.H. v2p0373c2s
v4p0043c1s v4p0288c1s v4p0318c2s
v4p0327c1s v4p0613c1s v5p0022c1s
v5p0323c1s v5p0380c2s v5p0438c1s
v5p0516c2s v6p0005c1s v6p0075c2s
v6p0714c2s
Wheeler, W.M. v5p0020c2s
v5p0021c2m v5p0022c1s v5p0282c1s
v5p0617c1s v6p0023c1s v6p0024c1s
v6p0024c2s v6p0152c2m v6p0153c1s
v6p0185c1s v6p0214c2m v6p0350c1s
v6p0444c1s v6p0464c1s
Wheeler, W.M. and Chapman, F.M.
v6p0386c1s
Wheeler, W.M. and Long, W.H.
v5p0174c2s
Wheeler, W.N. v5p0050c1s
Wheeler, W.R. v6p0529c1s
Wheeley, A.C. v1p0311c1s
v1p0786c1s v1p0984c1s v1p1172c1s
Wheelock, A. v1p0074c1s
Wheelock, C.F. v5p0198c2s
Wheelock, E.J. v6p0456c1s
Wheelock, E.M. v1p0247c1s
Wheelock, G.A. v1p0524c2s
Wheelock, J.A. v5p0414c1s
Wheelock, L. v4p0311c1s
Wheelock, L. et al. v4p0629c2s
Wheelock, R. v5p0528c1s
Wheelock, W. v5p0374c2s
v5p0504c2s
Wheelwright, E. v5p0350c1s
Wheelwright, E.C. v6p0311c2s
Wheelwright, E.G. v4p0197c2s
v5p0140c1s v5p0337c2s v5p0390c1s
v5p0456c1s v6p0281c1s v6p0355c1s
v6p0619c2s
Wheelwright, Edith G. v5p0555c1s
Wheelwright, J. v1p0151c2s
Wheelwright, J.T. v3p0348c2s
v4p0495c1s v6p0196c2s
Wheelwright, W.B. v5p0257c2s
Wheildon, W.W. v1p0283c2s
v1p0866c2s
Whelan, F. v6p0544c1s
Whelan, L.M. v5p0201c2s
Wheless, J. v5p0147c2s
v5p0550c1s v5p0559c2m
Wheless, J.F. v2p0453c1s
Whelpley, A.W. et al. v4p0408c2s
Whelpley, J.D. v1p0036c1s
v1p0072c1m v1p0074c1s v1p0186c2s
v1p0204c2s v1p0212c2m v1p0274c1s
v1p0344c2s v1p0533c1s v1p0592c1m
v1p0623c1s v1p0626c1s v1p0630c1s
v1p0639c2s v1p0640c2m v1p0716c1s
v1p0738c2s v1p0832c1m v1p0920c1m
v1p0947c2s v1p0976c1s v1p0999c1s
v1p0999c2s v1p1004c2s v1p1025c2s
v1p1048c1s v1p1062c2s v1p1199c1s
v1p1218c1s v1p1263c1s v1p1287c2s
v1p1303c1s v1p1361c1s v1p1368c1s
v1p1405c1m v4p0501c2s v5p0090c2s
v5p0091c1s v5p0147c2m v5p0161c1s
v5p0294c1s v5p0410c2s v5p0460c1s
v5p0460c2s v5p0627c2s v6p0202c2s
v6p0205c2s v6p0213c1s v6p0252c2s
v6p0263c1s v6p0308c2s v6p0309c1s
v6p0417c1s v6p0530c1s v6p0633c1s
Whelpley, J.D. and Wilson, R.R.
v5p0586c1s
Whelpley, James D. v6p0202c2s
Whelpley, P.B. v6p0018c1s
Whelpton, E. v2p0086c1s
v2p0322c1s v3p0440c2s v4p0571c2s
Whelpton, Edwin v4p0253c2s
Whelpton, M.W. v4p0181c2s
Wherry, A. v6p0164c1s
Wherry, Beatrix A. v6p0702c1s
Wherry, W.M. v1p1413c2s
v6p0163c2s v6p0513c1s
Whetham, C.D. v4p0177c1s
Whetham, W.C.D. v6p0199c1s
Whetham, W.G.B. v6p0471c1s
Whetstone, F.J. and Hardie, J.K.
v4p0214c1s
Whetstone, J.L. v2p0259c2s
Whewell, G. v2p0161c2s
Whewell, W. v1p0287c1s
v1p0506c2s v1p0508c1s v1p0600c2m
v1p0762c2s v1p1016c2s v1p1037c2s
v1p1310c1s
Whibley, C. v3p0195c1s
v3p0309c2s v4p0039c2s v4p0047c1s
v4p0073c2s v4p0091c1s v4p0218c1s
v4p0226c1s v4p0242c1s v4p0256c1s
v4p0293c2s v4p0322c1s v4p0369c1s
v4p0426c1s v4p0434c2s v4p0437c2s
v4p0447c2m v4p0467c2s v4p0473c2s
v4p0520c2s v4p0597c2s v4p0625c2s
v4p0628c1s v5p0038c2s v5p0049c1s
v5p0050c2s v5p0062c1s v5p0084c1s
v5p0170c1s v5p0212c2s v5p0325c1s
v5p0326c2s v5p0338c1s v5p0346c1s
v5p0350c2s v5p0358c2s v5p0398c1s
v5p0436c2s v5p0466c2s v5p0489c1s
v5p0505c1s v5p0532c1s v5p0558c2s
v5p0606c1s v5p0608c2s v5p0635c1s
v6p0058c2s v6p0076c1s v6p0086c1s
v6p0103c1s v6p0283c2s v6p0339c2s
v6p0379c1s v6p0380c1s v6p0451c2s
v6p0501c1m v6p0507c2s v6p0569c1s
v6p0575c2s v6p0640c2s v6p0661c1s
Whibley, C. and Barr, R. . v6p0084c2s
Whibley, Charles v4p0137c2s
v4p0406c1s
Whicher, G.M. v4p0241c2s
v4p0334c2s v4p0557c2s v4p0575c2s
v5p0542c1s v6p0320c1s
Whigham, H.J. v5p0239c1s
v5p0587c2m v5p0588c1m v6p0163c2s
Whilden, W.G. v3p0382c1s
Whilldin, J.K. v1p0257c2s
v1p0399c2s
Whinery, S. v4p0431c2s
Whipple, C.K. v1p0033c1s
v1p0119c2s v1p0241c1s v1p0252c2s
v1p0338c1s v1p0441c1s v1p0484c2s
v1p0486c1s v1p0619c2s v1p0646c1s
v1p0803c1s v1p0949c2m v1p1063c2s
v1p1094c1s v1p1095c1s v1p1103c1s
v1p1139c2m v1p1140c1s v1p1147c2s
v4p0109c1s v4p0262c2s v4p0463c1s
v4p0478c2s v4p0557c2s v4p0578c2s
Whipple, E.P. v1p0013c2s
v1p0032c2s v1p0085c1s v1p0086c2s
v1p0100c2s v1p0105c2s v1p0164c2s
v1p0166c2s v1p0182c1s v1p0218c1s
v1p0237c2m v1p0318c1s v1p0330c1s
v1p0349c2s v1p0350c1m v1p0350c2m
v1p0364c2m v1p0405c1s v1p0417c2s
v1p0418c2m v1p0451c2m v1p0511c2s
v1p0559c1s v1p0575c2s v1p0602c2s
v1p0676c2s v1p0695c2s v1p0707c2s
v1p0768c1s v1p0776c2s v1p0931c2s
v1p0932c1s v1p0993c1s v1p1047c2s
v1p1054c1s v1p1066c2s v1p1081c2s
v1p1184c2s v1p1185c1s v1p1187c1s
v1p1190c1s v1p1195c2s v1p1197c1s
v1p1208c1s v1p1211c2s v1p1223c1s
v1p1235c2s v1p1267c1s v1p1281c1s
v1p1298c1s v1p1309c2s v1p1348c2s
v1p1395c2s v1p1417c1s v1p1429c1s
v1p1429c2m v1p1438c2s v2p0022c1s
v2p0068c2s v2p0121c1s v2p0139c2s
v2p0140c1m v2p0175c1s v2p0405c1s
v2p0427c2s v2p0472c2s v3p0117c2s
v3p0254c2s
Whipple, G.C. v4p0573c2s
v5p0323c1s v5p0621c2m v5p0622c2s
Whipple, G.C. and Parker, H.N.
v5p0357c2s
Whipple, G.M. v2p0424c2s
v5p0123c1s v5p0369c2s v5p0486c1s
v5p0565c1s v6p0150c1s v6p0432c1s
v6p0500c2s v6p0532c1s
Whipple, H.B. v3p0213c2s
v4p0282c2s v5p0531c2s
Whipple, I.L. v6p0277c2s
Whipple, J. v1p1359c2s
Whish, C.W. v6p0312c2s
v6p0314c2s
Whishaw v1p1290c1s
Whishaw, E.M. v5p0575c1s
Whishaw, F. v4p0016c2s
v4p0048c1s v4p0048c2s v4p0060c2s
v4p0070c2s v4p0138c1s v4p0144c2s
v4p0178c1s v4p0199c2s v4p0275c2s
v4p0276c1s v4p0431c1s v4p0496c1m
v4p0496c2s v4p0624c1s v4p0624c2s
v4p0625c2m v5p0035c2s v5p0086c1s
v5p0158c2s v5p0186c2m v5p0207c2s
v5p0273c2s v5p0352c1m v5p0367c1s
v5p0389c1s v5p0489c1s v5p0500c2s
v5p0501c1s v5p0501c2s v5p0505c1s
v5p0516c2s v5p0561c1s v5p0593c2m
v5p0634c2s v6p0037c2s v6p0067c2s
v6p0181c1s v6p0246c2s v6p0381c2s
v6p0625c1s v6p0646c2s v6p0692c1s
Whishaw, Fred v5p0198c2s
v5p0406c1s v5p0617c2s
Whiskin, H. v5p0125c1s
Whistler, C.W. v5p0195c2s
Whistler, G.M. v5p0029c1s
v5p0033c1s
Whistler, G.W. v1p0267c2s
v1p0759c1s v1p0759c2s
Whistler, J.M. v3p0368c2s
Whistler, J.McN. v5p0095c1s
Whiston, E.A. v5p0305c2s
v5p0450c1s v5p0546c2s v6p0125c2s
Whitaker, A.C. v6p0260c1s
Whitaker, A.E. v5p0127c1s
Whitaker, A.P. v2p0276c2s
Whitaker, C.W. v1p1172c1s
Whitaker, D.K. v1p0701c2s
v1p0905c2s v1p1274c2s v1p1275c1s
v2p0238c1s
Whitaker, E. v1p0892c1s
v1p1219c1s v2p0221c1s v2p0277c1s
v2p0305c1s v2p0379c1s v5p0397c1m
v5p0562c2s
Whitaker, F.E. v5p0178c1s
v5p0249c1s v6p0273c1s
Whitaker, F.O. v4p0181c1s
v4p0608c2s
Whitaker, H. v5p0160c1s
v5p0169c2s v5p0219c2s v5p0532c2s
v5p0536c2s v6p0066c1s v6p0069c2s
v6p0085c2s v6p0172c2m v6p0201c1s
v6p0307c1s v6p0421c1s v6p0490c2s
v6p0517c2s v6p0518c1s v6p0597c2s
v6p0603c2m v6p0631c2s v6p0682c2s
v6p0685c2s v6p0696c2s
Whitaker, H.C. and Partridge, E.A.
v4p0218c2s
Whitaker, H.W. v3p0374c1s
Whitaker, Herman v5p0566c1s
v6p0014c1s
Whitaker, J.V. v2p0008c2s
v2p0010c2s v2p0068c1s
Whitaker, J.V. and Vinne, T.L.De.
v1p0743c1s
Whitaker, M.C. v5p0347c2s
Whitaker, M.S. v1p0668c2s
v2p0099c2s
Whitaker, M.S., Mrs. v1p0220c2s
Whitaker, N.T. v1p0881c2s
Whitaker, R. v4p0196c2s
Whitaker, T.D. v1p0520c2s
v1p1385c2m v1p1393c1s
Whitaker, W. v3p0089c1s
v4p0555c1s
v5p0229c1s
Whitbeck, Alice G. v6p0371c1s
Whitbeck, R.H. v6p0249c2s
v6p0250c1s v6p0441c1s
Whitby, J. v1p0048c1s
Whitby, J.E. v5p0053c1s
v6p0057c1m v6p0177c2s v6p0307c2s
v6p0630c2s
Whitby, J.E., Mrs. v5p0119c1s
v5p0156c2s v5p0307c1s v5p0634c2s
Whitcher, J. v1p1152c2s
Whitcher, W.F. v2p0311c1s
v2p0473c1s v3p0301c2s
Whitcomb, C. v5p0319c1s
v5p0378c2s v5p0559c2s v6p0524c1s
Whitcomb, G.A. v3p0441c2s
Whitcomb, Ida P. v6p0362c1s
Whitcomb, Jane v5p0341c1s
Whitcomb, M. v5p0428c1s
v6p0094c2s
Whitcomb, S.A. v3p0282c1s
Whitcomb, S.L. v5p0016c1s
v6p0306c1s
White, A. v1p0391c1s
v1p1027c1s v1p1236c1s v2p0093c2s
v2p0140c2s v2p0264c1s v2p0265c1s
v3p0092c2m v3p0136c1s v3p0209c1s
v3p0271c2s v4p0258c1s v4p0275c1s
v4p0302c2s v4p0501c1s v4p0590c2s
v5p0007c2s v5p0128c1s v5p0187c2s
v5p0244c2s v5p0245c2s v5p0307c1s
v5p0307c2m v5p0308c1s v5p0410c2s
v5p0502c1s v5p0586c2s v5p0645c2s
v6p0004c1s v6p0080c2s v6p0206c1s
v6p0254c2s v6p0265c1s v6p0268c2s
v6p0269c1s v6p0276c2m v6p0327c2s
v6p0352c2s v6p0387c2s v6p0456c2s
v6p0555c2s
White, A. and Hurd, A.S. . v6p0555c2s
White, A. and Lanin, E.B.. v3p0230c2s
White, A.D. v1p0386c1m
v1p0595c1s v1p0680c2s v1p1106c2s
v1p1137c1s v1p1150c2s v1p1163c1s
v1p1163c2s v1p1208c1s v2p0087c1s
v2p0095c2s v2p0131c1s v2p0390c2s
v3p0085c2s v3p0091c2s v3p0115c1s
v3p0131c2s v3p0197c1s v3p0216c2s

v3p0265c1s v3p0276c1s v3p0281c2s
v3p0295c1s v3p0329c2s v3p0337c2s
v3p0380c2s v3p0444c2m v3p0445c1s
v4p0018c1s v4p0123c2s v4p0144c1s
v4p0218c2s v4p0507c2s v4p0597c1s
v5p0054c1s v5p0310c2s v5p0455c1s
v5p0581c2m v6p0036c2s v6p0101c1s
v6p0158c1s v6p0174c2s v6p0275c1s
v6p0515c1s v6p0557c1s v6p0570c2s
v6p0644c1s v6p0661c1s v6p0686c1s
v6p0699c1s

White, A.D. and Rice, I.L.
v4p0596c1s

White, A.D. et al. v4p0596c1s
v5p0179c2s

White, A.E. v2p0396c1s
v5p0427c2s

White, A.H. v2p0436c2s

White, A.M. v4p0096c2s
v5p0490c2s v5p0587c1s

White, A.S. v3p0004c1s
v3p0424c1s v4p0005c1s v4p0005c2s
v4p0006c2s v4p0038c1s v4p0172c1s
v4p0237c1s v4p0403c2s v4p0404c1s
v4p0591c2s v5p0180c2s v6p0195c2s

White, A.Silva v4p0005c1s

White, A.T. v3p0074c1m
v4p0096c2s v4p0568c2s v6p0084c1s

White, A.W. v6p0344c1s

White, Alma G. v6p0543c2s

White, Arnold v4p0275c2s

White, B. v1p0071c1s
v1p0150c1s v1p0257c2m v1p0542c2s

White, C. v1p0242c1s
v1p0244c1s v1p0245c1s v1p0276c2s
v1p0530c1s v1p0558c1s v1p1057c2s
v1p1288c1s v1p1400c1s

White, C., Mrs. v1p1008c1m

White, C.A. v1p0035c2s
v1p0140c1s v1p0268c2s v1p0367c1s
v1p0462c2s v1p0508c2s v1p0638c2s
v1p0651c2s v1p0652c1m v1p0677c2s
v1p0718c2s v1p0814c1s v1p0817c2s
v1p0859c1s v1p0876c1s v1p0927c1s
v1p0960c1s v1p1041c2s v2p0024c1s
v2p0070c1s v2p0162c2s v2p0179c1s
v2p0224c1m v2p0240c1s v2p0294c1s
v2p0295c1s v2p0360c2s v2p0406c2s
v3p0104c2s v3p0243c1s v3p0275c1s
v3p0318c1s v3p0327c1s v3p0349c1s
v3p0361c2s v4p0048c1s v4p0060c1s
v5p0073c1s v5p0582c1s v6p0215c1s
v6p0233c1s v6p0478c2s v6p0649c2m

White, C.A., Mrs. v1p0139c1s
v1p0301c2s v1p0404c2s v1p0443c1m
v1p0494c1s v1p0569c1s v1p0659c2s
v1p0866c1s v1p1440c1s

White, C.C. v4p0134c2s

White, C.E. v3p0148c1s
v3p0451c1s v4p0135c1s v4p0516c2s

White, C.H. v2p0158c1s
v2p0216c1s v2p0310c1s v6p0045c1s
v6p0076c1s v6p0451c2s v6p0452c2m
v6p0491c2s

White, C.H.E. v5p0118c2s
v6p0127c1s

White, C.I. v1p0754c2s
v1p1119c1s v2p0371c2s

White, C.M. v5p0378c2m

White, C.W. v2p0143c1s
v2p0185c2s

White, Clara M. v5p0369c1s

White, D. v3p0104c2s
v4p0139c1s v4p0345c2s v5p0088c1s
v5p0251c2s v6p0620c2s

White, Diana v5p0299c1s

White, Douglas v5p0311c2s
v5p0508c2s

White, E. v1p0226c1s
v1p0347c2s v1p0384c2s v1p0641c1s
v1p0733c2s v1p0904c1s v2p0055c1s
v3p0043c2s v5p0140c1s v6p0387c1s
v6p0568c2s v6p0581c1s v6p0630c2s
v6p0687c2s

White, E.A. v6p0181c2s

White, E.C. v2p0132c1s

White, E.D. v4p0178c1s

White, E.E. v1p0386c2s
v1p1288c2s v1p1348c2s v2p0297c1s
v3p0146c1s v3p0378c1s v3p0379c1s
v4p0171c2s v5p0418c2s

White, E.G. v6p0074c1s
v6p0074c2s

White, E.L. v3p0243c1s
v4p0168c2s v6p0361c2s

White, E.M. v5p0226c2s

White, E.N. v1p1047c1s
v2p0034c2s v2p0085c1s v3p0175c1s
v5p0097c2s

White, E.O. v3p0057c2s
v3p0094c2s v3p0188c2s v4p0194c1s
v4p0469c1s v5p0342c1s

White, E.R. v5p0082c1s
v5p0550c2s v5p0558c2s v6p0112c2s
v6p0672c2s v6p0688c1s

White, E.S. v5p0152c2s

White, E.W. v4p0216c1s
v4p0311c1s

White, Esther G. v6p0074c2s
v6p0580c2s

White, F.A. v4p0428c1s
v5p0006c2s v5p0247c1s v5p0281c2s
v5p0437c1s v6p0107c2s v6p0655c1s

White, F.B. v1p0644c2s
v1p1015c1s v5p0629c1s

White, F.E. v1p1419c2s
v1p1423c1s v2p0117c1s v2p0274c1m
v2p0357c2s v3p0205c2s v3p0280c1s
v3p0292c2s v4p0076c1s v4p0135c2s
v4p0187c2s v4p0382c1s

White, F.H. v4p0104c1s
v6p0614c2s

White, F.I. v6p0509c2s

White, F.J. v5p0068c1s

White, F.M. v2p0062c2s
v2p0182c1s v3p0159c1s v3p0295c1s
v3p0311c2s v3p0394c1s v4p0382c2s
v5p0309c2s v5p0386c2s v5p0473c1s
v5p0508c1s v6p0655c2s

White, Fred M. v6p0041c1s

White, G. v4p0011c2s
v4p0072c2s v4p0089c2s v4p0090c2s
v4p0228c1s v4p0258c2s v4p0460c1s
v4p0460c2s v4p0474c1s v4p0539c1s
v5p0070c2s v5p0071c1m v5p0095c1s
v5p0151c2s v5p0186c2s v5p0234c1s
v5p0235c1s v5p0268c2s v5p0306c1s
v5p0310c1s v5p0312c1s v5p0330c1s
v5p0381c2s v5p0383c2s v5p0387c2s
v5p0411c1s v5p0435c2s v5p0441c2s
v5p0461c2s v5p0487c1s v5p0488c2s
v5p0490c2s v5p0507c2s v5p0524c2s
v5p0536c1s v5p0540c2s v5p0541c2s
v5p0560c2s v5p0578c1m v5p0619c2s
v5p0623c1m v6p0685c2s

White, G.A. v3p0266c1s

White, G.E. v6p0562c1s

White, G.F. v4p0588c1s
v5p0195c1s v5p0356c1s v5p0505c1s
v6p0415c2s

White, G.M. v2p0473c1s

White, G.R. v6p0016c1s

White, G.S. v6p0660c2s

White, G.W. v6p0233c1s
v6p0671c2s

White, Gleeson v4p0454c2s
v5p0129c1s v5p0273c2s v5p0466c1m
v5p0506c1s

White, Greenough v6p0088c2s

White, H. v1p0042c1s
v1p0133c2s v1p0144c2s v1p0180c1s
v1p0184c1s v1p0273c1s v1p0303c1s
v1p0326c2s v1p0343c2s v1p0356c2s
v1p0408c2s v1p0436c1s v1p0540c2s
v1p0556c2m v1p0650c2s v1p0735c1m
v1p0736c1s v1p0860c1m v1p0956c2m
v1p0963c2s v1p0974c2s v1p0976c1s
v1p1040c1s v1p1075c2s v1p1077c1s
v1p1108c2s v1p1110c2s v1p1190c2s
v1p1198c2m v1p1199c1m v1p1223c2s
v1p1232c2s v1p1256c2s v1p1261c1s
v1p1283c1m v1p1283c2m v1p1285c2s
v1p1342c2s v1p1350c1s v1p1352c2s
v1p1353c1s v1p1417c2s v2p0018c1s
v2p0033c1s v2p0033c2s v2p0036c2s
v2p0049c1s v2p0055c2s v2p0073c2s
v2p0102c1s v2p0103c2s v2p0104c1s
v2p0136c1s v2p0151c2s v2p0155c1s
v2p0157c2s v2p0181c2s v2p0188c1s
v2p0224c1s v2p0244c2s v2p0247c2m
v2p0306c2s v2p0321c1s v2p0328c1s
v2p0351c1s v2p0355c2s v2p0362c2s
v2p0363c1s v2p0363c2s v2p0373c2s
v2p0374c2s v2p0403c1m v2p0423c1s
v2p0423c2m v2p0430c2s v2p0431c2s
v2p0451c2s v2p0463c2s v2p0471c2m
v3p0006c2s v3p0031c2s v3p0032c1m
v3p0032c2s v3p0044c2m v3p0098c2s
v3p0112c1s v3p0113c1s v3p0127c2s
v3p0154c1s v3p0154c2s v3p0159c2s
v3p0176c2s v3p0218c2s v3p0225c2s
v3p0233c1s v3p0239c1s v3p0266c2s
v3p0298c1s v3p0305c1s v3p0316c2s
v3p0318c2s v3p0346c2s v3p0355c1s
v3p0374c1s v3p0393c1m v3p0393c2m
v3p0401c2s v3p0409c1s v3p0414c1m
v3p0420c1m v3p0421c1s v3p0422c1s
v3p0431c2s v3p0437c2m v3p0444c1m
v3p0461c2s v3p0465c2s v4p0022c2s
v4p0044c1s v4p0044c2m v4p0045c1s
v4p0059c1s v4p0059c2m v4p0063c1s
v4p0066c1m v4p0088c1s v4p0102c2s
v4p0131c1s v4p0143c2s v4p0144c1m
v4p0149c2s v4p0199c2s v4p0225c1s
v4p0230c1s v4p0242c2s v4p0262c2s
v4p0278c1s v4p0298c2s v4p0303c1s
v4p0332c2s v4p0342c1s v4p0354c1s
v4p0377c2m v4p0378c1s v4p0378c2s
v4p0423c2s v4p0434c1s v4p0504c1s
v4p0511c2s v4p0524c2m v4p0525c1s
v4p0525c2m v4p0526c1s v4p0526c2s
v4p0553c1s v4p0555c1s v4p0555c2s
v4p0559c1s v4p0563c1m v4p0563c2m
v4p0591c2s v4p0593c1m v4p0631c2s
v5p0010c1s v5p0021c2s v5p0024c2m
v5p0046c2s v5p0061c2m v5p0080c1s
v5p0080c2m v5p0109c1s v5p0110c1s
v5p0112c1s v5p0122c1s v5p0128c1s
v5p0132c1s v5p0146c2s v5p0147c1s
v5p0147c2s v5p0149c2m v5p0150c1s
v5p0158c1s v5p0181c2s v5p0194c2s
v5p0220c1s v5p0224c1s v5p0231c1s
v5p0237c2m v5p0238c1m v5p0238c2s
v5p0247c2s v5p0250c2s v5p0258c2s
v5p0294c1s v5p0326c2s v5p0333c2m
v5p0360c1m v5p0380c2s v5p0387c2s
v5p0403c1s v5p0410c1s v5p0410c2m
v5p0414c1s v5p0444c2s v5p0445c1s
v5p0445c2s v5p0457c2m v5p0460c1s
v5p0466c1s v5p0467c1s v5p0476c2s
v5p0480c2s v5p0502c1s v5p0526c2m
v5p0529c2s v5p0543c2s v5p0544c1m
v5p0557c1m v5p0557c2s v5p0558c2s
v5p0559c2s v5p0563c2s v5p0567c1m
v5p0568c2s v5p0571c2s v5p0592c1s
v5p0592c2s v5p0593c1s v5p0600c2m
v5p0604c1m v5p0619c2s v6p0011c2s
v6p0026c1s v6p0050c1s v6p0050c2s
v6p0051c1s v6p0068c2s v6p0071c2s
v6p0078c2s v6p0108c1s v6p0127c2s
v6p0130c2s v6p0133c1m v6p0138c1s
v6p0161c1s v6p0162c1m v6p0164c1s
v6p0166c2s v6p0231c1s v6p0289c1s
v6p0318c1s v6p0323c1s v6p0330c2m
v6p0346c2s v6p0355c1s v6p0357c1m
v6p0377c2m v6p0393c1s v6p0424c2s
v6p0431c1s v6p0447c1s v6p0454c2s
v6p0468c1s v6p0489c2s v6p0493c1s
v6p0493c2m v6p0494c2s v6p0518c1s
v6p0554c1s v6p0591c1s v6p0594c2s
v6p0616c1s v6p0621c2s v6p0652c2m
v6p0655c2s v6p0658c2s v6p0659c1s
v6p0663c1s v6p0701c2s

White, H. and Daniel, A.S.
v5p0407c1s

White, H. and Godkin, E.L.
v2p0068c1s

White, H. and Sedgwick, A.G.
v2p0049c1s

White, H.A. v2p0142c2s
v6p0053c2s

White, H.C. v2p0359c2s
v2p0471c1s v3p0074c1s

White, H.H. v3p0167c1s

White, H.K. v4p0420c2s

White, H.L. et al. v4p0427c2s

White, H.M. v3p0095c2s
v6p0089c1s v6p0215c1s

White, H.R. v5p0594c1s
v5p0599c2s

White, H.S. v2p0175c2s
v2p0395c2s v5p0126c1s

White, H.T. v1p0632c1s
v1p1021c2s v1p1022c2s v1p1368c1s
v4p0079c2s

White, H.W. v3p0096c2s

White, Horace v3p0023c2s
v3p0100c2s v6p0050c2s

White, I.C. v2p0171c2s
v2p0179c1s v3p0052c1s

White, I.H. v3p0013c1s

White, I.M. v5p0074c1s
v5p0460c1s

White, Ina M. v6p0509c2s

White, J. v1p0226c2s
v1p0385c1s v1p1100c2s v4p0012c2s

White, J.B. v1p0468c1s
v3p0421c2s

White, J.D. v4p0155c2s
v4p0170c2s v4p0356c2s v5p0083c1s
v5p0363c1s v5p0585c1s v6p0483c2s

White, J.E. v6p0605c1s

White, J.F. v1p0808c1s
v4p0550c1s

White, J.G. v1p1311c1s
v5p0183c2s

White, J.H. v5p0407c1s

White, J.L. v3p0288c2s

White, J.M. v4p0167c1s
v4p0602c2s

White, J.P. v4p0288c1s
v4p0338c1s v4p0388c2s v4p0389c1s
v4p0390c1m v4p0579c1s v6p0289c1s

White, J.S. v3p0025c1s
v3p0450c1s v4p0206c2s v5p0126c2s

White, J.W. v3p0025c2s
v3p0057c2s v3p0166c1s v3p0209c1s
v3p0273c2s v3p0316c1m v3p0425c1s
v4p0035c1s v4p0035c2s v4p0206c2s
v4p0248c1s v4p0508c1s v5p0177c2s
v5p0335c2s v5p0413c2s v6p0231c2s

White, J.W.F. v2p0008c1s

White, J.Z. v6p0634c1s

White, L. v1p0279c2s
v1p0799c2s v3p0163c1s v3p0464c1s

White, L.C. v1p0766c1s
v1p1267c1s

White, L.L. v1p0709c2s
v1p0716c2s v1p1228c1s v1p1312c1s
v1p1406c1s v1p1433c1s v2p0421c2s
v3p0092c1s v3p0154c2s v3p0286c2s
v3p0356c1s

White, L.W. v3p0366c1s

White, M. v1p0772c2s
v5p0006c2s v5p0254c1s v6p0066c1s
v6p0265c2s v6p0333c2s

White, M., jr. v4p0004c2s
v4p0052c1s v4p0151c2s v4p0217c2s
v4p0225c2s v4p0326c1s v4p0550c1s
v4p0581c2s v5p0151c2s v5p0422c1s

v5p0547c2s v6p0020c2s v6p0052c2s
v6p0053c2s v6p0102c2s v6p0201c1s
v6p0399c1s v6p0546c1s v6p0572c1s
v6p0604c1s
White, M.A. v5p0635c1s
White, M.C. v1p0236c1s
v1p0747c2s v1p0836c1s v1p1239c1s
White, M.E.D. v6p0450c1s
v6p0460c1s v6p0606c2s v6p0693c1s
v6p0706c1m
White, M.G. v6p0314c2s
White, M.L. v4p0503c1s
White, M.V. v5p0395c1s
White, Martha E.D. v5p0638c2s
White, Mary D. v3p0309c1s
White, Mrs. v1p0385c2s
v1p0446c2s v1p0500c2s v1p0560c2s
v1p0692c2s v1p0765c1s v1p0887c2s
v1p0904c1s v1p1108c2s v1p1389c2s
White, N. v1p0127c1s
v2p0044c2s
White, N.J.D. v5p0059c2m
v5p0306c1s v5p0306c2s v6p0064c2s
v6p0126c1s v6p0340c2s v6p0341c2s
v6p0342c1s v6p0342c2s v6p0657c1s
White, P. v2p0001c1s
v3p0107c1s v3p0395c1s v4p0087c1s
White, P.H. v1p0087c1s
v1p0226c1s v1p0272c1s v1p0561c1s
v1p0949c1s v1p0983c1s v1p1402c2m
v1p1429c1s
White, Percy v4p0219c2s
White, R. v4p0096c1s
v5p0313c1s v5p0498c1s
White, R.G. v1p0034c2m
v1p0108c1s v1p0115c1s v1p0163c2s
v1p0165c2s v1p0178c1s v1p0190c1s
v1p0197c2s v1p0200c2s v1p0266c2s
v1p0327c1s v1p0328c1s v1p0350c1s
v1p0354c2s v1p0364c1m v1p0366c2m
v1p0407c1s v1p0409c1s v1p0410c1s
v1p0413c2m v1p0414c1s v1p0414c2m
v1p0415c2m v1p0416c1m v1p0416c2m
v1p0417c1s v1p0419c1m v1p0419c2s
v1p0447c1m v1p0461c2s v1p0490c1s
v1p0493c2s v1p0539c2s v1p0568c2m
v1p0574c2s v1p0589c1s v1p0596c2s
v1p0621c1s v1p0649c1s v1p0696c2s
v1p0708c1s v1p0723c2s v1p0724c1s
v1p0751c1s v1p0752c1m v1p0763c2s
v1p0764c1s v1p0766c1m v1p0839c2s
v1p0879c2s v1p0882c1s v1p0883c2s
v1p0884c1s v1p0884c2s v1p0885c1s
v1p0916c1s v1p0926c2s v1p0954c1s
v1p0998c1s v1p0999c1s v1p1034c1s
v1p1063c1s v1p1065c2s v1p1076c2s
v1p1086c1s v1p1147c2s v1p1152c1s
v1p1181c2s v1p1183c2s v1p1184c1s
v1p1184c2m v1p1185c2m v1p1186c1m
v1p1186c2m v1p1187c1s v1p1187c2m
v1p1217c1s v1p1234c2m v1p1257c2s
v1p1258c2s v1p1260c1s v1p1276c1s
v1p1280c2s v1p1310c2s v1p1372c2m
v1p1379c2s v1p1387c1s v1p1396c2s
v1p1414c2s v1p1424c1s v1p1426c2s
v1p1429c1s v2p0012c2m v2p0031c1s
v2p0086c2s v2p0087c2s v2p0194c1s
v2p0275c2s v2p0301c1s v2p0303c1s
v2p0313c1s v2p0319c2s v2p0322c1s
v2p0358c2s v2p0378c1s v2p0397c1m
v2p0398c2s
White, R.L.C. v6p0525c2s
White, R.M. v6p0579c1s
White, R.S. v2p0372c2s
White, S. v6p0570c1s
White, S.D. v4p0097c2s
v4p0280c1s v4p0295c2s v5p0144c2s
v5p0286c1m v5p0563c1s
White, S.E. v5p0214c1s
v5p0234c1m v5p0475c1s v5p0509c2s
v5p0643c1s v6p0030c2s v6p0043c1s
v6p0066c1s v6p0095c2s v6p0123c2s
v6p0148c1s v6p0232c2m v6p0233c1s
v6p0297c1s v6p0376c2s v6p0433c2s
v6p0474c1s v6p0482c2s v6p0532c1s
v6p0544c2s v6p0571c2s v6p0594c2s
White, S.E. and Adam, S.H.
v6p0440c2s
White, S.J. v3p0130c1s
White, S.M. v5p0134c2s
v5p0258c2s
White, S.M. and McDonald, R.H., jr.
v6p0632c2s
White, Stewart E. v6p0088c1s
White, T. v1p0625c2m
v3p0065c2s v4p0373c1s
White, T.B. v4p0259c1s
White, T.G. v4p0583c2s
White, T.L. v4p0065c1s
White, T.M. v3p0201c2s
White, T.P. v3p0182c2s
v4p0209c2s v4p0417c2s v4p0508c2s
v4p0626c1s v5p0077c2s v5p0166c1s
White, T.W. v1p0466c2s
v1p1009c1s v3p0439c2s v4p0183c2s
White, Trumbull v6p0210c1s
White, W. v1p0787c1s
v1p1139c2s v2p0128c1s v3p0126c1m
v5p0500c1s v6p0686c1s
White, W. et al. v2p0046c1s
White, W.A. v2p0057c2s
v5p0074c2s v5p0080c2s v5p0144c2m
v5p0255c2m v5p0313c2m v5p0358c2s
v5p0364c1s v5p0370c2s v5p0379c2s
v5p0420c1s v5p0454c1s v5p0480c1s
v5p0496c1s v5p0591c1s v5p0602c1s
v5p0611c2s v5p0627c2s v5p0628c2s
v6p0099c2s v6p0131c1s v6p0160c2s
v6p0230c2s v6p0261c1s v6p0320c1s
v6p0500c1s v6p0507c1s v6p0550c1s
v6p0601c2s
White, W.F. v2p0016c1s
White, W.H. v1p0182c2s
v1p1077c1s v1p1189c2s v2p0028c2s
v2p0140c1s v2p0308c1s v2p0356c1s
v2p0442c2s v2p0467c2s v4p0023c1s
v4p0395c2s v5p0077c2s v5p0246c2s
v5p0526c1s v5p0546c1s v5p0551c1s
v6p0124c2s v6p0204c2s v6p0266c2s
v6p0268c1s v6p0268c2s v6p0623c1m
v6p0669c1s
White, W.H. and Jeans, J.H.
v6p0623c1s
White, W.H. and Smith, T.R.
v3p0125c1s
White, W.H., Sir v5p0619c1m
White, W.J. v6p0627c1s
White, W.L. v4p0031c2s
v5p0032c2s
White, W.O. v1p0027c1s
v1p0261c2s v1p0619c2s
White, W.W. v3p0274c1s
v5p0163c1s v5p0297c2s
White, W.W. et al. v1p0518c2s
White, Z.L. v3p0012c2s
v3p0047c1s v3p0051c1s v3p0154c1s
v3p0232c2m
Whiteaves, J.F. v1p0366c1m
v1p0470c1s v1p0910c2s v1p1144c1s
v2p0157c1s v2p0284c2s v5p0590c1s
v6p0664c1s
Whitechurch, V.L. v5p0096c1s
v5p0212c1s v5p0367c1s v5p0393c1s
v5p0451c1s v5p0474c2s v5p0494c2s
v5p0509c2s v5p0517c2s v5p0518c1s
v5p0544c2s v5p0563c1s v5p0590c2s
v5p0596c1s v6p0027c1s v6p0084c2s
v6p0154c2s v6p0423c1s v6p0462c1s
v6p0499c1s v6p0709c1s
Whitechurch, Victor L. ... v5p0302c1s
Whitefield, C.T. v6p0059c1s
v6p0298c2s
Whitefield, H.D. v6p0229c1s
Whitefoord, B. v5p0305c2s
v6p0063c2s v6p0364c2s v6p0679c1s
Whitefoord, P. v4p0252c2s
v4p0482c1s
Whiteford, R.N. v6p0208c2s
Whitehead, A.R. v5p0477c2s
Whitehead, B. v1p1398c1s
v2p0112c2s
Whitehead, C. v1p0176c1s
v1p0200c2s v1p0217c1s v1p0349c2s
v1p0393c2s v1p0398c1s v1p0547c1s
v1p0782c2s v1p0804c1s v1p0851c2s
v1p0878c2s v1p0896c2s v1p0948c2s
v1p1013c1s v1p1106c1s v1p1144c2s
v1p1156c1s v1p1383c2s v3p0062c1s
v4p0230c1s v4p0524c1s
Whitehead, C.B. et al. ... v4p0564c2s
Whitehead, C.E. v1p0559c2s
Whitehead, C.S. v5p0185c2s
Whitehead, F. v1p0406c1s
v1p0927c1s
Whitehead, H. v1p0238c1s
v1p0820c1s v2p0039c1s v3p0376c1s
v6p0315c1s
Whitehead, J. v3p0257c2s
v3p0301c2s v4p0180c1s v4p0559c2s
v5p0483c2s v5p0560c2s v6p0451c1s
v6p0628c2s
Whitehead, J.B. and Hill, H.D.
v6p0583c1s
Whitehead, J.B., jr. v6p0197c1s
Whitehead, L.G. v4p0364c2s
Whitehead, M. v4p0234c1s
Whitehead, Miss v3p0057c2s
Whitehead, T., Mrs. v1p0726c1s
Whitehead, W.A. v1p0912c1s
v1p1254c1s
Whitehouse, B. v6p0678c2s
Whitehouse, C. v2p0135c1s
v2p0156c1s v2p0293c2m v2p0360c2s
v2p0483c1s v3p0131c1s v4p0172c2s
v4p0555c1s
Whitehouse, F.C. v2p0156c1s
v2p0343c1s v6p0155c1s
Whitehouse, F.Cope v4p0404c2s
v4p0529c1s
Whitehouse, F.Cowley v6p0053c1s
Whitehouse, H.R. v5p0300c1s
v5p0300c2s
Whitehouse, J.H. v6p0078c1s
v6p0708c1s
Whitehouse, J.S. v6p0630c2s
Whitehouse, O.C. v4p0055c2s
v4p0143c1s v4p0252c2s v5p0042c1s
Whitehouse, R. v5p0591c1s
v6p0042c2s v6p0331c2s
Whitehouse, S.A. v2p0395c1s
Whitehouse, W. v1p1241c1s
v1p1289c2s
Whitehouse, W.F. v6p0002c1s
Whitehurst, A. v6p0572c2s
Whitehurst, F.M. v1p0478c2s
v1p0513c1s v1p0970c2m
Whiteing, R. v1p0924c2s
v2p0201c2s v2p0329c1s v4p0013c1s
v5p0430c2s v5p0431c2m v5p0432c1m
v6p0003c1s v6p0014c1s v6p0045c2s
v6p0071c1s v6p0108c1s v6p0110c2m
v6p0111c1s v6p0112c1s v6p0112c2s
v6p0121c1s v6p0361c1s v6p0382c1s
v6p0390c1s v6p0711c1s
Whitelaw, J. v1p1392c1s
Whitelaw, T. v3p0041c2s
v3p0142c2s v3p0195c1s v3p0196c1s
v3p0224c1s v3p0226c1s v3p0232c1s
v3p0289c1s v3p0418c2s v3p0424c1m
v3p0431c2s v4p0056c1s
Whitelaw-Houk, N. v5p0597c2s
Whiteley, B.M. v4p0388c2s
Whiteley, E.S. v5p0130c1s
v5p0222c1s v5p0637c2s
Whiteley, I.N. v5p0213c2s
Whiteley, J.G. v4p0072c1s
v4p0112c2s v4p0511c1s v5p0153c1s
v5p0162c1s v5p0259c2s v5p0294c1s
v5p0384c1s v5p0468c2s v5p0586c2s
v6p0146c2s v6p0401c1s v6p0508c2s
Whitelock, A. v1p0216c1s
v1p0265c1s v1p0713c1s
Whitelock, R.H. v1p0514c1s
v1p1221c2s
Whitelock, W.W. v5p0520c2s
v6p0056c1s v6p0153c1s v6p0252c2s
Whitely, I. v5p0620c1s
Whitely, W.G. v3p0344c1s
Whiteway, A.R. v4p0236c1s
v4p0402c1m v5p0143c2s v5p0223c1s
v5p0363c1s v5p0370c2s v5p0466c2s
v5p0473c2m v6p0055c1s v6p0241c2s
v6p0244c1s v6p0521c2s
Whiteway, C.P. v5p0049c1s
v5p0349c1s
Whiteway, P. v6p0585c1s
Whiteway, W., Sir et al. . v3p0301c1s
Whitfield, A.H. v5p0443c2s
v6p0605c2s
Whitfield, E.E. v5p0130c2s
Whitfield, H.S. v1p1316c2s
Whitfield, I.P. v4p0342c1s
Whitfield, J.E. v3p0050c2s
v3p0276c1s
Whitfield, J.E. and Merrill, G.P.
v3p0276c1s
Whitfield, J.H. v5p0590c1s
Whitfield, R.P. v1p0470c1s
v1p0751c1s v1p0859c1s v2p0391c1s
Whitford, H.N. v6p0077c2s
v6p0498c2s
Whitham, J.H. v2p0106c1s
Whitham, J.M. v2p0276c2m
Whitherby, H.F. v6p0416c1s
Whitin, E.S. v6p0078c2s
v6p0116c1s
Whiting, C. v1p1280c2s
Whiting, C.W. v4p0470c2s
Whiting, E. v5p0638c1s
v6p0531c1s
Whiting, E.M. v5p0604c1s
Whiting, F.J. v6p0056c2s
v6p0097c2s v6p0108c1s v6p0162c1s
v6p0206c1s v6p0216c2s v6p0323c1s
v6p0337c2s v6p0355c1s v6p0520c1s
v6p0523c1s v6p0557c1s v6p0591c2m
v6p0632c2s v6p0647c2s
v6p0667c2s
Whiting, H. v1p0461c2s
v1p0462c1s v1p0638c2s v1p0649c2s
v1p0666c2m v1p0838c1s v1p0839c1s
v1p0897c2s v1p0901c2s v1p0928c1s
v1p1009c2s v1p1160c1s v1p1287c1s
v1p1310c1s v1p1342c1s v1p1384c2s
v1p1401c2s
Whiting, J.D. v2p0057c2s
v2p0141c1s v2p0357c2s v2p0421c2s
v3p0003c1s v4p0266c2s
Whiting, J.J. v6p0275c1s
Whiting, L. v1p0254c2s
v1p0603c1s v3p0051c1s v3p0092c1s
v3p0148c1s v3p0203c2s v4p0046c2s
v4p0075c2s v4p0171c1s v4p0198c1s
v4p0198c2m v4p0464c1s v4p0542c1s
v4p0627c2s v5p0011c2s v5p0639c1s
v6p0229c1s v6p0276c2s v6p0595c1s
Whiting, M.B. v2p0261c2s
v3p0262c2s v3p0413c1s v4p0177c2s
v5p0351c1s v6p0350c1s
Whiting, M.C. v3p0326c2s
v4p0409c1s
Whiting, Marie L. v6p0617c2s
Whiting, Mary B. v4p0141c1s
v6p0055c1s v6p0056c2s v6p0085c1s
v6p0359c2s v6p0590c2s
Whiting, R. v2p0024c1s
v2p0482c2s
Whiting, S. v1p0160c1s
v1p0178c2s v1p0496c1s v1p0732c1s
Whiting, S.F. v5p0629c2s

v6p0496c2s v6p0609c1s
Whiting, Sarah F. v6p0037c2s
Whiting, W. v1p0910c2s
v1p1353c2s
Whitley, D.G. v3p0037c1s
v3p0148c2s v3p0265c2s v4p0177c2s
v4p0272c2m v4p0576c1s
Whitley, N. v1p0460c2s
Whitley, T.W. v1p0683c1s
Whitley, W.T. v5p0113c2s
v5p0371c2s v5p0462c1m
Whitling, H.J. v1p0930c1s
v1p0934c1m v1p1212c2s v1p1276c2s
v1p1386c2s
Whitlock, A.M. v4p0456c2s
v5p0562c2s
Whitlock, B. v6p0346c1s
v6p0513c2s v6p0642c1s
Whitlock, W.F. v3p0276c2s
v4p0365c1s v5p0255c1s
Whitlock, Will T. v5p0119c1s
Whitman, A. v1p0283c2s
v4p0073c2s v5p0208c1s v5p0521c1s
Whitman, A.M. v5p0528c1s
Whitman, Amy v4p0452c2s
Whitman, B. v3p0092c1s
v3p0109c2s v3p0128c2s v3p0235c1s
v3p0378c1s v3p0424c1s v3p0446c1s
v3p0469c1s
Whitman, B., Mrs. v3p0121c1s
v3p0188c1s v4p0353c1s
Whitman, C.O. v1p0463c2s
v1p0626c1s v2p0252c2s v2p0287c2s
v2p0483c2s v3p0044c2s v3p0296c1s
v4p0191c1s v4p0355c2m v4p0383c1s
v4p0441c2s v5p0020c2s v5p0062c1s
v5p0639c2s v6p0066c2s v6p0401c1s
v6p0706c2s
Whitman, E.A. v4p0442c1s
Whitman, E.A. and Alexander, W.J.
v3p0402c1s
Whitman, E.N. v2p0305c2s
Whitman, F.P. v5p0129c1s
v5p0321c2s v5p0613c1s v6p0617c1s
Whitman, H., Mrs. v1p1366c2s
Whitman, J. v1p0192c1s
v1p0238c2s v1p0436c2s v1p0457c2s
v1p0545c1s v1p0566c2s v1p0910c2s
v1p1158c1s v1p1270c1s
Whitman, J.S. v1p0409c2s
v2p0006c2s v2p0078c1s
Whitman, M.R. v6p0412c1s
Whitman, P.S. v1p0890c1s
Whitman, S. v3p0370c1s
v4p0062c1s v4p0207c2s v4p0223c2m
v4p0224c1m v4p0224c2s v4p0302c2s
v4p0312c1s v4p0377c1s v5p0054c1s
v5p0064c2s v5p0067c1s v5p0189c1s
v5p0231c1s v5p0231c2s v5p0330c2s
v5p0560c1s v6p0069c1s v6p0289c1s
v6p0367c2s v6p0424c2s
Whitman, S.F. v6p0167c1s
v6p0200c1s
Whitman, S.F. and Lyle, E.P., jr.
v6p0570c2s
Whitman, S.W. v1p0616c2s
v5p0030c2s
Whitman, S.W., Mrs. v2p0023c1s
Whitman, Sidney v4p0062c1s
Whitman, W. v1p0202c2s
v1p0992c2s v1p1022c1s v1p1042c1s
v1p1059c1s v1p1219c2s v1p1405c2s
v2p0041c2s v2p0062c1m v2p0068c2s
v2p0139c2s v2p0140c1s v2p0145c1s
v2p0260c2s v2p0265c2s v2p0297c2s
v2p0346c1s v2p0397c2s v2p0404c2s
v3p0294c1s v3p0335c2s v3p0421c2s
v3p0425c1s v4p0588c1s v6p0516c1s
Whitman, Walt v3p0020c2s
v3p0443c1s
Whitmarsh, H.P. v4p0432c1s
v4p0432c2s v5p0037c1s v5p0147c2s
v5p0169c2s v5p0438c1s v5p0446c1s
v5p0526c1s v5p0552c1s v5p0554c2s
v5p0627c2s v6p0108c2s
Whitmarsh, H.Phelps v4p0390c1s
Whitmarsh, P. v5p0023c2s
v5p0221c2s v5p0258c2s v5p0279c2s
v5p0351c2m v5p0360c1m v5p0377c1s
v5p0429c1s v5p0443c2m v5p0444c1m
v5p0444c2m v5p0445c1m v5p0445c2s
v5p0560c1s v5p0613c1s
Whitmee, S.J. v1p0790c2s
v1p1029c1m v1p1148c1s v2p0385c1s
Whitmer, C. v6p0470c1s
Whitmer, T.C. v5p0002c2s
v5p0050c2s v5p0304c1s v5p0395c1s
v5p0423c2s v5p0580c1s v5p0630c1m
Whitmore, C.A. v3p0182c2s
v3p0255c2s v3p0256c1s v3p0321c2m
v4p0238c2m v4p0338c1s v4p0338c2m
v4p0340c1s v4p0340c2s v5p0190c2s
v5p0419c1s v5p0433c1s v5p0624c1s
v6p0247c2s v6p0266c1s
Whitmore, F. v5p0211c1s
v5p0283c2s v5p0605c2s v5p0616c1s
Whitmore, H. v4p0069c1s
Whitmore, J. v4p0177c1s
Whitmore, M.T. v6p0150c1s
v6p0156c1s
Whitmore, O.S. v4p0631c1s
Whitmore, W.H. v1p0031c2s
v1p0059c1s v1p0083c1s v1p0154c2s
v1p0163c1s v1p0311c2m v1p0327c1s
v1p0329c2s v1p0337c2s v1p0402c2s
v1p0469c2s v1p0504c1m v1p0569c1s
v1p0586c1m v1p0587c1s v1p0618c1s
v1p0649c2s v1p0695c2s v1p0723c1m
v1p0761c1s v1p0767c2s v1p0785c1s
v1p0808c1s v1p0813c1s v1p0929c2s
v1p0941c2s v1p0990c2s v1p1041c1m
v1p1050c2s v1p1181c1s v1p1188c1s
v1p1223c1s v1p1293c2s v1p1330c1s
v1p1359c1m v1p1369c2s v1p1409c2s
v1p1416c2m v2p0102c1s v2p0212c2s
v2p0252c1s v2p0331c1s v2p0361c2s
v2p0444c1s v2p0475c2s v3p0051c1s
v3p0108c1s v3p0194c2s v3p0236c2s
v3p0456c1m v4p0291c2s v5p0215c2m
v5p0227c2s v5p0620c2s
Whitney, A. v1p0073c1s
v1p0956c1s
Whitney, A.D.T. v1p0244c2s
v1p0378c2s v1p1440c1s
Whitney, A.S. v4p0103c1s
v6p0574c1s
Whitney, A.W. v4p0477c2s
v5p0094c1s v5p0348c1s v5p0402c2s
v6p0214c2s
Whitney, Anna H. v6p0178c1s
Whitney, Anne K. v5p0219c2s
Whitney, C. v3p0005c2s
v5p0037c1s v5p0067c2s v5p0095c2s
v5p0145c2s v5p0239c2s v5p0508c1s
v5p0547c1m v6p0086c2s v6p0200c1m
v6p0304c1s v6p0332c2s v6p0357c2s
v6p0368c2s v6p0387c1s v6p0439c2s
v6p0542c1s v6p0593c1m v6p0611c2m
v6p0625c1s v6p0646c2s v6p0656c1s
v6p0663c2s
Whitney, C.A. and Shinn, M.W.
v3p0137c1s
Whitney, C.W. v4p0035c2s
v4p0046c1s v4p0073c2s v4p0136c2s
v4p0210c2m v4p0231c2s v5p0085c1s
v5p0136c1s v5p0259c2s v5p0275c2s
Whitney, Caspar v6p0396c1s
Whitney, E. v2p0035c1s
v2p0398c1s v3p0336c1s v3p0388c2s
v3p0410c2s
Whitney, E.B. v2p0096c2s
v2p0394c2s v2p0418c1s v4p0277c2s
v5p0147c2s v6p0151c1s v6p0436c1s
v6p0453c2s v6p0460c1s v6p0659c1s
Whitney, E.H. v5p0552c1s
Whitney, E.L. v4p0538c2s
Whitney, E.M. v1p1161c1s
Whitney, E.St.C. v4p0070c1s
Whitney, F.A. v1p1072c1s
Whitney, G.F. v6p0043c2s
Whitney, G.W. v1p1355c2s
v1p1399c1s
Whitney, H. v6p0706c2s
Whitney, H.A. v1p0842c1s
v1p1407c2s
Whitney, H.C. v5p0339c1s
v6p0377c2s
Whitney, H.H. v5p0061c1s
v5p0087c1s
Whitney, H.M. v1p0085c1s
v1p0646c2s v1p0649c1s v1p1150c1s
v2p0053c2s v3p0249c2s v6p0047c2s
v6p0060c1m v6p0189c2s v6p0207c2s
v6p0221c1s
Whitney, H.W. v2p0390c2s
v2p0477c2s
Whitney, J.A. v1p0231c2s
v1p0978c2s v1p1019c1s v1p1079c1s
v1p1320c2s
Whitney, J.C. v3p0463c1s
Whitney, J.D. v1p0187c2m
v1p0193c1s v1p0236c1s v1p0269c2s
v1p0368c2s v1p0376c2m v1p0506c2s
v1p0508c1s v1p0508c2s v1p0533c1s
v1p0533c2s v1p0844c2m v1p0908c1m
v1p0947c1s v1p0956c1s v1p1041c1s
v1p1196c1s v1p1377c1m v2p0293c1s
Whitney, J.D. and Foster, J.W.
v1p0509c1s v1p1271c1s
Whitney, J.D. and Silliman, B., jr.
v1p0300c1s
Whitney, J.E. v2p0060c1s
v4p0481c1s
Whitney, J.H.E. v3p0471c1s
Whitney, J.L. v1p0628c2s
v1p0743c2s v1p1061c2s v2p0051c2s
v2p0070c2s v2p0255c2s v2p0257c1s
v3p0249c2s v5p0072c2s v6p0076c2s
Whitney, J.S. v1p0049c1s
v1p0666c1s v1p1063c2s v1p1439c1s
v6p0706c2s
Whitney, J.S. and Silliman, B., jr.
v1p0163c2s
Whitney, L. v1p1064c1s
v2p0067c2s
Whitney, M. v3p0399c2s
v5p0123c1s
Whitney, M.A. and Block, L.J.
v6p0622c2s
Whitney, M.W. v3p0283c2s
v5p0537c2s
Whitney, Mary W. v4p0126c2s
v6p0625c2s
Whitney, Q. v1p0529c1s
v3p0345c1s
Whitney, S.B. v4p0107c2s
Whitney, S.W. v1p0096c1s
v1p0263c2s v3p0043c1s
Whitney, Travis H. v6p0367c1s
Whitney, W.A. v5p0592c1s
Whitney, W.B. v6p0483c2s
Whitney, W.C. v5p0640c2s
Whitney, W.D. v1p0231c1s
v1p0231c2s v1p0333c2s v1p0348c2s
v1p0377c2s v1p0390c1s v1p0415c2s
v1p0416c1s v1p0417c1m v1p0427c2s
v1p0496c2s v1p0539c2s v1p0555c1s
v1p0559c1s v1p0630c2s v1p0631c2s
v1p0649c1s v1p0723c2s v1p0724c1m
v1p0724c2m v1p0879c2s v1p0890c2s
v1p0898c1s v1p0992c1s v1p0998c2s
v1p0999c1m v1p1002c1s v1p1073c2s
v1p1095c1m v1p1108c1s v1p1151c1s
v1p1234c2s v1p1273c1s v1p1364c1m
v2p0024c1s v2p0071c1s v2p0203c1s
v2p0249c1s v2p0386c1s v2p0405c1s
v2p0456c2s v3p0445c2s v3p0447c2s
v4p0258c1s v4p0601c1s
Whiton, F. v6p0517c2s
Whiton, Grace v5p0040c2s
Whiton, J.G. v1p1181c2s
Whiton, J.M. v1p0253c2s
v1p0302c2s v1p0314c1s v1p0485c2s
v1p0689c2s v1p1038c2s v2p0042c1s
v2p0082c2s v2p0112c1s v2p0191c1s
v2p0426c1m v3p0143c1s v3p0336c2s
v4p0056c1s v4p0310c2s v4p0584c1s
v5p0055c1s v5p0257c2s v5p0372c2s
v5p0380c1m v5p0463c1s v5p0576c2s
v5p0644c2s v6p0211c2s v6p0341c1s
v6p0696c1s
Whiton, J.M. et al. v1p0496c1s
Whitridge, F. v3p0310c1s
Whitridge, F.W. v1p0291c2s
v1p1028c2s v2p0253c1s v3p0085c2s
v3p0367c2s v5p0169c1s v5p0646c1s
v6p0162c2s
Whitshed, A. v6p0054c1s
Whitsitt, W.H. v1p0096c1s
v1p0097c2s v2p0455c2s v5p0047c2s
Whittaker, D.K. v1p0238c1s
v1p0596c2s
Whittaker, E.T. v6p0406c1s
Whittaker, F. v1p0051c2s
v1p0314c1s v1p0327c1s v1p0364c1s
v1p0707c2s v1p0857c1s v1p1107c2s
v1p1342c1s v1p1395c1s
Whittaker, S. v3p0330c1s
Whittaker, T. v1p0843c2s
v2p0015c1s v2p0059c1s v2p0240c2s
v2p0262c2s v2p0346c2s v3p0145c2s
v3p0214c2s v3p0348c2s v4p0307c2s
v4p0450c2s v4p0575c1s v6p0024c2s
v6p0576c2s
Whittaker, T.P. v1p0649c1s
v1p0752c1s v5p0340c2s v6p0011c1s
v6p0637c2s
Whittaker, T.P. and Ecroyd, W.F.
v1p0486c1s
Whittaker, W.H. v1p1078c2s
v2p0420c2s
Whittall, E. v4p0145c1s
Whittall, J.W. v6p0484c1s
Whittall, O. v3p0054c2s
v3p0459c1s
Whittam, W.C. v5p0447c2s
v6p0496c2s
Whittan, W.C. v5p0254c1s
v5p0280c1s
Whittelsey, S.S. v5p0321c1s
v6p0217c2s v6p0600c1s
Whittemore, B.F. v2p0026c2s
v2p0081c1s v2p0389c2s v2p0403c2s
v2p0415c1s
Whittemore, G.H. v1p0122c1s
v1p0126c1s v1p0554c2s v1p0581c2s
Whittemore, J.G. v6p0643c1s
Whittemore, J.K. v6p0486c2s
Whittemore, J.O. v5p0210c2s
v5p0248c2s v5p0498c1s v6p0221c1s
v6p0565c2s
Whittemore, N.H. v4p0461c2s
v5p0475c1s
Whittemore, R.B. v4p0093c2s
v4p0459c1s
Whittemore, T. v1p1355c2s
Whitten, R.H. v5p0330c1m
v5p0568c2s v6p0196c2m v6p0367c1m
v6p0535c1s
Whitten, Robert H. v6p0373c1s
Whitten, W. v6p0352c2s
Whittet, R.C. v4p0143c2s
Whittier, C.B. v6p0627c2s
v6p0650c2s
Whittier, C.C. v6p0617c2s
Whittier, J.G. v1p0038c2s
v1p0098c1s v1p0105c2s v1p0160c1s
v1p0160c2s v1p0168c1s v1p0216c2s
v1p0270c1s v1p0343c1s v1p0359c1s
v1p0404c1s v1p0439c2s v1p0442c2s

v1p0491c1s v1p0534c1s v1p0541c2s v1p0598c1s v1p0619c2s v1p0627c2s v1p0693c2s v1p0701c2s v1p0708c1s v1p0722c1s v1p0735c2s v1p0797c2s v1p0800c1s v1p0817c2s v1p0841c1s v1p0857c1s v1p0872c1m v1p0901c2s v1p0903c1s v1p0910c1s v1p0925c2s v1p0960c1s v1p1042c2s v1p1127c1s v1p1174c2s v1p1175c1s v1p1176c1s v1p1202c2s v1p1220c1m v1p1286c1s v1p1320c2s v1p1375c2s v1p1408c2s v1p1417c2s v1p1433c2s v1p1436c2s v2p0003c1s v2p0035c2s v2p0036c2s v2p0206c2s v2p0209c2s v2p0346c1s v2p0427c1s v2p0449c2s v3p0191c1s v4p0261c1s v4p0491c1s v6p0166c2s v6p0677c2s
Whittingham, B. v1p1194c1s
Whittingham, R. v1p0240c1s v4p0190c2s
Whittingham, W.R. v1p0138c1s
Whittington, C.J. v5p0470c1s
Whittle, C.L. v4p0242c2s v4p0418c2s v5p0265c1s v5p0323c1s v5p0405c1s v5p0417c1s v5p0490c2s
Whittle, J. v1p0211c2s v1p0513c1s
Whittle, J., Mrs. v1p0347c2s
Whittle, J.L. v1p0659c1s v1p0660c2s v1p0714c1s v3p0345c2s v5p0080c2s v5p0180c2s v5p0233c1s v5p0354c1m
Whittle, R. v6p0124c1s v6p0568c2s v6p0603c2s
Whittle, W.C. v2p0299c2s
Whittlesey, C. v1p0267c2m v1p0367c1s v1p0458c2s v1p0500c2s v1p0556c1s v1p0621c1s v1p0938c2m v1p0939c1s v2p0080c1s v2p0109c2s v2p0127c1s v2p0184c2s v2p0219c2s v2p0243c2s v2p0250c1s v2p0252c2s v2p0280c1s v2p0320c1m v2p0324c1s v2p0343c1s v2p0400c2s v2p0465c1s v2p0466c1s v3p0325c2s
Whittlesey, C. and Bowen, F. v1p0725c1s
Whittlesey, C.C. v1p0339c1s v1p0373c1s v1p0855c1s
Whittlesey, F. v1p1077c2s
Whittlesey, H.C. v5p0256c2s
Whittlesey, L.M. v3p0301c1s
Whittlesey, M. v6p0322c1s
Whittlesey, M.K. v1p1140c1s v3p0259c2s
Whittlesey, M.R. v1p0950c1s
Whitton, F. v5p0517c2s
Whitwell, R.J. v6p0050c2s v6p0287c1s v6p0371c1s v6p0424c2s
Whitwell, W. v5p0066c2s
Whitwell, W.A. v1p1050c1s
Whitwick, M.C. v4p0316c2s
Whitworth, Grace v6p0420c1s v6p0661c2s
Whitworth, J. v1p0408c1s v1p0562c1s
Whitworth, J., Sir v1p0815c1s v1p1250c2m
Whitworth, W.A. v6p0126c1s
Whorf, E.H. and Faxon, W.. v6p0641c1s
Whymper, A. v5p0573c2s
Whymper, C. v2p0143c1s v2p0144c2s v2p0253c2s v3p0222c2s v4p0061c1s
Whymper, Charles v3p0051c1s v3p0471c1s
Whymper, E. v1p0025c1s v1p0025c2s v1p0524c2s v1p0557c1s v1p0877c1s v2p0009c1s v2p0020c2m v2p0072c2s v2p0191c2s v2p0426c2s v3p0078c1s v3p0102c1m v3p0318c2s v4p0050c2s v4p0063c2s v4p0257c2s v4p0385c2s v4p0410c1s v5p0002c2s v5p0018c2s v6p0451c2s
Whymper, F. v2p0032c1s v2p0078c1s v2p0406c2s
Whyte, A. v2p0482c2s v5p0140c2s v5p0625c2s
Whyte, E.T. v6p0693c2s
Whyte, Frederic v5p0003c1s v5p0134c1s
Whyte, H. v6p0655c1s
Whyte, W.H. v3p0396c1s
Whyte, W.P. v6p0687c1s
Whytock, A. v3p0069c1s
Whytock, W. v6p0599c2s
Wiatt, W.W. v5p0329c2s
Wicher, E.A. v6p0335c2s v6p0337c1s
Wichern, J.H. v1p1089c1s
Wichert, E. v1p0723c2s
Wick, J.H. v4p0467c2s
Wickam, W. v2p0337c1s
Wickel, Anna H. v5p0106c2s
Wickenden, R.J. v4p0148c1s
Wickersham, J. v4p0079c2s v4p0281c1s v4p0281c2s v4p0282c2s v4p0298c1s v4p0350c2s v4p0466c2s v5p0013c1s v5p0108c2s v5p0287c2s v5p0288c2s v5p0373c1s v5p0383c1s v5p0416c2s v5p0554c1s
Wickersham, J.P. v1p0323c1s v1p0390c2s v1p1087c1s
Wickersham, T. v6p0210c2s
Wickersham, W.B. v4p0100c1s
Wickes, W.H. v6p0225c2s
Wickes, W.K. v3p0140c1m v4p0116c2s v6p0630c2s
Wickett, S.M. v5p0119c2m v5p0130c2s v5p0175c2s v5p0512c2s v6p0435c2s
Wickett, S.Morley v6p0098c1s
Wickham, A.E. v5p0055c1s
Wickham, E.C. v5p0053c2s v5p0234c2s
Wickham, H.F. v4p0261c1s v4p0468c1s v6p0127c1s
Wickham, H.J. and Wyatt, H.F. v6p0267c2s
Wickham, W. v2p0308c1s v2p0313c2s v2p0319c2s v3p0013c2s v3p0476c2s v4p0243c1s
Wickliffe, J.C. v4p0342c1s v4p0396c2s
Wicklin, E.E. v6p0659c1s
Wicklin, E.S. v5p0437c1s v6p0319c2s
Wickoff, H. v1p0073c1s
Wickramasingha, F.M. v3p0279c1s
Wicks, F. v2p0186c2s v4p0039c1s v4p0088c1s v4p0237c1s v4p0445c1s v4p0482c2s v4p0581c1s
Wicks, H.S. v3p0311c1s v4p0304c2s v4p0637c1s v5p0289c2s
Wickson, E.J. v1p0329c1s v3p0063c1s v6p0502c1s
Wicksteed, C. v1p1083c2s v1p1340c2s
Wicksteed, J.H. v6p0518c2s
Wicksteed, P.H. v1p0126c2s v1p0347c1m v1p0591c1s v1p0597c2m v1p0668c2s v1p0850c1s v2p0042c1s v2p0067c1s v2p0092c1s v2p0199c2m v2p0236c2s v2p0260c2s v2p0278c2s v2p0430c2s v3p0207c1m v3p0238c1s v3p0337c1m v4p0313c2s v5p0153c1s v5p0364c1s v6p0085c1s v6p0342c2m
Wicksteed, R.J. v4p0356c2s v5p0467c1s
Widdrington, G. v4p0214c2s
Widdrington, George v4p0294c2s
Widney, J.P. v1p0185c1s v1p0279c2s v1p0286c1s v1p0878c1s v2p0079c2s v3p0317c1s v6p0092c1s v6p0093c1s
Widor, C.M. and Bovet, M.A.de. v4p0233c1s
Wiechmann, F.G. v5p0037c2s v5p0242c2s
Wiegand, C. v1p1099c2s
Wiegand, J. v1p0484c2s
Wiegand, K.M. v6p0400c1s
Wiegand, S.L. v2p0213c1s v2p0419c2s
Wiel, A. v6p0400c2s
Wiel, Alethea v6p0676c2s
Wieland, G.R. v4p0023c1s v5p0150c2s v5p0421c2s v5p0469c1s v5p0574c1s v5p0595c1s v5p0646c2s v6p0058c2s v6p0162c2s v6p0174c2s v6p0401c1s v6p0506c1s v6p0662c1m v6p0712c2s
Wielowiejski, H.R.von v2p0156c2s
Wiencke, J. v2p0328c1s
Wiener, H.M. v5p0460c1s
Wiener, L. v4p0170c2s v4p0305c2m v4p0625c2s v5p0068c2s v5p0532c2s v6p0558c1s v6p0559c2s
Wiener, L and Maude, A. .. v6p0649c1s
Wier, D.H. v1p0581c2s
Wier, J. v4p0582c1s
Wier, S. v5p0498c1s
Wierzbicki, Dr. v1p1023c2s
Wieseler, K. v1p0099c1s v1p0684c2s v1p0686c1s v1p0994c1s
Wieser, F. v3p0336c2s v3p0446c2s v4p0038c2s v4p0540c1s
Wieser, F.von v4p0599c2s
Wieser, G.A. v6p0464c2s
Wieting, S. v1p0584c1s v1p1190c1s
Wigan, G. v4p0175c1s
Wigeld, J. v2p0182c2s
Wiggin, J.H. v4p0068c2s v4p0144c2s v4p0226c1m
Wiggin, K.D. v3p0077c2s v4p0092c2s v4p0120c1s v4p0202c1s v4p0207c2s v4p0268c2s v4p0356c1s v4p0405c2s v4p0433c2s v4p0489c2s v4p0578c2s v4p0604c2m v4p0635c2s v5p0156c1s v5p0346c2s v5p0439c1m
Wiggin, Kate D. v4p0104c1s v5p0161c1s v6p0165c2s v6p0332c1s v6p0492c2s v6p0533c1s v6p0551c2s v6p0615c1s
Wiggin, P.G. v5p0522c2s v5p0523c2s v6p0693c1s
Wiggins, B.L. v5p0240c1s
Wiggins, Capt. v4p0522c2s
Wiggins, Frank v6p0416c1s
Wiggins, J. v4p0522c2s
Wigglesworth, E. v1p0005c2s v1p0010c1s v1p0023c1s v1p0074c2s v1p0151c2s v1p0213c2s v1p0285c1s v1p0388c2s v1p0419c1s v1p0555c1s v1p0690c1s v1p0796c2s v1p0809c2s v1p0849c2s v1p0867c1s v1p1088c2s
Wigglesworth, S. v1p0261c2s
Wiggs, R. v6p0008c2s
Wigham, J.R. v3p0251c1s
Wight, D. v1p0149c1s v1p0613c1s
Wight, D., jr. v1p0254c2s
Wight, J.G. v4p0184c1s
Wight, J.K. v1p0011c1s v1p0173c2s v1p0289c1s v1p0432c2s v1p0580c2s v1p0623c2s v2p0273c1s v2p0292c1s v2p0353c1s
Wight, O.W. v1p0189c1s v1p0305c1s v1p0312c1s v1p0594c1s v1p0777c1s v1p1000c2m v1p1088c1s v1p1119c2s
Wight, P.B. v1p0053c1s v1p0053c2s v1p0054c1s v1p0160c2s v1p0227c1s v1p0373c2s v1p0455c2s v1p1113c1s v1p1255c1s v4p0100c2s v4p0200c1s v5p0105c1s v6p0027c2s v6p0066c1s v6p0130c2s
Wight, W.W. v3p0463c2s
Wightman, J.C. v1p0082c2s v1p0254c1s v1p0335c2s v1p0640c2s v1p0825c1s v1p1093c1s v1p1364c1s v1p1432c2s v1p1440c1s v1p1441c2s v2p0034c2s
Wightman, J.W. v4p0041c2s v4p0331c2s
Wightman, M.T. v1p0038c2s
Wightwick, M.G. v2p0301c1s v2p0399c1s v2p0424c2s v3p0081c2s v3p0368c1s v5p0273c2s
Wigmore, J.H. v3p0031c2m v3p0052c2m v3p0098c1s v3p0227c1m v3p0227c2s v3p0259c1s v4p0029c2s v4p0068c1s v4p0164c2s v4p0193c2s v4p0247c1s v4p0297c1m v4p0297c2m v4p0298c1s v4p0325c1s v4p0426c2s v4p0507c2s v5p0098c1s v5p0101c2s v5p0132c2s v5p0303c2s v5p0350c2s v6p0285c1s v6p0582c2s
Wijnkoop, J.D. v5p0260c2s
Wikel, A.H. v6p0351c2s
Wikof, H. v1p0353c1s
Wikoff, H. v1p0482c2s v1p0855c2s v1p0895c2s
Wikoff, P. v3p0093c1s v3p0115c1s
Wilbar, L. v5p0213c2s v6p0655c1s
Wilber, W.A. v4p0536c2s
Wilberforce, B. v3p0220c2s v4p0606c2s
Wilberforce, B.A. v3p0177c1s
Wilberforce, E. v1p0282c1s v1p0338c2s v1p0541c2s v1p0914c1s v1p1066c1s v1p1397c1s
Wilberforce, F.B. v6p0009c1s
Wilberforce, H.W. v1p0247c1s v1p0912c2s
Wilberforce, R.G. v2p0473c2s v4p0354c1m v4p0468c1s v6p0190c2s
Wilberforce, S. v1p0016c2s v1p0018c2s v1p0197c2s v1p0249c1m v1p0425c1s v1p0473c2s v1p0574c2s v1p0704c1s v1p0900c1s v1p0912c2s v1p1130c2s v1p1149c2s v1p1205c2s v1p1233c1s v1p1263c2s
Wilberforce, W. v1p1205c2s v3p0195c1s v4p0611c1s
Wilberforce, Wilfred v6p0455c2s
Wilbert, M.I. v5p0448c2s v5p0492c1s v6p0111c2s v6p0496c2s
Wilbert, W.I. v6p0546c2s
Wilbraham, F.M. v2p0050c1s
Wilbraham, R. v1p0226c1s
Wilbrandt, A. v5p0365c2s
Wilbur, A.T. v1p0450c1s
Wilbur, C.L. v4p0453c1s v5p0599c2s v6p0680c2s
Wilbur, C.T. v6p0410c2s
Wilbur, E.M. v4p0263c1s
Wilbur, H.B. v1p0935c2s
Wilbur, H.H. v6p0356c1s
Wilbur, H.L. v5p0326c2s v6p0363c1s
Wilbur, H.W. v6p0105c1s
Wilbur, W.A. v5p0569c2s
Wilcocks, A. v1p0186c2s
Wilcocks, J. v3p0037c2s
Wilcox, A. v1p0955c1m v4p0315c2s
Wilcox, A.H. v3p0119c2s
Wilcox, A.M. v3p0088c1s
Wilcox, A.W. v6p0320c1s
Wilcox, B.C. v6p0573c2s
Wilcox, C.B. v5p0328c1s
Wilcox, C.F. v5p0313c2s
Wilcox, C.M. v1p0518c2s v1p0557c2s v1p0695c2s v1p0734c1s v1p0994c2s v1p1086c1s v1p1180c2s v3p0272c2s
Wilcox, C.M. et al. v6p0408c2s

Wilcox, C.S. v1p0326c2s
Wilcox, D.F. v5p0119c2s
v5p0392c1s v5p0406c2s v5p0407c1s
v5p0409c1s v5p0434c1s v6p0129c1s
Wilcox, E.H. v5p0434c2s
Wilcox, E.M. v5p0212c2s
Wilcox, E.V. v5p0214c2s
v6p0012c1s v6p0105c1s v6p0246c1s
v6p0265c1s v6p0709c2s
Wilcox, E.W. v4p0138c2s
v4p0247c1s v4p0334c2s v4p0542c1s
v4p0589c2s v5p0129c1s v5p0129c2s
v5p0430c1s v5p0454c2s v5p0480c2s
v5p0637c2s
Wilcox, Ella W. v5p0256c1s
v6p0376c1s
Wilcox, F.A. v6p0650c1s
Wilcox, F.M. v4p0078c2s
Wilcox, H.K.W. v1p0405c1s
v1p1242c2s
Wilcox, J. v1p0132c2s
v1p0203c2s v1p0366c2s v1p0647c2m
v1p0648c1s v1p0696c2s v1p0732c1s
v1p0942c2s v1p1007c2m v1p1154c1s
v1p1430c2s v6p0454c1s v6p0638c2s
Wilcox, L.C. v6p0701c2s
Wilcox, M. v2p0096c2s
v2p0314c2s v2p0316c1s v2p0337c2s
v2p0464c1s v4p0198c1s v4p0332c1s
v4p0386c1s v4p0406c1s v4p0414c1s
v4p0516c2s v5p0009c2s v5p0051c1s
v5p0173c1s v5p0444c2s v5p0445c2s
v5p0496c1s v5p0560c1s v6p0138c1s
v6p0160c2s v6p0161c1s v6p0169c1s
v6p0362c2s
Wilcox, M.A. v4p0286c1s
Wilcox, M.F. v6p0382c2s
Wilcox, M.O. v5p0214c1s
v5p0444c2s v5p0491c2s v6p0361c2s
Wilcox, R.W. v5p0368c1s
Wilcox, W.D. v4p0342c2s
v5p0091c2s v5p0509c1s v6p0546c2s
Wilcoxson, L.G. v5p0452c1s
Wilczynski, E.J. v5p0560c2s
v6p0505c1s
Wild, C. v3p0451c1s
Wild, H. v6p0083c2s
Wild, H.D. v4p0468c2s
Wild, J.J. v1p0073c1s
Wild, M. v5p0472c2s
Wilde, A. et al. v6p0635c1s
Wilde, A.H. v6p0249c1s
Wilde, E.S. v2p0313c1s
Wilde, H. v1p0399c1s
v1p0401c2s
Wilde, J.R. v1p0040c2s
Wilde, Lady v1p0613c2s
v1p0627c1s v1p1222c1s
Wilde, N. v4p0188c2s
v4p0308c1s v5p0359c2s v5p0386c1s
v6p0211c2s
Wilde, O. v1p0559c2s
v2p0397c1s v3p0021c1s v3p0106c1s
v3p0261c2s v3p0284c1s v3p0332c1s
v3p0340c1s v3p0355c1s v3p0399c1s
v4p0448c1s
Wilde, Oscar v2p0416c2s
v3p0388c2s v3p0453c1s
Wilde, W.C. v2p0230c2s
v4p0529c1s
Wilde, W.R. v1p0337c1s
v1p0465c2s v1p0661c1s v1p1039c1s
Wildeboer and Smith, J.M.P., tr.
v5p0056c2s
Wildenbruch, E.von v2p0253c1s
v3p0190c1s v5p0167c1s
Wildenhahn, Dr. v1p1336c1s
Wilder v1p1205c2s
Wilder, A. v2p0073c2s
Wilder, A.F. v1p1078c2s
Wilder, A.P. v3p0303c2s
v4p0322c2s v6p0358c2s
Wilder, B.G. v1p0037c2s
v1p0083c1s v1p0101c2s v1p0102c1s
v1p0136c1s v1p0205c1s v1p0280c2s
v1p0454c1s v1p0456c2s v1p0500c2s
v1p0569c1m v1p0618c1s v1p0619c1s
v1p0645c2s v1p0793c1s v1p0794c2s
v1p0898c2s v1p0901c1s v1p0986c2s
v1p1182c1m v1p1187c2s v1p1233c1s
v1p1236c1m v1p1314c2s v1p1368c1s
v1p1434c2s v2p0222c1s v2p0302c2s
v2p0462c2s v3p0053c1s v3p0448c2s
v5p0008c2s v5p0012c2s v5p0018c2s
v5p0075c1m v6p0019c2s
Wilder, B.G. and Coan, T.M.
v1p0392c2s
Wilder, C.F. v6p0649c1s
Wilder, D. v1p0094c2s
v1p1285c1s v1p1349c1s v1p1351c2s
Wilder, D., jr. v1p1049c2s
Wilder, E. v5p0235c1s
v6p0374c1s
Wilder, E.T. v3p0347c1s
Wilder, F.A. v6p0133c1s
Wilder, Frank A. v6p0518c1s
Wilder, G.A. v6p0051c2s
v6p0421c2s
Wilder, G.D. v6p0121c1s
Wilder, G.G. v6p0395c2s
Wilder, H.A. v6p0476c1s
Wilder, H.H. v5p0351c1s
v5p0505c1s v6p0171c2s v6p0201c2s
v6p0306c2s v6p0315c2s v6p0475c2m
v6p0486c2s v6p0648c1s
Wilder, H.J. v6p0025c2s
Wilder, J. v1p0462c1s
v1p1396c1s
Wilder, M.P. v1p0910c2s
v2p0046c1s v2p0310c2s v3p0139c2s
Wilder, R.G. v2p0291c2s
Wilder, S.Fanny G. v4p0110c2s
Wilder, S.H. v1p1336c2s
Wilder, W.E. v5p0029c1s
Wildey, L.R. v6p0494c1s
Wildig, G.L.B. v1p0490c2s
v1p1142c2s
Wilding, E. v1p0824c1s
Wildman, A.R. v2p0197c1s
Wildman, E. v4p0610c1s
v5p0041c1s v5p0112c1s v5p0206c2s
v5p0278c2s v5p0338c2s v5p0444c1s
v6p0119c2s v6p0334c2s v6p0538c2s
Wildman, L.D. v6p0568c1s
Wildman, M.W. v5p0265c1s
Wildman, R. v4p0016c2s
v4p0040c2m v4p0088c1s v4p0225c1s
v4p0267c2s v4p0276c1s v4p0304c1s
v4p0343c2s v4p0351c1m v4p0380c2s
v4p0392c1s v4p0399c2s v4p0415c1s
v4p0423c2s v4p0437c2s v4p0444c2s
v4p0476c1s v4p0485c1s v4p0501c2s
v4p0503c1s v4p0519c2s v4p0527c1m
v4p0578c2s v4p0636c1s v5p0078c2s
v5p0507c1s
Wildrick, M.W. v3p0228c1s
Wildridge, T.T. v4p0268c2s
Wile, F.W. v6p0080c1s
Wilenkin, G. v6p0558c1s
Wiles, C.P. v6p0419c1s
Wiley, C. v1p0198c2s
v1p1101c2s
Wiley, C.W. v4p0434c2s
v4p0526c1s v4p0629c2s
Wiley, D.C. and Arnold, R.
v6p0250c2s
Wiley, E. v6p0539c1s
Wiley, H.J. v6p0231c2s
Wiley, H.W. v1p0199c2s
v1p0399c2s v1p0452c2s v2p0005c1s
v2p0062c2m v2p0288c2s v2p0424c1s
v3p0061c2s v4p0004c1s v4p0049c1s
v4p0098c2s v4p0555c1s v5p0009c1s
v5p0034c2s v5p0075c2s v5p0104c1s
v5p0205c1s v5p0258c1s v5p0431c1s
v5p0537c2s v5p0559c2s v5p0567c1s
v6p0009c1s v6p0011c1s v6p0056c2s
v6p0111c2s v6p0112c1s v6p0118c1s
v6p0231c1m v6p0498c1s v6p0502c2s
v6p0515c1s v6p0669c2s
Wiley, I.W. v1p0233c1s
v1p1240c2s
Wiley, J.W. v1p0289c2s
v1p0629c1s
Wiley, S.K. v6p0255c1s
Wiley, W.H. v1p0527c1s
v4p0161c2s v4p0521c1s
Wilford, E.C. v3p0153c2s
Wilford, F. v1p0904c1s
Wilford, J.F. v5p0099c1s
Wilgus, H.L. v6p0670c1s
Wilgus, W.J. v6p0529c2s
Wilhelm, C. v4p0042c2s
v5p0211c2m
Wilhelm, L.W. v2p0030c1s
v2p0105c1s v2p0178c1s v2p0211c2s
v2p0247c2s v2p0262c1s v2p0279c1m
v2p0348c1s v2p0444c1s
Wilhelm, Thos., Col. v5p0399c1s
Wilholme, W. v2p0023c2s
Wilion, H.Schutz v5p0051c1s
Wilken, J.F. v1p0840c1s
Wilkens, H. v1p1338c1s
Wilker, V. v4p0320c1s
v4p0540c1s v5p0230c2s v5p0646c1s
v6p0302c1s v6p0713c1s
Wilkes, F.E. v4p0087c2s
Wilkes, G. v6p0127c2s
v6p0160c1s
Wilkes, R. v1p0465c1s
v1p0546c2s
Wilkeson, F. v2p0071c2s
Wilkie, Col. v1p0897c2s
Wilkie, D. v1p0341c1s
Wilkie, D.R. v4p0044c2s
v4p0085c2s
Wilkie, F.B. v1p0227c2s
Wilkins, A.L. v3p0234c1s
Wilkins, A.S. v1p0890c2s
v1p1067c1s v2p0040c1s v2p0086c1s
v2p0271c2s v2p0373c1s v2p0461c1s
v3p0200c2s v4p0263c1s v5p0196c1s
Wilkins, B. v5p0608c2s
Wilkins, B.S. v6p0315c2s
Wilkins, C. v5p0398c2s
v6p0085c2s v6p0140c1s
Wilkins, J. v1p0133c1s
v1p0360c2s v1p0423c1s v1p0572c2s
Wilkins, J.E. v5p0597c2s
Wilkins, M.E. v2p0098c2s
v2p0172c1s v2p0206c2s v2p0211c1s
v2p0320c2s v2p0412c1s v2p0421c2s
v3p0136c2s v3p0168c2s v3p0335c2s
v3p0360c1s v3p0439c1s v3p0454c1s
v4p0077c2s v4p0126c2s v4p0190c1s
v4p0226c1s v4p0296c2s v4p0335c2s
v4p0336c1s v4p0398c2s v4p0429c2s
v4p0523c2s v4p0575c2s v5p0096c2s
v5p0097c2s v5p0164c1s v5p0348c1s
v5p0349c2s v5p0383c2s v5p0421c1s
v5p0433c2s v5p0460c1s v5p0466c2s
v5p0520c1s v5p0547c2s v5p0585c1s
v5p0589c2s v5p0596c1s v5p0619c2s
Wilkins, M.F. v2p0017c1s
Wilkins, Mary E. v6p0083c2s
v6p0195c2s v6p0280c1s v6p0700c1s
Wilkins, T. v4p0441c2s
Wilkins, W. v1p0053c2s
v1p0404c2s v1p0818c2s v1p0930c1s
v1p1366c1s
Wilkins, W.F. v1p1265c2s
Wilkins, W.G. v4p0122c1s
Wilkins, W.H. v3p0207c2s
v3p0209c1s v3p0309c1s v3p0340c2s
v4p0247c2s v4p0630c1s v5p0539c2s
v6p0040c2s v6p0102c2s
Wilkins, W.J. v3p0196c2s
Wilkins, W.W. v1p0165c2s
Wilkinson, A. v4p0011c1s
v5p0156c2s v5p0276c2s v6p0504c1s
Wilkinson, A.E. v6p0363c2s
Wilkinson, A.G. v1p1146c2s
Wilkinson, B. v2p0184c2s
Wilkinson, C. v6p0350c2s
Wilkinson, C.C. v5p0641c1s
Wilkinson, C.S. v3p0302c2s
Wilkinson, Dr. v1p0268c1s
Wilkinson, E. v4p0308c1s
Wilkinson, E.T. v2p0055c2s
v5p0610c1s
Wilkinson, F. v3p0237c1s
v5p0088c2s v5p0342c1s v6p0218c1m
v6p0344c1s v6p0391c1s v6p0563c1s
Wilkinson, Florence v6p0456c2s
Wilkinson, G. v1p0165c2s
v1p0540c1s v6p0533c1s
Wilkinson, G.L. v5p0075c1s
Wilkinson, J. v1p1366c2s
v2p0403c2s
Wilkinson, J.B. v1p1106c1s
v5p0325c1s
Wilkinson, J.B., jr. v6p0624c1s
Wilkinson, J.F. v4p0007c1s
v4p0011c1s v4p0169c2s v4p0215c2m
v4p0411c2s v4p0412c1m v4p0428c2s
v4p0452c1m v5p0029c2s v5p0222c1s
Wilkinson, J.H. v5p0117c2s
v5p0366c2s
Wilkinson, J.W. v1p0062c1s
v1p0187c1s v4p0225c1s v5p0192c1s
v5p0287c2s v5p0290c2s v6p0105c2s
v6p0290c1s v6p0527c1s
Wilkinson, K. v4p0240c1m
v6p0048c1s
Wilkinson, M. v4p0076c1s
Wilkinson, Maurice v6p0489c1s
Wilkinson, R. v1p1106c1s
Wilkinson, R.A. v1p1265c2s
v2p0267c1s v2p0424c1s
Wilkinson, S. v3p0278c2s
v3p0454c1s v4p0009c2s v4p0107c1s
v4p0130c2m v4p0235c2m v4p0237c2s
v4p0239c2s v4p0244c2s v4p0310c2s
v4p0497c1s v4p0599c2s v4p0611c1s
v5p0005c1s v5p0197c1s v5p0243c2m
v5p0245c1s v5p0345c1s v5p0404c1s
v5p0563c1s v5p0587c1s v5p0588c2s
v6p0268c2s v6p0271c2m v6p0685c1s
Wilkinson, Spenser v4p0182c1s
Wilkinson, T.T. v1p0075c2s
v1p0464c1s v1p1140c1s
Wilkinson, T.W. v5p0075c1s
v5p0343c1s v5p0441c2s v5p0472c2s
v5p0585c2s v5p0606c2s v6p0279c2s
Wilkinson, W. v1p0292c2s
v6p0655c1s
Wilkinson, W.A. v1p1077c1s
Wilkinson, W.C. v1p0330c1s
v1p0420c1s v1p0423c2s v1p0447c2s
v1p0454c1s v1p0512c1s v1p0600c1s
v1p0774c2m v1p1064c2s v1p1355c1s
v1p1395c2s v2p0087c2m v2p0382c1s
v2p0469c1s v3p0033c2s v4p0074c1s
v4p0300c1s v5p0364c1s v5p0418c1s
v5p0420c2s v6p0342c1s
Wilkinson, W.F. v1p0578c2s
v1p1177c2s v2p0388c1s v2p0447c2s
v4p0231c1s v4p0483c1s v5p0487c2s
Wilkinson, W.G. v4p0300c1s
Wilkinson, W.H. v3p0078c2s
v3p0079c2s
Wilkinson, Warring v6p0166c2s
Wilks, E.V. v5p0409c1s
Wilks, H.M. v3p0067c2s
Wilks, S. v2p0420c1s
v4p0192c2s v5p0271c2s v6p0643c1s
v6p0679c2s
Wilks, S. et al. v1p1376c2s
Will, H. v1p0924c1s
Will, J. v5p0480c2s

Will, T.E. v4p0115c1s v4p0115c2s v4p0140c1s v4p0171c1s v4p0318c1s v4p0449c2s v4p0460c1s v4p0590c2s v4p0591c1s v4p0591c2s v5p0383c1s v5p0500c2s v6p0233c1s v6p0389c1s v6p0601c1s
Will, T.E. and Vrooman, H.C. v4p0610c1s
Will, T.E. et al. v4p0103c1s v4p0427c2s v6p0310c2s
Will, T.Elmer v6p0317c2s
Willaert, L. v6p0183c2s v6p0564c2s
Willan, J.N. v1p0437c2s v1p1382c1s
Willan, R. v1p1437c2s
Willard, A.J. v1p0453c1s
Willard, A.R. v3p0051c1s v3p0059c2s v3p0064c1s v3p0267c1s v3p0273c2s v3p0286c2s v3p0321c2s v3p0460c2s v4p0359c1s v5p0126c2s v5p0333c2s
Willard, Alice R. v5p0538c2s
Willard, B. v5p0183c2s v6p0360c1s
Willard, C.D. v3p0265c2s v6p0129c1s v6p0324c2s v6p0390c1s v6p0442c2s v6p0474c1s v6p0533c2s v6p0566c2s v6p0569c1s
Willard, C.F. v3p0238c2s
Willard, C.R. v4p0460c2s
Willard, C.W. v3p0393c1s v5p0458c2s
Willard, D.E. v4p0100c1s
Willard, Daniel v6p0129c1s
Willard, E.C. v5p0179c1s v5p0449c1s
Willard, E.P. v1p1196c1s v1p1438c1s
Willard, E.S. v6p0453c1s
Willard, E.S., Mrs. v3p0261c1s
Willard, F.B. v6p0419c1s
Willard, F.E. v1p0922c2s v1p1279c1s v1p1409c1s v3p0038c2s v3p0068c2s v3p0076c2s v3p0089c2s v3p0119c2s v3p0121c2s v3p0346c1m v3p0354c1s v3p0411c2s v3p0423c2s v3p0424c1m v3p0467c1s v3p0467c2m v3p0468c1s v3p0470c1s v4p0067c2s v4p0075c1s v4p0160c1s v4p0315c2s v4p0536c1s v4p0568c1m v4p0626c1m v4p0626c2s v5p0636c1s
Willard, F.E. et al. v3p0470c1s
Willard, H. v1p0247c1s
Willard, H.E. v6p0011c1s
Willard, H.M. v2p0388c2s v3p0378c2s
Willard, J. v1p0694c2s v1p0720c2s v1p0816c1s v1p1411c1m v4p0299c2s
Willard, J.F. v3p0218c1s v6p0316c1s v6p0355c1s
Willard, J.T. v4p0616c2s
Willard, M. v1p1340c2s
Willard, M.B. v1p0715c1m v1p1319c2s
Willard, S. v1p0005c2s v1p0034c2s v1p0116c2s v1p0120c1s v1p0123c2s v1p0256c2s v1p0373c2s v1p0389c2s v1p0416c2m v1p0481c2s v1p0506c1s v1p0555c1s v1p0581c2s v1p0808c2s v1p0809c1s v1p0842c1s v1p0882c2s v1p0899c1s v1p0921c2s v1p1058c2s v1p1106c2s v1p1159c1s v1p1275c1s v1p1396c1s v1p1429c1s v2p0171c2s v2p0455c2s v3p0167c2s v4p0226c1s v4p0306c2s v4p0620c2s v5p0597c2s v6p0071c1s
Willard, S.L. v6p0496c2s
Willbea, D.D. v1p0038c1s
Willcock, J. v6p0578c1s v6p0589c1s
Willcock, S. v6p0685c1s
Willcox, C.D. v5p0626c2s
Willcox, C.deW. v5p0375c2s
Willcox, D. v5p0592c2s v5p0593c1s v5p0593c2s v6p0132c2s v6p0529c1m
Willcox, E.G. v5p0080c1s
Willcox, E.S. v4p0362c2s
Willcox, F.W. v5p0283c2s
Willcox, G.B. v3p0427c2s
Willcox, J.M. v1p0644c1s v1p1238c2s
Willcox, L.C. v6p0075c1s v6p0085c2s v6p0262c1s v6p0309c2s v6p0461c2s v6p0472c1s v6p0694c1s v6p0697c1s
Willcox, Louise C. v6p0168c1s v6p0391c2s
Willcox, M.A. v4p0512c1s v5p0420c1s v6p0002c2m v6p0295c2s
Willcox, O.B. v5p0028c2s
Willcox, O.W. v6p0230c1s
Willcox, S.C. v6p0505c2s
Willcox, W.F. v4p0114c2m v4p0288c1s v4p0357c1m v4p0516c2s v5p0099c2m v5p0119c2s v5p0402c2s v5p0444c1s v5p0603c2s v6p0308c1s v6p0446c2s v6p0448c1s v6p0585c2s
Willcox, W.F. and Crum, F.S. v5p0559c1s
Willcox, Walter F. v6p0167c1s
Willeby, C. v3p0080c1s v3p0293c1s v4p0389c2s
Willdey, C.J. v4p0454c1m v5p0135c1s v5p0308c2s v5p0336c1s v5p0440c2s
Willement, T. v1p1143c1s
Willemoes-Suhm, R.v. v1p0444c2s
Willert, P.F. v2p0028c1s v2p0270c2s v3p0228c2s v3p0265c2s v3p0288c2s v3p0358c2s v6p0242c1s v6p0539c1s
Willet, J.E. v1p0638c2s v1p0828c1m
Willets, G. v4p0408c1s v4p0530c1s v5p0034c2s v5p0155c1s v5p0258c1s v5p0271c1s v5p0498c1s v5p0533c1s v6p0559c1s v6p0561c1s
Willets, Gilson v5p0636c2s v6p0043c1s
Willett, A.H. v6p0321c2s
Willett, E.M. v6p0397c2s v6p0434c1s
Willett, Edith M. v6p0025c2s v6p0111c1s v6p0421c2s
Willett, H.L. v5p0561c2s v6p0340c1s
Willett, R. v1p0547c1s v1p0901c2s v1p1051c2s
Willett, W.M. v1p0132c1s
Willett, W.P. v6p0471c1s
Willett, W.W. v1p0119c1s
Willey, A. v3p0159c2s v4p0395c1s v5p0318c1s
Willey, D.A. v5p0005c1s v5p0124c1s v5p0148c2s v5p0376c1s v5p0402c2s v5p0540c2s v5p0602c2s v5p0645c2s v6p0038c2s v6p0049c1s v6p0071c1s v6p0073c1m v6p0105c2s v6p0166c2s v6p0175c2s v6p0180c1s v6p0200c1s v6p0203c2s v6p0215c1s v6p0249c1s v6p0260c2m v6p0329c1s v6p0329c2s v6p0352c2s v6p0355c1s v6p0361c2s v6p0397c1s v6p0400c2s v6p0416c2s v6p0455c1s v6p0455c2s v6p0465c1s v6p0469c2s v6p0471c1s v6p0491c1s v6p0514c1s v6p0523c1s v6p0528c1m v6p0529c2m v6p0533c2s v6p0543c1s v6p0551c1m v6p0554c2s v6p0655c1s v6p0657c2s v6p0660c1s v6p0685c2s v6p0696c2s
Willey, D.A. and Gordon, S.B. v5p0009c2s
Willey, Day A. v6p0130c2s v6p0404c2s v6p0608c1s
Willey, H. v1p0744c1m
Willey, I. v2p0283c2s v2p0342c2s
Willey, J.H. v5p0114c2s v5p0475c2s
Willey, J.S. v5p0166c1s
Willey, S.H. v1p0567c1s v2p0064c1s v6p0093c2s
Willey, W.T. v1p0830c2s
Willi, O. v6p0296c1s
William, C.P. v1p0306c1s
William, G. v5p0314c1s
Williams, A. v1p0035c1s v1p0730c2s v1p0760c1s v2p0415c1s v3p0176c1s v3p0241c2s v3p0280c2s v3p0281c1s v4p0079c1s v4p0132c2m v4p0161c1s v4p0375c2s v4p0458c1s v4p0526c2s v5p0007c1s v5p0238c1s v5p0318c1s v5p0367c1s v5p0375c2s v5p0618c2s v6p0148c2m v6p0244c2s v6p0518c2s v6p0624c2s
Williams, A. and Vivian, H. v4p0314c1s v5p0136c1s
Williams, A. et al. v2p0398c2s
Williams, A., jr. v1p0506c2s v3p0390c2s v4p0138c2s v4p0230c1s v4p0347c1s v4p0372c2m v4p0416c2s v4p0526c2s v4p0617c1s v6p0419c1s
Williams, A.B. v3p0299c2s
Williams, A.M. v1p0088c1s v1p0225c2s v1p0275c1s v1p0452c1s v1p0541c2s v1p0638c2s v1p0661c2m v1p0662c2s v1p0939c2s v2p0076c2s v2p0209c2m v2p0211c2s v2p0219c1m v2p0228c2s v2p0302c2s v2p0319c1s v2p0324c1s v2p0374c1s v2p0464c2s v2p0469c2s v4p0063c2s v4p0074c1s v4p0308c1s v4p0452c2s v4p0483c1s v4p0511c2s v4p0594c1s
Williams, A.S. v6p0139c1s v6p0348c1m v6p0441c2s v6p0453c2s v6p0635c2s
Williams, A.W. v1p0796c1s v3p0030c1s
Williams, Alida S. v6p0217c1s
Williams, B. v1p0356c1s v1p0459c2s v1p0608c2s v1p0721c1s v1p0797c2m v1p0955c1s v4p0415c2s v5p0068c1s v5p0244c2s v5p0245c2s v5p0408c2s v5p0441c1s
Williams, B.J. v2p0113c1s
Williams, B.T. v1p1105c2s
Williams, B.W. v4p0109c2s v4p0275c1s v4p0318c2s v4p0461c2s v4p0497c1s
Williams, C. v1p0935c2s v2p0007c2s v2p0183c1m v3p0304c1s v4p0047c2s v5p0249c1s v5p0539c2s v5p0577c2s v6p0424c1s v6p0462c1s v6p0485c2s v6p0491c2m v6p0596c1s
Williams, C.A. v6p0152c2s v6p0245c2s v6p0676c1s v6p0711c1s
Williams, C.Arthur v6p0103c2s v6p0146c1s v6p0435c2s v6p0550c2s v6p0583c2s
Williams, C.B. v5p0015c1s
Williams, C.D. v6p0123c1s
Williams, C.E. v6p0055c2s
Williams, C.G. v1p0947c2s
Williams, C.H. v1p0023c2s v1p0673c2s v5p0090c2s v5p0091c2s v5p0323c1s v6p0095c2s v6p0097c1s v6p0546c2s v6p0678c2s
Williams, C.J.B. v2p0095c1s v2p0426c2s
Williams, C.M. v4p0185c2s v5p0124c2s v6p0103c1s v6p0182c2s v6p0203c2s v6p0292c1s v6p0386c1s v6p0397c2s v6p0506c2s v6p0544c1s v6p0622c1s
Williams, C.P. v1p1002c2s v1p1034c2s v1p1188c2s v1p1376c2s
Williams, C.P. and Blandy, J.F. v1p0300c1s v1p1271c1s
Williams, C.S. v5p0061c1s
Williams, C.T. v3p0128c1s v3p0196c1s v4p0582c1s
Williams, C.W. v1p0145c2s v1p1212c1s v4p0016c2s v5p0105c2s v5p0349c2s v5p0580c2s v6p0465c2s
Williams, Canning v5p0226c2s
Williams, Carrie v6p0594c2s
Williams, Churchill v6p0075c1s v6p0176c1s v6p0223c1s v6p0287c2s v6p0507c1s
Williams, D. v2p0335c1m v2p0393c2s
Williams, D.W. v4p0095c1s
Williams, E. v1p0204c1s v1p0660c1s v1p0663c2s v1p0878c2s v1p0888c2s v1p1075c1s v1p1368c2s v4p0197c2s v4p0234c2s v4p0474c1s
Williams, E.B. v3p0056c1s v3p0149c2s v5p0541c2s v6p0141c2s v6p0147c1s
Williams, E.C. v5p0294c2s v5p0543c2s
Williams, E.E. v4p0049c1s v4p0213c2s v4p0224c1s v4p0236c2s v4p0237c2s v4p0472c1s v5p0130c2m v5p0177c1s v5p0212c2s v5p0213c1s v5p0231c2m v5p0295c2s v5p0318c2s v5p0567c1s v5p0570c1s v6p0205c2s v6p0240c2s v6p0436c1s
Williams, E.F. v1p0380c2s v1p0900c1s v1p1233c1s v2p0236c1s v5p0436c2s v6p0059c1s v6p0678c2s
Williams, E.H. v4p0433c2s
Williams, E.H., jr. v3p0169c2s v4p0020c1s v4p0381c2s v4p0622c1s
Williams, E.H., jr. et al. v4p0180c2s
Williams, E.L. v3p0213c2s
Williams, E.R. v4p0234c1s
Williams, E.W. v6p0491c1s
Williams, Elisabeth M v4p0210c2s
Williams, Ernest E. v6p0100c1s
Williams, F. v1p0475c1s v1p0834c1s v2p0175c1s v5p0525c1s v6p0099c1s v6p0318c2s v6p0424c2s v6p0515c1s
Williams, F. et al. v4p0553c1s
Williams, F.C. v4p0124c2s v4p0348c1s v4p0361c2s v4p0520c1s v4p0598c1s v5p0141c1s v5p0442c1s v5p0533c2s v5p0547c2s v6p0145c2s v6p0507c1s
Williams, F.E. v6p0274c1s
Williams, F.H. v2p0073c1s v2p0169c1s v2p0374c2s v3p0057c1s v3p0057c2s v3p0100c1s v3p0151c2s v3p0430c1s v3p0462c2m v3p0463c1s v4p0042c2s v4p0076c1s v4p0076c2s v4p0120c1s v4p0178c2s v4p0309c2s v4p0434c1s v4p0443c1s v5p0280c2s v5p0492c1s v6p0166c2s v6p0380c2s v6p0653c1s
Williams, F.J. v2p0063c2s
Williams, F.S. v1p1080c1s v2p0306c1s v3p0311c2s v4p0375c1s
Williams, F.W. v2p0262c2s v3p0069c1s v3p0371c1s v4p0244c1s v5p0112c1s v5p0113c1s v5p0380c1s v6p0118c2s
Williams, Fannie B. v6p0446c2s
Williams, G. v1p1421c1s
Williams, G.D. v2p0260c1s v2p0355c2s
Williams, G.F. v2p0021c2s v4p0525c1s v5p0047c1s v5p0149c2s v5p0289c2s v6p0195c1s
Williams, G.H. v1p1412c1s v2p0173c2s v2p0336c1s v2p0360c2s

v2p0414c2s v3p0071c2s v3p0098c1s
v3p0101c2s v3p0107c1s v3p0169c2s
v3p0193c2s v3p0200c2s v3p0277c2s
v3p0306c2s v3p0350c1m v3p0385c2s
v4p0443c1s v4p0486c2s v4p0538c2s
v4p0607c1s v6p0173c1s v6p0324c2s
v6p0545c1s v6p0624c1s
Williams, G.W. v5p0283c1s
Williams, H. v3p0025c2s
v3p0089c1s v3p0182c1s v3p0182c2s
v3p0298c1s v3p0405c1s v4p0136c1s
v4p0180c2s v5p0114c1s v6p0169c1s
Williams, H. and Hicks, F.C.
v5p0588c2s
Williams, H.H. v4p0077c2s
v4p0308c1s v4p0504c2s v5p0114c2s
v5p0176c1s v5p0406c1s
Williams, H.L. v1p0359c1s
v1p0848c2s v3p0053c1s v3p0121c2s
v5p0159c2s v5p0213c1s
Williams, H.M. v2p0018c1s
v5p0353c2s v5p0598c1s
Williams, H.N. v5p0038c1s
v5p0440c1s v6p0245c2s
Williams, H.P. v5p0147c2s
v5p0258c2s v6p0457c1s
Williams, H.S. v1p0217c1s
v2p0247c1s v3p0116c1m v3p0169c2s
v4p0140c1m v4p0140c2s v4p0154c2s
v4p0255c2s v4p0273c2s v4p0285c1m
v4p0285c2s v4p0353c1s v4p0425c1s
v4p0479c2s v5p0018c2s v5p0035c1s
v5p0062c2s v5p0104c1s v5p0107c1s
v5p0160c1m v5p0210c2s v5p0229c1s
v5p0253c2s v5p0263c1s v5p0269c2s
v5p0362c1s v5p0368c2s v5p0372c1s
v5p0428c1m v5p0449c2m v5p0513c1s
v5p0514c2s v5p0529c2s v5p0607c2m
v6p0013c1s v6p0073c2s v6p0234c2s
v6p0273c1s v6p0540c1s v6p0575c2s
Williams, H.S. and Villard, O.G.
v6p0679c2s
Williams, H.T. v1p1128c1s
Williams, H.W. v1p0438c1s
v2p0348c2s v2p0369c2s v4p0135c1s
v4p0377c2s v5p0121c1s v6p0181c2s
v6p0557c2s
Williams, Helen v6p0261c2s
Williams, I.B. v6p0446c2s
Williams, I.P. v4p0243c2s
Williams, J. v1p0138c1s
v1p0178c2s v1p0230c1s v1p0242c2s
v1p0248c1s v1p0252c1s v1p0254c2s
v1p0291c1s v1p0412c1s v1p0421c2m
v1p0422c1s v1p0568c2s v1p0640c1s
v1p0646c1s v1p0667c2s v1p0690c1s
v1p0731c2s v1p0757c1s v1p0766c2s
v1p0769c2s v1p0847c1s v1p0910c1s
v1p0924c2s v1p0964c1s v1p0964c2s
v1p1033c2s v1p1045c1s v1p1053c1s
v1p1060c1s v1p1302c2s v1p1325c2s
v1p1326c1s v1p1377c2s v1p1431c2s
v2p0097c1s v2p0393c2s v3p0112c2s
v3p0124c1s v3p0199c1s v3p0211c1s
v3p0326c2s v3p0387c1s v3p0469c1s
v5p0181c2s v5p0386c2s v6p0032c2s
v6p0364c1s
Williams, J.A. v1p0830c1s
Williams, J.A., jr. v4p0138c2s
v4p0484c2s v4p0571c2s
Williams, J.B. v1p1078c1s
v3p0313c2s
Williams, J.C. v5p0637c2s
v6p0018c1s v6p0694c2s
Williams, J.C. and Haines, T.H.
v6p0680c2s
Williams, J.E. v1p0093c2s
v1p0453c1s v1p1232c2s v1p1388c1s
Williams, J.E.H. v5p0512c1s
Williams, J.E.H. and
Chesterton, G.K. v5p0450c2s
Williams, J.E.Hodder and
Chesterton, G. v5p0623c1s
Williams, J.E.T. v6p0180c1s
Williams, J.F. v2p0404c2s
v3p0143c2s v3p0281c2s v5p0371c1s
v6p0482c2s
Williams, J.F. and Brackett, R.N.
v3p0303c2s
Williams, J.H. v2p0169c2s
v5p0503c2s v5p0535c2s v5p0624c1s
v6p0119c2s v6p0356c1s v6p0562c2s
v6p0580c2s v6p0589c1s v6p0603c2s
v6p0604c2s v6p0610c2s v6p0618c2s
Williams, J.L. v3p0397c1s
v3p0431c1s v3p0434c2s v4p0206c2s
v4p0269c1s v4p0459c1s v4p0567c1s
v5p0120c1s v5p0146c2s v5p0234c1s
v5p0248c2s v5p0271c2s v5p0390c1s
v5p0406c1s v5p0408c1m v5p0480c1s
v5p0554c1s v6p0052c2s v6p0134c2s
v6p0231c2s v6p0257c1s v6p0359c1s
v6p0570c2s v6p0700c1s
Williams, J.L. and Warren, Arthur
v4p0031c2s v4p0110c2s
Williams, J.M. v1p0189c2s
v2p0099c2s v2p0462c1s v3p0175c1s
v3p0357c1s v3p0357c2s v3p0461c1s
v4p0193c2s v4p0343c1s v4p0572c2s
v4p0629c2s v6p0476c1s
Williams, J.N. v2p0211c1s
Williams, J.O. v6p0699c2m
Williams, J.R. v1p0283c2s
v1p0649c2s v1p0835c1s v1p1403c1s
v1p1404c1s v5p0368c1s
Williams, J.S. v6p0170c1s
Williams, J.Sharp v6p0170c1s
v6p0529c1s
Williams, J.W. v3p0152c2s
v4p0412c1s
Williams, James H. v6p0066c1s
v6p0420c2s v6p0518c1s
Williams, Jesse L. v5p0406c2s
v5p0407c2s v6p0282c2s
Williams, K.F. v1p1335c2s
Williams, L. v4p0115c2s
v4p0276c2s v4p0539c2s v5p0100c1s
v5p0148c1s v5p0233c1s v5p0542c1m
v6p0100c2s v6p0604c1s
Williams, L.A. v4p0465c1s
Williams, L.A., Miss v3p0070c1s
Williams, L.E. v6p0242c2s
Williams, L.W. v6p0148c2s
v6p0350c2s v6p0612c1s
Williams, Leonard v6p0604c1s
Williams, Lillie A. v4p0464c2s
v6p0707c1s
Williams, M. v1p0009c2s
v1p0173c2s v1p0633c2s v1p0634c1s
v1p0675c2s v1p0975c2s v1p1441c2s
v2p0293c2s v3p0058c2s v6p0362c1s
Williams, M.B. v1p0105c1s
v1p0185c2s v1p0246c1s v1p0462c1s
v1p0735c2s v1p0802c1s v1p1253c2s
Williams, M.C. v3p0107c2s
v3p0200c1s v5p0117c1s v5p0422c2s
Williams, M.C. and Seashore, C.E.
v5p0279c2s
Williams, M.F.S. v4p0386c1s
v4p0388c1s v4p0552c1s
Williams, M.G. v6p0347c2s
v6p0548c2s
Williams, M.M. v4p0134c1s
v4p0413c1s v5p0292c1s v5p0455c1s
v6p0155c1s
Williams, M.McC. v4p0317c1s
v4p0442c1s v5p0074c1s v5p0269c2s
Williams, M.P. v4p0089c1s
v4p0469c1s v5p0361c2s
Williams, M.S. v3p0444c1s
Williams, Martha M. v5p0267c2s
v6p0504c1s
Williams, Monier v4p0417c1s
Williams, N. v1p0662c1s
v5p0480c1s v5p0489c2s v5p0576c1s
Williams, N.M. v1p0047c2m
v1p0563c2s v1p0698c1s v1p0761c1s
v1p1017c1m v3p0066c2s
Williams, N.W. v4p0035c1s
v4p0092c1s v4p0189c1s v4p0241c1s
v4p0241c2s v4p0319c1s v4p0425c1s
v4p0551c2s v4p0562c1s v5p0036c1s
v5p0197c2s v5p0200c1s v5p0404c2s
v5p0532c1s v5p0555c2s v5p0556c2s
v5p0565c2s
Williams, Neil W. v5p0311c1s
Williams, Neil Wynn v5p0565c2s
Williams, O.C. v6p0212c2s
Williams, O.F. v6p0495c1s
Williams, P.S. v6p0383c1s
Williams, Prof. v1p0377c1s
v2p0190c1s
Williams, R. v1p0012c1s
v1p0159c1s v1p0264c2s v1p0543c2s
v1p0768c2s v1p1342c1m v2p0203c2s
v2p0460c2s v2p0468c1s
Williams, R.C. and Johnston, H.H.
v3p0004c1s
Williams, R.H. v3p0299c1s
v4p0453c1s v5p0613c2s v6p0635c1s
Williams, R.O. v1p0312c2s
v1p0395c1s v1p1062c2s v1p1101c2s
v1p1200c1s v1p1222c1s v1p1350c2s
v1p1355c2s v2p0371c1s v2p0403c2s
v3p0026c1s v3p0052c2s v3p0230c1s
v3p0239c1s v3p0412c2s
Williams, R.P. v1p0414c1s
v1p1078c1s v1p1290c2s v4p0472c2s
v5p0104c1s
Williams, R.P., Mrs. v5p0134c2s
Williams, R.R. v4p0036c1s
v6p0712c1s
Williams, S. v1p0610c2s
v1p1141c2s v1p1148c2s v1p1300c2s
v1p1322c2s v4p0239c2s
Williams, S. and Coolbrith, I.D.
v1p0082c2s
Williams, S., Mrs. v5p0614c1s
Williams, S.C. v4p0001c2s
v4p0137c1s
Williams, S.F. v1p0290c2s
v1p0291c1s v1p0793c1s v1p1167c2s
v2p0398c2s v3p0142c1s
Williams, S.G. v2p0194c1s
v2p0267c2s v4p0151c2s v4p0432c2s
v4p0507c2s
Williams, S.L. v6p0478c2s
Williams, S.M. v5p0245c2s
v6p0042c2s v6p0339c2s v6p0516c2s
v6p0554c2s v6p0593c1s
Williams, S.R. v5p0545c1s
Williams, S.W. v1p0009c2s
v1p0231c2s v1p0232c1s v1p0232c2m
v1p0233c1s v1p0234c2s v1p0235c1s
v1p0236c1m v1p0289c1s v1p0302c1s
v1p0638c1s v1p0678c1s v1p0830c1s
v1p0985c2s v1p1282c2s v5p0565c2s
v6p0285c1s
Williams, S.W.R. v4p0046c2s
Williams, T. v1p0320c2s
v1p1240c2s v3p0014c1s v3p0049c2s
v3p0302c2s v3p0326c1s v4p0104c2s
v4p0130c2s v4p0311c1s v4p0349c1s
v4p0478c1s v5p0028c2s v5p0034c1s
v5p0109c1s v5p0146c2s v5p0199c2s
v5p0206c1s v5p0381c1s v5p0383c2s
v5p0423c1s v5p0529c2s v5p0557c1m
v6p0015c1s v6p0160c2s v6p0206c2s
v6p0244c2s v6p0284c1s v6p0329c2s
v6p0352c2s v6p0407c2s v6p0430c1s
v6p0499c1m v6p0507c1s v6p0508c2s
v6p0560c1s v6p0573c1s v6p0576c2s
v6p0606c1s v6p0621c2s v6p0669c1s
v6p0692c2s
Williams, T. et al. v6p0170c2s
Williams, T.A. v3p0250c1s
v4p0330c2s
Williams, T.C. v2p0297c1s
v3p0472c1s v4p0108c1s v4p0133c1s
v4p0323c1s v4p0356c2s v4p0475c1s
v5p0277c1s v5p0485c2s v6p0132c1s
v6p0312c2s
Williams, T.H. v4p0623c1s
Williams, T.L. v3p0453c1s
Williams, T.M. v1p1032c1s
Williams, T.T. v6p0346c2s
Williams, Talcott v4p0438c1s
v6p0223c1s v6p0293c1s
Williams, W. v1p0669c2s
v1p0682c2s v2p0329c1s v2p0379c1s
v3p0333c1s v3p0372c1s v5p0154c2s
v5p0458c2s v6p0308c2s v6p0564c1s
Williams, W.C. v1p0487c1s
v6p0376c2s
Williams, W.F. v1p1167c1s
v3p0299c2s
Williams, W.G. v3p0007c1s
v3p0043c1s v3p0140c2s v4p0366c1s
Williams, W.G. et al. v3p0242c2s
Williams, W.H. v1p0687c2s
v1p0770c2s v2p0110c2s v5p0270c2s
v5p0459c1s
Williams, W.J. v5p0200c1s
v5p0462c2s
Williams, W.K. v3p0255c2s
Williams, W.L. v1p0851c1s
Williams, W.M. v1p0008c1s
v1p0044c1s v1p0055c2s v1p0399c2s
v1p0459c1s v1p0644c2m v1p0663c1s
v1p0663c2s v1p0664c1s v1p0666c1s
v1p0705c2s v1p0826c1s v1p0839c1s
v1p1006c2s v1p1162c1s v1p1306c2m
v1p1432c1s v2p0007c1m v2p0027c2s
v2p0047c2s v2p0089c2s v2p0090c1m
v2p0090c2s v2p0091c1s v2p0101c1s
v2p0124c2m v2p0136c2s v2p0137c1s
v2p0138c2s v2p0150c1s v2p0151c2s
v2p0157c1s v2p0158c1s v2p0173c2s
v2p0213c2s v2p0239c2s v2p0244c2s
v2p0296c2m v2p0317c1s v2p0336c1s
v2p0362c1s v2p0409c1s v2p0420c2s
v2p0424c2s v2p0425c1m v2p0459c1m
v2p0468c2s v2p0469c1s v3p0089c1s
v3p0089c2s v3p0098c2s v3p0167c1s
v3p0223c1s v3p0271c2s v3p0342c2s
v3p0382c2s v3p0397c1s v3p0409c1s
Williams, W.M.J. v4p0565c1m
v5p0120c2s v6p0150c1s v6p0270c2s
v6p0298c1s v6p0360c1s v6p0384c1s
v6p0385c1s v6p0385c2s v6p0541c1s
v6p0634c1s
Williams, W.R. v1p0977c1s
v1p1318c2s
Williams, W.W. v2p0322c2s
v2p0383c1s
Williams, Walker v6p0134c1s
Williamson and Russell ... v1p0502c2s
Williamson, A. v2p0079c1s
v3p0162c2s v4p0243c2s
Williamson, A.M. v6p0243c1s
Williamson, A.M. and
Williamson, C.N. v6p0012c1s
Williamson, A.W. v1p0539c1s
v2p0111c1s v3p0151c1s v3p0358c2s
Williamson, B. v6p0109c1s
Williamson, C.N. v4p0274c2s
v5p0301c1s v6p0699c2s
Williamson, C.N. and
Williamson, A.M. v6p0012c1s
Williamson, C.N., Mrs. ... v6p0699c2s
Williamson, D.B., Mrs. ... v5p0577c2s
Williamson, D.D. v1p1018c1s
Williamson, D.R. v1p1021c1s
Williamson, E.E. v6p0115c1s
v6p0348c2s v6p0451c1s
Williamson, E.S. v3p0126c2s
v5p0161c1s
Williamson, F. v4p0483c1s
v6p0710c2s
Williamson, F.S. and Davis, C.H.

v5p0184c1s
Williamson, G. v4p0337c1s
v6p0169c2s
Williamson, G.C. v3p0309c1s
v3p0372c2s v4p0091c1s v4p0495c1s
v5p0167c1s v5p0202c1s v5p0235c2s
v5p0351c2s v5p0552c1s v6p0148c1s
v6p0292c2s
Williamson, G.C. and Colles, W.M.
v6p0257c1s
Williamson, G.M. v5p0259c1s
Williamson, H. v1p0916c2s
v1p0965c2s
Williamson, H.M. v3p0016c1s
v3p0458c1s
Williamson, I.D. v1p0293c1s
v1p0684c1s v1p0761c1s v1p1203c2s
v1p1429c1s
Williamson, J. v1p0143c2s
v1p0165c2s v1p0281c1s v1p0618c1s
v1p0789c2s v1p1158c2s v1p1396c1s
v1p1412c1s v2p0272c2s v4p0070c2s
v4p0474c2s v5p0301c1s v5p0424c2s
Williamson, J.D. v1p0440c2m
v1p0486c2s v1p0789c2s v1p1094c2s
v1p1101c1s
Williamson, J.R. v4p0042c2s
Williamson, M.B. v5p0637c1s
v5p0638c1s
Williamson, M.B., Mrs. ... v4p0001c1s
v5p0155c1s
Williamson, Margaret M. .. v6p0631c2s
Williamson, Prof. v1p0982c1s
Williamson, R. v4p0498c1s
Williamson, R.B. and Klinck, J.H.
v5p0279c2s
Williamson, R.M. v6p0577c2s
Williamson, S. v1p1198c2s
v2p0005c2s v2p0096c1s v5p0212c2s
Williamson, S. and Patterson, R.H.
v1p1319c1s
Williamson, T. v2p0219c2s
Williamson, T.R. v4p0078c2s
Williamson, T.S. v1p0638c1s
Williamson, W.C. v1p0035c1s
v1p0102c2s v1p0208c1s v1p0267c1s
v1p0267c2s v1p0268c2s v1p0466c2s
v1p0470c2m v1p0750c1s v1p1156c1s
v1p1159c2s v1p1162c2s v1p1163c1s
v1p1212c1s v1p1236c1s v1p1239c1s
v1p1254c1s v2p0007c2s v2p0067c2s
v2p0458c1s v3p0334c1s v4p0541c2s
v6p0699c2s
Williamson, W.D. v1p0729c1m
v1p0777c2s
Williamson, W.E. v2p0338c1s
Williamson, W.H. v5p0067c2s
v6p0072c1s v6p0087c2s
Willian, J.N. v4p0505c1s
Williard, G.W. v1p0389c2s
v1p0514c2s
Willich, C.M. v1p0481c1s
v1p0550c1s
Willing, G.M. v1p0187c1s
Willing, J.F. v3p0054c2s
Willink, H.G. v2p0276c1s
Willis and Bray, W. v1p1122c2s
Willis, A. v1p1127c1s
Willis, A.I. v3p0188c1s
Willis, B. v1p0384c1s
v5p0078c2s v5p0094c1s v5p0601c1s
v6p0460c2s v6p0590c2s
Willis, B. and Hayes, C.W.
v4p0021c2s
Willis, Bailey v4p0032c2s
v6p0118c1s
Willis, C.W. v5p0383c1s
Willis, E.C. v1p0084c2s
v1p0998c1s v1p1337c2s v4p0044c2s
Willis, G.W. v1p0770c1s
Willis, H. v1p0110c2s
v1p0880c1s
Willis, H.A. v1p0203c1s
Willis, H.P. v4p0050c1s
v4p0059c1s v4p0059c2s v4p0138c2s
v4p0278c1m v4p0377c2s v4p0378c2m
v5p0046c1s v5p0046c2s v5p0093c1s
v5p0124c1m v5p0136c1s v5p0181c2s
v5p0382c2s v5p0391c2s v5p0408c2s
v5p0501c2s v5p0557c1m v5p0592c2s
v6p0141c1s v6p0152c2s v6p0159c2m
v6p0160c2s v6p0493c1m v6p0493c2s
v6p0523c1s
Willis, J. v6p0394c2s
Willis, J.B. and Farlow, A.
v5p0114c2s
Willis, J.C. v4p0019c2s
v4p0202c2s v4p0203c1s v4p0543c1s
v6p0554c1s
Willis, J.M. and Wells, H.L.
v5p0087c1m
Willis, L. v1p1022c2s
v2p0455c2s
Willis, N.P. v1p0112c2s
v1p0259c2s v1p0307c2s v1p0354c2s
v1p0405c1s v1p0460c2s v1p0716c2s
v1p0877c2s v1p1019c2s v1p1102c2s
v1p1257c1s v1p1313c1s
Willis, P. v5p0444c1s
v5p0556c2s
Willis, R.R. v6p0464c2s
Willis, R.S. v1p0161c1s
v1p1112c2s
Willis, S.T. v3p0346c2s
v5p0329c1m
Willis, T.F. v5p0135c1s
v5p0446c2s v5p0569c2s v5p0636c2s
v6p0495c2s
Willis, W. v1p0028c1s
v1p0483c2s v1p0692c2s v1p0784c1s
v1p0789c2m v1p0911c2s v1p0975c1s
v1p1164c2s
Willis, W.A. v3p0108c1s
v3p0353c2s v3p0417c1s
Willis-Burd, J.W. v3p0154c1m
Willison, J.S. v5p0421c2s
v6p0097c1s v6p0346c1s
Williston, A.L. v6p0464c2s
Williston, B., Sir v5p0353c1s
Williston, M.L. v1p1043c2s
Williston, S. v1p0598c2s
v3p0217c1s v6p0002c2s v6p0147c1m
v6p0489c2s v6p0540c1s
Williston, S.W. v1p0044c2s
v1p1041c2s v1p1084c1s v2p0046c2s
v3p0188c1s v3p0200c2s v3p0289c1s
v5p0096c2s v5p0142c1s v6p0174c1s
v6p0234c2s v6p0397c1m v6p0471c1s
v6p0504c1s v6p0520c2s v6p0539c2m
v6p0608c2s
Willits, A.B. v4p0065c1s
v5p0419c1s v5p0485c2s v5p0551c1s
Willmarth, J.W. v1p0095c2s
v1p0495c2s v1p1321c2s v3p0384c1s
v3p0467c1s v3p0469c1s v4p0127c2s
Willmer, F. v2p0243c1s
Willmot, A.B. v4p0414c2s
Willmott, R.A. v1p0753c2s
Willock, G.W. v5p0638c2s
Willock, H.B. v2p0364c1s
Willotte, M.H. v1p0377c1s
Willoughby, C.C. v5p0030c1s
v5p0462c1s v5p0463c2s v6p0053c1s
v6p0229c1s v6p0282c2s v6p0316c2m
v6p0317c1s v6p0369c2s v6p0412c1s
Willoughby, D. v3p0263c1s
Willoughby, E.F. v1p0487c2s
v1p1209c1s v2p0080c2s v4p0285c1s
Willoughby, H. v3p0027c2s
Willoughby, J. v3p0270c2s
Willoughby, J., Sir v4p0360c1s
Willoughby, J.C. v5p0302c1s
Willoughby, J.M. v6p0218c2s
Willoughby, W.F. v3p0408c1s
v3p0442c2s v4p0187c1s v4p0425c2s
v4p0593c2s v5p0047c1s v5p0273c1s
v5p0289c2s v5p0320c2m v5p0321c1s
v5p0396c1s v5p0598c1m v5p0602c1s
v5p0641c1s v6p0203c1s v6p0357c1s
v6p0510c1s
Willoughby, W.F. and
Graffenried, C.De v3p0077c2s
Willoughby, W.F. and
Willoughby, W.W. v3p0442c1s
Willoughby, W.J. v5p0321c1s
Willoughby, W.W. v4p0140c2m
v4p0252c1s v5p0131c1s v5p0457c2s
v5p0550c1s v6p0017c2m v6p0507c1s
Willoughby, W.W. and
Willoughby, W.F. v3p0442c1s
Wills, A. v1p0863c2s
v1p1053c1s
Wills, A.W. v1p0049c1s
Wills, B. v3p0023c2s
Wills, C. v1p1030c1s
v2p0045c2s
Wills, C.J. v3p0023c2s
v3p0069c2s v3p0284c1s v3p0470c2s
Wills, Evelyn v5p0499c1s
Wills, F. v2p0281c2s
Wills, F.L. v5p0507c1s
Wills, Frances L. v5p0507c1s
Wills, G.E. v6p0460c2s
Wills, J. v1p1432c2m
v2p0271c1s
Wills, J.C. v4p0436c1s
Wills, J.T. v2p0140c2s
v3p0136c2s v5p0043c1s v5p0093c1s
v5p0181c1s
Wills, L.M. v5p0044c2s
Wills, T. v1p0955c2s
v3p0089c2s v3p0167c2s
Wills, W.A. v4p0006c1s
Wills, W.G. v1p0334c2s
v2p0123c1s
Wills, W.H. v1p0090c2s
v1p0322c1s v1p0471c2s v1p0519c2s
v1p0623c2s v1p0923c2s v1p1337c1s
Willsie, H. v6p0058c2s
Willson, B. v5p0244c2s
v5p0275c1m v5p0327c1s v5p0347c1s
v5p0409c1s v5p0476c1s v6p0202c2s
Willson, E.B. v1p0338c2s
v1p1302c2s v4p0016c1s
Willson, M.J. v6p0098c1s
Willson, R.W. v3p0166c2s
v3p0228c1s v3p0264c1s
Willson, R.W. and Peirce, B.O.
v3p0036c1s v4p0355c1s v4p0529c1s
Willson, S.A. v2p0005c1s
v2p0035c1s v2p0055c1s v2p0101c2s
v2p0171c2s v2p0196c2s v2p0202c1s
v2p0238c1s v2p0289c1s v2p0343c1s
v2p0469c1s v3p0056c2s v3p0153c1s
v3p0188c1s v3p0196c1s v3p0234c1s
v3p0286c1s v3p0292c1s v3p0295c2s
v3p0374c2m v3p0376c2s v3p0383c1s
v3p0429c2s v3p0460c1s v3p0461c1s
v3p0474c2s
Willson, T.B. v2p0441c1s
v3p0231c1s v4p0612c2s v5p0580c1s
Willson, T.E. v4p0167c2s
Willson, T.L. and Suckert, J.J.
v4p0002c2s v4p0089c1s
Willson, T.R. v4p0232c2s
Willson, Z.G. v1p0385c2s
v1p0426c2s v1p0594c1s v1p0724c2s
Willyoung, E.G. v4p0176c1s
v4p0219c1s v4p0481c2s v4p0568c2s
Willyoung, E.G. and Sayen, H.L.
v5p0125c1s v5p0492c1s
Wilm, E.C. v6p0212c1s
Wilmar, C.B. v5p0171c1s
Wilmarth, J.W. v1p0834c1s
v1p0849c2s v1p1057c1s
Wilmer, H. v4p0440c2s
Wilmer, J. v1p0307c2s
v1p0495c1s v1p0857c1s v1p1280c2s
v1p1297c1s
Wilmer, L.A. v1p1174c2s
Wilmer, P.B. v2p0252c2s
Wilmer, W. v3p0036c2s
v3p0086c2s v3p0116c2s v3p0189c1s
Wilmerding, C.W. v2p0364c2s
Wilmeth, C.M. v2p0152c1s
Wilmot, A. v1p0011c2s
v1p0012c1s
Wilmot, A. and Wirgman, A.T.
v6p0099c2s
Wilmot, R.J. v1p0819c1s
v2p0303c2s
Wilmot, S.E. v3p0383c1s
v5p0246c2s
Wilmot, T. v4p0630c2s
Wilmot, V. v5p0486c2s
v6p0407c2s
Wilner, M.M. v6p0096c1s
v6p0098c2s v6p0210c2s
Wilse, A.B. v6p0460c2s
Wilson, A. v1p0041c2m
v1p0042c2m v1p0044c2s v1p0049c1s
v1p0134c2m v1p0137c1s v1p0156c1s
v1p0157c1s v1p0170c1s v1p0311c1s
v1p0327c2s v1p0333c2s v1p0340c1s
v1p0341c1m v1p0346c1s v1p0347c1s
v1p0358c1s v1p0373c1s v1p0375c2s
v1p0435c1s v1p0446c2s v1p0449c2s
v1p0466c2s v1p0470c1s v1p0520c2s
v1p0587c1s v1p0591c1s v1p0645c1s
v1p0681c2s v1p0701c2s v1p0745c1s
v1p0749c1m v1p0837c2s v1p0843c2s
v1p0852c1s v1p0856c2s v1p0877c2s
v1p0898c2s v1p0900c2s v1p0907c1s
v1p0936c2s v1p0967c1s v1p1004c2s
v1p1030c1s v1p1050c2s v1p1059c1s
v1p1101c2s v1p1131c1s v1p1163c2s
v1p1233c1s v1p1234c2s v1p1236c1s
v1p1244c1s v1p1280c1s v1p1403c1s
v1p1419c1s v1p1441c1m v2p0013c1s
v2p0015c1s v2p0046c1m v2p0050c1s
v2p0093c2s v2p0110c2s v2p0118c2s
v2p0119c2s v2p0123c1s v2p0130c1s
v2p0133c1s v2p0138c2s v2p0160c2s
v2p0175c2s v2p0177c2s v2p0199c1s
v2p0257c2s v2p0259c2s v2p0261c2s
v2p0274c2s v2p0291c2s v2p0295c1s
v2p0302c2s v2p0307c2s v2p0322c2s
v2p0328c2s v2p0341c1s v2p0344c1s
v2p0404c2s v2p0409c2s v2p0442c1s
v3p0150c1s v3p0216c1s v3p0233c1s
v4p0058c2s v4p0094c1s v4p0255c2s
v4p0299c1s v4p0327c2s v4p0500c1s
v5p0075c1s v5p0133c2s v5p0254c2s
v5p0394c2s v5p0441c2s v6p0198c2s
v6p0583c2s
Wilson, A., Dr.
v4p0336c1s
Wilson, A.D. v6p0173c1s
Wilson, A.E. v3p0050c1s
v4p0317c1s
Wilson, A.J. v1p0015c1s
v1p0079c2s v1p0087c1s v1p0092c2s
v1p0177c1s v1p0219c1s v1p0283c1s
v1p0299c2s v1p0395c2s v1p0414c1s
v1p0465c2s v1p0491c2s v1p0630c2s
v1p0832c2s v1p1038c2s v1p1057c1s
v1p1086c2s v1p1136c2s v1p1230c1s
v1p1331c2s v1p1383c2s v1p1401c1s
v2p0114c1s v2p0164c2s v2p0186c2s
v2p0218c2s v2p0306c2s v2p0407c1s
v3p0032c1s v5p0093c1s v5p0248c1s
v5p0399c1s v6p0143c2s
Wilson, A.M. v4p0147c2s
v6p0660c1s
Wilson, A.S. v1p0107c1s
v3p0039c2s v3p0045c1s v3p0109c2s
v3p0462c1s v4p0203c2m v4p0204c1m
v4p0210c1s v4p0217c2s v4p0285c2m
v4p0295c2s v4p0458c2s v4p0513c1s
v5p0299c1s v5p0329c1s v5p0389c1s

v5p0423c1s v5p0518c2s
v6p0503c1s
Wilson, Alice L. v4p0520c1s
v4p0603c1s
Wilson, Andrew, Dr. v6p0376c1s
Wilson, Anne C. v4p0281c1s
Wilson, Annie E. v3p0235c2s
v3p0236c1s
Wilson, Annie G. v4p0423c2s
Wilson, Archibald v6p0108c1s
Wilson, B. v5p0408c2s
v5p0421c1s
Wilson, B. and Farrington, F.L.
v5p0328c2s
Wilson, B.M. v6p0636c2s
Wilson, C. v1p0007c2s
v1p0558c2s v1p0749c2s v1p1255c1s
v2p0111c1s v3p0099c2s v3p0363c1s
v4p0008c1s v4p0144c1s v6p0703c2s
Wilson, C., Sir v2p0410c2s
Wilson, C.B. v2p0220c1s
v4p0216c1s v4p0223c2s v5p0331c2s
v6p0091c2s
Wilson, C.B. et al. v5p0170c2s
Wilson, C.C. v2p0385c2s
v5p0513c2s
Wilson, C.D. v4p0043c1s
v4p0072c1s v4p0128c1s v4p0137c2s
v4p0159c1s v4p0163c1s v4p0206c1s
v4p0217c1s v4p0362c2s v4p0468c2s
v4p0627c2s v5p0020c2s v5p0157c1s
v5p0341c2s v5p0364c2m v5p0426c2s
v5p0565c2s v5p0608c2s v6p0069c2s
v6p0410c2s v6p0523c2s v6p0597c1s
v6p0642c1s
Wilson, C.E. v2p0242c2s
v2p0324c2s v2p0336c2s v4p0390c1s
Wilson, C.E.A. v6p0663c2s
Wilson, C.G. et al. v4p0081c1s
v4p0108c1s
Wilson, C.H. v1p0063c1s
v1p0068c2s v1p0190c2s v1p0340c1s
v1p0671c2s v1p0874c1s v2p0450c2s
v5p0011c2s v5p0032c1m v5p0049c2s
v5p0252c2s v5p0255c2s v5p0296c2s
v5p0398c2s v5p0505c2s v5p0587c1s
v5p0587c2m v5p0614c2s v6p0007c1s
v6p0031c1s v6p0035c1m v6p0054c1s
v6p0248c1s v6p0448c2s v6p0462c1s
v6p0530c1s
Wilson, C.M. v2p0381c2s
Wilson, C.R. v5p0145c1s
Wilson, C.T.R. v6p0143c2s
v6p0199c1s
Wilson, C.U. v5p0007c2s
Wilson, C.W. v2p0067c2s
v3p0004c2s v3p0023c2s v3p0184c2s
v3p0434c1s v5p0007c1s v5p0371c1s
v6p0255c1s
Wilson, C.W., Sir v3p0305c2s
Wilson, D. v1p0018c1s
v1p0028c1s v1p0028c2s v1p0088c2s
v1p0106c1s v1p0162c2s v1p0170c1s
v1p0210c2m v1p0276c1s v1p0287c2s
v1p0300c1s v1p0300c2s v1p0312c1m
v1p0515c1s v1p0536c1s v1p0587c1s
v1p0592c1s v1p0617c1s v1p0636c2m
v1p0638c2s v1p0701c2s v1p0752c2s
v1p0844c1s v1p0896c2s v1p0912c2s
v1p1071c2s v1p1072c2s v1p1073c1m
v1p1103c1s v1p1105c2s v1p1108c1s
v1p1132c1s v1p1168c2s v1p1183c1s
v1p1204c1m v1p1271c1m v1p1316c2s
v1p1419c1s v1p1422c2s v6p0121c2s
v6p0147c2s v6p0165c2s v6p0579c2s
Wilson, D.H. v6p0094c1s
v6p0101c2s v6p0188c2s v6p0218c1s
v6p0307c2s v6p0484c2s v6p0682c1s
Wilson, D.J. and McCarthy, J.
v1p0599c2s
Wilson, D.L. v2p0244c2m
Wilson, D.M. v1p1121c2s
v2p0380c1s v5p0211c2s
Wilson, D.T. v6p0613c2s
Wilson, Dr. v1p0946c2s
v1p1046c1s
Wilson, E. v1p0660c1s
v1p1032c1s v1p1099c1s v4p0038c1s
v4p0250c2s v5p0178c2s v5p0273c1s
v5p0380c1s v5p0628c2s v5p0639c1s
v6p0228c2s
Wilson, E.B. v1p1098c2s
v3p0193c2s v3p0205c2s v5p0062c1s
v5p0400c1s v6p0022c2s v6p0172c1s
v6p0321c1s v6p0401c1s v6p0410c1s
v6p0585c2m
Wilson, E.B., Prof. v5p0469c1s
Wilson, E.C. v5p0352c1s
v5p0640c1s
Wilson, E.D. v6p0373c1s
Wilson, E.D.J. v1p0012c2s
v1p0208c1s v1p0478c2s v1p0491c1s
v1p0538c1s v1p0543c2m v1p0550c1s
v1p0578c1s v1p0657c2s v1p0659c1s
v1p0661c1s v1p0662c1s v1p0936c1s
v1p0973c2s v1p0976c1s v1p1352c2s
Wilson, E.D.J. et al. v1p0657c1s
Wilson, E.E. v4p0470c1s
v6p0446c2s
Wilson, E.F. v4p0409c1s
Wilson, E.L. v2p0337c2s
v3p0131c1s v3p0166c1m v3p0228c2s
v3p0305c2s v3p0316c2s v3p0318c1m
v3p0328c2s v3p0350c1s v3p0394c1m
v3p0456c2s
Wilson, E.S. v1p0074c2s
v1p0104c2s v1p0312c2s v1p0794c2s
v1p1325c1s v3p0218c1s
Wilson, E.T. v1p0836c1s
Wilson, E.V. v4p0045c2s
v4p0064c1s v4p0201c2s v4p0551c1s
Wilson, E.Y. v4p0485c2s
v4p0605c2s
Wilson, Ernest v6p0014c1s
Wilson, F. v1p0096c1s
v3p0220c1s v4p0305c1s v4p0333c2s
v4p0415c2s v5p0240c1s v5p0511c1s
v6p0223c1s v6p0339c2m
Wilson, F.B. v4p0095c2s
v4p0123c2s v4p0221c2s v4p0439c2s
Wilson, F.C. v1p0026c1s
Wilson, F.H. et al. v5p0603c1s
Wilson, F.J. v5p0491c2s
Wilson, F.L. v5p0081c2s
Wilson, F.M. v4p0276c1s
v4p0319c1s v4p0486c1s
Wilson, F.R. v2p0298c1s
Wilson, G. v1p0049c1s
v1p0224c1s v1p0278c2s v1p0362c2s
v1p0965c2s v1p1209c2s v1p1434c1s
v3p0210c1s v3p0394c2s v4p0616c2s
Wilson, G.A. v5p0447c1s
Wilson, G.B. v6p0334c2s
Wilson, G.G. v4p0532c1s
v6p0445c2s v6p0668c2s
Wilson, G.L. v3p0273c1s
Wilson, G.R. v6p0164c1s
Wilson, G.S. v2p0219c1s
v5p0029c1s v5p0038c1s
Wilson, G.W. v5p0107c1s
Wilson, H. v1p0306c2s
v1p0749c2s v1p0783c2s v1p1099c2s
v1p1134c1s v1p1217c2s v1p1243c2s
v1p1246c2s v1p1280c2s v2p0048c1s
v2p0051c2s v2p0151c1s v2p0182c2s
v2p0255c2s v2p0320c2s v2p0351c1s
v2p0417c1s v2p0464c2s v2p0467c2s
v3p0093c2s v4p0320c2s v4p0440c1s
v4p0496c2s v5p0128c2s v5p0187c2s
v6p0232c2s v6p0507c2s v6p0569c2s
v6p0601c2s
Wilson, H.B. v6p0630c2s
Wilson, H.C. v2p0095c1s
v2p0095c2m v2p0123c1s v2p0417c1s
v2p0417c2s v3p0093c2s v3p0094c1s
v3p0269c1s v4p0034c1s v4p0126c2m
v4p0306c2s v4p0357c2s v4p0396c1s
v4p0447c1m v4p0557c1m v5p0035c1m
v5p0074c2s v5p0174c2m v5p0202c1s
v5p0372c1m v5p0402c1m v5p0455c1s
v5p0549c2m v5p0556c1s v6p0261c2s
v6p0446c1s v6p0497c1s v6p0571c1s
v6p0613c2m v6p0614c2m v6p0625c2s
Wilson, H.C. and Barnard, E.E.
v2p0239c2s
Wilson, H.C. and Burnham, S.W.
v2p0417c1s
Wilson, H.C.N. v4p0142c1s
v4p0551c1s v4p0562c1s v6p0144c1s
Wilson, H.F. v3p0144c1s
v3p0275c1s v4p0026c2s v4p0189c2s
v4p0202c1s v4p0577c2s
Wilson, H.H. v2p0132c2s
v2p0240c1s v6p0351c1s
Wilson, H.J. v6p0002c2s
v6p0446c2s
Wilson, H.K. v1p0948c1s
v1p1103c1s
Wilson, H.L. v2p0436c1s
v5p0081c1s v5p0313c1s v5p0363c2s
v5p0373c1s v6p0014c1s v6p0562c1s
Wilson, H.M. v3p0223c2s
v3p0286c1s v4p0292c2s v4p0380c1s
v5p0214c1s v5p0460c1s v5p0622c2s
Wilson, H.N. v5p0139c2s
Wilson, H.S. v1p0024c2s
v1p0025c1s v1p0025c2s v1p0040c2s
v1p0062c1s v1p0116c2s v1p0150c1s
v1p0514c2s v1p0519c2s v1p0530c2m
v1p0531c1s v1p0531c2s v1p0680c1s
v1p0784c2s v1p0812c1s v1p0877c1s
v1p0941c2s v1p1073c2s v1p1156c2s
v1p1160c1s v1p1185c1s v1p1186c1s
v1p1322c1s v1p1397c1s v1p1440c2s
v2p0009c1s v2p0093c2s v2p0100c2s
v2p0118c1s v2p0122c1s v2p0139c1s
v2p0181c1s v2p0193c1s v2p0282c2s
v2p0311c1s v2p0384c1s v2p0387c2s
v2p0398c2s v2p0401c1s v2p0422c1s
v2p0428c2s v2p0448c2s v2p0465c1m
v3p0062c2s v3p0067c2s v3p0124c2s
v3p0175c2m v3p0237c2s v3p0381c2s
v3p0387c1s v3p0388c2s v3p0389c1s
v3p0426c1s v4p0046c2s v4p0089c2s
v4p0122c1s v4p0198c1s v4p0211c2s
v4p0229c2m v4p0243c1s v4p0313c1s
v4p0325c2s v4p0371c1s v4p0422c1s
v4p0517c2s v4p0544c1s v4p0572c1s
v4p0591c2s v4p0629c1s v5p0140c2s
v5p0174c1s v5p0365c2s v5p0374c1s
v5p0475c2s v5p0497c2s v5p0528c1s
v6p0259c2s
Wilson, H.Schultz v4p0088c1s
Wilson, H.Schutz v1p1437c1s
v2p0181c2s v2p0431c1s v4p0088c1s
v5p0237c1s v5p0624c2s v6p0588c1s
v6p0612c2s
Wilson, H.V. v4p0542c2s
v6p0611c1s
Wilson, H.W. v4p0022c2s
v4p0047c2s v4p0142c1m v4p0236c2s
v4p0237c2s v4p0238c1m v4p0297c2s
v4p0395c2s v4p0581c2s v4p0610c1s
v5p0028c2s v5p0050c1s v5p0054c1s
v5p0136c2s v5p0190c1s v5p0231c2m
v5p0243c1s v5p0246c1m v5p0246c2m
v5p0247c2s v5p0249c1s v5p0263c1s
v5p0302c2s v5p0308c2s v5p0345c1s
v5p0356c2s v5p0401c1s v5p0401c2m
v5p0433c1s v5p0508c1m v5p0508c2s
v5p0543c2s v5p0587c2s v5p0588c2m
v5p0592c2s v5p0598c2s v5p0618c1s
v6p0049c1s v6p0133c2m v6p0175c1s
v6p0235c1s v6p0254c2s v6p0266c1s
v6p0268c1s v6p0268c2m v6p0269c1s
v6p0337c1s v6p0429c2s v6p0442c1s
v6p0445c1s v6p0494c2s v6p0530c1s
v6p0560c2s v6p0572c2s v6p0580c1s
Wilson, H.W. and Taylor, B.
v5p0600c1s
Wilson, H.W.A. v5p0416c2s
Wilson, Henry v5p0223c1s
Wilson, Holt v1p0826c2s
v2p0453c2s
Wilson, I. v5p0288c1s
Wilson, J. v1p0101c1s
v1p0135c1s v1p0136c1s v1p0164c2s
v1p0208c1s v1p0223c1s v1p0245c2s
v1p0305c2s v1p0335c2s v1p0351c2s
v1p0368c2m v1p0397c2s v1p0433c1s
v1p0539c2s v1p0561c2s v1p0564c1s
v1p0577c1s v1p0596c2s v1p0697c1s
v1p0814c1s v1p0837c1s v1p0866c2s
v1p0924c2s v1p0949c1m v1p0949c2s
v1p1032c1s v1p1046c1s v1p1146c1s
v1p1209c2s v1p1263c1s v1p1273c2s
v1p1339c2s v1p1416c1s v1p1432c1s
v2p0217c1s v2p0391c2s v3p0066c1s
v5p0030c1s v5p0559c2s v6p0101c2s
v6p0262c2s v6p0329c1s v6p0329c2s
v6p0420c2s v6p0470c2s v6p0580c2s
Wilson, J. et al. v1p0214c2s
Wilson, J.A. v1p0037c2s
v1p0236c2s v1p0351c2s v1p0519c2s
v1p0619c1s v1p0675c2m v1p0676c1s
v1p0776c1s v1p0859c2s v1p0880c1s
v1p0886c2s v1p1081c2s v1p1144c1s
v1p1177c2s v1p1308c1s v1p1326c2s
v2p0068c1s v2p0069c2s v2p0077c1s
v2p0163c2s v2p0230c1s v2p0300c2s
v2p0304c2s v2p0333c2s v2p0357c2s
v2p0393c2s v2p0438c2s
Wilson, J.B. v4p0047c2s
v6p0519c1s
Wilson, J.C. v3p0443c2s
v5p0459c1s
Wilson, J.D. v1p1044c1s
v4p0291c2s v4p0322c2m v4p0357c1s
v4p0509c1m v5p0494c1s v5p0515c1s
v5p0586c2s v6p0364c1s
Wilson, J.F. v3p0352c1s
v4p0333c1s v6p0003c1s v6p0004c2s
v6p0111c1s v6p0219c1s v6p0310c2s
v6p0430c2s v6p0662c2s
Wilson, J.G. v1p0103c2m
v1p0119c1s v1p0154c1s v1p0160c1s
v1p0168c1s v1p0171c2s v1p0179c1s
v1p0201c1s v1p0215c2m v1p0271c2s
v1p0330c1s v1p0362c2s v1p0429c1s
v1p0444c2s v1p0504c1s v1p0505c1s
v1p0557c2s v1p0567c1s v1p0712c1s
v1p0891c1s v1p0894c2s v1p0989c2s
v1p0995c1s v1p1088c1m v1p1186c2s
v1p1259c2s v1p1337c1m v1p1369c1s
v1p1400c1s v1p1402c1s v1p1411c1s
v3p0108c1m v3p0285c1s v3p0319c2s
v4p0126c1s v4p0248c1s v4p0268c1s
v4p0343c2s v4p0400c2s v4p0401c1m
v4p0418c1s v4p0509c2s v4p0623c1s
v5p0242c1s v5p0271c1s v5p0455c2s
v5p0481c1s v5p0574c2s v6p0278c1s
v6p0294c2s v6p0590c2s v6p0656c2s
Wilson, J.G., Gen. v6p0686c2s
Wilson, J.H. v1p0059c2s
v1p1345c1s v2p0092c2s v2p0184c2s
v2p0263c2s v2p0292c1s v5p0108c2s
v5p0306c2s v5p0486c2s v5p0601c2s
v6p0050c2s v6p0186c2s v6p0521c2s
v6p0618c2s
Wilson, J.H. and Stedman, W.P.
v3p0111c2s
Wilson, J.H. et al. v3p0138c1s
Wilson, J.K. v6p0509c1s
Wilson, J.L. v1p0011c2s
v1p0012c1s v1p0289c2s v1p0561c2s
v1p1272c1s v2p0004c1s
Wilson, J.M. v1p0077c2s
v1p0161c2s v1p0162c1s v1p0510c1s
v1p1080c1s v2p0083c2s v2p0085c1s
v3p0378c2s v3p0434c1s v4p0506c2s

v6p0326c1s v6p0538c2s
Wilson, J.M. et al. v4p0170c1s
Wilson, J.P. v1p0253c1s
v1p1312c1s v6p0467c1s
Wilson, J.P., Miss v6p0168c1s
Wilson, J.R. v6p0054c2s
v6p0697c1s
Wilson, J.W. v6p0640c2s
Wilson, J., Prof. v1p0182c1s
Wilson, James v1p0039c1s
v6p0690c2s
Wilson, James M. v6p0191c2s
Wilson, Jas. v6p0690c2s
Wilson, John v1p0041c1s
Wilson, K. v6p0099c1s
Wilson, L. v2p0013c2s
v2p0197c2s
Wilson, L.G. v3p0031c2s
v3p0200c2s v4p0391c2s v6p0416c1s
Wilson, L.L.W. v5p0400c2s
Wilson, L.N. v5p0106c1s
v6p0115c2m v6p0129c2s v6p0400c1s
Wilson, Lucia W. v5p0555c1s
Wilson, M. v1p0354c1s
v1p0595c1s v1p0720c1s v1p0877c1s
v2p0096c2s v5p0641c1s v6p0184c2s
Wilson, M.C. v3p0016c2s
Wilson, M.F. v2p0030c2s
v3p0210c1s v3p0462c1s v5p0559c1s
Wilson, Mona v5p0187c2s
v6p0319c1s
Wilson, Mr. v5p0530c2s
Wilson, N. v3p0095c2s
Wilson, P. v5p0280c1s
v6p0326c1s v6p0663c2s
Wilson, P.B. v1p1197c2s
Wilson, Prof. v1p0664c2s
v1p0849c1s
Wilson, R. v1p0033c1s
v1p0033c2s v1p0615c1s v1p0617c1s
v1p0807c2s v1p0808c1s v1p0881c1s
v1p0962c2s v1p1225c2m v2p0178c1s
v2p0478c1s v4p0570c2s v6p0096c2s
v6p0320c1s v6p0399c1s v6p0455c2s
Wilson, R., Rev. v5p0405c1s
Wilson, R.B. v2p0201c2s
v3p0246c1m v3p0310c2s v4p0275c2s
v5p0019c1s v5p0559c1s
Wilson, R.D. v2p0022c1s
v3p0041c2s v5p0174c1s v6p0061c1s
v6p0285c2s v6p0482c2s
Wilson, R.E. v2p0384c2s
v3p0436c2s v6p0079c2s
Wilson, R.K. v4p0259c1s
v5p0286c2s v5p0500c2s v6p0313c2s
v6p0423c2s
Wilson, R.K., Sir v4p0324c1s
Wilson, R.P.C. et al. v4p0434c1s
Wilson, R.R. v3p0017c2s
v4p0011c2s v4p0084c1s v4p0168c2s
v4p0214c2s v4p0225c1s v4p0249c1s
v4p0300c2s v4p0371c1s v4p0404c1s
v4p0484c2s v4p0510c2s v4p0620c2s
v5p0040c2s v5p0259c1s v5p0339c1s
v5p0472c2s v5p0572c2s v5p0589c1s
v5p0599c1s v5p0603c1s v5p0620c2m
v6p0069c2s v6p0101c2s v6p0148c2s
v6p0468c1s v6p0513c1s v6p0598c1s
v6p0662c1s v6p0692c1s
Wilson, R.R. and Whelpley, J.D.
v5p0586c1s
Wilson, R.W. v6p0301c2s
v6p0598c1s
Wilson, R.W. and Peirce, B.O.
v4p0529c1s
Wilson, S. v1p0464c1s
v1p0499c1s v1p0610c1s v2p0078c1s
v3p0055c1s v3p0083c2s v3p0084c1s
v3p0216c2s v4p0113c2s v5p0106c2s
v5p0118c2s v5p0272c1s v5p0402c1s
Wilson, S., Sir v2p0186c2s
Wilson, S., Sir and Burrows, M.
v2p0215c2s
Wilson, S.A. v3p0460c1s
Wilson, S.C. v6p0304c1s
Wilson, S.D. v2p0074c1s
v3p0268c1s
Wilson, S.G. v4p0081c1s
v4p0497c2s v4p0615c2s v5p0088c1s
v5p0531c1s v6p0030c2s
Wilson, S.S. v1p0096c1s
Wilson, S.W. v5p0422c1s
Wilson, Sarah v5p0044c2s
v5p0226c1s v5p0227c1s v5p0260c1s
v5p0268c2s v5p0561c1s v5p0620c1s
v6p0030c2s v6p0139c2s v6p0345c1s
Wilson, T. v3p0019c2s
v3p0055c2s v3p0172c1s v3p0342c2m
v3p0396c2s v4p0016c2s v4p0020c1s
v4p0189c1s v4p0204c1m v4p0210c1s
v4p0444c1s v4p0456c2s v4p0468c2s
v5p0022c2s v5p0463c2s v5p0628c2s
Wilson, T.B. v6p0130c1s
v6p0685c2s v6p0711c1s
Wilson, T.D. v1p0664c1s
Wilson, T.H. v3p0231c1s
v3p0305c2s v3p0414c1s v4p0052c2s
v4p0267c1s v4p0444c1s v4p0585c2s
v6p0461c1s
Wilson, T.M. v4p0334c1s
Wilson, T.W. v1p1349c2s
Wilson, V. v4p0381c2s
Wilson, W. v1p0540c1s
v2p0192c1s v2p0452c1s v3p0003c1s
v3p0028c2s v3p0114c2s v3p0137c2s
v3p0337c2m v3p0396c1s v3p0441c2s
v4p0014c2s v4p0016c1s v4p0039c1s
v4p0041c2s v4p0116c1s v4p0119c1s
v4p0238c1s v4p0240c1s v4p0259c1s
v4p0335c1s v4p0459c1m v4p0530c1s
v4p0584c1s v4p0598c1s v5p0017c1s
v5p0043c1s v5p0083c2s v5p0123c1s
v5p0158c1s v5p0221c2s v5p0275c2s
v5p0356c2s v5p0436c1s v5p0480c2s
v5p0599c2s v5p0602c1s v5p0628c1s
v6p0306c2s v6p0516c2s v6p0668c1s
v6p0692c2s
Wilson, W.B. v6p0088c2s
Wilson, W.C. v1p0579c2s
v1p1233c1s
Wilson, W.D. v1p0171c1s
v1p0305c1s v1p0309c2s v1p0434c2s
v1p0528c2s v1p0641c2s v1p0692c1s
v1p0794c1s v1p0848c1s v1p0868c2s
v1p0972c2s v1p0999c2m v1p1025c2s
v1p1029c2s v1p1062c1s v1p1235c1s
v1p1398c2s v2p0042c1s v2p0129c1s
v2p0274c2s v2p0369c1s v3p0040c2s
v3p0238c2s v3p0258c2s v3p0359c2m
Wilson, W.E. v2p0191c1s
v2p0333c1s v3p0112c2s v3p0139c2s
v3p0184c2s v3p0330c1s v3p0366c2s
v4p0287c1s v4p0556c1s v4p0557c1s
v6p0613c2s
Wilson, W.H. v1p0997c2s
v1p1329c2s
Wilson, W.L. v4p0152c2s
v4p0278c1s v4p0475c2s v4p0563c1s
v4p0563c2s v5p0567c1s v6p0165c2s
v6p0235c1s v6p0277c1s v6p0303c1s
v6p0407c1s
Wilson, W.L. and Reed, T.B.
v4p0595c2s
Wilson, W.L. et al. v4p0567c1s
Wilson, W.P. v2p0344c1s
v4p0583c1s v5p0443c1m v5p0480c2s
v6p0140c2s v6p0493c2s v6p0494c2s
Wilson, W.R.A. v4p0035c1s
v5p0213c1s
Wilson, W.S. v3p0304c1s
Wilson, W.W. v5p0588c2s
v6p0544c2s
Wilson, W.W.W. v4p0397c1s
Wilson, Woodrow v4p0611c2s
v6p0516c2s
Wilson, Z.G. . v1p0385c2s v1p0426c2s
Wilson-Barker, D. v4p0120c1s
Wilson-Woodrow, N. v6p0311c1s
Wilstach, J.W. v3p0125c1s
v3p0130c2s v4p0224c2s v5p0325c2s
Wilstach, P. v5p0161c1s
v5p0167c1s v5p0497c2s v6p0180c2s
v6p0181c2s v6p0391c1s v6p0578c2s
v6p0640c2s
Wilsted, R. v5p0567c2s
v6p0001c1s
Wilt, A.D., jr. v6p0616c1s
v6p0649c2s
Wiltbank, E.W. v1p0504c2s
Wiltbank, W.W. v1p1345c2s
v1p1406c1s
Wiltberger, B.P. v4p0603c2s
Wilton, C. v1p0978c2s
Wilton, E. v1p0035c1s
v1p0120c1s v1p0125c1s
Wilton, G.W. v4p0211c1s
v4p0237c1s v6p0128c2s
Wilton, R. v1p1144c1s
Wilton, W. v5p0414c2s
Wiltse, H.M. v5p0015c2s
v5p0562c2s
Wiltse, S.E. v4p0103c1s
Wiltse, Sara E. v4p0103c1s
Wiltshire, F.H. v4p0566c1s
Wiltze, H.M. v6p0472c2s
Wiman, C. v4p0235c1s
Wiman, E. v3p0006c2s
v3p0055c1s v3p0064c2s v3p0065c1m
v3p0149c2s v3p0384c1s v4p0085c1s
v4p0086c1s v4p0108c1s v4p0175c1s
v4p0176c2s v4p0199c1m v4p0261c2s
v4p0313c1s v4p0475c2s v4p0478c1s
v4p0564c1s v6p0096c1s
Wiman, H.D. v3p0376c1s
Wimberly, F.C. v5p0028c1s
Wimborne, C. v5p0489c2s
v5p0490c1s v6p0126c1m v6p0191c1s
Wimborne, C. et al. v6p0126c1s
Wimmer, H. v1p0262c1s
v1p0389c1s v1p0518c1s
Wimperis, E.M. v4p0613c1s
Wimperis, H.E. v6p0412c2s
Wimshurst, J. v3p0214c2s
Winand, P.A.N. v4p0174c2s
Winans, E.B. v4p0595c2s
Winans, W. v5p0156c2s
v5p0487c1s
Winbolt, S.E. v3p0316c1m
Winbott, S.E. v3p0368c1s
Winch, F.W. v6p0055c2s
Winch, G.W. v6p0419c2s
Winch, W.H. v6p0503c2s
Winchell, A. v1p0045c2s
v1p0071c1s v1p0073c2s v1p0265c1s
v1p0295c2s v1p0434c1s v1p0469c2s
v1p0507c1s v1p0528c2m v1p0618c1s
v1p0794c1s v1p0810c1s v1p0826c2s
v1p0835c1m v1p0995c2s v1p1006c1s
v1p1041c1s v1p1096c2s v1p1097c1s
v1p1153c1s v1p1162c1s v1p1392c2m
v2p0010c2s v2p0016c2s v2p0097c1s
v2p0121c2s v2p0127c1s v2p0147c2s
v2p0149c2s v2p0174c1s v2p0206c1s
v2p0234c1s v2p0246c2s v2p0274c2s
v2p0300c2s v2p0307c2s v2p0389c2s
v2p0390c1s v2p0424c1s v2p0447c2s
v3p0093c2s v3p0145c2s v3p0173c2m
v3p0307c1s v3p0380c2s
Winchell, A. et al. v3p0129c2s
Winchell, F.M. v6p0374c2s
Winchell, H.V. v3p0418c1s v5p0377c2s
Winchell, J.M. v1p0750c2s v1p0610c2s
Winchell, N.H. v1p0300c1s
v1p0367c1s v1p0523c2s v1p0556c1s
v1p0621c1s v1p0938c2s v2p0108c2m
v2p0429c2s v3p0169c2s v3p0292c2s
Winchelsea, Earl of v1p0768c2s
Winchelsea, Lord and Curtis, G.B.
v4p0008c1s
Winchester, B. v4p0118c1s
v4p0439c1s v4p0546c1s v5p0120c1s
v5p0140c1s v5p0311c2s v5p0312c1s
v5p0464c2s v5p0479c2s v5p0519c2s
v5p0590c1s v5p0593c1s v6p0128c1s
v6p0130c2s v6p0425c1s v6p0703c1s
Winchester, B.S. v5p0484c1s
v6p0538c1s v6p0626c2s
Winchester, Boyd v5p0176c2s
Winchester, C.T. v1p1399c1s
v3p0061c2s v3p0260c1s v5p0500c1s
v6p0132c1s v6p0692c1s
Winchester, C.W. v2p0261c1s
Winchester, G.F. v3p0323c1s
v6p0483c2s
Winchester, M. v3p0307c1s
Winchester, Prof. v1p0419c1s
Winchester, S.G. v1p0989c2s
v1p1149c1s
Winchilsea, Lord v4p0150c1s
Winckler, H., Dr. v6p0026c1s
Winder, F.A. v3p0455c1s
Winder, J.R. v6p0429c1s
Winder, R.C. v5p0614c2s
Windes, R.D. v1p0600c1s
Windeyer, R.C. v1p0053c2s
Windeyer, W.C. v5p0570c1s
Windham, C. v6p0488c1s
v6p0647c2s
Windham, H. v6p0194c2s
Windham, J. v1p0349c1s
v1p1018c1s
Windham, L.R. v5p0069c1s
Windle, B.C.A. v6p0514c1s
v6p0547c2s v6p0596c2s v6p0691c1s
Windle, W.S. v4p0304c1s
Windmuller, L. v4p0078c1s
v4p0117c1s v4p0286c2s v4p0401c1s
v4p0411c1s v4p0423c2s v4p0514c2s
v4p0524c2s v4p0596c1s v5p0083c2s
v5p0212c2s v5p0292c2s v5p0432c2s
v5p0526c2s v6p0067c2s v6p0322c1s
v6p0486c2s v6p0684c1s
Windmuller, Louis v6p0321c2s
v6p0568c1s
Windscheid, K. v2p0476c2s
Windship, G.B. v1p1005c1s
Windsor, H.H. v4p0102c1s
Windsor, W. v5p0622c2s
Windt, H. v5p0505c1s
v6p0593c1s
Windt, H.De v5p0318c1s
v6p0058c2s v6p0480c1s
Windus, W.E. v4p0557c2s
Winecaff, J. v1p0248c2s
Wines, E.C. v1p0074c2s
v1p0075c1s v1p0117c1s v1p0315c1s
v1p0315c2s v1p0391c1s v1p0522c2s
v1p0537c2s v1p0688c2s v1p1052c2s
v1p1053c1m v1p1063c1s v1p1091c1s
Wines, F.H. v2p0107c2s
v2p0268c2s v4p0514c1s v4p0590c1s
v5p0018c1s v5p0072c1s v5p0099c2m
v5p0101c2s v5p0143c1s v5p0144c1s
v5p0340c2s v5p0392c2s v5p0406c1s
v5p0436c2s v5p0524c2s v5p0534c2s
v5p0535c1s v5p0537c1s v6p0109c1s
v6p0263c2s v6p0434c2s v6p0492c2s
Wines, W.B. v2p0200c1s
v2p0251c1m
Winfield, C.H. v2p0049c2s
Winfield, T.W. v6p0165c2s
Winfrey, R. v6p0360c1s
Wing, A.S. v6p0421c1m
Wing, C.P. v1p0241c1s
v1p0259c2s v1p0849c2s
Wing, D.E. v3p0241c1s
v6p0502c1s v6p0613c2s
Wing, D.W. v6p0708c2s
Wing, DeWitt C. v5p0009c1s
Wing, Dr. v1p0075c1s

Wing, F.E. ... v6p0331c2s
Wing, J. ... v2p0414c2s
Wing, J.E. ... v5p0387c1s
Wing, J.N. and Kelso, T.L., Miss v5p0542c1s
Wing, R.K. ... v3p0109c2s v5p0090c1s
Wing, W. ... v3p0076c1s
Wingate, A.M.S. ... v5p0110c2s
Wingate, A.W.S. ... v6p0369c2s
Wingate, C.E.L. ... v3p0087c2s v3p0195c1s v3p0313c1s v4p0276c1s v4p0530c2s
Wingate, C.F. ... v1p0566c2s v1p0916c2m v1p1334c2s v2p0198c2s v2p0386c1s v2p0434c2s v2p0468c1s v3p0304c1s v3p0375c1m v3p0424c1s v4p0502c2s v4p0556c1s v5p0292c2s v5p0407c2s
Wingate, D. ... v1p1313c1s v5p0330c2s v5p0422c2s
Wingate, F.R. ... v4p0310c2s
Wingate, G.W. ... v5p0032c2s v5p0488c2m v5p0599c1s
Wingate, U.O.B. ... v5p0259c2s
Wingfellde, A. and Oppenheim, M. v5p0633c1s
Wingfield, L. ... v1p0093c1s v2p0002c1s v2p0031c1s v2p0075c1s v2p0153c1s v2p0238c2s v2p0283c1s v2p0416c2s v3p0187c1s v3p0258c1s v3p0427c1s v4p0160c2s v4p0544c1s
Wingham, A. ... v3p0281c2s
Winkle, C. ... v3p0171c1s
Winkle, E.S.Van ... v1p1186c2s
Winkler, A. ... v1p1249c1s
Winkler, C. ... v5p0103c2s v6p0526c2s
Winkler, C., Dr. ... v4p0120c2s
Winkler, E.T. ... v1p0070c1s v1p0905c1s v1p1092c2s v2p0235c2s
Winkler, E.W. ... v6p0112c1s v6p0639c2s
Winkler, F.K. ... v5p0026c2s v6p0024c2s v6p0563c2s
Winkley, J.W. ... v5p0114c2s
Winkoop, H.S. ... v5p0208c1s
Winks, W.E. ... v3p0174c1s
Winkworth, C. ... v1p0297c1s
Winkworth, S. ... v1p0270c1s
Winkworth, T. ... v3p0058c1s v3p0094c1s
Winlock, W.C. ... v2p0095c1s v2p0095c2m v2p0204c2s v3p0024c2s
Winlock, W.C. et al. ... v2p0095c2s
Winn, C.D. ... v6p0394c2s
Winn, E.L. ... v5p0308c2m
Winn, Edith L. ... v5p0394c2s
Winn, F.L. ... v4p0404c1s v4p0554c2s v4p0579c2s
Winn, Frank L. ... v5p0375c1s
Winn, H. ... v4p0387c1s v5p0383c1s
Winn, J. ... v3p0144c1s v3p0224c1s v5p0121c1s v5p0125c2s v5p0302c1s
Winn, J.A. ... v1p0790c2s
Winn, Jan ... v3p0310c2s v4p0454c2s
Winn, T. ... v3p0239c1s
Winne, C.K. ... v5p0162c2s v5p0271c2s
Winnecker, A. ... v1p0017c2s
Winnington, L. ... v5p0317c2s
Winser, B. ... v6p0075c1s v6p0532c1s
Winser, Beatrice ... v6p0372c2s
Winser, R. ... v6p0372c1s
Winship, A. ... v1p1123c2s
Winship, A.E. ... v2p0131c1s v3p0253c1s v5p0365c1s v6p0410c2s v6p0443c1s v6p0451c1s
Winship, E.A. ... v6p0195c1s
Winship, G.P. ... v5p0086c2s v5p0645c2s v6p0139c2s v6p0140c1s v6p0150c2s v6p0455c2s v6p0650c2s v6p0683c2s
Winship, Margaret ... v6p0066c1s
Winship, W.E. ... v6p0619c1s
Winsloe, R.W.C. ... v2p0050c2s
Winsloe, R.W.C., Col. ... v2p0350c2s
Winslow, A. ... v2p0374c2s v2p0416c1s v4p0084c2s v4p0332c2s v4p0354c2s v4p0418c1s v4p0420c1s
Winslow, A.T. ... v4p0379c2s
Winslow, C.A. ... v6p0213c2s
Winslow, C.E.A. ... v6p0106c2s v6p0128c1s v6p0175c2m v6p0288c1s v6p0576c2s v6p0597c2s v6p0673c2m
Winslow, C.E.A. and Rogers, A.F. v6p0066c2s
Winslow, C.F. ... v1p0377c1s v1p0679c1s v1p1280c1s v1p1310c1s v1p1363c1s
Winslow, C.M. ... v5p0119c1s
Winslow, C.M.A. ... v1p0586c1s v1p1057c2s
Winslow, Clara A. ... v6p0432c1s
Winslow, E. ... v2p0183c2s v3p0051c1s v4p0068c2s v5p0281c2s v5p0603c2s v6p0310c1s v6p0700c2s
Winslow, F. ... v1p0273c2s v2p0325c2s v4p0285c1s v4p0285c2s v4p0518c2s
Winslow, F.E. ... v5p0013c2s v5p0469c1m v5p0521c1s v5p0590c2s v6p0399c1s
Winslow, Florence E. ... v6p0520c1s
Winslow, G.B. ... v4p0461c2s
Winslow, H. ... v1p0385c2s v1p0724c2s v1p0964c1s v1p1271c2s
Winslow, H.M. ... v3p0226c1s v3p0235c1s v3p0301c1s v4p0283c2s v4p0386c1s v4p0402c2s v6p0456c1s v6p0704c1s v6p0706c1s
Winslow, I.O. ... v5p0480c1s
Winslow, W. ... v5p0073c1s
Winslow, W.C. ... v1p1367c2s v2p0133c2s v2p0135c1s v2p0343c1s v2p0483c1m v3p0051c1s v3p0130c2m v3p0297c2s v4p0171c2s v5p0181c2s v6p0196c1s
Winslow, W.H. ... v1p0064c1s v3p0017c2s v3p0226c2s v4p0011c1s v5p0370c1s v5p0387c2s v5p0396c1s v5p0488c2s v5p0500c1s v5p0612c2s
Winsor, A.B. ... v3p0255c2s
Winsor, A.W. ... v5p0408c1s
Winsor, F. ... v1p1366c2s
Winsor, J. ... v1p0152c1m v1p0276c2s v1p0501c1s v1p0595c1s v1p0628c2s v1p0742c2m v1p0743c2m v1p0744c1s v1p1018c2s v1p1070c2s v1p1088c2s v2p0009c2s v2p0012c2s v2p0094c1s v2p0299c1s v2p0310c2s v3p0010c1s v3p0011c1s v3p0051c1s v3p0093c2m v3p0100c1s v3p0128c1s v3p0186c2s v3p0190c1s v3p0197c1s v3p0224c1s v3p0227c2s v3p0248c2m v3p0249c1m v3p0381c2s v3p0389c1s v3p0391c1s v3p0445c2s v4p0013c1m v4p0013c2s v4p0082c1s v4p0125c2s v4p0126c1s v4p0329c2m v4p0427c1s v4p0469c1s v4p0603c1s v4p0603c2s v4p0605c2s v4p0612c1s
Winsor, J. and Evans, E.P. v4p0125c2s
Winsor, J. and Brunt, H.Van v1p0743c2s
Winsor, Justin ... v3p0356c1s v3p0402c2s v3p0445c1s
Winsor, M. ... v5p0101c2s
Winstanley, D.A. ... v6p0251c1s
Winstedt, E.O. ... v6p0145c2s
Winstedt, R.O. ... v6p0396c1m
Winston, A.P. ... v4p0563c1s v5p0321c2s v5p0536c1s v5p0557c1s v5p0593c1s v6p0622c1s v6p0652c1s v6p0652c2s
Winston, A.S. ... v4p0132c2s v5p0088c2s v5p0202c1s v5p0205c2m v5p0251c1s v5p0379c2s v5p0390c1s v5p0520c1s
Winston, B. ... v4p0313c2s
Winston, E.M. ... v3p0378c1s v4p0015c2s v4p0017c1s v4p0489c1s v6p0347c1s
Winston, E.W. ... v4p0626c1s v4p0629c1s v4p0629c2s
Winston, G.T. ... v5p0403c2s
Winston, I. ... v5p0512c2s
Winston, Isaac ... v6p0525c2s
Winston, M.A. ... v4p0518c2s
Winston, N.B. ... v4p0201c1s v4p0611c2s
Winston, R.W. ... v6p0447c1s
Winston, W.R. ... v4p0172c2s v4p0292c2s v4p0327c1s
Wintemberg, W.J. ... v5p0091c1s v5p0288c2s v6p0252c2s
Winter, A. ... v3p0105c2s v4p0434c1s
Winter, A.A. ... v5p0069c1s
Winter, Arthur J.S., Mrs.. v3p0407c1s
Winter, C. ... v1p0091c1s
Winter, C.F. ... v4p0340c1s v4p0370c2s v5p0090c2s
Winter, E.C. ... v2p0442c1s
Winter, J., Sir et al. ... v3p0301c1s
Winter, J.G., jr. ... v5p0498c1s
Winter, J.S. ... v1p1014c2s v2p0062c2s v2p0077c2s v2p0402c1s v3p0263c2s v3p0315c1s v3p0344c1s v3p0392c1s v5p0201c2s v5p0465c1s v6p0613c1s
Winter, John Strange ... v4p0572c1s
Winter, K. ... v5p0102c2s
Winter, Leslie ... v6p0385c2s
Winter, W. ... v1p0150c1s v1p1259c2s v2p0230c1s v2p0234c1s v2p0474c2s v3p0002c2s v3p0389c1s v3p0453c2s v5p0380c2s v6p0003c1s v6p0339c2s
Winter, W. et al. ... v2p0123c1s
Winter, W.H.T. ... v2p0334c1s v2p0414c2m
Winterbotham, R. ... v5p0055c1s v5p0305c2s v5p0311c2s v5p0401c2s v5p0560c2s v6p0019c1s v6p0063c1s
Winterbotham, W. ... v1p0389c2s
Winterburn, F.H. ... v6p0115c2s
Winterburn, G. ... v6p0582c1s
Winterburn, G.W. ... v1p0885c1s v3p0330c1s v5p0164c2s
Winterburn, Rosa V. ... v5p0267c1m
Winterburn, Rose B. ... v3p0197c2s
Winterburn, W.G. ... v6p0347c2s
Winterfield, C. ... v1p0076c1s v1p0104c2s v1p0135c1m v1p0856c2s
Winterhalter, A.G. ... v3p0327c2s
Winternitz, M. ... v5p0265c2s v5p0368c2s v5p0634c1s v6p0661c1s
Winters, J.W. ... v6p0568c2s
Winters, W. ... v1p0705c2s v1p1305c1s v1p1320c1s v1p1391c1s v1p1434c2s v2p0121c1s v2p0139c1m v2p0164c1s v2p0196c2s v2p0342c1s v2p0465c1s
Wintersgill, H.G. ... v5p0116c2s
Winterton, F. ... v3p0228c2s v3p0377c2s
Winterwood, G. ... v4p0023c1s v4p0051c2s v4p0078c1s v4p0181c2s v4p0212c1s v4p0250c1s v4p0357c2s v4p0552c1s v4p0570c1s v4p0578c1s v4p0623c2s v4p0636c2s v5p0107c1s
Winther, C. ... v1p0604c2s
Winthrop, A.W. ... v4p0206c1s v5p0101c2s
Winthrop, B. ... v6p0509c2s v6p0510c1s
Winthrop, E. ... v1p0964c1s
Winthrop, E.W. ... v1p0229c1s
Winthrop, F.W. ... v1p0105c2s
Winthrop, H.A. ... v4p0394c1s
Winthrop, J. ... v1p0239c1s
Winthrop, Marion ... v6p0512c2s
Winthrop, R.C. ... v1p0283c1s v1p1385c2s v4p0003c2s v4p0616c1s
Winthrop, T. ... v1p0773c1s v1p0789c2s v1p1140c1s v1p1345c2s v1p1347c2s
Winthrop, W. ... v1p0710c2s v1p0791c2s v2p0394c1s v5p0445c1s v5p0460c1s v5p0573c2s
Wintle, Laura F. ... v5p0629c2s
Wintle, S.H. ... v1p0079c1s
Winton, A. ... v3p0172c2s
Winton, A.L. ... v5p0125c1s
Winton, F. ... v3p0169c1s
Winton, F.de, Sir ... v3p0004c1s
Winton, G.B. ... v6p0522c2s
Winton, I.C. ... v2p0378c1s
Winton, Maj. De ... v2p0021c2s v2p0288c2s
Winton, R. et al. ... v4p0557c2s
Wire, G.E. ... v4p0329c1s v4p0363c1s v5p0069c2m v5p0097c1s v5p0334c1m v5p0334c2s v5p0335c1m v5p0550c1s
Wirgman, A.T. ... v5p0006c2s v5p0007c1s v5p0068c1s v5p0068c2s v5p0588c2s
Wirgman, A.T. and Wilmot, A. v6p0099c2s
Wirner, A. ... v5p0005c2s
Wirt, G.H. ... v6p0233c1s
Wirt, W. ... v1p0730c1s
Wirth, A. ... v4p0446c2s
Wirth, B. ... v1p0639c2s v2p0062c2s v3p0392c2s v4p0344c2s
Wirth, M. ... v1p0080c1s v1p0326c2s v4p0199c1s
Wisby, H. ... v6p0005c1s v6p0043c2s v6p0095c2s v6p0122c1s v6p0164c1s v6p0277c1s v6p0318c1s v6p0518c1s v6p0572c1s
Wisby, J.H. ... v4p0062c1s v4p0153c1s v4p0485c2s v4p0498c1s v4p0610c1s v5p0109c2s v5p0130c2s v5p0167c1s v5p0531c2s v5p0587c1s
Wischnewetzky, F.K. ... v2p0132c1s v2p0429c1s v2p0448c2s v3p0077c2s
Wischnewetzky, Florence K. v3p0072c1s
Wise, A.G. ... v6p0107c1s v6p0107c2m v6p0563c1s
Wise, B. ... v2p0029c1s
Wise, B.H. ... v4p0538c1s
Wise, B.R. ... v2p0186c1s v3p0027c2s v3p0055c1s v5p0039c1s v5p0426c1s v6p0026c1s v6p0317c2s
Wise, B.R., Mrs. ... v6p0041c2s v6p0299c2s
Wise, D. ... v1p0018c1s v2p0164c1s v2p0241c2s v2p0280c2s v2p0406c1s v3p0240c2s v4p0125c2s
Wise, E.P. ... v5p0118c2s
Wise, Emma M. ... v5p0199c2s
Wise, F. ... v1p0145c2s
Wise, H. ... v1p1154c2s
Wise, H.A. ... v1p0201c1s v1p0949c2s v1p1064c1s v1p1388c1s
Wise, H.D. ... v5p0317c2s
Wise, J. ... v1p0089c1s v1p1310c1s
Wise, J.R. ... v1p0266c2s
Wise, J.S. ... v1p1196c2s

v3p0302c2s v3p0460c2s v5p0164c2s
v5p0188c1s v5p0224c2s v5p0225c1s
v5p0442c1s v6p0262c1s v6p0386c1s
Wise, J.S. and Chamberlain, D.H.
v2p0370c2s
Wise, K. and Severance, M.S.
v1p1315c1s
Wise, M.S. v4p0555c1s
Wise, P.M. v5p0291c2s
Wise, T. v1p0016c2s
v2p0443c2s
Wise, T.A. v1p0621c2s
v2p0422c1s
Wise, T.J. v4p0076c1s
v5p0079c2s v5p0573c1s
Wise, W.L. v3p0167c2s
Wisely, J.L. v1p1438c1s
Wiseman, Cardinal v1p0037c1s
v1p1102c1s v1p1142c1s v2p0390c1s
Wiseman, E.A. v5p0253c2s
Wiseman, Edith P. v6p0120c1m
Wiseman, H.E. v1p0735c2s
Wiseman, L.F. v4p0061c2s
Wiseman, L.H. v1p1103c2s
v1p1305c2s
Wiseman, N. v1p0599c1s
v1p1125c2s v1p1183c1s v2p0022c2s
v2p0023c2s v2p0377c1s v2p0423c1s
v2p0479c2s
Wiseman, W.J. v1p0120c1s
Wishard, M.N. v4p0347c2s
v4p0630c1s
Wishard, S.E. v6p0429c1s
Wishart, A. v4p0131c1s
Wishart, A.W. v6p0062c2s
Wishart, R.S. v5p0491c1s
Wishaw, F. v4p0562c1s
Wisker, J. v1p0078c1s
v1p0386c2s v1p1073c1s
Wislizenus, A. v5p0466c1s
Wisner, G.Y. v4p0072c2s
v4p0180c2m v4p0592c1m
Wisner, H.J. v1p1364c2s
Wisner, W.C. v1p1207c1s
Wisser, J.P. v3p0036c1s
v3p0278c2s v3p0279c1s v3p0412c1s
v3p0454c1s v3p0454c2s v4p0025c2s
v4p0065c2s v4p0411c1s v4p0444c2s
v5p0032c1s v5p0185c1s v5p0290c1s
v5p0375c2s v5p0418c1s v5p0565c2s
v6p0031c1s
Wissler, C. v5p0479c2s
v6p0212c1s v6p0275c1s v6p0585c2s
v6p0608c2s v6p0695c2s
Wissler, C. and Richardson, W.W.
v5p0389c1s
Wissler, H. v1p0286c1s
Wistar, I.A. v1p1251c2s
Wistar, I.J. v3p0089c2s
v5p0135c2s v5p0291c1s v6p0017c2s
Wister, C. v2p0475c2s
Wister, C.B. v4p0092c1s
Wister, J.B. v5p0342c1s
Wister, O. v2p0021c1s
v3p0326c1s v4p0041c2s v4p0137c2s
v4p0179c1s v4p0190c1s v4p0221c2s
v4p0267c1s v4p0332c2s v4p0390c1s
v4p0443c1s v4p0461c2s v4p0481c2s
v4p0501c1s v4p0512c1s v4p0515c2s
v4p0540c1s v4p0577c2s v4p0619c1s
v4p0624c1s v5p0062c2s v5p0159c2s
v5p0225c1s v5p0242c1s v5p0276c2s
v5p0427c1s v5p0447c1s v5p0458c1s
v5p0496c1s v5p0520c1s v5p0595c2s
Wister, Owen v5p0436c1s
v6p0223c1s v6p0311c2s
Wister, S.B. v1p0064c2s
v1p0109c2s v1p0115c1s v1p0202c1s
v1p0414c2s v1p0572c2s v1p0676c2s
v1p0886c1s v1p0971c2s v1p1036c1s
v1p1098c1s v1p1113c2s v1p1143c1s
v1p1202c2m v1p1338c1s v1p1367c2s
v1p1422c2s v3p0289c2s
Wiswall, J.T. v1p0057c1s
Witchell, C.A. v4p0060c2s
v5p0062c2m v5p0063c1s v5p0063c2s
v5p0064c1m v5p0564c1s
Witfield, J.E. v3p0276c1s
Withee, L.J.Young and
O'Donoghue, M.F. v6p0241c1s
Witherbee, F.D. v6p0496c1s
Witherbee, J.V. v4p0247c1s
Witherby, C. v6p0108c2s
Witherby, H.F. v4p0047c1s
v4p0061c1m v4p0310c1s v4p0508c2s
v4p0613c1s v4p0631c2s v5p0063c1s
v5p0063c2s v5p0251c2s v5p0397c2s
v5p0405c2s v5p0412c1s v5p0527c1s
v6p0361c2s
Witherly, H.F. v6p0067c2s
Witherow, J. v2p0003c1s
Witherow, T. v2p0109c2s
v2p0113c1s v2p0117c2s v2p0290c2s
v3p0016c1s v3p0084c2s v3p0104c1s
v3p0106c2s v3p0343c1s
Withers, C. v2p0117c1s
v3p0313c2s
Withers, H. v4p0181c2s
v4p0379c2s v4p0550c1s v4p0565c1s
v5p0175c2s v5p0295c1s v5p0383c1s
v5p0468c2s v6p0049c2s
Withers, H.W. v5p0178c1s
Withers, M.T. v6p0678c2s
Witherspoon, J. v1p0803c1s
Witherspoon, T.D. v1p0783c1s
Withey, E.A. and Hill, A.S.
v5p0192c1s
Withington, C.F. v2p0087c1s
Withington, E.T. v5p0021c1s
Withington, G. v5p0388c2s
Withington, L. v1p0036c2s
v1p0048c1s v1p0112c1s v1p0176c1s
v1p0179c2s v1p0189c2s v1p0217c1s
v1p0244c1s v1p0254c1s v1p0274c1s
v1p0289c1s v1p0296c1s v1p0352c2s
v1p0406c2s v1p0407c1s v1p0433c1s
v1p0465c2s v1p0520c2s v1p0528c1s
v1p0528c2s v1p0610c1s v1p0700c1s
v1p0754c1s v1p0826c2s v1p0978c1s
v1p1179c1s v1p1215c2s v1p1278c1s
v1p1302c1s v1p1303c1s v1p1368c1s
v1p1373c1s v1p1412c1s v5p0193c1s
v5p0366c2s v5p0426c1s v5p0632c1s
v6p0112c2s v6p0488c1m
Withington, M.S. v2p0140c1s
Withington, N.N. v1p0639c1s
v4p0560c2s v5p0150c2s v5p0451c1s
Withington, Nathan N. v6p0457c2s
Withington, V. v4p0176c1s
Withington, W. v1p1102c1s
Withrow, C.L. v6p0476c1s
Withrow, J.L. et al. v4p0054c1s
Withrow, T. v2p0083c2s
v2p0353c1s
Withrow, W.H. v1p0047c2s
v1p0061c2s v1p0205c2m v1p0206c1s
v1p0253c1s v1p0364c1s v1p0617c2s
v1p0806c1s v1p0948c1s v1p1277c2s
v1p1438c2s v3p0065c1s v3p0066c1s
v3p0080c1s v4p0085c1s v4p0160c2s
v4p0307c2s v4p0385c1s v4p0406c2s
v5p0594c2s v5p0625c2s v6p0294c2s
Withy, A. v4p0213c2s
v4p0239c2s v4p0283c1s v4p0289c2s
v4p0318c2s v4p0565c1s v4p0580c2s
v4p0591c1s v5p0584c2s v6p0240c2m
v6p0360c1s
Withy, E. v4p0318c2s
v4p0591c1s
Witmer, L. v4p0110c2s
v4p0465c2s v5p0470c2s
Witt, B.T.De v5p0329c2s
Witt, F., Dr. and Butterfield, H.S.
v3p0084c1s
Witt, G. v1p0102c1s
Witt, G.de v3p0173c2s
Witt, Guizot de, Mad. v2p0009c1s
v2p0215c2s
Witt, H.M. v1p0452c2s
Witt, J.De v1p0124c1s
v2p0352c1s v2p0479c2s v4p0042c1s
v4p0054c1s v4p0519c2s v5p0466c1m
v5p0627c1s
Witt, J.De and Beattie, F.R.
v5p0464c1s
Witt, J.De and Schaff, P.. v3p0461c1s
Witt, M.B.De v2p0041c2s
v2p0426c1s
Witt, M.de v1p0488c1s
v1p1329c1s
Witt, M.H. v5p0399c1s
v5p0610c2s v6p0228c2s v6p0276c1s
Witt, O.N. v5p0104c1s
Witt, R.C. v5p0230c1s
v5p0233c2s v5p0280c2s v5p0495c2s
v6p0034c1m v6p0542c1s
Witt, W.C.de v5p0407c1s
Witte, A. v4p0627c1s
v4p0628c1s
Witte, B. v4p0091c2s
Witte, B.B. v3p0151c2s
Witte, Sophie v6p0559c2s
v6p0702c1s
Wittelshofer, O. v4p0038c2s
Wittelshofer, P. v6p0011c1s
Wittmann, S. v2p0299c1s
Wittrock v2p0201c2s
Wittrock, V.B. v2p0020c2s
v2p0151c1s v2p0295c2s
Woad, E. v6p0046c2s
Woburn, R. v2p0343c2s
Wodehouse, E.A. v6p0495c1s
Wodehouse, E.R. v3p0174c1s
v4p0506c2s
Wodell, F.W. v4p0389c1s
v4p0566c2s v5p0524c1s
Woeikof, A. v1p1194c1s
v2p0035c1s v2p0089c1s v2p0364c1s
v2p0401c2s v2p0426c2s v4p0119c2s
Woeikoff, A.J. v3p0088c2s
Woerner, J.G. v2p0146c2s
v2p0356c1s v2p0425c2s v3p0216c2s
Wogan-Browne v5p0098c1s
Woglom, G.L. v5p0449c1s
Wohl, S. v1p0462c2s
Wohlfers, J.F.H. v1p0919c1s
Woker, P. v1p1118c1s
v2p0328c2s
Wolcott, C.D. v4p0064c2s
v4p0413c1s v5p0177c2s
Wolcott, E.O. v4p0593c2s
Wolcott, H.L.T. v3p0167c1s
Wolcott, J.D. v6p0548c2s
Wolcott, R. v1p0603c1s
Wolcott, R.H. v6p0233c1s
Wolcott, S. v1p0682c2s
v1p0871c1s v1p1218c1s v1p1419c1s
Wolcott, T. v4p0174c2s
Wolf, A. et al. v6p0343c1s
Wolf, Alice S. v4p0588c1s
Wolf, B. Colt de v5p0080c2s
Wolf, D.F.De v2p0096c2s
Wolf, Dr. v4p0218c2s
Wolf, E. v5p0010c1s
Wolf, E.J. v1p0777c2s
v2p0083c2s v2p0367c1s v3p0261c1m
v3p0291c2s v4p0053c2s v4p0057c2s
v4p0108c2s v4p0345c2s v5p0059c1s
Wolf, J.De v3p0242c1s
v3p0302c2s v4p0074c2s v4p0220c1s
v4p0462c1s v4p0556c1s
Wolf, L. v1p0689c2s
v2p0134c1s v2p0236c2s v2p0237c1s
v2p0239c1s v3p0015c2s v5p0168c2s
v6p0108c1s v6p0713c1s
Wolf, L.B. v3p0261c1s
Wolf, M. v5p0448c1s
v6p0417c1s v6p0446c1s
Wolf, M.C. v2p0258c2s
Wolf, Max v4p0445c1s
v6p0446c1s
Wolf, P. v1p0645c1s
Wolf, T. v4p0168c1s
Wolfe, A. v1p0426c1s
Wolfe, C. v1p0295c2s
v1p0866c2s
Wolfe, E.A.De v3p0093c2s
v4p0521c2s v5p0168c2s
Wolfe, E.F. v6p0020c2s
Wolfe, Elsie A.De v3p0075c1s
Wolfe, H.K. v3p0077c2s
v4p0171c2s v4p0465c1s v5p0531c1s
v5p0569c2s v6p0139c1s
Wolfe, L.E. v6p0207c1s
Wolfe, S.H. v6p0322c2s
Wolfe, S.Herbert v6p0322c2s
Wolfe, T. v2p0057c2s
v2p0059c1s
Wolfe, T.F. v5p0071c2s
v5p0080c2s v5p0084c1s v5p0407c1s
v5p0407c2s v5p0554c1s
Wolfe, W.M. v4p0160c1s
Wolfe, W.W. v3p0341c2s
Wolfenstein, M. v5p0279c1s
v5p0312c1s v5p0383c2s v5p0485c1s
v6p0595c2s
Wolfer, A. v6p0626c1s
Wolff, A. v3p0279c2s
v6p0098c2s
Wolff, A.R. v1p0580c1m
v2p0475c1m v3p0408c2s v3p0465c1s
v4p0252c2s v4p0602c2s
Wolff, B.C. v1p1090c2s
Wolff, Dr. v1p0001c1s
Wolff, G.D. v1p0247c2s
v1p0248c2s v1p0347c1s v1p0657c1s
v1p0794c1s v1p0823c2s v1p1058c1s
v1p1118c1s v1p1120c1s v1p1216c1s
v2p0225c1s v2p0244c2s v2p0359c1s
v2p0362c2s v2p0367c2s v2p0464c1s
v3p0342c2s v4p0488c2s
Wolff, H. v3p0264c2s
Wolff, H.D. v1p0786c2s
v3p0294c2s v6p0048c1s
Wolff, H.D., Sir v6p0295c1s
Wolff, H.F. v4p0633c2s
Wolff, H.W. v3p0009c1s
v3p0075c1s v3p0114c1s v3p0187c2s
v3p0274c2s v3p0325c1s v3p0436c1s
v4p0007c2s v4p0008c1m v4p0009c2s
v4p0044c1m v4p0044c2s v4p0045c1m
v4p0048c2s v4p0132c2m v4p0163c1s
v4p0286c2m v4p0287c1s v4p0312c1s
v4p0314c1s v4p0318c2s v4p0412c1s
v4p0458c1s v4p0504c1s v4p0544c2s
v4p0559c1s v4p0604c1s v4p0607c1s
v4p0617c1s v5p0136c1m v5p0187c2s
v5p0231c1s v5p0273c1s v5p0292c2s
v5p0293c1m v5p0419c1m v5p0457c1s
v5p0509c2m v5p0641c1m v6p0026c2s
v6p0050c2s v6p0058c2s v6p0148c1m
v6p0148c2m v6p0188c2s v6p0247c2s
v6p0300c1s v6p0331c1s v6p0360c2s
v6p0520c1s v6p0521c1s v6p0571c2s
v6p0708c1s
Wolff, J. v4p0633c2s
Wolff, J.E. v4p0135c2s
v4p0222c2s v4p0573c2s
Wolff, R.H. v4p0563c1s
Wolffsohn, L. v3p0224c2s
v3p0263c2s v3p0414c2s v5p0212c2s
v5p0299c2s v5p0397c2s v5p0458c2s
v5p0491c1s
Wolffsohn, Lily v4p0522c1s
v4p0599c2s v5p0351c1s v6p0049c1s
Wolffsohn, Lily and Woodward, Bettina
v5p0012c1s
Wolffsohn, M. v3p0013c1s
Wolffsohn, Max v3p0100c2s
Wolfson, A.M. v5p0044c1s

Wolfson, H.O. v2p0127c1s
Wolfsteig, Dr. v6p0375c1s
Wolikof, A. v2p0179c1s
Wolkenhauer, A. v6p0250c1s
Wolkins, G.G. v6p0076c1s
Wolkonsky, S. v4p0479c2s
v5p0582c1s v6p0410c1s
Woll, F.W. v4p0146c1s
Wollaston, A.N. v2p0281c2s
v2p0331c2s v3p0032c1s v3p0210c2s
Wollermann, O. v2p0175c2s
Wolley, C.P. v2p0107c2s
v6p0431c1s v6p0562c2s
Wollman, H. v4p0475c2s
v4p0594c2s
Wolmer, Lord v3p0180c2s
v3p0199c1s v3p0220c2s v4p0428c1s
Wolmer, S.L. v1p0205c2s
v1p0770c1s v1p1092c2s
Wolmer, Viscount v3p0344c1s
v3p0431c1s
Wolowski, L. v1p0474c2s
Wolowski, L.F.M.R. v1p0093c2s
Wolrige, W. v3p0286c2s
v3p0338c1s
Wolseley v3p0449c2s
v5p0617c2s
Wolseley, G. v4p0209c2s
v4p0377c1s v4p0512c1s v6p0106c1s
v6p0235c2s v6p0255c1s v6p0353c2s
v6p0361c2s
Wolseley, G., Sir v1p0480c1s
v1p0543c1s v1p0547c1s v3p0160c2s
v3p0245c2s v3p0395c2s v4p0391c1s
Wolseley, G.B. v4p0278c2s
v5p0303c1s v5p0645c1s
Wolseley, G.I. v1p0547c1s
v1p0629c1s
Wolseley, G.J. v3p0179c2s
Wolseley, Gen. v3p0278c2s
v3p0285c1s v3p0390c2s v3p0400c1s
v3p0454c1s
Wolseley, Gen. et al. v3p0406c2s
Wolseley, Lord v3p0102c2s
v3p0298c2s v3p0454c1s
Wolseley, Viscount v3p0443c1s
v4p0105c1s v4p0296c2s v6p0442c1s
Wolstenholme, H.J. v6p0355c2s
Wolter, F. v6p0367c2s
Wolters, P. v3p0475c2s
v4p0035c1s
Wolters, Paul v5p0036c2s
Woltmann, A. v1p0596c2s
Wolverton, Lady v3p0298c2s
Womack, T.B. v6p0459c2s
v6p0615c1s
Wong, Chin Foo v2p0079c1s
v2p0385c2s v3p0079c2m v3p0192c2s
Wong, Kai Kah v6p0666c2s
Wonnell, R. v5p0130c2s
Wood, A. v1p0037c2s
v1p0816c2s v5p0271c2s v6p0182c1s
v6p0275c1s
Wood, A.A. v3p0237c2s
v3p0387c2s v4p0616c2s
Wood, A.C. v5p0617c1s
Wood, A.D.W. v2p0201c2s
Wood, A.E. v3p0093c1s
Wood, A.F. v5p0419c1s
Wood, Aimee M. v5p0042c1s
Wood, Alex. v1p1273c1s
Wood, Amy v5p0161c2s
Wood, Arthur C. v6p0684c1s
Wood, B. v1p0184c2m
v4p0348c2s v5p0335c2s v5p0336c1s
v5p0595c2s
Wood, B.E. v6p0095c1s
Wood, B.M. v6p0698c1s
Wood, C. v1p0083c2s
v1p1204c2m v2p0079c1s v2p0083c2s
v2p0242c2s v2p0327c1s v2p0333c2s
v2p0334c2s v2p0404c2s v2p0442c2s
Wood, C.A. v4p0415c2s
Wood, C.E.S. v2p0006c2s
v2p0238c2s v2p0439c1s v3p0214c1m
v4p0282c1s
Wood, C.E.S. and Gibbon, J.
v5p0288c2s
Wood, C.H. v1p1070c1s
Wood, C.J. v3p0367c2s
v5p0087c1s v5p0181c2s v5p0185c2s
v5p0202c1s v5p0256c1s v5p0396c2s
v5p0632c1s
Wood, C.L. v2p0084c1s
Wood, C.T. v5p0152c2s
Wood, C.W. v1p0303c2s
v1p0347c2s v1p0413c2s v1p0558c1s
v1p0597c1s v1p0908c1s v1p0929c2s
v1p0948c2s v1p1143c2s v1p1146c1s
v1p1154c1s v1p1173c2s v1p1191c1s
v1p1256c1s v1p1434c2s v2p0048c2s
v2p0053c2s v2p0063c2s v2p0074c1s
v2p0109c1s v2p0183c2s v2p0193c1s
v2p0216c1s v2p0317c1s v2p0329c2s
v2p0348c2m v2p0464c2s v3p0054c1s
v3p0074c2s v3p0155c2s v3p0172c2s
v3p0193c2s v3p0228c2s v3p0264c2s
v3p0265c1s v3p0278c1s v3p0295c2s
v3p0306c2s v3p0320c2s v3p0366c1s
v3p0366c2s v3p0367c2s v3p0415c1s
v3p0470c2s v4p0006c1s v4p0045c2s
v4p0149c1s v4p0151c2s v4p0172c2s
v4p0212c2s v4p0225c1s v4p0307c1s
v4p0327c1s v4p0354c1s v4p0364c2s
v4p0380c2s v4p0384c1m v4p0418c1s
v4p0447c2s v4p0468c1s v4p0490c1s
v4p0503c1s v4p0539c2s v4p0564c1s
v4p0579c1s v4p0599c2s v4p0633c2s
v5p0048c2s v5p0186c1s v5p0188c1s
v5p0190c1s v5p0261c1m v5p0317c2s
v5p0345c2s v5p0346c2s v5p0414c2s
v5p0422c2s v5p0476c1s v5p0487c2s
v5p0504c1s v5p0504c2s v5p0564c2s
v5p0575c1s v5p0611c1s v5p0642c2s
Wood, D. v1p0051c1s
v1p0104c2s v1p0523c1s v1p0619c1s
v1p0640c2s v1p0859c1s v1p1272c2s
v1p1430c2s
Wood, D.G. v5p0356c1s
Wood, D.H. v3p0195c1s
Wood, D.J.H. v4p0479c1s
Wood, D.V. v1p1074c2m
v1p1100c2s
Wood, De V. v1p0466c2m
v1p0467c1s v2p0146c2s v2p0199c1s
v2p0365c1s v2p0378c1s v2p0382c2s
v2p0419c1s v2p0422c2s v2p0425c2m
v2p0434c1s v2p0438c1m v2p0448c2s
v3p0428c1s v3p0438c1s
Wood, De V. and Ericsson, J.
v2p0425c2s
Wood, E. v1p0703c1s
v4p0093c1s v4p0140c1s v5p0026c1s
v5p0030c2s v5p0031c1s v5p0116c1s
v5p0144c1s v5p0147c1s v5p0156c2s
v5p0176c1s v5p0243c2s v5p0268c2s
v5p0272c2s v5p0359c2s v5p0486c1s
v6p0053c2s v6p0078c2s v6p0105c1s
v6p0114c1s v6p0133c1s v6p0146c2s
v6p0177c1s v6p0185c2s v6p0208c1s
v6p0225c2s v6p0388c2s v6p0541c2s
v6p0561c2s v6p0629c1s v6p0647c1s
Wood, E. and Morris, G.L.. v6p0102c2s
Wood, E.E. v4p0431c2s
v5p0268c2s v5p0363c2s
Wood, E.G. v1p0564c2s
v3p0169c2s
Wood, E.H. v5p0410c1s
Wood, E.M. v3p0158c2s
Wood, E.P. v1p1144c1s
v2p0352c2s
Wood, E.W. v6p0232c2s
Wood, Edith E. v6p0045c2s
v6p0116c2s v6p0463c1s v6p0702c1s
Wood, Edith L. v5p0414c2s
Wood, Esther and Morris, G.L.
v6p0152c2s
Wood, Eugene v6p0124c1s
v6p0127c1s v6p0127c2s v6p0146c2s
v6p0154c2s v6p0258c2s v6p0456c2s
v6p0466c1s v6p0541c2s
Wood, F. v6p0540c1s
Wood, F.A. v5p0519c2s
v5p0608c1s v6p0212c2s v6p0405c1s
v6p0450c2s v6p0583c1s
Wood, F.M. v6p0550c1s
Wood, G v1p0324c2s
v5p0154c1s
v5p0531c1m
Wood, G.H. v2p0033c1s
v2p0114c2s v5p0584c2s v5p0615c1s
v5p0615c2s v6p0019c1s v6p0217c2s
v6p0405c2s
Wood, G.H. and Bowley, A.L.
v6p0682c2s
Wood, G.I. v1p0248c2s
v1p1344c1s v1p1359c1s
Wood, G.W. v4p0052c2s
v4p0083c1s v4p0185c2s v4p0299c2s
v4p0527c2s v5p0044c1s v5p0145c2s
Wood, H. v1p0010c1m
v1p0050c2s v1p0156c1s v1p0169c1s
v1p0204c1s v1p0333c1s v1p0444c2s
v1p0457c1s v1p0621c1s v1p0846c2s
v1p0975c2s v1p1011c2s v1p1396c1s
v1p1428c2s v2p0037c2s v3p0129c1s
v3p0218c2s v3p0280c1s v3p0437c1s
v4p0139c1s v4p0139c2s v4p0191c1s
v4p0194c1s v4p0229c1s v4p0229c2s
v4p0284c1s v4p0304c2s v4p0323c1s
v4p0352c1m v4p0358c1s v4p0363c2s
v4p0371c2m v4p0372c1s v4p0395c1s
v4p0578c2s v5p0230c2s
Wood, H., Mrs. v1p0043c1s
v1p0116c1s v1p0163c1s v1p0309c1s
v1p0343c2s v1p0378c2s v1p0383c1s
v1p0511c1s v1p0716c1s v1p0768c2s
v1p0805c2s v1p0809c2s v1p0878c2s
v1p0922c1s v1p0973c1s v1p1029c2s
v1p1081c2s v1p1111c1s v1p1114c2s
v1p1182c2s v1p1418c2s v2p0109c2s
v2p0129c1s v2p0237c2s v2p0272c2s
v2p0284c2s v2p0289c1s v2p0374c2s
v2p0427c1s v2p0444c2s v2p0451c1s
v3p0119c2s v3p0150c2s v3p0210c1s
v3p0240c1s v3p0411c1s v3p0439c2s
v4p0180c1s v5p0032c1s v5p0463c2s
Wood, H. and Adams, H.B. . v4p0125c2s
Wood, H. and Collins, J.A.
v5p0382c2s
Wood, H.A. v6p0220c1s
Wood, H.C. v1p0082c1s
v1p1376c2s v2p0026c2s v2p0365c2s
v3p0092c1s v3p0097c1s v3p0273c1s
v3p0274c1s v4p0248c2s v4p0271c2s
v5p0036c1s v6p0668c1s
Wood, H.C. et al. v2p0080c2s
Wood, H.C., jr. v1p0021c2s
v1p0152c2s v1p0406c2s v1p0450c1s
v1p0816c1m v1p1269c2s v6p0483c2s
Wood, H.G. v1p0648c1s
Wood, H.H. v1p0718c2s
v1p1368c2s
Wood, H.L. v6p0179c2s
Wood, H.O. and Palache, C.
v6p0417c2s
Wood, H.P. v6p0567c1s
Wood, H.R. v4p0227c1s
Wood, H.T. v1p0149c1s
v1p0304c2s v1p1182c1s v2p0150c1s
v2p0414c2s v3p0076c2s v3p0320c1s
v3p0434c1s v4p0100c2m v5p0129c1s
v5p0448c2s
Wood, H.T., Sir v5p0130c2s
Wood, Harriet A. v6p0106c1s
Wood, Henry, Mrs. v4p0386c1s
v5p0510c1s
Wood, I.F. v6p0060c1s
v6p0064c2m v6p0395c1s v6p0409c2s
v6p0513c1s
Wood, J. v1p1196c2s
v1p1340c1s v3p0394c1s v4p0010c2s
Wood, J.A.A. v1p0942c2s
Wood, J.B. v2p0273c2s
v2p0291c1s v4p0207c1s v6p0140c2s
v6p0413c1s
Wood, J.C. v2p0393c2s
Wood, J.E. v5p0140c1s
v5p0154c1s v5p0506c2s v5p0564c1s
Wood, J.G. v1p0044c1s
v1p0136c1s v1p0214c2s v1p0270c2s
v1p0311c1s v1p0439c2s v1p0604c1s
v1p0645c1s v1p0645c2m v1p0681c2s
v1p0858c2s v1p0899c2s v1p0901c1s
v1p1213c1s v1p1232c1s v1p1298c2s
v1p1313c2s v2p0001c2s v2p0009c2s
v2p0010c1s v2p0038c1m v2p0047c1m
v2p0110c2s v2p0146c2s v2p0202c2s
v2p0206c1s v2p0249c2s v2p0252c2s
v2p0259c2s v2p0283c1s v2p0288c1m
v2p0294c1s v2p0302c2s v2p0304c1s
v2p0393c1m v2p0401c1s v2p0413c1s
v2p0415c2s v2p0418c1s v2p0441c1s
v2p0463c2s v2p0471c1s v2p0475c2s
v2p0483c1s v3p0012c2s v3p0014c1s
v3p0015c1s v3p0029c1s v3p0045c1m
v3p0046c1s v3p0055c2s v3p0092c2s
v3p0119c2s v3p0154c1s v3p0195c1s
v3p0200c2s v3p0210c1s v3p0217c1s
v3p0219c1s v3p0292c2s v3p0391c1s
v3p0405c2s v3p0456c2s v3p0466c1s
v3p0467c1s
Wood, J.H. v5p0520c1s
Wood, J.Hickory v5p0396c1s
Wood, J.J. v4p0572c1s
Wood, J.L. v4p0564c1s
Wood, J.S. v3p0190c1s
v3p0211c2s v3p0301c1s v3p0411c1s
v4p0147c1s v4p0248c2s v5p0397c1s
v6p0369c1s
Wood, J.T. v1p0062c1s
v1p0135c2s v1p0742c1s v2p0295c1s
v4p0072c2s v5p0532c1s v5p0566c1s
Wood, J.Taylor v5p0254c2s
Wood, J.W. v3p0382c2s
v3p0391c1s
Wood, James v6p0675c2s
Wood, L. v1p0001c2s
v1p0039c1s v1p0466c1s v1p1315c2s
v5p0147c1s v5p0147c2s v5p0148c1s
v5p0491c1s v5p0508c1s v5p0508c2s
v6p0160c1s v6p0160c2s v6p0161c1s
Wood, L.C. v5p0222c2s
Wood, L.I. v6p0027c2s
Wood, L.P. v6p0136c2s
Wood, Lydia M. v3p0366c1s
Wood, M. v4p0290c1s
v5p0086c1s v5p0234c2s
Wood, M.N. v6p0119c2s
v6p0120c2s
Wood, N. v1p1249c1s
Wood, N.E. v3p0329c2s
Wood, N.M. v1p0687c1s
Wood, O.M. v6p0056c2s
Wood, R. v5p0364c2s
Wood, R.A. v2p0451c2s
v3p0233c2s v5p0476c1s
Wood, R.W. v4p0093c1s
v5p0174c2s v5p0338c2m v5p0423c1s
v5p0448c1m v5p0540c1s v5p0560c2m
v5p0614c2s v6p0527c2s v6p0654c1s
Wood, R.W., jr. v3p0167c2s
v3p0207c1s
Wood, S. v1p0101c1s
v3p0452c2m v4p0347c2s
Wood, S.A. v4p0203c2s
v4p0521c1s
Wood, S.T. v5p0082c2s
v5p0327c2s v5p0584c1s v6p0609c2s
Wood, S.V. and Elsden, J.V.

v2p0440c2s
Wood, T. v2p0030c1s
v2p0047c1s v2p0047c2s v2p0222c1m
v2p0445c2s v3p0045c2m v3p0217c1s
v3p0254c2s v3p0265c1m v3p0389c2s
v3p0390c1s v3p0391c1s v3p0457c2s
v4p0018c2s v4p0031c2s v4p0061c1s
v4p0107c2s v4p0273c1s v4p0379c1s
v4p0397c2s v4p0486c2s v5p0292c1s
v5p0546c1s
Wood, T.J. v1p0838c2s
Wood, T.M. v6p0143c2s
v6p0181c2s v6p0226c2s v6p0282c2s
v6p0369c1s v6p0409c2s v6p0425c2s
v6p0589c1s v6p0592c1s v6p0595c1s
Wood, T.McK. v5p0345c1s
Wood, T.Martin v6p0051c2s
v6p0181c2s v6p0211c1s v6p0229c2s
v6p0545c2s
Wood, T.W. v1p0135c2s
v1p0645c1s v1p0645c2s v1p0975c1s
Wood, V. v1p0162c1s
v5p0453c1s v5p0624c2s
Wood, W. v1p0094c2s
v1p0137c1m v1p0441c2m v1p0456c1s
v1p0575c1m v1p0578c2s v1p0938c2s
v1p0953c2s v3p0076c1s v3p0117c2s
v4p0421c2s v4p0480c2s v5p0029c2s
v5p0037c2s v5p0043c1s v5p0091c1s
v5p0096c1s v5p0222c1s v5p0243c1s
v5p0244c2s v5p0263c1s v5p0283c1s
v5p0414c1s v5p0416c1s v5p0612c1s
v5p0634c1s v6p0034c2s v6p0377c1s
v6p0480c2s v6p0525c1s v6p0580c1s
Wood, W.A. v2p0298c2s
v3p0193c1s v3p0240c1s v3p0302c2s
v3p0343c2s v3p0372c1s v3p0459c1s
v4p0164c1s v4p0375c1m
Wood, W.C. v1p0619c2s
v4p0102c1s v4p0592c2s v5p0139c1s
Wood, W.D. v1p0889c2s
v6p0354c2s v6p0368c1s v6p0634c2s
v6p0640c1s
Wood, W.H. v1p1288c1s
v6p0028c1s
Wood, W.M. v1p0280c2s
v1p0343c1s v1p0988c2s v1p1194c2s
v2p0383c1s v3p0212c2s v4p0278c2s
v5p0499c2s v5p0534c1s v6p0073c2s
v6p0121c1s v6p0313c1s v6p0339c1s
Wood, W.P. v1p0364c2s
v1p0573c2s
Wood, W.P., Sir v1p1328c1s
Wood, W.R. v4p0275c2s
Wood, Walter v5p0012c1s
v5p0098c2s v5p0199c1s v6p0105c1s
Wood-Lovejoy, E.M. v6p0572c2s
Wood-Samuel, R. v5p0610c2s
Wood-Smith, B. v3p0430c1s
Woodall, W. v3p0202c1s
v3p0340c2s
Woodard, H.D. v5p0080c1s
Woodberry, G.E. v1p0031c2s
v1p0060c2s v1p0179c2s v1p0311c1s
v1p0357c1s v1p0512c1s v1p0595c2s
v1p0840c2s v1p0898c1s v1p1189c1s
v1p1189c2s v1p1224c1s v2p0002c2s
v2p0003c2s v2p0061c1s v2p0092c1s
v2p0105c2s v2p0108c1s v2p0117c2s
v2p0144c2s v2p0198c1s v2p0248c2s
v2p0265c2s v2p0267c2m v2p0345c2s
v2p0378c2m v2p0397c1s v2p0398c1s
v2p0431c2s v2p0465c1s v2p0479c1s
v3p0011c2s v3p0057c1m v3p0061c2s
v3p0068c1s v3p0068c2s v3p0096c2s
v3p0115c2s v3p0135c1s v3p0140c2s
v3p0141c1s v3p0154c2s v3p0172c2s
v3p0179c2m v3p0188c2s v3p0191c2s
v3p0192c1s v3p0247c2s v3p0253c2s
v3p0259c2s v3p0289c2s v3p0292c2s
v3p0314c2s v3p0323c1s v3p0338c2s
v3p0373c1s v3p0387c1s v3p0390c1s
v3p0410c1s v3p0418c2s v3p0472c1m
v4p0180c2s v4p0223c2s v4p0260c2s
v4p0520c1s v4p0562c2s v4p0620c2s
v5p0067c1s v5p0251c1s v5p0517c1s
v6p0017c1s v6p0076c2s v6p0107c1s
v6p0202c2s v6p0283c2s v6p0353c1s
v6p0418c1s v6p0505c1s v6p0578c1s
v6p0605c1s v6p0689c1s
Woodbridge, A.A. v4p0487c1s
Woodbridge, A.L. v4p0283c2s
Woodbridge, A.L. et al. .. v4p0103c1s
Woodbridge, B. v4p0002c1s
v4p0503c1s v5p0592c1s
Woodbridge, D.E. v5p0562c1s
Woodbridge, Dwight E. v6p0184c1s
Woodbridge, E. v6p0145c1s
Woodbridge, F.J.E. v5p0447c1s
v5p0454c2s v6p0195c1s v6p0383c1s
v6p0412c2s v6p0609c2s
Woodbridge, H.T. v5p0076c1s
Woodbridge, J. v1p0103c2s
v1p0110c2s v1p0529c2s v1p0558c2s
v1p1410c1s
Woodbridge, J.L. v2p0448c2s
v5p0071c2s
Woodbridge, M.P. v1p0141c2s
v1p1410c1s
Woodbridge, S.H. v2p0199c2s
Woodbridge, S.M. v3p0229c1s
v5p0483c1s
Woodbridge, S.W. v3p0192c2s
Woodbridge, W. v1p1422c1s
v1p1423c1s
Woodbridge, W.C. v1p0315c2s
v1p0437c2s v1p0447c2s v1p0506c2s
v1p0884c2s v1p1159c2s v1p1276c2s
Woodbridge, W.E. v1p0563c1s
Woodbridge, W.S. v2p0384c2s
v2p0455c2s v3p0026c1s v3p0209c1s
Woodburn, B.F. v1p0708c2s
Woodburn, J.A. v3p0408c1s
v4p0015c2s v4p0379c2s v4p0451c1s
v4p0563c1s v4p0597c1s v5p0241c2s
v5p0601c1s v6p0597c1s
Woodburne, G.B.L. v2p0186c2s
v2p0206c1s v3p0364c2s v4p0003c1s
Woodbury, A. v1p0055c2m
v1p0103c1s v1p0203c2s v1p0402c2s
v1p0425c1s v1p0484c1s v1p0496c1s
v1p0709c1s v1p0715c1s v1p1041c2s
v1p1052c2s v1p1053c1s v1p1059c2s
v1p1101c1s v1p1102c1s v1p1246c1s
v1p1329c2s v1p1354c1s
Woodbury, A.K. v6p0638c2s
Woodbury, C.E. v4p0011c2s
Woodbury, C.J. v2p0443c1s
v3p0017c1s v3p0057c2s v3p0136c1s
v3p0313c2s v6p0463c1s
Woodbury, C.J.H. v1p0090c2s
v1p0840c1s v2p0137c1m v3p0059c1s
v3p0133c1s v3p0153c1s v3p0153c2s
v4p0175c2s v4p0200c1s v4p0543c1s
v5p0171c2s v5p0616c2s v6p0637c1s
Woodbury, C.L. v3p0154c1s
v4p0631c2s
Woodbury, D.P. v1p0093c1s
v1p0986c2s v1p1103c1s
Woodbury, H.E. v1p1424c1s
Woodbury, J.C. and Dresser, H.W.
v5p0114c2s v5p0176c1s
Woodbury, J.McC. v6p0687c2s
Woodbury, L. v1p0283c1s
v1p0486c1s
Woodbury, W.E. v4p0440c1s
Woodcock, G. v2p0419c2s
Woodcock, W. v1p1212c2s
Wooden, C.C. v6p0516c2s
Woodfall, T. v1p0277c1s
Woodford, A.B. v3p0067c2s
v3p0127c2s v4p0103c1s v4p0167c2m
v4p0182c2m v4p0387c2s v4p0394c1s
v4p0525c2m v4p0526c1s v4p0558c2s
v5p0179c2s
Woodford, C.M. v3p0400c1s
v4p0226c1s
Woodford, J.H. v2p0191c2s
Woodford, O.B. v5p0535c1s
Woodford, S.L. v6p0607c2s
Woodgate, W.B. v5p0067c2s
v6p0100c1s v6p0432c1s v6p0553c1s
v6p0641c1s
Woodgate, W.B. and Derby, R.A.
v6p0071c2s
Woodhams, G. v6p0203c1s
Woodhead, G.S. v4p0020c2m
v4p0429c2s v5p0042c2s v5p0594c1m
Woodhead, H. v6p0252c2s
v6p0435c2s v6p0436c2s
Woodhead, Sims v5p0521c1s
Woodhouse, John v5p0426c2s
Woodhull, A.A. v1p0637c2s
v1p1051c1s v1p1342c1s v1p1345c1s
v2p0089c1s v2p0255c2s v3p0185c2s
v3p0443c1s v3p0446c2s v4p0107c2s
v4p0325c1s v4p0327c1s v4p0516c2s
v4p0555c2s v4p0606c2s v5p0209c2s
v5p0219c2s v5p0244c1s v5p0263c1s
v5p0538c1s v5p0599c1s v6p0031c1s
v6p0305c1s v6p0398c2s v6p0474c1s
v6p0494c1s v6p0509c2s v6p0534c2s
v6p0561c1s v6p0668c1m
Woodhull, Anna M.W. and Graham, A.S.
v6p0696c2s
Woodhull, J.F. v3p0016c2s
v4p0394c2s v6p0112c1s v6p0498c2s
Woodhull, Mary E. v6p0153c1s
Wooding, M.I. v4p0340c1s
Woodlock, T.F. v4p0471c2s
v5p0476c1s v5p0476c2s v5p0477c1s
v6p0089c1s v6p0193c2s
Woodman, A.W. v5p0208c1s
Woodman, C.H. v1p0062c1s
v1p0396c2s v1p0459c1s v1p0657c1s
v1p0870c1s v1p0901c2s v1p1022c1s
v1p1266c1s
Woodman, D. v6p0375c2s
Woodman, H. v1p0237c2s
Woodridge, Alice L. v4p0630c2s
Woodriff, H. v1p1212c2s
Woodroffe, W.L. v4p0498c1s
v5p0259c2s v5p0311c2s
Woodrow, E.A. v3p0427c1s
Woodrow, E.A.E. v2p0156c2s
v3p0018c2s v4p0340c1s v4p0572c1m
Woodrow, E.A.E. and Bibby, G.H.
v4p0285c1s
Woodrow, F. v3p0035c2s
v4p0632c2s
Woodrow, J. v1p0931c1s
Woodrow, Nancy M.W. v6p0220c2s
Woodrow, S.G. v6p0566c1s
Woodrow, W., Mrs. v6p0541c1s
Woodrow, Wilson, Mrs. v6p0077c1s
v6p0103c2s v6p0182c1s v6p0209c1s
v6p0284c2s v6p0358c2s v6p0496c2s
v6p0604c2s v6p0611c2s v6p0682c2s
v6p0703c1s v6p0704c2s
Woodruff, C.A. v5p0424c2s
v5p0479c1s
Woodruff, C.E. v5p0042c2s
v6p0516c1s
Woodruff, C.H. v1p0211c1s
Woodruff, C.R. v4p0080c2s
v4p0115c1m v4p0115c2s v4p0135c1s
v4p0387c2s v5p0024c2m v5p0199c1s
v5p0391c2m v5p0399c2s v5p0443c1m
v5p0476c2s v5p0556c2s v5p0603c1s
v5p0641c1s v6p0014c2s v6p0055c2s
v6p0128c2s v6p0129c1s v6p0435c1s
v6p0435c2m v6p0436c1m v6p0443c2s
v6p0487c2m v6p0491c2s v6p0492c1m
v6p0585c1s v6p0690c2s
Woodruff, C.R. and McFarland, J.H.
v6p0127c2s
Woodruff, Clinton R. v6p0129c1s
v6p0366c1s
Woodruff, E. v1p0799c2s
Woodruff, E.B. v5p0335c1s
Woodruff, E.C. v6p0012c1s
Woodruff, E.H. v2p0051c2s
v2p0256c2s v3p0001c1s v3p0046c1s
v3p0070c1s v3p0130c1s v3p0381c2s
v4p0173c1s v4p0198c1s v4p0359c2s
Woodruff, F.E. v2p0045c1s
v2p0153c2s
Woodruff, J.A. v6p0354c1s
Woodruff, J.B. v1p0260c1s
v1p0990c2s v1p1344c2s
Woodruff, J.L. v4p0501c1s
Woodruff, J.P. v2p0054c2s
Woodruff, Judge v1p1084c1s
Woodruff, Paul H. v6p0185c1s
Woodruff, S. v1p0589c2s
Woodruff, T.M. v5p0222c2s
Woodruffe-Peacock, E.A. .. v6p0531c2s
Woods, A. v1p1342c1s
v6p0076c1s v6p0090c2s v6p0184c1s
v6p0331c1s v6p0564c1s v6p0579c2s
v6p0591c2s v6p0599c1s
Woods, A.F. v5p0080c2s
v5p0104c1s v6p0046c2s
Woods, A.T. v2p0362c1s
Woods, Amy v6p0660c2s
Woods, C.E. v3p0107c1s
Woods, C.F.F. v1p0352c2s
v1p0574c1s v1p0935c2s v1p1142c1s
Woods, E. v1p0759c2s
Woods, F.A. v6p0288c1s
v6p0410c2s v6p0428c2s
Woods, F.C. v5p0506c1s
Woods, F.H. v3p0023c1m
v4p0311c2s
Woods, G. v1p0464c1s
Woods, G.B. v1p0350c2s
v1p0447c1s v1p1352c2s
Woods, H. v6p0642c1s
Woods, H.B. v5p0199c1s
Woods, H.E. v6p0570c2s
Woods, J.E.T. v2p0273c1m
Woods, J.G. v3p0292c2s
Woods, J.H. v5p0236c2s
Woods, K.P. v3p0268c1s
v3p0470c2s v4p0193c1s v4p0216c1s
v5p0496c2s v6p0154c2s v6p0598c1s
Woods, K.T. v4p0461c2s
v5p0308c2s
Woods, K.T., Mrs. v4p0414c1s
Woods, Kate G. v3p0191c2s
Woods, Katharine P. v5p0053c1s
v5p0116c1s v5p0254c1s v5p0639c1s
Woods, L. v1p0118c1s
v1p0208c2s v1p0527c2s v1p0646c1s
v1p0989c2s v1p1378c1s v1p1410c2s
v2p0006c1s
Woods, L. and Plummer, W.S.
v1p0239c2s
Woods, L., jr. v1p0240c2s
v1p0241c2s v1p0530c1s v1p0843c2s
v1p1074c1s v1p1089c1s
Woods, M.L. v1p1141c2s
v2p0335c2s v3p0142c2s v4p0459c2s
v5p0268c2s v5p0426c2s v5p0548c2s
v5p0605c1s v5p0624c2s v6p0352c1s
Woods, M.L., Mrs. v5p0035c1s
v5p0053c2s v5p0331c1s v5p0355c1m
v5p0507c1s v5p0542c2s v5p0645c1s
v6p0622c2s
Woods, Margaret L. v6p0209c1s
Woods, Mrs. v4p0303c2s
v5p0301c2s v6p0086c2s v6p0276c1s
Woods, N.A. v1p1179c1s
Woods, R.A. v3p0050c2s
v3p0356c2s v3p0445c2s v4p0340c1s
v4p0598c1m v5p0120c1s v5p0520c2s
v5p0605c2s v6p0194c1s v6p0318c2s
v6p0584c2s v6p0585c1s v6p0600c2s
Woods, R.A. and Eastman, J.B.
v6p0076c2s

Woods, R.F. v6p0544c1s
Woods, S. v4p0553c1s v6p0050c2m v6p0233c2s
Woods, V. v4p0342c1s v4p0575c2s v5p0282c2s v5p0304c1s v5p0616c1s
Woods, W.G. v1p0143c2s
Woods, W.H. v3p0048c1s v4p0348c1s v5p0420c2s v5p0614c2s
Woods, W.J. v2p0201c1s v2p0349c1s v2p0414c2s v2p0427c2s v2p0443c2s v4p0129c1s
Woods, W.R. v1p1121c2s
Woodside, C.L. v2p0319c1s
Woodside, H.I. v4p0201c1s
Woodside, H.J. v4p0086c1s v4p0143c2s v4p0259c2s v4p0370c2s v4p0484c1s v4p0558c1s v5p0091c2s v5p0318c1s v5p0645c1s
Woodside, J.H. v4p0086c1s v4p0370c2s
Woodson, J.A. v4p0084c1s
Woodson, W.W. v4p0293c2s
Woodthorpe, R.G. v2p0305c1s v4p0364c1s v4p0519c2m
Woodville, J. v1p0188c2s v1p0216c2s v1p0359c1s v1p0608c2s v1p0755c2s v1p0904c2s v1p1339c1s
Woodville, J.L.Warren v6p0387c2s
Woodville, R.C. v4p0177c2s v4p0576c2s
Woodward, A. v1p0452c2m v1p0711c2m v1p0779c2s v2p0302c2m v2p0316c2s
Woodward, A.S. v4p0041c1s v4p0199c2s v4p0419c1s v4p0519c2s v5p0229c1s v5p0357c2s v6p0200c1s v6p0234c2s
Woodward, A.S. and Sherborn, C.D. v4p0584c1s
Woodward, B.B. v1p1040c1s v4p0433c1s
Woodward, B.D. v5p0430c2s
Woodward, Bettina and Wolffsohn, Lily v5p0012c1s
Woodward, C.L. v1p0905c1s
Woodward, C.M. v1p1236c1s v2p0006c1s v2p0275c2m v2p0299c2s v3p0266c2s v4p0354c2s v4p0499c1s v5p0015c1s v5p0177c1s v6p0039c1m v6p0111c1s v6p0193c2s v6p0564c1s v6p0581c2s
Woodward, C.N. v6p0399c2s
Woodward, Calvin M. v6p0399c2s
Woodward, E. v4p0362c2s v6p0446c1s
Woodward, Evelyn M. v5p0403c2s
Woodward, F.C. v4p0123c2s v4p0179c2s v6p0147c1s v6p0447c1s v6p0583c1s
Woodward, G. v6p0492c1s
Woodward, G.A. v3p0251c2s v3p0278c2s v4p0344c2s v5p0105c1s
Woodward, G.E. v5p0070c2s
Woodward, H. v1p0137c1s v1p0327c2s v1p0447c1s v1p0456c1s v1p0470c1s v1p0507c1s v1p0621c2s v1p0745c1s v1p0901c2s v1p0949c2s v1p1023c1s v1p1062c2s v1p1178c2s v1p1188c2m v2p0113c2s v2p0217c2s v4p0142c1s v4p0407c2s
Woodward, H.B. v1p0506c2s v1p0508c2s v1p0763c1s v2p0117c2s v4p0257c2s v4p0318c2s v4p0458c1s v5p0132c1s v5p0229c1s v6p0211c2s
Woodward, H.L. v4p0134c2s
Woodward, Horace B. v6p0304c2s
Woodward, J. v1p0394c2s v1p0691c1s v5p0321c2s v5p0330c1s v6p0214c1s v6p0347c1s
Woodward, J.J. v1p0399c1s v1p0787c1s v1p0835c2m v1p0955c1s v1p1003c1s v1p1004c1m v1p1342c1s
Woodward, K.S. v3p0054c2s
Woodward, L.J. v4p0529c2s
Woodward, M.C. v1p0848c2s
Woodward, M.S. v5p0438c2s
Woodward, M.V.M. v4p0628c1s
Woodward, P.H. v2p0479c1s v3p0367c1s v4p0011c1s
Woodward, R.F. v5p0182c1s
Woodward, R.S. v2p0319c1s v2p0322c2s v3p0125c2m v4p0273c1s v4p0363c1s v5p0417c1s v5p0513c2s v6p0102c1s v6p0190c1s v6p0263c1s v6p0323c2s v6p0408c1s v6p0498c1s
Woodward, S. v1p1122c2s v1p1434c2s
Woodward, S.P. v1p1188c2s v1p1189c1m
Woodward, S.W. v6p0114c2s
Woodward, T. v1p1152c1s
Woodward, T.R. v5p0076c2s v5p0639c2s
Woodward, W. v2p0224c1s v2p0424c1s v5p0077c2s
Woodward, W. and Gage, J.. v1p1129c1s
Woodward, W.E. v2p0219c2s
Woodward, W.H. v1p0247c1s
Woodwell, J.E. v6p0670c1s
Woodworth, C.L. v1p0432c2s v1p0709c2s v1p0817c2s v1p0847c1s
Woodworth, C.M. v6p0353c1s v6p0712c2s
Woodworth, C.W. v3p0141c2s
Woodworth, E. v5p0063c1s
Woodworth, E.B. v6p0570c1s
Woodworth, F. v5p0016c1s
Woodworth, F.C. v1p0438c1s
Woodworth, J.B. v4p0019c2s v4p0089c1s v4p0156c1s v4p0185c1s v4p0272c2s
Woodworth, M.B. v4p0116c1s v4p0553c2s v4p0592c2s v5p0120c1s
Woodworth, N.B. v3p0025c2s v3p0397c1s v3p0431c2s
Woodworth, R.S. v5p0061c1s v5p0164c1s v5p0168c1s v5p0614c2s
Woodworth, R.S. and Thorndike, E. v5p0356c1s
Woodworth, R.S. and Thorndike, E.L. v5p0370c1s
Woodworth, S. v6p0464c1s
Woodworth, W.J. v6p0500c2s v6p0509c2s
Woodworth, W.W. v1p0314c1s v1p1064c2s v1p1434c2s v3p0421c2s
Woof, R. v2p0075c1s
Wool, J.E. v1p1071c2s
Wool, T.J. v4p0116c2s
Woolbridge, J.L. v6p0198c2s
Woolbury, C.J.H. et al. .. v3p0132c2s
Woolcombe, H.S. v6p0708c1s
Wooldridge, C.W. v2p0173c2s
Wooldridge, W.B. v3p0450c2s
Woolery, W.H. v2p0400c2s
Wooley, C.P. v1p0610c2s v4p0247c2s v4p0373c2s
Wooley, J.G. et al. v6p0667c1s
Woolf, Alex. v5p0489c1s
Woolf, B.S. v5p0379c1s
Woolf, P. v5p0352c2s
Woolf, W.P. v5p0048c2s v5p0325c1s v6p0361c2s
Woolfe, H.D. v6p0118c1s v6p0119c1s
Woolhouse, W.S.B. v2p0271c2s v2p0418c2s v3p0217c2s v4p0287c1s
Woollcombe, W.G. v3p0284c2s
Woollen, E. v4p0313c2s v4p0315c2s
Woolley, C.P. v2p0001c2s v2p0098c2s v2p0151c2s v2p0317c1s v3p0080c2s v3p0112c1s v3p0468c2s v4p0050c1s v4p0112c1s v4p0165c2s v4p0267c2s v4p0467c2s v4p0561c1s v5p0459c1s
Woolley, J.G. v4p0116c1s v4p0461c2m v4p0467c1s v4p0476c2s v4p0500c2s
Woolley, M.E. v5p0510c2s
Woolley, R.W. v5p0271c1m v6p0276c1s v6p0297c1s
Woolley, T.C. v6p0548c2s
Woolman, M.S. v6p0257c1s
Woolman, Mary S. v6p0398c2s
Woolmer, S. v1p1287c2s
Woolmer, T. v1p0830c1s
Woolner, T. v3p0073c1s v3p0383c1s v4p0161c1s v4p0621c2s
Woolridge, A.S. v1p0269c1s
Woolridge, W.M. v6p0265c1s
Woolsey, J.D. v1p0244c1s v1p1342c1s
Woolsey, K.T., Mrs. v6p0703c1s
Woolsey, S.C. v1p0187c2s v1p0384c2s v1p0626c2s v1p1308c2s v1p1336c1s v3p0001c1s v3p0098c1s v3p0271c1s v4p0092c2s v4p0454c2s
Woolsey, T.C. v1p0143c1s
Woolsey, T.D. v1p0008c2s v1p0017c2s v1p0038c2s v1p0050c2s v1p0103c1s v1p0128c2s v1p0129c2s v1p0180c2s v1p0211c2s v1p0244c2s v1p0260c1s v1p0262c1s v1p0275c2s v1p0328c2s v1p0335c2s v1p0356c2s v1p0366c1s v1p0393c2s v1p0429c2s v1p0437c2s v1p0505c2s v1p0513c2s v1p0535c2s v1p0538c1s v1p0551c2m v1p0555c1s v1p0573c1s v1p0650c2m v1p0684c2s v1p0725c2s v1p0736c2s v1p0741c2s v1p0755c1s v1p0802c1s v1p0852c1s v1p0865c1s v1p0876c1s v1p0890c1s v1p0930c1s v1p0941c2s v1p0980c2s v1p0997c2s v1p1016c2m v1p1018c2s v1p1024c2s v1p1029c1s v1p1033c1s v1p1053c1s v1p1053c2s v1p1094c2s v1p1098c1s v1p1102c1s v1p1123c2s v1p1125c1s v1p1154c1s v1p1174c1s v1p1174c2s v1p1198c1s v1p1281c1s v1p1286c1s v1p1323c2s v1p1344c2s v1p1352c1s v1p1357c1s v1p1380c2s v2p0044c2m v2p0114c2s v2p0223c2s v2p0237c2s v2p0297c1s
Woolsey, T.D. and Jameson, J.A. v2p0119c2s
Woolsey, T.S. v2p0157c2s v4p0250c2s v4p0288c1m v4p0379c2s v4p0526c2s v4p0593c2m v5p0010c1s v5p0024c2s v5p0069c1s v5p0249c1s v5p0437c2s v5p0542c1s v6p0071c1s v6p0476c1s v6p0655c2s v6p0676c1s
Woolsey, T.S. et al. v4p0601c2s
Woolsey, Theo.S. v6p0277c2s
Woolson v6p0225c2s
Woolson, A.G. v2p0132c2s v2p0478c2s
Woolson, C.F. v1p0043c1s v1p0099c1s v1p0139c2s v1p0256c1s v1p0320c2s v1p0439c2s v1p0447c2s v1p0461c2s v1p0462c2s v1p0627c1s v1p0680c1s v1p0708c1m v1p0716c2s v1p0718c2m v1p0784c1s v1p0837c1s v1p0851c2m v1p0871c1s v1p0883c1s v1p0927c1s v1p0939c2s v1p0940c1s v1p0942c2s v1p0994c2s v1p1113c2s v1p1142c2s v1p1225c2m v1p1240c1s v1p1336c1s v1p1358c2s v1p1410c1s v1p1415c1s v2p0015c2s v2p0128c2s v2p0161c2s v2p0283c2s v2p0422c2s v2p0458c2s v3p0025c1s v3p0062c2s v3p0165c1s v3p0233c1s v3p0299c2s v3p0332c2s v4p0110c2s v4p0159c2s v4p0263c2s v4p0582c1s
Woolson, M.S. v6p0282c2s
Woolston, F. v6p0257c1s
Woolston, H. v6p0193c2s
Woolworth, J.M. v3p0298c1s
Wooster, E.W. v4p0444c1s
Wooster, W.H. v4p0449c1s v4p0531c1s
Wooten, D.G. v6p0545c2s
Wooton, E. v2p0309c2s
Wootton, A.C. v5p0143c1s
Worcester, A. v1p1178c1s v2p0194c1s v6p0462c2s
Worcester, B. v5p0236c1s v6p0538c1s
Worcester, C.P. v4p0104c1s
Worcester, D.C. v5p0328c1s v5p0444c2s v5p0445c1s
Worcester, D.C. and Bourns, F.S. v5p0445c2s
Worcester, D.G. v5p0444c2s
Worcester, J. v4p0096c2s v4p0410c1s v4p0636c1s v5p0055c2m v5p0057c2m v5p0173c1s v5p0236c1m v5p0358c2s v5p0463c1s v6p0060c2s v6p0341c1s
Worcester, J.H., jr. v3p0432c1s
Worcester, J.R. v6p0143c1s
Worcester, L. v1p0186c1s v1p0846c1s
Worcester, N. v1p0466c2s v1p0687c2s v1p0689c1s v1p1090c1s v1p1147c2s v1p1201c1s
Worcester, S.M. v1p0262c1s v1p0318c1s v1p0698c1s
Worcester, S.T. v1p0597c2s v2p0311c1s v2p0311c2s
Worcester, W.L. v4p0226c1s v4p0465c1s v5p0157c1s v5p0428c2s v6p0584c1s
Worden, G.H. v3p0437c1s
Worden, J.P. v4p0189c2s v5p0157c2s v6p0137c2s v6p0572c1s
Worden, O.N. v1p1105c1s
Wordsworth, C. v1p0240c2s v1p1165c2s v2p0325c2s v3p0025c2s v3p0322c1s v3p0332c2s
Wordsworth, C.F. and Wordsworth, F. v1p1260c1s
Wordsworth, F. and Wordsworth, C.F. v1p1260c1s
Wordsworth, J. et al. v3p0041c1s
Wordsworth, W. v3p0067c2s
Wores, T. v3p0226c2s v5p0211c1s
Wores, Theodore v5p0313c2s
Work, C.T. v4p0529c2s
Work, M.N. v5p0403c1s
Worker, L.R. v6p0678c1s
Workman, F.B. v3p0366c1s v3p0471c2s v4p0145c1s v6p0316c1s
Workman, Fanny B. v6p0291c1m
Workman, G.C. v4p0054c2s
Workman, J. v5p0092c1s v5p0163c2s v5p0390c1s v5p0480c1s v5p0629c1s v6p0485c2s
Workman, James v4p0511c2s v5p0064c2s
Workman, W.H. v5p0265c2s v5p0573c2s v6p0060c1s v6p0121c2s v6p0257c2s
Worley, D. v1p0097c1s v1p0848c1s v1p1088c2s v1p1089c1s v1p1292c2s
Worley, J.L. v6p0639c2s
Worlledge, C.W. v3p0362c1s
Wormald, J. v1p0493c1s
Wormald, R.B. v1p0609c2s v1p0951c2s
Worman, E.J. v6p0244c2s
Worman, J.H. v1p0998c2s
Wormeley, E., Miss v1p0088c1s
Wormeley, E., Mrs. v1p1272c1s
Wormely, E. v1p1238c1s
Wormer, J.R.Van v5p0304c2s
Wormley, T.G. v2p0274c1s

Worms, R. v4p0449c2s
v4p0534c2s
Worms, R. and Lindsay, S.McC.
v5p0293c2s
Wornum, R.N. v1p0203c2s
v1p0371c1s v1p0558c1s v1p0731c1s
v1p0898c1s v1p1104c2s v1p1195c2s
v1p1242c2s
Worsdell, W. v4p0337c2s
Worsfold, W.B. v2p0293c2s
v3p0027c2s v4p0006c1s v4p0086c1s
v4p0298c2s v4p0492c1s v4p0560c2s
v4p0582c1s v5p0078c1s v5p0093c1s
v5p0221c2s v5p0585c1s v5p0586c1s
v6p0610c2s
Worsfold, W.D. v6p0006c2s
Worsfold, W.R. v6p0505c1s
Worsley, H. v1p0595c1s
v2p0204c1s
Worsley, P.S. v1p0351c2s
v1p0424c1s v1p0896c2s v1p0996c1s
v1p1086c2s v1p1241c1s v1p1430c2s
Wortabit, J. v4p0312c2s
Worth, B. v1p0790c1s
Worth, G.C. v5p0140c1s
Worth, G.C. and Knott, G.H.
v5p0609c1s
Worth, J. v1p0612c2s
v4p0061c1s
Worth, R.N. v2p0052c2s
Wortham, B.H. v2p0036c1s
v2p0055c1s
Worthen, A.H. and Meek, F.B.
v1p0317c2s v1p0749c2s v1p1164c2s
Worthington, A.M. v1p0367c2m
v6p0636c2s
Worthington, A.M. et al. . v3p0270c2s
Worthington, A.W. v1p1034c2s
v1p1191c1s
Worthington, C. v4p0102c1s
Worthington, Daisy Lee ... v6p0704c1s
Worthington, E. v4p0225c2s
Worthington, E.B. v5p0043c1s
Worthington, J. v6p0441c1s
Worthington, L. v4p0190c1s
Worthington, R.H. v1p0675c2s
v5p0304c1s v5p0639c1s
Worthington, T. v1p0052c2s
Worthington, T.K. v3p0325c2s
Wortley, C.S. v4p0240c1s
Wortley, E.S. v5p0540c1s
Wortley, E.Stuart, Hon.Mrs.
v6p0390c1s
Wortley, H.G. v5p0535c2s
Wortley, J.S., Mrs. v3p0077c2s
v3p0386c2s
Wortley, J.Stuart, Mrs. .. v3p0040c1s
Wortley, Stuart, Hon.Mrs.. v6p0475c2s
Wortley, V.S. v6p0475c2s
Wortman, D. v1p0507c1s
Wortman, J.L. v2p0125c2s
v2p0207c2s v2p0435c2s v4p0168c1s
v5p0018c1s v5p0363c1s v5p0465c2s
v6p0209c2s v6p0580c2s
Wortman, J.S. v5p0193c2s
Wotherspoon, W.W. v4p0282c1s
v6p0603c1s
Wotquenne, M.A. v5p0043c2s
Wotton, H. v1p0391c1s
Wotton, M.E. v2p0252c2s
v3p0286c1s v4p0481c1s v4p0555c2s
Wotton, Mabel E. v4p0016c2s
v4p0265c2s
Woulfe-Flanagan, J. v3p0245c2s
Wozencraft, O.M. v2p0286c2s
v6p0164c2s v6p0414c2s
Wragge, C.L. v2p0039c2s
v2p0468c2s v3p0028c1s
Wragge, R. v3p0325c1s
Wraigh, X. v5p0425c2s
Wrangell, F.von v6p0235c2s
v6p0306c2s
Wratislaw, A.H. v1p0143c1s
v1p0145c1m v1p0594c1s v1p0617c2m
v1p0618c1m v1p1338c1s v2p0050c2s
v2p0086c1s v2p0124c2s v2p0237c2s
v2p0327c1s v2p0355c2s v2p0462c2s
v3p0043c1s v3p0043c2s v3p0231c1s
Wratislaw, T. v5p0170c2s
Wraxall, C.L., Sir v1p0908c2s
Wraxall, F.C.L. v1p0216c1s
Wraxall, F.C.L., Sir v1p0088c2s
v1p1016c2s
Wraxall, L. v1p0185c1s
v1p0200c1s v1p0202c2s v1p0209c2s
v1p0238c2s v1p0344c2s v1p0488c2s
v1p0498c2s v1p0710c1s v1p0907c2s
v1p1143c2s v1p1197c2s
Wray, D. v1p0554c2s
v1p1126c2s
Wray, Dr. v1p1265c2s
Wray, H. v3p0098c2s
Wray, H.R. v4p0012c1s
v4p0087c2s v4p0119c2s v5p0531c2s
v6p0139c2s
Wray, L. v1p1265c1s
v3p0102c1s v3p0391c1s v3p0421c2s
v4p0434c2s
Wray, N. v3p0084c2s
Wreford, H. v1p0038c1s
v1p0802c2s v1p1052c1s v1p1116c1s
Wren, J. v4p0269c1s
Wren, W. v3p0129c1s
v3p0278c2s v3p0439c1s v4p0120c2s
v4p0138c1s
Wren, W.C. v5p0294c2s
Wrench, F. v4p0264c1s
v4p0270c1s
Wrenshall, J. v2p0152c2s
Wrenshall, Letitia H. v6p0312c1s
Wrey, P. v1p0019c1s
v1p0183c2s v1p0521c1s
Wrey, Peyton v1p1242c1s
Wright v1p0200c2s
Wright, A. v3p0432c2s
v4p0056c2s v4p0142c1s v4p0424c2s
Wright, A.A. v4p0469c1s
Wright, A.B. v6p0696c2s
Wright, A.E. v4p0125c1m
v6p0175c2s
Wright, A.N. v1p0701c2s
Wright, A.O. v1p0594c2s
v2p0268c2s v3p0113c2s v4p0151c1s
Wright, A.W. v1p0019c2s
v1p0281c2s v1p0399c1s v1p0400c1s
v1p0401c2m v1p0502c2s v1p0824c1s
v1p0826c1s v1p0955c2m v1p1006c2s
v1p1055c1s v1p1234c1s v1p1440c2m
v2p0138c1s v2p0416c1s v2p0422c2s
v3p0475c2s v4p0487c1m v6p0158c1s
v6p0550c1s
Wright, A.W. and Kreider, D.A.
v5p0146c2s
Wright, B. v1p0424c1s
v2p0157c2s v2p0483c2s
Wright, B.H. v1p0424c1s
Wright, B.M., jr. v1p1239c1s
Wright, C. v1p0036c2s
v1p0070c1s v1p0083c1s v1p0104c2s
v1p0107c1s v1p0134c2s v1p0265c2s
v1p0287c1s v1p0333c2s v1p0340c2s
v1p0374c2s v1p0390c2s v1p0403c2s
v1p0434c1s v1p0568c1s v1p0587c1s
v1p0620c2s v1p0651c1s v1p0724c1s
v1p0760c2s v1p0779c1s v1p0782c2s
v1p0899c2s v1p0900c1s v1p0903c2s
v1p0953c1s v1p0999c2s v1p1001c1m
v1p1001c2s v1p1005c1s v1p1016c1s
v1p1037c1s v1p1052c1s v1p1053c2s
v1p1176c2s v1p1182c1s v1p1188c2s
v1p1216c2s v1p1233c1m v1p1234c1s
v1p1235c1s v1p1243c2s v1p1265c1s
v1p1303c2s v1p1395c1s
Wright, C. and Godkin, E.L.
v1p0839c1s
Wright, C. and March, F.A.
v1p1336c2s
Wright, C.B. v3p0139c2s
v5p0374c2s
Wright, C.D. v1p0212c1s
v1p0714c2s v2p0151c2s v2p0220c2s
v2p0245c1s v2p0354c1s v2p0359c1s
v2p0407c1s v2p0431c1s v2p0464c1s
v3p0071c2s v3p0072c1s v3p0119c1s
v3p0237c2s v3p0239c1s v3p0268c1s
v3p0345c1s v3p0398c1s v3p0408c2m
v3p0420c2s v4p0022c1s v4p0080c2s
v4p0094c1m v4p0102c2s v4p0114c2s
v4p0139c2s v4p0157c2s v4p0167c2s
v4p0179c2s v4p0194c1s v4p0288c2m
v4p0292c1s v4p0315c1m v4p0315c2m
v4p0316c1s v4p0336c2s v4p0356c2s
v4p0415c2s v4p0453c1s v4p0472c1s
v4p0473c2s v4p0532c2s v4p0546c2m
v4p0590c2s v4p0593c2s v4p0596c2s
v4p0608c1m v4p0630c1s v5p0014c1s
v5p0024c2s v5p0031c1s v5p0099c2s
v5p0289c1m v5p0320c2s v5p0353c2s
v5p0466c2s v5p0467c2s v5p0488c1s
v5p0600c1s v5p0601c1s v5p0616c2s
v5p0637c1s v6p0133c1s v6p0188c2s
v6p0355c1s v6p0356c2s v6p0472c1s
v6p0537c1s v6p0600c2s v6p0615c1s
v6p0622c1m v6p0651c2s v6p0687c1s
Wright, C.D. and Buchanan, J.R.
v5p0585c1s
Wright, C.D. et al. v5p0391c1s
v6p0690c1s
Wright, C.E. v1p1043c1s
v6p0252c2s v6p0272c2s v6p0290c2s
Wright, C.F. v5p0169c2s
Wright, C.G. v2p0083c2s
Wright, C.H. v3p0031c2s
v6p0560c1s
Wright, C.H.C. v3p0309c2s
Wright, C.H.H. v2p0115c1s
v2p0130c1s v2p0211c1m v2p0236c2s
v2p0268c2s v2p0269c1s v2p0382c2s
v3p0347c1s v3p0370c1s v4p0056c1s
v4p0057c2s v4p0469c2s
Wright, C.Q. v4p0537c1s
Wright, C.R.A. v1p0619c1s
v1p0664c1s v1p0825c2s v1p1218c1s
v1p1376c1s v1p1428c2s v3p0397c1s
Wright, C.T.H. v3p0370c1m
v4p0597c2s v5p0467c2s
Wright, C.W. v6p0295c1s
v6p0632c2s v6p0707c1s
Wright, Carroll D. v4p0193c1s
v6p0158c1s v6p0217c1s v6p0517c2s
Wright, D.T. v1p1346c1s
Wright, Dr. v1p0796c2s
Wright, E. v1p0236c2s
v1p0338c2s v1p0463c2s v1p0647c2m
v1p0651c2s v1p0729c1s v2p0223c1m
v6p0179c2s v6p0230c2s v6p0242c1s
v6p0258c1s v6p0280c1s v6p0281c1s
v6p0284c2s v6p0358c2s v6p0387c1s
v6p0428c2s v6p0472c1s v6p0478c1s
v6p0501c2s v6p0539c1s v6p0548c2s
v6p0596c1s v6p0707c2s
Wright, E.A. v5p0265c2s
Wright, E.B. v6p0470c2s
Wright, E.C. v1p0494c2s
Wright, E.J.D. v3p0006c2s
Wright, E.P. v1p0021c2s
v1p0035c2s v1p0267c1s v1p0381c2s
v1p0456c1s v1p0457c1s v1p0500c2s
v1p1028c2s v1p1144c2s v1p1187c2s
v1p1239c2s v1p1326c2s v2p0053c1s
Wright, E.W.H. v6p0595c2s
Wright, Elizabeth W. v6p0624c1s
Wright, F.A. v4p0596c2s
v5p0586c1s
Wright, F.B. v6p0372c1s
Wright, F.E. v6p0221c2s
v6p0323c1s v6p0415c2s v6p0418c2s
v6p0572c1s
Wright, F.H. v6p0085c2s
Wright, F.L. v5p0353c2s
Wright, F.M. v3p0291c2s
Wright, G.A. v5p0024c2s
v5p0082c2s v5p0440c2s
Wright, G.B. v2p0475c2s
Wright, G.C. v5p0391c2s
Wright, G.E. v1p1436c2s
Wright, G.F. v1p0096c1s
v1p0333c2m v1p0346c1s v1p0452c2s
v1p0454c2s v1p0523c2s v1p0639c2s
v1p0879c1s v1p1045c1s v1p1161c1m
v1p1164c1s v1p1232c2s v1p1233c1s
v2p0113c2s v2p0179c1m v2p0183c2s
v2p0257c2s v2p0273c2s v2p0314c1m
v2p0320c1s v2p0355c2s v2p0384c2s
v2p0389c1s v2p0390c1s v3p0054c2s
v3p0080c2s v3p0082c2s v3p0089c2s
v3p0111c1s v3p0114c2s v3p0173c2m
v3p0179c2s v3p0207c1s v3p0207c2s
v3p0265c1m v3p0265c2s v3p0288c1m
v3p0317c1s v3p0342c2s v3p0379c2s
v3p0400c2s v3p0404c1s v3p0418c2s
v4p0036c1s v4p0053c2s v4p0100c1s
v4p0114c1s v4p0120c2s v4p0151c2s
v4p0227c1m v4p0242c2s v4p0272c2m
v4p0273c1m v4p0317c2s v4p0352c1m
v4p0394c2m v4p0498c2s v5p0008c2s
v5p0033c2s v5p0043c1m v5p0043c2s
v5p0096c1s v5p0098c1s v5p0108c2s
v5p0110c1s v5p0114c2s v5p0157c2s
v5p0198c2s v5p0229c1s v5p0299c1s
v5p0299c2s v5p0303c1s v5p0306c2s
v5p0310c2s v5p0359c2m v5p0410c1s
v5p0417c1s v5p0428c2s v5p0432c2s
v5p0481c1s v5p0503c1s v5p0513c2s
v5p0557c1s v5p0567c2s v5p0585c2s
v5p0644c1s v5p0645c1s v6p0030c2s
v6p0036c2s v6p0105c1s v6p0158c1s
v6p0169c2s v6p0186c2s v6p0219c1s
v6p0335c1s v6p0397c1s v6p0398c1s
v6p0398c2m v6p0421c2s v6p0555c2s
v6p0559c2m v6p0561c1s v6p0593c1m
v6p0613c1s v6p0628c2s v6p0661c1s
v6p0662c1s
Wright, G.F. and Currier, A.H.
v3p0321c1s
Wright, G.F. and McGee, W.J.
v4p0273c1s
Wright, G.G. v5p0413c1s
Wright, G.S. v6p0567c1s
Wright, G.W. v2p0112c1s
v4p0607c1s
Wright, H. v1p0245c1s
v1p0460c1s v1p0663c1s v1p1183c2s
v1p1191c2s v1p1387c1s v5p0050c2s
v5p0129c1s v5p0156c2s v6p0329c1s
v6p0360c1s v6p0386c2s v6p0494c1s
v6p0567c2s v6p0594c1s v6p0667c2s
Wright, H.A. v4p0075c1s
Wright, H.B. v6p0136c1s
Wright, H.C. v5p0107c1s
v5p0581c1s
Wright, H.C.S. v4p0537c1s
v6p0604c2s
Wright, H.E. v6p0155c1s
v6p0217c1s v6p0461c1s v6p0513c2s
v6p0568c1s v6p0700c1s
Wright, H.L. v2p0014c1s
Wright, H.M. v6p0459c2s
v6p0493c1s
Wright, H.R. v6p0653c1s
Wright, H.W. v5p0033c2s
v6p0214c1s v6p0259c2s v6p0582c2s
Wright, Hamilton v6p0091c1s
v6p0092c1s v6p0280c2s
Wright, Helen E. v5p0531c1s
v5p0608c1s v6p0276c1s v6p0417c2s
v6p0697c2s
Wright, Irene A. v5p0131c2s
Wright, J. v1p0071c2s
v1p0127c2s v1p0264c2s v1p0687c1s

v1p0785c2s v1p0850c1s v1p0877c2s
v2p0035c2s v4p0202c2s v4p0343c1s
v6p0197c1m v6p0198c2s v6p0245c2s
Wright, J.A. v1p0650c1s
v1p0988c1s v2p0081c2s
Wright, J.C. v6p0444c2s
Wright, J.D. v5p0155c1s
v6p0043c2s v6p0045c1s
Wright, J.E. v5p0469c1s
Wright, J.F. v5p0236c2s
Wright, J.H. v1p0066c2s
v3p0019c2s v3p0246c2s v5p0126c2s
v6p0282c1s
Wright, J.J. v4p0176c1s
v6p0703c1s
Wright, J.L. v4p0422c1s
v5p0072c2s v5p0105c1s v5p0410c1s
v6p0102c2s
Wright, J.L. et al. v5p0158c2s
Wright, J.M. v2p0021c2s
v2p0336c2s v2p0457c2s v2p0470c2s
Wright, J.M.B. v5p0074c2s
Wright, J.McN. v1p0157c2s
v4p0612c2s v5p0174c2s v5p0548c2s
v5p0562c2s
Wright, J.McNair v3p0103c2s
Wright, J.O. v2p0324c1s
Wright, J.S. v1p1283c1s
v1p1428c2s
Wright, J.W. v1p1434c1s
v2p0323c1s v4p0478c1s
Wright, J.W.A. v2p0049c2m
v2p0075c2s v2p0113c1s v2p0266c1s
v2p0299c2s v2p0465c2s
Wright, L. v1p1037c2s
v3p0104c1s v3p0145c1s v3p0475c2s
v4p0286c1s v6p0070c2s v6p0253c2s
Wright, L.E. v6p0494c2s
Wright, L.W. v6p0668c1s
Wright, M. v3p0258c2s
v3p0306c1s v5p0340c1s v6p0499c2s
Wright, M.A.L. v4p0396c1s
Wright, M.B. v1p0031c1s
v1p0066c1s v1p0199c1s v1p0521c1s
v1p0855c1s v1p0958c2s v1p0960c1s
v1p1030c1s v1p1403c2s v2p0164c1s
v2p0203c2s v2p0230c2s v2p0315c2m
v2p0324c2s v2p0348c2s v2p0395c2s
v2p0470c2s v3p0253c1s v3p0267c2s
v3p0287c2s v3p0325c1s v3p0367c1s
v4p0132c1s v4p0511c2s v4p0609c1s
v5p0545c2s v5p0632c2s
Wright, M.E. v1p0191c1s
v1p1171c2s v1p1270c2s v5p0443c1s
Wright, M.J. v2p0053c2s
v2p0108c1s v2p0319c2s v2p0483c1s
v3p0201c2s v3p0248c1s v3p0321c2s
v4p0194c2s v4p0265c2s v4p0364c1s
Wright, M.O. v5p0064c1s
v6p0472c1s v6p0700c2s
Wright, M.T. v3p0023c1s
v3p0159c2s v4p0143c1s v4p0151c1s
v4p0216c1s v5p0155c1s v6p0682c1s
Wright, Marg.B. v3p0159c1s
Wright, Marie Robinson ... v6p0307c1s
Wright, Mary T. v3p0437c1s
v4p0453c2s v5p0154c2s v5p0315c2s
v6p0518c1s v6p0562c1s
Wright, N. v5p0278c2s
Wright, N.H. v1p0782c2s
Wright, P.B. v5p0025c2s
v5p0504c2s v6p0374c1m v6p0563c1s
Wright, P.C. v1p0133c1s
Wright, R.E. v1p1028c2s
Wright, R.H. v6p0372c1s
Wright, R.R. v1p0434c2s
v2p0087c2s v2p0194c2s v6p0446c2s
v6p0448c1s
Wright, R.R., jr. v6p0448c1s
Wright, R.W. v1p1107c1s
v1p1148c1s
Wright, S. v1p0928c1s
v1p1431c1s v1p1434c1s
Wright, S.H. v1p0070c1s
Wright, S.R. v6p0233c1s
Wright, T. v1p0019c2s
v1p0024c1s v1p0035c2s v1p0040c1s
v1p0040c2m v1p0041c2s v1p0046c1s
v1p0065c1s v1p0068c2s v1p0163c2s
v1p0200c2m v1p0223c1s v1p0285c2s
v1p0319c2s v1p0360c1s v1p0362c1s
v1p0363c2s v1p0390c1s v1p0412c2s
v1p0413c1s v1p0414c1s v1p0505c2s
v1p0584c2m v1p0587c2s v1p0715c1s
v1p0727c2s v1p0743c2s v1p0768c2s
v1p0776c2s v1p0797c1m v1p0880c2s
v1p0965c1s v1p0971c2s v1p0984c1s
v1p1039c2m v1p1050c1s v1p1070c2s
v1p1114c2s v1p1122c1m v1p1122c2m
v1p1141c2s v1p1142c2s v1p1148c1s
v1p1184c1s v1p1279c1s v1p1304c1s
v1p1322c2s v1p1359c1s v1p1420c2s
v1p1431c1s v2p0106c1s v2p0275c2s
v2p0432c2s v2p0456c1s v6p0120c2s
Wright, T. and Akerman, J.Y.
v1p1403c1s
Wright, T.D. v5p0621c2s
Wright, T.F. v4p0043c1s
v4p0053c2m v4p0054c1s v4p0055c1s
v4p0055c2s v4p0056c1s v4p0065c1s
v4p0077c2s v4p0081c1s v4p0261c1s
v4p0300c2s v4p0301c2s v4p0372c2s
v4p0397c1s v4p0456c1s v4p0476c1s
v4p0534c2s v4p0554c1s v4p0559c2m
v5p0001c1s v5p0056c1m v5p0056c2s
v5p0057c1s v5p0058c1s v5p0059c1s
v5p0060c2s v5p0084c2s v5p0116c2s
v5p0118c1s v5p0123c2s v5p0131c1s
v5p0132c2s v5p0142c1s v5p0232c2s
v5p0304c1s v5p0307c1s v5p0313c2m
v5p0372c2s v5p0380c1s v5p0402c1s
v5p0405c1m v5p0409c2s v5p0428c2s
v5p0437c2s v5p0453c2s v5p0458c1s
v5p0474c2s v5p0484c2s v5p0490c2s
v5p0544c1s v5p0546c2s v5p0548c1s
v5p0561c2s v5p0562c1m v5p0563c2m
v5p0565c1s v5p0577c1s v5p0590c2s
v5p0623c1s v5p0623c2s v5p0636c2s
v5p0640c1s v5p0641c2m v6p0021c2s
v6p0027c1s v6p0061c1s v6p0061c2m
v6p0064c2s v6p0073c2s v6p0126c1s
v6p0255c1s v6p0260c1s v6p0281c2s
v6p0339c2s v6p0347c1s v6p0359c2s
v6p0444c1s v6p0448c1s v6p0519c1s
v6p0524c1s v6p0628c2m v6p0708c2s
Wright, T.F. and Hay, H.C.
v5p0057c2s
Wright, T.H. v1p1263c1s
Wright, T.L. v1p0644c1s
Wright, T.W. v2p0252c1s
Wright, U. v1p0015c1s
Wright, W. v1p0246c2s
v1p0431c2s v1p0582c1s v1p0756c2s
v1p0806c1s v1p0831c1s v1p1243c2s
v1p1279c1s v1p1279c2s v1p1285c1s
v1p1394c2s v2p0041c2s v2p0201c2s
v2p0204c1m v2p0327c2s v2p0429c2s
v3p0040c2s v3p0042c2s v3p0078c2s
v3p0434c2s v4p0074c1s v4p0105c1s
v4p0469c1s v4p0561c1s v5p0060c2s
v5p0095c2s v6p0230c1m
Wright, W. and Tyler, T. . v2p0204c1s
Wright, W.A. v2p0108c2s
v3p0236c2s v3p0362c2s v6p0230c2s
v6p0531c2s
Wright, W.A. and Gardiner, S.R.
v2p0416c1s
Wright, W.A. et al. v2p0416c1s
Wright, W.B. v3p0046c1s
v4p0078c1s
Wright, W.C. v3p0217c2s
v4p0245c1s v5p0323c2s v5p0419c1s
v6p0240c2s
Wright, W.E.C. v3p0401c2s
v4p0108c2s v4p0524c1s v4p0534c2s
v5p0417c1s v5p0537c2s v6p0170c1s
Wright, W.G. v2p0062c2s
v2p0307c1s
Wright, W.H. v1p0810c1s
v6p0055c1s v6p0655c1s
Wright, W.H.K. v1p0742c2s
v2p0255c2s v2p0345c2s v3p0020c1s
v5p0333c1s v5p0336c1s
Wright, W.J. v5p0383c2s
Wright, W.K. v2p0481c1s
v3p0044c1s v3p0338c1s
Wright, W.M. v5p0252c2s
Wright, W.N. v6p0391c1s
Wright, W.R. v6p0312c1s
v6p0532c1s
Wright, W.W. v1p0026c1s
v1p0298c1s v1p0306c1s v1p0905c1m
v1p0905c2s v1p1401c1s
Wright-Henderson, P.A. ... v4p0420c1s
Wrightson, H.J. v5p0256c1s
Wrightson, J. v2p0005c2s
v2p0062c1s v2p0145c1s v2p0471c2m
v3p0006c1s v3p0006c2s
Wrightson, T. v1p0408c1s
Wrigley, E. v1p0174c2s
v1p0299c1s
Wrigley, H.E. v1p0995c2s
Wringe, R. v6p0710c1s
Wroblewski, S. v1p0502c1s
Wrong, G.M. v4p0086c1s
v4p0216c2s v6p0258c1s v6p0299c1s
Wroot, H.E. v4p0074c1s
Wroth, L.C. v6p0569c2s
Wroth, W. v2p0003c2s
v2p0091c2s v2p0291c1s v2p0318c1s
v3p0023c1s v3p0205c2s v3p0423c2s
Wrottesley, G. v3p0325c1s
Wrottesley, W. v1p0913c2s
Wu, Ting Fang v5p0108c2s
v5p0110c1s v5p0111c1s v5p0113c1s
v6p0120c1s v6p0120c2s v6p0144c1s
Wuarin, L. v4p0560c2s
v5p0227c2s
Wuarin, Louis v6p0176c2s
Wuensch, A.F. v4p0324c1s
Wuerpel, E.H. v4p0014c1s
v4p0032c1s v4p0425c1s v5p0626c2s
v6p0695c2s
Wuerpel, G.B. v6p0224c1s
Wuerpel, Gay B. v6p0155c1s
v6p0697c2s
Wundt, A. v2p0415c1s
Wundt, W. v1p0293c1s
v1p0907c1s v1p1000c2s v1p1238c1s
v4p0283c1s v4p0537c2s v4p0542c1s
Wunsch, J.R. v3p0210c1s
Wunsh, H. v5p0397c1s
Wurts, A.J. v3p0133c1s
v3p0251c1s v4p0176c1s v4p0332c1m
v5p0184c1s
Wurts, G. v1p0359c2s
Wurtz, A. v1p0074c1s
Wurtz, C.A. v1p0812c1s
Wurtz, H. v1p0143c1s
v1p0224c2s v1p0493c2s v1p0501c2s
v1p0502c1s v1p0527c1s v1p0977c1s
v1p1391c2s v4p0012c2s v4p0529c2s
Wurtz, H. and Silliman, B.
v1p0459c1s v1p0501c2s v1p1293c1s
Wurtzburg, C.A. v3p0057c1s
v3p0387c1s v4p0075c2s v4p0517c2s
v4p0518c2m
Wust, J. v4p0398c1s
Wuttke, Prof. v1p0427c1m
Wyat, T., Sir v4p0209c2s
v4p0343c2s
Wyatt, A.J. v4p0014c1s
Wyatt, C. v2p0478c1s
Wyatt, E. v5p0339c1s
v5p0366c2s v5p0524c1s v5p0585c1s
v6p0488c2s v6p0571c1s v6p0599c2s
Wyatt, Edith v6p0580c1s
Wyatt, F. v1p1388c2s
v4p0197c1s v4p0439c2s v4p0562c1s
v5p0052c1s
Wyatt, G.E. v4p0529c1s
Wyatt, H.F. v5p0006c2s
v5p0243c1s v5p0245c1s v5p0618c1s
v6p0266c2s v6p0417c1s v6p0445c2s
Wyatt, H.F. and Wickham, H.J.
v6p0267c2s
Wyatt, J.B.N. v5p0026c2s
Wyatt, M.D. v1p0948c1m
v1p1227c1s v3p0021c2s v3p0072c1s
v3p0281c2s
Wyatt, S. v3p0280c2m
Wyatt, T. v1p0305c2s
v1p0567c2s v1p0786c1s
Wyatt, V. v1p0963c1s
Wybergh, W. v6p0654c1s
Wychoff, E.G. v6p0696c2s
Wyck, C.Van v1p1408c1s
Wyckoff, A.B. v2p0213c1s
v3p0297c2s v4p0292c2s
Wyckoff, A.E. v4p0541c1s
Wyckoff, C.W. v1p0454c2s
Wyckoff, R.J. v6p0164c2s
Wyckoff, W.A. v5p0027c1s
v5p0084c2s v5p0295c1s v5p0518c2s
v5p0533c1s v5p0585c2s v6p0385c2s
v6p0652c1s
Wyckoff, W.C. v1p0457c1s
v2p0426c1s
Wyckoff, W.H. v5p0640c2s
Wycollar, F. v6p0557c1s
Wyczolkowska, A. v6p0055c1s
Wyer, J.I. v5p0179c2s
Wyer, J.I., jr. v5p0176c2s
v6p0190c1m v6p0375c1s
Wyer, J.I., jr. and
Leonard, Mabel, E. v6p0190c1s
Wyer, J.I., jr. and Lord, I.E.
v5p0176c2m
Wyer, J.I., jr. and
Lord, Isabel E.
v6p0190c1m
Wyer, S.S.
v6p0518c1s
Wyeth, J.A. v1p1213c2s
v3p0064c2s v3p0443c1s v4p0416c2s
v4p0634c1s v5p0076c1s v5p0214c2s
v5p0215c1m v5p0556c2s
Wyeth, J.A. and Holloway, W.R.
v3p0064c2s v3p0095c2s
Wyeth, M.E.C. v1p0875c1s
v1p0983c1s
Wyeth, N.C. v6p0553c1s
Wyeth, N.J. v1p0622c1s
Wyl, N. and Broadhead, G.C.
v1p0855c1s
Wylde, E.P. v3p0470c2s
Wylde, K. v3p0411c1s
v4p0126c2s v4p0267c1s v5p0282c1s
v6p0411c2s
Wylde, Katharine v5p0264c1s
v6p0095c1s v6p0234c1s
Wyley, F.N. v4p0536c1s
Wylie, A. v1p0589c1s
v2p0471c1s
Wylie, A.H. v3p0198c2s
Wylie, A.McE. v1p0107c2s
Wylie, A.R.T. v6p0070c2s
Wylie, D. v6p0235c1s
Wylie, D.G. v3p0378c1s
Wylie, J.A. v2p0120c2s
v2p0237c1s v2p0353c1s v2p0473c2s
v4p0353c1s
Wylie, J.C. v6p0490c2s
Wylie, J.H. v3p0326c2s
v6p0344c2s
Wylie, M.de v6p0556c1s
Wylie, R.C. v6p0128c1s
Wylie, W. v1p1154c2s
Wylie, W.G. v1p0606c1s
v1p0981c2s

Wylie, W.M. v1p0020c1s
v1p0211c1s v1p0314c1s v1p0680c1s
v1p0718c2s v1p0824c2s v1p0935c2s
v1p0996c1s v1p1122c1s v1p1178c2s
v1p1276c1s v1p1329c2s v2p0280c2s
v5p0428c2s
Wyllarde, D. v5p0007c1s
Wyllie, J.W.S. v1p0009c2m
v1p0067c2m
Wyllie, S.A. v1p0505c1s
Wyllie, W.L. v6p0490c1s
Wylly, H.C. v5p0050c2s
v5p0069c2s v6p0140c1s v6p0315c1m
v6p0369c2s v6p0396c2s v6p0645c2s
v6p0646c1s
Wyman, Aram v6p0450c1s
Wyman, B. v6p0078c2s
v6p0133c1s v6p0142c1s v6p0401c2s
v6p0460c1m v6p0522c1s v6p0555c2s
Wyman, Bruce v6p0102c2s
v6p0468c1m
Wyman, C.S. v1p0522c2s
Wyman, E. v1p0855c1s
Wyman, H.H. v2p0081c2s
v2p0132c2m v2p0324c1s v3p0033c2m
v3p0054c2s v3p0104c1s v3p0141c2s
v3p0365c1s v5p0493c2s v6p0547c2s
Wyman, J. v1p0178c2s
v1p0196c1s v1p0256c2s v1p0311c2s
v1p0312c1s v1p0318c2s v1p0456c1s
v1p0470c1m v1p0518c2s v1p0606c2s
v1p0638c2s v1p0642c1s v1p0792c1s
v1p0794c2s v1p0810c1s v1p0816c1s
v1p0876c1s v1p1007c2s v1p1189c1m
v1p1239c1s v1p1313c2s
Wyman, J.C. v4p0102c1s
v4p0483c1s
Wyman, L.B.C. v3p0046c2s
v3p0147c2m v3p0216c2s v4p0136c1s
v4p0226c2s v4p0496c2s v4p0586c1s
v5p0338c1s v5p0593c2s v6p0235c1s
Wyman, L.B.Chace v3p0167c1s
v3p0299c1s v3p0402c1s v3p0410c2s
v4p0022c1s
Wyman, L.C. v2p0056c1s
v2p0422c1s v2p0457c1s v3p0015c2s
v3p0164c2s v3p0233c1s
Wyman, Lillie B.C. v6p0495c1s
v6p0500c1s
Wyman, M. v1p1018c1s
v1p1323c1s v4p0265c1s v4p0634c1s
Wyman, M.B. v1p0116c2s
v1p0814c2s v1p1408c1s
Wyman, S.J. v1p1105c2s
v2p0050c1s
Wyman, T.B. v1p0155c2s
v1p1358c2s v1p1434c2s
Wyman, W. v5p0065c2s
v5p0194c1s v5p0474c1s v6p0668c2s
Wyman, W. et al. v4p0108c1s
Wyman, W.S. v4p0047c2s
Wyman, Walter v5p0644c1s
Wyndham, C. v3p0093c2s
Wyndham, Ch. et al. v3p0406c1s
Wyndham, F.M. v3p0231c1s
Wyndham, G. v3p0112c1s
v3p0221c2s v4p0138c1s v4p0448c2s
v4p0568c1s v4p0590c1s v5p0186c2s
v5p0618c1s
Wyndham, George v4p0609c1s
Wyndham, H. v5p0003c1s
v5p0073c2s v5p0115c2s v5p0167c2s
v5p0233c1s v5p0243c2s v5p0262c1s
v5p0538c1s v5p0556c1s v5p0597c2s
v6p0105c2s v6p0464c2s v6p0536c1s
v6p0584c2s v6p0629c2s v6p0704c2s
Wyndham, H.P. v1p1122c1s
v1p1386c2s
Wyndham, L. v4p0155c2s
v4p0366c1s v4p0578c2s v5p0207c1s
Wyndham, P. and Batson, H.M.
v5p0321c2s
Wynen, A.G. v5p0610c2s
Wynford, R. v1p0267c1s
v1p0368c2s v1p0409c2m v1p0413c2s
v1p0543c2s v1p0548c1s v1p0589c1s
v1p0763c2s v1p0985c1s v1p1370c1s
v3p0303c2s
Wynkoop, H.S. v5p0185c1s
v5p0226c1s
Wynkoop, J.D. v6p0285c2s
Wynkoop, W.C. v4p0230c1s
v4p0372c2s
Wynn, F.W. v5p0387c1s
Wynn, H.W. v1p0348c2s
v1p1065c1s
Wynn, W.H. v1p0530c2s
v1p0688c1s v1p0740c1s v1p0810c1s
v1p0907c2s v1p1090c1s v1p1094c2s
v1p1156c1s v1p1221c2s v1p1235c1s
v1p1308c1s v1p1325c2s v2p0054c2s
v2p0082c1s v2p0149c2s v2p0235c1s
v2p0346c2s v3p0037c1s v3p0040c2s
v3p0081c1s v3p0136c2s v3p0229c1s
v3p0229c2s v3p0325c1s v3p0427c1s
v4p0138c2s v4p0153c1s v4p0229c1s
v4p0301c1s v5p0106c1s v5p0306c2s
v5p0536c1s v5p0572c1s v6p0125c2s
v6p0505c1s v6p0639c1s
Wynne, A.S. v1p0583c2s
v1p1196c2s
Wynne, E.R. v6p0566c2s
Wynne, F. v3p0164c2s
Wynne, F.R. v1p1108c1s
v2p0008c1s v2p0376c2s
Wynne, G.R. v1p0264c1s
v1p0368c1s v1p0853c2s
Wynne, J. v1p0090c1s
v1p0667c1s v1p0705c2s v1p0873c1s
v1p0956c2s v1p1047c2s v1p1104c1s
v1p1198c1s v1p1296c1s v1p1407c1s
Wynne, J.F. v6p0166c1s
Wynne, J.G. v3p0068c2s
Wynne, J.H. v1p0423c2s
v1p1135c2s v3p0172c1s
Wynne, M.Y. v5p0188c1s
v5p0225c1s v5p0581c1s v6p0007c2s
Wynne, P.H. v4p0487c1s
Wynne, Stella F. v6p0617c2s
Wynne, W.P. v4p0340c2m
Wynter, A. v1p0007c1m
v1p0007c2s v1p0196c1m v1p0203c2s
v1p0267c1s v1p0329c1s v1p0353c2s
v1p0454c2s v1p0457c1s v1p0495c1s
v1p0604c2s v1p0606c1s v1p0643c2s
v1p0666c2s v1p0746c2s v1p0760c1s
v1p0763c1m v1p0764c1s v1p0766c1m
v1p0766c2s v1p0767c1s v1p0767c2s
v1p0809c2s v1p0815c1s v1p0869c2s
v1p0879c1s v1p0899c1s v1p0934c2s
v1p0942c1s v1p0968c1s v1p1003c2s
v1p1008c2s v1p1024c2s v1p1083c1s
v1p1192c2s v1p1218c2s v1p1227c1s
v1p1239c2s v1p1289c2s v1p1290c2s
v1p1297c2s v1p1299c1s v1p1312c1s
v1p1320c2s v1p1389c2m v1p1391c2s
v1p1428c2s v1p1440c2m
Wynter, J. v1p1431c1s
Wynyard, E.G. v5p0143c1s
Wyon, A. v5p0517c1s
Wyon, R. v6p0010c2m
v6p0087c1s v6p0311c2s v6p0392c1s
v6p0426c2m v6p0690c1s
Wyse, T. v1p0072c1s
Wyse, W.M. v1p0657c1s
v1p0968c1s v1p1243c1s v1p1276c2s
Wythe, J.H. v4p0138c2s
Wythe, J.W. v1p0746c1s
Wythe, W.T. v1p0018c1s
v1p0297c2s
Wyzewa, T.de v3p0226c2s

X, a working man and Lang, A.
v5p0480c1s
Xanthoudidis, S.A. v5p0291c2s
Yager, A. v2p0192c2s
Yale, C. v1p0618c2s
Yale, C.G. v2p0318c2s
v3p0176c2s v3p0473c2s v5p0378c2s
v6p0710c1m
Yale, E. v1p0168c1s
Yale, L.M. v4p0201c1m
v5p0597c2s
Yale, L.M. and Creighton, J.G.A.
v3p0465c1s
Yamagawa, K. v6p0079c1s
Yamaguchi, S. ....
v5p0303c1s
Yan, Phou Lee v3p0079c2s
v3p0192c2s
Yancey, D.W. v5p0288c1s
Yandell, D.W. v2p0145c2s
Yanos, V. v4p0513c2s
Yapp, G.W. v1p0535c1s
Yard, G. v5p0295c1s
v5p0429c1s v6p0131c2s v6p0345c2m
Yard, T.C. v5p0089c2s
Yardley, H.A. v2p0236c1s
Yardley, W. v2p0049c1s
Yarkes, R.M. v6p0470c1s
Yarnal, E.H. v1p0055c1s
Yarnall, E. v1p0954c2s
v2p0260c1s
Yarnell, E. v1p0709c1s
v1p1430c2s
Yarreo, V.S. v5p0019c1s
Yarros, V. v4p0017c1s
v4p0247c2s v4p0261c1s v4p0283c1s
v4p0307c1s v4p0307c2m v4p0314c1s
v4p0496c1s v4p0496c2m v4p0497c1s
v4p0578c2s
Yarros, V.S. v5p0373c2s
v5p0464c2s v5p0568c1s v5p0582c1s
v6p0113c1s v6p0356c2s v6p0435c2s
v6p0489c1s v6p0621c2s v6p0622c1s
v6p0659c2s
Yarrow, A.F. v5p0068c2s
v5p0582c2s
Yarrow, H.C. v1p1349c2s
v2p0219c2s
Yate, A.C. v2p0336c2s
v3p0060c2s v3p0214c2s v5p0384c2s
v5p0618c2s
Yate, C.E. v6p0057c2s
v6p0489c2s
Yates et al. v1p0831c2s
Yates, A.J. v2p0044c2s
Yates, E. v1p0005c1s
v1p0014c1s v1p0139c2s v1p0166c2s
v1p0204c2s v1p0318c2s v1p0351c1s
v1p0652c1s v1p0706c2s v1p0716c2s
v1p0722c1s v1p0739c1s v1p0761c2s
v1p0924c2s v1p0942c2s v1p0951c2s
v1p0952c2s v1p1017c1s v1p1067c2s
v1p1112c2s v1p1166c2s v1p1197c1s
v1p1266c2s v1p1276c2s v1p1301c1s
v1p1314c2s v1p1360c1s v1p1380c2s
v1p1433c2s v1p1437c1s v2p0242c1s
v4p0120c1s
Yates, E.H. v1p1071c2s
Yates, Edm. v4p0215c2s
Yates, G.F. v1p0593c2s
Yates, J. v1p0737c1s
v1p0743c1s v2p0252c2m
Yates, J. et al. v1p0627c2s
Yates, J.B. v1p0568c2s
Yates, J.T. v6p0128c1s
Yates, L.G. v1p0187c2s
v4p0363c2s v4p0442c2s v4p0503c1s
v4p0579c1s v4p0615c2s v5p0452c1s
v5p0525c1s
Yates, L.H. v5p0205c1s
v5p0208c1s v5p0213c1s v5p0464c1s
Yates, Margarita v6p0257c1s
v6p0379c2s
Yates, O.V. v4p0043c1s
Yates, W.W. v4p0074c1s
Yatsu, N. v6p0037c1s
v6p0648c2s
Yeakel, R. v3p0276c2s
Yealland, F.T. v6p0101c2s
Yeaman, G.H. v1p0353c1s
v1p0452c1s v1p1083c2s v1p1323c2s
Yearkes, R.M. v5p0595c1s
Yearsley, M. v5p0155c1s
Yeates, M.B. v4p0344c1s
Yeates, W.S. v3p0099c2s
v4p0446c2s
Yeatman, C.P. v4p0180c1s
v4p0538c2s v5p0586c1s
Yeatman, J.P. and Stokes, H.P.
v4p0517c1s v4p0517c2s
Yeatman, P. v2p0107c1s
v3p0190c1s
Yeatman, P. and Round, J.H.
v2p0107c1s
Yeatman, P. and Webb, H.H.
v5p0238c1s v5p0634c2s
Yeats, G.A.L. v5p0063c2s
Yeats, J. v1p0550c2s
v3p0094c1s v3p0129c1s v3p0186c2s
Yeats, S.L. v4p0088c2s
v4p0582c2s v5p0104c2s
Yeats, W.B. v3p0148c1s
v3p0412c1s v4p0624c2s v5p0066c1s
v5p0078c1s v5p0153c1s v5p0153c2s
v5p0206c1s v5p0295c2s v5p0296c2s
v5p0297c2s v5p0355c2s v5p0416c2s
v5p0467c1s v5p0634c1s v6p0045c2s
v6p0047c1s v6p0245c1s v6p0298c2s
v6p0379c2s v6p0430c2s v6p0505c2s
v6p0534c1s v6p0608c2s
Yegorevitsch, Y. v4p0583c2s
Yeigh, F. v4p0085c2s
v4p0385c2s v4p0407c2s v4p0579c2s
v5p0090c1s v5p0154c2s v5p0288c1s
v5p0533c1s v5p0607c2s v6p0083c1s
v6p0097c1s v6p0097c2m v6p0098c1s
v6p0114c2s v6p0150c2s v6p0359c1s
v6p0393c1s v6p0618c2s
Yeigh, Frank v5p0515c1s
Yeigh, K.W. v4p0091c1s
v4p0499c1s v5p0263c2s v6p0133c2s
Yeiser, J.O. v4p0318c2s
Yelverton, T. v1p0037c1s
v1p0173c1s v1p0232c2s v1p0803c1s
v1p1071c2s v1p1202c2s v2p0326c1s
Yendell, P.S. v4p0545c2m
v5p0210c1s v5p0549c2s v5p0550c1s
v6p0277c1s v6p0614c2m
Yendes, L.A. v5p0511c2s
Yendys, S. v1p0809c2s
Yenowine, G.H. v3p0280c1s
v4p0342c2s
Yeo, B. v1p0265c2s
v1p0579c1s v2p0160c2s
Yeo, G. v2p0462c2s
v5p0625c1s
Yeo, G.F. v2p0462c1s
Yeo, I.B. v1p0957c2s
Yeo, J. v2p0331c1s
v3p0278c1s
Yeo, J.B. v1p1068c2s
v1p1254c1s v1p1416c1s v2p0118c2s
v2p0290c1s v2p0300c2s v2p0373c2s
v2p0476c1s v3p0101c2s v4p0363c2s
Yeo, J.Burney v3p0257c2s
Yeoman, T.H. v1p0406c1s
v1p0599c1s
Yeomans, A. v2p0039c2s
v2p0179c1s v3p0338c2s
Yeomans, E.D. v1p0128c2s
v1p0684c2s
Yeomans, J.W. v1p0097c2s
v1p0111c2s v1p0117c2s v1p0179c2s
v1p0255c2s v1p0260c1s v1p0293c1s
v1p0424c1s v1p0443c1s v1p0686c2s
v1p0691c1s v1p0732c1s v1p0792c1s
v1p0850c1s v1p0895c2s v1p0964c2s
v1p0978c1s v1p1006c1s v1p1042c1s
v1p1042c2s v1p1047c1s v1p1101c1s
v1p1204c1s v1p1355c1s v1p1432c2s
Yerburgh, R. v5p0244c1s
Yerburgh, R.A. v4p0044c2s
v4p0234c1s v5p0111c1s
Yerger, E.N. v1p1224c2s
Yerkes, B.N. v6p0548c2s
Yerkes, R.M. v6p0079c2s
v6p0522c1s v6p0585c2s
Yerkes, Robert v6p0502c1s
Yerrington, A. v1p0496c2s
Yesse, O. v1p1421c2s
Yette, E. v1p0181c2s
v1p0805c1s v1p0886c2s
Yewens, H.L. v1p0853c1s
Yexley, L. v6p0268c2s
Yockney, A. v5p0254c1s
v6p0018c2s v6p0693c2s
Yockney, Alfred v6p0171c1s
v6p0385c2s
Yoder, A.H. v4p0071c1s
Yoe, F.E.De and Thurber, C.H.
v5p0264c2s
Yoe, J.B. v3p0192c2s
Yoe, L.De et al. v5p0348c1s
Yoe, S. v1p0173c2s
v1p0178c1m v2p0061c2s
Yoe, Shway v2p0240c1s
Yokoi, J.T. v4p0106c2s
v4p0298c1s
Yokoi, T. v4p0298c1s
v5p0302c1s v5p0303c1s
Yolland, E. v4p0039c2s
v4p0276c1s v4p0276c2s v4p0373c2s
v4p0414c2s v4p0512c2s
Yonce, G.V. v3p0380c1s
Yonge, C. v1p0603c1s
Yonge, C.F. v4p0206c1s
v5p0122c2s v5p0168c2s v5p0314c2s
v5p0496c1s v6p0022c2s v6p0242c2s
v6p0287c1s v6p0624c2s
Yonge, C.Fortescue v5p0205c2s
Yonge, C.M. v1p0217c2m
v1p0229c1s v1p0362c1s v2p0021c2s
v3p0102c1s
Yonge, E.S. v5p0143c2s
Yore, E.A. v4p0083c2s
York, E. v4p0365c2s
York, H.W. v4p0065c1s
York, J.O. v1p0083c1s
Yorke, A.C. v5p0408c1s
Yorke, C. v3p0040c1s
v3p0056c2s v3p0116c2s v3p0122c2s
v3p0210c1s v3p0312c2s v3p0315c1s
v3p0466c2s v4p0052c2s
Yorke, P.C. v4p0009c1s
v6p0193c1s
Yorke, R.S. v5p0624c2s
Yorke, S. v2p0151c1s
Yorke, V.W. v4p0189c1s
v5p0447c1s
Yorke-Davies, N.E. v3p0040c1s
v3p0127c1s v4p0155c2m v4p0252c1s
v4p0261c2s v4p0412c1s v4p0613c1s
v5p0055c1s v5p0633c1s v6p0151c2s
v6p0231c2s v6p0262c2s v6p0463c1s
Yorst, J.E. v2p0217c2s
Yorx, J.H.Van, jr. v6p0499c2s
Yos, G. v5p0236c2s
Yoshida, H. v6p0336c1s
Yost, H.M. v4p0288c1s
Yost, J.W. v4p0025c1s
Youatt, E. v1p0940c2s
Youl, E. v1p0144c1s
v1p0159c1s v1p0246c1s v1p1273c1s
Youmans, E.A. v1p0280c2s
v1p0588c2s v1p0716c1s v1p0945c1s
v1p1015c2s v1p1313c2s v2p0132c2s
v2p0344c1s v2p0368c1s v4p0589c1s
Youmans, E.L. v1p0298c1s
v1p0435c1m v1p0586c1s v1p0710c1s
v1p1163c2s v1p1235c1m v1p1235c2s
v1p1268c2s v2p0414c1s v2p0414c2s
v2p0439c1s
Youmans, E.L. et al. v2p0390c1s
Youmans, W.J. v1p0304c1s
v1p0580c1s v1p0747c1m v1p1234c2s
v2p0313c2s v4p0002c2s v5p0276c1s
Young, A. v1p0022c2s
v1p0084c1s v1p0085c2s v1p0135c2s
v1p0154c1s v1p0154c2m v1p0163c1s
v1p0201c2s v1p0232c1s v1p0242c2s
v1p0244c1s v1p0245c2s v1p0271c2s
v1p0288c1s v1p0370c1s v1p0389c2s
v1p0483c2s v1p0524c2s v1p0560c2s
v1p0756c1m v1p0756c2s v1p0765c1s
v1p0767c2s v1p0814c1s v1p0819c1s
v1p0877c2s v1p0882c2s v1p0883c1s
v1p0886c1s v1p0896c1s v1p0916c1s
v1p0929c1s v1p0937c2s v1p0951c1s
v1p0968c1s v1p0969c1s v1p0970c2s
v1p0971c2s v1p0975c2s v1p1030c2s
v1p1058c1s v1p1071c2s v1p1097c2s
v1p1108c2s v1p1109c2s v1p1117c1s
v1p1119c2s v1p1141c1s v1p1205c2s
v1p1296c1s v1p1312c1s v1p1372c2s
v1p1389c2s v1p1403c2m v1p1419c2s
v2p0152c2s v2p0199c2s v2p0237c2s
v3p0013c1s v3p0127c1s v3p0314c1s
v3p0318c1s v3p0342c1s v3p0347c1s
v3p0364c2s v3p0365c1s v3p0394c1s
v3p0398c1s v4p0170c1s v4p0428c1s
v4p0488c2s
Young, A.A. v2p0350c2s
v2p0385c2s v5p0008c2s v5p0107c1s
Young, A.D. v6p0245c1s
v6p0586c1s
Young, A.H. v4p0584c2s
v5p0354c2s
Young, A.M. v3p0472c1s
v4p0036c1s v5p0575c1s
Young, A.P. v4p0195c1s
Young, A.S. v5p0561c1s
Young, Allyn A. v6p0068c2s
v6p0450c2s
Young, B. v5p0028c1s
v6p0167c2s
Young, B.H. v1p0599c1s
v1p1167c2s
Young, Bicknell v5p0530c2s
v5p0614c1s
Young, C. v4p0064c1s
v4p0439c2s v5p0367c1s v5p0486c2s
Young, C.A. v1p0070c1s
v1p0246c1m v1p0278c2s v1p0281c1m
v1p0281c2s v1p0382c1m v1p0401c1s
v1p0804c1s v1p1233c2m v1p1267c2m
v1p1268c1m v1p1268c2m v1p1304c2s
v1p1375c1s v2p0014c1s v2p0025c2s
v2p0026c1m v2p0027c1s v2p0094c2s
v2p0095c1m v2p0123c2s v2p0138c2s
v2p0239c2m v2p0296c2s v2p0414c2s
v2p0424c2s v2p0425c1m v2p0426c2s
v2p0433c2s v2p0459c1s v3p0024c2m
v3p0231c2s v3p0269c1s v3p0298c2s
v3p0423c2s v4p0034c2s v4p0253c2s
v4p0357c2s v4p0540c2s v5p0035c2s
v5p0174c2s v5p0227c1s v5p0372c1s
v5p0545c1s v6p0187c2s
Young, C.A. and Brackett, C.F.
v1p0384c1s
Young, C.A. and Reed, T. . v4p0037c2s
Young, C.A. et al. v2p0285c1s
Young, C.C. v4p0329c1s
Young, C.F.T. v3p0155c1s
Young, C.G., Sir v1p0676c2s
Young, C.H. v4p0366c1s
Young, C.L. v1p0166c2s
v1p0881c1s
Young, C.L., Sir v1p0363c1s
Young, C.W. v6p0440c1s
Young, D. v1p0132c1s

v5p0151c2s
Young, D.B. and Felt, E.P.
v6p0362c1s
Young, E. v2p0436c1s
v5p0387c1s
Young, E.C. v6p0117c2s
Young, E.F. v6p0635c2s
Young, E.H. v5p0115c2s
v5p0174c1s v6p0151c1s
Young, E.J. v1p0513c2s
v1p0515c1s v1p0517c2s v1p0581c2s
v1p0686c2s v2p0042c2s v2p0082c2s
Young, E.R. v3p0065c2s
v5p0020c2s v6p0055c1s v6p0177c2s
Young, E.W. v2p0337c1s
v5p0569c1s
Young, F. v4p0236c2s
v6p0121c2s v6p0327c1s
Young, F.K. v5p0104c2s
Young, G. v4p0340c2s
v5p0539c2s v6p0619c2s
Young, G.C. and Young, W.H.
v5p0146c2s
Young, G.H. v5p0328c1s
Young, G.M. v4p0631c2s
Young, G.P. v1p0021c2s
v1p0467c1s v1p0541c2s v1p0711c1s
v1p0967c1s v1p1016c2s v1p1201c1s
v1p1307c2s v1p1325c1s v1p1375c1s
Young, G.W. v6p0433c1s
v6p0658c2s
Young, H.E. v2p0302c1s
v5p0084c2s
Young, H.E. et al. v5p0084c1s
Young, H.F. v4p0567c1s
Young, H.Selden v6p0073c1s
Young, H.W. v4p0523c2s
v5p0242c2s
Young, J. v1p0102c2s
v1p0189c1s v1p0192c2m v1p0207c2s
v1p0420c2s v1p0492c2s v1p0745c2s
v1p0747c2s v1p1010c2s v2p0261c2s
v2p0281c2s v3p0287c1s v3p0425c2s
v4p0086c1s
Young, J. and Gwynne, G. . v1p1265c1s
Young, J.B. v3p0043c1s
v5p0436c1s v6p0302c1s v6p0406c1s
v6p0692c1s
Young, J.C. v1p0080c2s
v1p0392c2s v1p0811c2s v6p0200c2s
Young, J.F. v1p0925c1s
v2p0096c2s v2p0261c1s
Young, J.H. v1p0946c1s
v1p1403c1s v2p0442c2s
Young, J.H. and Comfort, S.
v1p1152c1s
Young, J.I. v1p0883c1s
Young, J.J. v1p0213c1m
v1p0266c1s v1p0267c1s v1p0629c1s
v1p0887c2s v1p0996c2s v1p1039c1s
v1p1181c2s v2p0351c1s v4p0053c2s
v4p0300c1s v5p0307c1s v5p0351c1s
v6p0340c2s
Young, J.P. v4p0297c1s
v5p0109c2s v5p0124c2s v5p0189c2s
v5p0190c1s v5p0469c1s
Young, J.R. v1p0011c1s
v3p0079c1s v4p0051c1s v4p0106c1s
v4p0242c1s v4p0347c2s v4p0457c1s
v4p0474c1s v5p0259c1s
Young, J.S. v6p0128c1s
Young, J.T. v5p0099c2s
v5p0216c2s v5p0392c1s v5p0512c1s
v5p0603c2s v6p0138c2s v6p0535c1s
Young, J.W. v2p0085c1s
v2p0286c1s v6p0228c2s v6p0630c1s
Young, J.W. and Guthrie, W.N.
v5p0370c2s
Young, J.W.A. v6p0406c1s
v6p0576c1s
Young, James T. v6p0089c1s
Young, L. v1p0232c2s
v4p0148c2s
Young, M. v1p0493c2s
v2p0481c2s v4p0435c1s v5p0010c2s
v5p0267c2s v5p0546c2s
Young, M. and Kingsley, H.C.
v2p0481c2s
Young, M.De v6p0094c1s
Young, M.H.De v4p0083c2s
v4p0100c2s v6p0092c2s
Young, M.L. v4p0021c1s
v4p0373c1s v4p0456c2s v4p0535c1s
v5p0472c1s
Young, N. v3p0027c2s
v3p0166c2s v3p0286c1s v4p0037c2s
v4p0315c2s v4p0630c1s v6p0042c2s
v6p0138c2s
Young, N.B. v4p0046c2s
v5p0402c2s
Young, N.C. v5p0257c2s
Young, P. v5p0243c2s
v5p0404c1s v5p0618c1s
Young, R. v4p0297c1s
v5p0302c2s v6p0347c1s v6p0421c1s
v6p0491c1s v6p0652c1s v6p0709c2s
Young, R.A. v1p0154c1s
v3p0333c1s
Young, R.E. v5p0161c2s
v5p0562c2s v6p0117c2s v6p0249c2s
v6p0434c2s v6p0487c1s v6p0551c2s
v6p0653c1s v6p0689c2s
Young, R.M. v1p0095c1s
v5p0052c2s
Young, R.W. v5p0381c1s
Young, Rose v6p0279c1s
v6p0396c1s
Young, S. v3p0034c1s
v3p0080c1s v3p0428c1s v3p0456c2s
v5p0441c1s v5p0484c1s v5p0497c2s
Young, S. and Brauner, B.. v3p0009c2s
Young, S.B.M. v6p0666c1m
Young, S.G. v1p0032c1s
v1p0108c1s v1p0578c2s v1p0757c1s
v1p0801c1s v1p1365c1s v2p0036c1s
v2p0213c1s v3p0375c1s
v3p0126c2s v3p0411c2s
Young, S.W. v1p0658c2s
v4p0548c2s
Young, Sydney v6p0082c1s
Young, T. v1p0014c2s
v1p0224c2s v1p0278c2s v1p0279c1s
v1p0348c1s v1p0367c2s v1p0437c2s
v1p0555c2s v1p0586c2s v1p0587c2s
v1p0644c1s v1p0724c2m v1p0725c1m
v1p0747c1s v1p1091c1s v1p1310c1s
Young, T.E. v3p0157c2s
Young, T.R. v6p0422c2s
Young, T.U. v1p0385c2s
Young, W. v1p0082c1s
v1p0339c2s v1p1317c1s v6p0520c2s
Young, W.H. v6p0263c2s
v6p0575c1s
Young, W.H. and Young, G.C.
v5p0146c2s
Young, W.H.G.C. v5p0510c2s
Young, W.M. v6p0314c2s
Young, W.W. v1p0589c2s
v1p0728c1s v6p0456c1s
Young, William v4p0049c2s
Younger, E.F. v5p0274c1s
Younger, F.C. v5p0369c2s
Younghusband, F. v5p0034c1s
v5p0359c2s
Younghusband, F.E. v3p0175c1s
v3p0196c1s v4p0005c1s v4p0107c1m
v4p0258c1s v4p0278c1s v4p0423c1s
v5p0110c1m v5p0111c1s v6p0036c2s
Younghusband, Frank, Sir . v6p0645c2s
Younghusband, G.J. v4p0280c2s
v5p0286c2s v5p0323c2s
Younghusband, G.Y. v6p0105c2s
Youngman, A. v6p0050c2s
Youngman, D. v1p1439c1s
Youngs, S. v1p0179c1s
Yowell, E.I. v5p0363c1s
Yoxall, J.H. v2p0129c1m
v3p0377c2s v3p0378c1s v4p0566c1s
v5p0178c1s v6p0146c2s v6p0228c2s
v6p0299c1s v6p0385c1s v6p0511c2s
Ypsiloritis v4p0139c1s
Yriarte, C. v3p0050c2s
v4p0151c2s v4p0426c1s v5p0299c1s
v5p0368c2s v5p0376c2s v5p0452c1s
v5p0495c1s
Ysenburg, Princess v5p0636c2s
Ysendyck, J.van v4p0024c2s
Yturbide, A. v6p0477c2s
Yudelson, S. v6p0704c1s
v6p0705c1s
Yuen, T.Foo v6p0121c1s
Yule, A. v1p0231c2s
Yule, C. v1p1359c1s
Yule, G.U. v4p0431c2m
v4p0546c2s v5p0138c1s v5p0436c2s
Yule, G.U. and Vigor, H.D.
v6p0585c2s
Yule, G.Udny v6p0402c1s
Yule, H. v1p0231c2s
v1p0234c1s v1p0367c2s v1p0631c2s
v1p1015c1s v1p1165c1s v2p0058c1s
v2p0091c2s v2p0204c2s v2p0217c1s
v2p0276c1s v2p0446c2s v3p0115c1s
Yule, H.W. and Gwilliam, G.H.
v5p0083c2s
Yule, J.C. v1p0129c1s
v1p0404c1s
Yulli, Ord. v6p0623c1s
Yung, Kiung Yen v4p0105c2s
Yussuf v3p0031c1m
Yust, W.F. v5p0562c1s
v6p0372c1s v6p0374c2m
Yusuf, Zaida Ben v6p0489c1s
Yusuf-ali, A. v6p0260c1s
Yutzy, J. v5p0351c1s
Yvan and Callery, M.M. ... v5p0566c2s
Yvernes, E. v3p0007c2s
Yznaga, F.A. v5p0148c1s

Zabriskie, F.N. v1p1120c1s
v2p0121c1s v2p0154c2s v2p0216c1s
v2p0255c2s v2p0317c2s v3p0051c1s
v3p0056c2s v3p0142c2s v3p0449c2s
Zabriskie, P.D.O. v6p0236c1s
Zacharias, O. v3p0457c1s
Zack v5p0053c2s
v5p0531c1s
Zaddack, G. v2p0009c2s
Zahm, A.F. v4p0004c2m
Zahm, J.A. v3p0364c2s
v3p0379c2s v4p0064c1s v4p0326c2s
v4p0351c2s v4p0429c2s v4p0508c1s
v4p0601c1s v5p0198c1s v5p0571c1s
v6p0368c1s
Zahn, A. v3p0171c1s
v3p0427c2s v4p0021c1s v4p0138c2s
Zahn, I. v4p0300c1s
Zahn, T. v5p0024c1s
v6p0421c2s
Zahner, J.G. v1p1083c2s
Zahner, R. v1p1040c2s
Zalinski, E.L. v3p0413c2s
v3p0454c1s v5p0029c2s v5p0044c1s
v5p0172c2s v5p0458c2s v5p0478c2s
v5p0583c1m v5p0587c2s v6p0509c1s
Zallas, G. v6p0117c2s
Zamenhof, L.L. v6p0210c2m
Zander, Prof. v1p0388c1s
Zane, C.S. v3p0338c1s
Zane, J.M. v6p0221c2s
Zangwill, I. v4p0001c2s
v4p0077c2s v4p0098c2s v4p0107c2s
v4p0128c1s v4p0184c2s v4p0278c1s
v4p0286c1s v4p0305c1s v4p0306c1m
v4p0311c1s v4p0349c1s v4p0364c2s
v4p0469c1s v4p0480c2s v4p0497c2s
v4p0558c1s v4p0598c2s v5p0055c1s
v5p0250c2s v5p0261c2s v5p0360c2s
v5p0412c2s v5p0539c1s v5p0577c2s
v5p0581c1m v5p0586c1s v5p0595c1s
v5p0645c2s v6p0071c1s v6p0330c2s
v6p0332c1s v6p0343c1m v6p0344c1s
v6p0423c1s v6p0475c2s v6p0561c2s
v6p0711c2s v6p0713c1m
Zangwill, I., Mrs. v6p0673c1s
Zangwill, I., Mrs. and Ayrton, E.
v6p0631c1s
Zangwill, L. v5p0222c1s
v5p0361c2s v5p0531c1s v6p0431c2s
Zannoni, G. and Bonghi, R.
v4p0293c2m
Zappy, W.R. and Bangs, O.. v6p0068c1s
Zardetti, O. v3p0156c1s
Zartman, G.E. v3p0380c1s
Zeballos, E.S. v4p0538c2s
Zedlitz, Baroness von v4p0233c1s
v5p0421c2s
Zeeman, P. v6p0395c1s
Zeichmueller, H. v5p0199c1s
Zeisberger, D. v1p0638c2s
v3p0312c2s
Zeisler, S. v3p0233c2s
v5p0411c1s
Zeiss, H.L. v6p0579c2s
Zell, T.E. v3p0260c2s
Zeller, A.M. v6p0337c1s
Zeller, C. v2p0201c2s
Zeller, E. v1p0241c1s
v1p0271c2s v1p0320c2s v1p0397c2s
v1p0553c2s v1p0580c2s v1p0738c2s
v1p1215c2s v2p0295c2s
Zeller, W.H. v4p0226c2s
Zeltner, X. v1p0712c2s
Zendrini, P. v5p0542c2s
Zenos, A.C. v4p0058c1s
v4p0062c2s v4p0268c2s v4p0300c1s
v4p0311c1s v4p0457c1s v5p0201c2s
v5p0309c1s v5p0558c1s v6p0060c2s
v6p0065c1s v6p0123c1s v6p0237c2s
Zentmayer, J. v1p0737c1s
v1p0835c2s
Zerbe, A.S. v6p0279c1s
Zerbe, L.R. v3p0216c1s
Zerffi, Dr. v3p0021c2s
Zerffi, G.G. v2p0195c1s
v2p0204c1m v2p0212c1s v2p0214c2m
v2p0241c1s v2p0366c1s v2p0463c2s
Zervas, Josef v5p0473c2s
Zetetes v5p0181c2s
Zeuner, G. v1p0353c2s
Zick, H. v5p0232c1s
v5p0558c1s
Zieber, E. v4p0254c2s
Zieber, M. v6p0119c1s
Ziegler, E. v6p0620c2s
Ziegler, F.J. v5p0021c2s
v5p0047c1s v5p0050c2s v5p0052c1s
v5p0411c2s v5p0472c2s
Ziegler, H. v1p0121c1s
v1p1064c1s v1p1179c1s v1p1303c1s
v3p0070c1s v4p0193c2s v4p0477c2s
Ziegler, J.F. v5p0443c1s
Ziegler, T. v5p0178c1s
Zilcken, P. v5p0362c1s
Zimmer, A. v4p0597c1s
Zimmer, G.F. v6p0393c1s
Zimmer, H. v4p0422c2s
Zimmerman, A. v5p0058c2s
v5p0164c1s v6p0065c1s
Zimmerman, B. v4p0241c2s
Zimmerman, C.A. v1p0451c2s
v1p0848c2s
Zimmerman, C.H. v4p0111c2s
v4p0477c1s
Zimmerman, Helen v5p0299c2s
Zimmerman, J. v4p0489c2s
Zimmerman, J.E. v1p0337c1s
Zimmerman, J.H. v1p0307c2s
Zimmerman, O.B. v6p0372c1s
Zimmerman, R. v3p0170c2m
Zimmerman, W. v6p0562c2s
Zimmermann, I. v1p0955c2s
Zimmermann, R. v2p0175c2m
v4p0223c2m v5p0230c2m
Zimmermann, W. v2p0074c2s
Zimmern, A. v2p0072c2s
v4p0229c2s v4p0470c1s v4p0628c1s
v5p0273c1s v5p0638c2s v6p0199c1s
v6p0526c2s
Zimmern, A.E. v6p0473c1s
Zimmern, Alice v3p0334c1s
v3p0428c1s v4p0348c2s
Zimmern, H. v1p0181c2s
v1p0690c1s v1p0704c2s v1p0712c2s
v1p1140c1s v2p0069c1s v2p0080c1m
v2p0087c2s v2p0175c2s v2p0181c2s
v2p0234c2s v2p0241c2s v2p0249c2s
v2p0263c2s v2p0294c1s v2p0298c1s
v2p0301c2s v2p0385c1s v2p0399c1s
v2p0431c1s v2p0450c2s v2p0459c2s
v3p0035c1m v3p0048c2s v3p0109c1s
v3p0277c2s v3p0306c1s v3p0336c2s
v3p0344c2s v3p0367c1s v3p0413c1s
v4p0062c2s v4p0070c1s v4p0090c2s
v4p0134c1s v4p0137c2s v4p0151c2s
v4p0197c1s v4p0213c2s v4p0257c2s
v4p0262c2s v4p0294c1s v4p0312c1s
v4p0355c1s v4p0365c2m v4p0409c1s
v4p0428c1s v4p0437c2s v4p0460c1s
v4p0475c2s v4p0484c2s v4p0503c2s
v4p0513c2s v4p0517c1s v4p0523c2s
v4p0534c1s v4p0561c1s v4p0575c1s
v4p0603c1s v4p0627c2s v4p0630c2s
v5p0022c2s v5p0100c1s v5p0143c2s
v5p0171c2s v5p0300c1s v5p0610c2s
v6p0151c2s v6p0330c2s v6p0407c2s
v6p0484c2s v6p0546c2s v6p0566c2s
Zimmern, H.M. v4p0601c1s
Zimmern, Helen v2p0387c2s
v3p0026c2s v3p0048c2s v4p0482c2s
v5p0265c2s v5p0332c1s v5p0367c2s
v5p0573c2s v5p0578c1s v6p0022c2s
v6p0415c1s
Zincke, B. v1p0600c1s
Zincke, F.B. v1p0025c2s
v1p0217c1s v1p0479c2s v1p0720c2s
v1p0721c1s v1p0721c2m v1p0749c2s
v1p0981c2s v2p0157c2s v2p0166c1s
v2p0247c2s v2p0424c1s
Zingara, La v2p0475c2s
Zingg, C.J. v4p0005c1s
Zinkeisen, F. v4p0017c2s
v4p0130c2s
Zinkham, L.F. v6p0109c2s
Zinzendorf, Count v1p0870c1s
Zipser, Dr. v2p0395c1s
Zirngiebel, F. v5p0514c1s
v5p0569c2s v6p0230c1s
Zitkala-Sa v5p0287c2m
v5p0288c1s v5p0537c2s v5p0590c1s
v6p0697c2s
Ziwet, A. v6p0408c1s
v6p0498c2s
Zockler, O. v1p0047c2m
Zoeckler, O. v6p0280c2s
Zoellner, J.C.F. v1p1233c2m
Zogbaum, R.F. v2p0007c1s
v2p0105c2s v2p0164c1s v2p0176c1s
v2p0409c1s v2p0470c2s v3p0107c1s
v3p0443c2s v5p0599c2s v5p0601c2s
v6p0401c1s v6p0620c2s v6p0657c2s
v6p0669c1s
Zograff, N. v3p0167c1s
Zola, E. v4p0331c1s
v4p0334c2s v4p0611c1s v5p0153c2s
v5p0617c2s
Zollinger, G. v5p0437c2s
Zollner, F. v1p1228c1s
v1p1268c2s v1p1269c1m
Zollner, J.C.F. v2p0412c2s
Zolnay, G.J. v6p0509c2s
Zon, R.G. v6p0233c2s
v6p0458c2s
Zopke, H. v4p0482c2s
Zopritz, Prof. v1p0936c2s
Zorin v5p0215c1s
Zorn, P. v5p0231c2s
Zouche, Lord v1p0607c1s
Zozimus v6p0179c2s
Zozinskey, T.S. v1p0873c2s
Zozinsky, T.S. v2p0211c1s
Zschokke, H. v1p0143c2s
v1p0166c2s v1p0461c2s v1p0465c2s
v1p0668c2s v1p0695c1s v1p1383c1m
Zschokke, J.H.D. v1p0105c1s
Zuber, W.P. v6p0441c1s
v6p0617c1s
Zubof, R.I. v3p0197c1s
v4p0620c2s
Zucchi, M. v4p0373c2s
Zueblin, C. v5p0176c1s
v5p0289c1s v5p0454c2s v5p0536c2s
v6p0076c2s v6p0113c1s v6p0128c2s
v6p0129c1m v6p0193c2s v6p0216c2s
v6p0281c1s v6p0435c1s v6p0444c1s
v6p0452c2s v6p0585c1s v6p0687c1s
Zueblin, R.F. v4p0383c2s
v6p0034c2m v6p0035c2m v6p0146c2s
v6p0317c2m v6p0435c1s v6p0514c2s
v6p0522c2s
Zug, C.K. v6p0381c2s
v6p0532c2s
Zumpt, C.G. v1p0891c2s
Zumwalt, Clerin v6p0187c2s
Zuntz, Prof. v6p0498c2s
Zunz, Dr. v2p0236c2s
Zwemer, S.M. v3p0282c2s
v6p0423c2s v6p0466c2s
Zwingli, U. v1p0128c2s
v1p0935c1s